# Pseudonyms and Nicknames Dictionary

SECOND EDITION

# Pseudonyms and Nicknames Dictionary

A Guide to Aliases, Appellations, Assumed Names, Code Names, Cognomens, Cover Names, Epithets, Initialisms, Nicknames, Noms de Guerre, Noms de Plume, Pen Names, Pseudonyms, Sobriquets, and Stage Names of Contemporary and Historical Persons, Including the Subjects' Real Names, Basic Biographical Information, and Citations for the Sources from Which the Entries Were Compiled

Covers Actors, Aristocrats, Artists, Athletes, Authors, Clergymen, Criminals, Entertainers, Film Stars, Journalists, Military Leaders, Monarchs, Musicians, Playwrights, Poets, Politicians, Popes, Rogues, Saints, Theatrical Figures, and Other Prominent Personalities of All Nations Throughout the Ages

**Jennifer Mossman,**
Editor

Gale Research Company ● Book Tower ● Detroit, Michigan 48226

*Senior Editor:* Ellen T. Crowley
*Editor:* Jennifer Mossman
*Editorial Assistant:* Elwanda Houseworth
*Production Supervisor:* Carol Blanchard
*Cover Design:* Arthur Chartow

Computerized photocomposition by Computer Composition Corporation,
Madison Heights, Michigan

Gale's publications in the pseudonyms and nicknames field consist of the following:

**Pseudonyms and Nicknames Dictionary**

A Guide to Aliases, Appellations, Assumed Names, Code Names, Cognomens, Cover Names, Epithets, Initialisms, Nicknames, Noms de Guerre, Noms de Plume, Pen Names, Pseudonyms, Sobriquets, and Stage Names of Contemporary and Historical Persons, Including the Subjects' Real Names, Basic Biographical Information, and Citations for the Sources from Which the Entries Were Compiled

**New Pseudonyms and Nicknames**

(A Periodic Supplement to *Pseudonyms and Nicknames Dictionary*)

$ 125.00

0305-82-082-1 WAR

# Contents

# Preface to the Second Edition

A variety of circumstances may cause people to adopt or acquire new names. Whether the aim is to protect their privacy, promote a more glamorous image, or conceal a shameful past—inventing another name is often the ideal solution. Thus it is not uncommon to discover authors using pseudonyms or pen names, entertainers with stage names, and criminals taking aliases.

Unlike other types of assumed names, nicknames are usually bestowed by others, and may or may not be complimentary. The popularity enjoyed by a monarch can often be determined merely by examining the types of nicknames that he or she acquired. Alexander "the Great," Richard "the Lion-Hearted," and Ivan "the Terrible" are a few examples that come to mind.

It is the purpose of this publication to identify the original names behind these pseudonyms, stage names, aliases, nicknames, and other types of assumed names selected or acquired by prominent individuals. Basic biographical data, as well as the source(s) from which our information was obtained, are also included.

## Expanded Coverage

The first edition of *Pseudonyms and Nicknames Dictionary* (1980) provided a collection of 17,000 original names and 22,000 assumed names, and was limited to those persons who lived into the twentieth century. Two inter-edition supplements nearly doubled the original collection and included names that had received recent attention through the news media.

With the publication of this second edition, coverage has been expanded to include historical as well as contemporary personalities—a total of 90,000 entries. Listings can now be found for Napoleon Bonaparte, George Washington, Dante, Thomas Aquinas, Plato, William Shakespeare, Johann Sebastian Bach, Julius Caesar, Charlemagne, Confucius, Leonardo da Vinci, Jesus Christ, Michelangelo, Mohammed, and Sir Isaac Newton, as well as Ronald Reagan, Pope John Paul II, "Babe" Ruth, Ernest Hemingway, Elvis Presley, Marilyn Monroe, and Al Capone. Of the nearly 40,000 original names and over 50,000 assumed names to be found in this edition, authors, entertainers, and athletes continue to account for a large percentage of the total collection. The remaining entries cover personalities in a wide variety of fields—politicians, criminals, military leaders, monarchs, popes, clergymen, artistocrats, and business executives, among others.

## What's in a Name?

The variety of names collected for *Pseudonyms and Nicknames Dictionary* revealed that the methods of selecting new names are as varied as the reasons for their creation. Some rather unwieldy surnames were simply shortened so that they could be more easily pronounced and remembered (William Claude Dukinfield gained recognition as the talented comic actor W. C. Fields). Anagrams provided convenient disguises for others who wished to conceal their identities (Roger Caras wrote as Roger Sarac). In some instances, a surname was simply dropped, and the middle name used in its place (author Harry Arthur Bates was known as Harry Arthur). Names occasionally lent themselves to obvious punning and word associations. Surely Noel Young could not resist adopting Leon Elder as his pseudonym. Similarly, Robert L. Fish chose to write under the name A. C. Lamprey.

Nicknames, on the other hand, are not necessarily chosen. They may have been acquired because of some unique physical attribute (Big Jim), character trait (Honest Jack), or nationality (The Golden Greek). Professional athletes were frequently given nicknames that reflected their particular skills (Home Run Baker). Surnames have provided the basis for some rather amusing nicknames (Sugar Cain, Soupy Campbell, Boom Boom Cannon, Pickles Dillhoefer, and others). Whether complimentary or insulting, whimsical or pompous, the nicknames collected for this dictionary are usually quite colorful.

## Exclusions

Certain types of pseudonyms and nicknames were considered to be very closely related in form to the original names and, therefore, did not warrant inclusion as separate entries. These include common derivatives of given names (Bob for Robert), initials that replace a first or middle name (J. Paul Getty for Jean Paul Getty), and middle names used as pseudonyms (Taylor Caldwell for Janet Taylor Caldwell). Married/maiden name differences are not emphasized unless a woman chose to use her maiden name in some professional capacity.

## Acknowledgments

In addition to the reference sources and outside contributors cited in the entries and listed on pages 13-20, the editors received many helpful suggestions from a number of individuals and associations. Roger W. Hill, of the North American Radio Archives, Paul Everett, and Andrew C. McKay expanded our coverage of radio and film personalities. John G. Printz, the U.S. Auto Club National Championship Racing Historian, contributed a number of names in the auto racing field. Valuable additions to the sports collection were also provided by the National Basketball Hall of Fame, the National Football League, the Professional Pool Players Association, and the National Jockeys Hall of Fame at Pimlico. David Glagovsky supplied helpful information in a variety of subject areas.

Comments and suggestions for future editions are welcome.

# Editorial Policies and Arrangement of Names

*Pseudonyms and Nicknames Dictionary (PND)* and its supplements, *New Pseudonyms and Nicknames (NPN)*, index original and assumed names in one alphabetic sequence. Both contemporary and historical figures throughout the world are included.

Entries are coded to indicate the sources from which information was gathered. The List of Sources Cited decodes these symbols, and provides complete bibliographic data, where applicable, for users who wish to find additional information about a particular individual. Entries were frequently based on a compilation of information from several sources and do not necessarily represent an exact duplication of material found in any one source. Those entries without source-identification codes were collected through independent research by the editors.

## Form of Entries

Within *PND*'s single alphabet, there are two types of entry:

1. The main entry, which consists of six elements:

> Original name
> Dates of birth and (where applicable) death
> Up to three source-identification codes
> Nationality
> Occupation
> Assumed name (or names) by which the individual has become known, highlighted by an asterisk

> **Blair, Eric Arthur** 1903-1950
> [EWL, SF, TCL]
> *British author*
> *Orwell, George

Supplements *(New Pseudonyms and Nicknames)* contain the notation "See also base volume" at the end of each entry for which additional pseudonyms or nicknames can be found in the main edition.

2. The cross reference, which refers the user from the assumed name (pen name, nickname, stage name, etc.) to the original name:

> **Orwell, George**
> *See* Blair, Eric Arthur

## Source Conflicts

A variety of sources may have been used to compile an entry, and the editors sometimes found conflicting information. If additional research failed to resolve these discrepancies, various methods were employed to indicate that some uncertainty still exists:

When correct birth dates could not be determined, the earliest date was arbitrarily selected, and a question mark was added to show that some doubt remains. It was particularly necessary to use this procedure with some stage and screen personalities, whose age is traditionally a closely guarded secret.

If differences were found in the form or spelling of a name, both possibilities were incorporated into an entry: Badawi, Mohamed [or Muhammad] Mustafa.

Sources occasionally gave conflicting information in their description of nationalities. For example, one source might determine the nationality based upon place of birth, while a second source might consider length of residence to be of greater importance, and the actual legal status might be difficult to determine in any case. In these instances, *PND* would use a designation such as "British-born" to indicate that, while the place of birth may be known, the actual citizenship is unclear.

## Alphabetical Arrangement

All words and letters are considered in alphabetizing except those that are enclosed in brackets. Spacing generally affects alphabetical position, except in the case of surnames compounded of two or more names. These are arranged after the single surname. Particles (De, La, Von, etc.) are considered to be the first element of a surname and will, unless common usage dictates otherwise, be alphabetized as such:

> De Angelis, Alberto
> De Mille, Agnes
> Dean, Mary
> Dean, Robert George
> Dean-Andrews, Simon Paul
> Dean Norwood, Victor
> Deane, Joseph
> Deane, P. Virginia

Articles that begin a nickname, whether in English or other languages, are not considered for alphabetizing purposes. El Gato, for example, will be found in the G's.

Some common abbreviations (Mr., Dr., St., Ste.) are alphabetized as if they were spelled out (Mister, Doctor, Saint, Sainte).

## Name Reversals

Most names found in *PND* are alphabetized by surname, followed by the given name(s). There are some entries, however, that do not have the form of first and last names and must, therefore, be handled differently:

> Given names followed by a single initial can be found under the given name:
> *M*alcolm X,  *J*ackie O.

> Initials that replace the entire name are alphabetized under the first of the initials:
> *J*.F.K.,  *L*.B.J.

> When titles are combined with a given name, the entry will be found under the title:
> *U*ncle Miltie,  *M*iss Lillian.

## Treatment of Nicknames

Some nicknames are quite clearly meant to replace a given name, and thus fit the usual method of handling assumed names: Lefty Aber and Dusty Baker can be found under the surnames (in the A's and B's respectively).

Others cannot logically be made to fit this pattern since they are not commonly used in conjunction with a surname. These nicknames will stand alone: Calamity Jane, [The] Sultan of Swat.

It is not always immediately obvious whether a given nickname is generally used in combination with a surname or whether it should stand alone. In order to ensure that the user is able to locate the nickname, even though the surname may not be known, a double cross reference (by surname and by nickname) is given:

**Mehlhorn, Wild Bill**
*See* Mehlhorn, William

**Wild Bill Mehlhorn**
*See* Mehlhorn, William

In some cases, the editors had difficulty in deciding when a nickname should be combined with a surname and when it can correctly stand alone. In approaching this and other editorial problems, attempts were made to be as logical as circumstances permitted. Unfortunately, complete consistency was impossible, and the user who is unable to locate a particular name is encouraged to check other possible forms.

# List of Sources Cited

**AES**    Hollander, Zander. *The American Encyclopedia of Soccer.* New York: Everest House, 1980.

**ALR**    *American League Red Book.* 48th ed. Los Angeles: Baseball Fact Books, 1977.

**ALY**    Traub, Hamilton. *The American Literary Yearbook.* Reprint of the 1919 ed. Detroit: Gale Research Co., 1968.

**AM**    Vallance, Tom. *The American Musical.* New York: Castle Books, 1970.

**AN**    Nykoruk, Barbara. *Authors in the News.* Vol. 1. Detroit: Gale Research Co., 1976.

**ANT**    Warfel, Harry R. *American Novelists of Today.* Westport, Conn.: Greenwood Press, 1972.

**ART**    *Who's Who in Art.* 19th ed. Havant, Hants., England: Art Trade Press, 1980.

**AS**    Hickok, Ralph. *Who Was Who in American Sports.* New York: Hawthorn Books, Inc., 1971.

**ASC**    The Lynn Farnol Group Inc. *The ASCAP Biographical Dictionary of Composers, Authors and Publishers.* 3rd ed. New York: The American Society of Composers, Authors and Publishers, 1966.

**AW**    *The Author's and Writer's Who's Who.* 6th ed. Darien, Conn.: Hafner Publishing Co. Inc., 1971.

**BIO**    Louis, Rita Volmer, ed. *Biography Index.* Vol. 10. New York: The H. W. Wilson Co., 1977.

**BAB**    Appel, Martin, and Goldblatt, Burt. *Baseball's Best.* New York: McGraw-Hill, 1977.

**BB**    Mendell, Ronald L. *Who's Who in Basketball.* New Rochelle, N.Y.: Arlington House, 1973.

**BBD**    Slonimsky, Nicolas. *Baker's Biographical Dictionary of Musicians.* 5th ed. New York: G. Schirmer, 1971.

**BBH**    Soderberg, Paul, and Washington, Helen. *The Big Book of Halls of Fame in the United States and Canada.* New York: R. R. Bowker Co., 1977.

**BDF**    Thomson, David. *A Biographical Dictionary of Film.* New York: William Morrow and Co. Inc., 1976.

**BDW**    Tunney, Christopher. *A Biographical Dictionary of World War II.* New York: St. Martin's Press, 1972.

**BE**    *The Baseball Encyclopedia.* 3rd ed. New York: Macmillan Publishing Co. Inc., 1976.

**BEW**    Rigdon, Walter. *The Biographical Encyclopedia and Who's Who of the American Theatre.* New York: James H. Heineman, 1966.

**BF**    Gifford, Denis. *The Illustrated Who's Who in British Films.* London: B.T. Batsford Ltd., 1978.

**BL**    Wallechinsky, David; Wallace, Irving; and Wallace, Amy. *The People's Almanac Presents the Book of Lists.* New York: William Morrow and Co. Inc., 1977.

**BLB**    Nash, Jay Robert. *Bloodletters and Badmen.* New York: M. Evans and Co., 1973.

**BMH**    Busby, Roy. *British Music Hall,* Salem, N.H.: Paul Elek Inc., 1976.

**BN**    *Baseball Nicknames, 1870-1946.* Hingham, Mass.: Gates-Vincent Publications, 1946.

| | |
|---|---|
| **BR** | Marcin, Joe, and Byers, Dick, eds. *Official Baseball Register.* St. Louis: The Sporting News Publishing Co., 1977. |
| **BS** | Severn, Bill. *Bill Severn's Guide to Magic as a Hobby.* New York: David McKay Co. Inc., 1979. |
| **BTB** | Olan, Ben, ed. *Big-Time Baseball.* New York: Hart Publishing Co., 1958. |
| **BWG** | Bartlett, Michael, ed. *Bartlett's World Golf Encyclopedia.* New York: Bantam Books, 1973. |
| **BWW** | Harris, Sheldon. *Blues Who's Who.* New Rochelle, N.Y.: Arlington House, 1979. |
| **BX** | Burrill, Bob. *Who's Who in Boxing.* New Rochelle, N.Y.: Arlington House, 1974. |
| **CA** | *Contemporary Authors.* Vols. 1-102. New Revision Series, Vols. 1-4. Detroit: Gale Research Co., 1962-1981. |
| **CAA** | Millett, Fred B. *Contemporary American Authors.* Reprint of the 1940 ed. New York: AMS Press, 1970. |
| **CAL** | Foy, Felician A. *Catholic Almanac.* Huntington, Ind.: Our Sunday Visitor Inc., 1979. |
| **CAN** | Thomas, Clara. *Canadian Novelists, 1920-1945.* New York: Longmans, Green & Co., 1946. |
| **CAP** | *Contemporary Authors Permanent Series.* Vols. 1-2. Detroit: Gale Research Co., 1975, 1978. |
| **CAR** | Naylor, Colin, and P-Orridge, Genesis. *Contemporary Artists.* New York: St. Martin's Press, 1977. |
| **CAT** | Hoehn, Matthew. *Catholic Authors.* Newark: St. Mary's Abbey, 1948 and 1952. |
| **CBS** | Bacheller, Martin A., ed. *The CBS News Almanac, 1977.* Maplewood, N.J.: Hammond Almanac Inc., 1976. |
| **CC** | Barzun, Jacques, and Taylor, Wendell Hertig. *A Catalogue of Crime.* New York: Harper & Row Publishers, 1971. |
| **CD** | Smith, Horatio. *Columbia Dictionary of Modern European Literature,* New York: Columbia University Press, 1971. |
| **CEC** | Scott, Sir Harold. *The Concise Encyclopedia of Crime and Criminals.* New York: Hawthorn Books Inc., 1961. |
| **CED** | Rust, Brian. *The Complete Entertainment Discography.* New Rochelle, N.Y.: Arlington House, 1973. |
| **CEI** | Hollander, Zander, and Bock, Hal, eds. *The Complete Encyclopedia of Ice Hockey.* Rev. ed. Englewood Cliffs, N.J.: Prentice-Hall, 1974. |
| **CFH** | Smith, Larry, ed. *Canadian Football Hall of Fame.* Hamilton, Ontario: Canadian Football Hall of Fame. |
| **CLC** | *Contemporary Literary Criticism.* Vols. 1-14. Detroit: Gale Research Co., 1973-1980. |
| **CM** | *Country Music Who's Who.* Record World Publications, 1972. |
| **CME** | Shestack, Melvin. *The Country Music Encyclopedia.* New York: Thomas Y. Crowell Co., 1974. |
| **CN** | Vinson, James. *Contemporary Novelists.* 2nd ed. New York: St. Martin's Press, 1976. |
| **CND** | Ruffner, Frederick G., Jr., and Thomas, Robert C., eds. *Code Names Dictionary.* Detroit: Gale Research Co., 1974. |
| **CSH** | Wise, S. F., and Fisher, Douglas. *Canada's Sporting Heroes.* Don Mills, Ontario: General Publishing Co. Ltd., 1974. |
| **CU** | Finch, John R. *Close-Ups.* New York: A. S. Barnes and Co., 1978. |

| | |
|---|---|
| **CW** | Herdeck, Donald E. *Caribbean Writers.* Washington, D.C.: Three Continents Press, 1979. |
| **CWG** | Gentry, Linnell. *A History and Encyclopedia of Country, Western, and Gospel Music.* 2nd ed. Nashville, Tenn.: Clairmont Corp., 1969. |
| **DAM** | Claghorn, Charles Eugene. *Biographical Dictionary of American Music.* West Nyack, N.Y.: Parker Publishing Co. Inc., 1973. |
| **DBA** | Waters, Grant M. *Dictionary of British Artists Working 1900-1950.* 2 vols. Eastbourne, England: Eastbourne Fine Art, 1975. |
| **DC** | Sproat, Iain. *Debrett's Cricketers' Who's Who.* London: Debrett's Peerage Ltd., 1980. |
| **DEL** | Adams, W. Davenport. *Dictionary of English Literature.* Reprint of the 2nd ed. Detroit: Gale Research Co., 1966. |
| **DEP** | Hyamson, Albert M. *A Dictionary of English Phrases.* Reprint of the 1922 ed. Detroit: Gale Research Co., 1970. |
| **DGS** | Mac Farlane, Paul, ed. *Daguerreotypes of Great Stars of Baseball.* St. Louis: The Sporting News Publishing Co., 1971. |
| **DHA** | Harbottle, Thomas Benfield. *Dictionary of Historical Allusions.* Reprint of the 1904 ed. Detroit: Gale Research Co., 1968. |
| **DIL** | Hogan, Robert. *Dictionary of Irish Literature.* Westport, Conn.: Greenwood Press, 1979. |
| **DLE** | Myers, Robin. *A Dictionary of Literature in the English Language from 1940 to 1970.* New York: Pergamon Press, 1978. |
| **DNNF** | Wheeler, William A. *An Explanatory and Pronouncing Dictionary of the Noted Names of Fiction.* Reprint of the 1889 ed. Detroit: Gale Research Co., 1966. |
| **DNNS** | Latham, Edward. *A Dictionary of Names, Nicknames and Surnames of Persons, Places and Things.* Reprint of the 1904 ed. Detroit: Gale Research Co., 1966. |
| **EAR** | Cutter, Robert, and Fendell, Bob. *Encyclopedia of Auto Racing Greats.* Englewood Cliffs, N.J.: Prentice-Hall Inc., 1973. |
| **EC** | Golesworthy, Maurice. *Encyclopaedia of Cricket.* 1st and 6th eds. London: Robert Hale, 1962 and 1977. |
| **ECM** | Dellar, Fred; Thompson, Roy; and Green, Douglas B. *The Illustrated Encyclopedia of Country Music.* New York: Harmony Books, 1977. |
| **EE** | Seth, Ronald. *Encyclopedia of Espionage.* London: New English Library, 1972. |
| **EG** | Evans, Webster. *Encyclopedia of Golf.* 2nd ed. New York: St. Martin's Press Inc., 1974. |
| **EJ** | Feather, Leonard. *The Encyclopedia of Jazz.* Rev. ed. New York: Horizon Press, 1960. |
| **EJ7** | Feather, Leonard, and Gitler, Ira. *The Encyclopedia of Jazz in the Seventies.* New York: Horizon Press, 1976. |
| **EJS** | Postal, Bernard; Silver, Jesse; and Silver, Roy. *Encyclopedia of Jews in Sports.* New York: Bloch, 1965. |
| **EMD** | Steinbrunner, Chris, and Penzler, Otto, eds. *Encyclopedia of Mystery and Detection.* New York: McGraw-Hill Book Co., 1976. |
| **EMT** | Green, Stanley. *Encyclopaedia of the Musical Theatre.* New York: Dodd, Mead & Co., 1976. |
| **EPM** | Stambler, Irwin. *Encyclopedia of Popular Music.* New York: St. Martin's Press, 1965. |
| **ESF** | Nicholls, Peter. *The Encyclopedia of Science Fiction.* New York: Granada Publishing Ltd., 1979. |

| | |
|---|---|
| *ET* | Brown, Les. *The New York Times Encyclopedia of Television.* New York: Times Books, 1977. |
| *EWL* | Fleischmann, Wolfgang Bernard, ed. *Encyclopedia of World Literature in the 20th Century.* Vols. 1-3. New York: Frederick Ungar Publishing Co., 1967. |
| *F1* | Stewart, John. *Filmarama.* Vol. 1: The Formidable Years, 1893-1919. Metuchen, N.J.: The Scarecrow Press Inc., 1975. |
| *F2* | Stewart, John. *Filmarama.* Vol. 2: The Flaming Years, 1920-1929. Metuchen, N.J.: The Scarecrow Press Inc., 1977. |
| *FAP* | Kane, Joseph Nathan. *Facts about the Presidents.* 4th ed. New York: The H. W. Wilson Co., 1981. |
| *FB* | Mendell, Ronald L., and Phares, Timothy B. *Who's Who in Football.* New Rochelle, N.Y.: Arlington House, 1974. |
| *FBJ* | De Montreville, Doris, and Crawford, Elizabeth D. *Fourth Book of Junior Authors and Illustrators.* New York: The H. W. Wilson Co., 1978. |
| *FC* | Halliwell, Leslie. *The Filmgoer's Companion.* 3rd ed. New York: Avon Books, 1970. |
| *FCW* | Stambler, Irwin, and Landon, Grelun. *Encyclopedia of Folk, Country and Western Music.* New York: St. Martin's Press, 1969. |
| *FD* | Parish, James Robert, and Pitts, Michael R. *Film Directors: A Guide to Their American Films.* Metuchen, N.J.: The Scarecrow Press Inc., 1974. |
| *FDG* | Parish, James Robert. *Film Directors Guide — Western Europe.* Metuchen, N.J.: The Scarecrow Press Inc., 1976. |
| *FF* | Phyfe, William Henry P. *5,000 Facts and Fancies.* Reprint of the 1901 ed. Detroit: Gale Research Co., 1966. |
| *FFA* | Lawless, Ray M. *Folksingers and Folksongs in America.* 2nd ed. New York: Duell, Sloan & Pearce, 1965. |
| *FFF* | Reddall, Henry Frederic. *Fact, Fancy, and Fable.* Reprint of the 1889 ed. Detroit: Gale Research Co., 1968. |
| *FHE* | Fischler, Stan, and Fischler, Shirley. *Fischler's Hockey Encyclopedia.* New York: Thomas Y. Crowell Co., 1975. |
| *FIR* | *Films in Review.* New York: National Board of Review of Motion Pictures Inc., Feb., 1972-Oct., 1981. |
| *GA* | Amstutz, Walter. *Who's Who in Graphic Art.* Zurich: Amstutz & Herdeg Graphis Press, 1962. |
| *GF* | Elliott, Len, and Kelly, Barbara. *Who's Who in Golf.* New Rochelle, N.Y.: Arlington House, 1976. |
| *GLET* | Lee, Frederick George. *A Glossary of Liturgical and Ecclesiastical Terms.* Reprint of the 1877 ed. Detroit: Gale Research Co., 1971. |
| *GME* | Scharff, Robert, ed. *Golf Magazine's Encyclopedia of Golf.* New York: Harper & Row Publishers, 1970. |
| *GS* | Smith, George B. Taurine Bibliophiles of America. Private communication. |
| *GSH* | Davis, Mac. *100 Greatest Sport Heroes.* Rev. ed. New York: Grosset & Dunlap, 1958. |
| *GW* | Willams, George. National Cowboy Hall of Fame, Rodeo Division. Private communication. |
| *GWP* | Nares, Robert. *A Glossary of Words, Phrases, Names and Allusions in the Works of English Authors.* Reprint of the 1905 ed. Detroit: Gale Research Co., 1966. |

| | |
|---|---|
| *A* | Parish, James Robert. *Hollywood Character Actors*. New Rochelle, N.Y.: Arlington House, 1978. |
| *HDM* | Bullock, Alan, and Stallybrass, Oliver, eds. *The Harper Dictionary of Modern Thought*. New York: Harper & Row Publishers, 1977. |
| *HFF* | Ashley, Mike. *Who's Who in Horror and Fantasy Fiction*. New York: Taplinger Publishing Co., 1977. |
| *HHF* | Walsh, William S. *Heroes and Heroines of Fiction*. Reprint of the 1914 ed. Detroit: Gale Research Co., 1966. |
| *HK* | Kariher, Harry C. *Who's Who in Hockey*. New Rochelle, N.Y.: Arlington House, 1973. |
| *HN* | Brewer, E. Cobham. *The Historic Note-Book*. Reprint of the 1891 ed. Detroit: Gale Research Co., 1966. |
| *HR* | Elk, Herb. *The Hockey Register, 1976-77*. St. Louis: The Sporting News Publishing Co., 1976. |
| *HT* | Billings, Pat, and Eyles, Allen. *Hollywood Today*. New York: A.S. Barnes & Co., 1971. |
| *IA* | Thompson, Donald E. *Indiana Authors and Their Books, 1917-1966*. Crawfordsville, Ind.: Wabash College, 1974. |
| *IAW* | Gaster, Adrian. *The International Authors and Writers Who's Who*. 8th ed. Cambridge, England: Melrose Press Ltd., 1977. |
| *IBW* | Spradling, Mary Mace. *In Black and White*. 3rd ed. Detroit: Gale Research Co., 1980. |
| *IBY* | Ward, Martha E., and Marquardt, Dorothy A. *Illustrators of Books for Young People*. 2nd ed. Metuchen, N.J.: Scarecrow Press, 1975. |
| *ICB* | *Illustrators of Children's Books, 1946-56, 1957-66, 1967-76*. Boston: The Horn Book Inc., 1958, 1968, and 1978. |
| *IEJ* | Case, Brian. *The Illustrated Encyclopedia of Jazz*. New York: Harmony Books, 1978. |
| *IPA* | Golenpaul, Ann, ed. *Information Please Almanac, Atlas and Yearbook, 1977*. New York: Information Please Almanac, 1976. |
| *ITA* | Gertner, Richard, ed. *International Television Almanac, 1977*. New York: Quigley Publishing Co., Inc., 1977. |
| *IWM* | Gaster, Adrian. *International Who's Who in Music and Musicians' Directory*. 8th ed. Cambridge, England: Melrose Press Ltd., 1977. |
| *JL* | Greenberg, Martin H. *The Jewish Lists*. New York: Schocken Books, 1979. |
| *LAO* | Lawrence, A. ed. *Who's Who Among Living Authors of Older Nations*. Reprint of the 1931 ed. Detroit: Gale Research Co., 1966. |
| *LBA* | Shockley, Ann Allen, and Chandler, Sue P. *Living Black American Authors*. New York: R. R. Bowker Co., 1973. |
| *LC* | Ward, A. C. *Longman Companion to Twentieth Century Literature*. London: Longman Group Ltd., 1970. |
| *LRR* | *Lillian Roxon's Rock Encyclopedia*. New York: Grosset & Dunlap Inc., 1971. |
| *MBF* | Lofts, W. O. G., and Adley, D. J. *The Men Behind Boys' Fiction*. London: Howard Baker, 1970. |
| *MBL* | Temple, Ruth Z., and Tucker, Martin. *Modern British Literature. A Library of Literary Criticism*. Vols. 1-3. New York: Frederick Ungar Publishing Co., 1966. |
| *MEB* | Hollander, Zander, ed. *The Modern Encyclopedia of Basketball*. New York: Four Winds Press, 1969. |

| | |
|---|---|
| *MGL* | Domandi, Agnes Koerner. *Modern German Literature. A Library of Literary Criticis.* 2 Vols. New York: Frederick Ungar Publishing Co., 1972. |
| *MJA* | Fuller, Muriel. *More Junior Authors.* New York: The H. W. Wilson Co., 1963. |
| *MK* | Kleinknecht, Merl F. Society for American Baseball Research, Negro Leagues Research Committee. Private communication. |
| *MM* | Messick, Hank, and Goldblatt, Burt. *The Mobs and the Mafia.* New York: Thomas Y. Crowell Co., 1972. |
| *MS* | Ewen, David. *Musicians Since 1900.* New York: The H.W. Wilson Co., 1978. |
| *MWD* | Matlaw, Myron. *Modern World Drama.* New York: E. P. Dutton & Co. Inc., 1972. |
| *MY* | Miller, Paul Eduard. *Miller's Yearbook of Popular Music.* Chicago: Pem Publications, 1943. |
| *NAA* | Lawrence, Alberta, ed. *Who Was Who Among North American Authors 1921-1939.* Reprint of the 1921-1939 series. Detroit: Gale Research Co., 1976. |
| *NAD* | Jack, Alex, ed. *The New Age Dictionary.* Brookline, Mass.: Kanthaka Press, 1976. |
| *NBA* | Winick, Matt, ed. *National Basketball Association Official Guide for 1976-77.* St. Louis: The Sporting News Publishing Co., 1976. |
| *NBB* | Leadbitter, Mike. *Nothing but the Blues.* London: Hanover Books, 1971. |
| *NLG* | *National League Green Book-1977.* Los Angeles: Baseball Fact Books, 1977. |
| *NN* | Noble, Vernon. *Nicknames Past and Present.* London: Hamish Hamilton Ltd., 1976. |
| *NND* | Attwater, Donald. *Names and Name-Days.* Reprint of the 1939 ed. Detroit: Gale Research Co., 1968. |
| *NOJ* | Rose, Al, and Souchon, Edmond. *New Orleans Jazz.* Baton Rouge, La.: Louisiana State University Press, 1978. |
| *NP* | Wells, Dicky. *The Night People.* London: Robert Hale & Co., 1971. |
| *OBW* | Peterson, Robert. *Only the Ball Was White.* Englewood Cliffs, N.J.: Prentice-Hall Inc., 1970. |
| *OCF* | Bawden, Liz-Anne, ed. *The Oxford Companion to Film.* New York: Oxford University Press, 1976. |
| *OCS* | Arlott, John, ed. *The Oxford Companion to Sports and Games.* New York: Oxford University Press, 1975. |
| *OET* | *United States Lawn Tennis Association Official Encyclopedia of Tennis.* New York: Harper & Row Publishers, 1972. |
| *OP* | Rich, Maria F., ed. *Who's Who in Opera.* New York: Arno Press Inc., 1976. |
| *PA* | Haynes, John Edward. *Pseudonyms of Authors.* Reprint of the 1882 ed. Detroit: Gale Research Co., 1969. |
| *PAC* | Ewen, David. *Popular American Composers.* 1st suppl. New York: The H. W. Wilson Co., 1972. |
| *PB* | Karst, Gene, and Jones, Martin J. Jr. *Who's Who in Professional Baseball.* New Rochelle, N.Y.: Arlington House, 1973. |
| *PHM* | Maclean, Don. *Pictorial History of the Mafia.* New York: Pyramid Books, 1974. |
| *PMJ* | Kinkle, Roger D. *The Complete Encyclopedia of Popular Music and Jazz, 1900-1950.* New Rochelle, N.Y.: Arlington House, 1974. |
| *PRS* | Stambler, Irwin. *Encyclopedia of Pop, Rock and Soul.* New York: St. Martin's Press, 1974. |

| | |
|---|---|
| *RBE* | Loubet, Nat, and Ort, John. *The Ring Boxing Encyclopedia and Record Book*. 1977 ed. New York: The Ring Book Shop, 1976. |
| *RH* | Brewer, E. Cobham. *The Reader's Handbook of Famous Names in Fiction, Allusions, References, Proverbs, Plots, Stories, and Poems*. Reprint of the 1899 ed. Detroit: Gale Research Co., 1966. |
| *RM* | York, William. *Who's Who in Rock Music*. Seattle: Atomic Press, 1978. |
| *RO1* | Nite, Norm N. *Rock On*. Vol. 1: The Solid Gold Years. New York: Thomas Y. Crowell Co., 1974. |
| *RO2* | Nite, Norm N. *Rock On*. Vol. 2: The Modern Years. New York: Thomas Y. Crowell Co., 1978. |
| *SA* | *The Official Associated Press Sports Almanac 1975*. New York: Dell Publishing Co. Inc., 1975. |
| *SAT* | Commire, Anne. *Something about the Author*. Vols. 1-23. Detroit: Gale Research Co., 1971-1981. |
| *SC* | Truitt, Evelyn Mack. *Who Was Who on Screen*. 2nd ed. New York: R.R. Bowker Co., 1977. |
| *SF* | Ash, Brian. *Who's Who in Science Fiction*. New York: Taplinger Publishing Co., 1976. |
| *SFL* | Reginald, R. *Science Fiction and Fantasy Literature*. 2 Vols. Detroit: Gale Research Co., 1979. |
| *SFP* | McGhan, Barry. *Science Fiction and Fantasy Pseudonyms*. Dearborn, Mich.: Howard DeVore, 1978. |
| *SG* | Gallelo, Al "Scoop." International Veteran Boxers Association. Private communication. |
| *SMG* | Sports Media Guides. Official press guides for professional baseball, basketball, football, and hockey teams. |
| *SN* | Frey, Albert R. *Sobriquets and Nicknames*. Reprint of the 1888 ed. Detroit: Gale Research Co., 1966. |
| *SR* | Frommer, Harvey. *Sports Roots*. New York: Atheneum, 1979. |
| *SSS* | Wieder, Judy, and Mattern, Lynn. *Right On's 100 Super-Soul Stars*. Hollywood, Calif.: Laufer Co., 1972. |
| *SW* | Willis, John, ed. *Screen World*. Vol. 27. New York: Crown Publishers Inc., 1976. |
| *SWI* | Besford, Pat. *Encyclopaedia of Swimming*. New York: St. Martin's Press, 1971. |
| *TBJ* | De Montreville, Doris, and Hill, Donna. *Third Book of Junior Authors*. New York: The H. W. Wilson Co., 1972. |
| *TC* | Kunitz, Stanley J., and Haycraft, Howard, eds. *Twentieth Century Authors*. New York: The H. W. Wilson Co., 1942. |
| *TC1* | Kunitz, Stanley J., and Colby, Vineta, eds. *Twentieth Century Authors*. First Supplement. New York: The H. W. Wilson Co., 1955. |
| *TCC* | Kirkpatrick, D. L. *Twentieth-Century Children's Writers*. New York: St. Martin's Press, 1978. |
| *TCL* | Seymour-Smith, Martin. *Who's Who in Twentieth Century Literature*. New York: Holt, Rinehart and Winston, 1976. |
| *TF* | Hanley, Reid M. *Who's Who in Track and Field*. New Rochelle, N.Y.: Arlington House, 1973. |
| *THR* | *Who Was Who in the Theatre: 1912-1976*. 4 Vols. Reprint of the 1912-1972 eds. Detroit: Gale Research Co., 1978. |

| | |
|---|---|
| **TLC** | *Twentieth-Century Literary Criticism.* Vols. 1-3. Detroit: Gale Research Co., 1978-1980. |
| **TR** | Herbert, Ian. *Who's Who in the Theatre.* 16th ed. Detroit: Gale Research Co., 1977. |
| **WA** | Delury, George E., ed. *The World Almanac and Book of Facts 1977.* New York: Newspaper Enterprise Association Inc., 1976. |
| **WBC** | McCallum, John D. *The Encyclopedia of World Boxing Champions Since 1882.* Radnor, Pa.: Chilton Book Co., 1975. |
| **WBD** | *Webster's Biographical Dictionary.* Springfield, Mass.: G. & C. Merriam Co., 1974. |
| **WD** | *The Writers Directory, 1974-76.* New York: St. Martin's Press, 1974. |
| **WEC** | Horn, Maurice. *The World Encyclopedia of Cartoons.* 2 Vols. New York: Chelsea House Publishers, 1980. |
| **WECO** | Horn, Maurice. *The World Encyclopedia of Comics.* 2 Vols. New York: Chelsea House Publishers, 1976. |
| **WEF** | Cawkwell, Tim, and Smith, John M. *The World Encyclopedia of Film.* New York: World Publishing, 1972. |
| **WF** | Cowie, Peter. *World Filmography,* 1967 and 1968. New York: A. S. Barnes and Co., 1977. |
| **WFA** | Lambert, Eleanor. *World of Fashion.* New York: R. R. Bowker Co., 1976. |
| **WGT** | Rock, James A. *Who Goes There.* Bloomington, Ind.: James A. Rock and Co., 1979. |
| **WOA** | Wakeman, John. *World Authors, 1950-1970* and *1970-1975.* New York: The H. W. Wilson Co., 1975 and 1980. |
| **WW** | Gribbin, Lenore S. *Who's Whodunit.* University of North Carolina Library Studies, No. 5. Reprint of the 1969 ed. Ann Arbor, Mich: University Microfilms International, 1978. |
| **WWB** | Siwoff, Seymour, ed. *Who's Who in Baseball.* 62nd ed. New York: Who's Who in Baseball Magazine Co. Inc., 1977. |
| **WWJ** | Chilton, John. *Who's Who of Jazz.* New York: Chilton Book Co., 1970. |
| **WWL** | *Who Was Who in Literature, 1906-1934.* 2 Vols. Reprint of *Literary Yearbook* (1906-1922) and *Who's Who in Literature* (1924-1934). Detroit: Gale Research Co., 1979. |
| **WWS** | McCormick, Donald. *Who's Who in Spy Fiction.* New York: Taplinger Publishing Co. Inc., 1977 |
| **WWW** | Keegan, John. *Who Was Who in World War II.* London: Arms and Armour Press, 1978. |
| **WYA** | Sarkissian, Adele. *Writers for Young Adults: Biographies Master Index.* 1st ed. Detroit: Gale Research Co., 1979. |
| **YAB** | Commire, Anne, ed. *Yesterday's Authors of Books for Children,* Vol. 1. Detroit: Gale Research Co., 1977. |

Additional entries were compiled from a variety of newspaper and periodical articles. Several associations and individuals who provided valuable contributions have been acknowledged in the preface.

# A

**A.**
*See* Arnold, Matthew

**A.**
*See* Brierley, Robert Benjamin

**A. A.**
*See* Willis, [George] Anthony Armstrong

**A. A. M.**
*See* Milne, Alan Alexander

**A. B.**
*See* Beaty, Annie

**A. B.**
*See* Boyle, Alicia

**A. B.**
*See* Broadfield, Aubrey Alfred [Alan]

**A. B. G.**
*See* Airy, [Sir] George Biddell

**A. B. G.**
*See* Granville, Augustus Bozzi

**A. B. H.**
*See* Harris, Amanda Bartlett

**A. B. S.**
*See* Sharrocks, Alfred Burgess

**A. C.**
*See* Carr, Austin

**A. C.**
*See* Christopher, Ann

**A. C. H.**
*See* Haeselbairth, A. C.

**A. D.**
*See* Daintrey, Adrian Maurice

**A. D.**
*See* Dantley, Adrian

**A. D.**
*See* Down, Avril

**A. D. S.**
*See* De Maune, Edward

**A. E.**
*See* Earhart, Amelia

**A. E.**
*See* Russell, George William

**A. E. L.**
*See* Lee, A. E. L.

**A. E. T.**
*See* Henry, Ainsley E. T.

**A. F.**
*See* Fleischmann, Arthur John

**A. F. S.**
*See* Silvani, Anita

**A. F. T.**
*See* Tytler, Anne Fraser

**A. G. A. P.**
*See* Paine, A. G. Amye

**A. G. G.**
*See* Grinling, Antony Gibbons

**A. G. J.**
*See* Gwynne-Jones, Allan

**A. H. R.**
*See* Rhine, Alice Hyneman

**A. J.**
*See* Johnson, Anderson Sidney

**A. J. O.**
*See* Ogilvy, Arthur James

**A. K.**
*See* Kindberg, Agnes Marie

**A. K. H.**
*See* Hopkins, Alice K[imball]

**A. K. H. B.**
*See* Boyd, Andrew Kennedy Hutchinson

**A. L. O. E. [A Lady of England]**
*See* Tucker, Charlotte Maria

**A. L. S.**
*See* Schoenduv, A. L.

**A. M.**
*See* Megged [or Meged], Aharon [or Aron]

**A. M.**
*See* O'Mahoney, Thaddeus

**A. M. B.**
*See* Bulkley, Annette Mabel

**A. M. D.**
*See* Daintrey, Adrian Maurice

**A. N.**
*See* Nyvall, David

**A. P. F.**
*See* Forbes, Alexander P.

**A. P. H.**
*See* Herbert, [Sir] Alan Patrick

**A. R.?**
*See* Jimenez Sola, Enrique

**A. R.**
*See* Rossiter, Anthony

**A. R.**
*See* Rothstein, Arnold

**A. R. A.**
*See* Lees, James Cameron

**A. R. C.**
*See* Cooke, Anthony R.

**A. R. P. - M.**
*See* Galsworthy, John

**A. S.**
*See* Shipton, Anna

**A. S.**
*See* Swanwick, Anna

**A. T.**
*See* Cudlip, Annie Thomas

**A. U.**
*See* Urbanczyk, Andrew Andrzej

**A. W., Sir**
*See* Weldon, [Sir] Anthony

**Aachen, C. V.**
*See* Melcher, Gilbert W[ayne]

**Aakjaer, Jeppe**
*See* Jensen, Jeppe

**Aalben, Patrick**
*See* Jones, Noel

**Aaltonen, [Ilta] Annikki [Tyyne]** 1911-   [IAW]
*Finnish author and playwright*
* Maruna, Annikki

**Aardema, Verna**
*See* Vugteveen, Verna Aardema

**Aarigapudi**
*See* Aarigapudi, Ramesh Choudhary

**Aarigapudi, Ramesh Choudhary** 1922-   [IAW]
*Indian author*
* Aarigapudi

**Aaron, Abe**
*See* Aaron, Alvin

**Aaron, Alvin** 1910-   [EJ]
*American jazz musician*
* Aaron, Abe

**Aaron, Barney** 1836-1907 [AS, RBE]
*British-born boxer*
* Aaron, Young Barney

**Aaron, Hammerin' Henry [or Hank]**
*See* Aaron, Henry Louis [Hank]

**Aaron, Henry Louis [Hank]** 1934- [SA]
*American baseball player*
* Aaron, Hammerin' Henry [or Hank]
* [The] Hammer

**Aaron, Sidney**
*See* Chayefsky, Sidney

**Aaron, Young Barney**
*See* Aaron, Barney

**Aarons, Edward S[idney]** 1916-1975 [CC, EMD, WW]
*American author*
* Ayres, Paul
* Ronns, Edward

**Aaronson, Max** 1882?-1970? [F1, OCF, WEF]
*American actor, director, producer*
* Anderson, Bronco Billy
* Anderson, Gilbert M.

**Aartsen, Peter** 1507-1573 [DNNS, FFF, RH]
*Flemish painter*
* Long Peter

**Ab Originee**
*See* Clemens, Samuel Langhorne

**Ab-O'Th'-Yate**
*See* Brierley, Robert Benjamin

**Abacrombi, Signor**
*See* Abercrombie, James [Baron Dunfermline]

**Abadi, Henry**
*See* Youssef-Ahmabadabi, Henry

**Abafi, Lajos**
*See* Aigner, Lajos

**Abarbanell, Jacob**   [PA]
*Author*
* Revere, Paul
* Royal, Ralph

**Abatematteo, John Anthony** 1938- [IWM]
*American composer, producer, arranger*
* Abbott, John Anthony

**Abati, Francesco**
*See* Reade, William Winwood

**Abba Arika** ?- 247 [WBD]
*Babylonian clergyman*
* Rab

**Abba Salamah [Father of Peace]**
See Frumentius

**Abbandando, Dasher**
See Abbandando, Frank

**Abbandando, Frank** ?-1942 [PHM]
*American underworld figure*
* Abbandando, Dasher

**Abbas, Abu-al-** 721?- 754 [WBD]
*Caliph of the Abbasside dynasty*
* Saffah, al- [The Bloodshedder]

**Abbas Effendi** 1844-1921 [WBD]
*Persian religious leader*
* Abdul Baha [Servant of Baha]

**Abbas, Syed Zaheer** 1947- [DC]
*Pakistani cricketer*
* Abbas, Zed

**Abbas, Zed**
See Abbas, Syed Zaheer

**Abbas I** 1557-1628
[FFF, SN, WBD]
*Shah of Persia*
* [The] Great

**Abbasi, Najam**
See Abbasi, Najmuddin

**Abbasi, Najmuddin** 1927- [IAW]
*Pakistani author*
* Abbasi, Najam

**[The] Abbe**
See Barruel, Augustin

**Abbe**
See Cagnoli, Belmonti

**Abbe de La Tour**
See Charriere, Isabelle de

**Abberley, Grabbers**
See Abberley, Robert Neal

**Abberley, Robert Neal** 1944- [DC]
*British cricketer*
* Abberley, Grabbers

**Abbey, Kieran**
See Reilly, Helen [Abby Kieran]

**Abbey, Mrs. Henry E.** [FFF]
*Entertainer*
* Girard, Florence

**Abbot, Anthony**
See Oursler, [Charles] Fulton

**Abbot, Jacob** 1803- ? [PA]
*Author*
* Paul, Marco

**Abbot, Rick**
See Sharkey, John Michael

**Abbot, Sara**
See Zolotow, Charlotte [Shapiro]

**Abbot-Anderson, Louis**
1873?-1945 [BEW]
*British-born actor*
* Goodrich, Louis

**Abbott, A. A.**
See Spewack, Samuel

**Abbott, Alice** [joint pseudonym with
Helen Ross (Smith) Speicher]
See Borland, Kathryn Kilby

**Abbott, Alice** [joint pseudonym with
Kathryn Kilby Borland]
See Speicher, Helen Ross [Smith]

**Abbott, Alice Irving**
See Burdick, H. H.

**Abbott, Big Dan**
See Abbott, Leander Franklin

**Abbott, Brook**
See Davies, Blodwen

**Abbott, Bruce**
See Reach, James

**Abbott, Bud**
See Abbott, William A.

**Abbott, Charles Edwards**
[FFF, PA]
*Clergyman and author*
* Old Harlo

**Abbott, Charles Henry** 1865-1946
*American educator*
* Abbott, Chip
* Abbott, Habit

**Abbott, Chip**
See Abbott, Charles Henry

**Abbott, Dan**
See Abbott, Leander Franklin

**Abbott, Dolly**
See Horn, Emily

**Abbott, Edward S.**
See Sanders, Edward S.

**Abbott, Edwin Abbott** 1838-1926
[ESF, PA, WGT]
*British author and clergyman*
* Philochristus
* [A] Square

**Abbott, Emma**
See Wetherell, Mrs. E.

**Abbott, Evelyn**
See Reyna, Ruth

**Abbott, Fred**
See Vandemann, Frederick H.

**Abbott, Grace Barrett Hartman**
1907?-1955 [BEW]
*American dancer*
* Hartman, Grace

**Abbott, Habit**
See Abbott, Charles Henry

**Abbott, Helen Raymond**
See Beals, Helen Raymond Abbott

**Abbott, [Manager] Henry**
See Stratemeyer, Edward L.

**Abbott, Jack Henry** 1944?-
*Convicted bankrobber, murderer,
author*
* Eastman, Jack

**Abbott, Jacob** 1803- ? [PA]
*Author*
* Erodore

**Abbott, Jennie A.** 1808-1872 [PA]
*Author*
* Bourne, Margaret

**Abbott, John Anthony**
See Abatematteo, John Anthony

**Abbott, John G.** [FFF]
*Author*
* Augustine, Van

**Abbott, Lawrence**
See Lawrence, Christopher George
Holman

**Abbott, Lawrence Fraser**
1859-1933 [PA]
*Author*
* Frazer, Lawrence

**Abbott, Leander Franklin**
1862-1930 [BE]
*American baseball player*
* Abbott, Big Dan
* Abbott, Dan

**Abbott, Lyman** 1835-1922
[DEL, FFF, PA]
*American clergyman and author*
* Benauly
* Laicus

**Abbott, Ody Cleon** 1886-1933 [BE]
*American baseball player*
* Abbott, Toby

**Abbott, Orrina**
See Reyna, Ruth

**Abbott, Philip**
See Alexander, Philip Abbott

**Abbott, Richard**
See Vandenberg, Simon

**Abbott, Rosa**
See Parker, Rosa Abbott

**Abbott, Thomas C.** [PA]
*Author*
* Recapper

**Abbott, Toby**
See Abbott, Ody Cleon

**Abbott, Wenonah Stevens** 1865- ?
[NAA]
*American author and clergywoman*
* Cricket
* Sunshine
* Zale Gale

**Abbott, William A.** 1895?-1974
[FC, IPA, TR]
*American actor and comedian*
* Abbott, Bud

**Abbott Willie Nelson**
See Nelson, Willie

**Abbott-Anderson, E.** 1864-1959
[BEW]
*British actor*
* Aynesworth, Allen

**Abd-el-Kader** 1808?-1883 [HN]
*Emir of Mascara*
* [The] Modern Jugurtha

**Abd-er Rahman I** 731?- 788?
[HN]
*Caliph of Cordova*
* [The] Calif of the West

**Abd-er-Rahman III** 891- 961
[DNNS]
*Caliph of Cordova*
* Defender of the Faith of God

**Abdallah**
See Curry, Otway

**Abdallah**
See Pereria Saromenho, Auguste

**Abdallah, Omar**
See Humbaraci, D[emir] Arslan

**Abdel-Malek, Anouar** 1924- [CA]
*Egyptian-born author*
* Ebn El-Nil

**Abdel-Rahmen, Aisha** 1912- [IAW]
*Egyptian author*
* El Shati, Bent

**[The] Abderite**
See Democritus

**Abderrahman**
See Duvalier, Francois

**Abdiel**
See Brooks, Joshua William

**Abdiel**
See Hull, Samuel

**Abdou, [Dr.] N. T.**
See Abdou, Nagib Antonius

**Abdou, Nagib Antonius** 1876- ?
[NAA]
*Syrian physician and author*
* Abdou, [Dr.] N. T.

**Abdul-Aleem, Shaheed**
See Scott, Charlie

**Abdul-Aziz, Zaid**
See Smith, Don[ald A.]

**Abdul Baha [Servant of Baha]**
See Abbas Effendi

**Abdul Ghafur** 1794-1874 [WBD]
*Saint*
* Akhund of Swat

**Abdul-Hamid, Sufi**
See Brown, Eugene

**Abdul-Hamid II** 1842-1918 [DEP]
*Sultan of Turkey*
* Abdul the Damned
* [The] Red Sultan

**Abdul-Jabbar, Kareem**
See Alcindor, [Ferdinand] Lew[is,
Jr.]

**Abdul Khaalis, Hamaas**
See McGee, Ernest Timothy

**Abdul-Rahman, Mahdi**
See Hazzard, Walt

**Abdul the Damned**
See Abdul-Hamid II

**Abdullah, Achmed**
See Romanoff, Alexander
Nicholayevitch

**Abdullah, Ahmed**
See Bland, Leroy

**Abdullah et Taaisha** 1846?-1899
[WBD]
*Arab leader*
* [The] Khalifa [Adviser]

**Abdullah, Mohammed**
See Howk, Joseph, Jr.

**Abdullah, Shakur**
See Weaver, Charles

**Abdulmajid, Iman Mohamed** 1955-
[IBW]
*Kenyan-born fashion model*
* Iman

**[The] Abe Lincoln of Baseball**
See Flood, Curtis Charles

**Abe the Newsboy**
See Hollandersky, Abraham

**Abel, Abe**
See Abel, Iorwith Wilbur

**Abel, Alan [Irwin]** 1928- [CA]
*American author*
* Bristol, Julius

**Abel, Alfred** 1880-1939 [F2]
*Actor*
* Schreck, Max

**Abel, Clarence John** 1900-1964
[CEI, FHE, HK]
*American hockey player*
\* Abel, Taffy

**Abel, Frederic Michel Maurice**
1903- [CA]
*Hungarian-born author and actor*
\* O'Brady, Frederic Michel
Maurice

**Abel, I. W.**
*See* Abel, Iorwith Wilbur

**Abel, Iorwith Wilbur** 1908-
*American labor leader*
\* Abel, Abe
\* Abel, I. W.

**Abel, Jeanne** 1937- [CA]
*American author*
\* Bronstein, Yetta

**Abel, Lionel**
*See* Abelson, Lionel

**Abel, Mrs. Peter E.** [FFF]
\* Hilda

**Abel, Ole Bootnose**
*See* Abel, Sid[ney Gerald]

**Abel, Robert** 1857-1936 [OCS]
*British cricketer*
\* [The] Guv'nor

**Abel, Rudolf Ivanovich** 20th c. [EE]
*Russian intelligence agent*
\* Goldfus, Emil R.

**Abel, Sid[ney Gerald]** 1918- [FHE]
*Canadian-born hockey player and
coach*
\* Abel, Ole Bootnose

**Abel, Taffy**
*See* Abel, Clarence John

**Abelin, Johann Philipp** 17th c.
[WBD]
*German historian*
\* Arlanibaus, Philipp
\* Gothofredus
\* Gottfried, Johann Ludwig

**Abell, Earl C.** 1892- [FB]
*American football player and coach*
\* Abell, Toughey

**Abell, Toughey**
*See* Abell, Earl C.

**Abell, William** [SN]
*British politician*
\* Alderman Medium

**Abels, Marcella Ruth** 20th c.
[BEW]
*American actress, theatre
administrator, director*
\* Cisney, Marcella

**Abelsohn, Frank** 1928- [FC]
*British entertainer and actor*
\* Vaughan, Frankie

**Abelson, Ann**
*See* Cavallaro, Ann [Abelson]

**Abelson, Lionel** 1910- [JL]
*Playwright and critic*
\* Abel, Lionel

**Abelson, Robert** 20th c. [OP]
*American opera singer*
\* Paul, Robert

**Aben-Ezra [or Esra]** 12th c.
[FFF, SN]
*Spanish clergyman*
\* [The] Wise

**Aber**
*See* Grundy, Wilfred Walker

**Aber, Albert Julius** 1927- [BE]
*American baseball player*
\* Aber, Lefty

**Aber, Lefty**
*See* Aber, Albert Julius

**Abercrombie, James [Baron
Dunfermline]** [FFF]
*British author*
\* Abacrombi, Signor

**Abercrombie, John** 1726-1806
[SN]
*Scottish author*
\* [The] Great Teacher of
Gardening

**Abercrombie, Lascelles** 1881-1938
[TC]
*British poet, critic, scholar*
\* [The] Georgian Laureate

**Aberdeen**
*See* McIntyre, Hugh D.

**[The] Aberdeen Assassin**
*See* Lomski, Leo

**Aberle, Kathleen Gough** 1925-
[CA]
*British-born anthropologist and
author*
\* Gough, Kathleen

**Abernathy, Tal**
*See* Abernathy, Talmadge
Lafayette

**Abernathy, Talmadge Lafayette**
1921- [BE]
*American baseball player*
\* Abernathy, Tal

**Abernathy, Virgil Woodrow** 1915-
[BE]
*American baseball player*
\* Abernathy, Woody

**Abernathy, Woody**
*See* Abernathy, Virgil Woodrow

**Abernethy, John** 1764?-1831?
[HN, RH, SN]
*British surgeon*
\* My Book, Doctor

**Abiatt, Roland** 20th c. [EE]
*Intelligence agent*
\* Rossi, Francois

**Abingdon, W. L.**
*See* Pilgrim, William Lepper

**Abisch, Roslyn Kroop [Roz]** 1927-
[CA, SAT]
*American author*
\* McGillicuddy, Mr.
\* Roche, A. K. [joint pseudonym
with Boche Kaplan]
\* Sniff, Mr.

**Ables, Hal**
*See* Ables, Harry Terrell

**Ables, Hans**
*See* Ables, Harry Terrell

**Ables, Harry Terrell** 1884-1951
[BE]
*American baseball player*
\* Ables, Hal
\* Ables, Hans

**Ablitzer, Alfred G.** 1889-1968
[WEC]
*American artist*
\* Zere, Al

**Abner, Gerald**
*See* Owen, Frank

**Abou Bekr** 573- 634 [SN]
*Founder of Islamic sect*
\* [The] Father of the Virgin

**Abou Giafar Abdallah** 712?- 775
[HHF, RH]
*Abbasside caliph*
\* Almansor [or Almanzor] [The
Invincible]

**Abou Hanifa** 699- 757? [HN]
*Founder of school of Moslem law*
\* [The] Socrates of the Musulmans

**About, Edmond Francois Valentin**
1828-1885 [SN]
*French journalist, author,
playwright*
\* [Le] Petit Fils de Voltaire

**Abrabanel, Judah Leon** ?-1535
[WBD]
*Spanish physician and poet*
\* Leo Hebraeus
\* Leon Hebreo

**Abrabanel, Solomon**
*See* Arnall, William

**Abrahall, C. H.**
*See* Hoskyns-Abrahall, Clare
[Constance Drury]

**Abrahall, Clare Hoskyns**
*See* Hoskyns-Abrahall, Clare
[Constance Drury]

**Abraham**
*See* Norwood, Abraham

**Abraham a Sancta [or Santa] Clara**
*See* Megerle, Hans Ulrich

**Abraham, David** 1909- [JL]
*Indian actor*
\* David

**Abraham, Gus** 1884-1933 [SC]
*American actor*
\* Orman, Felix

**Abraham, Irvin** 1909- [BEW]
*American composer, lyricist, writer*
\* Graham, Irvin

**Abraham, John** 1774?-1856 [WBD]
*British singer*
\* Braham, John

**Abraham, Martin** 1886- [WWJ]
*American jazz musician*
\* Martin, Chink

**Abraham, Martin, Jr.** 1918-
*American jazz musician*
\* Martin, Little Chink

**Abrahamian, Arousiak**
*See* Hashashian, Arousiak

**Abrahams, Abey**
*See* Abrahams, John

**Abrahams, Alan** 1926?-
*American business executive and
fraud suspect*
\* Carr, James

**Abrahams, Doris Caroline** 1901-
[WW]
*Author*
\* Brahms, Caryl
\* Linden, Oliver

**Abrahams, John** 1952- [DC]
*South African-born cricketer*
\* Abrahams, Abey

**Abrahams, Maurice** 1883-1931
[ASC, DAM]
*Russian-born composer and music
publisher*
\* Abrams, Maurie

**Abrahams, Sidney** 1885-1957
[EJS]
*British track and field athlete*
\* Abrahams, Solly

**Abrahams, Solly**
*See* Abrahams, Sidney

**Abrahamsen, Christine Elizabeth**
1916- [ESF, SFL, WGT]
*American author*
\* Cristabel
\* Westcott, Kathleen

**Abrahamsohn, Otto** 1856-1912
[BEW]
*German director, journalist, literary
historian*
\* Brahm, Otto

**Abrahamson, Mayer Ellis** 1917-
[BEW]
*American producer*
\* Ellis, Michael

**Abrhms, Terri**
*See* Ackerman, Forrest J[ames]

**Abram**
*See* Krylenko, Nikolai Vasilievich

**Abram, Eddie** 20th c. [RBE]
*American boxer*
\* Owens, Eddie

**Abramov, Emil**
*See* Draitser, Emil

**Abramovic, Brooms**
*See* Abramovic, John

**Abramovic, John** 1919- [BB]
*American basketball player*
\* Abramovic, Brooms

**Abramovitz, Anita [Zeltner Brooks]**
1914- [CA]
*American author*
\* Brooks, Anita

**Abramowicz, Abe**
*See* Abramowicz, Daniel [Danny]

**Abramowicz, Daniel [Danny]** 1945-
[FB]
*American football player*
\* Abramowicz, Abe

**Abramowitz, Joseph** 1911- [BEW]
*American entertainer*
\* Adams, Joey

**Abrams, George J[oseph]** 1918-
[CA]
*American author*
\* Hipp, George

**Abrams, Herbert Edward** 1937-
[OP]
*American opera singer*
* Ames, Richard

**Abrams, Lee**
*See* Abramson, Leon

**Abrams, Maurie**
*See* Abrahams, Maurice

**Abrams, Ray**
*See* Abramson, Raymond

**Abrams, Sam[uel]** 1935-   [CA]
*American poet*
* Newman, Frank

**Abramson, Leon** 1925-   [EJ]
*American jazz musician*
* Abrams, Lee

**Abramson, Raymond** 1920-   [EJ]
*American jazz musician*
* Abrams, Ray

**Abramson, Stanley J.** 20th c.
*Actor*
* Kramer, Stanley

**Abreu, Joseph Lawrence [Joe]**
1916-   [BE]
*American baseball player*
* [The] Magician

**Abrial, [Vice Admiral]** 20th c.
[CND]
*French military leader*
* Nord, Amiral [code name used
during World War II]

**Abricht, Johann**
*See* Birch, Jonathan

**Abromowitz, Sholem Yakob**
1836-1917   [CD, MWD]
*Russian-born Yiddish author*
* [The] Grandfather of Yiddish
Literature
* Mendele Mocher Sforim
[Mendele the Bookseller]

**Abruzzo, Raffaella Julia Theresa**
1926-   [BEW, TR]
*American actress and director*
* Allen, Rae

**Absolute Wisdom**
*See* Wood, [Sir] Matthew

**Abstein, Big Bill**
*See* Abstein, William Henry [Bill]

**Abstein, William Henry [Bill]**
1885-1940   [BE]
*American baseball player*
* Abstein, Big Bill

**Abu Abdallah [or Abdullah]**
?-1533?   [HN, WBD]
*King of Granada*
* Assaghir [Small]
* Boabdil
* [El] Chico [The Little]
* Mohammed XI

**Abu Daoud** [code name]
*See* Audeh, Muhammad Daoud

**Abu Hassan**
*See* Salameh, Ali Hassan

**Abu Iyad**
*See* Khalaf, Salah

**Abu Nadaar**
*See* Morrough, E. R.

**Abu Nidal**
*See* Banna, Sabri al-

**Abu Nuwas**
*See* Hasan ibn-Hani, al-

**Abu Sharein [Father of the Double
Evil]**
*See* Mohammed

**Abu Walid**
*See* Sayel, Saed

**Abubakari, Dara**
*See* Collins, Virginia E. V.

**Abullah, Zakariya** 1921-1969   [SC]
*American actor and singer*
* Scott, Leslie

**Abuna [Our Father]**
*See* Frumentius

**Aburthnot, John** 1675-1735   [PA]
*Author*
* P. P., Clerk of this Parish

**Abuza, Sophie** 1884?-1966
[BEW, BMH, NN]
*American entertainer*
* America's Foremost Jewish
Actress
* [The] Last of the Red Hot
Mamas
* [The] Mary Garden of Ragtime
* Tucker, Sophie
* [The] World Renowned Coon
Shouter

**Aby, Joe C.**   [PA]
*Author*
* Saw, Buck

**[The] Abyssinian Prince**
*See* Bridgetower, George Augustus
Polgreen

**Abzug, Battling Bella**
*See* Abzug, Bella Savitzky

**Abzug, Bella Savitzky** 1920-
*American politician*
* Abzug, Battling Bella

**Acacia**
*See* Clarens, Angel

**Academic Investor**
*See* Reddaway, W[illiam] Brian

**Academicus**
*See* Alison, William Pulteney

**Academicus**
*See* Loveday, John

**Academicus**
*See* Macaulay, Aula

**Academicus**
*See* Seager, Charles

**Acal, Luis Jacobo**
*See* Dominguez Aragones,
Edmundo

**Acante**
*See* Racine, Jean Baptiste

**Accardo, Anthony Joseph**
*See* Accardo, Antonio Leonardo

**Accardo, Antonio Leonardo** 1906-
[BLB, PHM]
*American underworld figure*
* Accardo, Anthony Joseph
* Accardo, Big Tuna
* Batters, Joe
* Batty, Joe

**Accardo, Big Tuna**
*See* Accardo, Antonio Leonardo

**[The] Accidental President**
*See* Adams, John Quincy

**[The] Accidental President**
*See* Fillmore, Millard

**[The] Accidental President**
*See* Tyler, John

**Accolti, Bernardo** 1465-1536   [FFF]
*Italian poet*
* [The] Only Aretino

**[The] Accomplished**
*See* Orsini, Giovanni Gaetano

**Accurate Angelo Bertelli**
*See* Bertelli, Angelo B.

**[The] Accusative**
*See* Chauvin [or Caulvin?], Jean

**Ace Clubs**
*See* Loftin, J. C.

**Ace, Johnny**
*See* Alexander, John M., Jr.

**Ace of Aces**
*See* Richenbacher, Edward

**Acfield, Ackers**
*See* Acfield, David Laurence

**Acfield, David Laurence** 1947-
[DC]
*British cricketer*
* Acfield, Ackers

**Acha Sanz, Raul** 1920-   [GS]
*Argentinian-born bullfighter*
* Rovira

**Achad Haam**
*See* Ginzberg, Asher

**Achaicus**
*See* Mummius, Lucius

**Acham, Bernard Ivan Felix** 1908-
[CA]
*Author*
* Chen, Jack

**Achard, George**
*See* Torres, Tereska [Szwarc]

**Achard, Louis Amede Eugene**
1814-1875   [PA]
*Author*
* Grimm

**Achard, Marcel**
*See* Ferreol, Marcel Auguste

**Achard, Marcel** 1892-1950   [CW]
*West Indian-born poet*
* Foyal, Jean

**Acharius**
*See* Scholander, Fredrik Wilhelm

**Ache, Jean**
*See* Huet, Jean

**Achebe, Chinua**
*See* Chinualumogu, Albert

**Achelis, Thomas** 1886-1929   [SC]
*American actor*
* Gordon, Paul

**Acher, Mathias**
*See* Birnbaum, Nathan

**Aches and Pains**
*See* Appling, Lucius Benjamin

**Acheta Domestica**
*See* Budgen, L. M.

**Achilles**
*See* Lamb, Charles Bentall

**[The] Achilles of England**
*See* Talbot, John

**[The] Achilles of England**
*See* Wellesley, Arthur

**[The] Achilles of Germany**
*See* Albert III [or Albrecht]

**[The] Achilles of Rome**
*See* Dentatus, Sicinius

**Achillini, Alessandro** 1463-1512
[DNNS]
*Italian physician and philosopher*
* [The] Second Aristotle

**Achte, Aino** 1876-1944   [BBD]
*Finnish opera singer*
* Ackte, Aino

**Achyut**
*See* Birla, Lakshminiwas N.

**Ack Ack, Sgt.**
*See* Ackerman, Forrest J[ames]

**Ack-Lak, General**
*See* Perry, A. T.

**Acker, Shoulders**
*See* Acker, Thomas James [Tom]

**Acker, Thomas James [Tom]** 1930-
[BE]
*American baseball player*
* Acker, Shoulders

**Ackerley, J. R.**
*See* Ackerley, Joe Randolph

**Ackerley, Joe Randolph** 1896-1967
[LC]
*British author*
* Ackerley, J. R.

**Ackerlos, John**
*See* Smith, John Stores

**Ackerman, Forrest J[ames]** 1916-
[ESF, SFP, WGT]
*American author*
* Abrahms, Terri
* Ack Ack, Sgt.
* Ackerman, Forry
* [The] Ackermonster
* Acula, Dr.
* Agricola, Sylvius
* Aldeano, Silvestre
* Angeleno, Les
* Ankh-er-man, Pharaoh J.
* Balboa, S. F.
* Beal, Nick
* Benson, Bobby
* Burke, Carl F.
* Carnell, Richard
* Chapnick, Norris
* Chinwell, Walter
* DM-92
* Eckman, J. Forester
* Eeee
* Efjay
* Erdstelulov
* Erman, Jack
* Erman, Jacques deForest
* Ermayne, Laurajean
* Farmington, Stone T.
* Farwest
* Filmonster, Mr.
* Fojak
* Ford, Garret [joint pseudonym
with Margaret Crawford, William
L. Crawford, etc.]
* Forijay
* 4 e

**Ackerman, Forrest J[ames]**
(Continued)
* 4 sJ
* GaPersono, Stran
* Giles, Geoffrey [joint pseudonym with Walter Gillings]
* Graystark, Chon
* Helding, Clair
* Hori
* Kamdois, Kurt
* Katolique, A. DeFout
* Kay, Marlene
* Kepac, Coil
* Kerlay, Allis
* Kerr, Joe
* Kover, Joe
* Lark, J. C.
* Lorraine, Alden
* Merrit, Katarin Markov
* Merritt, Aime
* Nader, Owen
* Nader, Seena
* Ornig, Graef
* Ralph 124E41
* Ralph 124TL41
* Rhodan, Forry
* Science Fiction, Mr.
* Strong, Spencer
* Torgosi, Karlon
* Torgosi, Vespertina
* Trentworth, Fisher
* Villette, Allis
* Virlup, A. Kvazau
* Voyant, Clair
* Wells, Hubert George
* Wright, Damon
* Wright, Robert [joint pseudonym with Robert Augustine Ward Lowndes]
* Wright, Weaver

**Ackerman, Forry**
*See* Ackerman, Forrest J[ames]

**Ackerman, Wendayne** 20th c.
[WGT]
*German-born American author*
* Dane, W. N.?
* Mondelle, Wendayne

**Ackermann, Alexander**
1446?-1506 [WBD]
*German composer*
* Agricola, Alexander

**Ackermann, Gottlieb**
*See* Mayer, Franz Xaver

**[The] Ackermonster**
*See* Ackerman, Forrest J[ames]

**Ackley, Florian Frederick** 1937-
[BE]
*American baseball player*
* Ackley, Fritz

**Ackley, Fritz**
*See* Ackley, Florian Frederick

**Acklom, Rauff De Ryther Duan**
1900?- [F2, FC]
*Canadian actor*
* Manners, David

**Ackte, Aino**
*See* Achte, Aino

**Ackworth, John**
*See* Smith, F. R.

**Acland, Alice**
*See* Wignall, Anne

**Aclea, Damaso Gil**
*See* Marquez y Gispert, Matias Felipe

**Aco, Lucas**
*See* Giarraputo, Lucas Thomas Aco

**Acomb, Evelyn Martha**
*See* Acomb-Walker, Evelyn

**Acomb-Walker, Evelyn** 1910- [CA]
*American historian and author*
* Acomb, Evelyn Martha

**Acontius, Jacobus** 1492?-1565?
[SN]
*Italian-born author*
* Intendente de Fortificazione

**Acorn**
*See* Oakes, James

**Acosta, Balmadero Pedro**
1896-1963 [BE]
*Cuban-born baseball player*
* Acosta, Merito

**Acosta, Cy**
*See* Acosta Miranda, Cecilio

**Acosta, Ed**
*See* Acosta, Eduardo Elixbeth Lopez

**Acosta, Eduardo Elixbeth Lopez**
1944- [BE]
*Panamanian-born baseball player*
* Acosta, Ed

**Acosta, Gabriel** 1587-1647
[PA, WBD]
*Portuguese philosopher and author*
* Acosta, Uriel
* Da Costa, Uriel
* Jurista

**Acosta, Merito**
*See* Acosta, Balmadero Pedro

**Acosta, Rodolfo**
*See* Hernandez, Rodolfo

**Acosta, Uriel**
*See* Acosta, Gabriel

**Acosta Miranda, Cecilio** 1946-
[SMG]
*Mexican-born baseball player*
* Acosta, Cy

**Acquanetta**
*See* Davenport, Burnu

**Acre, Stephen**
*See* Gruber, Frank

**Actaea**
*See* Agassiz, Elizabeth Cary

**Action Man**
*See* Sharp, Kevin

**Actius Sincerus**
*See* Sannazaro, Jacopo [or Giacomo]

**Acton, Edward J.** 1949- [CA]
*American author*
* Acton, Jay

**Acton, Jay**
*See* Acton, Edward J.

**Acton, Llewellin**
*See* Baxter, Wynne Edwin

**Acton, Thomas** 1662-1721 [PA]
*Author*
* Dupuy

**[The] Actor**
*See* Sutton, William Francis [Willie]

**[The] Actor Mimic**
*See* Williams, Bransby

**[The] Actress of One Hundred Voices**
*See* Wentworth, Verna

**Acuff, Roy** 1903- [CME, PMJ]
*American country-western performer*
* [The] King of Country Music

**Acula, Dr.**
*See* Ackerman, Forrest J[ames]

**Acuto, John** ?-1390 [PA]
*Author*
* Harkwood

**Adachi, Barbara [Curtis]** 1924-
[CA]
*Chinese-born columnist*
* Anthony, Catherine

**Adail, Terry** 1921- [BWW]
*American singer*
* Terry, Doc

**Adair, Bill**
*See* Adair, Marion Danne

**Adair, Cecil**
*See* Everett-Green, Evelyn

**Adair, Choppy**
*See* Adair, James Audrey [Jimmy]

**Adair, Dennis**
*See* Cronin, Bernard [Charles]

**Adair, Hazel**
*See* Addis, Hazel Iris Wilson

**Adair, James**
*See* Phillips, [Sir] Richard

**Adair, James Audrey [Jimmy]**
1907- [BE]
*American baseball player*
* Adair, Choppy

**Adair, Janice**
*See* Duffy, Beatrice

**Adair, Jean**
*See* McNaughton, Violet

**Adair, Marie**
*See* Loftus, Mrs. W. F.

**Adair, Marion Danne** 1916- [BE]
*American baseball manager*
* Adair, Bill

**Adair, Paul Neal** 1916-
*American oilwell troubleshooter*
* Adair, Red

**Adair, Red**
*See* Adair, Paul Neal

**Adair, Towle**
*See* Jagendorf, M.

**Adair, Yvonne**
*See* Bornshine, Yvonne Vivienne

**Adalbert** ?-981 [DNNS]
*Saint*
* [The] Apostle of the Slavs

**Adalbert [or Adelbert]** 955?-997
[DNNS, WBD]
*Saint*
* [The] Apostle of the Prussians
* Vojtech

**Adalbert, Max**
*See* Krampf, Max

**Adam**
*See* Clough, Arthur Hugh

**Adam, Ben**
*See* Drachman, Julian M[oses]

**Adam, Christian**
*See* Andersen, Carl Christian Thorvaldus

**Adam, Cornel**
*See* Lengyel, Cornel Adam

**Adam de la Halle** 1235?-1285
[WBD]
*French musician and playwright*
* Adam le Bossu

**Adam, Don**
*See* Sellers, Connie Leslie, Jr.

**Adam, Juliette** 1836-1936 [WBD]
*French author*
* Lamber, Juliette
* [La] Messine
* Vasili, [Comte] Paul

**Adam le Bossu**
*See* Adam de la Halle

**Adam of Bremen** ?-1076 [HN]
*German ecclesiastical historian*
* Adamus Magister

**Adam, Robert James** 1924-
[ESF, SFL]
*Scottish author*
* MacTyre, Paul

**Adamantius**
*See* Origen

**Adamberger, Valentin** 1743-1804
[WBD]
*Austrian opera singer*
* Adamonti

**Adamonti**
*See* Adamberger, Valentin

**Adamowicz, Adam** 1760-1812 [PA]
*Author*
* Woyda

**Adams, A. Don**
*See* Cleveland, Philip Jerome

**Adams, Abigail** ?-1955 [SC]
*Actress*
* Adams, Tommye

**Adams, Abigail Smith** 1744-1818
[FFF]
*American writer and wife of President John Adams*
* Diana
* Portia

**Adams, Ace**
*See* Adams, Emery

**Adams, Ace**
*See* Adams, James Frederic

**Adams, Ace**
*See* Adams, Stanley

**Adams, Ada** 1862-1953 [THR]
*British actress*
* Blanche, Ada

**Adams, Agnes** 1891- [WWL]
*British author*
* Logan, Agnes

**Adams, Alexander Maxwell** [PA]
*Author*
* [An] Antiquary

**Adams, Annette**
*See* Rowland, D[onald] S[ydney]

**Adams, Anthony L.** 1950-   [FB]
*American football player*
* Adams, Touchdown Tony

**Adams, Arthur Henry** 1872-1936
[WWL]
*New Zealand-born author,
playwright, poet*
* James, James

**Adams, Atomic**
See  Scruggs, Faye

**Adams, Babe**
See  Adams, Charles Benjamin

**Adams, Bart**
See  Bingley, David Ernest

**Adams, Bertram Martin** 1879- ?
[WBD]
*British-born author and poet*
* Adams, Bill

**Adams, Betsy**
See  Pitcher, Gladys

**Adams, Betty May** 1926?-
[FC, ITA, SW]
*American actress*
* Adams, Julie [or Julia]

**Adams, Bill**
See  Adams, Bertram Martin

**Adams, Bret**
See  Adams, John Wallace

**Adams, Bud**
See  Adams, Kenneth Stanley, Jr.

**Adams, Buster**
See  Adams, Elvin Clark

**Adams, Carol Wayne** 1936-1967
[SC]
*American actor*
* Adams, Jeff

**Adams, Casey**
See  Showalter, Max

**Adams, Charles Baker** 1814-1853
[FFF, PA]
*American naturalist and author*
* Templeton, Timothy

**Adams, Charles Benjamin**
1882?-1968   [AS, DGS, PB]
*American baseball player*
* Adams, Babe

**Adams, Charles Dwight** 1921-
[SMG]
*American baseball coach*
* Adams, Red

**Adams, Charles Follen**   [PA]
*Author*
* Strauss, Yawcob

**Adams, Christopher**
See  Hopkins, Kenneth

**Adams, Chuck**
See  Tubb, Edwin Charles

**Adams, Clayton**
See  Holmes, Charles Henry

**Adams, Cleve F[ranklin]**
1895-1949?  [CC, EMD, WW]
*American author*
* Charles, Franklin
* Spain, John

**Adams, Clifton** 1919-   [CA]
*American author*
* Gant, Jonathan
* Kinkaid, Matt

**Adams, Clifton** (Continued)
* Randall, Clay

**Adams, Cyrus C.**   [PA]
*Author*
* C. C. A.

**Adams, Dale**
See  Quinn, Elisabeth

**Adams, Dan[iel Leslie]** 1889-1964
[BE]
*American baseball player*
* Adams, Rube

**Adams, Derek John** 1942-   [IAW]
*British journalist and author*
* [The] Squire

**Adams, Derroll**
See  Thompson, Derroll Lewis

**Adams, Donna**
See  Mullenger, Donna

**Adams, Dooley**
See  Adams, Frank David

**Adams, Earl John** 1894-   [BE, BN]
*American baseball player*
* Adams, Spark Plug
* Adams, Sparky

**Adams, Edie**
See  Enke, Elizabeth Edith

**Adams, Elvin Clark** 1915-   [BE]
*American baseball player*
* Adams, Buster

**Adams, Emery** 20th c.   [OBW]
*American baseball player*
* Adams, Ace

**Adams, F[rank] Ramsay**
1883-1963   [CA]
*American author*
* Dane, Carl

**Adams, F. W.**   [PA]
*Author*
* Shaker

**Adams, Faye**
See  Scruggs, Faye

**Adams, Florence Victoria** ?-1979
[IBW]
*American educator*
* Adams, Frankie V.

**Adams, Frank David** 20th c.   [BBH]
*American jockey*
* Adams, Dooley

**Adams, Frankie V.**
See  Adams, Florence Victoria

**Adams, Franklin Pierce** 1881-1960
[NAA, TC]
*American journalist and author*
* F. P. A.

**Adams, George**
See  Lengyel, Geza

**Adams, George** 20th c.   [BE]
*American baseball player*
* Adams, Partridge

**Adams, Georgia Sachs** 1913-   [CA]
*American educator and author*
* Sachs, Georgia

**Adams, Harriet S[tratemeyer]** 20th
c.  [B10, CA, SAT]
*American author*
* Appleton, Victor, II [house
  pseudonym] [Stratemeyer
  Syndicate]

**Adams, Harriet S[tratemeyer]**
(Continued)
* Barton, May Hollis [house
  pseudonym] [Stratemeyer
  Syndicate]
* Dixon, Franklin W. [house
  pseudonym] [Stratemeyer
  Syndicate]
* Hope, Laura Lee [house
  pseudonym] [Stratemeyer
  Syndicate]
* Keene, Carolyn [house
  pseudonym] [Stratemeyer
  Syndicate]

**Adams, Harrison**
See  Rathborne, St. George

**Adams, Harrison**
See  Stratemeyer, Edward L.

**Adams, Henry H[itch]** 1917-   [CA]
*American author*
* Allen, Henry [joint pseudonym]

**Adams, Henry Joseph** 20th c.
[LAO]
*Australian clergyman and author*
* Ignotus

**Adams, Henry T.**
See  Ransom, Jay Ellis

**Adams, Herbert** 1874-1952
[CC, EMD, WW]
*British author*
* Gray, Jonathan

**Adams, J.** 20th c.   [SFL, WGT]
*Author*
* Kuppord, Skelton

**Adams, J. B.**   [FFF]
*American author*
* Kit

**Adams, J. T.**
See  Adams, John Tyler

**Adams, Jack**
See  Grigsby, Alcanoan O.

**Adams, James Frederic** 1928-
[BBH]
*American lacrosse player and coach*
* Adams, Ace

**Adams, James Irwin** 1890-1937
[BE]
*American baseball player*
* Adams, Willie

**Adams, Jeff**
See  Adams, Carol Wayne

**Adams, Joey**
See  Abramowitz, Joseph

**Adams, John**
See  McLaren, J. A.

**Adams, John** 1735-1826
[DEP, FAP, SN]
*American president*
* [The] Atlas of Independence
* [The] Colossus of Debate
* [The] Colossus of Independence
* [The] Duke of Braintree
* [The] Father of American
  Independence
* [The] Father of the American
  Navy
* His Rotundity
* Novanglus
* Old Sink and Swim
* [The] Partisan of Independence

**Adams, John** 1760?-1829   [WBD]
*British seaman*
* Smith, Alexander

**Adams, John J. [Jack]** 1895-1968
[FHE]
*Canadian-born hockey player,
coach, league official*
* Adams, Jovial Jawn

**Adams, John Paul**
See  Kinnaird, Clark

**Adams, John Quincy** 1767-1848
[DEP, FAP, PA]
*American president*
* [The] Accidental President
* Old Man Eloquent
* Publicola
* [The] Second John

**Adams, John Tyler** 1911-   [BWW]
*American singer*
* Adams, J. T.

**Adams, John W.** 1921-1969
[AS, SMG]
*American football player*
* Adams, Tree

**Adams, John Wallace** 1930-   [BEW]
*American producer and talent
representative*
* Adams, Bret

**Adams, Joseph Edward [Joe]**
1877-1952   [BE]
*American baseball player*
* Adams, Wagon Tongue

**Adams, Jovial Jawn**
See  Adams, John J. [Jack]

**Adams, Judith**
See  Morgan, Judith A[dams]

**Adams, Julie [or Julia]**
See  Adams, Betty May

**Adams, Justin**
See  Cameron, Lou

**Adams, Karl Tutwiler** 1891-1967
[BE]
*American baseball player*
* Adams, Rebel

**Adams, Kenneth Stanley, Jr.** 20th
c.  [SMG]
*American football executive*
* Adams, Bud

**Adams, Laurie** 1941-   [CA]
*American art historian and author*
* Schneider, Laurie

**Adams, Louis J. A.** [joint pseudonym
with Alexei Panshin]
See  Hensley, Joe Louis

**Adams, Louis J. A.** [joint pseudonym
with Joe Louis Hensley]
See  Panshin, Alexei

**Adams, Lowell**
See  Joseph, James Herz

**Adams, Lynn**
See  Boudin, Katherine [Kathy]

**Adams, Mary**
See  Ward, Elizabeth Stuart
[Phelps]

**Adams, Maud**
See  Wikstrom, Maud

**Adams, Moses**
See  Bagby, George W.

**Adams, Mrs. Mark**   [FFF]
*Entertainer*
* Wilde, Susie

**Adams, Nicholas**
*See* Anspach, Nathan

**Adams, Nick**
*See* Adamschock, Nicholas

**Adams, Park** 1930-   [DAM, EJ]
*American jazz musician*
* Adams, Pepper

**Adams, Partridge**
*See* Adams, George

**Adams, Pepper**
*See* Adams, Park

**Adams, Rebel**
*See* Adams, Karl Tutwiler

**Adams, Red**
*See* Adams, Charles Dwight

**Adams, Reuben Alexander**
1878-1955   [BE]
*American baseball player*
* Adams, Rick

**Adams, Rich**
*See* Sellers, Connie Leslie, Jr.

**Adams, Richard N[ewbold]** 1924-
[CA]
*American anthropologist and author*
* Newbold, Stokes

**Adams, Rick**
*See* Adams, Reuben Alexander

**Adams, Robert [Franklin]** 1932-
[CA]
*American author*
* Adamson, Frank
* Eberhardt, Peter

**Adams, Robert** 20th c.   [THR]
*British actor and wrestler*
* Black Eagle

**Adams, Robert Martin**
*See* Krapp, R. M.

**Adams, Rube**
*See* Adams, Dan[iel Leslie]

**Adams, Samuel** 1722-1803
[FFF, HN, SN]
*American statesman and
revolutionary leader*
* Alfred
* [The] American Cato
* [The] Cromwell of New England
* [The] Father of America
* [The] Last of the Puritans
* [The] Man of the Revolution
* Sammy the Publican

**Adams, Samuel Hopkins**
1871-1958   [WW]
*American author*
* Fabian, Warner

**Adams, Spark Plug**
*See* Adams, Earl John

**Adams, Sparky**
*See* Adams, Earl John

**Adams, Stanley** 1926-   [IBW]
*American music publisher and
songwriter*
* Adams, Ace

**Adams, Stephen**
*See* Maybrick, Michael

**Adams, Tommye**
*See* Adams, Abigail

**Adams, Touchdown Tony**
*See* Adams, Anthony L.

**Adams, Tree**
*See* Adams, John W.

**Adams, W. H. D.** 19th c.   [PA]
*Author*
* Clinton, Walter

**Adams, Wagon Tongue**
*See* Adams, Joseph Edward [Joe]

**Adams, Weld**
*See* Bank, Theodore P[aul], II
[Ted]

**Adams, Will**
*See* Neal, John

**Adams, Will** 1575?-1620   [WBD]
*British navigator*
* Anjin Sama [Mr. Pilot]

**Adams, William Edward** 1866- ?
[NAA]
*American educator and author*
* Gardiner, Clarke

**Adams, William Taylor** 1822-1897
[PA, SAT]
*American author*
* Ashton, Warren T.
* Optic, Oliver [joint pseudonym
with Edward L. Stratemeyer]

**Adams, Willie**
*See* Adams, James Irwin

**Adamschock, Nicholas** 1931-1968
[FC]
*American actor*
* Adams, Nick

**Adamson, Frances A.** 20th c.
[WWL]
*British author*
* Gray, Esca

**Adamson, Frank**
*See* Adams, Robert [Franklin]

**Adamson, Graham**
*See* Groom, Arthur William

**Adamson, Iaian Beaton** 1928-
[IAW]
*Scottish-born author*
* Beaton, Chris
* Macadam, Ian

**Adamson, Joseph, III [Joe]** 1945-
[CA]
*American author and screenwriter*
* Wintergreen, Warren

**Adamson, Penrhyn Stanley**
1877-1923   [FD]
*Scottish-born director*
* Stanlaws, Penrhyn

**Adamson, Victor**
*See* Dixon, Denver

**Adamus, Franz**
*See* Bronner, Ferdinand

**Adamus Magister**
*See* Adam of Bremen

**Adani, Laura** 1934-   [OP]
*Italian opera singer*
* Adani, Mariella

**Adani, Mariella**
*See* Adani, Laura

**Aday, Marvin Lee** 1949?-
*American singer*
* Meat Loaf

**Adcock, Almey St. John** 1894-
[CA]
*British author*
* March, Hilary

**Adcock, [Arthur] St. John**
1864-1930   [LAO, LC]
*British author*
* Flecknor, Richard
* Rutland, Arthur

**Adderley, Cannonball**
*See* Adderley, Julian Edwin

**Adderley, Julian Edwin** 1928-1975
[B10, DAM, EJ]
*American jazz musician*
* Adderley, Cannonball

**Addie**
*See* Cooley, Adelaide J.

**Addington, Henry [First Viscount
Sidmouth]** 1757-1844
[DNNF, DNNS, FFF]
*British statesman*
* [The] Doctor

**Addington, Sarah**
*See* Reid, Sarah Addington

**Addis, Eric Elrington** 20th c.   [WW]
*Author*
* Drax, Peter

**Addis, H. I.**
*See* Addis, Hazel Iris Wilson

**Addis, Hazel Iris Wilson** 1900-
[SFL, WGT]
*British author*
* Adair, Hazel
* Addis, H. I.
* Heritage, A. J.
* Mao?

**Addiscombe, John**
*See* Hunter, [Alfred] John

**Addison**
*See* Walker, [Addison] Mort[imer]

**Addison, Carol**
*See* Clarke, J. Calvitt

**Addison, D. C.**
*See* Daniell, Charles Addison

**Addison, Fannie**
*See* Pitt, Mrs. H. M.

**Addison, Gwen**
*See* Harris, Alf[red]

**Addison, Hugh**
*See* Owen, [Harry] Collinson

**Addison, Joseph** 1672-1719
[DEL, HN, PA]
*British author, poet, statesman*
* Atticus
* Clio
* [The] English Atticus
* [A] Literary Machiavel

**Addison, Katharine** 20th c.   [WWL]
*British author*
* Anson, Kathleen

**[The] Addison of America**
*See* Dennie, Joseph

**[The] Addison of the North**
*See* Mackenzie, Henry

**Addums, Mozis**
*See* Bagby, George W.

**Addy, Robert Edward [Bob]**
1838-1910   [BE]
*American baseball player and
manager*
* [The] Magnet

**Addy, Ted**
*See* Winterbotham, Russell Robert

**Adelaer [or Adeler]**
*See* Sivertsen, Cort

**Adelaide**
*See* Bogart, Elizabeth

**Adelberg, Doris**
*See* Orgel, Doris

**Adeler, Max**
*See* Clark, Charles Heber

**Adeline**
*See* Sergeant, Emily Frances
Adeline

**Adell, Ilunga**
*See* Stevenson, William Adell

**Adelstein, Milton** 1925-   [ASC]
*American composer, pianist,
conductor*
* Rogers, Milt

**Adeodatus I**
*See* Deusdedit

**Ader, Paul [Fassett]** 1919-
[ANT, CA]
*American author*
* Allen, James

**Adersey Curiosibhoy**
*See* Moore, Joseph Solomon

**Adirondack**
*See* Chittenden, L. E.

**Adix, LaVern** 1912-   [BEW]
*American theatrical educator,
director, designer*
* Adix, Vern

**Adix, Vern**
*See* Adix, LaVern

**Adkin, Knight**
*See* Knight-Adkin, James Harry

**Adkins, Babe**
*See* Adkins, Merle Theron

**Adkins, Butcher Boy**
*See* Adkins, Grady Emmett

**Adkins, Doc**
*See* Adkins, Merle Theron

**Adkins, Dorothy C.** 1912-   [CA]
*American educator and author*
* Wood, Dorothy Adkins

**Adkins, Grady Emmett** 1897-1966
[BE]
*American baseball player*
* Adkins, Butcher Boy

**Adkins, Merle Theron** 1872-1934
[BE]
*American baseball player*
* Adkins, Babe
* Adkins, Doc

**Adlam, Basil G.** 20th c.   [ASC]
*British-born composer, conductor,
musician*
* Adlam, Buzz

**Adlam, Buzz**
*See* Adlam, Basil G.

**Adlard, Mark**
*See* Adlard, Peter Marcus

**Adlard, Peter Marcus** 1932-
[ESF, SFL]
*British author*
* Adlard, Mark

**Adler, Buddy**
*See* Adler, Maurice

**Adler, Irene**
*See* Penzler, Otto

**Adler, Irene**
*See* Storr, Catherine [Cole]

**Adler, Irving** 1913-
[CA, SAT, TBJ]
*American author and educator*
* Irving, Robert

**Adler, Jacob** 1873?-1974
[B10, CA, NAA]
*Austrian-born American Yiddish
humorist and writer*
* Kovner, B.

**Adler, Jacob Pavlovitch** ?-1926
*Russian-born American actor*
* [The] Great Eagle

**Adler, Kaspar** 1488-1560 [WBD]
*Bavarian theologian*
* Aquila, Kaspar

**Adler, Kathleen**
*See* Jones, Kathleen Eve

**Adler, Lulla**
*See* Rosenfeld, Lulla

**Adler, Lutha** 1903- [BEW, TR]
*American actor and director*
* Adler, Luther

**Adler, Luther**
*See* Adler, Lutha

**Adler, Maurice** 1908?-1960
[BEW, FC, WEF]
*American producer, film executive,
writer*
* Adler, Buddy

**Adler, Philip** 1484-1539 [PA]
*Author*
* Patricius

**Adler, Sarah**
*See* Levitzka, Sarah

**Adler, William [Bill]** 1929- [CA]
*American author*
* David, Jay

**Adlersparre, Carl August** [FFF]
*German poet and author*
* Albano

**[The] Admirable Crichton**
*See* Crichton, James

**[The] Admirable Doctor**
*See* Bacon, Roger

**[The] Admiral of the Lakes**
*See* Newberry, Oliver

**Admiral Q** [code name used during
World War II]
*See* Roosevelt, Franklin Delano

**Adnopoz, Elliott Charles** 1931-
[DAM, FCW]
*American singer and guitarist*
* Elliott, Buck

**Adnopoz, Elliott Charles** (Continued)
* Elliott, Jack
* Elliott, Ramblin' Jack

**Adoian, Vosdanik** 1904?-1948
*Armenian-born painter*
* Gorky, Arshile

**Adolbert, Bela**
*See* Turpinszky, Bela

**Adolf of Nassau**
*See* William August Charles
Frederick Adolf

**Adolfo**
*See* Sardina, Adolfo

**Adone, Joe**
*See* Doto, Giuseppe

**Adonis**
*See* Sa'id, Ali Ahmad

**Adonis, Joe**
*See* Doto, Giuseppe

**Adonis, Michael**
*See* Sellers, Connie Leslie, Jr.

**Adony, Raoul**
*See* Launay, Andrew [Joseph]

**Adoree, Renee**
*See* De La Fonte, Jeanne

**Adorno, Theodor**
*See* Wiesengrund, Theodor

**Adri**
*See* Steckling, Adri

**Adriaanszoon, Adriaan**
*See* Metius, Adriaan

**Adrian**
*See* Greenburgh, Gilbert Adrian

**Adrian, Frances**
*See* Polland, Madeleine A[ngela]

**Adrian, Iris**
*See* Hostetter, Iris Adrian

**Adrian, Mary**
*See* Jorgensen, Mary Venn

**Adrian, Max**
*See* Bor, Max

**Adrian IV**
*See* Breakspear, Nicholas

**Adrian V**
*See* Fieschi, Ottobono

**Adrian VI**
*See* Florensz, Adrian

**Adriance, Jane Sterling** 1923-
[BEW, FC, TR]
*American actress*
* Sterling, Jan [or Jane]

**Adrienne, Jean**
*See* Armstrong, Jean

**Adry-Carene**
*See* Carrenard, Adrien

**Advena**
*See* Starkey, Digley Pilot

**Adytum**
*See* Curl, James Stevens

**Adzak, Roy**
*See* Wright, Royston

**Aeby, Jacquelyn** 20th c. [CA]
*American author*
* Carew, Jocelyn

**Aeby, Jacquelyn** (Continued)
* Gray, Vanessa

**Aegidius of Assisi** ?-1262 [WBD]
*Companion of St. Francis of Assisi*
* Blessed Giles

**Aegidius [or Giles] of Colonna**
1247-1316 [HN, RH, SN]
*Archbishop of Bourges*
* [The] Doctor with Good
Foundations
* Fundatissimus, Doctor
* [The] Most Profound Doctor
* Princeps Theologorum
* Profundissimus, Doctor
* [The] Well Founded Doctor

**Aegocerus**
*See* Brown, Edgar Rogers

**Aelfgifu**
*See* Emma

**Aelfric** ?-1051 [SN]
*Archbishop of York*
* [The] Kite

**Aelfric** 955?-1020? [SN]
*British abbot and author*
* Grammaticus

**Aemilius Paulus, Lucius** 2nd c. BC
[FFF, RH, WBD]
*Roman general*
* Macedonicus

**Aerbel, Dan**
*See* Ert, Dan

**Aeron, Idris**
*See* Williams, Idris Elgina

**Aeschines**
*See* Blagdon, Francis William

**Aeschylus** 5th c. BC
[DEP, HN, SN]
*Greek playwright*
* [The] Father of Greek Drama
* [The] Father of Greek Tragedy
* [The] Father of Tragedy
* [The] Founder of the Greek
Drama

**Aesop**
*See* Blake, Lillie Devereux

**Aesop, George Washington**
*See* Lanigan, George Thomas

**[The] Aesop of England**
*See* Gay, John

**[The] Aesop of France**
*See* La Fontaine, Jean de

**[The] Aesop of Germany**
*See* Lessing, Gotthold Ephraim

**Aethelflaed [Aethelfled or Elflida]** ?-
918? [DHA, DNNS, RH]
*Daughter of King Alfred of England*
* [The] Lady of the Mercians

**[The] Aetheling**
*See* Edgar [or Eadgar]

**Aetion**
*See* Shakespeare, William

**Aetius, Flavius** 396?-454
[DEP, RH, SN]
*Roman general*
* [The] Last of the Romans

**Aetius of Antioch** ?-367 [WBD]
*Syrian theologian*
* [The] Atheist
* [The] Ungodly

**Afer**
*See* Arnobius

**[L']Affable**
*See* Charles VIII

**[The] Affable**
*See* Santi [or Sanzio?], Raffaello

**Affable Hawk**
*See* MacCarthy, [Sir] Desmond

**Affable, Sir**
*See* Knowles, Alec

**Affif, Charles** 20th c. [SG]
*Boxer*
* Zivic, Charlie

**Afflis, Richard** 20th c.
*American wrestler*
* Dick the Bruiser

**Afonski, Nicholas** 20th c. [WECO]
*American cartoonist*
* Afonsky, N.

**Afonsky, N.**
*See* Afonski, Nicholas

**Africa, Ben**
*See* Swemmer, B. Northling

**[The] African**
*See* Leo, Juan

**[The] African Flying Queen**
*See* Annum, Alice

**[The] African Roscius**
*See* Aldridge, Ira Frederick

**[The] African Tragedian**
*See* Aldridge, Ira Frederick

**[O] Africano**
*See* Alfonso V [or Affonso]

**Africano, Lillian** 1935- [CA]
*American writer, columnist, critic*
* Atallah, Lillian

**Africanus**
*See* Gordianus I, Marcus Antonius

**Africanus**
*See* Melland, Frank Hulme

**Afrique**
*See* Witkins, Alexander

**Afton, Effie**
*See* Harper, Frances Ellen Watkins

**Aga Khan I**
*See* Hasan Ali Shah

**Aga Khan III**
*See* Aga Sultan Sir Mahomed
Shah

**Aga Sultan Sir Mahomed Shah**
1877-1957 [WBD]
*Moslem religious leader*
* Aga Khan III

**Agajanian, Automatic**
*See* Agajanian, Benjamin

**Agajanian, Benjamin** 1919- [FB]
*American football player*
* Agajanian, Automatic

**Agajanian, Joshua James** [EAR]
*Auto racer*
* J. C.

**Agam, Yaacov**
*See* Gipstein, Yaacov

**Agapida, [Friar] Antonio**
*See* Irving, Washington

**Agar, Brian**
*See* Ballard, [Willis] Todhunter

**Agar, Dan**
*See* Davis, Dan

**Agard, Clifford** 1942?-  [CW]
*Guyanese playwright and poet*
* Ali, Jamal

**Agard, H. E.**
*See* Evans, Hilary

**Agarossi, Elena** 1940-  [CA]
*Italian historian and author*
* Rossi, Aga

**Agassiz, Elizabeth Cary**
1822-1907  [FFF, PA]
*American author and educator*
* Actaea

**Agate**
*See* Reid, Whitelaw

**Agatha**
*See* Lawrence, Bessie

**Agathon**
*See* Massis, Henri

**Agati, James** 20th c.  [SG]
*Boxer*
* [The] East Side Assassin
* O'Gatty, Jimmy

**Agati, Pasquale** 1900-1966  [BX]
*Italian-born boxer*
* O'Gatty, Packey
* Speed Demon

**Agatstein, Mieczyslaw** 1903-
[EWL]
*Polish author*
* Jastrun, Mieczyslaw

**Agca, Mehmet Ali** 20th c.
*Turk accused of attempted
assassination of Pope John Paul II*
* Ozgun, Faruk

**Age**
*See* Incrocci, Agenore

**Aged Eagle**
*See* Eliot, Thomas Stearns

**Agee, Ray[mond Clinton]** 1930-
[BWW]
*American singer*
* Agee, Roy
* Egge, Ray
* Little Ray
* Ray, Isom

**Agee, Roy**
*See* Agee, Ray[mond Clinton]

**Agent 55**
*See* Longhurst, Percy William

**Agganis, Greek**
*See* Agganis, Harry

**Agganis, Harry** 1930-1955
[AS, FB]
*American football and baseball
player*
* Agganis, Greek
* [The] Golden Greek

**[The] Aggressor**
*See* Charles X

**Aggrey, James Emman Kodwo Mensa
Humanfunsam Kwegyir** 1872-1927
[IBW]
*African educator*
* [The] Father of African
Education

**Aghill, Gordon** [joint pseudonym
with Robert Silverberg]
*See* Garrett, [Gordon] Randall
[Philip David]

**Aghill, Gordon** [joint pseudonym
with Randall Garrett]
*See* Silverberg, Robert

**Aginsky, Bernard W[illard]** 1905-
[CA]
*American anthropologist and author*
* Aginsky, Burt W.

**Aginsky, Burt W.**
*See* Aginsky, Bernard W[illard]

**Aglassinger, Andreas** 1895-1940
[SC]
*Austrian-born actor and circus
performer*
* Raffles Bill

**Agle, Anna Bradford Hayden**
1905-  [FBJ]
*American author*
* Agle, Nan

**Agle, Nan**
*See* Agle, Anna Bradford Hayden

**Agnes**
*See* McClintock, Minda Agnes

**Agnesi, Maria Gaetana** 1718-1799
[FFF]
*Italian mathematician*
* [The] Walking Polyglot

**Agnew, Agnes**
*See* Agnew, Jonathan Philip

**Agnew, Edith J[osephine]** 1897-
[CAP, SAT]
*American author*
* Marcelino

**Agnew, Emily C.**  [PA]
*Author*
* E. C. A.

**Agnew, Jonathan Philip** 1960-
[DC]
*British cricketer*
* Agnew, Agnes
* Agnew, Spiro

**Agnew, Spiro**
*See* Agnew, Jonathan Philip

**Agnew, Stephen Hamilton**  ?-1915
[MBF]
*British author*
* Allyne, Roy
* Stephens, Arthur
* Stephens, Kenneth
* Summers, Colin

**Agnew, Walter L.** 1884-1941  [FC]
*American actor*
* Fields, Stanley

**Agnon, S[hmuel] Y[osef]**
*See* Czaczkes, Shmuel Yosef

**Ago, Felix**
*See* Haldeman, Samuel Stehman

**Agogas**
*See* Davy, Charles William

**Agoglia, Fiore** 20th c.  [BLB]
*American underworld figure*
* Agoglia, Fury

**Agoglia, Fury**
*See* Agoglia, Fiore

**Agoult, Comtesse d'**
*See* De Flavigny, Marie Catherine
Sophie

**Agreda, Maria de**
*See* Fernandez Coronel, Maria

**Agress, Mitchell** 1910-1969  [PMJ]
*American bandleader*
* Ayres, Mitch[ell]

**Agricola**
*See* Anderson, James

**Agricola**
*See* Elliott, William

**Agricola**
*See* Nicholas, Philip Norborne

**Agricola**
*See* Stockdale, Percival

**Agricola**
*See* Whitehouse, W. F.

**Agricola**
*See* Young, John

**Agricola, Alexander**
*See* Ackermann, Alexander

**Agricola, Georgius**
*See* Bauer, Georg

**Agricola, Johannes**
*See* Sneider, Johannes

**Agricola, Martin**
*See* Sohr [or Sore], Martin

**Agricola, Rodolphus**
*See* Huysman [or Huysmann],
Roelof

**Agricola, Sylvius**
*See* Ackerman, Forrest J[ames]

**Agrikler**
*See* Edwards, Joseph

**Agrilupo**
*See* Trissino, Giulio

**Agrippa**
*See* Herod Agrippa I [or Julius
Agrippa I]

**Agrippa, [Cornelius] Heinrich**
1486?-1535  [SN, WBD]
*German physician and theologian*
* Agrippa von Nettesheim
* [The] Omniscious Doctor

**Agrippa von Nettesheim**
*See* Agrippa, [Cornelius] Heinrich

**Agrippina**  ?- 33  [WBD]
*Roman heroine*
* Vipsania Agrippina

**Agudo, Angel** 1946-  [GS]
*Spanish bullfighter*
* [El] Greco [The Greek]

**Aguecheek**
*See* Fairbanks, Charles Bullard

**Aguesseau, Henri Francois d'**
*See* Daguesseau, Henri Francois

**Aguilar Gonzalez, Jorge** 1927-
[GS]
*Mexican bullfighter*
* [El] Ranchero [The Rancher]

**Aguirre Garcia, Antonio**
1885-1954  [GS]
*Mexican bullfighter*
* Conejo Grande [Big Rabbit]

**Agujari, Lucrezia** 1743-1783  [SN]
*Italian opera singer*
* [La] Bastardina

**Agus, Irving A[braham]**
*See* Agushewitz, Irving A[braham]

**Agushewitz, Irving A[braham]**
1910-  [CAP]
*Polish-born American author and
educator*
* Agus, Irving A[braham]

**Agyeman, Jaramogi Abebe**
*See* Cleage, Albert Buford, Jr.

**[The] Ahab of the Nation**
*See* Charles I

**Ahasuerus [Lion-Hearted]**
*See* Cambyses

**Ahasuerus [Lion-Hearted]**
*See* Darius I

**Ahearn, Jacques** 1934-  [AM]
*American dancer and choreographer*
* D'Amboise, Jacques

**Ahearn, James A.** 1839-1901
[BEW]
*American-born actor, playwright,
producer*
* Herne, James A.

**Ahearne, Bunny**
*See* Ahearne, John F.

**Ahearne, Burt**
*See* Hernhuter, Albert

**Ahearne, John F.** 20th c.  [FHE]
*International Ice Hockey Federation
president*
* Ahearne, Bunny

**Ahern, Margaret McCrohan** 1921-
[CA, SAT]
*American writer and illustrator*
* O'Connell, Peg

**Ahern, Thomas**
*American narcotics investigator with
alleged CIA connections*
* Penguin [code name]

**Aherne, Owen**
*See* Cassill, Ronald Verlin

**Ahijado del Matadero [God-Child of
the Slaughter-House]**
*See* Ramos Lopez, Leopoldo

**Ahlgren, Ernst**
*See* Benedictsson, Victoria Maria

**Ahmed Arabi** 1841?-1911  [WBD]
*Egyptian revolutionist*
* Arabi Pasha

**Ahmed Bey Zogu** 1895-1961
[WBD]
*King of the Albanians*
* Scanderbeg III
* Zog I [or Zogu]

**Ahmed Fuad Pasha** 1868-1936
[WBD]
*Sultan of Egypt*
* Fuad I

**Ahmed [or Achmet] Pasha**
See Bonneval, Claude Alexandre de

**Ahmed [or Achmed] Pasha** 1735?-1804 [FFF, HN, WBD]
*Turkish official*
* [The] Butcher
* Djezzar

**Ahmed, Raju** 1937-1972 [SC]
*Indian actor*
* Raju

**Ahmed Shah** 1724-1773 [HN]
*Amir of Afghanistan*
* Duri Durani [Pearl of Pearls]

**Ahn, Soo-gil** 1911- [IAW]
*Korean author*
* Nam Suk

**Aho, Juhani**
See Brofeldt, Juhani

**Ahola, Hooley**
See Ahola, Sylvester

**Ahola, Sylvester** 1902- [WWJ]
*American musician*
* Ahola, Hooley

**Ahrens, Thomas**
See Wilson, Roger C.

**Ahriman**
See Martinez Ruiz, Jose

**Ai [Love]**
See Anthony, Florence

**Aiello, Antonio** 1937- [RO1]
*American singer*
* Aiello, Nino

**Aiello, Nino**
See Aiello, Antonio

**[L']Aiglon [The Eaglet]**
See Bonaparte, Francois Charles Joseph [Duc de Reichstadt]

**Aigner, Lajos** [FFF]
*Hungarian author*
* Abafi, Lajos

**Aiguillette**
See Hargreaves, Reginald [Charles]

**Aiken, Chief**
See Aiken, Walter H.

**Aiken, Clementina Edith** 19th c. [PA]
*Author*
* C. E. A.

**Aiken, Conrad [Potter]** 1889-1973 [CA, SAT]
*American author*
* Jeake, Samuel, Jr.

**Aiken, Elizabeth** 1805- ? [PA]
*Author*
* Nora [or Norma]

**Aiken, Henry**
See Gardner, William Henry

**Aiken, Joan Delano** 1924- [HFF, WGT]
*British author*
* Dee, Nicholas
* Lee, Rosie

**Aiken, John [Kempton]** 1913- [SFL]
*Author*
* Paget, John

**Aiken, Loretta Mary** 1897?-1975 [SW, TR]
*American comedienne*
* Mabley, Jackie
* Mabley, Moms

**Aiken, Margaret** 16th c. [DNNF, DNNS]
*Scottish woman accused of witchcraft*
* [The] Great Witch of Balwery

**Aiken, Mrs. Frank E.** [FFF]
*Entertainer*
* Rogers, Genevieve

**Aiken, Walter H.** 20th c. [IBW]
*American realtor*
* Aiken, Chief

**Aikin, Francis** [SN]
*Irish actor*
* Aikin, Tyrant

**Aikin, Tyrant**
See Aikin, Francis

**Aikman, Ann**
See McQuade, Ann Aikman

**Ailly, Pierre d'** 1350-1420 [DEP, HN, RH]
*French cardinal and astrologer*
* Aquila Doctorum
* [The] Eagle of France
* [The] Eagle of the Doctors of France
* [The] Hammer of Heretics
* Malleus Hereticorum
* [Le] Marteau des Heretiques

**Aimard, Gustave**
See Gloux, Olivier

**Aimee, [Sister]**
See McPherson, Aimee Semple

**Aimee, Anouk**
See Sorya, Francoise

**Aimwell, Walter**
See Simonds, William

**Ain**
See Stevens, William

**Aina**
See Olsson, Anna

**Ainley, Richard** 1910-1967 [SC]
*British actor*
* Riddle, Richard

**Ainsbury, Ray**
See Verrill, A[lpheus] Hyatt

**Ainslie, D. Grant Duff**
See Ainslie, Douglas

**Ainslie, Douglas** 1865- ? [LAO]
*French-born author*
* Ainslie, D. Grant Duff

**Ainslie, Herbert**
See Maitland, E.

**Ainslie, Peter** 1925- [ART]
*British potter*
* P. A.

**Ainslie, Tom**
See Carter, Richard

**Ainsworth, Harriet**
See Cadell, [Violet] Elizabeth

**Ainsworth, Leonard Victor, Jr.** 1942- [RO2]
*American singer*
* Gray, Dobie

**Ainsworth, Mary D[insmore] Salter** 1913- [CA, WD]
*American author*
* Salter, Mary D.

**Ainsworth, Norma** 20th c. [CA, SAT]
*American editor and author*
* Ruedi, Norma Paul

**Ainsworth, Oliver**
See Sharp, [Sir] Henry

**Ainsworth, Patricia**
See Bigg, Patricia Nina

**Ainsworth, Ruth**
See Gilbert, Ruth Gallard Ainsworth

**Ainsworth, Sydney**
See Sydney, Charles

**Ainsworth, W. H.** 1805- ? [PA]
*Author*
* Tichborne, Cheviot

**Aintree**
See Wallace, John

**[An] Air Pilot**
See Middleton, Edgar Charles

**Aird, Alisdair** 1940- [IAW]
*Scottish-born writer*
* Fairley, Alisdair

**Aird, Catherine**
See McIntosh, Kinn Hamilton

**Airdale**
See Drysdale, Donald Scott

**[The] Airedale Poet**
See Nicholson, John

**Airlie, Catherine**
See Macleod, Jean Sutherland

**Airto**
See Guimorva Moreira, Airto

**Airy, [Sir] George Biddell** 1801- ? [PA]
*Author*
* A. B. G.

**Aislin**
See Mosher, [Christopher] Terry

**Aistis, Jonas**
See Alexandravicius, Kossu

**Aitchess, A.**
See Sulzberger, Arthur Hays

**Aitchison, George** 1877- ? [WWL]
*British author*
* Thyson, A. C.

**Aitchison, Ivy** ?-1971 [SC, TR]
*British actress and singer*
* St. Helier, Ivy

**Aitchison, Raleigh Leonidas** 1887-1958 [BE]
*American baseball player*
* Aitchison, Redskin

**Aitchison, Redskin**
See Aitchison, Raleigh Leonidas

**Aitiaiche**
See Howells, Annie T.

**Aitken, A. Donnelly** 1892-1962 [MBF]
*British author*
* Donnelly, A.
* Shannon, A. Donnelly

**Aitken, Frank** 1869-1933 [SC]
*American actor*
* Aitken, Spottiswoode

**Aitken, Grover Robert** 1936- [BEW]
*American singer and dancer*
* Dale, Grover

**Aitken, James** ?-1777? [SN]
*American patriot*
* Jack the Painter

**Aitken, Mary** 1898-1954 [THR]
*British actress*
* Glynne, Mary

**Aitken, Mrs.** ?-1888 [FFF]
*Sister of Scottish historian, Thomas Carlyle*
* [The] Crow

**Aitken, Robert** 1872- ? [WGT, WWL]
*Author*
* Douglas, Hudson

**Aitken, Spottiswoode**
See Aitken, Frank

**Aitken, William Russell** 1913- [CA]
*Scottish author, editor, reviewer*
* Scott, Stuart

**Aiton, Bill**
See Aiton, George Wilson

**Aiton, George Wilson** 1890- [BE]
*American baseball player*
* Aiton, Bill

**Aiuppa, Joseph John [Joe]** 1907?-
*American underworld figure*
* Buonoma, J.
* [The] Doves
* O'Brien, Joey
* O'Brien, Tom
* Spano, James

**Aiverum, Timothy Louis** 1915- [EJ, IBW]
*American jazz musician, songwriter, comedian*
* Rogers, Oh Yeah
* Rogers, Timmie

**Aiwas, Dzati** [PA]
*Author*
* Roumi

**Aizpuru, Mario**
See Mendoza, Mario

**Aja, Frau**
See Goethe, Katharina Elizabeth

**Ajar, Emile**
See Kacew, Romain

**Ajax**
See Besant, Annie

**[An] Ajax Flagellifer**
See Rive, Jean Joseph

**[The] Ajax of the East**
See Leo

**Ajzenberg, Harold** 1947- [SW]
*Puerto Rican-born actor*
* Woodlawn, Holly

**AKA, Miss**
See Mitchell, Lottie Pearl

**Akakia, Martin** ?-1551 [PA]
*Author*
* Sans Malice

**Akanji, Sangodare**
See Beier, Ulli

**Akast, Doris** 1903- [THR]
*British actress and singer*
* Francis, Doris

**Akbar** 1542-1605 [WBD]
*Emperor of Hindustan*
* [The] Great

**Akeman, David** 1915-1973
[CME, ECM, FCW]
*American country-western performer*
* [The] Kentucky Wonder
* Stringbean

**Akenside, Mark** 1721-1770
[HN, RH, SN]
*British poet*
* [The] Bard of the Imagination

**Aker, Chief**
See Aker, Jack Delane

**Aker, Jack Delane** 1940- [BE, PB]
*American baseball player*
* Aker, Chief

**Akerman, John Yonge** 1800- ?
[FFF, PA]
*British numismatist and author*
* J. Y. A.
* Pindar, Paul

**Akerman, Richard**
See Noel Hume, Ivor

**Akers, Alan Burt**
See Bulmer, [Henry] Kenneth

**Akers, Albert Earl** 1887- [BE]
*American baseball player*
* Akers, Jerry

**Akers, Bill**
See Akers, Thomas Ernest

**Akers, Floyd**
See Baum, L[yman] Frank

**Akers, Jerry**
See Akers, Albert Earl

**Akers, Thomas Ernest** 1904-1962
[BE]
*American baseball player*
* Akers, Bill

**Akhmatova, Anna**
See Gorenko, Anna Andreyevna

**Akhnaton, Askia**
See Eckels, Jon

**Akhtal, al-**
See Ghiyath ibn-Harith

**Akhund of Swat**
See Abdul Ghafur

**Akiba, Ben**
See Nusic, Branislav

**Akilandam, Perungalur
Vaithialingam** 1922- [IAW]
*Indian producer and author*
* Akilon

**Akilon**
See Akilandam, Perungalur
Vaithialingam

**Akira**
See Moore, Erica Maria

**[The] Al Capone of Los Angeles**
See Dragna, Jack

**Al-Van-Gar**
See Radwanski, Pierre A[rthur]

**[The] Alabama Antelope**
See Hutson, Donald M.

**[The] Alabama Cowboy**
See Clements, Zeke

**[The] Alabama Kid**
See Reeves, Clarence

**Aladdin**
See Pallante, Aladdin Abdullah
Achmed Anthony

**Alagan, Koodal**
See Naa Parthasarathy,
Naarayana-Parthasarathy

**Alailima, Fay C.** 1921- [CA]
*American author*
* Calkins, Fay

**Alain**
See Brustlein, Daniel

**Alain**
See Chartier, Emile-Auguste

**Alain de Lille [or Alan de l'Isle]**
1114-1203 [DNNF, FFF, HN]
*French philosopher, theologian,
alchemist*
* [The] Universal Doctor
* Universalis, Doctor

**Alain-Fournier**
See Fournier, Henri Alban

**Alais, Ernest W.** 1864-1922 [MBF]
*British author*
* Miller, Lawrence
* Wolfe, Cedric

**Alam**
See Bahadur Shah I

**Alamgir [Conqueror of the World]**
See Aurungzebe [Aurangzeb or
Aurungzeb]

**Alan, A. J.**
See Lambert, Leslie Harrison

**Alan, Jack**
See Green, Alan [Baer]

**Alan, Marjorie**
See Bumpus, Doris Marjorie

**Alan Turner, Violet Prudence**
1906- [AW, WD]
*British author*
* Summerhayes, Prudence

**Alane, Alexander**
See Aless, Alexander

**Alanus**
See Bardzinski, Jan

**Alarcon, Tomas** 1879-1916 [GS]
*Spanish bullfighter*
* Mazzantinito [Little Mazzantino]

**Alaric Cottin**
See Frederick II

**Alas, Leopold** 1852-1901 [WBD]
*Spanish author*
* Clarin

**Alaska Jack Giniva**
See Giniva, John

**Alaster**
See Orton, James

**Alatri, Paolo** 1918- [IAW]
*Italian author*
* Romano, Paolo

**[El] Alba [The Dawn]**
See Gomez, Jose

**Alba**
See White, Alexina B.

**Alba, Patricio**
See Castillo Velasquez, Luis
Alberto

**Alba, Victor**
See Pages, Pedro

**Alba De Gamez, Cielo Cayetana**
1920- [CA]
*Spanish-born American author*
* De Gamez, Tana

**Albach-Retty, Rosemarie** 1938-
[BDF, FC, WEF]
*Austrian actress*
* Schneider, Romy

**Albam, Emmanuel** 1922- [DAM]
*Dominican-born composer and
music teacher*
* Albam, Manny

**Albam, Manny**
See Albam, Emmanuel

**Alban, Anthony**
See Thompson, Anthony A.

**Albanesi, [Madame] Effie Maria
[Henderson]** 1859-1936 [LC]
*Author*
* Rowlands, Effie Adelaide

**Albanesi, Margherita** 1899-1923
[THR]
*British actress*
* Albanesi, Meggie

**Albanesi, Meggie**
See Albanesi, Margherita

**Albani, Emma**
See Lajeunesse, Marie Louise
Cecilia Emma

**Albani [or Albano], Francesco**
1578-1660 [HN, RH, SN]
*Italian painter*
* [The] Anacreon of Painters

**Albani, Giovanni Francesco**
1649-1721 [WBD]
*Pope*
* Clement XI

**Albani, Joseph** 1924- [EJ7]
*American jazz musician*
* Albany, Joe

**[The] Albanian Alexander**
See Castriot [or Castriota?],
George

**Albano**
See Adlersparre, Carl August

**Albany, Joe**
See Albani, Joseph

**Albe [or Albaneser]**
See Byron, George Gordon Noel

**Albeck, Stan** 1931- [SMG]
*American basketball coach*
* [The] Miracle Man of the
Rockies

**Alberdingk Thijm, Karel Joan
Lodewijk** 1864-1952 [CD, EWL]
*Dutch critic and author*
* Deyssel, Lodewijk Van

**Alberge, Ernest** 1893-1957 [THR]
*British actor*
* Jay, Ernest

**Albershart, Harry** 1901?-1973
[FC, SC]
*American actor*
* Lane, Allan
* Lane, Rocky

**Albert**
See Fortis, Giovanni Battista

**Albert**
See Markes, Albert Ernest

**Albert** ?-1215 [WBD]
*Patriarch of Jerusalem*
* [The] Blessed

**Albert** ?-1314 [DNNS]
*Landgrave of Thuringia and
margrave of Meissen*
* [The] Bad

**Albert [Count of Bollstadt]**
1193?-1280 [FF, SN, WBD]
*German scholastic philosopher*
* Albertus Magnus
* [The] Great
* [Le] Petit Albert
* Universalis, Doctor

**Albert [or Albrecht]** 1236-1279
[DNNS, SN]
*Duke of Brunswick and Luneburg*
* [The] Great
* [The] Tall

**Albert [or Albrecht]** 1522-1557
[HN, RH]
*Margrave of Brandenburg*
* [The] Alcibiades of Germany

**Albert [or Albrecht]** 1559-1621
[WBD]
*Archduke of Austria*
* [The] Pious

**Albert, Ben**
See Sibley, Ben

**Albert, Bessie**
See Gayton, Mrs. Edmund

**Albert, Burton Jr.** 1936- [SAT]
*American author*
* Healey, Brooks

**Albert, Don**
See Dominique, Albert

**Albert, Eddie**
See Heimberger, Edward Albert

**Albert Francis Charles Augustus
Emmanuel of Saxe-Coburg-Gotha**
1819-1861 [DNNS, FFF, WBD]
*Prince consort of England*
* [The] Good

**Albert, Heinrich** 1604-1651 [SN]
*German musician and poet*
* [Der] Vater des Deutschen Liedes
[The Father of German Songs]

**Albert i Paradis, Catalina** 1873- ?
[CD]
*Spanish author*
* Catala, Victor

**Albert, Louis**
See Regnier, Michel

**Albert, Marvin H.** 20th c.
[CA, WW]
*American author and editor*
* Rome, Anthony

**Albert, Morris**
See Kaiserman, Mauricio Alberto

**Albert the Great**
See Thurgood, Albert

**Albert the Workingman**
See Martin, Alexandre

**Albert, William**
See Wakeford, William

**Albert with the Tress**
See Albert III

**Albert I [or Albrecht]** 1100?-1170
[FFF, HN, SN]
*Margrave of Brandenburg*
* [The] Bear
* [The] Fair
* [The] Handsome
* [The] Second Romulus of Brandenburg

**Albert I [or Albrecht]** 1158-1195
[DNNS, SN]
*Margrave of Meissen*
* [The] Proud

**Albert II** 1298-1358
[FFF, RH, SN]
*Duke of Austria*
* [The] Lame
* [The] Wise

**Albert III** 1349?-1395 [SN]
*Duke of Austria*
* Albert with the Tress
* [The] Astrologer

**Albert III [or Albrecht]** 1414-1486
[DNNS, HN, SN]
*Elector of Brandenburg*
* [The] Achilles of Germany
* [The] Ulysses

**Albert III [or Albrecht]** 1443-1500
[DNNS, WBD]
*Duke of Saxony*
* [The] Bold

**Albert IV** 1377?-1404
[DNNS, FFF, SN]
*Duke of Austria*
* [The] Patient
* [The] Pious
* [The] Wonder of the World

**Albert IV** 1447-1508 [DNNS]
*Duke of Bavaria*
* [The] Wise

**Albert V [or Albrecht]** 1397-1439
[DNNS, FFF, SN]
*Duke of Austria and King of Germany*
* [The] Illustrious
* [The] Magnanimous

**Albert VI** 1418?-1463
[FFF, RH, SN]
*Duke of Austria*
* [The] Prodigal

**Albertini, Adalberto** 20th c. [WF]
*Italian director*
* Mitchell, Stanley

**Alberts, August P.** 1861-1912 [BE]
*American baseball player*
* Alberts, Gus

**Alberts, Cy**
See Alberts, Frederick Joseph

**Alberts, Frederick Joseph**
1882-1917 [BE]
*American baseball player*
* Alberts, Cy

**Alberts, Gus**
See Alberts, August P.

**Alberts, James** 1882-1958 [BE]
*American baseball player*
* Dolan, Alvin James
* Dolan, Cozy

**Alberts, William** 1882-1912 [BLB]
*American underworld figure*
* Zelig, Big Jack
* Zelig, Jack

**Albertus Magnus**
See Albert [Count of Bollstadt]

**Albery, Nobuko** 20th c. [CA]
*Japanese-born author*
* Morris, Nobuko

**Albicante, Giovanni Alberto** 16th c.
[SN]
*Milanese poet*
* Bestiale
* Furibondo

**Albina, Giuseppe** ?-1611 [PA]
*Author*
* Sozzo

**Albinson, Jack**
See Albinson, James P.

**Albinson, James P.** 1932- [CA]
*American author*
* Albinson, Jack

**Albinus**
See Brutus, Decimus Junius

**Albinus, Giovanni** ?-1480 [PA]
*Author*
* Albinus, Joannes

**Albinus, Joannes**
See Albinus, Giovanni

**Albion**
See Stephenson, George James

**Alborough, Edward Morgan** 20th
c. [WWL]
*British author*
* De Burgh, A.

**Albosta, Ed[ward John]** 1918- [BE]
*American baseball player*
* Albosta, Rube

**Albosta, Rube**
See Albosta, Ed[ward John]

**Albran, Kehlog** [joint pseudonym
with Sheldon R(ubin) Shacket]
See Cohen, Martin A.

**Albran, Kehlog** [joint pseudonym
with Martin A. Cohen]
See Shacket, Sheldon R[ubin]

**Albrand, Martha**
See Freybe, Heidi Huberta

**Albrecht, Hardy** 1903-1975 [FC]
*American actor*
* Albright, Hardie

**Albrecht, Joyce Marie** 20th c. [OP]
*American opera singer*
* Clements, Joy

**Albright, Bob** 1884-1971 [SC]
*American actor*
* Albright, Oklahoma Bob

**Albright, Hardie**
See Albrecht, Hardy

**Albright, Joseph [Medill Patterson]**
See Reeve, Joseph

**Albright, Oklahoma Bob**
See Albright, Bob

**Albright, Pistol Pete**
See Albright, Thomas

**Albright, Thomas** 1909- [MK]
*American baseball player*
* Albright, Pistol Pete

**Albritton, Carol** 20th c. [WD]
*Author*
* Trehearne, Elizabeth [joint
pseudonym with Patricia Anne
Maxwell]

**Albrizzi, Almoro** ?-1722 [PA]
*Author*
* Hermolaus

**Albuquerque, Alfonso [or Affonso] de**
1453-1515 [DEP, DNNS, RH]
*Viceroy of India*
* [The] Great
* [The] Mars of Portugal
* [The] Portuguese Mars

**Alcaeus**
See Montgomery, James

**Alcaeus** 6th c. BC [DEP, SN]
*Greek poet*
* [The] Indignant Bard
* [The] Lesbian Citizen

**Alcaforada, Mariana** ?-1700?
[DNNF, DNNS]
*Portuguese writer*
* [The] Portuguese Nun

**Alcalareno [Man from Alcala]**
See Garcia Rodriguez, Jose

**Alcalde, E. L.**
See Chaij, Fernando

**Alcazar, Victor**
See Mora, Victor

**Alcibiade**
See Praz, Mario

**Alcibiades**
See Anderson, James

**Alcibiades**
See Tennyson, Alfred [First Baron
Tennyson]

**[The] Alcibiades of Germany**
See Albert [or Albrecht]

**[The] Alcibiades of his Time**
See Villiers, George

**Alcindor, [Ferdinand] Lew[is, Jr.]**
1947- [BB, OCS, SMG]
*American basketball player*
* Abdul-Jabbar, Kareem

**Alciphron**
See Doyle, Rosina [Wheeler]

**Alcium**
See Chauvin [or Caulvin?], Jean

**Alcman** 7th c. BC [FFF, RH, SN]
*Lydian poet*
* [The] Lydian Poet

**Alcock, John Forbes** 1885-1973
[BE]
*American baseball player*
* Alcock, Scotty

**Alcock, Josephine** 1883?-1971
[THR]
*American-born actress*
* Middleton, Josephine

**Alcock, Scotty**
See Alcock, John Forbes

**Alcott, John S.** 1873-1949
[BEW, FC, FD]
*Canadian-born director*
* Olcott, Sidney

**Alcott, Julia**
See Cudlipp, Edythe

**Alcott, Ten**
See Totten, Charles Adiel Lewis

**Alcuin [or Albinus]** 735- 804
[WBD]
*British scholar*
* Ealhwine
* Flaccus

**Alcyone**
See Krishnamurti, Jiddu

**Alda, Alan**
See D'Abruzzo, Alphonso

**Alda, Frances**
See Davies, Frances

**Alda, Robert**
See D'Abruzzo, Alphonso
Giovanni Giusseppi Roberto

**Aldanov, Mark Aleksandrovich**
See Landau, Mark Aleksandrovich

**Aldeano, Silvestre**
See Ackerman, Forrest J[ames]

**Aldebert, Monique**
See Dozo, Monique

**Aldegrever, Heinrich**
See Trippenmeker, Heinrich

**Alden, Betty** [house pseudonym?]
See Reynolds, Myra Rolfe

**Alden, Betty** [house pseudonym?]
See Tracy, Lucy Bradshaw

**Alden, Carella**
See Remington, Ella-Carrie

**Alden, Darius Adner** ?-1926 [SC]
*American actor and circus performer*
* Thumb, Tom

**Alden, Isabella Macdonald**
1841-1930 [LC]
*American author*
* Pansy

**Alden, Jack**
See Barrows, [Ruth] Marjorie

**Alden, Michele**
See Avallone, Michael [Angelo],
Jr.

**Alden, William L.** 1837- ?
[FFF, PA]
*American journalist*
* Brown, Jimmy
* [The] Funny Man of the Times
* Metador
* N. Y. Times Man

**Alderdice, Alfred** 1919- [FC, ITA]
*American actor*
* Drake, Tom

**Alderisio, Felix Anthony**
1922-1971 [BLB]
*American underworld figure*
* Alderisio, Milwaukee Phil
* Aldi, Philip
* Alerise, Felix
* Elderise, Phil
* Gato, Phil

**Alderisio, Milwaukee Phil**
See   Alderisio, Felix Anthony

**Alderman Medium**
See   Abell, William

**Alderson, Floyd Taliaferro**
1895?-1980
*American actor*
* Wales, Wally

**Aldert, Joseph Bennett** 1889-1967
[SC]
*American entertainer*
* Bennett, Joe

**[The] Aldgate Sphinx**
See   Mendeloff, Gershon

**Aldi, Philip**
See   Alderisio, Felix Anthony

**Aldiborontiphoscophornio**
See   Ballantyne, James

**Alding, Peter**
See   Jeffries, Roderic [Graeme]

**Aldiss, Brian W[ilson]** 1925-
[CA, ESF, WGT]
*British author and critic*
* Cracken, Jael
* Mendicant, Arch?
* Pica, Peter
* Runciman, John
* Shackleton, C. C.

**Aldiss, Margaret [Christie]** 1933-
[SFL]
*British author*
* Manson, Margaret

**Aldo, G. R.**
See   Graziati, Aldo

**Aldobrandini, Ippolito** 1536-1605
[WBD]
*Pope*
* Clement VIII

**Aldon, Adair**
See   Meigs, Cornelia Lynde

**Aldouby, Zwy H[erbert]**
See   Dubensky, Herbert

**Aldred** ?-1069   [SN]
*Archbishop of York*
* [The] Glossator

**Aldred, Eben**   [PA]
*Author*
* Eben-ezer

**Aldrich, Ann**
See   Meaker, Marijane

**Aldrich, Bess Streeter** 1881-1954
[ANT, TC]
*American author*
* Stevens, Margaret Dean

**Aldrich, Charles C.** 20th c.   [FB]
*American football player*
* Aldrich, Ki

**Aldrich, Charles T., Jr.** 1906-
[ITA, SW]
*American actor*
* Gordon, Gale

**Aldrich, Clara Chapine Thomas** 20th
c.   [NAA]
*American author*
* Aldrich, Darragh

**Aldrich, Darragh**
See   Aldrich, Clara Chapine
Thomas

**Aldrich, Earl Augustus** 1886-
[WW]
*Author*
* Leonard, A. B.

**Aldrich, Ki**
See   Aldrich, Charles C.

**Aldrich, Louis**
See   Moses, Louis

**Aldridge, Ira Frederick** 1807-1867
[DEP, IBW]
*American actor*
* [The] African Roscius
* [The] African Tragedian

**Aldridge, Victor Eddington**
1894-1973   [PB]
*American baseball player*
* [The] Hoosier Schoolmaster

**Aldrin, Buzz**
See   Aldrin, Edwin E., Jr.

**Aldrin, Edwin E., Jr.** 1930-   [WA]
*American astronaut*
* Aldrin, Buzz

**Aldyne, Nathan** [joint pseudonym
with Dennis Schuetz]
See   McDowell, Michael

**Aldyne, Nathan** [joint pseudonym
with Michael McDowell]
See   Schuetz, Dennis

**Aleardi, Aleardo**
See   Gaetano, Aleardo

**Aleck**
See   Alexander, F. Russell

**Aleichem, Shalom**
See   Rabinowitz, Solomon J.

**Alejandro**
See   Canedo, Alejandro

**Alek** [code name]
See   Nunn May, Allan

**Aleman, Harry** 20th c.
*American underworld figure*
* [The] Hook

**Alemanicus, Alexander**   [HN]
*Medieval scholar*
* Illibatus, Doctor

**Alembert, Jean Le Rond d'**
1717?-1783   [HN, RH, SN]
*French mathematician and
philosopher*
* Anaxagoras
* [Le] Chancelier du Parnasse
* [The] Father of French
  Philosophy
* [The] Mazarin of Letters

**Alep Arslan** ?-1072   [HN, RH, SN]
*Perso-Turkish king*
* [The] Valiant Lion

**Aleph**
See   Harvey, William

**Alepoudelis, Odysseus** 1911-   [B10]
*Greek poet*
* Elytis, Odysseus

**Aleramo, Sibilla**
See   Faccio, Rina

**Alerise, Felix**
See   Alderisio, Felix Anthony

**Alesius**
See   Aless, Alexander

**Aless, Alexander** 1500-1565
[WBD]
*Scottish theologian*
* Alane, Alexander
* Alesius

**Aless, Tony**
See   Alessandrini, Anthony

**Alessandrini, Anthony** 1921-   [EJ]
*American jazz musician*
* Aless, Tony

**Alessandro, Romano** 16th c.   [SN]
*Musician*
* Della Viola

**Aleter, Esq.**
See   Strahorn, Robert E.

**Aletes**
See   Sanchez Morales, Narciso

**Alethes**
See   Baird, Thomas H.

**Alethitheras**
See   Osborn, Laughton

**Alex**
See   White, Eliza A.

**Alex, Gus** 1916-   [BLB]
*American underworld figure*
* Benson, Paul
* Johnson, Gus
* Taylor, Sam

**Alex the Great**
See   Alexander, Grover Cleveland

**Alexander, Adolphe, Jr.** 1898-1968
[NOJ]
*American jazz musician*
* Alexander, Tats

**Alexander, Alex**
See   Alexander, Grover Cleveland

**Alexander, Alger** 1880?-1955?
[BWW]
*American singer*
* Alexander, Texas
* Oliver, Kine

**Alexander, Anna B[arbara Cooke]**
1913-   [CA]
*American author*
* Cooke, Barbara

**Alexander, Archie Alphonso**
1888-1958   [IBW]
*American engineer and government
official*
* [The] Great

**Alexander, Ben**
See   Alexander, Nicholas Benton

**Alexander, Boyd** 1913-1980   [CA]
*British author, editor, translator*
* Lacey, John

**Alexander, Bruce**
See   Montague, Bruce Alexander

**Alexander, Buck**
See   Alexander, Grover Cleveland

**Alexander, C. K.**
See   Alexander, Charles K.

**Alexander, Charles**
See   Hadfield, [Ellis] Charles
[Raymond]

**Alexander, Charles K.** 1923-
[BEW]
*Egyptian-born actor*
* Alexander, C. K.

**Alexander, Charles Wesley**
1837-1927   [PA]
*American author*
* Bradshaw, Wellesley
* Bradshaw, Wesley

**Alexander, Colin James** 1920-
[CA, CC]
*New Zealand author*
* Jay, Simon

**Alexander, Dair**
See   Thomson, Christine Campbell

**Alexander, [David] Dale** 1903-
[BE, PB]
*American baseball player*
* Alexander, Moose

**Alexander, Dave** 1938-   [BWW]
*American singer*
* Khayyam, Omar Hakim

**Alexander, Dave** 20th c.   [BWW]
*American singer*
* [The] Black Ivory King

**Alexander, David**
See   Cunliffe, Dave

**Alexander, David** 20th c.   [BWW]
*American singer*
* Alexander, Little David

**Alexander, Dode**
See   Alexander, Grover Cleveland

**Alexander, Doyle Lafayette** 1950-
[SMG]
*American baseball player*
* Alexander, Gabby

**Alexander, Ed?**
See   Emshwiller, Ed[mund
Alexander]

**Alexander, Eleanor Jane** 20th c.
[LAO]
*British author*
* E. A.

**Alexander, Elmer** 1922-   [EJ]
*American jazz musician*
* Alexander, Mousie

**Alexander, F. Russell** 1902-   [NAA]
*American journalist*
* Aleck

**Alexander, Fatty**
See   Alexander, Frank

**Alexander, Frank** 1879-1937   [SC]
*American actor*
* Alexander, Fatty

**Alexander, Franz C. M.** 1928-   [EC]
*West Indian cricketer*
* Alexander, Gerry

**Alexander, Gabby**
See   Alexander, Doyle Lafayette

**Alexander, Georg**
See   Luddeckens, Werner Louis
Georg

**Alexander, [Sir] George**
See   Samson, George Alexander
Gibb

**Alexander, Gerry**
See   Alexander, Franz C. M.

**Alexander, Gil**
See   Ralston, Gilbert A[lexander]

**Alexander, Grover Cleveland**
1887-1950 [AS, OBW, PB]
*American baseball player*
* Alex the Great
* Alexander, Alex
* Alexander, Buck
* Alexander, Dode
* Alexander, Old Pete
* Alexander, Pete

**Alexander, Harold Lee** 1934- [CA]
*American author and marriage counselor*
* Alexander, Zane

**Alexander, James** 1768-1851
[DNNS]
*Scottish clergyman*
* [The] Scottish Boanerges

**Alexander, James Waddell**
1804-1859 [FFF, PA]
*American writer*
* Caesariensis

**Alexander, Jan**
*See* Banis, Victor J[erome]

**Alexander, Jane**
*See* Quigley, Jane

**Alexander, Janet** 1907- [AW, WD]
*British author*
* McNeill, Janet

**Alexander, Joan**
*See* Wetherell-Pepper, Joan
Alexander

**Alexander, Jocelyn Anne Arundel**
1930- [CA]
*American author*
* Arundel, Jocelyn

**Alexander, Joe**
*See* Allesandra, Giuseppe

**Alexander, John**
*See* Ruler, Alexander John

**Alexander, John**
*See* Vlasto, John Alexander

**Alexander, John M., Jr.** 1932-1954
[EJ, NBB]
*American singer*
* Ace, Johnny
* [The] Colored James Dean

**Alexander, Justin**
*See* Smith, Robert Dickie

**Alexander, Kathryn**
*See* Caldwell, Kathryn [Smoot]

**Alexander Leopold** 1794-1849
[RH]
*Prince of Hohenlohe-Waldenburg-Schillingsfuerst*
* Thaumaturgus

**Alexander, Little David**
*See* Alexander, David

**Alexander, Mara**
*See* Levine, Mara

**Alexander, Marge**
*See* Edwards, Roselyn

**Alexander, Montgomery Bernard**
1944- [EJ7]
*Jamaican-born jazz musician*
* Alexander, Monty

**Alexander, Monty**
*See* Alexander, Montgomery
Bernard

**Alexander, Moose**
*See* Alexander, [David] Dale

**Alexander, Mousie**
*See* Alexander, Elmer

**Alexander, Mrs.**
*See* Hector, Annie [French]

**Alexander, Muriel**
*See* Marsh, Muriel

**Alexander, Nicholas Benton**
1911-1969 [F1, F2]
*American actor*
* Alexander, Ben

**Alexander, Nin**
*See* Alexander, William Henry

**Alexander of Hales** ?-1245
[DEP, HN, SN]
*British theologian and philosopher*
* Doctorum, Doctor
* Fons Vitae
* [The] Fountain of Life
* Irrefragabilis, Doctor
* [The] Irrefragable Doctor

**[The] Alexander of Persia**
*See* Sandjar

**[The] Alexander of the North**
*See* Charles XII

**Alexander, Old Pete**
*See* Alexander, Grover Cleveland

**Alexander, Patrick Proctor** [PA]
*Author*
* Smelfungus

**Alexander, Pete**
*See* Alexander, Grover Cleveland

**Alexander, Philip Abbott** 1924-
[BEW]
*American actor*
* Abbott, Philip

**Alexander, R. W.**
*See* Alexander, Robert William

**Alexander, Rae Pace**
*See* Alexander, Raymond Pace

**Alexander, Raymond Pace**
1898-1974 [CA]
*American author and civil rights activist*
* Alexander, Rae Pace

**Alexander, Ric**
*See* Long, Richard A[lexander]

**Alexander, Robert**
*See* Gross, Michael [Robert]

**Alexander, Robert William**
1905-1980 [ESF, SFL, WGT]
*British author*
* Alexander, R. W.
* Butler, Joan
* Temple, Ralph

**Alexander, Ross**
*See* Smith, Ross Alexander

**Alexander, Ruth**
*See* Rogers, Ruth

**Alexander Severus, Marcus Aurelius**
*See* Bassianus, Alexianus

**Alexander, Skip**
*See* Alexander, Stewart

**Alexander, Stanley Walter**
1895-1980 [CA]
*British author and editor*
* Hannibal

**Alexander, Stewart** 1918- [GF]
*American golfer*
* Alexander, Skip

**Alexander, Tats**
*See* Alexander, Adolphe, Jr.

**Alexander, Texas**
*See* Alexander, Alger

**Alexander, [Sir] William [First Earl of Stirling]** 1567?-1640
[SN, WBD]
*Scottish poet*
* My Philosophical Poet

**Alexander, William Henry**
1858-1933 [BE]
*American baseball player*
* Alexander, Nin

**Alexander, Zane**
*See* Alexander, Harold Lee

**Alexander I**
*See* Ptolemy X [IX or XI]

**Alexander I** 1078?-1124 [RH, SN]
*King of Scotland*
* [The] Fierce

**Alexander I [Aleksandr Pavlovich]**
1777-1825 [HN, WBD]
*Russian emperor*
* [The] Northern Telemaque

**Alexander II**
*See* Anselmo

**Alexander II**
*See* Ptolemy XI [X or XII]

**Alexander II** 1198-1249 [SN]
*King of Scotland*
* [The] Little Red Fox

**Alexander III**
*See* Bandinelli, Orlando

**Alexander III** 4th c. BC
[FFF, RH, SN]
*King of Macedonia*
* [The] Conqueror of the World
* [The] Emathian Conqueror
* [The] Great
* Macedonia's Madman

**Alexander IV**
*See* Conti, Rinaldo

**Alexander V**
*See* Philargos, Petros

**Alexander VI**
*See* Borgia, Rodrigo [or Rodriguez]

**Alexander VII**
*See* Chigi, Fabio

**Alexander VIII**
*See* Ottoboni, Pietro

**Alexandra [or Aleksandra] Feodorovna**
*See* Alix Victoria Helene Luise Beatrix

**Alexandravicius, Kossu** 1904-
[EWL]
*Lithuanian poet*
* Aistis, Jonas

**Alexandre**
*See* Raimon, Louis Albert
Alexandre

**Alexandros, Alexis**
*See* Winn, William Edwin

**Alexandrov, Grigori**
*See* Mormonenko, Grigori

**Alexeyev, Konstantin Sergeivitch**
1863?-1938 [BEW, LC]
*Russian actor, producer, teacher*
* Stanislavsky, Konstantin
Sergeivitch

**Alexis [or Alexius]** 5th c. [NND]
*Saint*
* [The] Man of God

**Alexis, Wilibald**
*See* Haring [or Haering], Wilhelm

**Alexius I** 1180?-1222 [WBD]
*Emperor of Trebizond*
* Grand Comnenus

**Alexius V** ?-1204 [WBD]
*Byzantine emperor*
* Ducas Mourtzuphlos

**Alfalfa Bill Murray**
*See* Murray, William H.

**Alfidi, Giuseppe Arturo** 20th c.
[ASC]
*Composer, conductor, pianist*
* Alfidi, Joseph [Joey]

**Alfidi, Joseph [Joey]**
*See* Alfidi, Giuseppe Arturo

**Alfonso I [or Alphonso]** ?-1134
[DNNS, WBD]
*King of Aragon and Navarre*
* [El] Batallador
* [The] Fighter

**Alfonso I [Alonzo or Alphonso]** 693-
757 [DNNS, FFF, SN]
*King of Leon and Asturias*
* [The] Catholic

**Alfonso I [Affonso or Alphonso]**
1112-1185 [DNNS, RH, SN]
*King of Portugal*
* [The] Conqueror

**Alfonso II [or Alphonso]** 758- 842
[DNNS, FFF, RH]
*King of Leon and Asturias*
* [The] Chaste

**Alfonso II [Affonso, Alonzo or Alphonso]** 1185-1223
[DNNS, FFF, WBD]
*King of Portugal*
* [The] Fat
* [O] Gordo

**Alfonso III [or Alphonso]** 848- 912
[DNNS, FFF, SN]
*King of Leon and Asturias*
* [The] Great

**Alfonso III [or Alphonso]**
1265-1291 [DNNS]
*King of Aragon*
* [The] Magnificent

**Alfonso IV [or Alphonso]** ?- 933
[DNNS]
*King of Leon and Asturias*
* [The] Monk

**Alfonso IV [Affonso, Alfonzo, or Alphonso]** 1290-1357
[DNNS, RH, SN]
*King of Portugal*
* [The] Brave
* [The] Fierce

**Alfonso IV [or Alphonso]**
1299-1336   [DNNS]
*King of Aragon*
* [The] Good

**Alfonso V [or Alphonso]** 1385-1458
[DNNS, SN, WBD]
*King of Aragon*
* [El] Magnanimo
* [The] Magnanimous

**Alfonso V [or Affonso]** 1432-1481
[WBD]
*King of Portugal*
* [O] Africano

**Alfonso VI [or Alphonso]**
1030-1109   [DNNS]
*King of Leon and Castile*
* [The] Valiant

**Alfonso VII [Alphonso or Alonso]**
?-1157   [WBD]
*King of Leon and Castile*
* [El] Emperador [The Emperor]

**Alfonso VIII [or Alphonso]**
1155?-1214   [DNNS, FFF, SN]
*King of Leon and Castile*
* [The] Good
* [The] Noble

**Alfonso X [or Alphonso]**
1226?-1284   [FFF, SN, WBD]
*King of Leon and Castile*
* [The] Astronomer
* [The] Philosopher
* [El] Sabio [The Learned]
* [The] Wise

**Alfonso XI [or Alphonso]** ?-1350
[DNNS]
*King of Leon and Castile*
* [The] Avenger

**Alfonso XII** 1857-1885   [HN]
*King of Spain*
* [The] Uhlan King

**Alford, Michael** 1582-1652   [PA]
*Author*
* Griffith

**Alfragan** 9th c.   [SN]
*Arabian astronomer*
* [The] Calculator

**Alfred**
*See*   Adams, Samuel

**Alfred**
*See*   Girardin, Dr.

**Alfred**
*See*   Sackett, Grenville A.

**Alfred [or Alured]** ?-1270
[HN, RH]
*British scholar*
* Anglicus [or Anglicanus]
* [The] Philosopher
* Scolasticus, Doctor

**Alfred** 849- 899   [DNNS, FFF, SN]
*King of England*
* [The] Great

**Alfred, Richard** [joint pseudonym
with Richard C. Schroeder]
*See*   Haverstock, Nathan Alfred

**Alfred, Richard** [joint pseudonym
with Nathan Alfred Haverstock]
*See*   Schroeder, Richard C.

**Alfur Utangaros**
*See*   Robertsson, Sigurdur

**Alfven, Hannes O[lof] G[oesta]**
1908-   [CA]
*Swedish physicist and author*
* Johannesson, Olof

**[El] Algabeno [The Man from La
Algaba]**
*See*   Garcia y Rodriguez, Jose

**Algabeno-Chico [Little One from
Algaba]**
*See*   Molina, Manuel

**Algarotti, Francesco** 1712-1764
[DEP, RH, SN]
*Italian author*
* [The] Swan of Padua

**Alger, Edwin, Jr.**
*See*   Williams, Jay Jerome

**Alger, Leclaire [Gowans]**
1898-1969   [CA, TBJ]
*American author and librarian*
* Nic Leodhas, Sorche

**Algery, Andre**
*See*   Coulet Du Gard, Rene

**Algren, Nelson** 1909-1981   [CLC]
*American author*
* Poet of the Chicago Slums

**Ali** 600?- 661   [DNNS, RH, SN]
*Caliph and son-in-law of
Mohammed*
* [The] Lion of God
* [The] Rugged Lion [Al Haidara]

**Ali** 1741-1822   [HN, RH, SN]
*Turkish pasha*
* Ali Pasha
* [The] Lion of Janina

**Ali Baba**
*See*   Babartsky, Albert J.

**Ali Baba**
*See*   Mackaye, Alberigh

**Ali, Belinda [Boyd]** 1950-   [B10]
*Former wife of American boxer
Muhammad Ali*
* Ali, Khalilah

**Ali, [Sheik] Ben** 1906-   [BMH]
*Indian-born entertainer*
* [The] Comedy Prince of Magic

**Ali Bey el-Abbassi**
*See*   Badia y Leblich, Domingo

**Ali, George**
*See*   Bolingbroke, George

**Ali, Hadji** 1892-1937   [BMH]
*Egyptian-born entertainer*
* [The] Egyptian Enigma

**Ali, Jamal**
*See*   Agard, Clifford

**Ali, Khalilah**
*See*   Ali, Belinda [Boyd]

**Ali Mohammed of Shiraz**
1819-1850   [WBD]
*Founder of Persian religious sect*
* [The] Bab [The Gate]

**Ali, Muhammad**
*See*   Clay, Cassius Marcellus, Jr.

**[The] Ali of Baseball**
*See*   Ellis, Dock Phillip, Jr.

**Ali Pasha**
*See*   Ali

**Ali, Rahaman**
*See*   Clay, Rudolph Valentino

**Ali Vardi Khan**
*See*   Mirza Muhammad Ali

**Alice**
*See*   Neale, Alice Clay

**Alice**
*See*   Rhine, Alice Hyneman

**Alida**
*See*   Ladd, Catherine Stratton

**Aliff, Hamilton C.** 1899-1966
[CM]
*American country-western performer*
* Big Slim
* [The] Lone Cowboy

**Alighieri, Dante**
*See*   Alighieri, Durante

**Alighieri, Durante** 1265-1321
[DEP, SN, WBD]
*Italian poet*
* Alighieri, Dante
* Dante
* [The] Poet Sire of Italy
* [The] White Flower

**Aligny, Claudo Felix Theodore** 1798-
?   [PA]
*Author*
* Carnelle

**Aliki**
*See*   Brandenberg, Aliki Liacouras

**Alimayo, Chikuyo**
*See*   Franklin, Harold L[eroy]

**Alin, Morris** 1905-   [ASC]
*Russian-born songwriter, editor,
publicist*
* Allen, Morrie

**Alinder, Martha Wheelock**
*See*   Wheelock, Martha E.

**Alington, Argentine Francis** 1898-
[AW]
*British author*
* Talbot, Hugh

**Alington, Cyril Argentine**
1872-1955   [CC, WW]
*British author and clergyman*
* Westerham, S. C.

**Aliomar, Latif**
*See*   Robinson, Jimmy Lee

**Aliqua**
*See*   Peerson, Eliza O.

**Aliquis**
*See*   Marks, Richard

**Alison, William Pulteney**
1790-1856   [FFF]
*Scottish physician*
* Academicus

**Alithinas**
*See*   Ivers, Hardinge Furenzo

**Alix, Juan Antonio** 1833-1918
[CW]
*Dominican poet*
* Papa Tono

**Alix, Liza Mae** 1904-   [BWW]
*American singer*
* [The] Queen of the Night Clubs

**Alix, Mae**
*See*   Hicks, Edna

**Alix, May**
*See*   Hunter, Alberta

**Alix Victoria Helene Luise Beatrix**
1872-1918   [WBD]
*Empress of Russia*
* Alexandra [or Aleksandra]
Feodorovna

**Alkalamit, Abdul**
*See*   McWorter, Gerald

**Alkali Ike Thomason**
*See*   Thomason, Ike

**[The] All American Out**
*See*   Durocher, Leo Ernest

**All Pride, Lord**
*See*   Sheffield, John [Duke of
Buckingham and Earl of Mulgrave]

**All World**
*See*   Free, Lloyd

**Allahvardi Khan**
*See*   Mirza Muhammad Ali

**Allain, Soulouque**
*See*   Allain, Theophile T.

**Allain, Theophile T.** 1846- ?   [IBW]
*American politician*
* Allain, Soulouque

**Allan, Allan Alexander** 20th c.
[BBH]
*American sled dog racer*
* Allan, Scotty

**Allan, Ann**
*See*   Lilly, Isabella Purvis

**Allan, David** 1744-1796
[DEP, DNNS, SN]
*Scottish painter*
* [The] Scottish Hogarth

**Allan, Dennis**
*See*   Denniston, Elinore

**Allan, Ella**
*See*   Armour-Allan, Ella

**Allan, Eva Dorothy** 1892-   [DBA]
*British sculptor*
* Allan, Julian Phelps

**Allan, F. Carney** 20th c.   [MBF]
*British author*
* MacDonald, Eric
* Neish, Duncan

**Allan, Frederick William**
1860-1918   [NAD]
*British astrologer*
* Leo, Alan

**Allan, George**
*See*   Kremnitz, Marie

**Allan, Julian Phelps**
*See*   Allan, Eva Dorothy

**Allan, Lewis**
*See*   Meeropol, Abel

**Allan, Luke**
*See*   Amy, [William] Lacey

**Allan, Mabel Esther** 1915-
[CA, SAT, WD]
*British author*
* Estoril, Jean

**Allan, Mabel Esther** (Continued)
* Hagon, Priscilla
* Pilgrim, Anne

**Allan, Patricia Colinaka** 1935-
[ITA]
*American entertainer*
* Collins, Pat

**Allan, Robert M., Jr.** 20th c.   [BBH]
*American sailboat racer*
* Allan, Skip

**Allan, Scotty**
*See*  Allan, Allan Alexander

**Allan, Skip**
*See*  Allan, Robert M., Jr.

**Allan, Ted**
*See*  Herman, Alan

**Allandale, Fred**
*See*  Arnold, Fred

**Allardice, Robert Barclay** 19th c.
[DNNS]
*British officer*
* Captain Barclay

**Allardyce, Paula**
*See*  Torday, Ursula

**Allarmet [or D'Alouzier], Jean**
1342-1426   [WBD]
*French ecclesiastic*
* Brogny [or Brogni], Cardinal de
* De Viviers, Cardinal
* D'Ostie, Cardinal

**Allbeury, Theodore Edward Le
Bouthillier [Ted]** 1917-
[CA, WD, WWS]
*British author*
* Butler, Richard

**Allbut, Jiggs**
*See*  Allbut, Phyllis

**Allbut, Phyllis** 1942-   [RO1]
*American singer*
* Allbut, Jiggs

**Allderice, Eliza Winslow**   [PA]
*Author*
* E. W. A.

**Alldridge, John Stratten** 1914-
[AW]
*British author*
* Stratten, John

**Allegri da Correggio, Antonio**
1494-1534   [HN, WBD]
*Italian painter*
* [The] Apelles of Europe
* Correggio

**Allegro, John Marco** 1923-   [CA]
*British-born author and
archaeologist*
* McGill, Ian

**Allen, Adam** [joint pseudonym with
Samuel Epstein]
*See*  Epstein, Beryl [Williams]

**Allen, Adam** [joint pseudonym with
Beryl (Williams) Epstein]
*See*  Epstein, Samuel

**Allen, Adams**
*See*  Gale, Linn A. E.

**Allen, Alex B.**
*See*  Heide, Florence Parry

**Allen, Allyn**
*See*  Eberle, Irmengarde

**Allen, Angus J.** 20th c.   [CSH]
*Canadian lacrosse player*
* Allen, Bones

**Allen, Anita**
*See*  Schenck, Anita A[llen]

**Allen, Artemus Ward** 1888-1939
[BE]
*American baseball player*
* Allen, Nick

**Allen, Arthur Bruce** 1903-1975
[CAP]
*British author*
* Trice, Borough

**Allen, Barbara**
*See*  Stuart, Vivian [Finlay]

**Allen, Barbara**
*See*  Tunnell, Peggy Joye

**Allen, Barbara Jo** 1904?-1974
[B10, FC, TR]
*American actress*
* Vague, Vera

**Allen, Bessie Bacon** 1886-1952
[SC]
*American actress and author*
* Bacon, Bessie

**Allen, Betsy**
*See*  Cavanna, Elizabeth Allen
[Betty]

**Allen, Bingo**
*See*  Allen, Courtney Keith

**Allen, Bones**
*See*  Allen, Angus J.

**Allen, Buddy**
*See*  Allen, Elihu

**Allen, Bugs**
*See*  Allen, Leslie

**Allen, C. K.**
*See*  Allen, [Sir] Carleton Kemp

**Allen, [Sir] Carleton Kemp**
1887-1966   [LC]
*Australian-born author*
* Allen, C. K.

**Allen, Cecil J[ohn]** 1886-1973   [CA]
*British writer and editor*
* Mercury
* Voyageur

**Allen, Charlie**
*See*  Palermo, Charles

**Allen, Chesney**
*See*  Allen, William E.

**Allen, Clifford** 20th c.   [OBW]
*American baseball player*
* Allen, Crooks

**Allen, Colt**
*See*  Allen, Newton Henry

**Allen, Courtney Keith** 1923-
[CEI, HK]
*Canadian-born hockey player,
coach, general manager*
* Allen, Bingo

**Allen, Crooks**
*See*  Allen, Clifford

**Allen, Cyrus Alban** 1855-1915   [BE]
*American baseball player*
* Allen, Jack

**Allen, Dale**
*See*  Saunders, Allen

**Allen, Deryck Neil** 1925-   [BMH]
*British theatre organist*
* Allen, Jerry

**Allen, Don B.**   ?-1966   [CA]
*American author*
* Allen, T. D. [joint pseudonym
with Terril Diener Allen]

**Allen, E. C.**
*See*  Ward, Elizabeth Campbell

**Allen, Edmund**
*See*  Reeve-Jones, Alan Edmond

**Allen, Elihu** 20th c.   [SMG]
*American football player*
* Allen, Buddy

**Allen, Elizabeth**
*See*  Gillease, Elizabeth Ellen

**Allen, Elizabeth Akers** 1832-1911
[FFF, PA, WBD]
*American poet*
* Percy, Florence

**Allen, F. M.**
*See*  Downey, Edmund

**Allen, Fletcher Manson** 1886-1959
[BE]
*American baseball player*
* Allen, Sled

**Allen, [Dr.] Forrest** 1885?-
[BB, OCS]
*American basketball coach*
* Allen, Phog

**Allen, Fred**
*See*  Sullivan, John Florence

**Allen, Frederick G[arfield]** 1936-
[CA]
*American author*
* Allen, Gary

**Allen, Fulton** 1908-1941   [BWW]
*American singer*
* Brother George
* Fuller, Blind Boy

**Allen, Gary**
*See*  Allen, Frederick G[arfield]

**Allen, Gene**
*See*  Sufana, Eugene

**Allen, George**
*See*  Smith, George

**Allen, George** 1922-
*American football coach*
* Allen, Ice Cream

**Allen, George Oswald Browning**
1902-   [OCS]
*British cricketer*
* Allen, Gubby

**Allen, Glen**
*See*  Montgomery, Roselle Mercier

**Allen, Grace**
*See*  Hogarth, Grace Weston

**Allen, [Charles] Grant [Blairfindie]**
1848-1899   [FFF, WBD]
*British author*
* Power, Cecil
* Wilson, J. Arbuthnot

**Allen, Gubby**
*See*  Allen, George Oswald
Browning

**Allen, H. Fredericka**
*See*  Allen, Helena Gronlund

**Allen, Ham**
*See*  Allen, Homer

**Allen, Hank**
*See*  Allen, Harold Andrew

**Allen, Harold Andrew** 1940-   [BE]
*American baseball player*
* Allen, Hank

**Allen, Harriette Bias** 20th c.   [IBW]
*American poet and educator*
* [The] Ambassador of Letters of
Tennessee

**Allen, Hazel**
*See*  Hershberger, Hazel Kuhns

**Allen, Helena Gronlund** 20th c.
[CA]
*American author*
* Allen, H. Fredericka

**Allen, Henry** [joint pseudonym]
*See*  Adams, Henry H[itch]

**Allen, Henry Francis** 20th c.
[SFL, WGT]
*American author*
* Pruning Knife

**Allen, Henry James, Jr.**
1900?-1967?   [ASC, DAM, WWJ]
*American jazz musician*
* Allen, Red

**Allen, Henry Wilson** 1912-
[CA, ESF, WGT]
*American author*
* Fisher, Clay
* Henry, Will

**Allen, Heywood**
*See*  Konigsberg, Allen Stewart

**Allen, Homer** 19th c.   [BE]
*American baseball player*
* Allen, Ham

**Allen, Horace Tanner** 1899-   [BE]
*American baseball player*
* Allen, Pug

**Allen, Hubert Raymond** 1919-
[IAW]
*British author*
* Guthrie, David
* Helley, Denis
* Jones, Llewelly

**Allen, Hugh**
*See*  Morris, Charles Smith

**Allen, Ice Cream**
*See*  Allen, George

**Allen, J. Mord**
*See*  Allen, Junius Mordecai

**Allen, Jack**
*See*  Allen, Cyrus Alban

**Allen, Jack**
*See*  Panzram, Carl

**Allen, James**
*See*  Ader, Paul [Fassett]

**Allen, James** 19th c.   [SN]
*British author*
* [The] Northumberland Piper

**Allen, James Browning** 1913?-1978
*American politician*
* [The] Great Obstructionist

**Allen, James L[ovic], Jr. [Jim]**
1929-   [CA]
*American author*
* James, Allen

**Allen, Jap**
See Allen, Jasper

**Allen, Jasper** 1899- [WWJ]
*American jazz musician*
* Allen, Jap

**Allen, Jerry**
See Allen, Deryck Neil

**Allen, Jesse Hall** 1868-1946 [BE]
*American baseball player*
* Allen, Pete

**Allen, Jimmy** 20th c.
*American football player*
* Allen, Spiderman
* [The] Spiderman

**Allen, John**
See Garbutt, John L.

**Allen, John**
See Perry, Ritchie [John Allen]

**Allen, John E[lliston]** 1921-
[IAW, WD]
*British technical writer*
* Aquarius
* Bisonius
* Danforth, Paul M.

**Allen, John Edward** 1889- [NAA]
*American journalist and author*
* Edwards, Jack

**Allen, Joseph**
See McGurn, Joseph

**Allen, Judith Evelyn** 1913-1967
[BEW, FC]
*American actress*
* Evelyn, Judith

**Allen, Junius Mordecai** 1875-1906
[IBW]
*American poet and playwright*
* Allen, J. Mord

**Allen, Kelcey**
See Kuttner, Eugene

**Allen, Kenneth S[ydney]** 1913-
[WD]
*British author*
* Carter, Avis Morton
* Scott, Alastair

**Allen, Leslie** 20th c. [EAR]
*American auto racer*
* Allen, Bugs

**Allen, Louise** [FFF]
*Entertainer*
* Hanley, Emma

**Allen, Mack**
See Slaughter, Marion T.

**Allen, Marcus**
See Donicht, Mark Allen

**Allen, Marion C.** 1914- [CA]
*American clergyman, author, columnist*
* Allen, Sam

**Allen, Marjory [Gill]** 1897- [CAP]
*British author*
* Allen of Hurtwood, Lady

**Allen, Mark**
See Donicht, Mark Allen

**Allen, Mary** 1877-1955 [FC]
*British actress*
* Jerrold, Mary

**Allen, Maude**
See Giannone, Maude Allen

**Allen, Maxine Alton** 1890- [NAA]
*American author*
* Alton, Maxine

**Allen, Maybelle**
See Johnson, Edith North

**Allen, Mel**
See Israel, Melvin

**Allen, Morrie**
See Alin, Morris

**Allen, Mrs. George W.** [FFF]
*Entertainer*
* Delmaine, Lottie

**Allen, Mrs. William W.** [FFF]
*Entertainer*
* Rees, Stella

**Allen, Newt**
See Allen, Newton Henry

**Allen, Newton Henry** 1903-
[IBW, MK]
*American baseball player*
* Allen, Colt
* Allen, Newt

**Allen, Nick**
See Allen, Artemus Ward

**Allen of Hurtwood, Lady**
See Allen, Marjory [Gill]

**Allen, Paul**
See Neal, John

**Allen, Pete**
See Allen, Jesse Hall

**Allen, Phog**
See Allen, [Dr.] Forrest

**Allen, Pug**
See Allen, Horace Tanner

**Allen, Rae**
See Abruzzo, Raffaella Julia
Theresa

**Allen, Ralph** 1694-1764
[DNNS, FFF, SN]
*British philanthropist*
* [The] Man of Bath

**Allen, Red**
See Allen, Henry James, Jr.

**Allen, Red**
See Allen, V. O.

**Allen, Rex** 1924- [CWG]
*American country-western performer*
* [The] Arizona Cowboy

**Allen, Richard**
See Markowitz, Richard

**Allen, Richard** ?-1940 [SC]
*American actor*
* Barnes, Frank

**Allen, Richard C.**
See Taylor, John M[axwell]

**Allen, Robert**
See Dodd, Allen Robert

**Allen, Robert**
See Garfinkel, Bernard

**Allen, Rod**
See Bainbridge, Rod

**Allen, Ronald**
See Ayckbourn, Alan

**Allen, Rosalie**
See Bedra, Julie Marlene

**Allen, Sam**
See Allen, Marion C.

**Allen, Samuel [Washington]** 1917-
[CA, SAT]
*American poet and essayist*
* Vesey, Paul

**Allen, Shep**
See Allen, Shepard

**Allen, Shepard** 1891- [IBW]
*American movie chain supervisor*
* Allen, Shep
* [The] Dean of Show Biz

**Allen, Sled**
See Allen, Fletcher Manson

**Allen, Spiderman**
See Allen, Jimmy

**Allen, Squee**
See Allen, Vivan Mariner

**Allen, Stephen Valentine [Steve]**
1921- [WD]
*American entertainer, composer, author*
* Stevens, William Christopher

**Allen, Sydney [Earl], Jr.** 1929-
[CA]
*American author*
* Currie, David

**Allen, T. D.** [joint pseudonym with
Terril Diener Allen]
See Allen, Don B.

**Allen, T. D.** [joint pseudonym with
Don B. Allen]
See Allen, Terril Diener

**Allen, Ted**
See Tedmon, Allyn Henry

**Allen, Terril Diener** 1908- [CA]
*American author*
* Allen, T. D. [joint pseudonym
with Don B. Allen]
* Allen, Terry D.

**Allen, Terry**
See Govier, Edward

**Allen, Terry D.**
See Allen, Terril Diener

**Allen, Thomas** 1542-1632 [SN]
*British mathematician*
* [The] Coryphaeus of
Mathematicians

**Allen, Thomas Sylvester** 1931-
[PRS, RO2]
*American musician*
* Dee, Papa

**Allen, Tom**
See Allen, Toussaint

**Allen, Toussaint** 20th c. [OBW]
*American baseball player*
* Allen, Tom

**Allen, V. O.** [BBH]
*American golfer*
* Allen, Red

**Allen, Vera**
See Klopman, Vera

**Allen, Vivan Mariner** 1916- [CEI]
*Canadian-born hockey player*
* Allen, Squee

**Allen, William** 1806-1879 [FFF]
*American statesman*
* [The] Ohio Gong

**Allen, William E.** 1896- [THR]
*British comedian*
* Allen, Chesney

**Allen, William Francis** 1830-1889
[FFF]
*American editor*
* Marcel

**Allen, Woody**
See Konigsberg, Allen Stewart

**Allenby, Enos Will**
See Bixler, William Allen

**Allenby, Frank**
See Gatehouse, Frank

**Allenby, Peggy**
See Fox, Eleanor Byrne

**Allerton, Mark**
See Cameron, William Ernest

**Allerton, Mary**
See Govan, [Mary] Christine
Noble

**Allesandra, Giuseppe** 1865-1950
[NOJ]
*Italian-born jazz musician*
* Alexander, Joe

**Alleyn, Simon** [PA]
*Author*
* Vicar of Bray

**Alleyne [or Allyn?], Ellen**
See Rossetti, Christina Georgina

**Allgood, Marie** 1885?-1952
[BEW, FC]
*Irish actress*
* O'Neill, Marie

**Allibone, Samuel Austin** 1816-1889
[DEL, FFF]
*American lexicographer and
bibliographer*
* Bibliophile
* [A] Layman

**Alliette** 18th c. [RH]
*French fortuneteller and author*
* Etteilla

**Allihn, Heinrich** 1841-1910
*German musicologist*
* Anders, Fritz

**Allin, Abby** 19th c. [PA]
*Author*
* Nilla

**Allingham, John W.** 20th c. [MBF]
*British editor and publisher*
* Rollington, Ralph

**Allingham, Margery**
See Carter, Margery Louise
Allingham

**Allison, Clay**
See Keevill, Henry J[ohn]

**Allison, Clyde**
See Knoles, William

**Allison, Jerry** 20th c. [RO1]
*American musician and singer*
* Ivan

**Allison, Joy**
See Cragin, Mary A.

**Allison, Marian**
See Reid, Frances P[ugh]

**Allison, Milo Henry** 1890-1957
[BE]
*American baseball player*
* Allison, Pete

**Allison, Norma** 1904-    [EMT]
*American actress and singer*
* Terris, Norma

**Allison, Pete**
See   Allison, Milo Henry

**Allison, Rand**
See   McCormick, Wilfred

**Allison, Ruth** 20th c.    [WGT]
*Author*
* Rice, Allison [joint pseudonym
   with Jane Rice]

**Allison, Sam**
See   Loomis, Noel M[iller]

**Allister, Claud**
See   Palmer, William Claud Michel

**Alliston, Buddy**
See   Alliston, Vaughn S.

**Alliston, Vaughn S.** 20th c.    [SMG]
*American football player*
* Alliston, Buddy

**Allman, [Howard] Duane**
1946-1971    [RM]
*American musician*
* Allman, Skydog

**Allman, Skydog**
See   Allman, [Howard] Duane

**Allmendinger, Aqua**
See   Allmendinger, Ernest

**Allmendinger, Ernest** 20th c.
*American football player*
* Allmendinger, Aqua

**Allon, Yigal**
See   Paicovich, Yigal

**Allotey, Bob**
See   Wago, Bob Allotey

**Allport, Arthur**
See   Gallun, Raymond Z[inke]

**Allsop, Thomas** 19th c.    [SN]
*Author*
* [The] Favorite Disciple of
   Coleridge

**Allsopp, Bruce** 1912-    [ART]
*British painter and designer*
* B. A.

**Allsopp, Fred W.** 1868- ?    [NAA]
*British-born author*
* Erick, Fred

**Allspice, Zekel**
See   Vail, John Cooper

**Allucingoli, Ubaldo** ?-1185    [CAL]
*Pope*
* Lucius III

**Allured, Lloyd**
See   Hoffmann, Donald

**Allut, Jean**
See   Marion, Elias

**Allward, Maurice Frank** 1923-
[IAW]
*British author*
* Commentator

**Allwood, Edith**
See   Mosser, Ann J.

**Allyn, Enylla**
See   Spencer, Mr.

**Allyn, Lilly**
See   Tatu, Elizabeth A.

**Allyn, Paul**
See   Schosberg, Paul A.

**Allyne, Kitty**
See   Huber, Mrs. Fred J.

**Allyne, Roy**
See   Agnew, Stephen Hamilton

**Allyson, June**
See   Geisman, Ella

**Allyson, Kym**
See   Kimbro, John M.

**Alm, Monica**
See   Olausson, Rune Erland

**Almada, Baldomero Melo** 1913-
[BE]
*Mexican-born baseball player*
* Almada, Mel

**Almada, Mel**
See   Almada, Baldomero Melo

**Almadovar, Sanchez de**
See   Del Monte y Aponte, Domingo

**Almagro, Diego de** 1520-1542
[DNNS]
*Panamanian-born Governor of Peru*
* [The] Lad
* [The] Youth

**Alman, David** 1919-    [CA, WD]
*American author*
* David, Emily [joint pseudonym
   with Emily Alman]

**Alman, Emily** 20th c.    [CA, WD]
*American author*
* David, Emily [joint pseudonym
   with David Alman]

**[The] Almanack Maker**
See   Harvey, Richard

**Almanseno [Man from Almansa]**
See   Gonzalez y Saus, Pascual

**Almansor [or Almanzor] [The
Invincible]**
See   Abou Giafar Abdallah

**Almanzor**
See   Ashton, Thomas

**Almar the Clown**
See   Marx, Albert A.

**Almas, Ralph Clayton** 1924-    [CEI]
*Canadian-born hockey player*
* Almas, Red

**Almas, Red**
See   Almas, Ralph Clayton

**Almaviva**
See   Scott, Clement William

**Almaviva**
See   St. Maur, Harry

**Almayne, Nard**
See   Decker, Mrs. Nelson

**Almedingen, E. M.**
See   Almedingen, Martha Edith
Von

**Almedingen, Martha Edith Von**
1898-1971    [CA, LC, SAT]
*Russian-born author*
* Almedingen, E. M.

**Almeida, Brites de** 14th c.    [WBD]
*Portuguese heroine*
* [The] Portuguese Joan of Arc

**Almeida Prado, Joao Fernando**
1898-    [IAW]
*Brazilian author*
* Yan

**Almereyda, Jean** 1905-1934    [FC]
*French director*
* Vigo, Jean

**[The] Almighty Nose**
See   Cromwell, Oliver

**Almohadilla [Little Pillow]**
See   Caro Aviles, Manuel

**Almon, Caspar**
See   Leasley, F. W.

**[The] Almoner**
See   John

**[The] Alnaschar of Modern Literature**
See   Coleridge, Samuel Taylor

**Alo, Vincent** 20th c.
[BLB, MM, PHM]
*American underworld figure*
* Jimmy Blue Eyes

**Aloma, Luis Barba** 1923-    [BE]
*Cuban-born baseball player*
* Aloma, Witto

**Aloma, Witto**
See   Aloma, Luis Barba

**Alomar, Sandy**
See   Alomar, Santos

**Alomar, Santos** 1943-    [BE, SMG]
*Puerto Rican-born baseball player*
* Alomar, Sandy

**Alonso, Julius G.** 1905-    [BBH]
*Spanish-born soccer player, coach,
manager*
* American Soccer League, Mr.

**Alonso, Manuel** 20th c.    [GS]
*Spanish bullfighter*
* Herrerita [Little Blacksmith]

**Alou, Felipe Rojas** 1935-    [PB]
*Dominican-born baseball player*
* Alou, Panque

**Alou, Jay**
See   Alou, Jesus Maria Rojas

**Alou, Jesus Maria Rojas** 1942-
[BE]
*Dominican-born baseball player*
* Alou, Jay

**Alou, Mateo Rojas** 1938-
[BE, SMG]
*Dominican-born baseball player*
* Alou, Matty

**Alou, Matty**
See   Alou, Mateo Rojas

**Alou, Panque**
See   Alou, Felipe Rojas

**Alp Arslan [Courageous Lion]**
See   Mohammed

**Alperman, Charles Augustus**
1879-1942    [BE]
*American baseball player*
* Alperman, Whitey

**Alperman, Whitey**
See   Alperman, Charles Augustus

**Alpert, Alex** ?-1934    [PHM]
*American underworld figure*
* Alpert, Red

**Alpert, Herman** 1916-
[DAM, EJ, PMJ]
*American jazz musician*
* Alpert, Trigger

**Alpert, Mickey**
See   Alpert, Milton I.

**Alpert, Milton I.** 1904-1965    [ASC]
*American conductor, personal
manager, agent*
* Alpert, Mickey

**Alpert, Red**
See   Alpert, Alex

**Alpert, Richard** 1932-    [NAD]
*American educator and spiritual
leader*
* Ram Dass, [Baba] [Servant of
   God]

**Alpert, Trigger**
See   Alpert, Herman

**Alpha**
See   Phelps, L. L.

**Alpha of the Plough**
See   Gardiner, Alfred George

**Alphonsa, [Mother]**
See   Hawthorne, Rose

**Alphonso, John B.** 1923-    [CA]
*American educator and author*
* Alphonso-Karkala, John B.

**Alphonso-Karkala, John B.**
See   Alphonso, John B.

**Alpin**
See   Wilson, William

**Alplaus, N. Y.** [joint pseudonym with
Jerome Rubin]
See   Rubin, Cynthia Elyce

**Alplaus, N. Y.** [joint pseudonym with
Cynthia Elyce Rubin]
See   Rubin, Jerome

**Alsop, Mary O'Hara** 1885-1980
[CA, SAT, TCC]
*American author and composer*
* O'Hara, Mary
* Sture-Vasa, Mary

**Alsterlund, Betty**
See   Pilkington, Betty

**Alstern, Fred**
See   Stern, Alfred

**Alston, Charles**
See   Mott, Michael

**Alston, Charles Henry** 1907-1977
[IBW]
*American painter, sculptor,
illustrator*
* Alston, Spinky

**Alston, Dell**
See   Alston, Wendell

**Alston, Edith**
See   Goodale, Mary Green

**Alston, Mary Niven** 1918-    [CA]
*American author*
* Niven, Marian

**Alston, Overton** 1906?-    [WWJ]
*American jazz musician*
* Alston, Ovie

**Alston, Ovie**
See   Alston, Overton

**Alston, Smokey**
See   Alston, Walter Emmons

**Alston, Spinky**
See   Alston, Charles Henry

**Alston, Walter Emmons** 1911-
[B10, BE, PB]
*American baseball manager*
* Alston, Smokey

**Alston, Wendell** 1952-   [ALR]
*American baseball player*
* Alston, Dell

**Altair**
See   Griffin, Anthony Jerome

**Altamura, Tullio** 20th c.   [WF]
*Italian actor*
* Altmayer, Tor

**Altan, Francesco Tullio**
See   Marquis, Jean-Robert

**Altares Saura, Carlos** 1932-   [FDG]
*Spanish director*
* Saura, Carlos

**[Der] Alte Dessauer**
See   Leopold I

**[Der] Alte Fritz**
See   Frederick II

**Alten, Ernest Matthias [Ernie]**
1894-   [BE]
*American baseball player*
* Alten, Lefty

**Alten, Lefty**
See   Alten, Ernest Matthias [Ernie]

**Altenberg, Peter**
See   Englaender, Richard

**Altenburger, Alida Maria** 1921-
[BDF, OCF, WEF]
*Italian actress*
* Valli, Alida

**Alter**
See   Owen, Joseph B.

**Alter Ego of Richelieu**
See   Leclerc du Tremblay, Francois

**Alter, Robert Edmond** 1925-1965
[CA, SAT]
*American author*
* Raymond, Robert
* Retla, Robert

**Alterego**
See   Jaffe, Hyman

**Alterie, Leland Verain** 1892-1935
[BLB, PHM]
*American underworld figure*
* Alterie, Louis
* Alterie, Two Gun
* [The] Cowboy

**Alterie, Louis**
See   Alterie, Leland Verain

**Alterie, Two Gun**
See   Alterie, Leland Verain

**Alth, Max O[ctavious]**
See   Becker, Max O[ctavious]

**Althea**
See   Braithwaite, Althea

**Altieri, Emilio** 1590-1676   [CAL]
*Pope*
* Clement X

**Altizer, David Tildon** 1876-1964
[BE]
*American baseball player*
* Altizer, Filipino

**Altizer, Filipino**
See   Altizer, David Tildon

**Altizer, Jim Bob** 20th c.   [GW]
*American rodeo performer*
* Altizer, Jinglebob

**Altizer, Jinglebob**
See   Altizer, Jim Bob

**Altman, Irwin** 1928-   [CA]
*American author*
* Altman, Larry

**Altman, Larry**
See   Altman, Irwin

**Altman, Thomas**
See   Black, Campbell

**Altmann, Klaus** 20th c.
*German Nazi government official*
* [The] Butcher of Lyon

**Altmayer, Tor**
See   Altamura, Tullio

**Altobelli, Alto**
See   Altobelli, Joseph Salvador

**Altobelli, Joseph Salvador** 1932-
[BR]
*American baseball manager*
* Altobelli, Alto

**Alton, Maxine**
See   Allen, Maxine Alton

**Alton, Robert**
See   Hart, Robert Alton

**Altreuter, Roger W.** 20th c.   [BBH]
*American sailboat racer*
* Altreuter, Sam

**Altreuter, Sam**
See   Altreuter, Roger W.

**Altshuler, Harry**   [WGT]
*Author*
* Faust, Alexander

**Altstock, Igal** 1942-   [CA]
*Israeli author*
* Ayal, Igal

**Altwerger, John** 1919-
[EJ, PMJ, WWJ]
*Canadian-born jazz musician*
* Auld, George

**Alunni, Corrado** 1948?-
*Italian terrorist*
* Turicchia, Signor

**Alurista**
See   Urista, Alberto H.

**Alusik, George Joseph** 1935-   [BE]
*American baseball player*
* Alusik, Glider
* Alusik, Turk

**Alusik, Glider**
See   Alusik, George Joseph

**Alusik, Turk**
See   Alusik, George Joseph

**Aluta, Juan De**
See   Uscatescu, George

**Alva, Martin**
See   Martinez Alvarez, Rafael

**Alvarado, Don**
See   Paige, Jose

**Alvarado, Luis Cesar** 1949-   [BE]
*Puerto Rican-born baseball player*
* Alvarado, Pimba

**Alvarado, Pimba**
See   Alvarado, Luis Cesar

**Alvarado Luvianos, Victor** 1929-
[GS]
*Mexican bullfighter*
* [El] Papelero [The Paper Seller]

**Alvarez, Albert Raymond**
See   Gourron, Albert

**Alvarez, Alfred** 1920-   [EJ]
*Canadian-born jazz musician*
* Alvarez, Chico

**Alvarez, Carmen**
See   Alvarez, Carmencita Louise

**Alvarez, Carmencita Louise** 20th c.
[BEW]
*American singer, dancer, actress*
* Alvarez, Carmen

**Alvarez, Chico**
See   Alvarez, Alfred

**Alvarez, Gorrego**
See   Alvarez, Rogelio Hernandez

**Alvarez, Ivan**
See   De Jesus, Ivan

**Alvarez, John**
See   Alvarez Del Rey, Ramon
Felipe San Juan Mario Silvio Enrico

**Alvarez, Manuel** ?-1797
[FFF, SN]
*Spanish sculptor*
* [The] Greek
* [El] Griego

**Alvarez, Ossie**
See   Alvarez, Oswaldo Gonzalez

**Alvarez, Oswaldo Gonzalez** 1933-
[BE]
*Cuban-born baseball player*
* Alvarez, Ossie

**Alvarez, Rogelio Hernandez** 1938-
[BE]
*Cuban-born baseball player*
* Alvarez, Gorrego

**Alvarez Del Rey, Ramon Felipe San
Juan Mario Silvio Enrico** 1915-
[CA, SF, SFL]
*American author*
* Alvarez, John
* Del Rey, Lester [joint pseudonym
  with Paul W. Fairman]
* Hall, Cameron [joint pseudonym
  with Henry Dempsey]
* Henry, Marion
* James, Philip [joint pseudonym
  with James H. Beard]
* Kaempfert, Wade
* Marion, Henry
* McCann, Edson [joint pseudonym
  with Frederik Pohl]
* St. John, Philip
* Satterfield, Charles [joint
  pseudonym with Frederik Pohl]
* Van Lhin, Erik
* Vincent, John
* Wright, Kenneth

**Alvarez Martin, Casimir** 1873- ?
[NAA]
*Spanish-born columnist*
* Alvaro

**Alvarez Quintero, Joaquin**
1873-1944   [TC]
*Spanish playwright*
* Diablo Cojuelo [Limping Devil]
  [joint pseudonym with Serafin
  Alvarez Quintero]

**Alvarez Quintero, Serafin**
1871-1938   [TC]
*Spanish playwright*
* Diablo Cojuelo [Limping Devil]
  [joint pseudonym with Joaquin
  Alvarez Quintero]

**Alvaro**
See   Alvarez Martin, Casimir

**Alvarus**
See   Cotrim, Alvaro

**Alverio, Rosita Dolores** 1931-
[FC, SW, TR]
*Puerto Rican actress and dancer*
* Moreno, Rita

**Alvero Cruz, Jose Medrano** 20th c.
*Cuban drug dealer*
* [El] Padrino

**Alves, Antonio De Castro**
1847-1871   [IBW]
*Brazilian abolitionist and poet*
* Poet of the Slaves

**Alvin, Danny**
See   Viniello, Danny

**Alvin, John**
See   Hoffstadt, John Alvin

**Alvirez, Pablos Alfonso** 1911-   [GS]
*Mexican bullfighter*
* Guero Alvirez [Blonde Alvirez]

**Alvord, William C.** 20th c.   [BE]
*American baseball player*
* Uncle Bill

**Always in Front, Prince**
See   Frederick Charles

**Alworth, Bambi**
See   Alworth, Lance D.

**Alworth, Lance D.** 1940-   [FB]
*American football player*
* Alworth, Bambi

**Alyagrov**
See   Jakobson, Roman [Osipovich]

**Alyea, Brant**
See   Alyea, Garrabrant Ryerson

**Alyea, Garrabrant Ryerson** 1940-
[BE]
*American baseball player*
* Alyea, Brant

**Alzee, Grendon?**
See   Zagat, Arthur Leo

**Amabile, George** 1936-   [CA]
*American-born poet*
* Los, George

**Amadeus** 1383-1451   [WBD]
*Antipope*
* Felix V

**Amadeus** 1845-1890
[DEP, HN, RH]
*King of Spain and Duke of Aosta*
* [The] Duke of Langosta [Locust]
* [The] Summer King

**Amadeus V** 1249-1323
[DNNS, WBD]
*Count of Savoy*
* [The] Great

**Amadeus VI** 1334-1383
[DNNS, HN]
*Count of Savoy*
* [The] Green Count

**Amadeus VII** 1360-1391
[DNNS, HN]
*Count of Savoy*
* [The] Red

**Amadeus VIII** 1383-1451
[FFF, RH, SN]
*Duke of Savoy*
* [The] Hermit of La Ripaille
* [The] Pacific

**Amador, Americo**
*See* De Elzaburu, Manuel

**Amalie Marie Friederike Auguste
[Duchess of Saxony]** 1794-1870
[WBD]
*German playwright and composer*
* Heiter, Amalie

**Amalrich** [SN]
*Earl of Flanders*
* [The] Leper

**Amamoo, Joseph Godson** 1931-
[CA]
*Ghanaian author*
* Kambu, Joseph

**Amand [or Amandus]** 594?- 667?
[DNNF, HN]
*Saint*
* [The] Apostle of the Netherlands

**Amanda**
*See* Dennis, Amanda E.

**Amanda**
*See* Wynne-Tyson, Esme

**Amara, Lucine**
*See* Armaganian, Lucine Tockqui

**Amare, Rothayne**
*See* Byrne, Stuart J[ames]

**Amarillo Slim**
*See* Preston, Thomas Austin

**Amarnath**
*See* Oak, Purushottam Nagesh

**Amaryllis**
*See* Deshoulieres, Antoinette du
Ligier de la Garde

**[An] Amateur**
*See* Cox, W.

**[An] Amateur**
*See* De Kay, James E.

**[An] Amateur**
*See* Egan, Pierce

**[An] Amateur**
*See* Sharpe, Charles Kirkpatrick

**Amateur Angler**
*See* Marston, Edward

**[The] Amateur Casual**
*See* Greenwood, James

**Amati, Orlanda**
*See* D'Amato, Elinor Barbara

**Amato, Giovanni Antonio d'**
1475-1555 [WBD]
*Neapolitan painter*
* [Il] Vecchio

**Amato, Giuseppe**
*See* Vasaturo, Giuseppe

**Amato, Peppino**
*See* Vasaturo, Giuseppe

**Amatora, [Sister] Mary**
*See* Fleury, Delphine

**Amatthey**
*See* Arnould, Arthur

**Amatuna, Samoots**
*See* Amatuna, Samuzzo

**Amatuna, Samuzzo** ?-1925 [BLB]
*American underworld figure*
* Amatuna, Samoots

**Amaury-Duval, Eugene Emmanuel**
*See* Pineux-Duval, Eugene
Emmanuel

**[The] Amazing Fogel**
*See* Fogel, Maurice

**[The] Amazing Kildon**
*See* Kill, Don

**[The] Amazing Kreskin**
*See* Kresge, George Joseph, Jr.

**[The] Amazing Randi**
*See* Randi, James

**[The] Amazon of Liberty**
*See* Terwagne, Anne Joseph

**[The] Amazon of the Revolution**
*See* Terwagne, Anne Joseph

**[The] Ambassador of Basketball**
*See* Taylor, Charles H. [Chuck]

**[The] Ambassador of Letters of
Tennessee**
*See* Allen, Harriette Bias

**Amber, Gracie**
*See* Koontz, Gerda

**Amberg, Louis** ?-1935 [BLB]
*American underworld figure*
* Amberg, Pretty

**Amberg, Pretty**
*See* Amberg, Louis

**Amberley, Richard**
*See* Bourquin, Paul Henry James

**Amberley, Simon**
*See* Hoar, Peter

**Ambers, Lou**
*See* D'Ambrosio, Luigi

**Ambhanwong, Suthilak** 1924-   [CA]
*Thai educator and author*
* Suthinee

**Ambient, Mark**
*See* Harley, Mark

**Ambler, Eric** 1909-
[CA, WD, WW]
*British author*
* Reed, Eliot [joint pseudonym with
Charles Rodda]

**[The] Ambling Alp**
*See* Carnera, Primo

**Ambree, Mary** 16th c.
[DNNS, RH]
*British heroine*
* [The] English Joan of Arc

**Ambrogini, Angelo** 1454-1494
[SN, WBD]
*Italian poet and playwright*
* Politian
* Poliziano, Angelo
* [The] Ruler of the Ausonian Lyre

**Ambroise**
*See* Catarino, Launcelot-Polite

**Ambroise, Fernand** 1881-1938
[CW]
*Haitian poet*
* Saint Laurent, Felix de

**Ambroise, Lys** 1911-   [CW]
*Haitian poet*
* Libose, Jean

**Ambros**
*See* Ambrosio Zaragoza, Miguel

**Ambrose**
*See* Wight, James Ambrose

**Ambrose, Alice**
*See* Lazerowitz, Alice Ambrose

**Ambrose, Bam-Bam**
*See* Ambrose, Dick

**Ambrose, Dick** 1953-   [SMG]
*American football player*
* Ambrose, Bam-Bam

**Ambrose, Eric [Samuel]** 1908-
[CAP]
*British author and playwright*
* MacIre, Esor B.
* Rennie, Christopher
* Vance, Edgar

**Ambrose, James** 20th c.   [SG]
*Boxer*
* Sullivan, Yankee

**Ambrosio Zaragoza, Miguel** 20th
c.   [WECO]
*Spanish cartoonist*
* Ambros

**Ambrus, Gyozo Laszlo** 1935-   [CA]
*Hungarian-born author and
illustrator*
* Ambrus, Victor G.

**Ambrus, Victor G.**
*See* Ambrus, Gyozo Laszlo

**Ameche, Alan D.** 1933-   [FB]
*American football player*
* [The] Horse

**Ameche, Don**
*See* Amici, Dominic Felix

**Amelunghi, Geronimo [Girolamo]**
16th c.   [FFF, RH, SN]
*Italian poet*
* [Il] Gobbo di Pisa
* [The] Humpback

**Amemiya, Yuriko** 1920-   [BEW]
*American dancer*
* Yuriko

**Amender**
*See* Burnham, Benjamin F.

**Amendola, Mario** 1910-   [FDG]
*Italian director*
* Jacobs, Irving

**Amenhotep IV**
*See* Ikhnaton [or Akhenaten]

**[An] American**
*See* Biddle, Richard

**[An] American**
*See* Calvert, George Henry

**[An] American**
*See* Cass, Lewis

**[An] American**
*See* Cooper, James Fenimore

**[The] American**
*See* Fournier, Claude

**[The] American Addison**
*See* Dennie, Joseph

**[The] American Beauty**
*See* MacDonald, Katherine

**American Beauty Rose**
*See* Shearer, [Edith] Norma

**[The] American Bewick**
*See* Anderson, Alexander

**[The] American Blackstone**
*See* Kent, James

**[The] American Bulldog**
*See* Smith, Walter Bedell

**[The] American Caesar**
*See* Grant, Hiram Ulysses

**[The] American Cato**
*See* Adams, Samuel

**[The] American Charles Lamb**
*See* Curtis, George William

**[The] American Cincinnatus**
*See* Washington, George

**[An] American Citizen**
*See* Lawrence, William Beach

**[The] American Eagle**
*See* Clark, Mark Wayne

**[The] American Fabius**
*See* Washington, George

**[The] American Fat Man**
*See* Dunlop, Bobby

**[The] American Florence Nightingale**
*See* Maxwell, Anna Caroline

**[An] American Gentleman**
*See* Coxe, Richard S.

**American Girl Abroad**
*See* Trafton, Adelina

**[The] American Goldsmith**
*See* Woodworth, Samuel

**[An] American in London**
*See* Colton, Calvin

**[The] American Louis Philippe**
*See* Fillmore, Millard

**[The] American Montaigne**
*See* Emerson, Ralph Waldo

**[The] American Mrs. Montague**
*See* Morton, Sarah Wentworth

**[The] American Newton**
*See* Rittenhouse, David

**[The] American Peasant**
*See* Pipgras, George

**[The] American Prodigy**
*See* Lemoine, Sauvelle

**[The] American Prophet**
*See* Miller, William

**[The] American Richard Savage**
*See* Poe, Edgar Allan

**[The] American Sappho**
*See* Appleton, Sarah Wentworth

**American Soccer League, Mr.**
See Alonso, Julius G.

**[The] American Socrates**
See Franklin, Benjamin

**[The] American Stuart**
See Stuart, Gilbert Charles

**[The] American Talleyrand**
See Van Buren, Martin

**[The] American Tupper**
See Holland, Josiah Gilbert

**Americanus**
See Baird, Robert

**Americanus**
See Evans, Caleb

**America's Beloved Gospel Singer**
See Shea, George Beverly

**America's Blue Yodeler**
See Rodgers, James Charles [Jimmie]

**America's Favorite Cowboy**
See Autry, [Orvon] Gene

**America's First Gentleman**
See Arthur, Chester Alan

**America's Foremost Brown Blues Singer**
See Hunter, Alberta

**America's Foremost Ebony Comedienne**
See Waters, Ethel

**America's Foremost Folk Singer**
See Kincaid, Bradley

**America's Foremost Jewish Actress**
See Abuza, Sophie

**America's Sweetheart**
See Smith, Gladys Mary

**America's Toastmaster General**
See Jessel, George

**Americus**
See Lieber, Francis

**Amery, L. S.**
See Amery, Leopold Stennett

**Amery, Leopold Stennett** 1873-1955 [LC]
*British statesman and author*
* Amery, L. S.

**Ames**
See Stephenson, Andrew M.

**Ames, Adrienne**
See McClure, Adrienne Ruth

**Ames, Amy**
See Hennessy, Mrs. Augustus

**Ames, Charles** 1907?-1964 [BEW]
*Dancer*
* Conkling, Charles

**Ames, Clinton**
See Graham, Roger Phillips

**Ames, Clyde**
See Knoles, William

**Ames, Ed**
See Urick, Ed

**Ames, Eleanor Maria [Easterbrook]** 1831-1905 [FFF, SFL, WGT]
*American author*
* Kirk, Eleanor

**Ames, Elinor**
See Ranzini, Addis Durning

**Ames, Felicia**
See Burden, Jean

**Ames, Fisher** 1758-1808 [FFF]
*American statesman and writer*
* Camillus

**Ames, Francis H.** 1900- [CA]
*American author*
* Watson, Frank

**Ames, Gene**
See Urick, Gene

**Ames, Jennifer**
See Greig, Maysie

**Ames, Joe**
See Urick, Joe

**Ames, Knowlton L.** 1868-1931 [AS, FB]
*American football player*
* Ames, Snake

**Ames, Lee J[udah]** 1921- [SAT]
*American illustrator*
* David, Jonathan

**Ames, Leon**
See Wycoff, Leon

**Ames, Leon Kessling** 1882?-1936 [AS, DGS, PB]
*American baseball player*
* Ames, Red

**Ames, Leslie**
See Rigoni, Orlando [Joseph]

**Ames, Leslie**
See Ross, William Edward Daniel

**Ames, Noel**
See Barrows, [Ruth] Marjorie

**Ames, Norma** 1920- [CA]
*American author*
* Norman, Ames

**Ames, Rachel** 1922- [CA]
*British author*
* Gainham, Sarah

**Ames, Red**
See Ames, Leon Kessling

**Ames, Richard**
See Abrams, Herbert Edward

**Ames, Rose Wyler** 1909- [TBJ]
*American author*
* Thayer, Peter
* Wyler, Rose

**Ames, Snake**
See Ames, Knowlton L.

**Ames, Tessie**
See Smith, Trixie

**Ames, Vic**
See Urick, Vic

**Ames, Woodforde**
See Ramp, James

**Amey, Ian** 20th c. [RM]
*Musician*
* Tich

**Amfrye, Guillaume** 1639-1720 [HN, RH, SN]
*French poet*
* [The] Anacreon of the People of Quality
* [The] Anacreon of the Temple
* Chaulieu, Abbe de

**Amfrye, Guillaume** (Continued)
* [The] Horace of France
* [The] Tom Moore of France

**Amherst, Nicholas** ?-1742 [FFF, HN]
*British editor*
* Bolingbroke
* D'Anvers, Caleb
* Philalethes
* Pulteney

**Amherst, Wes**
See Shaver, Richard S[harpe]

**[L']Ami des Hommes**
See Riquetti, Victor

**Ami du Peuple**
See Marat, Jean Paul

**Amici, Dominic Felix** 1908- [FC, PMJ, TR]
*American actor*
* Ameche, Don

**Amicus**
See Fairbairn, [Sir] Thomas

**Amicus**
See Wildbore, Charles

**Amicus Curiae**
See Collier, John Payne

**Amicus Curiae?**
See Francis, [Sir] Philip

**Amicus Curiae**
See Fuller, Edmund [Maybank]

**Amid, John**
See Stearns, Myron Morris

**Amidon, Bill [Vincent]** 1935- [CA]
*American author*
* Taylor, Jesse

**Amigo**
See Skinner, Salmon

**[Un] Amigo de la Juventud**
See Zenea, Juan Clemente

**Amin, Big Daddy**
See Amin Dada, Idi

**Amin, Masha Allah Jamil Abdullah al-**
See Brown, Hubert Geroid

**Amin Dada, Idi** 1925-
*Ugandan head of state*
* Amin, Big Daddy

**Aminedi [Invisible One]**
See Ben Bella, Ahmed

**Amini, Johari**
See Latimore, Jewel C.

**Amir Chand** ?-1767 [WBD]
*Indian banker*
* Omichund

**Amis, Breton**
See Best, Rayleigh Breton Amis

**Amis, Kingsley [William]** 1922- [CA, CC, ESF]
*British author*
* Angry Young Man
* Markham, Robert

**Amishai, M. H.**
See Maisels, Misha

**Amishai-Maisels, Ziva**
See Maisels, Maxine S.

**Amiss, Dennis Leslie** 1943- [DC]
*British cricketer*
* Amiss, Sacker

**Amiss, Sacker**
See Amiss, Dennis Leslie

**Ammonius** 3rd c. BC [WBD]
*Greek surgeon*
* Lithotomus

**Ammonius** 3rd c. [WBD]
*Alexandrian philosopher*
* Saccas [Sack Bearer]

**Ammons, [Eu]gene** 1925-1974 [B10, DAM, PMJ]
*American jazz musician*
* Ammons, Jug

**Ammons, Jug**
See Ammons, [Eu]gene

**Amner**
See Steevens, George

**Amner, Ralph** 17th c. [SN]
*British composer*
* [The] Bull Speaker

**Amnon III**
See Evans, William

**Amoenus, Doctor**
See Couton, Robert

**Amole, Doc**
See Amole, Morris George

**Amole, Morris George** 1878-1912 [BE]
*American baseball player*
* Amole, Doc

**Amond, Nellie**
See Putnam, Mrs. S. W.

**Amor, Amos**
See Harrell, Irene B[urk]

**[The] Amorian**
See Michael II

**Amoros, Edmundo Isasi** 1932- [BE, PB]
*Cuban-born baseball player*
* Amoros, Sandy

**Amoros, Juan Bautista** 1856-1912 [CD]
*Spanish author*
* Lanza, Silverio

**Amoros, Sandy**
See Amoros, Edmundo Isasi

**[The] Amorous**
See Philip I [or Philippe]

**Amory, Arthur R.**
See Sarle, Charles Spenser

**Amory, Guy**
See Bradbury, Ray [Douglas]

**Amory, Thomas** 1691?-1788 [DEL, PA, SN]
*British author*
* Buncle, John
* [The] English Rabelais

**Amos, Alan**
See Knight, Kathleen Moore

**Amos, Famous**
See Amos, Wally

**Amos, Wally** 20th c.
*American cookie manufacturer*
* Amos, Famous

**Amos, Wally** (Continued)
* [The] Chocolate Chip Cookie
   King

**Amouzegar, Jamshid** 1923?-
*Iranian oil negotiator*
* [The] 12 Million Dollar Man

**Amphibian**
*See* Ashton, [Sir] George Grey

**Amphilogist**
*See* Sands, Robert Charles

**Amplegirth, Anthony**
*See* Dent, Anthony Austen

**Amr Bey, F. D.** 1910-   [OCS]
*Egyptian squash rackets player*
* Amr Pasha

**Amr ibn-Bahr** 773?- 869   [WBD]
*Arabic author*
* Jahiz, al- [The Goggle-Eyed]

**Amr Pasha**
*See* Amr Bey, F. D.

**Amy, [William] Lacey** 20th c.
[WW, WWL]
*Canadian author*
* Allan, Luke

**Amyand, Arthur** 1860-1925   [SFL]
*Author*
* Haggard, [Captain] Edward
   Arthur

**An Craoibhin Aoibhinn [Delightful
Little Branch]**
*See* Hyde, Douglas

**Ana, Ray**
*See* Reyna, Ruth

**Anacletus II**
*See* Pierleoni, Pietro

**Anacreon** 6th c. BC
[DEP, DNNS, RH]
*Greek poet*
* [The] Teian Muse [or Poet]

**[The] Anacreon of Ancient Scottish
Poetry**
*See* Scot, Alexander

**[The] Anacreon of France**
*See* Thiard, Pontus de

**[The] Anacreon of Germany**
*See* Fleming [or Flemming], Paul

**[The] Anacreon of His Day**
*See* Basselin, Olivier

**[The] Anacreon of Painters**
*See* Albani [or Albano], Francesco

**[The] Anacreon of Painting**
*See* Boucher, Francois

**[The] Anacreon of Persia**
*See* Hafiz, Mohammed

**[The] Anacreon of Sicily**
*See* Meli, Giovanni

**[The] Anacreon of the French**
*See* Laujon, Pierre

**[The] Anacreon of the French**
*See* Tyard, Pontus de

**[The] Anacreon of the Guillotine**
*See* Barere de Vieuzac, Bertrand

**[The] Anacreon of the People of
Quality**
*See* Amfrye, Guillaume

**[The] Anacreon of the Temple**
*See* Amfrye, Guillaume

**[The] Anacreon of the Twelfth
Century**
*See* Mapes, Walter

**[The] Anak of Publishers**
*See* Murray, John

**Analyticus**
*See* Wise, James Waterman

**Anand, Mulk Raj** 1905-   [IAW]
*Indian author*
* Muni, Narad

**Anand, Valerie** 1937-   [CA]
*British editor and author*
* Buckley, Fiona

**Anastasia, Albert** 1903-1957   [BLB]
*American underworld figure*
* [The] Lord High Executioner
* [The] Mad Hatter

**Anastasio, Anthony** ?-1963
*American underworld figure*
* Anastasio, Tough Tony

**Anastasio, Tough Tony**
*See* Anastasio, Anthony

**Anastasius**
*See* Radla, Astrik

**Anastasius** 7th c.   [DNNF, FFF]
*Monk of Mt. Sinai*
* [The] New Moses

**Anastasius** 9th c.   [WBD]
*Librarian of the Vatican*
* Bibliothecarius

**Anastasius I** 430?- 518   [HN]
*Byzantine emperor*
* [The] Silentiary

**Anastasius IV**
*See* Corrado

**Anati, Emmanuel** 1930-   [IAW]
*Italian archaeologist and author*
* E. A.
* Emmanuel

**Anatol, A.**
*See* Kuznetsov, Anatoli

**[L']Anatomie Vivante [The Living
Anatomy]**
*See* Arouet, Francois Marie

**[The] Anatomist of Humanity**
*See* Poquelin, Jean Baptiste

**Anaxagoras**
*See* Alembert, Jean Le Rond d'

**Ancel, Martin**
*See* Martin, Lance

**Ancey, Georges**
*See* De Curnieu, Georges

**Anchieta, Jose de** 1533-1597
[DEP, DNNS, HN]
*Portuguese missionary*
* [The] Apostle of Brazil
* [The] Apostle of the New World

**Anchor**
*See* De Peyster, John Watts

**[The] Anchor**
*See* Maple, Eddie

**Anchowitz, Charles** 1891-
[BX, EJS, RBE]
*British-born boxer*
* White, Charley

**Anchusa**
*See* Spicer, Anne Higginson

**[The] Ancient**
*See* Lincoln, Abraham

**[The] Ancient Mariner of the Wabash**
*See* Thompson, Richard Wigginton

**Ancient, Oliver**
*See* McAlpine, Robert W.

**Ancker, Gee**
*See* Ancker, Walter

**Ancker, Liver**
*See* Ancker, Walter

**Ancker, Walter** 1894-1954   [BE]
*American baseball player*
* Ancker, Gee
* Ancker, Liver

**Ancklitzer [Anklitzen or Angelisen],
Konstantin** 13th c.   [WBD]
*German monk*
* Berthold, Meister

**Ander, Lee**
*See* Hershberger, Leander Leonard

**Andereich, Justus**
*See* Steiner, Gerolf

**Anders, Edith [Mary] England**
1899-   [CAP, IAW, WD]
*Australian author*
* England, E. M.
* England, Edith

**Anders, Fritz**
*See* Allihn, Heinrich

**Anders, Pete**
*See* Andreoli, Peter

**Anders, Peter**
*See* Seadlund, John Henry

**Andersen, Carl Christian
Thorvaldus**   [FFF]
*Danish author*
* Adam, Christian

**Andersen, Hans Christian**
1805-1875   [DEP, RH]
*Danish author*
* [The] Danish Lafontaine

**Andersen, Martin** 1869-1954
[EWL]
*Danish author*
* Andersen Nexo, Martin

**Andersen, Ted**
*See* Boyd, Waldo T.

**Andersen Nexo, Martin**
*See* Andersen, Martin

**Anderson, Alexander** 1775-1870
[SN]
*American engraver*
* [The] American Bewick

**Anderson, Alexander** 1845-1909
[LC]
*Scottish poet*
* Surfaceman

**Anderson, Alfred**
*See* Pulos, William Leroy

**Anderson, Andy**
*See* Anderson, Edgar W.

**Anderson, Andy**
*See* Anderson, Edward

**Anderson, Andy**
*See* Anderson, Edwin J.

**Anderson, Andy**
*See* Anderson, Glenn

**Anderson, Andy**
*See* Anderson, Paul T.

**Anderson, Andy**
*See* Anderson, William C[harles]

**Anderson, Arnold Revola** 1912-
[BE]
*American baseball player*
* Anderson, Red

**Anderson, Arthur Henry** 1867- ?
[WWL]
*British author*
* Henry, Arthur
* [The] Tramp

**Anderson, Bernard Hartwell** 1919-
[WWJ]
*American jazz musician*
* Anderson, Buddy

**Anderson, Betty** 20th c.   [WW]
*Author*
* Canyon, Claudia

**Anderson, Bill** 1937-   [ECM]
*American country-western performer*
* Anderson, Whispering Bill
* [The] Pat Boone of Country
   Music

**Anderson, Bronco Billy**
*See* Aaronson, Max

**Anderson, Bubbles**
*See* Anderson, Theodore

**Anderson, Buddy**
*See* Anderson, Bernard Hartwell

**anderson, c. v. j.**
*See* Anderson, Chester

**Anderson, C. W.**
*See* Anderson, Clarence William

**Anderson, Candice** ?-1959   [IBW]
*American singer*
* Anderson, Queen

**Anderson, Cat**
*See* Anderson, William Alonzo

**Anderson, Catherine** 1905?-1962
[BEW]
*Theatrical performer*
* Gallimore, Catherine

**Anderson, Charles** 20th c.   [CSH]
*Canadian lacrosse promoter*
* Anderson, Chick

**Anderson, Chester** 20th c.   [ESF]
*American author and poet*
* anderson, c. v. j.

**Anderson, Chick**
*See* Anderson, Charles

**Anderson, Clarence** 20th c.   [BWW]
*American singer*
* Williamson, Sonny Boy, Jr.

**Anderson, Clarence William**
1891-1971   [WYA]
*Author*
* Anderson, C. W.

**Anderson, Clifford** [joint pseudonym
with Richard Gardner and Clifford
Irving]
*See* Anderson, Robert

**Anderson, Clifford** [joint pseudonym with Robert Anderson and Richard Gardner]
*See* Irving, Clifford Michael

**Anderson, Clifford** [joint pseudonym with Robert Anderson and Clifford Irving]
*See* Orth, Richard

**Anderson, Coochie**
*See* Anderson, Leo

**Anderson, Cowboy**
*See* Anderson, Thomas Linton

**Anderson, Daphne**
*See* Scrutton, Daphne

**Anderson, David**
*See* Jones, Raymond F.

**Anderson, Dutch**
*See* Anderson, John D.

**Anderson, Dutch**
*See* Von Teller, Ivan Dahl

**Anderson, Edgar** 1920- [CA]
*Latvian-born American author*
* Andersons, Edgars

**Anderson, Edgar W.** 1931- [IWM]
*American musician*
* Anderson, Andy

**Anderson, Edmund Lincoln [Eddie]** 1905-1977 [FC, IPA, WA]
*American entertainer*
* Rochester

**Anderson, Edward** 1910- [WWJ]
*American jazz musician*
* Anderson, Andy

**Anderson, Edward Hall** [PA]
*Author*
* [A] Layman

**Anderson, Edward John** 1880-1923 [BE]
*American baseball player*
* Anderson, Goat

**Anderson, Edwin J.** 20th c. [SMG]
*American football team consultant*
* Anderson, Andy

**Anderson, Ella**
*See* MacLeod, Ellen Jane

**Anderson, [Lady] Flavia** 1910- [WD]
*British author*
* Portobello, Petronella

**Anderson, Forddy**
*See* Anderson, Forrest

**Anderson, Forrest** 1919- [BB]
*American basketball coach*
* Anderson, Forddy

**Anderson, Frank** 20th c. [MBF]
*British editor*
* Uncle Dan

**Anderson, G. J. B.** 20th c. [MBF]
*British author*
* Dangerfield, Captain
* Fielding, Howard
* Lynn, Max
* Whyte, [Viscount] Y. Melton

**Anderson, Gary** 1939- [RO1]
*American singer*
* Bonds, Gary U. S.
* Bonds, Ulysses Samuel

**Anderson, George**
*See* Groom, Arthur William

**Anderson, George**
*See* Miner, William

**Anderson, George**
*See* Von Teller, Ivan Dahl

**Anderson, George**
*See* Weissman, Jack

**Anderson, George Lee** 1934- [IPA, PB, SMG]
*American baseball manager*
* Anderson, Sparky

**Anderson, Gertrud** 1900- [OCF]
*German dancer and singer*
* Gert, Valeska

**Anderson, Gertrude** 1898-1955 [SC]
*Canadian-born actress*
* Hoffman, Gertrude

**Anderson, Gilbert M.**
*See* Aaronson, Max

**Anderson, Glenn** 1960- [SMG]
*Canadian-born hockey player*
* Anderson, Andy

**Anderson, Goat**
*See* Anderson, Edward John

**Anderson, Goings**
*See* Anderson, Ronald Chester

**Anderson, Heartley** 1899?-1978 [FB]
*American football player and coach*
* Anderson, Hunk

**Anderson, Honest John**
*See* Anderson, John Joseph

**Anderson, Hunk**
*See* Anderson, Heartley

**Anderson, J. N.**
*See* Anderson, [James] Norman [Dalrymple]

**Anderson, James** 1739-1808 [FFF, PA]
*Editor*
* Agricola
* Alcibiades
* Hairbrain, Timothy
* Senex

**Anderson, John Bayard** 1922-
*American politician*
* Saint John the Righteous

**Anderson, John D.** 20th c. [SMG]
*American baseball scout*
* Anderson, Dutch

**Anderson, John Fred** 1885-1957 [BE]
*American baseball player*
* Anderson, Spitball

**Anderson, John Joseph** 1873-1949 [BE]
*Norwegian-born baseball player*
* Anderson, Honest John

**Anderson, John Larnicourt** [PA]
*Author*
* [A] Layman

**Anderson, John W.** 1937- [IBW]
*American poet, songwriter, singer*
* Kasandra, John

**Anderson, [Dame] Judith**
*See* Anderson-Anderson, Frances Margaret

**Anderson, Julia**
*See* Lueth, Julia

**Anderson, Karen** 20th c. [SFP]
*Author*
* Kruse, June Millichamp

**Anderson, Kathleen Agness Cicely** [SFL]
*British author*
* Mary Catherine, [Sister]
* S. M. C.

**Anderson, Laura** 1853-1939 [SC]
*American actress*
* La Vernie, Laura

**Anderson, Lefty**
*See* Anderson, Walter Carl

**Anderson, Lefty**
*See* Anderson, William Edward [Bill]

**Anderson, Leo** 20th c. [GW]
*American rodeo performer*
* Anderson, Coochie

**Anderson, Little Milton**
*See* Anderson, Milton

**Anderson, Lucia [Lewis]** 1922- [CA, SAT]
*American biologist and scientific writer*
* Lewis, Lucia Z.

**Anderson, Madeleine Paltenghi** 1899- [CAP]
*American author*
* Paltenghi, Madeleine

**Anderson, Martin** 1854-1932 [DBA, LAO]
*Scottish satirist and cartoonist*
* Cynicus

**Anderson, Mary Antoinette** 1859-1940 [FFF]
*American actress*
* Our Mary

**Anderson, Milton** 20th c. [BWW]
*American musician*
* Anderson, Little Milton

**Anderson, Mrs. Galusha** [PA]
*Author*
* Doe, Dorothy

**Anderson, Mrs. Oscar** [FFF]
*Entertainer*
* Melville, Maud

**Anderson, [James] Norman [Dalrymple]** 1908- [CA]
*British author and legal advisor*
* Anderson, J. N.

**Anderson, O. J.**
*See* Anderson, Ottis Jerome

**Anderson, Olive San Louie** [PA]
*Author*
* Sola

**Anderson, Ottis Jerome** 20th c.
*American football player*
* Anderson, O. J.

**Anderson, Paul** 1933- [OCS]
*American weight lifter*
* [The] Dixie Derrick

**Anderson, Paul T.** 1918- [IBW]
*American pilot and flight instructor*
* Anderson, Andy

**Anderson, Poul [William]** 1926- [CA, ESF, HFF]
*American author*
* Craig, A. A.
* Karageorge, Michael?
* Sanders, Winston P.

**Anderson, Queen**
*See* Anderson, Candice

**Anderson, Rachel**
*See* Bradby, Rachel

**Anderson, Red**
*See* Anderson, Arnold Revola

**Anderson, Robert** 1770-1833 [DNNF]
*British poet*
* [The] Cumbrian Poet

**Anderson, Robert** 20th c. [CA]
*Author*
* Anderson, Clifford [joint pseudonym with Richard Gardner and Clifford Irving]

**Anderson, Robert C[harles]** 1930- [CA]
*American author*
* Cottle, Charles

**Anderson, Roberta Joan** 1943- [CLC]
*Canadian songwriter and musician*
* Mitchell, Joni

**Anderson, Ronald Chester** 1945- [CEI, HK]
*Canadian-born hockey player*
* Anderson, Goings

**Anderson, Rosa** 1881- [LAO]
*German author*
* Kaulitz-Niedeck, R.

**Anderson, Sam**
*See* Miner, William

**Anderson, Sarah**
*See* Coxer, Sarah

**Anderson, Shirley Lord** 1934- [CA]
*British-born beauty consultant, editor, author*
* Lord, Shirley

**Anderson, Sparky**
*See* Anderson, George Lee

**Anderson, Spitball**
*See* Anderson, John Fred

**Anderson, Stella Benson** 1892-1933 [WGT]
*Author*
* Benson, Stella

**Anderson, Teresa** 1944- [CA]
*American poet and playwright*
* McCarthy, Teresa

**Anderson, Theodore** 20th c. [OBW]
*American baseball player*
* Anderson, Bubbles

**Anderson, Thomas Linton** 1911- [CEI]
*Scottish-born hockey player*
* Anderson, Cowboy

**Anderson, Vilhelm Carl Emil** 1875-1955 [WBD]
*Swedish sculptor*
* Milles, [Vilhelm] Carl [Emil]

**Anderson, Virginia [R. Cronin]**
1920-   [CA, WD]
*American poet*
* Hill, Hyacinthe

**Anderson, Vivian** 1895-1958
[F2, FC]
*American actress*
* Oakland, Vivian

**Anderson, W. B.**
*See* Schultz, James Willard

**Anderson, Walter Carl** 1897-   [BE]
*American baseball player*
* Anderson, Lefty

**Anderson, Whispering Bill**
*See* Anderson, Bill

**Anderson, William** 1929-   [FC]
*American actor*
* West, Adam

**Anderson, William Alonzo**
1916-1981   [DAM, EJ, PMJ]
*American jazz musician*
* Anderson, Cat

**Anderson, William C[harles]** 1920-
[ESF, WGT]
*American author*
* Anderson, Andy

**Anderson, William Edward [Bill]**
1895-   [BE]
*American baseball player*
* Anderson, Lefty

**Anderson, William Wycliffe** 1911-
[BEW, FC]
*American actor*
* Erickson, Leif

**Anderson-Anderson, Frances
Margaret** 1898-   [BEW, TR]
*Australian-born actress*
* Anderson, [Dame] Judith

**Andersons, Edgars**
*See* Anderson, Edgar

**Andersson, Annifrid Lyngstad**
1945-   [RO2]
*Swedish singer*
* Andersson, Frida

**Andersson, Frida**
*See* Andersson, Annifrid Lyngstad

**Andersson, Nic**
*See* Tofte, Arthur

**Andersson, Oskar Emil** 1877-1906
[WECO]
*Swedish cartoonist*
* O. A.

**Anderton, Joanne [Marie] Gast**
1930-   [CA]
*American author*
* Anderton, Johana Gast

**Anderton, Johana Gast**
*See* Anderton, Joanne [Marie]
Gast

**Anderton, Laurence**   [SN]
*Jesuit scholar*
* Golden Mouth

**Andes, John Charles** 1920-   [BEW]
*American actor and singer*
* Andes, Keith

**Andes, Keith**
*See* Andes, John Charles

**Andom, R.**
*See* Barrett, Alfred Walter

**Andonian, Jeanne [Beghian]**
1890-1976   [B10]
*American author*
* May, Janine

**Andouard**
*See* Giraudoux, Jean [Hippolyte]

**Andrada e Silva, Jose Bonifacio de**
1763?-1838   [WBD]
*Brazilian statesman and geologist*
* Bonifacio, Jose

**Andrade, A.** 20th c.   [WF]
*Author*
* Haskins, Dick

**Andrade, Daniel Ray** 1929-
[CWG, DAM]
*American country-western performer*
* Hank the Drifter

**Andrade, E. N. Da C.**
*See* Andrade, Edward Neville Da
Costa

**Andrade, Edward Neville Da Costa**
1887-1971   [LC]
*British physicist and author*
* Andrade, E. N. Da C.

**Andre**
*See* Marville, Pierre Nicolas

**Andre, John Edward** 1923-   [BE]
*American baseball player*
* Andre, Long John

**Andre, Lee**
*See* Andrus, L. R.

**Andre, Long John**
*See* Andre, John Edward

**Andre the Giant**
*See* Roussimoff, Andre

**Andre, W. J.**
*See* Jordan, W.

**Andrea da Salerno**
*See* Sabbatini, Andrea

**Andreae, Otto Stuart** 1865-1930
[BEW]
*Actor and producer*
* Stuart, Otho

**Andreas, Antonio [or Anthony]**
?-1320   [HN, RH, SN]
*Spanish theologian*
* [The] Dulcifluous Doctor

**Andreas, Thomas**
*See* Williams, Thomas [Andrew]

**Andree, Madame**
*See* Wake, Nancy

**Andreev, Georgy** 1918-   [IAW]
*Bulgarian poet*
* Andreev, Vesselin

**Andreev, Vesselin**
*See* Andreev, Georgy

**Andreeva-Babakhan, Anna
Misaakovna**
*See* Babakhan, Anna Misaakovna

**Andreino degl'Impiccati**
*See* Castagno, Andrea del

**Andrenio**
*See* Gomez De Baquero, Eduardo

**Andreoli, Peter** 1941-   [RO2]
*American singer and songwriter*
* Anders, Pete

**Andres, Ernest Henry [Ernie]** 1918-
[BE]
*American baseball player*
* Andres, Junie

**Andres, Junie**
*See* Andres, Ernest Henry [Ernie]

**Andreski, Iris**
*See* Gillespie, Iris Sylvia

**Andreva, Stella**
*See* Brown, Stella

**Andrevon, Jean-Pierre** 1937-   [ESF]
*French author and illustrator*
* Brutsche, Alphonse

**Andrew** 1960?-
*British prince*
* Randy Andy

**Andrew, Nicholas Jeffery**   [FFF]
*American writer*
* Aquarist

**Andrew, [Dr.] Robert**
*See* Cooper, Robert Andrew

**Andrew, Stephen**
*See* Layton, Frank George

**Andrew, Thomas**
*See* Wright, Sewell Peaslee

**Andrew III** ?-1301   [WBD]
*King of Hungary*
* [The] Venetian

**Andrewes, Patience**
*See* Bradford, Patience Andrewes

**Andrews, Allen** 1913-   [WD]
*British author*
* Cotton, Billy
* Pierrepoint, Albert

**Andrews, Arthur [Douglas, Jr.]**
1923-   [CA]
*American writer and poet*
* Ort, Ana

**Andrews, Carrie**
*See* Richardson, Mrs. Leander

**Andrews, Carver Daniel** 1909-   [FC]
*American actor*
* Andrews, Dana

**Andrews, Claire** 1940-   [AW, CA]
*British author*
* Claire, Keith [joint pseudonym
with Keith Andrews]

**Andrews, Clarence A[delbert]**
1912-   [CA]
*American author*
* Randall, Steven

**Andrews, Dana**
*See* Andrews, Carver Daniel

**Andrews, E. L.**
*See* Andrews, Edith Lovell

**Andrews, Edith Lovell** 1886-   [ART]
*British painter and poster designer*
* Andrews, E. L.

**Andrews, Elisha Benjamin**
1844-1917   [FFF]
*American educator and author*
* Gimel

**Andrews, Eliza Frances [Fanny]**
1840?-
*American author*
* Hay, Elzey

**Andrews, Elizabeth** 1874-1901
[BMH]
*Singer*
* Wentworth, Bessie

**Andrews, Elizabeth** 1940-   [IAW]
*American author*
* Hainstock, Elizabeth

**Andrews, Elton V.**
*See* Pohl, Frederik

**Andrews, George Augustus**
1868-1946   [F2, FC, WEF]
*British actor*
* Arliss, George

**Andrews, Herman** 20th c.   [OBW]
*American baseball player*
* Andrews, Jabo

**Andrews, Hub**
*See* Andrews, Hubert Carl

**Andrews, Hubert Carl** 1922-   [BE]
*American baseball player*
* Andrews, Hub
* Andrews, Tuny

**Andrews, Ivy Paul** 1907-   [BE]
*American baseball player*
* Andrews, Poison Ivy

**Andrews, J. S.**
*See* Andrews, James Sydney

**Andrews, Jabo**
*See* Andrews, Herman

**Andrews, James Sydney** 1934-
[SFL]
*Irish author*
* Andrews, J. S.

**Andrews, John Urkhardt**
1825-1883   [FFF]
*American orator and leader of 1863
draft riots*
* [The] Passion Orator

**Andrews, Julie**
*See* Wells, Julia Elizabeth

**Andrews, Keith** 1930-   [AW, CA]
*British author*
* Claire, Keith [joint pseudonym
with Claire Andrews]

**Andrews, Leslie** 1901-
[FDG, WEF]
*British director*
* Arliss, Leslie

**Andrews, Lois**
*See* Gourley, Lorraine

**Andrews, Marcia** 20th c.   [ART]
*British painter*
* M. A.

**Andrews, Mrs. C. R.**   [FFF]
*Entertainer*
* Colville, Violetta

**Andrews, Mrs. Charles A.**   [FFF]
*Entertainer*
* Arnold, Florine

**Andrews, Muriel** 20th c.   [THR]
*British actress and dancer*
* Montrose, Muriel

**Andrews, Poison Ivy**
*See* Andrews, Ivy Paul

**Andrews, Polo**
*See* Andruskewicz, Stanley Joseph

**Andrews, Richard** 1831-1909
[WBD]
*British-born musician and composer*
* Hoffman, Richard

**Andrews, Robert**
*See* Zanchin, Nino

**Andrews, [Charles] Robert D[ouglas Hardy]** 1908- [CAP]
*American author*
* Douglas, Robert
* Hardy, Douglas

**Andrews, Ruby**
*See* Stackhouse, Ruby

**Andrews, Sonny**
*See* Andrietta, Carmine

**Andrews, Stan[ley Joseph]**
*See* Andruskewicz, Stanley Joseph

**Andrews, Stephen Pearl** 1812- ?
[PA]
*Author*
* Pantarch

**Andrews, Ted** 1907- [BMH]
*Canadian-born singer*
* [The] Canadian Troubador

**Andrews, Tige**
*See* Androwaous, Tiger

**Andrews, Tuny**
*See* Andrews, Hubert Carl

**Andrews, Wayne** 1913- [CA]
*American author*
* O'Reilly, Montagu

**Andrews, William Forrest** 1924-
[FC]
*American actor*
* Forrest, Steve

**Andrews, William Linton** 1886-
[CA]
*British author and journalist*
* Settle, Edith

**Andreyev, Leonid [Nikolaevich]**
1871-1919 [TLC]
*Russian author and playwright*
* [The] Edgar Allan Poe of Russian
  Literature
* Lynch, James

**Andrezel, Pierre**
*See* Blixen, Karen [Christentze
Dinesen]

**Andrianus Romanus**
*See* Van Roomen, Adrian

**Andrietta, Carmine** 1924- [IWM]
*American jazz musician*
* Andrews, Sonny

**Andrieux, Nicole** 1930- [FC]
*French actress*
* Courcel, Nicole

**Andriola, Alfred** 1912- [WECO]
*American cartoonist*
* James, Alfred

**Andronicus II Palaeologus**
1260-1332 [DNNF, FFF, RH]
*Byzantine emperor*
* [The] Father of His Country

**Andros, [Sir] Edmund** 1637-1714
[SN]
*British colonial governor in America*
* [The] Tyrant of the New England

**Androuet, Jean** 17th c. [WBD]
*French architect*
* [The] Architect of Louis XIII

**Androwaous, Tiger** 1923?- [FC]
*Greek-American actor*
* Andrews, Tige

**Andrus, Dutch**
*See* Andrus, Merwin

**Andrus, L. R.** 20th c. [SFL]
*Author*
* Andre, Lee

**Andrus, Merwin** 1912- [NOJ]
*American jazz musician*
* Andrus, Dutch

**Andruskewicz, Stanley Joseph**
1917- [BE]
*American baseball player*
* Andrews, Polo
* Andrews, Stan[ley Joseph]

**Andrzejewski, Jerzy** 1909- [CA]
*Polish author*
* Andrzeyevski, George

**Andrzeyevski, George**
*See* Andrzejewski, Jerzy

**Andujar, Jack**
*See* Andujar, Joaquin

**Andujar, Joaquin** 1952- [BR]
*Dominican-born baseball player*
* Andujar, Jack

**Anduze-Dufy, Raphael**
*See* Coulet Du Gard, Rene

**Anet, Claude**
*See* Schopfer, Jean

**[El] Anfibio**
*See* Crespo y Borbon, Bartolome
Jose

**Anfriso**
*See* De Navarrete, Manuel Maria

**[L']Ange, Madame**
*See* Becu, Marie Jeanne

**Angebert, Jean**
*See* Bertrand, Michel

**Angebert, Jean-Michel**
*See* Bertrand, Michel

**Angebert, Michel**
*See* Bertrand, Michel

**[The] Angel of Assassination**
*See* Corday d'Armont, [Marie
Anne] Charlotte

**[The] Angel of Death**
*See* Mengele, [Dr.] Josef

**[The] Angel of the Schools**
*See* Aquinas, Thomas [Thomas of
Aquino]

**[The] Angel of the Sun**
*See* Santi [or Sanzio?], Raffaello

**Angel Sleeves Jones**
*See* Jones, Ryerson L.

**Angel, Zuzu**
*See* Joines, Zuleika Angel

**Angeleno, Les**
*See* Ackerman, Forrest J[ames]

**Angeles, Peter A.**
*See* Angelos, Peter A.

**Angelete [Big Angel]**
*See* Fernandez y Pedraza, Angel

**Angeli, Pier**
*See* Pierangeli, Anna Maria

**[The] Angelic Doctor**
*See* Aquinas, Thomas [Thomas of
Aquino]

**Angelico, [Fra]**
*See* Di Pietro, Guido

**Angelico**
*See* Schmalz, Herbert Gustave

**Angelillo [Little Angel]**
*See* Gonzalez y Mazon, Angel

**Angelillo de Triana [Little Angel of
Triana]**
*See* Perez y Hoyos, Angel

**Angelina**
*See* Martineau, Harriet

**Angelina**
*See* Prest, T.

**Angelique, [Mere]**
*See* Arnauld, Jacqueline Marie

**Angelique, Pierre**
*See* Bataille, Georges

**Angell, [Sir] Norman**
*See* Lane, Ralph Norman Angell

**Angelo, [Fra]**
*See* Pezza, Michele

**Angelo, Nancy Carolyn Harrison**
1928- [IA]
*American author*
* DeAngelis, Nancy

**Angeloni, Battista**
*See* Shebbeare, John

**Angelos, Peter A.** 1931- [CA]
*American educator and author*
* Angeles, Peter A.

**Angelou, Maya**
*See* Johnson, Marguerita

**Angelus, Muriel**
*See* Findlay, Muriel Angelus

**Angelus Silesius**
*See* Scheffler, Johannes

**Angerer, Mea** 1905- [ART]
*Austrian-born artist*
* Mea

**Angermayer, Fred Antoine** 1889-
[LAO]
*Austrian playwright and critic*
* LYNX

**Angersola, John** 20th c. [PHM]
*American underworld figure*
* King, John

**Anghiera, Pietro Martire**
1455-1526 [PA]
*Author*
* Martyr, Peter

**Angier, Belle Sumner**
*See* Burn, Belle Sumner Angier

**Angilbert** 740?- 814
[DEP, DNNS, HN]
*Saint*
* [The] Homer of His Age
* [The] Homer of the Franks

**[An] Angler**
*See* Davy, [Sir] Humphrey

**Anglesey, Marquess of**
*See* Paget, George Charles Henry
Victor

**Anglicanus**
*See* Ellis, R. S.

**Anglicanus**
*See* Stanley, Dean

**Anglicus [or Anglicanus]**
*See* Alfred [or Alured]

**Anglo, Maurice** 1916- [WECO]
*British cartoonist, writer, editor*
* Anglo, Mick

**Anglo, Mick**
*See* Anglo, Maurice

**[The] Anglo Saxon Milton**
*See* Caedmon

**Anglus, Thomas** 1582-1676 [PA]
*Author*
* White

**Ango, Fan D.**
*See* Longyear, Barry Brookes

**Angoff, Charles** 1902-1979
[CA, NAA]
*Russian-born American author and
editor*
* Hinton, Richard W.

**Angold, Edit**
*See* Goldstandt, Edit

**Angone, Frank** 1882-1958 [BX]
*American boxer*
* [The] Tipton Slasher
* Yanger, Benny

**Angott, Sammy**
*See* Engotti, Samuel

**Angouleme, Duchesse d'**
*See* Bourbon, Marie Therese
Charlotte de

**Angoulevant** 16th c. [DNNF]
*French court jester*
* [The] Prince of Fools

**Angremy, Jean-Pierre**
*See* Remy, Pierre-Jean

**Angry Young Man**
*See* Amis, Kingsley [William]

**Angus, Carl**
*See* Burpee, Charles W[inslow]

**Angus, Ian**
*See* Mackay, James [Alexander]

**Angus, Tom**
*See* Powell, Geoffrey Stewart

**Angus-Butterworth, Lionel Milner**
*See* Butterworth, Lionel Milner

**Anhalt, Edward** 1914- [CA, HT]
*American screenwriter*
* Holt, Andrew

**Anicar, Tom**
*See* Racina, Thom

**Anicetus**
*See* Clarke, William A.

**Aniello, Tommaso** 1622?-1647
[DHA, HN, SN]
*Neapolitan insurrectionist*
* Masaniello
* [The] Seven Days' King

**Anikulapo-Kuti, Fela** 20th c.　[IBW]
*Nigerian singer and musician*
* [The] King of Afro Beat

**[The] Animal**
*See* Duran, Roberto

**Animuccia, Giovanni** 1500?-1571
[SN, WBD]
*Italian composer*
* [The] Father of the Oratorio

**Anita**
*See* Daniel, Anita

**Anjin Sama [Mr. Pilot]**
*See* Adams, Will

**Anjou, Marguerite d'**
*See* Margaret [or Marguerite]

**Anjou, Rene d'** 1408-1480　[DNNF]
*Duke of Lorraine*
* Good King Rene

**Ankenman, Fred Norman** 1912-
[PB]
*American baseball player*
* Ankenman, Pat

**Ankenman, Pat**
*See* Ankenman, Fred Norman

**Ankerson, Ardis** 1915-　[FC]
*American actress*
* Marshall, Brenda

**Ankewich, Camille** 20th c.　[F1, F2]
*Actress*
* Manon, Marcia

**Ankh-er-man, Pharaoh J.**
*See* Ackerman, Forrest J[ames]

**Ankrum, Morris**
*See* Nussbaum, Morris

**Anllo y Orrio, Juan** 1898-1925
[GS]
*Spanish bullfighter*
* Nacional II [National, the
　Second]

**Anllo y Orrio, Ricardo** 1891-　[GS]
*Spanish bullfighter*
* Nacional [National]

**Anmar, Frank**
*See* Nolan, William F[rancis]

**Ann Margret**
*See* Olson, Ann Margret

**Ann the Word**
*See* Lee, Ann

**Anna Karlovna**
*See* Elisabeth Katharina Christine

**Anna Leopoldovna**
*See* Elisabeth Katharina Christine

**Annabella**
*See* Charpentier, Suzanne

**Annaeus Novatus, Marcus**　[WBD]
*Roman jurist*
* Gallio

**Annandale, Barbara**
*See* Bowden, Jean

**Anne** ?-1716　[DNNS, FFF, SN]
*Countess of Sunderland*
* [The] Little Whig

**Anne** 1665-1714　[DEP, FFF, RH]
*Queen of England*
* Brandy Nan
* [The] Church's Wet Nurse
* Morley, Mrs.

**Anne Mariel**
*See* Goud, Anne

**Anne of Bohemia** 1366-1394　[HN]
*Queen of England*
* Good Queen Anne

**Anne of Cleves** 1515-1557
[HN, RH]
*Wife of King Henry VIII of England*
* [A] Flanders Mare

**Anne of Denmark** 1574-1619
[DNNF, FFF]
*Wife of King James I of England*
* Oriana

**Anneman the Enigma**
*See* Squires, Theodore

**Annemann, Theodore**
*See* Squires, Theodore

**Annesley, Maude**
*See* Brownlow, Maude Annesley

**Annett, Cora**
*See* Scott, Cora Annett [Pipitone]

**Annette**
*See* Funicello, Annette

**Anni, Makituvan**
*See* Honkanen, Hilja Loviisa
Valkeapaa

**Annibale**
*See* Ballard, Anna

**Annichiarico, Walter** 1924-　[FC]
*Italian actor*
* Chiari, Walter

**Annie Laurie**
*See* Black, Winifred

**Anniseed**
*See* Edwards, Lionel Dalhousie
Robertson

**Annius of Viterbo** 1432-1502　[PA]
*Author*
* Nanni, Giovanni

**Annius Verus, Marcus** 121- 180
[HN, RH, WBD]
*Roman emperor*
* Antoninus, Marcus Aurelius
* [The] Augustine of Philosophy
* Marcus Aurelius
* [The] Philosopher
* [The] Pious
* Verissimus

**Annixter, Jane**
*See* Sturtzel, Jane Levington

**Annixter, Julius** 20th c.　[BLB]
*American underworld figure*
* Annixter, Lovin' Putty

**Annixter, Lovin' Putty**
*See* Annixter, Julius

**Annixter, Paul**
*See* Sturtzel, Howard A[llison]

**Annum, Alice** 20th c.　[IBW]
*Track and field athlete*
* [The] African Flying Queen

**Anonym, Walter**
*See* Sargent, Henry Jackson

**Anonymous**
*See* Talbot, John William

**Another Proteus**
*See* Rous [or Rowse], Francis

**Anouk**
*See* Sorya, Francoise

**Anoushavan**
*See* Shiroyan, Haig Krikor

**Anschel, Eugene** 1907-　[CA]
*German-born business executive,
writer, book reviewer*
* Polcher, Egon

**Ansdell, Richard** 1815-1885　[FFF]
*British painter*
* [The] Landseer of the Present

**Ansell, Norah** 1906-　[ART]
*British sculptor*
* N. A.

**Anselm, Felix**
*See* Pollak, Felix

**Anselm of Laon** 1030?-1117
[DNNS, FFF, PA]
*French theologian*
* [The] Scholastic Divine
* [The] Scholastic Doctor

**Anselmi, Teodero**　[PA]
*Author*
* Valleita, Leo

**Anselmo**
*See* Francesconi, Anselmo

**Anselmo** ?-1073　[CAL]
*Pope*
* Alexander II

**Ansgar** 801- 864　[DEP, HN, SN]
*Saint*
* [The] Apostle of the North

**Ansky, S. A.**
*See* Rappaport, Solomon

**Ansle, Dorothy Phoebe** 20th c.
[SFL]
*British author and playwright*
* Conway, Laura
* Elsna, Hebe
* Snow, Lyndon

**Anson, Adrian Constantine**
1851-1922　[AS, BAB, BN]
*American baseball player and
manager*
* Anson, Baby
* Anson, Cap
* Anson, Cry Baby
* Anson, Pop
* [The] Grand Old Man of Baseball
* [The] Marshalltown Infant
* Uncle Constantchin

**Anson, Baby**
*See* Anson, Adrian Constantine

**Anson, Cap**
*See* Anson, Adrian Constantine

**Anson, Cry Baby**
*See* Anson, Adrian Constantine

**Anson, Kathleen**
*See* Addison, Katharine

**Anson, Piers**
*See* Dell, Draycot Montagu

**Anson, Pop**
*See* Anson, Adrian Constantine

**Anspach, Nathan** 1871?-1935
[BEW]
*American actor*
* Adams, Nicholas

**Ansted, Hope**
*See* Burdett, Miss

**Anstey, Edgar**
*See* Slusser, George Edgar

**Anstey, F.**
*See* Guthrie, Thomas Anstey

**Anstey, John** 1796-1867
[DEL, FFF]
*Irish poet*
* Surrebutter, John, Esq.

**Anstruther, Harold**
*See* Archer, Harold Edward

**Anstruther, James**
*See* Maxtone Graham, James
Anstruther

**Antel, Franz** 20th c.　[WF]
*Austrian director*
* Legrand, Francois

**[The] Antelope**
*See* Verban, Emil Matthew

**Antennae Jimmy Simmons**
*See* Simmons, Jimmy

**Anteo**
*See* Sanchez Morales, Narciso

**Anthony, [Father]**
*See* McCabe, Joseph

**Anthony, Barbara** 1932-　[AW]
*British author*
* Barber, Antonia

**Anthony, C. L.**
*See* Smith, Dorothy Gladys

**Anthony, Catherine**
*See* Adachi, Barbara [Curtis]

**Anthony, Charles**
*See* Caruso, Calogero Anthony

**Anthony, David**
*See* Smith, William Dale

**Anthony, [Dr.] E.** 1907-　[AW]
*British physician and author*
* Parr, [Dr.] John Anthony

**Anthony, Evelyn**
*See* Ward Thomas, Evelyn Bridget
Patricia

**Anthony, Florence** 1947-
[CA, CLC]
*American poet*
* Ai [Love]
* Ogawa, Pelorhanke Ai

**Anthony, Gordon**
*See* Stannus, [James] Gordon
[Dawson]

**Anthony, Jack**
*See* Herbertson, John Anthony

**Anthony, John**
*See* Beckett, Ronald Brymer

**Anthony, John**
*See* Ciardi, John

**Anthony, John**
*See* Connor, Tony

**Anthony, John**
*See* Roberts, John S[torm]

**Anthony, John**
*See* Sabini, John Anthony

**Anthony, Joseph**
*See* Deuster, Joseph Anthony

**Anthony, Leo**
*See* Antonini, Leo

**Anthony, Mike**
See Micantoni, Adriano

**Anthony of Padua**
See De Bulhoes, Fernando

**Anthony, Peter** [joint pseudonym
with Peter (Levin) Shaffer]
See Shaffer, Anthony [Joshua]

**Anthony, Peter** [joint pseudonym
with Anthony (Joshua) Shaffer]
See Shaffer, Peter [Levin]

**Anthony, Piers**
See Jacob, Piers A[nthony]
D[illingham]

**Anthony, Ray**
See Antonini, Raymond

**Anthony, Robert**
See Santoni, Espartaco B.

**Anthropophagus Minor**
See Conniff, James C[lifford]
G[regory]

**Anti Harmonicus**
See Peterkin, Alexander

**Anti Scriblerus Histronicus**
See Roberts, John

**Antido**
See Saussure, Rene de

**Antigonus I** 4th c. BC [WBD]
*King of Macedonia*
* Cyclops
* Monophthalmos [The One-Eyed]

**Antigonus II** 1st c. BC [WBD]
*King of Judea*
* Mattathias

**Antiochus I** 3rd c. BC [WBD]
*King of Syria*
* Soter [The Preserver]

**Antiochus II** 3rd c. BC [WBD]
*King of Syria*
* Theos [The Divine]

**Antiochus III** 3rd c. BC [WBD]
*King of Syria*
* [The] Great

**Antiochus IV** 2nd c. BC [WBD]
*King of Syria*
* Epiphanes [The Illustrious]

**Antiochus IX** 2nd c. BC [WBD]
*King of Syria*
* Cyzicenus
* Philopator

**Antiochus V** 2nd c. BC [WBD]
*King of Syria*
* Eupator [Of a Good Father]

**Antiochus VI** 2nd c. BC [WBD]
*King of Syria*
* Epiphanes Dionysus
* Theos

**Antiochus VII** 2nd c. BC
[HN, WBD]
*King of Syria*
* Euergetes
* Sidetes

**Antiochus VIII** 2nd c. BC
[HN, WBD]
*King of Syria*
* Grypus [Hooked Nose]
* Philometor

**Antiochus X** 2nd c. BC [WBD]
*King of Syria*
* Eusebes [The Pious]

**Antiochus XI** 2nd c. BC [WBD]
*King of Syria*
* Epiphanes Philadelphus

**Antiochus XII** 2nd c. BC [WBD]
*King of Syria*
* Dionysus

**Antiochus XIII** 1st c. BC [WBD]
*King of Syria*
* Asiaticus

**Antipas** ?- 39 [RH, WBD]
*Ruler of Judea*
* Herod Antipas
* That Fox

**Antipater** 1st c. BC [WBD]
*Procurator of Judea*
* [The] Idumaean

**[The] Antiquarian King**
See Nabonidus

**[An] Antiquary**
See Adams, Alexander Maxwell

**[An] Antiquary**
See De la Moote, Col.

**[An] Antiquary**
See Thomson, Richard

**Antley, Pinball**
See Antley, Warren

**Antley, Warren** 20th c. [GW]
*American rodeo performer*
* Antley, Pinball

**Antoine, [Pere]**
See Antonio de Sedilla

**Antoine, Lionel Sylvester** 1950-
[SMG]
*American football player*
* Antoine, Twine

**Antoine, Paul**
See Closson, Ernest

**Antoine, Twine**
See Antoine, Lionel Sylvester

**Anton** [joint pseudonym with Harold
Thompson]
See Thompson, Beryl Antonia

**Anton** [joint pseudonym with Beryl
Antonia Thompson]
See Thompson, Harold

**Anton, Amerigo**
See Bocca, Tonio

**Anton the Greek**
See Antopoulis, Theodore

**Antonete [Big Antonio]**
See Chenel y Albaldejo, Antonio

**Antoni**
See Iranek-Osmecki, Kazimierz

**Antonia**
See Erskine, Gladys [Shaw]

**Antonick, Robert J.** 1939- [CA]
*American author*
* Kamin, Nick

**Antonietti, Hilda** 1886- [THR]
*British actress*
* Antony, Hilda

**Antonietti, Vernon** 1882-1955
[THR]
*Chilean-born actor*
* Steel, Vernon

**Antonini, Leo** 1925- [EJ]
*American jazz musician*
* Anthony, Leo
* Roy, Lee

**Antonini, Raymond** 1922-
[EJ, PMJ]
*American jazz musician*
* Anthony, Ray

**Antoninus, [Brother]**
See Everson, William [Oliver]

**Antoninus**
See Pierozzi, Antonio

**Antoninus, Marcus Aurelius**
See Annius Verus, Marcus

**Antoninus, Marcus Aurelius**
See Avitus Bassianus, Varius

**Antoninus, Marcus Aurelius**
See Bassianus

**Antoninus Pius**
See Titus Aurelius Fulvus Boionius
Arrius

**Antonio de Sedilla** 1748-1829
[WBD]
*Spanish-born clergyman*
* Antoine, [Pere]

**Antoniorrobles**
See Robles Soler, Antonio

**Antonius, Gaius** 1st c. BC [WBD]
*Roman politician and administrator*
* Hybrida, Antonius

**Antonowsky, Marvin** 20th c. [ET]
*American television executive*
* [The] Mad Programmer

**Antony**
See Berand, Antoine Nicolas

**Antony, Hilda**
See Antonietti, Hilda

**Antopoulis, Theodore** 20th c. [SG]
*Boxer*
* Anton the Greek

**Antrim, Henry**
See McCarty, Henry

**Antrim, Kid**
See McCarty, Henry

**Antrim, William**
See McCarty, Henry

**Antschel, Paul** 1920-1970
[B10, TCL]
*Austrian poet*
* Celan, Paul

**Antwine, Houston** 1939- [FB]
*American football player*
* Antwine, Twine

**Antwine, Twine**
See Antwine, Houston

**Anushirvan [Having an Immortal
Soul]**
See Khosru I [or Chosroes]

**Anvari** 12th c. [FFF, SN]
*Persian poet*
* [The] King of Khorassan

**Anvic, Frank**
See Sherman, Jory [Tecumseh]

**Anvil, Christopher**
See Crosby, Harry C.

**Anwyl, John Bodvan** 1875- ? [LAO]
*Welsh lexicographer and poet*
* Bodfan

**Anzelevitz [or Anzelwitz], Benjamin**
1891?-1943 [BEW, PMJ]
*American entertainer and
bandleader*
* Bernie, Ben

**Aoki, Hiroaki** 1938- [B10]
*Japanese-American restaurateur
and wrestler*
* Aoki, Rocky

**Aoki, Rocky**
See Aoki, Hiroaki

**Aonyx**
See Brown, Leslie Hilton

**Aos, Foel**
See Ter Balkt, Herman Hendrik

**Ap Evans, Humphrey**
See Drummond, Humphrey

**Apa**
See Elies i Bracons, Feliu

**Aparici y Pascual,** 1866- ? [GS]
*Spanish bullfighter*
* Fabrilo [Workman]

**Aparicio, Little Looie**
See Aparicio, Luis Ernesto

**Aparicio, Luis Ernesto** 1934-
[BE, SMG]
*Venezuelan-born baseball player*
* Aparicio, Little Looie

**Ape**
See Pellegrini, Carlo

**[The] Ape of Envie**
See Lyly, John

**[The] Ape of Euphues**
See Greene, Robert

**[The] Ape of Greene**
See Nash [or Nashe?], Thomas

**[The] Ape of Scarron**
See Coypeau, Charles [Sieur
d'Assouci]

**Apelian, Albert S.** 1893- [NAA]
*Syrian-born physician and author*
* Apilentz

**Apelles** 4th c. BC
[DEP, DNNF, RH]
*Greek painter*
* [The] Prince of Painters

**[The] Apelles of Europe**
See Allegri da Correggio, Antonio

**[The] Apelles of His Age**
See Cooper, Samuel

**Apesteguy, Joseph** 1881-1956
[OCS]
*French-Basque pelota player*
* Chiquito de Cambo

**Apfelbaum, Hirsch** 1883-1936
*Russian Communist leader*
* Zinoviev, Grigori Evseevich

**Apianus, Petrus**
See Bienewitz [or Bennewitz],
Peter

**Apicius, [Marcus] Gavius** 1st c.
[RH]
*Roman epicure*
* [The] Glutton

**Apikuni [Far-Off White Robe]**
*See*   Schultz, James Willard

**Apilentz**
*See*   Apelian, Albert S.

**Apis**
*See*   Dimitrijevic, Dragutin

**Apollinaire, Guillaume**
*See*   Kostrowitski, Wilhelm [or
Guillaume?]

**Apollinaris Sidonius, Gaius Sollius**
430?- 487?   [SN, WBD]
*French prelate, politician, writer*
* [The] Sydney Smith of the Gallic
   Church

**[The] Apollo of Portugal**
*See*   Camoens, Luis de

**[The] Apollo of the Box**
*See*   Mullane, Anthony John

**Apollodorus** 5th c. BC   [HN, WBD]
*Athenian painter*
* [The] Madman
* [The] Shadower
* Skiagraphos

**[L']Apollon de la Source des Muses**
**[The Apollo of the Fountain of Muses]**
*See*   Ronsard, Pierre de

**Apollonius** 1st c. BC   [WBD]
*Greek rhetorician*
* Molon

**Apollonius of Tyana** 1st c.   [RH]
*Greek philosopher*
* Thaumaturgus

**Apollo's Messenger**
*See*   Massinger, Philip

**[The] Apologist for the Quakers**
*See*   Barclay, Robert

**[The] Apostate**
*See*   Julian [Flavius Claudius
Julianus]

**[The] Apostate**
*See*   Julien, Simon

**[The] Apostate**
*See*   Mackintosh, [Sir] James

**[The] Apostle of Andalusia**
*See*   Avila, Juan de

**[The] Apostle of Beauvais**
*See*   Lucian

**[The] Apostle of Brazil**
*See*   Anchieta, Jose de

**[The] Apostle of Caledonia**
*See*   Columba

**[The] Apostle of Cheerfulness**
*See*   Kenyon, John

**[The] Apostle of Culture**
*See*   Arnold, Matthew

**[The] Apostle of England**
*See*   Latimer, Hugh

**[The] Apostle of Enlightenment**
*See*   Thomasius, Christian

**[The] Apostle of Ethiopia**
*See*   Frumentius

**[The] Apostle of France**
*See*   Denys

**[The] Apostle of Free Trade**
*See*   Bright, John

**[The] Apostle of Free Trade**
*See*   Cobden, Richard

**[The] Apostle of Gaul**
*See*   Martin

**[The] Apostle of Germany**
*See*   Winfrid [or Winfrith]

**[The] Apostle of Greenland**
*See*   Egede, Hans

**[The] Apostle of Hungary**
*See*   Radla, Astrik

**[The] Apostle of Hungary**
*See*   Stephen I

**[The] Apostle of Infidelity**
*See*   Arouet, Francois Marie

**[The] Apostle of Ireland**
*See*   Patrick

**[The] Apostle of Liberty**
*See*   Clay, Henry

**[The] Apostle of Liberty**
*See*   Jefferson, Thomas

**[The] Apostle of Massacre**
*See*   Marat, Jean Paul

**[The] Apostle of Molasses and**
**Moonshine**
*See*   Arnold, Matthew

**[The] Apostle of New Zealand**
*See*   Marsden, Samuel

**[The] Apostle of Persia**
*See*   Perkins, Justin

**[The] Apostle of Peru**
*See*   De Barcena [or Barzena],
Alonso

**[The] Apostle of Presbytery**
*See*   Knox, John

**[The] Apostle of Ragged Schools**
*See*   Guthrie, Thomas

**[The] Apostle of Silence**
*See*   Carlyle, Thomas

**[The] Apostle of Spain**
*See*   James

**[The] Apostle of Sweetness and Light**
*See*   Arnold, Matthew

**[The] Apostle of Temperance**
*See*   Mathew, Theobald

**[The] Apostle of the Abyssinians**
*See*   Frumentius

**[The] Apostle of the Allemanian**
**Nations**
*See*   Cellach [or Caillech]

**[The] Apostle of the Alps**
*See*   Neff, Felix

**[The] Apostle of the Anglo-Saxons**
*See*   Augustine [or Austin]

**[The] Apostle of the Ardennes**
*See*   Hubert

**[The] Apostle of the Armenians**
*See*   Gregory

**[The] Apostle of the Bavarians**
*See*   Rupert [Rupertus or
Ruprecht]

**[The] Apostle of the English**
*See*   Augustine [or Austin]

**[The] Apostle of the English**
*See*   George

**[The] Apostle of the English**
*See*   Gregory I

**[The] Apostle of the Franks**
*See*   Remi [or Remigius]

**[The] Apostle of the French**
*See*   Denis [or Denys]

**[The] Apostle of the Frisians**
*See*   Willibrord

**[The] Apostle of the Gauls**
*See*   Denis [or Denys]

**[The] Apostle of the Gauls**
*See*   Irenaeus

**[The] Apostle of the Gentiles**
*See*   Saul of Tarsus

**[The] Apostle of the Goths**
*See*   Ulfilas [or Uphilas]

**[The] Apostle of the Highlanders**
*See*   Columba

**[The] Apostle of the Hungarians**
*See*   Radla, Astrik

**[The] Apostle of the Indians**
*See*   Eliot, John

**[The] Apostle of the Indians**
*See*   Las Casas, Bartolome de

**[The] Apostle of the Indies**
*See*   Xavier, Francis [or Francisco]

**[The] Apostle of the Iroquois**
*See*   Piquet, Francois

**[The] Apostle of the Isle of Ely**
*See*   Sedgwick, William

**[The] Apostle of the Lowlands**
*See*   Cuthbert

**[The] Apostle of the Negroes**
*See*   Peter Claver

**[The] Apostle of the Netherlands**
*See*   Amand [or Amandus]

**[The] Apostle of the New Jerusalem**
*See*   Svedberg, Emanuel

**[The] Apostle of the New World**
*See*   Anchieta, Jose de

**[The] Apostle of the North**
*See*   Ansgar

**[The] Apostle of the North**
*See*   Gilpin, Bernard

**[The] Apostle of the North**
*See*   Hyacinth

**[The] Apostle of the North**
*See*   Macdonald, John

**[The] Apostle of the Peak**
*See*   Bagshaw, William

**[The] Apostle of the Picts**
*See*   Ninian

**[The] Apostle of the Prussians**
*See*   Adalbert [or Adelbert]

**[The] Apostle of the Scottish**
**Reformers**
*See*   Knox, John

**[The] Apostle of the Slavs**
*See*   Adalbert

**[The] Apostle of the Slavs**
*See*   Constantine

**[The] Apostle of the Slavs**
*See*   Methodius

**[The] Apostle of the Sword**
*See*   Mohammed [or Mahomet]

**[The] Apostle of Unitarianism**
*See*   Channing, William Ellery

**[The] Apostle of Virginia**
*See*   Harris, Samuel

**[The] Apostle of Virginia**
*See*   Whittaker, A.

**[The] Apostle of Wales**
*See*   David

**[The] Apostle to the Blind**
*See*   Hawy, Valentine

**[The] Apostle to the Prussians**
*See*   Bruno [or Brun] of Querfurt

**[The] Apostle to the Sioux**
*See*   Hare, William Hobart

**[An] Apothecary**
*See*   Pope, Alexander

**Appe**
*See*   Pedrosa, Amilde

**Appel, Anna**
*See*   Bercovici, Anna

**Appel, Augusta** 1902?-1973
[F1, F2, FC]
*American actress*
* Lee, Lila

**Apperley, Charles James**
1777-1843   [DEL, PA, WBD]
*Welsh author*
* Cecil
* Nimrod

**Appiani, Andrea** 1754-1817
[DEP, DNNS, RH]
*Italian painter*
* [The] Painter of the Graces

**Apple Cheeks Lumley**
*See*   Lumley, Harry

**Apple, Johnny**
*See*   Apple, R. W.

**Apple, R. W.** 20th c.
*American journalist*
* Apple, Johnny

**Applebaum, Stan** 1929-   [CA]
*American author, playwright,*
*composer*
* Keith, Robert

**Applebaum, Stella Balaban** 1897-
[NAA]
*American educator and writer*
* Slatoff, Stella B.

**Applebud, Adam**
*See*   Pierce, Carl Webster

**Applegate, Fred[erick Romaine]**
1879-1968   [BE]
*American baseball player*
* Applegate, Snitz

**Applegate, Snitz**
See Applegate, Fred[erick Romaine]

**Appleman, John Alan** 1912- [CA]
*American attorney and author*
* Daley, Bill
* Montrose, James St. David

**Appleman, Mark J[erome]** 1917-
[CA]
*American business executive and author*
* Jerome, Mark

**Appleseed, Johnny**
See Chapman, John

**Appleton, Ed[ward Sam]**
1892-1932 [BE]
*American baseball player*
* Appleton, Whitey

**Appleton, Jake**
See Jablonowski, Peter William

**Appleton, Jesse** 1772-1819
[FFF, PA]
*American author*
* Leighton

**Appleton, Laurence**
See Lovecraft, Howard Phillips

**Appleton, Peter William**
See Jablonowski, Peter William

**Appleton, Sarah**
See Weber, Sarah Appleton

**Appleton, Sarah Wentworth**
1759-1846 [FFF]
*American poet*
* [The] American Sappho

**Appleton, Victor** [house pseudonym]
[Stratemeyer Syndicate]
See Garis, Howard Roger

**Appleton, Victor** [house pseudonym]
[Stratemeyer Syndicate]
See Stratemeyer, Edward L.

**Appleton, Victor, II** [house pseudonym] [Stratemeyer Syndicate]
See Adams, Harriet S[tratemeyer]

**Appleton, Victor, II** [house pseudonym] [Stratemeyer Syndicate]
See Stratemeyer, Edward L.

**Appleton, Whitey**
See Appleton, Ed[ward Sam]

**Applewhite, Bo**
See Applewhite, Marshall Herff

**Applewhite, Eric Leon** 1897-1973
[SC]
*American actor*
* Applewhite, Ric

**Applewhite, Marshall Herff** 20th c.
*American religious cult leader*
* Applewhite, Bo

**Applewhite, Ric**
See Applewhite, Eric Leon

**Appley, M[ortimer] H[erbert]**
See Applezweig, Mortimer Herbert

**Appleyard, Ernst Sylvanus** [PA]
*Author*
* E. S. A.

**Applezweig, Mortimer Herbert**
1921- [CA]
*American psychologist and author*
* Appley, M[ortimer] H[erbert]

**Applin, Arthur** 1883- [WW]
*Author*
* Swift, Julian

**Appling, Lucius Benjamin** 1908?-
[BAB, BE, CBS]
*American baseball player and coach*
* Aches and Pains
* Appling, Luke
* Boots, Kid
* Old Aches and Pains

**Appling, Luke**
See Appling, Lucius Benjamin

**Appollonius of Alexandria** 3rd c.
BC [DEP, RH, WBD]
*Alexandrian scholar*
* Dyscolus [The Crabbed]
* Grammaticorum Princeps
* [The] Prince of Grammarians

**Apps, Joseph Sylvanus** 1915-
[FHE]
*Canadian-born hockey player*
* Apps, Syl

**Apps, Syl**
See Apps, Joseph Sylvanus

**Apps, Syl, Jr.**
See Apps, Sylvanus Marshall

**Apps, Sylvanus Marshall** 1947-
[CEI, FHE]
*Canadian-born hockey player*
* Apps, Syl, Jr.

**Apricott, Albert Alfred**
See Berlin, Isaiah

**Apstein, Tevyeh** 1918- [BEW]
*Russian-born playwright*
* Apstein, Theodore

**Apstein, Theodore**
See Apstein, Tevyeh

**Apter, Michael J[ohn]**
See Smith, Michael

**Aptomas**
See Thomas, M.

**Aquarist**
See Andrew, Nicholas Jeffery

**Aquarius**
See Allen, John E[lliston]

**Aquarius**
See Oppenheim, Joel Lester

**Aquarius, Qass**
See Buskirk, Richard H[obart]

**Aquila** 2nd c. BC [WBD]
*Translator*
* Aquila of Pontus
* Ponticus

**Aquila Doctorum**
See Ailly, Pierre d'

**Aquila Doctorum**
See Aquinas, Thomas [Thomas of Aquino]

**Aquila, Kaspar**
See Adler, Kaspar

**Aquila of Pontus**
See Aquila

**Aquillo, Don**
See Prince, Jack Harvey

**Aquinas, Thomas [Thomas of Aquino]**
1224-1274 [DEL, HN, RH]
*Italian scholastic philosopher and saint*
* [The] Angel of the Schools
* [The] Angelic Doctor
* Aquila Doctorum
* [The] Aristotle of Christianity
* Communis, Doctor
* [The] Dumb Ox
* [The] Eagle of Divines
* [The] Father of Moral Philosophy
* [The] Fifth Doctor of the Church
* [The] Second Augustine
* [The] Sicilian Ox
* [The] Stupid Boy
* [The] Universal Doctor
* Universalis, Doctor

**[The] Aquinian Sage**
See Juvenal [Decimus Junius Juvenalis]

**Aquino, Benigno** 20th c.
*Filipino politician*
* Aquino, Ninoy

**Aquino, Frank J.** 1906- [ASC]
*American composer, conductor, musician*
* Kane, Bernie

**Aquino, Ninoy**
See Aquino, Benigno

**Arabi Pasha**
See Ahmed Arabi

**[The] Arabian**
See Philip [Marcus Julius Philippus]

**[The] Arabian Tailor**
See Wild, Henry

**Arabius**
See Phrynicus

**Aracelis, Gabriel**
See Corretjer, Juan Antonio

**Arachnophilus**
See White, Adam

**Aragall, Giacomo**
See Aragall y Garriga, Jaime

**Aragall y Garriga, Jaime** 1939-
[OP]
*Spanish opera singer*
* Aragall, Giacomo

**Aragbabalu, Omidiji**
See Beier, Ulli

**Aragon, Angel Valdes, Jr.** 1915-
[BE]
*Cuban-born baseball player*
* Aragon, Jack

**Aragon, Angel Valdes, Sr.**
1893-1952 [BE]
*Cuban-born baseball player*
* Aragon, Pete

**Aragon, Jack**
See Aragon, Angel Valdes, Jr.

**Aragon, Louis** 1897- [CA]
*French poet and author*
* Arnaud, Saint Romain
* La Colere [or Lacolere], Francois

**Aragon, Pete**
See Aragon, Angel Valdes, Sr.

**Arambillet, Fernando** 1915- [FC]
*Spanish actor*
* Rey, Fernando

**Arana, Ric**
See Sellers, Connie Leslie, Jr.

**Arana Carmona, Antonio**
1868-1928 [GS]
*Spanish bullfighter*
* Jarana [Merrymaker]

**Arango, Doroteo** 1877-1923
[B10, IPA]
*Mexican bandit and revolutionist*
* Villa, Francisco
* Villa, Pancho

**Arantes Do Nascimento, Edson**
1940- [B10, IBW, OSC]
*Brazilian soccer player*
* [The] Black Pearl
* Pele
* [Il] Re

**Arap Moi, Daniel Torotich** 1924?-
*Kenyan president*
* [The] Father of the House

**Araphil [or Araphill]**
See Habington, William

**Arata, Carol Jane** 1935- [BEW]
*American actress, singer, comedienne*
* Arthur, Carol

**Arbanas, Frederick V.** 1939- [FB]
*American football player*
* Arbanas, Fritz

**Arbanas, Fritz**
See Arbanas, Frederick V.

**Arbeiter, Petronius**
See Ruckstull, F[red] Wellington

**Arbenina, Stella**
See Whitshaw, Stella

**Arbiter Elegantiae [or Elegantiarum]**
See Petronius, Caius [or Gaius]

**Arbory, John**
See Macfarlane, John

**Arbour, Al**
See Arbour, Alger

**Arbour, Alger** 1932-
[CEI, FHE, HK]
*Canadian-born hockey player*
* Arbour, Al

**Arbour, Ernest** 20th c. [CEI]
*Hockey player*
* Arbour, Ty

**Arbour, Ty**
See Arbour, Ernest

**Arbuckle, Fatty**
See Arbuckle, Roscoe Conklin

**Arbuckle, Roscoe Conklin**
1887-1933 [FC, SC, WEF]
*American actor and director*
* Arbuckle, Fatty
* Good, Will B.
* Goodrich, William

**Arbuthnot, John** 1667-1735
[DEL, SN]
*British author and physician*
* P. P., A Parish Clerk
* [The] Queen's Favorite Physician

**Arcady, Jean**
See Brachlianoff, Arcady

**Arcano, Giovanni** 1500-1535 [PA]
*Author*
* [Il] Mauro

**Arcaro, George Edward [Eddie]** 1916-
*American jockey*
* Banana Nose

**Arce, Jose de**
*See* Martinez Davila, Manuel

**Arce Robledo, Carlos De** 1932-
[IAW]
*Spanish author*
* Reader, Paul

**Arcesi, John** 1918- [PMJ]
*American singer*
* Darcy [or D'Arcy], Don

**[The] Arch**
*See* Turrell, James Archie [Jim]

**[The] Arch Druid**
*See* Stukeley, William

**Arch, E. L.**
*See* Payes, Rachel C[osgrove]

**[The] Arch Monarch of the World**
*See* Bonaparte, Charles Louis
Napoleon

**Archcarnifex**
*See* Norton, Thomas

**Archdeacon, Flash**
*See* Archdeacon, Maurice Bruce

**Archdeacon, Maurice Bruce**
1897-1954 [BE]
*American baseball player*
* Archdeacon, Flash

**Archdekin, Richard** 1619-1690
[PA]
*Author*
* Mac Gilla Cuddy

**Archdiavolo**
*See* Strunck, Nicolas Adam

**Archelaus** ?- 17 [WBD]
*King of Cappadocia*
* Sisines

**Archelaus** 1st c. [WBD]
*Ruler of Palestine*
* Herod Archelaus

**Archer**
*See* Stockwell, George A.

**Archer, A[rchie] A[lexander]**
*See* Joscelyn, Archie Lynn

**Archer, Belle**
*See* Mingle, Belle

**Archer, Frank**
*See* O'Connor, Richard

**Archer, Fred[erick Marvin]** 1912-
[BE]
*American baseball player*
* Archer, Lefty

**Archer, George**
*See* Hardwick, Archer

**Archer, George B.** 1939- [GF]
*American golfer*
* [The] Gilroy Cowboy

**Archer, Harold Edward** 20th c.
[THR]
*British actor*
* Anstruther, Harold

**Archer, Harry**
*See* Auracher, Harry

**Archer, Insatiate**
*See* Archer, William S.

**Archer, John B.**
*See* Bowman, Ralph Skipwith

**Archer, Lane**
*See* Hauck, Louise [Platt]

**Archer, Lee** [house pseudonym,
Ziff-Davis]
*See* Ellison, Harlan [Jay]

**Archer, Lefty**
*See* Archer, Fred[erick Marvin]

**Archer, Lily** 1879- ? [THR]
*British comedienne*
* Lena, Lily

**Archer, Ron** [joint pseudonym with
Theodore Edwin (Ted) White]
*See* Van Arnam, Dave

**Archer, Ron** [joint pseudonym with
Dave Van Arnam]
*See* White, Theodore Edwin [Ted]

**Archer, S. E.**
*See* Soderberg, Percy Measday

**Archer, William S.** 1789-1855
[SN]
*American politician*
* Archer, Insatiate

**Archer-Batten, S.**
*See* Walker, Stella Archer

**Archerd, Armand** 20th c. [ITA]
*American columnist and television
commentator*
* Archerd, Army

**Archerd, Army**
*See* Archerd, Armand

**Archestratus**
*See* Driver, Christopher Prout

**Archette, Guy**
*See* Geier, Chester S.

**Archeus**
*See* Sterling, John

**Archibald**
*See* Gross, Leon T.

**Archibald, Edith Jessie** 1854- ?
[NAA]
*Canadian author*
* Morien, Sydney

**Archibald, Nathaniel [Nate]** 1948-
[BB, IBW, SMG]
*American basketball player*
* Archibald, Tiny
* [The] Skate

**Archibald, Tiny**
*See* Archibald, Nathaniel [Nate]

**Archie Boy**
*See* Gross, Leon T.

**Archilochus** 7th c. BC
[HN, RH, SN]
*Greek poet*
* [The] Father of Iambic Verse
* [The] Father of Satire

**[An] Archimagus**
*See* Dyer, George

**[An] Archimedes**
*See* Dyer, George

**Archimedes** 3rd c. BC [HN, SN]
*Greek mathematician and inventor*
* [The] Father of Statics

**Archimedes** (Continued)
* [The] Homer of Geometry
* [The] Sage of Syracuse

**[The] Architect Earl**
*See* Herbert, Henry

**[The] Architect of Louis XIII**
*See* Androuet, Jean

**Archmere, Halie**
*See* Lucier, Mrs. Frederick

**[The] Archpriest of Hita**
*See* Ruiz, Juan

**Arcia, Flaco**
*See* Arcia, Jose Raimundo Orta

**Arcia, Jose Raimundo Orta** 1943-
[BE]
*Cuban-born baseball player*
* Arcia, Flaco

**Arco, Alonso del** 1625-1700 [WBD]
*Spanish painter*
* [El] Sordillo de Pereda

**Arcone, Sonya** 1925-1978 [CA]
*American author*
* Goodman, Sonya

**Arcot, Roger**
*See* Locke, Robert Donald

**Arcturus**
*See* Ladd, Catherine Stratton

**Arcularius, Henry W.** [PA]
*Author*
* Larius, R. Q.
* Sulky

**Ard, William [Thomas]**
1922-1962? [CA, CC, WW]
*American author*
* Kerr, Ben
* Moran, Mike
* Ward, Jonas
* Wills, Thomas

**Ardashir I** ?- 241 [DNNF, FFF]
*King of Persia*
* King of Kings
* King of Men

**Ardboe**
*See* Miller, F. F.

**Arden, Barbie** [joint pseudonym with
Adrien (Pearl) Stoutenburg]
*See* Ritchie, Barbara

**Arden, Barbie** [joint pseudonym with
Barbara Ritchie]
*See* Stoutenburg, Adrien [Pearl]

**Arden, Clive**
*See* Nutt, Lily Clive

**Arden, Eve**
*See* Quedens, Eunice

**Arden, J. E. M.**
*See* Conquest, [George] Robert
[Acworth]

**Arden, Rice**
*See* Weekley, Maurice Arden

**Arden, Toni**
*See* Aroizzone, Antoinette

**Arden, Victor**
*See* Fuiks, Lewis J.

**Arden, William**
*See* Lynds, Dennis

**Ardesier-Macdonald, Charles**
*See* Boyd, Andrew Kennedy
Hutchinson

**Ardigo, Isabella**
*See* Lanza, Isabel

**Ardizola, Rinaldo Joseph** 1919-
[BE]
*Italian-born baseball player*
* Ardizola, Rugger

**Ardizola, Rugger**
*See* Ardizola, Rinaldo Joseph

**Ardizzone, Edward** 1900- [ART]
*British painter*
* Diz
* E. A.

**Ardmore, Jane Kesner** 1915- [CA]
*American author*
* Morris, Jane

**Ardner, Joseph A. [Joe]** 1858-1935
[BE]
*American baseball player*
* Ardner, Old Hoss

**Ardner, Old Hoss**
*See* Ardner, Joseph A. [Joe]

**Ardo the Frog**
*See* Cash, William F.

**Ardoin, Amedie** 20th c. [NBB]
*American singer*
* Ardoin, Tite Amedie

**Ardoin, Tite Amedie**
*See* Ardoin, Amedie

**Ardon, Mordecai**
*See* Bronstein, Max

**Ardura, Adaljina** 1915-1970 [SC]
*American actress and dancer*
* Reyes, Eva

**Arena, Maurizio**
*See* Li Lorenzo, Maurizio

**Arenberg, Auguste Marie Raymond
d'** 1753-1834 [WBD]
*French politician*
* De La Marck, Comte

**Arenenberg, Comte d'**
*See* Bonaparte, Charles Louis
Napoleon

**Arequipeno [Man from Arequipa]**
*See* Chaves, Elias

**[The] Aresbys** [joint pseudonym with
Raymond S. Bamberger]
*See* Bamberger, Helen R.

**[The] Aresbys** [joint pseudonym with
Helen R. Bamberger]
*See* Bamberger, Raymond S.

**Areta, Mavis**
*See* Winder, Mavis Areta

**Aretaeos of Cappadocia** 1st c.
[DEP, RH]
*Greek physician and author*
* [The] Father of Medicine

**Aretino, Leonardo**
*See* Bruni [or Bruno], Leonardo

**Aretino, Pietro** 1492-1557?
[HN, RH, SN]
*Italian author*
* [The] Censor of the World
* [Il] Divino
* [The] Scourge of Princes

**Aretius Felinus**
See   Kuhhorn, Martin

**Areton, Buck**
See   Areton, William

**Areton, William**   [RBE]
*American boxing manager*
* Areton, Buck

**Arfe y Villafane, Juan de**
1535-1603?   [WBD]
*Spanish silversmith*
* [The] Spanish Cellini

**Arft, Bow Wow**
See   Arft, Henry Irven

**Arft, Henry Irven** 1922-   [BE]
*American baseball player*
* Arft, Bow Wow

**Argensola, Bartolome Leonardo de**
1562-1631   [DEP, DNNS, RH]
*Spanish poet*
* [The] Horace of Spain
* [The] Spanish Horace

**Argensola, Lupercio Leonardo de**
1559-1613   [DEP, DNNS, RH]
*Spanish poet*
* [The] Horace of Spain
* [The] Spanish Horace

**Argenson, Rene Louis de Voyer d'**
18th c.   [WBD]
*French diplomat*
* [La] Bete

**Argentina**
See   Merce, Antonia

**[The] Argentine Firecracker**
See   Battistella, Annabella

**Argentinita**
See   Lopez, Encarnacion

**Arghezi, Tudor**
See   Teodorescu, Ion N.

**Argles, Margaret**   [DNNF, FF]
*Author*
* [The] Duchess

**Argove, Debbie**
See   Buckholtz, Wanda

**Arguelles, Agustin** 1776-1844
[WBD]
*Spanish statesman*
* [The] Spanish Cicero

**Argus**
See   Osusky, Stefan

**Argus**
See   Phillips-Birt, Douglas

**Argus**
See   Willes, Irwin

**Argus the Exile**
See   Willes, Irwin

**Argyle, Pearl**
See   Wellman, Pearl

**Argyll, Marquis of**
See   Campbell, Archibald

**Argyll, Second Duke of**
See   Campbell, John

**Arias, Rodolfo Martinez** 1931-
[BE]
*Cuban-born baseball player*
* Arias, Rudy

**Arias, Rudy**
See   Arias, Rodolfo Martinez

**Arid, Ben**
See   Barnard, Melville Clemens

**Arie, Norman Joseph** 1928?-
[PMJ]
*Canadian singer*
* Brooks, Norman

**Ariel**
See   Canning, E. B.

**Ariel**
See   Fiske, Stephen R.

**Ariel**
See   Payne, Buckner H.

**Ariel**
See   Shelley, Percy Bysshe

**Ariel, Guido de**
See   Fernandez Sanchez, Angel

**Arioch al Asser**   [FFF, HN, RH]
*King of Assyria*
* [The] Lion King of Assyria

**Arion**
See   Falconer, William

**Arion** 7th c. BC   [RH, SN]
*Greek poet*
* [The] Father of Dithyrambic
  Poetry

**Arion, F. M.**
See   Martinus, [Efraim] Frank

**[The] Arioso of the North**
See   Scott, [Sir] Walter

**Ariosto, Lodovico** 1474-1533
[DEP, HN, SN]
*Italian poet*
* [The] Divine
* [The] Homer of Ferrara
* [The] Sir Walter Scott of Italy
* [The] Southern Scott
* [The] Tuscan Poet

**[The] Aristarch of British Criticism**
See   Lockhart, John Gibson

**Aristarchus** 2nd c. BC
[DEP, DNNS, SN]
*Greek grammarian and critic*
* [The] Coryphaeus of
  Grammarians
* [The] Prince of Critics

**[The] Aristarchus of Cambridge**
See   Bentley, Richard

**[The] Aristarchus of his Day**
See   Harvey, Gabriel

**[The] Aristarchus of the Edinburgh
Review**
See   Jeffrey, Francis

**Ariste**
See   Boileau-Despreaux, Nicolas

**Aristides**
See   Blagdon, Francis William

**Aristides**
See   McKinney, T. L.

**Aristides [or Aristeides]** 5th c. BC
[FFF, RH, WBD]
*Athenian statesman*
* [The] Just

**Aristides, Othon** 20th c.   [WECO]
*French cartoonist*
* Fred

**Aristides [or Aristeides], Publius
Aelius** 2nd c.   [WBD]
*Greek rhetorician*
* Theodorus

**Aristobulus I** 2nd c. BC   [WBD]
*King of Judea*
* Judah

**Aristocles** 4th c. BC
[HN, SN, WBD]
*Greek philosopher*
* [The] Athenian Bee
* [The] Athenian Moses
* [The] Attic Bee
* [The] Attic Moses
* [The] Bee Lipped Oracle
* [The] Bee of Athens
* Deus Philosophorum [God of
  Philosophers]
* [The] God of All Philosophers
* [The] Homer of Philosophers
* [The] Moses of Athens
* [The] Philosopher of the
  Christians
* Plato
* [The] Prince of Philosophers
* [The] Secretary of Nature

**[The] Aristocrat of Swing**
See   Ellington, Edward Kennedy

**Aristophanes**
See   Boyrie, Arthur

**Aristophanes** 5th c. BC
[DEP, RH, SN]
*Greek playwright*
* [The] Darling of the Graces
* [The] Father of Comedy
* [The] Prince of Ancient Comedy

**[The] Aristophanes of Caricature**
See   Daumier, Honore Victorin

**[The] Aristophanes of His Age**
See   Poquelin, Jean Baptiste

**[The] Aristophanes of the Revolution**
See   Desmoulins, [Lucie Simplice]
Camille [Benoit]

**Aristotle** 4th c. BC
[DEP, HN, RH]
*Greek philosopher*
* [The] Father of Greek Philosophy
* [The] Master of Those Who
  Knew
* [The] Mind of the School
* [The] Pope of Philosophy
* [The] Secretary of Nature
* [The] Stagirite
* [The] Talent of the Academy

**[The] Aristotle of China**
See   Tehuhe

**[The] Aristotle of Christianity**
See   Aquinas, Thomas [Thomas of
Aquino]

**[The] Aristotle of the Arabs**
See   Avicenna [or Abou-ibn-Sina]

**[The] Aristotle of the Nineteenth
Century**
See   Cuvier, Georges Leopold
Chretien Frederic Dagobert

**Arizmendi, Alberto** 1914-1963
[BX, RBE]
*Mexican-born boxer*
* Arizmendi, Baby

**Arizmendi, Baby**
See   Arizmendi, Alberto

**[The] Arizona Cowboy**
See   Allen, Rex

**Arjunwadkar, Krishna S.** 1926-
[IAW]
*Indian author*
* Kantakarjuna

**[The] Arkansas Humming Bird**
See   Warneke, Lonnie

**[The] Arkansas Philosopher**
See   Burns, Bob

**[The] Arkansas Razorback**
See   Freeman, Tommy

**[The] Arkansas Traveler**
See   Harrison, Ernest Joseph

**[The] Arkansas Traveler**
See   Jackson, Travis Calvin

**[The] Arkansas Woodchopper**
See   Ossenbrink, Luther W.

**Arkell, Monique** ?-1957   [BEW]
*French actress*
* Berendt, Rachel

**Arkhipova, Irina**
See   Veloshkina, Irina

**Arkie**
See   Ossenbrink, Luther W.

**Arkwright, Peleg**
See   Proudfit, David L.

**Arlandson, Leone** 1917-   [CA]
*American author*
* Ryland, Lee

**Arlanibaus, Philipp**
See   Abelin, Johann Philipp

**Arlaz, Regine** 1894-1926   [THR]
*French actress and dancer*
* Flory, Regine

**Arledge, John**
See   Arledge, Johnson Lundy

**Arledge, Johnson Lundy**
1906-1947   [SC]
*American actor*
* Arledge, John

**Arlen, Harold**
See   Arluck, Hyman

**Arlen, Jerry**
See   Arluck, Jerry

**Arlen, Judith**
See   Rutherford, Laurette

**Arlen, Michael**
See   Kuyumjian, Dikran

**Arlen, Richard**
See   Van Mattimore, Richard

**Arlen, Stephen**
See   Badham, Stephen

**Arlesienne**
See   Couet, Yvonne

**Arlett, Buzz**
See   Arlett, Russell Loris

**Arlett, Russell Loris** 1899-1964
[PB]
*American baseball player*
* Arlett, Buzz

**Arletty**
See   Bathiat, Arlette-Leonie

**Arley, Catherine**
See Mourer, Marie-Louise-Jeanne

**Arley, Cecile**
See Arnold, Cecile

**Arley, Maryse**
See Mourer, Marie-Louise-Jeanne

**Arling, Joyce**
See Burge, Doris Marie

**Arlington**
See Baxter, Robert M.

**Arliss, Florence**
See Montgomery, Florence

**Arliss, George**
See Andrews, George Augustus

**Arliss, Leslie**
See Andrews, Leslie

**Arlotto Mainardi** 1395-1483
[WBD]
*Italian poet*
* [Il] Piovano

**Arluck, Hyman** 1905-
[CED, OCF, TR]
*American composer*
* Arlen, Harold

**Arluck, Jerry** 20th c. [BEW]
*American musical director*
* Arlen, Jerry

**[The] Arm**
See Hafey, Thomas Francis [Tom]

**Arma, Paul**
See Weisshaus, Imre

**Armaganian, Lucine Tockqui**
1927- [OP]
*American opera singer*
* Amara, Lucine

**Arman**
See Fernandez, Armand

**Armand** [code name used during
World War II]
See Czeniawski, Romain

**Armand**
See Strubberg, Friedrich Armand

**Armand, Francais** 1699-1765 [PA]
*Author*
* Huguet

**Armand, Jacqueline**
See Skarbek, Krystyne

**Armand, Teddy V.**
See Winscott, Edwin C.

**Armas y Cardenas, Jose de**
1866-1919 [CW]
*Cuban critic, author, playwright*
* Justo de Lara

**Armbrister, Ed**
See Armbrister, Edison Rosanda

**Armbrister, Edison Rosanda** 1948-
[BE, BR]
*Bahamian-born baseball player*
* Armbrister, Ed

**Armbruster, Buster**
See Armbruster, Herman

**Armbruster, Herman** 1882-1953
[BE]
*American baseball player*
* Armbruster, Buster

**[The] Armed Soldier of Democracy**
See Bonaparte, Napoleon

**Armenheim, Gregory**
See Gray, Whitley

**[The] Armenian**
See Leo V

**Armes, Blackie**
See Armes, Monroe

**Armes, Monroe** 20th c. [BLB]
*American underworld figure*
* Armes, Blackie

**Armeth, Auguste** 1939- [CW]
*West Indian playwright, author, poet*
* Macouba, Auguste

**Armfield, Diana M.** 1920- [ART]
*British painter*
* D. M. A.

**Armhold, Adelheid**
See Domsaitis, Adelheid Agathe
Marie

**Armicus**
See Gee, Herbert Leslie

**Armida**
See Louisa Henrietta

**Armillita Chico [Little Armillita]**
See Espinosa Saucedo, Fermin

**Armillita de Venezuela [Armillita
from Venezuela]**
See Figueras Alvarez, Rafael
Antonio

**Armin, Georg**
See Hermann, Georg

**Arminius [or Armin]** ?- 21
[SN, WBD]
*German chieftain*
* [The] German Cid
* Hermann

**Arminius, Jacobus**
See Harmensen [or Hermansz],
Jacob

**Armitage, Alfred**
See Graydon, William Murray

**Armitage, John** 20th c. [CAN]
*Australian-born author*
* Hin me Geong

**Armitage, Joshua Charles** 1913-
[ART]
*British artist*
* Ionicus

**Armitage, Norman C.**
See Cohn, Norman

**Armitage, Reginald Moxon**
1898-1954 [BEW, EMT]
*British composer*
* Gay, Noel

**Armitage, Vincent**
See Wheway, John W.

**Armour, Alfred** 20th c. [OBW]
*American baseball player*
* Armour, Buddy

**Armour, Buddy**
See Armour, Alfred

**Armour, Margaret**
See Macdougall, Margaret

**Armour, R. Coutts** 20th c.
[MBF, WGT]
*Australian author*
* Brisbane, Coutts
* Tremayne, Hartley
* Whitney, Reid

**Armour, Thomas Dickson [Tommy]**
1895-1968 [EG, GF]
*Scottish-born golfer*
* [The] Silver Scot

**Armour-Allan, Ella** 1913-1969
[BEW, PMJ]
*Scottish singer and actress*
* Allan, Ella
* Logan, Ella

**Arms, Johnson**
See Halliwell, David [William]

**Armstrong, Anthony**
See Tubb, Edwin Charles

**Armstrong, Anthony**
See Willis, [George] Anthony
Armstrong

**Armstrong, Anthony C.**
See Armstrong, Christopher J[ohn]
R[ichard]

**Armstrong, April**
See Oursler, [Charles] Fulton

**Armstrong, Bob**
See Armstrong, Sinclair

**Armstrong, Catherine** [FFF]
*Author*
* De Courcy, Kate

**Armstrong, Cathleen**
See Page, Catherine

**Armstrong, Charles Wicksteed** 1871-
? [WGT]
*British author*
* Strongi'th'arm, Charles

**Armstrong, Charlotte** 1905-1969
[CA, CC, EMD]
*American author*
* Valentine, Jo

**Armstrong, Christopher J[ohn]
R[ichard]** 1935- [CA]
*British clergyman, translator, editor*
* Armstrong, Anthony C.

**Armstrong, Dodo**
See Armstrong, George Noble

**Armstrong, Douglas Albert** 1920-
[CA]
*British author and journalist*
* Douglas, Albert
* Tribune
* Windsor, Rex

**Armstrong, [Annette] Elizabeth**
1917- [CA]
*British author*
* Tyler, A. E.

**Armstrong, Geoffrey**
See Fearn, John Russell

**Armstrong, George Edward** 1930-
[CEI, FHE, HK]
*Canadian-born hockey player*
* [The] Chief

**Armstrong, George Noble** 1924-
[BE]
*American baseball player*
* Armstrong, Dodo

**Armstrong, Hammerin' Hank**
See Jackson, Henry

**Armstrong, Harold Barry** 1902-
[WEC]
*Australian cartoonist*
* Armstrong, Mick

**Armstrong, Harry**
See Armstrong, Henry W.

**Armstrong, Henry**
See Jackson, Henry

**Armstrong, Henry W.** 1879-1951
[BEW]
*American songwriter*
* Armstrong, Harry

**Armstrong, Homicide Hank**
See Jackson, Henry

**Armstrong, Hurricane Henry**
See Jackson, Henry

**Armstrong, Jack**
See Felton, Frederick A.

**Armstrong, Jean** 1905- [THR]
*British actress, singer, dancer*
* Adrienne, Jean

**Armstrong, John** 1709-1779
[DEL, FFF, RH]
*Scottish physician and poet*
* Temple, Launcelot

**Armstrong, John** 1826- ? [PA]
*Author*
* Tombo, Monsieur

**Armstrong, John Byron** 1917- [CA]
*American author*
* Byron, John
* Willard, Charles

**Armstrong, Keith F[rancis]
W[hitfield]** 1950- [CA]
*British poet*
* Carm Mac
* Keith X

**Armstrong, [Daniel] Louis**
1900-1971 [BBD, DAM, NN]
*American jazz musician*
* Armstrong, Pops
* [The] Einstein of Jazz
* Satchmo

**Armstrong, Marie G.** 1922-1952
[SC]
*American actress*
* Forsythe, Mimi

**Armstrong, Mick**
See Armstrong, Harold Barry

**Armstrong, Norman** 1938- [CEI]
*Canadian-born hockey player*
* Armstrong, Red

**Armstrong, Paul** 1869-1915 [TC]
*American playwright and journalist*
* Right Cross

**Armstrong, Pops**
See Armstrong, [Daniel] Louis

**Armstrong, R. L.** ?-1978 [FIR]
*Actor*
* Armstrong, Tex

**Armstrong, Raymond**
See Lee, Norman

**Armstrong, Red**
See Armstrong, Norman

**Armstrong, Richard** 1903-
[CA, TCC]
*British author*
* Renton, Cam

**Armstrong, Robert**
See Smith, Donald Robert

**Armstrong, Shelley**
See Easton, Amos

**Armstrong, Sinclair** 1912- [ASC]
*American composer, conductor, arranger*
* Armstrong, Bob

**Armstrong, Sybil**
See Edmondson, Sybil
[Armstrong]

**Armstrong, T. I. F.**
See Armstrong, Terence Ian Fytton

**Armstrong, Terence Ian Fytton**
1912-1970 [AW, CA, WGT]
*British poet, editor, bibliographer*
* Armstrong, T. I. F.
* Gawsworth, John
* Scrannel, Orpheus

**Armstrong, Tex**
See Armstrong, R. L.

**Armstrong, Warren**
See Bennett, William Edward

**Armstrong, Warren** 1946- [BB]
*American basketball player*
* Jabali, Warren

**Armstrong, Warwick Windridge**
1879-1947 [EC]
*Australian cricketer*
* [The] Big Ship

**Armstrong, William [Billy]**
See Devine, William M.

**Armstrong, William** 16th c.
[DHA, DNNF, RH]
*Scottish border raider*
* Kinmont Willie

**Armstrong, William A[lexander]**
1912- [CA]
*Scottish author*
* Hazelton, Alexander

**Armstrong, Willimina Leonora** 1866-
? [SFL]
*Author*
* Ki Dost, Zamin

**Armuna, Ezequiel**
See Zequiera y Arango, Manuel de

**Arnade, Charles W[olfgang]** 1927-
[CA]
*German-born author*
* Giersch, Julius

**Arnal, Claude**
See Cabrero Arnal, Jose

**Arnall, William** [FFF]
*Author*
* Abrabanel, Solomon

**Arnao, Gabriel** 20th c. [WECO]
*Spanish cartoonist*
* Gabi

**Arnarson, Oern**
See Stefansson, Magnus

**Arnaud de Villeneuve** 1238?-1314?
[DEP, DNNS, HN]
*French chemist, astrologer, theologian*
* [The] Father of Chemistry

**Arnaud de Villeneuve** (Continued)
* [The] Father of French
  Chemistry

**Arnaud, Henrietta** 1800- ? [PA]
*Author*
* Reyhaud, [Madam] C.

**Arnaud, Saint Romain**
See Aragon, Louis

**Arnauld, Antoine** 1612-1694
[WBD]
*Philosopher and theologian*
* [The] Great Arnauld

**Arnauld, Antoine Vincent**
1766-1834 [PA]
*Author*
* [L']Avocat

**Arnauld, Jacqueline Marie**
1591-1661 [WBD]
*French abbess*
* Angelique, [Mere]

**Arnaz, Desi**
See Arnaz y De Acha, Desiderio
Alberto

**Arnaz y De Acha, Desiderio Alberto**
1915- [FC]
*Cuban-born actor and musician*
* Arnaz, Desi

**Arnd [or Arndt], Johann** 1555-1621
[DNNS, HN, RH]
*German theologian*
* [The] Fenelon of the Reformation

**Arne, Aaron**
See Jorgenson, Alf A.

**Arneson, Hike**
See Arneson, Jim

**Arneson, Jim** 20th c.
*American football player*
* Arneson, Hike

**Arness, James**
See Aurness, James

**Arnet**
See Hannet, John

**Arnett, Caroline**
See Cole, Lois Dwight

**Arnett, Carroll** 1927- [CA]
*American poet*
* Gogisgi

**Arnett, Jaguar Jon**
See Arnett, Jon D.

**Arnett, Jon D.** 1934- [FB]
*American football player*
* Arnett, Jaguar Jon

**Arnette, Robert** [house pseudonym,
Ziff-Davis]
See Graham, Roger Phillips

**Arnette, Robert** [house pseudonym,
Ziff-Davis]
See Silverberg, Robert

**Arnim, Bettina Brentano von**
1785-1859 [RH]
*German author*
* [The] Child

**Arno, Elroy**
See Yerxa, Leroy

**Arno, Peter**
See Peters, Curtis Arnoux, Jr.

**Arno, Sig**
See Aron, Siegfried

**Arnobius** 4th c. [WBD]
*Author*
* Afer

**Arnold, Adlai F[ranklin]** 1914-
[CA]
*American agricultural writer*
* Franklin, A.

**Arnold, Arlo**
See Arnold, Christopher Paul

**Arnold, Augustus [Gus]** 20th c.
[BWW]
*American musician*
* Finn, Julio

**Arnold, Benjamin**
See Kilpatrick, Ben

**Arnold, Bernard** 1915- [ASC]
*American composer and writer*
* Arnold, Buddy

**Arnold, Billy Boy**
See Arnold, William [Billy]

**Arnold, Birch**
See Bartlett, Alice Elinor Bowen

**Arnold, Buddy**
See Arnold, Bernard

**Arnold, Buddy**
See Grishaver, Arnold Buddy

**Arnold, C. G.**
See Arnold, Charles Geoffrey

**Arnold, Carl**
See Raknes, Ola

**Arnold, Cecile** 1931- [SC]
*American actress*
* Arley, Cecile

**Arnold, Charles Geoffrey** 1915-
[ART]
*British painter*
* Arnold, C. G.

**Arnold, Christopher Paul** 1947-
[SMG]
*American baseball player*
* Arnold, Arlo

**Arnold, Clement**
See Panting, Arnold Clement

**Arnold, Danny**
See Rothman, Arnold

**Arnold, Eddie**
See Wendorff, Arnold

**Arnold, Edward**
See Schneider, Guenther

**Arnold, Edwin Lester** 1856- ?
[LAO]
*British author*
* Phra

**Arnold, Elizabeth** 20th c. [WWL]
*British author*
* Kaumudi, Kavita

**Arnold, Faith Stewart**
See Miles, Gertrude Elizabeth

**Arnold, Florine**
See Andrews, Mrs. Charles A.

**Arnold, Frank**
See Young, Fred W.

**Arnold, Fred** 1872- ? [THR]
*British comedian*
* Allandale, Fred

**Arnold, Frederick** 19th c. [PA]
*Author*
* F. A.

**Arnold, G. L.**
See Lichtheim, George

**Arnold, Gail Einhart Haley** 1939-
[TBJ]
*American author and illustrator*
* Haley, Gail E.

**Arnold, Geoffrey Graham** 1944-
[DC]
*British cricketer*
* Arnold, Horse

**Arnold, George** 1834-1865
[FFF, PA]
*American comic poet*
* Garrulous, George
* Grahame, Allen
* Macarone
* Pierrot
* [The] Undersigned

**Arnold, Grace**
See Wupperman, Georgiana
[Iversen]

**Arnold, Hap**
See Arnold, Henry Harley

**Arnold, Harry**
See Persson, Harry Arnold

**Arnold, Henry Harley** 1886-1950
[CND, WA]
*American military leader*
* Arnold, Hap
* Colter [code name used during
  World War II]

**Arnold, Horse**
See Arnold, Geoffrey Graham

**Arnold, Ian**
See Crump, Spencer

**Arnold, Jack**
See Gluck, Arnold Jack

**Arnold, James** 1901-1968 [BWW]
*American singer*
* Arnold, Kokomo
* Gitfiddle Jim

**Arnold, John**
See Kummer, Frederic Arnold

**Arnold, Joseph H.**
See Hayes, Joseph [Arnold]

**Arnold, June [Davis]** 1926- [CA]
*American author*
* Carpenter

**Arnold, Kokomo**
See Arnold, James

**Arnold, L. J.**
See Cameron, Lou

**Arnold, Malcolm**
See Murray, Andrew Nicholas

**Arnold, Margot**
See Cook, Petronelle Marguerite
Mary

**Arnold, Marie**
See Arnold, Phyl

**Arnold, Matthew** 1822-1888
[DEL, DNNS, FFF]
*British poet and critic*
* A.
* [The] Apostle of Culture
* [The] Apostle of Molasses and
  Moonshine
* [The] Apostle of Sweetness and
  Light
* [The] Saint Beuve of English
  Criticism
* Thundertentronckh, Arminius
  Von

**Arnold, Maurice**
*See* Strothotte, Maurice Arnold

**Arnold, Phyl** 1903?-1941   [THR]
*British actress*
* Arnold, Marie

**Arnold, Richard** 1912-   [CA]
*Scottish-born author*
* Coch-y-Bonddhu

**Arnold, Richard Edward [Eddy]**
1918-   [CME, CWG, ECM]
*American country-western performer*
* [The] Tennessee Plowboy

**Arnold, William [Billy]** 1935-
[BWW, NBB]
*American singer*
* Arnold, Billy Boy

**Arnold, Winifred**
*See* May, Winifred Arnold

**Arnoldy, Julie**
*See* Bischoff, Julia Bristol

**Arnolfo di Cambio** 1232?-1300?
[SN]
*Italian sculptor and architect*
* Arnolfo di Lapo
* [The] Michael Angelo of the
  Middle Ages

**Arnolfo di Lapo**
*See* Arnolfo di Cambio

**Arnondrin, Sidney J.** 1901-1948
[WWJ]
*American jazz musician*
* Arodin, Sidney J.

**Arnot, Florence**
*Actress*
* Doran, Mary

**Arnot, Robin Page** 1890-   [IAW]
*British author*
* Cade, Jack

**Arnott, Edwin**
*See* Job, Edwin

**Arnoul, Francoise**
*See* Gautsch, Francoise Annette

**Arnould, Arthur** 19th c.   [PA]
*Author*
* Amatthey

**Arnould, Jean-Francois** 1734-1795
[PA]
*Author*
* Mussot

**Arnould, Rigo**
*See* Arnould, Rigobert

**Arnould, Rigobert** 1925-   [FDG]
*Belgian director*
* Arnould, Rigo

**Arnovich, Morris** 1910-1959   [BE]
*American baseball player*
* Arnovich, Snooker

**Arnovich, Snooker**
*See* Arnovich, Morris

**Arnstein, Nicky**
*See* Stein, Jules W. Arndt

**Arntzen, Old Folks**
*See* Arntzen, Orie Edgar

**Arntzen, Orie Edgar** 1909-   [BE]
*American baseball player*
* Arntzen, Old Folks

**Arodin, Sidney J.**
*See* Arnondrin, Sidney J.

**Aroizzone, Antoinette** 20th c.
[RO1]
*American singer*
* Arden, Toni

**Aron, Siegfried** 1895-1975
[BEW, FC]
*German actor, singer, director*
* Arno, Sig

**Aronin, Ben**
*See* Herron, Edna

**Aronstam, Noah E.** 1872- ?   [NAA]
*Latvian-born physician and author*
* De Chevette, J.

**Arora, Ramesh Chandra** 1933-
[IAW]
*Indian author*
* Don

**Arouet**
*See* Ladd, Joseph Brown

**Arouet, Francois Marie** 1694-1778
[DNNS, FFF, SN]
*French author*
* [L']Anatomie Vivante [The
  Living Anatomy]
* [The] Apostle of Infidelity
* [The] Audacious Gaul
* [The] Coryphaeus of Deism
* [The] Devil's Missionary
* [The] Dictator of Letters
* [The] French Virgil
* [Le] Grand Pan
* [The] Great Pan
* [The] Patriarch of Ferney
* [The] Philosopher of Ferney
* [The] Plato of the Eighteenth
  Century
* [The] Prince of Scoffers
* Voltaire

**Arp, Bill**
*See* Smith, Charles Henry

**Arp, Hans**
*See* Arp, Jean

**Arp, Jean** 1887-1966   [CA]
*French sculptor, painter, author,*
*poet*
* Arp, Hans
* Seuphor, Michel

**Arpel, Adrien**
*See* Newman, Adrien Ann

**Arquette, Cliff[ord]** 1905-1974
[CA, TR, WA]
*American entertainer*
* Weaver, Charley

**Arquette, Lois S[teinmetz]** 1934-
[SAT, WYA]
*American author*
* Cardozo, Lois S.
* Duncan, Lois
* Kerry, Lois

**Arr, E. H.**
*See* Rollins, Ellen H.

**Arr, Stephen**
*See* Rynas, Stephen A.

**Arrand, Dick**
*See* Arrand, Richmond Henry

**Arrand, Richmond Henry** 1929-
[IWM]
*British musician*
* Arrand, Dick

**Arre, Helen**
*See* Ross, Zola Helen

**Arre, John**
*See* Holt, John [Robert]

**Arrebo, Anders Christensen**
1587-1637   [SN]
*Danish poet*
* [The] Father of Scandinavian
  Poetry

**Arrelsee**
*See* Cope, Robert L.

**Arria**
*See* Pugh, Eliza Lofton [Phillips]

**Arrich, Josephine** 1904-1951   [SC]
*Austrian-born actress*
* Norman, Josephine

**Arrigoni, Carlo** 18th c.   [SN]
*Italian musician*
* [The] King of Arragon

**Arrington, Alfred W.** 1810-1867
[FFF, PA]
*Author*
* Summerfield, Charles

**Arrington, Joseph, Jr.** 1933-
[IBW, RO2]
*American singer*
* Hazziez, Yusef
* Joseph X
* Tex, Joe

**Arriola, Gus**
*See* Montano Arriola, Gustavo

**Arrom, Cecilia Francisca Josefa**
1797-1877   [DNNF, FFF, WBD]
*Spanish author*
* Caballero, Fernan

**Arrow, William** [house pseudonym,
Ballantine Books]
*See* Pfeil, Donald J.

**Arrow, William** [house pseudonym,
Ballantine Books]
*See* Rotsler, William

**Arrowsmith, Robert** 1953-   [DC]
*British cricketer*
* Barrow, Joe

**Arroyo, Fernando** 1952-
[BR, SMG]
*American baseball player*
* Arroyo, Fred
* Arroyo, Mex
* Arroyo, Nando

**Arroyo, Fred**
*See* Arroyo, Fernando

**Arroyo, Luis Enrique** 1927-
[BE, BTB]
*Puerto Rican-born baseball player*
* Arroyo, Yo-Yo

**Arroyo, Mex**
*See* Arroyo, Fernando

**Arroyo, Nando**
*See* Arroyo, Fernando

**Arroyo, Yo-Yo**
*See* Arroyo, Luis Enrique

**Arrugado**
*See* Roquero Dominguez, Juan

**Arruza, Carlos**
*See* Ruiz Camino, Carlos

**Arruza, Manolo** 20th c.   [GS]
*Mexican bullfighter*
* Nuevo Ciclon de Mexico [New
  Cyclone of Mexico]

**Arsaces VI**
*See* Mithridates I

**Arsaces XXIV**
*See* Firuz I

**Arshawsky, Arthur Jacob** 1910-
[BBD, EJ, WWJ]
*American jazz musician*
* Shaw, Artie

**Art[hur] the Great**
*See* Shires, [Charles] Art[hur]

**Artamonov, Nikolai** 20th c.
*Russian-born intelligence agent*
* Shadrin, Nicholas

**Artaud, Antonin** 1896-1948   [TLC]
*French playwright, poet, author*
* [Le] Revele

**Artax**
*See* Eden, John Lancelot

**Artaxerxes I** 5th c. BC
[HN, WBD]
*King of Persia*
* Longimanus [The Long-Handed]

**Artaxerxes II** 4th c. BC   [WBD]
*King of Persia*
* Mnemon

**Artaxerxes III**
*See* Ochus

**Artemas**
*See* Mason, Arthur Telford

**Artemisia**
*See* Montagu, Mary Wortley

**Arter, Wallace E.** 20th c.   [MBF]
*British author and journalist*
* Kay, Wallace

**Artevelde, Jacob van** 1290?-1345
[DNNF, DNNS, FF]
*Flemish statesman*
* [The] Brewer of Ghent

**[The] Artful Dodger**
*See* Needham, David

**Arthaud, Robert** 1925-
[FC, ITA, SW]
*American actor*
* Arthur, Robert

**Arthenice**
*See* De Rambouillet, Mme.

**Arthfab**
*See* Williams, Jac Lewis

**Arthgal** 6th c.   [SN]
*First Earl of Warwick*
* [The] Bear

**Arthur** 6th c.   [DEP, DNNS, RH]
*King of England*
* [The] Flower of Kings

**Arthur, Ada** [FFF]
* Arturi, Mademoiselle

**Arthur, Alan**
See Edmonds, Arthur Denis

**Arthur, Beatrice**
See Frankel, Bernice

**Arthur, Budd**
See Shappiro, Budd

**Arthur, Burt**
See Shappiro, Herbert [Arthur]

**Arthur, Carol**
See Arata, Carol Jane

**Arthur, Chester Alan** 1830-1886
[FAP]
*American president*
* America's First Gentleman
* Arthur, Prince
* Arthur the Gentleman
* [The] Dude President
* Elegant Arthur
* [The] First Gentleman of the Land
* His Accidency
* Our Chet

**Arthur, Frank**
See Ebert, Arthur Frank

**Arthur, Frederick**
See Lambert, F. A. Heygate

**Arthur, George K.**
See Brest, George K. A.

**Arthur, Gladys**
See Osborne, Dorothy [Gladys]
Yeo

**Arthur, H. Preston**
See Hankins, Arthur Preston

**Arthur, Harry**
See Base, A. H.

**Arthur, Harry**
See Bates, Harry Arthur

**Arthur, Herbert**
See Shappiro, Herbert [Arthur]

**Arthur, Hugh**
See Christie-Murray, David [Hugh Arthur]

**Arthur, Jean**
See Greene, Gladys Georgianna

**Arthur, Johnny**
See Williams, John

**Arthur, Joseph**
See Smith, Arthur F.

**Arthur, Joseph**
See Smith, Joseph Arthur

**Arthur, Julia**
See Lewis, Ida

**Arthur, Peter**
See Porges, Arthur

**Arthur, Prince**
See Arthur, Chester Alan

**Arthur, Robert**
See Arthaud, Robert

**Arthur, Robert**
See Feder, Robert Arthur

**Arthur, Ruth M.** 1905- [AW]
*Scottish author*
* Huggins, Ruth Mabel

**Arthur the Gentleman**
See Arthur, Chester Alan

**Arthur, Tiffany**
See Pelton, Robert W[ayne]

**Arthur, Timothy Shay** 1809- ?
[PA]
*Author*
* Uncle Herbert

**Arthur, William**
See Baker, William Arthur
Howard

**Arthur, William**
See Neubauer, William Arthur

**Arthurs, Harry**
See Base, A. H.

**[The] Artichoke King**
See Terranova, Ciro

**Artifex**
See Green, Peter

**Artis, Oda Bell** 20th c. [IBW]
*American parakeet exhibitor*
* [The] Bird Lady

**Artis Gener, Aveli** 1912- [WEC]
*Spanish cartoonist*
* Tisner

**[The] Artist of the Revolution**
See David, Jacques Louis

**Arto, Florence** 1895- [F2, FC]
*American actress*
* Vidor, Florence

**Artur**
See Soares Correia, Artur Manuel

**Arturi, Mademoiselle**
See Arthur, Ada

**Aruego, Ariane**
See Dewey, Ariane

**Arundel, Jocelyn**
See Alexander, Jocelyn Anne
Arundel

**Arundel, John Thomas** 1863-1912
[BE]
*American baseball player*
* Arundel, Tug

**Arundel, Tug**
See Arundel, John Thomas

**Arveco**
See Coster, Arthur Vennell

**Arvede Barine**
See Vincens, Mme. Charles

**Arvidson, Linda**
See Johnson, Linda

**Arvill, Robert**
See Boote, Robert Edward

**Arvonen, Helen** 20th c. [SFL]
*Author*
* Worth, Margaret

**Ary, Sheila M[ary Littleboy]** 1929-
[CA]
*British-born author*
* Littleboy, Sheila M.

**Arzhak, Nikolai**
See Daniel, Julii [or Yuli]

**Asabore**
See King, Carroll E.

**Asafiev, Boris Vladimirovitch**
1884-1949 [BBD]
*Russian composer and writer on music*
* Glebov, Igor

**Asante, Molefi K.**
See Smith, Arthur L.

**Asare, Bediako**
See Konadu, Samuel Asare

**Asbell, Bernard** 1923- [CA]
*American author*
* Max, Nicholas

**Asbjornson, Asby**
See Asbjornson, Robert Anthony

**Asbjornson, Robert Anthony** 1909-
[BE]
*American baseball player*
* Asbjornson, Asby

**Asch, Sholem [or Shalom]**
1880-1957 [TC]
*Polish-born Yiddish author and playwright*
* Ash, Sholem [or Shalom]

**Asch, Stan**
See Aschmeier, Stanley

**Ascham, Roger** 1515-1568
[DEL, RH, SN]
*British author and scholar*
* [The] Father of English Prose

**Asche, Oscar**
See Heiss, John Strange

**Aschenbach, Charles S.** 1883- [BE]
*American baseball player*
* Charles, Chappy
* Charles, Raymond

**Ascher, Sheila** 1944- [IAW]
*American author*
* Ascher/Straus

**Ascher/Straus**
See Ascher, Sheila

**Ascherson, Renee** 1920- [BF]
*British actress*
* Asherson, Renee

**Aschmann,** 1921- [CA]
*American author and playwright*
* Clare, Francis D.
* Mary Francis, [Mother]

**Aschmeier, Stanley** 20th c.
[WECO]
*American cartoonist*
* Asch, Stan

**Aschwanden, Peter** 20th c.
*American illustrator*
* Scopulorum, Junipero

**Asclepius, Nicolas** ?-1571 [PA]
*Author*
* Barbatus

**Ascott, Adelie**
See Bobin, John William [Jack]

**Ascott, Anthony**
See Carmineo, Giuliano

**Ascott, John**
See Bobin, John William [Jack]

**[The] Ascraean Poet**
See Hesiod

**[The] Ascraean Sage**
See Hesiod

**Ash**
See Cannell, Edward Ashton

**Ash Can Joe**
See Del Rio, James Cohen

**Ash, Derek**
See Bolton, F. T.

**Ash, Edward Cecil** 1888- [WWL]
*British author*
* Brasset, A. D.
* Fielding, A. D.
* Syntax

**Ash, Fenton**
See Atkins, Frank

**Ash, Marvin**
See Ashbaugh, Marvin

**Ash, Pauline**
See Walker, Emily Kathleen

**Ash, Peter**
See Hauck, Louise [Platt]

**Ash, Rene Lee** 1939- [CA]
*Belgian-born American editor and writer*
* Lee, A. R.

**Ash, Robert John** 1943- [SMG]
*Canadian-born hockey player*
* Ash, Squeaky

**Ash, Roberta**
See Garner, Roberta

**Ash, Sholem [or Shalom]**
See Asch, Sholem [or Shalom]

**Ash, Squeaky**
See Ash, Robert John

**Ashbaugh, Marvin** 1914-
[EJ, PMJ]
*American jazz musician*
* Ash, Marvin

**Ashbee, C. R.**
See Ashbee, Charles Robert

**Ashbee, Charles Robert** 1863-1942
[WGT]
*British author*
* Ashbee, C. R.

**Ashbrook, Harriette [Cora]**
1898-1946 [WW]
*Author*
* Shane, Susannah

**Ashburn, Don Richie** 1927- [BE]
*American baseball player*
* Ashburn, Whitey

**Ashburn, Whitey**
See Ashburn, Don Richie

**Ashburton, Sarah Frances**
See Mannix, Mary Walsh

**Ashby, Ash**
See Ashby, Don

**Ashby, Don** 1955- [SMG]
*Canadian-born hockey player*
* Ashby, Ash

**Ashby, George** [PA]
*Author*
* T. F.

**Ashby, John**
See Tooley, John

**Ashby, Rubie Constance** 1899-
[EMD]
*British author*
* Freugon, Ruby

**Ashdown, Clifford** [joint pseudonym with John James Pitcairn]
*See* Freeman, Richard

**Ashdown, Clifford** [joint pseudonym with Richard Freeman]
*See* Pitcairn, John James

**Ashe, Douglas**
*See* Bardin, John Franklin

**Ashe, Faith**
*See* Winter, Faith

**Ashe, Gordon**
*See* Creasey, John

**Ashe, Mary Ann**
*See* Lewis, Mary Christianna [Milne]

**Ashe, Penelope** [joint pseudonym]
*See* Young, Billie

**Ashe, Susan**
*See* Best, Carol Ann

**Ashenfelter, Ash**
*See* Ashenfelter, Horace

**Ashenfelter, Horace** 1923-
[BBH, TF]
*American track and field athlete*
* Ashenfelter, Ash
* Ashenfelter, Nip

**Ashenfelter, Nip**
*See* Ashenfelter, Horace

**Asher, Robert Dabney** 1948-
[SMG]
*American football player*
* Asher, Smasher

**Asher, Smasher**
*See* Asher, Robert Dabney

**Asherson, Renee**
*See* Ascherson, Renee

**Ashey, Bella**
*See* Breinburg, Petronella

**Ashford, Daisy**
*See* Ashford, Margaret Mary

**Ashford, Jeffrey**
*See* Jeffries, Roderic [Graeme]

**Ashford, Margaret Mary**
1881-1972 [LC, SAT]
*British author*
* Ashford, Daisy

**Ashford, Thomas Steven** 1954-
[SMG]
*American baseball player*
* Ashford, Tucker

**Ashford, Tucker**
*See* Ashford, Thomas Steven

**Ashkenazy, Irwin** 20th c. [WGT]
*Author*
* Garnet, G.

**Ashley**
*See* Havinden, Ashley Eldrid

**Ashley, Annie**
*See* Drolet, Annie

**Ashley, Barbara**
*See* Barbieri, G. M.

**Ashley, Clarence** 1895-1967
[CME]
*American country-western performer*
* Ashley, Tom

**Ashley, Edward**
*See* Cooper, E. A.

**Ashley, Elizabeth**
*See* Cole, Elizabeth

**Ashley, Elizabeth**
*See* Salmon, Annie Elizabeth [Martin]

**Ashley, [Arthur] Ernest** 1906-
[CAP, CC, WW]
*British author*
* Vivian, Francis

**Ashley, Fred**
*See* Atkins, Frank

**Ashley, Gladys**
*See* Ewens, Gwendoline Wilson

**Ashley, Graham**
*See* Organ, John

**Ashley, Helen**
*See* Hurt, Helen

**Ashley, Iris**
*See* Stafford-Northcote, Iris

**Ashley, John**
*See* Atchley, John

**Ashley, Lud**
*See* Ashley, Thomas Ludlow

**Ashley, Merrill**
*See* Merrill, Linda

**Ashley, Mrs. Warren** [FFF]
*Entertainer*
* Heath, Marie

**Ashley, Thomas Clarence**
*See* McCurry, Clarence Earl

**Ashley, Thomas Ludlow**
*American politician*
* Ashley, Lud

**Ashley, Tom**
*See* Ashley, Clarence

**Ashlin, John**
*See* Cutforth, John Ashlin

**Ashmind, Kim**
*See* Van Laerhoven, Robert Victor Flora

**Ashmole, Elias** 1617-1692 [FFF]
*British antiquary and alchemist*
* Hasolle, James

**Ashmore, Basil Norton** 1915- [AW]
*British author*
* Marlin, Roy

**Ashok**
*See* Konishi, Masatoshi A.

**Ashraf, [Princess]** 1920?-
*Sister of Iranian shah, Mohammed Reza Pahlavi*
* [The] Black Panther

**Ashtock**
*See* Ashton-Bostock, David

**Ashton, Alfred**
*See* Forman, William Henry

**Ashton, Ann**
*See* Kimbro, John M.

**Ashton, [Sir] George Grey** 1861- ?
[LAO]
*British author*
* Amphibian
* Southcote, George

**Ashton, Howard**
*See* Barton, James Levi

**Ashton, Knight** [PA]
*Author*
* Sarti, Signor

**Ashton, Lucy**
*See* Martin, Netta

**Ashton, Thomas** [SN]
* Almanzor

**Ashton, Warren T.**
*See* Adams, William Taylor

**Ashton, William** 1943- [RM, RO2]
*British singer*
* Kramer, Billy J.

**Ashton, Winifred** 1888-1965
[CC, EMD, MWD]
*British author and playwright*
* Cortis, Diana
* Dane, Clemence

**Ashton-Bostock, David** 1932-
[ART]
*British painter and interior decorator*
* Ashtock

**Ashton-Gwatkin, Frank Trelawny Arthur** 1889- [SFL, WGT]
*Author*
* Paris, John

**Ashton-Warner, Sylvia [Constance]**
*See* Henderson, Sylvia

**Ashwell, Lena**
*See* Simson, Lena Margaret

**[The] Asian Great Gatsby**
*See* Park, Tongsun

**Asia's Queen of Jazz**
*See* Din, Dulce

**Asiaticus**
*See* Antiochus XIII

**Asimov, Isaac** 1920-
[CA, ESF, WGT]
*Russian-born American author*
* Dale, George E.
* Dr. A
* French, Paul

**Aska the Magician**
*See* Musselman, Johnson J.

**Askari, Hussaini Muhammad**
*See* Pereira, Harold Bertram

**Askew, Jack**
*See* Hivnor, Robert

**Askew, John** 1957- [AES]
*American soccer player*
* Askew, Sonny

**Askew, Sonny**
*See* Askew, John

**Askey, Arthur** 1900- [BMH]
*British comedian*
* Big Hearted Arthur

**Askham, Francis**
*See* Greenwood, Julia Eileen Courtney

**Aslan, Gregoire**
*See* Aslanian, Kridor

**Aslanian, Kridor** 1908- [FC]
*French-Turkish actor*
* Aslan, Gregoire

**Asmodeus**
*See* Meighan, Thaddeus W.

**Asmodeus**
*See* Nichols, Thomas

**Asmus**
*See* Claudius, Matthias

**Asmussen, Andreas** 1913- [WEC]
*Danish cartoonist*
* Asmussen, Des
* Des

**Asmussen, Des**
*See* Asmussen, Andreas

**Asnyk, Adam** 1838-1897 [WBD]
*Polish poet and playwright*
* El y

**Asoka [or Acoka]** 3rd c. BC [WBD]
*King of Magadha*
* [The] Great

**Aspasia**
*See* Milto

**[The] Aspasia of France**
*See* L'Enclos, Anne

**[The] Aspasia of Lyons**
*See* Labe, Louise

**[The] Aspasia of the Seventeenth Century**
*See* L'Enclos, Anne

**Asquith, Anthony** 1902-1968 [FC]
*British director*
* Asquith, Puffin

**Asquith, Nan**
*See* Pattinson, Nancy Evelyn

**Asquith, Puffin**
*See* Asquith, Anthony

**Assad, Hafez** 1930?-
*Syrian president*
* [The] Tito of the Arab World

**Assaghir [Small]**
*See* Abu Abdallah [or Abdullah]

**Asse, Jack**
*See* Chauvin [or Caulvin?], Jean

**Asselineau, Roger [Maurice]** 1915-
[CA]
*French author*
* Maurice, Roger

**Assiac**
*See* Fraenkel, Heinrich

**[The] Assistant President**
*See* Roosevelt, [Anna] Eleanor

**Assollant, Jean-Baptiste-Alfred**
1827-1886
*Author*
* Cumbermere, [Lord] Claudius Hastings

**Assunto, Jacob** 1905- [DAM, EJ]
*American jazz musician*
* Papa Jac

**[Die] Asta**
*See* Nielsen, Asta

**Astaire, Adele**
*See* Austerlitz, Adele

**Astaire, Fred**
*See* Austerlitz, Frederick

**Astan, Laurence**
*See* Astangov, Mikhail

**Astangov, Mikhail** 1901-1965   [SC]
*Russian actor*
* Astan, Laurence

**Astbury, Gertrude Mary**
1887-1957   [BEW]
*British theatrical performer*
* Gitana, Gertie

**Astell, Mary** 1668-1731
[SN, WBD]
*British author*
* Madonilla [or Madonella]

**Astericus**
*See* Radla, Astrik

**Asterisk**
*See* Fletcher, Robert James

**Astles, Robert** 20th c.
*British-born aide to Ugandan
president, Idi Amin*
* Major Bob

**Astley, Juliet**
*See* Lofts, Norah [Robinson]

**Aston, Anthony**   [SN]
*British actor and playwright*
* Trusty Anthony

**Aston, James**
*See* White, Terence Hanbury

**Astor, Bob**
*See* Dade, Robert E.

**Astor, Mary**
*See* Langhanke, Lucille
Vasconcellos

**[The] Astoria Assassin**
*See* Berlenbach, Paul

**[The] Astoria Eagle**
*See* McQuillan, Hugh A.

**Astraea**
*See* Behn, Aphra

**Astrid, [Princess] Marie** 20th c.
*Princess of Luxembourg*
* Asty

**[The] Astrologer**
*See* Albert III

**Astrological Richard**
*See* Harvey, Richard

**[The] Astronomer**
*See* Alfonso X [or Alphonso]

**[The] Astronomer Poet**
*See* Omar Khayyam

**Astrophel**
*See* Oldham, John

**Astrophel**
*See* Sidney, [Sir] Philip

**Asty**
*See* Astrid, [Princess] Marie

**Asunsolo De Martinez, Lolita
Dolores** 1905-   [BDF, FC, WEF]
*Mexican actress*
* Del Rio, Dolores

**Asuque, Okon Bassey** 1932-
[BX, RBE]
*Nigerian-born boxer*
* Bassey, Hogan
* Bassey, Kid

**Aswad, al-**   [RH]
*Islamic prophet*
* [The] Imposter
* [The] Liar

**Aswad, al-** (Continued)
* [The] Weathercock

**Aswell, Mary Louise**   [EMD]
*Author*
* Patrick, Q. [joint pseudonym with
Richard Wilson Webb]

**Aswin**
*See* Nandakumar, Prema

**Atacinus**
*See* Varro, Publius Terentius

**Atahualpa [or Atahuallpa]**
1495?-1533   [DNNS]
*King of Peru*
* [The] Last of the Incas

**Atallah, Lillian**
*See* Africano, Lillian

**Atanas, Ants**
*See* Atanas, Walter

**Atanas, Walter** 1922-   [CEI]
*Canadian-born hockey player*
* Atanas, Ants

**Atano III**
*See* Juaristi Mendizabal, Mariano

**Atchby, El**
*See* Bazy, Lyman Hotchkiss

**Atcheson, Richard** 1934-   [CA]
*American author and journalist*
* Tressilian, Charles

**Atchison, Sandra Dallas** 1939-
[CA]
*American author*
* Dallas, Sandra

**Atchison, Shelby David** 1912-
[CWG, DAM]
*American country-western performer*
* Atchison, Tex

**Atchison, Tex**
*See* Atchison, Shelby David

**Atchley, John** 1934-   [ITA]
*American actor*
* Ashley, John

**Athanas, George**
*See* Athanasiadis-Novas, Georgios

**Athanas, W. V.**
*See* Athanas, William Verne

**Athanas, William Verne**
1918-1962   [WGT]
*Author*
* Athanas, W. V.
* Colson, Bill

**Athanasiadis-Novas, Georgios**
1893-   [IAW]
*Greek politician and author*
* Athanas, George

**Athanasius** 296?- 373
[DEP, SN, WBD]
*Saint*
* Athanasius Contra Mundum
* [The] Father of Orthodoxy
* [The] Great

**Athanasius Contra Mundum**
*See* Athanasius

**[The] Atheist**
*See* Aetius of Antioch

**[The] Atheist**
*See* Diagoras

**[The] Atheist**
*See* Hobbes, Thomas

**[The] Atheist**
*See* Shelley, Percy Bysshe

**[That] Atheist Tamburian**
*See* Marlowe, Christopher

**Athelard of Bath** 12th c.
[DEL, SN]
*British scholar*
* Philosophus Anglorum

**Atheling, William**
*See* Pound, Ezra [Loomis]

**Atheling, William, Jr.**
*See* Blish, James [Benjamin]

**Athelstan** 895- 940   [DNNS]
*King of England*
* [The] Glorious

**Athenais** 401?- 460?   [WBD]
*Wife of Byzantine emperor,
Theodosius II*
* Eudocia

**[The] Athenian Aberdeen**
*See* Gordon, George Hamilton
[Fourth Earl of Aberdeen]

**[The] Athenian Bee**
*See* Aristocles

**[The] Athenian Moses**
*See* Aristocles

**Atherton, Alfred Leroy, Jr.** 1921-
*American diplomat*
* Atherton, Roy

**Atherton, Alice**
*See* Hogan, Mary Alice

**Atherton, Charles Morgan Herbert
[Charlie]** 1873-1934   [BE]
*American baseball player*
* Atherton, Prexy

**Atherton, Gertrude [Franklin Horn]**
1857-1948   [CAA, TLC]
*American author and historian*
* Lin, Frank

**Atherton, Lucius**
*See* Masters, Edgar Lee

**Atherton, Prexy**
*See* Atherton, Charles Morgan
Herbert [Charlie]

**Atherton, Roy**
*See* Atherton, Alfred Leroy, Jr.

**Atherton, Sarah**
*See* Bridgman, Sarah Atherton

**Athey, Bumper**
*See* Athey, Charles William
Jeffrey

**Athey, Charles William Jeffrey**
1957-   [DC]
*British cricketer*
* Athey, Bumper

**[The] Athlete of Christendom**
*See* Castriot [or Castriota?],
George

**Athos**
*See* Dawson, Ernest

**Athos**
*See* Walkerley, Rodney Lewis [De
Burgh]

**Atkey, Philip** 1908-   [EMD]
*British author*
* Merriman, Pat
* Perowne, Barry

**Atkin, Ann** 1937-   [ART]
*British artist*
* Fawssett
* G. C. [Gnome Club]

**Atkin, Charles**
*See* Griffin, Frank

**Atkins, Buddy**
*See* Atkins, James Curtis [Jim]

**Atkins, Charles** 20th c.   [IBW]
*American dancer and choreographer*
* Atkins, Cholly

**Atkins, Cholly**
*See* Atkins, Charles

**Atkins, Francis Montgomery**
1887-1956   [BE]
*American baseball player*
* Atkins, Tommy

**Atkins, Frank** 20th c.
[ESF, SFL, WGT]
*British author*
* Ash, Fenton
* Ashley, Fred
* Aubrey, Frank

**Atkins, Frank, Jr.** 20th c.   [ESF]
*British author*
* St. Mars, F.

**Atkins, Frederick Anthony** 1864- ?
[LAO]
*British author and journalist*
* Quousque

**Atkins, Jack**
*See* Finkelstein, Mark

**Atkins, James Curtis [Jim]** 1921-
[BE]
*American baseball player*
* Atkins, Buddy

**Atkins, Meg Elizabeth** 20th c.
[CA]
*British author*
* Moore, Elizabeth

**Atkins, Oliver F.** 1916-1977   [CA]
*American photographer*
* Atkins, Ollie

**Atkins, Ollie**
*See* Atkins, Oliver F.

**Atkins, Tommy**
*See* Atkins, Francis Montgomery

**Atkinson, A. K.** 1922-   [EJ]
*American composer and jazz
musician*
* Salim, Ahmad Khatab

**Atkinson, Alan E.** 1943-   [FB]
*American football player*
* Atkinson, Hombre

**Atkinson, Alice M.**
*See* Kirson, Alice Atkinson

**Atkinson, Butch**
*See* Atkinson, George Henry

**Atkinson, Eleanor [Stackhouse]**
1863-1942   [TC]
*American author and journalist*
* Marks, Nora

**Atkinson, Eleanor Blake**
*See* Pratt, Eleanor Blake
[Atkinson]

**Atkinson, George Henry** 1947-
[FB]
*American football player*
* Atkinson, Butch

**Atkinson, Harry**
See Fitts, Harry

**Atkinson, Hombre**
See Atkinson, Alan E.

**Atkinson, Hubert Burley**
1904-1961 [BE]
*American baseball player*
* Atkinson, Lefty

**Atkinson, John** 1877- ? [WWL]
*British author*
* Aye, John

**Atkinson, Lefty**
See Atkinson, Hubert Burley

**Atkinson, Louisa**
See Calvert, Caroline Louisa
Waring

**Atkinson, M. E.**
See Frankau, Mary Evelyn
Atkinson

**Atkinson, Marshall Foster** 1913-
[ART]
*British painter*
* M. F. A.

**Atkinson, Mary**
See Hardwick, Mollie

**Atkinson, Maude**
See Johnston, Mrs. R. J.

**Atkinson, Mrs. Charles** [FFF]
*Entertainer*
* Bate, Lily

**Atkinson, Mrs. Paul** [FFF]
*Entertainer*
* Hurst, Lulu

**Atkinson, Nancy** 1910- [WD]
*Australian author*
* Benko, Nancy

**Atkinson, Reginald**
See Carlton, G. E. L.

**Atkinson, Ted** 1916- [BBH]
*Canadian-born jockey*
* Atkinson, Teddy Boy

**Atkinson, Teddy Boy**
See Atkinson, Ted

**Atlas**
See Roberts, William Hedley

**Atlas**
See Van Vechten, Carl

**Atlas, Charles**
See Siciliano, Angelo

**[The] Atlas of America**
See Washington, George

**[The] Atlas of Independence**
See Adams, John

**[The] Atlas of Poetrie**
See Peele, George

**Atlee, Howard**
See Heinlen, Howard Atlee

**Atlee, Phil**
See Hammack, Robert Dean
Michael

**Atomcracker, Buzz-Bolt**
See Wilcox, Don

**[The] Atomic Bombshell**
See Echols, Anita

**Atossa**
See Churchill, Sarah Jennings

**Atrakhovich, Kondrat Kondratyevich**
1896- [IAW]
*Russian author, poet, playwright*
* Krapiva

**Attaboy**
See Hetherington, John Rowland

**Attalik Ghazi**
See Yakoub Beg

**Attalo**
See Colizzi, Gioacchino

**Attalus I** 3rd c. BC [WBD]
*King of Pergamum*
* Soter

**Attalus II** 2nd c. BC [WBD]
*King of Pergamum*
* Philadelphus

**Attalus III** 2nd c. BC [WBD]
*King of Pergamum*
* Philometor

**Attar [Druggist]**
See Mohammed ibn-Ibrahim

**Attean, Elmer** ?-1975 [SC]
*American actor*
* Black Hawk, Chief

**Attell, Abraham Washington** 1884-
[EJS]
*American boxer*
* [The] Little Hebrew

**Attell, Monte** 1885-1960 [EJS, SG]
*American boxer*
* [The] Knob Hill Terror

**Attenborough, Bernard George** 20th
c. [CA]
*British author*
* Rand, James S.

**Attendolo, Giacomuzo d'**
1369-1424 [HN]
*Italian soldier and founder of ruling
Milanese family*
* [The] Peasant of Cotignola
* Sforza

**Atterbury, Duke**
See Atterbury, R. E.

**Atterbury, R. E.**
*Radio scriptwriter*
* Atterbury, Duke

**Atterbury's Pad**
See Coningsby, Thomas

**Atthill, Robert Anthony** 1912-
[WD]
*British writer and poet*
* Atthill, Robin

**Atthill, Robin**
See Atthill, Robert Anthony

**[The] Attic Bee**
See Aristocles

**[The] Attic Bee**
See Sophocles

**[The] Attic Homer**
See Sophocles

**[The] Attic Moses**
See Aristocles

**[The] Attic Muse**
See Xenophon

**Atticus**
See Addison, Joseph

**Atticus**
See Fleming, Ian [Lancaster]

**Atticus?**
See Francis, [Sir] Philip

**Atticus**
See Heber, Richard

**Atticus**
See Maccall, William

**Atticus**
See Pawle, Gerald

**[The] Atticus of Midlothian**
See Gladstone, William Ewart

**Attila** 406?- 453
[DNNF, HN, RH]
*King of the Huns*
* [The] Scourge of God
* [The] Sword of Mars
* [The] Terror of the World

**Attila le Petit**
See Thiers, Louis Adolphe

**[The] Attila of the Piano**
See Thalberg, Sigismund

**Attila the Hen**
See Byrne, Jane

**Attila the Hen**
See Thatcher, Margaret Hilda
[Roberts]

**Attila the Nun**
See Pfeiffer, Jane Cahill

**Attle, John C.**
See Welker, John Paul Pater

**Attles, Alvin J., Jr.** 1936-
[IBW, SMG]
*American basketball player, coach,
manager*
* [The] Brother
* [The] Destroyer

**Attmore, Billy** 1965- [IBW]
*German-born actor*
* Attmore, Pop

**Attmore, Pop**
See Attmore, Billy

**[An] Attorney**
See Stephen, [Sir] George

**[The] Attorney General of the Lantern**
See Desmoulins, [Lucie Simplice]
Camille [Benoit]

**[The] Attorney General of the
Republic of Letters**
See Peiresc, Nicolas Claude Fabi
de

**Atuegbu, Andy**
See Atuegbu, Fidelus

**Atuegbu, Fidelus** 1949- [AES]
*Nigerian soccer player*
* Atuegbu, Andy

**Atwater, Caroline Lobdell**
See Pynchon, Adeline Lobdell
Atwater

**Atwater, Richard Tupper** 1892-1948
*American author and columnist*
* Riq

**Atwell, John Leroy** 1879?-1962
[BEW]
*American actor and writer*
* Atwell, Roy

**Atwell, Maurice Dailey** 1924- [BE]
*American baseball player*
* Atwell, Toby

**Atwell, Roy**
See Atwell, John Leroy

**Atwell, Toby**
See Atwell, Maurice Dailey

**Atwell, Winifred** 1921- [IBW]
*Trinidad-born musician*
* [The] Liberace of London

**Atwood, Drucy**
See Morrison, Eula Atwood

**Atwood, Mrs.** [FFF]
*Entertainer*
* Randel, Adelaide

**Au H2O**
See Goldwater, Barry [Morris]

**Auber, Forrestier**
See Woodward, A. A.

**Aubert, Etienne** ?-1362 [WBD]
*Pope*
* Innocent VI

**Aubert, Jeanne**
See Perrinot, Jeanne

**Aubert, [Mother] Marie Joseph**
See Aubert De Laye, Suzanne

**Aubert, Rene** 1655-1735
[HN, WBD]
*French historian*
* [The] Modern Quintus Curtius
* Vertot, Abbe de

**Aubert De Laye, Suzanne**
1835?-1926 [B10]
*French missionary*
* Aubert, [Mother] Marie Joseph

**Aubrey, Frank**
See Atkins, Frank

**Aubrey, James T.** 1918- [ET]
*American television executive*
* Aubrey, Jungle Jim
* [The] Cobra
* [The] Smiling Cobra

**Aubrey, John** 1626-1697 [SN]
*British antiquary*
* [The] Little Boswell of His Day

**Aubrey, Jungle Jim**
See Aubrey, James T.

**Aubrey, Madge**
See Witham, Marjorie Alexandra

**Aubrey-Fletcher, [Sir] Henry
Lancelot** 1887-1969
[CC, EMD, WW]
*British author*
* Wade, Henry

**Aubry, Cecile**
See Benard, Anne-Jose

**Aubry, Clodagh** 1937- [WFA]
*Irish fashion designer*
* Clodagh

**Auburn, Joy**
See McCormick, Alyce

**Auch, Lord**
See Bataille, Georges

**Auchincloss, Louis Stanton** 1917-
[B10, CA, WD]
*American author*
* Lee, Andrew

**Auchinleck, [Sir] Claude**
1884-1981    [BDW, WWW]
*British army officer*
* [The] Auk

**Auchterlonie, Dorothy**
*See* Green, Dorothy

**Auclair, Michel**
*See* Vujovic, Vladimir

**Auctor Ignotus?**
*See* Legg, W. Dorr

**[The] Audacious**
*See* Charles

**[The] Audacious Gaul**
*See* Arouet, Francois Marie

**Audax**
*See* Beesley, Thomas Quinn

**Audax**
*See* Oaksey, [Lord] John Geoffrey
Tristram

**Audax**
*See* Portman, Arthur Fitzhardinge

**Audax Minor**
*See* Ryall, George Francis Trafford

**Audeh, Muhammad Daoud** 1938-
*Palestinian terrorist*
* Abu Daoud [code name]
* Mahdi, Tarik Shakir

**Audemars, Pierre** 20th c.
[CC, WW]
*Author*
* Hodemart, Peter

**Auden, Renee**
*See* West, Uta

**Auden, W. H.**
*See* Auden, Wystan Hugh

**Auden, Wystan Hugh** 1907-1973
[ASC, BEW, LC]
*British-born American poet*
* Auden, W. H.

**Auen, Signe** 1894?-1966
[F1, F2, FC]
*American actress*
* Owen, Seena

**Auer, Anna** 1860-1944    [SC]
*American actress*
* Baker, Anna Willis

**Auer, Gaylord R.** 20th c.    [BBH]
*American lacrosse promoter*
* Auer, Peck

**Auer, Josef** 1928-    [EJ]
*American composer and jazz
musician*
* Auer, Pepsi

**Auer, Mischa**
*See* Ounskowsky, Mischa

**Auer, Peck**
*See* Auer, Gaylord R.

**Auer, Pepsi**
*See* Auer, Josef

**Auerbach, Arnold** 1917?-
[BB, EJS, OCS]
*American basketball coach and
executive*
* Auerbach, Red

**Auerbach, Red**
*See* Auerbach, Arnold

**Auerbach, Stevanne** 1938-    [CA]
*American educator and author*
* Fink, Stevanne Auerbach

**Auersperg, Anton Alexander von**
1806-1876    [DNNF, FFF, RH]
*German poet*
* Gruen, Anastasius

**Auger, Edmond**    [SN]
*French theologian*
* [The] French Chrysostom

**Auger, Ginette Marguerite** 1930-
[BEW, IPA]
*French entertainer*
* Genevieve

**Augur**
*See* Feist, Henry Mort

**Augur?**
*See* Francis, [Sir] Philip

**August, Edwin**
*See* Von Der Butz, Philip

**August, Garry J.** 1894-    [IA]
*American clergyman and columnist*
* Garrett, Myron H.

**August, Jan**
*See* Augustoff, Jan

**August, John**
*See* De Voto, Bernard [Augustine]

**August, Leo**
*See* Segall, Don

**Augusta, Clara**
*See* Trask, Kate

**Augusta, Clara**
*See* Winthorpe, Winifred

**Augustabernard**
*See* Bernard, Augusta

**Auguste, Arsene** 20th c.
*Haitian-born soccer player*
* Pelau

**Augustina** 19th c.    [FFF, RH, SN]
*Spanish heroine*
* [The] Maid of Saragossa [or
Saragoza]

**Augustine [or Austin]** ?- 604
[DNNS, HN, SN]
*First Archbishop of Canterbury and
Saint*
* [The] Apostle of the
Anglo-Saxons
* [The] Apostle of the English
* [The] Bishop of the English

**Augustine** 354- 430
[DNNS, GLET, HN]
*Saint*
* [The] Bishop of Hippo
* [The] Cicero of Latin Christianity
* [The] Doctor of Grace
* [The] Hammer of Heresies [or
Heretics]

**Augustine, Augie**
*See* Augustine, Gerald Lee

**Augustine, Erich**
*See* Stoil, Michael Jon

**Augustine, Gerald Lee** 1952-
[SMG]
*American baseball player*
* Augustine, Augie

**[The] Augustine of his Age**
*See* Fulgentius, Fabius Claudius
Gordianus

**[The] Augustine of Philosophy**
*See* Annius Verus, Marcus

**Augustine, Richard** ?-1568    [PA]
*Author*
* Sexten

**Augustine, Van**
*See* Abbott, John G.

**Augustoff, Jan** 1912?-1976    [PMJ]
*American musician*
* August, Jan

**Augustsohn, W.**
*See* Kotzebue, Wilhelm

**Augustson, Ernest**
*See* Ryden, Ernest Edwin

**Augustus**
*See* Lynn, Elwyn Augustus

**Augustus**
*See* Octavius, Gaius

**Augustus**
*See* Philip II [or Philippe]

**Augustus**
*See* Sigismund II

**Augustus**
*See* Stoddard, Charles Augustus

**Augustus, Albert, Jr.**
*See* Nuetzel, Charles [Alexander]

**[The] Augustus of Arabian Literature**
*See* Mamoun, al-

**Augustus II** 1670-1733
[DNNS, WBD]
*King of Poland*
* [The] Strong

**[The] Auk**
*See* Auchinleck, [Sir] Claude

**Auker, Eldon LeRoy** 1910-    [BE]
*American baseball player*
* Big Six

**Auld, George**
*See* Altwerger, John

**Auld, J. L.**
*See* Auld, John Leslie M.

**Auld, John Leslie M.** 1914-    [ART]
*Irish-born artist*
* Auld, J. L.

**Auld, Philip**
*See* Burns, Bernard

**Aulds, Leycester Doyle** 1920-    [BE]
*American baseball player*
* Aulds, Tex

**Aulds, Tex**
*See* Aulds, Leycester Doyle

**Auletes [Flute Player]**
*See* Ptolemy XII [or X]

**Aulicus**
*See* Thynne [or Boteville?],
William

**Ault, Marie**
*See* Cragg, Mary

**Aumbry, Alan**
*See* Bayley, Barrington J[ohn]

**Aumont, Jean-Pierre**
*See* Salomons, Jean-Pierre

**Aung, [Maung] Htin** 1909-    [CA]
*Burmese educator and author*
* [The] Fourth Brother

**Aungerville [or Aungervyle], Richard**
1287-1345    [WBD]
*British scholar and book collector*
* Bury, Richard de

**Aunt Abby**
*See* Skinner, Abby

**Aunt Adna**
*See* Dana, Mrs. J. M.

**Aunt Bee**
*See* Middleton, Julia

**Aunt Carrie**
*See* Smith, Caroline L.

**Aunt Carry**
*See* Norton, Caroline Elizabeth
Sarah

**Aunt Charity**
*See* Yeiser, Sarah C. [Smith]

**Aunt Effie**
*See* Harkshaw, Mrs.

**Aunt Este**
*See* Deihl, Edna Groff

**Aunt Esther**
*See* Smith, Mrs. John A.

**Aunt Fanny**
*See* Barrow, Fanny

**Aunt Fanny**
*See* Gage, Frances Dana Barker

**Aunt Florida**
*See* Travers, Phebe

**Aunt Hattie**
*See* Baker, Harriette Newell

**Aunt Jemima**
*See* Gardella, Tess

**Aunt Jemima**
*See* Wilson, Edith

**Aunt Judy**
*See* Gatty, Mrs. Alfred

**Aunt Julia**
*See* Colman, Julia

**Aunt Kitty**
*See* McIntosh, Maria Jane

**Aunt Kitty**
*See* Windsor, Mary Catherine

**Aunt Louisa**
*See* Valentine, Mrs.

**Aunt Lucy**
*See* Bather, Mrs. L. E. B.

**Aunt Maggie**
*See* Blaythwait, Mrs. Raymond

**Aunt Maggie**
*See* Henshaw, Mrs.

**Aunt Margaret**
*See* Buchan, Margaret

**Aunt Marian**
*See* Hill, Agnes Isabel Aston

**Aunt Mary**
See   Hodgson, M. A.

**Aunt Mary**
See   Hughes, Mary

**Aunt Mary**
See   Lathbury, Mary Artemisia

**Aunt Maysie**
See   Jeffrey-Smith, May Thornton

**Aunt Mollie Jackson**
See   Garland, Mary Magdalene

**Aunt Patty**
See   Hentz, Caroline Lee

**Aunt Peggy**
See   Britton, Mary E.

**Aunt Prudence**
See   Muzzy, L. R.

**Aunt Sap**
See   Brasfield, Neva Inez

**Aunt Sophronia**
See   Wright, Julia McNair

**Aunt Yvonne**
See   De Gaulle, Yvonne

**Auntie**
See   Clark, P. L.

**Auntie Io**
See   Luahne, Iolani

**Auntie Lizzie**
See   MacKenzie, Rhoda Elizabeth

**Aura**
See   Gale, William

**Aura**
See   Urziceanu, Aura

**Auracher, Harry** 1888-1960
[ASC, PMJ]
*American composer, conductor,
musician*
* Archer, Harry

**Aurandt, Paul Harvey** 1918-   [CA]
*American author and journalist*
* Harvey, Paul

**Auratus**
See   Daurat, Jean

**Auratus, Petrus**
See   Dore, Pierre

**Aurel**
See   Mortier, Marie Antoinette

**Aureli, Andrea** 20th c.   [WF]
*Italian actor*
* Ray, Andrew

**Aurelian [Claudius Lucius Valerius
Domitius Aurelianus]** 212?- 275
[DNNS, WBD]
*Roman emperor*
* Restitutor Orbis
* [The] Restorer of the Roman
Empire

**Aureolus, Peter** 14th c.
[DEP, HN, RH]
*Archbishop of Aix*
* [The] Eloquent Doctor

**Auriol**
See   Butler, Auriol

**Aurive, Jean Charles**
See   Rieger, August

**Aurness, James** 1923-
[FC, IPA, SW]
*American actor*
* Arness, James

**Aurness, Peter** 1926-   [FC, SW]
*American actor*
* Graves, Peter

**Aurungzebe [Aurangzeb or
Aurungzeb]** 1618-1707
[DEP, RH, WBD]
*Mogul emperor*
* Alamgir [Conqueror of the
World]
* [The] Charlemagne of the East
* [The] Conqueror
* [The] Great

**Ausman, Oz**
See   Ausman, Paul David

**Ausman, Paul David** 1955-   [SMG]
*American baseball player*
* Ausman, Oz

**Austen, Jane** 1775-1817   [SN]
*British author*
* [The] Shakespeare of Prose

**Austerlitz, Adele** 1898-1981
[BEW, CED, EMT]
*American dancer and actress*
* Astaire, Adele

**Austerlitz, Frederick** 1899-
[BDF, FC, WEF]
*American dancer and actor*
* Astaire, Fred

**Austin, Adam**
See   Colan, Eugene

**Austin, Anna R.** 1853-1944   [SC]
*American actress*
* Austin, Johanna

**Austin, Augusta Marie** 1918-   [EJ]
*American singer*
* Austin, Claire

**Austin, Baby Cassius**
See   Austin, Laurie Loche

**Austin, Barbara Leslie**
See   Linton, Barbara Leslie

**Austin, Benjamin** 1752-1820
[DNNF, FFF, PA]
*American author*
* Honestus
* Old South

**Austin, Brett**
See   Floren, Lee

**Austin, Bud**
See   Austin, Harold M.

**Austin, Bunny**
See   Austin, Henry Wilfred

**Austin, Charles**
See   Reynolds, Charles

**Austin, Claire**
See   Austin, Augusta Marie

**Austin, Colonel**
See   Austin, Darrell

**Austin, Darrell** 20th c.   [SMG]
*American football player*
* Austin, Colonel

**Austin, Evelyn Page** 1922-   [BEW]
*American producer*
* Austin, Lyn

**Austin, Frank**
See   Faust, Frederick [Schiller]

**Austin, Gene**
See   Lucas, Eugene

**Austin, Harold M.** 20th c.   [ITA]
*American film executive*
* Austin, Bud

**Austin, Harry**
See   McInerny, Ralph

**Austin, Henry Wilfred** 1906-
[OCS]
*British tennis player*
* Austin, Bunny

**Austin, Henry Willard**   [PA]
*Author*
* [The] Devil's Football

**Austin, Hugh**
See   Evans, Hugh Austin

**Austin, J. L.**
See   Austin, John Langshaw

**Austin, James Philip** 1879-1965
[BE, PB]
*Welsh-born baseball player and
manager*
* Austin, Pepper

**Austin, Jane Goodwin**   [PA]
*Author*
* [A] Nameless Nobleman

**Austin, Jo** 1929-   [IBW]
*American sculptor*
* Fundi, Ibibio

**Austin, Johanna**
See   Austin, Anna R.

**Austin, John** 1898-1968   [SC]
*British-born actor*
* Stafford, Hanley

**Austin, John Langshaw** 1911-1960
[LC]
*British author and philosopher*
* Austin, J. L.

**Austin, Laurie Loche** 20th c.   [RBE]
*Australian boxer*
* Austin, Baby Cassius

**Austin, Lovie**
See   Calhoun, Cora

**Austin, Lyn**
See   Austin, Evelyn Page

**Austin, Mary**
See   Rice, Jane

**Austin, Mary [Hunter]** 1868-1934
[CAA, SFL, WGT]
*American author*
* Stairs, Gordon

**Austin, Mortimer**
See   Rowe, John Gabriel

**Austin, Pepper**
See   Austin, James Philip

**Austin, Ping Pong**
See   Austin, Sylvester

**Austin, Ramie**
See   Davidson, Dora

**Austin, Sil**
See   Austin, Sylvester

**Austin, Stanley E.** 20th c.   [MBF]
*British author*
* Clifford, Martin [house
pseudonym]

**Austin, Stanley E.** (Continued)
* Conquest, Owen [house
pseudonym]
* Richards, Frank [house
pseudonym]

**Austin, Stuart**
See   Wier, Stuart Austin

**Austin, Sylvester** 1929-   [RO1]
*American singer*
* Austin, Ping Pong
* Austin, Sil

**Austin, Tom**
See   Jacobs, Linda C.

**Austral**
See   Howard-Ellis, Charles

**Austral, Florence**
See   Wilson, Florence

**[The] Australian Entertainer**
See   Waxman, Albert

**[The] Australian Marie Lloyd**
See   Flanagan, Florence

**[The] Australian Orpheus**
See   Fitts, Harry

**[The] Australian Patriot**
See   Wentworth, William Charles

**Australia's Angela Davis**
See   Sykes, Bobbi

**Australie**
See   Herron, Mrs. Henry

**[The] Austrian**
See   [Josephe Jeanne] Marie
Antoinette

**[The] Austrian Hyena**
See   Haynau, Julius Jakob von

**[The] Austrian Oak**
See   Schwarzeneggar, Arnold

**Austwick, John**
See   Lee, Austin

**[The] Authentic Doctor**
See   Gregory of Rimini

**Authenticus, Doctor**
See   Gregory of Rimini

**[The] Autocrat**
See   Holmes, Oliver Wendell

**[The] Autocrat of Austria**
See   Metternich, Clemens Wenzel
Lothar

**[The] Autocrat of the Breakfast Table**
See   Holmes, Oliver Wendell

**Autograph**
See   Coburn, Charles F.

**Automatic Jack Manders**
See   Manders, John

**Automatic Otto Graham**
See   Graham, Otto

**[L']Autre**
See   Bonaparte, Napoleon

**Autrichienne**
See   [Josephe Jeanne] Marie
Antoinette

**Autry, Chick**
See   Autry, Martin Gordon

**Autry, Chick**
See   Autry, William Askew

**Autry, [Orvon] Gene** 1907-
[CWG, DAM, ECM]
*American singer and actor*
* America's Favorite Cowboy
* Oklahoma's Singing Cowboy

**Autry, Martin Gordon** 1903-1950
[BE]
*American baseball player*
* Autry, Chick

**Autry, Mel** 20th c.   [GW]
*American rodeo performer*
* Autry, Philly

**Autry, Philly**
*See* Autry, Mel

**Autry, William Askew** 1885-   [BE]
*American baseball player*
* Autry, Chick

**Auty, Phyllis** 1910-   [CA]
*British author*
* Richards, Phyllis

**Avai, Caesar**
*See* Caesar, Kurt

**Avalle-Arce, Juan Bautista** 1927-
[CA]
*Argentinian-born educator and author*
* Galvez De Montalvo, Luis
* Goyeneche, Gabriel

**Avallone, Francis Thomas** 1939?-
[FC, ITA, SW]
*American entertainer*
* Avalon, Frankie

**Avallone, Michael [Angelo], Jr.**
1924-   [CA, ESF, WW]
*American author*
* Alden, Michele
* Blaine, James
* Carter, Nick [house pseudonym]
* Conway, Troy [house pseudonym,
   Paperback Library]
* Dalton, Priscilla
* Dane, Mark
* De Pre, Jean-Anne
* Frazer, Fred
* Highland, Dora
* Jason, Stuart
* Michaels, Steve
* Morgan, Memo
* Nile, Dorothea
* Noon, Ed
* Noone, Edwina
* Patrick, John
* St. George, Philip
* Sidney, Stuart?
* Stanton, Vance
* Stuart, Sidney

**Avalon**
*See* Blaser, Robin

**Avalon, Frankie**
*See* Avallone, Francis Thomas

**Avant, Sleepy**
*See* Avant, Vernon

**Avant, Vernon**   [B10]
*American cowboy*
* Avant, Sleepy

**Avaricious Tyrant**
*See* Mauricius [or Mauritius],
Flavius Tiberius

**Ave**
*See* Poggel, Mary

**Aveling, Mrs. Henry**   [FFF]
*Entertainer*
* Willet, Mittens

**Avellaneda, Luis**
*See* Bolio Cantarell De Peon,
Dolores

**Avellaneda y Arteaga, Gertrudis
Gomez de** 1814-1873   [WBD]
*Spanish author*
* [La] Peregrina

**Avellano, Alberto**
*See* Nussbaum, Al[bert F.]

**Avempace [or Avenpace]**   ?-1138
[WBD]
*Spanish-Arabian philosopher,
scientist, poet*
* Ibn-al-Saigh
* Ibn-Bajjah

**Avena, Rolf**
*See* Kunze, Rolf

**[The] Avenger**
*See* Alfonso XI [or Alphonso]

**Aventinus, Johannes**
*See* Turmair [or Thurmayr],
Johannes

**Avenzoar [or Abumeron]**
1091?-1162   [WBD]
*Arab physician*
* Ibn-Zuhr [or Ibn-Zohr]

**Averill, [Howard] Earl** 1902-
[BAB, DGS, PB]
*American baseball player*
* [The] Earl of Snohomish
* [The] Rock

**Averill, Esther [Holden]** 1902-
[TCC]
*American author and illustrator*
* Domino, John

**Averill, H. C.**
*See* Snow, Charles Horace

**Averitt, Bird**
*See* Averitt, William

**Averitt, William** 1952-
[NBA, SMG]
*American basketball player*
* Averitt, Bird

**Averroes [or Averrhoes]**
1126?-1198?   [HN, SN, WBD]
*Moorish philosopher and physician*
* [The] Commentator
* [The] Expositor
* Ibn-Rushd

**Avery, A. A.**
*See* Montgomery, Rutherford
George

**Avery, Al**
*See* Montgomery, Rutherford
George

**Avery, Frederick Bean** 1907-
[FC, WEC]
*American animator*
* Avery, Tex

**Avery, Harold** 1903-   [AW]
*British physician and author*
* Westridge, Harold

**Avery, Ira** 1914-   [CA]
*American author*
* Hathaway, Mavis

**Avery, Jane G.**   [PA]
*Author*
* Greenough, A. J.

**Avery, Joseph** 1892-1955   [NOJ]
*American jazz musician*
* Avery, Kid

**Avery, June**
*See* Rees, Joan

**Avery, Kid**
*See* Avery, Joseph

**Avery, Lynn**
*See* Cole, Lois Dwight

**Avery, Richard**
*See* Cooper, Edmund

**Avery, Samuel P.**   [PA]
*Author*
* Partington, Mrs.

**Avery, Tex**
*See* Avery, Frederick Bean

**Avey, Ruby** 1927-   [CA]
*British author and broadcaster*
* Page, Vicki

**Avi**
*See* Wortis, Avi

**Avice, Claude** 1925-   [CA]
*French author and pharmacist*
* Barbet, Pierre
* Maine, David
* Sprigel, Olivier

**Avicenna [or Abou-ibn-Sina]**
980-1037   [DEP, DNNS, RH]
*Arabian physician and philosopher*
* [The] Aristotle of the Arabs
* [The] Father of Geology
* [The] Hippocrates of the Arabs
* [The] Philosopher of Persia
* [The] Prince of Physicians

**Avicus**
*See* Fulljames, Henry J.

**Avid, Alan**
*See* Stevens, Lee

**Avidom, Menahem**
*See* Mahler-Kalkstein, Menahem

**Avidor, Ben Moise** ?-1591   [PA]
*Author*
* Itzmunsh

**Avila, Beto**
*See* Avila, Roberto Gonzalez

**Avila, Juan de** 1500-1569
[DEP, DNNS, SN]
*Spanish clergyman*
* [The] Apostle of Andalusia

**Avila, Roberto Gonzalez** 1924-
[BE]
*Mexican-born baseball player*
* Avila, Beto

**Avitus Bassianus, Varius** 204- 222
[WBD]
*Roman emperor*
* Antoninus, Marcus Aurelius
* Heliogabalus [or Elagabalus]

**Avni, Abraham Albert**
*See* Steiner, Abraham Albert

**[L']Avocat**
*See* Arnauld, Antoine Vincent

**[L']Avocat des Pauvres**
*See* Yves of Brittany

**Avon, Margaret**
*See* Keatley, Sheila Marjorie

**Avon, Violet**
*See* LaPlante, Violet Virginia

**Avrelin, M.**
*See* Steinberg, Aaron Zacharovich

**Away, Caesar**
*See* Caesar, Kurt

**Awdry, Richard Charles** 1929-
[WD]
*British author*
* Charles, Richard

**Awoonor, Kofi** 1935-   [B10]
*Ghanaian author*
* Awoonor-Williams, George

**Awoonor-Williams, George**
*See* Awoonor, Kofi

**Awrey, Donald William** 1943-
[FHE]
*Canadian-born hockey player*
* Awrey, Elbows

**Awrey, Elbows**
*See* Awrey, Donald William

**[The] Ax**
*See* Martin, Lynn

**Axis Sally**
*See* Gillars, Mildred Elizabeth

**Axton, David**
*See* Koontz, Dean R[ay]

**Ay-O**
*See* Iijima, Takao

**Aya**
*See* Broughton, Aya

**Ayal, Igal**
*See* Altstock, Igal

**Ayala, Benigno Felix** 1951-   [SMG]
*Puerto Rican-born baseball player*
* Ayala, Benny

**Ayala, Benny**
*See* Ayala, Benigno Felix

**Ayala, Reginald** 1932-   [IBW]
*American basketball player*
* Ayala, Rick

**Ayala, Rick**
*See* Ayala, Reginald

**[The] Ayatullah**
*See* Pfeiffer, Jane Cahill

**Aybar o Rodriguez, Manuela**
1790-1850?   [CW]
*Dominican poet and author*
* [La] Deana

**Ayckbourn, Alan** 1939-   [DLE]
*British playwright*
* Allen, Ronald

**Aycock, Roger Dee** 1914-
[ESF, SFL, WGT]
*American author*
* Dee, Roger
* Starr, John

**Aydy, Catherine**
*See* Tennant, Emma

**Aye, John**
*See* Atkinson, John

**Ayer, Alberta Constance [Chapman]**
20th c.   [B10]
*American author and columnist*
* Wells, Dee

**Ayer, Lewis** 1908-
[BDF, FC, WEF]
*American actor*
* Ayres, Lew

**Ayers, Alfred**
*See*   Osman, T. Embly

**Ayers, Doc**
*See*   Ayers, Yancy Wyatt

**Ayers, William [Bill]** 20th c.
*American political organizer*
* Lee, Anthony

**Ayers, Yancy Wyatt** 1890-1968
[AS, BE]
*American baseball player*
* Ayers, Doc

**Ayes, Anthony**
*See*   Sambrot, William [Anthony]

**Ayes, William**
*See*   Sambrot, William [Anthony]

**Ayesha [or Ayeshah]** 611- 678
[DEP, DNNS, RH]
*Wife of the prophet, Mohammed*
* [The] Mother of Believers
* [The] Prophetess

**Aylen, Elise**
*See*   Scott, Elise Aylen

**Aylesworth, Allison**
*See*   Martin, Lawrence

**Aylesworth, Deac**
*See*   Aylesworth, Merlin Hall

**Aylesworth, Merlin Hall**  ?-1952
[ET]
*American television executive*
* Aylesworth, Deac

**Ayling, Joan** 1907-   [ART]
*Scottish-born painter*
* J. A.

**Aylmer, Felix**
*See*   Aylmer-Jones, Felix Edward

**Aylmer-Jones, Felix Edward**
1889-1964   [CAP, FC, THR]
*British actor and author*
* Aylmer, Felix

**Aymar, Patterson**
*See*   Knight, Charles

**Aynes, Edith A[nnette]** 1909-   [CA]
*American nurse and author*
* Aynes, Pat Edith

**Aynes, Pat Edith**
*See*   Aynes, Edith A[nnette]

**Aynesworth, Allen**
*See*   Abbott-Anderson, E.

**Aynsworth, Cecil**
*See*   Childs, Edmund Burton

**Ayraud, Pierre** 1908-   [B10]
*French author and playwright*
* Narcejac, Thomas

**Ayre, Thorton**
*See*   Fearn, John Russell

**Ayres, Agnes**
*See*   Hinkle, Agnes

**Ayres, Alfred**
*See*   Osmun, Thomas Embly

**Ayres, Alison**
*See*   Carter, Robert A[yres]

**Ayres, Frederic**
*See*   Johnson, Frederick Ayres

**Ayres, Lew**
*See*   Ayer, Lewis

**Ayres, Mitch[ell]**
*See*   Agress, Mitchell

**Ayres, Paul**
*See*   Aarons, Edward S[idney]

**[The] Ayrshire Bard**
*See*   Burns, Robert

**[The] Ayrshire Poet**
*See*   Burns, Robert

**Ayrton, Michael** 1921-1975   [CA]
*British painter, sculptor, writer*
* Gould, Michael

**Ayrton, William Edward**
1847-1908   [WWL]
*British engineer and writer*
* [A] Friend of the Family

**Ayscough, John**
*See*   Bickerstaffe-Drew, Francis
Browning Drew

**Aytoun, William Edmonstoune**
1813-1865   [DEL, WWL]
*Scottish author and poet*
* Dunshunner, Augustus
* Gaultier, Bon [joint pseudonym
   with (Sir) Theodore Martin]
* Jones, T. Percy

**Ayvazian, L. Fred** 1919-   [CA]
*Turkish-born American author and
physician*
* Flagg, Kenneth
* Levon, Fred

**Azamat Batuk**
*See*   Thieblin, Napoleon [or
Nicolas?] Leon

**Azarch, Abraham** 1890-1937
[BEW]
*Russian actor, producer, director*
* Granovsky, Alexander

**Azcue, Jose Joaquin** 1939-   [BE]
*Cuban-born baseball player*
* [The] Immortal Azcue

**Azelee**
*See*   Yeiser, Sarah C. [Smith]

**Azikiwe, Nnamdi** 1909-   [IBW]
*Nigerian president*
* Azikiwe, Zik
* [The] Father of Modern Nigerian
   Nationalism

**Azikiwe, Zik**
*See*   Azikiwe, Nnamdi

**Aznavour, Charles**
*See*   Aznavurian, Charles

**Aznavurian, Charles** 1924-
[BBD, FC, WEF]
*French singer and actor*
* Aznavour, Charles

**Azorin**
*See*   Martinez Ruiz, Jose

**Azpeleneta, Martimius ab**
1493-1586   [PA]
*Author*
* Navarrus

**Azteca, Kid**
*See*   Villanueva Parma, Luis

**Azucena, Adolfo de la**
*See*   Zenea, Juan Clemente

**Azuela, Mariano** 1873-1952   [TLC]
*Mexican author*
* Beleno

**Azzara, Pat** 1944-   [EJ7]
*American jazz musician*
* Martino, Pat

# B

**B.**
See Banbury, Henry Charles

**B.**
See Canning, George

**B.**
See Chichester, F. R.

**B. A.**
See Allsopp, Bruce

**B. A. M.**
See Mullany, Azarius

**B. B.**
See Long, John

**B. B.**
See Valvrojenski, Bernard

**B B**
See Watkins-Pitchford, Denys James

**B. B. Jr.**
See Odom, Andrew

**B. B., Mr.**
See Brandon, Brumsic, Jr.

**B. D.**
See Dunstan, Bernard

**B. G.**
See Gay, Bernard

**B. G. A.**
See Crooks, Barbara Gwendolen Anne

**B. J.**
See Johnston, Brenda

**B. L.**
See Levene, Ben

**B. L. T.**
See Taylor, Bert Leston

**B. M.**
See Mathews, Benjamin Kenny Ollard

**B. M.**
See Miller, B.

**B. P. B.**
See Batchelor, Bernard Philip

**B. R.**
See Randall, Robert Lee

**B. T.**
See Torrey, Amos

**B. T. B.**
See Blackwell, Basil T.

**B. T. N. B.**
See Bennett, Brian Theodore Norton

**B. V.**
See Thomson, James

**B. W.**
See Weller, Bernard Williams

**BA**
See Barrett, Katharine Ruth Ellis

**Baal Shem-Tov [Kind Master of the Holy Name]**
See Ben Eliezer, Israel

**Baastad, Babbis Friis**
See Friis-Baastad, Babbis Ellinor

**[The] Bab [The Gate]**
See Ali Mohammed of Shiraz

**Bab**
See Gilbert, [Sir] William Schwenck

**Babakhan, Anna Misaakovna** 1923- [THR]
*Russian actress*
* Andreeva-Babakhan, Anna Misaakovna

**Babartsky, Albert J.** 1895- [FB]
*American football player*
* Ali Baba

**Babb, Janice B.**
See Bentley, Janice Babb

**Babbis, Eleanor**
See Friis-Baastad, Babbis Ellinor

**Babbitt, Robert**
See Bangs, Robert Babbitt

**Babble Brook**
See McNaughton, John H.

**Babbler**
See Kelley, Hugh

**Babbler**
See Trumble, Alfred

**Babbo, Joan Carmello** 1930- [PMJ]
*American singer*
* James, Joni

**Babcock, Edward Chester** 1913- [BEW, PMJ, TR]
*American composer*
* Van Heusen, James [Jimmy]

**Babcock, Florence**
See Tofte, Arthur

**Babcock, Frederic** 1896- [CA]
*American author and journalist*
* Mark, Matthew

**Babcock, Winnifred Eaton** 1879- ? [WBD]
*American author*
* Onoto Watanna

**[The] Babe**
See Ruth, George Herman

**Babe, Bee Bee**
See Babe, Loren Rolland

**Babe, Loren Rolland** 1928- [BE]
*American baseball player*
* Babe, Bee Bee

**[The] Babe Ruth of Bank Robbers**
See Sutton, William Francis [Willie]

**[The] Babe Ruth of Basketball**
See Beckman, John

**[The] Babe Ruth of Cuba**
See Orta, Pedro

**[The] Babe Ruth of Hockey**
See Morenz, Howarth William

**[The] Babe Ruth of Hockey**
See Richard, [Joseph Henri] Maurice

**[The] Babe Ruth of Hockey**
See Shore, Edward William [Eddie]

**[The] Babe Ruth of Lacrosse**
See Turnbull, John Iglehart

**[The] Babe Ruth of Skiing**
See Tokle, Torger

**Babe Ruth's Legs**
See Byrd, Samuel Dewey [Sammy]

**Babel**
See Nogues i Cases, Xavier

**Babel, Seymour** 1912- [MY]
*American jazz musician*
* Baker, Cy

**Baber [Babur or Babar]**
See Zahir ud-Din Muhammad

**Baber, Monica Mary** 1917- [IAW]
*Welsh-born author*
* Hutchings, Monica
* Scott, Monica

**Babeuf, Francois Noel** 1764?-1797 [FFF, HN, SN]
*French journalist and political agitator*
* Gracchus, Caius
* [The] Tribune of the People

**Babic, Ljubomir** 1854-1935 [WBD]
*Yugoslav author and patriot*
* Djalski, Ksaver Sandor

**Babilee, Jean**
See Gutmann, Jean

**Babinecz, John Michael** 1950- [SMG]
*American football player*
* Babinecz, Nez

**Babinecz, Nez**
See Babinecz, John Michael

**Babinot, Albert** [SN]
*Disciple of French theologian, John Calvin*
* [La] Ministerie

**Babitt, Mack** 20th c.
*American baseball player*
* Babitt, Shooty

**Babitt, Shooty**
See Babitt, Mack

**Babo, Edward** 1910?-1962
*American football player*
* Babo, Green Pants

**Babo, Green Pants**
See Babo, Edward

**Baboon, Lewis**
See Louis XIV

**Baboon, Philip**
See Philip V

**Babou, Hippolyte** 1824-1878 [FFF]
*French writer*
* Lorrain, Camille
* Sans Peur, Jean

**Babs, Alice**
See Nilson, Alice

**Babson, Joseph E.** [FFF, PA]
*American writer*
* Folio, Tom

**Babson, Mrs. E. M.** [FFF, PA]
*Author*
* Kenneth, Esther Sarah

**Babushka**
See Breshkovsky, Catherine

Baharam 220?- 296
[FFF, RH, SN]
*King of Persia*
* [The] Just King [Shah Endeb]

Bahaullah [Splendor of God]
*See* Husayn Ali

Bahl, Franklin
*See* Graham, Roger Phillips

Bahlke, Valerie Worth 1933- [CA]
*American poet*
* Worth, Valerie

Bahram V 5th c. [WBD]
*King of Persia*
* Gor [Wild Ass]

Baier, Eric
*See* Glaser, Karl Georg Hermann

Baikoro
*See* Sillah, Mododou Baikoro

Bailey
*See* Douglas, Fred

Bailey, Abraham Lincoln 1895-1939
*American baseball player*
* Bailey, Sweetbreads

Bailey, Ace
*See* Bailey, Garnet Edward

Bailey, Ace
*See* Bailey, Irvine Wallace

Bailey, Albert 20th c. [RO2]
*Singer*
* Hope

Bailey, Alfred Goldsworthy 1905-
[CA]
*Canadian author*
* Clayton, Susan

Bailey, Arthur Buckner 20th c.
[BBH]
*American baseball coach*
* Bailey, Buck

Bailey, Beetles
*See* Bailey, Robert Sherwood

Bailey, Benny
*See* Bailey, Ernest Harold

Bailey, Betty
*See* Hickey, Madelyn Eastlund

Bailey, Bill
*See* Bailey, Harry Lewis

Bailey, Bill
*See* Bailey, Percy

Bailey, Bill
*See* Stanley, Milton O.

Bailey, Buck
*See* Bailey, Arthur Buckner

Bailey, Buck
*See* Bailey, Paul

Bailey, Buddy
*See* Bailey, John

Bailey, Buster
*See* Bailey, William C.

Bailey, By
*See* Bailey, Byron L.

Bailey, Byron L. 20th c. [CFH]
*American-born football player*
* Bailey, By

Bailey, D[avid] R[oy] Shackleton
1917- [CA, WD]
*British author and editor*
* Shackleton-Bailey, D[avid] R[oy]
]

Bailey, Donald Orlando 1934-
[DAM]
*American jazz musician*
* Duck, Donald

Bailey, Dude
*See* Bailey, James A.

Bailey, Dulcie 1919- [FC]
*British actress*
* Gray, Dulcie

Bailey, Ernest Harold 1925-
[DAM, EJ]
*American jazz musician*
* Bailey, Benny

Bailey, Eugene Marcus 1901-1956
[SC]
*American actor*
* La Rue, Jean

Bailey, Evangeline Geraldine 1949-
[IBW]
*American singer*
* Bailey, Vangie

Bailey, Frankie
*See* Walters, Frankie

Bailey, Fred Middleton 1895- [BE]
*American baseball player*
* Bailey, Penny

Bailey, Frederick Augustus
Washington 1817?-1895 [WBD]
*American lecturer and author*
* Douglass, Frederick

Bailey, Garnet Edward 1948-
[CEI, HK, SMG]
*Canadian-born hockey player*
* Bailey, Ace

Bailey, George W. [FFF]
*Magician*
* Tan Ku

Bailey, Gordon 1936- [AW]
*British writer*
* Gordon, Keith

Bailey, H. C.
*See* Bailey, Henry Christopher

Bailey, Hannah
*See* Sargent, Mrs. H. J.

Bailey, Harry Lewis 1881-1967
[BE]
*American baseball player*
* Bailey, Bill

Bailey, Harvey 1889- [BLB]
*American bank robber*
* Bailey, Old Harve

Bailey, Henry Christopher
1878-1961 [LC]
*British author*
* Bailey, H. C.

Bailey, Herman 1931- [IBW]
*American artist*
* Bailey, Kofi

Bailey, Hilea
*See* Marting, Ruth Lenore

Bailey, Irvine Wallace 1903-
[CEI, FHE, HK]
*Canadian-born hockey player*
* Bailey, Ace

Bailey, Isaac H. [PA]
*Author*
* Yarmouth

Bailey, J. O.
*See* Bailey, James Osler

Bailey, James A. 1927- [IBW]
*American football player, track and
field athlete, physician*
* Bailey, Dude

Bailey, James Montgomery
1841-1894 [DEL, DNNF, WBD]
*American journalist*
* [The] Danbury Newsman

Bailey, James Osler 1903- [SFL]
*American author*
* Bailey, J. O.

Bailey, John 20th c. [RO1]
*American singer*
* Bailey, Buddy

Bailey, Josephine
*See* Eytinge, Mrs. Walter

Bailey, King
*See* Bailey, Lemuel

Bailey, Kofi
*See* Bailey, Herman

Bailey, Lemuel 19th c. [BE]
*American baseball player*
* Bailey, King

Bailey, Matilda
*See* Radford, Ruby L[orraine]

Bailey, Matilda A. [FFF]
*American writer*
* Forlorn Hope

Bailey, Mildred
*See* Rinker, Mildred

Bailey, Mrs. V. L. [PA]
*Author*
* Locke, Una

Bailey, Nathan ?-1742 [SN]
*British lexicographer*
* Philologos [A Lover of Words]

Bailey, Old Harve
*See* Bailey, Harvey

Bailey, Paul 20th c.
*American baseball player*
* Bailey, Buck

Bailey, Penny
*See* Bailey, Fred Middleton

Bailey, Percy 20th c. [OBW]
*American baseball player*
* Bailey, Bill

Bailey, Philip James 1816-1902
[DEL, FFF, SN]
*British poet*
* [The] Nottingham Poet

Bailey, Prentiss 1873- ? [NAA]
*American publisher and author*
* Rexford, John

Bailey, Robert Sherwood 1942-
[PB]
*American baseball player*
* Bailey, Beetles

Bailey, Robin
*See* Bailey, William Henry
Mettam

Bailey, Ruth
*See* Robison, Ruth

Bailey, Sweetbreads
*See* Bailey, Abraham Lincoln

Bailey, Thomas
*See* Partridge, Edward Bellamy

Bailey, Vangie
*See* Bailey, Evangeline Geraldine

Bailey, William C. 1902-1967
[DAM, PMJ, WWJ]
*American jazz musician*
* Bailey, Buster

Bailey, William Henry Mettam
1919- [BEW]
*British actor*
* Bailey, Robin

Bailhe, Edilou 1922- [BEW]
*American actress*
* Claire, Ludi

Baillen, Claude
*See* Delay-Baillen, Claude

Baillie, Joanna 1762-1851
[DNNS, HN]
*Scottish playwright and poet*
* Bountiful, Lady
* [The] Sister of Shakespeare

Baillie, Robert ?-1684 [FFF, SN]
*Scottish politician and conspirator*
* [The] Scottish Sidney

Bain, Dan
*See* Bain, Donald H.

Bain, Donald H. 1874-1962
[FHE, HK]
*Canadian-born hockey player*
* Bain, Dan

Bain, Frank 20th c. [BBH, CSH]
*Canadian lacrosse player*
* Bain, Piper

Bain, Kenneth Bruce Findlater
1921- [CA]
*British author*
* Findlater, Richard

Bain, Piper
*See* Bain, Frank

Bain, Ted
*See* Tubb, Edwin Charles

Bainbridge, Bains
*See* Bainbridge, Philip

Bainbridge, Harriette Smith 19th
c. [FFF]
*American poet and writer*
* Laker, Cecil

Bainbridge, Philip 1958- [DC]
*British cricketer*
* Bainbridge, Bains

Bainbridge, Rod 1944- [RO2]
*British musician*
* Allen, Rod

Bair, Patrick 20th c. [SFL]
*Author*
* Gurney, David

Bairaktar [Standard Bearer]
*See* Mustapha

Baird, Butch
*See* Baird, Fred

Baird, Dorothy
*See* Vernon, Dorothy

**Baird, Fred** 1936-    [GF]
*American golfer*
* Baird, Butch

**Baird, George D.**    [FFF]
*American editor*
* Mercury

**Baird, Henry** 20th c.    [PA, WWL]
*British editor*
* Hogg, Nathan

**Baird, Madame**    [PA]
*Author*
* D'Aunet, Leonie

**Baird, Robert** 1798-1863    [FFF]
*American clergyman and writer*
* Americanus

**Baird, Roland** 20th c.    [CA, WD]
*Author*
* Brennan, Christopher [joint
  pseudonym with Christopher
  Kininmonth]

**Baird, Thomas H.** 19th c.    [FFF]
*American writer*
* Alethes

**Bairstow, Bluey**
*See* Bairstow, David Leslie

**Bairstow, David Leslie** 1951-    [DC]
*British cricketer*
* Bairstow, Bluey

**Bajazet I [Bayazid or Bajasid]**
1347-1403    [DNNS, HN, WBD]
*Sultan of the Turks*
* Ilderim [or Yilderim] [Lightning]
* [The] Thunderbolt

**Bak, Albert** 1844-1912    [BBD]
*Hungarian singer*
* Bach, Albert

**Bakely, Edward Enoch** 1864-1915
[BE]
*American baseball player*
* Bakely, Jersey

**Bakely, Jersey**
*See* Bakely, Edward Enoch

**[The] Baker**
*See* Liberito, Joe

**[The] Baker**
*See* Louis XVI

**Baker, Adelaide Nichols** 1894-
[NAA]
*American author*
* Nichols, Adelaide

**Baker, Al** 20th c.    [IBW]
*American football player*
* Baker, Bubba

**Baker, Alfred Zantzinger**
1870-1933    [WEC]
*American cartoonist*
* Baker Baker

**Baker, Allison**
*See* Crumbaker, Alice

**Baker, Anna Willis**
*See* Auer, Anna

**Baker, Asa**
*See* Dresser, Davis

**Baker, Augustus** 20th c.    [MBF]
*British author and editor*
* Baron, Anthony
* Baron, John

**Baker Baker**
*See* Baker, Alfred Zantzinger

**Baker, Belle**
*See* Becker, Belle

**Baker, Betty**
*See* Venturo, Betty Lou Baker

**Baker, Betty D[oreen Flook]** 1916-
[CA]
*British author*
* Renier, Elizabeth

**Baker, Bob**
*See* Weed, Leland T.

**Baker, Bock**
*See* Baker, Charles

**Baker, Bones**
*See* Baker, Norm[an Leslie]

**Baker, Bonnie**
*See* Nelson, Evelyn

**Baker Boy Mandot**
*See* Mandot, Joe

**Baker, Bubba**
*See* Baker, Al

**Baker, Buck**
*See* Baker, Elzie Wylie, Sr.

**Baker, Buck**
*See* Baker, Jack Edward

**Baker, Buck**
*See* Baker, Sam A., Jr.

**Baker, Buddy**
*See* Baker, Elzie Wylie, Jr.

**Baker, C[harles] William [Bill]**
*See* Baecker, Wilhelm C.

**Baker, Cannon Ball**
*See* Baker, Erwin George

**Baker, Cannonball**
*See* Baker, John

**Baker, Charles** 1878- ?    [BN]
*American baseball player*
* Baker, Bock
* Baker, Smiling Bock

**Baker, Charles William** 1923-
[BEW]
*American director and producer*
* Baker, Word

**Baker, Charlotte**
*See* Montgomery, Charlotte Baker

**Baker, Chesney H.** 1929-
[DAM, EJ]
*American jazz musician*
* Baker, Chet

**Baker, Chet**
*See* Baker, Chesney H.

**Baker, Cy**
*See* Babel, Seymour

**Baker, Dusty**
*See* Baker, Johnnie B., Jr.

**Baker, Eddie**
*See* King, Edward

**Baker, Elizabeth W.** 20th c.    [NAA]
*American educator and author*
* Dutton, Margaret Payne

**Baker, Elsie** 1929-    [CA]
*American writer*
* Woodson, Meg

**Baker, Elzie Wylie, Jr.** 20th c.
[EAR]
*American auto racer*
* Baker, Buddy

**Baker, Elzie Wylie, Sr.** 1919-
[EAR]
*American auto racer*
* Baker, Buck

**Baker, Ernest A.** 1869- ?    [WWL]
*British author and librarian*
* E. A. B.

**Baker, Erwin George** 1882-1960
[EAR]
*American auto racer*
* Baker, Cannon Ball

**Baker, Evelyn Greenleaf**
1855-1908    [BEW, WWL]
*American-born playwright*
* Rutherford, John
* Sutherland, Evelyn Greenleaf

**Baker, Fannie**
*See* Thomas, Lillian

**Baker, Fanny**
*See* Hegamin, Lucille

**Baker, Fay** 1894-1954    [SC]
*American actress*
* Kirk, Fay B.

**Baker, [John] Frank[lin]** 1886-1963
[AS, BE, PB]
*American baseball player*
* Baker, Home Run

**Baker, Frank Leslie**    [FFF]
*American writer*
* Grip Fast

**Baker, G. P.**
*See* Baker, George Pierce

**Baker, George**
*See* Bouwens, Johannes

**Baker, George** 1874?-1965
[CBS, NAD]
*American clergyman*
* Divine, [Father]

**Baker, George** 20th c.    [SFL]
*Author*
* Olemy, P. T.

**Baker, George** 20th c.    [PHM]
*American underworld figure*
* Baker, Red

**Baker, George Cornelius** 1881- ?
[NAA]
*American author*
* Kerba, Buck

**Baker, George Pierce** 1866-1935
[LC]
*American educator and author*
* Baker, G. P.

**Baker, Ginger**
*See* Baker, Peter

**Baker, Guitar**
*See* Baker, McHouston

**Baker, Harold** 1914-1966
[DAM, PMJ, WWJ]
*American jazz musician*
* Baker, Shorty

**Baker, Harriette Newell** 19th c.
[FFF]
*American author*
* Aunt Hattie

**Baker, Hobart Amery Hare**
1892-1918    [FHE, HK]
*American amateur hockey player*
* Baker, Hobey

**Baker, Hobey**
*See* Baker, Hobart Amery Hare

**Baker, Home Run**
*See* Baker, [John] Frank[lin]

**Baker, Home Run**
*See* Baker, Howard

**Baker, Howard** 20th c.    [OBW]
*American baseball player*
* Baker, Home Run

**Baker, Iris**
*See* Stuart-Baker, Iris

**Baker, Jack**
*See* Jones, Ernest Mahlon

**Baker, Jack Edward** 1950-    [SMG]
*American baseball player*
* Baker, Buck

**Baker, James Britt** 1912?-1972
[CME, CWG, PMJ]
*American country-western performer*
* Britt, Elton

**Baker, Jesse Ormand**
*See* Silverman, Jesse Ormand

**Baker, John** 20th c.    [BBH]
*American softball player*
* Baker, Cannonball

**Baker, John Clifford Yorke** 1905-
[WD]
*British technical writer*
* Circuit Breaker

**Baker, Johnnie B., Jr.** 1949-
[PB, SMG, WWB]
*American baseball player*
* Baker, Dusty

**Baker, Josephine Carson**
1906-1975    [BMH, IBW]
*American-born entertainer*
* Black Venus
* [The] St. Louis born Flame of
  Paris

**Baker, Katie**
*See* Handysides, Mrs. Clarence

**Baker, L. H.**
*See* Levy, Louis Henry

**Baker, Laura Nelson** 1911-    [AW]
*American author*
* Minier, Nelson [joint pseudonym
  with Adrien (Pearl) Stoutenburg]

**Baker, LaVern** 1928-    [PRS, RO1]
*American singer*
* Little Miss Sharecropper

**Baker, Lee, Jr.** 1933-    [BWW]
*American singer*
* Brooks, Lonnie
* Guitar Jr.

**Baker, Lefty**
*See* Britchforth, Eustace

**Baker, Lon**
*See* Wood, Richard Kennedy
[Dick]

**Baker, Loris H.** 1929-    [FB]
*American football player*
* Baker, Sam

**Baker, Lucia Adelaide Victor** 20th
c.　[BEW]
*American production stage manager,
director, playwright*
* Victor, Lucia

**Baker, Mac**
See　Baker, Maclyn

**Baker, Maclyn** 1898-　[EJS]
*American basketball player*
* Baker, Mac

**Baker, Mae Rose** 1878-1933
[BMH, THR]
*American-born dancer*
* My Fancy

**Baker, Marc**
See　Baker, Marceil Genee
[Kolstad]

**Baker, Marceil Genee** [Kolstad]
1911-　[AN, B10, WW]
*American author*
* Baker, Marc
* Miller, Marc
* Miller, Marsha

**Baker, Mary Gladys Steel**
1892-1974　[CAP, SAT]
*Scottish author and journalist*
* Stuart, Sheila

**Baker, McHouston** 1925-
[BWW, EJ, RO1]
*American entertainer*
* Baker, Guitar
* Baker, Mickey
* McHouston, Ed

**Baker, Mickey**
See　Baker, McHouston

**Baker, Miriam Hawthorn**
See　Nye, Miriam [Maurine
Hawthorn] Baker

**Baker, Moon**
See　Baker, Ralph

**Baker, Mrs. H. N. Woods** 1815- ?
[PA]
*Author*
* Leslie, Madeline

**Baker, Norah** 1907-　[F2]
*Actress*
* Baring, Norah

**Baker, Norm[an Leslie]** 1862- ?
[BE]
*American baseball player*
* Baker, Bones

**Baker [or Mortenson?], Norma Jean**
1926-1962　[BDF, FC, WEF]
*American actress*
* M. M.
* Monroe, Marilyn

**Baker, P.** 19th c.　[PA]
*Author*
* Delphine

**Baker Pasha**
See　Baker, Valentine

**Baker, Penriel** 20th c.　[SG]
*Boxer*
* Baker, Sammy

**Baker, Peter** 1940-
[EJ7, PRS, RO2]
*British musician*
* Baker, Ginger

**Baker, Phil** 1899?-　[PE]
*American entertainer*
* [The] Great American Trouper

**Baker, Philip John** 1889-　[WBD]
*British statesman and author*
* Noel-Baker, Philip John

**[The] Baker Poet**
See　Reboul, Jean

**Baker, Rachel Maddux** 1912-
[WGT]
*American author*
* Maddux, Rachel

**Baker, Ralph** 20th c.　[FB]
*American football player*
* Baker, Moon

**Baker, Rattlesnake**
See　Baker, Thomas Calvin [Tom]

**Baker, Ray Stannard** 1870-1946
[LC, NAA, TC]
*American journalist and essayist*
* Grayson, David

**Baker, Red**
See　Baker, George

**Baker, Richard E.** 1916-　[ASC]
*American composer, musician,
singer*
* Baker, Two Ton

**Baker, Sam**
See　Baker, Loris H.

**Baker, Sam A., Jr.**　[SMG]
*American football player*
* Baker, Buck

**Baker, Sammy**
See　Baker, Penriel

**Baker, Sarah S. Tuthill**　[FFF, PA]
*Author*
* Friendly, Aunt

**Baker, Shorty**
See　Baker, Harold

**Baker, Smiling Bock**
See　Baker, Charles

**Baker, Thomas** 1656-1740
[FFF, SN]
*British antiquary*
* [The] Hermit of Literature
* Socius Ejectus

**Baker, Thomas** 19th c.　[PA]
*Author*
* Pikestaff

**Baker, Thomas Calvin [Tom]** 1915-
[BE]
*American baseball player*
* Baker, Rattlesnake

**Baker, Tony** 1945-　[SMG]
*American football player*
* Baker, Touchdown Tony

**Baker, Touchdown Tony**
See　Baker, Tony

**Baker, Two Ton**
See　Baker, Richard E.

**Baker, Valentine** 1827-1887
[WBD]
*British army officer*
* Baker Pasha

**Baker, W[illiam] Howard**
See　McNeilly, Wilfred Glassford

**Baker, Wee Bonnie**
See　Nelson, Evelyn

**Baker, William** 1912-1962　[SC]
*American actor and dancer*
* Daniel, Billy

**Baker, William Arthur Howard**
1925-　[MBF, SFP]
*Irish-born author*
* Arthur, William
* Ballinger, W. A.
* Saxon, Peter [house pseudonym]
* Williams, Richard [house
pseudonym]

**Baker, Word**
See　Baker, Charles William

**[The] Baker's Boy of Anduze**
See　Cavalier, Jean

**[The] Baker's Wife**
See　[Josephe Jeanne] Marie
Antoinette

**Bakken, Bak**
See　Bakken, James L.

**Bakken, James L.** 1940-　[FB]
*American football player*
* Bakken, Bak

**Bakker, Jacob Marinus** 1938-　[OP]
*Dutch opera singer*
* Bakker, Marco

**Bakker, Marco**
See　Bakker, Jacob Marinus

**Bakker-Rabdau, Marianne
K[atherine]** 1935-　[CA]
*American nurse and author*
* Rabdau, Marianne

**Bakst, Leon Nikolaevich**
See　Rosenberg, Leon Nikolaevich

**Bakus, Donald** 20th c.　[RO1]
*American singer*
* Bakus, Gus

**Bakus, Gus**
See　Bakus, Donald

**Balaam**
See　Lamb, Geoffrey Frederick

**[The] Balaam of Modern History**
See　Sigismund

**Balaban, Leonard J.** 1929-　[EJ7]
*American jazz musician*
* Balaban, Red

**Balaban, Red**
See　Balaban, Leonard J.

**[Le] Balafre [The Scarred]**
See　Lorraine, Francois de

**[Le] Balafre [The Scarred]**
See　Lorraine, Henry I [or Henri]
de

**Balanchine, George**
See　Balanchivadze, Gyorgi
Melitonovitch

**Balanchivadze, Gyorgi Melitonovitch**
1904-　[BEW, EMT]
*Russian-born choreographer*
* Balanchine, George
* Mr. B

**Balas, Mike**
See　Balaski, Mitchell Francis

**Balas, Mitchell Francis**
See　Balaski, Mitchell Francis

**Balaski, Mitchell Francis** 1910-
[BE]
*American baseball player*
* Balas, Mike
* Balas, Mitchell Francis

**Balassoni, Louis** 1924-　[EJ, PMJ]
*American jazz musician*
* Bellson, Louis

**Balazs, Bela**
See　Bauer, Herbert

**Balboa, S. F.**
See　Ackerman, Forrest J[ames]

**Balbulus**
See　Notger [or Notker]

**Balbus**
See　Huxley, Julian [Sorell]

**Balchin, Nigel [Marlin]** 1908-1970
[LC]
*British author*
* Spade, Mark

**Balcys, Wilhelm** 20th c.
*German Nazi government official*
* [The] Hangman of the East

**[The] Bald**
See　Charles I

**Bald Billy Barnie**
See　Barnie, William Harrison
[Billy]

**[The] Bald Eagle**
See　Botha, Pieter

**Bald Eagle**
See　Isbell, William Frank

**Bald Eagle**
See　Tittle, Yelberton Abraham

**[The] Bald Eagle of Westchester**
See　Husted, James William

**Bald Head Byrd**
See　Byrd, Henry Roeland

**Bald, Kenneth** 1920-　[WECO]
*American cartoonist*
* Bruce, K.

**Baldanello, Gianfranco** 20th c.
[WF]
*Italian director*
* Carroll, Frank G.

**Baldelli, Ecola** ?-1926
[BLB, PHM]
*American underworld figure*
* Baldelli, Eddie
* [The] Eagle

**Baldelli, Eddie**
See　Baldelli, Ecola

**Baldenne, Fernand**
See　Baldensperger, Fernand

**Baldensperger, Fernand** 1871- ?
[CD]
*French author*
* Baldenne, Fernand

**Balderston, J. L.**
See　Balderston, John Lloyd

**Balderston, John Lloyd** 1889-1954
[LC]
*American journalist, editor,
playwright*
* Balderston, J. L.

**Balderstone, Baldy**
See　Balderstone, John Christopher

**Balderstone, John Christopher**
1940- [DC]
*British cricketer*
* Balderstone, Baldy

**Baldiccini, Cesar** 1921- [CAR]
*French sculptor*
* Cesar

**Baldini, Renato** 20th c. [WF]
*Italian actor*
* Baldwin, Rajan

**Baldrick** [SN]
*Defended his territory against the lawless Algar*
* [The] King of the Teign

**Baldrige, Mac**
See Baldrige, Malcolm

**Baldrige, Malcolm** 1922?-
*American business executive and government official*
* Baldrige, Mac

**Baldry, Enid**
See Citovich, Enid Sarah Kortright

**Baldry, John** 1940?- [PRS]
*British musician*
* Baldry, Long John

**Baldry, Long John**
See Baldry, John

**Baldung, Hans** 1470-1545
[DNNF, WBD]
*German painter, engraver, designer*
* Grien [or Gruen], Hans

**Baldwin, Basil**
See Ritchie, Balfour

**Baldwin, Bates**
See Jennings, John [Edward, Jr.]

**Baldwin, Billy**
See Baldwin, Robert Harvey

**Baldwin, Charles Busted**
1859-1937 [AS, BE]
*American baseball player*
* Baldwin, Lady

**Baldwin, Clarence Geoghan**
1864-1897 [BE]
*American baseball player*
* Baldwin, Kid

**Baldwin de Burgh**
See Baldwin II

**Baldwin, Dorothy Anne Clare**
1934- [AW]
*British author*
* Jones, Clara

**Baldwin, Douglas**
See Morse, Irl

**Baldwin, [Rev.] Edward**
See Godwin, William

**Baldwin, Faith** 1893-1978 [CA]
*American author*
* Lee, Amber

**Baldwin, Florence**
See Robinson, Mrs. George

**Baldwin, George**
See Schick, George Baldwin Powell

**Baldwin, Gordo**
See Baldwin, Gordon C.

**Baldwin, Gordon C.** 1908-
[CA, SAT]
*American author*
* Baldwin, Gordo
* Gordon, Lew

**Baldwin, Harry**
See Baldwin, Howard Edward

**Baldwin, Henry Clay** 1894-1964
[BE]
*American baseball player*
* Baldwin, Ted

**Baldwin, Howard Edward**
1900-1958 [BE]
*American baseball player*
* Baldwin, Harry

**Baldwin, Jeff**
See Panzram, Carl

**Baldwin, John** 1946- [B10]
*British musician*
* Jones, John Paul

**Baldwin, John Loraine** [PA]
*Author*
* Glow-Worm

**Baldwin, Kid**
See Baldwin, Clarence Geoghan

**Baldwin, Lady**
See Baldwin, Charles Busted

**Baldwin, Marcus Elmore**
1865-1929 [BE]
*American baseball player*
* Baldwin, Mark

**Baldwin, Mark**
See Baldwin, Marcus Elmore

**Baldwin, Michael** 1930- [CA]
*British poet*
* Jesse, Michael

**Baldwin, Mrs. Walter S.** [FFF]
*Entertainer*
* Melville, Pearl

**Baldwin, Oliver Ridsdale** 1899-
[SFL, WGT]
*British author*
* Hussingtree, Martin

**Baldwin, Rajan**
See Baldini, Renato

**Baldwin, Robert** 1804-1858 [SN]
*Canadian statesman*
* [The] Nestor of Canadian Politicians

**Baldwin, Robert Harvey** 1951-
[SMG]
*American baseball player*
* Baldwin, Billy

**Baldwin, Ted**
See Baldwin, Henry Clay

**Baldwin I** ?- 879 [DHA, WBD]
*First Count of Flanders*
* Bras de Fer [Iron Arm]

**Baldwin II** ?-1131 [WBD]
*King of Jerusalem*
* Baldwin de Burgh

**Baldwin IV** 988-1035
[FFF, RH, SN]
*Earl of Flanders*
* Handsome Beard

**Baldwin IV** 1160-1183? [DNNS]
*King of Jerusalem*
* [The] Leper

**Baldwin V** ?-1067 [WBD]
*Count of Flanders*
* [Le] Debonnaire

**Bale, Bilious**
See Bale, John

**Bale, John** 1495-1563 [SN]
*British author and Bishop of Ossory*
* Bale, Bilious

**Bales, Granny**
See Bales, R. C.

**Bales, Lee**
See Bales, Wesley Owen

**Bales, R. C.** 20th c. [GW]
*American rodeo performer*
* Bales, Granny

**Bales, Wesley Owen** 1944- [BE]
*American baseball player*
* Bales, Lee

**Balestier, Charles Wolcott**
1861-1891 [FFF]
*American publisher and writer*
* Crepin

**Baletti, Giuseppe** ?-1728 [PA]
*Author*
* Mario

**Balewa, [Sir] Alhaji Abukakar
Tafewa** 1912- [IBW]
*Nigerian prime minister*
* [The] Golden Voice of the North

**Balfe, Louise**
See Harcourt, Mrs. William

**Balfe, Veronica** 20th c. [SC]
*Actress*
* Shaw, Sandra

**Balfort, Neil**
See Fanthorpe, R[obert] Lionel

**Balfour, A. J.**
See Balfour, Arthur James

**Balfour, Arthur James** 1848-1930
[EG, LC]
*British statesman and philosopher*
* Balfour, A. J.
* [The] Father of English Golf

**Balfour, Clara**
See Hemans, Felicia Dorothea

**Balfour, Eva** 20th c. [WW]
*Author*
* Balfour, Hearnden [joint pseudonym with Beryl Hearnden]

**Balfour, Fairfax**
See Phillips, Watts

**Balfour, Frederic H[enry]** 20th c.
[WGT]
*Author*
* Dering, Ross George

**Balfour, Grant**
See Grant, James Miller

**Balfour, Hearnden** [joint pseudonym
with Beryl Hearnden]
See Balfour, Eva

**Balfour, Hearnden** [joint pseudonym
with Eva Balfour]
See Hearnden, Beryl

**Balfour, John**
See Moore, James

**Balfour, Maria** 1934- [ART]
*British painter*
* M. B.

**Balfour, Patrick**
See Kinross, Patrick

**Balfour, William Raymond John
Evelyn** 1923- [AW]
*British writer*
* Russell, Raymond

**Balin, Ina**
See Rosenberg, Ina

**Balin, Marty**
See Buchwald, Martin

**Baline, Israel** 1888-
[FC, ITA, OCF]
*American composer*
* Berlin, Irving
* [The] Last of the Troubadours

**Balint, Emery**
See Balint, Imre

**Balint, Imre** 1892- [SFL]
*Author*
* Balint, Emery

**Baliol [or Balliol], John** 1259-1314
[DHA, HN, RH]
*King of Scotland*
* Toom Tabard [Empty Jacket]

**Ball, Armine** 1899- [NAA]
*American author*
* Von Tempski, Armine

**Ball, B. N.**
See Ball, Brian N[eville]

**Ball, Brian N[eville]** 1932- [CA]
*British author*
* Ball, B. N.
* Kinsey-Jones, Brian

**Ball, Charles Chester Everett** 1913-
[IBW]
*American clergyman*
* Chet, [Father]

**Ball, Cornelius** 1881-1957 [BE]
*American baseball player*
* Ball, Neal

**Ball, Doris Bell [Collier]** 1897-
[AW, CA, CC]
*British physician and author*
* Bell, Josephine

**Ball, Edward** 1792-1873
[FFF, PA, WBD]
*British playwright*
* Fitzball, Edward

**Ball, Frances** 1794-1861 [WBD]
*Founder of English religious order*
* Frances Mary Theresa, [Mother]

**Ball, Frank** 1921- [TR]
*British actor*
* Thornton, Frank

**Ball, George W.** 20th c. [OBW]
*American baseball player*
* [The] Georgia Rabbit

**Ball, Harry**
See Powles, Harry

**[The] Ball Hawk**
See Douthit, Taylor Lee

**Ball, Jane Eklund** 1921- [CA]
*American author*
* Eklund, Jane Mary

**Ball, John** ?-1381 [DNNS, HN]
*British clergyman*
* [The] Mad Priest of Kent

**Ball, John** 1585-1640 [PA]
*Author*
* Lucifer

**Ball, Neal**
*See* Ball, Cornelius

**Ball, Oona Howard** 1867- ?
[WWL]
*Irish author*
* Burke, Barbara

**Ball, Pat**
*See* Ball, Robert

**Ball, Robert** 20th c. [IBW]
*American golfer*
* Ball, Pat

**Ball, Susan** 1933-1955 [SC]
*American actress*
* Ball, Suzan

**Ball, Suzan**
*See* Ball, Susan

**Ball, Sylvia Patricia** 1936- [CA]
*British author*
* England, E Squires
* Squires, Eric
* Squires, Patricia

**Ball, Zachary**
*See* Masters, Kelly R.

**Ballagi, Mor**
*See* Bloch, Moritz

**Ballantine, John**
*See* Da Cruz, Daniel, Jr.

**Ballantyne, Colin, R.N.**
*See* Dunlop, William

**Ballantyne, James** 1772-1833
[HHF, PA, RH]
*Scottish printer*
* Aldiborontiphoscophornio
* Miller, Joe, II

**Ballantyne, John** 1774-1821
[DEL, FFF, SN]
*Scottish publisher*
* [The] Dey of Algiers
* Fidus Achates
* Jocund Johnny
* Our Scottish Bodoni
* Picaroon
* Rigdum Funnidos

**Ballard, Anna** [PA]
*Author*
* Annibale

**Ballard, Butch**
*See* Ballard, George

**Ballard, Cyrus**
*See* Miller, Carl Grover

**Ballard, Dean**
*See* Wilkes-Hunter, Richard

**Ballard, Edward** 18th c. [PA]
*Author*
* Sabino

**Ballard, Eric Alan** 20th c. [MBF]
*British author*
* Harrison, Edwin

**Ballard, Francis Drake** 1899-1960
[ASC]
*American composer and writer*
* Ballard, Pat

**Ballard, George** 1918- [EJ]
*American jazz musician*
* Ballard, Butch

**Ballard, J. D.**
*See* Morris, Charles Smith

**Ballard, J. G.**
*See* Ballard, James Graham

**Ballard, James Graham** 1930- [SF]
*British author*
* Ballard, J. G.

**Ballard, K. G.**
*See* Roth, Holly

**Ballard, Kaye**
*See* Balotta, Catherine Gloria

**Ballard, Morton D.**
*See* Leopold, Nathan F.

**Ballard, P. D.**
*See* Ballard, [Willis] Todhunter

**Ballard, Pat**
*See* Ballard, Francis Drake

**Ballard, [Willis] Todhunter** 1903-
[CA, WD, WW]
*American author*
* Agar, Brian
* Ballard, P. D.
* Ballard, W. T.
* Bonner, Parker
* Bowie, Sam
* Carter, Nick
* D'Allard, Hunter
* Fox, Brian
* Hunt, Harrison
* Hunter, John
* MacNeil, Neil
* Reno, Clint
* Shepherd, John
* Slade, Jack
* Turner, Clay

**Ballard, W. T.**
*See* Ballard, [Willis] Todhunter

**Ballard, Wolfe**
*See* Slaughter, Marion T.

**Ballardo, Ricardo** 1921?- [B10]
*French musician*
* De Plata, Manitas

**Ballew, Charles**
*See* Snow, Charles Horace

**Ballinger, [Violet] Margaret**
**[Livingstone]** 1894- [CA]
*South African author*
* Hodgson, Margaret

**Ballinger, W. A.**
*See* Baker, William Arthur
Howard

**Ballinger, W. A.**
*See* McNeilly, Wilfred Glassford

**Ballinger, William Sanborn [Bill]**
1912-1980 [CA, EMD, WD]
*American author and screenwriter*
* Freyer, Frederic
* Sanborn, B. X.

**Balloon, Buddy**
*See* Boone, Carl George

**Balloonist**
*See* Ford, Alfred

**Ballou, Hosea** 1771-1852
[FFF, PA]
*American clergyman*
* Gilman, Mrs.

**Ballou, Noble Winfield** 1897-1963
[BE]
*American baseball player*
* Ballou, Win
* Old Pard

**Ballou, Win**
*See* Ballou, Noble Winfield

**Balluseck, Daniel J. Von** 1895-
[IAW]
*Dutch journalist, diplomat, author*
* Bricklayer, Peter
* Schakel, Pieter

**Balmer, Earl Franklin** 1935- [EAR]
*American auto racer*
* [The] Bomber

**Balogh, Penelope** 1916- [AW, WD]
*British author*
* Fox, Petronella

**Balons, Earl**
*See* Kornbluth, Cyril M.

**Balotta, Catherine Gloria** 1926-
[BEW, FC, TR]
*American actress and singer*
* Ballard, Kaye

**Balsamo, Giuseppe** 1743-1795
[FFF, SN, WBD]
*Italian imposter*
* [The] Bull Necked Forger
* Cagliostro, [Count] Alessandro di

**Balsiger, David W[ayne]** 1945-
[CA]
*American writer*
* Wayne, David

**Baltazarini** 16th c. [WBD]
*Italian violinist*
* Balthazar de Beaujoyeulx

**Balter, Elsie** 20th c. [ESF, WGT]
*Author*
* Cooke, Arthur [joint pseudonym
with C. Kornbluth, R. Lowndes, J.
Michel, D Wollheim]

**Balterman, Marcia Ridlon** 1942-
[CA, SAT]
*American author*
* Carafoli, Marci
* McGill, Marci
* Ridlon, Marcia

**Balthazar de Beaujoyeulx**
*See* Baltazarini

**Balthus**
*See* Klossowski De Rola, Balthasar

**Baltimore, J.**
*See* Catherall, Arthur

**Balucki, Michal** 1837-1901
[CD, WBD]
*Polish playwright and author*
* Elpidon
* Zalega

**Balwhidder, [Rev] Micah**
*See* Galt, John

**Balzac, Honore de** 1799-1850
[FFF, PA]
*French author*
* Coudreux, Alfred
* De Viellerge, M.
* Saint Albin

**Balzac, Jean Louis Guez de**
1596?-1655? [DEP, DNNS, HN]
*French author*
* [Le] Grand Epistolier de France
* [The] Solon of French Prose

**Balzano, Jeanne [Koppel]**
*See* Iannone, Jeanne [Koppel]

**Bam, Brigalia** 1933- [IBW]
*South African social worker*
* Brave Woman of South Africa

**Bam, Charlie**
*See* Bambridge, E. Charles

**Bambara, Toni Cade** 20th c. [CA]
*American writer and editor*
* Cade, Toni

**Bamber, Wallace Eugene** 1895-
[NAA]
*American writer*
* Williams, Ace

**Bamberger, Dutch**
*See* Bamberger, Harold Earl [Hal]

**Bamberger, Harold Earl [Hal]**
1924- [BE]
*American baseball player*
* Bamberger, Dutch

**Bamberger, Helen R.** 1888- [WW]
*Author*
* [The] Aresbys [joint pseudonym
with Raymond S. Bamberger]
* Berger, Helen

**Bamberger, Hermann** 1832?-1913
[WBD]
*Hungarian author*
* Vambery, Armin

**Bamberger, Laura Owen Miller**
1914- [IA]
*American writer*
* Miller, Laura Owen

**Bamberger, Ludwig** 1892-1969
[FC, FD, FDG]
*German director*
* Berger, Ludwig

**Bamberger, Raymond S.** 20th c.
[WW]
*Author*
* [The] Aresbys [joint pseudonym
with Helen R. Bamberger]

**[The] Bambino**
*See* Ruth, George Herman

**[Il] Bamboccio [The Deformed]**
*See* Laar [or Laer], Pieter van

**Bambridge, E. Charles** 1862- ?
[OCS]
*British soccer player*
* Bam, Charlie

**Bamdad, A.**
*See* Shamlu, Ahmad

**Bamfield, Veronica [Grissell]** 1908-
[AW]
*British author*
* Wood, Mary

**Bamford, Joseph** 1908-1971 [SG]
*British boxer*
* McAvoy, Jock
* [The] Rochdale Thunderbolt

**Bamm, Peter**
*See* Emmrich, Curt [or Kurt]

**Ban**
*See* Bannister, Geoffrey Ernest
John

**Bana, Dan**
*See* White, Stanhope

**Banana**
*See* Levinger, Lowell

**Banana, Azijn**
See Van Kampen, Oscar

**Banana Nose**
See Arcaro, George Edward
[Eddie]

**Banana Nose**
See Barazzutti, Corrado

**Bananas, Joe**
See Bonanno, Joseph, Sr.

**Bananas, Joe**
See Petroselli, Luigi

**Banash, Joseph** 1910- [ASC]
German-born composer
* Nash, B. A.

**Banat, D. R.**
See Bradbury, Ray [Douglas]

**Banbury, Henry Charles** [PA]
Author
* B.

**Banchard, E. Quentin** 19th c. [PA]
Author
* E. Q. B.

**Bancker, John** 19th c. [BE]
American baseball player
* Bancker, Stud

**Bancker, Stud**
See Bancker, John

**Bancroft, Anne**
See Italiano, Anna Maria Luisa

**Bancroft, Banny**
See Bancroft, David James [Dave]

**Bancroft, Beauty**
See Bancroft, David James [Dave]

**Bancroft, Charles**
See Bently, Fred

**Bancroft, David James [Dave]**
1892-1972 [BAB, BE, PB]
American baseball player
* Bancroft, Banny
* Bancroft, Beauty

**Bancroft, G. P.**
See Bancroft, George Pleydell

**Bancroft, George Pleydell**
1868-1956 [LC, WW]
British author and playwright
* Bancroft, G. P.
* Pleydell, George

**Bancroft, Iris [Nelson]** 1922- [CA]
American author
* Layton, Andrea
* Nielson, Ingrid

**Bancroft, Laura**
See Baum, L[yman] Frank

**Bancroft, Marie Constant** 1916-
[DLE]
British-born poet
* O'Connor, Philip

**Bancroft, Robert**
See Kirsch, Robert R.

**Banda, Hastings Kamuzu** 1906-
[IBW]
Prime minister of Nyasaland
* Chief of Chiefs

**Bandarra, Goncalo Annes** ?-1556
[FFF, RH, SN]
Portuguese poet
* [The] Nostradamus of Portugal

**Bandarra, Goncalo Annes**
(Continued)
* [The] Portuguese Nostradamus

**Bandello, Matteo [or Matthew]**
1480?-1562 [SN]
Italian author
* [A] Prose Ariosto

**Bander, Peter** 1930- [WD]
British author
* Jones, Melville

**Bandera, Stefan** ?-1959 [EE]
Russian-born exile leader
* Popel, Stefan

**Bandinelli, Orlando** ?-1181 [WBD]
Pope
* Alexander III

**[The] Bandit**
See Berry, Allen Ken

**Bando, Sal**
See Bando, Salvatore Leonard

**Bando, Salvatore Leonard** 1944-
[BE, BR]
American baseball player
* Bando, Sal

**Bandovin, E.** [PA]
Author
* Peccadille

**Bandrowski, Juljusz** 1885-1945
[CD]
Polish author
* Kaden

**Bands, Paul**
See Newsons, Albert

**Bandy, Eugene Franklin, Jr.** 1914-
[CA]
American business executive and
author
* Franklin, Eugene

**Bandy, Joe**
See Biondo, Joseph

**Bandy Legged**
See Gouffe, Armand

**Bandy De Naleche, Francoise**
1891-1974 [BEW, OCF, WEF]
French actress
* Rosay, Francoise

**Baner [Banier or Banner], Johan**
1596?-1641 [DHA, HN, SN]
Swedish army officer
* [The] Lion of Sweden

**Banerjee [or Bandyopadhyay], Abani
Mohan** 1901- [IAW]
Indian author
* Devala

**Banfield, Britt Annika** 1952-
[IAW]
Swedish-born author
* Skoglund, Annika

**Bang**
See Banger, Edgar Henry

**Banger, Edgar Henry** 1897-1968
[WECO]
British cartoonist
* Bang

**Banghart, Basil** 20th c. [BLB]
American burglar
* [The] Owl

**Bangs, John Kendrick** 1862-1922
[SFL, WGT]
American author
* Two Wags [joint pseudonym with
Frank Dempster Sherman]
* Witherup, Anne Warrington

**Bangs, Mrs. F. C.** [FFF]
Entertainer
* Leonard, Agnes

**Bangs, Robert Babbitt** 1914- [WD]
American author
* Babbitt, Robert

**Banim, John** 1798-1842 [WBD]
Irish poet, playwright, author
* [The] Scott of Ireland

**Banim, Michael, Jr.** [PA]
Author
* O'Hara, Barnes

**Banis, Victor J[erome]** 1937-
[CA, SFL]
American author
* Alexander, Jan
* Benedict, Lynn
* Samuels, Victor

**Banjamin, Gladys**
See Lanphere, Gladys

**[The] Banjo**
See Paterson, Andrew Barton

**Banjo Bill Cornett**
See Cornett, Bill

**[The] Banjo Boy**
See Nash, Lemoine

**Banjo Eyes**
See Iskowitz, Edward Israel

**Banjo Joe**
See Cannon, Gus

**[The] Banjo King of the Southland**
See Guesnon, George

**Bank, Theodore P[aul], II [Ted]**
1923- [CA, IAW]
American anthropologist, explorer,
filmmaker, author
* Adams, Weld
* Kirk, Ted

**Bank, W. Dane**
See Williamson, William Henry

**Bank-Jensen, Thea**
See Ottesen, Thea Tauber

**[The] Banker Poet**
See Rogers, Samuel

**[The] Banker Poet**
See Sprague, Charles

**[The] Banker Poet**
See Stedman, Edmund Clarence

**Bankoff, George Alexis**
See Milkomane, George Alexis
Milkomanovich

**Banks, Chocolate**
See Banks, Patryce

**Banks, David** 1901-1952 [EJS]
American basketball player
* Banks, Pretzel

**Banks, Earl** 20th c. [IBW]
American football coach
* Banks, Papa Bear

**Banks, Edward**
See Bradbury, Ray [Douglas]

**Banks, Elizabeth** 20th c. [WWL]
British author
* Enid
* Maxwell, Mary Mortimer

**Banks, Ernest [Ernie]** 1931-
[BAB, IBW]
American baseball player
* Cub, Mr.
* [The] Greatest Cub
* Sunshine, Mr.

**Banks, Eugene** 1959- [IBW]
American basketball player
* Banks, Tinkerbell

**Banks, Jane** 1913- [CA]
American author
* Banks, Taylor

**Banks, Montague**
See Bianchi, Mario

**Banks, Monty**
See Bianchi, Mario

**Banks, Nathaniel Prentiss**
1816-1894 [DNNS]
American politician and army
officer
* [The] Bobbin Boy

**Banks, Papa Bear**
See Banks, Earl

**Banks, Patryce** 20th c. [RO2]
American singer
* Banks, Chocolate

**Banks, Percival Weldon** 1806-1850
[DEL, PA]
British writer
* Rattler, Morgan

**Banks, Pretzel**
See Banks, David

**Banks, Taylor**
See Banks, Jane

**Banks, Tinkerbell**
See Banks, Eugene

**Banks, William John [Bill]**
See Yerrick, William John

**Bankston, Bill**
See Bankston, Wilborn Everett

**Bankston, Wilborn Everett** 1893-
[BE]
American baseball player
* Bankston, Bill

**Banky, Vilma**
See Baulsy, Banky Vilma

**Banna, Sabri al-** 20th c.
Palestinian terrorist
* Abu Nidal

**Bannarn, Henry W.** 1910- [IBW]
American sculptor and painter
* Bannarn, Mike

**Bannarn, Mike**
See Bannarn, Henry W.

**Bannatyne, Jack**
See Gaston, William James [Bill]

**Banner, Angela**
See Maddison, Angela Mary

**Banner, Hubert Stewart** 1891-1964
[CAP]
British author
* Vexillum

**Bannerman, Alexander Chambers**
1854-1924  [EC]
*Australian cricketer*
* Bannerman, Little Alec

**Bannerman, Little Alec**
*See* Bannerman, Alexander
Chambers

**Bannerman, Margaret**
*See* Le Grand, Margaret

**Bannerman, Mark**
*See* Lewing, Anthony Charles

**Banning, E. P.** [FFF]
*American writer*
* Goldlace

**Bannion, Della**
*See* Sellers, Connie Leslie, Jr.

**Bannisdale, V. E.**
*See* Portal, V. E.

**Bannister, Annie Bethel Scales**
1880-1975  [IBW]
*American poet*
* Spencer, Anne

**Bannister, Geoffrey Ernest John**
1924-  [ART]
*British artist*
* Ban

**Bannister, Pat**
*See* Davis, Lou Ellen

**Bannon, Foxy Grandpa**
*See* Bannon, James Henry
[Jimmy]

**Bannon, James Henry [Jimmy]**
1871-1948  [BE]
*American baseball player*
* Bannon, Foxy Grandpa

**Bannon, Mark**
*See* King, Albert

**Bannon, Peter**
*See* Durst, Paul

**Bannon, Thomas Edward [Tom]**
1869-1950  [BE]
*American baseball player*
* Uncle Tom

**Banshuck, Grego**
*See* Gernsback, Hugo

**Bantam Ben Hogan**
*See* Hogan, Benjamin William

**Banti, Anna**
*See* Lopresti, Lucia Longhi

**Bantock, [Lady] Helen Francesca**
1868- ?  [WWL]
*British author*
* H. F. B.

**Banton, Coy**
*See* Norwood, Victor G[eorge]
C[harles]

**Banu, Eugenia** 1910-  [IAW]
*Rumanian author*
* Postelnich, Joana

**Baptiste, Jean**
*See* Du Tertre, Jacques

**Baptiste, John Phillip** 1931-  [RO1]
*American singer and songwriter*
* Phillips, Phil

**Bapu**
*See* Gandhi, Mohandas
Karamchand

**Bapu**
*See* Khare, Narayan Bhaskar

**Bar-Natan, Moshe**
*See* Louvish, Misha

**Bara**
*See* Herzog, Guy

**Bara, Theda**
*See* Goodman, Theodosia

**Barajitas [The Little Card Player]**
*See* Sanchez, Pablo

**Baraka, Imamu Amiri**
*See* Jones, [Everett] LeRoi

**Baraniev, Sacha** 1909-  [FC]
*American screenwriter and producer*
* Bartlett, Sy

**Baranovius**
*See* Barowski, Albert

**Barany, Istvan** 1907-  [SWI]
*Hungarian swimmer*
* Barany, Pista

**Barany, Pista**
*See* Barany, Istvan

**Baratier, Jacques**
*See* Baratier De Rey, Jacques

**Baratier De Rey, Jacques** 1918-
[FDG]
*French director*
* Baratier, Jacques

**Baratto, Luisa** 20th c.  [WF]
*Italian actress*
* Barrett, Liz

**Barazzutti, Corrado**
*Italian tennis player*
* Banana Nose
* [Il] Soldatino [The Little Soldier]

**Barba, Harry** 1922-  [CA]
*American author and educator*
* Mikan, Baron
* Ohon

**[The] Barbados Demon**
*See* Walcott, Joe

**Barbara**
*See* Wright, Mabel Osgood

**Barbara of Cilley** 15th c.  [DEP]
*Wife of Emperor Sigismund*
* [The] Messalina of Germany

**Barbara, Paulo Henrique**
*See* Pinheiro, Paulo Henrique
Barbara

**Barbare, Dinty**
*See* Barbare, Walter Lawrence

**Barbare, Rholf**
*See* Volkoff, Vladimir

**Barbare, Walter Lawrence**
1891-1965  [BE]
*American baseball player*
* Barbare, Dinty

**Barbarelli, Giorgio** 1478?-1511
[WBD]
*Venetian painter*
* Castelfranco Giorgione da
* [Il] Giorgione

**Barbari, Jacopo de'** 1440?-1516?
[WBD]
*Italian painter and engraver*
* Walch, Jakob

**Barbarossa**
*See* Frederick I [or Friedrich]

**Barbarossa**
*See* Scott, John

**Barbarossa I**
*See* Horush [Arouj, Horuc or
Koruk]

**Barbarossa II**
*See* Khizr

**Barbary, Donald Odell** 1920-  [BE]
*American baseball player*
* Barbary, Red

**Barbary, James** [joint pseudonym
with Jack Beeching]
*See* Baumann, Amy [Brown]
Beeching

**Barbary, James** [joint pseudonym
with Amy (Brown) Beeching
Baumann]
*See* Beeching, Jack

**Barbary, Red**
*See* Barbary, Donald Odell

**[The] Barbasol Man**
*See* Frankel, Harry

**Barbatelli, Bernardino [or Bernardo]**
1548?-1612  [WBD]
*Italian painter*
* Poccetti, Bernardino

**Barbatus**
*See* Asclepius, Nicolas

**Barbatus**
*See* Han, Ulrich

**Barbatus**
*See* Scipio, Lucius Cornelius

**Barbazan, Arnaud Guillaume [or
Arnauld Guilhelm]** 1360?-1432
[DNNS, WBD]
*French army officer*
* Chevalier sans Reproche
* Knight without Reproach

**Barbeau, Jap**
*See* Barbeau, William Joseph

**Barbeau, William Joseph**
1882-1969  [BE]
*American baseball player*
* Barbeau, Jap

**Barbecue Bob**
*See* Hicks, Robert [Bob]

**Barbee, John Henry**
*See* Tucker, William George

**Barbee, Phillips**
*See* Sheckley, Robert

**Barbella, Rocco** 1922-  [BX, RBE]
*American boxer*
* Graziano, Rocky

**Barbellion, W. N. P.**
*See* Cummings, Bruce Frederick

**[The] Barber**
*See* Maglie, Salvatore Anthony

**Barber, Anna-Ottilie Patterson**
1932-  [EJ]
*Irish-born singer*
* Patterson, Ottilie

**Barber, Antonia**
*See* Anthony, Barbara

**Barber, Dulan F.** 1940-  [CA, WD]
*British author*
* Fletcher, David

**Barber, Harriet Booner** 19th c.
[PA]
*Author*
* Templeton, Faith

**Barber, Joseph** 1798- ?  [PA]
*American author*
* [The] Disbanded Volunteer

**Barber, Luis**
*See* Barbieri, Luigi

**Barber, Margaret Fairless**
1869-1901  [LC, TC]
*British author*
* Fairless, Michael

**Barber, Miller** 1931-  [BWG]
*American golfer*
* Mr. X

**[The] Barber Poet**
*See* Boe, Jacques

**Barber, Raymond** 1921-  [ART]
*British artist*
* Renny

**Barber, Red**
*See* Barber, Walter Lanier

**Barber, Stephen Guy** 1921-1980
[CA]
*Egyptian-born American journalist*
* Bernard, Guy

**Barber, W. R.** [FFF]
*American writer*
* Chincapin

**Barber, Walter Lanier** 1908-  [B10]
*American sportscaster*
* Barber, Red

**Barberini, Maffeo** 1568-1644
[WBD]
*Pope*
* Urban VIII

**Barberis**
*See* Barberis, Franco

**Barberis, Franco** 1905-  [CA]
*Swiss author and illustrator*
* Barberis

**Barbet, Pierre**
*See* Avice, Claude

**Barbette**
*See* Broodway, Van der Clyde

**Barbette, Jay**
*See* Spicer, Bart

**Barbette the Enigma**
*See* Broodway, Van der Clyde

**Barbiere, Domenico del** 1501-1565
[WBD]
*Italian painter, sculptor, engraver*
* Domenico Fiorentino

**Barbieri, G. M.** [BEW]
*American singer and actress*
* Ashley, Barbara

**Barbieri, Gato**
*See* Barbieri, Leandro

**Barbieri, Giovanni [or Gian]
Francesco** 1590?-1666
[FFF, RH, SN]
*Bolognese painter*
* Guercino
* [The] Squint-Eyed

**Barbieri, Leandro** 1933- [DAM]
*Argentinian musician*
* Barbieri, Gato

**Barbieri, Luigi** 20th c. [WF]
*Italian actor*
* Barber, Luis

**Barbilian, Dan** 1895-1961 [EWL]
*Rumanian poet*
* Barbu, Ion

**Barbirolli, Giovanni Battista**
1899-1970 [MS]
*British conductor*
* Barbirolli, [Sir] John

**Barbirolli, [Sir] John**
See Barbirolli, Giovanni Battista

**Barbo, Pietro** 1417-1471
[CAL, WBD]
*Pope*
* Paul II

**Barboni, Enzo** 1922- [FDG]
*Italian director*
* Clucher, E. B.

**Barbour, Ralph Henry** 1870-1944
[SAT, WW]
*American author*
* Powell, Richard Stillman

**Barbour, Robert MacDermot**
1910-1964 [THR]
*British playwright*
* MacDermot, Robert

**Barbour, Thomas L.**
See Lesure, Thomas B[arbour]

**Barboza, Baron**
See Barboza, Joseph

**Barboza, Joseph** 20th c. [BLB]
*American underworld figure and government witness*
* Barboza, Baron
* Bently, Joseph [assumed name]

**Barbu, Ion**
See Barbilian, Dan

**Barbus, Paolo** [PA]
*Author*
* Soncinus

**Barca**
See Hamilcar

**Barclay, Alan**
See Tait, George B.

**Barclay, Ann**
See Greig, Maysie

**Barclay, Arthur**
See Jones, Arthur Barclay

**Barclay, Bill**
See Moorcock, Michael John

**Barclay, David**
See Fronabarger, David Poole

**Barclay, Deerfoot**
See Barclay, George Oliver

**Barclay, Florence Louisa**
**Charlesworth** 1862-1921
[WGT, WWL]
*British author*
* Roy, Brandon

**Barclay, Gabriel** [house pseudonym]
See Kornbluth, Cyril M.

**Barclay, Gabriel** [house pseudonym]
See Wellman, Manly Wade

**Barclay, George** 20th c. [AW]
*Scottish-born author and screenwriter*
* Kinnoch, R. G. B.

**Barclay, George Oliver** 1875-1909
[BE]
*American baseball player*
* Barclay, Deerfoot

**Barclay, Isabel**
See Dobell, Isabel Marian Barclay

**Barclay, John Robert Troutbeck**
1954- [DC]
*German-born cricketer*
* Barclay, Trouters

**Barclay, Lester**
See Livingston, Berkeley

**Barclay, Oliver R[ainsford]** 1919-
[CA]
*British author*
* Triton, A. N.

**Barclay, Robert** 1648-1690 [SN]
*Scottish Quaker*
* [The] Apologist for the Quakers

**Barclay, Trouters**
See Barclay, John Robert Troutbeck

**Barclay, Vera** 1893- [WWL]
*Author*
* Beech, Margaret

**Barcroft, Roy**
See Ravenscroft, Howard H.

**Barcynska, Countess**
See Evans, Marguerite Florence Helene Jervis

**Barcynski, Leon Roger** 1949- [CA]
*British author*
* Phillips, Osborne

**[The] Bard**
See Jerningham, Edward

**Bard, Maria** 1901-1944 [SC]
*German actress*
* Bard, Migo

**Bard, Migo**
See Bard, Maria

**Bard Nantglyn**
See Davies, Robert

**[The] Bard of all Time**
See Shakespeare, William

**[The] Bard of Arthurian Romance**
See Tennyson, Alfred [First Baron Tennyson]

**[The] Bard of Avon**
See Shakespeare, William

**[The] Bard of Avondale**
See Jacobs, Howard

**[The] Bard of Ayrshire**
See Burns, Robert

**[The] Bard of Bronzevilla**
See Brooks, Inez Gwendolyn Elizabeth

**[The] Bard of Erin**
See Moore, Thomas

**[The] Bard of Hope**
See Campbell, Thomas

**[The] Bard of Hyde**
See Prince, John Critchley

**[A] Bard of Martial Lay**
See Scott, [Sir] Walter

**[The] Bard of Memory**
See Rogers, Samuel

**[The] Bard of Mulla's Silver Stream**
See Spenser, Edmund

**[The] Bard of Olney**
See Cowper, William

**[The] Bard of Prose**
See Boccaccio, Giovanni

**[The] Bard of Rydal Mount**
See Wordsworth, William

**[The] Bard of Sheffield**
See Montgomery, James

**[The] Bard of Staten Island**
See Shakespeare, William V.

**[The] Bard of the British Navy**
See Dibdin, Charles

**[The] Bard of the Forest**
See Wickenden, William

**[The] Bard of the Imagination**
See Akenside, Mark

**[The] Bard of Twickenham**
See Pope, Alexander

**[The] Bard of Woodstock**
See Chaucer, Geoffrey

**Bard, Samuel A.**
See Squier, Ephraim George

**Bard, Wilkie**
See Smith, William Augustus

**Bardanes** 8th c. [WBD]
*Byzantine emperor*
* Philippicus

**Bardella, Antonio Naldi** 16th c.
[SN]
*Italian musician*
* [Il] Bardello

**[Il] Bardello**
See Bardella, Antonio Naldi

**Bardem, Juan Antonio**
See Munoz, Juan Antonio

**Bardens, Dennis [Conrad]** 1911-
[CA]
*British author and journalist*
* Farel, Conrad
* Roberts, Julian

**Bardin, John Franklin** 1916- [CA]
*American author*
* Ashe, Douglas
* Tree, Gregory

**Bardon, Henry**
See Bardon, Jindrich

**Bardon, Jindrich** 1923- [OP]
*Czech-born scenic designer*
* Bardon, Henry

**Bardot, Brigitte**
See Javal, Camille

**Bardot, Louis** 1896-1975
[B10, CA]
*French industrialist and poet*
* Pilou

**Bardwell, Denver**
See Sayers, James Denson

**Bardzinski, Jan** [PA]
*Author*
* Alanus

**Barefoot**
See Magnus III

**[The] Barefoot Boy from Pena Blanca**
See Montoya, Joseph M.

**Barek, Larbi Ben** 20th c. [IBW]
*Moroccan-born soccer player*
* [The] Black Pearl

**Barent, Ralph** 1869?-1944 [THR]
*British actor*
* Roberts, Ralph

**Barere de Vieuzac, Bertrand**
1755-1841 [DNNF, RH, SN]
*French attorney and revolutionary leader*
* [The] Anacreon of the Guillotine
* [The] Witling of Terror

**Baretti, Giuseppe Marc'Antonio**
1719-1789 [WBD]
*Italian critic*
* Scannabue, Aristarco

**Barfield, [Arthur] Owen** 1898-
[AW, CA]
*British author*
* Burgeon, G. A. L.

**Barfod**
See Magnus III

**Barge, Gillian**
See Bargh, Gillian

**Barger, Cy**
See Barger, Eros Bolivar

**Barger, Eros Bolivar** 1885-1964
[BE, BN]
*American baseball player*
* Barger, Cy
* [The] Old Home Remedy

**Barger, Ralph** 1939?-
*American motorcycle gang leader*
* Barger, Sonny

**Barger, Sonny**
See Barger, Ralph

**Bargh, Gillian** 1940- [TR]
*British actress*
* Barge, Gillian

**Bargone, [Frederic] Charles [Pierre Edouard]** 1876-1957 [EWL]
*French author*
* Farrere, Claude

**Bargordes, Benjamin** 20th c. [SG]
*Boxer*
* Troubles, Kid

**Barham, Richard Harris**
1788-1845 [DEL, DNNF, RH]
*British author and poet*
* Ingoldsby, Thomas
* Peppercorn, H., M.D.

**Barham, Samuel, Jr.** [PA]
*Author*
* Uncle Paul

**Barhebroeus**
See Faradge, Aboul

**Bari, Joe**
See Benedetto, Anthony Dominick

**Bari, Lynn**
See Bitzer, Marjorie

**Barimbaum, Robert H.** 1920-
[BEW]
*American theatrical manager and director*
* Baron, Robert Alex

**Baring, Max**
*See* Messent, Charles

**Baring, Norah**
*See* Baker, Norah

**Barios, Joe** 20th c. [RO1]
*American singer*
* Barry, Joe

**Barizan, Louis Martial** 1800-1883
[FFF]
*French actor*
* Monrose, Louis

**Barkan, Stanley Howard** 1936-
[ASC]
*American composer*
* Hendrix, Sonny

**Barkee, Asouff**
*See* Strung, Norman

**Barker, A. J.**
*See* Barker, Arthur James

**Barker, Albert W.** 1900- [SAT]
*American author*
* King, Reefe
* Macrae, Hawk

**Barker, Alexander Crichlow, Jr.**
1919-1973 [SC]
*American actor*
* Barker, Lex

**Barker, Arizona Donnie Clark**
1872-1935 [BLB]
*American underworld figure*
* Barker, Kate
* Barker, Ma

**Barker, Arthur** 1899-1939 [BLB]
*American murderer and bank robber*
* Barker, Doc

**Barker, Arthur James** 1918-
[WYA]
*Author*
* Barker, A. J.

**Barker, Blue Lu**
*See* Barker, Louisa

**Barker, Buddy**
*See·* Barker, Ray[mond Herrell]

**Barker, Doc**
*See* Barker, Arthur

**Barker, Dudley** 1910-
[AW, CA, WD]
*British author*
* Black, Lionel
* Matthews, Anthony

**Barker, E. M.**
*See* Barker, Elsa [McCormick]

**Barker, Edmund Henry** 1788-1839
[FFF]
*British scholar*
* Vindex

**Barker, Elsa [McCormick]** 1906-
[CAP, WD]
*American author*
* Barker, E. M.
* Jordan, Nell

**Barker, Elver A.** 1920- [CA]
*American artist and author*
* Harding, Carl B.

**Barker [or Hurd?], Francine** 20th
c. [PRS, RO2]
*American singer*
* Peaches

**Barker, George William Michael
Jones** ?-1855 [DEL]
*British poet*
* [The] Wensleydale Poet

**Barker, H[arley] Granville**
1877-1946 [LC]
*British playwright, producer, author*
* Granville-Barker, Harley

**Barker, Kate**
*See* Barker, Arizona Donnie Clark

**Barker, Laura**
*See* Taylor, Mrs. Tom

**Barker, Leonard Noel** 1882- [WW]
*Author*
* Noel, L.

**Barker, Lex**
*See* Barker, Alexander Crichlow,
Jr.

**Barker, Louisa** 1913- [BWW]
*American singer*
* Barker, Blue Lu
* Blue, Lu

**Barker, Ma**
*See* Barker, Arizona Donnie Clark

**Barker, Matthew Henry**
1790-1846 [FFF, PA]
*British author and journalist*
* Father Ambrose
* Old Sailor
* [The] Wanderer

**Barker, Ray[mond Herrell]** 1936-
[BE]
*American baseball player*
* Barker, Buddy

**Barker, Reginald Charles** 1881- ?
[NAA]
*British-born American author*
* Harrington, Lee

**Barker, Ronald Ernest** 1920-
[AW, WW]
*British author*
* Ronald, E. B.

**Barker, S[quire] Omar** 1894-
[CAP, SAT, WD]
*American author*
* Canusi, Jose
* Scott, Dan [house pseudonym]
  [Stratemeyer Syndicate]
* Squires, Phil

**Barker, Stanley** 1870- ? [NAA]
*Canadian writer on lumber industry*
* Vigilant

**Barker, Will** 1908?-
[AW, CA, SAT]
*American author*
* Demarest, Doug

**Barkley, John Duncan** 1913- [BE]
*American baseball player*
* Barkley, Red

**Barkley, Lil Ty**
*See* Barkley, Tyrone

**Barkley, Red**
*See* Barkley, John Duncan

**Barkley, Tyrone** 20th c. [RO2]
*American singer*
* Barkley, Lil Ty

**Barko, Louis** 20th c. [BLB]
*American underworld figure*
* Valerie, Louis

**Barkton, S. Rush**
*See* Brav, Stanley R[osenbaum]

**Barkum, Gee**
*See* Barkum, Jerome

**Barkum, Jerome** 20th c. [SMG]
*American football player*
* Barkum, Gee

**Barlass, Kate**
*See* Douglas, Catherine

**Barlay, Bennett**
*See* Crossen, Ken[dell Foster]

**Barlesio, Marvin** ?-1480 [PA]
*Author*
* Barletius

**Barletius**
*See* Barlesio, Marvin

**Barling, Charles**
*See* Barling, Muriel Vere Mant

**Barling, Muriel Vere Mant** 1904-
[CA, WW]
*British author*
* Barling, Charles
* Barrington, P. V.
* Barrington, Pamela

**Barling, Philip** 1857-1936 [CED]
*British actor*
* Greet, Ben
* Greet, [Sir] Philip

**Barloeus**
*See* Van Bairle, Gaspard

**Barlow, Billie**
*See* Barlow, Minnie

**Barlow, Duncan**
*See* Barlow, Graham Derek

**Barlow, Eddy**
*See* Barlow, Graham Derek

**Barlow, Emma** [FFF]
*American writer*
* Leila

**Barlow, Gladys**
*See* Barlow, Graham Derek

**Barlow, Graham Derek** 1950- [DC]
*British cricketer*
* Barlow, Duncan
* Barlow, Eddy
* Barlow, Gladys

**Barlow, James Henry Stanley**
1921- [DLE]
*British author*
* Forden, James

**Barlow, James William** 1826-1913
[SFL, WGT]
*Irish author*
* Skorpios, Antares

**Barlow, Klara**
*See* Williams, Alma Claire

**Barlow, Maud** 1882-1967 [BMH]
*British comedienne*
* Barr, Ida
* Laverne, Maud
* [The] Ragtime Girl

**Barlow, Minnie** 1862-1937 [THR]
*British actress and singer*
* Barlow, Billie

**Barlow, Robert O.**
*See* Meyer, Heinrich

**Barlow, Roger**
*See* Leckie, Robert [Hugh]

**Barlow, Roger**
*See* West, Wallace

**Barlow, Sanna Morrison**
*See* Rossi, Sanna Morrison Barlow

**Barltrop, Robert** 1922- [CA]
*British author*
* Coster, Robert

**Barmby, Katherine R.** [FFF]
*Writer*
* Kate

**Barmes, Bruce Raymond** 1929-
[BE]
*American baseball player*
* Barmes, Squeaky

**Barmes, Squeaky**
*See* Barmes, Bruce Raymond

**Barna, Babe**
*See* Barna, Herbert Paul

**Barna, Herbert Paul** 1915-1972
[BE]
*American baseball player*
* Barna, Babe

**Barnabas**
*See* West, Charles Converse

**Barnabas, Brother**
*See* O'Nuallain, Brian

**Barnaby, Hugo**
*See* Fitzpatrick, Ernest Hugh

**Barnacle**
*See* Barnes, Albert Coombs

**Barnacle, [Captain] B.**
*See* Newell, Charles M.

**Barnacle Bill Posedel**
*See* Posedel, William John

**Barnard, Alfred J.** 1878- ? [MBF]
*British author and editor*
* Clifford, Martin [house
  pseudonym]
* Hart, Leonard

**Barnard, Amy B.** 20th c. [WWL]
*British author*
* Barr, Maynard

**Barnard, C. F., Jr.** [PA]
*Author*
* Gilman, [Mrs.] Maria
* Kingsford, Jane

**Barnard, Caroline** 19th c.
[DEL, FFF, RH]
*Author and songwriter*
* Claribel

**Barnard, Charles** [PA]
*Author*
* De Bernhard, Charles

**Barnard, H. H.**
*See* Skinner, George

**Barnard, [Sir] John** 1685-1764
[HN, RH, SN]
*British politician*
* Cato the Younger
* [The] Father of London
* [The] Great Commoner

**Barnard, Judith** 20th c.
*American author*
* Michael, Judith [joint pseudonym
  with Michael Fain]

**Barnard, Marjorie Faith** 1897-
[SFL]
*Australian author*
* Eldershaw, M. Barnard [joint
  pseudonym with Flora Sydney
  Patricia Eldershaw]

**Barnard, Melville Clemens** 20th c.
[WW]
*Author*
* Arid, Ben

**Barnard, Richard Innes** 20th c.
[MBF]
*British author*
* Richards, Frank [house
  pseudonym]

**Barnard, T. H.**
*See* Barnard, Thomas Henslow

**Barnard, Thomas Henslow** 1898-
[ART]
*British painter and engraver*
* Barnard, T. H.

**Barnato, Barnett [Barney]**
*See* Isaacs, Barnett

**Barndt, H. G.**
*See* Barndt, Helen Grace

**Barndt, Helen Grace** 20th c. [ART]
*American painter*
* Barndt, H. G.

**Barne, Kitty**
*See* Barne, Marion Catherine

**Barne, Marion Catherine**
1883-1957 [TCC]
*British author and playwright*
* Barne, Kitty

**Barner, Juke Boy**
*See* Bonner, Weldon H. Philip

**Barnes, Albert Coombs** 1873-1951
[FFF]
*American art collector and physician*
* Barnacle

**Barnes, Arthur K[elvin]**
1909?-1969 [ESF, NAA, WGT]
*American writer*
* Barnes, Dave
* Kent, Kelvin [joint pseudonym
  with Henry Kuttner]

**Barnes, Bad News**
*See* Barnes, Jim

**Barnes, Bad News**
*See* Barnes, Marvin

**Barnes, Barnsey**
*See* Barnes, Blair

**Barnes, Barry K.**
*See* Barnes, Nelson

**Barnes, Bill** 20th c. [NBB]
*American musician*
* Guitar Papa

**Barnes, Binnie**
*See* Barnes, Gertrude Maude

**Barnes, Blair** 1960- [SMG]
*Canadian-born hockey player*
* Barnes, Barnsey

**Barnes, Bud**
*See* Barnes, Francis

**Barnes, Chesley Virginia**
*See* Young, Chesley Virginia

**Barnes, Clara Ernst** 1895- [CA]
*German-born artist and author*
* Ernst, Clara

**Barnes, Dave**
*See* Barnes, Arthur K[elvin]

**Barnes, Djuna** 1892- [CA]
*American author*
* Steptoe, Lydia

**Barnes, Emile Deering** 1903-1959
[BE]
*American baseball player*
* Barnes, Red

**Barnes, Eppie [or Eppy]**
*See* Barnes, Everett Duane

**Barnes, Everett Duane** 1900-
[BBH, BE]
*American baseball coach*
* Barnes, Eppie [or Eppy]

**Barnes, Fae** 1900?- [BWW]
*American singer*
* Jones, Maggie
* [The] Texas Nightingale

**Barnes, Florence**
*See* Lowe, Florence

**Barnes, Francis** 20th c.
*American politician*
* Barnes, Bud

**Barnes, Frank**
*See* Allen, Richard

**Barnes, Frank Samuel** 1900-1967
[BE]
*American baseball player*
* Barnes, Lefty

**Barnes, Gertrude Maude** 1905-
[THR]
*British actress*
* Barnes, Binnie

**Barnes, Good News**
*See* Barnes, Marvin

**Barnes, Honey**
*See* Barnes, John Francis

**Barnes, Irene** 1872-1949 [THR]
*British actress*
* Vanbrugh, [Dame] Irene

**Barnes, James M.** 1887-1966
[AS, EG]
*British-born golfer*
* Barnes, Long Jim

**Barnes, Jim** 1941- [BB]
*American basketball player*
* Barnes, Bad News

**Barnes, Jim Weaver** 1933- [IAW]
*American poet*
* Tisserand, Jacques

**Barnes, Joe** 1905?-1964 [BEW]
*Theatrical performer*
* Uncle Joe

**Barnes, John**
*See* O'Donnell, Peter

**Barnes, John Francis** 1900- [BE]
*American baseball player*
* Barnes, Honey

**Barnes, June Shoaf** 1911-1963
[BE]
*American baseball player*
* Barnes, Junie

**Barnes, June Shoaf** (Continued)
* Barnes, Lefty

**Barnes, Junie**
*See* Barnes, June Shoaf

**Barnes, Kate D. W.** [FFF, PA]
*Author*
* Cameron, Kate

**Barnes, Lefty**
*See* Barnes, Frank Samuel

**Barnes, Lefty**
*See* Barnes, June Shoaf

**Barnes, Lefty**
*See* Barnes, Robert Avery [Bob]

**Barnes, Leroy** 1932?-
*American underworld figure*
* Barnes, Nicky
* Brown, Bad Bad Leroy
* Untouchable, Mr.

**Barnes, Long Jim**
*See* Barnes, James M.

**Barnes, Lute**
*See* Barnes, Luther Owen

**Barnes, Luther Owen** 1947- [BE]
*American baseball player*
* Barnes, Lute

**Barnes, Mae**
*See* Stith, Edith Mae

**Barnes, Marvin** 1952- [BB]
*American basketball player*
* Barnes, Bad News
* Barnes, Good News
* Barnes, News
* Marvin the Magnificent

**Barnes, Mrs. J. H.** [FFF]
*Entertainer*
* Williams, Mary

**Barnes, Nelson** 1906-1965
[BF, SC]
*British actor*
* Barnes, Barry K.

**Barnes, News**
*See* Barnes, Marvin

**Barnes, Nicky**
*See* Barnes, Leroy

**Barnes, Pancho**
*See* Lowe, Florence

**Barnes, Paul D.** 1901?-
[DAM, WWJ]
*American jazz musician*
* Barnes, Polo

**Barnes, Polo**
*See* Barnes, Paul D.

**Barnes, Red**
*See* Barnes, Emile Deering

**Barnes, Robert** 1495-1540 [RH]
*British martyr*
* [The] Hot Gospeller

**Barnes, Robert Avery [Bob]** 1902-
[BE]
*American baseball player*
* Barnes, Lefty

**Barnes, Roscoe Conkling**
1850-1915 [BE]
*American baseball player*
* Barnes, Ross

**Barnes, Ross**
*See* Barnes, Roscoe Conkling

**Barnes, Thomas** 1785-1841 [FFF]
*British editor*
* Criticus

**Barnes, Violet** 1867-1942 [THR]
*British actress*
* Vanbrugh, Violet

**Barnes, Virgil Jennings** 1897-1958
[AS, BE]
*American baseball player*
* Barnes, Zeke

**Barnes, W. Therold** 1913?-1965
[CW]
*Barbadian poet, author, editor*
* Bendix

**Barnes, Zeke**
*See* Barnes, Virgil Jennings

**Barnet, Charles Daly [Charlie]**
1913- [PMJ]
*American jazz musician*
* Barnet, Mad Mab

**Barnet, John**
*See* Stagg, J. R.

**Barnet, Mad Mab**
*See* Barnet, Charles Daly [Charlie]

**Barnett, Adam**
*See* Fast, Julius

**Barnett, Bones**
*See* Barnett, Everett

**Barnett, Charis**
*See* Frankenburg, Charis Ursula

**Barnett, Everett** 20th c. [GW]
*American rodeo performer*
* Barnett, Bones

**Barnett, Helen Isabel** 20th c.
[EMT]
*American actress and singer*
* Ford, Helen

**Barnett, Ida Baker Wells**
1862-1931 [IBW]
*American journalist*
* Princess of the Press

**Barnett, L. David**
*See* Laschever, Barnett D.

**Barnett, Samuel** 1863-1927 [SC]
*British-born American actor*
* Bernard, Sam

**Barney, Jay**
*See* Schmide, John Bernhardt
Vander Kleine

**Barney, Lem[uel J.]** 1945- [FB]
*American football player*
* Barney, Stroll

**Barney, Rex** 1924-
*American baseball player*
* [The] Wild Man of Brooklyn

**Barney, Stroll**
*See* Barney, Lem[uel J.]

**Barnfield, Richard** [PA]
*Author*
* Ignoto

**Barnhart, Clyde Lee** 1895- [BE]
*American baseball player*
* Barnhart, Pooch

**Barnhart, Pooch**
*See* Barnhart, Clyde Lee

**Barnhill, David** 1914-    [MK]
*American baseball player*
* Barnhill, Impo

**Barnhill, Impo**
*See*  Barnhill, David

**Barnhill, John** 1938-    [BB]
*American basketball player*
* Barnhill, Rabbit

**Barnhill, Rabbit**
*See*  Barnhill, John

**Barnhisel, Ethel Keeler Betts** 1880-
?    [NAA]
*American writer*
* Betts, Nancy K.

**Barnhurst, Laura Nelson** 1876- ?
[THR]
*American actress*
* Hall, Laura Nelson

**Barnie, Bald Billy**
*See*  Barnie, William Harrison
[Billy]

**Barnie, William Harrison [Billy]**
1853-1900    [BE]
*American baseball manager*
* Barnie, Bald Billy

**Barnitt, Nedda Lemmon** 20th c.
[CA]
*British-born author*
* Lamont, N. B.
* Lamont, Nedda

**Barnsley, Alan Gabriel** 1916-
[B10, CA, WD]
*British author and physician*
* Fielding, Gabriel

**[The] Barnum of Basketball**
*See*  Saperstein, Abraham M.
[Abe]

**[The] Barnum of Bread**
*See*  Weston, W. Garfield

**Barnum, P. T.**
*See*  Barnum, Phineas Taylor

**Barnum, Phineas Taylor**
1810-1891    [DNNF, DNNS, SN]
*American showman*
* Barnum, P. T.
* [The] Prince of Showmen

**Barnum, Richard** [house pseudonym]
[Stratemeyer Syndicate]
*See*  Stratemeyer, Edward L.

**Barnum, W[illiam] Paul** 1933-
[CA]
*American journalist*
* O'Brynt, Jon
* O'Neil, Eric

**Barnwell**
*See*  Roosevelt, Robert Barnwell

**Barnwell, Annie M.**    [FFF]
*Writer*
* Leroy

**Baro, Bonaventura** 1600-1696    [PA]
*Author*
* FitzGerald

**Barocchio [or Barozzi], Giacomo**
1507-1573    [WBD]
*Italian architect*
* Vignola, Giacomo da

**Baromeo, Cesare**
*See*  Baromeo, Chase

**Baromeo, Chase** 1893-    [DAM]
*American opera singer*
* Baromeo, Cesare

**[The] Baron**
*See*  Ricasoli, Bettino [Baron of
Brolio]

**[The] Baron**
*See*  Rupp, Adolph

**[The] Baron**
*See*  Worfel, W. G.

**Baron, [Joseph] Alexander**
*See*  Bernstein, Alec

**Baron, Anthony**
*See*  Baker, Augustus

**Baron, David**
*See*  Pinter, Harold

**Baron, Hyacinthe-Theodore**
1707-1787    [PA]
*Author*
* Junior

**Baron, John**
*See*  Baker, Augustus

**Baron, Michel**
*See*  Boyron, Michel [or Michael]

**Baron of the Holy Sepulchre**
*See*  Godfrey of Bouillon

**Baron, Oscar** 1908?-1976    [B10]
*American author and publisher*
* Borden, Orson T.

**Baron, Othello**
*See*  Fanthorpe, R[obert] Lionel

**Baron, Peter**
*See*  Clyde, Leonard Worswick

**Baron, Pierre** ?-1535    [PA]
*Author*
* Stempasius

**Baron, Robert Alex**
*See*  Barimbaum, Robert H.

**Baron, Vic**
*See*  Baroni, Vasco

**Baron, [Ora] Wendy** 1937-    [CA]
*British art historian and author*
* Dimson, Wendy

**Barondess, Sue K[aufman]**
1926-1977    [CA]
*American author*
* Kaufman, Sue

**Barone, Nick**
*See*  Barrone, Carmine

**Baroni, Vasco** 1910-    [ASC]
*Italian-born composer and arranger*
* Baron, Vic

**Barowski, Albert** ?-1615    [PA]
*Author*
* Baranovius

**Barr, Alfred Hamilton, Jr.** 1902-1981
*American museum curator*
* [The] Pope

**Barr, Andros**
*See*  Barr, Ernie

**Barr, Anthony**
*See*  Yaffe, Morris

**Barr, Betty** 1932-    [CA]
*British author*
* Skipper, Betty

**Barr, Byron Ellsworth** 1913?-1978
[BEW, FC, HT]
*American actor*
* Fleming, Bryant
* Young, Gig

**Barr, Densil Neve**
*See*  Buttrey, Douglas Norton

**Barr, Ernie** 1955?-    [RBE]
*Bahamian-born boxer*
* Barr, Andros

**Barr, Hyder Edward** 1886-1934
[BE]
*American baseball player*
* Barr, Scotty

**Barr, Ida**
*See*  Barlow, Maud

**Barr, James Leland** 1948-    [SMG]
*American baseball player*
* J. B.

**Barr, Maynard**
*See*  Barnard, Amy B.

**Barr, Nat**
*See*  Goddard, Norman Molyneux

**Barr, Richard**
*See*  Baer, Richard Alphonse

**Barr, Robert** 1850-1912
[CC, EMD, WW]
*British journalist*
* Sharp, Luke

**Barr, Scotty**
*See*  Barr, Hyder Edward

**Barraclough, David Pearson** 1928-
[EJ]
*American-born jazz musician*
* Pearson, Dave

**[The] Barracuda**
*See*  Regan, Donald Thomas

**Barracuda, John**
*See*  Serato, Massimo

**Barradell-Smith, Walter** 1881- ?
[WWL]
*Scottish author*
* Bird, Richard

**Barragan, Cuno**
*See*  Barragan, Facundo Anthony

**Barragan, Facundo Anthony** 1932-
[BE]
*American baseball player*
* Barragan, Cuno

**Barratt, Krome** 1924-    [ART, DBA]
*British painter and mural designer*
* K. B.
* Krome

**Barratt, Percy Ernest** 1874?-1937
[BEW]
*Comedian*
* Mayne, Ernie

**Barraud, Danielle-Jeanne** 1940-
[OP]
*French opera singer*
* Barraud, Dany

**Barraud, Dany**
*See*  Barraud, Danielle-Jeanne

**Barrelhouse Sammy**
*See*  McTell, Willie Samuel

**Barrelhouse Tommy**
*See*  Dorsey, Thomas A[ndrew]

**Barrell, M. E.** 1883-1945    [SC]
*American actor*
* Edwards, Ted

**Barren, Charles** 1913-    [CA]
*British author*
* Rainham, Thomas

**Barrera, Giulia**
*See*  DeCurtis, Julia A.

**Barrera, Laz**
*See*  Barrera, Lazaro

**Barrera, Lazaro** 1925?-
*Cuban-born horse trainer*
* Barrera, Laz

**[El] Barrero [The Potter]**
*See*  Fernandez, Antonio

**Barret, E. S.** ?-1820    [PA]
*Author*
* Hogg, Cervantes

**Barreto, Benedito Bastos**
1897-1947    [WEC]
*Brazilian cartoonist and journalist*
* Belmonte

**Barrett, Alfred Walter** 1869- ?
[WW, WWL]
*British author*
* Andom, R.

**Barrett, Bird Man**
*See*  Barrett, Mike

**Barrett, C. Lindsay** 1941-    [CW]
*Jamaican author, poet, playwright*
* Eseoghene

**Barrett, Charles Frederick**
1869-1935    [BEW]
*British-born actor*
* Barrett, George

**Barrett, Charles Henry** 1915-    [BE]
*American baseball player*
* Barrett, Red

**Barrett, Dean** 1942-    [CA]
*American author and journalist*
* Char, Yum

**Barrett, Dick**
*See*  Barrett, Tracey Souter

**Barrett, Eaton Stannard**
1785-1820    [PA]
*Author*
* Polypus

**Barrett, Edith**
*See*  Williams, Edith

**Barrett, Elise Barbara Alleyne**
1898-    [THR]
*British actress*
* Craven, Elise

**Barrett, Emma** 1905-    [DAM]
*American singer*
* Sweet Emma
* Sweet Emma the Bell Gal

**Barrett, Francis Joseph** 1913-    [BE]
*American baseball player*
* Barrett, Red

**Barrett, G. J.**
*See*  Barrett, Geoffrey John

**Barrett, Geoffrey John** 1928-
[ESF, SFL]
*British author*
* Barrett, G. J.
* Rickard, Cole
* Wade, Bill

**Barrett, George**
See Barrett, Charles Frederick

**Barrett, George Hooker** 1794-1860
[FFF]
*British-born American actor*
* Gentleman George

**Barrett, Harry B[emister]** 1922-
[CA]
*Canadian author and columnist*
* Bemister, Henry

**Barrett, Hugh Gilchrist** 1917-
[AW]
*British author*
* Bellman, Walter

**Barrett, Jumbo**
See Barrett, Robert Schley

**Barrett, Katharine Ruth Ellis** 20th c.
*Author*
* BA

**Barrett, Kewpie**
See Barrett, Tracey Souter

**Barrett, Lawrence**
See Brannigan, Larry

**Barrett, Liz**
See Baratto, Luisa

**Barrett, Mary**
See Nutting, Mary O.

**Barrett, Max** 20th c. [CA]
*Australian-born author*
* Barrett, Maye

**Barrett, Maye**
See Barrett, Max

**Barrett, Mike** 1943- [BB]
*American basketball player*
* Barrett, Bird Man

**Barrett, Monte**
See Barrett, Montgomery

**Barrett, Montgomery** 1897- [NAA]
*American author*
* Barrett, Monte

**Barrett, Patrick J.** 1887-1959
[CWG]
*American country-western performer*
* Uncle Ezra

**Barrett, Raina**
See Kelly, Pauline Agnes

**Barrett, Red**
See Barrett, Charles Henry

**Barrett, Red**
See Barrett, Francis Joseph

**Barrett, Rice** 20th c. [FI]
*Actress*
* Crosthwaite, Ivy

**Barrett, Robert Schley** 1899- [BE]
*American baseball player*
* Barrett, Jumbo

**Barrett, Roderic** 20th c. [ART]
*British painter*
* R. B.

**Barrett, Rona**
See Burstein, Rona

**Barrett, T. W.** 1851-1935 [BMH]
*British comedian*
* [A] Nobleman's Son

**Barrett, Thomas Augustine**
1864?-1928 [BBD, EMT, PMJ]
*British composer*
* Stuart, Leslie

**Barrett, Tracey Souter** 1906-1966
[BE]
*American baseball player*
* Barrett, Dick
* Barrett, Kewpie
* Oliver, Dick

**Barrett, Walter, Clerk**
See Scoville, Joseph A.

**Barrett, Whispering Bill**
See Barrett, William Joseph

**Barrett, William Henry** 1846-1904
[LC]
*Actor and playwright*
* Barrett, Wilson

**Barrett, William Joseph**
1900-1951 [BE]
*American baseball player*
* Barrett, Whispering Bill

**Barrett, Wilson**
See Barrett, William Henry

**Barretto, Larry** 1890- [WWL]
*American author*
* Brevoort, Laurence

**Barretton, Grandall**
See Garrett, [Gordon] Randall
[Philip David]

**Barrheus**
See Cellarius, Martin

**Barrie, Amanda**
See Broadbent, Amanda

**Barrie, J. M.**
See Barrie, [Sir] James Matthew

**Barrie, [Sir] James Matthew**
1860-1937 [LC, YAB]
*Scottish author*
* Barrie, J. M.
* Ogilvy, Gavin

**Barrie, Jane**
See Savage, Mildred [Spitz]

**Barrie, Jane**
See Woodford, [Irene] Cecile

**Barrie, Mona**
See Smith, Mona

**Barrie, S.** 20th c. [MBF]
*British author*
* Richards, Frank [house
   pseudonym]

**Barrie, Wendy**
See Jenkins, Wendy

**Barrington, E.**
See Beck, Eliza Louisa Moresby

**Barrington, F. Clinton**
See Lewis, Julius Warren

**Barrington, George**
See Waldron, George

**Barrington, H. W.**
See Brannon, William T.

**Barrington, Herbert**
See Hollingsworth, Herbert
Barrington

**Barrington, Howard** 1906- [WW]
*Author*
* Stone, Simon

**Barrington, Maurice**
See Brogan, [Sir] Denis William

**Barrington, Michael** [joint
pseudonym with Michael John
Moorcock]
See Bayley, Barrington J[ohn]

**Barrington, Michael** [joint
pseudonym with Barrington J(ohn)
Bayley]
See Moorcock, Michael John

**Barrington, Nicholas**
See Whittington-Egan, Richard

**Barrington, P. V.**
See Barling, Muriel Vere Mant

**Barrington, Pamela**
See Barling, Muriel Vere Mant

**Barrington, Rutland**
See Fleet, George Rutland

**Barrios, Francisco Javier** 1953-
[BE]
*Mexican-born baseball player*
* Jimenez, Francisco Javier

**Barriscale, Bessie**
See Scale, Elizabeth Barry

**[A] Barrister**
See Stephen, [Sir] James
Fitzjames

**Barrois, Raymond N.** 1904-
[EJ, WWJ]
*American jazz musician*
* Burke, Raymond N.

**Barrol, Grady**
See Bograd, Larry

**Barron, A. Elton**
See Burrage, Edwin Harcourt

**Barron, Ann Forman** 20th c. [CA]
*American author*
* Erwin, Annabel

**Barron, Blue**
See Freedlin, Harry

**Barron, Charles**
See Brown, Charles

**Barron, David Irenus** 1900- [BE]
*American baseball player*
* Barron, Red

**Barron, Ed**
See Bernhardt, Clyde Edric Barron

**Barron, Oswald** 1868-1939 [LC]
*British author*
* [The] Londoner

**Barron, Red**
See Barron, David Irenus

**Barron, Rusty**
See Hevelin, James

**Barron, William Gilbert** 1894-1971
[BEW]
*American actor, director, writer*
* Gilbert, Billy

**Barrone, Carmine** 20th c. [SG]
*Boxer*
* Barone, Nick

**Barros, Joao de** 1496-1570
[DNNF, HN, SN]
*Portuguese historian*
* [The] Livy of Portugal
* [The] Portuguese Livy

**Barrow, Clyde** 1909-1934 [BLB]
*American murderer and robber*
* [The] Texas Rattlesnake

**Barrow, Edward Grant** 1868-1953
[BE, DGS]
*American baseball manager and
executive*
* Cousin Ed
* Cousin Egbert
* [The] Yankee Empire Builder

**Barrow, Fanny** [PA]
*Author*
* Aunt Fanny

**Barrow, Isaac** 1630-1677
[DNNS, HN, RH]
*British theologian, scholar,
mathematician*
* [The] Unfair Preacher

**Barrow, Joe**
See Arrowsmith, Robert

**Barrow, Joseph Louis** 1914-1981
[BX, IPA, OCS]
*American boxer*
* [The] Brown Bomber
* Louis, Joe

**Barrow, Pamela**
See Howarth, Pamela

**Barrow, [Rev.] S.**
See Phillips, [Sir] Richard

**Barrow, William**
See Fuller, Hoyt [William]

**Barrowcliffe, A. J.**
See Mott, Alfred Julius

**Barrows, Catherine Isabel**
1845-1913 [FFF]
*American editor and author*
* Shayback, Mrs.

**Barrows, Cuke**
See Barrows, Roland

**Barrows, [Ruth] Marjorie** 20th c.
[CAP, NAA]
*American author and editor*
* Alden, Jack
* Ames, Noel
* Barrows, R. M.
* Boojum
* Dixon, Ruth
* Graham, Hugh
* Psycho Ann

**Barrows, P. S.** 20th c. [SFL]
*Author*
* Sarbrow, Cepre

**Barrows, R. M.**
See Barrows, [Ruth] Marjorie

**Barrows, Roland** 1883-1955 [BE]
*American baseball player*
* Barrows, Cuke

**Barrows, Samuel June** 1845-1909
[FFF]
*American clergyman and author*
* Shayback, Mr.

**Barruel, Augustin** 1741-1820 [PA]
*Author*
* [The] Abbe

**Barry, Alice Montgomery**
See Norton, Alice Whitson

**Barry, Ann**
See Byers, Amy Irene

**Barry, B. X.**
See Giles, R. A.

**Barry, Charles**
See Bryson, Charles

**Barry, Christine**
See Underwood, Grace

**Barry, Don**
See De Acosta, Donald Barry

**Barry, Ed[ward]** 20th c.   [BE]
*American baseball player*
* Barry, Jumbo

**Barry, Eleanor**
See Chesley, Mrs. J. G.

**Barry, Gene**
See Klass, Eugene

**Barry, Georgetta** 1915-   [FC, ITA]
*French-born actress*
* King, Andrea

**Barry, Girald** 1146-1224   [PA]
*Author*
* Canderensis, Giraldus

**Barry, Helen**
See Holman, Mrs. H. S.

**Barry, J. A.**
See Barry, John Arthur

**Barry, Jocelyn**
See Bowden, Jean

**Barry, Joe**
See Barios, Joe

**Barry, Joe**
See Lake, Joe Barry

**Barry, John** 1896-1968   [BB]
*American basketball player*
* Barry, Pete

**Barry, John Arthur** 1850-1911
[HFF]
*British-born author*
* Barry, J. A.

**Barry, John C.** 1876-1936
[AS, BE]
*American baseball player*
* Barry, Shad

**Barry, Jumbo**
See Barry, Ed[ward]

**Barry, Justin** 1892-1950   [BB]
*American basketball player*
* Barry, Sam

**Barry, Kevin**
See Laffan, Kevin [Barry]

**Barry, Len**
See Borisoff, Leonard

**Barry, Mrs. Shiel**   [FFF]
*Entertainer*
* Stewart, Geraldine

**Barry, Nancy Rosamond**
See Corbett, Arleigh Jean

**Barry, Patrick** 1912-
[FC, HT, ITA]
*American actor*
* Sullivan, Barry

**Barry, Pete**
See Barry, John

**Barry, Ray**
See Hughes, Den[n]is [Talbot]

**Barry, Sam**
See Barry, Justin

**Barry, Shad**
See Barry, John C.

**Barry, Spranger**
See Kauffmann, Stanley

**Barry, Spranger** 1719-1777
[DEP, HN, RH]
*Irish actor*
* [The] Irish Roscius
* [The] Silver Tongued

**Barry, Tom**
See Donahue, Hal

**Barrymore, Al** 1923-   [EJ]
*Antiguan-born jazz musician*
* Dawud, Talib Ahmad

**Barrymore, Diana**
See Blythe, Diana Blanche
Barrymore

**Barrymore, Ethel**
See Blythe, Ethel

**Barrymore, Georgiana Emma**
1856-1893   [FFF]
*American actress*
* Drew, Georgie

**Barrymore, John**
See Blythe, John

**Barrymore, Lionel**
See Blythe, Lionel

**Barrymore, Maurice**
See Blythe, Herbert

**Barsha, John**
See Barshofsky, Abraham

**Barshofsky, Abraham** 1900-   [EJS]
*Russian-born American football player*
* Barsha, John

**Barshofsky, Philip**
See Kaplan, M. M.

**Barstow, Emma Magdalena Rosalina Marie Josepha Barbara** 1865-1947
[WWS]
*Hungarian-born author*
* Orczy, Baroness

**Barstow, Norah Lee Haymond Bradley** 1898-1941   [ASC]
*American composer*
* Lee, Norah

**Barstow, Paul**
See DeLucia, Felice

**Bart [or Barth?], Jean** 1650?-1702
[DNNS, FFF, SN]
*French naval commander*
* [The] French Devil

**Bart, Lionel**
See Begleiter, Lionel

**Bartas, Seigneur de**
See De Salluste [or Salustius?],
Guillaume

**Bartek, E[dward] J[ohn]**
See Bartosiewicz, Edward John

**Bartel, Philip Jacques**
See Kaplan, M. M.

**Bartell, Richard William** 1907-
[BE, DGS, PB]
*American baseball player*
* Bartell, Rowdy

**Bartell, Richard William**
(Continued)
* Bartell, Rowdy Richard

**Bartell, Rowdy**
See Bartell, Richard William

**Bartell, Rowdy Richard**
See Bartell, Richard William

**Barter, W. G. T.**   [PA]
*Author*
* Cour, T. E.

**Bartet, Jeanne Julia**
See Regnault, Jeanne Julia

**Barteville, Alexis**
See De Maune, Edward

**Bartfield, Jacob** 1892-   [BX, EJS]
*Austrian-born boxer*
* Bartfield, Soldier

**Bartfield, Soldier**
See Bartfield, Jacob

**Barth, Alan** 1906?-1979
*American journalist and author*
* [The] Liberal Conscience of
Washington

**Barth, Arthur J.** ?-1956   [BBH]
*American skiing organization founder*
* Barth, Red

**Barth, Cecil**
See Walenn, Cecil

**Barth, Charles P.** 1895-   [CA]
*American journalist*
* Buffalo Chuck

**Barth, Edna** 1914-   [CA]
*American author*
* Weiss, Edna

**Barth, Lois**
See Freihofer, Lois Diane

**Barth, Red**
See Barth, Arthur J.

**Barthelmes, [Albert] Wes[ley, Jr.]**
1922-1976   [B10, CA]
*American journalist*
* Sisyphus

**Bartholemew, Freddie**
See Llewellyn, Frederick

**Bartholomew, Annie E.** 1807-1862
[FFF, PA]
*Author*
* Fagerman

**Bartholomew, Ed[ward Ellsworth]**
1914-   [CA]
*American author*
* Rascoe, Jesse Ed

**Bartholomew, [John] Eric** 1926-
[BMH, FC]
*British entertainer*
* Morecambe, Eric

**Bartholomew, Jean**
See Beatty, Patricia

**Bartholomew, John** 1888-1942
[BEW, BMH]
*British comedian*
* Barty, Jack
* [The] Burly Burlesquer

**Bartier, Pierre** 1945-   [CA]
*Belgian author, cartoonist, film critic*
* Pan, Peter

**Bartimeus**
See Da Costa Ricci, Lewis
Anselmo

**Bartine, Jennie**
See David, Mrs. Frank

**Bartkowicz, Christine** 1954-
*American tennis player*
* Bartkowicz, Plums

**Bartkowicz, Jane** 1949-   [OET]
*American tennis player*
* Bartkowicz, Peaches

**Bartkowicz, Peaches**
See Bartkowicz, Jane

**Bartkowicz, Plums**
See Bartkowicz, Christine

**Bartle, L. E.** 20th c.   [WGT]
*Author*
* Lawrence, Richard
* Richardson, Francis [joint
pseudonym with Frank Parnell]

**Bartlemy**
See Windsor, Ernest Victor

**Bartlett, Alice Elinor Bowen**
1848-1920   [WGT]
*Author*
* Arnold, Birch

**Bartlett, David**
See Mason, Madeline

**Bartlett, David W.**   [FFF]
*American writer*
* Van

**Bartlett, Elise**
See Porter, Elise

**Bartlett, Elsa Jaffe** 1935-   [CA]
*American educator and author*
* Jaffe, Elsa

**Bartlett, Frederick Orin** 1876- ?
[NAA]
*American author*
* Carleton, William
* [The] Old Dog

**Bartlett, J.**   [FFF]
*Author*
* Maitland

**Bartlett, J. R.**
See Bartlett, June Rosalyn

**Bartlett, June Rosalyn** 1947-
[ART]
*British artist*
* Bartlett, J. R.

**Bartlett, Marie [Swan]** 1918-   [CA]
*British author*
* Lee, Rowena
* Linden, Sara
* Rift, Valerie
* Swan, Marie

**Bartlett, Nancy**
See Strong, Charles Stanley

**Bartlett, Philip A.** [house
pseudonym] [Stratemeyer
Syndicate]
See Stratemeyer, Edward L.

**Bartlett, Stephen** 20th c.   [WWL]
*British author*
* Slade, Gurney

**Bartlett, Sy**
See Baraniev, Sacha

**Bartlett, Vernon** 1894-
[CA, LAO, WD]
*British author*
* Oldfeld, Peter [joint pseudonym with P. Jacobsson]

**Bartlett-Merriman, Horace** 1914-
[ART]
*British industrial designer*
* H. B. M.

**Bartling, Ada**
*See* Levick, Mrs. Gustavus

**Bartok, Eva**
*See* Sjoeke, Eva

**Bartoli** [or Bartolus] 1312?-1356?
[HN]
*Italian jurist*
* [The] Coryphaeus of the Interpreters of Law
* [The] Star and Luminary of Law and Latern of Equity

**Bartoli, Pietro Santi** 1635?-1700
[WBD]
*Italian painter and engraver*
* [Il] Perugino

**Bartolome, Johan**
*See* Jongh, Edward A. de

**Bartolommeo, [Fra]**
*See* Di Pagolo del Fattorino, Bartolommeo

**Barton, Alix Gres** 20th c. [WFA]
*French fashion designer*
* Gres, Mme.

**Barton, Bernard** 1784-1849
[DEL, WBD]
*British poet*
* [The] Quaker Poet

**Barton, Dora**
*See* Brockbank, Dora

**Barton, Elizabeth** 1506?-1534
[DNNS, FFF, SN]
*British religious leader*
* [The] Holy Maid of Kent
* [The] Nun of Kent

**Barton, Erle**
*See* Fanthorpe, R[obert] Lionel

**Barton, [Dr.] Eustace Robert** 1854-
? [CC, EMD]
*Author*
* Eustace, Robert
* Rawlins, E[ustace]

**Barton, George** 1866-1940 [CAT]
*American author and columnist*
* [The] Rambler

**Barton, J. A. G.**
*See* Dutt, Shosher Chunder

**Barton, James Levi** 1855- ? [NAA]
*American writer*
* Ashton, Howard

**Barton, Lee**
*See* Fanthorpe, R[obert] Lionel

**Barton, May Hollis** [house pseudonym] [Stratemeyer Syndicate]
*See* Adams, Harriet S[tratemeyer]

**Barton, May Hollis** [house pseudonym] [Stratemeyer Syndicate]
*See* Stratemeyer, Edward L.

**Barton, Mrs. Charles** [FFF]
*Entertainer*
* Forrest, Gail

**Barton, S. W.**
*See* Whaley, Barton Stewart

**Barton, Tippy**
*See* White, Josh[ua Daniel]

**Bartos, Eloise C[olleen]** 1928- [CA]
*American sociologist and author*
* Snyder, Eloise C[olleen]

**Bartosiewicz, Edward John** 1921-
[CA]
*American author*
* Bartek, E[dward] J[ohn]

**Barty, Jack**
*See* Bartholomew, John

**Bartz, Patricia McBride** 1921-
[CA]
*Australian-born geographer and author*
* McBride, Patricia

**Baruch, Bernard Mannes**
1870-1965 [BDW]
*American businessman and government adviser*
* Elder Statesman Number One

**Baruch, Hugo** 1907- [WGT]
*British author*
* Bilbo, Jack

**Baruch, Loeb** 1786-1837 [WBD]
*German author*
* Boerne, Ludwig

**Baruch de la Pardo, Rosa Lily Odette**
1912- [FCW]
*Dutch-born American singer*
* Marais, Miranda

**Baryshnikov, Mikhail** 1948?-
*Russian-born ballet dancer*
* Baryshnikov, Misha

**Baryshnikov, Misha**
*See* Baryshnikov, Mikhail

**Barzilauskas, Barzo**
*See* Barzilauskas, Carl

**Barzilauskas, Brontosaurus**
*See* Barzilauskas, Carl

**Barzilauskas, Carl** 20th c. [SMG]
*American football player*
* Barzilauskas, Barzo
* Barzilauskas, Brontosaurus

**Bas, Rutger**
*See* Rutgers van der Loeff, An[na] Basenau

**Basauri Paguaga, Pedro** 1893-
[GS]
*Spanish bullfighter*
* Pedrucho [Big Pedro]

**Bascom, David** 1912- [CA]
*American author*
* Poltroon, Milford

**Bascomb, Dud**
*See* Bascomb, Wilbur Odell

**Bascomb, Wilbur Odell** 1916-1972
[B10, PMJ, WWJ]
*American jazz musician*
* Bascomb, Dud

**Base, A. H.** 20th c. [MBF]
*British author*
* Arthur, Harry
* Arthurs, Harry

**[The] Base Burglar**
*See* Brock, Lou[is Clark]

**Baseball's Paul Bunyan**
*See* Hartung, Clinton Clarence

**Basgall, Monty**
*See* Basgall, Romanus

**Basgall, Romanus** 1923- [SMG]
*American baseball coach*
* Basgall, Monty

**Bashevis, Isaac**
*See* Singer, Isaac Bashevis

**Bashford, H. H.**
*See* Bashford, [Sir] Henry Howarth

**Bashford, [Sir] Henry Howarth**
1880-1961 [LC]
*British physician and author*
* Bashford, H. H.

**Bashful Brother Oswald**
*See* Kirby, Beecher

**[The] Bashful Limit**
*See* Pleasants, Jack

**Bashibazouk**
*See* Harding, William

**Bashiri, Chungulia Kwakwa**
*See* Hill, Roy Leeuwenhoek Aloysius

**Basho**
*See* Matsuo Munefusa

**Basie, Count**
*See* Basie, William

**Basie, William** 1904?-
[ASC, NP, WWJ]
*American jazz musician*
* Basie, Count
* [The] Holy Main

**Basil** [or Basilius] 330?- 379?
[FFF, SN, WBD]
*Saint*
* [The] Great

**Basil, Theodore**
*See* Becon, Thomas

**Basil I** [or Basilius] 812?- 886
[DNNS, WBD]
*Byzantine emperor*
* [The] Macedonian

**Basil II** 958?-1025 [DNNS, WBD]
*Byzantine emperor*
* [The] Slayer of the Bulgarians [Bulgaroctonus]

**Basil II** [or Vasili] 1415-1462
[DNNS, WBD]
*Grand Prince of Moscow*
* [The] Blind
* Temny

**Basile, Gloria Vitanza** 1929- [CA]
*American author and composer*
* Morgan, McKayla
* Morgan, Michaela

**Basile, Mathieu** 1845-1922 [WBD]
*French Socialist leader*
* Guesde, Jules

**Basilea, [Mother]**
*See* Schlink, Klara

**Basilio, Carmen**
*See* Basilio, Italiano

**Basilio, Italiano** 1927- [WBC]
*American boxer*
* Basilio, Carmen

**Basinski, Edwin Frank** [Eddie]
1922- [BE]
*American baseball player*
* Basinski, Fiddler

**Basinski, Fiddler**
*See* Basinski, Edwin Frank [Eddie]

**Baskerville, John** 1706-1775 [SN]
*British printer and type-founder*
* [The] Jenson of His Day

**[The] Basket Maker**
*See* Miller, Thomas

**Basketball, Mr.**
*See* Cousy, Robert J. [Bob]

**Basketball, Mr.**
*See* Holman, Nat

**Basketball, Mr.**
*See* Hoyt, George H.

**Basketball, Mr.**
*See* Russell, William Felton [Bill]

**Baskette, Big Jim**
*See* Baskette, James Blaine [Jim]

**Baskette, James Blaine** [Jim]
1887-1942 [BE]
*American baseball player*
* Baskette, Big Jim

**Baskin, Marjorie Kinnan Rawlings**
1896-1953 [TBJ]
*American author*
* Rawlings, Marjorie Kinnan

**Basko, Maurice P. Duviella** 1921-
[ART]
*French painter*
* Duviella

**Basloe, Frank J.**
*See* Breslau, Frank J.

**Bason, Fred[erick Thomas]**
1907-1973 [CA]
*British author, bookseller, lecturer*
* [The] Gallerite

**[The] Basque Woodchopper**
*See* Uzcudun, Paolino

**Basquette, Lina**
*See* Belcher, Lina

**Bass, Charlotta A.** 1890- [IBW]
*American politician and journalist*
* [The] Dean of California Journalists

**Bass, Clara May** 1910- [AW, WD]
*British poet*
* Overy, Claire May

**Bass, Doc**
*See* Bass, William C.

**Bass John**
*See* Spreull, John

**Bass, Josef** 1852- ? [LAO]
*Moravian-born educator and author*
* Job

**Bass, Kingsley B., Jr.**
*See* Bullins, Ed

**Bass, Lee Oddis, III** 1943- [EJ7]
*American jazz musician*
* Bass, Mickey

**Bass, Mickey**
*See* Bass, Lee Oddis, III

**Bass, Oak**
See Bass, Randy William

**Bass, Randy William** 1954- [SMG]
*American baseball player*
* Bass, Oak

**Bass, Rochelle** 1936- [TR]
*American playwright*
* Owens, Rochelle

**Bass, T. J.**
See Bassler, Thomas Joseph

**Bass, William C.** 20th c. [BE]
*American baseball player*
* Bass, Doc

**Bassani, Giorgio** 1916- [CA]
*Italian author and poet*
* Marchi, Giacomo

**Bassano, Jacopo [or Giacomo] da**
See Ponte, Jacopo [or Giacomo] da

**Basselin, Olivier** 15th c.
[FFF, RH, SN]
*French songwriter*
* [The] Anacreon of His Day
* [The] Father of the Vaudeville

**Basserman, Else**
See Schiff, Else

**Bassermann, Lujo**
See Schreiber, Hermann O. L.

**Basset, Arthur Ward**
See Bull, Albert E.

**Bassett, E. B.** 19th c. [PA]
*Author*
* Beta

**Bassett, Flora Marjorie**
1890?-1980 [CA]
*Australian author*
* wbassett, Marnie

**Bassett, Jack**
See Rowland, D[onald] S[ydney]

**Bassett, John Keith**
See Keating, Lawrence A.

**Bassett, Lloyd** 20th c. [OBW]
*American baseball player*
* Bassett, Pepper

**Bassett, Pepper**
See Bassett, Lloyd

**Bassett, Ronald Leslie** 1924- [WD]
*British author*
* Clive, William

**Bassett, William B. K.** 1908-
[CAP]
*American poet*
* Darien, Peter

**Bassevi, Giacomo** 18th c. [SN]
*Musician*
* Cervetto

**Bassey, Hogan**
See Asuque, Okon Bassey

**Bassey, Kid**
See Asuque, Okon Bassey

**Basshe, Emanuel Jo** 1900-1939
[TC]
*Russian-born American playwright*
* Basshe, Emjo

**Basshe, Emjo**
See Basshe, Emanuel Jo

**Bassianus** 188- 217
[FFF, HN, WBD]
*Roman emperor*
* Antoninus, Marcus Aurelius
* Caracalla
* [The] Ferocious Beast of Ausonia
* Oedipus

**Bassianus, Alexianus** 208?- 235
[WBD]
*Roman emperor*
* Alexander Severus, Marcus
 Aurelius

**Bassler, Thomas Joseph** 1932-
[ESF, SFL, WGT]
*American author*
* Bass, T. J.

**Bassol, John** ?-1347
[FFF, HN, SN]
*Scottish philosopher*
* Methodicus, Doctor
* [The] Most Methodical Doctor
* Ordinatissimus, Doctor

**[The] Bastard**
See John I [or Joao]

**[The] Bastard**
See William I

**[The] Bastard from the Bush**
See Robinson, Roland Edward

**Bastard, Lucien** 1911- [B10, EWL]
*French poet and author*
* Estang, Luc

**[The] Bastard of Orleans**
See Dunois, Jean

**[La] Bastardina**
See Agujari, Lucrezia

**Baste**
See Grange, Pierre Eugene

**Bastide, Jenny** 1792- ? [PA]
*Author*
* Dufourquet

**Bastien, Aldege** 1920- [CEI, FHE]
*Canadian-born hockey player*
* Bastien, Baz

**Bastien, Baz**
See Bastien, Aldege

**Bastien, Marie** 20th c. [THR]
*French actress*
* Lender, Marcelle

**Basu, Kanu**
See Basu, Shovendu

**Basu, Shovendu** 1924- [GA]
*Indian graphic artist*
* Basu, Kanu

**[The] Bat**
See Battalino, Christopher

**Bat 'em Bob**
See Kinney, Robert

**Bat, Mr.**
See Batiste, Alvin

**Bat the Humming-Bird**
See Robinson, James

**Bat the Hummingbird**
See Davenport, Charles [Edward]

**Bataille, Georges** 1887-1962 [CA]
*French author and poet*
* Angelique, Pierre
* Auch, Lord

**[Des] Batailles [Of Battles]**
See Martin, Jean Baptiste

**[El] Batallador**
See Alfonso I [or Alphonso]

**Batard d'Orleans**
See Dunois, Jean

**[The] Batavian Buffoon**
See Gerhards, Gerhard [or Geert]

**Batbedat, Jean** 1926- [CA]
*French author*
* Larneuil, Michel

**Batch, Emil Henry** 1880- ? [BE]
*American baseball player*
* Batch, Heinie

**Batch, Heinie**
See Batch, Emil Henry

**Batchelder, Joseph Edmund [Joe]**
1898- [BE]
*American baseball player*
* Batchelder, Win

**Batchelder, Win**
See Batchelder, Joseph Edmund
[Joe]

**Batchelor, Bernard Philip** 1924-
[ART]
*British painter*
* B. P. B.

**Batchelor, Paula**
See Lansberry, Paula Vivien

**Batchelor, Richard A. C.** 20th c.
[MBF]
*British author*
* Henton, Collett
* Mayne, Arthur

**Bate, Lily**
See Atkinson, Mrs. Charles

**Bate, Parson**
See Dudley, [Sir] Henry Bate

**Bateman, Chick**
See Bateman, John Alvin

**Bateman, John Alvin** 1942- [PB]
*American baseball player*
* Bateman, Chick

**Bateman, Leah**
See Hunter, Leah

**Bateman, Virginia F.** 1853-1940
[FFF]
*British actress*
* Francis, Virginia

**Baten, Charles Edwin** 1890- [NAA]
*American author and educator*
* Baen, Chadwyn

**Bates, Barbara S[nedeker]** 1919-
[CA, SAT]
*American author*
* Cuyler, Stephen
* Roberts, Jim

**Bates, Bud**
See Bates, Hubert Edgar

**Bates, Clayton** 1907?- [B10]
*American dancer*
* Bates, Peg-Leg

**Bates, Clive** 1933- [CA]
*British author*
* Irving, Clive

**Bates, Fanny D.** [PA]
*Author*
* Beulah

**Bates, Florence**
See Rabe, Florence

**Bates, H. E.**
See Bates, Herbert Ernest

**Bates, Harriet L. Vose** [FFF]
*American writer*
* Putnam, Eleanor

**Bates, Harry Arthur** 1900-
[ESF, WGT, WW]
*American author and editor*
* Arthur, Harry
* Gilmore, Anthony [joint
 pseudonym with Desmond W.
 Hall]
* Holmes, A. R.
* Quien Sabe?
* Winter, H. G. [joint pseudonym
 with Desmond W. Hall]

**Bates, Helen L. Z.**
See Yakobson, Helen B[ates]

**Bates, Herbert Ernest** 1905-1974
[CA, LC]
*British author*
* Bates, H. E.
* Flying Officer X
* Gawsworth, John

**Bates, Hubert Edgar** 1912- [BE]
*American baseball player*
* Bates, Bud

**Bates, L. C.**
See Bates, Lucius Christopher

**Bates, [Deacon] L. J.**
See Jefferson, Lemon

**Bates, L. J.** [FFF]
*American journalist*
* Bates, President

**Bates, Lucius Christopher**
1901?-1980
*American civil rights activist and
publisher*
* Bates, L. C.

**Bates, Lulu**
See Ries, Lulu

**Bates, Mickey** 20th c. [IBW]
*American football player*
* Inside, Mr.
* [The] Touchdown Twin

**Bates, Mrs. M. V.** [PA]
*Author*
* Holmes, Margaret

**Bates, Norman**
See Sellers, Connie Leslie, Jr.

**Bates, Otha Ellas** 1928-
[BWW, NBB]
*American singer*
* [The] Black Gladiator
* Diddley, Bo
* 500 Per Cent More Man
* McDaniel, Ellas

**Bates, Peg-Leg**
See Bates, Clayton

**Bates, President**
See Bates, L. J.

**Bates, Thomas** 19th c. [PA]
*Author*
* T. B.

**Bates, William** 1625-1699
[DNNF, DEL, RH]
*Clergyman*
* [The] Silver Tongued

**Bateson, F. W.**
*See* Bateson, Frederick Wilse

**Bateson, Frederick Wilse** 1901-
[MBL]
*British author*
* Bateson, F. W.

**Bath, Albert J.** 1879?-1964 [BEW]
*Theatrical performer*
* Bath, Pop

**Bath, Oliver**
*See* Giffard, Hardinge Goulburn

**Bath, Pop**
*See* Bath, Albert J.

**[The] Bath Roscius**
*See* Henderson, John

**Bather, Mrs. L. E. B.** [FFF]
*Author*
* Aunt Lucy

**Batherman, Muriel**
*See* Sheldon, Muriel

**[The] Bathhouse**
*See* Coughlin, John

**Bathhouse John**
*See* Coughlin, John

**Bathiat, Arlette-Leonie** 1898-
[BDF, FC, WEF]
*French actress*
* Arletty

**[The] Bathing Belle on the Bicycle**
*See* Selbini, Lalla

**Bathurst, Charles** [PA]
*Author*
* C. B.

**Bathurst, Sheila**
*See* Sullivan, Sheila

**Batiste, Alvin** 20th c. [IBW]
*American educator, author,
bandleader*
* Bat, Mr.

**Batley, Ernest G.**
*See* Batley, Ethyle

**Batley, Ethyle** 1879-1917 [F1]
*Actor*
* Batley, Ernest G.

**Baton, Rene** 1879-1940 [BBD]
*French conductor*
* Rhene Baton

**Batstein, William**
*See* Ebel, Henry

**Battaglia, Sam** 1908- [BLB]
*American underworld figure*
* Battaglia, Teets

**Battaglia, Teets**
*See* Battaglia, Sam

**[El] Battalador [The Battler]**
*See* Hill, Philip Toll

**Battalino, Battling**
*See* Battalino, Christopher

**Battalino, Christopher** 1908-
[BX, RBE, WBC]
*Russian-born American boxer*
* [The] Bat
* Battalino, Battling

**Battay, Emily Verdery** [PA]
*Author*
* Verdery, Emily

**Battcock, Marshall King** 1920-
[IAW]
*British playwright*
* Marshall, Henry

**Battelle, Adah Fairbanks**
*See* Everett, Laura Bell

**Battelle, Kenneth** 20th c. [WFA]
*American hairstylist*
* Kenneth

**Batten, Joyce Mortimer**
*See* Mankowska, Joyce Kells
Batten

**Batters, Joe**
*See* Accardo, Antonio Leonardo

**Battersby, William J[ohn]**
1904-1976 [CA]
*British-born educator and author*
* Clair Stanislaus, [Brother]

**Battier, Alcibiade Fleury**
1841-1883 [CW]
*Haitian poet*
* Fleury-Battier, Alcibiade

**Battiscombe, E[sther] Georgina
[Harwood]** 1905- [AW, CAP]
*British author*
* Harwood, Gina

**Battistella, Annabella** 1936?- [B10]
*Argentinian entertainer involved in
U.S. political scandal*
* [The] Argentine Firecracker
* Foxe, Fanne

**Battisti, Eugenio** 1924- [CA]
*Italian-born art historian and author*
* Rinaldini, Angiolo

**Battistini, Mattia** 1856-1928 [MS]
*Italian opera singer*
* [The] Glory of Italy
* [The] King of Baritones

**[The] Battlin' Shoeshine Boy**
*See* Walker, Sidney

**Battling Beau Jack**
*See* Walker, Sidney

**Battling Bella Abzug**
*See* Abzug, Bella Savitzky

**Batton, Clyde** 20th c. [RO1]
*American singer*
* Skip

**Batty, Joe**
*See* Accardo, Antonio Leonardo

**Battye, Gladys** 1915- [AW]
*British author*
* Lynn, Margaret

**Bauchart**
*See* Camus, Albert

**Baudouin, Charles Pierre**
*See* Peguy, Charles Pierre

**Baudovy, Michel-Aime** 1909-
[IAW]
*French author*
* Vernieres, Francois

**Bauer, Britta** 1944- [WFA]
*German-born fashion model and
designer*
* Britta

**Bauer, Carl Otto** 20th c. [BBH]
*German-born swimming and water
polo coach*
* [The] Father of Age-Group
Swimming

**Bauer, Erwin A.** 1919- [CA]
*American author*
* Bourbon, Ken
* Franklin, Nat
* Hardin, Tom
* North, Charles W.
* Peters, Barney

**Bauer, Franz Ferdinand** 1928- [OP]
*Austrian conductor*
* Bauer-Theussl, Franz Ferdinand

**Bauer, Georg** 1494-1555 [WBD]
*German mineralogist*
* Agricola, Georgius

**Bauer, Herbert** 1884-1949 [WBD]
*Hungarian journalist and poet*
* Balazs, Bela

**Bauer, Klara** 1836-1876 [PA]
*Author*
* Detlef, Karl

**Bauer, Lou**
*See* Bierbauer, Louis W.

**Bauer-Theussl, Franz Ferdinand**
*See* Bauer, Franz Ferdinand

**Bauersfeld, Marjorie** 1890-1974
[SC]
*American actress*
* Bauersfeld, Mirandy

**Bauersfeld, Mirandy**
*See* Bauersfeld, Marjorie

**Baugh, Samuel A.** 1914- [FB]
*American football player*
* Baugh, Slingin' Sammy

**Baugh, Slingin' Sammy**
*See* Baugh, Samuel A.

**Baughan, Edward Algernon** 1865-
? [LAO]
*British journalist*
* E. A. B.

**Baujan, Harry Clifford** 20th c.
[BBH]
*American football coach and
collegiate athletic director*
* [The] Blond Beast

**Baukhage, H. R.**
*See* Baukhage, Hilmar Robert

**Baukhage, Hilmar Robert**
*Newscaster*
* Baukhage, H. R.

**Baulat, Paul**
*See* Valmain, Frederic

**Bauld Willie**
*See* Howard, [Lord] William

**Bauler, Mathius** 20th c. [BLB]
*American politician*
* Bauler, Paddy

**Bauler, Paddy**
*See* Bauler, Mathius

**Baulsy, Banky Vilma** 1903-
*Hungarian-born actress*
* Banky, Vilma
* [The] Hungarian Rhapsody
* Lonchit [or Loncit], Vilma?

**Baum, Allen**
*See* Bunn, Alden

**Baum, Jacob Kestem** 1893- [BEW]
*American actor*
* Waldron, Jack

**Baum, L[yman] Frank** 1856-1919
[TBJ, TC, TCC]
*American author*
* Akers, Floyd
* Bancroft, Laura
* Baum, Louis F.
* Brooks, George
* Cook, John Estes
* Fitzgerald, [Captain] Hugh
* Metcalf, Suzanne
* Staunton, Schuyler
* Van Dyne, Edith

**Baum, Loren**
*See* Hintz, Loren E.

**Baum, Louis F.**
*See* Baum, L[yman] Frank

**Baum, Robert** 1913- [CA]
*German-born American author*
* Jungk, Robert

**Bauman, Bowser**
*See* Bauman, John

**Bauman, John** 1947- [RO2]
*American singer*
* Bauman, Bowser

**Baumann, Amy [Brown] Beeching**
1922- [CA, SAT]
*British author*
* Barbary, James [joint pseudonym
with Jack Beeching]
* Brown, Alexis

**Baumann, Charles John** 1885-1969
[BE]
*American baseball player*
* Baumann, Paddy

**Baumann, Frank Matt** 1933- [BE]
*American baseball player*
* [The] Beau

**Baumann, Paddy**
*See* Baumann, Charles John

**Baumbach, Rudolf** 1840-1905
[WBD]
*German poet*
* Bach, Paul

**Baume Le Blanc, Francoise Louise de
la** 1644-1710 [HN]
*Mistress of King Louis XIV*
* La Valliere, Duchesse de
* Soeur Louise de la Misericorde

**Baumfree, Betsy** 18th c. [IBW]
*Mother of American abolitionist,
Sojourner Truth*
* Mau-Mau Bett

**Baumgardtner, Claude Chalmers**
1883-1942 [IA]
*American columnist and songwriter*
* Coxie

**Baumgarner, James** 1928-
[FC, HT, SW]
*American actor*
* Garner, James

**Baumgartner, Stan**
*See* Baumgartner, Stanwood
Fulton

**Baumgartner, Stanwood Fulton**
1894-1955 [BE]
*American baseball player*
* Baumgartner, Stan

**Baumrin, Bernard H[erbert]** 1934-
[CA]
*American educator and author*
* Baumrin, Stefan
* Bernard, Stefan

**Baumrin, Stefan**
*See* Baumrin, Bernard H[erbert]

**Baun, Kit, Mariner**
*See* Novello, Mary

**Bausch, James** 1906-　　[TF]
*American track and field athlete*
* Bausch, Jarring Jim

**Bausch, Jarring Jim**
*See* Bausch, James

**Bauta, Ed**
*See* Bauta, Eduardo Galvez

**Bauta, Eduardo Galvez** 1935-　　[BE]
*Cuban-born baseball player*
* Bauta, Ed

**Bava, Mario** 1914-　　[FDG]
*Italian director*
* Old, John M.

**[The] Bavarian**
*See* Louis IV

**Bavasi, Buzzie**
*See* Bavasi, Emil J.

**Bavasi, Emil J.** 1915-　　[PB, SMG]
*American baseball executive*
* Bavasi, Buzzie

**Bavin, John**　　[PA]
*Author*
* [A] Traveler

**Bawden, Nina**
*See* Kark, Nina Mary [Mabey]

**Bawn, Harry**
*See* Beales, Harry

**Bawn, Mary**
*See* Wright, Mary Pamela
[Godwin]

**Bax**
*See* Baxter, Gordon F[rancis], Jr.

**Bax, [Sir] Arnold [Edward Trevor]**
1883-1953　　[LC]
*British author and composer*
* O'Byrne, Dermot

**Bax, Roger**
*See* Winterton, Paul

**Baxes, Dimitrios S.** 1928-　　[BE]
*American baseball player*
* Baxes, Jim

**Baxes, Jim**
*See* Baxes, Dimitrios S.

**Baxter, Beryl**
*See* Ivory, Beryl

**Baxter, Clarice Howard** 20th c.
*American songwriter*
* Baxter, Ma

**Baxter, Denis Charles Trevor** 20th
c.　　[ART]
*British painter and printmaker*
* D. B.

**Baxter, Elizabeth** ?-1534　　[PA]
*Author*
* [The] Holy Maid of Kent

**Baxter, George Owen**
*See* Faust, Frederick [Schiller]

**Baxter, Gillian**
*See* Hirst, Gillian Jose Charlotte

**Baxter, Gordon F[rancis], Jr.** 1923-
[CA]
*American columnist, television
producer, editor*
* Bax

**Baxter, Gregory** [joint pseudonym
with John Sellar Matheson Ressich]
*See* De Banzie, Eric

**Baxter, Gregory** [joint pseudonym
with Eric De Banzie]
*See* Ressich, John [Sellar
Matheson]

**Baxter, Hazel**
*See* Rowland, D[onald] S[ydney]

**Baxter, J. R.** ?-1960
*American songwriter*
* Baxter, Pap

**Baxter, Jane**
*See* Forde, Feodora

**Baxter, Jeff[rey Allen]** 20th c.
[RM, RO2]
*American musician*
* Baxter, Skunk

**Baxter, John**
*See* Hunt, E[verette] Howard, Jr.

**Baxter, John** 1939-　　[CA]
*Australian author*
* Loran, Martin [joint pseudonym
with Ron Smith]

**Baxter, Keith**
*See* Baxter-Wright, Keith

**Baxter, Larry**
*See* Setaro, Peter D.

**Baxter, Lucy E.** 1837-1902　　[FFF]
*Writer*
* Leader Scott

**Baxter, Ma**
*See* Baxter, Clarice Howard

**Baxter, Mrs. William R.**　　[FFF]
*Entertainer*
* Granger, Maude

**Baxter, Olive**
*See* Eastwood, Helen

**Baxter, Pap**
*See* Baxter, J. R.

**Baxter, Phyllis**
*See* Wallmann, Jeffrey M[iner]

**Baxter, Richard** 1615-1691　　[SN]
*British author and scholar*
* [The] English Demosthenes

**Baxter, Robert M.** 1851- ?　　[PA]
*Author*
* Arlington

**Baxter, Shane V.**
*See* Norwood, Victor G[eorge]
C[harles]

**Baxter, Skunk**
*See* Baxter, Jeff[rey Allen]

**Baxter, Valerie**
*See* Meynell, Laurence [Walter]

**Baxter, Wynne Edwin**　　[FFF]
*Author*
* Acton, Llewellin

**Baxter, Young**
*See* James W. I.

**Baxter-Wright, Keith** 1933?-
[BEW, TR]
*Welsh-born actor*
* Baxter, Keith

**Bay Boy Williams**
*See* Williams, Matthew

**Bay, Deerfoot**
*See* Bay, Harry Elbert

**Bay, Harry Elbert** 1878-1952　　[BE]
*American baseball player*
* Bay, Deerfoot

**Bay, James**
*See* Clark, James Bayard

**Bay, Magdalena** 1922-　　[IAW]
*German-born poet and author*
* Magdalena

**[The] Bayard of India**
*See* Outram, [Sir] James

**[The] Bayard of Poland**
*See* Poniatowski, Joseph

**[The] Bayard of the Confederate
Army**
*See* Lee, Robert Edward

**[The] Bayard of the East**
*See* Outram, [Sir] James

**[The] Bayard of the Indian Army**
*See* Outram, [Sir] James

**[The] Bayard of the Netherlands**
*See* Louis of Nassau

**[The] Bayard of the Revolution**
*See* Laurens, John

**Bayard, Seigneur de**
*See* Terrail, Pierre du

**Baybars, Taner** 1936-　　[CA, WD]
*British author and poet*
* Bayliss, Timothy

**Bayer, Burley**
*See* Bayer, Christopher A.

**Bayer, Christopher A.** 1875-1933
[BE]
*American baseball player*
* Bayer, Burley

**Bayer, Eleanor [Rosenfeld]** 20th c.
[WW]
*Author*
* Bayer, Oliver Weld [joint
pseudonym with Leo G. Bayer]

**Bayer [or Beyer?], Hanne Karin
Blarke** 1940-　　[BDF, FC]
*Danish actress*
* Karina, Anna

**Bayer, Karl Robert Emmerich von**
1835-1902　　[WBD]
*Austrian author*
* Byr, Robert

**Bayer, Leo G.** 20th c.　　[WW]
*Author*
* Bayer, Oliver Weld [joint
pseudonym with Eleanor
(Rosenfeld) Bayer]

**Bayer, Oliver Weld** [joint pseudonym
with Leo G. Bayer]
*See* Bayer, Eleanor [Rosenfeld]

**Bayer, Oliver Weld** [joint pseudonym
with Eleanor (Rosenfeld) Bayer]
*See* Bayer, Leo G.

**Bayer, Sylvia**
*See* Glassco, John [Stinson]

**Bayer, William** 1939-　　[CA, WD]
*American author and screenwriter*
* St. John, Leonie [joint pseudonym
with Nancy Harmon]

**Bayes, Nora**
*See* Goldberg, Dora

**Bayete**
*See* Cochran, Todd

**Bayfield, William John** 1871-1958
[MBF]
*British author*
* Blair, Allan
* Carr, Gordon
* Jardine, Warwick [house
pseudonym]
* Maxwell, Allan
* Osborne, Mark
* Wing, James Egerton

**Bayle, Marc Antoine** 1825- ?　　[PA]
*Author*
* Theotine

**Bayle, Pierre** 1647-1706
[DEP, HN, SN]
*French philosopher*
* [The] Father of Modern
Scepticism

**Bayless, Dick**
*See* Bayless, Harry Owen

**Bayless, Harry Owen** 1882-1920
[BE]
*American baseball player*
* Bayless, Dick

**Bayley, Barrington J[ohn]** 1937-
[CA, ESF, WD]
*British author*
* Aumbry, Alan
* Barrington, Michael [joint
pseudonym with Michael John
Moorcock]
* Diamond, John
* Woods, P. F.

**Bayley, Peter** 1778?-1823
*British author*
* Castel Chiuso, Giorgione di

**Bayliss, J. C.**
*See* Bayliss, John Clifford

**Bayliss, John Clifford** 1919-
[CA, SFL]
*British author*
* Bayliss, J. C.
* Clifford, John

**Bayliss, Timothy**
*See* Baybars, Taner

**Baylor, Byrd** 1924-　　[CA]
*American author*
* Schweitzer, Byrd Baylor

**Baylor, Elgin** 1934-　　[BBH, IBW]
*American basketball player*
* Everything, Mr.
* [The] Man of a Thousand Moves

**Baylor, Jack**
*See* Baylor, Julius A.

**Baylor, Julius A.** 1928-　　[IBW]
*American business executive*
* Baylor, Jack

**Bayly, Ada Ellen** 1857-1903
[FFF, LC, WBD]
*British author*
* Lyall, Edna

**Bayne, Beverly**
See Bayne, William Lear

**Bayne, Henry Wyndel**
See Bromley, Henry Walter

**Bayne, Peter**
See Brindle, Ernest

**Bayne, William Lear** 1899- [BE]
*American baseball player*
* Bayne, Beverly

**Baynes, Arthur Clifford**
1892?-1971 [BDW, BMH]
*British comedian*
* Stainless Stephen

**Bayo**
See Rodriguez, Braulio

**Baz, Irineo** 20th c. [GS]
*Spanish bullfighter*
* [El] Charro [The Horseman]

**Bazin, Herve**
See Herve-Bazin, Jean Pierre

**Bazna, Elyesa** 1904-1970 [B10]
*German intelligence agent*
* Cicero [code name used during World War II]

**Bazooka Bob Burns**
See Burns, Bob

**Bazuky, Maya**
See Michel, Maria Johanna

**Bazy, Lyman Hotchkiss** 19th c.
[FFF]
*Writer*
* Atchby, El

**Bazzano, Tommy**
See Pario, James

**Bazzi, Giovanni Antonio de**
1477?-1549 [SN, WBD]
*Italian painter*
* [Il] Sodoma

**Bazzoni, Camillo** 20th c. [WF]
*Italian director*
* Burks, Alex

**Beach, Charles** [PA]
*Author*
* Cannibal Jack

**Beach, Charles Amory** [house
pseudonym] [Stratemeyer
Syndicate]
See Stratemeyer, Edward L.

**Beach, Clyde**
See Beach, Robert M.

**Beach, Jack**
See Beach, Jackson

**Beach, Jackson** 20th c. [BE]
*American baseball player*
* Beach, Jack

**Beach, John Wesley** 1825- ? [FFF]
*Writer*
* John

**Beach, Robert M.** 1933- [IBW]
*American zoo director*
* Beach, Clyde

**Beach, S. B.** [PA]
*Author*
* Ploughshare, Peter

**Beach, Thomas Miller** 1841-1894
[WBD]
*British intelligence agent*
* Le Caron, Henry

**Beach, Tom**
See Harris, Larry M[ark]

**Beachboard, Molly** 1939- [CME]
*American country-western performer*
* Bee, Molly

**Beachcomber** [newspaper column
pseudonym, 1919-1924]
See Lewis, Dominic Bevan
Wyndham

**Beachcomber** [newspaper column
pseudonym, 1924- ]
See Morton, John [Cameron
Andrieu] Bingham [Michael]

**Beadle, Gwyneth Gordon** 1908-
[AW]
*Ceylonese-born author*
* Gordon, Glenda

**Beadnell, Charles Marsh** 1872- ?
[LAO]
*British author and physician*
* Javali

**Beaglehole, J. C.**
See Beaglehole, John Cawte

**Beaglehole, John Cawte** 1901-1971
[LC]
*New Zealand-born historian and
writer*
* Beaglehole, J. C.

**[The] Beak**
See Stratton, Richard A.

**Beaky**
See Dymond, John

**Beal, Andrew Edward** [PA]
*Author*
* [A] Detective

**Beal, Gwyneth Morgan** 1943- [CA]
*British author and educator*
* Morgan, Gwyneth

**Beal, John**
See Bliedung, James Alexander

**Beal, Nick**
See Ackerman, Forrest J[ames]

**Bealby, George**
See Wright, George

**Beale, Anne?**
See Tremaine, F[rederick] Orlin

**Beale, Elizabeth Helen** 1946-
[ART]
*British painter*
* Green, E. Helen

**[The] Beale Street Blues Boy**
See King, Riley B.

**Beale, Thomas Willert** 1831- ?
[DEL]
*British author*
* Maynard, Walter

**Beales, Harry** 1872- ? [THR]
*British theatrical manager*
* Bawn, Harry

**Beals, Helen Raymond Abbott**
1888- [NAA]
*American author*
* Abbott, Helen Raymond
* H. B.

**Beaman, Lottie Kimbrough** 1900?-
[BWW]
*American singer*
* Brooks, Jennie
* Brown, Lottie
* Cary, Clara
* Everson, Lottie
* Johnson, Martha
* [The] Kansas City Butterball
* Kimbrough, Lena
* Moran, Mae

**Beamish, Annie O'Meara de Vic**
1883- [CA, SFL]
*British author*
* Beamish, Noel De Vic
* Bernard, John

**Beamish, Noel De Vic**
See Beamish, Annie O'Meara de
Vic

**Beamish, Tufton Victor Hamilton**
See Chelwood, Tufton Victor
Hamilton

**Beamiss, Frederick Harold** 1898-
[ART]
*British artist*
* Calbeam

**Bean, Belve**
See Bean, Beveric Benton

**Bean, Beveric Benton** 1905- [BE]
*American baseball player*
* Bean, Belve
* Bean, Bill

**Bean, Bill**
See Bean, Beveric Benton

**Bean, Keith F[enwick]** 1911- [CAP]
*British author*
* Fenwick, Kay
* Harrington, K.

**Bean, Mabel Greene** 1898?-1977
[CA]
*American journalist*
* Greene, Mabel

**Bean, Norman**
See Burroughs, Edgar Rice

**Bean, Orson**
See Burrows, Dallas Frederick

**Bean Pole**
See Jones, James Chamberlain

**Beane, Fannie**
See Gilday, Mrs. Charles

**Beane, Mrs. George A., Jr.** [FFF]
*Entertainer*
* Semon, Ray

**Beaney, Jan**
See Udall, Jan Beaney

**[The] Bear**
See Albert I [or Albrecht]

**[The] Bear**
See Arthgal

**[The] Bear**
See Brady, James S. [Jim]

**[The] Bear**
See Hite, Robert, Jr.

**[The] Bear**
See Hobbes, Thomas

**[The] Bear**
See Liston, Charles

**Bear, Bullen**
See Donnelly, Augustine Stanislaus

**Bear, Joan** 1918- [CA]
*British author*
* Mayhew, Elizabeth

**Bear, Joe**
See Sellers, Connie Leslie, Jr.

**Bear, June** 1918- [THR]
*British dancer*
* Brae, June

**[The] Bear Leader**
See Boswell, James

**Bear Man Davenport**
See Davenport, Lloyd

**Bear Tracks Javery**
See Javery, Alva William

**Bear Tracks Schmitz**
See Schmitz, John Albert

**Beard, Beardo**
See Beard, Michael Richard

**Beard, James H.** 20th c. [WGT]
*Author*
* James, Philip [joint pseudonym
with Ramon Felipe San Juan
Mario Alvarez Del Rey]

**Beard, Matthew** 1925-1981 [B10]
*American actor*
* Stymie

**Beard, Michael Richard** 1950-
[SMG]
*American baseball player*
* Beard, Beardo

**[The] Bearded**
See Constantine IV

**[The] Bearded**
See Geoffrey [or Geoffroy?]

**[The] Bearded**
See George

**[The] Bearded**
See Killingworthe, George

**[The] Bearded**
See Mayo, Johann

**[The] Bearded Master**
See Socrates

**Bearden, Anthony**
See Linebarger, Paul M[yron]
A[nthony]

**Beardless Barbara**
See Collins, Barbara Ines

**Beardmore, Cedric**
See Beardmore, George

**Beardmore, George** 1908-1979
[CA, SAT]
*British author*
* Beardmore, Cedric
* Stokes, Cedric
* Wolfenden, George

**Beardslee, L. A.** 1836- ? [PA]
*Author*
* Pieseio

**[The] Bearnais**
See Henry IV [or Henri]

**Bearne, C. G.**
*See* Bearne, Colin Gerald

**Bearne, Colin Gerald** 1939-    [SFL]
*British author*
* Bearne, C. G.

**Beasler, Norma Jean** 1938-    [ECM]
*American country-western performer*
* Norma Jean

**[The] Beast**
*See* Crowley, Edward Alexander

**[The] Beast**
*See* Foxx, James Emory

**[The] Beast**
*See* Jeffries, James Jackson

**[The] Beast of Belsen**
*See* Kramer, Josef

**Beatin, Ebenezer Ambrose**
1866-1925    [BE]
*American baseball player*
* Beatin, Ed

**Beatin, Ed**
*See* Beatin, Ebenezer Ambrose

**Beaton, Anne**
*See* Washington, [Catherine]
Marguerite Beauchamp

**Beaton, Cecil**
*See* Hardy, Walter

**Beaton, Chris**
*See* Adamson, Iaian Beaton

**Beaton, George**
*See* Brenan, [Edward Fitz-] Gerald

**Beatson, Evelyn May** 1943-    [RO2]
*Scottish singer*
* Graham, Eve

**Beattie, John** 1907-    [CEI, HK]
*British-born hockey player*
* Beattie, Red

**Beattie, John McIntosh** 1905-1972
[FC, SC]
*Australian actor*
* Warwick, John

**Beattie, Red**
*See* Beattie, John

**Beatty, Aloysius Desmond**
1893-1969    [BE]
*American baseball player*
* Beatty, Des
* Beatty, Desperate

**Beatty, Baden**
*See* Casson, Frederick Ronald
Christopher

**Beatty, Des**
*See* Beatty, Aloysius Desmond

**Beatty, Desperate**
*See* Beatty, Aloysius Desmond

**Beatty, Elizabeth**
*See* Holloway, Teresa [Bragunier]

**Beatty, Josephine**
*See* Hunter, Alberta

**Beatty, Patricia** 1922-    [TCC]
*American author*
* Bartholomew, Jean

**Beatty, Warren**
*See* Beaty, Henry Warren

**Beaty, Annie**    [PA]
*Author*
* A. B.

**Beaty, Betty** 20th c.    [CA]
*British author*
* Campbell, Karen
* Ross, Catherine

**Beaty, [Arthur] David** 1919-    [WD]
*British author*
* Stanton, Paul

**Beaty, Henry Warren** 1937-
[BDF, BEW, WEF]
*American actor*
* Beatty, Warren

**Beaty, Shirley Maclean** 1934-
[BDF, FC, HT]
*American actress*
* MacLaine, Shirley

**Beaty, Zelmo** 1941-    [BB]
*American basketball player*
* [The] Big Z

**[The] Beau**
*See* Baumann, Frank Matt

**[The] Beau Brummel of Language**
*See* Opitz, Martin

**[The] Beau Brummel of Living
Authors**
*See* Dibdin, Thomas Frognall

**[The] Beau Brummell of the Halls**
*See* Lashwood, George

**Beau, Heinie**
*See* Beau, Henry John

**Beau, Henry John** 1911-    [ASC, EJ]
*American composer, arranger,
musician*
* Beau, Heinie

**Beau, Jack**
*See* Walker, Sidney

**[A] Beau Nasty**
*See* Foote, Samuel

**[The] Beau of Princes**
*See* George IV

**[Le] Beau Sabreur**
*See* Murat, Joachim

**Beaubien**
*See* Mooreau, M.

**Beaubien, Julien**
*See* Dolenzai, Julien A.

**Beaubrun, Theodore** 1923-    [CW]
*Haitian playwright and actor*
* Languichatte

**Beauchamp, Al** 1944-    [SMG]
*American football player*
* Beauchamp, Big Al

**Beauchamp, Big Al**
*See* Beauchamp, Al

**Beauchamp, Bold**
*See* Beauchamp, Thomas de

**Beauchamp, Kathleen Mansfield**
1888-1923    [EWL, LC, TC]
*British author and critic*
* K. M.
* Mansfield, Katherine

**Beauchamp, Mary Annette**
1866-1941    [LC]
*Australian-born author*
* Cholmondeley, Alice

**Beauchamp, Mary Annette**
(Continued)
* Elizabeth

**Beauchamp, Pat**
*See* Washington, [Catherine]
Marguerite Beauchamp

**Beauchamp, Richard de** 1382-1439
[FFF, SN]
*12th Earl of Warwick*
* [The] Father of Curtesie
* [The] Good

**Beauchamp, Shelsley**
*See* Bradley, T. Waldron

**Beauchamp, Thomas de** 14th c.
[DNNS, GWP, RH]
*First Earl of Warwick*
* Beauchamp, Bold

**Beauchamps** ?-1695    [HN]
*French dancing teacher*
* [The] Doctor of Dancing
* [The] Father of all
  Dancing-Masters

**Beauclerc [Good Scholar]**
*See* Henry I

**Beauclerk, Helen De Vere**
*See* Bellingham, Helen Mary
Dorothea

**Beaudoin, Jethro**
*See* Beaudoin, Serge

**Beaudoin, Kenneth Lawrence**
1913-    [CA]
*American poet*
* De Chatellerault, Victor
* De Todany, James

**Beaudoin, Serge** 1952-    [SMG]
*Canadian-born hockey player*
* Beaudoin, Jethro

**Beaufitz, William**
*See* Critchley, Julian [Michael
Gordon]

**Beaufort, Duc de**
*See* Vendome, Francois de

**Beaujon, Paul**
*See* Warde, Beatrice Lamberton

**Beaulien**
*See* Wood, Roland A.

**Beaulieu, Big Rudolph**
*See* Beaulieu, Rudolph

**Beaulieu, Rudolph** 1900-1972
[NOJ]
*American jazz musician*
* Beaulieu, Big Rudolph

**Beaumanoir, Sire de**
*See* Remi, Philippe de

**Beaumarchais, Pierre Augustin
Caron**
*See* Caron, Pierre Augustin

**Beaumesnil, Henrietta Adelaide**
1748-1803    [PA]
*Author*
* Villaard

**Beaumont, Beverly**
*See* Von Block, Sylvia

**Beaumont, Binkie**
*See* Beaumont, Hugh

**Beaumont, Brenchley**
*See* Viles, Walter

**Beaumont, Charles**
*See* Nutt, Charles

**Beaumont, Clarence Howeth**
1876-1956    [AS, BE, DGS]
*American baseball player*
* Beaumont, Ginger

**Beaumont, Donna Brooks** 20th c.
[SFL]
*Author*
* Claxton, John G.

**Beaumont, E. J.**
*See* Nutt, Charles

**Beaumont, Edgar** 20th c.
[CC, EMD, WW]
*Author*
* Halifax, [Dr.] Clifford

**Beaumont, Ginger**
*See* Beaumont, Clarence Howeth

**Beaumont, [Sir] Harry**
*See* Spence, Joseph

**Beaumont, Hugh** 1908-1973    [EMT]
*Welsh-born producer*
* Beaumont, Binkie

**Beaumont, Lottie**
*See* Chapelle, Mrs. Charles

**Beaumont, Ralph**
*See* Bergendorf, Ralph Wallace

**Beauregard, Pierre Gustave Toutant**
1818-1893    [DNNS, SN]
*American army officer*
* [The] Little Napoleon
* Old Bory

**[The] Beautiful Blonde of Antwerp**
*See* Schragmueller, Elsbeth

**[The] Beautiful Corisande**
*See* D'Andouins, Diane

**[The] Beautiful Gardener**
*See* Estrees, Gabrielle d'

**[The] Beautiful One**
*See* Castellotti, Eugene

**[The] Beautiful Parricide**
*See* Cenci, Beatrice

**[The] Beautiful Ropemaker**
*See* Labe, Louise

**[The] Beautifyer**
*See* Hogarth, William

**[The] Beauty of Buttermere**
*See* Robinson, Mary

**[The] Beauty of Holiness**
*See* Taylor, Jeremy

**Beauvoir, Roger de**
*See* De Bully, Edouard Roger

**Beaver Felt Emmerson**
*See* Emmerson, Bruce

**Beaver, Flash**
*See* West, Virgil Clifford

**Beaver, John** ?-1395    [PA]
*Author*
* Castor [or Castorius]
* Fiber [or Fiberius]

**Beaver, Lee**
*See* Lizzani, Carlo

**Beaver, [Jack] Patrick** 1923-    [CA]
*British author*
* Billington, John

**Beaver, Robert Atwood** 1906-
[ART]
*British painter*
* R. B.

**Beaver, W. H.** [PA]
*Author*
* Pimpernel

**Bebe Chico [Little Baby]**
*See* Rodriguez Sanchez, Jose

**Bebop, Ralph** 20th c. [OBW]
*American baseball player*
* Bebop, Spec

**Bebop, Spec**
*See* Bebop, Ralph

**Bec, Marie**
*See* Colimon, Marie-Therese

**Becannon, Buck**
*See* Becannon, James Melville

**Becannon, James Melville**
1859-1923 [BE]
*American baseball player*
* Becannon, Buck

**Beccadelli, Antonio** 1394-1471
[PA]
*Author*
* Panomita

**Beccafumi, Domenico**
*See* Di Pace, Domenico

**Becerra, Joe**
*See* Becerra Covarrubias, Jose

**Becerra Covarrubias, Jose** 1936-
[BX, RBE]
*Mexican boxer*
* Becerra, Joe

**Bechhofer, C. E.**
*See* Roberts, [Carl Eric] Bechhofer

**Bechko, Peggy Anne** 1950- [CA]
*American author*
* Haller, Bill

**Beck, Allen**
*See* Cave, Hugh B[arnett]

**Beck, Boom-Boom**
*See* Beck, Walter William

**Beck, Christopher**
*See* Bridges, Thomas Charles

**Beck, Dutch**
*See* Beck, Erwin Thomas

**Beck, Eliza Louisa Moresby**
?-1931 [LC, TC]
*British author*
* Barrington, E.
* Beck, Lily Adams
* Moresby, Louis

**Beck, Erve**
*See* Beck, Erwin Thomas

**Beck, Erwin Thomas** 1878-1916
[BE]
*American baseball player*
* Beck, Dutch
* Beck, Erve

**Beck, Joe**
*See* Dipalermo, Joseph

**Beck, Lily Adams**
*See* Beck, Eliza Louisa Moresby

**Beck, Phineas**
*See* Chamberlain, Samuel

**Beck, Pia**
*See* Beck, Pieternella

**Beck, Pieternella** 1925- [EJ]
*Dutch musician*
* Beck, Pia

**Beck, Robert** 1918- [IBW, LBA]
*American author*
* Iceberg Slim

**Beck, Thomas** 1765-1808 [PA]
*Author*
* Touch'em, Timothy

**Beck, Walter William** 1904-
[BE, BN]
*American baseball player*
* Beck, Boom-Boom
* Elmer the Great

**Beckenbauer, Franz** 1945- [AES]
*German soccer player*
* [The] Kaiser

**Beckendorf, Heinie**
*See* Beckendorf, Henry Ward

**Beckendorf, Henry Ward**
1884-1949 [BE]
*American baseball player*
* Beckendorf, Heinie

**Becker, Belle** 1895?-1957 [BEW]
*American theatrical performer*
* Baker, Belle

**Becker, Buck**
*See* Becker, Charles S. [Charlie]

**Becker, Carl Edward Clarence Paul**
20th c.
*American author*
* Becker, Freckle

**Becker, Charles S. [Charlie]**
1890-1928 [BE]
*American baseball player*
* Becker, Buck

**Becker, Dutch**
*See* Becker, Heinz Reinhard

**Becker, Florence**
*See* Lennon, Florence Becker
[Tanenbaum]

**Becker, Freckle**
*See* Becker, Carl Edward Clarence
Paul

**Becker, Heinz Reinhard** 1915-
[BE]
*German-born baseball player*
* Becker, Dutch

**Becker, Helen** 1905-1966
[BEW, EMT]
*American choreographer*
* Tamiris, Helen

**Becker, Herman Heinrich** 1829- ?
[FFF]
*German politician*
* Becker, Red

**Becker, Leah** 1933- [BEW]
*American choreographer, dancer,
actress*
* Becker-Theodore, Lee

**Becker, Max O[ctavious]** 1927-
[CA, IAW]
*American author*
* Alth, Max O[ctavious]
* Collins, Harry C.
* Hardforth, Carrie

**Becker, Red**
*See* Becker, Herman Heinrich

**Becker, Stephen [David]** 1927-
[CA]
*American author*
* Dodge, Steve

**Becker-Theodore, Lee**
*See* Becker, Leah

**Beckert, Bruno**
*See* Beckert, Glenn Alfred

**Beckert, Glenn Alfred** 1940- [PB]
*American baseball player*
* Beckert, Bruno

**Becket, Gilbert** 1810-1856 [PA]
*Author*
* Beichan, Lord

**Becket, Lavinia**
*See* Course, Pamela Mary

**Beckett, Arthur** 20th c. [WWL]
*British author*
* Vyse, Bertie

**Beckett, Gillian** 1935- [IAW]
*British author*
* Bower, Alison

**Beckett, Kenneth A[lbert]** 1929-
[CA]
*British author*
* Bower, Keith

**Beckett, Mark**
*See* Truman, Marcus George

**Beckett, Ronald Brymer** 1891-
[CA]
*British author*
* Anthony, John

**Beckley, Gilbert Lee** 20th c. [MM]
*American underworld figure*
* Gil the Brain

**Beckley, Jacob Peter [Jake]**
1867-1918 [AS, BE, PB]
*American baseball player*
* Eagle Eye
* Old Eagle Eye

**Beckman, Becky**
*See* Beckman, John

**Beckman, Dee**
*See* Boeckmann, Dolores A.

**Beckman, Elizabeth Hurlock** 1898-
[NAA]
*American educator and author*
* Hurlock, Elizabeth B.

**Beckman, John** 1895-1968 [BB]
*American basketball player*
* [The] Babe Ruth of Basketball
* Beckman, Becky

**Beckman, Ross**
*See* Dey, Frederic Van Rensselaer

**Beckner, S. W. E.** 1838- ? [PA]
*Author*
* Bubb, Belle Z.
* O'Pake, Mr.

**Beckwith, Burnham Putnam** 1904-
[CA, WD]
*American author*
* Burnham, John
* Putnam, John

**Beckwith, Chargin' Charlie**
*See* Beckwith, Charles

**Beckwith, Charles** 1929?-
*American army officer*
* Beckwith, Chargin' Charlie

**Beckwith, Lillian**
*See* Comber, Lillian

**Beckwith, Roger**
*See* Von Brincken, Wilhelm

**Becold [Boccold, or Bockholdt], John**
1510-1536 [HN, RH]
*Dutch Anabaptist*
* Becold, King
* John of Leyden
* [The] King of Sion

**Becold, King**
*See* Becold [Boccold, or
Bockholdt], John

**Becon, Thomas** 1510?-1570
[DEL, PA]
*British author*
* Basil, Theodore

**Becraft, Ann Marie** 1805-1833
[IBW]
*American educator*
* Mary Aloysius, [Sister]

**Becton, George W.** ?-1933
*American clergyman*
* [The] Dancing Evangelist

**Becu, Marie Jeanne** 1746?-1793
[HN]
*Mistress of King Louis XV of France*
* [L']Ange, Madame
* Du Barry, Comtesse

**Beda, Noel** [SN]
*French theologian*
* [The] Great Sopper [Gros
Soupier]

**Bedard, Michelle**
*See* MacKenzie, Joan

**Beddoe, Ellaruth**
*See* Elkins, Ella Ruth

**Bede [Baeda, or Beda]** 673- 735
[DNNF, DNNS, HN]
*Saint*
* [The] Father of Ecclesiastical
History
* [The] Father of English Learning
* Venerabilis, Doctor
* [The] Venerable Bede

**Bede, Andrew**
*See* Beha, Ernest

**Bede, Cuthbert**
*See* Bradley, Edward

**Bede, Seth**
*See* Evans, Samuel

**Bedell, Lew** 1919- [ASC]
*American composer, comedian,
publisher*
* Bideu, Lou

**Bedell, William** 1571-1642 [HN]
*British prelate*
* Ultimus Anglorum

**Bedford, A. N.**
*See* Watson, Jane Werner

**Bedford, Ann**
*See* Rees, Joan

**Bedford, Annie North**
*See* Watson, Jane Werner

**Bedford Bill Rariden**
*See* Rariden, William Angel

**Bedford, Donald F.** [joint pseudonym with Kenneth Fearing and Donald Friede]
*See* Bedford-Jones, Henry [James O'Brien]

**Bedford, Donald F.** [joint pseudonym with Donald Friede and Henry Bedford-Jones]
*See* Fearing, Kenneth [Flexner]

**Bedford, Donald F.** [joint pseudonym with Henry Bedford-Jones and Kenneth Fearing]
*See* Friede, Donald

**Bedford, Harry** 1873-1939　[BMH]
*British comedian*
* City, Fred

**Bedford, John**
*See* Hastings, Phyllis Dora Hodge

**Bedford-Jones, Henry [James O'Brien]** 1887-1949
[HFF, SFP, WGT]
*Canadian-born American author*
* Bedford, Donald F. [joint pseudonym with Kenneth Fearing and Donald Friede]
* Bedrod-Foran, Capt. [joint pseudonym with (Capt.) William Robert Foran]
* Brissard, Montague
* Chase, Cleveland B.
* De Mourant, George Souli
* Ferval, Paul
* Gallister, Michael
* Hawkwood, Allan
* Keyne, Gordon
* Lassez, M.
* Pamjean, Louis
* Pemjean, Lucian
* Sangerson, Margaret Love
* Seabrooke, David
* Souli, Charles George
* Stuart, Gordon
* Trevision, Torquay
* Whitney, Elliott [joint pseudonym with Harry Lincoln Saylor]
* Wycliffe, John

**Bediako, K. A.**
*See* Konadu, Samuel Asare

**Bednarik, Chuck** 20th c.
*American football player*
* [The] Clutch

**Bednarski, John Severn** 1952-
[SMG]
*Canadian-born hockey player*
* Bednarski, Ski

**Bednarski, Ski**
*See* Bednarski, John Severn

**Bedny, Demyan**
*See* Pridvorov, Yefim

**Bedon, Peter** ?-1561　[FFF]
*Ecuadoran clergyman and painter*
* [The] Fra Angelico of Equador

**Bedott, [Widow] Priscilla P.**
*See* Whitcher, Frances Miriam

**Bedra, Julie Marlene** 1924-　[ECM]
*American country-western performer*
* Allen, Rosalie
* [The] Prairie Star
* [The] Queen of the Yodelers

**Bedrod-Foran, Capt.** [joint pseudonym with (Capt.) William Robert Foran]
*See* Bedford-Jones, Henry [James O'Brien]

**Bedrod-Foran, Capt.** [joint pseudonym with Henry Bedford-Jones]
*See* Foran, [Capt.] William Robert

**Bedwell, Hard Guy**
*See* Bedwell, Harvey Guy

**Bedwell, Harvey Guy** 1876-1950
[BBH]
*American horse trainer*
* Bedwell, Hard Guy

**Bee, Betty**
*See* Lanham, Ceora B.

**Bee, Clair F.** 1900-　[BBH]
*American basketball coach*
* Bee, Hillbilly

**Bee, Helen L.** 1939-　[CA]
*American author and psychologist*
* Douglas, Helen Bee

**Bee, Hillbilly**
*See* Bee, Clair F.

**Bee, Hookanit, Esq.**
*See* Wigram, S. R.

**Bee, Jay**
*See* Brainerd, John W[hiting]

**Bee, Johnny**
*See* Badanjek, John

**Bee, Jon**
*See* Badcock, John

**Bee, Joyce**
*See* Mansfield, Joyce

**[The] Bee Lipped Oracle**
*See* Aristocles

**Bee, Molly**
*See* Beachboard, Molly

**[The] Bee of Athens**
*See* Aristocles

**[The] Bee of Attica**
*See* Sophocles

**[The] Bee of France**
*See* Rollin, Charles

**Beebe, B. F.**
*See* Johnson, Burdetta Fay Beebe

**Beebe, Ella**
*See* Fitzpatrick, Mrs. M. J.

**Beebe, Ethel Fairmont** 1881- ?
[NAA]
*American author*
* Fairmont, Ethel
* Snyder, Fairmont

**Beebe, Henrietta**
*See* Lawton, Mrs. W. H.

**Beebe, Rachel Irene** 1903-
[CA, SAT]
*American author*
* Ray, Irene
* Sutton, Margaret [Beebe]

**Beebee, Charles Washington**　[PA]
*Author*
* Ravenswood

**Beech, Margaret**
*See* Barclay, Vera

**Beech, Webb**
*See* Butterworth, William Edmund, III

**Beecham, Alice**
*See* Tubb, Edwin Charles

**Beecham, Justin**
*See* Wintle, Justin [Beecham]

**Beechcroft, T. O.**
*See* Beechcroft, Thomas Owen

**Beechcroft, Thomas Owen** 1902-
[LC]
*British author*
* Beechcroft, T. O.

**Beecher, Colonel**
*See* Beecher, LeRoy

**Beecher, Ed[ward]** 1873- ?　[BE]
*American baseball player*
* Beecher, Scrap Iron

**Beecher, Elizabeth [Betty]**
*See* Miller, Elizabeth Beecher

**Beecher, Henry Ward** 1813- ?　[PA]
*Author*
* [The] Man Who Keeps his Eyes and Ears Open

**Beecher, Janet**
*See* Meysenburg, Janet B.

**Beecher, Lee**
*See* Mullen, Stanley [B.]

**Beecher, LeRoy** 1884-1952　[BE]
*American baseball player*
* Beecher, Colonel
* Beecher, Roy

**Beecher, Roy**
*See* Beecher, LeRoy

**Beecher, Scrap Iron**
*See* Beecher, Ed[ward]

**Beecher, Stanley**
*See* Mullen, Stanley [B.]

**Beechhold, Henry F[rank]** 1928-
[CA]
*American educator and author*
* O'Doire, Annraoi

**Beeching, H. C.**
*See* Beeching, Henry Charles

**Beeching, Henry Charles** 1859-1919　[LC]
*British clergyman, poet, author*
* Beeching, H. C.
* Sylvan, Urbanus

**Beeching, Jack** 1922-　[CA]
*British author*
* Barbary, James [joint pseudonym with Amy (Brown) Beeching Baumann]

**Beeding, Francis** [joint pseudonym with Hilary Aidan St. George Saunders]
*See* Palmer, John Leslie

**Beeding, Francis** [joint pseudonym with John Leslie Palmer]
*See* Saunders, Hilary Aidan St. George

**Beedle, William Franklin, Jr.** 1918-1981　[BDF, FC, WEF]
*American actor*
* Holden, William

**Beef Eater**
*See* Vesey, George

**Beefheart, Captain**
*See* Van Vliet, Don

**Beege**
*See* Gillman, Margaret C.

**Beehan, Jack Rogers**
*See* Jamieson, Leland Shattuck

**Beeks, Clarence** 1922-　[EJ]
*American jazz musician*
* Pleasure, King

**Beeler, Jodie**
*See* Beeler, Joseph Sam

**Beeler, Joseph Sam** 1921-　[BE]
*American baseball player*
* Beeler, Jodie

**Beer, Eloise C. S.** 1903-　[CA]
*American author*
* Beer, Lisl
* Drake, Lisl

**Beer, Jakob Liebmann** 1791-1864
[WBD]
*German composer*
* Meyerbeer, Giacomo

**Beer, Lisl**
*See* Beer, Eloise C. S.

**Beer, Rachel**
*See* Sassoon, Richa

**Beer, Vic**
*See* Bird, Vivian

**Beer [or Baer], Zacharias** 1534-1583　[WBD]
*German theologian and author*
* Ursinus, Zacharias

**Beerbohm, Herbert** 1853-1917
[BEW]
*British-born actor, producer, playwright*
* Tree, [Sir] Herbert Draper Beerbohm

**Beers, Ethel Lynn**
*See* Beers, Ethelinda Elliot

**Beers, Ethelinda Elliot** 1827-1879
[PA]
*American author*
* Beers, Ethel Lynn
* E. B.

**Beers, Evelyne Christine Sauer** 1925-　[FFA]
*American folk singer*
* Fiddler, Mrs.

**Beers, Mrs. J. Newton**　[FFF]
*Entertainer*
* Randolph, Josie Lee

**Beers, Robert Harlan** 1920-　[FFA]
*American folk singer*
* Fiddler

**Beers, William George** 1843-1900
[BBH]
*Canadian lacrosse pioneer*
* [The] Father of Lacrosse

**Beesley, Thomas Quinn** 1891-
[NAA]
*American business executive and author*
* Audax

**Beeson**
*See* Vestal, Herman Beeson

**Beeston, L. J.** 20th c.　[MBF]
*British author*
* Camden, Richard
* Davies, Lucian

**Beets, Nikolaas** 1814-1903　[WBD]
*Dutch poet and author*
* Hildebrand

**Beevers, John [Leonard]** 1911-1975
[CA]
*British author and journalist*
* Clayton, John

**Beffroy de Reigny, Louis Abel**
1757-1811 [WBD]
*French author*
* Cousin Jacques

**Befumo, Joseph A.** 1925- [EJ]
*Italian-born jazz musician*
* Holiday, Joe

**Beg, Toran**
See McKillop, Norman

**Begbie, [Edward] Harold**
1871-1929 [LC, SFL, WGT]
*British author*
* [A] Gentleman with a Duster
* Lewis, Caroline [joint pseudonym
  with (James) Stafford Ransome
  and M. H. Temple]
* [The] Man Who was Warned

**Begg, Walter** [FFF]
*Entertainer*
* Bentley, Walter

**Beggarstaff, J.**
See Pryde, James Ferrier

**Beggarstaff, W.**
See Nicholson, [Sir] William
Newzam Prior

**Beghtol, Gene** 20th c. [GW]
*American rodeo performer*
* Beghtol, Mop

**Beghtol, Mop**
See Beghtol, Gene

**Begleiter, Lionel** 1930-
[BEW, EMT, FC]
*British lyricist, composer,
playwright, director*
* Bart, Lionel

**Begley, Imp**
See Begley, James Lawrence [Jim]

**Begley, James Lawrence [Jim]**
1903-1957 [BE]
*American baseball player*
* Begley, Imp

**Begon, F.** [PA]
*Author*
* De Stolz, Madam

**Begovic, Milan** 1876-1948 [EWL]
*Croatian author, poet, playwright*
* De La Maraja, Xeres
* Dusic, Stanko

**Begovich, Matthew** 1910-1966
[BB]
*American basketball player*
* Begovich, Matty

**Begovich, Matty**
See Begovich, Matthew

**[Le] Begue**
See Louis II

**[Le] Begue**
See Michael II

**[Le] Begue**
See Notger [or Notker]

**Begum, Mehzabeenara** 1932-1972
[SC]
*Indian actress and screenwriter*
* Kumari, Meena

**Beha, Ernest** 1908- [CAP]
*British journalist*
* Bede, Andrew
* Elvin, Drake

**Behadour**
See Tippou-Saib

**Beham, Hans Sebald** 1500-1550
[DNNF, DNNS, SN]
*German painter and engraver*
* [The] Little Master

**Behan, Charles Frederick**
1887-1957 [BE]
*American baseball player*
* Behan, Petie

**Behan, Leslie**
See Gottfried, Theodore Mark

**Behan, Petie**
See Behan, Charles Frederick

**Behar, George** 1922- [JL]
*Dutch-born intelligence agent*
* Blake, George

**Behn, Aphra** 1640-1689
[DEL, FFF, SN]
*British author and playwright*
* Astraea

**Behnji [Honored Sister]**
See Gandhi, Indira Nehru

**Behrman, Lucy Creevey**
See Creevey, Lucy E.

**Behrman, S. N.**
See Behrman, Samuel Nathaniel

**Behrman, Samuel Nathaniel**
1893-1973 [BEW, LC]
*American playwright*
* Behrman, S. N.

**Behymer, L. E.**
See Behymer, Lynden Ellsworth

**Behymer, Lynden Ellsworth**
1862?-1947 [BEW]
*American impresario*
* Behymer, L. E.

**Beichan, Lord**
See Becket, Gilbert

**Beiderbecke, Bix**
See Beiderbecke, Leon Bismarck

**Beiderbecke, Leon Bismarck**
1903-1931 [BBD, DAM, EJ]
*American jazz musician*
* Beiderbecke, Bix

**Beier, Ulli** 1922- [CA, IAW]
*German-born author*
* Akanji, Sangodare
* Aragbabalu, Omidiji
* Obotunde, Ijimere

**Beilenson, Edna** 1909- [CA]
*American author*
* Deane, Elisabeth

**Beith, [Sir] John Hay** 1876-1952
[BEW, LC, WWL]
*British author and playwright*
* Hay, Ian
* Junior Sub
* K (1)

**Bejarano y Carrasco, Rafael**
1863-1900 [GS]
*Spanish bullfighter*
* Torerito [Little Bullfighter]

**Bejart, Louis** 1630-1678 [SN]
*French comedian*
* [The] Sharp One

**Bejart, Maurice**
See Berger, Maurice

**Bejma, Aloysius Frank** 1907- [BE]
*American baseball player*
* Bejma, Ollie

**Bejma, Ollie**
See Bejma, Aloysius Frank

**Bek, Anthony** ?-1310? [SN]
*Bishop of Durham*
* King of the Isle of Man

**Beke, X.**
See Hawtayne, G. H.

**Bekessy, Jean** 1911-1977
[CA, TC1]
*Hungarian-born journalist and
author*
* Habe, Hans

**Bekker, Betje**
See Bekker, Elizabeth

**Bekker, Elizabeth** 1738-1804
[WBD]
*Dutch author*
* Bekker, Betje

**Bekker, Petrus Jakobus** 1935-
[IAW]
*South African author*
* Bekker, Pirow

**Bekker, Pirow**
See Bekker, Petrus Jakobus

**[Le] Bel**
See Charles IV

**[Le] Bel**
See Philip IV [or Philippe]

**[Le] Bel Anglais**
See Churchill, John [First Duke of
Marlborough]

**Bel Geddes, Barbara**
See Geddes, Barbara

**Belalcazar [or Benalcazar], Sebastian
de**
See Moyano, Sebastian

**Belan, Cliff**
See Bielinski, Clifford Martin

**Belane, George**
See Boas, George

**Belaney, Archibald Stansfeld**
1888-1938 [LC]
*Canadian author and lecturer*
* Grey Owl

**Belanger, Albert** 1906-1969
[BBH, BX, CSH]
*Canadian boxer*
* Belanger, Frenchy

**Belanger, Frenchy**
See Belanger, Albert

**Belanger-Gill, Georgiana** 20th c.
[NAA]
*Canadian author and journalist*
* De Montreuil, Gaetane

**Belangio, Prosper Albert** 1909-
[BE]
*American baseball player*
* Blanche, [Prosper] Al[bert]

**Belardi, Carroll Wayne** 1930- [BE]
*American baseball player*
* Belardi, Footsie

**Belardi, Footsie**
See Belardi, Carroll Wayne

**Belarius of Cymbeline**
See Evans, Eastwick

**Belasco, David**
See Valasco, David

**Belasco, F.**
See Rosenfeld, Monroe H.

**Belasco, Mrs. Isaac** [FFF]
*Entertainer*
* Dolaro, Selina

**Belbin, Harry**
See Garrish, Harold J.

**Belcastro, James** 20th c. [BLB]
*American underworld figure*
* King of the Bombers

**Belcher, Fannie**
See Belcher, Fannin Saffore

**Belcher, Fannin Saffore** 1909-1967
[IBW]
*American drama coach*
* Belcher, Fannie

**Belcher, James** 1781-1811 [WBD]
*British prize fighter*
* Belcher, Jem

**Belcher, Jem**
See Belcher, James

**Belcher, Lina** 1907- [F1, F2]
*Actress*
* Basquette, Lina

**Belcher, Lynda Susan** 1949- [RO2]
*British singer*
* Paul, Lyn

**Belcheva, Elisaveta** 1893- [CLC]
*Bulgarian poet, author, editor*
* Bagryana [or Bagrjana],
  Elisaveta

**Beldam [or Belden?], George F.**
1905-1962 [BEW, F2, FC]
*American actor and politician*
* Bell, Rex

**Belden, Clara**
See Trippetts, Mrs. Henry

**Belden, N. H.**
See Clarke, N. B.

**Beldon, Phil Cheech**
See Ellison, Harlan [Jay]

**Belenguer Hevoas, Baltazar** 1911-
[BX, RBE]
*Spanish-born boxer*
* Sangchilli, Baltazar

**Beleno**
See Azuela, Mariano

**[The] Belfast Spider**
See Weir, Ike O'Neil

**Belfield, David** 1951?-
*American security guard, suspected
of murdering Iranian press attache*
* Salahuddin, Daoud

**Belfield, Harry Wedgwood** 20th c.
[MBF]
*British writer*
* Drake, Rupert
* Grimshaw, Mark

**Belfield, Harry Wedgwood**
(Continued)
* Wroxham, Cecil

**Belford, Senator** [FFF]
*American politician*
* [The] Red Headed Rooster of the Rockies

**Belgarde, Adele**
*See* Levy, Adele

**[The] Belgian Shakespeare**
*See* Maeterlinck, Maurice [Polydore Marie Bernard]

**Belime, Jean** 1891- [BBD]
*French music critic*
* Coeuroy, Andre

**Belinda**
*See* Fermor, Arabella

**Beling, Richard** 1613-1677 [FFF]
*Irish author*
* Irenaeus, Philopater

**Belinsky, Bo**
*See* Belinsky, Robert

**Belinsky, Robert** 1936-
[BE, EJS, PB]
*American baseball player*
* Belinsky, Bo

**Belisario**
*See* Vieira da Cunha, Antonio Belisario

**Belita**
*See* Jepson-Turner, Gladys

**Beliveau, Jean** 1931- [FHE]
*Canadian-born hockey player*
* [Le] Gros Bill

**Belkine, Ivan**
*See* Pushkin, Alexander Sergeivitch

**Belknap, B. H.**
*See* Ellis, Edward S[ylvester]

**Bell, Acton**
*See* Bronte, Anne

**Bell, Archie**
*See* Sapon, Archie

**Bell, Beau**
*See* Bell, Roy Chester

**Bell, Bert**
*See* Bell, DeBenneville

**Bell, Brian** 1937- [TR]
*South African-born actor*
* Murray, Brian

**Bell, Bubba**
*See* Bell, Herbert

**Bell, Buddy**
*See* Bell, David Gus

**Bell, C. F. Moberly**
*See* Bell, Charles Frederick Moberly

**Bell, Carey**
*See* Harrington, Carey Bell

**Bell, Carol**
*See* Flavell, Carol Willsey Bell

**Bell, Caroline**
*See* Hearne, Mrs. George

**Bell, Carolyn**
*See* Rigoni, Orlando [Joseph]

**Bell, Catherine**
*See* Weir, Rosemary

**Bell, Catherine D.** [DEL, FFF]
*American author*
* Cousin Kate

**Bell, Charles** 20th c. [OBW]
*American baseball player*
* Bell, Lefty

**Bell, Charles Frederick Moberly**
1847-1911 [LC]
*British author and journalist*
* Bell, C. F. Moberly

**Bell, Colin Alexander** 1919- [IAW]
*New Zealand author*
* Bell, Colin Kane

**Bell, Colin Kane**
*See* Bell, Colin Alexander

**Bell, Cool Papa**
*See* Bell, James Thomas

**Bell, Currer**
*See* Bronte, Charlotte

**Bell, Danny**
*See* Bell, Fern Lee

**Bell, David Gus** 1951-
[PB, SMG, WWB]
*American baseball player*
* Bell, Buddy

**Bell, David Russell** 1928-
[BE, DGS, PB]
*American baseball player*
* Bell, Gus

**Bell, DeBenneville** 1895-1959
[AS, FB]
*American football executive*
* Bell, Bert

**Bell, Ding Dong**
*See* Bell, William Samuel [Bill]

**Bell, Douglas**
*See* Douglass, Miss

**Bell, E. T.**
*See* Bell, Eric Temple

**Bell, Ed**
*American football player*
* [The] Flea

**Bell, Ed[ward]** 1905?-1960 [BWW]
*American singer*
* [The] Weird Guitar Player

**Bell, Elizabeth**
*See* Brentnall, Margaret Elizabeth

**Bell, Ellis**
*See* Bronte, Emily Jane

**Bell, Elmon** 20th c. [BWW]
*American entertainer*
* Bell, Shorty

**Bell, Emerson**
*See* Patten, William George

**Bell, Emily Mary**
*See* Cason, Mabel Earp

**Bell, Eric Temple** 1883-1960
[NAA, SF, WGT]
*Scottish American author and mathematician*
* Badger, Richard C.
* Bell, E. T.
* J. T.
* Taine, John
* Temple, James

**Bell, Evans** [PA]
*Author*
* Indicus

**Bell, Fern Lee** 1913- [BE]
*American baseball player*
* Bell, Danny

**Bell, Fred** 20th c. [OBW]
*American baseball player*
* Bell, Lefty

**Bell, George Glenn** 1874-1941 [BE]
*American baseball player*
* [The] Farmer

**Bell, Gina**
*See* Iannone, Jeanne [Koppel]

**Bell, Gus**
*See* Bell, David Russell

**Bell, Harry** 1925- [FHE]
*Canadian-born hockey player*
* Bell, Huddie

**Bell, Herbert** 20th c. [IBW]
*American fashion designer*
* Bell, Bubba

**Bell, Herman S.** 1895-1949 [BE]
*American baseball player*
* Bell, Hi

**Bell, Hi**
*See* Bell, Herman S.

**Bell, Huddie**
*See* Bell, Harry

**Bell, Ida**
*See* Eustis, Mrs. Frederick J.

**Bell, J. J.**
*See* Bell, John Jay

**Bell, James Thomas** 1903-
[B10, CBS, MK]
*American baseball player*
* Bell, Cool Papa
* Bell, Papa

**Bell, Jane** [PA]
*Author*
* Gertrude

**Bell, Janet**
*See* Clymer, Eleanor

**Bell, Jeanne**
*See* Bell, Lily

**Bell, Jessie** 20th c. [BWW]
*American musician*
* Red Eye Jessie

**Bell, John**
*See* Johnson, Victor Hugo

**Bell, John Jay** 1871-1934 [LC]
*Author*
* Bell, J. J.

**Bell, John Keble** 1875-1928
[BEW, MBF]
*British-born playwright and author*
* Howard, Keble
* Methuen, John

**Bell, Josephine**
*See* Ball, Doris Bell [Collier]

**Bell, Joyce** 1920- [CA, WD]
*British author*
* Colin, Jean

**Bell, Kitty**
*See* Bloom, Mrs. Lewis

**Bell, Kool**
*See* Bell, Robert

**Bell, Lefty**
*See* Bell, Charles

**Bell, Lefty**
*See* Bell, Fred

**Bell, Lefty**
*See* Bell, William Samuel [Bill]

**Bell, [Prof.] Leo D.**
*See* Lebo, Dell

**Bell, Lily** 1955- [IBW]
*American actress*
* Bell, Jeanne

**Bell, Louise Price** 20th c. [CAP]
*American author*
* Bronson, Lita
* Jeffrey, Ruth

**Bell, Madison** 20th c. [FB]
*American football coach*
* Bell, Moanin' Matty

**Bell, Marie**
*See* Bellon-Downey, Marie Jeanne

**Bell, Mark** 20th c.
*American musician*
* Ramone, Marky

**Bell, Martin** 1918- [DLE]
*British poet*
* Oates, Titus

**Bell, Mary Hayley**
*See* Hayley Bell, Mary

**Bell, Moanin' Matty**
*See* Bell, Madison

**Bell, Mrs. A. M.** [FFF]
*Entertainer*
* Mulle, Maude

**Bell, Mrs. C. M.** [PA]
*Author*
* Materfamilias

**Bell, Mrs. Digby** [FFF]
*Entertainer*
* Joyce, Laura

**Bell, Mrs. S. May** [PA]
*Author*
* Lawton, Effie

**Bell, Neil**
*See* Southwold, Stephen

**Bell, Papa**
*See* Bell, James Thomas

**Bell, R. C.**
*See* Bell, Robert Charles

**Bell, Rex**
*See* Beldam [or Belden?], George F.

**Bell, Robert** 20th c. [RO2]
*American musician*
* Bell, Kool

**Bell, Robert Charles** 1917- [WYA]
*Author*
* Bell, R. C.

**Bell, Robert Stanley Warren**
1871-1921 [MBF]
*British author*
* Brett, Hawkesley

**Bell, Roy Chester** 1907- [BE]
*American baseball player*
* Bell, Beau

**Bell, Rudolph Fred [Rudy]**
*See* Baerwald, John

**Bell, Shorty**
*See* Bell, Elmon

**Bell, Solomon**
*See* Snelling, William Joseph

**Bell, Ted**
*See* Bell, Terrel H.

**Bell, Terrel H.** 1922?-
*American educator and government
official*
* Bell, Ted

**Bell the Cat**
*See* Douglas, Archibald

**Bell, Thornton**
*See* Fanthorpe, R[obert] Lionel

**Bell, William Samuel [Bill]**
1933-1962   [BE, OBW]
*American baseball player*
* Bell, Ding Dong
* Bell, Lefty

**Bell-Zano, Gina**
*See* Iannone, Jeanne [Koppel]

**[La] Bella Ella**
*See* Fitzgerald, Ella

**Bella, John** 1930-   [BE]
*American baseball player*
* Bella, Zeke

**Bella, Zeke**
*See* Bella, John

**Bellairs, George**
*See* Blundell, Harold

**Bellamy, Bells**
*See* Bellamy, Walt[er]

**Bellamy, George Anne**
*See* Bellamy, Georgiana

**Bellamy, Georgiana** 1731?-1788
[WBD]
*British actress*
* Bellamy, George Anne

**Bellamy, Harmon**
*See* Bloom, Herman Irving

**Bellamy, Madge**
*See* Philpott, Margaret

**Bellamy, Mrs. E. W.**   [PA]
*Author*
* Thorpe, Kampa

**Bellamy, Walt[er]** 1939-   [BB, IBW]
*American basketball player*
* Bellamy, Bells

**Bellan, Esteban Enrique** 1850-1932
[BE]
*Cuban-born baseball player*
* Bellan, Steve

**Bellan, Steve**
*See* Bellan, Esteban Enrique

**Bellasis, Margaret Rosa** 20th c.
[AW]
*British author*
* Marton, Francesca

**Bellaut, Adam** ?-1662   [RH]
*Poet*
* [Le] Virgile au Rabot [The Virgil
of the Plane]

**Bellaver, Enrico** 1905-   [BEW]
*American actor*
* Bellaver, Harry

**Bellaver, Harry**
*See* Bellaver, Enrico

**Bellay, Joachim du** 1524?-1560
[DNNF, FFF, SN]
*French poet*
* [The] Father of Grace and
Elegance
* [The] French Ovid
* [The] Ovid of France
* [The] Prince of the Sonnet

**[La] Belle Bretonne**
*See* Eleanor

**Belle, Clara**
*See* Browne, Junius Henri

**Belle, Clara**
*See* Fiske, Mary Hewins

**Belle, Clara**
*See* Logan, Olive

**[La] Belle Cordiere**
*See* Labe, Louise

**[La] Belle Corisande**
*See* D'Andouins, Diane

**[La] Belle et Vertueuse Huguenotte**
*See* De Rouvigny, Rachel

**[La] Belle Gabrielle**
*See* Estrees, Gabrielle d'

**[La] Belle Indienne**
*See* D'Aubigne, Francoise

**[La] Belle Jardiniere**
*See* Estrees, Gabrielle d'

**[La] Belle Liegeoise**
*See* Terwagne, Anne Joseph

**Belle Lumiere des Pasteurs**
*See* De l'Espagne, Jean

**Belle, Nancy**
*See* Leonhardt, Anna

**Belle of Indiana**
*See* Gunness, Belle

**[La] Belle Parricide**
*See* Cenci, Beatrice

**[La] Belle Stuart**
*See* Stuart [or Stewart], Frances
Teresa

**Belleau, Remi** 1528-1577
[DNNS, FFF, HN]
*French poet*
* [Le] Gentil Belleau
* [The] Painter of Nature

**Bellemere, Jean** 1897-   [MWD]
*French actor and playwright*
* Sarment, Jean

**Bellenden, William** ?-1633   [FFF]
*Scottish author*
* Bellendenus, Gulielmo

**Bellendenus, Gulielmo**
*See* Bellenden, William

**Bellerby, [Mary Eireen] Frances**
1899-1975   [CA, WWL]
*British author and poet*
* Parker, M. E. Frances

**Belleville, Henri** ?-1634   [PA]
*Author*
* Legrand

**Bellew, Dorothy**
*See* Falck, Dorothy

**Bellew, Frank P. W.**   [FFF, PA]
*American author and artist*
* Chip
* Triangle

**Bellew, Henry Walter**   [FFF]
*British writer*
* Spectator

**Bellew, John Chippendall
Montesquieu**
*See* Higgin, John Chippendall
Montesquieu

**Bellew, Kyrle**
*See* Falck, Kyrle

**Bellicour, Gillis** 1725-1778   [PA]
*Author*
* Colson

**Bellin, Edward J.** [house pseudonym]
*See* Kuttner, Henry

**Bellin, Olga**
*See* Bielinski, Olga Helena

**Bellingham, Helen Mary Dorothea**
1892-1969   [LC, TC]
*British author*
* Beauclerk, Helen De Vere

**Bellini, Laura**
*See* Woolwine, Laura

**Bellini, Tina** 20th c.   [SFL]
*Author*
* Forest, Salambo

**Bellino** ?-1851   [RH]
*Italian bandit*
* [Il] Passatore

**[Le] Belliqueux**
*See* Henry II [or Henri]

**Bellman, Erik Maria**
*See* Falkner, Annemy

**Bellman, Walter**
*See* Barrett, Hugh Gilchrist

**Bello, Francesco**   [SN]
* [Il] Cieco [The Blind]

**Belloc, Hilaire**
*See* Belloc, [Joseph] Hilary
[Pierre]

**Belloc, [Joseph] Hilary [Pierre]**
1870-1953   [WBD]
*British author*
* Belloc, Hilaire

**Bellocq, Louise**
*See* Boudat, Marie-Louise

**Bellon-Downey, Marie Jeanne**
1900-   [F2, FC]
*French actress*
* Bell, Marie

**Belloy, Dormont de**
*See* Buyrette, Pierre Laurent

**Bellson, Louis**
*See* Balassoni, Louis

**Bellwood, Bessie**
*See* Mahony, Elizabeth Ann
Katherine

**Bellwood, Herbert**
*See* Patten, William George

**Belmeys, John**   [PA]
*Author*
* Eboracensis, Joannes

**Belmont, Clara**
*See* Calvert, Mrs. C. H.

**Belmonte**
*See* Barreto, Benedito Bastos

**Belmonte y Garcia, Juan**
1892-1962   [GS]
*Spanish bullfighter*
* [El] Fenomeno de Triana [The
Phenomenon of Triana]
* [El] Revolucionario del Toreo
[The Revolutionary Bullfighter]

**Belmood, Husny**
*See* Neagu, Paul

**Belmore, Alice**
*See* Cliffe, Alice

**Belmore, Daisy**
*See* Garstin, Daisy

**Belotto [or Bellotto], Bernardo**
1720-1780   [WBD]
*Venetian painter*
* Canaletto [or Canale], Bernardo

**[The] Beloved Disciple**
*See* John

**[The] Beloved Merchant**
*See* Pole, Michael de la

**[The] Beloved Physician**
*See* Luke

**Belshazzar**
*See* Waters, Augustus

**Belted Will**
*See* Howard, [Lord] William

**Belting Bert Wilson**
*See* Wilson, Bertwin Hilliard

**Belt'n Melt'n**
*See* Melton, William Edwin

**[La] Beltraneja**
*See* Juana

**Belvedere, Lee**
*See* Grayland, Valerie Merle
[Spanner]

**Bely [or Belyi], Andrei**
*See* Bugaev [or Bugayev], Boris
Nikolaevich

**Belyavin, Vasili Ivanovich**
1865?-1925   [WBD]
*Patriarch of Moscow and head of
Russian Orthodox Church*
* Tikhon

**Bembo, Pietro** 1470-1547   [SN]
*Italian cardinal and poet*
* [The] Foster Father of Our
Language
* [The] Guide and Master of Our
Tongue

**Bement, Dwight** 1940?-   [RO2]
*American musician*
* Bement, Sergeant
* Bement, Spider

**Bement, Sergeant**
*See* Bement, Dwight

**Bement, Spider**
*See* Bement, Dwight

**Bemiller, Albert D.** 1939-   [FB]
*American football player*
* Bemiller, Tombstone

**Bemiller, Tombstone**
*See* Bemiller, Albert D.

**Bemister, Henry**
*See* Barrett, Harry B[emister]

**Ben, Ilke**
*See* Harper, Carol Ely

**Ben Ali, Achmed**
See Robinson, William Ellsworth

**Ben Ami**
See Eliav, Arie L[ova]

**Ben-Ami, Jacob**
See Shtchirin, Jacob

**Ben Asher, Judah Loeb** 1830-1892
[WBD]
*Russian poet and author*
* Gordon, Jehuda Leb

**Ben Avraham, Chofetz Chaim**
See Pickering, Stephen

**Ben Avraham, Elisha**
See Perry, Aulcie

**Ben Bella, Ahmed** 20th c.
*Algerian president*
* Aminedi [Invisible One]

**Ben Chaim**
See Kahn, Yitzhak

**Ben Dov, Meir**
See Bernet, Michael M.

**Ben Eliezer, Israel** 1700?-1760
[WBD]
*Polish educator and religious leader*
* Baal Shem-Tov [Kind Master of the Holy Name]
* BEShT

**Ben-Ezra, Juan J.**
See Lacanza, Manuel

**Ben-Fares, Almed** [PA]
*Author*
* [El] Razi

**Ben Gurion, David**
See Green, David

**Ben-Haim, Paul**
See Frankenburger, Paul

**Ben Horav, Naphthali**
See Krivitsky, Nathaniel

**Ben Horin, Meir**
See Schiffmann, Meir

**Ben Issa, Isuf**
See Lopez-Portillo y Rojas, Jose

**Ben-Nez**
See Novachovitch, Lippe Benzion

**Ben-Schachar, Mordecai Enric**
See Stern, Maximilian Enric

**Ben Solomon, Elijah [or Elias]**
See Wilna, Elijah [or Elias]

**Ben Yosef, Avraham Chaim** 1917-
[WD]
*Israeli author*
* Matsuba, Moshe

**Benard, Anne-Jose** 1929- [FC]
*French actress*
* Aubry, Cecile

**Benard, Ray** 1907- [FC]
*American actor*
* Corrigan, Crash
* Corrigan, Ray

**Benarria, Allan**
See Goldenthal, Allan Benarria

**Benary, Margot**
See Benary-Isbert, Margot

**Benary-Isbert, Margot** 1889-1979
[SAT]
*German-born American author*
* Benary, Margot

**Benauly**
See Abbott, Lyman

**Bence, Gretchen Anne** 1930- [OP]
*American opera singer*
* Bence, Margarethe

**Bence, Margarethe**
See Bence, Gretchen Anne

**Bench, Hands**
See Bench, Johnny Lee

**Bench, Johnny Lee** 1947- [PB]
*American baseball player*
* Bench, Hands

**Bencur, Matej** 1860-1928 [EWL]
*Slovakian author*
* Kukucin, Martin

**Benda, Pauline** 1880- ? [WBD]
*French actress*
* Simone

**Benda, Simone** 1880- ? [THR]
*French actress*
* Le Bargy, Simone
* Madame Simone

**Bender, Ariel**
See Grosvenor, Luther

**Bender, Arnold** 1904- [AW]
*German-born author*
* Philippi, Mark

**Bender, Charles Albert**
1883?-1954 [AS, BAB, PB]
*American baseball player*
* Bender, Chief
* [The] Chief

**Bender, Chief**
See Bender, Charles Albert

**Bender, Chief**
See Bender, Sheldon

**Bender, D. C.** 1919- [BWW]
*American singer*
* Bender, Wine Head
* Dee, Bobby
* Washington, D. C.

**Bender, Jay**
See Deindorfer, Robert Greene

**Bender, Louis** 1910- [EJS]
*American basketball player*
* Bender, Lulu

**Bender, Lulu**
See Bender, Louis

**Bender, Sheldon** 20th c. [SMG]
*American football executive*
* Bender, Chief

**Bender, Tony**
See Strollo, Anthony C.

**Bender, Wine Head**
See Bender, D. C.

**Bendit, Gladys Williams**
1889-1975 [AW, CAP, SFL]
*British author*
* Presland, John

**Bendix**
See Barnes, W. Therold

**Bendow, Josef**
See Tenenbaum, Joseph

**Benedetto, Anthony Dominick**
1926- [EJ7, EPM, RO1]
*American singer*
* Bari, Joe
* Bennett, Tony

**Benedetto, Giovanni**
See Mittarilli, Nicolo Gracome

**Benedetto, Riccardo** 1916- [FC]
*American actor*
* Benedict, Richard

**Benedict**
See Dawson, Edward Walter

**Benedict**
See Jouvin, B.

**Benedict** 480?- 543? [DNNS]
*Saint*
* Founder of Peace

**Benedict, Benny**
See Benedict, Clint[on]

**Benedict, Clarence W.** 1903- [GF]
*American golf executive*
* Benedict, Gus

**Benedict, Clint[on]** 1894-
[BBH, HK]
*Canadian-born hockey player*
* Benedict, Benny

**Benedict, Gus**
See Benedict, Clarence W.

**Benedict, Hester A.**
See Dickinson, Hester A.

**Benedict, I.**
See Forster, Bobbie Hughes

**Benedict, Joseph**
See Dollen, Charles Joseph

**Benedict, Leopold**
See Novachovitch, Lippe Benzion

**Benedict, Lynn**
See Banis, Victor J[erome]

**Benedict, Margaret**
See Fisher, Margaret Trusler

**Benedict, Myrle**
See Sallaska, Georgia Myrle

**Benedict, Richard**
See Benedetto, Riccardo

**Benedict, Steve** 1899- [WGT]
*American author*
* Marius

**Benedict IV** 1012?-1056 [WBD]
*Pope*
* [The] Boy Pope

**Benedict IX**
See Theophylactus

**Benedict V** ?- 965 [DNNS]
*Pope*
* Grammaticus

**Benedict VIII**
See Theophylactus

**Benedict X**
See Mincius, John

**Benedict XI**
See Boccasini, Niccolo

**Benedict XII**
See Fournier, Jacques

**Benedict XIII**
See De Luna, Pedro

**Benedict XIII**
See Orsini, Pietro Francesco

**Benedict XIV**
See Lambertini, Prospero

**Benedict XV**
See Chiesa, Giacomo della

**Benedictsson, Victoria Maria**
1850-1888 [WBD]
*Swedish author*
* Ahlgren, Ernst

**Beneke, Gordon** 1914- [EJ, PMJ]
*American musician and bandleader*
* Beneke, Tex

**Beneke, Tex**
See Beneke, Gordon

**Benengeli, Cid Hamet**
See Macaulay, Thomas Babington
[First Baron Macaulay]

**Benes, Bananas**
See Benes, Joseph Anthony [Joe]

**Benes, Jan** 1936- [CA]
*Czech-born author*
* Stepka, Milan

**Benes, Joseph Anthony [Joe]** 1901-
[BE]
*American baseball player*
* Benes, Bananas

**Benet, Edouard**
See Edwards, William B[ennett]

**Benete, Antonio** [GS]
*Spanish bullfighter*
* [El] Mesias [The Messiah]

**Benevides, Marco** 1489-1582 [PA]
*Author*
* Mantuano, Marco

**Benge, Cal**
See Benge, Ray Adelphia

**Benge, Ray Adelphia** 1902-
[BE, BN]
*American baseball player*
* Benge, Cal
* Benge, Silent Cal

**Benge, Silent Cal**
See Benge, Ray Adelphia

**Bengough, Benny**
See Bengough, Bernard Oliver

**Bengough, Bernard Oliver**
1898-1968 [BE, PB]
*American baseball player*
* Bengough, Benny

**Benham, William** 1831-1910
[WWL]
*British clergyman and author*
* Lombard, Peter

**Beni, Gimi**
See Beni, James J.

**Beni, James J.** 20th c. [OP]
*American opera singer*
* Beni, Gimi

**[The] Benicia Boy**
See Heenan, John C.

**Benisius**
See Boten, Giovanni

**Benitez, Gaspar** 1935- [BX]
*Mexican boxer*
* [The] Indian
* Ortega, Gaspar

**Benitez Perez, Manuel** 1937-
[GS, IPA, OCS]
*Spanish bullfighter*
* [El] Cordobes [The Cordovan]

**Benitez Trevino, Christina**
1930-1956   [SC]
*Mexican actress and opera singer*
* Trevi, Christina

**Benjamin, Alice**
*See* Brooke, Avery [Rogers]

**Benjamin, Bea** 20th c.   [EJ7]
*South African singer*
* Sathima

**Benjamin, Buck**
*See* Benjamin, Jason

**Benjamin, Bud**
*See* Benjamin, Burton

**Benjamin, Burton** 20th c.   [ET]
*American television producer*
* Benjamin, Bud

**Benjamin, Cicero**
*See* Benjamin, Robert Charles
O'Hara

**Benjamin, Claude**
*See* Pohlman, Max Edward

**Benjamin, Elbert** 1882-1951
[NAD]
*Author*
* Zain, C. C.

**Benjamin, Fish**
*See* Benjamin, James

**Benjamin, James** 20th c.   [IBW]
*American jazz musician*
* Benjamin, Fish

**Benjamin, Jason** 1928?-
*American baseball player*
* Benjamin, Buck

**Benjamin, Lewis Saul** 1874- ?
[SFP]
*British author*
* Melville, Lewis [joint pseudonym
    with Reginald Hargreaves]

**Benjamin, Nora**
*See* Kubie, Nora Gottheil
Benjamin

**Benjamin, Park** 1809-1864   [PA]
*Author*
* Flaneur
* Parker, Bently

**Benjamin, Robert Charles O'Hara**
1855- ?   [IBW]
*American author and journalist*
* Benjamin, Cicero

**Benjamin, Walter** 1892-1940
[EWL]
*German author*
* Conrad, C.
* Holz, Detlev

**Benjamin, Walter Romeyn** 1854- ?
[PA]
*Author*
* Jermyn, Dud

**Benjamins, Mr.**
*See* Hart, Charles B.

**Benji, Thomas**
*See* Robinson, Frank M[alcolm]

**Benko, Nancy**
*See* Atkinson, Nancy

**Benn, Matthew**
*See* Siegel, Benjamin

**Benner, Bill**
*See* Fletcher, Tex

**Benners, Isaac [Ike]** 20th c.   [BE]
*American baseball player*
* Benners, Windy

**Benners, Windy**
*See* Benners, Isaac [Ike]

**Bennet, Robert A[mes]**
*See* Browne, F. G.

**Bennett, [Enoch] Arnold** 1867-1931
[LC, TC]
*British author and playwright*
* Gwendolyn
* Tonson, Jacob

**Bennett, Brian Theodore Norton**
1927-   [ART]
*British painter*
* B. T. N. B.

**Bennett, Bruce**
*See* Brix, Herman

**Bennett, Bugs**
*See* Bennett, Joseph Harley

**Bennett, C. N.** 20th c.   [MBF]
*British author*
* Collier, Norman

**Bennett, Chip**
*See* Bennett, Francis Allen [Frank]

**Bennett, Christine**
*See* Neubauer, William Arthur

**Bennett, Compton**
*See* Compton-Bennett, Robert

**Bennett, Daniel**
*See* Gilmore, Joseph L[ee]

**Bennett, Doc**
*See* Bennett, E. S.

**Bennett, Dorothea**
*See* Young, Dorothea Bennett

**Bennett, Dwight**
*See* Newton, Dwight Bennett

**Bennett, E. S.** 20th c.   [SMG]
*American baseball scout*
* Bennett, Doc

**Bennett, Faith**
*See* Riddick, Margaret

**Bennett, Francis Allen [Frank]**
1904-1966   [BE]
*American baseball player*
* Bennett, Chip

**Bennett, [James] Fred** 1902-1957
[BE]
*American baseball player*
* Bennett, Red

**Bennett, Geoffrey [Martin]** 1909-
[AW, CA, WD]
*British author*
* Sea Lion

**Bennett, George** 20th c.   [IBW]
*American author*
* Bennett, Hal

**Bennett, Gertrude Barrows**
1884-1940?   [ESF, SFL, WGT]
*American author*
* Stevens, Francis

**Bennett, H. O.**
*See* Hardison, Osborne B.

**Bennett, H. S.**
*See* Bennett, Henry Stanley

**Bennett, Hal**
*See* Bennett, George

**Bennett, Hall**
*See* Hall, Bennie Caroline
[Humble]

**Bennett, Harve**
*See* Fischman, Harve

**Bennett, Helen Christine**
*See* Maupin, Helen Christine
Bennett

**Bennett, Henry Stanley** 1889-1972
[LC]
*British author*
* Bennett, H. S.

**Bennett, Isadora** 1900-1980   [CA]
*American publicity agent,
playwright, author*
* Morgan, Wesley

**Bennett, Jean Frances**
*See* Dorcy, Mary Jean

**Bennett, Jeremy**
*See* Bennett, John Jerome Nelson

**Bennett, Joe**
*See* Aldert, Joseph Bennett

**Bennett, John [Frederic]**
*See* Garrigan, John Frederic

**Bennett, John Jerome Nelson**
1939-   [CA]
*British author and broadcaster*
* Bennett, Jeremy

**Bennett, John Michael** 1942-
[IAW]
*American poet*
* Nips, Nick

**Bennett, Joseph Harley** 1892-1957
[BE]
*American baseball player*
* Bennett, Bugs
* Morris, Bugs
* Morris, Joseph Harley

**Bennett, Justin Titus** 1874-1935
[BE]
*American baseball player*
* Bennett, Pug

**Bennett, Lavinia**
*See* Mackay, Mrs. John A.

**Bennett, Lou**
*See* Benoit, Louis

**Bennett, Louise Simone** 1919-
[CW, IBW]
*Jamaican poet, actress, singer*
* Miss Lou

**Bennett, Michael**
*See* DiFiglia, Michael Bennett

**Bennett, Mrs. Clement**   [FFF]
*Entertainer*
* Murielle, Constance

**Bennett, Mrs. Frank**   [FFF]
*Entertainer*
* Bowers, May

**Bennett, Mrs. William**   [PA]
*Author*
* Gay, Getty

**Bennett, Pug**
*See* Bennett, Justin Titus

**Bennett, Rachel**
*See* Hill, Margaret [Ohler]

**Bennett, Red**
*See* Bennett, [James] Fred

**Bennett, Red**
*See* Houghton, William

**Bennett, Tony**
*See* Benedetto, Anthony Dominick

**Bennett, William** 1824-1887   [PA]
*Author*
* Wilmshurst, Zavarr

**Bennett, William Edward** 1898-
[WGT]
*British author*
* Armstrong, Warren

**Bennette, George** 1901-   [MK]
*American baseball player*
* Bennette, Jewbaby

**Bennette, Jewbaby**
*See* Bennette, George

**Benning, Howe**
*See* Henry, Mary H.

**Bennis, Wessel Johannes** 1933-
[IAW]
*Dutch author and poet*
* Lucullus
* Sinbeth, Lesly

**Benno, Alex**
*See* Bonefang, Benjamin

**Benny, Benny K.**
*See* Kubelsky, Benjamin [Benny]

**Benny, Jack**
*See* Kubelsky, Benjamin [Benny]

**Benoit, Alice P.** 20th c.   [NAA]
*Canadian author and playwright*
* Monique

**Benoit, Francois Pierre Joseph**
*See* Bobo, [Dr.] Rosalvo

**Benoit, Louis** 1926-   [DAM]
*American organist and composer*
* Bennett, Lou

**Benoit, Norbert**
*See* Vanpeperstraete, Norbert

**Benoliel, Jeanne Quint** 1919-   [CA]
*American nurse and author*
* Quint, Jeanne

**Benrath, Frederic**
*See* Gerard, Philippe

**Bensley, Robert** 1738?-1817?   [SN]
*British actor*
* Roaring Bob of the Garden

**Bensman, Joseph** 1922-   [CA]
*American sociologist and author*
* Bentham, Jay
* Lewis, Ian

**Bensol, Oscar**
*See* Gomberg, William Gilbert

**Benson, A. C.**
*See* Benson, Arthur Christopher

**Benson, Allan Ingvald** 20th c.
[WGT]
*Author*
* Valding, Victor [joint pseudonym
    with John Victor Peterson]

**Benson, Allen Wilbert** 1908-   [BE]
*American baseball player*
* Benson, Bullet Ben

**Benson, Arthur Christopher**
1862-1925   [HFF]
*British author*
* Benson, A. C.

**Benson, B. A.**
*See*   Beyea, Basil

**Benson, Benee**
*See*   Benson, George

**Benson, Bennie**
*See*   Benson, Kent

**Benson, Bobby**
*See*   Ackerman, Forrest J[ames]

**Benson, Bullet Ben**
*See*   Benson, Allen Wilbert

**Benson, Carl**
*See*   Bristed, Charles Astor

**Benson, Daniel**
*See*   Cooper, Colin Symons

**Benson, E. F.**
*See*   Benson, Edward Frederic

**Benson, Edward Frederic**
1867-1940   [HFF, MBL]
*British author*
* Benson, E. F.

**Benson, Edwin**
*See*   Shaver, Richard S[harpe]

**Benson, Eugene** 1913-   [MK]
*American baseball player*
* Benson, Spider

**Benson, Frederick William** 1948-
[CA]
*American author and photographer*
* Benson, Ted

**Benson, George** 1943-   [IBW]
*American jazz musician*
* Benson, Benee

**Benson, Godfrey**
*See*   Charnwood, Godfrey
Rathbone Benson

**Benson, Hamilton** 1885-   [NOJ]
*American jazz musician*
* Benson, Hamp

**Benson, Hamp**
*See*.  Benson, Hamilton

**Benson, Jennie**
*See*   Fish, Mrs. M. J.

**Benson, John**
*See*   Sebastian, John

**Benson, Kent** 1954-
*American basketball player*
* Benson, Bennie

**Benson, Nathaniel Anketell** 1903-
[NAA]
*Canadian author, poet, journalist*
* Pegasus

**Benson, Obie**
*See*   Benson, Renaldo

**Benson, P., Sr.**
*See*   Miller, Charles C.

**Benson, Paul**
*See*   Alex, Gus

**Benson, R. H.**
*See*   Benson, Robert Hugh

**Benson, Renaldo** 20th c.   [RO2]
*American singer*
* Benson, Obie

**Benson, Richard**
*See*   Cooper, Saul

**Benson, Robert Hugh** 1871-1914
[HFF]
*British author*
* Benson, R. H.

**Benson, Sally**
*See*   Benson, Sara Mahala Redway
[Smith]

**Benson, Sara Mahala Redway**
[Smith] 1897?-1972
[BEW, CA, CAP]
*American author and playwright*
* Benson, Sally
* Evarts, Esther

**Benson, Spider**
*See*   Benson, Eugene

**Benson, Stella**
*See*   Anderson, Stella Benson

**Benson, Ted**
*See*   Benson, Frederick William

**Benson, Therese**
*See*   Knipe, Emilie Benson

**Bent, M. H.**
*See*   Bent, Medora Heather

**Bent, Medora Heather** 20th c.
[ART]
*British painter and potter*
* Bent, M. H.

**Benteen, John**
*See*   Haas, Ben[jamin] L[eopold]

**Bentein, Jean-Marie Georges Joseph**
1913-   [IAW]
*Belgian author*
* Dorchato, Jean
* Georges, Jean

**Bentham, Jay**
*See*   Bensman, Joseph

**Bentham, Jeremy** 1748-1832
[DEP, FFF, RH]
*British jurist and philosopher*
* [The] Queen Square Hermit
* Smith, Gamaliel

**Benthic, Arch E.**
*See*   Stewart, Harris B[ates], Jr.

**Benthien, Fritz**
*See*   Bonus, Arthur

**Bentinck, [Lord] George** 1802-1848
[HN]
*British statesman*
* [The] Napoleon of the Turf

**Bentinck, William John Cavendish
Scott** 1800-1879   [HN]
*Fifth Duke of Portland*
* [The] Invisible Prince

**Bentivoglio, Guido** 1579-1644   [SN]
*Italian cardinal, diplomat, historian*
* [An] Ornament of Italy

**Bentley, Alexina** 1904-1965   [SC]
*American actress*
* Bentley, Irene

**Bentley, Edmund Clerihew**
1875-1956   [EMD, TC]
*British author*
* Clerihew, E.

**Bentley, Gladys Alberta** 1907-1960
[BWW]
*American singer*
* Broadway's Queen of Song and
Jazz

**Bentley, Grendon**
*See*   Bentley-Taylor, Grendon

**Bentley, Irene**
*See*   Bentley, Alexina

**Bentley, James William Benedict**
1914-   [AW]
*British author*
* Claughton-James, James
* Nostalgia

**Bentley, Janice Babb** 1933-   [CA]
*American librarian and author*
* Babb, Janice B.

**Bentley, Margaret** 1926-   [WD]
*British author*
* Stephens, Frances

**Bentley, Richard**
*See*   Browning, Alice C.

**Bentley, Richard** 1662-1742
[FFF, SN]
*British critic and scholar*
* [The] Aristarchus of Cambridge
* Phileleutherus Lipsiensis

**Bentley, Sarah** 1946-   [CA]
*American editor*
* Doely, Sarah Bentley

**Bentley, Walter**
*See*   Begg, Walter

**Bentley-Taylor, Grendon**
1877-1956   [THR]
*British actor*
* Bentley, Grendon

**Bently, Fred** 1911-1969   [SC]
*American actor*
* Bancroft, Charles

**Bently, J.**   [PA]
*Author*
* Oldest Inspector

**Bently, Joseph** [assumed name]
*See*   Barboza, Joseph

**Benton, Al**
*See*   Benton, John Alton

**Benton, Alfred Lee** 1957-   [SMG]
*American baseball player*
* Benton, Butch

**Benton, Brook**
*See*   Peay, Benjamin Franklin

**Benton, Butch**
*See*   Benton, Alfred Lee

**Benton, Caroline French**
*See*   Burrell, Caroline Benedict

**Benton, John**
*See*   Daniels, Norman [A.]

**Benton, John Alton** 1911-   [BE]
*American baseball player*
* Benton, Al

**Benton, John Clebon** 1887?-1937
[AS, BE, PB]
*American baseball player*
* Benton, Rube

**Benton, Joseph Horace**
1898?-1975   [B10, BBD]
*American opera singer*
* Bentonelli, Joseph [or Giuseppe]

**Benton, Karla**
*See*   Rowland, D[onald] S[ydney]

**Benton, Peggie** 1906?-
[AW, CA, WD]
*British author*
* Burke, Shifty

**Benton, Robert**
*See*   Buse, Renee

**Benton, Rube**
*See*   Benton, John Clebon

**Benton, Thomas Hart** 1782-1848
[DEP, DNNF, FFF]
*American statesman*
* Old Bullion

**Bentonelli, Joseph [or Giuseppe]**
*See*   Benton, Joseph Horace

**Bentzon, Therese**
*See*   Blanc, Marie Therese [De
Solms]

**Beny, Roloff**
*See*   Beny, Wilfred Roy

**Beny, Wilfred Roy** 1924-   [CA]
*Canadian artist and photographer*
* Beny, Roloff

**Benyehuda, Yoseh Ben Moshea**
1892-1973   [IBW]
*Nigerian-born American religious
leader*
* Matthew, Wentworth Arthur

**Benz, Blitzen Joe**
*See*   Benz, Joseph Louis

**Benz, Joseph Louis** 1886-1957
[BE]
*American baseball player*
* Benz, Blitzen Joe

**Benzell, Mimi**
*See*   Benzell, Miriam Ruth

**Benzell, Miriam Ruth** 1924-1970
[BEW, IPA]
*American singer*
* Benzell, Mimi

**Beolco, Angelo** 1502-1542
[FFF, SN, WBD]
*Italian playwright*
* [The] Farceur
* [Il] Ruzzante

**Beorse, Bryn** 1896-   [CA]
*Norwegian-born American author*
* Bjorset, Brynjolf

**Bera, Sudhir** 1933-   [IAW]
*Indian author*
* Sri-Rajputra

**Beraldus Aurelius**
*See*   Berauld, Nicolas

**Berand, Antoine Nicolas** 1792- ?
[PA]
*Author*
* Antony

**Beranger, Emily**   [PA]
*Author*
* De Chandeneux, Claire

**Beranger, Paul**
*See*   Collin, Jacques Albin Simon

**Beranger, Pierre Jean de**
1780-1857   [DNNS, FFF, SN]
*French poet*
* [The] Burns of France
* [The] French Burns
* [The] French Horace

**Beranger, Pierre Jean de** (Continued)
* [The] Horace of France
* [The] Poet of St. Honore

**Berardinelli, Guiseppe Antonio**
1922-   [BX, RBE]
*American boxer*
* Maxim, Joey

**Berauld, Nicolas** 1473-1550   [PA]
*Author*
* Beraldus Aurelius

**Berch, William O.**
*See* Coyne, Joseph E.

**Berchtenbreiter, Marie** 1892-
[BBD]
*German opera singer*
* Olczewska, Maria

**Berckman, Evelyn Domenica** 1900-
[CA]
*American-born author and composer*
* Wade, Joanna

**Bercoff, Andre** 1941?-
*French author*
* De Commines, Philippe

**Bercovici, Anna** ?-1963   [BEW]
*Rumanian-born actress*
* Appel, Anna

**Berdell, Lucille** 1871-1964   [SC]
*American actress*
* Page, Lucille

**Berdoe, Edward** 1836-1916   [WWL]
*British author*
* Scalpel, Aesculapius

**Berek, Augustus** 1882?-1964
[BEW]
*Theatrical performer*
* Burt, Frank A.

**Berend, Alice**
*See* Breinlinger, Alice Berend

**Berendt, Rachel**
*See* Arkell, Monique

**Berenger, Rene** 1830-1915   [WBD]
*French jurist and politician*
* Pere la Pudeur

**Berenson, Bernard**
*See* Valvrojenski, Bernard

**Berenson, Gordon Arthur** 1939-
[FHE, HK, SMG]
*Canadian-born hockey player and coach*
* Berenson, Red
* [The] Red Baron

**Berenson, Harold** 1939-
*American business executive*
* [The] Red Baron

**Berenson, Red**
*See* Berenson, Gordon Arthur

**Bereny, Gail Rubin**
*See* Rubin, Gail

**Berenyi, Maria** 1885-   [THR]
*French-born entertainer*
* Klio
* Lorraine, Irma

**Beresford**
*See* Hamburger, Anne Ellen

**Beresford, J. D.**
*See* Beresford, John Davys

**Beresford, John**
*See* Rochester, George Ernest

**Beresford, John Claudius** 18th c.
[SN]
*Tortured suspected rebels during the 1798 Irish revolt*
* [The] Court Historian
* [The] State Apothecary

**Beresford, John Davys** 1873-1947
[LC]
*British author*
* Beresford, J. D.

**Beresford, Leslie** 20th c.
[SFL, WW, WWL]
*British author*
* Pan

**Beresford, Marcus** 1919-
[ANT, WW]
*British-born American author*
* Brandel, Marc

**Beresford, Russell**
*See* Roberts, Cecil Edric Mornington

**Beresford-Williams, Mary E.**
1931-   [ART]
*British painter and printmaker*
* Williams, M. B.

**Berg, David Brandt** 1919?-
*Founder of religious cult, Children of God*
* David, Moses

**Berg, Gene**
*See* Berg, Leander

**Berg, Gertrude**
*See* Edelstein, Gertrude

**Berg, Heinrich** 1300?-1366   [WBD]
*German mystic*
* Suso [or Seuse], Heinrich

**Berg, Jack [or Jackie]**
*See* Bergman, Judah

**Berg, Joan**
*See* Victor, Joan Berg

**Berg, Kid**
*See* Bergman, Judah

**Berg, Leander** 1920-
[FC, ITA, TR]
*American actor, dancer, singer*
* Berg, Gene
* Nelson, Gene

**Berg, Moe**
*See* Berg, Morris

**Berg, Morris** 1902-1972
[B10, BE, EJS]
*American baseball player*
* Berg, Moe

**Berg, Patricia J. [Patty]** 1918-
[BBH]
*American golfer*
* [The] Minneapolis Tomboy
* [The] Red Headed Tomboy

**Berg, Rilla**
*See* France, Thelma Edith Minnie

**Berg, Solomon** 1924-   [FC]
*American actor*
* Hill, Steven

**[Il] Bergamasco**
*See* Castello, Giovanni Battista

**Bergamo, Augie**
*See* Bergamo, August Samuel

**Bergamo, August Samuel** 1918-
[BE]
*American baseball player*
* Bergamo, Augie

**Bergamonti, Rosella** 20th c.   [WF]
*Italian actress*
* Carr, Patricia

**Berganza, Teresa**
*See* Vargas, Teresa

**Bergauer, Johannes**
*See* Tschernek, Viktor

**Bergdahl, Enid**
*See* Gillette, Leland J.

**Bergen, Polly**
*See* Burgin, Nellie Paulina

**Bergen, Red Hott**
*See* Bergen, Stuart

**Bergen, Stuart** 1911-   [NOJ]
*American jazz musician*
* Bergen, Red Hott

**Bergendorf, Ralph Wallace** 1926-
[BEW]
*American choreographer and dancer*
* Beaumont, Ralph

**Berger, [Colonel] A.**
*See* Malraux, [Georges-] Andre

**Berger, Bilbo**
*See* Berger, Ernest

**Berger, Bobby** 20th c.   [GW]
*American rodeo performer*
* Berger, Bugs

**Berger, Boze**
*See* Berger, Louis William

**Berger, Bugs**
*See* Berger, Bobby

**Berger, Charles** 1882-1954   [BE]
*American baseball player*
* Berger, Heinie

**Berger, Elizabeth**
*See* Sheppard, Elizabeth Sara

**Berger, Ernest** 20th c.   [RO2]
*Czech musician*
* Berger, Bilbo

**Berger, Evelyn Miller** 1896-   [WD]
*American educator and author*
* Miller, Evelyn

**Berger, Fats**
*See* Berger, Joseph August [Joe]

**Berger, Hans**
*See* Eisler, Gerhard

**Berger, Heinie**
*See* Berger, Charles

**Berger, Helen**
*See* Bamberger, Helen R.

**Berger, Henry David** 1920-   [BEW]
*American actor, singer, director, producer*
* Brooks, David

**Berger, Ike L.**
*See* Eichelberger, Thomas W.

**Berger, Ivan [Bennett]** 1939-   [CA]
*American author*
* Evans, Bennett
* Leynard, Martin

**Berger, John Henry** 1867-1907
[BE]
*American baseball player*
* Berger, Tun

**Berger, Josef** 1903-1971   [CA]
*American author and speechwriter*
* Digges, Jeremiah

**Berger, Joseph August [Joe]**
1886-1956   [BE]
*American baseball player*
* Berger, Fats

**Berger, Louis William** 1910-   [BE]
*American baseball player*
* Berger, Boze

**Berger, Ludwig**
*See* Bamberger, Ludwig

**Berger, Maurice** 1927-   [OP]
*French opera producer, dancer and choreographer*
* Bejart, Maurice

**Berger, Siegfried**
*See* Von Chelius, Oskar

**Berger, Tun**
*See* Berger, John Henry

**Bergerac, Catfish**
*See* Bergerac, Michel

**Bergerac, Michel** 1932-
*French-born business executive*
* Bergerac, Catfish

**Bergere, Dorothy**
*See* Resetar, Dorothy L.

**Bergeret, Ida Treat** 1889?-1978
[CA]
*American educator, journalist, author*
* Treat, Ida

**Bergeron, Victor** 1903-   [B10]
*American restaurateur*
* Trader Vic

**Bergh, A. E.** 1855- ?   [PA]
*Author*
* Snap, Sylvanus

**Bergin, Osborn J.** 20th c.   [WWL]
*Irish author and poet*
* O hAimhirgin, Osborn

**Bergius, Elsa Britt**
*See* Olenius, Elsa Victoria

**Bergman, Al[fred Henry]**
1890-1961   [BE]
*American baseball player*
* Bergman, Dutch

**Bergman, Arthur** 20th c.   [SMG]
*American football coach*
* Bergman, Dutch

**Bergman, Bergie**
*See* Bergman, Bernard A.

**Bergman, Bernard A.** 1895?-1980
*American editor*
* Bergman, Bergie

**Bergman, Dutch**
*See* Bergman, Al[fred Henry]

**Bergman, Dutch**
*See* Bergman, Arthur

**Bergman, Hjalmar [Fredrik Elgerus]**
1883-1931   [MWD]
*Swedish author and playwright*
* [The] Swedish Dickens

**Bergman, [Ernst] Ingmar** 1918-
[CA]
*Swedish screenwriter, director,
producer*
* Eriksson, Buntel
* Riffe, Ernest

**Bergman, Jonas**
*See* Soederhjelm, Kai

**Bergman, Judah** 1909-
[BX, EJS, RBE]
*British boxer*
* Berg, Jack [or Jackie]
* Berg, Kid
* [The] Whitechapel Whirlwind
* [The] Whitechapel Windmill

**Bergman, Richard Thomas** 1947-
*British author*
* Richards, Thomas

**Bergman, Teddy**
*Actor*
* Reed, Alan

**Bergner, Elisabeth**
*See* Ettel, Elizabeth

**Bergon, Serge**
*See* Bergonzelli, Sergio

**Bergonzelli, Sergio** 20th c.    [FDG]
*Director*
* Bergon, Serge

**Bergson, Leo**
*See* Stebel, Sidney Leo

**Berigan, Bunny**
*See* Berigan, Roland Bernard

**Berigan, Roland Bernard**
1908?-1942    [DAM, EJ, PMJ]
*American jazz musician*
* Berigan, Bunny

**Berindey, Stephanie** 1913-    [FC]
*Hungarian dancer and actress*
* Duna, Steffi

**Beringer, Carroll James** 1928-
[SMG]
*American baseball player and coach*
* C. B.

**Beringer, Joseph August** 1862- ?
[LAO]
*German author*
* J. A. B.

**Berk, Artie**
*See* Berkowitz, Artie

**Berkebile, Fred D[onovan]** 1900-
[CA]
*American educator and author*
* Donovan, William
* Ernest, William
* Stauffer, Don

**Berkeley**
*See* Lester, Charles Edward

**Berkeley, Anthony**
*See* Cox, Anthony Berkeley

**Berkeley, Ballard**
*See* Blascheck, Ballard

**Berkeley, Busby**
*See* Enos, William Berkeley

**Berkeley, Everard**
*See* Edwards, Tryon

**Berkeley, F. Grantley**    [PA]
*Author*
* Huntsman

**Berkeley, George** 1685-1753    [SN]
*Irish philosopher*
* [The] Irish Plato

**Berkeley, Helen**
*See* Ogden, Anna Cora

**Berkely, Olive**
*See* Dickson, Olive

**Berkley, Lady**    [FFF, RH]
*British jurist*
* [The] Lady Magistrate

**Berkley, Tom**
*See* Geen, Clifford

**Berkoff, Nerik**
*See* Bernardi, Nerio

**Berkowitz, Artie** 20th c.    [RO1]
*American singer*
* Berk, Artie

**Berkowitz, David R.** 1953?-
*American murderer*
* [The] 44-Caliber Killer
* Son of Sam

**[The] Berkshire Lady**
*See* Kendrick, Frances

**Berl-Lee, Maria**
*See* Lee, Maria Berl

**Berle, Milton**
*See* Berlinger, Milton

**Berle, Sandra**
*See* Glanz, Sarah

**Berlenbach, Paul** 1901-    [BX, RBE]
*American boxer and wrestler*
* [The] Astoria Assassin

**Berlichingen, Goetz [or Gottfried] von**
1480-1562    [DNNS, FFF, HHF]
*German feudal knight*
* Goetz with the Iron Hand
* Iron Hand

**[The] Berlin Bach**
*See* Bach, Karl Philipp Emanuel

**Berlin, Elaine** 1932-    [SW]
*American entertainer*
* May, Elaine

**Berlin Guy Chamberlin**
*See* Chamberlin, Guy

**Berlin, Irving**
*See* Baline, Israel

**Berlin, Isaiah** 1910?-
*Latvian-born historian and author*
* Apricott, Albert Alfred

**Berliner**
*See* Thompson, Joseph Parrish

**Berlinger, Milton** 1908-
[ITA, SW, TR]
*American comedian*
* Berle, Milton
* Television, Mr.
* Uncle Miltie

**Berlinguer, Enrico** 1922-
*Italian politician*
* Culo di Ferro [Iron Bottom]

**Berman, A. L.**
*See* Berman, Abraham Lincoln

**Berman, Abbadabba**
*See* Berman, Otto

**Berman, Abraham Lincoln** 1890-
[BEW]
*American attorney and theatrical
manager*
* Berman, A. L.

**Berman, Leonide [or Leonid]** 1896-
[WBD]
*Russian-born painter*
* Leonide [or Leonid]

**Berman, Otto** 20th c.    [BLB]
*American underworld figure*
* Berman, Abbadabba

**Berman, Saul** 1924-1947
[DAM, EJ, PMJ]
*American jazz musician*
* Berman, Sonny

**Berman, Sheila Phylis** 1928-
[BEW]
*American actress, dancer, singer*
* Bond, Sheila

**Berman, Sonny**
*See* Berman, Saul

**Bermann, Richard Arnold**
1883-1939    [SFL]
*Author*
* Hoellriegel, Arnold

**Bermudas**
*See* Harris, Charles T.

**Bermudo I** ?- 791    [WBD]
*King of Asturias and Leon*
* [El] Diacono [The Deacon]

**Bern, Maria Rasputin Soloviev**
1900?-1977    [CA]
*Russian-born dancer, circus
performer, author*
* Rasputin, Maria

**Bern, Paul**
*See* Levy, Paul

**Bernac, Pierre**
*See* Bertin, Pierre

**Bernacchi, Antonio** 1685-1756
[SN]
*Italian singer*
* [Il] Re dei Cantatori

**Bernadette**
*See* Watts, [Anna] Bernadette

**Bernadette of Lourdes**
*See* Soubirous, Bernadette

**Bernadillo**
*See* Fournet, Victor

**Bernadino**
*See* Chrystal, Thomas B.

**Bernadotte, Jean Baptiste Jules**
1763?-1844    [WBD]
*King of Sweden and Norway*
* Charles XIV John

**Bernal, John Desmond** 1901-1971
[CA]
*Irish-born physicist,
crystallographer, author*
* Old Chrysanthemum
* [The] Sage

**Bernal, Judith F.** 1939-    [CA]
*British psychologist and author*
* Dunn, Judith F.

**Bernard, Augusta** 20th c.    [WFA]
*French fashion designer*
* Augustabernard

**Bernard, Bert**
*See* Maxwell, Bert

**Bernard, Bessie**
*See* Shields, Mrs. Bernard G.

**Bernard, Camille**
*See* Katazzi, Mme.

**Bernard, Claude** 1588-1641
[DNNS, FFF, SN]
*French monk*
* Bernard the Poor
* Poor Bernard
* [The] Poor Priest

**Bernard de Chartres** 12th c.    [WBD]
*French philosopher*
* Sylvestris

**Bernard, Guy**
*See* Barber, Stephen Guy

**Bernard, Hattie**
*See* Chase, Mrs. C. W.

**Bernard, John**
*See* Beamish, Annie O'Meara de
Vic

**Bernard, Marley**
*See* Graves, Susan B[ernard]

**Bernard of Clairvaux** 1091-1153
[DNNF, HN, RH]
*Saint*
* [The] Honeyed Teacher
* [The] Last of the Fathers
* [The] Mellifluous Doctor
* [The] Oracle of France
* [The] Oracle of the Church
* [The] River of Paradise
* [The] Thaumaturgus of the West

**Bernard, Paul** 1866-1947
[CD, LC, WBD]
*French playwright and author*
* Bernard, Tristan

**Bernard, Pierre Joseph** 1710-1775
[FFF, RH, SN]
*French poet*
* [Le] Gentil Bernard

**Bernard, Robert**
*See* Martin, Robert Bernard

**Bernard, Roger** 1223-1241
[DNNS]
*Count of Foix*
* [The] Great

**Bernard, [Henriette] Rosine**
1844-1923    [CED, LC, WEF]
*French actress*
* Bernhardt, Sarah
* [The] Divine Sarah

**Bernard, Sam**
*See* Barnett, Samuel

**Bernard, Samuel** 1651-1739
[FFF, SN]
*Capitalist*
* Lucullus

**Bernard, Solomon** 16th c.
[FFF, RH, SN]
*French engraver*
* Bernard the Little
* [Le] Petit Bernard

**Bernard, Stefan**
*See* Baumrin, Bernard H[erbert]

**Bernard the Little**
*See* Bernard, Solomon

**Bernard the Poor**
See Bernard, Claude

**Bernard, Tristan**
See Bernard, Paul

**Bernardi, Nerio** 20th c. [WF]
*Italian actor*
* Berkoff, Nerik

**Bernardo, Cardinal** 1470-1520
[FFF, SN]
*Italian author*
* [Il] Bibbiena

**Bernardone, Giovanni Francesco**
1182-1226 [DEP, RH, WBD]
*Saint*
* Francis d'Assisi
* [The] Seraphic Saint
* Thaumaturgus

**Bernarn, Terrave**
See Burnett, David [Benjamin Foley]

**Bernat, Julie** 1827?-1912 [BEW]
*Actress*
* Mademoiselle Judith

**Bernauer, Evelyn Rudie** 20th c.
[ITA]
*American actress, singer, songwriter*
* Rudie, Evelyn

**Bernays, Anne**
See Kaplan, Anne Bernays

**Bernazza, Ann Marie**
See Haase, Ann Marie Bernazza

**Bernd, Aaron Blum** 1894- [NAA]
*American journalist*
* Hill, Coleman

**Berne, Arlene**
See Zekowski, Arlene

**Berne, Eric**
See Bernstein, Eric [Lennard]

**Berne, Leo**
See Davies, Leslie Purnell

**Bernert, Eleanor H.**
See Sheldon, Eleanor Bernert

**[The] Bernese Friedli**
See Mind, Gottfried [or Godefroi]

**Bernet, Michael M.** 1930- [CA]
*German-born journalist*
* Ben Dov, Meir

**Bernetta, [Mlle.] Clara**
See Johnson, Clara

**Bernhard, Karl**
See Saint Aubain, Andreas Nicolai de

**Bernhard, Strawberry Bill**
See Bernhard, William Henry

**Bernhard, William Henry**
1871-1949 [BE]
*American baseball player*
* Bernhard, Strawberry Bill

**Bernhardsen, Bris**
See Bernhardsen, [Einar] Christian [Rosenvinge]

**Bernhardsen, [Einar] Christian**
[Rosenvinge] 1923- [CA]
*Norwegian-born author*
* Bernhardsen, Bris

**Bernhardt, Clyde Edric Barron**
1905- [BWW]
*American singer*
* Barron, Ed

**Bernhardt, Curtis**
See Bernhardt, Kurt

**Bernhardt, Juan Ramon** 20th c.
[BR]
*Dominican-born baseball player*
* Bernhardt, Moncho

**Bernhardt, Kurt** 1899-
[BDF, FD, FDG]
*German actor and director*
* Bernhardt, Curtis

**Bernhardt, Moncho**
See Bernhardt, Juan Ramon

**[The] Bernhardt of the Klondike**
See Rambeau, Marjorie

**[The] Bernhardt of the Music Halls**
See Wood, Matilda Alice Victoria

**Bernhardt, Sarah**
See Bernard, [Henriette] Rosine

**Berni, Francesco** 1497?-1535 [SN]
*Italian poet*
* Sbernia

**Bernich, Ken** 20th c. [SMG]
*American football player*
* [The] Corn Bread Man

**Bernie, Ben**
See Anzelevitz [or Anzelwitz], Benjamin

**Bernis, Francois Joachim de Pierre**
de 1715-1794 [SN]
*French prelate*
* [The] King of Rome

**Bernstein, Alec** 1917- [CA]
*British author*
* Baron, [Joseph] Alexander

**Bernstein, Aline**
See Frankau, Aline

**Bernstein, Benjamin** 1900?-1975
[F2, FC, TR]
*American comedian*
* Blue, Ben

**Bernstein, Bonecrusher**
See Bernstein, Joseph

**Bernstein, Elsa** 1866- ? [WBD]
*Austrian playwright*
* Rosmer, Ernst

**Bernstein, Eric [Lennard]**
1910-1970 [CA, JL]
*Canadian-born American psychologist and author*
* Berne, Eric
* [The] Father of Transactional Analysis
* Gandalac, Lennard
* Horsely, Ramsbottom
* Pinto, Peter
* St. Cyr, Cyprian

**Bernstein, Jack**
See Dodick, John

**Bernstein, Jerry Marx** 1908-1969
[CA]
*American writer on public safety*
* Marx, Jerry

**Bernstein, Joe** 1877-1931 [EJS]
*American boxer*
* [The] Pride of the Ghetto

**Bernstein, Joseph** [EJS]
*American football player*
* Bernstein, Bonecrusher

**Bernstein, Julius** 1839-1917 [JL]
*German physician*
* [The] Father of Modern Neurophysiology

**Bernstein, Meyer Y.** 1852-1925
[JL]
*Russian opera singer*
* Medvedev, Mikhail

**Bernstein, Morris Louis** 1912-1962
[CAR]
*American painter*
* Louis, Morris

**Bernstein, Mrs. Jefferson F.** [FFF]
*Entertainer*
* Jarbeau, Vernona

**Bernstein-Namierowski, Lewis**
1888-1960 [JL]
*Polish-born historian*
* Namier, [Sir] Lewis

**Bernstorff, Johann Hartwig Ernst von**
1712-1772 [DNNS]
*Danish statesman*
* [The] Oracle of Denmark

**Berold, Basil** [house pseudonym]
See Fine, Louis

**Berolzheimer, Daniel Deronda** 1877-
? [NAA]
*American chemist and technical writer*
* D. D.

**Berquin, Arnaud** 1749?-1791
[WBD]
*French author*
* [The] Children's Friend

**Berquist, Bernard H.** 1903-1962
[ASC]
*American composer*
* Berquist, Whitey

**Berquist, Whitey**
See Berquist, Bernard H.

**Berra, Lawrence Peter** 1925-
[DGS, IPA, PB]
*American baseball player and manager*
* Berra, Yogi

**Berra, Yogi**
See Berra, Lawrence Peter

**Berrell, George** 1849-1933 [SC]
*American actor*
* Burrell, George

**Berrettini, Pietro** 1596-1669
[WBD]
*Italian painter and architect*
* Cortona, Pietro da

**Berri, Claude**
See Langmann, Claude

**Berrien, Edith Heal**
See Heal, Edith

**Berrill, N. J.**
See Berrill, Norman John

**Berrill, Norman John** 1903- [WYA]
*Author*
* Berrill, N. J.

**Berrinches [Bad-Tempered]**
See Olvero Lara, Francisco

**Berrington, John**
See Brownjohn, Alan Charles

**Berrisford, Judith M.** [joint pseudonym with Judith Mary (Berrisford) Lewis]
See Lewis, Clifford

**Berrisford, Judith M.** [joint pseudonym with Clifford Lewis]
See Lewis, Judith Mary [Berrisford]

**Berry**
See Le Bouvier, Gillies

**Berry, Admiral**
See Berry, Claude Elzy

**Berry, Allen Ken** 1941- [BE, SMG]
*American baseball player*
* [The] Bandit

**Berry, B. J.**
See Berry, Barbara J.

**Berry, Barbara J.** 1937- [CA]
*American author*
* Berry, B. J.

**Berry, Bill**
See Berry, Edwin Carlos

**Berry, Bryan** 1930-1955
[ESF, SFL, WGT]
*British author*
* Garner, Rolf

**Berry, Chu [or Chew]**
See Berry, Leon

**Berry, Claude Elzy** 1880- ? [BE]
*American baseball player*
* Berry, Admiral

**Berry, Cornelius John** 1922- [BE]
*American baseball player*
* Berry, Neil

**Berry, Crease**
See Berry, Robert Victor

**Berry, Douglas Bruce** 20th c. [SFL]
*Author*
* Douglas, Jeff [joint pseudonym with Andrew Jefferson Offutt]
* Drake, Morgan

**Berry, Duc de**
See Bourbon, Charles Ferdinand de

**Berry, Edwin Carlos** 1910- [IBW]
*American sociologist and business executive*
* Berry, Bill

**Berry, Emmett** 20th c. [NP]
*American jazz musician*
* Berry, Rev

**Berry, Erick**
See Best, [Evangel] Allena Champlin

**Berry, Frances Miriam** [FFF]
*Writer*
* Maguire, Aunt

**Berry, Helen**
See Rowland, D[onald] S[ydney]

**Berry, Hodge**
See Berry, Joseph Howard, Sr.
[Joe]

**Berry, Jane Cobb** 1915?-1979 [CA]
*American columnist, critic, author*
* Cobb, Jane

**Berry, Jittery Joe**
See Berry, Jonas Arthur

**Berry, Joe**
See Berry, Jonas Arthur

**Berry, Jonas Arthur** 1904-1958
[BE]
*American baseball player*
* Berry, Jittery Joe
* Berry, Joe

**Berry, Joseph Howard, Sr. [Joe]**
1872-1961 [BE]
*American baseball player*
* Berry, Hodge

**Berry, Jules**
See Paufichet, Jules

**Berry, Julian**
See Gastoldi, Ernesto

**Berry, Leon** 1910-1941
[DAM, PMJ, WWJ]
*American jazz musician*
* Berry, Chu [or Chew]

**Berry, Martha Eugenia** [PA]
*Author*
* St. John, Eugenia

**Berry, Mrs. Charles** [FFF]
*Entertainer*
* Darling, Bessie

**Berry, Neil**
See Berry, Cornelius John

**Berry, Rev**
See Berry, Emmett

**Berry, Robert Victor** 1943- [SMG]
*Canadian-born hockey player*
* Berry, Crease

**Berry-Hart, David James** 1940-
[ART]
*British sculptor*
* D. J. B-H.

**Bershad, Sheldon Leonard** 1907-
[FC, ITA, SW]
*American actor and producer*
* Leonard, Sheldon

**Bert, Mabel**
See Johnston, Mabel

**Bertall**
See D'Carnoux, C. Albert

**Berte, Marie** 1893- [CW]
*West Indian author*
* Emmbe

**Bertelli, Accurate Angelo**
See Bertelli, Angelo B.

**Bertelli, Angelo B.** 20th c. [FB]
*American football player*
* Bertelli, Accurate Angelo

**Bertelson, Emily Marie** 1923-
[FC, SW]
*American actress*
* Windsor, Marie

**Bertha** ?- 783
[DNNF, DNNS, RH]
*Mother of Charlemagne*
* Bertha au Grand-Pied
* Bertha with the Great Foot

**Bertha au Grand-Pied**
See Bertha

**Bertha with the Great Foot**
See Bertha

**Berthault, Jean Louis** 1907- [WFA]
*French-born fashion designer*
* Louis, Jean

**Berthiaume, Roland** 1927- [WEC]
*Canadian cartoonist*
* Berthio

**Berthio**
See Berthiaume, Roland

**Berthold**
See Dunne, Berthold

**Berthold, Meister**
See Ancklitzer [Anklitzen or
Angelisen], Konstantin

**Berthollet, Claude Louis**
1748-1822 [DEP, FFF, SN]
*French chemist*
* [The] Martyr to Science

**Berthoud, Eugene** [PA]
*Author*
* Borys, Gontrau

**Bertignono, Giovanni, Jr.**
1904-1963 [SFL]
*Italian-born writer*
* Bertin, Jack

**Bertin, Antoine** 1752-1790 [HN]
*French poet*
* [The] French Propertius

**Bertin, Eddy C[harly]** 1944-
[HFF, IAW, WGT]
*Belgian author*
* Brendall, Edith
* Greysun, Doriac

**Bertin, Jack**
See Bertignono, Giovanni, Jr.

**Bertin, Jack** [house pseudonym]
See Germano, Peter B.

**Bertin, Pierre** 1899- [BBD]
*French singer*
* Bernac, Pierre

**Bertocci, Chiarina Francesca**
1924- [EJ, PMJ]
*American singer*
* Wayne, Frances

**Bertocci, Nicholas** 1921- [EJ]
*American jazz musician*
* Jerret, Nick

**Berton, Guy** [joint pseudonym with
Guy Robert La Coste]
See Bingham, Eadfrid A.

**Berton, Guy** [joint pseudonym with
Eadfrid A. Bingham]
See La Coste, Guy Robert

**Berton, Vic**
See Cohen, Victor

**Bertram, J. G.** [PA]
*Author*
* Cooper, [Rev] W.

**Bertram, Minnie**
See Cross, Mrs. Edward J.

**Bertram, Noel**
See Fanthorpe, R[obert] Lionel

**Bertram, Vedah**
See Buck, Adele

**Bertram, William**
See Switzer, Benjamin

**Bertrand, Charles**
See Carter, David C[harles]

**Bertrand, Lefty**
See Bertrand, Roman Mathias

**Bertrand, Michel** 1944- [CA]
*French author*
* Angebert, Jean
* Angebert, Jean-Michel
* Angebert, Michel

**Bertrand, Roman Mathias** 1909-
[BE]
*American baseball player*
* Bertrand, Lefty

**Berwick**
See Redpath, James

**Berwick, Jean**
See Meyer, Jean Shepherd

**Berwick, Mary**
See Procter, Adelaide Anne

**Berwick, Pee Wee**
See Berwick, Warren

**Berwick, Warren** 20th c. [RBE]
*Boxing agent*
* Berwick, Pee Wee

**Berwickshire Sandie**
See Brown, Alexander

**Besant, Annie** 1847-1933 [WBD]
*British-born political leader in India*
* Ajax

**Beschitay, Elie** 1420-1490 [PA]
*Author*
* [The] Byzantine

**Besemeres, John** [PA]
*Author*
* Daly, John

**BEShT**
See Ben Eliezer, Israel

**Besieged Resident**
See Labouchere, Henry

**[The] Besieger**
See Demetrius I

**Bess, Larry** 1935- [ITA]
*American actor*
* Blair, Larry

**Bess of Hardwick**
See Talbot, Elizabeth

**Bessarion**
See Prince, Edward Ernest

**Besse, Herman** 1915-1972 [BE]
*American baseball player*
* Besse, Long Herm

**Besse, Long Herm**
See Besse, Herman

**Besselo, George** 1914-1959 [FC]
*American actor*
* Reeves, George

**Bessent, Fred Donald** 1931- [BE]
*American baseball player*
* [The] Weasel

**Bessie, Alvah** 1904- [WD]
*American author*
* Young, Nedrick

**[The] Best Abused Man in England**
See Dennis, John

**Best, Adam**
See Carmichael, William Edward

**Best, [Evangel] Allena Champlin**
1892-1974 [CAP, SAT]
*American author and illustrator*
* Berry, Erick
* Maxon, Anne

**Best, Carol Ann** 20th c. [AW]
*British author*
* Ashe, Susan

**Best, Cecil** 20th c. [IBW]
*American soccer player*
* Best, Clyde

**Best, Clifton** 1914- [EJ]
*American jazz musician*
* Best, Skeeter

**Best, Clyde**
See Best, Cecil

**Best, Edna**
See Hove, Edna

**Best, Katherine** 1873-1950 [THR]
*American actress*
* Grey, Katherine

**Best, Marc**
See Lemieux, Marc

**[The] Best Poet of England**
See Pope, Alexander

**Best, Rayleigh Breton Amis** 1905-
[AW, CAP]
*British author*
* Amis, Breton

**Best, Skeeter**
See Best, Clifton

**Best, Tharratt Gilbert** 1892-
[NAA]
*American author*
* Tarasc, Gilbert

**Best, Willie** 1916-1962 [SC]
*American actor*
* Sleep 'n Eat

**Bestall, A. E.**
See Bestall, Alfred Edmeades

**Bestall, Alfred Edmeades** 1892-
[ART]
*British illustrator and painter*
* Bestall, A. E.

**Bester, Alfred** 1913- [WGT]
*American author*
* Powell, Sonny

**Besterman, Henry** 1886?-1956
[BX, EJS, RBE]
*American boxer*
* Lewis, Harry

**Bestiale**
See Albicante, Giovanni Alberto

**Beston, Henry**
See Sheahan, Henry Beston

**Bestuzhev [or Bestuschew], Aleksandr
Aleksandrovich** 1795-1837
[FFF, WBD]
*Russian author and poet*
* Marlinski, Cossack

**Beswick, Harry** 1868- ? [WWL]
*British journalist, critic, author*
* Bezique
* Busy Bee
* Egerton, Randolph

**Bet-You-A-Million Gates**
See Gates, John Wayne

**Beta**
See Bassett, E. B.

**Beta**
See Boyle, Wilfred

**Betancourt Cisneros, Gaspar**
1803-1866 [CW]
Cuban author
* [El] Lugareno

**Betcher, Frank[lin Lyle]**
See Bettger, Franklin Lyle

**[La] Bete**
See Argenson, Rene Louis de Voyer d'

**Beth**
See Winship, Elizabeth

**Bethancourt, T. Ernesto**
See Passailaigue, Thomas E.

**Bethea, Elvin** 1946- [SMG]
American football player
* [The] Big E

**Bethea, Spot**
See Bethea, William Lamar [Bill]

**Bethea, William Lamar [Bill]** 1942-
[BE]
American baseball player
* Bethea, Spot

**Bethel, Dawn** 1932?-
[FC, HT, SW]
American actress
* North, Sheree

**Bethel, Marion Ross** 1929- [ART]
German-born artist
* M. R. B.

**Bethell, Mary Ursula** 1874-1945
British-born poet
* Hayes, Evelyn

**Bethge, Pete**
See Bethge, Victor W.

**Bethge, Victor W.** 20th c. [BBH]
American sailboat racer
* Bethge, Pete

**Bethlen, T. D.**
See Silverberg, Robert

**Bethune, Blind Tom**
See Bethune, Thomas Greene

**Bethune, J. G.**
See Ellis, Edward S[ylvester]

**Bethune, Mary** 20th c. [AW]
British author
* Clopet, Lilane M. C.

**Bethune, Maximilien de [Duc de Sully]** 1560-1641 [HN, SN]
French statesman
* [The] Iron Calvinist of Rosny
* [The] Iron Duke

**Bethune, Thomas Greene**
1849-1908 [B10, DAM]
American pianist and composer
* Bethune, Blind Tom

**Beti, Mongo**
See Biyidi, Alexandre

**[The] Betisian Menander**
See Malara

**Betjeman, [Sir] John** 1906-
[CA, WD]
British poet and author
* Epsilon

**Betjeman, [Sir] John** (Continued)
* Farren, Richard J.

**[The] Betrayer of the Fatherland**
See Wergeland, Henrik Arnold

**Betruz, Miguel** 20th c. [RBE]
Colombian boxer
* Turquito

**Bettenhausen, Melvin E.**
1916-1961 [AS, EAR]
American auto racer
* Bettenhausen, Tony
* [The] Tinley Park Express

**Bettenhausen, Tony**
See Bettenhausen, Melvin E.

**Betteridge, Anne**
See Potter, Margaret [Newman]

**Betteridge, Don**
See Newman, Bernard [Charles]

**Betterson, Boom Boom**
See Betterson, James

**Betterson, James** 1954- [SMG]
American football player
* Betterson, Boom Boom

**Betterton, Thomas** 1635-1710
[FFF, HN, RH]
British actor
* [The] British Roscius
* Roscius Britannicus
* [The] Roscius of England

**Bettger, Franklin Lyle** 1888- [BE]
American baseball player
* Betcher, Frank[lin Lyle]

**Betti [or Di Biagio?], Bernardino**
1454-1513 [SN, WBD]
Italian painter
* Pinturicchio, Bernardo
* [An] Umbrian Gozzoli

**Bettina**
See Brentano, Elizabeth

**Bettina**
See Ehrlich, Bettina [Bauer]

**Bettinsoli, Enzo** 1951- [RBE]
Italian boxer
* Bettinzoli, Elia

**Bettinzoli, Elia**
See Bettinsoli, Enzo

**Betts, Huck**
See Betts, Walter Martin

**Betts, Keter**
See Betts, William Thomas

**Betts, Nancy K.**
See Barnhisel, Ethel Keeler Betts

**Betts, Walter Martin** 1897- [BE]
American baseball player
* Betts, Huck

**Betts, William Thomas** 1928- [EJ]
American jazz musician
* Betts, Keter

**Betty**
See Olson, Helene Dean

**Betty Be-Bop Carter**
See Jones, Lillie Mae

**[The] Betty Boop Girl**
See Questal, Mae

**Betty, William Henry West**
1791-1874 [DEP, HN, RH]
British actor
* [The] Infant Roscius
* [The] Modern Roscius
* [The] Young Roscius

**Betz, Eva Kelly** 1897-1968
[CAP, SAT]
American author
* Peters, Caroline

**Betz, Matthew**
See Von Betz, Matthew

**Betzel, Bruno**
See Betzel, Christian Frederick Albert John Henry David

**Betzel, Christian Frederick Albert John Henry David** 1894-1965 [BE]
American baseball player
* Betzel, Bruno

**Beulah**
See Bates, Fanny D.

**Beulah**
See Kershau, Beulah Sevenney

**Beum, Robert [Lawrence]** 1929-
[CA]
American poet and author
* Lawrence, Robert

**Beurling, George** 1922-1948
[BDW, WWW]
Canadian-born fighter pilot
* Beurling, Screwball

**Beurling, Screwball**
See Beurling, George

**Beuttler, Edward Ivan Oakley** 20th c. [CA]
British author
* Butler, Ivan

**Bevan, Alistair**
See Roberts, Keith [John Kingston]

**Bevan, Billy**
See Harris, William Bevan

**Bevans, J.** 19th c. [PA]
Author
* [A] Layman

**Bevans, Torre**
See Chanslor, Marjorie Torrey [Hood]

**Bevard, Camille** 20th c. [IA]
American author
* Hume, Mickey

**Bevens, Bill**
See Bevens, Floyd Clifford

**Bevens, Floyd Clifford** 1916-
[B10, PB]
American baseball player
* Bevens, Bill

**Bevere, Maurice** 1923- [WECO]
Belgian cartoonist
* Morris

**Beveridge, Meryle Secrest** 1930-
[CA]
British-born American author
* Doman, June
* Secrest, Meryle

**Beverley**
See Cox, Mrs. S. B. Hughes

**Beverly**
See Freeland, Beverly

**Beverly, Robert** [PA]
Author
* R. B.

**Beverly, Vivian**
See Brown, Grace Evelyn

**Beverovicus**
See Von Benewyck, Jan

**Bevil, Lou[is Eugene]**
See Bevilacqua, Louis Eugene

**Bevilacqua, Louis Eugene**
1921-1973 [BE]
American baseball player
* Bevil, Lou[is Eugene]

**Beville, Candy**
See Beville, Charles E. [Charlie]

**Beville, Charles E. [Charlie]** 20th c.
[BE]
American baseball player
* Beville, Candy

**Bevin, Ernest** 1881-1951 [NN]
British politician
* [The] Dockers' K. C.

**Bevis, H. U.**
See Bevis, Herbert Urlin

**Bevis, Herbert Urlin** 1902- [SFL]
American author
* Bevis, H. U.

**Bevis, James** [joint pseudonym with B. V. Shann]
See Cumberland, Marten

**Bevis, James** [joint pseudonym with Marten Cumberland]
See Shann, B. V.

**[The] Bewildered**
See Dati, Carlo Roberto

**Bey, Isabelle**
See Bosticco, Isabel Lucy Mary

**Bey, Iverson**
See Minter, Iverson

**Bey, Roosevelt Sykes**
See Sykes, Roosevelt

**Beyea, Basil** 1910- [CA]
American author
* Benson, B. A.

**Beyer, Ernestine Cobern** 1893-
[NAA]
American singer and author
* Conde, Maria

**Beyle, Marie Henri** 1783-1842
[FFF, PA, WBD]
French author
* Birkbeck
* Bombet, Louis Alexander Cesar
* Stendhal

**Beynon, John**
See Harris, John [Wyndham Parkes Lucas] Beynon

**Bezdek, Hugo F.** 1884-1952 [FB]
Czech-born football coach and baseball manager
* [The] Thirteen Inch Shell

**Bezique**
See Beswick, Harry

**Bezruc, Petr**
See Vasek, Vladimir

**Bhagwan Shree Rajneesh [Good Sir Rajneesh]**
See Mohan, Rajneesh Chandra

**Bhajan, Yogi**
See Yogiji, Harbhajan Singh Khalsa

**Bhaktivedanta, A. C.**
See Prabhupada, Bhaktivedanta

**Bhaktivedanta Swami, A. C.**
See Prabhupada, Bhaktivedanta

**Bhanubandh, Birabongse Bhanudej** 1914- [EAR]
*Prince of Siam and auto racer*
* Bira, B.

**Bharati, Agehananda**
See Fischer, Leopold

**Bharti, Ma Satya**
See Jacobs, Jill

**Bhaskar**
See Chowdhury, Bhaskar Roy

**Bhatia, Jamunadevi** 1919- [AW, WD]
*British author*
* Bhatia, June
* Edwards, June
* Forrester, Helen
* Rana, J.

**Bhatia, June**
See Bhatia, Jamunadevi

**Bhatt, Janardan T.** 1941- [ART]
*Kenyan-born painter*
* Janardan

**Bhosale, Yeshwantrao P.** 1904- [LAO]
*Indian author and agriculturist*
* Roy, Ramala Pratap

**Biagoli, Nicola-Giuseppe** 1768-1860 [PA]
*Author*
* Biascoli

**Bialk, Elisa**
See Krautter, Elisa [Bialk]

**Bianchi, Bianca**
See Schwarz, Bertha

**Bianchi, Giovanni** 1693-1775 [PA]
*Author*
* Plancus, Janus

**Bianchi, Mario** 1897-1950 [BEW, FC, SC]
*French-born actor and director*
* Banks, Montague
* Banks, Monty

**Bianchi, Martha Dickinson** 20th c. [NAA]
*American author*
* Dickinson, Martha Gilbert

**Bianchi-Ferrari, Francesco** 1460?-1510 [WBD]
*Italian painter*
* [Il] Frare

**Biascoli**
See Biagoli, Nicola-Giuseppe

**Biba**
See Hulanicki, Barbara

**Bibalitsch, Antonio** 1922- [BBD]
*Italian composer*
* Bibalo, Antonio

**Bibalo, Antonio**
See Bibalitsch, Antonio

**[Il] Bibbiena**
See Bernardo, Cardinal

**Bibesco, Marthe-Lucile [Lahovary]** 1887?-1973 [CA, EWL, TC]
*Rumanian-born author and playwright*
* Decaux, Lucile

**[The] Bible Printer**
See Lufft, Hans

**Bibliander**
See Buchmann, Theodor

**Biblicus**
See Tilloch, Alexander

**Bibliophile**
See Allibone, Samuel Austin

**Bibliophile Jacob**
See Lacroix, Paul

**Bibliophobia**
See Dibdin, Thomas Frognall

**[Il] Biblioteca Animata [The Living Library]**
See Magliabecchi, Antonio [or Anthony]

**Bibliothecarius**
See Anastasius

**Bibolet, R. H.**
See Kelly, Tim

**Bicchieri, Theresa F.** 1908- [CA]
*American author*
* Bucchieri, Theresa F.

**Bickel, Frederick McIntyre** 1897-1975 [BDF, BEW, FC]
*American actor*
* March, Fredric

**Bicker-Caarten, Audrey** 1900- [THR]
*British actress*
* Carten, Audrey

**Bickerdyke, John**
See Cook, Charles Henry

**Bickers, Richard Leslie Townshend** 1917- [CA]
*British author*
* Charles, Mark
* Cittafino, Ricardo
* Dukes, Philip
* Kapusta, Paul
* Keene, Burt
* Kirschner, Fritz
* Lefevre, Gui
* Mueller, Gerhardt
* Richards, David
* Townshend, Richard

**Bickerstaff, Isaac**
See Steele, [Sir] Richard

**Bickerstaff, Isaac, Esq.**
See Swift, Jonathan

**Bickerstaffe, Isaac, Jr.**
See Lovecraft, Howard Phillips

**Bickerstaffe-Drew, Francis Browning Drew** 1858-1928 [LC, TC]
*British clergyman and author*
* Ayscough, John

**Bickham, Jack M[iles]** 1930- [CA, WD]
*American author*
* Clinton, Jeff

**Bickham, Jack M[iles]** (Continued)
* Miles, John

**Bickle, Judith Brundrett** [AW, CAP]
*British author*
* Tweedale, J.

**Bickle, Phyllis** 1915- [FC, OCF]
*British actress*
* Calvert, Phyllis

**Bickley, Samuel Felton** 1908-1976 [B10]
*American actor*
* Bickley, Tony

**Bickley, Tony**
See Bickley, Samuel Felton

**Bicknell, Bud**
See Bicknell, Charles Stephen [Charlie]

**Bicknell, Charles Stephen [Charlie]** 1928- [BE]
*American baseball player*
* Bicknell, Bud

**Bidder, George** [SN]
*Mathematician*
* [The] Calculator

**Biddle, Clement** 1740-1814 [DNNS, FFF]
*American army officer*
* [The] Quaker Soldier

**Biddle, Jasper**
See Smith, Albert Richard

**Biddle, John** 1615-1662 [DEL, DNNS, SN]
*British clergyman and author*
* [The] Father of English Unitarianism

**Biddle, Katherine Garrison Chapin** 1890-1977 [CA]
*American poet, playwright, critic*
* Chapin, Katherine G[arrison]

**Biddle, Richard** 1796-1847 [PA]
*American author*
* [An] American

**Biddles [or Bedells], Adelaide Helen** 1837-1921 [BEW]
*Actress and playwright*
* Calvert, Adelaide Helen

**[The] Bideford Postman**
See Capern, Edward

**Biden, Edmond P.** 1898-1959 [BDF, FC, OCF]
*American writer and director*
* Sturges, Preston

**Bidermanas, Israel** 1911- [JL]
*French photographer*
* Izis

**Bideu, Lou**
See Bedell, Lew

**Bidston, Lester** 1884- [MBF]
*British author*
* Hotspur, Paul

**Bidwell, Marjory Elizabeth Sarah** 20th c. [CA]
*British author*
* Ford, Elizabeth
* Gibbs, Mary Ann

**Bieber, Colonel**
See Bieber, Isador

**Bieber, Isador** 1887- [EJS]
*American horse owner and breeder*
* Bieber, Colonel

**Biederman, Charles**
See Biederman, Kerel

**Biederman, Kerel** 1906- [CAR]
*American artist*
* Biederman, Charles

**Biedermann, Felix** 1876-1928 [WBD]
*Austrian author*
* Doermann, Felix

**Biel [or Byll], Gabriel** 1425?-1495 [DNNS, HN]
*German scholastic philosopher*
* [The] Last of the Schoolmen
* Ultimus Scholasticorum, Doctor

**Bielby, Mrs.** [PA]
*Author*
* Le Baron, Marie

**Bielinski, Clifford Martin** 1921- [ASC]
*American composer, arranger, musician*
* Belan, Cliff

**Bielinski, Olga Helena** 1935- [BEW]
*Actress*
* Bellin, Olga

**Bielski, Feliks**
See Giergielewicz, Mieczyslaw

**Bielyi, Sergei**
See Hollo, Anselm

**[Le] Bien Aime**
See Charles VI

**[Le] Bien Aime**
See Louis XV

**[Le] Bien Fortune**
See Philip VI [or Philippe]

**Bien, Robert Taylor** 1878?-1964? [BEW, F1, FC]
*American actor*
* Warwick, Robert

**[Le] Bien Servi [The Well Served]**
See Charles VII

**Bienewitz [or Bennewitz], Peter** 1501?-1552 [WBD]
*German astronomer, mathematician, geographer*
* Apianus, Petrus

**Bienstock, Mike**
See Bienstock, Myron Joseph

**Bienstock, Myron Joseph** 1922- [CA]
*American-born writer*
* Bienstock, Mike

**Bienvenida [Welcome]**
See Mejias y Jimenez, Antonio

**Bienvenida [Welcome]**
See Mejias y Jimenez, Manuel

**Bienvenida [Welcome]**
See Mejias y Rapela, Manuel

**Bienvenu, Leon** [PA]
*Author*
* Touchatout

Bierbauer, Louis W. 1865-1926
[BE]
*American baseball player*
* Bauer, Lou

Bierbower [or Bierbauer], Elsie
1889-1956    [EMT, FC, PMJ]
*American actress, singer, lyricist,*
*producer*
* Janis, Elsie
* Little Elsie

Bierce, Ambrose [Gwinett]
1842-1914?    [EMD, TLC, WGT]
*American author*
* Grile, Dod
* Herman, William [joint
  pseudonym with Thomas A.
  Harcourt]
* Sloluck, J. Milton
* [The] Wickedest Man in San
  Francisco

Bierle, Natalie 1908-    [FC]
*Polish-Austrian actress*
* Birell, Tala

Bierman, Bernard W. [Bernie]
1894-1977    [FB]
*American football coach*
* [The] Silver Fox
* [The] Silver Fox of the Northland

Biermann, Lillian
See   Wehmeyer, Lillian [Mabel]
Biermann

Bifone, Carlo 20th c.    [OP]
*Italian opera singer*
* Bini, Carlo

Bifrons?
See   Francis, [Sir] Philip

[The] Big
See   Leopold II

Big Al Beauchamp
See   Beauchamp, Al

Big Al Capone
See   Capone, Al[phonse]

Big Al Libke
See   Libke, Al[bert Walter]

Big Al Polizzi
See   Polizzi, Alfred

Big Back Grant
See   Grant, Ike

[The] Big Bankroll
See   Rothstein, Arnold

Big Bates Karl
See   Karl, George

[The] Big Bear
See   Garcia, Edward Miguel

Big Bear Hutchinson
See   Hutchinson, Frederick Charles

Big Bear Kiser
See   Kiser, Larry Grant

[The] Big Beggarman
See   O'Connell, Daniel

Big Ben Cardoni
See   Cardoni, Armond Joseph

Big Ben Shields
See   Shields, Ben[jamin Cowan]

Big Bill Abstein
See   Abstein, William Henry [Bill]

Big Bill Bagwell
See   Bagwell, William Mallory
[Bill]

Big Bill Blaisell
See   Blaisell, Charles

Big Bill Bolden
See   Bolden, William Horace [Bill]

Big Bill Broomsley
See   Broonzy, William Lee Conley

Big Bill Broonzy
See   Broonzy, William Lee Conley

Big Bill Brown
See   Brown, Willard

Big Bill Byers
See   Byers, John William [Bill]

Big Bill Campbell
See   Campbell, Bill

Big Bill Chappelle
See   Chappelle, William Hogan
[Bill]

Big Bill Dinneen
See   Dinneen, William Henry

Big Bill Duffy
See   Duffy, William J.

Big Bill Dwyer
See   Dwyer, William Vincent

Big Bill Edwards
See   Edwards, William H.

Big Bill Hanlon
See   Hanlon, William [Bill]

Big Bill Henry
See   Henry, Bill

Big Bill Hollenback
See   Hollenback, William M.

Big Bill James
See   James, William Henry

Big Bill Johnson
See   Broonzy, William Lee Conley

Big Bill Kelly
See   Kelly, William Henry [Bill]

Big Bill Knudsen
See   Knudsen, Signius Wilhelm
Paul

Big Bill Lee
See   Lee, William Crutcher

Big Bill Lingley
See   Lingley, William

Big Bill Massey
See   Massey, William Harry [Bill]

Big Bill McGilvray
See   McGilvray, William Alexander
[Bill]

Big Bill Renna
See   Renna, William Beneditto

Big Bill Schardt
See   Schardt, Wilburt

Big Bill Steele
See   Steele, William Mitchell

Big Bill Thompson
See   Thompson, William Hale

Big Bill Tilden
See   Tilden, William Tatem, II

Big Bill Voiselle
See   Voiselle, William Symmes

Big Bird Garner
See   Garner, Joel

Big Bird Restani
See   Restani, Kevin

Big Black Ray
See   Ray, Danny

Big Bloke
See   Oden, James Burke [Jimmy]

[The] Big Blonde
See   Gilchrist, Connie

Big Bob McCullough
See   McCullough, Robert

Big Bobby Marino
See   Marino, Francis

[The] Big Bopper
See   Richardson, Jape

Big Bow Bowman
See   Bowman, Elmer William

Big Boy Crudup
See   Crudup, Arthur

Big Boy Ellis
See   Ellis, Wilbert Thirkield

Big Boy Goudie
See   Goudie, Frank

Big Boy Kraft
See   Kraft, Clarence Otto

Big Boy Spires
See   Spires, Arthur

Big Boy Williams
See   Williams, Guinn

Big Boy Woods
See   Collins, Samuel

Big Burley Bonner
See   Bonner, William

Big Bus Mathis
See   Mathis, Buster

Big C
See   Lloyd, Clive Hubert

[The] Big Cat
See   Mize, John Robert

[The] Big Cat
See   Wright, Rayfield

Big Cat Williams
See   Williams, Clarence

[The] Big Chef
See   Trepper, Leopold

Big Cherry
See   Scolnick, Sylvan

Big Chief Ellis
See   Ellis, Wilbert Thirkield

Big Chief Feathers
See   Feathers, William B.

Big Chief Moore
See   Moore, Russell

Big Chief Stallings
See   Stallings, George Tweedy

Big D
See   Drysdale, Donald Scott

Big D
See   Imhoff, Darrall

Big D
See   Lewis, Edward

Big D
See   Minor, Dan

Big Daddy Amin
See   Amin Dada, Idi

Big Daddy Crowe
See   Crowe, George

Big Daddy Garlits
See   Garlits, Donald Glenn

Big Daddy Haskins
See   Haskins, Clem

Big Daddy Kirby
See   Kirby, George

Big Daddy Lattin
See   Lattin, David

Big Daddy Lipscomb
See   Lipscomb, [Eu]gene

Big Daddy Nievens
See   Nievens, Roosevelt

Big Dan Abbott
See   Abbott, Leander Franklin

Big Dan Brouthers
See   Brouthers, Dennis Joseph

Big Dan Tipple
See   Tipple, Dan[iel Slaughter]

Big Dee Irwin
See   Irwin, Dee

Big Dee Spencer
See   Spencer, Daryl Dean

Big Devil Little
See   Little, John

Big Do Doherty
See   Doherty, Reginald Frank

Big Dog Gray
See   Gray, Leon

Big Dog Pihos
See   Pihos, Peter L.

[The] Big E
See   Bethea, Elvin

[The] Big E
See   Hayes, Elvin

Big Ed
See   Burns, Eddie

Big Ed Delahanty
See   Delahanty, Edward James

Big Ed Harmon
See   Harmon, Ed

Big Ed Hendricks
See   Hendricks Ed[ward]

Big Ed Klepfer
See   Klepfer, Edward Lloyd

Big Ed Konetchy
See   Konetchy, Edward Joseph

Big Ed Lewis
See   Lewis, Edward

Big Ed Munns
See   Munns, Les[lie Ernest]

Big Ed Reulbach
See   Reulbach, Edward Marvin

Big Ed Stevens
See   Stevens, Edward Lee

**Big Ed Vogel**
See Vogel, Eddie

**Big Ed Walsh**
See Walsh, Edward Augustine

**Big Eye Nelson**
See Nelson, Louis Delisle

**Big Finn Fiene**
See Fiene, Lou[is Henry]

**Big Foot**
See Burnett, Chester Arthur

**Big Frenchy DeMange**
See DeMange, George

**Big G**
See Crowe, George D.

**Big G**
See Gianelli, John

**Big Game Hunter**
See Hunter, Les

**Big George Meany**
See Meany, [William] George

**Big George Nelson**
See Gillis, Lester

**Big Girl**
See Gilchrist, Connie

**Big Greenie Greenberg**
See Greenberg, Harry

**Big Hands Johnson**
See Johnson, Gary

**Big Hayes**
See Hrubec [or Hubacek], Charles

**Big Hearted Arthur**
See Askey, Arthur

**Big House Gaines**
See Gaines, Clarence

**Big Ike Darby**
See Darby, Ike

**Big Ike Robinson**
See Robinson, Isaiah

**Big Irish Sheeran**
See Sheeran, Frank

**Big Jack McGill**
See McGill, John George

**Big Jack Valiquette**
See Valiquette, Jack

**Big Jack Zelig**
See Alberts, William

**Big Jay McNeely**
See McNeely, Cecil

**Big Jeff Pfeffer**
See Pfeffer, Francis Xavier

**Big Jim Baskette**
See Baskette, James Blaine [Jim]

**Big Jim Braid**
See Braid, James

**Big Jim Clinton**
See Clinton, James Lawrence

**Big Jim Colosimo**
See Colosimo, James

**Big Jim Fridley**
See Fridley, James Riley [Jim]

**Big Jim Lawson**
See Lawson, Harry

**Big Jim Martin**
See Martin, James

**Big Jim Murray**
See Murray, James Francis [Jim]

**Big Jim O'Leary**
See O'Leary, Jim

**Big Jim Parker**
See Parker, Jim

**Big Jim Randolph**
See Randolph, James Lyle

**Big Jim Roberts**
See Roberts, James Newson [Jim]

**Big Jim Robinson**
See Robinson, Nathan

**Big Jim Russell**
See Russell, James Wyman

**Big Jim Sheehan**
See Sheehan, James Thomas [Jim]

**Big Jim Thompson**
See Thompson, James R.

**Big Jim Turrell**
See Turrell, James Archie [Jim]

**Big Jim Weaver**
See Weaver, James Dement

**Big Jim West**
See West, Jim

**Big Jim Wiggs**
See Wiggs, James Alvin [Jimmy]

**Big Joe**
See McCoy, Joe

**Big Joe Henderson**
See Henderson, Joe

**Big Joe Lonardo**
See Lonardo, Joseph

**Big Joe Mulligan**
See Mulligan, Joseph Ignatius [Joe]

**Big Joe Turner**
See Turner, Joseph [Vernon]

**Big Joe Williams**
See Williams, Joe

**Big John Bogart**
See Bogart, John Renzie

**Big John Connally**
See Connally, John Bowden, Jr.

**Big John Davidson**
See Davidson, John Arthur

**Big John Johnson**
See Johnson, John Henry

**Big John Mayberry**
See Mayberry, John Claiborn

**Big John Mecom**
See Mecom, John W., Sr.

**Big John Niland**
See Niland, John H.

**Big John Patton**
See Patton, John

**Big John Rayford**
See Rayford, John

**Big John Wrencher**
See Wrencher, John Thomas

**Big Klu Kluszewski**
See Kluszewski, Theodore Bernard [Ted]

**Big Knife**
See Jackson, Andrew

**Big Leroy Ostransky**
See Ostransky, Leroy

**Big Lewie Lewis**
See Lewis, David R.

**Big Lis Liston**
See Liston, Emil S.

**[The] Big M**
See Mahovlich, Francis William [Frank]

**Big Mac McGinnis**
See McGinnis, George

**Big Mac McNamara**
See McNamara, Gerry

**Big Maceo**
See Merriweather, Major

**Big Mama Bev**
See Hill, Bev[erly Jean]

**Big Mama Thornton**
See Thornton, Willie Mae

**Big Maxey Greenberg**
See Greenberg, Max

**Big Maybelle**
See Smith, Mabel Louise

**Big Meade Carlton**
See Carlton, Darryl

**Big Mike McKendrick**
See McKendrick, Reuben Michael

**Big Mike Michael**
See Michael, J. E.

**Big Mike Sullivan**
See Sullivan, Michael Joseph

**Big, Mr.**
See Mottola, Tony

**Big, Mr.**
See Rothstein, Arnold

**Big Mo Modzelewski**
See Modzelewski, Ed

**Big Mo Stokes**
See Stokes, Maurice

**Big Moose**
See Walker, John Mayon [Johnny]

**Big Nick Nicholas**
See Nicholas, George Walker

**Big Nose Curry**
See Parrott, George

**[The] Big O**
See Robertson, Oscar

**[The] Big One**
See Dougherty, Nathan W.

**Big Play, Mr.**
See Johnson, Essex

**Big Poison**
See Waner, Paul Glee

**Big Potatoes Wilson**
See Wilson, Homer

**Big Red Drew**
See Drew, Charles Richard

**Big Red McPeake**
See McPeake, William Curtis

**Big Red Powell**
See Powell, Edward D.

**Big Rich**
See Richardson, Emory Aaron

**Big Rudolph Beaulieu**
See Beaulieu, Rudolph

**Big Sal Sinno**
See Sinno, Salvatore

**Big Sam Thompson**
See Thompson, Samuel L.

**[The] Big Serb**
See Miljus, John Kenneth

**[The] Big Ship**
See Armstrong, Warwick Windridge

**Big Sid Catlett**
See Catlett, Sidney

**Big Six**
See Auker, Eldon LeRoy

**Big Six**
See Mathewson, Christopher

**Big Skee**
See Cukoschay [or Zukauskas], Joseph Paul

**Big Slim**
See Aliff, Hamilton C.

**Big Smoke**
See Johnson, John Arthur [Jack]

**Big Sol Moore**
See Moore, Wayne

**Big Sonny Edwards**
See Edwards, Robert

**Big Stan Walters**
See Walters, Stan

**Big T Teagarden**
See Teagarden, Weldon Leo

**Big Tank Conrad**
See Conrad, Thomas

**Big Tim Murphey**
See Murphey, Timothy

**Big Tiny Little**
See Little, Dudley

**Big Tom Collins**
See Dupree, William Thomas

**Big Tom Collins**
See McGhee, Walter Brown

**Big Tom Gorman**
See Gorman, Thomas David [Tom]

**[The] Big Train**
See Conacher, Lionel Pretoria

**[The] Big Train**
See Johnson, Walter Perry

**[The] Big Train**
See Lawson, Smirle

**Big Train Moody**
See Moody, John Clifford

**Big Train Parker**
See Parker, Thomas [Tom]

**Big Tree, [Chief] John**
See John, Isaac Johnny

**Big Tubby Raskin**
See Raskin, Morris

**Big Tuna Accardo**
See Accardo, Antonio Leonardo

**Big 'Un Page**
See Page, Walter

**Big Vernon**
See Turner, Joseph [Vernon]

**Big Vinnie Teresa**
See Teresa, Vincent

**Big Voice**
See Odom, Andrew

**Big Walter**
See Horton, Walter

**Big Walter**
See Price, Walter Travis

**Big Walter**
See Smith, George

**[The] Big Warrior**
See Drysdale, Donald Scott

**[The] Big Whistle**
See Chadwick, William L. [Bill]

**Big Willie**
See Mabon, Willie

**Big Willie Dixon**
See Dixon, Willie James

**Big Yellow Dorsey**
See Dorsey, Bob

**[The] Big Z**
See Beaty, Zelmo

**Bigard, Barney**
See Bigard, Leon Albany

**Bigard, Leon Albany** 1906-
[EJ, PMJ, WWJ]
*American jazz musician*
* Bigard, Barney

**Bigbee, Al**
See Bigbee, Lyle Randolph

**Bigbee, Carson Lee** 1895-1964
[AS, BE]
*American baseball player*
* Bigbee, Skeeter

**Bigbee, Lyle Randolph** 1893-1942
[BE]
*American baseball player*
* Bigbee, Al

**Bigbee, Skeeter**
See Bigbee, Carson Lee

**Bigelow, Elliott Allardice**
1898-1933 [BE]
*American baseball player*
* Bigelow, Gilly

**Bigelow, Gilly**
See Bigelow, Elliott Allardice

**Bigelow, Jacob** 1787- ? [PA]
*Author*
* Eolopoesis

**Bigeou, Boy**
See Bigeou, Clifford

**Bigeou, Clifford** 20th c. [NOJ]
*American jazz musician*
* Bigeou, Boy

**Bigeou, Esther** 1895?-1936?
[BWW]
*American singer and dancer*
* [The] Creole Songbird
* [The] Girl with the Million Dollar
  Smile

**Bigg, Patricia Nina** 1932-
[AW, WD]
*Australian author*
* Ainsworth, Patricia

**Biggers, Doc**
See Biggers, John Thomas

**Biggers, John Thomas** 1924- [IBW]
*American painter, sculptor,
printmaker*
* Biggers, Doc

**Biggs, Peter**
See Rimel, Duane [Weldon]

**Biggs, Ronald Arthur** 1929- [B10]
*British robber*
* Cooke, Terry
* [The] Great Train Robber

**Biglow, Hosea**
See Lowell, James Russell

**Bigly, Cantell A.**
See Peck, George W.

**Bigot**
See Carnuel, Anne

**Bihalji-Merin, Oto** 1904-
[CA, IAW]
*Yugoslav author*
* Merin, Peter
* Thoene, Peter

**Bijns [or Byns], Anna** 1494?-1575
[WBD]
*Flemish poet*
* [The] Sappho of Brabant

**Bilbo, Jack**
See Baruch, Hugo

**Bilbrooke, Lydia**
See Macbeth, Lydia

**Bildilli, Emil** 1912-1946 [BE]
*American baseball player*
* Bildilli, Hill Billy

**Bildilli, Hill Billy**
See Bildilli, Emil

**Bildsoe, J. A. D. J.**
See Jensen, Jens Arnold Diederich

**Bildstein, Youry** 1887-1947 [BBD]
*Russian cellist*
* Bilstin, Youry

**Bilenkin, Miriam** 1911- [F2]
*Actress*
* Byron, Marion

**Bilk, Acker**
See Bilk, Bernard Stanley

**Bilk, Bernard Stanley** 1929- [IWM]
*British musician and composer*
* Bilk, Acker

**Billaber, She P.**
See Shillaber, Benjamin Penhallow

**Billaut, Adam** 1602-1662
[DNNF, DNNS, FFF]
*French poet*
* Maitre Adam
* Master Adam

**Billcard, Denise** 1925-
[FC, IPA, SW]
*French actress*
* Darcel, Denise

**Billemaz, Francois** 1750-1793 [PA]
*Author*
* Billiemas

**Billerbeck, Herbert Schussler**
1884?-1936 [BEW]
*American comedian*
* Williams, Herb

**Billiard Ball Jack**
See Rose, Jack

**Billiards, Mr.**
See Hoppe, Willie

**Billiart, Marie R. J.** 19th c. [PA]
*Author*
* Mother Julia

**Billiemas**
See Billemaz, Francois

**Billingham, Cactus**
See Billingham, John Eugene
[Jack]

**Billingham, John Eugene [Jack]**
1943- [BE, NLG]
*American baseball player*
* Billingham, Cactus
* [The] Blade

**Billingkoff, Morris** 1898-
[BX, EJS, RBE]
*Russian-born boxer*
* Montreal, Young

**Billings, Edith S.** 20th c. [SFL]
*Author*
* Billings, Maris Herrington
* Warrington, Maris

**Billings, Ezra**
See Halla, Robert Christian

**Billings, Frank R.** 1904-1957 [EJ]
*American jazz musician*
* Billings, Josh

**Billings, John Augustus** 1891- [BE]
*American baseball player*
* Billings, Josh

**Billings, Josh**
See Billings, Frank R.

**Billings, Josh**
See Billings, John Augustus

**Billings, Josh**
See Shaw, Henry Wheeler

**Billings, Kathleen Wyatt** 20th c.
[ART]
*New Zealand artist*
* K. W. B.

**Billings, Maris Herrington**
See Billings, Edith S.

**Billington, John**
See Beaver, [Jack] Patrick

**Billiu, Russell**
See Long, Huey Pierce, Jr.

**Billouin, Crystal Joy** 1938- [IBW]
*Canadian-born singer*
* Joy, Crystal

**Billsbury, Rye**
*Actor*
* Rye, Michael

**Billy Boy Arnold**
See Arnold, William [Billy]

**Billy Crash Craddock**
See Craddock, Billy

**Billy G.**
See Grabarkewitz, Bill Cordell

**Billy Jack Hudson**
See Hudson, Rex Haughton

**Billy No-No**
See Singer, William Robert

**Billy the Butcher**
See William Augustus

**Billy the Kid**
See Emerson, William Robert

**Billy the Kid**
See McCarty, Henry

**Billy the Kid**
See Olson, Willis S.

**Billy the Kid**
See Southworth, Billy

**Bilsland, Bilko**
See Bilsland, Ernest Charles

**Bilsland, Ernest Charles** 1931-
[CA]
*American writer and cartoonist*
* Bilsland, Bilko

**Bilstin, Youry**
See Bildstein, Youry

**Bimbi, Meste**
See Dos Reis Machado, Manuel

**Bimbo Boy**
See Reeves, James Travis [Jim]

**Bimstein, Morris** 1897-1969
[AS, EJS]
*American boxer and trainer*
* Bimstein, Whitey
* White, Johnny

**Bimstein, Whitey**
See Bimstein, Morris

**Binder, Eando** [joint pseudonym with
Otto O(scar) Binder]
See Binder, Earl Andrew

**Binder, Eando** [joint pseudonym with
Earl Andrew Binder]
See Binder, Otto O[scar]

**Binder, Earl Andrew** 1904-1965
[ESF, SF, WGT]
*American author*
* Binder, Eando [joint pseudonym
  with Otto O(scar) Binder]
* Coleridge, John [joint pseudonym
  with Otto O(scar) Binder]
* Giles, Gordon A. [joint
  pseudonym with Otto O(scar)
  Binder]
* O'Brien, Dean D. [joint
  pseudonym with Otto O(scar)
  Binder]

**Binder, Fred**
See Falls, Fred

**Binder, Frederick Moore** 1920-
[CA]
*American author and educator*
* Moore, Andrew

**Binder, Otto O[scar]** 1911-1974
[ESF, SF, WGT]
*American author*
* Binder, Eando [joint pseudonym with Earl Andrew Binder]
* Coleridge, John [joint pseudonym with Earl Andrew Binder]
* Garth, Will [house pseudonym]
* Giles, Gordon A. [joint pseudonym with Earl Andrew Binder]
* O'Brien, Dean D. [joint pseudonym with Earl Andrew Binder]

**Bindley, James** 1740- ?    [PA]
*Author*
* Leontes

**Binek, Izabella** 1943-    [OP]
*Polish opera singer*
* Nawe, Izabella

**Binet, Satane**
See   Sarcey, Francisque

**Bing, Gus** 1893-1967    [SC]
*American actor*
* Bingham, George

**Bing, Jon** 1944-    [IAW]
*Norwegian author*
* Catamaran

**Bingay, Malcolm** 1884-1953
*American sportswriter*
* Iffy the Dopester

**Bingham, [Major] Arthur**
See   Rowe, W.

**Bingham, Carson**
See   Cassiday, Bruce [Bingham]

**Bingham, Eadfrid A.** 20th c.    [WW]
*Author*
* Berton, Guy [joint pseudonym with Guy Robert La Coste]

**Bingham, Evangeline M[arguerite] L[adys] [Elliot]** 1899-    [CA]
*British author*
* Elliot, Geraldine

**Bingham, George**
See   Bing, Gus

**Bingham, Jocelyn** 20th c.    [IBW]
*Panamanian-born nightclub owner*
* Frisco

**Bingham, Madeleine** 1912-    [CA]
*British author and playwright*
* Mannering, Julia

**Bingham, Sallie**
See   Ellsworth, Sallie Bingham

**[Der] Bingle**
See   Crosby, Harry Lillis

**Bingley, D. E.**
See   Bingley, David Ernest

**Bingley, David Ernest** 1920-    [CA]
*British author*
* Adams, Bart
* Bingley, D. E.
* Bridger, Adam
* Camber, Andrew
* Canuck, Abe
* Carver, Dave
* Chatham, Larry
* Chesham, Henry
* Coltman, Will
* Coniston, Ed
* Dorman, Luke
* Fallon, George
* Horsely, David

**Bingley, David Ernest** (Continued)
* Jefford, Bat
* Kingston, Syd
* Lynch, Eric
* Martell, James
* North, Colin
* Plummer, Ben
* Prescott, Caleb
* Remington, Mark
* Roberts, John
* Romney, Steve
* Silvester, Frank
* Starr, Henry
* Tucker, Link
* Wigan, Christopher
* Yorke, Roger

**Bingley, Richard**
See   Smith, Leonard B.

**Bini, Carlo**
See   Bifone, Carlo

**Binion, Benny**
See   Binion, Lester

**Binion, Lester** 20th c.    [PHM]
*American underworld figure*
* Binion, Benny

**Binkowski, George Eugene** 1914-
[BE]
*American baseball player*
* Binks, Bingo
* Binks, George Eugene

**Binks, Bingo**
See   Binkowski, George Eugene

**Binks, George Eugene**
See   Binkowski, George Eugene

**Binnacle**
See   Lewis, W. W.

**Binney, Cecil** 1897-    [LAO]
*British barrister and writer*
* Hoopington, Ambrose

**Binney, Mrs. J. G.**
See   Binny, Juliette Pattison

**Binns, Ottwell** 1872- ?
[WW, WWL]
*British author*
* Bolt, Ben

**Binny, Juliette Pattison**    [PA]
*Author*
* Binney, Mrs. J. G.

**Bioff, Willie** 1900?-1955    [PHM]
*American underworld figure*
* [The] Squealer

**[The] Biograph Baby**
See   Seabury, Ynez

**[The] Biograph Blonde**
See   Wayne, Daphne

**[The] Biograph Girl**
See   Lawrence, Florence

**Bion**
See   Southey, Robert

**Biondetti, Clemente** 1898-    [EAR]
*Italian auto racer*
* [The] King of the Mille Miglia

**Biondi, Ray**
See   Biondi, Remo

**Biondi, Remo** 1905-    [WWJ]
*American musician*
* Biondi, Ray

**Biondo, Joseph** 20th c.
[BLB, PHM]
*American underworld figure*
* Bandy, Joe

**Biondolillo, Gaspare** 1903-    [FC]
*American actor*
* La Rue, Jack

**Bioy-Casares, Adolfo** 1914-    [CA]
*Argentinian author*
* Bustos Domecq, H[onorio] [joint pseudonym with Jorge Luis Borges]
* Miranda, Javier
* Sacastru, Martin
* Suarez Lynch, B. [joint pseudonym with Jorge Luis Borges]

**Bira, B.**
See   Bhanubandh, Birabongse Bhanudej

**Birch, Flash**
See   Birch, Gaylord

**Birch, Gaylord** 20th c.    [RO2]
*American musician*
* Birch, Flash

**Birch, Harry**
See   White, Charles Albert

**Birch, Jonathan** 1783-1847    [FFF]
*British translator*
* Abricht, Johann

**Birch, Leo Bedrich**
See   Bischitzky, Leo Bedrich

**Birch, Paul** 1911-    [BB]
*American basketball player*
* Birch, Polly

**Birch, Percival Lea** 20th c.    [WWL]
*British writer*
* Fleur de Lys

**Birch, Polly**
See   Birch, Paul

**Birch, Reginald Bathurst**
1856-1943    [WEC]
*British-born American artist*
* [The] Children's Gibson

**Birch, Woody**
See   Bjorksten, Gunnar O.

**Birchall, Ian H[arry]** 1939-    [CA]
*British political theorist and author*
* McNally, Curtis

**Birchansky, Leo**
See   Birchansky, Lev

**Birchansky, Lev** 1887-1949    [WEC]
*Russian-born American cartoonist*
* Birchansky, Leo

**[The] Bird**
See   Fidrych, Mark Steven

**[The] Bird**
See   Saleski, Don

**Bird, Brandon** [joint pseudonym with Kay Harris Evans]
See   Evans, George Bird

**Bird, Brandon** [joint pseudonym with George Bird Evans]
See   Evans, Kay Harris

**Bird, C[ordwainer]**
See   Ellison, Harlan [Jay]

**Bird, Dennis Leslie** 1930-
[AW, WD]
*British writer on ice skating*
* Noel, John

**Bird, Dodo**
See   Bird, Frank Zepherin

**Bird Dog Correll**
See   Correll, Victor Crosby

**Bird Dog Hopper**
See   Hoppper, William Booth [Bill]

**Bird Eye Truby**
See   Truby, Harry Garvin

**Bird, Florence [Bayard]** 1908-    [CA]
*American-born author*
* Francis, Anne

**Bird, Frank Zepherin** 1869-1958
[BE]
*American baseball player*
* Bird, Dodo

**Bird, George T.** 20th c.    [SMG]
*American football executive*
* Bird, Red

**Bird, J.**
See   Royster, Jeron Kennis

**Bird, James Edwin** 1890-    [BE]
*American baseball player*
* Bird, Red

**Bird, [Cyril] Kenneth** 1887-1965
[CAP, LAO, LC]
*British artist, author, cartoonist*
* Fougasse

**[The] Bird Lady**
See   Artis, Oda Bell

**Bird, Lewis**
See   Hayter, Cecil Goodenough

**Bird Man Barrett**
See   Barrett, Mike

**Bird, Red**
See   Bird, George T.

**Bird, Red**
See   Bird, James Edwin

**Bird, Richard**
See   Barradell-Smith, Walter

**Bird, Robert Montgomery**
1803-1854    [PA]
*Author*
* Pilgrim, Peter

**Bird, Sarah**    [PA]
*Author*
* [A] Mother

**Bird, Vivian** 1910-    [CA]
*British author and journalist*
* Beer, Vic

**Bird, William Henry Fleming**
1896-1971    [SFL]
*British author*
* Blair, Adrian
* Elliot, Lee [house pseudonym, Curtis Warren]
* Fleming, Harry
* Le Page, Rand [house pseudonym, Curtis Warren]
* Lorraine, Paul [house pseudonym, Curtis Warren]
* Luna, Kris [house pseudonym, Curtis Warren]

**[The] Bird with the Feathers**
See   Stevens, Lee

**[The] Birdman**
See   Parrott, Michael Everett Arch

**[The] Birdman of Alcatraz**
See   Stroud, Robert Franklin

**Birdsall, A. F.** 1858- ?   [PA]
*Author*
* Hildebrand, Hall

**Birell, Tala**
See   Bierle, Natalie

**Birkbeck**
See   Beyle, Marie Henri

**Birkenhead, Edward**
See   Birkenhead, Elijah

**Birkenhead, Elijah** 1903-   [AW]
*British author*
* Birkenhead, Edward

**Birkenhead, Frank** 20th c.   [BMH]
*British comedian*
* Cowley, Frank

**Birkenhead, Harry** 20th c.   [BMH]
*British comedian*
* Morris, Harry

**Birkenshaw, Birky**
See   Birkenshaw, Jack

**Birkenshaw, Jack** 1940-   [DC]
*British cricketer*
* Birkenshaw, Birky

**Birkin, Charles [Lloyd]** 1907-   [CA]
*British author*
* Lloyd, Charles

**Birkin, Henry R. S.** 1896-   [EAR]
*British auto racer*
* Birkin, Tim

**Birkin, Tim**
See   Birkin, Henry R. S.

**Birkley, Dolan**
See   Hitchens, Dolores [Birk]

**Birkofer, Lefty**
See   Birkofer, Ralph Joseph

**Birkofer, Ralph Joseph** 1908-1971
[BE]
*American baseball player*
* Birkofer, Lefty

**Birksted-Breen, Dana** 1946-   [CA]
*American-born author*
* Breen, Dana

**Birla, Lakshminiwas N.** 1909-
[CAP]
*Indian author*
* Achyut

**[The] Birmingham Doctor**
See   Parr, Samuel

**Birmingham, Dode**
See   Birmingham, Joseph Lee

**Birmingham, George A.**
See   Hannay, James Owen

**Birmingham, Joseph Lee**
1884-1946   [AS, BE]
*American baseball player*
* Birmingham, Dode

**[The] Birmingham Milton**
See   Klopstock, Friedrich Gottlieb

**[The] Birmingham Poet**
See   Freeth, John

**Birmingham Sam**
See   Hooker, John Lee

**Birmingham, Wright** 1937-   [BWW]
*American singer*
* Jones, Birmingham

**Birnage, Derek A. W.** 20th c.
[MBF]
*British author and editor*
* Birnage, Dick
* Windsor, Frank

**Birnage, Dick**
See   Birnage, Derek A. W.

**Birnbaum, Nathan** 1864- ?   [LAO]
*Austrian-born author*
* Acher, Mathias

**Birnbaum, Nathan** 1896-
[FC, ITA, SW]
*American comedian*
* Burns, George

**Birney, [Alfred] Earle** 1904-   [CLC]
*Canadian poet, author, critic*
* [The] Chronicler of Canada

**Birney, [Herman] Hoffman** 1891-
[WW]
*Author*
* Kent, David

**Biro, Balint Stephen** 1921-   [CA]
*Hungarian-born illustrator*
* Biro, Val

**Biro, Lajos**
See   Blau, Lajos

**Biro, Val**
See   Biro, Balint Stephen

**Biron, Baron de**
See   De Gontaut, Armand

**Biron, Duc de**
See   De Gontaut, Charles

**Biron, Ernst Johann**
See   Buehren, Ernst Johann

**Biron, [Sir] Henry Chartres**
1863-1940   [SFL, WGT]
*Author*
* Ragged, Hyder

**Birren, Faber** 1900-   [CA]
*American author*
* Lang, Gregor
* Lang, Martin

**Birrer, Babe**
See   Birrer, Werner

**Birrer, Werner** 1928-   [BE, SMG]
*American baseball player*
* Birrer, Babe

**Birtill, George Arthur** 1912-   [IAW]
*British author*
* Pendle, Nicholas

**Bisbee, Aileen** 1895-   [F2, FC]
*American actress*
* Pringle, Aileen

**Biscan, Frank Stephen** 1920-1959
[BE]
*American baseball player*
* Biscan, Porky

**Biscan, Porky**
See   Biscan, Frank Stephen

**Bisch, Edith** 20th c.   [IAW]
*Austrian-born author*
* De Born, Edith

**Bischitzky, Leo Bedrich** 1902-
[CA]
*Czech-born author and poet*
* Birch, Leo Bedrich

**Bischoff, John George** 1894-   [BE]
*American baseball player*
* Bischoff, Smiley

**Bischoff, Joseph E. Carl**   [PA]
*Author*
* Von Bolanden, Conrad

**Bischoff, Julia Bristol** 1909-1970
[CAP, SAT]
*American author*
* Arnoldy, Julie

**Bischoff, Marie** 1842-1921   [BBD]
*Austrian opera singer*
* Brandt, Marianne

**Bischoff, Smiley**
See   Bischoff, John George

**Bischoff, William G.** 20th c.
[PHM]
*American underworld figure*
* Clark, Lefty

**Bischop**
See   Episcopus, Simon

**Biscuit Pants Gehrig**
See   Gehrig, [Henry] Lou[is]

**[The] Bishop**
See   Davis, Shawn

**Bishop, Bish**
See   Bishop, Don

**Bishop, Bish**
See   Bishop, Wallace Henry

**Bishop, Bish**
See   Bishop, Walter, Jr.

**Bishop, Camera Eye**
See   Bishop, Max Frederick

**Bishop, Claire Huchet** 20th c.
[TCC]
*American author*
* Huchet, Claire

**Bishop, Curtis [Kent]** 1912-1967
[CAP, SAT]
*American author*
* Brandon, Curt
* Carroll, Curt

**Bishop, Don** 20th c.
*American football player*
* Bishop, Bish

**Bishop, E. Morchard**
See   Stonor, Oliver

**Bishop, Frances**
See   McKeever, Mrs. John T., Jr.

**Bishop, [Sir] Henry** 1780?-1855
[DEP, RH]
*British composer*
* [The] English Mozart

**Bishop, Joey**
See   Gottlieb, Joseph Abraham

**Bishop, Julie**
See   Wells, Jacqueline

**Bishop, Lefty**
See   Bishop, William H. [Bill]

**Bishop, Max Frederick** 1899-1962
[BE, BTB]
*American baseball player*
* Bishop, Camera Eye

**Bishop, Max Frederick** (Continued)
* Bishop, Tilly

**Bishop, Morchard**
See   Stonor, Oliver

**Bishop, Morris Gilbert** 1893-1973
[CA, CC, WW]
*American scholar, critic, author*
* Johnson, W. Bolingbroke

**Bishop of all the Denominations**
See   Fraser, Rev. Dr.

**[The] Bishop of Broadway**
See   Valasco, David

**[The] Bishop of Hippo**
See   Augustine

**[The] Bishop of London**
See   Tait, Archibald Campbell

**[The] Bishop of the English**
See   Augustine [or Austin]

**Bishop, Percy Cook** 20th c.   [MBF]
*British editor*
* Cooke, Percival

**Bishop, Stanley E.** 1913-   [GF]
*American golfer*
* Bishop, Ted

**Bishop, Stanley Walter Edgar**
1906-   [AW]
*British author and journalist*
* Edgar, Icarus Walter

**Bishop, Tania Kroitor**
See   Shevchuk, Tetiana

**Bishop, Ted**
See   Bishop, Stanley E.

**Bishop, Thomas**
See   Hayes, M.

**Bishop, Tilly**
See   Bishop, Max Frederick

**Bishop, Wallace Henry** 1906-
[WWJ]
*American jazz musician*
* Bishop, Bish

**Bishop, Walter, Jr.** 20th c.   [IBW]
*American songwriter*
* Bishop, Bish

**Bishop, William H. [Bill]** 1900-
[BE]
*American baseball player*
* Bishop, Lefty

**Bishop, Zealia Brown Reed** 20th c.
[WGT]
*Author*
* Heald, Hazel

**[The] Bismarck of Asia**
See   Li Hung-chang

**Bismarck, Otto Eduard Leopold von**
1815-1898   [DHA, DNNS, HN]
*German statesman*
* [The] Honest Broker
* [The] Iron Chancellor
* [The] Man of Blood and Iron
* [The] Prussian Boot

**Bisonius**
See   Allen, John E[lliston]

**Bisque, Anatole**
See   Bosquet, Alain

**Bisset-Smith, George Tulloch** 1863-
?   [WWL]
*Scottish sociologist and author*
* Bizet, George

**Bissonette, Adelphia Louis**
1899-1972   [BE]
*American baseball player*
* Bissonette, Del

**Bissonette, Del**
*See* Bissonette, Adelphia Louis

**Bissoondoyal, Basdeo** 1906-
[IAW, WD]
*Mauritian author and critic*
* Gotama, Ramta Yogi
* Vasudeva, Vishnudayal

**Biswas, Chittaranjan** 1939-   [IAW]
*Indian journalist and author*
* Chiranjib

**[The] Bitch Queen**
*See* O'Connor, Sandra Day

**Bite, Ben**
*See* Schneck, Stephen

**Bite 'em**
*See* Morellet, Andre

**Bithorn, Hi**
*See* Bithorn, Hiram Gabriel

**Bithorn, Hiram Gabriel** 1916-1952
[BE]
*Puerto Rican-born baseball player*
* Bithorn, Hi

**Bitter, Arthur**
*See* Haberstitch, Samuel

**Bitter Herb Ross**
*See* Ross, Herbert George

**Bittman, Henry** 20th c.   [BE]
*American baseball player*
* Bittman, Red

**Bittman, Red**
*See* Bittman, Henry

**Bitzer, Billy**
*See* Bitzer, G. Wilhelm

**Bitzer, G. Wilhelm** 1870?-1944
[FC, OCF, WEF]
*American cinematographer*
* Bitzer, Billy

**Bitzer, Marjorie** 1915?-   [FC, ITA]
*American actress*
* Bari, Lynn

**Bitzius, Albert** 1797-1854
[FFF, PA, WBD]
*Swiss author*
* Gotthelf, Jeremias

**Bivens, Edward** 1942-   [RO2]
*American singer*
* Bivens, Sonny

**Bivens, Sonny**
*See* Bivens, Edward

**Bix**
*See* Bixby, Ammi [or Amsori?]
Leander

**Bixby, Ammi [or Amsori?] Leander**
1856- ?   [NAA]
*American poet and journalist*
* Bix

**Bixby, Jay Lewis**
*See* Bixby, Jerome Lewis

**Bixby, Jerome Lewis** 1923-
[CA, ESF, WGT]
*American author and screenwriter*
* Bixby, Jay Lewis
* Drexel, Jay B.
* Herrick, Thornecliff [house
pseudonym]
* Jan, Emerson
* Lewis, D. B.
* Neal, Harry
* Rome, Alger [joint pseudonym
with Algirdas Jonas Budrys]
* Russell, Albert
* Russell, J.
* St. Vivant, M.

**Bixby, Ray Z.**
*See* Tralins, S[andor] Robert
[Bob]

**Bixler, William Allen** 1876- ?
[NAA]
*American author and artist*
* Allenby, Enos Will

**Biyidi, Alexandre** 1932-
*Cameroonian author*
* Beti, Mongo
* Boto, Eza

**Bizardel, Yvon** 1891-   [CA]
*French author*
* Lapaquellerie, Yvon

**Bizarre**
*See* Young, John Russell

**Bizet, Alexandre Cesar Leopold**
1838-1875   [WBD]
*French composer*
* Bizet, Georges

**Bizet, George**
*See* Bisset-Smith, George Tulloch

**Bizet, Georges**
*See* Bizet, Alexandre Cesar
Leopold

**Bjarme, Brynjolf**
*See* Ibsen, Henrik [Johan]

**Bjerke, Jarl Andre** 1918-   [EWL]
*Norwegian poet and author*
* Borge, Bernhard

**Bjerregaard-Jensen, Wilhelm Hans**
1900-   [CA]
*Danish-born American author*
* Green Bar Bill
* Hillcourt, William

**Bjoerling, John Jonaton** 1911-1960
[MS]
*Swedish opera singer*
* Bjoerling, Jussi

**Bjoerling, Jussi**
*See* Bjoerling, John Jonaton

**Bjorkland, Penny**
*See* Bjorkland, Rosemarie Diane

**Bjorkland, Rosemarie Diane** 1941-
[BLB]
*American murderer*
* Bjorkland, Penny

**Bjorkman, Carol** 1929-1967   [SC]
*American actress*
* Yorke, Carol

**Bjorksten, Gunnar O.** 1934-   [EJ]
*Finnish jazz musician*
* Birch, Woody
* Bjorksten, Hacke

**Bjorksten, Hacke**
*See* Bjorksten, Gunnar O.

**Bjornard, Reidar B[ernhard]**
*See* Kallestad, Reidar B[ernhard]

**Bjornstad, Marianne**
*See* Engh, Bjorg Larsen

**Bjorset, Brynjolf**
*See* Beorse, Bryn

**[The] Black**
*See* Cameron, [Sir] Evan

**[The] Black**
*See* Clitus

**[The] Black**
*See* Henry IX

**[The] Black**
*See* Radziwill, Nicholas

**Black Ace**
*See* Turner, Babe Kyro Lemon

**Black, Adam** 1784- ?   [PA]
*Author*
* Scribe, Simeon

**Black Agnes**
*See* Dunbar, Agnes

**Black, Alexander** 1858- ?
[FFF, PA]
*American writer*
* Brick, Jefferson

**[The] Black American Rimbaud**
*See* Kaufman, Bob

**Black Arthur**
*See* Blythe, Arthur Murray

**[The] Black Avenger**
*See* Johnson, John Arthur [Jack]

**[The] Black Babe Ruth**
*See* Gibson, Joshua

**[The] Black Baron**
*See* Munro [or Monro], Robert

**Black, Betty**
*See* Schwartz, Betty

**Black, Blackie**
*See* Black, Clayton

**Black, Bud**
*See* Black, William Carroll [Bill]

**Black, Campbell** 1944-   [CA]
*Scottish-born author*
* Altman, Thomas
* Campbell, Jeffrey [joint
pseudonym with Jeffrey Caine]

**[The] Black Captain**
*See* Davidov [or Davidoff], Denis
Vassilievitch

**Black Cat Gagnon**
*See* Gagnon, John

**Black Cat Mendes**
*See* Mendes, Joe

**Black Charlie Harris**
*See* Harris, Charlie

**Black, Cilla**
*See* White, Priscilla

**Black, Clara Ella** 1871-1961
[CED]
*American entertainer*
* Vance, Clarice

**[The] Black Clarence Darrow**
*See* Harris, De Long

**Black, Clayton** 20th c.   [CSH]
*Canadian lacrosse player*
* Black, Blackie

**[The] Black Clifford**
*See* Clifford, John de

**Black, Clinton** 1918-   [CW]
*Jamaican author, folklorist,
archivist*
* Brosse, Vane de

**Black, Clinton R., Jr.** 1894-1963
[AS]
*American football player*
* Black, Cupe

**Black Cloud, Chief**
*See* Breeden, Leon

**Black, Cupe**
*See* Black, Clinton R., Jr.

**[The] Black Cyclone from Wooster**
*See* Follis, Charles W.

**Black, D. M.**
*See* Black, David [Macleod]

**Black, David**
*See* Way, Robert E[dward]

**Black, David [Macleod]** 1941-   [CA]
*British poet*
* Black, D. M.

**Black, Dorothy** 1914-   [AW]
*British translator*
* Black, Kitty

**[The] Black Douglas**
*See* Douglas, [Sir] James

**[The] Black Douglas**
*See* Douglas, Archibald

**[The] Black Dunlap**
*See* Grant, Frank

**[The] Black Duse**
*See* McClendon, Rosalie Virginia
Scott [Rose]

**Black Dwarf**
*See* Wooler, Thomas Jonathan

**Black Eagle**
*See* Adams, Robert

**[The] Black Englishman**
*See* Burns, Isaac Murphy

**Black Eyed Susan**
*See* Ledford, Minnie Lena

**Black, F. R.**   [PA]
*Author*
* M. D.

**[The] Black Flash**
*See* Moseley, Hallam Reynold

**[The] Black Flo Ziegfeld**
*See* Steele, Larry

**Black, Frankie**
*See* Blackwell, Francis Hillman

**Black, Gavin**
*See* Wynd, Oswald [Morris]

**[The] Black Gazelle**
*See* Rudolph, Wilma Glodean
Ward

**Black George**
*See* Petrovitsch [or Petrovic],
George

**[The] Black Gladiator**
*See* Bates, Otha Ellas

[The] Black Globetrotter
See McVea, Samuel

Black Happy Goldston
See Goldston, Christopher

Black Hawk
See Ma-ka-tae-mish-kia-kiak

Black Hawk, Chief
See Attean, Elmer

Black Helmet
See Peek, Coyle, Jr.

Black, Hobart
See Sanders, Ed

Black Hoss Weeks
See Weeks, Guy

[The] Black Houdini
See Potter, Richard

Black, Ian 1929- [ART]
British artist
* I. B.

[The] Black Ivory King
See Alexander, Dave

Black Jack Burdock
See Burdock, John Joseph

Black Jack Fletcher
See Fletcher, Frank

Black Jack Ketchum
See Ketchum, Thomas

Black Jack Pershing
See Pershing, John Joseph

Black Jack Stewart
See Stewart, John Sherratt

Black Jack Wilson
See Wilson, John Francis

Black, James 1728-1799
[DNNS, FFF, SN]
French-born chemist
* [The] Nestor of the Chemical
Revolution

[The] Black Jerry West
See Tatum, Earl

[The] Black Jesse James
See Fields, Ross Eugene

Black, Jigger
See Black, John William [Bill]

Black, John Falcnor
See Haddow, John Falcnor

Black, John William [Bill]
1899-1968 [BE]
American baseball player
* Black, Jigger

Black Jr.
See Johnson, Luther, Jr.

Black, Karen
See Ziegler, Karen

[The] Black King
See Henry III [or Heinrich]

Black, Kitty
See Black, Dorothy

Black, Ladbroke Lionel Day
1877-1940 [MBF]
British author
* Day, Lionel
* Urquhart, Paul

Black Lightning
See Patrick, Ted

Black, Lillian 20th c. [BMH]
British trapeze performer
* Lady

Black, Lionel
See Barker, Dudley

[The] Black Lou Gehrig
See Leonard, Walter Fenner

Black, M. Dana
See Butler, H. B.

Black, Mansell
See Dudley-Smith, Trevor

Black, Margaret K[atherine] 1921-
[CA, IAW]
British author
* Howard, Katherine
* Howorth, M. K.
* Howorth, Margaret

Black Mario
See Bowers, Thomas J.

Black Mike Cochrane
See Cochrane, Gordon Stanley

[The] Black Milton Berle
See Drew, Allan

Black Monocle
See Canal, Andre

[The] Black Moses
See Hayes, Isaac

Black Moses of the Black Press
See Jackson, Emory O.

[The] Black Nightingale
See Rainey, Gertrude Malissa Nix
[Pridgett]

[The] Black Panther
See Ashraf, [Princess]

[The] Black Panther
See James, Daniel, Jr.

[The] Black Panther
See Wills, Harry

[The] Black Pearl
See Arantes Do Nascimento,
Edson

[The] Black Pearl
See Barek, Larbi Ben

[The] Black Pearl
See Rudolph, Wilma Glodean
Ward

[The] Black Pearl of the 1960
Olympiad
See Coachman, Alice

[The] Black Pie Traynor
See Johnson, William Julius

[The] Black Pope
See Potter, Phillip A.

[The] Black Prince
See Edward

[The] Black Prince of the Ring
See Jackson, Peter

[The] Black Puritan
See Grimke, Francis James

Black Rabbit Smith
See Smith, Billy Ray

Black, Robert
See Holdstock, Robert P.

Black, Roberta [joint pseudonym
with Sandra Miesel]
See Coulson, Robert [Stratton]

Black, Roberta [joint pseudonym
with Robert (Stratton) Coulson]
See Miesel, Sandra

[The] Black Robin Hood of Harlem
See Johnson, Ellsworth Raymond

Black, Ruby Aurora
See Little, Ruby A. Black

Black Rusie Robinson
See Robinson, James

Black Satan
See Patrick, Ted

[The] Black Shoemaker
See Long, James Sebastian

[The] Black Swallow
See Bullard, Eugene Jacques

[The] Black Swan
See Greenfield, Elizabeth Taylor

[The] Black Swan of Lac Leman
See Nabokov, Vladimir
Vladimirovich

[The] Black Terror
See Richmond, Bill

[The] Black Tiger
See Reed, Donald

Black, Tom 1885-1955 [BEW]
Irish-born comedian
* Howard, Tom

[The] Black Tornado
See Mooney, Paul

[The] Black Tuna
See Davila-Jimeno, Raul

[The] Black Uhlan
See Schmeling, Max[imilian
Adolph Otto Siegfried]

[The] Black Valentino
See Tucker, Lorenzo

Black Venus
See Baker, Josephine Carson

Black Venus
See Bumbry, Grace Ann Melzia

Black, Veronica
See Peters, Maureen

[The] Black Wagner
See Lloyd, John Henry

Black, Wendy 1925-1972 [SC]
American actress
* Howard, Wendy

Black Widow Owens
See Owens, Milton

Black, William 1840?-1898
[FFF, PA]
British author
* Brown, Pisistratus

Black, William Carroll [Bill] 1932-
[BE]
American baseball player
* Black, Bud

Black, Winifred 1863?-1936 [B10]
American journalist
* Annie Laurie

[The] Black Wolf of Wall Street
See George, H. R.

Blackall, Christopher Rubey 1830-
? [ALY]
American author and editor
* Quad, Doctor

Blackbeard
See Teach, Edward

Blackburn, Babe
See Blackburn, Foster Edwin

Blackburn, Barbara
See Leader, [Evelyn] Barbara
[Blackburn]

Blackburn, Bones
See Blackburn, James Ray [Jim]

Blackburn, Bunkie
See Blackburn, James R.

Blackburn, Charles Henry
1883-1942 [BX, RBE]
American boxer
* Blackburn, Jack

Blackburn, Claire
See Jacobs, Linda C.

Blackburn, Dorothy
See Smith, Dorothy Loraine
Blackburn

Blackburn, E. Owens
See Casey, Elizabeth

Blackburn, Foster Edwin 1895-
[BE]
American baseball player
* Blackburn, Babe

Blackburn, Jack
See Blackburn, Charles Henry

Blackburn, James R. 1936- [EAR]
American auto racer
* Blackburn, Bunkie

Blackburn, James Ray [Jim] 1924-
[BE]
American baseball player
* Blackburn, Bones

Blackburn, Laura
See Blanden, Charles Granger

Blackburn, Victoria Grace ?-1928
[CAN]
Canadian journalist
* Fan Fan

Blackburne, Lena
See Blackburne, Russell Aubrey

Blackburne, Russell Aubrey
1886-1968 [BE, PB]
American baseball player and
manager
* Blackburne, Lena
* Blackburne, Slats

Blackburne, Slats
See Blackburne, Russell Aubrey

Blacker, Hereth
See Chalke, Herbert Davis

Blacker, Tina 1934?- [BEW, SW]
American actress
* Louise, Tina

Blackett, Veronica Heath Stuart
[Tegner] 1927- [AW, CA, WD]
British author
* Heath, Veronica

**Blackham, John McCarthy**
1853-1932   [OCS]
*Australian cricketer*
* [The] Prince of Wicket-Keepers

**Blackie, Kid**
See   Dempsey, William Harrison

**Blackledge, Ethel H.** 1920-   [CA]
*American author*
* Hale, Allison

**Blackley, Douglas** 1908-1955   [SC]
*American actor*
* Kent, Robert

**Blacklin, Malcolm**
See   Chambers, Aidan

**Blackmantle, Bernard**
See   Westmacott, Charles Malloy

**Blackmore, Amos** 1934-
[BWW, NBB]
*American singer*
* [The] Little Giant of the Blues
* Wells, Amos
* Wells, Junior
* Wells, Little Junior

**Blackmore, [Sir] Richard**
1650-1729   [DEL, HN, SN]
*British physician and author*
* [The] Cheapside Knight

**Blackmun, Harry A.** 1908-
*American Supreme Court Justice*
* Hip Pocket Harry

**Blackmur, Richard Palmer**
1904-1965   [CAP]
*American author*
* Hobbs, Perry

**Blackrobe**
See   De Smet, Pierre Jean

**[The] Blacksmith of Antwerp**
See   Matsys, Quentin

**Blacksnake, George**
See   Richardson, Gladwell

**Blackstock, Charity**
See   Torday, Ursula

**Blackstock, Lee**
See   Torday, Ursula

**Blackstone, Harry**
See   Bouton, Harry

**Blackstone, Robert J.** 1855-1918
[BE]
*American baseball player*
* Blakiston, Robert J. [Bob]

**Blackstone, Valerius D.**
See   Galpin, J. A.

**Blackton, Jay**
See   Schwartzdorf, Jacob

**Blackwell, Basil T.** 20th c.   [YAB]
*Illustrator*
* B. T. B.

**Blackwell, Ewell** 1922-   [BE, PB]
*American baseball player*
* [The] Whip

**Blackwell, Francis Hillman**
1903-1962   [BWW]
*American singer*
* Black, Frankie
* Blackwell, Scrapper

**Blackwell, John**
See   Collings, Edwin Geoffrey

**Blackwell, Mr.**
See   Blackwell, Richard

**Blackwell, Richard** 20th c.   [WFA]
*American fashion designer and radio commentator*
* Blackwell, Mr.
* Ellis, Dick

**Blackwell, Scrapper**
See   Blackwell, Francis Hillman

**Blackwood, William** 1776-1834
[DEL, PA]
*Scottish publisher*
* Ebony
* Maga
* Old Ebony

**[The] Blade**
See   Billingham, John Eugene
[Jack]

**[The] Blade**
See   Dyer, Ken

**[The] Blade**
See   Hall, Tom Edward

**Blade, Alexander** [house pseudonym, Ziff-Davis]
See   Browne, Howard

**Blade, Alexander** [house pseudonym, Ziff-Davis]
See   Cooke, Millen

**Blade, Alexander** [joint pseudonym with Robert Silverberg] [house pseudonym, Ziff-Davis]
See   Garrett, [Gordon] Randall [Philip David]

**Blade, Alexander** [house pseudonym, Ziff-Davis]
See   Geier, Chester S.

**Blade, Alexander** [house pseudonym, Ziff-Davis]
See   Graham, Roger Phillips

**Blade, Alexander** [house pseudonym, Ziff-Davis]
See   Hamilton, Edmond [Moore]

**Blade, Alexander** [house pseudonym, Ziff-Davis]
See   Hauser, Heinrich

**Blade, Alexander** [house pseudonym, Ziff-Davis]
See   Livingston, Berkeley

**Blade, Alexander** [house pseudonym, Ziff-Davis]
See   Livingston, Herb

**Blade, Alexander** [house pseudonym, Ziff-Davis]
See   McGivern, William P[eter]

**Blade, Alexander** [house pseudonym, Ziff-Davis]
See   O'Brien, David Wright

**Blade, Alexander** [house pseudonym, Ziff-Davis]
See   Sampliner, Louis H.

**Blade, Alexander** [house pseudonym, Ziff-Davis]
See   Shaver, Richard S[harpe]

**Blade, Alexander** [joint pseudonym with Randall Garrett] [house pseudonym, Ziff-Davis]
See   Silverberg, Robert

**Blade, Alexander** [house pseudonym, Ziff-Davis]
See   Vern, David

**Blade, Alexander** [house pseudonym, Ziff-Davis]
See   Wilcox, Don

**Blade, Alexander** [house pseudonym, Ziff-Davis]
See   Yerxa, Leroy

**Blades, Kitty** 1878?-1974
[SC, THR]
*British actress and singer*
* Gordon, Constance
* Gordon, Kitty

**Bladon, Bomber**
See   Bladon, Tom

**Bladon, Tom** 1952-   [SMG]
*Canadian-born hockey player*
* Bladon, Bomber

**Blaffer, Sarah C.**
See   Blaffer-Hrdy, Sarah C[ampbell]

**Blaffer-Hrdy, Sarah C[ampbell]**
1946-   [CA]
*American author*
* Blaffer, Sarah C.

**Blagdon, Francis William** 19th c.
[DEL, PA]
*British writer*
* Aeschines
* Aristides
* M. A.

**Blaich, Hans Erich** 1873-1945
[WBD]
*German author and translator*
* Owlglass, Dr.
* Ratatoskr

**Blaik, Earl Henry** 1897-   [B10, FB]
*American football coach*
* Blaik, Red

**Blaik, Red**
See   Blaik, Earl Henry

**Blaiklock, Edward Musgrave** 1903-
[CA]
*British author and journalist*
* Grammaticus

**Blaine, James**
See   Avallone, Michael [Angelo], Jr.

**Blaine, James Gillespie** 1830-1893
[DHA, FFF, SN]
*American statesman*
* [The] Gladstone of America
* [The] Magnetic Statesman
* [The] Plumed Knight
* [The] Tattooed Man

**Blaine, John** [joint pseudonym with Philip Harkins]
See   Goodwin, Harold Leland [Hal]

**Blaine, John** [joint pseudonym with Harold Leland Goodwin]
See   Harkins, Philip

**Blaine, Vivian**
See   Stapleton, Vivian S.

**Blair**
See   Blair-Fish, Wallace Wilfrid

**Blair, Adrian**
See   Bird, William Henry Fleming

**Blair, Allan**
See   Bayfield, William John

**Blair, Andrew James Fraser**
1872-1935   [ESF, SFL, WGT]
*Scottish author, journalist, editor*
* Blair, Hamish

**Blair, Anthony**
See   Walker, Rowland

**Blair, Betsy**
See   Boger, Elizabeth Winifred

**Blair, Buddy**
See   Blair, Louis Nathan

**Blair, Caroline** 1816-1869   [FFF]
*Writer*
* Woodland, Waif

**Blair, Clarence Vick** 1903-   [BE]
*American baseball player*
* Blair, Footsie

**Blair, David**
See   Goyne, Richard

**Blair, [Rev.] David**
See   Phillips, [Sir] Richard

**Blair, Dorothy** 20th c.   [WW]
*Author*
* Scarlett, Roger [joint pseudonym with Evelyn Page]

**Blair, Dorothy Sara [Greene]** 1913-
[AW]
*British author*
* Bolitho, Ray D.

**Blair, Dusty**
See   Blair, George

**Blair, Eric Arthur** 1903-1950
[EWL, SF, TCL]
*British author*
* Orwell, George

**Blair, Eugenia**
See   Robinson, Mrs. Forrest

**Blair, Ezell, Jr.** 1942-   [IBW]
*American civil rights activist*
* Khazan, Jibreel

**Blair, Footsie**
See   Blair, Clarence Vick

**Blair, George** 1929-   [CEI, SMG]
*Canadian-born hockey player*
* Blair, Dusty

**Blair, Hamish**
See   Blair, Andrew James Fraser

**Blair, Heavy**
See   Blair, Walter Allan

**Blair, Janet**
See   Lafferty, Martha Janet

**Blair, Joyce**
See   Ogus, Joyce

**Blair, Larry**
See   Bess, Larry

**Blair, Lionel**
See   Ogus, Lionel

**Blair, Lottie**
See   Parker, Mrs. Harry D.

**Blair, Louis Nathan** 1910-   [BE]
*American baseball player*
* Blair, Buddy

**Blair, Lucile**
See   Yeakley, Marjory Hall

**Blair, Mary**
See  Eakin, Mary Blair

**Blair, Motormouth**
See  Blair, Paul L. D.

**Blair, Paul L. D.** 1944-    [BE, PB]
*American baseball player*
* Blair, Motormouth

**Blair, Peggy** 1927-1973    [FIR]
*American actress*
* Call, Peggy
* Castle, Peggy

**Blair, Peter**
See  Hunter Blair, Peter

**Blair, Sylvia**
See  Jacobs, Alma Sylvia

**Blair, Walter** 1900-    [WD]
*American author and critic*
* Post, Mortimer

**Blair, Walter Allan** 1883-1948
[BE]
*American baseball player and
manager*
* Blair, Heavy

**Blair, Wilfrid**
See  Blair-Fish, Wallace Wilfrid

**Blair-Fish, Wallace Wilfrid**
1889-1968    [CAP, WWL]
*British journalist and playwright*
* Blair
* Blair, Wilfrid
* Vexatus

**Blairman, Jacqueline**
See  Pinto, Jacqueline

**Blais, George** 1856-1918
[RBE, SG]
*Canadian-born boxer*
* LaBlanche, George
* [The] Marine

**Blaisdell, Anne**
See  Linington, Elizabeth

**Blaisdell, Anne**
See  Rosenberg, Elinor Blaisdell

**Blaisdell, Dick**
See  Blaisdell, Howard Carleton

**Blaisdell, Elinor**
See  Rosenberg, Elinor Blaisdell

**Blaisdell, George G.** 1895?-1978
*American business executive*
* Zippo, Mr.

**Blaisdell, Howard Carleton**
1862-1886    [BE]
*American baseball player*
* Blaisdell, Dick

**Blaisdell, Paul** 20th c.    [SFP]
*Author*
* Dell, Paul

**Blaise, Ed** 1895?-1944    [NOJ]
*American jazz musician*
* Totts, Kid

**Blaisell, Big Bill**
See  Blaisell, Charles

**Blaisell, Charles** 1874-1930    [SC]
*American actor*
* Blaisell, Big Bill

**Blake, Al**
See  Blake, Alva D.

**Blake, Alfred**
See  Harris, Larry M[ark]

**Blake, Alva D.** 1877-1966    [EE, SC]
*American entertainer involved in
Japanese intelligence activities*
* Blake, Al
* King of the Robots

**Blake, Amanda**
See  Neill, Beverly Louise

**Blake, Andrea** 1929-    [AW]
*British author*
* Weale, Anne

**Blake, Andrew**
See  Harris, Larry M[ark]

**Blake, Anthony**
See  Tubb, Edwin Charles

**Blake, Arthur** 1890?- ?    [EJ]
*American singer and guitarist*
* Blake, Blind

**Blake, Betty**
See  Gibbs, Betty

**Blake, Blind**
See  Blake, Arthur

**Blake, Bud**
See  Blake, Julian Watson

**Blake, Buddy**
See  Blasingame, Gilbert, Jr.

**Blake, Cameron**
See  Mason, Michael Henry

**Blake, Doris**
See  Donnelly, Antoinette

**Blake, Dude**
See  Blake, Harry Cooper

**Blake, E. A.**
See  Pratt, Eleanor Blake
[Atkinson]

**Blake, Eleanor**
See  Pratt, Eleanor Blake
[Atkinson]

**Blake, Eric**
See  Boardman, John

**Blake, Eubie**
See  Blake, James Hubert

**Blake, Everett**
See  Everett, Bill

**Blake, Francis J.** 1912-    [CEI]
*Canadian-born hockey player*
* Blake, Mickey

**Blake, George**
See  Behar, George

**Blake, George** 1893-1961    [TC]
*Scottish author*
* Vagabond

**Blake, Harry Cooper** 1874-1919
[BE]
*American baseball player*
* Blake, Dude

**Blake, Hector** 1912-
[CEI, FHE, HK]
*Canadian-born hockey player*
* Blake, Toe
* [The] Old Lamplighter

**Blake, Hume** 1911-    [FC]
*Canadian-born actor*
* Cronyn, Hume

**Blake, James Hubert** 1883-
[DAM, IPA, WWJ]
*American jazz musician and
composer*
* Blake, Eubie

**Blake, Jennifer**
See  Maxwell, Patricia Anne

**Blake, Jerry**
See  Chabania, Jacinto

**Blake, John Frederick** 1899-    [BE]
*American baseball player*
* Blake, Sheriff

**Blake, Jonas**
See  Hardy, C. Colburn

**Blake, Joseph** ?-1723
[DNNF, DNNS, FFF]
*British burglar*
* Blueskin

**Blake, Julian Watson** 1918-    [CA]
*American cartoonist*
* Blake, Bud

**Blake, Justin** [joint pseudonym with
Jeremy Bullmore]
See  Bowen, John [Griffith]

**Blake, Justin** [joint pseudonym with
John (Griffith) Bowen]
See  Bullmore, Jeremy

**Blake, Justin**
See  Hodges, Donald Clark

**Blake, Katherine**
See  Walter, Dorothy Blake

**Blake, Kay**
See  Walter, Dorothy Blake

**Blake, Leslie**
See  Duckworth, Leslie Blakey

**Blake, Leslie James** 1913-
[AW, CA]
*Australian author*
* Lester, James
* Tabard, Peter

**Blake, Lillie Devereux** 1835-1913
[PA]
*American author*
* Aesop
* Tiger Lily

**Blake, Lowell**
See  Schoenfeld, William C.

**Blake, Marie** ?-1978    [FIR]
*Actress*
* Rock, Blossom

**Blake, Mary**
See  Blakeslee, Mary N.

**Blake, Mickey**
See  Blake, Francis J.

**Blake, Minden V[aughan]** 1913-
[CA]
*New Zealand-born author and
inventor*
* Blake, Mindy

**Blake, Mindy**
See  Blake, Minden V[aughan]

**Blake, Monica**
See  Muir, Marie Agnes

**Blake, Mrs. O. W.**    [FFF]
*Entertainer*
* Worthington, Mabel

**Blake, Nicholas**
See  Day-Lewis, C[ecil]

**Blake, Olive**
See  Supraner, Robyn

**Blake, Paul**
See  Paull, Harry Major

**Blake, Redmond?**
See  Morris, Charles Smith

**Blake, Robert**
See  Davies, Leslie Purnell

**Blake, Robert**
See  Gubitosi, Michael

**Blake, Royston**
See  Childs, Edmund Burton

**Blake, Sally**
See  Saunders, Jean

**Blake, Sally Mirliss** 1925-
[CA, WD]
*American author*
* Sara

**Blake, Sheriff**
See  Blake, John Frederick

**Blake, Toe**
See  Blake, Hector

**Blake, Vanessa**
See  Brown, Mary

**Blake, Walker E.**
See  Butterworth, William
Edmund, III

**Blake, Wendon**
See  Holden, Donald

**Blake, William**
See  Everett, Bill

**Blake, [Captain] Wilton**
See  Parry, David Harold

**Blakely, Delois** 20th c.    [IBW]
*American fashion model*
* Noelita Marie, [Sister]

**Blakely, Lincoln Howard** 1912-
[BE]
*American baseball player*
* Blakely, Link

**Blakely, Link**
See  Blakely, Lincoln Howard

**Blakely, Paul Lendrum** 1880-1943
[CAT]
*American journalist*
* Wainscott, Cricket
* Wiltbye, John

**Blakely, Robert** 19th c.    [PA]
*Author*
* Hackle, Palmer

**Blakeslee, Mary N.**    [FFF]
*Writer*
* Blake, Mary

**Blakesley, Joseph Williams** 1808-
?    [DEL]
*British author and clergyman*
* [A] Hertfordshire Incumbent

**Blakesley, Stephen**
See  Bond, F.

**Blakeston, Oswell** 1907-    [WW]
*Author*
* Simon [joint pseudonym with
Roger D'Este Burford]

**Blakey, Art** 1919- [EJ]
*American jazz musician*
* Ibn-Buhaina, Abdullah

**Blakiston, Robert J. [Bob]**
*See* Blackstone, Robert J.

**Blaman, Anna**
*See* Vrugt, J. P.

**Blamauer, Karoline** 1900-1981
[EMT, OCF, TR]
*Austrian actress and singer*
* Lenya, Lotte

**Blamire, Susanna** 1747-1794
[WBD]
*British poet*
* [The] Muse of Cumberland

**Blanc, Antonio**
*See* De Guillet, Leblanc

**Blanc, Jean Joseph Louis** 1813- ?
[PA]
*Author*
* [A] Freeman

**Blanc, Marie Therese [De Solms]**
1840-1907 [B10]
*French author*
* Bentzon, Therese

**Blanchan, Neltje**
*See* Doubleday, Neltje de Graff

**Blanchard, Bernard** 20th c. [BBH]
*Canadian lacrosse promoter*
* Blanchard, CoCo

**Blanchard, CoCo**
*See* Blanchard, Bernard

**Blanchard, Doc**
*See* Blanchard, Felix Anthony

**Blanchard, Donald F.** 1914-
[CWG, DAM]
*American country-western performer*
* Blanchard, Red

**Blanchard, E. E.** [PA]
*Author*
* Old Boy

**Blanchard, Felix Anthony** 1924-
[B10, FB]
*American football coach*
* Blanchard, Doc
* Inside, Mr.

**Blanchard, Jacques** 1600-1638
[DEP, DNNS, FFF]
*French painter*
* [The] French Titian
* [The] Titian of France

**Blanchard, Kittie**
*See* Rankin, Mrs. McKee

**Blanchard, Red**
*See* Blanchard, Donald F.

**Blanchard, Theresa Weld**
1894?-1978
*American figure skater*
* [The] Queen of the Ice

**Blanche**
*See* Field, Mrs. E. B.

**Blanche, Ada**
*See* Adams, Ada

**Blanche, [Prosper] Al[bert]**
*See* Belangio, Prosper Albert

**Blanche, Belle**
*See* Minzesheimer, Blanche

**Blanche, Margaret**
*See* Jessen, M.

**Blanche, Marie**
*See* Peacock, Marie

**Blanchot, Gustave** 1885-1968
[WEC]
*French cartoonist, illustrator,
publisher*
* Bofa, Gus

**Blanco, Carlos Osvaldo J.** 1945-
[BE]
*Venezuelan-born baseball player*
* Blanco, Ossie

**Blanco, Jose** 1905- [GS]
*Spanish bullfighter*
* Blanquito [Little Blanco]

**Blanco, Ossie**
*See* Blanco, Carlos Osvaldo J.

**Bland, Bobby Blue**
*See* Bland, Robert Calvin [Bobby]

**Bland, Dorothea** 1762-1816 [WBD]
*Irish actress*
* Jordan, Dorothea [or Dorothy]

**Bland, Edith**
*See* Brereton, Mrs. Austin

**Bland, Fabian** [joint pseudonym with
Edith Nesbit]
*See* Bland, Hubert

**Bland, Fabian** [joint pseudonym with
Hubert Bland]
*See* Nesbit, Edith

**Bland, Hubert** 1856-1914 [LC]
*Author*
* Bland, Fabian [joint pseudonym
with Edith Nesbit]

**Bland, Jennifer**
*See* Bowden, Jean

**Bland, John** 20th c. [GW]
*American rodeo performer*
* Bland, Twigs

**Bland, John O. P.** 1863- ? [WWL]
*British author*
* Hubert

**Bland, Leroy** 1948- [IBW]
*American jazz musician*
* Abdullah, Ahmed

**Bland, Mrs. Lionel E.** [FFF]
*Entertainer*
* Dean, Maggie

**Bland, Robert Calvin [Bobby]** 1930-
[BWW, NBB, PRS]
*American singer*
* Bland, Bobby Blue
* [The] Soul Man

**Bland, Twigs**
*See* Bland, John

**Blanden, Charles Granger** 1857- ?
[ALY]
*American author*
* Blackburn, Laura
* Rhuddlau, John

**Blandina, [Sister]**
*See* Segale, Rose

**Blanding, Fred James** 1888-1950
[BE]
*American baseball player*
* Blanding, Fritz

**Blanding, Fritz**
*See* Blanding, Fred James

**Blane, Ralph**
*See* Hunsecker, Ralph Uriah

**Blane, Sally**
*See* Young, Elizabeth Jane

**Blaney, Walter** 20th c. [BS]
*American magician*
* Blaney, Zaney

**Blaney, Zaney**
*See* Blaney, Walter

**Blankenhorn, Lulu**
*See* Cornu, Mrs. Louis J.

**Blankenship, Homer** 1902- [BE]
*American baseball player*
* Blankenship, Si

**Blankenship, Si**
*See* Blankenship, Homer

**Blanks, Larvell** 20th c.
*American baseball player*
* Blanks, Sugar Bear

**Blanks, Sugar Bear**
*See* Blanks, Larvell

**Blanquito [Little Blanco]**
*See* Blanco, Jose

**Blanton, Cy**
*See* Blanton, Darrell Elijah

**Blanton, Darrell Elijah** 1908-1945
[AS, BE]
*American baseball player*
* Blanton, Cy

**Blas, Ruy**
*See* Mimenza Castillo, Ricardo

**Blascheck, Ballard** 1904- [THR]
*British actor*
* Berkeley, Ballard

**Blaser, Robin** 1925- [DLE]
*American poet*
* Avalon

**Blasingame, Blazer**
*See* Blasingame, Wade Allen

**Blasingame, Don Lee** 1932- [BE]
*American baseball player*
* [The] Blazer

**Blasingame, Gilbert, Jr.** 1935-
[CM]
*American radio executive*
* Blake, Buddy

**Blasingame, Wade Allen** 1943-
[PB]
*American baseball player*
* Blasingame, Blazer

**Blasko, Bela Lugosi** 1882?-1956
[BDF, FC, WEF]
*Hungarian actor*
* Lugosi, Bela
* Olt, Arisztid

**Blassen, Sal**
*See* Bonnekamp, Sonja Maria

**Blassey, Classy Freddie**
*See* Blassey, Frederick

**Blassey, Frederick** 20th c.
*American wrestler*
* Blassey, Classy Freddie

**Blassingame, Wyatt Rainey** 1909-
[HFF, WGT]
*American author*
* Rainey, W. B.

**Blast, Kid**
*See* Gallo, Albert

**Blaszko**
*See* Blaszkowski, Martin

**Blaszkowski, Martin** 1920- [ART]
*German-born Argentinian painter
and sculptor*
* Blaszko

**Blatnik, Chief**
*See* Blatnik, John Louis [Johnny]

**Blatnik, John Louis [Johnny]** 1921-
[BE]
*American baseball player*
* Blatnik, Chief

**Blattner, Buddy**
*See* Blattner, Robert Garnett

**Blattner, Robert Garnett** 1920-
[BE, PB]
*American baseball player*
* Blattner, Buddy

**Blatty, William Peter** 1928- [CA]
*American author*
* Clyne, Terence

**Blau, Eric** 1921- [CA]
*American author, producer, lyricist*
* Blau, Milton

**Blau, Eugene** 1899- [BBD]
*Hungarian-born conductor*
* Ormandy, Eugene

**Blau, Joshua** 1919- [CA]
*Rumanian-born author*
* Blau, Yehoshua

**Blau, Lajos** 1880-1948 [JL]
*Austrian-born film executive and
screenwriter*
* Biro, Lajos

**Blau, Milton**
*See* Blau, Eric

**Blau, Sebastian**
*See* Eberle, Josef

**Blau, Yehoshua**
*See* Blau, Joshua

**Blau Gisbert, Vicente** 1932- [GS]
*Spanish bullfighter*
* [El] Tino [The Tank]

**Blauschild, Marcel Benoit** 1900-
*French-born actor*
* Dalio, Marcel

**Blaustein, Albert P[aul]** 1921-
[WD]
*American author and editor*
* De Graeff, Allen

**Blauth, Christopher**
*See* Blauth-Muszkowski, Peter
Christopher

**Blauth-Muszkowski, Peter
Christopher** 1919- [AW]
*Polish-born author and translator*
* Blauth, Christopher

**Blaylock, Travis L.** 1934- [BWW]
*American singer*
* Harmonica Slim

**Blayn, Hugo**
*See* Fearn, John Russell

**Blayre, Christopher**
See Heron-Allen, Edward

**Blaythwait, Mrs. Raymond** [FFF]
*Author*
* Aunt Maggie

**Blaze, Ange Henri** 1813-1888
[WBD]
*German poet, critic, translator*
* Blaze de Bury

**Blaze de Bury**
See Blaze, Ange Henri

**Blaze de Bury, Yetta** ?-1902 [FFF]
*French author*
* Brown, Jane

**Blaze, Francois Henri Joseph**
1784-1857 [WBD]
*French musician and critic*
* Castil-Blaze

**[The] Blazer**
See Blasingame, Don Lee

**Blazin' Ben Chapman**
See Chapman, [William]
Ben[jamin]

**Blazing Ben Eastman**
See Eastman, Ben

**Bleakley, Horace William** 1868- ?
[WWL]
*British author*
* Tivoli

**Blech, Aimee**
See Dalsace, Lionel

**Bledlow, John**
See Vale, [Henry] Edmund
[Theodoric]

**Bleeck, Oliver**
See Thomas, Ross

**Bleecker, Mary Noel** 19th c. [PA]
*Author*
* M. N. M.

**Bleeker, Mordecia**
See Morgan, Fred Troy

**Bleeker, Sonia**
See Zim, Sonia Bleeker

**Blees, David Hughes** 1924-1945
[SC]
*American actor*
* Hughes, David

**Blefary, Buff**
See Blefary, Curtis Leroy

**Blefary, Curtis Leroy** 1943- [PB]
*American baseball player*
* Blefary, Buff

**Blegen, Julius P.** 20th c. [BBH]
*Norwegian-born skier, coach, skiing
organization founder*
* Uncle Yoolus

**Bleicher, Hugo** 1899-
[BDW, WWW]
*German counter-intelligence agent*
* Henri, Colonel
* Jean, Monsieur

**Bleier, Robert Patrick** 1946- [CA]
*American football player and author*
* Bleier, Rockey

**Bleier, Rockey**
See Bleier, Robert Patrick

**Bleiler, E. F.**
See Bleiler, Everett Franklin

**Bleiler, Everett Franklin** 1920-
[SF]
*American anthologist*
* Bleiler, E. F.

**Blemker, Buddy**
See Blemker, Ray

**Blemker, Ray** 1937- [BE]
*American baseball player*
* Blemker, Buddy

**Blenkinsop, Vicesimus**
See Hook, Theodore Edward

**Bles, Henri Met de** 1480?-1550?
[WBD]
*Flemish painter*
* Blessius, Henricus

**[The] Blessed**
See Albert

**[The] Blessed**
See Gerard

**Blessed Giles**
See Aegidius of Assisi

**[The] Blessed Virgin**
See Mary

**Blessitt, Ike**
See Blessitt, Isaiah

**Blessitt, Isaiah** 1949- [SMG]
*American baseball player*
* Blessitt, Ike

**Blessius, Henricus**
See Bles, Henri Met de

**Blethen, Clarence Waldo** 1893-
[BE]
*American baseball player*
* Blethen, Climax

**Blethen, Climax**
See Blethen, Clarence Waldo

**Blevins, Rubye** 1914-
[CME, FCW, PMJ]
*American country-western performer*
* Montana, Patsy
* [The] Yodeling Cowgirl

**Blewitt, Octavius** 19th c. [PA]
*Author*
* Jonathan, [Brother]
* Peregrine, [Brother]

**Blick, Elsa** 1896?-1970
[EWL, WOA]
*French author*
* Daniel, Laurent
* Triolet, Elsa

**Blieden, Ivan Lawrence** 1925-1975
[BEW, TR]
*American actor, director, producer*
* Blyden, Larry

**Bliedung, James Alexander** 1909-
[BEW, ITA, SW]
*American actor*
* Beal, John

**Bligh, Norman**
See Neubauer, William Arthur

**Blinco, Beaver**
See Blinco, Russell Percival

**Blinco, Russell Percival** 1908-
[CEI]
*Canadian-born hockey player*
* Blinco, Beaver

**[The] Blind**
See Basil II [or Vasili]

**[The] Blind**
See Didymus

**[The] Blind**
See John [or Johann]

**[The] Blind**
See Louis III [or Ludwig]

**[The] Blind**
See Magnus IV

**Blind Arthur**
See Phelps, Arthur

**Blind Arvella Gray**
See Gray, Arvella

**[The] Blind Bard**
See Homer

**[The] Blind Beak**
See Fielding, [Sir] John

**Blind Ben Covington**
See Covington, Ben

**Blind Blake**
See Higgs, Blake

**Blind Blake**
See Phelps, Arthur

**Blind Blues Darby**
See Darby, Theodore [Teddy]

**[The] Blind Bomber**
See Glamack, George

**Blind Boy Fuller**
See Allen, Fulton

**Blind Boy Fuller's Buddy**
See Council, Floyd

**Blind Boy Johnson**
See Dupree, William Thomas

**Blind Boy Williams**
See McGhee, Walter Brown

**Blind Curley Weaver**
See Weaver, Curley James

**Blind Doogie**
See McTell, Willie Samuel

**Blind Freddie Small**
See Small, Freddie

**Blind Gary Davis**
See Davis, Gary

**Blind George Martin**
See Phelps, Arthur

**Blind Gilbert**
See Meistier, Gilbert

**Blind Harry**
See Henry the Mistrel

**Blind James Campbell**
See Campbell, James

**Blind Jimmy Brewer**
See Brewer, James [Jimmy]

**Blind John Davis**
See Davis, John Henry

**Blind Lemon Jefferson**
See Jefferson, Lemon

**Blind Lemon's Buddy**
See Holmes, Joe

**[The] Blind Man of Cambassi**
See Gonelli, Giovanni

**Blind, Mathilde** [PA]
*Author*
* Lake, Claude

**[The] Blind Old Man of Scio's Rocky
Isle**
See Homer

**[The] Blind Preacher**
See Milburn, William Henry

**[The] Blind Preacher**
See Waddell, James

**[The] Blind Preacher**
See Woodbridge, Timothy

**[The] Blind Prebendary of
Westminster**
See Lucas, Richard

**Blind Sammy**
See McTell, Willie Samuel

**[The] Blind Scholar**
See Fisher, Ambrose

**[The] Blind Sculptor**
See Gonelli, Giovanni

**Blind Simmie Dooley**
See Dooley, Simmie

**[The] Blind Singer**
See Shaw, Oliver

**Blind Snooks Eaglin**
See Eaglin, Fird

**Blind Squire Turner**
See Darby, Theodore [Teddy]

**[The] Blind Tiresias of Modern Times**
See Milton, John

**Blind Tom Bethune**
See Bethune, Thomas Greene

**Blind Traveler**
See Cranborne, Janus Emilius W.
E.

**[The] Blind Traveller**
See Holman, James

**Blind Willie Johnson**
See Johnson, Willie

**Blind Willie McTell**
See McTell, Willie Samuel

**Blind Willie Walker**
See Walker, Willie

**Blinder, Oda**
See Corsen, Yolanda

**Blinders, Belinda**
See Coke, Desmond

**Blinking Sam**
See Johnson, Samuel

**Blinky**
See Williams, Sandra

**Blinn, Genevieve**
See Namary, Genevieve

**Blinn, Mrs. Henry G.** 19th c. [PA]
*Author*
* Yewrownckie, Aunt

**Bliokh, Ivan** 1836-1901 [JL]
*Polish-born author and social critic*
* Bloch, Ivan

**Blish, James [Benjamin]** 1921-1975
[ESF, WD, WGT]
*American author, poet, playwright*
* Atheling, William, Jr.

**Blish, James [Benjamin]** (Continued)
* Laverty, Donald [joint pseudonym with Damon F(rancis) Knight]
* Lyons, Marcus
* MacDougal, John [joint pseudonym with Robert Augustine Ward Lowndes]
* Merlyn, Arthur
* Torley, Luke

**Blish, Virginia**
See Kidd, Mildred Virginia

**Bliss, Adam** [joint pseudonym with Robert Ferdinand Burkhardt]
See Burkhardt, Eve

**Bliss, Adam** [joint pseudonym with Eve Burkhardt]
See Burkhardt, Robert Ferdinand

**Bliss, Carlyse**
See Brechin, Carlyse Bliss

**Bliss, Helena**
See Lipp, Helen Louise

**Bliss, Lena Edith** 20th c.    [NAA]
*American educator and author*
* Le Noire, Felicia

**Bliss, Louise**
See Hedges, Bonny

**Bliss, Pauline** 1885-1962    [THR]
*American actress*
* Chase, Pauline

**Bliss, Reginald**
See Wells, Herbert George

**Blisterfeet**
See Hareen, Malcolm

**Blitzen Joe Benz**
See Benz, Joseph Louis

**Blitzer, Harry** 1892-1958    [BEW]
*American-born comedian*
* Green, Harry

**Blixen, Karen [Christentze Dinesen]** 1885-1962    [CA, EWL, WGT]
*Danish author*
* Andrezel, Pierre
* Blixen, Tania
* Blixen-Finecke, Karen
* Dinesen, Isak
* Osceola
* Tania B.
* Titania

**Blixen, Tania**
See Blixen, Karen [Christentze Dinesen]

**Blixen-Finecke, Karen**
See Blixen, Karen [Christentze Dinesen]

**Bloch, Darius P.** 1882-    [JL]
*French army officer*
* Dassault, Darius P.

**Bloch, David** ?-1916    [EE]
*French intelligence agent*
* Sprecher, Karl

**Bloch, Ivan**
See Bliokh, Ivan

**Bloch, Marcel** 1892-    [JL]
*French aircraft designer*
* Dassault, Marcel

**Bloch, Moritz** 1818-1891    [WBD]
*Hungarian theologian and grammarian*
* Ballagi, Mor

**Bloch, Robert [Albert]** 1917-    [EMD, ESF, WGT]
*American author*
* Fiske, Tarleton
* Folke, Will [house pseudonym]
* Hindin, Nathan
* Jarvis, E. K. [house pseudonym, Ziff-Davis]
* Kane, Wilson [house pseudonym, Ziff-Davis]
* Sheldon, John [house pseudonym]
* Young, Collier

**Blochowitz, James John** 1885-1937    [BE]
*American baseball player*
* Block, Bruno
* Block, James John

**Block, Bruno**
See Blochowitz, James John

**Block Buster Roberts**
See Roberts, Lenerte

**Block, Cy**
See Block, Seymour

**Block, Herbert Lawrence** 1909-    [B10, IPA, WA]
*American cartoonist*
* Herblock

**Block, James John**
See Blochowitz, James John

**Block, Maurice**
See Block, Moritz

**Block, Moritz** 1816-1901    [WBD]
*German-born French economist*
* Block, Maurice

**Block, Rudolph** 1870- ?    [ALY]
*American author and journalist*
* Lessing, Bruno

**Block, Sanford** 1928-    [BEW]
*American talent representative*
* Block, Steven

**Block, Seymour** 1922-    [EJS]
*American baseball player*
* Block, Cy

**Block, Steven**
See Block, Sanford

**Block, William Norris** 1870-1929    [BEW]
*American actor*
* Norris, William

**Blocklinger, Betty**
See Blocklinger, Peggy O'More

**Blocklinger, Peggy O'More** 1895-    [CA]
*American author*
* Blocklinger, Betty
* Bowman, Jeanne
* O'More, Peggy

**Blodgett, Levi**
See Parker, Theodore

**Bloede, Gertrude** 19th c.    [PA]
*Author*
* Sterne, Stuart

**Bloemen, Pieter van** 1651-1720    [WBD]
*Flemish painter*
* Standaert

**Blofeld, John [Eaton Calthorpe]** 1913-    [AW, CA]
*British-born author*
* Chu Ch'an
* Chu Feng

**Blom, Eric Walter** 20th c.    [WW]
*Author*
* Farr, Sebastian

**Blom, Karl Arne** 1946-    [CA]
*Swedish author*
* Lagevi, Bo

**Blomberg, Werner von** 1878-1943    [WWW]
*German army officer*
* [The] Rubber Lion

**Blomstedt, Jussi** 1908-    [BBD]
*Finnish conductor*
* Jalas, Jussi

**[The] Blond**
See Gallo, Larry

**[The] Blond Beast**
See Baujan, Harry Clifford

**[The] Blond Blizzard**
See Fenimore, Robert

**[The] Blond Bomber**
See Cook, Gregory L.

**[The] Blond Panther**
See Platak, Joseph

**[The] Blond Terror**
See Triplett, Ernie

**[The] Blond Terror of Terre Haute**
See Taylor, Charles B.

**[The] Blonde Bomber**
See Grayson, Betty Evans

**[The] Blonde Bombshell**
See Thornburg, Elizabeth June

**[The] Blonde Bombshell of Rhythm**
See Cowan, Odessa

**[The] Blonde of Antwerp**
See Schragmueller, Elsbeth

**Blondeau, Georges** 1929-    [WEC]
*French cartoonist*
* Gebe

**Blondel, Maurice** 1861-1949    [CAT]
*French author*
* Testis

**Blondel, Roger** 1895-    [ESF]
*French author*
* Bruss, B. R.

**Blondell**
See Williams, W. F.

**Blondin, Charles**
See Gravelet, Jean Francois

**Blood, Ernest A.** 1872-1955
*American basketball coach*
* [The] Prof

**Blood, Johnny**
See McNally, John V.

**Blood, Marje** 20th c.    [CA, WD]
*American author*
* McKenzie, Paige

**Blood, Matthew**
See Dresser, Davis

**Blood, Thomas** 1628?-1680    [HN]
*Irish adventurer*
* [The] Irish Judas

**Bloodgood, Clara**
See Stephens, Clara

**Bloodgood, Harry**
See Moran, Carlo

**Bloodstone, John**
See Byrne, Stuart J[ames]

**[The] Bloody**
See Otto II [or Otho]

**Bloody Angelo Genna**
See Genna, Angelo

**[The] Bloody Butcher**
See William Augustus

**Bloody Jake Evans**
See Evans, Jacob

**Bloody Mary**
See Mary I

**[The] Bloody One-Handed**
See Loison, Louis Henri

**Bloody Queen Bess**
See Elizabeth I

**Bloom, Bloomer**
See Bloom, Michael Carroll

**Bloom, David Victor** 1900-    [BMH]
*British comedian*
* Wise, Vic

**Bloom, Herman Irving** 1908-    [CA]
*American author and columnist*
* Bellamy, Harmon
* Hart, Barry

**Bloom, Jack Don** 1920-    [AW]
*British author*
* Donne, Jack

**Bloom, Meyer** 1915-    [BB, EJS]
*American basketball player*
* Bloom, Mike

**Bloom, Michael Carroll** 1952-    [SMG]
*Canadian-born hockey player*
* Bloom, Bloomer

**Bloom, Mickey**
See Bloom, Milton

**Bloom, Mike**
See Bloom, Meyer

**Bloom, Milton** 1906-    [ASC, DAM, WWJ]
*American jazz musician and composer*
* Bloom, Mickey

**Bloom, Mrs. Lewis**    [FFF]
*Entertainer*
* Bell, Kitty

**Bloom, Murray** 1889-    [ASC]
*American composer, writer, publisher*
* Murray, Donald

**Bloom, Phil** 1894-    [BX, EJS]
*British-born boxer*
* [The] Ring Gorilla

**Bloom, Seymour L.** 1911-    [ASC]
*American writer*
* Bloom, Si

**Bloom, Si**
See Bloom, Seymour L.

**Bloom, Ursula [Harvey]** 1896?-
[CA, SFL]
*British author and journalist*
* Burns, Sheila
* Essex, Mary
* Harvey, Rachel
* Mann, Deborah
* Prole, Lozania [joint pseudonym
  with Charles Eade]
* Sloane, Sara

**Bloom, William** 1948-   [SFL]
*Author*
* W. W.

**Blooman, Percy A.** 1906-   [CAP]
*British editor*
* Pab

**Bloomberg, Marty**
*See* Bloomberg, Max Arthur

**Bloomberg, Max Arthur** 1938-
[CA]
*American librarian and author*
* Bloomberg, Marty

**Bloomer, Arnold Euston More**
1928-   [AW]
*British author*
* More, Euston

**Bloomer, Ben**
*See* Whittlesey, Oscar C.

**Bloomer, Jack**
*See* Lynch, John Gilbert Bohun

**Bloomer, Steve**
*See* Jones, J. G.

**Bloomfield, Anthony John Westgate**
1922-   [AW, WD]
*British author and playwright*
* Westgate, John

**Bloomfield, Bud**
*See* Bloomfield, Clyde Stalcup

**Bloomfield, Clyde Stalcup** 1937-
[BE]
*American baseball player*
* Bloomfield, Bud

**Bloomfield, Gordon Leigh** 1933-
[SMG]
*American baseball coach*
* Bloomfield, Jack

**Bloomfield, Jack**
*See* Bloomfield, Gordon Leigh

**Bloomfield, Robert**
*See* Edgley, Leslie

**BLoomfield, Robert**
*See* Flagg, Elizabeth

**Bloomfield, Robert** 1766-1823
[HN]
*British poet*
* [The] Peasant Poet of Suffolk

**Bloor, Ella Reeve** 1862-1951
[WBD]
*American Communist leader and
author*
* Bloor, Mother

**Bloor, Mother**
*See* Bloor, Ella Reeve

**Blossom**
*See* Schuman, Karen

**Blossom, Bun**
*See* Blossom, Dudley S., III

**Blossom, Dudley S., III** 1942-
[SMG]
*American baseball executive*
* Blossom, Bun

**Blot, Thomas**
*See* Simpson, William

**Blotter, Samuel**
*See* Doe, Charles Henry

**Blouet, Paul** 1848-1903
[FFF, HN, WBD]
*French author*
* O'Rell, Max

**Blount, Anna**
*See* Gallichan, Walter M.

**Blount, Herman** 1915?-   [EJ7]
*American jazz musician*
* Blount, Sonny
* [Le] Sony'r Ra
* Sun Ra

**Blount, Jeb**
*See* Blount, John Eugene

**Blount, John Eugene** 20th c.   [SMG]
*American football player*
* Blount, Jeb

**Blount, John T.** 20th c.   [OBW]
*American baseball executive*
* Blount, Tenny

**Blount, Margaret**
*See* O'Francis, Mary

**Blount, Red**
*See* Blount, Winton

**Blount, Roy [Alton], Jr.** 1941-   [CA]
*American journalist*
* Sanders, Noah
* Ways, C. R.

**Blount, Sonny**
*See* Blount, Herman

**Blount, Tenny**
*See* Blount, John T.

**Blount, William [Fourth Baron
Mountjoy]** ?-1534   [SN]
*British statesman*
* [A] Maecenas

**Blount, Winton** 1921?-
*American industrialist*
* Blount, Red

**Blow, Marya Mannes** 1904-
[WGT, WOA]
*American author, poet, playwright*
* Mannes, Marya
* Sec

**Blow, Sidney**
*See* Jellings-Blow, Sidney

**Blowtorch Bob Komer**
*See* Komer, Robert

**Blue, Ben**
*See* Bernstein, Benjamin

**Blue, Bert**
*See* Blue, Bird Wayne

**Blue, Billy**
*See* Jervis, John

**Blue, Bird Wayne** 1876-1928   [BE]
*American baseball player*
* Blue, Bert

**Blue Bonnet**
*See* Fenwick, Thomas

**Blue, David**
*See* Cohen, David

**[The] Blue Devil**
*See* Tipton, Eric Gordon

**Blue Dick of Thanet**
*See* Culmer, Richard

**[The] Blue Duke**
*See* Wenceslas of Luxembourg

**Blue Eagle, Acee**
*See* McIntosh, Alec

**Blue Goose Moore**
*See* Moore, Eugene, Sr.

**Blue, Guy**
*See* Britton, Rollin J.

**Blue Jacket**
*See* Dahlgren, John Adolphus
Bernard

**Blue Jacket, Uncle**
*See* McEntee, Maurice Wurts

**Blue Jay**
*See* Williams, Charles J.

**Blue, Joe**
*See* Valery, Joseph, Jr.

**Blue, Little Joe**
*See* Valery, Joseph, Jr.

**Blue, Lu**
*See* Barker, Louisa

**Blue, Lu**
*See* Blue, Luzerne Atwell

**Blue Lu Barker**
*See* Barker, Louisa

**Blue, Luzerne Atwell** 1897-1958
[BE]
*American baseball player*
* Blue, Lu

**[The] Blue Prince**
*See* Salazar, Lazaro

**Blue Ridge Rangers**
*See* Fogerty, John

**Blue, Rose**
*See* Bluestone, Rose

**Blue Sky**
*See* Johnson, Warren

**Blue Sleeve Harper**
*See* Harper, William Homer [Bill]

**Blue Smitty Smith**
*See* Smith, Claude

**Blue Tooth**
*See* Harold

**Blue, Wallace**
*See* Kraenzel, Margaret [Powell]

**Blue Wolf**
*See* Scott, Robert

**Bluecher, Gebhard Leberecht von**
1742-1819   [DEP, RH, WBD]
*Prussian army officer*
* Forwards, Marshal
* Vorwarts, Marschall

**Bluege, Otto Adam** 1909-   [BE]
*American baseball player*
* Bluege, Squeaky

**Bluege, Squeaky**
*See* Bluege, Otto Adam

**Bluejacket, James [Jim]**
*See* Smith, James

**Bluenose**
*See* Smith, Norma E[thel]

**[The] Blues Boy**
*See* King, Riley B.

**Blues Boy**
*See* Odom, Andrew

**Blues Boy**
*See* Seward, Alexander T. [Alec]

**Blues Boy Bill**
*See* Broonzy, William Lee Conley

**[The] Blues Doctor**
*See* Clayton, Peter Joe

**Blues King**
*See* Seward, Alexander T. [Alec]

**[The] Blues Man**
*See* Kirkland, Eddie

**[The] Blues Man**
*See* Sykes, Roosevelt

**Blues, Mr.**
*See* Harris, Wynonie

**Blues, Mr.**
*See* Moore, Arnold Dwight

**[The] Blues Sensation from the West**
*See* Dunn, Sara

**[The] Blues Singer Supreme**
*See* Hegamin, Lucille

**Blueskin**
*See* Blake, Joseph

**Bluestein, Daniel Thomas** 1943-
[CA]
*American author and poet*
* Thomas, Daniel B.

**Bluestone, Rose** 1931-   [CA]
*American author*
* Blue, Rose

**Bluestring, Robin**
*See* Walpole, [Sir] Robert [First
Earl of Orford]

**Bluethenthal, Arthur** 1891-1918
[EJS]
*American football player*
* Bluethenthal, Bluey

**Bluethenthal, Bluey**
*See* Bluethenthal, Arthur

**Bluff, Bachelor**
*See* Bunce, Oliver Bell

**Bluff, Harry**
*See* Maury, Matthew Fontaine

**Bluff King Hal**
*See* Henry VIII

**Bluhm, Harvey Fred** 1894-1952
[BE]
*American baseball player*
* Bluhm, Red

**Bluhm, Red**
*See* Bluhm, Harvey Fred

**Blum, Mousy**
*See* Blum, Walter

**Blum, Tamas** 1927-   [OP]
*Hungarian conductor*
* Blum, Thomas

**Blum, Thomas**
See Blum, Tamas

**Blum, Walter** 1934- [EJS]
*American jockey*
* Blum, Mousy

**Blum, William David** 1923- [BEW]
*American producer*
* Darrid, William

**Blumberg, Barry**
See Blumberg, Baruch

**Blumberg, Baruch** 1926?-
*American medical researcher*
* Blumberg, Barry

**Blumberg, Gary** 1938- [CA]
*American author*
* Bradley, Michael

**Blumenfeld, Isadore** 1901?-1981
[BLB, MM]
*American underworld figure*
* Cann, Kid

**Blumenfeld, R. D.**
See Blumenfeld, Ralph David

**Blumenfeld, Ralph David**
1864-1948 [LC]
*American journalist*
* Blumenfeld, R. D.

**Blumenthal, Nathaniel** 1930-
[CA, JL]
*Canadian-born American
psychologist, author, philosopher*
* Branden, Nathaniel

**Blumgarten, Solomon** 1872-1927
[EWL]
*Lithuanian-born Yiddish poet*
* Yehoash

**Blundell, Harold** 1902- [CC, EMD]
*British author and banker*
* Bellairs, George

**Blundell, Peter**
See Butterworth, Frank Nestle

**Blunden, Joan** 1949-
*American television performer*
* Lunden, Joan

**Blunt, Don**
See Booth, Edwin

**Blunt, George W.** 1802- ? [PA]
*Author*
* G. W. B.

**Blunt, Paul** ?-1978 [FIR]
*American country-western performer*
* Parker, Paul

**Bluphocks, Lucien**
See Seldes, Gilbert [Vivian]

**Bluth, Bloop**
See Bluth, Raymond Albert

**Bluth, Raymond Albert** 1927-
[BBH]
*American bowler*
* Bluth, Bloop

**Bluthgen, Clara** 1856- ? [LAO]
*German author*
* Kilburger, C. Eyna

**Blutig, Eduard**
See Gorey, Edward [St. John]

**Bly, Nellie**
See Seaman, Elizabeth [Cochrane]

**Blyden, Larry**
See Blieden, Ivan Lawrence

**Blyleven, Bert**
See Blyleven, Rik Aalbert

**Blyleven, Rik Aalbert** 1951-
[BR, PB, SMG]
*Dutch-born baseball player*
* Blyleven, Bert

**Blyth, Edward** [FFF]
*Author*
* Zoophilus

**Blyth, Harry** 1852-1898
[EMD, MBF]
*British author*
* Meredith, Hal
* Policeman Paul

**Blyth, John**
See Hibbs, John Alfred Blyth

**Blythe, Arthur Murray** 1940- [EJ7]
*American jazz musician*
* Black Arthur

**Blythe, Betty**
See Slaughter, Elizabeth Blythe

**Blythe, Charlie**
See Blythe, Colin

**Blythe, Colin** 1879-1917 [OCS]
*British cricketer*
* Blythe, Charlie

**Blythe, Diana Blanche Barrymore**
1921-1960 [SC]
*American actress and author*
* Barrymore, Diana

**Blythe, Ethel** 1879-1959
[OCF, WEF]
*American actress*
* Barrymore, Ethel

**Blythe, Herbert** 1847-1905
[BEW, LC]
*British actor*
* Barrymore, Maurice

**Blythe, Herbert** 1877-1950
[F1, F2]
*Actor*
* Costello, Maurice

**Blythe, John** 1882-1942
[BDF, F2, WEF]
*American actor*
* Barrymore, John
* Great Profile

**Blythe, Joyce**
See Trent, Ann

**Blythe, Lionel** 1878-1954
[BDF, WEF]
*American actor*
* Barrymore, Lionel

**Blythe, Vernon Castle** 1885?-1918
[BEW, EMT, F1]
*British-born dancer and actor*
* Castle, Vernon

**Blythe, White, Jr.**
See Robinson, Solon

**Blyton, Enid [Mary]** 1897-1968
[CA, TCC]
*British author, poet, playwright*
* Pollock, Mary

**Bo Bo Junior**
See Bonds, Bobby Lee

**Bo-Peep**
See Drummond, William

**Boabdil**
See Abu Abdallah [or Abdullah]

**Boaistnan, Pierre** 1500-1566 [PA]
*Author*
* Launay

**Boak, Alfred Brydone** 1863-1920
[THR]
*Scottish-born actor*
* Brydone, Alfred

**[The] Boar**
See Richard III

**Boardman, Eunice**
See Meske, Eunice Boardman

**Boardman, Gwenn R.**
See Petersen, Gwenn Boardman

**Boardman, John** 20th c. [SFP]
*Author*
* Blake, Eric

**Boas, F. S.**
See Boas, Frederick Samuel

**Boas, Frederick Samuel** 1862-1957
[LC]
*Author*
* Boas, F. S.

**Boas, George** 1891- [NAA]
*American educator and author*
* Belane, George

**Boas, Guy [Herman Sidney]**
1896-1966 [CAP]
*British author*
* G. B.

**Boas, Marie**
See Hall, Marie Boas

**Boatfield, Jeffrey Montagu** 1924-
[AW]
*British author and journalist*
* Jeffries, Jeff

**Bobadilla, Pepita**
See Burton, Nelly

**Bobadilla y Lunar, Emilio**
1862-1921 [CW]
*Cuban poet, author, playwright*
* Candil, Fray
* Marmora, Dagoberto

**[The] Bobbin Boy**
See Banks, Nathaniel Prentiss

**Bobbin, Tim**
See Collier, John

**Bobbing John**
See Erskine, John

**Bobby Blue Bland**
See Bland, Robert Calvin [Bobby]

**Bobette**
See Simenon, Georges [Joseph
Christian]

**Bobillier, Marie** 1858-1918 [BBD]
*French musicologist*
* Brenet, Michel

**Bobin, Donald E. M.** 20th c. [MBF]
*British author*
* Halliday, Shirley
* Lawson, Warren J.

**Bobin, John William [Jack]** ?-1935
[MBF]
*British author*
* Ascott, Adelie
* Ascott, John
* Ironside, Matthew

**Bobin, John William [Jack]**
(Continued)
* Nelson, Gertrude
* Nelson, Steve
* Nelson, Victor
* Osborne, Mark

**Bobo, [Dr.] Rosalvo** 1873-1929
[CW]
*Haitian poet and author*
* Benoit, Francois Pierre Joseph

**Bobo, Willie**
See Correa, William

**Bobone, Giacinto** 1106?-1198
[WBD]
*Pope*
* Celestine III

**Bobri, V.**
See Bobritsky, Vladimir

**Bobritsky, Vladimir** 1898-
[IBY, ICB]
*Russian-born illustrator, editor,
musician*
* Bobri, V.

**Bobroff, Edith**
See Marks, Edith Bobroff

**Bobs**
See Roberts, Frederick Sleigh

**Bobs Bahadur**
See Roberts, Frederick Sleigh

**Bocadelot, Abbe**
See Michon, Pierre

**Bocage [or Boccage], Manuel Maria
Barbosa du** 1765-1805 [WBD]
*Portuguese poet*
* Sadino, Elmano

**Bocca, Al**
See Winter, Bevis

**Bocca, Tonio** 20th c. [FDG]
*Director*
* Anton, Amerigo

**Boccaccio, Giovanni** 1313-1375
[DEP, DNNS, SN]
*Italian author*
* [The] Bard of Prose
* [The] Father of Italian Novelists
* [The] Father of Italian Prose
* [The] Prince of Story-Tellers

**[The] Boccaccio of the Nineteenth
Century**
See Quivogne de Montifaud, Marie
Amelie

**[The] Boccaccio of the Provencal
Language**
See Martorell, John

**Boccage, Marie Anne** 1710-1802
[PA]
*Author*
* Lapage

**Boccasini, Niccolo** 1240-1304
[CAL]
*Pope*
* Benedict XI

**Bocciardo, Clement** 1620-1658
[PA]
*Author*
* Clemastone

**Bochenski, Innocentius M.**
See Bochenski, Joseph M.

**Bochenski, Joseph M.** 1902- [CA]
*Polish author and clergyman*
* Bochenski, Innocentius M.
* Miche, Giuseppe

**Bocher, Joan** ?-1550 [HN]
*British Anabaptist*
* Joan of Kent
* [The] Maid of Kent

**Bocher, Main Rousseau** 1890-
[B10, BEW, IPA]
*American costume designer*
* Mainbocher

**Bock, Fred** 1939- [CA]
*American composer and author*
* Richards, Jason

**Bock, Hieronymus** 1498-1554 [PA]
*Author*
* Tragus

**Bock, William Sauts** 20th c. [IBY]
*American illustrator*
* Netamuxwe

**Bockhorn, Arlen** 1933- [BB]
*American basketball player*
* Bockhorn, Bucky

**Bockhorn, Bucky**
See Bockhorn, Arlen

**Bocock, Willis H.** [FFF]
*American writer*
* Erceldoune

**Bod, Peter**
See Vesenyi, Paul E.

**Bodecker, N. M.**
See Bodecker, Niels Mogens

**Bodecker, Niels Mogens** 1922-
[TCC]
*Danish-born author and poet*
* Bodecker, N. M.

**Bodell, Mary**
See Pecsok, Mary Bodell

**Boden, Hilda**
See Bodenham, Hilda Morris

**Bodenger, Bodie**
See Bodenger, Morris

**Bodenger, Morris** 1909- [EJS]
*American football player*
* Bodenger, Bodie

**Bodenham, Hilda Morris** 1901-
[CA, SAT]
*British author*
* Boden, Hilda
* Welch, Pauline

**Bodenheim, Maxwell**
See Bodenheimer, Maxwell

**Bodenheimer, Maxwell** 1893-1954
[BEW]
*American poet, author, performer*
* Bodenheim, Maxwell

**Bodenstein, Andreas Rudolf**
1480?-1541 [WBD]
*German religious reformer*
* Karlstadt [Carlstadt or
Karolstadt]

**Bodenstein, Charlotte** 1891- [JL]
*Austrian-born opera singer*
* Schoene, Lotte

**Boderianus, Fabricus**
See De la Boderie, Gui Lefevre

**Bodfan**
See Anwyl, John Bodvan

**Bodger, Joan**
See Mercer, Joan Bodger

**Bodhidharma** 6th c. [WBD]
*Buddhist monk*
* Tamo

**Bodie, Frank Stephan**
See Pezzolo, Francesco Stefano

**Bodie, Ping**
See Pezzolo, Francesco Stefano

**Bodie, Sam** 1870-1939 [BMH]
*Scottish-born entertainer*
* Bodie, Walford
* [The] Great Healer
* [The] Merry Monarch
* [The] Modern Miracle Worker
* [The] Most Remarkable Man on
Earth
* [The] Talkies Only Rival

**Bodie, Walford**
See Bodie, Sam

**Bodine, Helen Koues** 20th c.
[NAA]
*American author and editor*
* Koues, Helen

**Bodington, Nancy [Hermione]**
1912?- [CA, CC, WD]
*British author*
* Smith, Shelley

**Bodkin, Matthias McDonnell**
1850-1933 [WW]
*Author*
* Crom a Boo

**Bodnar, August** 1925-
[CEI, FHE, HK]
*Canadian-born hockey player*
* Bodnar, Gus

**Bodnar, Gus**
See Bodnar, August

**Bodwell, Richard**
See Spring, Gerald M[ax]

**[The] Body**
See Frye, Marie

**Boe, Jacques** 1798-1864
[DNNF, RH, WBD]
*French poet*
* [The] Barber Poet
* [The] Burns of France
* Jasmin d'Agen
* Jasmin, Jacques
* [The] Last of the Troubadours
* [The] Poet of Languedoc

**Boeckel, Mary**
See Reed, Mrs. Samuel

**Boeckel, Norman D.** 1894-1924
[BE]
*American baseball player*
* Boeckel, Tony

**Boeckel, Tony**
See Boeckel, Norman D.

**Boeckmann, Dolores A.** 20th c.
[BBH]
*American track and field athlete and
coach*
* Beckman, Dee

**Boegehold, Betty [Doyle]** 1913-
[CA]
*American author*
* Doyle, Donovan

**Boehm, Herb**
See Varley, John

**Boehm, Karl [or Carl]**
See Boehm, Karlheinz

**Boehm, Karlheinz** 1928- [FC]
*German actor*
* Boehm, Karl [or Carl]

**Boehme, Jacob** 1575-1624 [SN]
*German mystic*
* Philosophus Teutonicus
* [The] Teutonic Theosopher

**Boehme, Lillian R.**
See Rodberg, Lillian

**[The] Boehme of England**
See Fox, George

**Boehnel, Molly** 1907?-1963 [BEW]
*Playwright and actress*
* Ricardel, Molly

**[Il] Boemo**
See Myslivecek [or Mysliweczek],
Josef

**Boerhaave, Hermann** 1668-1738
*Dutch physician and philosopher*
* [The] Voltaire of Science

**Boerne, Ludwig**
See Baruch, Loeb

**Boesen, Victor** 1908- [CA]
*American journalist*
* Hall, Jesse
* Harald, Eric

**Boethius, Anicius Manlius Severinus**
470?- 524
*Roman philosopher*
* [The] Last of the Romans

**Boetticher, Budd**
See Boetticher, Oscar, Jr.

**Boetticher, Hans** 1883-1934
[MGL]
*German poet*
* Ringelnatz, Joachim

**Boetticher, Oscar, Jr.** 1916?-
[BDF, FC, ITA]
*American director*
* Boetticher, Budd

**Boex, Joseph-Henri Honore**
1856-1940 [ESF, SFL, WGT]
*French author*
* Enacryos
* Rosny, J. H. [joint pseudonym
with Seraphin Justin Francois
Boex]
* Rosny aine, J. H.

**Boex, Seraphin Justin Francois**
1859-1948 [ESF, WGT]
*French author*
* Rosny, J. H. [joint pseudonym
with Joseph-Henri Honore Boex]
* Rosny jeune, J. H.

**Bofa, Gus**
See Blanchot, Gustave

**Bogaduck**
See Lindsay, Harold Arthur

**[The] Bogalusa Bomber**
See Spikes, Charley

**Bogan, Gulam** 20th c. [IBW]
*American Black Muslim leader*
* Mohammed, Elijah
* Rassoul, Mohammed

**Bogan, Lucille** 1897-1948 [BWW]
*American singer*
* Jackson, Bessie

**Bogar, Jeff**
See Thomas, Ronald Wills

**Bogard, Carole Christine**
See Geistweit, Carole Christine

**Bogarde, Dirk**
See Van Den Bogaerde, Derek
Niven

**Bogart, Big John**
See Bogart, John Renzie

**Bogart, Elizabeth** 1836- ?
[FFF, PA]
*American poet*
* Adelaide
* Estelle

**Bogart, Humphrey** 1899-1957
[BDF]
*American actor*
* Bogie

**Bogart, John Renzie** 1900- [BE]
*American baseball player*
* Bogart, Big John

**Bogart, William G.** 20th c. [SFP]
*Author*
* Robeson, Kenneth [house
pseudonym, Street & Smith]

**Bogart, William H.** 1810?-1888
[FFF, PA]
*Journalist*
* Sentinel

**Bogash, Lou**
See Bogassi, Luigi

**Bogassi, Luigi** 1901- [BX]
*Italian-born boxer*
* Bogash, Lou

**Bogat, Shatan**
See Kacew, Romain

**Bogdanov, Alexander**
See Malinovsky, Alexander

**Boger, Elizabeth Winifred** 1923-
[BEW, FC, ITA]
*American actress*
* Blair, Betsy

**Boggs, Corinne Claiborne** 1916-
*American politician*
* Boggs, Lindy

**Boggs, Dock**
See Boggs, Moran L.

**Boggs, Lefty**
See Boggs, Ray[mond Joseph]

**Boggs, Lindy**
See Boggs, Corinne Claiborne

**Boggs, Moran L.** 1898- [CME]
*American banjoist*
* Boggs, Dock

**Boggs, Ray[mond Joseph]** 1904-
[BE]
*American baseball player*
* Boggs, Lefty

**Boggs, Robert**
See Clark, H. A.

**Boggs, Winifred** 20th c. [WWL]
*British author*
* Burke, Edward

**Bogie**
See Bogart, Humphrey

**Bogle, Charles**
See Dukinfield, William Claude

**Bogoras, Waldemar**
See Bogoraz, Vladimir
Germanovich

**Bogoraz, Vladimir Germanovich**
1865-1936 [SFL]
*Author*
* Bogoras, Waldemar

**Bograd, Larry** 1953- [CA]
*American author*
* Barrol, Grady

**Bogue, Lucile Maxfield** 1911- [CA]
*American playwright, poet, educator*
* Bogue, Max
* Max, Lucy

**Bogue, Max**
See Bogue, Lucile Maxfield

**Bogue, Merwyn** [PMJ]
*Musician and comedian*
* Ish Kabibble

**Bogus Ben Covington**
See Covington, Ben

**Bogza, Nicolae** 1910- [IAW]
*Rumanian author*
* Tudoran, Radu

**Bohan, Francois-Phillippe**
1751-1804 [PA]
*Author*
* Loubat

**Bohannon, Bo**
See Bohannon, E. J.

**Bohannon, E. J.** 1896-1966 [SC]
*American actor and stunt performer*
* Bohannon, Bo

**Bohemian**
See Channing-Renton, Ernest
Matthews

**Bohemond I** 1056?-1111 [HN]
*Prince of Antioch*
* [The] Latin Ulysses

**Bohen, Leo J.** 1891-1942 [BE]
*American baseball player*
* Bohen, Pat

**Bohen, Pat**
See Bohen, Leo J.

**Bohlman, [Mary] Edna McCaull**
1897- [CAP]
*American author and educator*
* McCaull, M. E.

**Bohme, David M.** 1916- [ASC]
*Polish-born composer and musician*
* Romaine, David

**Bohne, Sammy**
See Cohen, Samuel Arthur

**Bohney, Lillian** 1901-
[F2, FC, FIR]
*American actress*
* [The] Dove
* Dove, Billie

**Bohr, Russell LeRoi** 1916- [CA]
*American artist and author*
* Riis

**Bohr, Theophilus**
See Thistle, Mel[ville William]

**Bohse, August** 1661-1751 [PA]
*Author*
* Talender

**Boido, Federico** 20th c. [WF]
*Italian actor*
* Boyd, Rick

**Boigne, Beuvit** 1741-1830 [PA]
*Author*
* Leborgne

**Boileau-Despreaux, Nicolas**
1636-1711 [DNNS, HN, SN]
*French critic and poet*
* Ariste
* [The] Flatterer of Louis XIV
* [The] Lawgiver of Parnassus
* [The] Legislator of Parnassus
* Our Champion for Homer
* [The] Solon of Parnassus
* [The] Zoilos of Quinault

**[The] Boilermaker**
See Jeffries, James Jackson

**Boiles, Charles Lafayette, Jr.**
1932- [CA]
*American author*
* Lafayette, Carlos

**Boisgilbert, Edmund**
See Donnelly, Ignatius [Loyola]

**Boispreaux**
See Dujardin, Benigne

**Boissier, Jeane B. Prudence** [PA]
*Author*
* Sierbois, R. Q.

**Boissonnault, Marie D.** 1875- ?
[NAA]
*Canadian journalist*
* D'Iberville, Berthe

**Boitel, Leonard** 1806-1855 [PA]
*Author*
* Leon

**[Le] Boiteux**
See De Gontaut, Armand

**Boito, Arrigo** 1842-1918
[FFF, WBD]
*Italian composer and librettist*
* Gorria, Tobio

**Bojangles**
See Robinson, Luther

**Bojaxhiu, Agnes Gonxha** 1910-
[B10, NAD]
*Yugoslav-born missionary*
* [The] Mother of the World
* [The] Saint of the Gutters
* Teresa, [Mother]

**Bojorski, Walter** 1904- [BMH]
*German contortionist and acrobat*
* Colberg, Walter

**Bojtler, Arcadij** 1895- [FIR]
*Russian-born actor and director*
* Boytler, Arcady

**Bok, Hannes Vajn** 1914-1964
[HFF]
*American author and artist*
* Dolbokov [joint pseudonym with
Boris Dolgov]

**Bok, Kooshti**
See Mair, George Brown

**Bokassa, Jean-Bedel** 1921?-
*Ruler of the Central African Empire*
* Bokassa I
* [The] Butcher of Bangui

**Bokassa I**
See Bokassa, Jean-Bedel

**Bokenham, Jane** 1886- [THR]
*British actress*
* Wood, Jane

**Boker, George Henry** 1823-1890
[HN]
*American poet, playwright, diplomat*
* [The] War Poet

**Bokum, Fanny Butcher** 1888- [CA]
*American author*
* Butcher, Fanny

**Boky, Colette**
See Giroux, Colette

**Bolam, Margaret** 1922- [THR]
*British dancer*
* Dale, Margaret

**Bolan, Marc**
See Feld, Marc

**Boland, Francois** 1929- [EJ7]
*Belgian jazz musician*
* Boland, Francy

**Boland, Francy**
See Boland, Francois

**Boland, Jesse Lee** 1914- [IBW]
*American cult leader*
* Master X

**Bolasni, Saul**
See Bolasny, Saul Harold

**Bolasny, Saul Harold** 1923- [BEW]
*American costume designer*
* Bolasni, Saul

**Bolay, Karl H.** 1914- [IAW]
*German-born author and critic*
* Da Bayola, Ugo
* Svensson, Sven

**[The] Bold**
See Albert III [or Albrecht]

**[The] Bold**
See Boleslav II

**[The] Bold**
See Charles

**[The] Bold**
See Charles II

**[The] Bold**
See Michael of Walachia

**[The] Bold**
See Philip [or Philippe]

**[The] Bold**
See Philip III [or Philippe]

**Bold Bean-Hiller**
See Durkee, John

**Bold Briareus**
See Handel, Georg Friedrich

**[The] Bold Eagle**
See Whittingham, Charlie

**[The] Bold Lady of Cheshire**
See Cholmondeley, Mary

**Bold, Ralph**
See Griffiths, Charles Tom Watson

**Bold, Roger**
See Harley, Robert [First Earl of
Oxford]

**Boldao y Castilla, Maria Marguerita**
**Guadalupe** 1918?- [BEW, FC, ITA]
*Mexican-born dancer and actress*
* Margo

**Bolden, Big Bill**
See Bolden, William Horace [Bill]

**Bolden, Buddy**
See Bolden, Charles

**Bolden, Charles** 1868-1931
[DAM, EJ, IBW]
*American jazz musician*
* Bolden, Buddy
* Bolden, King
* Buddy the King

**Bolden, Jody**
See Henderson, Robert Bolden
[Bobby]

**Bolden, King**
See Bolden, Charles

**Bolden, William Horace [Bill]**
1893-1966 [BE]
*American baseball player*
* Bolden, Big Bill

**Boldrewood, Rolf**
See Browne, Thomas Alexander

**Boles, Nick**
See Tofte, Arthur

**Boles-Watson, Elizabeth** ?-1931
[THR]
*British actress*
* Watson, Elizabeth

**Boles-Watson, Henrietta**
1873-1964 [THR]
*British actress*
* Watson, Henrietta

**Boles-Watson, Margaret**
1875?-1940 [THR]
*British actress*
* Watson, Margaret

**Boleslav I [or Boleslas]** 960-1025
[HN, SN, WBD]
*King of Poland*
* Chrobry [The Mighty]
* Coeur de Lion [Lion-Hearted]
* [The] Father of Poland
* [The] Intrepid

**Boleslav II** 1039?-1083 [WBD]
*King of Poland*
* [The] Bold

**Boleslav III** 1086-1138 [WBD]
*King of Poland*
* Wry-Mouthed

**Boleslav V** 1221-1279 [WBD]
*King of Poland*
* [The] Chaste

**Boleslavsky [or Boleslawski], Richard**
See Boleslavsky, Ryszard
Srzednicki

**Boleslavsky, Ryszard Srzednicki**
1889-1937 [BDF, FD, WEF]
*Polish-born director*
* Boleslavsky [or Boleslawski],
Richard

**Boleslawita**
See Kraszewski, Jozef Ignacy

**Boley, Joe**
See Bolinsky, John Peter

**Boley, John Peter**
See Bolinsky, John Peter

**Bolger, Bo**
See Bolger, Robert Erin

**Bolger, Dutch**
See Bolger, James Cyril

**Bolger, James Cyril** 1932- [BE]
*American baseball player*
* Bolger, Dutch

**Bolger, Philip C[unningham]** 1927-
[CA]
*American author and boat designer*
* Trim, Corporal

**Bolger, Robert Erin** 1937-1969
[SC]
*American actor and stunt performer*
* Bolger, Bo

**Bolinbroke, William**
See Home-Gall, William
Bolinbroke

**Bolinder, Jean Adolf** 1935- [IAW]
*Swedish author*
* Borghamn, Jesper
* Lagevi, Bo

**Bolingbroke**
See Amherst, Nicholas

**Bolingbroke**
See Henry IV

**Bolingbroke, George** 1866?-1947
[BEW]
*Animal impersonator*
* Ali, George

**Bolingbroke, Proud**
See St. John, Henry

**Bolingbroke, Viscount**
See St. John, Henry

**Bolinsky, John Peter** 1896-1962
[BE]
*American baseball player*
* Boley, Joe
* Boley, John Peter

**Bolio, Dolores**
See Bolio Cantarell De Peon,
Dolores

**Bolio Cantarell De Peon, Dolores**
1882- [NAA]
*Mexican author*
* Avellaneda, Luis
* Bolio, Dolores

**Bolitho, [Henry] Hector**
1897?-1974 [CA, LC, TC]
*New Zealand-born author*
* Ney, Patrick

**Bolitho, Ray D.**
See Blair, Dorothy Sara [Greene]

**Bolitho, William**
See Ryall, William Bolitho

**Bolivar, Simon** 1783-1830
[DHA, DNNS, SN]
*Venezuelan general and statesman*
* [The] Liberator
* [El] Libertador
* [El] Tio Porsupuesto
* [The] Washington of Colombia
* [The] Washington of South
America

**Boll, Buzz**
See Boll, Frank Thurman

**Boll, Ernest**
See Boll, Theophilus E[rnest]
M[artin]

**Boll, Frank Thurman** 1911-
[CEI, FHE, HK]
*Canadian-born hockey player*
* Boll, Buzz

**Boll, Theo**
See Boll, Theophilus E[rnest]
M[artin]

**Boll, Theophilus E[rnest] M[artin]**
1902- [CA]
*American educator and author*
* Boll, Ernest
* Boll, Theo

**Boll Weenie Bill**
See Moore, Willie C.

**Boll Weevil Bill**
See Moore, Willie C.

**Bollerman, Howard** 1907-1966
[BB]
*American basketball player*
* Superman

**Bolling, Claude** 20th c. [WF]
*Composer*
* Bolling, Klaus

**Bolling, Hal**
See Schwalberg, Carol[yn
Ernestine Stein]

**Bolling, Klaus**
See Bolling, Claude

**Bolo, Solomon**
See Whiton, James Nelson

**[Il] Bolognese**
See Grimaldi, Giovanni Francesco

**Bolognese, Elaine Raphael
[Chionchio]** 1933- [CA]
*American author and illustrator*
* Raphael, Elaine

**Bolster, Evelyn**
See Bolster, [Sister] M. Angela

**Bolster, [Sister] M. Angela** 1925-
[AW]
*Irish author*
* Bolster, Evelyn

**Bolt, Ben**
See Binns, Ottwell

**[The] Bolt Court Philosopher**
See Johnson, Samuel

**Bolt, Lee**
See Faust, Frederick [Schiller]

**Bolt, Terrible Tommy**
See Bolt, Tommy

**Bolt, Thunder**
See Bolt, Tommy

**Bolt, Tommy** 1918- [BWG, EG]
*American golfer*
* Bolt, Terrible Tommy
* Bolt, Thunder

**Bolton, Cecil Glenford** 1904- [BE]
*American baseball player*
* Bolton, Lefty

**Bolton, Evelyn**
See Bunting, Anne Evelyn

**Bolton, F. T.** 20th c. [MBF]
*British author*
* Ash, Derek
* Hammond, Wally

**Bolton, Isabel**
See Miller, Mary Britton

**Bolton, Lefty**
See Bolton, Cecil Glenford

**Bolton, Maisie Sharman** 1915-
[CA]
*Scottish-born author*
* Davis, Stratford
* Sharman, Maisie
* Sharman, Miriam

**Bolton, St. George Guy Reginald**
1886- [BEW]
*British author and playwright*
* Saisson, Pierre [joint pseudonym
with George Middleton]

**Bolyer, Maurice** 1921?-1978 [FIR]
*Canadian musician*
* King of the Banjo

**Bomar, Buddy**
See Bomar, Herbert Booth

**Bomar, Herbert Booth** 1916-
[BBH]
*American bowler*
* Bomar, Buddy

**Bomba**
See Ferdinand II

**Bomba II**
See Francis II

**Bombalino**
See Francis II

**Bombardier Billy Wells**
See Wells, Billy

**Bombardinio**
See Maginn, William

**[The] Bomber**
See Balmer, Earl Franklin

**Bomberger, Alva**
*Singer*
* Bomberger, Bomby

**Bomberger, Bomby**
See Bomberger, Alva

**Bombet, Louis Alexander Cesar**
See Beyle, Marie Henri

**Bombita [Little Bomb]**
See Torres y Reina, Emilio

**Bombita [Little Bomb]**
See Torres y Reina, Ricardo

**Bombita III [Little Bomb the Third]**
See Torres y Reina, Manuel

**Bomeair, D. H.**
See Mitchell, Robert

**Bomeisler, Bo**
See Bomeisler, Douglass M.

**Bomeisler, Douglass M.** 1892-1953
[FB]
*American football player*
* Bomeisler, Bo

**Bomkauf**
See Kaufman, Bob

**[The] Bomp**
See Bompensiero, Frank

**Bompensiero, Frank** 1906-1977
*American underworld figure*
* [The] Bomp

**[Le] Bon**
See John II [or Jean]

**[Le] Bon**
See John III [or Jean]

**[Le] Bon**
See Philip [or Philippe]

**Bon Bon**
See Tunnell, George N.

**[Le] Bon Roi Rene**
See Rene I

**Bon Ton Garlow**
See Garlow, Clarence Joseph

**Bona, Mercy**
See Ziegler, Alan

**Bonal y Casado, Francisco**
1871-1955 [GS]
*Spanish bullfighter*
* Bonarillo [The Little Good One]

**Bonaldi, Bert** 20th c.
*American entertainer*
* Holiday, Bert

**Bonanno, Bill**
See Bonanno, Salvatore

**Bonanno, Joseph, Jr.** 20th c.
*American underworld figure*
* Bonanno, Little Joe

**Bonanno, Joseph, Sr.** 1905-
*American underworld figure*
* Bananas, Joe

**Bonanno, Little Joe**
See Bonanno, Joseph, Jr.

**Bonanno, Salvatore** 1932- [PHM]
*American underworld figure*
* Bonanno, Bill

**Bonano, Joseph G.** 1900?-1972
[DAM, EJ, WWJ]
*American jazz musician*
* Bonano, Sharkey

**Bonano, Sharkey**
See Bonano, Joseph G.

**Bonaparte, Carlotta** 1780-1825
[WBD]
*Duchess of Guastalla*
* Bonaparte, Maria Paulina

**Bonaparte, Carolina**
See Bonaparte, Maria Annunciata

**Bonaparte, Charles Louis Napoleon**
1808-1873 [DEP, HN, SN]
*Emperor of France*
* [The] Arch Monarch of the
World
* Arenenberg, Comte d'
* Badinguet
* Boustrapa
* Carbonaro
* Conscience Tranquelle
* Good Friend
* Grosbec
* [L']Homme de Decembre
* Louis Napoleon
* [The] Man of December
* [The] Man of Sedan
* [The] Man of Silence
* [The] Man of the Third Republic
* Napoleon le Petit
* Napoleon the Little
* Napoleon III
* Nero
* [The] Prisoner of Ham
* Rantipole
* [The] Saviour of Society
* Soulouque
* Thumb, Tom
* Verhuel

**Bonaparte, Francois Charles Joseph**
**[Duc de Reichstadt]** 1811-1832
[DNNS, HHF, WBD]
*Son of Napoleon I of France*
* [L']Aiglon [The Eaglet]
* [The] King of Rome
* Napoleon I

**Bonaparte, Maria Annunciata**
1782-1839 [WBD]
*Queen of Naples*
* Bonaparte, Carolina

**Bonaparte, Maria Paulina**
See Bonaparte, Carlotta

**Bonaparte, Napoleon** 1769-1821
[DNNS, HN, SN]
*Emperor of France*
* [The] Armed Soldier of
  Democracy
* [L']Autre
* Boney
* Caporal la Violette
* [The] Colossus of the Nineteenth
  Century
* Corporal Violet
* [The] Corsican
* [The] Corsican General
* [The] Corsican Ogre
* [The] Corsican Sesostris
* [The] Emperor of Elba
* [L']Enfant de Miracle
* Father Violet
* [The] Gallic Caesar
* [Le] General Entrepreneur
* [The] General Undertaker
* [Le] Grand
* [The] Great
* [The] Heir of the Republic
* [The] Hero of Austerlitz
* Jean d'Epee [John with the
  Sword]
* Jonathan Wild the Second
* Jupiter Scapin
* Kaiser Klaes
* [The] King of Fire
* [The] Little Corporal
* [The] Man of Destiny
* [The] Modern Charlemagne
* [The] Modern Nimrod
* [The] Modern Sesostris
* Nap
* Napoleon I
* [The] Nightmare of Europe
* [The] Other One
* Papa la Violette
* [Le] Petit Caporal
* [The] Plebeian Child of the
  Revolution
* [The] Scourge of Europe
* [The] Victor of a Hundred Battles

**Bonaparte, Napoleon Eugene Louis**
**Jean Joseph** 1856-1879
[RH, WBD]
*Son of Napoleon III of France*
* Lulu
* [The] Prince Imperial

**Bonaparte, Napoleon Joseph Charles**
**Paul** 1822-1891
[DEP, DHA, DNNS]
*French army officer*
* Napoleon, Prince
* Plon-Plon

**Bonarillo [The Little Good One]**
See Bonal y Casado, Francisco

**Bonaventura**
See Di Fidanza, Giovanni

**Bonavino, Cristoforo** 1821-1895
[WBD]
*Italian philosopher*
* Franchi, Ausonio

**Bonavino, Francesco** 1634-1709
[RH]
*Italian philosopher*
* Franchi, Antonio

**Bond**
See Price, Charles

**Bond, Alphabetical**
See Bond, William Joseph J. C.

**Bond, Bert**
See Rowley, Herbert

**Bond, Christopher** 1939?-
*American politician*
* Bond, Kit

**Bond, Cyrus Whitfield** 1915-
[CME, CWG, DAM]
*American country-western performer
and songwriter*
* Bond, Johnny

**Bond, Evelyn**
See Hershman, Morris

**Bond, F.** 20th c. [MBF]
*British author*
* Blakesley, Stephen

**Bond, Florence Demarest [Foos]** 20th
c. [WW]
*Author*
* Demarest, Ann

**Bond, Gladys Baker** 1912-
[CA, SAT]
*American author*
* Mendel, Jo [house pseudonym,
  Albert Whitman & Co.]
* Walker, Holly Beth

**Bond, J. Harvey**
See Winterbotham, Russell Robert

**Bond, Jack**
See Welch, Alfred

**Bond, Johnny**
See Bond, Cyrus Whitfield

**Bond, Kit**
See Bond, Christopher

**Bond, Mary Fanning Wickham**
1898- [CA]
*American author*
* Bond, Mrs. James
* Lewis, Mary F. W.
* Porcher, Mary F. Wickham
* Wickham, Mary Fanning

**Bond, Mrs. James**
See Bond, Mary Fanning Wickham

**Bond, Nelson S[lade]** 1908-
[ESF, WGT]
*American author*
* Danzell, George
* Mavity, Hubert

**Bond, Ray**
See Smith, Richard Rein

**Bond, Sheila**
See Berman, Sheila Phylis

**Bond, Stephen** 20th c. [WGT]
*Author*
* Lloyd, Stephen

**Bond, Walter** 1896- [BEW, FC]
*British actor*
* Fitzgerald, Walter

**Bond, William Joseph J. C.**
1833-1926 [DBA]
*British painter*
* Bond, Alphabetical

**Bondhill, Gertrude**
See Schafer, Gertrude

**Bondi, Beulah**
See Bondy, Beulah

**Bondino, Guerrino** 1930- [OP]
*Italian opera singer*
* Bondino, Ruggero

**Bondino, Ruggero**
See Bondino, Guerrino

**Bonds, Bobby Lee** 1946- [PB]
*American baseball player*
* Bo Bo Junior

**Bonds, Brother**
See Bonds, Son

**Bonds, Brownsville**
See Bonds, Son

**Bonds, Gary U. S.**
See Anderson, Gary

**Bonds, Son** 1909-1947 [BWW]
*American singer*
* Bonds, Brother
* Bonds, Brownsville

**Bonds, Ulysses Samuel**
See Anderson, Gary

**Bondu, David [Dave]** ?-1979 [IBW]
*American disc jockey, interviewer,
inventor*
* Swing, Mr.

**Bondu, Mayme** 20th c. [IBW]
*American disc jockey, interviewer,
inventor*
* Swing, Mrs.

**Bondy, Beulah** 1892- [BEW, FC]
*American actress*
* Bondi, Beulah

**Bone, J. F.**
See Bone, Jesse Franklin

**Bone, Jesse Franklin** 1916- [SF]
*American author and veterinary
surgeon*
* Bone, J. F.

**Bonefang, Benjamin** 1873-1952
[FDG]
*German director*
* Benno, Alex

**Bonehill, [Captain] Ralph**
See Stratemeyer, Edward L.

**Bonelli, Richard**
See Bunn, Richard

**Bonemelus**
See Von Bonewell, Hendrick

**Bones, Mr.**
See Morton, Henry Sterling

**Bones, Sherlock**
See Keane, John

**Bonesteele, Laura Justine**
1866?-1932 [BEW]
*American actress*
* Bonstelle, Jessie

**Bonet, Nicholas** ?-1360 [HN]
*Scholar*
* Perspicuus, Doctor
* Profitabilis, Doctor

**Bonett, Emery**
See Coulson, Felicity Winifred
Carter

**Bonett, John**
See Coulson, John H[ubert]
A[rthur]

**Boney**
See Bonaparte, Napoleon

**Boney, Mary Lily**
See Sheats, Mary Boney

**Bonfanti, Mlle.**
See Hoffman, Mrs.

**Bonfire, Mars**
See Edmonton, Dennis

**Bonfrere, Jacques** 1573-1643 [PA]
*Author*
* Bonfrerius

**Bonfrerius**
See Bonfrere, Jacques

**Bongartz, Heinz** 1916- [CA]
*German-born author*
* Thorwald, Juergen

**Bongiovanni, Anthony Thomas**
1911- [BE]
*American baseball player*
* Bongiovanni, Nino

**Bongiovanni, Nino**
See Bongiovanni, Anthony Thomas

**Bongo, Albert-Bernard** 20th c.
*Gabonese president*
* Bongo, Omar

**Bongo, Omar**
See Bongo, Albert-Bernard

**Bonham, Bonzo**
See Bonham, John

**Bonham, Ernest Edward**
1913-1949 [BE, PB]
*American baseball player*
* Bonham, Tiny

**Bonham, John** 1947-1980 [RO2]
*British musician*
* Bonham, Bonzo

**Bonham, Ron** 1942- [BB]
*American basketball player*
* [The] Muncie Mortar

**Bonham, Tiny**
See Bonham, Ernest Edward

**Bonheur, Rosalie** 1822- ? [PA]
*Author*
* Rosa

**[A] Bonhomme**
See Francis de Paule

**Bonhomme, Arthur** 1910- [CW]
*Haitian poet and diplomat*
* Fabry, Claude

**Bonhomme, Jacques**
See Caillet, Guillaume

**Boniface**
See Winfrid [or Winfrith]

**Boniface, Joseph Xavier**
1797?-1865 [DNNF, FFF, PA]
*French author and playwright*
* Saintine
* Xavier

**Boniface IX**
See Tomacelli, Pietro

**Boniface VIII**
See Gaetano [or Caetani], Benedetto

**Bonifacio, Jose**
See Andrada e Silva, Jose Bonifacio de

**Bonifacius**
See Bruno [or Brun] of Querfurt

**Bonifacius** ?- 432 [DEP]
*Roman governor of Africa*
* [The] Last of the Romans

**Bonifazio di Pitati** 1487-1553 [WBD]
*Italian painter*
* Bonifazio Veneziano
* Bonifazio Veronese

**Bonifazio Veneziano**
See Bonifazio di Pitati

**Bonifazio Veronese**
See Bonifazio di Pitati

**Bonime, Florence** 1907- [CA]
*American author*
* Cummings, Florence

**Bonn, Issy**
See Levin, Benjamin

**Bonn, Skeeter**
See Bougham, Junior Lewis

**Bonnamy, Francis**
See Walz, Audrey

**Bonnard, Isabel Stewart Way** 1904- [NAA]
*American writer*
* Way, Isabel Stewart

**[La] Bonne Reine**
See Claude

**Bonnekamp, Sonja Maria** 1930- [IAW]
*Dutch-born author, translator, journalist*
* Blassen, Sal

**Bonnell, Kenneth** 20th c. [SFP]
*Author*
* Leone, Scott

**Bonner, Big Burley**
See Bonner, William

**Bonner, Bloody**
See Bonner, Edmund

**Bonner, Edmund** 1500-1569 [HN]
*Bishop of London*
* Bonner, Bloody

**Bonner, Frank J.** 1869-1905 [BE]
*American baseball player*
* [The] Human Flea

**Bonner, Geraldine** 1870-1930 [WW]
*Author*
* Hard Pan

**Bonner, Juke Boy**
See Bonner, Weldon H. Philip

**Bonner, Leroy** 20th c. [RO2]
*American musician*
* Bonner, Sugar

**Bonner, Michael**
See Glasscock, Anne Bonner

**Bonner, Parker**
See Ballard, [Willis] Todhunter

**Bonner, Raleigh**
See Price, William Raleigh

**Bonner, Sherwood**
See McDowell, Kate Sherwood

**Bonner, Sugar**
See Bonner, Leroy

**Bonner, Weldon H. Philip** 1932-1978 [BWW, NBB]
*American singer*
* Barner, Juke Boy
* Bonner, Juke Boy
* [The] One Man Trio

**Bonner, William** 1924- [IBW]
*American educator*
* Bonner, Big Burley

**Bonnesen, Edith** 20th c. [EE]
*Danish intelligence agent*
* Lotte [code name used during World War II]

**Bonness, Lefty**
See Bonness, William John [Bill]

**Bonness, William John [Bill]** 1923- [BE]
*American baseball player*
* Bonness, Lefty

**Bonnet, Amedee** 1795- ? [PA]
*Author*
* Bonnet de Lyon

**Bonnet de Lyon**
See Bonnet, Amedee

**Bonnette, Jeanne** 1907- [CA]
*American poet*
* DeLamarter, Jeanne

**Bonnette, Victor**
See Roy, Ewell Paul

**Bonneval, Claude Alexandre de** 1675-1747 [WBD]
*French soldier*
* Ahmed [or Achmet] Pasha

**Bonney, Bill**
See Keevill, Henry J[ohn]

**Bonney, William**
See McCarty, Henry

**[The] Bonnie Chevalier**
See Stuart, Charles Edward Louis Philip Casimir

**Bonnie Lou**
See Carson, Sally

**Bonnie Prince Charlie**
See Rayner, Claude Earl

**Bonnie Prince Charlie**
See Stuart, Charles Edward Louis Philip Casimir

**Bonnier, Jo**
See Bonnier, Joakim

**Bonnier, Joakim** 1930- [EAR]
*Swedish auto racer*
* Bonnier, Jo

**Bonnivard, Francois de** 1496-1570 [DHA, DNNS, FFF]
*French historian*
* [The] Montaigne of Geneva
* [The] Prisoner of Chillon
* [The] Rabelais of Geneva

**Bonny Black Boy**
See Charles II

**[The] Bonny Earl**
See Stewart [or Stuart], James

**Bonnye, J. H.** [PA]
*Author*
* Carlin, Michel

**Bono, Adlai Wendell** 1894-1948 [BE]
*American baseball player*
* Bono, Gus

**Bono, Gus**
See Bono, Adlai Wendell

**Bono, Joe**
See Riccobono, Joseph S.

**Bono, Salvatore** 1935- [B10, DAM, ITA]
*American entertainer*
* Bono, Sonny

**Bono, Sonny**
See Bono, Salvatore

**Bonomo, Joe** 1902?-1978 [FIR]
*Actor and stunt performer*
* [The] Hercules of the Screen

**Bononiensis [Of Bononia]**
See Pomponius, Lucius

**Bonpland, Aime Jacques Alexandre**
See Goujaud, Aime Jacques Alexandre

**Bonsall, Crosby Barbara [Newell]** 1921- [CA, TBJ]
*American author and illustrator*
* Newell, Crosby

**Bonstelle, Jessie**
See Bonesteele, Laura Justine

**Bontemps, Arna**
See Bontemps, Arnaud Wendell

**Bontemps, Arnaud Wendell** 1902-1973 [WOA]
*American author, poet, playwright*
* Bontemps, Arna

**Bontemps, Roger**
See Collerye, Roger de

**Bontine, Robert** 1852-1936 [LC, TC]
*British author*
* Cunninghame Graham, R[obert] B[ontine]
* Don Roberto

**Bonura, Henry John** 1908- [BE, PB]
*American baseball player*
* Bonura, Zeke

**Bonura, Zeke**
See Bonura, Henry John

**Bonus, Arthur** 1864- ? [LAO]
*German author*
* Benthien, Fritz
* Brand, Franz
* Stolterfoth, Georg

**Bonvi**
See Bonvicini, Franco

**Bonvicini, Franco** 1941- [WECO]
*Italian cartoonist*
* Bonvi

**Bonvicino, Alessandro [or Alexander]** 1498-1554 [FFF, RH, SN]
*Italian painter*
* [Il] Moretto da Brescia
* [The] Tawny

**Bonzi, Peter Paul** 1580-1640 [HN]
*Italian painter*
* [Il] Gobbo [The Hunchback]

**Boo, Billy**
See Boozer, Emerson

**Booger Red Nobis**
See Nobis, Thomas H., Jr.

**Booger Red Privett**
See Privett, Sam

**Boogie Bill Webb**
See Webb, Bill

**Boogie Jake**
See Jacobs, Matthew

**Boogie Man**
See Hooker, John Lee

**Boogie 'n' Blues, Mr.**
See Perryman, William Lee [Willie]

**Boogie Woogie Red**
See Harrison, Vernon

**Boojum**
See Barrows, [Ruth] Marjorie

**[A] Book Collector**
See Ellis, E. T.

**[A] Book in Breeches**
See Macaulay, Thomas Babington [First Baron Macaulay]

**[The] Book Prodigy of His Age**
See Magliabecchi, Antonio [or Anthony]

**Bookchin, Murray** 1921- [B10, CA]
*American author*
* Herber, Lewis

**Booker, Buddy**
See Booker, Richard Lee

**Booker, James** 20th c. [OBW]
*American baseball player*
* Booker, Pete

**Booker, James Carroll** 1939- [BWW, NBB]
*American singer*
* Booker, Little

**Booker, John Lee**
See Hooker, John Lee

**Booker, Little**
See Booker, James Carroll

**Booker, Mease** 1937- [IBW]
*American fashion model*
* Golden Girl

**Booker, Pete**
See Booker, James

**Booker, Richard Lee** 1942- [BE]
*American baseball player*
* Booker, Buddy

**Booker T.**
See Jones, Booker T.

**Bookman, Charlotte**
See Zolotow, Charlotte [Shapiro]

**[The] Booktaster**
See Tullock, W. W.

**Bookworm**
See Donnelly, Thomas F.

**Bookworm**
See Ellis, E. T.

**Booles, Red**
See Booles, Seabron Jesse

**Booles, Seabron Jesse** 1880-1955
[BE]
*American baseball player*
* Booles, Red

**[The] Boomer**
See Geoffrion, Bernard

**[The] Boomer**
See Scott, George C., Jr.

**Boon, Francis**
See Bacon, Edward

**Boon, Louis-Paul** 1912- [CA]
*Belgian author and artist*
* Boontje

**Boon, Violet Mary** 20th c. [AW]
*British author and illustrator*
* Williams, Violet M.

**Boone, Alonzo D.** 1910- [MK]
*American baseball player*
* Boone, Buster

**Boone, Blind**
See Boone, John William

**Boone, Buddy**
See Boone, Carl George

**Boone, Buster**
See Boone, Alonzo D.

**Boone, Carl George** 1932-
[CEI, FHE, SMG]
*Canadian-born hockey player*
* Balloon, Buddy
* Boone, Buddy

**Boone, Charles** 20th c. [OBW]
*American baseball player*
* Boone, Lefty

**Boone, Charles Eugene** 1934-
[ASC, CA, DAM]
*American singer*
* Boone, Pat

**Boone, Daniel**
See Stirling, Peter Lee

**Boone, Dan'l**
See Davis, Curt[is Benton]

**Boone, Danny**
See Boone, James Albert

**Boone, Danny**
See Boone, Lute Joseph

**Boone, Ike**
See Boone, Raymond Otis

**Boone, James Albert** 1895-1968
[BE]
*American baseball player*
* Boone, Danny

**Boone, John William** 1864-1927
[IBW]
*American musician*
* Boone, Blind

**Boone, Lefty**
See Boone, Charles

**Boone, Lefty**
See Boone, Steve

**Boone, Luke**
See Boone, Lute Joseph

**Boone, Lute Joseph** 1890- [BE]
*American baseball player*
* Boone, Danny
* Boone, Luke

**Boone, Nick** 20th c. [RO1]
*American singer*
* Todd, Nick

**Boone, Pat**
See Boone, Charles Eugene

**Boone, Raymond Otis** 1923- [BE]
*American baseball player*
* Boone, Ike

**Boone, Steve** 20th c. [OBW]
*American baseball player*
* Boone, Lefty

**Boontje**
See Boon, Louis-Paul

**[The] Boop Boop A Doop Girl**
See Schroder, Helen

**Boorman, Arthur** 1896-1954
[THR]
*British actor*
* Riscoe, Arthur

**Boorstin, Daniel Joseph** 1914-
[DLE]
*American historian and author*
* Professor X

**Boosey, Philip Harold** 1865- ?
[THR]
*British actor*
* Cuningham, Philip

**[The] Boot**
See Geffin, Aaron

**Boot Jack**
See Stuart, John [Third Earl of Bute]

**Boote, Henry Ernest** 20th c.
[WWL]
*Australian author*
* Touchstone

**Boote, Robert Edward** 1920- [CA]
*British author*
* Arvill, Robert

**[The] Booted Head**
See Comines [or Commines], Philippe de

**Booth, Adrian**
See Gray, Lorna

**Booth, Agnes**
See Shoeffel, Mrs. John

**Booth, Albert J.**
See Burleigh, Cecil

**Booth, Albert James, Jr.**
1908-1959 [FB]
*American football player*
* Booth, Albie
* Booth, Little Albie
* Little Boy Blue
* [The] Mighty Atom
* [The] Mighty Mite
* Number 48

**Booth, Albie**
See Booth, Albert James, Jr.

**Booth, Alice**
See Hartwell, Alice Booth

**Booth, Amos Smith** 1852-1921
[BE]
*American baseball player*
* Booth, Darling Amos
* [The] Darling

**Booth, Andrew Donald** 1918-
[IAW]
*British-born physicist and author*
* Gamma

**Booth, Barton** 1681-1733 [DNNF]
*British actor*
* Silver Tongued

**Booth, Catherine Mumford**
1829-1890 [WBD]
*British religious leader*
* [The] Mother of the Salvation Army

**Booth, Darling Amos**
See Booth, Amos Smith

**Booth, Edwin** 20th c. [CA]
*American author*
* Blunt, Don
* Hazard, Jack

**Booth, Edwina**
See Woodruff, Josephine Constance

**Booth, General**
See Booth, William

**Booth, George Hoy** 1904-1961
[BF, BMH]
*British comedian*
* Formby, George, Jr.
* Hoy, George

**Booth, Henry** 1652-1694 [SN]
*First Earl of Warrington*
* Turn Coat Meres

**Booth, Henry Spencer** 20th c.
[SFL]
*Author*
* Craig, Colin

**Booth, Irwin**
See Hoch, Edward D.

**Booth, James**
See Geeves-Booth, James

**Booth, James** 1877-1921 [BMH]
*British comedian*
* Formby, George, Sr.
* [The] Lad from Wigan
* [The] Wigan Nightingale

**Booth, Little Albie**
See Booth, Albert James, Jr.

**Booth, Mary** 1831- ? [PA]
*Author*
* Carleton, Carrie

**Booth, Peter** 1952- [DC]
*British cricketer*
* Booth, Shaker

**Booth, Polly**
See Foster, Mrs. Frank

**Booth, Rachel**
See Powers, Mrs. William

**Booth, Rosemary Frances** 1928-
[CA, WD]
*Scottish author*
* Murray, Frances

**Booth, Shaker**
See Booth, Peter

**Booth, Shirley**
See Ford, Thelma Booth

**Booth, William** 1829-1912 [WBD]
*British religious leader*
* Booth, General

**Boothby, Frederick Lewis Maitland**
20th c. [LAO]
*British aeronautical writer*
* Per Aera
* Per Mare

**Boothe, [Ann] Clare** 1903- [TC]
*American author, playwright, diplomat*
* Brokaw, Clare Boothe

**Boots, Bonny**
See Devereux, Robert [Second Earl of Essex]

**Boots, Kid**
See Appling, Lucius Benjamin

**Booze, Beatrice**
See Nicholls, Muriel

**Booze, Courtland** 1944- [IBW]
*American auto racer*
* Booze, Crazy Corky

**Booze, Crazy Corky**
See Booze, Courtland

**Booze, Wee Bea**
See Nicholls, Muriel

**Boozer, Emerson** 1943- [FB]
*American football player*
* Boo, Billy

**Bops Junior**
See Jackson, Oliver, Jr.

**Bor** [code name used during World War II]
See Komorowski, Tadeusz

**Bor, Matei**
See Pavsic, Vladimir

**Bor, Max** 1903-1973 [EMT]
*Irish-born actor*
* Adrian, Max

**Borach, Fannie** 1891-1951
[BEW, EMT, FC]
*American actress and singer*
* Brice, Fanny

**Borah, Leo Arthur** 1889- [NAA]
*American journalist*
* Kelly, James

**Borch, Ted**
See Lund, A. Morten

**Borch-Johansen, Eigil** 20th c. [EE]
*Danish intelligence agent*
* [The] Duke [code name used during World War II]

**Borchard, Ruth [Berendsohn]** 1910-
[CA]
*German-born author*
* Medley, Anne

**Borchers, Cornell**
See Bruch, Cornelia

**Bordagaray, Frenchy**
See Bordagaray, Stanley George

**Bordagaray, Stanley George** 1912-
[BE, PB]
*American baseball player*
* Bordagaray, Frenchy

**Borde, Andrew** 1500-1549
[DNNF, DNNS, PA]
*British physician*
* Merry Andrew
* Perforatus
* [The] Vicar of Hell

**Bordeaux**
See Richard II

**Bordeaux, Ella**
See Ransome, Mrs. J. W.

**Borden, Lee [or Leigh]**
See Deal, Borden

**Borden, M.**
See Saxon, Gladys Relyea

**Borden, Mary** 1886-1968
[CAP, LC]
*American author*
* Maclagan, Bridget

**Borden, Olive**
See Trinkle, Sybil

**Borden, Orson T.**
See Baron, Oscar

**[The] Border Minstrel**
See Scott, [Sir] Walter

**Bordes, Francois** 1919-1977 [ESF]
*French author*
* Carsac, Francis

**Bordetzki, Antonio** 1892-1963
[BE]
*American baseball player*
* Brief, Anthony Vincent
* Brief, Bunny

**Bordewijk, Ferdinand** 1884- [EWL]
*Dutch author and poet*
* Ton Ven

**Bordino, Pietro** 20th c.
*Auto racer*
* [The] Mad Mullah

**Bordow, Joan [Wiener]** 1944- [CA]
*American author*
* Wiener, Joan

**Bore, Michael Kenneth** 1947- [DC]
*British cricketer*
* Bore, Noddy

**Bore, Noddy**
See Bore, Michael Kenneth

**Borel**
See Hugh II

**Borel, Helene**
See Hegeler, Sten

**Borel, Marguerite [Appell]** 1883-
[WGT]
*French author*
* Marbo, Camille

**Borel, Pierre Bord d'Hautoine** 1809-
? [PA]
*Author*
* De Petrus

**Borel-Clerc, Charles**
See Clerc, Charles

**Borge, Bernhard**
See Bjerke, Jarl Andre

**Borge, Victor**
See Rosenbaum, Borge

**Borges, Jorge Luis** 1899- [CA]
*Argentinian author*
* Bustos Domecq, H[onorio] [joint pseudonym with Adolfo Bioy-Casares]
* Suarez Lynch, B. [joint pseudonym with Adolfo Bioy-Casares]

**Borghamn, Jesper**
See Bolinder, Jean Adolf

**Borghese, Camillo** 1552-1621
[RH, WBD]
*Pope*
* Lord God the Pope
* Monarch of Christendom
* Paul V
* Supporter of the Papal Omnipotence
* Vice God

**Borghese, Scipione**
See Caffarelli

**Borgia, Alfonso** 1378-1458 [WBD]
*Pope*
* Calixtus III

**Borgia, Rodrigo [or Rodriguez]**
1431?-1503 [HN, WBD]
*Pope*
* Alexander VI
* [The] Worst Pope

**Borgmann, Benny**
See Borgmann, Bernhard

**Borgmann, Bernhard** 1899- [BB]
*American basketball player and coach*
* Borgmann, Benny

**Borgmann, Borgy**
See Borgmann, Glenn Dennis

**Borgmann, Dmitri A[lfred]** 1927-
[CA]
*German-born American author and word game inventor*
* Houdini, [Prof.] Merlin X.
* Quincunx, [Ms.] Ramona J.
* [El] Uqsor
* Xixx, [Ms.] Jezebel Q.

**Borgmann, Glenn Dennis** 1950-
[SMG]
*American baseball player*
* Borgmann, Borgy

**Borgnine, Ernest**
See Borgnino, Ermes

**Borgnino, Ermes** 1915?- [FC, SW]
*American actor*
* Borgnine, Ernest

**Borgognone, Ambrogio**
See Stefani [or di Stefano], Ambrogio

**Borgudd, Slim**
See Borgudd, Tommy

**Borgudd, Tommy** 1946- [IWM]
*Swedish musician and composer*
* Borgudd, Slim

**Bori, Lucrezia**
See Gonzalez de Riancho, Lucrecia Borja

**Borin, Barbara** 1950- [B10]
*American sportscaster*
* Borin, Biff

**Borin, Biff**
See Borin, Barbara

**Boring, Wayne** 1916- [WECO]
*American cartoonist*
* Harmon, Jack

**[El] Boris**
See Figueras, Fermin

**Borisoff, Leonard** 1942- [RO2]
*American singer*
* Barry, Len

**Borken, Samuel** 1903-1968 [SC]
*American actor*
* Bagley, Sam

**Borkh, Inge**
See Simon, Inge

**Borkowski, Bush**
See Borkowski, Robert Vilarian

**Borkowski, Robert Vilarian** 1926-
[BE]
*American baseball player*
* Borkowski, Bush

**Borland, Harold Glen [Hal]**
1900-1978 [CA, SAT]
*American author*
* West, Ward

**Borland, Kathryn Kilby** 1916- [CA]
*American author*
* Abbott, Alice [joint pseudonym with Helen Ross (Smith) Speicher]
* Land, Jane and Ross [joint pseudonym with Helen Ross (Smith) Speicher]

**Borland, Spike**
See Borland, Thomas Bruce [Tom]

**Borland, Thomas Bruce [Tom]**
1933- [BE]
*American baseball player*
* Borland, Spike

**Borland, William Armstrong** 1893-
[WW]
*Author*
* Dixon, Bingham

**Borlase, Skip**
See Bradley, J. J. G.

**Born, B. H.**
See Born, Bertram H.

**Born, Bertram H.** 1932- [BB]
*American basketball player*
* Born, B. H.

**Borne, Dorothy**
See Rice, Dorothy Mary

**Borneman, Ernest Wilhelm Julius**
1915- [CA, CC, WW]
*German-born author*
* McCabe, Cameron

**Borneman, H.**
See Gottshall, Franklin Henry

**Bornemann, Mary** [FFF]
*American author*
* Oraquill

**Bornet, Francois** 1915- [ASC]
*Dutch-born composer, director, singer*
* Bornet, Fred

**Bornet, Fred**
See Bornet, Francois

**Bornshine, Yvonne Vivienne** 1925-
[BEW]
*American singer, dancer, actress*
* Adair, Yvonne

**Bornstein, Flora-Jean** 1929- [OP]
*American opera singer*
* Warfield, Sandra

**Bornstein, Marguerita** 1950-
[WEC]
*Brazilian cartoonist and animator*
* Marguerita

**Borodin, George**
See Milkomane, George Alexis Milkomanovich

**Borodin, Mikhail Markovich**
See Grusenberg, Mikhail Markovich

**Borom, Edward Jones** 1915- [BE]
*American baseball player*
* Borom, Red

**Borom, Red**
See Borom, Edward Jones

**Boroniecki, Miroslaw**
See Stoberski, Zygmunt Julian

**Boros, Julius Nicholas** 1920-
[BBH, BWG, GF]
*American golfer*
* [The] Moose
* Old Man River

**Boroson, Warren** 1935- [CA]
*American writer and editor*
* Brown, Warner

**Borotra, Jean** 1898- [BBH]
*French tennis player*
* [The] Bounding Basque

**Borough, Reuben Warriner** 1883-
[NAA]
*American journalist*
* Borough, Rube

**Borough, Rube**
See Borough, Reuben Warriner

**Borovsky, Havel**
See Havlicek, Karel

**Borowitz, Abram Solman** 1910-
[EMT]
*American librettist and director*
* Burrows, Abe

**Borrego Ruiz, Carlos** 1862- ? [GS]
*Spanish bullfighter*
* Zocato [Left-Handed]

**Borrero Morano, Antonio** 1935-
[GS]
*Spanish bullfighter*
* Chamaco [The Kid]

**Borries, Buzz**
See Borries, Fred, Jr.

**Borries, Fred, Jr.** 1911-1969
[AS, BB, FB]
*American football player*
* Borries, Buzz

**Borrington, Anthony John [Tony]**
1948- [DC]
*British cricketer*
* Borrington, Borrers

**Borrington, Borrers**
See Borrington, Anthony John [Tony]

**Borrini, Angelo** 1919- [FIR]
*Italian actor*
* Ventura, Lino

**Borrow, George** 1803-1881 [PA]
*Author*
* Lavengro

**Borth, Willan G.**
See Bosworth, Willan George

**Bortniansky, Dmitri** 1752-1825
[SN]
*Russian composer*
* [The] Russian Palestrina

**Borto, Dewey**
*See* Swoyer, Dewey Stewart

**Borton, Babe**
*See* Borton, William Baker

**Borton, John C., Jr.** 1938-    [CA]
*American author and educator*
* Borton, Terry

**Borton, Terry**
*See* Borton, John C., Jr.

**Borton, William Baker** 1888-1954
[BE]
*American baseball player*
* Borton, Babe

**Borum, William [Willie]** 1911- ?
[BWW]
*American singer*
* Memphis Willie B
* Willie B

**Borys, Gontrau**
*See* Berthoud, Eugene

**Bos**
*See* Reynolds, George W. M.

**Bosabalian, Luisa Anais**
*See* Yeghiayan, Luisa Anais

**Boscawen, Edward** 1711-1761
[FFF, WBD]
*British naval officer*
* Old Dreadnought

**Bosch, Hieronymus**
*See* Van Aeken [or Van Aken],
Hieronymus

**Bosco**
*See* Moore, Harry R.

**Bosco, Gianfabio** 20th c.    [WF]
*Italian actor*
* Gian

**Bosco, Jack**
*See* Holliday, Joseph [Joe]

**Bosco, Joannes A.**
*See* Dubois, Jean

**Bose, Bozo**
*See* Bose, Sterling Belmont

**Bose, Nirmal Kumar** 1901-1972
[CAP]
*Indian anthropologist and author*
* Vasu, Nirmala-Kumara

**Bose, Sterling Belmont** 1906-1958
[WWJ]
*American jazz musician*
* Bose, Bozo

**Bosen, Jens Cruz** 1884-1942
[BDF, BEW, WEF]
*American director*
* Cruze, James

**Boshell, Ada**
*See* Grath, Mrs. J. W.

**Bosquet, Alain** 1919-    [CA]
*Russian-born American author*
* Bisque, Anatole

**[The] Boss**
*See* Friedhofer, Hugo Wilhelm

**[The] Boss**
*See* Masseria, Giuseppe

**[The] Boss**
*See* Roosevelt, Franklin Delano

**Boss, [Elmer] Harley** 1908-1964
[BE]
*American baseball player*
* Boss, Lefty

**Boss, Lefty**
*See* Boss, [Elmer] Harley

**Boss Man**
*See* Morganfield, McKinley

**[The] Boss of the Blues**
*See* Turner, Joseph [Vernon]

**Bossard, Frank Clifton** 1912-    [EE]
*British-born intelligence agent for
Russia*
* Hathaway, J.

**Bosse, Harriet Sofie** 1878- ?
[THR]
*Swedish actress*
* Bosse-Vingard, Harriet Sofie

**Bosse-Vingard, Harriet Sofie**
*See* Bosse, Harriet Sofie

**Bossman of the Blues**
*See* King, Riley B.

**Bossolus**
*See* Le Bossu, Jacques

**Bossu**
*See* Brierley, Robert Benjamin

**Bossuet, Jacques Benigne**
1627-1704    [DEP, HN, SN]
*Bishop of Meaux*
* [The] Eagle of Meaux
* [The] Father of the Church
* [The] Rhone of Christian
Eloquence

**Bossut, M. L'Abbe**
*See* Phillips, [Sir] Richard

**Bosticco, Isabel Lucy Mary**    [WD]
*British author*
* Bey, Isabelle

**Bostock, Bos**
*See* Bostock, Lyman Wesley, Jr.

**Bostock, Lyman Wesley, Jr.**
1950-1978    [SMG]
*American baseball player*
* Bostock, Bos

**[The] Boston Bard**
*See* Coffin, Robert

**Boston Blackie**
*See* Connolly, Thomas Francis
[Tom]

**[The] Boston Bomber**
*See* Liotta, Leonardo

**Boston, Charles K.**
*See* Gruber, Frank

**Boston, Cynthia Priscilla** 1948?-
*American political activist*
* Sunni-Ali, Fulani

**Boston, Mr.**
*See* Whitehill, Walter Muir

**[The] Boston Rebel**
*See* Lowell, John

**[The] Boston Siege Gun**
*See* Guilford, Jesse P.

**[The] Boston Strangler**
*See* DeSalvo, Albert

**[The] Boston Strong Boy**
*See* Sullivan, John L[awrence]

**[The] Boston Tar Baby**
*See* Langford, Sam

**[A] Bostonian**
*See* Lowell, John

**[A] Bostonian**
*See* Poe, Edgar Allan

**Boswell**
*See* Gordon, Giles [Alexander
Esme]

**Boswell, Clementine**
*See* Collett, Beryl Bishop

**Boswell, Connee**
*See* Boswell, Connie

**Boswell, Connie** 1912?-
[PMJ, WWJ]
*American singer*
* Boswell, Connee

**Boswell, Corsica**
*See* Boswell, James

**Boswell, James**
*See* Kent, Arthur [William
Charles]

**Boswell, James** 1740-1795
[FFF, SN, WBD]
*Scottish attorney and author*
* [The] Bear Leader
* Boswell, Corsica
* Bozzy
* Johnson's Spitting-Pot

**Boswell, John**
*See* King, John Boswell

**Bosworth, Allan R[ucker]** 1901-
[CA]
*American author*
* Boyd, Alamo

**Bosworth, John** 19th c.    [PA]
*Author*
* John of Manchester

**Bosworth, Willan George** 1904-
[WW]
*Author*
* Borth, Willan G.
* Leonid

**[The] Botanist of Ziegenhain**
*See* Dietrich, Adam

**Botelho, Francis Martin** 1893-
[NAA]
*Author, linguist, editor*
* Letob, O. H.

**Botelho de Magalhaes, Benjamin
Constant** 1833-1891    [WBD]
*Brazilian diplomat*
* Constant, Benjamin

**Boten, Giovanni** 1540-1617    [PA]
*Author*
* Benisius

**Both, L. W.**
*See* Schneider, Louis

**Botha, Peevee**
*See* Botha, Pieter

**Botha, Piet**
*See* Botha, Pieter

**Botha, Pieter** 1916?-
*South African prime minister*
* [The] Bald Eagle
* Botha, Peevee

**Botha, Pieter** (Continued)
* Botha, Piet
* [The] J. R. of the National Party
* Wapens, Piet [Pete Weapons]

**Botha, Pik**
*See* Botha, Roelof

**Botha, Roelof** 1932?-
*South African diplomat*
* Botha, Pik

**Botham, Both**
*See* Botham, Ian Terrance

**Botham, Ian Terrance** 1955-    [DC]
*British cricketer*
* Botham, Both
* Guy the Gorilla

**Bothner, Mrs. A.**    [FFF]
*Entertainer*
* Stanhope, Ada

**[El] Boto [The Dull One]**
*See* Escobar y Mellado, Antonio

**Boto, Eza**
*See* Biyidi, Alexandre

**Boto y Recatero, Antonio**
1876-1938    [GS]
*Spanish bullfighter*
* Regaterin [The Little Bargainer]

**Bott, Elizabeth**
*See* Spillius, Elizabeth Jane [Bott]

**Bott, Henry** 20th c.    [WGT]
*Author*
* Recour, Charles

**Botterill, H.**
*See* Thompson, Harold

**Botterill, Joyce** 1939-    [SW]
*British-born actress*
* Carne, Judy

**Botticelli, Sandro**
*See* Dei Filipepi, Alessandro di
Mariano

**Bottle, J. M.** 1876- ?    [THR]
*British entertainer*
* Datas
* [The] Memory Man

**Botto, Jan** 1876-1958    [EWL]
*Slovak poet*
* Krasko, Ivan
* Potokinova, Bohd. J.

**Bottom Line Ed**
*See* Griffiths, Edgar H.

**Bottome, Phyllis**
*See* Forbes-Dennis, Phyllis

**Bottomley, James Leroy**
1900-1959    [AS, DGS, PB]
*American baseball player*
* Bottomley, Sunny Jim

**Bottomley, Sunny Jim**
*See* Bottomley, James Leroy

**Bottrell, W.** ?-1881    [PA]
*Author*
* Old Celt

**Botts, Randolph**    [FFF]
*American author*
* Spikes

**Botyov, Khristo**
*See* Petkov, Khristo Botyov

**Botz, Butterball**
*See* Botz, Robert Allen [Bob]

**Botz, Robert Allen [Bob]** 1935-
[BE]
*American baseball player*
* Botz, Butterball

**Bouchard, Butch**
See Bouchard, Emile Joseph

**Bouchard, Daniel** 1950- [SMG]
*Canadian-born hockey player*
* Bouchard, Flake

**Bouchard, Emile Joseph** 1919?-
[CEI, FHE, HK]
*Canadian-born hockey player*
* Bouchard, Butch

**Bouchard, Emilie Marie**
1879-1939 [BEW]
*Algerian-born actress and singer*
* Polaire, Mademoiselle

**Bouchard, Flake**
See Bouchard, Daniel

**Bouchard, William**
See Wright, W. George

**Bouchard De Montmerency, William Geoffrey** 1872-1936 [MBF]
*Irish author*
* Morris, Patrick

**Bouche-Villeneuve, Christian Francois** 1921- [BDF, OCF]
*French director*
* Marker, Chris

**Boucher, Al[exander Francis]**
1881-1974 [BE]
*American baseball player*
* Boucher, Bo

**Boucher, Anthony**
See White, William A[nthony] P[arker]

**Boucher, Bo**
See Boucher, Al[exander Francis]

**Boucher, Buck**
See Boucher, George

**Boucher, Francois** 1703-1770 [SN]
*French painter*
* [The] Anacreon of Painting
* [The] French Raphael
* [The] Painter of the Graces
* [The] Raphael of the Parc-aux-Cerfs

**Boucher, Frank** 1901- [CEI, HK]
*Canadian-born hockey player*
* Boucher, Raffles

**Boucher, George** 1896-1960
[CEI, FHE, HK]
*Canadian-born hockey player and coach*
* Boucher, Buck

**Boucher, Raffles**
See Boucher, Frank

**Bouchier, Chili**
See Bouchier, Dorothy

**Bouchier, Dorothy** 1909?-
[F2, FC, TR]
*British actress*
* Bouchier, Chili

**Boucicault, Agnes Kelly Robertson**
1833-1916 [FFF]
*Scottish-born actress*
* Robertson, Agnes
* Thorndyke, Louise

**Boucicault, Darley George**
1859-1929 [BEW]
*American-born director, actor, producer*
* Boucicault, Dion George

**Boucicault [or Bourcicault], Dion**
See Boursiquot, Dionysius Lardner

**Boucicault, Dion George**
See Boucicault, Darley George

**Boucicault, Eva**
See Clayton, Mrs. John

**Bouciquaut**
See Le Meingre, Jean

**Boudat, Marie-Louise** 1909- [CAP]
*French author*
* Bellocq, Louise

**Boudin, Katherine [Kathy]** 1943?-
*American political activist*
* Adams, Lynn

**Boudin y Martin, Pierre** 1899-
[GS]
*French bullfighter*
* Pouly

**Boudreau, Lou[is]** 1917- [BAB]
*American baseball player and manager*
* [The] Boy Manager

**Boufflers, Chevalier de**
See Boufflers, Louis Francois de

**Boufflers, Louis Francois de**
1644-1711 [WBD]
*Marshal of France*
* Boufflers, Chevalier de

**Boufflers, Mme. de** [RH]
* [The] Nursing Mother of Philosophy

**Bougal, David** 1911-1973 [SC]
*American actor*
* Carney, Alan

**Bougham, Junior Lewis** 1923-
[CWG]
*American country-western performer*
* Bonn, Skeeter

**Bouhelier, Saint-Georges de**
See De Bouhelier-Lepelletier, Georges

**Bouillon, Comte de**
See La Marck, Robert III de

**Boukharouba, Mohammed Ben Brahim** 1925?-
*Algerian president*
* Boumedienne, Houari

**[Le] Boulanger de Nimes**
See Reboul, Jean

**Boulanger, Georges Ernest Jean Marie** 1837-1891
[DNNS, FFF, WBD]
*French general and politician*
* [The] Man on Horseback

**Boulanger, Lili**
See Boulanger, Marie-Juliette

**Boulanger, Louise** 1900- ? [WFA]
*French fashion designer*
* Louiseboulanger

**Boulanger, Marie-Juliette**
1893-1918 [BBD]
*French composer*
* Boulanger, Lili

**Boulanger, Robert F.** 1940- [ASC]
*American musician*
* Trevor, Van

**Boularan, Jacques** 1890-1972 [CA]
*French playwright*
* Deval, Jacques

**Boulger, Theodora Henrietta [Havers]**
1847-1923 [FFF]
*British author*
* Gift, Theo

**Boullioun, E. H.** 20th c.
*American aircraft salesman*
* Boullioun, Tex

**Boullioun, Tex**
See Boullioun, E. H.

**Boult, S. Kye**
See Cochrane, William E.

**Boulting, Sydney** 1912- [CA, TR]
*British actor, producer, director*
* Cotes, Peter
* Northcote

**Boulton, Anna** [PA]
*Author*
* Severne, Christian

**Boum, General**
See Thiers, Louis Adolphe

**Boumedienne, Houari**
See Boukharouba, Mohammed Ben Brahim

**[The] Bounding Basque**
See Borotra, Jean

**Bounds, S. J.** 20th c. [MBF]
*British author*
* Reid, Desmond [house pseudonym]
* Sidney, George

**Bounds, Sydney J[ames]** 1920-
[HFF, WGT]
*British author*
* Marshal, James
* Saunders, Wes

**Bountiful, Lady**
See Baillie, Joanna

**Bouquet, Johnny**
See Townsend, George Alfred

**Bourbon, Charles Ferdinand de**
1778-1820 [DNNS]
*Son of King Charles X of France*
* Berry, Duc de
* [L']Enfant du Miracle

**Bourbon, Henri Jules de** 1643-1709
[FFF, HN]
*French soldier*
* Monsieur le Duc

**Bourbon, Ken**
See Bauer, Erwin A.

**Bourbon, Louis Henri de**
1692-1740 [RH, WBD]
*French prime minister*
* Monsieur le Duc

**Bourbon, Louis I de [Prince de Conde]**
1530-1569 [DHA, DNNS, FF]
*French army officer*
* [The] Dumb Captain

**Bourbon, Louis II de [Prince de Conde]** 1621-1686 [HN, WBD]
*French army officer*
* [The] Great Conde
* Monsieur le Prince

**Bourbon, Marie Therese Charlotte de**
1778-1851 [DEP, FFF, SN]
*Daughter of King Louis XVI of France*
* Angouleme, Duchesse d'
* Filia Dolorosa [Grieving Daughter]
* [The] Modern Antigone
* [The] Orphan of the Temple

**Bourchier, Prudence** 1902- [THR]
*British actress*
* Vanbrugh, Prudence

**Bourdaloue, Louis** 1632-1704
[DNNS, FFF, RH]
*French clergyman*
* [The] Founder of Christian Eloquence
* [The] King of Preachers
* [Le] Roi des Predicateurs

**Bourde, Paul** [PA]
*Author*
* Dilion, Paul

**Bourdin, Maurice** ?-1125 [WBD]
*Antipope*
* Gregory VIII

**Bourdon, Madam**
See Froment, Mathilde

**Bourette, Charlotte** 1714-1784
[DNNF, DNNS, SN]
*French poet*
* [The] Coffee House Muse
* [La] Muse Limonadiere

**Bourgeau, Fan**
See Bourgeau, Joseph

**Bourgeau, Joseph** 1891-1970
[NOJ]
*American jazz musician*
* Bourgeau, Fan

**Bourgeois, Bill**
See Bourgeois, Wilfred S.

**Bourgeois, Jeanne Marie**
1875?-1956 [BEW, BMH]
*French theatrical performer*
* Mistinguett
* Tinquette, Miss

**Bourgeois, Wilfred S.** 1907- [NOJ]
*American jazz musician*
* Bourgeois, Bill

**Bourgogne, Duc de**
See Louis de France

**[Le] Bourguignon**
See Courtois, Jacques

**Bourguignon, Hubert Francois**
1699-1773 [WBD]
*French engraver*
* Gravelot, Hubert Francois

**Bourguignon, Louis Dominique**
1693-1721 [DNNS, RH, WBD]
*French robber*
* Cartouche
* [The] Dick Turpin of France
* [The] French Dick Turpin

**Bourillon, Pierre** 1876- ? [CD]
*French author and sociologist*
* Hamp, Pierre

**Bourn, Dale**
See Bourn, T. A.

**Bourn, T. A.** 1904- ? [EG]
*British golfer*
* Bourn, Dale

**Bourne, Bournie**
See Bourne, Robert Glen

**Bourne, George**
See Sturt, George

**Bourne, J. F.**
See Bourne, John Frye

**Bourne, John Frye** 1912- [ART]
*British painter*
* Bourne, J. F.

**Bourne, Lesley**
See Marshall, Evelyn

**Bourne, Margaret**
See Abbott, Jennie A.

**Bourne, Peter**
See Jeffries, Graham Montague

**Bourne, Robert Glen** 1954- [SMG]
*Canadian-born hockey player*
* Bourne, Bournie

**Bourne, St. Clair** 1943- [IBW]
*American publisher and community organizer*
* Bourne, Santo

**Bourne, Santo**
See Bourne, St. Clair

**Bourne, Sweet Vinny**
See Bourne, Vincent

**Bourne, Vincent** 1695-1747 [SN]
*British author*
* Bourne, Sweet Vinny

**Bourque, Napoleon** 1885?-1963
[AS]
*Canadian auto racer*
* Bourque, Pit

**Bourque, Pit**
See Bourque, Napoleon

**Bourquin, Paul Henry James** 1916-
[AW, WD]
*British author*
* Amberley, Richard

**Bourrette, G. V.** 20th c. [SMG]
*Baseball team physical coordinator*
* Bourrette, Pee Wee

**Bourrette, Pee Wee**
See Bourrette, G. V.

**Boursiquot, Dionysius Lardner**
1820?-1890 [WBD]
*Irish-born actor and playwright*
* Boucicault [or Bourcicault], Dion

**Bourvil**
See Raimbourg, Andre

**Boussac, Marcel** 1889?-
*French business executive*
* [The] Cotton King

**Boustrapa**
See Bonaparte, Charles Louis
Napoleon

**Boutelleau, Jacques** 1884-1968
[CD, EWL, TC]
*French author*
* Chardonne, Jacques

**Boutet, Anne Francoise Hippolyte**
1779-1847 [WBD]
*French actress*
* Mars, Mlle.

**Boutet, Jacques Marie** 1745-1812
[WBD]
*French actor and playwright*
* Monvel

**Bouthillier, Arthur Edward** 1887-
[BE]
*American baseball player*
* Butler, Art

**Bouton, Bulldog**
See Bouton, James Alan [Jim]

**Bouton, Harry** ?-1965 [BS]
*American magician*
* Blackstone, Harry
* [The] Great Blackstone

**Bouton, James Alan [Jim]** 1939-
[BE]
*American baseball player*
* Bouton, Bulldog

**Bouverie, Bartholomew**
See Gladstone, William Ewart

**Bouvier, Mme.** [PA]
*Author*
* Vignon, Claude

**Bouwens, Johannes** 20th c. [RO2]
*Dutch singer*
* Baker, George

**Bouwmeester, Theo**
See Frenkel, Theodorus

**Bovet, Marie Anne de**
See De Bois-Hebert, Guy

**Bow, Clara** 1905-1965 [NN]
*American actress*
* [The] It Girl

**Bowden, David Timon** 1891-1949
[BE]
*American baseball player*
* Bowden, Tim

**Bowden, Jean** 1925-
[AW, CA, IAW]
*British author*
* Annandale, Barbara
* Barry, Jocelyn
* Bland, Jennifer
* Curry, Avon
* Dell, Belinda

**Bowden, Jim**
See Spence, William John Duncan

**Bowden, Joan Chase** 1925- [CA]
*British-born American author*
* Godfrey, Jane
* Graham, Charlotte
* Kenny, Kathryn

**Bowden, Tim**
See Bowden, David Timon

**Bowditch, Edward, Jr.** 1881-1965
[AS, FB]
*American football player*
* Bowditch, Pete

**Bowditch, Frederick W.** 1906-1973
[FC, SC]
*American actor*
* Richmond, Kane

**Bowditch, Nathaniel Ingersoll**
1805-1861 [FFF, PA]
*American writer*
* Gleaner

**Bowditch, Pete**
See Bowditch, Edward, Jr.

**Bowdoin, William Goodrich** 1860-
? [NAA]
*American journalist*
* Stone, Oliver

**Bowduoin, William**
See Brannon, William T.

**Bowe, Bob**
See Bowe, Randolph

**Bowe, Kate**
See Taylor, Mary Ann

**Bowe, Lefty**
See Bowe, Randolph

**Bowe, Randolph** 20th c. [OBW]
*American baseball player*
* Bowe, Bob
* Bowe, Lefty

**Bowen, Betty Morgan**
See West, Betty

**Bowen, Chick**
See Bowen, Emmons Joseph

**Bowen, Cy**
See Bowen, Sutherland McCoy

**Bowen, Elizabeth**
See Cameron, Elizabeth Dorothea
Cole Bowen

**Bowen, Emmons Joseph** 1897-1948
[BE]
*American baseball player*
* Bowen, Chick

**Bowen, George** 1816-1888 [WBD]
*American missionary*
* [The] White Saint of India

**Bowen, [Sir] George Ferguson**
1821-1899 [FFF]
*British colonial administrator*
* Jawbone, Sir

**Bowen, John [Griffith]** 1924- [WD]
*British author*
* Blake, Justin [joint pseudonym
with Jeremy Bullmore]

**Bowen, Leonard Claude** 1924-
[CA]
*American author*
* Keith, K. Wymand

**Bowen, Marjorie**
See Long, Gabrielle Margaret Vere
[Campbell]

**Bowen, Mary**
See Hall, Mary Bowen

**Bowen, Reuben Bochert** 1917-1980
[BEW]
*American entertainer*
* Kajar the Magician

**Bowen, Robert Sydney** 1900-1977
[CA]
*American author, editor, journalist*
* Richard, James Robert

**Bowen, Ruth J. Baskerville** 1930-
[IBW]
*American business executive*
* Mother Goose

**Bowen, Sutherland McCoy**
1871-1925 [BE]
*American baseball player*
* Bowen, Cy

**Bowen, William Abraham** 1856- ?
[ALY]
*American author and editor*
* Philkins, Ike

**Bowen-Graves, Mrs.** [DEL, HN]
*Author*
* Stella

**Bowen-Judd, Sara [Hutton]** 1922-
[CA, CC, EMD]
*British author*
* Woods, Sara

**Bowen-Rowlands, Ernest Bowen
Brown** 20th c. [LAO]
*British barrister and writer*
* Member for Treorky

**Bower, Alison**
See Beckett, Gillian

**Bower, B. M.**
See Sinclair, Bertha M[uzzy]

**Bower, Barbara**
See Todd, Barbara Euphan

**Bower, Bugs**
See Bower, Maurice

**Bower, Donald E[dward]** 1920-
[CA]
*American author*
* Tower, Don

**Bower, George Collier** [PA]
*Author*
* Col

**Bower, [Sir] Graham John** 1848- ?
[LAO]
*British naval officer and writer*
* Centurion

**Bower, John Graham** 1886-1940
[SFL, WGT]
*British author*
* Klaxon

**Bower, John William** 1924- [CEI]
*Canadian-born hockey player*
* [The] China Wall

**Bower, Keith**
See Beckett, Kenneth A[lbert]

**Bower, Maurice** 1922- [ASC]
*American musician*
* Bower, Bugs

**Bower, Philip** 1891-1954 [THR]
*British theatrical producer*
* Ridgeway, Philip

**Bower [or Bowmaker?], Robert**
1385-1449 [FFF]
*Scottish historian and author*
* [The] Continuator of Fordun

**Bowering, George** 1935- [DLE]
*Canadian poet*
* [The] Panavision Kid

**Bowerman, Frank Eugene**
1868-1948 [AS, BE]
*American baseball player*
* Bowerman, Mike

**Bowerman, Mike**
See Bowerman, Frank Eugene

**Bowerman, Paul** 1898- [NAA]
*American writer and educator*
* Ingersoll, Drake

**Bowers, Doc**
See Bowers, Stew[art Cole]

**Bowers, Kathleen** 1917- [TR]
*British actress*
* Bowers, Lally

**Bowers, Lally**
See Bowers, Kathleen

**Bowers, May**
See   Bennett, Mrs. Frank

**Bowers, Pete**
See   Seeger, Pete[r R.]

**Bowers, Robert Hood** 1877-1941
[PMJ]
*American composer and conductor*
* Bowers, Robin Hood

**Bowers, Robin Hood**
See   Bowers, Robert Hood

**Bowers, Santha Rama Rau** 1923-
[CA]
*Indian author*
* Rama Rau, Santha

**Bowers, Stew[art Cole]** 1915-   [BE]
*American baseball player*
* Bowers, Doc

**Bowers, Thomas J.** 1826-1885
[IBW]
*American singer*
* Black Mario

**Bowers, Warner Fremont** 1906-
[CA]
*American physician and writer*
* Fremont, W. B.
* Warner, B. F.

**Bowes, Anne LaBastille**
See   LaBastille, Anne

**Bowes, James Stuart**   [FFF]
*British playwright*
* Dubois, Alfred

**Bowick, Dorothy Mueller**
See   Mueller, Dorothy

**Bowie, David**
See   Jones, David Robert Hayward

**Bowie, Dubbie**
See   Bowie, Russell

**Bowie, Edith Charlotte [Habback]**
1876- ?   [WWL]
*British author*
* Habbacknee

**Bowie, Jim**
See   Bowie, Larry

**Bowie, Jim**
See   Norwood, Victor G[eorge]
C[harles]

**Bowie, Jim**
See   Stratemeyer, Edward L.

**Bowie, Larry** 20th c.
*American football player*
* Bowie, Jim

**Bowie, Lester** 20th c.   [IBW]
*American jazz musician*
* Bowie, Maverick

**Bowie, Maverick**
See   Bowie, Lester

**Bowie, Russell** 1880-1959   [HK]
*Canadian-born hockey player*
* Bowie, Dubbie

**Bowie, Sam**
See   Ballard, [Willis] Todhunter

**Bowker, Joe**
See   Mahon, Tommy

**[The] Bowlegged One**
See   Fangio, Juan Manuel

**Bowler, Grant Tierney** 1907-1968
[BE]
*American baseball player*
* Bowler, Moose

**Bowler, Moose**
See   Bowler, Grant Tierney

**Bowles, Caroline Annie** 1787-1854
[PA]
*Author*
* C.

**Bowles, Chief**
See   Bowles, Emmett Jerome

**Bowles, Emmett Jerome**
1898-1959   [BE]
*American baseball player*
* Bowles, Chief

**Bowles, William Augustus**
1763-1805   [PA]
*Author*
* Indian Agent

**Bowlin, Hoss**
See   Bowlin, Lois Weldon

**Bowlin, Lois Weldon** 1940-   [BE]
*American baseball player*
* Bowlin, Hoss

**Bowline, Billy**
See   Raymond, Henry S.

**Bowman, Abe**
See   Bowman, Alvah Edson

**Bowman, Alvah Edson** 1893-   [BE]
*American baseball player*
* Bowman, Abe

**Bowman, Big Bow**
See   Bowman, Elmer William

**Bowman, Don** 1937-   [FCW]
*American country-western performer*
* [The] World's Worst Guitarist

**Bowman, Elmer William** 1897-
[BE]
*American baseball player*
* Bowman, Big Bow

**Bowman, Emmett** 20th c.   [OBW]
*American baseball player*
* Bowman, Scotty

**Bowman, Gerald** ?-1967   [MBF]
*British author*
* Bowman, J. M.
* Hawke, [Captain] Robert
* Lynk, Warder
* Magnus, Gerald

**Bowman, Helen** 1878- ?   [THR]
*British actress*
* Bowman, Nellie

**Bowman, J. L.**   [PA]
*Author*
* Le Conner, Hans Patrick

**Bowman, J. M.**
See   Bowman, Gerald

**Bowman, Jeanne**
See   Blocklinger, Peggy O'More

**Bowman, John** 20th c.   [GW]
*American rodeo performer*
* Bowman, Tackhead

**Bowman, Nellie**
See   Bowman, Helen

**Bowman, Ralph** 1911-   [CEI]
*Canadian-born hockey player*
* Bowman, Scotty

**Bowman, Ralph Skipwith** 1915-
[BEW, FC, ITA]
*American actor*
* Archer, John B.

**Bowman, Scotty**
See   Bowman, Emmett

**Bowman, Scotty**
See   Bowman, Ralph

**Bowman, Scotty**
See   Bowman, William Scott

**Bowman, Tackhead**
See   Bowman, John

**Bowman, William Scott** 1933-
[SMG]
*Canadian hockey coach*
* Bowman, Scotty

**Bowne, Ford**
See   Brown, Forrest

**Bowood, Richard**
See   Daniell, Albert Scott

**Bowran, John George** 1869- ?
[LAO]
*British author and clergyman*
* Guthrie, Ramsay

**Bowrey, Bill** 1943-   [OET]
*Australian tennis player*
* Bowrey, Tex

**Bowrey, Tex**
See   Bowrey, Bill

**Bowser, James H.** 1886-   [BE]
*American baseball player*
* Bowser, Red

**Bowser, Joan**
See   Bowser, Pearl

**Bowser, L.**   [PA]
*Author*
* Lucinda B.

**Bowser, Pearl** 1931-   [CA]
*American author and editor*
* Bowser, Joan

**Bowser, Red**
See   Bowser, James H.

**Bowskill, Derek** 1928-   [IAW]
*British author and playwright*
* Clewes, Jeremy
* Edwardes, Pauline

**Bowstead, Kenneth** 1896-1961
[SC]
*American actor*
* Dillon, Dick

**Bowyer, William** 1699-1777
[WBD]
*British printer*
* [The] Learned Printer

**Box, Ab**
See   Box, Albert

**Box, Albert** 20th c.   [BBH, CSH]
*Canadian football player*
* Box, Ab

**Box, Edgar**
See   Vidal, Eugene Luther, Jr.

**[The] Boxing Marvel**
See   Breslin, William J.

**Boxing, Mr.**
See   Fleischer, Nat[haniel Stanley]

**Boy**
See   Zelenski, Tadeusz

**[The] Boy Baritone**
See   Smith, Norris

**[The] Boy Barry Sullivan of the Music
Halls**
See   Brandon, Sydney Edward

**Boy Bruce, the Mighty Atom**
See   Johnson, Bruce Forsyth

**[The] Boy Commissioner**
See   Rozelle, Alvin Ray

**[The] Boy Earthquake**
See   Califano, Joseph Anthony, Jr.

**[The] Boy from Alabam**
See   Childre, Lew

**[The] Boy from Beale Street**
See   King, Riley B.

**[The] Boy in Blue**
See   Hanlan, Edward [Ned]

**[The] Boy in the Glass Cage**
See   DeVita, Teddy

**[The] Boy Manager**
See   Boudreau, Lou[is]

**[The] Boy Manager**
See   Harris, Stanley Raymond

**[The] Boy Mayor**
See   Patton, John

**[The] Boy Pope**
See   Benedict IV

**[The] Boy Pope**
See   John XII

**Boy Scout Bill**
See   Milliken, William Grawn

**[The] Boy Wonder**
See   Jones, Robert Tyre, Jr.

**[The] Boy Wonder**
See   Lockhart, Frank

**[The] Boy Wonder**
See   Patterson, Roy Lewis

**[The] Boy Wonder of Hollywood**
See   Schary, Isidore

**[The] Boy Wonder of the Clarinet**
See   Herman, Woodrow Wilson

**Boyajian, Cecile**
See   Starr, Cecile

**Boyar, Monica**
See   Gonzalez, Argentina Mercedes
Maria

**Boyce, Buck**
See   Boyce, Gordon

**Boyce, Christopher John** 1953?-
*Convicted of selling spy satellite
secrets to the Soviet Union*
* Lester, Anthony

**Boyce, Gordon** 20th c.   [GW]
*American rodeo performer*
* Boyce, Buck

**Boyce, J.** 19th c.   [PA]
*Author*
* Peppergrass, Paul

**Boyce, John Coxe**   [PA]
*Author*
* J. C. B.

**Boyce, Morton**
See   Fearn, John Russell

**Boycott, Boycs**
See Boycott, Geoffrey

**Boycott, Fiery**
See Boycott, Geoffrey

**Boycott, Geoffrey** 1940- [DC]
*British cricketer*
* Boycott, Boycs
* Boycott, Fiery
* Boycott, Thatch

**Boycott, Thatch**
See Boycott, Geoffrey

**Boycott-Brown, Hugh** 1909- [ART]
*British painter*
* Brown, Hugh
* H. B. B.

**Boyd, Alamo**
See Bosworth, Allan R[ucker]

**Boyd, Andrew Kennedy Hutchinson**
1825-1899 [DEL, DNNF, FFF]
*Scottish clergyman and author*
* A. K. H. B.
* Ardesier-Macdonald, Charles
* [A] Country Parson

**Boyd, Ann S.**
See Schoonmaker, Ann

**Boyd, Barbara**
See Burr, Agnes Rush

**Boyd, Belle**
See Hardinge, Belle Boyd

**Boyd, Blanche** 1889-1959 [SC]
*American actress*
* Boyd, Deedee

**Boyd, Deedee**
See Boyd, Blanche

**Boyd, Edna McGuire** 1899- [IA]
*American author*
* McGuire, Edna

**Boyd, Edward Riley** 1914- [BWW]
*American singer*
* Boyd, Ernie
* Boyd, Little Eddie

**Boyd, Elizabeth Orr** 1912- [AW]
*Scottish author*
* Maccall, Isobel

**Boyd, Ernie**
See Boyd, Edward Riley

**Boyd, Eva Narcissus** 1944- [RO1]
*American singer*
* Little Eva

**Boyd, Felix**
See Dempsey, Henry

**Boyd, Frank**
See Kane, Frank

**Boyd, Frank C.** 20th c. [BE]
*American baseball player*
* Boyd, Jake

**Boyd, George** 1904?-1931? [NOJ]
*American jazz musician*
* Georgia Boy

**Boyd, Gregory Earl** 1952- [SMG]
*American football player*
* Boyd, Too Strong

**Boyd, Heavy**
See Boyd, Rufus

**Boyd, Irvin** 1908- [CEI, SMG]
*American hockey player*
* Boyd, Yank

**Boyd, Jake**
See Boyd, Frank C.

**Boyd, John**
See Upchurch, Boyd Bradfield

**Boyd, Little Eddie**
See Boyd, Edward Riley

**Boyd, Lyle G[ifford]** 20th c. [WGT]
*American author*
* Ellanbee, Boyd [joint pseudonym with William C(louser) Boyd]
* Ellanby, Boyd [joint pseudonym with William C(louser) Boyd]

**Boyd, Martin** 1893- [B10]
*Australian author*
* Mills, Martin

**Boyd, Nancy**
See Millay, Edna St. Vincent

**Boyd, Neil**
See De Rosa, Peter

**Boyd, Ray** ?-1962 [BEW]
*Theatrical performer*
* Rajah, Raboid

**Boyd, Rick**
See Boido, Federico

**Boyd, Robert**
See Byrd, Henry Roeland

**Boyd, Robert Richard** 1926- [BE]
*American baseball player*
* [The] Rope

**Boyd, Rufus** 20th c. [IBW]
*American auto racer*
* Boyd, Heavy

**Boyd, Shylah** 1945- [CA]
*American poet*
* Whyatt, Frances

**Boyd, Stage**
See Boyd, William

**Boyd, Stephen**
See Miller, William

**Boyd, Too Strong**
See Boyd, Gregory Earl

**Boyd, Waldo T.** 1918- [CA]
*American author*
* Andersen, Ted
* Parker, Robert

**Boyd, William** 1890-1935 [SC]
*American actor*
* Boyd, Stage

**Boyd, William [Bill]** 20th c.
[CWG, FCW]
*American country-western performer*
* [The] Cowboy Rambler

**Boyd, William C[louser]** 1903-
[WGT]
*American author*
* Ellanbee, Boyd [joint pseudonym with Lyle G(ifford) Boyd]
* Ellanby, Boyd [joint pseudonym with Lyle G(ifford) Boyd]

**Boyd [or Gitry?], Willie** 1946-
[BWW]
*American singer*
* Harris, Hi Tide

**Boyd, [Margaret] Woodward [Smith]**
1898- [NAA]
*American author*
* Shane, Peggy

**Boyd, Yank**
See Boyd, Irvin

**Boyden, Simeon** [FFF]
*American hotel owner*
* [The] Father of the Hotel System of the United States

**Boyer, Bruce Hatton** 1946- [CA]
*American author*
* Tate, B. H.

**Boyer, Clete**
See Boyer, Cletis Leroy

**Boyer, Cletis Leroy** 1937- [BE]
*American baseball player*
* Boyer, Clete

**Boyer, Cloyd Victor** 1927- [BE]
*American baseball player*
* Boyer, Junior

**Boyer, Columbia**
See Martin, Nell Columbia Boyer

**Boyer d'Agen, Augustin**
See Boyer, Jean Auguste

**Boyer, Jean Auguste** 1857-1943?
[WBD]
*French author*
* Boyer d'Agen, Augustin

**Boyer, Junior**
See Boyer, Cloyd Victor

**Boyer, Ken**
See Boyer, Kenton Lloyd

**Boyer, Kenton Lloyd** 1931- [BE]
*American baseball player*
* Boyer, Ken

**Boyer, Louis** [FFF]
*French entertainer*
* La Roque

**Boyer, Robert**
See Lake, Kenneth R[obert]

**Boyer, William Frederick**
1846-1908 [BEW]
*Theatrical performer*
* Edouin, Willie

**Boykoff, Harry**
See Boykoff, Heshie

**Boykoff, Heshie** 1922- [BB]
*American basketball player*
* Boykoff, Harry

**Boylan, Boyd**
See Whiton, James Nelson

**Boylan, Estelle** 1899-1958
[F2, FC]
*American actress*
* Taylor, Estelle

**Boyle, Acland** [FFF]
*Entertainer and writer*
* Von Boyle, Ackland

**Boyle, Alicia** 20th c. [ART]
*British painter*
* A. B.

**Boyle, Buzz**
See Boyle, Ralph Francis

**Boyle, Catherine**
See Di Francavilla, Caterina

**Boyle, Charles [Fourth Earl of Orrery]** 1676-1731 [SN]
*British statesman, soldier, author*
* Phalaris Junior

**Boyle, Eleanor Vere** 19th c. [PA]
*Artist*
* E. V. B.

**Boyle, Handsome Henry**
See Boyle, Henry J.

**Boyle, Henry** [FFF]
*Entertainer*
* Richmond, Harry

**Boyle, Henry J.** 1860- ? [BE]
*American baseball player*
* Boyle, Handsome Henry

**Boyle, Honest Jack**
See Boyle, John Anthony

**Boyle, John Anthony** 1866-1913
[BE]
*American baseball player*
* Boyle, Honest Jack

**Boyle, Kay**
See Vail, Kay Boyle

**Boyle, Mark**
See Kienzle, William X[avier]

**Boyle, Mrs. Charles H.** [FFF]
*Entertainer*
* Fox, Stella
* Marion, Stella

**Boyle, Paul**
See Graves, Robert Von Ranke

**Boyle, Ralph Francis** 1908- [BE]
*American baseball player*
* Boyle, Buzz

**Boyle, Richard [First Earl of Cork]**
1566-1643 [DNNF, DNNS, FFF]
*Lord treasurer of Ireland*
* [The] Great Earl of Cork

**Boyle, Wilfred** 20th c. [IAW]
*British actor, singer, author*
* Beta

**Boyles, Clarence Scott, Jr.** 1905-
[CA]
*American author*
* Brown, Will C.

**Boyles, Harry** 1911- [BE]
*American baseball player*
* Boyles, Stretch

**Boyles, Stretch**
See Boyles, Harry

**Boylesve, Rene**
See Tardiveau, Rene Marie Auguste

**Boyne, Don**
See Kevin, Neil

**Boyne, Eva** 1885-1960 [BEW]
*British-born actress*
* Leonard-Boyne, Eva

**Boynton, Ben L.** 1898-1963 [FB]
*American football player*
* [The] Purple Streak

**Boynton, Charles** 1921-1968 [SC]
*Actor*
* Boynton, Ted

**Boynton, Harry F.** [PA]
*Author*
* Free, Harry B.

**Boynton, Ted**
See Boynton, Charles

**Boyrie, Arthur** 19th c.   [PA]
*Author*
* Aristophanes

**Boyron, Michel [or Michael]**
1653-1729   [DNNF, SN, WBD]
*French actor*
* Baron, Michel
* [The] French Garrick
* [The] French Roscius
* [The] Roscius of France

**Boytler, Arcady**
*See*  Bojtler, Arcadij

**Boyum, Joy Gould** 1934-   [CA]
*American film critic and poet*
* Gould, Joy

**Boz**
*See*  Dickens, Charles

**Bozeman, Beverley**
*See*  Fuller, Beverley Bozeman

**Bozzaris, Marco** 1788?-1823
[DEP, DNNF, FFF]
*Greek soldier*
* [The] Leonidas of Modern Greece

**Bozzy**
*See*  Boswell, James

**Brabazon, James**
*See*  Seth-Smith, Leslie James

**[Il] Braccatone**
*See*  Ricciarelli, Daniele

**Bracciolini, Francis** 1566-1645
[SN]
*Italian clergyman and poet*
* Delle Ape [Of the Bees]

**Brace, Ellis** 20th c.   [BBH]
*Boxer*
* Brace, Jackie

**Brace, Jackie**
*See*  Brace, Ellis

**Brace, Timothy**
*See*  Pratt, Theodore

**Bracegirdle, Anne** 1663-1748
[DNNS, RH]
*British actress*
* [The] Diana of the Stage

**Brachard, Paul, Jr.** 1910-1959
[SC]
*American actor*
* Cameron, Bruce

**Brachlianoff, Arcady** 1912-   [WEC]
*French animator and producer*
* Arcady, Jean

**Brack, Gib [or Gibby]**
*See*  Brack, Gilbert Herman

**Brack, Gilbert Herman** 1912-1960
[BE]
*American baseball player*
* Brack, Gib [or Gibby]

**Brack, Vektis** [house pseudonym,
Gannet Press]
*See*  Humphrys, Leslie George

**Brackeen, Joanne**
*See*  Grogan, Joanne

**Brackenbury, Curt**
*See*  Brackenbury, John Curtis

**Brackenbury, John Curtis** 1952-
[HR]
*Canadian-born hockey player*
* Brackenbury, Curt

**Brackett, Leigh**
*See*  Hamilton, Leigh Brackett
Douglass

**Bradburne, E[lizabeth] Sutton**
1915-   [AW, CA]
*British author and educator*
* Lawrence, E. S.

**Bradbury, E[dward] P.**
*See*  Moorcock, Michael John

**Bradbury, Edward**   [PA]
*Author*
* Strephon

**Bradbury, Irene**   [FFF]
*Author*
* Lunt, Irene

**Bradbury, Parnell** 1904-   [AW]
*British author and osteopath*
* Dermott, Stephen

**Bradbury, Ray [Douglas]** 1920-
[ESF, HFF, WGT]
*American author*
* Amory, Guy
* Banat, D. R.
* Banks, Edward
* Corvais, Anthony
* Cunningham, Cecil Claybourne
* Cunningham, E.
* Douglas, Leonard
* Eldred, Brian
* Elliott, William
* Hollerbochen
* Omega
* Reynolds, Ron
* Rogers, Doug
* Spaulding, Douglas
* Sterling, Brett [house
pseudonym]
* Tremaine, D. Lerium

**Bradbury, Robert** 1906?-1966
[F2, FC]
*American actor*
* Steele, Bob

**Bradbury, Stephen Henry**  ?-1865
[DEL]
*Poet*
* Quallon

**Bradby, G. F.**
*See*  Bradby, Godfrey Fox

**Bradby, Godfrey Fox** 1863-1947
[LC]
*British author and poet*
* Bradby, G. F.

**Bradby, Rachel** 1943-   [WD]
*British author, playwright, critic*
* Anderson, Rachel

**Braddix, Ben** 1948-   [IBW]
*American entertainer*
* Little Daddy

**Braddock, James Joseph [Jim]**
1905-   [BX, RBE]
*American boxer*
* [The] Cinderella Man

**Braddon, George**
*See*  Milkomane, George Alexis
Milkomanovich

**Braddon, Gerald**   [FFF]
*Entertainer*
* Maxwell, Gerald

**Braddon, [Sir] Henry Yule** 1863- ?
[DEL, FFF, WWL]
*Australian author*
* Forrester, Gilbert

**Braddon, [Sir] Henry Yule**
(Continued)
* Member of the Burton Hunt

**Braddon, [Miss] Mary E.**
*See*  Maxwell, Mary Elizabeth
[Braddon]

**Braddon, Paul**
*See*  Van Arden, J. Howard

**Bradds, Gary** 1942-   [BB]
*American basketball player*
* Bradds, Tex

**Bradds, Tex**
*See*  Bradds, Gary

**Braden, Irene A.**
*See*  Hoadley, Irene Braden

**Braden, Paul** 1901-1958   [SC]
*American actor, magician, author*
* Le Paul, Paul

**Braden, Walter**
*See*  Finney, Walter Braden

**Bradfield, Jolly Roger**
*See*  Bradfield, Roger

**Bradfield, Nancy**
*See*  Sayer, Nancy Margetts

**Bradfield, Roger** 1924-   [CA]
*American author and illustrator*
* Bradfield, Jolly Roger

**Bradford [M.D.], Adam**
*See*  Wassersug, Joseph D.

**Bradford, Buddy**
*See*  Bradford, Charles William

**Bradford, Charles William** 1944-
[BE, SMG]
*American baseball player*
* Bradford, Buddy

**Bradford, David** 1954-
*British soccer player*
* [The] Mighty Atom

**Bradford, [Captain] L.**
*See*  Carson, [Captain] L. B.

**Bradford, Mule**
*See*  Bradford, Perry

**Bradford, Patience Andrewes**
1918-   [CA]
*British author*
* Andrewes, Patience

**Bradford, Perry** 1895-1970   [WWJ]
*American jazz musician and
composer*
* Bradford, Mule

**Bradford, Robert** 1945-   [ART]
*British artist*
* R. B.

**Bradford, William** 1722-1791
[WBD]
*American printer*
* [The] Patriot Printer of 1776

**Bradford, William** 1879- ?   [WWL]
*British author*
* Ford, Nox

**Bradlaugh, Charles** 1833-1891
[PA, WBD]
*British political reformer and
lecturer*
* Iconoclast

**Bradley, A. C.**
*See*  Bradley, Andrew Cecil

**Bradley, Albert W.** 20th c.   [MBF]
*British author*
* Wentworth, Charles [house
pseudonym]

**Bradley, Alice**
*See*  Sheldon, Alice Bradley

**Bradley, Andrew Cecil** 1851-1935
[LC]
*British author and educator*
* Bradley, A. C.

**Bradley, Bill**
*See*  Silbert, William M.

**Bradley, Brian K.**
*See*  Schuyler, Keith C.

**Bradley, Buddy**
*See*  Bradley, Robert

**Bradley, Buddy**
*See*  Epps, Clarence Bradley

**Bradley, Curley**
*See*  Bradley, Joe

**Bradley, Doc**
*See*  Bradley, Harold C.

**Bradley, Dollar Bill**
*See*  Bradley, William [Bill]

**Bradley, Duane**
*See*  Sanborn, Duane

**Bradley, Edward** 1827-1889
[DEL, PA, WBD]
*British author, clergyman,
illustrator*
* Bede, Cuthbert

**Bradley, Emily** 1828-1863
[FFF, PA]
*Author*
* Cushman, Clara
* Lee, Alice G.

**Bradley, F. H.**
*See*  Bradley, Francis Herbert

**Bradley, Foghorn**
*See*  Bradley, George H.

**Bradley, Francis Herbert**
1846-1924   [LC]
*British author and educator*
* Bradley, F. H.

**Bradley, George H.** 1853-1900
[BE]
*American baseball player*
* Bradley, Foghorn

**Bradley, George Washington**
1852-1931   [BE]
*American baseball player*
* Bradley, Grin

**Bradley, Grin**
*See*  Bradley, George Washington

**Bradley, Harold C.** 1879- ?   [BBH]
*American skiing organization officer*
* Bradley, Doc

**Bradley, Harriet M.**   [PA]
*Author*
* Marietta

**Bradley, Ian [Roberts Ambrose]**
1900-   [WD]
*British writer*
* Duplex [joint pseudonym with N.
F. Hallows]

**Bradley, J. J. G.** 20th c.   [MBF]
*British author*
* Borlase, Skip

**Bradley, J. J. G.** (Continued)
* Leslie, Captain

**Bradley, Joe**
*Singer*
* Bradley, Curley

**Bradley, Katharine Harris**
1848-1914   [LC]
*British author and poet*
* Field, Michael [joint pseudonym
   with Edith Emma Cooper]

**Bradley, Marion Zimmer** 1930-
[SFP, WGT]
*American author*
* Morley, Brian
* O'Brien, Dee
* Wells, John Jay [joint pseudonym
   with Juanita Ruth Wellons
   Coulson]

**Bradley, Michael**
*See*   Blumberg, Gary

**Bradley, Omar Nelson** 1893-1981
*American military leader*
* [The] GI's General

**Bradley, Robert** 1908-   [THR]
*American-born dancer*
* Bradley, Buddy

**Bradley, Shelland**
*See*   Bradley-Birt, Francis Bradley

**Bradley, T. Waldron**   [PA]
*Author*
* Beauchamp, Shelsley

**Bradley, Velma**
*See*   Cox, Ida

**Bradley, Vera Jeanne** 1931-   [IBW]
*American singer*
* Karter, Kim
* Karter, Kissing Kim

**Bradley, Warren S.**   [PA]
*Author*
* Gaylord, Glance

**Bradley, Will**
*See*   Schwichtenberg, Wilbur

**Bradley, William**   [PA]
*Author*
* [A] Retired Guardian

**Bradley, William [Bill]** 1943-
[BB, BBH]
*American basketball player*
* Bradley, Dollar Bill

**Bradley, William Aspenwall** 1878-
?   [ALY]
*American author and editor*
* Palmer, Cleveland

**Bradley-Birt, Francis Bradley** 1874-
?   [LAO]
*British author*
* Bradley, Shelland

**[The] Bradman of the Caribbeans**
*See*   Headley, George Alphonso

**Bradshaw, Brad**
*See*   Bradshaw, Thornton

**Bradshaw, Brum**
*See*   Bradshaw, J. B.

**Bradshaw, Dallas Carl** 1895-1939
[BE]
*American baseball player*
* Bradshaw, Rabbit

**Bradshaw, J. B.** 20th c.   [GW]
*American rodeo performer*
* Bradshaw, Brum

**Bradshaw, James** 1898-   [FB]
*American football player*
* Bradshaw, Rabbit

**Bradshaw, Myron** 1905-1958
[WWJ]
*American jazz musician*
* Bradshaw, Tiny

**Bradshaw, Percival Vanner**
1878-1965   [WEC]
*British cartoonist*
* P. V. B.

**Bradshaw, Rabbit**
*See*   Bradshaw, Dallas Carl

**Bradshaw, Rabbit**
*See*   Bradshaw, James

**Bradshaw, Thornton** 1918?-
*American business executive*
* Bradshaw, Brad
* [The] Mountie of American
   Corporate Chiefs

**Bradshaw, Tiny**
*See*   Bradshaw, Myron

**Bradshaw, Wellesley**
*See*   Alexander, Charles Wesley

**Bradshaw, Wesley**
*See*   Alexander, Charles Wesley

**Bradstreet, Anne** 1612-1672   [FFF]
*American poet*
* [The] Tenth Muse

**Bradwardine, Thomas** 1290?-1349
[DEL, HN, SN]
*British prelate and mathematician*
* [The] Profound Doctor
* Profundus, Doctor

**Bradwell, James**
*See*   Kent, Arthur [William
Charles]

**Brady, Alice** 1893-1939   [F1]
*Actress*
* Rose, Marie

**Brady, Big**
*See*   Brady, Xernona Brewster
Clayton

**Brady, Diamond Jim**
*See*   Brady, James Buchanan [Jim]

**Brady, Diamond Jim**
*See*   Brady, James Joseph [Jim]

**Brady, Esther Wood** 1905-   [CA]
*American author*
* Wood, Esther

**Brady, Floyd Maurice** 1910-
[WWJ]
*American jazz musician*
* Brady, Stumpy

**Brady, Fred**
*See*   Kopf, William Lorenz

**Brady, Fred**
*See*   Kress, Frederick

**Brady, Hal**
*See*   Miraglia, Emilio

**Brady, Helen**   [FFF]
*Entertainer*
* Sedgewick, Helen

**Brady, Irene**   [FFF]
*Entertainer*
* Perry, Irene

**Brady, Ish**
*See*   Brady, Kenneth

**Brady, James Buchanan [Jim]**
1856-1917
*American financier*
* Brady, Diamond Jim

**Brady, James Joseph [Jim]** 1936-
[BE]
*American baseball player*
* Brady, Diamond Jim

**Brady, James S. [Jim]** 1941?-
*American presidential press
secretary*
* [The] Bear

**Brady, James T.** 1815-1869   [PA]
*Author*
* Query

**Brady, James Ward** 1881-1947
[BE]
*American baseball player*
* Brady, King

**Brady, John Walter** 1933-   [OP]
*Australian opera singer*
* Sydney, Jon

**Brady, Kenneth** 1947?-1974   [FIR]
*Musician*
* Brady, Ish

**Brady, King**
*See*   Brady, James Ward

**Brady, Nicholas**
*See*   Turner, John Victor

**Brady, Peter**
*See*   Daniels, Norman [A.]

**Brady, Raccoon**
*See*   Brady, Sarah

**Brady, Sarah** 20th c.
*Wife of American presidential press
secretary, James Brady*
* Brady, Raccoon

**Brady, Scott**
*See*   Tierney, Gerald

**Brady, Stumpy**
*See*   Brady, Floyd Maurice

**Brady, Xernona Brewster Clayton**
1932-   [IBW]
*American television performer and
columnist*
* Brady, Big

**Brae, June**
*See*   Bear, June

**Braeme, Charlotte Monica**
1836-1884   [FFF, WBD]
*British author*
* Clay, Bertha M.

**Braff, Reuben** 1927-   [DAM, EJ]
*American jazz musician*
* Braff, Ruby

**Braff, Ruby**
*See*   Braff, Reuben

**Brag, [Sir] Jack**
*See*   Burgoyne, John

**Braganza**
*See*   Bragg, H. A.

**Bragdon, Elspeth [MacDuffie]**
1897-   [CA, SAT]
*American author and poet*
* Elspeth

**Bragg, Dobby**
*See*   Sykes, Roosevelt

**Bragg, Don** 1935-   [TF]
*American pole vaulter*
* Bragg, Tarzan

**Bragg, Grumps**
*See*   Bragg, Mike

**Bragg, H. A.**   [PA]
*Author*
* Braganza

**Bragg, Mike** 20th c.
*American football player*
* Bragg, Grumps

**Bragg, Tarzan**
*See*   Bragg, Don

**Braha, George**
*See*   Robinson, Lewis George

**Braham, John**
*See*   Abraham, John

**Braham, Leonora**
*See*   Young, Mrs. Duncan

**Brahe, Tycho** 1546-1601
[DNNS, RH]
*Danish astronomer*
* Golden Nose

**Brahm, Hans** 1893?-
[BDF, FC, FD]
*German director*
* Brahm, John

**Brahm, John**
*See*   Brahm, Hans

**Brahm, Otto**
*See*   Abrahamsohn, Otto

**Brahms, Caryl**
*See*   Abrahams, Doris Caroline

**Braid** [code name used during World
War II]
*See*   Marshall, George Catlett

**Braid, Big Jim**
*See*   Braid, James

**Braid, James** 1870-1950   [GF]
*Scottish-born golfer*
* Braid, Big Jim

**Brailsford, Frances**
*See*   Wosmek, Frances

**Braiman, Susan** 1943-   [CA]
*American author and
psychotherapist*
* Gettleman, Susan

**[The] Brain**
*See*   Rothstein, Arnold

**Brain, Brainy**
*See*   Brain, Brian Maurice

**Brain, Brian Maurice** 1940-   [DC]
*British cricketer*
* Brain, Brainy

**Brainard, Asa** 1841-1888   [BE]
*American baseball player*
* Brainard, Count

**Brainard, Count**
*See*   Brainard, Asa

**Brainerd, Chauncey Corey**
1874-1922 [SFL, WW]
*Author*
* Rath, E. J. [joint pseudonym with Edith Rathbone (Jacobs) Brainerd]

**Brainerd, Edith Rathbone [Jacobs]**
?-1922 [SFL, WW]
*Author*
* Rath, E. J. [joint pseudonym with Chauncey Corey Brainerd]

**Brainerd, John W[hiting]** 1918-
[CA]
*American biologist, author, poet*
* Bee, Jay

**Braith, George**
See Braithwaite, George

**Braithwaite, Althea** 1940- [IAW]
*British author and illustrator*
* Althea

**Braithwaite, Coulton**
See Brown, G. W.

**Braithwaite, E. E.**
See Braithwaite, Eustace Edward

**Braithwaite, Eustace Edward**
1920- [LC]
*Guyanese diplomat, educator, author*
* Braithwaite, E. E.

**Braithwaite, George** 1937- [IBW]
*Guyanese-born table tennis player*
* [The] Ping Pong Diplomat

**Braithwaite, George** 1939- [DAM]
*American jazz musician*
* Braith, George

**Braithwaite, J. Ashton** 1945?-
[CW]
*Barbadian poet and author*
* Kwamdela, Odimumba

**Braithwaite, Raymond**
See Owen, Frank

**Braithwaite, Richard** [SN]
*British poet*
* Drunken Barnaby
* Famous Barnaby

**Bramah, Ernest**
See Smith, Ernest Brammah

**Bramante**
See D'Agnolo [or D'Angelo], Donato

**[Il] Bramantino**
See Suardi, Bartolommeo

**Bramble, Matthew**
See MacDonald, Andrew

**Brambleby, Ailsa** 1915- [AW]
*Scottish author and educator*
* Craig, Jennifer

**Bramer, Jennie [Perkins]** 1900-
[CAP]
*American writer*
* Perkins, Faith

**Bramlett, Bull**
See Bramlett, John C.

**Bramlett, George** 1895- [BMH]
*British entertainer*
* Wood, Wee Georgie

**Bramlett, John**
See Pierce, John Leonard, Jr.

**Bramlett, John C.** 1941- [FB]
*American football player and baseball player*
* Bramlett, Bull

**Brammer, L. G.**
See Brammer, Leonard Griffiths

**Brammer, Leonard Griffiths** 1906-
[ART]
*British painter, etcher, engraver*
* Brammer, L. G.

**Brampton, James?**
See Williams, John Babington

**Bramwahld, Theodore**
See Kent, George

**Bramwell, Charlotte**
See Kimbro, John M.

**Bramwell, James Guy** 1911-
[CA, CC, WW]
*British author and poet*
* Byrom, James

**Branca, Hawk**
See Branca, Ralph Theodore Joseph

**Branca, Ralph Theodore Joseph**
1926- [BE]
*American baseball player*
* Branca, Hawk

**Branch, Norm[an Downs]** 1915-
[BE]
*American baseball player*
* Branch, Red

**Branch, Red**
See Branch, Norm[an Downs]

**Brand, Adolph Johannes** 1934-
[EJ7]
*South African jazz musician*
* Brand, Dollar
* Ibrahim, Abdullah

**Brand, Christianna**
See Lewis, Mary Christianna [Milne]

**Brand, Clay**
See Norwood, Victor G[eorge] C[harles]

**Brand, Dollar**
See Brand, Adolph Johannes

**Brand, Dudley**
See Hild, H.

**Brand, Franz**
See Bonus, Arthur

**Brand, Garrison**
See Brandner, Gary

**Brand, Max**
See Faust, Frederick [Schiller]

**Brand, Mona**
See Fox, Mona Alexis [Brand]

**Brand, [Charles] Neville** 1895-
[WW]
*Author*
* Lorne, Charles

**Brand, Pauline**
See Hall, Pauline

**Brand, Peter**
See Larsen, Erling

**Brand, Roma** 1918- [CA]
*Austrian-born American author*
* Brand, Sandra

**Brand, Sandra**
See Brand, Roma

**Brand, Susan**
See Roper, Susan Bonthron

**Brandane, John**
See McIntyre, John

**Brandel, Marc**
See Beresford, Marcus

**Branden, Nathaniel**
See Blumenthal, Nathaniel

**Branden, Victoria [Fremlin]** 20th c.
[CA]
*Canadian author and playwright*
* Stylla, Joanne

**Brandenberg, Aliki Liacouras**
1929- [CA, SAT, TBJ]
*American author and illustrator*
* Aliki

**Brandenburg, Margaret Johnston**
20th c. [NAA]
*American journalist*
* Snow, Jane

**Brandes, Carl E.**
See Cohen, Carl E.

**Brandes, Georg**
See Cohen, Morris

**Brandmuller, Johannes**
See Christ, Robert Balthasar

**Brandner, Gary** 1933- [CA]
*American author*
* Brand, Garrison
* Moore, Clayton
* Quill, Barnaby

**Brandolini, Aurelius** 1440?-1497
[SN]
*Italian poet*
* [Il] Lippo [The Blear-Eyed]

**Brandom, Chester Milton**
1887-1958 [BE]
*American baseball player*
* Brandom, Chick

**Brandom, Chick**
See Brandom, Chester Milton

**Brandon, Beatrice**
See Krepps, Robert W[ilson]

**Brandon, Brumsic, Jr.** 1927- [IBW]
*American cartoonist and illustrator*
* B. B., Mr.

**Brandon, Bucky**
See Brandon, Darrell G.

**Brandon, Carl**
See Carr, Terry [Gene]

**Brandon, Carl, Jr.**
See Holmberg, John-Henri

**Brandon, Curt**
See Bishop, Curtis [Kent]

**Brandon, Darrell G.** 1940- [BE]
*American baseball player*
* Brandon, Bucky

**Brandon, Dorothy** 1918- [MY]
*American singer*
* Dunn, Dorothy

**Brandon, Ethel**
See Stockwell, Mrs. L. R.

**Brandon, Frank**
See Bulmer, [Henry] Kenneth

**Brandon, Henry**
See Kleinbach, Henry

**Brandon, Joe**
See Davis, Robert Prunier

**Brandon, Michael** 1906-1957 [SC]
*American actor*
* Twitchell, A. R.
* Twitchell, Archie

**Brandon, Philip**
See Leaver, Philip

**Brandon, Roy**
See Hooper, Stanley

**Brandon, Sheila**
See Rayner, Claire

**Brandon, Sydney Edward** 1890-
[BMH]
*British actor and comedian*
* [The] Boy Barry Sullivan of the Music Halls
* Carrol, Norman

**Brandreth, Jeremiah** ?-1817 [HN]
*Leader of rebellion against British government*
* [The] Nottingham Captain

**Brandsten, Ernst** 20th c. [BBH]
*Swedish-born diver and coach*
* [The] Father of Modern Diving

**Brandt, Flakey**
See Brandt, John George, Jr.
[Jackie]

**Brandt, Harvey**
See Edwards, William B[ennett]

**Brandt, Ivan**
See Cook, Roy Francis

**Brandt, Jane Lewis** 1915- [CA]
*American author*
* Lewis, Lange

**Brandt, Johanna** 1876- ? [WWL]
*South African author*
* Romondt, Marcus

**Brandt, John George, Jr. [Jackie]**
1934- [PB]
*American baseball player*
* Brandt, Flakey

**Brandt, Lucile [Long Strayer]**
1900- [CA]
*American author and educator*
* Long, Lucile

**Brandt, Marianne**
See Bischoff, Marie

**Brandt, Paul** 20th c.
*German author*
* Licht, Hans

**Brandt, Roger**
See Crawford, William [Elbert]

**Brandt, Tom**
See Dewey, Thomas B[lanchard]

**Brandt, Willy**
See Frahm, Herbert Ernst Karl

**Brandwein, Chaim N[aftali]** 1920-
[CA]
*Israeli-born author and journalist*
* Naftali, Ch.

**Brandy Nan**
See Anne

**Brandywine**
See McGrew, Alex

**Brangwyn, Charles**
See Reed, Edward Charles

**Brank**
See Price, Charles

**Brannigan, Larry** 1838-1891
[FFF, PA]
*American actor*
* Barrett, Lawrence

**Brannon, Humphrey J.** 1916- [EJ]
*American jazz musician*
* Brannon, Teddy

**Brannon, Teddy**
See Brannon, Humphrey J.

**Brannon, William Penn** 1825-1866
[PA]
*Author*
* Brown, Vandyke

**Brannon, William T.** 1906-
[CAP, WD]
*American author*
* Barrington, H. W.
* Bowduoin, William
* Bronston, William
* Gardner, Lawrence
* Hamilton, Jack
* Hermanns, Peter
* Lebert, Randy
* McGlinn, Dwight
* Oberholtzer, Peter
* Peters, S. T.
* Randolph, Jerry
* Swanstrom, Nils
* Tibbetts, William

**Brannum, Hugh** 1910?-
*American television performer*
* Brannum, Lumpy

**Brannum, Lumpy**
See Brannum, Hugh

**Branquinho Da Fonseca, Antonio Jose**
See Madeira, Antonio

**Bransby, Emma Lindsay Squier**
1892- [WGT]
*American author*
* Squier, Emma Lindsay

**Branscombe, Maud**
See Stuart, Mrs. Everard

**Bransfield, Kitty**
See Bransfield, William Edward

**Bransfield, William Edward**
1875-1947 [AS, BE]
*American baseball player*
* Bransfield, Kitty

**Bransom, Paul** 1885- [IBY]
*American illustrator*
* [The] Dean of American Animal Artists

**Brant, Joseph**
See Thayendanegea

**Brant, Lewis**
See Rowland, D[onald] S[ydney]

**Brant, Mrs. Luke** [FFF]
*Entertainer*
* Vernon, Rose

**Brant, Remington**
See Briefer, Richard [Dick]

**Brantsch, Ingmar** 1946- [IAW]
*Rumanian-born author*
* Eris, Hermann

**Bras de Fer [Iron Arm]**
See Baldwin I

**Bras de Fer**
See Cole, Comyns

**Bras de Fer**
See Lanoue, Francois de

**Bras Droit du Cardinal**
See Leclerc du Tremblay, Francois

**Braschi, Giovanni Angelo**
1717-1799 [SN, WBD]
*Pope*
* [The] Last of Monsters
* Pius VI

**Brasfield, Boob**
See Brasfield, L. L.

**Brasfield, L. L.** ?-1966 [CWG]
*American country-western performer*
* Brasfield, Boob
* Uncle Cyp

**Brasfield, Neva Inez** 1889- [CWG]
*American country-western performer*
* Aunt Sap

**Brasfield, Rodney Leon** 1910-1958
[CWG]
*American country-western performer*
* [The] Hohenwald Flash

**Brash, Margaret Maud** 1880- ?
[ESF, SFL, WGT]
*British author*
* Kendall, John

**Brashear, Kitty**
See Brashear, Robert Norman

**Brashear, Robert Norman**
1878-1934 [BE]
*American baseball player*
* Brashear, Kitty

**Brasier-Creagh, Patrick** 1930-
[CA]
*British poet and translator*
* Creagh, Patrick

**Brass, Dee Shirley** 1928- [CA]
*American author*
* Deane, Dee Shirley

**Brass, Giovanni** 1933- [FDG]
*Italian director*
* Brass, Tinto

**Brass, Tinto**
See Brass, Giovanni

**Brassai**
See Halasz, Gyula

**Brasselle, Keefe**
See Brasselli, John J.

**Brasselli, John J.** 1923?-
*American actor, producer, author*
* Brasselle, Keefe

**Brasset, A. D.**
See Ash, Edward Cecil

**Brasseur, Pierre**
See Espinasse, Albert

**Brassington, Andrew James** 1954-
[DC]
*British cricketer*
* Brassington, Imma

**Brassington, Imma**
See Brassington, Andrew James

**Braswell, Braz**
See Braswell, Charles

**Braswell, Charles** 1952- [SMG]
*American football player*
* Braswell, Braz

**[The] Brat**
See Stanky, Edward Raymond

**Bratcher, Goobers**
See Bratcher, Joseph Warlick [Joe]

**Bratcher, Joseph Warlick [Joe]**
1898- [BE]
*American baseball player*
* Bratcher, Goobers

**Bratchi, Fred[erick Oscar]**
1892-1962 [BE]
*American baseball player*
* Bratchi, Fritz

**Bratchi, Fritz**
See Bratchi, Fred[erick Oscar]

**Brathwaite, Edward Kamau**
See Brathwaite, L. Edward

**Brathwaite, L. Edward** 1930- [CW]
*Barbadian poet, critic, author*
* Brathwaite, Edward Kamau

**Bratkowski, Edmund Raymond**
1931- [FB, SMG]
*American football player and coach*
* Bratkowski, Zeke

**Bratkowski, Zeke**
See Bratkowski, Edmund
Raymond

**Bratsburg, Harry** 1915-
[FC, HT, ITA]
*American actor*
* Morgan, Harry

**Braud, Wellman**
See Breaux, Wellman

**Brauer-Tuchorze, Johann Ernst**
1863- ? [LAO]
*German editor and author*
* Lemmitz, Hans

**Braughal, Michael** 1878-1936 [SC]
*American actor*
* Hall, John

**Braun, Augusta-Johanna** 1931-
[OP]
*German opera singer*
* Braun, Gustl

**Braun, Bob**
See Brown, Robert Earl

**Braun, Gustl**
See Braun, Augusta-Johanna

**Braun, Meyer** 20th c. [RBE]
*Boxing promoter*
* Braun, Rex

**Braun, Rex**
See Braun, Meyer

**Braun, Thomas Eugene** 1945-
[BLB]
*American murderer*
* Ford, Mike

**Braun, Valentine** 1891-1948
[RBE, SG]
*American boxer*
* Brown, Knockout

**Braun-Vogelstein, Julie** 1883-
[LAO]
*German archaeologist and author*
* Vogelstein, Julie

**Brav, Stanley R[osenbaum]** 1908-
[CA]
*American clergyman and author*
* Barkton, S. Rush

**[The] Brave**
See Alfonso IV [Affonso, Alfonzo, or Alphonso]

**[The] Brave**
See Canute II

**[The] Brave**
See Mohammed X

**[Le] Brave des Braves**
See De Balbe de Crillon, Louis

**[The] Brave Fleming**
See Van der Mersch, Jean Andre

**Brave Woman of South Africa**
See Bam, Brigalia

**[The] Bravest of the Brave**
See De Balbe de Crillon, Louis

**[The] Bravest of the Brave**
See Ney, Michel [Duc
d'Elchingen]

**[El] Bravo**
See Sancho IV

**Bray, Adele**
See Kendrick, Mrs. F. M.

**Bray, Alison**
See Rowland, D[onald] S[ydney]

**Bray, Buster**
See Bray, Clarence Wilbur

**Bray, Clarence Wilbur** 1913- [BE]
*American baseball player*
* Bray, Buster

**Brayce, William**
See Rowland, D[onald] S[ydney]

**Braymer, Marguerite**
See Dodd, Marguerite

**Brayton, Gertrude E.** 20th c. [SFL]
*Author*
* Bryat, Edith

**Braza, Jacque**
See McKeag, Ernest L[ionel]

**Brazeau, Buzz**
See Brazeau, Philip H.

**Brazeau, Philip H.** 1949- [SMG]
*American football player*
* Brazeau, Buzz

**Brazelton, Ethel M. Colson** 20th c.
[NAA]
*British-born American author and lecturer*
* Colson, Ethel M.

**[The] Brazilian Bombshell**
See Da Cunha, Maria Do Carmo

**[The] Brazilian Humboldt**
See Rodrigues Ferreira, Alexander

**Brazle, Al**
See Brazle, Alpha Eugene

**Brazle, Alpha Eugene** 1914-1973
[BE]
*American baseball player*
* Brazle, Al
* Brazle, Cotton

**Brazle, Cotton**
See Brazle, Alpha Eugene

**Brazos, Waco**
See   Jennings, Michael

**Brdlbrmpft**
See   Roth, Christian

**[The] Break Away Kid**
See   Lefley, Charles Thomas

**Breakspear, Nicholas** 1100-1159
[HN, WBD]
*Pope*
* Adrian IV
* [The] English Pope

**Breakwell, Breakleg**
See   Breakwell, Dennis

**Breakwell, Dennis** 1948-   [DC]
*British cricketer*
* Breakwell, Breakleg

**Brearley, John**
See   Garbutt, John L.

**Brearley, John Michael** 1942-   [DC]
*British cricketer*
* Brearley, Scagg

**Brearley, Scagg**
See   Brearley, John Michael

**Breau, Harold** 1916-   [CWG]
*American country-western performer*
* Lone Pine, Hal

**Breaux, Wellman** 1891-1966
[WWJ]
*American jazz musician*
* Braud, Wellman

**Brebner, Percy James** 1864-1922
[SFL, WGT, WWL]
*British author*
* Lys, Christian

**Brecheen, Harry David** 1914-
[BE, BN, PB]
*American baseball player*
* Brecheen, Weasel
* [The] Cat

**Brecheen, Weasel**
See   Brecheen, Harry David

**Brechin, Carlyse Bliss** 20th c.
[IAW]
*American poet*
* Bliss, Carlyse

**[The] Brechin Poet**
See   Laing, Alexander

**Brecht, Bertolt**
See   Brecht, Eugen Berthold
Friedrich

**Brecht, Eugen Berthold Friedrich**
1898-1956   [BEW]
*German playwright*
* Brecht, Bertolt

**Breck, Vivian**
See   Breckenfeld, Vivian Gurney

**Breckenfeld, Vivian Gurney** 1895-
[CA, MJA, SAT]
*American author*
* Breck, Vivian

**Breckinridge, John** 19th c.   [FFF]
*Canadian author*
* Halcro, Claud

**Breckler, Rosemary** 1920-   [CA]
*American author and playwright*
* Winters, Rosemary

**Breda, Tjalmar**
See   DeJong, David C[ornel]

**Bredon, John**
See   Taylor, W. T.

**Bredow, Miriam**
See   Wolf, Miriam Bredow

**[The] Breeches Maker**
See   Ricciarelli, Daniele

**Breeden, Brick**
See   Breeden, John

**Breeden, John** 1904-   [BB]
*American basketball coach*
* Breeden, Brick

**Breeden, Leon** 1921-
*American jazz musician and
educator*
* Black Cloud, Chief

**Breedlove, Craig**
See   Breedlove, Norman

**Breedlove, Norman** 1938-   [IPA]
*American auto racer*
* Breedlove, Craig

**Breen, Dana**
See   Birksted-Breen, Dana

**Breen, Hurley** 1913-1963   [SC]
*American actor and boxer*
* Breen, Red

**Breen, Red**
See   Breen, Hurley

**Breese, Lou**
See   Calabreese, Lou

**Breetveld, Jim Patrick** 1925-   [CA]
*American author and editor*
* Mann, Avery

**[Le] Bref**
See   Pepin III

**Breinburg, Petronella** 1927-
[CA, SAT]
*Surinamese-born author and
playwright*
* Ashey, Bella
* Totham, Mary

**Breinlinger, Alice Berend** 1878- ?
[LAO]
*German author*
* Berend, Alice

**Breit, William [Leo]** 1933-   [CA]
*American economist and author*
* Jevons, Marshall [joint
    pseudonym with K. G. Elzinga]

**Breitberg, Louis** 1910-   [BEW]
*American director, writer, educator*
* Warren, Brett

**Breitenberger, Edward** 1933-   [FC]
*American actor*
* Byrnes, Edd

**Breitenfeld, Paul Emile** 1924-1977
[EJ, PMJ]
*American jazz musician*
* Desmond, Paul

**Breitmann, Hans**
See   Leland, Charles Godfrey

**Brema, Marie**
See   Fehrman, Minny

**Bremer, B. E.** 1904-1974   [B10]
*American petroleum geologist*
* Bremer, Boots

**Bremer, Boots**
See   Bremer, B. E.

**Bremer, Ward**
See   Reach, James

**Bremyer, Jayne Dickey** 1924-   [CA]
*American writer*
* Dickey, Lee

**Brenan, [Edward Fitz-] Gerald**
1894-   [CA, SFL]
*Maltese-born author*
* Beaton, George

**Brenda**
See   Smith, Mrs. Castle

**Brendall, Edith**
See   Bertin, Eddy C[harly]

**Brenegan, Olaf Selmer** 1890-1956
[BE]
*American baseball player*
* Brenegan, Sam

**Brenegan, Sam**
See   Brenegan, Olaf Selmer

**Brenet, Michel**
See   Bobillier, Marie

**Brengle, William** [house pseudonym]
See   Browne, Howard

**Brennan, Ad**
See   Brennan, Addison Foster

**Brennan, Addison Foster**
1881-1962   [BE]
*American baseball player*
* Brennan, Ad

**Brennan, Bill**
See   Schenck, William

**Brennan, Charles** 1895-1961   [SC]
*American actor and circus performer*
* O'Brien, Shots

**Brennan, Charles** 20th c.   [WWL]
*Irish poet and author*
* O Breanndain, Cathaoir

**Brennan, Christopher** [joint
pseudonym with Christopher
Kininmonth]
See   Baird, Roland

**Brennan, Christopher** [joint
pseudonym with Roland Baird]
See   Kininmonth, Christopher

**Brennan, John N[eedham] H[uggard]**
1914-   [AW, CA, CC]
*Irish author*
* Welcome, John

**Brennan, Joseph L[omas]** 1903-
[CA, SAT]
*American author*
* Graystone, Lynn
* Lomas, Steve

**Brennan, Joseph R.** 1900-   [BBH]
*American basketball player*
* Brennan, Poison Joe

**Brennan, Poison Joe**
See   Brennan, Joseph R.

**Brennan, Rudolph Cameron**
1894-1958   [SC]
*American actor*
* Cameron, Rudolph [Rudy]

**Brennan, Tim**
See   Conroy, John Wesley [Jack]

**Brennand, Frank**
See   Lambert, Eric

**Brenner, Bert**
See   Brenner, Delbert Henry

**Brenner, Delbert Henry** 1887-   [BE]
*American baseball player*
* Brenner, Bert
* Brenner, Dutch

**Brenner, Dutch**
See   Brenner, Delbert Henry

**Brenner, Isabel**
See   Schuchman, Joan

**Brenner, Peter**
See   Felsenstein, Peter

**Brennglas, Adolf**
See   Glassbrenner, Adolf

**Brenning, L. H.**
See   Hunter, [Alfred] John

**Brent, Calvin**
See   Hornby, John [Wilkinson]

**Brent, Evelyn**
See   Riggs, Mary Elizabeth

**Brent, Francis**
See   Hunter, [Alfred] John

**Brent, George**
See   Nolan, George Brent

**Brent, Harold Patrick** 1943-   [CA]
*American author*
* Brent, Harry

**Brent, Harry**
See   Brent, Harold Patrick

**Brent, Henry J.**   [FFF]
*Author*
* Stirrup

**Brent, Herel**
See   Brown, Ralph Lawrence

**Brent, Linda**
See   Jacobs, Harriet

**Brent, Loring**
See   Worts, George Frank

**Brent, Marion**
See   Elroy, Mrs. Edwin

**Brent, Nigel**
See   Wimhurst, Cecil Gordon
[Eugene]

**Brent, Peter [Ludwig]** 1931-
[CA, WD]
*British author*
* Peters, Ludovic

**Brent, Romney**
See   Larralde, Romulo, Jr.

**Brent, Stuart**
See   Brodsky, Stuart

**Brentano, Elizabeth** 1785-1859
[DNNF, PA]
*German author*
* Bettina

**Brentford, Burke**
See   Urner, Nathan D.

**Brentnall, Margaret Elizabeth**
1912-   [IAW]
*British author and journalist*
* Bell, Elizabeth

**Brenton, Buck**
See   Brenton, Lynn Davis

**Brenton, Herb**
See   Brenton, Lynn Davis

**Brenton, Lynn Davis** 1889-1968
[BE]
*American baseball player*
* Brenton, Buck
* Brenton, Herb

**Breon, Edmund**
See McLaverty, Edmund

**Brereton, Jane Hughes** 1685-1740
[FFF]
*British poet*
* Melissa

**Brereton, John Le Gay** 1871- ?
[LAO]
*Australian educator and poet*
* Garstang, Basil

**Brereton, Mrs. Austin** [FFF]
*Entertainer*
* Bland, Edith

**Breshkovsky, Catherine** 1844-1934
[WBD]
*Russian revolutionist*
* Babushka
* [The] Grandmother of the
Russian Revolution

**Breslau, Frank J.** 1887- [EJS]
*Austrian-born American basketball
coach and promoter*
* Basloe, Frank J.

**Breslin, William J.** 1885-1962
[BX, RBE]
*American boxer*
* [The] Boxing Marvel
* Britton, Jack

**Bresnahan, Duke**
See Bresnahan, Roger Philip

**Bresnahan, Roger Philip**
1879?-1944 [BAB, BE, PB]
*American baseball player*
* Bresnahan, Duke
* [The] Duke
* [The] Duke of Tralee

**Bresnan, Catharine Mary** 1904-
[NAA]
*American lyricist and writer*
* Canty, Cathal

**Bressano [or Brescianino], Girolamo**
See Muziano, Girolamo

**Bressler, Raymond Bloom**
1894-1966 [AS, DGS, PB]
*American baseball player*
* Bressler, Rube

**Bressler, Rube**
See Bressler, Raymond Bloom

**Brest, George K. A.** 1884?-1952
[F2, FC]
*British actor*
* Arthur, George K.

**Brestowski, Carl August** 1861- ?
[LAO]
*Austrian chemist and author*
* Troll, Gustav

**Bretagne**
See Cheque, Pierre

**Bretherton, Fred Spencer** ?-1952
[SC]
*American actor*
* Spencer, Fred

**Bretherton, Ralph Harold** 1877- ?
[WWL]
*British author*
* Ralp, Howard

**Bretnor, Reginald** 1911- [CA]
*Russian-born American author and
editor*
* Briarton, Grendel

**Breton-Smith, Clare** 1906- [AW]
*British author*
* Caldwell, Elinor
* Vernon, Claire
* Wilde, Hilary

**Brett, Anthony** 1861-1948 [BF]
*British actor*
* Norwood, Ellie

**Brett, David**
See Campbell, Will D[avis]

**Brett, Duke**
See Brett, Herb[ert James]

**Brett, George Howard** 1953- [BE]
*American baseball player*
* Brett, Kemer

**Brett, George Ira**
See Crawfurd, Oswald John
Frederick

**Brett, Hawkesley**
See Bell, Robert Stanley Warren

**Brett, Herb[ert James]** 1900- [BE]
*American baseball player*
* Brett, Duke

**Brett, Jeremy**
See Huggins, Jeremy

**Brett, John Michael**
See Tripp, Miles [Barton]

**Brett, Kemer**
See Brett, George Howard

**Brett, Leo**
See Fanthorpe, R[obert] Lionel

**Brett, Martin**
See Sanderson, [Ronald] Douglas

**Brett, Mary Elizabeth** 20th c.
[AW, CA]
*British author and illustrator*
* Brett, Molly

**Brett, Michael**
See Tripp, Miles [Barton]

**Brett, Molly**
See Brett, Mary Elizabeth

**Brett, Stanley**
See Hicks, Stanley

**Breuer, Adonis**
See Breuer, Marvin Howard

**Breuer, Baby Face**
See Breuer, Marvin Howard

**Breuer, Marvin Howard** 1914-
[BE, BN]
*American baseball player*
* Breuer, Adonis
* Breuer, Baby Face

**Breuer, Theresa** 1931- [RO1]
*American singer*
* Brewer, Teresa

**Breval, Lucienne**
See Schilling, Bertha

**Breville, Pierre**
See Hippolyte, Dominique

**Brevoort, Laurence**
See Barretto, Larry

**[The] Brewer**
See Whitbread, Samuel

**Brewer, Blind Jimmy**
See Brewer, James [Jimmy]

**Brewer, Brew**
See Brewer, James Thomas

**Brewer, Brew**
See Brewer, Jim

**Brewer, Buddy**
See Brewer, John Herndon [Jack]

**Brewer, Fireball**
See Brewer, James Thomas

**Brewer, Fredric [Aldwyn]** 1921-
[CA]
*American writer and editor*
* Wynn, Alfred

**Brewer Gabriel**
See Richardson, Gabriel

**Brewer, James [Jimmy]** 1921-
[BWW, NBB]
*American singer*
* Brewer, Blind Jimmy

**Brewer, James Thomas** 1937-
[SMG]
*American baseball player*
* Brewer, Brew
* Brewer, Fireball

**Brewer, Jim** 1951- [BB, SMG]
*American basketball player*
* Brewer, Brew
* Brewer, Papa

**Brewer, John Herndon [Jack]**
1919- [BE]
*American baseball player*
* Brewer, Buddy

**Brewer, John L.** 1937- [FB]
*American football player*
* Brewer, Tonto

**Brewer, Mike**
See Guinness, Maurice C.

**[The] Brewer of Ghent**
See Artevelde, Jacob van

**Brewer, Papa**
See Brewer, Jim

**Brewer, Peaches**
See Brewer, Sherry

**Brewer, Sherry** 20th c. [IBW]
*American actress, dancer, costume
designer*
* Brewer, Peaches

**Brewer, Teresa**
See Breuer, Theresa

**Brewer, Tonto**
See Brewer, John L.

**Brewer, William A.** [FFF]
*American writer*
* Mercator
* Wilhelm

**Brewery Jack Taylor**
See Taylor, John B.

**Brewster, Benjamin** [joint
pseudonym with Franklin (Brewster)
Folsom]
See Elting, Mary

**Brewster, Benjamin** [joint
pseudonym with Mary Elting]
See Folsom, Franklin [Brewster]

**Brewster, Darrell** 20th c. [SMG]
*American football coach*
* Brewster, Pete

**Brewster, Kingman, Jr.** 1920-
*American college president and
diplomat*
* [The] King

**Brewster, Pete**
See Brewster, Darrell

**Breydel, Charles** 1677-1744
[FFF, RH, SN]
*Flemish painter*
* [The] Cavalier
* [Le] Chevalier

**Brezin, Fred**
See Brezinski, Max Frederick

**Brezina, Greg** 20th c.
*American football player*
* [The] Reverend

**Brezina, Otokar**
See Jebavy, Vaclav Ignac

**Brezinski, Max Frederick** 1886-
[BMH]
*British magician*
* Brezin, Fred
* Prince Kuroki

**Brial, Michel-Jean-Joseph**
1743-1828 [SN]
*French historian and author*
* [The] Father of French History

**Brian**
See Powell, Brian

**Brian, Alan B.**
See Parulski, George R[ichard], Jr.

**Brian, B.**
See Speck, Richard Franklin

**Brian Boru** 926-1014 [HN]
*King of Ireland*
* [The] Conqueror of the Danes

**Brian, James**
See Street, Arthur George

**Brian, Mary**
See Dantzler, Louise

**Briand, Rena**
See Huxley, Rena

**[The] Briareus of Languages**
See Mezzofanti, Giuseppe

**[The] Briareus of Music**
See Handel, Georg Friedrich

**Briarly, Mary**
See Ritchie, [Mary] Lily Munsell

**Briarton, Grendel**
See Bretnor, Reginald

**Brice, Betty** 1892-1935 [SC]
*American actress*
* Brice, Rosetta

**Brice, Douglas Francis Aloysius**
1916- [IAW]
*British author and clergyman*
* Forest, John
* Jackson, Peter

**Brice, Fanny**
See Borach, Fannie

**Brice, Marvelle** 1891?-1962 [BEW]
*American-born writer, producer,
director*
* Brice, Monte

**Brice, Monte**
See Brice, Marvelle

**Brice, Rosetta**
See Brice, Betty

**[The] Brick and Mortar Priest**
See McIntyre, James Francis

**Brick, George Washington**
See Hatcher, John E.

**Brick, Jefferson**
See Black, Alexander

**Brick, Richard**
See Duncan, J.

**Brick, Titus**
See Seaman, Augustus

**Brick, Titus A.**
See File, Charles E.

**Brick, Titus A.**
See Hotten, John Camden

**Brick Top Smith**
See Smith, Ada Beatrice Queen
Victoria Louisa Virginia Du Conge

**[The] Bricklayer**
See Jonson, Ben[jamin]

**Bricklayer, Peter**
See Balluseck, Daniel J. Von

**Brickman, William W.** 1913-
[IAW]
*American author*
* Paidagogos, Petros

**Brickner, Brick**
See Brickner, Ralph Harold

**Brickner, Gustave** 20th c. [BBH]
*Swimmer*
* [The] Human Polar Bear

**Brickner, Ralph Harold** 1925- [BE]
*American baseball player*
* Brickner, Brick

**Bricktop**
See Small, George

**Bricuth, John**
See Irwin, John T[homas]

**Bride, St.**
See Bridget [or Brigette]

**Bridge, Ann**
See O'Malley, Mary Dolling
[Sanders]

**Bridge, Bonar**
See Tullock, W. W.

**Bridge, Frank J.**
See Brueckel, Francis J.

**Bridge, James Howard** 1858-1939
[SFL]
*Author*
* Brydges, Harold

**Bridgecross, Peter**
See Cardinal, Roger [Thomas]

**Bridgeman, Irene**
See Dancyger, Irene

**Bridgeman, Junior**
See Bridgeman, Ulysses

**Bridgeman, Richard**
See Davies, Leslie Purnell

**Bridgeman, Ulysses** 1953- [SMG]
*American basketball player*
* Bridgeman, Junior

**Bridger, Adam**
See Bingley, David Ernest

**Bridger, John**
See Gibson, Joe

**Bridges, Everett Lamar** 1927-
[BE, PB]
*American baseball player*
* Bridges, Rocky

**Bridges, Howard**
See Staples, Reginald Thomas

**Bridges, Marshall** 1931- [BE]
*American baseball player*
* Bridges, Sheriff

**Bridges, Robert** 1844-1930 [TC]
*British poet*
* [The] Silent Laureate

**Bridges, Robert** 1858- ? [NAA]
*American critic and editor*
* Droch

**Bridges, Rocky**
See Bridges, Everett Lamar

**Bridges, Sallie**
See Stebbins, Mrs. S. B.

**Bridges, Sheriff**
See Bridges, Marshall

**Bridges, T. C.**
See Bridges, Thomas Charles

**Bridges, Thomas Charles**
1868-1944 [MBF, SFL, WGT]
*British author*
* Beck, Christopher
* Bridges, T. C.
* T. C. B.

**Bridges, Victor** 20th c. [MBF]
*British author*
* James, Vernon

**Bridget [or Brigette]** 450?- 523
[DNNS, HN, RH]
*Saint*
* Bride, St.
* [The] Mary of the Gael
* [The] Pearl of Ireland

**Bridgetower, George Augustus
Polgreen** 1779-1860 [SN]
*Polish-born composer and musician*
* [The] Abyssinian Prince

**Bridgewater, Dee Dee**
See Bridgewater, Denise

**Bridgewater, Denise** 1950- [EJ7]
*American singer*
* Bridgewater, Dee Dee

**Bridgewater, John William Stevenson**
1893- [THR]
*British actor*
* Kove, Kenneth

**Bridgman, Geraldine**
See Jerrold, Ianthe

**Bridgman, Sarah Atherton**
1889?-1975 [CA]
*American author*
* Atherton, Sarah

**Bridie, James**
See Mavor, Osborne Henry

**Brief, Anthony Vincent**
See Bordetzki, Antonio

**Brief, Bunny**
See Bordetzki, Antonio

**Briefer, Richard [Dick]** 1915-
[WECO]
*American cartoonist*
* Brant, Remington
* Norman, Richard
* Stein, Frank N.

**Briegleb, Gus**
See Briegleb, William G.

**Briegleb, William G.** 20th c. [BBH]
*American airplane designer and
aviator*
* Briegleb, Gus

**Brien, Raley**
See McCulley, Johnston

**Brierley, Robert Benjamin** 1875- ?
[WWL]
*British author*
* A.
* Ab-O'Th'-Yate
* Bossu

**Brierwood, Frank**
See Clifton, Mabel

**Brigance**
See Brigance, Thomas F.

**Brigance, Thomas F.** 1913- [WFA]
*American fashion designer*
* Brigance

**Briggs, Buttons**
See Briggs, Herbert Theodore

**Briggs, Charles Frederick**
1804-1877 [DEL, FFF, PA]
*American author and journalist*
* Franco, Harry

**Briggs, Emily Edson** 1831-1910
[FFF, PA]
*American author*
* Olivia

**Briggs, Hedley**
See Gawthorne-Briggs, Hedley

**Briggs, Helen Virginia** 1910-
[CED, F2, FC]
*American actress*
* Bruce, Virginia

**Briggs, Herbert Theodore**
1875-1911 [BE]
*American baseball player*
* Briggs, Buttons

**Briggs, Jimuel**
See Thompson, Phillips

**Briggs, Philip**
See Briggs, Phyllis

**Briggs, Phyllis** 20th c. [SFL]
*Author*
* Briggs, Philip

**Bright Eyes** 1854-1903 [B10]
*Advocate of American Indian rights*
* La Flesche, Susette

**Bright Eyes Delaney**
See Chapdelaine, Ovila

**Bright, Gerald** 1904-1974 [PMJ]
*British bandleader*
* Geraldo

**Bright, J. H.** 1804-1837 [FFF, PA]
*American poet*
* Viator

**Bright, James**
See Rowe, John Gabriel

**Bright, John** 1811-1889
[DEP, DHA, RH]
*British orator and statesman*
* [The] Apostle of Free Trade
* [The] Tribune of the People

**Bright, Mary Chavelita [Dunne]**
1860-1945 [TC]
*British author, playwright,
translator*
* Egerton, George

**Bright, Matilda A.** [PA]
*Author*
* Lyndon

**Bright, Robert** 1902- [TCC]
*American author and poet*
* Douglas, Michael

**Brighte, John**
See Duncan, J.

**Brighton, Wesley, Jr.**
See Lovin, Roger Robert

**Brightwell, Richard**
See Frith, John

**Brightwell, Thomas** [PA]
*Author*
* T. B.

**Briguglio, Sally Bugs**
See Briguglio, Salvatore

**Briguglio, Salvatore** 20th c.
*American underworld figure*
* Briguglio, Sally Bugs

**Briles, Nellie**
See Briles, Nelson Kelley

**Briles, Nelson Kelley** 1943- [SMG]
*American baseball player*
* Briles, Nellie

**Brilhante, Patricia** 1923-1963 [SC]
*American actress and dancer*
* Brill, Patti
* Paige, Patsy

**Brill, Ethel Claire** 20th c. [NAA]
*American author*
* Burritt, Edwin C.

**Brill, Patti**
See Brilhante, Patricia

**Brillheart, Buck**
See Brillheart, James Benson [Jim]

**Brillheart, James Benson [Jim]**
1903-1972 [BE]
*American baseball player*
* Brillheart, Buck

**[The] Brilliant Madman**
See Charles XII

**[El] Brilliantino [The Little Shiny
One]**
See Gomez, Alfredo

**Brimmer, Ernest Carlton**
1894-1949 [BDF, BEW, FC]
*American actor*
* Dix, Richard

**Brimmer, Son**
See Shade, Will

**Brimsek, Francis Charles [Frank]**
1915- [CEI, FHE, SR]
*American hockey player*
* Brimsek, Frigid Frankie
* Zero, Kid

**Brimsek, Francis Charles [Frank]**
(Continued)
* Zero, Mr.

**Brimsek, Frigid Frankie**
See Brimsek, Francis Charles
[Frank]

**Brind, Smylla** 1928- [FC, IPA]
*American actress*
* Brown, Vanessa

**Brindamour**
See Collin, Jacques Albin Simon

**Brindle, Ernest** 20th c. [MBF]
*British author*
* Bayne, Peter

**Brindley, Charles** [PA]
*Author*
* Hieover, Harry

**Brindmour, George** 1870-1941
[SC]
*American actor*
* [The] Handcuff King

**Briney, Robert E[dward]** 1933-
[WGT]
*American author*
* Duane, Andrew

**Brinitzer, Carl** 1907-1974 [CA]
*German-born British author,*
*translator, broadcaster*
* Usikota

**Brinker, Dode**
See Brinker, William Hutchinson
[Bill]

**Brinker, Martin**
See Walters, Marvin M.

**Brinker, William Hutchinson [Bill]**
1883-1965 [BE]
*American baseball player*
* Brinker, Dode

**Brinkman, Brink**
See Brinkman, Edwin Albert
[Eddie]

**Brinkman, Edwin Albert [Eddie]**
1941- [SMG]
*American baseball player*
* Brinkman, Brink

**Brinsmead, H. F.**
See Brinsmead, Hesba Fay

**Brinsmead, Hesba Fay** 1922- [CA]
*Australian writer*
* Brinsmead, H. F.
* Hungerford, Pixie

**Brinton, Henry** 1901-
[CA, CC, WW]
*British author*
* Fraser, Alex

**Briody, Alderman**
See Briody, Charles F.

**Briody, Charles F.** 1858- ? [BE]
*American baseball player*
* Briody, Alderman
* Briody, Fatty

**Briody, Fatty**
See Briody, Charles F.

**Brion, Guy**
See Madsen, Axel

**Briony, Henry**
See Ellis, Oliver C. De C.

**Briosco, Andrea** 1470?-1532
[WBD]
*Italian sculptor and architect*
* Riccio, Andrea

**Briquet, Jean**
See Philipp, Adolph

**Brisbane, Coutts**
See Armour, R. Coutts

**Brisbois, Austin Dean** 1937?-1978
[FIR]
*American jazz musician*
* Brisbois, Bud

**Brisbois, Bud**
See Brisbois, Austin Dean

**Brisco, Pat A.**
See Matthews, Patricia [Brisco]

**Brisco, Patty** [joint pseudonym with
Patricia (Brisco) Matthews]
See Matthews, Clayton

**Brisco, Patty** [joint pseudonym with
Clayton Matthews]
See Matthews, Patricia [Brisco]

**Briscoe, Arthur John Trevor**
1873-1943 [DBA]
*British painter, yachtsman, author*
* Hitch, Clove

**Briscoe, Margaret Sutton**
See Hopkins, Margaret Briscoe

**Briscoe, Marlin** 1945- [FB]
*American football player*
* [The] Magician

**Brissard, Montague**
See Bedford-Jones, Henry [James
O'Brien]

**Brissie, Leland Victor, Jr.** 1924-
[BE, PB]
*American baseball player*
* Brissie, Lou

**Brissie, Lou**
See Brissie, Leland Victor, Jr.

**Brisson, Carl**
See Pederson, Carl

**Brissot, Jean-Pierre** 1754-1793
[HN]
*French journalist and revolutionary*
*leader*
* De Warville

**Brissot, Roland** 1560-1643 [PA]
*Author*
* Sauvage, Sieur du

**Bristed, Charles Astor** 1820-1874
[FFF, PA]
*American author*
* Benson, Carl

**Brister, Richard** 1915- [CA]
*American author*
* Grove, Will O.
* Lewin, C. L.
* Richmond, George

**[The] Bristol Boy**
See Chatterton, Thomas

**Bristol, James David** 1933- [SMG]
*American baseball player*
* Double O

**Bristol, John A.**
See Speer, Jack

**Bristol, Julius**
See Abel, Alan [Irwin]

**Britain, Dan**
See Pendleton, Don[ald Eugene]

**Britannicus**
See Germanicus, Claudius Tiberius

**Britchforth, Eustace** 20th c. [RO2]
*American musician*
* Baker, Lefty

**Britindian**
See Solomon, Samuel

**[The] British Aristides**
See Marvell, Andrew

**[The] British Bayard**
See Sidney, [Sir] Philip

**[The] British Cicero**
See Pitt, William [Earl of
Chatham]

**[The] British Hector**
See Nennius

**[The] British Hippocrates**
See Sydenham, Thomas

**[The] British Homer**
See Chaucer, Geoffrey

**[The] British Homer**
See Milton, John

**[The] British Jeremiah**
See Gildas [or Gildus]

**[The] British Pausanias**
See Camden, William

**[The] British Pindar**
See Gray, Thomas

**[The] British Poussin**
See Cooper, Richard

**[The] British Roscius**
See Betterton, Thomas

**[The] British Roscius**
See Burbage, Richard

**[The] British Roscius**
See Garrick, David

**[The] British Samson**
See Topham, Thomas

**[The] British Spy**
See Wirt, William

**[The] British Strabo**
See Camden, William

**[The] British Varro**
See Tusser, Thomas

**Brito, Phil**
See Colombrito, Philip

**Brito e Cunha, Jose Carlos de**
1884-1950 [WEC]
*Brazilian cartoonist*
* Carlos, J.

**Britt, Chippy**
See Britt, George

**Britt, Elton**
See Baker, James Britt

**Britt, George**
See Sealey, Leonard George
William

**Britt, George** 20th c. [OBW]
*American baseball player*
* Britt, Chippy

**Britt, May**
See Wilkens, Maybritt

**Britt, Sappho Henderson**
See Woolfolk, Josiah Pitts

**Britta**
See Bauer, Britta

**Brittain, Noel**
See Lumb, Emmeline

**Brittain, William** 1930- [CA]
*American author*
* Knox, James

**Brittan, Belle**
See Fuller, Hiram

**Brittany, Louis**
See Teed, George Heber Hamilton

**Brittle, Gath**
See McAlpine, Robert W.

**Britton, Barbara**
See Czukor, Barbara Brantingham

**Britton, Colonel**
See Ritchie, Douglas

**Britton, Herbert**
See Eves, Reginald T.

**Britton, Jack**
See Breslin, William J.

**Britton, Keith**
See Britza, Eli

**Britton, Mary E.** 1873- ? [IBW]
*American columnist*
* Aunt Peggy
* Britton, Meb

**Britton, Mattie Lula Cooper** 1914-
[CA]
*American author and educator*
* Cooper, Mattie Lula
* Patterson, Jane

**Britton, Meb**
See Britton, Mary E.

**Britton, Milt**
See Levy, Milton

**Britton, Peter Ewart** 1936- [CA]
*British author*
* Lemesurier, Peter

**Britton, Rollin J.** 1863- ? [NAA]
*American attorney and author*
* Blue, Guy

**Britton, Thomas** 1650?-1714
[HN, RH, SN]
*British musician and coal dealer*
* [The] Musical Small-Coal Man

**Britza, Eli** 1919-1970 [SC]
*American actor*
* Britton, Keith

**Britzius, Albert** [PA]
*Author*
* Gotthelf, Geremias

**Briusov, Valeri Yakovlevich**
1873-1924 [WGT]
*Russian author*
* Brussof, Valery

**Brix, Herman** 1909- [FC, ITA, TF]
*American actor and athlete*
* Bennett, Bruce

**Brkovich, Mike** 20th c.
*Canadian-born basketball player*
* [The] Golden Arm

**Broad, Broadie**
See Broad, [Brian] Chris[topher]

**Broad, [Brian] Chris[topher]** 1957-
[DC]
*British cricketer*
* Broad, Broadie

**Broad, Kid**
*See* Thomas, William M.

**Broadbent, Amanda** 1939-
[FC, TR]
*British actress*
* Barrie, Amanda

**Broadbent, Charles**
*See* Halpine, Charles Graham

**Broadbent, Dora** 1923?-
[EMT, FC, TR]
*British actress and singer*
* Bryan, Dora

**Broadbent, Harry L.** 1892?-1971
[CEI, FHE, HK]
*Canadian-born hockey player*
* Broadbent, Punch

**Broadbent, Punch**
*See* Broadbent, Harry L.

**Broadbottom, Geffery**
*See* Stanhope, Philip Dormer

**Broadfield, Aubrey Alfred [Alan]**
1910- [ART]
*British author and librarian*
* A. B.

**Broadfield, Robina Margaret** 20th
c. [ART]
*British painter*
* R. M. B.

**Broadwater, C. C.** 20th c.
*American business executive*
* Broadwater, Pete

**Broadwater, Pete**
*See* Broadwater, C. C.

**Broadway Aleck Smith**
*See* Smith, Alexander Benjamin

**Broadway Joe Namath**
*See* Namath, Joseph W.

**Broadway's Cockney Star**
*See* Hicks, Thomas

**Broadway's Queen of Song and Jazz**
*See* Bentley, Gladys Alberta

**Broccoli, Albert R.** 1909- [FC]
*American producer*
* Broccoli, Cubby

**Broccoli, Cubby**
*See* Broccoli, Albert R.

**Broch**
*See* Sonsteby, Gunnar

**Brochet, Jean-Alexandre**
1921-1963 [CC]
*French author*
* Bruce, Jean

**Brock, Alan St. Hill** 1886- [WW]
*Author*
* Dewdney, Peter

**Brock, Gavin**
*See* Lindsay, [John] Maurice

**Brock, [Sir] Isaac** 1769-1812
[WBD]
*British army officer*
* [The] Hero of Upper Canada

**Brock, Lou[is Clark]** 1939-     [SMG]
*American baseball player*
* [The] Base Burglar

**Brock, Lynn**
*See* McAllister, Alister

**Brock, Rose**
*See* Hansen, Joseph

**Brock, Sallie A.**
*See* Putnam, Sarah A.

**Brock, Stuart**
*See* Trimble, Louis P[reston]

**Brockbank, Dora** ?-1966     [THR]
*British actress*
* Barton, Dora

**Brockett, King**
*See* Brockett, Lew[is Albert]

**Brockett, Lew[is Albert]** 1880-1960
[BE]
*American baseball player*
* Brockett, King

**Brockett, O. G.**
*See* Brockett, Oscar Gross

**Brockett, Oscar Gross** 1923-
[BEW]
*American educator and writer*
* Brockett, O. G.

**Brockies, Enid Florence** 1911-
[SFL, WGT]
*Author*
* Magriska, Helene

**Brockley, Fenton**
*See* Rowland, D[onald] S[ydney]

**[The] Brockton Blockbuster**
*See* Marchegiano, Rocco

**Brod, Ruth Hagy** 1911-1980     [CA]
*American author, journalist, literary
agent*
* Hagy, Ruth Geri

**Broda, Turk**
*See* Broda, Walter

**Broda, Walter** 1914-1972
[CEI, FHE, HK]
*Canadian-born hockey player*
* Broda, Turk

**Brodell, Joan** 1925-
[FC, PMJ, SW]
*American actress*
* Leslie, Joan

**Broderick, Mark**
*See* Thompson, Mrs. E. S. L.

**Broderick, Richard L[awrence]**
1927- [CA]
*American executive and author*
* Richards, Kenny

**Brodie, Julian Paul** 20th c.
[CC, WW]
*American author and advertising
executive*
* Denbie, Roger [joint pseudonym
with Alan (Baer) Green]

**Brodie, Steve**
*See* Brodie, Walter Scott

**Brodie, Steve**
*See* Stevens, John

**Brodie, Walter Scott** 1868-1935
[BE, DGS, PB]
*American baseball player*
* Brodie, Steve

**Brodin, Norbert** 1897-     [WEF]
*American cinematographer*
* Brodine, Norbert

**Brodine, Norbert**
*See* Brodin, Norbert

**Brodine, Virginia Warner** 1915-
[CA]
*American author*
* Warner, Virginia

**Brodnax, John W.** 20th c.     [SMG]
*American football player*
* Brodnax, Red

**Brodnax, Red**
*See* Brodnax, John W.

**Brodribb, Sydney** 1872-1914
[WBD]
*British actor and theatre manager*
* Irving, Lawrence

**Brodsky, Iosif Alexandrovich**
1940- [CA]
*Russian-born poet*
* Brodsky, Joseph

**Brodsky, Joseph**
*See* Brodsky, Iosif Alexandrovich

**Brodsky, Stuart** 20th c.     [CA]
*American author and critic*
* Brent, Stuart

**Brodt, Dottsy** 20th c.     [ECM]
*American country-western performer*
* Dottsy

**Brody, Ann**
*See* Goldstein, Ann Brody

**Brody, Marc**
*See* Wilkes-Hunter, Richard

**Broekel, Rainer Lothar** 1923-     [CA]
*German-born American author*
* Broekel, Ray

**Broekel, Ray**
*See* Broekel, Rainer Lothar

**Broemel, Rose** [WW]
*Author*
* D'Evelyn, Rose

**Brofeldt, Juhani** 1861-1921     [WBD]
*Finnish author*
* Aho, Juhani

**Brogan, [Sir] Denis William**
1900-1974 [LC]
*Scottish-born author and educator*
* Barrington, Maurice

**Brogan, Elise**
*See* Urch, Elizabeth

**Brogan, James**
*See* Hodder-Williams, John
Christopher Glazebrook

**Brogan the Scribe**
*See* Spickler, Charles A[braham]

**Brogdon, Roseea Arbana** 1926-
[CME]
*American country-western performer*
* Maddox, Rose

**Brogny [or Brogni], Cardinal de**
*See* Allarmet [or D'Alouzier], Jean

**Brogue, Roslyn**
*See* Henning, Roslyn Brogue

**Broido, Vera**
*See* Cohn, Vera

**Broil, Arlette B.** 20th c.     [IBW]
*American singer*
* Griffin, Bessie
* Queen of the South

**Brokamp, Marilyn** 1920-
[CA, SAT]
*American author and educator*
* Lynn, Mary

**Brokaw, Clare Boothe**
*See* Boothe, [Ann] Clare

**Bromberg, Gabriel** 20th c.     [EJS]
*American football player*
* Bromberg, Gay

**Bromberg, Gay**
*See* Bromberg, Gabriel

**Bromberg, J. Edward**
*See* Bromberger, J. Edward

**Bromberger, J. Edward** 1904-1951
[THR]
*American actor*
* Bromberg, J. Edward

**Brome, Alexander** 1620-1666     [SN]
*British poet and playwright*
* [The] English Anacreon

**Bromfield, Farron** 1922-
[FC, ITA, SW]
*American actor*
* Bromfield, John

**Bromfield, John**
*See* Bromfield, Farron

**Bromley, Henry Walter** 1879-
[NAA]
*American clergyman and author*
* Bayne, Henry Wyndel

**Bronc Man Walker**
*See* Walker, Enoch

**Bronco Billy Anderson**
*See* Aaronson, Max

**Bronkie, Dutch**
*See* Bronkie, Herman Charles

**Bronkie, Herman Charles**
1885-1968 [BE]
*American baseball player*
* Bronkie, Dutch

**Bronner, Ferdinand** 1867- ?     [LAO]
*German educator and author*
* Adamus, Franz

**Bronsart, Hans von**
*See* Bronsart von Schellendorf,
Hans

**Bronsart von Schellendorf, Hans**
1830-1913 [WBD]
*German musician and composer*
* Bronsart, Hans von

**Bronson, Charles**
*See* Buchinsky, Charles

**Bronson, Doctor**
*See* Peters, W. A.

**Bronson, Donna**
*See* Edelstein, Scott

**Bronson, Lita**
*See* Bell, Louise Price

**Bronson, Lynn**
*See* Lampman, Evelyn Sibley

**Bronson, Oliver**
*See* Rowland, D[onald] S[ydney]

**Bronstein, Lev Davidovich**
1879-1940 [F1, IPA, LC]
*Russian political leader*
* Trotsky, Leon

**Bronstein, Max** 1896- [JL]
*Israeli painter*
* Ardon, Mordecai

**Bronstein, Yetta**
*See* Abel, Jeanne

**Bronston, William**
*See* Brannon, William T.

**Bronte, Anne** 1820-1849 [DEL]
*British author*
* Bell, Acton

**Bronte, Charlotte** 1816-1855
[DEL]
*British author*
* Bell, Currer

**Bronte, Emily Jane** 1818-1848
[DEL]
*British author and poet*
* Bell, Ellis

**Bronte, Louisa**
*See* Roberts, Janet Louise

**[The] Bronx Beauty**
*See* Singer, Al

**[The] Bronx Bone-Crusher**
*See* Sloves, Herman

**[The] Bronx Bull**
*See* LaMotta, Jacob [Jake]

**Bronx, Pat**
*See* Schilperoort, Peter

**[The] Bronze Buckaroo**
*See* Jeffries, Herb[ert Jeffrey]

**[The] Bronze Goddess of Fire**
*See* Page, La Wanda

**[The] Bronze Titan**
*See* Maceo, Antonio

**Broodway, Van der Clyde**
1899-1972 [BMH]
*American female impersonator and trapeze artist*
* Barbette
* Barbette the Enigma

**Brook, Barnaby**
*See* Brooks, [William] Collin

**Brook, Clifford** 1887?-1974
[BDF, F2, FC]
*British actor*
* Brook, Clive

**Brook, Clive**
*See* Brook, Clifford

**Brook, Eric F.** 1908-1965 [OCS]
*British soccer player*
* Brook, Wandering Eric

**Brook, Fanshawe**
*See* Wyvill, Fanny Susan

**Brook, Nelsie**
*See* Ross, Ellen

**Brook Trout Lee**
*See* Lee, Bob

**Brook, Wandering Eric**
*See* Brook, Eric F.

**Brooke, A. B.**
*See* Jennings, Leslie Nelson

**Brooke, Arthur**
*See* Marshall, Arthur C.

**Brooke, Avery [Rogers]** 1923- [CA]
*American author and editor*
* Benjamin, Alice

**Brooke, Carol**
*See* Ramskill, Valerie Patricia
Roskams

**Brooke, F.** [PA]
*Author*
* Singleton, Mary, Spinster

**Brooke, Geoffrey Arthur George**
1920- [ART]
*British painter*
* G. A. G. B.

**Brooke, Gilbert Edward** 1873- ?
[LAO]
*British health officer and author*
* Sungei, Anak

**Brooke, Gustavus Vaughan**
1819-1862 [HN]
*Actor*
* [The] Hibernian Roscius

**Brooke, Hillary**
*See* Peterson, Beatrice

**Brooke, Magdalen**
*See* Capes, M. Harriet

**Brooke, Ralph**
*See* Brooks, Ralph Tweer

**Brooke, Ralph** 17th c. [SN]
*British politician*
* [A] Choleric Herault

**Brooke, Tyler**
*See* De Biere, Victor Huge

**Brooke, Valentine** 1912- [THR]
*British actor*
* Rooke, Valentine

**Brooke, Wesley**
*See* Lunt, George

**Brooke-Haven, P.**
*See* Wodehouse, Pelham Grenville

**Brookens, Edward Dwain** 1949-
[SMG]
*American baseball player*
* Brookens, Ike

**Brookens, Ike**
*See* Brookens, Edward Dwain

**Brooker, Bertram** 1888-1955
[B10, WW]
*Canadian advertising executive, author, artist*
* Herne, Huxley
* Surrey, Richard

**Brooker, Clark**
*See* Fowler, Kenneth A[brams]

**Brooker, Wallace**
*See* Daniels, Norman [A.]

**Brookholt, Henry**
*See* Buchholz [or Bucholz], Horst

**Brooklyn**
*See* Kinsella, Thomas

**[The] Brooklyn Billygoat**
*See* DeMarco, Pat

**[The] Brooklyn Kid**
*See* Murphy, Cicero

**[The] Brooklyn Schoolboy**
*See* Hoyt, Waite Charles

**Brookman, Rosina Francesca**
1932- [CA]
*Hungarian-born author*
* Francesca, Rosina

**Brooks, Alan**
*See* Fowler, Irving

**Brooks, Amy** 20th c. [ALY]
*American author*
* Loomis, Amy

**Brooks, Anita**
*See* Abramovitz, Anita [Zeltner
Brooks]

**Brooks, Anne Sooy** 1911- [ASC]
*American composer and singer*
* Savoy, Anne

**Brooks, Anne Tedlock** 1905- [CA]
*American author*
* Carter, Anne
* Millburn, Cynthia

**Brooks, Baby**
*See* Brooks, Roosevelt

**Brooks, Budda**
*See* Brooks, Charlie

**Brooks, Bully**
*See* Brooks, Preston Smith

**Brooks, C. W., Jr.** 20th c. [SFL]
*Author*
* Brooks, Ned

**Brooks, C. Wayland** ?-1957
*American politician*
* Brooks, Curly

**Brooks, Charlie** 20th c. [IBW]
*American horseman*
* Brooks, Sonny

**Brooks, Charlie** 20th c. [RBE]
*American boxer*
* Brooks, Budda

**Brooks, Chatty**
*See* Rice, Rosella

**Brooks, [William] Collin** 1893-
[WW, WWL]
*British author*
* Brook, Barnaby

**Brooks, Curly**
*See* Brooks, C. Wayland

**Brooks, David**
*See* Berger, Henry David

**Brooks, Douglas** 1942- [CA]
*British author and educator*
* Brooks-Davies, Douglas

**Brooks, Dynamite**
*See* Brooks, Joseph

**Brooks, Edwy Searles** 1889-1965
[EMD, MBF, WW]
*British author*
* Browne, Reginald
* Clifford, Martin [house
pseudonym]
* Comrade, Robert W.
* Gosfield, C. Heddingham
* Gray, Berkeley
* Greaves, Norman
* Gunn, Victor
* Halstead, E. Sinclair
* Halstead, S. B.
* Richards, Frank [house
pseudonym]
* Thornton, Edward

**Brooks, Erastus** 1815- ? [PA]
*Author*
* E. B.
* Erao
* M. D. C.

**Brooks, Garnet** 1937- [IBW]
*Canadian opera singer*
* Canada's Caruso

**Brooks, George**
*See* Baum, L[yman] Frank

**Brooks, Geraldine**
*See* Stroock, Geraldine

**Brooks, Inez Gwendolyn Elizabeth**
1917- [IBW]
*American author and poet*
* [The] Bard of Bronzevilla

**Brooks, James Gordon** 1801-1841?
[FFF, PA]
*American poet and journalist*
* Florio

**Brooks, Janice Young** 1943- [CA]
*American author*
* Singer, Amanda

**Brooks, Jennie**
*See* Beaman, Lottie Kimbrough

**Brooks, Jeremy** 1926- [AW, CA]
*British author*
* Meikle, Clive

**Brooks, John**
*See* Sugar, Bert Randolph

**Brooks, Jonathan**
*See* Mellett, John Calvin

**Brooks, Jonathan Joseph**
*See* Brozek, Jonathan Joseph

**Brooks, Joseph** ?-1925
[BLB, PHM]
*American underworld figure*
* Brooks, Dynamite

**Brooks, Joshua William** [FFF]
*Author*
* Abdiel

**Brooks, Lawrence**
*See* Huard, Emile

**Brooks, Leonard Harold** ?-1950
[MBF]
*British author*
* Steele, Howard [house
pseudonym]

**Brooks, Leslie**
*See* Gettman, Leslie

**Brooks, Lonnie**
*See* Baker, Lee, Jr.

**Brooks, Mandy**
*See* Brozek, Jonathan Joseph

**Brooks, Maria Gowen** 1795?-1845
[DEL, FFF, WBD]
*American poet*
* Lover of the Fine Arts
* Occidente, Maria dell'

**Brooks, Mary Elizabeth [Aiken]**
[FFF]
*American poet*
* Norna

**Brooks, Mel**
*See* Kaminsky, Melvin

**Brooks, Ned**
*See* Brooks, C. W., Jr.

**Brooks, Norman**
See Arie, Norman Joseph

**Brooks, Phyllis**
See Weiler, Phyllis

**Brooks, Preston Smith** 1819-1857
[FFF]
*American politician*
* Brooks, Bully

**Brooks, Ralph Tweer** 1920-1963
[SC]
*American actor, screenwriter,*
*producer, director*
* Brooke, Ralph

**Brooks, Roosevelt** 20th c.    [BWW]
*American singer*
* Brooks, Baby

**Brooks, Shirley**    [FFF]
*British writer*
* Epicurus Rotundus

**Brooks, Sonny**
See Brooks, Charlie

**Brooks, Vincent**    [PA]
*Author*
* V. B.

**Brooks, Vivian Collin** 1922-
[AW, CC, WW]
*British author*
* Mills, Osmington

**Brooks, W. H.**
See Sharp, William

**Brooks-Davies, Douglas**
See Brooks, Douglas

**Broom, W. W.** 19th c.    [PA]
*Author*
* Eboracus

**Broome, Adam**
See James, Godfrey Warden

**Broome, George** 1886-1946    [THR]
*British actor*
* Clarke, George

**Broome, Sutton**
See Smith, Alice Maude

**Broome, William** 1694-1745    [FFF]
*British poet and clergyman*
* Chester

**Broomsley, Big Bill**
See Broonzy, William Lee Conley

**Broonzy, Big Bill**
See Broonzy, William Lee Conley

**Broonzy, William Lee Conley**
1893-1958    [BWW, FFA, PMJ]
*American singer*
* Blues Boy Bill
* Broomsley, Big Bill
* Broonzy, Big Bill
* Chicago Bill
* Hunter, Slim
* Johnson, Big Bill
* Little Sam
* Little Son
* Natchez
* Sampson, Sammy

**Brophy, Brigid**
See Levy, Brigid Antonia Brophy

**Brophy, Robert**    [DIL]
*Irish playwright*
* Ray, R. J.

**Brosch, Alfred** 1911-1975    [GF]
*American golfer*
* Brosch, Red

**Brosch, Red**
See Brosch, Alfred

**Broschi, Carlo** 1705-1782    [WBD]
*Italian singer*
* Farinelli, Carlo
* [Il] Ragazzo

**Broskie, Chops**
See Broskie, Sigmund Theodore

**Broskie, Siggy**
See Broskie, Sigmund Theodore

**Broskie, Sigmund Theodore**
1911-1975    [BE]
*American baseball player*
* Broskie, Chops
* Broskie, Siggy

**Brosman, Catharine Savage** 1934-
[CA]
*American author and educator*
* Savage, Catharine

**Brosnahan, Katherine Mary**
1890-1940    [CAT]
*American author*
* Eleanor, [Mother]
* Mary Eleanor, [Sister]

**Brosnan, James Patrick** 1929-    [BE]
*American baseball player*
* Brosnan, Professor

**Brosnan, Professor**
See Brosnan, James Patrick

**Brossard, Chandler** 1922-
[CA, WD]
*American author, playwright, editor*
* Harper, Daniel

**Brosse, Vane de**
See Black, Clinton

**Brost, Raymond** 1896-1970
[BEW, EMT]
*American composer*
* Henderson, Ray

**Broster, D. K.**
See Broster, Dorothy Kathleen

**Broster, Dorothy Kathleen**
1877-1950    [HFF, WGT]
*British author*
* Broster, D. K.

**[The] Brother**
See Attles, Alvin J., Jr.

**Brother Blues**
See Dupree, William Thomas

**Brother Bob**
See Buell, Robert Kingery

**Brother Bones**
See Davis, Freeman

**Brother Choleric**
See Van Zeller, Claud

**Brother Cornbread**
See Thomas, Joe

**Brother George**
See Allen, Fulton

**Brother George**
See McGhee, Walter Brown

**Brother Jack McDuff**
See McDuffy, Eugene

**Brother Joe**
See May, Joseph

**Brother John**
See Sellers, John

**Brother Jonathan**
See Trumbull, Jonathan

**Brother Joshua**
See Joseph, Pleasant

**Brothers, Buster**
See Brothers, Leo Vincent

**Brothers, Leo Vincent** 1899-1951
[BLB]
*American underworld figure*
* Bader, Leo
* Brothers, Buster

**Brothers, Richard** 1757-1824
*British leader of religious sect*
* [The] Prophet

**Brotherton, Alice Williams** 20th c.
[ALY]
*American author*
* Lloyd, Richard

**Brottem, Anton Christian**
1892-1929    [BE]
*American baseball player*
* Brottem, Tony

**Brottem, Tony**
See Brottem, Anton Christian

**Brough, Charles Hillman** 1876- ?
[NAA]
*American author, politician,*
*educator*
* Brough, Dr.
* Brough, Governor

**Brough, Dr.**
See Brough, Charles Hillman

**Brough, Fanny**
See Frost, Sarah Frances

**Brough, Governor**
See Brough, Charles Hillman

**Brough, Spangler Arlington**
1911-1969    [BDF, FC, IPA]
*American actor*
* Taylor, Robert

**Brougham, Henry Peter** 1778-1868
[DEP, DNNS, HN]
*Scottish statesman and jurist*
* [The] Stormy Petrel of Politics
* Twitcher, Harry

**Brougham, John** 1810-1880    [PA]
*Author*
* Diogenes Jr.

**Brougham, Lord** 1779-1868    [PA]
*Author*
* Gent, Isaac Tompkins

**Broughton, Aya** 20th c.    [ART]
*Japanese-born painter*
* Aya

**Brouillard, Andre Leon** 20th c.
[WWS]
*French author*
* Nord, Pierre

**Brouillard, Lou**
See Brouillard, Lucien

**Brouillard, Lucien** 1911-
[BX, RBE, SG]
*Canadian-born boxer*
* Brouillard, Lou

**Broun, Emily**
See Sterne, Emma Gelders

**Broussard, Vivian L.**
See Martinetz, Vivian L.

**Brouthers, Big Dan**
See Brouthers, Dennis Joseph

**Brouthers, Dan**
See Brouthers, Dennis Joseph

**Brouthers, Dennis Joseph**
1858-1932    [AS, BE, PB]
*American baseball player*
* Brouthers, Big Dan
* Brouthers, Dan

**Brovia, Joseph John [Joe]** 1922-
[BE]
*American baseball player*
* Brovia, Ox

**Brovia, Ox**
See Brovia, Joseph John [Joe]

**[The] Brow**
See Pafko, Andrew

**Broward, Donn**
See Halleran, Eugene E[dward]

**Browder, Bill** 20th c.    [ECM]
*American musician and record*
*promoter*
* Sheppard, T. G.
* Stacy, Brian

**Brower, Cyril De Cordova**
1898-1954    [BBH]
*American lacrosse player and*
*official*
* Brower, Darb

**Brower, Darb**
See Brower, Cyril De Cordova

**Brower, Francis Willard**
1893-1960    [BE, BN]
*American baseball player*
* Brower, Turk
* Brower, Turkeyfoot

**Brower, Linda A.** 1945-    [CA]
*American educator and editor*
* Meeks, Linda A.

**Brower, Roy**
*Singer*
* Johnson, Ornamental

**Brower, Turk**
See Brower, Francis Willard

**Brower, Turkeyfoot**
See Brower, Francis Willard

**Browin, Frances Williams** 1898-
[CAP, SAT]
*American author*
* Williams, Frances B.

**Brown, Aaron L.** 1883-1935?
[AS, BX, RBE]
*American boxer*
* [The] Dixie Kid

**Brown, Ab**
See Brown, Albert

**Brown, Ada** 1890-1950    [BWW]
*American singer*
* [The] Queen of Blues

**Brown, Ada** 20th c.    [THR]
*British comedienne*
* Cerito, Ada

**Brown, Adam George** 1893-1971
[BMH]
*British comedian*
* Russell, Billy
* [The] Son of Toil

**Brown, Adeline E.** [ASC]
*American composer*
* Brown, Pat

**Brown, Al**
*See* Brown, Alphonse Theo

**Brown, Al**
*See* Capone, Al[phonse]

**Brown, Albert** 20th c. [BBH, CSH]
*Canadian lacrosse promoter*
* Brown, Ab

**Brown, Albert Thacker** 1887-1974
[WECO]
*British cartoonist*
* Brown, Bertie

**Brown, Alexander** 19th c. [FFF]
*Scottish poet*
* Berwickshire Sandie

**Brown, Alexander** 1929-1975 [EJ]
*British jazz musician*
* Brown, Sandy

**Brown, Alexis**
*See* Baumann, Amy [Brown]
Beeching

**Brown, Alice** 1857-1948 [TC, WW]
*American author and playwright*
* Redfield, Martin

**Brown, Alphonse Theo** 1902-1951
[BX, RBE]
*Panamanian-born boxer*
* Brown, Al
* Brown, Panama Al

**Brown, Alton Leo** 1925- [BE]
*American baseball player*
* Brown, Deacon

**Brown, Altyrone** 20th c. [IBW]
*American singer, dancer, actor*
* Brown, Deno

**Brown, Amanda**
*See* McCoy, Viola

**Brown, Andy** 20th c. [IBW, RBE]
*American boxer, trainer, manager*
* Brown, Pop

**Brown, Angeline** 1931- [IPA]
*American actress*
* Dickinson, Angie

**Brown, Arthur**
*See* Wilton, Arthur

**Brown, Audrey** 1936- [RO1]
*American singer*
* Grant, Gogi

**Brown, Babe**
*See* Brown, John H., Jr.

**Brown, Bad Bad Leroy**
*See* Barnes, Leroy

**[The] Brown Bambino**
*See* Gibson, Joshua

**Brown, Barnsley**
*See* Brown, David John

**Brown, Bear**
*See* Brown, Troy

**Brown, Beatrice Bradshaw** 20th c.
[CAT]
*American author*
* Kent, Michael

**Brown, Bertie**
*See* Brown, Albert Thacker

**Brown, Bessie** 1895?- [BWW]
*American singer*
* Green, Sadie
* Lee, Caroline

**Brown, Beth** 20th c. [CAP]
*American author*
* Retner, Beth A.

**Brown, Betty**
*See* Jones, Elizabeth B[rown]

**Brown, Big Bill**
*See* Brown, Willard

**Brown, Billye Walker**
*See* Cutchen, Billye Walker

**Brown, Blower**
*See* Brown, Lewis J.

**Brown, Boardwalk**
*See* Brown, Carroll William

**[The] Brown Bomber**
*See* Barrow, Joseph Louis

**Brown, Boomer**
*See* Brown, Robert S.

**Brown, Box**
*See* Brown, Henry

**Brown, Brownie**
*See* Brown, Clifford

**Brown, Brownie**
*See* Brown, Larry Wayne

**Brown, Bubba**
*See* Brown, John Henry

**Brown, Buckshot**
*See* Brown, Thomas Michael

**Brown, Bud**
*See* Brown, Kenneth J.

**Brown, Buddy**
*See* Brown, Victor J.

**Brown, Bundini**
*See* Brown, Drew

**Brown, Buster**
*See* Brown, Charles Edward

**Brown, Buster**
*See* Brown, Ulysses

**Brown, California**
*See* Brown, Willard

**Brown, Campbell**
*See* Brown, G. W.

**Brown, Capability**
*See* Brown, Lancelot

**Brown, Carroll William** 1887- [BE]
*American baseball player*
* Brown, Boardwalk

**Brown, Carter**
*See* Yates, Alan Geoffrey

**Brown, Charles**
*See* Cadet, John

**Brown, Charles** [FFF]
*Entertainer*
* Barron, Charles

**Brown, Charles Edward** 1881-1914
[AS, BE]
*American baseball player*
* Brown, Buster

**Brown, Charles M.** 1939- [EJ7]
*American jazz musician*
* Owens, Charles M.

**Brown, Charles Roy** 1888-1968
[BE]
*American baseball player*
* Brown, Curly
* Brown, Lefty

**Brown, Charlie** 20th c. [MEB]
*American basketball player*
* Brown, Sweet Charlie

**Brown, Charlotte Elizabeth**
1792-1846 [PA]
*Author*
* C. E.

**Brown, Chocolate**
*See* Scruggs, Irene

**Brown, Clarence** 1924-
[BWW, NBB]
*American singer*
* Brown, Gatemouth

**Brown, Clifford** 1930-1956 [IBW]
*American jazz musician*
* Brown, Brownie

**Brown, Cochise**
*See* Brown, Tommy

**[The] Brown Condor**
*See* Robinson, John C.

**Brown, Conny**
*See* Brown, Patrick Cornelius

**Brown, Curly**
*See* Brown, Charles Roy

**Brown, D.** ?-1962 [BBH]
*Canadian football club officer*
* Brown, Wes

**Brown, Daniel Russell** 20th c. [CA]
*American author, playwright, poet*
* Curzon, Daniel

**Brown, David** ?-1873 [FFF]
*American book-collector*
* [The] Hermit of Newfane

**Brown, David [Dave]** 20th c.
[IBW, OBW]
*American baseball player*
* Brown, Lefty

**Brown, David John** 1942- [DC]
*British cricketer*
* Brown, Barnsley

**Brown, Deacon**
*See* Brown, Alton Leo

**Brown, Demetra Kenneth** 20th c.
[NAA]
*Turkish-born author*
* Vaka, Demetra

**Brown, Denise Scott** 1931- [CA]
*Zambian-born architect, educator,
author*
* Venturi, Denise Scott Brown

**Brown, Deno**
*See* Brown, Altyrone

**Brown, Diana Elizabeth** 1929-
[ART]
*British painter and illustrator*
* D.
* D. A.

**Brown, Diana Elizabeth** (Continued)
* D. B.

**Brown, Doc**
*See* Brown, Robert William

**Brown, Downtown**
*See* Brown, Ollie Lee

**Brown, Drew** 1928- [IBW]
*American boxing trainer*
* Brown, Bundini

**Brown, Duncan**
*See* Nelson, T.

**Brown, Dunn**
*See* Fiske, Samuel

**Brown, Edgar Rogers** 1903-
[WWL]
*British author*
* Aegocerus

**Brown, Edmund Gerald** 1905-
*American politician*
* Brown, Pat

**Brown, Edmund Gerald, Jr.[Jerry]**
1938-
*American politician*
* Moonbeam, Governor
* [The] Peter Pan of Politics

**Brown, Edward William**
1891-1956 [BE]
*American baseball player*
* Brown, Glass Arm Eddie

**Brown, Elijah** 1867- ? [WWL]
*British author*
* Raleigh, Alan

**Brown, Elizabeth Ann** 1848-1880
[WBD]
*British actress*
* Neilson, Lilian Adelaide

**Brown, Ellison** 1914?-1975 [B10]
*American runner*
* Brown, Tarzan

**Brown, Elmer Young** 1883-1955
[BE]
*American baseball player*
* Brown, Shook

**Brown, Eugene** 20th c. [IBW]
*American religious leader and
community organizer*
* Abdul-Hamid, Sufi
* Conshankin, Bishop
* Mu Minin, Ameru al-

**Brown, Fast Black**
*See* Brown, Percy

**Brown, Forrest** 20th c. [CA]
*American author*
* Bowne, Ford
* Brown, Rae

**Brown, Frankie**
*See* Daffan, Theron Eugene

**Brown, Frankie Dee** 1919- [IBW]
*American entertainer*
* Dee, Frankie

**Brown, Freckles**
*See* Brown, Warren

**Brown, Frederick Kenyon** 1882-
[NAA]
*British-born author*
* Priddy, Al

**Brown, Fredric** 1926-1972 [WGT]
*American author*
* Graham, Felix

**Brown, Funky**
See   Brown, George

**Brown, G. W.** 20th c.   [MBF]
*British author*
* Braithwaite, Coulton
* Brown, Campbell
* Campbell, G. W.
* Graham, Alexis

**Brown, Gatemouth**
See   Brown, Clarence

**Brown, Gates**
See   Brown, William James

**Brown, Gator**
See   Brown, William James

**Brown, Gavin** 1901-1970   [THR]
*Scottish-born actor, singer, composer*
* Gordon, Gavin

**Brown, George**
See   Jenkins, Norman

**Brown, George**
See   Wertmueller Von Elgg, Arcangela

**Brown, George** 20th c.   [RO2]
*American musician*
* Brown, Funky

**Brown, George Douglas** 1869-1902
[LC]
*Scottish author and educator*
* Douglas, George

**Brown, Georgia**
See   Klot, Lillian Claire Laizer Getel

**Brown, Gerald** 1936-   [EJ7]
*American jazz musician*
* Brown, Sonny

**[The] Brown Giant**
See   Davis, John

**Brown, Gimpy**
See   Brown, Lloyd Andrew

**Brown, Ginger**
See   Brown, Virginia Anne

**Brown, Glass Arm Eddie**
See   Brown, Edward William

**Brown, Good Rockin**
See   Brown, Roy James

**Brown, Gordon F.** 1880-1911   [FB]
*American football player*
* Brown, Skim

**Brown, Grace Evelyn** 1873- ?
[NAA]
*American author, artist, lecturer*
* Beverly, Vivian

**Brown, H. Clark** 1898-   [NAA]
*American author*
* Thistle, Donald

**Brown, H. Rap**
See   Brown, Hubert Geroid

**Brown, Harold, Jr.** 20th c.   [BBH]
*American sailboat racer*
* Brown, Hatch

**Brown, Harry**
See   Samek, Viktor Oliver

**Brown, Harry [Peter McNab]**
1917-   [CA]
*American author, poet, playwright*
* Greengroin, Artie

**Brown, Harry** 20th c.   [EJS]
*American boxer*
* Brown, Kid

**Brown, Hatch**
See   Brown, Harold, Jr.

**Brown, Hazel Crosby** 1890?-1964
[BEW]
*Theatrical performer*
* Crosby, Hazel

**Brown, Hector Harold** 1924-   [BE]
*American baseball player*
* Brown, Skinny

**Brown, Helen** 1916-1974   [SC]
*American actress*
* Brown, Mina

**Brown, Helen Hayes** 1900-
[BEW, CED, F2]
*American actress*
* [The] First Lady of the American Stage
* Hayes, Helen

**Brown, Henry** 1816- ?   [IBW]
*American author*
* Brown, Box

**Brown, Henry** 1906-   [BWW]
*American singer*
* Brown, Papa Henry
* Charles, Henry

**Brown, Henry** 20th c.   [BWW]
*American musician*
* Brown, Hi

**Brown, Hi**
See   Brown, Henry

**Brown, Hubert Geroid** 1943-   [IBW]
*American political organizer*
* Amin, Masha Allah Jamil Abdullah al-
* Brown, H. Rap

**Brown, Hugh**
See   Boycott-Brown, Hugh

**Brown, Ida G.** 1900?-   [BWW]
*American singer and actress*
* Baby Blues
* Dale, Flora
* Jones, Sadie

**Brown, Iron Man**
See   Brown, Larry

**Brown, Irwin**
See   Murray, David Stark

**Brown, [Elder] J. C.**
See   Jefferson, Lemon

**Brown, J. G.**
See   Brown, James Goldie

**Brown, Jake**
See   Brown, Jerald Ray

**Brown, James**   [BWW]
*American singer*
* Brown, Widemouth

**Brown, James** 1709-1787   [PA]
*Author*
* Selkirk, J. B.

**Brown, James** 1897?-1940
[F2, FC]
*American actor*
* Hall, James

**Brown, James** 1928?-
[DAM, IBW, RO1]
*American singer and songwriter*
* Dynamite, Mr.

**Brown, James** (Continued)
* [The] Godfather of Soul
* Soul Brother Number 1

**Brown, James** 20th c.   [SMG]
*American baseball scout*
* Brown, Red

**Brown, James Donaldson [Jim]**
1897-   [BE]
*American baseball player*
* Brown, Moose

**Brown, James Goldie** 1901-   [SFL]
*New Zealand author*
* Brown, J. G.

**Brown, James H.**   [PA]
*Author*
* Junius

**Brown, James Ostend** 1906-1963
[DAM, EJ, PMJ]
*American jazz musician*
* Brown, Pete

**Brown, Jane**
See   Blaze de Bury, Yetta

**Brown, Jerald Ray** 1946-
[BE, IBW]
*American baseball player*
* Brown, Jake
* [The] Miracle Man

**Brown, Jimmy**
See   Alden, William L.

**Brown, Jimmy** 20th c.   [RO2]
*American singer and musician*
* Brown, Lord

**Brown, Joe** 1926-   [BX, RBE]
*American boxer*
* Brown, Old Bones

**Brown, John** 1800-1859   [WBD]
*American abolitionist*
* Old Brown of Osawatomie

**Brown, John H.** 1904-1957   [SC]
*American actor*
* O'Dell, Digger

**Brown, John H., Jr.** 1891-1963
[AS, FB]
*American football player*
* Brown, Babe

**Brown, John Henry** 1902-   [BWW]
*American singer*
* Brown, Bubba

**Brown, John J.** 1916-   [CA]
*Canadian author and educator*
* Sherashevski, Boris

**Brown, John Macmillan** 1846-1935
[ESF, SFL, WGT]
*Scottish author*
* Sweven, Godfrey

**Brown, John Mason**
See   Mason, John

**Brown, Jones, and Robinson**
See   Doyle, Richard

**Brown, Jumbo**
See   Brown, Walter George

**Brown, Kenneth J.** 20th c.   [BBH]
*American basketball player*
* Brown, Bud

**Brown, Kid**
See   Brown, Harry

**Brown, Knockout**
See   Braun, Valentine

**Brown, L. J.**
See   DuBreuil, Elizabeth Lorinda

**Brown, Lancelot** 1715-1783
[FFF, HN, WBD]
*British gardener*
* Brown, Capability

**Brown, Larry** 1905-1972   [IBW]
*American baseball player*
* Brown, Iron Man

**Brown, Larry** 20th c.
*American football player*
* Brown, Rap

**Brown, Larry Wayne** 1947-   [SMG]
*Canadian-born hockey player*
* Brown, Brownie

**Brown, LaVerne** 1906-1966   [SC]
*American aviator and actor*
* Trent, John

**Brown, Lefty**
See   Brown, Charles Roy

**Brown, Lefty**
See   Brown, David [Dave]

**Brown, Leslie Hilton** 1917-   [IAW]
*British author*
* Aonyx

**Brown, Lew**
See   Brownstein, Louis

**Brown, Lewis J.** 1856-1889   [BE]
*American baseball player*
* Brown, Blower

**Brown, Lilian Rowland** 20th c.
[WWL]
*British author*
* Grey, Rowland

**Brown, Lillian [or Lillyn]**
See   Thomas, Lillian

**Brown, [John] Lindsay** 1911-1967
[BE]
*American baseball player*
* Brown, Red

**Brown, Little Sonny**
See   Brown, Samuel

**Brown, Lloyd Andrew** 1904-   [BE]
*American baseball player*
* Brown, Gimpy

**Brown, Lord**
See   Brown, Jimmy

**Brown, Lottie**
See   Beaman, Lottie Kimbrough

**Brown, Louis** 20th c.   [RBE]
*American boxer*
* Brown, Piggy

**Brown, M. E.**
See   Mosser, Ann J.

**Brown, Mandy**
See   Brown, Mary

**Brown, Marel**
See   Brown, Margaret Elizabeth

**Brown, Margaret Elizabeth** 1899-
[WD]
*American author and poet*
* Brown, Marel

**Brown, Margaret Wise** 1910-1952
[CA, SAT, TCC]
*American author and poet*
* Hay, Timothy
* MacDonald, Golden

**Brown, Margaret Wise** (Continued)
* Sage, Juniper [joint pseudonym with Edith (Thacher) Hurd]

**Brown, Marjorie** 1903-   [THR]
*British actress*
* Mars, Marjorie

**Brown, Mary** 1913-   [AW]
*British author*
* Blake, Vanessa
* Brown, Mandy

**Brown, Mary Rachel** 1921-   [ART]
*American painter*
* Marais

**Brown, Mary Richardson** 1944-
[IBW]
*American journalist and television broadcaster*
* [The] Multi-Media Person

**Brown, Mina**
*See* Brown, Helen

**Brown, Miner**
*See* Brown, Mordecai Peter Centennial

**Brown, Mr.**
*See* Thackeray, William Makepeace

**Brown, Moose**
*See* Brown, James Donaldson [Jim]

**Brown, Mordecai Peter Centennial** 1876-1948   [AS, BE, PB]
*American baseball player*
* Brown, Miner
* Brown, Three Finger

**Brown, Morna Doris [MacTaggart]** 1907-   [CA, CC, EMD]
*British author*
* Ferrars, E. X.
* Ferrars, Elizabeth

**Brown, Morris Cecil** 1943-   [CA]
*American author and educator*
* Goslovich, Marianne

**Brown, Mrs. C. R.**   [PA]
*Author*
* May, Mattie

**Brown, Mrs. George C.**   [FFF]
*Author*
* Celeste

**Brown, Mrs. Sedley**   [FFF]
*Entertainer*
* Crossman, Henrietta

**Brown, Napoleon** 20th c.   [RO1]
*American singer*
* Brown, Nappy

**Brown, Nappy**
*See* Brown, Napoleon

**Brown, Newsboy**
*See* Montrose, David

**Brown, Old Bones**
*See* Brown, Joe

**Brown, Olive** 1922-   [BWW]
*American singer*
* Foxy GGM [Great-Grandmother]
* [The] New Empress of the Blues
* [The] Princess of the Blues

**Brown, Ollie Lee** 1944-   [BE, SMG]
*American baseball player*
* Brown, Downtown

**Brown, Ollie Lee** (Continued)
* O. B.

**Brown, Panama Al**
*See* Brown, Alphonse Theo

**Brown, Papa Henry**
*See* Brown, Henry

**Brown, Pat**
*See* Brown, Adeline E.

**Brown, Pat**
*See* Brown, Edmund Gerald

**Brown, Patrick Cornelius** 1917-
[CEI]
*Canadian-born hockey player*
* Brown, Conny

**Brown, Paul Percival** 1889-   [BE]
*American baseball player*
* Brown, Ray

**Brown, Percy** 20th c.   [BWW]
*American musician*
* Brown, Fast Black

**Brown, Pete**
*See* Brown, James Ostend

**Brown, Piggy**
*See* Brown, Louis

**Brown, Pisistratus**
*See* Black, William

**Brown, Polly**   [RO2]
*Singer*
* Leone, Sarah

**Brown, Pop**
*See* Brown, Andy

**Brown, Pop**
*See* Brown, William T.

**Brown, Rabbit**
*See* Brown, Richard

**Brown, Rae**
*See* Brown, Forrest

**Brown, Ralph Lawrence** 1913-
[NAA]
*American poet*
* Brent, Herel

**Brown, Rap**
*See* Brown, Larry

**Brown, Ray**
*See* Brown, Paul Percival

**Brown, Red**
*See* Brown, [John] Lindsay

**Brown, Red**
*See* Brown, James

**Brown, Red**
*See* Brown, Robert N.

**Brown, Richard** 1880?-1937   [EJ]
*American singer*
* Brown, Rabbit

**Brown, Richard P.** 1870-1948   [BE]
*American baseball player*
* Brown, Stub

**Brown, Robert** 1910-1966
[BWW, EJ]
*American jazz musician*
* Ham Gravy
* Shufflin' Sam
* Washboard Sam

**Brown, Robert** 1927-1975   [BWW]
*American singer*
* Smoky Babe

**Brown, Robert Earl** 1929-   [RO1]
*American singer*
* Braun, Bob

**Brown, Robert Howell** 1925-
[BEW, SW]
*American actor*
* Lansing, Robert

**Brown, Robert McAfee** 1920-   [CA]
*American clergyman, educator, author*
* St. Hereticus

**Brown, Robert N.** 20th c.   [BBH]
*American collegiate athletic director*
* Brown, Red

**Brown, Robert S.** 1941-   [FB]
*American football player*
* Brown, Boomer

**Brown, Robert William** 1924-
[BE, PB]
*American baseball player*
* Brown, Doc
* [The] Golden Boy

**Brown, Roger** 1950-
*American basketball player*
* Brown, Tipper

**Brown, Roosevelt** 1932-
[BBH, IBW]
*American football player*
* Brown, Rosie [or Rosey]

**Brown, Rosalie [Gertrude] Moore** 1910-   [CA, SAT]
*American poet and educator*
* Moore, Rosalie

**Brown, Rosie [or Rosey]**
*See* Brown, Roosevelt

**Brown, Roy James** 1925-1981
[BWW]
*American singer*
* Brown, Good Rockin
* Brown, Tommy

**Brown, Ruth** 1928-   [RO1]
*American singer*
* Rhythm, Miss

**Brown, Samuel**   [PA]
*Author*
* Crito

**Brown, Samuel** 20th c.   [RO2]
*American singer*
* Brown, Little Sonny

**Brown, Sandy**
*See* Brown, Alexander

**Brown, Shook**
*See* Brown, Elmer Young

**Brown, Sidney** 1894-1968   [NOJ]
*American jazz musician*
* Little, Jim

**Brown, Skim**
*See* Brown, Gordon F.

**Brown, Skinny**
*See* Brown, Hector Harold

**Brown, Sonny**
*See* Brown, Gerald

**Brown, Sonny**
*See* Brown, William

**Brown, Stella** 20th c.
*British singer*
* Andreva, Stella

**Brown, Steve**
*See* Brown, Theodore

**Brown, Stub**
*See* Brown, Richard P.

**Brown, Sweet Charlie**
*See* Brown, Charlie

**Brown, T. Allston**   [PA]
*Author*
* Rapid, Young

**Brown, Tarzan**
*See* Brown, Ellison

**Brown, Tarzan**
*See* Brown, Tony Ersic

**Brown, Teddy**
*See* Himmebrand, Abraham

**Brown, Theodore** 1890-1965
[WWJ]
*American jazz musician*
* Brown, Steve

**Brown, Thomas A.** 1937-   [FB]
*American football player*
* Brown, Tim

**Brown, Thomas Michael** 1927-
[BE]
*American baseball player*
* Brown, Buckshot

**Brown, Thomas, the Younger**
*See* Moore, Thomas

**Brown, Three Finger**
*See* Brown, Mordecai Peter Centennial

**Brown, Three Finger**
*See* Lucchese, Thomas Gaetano

**Brown, Tim**
*See* Brown, Thomas A.

**Brown, Tipper**
*See* Brown, Roger

**Brown, Tom**
*See* Hughes, Thomas

**Brown, Tommy**
*See* Brown, Roy James

**Brown, Tommy** 20th c.
*American basketball player*
* Brown, Cochise

**Brown, Tony Ersic** 1946-   [CWG]
*American country-western performer*
* Brown, Tarzan

**Brown, Troy** 20th c.   [BWW]
*American entertainer*
* Brown, Bear

**Brown, Ulysses** 20th c.   [OBW]
*American baseball player*
* Brown, Buster

**Brown, Vandyke**
*See* Brannon, William Penn

**Brown, Vandyke**
*See* Cook, Marc E.

**Brown, Vandyke**
*See* Prouting, Frederick James

**Brown, Vanessa**
*See* Brind, Smylla

**Brown, Velma Darbo** 1921-   [CA]
*American author and columnist*
* Lynn

**Brown, Victor J.** ?-1968 [BBH]
*American roller skating organization officer*
* Brown, Buddy

**Brown, Virginia Anne** 20th c. [IBW]
*American dancer, exercise and grooming consultant*
* Brown, Ginger

**Brown, Walter George** 1907-1966 [BE]
*American baseball player*
* Brown, Jumbo

**Brown, Warner**
See   Boroson, Warren

**Brown, Warren** 20th c. [GW]
*American rodeo performer*
* Brown, Freckles

**Brown, Wes**
See   Brown, D.

**Brown, Widemouth**
See   Brown, James

**Brown, Will C.**
See   Boyles, Clarence Scott, Jr.

**Brown, Willard** 1866-1897 [BE]
*American baseball player*
* Brown, Big Bill
* Brown, California

**Brown, William**
See   Richter, Ernst H.

**Brown, William** 1928- [DAM]
*American musician*
* Brown, Sonny

**Brown, William James** 1939-
[BE, IBW, PB]
*American baseball player*
* Brown, Gates
* Brown, Gator

**Brown, William Perry** 1847-1923 [WW]
*Author*
* Perry, [Captain] William B.

**Brown, William T.** 20th c. [BBH]
*American roller skating organization officer*
* Brown, Pop

**Brown, Willie**
See   Sissle, Noble

**Brown, Zenith [Jones]** 1898-
[CA, EMD, TC]
*American author*
* Conrad, Brenda
* Ford, Leslie
* Frome, David

**Brownbill, Thomas Robson** 1821-1864 [BMH]
*British actor and singer*
* [The] Great Little Robson
* Robson, Frederick

**Browne, Billie**
See   Brune, Phyllis Caroline

**Browne, By**
See   Browne, Byron Ellis

**Browne, Byron Ellis** 1942- [SMG]
*American baseball player*
* Browne, By

**Browne, Charles Farrar** 1832-1867 [DEL, SN]
*American author*
* [The] Delicious
* Ward, Artemus

**Browne, Charles Thomas** [PA]
*Author*
* De Comyne, Alexander

**Browne, Dik**
See   Browne, Richard

**Browne, Dorothy Margaret Stuart** 1889-1963 [LAO, LC, WWL]
*British author*
* D. M. S.
* Stuart, D[orothy] M[argaret]

**Browne, Earl James** 1911- [BE]
*American baseball player*
* Browne, Snitz

**Browne, Ernest D.** 1900- [ASC]
*American composer*
* Rose, Irving

**Browne, F. G.** 1870-1954 [WGT]
*American author*
* Bennet, Robert A[mes]
* Robinet, Lee

**Browne, George N.**
See   McKnight, Harmen Packard

**Browne, George Waldo** 1851- ? [NAA]
*American author*
* St. Clair, Victor

**Browne, Hablot Knight** 1815-1882 [SAT]
*British illustrator*
* Damocles
* Nemo
* Phiz

**Browne, Helen de Guerry Simpson** 1897-1940 [WGT]
*British author*
* Simpson, Helen [de Guerry]

**Browne, Howard** 1908-
[CA, ESF, WGT]
*American author, editor, screenwriter*
* Blade, Alexander [house pseudonym, Ziff-Davis]
* Brengle, William [house pseudonym]
* Carleton, H. B. [house pseudonym]
* Chandler, Lawrence
* Evans, John
* Francis, Lee [house pseudonym]
* Phillips, Peter [house pseudonym]
* Pollard, John X. [house pseudonym]

**Browne, Isaac Hawkins** 1705-1760 [SN]
*British poet*
* Browne, Tobacco

**Browne, Junius Henri** 1833-1902 [FFF]
*American journalist*
* Belle, Clara

**Browne, Matthew**
See   Rands, William Brightly

**Browne, Nicholas Simon Fitz-Gerald** 1948- [IAW]
*British journalist and author*
* Hammerbeck, Nick

**Browne, Noel** 20th c. [MBF]
*British author*
* Reid, Desmond [house pseudonym]

**Browne, Pidge**
See   Browne, Prentice Almont

**Browne, Prentice Almont** 1929- [BE]
*American baseball player*
* Browne, Pidge

**Browne, Reginald**
See   Brooks, Edwy Searles

**Browne, Richard** 1918- [WECO]
*American cartoonist*
* Browne, Dik

**Browne, Sam**
See   Smith, Ronald Gregor

**Browne, Scoville** 1909- [WWJ]
*American jazz musician*
* Browne, Toby

**Browne, Snitz**
See   Browne, Earl James

**Browne, Thomas Alexander** 1826-1915 [WBD]
*Australian author*
* Boldrewood, Rolf

**Browne, Tobacco**
See   Browne, Isaac Hawkins

**Browne, Toby**
See   Browne, Scoville

**Brownell, Amanda Benjamin Hall** 1890- [NAA]
*American author*
* Hall, Amanda Benjamin

**Brownell, Anna Gertrude [Hall]** 1863- ? [WGT]
*American author*
* Hall, Gertrude

**Browning, A. K.**
See   Browning, Amy Katherine

**Browning, Alice C.** 20th c. [IBW]
*American editor and publisher*
* Bentley, Richard

**Browning, Amy Katherine** 20th c. [ART]
*British artist*
* Browning, A. K.

**Browning, Arthur** 1902- [BB]
*American basketball player*
* Browning, Bun

**Browning, Boy**
See   Browning, Frederick

**Browning, Bud**
See   Browning, Omar

**Browning, Bun**
See   Browning, Arthur

**Browning, Craig**
See   Graham, Roger Phillips

**Browning, Daphne Du Maurier** 1907- [WGT]
*British author*
* Du Maurier, Daphne

**Browning, David** 20th c. [BBH]
*American diver*
* Browning, No Splash
* Browning, Skippy

**Browning, Frederick** 1896-1966 [BDW, WWW]
*British military leader*
* Browning, Boy

**Browning, George** 1899- [BB]
*American boxer*
* Browning, Pidge

**Browning, John S.**
See   Williams, Robert Moore

**Browning, L. J.**
See   DuBreuil, Elizabeth Lorinda

**Browning, Louis Rogers** 1858?-1905 [AS, BE, PB]
*American baseball player*
* Browning, Pete
* [The] Gladiator

**Browning, No Splash**
See   Browning, David

**Browning, Omar** 1911- [BB]
*American basketball player*
* Browning, Bud

**Browning, Pete**
See   Browning, Louis Rogers

**Browning, Pidge**
See   Browning, George

**Browning, Robert** 1812-1889 [SN]
*British poet*
* [The] Danton of Modern Poetry

**Browning, S. J.**
See   Browning, Stephen James

**Browning, Skippy**
See   Browning, David

**Browning, Stephen James** 1953- [ART]
*British painter*
* Browning, S. J.

**Browning, Sterry**
See   Gribble, Leonard R[eginald]

**Brownjohn, Alan Charles** 1931- [AW, CA, SAT]
*British author, poet, critic*
* Berrington, John

**Brownjohn, John**
See   Talbot, Charles R.

**Brownlow, Maude Annesley** 20th c. [WWL]
*British author*
* Annesley, Maude

**Brownlow, Parson**
See   Brownlow, William Gannaway

**Brownlow, William Gannaway** 1805-1877 [DNNS, FFF, WBD]
*American journalist and politician*
* Brownlow, Parson
* [The] Fighting Parson

**Brownrigg, Henry**
See   Jerrold, Douglas William

**Brownskin Mama**
See   Stith, Edith Mae

**Brownstein, Louis** 1893-1958 [EMT]
*Russian-born lyricist, librettist, producer*
* Brown, Lew

**Broxholme, John Franklin** 1930- [CA, WD]
*British author, editor, journalist*
* Kyle, Duncan

**Broxholme, John Franklin**
(Continued)
* Meldrum, James

**Broz, Josip** 1892-1980    [B10]
*Yugoslav premier*
* [The] Old Man
* Tito, Josip Broz

**Broza, Elliot Lawrence** 1925?-
[ASC, BEW, EJ]
*American composer and conductor*
* Lawrence, Elliot

**Brozek, Jonathan Joseph**
1898-1962    [BE]
*American baseball player*
* Brooks, Jonathan Joseph
* Brooks, Mandy

**Brubaker, Bill**
*See* Brubaker, Wilbur Lee

**Brubaker, Bru**
*See* Brubaker, Bruce Ellsworth, Jr.

**Brubaker, Bruce Ellsworth, Jr.**
1941-    [SMG]
*American baseball player*
* Brubaker, Bru

**Brubaker, Wilbur Lee** 1910-    [BE]
*American baseball player*
* Brubaker, Bill

**Bruce, [Father]**
*See* Medaris, John B.

**[The] Bruce**
*See* Robert I

**Bruce, Abyssinian**
*See* Bruce, James

**Bruce, Authur Loring**
*See* Crowninshield, Francis Welch

**Bruce, Benjamin**    [PA]
*Author*
* Neptunus
* Observer

**Bruce, Betty**
*See* Eisner, Betty

**Bruce, David**
*See* McBroom, Marden

**Bruce, David**
*See* Patchett, Mary Osborne Elwyn

**Bruce, James** 1730-1794    [SN]
*Scottish explorer and author*
* Bruce, Abyssinian
* [The] Sagacious Terrier

**Bruce, Jean**
*See* Brochet, Jean-Alexandre

**Bruce, John Edward** 1856-1924
[IBW]
*American journalist*
* [The] Duke of Uganda
* Grit

**Bruce, K.**
*See* Bald, Kenneth

**Bruce, Kenneth** 1876-1916
[SFL, WGT]
*Author*
* Crayon, Diedrick, Jr.

**Bruce, L. C.**    [FFF, PA]
*American writer*
* Mercury

**Bruce, Lenny**
*See* Schneider, Leonard Alfred

**Bruce, Leo**
*See* Croft-Cooke, Rupert

**Bruce, Martin**
*See* Montague, Bruce Alexander

**Bruce, Monica**
*See* Melaro, Constance L[oraine]

**Bruce, Robert**
*See* Wright, Robert B.

**Bruce, Robert VI** 1210-1295
[WBD]
*Scottish aristocrat*
* [The] Competitor

**Bruce, Rose Evelyn** 20th c.    [WWL]
*British writer*
* Hounsfield, Thirza M.

**Bruce, Sanders D.**    [FFF, PA]
*Author*
* Occasional
* S. D. B.

**Bruce, Sybil Etonia** 1892-1966
[THR]
*British actress*
* Bruce, Tonie Edgar

**Bruce, Tonie Edgar**
*See* Bruce, Sybil Etonia

**Bruce, Virginia**
*See* Briggs, Helen Virginia

**Bruce, Wallace** 19th c.    [PA]
*Author*
* McQuail, Thursty

**Bruce, William** 19th c.    [PA]
*Author*
* [The] Scotts Irishman

**Bruce-Okine, Emanuel** 20th c.
[IBW]
*Ghanaian-born soccer and cricket player*
* Bruce-Okine, Mannie

**Bruce-Okine, Mannie**
*See* Bruce-Okine, Emanuel

**Bruce-Potter, Hilda**
*See* Potter, Hilda

**Bruce-Smith, Cyril** 1892-1963
[THR]
*Scottish-born actor*
* Smith, Cyril

**Bruch, Cornelia** 1925-    [FC]
*German actress*
* Borchers, Cornell

**Brucker, Roger W[arren]** 1929-
[CA]
*American author and advertising executive*
* Rogers, Warren

**Bruckner, Ferdinand**
*See* Tagger, Theodor

**Bruckner, John** 1726-1804    [FFF]
*French clergyman and author*
* Cassander

**Bruder, Hank** 20th c.    [BBH]
*American football player*
* Hard Luck Hank

**Bruder Klaus**
*See* Loewenbrugger, Nikolaus

**Brueckel, Francis J.** 20th c.    [WGT]
*Author*
* Bridge, Frank J.

**Bruegel, Johann Wolfgang** 1905-
[CA]
*Austrian-born author*
* Bruegel, John Wolfgang

**Bruegel, John Wolfgang**
*See* Bruegel, Johann Wolfgang

**Brueghel, Flower**
*See* Brueghel [or Bruegel], Jan

**Brueghel, Hell**
*See* Brueghel [or Bruegel], Pieter

**Brueghel [or Bruegel], Jan**
1568-1625    [WBD]
*Flemish painter*
* Brueghel, Flower
* Brueghel, Velvet

**Brueghel, Peasant**
*See* Brueghel [or Bruegel], Pieter

**Brueghel [or Bruegel], Pieter**
1520?-1569    [WBD]
*Flemish painter*
* Brueghel, Peasant
* [The] Droll

**Brueghel [or Bruegel], Pieter**
1564?-1638?    [WBD]
*Flemish painter*
* Brueghel, Hell

**Brueghel, Velvet**
*See* Brueghel [or Bruegel], Jan

**Bruel, Joachim** ?-1653    [PA]
*Author*
* Brulius

**Bruff, Nancy**
*See* Gardner, Nancy Bruff

**Brugensis**
*See* Lucas, Francois

**Brugnon, Jacques** 1895-1978
[BBH]
*French tennis player*
* Brugnon, Toto

**Brugnon, Toto**
*See* Brugnon, Jacques

**Bruhn, Carl** 1869- ?    [NAA]
*Swedish-born playwright and editor*
* Graa

**Bruhns, Arthur**
*See* Bruhns, George Frederick William

**Bruhns, George Frederick William**
1874-1963    [ASC]
*German-born composer*
* Bruhns, Arthur

**Bruin, John**
*See* Brutus, Dennis [Vincent]

**[El] Brujo [The Wizard]**
*See* Cabello, Juan

**Brulius**
*See* Bruel, Joachim

**Bruller, Jean Marcel** 1902-
[CA, SF, TC]
*French author and graphic artist*
* Vercors [code name used during World War II]

**Brulls, Christian**
*See* Simenon, Georges [Joseph Christian]

**Brumbaugh, Brummie**
*See* Brumbaugh, Carl L.

**Brumbaugh, Carl L.** 1907-1969
[AS]
*American football player*
* Brumbaugh, Brummie

**Brumm, Boomer**
*See* Brumm, Donald D.

**Brumm, Donald D.** 1941-    [FB]
*American football player*
* Brumm, Boomer

**Brummel, Beau**
*See* Brummel, George Bryan

**Brummel, Belle**
*See* Worden, Helen

**Brummel, George Bryan**
1778-1840    [FF, RH, SN]
*British leader of fashionable society*
* Brummel, Beau
* [The] Dandy Killer
* George the Lesser
* [The] Prince of Beaux
* [The] Prince of Dandies

**Brundage, John Herbert** 1926-
[B10, WD]
*Canadian actor, playwright, director*
* Herbert, John

**Brundtland, Gro Harlem** 1940?-
*Norwegian prime minister*
* [The] Green Goddess

**Brune, Adrienne**
*See* Brune, Phyllis Caroline

**Brune, Gabrielle**
*See* Hudson, Gabrielle

**Brune, Phyllis Caroline** 1892-
[THR]
*Australian-born actress and singer*
* Browne, Billie
* Brune, Adrienne

**Bruneau, Jean**
*See* Sylvestre, [Joseph Jean] Guy

**[The] Brunel of America**
*See* Ellet, Charles

**Bruner, Bud**
*See* Bruner, E. L.

**Bruner, E. L.**    [RBE]
*Boxing manager*
* Bruner, Bud

**Bruner, Jack Raymond** 1924-    [BE]
*American baseball player*
* Bruner, Pappy

**Bruner, Pappy**
*See* Bruner, Jack Raymond

**Brunet, Bob** 20th c.
*American football player*
* Brunet, Y. A.

**Brunet, George Stuart** 1935-    [BE]
*American baseball player*
* Brunet, Lefty

**Brunet, Gustave** 19th c.    [PA]
*Author*
* Philomneste, Junior

**Brunet, Jean Joseph** 1766-1853
[PA]
*Author*
* Mira

**Brunet, Lefty**
*See* Brunet, George Stuart

**Brunet, Y. A.**
*See* Brunet, Bob

**Bruneteau, Modere** 1914-
[CEI, FHE]
*Canadian-born hockey player*
* Bruneteau, Mud

**Bruneteau, Mud**
See   Bruneteau, Modere

**Brunfels, Otto** 1488?-1534   [WBD]
*German physician and botanist*
* [The] Father of Botany

**Brunglas, Adolph**
See   Glaisbrunner, Adolph

**Bruni [or Bruno], Leonardo**
1369-1444   [WBD]
*Italian humanist*
* Aretino, Leonardo

**Brunies, Abbie**
See   Brunies, Albert

**Brunies, Albert** 1900-1978   [WWJ]
*American jazz musician*
* Brunies, Abbie

**Brunies, Albert** 1914-1955   [NOJ]
*American jazz musician*
* Brunies, Little Abbie

**Brunies, George Clarence**
1900-1974   [EJ, PMJ, WWJ]
*American jazz musician*
* Brunis, Georg

**Brunies, Henny**
See   Brunies, Henry

**Brunies, Henry** 1882?- ?   [NOJ]
*American jazz musician*
* Brunies, Henny

**Brunies, Little Abbie**
See   Brunies, Albert

**Brunious, John** 1920-1976   [NOJ]
*American jazz musician*
* Brunious, Pickett

**Brunious, Pickett**
See   Brunious, John

**Brunis, Georg**
See   Brunies, George Clarence

**Brunken, Ernest** 1865- ?   [NAA]
*German-born attorney and author*
* Van Velthus, Jan

**Brunner, Adrah** 1897-   [THR]
*American-born actress and singer*
* Fair, Adrah

**Brunner, Constantin**
See   Wertheimer, Leo

**Brunner, John [Kilian Houston]**
1934-   [CA, ESF, SFL]
*British author, poet, songwriter*
* Hunt, Gill [house pseudonym,
    Curtis Warren]
* Loxmith, John
* Sheldon, Roy [house pseudonym,
    Hamilton]
* Staines, Trevor
* Woodcott, Keith

**Bruno** 1002-1054   [WBD]
*Pope*
* Leo IX

**Bruno, Frank**
See   St. Bruno, Albert Francis

**Bruno, Giordano** 1550-1600   [HN]
*Italian philosopher*
* [The] Nolan

**Bruno, Guido** 1884-   [ALY]
*Czech-born author and editor*
* Martin, Maude
* Meeker, Mildred

**Bruno, Harry A.** 1893-   [NAA]
*British-born public relations counsel
and writer*
* Flight

**Bruno, James Edward** 1940-   [CA]
*American educator and writer*
* Sumner, Eldon

**Bruno of Carinthia** ?- 999   [WBD]
*Pope*
* Gregory V

**Bruno [or Brun] of Querfurt**
970?-1009   [DNNS, WBD]
*Saint*
* [The] Apostle to the Prussians
* Bonifacius

**Bruno I [or Brun]** 925- 965
[DNNS, WBD]
*Saint*
* [The] Great

**Brunson, Doyle** 20th c.
*American poker player*
* Brunson, Texas Dolly

**Brunson, Texas Dolly**
See   Brunson, Doyle

**Brunstroem, Rita** 1909-1957
[BEW, FC]
*British actress*
* Carr, Jane

**Brunswick, James**
See   Stitt, J. M.

**[Il] Brusasorci**
See   Riccio, Domenico

**Brush, Katharine**
See   Winans, Katharine Brush

**Bruss, B. R.**
See   Blondel, Roger

**Brusso, Noah** 1881-1955
[BX, RBE, SG]
*Canadian-born boxer*
* Burns, Tommy

**Brussof, Valery**
See   Briusov, Valeri Yakovlevich

**Brustlein, Daniel** 20th c.
[IBY, ICB]
*French-born American illustrator*
* Alain

**Brustlein, Janice Tworkov**   [CA]
*Author*
* Janice

**[The] Brute**
See   Trafton, George

**Brute Force Thompson**
See   Thompson, George

**Brute, Q.**
See   Smith, Robert Edward

**Bruto, Cesar**
See   Warnes, Carlos

**Brutsche, Alphonse**
See   Andrevon, Jean-Pierre

**Brutus**
See   Gramsch, Walter

**Brutus**
See   Simpson, Stephen

**Brutus**
See   Spooner, John D.

**Brutus**
See   Turnbull, Robert James

**Brutus, Decimus Junius** 1st c. BC
[WBD]
*Roman general*
* Albinus

**Brutus, Dennis [Vincent]** 1924-
[CA, WD]
*South African poet*
* Bruin, John

**Brutus, Marcus Junius** 1st c. BC
[FFF, RH]
*Roman politician and conspirator*
* [The] Last of the Romans

**Bruun, Malte Conrad** 1775-1826
[WBD]
*Danish-born geographer*
* Malte-Brun [or Maltebrun],
    Conrad

**Bryan, C. D. B.**
See   Bryan, Courtlandt Dixon
Barnes

**Bryan, Courtlandt Dixon Barnes**
1936-   [WYA]
*Author*
* Bryan, C. D. B.

**Bryan, Dora**
See   Broadbent, Dora

**Bryan, E.**
See   Latham, Edward Bryan

**Bryan, Evelyn McDaniel Frazier**
1911-   [IAW]
*American author*
* Frazier, Evelyn McDaniel
* McDaniel, Evelyn

**Bryan, [Sir] Francis** ?-1550   [WBD]
*British soldier and poet*
* [The] Vicar of Hell

**Bryan, Hal**
See   Clark, Johnson

**Bryan, Jack**
See   Bryan, Jackson Lee

**Bryan, Jackson Lee** 1909-1964
[SC]
*American actor*
* Bryan, Jack

**Bryan, Jane**
See   O'Brien, Jane

**Bryan, Jimmy** 20th c.
*Auto racer*
* [The] Cowboy
* [The] Motorized Cowboy

**Bryan, Kim**
See   Klein, Joanne Kim

**Bryan, Mavis**
See   O'Brien, Marian P[lowman]

**Bryan, Ralph Burgess** 1899-
[NAA]
*American business executive and
writer*
* Henderson, Alfred

**Bryan, Sarah M. L.**   [PA]
*Author*
* Myrtle, Minnie

**Bryan, Walter**
See   Willis, Walt

**Bryan, William Jennings**
1860-1925   [WBD]
*American attorney and political
leader*
* [The] Commoner

**Bryans, Robert Harbinson [Robin]**
1928-   [AW, CA, WD]
*Irish-born author and poet*
* Cameron, Donald
* Harbinson, Robert

**Bryant, Ada Bevan ap Rees** 20th c.
[THR]
*British actress*
* Grey, Mary

**Bryant, Adrian** [joint pseudonym]
See   Cole, Adrian Christopher
Synnot

**Bryant, Anita** 1940-   [RO1]
*American singer*
* [The] Red Feather Girl

**Bryant, Bear**
See   Bryant, Paul William

**Bryant, Bear**
See   Bryant, Ronald Raymond

**Bryant, Bruce**
See   Wright, W. George

**Bryant, Claiborne Henry** 1911-
[BE]
*American baseball player*
* Bryant, Clay

**Bryant, Clay**
See   Bryant, Claiborne Henry

**Bryant, Dena** 1930-   [ART]
*British painter*
* D. B.
* Dena

**Bryant, Edward [Winslow, Jr.]**
1945-   [CA]
*American author*
* Talbot, Lawrence

**Bryant, Ivy** 1925-   [CWG, DAM]
*American country-western performer*
* Bryant, Jimmy

**Bryant, Jimmy**
See   Bryant, Ivy

**Bryant, Katherine Cliffton** 1912-
[CA]
*American author and educator*
* Cliffton, Katherine Potter

**Bryant, M.**
See   Munn, Marguerite

**Bryant, Paul William** 1913-   [FB]
*American football coach*
* Bryant, Bear

**Bryant, Peter**
See   George, Peter [Bryan]

**Bryant, Raphael** 1931-   [DAM, EJ]
*American jazz musician*
* Bryant, Ray

**Bryant, Ray**
See   Bryant, Raphael

**Bryant, Ronald Raymond** 1947-
[BE]
*American baseball player*
* Bryant, Bear

**Bryant, Royal G.** 1929-   [EJ7]
*American jazz musician*
* Bryant, Rusty

**Bryant, Rusty**
See   Bryant, Royal G.

**Bryant, Slim**
See   Bryant, Thomas Hoyt

**Bryant, Thomas Hoyt** 1908-
[CWG, DAM]
*American country-western performer*
* Bryant, Slim

**Bryant, William Cullen** 1794-1880
[PA]
*Author*
* Herbert, Francis

**Bryat, Edith**
See   Brayton, Gertrude E.

**Bryce, Ronald**
See   Rockey, Howard

**Brydges, [Sir] Edgerton** 1762-1867
[PA]
*Author*
* Gordon, [Sir] Cosmo

**Brydges, Grey** ?-1621   [FFF, SN]
*Earl of Chandos*
* [The] King of Cotswold

**Brydges, Harold**
See   Bridge, James Howard

**Brydges, Mrs. Castel**   [FFF]
*Entertainer*
* Freeman, Ida

**Brydges, Samuel Egerton**
1762-1837   [PA]
*Author*
* S. E. B.

**Brydone, Alfred**
See   Boak, Alfred Brydone

**Bryher, Winifred**
See   Ellerman, Annie Winifred

**Brymn, James** 1881-1946   [IBW]
*American orchestra leader and
composer*
* Brymn, Tim

**Brymn, Tim**
See   Brymn, James

**Bryner, Edna**
See   Bryner-Schwab, Edna

**Bryner, Youl** 1915-   [EMT, FC]
*Russian-born actor*
* Brynner, Yul

**Bryner-Schwab, Edna** 1886-
[NAA]
*American author*
* Bryner, Edna

**Brynner, Yul**
See   Bryner, Youl

**Bryson, Bernarda** 1905?-
[CA, SAT, TBJ]
*American author and illustrator*
* Shahn, Bernarda Bryson

**Bryson, Charles** 1887- ?   [CC, WW]
*Irish-born author*
* Barry, Charles

**Bryson, Leigh**
See   Rutledge, Nancy

**Bryson, Peabo**
See   Bryson, Robert

**Bryson, Robert** 1952-   [IBW]
*American singer*
* Bryson, Peabo

**Brzezinski, Emilie Anna [Benes]**
*Wife of American national security
advisor Zbigniew Brzezinski*
* Brzezinski, Muska

**Brzezinski, Muska**
See   Brzezinski, Emilie Anna
[Benes]

**Brzezinski, Zbig**
See   Brzezinski, Zbigniew

**Brzezinski, Zbigniew** 1926?-
*National security advisor to
American president, Jimmy Carter*
* Brzezinski, Zbig
* Vitamin Z
* Woodpecker, Woody

**Bschliessmayer, Josef** 1922-
[BDF, FC, WEF]
*Austrian actor*
* Werner, Oskar

**Bubb, Belle Z.**
See   Beckner, S. W. E.

**Bubb, Mel**
See   Whitcomb, Ian

**Bubba Free John**
See   Jones, Franklin

**[The] Bubblegum Bomber**
See   O'Grady, Sean

**Bubbles**
See   Silverman, Belle Miriam

**Bucca Porci [Pig's Snout]**
See   Peter

**Bucchieri, Theresa F.**
See   Bicchieri, Theresa F.

**Bucci, Vincent** 1921-   [EJ]
*American jazz musician*
* Burke, Vinnie

**Buccieri, Fifi**
See   Buccieri, Fiore

**Buccieri, Fiore** 1904-1973   [BLB]
*American underworld figure*
* Buccieri, Fifi

**Bucer [or Butzer], Martin**
See   Kuhhorn, Martin

**Buchalter, Lepke**
See   Buchalter, Louis

**Buchalter, Louis** 1897-1944
[BLB, CEC, MM]
*American underworld figure*
* Buchalter, Lepke
* Judge Louis

**Buchan, A. W.**   [PA]
*Author*
* Esther

**Buchan, Annabelle Whitford**
1878-1961   [SC]
*American actress*
* Peerless Annabelle

**Buchan, David**
See   Womack, David A[lfred]

**Buchan, John** 1875-1940   [WGT]
*British author*
* Cadmus and Harmonia [joint
   pseudonym with Susan Buchan]
* Erskine, Douglas

**Buchan, Margaret**   [FFF]
*Writer*
* Aunt Margaret

**Buchan, Susan** 1882-   [WGT]
*Author*
* Cadmus and Harmonia [joint
   pseudonym with John Buchan]

**Buchanan, Betty [Joan]** 1923-
[CA, WW]
*American author*
* Shepherd, Joan

**Buchanan, Buck**
See   Buchanan, Chester

**Buchanan, Buck**
See   Buchanan, Junious

**Buchanan, Buck**
See   Buchanan, William T.

**Buchanan, Bucky**
See   Buchanan, Ralph L.

**Buchanan, Chester** 20th c.   [OBW]
*American baseball player*
* Buchanan, Buck

**Buchanan, Chuck**
See   Rowland, D[onald] S[ydney]

**Buchanan, Fannie** 1872-1952
[THR]
*American actress*
* Ward, Fannie

**Buchanan, Goober**
See   Buchanan, James Gilbert

**Buchanan, James** 1791-1868
[DEP, FFF, SN]
*American president*
* [The] Bachelor President
* O. P. F.
* Old Buck
* [The] Old Public Functionary
* Old Zach
* [The] Sage of Wheatland
* Ten Cent Jimmy

**Buchanan, James Gilbert** 1917-
[CWG, DAM]
*American country-western performer*
* Buchanan, Goober

**Buchanan, Junious** 1940-   [B10, FB]
*American football player*
* Buchanan, Buck

**Buchanan, Marie**   [CA]
*British author*
* Petrie, Rhona

**Buchanan, Mary Estill** 1935?-
*American politician*
* Give-'em-Hell Mary

**Buchanan, Patrick**
See   Corley, Edwin

**Buchanan, Ralph L.** 1922-   [CEI]
*Canadian-born hockey player*
* Buchanan, Bucky

**Buchanan, Robert Angus** 1930-
[IAW]
*British author*
* Janus

**Buchanan, Robert Williams**
1841-1901   [DEL, FFF, RH]
*British author and poet*
* Caliban
* Maitland, Thomas

**Buchanan, Virginia**
See   Parker, Mrs. Benton

**Buchanan, William**
See   Buck, William Ray

**Buchanan, William T.** 1933-
[SMG]
*American football team staff
member*
* Buchanan, Buck

**Buchanan-Brown, John** 1929-   [CA]
*British author, translator, editor*
* Warland, John

**Bucharoff, Simon**
See   Buchhalter, Simon

**Bucheim**
See   Fagius, Paul

**Bucher, George** ?-1923
[BLB, PHM]
*American bootlegger*
* Bucher, Spot

**Bucher, Spot**
See   Bucher, George

**Buchhalter, Simon** 1881-1955
[BBD]
*Russian-born American pianist and
composer*
* Bucharoff, Simon

**Buchholz, Butch**
See   Buchholz, Earl, Jr.

**Buchholz, Earl, Jr.**   [OET]
*American tennis player*
* Buchholz, Butch

**Buchholz [or Bucholz], Horst** 1933-
[WEF]
*German-born actor*
* Brookholt, Henry

**Buchinsky, Charles** 1922-
[HT, IPA, SW]
*American actor*
* Bronson, Charles

**Buchmann, Theodor** 1500?-1564
[WBD]
*Swiss theologian and scholar*
* Bibliander

**Buchwald, Martin** 1943-   [RO2]
*American singer*
* Balin, Marty

**Buck, Adele** 1891-1912   [SC]
*American actress*
* Bertram, Vedah

**Buck, Billy**
See   Buckner, William Joseph

**Buck, Charlie**
See   Palermo, Charles

**Buck, Cub**
See   Buck, Howard

**Buck, Doug**
See   Filer, Thomas Hanford

**Buck, Ford**
See   Washington, Ford Lee

**Buck, Henry**   [FFF, PA]
*British writer*
* Hotspur

**Buck, Howard**   [SMG]
*American football player*
* Buck, Cub

**Buck, Laura A.**   [PA]
*Author*
* Williams, Katherine

**Buck, Marilyn Jean** 1947?-
*American political activist*
* Lewis, Nina?

**Buck, Pearl S[ydenstricker]**
1892-1973 [CA, SAT]
*American author*
* Sedges, John

**Buck, Ruth**
See Lamb, Ruth

**Buck, William Ray** 1930-
[CA, WD]
*American author*
* Buchanan, William

**Bucketfoot Al Simmons**
See Szymanski, Aloysius Harry

**Buckeye**
See Cox, Samuel Sullivan

**Buckeye, Garland Maiers**
1897-1975 [B10, BE]
*American baseball and football
player*
* Buckeye, Gob

**Buckeye, Gob**
See Buckeye, Garland Maiers

**Buckholtz, Wanda** 1870-1923
*American actress*
* Argove, Debbie

**Buckingham, Bruce** [joint pseudonym
with Anthony Stansfeld]
See Lilley, Peter

**Buckingham, Bruce** [joint pseudonym
with Peter Lilley]
See Stansfeld, Anthony

**Buckingham, Fanny Louise**
See Pettitt, Mrs.

**Buckingham, James [William]**
1932- [CA]
*American author and columnist*
* Buckingham, Jamie

**Buckingham, Jamie**
See Buckingham, James [William]

**Buckingham, Jessie** [FFF]
*Entertainer*
* Rosa, Patti

**Buckland, Francis Trevelyan**
1826-1880 [FFF]
*British naturalist and author*
* Irondequoit

**Buckland, Raymond** 1934- [CA]
*British-born author and illustrator*
* Earll, Tony
* Wells, Jessica

**Buckland-Wright, Mary Elizabeth**
[AW]
*Canadian-born author*
* Hume, Frances

**Buckle, G. E.**
See Buckle, George Earle

**Buckle, George Earle** 1854-1935
[LC]
*British author and journalist*
* Buckle, G. E.

**Buckles, Jess Robert** 1890- [BE]
*American baseball player*
* Buckles, Jim

**Buckles, Jim**
See Buckles, Jess Robert

**Buckley, Fergus Reid** 1930- [CA]
*French-born business executive and
author*
* Crumpet, Peter

**Buckley, Fiona**
See Anand, Valerie

**Buckley, Theodore William Alois**
1825-1856 [PA]
*Author*
* Hawkins, Tom

**Buckmaster, Henrietta**
See Henkle, Henrietta

**Buckner, Brad**
See Repp, Ed[ward] Earl

**Buckner, Buck**
See Buckner, William Joseph

**Buckner, Quinn** 1954- [SMG]
*American basketball player*
* Q
* Q. B.

**Buckner, William Joseph** 1949-
[PB, SMG]
*American baseball player*
* Buck, Billy
* Buckner, Buck

**Buckrose, J. E.**
See Jameson, Annie Edith

**Buckskin Bill**
See Hart, Sylvan Ambrose

**Buckskin Joe**
See Hoyt, Edward Jonathan

**Buckstone, Mrs. J. C.** [FFF]
*Entertainer*
* Measor, Adele

**Buckton, Florence**
See Wollersen, Florence

**Bucyk, Chief**
See Bucyk, John Paul

**Bucyk, John Paul** 1935-
[FHE, SMG]
*Canadian-born hockey player*
* Bucyk, Chief

**Budd, Jackson**
See Budd, William John

**Budd, John** 1913- [AW]
*British author*
* Prescot, Julian

**Budd, Mavis** 20th c. [CA]
*British author and poet*
* Denham, Sully

**Budd, William John** 1898- [WW]
*Author*
* Budd, Jackson
* Jackson, Wallace

**Budde, Gerhard August** 1865- ?
[LAO]
*German educator and author*
* Friese, [Dr.] Edzard

**Budde, Johann Franz** 1667-1729
[WBD]
*German theologian and scholar*
* Buddeus, Johann Franz

**Buddee, Paul Edgar** 1913- [AW]
*Australian author, educator,
musician*
* Richards, Paul

**Buddeus, Johann Franz**
See Budde, Johann Franz

**[The] Buddhist St. Augustine**
See Shonin, Shodo

**Buddicom, Jacintha Laura May**
[LAO]
*British poet*
* Dering, Cini Willoughby

**Buddy Boy**
See Guy, George

**Buddy the King**
See Bolden, Charles

**Bude, Guillaume** 1467-1540
[DEP, DNNS, RH]
*French scholar*
* [The] Prodigy of France

**Budgell, Eustace** 1685-1736 [PA]
*Author*
* X.

**Budgen, L. M.** 19th c. [DEL, FFF]
*American poet*
* Acheta Domestica

**Budlong, Pharaoh**
See Perkins, Frederick Beecher

**Budnitz, Buzzy**
See Budnitz, Emil A., Jr.

**Budnitz, Emil A., Jr.** 20th c. [BBH]
*American lacrosse player and coach*
* Budnitz, Buzzy

**Budry, Chester** 1921?-1975 [FIR]
*Orchestra leader*
* [The] Polka King

**Budrys, Algirdas Jonas** 1931-
[ESF, SFL, WGT]
*American author and editor*
* Budrys, Algis
* Hodgkins, David C.
* Janvier, Ivan
* Janvier, Paul
* Marner, Robert
* Rome, Alger [joint pseudonym
  with Jerome Lewis Bixby]
* Scarff, William
* Sentry, John A.
* Stroud, Albert
* Van Dall, Harold?

**Budrys, Algis**
See Budrys, Algirdas Jonas

**[The] Bueckburg Bach**
See Bach, Johann Christoph
Friedrich

**Buehnau, Ludwig**
See Schreiber, Hermann O. L.

**Buehren, Ernst Johann** 1690-1772
[WBD]
*Russian statesman*
* Biron, Ernst Johann

**Buek, Richard** 1929-1957 [BBH]
*American skier*
* [The] Madman of Donner
  Summit

**Buell, Marjorie Henderson** 20th c.
[WECO]
*American cartoonist*
* Marge

**Buell, Robert Kingery** 1908-1971
[CAP]
*American author and poet*
* Brother Bob

**Buell, Wilder**
See Wilder, Katherine Loving
Buell

**Buelow, Bernhard-Viktor von**
1923- [WECO]
*German cartoonist*
* Loriot

**Buelow, Frederick William**
1876-1933 [BE]
*German-born baseball player*
* Buelow, Fritz

**Buelow, Fritz**
See Buelow, Frederick William

**Buenamar, Ricardo**
See Cabrera, Raimundo

**[El] Bueno**
See Perez de Guzman, Alphonso
[or Alonso]

**Bueno, Bill**
See Bueno, Jose de la Torre

**Bueno, Jose** 1937- [CAR]
*American painter*
* Goode, Joe

**Bueno, Jose de la Torre** 1905?-1980
*American editor*
* Bueno, Bill

**Buerger, Lucian**
See Niese, Charlotte

**Buet, Charles** [PA]
*Author*
* Vindex

**Buff, Johnny**
See Lesky, John

**Buffalo Bill**
See Cody, William Frederick

**Buffalo Bill Hogg**
See Hogg, William [Bill]

**Buffalo Bill, Jr.**
See Wilsey, Jay

**Buffalo Chuck**
See Barth, Charles P.

**[The] Buffalo Hangman**
See Cleveland, [Stephen] Grover

**[The] Buffalo Sheriff**
See Cleveland, [Stephen] Grover

**Buffon, Georges Louis Leclerc de**
1707-1788 [SN]
*French naturalist*
* [The] King of Phrases

**[The] Buffoon**
See Lincoln, Abraham

**Bufman, Zeev** 1930- [BEW]
*Israeli producer*
* Bufman, Zev

**Bufman, Zev**
See Bufman, Zeev

**Buford, George** 1929-
[BWW, NBB]
*American singer*
* Buford, Little George
* Mojo
* Waters, Muddy, Jr.

**Buford, Little George**
See Buford, George

**[The] Bug**
See Workman, Charles

**Bugaev [or Bugayev], Boris Nikolaevich** 1880-1934
[CD, EWL, TCL]
*Russian author, poet, critic*
* Bely [or Belyi], Andrei

**Bugbee, Ruth Carson** 1903-   [CA]
*American writer*
* Carson, Ruth

**Bugenhagen, Johann** 1485-1558
[PA, WBD]
*German religious reformer*
* Pomeranus
* Pommer, Dr.

**Buggy Whip Maddox**
*See* Maddox, Garry Lee

**Buglin Sam, the Waffle Man**
*See* Dekemel, Matthew Antoine Desire

**Bugs Bunny Ford**
*See* Ford, Phil

**Buist, Charlotte**
*See* Patterson, Charlotte [Buist]

**Buker, Cy**
*See* Buker, Cyril Owen

**Buker, Cyril Owen** 1919-   [BE]
*American baseball player*
* Buker, Cy

**Buker, Happy**
*See* Buker, Harry L.

**Buker, Harry L.** 20th c.   [BE]
*American baseball player*
* Buker, Happy

**Bukich, Rifle**
*See* Bukich, Rudolph A.

**Bukich, Rudolph A.** 1932-   [FB]
*American football player*
* Bukich, Rifle

**Buley, Bernard** 20th c.   [MBF]
*British editor*
* Masters, Bat
* McRae, Roy

**Bulgakov, Mikhail Ivanovich** ?-1554   [WBD]
*Russian aristocrat*
* Golitsa

**Bulkeley, Morgan Gardner** 1837-1922   [BAB]
*American business executive, politician, baseball financier*
* [The] Crow Bar Governor

**Bulkley, Annette Mabel** 1868- ?
[WWL]
*British author*
* A. M. B.

**Bulkley, Mrs. Edward A.**   [FFF]
*Entertainer*
* Thropp, Florence

**[The] Bull**
*See* Ferrara, Alfred John

**[The] Bull**
*See* Lawrence, Ulysses Brooks

**[The] Bull**
*See* Luzinski, Gregory Michael

**[The] Bull**
*See* Montagna, Luigi

**[The] Bull**
*See* Ohira, Masayoshi

**[The] Bull**
*See* Pennochio, Tommy

**[The] Bull**
*See* Simons, Arthur D.

**[The] Bull**
*See* Sobhuza II

**[The] Bull**
*See* Uhle, George Ernest

**Bull, Albert E.** 20th c.
[MBF, WWL]
*British author and editor*
* Basset, Arthur Ward
* Cromwell, Victor

**Bull Cow**
*See* Burnett, Chester Arthur

**Bull, David** 1955?-
*American magician*
* [Le] Grand David

**[The] Bull Dog of la Valliere**
*See* Rive, Jean Joseph

**Bull Face Double-Fee, Sir**
*See* Norton, Fletcher [First Baron Grantley]

**Bull Faced Jones**
*See* Jones, [Sir] William

**Bull, Lois** 1900-   [WW]
*Author*
* Burt, Melville
* Wright, Judith Grovner

**[The] Bull Moose**
*See* Roosevelt, Theodore [Teddy]

**Bull Moose Jackson**
*See* Jackson, Benjamin Clarence

**Bull, Mrs.**   [PA]
*Author*
* E. Q. A. B.

**[The] Bull Necked Forger**
*See* Balsamo, Giuseppe

**Bull Run Russell**
*See* Russell, [Sir] William Howard

**[The] Bull Speaker**
*See* Amner, Ralph

**Bull, [Sergeant] Terry**
*See* Triplet, William Samuel

**Bull-us, Hector**
*See* Paulding, James Kirke

**Bullard, Arthur** 1880- ?   [ALY]
*American author*
* Edwards, Albert

**Bullard, Eugene Jacques** 1894-1961   [IBW]
*American fighter pilot*
* [The] Black Swallow

**Bullas, Derby**
*See* Bullas, Simeon Edward

**Bullas, Sim**
*See* Bullas, Simeon Edward

**Bullas, Simeon Edward** 1861-1908
[BE]
*American baseball player*
* Bullas, Derby
* Bullas, Sim

**[The] Bulldozer**
*See* Sharon, Ariel

**Bulleid, Henry Anthony Vaughan** 1912-   [AW, CAP]
*British engineer, cinematographer, author*
* Collins, D.

**Buller, Hy**
*See* Buller, Hyman

**Buller, Hyman** 1926-1968   [FHE]
*Canadian-born hockey player*
* Buller, Hy

**Buller of Brazenose**
*See* Hughes, John

**Buller, [Sir] Redvers Henry** 1839-1908   [NN]
*British military leader*
* Reverse, Sir

**Bullet Ben Benson**
*See* Benson, Allen Wilbert

**Bullet Bill Dudley**
*See* Dudley, William M.

**Bullet Bill Singer**
*See* Singer, William Robert

**Bullet Bob Burns**
*See* Burns, Bob

**Bullet Bob Hayes**
*See* Hayes, Robert L.

**Bullet Bob Turley**
*See* Turley, Robert Lee

**Bullet Jack Thoney**
*See* Thoeny, John

**Bullet Joe Bush**
*See* Bush, Leslie Ambrose

**Bullet Joe Rogan**
*See* Rogan, Wilbur

**Bullet Joe Silverstein**
*See* Silverstein, Joseph L.

**Bullet Joe Simpson**
*See* Simpson, Harold Joseph

**Bulletin**
*See* Guild, Mr.

**Bullett, Gerald [William]** 1894-1958   [CC, WW]
*Author*
* Fox, Sebastian

**Bullface Doubleface, Sir**
*See* Fletcher, [Sir] Norton

**[The] Bullfrog of the Pontine Marshes**
*See* Mussolini, Benito

**Bulliet, Richard W[illiams]** 1940-
[CA]
*American author and historian*
* Jackson, Clarence J. L.

**Bullingham, Rodney**
*See* Sladen, Norman St. Barbe

**Bullins, Ed** 1943-   [IBW]
*American author*
* Bass, Kingsley B., Jr.

**Bullion, Laura** 20th c.   [BLB]
*American train robber*
* Rose, Della

**Bullivant, Cecil Henry** 1882-
[MBF, WWL]
*British author and editor*
* Dixon, Robert W.
* Everard, Maurice
* Grey, Carlton

**Bullivant, Cecil Henry** (Continued)
* Millard, Alice
* North, Colonel
* Turville, Henry

**Bullivant, Margaret D.** 1886-
[WWL]
*British author*
* Templeton, Ruth

**Bullmore, Jeremy** 20th c.   [WD]
*British author*
* Blake, Justin [joint pseudonym with John (Griffith) Bowen]

**Bulloch, John Malcolm** 1867- ?
[WWL]
*British author*
* J. M. B.

**Bullock, Barbara**
*See* Bullock-Wilson, Barbara

**Bullock, Malton Joseph** 1912-   [BE]
*American baseball player*
* Bullock, Red

**Bullock, Michael [Hale]** 1918-
[CA, WD]
*British author, poet, playwright*
* Hale, Michael

**Bullock, Red**
*See* Bullock, Malton Joseph

**Bullock, William** ?-1964   [BEW]
*Theatrical performer*
* Seth, Will

**Bullock-Webster, Llewelyn** 1879- ?
[NAA]
*Welsh playwright and poet*
* Sultan El Osman, Chareh
* Tua Fault, Frank

**Bullock-Wilson, Barbara** 1945-
[CA]
*American author and educator*
* Bullock, Barbara

**Bullocks, Amos** 20th c.
*American football player*
* Bullocks, Bull

**Bullocks, Bull**
*See* Bullocks, Amos

**Bulmer, [Henry] Kenneth** 1921-
[CA, ESF, WD]
*British author*
* Akers, Alan Burt
* Brandon, Frank
* Clinton, Rupert
* Corley, Ernest
* Frazier, Arthur
* Green, Peter
* Hardy, Adam
* Johns, Kenneth [joint pseudonym with John Newman]
* Kent, Philip
* Langholm, Neil
* Maras, Karl [house pseudonym, Comyns]
* Quiller, Andrew
* Scot, Chesman
* Sherwood, Nelson
* Stratford, Philip
* Zetford, Tully

**Bulmer-Thomas, Ivor** 1905-   [WD]
*British author and politician*
* Thomas, Ivor

**Bulsara, Frederick** 1946-   [RO2]
*British singer*
* Mercury, Fred

**Bulwer-Lytton, Edward George Earle Lytton** 1805?-1873
[DEL, FFF, RH]
*British author and playwright*
* Caxton, Pisistratus

**Bulwer-Lytton, Edward Robert** 1831-1891   [DEL, SFP]
*British statesman and poet*
* Meredith, Owen
* Trevor, Edward

**Bulyga** 1901-1956   [EWL]
*Russian author*
* Fadeyev, Alexander [Alexandrovich]

**Bumble Bee Slim**
See   Easton, Amos

**Bumbry, Al**
See   Bumbry, Alonza Benjamin

**Bumbry, Alonza Benjamin** 1947-
[BE, SMG]
*American baseball player*
* Bumbry, Al

**Bumbry, Grace Ann Melzia** 1937-
[IBW]
*American opera singer*
* Black Venus

**Bump, Franklin E., Jr.** 1898-
[NAA]
*American writer, journalist, editor*
* Kilby, Morgan

**Bumpas, Bob**
See   Bumpas, H. W.

**Bumpas, H. W.** 1911-1959   [SC]
*Actor and screenwriter*
* Bumpas, Bob

**Bumppo, Nathaniel John Balthazar**
See   Dean, John Edwin

**Bumppo, Natty**
See   Dean, John Edwin

**Bumpus, Doris Marjorie** 1905-
[WW]
*Author*
* Alan, Marjorie

**Bun**
See   Sheahan, D. B.

**Bunbury, Henry William**
1750-1811   [DEP, SN]
*British artist*
* [The] Second Hogarth

**Bunce, Corajane Diane** 1919-
[ASC]
*American musician*
* Ward, Diane

**Bunce, Oliver Bell** 1828-1890
[FFF]
*American author, playwright, editor*
* Bluff, Bachelor
* Censor

**Bunch, David R.** 20th c.   [CA]
*American author and poet*
* Groupe, Darryl R.

**Bunch, William** 1902-1941   [BWW]
*American singer*
* [The] Devil's Son-in-Law
* [The] High Sheriff from Hell
* Wheatstraw, Peetie

**Buncle, John**
See   Amory, Thomas

**Bundrick, John** 20th c.   [RM, RO2]
*Musician*
* Bundrick, Rabbit

**Bundrick, Rabbit**
See   Bundrick, John

**Bundsmann, Anton [or Emil]**
1906-1967   [BDF, FD, WEF]
*American director*
* Mann, Anthony [or Anton]

**[El] Bundukhari**
See   Dent, Anthony Austen

**Bungay, E. Newton** 20th c.   [MBF]
*British writer*
* Lance, John
* Richmond, H. B.

**Buning, Sietze**
See   Wiersma, Stanley M[arvin]

**Bunke, Haydee Tamara** 1937-1967
[B10, EE]
*Argentinian-born intelligence agent for Russia*
* Guterrez, Laura
* Tania

**Bunker, Buddy**
See   Bunker, Earle L.

**Bunker, Earle L.** 1912?-1975   [B10]
*American photographer*
* Bunker, Buddy

**Bunker Hill**
See   De Costa, Benjamin Franklin

**Bunker, Max**
See   Secchi, Luciano

**Bunker, Tim**
See   Clift, William

**Bunn, Alden** 1924-1977   [BWW]
*American singer*
* Baum, Allen
* Bunn, Allen
* Tarheel Slim

**Bunn, Alfred** 1796?-1860
[DEP, DNNS, PA]
*British theatrical manager and playwright*
* Bunn, Poet
* Conrad
* [The] Napoleon of the Drama

**Bunn, Allen**
See   Bunn, Alden

**Bunn, Ann**   [BWW]
*American singer*
* Bunn, Little Ann

**Bunn, Little Ann**
See   Bunn, Ann

**Bunn, Poet**
See   Bunn, Alfred

**Bunn, Richard** 1894-   [BBD, WBD]
*American opera singer*
* Bonelli, Richard

**Bunner, Henry Cuyler** 1855-1896
[FFF, PA]
*American writer*
* Dusenberry, V. Hugo
* Lot, Arthur
* Oakes, A. H.
* Penn, Arthur

**Bunny**
See   Schultze, Carl Edward

**Bunsby, Jack**
See   Vandenburgh, Theodore H.

**Bunston, Anna**
See   De Bary, Anna

**Bunting, A. E.**
See   Bunting, Anne Evelyn

**Bunting, Anne Evelyn** 1928-   [CA]
*Irish-born author*
* Bolton, Evelyn
* Bunting, A. E.
* Bunting, Eve

**Bunting, Daniel George** 1890-1967
[LC]
*Author and critic*
* George, Daniel

**Bunting, Eve**
See   Bunting, Anne Evelyn

**Buntline, Ned**
See   Judson, Edward Zane Carroll

**Bunyan, Bishop**
See   Bunyan, John

**Bunyan, John** 1628-1688
[DEP, FFF, SN]
*British clergyman and author*
* Bunyan, Bishop
* [The] Immortal Dreamer
* [The] Immortal Tinker
* [The] Inspired Tinker

**Buonaccorsi, Filippo** 1437-1496
[RH, SN]
*Italian sculptor*
* [The] Italian Callimachus

**Buonaccorsi, Pietro** 1501-1547
[WBD]
*Italian painter*
* Vaga, Perino del

**Buonarroti, Michelangelo [or Michael Angelo]** 1475-1564
[DNNS, FF, SN]
*Italian sculptor, painter, architect*
* [The] Divine Madman
* [The] Interpreter of the Renaissance
* Michelangelo [or Michael Angelo]
* [The] Salt of Art

**Buoncompagni, Ugo** 1502-1585
[WBD]
*Pope*
* Gregory XIII

**Buonconciglio, Ian** 1947-   [RO2]
*American musician*
* Lloyd, Ian

**Buoniconti, Nicholas** 1940-   [FB]
*American football player*
* Buoniconti, Skip

**Buoniconti, Skip**
See   Buoniconti, Nicholas

**Buonoma, J.**
See   Aiuppa, Joseph John [Joe]

**Bupp, Walter**
See   Garrett, [Gordon] Randall [Philip David]

**Burack, Sylvia** 1916-   [CA]
*American editor and author*
* Kamerman, Sylvia E.

**Burain, Paul**   [PA]
*Author*
* Cocambo
* Strapontin

**Buranelli, Agnes Wallace** 1917-
[IAW]
*British-born author and translator*
* Gillespie, Nan

**Buranelli, Prosper** 20th c.   [CA]
*Author*
* Prosper, John [joint pseudonym with John C(hipman) Farrar]

**[Il] Buranello**
See   Galuppi, Baldassare

**Burbage, Benjamin** 20th c.   [OBW]
*American baseball player*
* Burbage, Buddy

**Burbage, Buddy**
See   Burbage, Benjamin

**Burbage, Buddy**
See   Burbage, Knowlington O.

**Burbage, Knowlington O.** 1907-
[MK]
*American baseball player*
* Burbage, Buddy

**Burbage, Richard** 1566-1619?
[DNNF, HF]
*British actor*
* [The] British Roscius
* [The] English Roscius

**Burbeck, Mrs. F. M.**   [FFF]
*Entertainer*
* Lingard, Nellie

**Burbidge, Eric** 1904-   [THR]
*British actor and singer*
* Fawcett, Eric

**Burce, Suzanne** 1929-
[FC, ITA, PMJ]
*American actress and singer*
* Powell, Jane

**Burch, Allene** 20th c.
*Actress*
* Ray, Allene

**Burchard, S. H.**
See   Burchard, Sue

**Burchard, Sue** 1937-   [CA]
*American author and librarian*
* Burchard, S. H.

**Burchell, Frederick** 1931-   [CEI]
*Canadian-born hockey player*
* Burchell, Skippy

**Burchell, Skippy**
See   Burchell, Frederick

**[Il] Burchiello**
See   Di Giovanni, Domenico

**Burchiello, Domenico**
See   Di Giovanni, Domenico

**Burchstein, Rosa Raisa** 1893-1963
[MS]
*Polish-born opera singer*
* Raisa, Rosa

**Burckhardt, Georg** 1484-1545
[WBD]
*German religious reformer*
* Spalatin, Georg

**Burden, Jean** 1914-
[CA, IAW, WD]
*American author and poet*
* Ames, Felicia
* Prussing, M. Jean

**Burden, Luther** 1953-   [NBA]
*American basketball player*
* Burden, Ticky

**Burden, Ticky**
See Burden, Luther

**Burdett, [Sir] Francis** 1770-1844
[FFF, HN, SN]
*British political leader*
* England's Pride and
  Westminster's Glory
* Old Glory
* [The] Piccadilly Patriot

**Burdett, Miss** [PA]
*Author*
* Ansted, Hope

**Burdette, Robert J.** 1831- ? [PA]
*Author*
* Hawkeye Man

**Burdick, H. H.** 19th c. [FFF, PA]
*Author*
* Abbott, Alice Irving

**Burdick, Jennie Ellis**
See Webster, Jennie Ellis Burdick

**Burdock, Black Jack**
See Burdock, John Joseph

**Burdock, John Joseph** 1851-1931
[BE]
*American baseball player*
* Burdock, Black Jack

**Burfield, Eva**
See Ebbett, Frances Eva

**Burford, Eleanor**
See Hibbert, Eleanor Alice
[Burford]

**Burford, Roger D'Este** 1904-
[WW]
*Author*
* East, Roger
* Simon [joint pseudonym with
  Oswell Blakeston]

**Burg, David**
See Dolberg, Alexander

**Burg, Paul**
See Schaumburg, Paul

**Burge, Doris Marie** 1911- [BEW]
*American actress*
* Arling, Joyce

**Burge, Milward Rodon Kennedy**
1884?-1968 [CC, EMD, WW]
*British author, civil servant,*
*journalist*
* Cabot, Joseph
* Elder, Evelyn
* Kennedy, Milward

**Burgeon, G. A. L.**
See Barfield, [Arthur] Owen

**Burger, John**
See Marquard, Leo[pold]

**Burgess, Ann Marie**
See Gerson, Noel Bertram

**Burgess, Anthony**
See Wilson, John [Anthony]
Burgess

**Burgess, Em**
See Burgess, Mary Wyche

**Burgess, Forrest Harrill** 1927-
[B10, BE, PB]
*American baseball player*
* Burgess, Smoky

**Burgess, George** 1809-1866 [PA]
*Author*
* Cato

**Burgess, George** 1908- [FC]
*American actor*
* Meredith, Burgess

**Burgess, Joseph** 1853- ? [WWL]
*British author*
* Joe

**Burgess, Lord**
See Burgie, Irving

**Burgess, Marlena** 1944- [EJ7]
*American singer and songwriter*
* Shaw, Marlena

**Burgess, Mary** 1909- [WD]
*Australian writer*
* Burgess, Sally

**Burgess, Mary Wyche** 1916- [CA]
*American journalist*
* Burgess, Em

**Burgess, Michael**
See Gerson, Noel Bertram

**Burgess, Michael Roy** 1948-
[ESF, SFL]
*American publisher and author*
* Cooper, C. Everett
* Reginald, R[obert]
* Webb, Lucas

**Burgess, Paul** 1886- [NAA]
*American-born missionary and*
*author*
* Cuidano, P.

**Burgess, Sally**
See Burgess, Mary

**Burgess, Smoky**
See Burgess, Forrest Harrill

**Burgess, Starling** 1915- [CA]
*American author and illustrator*
* Tudor, Tasha

**Burgess, Thomas Roland [Tom]**
1927- [BE]
*Canadian-born baseball player*
* Burgess, Tim

**Burgess, Thornton Waldo**
1874-1965 [CA]
*American author and editor*
* Thornton, W. B.

**Burgess, Tim**
See Burgess, Thomas Roland
[Tom]

**Burgess, Trevor**
See Dudley-Smith, Trevor

**Burgie, Irving** 1924- [ASC]
*American singer and songwriter*
* Burgess, Lord

**Burgin, G. B.**
See Burgin, George Brown

**Burgin, George Brown** 1856-1944
[LC]
*British author*
* Burgin, G. B.

**Burgin, Nellie Paulina** 1930-
[BEW, CA, FC]
*American actress and singer*
* Bergen, Polly

**Burgmeier, Bugs**
See Burgmeier, Thomas Henry

**Burgmeier, Thomas Henry** 1943-
[BE]
*American baseball player*
* Burgmeier, Bugs

**Burgmein**
See Ricordi, Giulio

**Burgoyne, Elizabeth**
See Pickles, M[abel] Elizabeth

**Burgoyne, John** 1722?-1792
[DNNS, FF, FFF]
*British army officer and playwright*
* Brag, [Sir] Jack
* Chrononhotonthologos

**Burian, Jarka M.**
See Burian, Jaroslav Marsano

**Burian, Jaroslav Marsano** 1927-
[BEW, CA]
*American actor, director, educator*
* Burian, Jarka M.

**Buridan, Jean** 1295-1360 [HN]
*French philosopher*
* Scolasticus, Doctor

**Burk, Clyde** 1913-1945 [GW]
*American rodeo performer*
* Burk, Sagey

**Burk, Sagey**
See Burk, Clyde

**Burkart, Elmer Robert** 1917- [BE]
*American baseball player*
* Burkart, Swede

**Burkart, Swede**
See Burkart, Elmer Robert

**Burkauskus, Billy** 1902- [GME]
*American golfer*
* Burke, Billy

**Burke, Aileen** 1877-1939 [THR]
*British actress and singer*
* D'Orme, Aileen

**Burke, Arleigh** 1901-
[BDW, WWW]
*American naval officer*
* Burke, 31 Knot

**Burke, Barbara**
See Ball, Oona Howard

**Burke, Billie**
See Burke, Mary William
Ethelbert Appleton

**Burke, Billy**
See Burkauskus, Billy

**Burke, Blanche E.** ?-1935 [SC]
*American actress*
* McCormack, Billie

**Burke, Buck**
See Burke, Les[lie Kingston]

**Burke, Carl F.**
See Ackerman, Forrest J[ames]

**Burke, Charles F.** 20th c. [BLB]
*American train robber*
* Burke, Dink

**Burke, Dink**
See Burke, Charles F.

**Burke, Edmund** 1729-1797
[HN, RH, SN]
*British statesman, orator, author*
* [The] Dinner Bell
* [The] Scientific Statesman

**Burke, Edward**
See Boggs, Winifred

**Burke, Elmer** 1917-1958 [BLB]
*American underworld figure*
* Burke, Trigger

**Burke, Fielding**
See Dargan, Olive [Tilford]

**Burke, Fred R.** 20th c. [BLB]
*American underworld figure*
* Burke, Killer

**Burke, Georgia**
See Burke, Gracie Maedell

**Burke, Gracie Maedell** 1906-
[BEW]
*American actress*
* Burke, Georgia

**Burke, James** 19th c. [FFF]
*American author*
* Dooley, Dan de le

**Burke, James [Jimmy]** 20th c.
*American underworld figure*
* [The] Gent

**Burke, James Timothy** 1874-1942
[BE]
*American baseball player*
* Burke, Sunset Jimmy

**Burke, John**
See O'Connor, Richard

**Burke, John [Frederick]** 1922-
[AW, CA, MBF]
*British author*
* Burke, Jonathan
* Esmond, Harriet
* George, Jonathan [joint
  pseudonym with George Theiner]
* Jones, Joanna
* Miall, Robert
* Morris, Sara
* Reid, Desmond [house
  pseudonym]
* Sands, Martin

**Burke, Jonathan**
See Burke, John [Frederick]

**Burke, Joseph Francis** 1914-
[ASC, EJ, PMJ]
*American conductor, arranger,*
*composer*
* Burke, Sonny

**Burke, Killer**
See Burke, Fred R.

**Burke, Leda**
See Garnett, David

**Burke, Lefty**
See Burke, Robert James

**Burke, Les[lie Kingston]** 1902-
[BE]
*American baseball player*
* Burke, Buck

**Burke, Marie**
See Holt, Marie

**Burke, Martha Jane [Canary]**
1848?-1903 [B10, FC, LC]
*American frontier figure*
* Calamity Jane

**Burke, Mary William Ethelbert**
**Appleton** 1884?-1970
[BEW, F2, SN]
*American actress*
* Burke, Billie

**Burke, Noel**
See Hitchens, Dolores [Birk]

**Burke, Ralph** [joint pseudonym with
Robert Silverberg]
See Garrett, [Gordon] Randall
[Philip David]

**Burke, Ralph** [joint pseudonym with Randall Garrett]
See Silverberg, Robert

**Burke, Raymond N.**
See Barrois, Raymond N.

**Burke** [or Burgo?], **Richard** 13th c.
[HN]
*Earl of Ulster*
* [The] Red Earl

**Burke, Robert James** 1907- [BE]
*American baseball player*
* Burke, Lefty

**Burke, Sailor**
See Presser, Charles

**Burke, Samson**
See Scortichini, Guido

**Burke, Shifty**
See Benton, Peggie

**Burke, Solomon** 1935- [PRS, RO1]
*American singer and songwriter*
* [The] Wonder Boy Preacher

**Burke, Sonny**
See Burke, Joseph Francis

**Burke, Sunset Jimmy**
See Burke, James Timothy

**Burke, 31 Knot**
See Burke, Arleigh

**Burke, Thomas** 1867- ? [MBF]
*British author*
* Rhodes, Oakmead

**Burke, Trigger**
See Burke, Elmer

**Burke, Vee**
See Burke, Velma Whitgrove

**Burke, Velma Whitgrove** 1921-
[CA]
*American author*
* Burke, Vee

**Burke, Vinnie**
See Bucci, Vincent

**Burke, Warren**
See Wilson, Warren

**Burkemo, Sarge**
See Burkemo, Walter

**Burkemo, Walter** 1918- [GF]
*American golfer*
* Burkemo, Sarge

**Burkett, Jesse Cail** 1868?-1953
[AS, BE, PB]
*American baseball player*
* [The] Crab

**Burkhardt, Eve** 1899- [WW]
*Author*
* Bliss, Adam [joint pseudonym with Robert Ferdinand Burkhardt]
* Eden, Rob [joint pseudonym with Robert Ferdinand Burkhardt]
* Jardin, Rex [joint pseudonym with Robert Ferdinand Burkhardt]

**Burkhardt, Kenneth William** 1916-
[BE]
*American baseball player*
* Burkhart, Ken

**Burkhardt, Robert Ferdinand**
1892-1947 [WW]
*Author*
* Bliss, Adam [joint pseudonym with Eve Burkhardt]
* Eden, Rob [joint pseudonym with Eve Burkhardt]
* Jardin, Rex [joint pseudonym with Eve Burkhardt]

**Burkhart, Kathryn Watterson**
1942- [CA]
*American author and editor*
* Burkhart, Kitsi

**Burkhart, Ken**
See Burkhardt, Kenneth William

**Burkhart, Kitsi**
See Burkhart, Kathryn Watterson

**Burkhilder, Edwin** 20th c. [SFP]
*Author*
* Jones, G. Wayman [house pseudonym]

**Burkholz, Herbert** 1932-
*Author*
* Luckless, John [joint pseudonym with Clifford Irving]

**Burkitt, Frederick Evelyn** 20th c.
[WGT]
*Author*
* Saben, Gregory [joint pseudonym with Gertrude Chetwynd Shallcross Saben]

**Burks, Alex**
See Bazzoni, Camillo

**Burks, Arthur J.** 1898-1974
[HFF, WGT]
*American author*
* Critchie, Estil
* MacArthur, Burke
* Speed Merchant of the Pulps
* Whitney, Spencer

**Burks, Jesse D.** 1923- [IBW]
*American disc jockey*
* Burks, Spider

**Burks, Spider**
See Burks, Jesse D.

**Burland, C. A.**
See Burland, Cottie [Arthur]

**Burland, Cottie** [Arthur] 1905-
[CA, SAT]
*British museum curator and author*
* Burland, C. A.

**Burland, Granville Alexander**
1927- [EJ]
*American jazz musician*
* Burland, Sascha

**Burland, Harris**
See Harris-Burland, John Burland

**Burland, Sascha**
See Burland, Granville Alexander

**Burleigh**
See Smith, Matthew Hale

**Burleigh, Cecil** 1850- ? [FFF, PA]
*Author*
* Booth, Albert J.
* Burt, Caleb
* Dayton, [Captain] Will
* No Name

**Burleigh, F. J. Le Moyne** 1845- ?
[PA]
*Author*
* Donatello

**Burleigh, Harriet E.** 1813-1864
[PA]
*Author*
* Munster, Minnie

**Burleigh, Mary Lou**
See Winn, Mary Elfrieda

**Burleigh, Mrs. C. M.** [FFF]
*Writer*
* Celia

**Burleigh,** [or Burley?], **Walter**
1275-1338 [FFF, HN, SN]
*British scholar*
* [The] Perspicuous Doctor
* [The] Plain and Perspicuous Doctor
* Planus et Perspicuus, Doctor

**Burleigh, William Henry**
1812-1871 [FFF, PA]
*American poet and journalist*
* Fuzzy Guzzy
* Ligonier

**Burleson, Richard Paul** 1951-
*American baseball player*
* Burleson, Rooster

**Burleson, Rooster**
See Burleson, Richard Paul

**Burley, Daniel Gardner** 1907-1971
[IBW]
*American editor, musician, composer*
* De Leighbur, Don

**Burlingame, Virginia** [Struble]
1900- [CAP]
*American author*
* Struble, Virginia

**Burlington**
See Saunders, Robert

**[The] Burly Burlesquer**
See Bartholomew, John

**Burly King Harry**
See Henry VIII

**Burly Mike Souchak**
See Souchak, Mike

**Burmeister, Harold** 1900-1933
[SC]
*American actor*
* Burney, Hal

**Burmister, A. H.** 20th c. [GW]
*American rodeo performer*
* Burmister, Hippy

**Burmister, Hippy**
See Burmister, A. H.

**Burn, Belle Sumner Angier** 1870- ?
[NAA]
*American landscape architect and author*
* Angier, Belle Sumner

**Burn, Cly**
See Fischer, Axel

**Burn, R. J.**
See Burn, Rodney Joseph

**Burn, Rodney Joseph** 1899- [ART]
*British painter*
* Burn, R. J.

**Burnaby, Nigel**
See Ellett, Harold Pincton

**Burnand, F. C.**
See Burnand, Francis Cowley

**Burnand, Francis Cowley**
1836-1917 [LC]
*British author and editor*
* Burnand, F. C.

**Burnbill**
See De Londres, Henry

**Burncoat, Nancy**
See Emerson, Marion Winslow

**Burne, Glen** [joint pseudonym with Gladys Elizabeth (Blun) Green]
See Green, Alan [Baer]

**Burne, Glen** [joint pseudonym with Alan (Baer) Green]
See Green, Gladys Elizabeth [Blun]

**Burne, Philip Lauraine** 1892-
[WWL]
*Author*
* Douglas, Brain

**Burne-Jones,** [Sir] **Edward Coley**
See Jones, Edward Coley

**Burnes, Leroy** 1935- [EJ]
*American jazz musician*
* Burnes, Roy

**Burnes, Roy**
See Burnes, Leroy

**Burness, Tad**
See Burness, Wallace B[inny]

**Burness, Wallace B[inny]** 1933-
[CA]
*American author and columnist*
* Burness, Tad

**Burnet, Dr.** [SN]
* [The] Noble Buzzard

**Burnet, Gilbert** 1643-1715 [SN]
*Scottish-born historian and clergyman*
* [The] Busy Scotch Parson
* [The] English Eusebius
* [The] Lying Scot

**Burnett, Bob**
See Miller, Bob

**Burnett, Carl** 1944- [RO1]
*American singer*
* Little Caesar

**Burnett, Chester Arthur** 1910-1976
[BWW, DAM, LRR]
*American singer*
* Big Foot
* Bull Cow
* Howlin' Wolf

**Burnett, David** [Benjamin Foley]
1931-1971 [CA]
*American author and editor*
* Bernarn, Terrave
* Pace, Peter

**Burnett, Fred** 20th c. [OBW]
*American baseball player*
* Burnett, Tex

**Burnett, Ivy Compton** 1892-1969
[LC]
*British author*
* Compton-Burnett, I.

**Burnett, J. Henry** 20th c. [RM]
*Musician*
* Burnett, T Bone

**Burnett, James Kelvin** 1926- [CEI]
*Canadian-born hockey player*
* Burnett, Kelly

**Burnett, John** 20th c.    [GW]
*American rodeo performer*
* Burnett, Nocona Slim

**Burnett, Kelly**
See  Burnett, James Kelvin

**Burnett, Mrs. John**    [FFF]
*Entertainer*
* Glassford, Kate

**Burnett, Nocona Slim**
See  Burnett, John

**Burnett, T Bone**
See  Burnett, J. Henry

**Burnett, Tex**
See  Burnett, Fred

**Burnett, W. R.**
See  Burnett, William Riley

**Burnett, William Riley** 1899-
[CA, LC]
*American author*
* Burnett, W. R.
* Updyke, James

**Burnette, Frog**
See  Burnette, Lester Alvin

**Burnette, Lester Alvin** 1911-1967
[CWG]
*American actor and songwriter*
* Burnette, Frog
* Burnette, Smiley

**Burnette, Smiley**
See  Burnette, Lester Alvin

**Burney, Anton**
See  Hopkins, Kenneth

**Burney, Hal**
See  Burmeister, Harold

**Burnford, S. D.**
See  Burnford, Sheila [Philip
Cochrane Every]

**Burnford, Sheila [Philip Cochrane
Every]** 1918-    [CA, FBJ, SAT]
*Scottish-born author*
* Burnford, S. D.
* Every, Philip Cochrane

**Burnham, Bee**
See  Burnham, Willie

**Burnham, Benjamin F.** 19th c.    [PA]
*Author*
* Amender

**Burnham, C. A.**
See  Burnham, Christopher
Anthony

**Burnham, Christopher Anthony**
1956-    [ART]
*British artist*
* Burnham, C. A.

**Burnham, Clara Louise [Root]**
1854-1927    [WW]
*Author*
* Douglas, Edith

**Burnham George P.** 1815- ?    [PA]
*Author*
* [The] Young 'Un

**Burnham, George Walter**
1860-1902    [BE]
*American baseball manager*
* Burnham, Watch

**Burnham, John**
See  Beckwith, Burnham Putnam

**Burnham, Mary Hewins**    [PA]
*Author*
* M. H. B.
* Satanella

**Burnham, Watch**
See  Burnham, George Walter

**Burnham, Willie** 20th c.    [OBW]
*American baseball player*
* Burnham, Bee

**Burnier, Andreas**
See  Dessaur, Catherine Irma

**Burningham, Helen Oxenbury**
1938-    [TBJ]
*British author*
* Oxenbury, Helen

**Burns, Alma** 1919-    [CA]
*American author*
* Dalton, Claire

**Burns, Bazooka**
See  Burns, Bob

**Burns, Bazooka Bob**
See  Burns, Bob

**Burns, Bernard** 1915-    [WD]
*British author and physician*
* Auld, Philip

**Burns, Bob** 1893-1956    [FC, SC]
*American comedian*
* [The] Arkansas Philosopher
* Burns, Bazooka

**Burns, Bob** 20th c.    [SMG]
*American football player*
* Burns, Bazooka Bob
* Burns, Bullet Bob

**Burns, Bobby**
See  Burns, Vincent Godfrey

**Burns, Bullet Bob**
See  Burns, Bob

**Burns, Dorothy**
See  Vernon, Dorothy

**Burns, Eddie** 1928-    [BWW]
*American singer*
* Big Ed
* Burns, Guitar
* Burns, Little Eddie
* Pickens, Slim
* Swing Brother

**Burns, Eedson Louis Millard** 1897-
[CA]
*Canadian army officer and author*
* Conway, Arlington B.

**Burns, Farmer**
See  Burns, James

**Burns, George**
See  Birnbaum, Nathan

**Burns, George Henry** 1893-
[BE, DGS, PB]
*American baseball player*
* Burns, Tioga George

**Burns, Guitar**
See  Burns, Eddie

**Burns, Isaac Murphy** 1856-1896
[IBW]
*American-born jockey*
* [The] Black Englishman
* Murphy, Ike
* Murphy, Isaac

**Burns, James** 20th c.    [BE]
*American baseball player*
* Burns, Farmer

**Burns, Jerry** 1889?-1962    [BEW]
*Theatrical performer*
* Burns, Pop

**Burns, John Irving** 1907-1975    [BE]
*American baseball player*
* Burns, Slug

**Burns, Kenneth C.** 1920?-
[CME, CWG, DAM]
*American country-western performer*
* Jethro

**Burns, Little Eddie**
See  Burns, Eddie

**Burns, Nat**
See  Haines, Nat Burden

**[The] Burns of France**
See  Beranger, Pierre Jean de

**[The] Burns of France**
See  Boe, Jacques

**Burns, Oyster**
See  Burns, Thomas P.

**Burns, Pop**
See  Burns, Jerry

**Burns, Ralph J.** 1901-    [CAP]
*American author*
* Byrne, Ralph

**Burns, Robert** 1759-1796
[FF, RH, SN]
*Scottish poet*
* [The] Ayrshire Bard
* [The] Ayrshire Poet
* [The] Bard of Ayrshire
* [The] Glory and Reproach of
Scotland
* [The] Peasant Bard
* Sylvander

**Burns, Robert Arthur** 1946-
[CEI, FHE]
*Canadian-born hockey player*
* Burns, Robin

**Burns, Robert M[ilton] C[lark], Jr.**
1940-    [CA]
*American author and columnist*
* Burns, Scott

**Burns, Robin**
See  Burns, Robert Arthur

**Burns, Scott**
See  Burns, Robert M[ilton]
C[lark], Jr.

**Burns, Sheila**
See  Bloom, Ursula [Harvey]

**Burns, Sleepy Bill**
See  Burns, William Thomas

**Burns, Slug**
See  Burns, John Irving

**Burns, Tex**
See  LaMoore, Louis [Dearborn]

**Burns, Thomas P.** 1862-1928
[AS, BE, DGS]
*American baseball player*
* Burns, Oyster

**Burns, Tioga George**
See  Burns, George Henry

**Burns, Tommy**
See  Brusso, Noah

**Burns, Vincent Godfrey** 1893-1979
[AW, CA]
*American author*
* Burns, Bobby

**Burns, William Thomas** 1880-1953
[BE]
*American baseball player*
* Burns, Sleepy Bill

**Burnside, Ambrose Everett**
1824-1881    [FFF, SN]
*American army officer*
* Kaiser William
* Rhody

**Burnside, Jean**
See  Carr, Jean B.

**Burnside, R. H.**
See  Burnside, Richard

**Burnside, Richard** 1870-1952
[BEW]
*Scottish-born producer and director*
* Burnside, R. H.

**Burnstein, George** 1920-    [BBD]
*Canadian-born opera singer*
* London, George

**Burpee, Charles W[inslow]** 1859- ?
[NAA]
*American author and journalist*
* Angus, Carl

**Burpee, David** 1893?-
*American business executive*
* D. B.

**Burr, Aaron Ainsworth**
See  Dey, Frederic Van Rensselaer

**Burr, Agnes Rush** 20th c.    [NAA]
*American author*
* Boyd, Barbara

**Burr, Dangerfield**
See  Ingraham, Prentiss

**Burr, Henry**
See  McClaskey, Harry

**Burr, Raymond**
See  Burr, William Stacey

**Burr, William Stacey** 1917-    [IPA]
*Canadian-born actor*
* Burr, Raymond

**Burrage, A. M.**
See  Burrage, Alfred McLelland

**Burrage, Alfred McLelland**
1889-1956    [CC, MBF, WGT]
*British author*
* Burrage, A. M.
* Ex Private X
* Lancaster, Jack
* Lelland, Frank
* Young, Stewart

**Burrage, Alfred Sherrington** 20th
c.    [MBF]
*British author and editor*
* Hatherway, Cyril
* Hood, Aldine Robin
* Jackson, Philander
* Sherrington, Alf

**Burrage, Edwin Harcourt**
1839-1916    [MBF]
*British author*
* Barron, A. Elton
* Darrell, Walter
* Morland, Bart

**Burrell, Boz**
See  Burrell, Raymond

**Burrell, Buster**
See  Burrell, Frank Andrew

**Burrell, Caroline Benedict** 20th c.
[NAA]
*American author*
* Benton, Caroline French

**Burrell, Dave**
*See* Burrell, Herman Davis, II

**Burrell, Frank Andrew** 1866-1962
[BE]
*American baseball player*
* Burrell, Buster

**Burrell, George**
*See* Berrell, George

**Burrell, Herman Davis, II** 1940-
[EJ7]
*American jazz musician*
* Burrell, Dave

**Burrell, Raymond** 1946- [RO2]
*British musician*
* Burrell, Boz

**Burrell, Stanley** 1962?-
*American sportscaster*
* [The] Hammer

**Burright, Larry Allen** 1937- [BE]
*American baseball player*
* Burright, Possum

**Burright, Possum**
*See* Burright, Larry Allen

**Burris, Al**
*See* Burris, Alva Burton

**Burris, Alva Burton** 1874-1938
[BE]
*American baseball player*
* Burris, Al

**Burris, Buddy**
*See* Burris, Paul

**Burris, Paul** 20th c. [BBH]
*American football player*
* Burris, Buddy

**Burritt, Edwin C.**
*See* Brill, Ethel Claire

**Burritt, Elihu** 1810-1879
[DEL, PA]
*American author and linguist*
* [The] Learned Blacksmith
* OLd Burchell

**Burro-Fleta, Anatole** 1925- [OP]
*French operatic stage director*
* Fleta, Pierre

**Burrough, Helen Mary** 1917-
[ART]
*British painter*
* Helen

**Burroughs, Alvin** 1911-1950
[WWJ]
*American jazz musician*
* Burroughs, Mouse

**Burroughs, Edgar Rice** 1875-1950
[ESF, SF, WGT]
*American author*
* Bean, Norman
* E. R. B.
* McCulloch, John Tyler

**Burroughs, Jeremiah** 1599-1646
[SN]
*British clergyman and author*
* [The] Morning Star of Stepney

**Burroughs, Margaret Taylor** 1917-
[CA]
*American author*
* Taylor, Margaret

**Burroughs, Marie**
*See* Massen, Mrs. L. F.

**Burroughs, Mouse**
*See* Burroughs, Alvin

**Burroughs, William [Seward]** 1914-
[AW, CA, WD]
*American author, poet, playwright*
* Lee, William [or Willy]

**Burroughs-Fowler, Walter John**
*See* Fowler, Walter

**Burrow, Diana Wynne** 1934- [WD]
*British author*
* Jones, Diana Wynne

**Burrow, Ken** 20th c.
*American football player*
* Burrow, Mule

**Burrow, Mule**
*See* Burrow, Ken

**Burrowes, Peter** [SN]
*Irish jurist*
* [The] Goldsmith of the Bar

**Burrows, Abe**
*See* Borowitz, Abram Solman

**Burrows, Dallas Frederick** 1928-
[BEW, IPA, TR]
*American actor*
* Bean, Orson

**Burrows, Hermann** 1896- [AW]
*British author and business executive*
* [The] Rag Man

**Burrows, [Colonel] Jon [FBI code name]**
*See* Presley, Elvis Aaron

**Burrows, Stephen** 1944- [IBW]
*American fashion designer*
* [The] King of Cling

**Burrus, Dick**
*See* Burrus, Maurice Lennon

**Burrus, Maurice Lennon** 1898-
[BE]
*American baseball player*
* Burrus, Dick

**Burse, Charlie** 1901-1965 [BWW]
*American singer*
* Burse, Uke
* Ukelele Kid

**Burse, Uke**
*See* Burse, Charlie

**Burstein, Joseph** 1913- [EJS]
*Polish-born Israeli Olympic committee chairman*
* Inbar, Joseph

**Burstein, Rona** 1937-
*American columnist*
* Barrett, Rona

**Burstenbinder, Elisabeth**
1838-1918 [WGT]
*German author*
* Werner, E.

**Burstyn, Ellen**
*See* Gillooly, Edna Rae

**Burt, Bessie**
*See* Imson, Mrs.

**Burt, Caleb**
*See* Burleigh, Cecil

**Burt, [Sir] Cyril** 1883-1971
*British psychologist*
* Conway, J.?
* Howard, Margaret?

**Burt, Frank A.**
*See* Berek, Augustus

**Burt, Gill**
*See* Melcher, Gilbert W[ayne]

**Burt, Katharine Newlin** 1882-
[ANT]
*American author*
* Scarlet, Rebecca

**Burt, Melville**
*See* Bull, Lois

**Burte, Hermann**
*See* Struebe, Hermann

**Burton, Alfred**
*See* Mitford, John

**Burton, Andy**
*See* Rathborne, St. George

**Burton, Barry** 20th c. [ECM]
*American musician*
* Burton, Byrd

**Burton, Byrd**
*See* Burton, Barry

**Burton, Charles**
*See* Chadwick, A. Burton

**Burton, Claude Edward Cole-Hamilton** 1869- ? [WWL]
*British poet*
* C. E. B.
* E. C. B.
* Touchstone

**Burton, Doris** 20th c. [CAT]
*British author*
* Lucis Amator

**Burton, Edmund**
*See* Childs, Edmund Burton

**Burton, Edward** 18th c. [PA]
*Author*
* Du Mort, Reuben

**Burton, Edward J.** 1917- [CA]
*American police officer and author*
* Carey, Michael

**Burton, [Alice] Elizabeth** 1908-
[CA]
*British author*
* Kerby, Susan Alice

**Burton, Eric**
*See* Burton, Jim Scott

**Burton, H. A.**
*See* Habberton, John

**Burton, Harry McGuire** 1898-
[IAW]
*British author*
* MacGuire, Philip

**Burton, Jim Scott** 1949- [SMG]
*American baseball player*
* Burton, Eric

**Burton, Lee**
*See* Lollobrigida, Guido

**Burton, Leonard Lamming** 1872- ?
[WWL]
*British author*
* Keloid

**Burton, Leonard Lamming**
(Continued)
* Ship Surgeon

**Burton, Lizzie**
*See* Morsell, Mrs. Herndon

**Burton, Mike** 1947- [SWI]
*American swimmer*
* Machine, Mr.

**Burton, Miles**
*See* Street, Cecil John Charles

**Burton, Nelly** 20th c. [THR]
*British actress*
* Bobadilla, Pepita

**Burton, P. M.**
*See* Pemberton, Edgar

**Burton, Richard**
*See* Jenkins, Richard Walter, Jr.

**Burton, Richard** 1821-1890 [SN]
*British explorer*
* [The] Modern Admirable Crichton

**Burton, [Sir] Richard Francis**
1821-1920 [WGT]
*British author*
* F. B.

**Burton, Robert**
*See* Crouch, Nathaniel

**Burton, Robert** 1576?-1640?
[DEP, FFF, RH]
*British author and philosopher*
* Democritus Junior

**Burton, Robert G.**
*See* Hall, Robert G.

**Burton, S. H.**
*See* Burton, Samuel Holroyd

**Burton, Samuel Holroyd** 1919-
[SFL]
*British author*
* Burton, S. H.
* Holroyd, Sam

**Burton, Thomas**
*See* Longstreet, [Henry] Stephen [Weiner]

**Burton, Willard** 20th c. [NBB]
*American musician*
* Piano Slim

**Burtschy, Edward Frank** 1922-
[BE]
*American baseball player*
* Burtschy, Moe

**Burtschy, Moe**
*See* Burtschy, Edward Frank

**Burvik, Mabel Odin** 20th c.
[WECO]
*American cartoonist*
* Odin

**Bury, Frank**
*See* Harris, Herbert

**Bury, J. B.**
*See* Bury, John Bagnell

**Bury, John Bagnell** 1861-1927
[LC]
*Historian and author*
* Bury, J. B.

**Bury, Margaret** 1882-1942 [THR]
*Scottish-born actress*
* Moffat, Margaret

**Bury, Richard de**
See Aungerville [or Aungervyle],
Richard

**Busby, Buzz**
See Busby, Steven Lee

**Busby, F. M.** 20th c. [SFP]
*Author*
* Pemberton, Renfrew

**Busby, Hamilton** [PA]
*Author*
* H. B.

**Busby, Lefty**
See Busby, Maurice

**Busby, Mabel Janice** 1903-1982
*American politician and former
madam*
* Owen, Marsha
* Stanford, Sally

**Busby, Maurice** 20th c. [OBW]
*American baseball player*
* Busby, Lefty

**Busby, Paul Miller** 1918- [BE]
*American baseball player*
* Busby, Red

**Busby, Red**
See Busby, Paul Miller

**Busby, Steven Lee** 1949- [SMG]
*American baseball player*
* Busby, Buzz

**Buschbom, Bushy**
See Buschbom, Jack

**Buschbom, Jack** 20th c. [GW]
*American rodeo performer*
* Buschbom, Bushy

**Busche, Hermann von dem**
1468-1534 [WBD]
*German scholar and author*
* Pasiphilus

**Buscher, Ella** 1879- ? [THR]
*American comedienne*
* Shields, Ella

**Buscon, Juan**
See Troncoso de la Concha,
Manuel de Jesus

**Buse, R. F.**
See Buse, Renee

**Buse, Renee** 1914?-1979 [CA]
*Italian-born editor, executive,
author*
* Benton, Robert
* Buse, R. F.
* King, Michael

**Busey, Gary** 1944-
*American actor and musician*
* Eddy, Teddy Jack

**Bush, Anita** 1883-1974 [IBW]
*American drama company organizer*
* [The] Little Mother of Colored
  Drama

**Bush, Bullet Joe**
See Bush, Leslie Ambrose

**Bush, Charlie Christmas**
1885?-1973 [CC, EMD, WW]
*British author*
* Bush, Christopher
* Home, Michael

**Bush, Christopher**
See Bush, Charlie Christmas

**Bush, Donie**
See Bush, Owen Joseph

**Bush, Frances Cleveland**
1889-1967 [SC]
*American actress*
* Chaney, Frances
* Creighton, Cleva

**Bush, Guy Terrell** 1903- [BE, PB]
*American baseball player*
* [The] Mississippi Mudcat

**Bush, H. R.** [PA]
*Author*
* [A] Layman

**Bush, Joe**
See Bush, Leslie Ambrose

**Bush, Leslie Ambrose** 1892-
[BE, DGS, PB]
*American baseball player*
* Bush, Bullet Joe
* Bush, Joe

**Bush, Louis F.** 1910-1979
[ASC, EJ, PMJ]
*American jazz musician*
* Carr, Fingers
* Carr, Joe Fingers

**Bush, Owen Joseph** 1888-1972
[BE, PB]
*American baseball player and
manager*
* Bush, Donie

**Bush, Robert Finlay** 1888-1929
[SC]
*American actor*
* Finlay, Robert [Bob]

**Bush, Rose**
See Turner, Lily

**Bush-Fekete, Laszlo** 1896- [BEW]
*Hungarian-born playwright and
author*
* Bush-Fekete, Leslie

**Bush-Fekete, Leslie**
See Bush-Fekete, Laszlo

**Bushel Basket Keeler**
See Keeler, William Henry

**Bushman, Francis X., Jr.**
See Bushman, Ralph E.

**Bushman, Ralph E.** 1903- [F2]
*American actor*
* Bushman, Francis X., Jr.

**Bushong, Albert John** 1856-1908
[BE]
*American baseball player*
* Bushong, Doc

**Bushong, Doc**
See Bushong, Albert John

**Busillo, Anthony** 1942- [RO1]
*American singer*
* Valentino, Mark

**Businsky, Madlaine** 1876?-1964
[BEW]
*American actress*
* Traverse, Madlaine

**Buskirk, Richard H[obart]** 1927-
[CA]
*American author and educator*
* Aquarius, Qass

**Buss, Frances** 1902- [CA]
*British-born author*
* Fleetwood, Frances

**Buss, Frances** (Continued)
* Fleetwood, Frank

**Bussa di Leoni, Francesca**
1384-1440 [WBD]
*Saint*
* Frances of Rome

**Bussone, Francesco [Conte di
Castelnuovo]** 1390?-1432 [WBD]
*Italian soldier*
* Carmagnola

**Busta, Christine**
See Dimt, Christine

**Bustamante, [Sir] William Alexander**
1884?-1977
*Jamaican prime minister*
* [The] Lion of the Caribbean

**Busteed, William** 1893-1938
[THR]
*Irish-born actor*
* Daunt, William

**Bustos Domecq, H[onorio]** [joint
pseudonym with Jorge Luis Borges]
See Bioy-Casares, Adolfo

**Bustos Domecq, H[onorio]** [joint
pseudonym with Adolfo
Bioy-Casares]
See Borges, Jorge Luis

**Busvine**
See Busvine, Richard

**Busvine, Richard** 20th c. [WFA]
*British fashion designer*
* Busvine

**Busy Bee**
See Beswick, Harry

**[The] Busy Scotch Parson**
See Burnet, Gilbert

**[The] Butch**
See Sgroi, Alfonso

**[The] Butcher**
See Ahmed [or Achmed] Pasha

**[The] Butcher**
See Calleja del Rey, Felix Maria

**[The] Butcher**
See Clifford, John de

**[The] Butcher**
See Clisson, Olivier de

**[The] Butcher**
See Fowler, William

**[The] Butcher**
See Serov, Ivan A.

**Butcher, Alan Raymond** 1954-
[DC]
*British cricketer*
* Butcher, Budgie
* Butcher, Butch

**Butcher, Albert Maxwell**
1910-1957 [BE]
*American baseball player*
* Butcher, Max

**Butcher Boy Adkins**
See Adkins, Grady Emmett

**Butcher, Budgie**
See Butcher, Alan Raymond

**Butcher, Butch**
See Butcher, Alan Raymond

**Butcher, Butch**
See Butcher, Roland Orlando

**Butcher, Fanny**
See Bokum, Fanny Butcher

**[The] Butcher from Galena**
See Grant, Hiram Ulysses

**Butcher, Max**
See Butcher, Albert Maxwell

**[The] Butcher of Baghdad**
See Hussein, Saddam

**[The] Butcher of Bangui**
See Bokassa, Jean-Bedel

**[The] Butcher of Culloden**
See William Augustus

**[The] Butcher of England**
See Tiptoft, John

**[The] Butcher of Lyon**
See Altmann, Klaus

**[The] Butcher of Prague**
See Heydrich, Reinhard

**[The] Butcher of Teheran**
See Oveissi, Gholam Ali

**[The] Butcher of Vassy**
See Lorraine, Francois de

**Butcher, Roland Orlando** 1953-
[DC]
*West Indian cricketer*
* Butcher, Butch

**Butcher, S. H.**
See Butcher, Samuel Henry

**Butcher, Samuel Henry** 1850-1910
[LC]
*Irish-born scholar and translator*
* Butcher, S. H.

**Butck, Zulie**
See Jones, Thomas W[arren]

**Bute, Earl** 20th c. [BBH]
*American collegiate athletic director*
* Bute, Skip

**Bute, Skip**
See Bute, Earl

**Butera, Lou** 20th c.
*American billiard player*
* Butera, Machine Gun

**Butera, Machine Gun**
See Butera, Lou

**Butka, Babe**
See Butka, Ed[ward Luke]

**Butka, Ed[ward Luke]** 1916- [BE]
*American baseball player*
* Butka, Babe

**Butland, Bill**
See Butland, Wilburn Rue

**Butland, Wilburn Rue** 1918- [BE]
*American baseball player*
* Butland, Bill

**Butler, Al**
See Butler, Elbert

**Butler, Art**
See Bouthillier, Arthur Edward

**Butler, Auriol** 20th c. [ART]
*British painter*
* Auriol

**Butler, Benjamin Franklin**
1818-1893 [FF, FFF, SN]
*American army officer*
* Butler, Picayune

**Butler, Benjamin Franklin**
(Continued)
* Cockeye

**Butler, Bill**
See Butler, Ernest Alton

**Butler, Butts**
See Butler, Robert P.

**Butler, Cecil Dean** 1937- [BE]
*American baseball player*
* Butler, Slewfoot

**Butler, Charles Dawson** 1916-
[ITA]
*American actor*
* Butler, Daws

**Butler, Charles Thomas** 1905-1964
[BE]
*American baseball player*
* Butler, Lefty

**Butler, Daddy**
See Butler, William J.

**Butler, Daws**
See Butler, Charles Dawson

**Butler, Diana**
See Tindale, Mrs. Acton

**Butler, E. M.**
See Butler, Eliza Marian

**Butler, Elbert** 20th c. [SMG]
*American basketball player*
* Butler, Al

**Butler, Eliza Marian** 1885- [TC1]
*British critic and scholar*
* Butler, E. M.

**Butler, Ernest Alton** 1926- [CA]
*American business executive and
author*
* Butler, Bill

**Butler, Frank Dean** 1860-1945
[BE]
*American baseball player*
* Butler, Stuffy

**Butler, Frank E.** 20th c. [BE]
*American baseball player*
* Butler, Kid

**Butler, G. M.**
See Butler, Gurdon Montague

**Butler, Geezer**
See Butler, Terry

**Butler, George** 1936- [BWW]
*American singer*
* Butler, Wild Child

**Butler, George H.** [PA]
*Author*
* Rifle
* Zena, Harry

**Butler, Gurdon Montague** 1881- ?
[NAA]
*American educator, engineer, author*
* Butler, G. M.

**Butler, Gwendoline [Williams]** 20th
c. [IAW]
*British author*
* Melville, Jennie

**Butler, H. B.** 20th c. [WW]
*Author*
* Black, M. Dana

**Butler, Ivan**
See Beuttler, Edward Ivan Oakley

**Butler, James** 1610-1688 [SN]
*British royalist leader*
* Butler, Jemmy
* Ormonde, Duke of

**Butler, Jean Rouverol** 1916- [CA]
*American author and screenwriter*
* Rouverol, Jean

**Butler, Jemmy**
See Butler, James

**Butler, Jerry** 1939- [IBW]
*American singer and former ice
sculptor*
* [The] Iceman

**Butler, Joan**
See Alexander, Robert William

**Butler, John Stephen [Johnny]**
1894-1967 [BE]
*American baseball player*
* Butler, Trolley Line

**Butler, Joseph** 1692-1752
[DNNS, FF, SN]
*British theologian and author*
* [The] Bacon of Theology

**Butler, Kid**
See Butler, Frank E.

**Butler, Kid**
See Butler, Willis Everett

**Butler, L. C.** 20th c. [BBH]
*American baseball coach*
* Butler, Pete

**Butler, Lefty**
See Butler, Charles Thomas

**Butler, Louise**
See Fiske, Estelle Louise

**Butler, Mrs.**
See Kemble, Frances A.

**Butler, Mrs. Benjamin** [FFF]
*Entertainer*
* Hildreth, Sarah

**Butler, Nathan**
See Sohl, Gerald Allan [Jerry]

**Butler, O'Brien**
See Whitwell, O'Brien

**Butler, Patrick**
See Dunboyne, [Lord]

**Butler, Pete**
See Butler, L. C.

**Butler, Picayune**
See Butler, Benjamin Franklin

**Butler, Richard**
See Allbeury, Theodore Edward Le
Bouthillier [Ted]

**Butler, Robert P.** 1891-1959 [FB]
*American football player*
* Butler, Butts

**Butler, Roy**
See Butler, Royal Edwin

**Butler, Royal Edwin** 1895-1973
[SC]
*American actor*
* Butler, Roy

**Butler, Samuel** 1835-1902 [LC]
*British author*
* Owen, John Pickard

**Butler, Slewfoot**
See Butler, Cecil Dean

**Butler, Stuffy**
See Butler, Frank Dean

**Butler, Susan Ruth** 1937- [IAW]
*Canadian-born psychologist and
author*
* Butler, Susanne

**Butler, Susanne**
See Butler, Susan Ruth

**Butler, Terry** 1949- [RO2]
*British musician*
* Butler, Geezer

**Butler, Trolley Line**
See Butler, John Stephen [Johnny]

**Butler, Walter** 1901- [F2]
*Actor*
* Byron, Walter

**Butler, Walter C.**
See Faust, Frederick [Schiller]

**Butler, Wild Child**
See Butler, George

**Butler, [Sir] William Francis**
1838-1910 [SFL]
*Author*
* [An] Old Soldier

**Butler, William Huxford [Bill]**
1934- [CA, IAW, WD]
*American author, poet, critic*
* Deast, Basil
* I Sabbah, Hassan

**Butler, William J.** 1860-1927
[F1, SC]
*American actor*
* Butler, Daddy

**Butler, William M.** [FFF]
*American writer*
* Mill

**Butler, Willis Everett** 1887-1964
[BE]
*American baseball player*
* Butler, Kid

**Butlin, [Sir] Billy** 1900?-1980
*British business executive*
* [The] Oliday King

**Butt, George** 18th c. [PA]
*Author*
* One Who is But an Attorney

**Butt, Isaac** 1813- ? [PA]
*Author*
* O'Brien, Edward Stephenson

**Buttermilk Tommy Dowd**
See Dowd, Thomas Jefferson

**Butters, Dorothy Gilman** 1923-
[AW, CA, SAT]
*American author*
* Gilman, Dorothy

**Butters, Francis** 1867-1961 [THR]
*British playwright*
* Neilson, Francis

**Butters, Paul Theophilus William**
1908- [AW]
*British barrister and writer*
* Williamson, Paul

**Butterscotch, Mr.**
See Torme, Mel[vin Howard]

**Butterworth, Frank Nestle** [WW]
*Author*
* Blundell, Peter

**Butterworth, John Malcolm** 1945-
[ART]
*British artist*
* J. M. B.

**Butterworth, Lionel Milner** 1900-
[CA]
*British author*
* Angus-Butterworth, Lionel
Milner

**Butterworth, William Edmund, III**
1929- [CA, SAT]
*American author*
* Beech, Webb
* Blake, Walker E.
* Douglas, James McM.
* Hughes, Eden
* Scholefield, Edmund O.
* Williams, Patrick J.

**Buttimer, Anne** 1938- [CA]
*Irish-born educator and author*
* Mary Annette, [Sister]

**Buttlar, Johannes**
See Von Buttlar-Brandenfels,
Johannes

**Buttle, Myra**
See Purcell, Victor William
Williams Saunders

**Button, Margaret Helen** 1906-
[AW]
*British author, actress, educator*
* Leona

**Buttons**
See Cowles, T. Z. C.

**Buttons, Red**
See Chwatt, Aaron

**Buttrey, Douglas Norton** 1918-
[ESF, SFL]
*Author*
* Barr, Densil Neve

**Butts, Jane Roberts**
See Roberts, Jane

**Butts, Pee Wee**
See Butts, Thomas

**Butts, Thomas** 1919-1973
[B10, MK]
*American baseball player*
* Butts, Pee Wee

**Buxbaum, Martin**
See Noll, Martin David

**Buxton, Buck**
See Buxton, Ralph Stanley

**Buxton, C.**
See Hersey, Harold

**Buxton, Jedediah** 1705-1772
[DNNS, SN]
*British mathematical prodigy*
* [The] Calculator

**Buxton, Ralph Stanley** 1911- [BE]
*Canadian-born baseball player*
* Buxton, Buck

**Buyana, Mohamed** 20th c. [RBE]
*Spanish boxer*
* Rubio, Julio

**Buyrette, Pierre Laurent**
1727-1775 [WBD]
*French actor and playwright*
* Belloy, Dormont de

**Buzurg-Mihir** 6th c.  [HN]
*Persian scholar*
* [The] Seneca of the East

**Buzurin, Maria** 1938-  [OP]
*Rumanian opera singer*
* Slatinaru, Maria

**[The] Buzzer Beater**
*See* Sparrow, Rory

**Buzzle, Buck**
*See* Rubin, Charles J.

**Byard, Carole** 1941-  [IBW]
*American artist*
* Byard, Sugar

**Byard, Edithe** ?-1934  [SC]
*British actress*
* Yorke, Edith

**Byard, Jaki**
*See* Byard, John A., Jr.

**Byard, John A., Jr.** 1922-
[DAM, EJ]
*American jazz musician*
* Byard, Jaki

**Byard, Sugar**
*See* Byard, Carole

**Byars, William Vincent** 1857- ?
[ALY]
*American poet*
* Lewis, Fielding
* Warner, Augustine

**Byas, Carlos Wesley** 1912-1972
[DAM, EJ, PMJ]
*American jazz musician*
* Byas, Don

**Byas, Don**
*See* Byas, Carlos Wesley

**Byas, Richard Thomas** 1910-  [MK]
*American baseball player*
* Byas, Subby

**Byas, Subby**
*See* Byas, Richard Thomas

**Byatt, A. S.**
*See* Duffy, Antonia Susan

**Byerley, John Scott** 19th c.  [PA]
*Author*
* Ripon, John Scott

**Byerley, Thomas** 1788-1826
[FFF, PA]
*British editor*
* Collet, Stephen
* Percy, Reuben

**Byerly, Bud**
*See* Byerly, Eldred William

**Byerly, Eldred William** 1920-  [BE]
*American baseball player*
* Byerly, Bud

**Byers, Amy Irene** 1906-  [AW]
*British author, journalist,
broadcaster*
* Barry, Ann

**Byers, Big Bill**
*See* Byers, John William [Bill]

**Byers, Charles Alma** 1879- ?
[NAA]
*American writer*
* Mala, Yenomdrah

**Byers, Dolly**
*See* Byers, J. Dallet

**Byers, J. Dallet** ?-1966  [BBH]
*American horse trainer*
* Byers, Dolly

**Byers, John William [Bill]** 20th c.
[BE]
*American baseball player*
* Byers, Big Bill

**Bygraves, Max**
*See* Bygraves, Walter

**Bygraves, Walter** 1922-  [BF]
*British actor and comedian*
* Bygraves, Max

**Byk, Jan**
*See* Starowieyski, Franciszek

**Bykovsky, Valery Feodorovich** 20th
c.  [CND]
*Russian cosmonaut*
* Hawk [code name]

**Byles**
*See* Quincy, Edmund

**Bynner, Witter** 1881-1968
[CA, TC]
*American poet*
* Morgan, Emanuel

**Byr, Robert**
*See* Bayer, Karl Robert Emmerich
von

**Byrd, Bald Head**
*See* Byrd, Henry Roeland

**Byrd, Butch**
*See* Byrd, George E.

**Byrd, Curly**
*See* Byrd, Harold C.

**Byrd, Fess**
*See* Byrd, Henry Roeland

**Byrd, Francis Alfred** 1905-  [IBW]
*American college athletic director*
* Byrd, Jazz

**Byrd, Gene** 1933-  [DAM]
*American musician*
* Byrd, Joe

**Byrd, George E.** 1941-  [FB, SMG]
*American football player*
* Byrd, Butch

**Byrd, Hammer**
*See* Byrd, Leland

**Byrd, Harold C.** 1889-1970  [AS]
*American football coach and
university president*
* Byrd, Curly

**Byrd, Henry Roeland** 1918-1980
[BWW, IBW]
*American singer*
* Boyd, Robert
* Byrd, Bald Head
* Byrd, Fess
* Byrd, Roy
* Little Loving Henry
* Longhair, Dr.
* Longhair, Professor

**Byrd, Jazz**
*See* Byrd, Francis Alfred

**Byrd, Joe**
*See* Byrd, Gene

**Byrd, John**
*See* Moffa, Paolo

**Byrd, L. Ella** 19th c.  [FFF]
*American author*
* Carr, Beryl

**Byrd, Lefty**
*See* Byrd, Leland

**Byrd, Leland** 1927-  [BB]
*American basketball player*
* Byrd, Hammer
* Byrd, Lefty

**Byrd, Martha** 1930-  [CA]
*American author*
* Hoyle, Martha Byrd

**Byrd, Robert** 1934-  [RO1]
*American singer*
* Day, Bobby

**Byrd, Robert Carlyle**
*See* Sale, Cornelius, Jr.

**Byrd, Roy**
*See* Byrd, Henry Roeland

**Byrd, Samuel Dewey [Sammy]**
1906-  [ALR, BE]
*American baseball player*
* Babe Ruth's Legs

**Byrem, Jill** 1947?-
*American country-western performer*
* Dalton, Lacy J.

**Byrne, Charles A.**  [PA]
*Author*
* Town Crier

**Byrne, Charlotte Dacre** 1782- ?
[FFF]
*Author*
* Dacre, Charlotte
* Matilda, Rosa

**Byrne, Donn**
*See* Donn-Byrne, Brian Oswald

**Byrne, James**
*See* Garnett, Edward William

**Byrne, Jane** 20th c.
*American politician*
* Attila the Hen

**Byrne, John [Patrick]** 1940-  [ART]
*Scottish painter*
* Patrick

**Byrne, John K.** 1860-1910  [BE]
*American baseball player*
* O'Brien, John K.

**Byrne, John Keyes** 1926-
[B10, TR, WD]
*Irish playwright*
* Leonard, Hugh

**Byrne, Laurence Patrick**
1888-1939  [DIL]
*Irish drama critic and journalist*
* Malone, Andrew E.

**Byrne, Oliver**  [PA]
*Author*
* Revile, E. B.

**Byrne, Ralph**
*See* Burns, Ralph J.

**Byrne, Stuart J[ames]** 1913-
[CA, SFL, WGT]
*American author and screenwriter*
* Amare, Rothayne
* Bloodstone, John
* Dare, Howard
* Kaye, Marx [house pseudonym]

**Byrnes, Edd**
*See* Breitenberger, Edward

**Byrnes, James F.** 20th c.  [CND]
*American diplomat*
* Iceblink [code name used during
World War II]

**Byrnes, Milt[on John]** 1916-  [BE]
*American baseball player*
* Byrnes, Skippy

**Byrnes, Mrs. J. H. W.**  [FFF]
*Entertainer*
* Edwards, Flossie

**Byrnes, Skippy**
*See* Byrnes, Milt[on John]

**Byrom, James**
*See* Bramwell, James Guy

**Byrom, John** 1691-1763
[DEL, FFF]
*British poet*
* Shadow, John

**Byron**
*See* Pellerano Castro, Arturo
Bautista

**Byron and Moore**
*See* Collin, Jacques Albin Simon

**Byron, Clara**
*See* Lake, Mrs. W. P.

**Byron, George Gordon Noel**
1788-1824  [DEL, HN, SN]
*British poet*
* Albe [or Albaneser]
* [The] Comus of Poetry
* Hornem, Horace

**Byron, James** 1931-1955  [FC]
*American actor*
* Dean, James

**Byron, John**
*See* Armstrong, John Byron

**Byron, John**
*See* Heanley, John

**Byron, John** 1723-1786
[DEP, DNNF, SN]
*British naval officer*
* Foul Weather Jack

**Byron, Lord**
*See* Byron, William

**Byron, Marion**
*See* Bilenkin, Miriam

**Byron, Oliver Doud**
*See* Doud, Oliver B.

**Byron, Red**
*See* Byron, Robert

**Byron, Robert** ?-1960  [EAR]
*American auto racer*
* Byron, Red

**Byron, Robert** 20th c.  [CA]
*Author*
* Waughburton, Richard [joint
pseudonym with Christopher
(Hugh) Sykes]

**Byron, Walter**
*See* Butler, Walter

**Byron, William** 1872-1955  [PB]
*American baseball umpire*
* Byron, Lord
* [The] Singing Umpire

**Bysshe Vanolis**
*See* Thomson, James

**[The] Bystander**
*See* Smith, Goldwin

**Bystrzycki, Przemyslaw** 1923-
[IAW]
*Polish author*
* Stankiewicz, Michal

**[The] Byzantine**
*See* Beschitay, Elie

**Byzantinus**
*See* Leontius of Byzantium

**Byzantinus, Josephus**
*See* Genesius, Josephus

# C

**C.**
*See* Bowles, Caroline Annie

**C**
*See* Carew, Hugh

**C.**
*See* Cogan, John

**C.**
*See* Coxe, Arthur Cleveland

**C.**
*See* Croker, John Wilson

**C. A. C.**
*See* Cary, Caroline Anne

**C. A. M. W.**
*See* Wooley [or Woodley?], Charles

**C. A. R.**
*See* Roberts, Catherine Alice

**C. B.**
*See* Bathurst, Charles

**C. B.**
*See* Beringer, Carroll James

**C. C.**
*See* Cabrera, Raimundo

**C. C.**
*See* Clarke, Charles Baron

**C. C. A.**
*See* Adams, Cyrus C.

**C. D.**
*See* Deakins, Cyril Edward

**C. E.**
*See* Brown, Charlotte Elizabeth

**C. E.**
*See* Edwards, Carl J.

**C. E. A.**
*See* Aiken, Clementina Edith

**C. E. B.**
*See* Burton, Claude Edward Cole-Hamilton

**C. E. K.**
*See* Kelly, Caroline E.

**C. F.**
*See* File, Charles E.

**C. F. D.**
*See* Deems, Charles Force

**C. F. G.**
*See* Grace, Catherine Frances

**C. G. H.**
*See* Hamilton, C. G.

**C. H.**
*See* Hutton, Clarke

**C. H. D.**
*See* Duranty, Charles Henry

**C. I. de B. K.**
*See* Kinahan, [Lady] Coralie

**C. J.**
*See* Dorji, Paljore

**C. K.**
*See* Kingsley, Charles

**C. L.**
*See* Logan, Celia

**C. L. C.**
*See* Cunnington, Charles Leslie

**C. M. C.**
*See* Clark, Charlotte Moon

**C. M. G.**
*See* Garrett, Clara Maud

**C. M. I. H.**
*See* Halliday, Charlotte Mary Irvine

**C. R.**
*See* Rajagopalacharia, Chakravarti

**C. S.**
*See* Sotheran, Charles

**C. S.**
*See* Stanton, C.

**C. S. C.**
*See* Caverley, Charles S.

**C. V. T.**
*See* Tench, Charles Victor

**C. W. B.**
*See* Bacon, Cecil Walter

**C. W. S.**
*See* Short, Charles Williams

**Caballero, Fernan**
*See* Arrom, Cecilia Francisca Josefa

**Caballero, Putsy**
*See* Caballero, Ralph Joseph

**Caballero, Ralph Joseph** 1927- [BE]
*American baseball player*
* Caballero, Putsy

**[El] Caballo [The Horse]**
*See* Casanas, Alejandro

**Cabaret Tess**
*See* Wheeler, Teresa

**Cabassou, Lionel George Andre**
*See* Damas, Leon Gontran

**Cabby with Camera**
*See* Green, Maxwell Revenell

**Cabell, James Branch** 20th c. [SFP]
*Author*
* Jefferson, Henry Lee
* Washington, Berwell

**Cabellera**
*See* Machado y Ruiz, Antonio

**Cabello, Juan** [GS]
*Spanish bullfighter*
* [El] Brujo [The Wizard]

**Cable, Boyd**
*See* Ewart, Ernest Andrew

**Cable, George Washington** 1844- ? [FFF]
*American author*
* Drop Shot

**Cabot, Bruce**
*See* Pelissier De Bujac, Jacques Etienne

**Cabot, John York**
*See* O'Brien, David Wright

**Cabot, Joseph**
*See* Burge, Milward Rodon Kennedy

**Cabral, Alberto**
*See* White, Richard Alan

**Cabral, Ce'sar Augusto** 1917- [IAW]
*Argentinian psychiatrist and author*
* Villagran, Ce'sar

**Cabral, O. M.**
*See* Cabral, Olga

**Cabral, Olga** 1909- [CA]
*American author and poet*
* Cabral, O. M.

**Cabre, Teresa** 1890-1942 [SC]
*Argentinian-born actress and dancer*
* Gerard, Teddie

**Cabrera, Al**
*See* Cabrera, Alfredo A.

**Cabrera, Alfredo A.** 1883- [BE]
*American baseball player*
* Cabrera, Al

**Cabrera, Miguel** ?-1730? [FFF]
*Mexican artist*
* [The] Michael Angelo of America

**Cabrera, Raimundo** 1852-1923 [ALY, CW]
*Cuban author*
* Buenamar, Ricardo
* C. C.

**Cabrera Infante, Guillermo** 1929- [CA, WOA]
*Cuban-born critic and author*
* Cain, Guillermo

**Cabrero Arnal, Jose** 20th c. [WECO]
*Cartoonist*
* Arnal, Claude

**Cabrie, Therese Theodora Gerard** 1892-1942 [BEW]
*Argentinian-born actress*
* Gerrard, Teddie

**Cabrini, Frances Xavier** 1850-1917 [WBD]
*Saint*
* Cabrini, Mother

**Cabrini, Mother**
*See* Cabrini, Frances Xavier

**Caccianemici, Gerardo** ?-1145 [CAL]
*Pope*
* Lucius II

**Caccini, Giulio** 1550?-1618 [WBD]
*Italian singer and composer*
* Giulio Romano

**Caceres, Ernesto** 1911- [EJ]
*American jazz musician*
* Caceres, Ernie

**Caceres, Ernie**
*See* Caceres, Ernesto

**Cacheta [Lever]**
*See* Sanchez De Leon, Leandro

**Cachorro [The Cub]**
*See* Gorraez Arcante, Francisco

**Cacioppo, Joseph** 1936- [CA]
*American journalist*
* Cappo, Joseph

**Cacoyannis, Michael** 1922- [THR]
*Greek-born actor*
* Yannis, Michael

**Cactus**
*See* Foster, Mary F.

**[The] Cactus Comet**
See Robinson, Paul

**Cactus Jack Curtice**
See Curtice, Jack C.

**Cactus Jack Garner**
See Garner, John Nance

**Cactus Jack Turner**
See Turner, Jack

**Cadalous, Pietro** ?-1072 [WBD]
*Antipope*
* Honorius II

**Cade, Alexander**
See Methold, Kenneth Walter

**Cade, Jack**
See Arnot, Robin Page

**Cade, John [Jack]** ?-1450
[DNNS, HN, SN]
*Irish-born rebellion leader*
* [The] Captain of Kent
* Jack Amend-All
* Mortimer

**Cade, Robin**
See Nicole, Christopher Robin

**Cade, Toni**
See Bambara, Toni Cade

**Cadell, [Violet] Elizabeth** 1903-
[CA]
*British author*
* Ainsworth, Harriet

**Cadell, James**
See Thomas, Ronald Wills

**Cadenus**
See Swift, Jonathan

**Cadet, John** 1935- [CA]
*British author*
* Brown, Charles
* Greene, Fred

**Cadet la Perle [The Pearl Son]**
See De Harcourt, Henri

**Cadillac Baby**
See Eatmon, Narvell

**Cadillac, Captain**
See Nasworthy, Frank

**Cadillac Jake**
See Harris, James D. [Jimmie]

**[The] Cadillac Wildcat**
See Wolgust, Adolphus

**Cadmus**
See Zachos, John C.

**Cadmus and Harmonia** [joint
pseudonym with Susan Buchan]
See Buchan, John

**Cadmus and Harmonia** [joint
pseudonym with John Buchan]
See Buchan, Susan

**Cadoudal, Georges** 1769-1804
[FFF, HN, SN]
*French royalist leader*
* [The] Great Bullet-Head

**Cadreau, William** 1889-1948 [BE]
*American baseball player*
* Chouneau, Chief
* Chouneau, William

**Cadry, Jean Baptiste** 1680-1756
[PA]
*Author*
* Darcy

**Cadwr**
See Palsson, Hermann

**Cady, Forrest Leroy** 1886-1946
[BE, PB]
*American baseball player*
* Cady, Hick

**Cady, Hick**
See Cady, Forrest Leroy

**Caecus**
See Claudius, Appius

**Caedmon, [Father]**
See Wahl, Thomas [Peter]

**Caedmon** 7th c. [DEP, FFF, SN]
*British poet*
* [The] Anglo Saxon Milton
* [The] Dreamer of Whitby
* [The] Father of English Song
* [The] Saxon Milton

**Caeiro, Alberto**
See Pessoa, Fernando [Antonio
Nogueira]

**Caesar**
See Lincoln, Abraham

**Caesar, Dionaean**
See Caesar, [Gaius] Julius

**Caesar, [Eu]gene [Lee]** 1927- [CA]
*American author*
* Laredo, Johnny
* Sterling, Anthony

**Caesar, Irving**
See Caesar, Isaac

**Caesar, Isaac** 1895- [BEW, TR]
*American lyricist*
* Caesar, Irving

**Caesar, [Gaius] Julius** 1st c. BC
[DEP, HN, RH]
*Roman general and statesman*
* Caesar, Dionaean
* [The] Father of His Country
* [The] Loose Girt Boy
* [The] Pisistratos of Rome

**Caesar, Kurt** 1906-1974 [WECO]
*Italian cartoonist and illustrator*
* Avai, Caesar
* Away, Caesar

**[The] Caesar of Caesars**
See Frederick II

**Caesar, R. D.** 20th c. [TBJ]
*Author*
* James, Dynely [joint pseudonym
  with William (James Carter)
  Mayne]

**Caesariensis**
See Alexander, James Waddell

**Cafego, Bad News**
See Cafego, George

**Cafego, George** 1915- [FB]
*American football player*
* Cafego, Bad News

**Caffarelli**
See Majorano, Gaetano

**Caffarelli** ?-1633 [WBD]
*Italian art collector and prelate*
* Borghese, Scipione

**Caffie, Joseph Clifford [Joe]** 1931-
[BE]
*American baseball player*
* Caffie, Rabbit

**Caffie, Rabbit**
See Caffie, Joseph Clifford [Joe]

**Caffrey, Kate** 20th c. [CA]
*British author and educator*
* Toller, Kate Caffrey

**Caffyn, Kathleen Mannington** 20th
c. [WWL]
*Author*
* Iota

**Cagancho**
See Rodriguez y Ortega, Joaquin

**Cage, Butch**
See Cage, James

**Cage, James** 1894-1975 [BWW]
*American singer*
* Cage, Butch

**[The] Cage Queen**
See Harris, Lusia

**Cagle, Christian K.** 1905-1942
[FB]
*American football player*
* Cagle, Red

**Cagle, Red**
See Cagle, Christian K.

**Cagliari [or Caliari?], Paolo**
1528?-1588 [HN, WBD]
*Italian painter*
* [The] Painter of Pageants
* Veronese, Paolo

**Cagliostro, [Count] Alessandro di**
See Balsamo, Giuseppe

**[The] Cagliostro of Literature**
See De Courchamps, Comte

**Cagney, James Francis [Jimmy]**
1899-
*American actor*
* Cagney, Little Red

**Cagney, Jean** 1919- [FC]
*American actress*
* Cagney, Jeanne

**Cagney, Jeanne**
See Cagney, Jean

**Cagney, Little Red**
See Cagney, James Francis
[Jimmy]

**Cagney, Peter**
See Winter, Bevis

**Cagnoli, Belmonti** [PA]
*Author*
* Abbe

**Cago, Joe**
See Valachi, Joseph Michael

**Cahill, Frank** [FFF]
*American writer*
* Conway, Mark

**Cahill, Mike?**
See Nolan, William F[rancis]

**Cahlman, Robert**
See Kalman, Bernard

**Cahn, Bobie**
See Cahn, Norman

**Cahn, Jake**
See Cahn, Julius Charles

**Cahn, Julius Charles** 1864-1941
[EJS]
*American horse owner and trainer*
* Cahn, Jake

**Cahn, Norman** 1892-1965 [EJS]
*American football player*
* Cahn, Bobie

**Cahn, Sammy**
See Cohen, Samuel

**Cahn, Zvi** 1896- [CAP]
*Polish-born author*
* Laurie, Harry C.

**Caiani, Joe** 1929- [ASC]
*American musician*
* Cain, Joe

**Caiano, Mario** 20th c. [WF]
*Italian director*
* Hawkins, William

**Caillet, Guillaume** ?-1358
[DNNS, HN, SN]
*French peasant rebellion leader*
* Bonhomme, Jacques
* [The] Jack Cade of France

**Cain, Arthur H[omer]** 1913-
[CA, SAT]
*American author*
* King, Arthur

**Cain, Christopher**
See Fleming, Thomas J[ames]

**Cain, Dutch**
See Cain, James F.

**Cain, Guillermo**
See Cabrera Infante, Guillermo

**Cain, Henri Louis** 1728-1778
[WBD]
*French actor*
* Lekain, Henri Louis

**Cain, J. M.**
See Cain, James Mallahan

**Cain, J. V.**
See Cain, James Victor

**Cain, James F.** 20th c. [CEI]
*Canadian-born hockey player*
* Cain, Dutch

**Cain, James Mallahan** 1892- [LC]
*American author*
* Cain, J. M.

**Cain, James Victor** 1951-1979
[IBW, SMG]
*American football player*
* Cain, J. V.

**Cain, Joe**
See Caiani, Joe

**Cain, John L.** 20th c. [FB]
*American football player*
* Cain, Sugar

**Cain, Leslie** 1948- [SMG]
*American baseball player*
* Cain, Sugar

**Cain, Marlon** 20th c. [OBW]
*American baseball player*
* Cain, Sugar

**Cain, Merritt Patrick** 1907-1975
[BE]
*American baseball player*
* Cain, Sugar

**Cain, Murray** 20th c. [SG]
*Boxer*
* Davis, Redtop
* Davis, Ted

**[The] Cain of America**
See Durand, Nicholas

**[The] Cain of Literature**
See Henley, John

**[The] Cain of Literature**
See Hill, [Sir] John

**Cain, Paul**
See Ruric, Peter

**Cain, Perry** 1929-   [BWW, NBB]
*American singer*
* Daddy Deep Throat

**Cain, Robert Max** 1924-
[BE, GSH]
*American baseball player*
* Cain, Sugar

**Cain, Sugar**
See Cain, John L.

**Cain, Sugar**
See Cain, Leslie

**Cain, Sugar**
See Cain, Marlon

**Cain, Sugar**
See Cain, Merritt Patrick

**Cain, Sugar**
See Cain, Robert Max

**Cain, Sugar**
See McCain, Constance

**Caine, Henry**
See Hawken, Henry

**Caine, Jeff**
See Eisfeld, Rainer

**Caine, Jeffrey** 20th c.   [CA]
*Author*
* Campbell, Jeffrey [joint
   pseudonym with Campbell Black]

**Caine, Mark** [joint pseudonym with
Frederic (Michael) Raphael]
See Maschler, Tom

**Caine, Mark** [joint pseudonym with
Tom Maschler]
See Raphael, Frederic [Michael]

**Caine, Michael**
See Micklewhite, Maurice

**Caine, Mitchell**
See Sparkia, Roy [Bernard]

**Caines, John** 1886-1953   [BF]
*British director*
* Raymond, Jack

**Cains, G. A.**
See Cains, Gerald Albert

**Cains, Gerald Albert** 1932-   [ART]
*British painter*
* Cains, G. A.

**Cairnes, Maud**
See Curzon-Herrick, Maud
Kathleen Cairnes Plantagenet
Hastings

**Cairns, Huntington** 1904-   [CA]
*American author and attorney*
* Utley, Ralph

**Cairo, Francesco** 1598-1674
[FFF, SN]
*Italian painter*
* [The] Cavalier
* [El] Chevaliere del Cairo

**Cairo, Jon**
See Romano, Deane Louis

**Caito, Estelle** 20th c.   [BBH]
*American softball player*
* Caito, Ricki

**Caito, Ricki**
See Caito, Estelle

**Caius**
See Mitchell, Donald Grant

**Caius, John**
See Kees [Keys, Kay or Key], John

**Cajetan, Cardinal**
See De Vio, Tommaso

**Cajun Gib Guilbeau**
See Guilbeau, Gib

**Cajun Pete**
See Vidacovich, Irving J.

**[The] Cajun Whip**
See Guidry, Ron[ald Ames]

**Cake, Patrick**
See Welch, Timothy L.

**[The] Cakewalk King**
See Johnson, Charles E.

**Calabreese, Lou** 20th c.   [PMJ]
*American bandleader*
* Breese, Lou

**[Il] Calabrese**
See Preti, Mattia

**Calabriese, Joseph** ?-1925   [PHM]
*American underworld figure*
* Calabriese, Little Joe

**Calabriese, Little Joe**
See Calabriese, Joseph

**Calabro, John A.** 1909-   [ASC]
*American composer*
* Cale, Johnny

**Calamity Jane**
See Burke, Martha Jane [Canary]

**[El] Calatraveno [The Man from
Calatrava]**
See Ruiz, Jose

**Calbeam**
See Beamiss, Frederick Harold

**[The] Calculator**
See Alfragan

**[The] Calculator**
See Bidder, George

**[The] Calculator**
See Buxton, Jedediah

**[The] Calculator**
See Colburn, Zerah

**Caldara, Polidoro** 1495?-1543
[WBD]
*Italian painter*
* Caravaggio, Polidoro da

**Caldarelli, Nazarene** 1887-1959
[EWL]
*Italian poet, author, journalist*
* Cardarelli, Vincenzo

**Calder, Alma**
See Johnston, Alma Calder

**Calder, Peter Ritchie** 1906-   [CA]
*Scottish-born author*
* Ritchie-Calder, Peter Ritchie

**Calderon, Fernando Juan Iglesias**
1856- ?   [ALY]
*Mexican historian and author*
* Guillermo

**Calderon, George** 1868-1915?
[WWL]
*Author and playwright*
* Tihoti

**Calderon de la Barca, Pedro**
1600?-1681?   [DEP, HN]
*Spanish poet and playwright*
* [The] Poet of the Inquisition
* [The] Spanish Shakespeare

**Caldwell, Albert W.** 1903-
[DAM, EJ, WWJ]
*American jazz musician*
* Caldwell, Happy

**Caldwell, Anne**
See O'Dea, Anne Caldwell

**Caldwell, Earl Welton** 1905-   [BE]
*American baseball player*
* Caldwell, Teach

**Caldwell, Elinor**
See Breton-Smith, Clare

**Caldwell, Ella**   [FFF]
*American poet*
* Leila

**Caldwell, Happy**
See Caldwell, Albert W.

**Caldwell, James**
See Lowry, Robert [James Collas]

**Caldwell, Joe** 1941-   [BB]
*American basketball player*
* Caldwell, Pogo

**Caldwell, Kathryn [Smoot]** 1942-
[CA]
*American author*
* Alexander, Kathryn

**Caldwell, Lefty**
See Caldwell, Ralph Grant

**Caldwell, Mack M.** 1896-   [NAA]
*American clergyman and writer*
* Doe, Deadrick

**Caldwell, Marianne**
See Lipsett, Marianne

**Caldwell, Mary** 1901-1957   [BEW]
*American actress*
* Hay, Mary

**Caldwell, Pogo**
See Caldwell, Joe

**Caldwell, Ralph Grant** 1884-   [BE]
*American baseball player*
* Caldwell, Lefty

**Caldwell, Raymond Benjamin**
1888-1967   [AS, BE]
*American baseball player*
* Caldwell, Slim

**Caldwell, Slim**
See Caldwell, Raymond Benjamin

**Caldwell, [Janet] Taylor** 1900-
[ANT, CA, WD]
*British-born American author*
* Reiner, Max

**Caldwell, Teach**
See Caldwell, Earl Welton

**Caldwell, Web**
See Caldwell, Wilbur

**Caldwell, Wilbur** 1910-   [BBH]
*American volleyball player*
* Caldwell, Web

**Caldwell, William A.** 20th c.   [SFP]
*Author*
* Stylites, Simeon

**Cale, Johnny**
See Calabro, John A.

**Caledfryn, Gwilym**
See Williams, William

**[The] Caledonian Vandyck**
See Jamesone, George

**Calerito [Little Lime Dealer]**
See Calero y Berdejo, Joaquin

**Calero y Berdejo, Joaquin**
1876-1942   [GS]
*Spanish bullfighter*
* Calerito [Little Lime Dealer]

**Cales, Claude**
See Calestreme, Jean-Claude

**[El] Calesero [The Buggy Driver]**
See Ramirez Alonso, Alfonso

**Calestreme, Jean-Claude** 1934-
[OP]
*French opera singer*
* Cales, Claude

**Caletti-Bruni, Pietro Francesco**
1602?-1676   [WBD]
*Italian composer*
* Cavalli, Francesco

**Caley, J. C.** 1763-1834   [PA]
*Author*
* Ill-Used Candidate

**Caley, Rod**
See Rowland, D[onald] S[ydney]

**Calgary Red Seward**
See Seward, Roy

**Calhern, Louis**
See Vogt, Carl Henry

**Calhoun, Alfred R.**   [FFF, PA]
*American writer*
* Edwards, Leon
* Lawrence, [Lieut.] Ashbury
* Rochfort, Alfred

**Calhoun, Cora** 1887?-1972
[EJ, PMJ]
*American jazz musician*
* Austin, Lovie

**Calhoun, Corky**
See Calhoun, David

**Calhoun, David** 1950-   [BB, SMG]
*American basketball player*
* Calhoun, Corky
* [The] Stopper

**Calhoun, Eric**
See Turner, Robert [Harry]

**Calhoun, Fred** 20th c.   [ECM]
*American country-western performer*
* Calhoun, Papa

**Calhoun, Herman** 1934-   [BX]
*American boxer*
* Calhoun, Rory

**Calhoun, Jeff**
See Slaughter, Marion T.

**Calhoun, John Caldwell** 1782-1850
[DNNS]
*American politician*
* Squatter Sovereignty

**Calhoun, John Charles** 1879-1947
[BE]
*American baseball player*
* Calhoun, Red

**Calhoun, Lefty**
*See* Calhoun, Walter

**Calhoun, Mary**
*See* Calhoun, William Davitte
[Bill]

**Calhoun, Mary**
*See* Wilkins, Mary Huiskamp
Calhoun

**Calhoun, Mr.**
*See* Vincent, Monroe

**Calhoun, Moon**
*See* Calhoun, Richard

**Calhoun, Mrs.**
*See* Runkle, Lucia Gilbert

**Calhoun, Papa**
*See* Calhoun, Fred

**Calhoun, Red**
*See* Calhoun, John Charles

**Calhoun, Richard** 20th c. [RO2]
*American musician*
* Calhoun, Moon

**Calhoun, Rory**
*See* Calhoun, Herman

**Calhoun, Rory**
*See* Durgin, Francis Timothy

**Calhoun, Walter** 20th c. [OBW]
*American baseball player*
* Calhoun, Lefty

**Calhoun, William Davitte** [Bill]
1890-1955 [BE]
*American baseball player*
* Calhoun, Mary

**[EL] Cali [The Man from Cali,
Colombia]**
*See* Calvo, Enrique

**Cali, Charles** 1903-1960 [SC]
*American actor*
* Cooley, Charles

**Caliban**
*See* Buchanan, Robert Williams

**Caliban**
*See* Gonzales, Louis Jean
Emmanuel

**Caliban**
*See* Nordhausen, Richard

**Caliban**
*See* Reid, John Cowie

**[The] Caliban of Science**
*See* Ramsay, Alexander

**Calicott, Joe**
*See* Callicott, Joe

**[The] Calif of the West**
*See* Abd-er Rahman I

**[El] Califa de Leon [The Caliph of
Leon]**
*See* Gaona y Jimenez, Rodolfo

**Califano, Crazy**
*See* Califano, Joseph Anthony, Jr.

**Califano, Joseph Anthony, Jr.** 1931?-
*HEW secretary under American
president Jimmy Carter*
* [The] Boy Earthquake
* Califano, Crazy
* Califano, Mad Mad Joe
* [The] Dynamo

**Califano, Mad Mad Joe**
*See* Califano, Joseph Anthony, Jr.

**California Billy Miner**
*See* Miner, William

**[The] California Comet**
*See* McLoughlin, Maurice E.

**[The] California Grizzly**
*See* Jeffries, James Jackson

**Caligny, Jean Antenor Huede**
1657-1731 [PA]
*Author*
* De Luc

**Caligula**
*See* Gaius Caesar

**Caliniff, Martin** 1935- [FC, SW]
*American actor*
* Callan, Michael

**[The] Caliph of Cordoba**
*See* Rodriguez Sanchez, Manuel

**Caliste, Jean** 1943- [IBW]
*American singer and songwriter*
* Knight, Jean

**Calixtus [or Calixt], Georg**
*See* Callisen, Georg

**Calixtus II**
*See* Guido of Vienne [or
Burgundy]

**Calixtus III**
*See* Borgia, Alfonso

**[The] Calker**
*See* Michael V Calaphrates

**Calkins, Fay**
*See* Alailima, Fay C.

**Calkins, Franklin**
*See* Stratemeyer, Edward L.

**Calkins, Hiram** [FFF]
*American journalist*
* Deacon

**[The] Call Boy**
*See* Smith, Charles J.

**Call, Peggy**
*See* Blair, Peggy

**Callaghan, Dennis** 20th c. [BBH]
*Irish-born greyhound racing
organization officer*
* NCA, Mr.

**Callaghan, Leonard James** 1913?-
[NN]
*British prime minister*
* Callaghan, Sunny Jim

**Callaghan, Sunny Jim**
*See* Callaghan, Leonard James

**Callahan, Bill**
*See* Callahan, Homer C.

**Callahan, Claire Wallis** 1890- [CA]
*American author*
* Cole, Ann Kilborn
* Hartwell, Nancy

**Callahan, Homer C.** 1912-1971
[ECM]
*American country-western performer*
* Callahan, Bill

**Callahan, James Joseph** 1874-1934
[AS, BE]
*American baseball player and
manager*
* Callahan, Nixey

**Callahan, Joe**
*See* Callahan, Walter T.

**Callahan, John**
*See* Gallun, Raymond Z[inke]

**Callahan, Mushi [or Mushy]**
*See* Scheer, Vincent Morris

**Callahan, Nixey**
*See* Callahan, James Joseph

**Callahan, Pat**
*See* Callahan, Ray James

**Callahan, Ray James** 1891- [BE]
*American baseball player*
* Callahan, Pat

**Callahan, Walter T.** 1910- [ECM]
*American country-western performer*
* Callahan, Joe

**Callahan, William**
*See* Gallun, Raymond Z[inke]

**Callan, Michael**
*See* Caliniff, Martin

**Callao [Pebble]**
*See* Reyes, Fernando De Los

**Callard, Thomas Henry** 1912-
[AW, CA]
*British author*
* Ross, Sutherland

**Callas, Maria**
*See* Kalogeropoulos, Maria Anna
Sofia Cecilia

**Callas, Theo**
*See* McCarthy, Shaun [Lloyd]

**Callaway, Bo**
*See* Callaway, Howard Hollis

**Callaway, Howard Hollis** 1927-
*American political campaign
manager and former secretary of the
army*
* Callaway, Bo

**[The] Callaway Kid**
*See* McBride, Arnold Ray

**Callcott, Maria** 1788-1842 [PA]
*Author*
* Graham, Lady

**Calle, Paul** 20th c. [SFP]
*Author*
* Pierre, Paul

**Calleia, Joseph**
*See* Spurin-Calleia, Joseph

**Calleja del Rey, Felix Maria**
1750-1820 [WBD]
*Spanish army officer*
* [The] Butcher

**Callender, George** 1918-
[ASC, DAM, EJ]
*American jazz musician*
* Callender, Red

**Callender, Julian**
*See* Lee, Austin

**Callender, Red**
*See* Callender, George

**Calliam, Selma**
*See* Kalichmam, Claire

**Callicott, Joe** 1901?-1969 [BWW]
*American singer*
* Calicott, Joe
* Callicott, Mississippi Joe
* Callicutt, Joe

**Callicott, Mississippi Joe**
*See* Callicott, Joe

**Callicutt, Joe**
*See* Callicott, Joe

**Callighen, Brett** 1953- [SMG]
*Canadian-born hockey player*
* Callighen, Key

**Callighen, Francis Charles Winslow**
1906- [CEI]
*Canadian-born hockey player*
* Callighen, Patsy

**Callighen, Key**
*See* Callighen, Brett

**Callighen, Patsy**
*See* Callighen, Francis Charles
Winslow

**[The] Calligrapher**
*See* Theodosius II

**Callihou, James**
*See* Morin, Leo-Pol

**Callimides** [HN]
*Athenian wit*
* [The] Grasshopper

**Callinicus**
*See* Seleucus II

**Callisen, Georg** 1586-1656 [WBD]
*German theologian*
* Calixtus [or Calixt], Georg

**Callistus, Nicephorus** [PA]
*Author*
* Xanthopalus

**Calloway, Cab**
*See* Calloway, Cabell

**Calloway, Cabell** 1907-
[DAM, FC, IBW]
*American bandleader and singer*
* Calloway, Cab
* [The] King of Hi-De-Ho

**Callwood, June**
*See* Frayne, June

**Calm Daddy McWilliams**
*See* McWilliams, Stanley W.

**Calmes, Neville**
*See* Everett, Katherine Calmes

**Calnan, T. D.**
*See* Calnan, Thomas Daniel

**Calnan, Thomas Daniel** 1915-
[IAW]
*Italian author*
* Calnan, T. D.

**Calojoannes [Handsome]**
*See* John II Comnenus

**[The] Calomniographe of His Age**
*See* Des Reaux, Gedeon Tallemant

**Calov, Abraham**
*See* Kalau, Abraham

**Calpurnius Piso, Lucius** 2nd c. BC
[WBD]
*Roman politician*
* Frugi

**Calson, Isaac**
See Ledoux, John Walter

**Calster, Og**
See Van Calster, A. M.

**Calvaert [or Calvart], Denis**
1540?-1619 [WBD]
*Flemish painter*
* Denis le Flamand

**Calve, Emma**
See Calvet, Rosa Emma

**Calvert, Adelaide Helen**
See Biddles [or Bedells], Adelaide
Helen

**Calvert, Caroline Louisa Waring**
1834-1872 [WBD]
*Australian author*
* Atkinson, Louisa

**Calvert, Catherine**
See Cassidy, Catherine

**Calvert, Elinor H.** 1929- [CA]
*German-born author*
* Lasell, Fen H.

**Calvert, George Henry** 1803- ?
[PA]
*American author*
* [An] American

**Calvert, John**
See Leaf, [Wilbur] Munro

**Calvert, Mad Mike**
See Calvert, Michael

**Calvert, Mary** 1941- [WD]
*British author*
* Danby, Mary

**Calvert, Michael** 1913- [BDW]
*British soldier*
* Calvert, Mad Mike

**Calvert, Mrs. C. H.** [FFF]
*Entertainer*
* Belmont, Clara

**Calvert, Mrs. Louis** [FFF]
*Entertainer*
* Roberts, Rose

**Calvert, Phyllis**
See Bickle, Phyllis

**Calvert, William Robinson** 1882- ?
[MBF]
*British author and editor*
* Croft, Roy
* Dale, Austin

**Calvert-Langton, Basil** 1912-
[THR]
*British actor, theatrical manager,
producer*
* Langton, Basil C.

**Calverton, Victor Francis**
See Goetz, George

**Calvet, Corinne**
See Dibos, Corinne

**Calvet, Rosa Emma** 1858-1942
[BBD]
*French opera singer*
* Calve, Emma

**Calvin, Henry**
See Goodman, Wimberley Calvin,
Jr.

**Calvin, Henry**
See Hanley, Clifford

**Calvin, John**
See Chauvin [or Caulvin?], Jean

**Calvinus, Johann** ?-1630 [PA]
*Author*
* Kahl

**Calvisius, Sethus**
See Kallwitz, Seth

**Calvo, Enrique** 20th c. [GS]
*Colombian bullfighter*
* [EL] Cali [The Man from Cali,
Colombia]

**Calvo, Jacinto** 1894-1965 [BE]
*Cuban-born baseball player*
* Calvo, Jack

**Calvo, Jack**
See Calvo, Jacinto

**Cam**
See Campbell, Barbara

**Cam**
See Lewis, Waller

**Camand, Richard**
See Coekelberghs, Amand Joseph
Richard

**Camara, Helder Pessoa** 1909-
[CA]
*Brazilian clergyman and author*
* Dom Helder
* [The] Red Bishop

**Camarata, Salvador Tutti** 1913-
[ASC, PMJ]
*American composer and conductor*
* Camarata, Toots

**Camarata, Toots**
See Camarata, Salvador Tutti

**Camaso, Claudio**
See Volonte, Claudio

**Camber, Andrew**
See Bingley, David Ernest

**Camblos, Lillian** [FFF]
*Entertainer*
* Conway, Lillian

**Cambridge, Elizabeth**
See Hodges, Barbara K. [Webber]

**Cambyses** [SN]
*King of Persia*
* Ahasuerus [Lion-Hearted]

**[The] Camden of the Eighteenth
Century**
See Gough, Richard

**Camden, Richard**
See Beeston, L. J.

**Camden, School Master**
See Camden, William

**Camden, William** 1551-1623
[PA, RH, SN]
*British historian*
* [The] British Pausanias
* [The] British Strabo
* Camden, School Master
* [The] English Strabo
* [The] Nurse of Antiquity
* [The] Pausanias of Britain
* [The] Strabo of Britain

**Camden, William** (Continued)
* [The] Varro of Britain

**[The] Camel**
See Humphreys [or Humphries],
Murray

**[The] Camel Driver of Mecca**
See Mohammed [or Mahomet]

**Cameleon**
See Thiers, Louis Adolphe

**Camelinat, Hermine** 1924- [THR]
*British actress, dancer, singer*
* French, Hermene

**[The] Cameo Girl**
See Hegamin, Lucille

**Camera Eye Bishop**
See Bishop, Max Frederick

**Camerlengo, Anthony** 20th c. [SG]
*Boxer*
* Gans, Italian Joe

**Camero de Guerra, Candido** 1921-
[EJ, IBW]
*Cuban-born jazz musician*
* Candido

**Cameron, Angus** 1921- [CEI]
*Canadian-born hockey player*
* Cameron, Scotty

**Cameron, Berl** [joint pseudonym with
Arthur O. Roberts] [house
pseudonym, Curtis Warren]
See Glasby, John [Stephen]

**Cameron, Berl** [house pseudonym,
Curtis Warren]
See Holloway, Brian

**Cameron, Berl** [house pseudonym,
Curtis Warren]
See Hughes, Den[n]is [Talbot]

**Cameron, Berl** [house pseudonym,
Curtis Warren]
See O'Brien, David

**Cameron, Berl** [joint pseudonym with
John (Stephen) Glasby] [house
pseudonym, Curtis Warren]
See Roberts, Arthur O.

**Cameron, Brett**
See Martin, Reginald Alec

**Cameron, Bruce**
See Brachard, Paul, Jr.

**Cameron, Clifford**
See Garbutt, John L.

**Cameron, D. A.**
See Cameron, Donald [Allan]

**Cameron, D. Y.**
See Cook, Dorothy Mary

**Cameron, Donald**
See Bryans, Robert Harbinson
[Robin]

**Cameron, Donald** 1695?-1748
[DNNF, DNNS, SN]
*Scottish chieftain*
* [The] Gentle Lochiel

**Cameron, Donald [Allan]** 1937-
[CA]
*Canadian writer and editor*
* Cameron, D. A.
* Cameron, Silver Donald

**Cameron, Elizabeth**
See Nowell, Elizabeth Cameron

**Cameron, Elizabeth Dorothea Cole
Bowen** 1889-1973 [WGT]
*Irish author*
* Bowen, Elizabeth

**Cameron, Elizabeth Jane**
1910-1976 [CA, WD]
*British author*
* Duncan, Jane
* Sandison, Janet

**Cameron, [Sir] Evan** 1629-1719
[DNNF, HN, SN]
*Scottish chieftain*
* [The] Black
* Ewan Dhu
* [The] Ulysses of the Highlands

**Cameron, G. S.**
See Cameron, Gordon Stewart

**Cameron, Gordon Stewart** 1916-
[ART]
*Scottish painter*
* Cameron, G. S.

**Cameron, Harold Hugh** 1890-1953
[FHE, HK]
*Canadian-born hockey player*
* Cameron, Harry

**Cameron, Harry**
See Cameron, Harold Hugh

**Cameron, Ian**
See Payne, Donald Gordon

**Cameron, John**
See Macdonell, Archibald Gordon

**Cameron, Julia** [FFF]
*Opera singer*
* Valda, [Mme.] Giulia

**Cameron, Julie**
See Cameron, Lou

**Cameron, Kate**
See Barnes, Kate D. W.

**Cameron, Kate**
See DuBreuil, Elizabeth Lorinda

**Cameron, Kenneth Neill** 1908-
[CA]
*British-born author and educator*
* Madden, Warren

**Cameron, Leigh**
See Wright, Sewell Peaslee

**Cameron, Leila**
See DuBose, Catherine A.
[Richards]

**Cameron, Lou** 1924- [CA, SFL]
*American author*
* Adams, Justin
* Arnold, L. J.
* Cameron, Julie
* Cartier, Steve
* Dagmar
* Evans, Tabor
* Manning, Mary Louise
* Marvin, W. R.
* Thorne, Ramsay

**Cameron, Ludovick Charles Richard**
1866- ? [WWL]
*British author*
* Hewson, Charles

**Cameron, Margaret**
See Lewis, Margaret Cameron

**Cameron, Margaret**
See Lindsay, Kathleen

**Cameron, Rod**
See Cox, Nathan

**Cameron, Rudolph [Rudy]**
See Brennan, Rudolph Cameron

**Cameron, Scotty**
See Cameron, Angus

**Cameron, Silver Donald**
See Cameron, Donald [Allan]

**Cameron, Violet**
See De Bensaude, Mrs.

**Cameron, Ward**
See Hallbing, Kjell Kare

**Cameron, William Ernest** 1881- ?
[WW, WWL]
*British author*
* Allerton, Mark

**Cameroy**
See Lane, James Woods

**Camgan, Bill** 1883-1969
*American baseball player*
* Holy Cross Bill

**Camille, Roussan** 1912-1961 [CW]
*Haitian poet and journalist*
* El Limac, Nassour

**Camilli, Adolph Louis** 1908-
[BE, DGS]
*American baseball player*
* Camilli, Dolph

**Camilli, Dolph**
See Camilli, Adolph Louis

**Camillo, Giulio** 1497-1550 [PA]
*Author*
* Delminio

**Camillus**
See Ames, Fisher

**Camillus**
See Hamilton, Alexander

**Camillus, Marcus Furius** 4th c. BC
[FFF, HN]
*Roman soldier and statesman*
* [The] Founder of Rome
* [The] Second Romulus

**Camino, Leon Felipe** 1884- [CD]
*Spanish poet*
* Leon Felipe

**Camino Sanchez, Francisco** 1941-
[GS]
*Spanish bullfighter*
* [El] Nino Sabio [The Wise Child]

**[El] Camisero [The Shirt Maker]**
See Carmona y Gonzalez, Angel

**Camnitz, Red**
See Camnitz, Samuel Howard

**Camnitz, Samuel Howard**
1881-1960 [BE]
*American baseball player*
* Camnitz, Red
* [The] Kentucky Rosebud

**Camoens, Luis de** 1524-1580
[DNNF, FFF, SN]
*Portuguese poet*
* [The] Apollo of Portugal
* [The] Great
* [The] Homer and Virgil of
Portugal
* [The] Homer of Portugal
* [The] Portuguese Apollo

**Camors, Conde de**
See Casal, Julian del

**Camp, Candace P[auline]** 1949-
[CA]
*American author*
* Gregory, Lisa
* James, Kristin

**Camp, Kid**
See Camp, Winfield Scott

**Camp, Madeleine L'Engle** 1918-
[MJA, SAT]
*American author*
* Franklin, Madeleine
* L'Engle, Madeleine

**Camp, Phineas**
See Duane, W. N.

**Camp, Walter Chauncey**
1859-1925 [OCS]
*American football player and coach*
* [The] Father of American
Football

**Camp, Winfield Scott** 1870-1895
[BE]
*American baseball player*
* Camp, Kid

**Campagna, Louis** 1906?-1963?
[BLB, PHM]
*American underworld figure*
* Little New York

**Campana, Pedro de**
See Kempener [or Kempeneer],
Peter de

**Campanella, Campy**
See Campanella, Roy

**Campanella, Giovanni Domenico**
1568-1639 [WBD]
*Italian philosopher*
* Campanella, Tommaso

**Campanella, Roy** 1921- [BBH]
*American baseball player*
* Campanella, Campy

**Campanella, Tommaso**
See Campanella, Giovanni
Domenico

**Campaneris, Bert**
See Campaneris, Dagoberto Blanco

**Campaneris, Campy**
See Campaneris, Dagoberto Blanco

**Campaneris, Dagoberto Blanco**
1942- [BE, PB, SMG]
*Cuban-born baseball player*
* Campaneris, Bert
* Campaneris, Campy

**Campanini, Cleofonte** 1860-1919
[FFF]
*Italian conductor*
* Fetrazzini, Eva

**Campanora, Peter** ?- 984 [CAL]
*Pope*
* John XIV

**Campari, Darkie**
See Campari, Giuseppe

**Campari, Giuseppe** 1892-1933
[EAR]
*Italian auto racer*
* Campari, Darkie
* Campari, Negher

**Campari, Negher**
See Campari, Giuseppe

**Campau, Charles C.** 1863-1938
[BE]
*American baseball player and
manager*
* Campau, Count

**Campau, Count**
See Campau, Charles C.

**Campbell, Ada** 1862-1938 [CED]
*Canadian-born singer*
* Irwin, May

**Campbell, Alexander** [SN]
*Editor*
* Dunnie-Wassail

**Campbell, Angus**
See Chetwynd-Hayes, Ronald
Henry Glynn

**Campbell, Archer Stewart** 1903-
[BE]
*American baseball player*
* Campbell, Archie

**Campbell, Archibald** 1598-1661
[SN]
*Scottish aristocrat*
* Argyll, Marquis of
* [The] Presbyterian Ulysses

**Campbell, Archie**
See Campbell, Archer Stewart

**Campbell, B. F.** 20th c.
*Actress*
* Friderici, Blanche

**Campbell, Bad Earl**
See Campbell, Earl

**Campbell, Barbara** 1913- [ICB]
*British illustrator*
* Cam

**Campbell, Beatrice Murphy**
See Murphy, Beatrice M.

**Campbell, Beth**
See Short, Beth Campbell

**Campbell, Big Bill**
See Campbell, Bill

**Campbell, Bill** 1893- [BMH]
*Canadian-born entertainer*
* Campbell, Big Bill
* [The] Happy Philosopher

**Campbell, Blanche** 1902- [CA]
*American writer*
* Fish, Julian

**Campbell, Blanche Friderici**
1878-1933 [SC]
*American actress*
* Frederici, Blanche

**Campbell, Blind James**
See Campbell, James

**Campbell, Bridget**
See Sanctuary, Brenda

**Campbell, Bruce**
See Epstein, Samuel

**Campbell, Bus**
See Campbell, Robert

**Campbell, C. J.**
See Stuart, Morna

**Campbell, C[larence] Samuel** 1900-
[NAA]
*American author*
* Roane, Peter

**Campbell, Camrod**
See Campbell, Willie

**Campbell, Charlotte [Countess of
Bury]** 1775-1861 [FFF]
*Author*
* Dudley, Arthur

**Campbell, Clarence** 1915- [BE]
*American baseball player*
* Campbell, Soup

**Campbell, Clementina Dinah** 1927-
[EJ7]
*British singer*
* Laine, Cleo

**Campbell, Clive**
See MacRae, Donald G.

**Campbell, Clyde Crane**
See Gold, Horace Leonard

**Campbell, Colin**
See Christie, Douglas

**Campbell, [Sir] Colin**
See Macliver, Colin

**Campbell, Colin John** 1953- [SMG]
*Canadian-born hockey player*
* Campbell, Soupy

**Campbell, Donald**
See Carpenter, Stephen Cullen

**Campbell, Donald**
See Gilford, Charles Bernard

**Campbell, Earl** 1953- [IBW]
*American football player*
* Campbell, Bad Earl

**Campbell, Earl** 20th c. [CEI]
*Hockey player*
* Campbell, Spiff

**Campbell, Ellen A. F.**
See Flanner, Abbe

**Campbell, Flora** 1859?-1930
[BEW]
*Canadian-born theatrical performer*
* Irwin, Flo

**Campbell, Francis Stuart**
See Kuehnelt-Leddihn, Erik
[Ritter Von]

**Campbell, Fred**
See Sellers, Connie Leslie, Jr.

**Campbell, G. W.**
See Brown, G. W.

**Campbell, Gilly**
See Campbell, William Gilthorpe

**Campbell, Hannah** 20th c. [CA]
*American writer and editor*
* Franklin, Elizabeth

**Campbell, Harry**
See Smith, Bernard

**Campbell, Helen**
See Weeks, Helen C.

**Campbell, Herbert J.** 1925-
[ESF, SFL]
*British author and editor*
* Deegan, Jon J. [house
pseudonym, Hamilton]
* Sheldon, Roy [house pseudonym,
Hamilton]

**Campbell, Hope**
See Wallis, Geraldine McDonald

**Campbell, Hutch**
See Campbell, Marc Thaddeus

**Campbell, James** 1906- [BWW]
*American singer*
* Campbell, Blind James

**Campbell, Jane**
*See* Edwards, Jane Campbell

**Campbell, Jeffrey** [joint pseudonym with Jeffrey Caine]
*See* Black, Campbell

**Campbell, Jeffrey** [joint pseudonym with Campbell Black]
*See* Caine, Jeffrey

**Campbell, Jock**
*See* Campbell, John

**Campbell, John** 1678-1743 [HN]
*Scottish general and statesman*
* Argyll, Second Duke of
* [The] Good Duke of Argyll

**Campbell, John** 1708-1775 [DNNF, FFF, RH]
*Scottish author*
* Shepherd, John Claridge
* [The] Shepherd of Banbury

**Campbell, John** 1894-1942 [BDW, WWW]
*British artillery officer*
* Campbell, Jock

**Campbell, John Beautiste** 1848- ? [NAA]
*American author*
* Strong Bow
* Tuan

**Campbell, John Lorne** 1906- [AW, CA]
*Scottish author, folklorist, translator*
* Chanaidh, Fear

**Campbell, John Patrick** 20th c. [DBA]
*Irish illustrator*
* MacCathmhaoil, Seaghan

**Campbell, John Ramsey** 1946- [CA, HFF, WGT]
*British author*
* Comfort, Montgomery
* Dreadstone, Carl [house pseudonym]
* Undercliffe, Errol

**Campbell, John W[ood], Jr.** 1910-1971 [B10, CAP, SF]
*American author and editor*
* McCann, Arthur
* Stuart, Don A.
* Van Campen, Karl

**Campbell, Joseph** 1879-1944 [CAT]
*Irish poet, playwright, editor*
* MacCathmhaoil, Seosamh

**Campbell, Judith**
*See* Pares, Marion Stapylton

**Campbell, Judy**
*See* Gamble, Judy

**Campbell, Karen**
*See* Beaty, Betty

**Campbell, Kate**
*See* Lincoln, Jane Elizabeth [Larcombe]

**Campbell, Katherine Roger** 1886-1957 [BEW]
*Scottish-born actress and director*
* Fawcett, Marion

**Campbell, Keith**
*See* West-Watson, Keith Campbell

**Campbell, Ken** 1941- [CA]
*British actor, director, playwright*
* Pilk, Henry

**Campbell, Lizzie**
*See* Little, Mrs. J. Z.

**Campbell, Luke**
*See* Madison, Thomas A[lvin] [Tom]

**Campbell, Marc Thaddeus** 1884- [BE]
*American baseball player*
* Campbell, Hutch

**Campbell, Margaret**
*See* Long, Gabrielle Margaret Vere [Campbell]

**Campbell, Mary** ?-1786 [DNNF, SN]
*First love of Scottish poet, Robert Burns*
* Highland Mary

**Campbell, Milton James** 1934- [BWW, NBB, RO2]
*American singer*
* Little Milton

**Campbell, Molly**
*See* Thomson, Christine Campbell

**Campbell, R. J.**
*See* Campbell, Reginald John

**Campbell, R. T.**
*See* Todd, Ruthven

**Campbell, R. W.**
*See* Campbell, Rosemae Wells

**Campbell, Reginald John** 1867-1956 [LC]
*British clergyman and author*
* Campbell, R. J.

**Campbell [or Macgregor?], Robert** 1671-1734 [HN, SN, WBD]
*Scottish chieftain*
* Rob Roy
* Robert the Red
* [The] Robin Hood of the Lowlands

**Campbell, Robert** 20th c. [SMG]
*Baseball scout*
* Campbell, Bus

**Campbell, Rosemae Wells** 1909- [SAT]
*American author and librarian*
* Campbell, R. W.

**Campbell, S. Brunson** 1884- [DAM]
*American pianist*
* [The] Ragtime Kid

**Campbell, Scott**
*See* Davis, Frederick William

**Campbell, Soup**
*See* Campbell, Clarence

**Campbell, Soupy**
*See* Campbell, Colin John

**Campbell, Spiff**
*See* Campbell, Earl

**Campbell, Sydney G.** 20th c. [MBF]
*British author*
* Lawrence, Chester

**Campbell, Thomas** 1777-1844 [DNNF, DNNS, SN]
*British poet*
* [The] Bard of Hope

**Campbell, Thomas F.** 1924- [CA]
*Irish-born author, columnist, editor*
* Crosscountry

**Campbell, Violet**
*See* Shelton, Violet

**Campbell, Walter Stanley**
*See* Vestal, Stanley

**Campbell, Will D[avis]** 1924- [CA]
*American clergyman and writer*
* Brett, David

**Campbell, William** 20th c. [OBW]
*American baseball player*
* Campbell, Zip

**Campbell, William Edward March** 1893-1954 [ANT, LC, TC1]
*American author*
* March, William

**Campbell, William Gilthorpe** 1907-1973 [BE]
*American baseball player*
* Campbell, Gilly

**Campbell, William V.** 1891-1961 [SC]
*American actor*
* Gilbert, Billy

**Campbell, Willie** 20th c. [IBW]
*American auto racer*
* Campbell, Camrod

**Campbell, Zip**
*See* Campbell, William

**Campbell-Quine, Nina** 1911- [ART]
*South African artist*
* Nina

**Campeador [Champion]**
*See* Diaz de Vivar, Rodrigo

**Campeau, Jean Claude** 1923- [CEI]
*Canadian-born hockey player*
* Campeau, Tod

**Campeau, Tod**
*See* Campeau, Jean Claude

**Camper, Shirley**
*See* Soman, Shirley

**[El] Campesino**
*See* Gonzales, Valentin

**Campfield, Sal**
*See* Campfield, William Holton

**Campfield, William Holton** 1868-1952 [BE]
*American baseball player*
* Campfield, Sal

**Campi, Bernardino** 1522-1590 [FFF]
*Italian painter*
* [The] Caracci of the Eclectic School

**Campi, Eddie**
*See* De Campus, Eddie

**Campion, Katherine** 1868- ? [NAA]
*American author, editor, lecturer*
* King, Caroline Blanche
* Warren, Mary

**Campion, Rose** [joint pseudonym with Jean Lee Latham and Ruth Perry]
*See* Kaser, Arthur LeRoy

**Campion, Rose** [joint pseudonym with Arthur LeRoy Kaser and Ruth Perry]
*See* Latham, Jean Lee

**Campion, Rose** [joint pseudonym with Arthur LeRoy Kaser and Jean Lee Latham]
*See* Perry, Ruth

**Campion, Sarah**
*See* Coulton, Mary Rose

**Campion, Sidney Ronald** 1891- [AW, CAP]
*British author*
* Swayne, Geoffrey

**Campionissimo [Champion of Champions]**
*See* Coppi, Fausto

**Campistron, Jean Galbert de** 1656-1723 [DNNS, HN, RH]
*French playwright*
* Racine's Monkey
* [Le] Singe de Racine

**Campling, F. Knowles** ?-1940 [MBF]
*British author and editor*
* Wood, Eric

**Campo, John [Johnny]** 1938?-
*American horse trainer*
* [The] Fat Man

**Campos, Francisco Jose Lopez** 1925- [BE]
*Cuban-born baseball player*
* Campos, Frank

**Campos, Frank**
*See* Campos, Francisco Jose Lopez

**Camus**
*See* Merville, Pierre Francois

**Camus, Albert** 1913-1960 [CA]
*Algerian-born author and playwright*
* Bauchart
* Mathe, Albert
* Saetone [joint pseudonym]

**Camus in Shoulder Pads**
*See* Saimes, George

**Canada, Cat**
*See* Canada, James

**Canada, James** 1912- [MK]
*American baseball player*
* Canada, Cat

**Canada Kid Ferris**
*See* Ferris, Lee

**Canada's Caruso**
*See* Brooks, Garnet

**Canada's Eddie Guest**
*See* Clark, Greg

**Canadas, Enrique**
*See* Higgins, Henry

**Canaday, John [Edwin]** 1907- [CA, CC, EMD]
*American art critic and author*
* Head, Matthew

**Canadeo, Anthony [Tony]** 1919-
[FB, SMG]
*American football player*
* [The] Gray Ghost of Gonzaga

**[The] Canadian Burl Ives**
*See* Miller, Albert

**[The] Canadian Catapault**
*See* Morenz, Howarth William

**[The] Canadian Crosby**
*See* Todd, Arthur

**[The] Canadian O'Connell**
*See* Papineau, Louis Joseph

**[The] Canadian Troubador**
*See* Andrews, Ted

**Canal, Andre** [CND]
*French OAS leader, 1961-62*
* Black Monocle

**[The] Canal Boy**
*See* Garfield, James Abram

**Canale [or Canal], Antonio**
1697-1768 [WBD]
*Venetian painter*
* Canaletto, Antonio

**Canales, J. A.** 20th c.
*American federal investigator*
* Canales, Tony

**Canales, Tony**
*See* Canales, J. A.

**Canaletto, Antonio**
*See* Canale [or Canal], Antonio

**Canaletto [or Canale], Bernardo**
*See* Belotto [or Bellotto], Bernardo

**Canary**
*See* Conn, Canary Denise

**Canavan, Hugh Edward** 1897-1967
[BE]
*American baseball player*
* Canavan, Hugo

**Canavan, Hugo**
*See* Canavan, Hugh Edward

**Canaway, William Hamilton [Bill]**
1925- [WD]
*British author, playwright,
screenwriter*
* Hamilton, William
* Hermes

**Canby, H. S.**
*See* Canby, Henry Seidel

**Canby, Henry Seidel** 1878-1961
[LC]
*American journalist*
* Canby, H. S.

**Candelaria, Candy**
*See* Candelaria, John Robert

**Candelaria, John Robert** 1953-
[SMG]
*American baseball player*
* Candelaria, Candy
* [The] Candy Man

**Candelin, Catherine** 1852?-1903
[BEW]
*Actress and dancer*
* Vaughan, Kate

**Candelin, Susan Mary Charlotte**
1853-1950 [BEW]
*British-born actress*
* Vaughan, Susie

**Canderensis, Giraldus**
*See* Barry, Girald

**Candida**
*See* Hoffman, Lisa

**Candide**
*See* Claretie, Arsene Arnaud

**Candido**
*See* Camero de Guerra, Candido

**Candido**
*See* Martinez Ruiz, Jose

**Candido, Pepe**
*See* Deligne y Figueroa, Rafael
Alfredo

**Candido, Pietro**
*See* De Wit [or de Witte], Pieter

**Candidus**
*See* White, Thomas

**Candil, Fray**
*See* Bobadilla y Lunar, Emilio

**Candoli, Conte**
*See* Candoli, Secondo

**Candoli, Pete**
*See* Candoli, Walter Joseph

**Candoli, Secondo** 1927-
[DAM, EJ, PMJ]
*American jazz musician*
* Candoli, Conte

**Candoli, Walter Joseph** 1923-
[DAM, EJ, PMJ]
*American jazz musician*
* Candoli, Pete

**Candor**
*See* Webster, Noah

**Candy, Edward**
*See* Neville, B[arbara] Alison
[Boodson]

**[The] Candy Man**
*See* Candelaria, John Robert

**Cane, Charlie**
*See* Koppelman, Charlie

**Canedo, Alejandro** 20th c. [WGT]
*Author*
* Alejandro

**Canegata, Leonard Lionel Cornelius**
1907-1952 [BEW, FC]
*American actor and producer*
* Lee, Canada

**Canevaro, Barbara** 1954?-
*Leader of religious cult, Children of
God*
* Queen Rachel

**Canfield, Arthur Graves** 1859- ?
[NAA]
*American educator and writer*
* Gervas, Thaurr

**Canfield, Dorothy**
*See* Fisher, Dorothea [Frances]
Canfield

**Canfield, Mrs. Eugene** [FFF]
*Entertainer*
* Richmond, Hattie L.

**Caniff, Milton** 20th c. [WECO]
*American cartoonist and writer*
* [The] Rembrandt of the Comic
Strip

**Canisius, Peter**
*See* De Hondt, Pieter

**Canmore**
*See* Malcolm III

**Cann, Kid**
*See* Blumenfeld, Isadore

**Cann, Teddy**
*See* Cann, Tedford

**Cann, Tedford** ?-1963 [BBH]
*American swimmer*
* Cann, Teddy

**Cannady, Rev**
*See* Cannady, Walter

**Cannady, Walter** 1904- [MK]
*American baseball player*
* Cannady, Rev

**Cannan, Denis**
*See* Pullein-Thompson, Denis

**Cannell, Charles**
*See* Vivian, Evelyn Charles H.

**Cannell, Edward Ashton** 1927-
[ART]
*British painter and illustrator*
* Ash

**Cannell, Rip**
*See* Cannell, Virgin Wirt

**Cannell, Virgin Wirt** 1880-1948
[BE]
*American baseball player*
* Cannell, Rip

**Cannibal Jack**
*See* Beach, Charles

**Canning, Charles John [Earl Canning]**
1812-1862 [DEP, DHA, WBD]
*British colonial administrator*
* Canning, Clemency

**Canning, Clemency**
*See* Canning, Charles John [Earl
Canning]

**Canning, E. B.** [PA]
*Author*
* Ariel

**Canning, Effie**
*See* Carlton, Effie

**Canning, George** 1770-1827
[DEL, DEP, PA]
*British prime minister*
* B.
* [The] Cicero of the British Senate
* Griffin, Gregory
* [The] Zany of Debate

**Canning, John**
*See* Shushtary, John

**Canning, Josiah D., of Gill** [PA]
*Author*
* [The] Peanut Bard

**Canning, [Sir] Stratford [First
Viscount Stratford de Redcliffe]**
1786-1880 [DEP, DHA, HN]
*British diplomat*
* [The] Great Eltchi [or Elchi]
* [The] Padishah of the Padishah

**Canning, Victor** 1911- [CA, EMD]
*British author*
* Gould, Alan

**Cannirt, Charles** [PA]
*Author*
* De Vivelle, Jean

**Cannon, Anthony J.** 1855- ? [FFF]
*American actor*
* Hart, Tony

**Cannon, Boom Boom**
*See* Cannon, Larry

**Cannon, Boom-Boom**
*See* Cannon, Otey

**Cannon, Boom Boom**
*See* Picariello, Fredrick Anthony

**Cannon, Curt**
*See* Lombino, Salvatore A.

**Cannon, Dyan**
*See* Friesen, Samile Diane

**Cannon, Freddy**
*See* Picariello, Fredrick Anthony

**Cannon, Gus** 1883- [BWW]
*American singer*
* Banjo Joe

**Cannon, Helen** 1921- [CA]
*American author*
* Prosper, Lincoln

**Cannon, J. D.**
*See* Cannon, John Donovan

**Cannon, J. R.**
*See* Goddard, Norman Molyneux

**Cannon, John Donovan** 1922-
[BEW]
*American actor*
* Cannon, J. D.

**Cannon, Joseph Gurney** 1836-1926
[WBD]
*American politician*
* Uncle Joe

**Cannon, Larry** 20th c.
*Auto racer*
* Cannon, Boom Boom

**Cannon, Noel**
*American jurist*
* [The] Dragon Lady

**Cannon, Otey** 20th c. [AES]
*American soccer player*
* Cannon, Boom-Boom

**Cannon, Richard** 20th c. [OBW]
*American baseball player*
* Cannon, Speed Ball

**Cannon, Sarah Ophelia Colley**
1912- [CME, CWG, IPA]
*American country-western performer*
* Pearl, Minnie

**Cannon, Speed Ball**
*See* Cannon, Richard

**Cano, Alonso [or Alonzo]**
1601-1667 [SN, WBD]
*Spanish painter, sculptor, architect*
* [El] Granadino
* [The] Michael Angelo of Spain

**Cano e Iriborne, Enrique**
1890-1927 [GS]
*Spanish bullfighter*
* Gavira

**Cano Ruiz, Manuel** 1943- [GS]
*Spanish bullfighter*
* [El] Pireo

**Canoe, John**
*See* Kirkpatrick, Oliver Austin

**Canova, Judy**
*See* Canova, Juliet

**Canova, Juliet** 1916-   [FC]
*American comedienne*
* Canova, Judy

**Canovas del Castillo, Antonio**
1908-   [WFA]
*Spanish-born fashion designer*
* Castillo

**Cansino, Margarita Carmen** 1918-
[BDF, FC, IPA]
*American actress*
* Hayworth, Rita
* [The] Love Goddess

**Cantabrigiensis**
*See* Porson, Richard

**Cantabrigiensis, Crito**
*See* Turton, Thomas

**Cantarini [or da Pesaro], Simone**
1612-1648   [WBD]
*Italian painter and etcher*
* [Il] Pesarese

**Canter, Lynn**
*See* Castile, Lynn

**Canth, Minna**
*See* Canth, Ulrika Vilhelmina

**Canth, Ulrika Vilhelmina**
1844-1897   [WBD]
*Finnish author*
* Canth, Minna

**Cantianus**
*See* Marshall, Edmund

**Cantillon, Joe** 1861-1930   [BE]
*American baseball manager*
* Cantillon, Pongo

**Cantillon, Pongo**
*See* Cantillon, Joe

**Cantinflas**
*See* Moreno, Mario

**Cantiuncula, M.** ?-1560   [PA]
*Author*
* Chansonetti, Claude

**Cantlon, Shorty**
*See* Cantlon, William

**Cantlon, William** ?-1947   [EAR]
*American auto racer*
* Cantlon, Shorty

**Cantonwine, Howard** 20th c.
*American wrestler*
* [The] Hangman

**[The] Cantor**
*See* Hensel, Fanny Cecile

**Cantor, Eddie**
*See* Iskowitz, Edward Israel

**Cantor, Eli** 1913-   [CA]
*American author and playwright*
* Wheatley, Agnes

**Cantrell, Gunner**
*See* Cantrell, [Dewey] Guy

**Cantrell, [Dewey] Guy** 1904-1961
[BE]
*American baseball player*
* Cantrell, Gunner

**Canty Carl**
*See* Sawyer, Frederick William

**Canty, Cathal**
*See* Bresnan, Catharine Mary

**Canuck, Abe**
*See* Bingley, David Ernest

**Canuck, Janey**
*See* Murphy, Emily F.

**Canuni**
*See* Suleiman II [or Soliman]

**Canusi, Jose**
*See* Barker, S[quire] Omar

**Canute II** 995-1035?
[FFF, HN, SN]
*King of Denmark*
* [The] Brave
* [The] Great
* [The] Pious
* [The] Rich

**Canute IV** ?-1086   [WBD]
*King of Denmark*
* [The] Saint

**Canutt, Enos Edward** 1895-
[F2, FC, OCF]
*American actor, stuntman, director*
* Canutt, Yakima

**Canutt, Yakima**
*See* Canutt, Enos Edward

**Canyon, Claudia**
*See* Anderson, Betty

**Canzano, Joe** 1943-   [RO1]
*American singer*
* Vann, Joe

**Cap de Vielle, Maria** 1908-
[F2, FC]
*Argentinian-born actress*
* Maris, Mona

**Cap, Paul Antoine** 1788- ?   [PA]
*Author*
* Gratacap

**Cap the Cup**
*See* Weinberger, Caspar

**Cap the Knife**
*See* Weinberger, Caspar

**Cap the Shovel**
*See* Weinberger, Caspar

**Cap the Suitcase**
*See* Weinberger, Caspar

**Capa, Robert**
*See* Friedmann, Andrei

**Capa y Garcia, Joaquin** 1873-1949
[GS]
*Spanish bullfighter*
* Capita [Little Capa]

**[El] Capacho**
*See* Rodriguez Ucares, Fray Jose

**Capacho, Padre**
*See* Rodriguez Ucares, Fray Jose

**[The] Cape Cod Bard**
*See* Ellenwood, Henry S.

**Cape, Judith**
*See* Page, Patricia Kathleen

**Capel, Roger**
*See* Sheppard, Lancelot C[apel]

**Capelo**
*See* Sancho II

**Capern, Edward** 1819-1894
[DEL, DEP, FFF]
*British poet*
* [The] Bideford Postman
* [The] Postman Poet
* [The] Rural Postman of Bideford

**Capes, M. Harriet** 20th c.   [WWL]
*British author*
* Brooke, Magdalen

**Capezio, Anthony** 20th c.   [PHM]
*American underworld figure*
* Capezio, Tough Tony

**Capezio, Tough Tony**
*See* Capezio, Anthony

**Capita [Little Capa]**
*See* Capa y Garcia, Joaquin

**[Le] Capitaine Noir**
*See* Davidov [or Davidoff], Denis
Vassilievitch

**[The] Capital Mover**
*See* Reavis, T. M.

**[The] Capital Punisher**
*See* Howard, Frank Oliver

**Capitani, Giorgio** 20th c.   [WF]
*Italian director*
* Holloway, George

**[Il] Capitano del Popolo**
*See* Garibaldi, Giuseppe

**Capito, Wolfgang Fabricius**
*See* Koepfel, Wolfgang Fabricius

**Capitola, Jack** 1893-1956   [SC]
*American actor*
* Lamont, Jack

**Capli, Erdogan** 1926-   [ASC]
*Turkish-born musician*
* Capli, Pasha

**Capli, Pasha**
*See* Capli, Erdogan

**Caplin, Alfred Gerald** 1909-1979
[CA, IPA]
*American cartoonist*
* Capp, Al

**Cap'n Bill**
*See* Vinal, William Gould

**Capon, Peter**
*See* Oakley, Eric Gilbert

**Capone, Al[phonse]** 1899-1947
[BLB]
*American underworld figure*
* Brown, Al
* Capone, Big Al
* Caponi, Alfred
* Costa, A.
* [The] Millionaire Gorilla
* Scarface

**Capone, Big Al**
*See* Capone, Al[phonse]

**Capone, Bottles**
*See* Capone, Ralph

**Capone, Ralph** 20th c.   [PHM]
*American underworld figure*
* Capone, Bottles

**Caponi, Alfred**
*See* Capone, Al[phonse]

**Capooch, Tony**
*See* Vawter, L. P.

**[The] Caporal King**
*See* Frederick William I

**Caporal la Violette**
*See* Bonaparte, Napoleon

**Capp, Al**
*See* Caplin, Alfred Gerald

**Cappel, Constance** 1936-   [SAT]
*American author and poet*
* Montgomery, Constance

**Cappeletti, Cappy**
*See* Cappeletti, Gino

**Cappeletti, Duke**
*See* Cappeletti, Gino

**Cappeletti, Gino** 1934-   [FB]
*American football player*
* Cappeletti, Cappy
* Cappeletti, Duke

**Cappellari, Bartolommeo Alberto**
1765-1846   [WBD]
*Pope*
* Gregory XVI

**Cappo, Joseph**
*See* Cacioppo, Joseph

**Cappon, Cappy**
*See* Cappon, Franklin

**Cappon, Franklin** 1900-1961   [BB]
*American basketball coach*
* Cappon, Cappy

**Capponi, Pier Paolo** 20th c.   [WF]
*Italian actor*
* Clark, Norman

**Capponi, Raffaello** 1466-1524
[WBD]
*Florentine painter*
* Raffaelino del Garbo

**Capps, Carroll M.** 1917?-1971
[ESF, SFL, WGT]
*Author*
* MacApp, C. C.

**Cappy, Ted**
*See* Capuozzo, Ted

**Capra, Buzz**
*See* Capra, Lee William

**Capra, Lee William** 1947-
[BE, SMG, WWB]
*American baseball player*
* Capra, Buzz

**Capranica del Grillo, Marchioness**
1822-1906   [BEW, FFF]
*Italian actress*
* Ristori, Adelaide

**Caprice, June**
*See* Millarde, June Elizabeth

**Capron, M. J.**   [PA]
*Author*
* Fell, Archie

**Capsadell, Louise**
*See* Hammond, Mrs.

**[The] Capsize Kid**
*See* Turner, Robert Edward, III

**[The] Captain**
*See* Colaabavala, Firooze
Darashaw

**[The] Captain**
*See* Dragon, Daryl

**[The] Captain**
*See* Gover, William C.

**Captain**
*See* Manuel I Comnenus

**Captain Barclay**
*See* Allardice, Robert Barclay

**Captain Eddie**
*See* Knipschield, Edward Henry

**[The] Captain in Lace**
See Horneck, Charles

**Captain Jack**
See Crawford, J. W.

**Captain Louisa**
See Labe, Louise

**[The] Captain of Kent**
See Cade, John [Jack]

**[A] Captain of Koepenick**
See Voigt

**[The] Captain of the Age**
See Wellesley, Arthur

**Captain X**
See Power-Waters, Brian

**Capuano, Luigi** 1904- [FDG]
*Italian director*
* King, Lewis

**[Il] Capuccino**
See Strozzi [or Strozza], Bernardo

**Capucine**
See Lefebvre, Germaine

**Capuozzo, Ted** 20th c. [BEW]
*American choreographer and director*
* Cappy, Ted

**Capurro, Alfred** 1914-
[BEW, EMT, FC]
*American singer, actor, director*
* Drake, Alfred

**Capuzzi, Nick** 20th c. [PHM]
*American underworld figure*
* [The] Thief

**Caqueteur**
See Webb, Charles Hull

**Cara Ancha [Wide-Face]**
See Sanchez Del Campo, Jose

**Caracalla**
See Bassianus

**[The] Caracci of France**
See Jouvenet, Jean

**[The] Caracci of the Eclectic School**
See Campi, Bernardino

**Caracciola, Rudi** 20th c.
*Auto racer*
* Regenmeister

**Caraccioli, Lardolpho** [HN]
*Medieval scholar*
* Collectivus, Doctor

**[El] Caracol [The Snail]**
See Fernandez Bernabe, Vicente

**Caractacus**
See Sendall, E.

**Caradonna, Elisabetta** [OP]
*American opera singer*
* Carron, Elisabeth

**Carados**
See Newton, Henry Chance

**Caraffa, Giovanni Pietro**
1476-1559 [WBD]
*Pope*
* Paul IV

**Carafoli, Marci**
See Balterman, Marcia Ridlon

**Caras, Roger A[ndrew]** 1928-
[SAT]
*American author*
* Sarac, Roger

**Carausius, Marcus Aurelius Valerius**
250?- 293 [RH, SN]
*Roman insurgent*
* [The] Dutch Augustus
* [The] King of Ships

**Caravaggio, Michelangelo da**
See Merisi [or Merisio],
Michelangelo

**Caravaggio, Polidoro da**
See Caldara, Polidoro

**Caravane, Pietro** ?-1236 [PA]
*Author*
* Della Caravauna

**Carawan, Candie**
See Carawan, Carolanne M.

**Carawan, Carolanne M.** 1939-
[CA]
*American author*
* Carawan, Candie

**Caraway, Cecil Bradford**
1906-1974 [BE]
*American baseball player*
* Caraway, Pat

**Caraway, Pat**
See Caraway, Cecil Bradford

**Carbasse, Louise**
See Welch, Louise

**Carbery, Ethna**
See Johnston, Anna Isabel

**Carbet, Claude** 1893- [CW]
*West Indian author*
* Claude

**Carbet, Marie-Magdalene** 1906?-
[CW]
*West Indian author and poet*
* Magdeleine

**Carbo, Bernardo** 1947- [BE, BR]
*American baseball player*
* Carbo, Bernie

**Carbo, Bernie**
See Carbo, Bernardo

**Carbon**
See Labrousse, M.

**Carbonaro**
See Bonaparte, Charles Louis
Napoleon

**Carboy, John**
See Harrington, John A.

**Carbury, A. B.**
See Carr, Albert H. Z[olotkoff]

**Carco, Francis**
See Carcopino-Tusoli, Francois
Marie Alexandre

**Carcopino-Tusoli, Francois Marie Alexandre** 1886-1958
[CD, LC, TC]
*French author, poet, art critic*
* Carco, Francis

**Cardarelli, Vincenzo**
See Caldarelli, Nazarene

**Cardeilhac, Augustin** ?-1876 [PA]
*Author*
* Lagrange

**Cardena, Clement** 1914- [AW]
*Spanish poet and playwright*
* DeLaube

**Cardenal, Che**
See Cardenal, Jose Domec

**Cardenal, Jose Domec** 1943- [PB]
*Cuban-born baseball player*
* Cardenal, Che

**Cardenal [or Cardinal?], Pierre**
?-1305? [DNNS, WBD]
*French poet*
* [The] Juvenal of the Provencals

**Cardenas, Chico**
See Cardenas, Leonardo Lazaro

**Cardenas, Leonardo Lazaro** 1938-
[BE]
*Cuban-born baseball player*
* Cardenas, Chico

**Cardenas y Rodriguez, Nicolas**
1814-1868 [CW]
*Cuban poet, playwright, author*
* Teodomofilo

**Cardiff, Albert**
See Cardone, Alberto

**Cardijn, Josef** 1907-1951 [EWL]
*French author*
* Van Der Meersch, Maxence

**[Le] Cardinal de l'Ignominie**
See Lomenie de Brienne, Etienne
Charles

**Cardinal, Jane**
See Williamson, Ethel

**[The] Cardinal of Atheists**
See Du Plessis, Armand Jean

**[The] Cardinal of Huguenots**
See Du Plessis, Armand Jean

**[The] Cardinal of La Rochelle**
See Du Plessis, Armand Jean

**Cardinal, Roger [Thomas]** 1940-
[CA]
*British author*
* Bridgecross, Peter

**[The] Cardinal's Hangman**
See De Laffemas, Isaac

**[The] Cardinal's Right Arm**
See Leclerc du Tremblay, Francois

**Cardini**
See Pitchford, Richard Valentine

**Cardona, Florencia Bisenta De Casillas Martinez** 1938?-
[PRS, RO2, SW]
*American singer*
* Carr, Vikki

**Cardone, Alberto** 20th c. [WF]
*Italian director*
* Cardiff, Albert

**Cardoni, Armond Joseph**
1920-1969 [BE]
*American baseball player*
* Cardoni, Ben
* Cardoni, Big Ben

**Cardoni, Ben**
See Cardoni, Armond Joseph

**Cardoni, Big Ben**
See Cardoni, Armond Joseph

**Cardozo, Lois S.**
See Arquette, Lois S[teinmetz]

**Cardrac, Verdillo**
See Harris, Richard

**Carducci, Giosue** 1835-1907
[WBD]
*Italian poet*
* Enotrio Romano

**Cardui, Van**
See Wayman, Tony Russell

**Cardui, Vanessa**
See Wayman, Tony Russell

**Cardwell, Ann**
See Powley, Jean [Makins]

**Cardy**
See Viskardy, Nicholas

**Careddu, Stefania** 20th c. [WF]
*Italian actress*
* O'Hara, Kareen

**Careless, Franck**
See Head, Richard

**Careme, Jean de**
See Jean

**Careme, Marie Antoine** 1783-1833
[FFF]
*French cook*
* [The] Regenerator of Cookery

**Carette**
See Carette, Julien

**Carette, Julien** 1897-1966 [FC]
*French actor*
* Carette

**Carette, Louis Albert** 1913-
[B10, BEW, CA]
*French author and playwright*
* Marceau, Felicien

**Carew, Bamfylde Moore**
1693-1770 [DEP, DNNS, FFF]
*British vagabond*
* [The] King of the Beggars
* [The] King of the Gypsies

**Carew, Burleigh**
See Cook, Fred Gordon

**Carew, Hugh** [PA]
*Author*
* C

**Carew, James**
See Usselmann, James

**Carew, Jean**
See Corby, Jane

**Carew, Jocelyn**
See Aeby, Jacquelyn

**Carew, John Mohun** 1921- [CA]
*British author*
* Carew, Tim

**Carew, Junior**
See Carew, Rod[ney Cline]

**Carew, Leslie**
See Priestley, Leslie Avoca

**Carew, Ora**
See Whytock, Ora

**Carew, Rod[ney Cline]** 1945-
[SMG]
*Panamanian-born baseball player*
* Carew, Junior

**Carew, Tim**
See Carew, John Mohun

**Carew, Wynter**
See Wynter, Sylvia

**Carew-Slater, Harold James** 1909-
[AW, WD]
*British author, playwright, poet*
* Carey, James

**Carewe, Edwin**
See Fox, Jay J.

**Carewe, S. C.**
See DuBreuil, Elizabeth Lorinda

**Carey, Alice** 1820-1871 [PA]
*American poet*
* Lee, Patty

**Carey, Andy**
See Nordstrom, Andrew Arthur

**Carey, Blue**
See Carey, Burgess

**Carey, Burgess** 1905-1961 [BB]
*American basketball player*
* Carey, Blue

**Carey, Charles**
See Waddel, Charles Carey

**Carey, Elisabeth** 20th c. [WW]
*Author*
* Magoon, Carey [joint pseudonym
with Marian Austin (Waite)
Magoon]

**Carey, George C.** 1870-1916 [BE]
*American baseball player*
* Carey, Scoops

**Carey, Henry** ?-1743 [FFF]
*British poet and musician*
* Waters, John

**Carey, James**
See Carew-Slater, Harold James

**Carey, John** 20th c. [EG]
*Golf caddie*
* Fiery

**Carey, Joyce**
See Lawrence, Joyce

**Carey, Julian**
See Tubb, Edwin Charles

**Carey, Laughing Sam**
See Carey, Sam

**Carey, Matthew**
See Cazauran, Augustus R.

**Carey, Max George**
See Carnarius, Maximilian

**Carey, Michael**
See Burton, Edward J.

**Carey, Mutt**
See Carey, Thomas

**Carey, Papa Mutt**
See Carey, Thomas

**Carey, Sam** 20th c. [BLB]
*American bandit*
* Carey, Laughing Sam

**Carey, Scoops**
See Carey, George C.

**Carey, Scoops**
See Carey, Thomas Francis
Aloysius

**Carey, Scoops**
See Carnarius, Maximilian

**Carey, Thomas** 1891?-1948
[EJ, PMJ, WWJ]
*American jazz musician*
* Carey, Mutt
* Carey, Papa Mutt

**Carey, Thomas Francis Aloysius**
1908- [BE]
*American baseball player*
* Carey, Scoops

**Carey, Thomas John [Tom]**
See Norton, J. J.

**Carfagne, Cyril**
See Jennings, Leslie Nelson

**Carfano, Anthony** ?-1958
[BLB, MM, PHM]
*American underworld figure*
* Carfano, Little Augie
* Pisano, Little Augie

**Carfano, Little Augie**
See Carfano, Anthony

**Carfax, Bruce**
See Gardner-Ballinger, Bruce

**Carfax, Catherine**
See Fairburn, Eleanor

**Carghill, Ralph**
See Cox, Arthur Jean

**Cargill, Morris** 1914- [CW, WD]
*Jamaican author and columnist*
* Morris, John [joint pseudonym
with John Hearne]

**Cargo, Chick**
See Cargo, Robert J.

**Cargo, Joe**
See Valachi, Joseph Michael

**Cargo, Robert J.** 1871-1970 [BE]
*American baseball player*
* Cargo, Chick

**Cargoe, Richard**
See Payne, [Pierre Stephen]
Robert

**Carhart, Arthur Hawthorne** 1892-
[CAP, NAA]
*American author*
* Thorne, Hart
* VanSickle, V. A.

**[El] Caribe**
See Padilla, Jose Gualberto

**Carini, Nina**
See Scalisi, Josefina

**Carisbrooke**
See Nesbit, Edith

**Cariveac, Denis** 1930-1950 [SC]
*Belgian-born actress*
* Daix, Daisy

**Cariveau, Robert Edward** 20th c.
[NAA]
*American author, poet, inventor*
* Cary, Robert

**Carl**
See Newhall, C. S.

**Carl**
See Sawyer, Frederick William

**Carl**
See Williams, Charles Hanbury

**Carl** 1872-1957 [WBD]
*King of Norway*
* Haakon VII

**Carl, Hersh**
See Carl, Howard [Howie]

**Carl, Howard [Howie]** 1938- [BB]
*American basketball player*
* Carl, Hersh

**Carle**
See Sardon, F. J.

**Carle, C. E.** 20th c. [WW]
*Author*
* Morgan, Michael [joint
pseudonym with Dean M. Dorn]

**Carle, Richard**
See Carleton, Charles Nicholas

**Carleton**
See Charlton, Walter

**Carleton**
See Coffin, Charles Carleton

**Carleton, Captain** [PA]
*Author*
* Craven

**Carleton, Carrie**
See Booth, Mary

**Carleton, Charles Nicholas**
1871-1941 [THR]
*American actor and playwright*
* Carle, Richard

**Carleton, Cousin May**
See Fleming, May Agnes

**Carleton, [Admiral] George**
See George IV

**Carleton, H. B.** [house pseudonym]
See Browne, Howard

**Carleton, James Otto** 1906-
[BE, PB]
*American baseball player*
* Carleton, Tex

**Carleton, [Captain] L. C.**
See Ellis, Edward S[ylvester]

**Carleton Milecete**
See Jones, Susan Carleton

**Carleton, S.**
See Jones, Susan Carleton

**Carleton, Tex**
See Carleton, James Otto

**Carleton, William**
See Bartlett, Frederick Orin

**Carleton, William** 1794-1869 [SN]
*Irish author*
* [The] Prose Burns of Ireland

**Carlfried**
See Wingate, Charles F.

**Carlier, Lucienne**
See Wake, Nancy

**Carlile, John Charles** 20th c.
[LAO]
*British author*
* Iron, John

**Carlin, Emelia F.** 1810- ? [PA]
*Author*
* Flaggare, Madam
* Klein, Waldemir

**Carlin, Francis**
See MacDonnell, James Francis
Carlin

**Carlin, Michel**
See Bonnye, J. H.

**Carlisle, Alexandra**
See Swift, Alexandra

**Carlisle, Clark**
See Holding, James [Clark
Carlisle, Jr.]

**Carlisle, Fred** 1915- [CA]
*British-born author*
* Murray, K. F.

**Carlisle, Helen Grace**
See Reid, Helen Grace

**Carlisle, Kitty**
See Conn, Catharine

**Carlisle, Lick**
See Carlisle, Matthew

**Carlisle, Matthew** 1910-1972 [MK]
*American baseball player*
* Carlisle, Lick

**Carlisle, R. H.** 1864- ? [WWL]
*British author*
* Hawkeye

**Carlisle, Rosy**
See Carlisle, Walter G.

**Carlisle, Thomas [Fiske]** 1944-
[CA]
*American writer and editor*
* Kahn, Balthazar

**Carlisle, Walter G.** 1883-1945 [BE]
*British-born baseball player*
* Carlisle, Rosy

**Carllile, Kenneth Ray** 1931-
[CWG, DAM]
*American country-western performer*
* Carllile, Thumbs

**Carllile, Thumbs**
See Carllile, Kenneth Ray

**Carlo, Johnny**
See Selvaggio, John R.

**Carlo-Rim**
See Richard, Jean-Marius

**Carlock, E.** 1923- [CM]
*American record distributor*
* Carlock, Hutch

**Carlock, Hutch**
See Carlock, E.

**Carlopago**
See Zwingli, Carl

**Carlos**
See Ramirez-Sanchez, Ilyich

**Carlos, Cisco**
See Carlos, Francisco Manuel

**Carlos, Francisco Manuel** 1940-
[BE]
*American baseball player*
* Carlos, Cisco

**Carlos, J.**
See Brito e Cunha, Jose Carlos de

**[Don] Carlos of Bourbon**
See Charles III

**Carlsen, Chris**
See Holdstock, Robert P.

**Carlson, Adloph D.** 1897-1967
[AS]
*Swedish-born bowler*
* Carlson, Swede

**Carlson, Doc**
See Carlson, Harold C.

**Carlson, Harold C.** 1894-1964
[AS]
*American basketball player*
* Carlson, Doc

**Carlson, John Roy**
*See* Derounian, Avodis Arthur

**Carlson, Joseph Martin Napoleon**
1899- [BE]
*American baseball player*
* Munson, Joseph Martin Napoleon
[Joe]

**Carlson, Jules** 20th c. [SMG]
*Football player*
* Carlson, Zuck

**Carlson, Leon Alton** 1895-1961
[BE]
*American baseball player*
* Carlson, Swede

**Carlson, Lewis H[erbert]**
*See* Lavine, Lewis H[erbert]

**Carlson, Ruth [Elizabeth] Kearney**
1911- [CA]
*American author*
* Kearney, Ruth Elizabeth

**Carlson, Swede**
*See* Carlson, Adloph D.

**Carlson, Swede**
*See* Carlson, Leon Alton

**Carlson, Vada F.** 1897- [CA]
*American author*
* Rose, Florella

**Carlson, Zuck**
*See* Carlson, Jules

**Carlstrom, Albin Oscar** 1890-1935
[BE]
*American baseball player*
* Carlstrom, Swede

**Carlstrom, Swede**
*See* Carlstrom, Albin Oscar

**Carlton**
*See* Philps, Arthur Carlton

**Carlton, Alva**
*See* Delk, Robert Carlton

**Carlton, Ann**
*See* Trent, Ann

**Carlton, Big Meade**
*See* Carlton, Darryl

**Carlton, Captain** 19th c. [PA]
*Author*
* Marston, Hyde

**Carlton, Carl** 20th c. [RO2]
*American singer*
* Carlton, Little Carl

**Carlton, Carrie**
*See* Chamberlain, Mary Booth

**Carlton, Darryl** 1953- [SMG]
*American football player*
* Carlton, Big Meade

**Carlton, Effie** 1857-1940 [WBD]
*American actress and author*
* Canning, Effie

**Carlton, Ethel**
*See* King, Oliver

**Carlton, G. E. L.** 1886?- [MBF]
*British author and editor*
* Atkinson, Reginald
* Carlton, Lewis

**Carlton, G. E. L.** (Continued)
* Clifford, Martin [house
pseudonym]

**Carlton, Grace [Greenwood]** 1878-
? [AW]
*British author, playwright,
journalist*
* Garth, Cecil

**Carlton, Jay**
*See* Goldsmith, Jay Carlton

**Carlton, Joseph**
*See* McMullen, Joseph Carl

**Carlton, Lefty**
*See* Carlton, Stephen Norman

**Carlton, Lewis**
*See* Carlton, G. E. L.

**Carlton, Little Carl**
*See* Carlton, Carl

**Carlton, Mary** ?-1673 [FFF]
* [The] German Princess
* [The] Kentish Moll

**Carlton, [Cousin] May**
*See* Earle, M. A.

**Carlton, Robert**
*See* Hall, Barnard R.

**Carlton, Roger**
*See* Rowland, D[onald] S[ydney]

**Carlton, Stephen Norman** 1944-
[BE, SMG]
*American baseball player*
* Carlton, Lefty

**Carlyle, Alexander** 1722-1805
[DNNS, FFF, SN]
*Scottish clergyman*
* Carlyle, Jupiter

**Carlyle, Anthony**
*See* Milton, Gladys Alexandra

**Carlyle, Dizzy**
*See* Carlyle, Roy Edward

**Carlyle, Jupiter**
*See* Carlyle, Alexander

**Carlyle, Roy Edward** 1900-1956
[BE]
*American baseball player*
* Carlyle, Dizzy

**Carlyle, Thomas** 1795-1881
[DEL, FFF, HN]
*Scottish author and historian*
* [The] Apostle of Silence
* [The] Censor of the Age
* [The] Chelsea Philosopher
* [The] Philosopher of Chelsea
* [The] Sage of Chelsea
* Teufelsdroeckh, Herr

**Carlyon, John** 1917- [ART]
*British sculptor*
* J. C.

**Carm Mac**
*See* Armstrong, Keith F[rancis]
W[hitfield]

**Carmagnola**
*See* Bussone, Francesco [Conte di
Castelnuovo]

**Carman, Dulce**
*See* Drummond, Edith Marie
Dulce Carman

**Carman, Jenks** 1911- [CWG]
*American country-western performer*
* Carman, Tex

**Carman, Tex**
*See* Carman, Jenks

**Carmel, Duke**
*See* Carmel, Leon James

**Carmel, Leon James** 1937- [BE]
*American baseball player*
* Carmel, Duke

**Carmendolla, Anthony**
*See* Cebulash, Mel

**Carmi, T.**
*See* Charny, Carmi

**Carmichael, Albert R.** 1929- [FB]
*American football player*
* Carmichael, Hoagy

**Carmichael, Ann**
*See* MacAlpine, Margaret
H[esketh Murray]

**Carmichael, Anne Jeffreys** 1923?-
[BEW, SW, TR]
*American actress and singer*
* Jeffreys, Anne

**Carmichael, Dozie**
*See* Carmichael, Harold Lee

**Carmichael, Geraldine Elizabeth**
*See* Michael, Jerry Dean

**Carmichael, Harold Lee** 20th c.
*American football player*
* Carmichael, Dozie

**Carmichael, Harry**
*See* Ognall, Leopold Horace

**Carmichael, Herbert**
*See* Schmalz, Herbert Gustave

**Carmichael, Hoagland Howard**
1899-1981 [ASC, DAM, FC]
*American composer and lyricist*
* Carmichael, Hoagy

**Carmichael, Hoagy**
*See* Carmichael, Albert R.

**Carmichael, Hoagy**
*See* Carmichael, Hoagland
Howard

**Carmichael, Marie**
*See* Stopes, Marie Carmichael

**Carmichael, Stokeley** 1941- [IBW]
*West Indian-born political organizer*
* Toure, Kwame

**Carmichael, William Edward**
1922- [CA]
*American author and columnist*
* Best, Adam

**Carmilly, Moshe**
*See* Weinberger, Moshe

**Carminati, Tullio**
*See* Carminati De Brambilla,
Tullio

**Carminati De Brambilla, Tullio**
1894-1971 [FC]
*Italian actor*
* Carminati, Tullio

**Carmineo, Giuliano** 20th c. [FDG]
*Italian director*
* Ascott, Anthony

**Carmody, Gareth** 1938- [FC]
*American actor*
* Conway, Gary

**Carmona, Antonio** 1838-1920
[GS, OCS]
*Spanish bullfighter*
* Gordito [Little Fat One]

**Carmona y Garcia, Jose** 1883-1951
[GS]
*Spanish bullfighter*
* Gordito [Little Fat One]

**Carmona y Gonzalez, Angel**
1874-1960 [GS]
*Spanish bullfighter*
* [El] Camisero [The Shirt Maker]

**Carmontelle, Louis**
*See* Carrogis, Louis

**Carn, Doug** 1948- [EJ7]
*American jazz musician*
* Ibrahim, Abdul Rahim

**Carnac, Carol**
*See* Rivett, Edith Caroline

**Carnac, Levin**
*See* Griffith-Jones, George
Chetwynd

**Carnahan, Suzanne** 1921?-1952
[BEW, FC]
*American actress*
* Peters, Susan

**Carnarius**
*See* Vieschouwer, Johann

**Carnarius, Maximilian** 1890-
[BE, PB]
*American baseball player*
* Carey, Max George
* Carey, Scoops

**Carne, Judy**
*See* Botterill, Joyce

**Carnegie, Arthur** 20th c. [RO2]
*American musician*
* Carnegie, Lorenzo

**Carnegie, Hattie**
*See* Kannengiser, Henriette

**Carnegie, Lorenzo**
*See* Carnegie, Arthur

**Carnegie, Raymond Alexander**
1920- [CA]
*Scottish author*
* Carnegie, Sacha

**Carnegie, Sacha**
*See* Carnegie, Raymond Alexander

**Carnell, E. J.**
*See* Carnell, [Edward] John

**Carnell, [Edward] John** 1912-
[CA, SF]
*British editor*
* Carnell, E. J.

**Carnell, Richard**
*See* Ackerman, Forrest J[ames]

**Carnelle**
*See* Aligny, Claude Felix Theodore

**Carnera, Primo** 1906-1967
[BX, RBE]
*Italian boxer*
* [The] Ambling Alp

**Carnes, Captain**
*See* Cumming, M. I.

**Carnett, Edwin Elliott [Eddie]**
1916- [BE]
*American baseball player*
* Carnett, Lefty

**Carnett, Lefty**
*See* Carnett, Edwin Elliott [Eddie]

**Carnevale, Ben**
*See* Carnevale, Bernard L.

**Carnevale, Bernard L.** 1915-
*American basketball coach*
* Carnevale, Ben

**Carney, Alan**
*See* Bougal, David

**Carney, Doc**
*See* Carney, Pat[rick Joseph]

**Carney, Don**
*See* Rice, Howard

**Carney, Handsome Jack**
*See* Carney, John Joseph [Jack]

**Carney, James [Patrick]** 1914-
[CA]
*Irish writer*
* O Ceithearnaigh, Seamus

**Carney, John Joseph [Jack]**
1867-1925 [BE]
*American baseball player*
* Carney, Handsome Jack

**Carney, Kate** 1869-1950 [BMH]
*British comedienne*
* [The] Cockney Queen

**Carney, Pat[rick Joseph]**
1876-1953 [BE]
*American baseball player*
* Carney, Doc

**Carnicerito [Little Butcher]**
*See* Munoz y Marin, Bernardo

**Carnicerito de Mejico [Little Butcher from Mexico]**
*See* Gonzalez Lopez, Jose

**Carnicerito de Ubeda [Little Butcher from Ubeda]**
*See* Millan Diaz, Antonio

**Carnoli, Luigi** 1618-1693 [PA]
*Author*
* Nolarci, Vigilio

**Carnot, Lazare-Nicolas-Marquerite**
1753-1823 [DEP, DNNS, WBD]
*French statesman*
* [Le] Grand Carnot
* [The] Organizer of Victory

**Carnuel, Anne** ?-1694 [PA]
*Author*
* Bigot

**Caro**
*See* Mason, Mrs. C. A. B.

**[Il] Caro Sassone**
*See* Hasse, Johann Adolf

**Caro Aviles, Manuel** 1907- [GS]
*Spanish bullfighter*
* Almohadilla [Little Pillow]

**Caroe, William Douglas** 1857- ?
[LAO]
*British architect and writer*
* Wedecee

**Carol, Bill J.**
*See* Knott, William Cecil, Jr. [Bill]

**Carol, Martine**
*See* Mourer, Marie-Louise-Jeanne

**Carol, Sue**
*See* Lederer, Evelyn

**[The] Carolina Game-Cock**
*See* Sumter, Thomas

**Carolina Slim**
*See* Harris, Ed[ward P.]

**Caroline**
*See* Minter, Davide C.

**Caroline** 1768-1821 [HN]
*Queen of England*
* [The] Dreadful Woman
* [The] Kensington Martyr
* [The] Kensington Megaera

**Caroline, J. C.**
*See* Caroline, James Calvin

**Caroline, James Calvin** 1933-
[FB, IBW]
*American football player*
* Caroline, J. C.
* Outside, Mr.
* [The] Touchdown Twin

**Carolus**
*See* Wolff, Carl [or Karl?]

**Carolus Magnus**
*See* Charles I [or Karl]

**Caron, Alain Luc** 1938- [CEI]
*Canadian-born hockey player*
* Caron, Boom-Boom

**Caron, Boom-Boom**
*See* Caron, Alain Luc

**Caron, Christine** 1948- [SWI]
*French swimmer*
* Caron, Kiki

**Caron, Kiki**
*See* Caron, Christine

**Caron, Pierre Augustin** 1732-1799
[HN, SN]
*French playwright*
* Beaumarchais, Pierre Augustin
  Caron
* De Beaumarchais, Pierre
  Augustin Caron
* [The] Figaro of His Age
* [The] Prince of Quarrellers

**Caross, Mark** [DNNF]
*Scottish landowner*
* [The] Laird of Cockpen

**Carp**
*See* Carpenter, Frank

**Carpenter**
*See* Arnold, June [Davis]

**Carpenter, Donald G.** 20th c. [SFL]
*Author*
* Merlino, Merlin Mesmer

**Carpenter, Dutch**
*See* Carpenter, Frank

**Carpenter, Eddie**
*See* Carpenter, Everar Lorne

**Carpenter, Everar Lorne** 20th c.
[CEI]
*American hockey player*
* Carpenter, Eddie

**Carpenter, Frank** [FFF]
*American journalist*
* Carp

**Carpenter, Frank** 20th c. [BLB]
*American underworld figure*
* Carpenter, Dutch

**Carpenter, Fred**
*See* Hand, [Andrus] Jackson

**Carpenter, Gordon** 1919- [BB]
*American basketball player*
* Carpenter, Shorty

**Carpenter [or Carpentier?], Harlean**
1911-1937 [BDF, BEW, F2]
*American actress*
* Harlow, Jean

**Carpenter, Hick**
*See* Carpenter, Warren William

**Carpenter, John Jo**
*See* Reese, John [Henry]

**Carpenter, Morley**
*See* Tubb, Edwin Charles

**Carpenter, Patricia [Healy Evans]**
1920- [CA, SAT]
*American author and illustrator*
* Evans, Patricia Healy

**Carpenter, R. R. M., III** 1940-
[SMG]
*American baseball executive*
* Carpenter, Ruly

**Carpenter, Ruly**
*See* Carpenter, R. R. M., III

**Carpenter, Shorty**
*See* Carpenter, Gordon

**Carpenter, Stephen Cullen** ?-1820
[PA]
*Author*
* Campbell, Donald

**Carpenter, Theodore** 1898- [WWJ]
*American jazz musician*
* Carpenter, Wingie

**Carpenter, Warren William**
1855-1937 [AS, BE]
*American baseball player*
* Carpenter, Hick

**Carpenter, Wingie**
*See* Carpenter, Theodore

**Carpentier, Gentleman George**
*See* Carpentier, Georges

**Carpentier, Georges** 1894-1975
[BX, NN, RBE]
*French boxer*
* Carpentier, Gentleman George
* [The] Orchid Man

**[Il] Carpentrasso**
*See* Genet, Eliazar

**Carpi, Girolamo da**
*See* Sellari, Girolamo de'

**Carr, A. H. Z.**
*See* Carr, Albert H. Z[olotkoff]

**Carr, Adams**
*See* Walshe, Douglas

**Carr, Albert H. Z[olotkoff]**
1902-1971 [CA, EMD]
*American economist and author*
* Carbury, A. B.
* Carr, A. H. Z.

**Carr, Alfred** 20th c. [CEI]
*Canadian-born hockey player*
* Carr, Red

**Carr, Austin** 1948- [SMG]
*American basketball player*
* A. C.

**Carr, Beryl**
*See* Byrd, L. Ella

**Carr, Burgess** 1936?-
*Liberian clergyman*
* [The] Pope of Africa

**Carr, Catharine**
*See* Wade, Rosalind Herschel

**Carr, Dorothy Stevenson Laird**
1912- [CA]
*British author*
* Laird, Dorothy

**Carr, E. H.**
*See* Carr, Edward Hallett

**Carr, Edward Hallett** 1892- [LC]
*British historian and author*
* Carr, E. H.

**Carr, Elias F.** [FFF, PA]
*Author*
* Hari Kari

**Carr, Eugene William** 1951-
[SMG]
*Canadian-born hockey player*
* Carr, Geno

**Carr, F.** 20th c. [SMG]
*American baseball scout*
* Carr, Kid

**Carr, Fingers**
*See* Bush, Louis F.

**Carr, Geno**
*See* Carr, Eugene William

**Carr, George** 1895- [MK]
*American baseball player*
* Carr, Tank

**Carr, Georgia**
*See* Carr, Marie Louise

**Carr, Glyn**
*See* Styles, Frank Showell

**Carr, Gordon**
*See* Bayfield, William John

**Carr, Gordon** 20th c. [MBF]
*British author*
* West, Edgar
* Westcombe, Charles

**Carr, Governor** [PA]
*Author*
* Epistographas

**Carr, Gunter Lee**
*See* Gant, Cecil

**Carr, James**
*See* Abrahams, Alan

**Carr, Jane**
*See* Brunstroem, Rita

**Carr, Jean**
*See* Field, Joan

**Carr, Jean B.** [FFF]
*Entertainer*
* Burnside, Jean

**Carr, Joan**
*See* Sanderson, H. P.

**Carr, Joe Fingers**
*See* Bush, Louis F.

**Carr, [Sir] John** 1772-1832 [SN]
*British author*
* [The] Jaunting Carr

**Carr, John Dickson** 1906-1977
[CA, EMD, WGT]
*American author*
* Dickson, Carr
* Dickson, Carter
* Fairbairn, Roger

**Carr, Kent**
*See* Oliver, Gertrude Kent

**Carr, Kid**
*See* Carr, F.

**Carr, Leroy** 1905-1935 [BWW]
*American singer*
* Johnson, Blues

**Carr, M. Frank** [PA]
*Author*
* Crosse, Launcelot

**Carr, Mancy** 1900?- ? [WWJ]
*American jazz musician*
* Carr, Peck

**Carr, Margaret** 1935- [AW]
*British author*
* Carroll, Martin

**Carr, Marie Louise** 1926- [IBW]
*American singer*
* Carr, Georgia
* [The] Girl with the Golden
Throat

**Carr, Michael**
*See* Cohen, Michael

**Carr, Pat M[oore]** 1932- [CA]
*American author*
* Esslinger, Pat M.

**Carr, Patricia**
*See* Bergamonti, Rosella

**Carr, Peck**
*See* Carr, Mancy

**Carr, Philippa**
*See* Hibbert, Eleanor Alice
[Burford]

**Carr, Red**
*See* Carr, Alfred

**Carr, Roberta**
*See* Roberts, Irene M.

**Carr, Russ**
*See* Parnell, Frederick Russell

**Carr, S.**
*See* Carraway, Gertrude S.

**Carr, Sade**
*See* Latham, Sade

**Carr, Sam**
*See* Kogan, Schmil

**Carr, Stephen J.**
*See* Palickar, Stephen J.

**Carr, Tank**
*See* Carr, George

**Carr, Terry [Gene]** 1937-
[CA, WGT]
*American author*
* Brandon, Carl
* Edwards, Norman [joint
pseudonym with Theodore Edwin
White]

**Carr, Vikki**
*See* Cardona, Florencia Bisenta De
Casillas Martinez

**Carradine, John**
*See* Carradine, Richmond Reed

**Carradine, Richmond Reed** 1906-
[BEW, FC, HT]
*American actor*
* Carradine, John
* Richmond, John Peter

**Carradine, William** 1896?-1958?
[BWW]
*American singer*
* Cat-Iron

**Carrasquel, Alfonso Colon** 1928-
[BE]
*Venezuelan-born baseball player*
* Carrasquel, Chico

**Carrasquel, Chico**
*See* Carrasquel, Alfonso Colon

**Carraway, Gertrude S.** 1896-
[NAA]
*American journalist*
* Carr, S.

**Carre, Chuck**
*See* Sellers, Connie Leslie, Jr.

**Carre, Freddy** ?-1978 [FIR]
*Clown*
* Pepino

**Carre, Lilliane** 1901?- [F2, FC]
*French actress*
* Damita, Lili

**Carre, Mathilde [Belard]** 1910-
[B10, BDW, EE]
*French-born intelligence agent*
* [The] Cat
* Lily [code name used during
World War II]
* Victoire [code name used during
World War II]

**Carre, Thomas** 1600-1674 [FFF]
*British monk and writer*
* Pinkney, Miles

**Carrel, Mark**
*See* Paine, Lauran [Bosworth]

**Carrell, Lenore Kathrin Cary
Gregory** 1859-1911 [IA]
*American author*
* Gregory, Kate

**Carrenard, Adrien** 1880-1971
[CW]
*Haitian poet*
* Adry-Carene

**Carreno, Teresa**
*See* Tagliapetra, Madame

**Carreon, Cam**
*See* Carreon, Camilo Garcia

**Carreon, Camilo Garcia** 1937- [BE]
*American baseball player*
* Carreon, Cam

**Carrick, A. B.**
*See* Lindsay, Harold Arthur

**Carrick, Doughnut Bill**
*See* Carrick, William Martin

**Carrick, Edward**
*See* Craig, Edward Anthony

**Carrick, Fergus**
*See* Carrick, Phillip

**Carrick, John**
*See* Crosbie, [Hugh] Provan

**Carrick, Phillip** [DC]
*British cricketer*
* Carrick, Fergus

**Carrick, William Martin**
1873-1932 [BE]
*American baseball player*
* Carrick, Doughnut Bill

**Carrier, Robert**
*See* MacMahon, Robert Carrier

**Carriere, Hawk**
*See* Carriere, Larry

**Carriere, Larry** 1952- [SMG]
*Canadian-born hockey player*
* Carriere, Hawk

**Carrigan, Rough**
*See* Carrigan, William Francis

**Carrigan, William Francis**
1883-1969 [AS, BE, PB]
*American baseball player and
manager*
* Carrigan, Rough

**Carrigio, Jimmy** 20th c. [BLB]
*American gangster*
* Gold Mine Jimmy

**Carrillo, Santiago** 1915?-
*Spanish Communist leader*
* Don Santiago
* Giscard, Monsieur

**Carringford, Arthur** 1882-1959
[SC]
*American actor*
* Fox, Harry

**Carrington, Charles Edmund** 1897-
[AW, CA, WD]
*British historian and author*
* Edmonds, Charles

**Carrington, Dorothy**
*See* Rose, [Lady] Dorothy Violet
Frederica

**Carrington, Hereward Hubert
Lavington** 1880- ? [WGT]
*British-born American author*
* Fodor, Nandor?
* Lavington, Hubert?

**Carrington, Michael**
*See* Williams, Meurig Mon

**Carrington, Molly**
*See* Matthews, Constance Mary

**Carrington, Murray**
*See* Hamer, Murray

**Carritt, E. F.**
*See* Carritt, Edgar Francis

**Carritt, Edgar Francis** 1876-1964
[LC]
*British philosopher*
* Carritt, E. F.

**Carroder, C. H.**
*See* Tripp, Walter John

**Carrogis, Louis** 1717-1806 [WBD]
*French painter, engraver, author*
* Carmontelle, Louis

**Carrol, Norman**
*See* Brandon, Sydney Edward

**Carrol, Shana** [joint pseudonym with
Frank Schaefer]
*See* Newcomb, Kerry

**Carrol, Shana** [joint pseudonym with
Kerry Newcomb]
*See* Schaefer, Frank

**Carroll**
*See* Tillinghast, Joseph Leonard

**Carroll, Alice Viola** 20th c. [CAT]
*American author*
* Mary Consolata, [Sister]

**Carroll, Andrea**
*See* DeCapite, Andrea Lee

**Carroll, Anne Kristin**
*See* Denis, Barbara J.

**Carroll, Barbara**
*See* Coppersmith, Barbara Carole

**Carroll, Bebop**
*See* Carroll, Joe

**Carroll, Clay Palmer** 1941-
[BE, PB]
*American baseball player*
* Carroll, Hawk

**Carroll, Curt**
*See* Bishop, Curtis [Kent]

**Carroll, Daniel Patrick** 1928- [FC]
*British female impersonator*
* La Rue, Danny

**Carroll, Diahann**
*See* Johnson, Carol Diahann

**Carroll, Dixie**
*See* Carroll, Dorsey Lee

**Carroll, Doc**
*See* Carroll, Ralph Arthur

**Carroll, Dorsey Lee** 1891- [BE]
*American baseball player*
* Carroll, Dixie

**Carroll, Earl** 1937- [RO1]
*American singer*
* Carroll, Speedo

**Carroll, Frank G.**
*See* Baldanello, Gianfranco

**Carroll, Hal**
*See* Carroll, Horace

**Carroll, Hawk**
*See* Carroll, Clay Palmer

**Carroll, Horace** 1941- [RBE]
*American boxer*
* Carroll, Hal

**Carroll, Howard** [PA]
*Author*
* H. C.

**Carroll, Irv**
*See* Gellers, Irving

**Carroll, Joe** 1919- [DAM, EJ]
*American singer*
* Carroll, Bebop

**Carroll, John**
*See* La Faye, Julian

**Carroll, John E.** 1863-1942 [BE]
*American baseball player*
* Carroll, Scrappy

**Carroll, Julian** 20th c.
*American politician and lay
preacher*
* [The] Flying Deacon

**Carroll, Laura**
*See* Parr, Lucy

**Carroll, Lewis**
See Dodgson, Charles Lutwidge

**Carroll, Madeleine**
See O'Carroll, Marie-Madeleine Bernadette

**Carroll, Margot**
See Cavell, F. Margaret Strutt

**Carroll, Martin**
See Carr, Margaret

**Carroll, Nancy**
See La Hiff, Anne Veronica

**Carroll, Owen Thomas** 1902-1975 [B10, BE]
*American baseball player and coach*
* Carroll, Ownie

**Carroll, Ownie**
See Carroll, Owen Thomas

**Carroll, Ralph Arthur** 1891- [BE]
*American baseball player*
* Carroll, Doc
* Carroll, Red

**Carroll, Red**
See Carroll, Ralph Arthur

**Carroll, St. Thomas Marion**
See Carroll, Tom M.

**Carroll, Scrappy**
See Carroll, John E.

**Carroll, Shelley**
See Shelly, Carol Lee

**Carroll, Speedo**
See Carroll, Earl

**Carroll, Sydney W.**
See Whiteman, Sydney

**Carroll, Tom M.** 1950- [CA]
*American columnist*
* Carroll, St. Thomas Marion

**Carroll-Held, Peter** 1937- [IWM]
*Irish-born musician*
* Held, Peter

**Carron, Elisabeth**
See Caradonna, Elisabetta

**Carrouges, Michel**
See Couturier, Louis [Joseph]

**Carrucci, Jacopo** 1494-1557 [WBD]
*Italian painter*
* Pontormo, Jacopo da

**Carruth, Agnes K.**
See Tucker, Agnes Kent Carruth

**Carruthers, Earl Malcolm** 1910-1971 [EJ, WWJ]
*American jazz musician*
* Carruthers, Jock

**Carruthers, Jock**
See Carruthers, Earl Malcolm

**Carruthers, Rose**
See Ellenby, Rose

**Carry, George Dorman** 1915-1970 [EJ, WWJ]
*American jazz musician*
* Carry, Scoops

**Carry, Scoops**
See Carry, George Dorman

**Carryaway, Nick**
See Murray, John F[rancis]

**Carsac, Francis**
See Bordes, Francois

**Carsey, Kid**
See Carsey, Wilfred

**Carsey, Wilfred** 1870- ? [AS, BE]
*American baseball player*
* Carsey, Kid

**Carson, Alex[ander James]** 20th c. [BE]
*American baseball player*
* Carson, Soldier

**Carson, Bud**
See Carson, Leon

**Carson, Christopher** 1809-1868 [DNNS, HHF, WBD]
*American trapper and mountain guide*
* Carson, Kit

**Carson, Eldridge Franklin** 1909?-1978 [FIR]
*Television performer*
* Carson, Kit

**Carson, Fiddlin' John**
See Carson, John

**Carson, Gerald** 1905- [CEI]
*Canadian-born hockey player*
* Carson, Stub

**Carson, James**
See Roberts, James William

**Carson, [Captain] James** [house pseudonym] [Stratemeyer Syndicate]
See Stratemeyer, Edward L.

**Carson, Jeannie**
See Shuff, Jean

**Carson, John** 1868-1949 [CME, CWG, ECM]
*American country-western performer*
* Carson, Fiddlin' John

**Carson, Kit**
See Carson, Christopher

**Carson, Kit**
See Carson, Eldridge Franklin

**Carson, Kit**
See Carson, L. M.

**Carson, Kit**
See Carson, Walter Lloyd

**Carson, Kit**
See Carson, Xanthus

**Carson, Kris**
See Kristofferson, Kris

**Carson, [Captain] L. B.** 20th c. [MBF]
*British author*
* Bradford, [Captain] L.

**Carson, L. M.** 1942?- [B10]
*American writer and filmmaker*
* Carson, Kit

**Carson, Leon** 20th c. [SMG]
*American football coach*
* Carson, Bud

**Carson, Lettie Gay** 1901- [NAA]
*American editor*
* Gay, Lettie

**Carson, Moonshine Kate**
See Carson, Rosa Lee

**Carson, Nelson** 1917- [BWW]
*American singer*
* Carter, Nelson

**Carson, Rosa Lee** 20th c. [ECM]
*American country-western performer*
* Carson, Moonshine Kate

**Carson, Ruth**
See Bugbee, Ruth Carson

**Carson, Sally** 1926- [DAM]
*American country-western performer*
* Bonnie Lou

**Carson, Soldier**
See Carson, Alex[ander James]

**Carson, Stub**
See Carson, Gerald

**Carson, Sylvia**
See Dresser, Davis

**Carson, Walter Lloyd** 1912- [BE]
*American baseball player*
* Carson, Kit

**Carson, Xanthus** 1910- [CA]
*American writer*
* Carson, Kit
* Wade, Kit

**Carstairs, Cardinal**
See Carstairs, William

**Carstairs, John Paddy**
See Keys, John

**Carstairs, Kathleen**
See Pendower, Jacques

**Carstairs, Rod**
See Dalton, Gilbert

**Carstairs, William** 1649-1715 [HN, SN]
*Scottish clergyman and government advisor*
* Carstairs, Cardinal

**Carsten, Peter**
See Ransenthaler, Peter

**Carstens, Netta**
See Laffeaty, Christina

**Carswell, Frank Willis** 1919- [BE]
*American baseball player*
* Carswell, Tex
* Carswell, Wheels

**Carswell, Leslie**
See Stephens, Rosemary

**Carswell, Tex**
See Carswell, Frank Willis

**Carswell, Wheels**
See Carswell, Frank Willis

**Carten, Audrey**
See Bicker-Caarten, Audrey

**Carten, Laura Paty** 20th c. [NAA]
*Canadian editor and columnist*
* Smith, Farmer

**Carter, A. P.**
See Carter, Alvin Pleasant

**Carter, Ad**
See Carter, Augustus Daniels

**Carter, Alvin Pleasant** 1891-1960 [CWG, ECM]
*American country-western performer*
* Carter, A. P.

**Carter, Anne**
See Brooks, Anne Tedlock

**Carter, Arnold Lee** 1920- [BE]
*American baseball player*
* Carter, Lefty

**Carter, Augustus Daniels** 1895-1957 [WECO]
*American cartoonist*
* Carter, Ad

**Carter, Avis Morton**
See Allen, Kenneth S[ydney]

**Carter, Bennett Lester** 1907- [ASC, IBW, NP]
*American jazz musician*
* Carter, Benny
* Carter, King
* [The] Elder Statesman of Jazz

**Carter, Benny**
See Carter, Bennett Lester

**Carter, Betty**
See Jones, Lillie Mae

**Carter, Betty Be-Bop**
See Jones, Lillie Mae

**Carter, Blackie**
See Carter, Otis Leonard

**Carter, Bo**
See Chatmon, Armenter

**Carter, Bob**
See Kahakalau, Robert

**Carter, Bosco**
See Carter, Donald James

**Carter, Bruce**
See Hough, Richard [Alexander]

**Carter, Bryan** 1917- [AW]
*Scottish-born author*
* Carter, Nick

**Carter, Buck**
See Carter, Sol[omon Mobley]

**Carter, Bunny**
See Collins, Samuel

**Carter, Charles** 20th c. [OBW]
*American baseball player*
* Carter, Kid

**Carter, Charles J.** 1875-1936 [BMH, BS]
*American-born magician*
* Carter the Boy Magician
* Carter the Great
* [The] Great Carter

**Carter, Charlie**
See Jackson, Charlie

**Carter, Charlton** 1922?- [BEW, TR]
*American actor*
* Heston, Charlton

**Carter, Chip**
See Carter, James Earl, III

**Carter, Conrad Powell** 1879-1961 [BE]
*American baseball player*
* Carter, Nick

**Carter, David C[harles]** 1946- [CA]
*American sales manager and writer*
* Bertrand, Charles
* Doyle, David
* Reade, Lang

**Carter, Dee**
See Hughes, Den[n]is [Talbot]

**Carter, Donald James** 1926-  [BBH]
*American bowler*
* Carter, Bosco

**Carter, Elizabeth** 1717-1806
[DEL, PA]
*British poet*
* Eliza

**Carter, Ernest** 20th c.  [OBW]
*American baseball player*
* Carter, Spoon

**Carter, Ernest Frank** 1899-  [AW]
*British author*
* Giffin, Frank

**Carter, Frances Monet** 1923-  [CA]
*American educator and author*
* Evans, Frances Monet Carter

**Carter, Fred** 20th c.  [SMG]
*American basketball player*
* Carter, Mad Dog

**Carter, Hanson** 1878-1948  [EC]
*British-born cricketer*
* Carter, Sammy
* Carter, Sep

**Carter, Helena**
See   Rickerts, Helen

**Carter, Henry** 1821-1880  [WBD]
*British-born illustrator, journalist, publisher*
* Leslie, Frank

**Carter, Herbert**
See   Rathborne, St. George

**Carter, [John] Howard** 1904-  [BE]
*American baseball player*
* Carter, Nick

**Carter, Hugh** 1921?-
*Politician and cousin of American president, Jimmy Carter*
* Cousin Beedie

**Carter, Hugh, Jr.** 20th c.
*Aide to, and cousin of, American president, Jimmy Carter*
* Cousin Cheap

**Carter, Hurricane**
See   Carter, Rubin

**Carter, Jack**
See   Chakrin, Jack

**Carter, James**
See   Valmain, Frederic

**Carter, James Earl, III** 1950-
*Son of American president, Jimmy Carter*
* Carter, Chip

**Carter, James Earl, Jr. [Jimmy]** 1924-
*American president*
* Cousin Hot
* Deacon [Secret Service code name]
* [The] Peanut Farmer

**Carter, Janis**
See   Dremann, Janis

**Carter, John Franklin** 1897-1967
[EMD, TC, WW]
*American author and journalist*
* Diplomat
* Franklin, Jay
* Unofficial Observer

**Carter, John Hanson**  [PA]
*Author*
* Rolling-Pin, Commodore

**Carter, John L[ouis Justin]** 1880- ?
[SFL, WGT]
*Author*
* Irving, Compton

**Carter, Kid**
See   Carter, Charles

**Carter, King**
See   Carter, Bennett Lester

**Carter, King**
See   Carter, Robert

**Carter, Lefty**
See   Carter, Arnold Lee

**Carter, Lillian [Gordy]** 1898-
*Mother of American president, Jimmy Carter*
* Miss Lillian

**Carter, Lin**
See   Carter, Linwood Vrooman

**Carter, Linwood Vrooman** 1930-
[HFF, SFL, WGT]
*American author*
* Carter, Lin

**Carter, M. L.**
See   Carter, Margaret Louise

**Carter, Mad Dog**
See   Carter, Fred

**Carter, Manley** 1947-  [AES]
*American soccer player*
* Carter, Sonny

**Carter, Margaret Louise** 1948-
[SFL]
*American author*
* Carter, M. L.

**Carter, Margery Louise Allingham**
1904-1966  [WGT]
*British author*
* Allingham, Margery

**Carter, Marlin Theodore** 1912-
[MK]
*American baseball player*
* Carter, Mel
* Carter, Pee Wee

**Carter, Maybelle** 1909-1978
[ECM]
*American country-western performer*
* Mother Maybelle
* [The] Queen of the Autoharp

**Carter, Mel**
See   Carter, Marlin Theodore

**Carter, Mrs.**  [PA]
*Author*
* Gorham, Elsie

**Carter, Nancy**
See   Gombell, Minna

**Carter, Nelson**
See   Carson, Nelson

**Carter, Nicholas?**
See   Cook, William Wallace

**Carter, Nicholas**
See   Coryell, John Russell

**Carter, Nicholas**
See   Davis, Frederick William

**Carter, Nicholas**
See   Dey, Frederic Van Rensselaer

**Carter, Nicholas?**
See   Foster, W. Bert

**Carter, Nicholas?**
See   Hanshew, Thomas W.

**Carter, Nicholas?**
See   Harbaugh, Thomas Chalmers

**Carter, Nicholas**
See   Jenks, George Charles

**Carter, Nicholas?**
See   McCulley, Johnston

**Carter, Nicholas**
See   Sawyer, Eugene T.

**Carter, Nicholas?**
See   Whitson, John H.

**Carter, Nick** [house pseudonym]
See   Avallone, Michael [Angelo], Jr.

**Carter, Nick**
See   Ballard, [Willis] Todhunter

**Carter, Nick**
See   Carter, [John] Howard

**Carter, Nick**
See   Carter, Bryan

**Carter, Nick**
See   Carter, Conrad Powell

**Carter, Nick**
See   Carter, Paul Warren

**Carter, Nick** [house pseudonym]
See   Chambliss, John

**Carter, Nick** [house pseudonym]
See   Clark, Philip

**Carter, Nick** [joint pseudonym with Ormond G. Smith] [house pseudonym]
See   Coryell, John Russell

**Carter, Nick** [house pseudonym]
See   Granbeck, Marilyn

**Carter, Nick**
See   Hayes, Ralph E[ugene]

**Carter, Nick** [joint pseudonym with John Russell Coryell] [house pseudonym]
See   Smith, Ormond G.

**Carter, Nick** [house pseudonym]
See   Wallmann, Jeffrey M[iner]

**Carter, Nick** [house pseudonym]
See   Wormser, Richard [Edward]

**Carter, Otis Leonard** 1902-  [BE]
*American baseball player*
* Carter, Blackie

**Carter, Paul A.** 20th c.  [WGT]
*Author*
* Carter, Philip

**Carter, Paul Warren** 1894-  [BE]
*American baseball player*
* Carter, Nick

**Carter, Pee Wee**
See   Carter, Marlin Theodore

**Carter, Philip**
See   Carter, Paul A.

**Carter, Phyllis Ann**
See   Eberle, Irmengarde

**Carter, Ralph**
See   Neubauer, William Arthur

**Carter, Ray**
See   Krumbein, Maurice

**Carter, Richard** 1918-  [CA]
*American author*
* Ainslie, Tom

**Carter, Robert**
*American plantation owner and banker*
* Carter, King

**Carter, Robert A[yres]** 1923-  [CA]
*American author and playwright*
* Ayres, Alison

**Carter, Rosalynn Smith** 1927-
*Wife of American president, Jimmy Carter*
* [The] Steel Magnolia

**Carter, Rubin** 1937-  [B10]
*American boxer*
* Carter, Hurricane

**Carter, Sammy**
See   Carter, Hanson

**Carter, Sep**
See   Carter, Hanson

**Carter, Sol[omon Mobley]** 1908-
[BE]
*American baseball player*
* Carter, Buck

**Carter, Sonny**
See   Carter, Manley

**Carter, Spoon**
See   Carter, Ernest

**Carter the Boy Magician**
See   Carter, Charles J.

**Carter the Great**
See   Carter, Charles J.

**Carter, Tracy**
See   Olsen, Tracy

**Carter, Wilf** 1904-
[CME, CWG, PMJ]
*Canadian-born country-western performer*
* Montana Slim

**Carteret, Anna**
See   Wilkinson, Anna

**Carteromaco**
See   Forteguerri [or Fortiguerra], Niccolo

**[The] Carthaginian Lion**
See   Hannibal

**Cartier**
See   Villemessant, Jean Hippolyte

**Cartier, Alfred** 1924-  [RBE]
*American boxer*
* Cartier, Walter

**Cartier, Steve**
See   Cameron, Lou

**Cartier, Walter**
See   Cartier, Alfred

**Cartland, Barbara [Hamilton]**
1904-  [CA, WD]
*British author*
* McCorquodale, Barbara

**Cartmell, Robert** 1877- ?
[SFL, WGT]
*Author*
* Tarnacre, Robert

**Cartmill, Cleve** 1908-1964 [WGT]
*American author*
* Corbin, Michael

**Carton, Richard Claude**
*See* Critchett, Richard Claude

**Cartouche**
*See* Bourguignon, Louis
Dominique

**Cartwright, A.**
*See* Twyman, Harold William

**Cartwright, Alexander Joy, Jr.**
1820-1892 [BBH, PB]
*American surveyor and amateur
athlete*
* [The] Father of Modern Baseball
* [The] Father of Organized
Baseball

**Cartwright, Charles**
*See* Morley, Charles

**Cartwright, Edward H.** 1859- ?
[BE]
*American baseball player*
* Cartwright, Jumbo

**Cartwright, Harold** 1951- [DC]
*British cricketer*
* Cartwright, Harry

**Cartwright, Harry**
*See* Cartwright, Harold

**Cartwright, James McGregor**
*See* Jennings, Leslie Nelson

**Cartwright, John** 1740-1824
[DEP, DNNS, WBD]
*British politician*
* [The] Father of Reform

**Cartwright, Jumbo**
*See* Cartwright, Edward H.

**Cartwright, Rosalind Dymond**
1922- [CA]
*American psychologist and author*
* Dymond, Rosalind

**Cartwright, William** 1611-1643
[PA]
*Author*
* Clericus

**Carty, Ricardo Adolpho Jacabo**
1941?- [BE, SMG]
*Dominican-born baseball player*
* Carty, Rico

**Carty, Rico**
*See* Carty, Ricardo Adolpho
Jacabo

**Caruba, Alan** 1937- [CA]
*American writer*
* Jordan, Monica

**Carus Sterne**
*See* Krause, Ernst Ludwig

**Caruso, Calogero Anthony** 1929-
[OP]
*American opera singer*
* Anthony, Charles

**Caruso, Enrico**
*See* Caruso, Errico

**Caruso, Errico** 1873-1921 [IPA]
*Italian opera singer*
* Caruso, Enrico

**[The] Caruso in Petticoats**
*See* Ponzillo, Rosa Melba

**Caruthers, Earl Malcolm** 1910-
[MY]
*American jazz musician*
* Caruthers, Jock

**Caruthers, Jock**
*See* Caruthers, Earl Malcolm

**Caruthers, Parisian Bob**
*See* Caruthers, Robert Lee

**Caruthers, Robert Lee** 1864-1911
[BE, DGS]
*American baseball player*
* Caruthers, Parisian Bob

**Caruthers, William** ?-1845 [PA]
*American author*
* [A] Virginian

**Carvaille, Leon** 1825-1897 [WBD]
*French opera singer and theatre
director*
* Carvalho, Leon

**Carvajal, Ricardo**
*See* Meneses, Enrique

**Carvalho, E. N.** 1817- ? [FFF, PA]
*Author*
* Falconer, Frank

**Carvalho, Leon**
*See* Carvaille, Leon

**Carvalho, S. S.** [PA]
*Author*
* Proteus

**Carvalho e Mello, Sebastiao Jose de**
1699-1782 [DNNS, HN, RH]
*Portuguese statesman*
* [The] Great Marquis
* Pombal, Marques de

**Carver, Al**
*See* Slaughter, Marion T.

**Carver, Dave**
*See* Bingley, David Ernest

**Carver, Doc**
*See* Carver, W. F.

**Carver, George Washington**
1860-1943 [IBW]
*American agronomist*
* [The] Goober Genius
* [The] Old Wizard
* Peanut, Mr.

**Carver, John**
*See* Orth, Richard

**Carver, Kathryn** 1906-1947 [SC]
*American actress*
* Hill, Kathryn

**Carver, Louise**
*See* Murray, Louise Spigler

**Carver, Lynn**
*See* Sampson, Virginia Reid

**Carver, Mrs. J. H.** [FFF]
*Entertainer*
* Neilson, Cora

**Carver, W. F.** 1840-1927 [AS]
*American trapshooter*
* Carver, Doc

**Cary**
*See* Cary, Louis F[avreau]

**Cary, Caroline Anne** 1940- [ART]
*British painter*
* C. A. C.

**Cary, Clara**
*See* Beaman, Lottie Kimbrough

**Cary, D. M.**
*See* Macmillan, Douglas

**Cary, Diana Serra**
*See* Cary, Peggy-Jean Montgomery

**Cary, Jud**
*See* Tubb, Edwin Charles

**Cary, Louis F[avreau]** 1915- [SAT]
*American illustrator*
* Cary

**Cary, Peggy-Jean Montgomery**
1918- [CA]
*American writer*
* Cary, Diana Serra
* Serra, Diana

**Cary, Red**
*See* Cary, Scott Russell

**Cary, Robert**
*See* Cariveau, Robert Edward

**Cary, Scott Russell** 1923- [BE]
*American baseball player*
* Cary, Red

**Cary, Webster**
*See* Fleischer, Leonore

**Caryl, Jean**
*See* Kaplan, Jean Caryl Korn

**Caryl, Warren** 1920- [CA]
*American author*
* Tadrack, Moss

**Caryll, Ivan**
*See* Tilken, Felix

**Caryophilus**
*See* Grofalo, Blasio

**[The] Casablanca Clouter**
*See* Cerdan, Marcel

**Casal, Julian del** 1863-1893 [CW]
*Cuban poet, author, journalist*
* Camors, Conde de
* Vasili, Paul

**Casalandra, Estelle** 1907- [CAP]
*American author*
* Mary Estelle, [Sister]

**Casale, Joan T[herese]** 1935- [CA]
*American author*
* Watkins, Joan C.

**Casalegno, Mario Terenzio Enrico**
1884- [WBD]
*Italian-born aeronautics authority,
publisher, author*
* Woodhouse, Henry

**Casalis De Pury, Jeanne**
1897-1966 [THR]
*South African-born actress*
* De Casalis, Jeanne

**Casals, Pablo**
*See* Defillo De Casals, Pau Carlos
Salvador

**Casanas, Alejandro** 1952?-
*American track and field athlete*
* [El] Caballo [The Horse]

**Casanova, Baby**
*See* Casanova, Rodolfo

**Casanova, Ortiz Paulino** 1941-
[BE]
*Cuban-born baseball player*
* Casanova, Paul

**Casanova, Paul**
*See* Casanova, Ortiz Paulino

**Casanova, Rodolfo** 20th c. [RBE]
*Mexican boxer*
* Casanova, Baby

**Casanova, Young**
*See* Medina, Hector

**Casares, Maria**
*See* Casares Quiroga, Maria

**Casares Quiroga, Maria** 1922-
[FC]
*French-Spanish actress*
* Casares, Maria

**Casca**
*See* Thompson, John

**Cascadananda, Anagaraca**
*See* Smiley, Charles Wesley

**Cascales, John** 1911-1968
[EJ, PMJ]
*American jazz musician and
composer*
* Richards, Johnny

**Cascarella, Crooning Joe**
*See* Cascarella, Joseph Thomas

**Cascarella, Joseph Thomas** 1907-
[BE]
*American baseball player*
* Cascarella, Crooning Joe

**Case, Everett** 1900-1966 [BB]
*American basketball coach*
* [The] Old Gray Fox

**Case, John Francis** 1876- ? [NAA]
*American author and editor*
* Kane, Philip

**Case, Justin**
*See* Cave, Hugh B[arnett]

**Case, Justin**
*See* Gleadow, Rupert Seeley

**Case, L. L.**
*See* Lewin, Leonard C[ase]

**Case, Michael**
*See* Howard, Robert West

**Casei, Nedda**
*See* Casey, Nedda-Jane

**Casel, Tyari** 20th c. [IBW]
*Martial arts expert*
* Kung Fu, Mr.

**Caseleyr, Cam[ille Auguste Marie]**
1909- [AW, CAP, WW]
*Belgian-born Australian author*
* Danvers, Jack

**Caselius, Johann** 1533-1613 [PA]
*Author*
* Chessel

**Casellato, Giorgio** 1938- [OP]
*Italian opera singer*
* Casellato Lamberti, Giorgio

**Casellato Lamberti, Giorgio**
*See* Casellato, Giorgio

**Caselli, Jean**
*See* Cazalis, Henry

**Casement, Christina** 1933- [AW]
*British author*
* Maclean, Christina

**Casewit, Curtis** 1922- [SAT]
*German-born American author*
* Green, D.

**Casewit, Curtis** (Continued)
* Vernor, D.
* Werner, K.

**Casey Bill Weldon**
See Weldon, Will

**Casey, Bob**
See Casey, O. Robinson

**Casey, Citation**
See Casey, Thomas

**Casey, Daniel J[oseph]** 1937-    [CA]
American author and editor
* O'Cathasaigh, Donal

**Casey, Doc**
See Casey, Edward

**Casey, Doc**
See Casey, James Peter

**Casey, Edward** ?-1966    [AS]
American boxer and trainer
* Casey, Doc

**Casey, Edward L.** 1894-1966    [FB]
American football player
* Casey, Natick Eddie

**Casey, Elizabeth**    [PA]
Author
* Blackburn, E. Owens

**Casey, Harry Wayne** 1951-    [RO2]
American singer, songwriter,
musician
* K. C.

**Casey, J. K.**    [PA]
Author
* Leo

**Casey, James** 1892-1965    [BMH]
British comedian
* James, Jimmy
* Terry the Blue-Eyed Irish Boy

**Casey, James Peter** 1871-1936
[AS, BE]
American baseball player
* Casey, Doc

**Casey, John** 1880-1964
[BEW, CA, EWL]
Irish playwright
* O'Casey, Sean
* O'Cathasaigh, Shaun

**Casey, John E.** 1876- ?    [NAA]
American editor
* De Field, Edward

**Casey, Kent**
See McIntosh, Kenneth

**Casey, Mart**
See Casey, Michael T.

**Casey, Michael T.** 1922-    [CA]
American author
* Casey, Mart

**Casey, Mickey**
See Casey, William

**Casey, Natick Eddie**
See Casey, Edward L.

**Casey, Nedda-Jane** 1935-    [OP]
American opera singer
* Casei, Nedda

**Casey, O. Robinson** 1936-    [BE]
American baseball player
* Casey, Bob

**Casey, Richard** [house pseudonym,
Ziff-Davis]
See Yerxa, Leroy

**Casey, Thomas** 1924-    [BBH]
American-born football player
* Casey, Citation

**Casey, William** 20th c.    [OBW]
American baseball player
* Casey, Mickey

**Cash and Carry Pyle**
See Pyle, Charles C.

**Cash, Grace [Savannah]** 1915-
[CA]
American writer
* Cash, Grady

**Cash, Grady**
See Cash, Grace [Savannah]

**Cash, Helen**
See Stocker, Helen

**Cash, John R. [Johnny]** 1932-
[PAC]
American singer and songwriter
* [The] Hag
* [The] King of Country and
Western Music

**Cash, Morny** 1872-1938    [BMH]
British comedian
* [The] Lancashire Lad

**Cash, Ready**
See Cash, William Walker

**Cash, Sebastian**
See Smithells, Roger [William]

**Cash, William F.** ?-1963    [BEW]
Theatrical performer
* Ardo the Frog

**Cash, William Walker** 1919-    [MK]
American baseball player
* Cash, Ready

**Cashman, Cash**
See Cashman, Wayne John

**Cashman, John**
See Davis, Timothy Francis Tothill

**Cashman, Terry**
See Minogue, Dennis

**Cashman, Wayne John** 1945-
[SMG]
Canadian-born hockey player
* Cashman, Cash

**Casias, Rose-Marie Perrier** 1944?-
[CW]
Haitian poet and author
* Perrier, Rose-Marie

**Casimir, Camello** 1917-    [IBW]
Haitian-born hair stylist
* Casimir, Frenchie

**Casimir, Frenchie**
See Casimir, Camello

**Casimir Perier, Auguste**
See Perier, Auguste Casimir

**Casimir I** 1015-1058
[DNNS, WBD]
King of Poland
* [The] Monk
* [The] Peaceful
* [The] Red Fox
* [The] Restorer of Poland

**Casimir II** 1138-1194
[DNNS, FFF, SN]
King of Poland
* [The] Just

**Casimir III** 1309-1370
[DNNS, FFF, WBD]
King of Poland
* [The] Great
* [The] Peasants' King

**Casimir V**
See John II Casimir

**Caskoden, [Sir] Edwin**
See Major, Charles

**Casley, Leonard** 1927?-    [B10]
Australian eccentric
* Prince Leonard

**Caslon, William** 1692-1766    [SN]
British type founder
* [The] Coryphaeus of
Letter-Founders

**Casner, Lloyd** 1926-1965    [EAR]
American auto racer
* Casner, Lucky

**Casner, Lucky**
See Casner, Lloyd

**Cason, Buzz**
See Cason, James

**Cason, James** 20th c.    [RO1]
American singer
* Cason, Buzz
* Miles, Garry

**Cason, Mabel Earp** 1892-1965
[CAP, SAT]
American author
* Bell, Emily Mary

**Cason, Pedro** 1525-1581    [PA]
Author
* Ciaconicus

**Casona, Alejandro**
See Rodriguez Alvarez, Alejandro

**Casque, Sammy**
See Davis, Sydney Charles
Houghton

**Cass, Guy**
See Gay, Caster Abney, Jr.

**Cass, Lewis** 1782-1860    [PA]
American author
* [An] American

**Cassaba, Carlos**
See Parry, Michel Patrick

**Cassady, Hopalong**
See Cassady, Howard

**Cassady, Howard** 1934-
[FB, SMG]
American football player
* Cassady, Hopalong

**Cassady, James**
See Cassidy, James J.

**Cassander**
See Bruckner, John

**Cassandra**
See Connor, [Sir] William Neil

**Cassandre, A. M.**
See Mouron, Adolphe Jean Marie

**Cassel, Jean-Pierre**
See Crochon, Jean-Pierre

**Cassel, Lili**
See Wronker, Lili Cassel

**Cassells, John**
See Duncan, W[illiam] Murdoch

**Cassianus, Johannes** 360?- 435?
[WBD]
Monk and theologian
* Johannes Eremita
* Johannes Massiliensis

**Cassiday, Bruce [Bingham]** 1920-
[CA, SFL, WW]
American editor and author
* Bingham, Carson
* Day, Max
* Steffanson, Con [house
pseudonym]

**Cassidy, Butch**
See Kiick, James F. [Jim]

**Cassidy, Butch**
See Parker, Robert LeRoy

**Cassidy, Catherine** 1890-1971
[THR]
American actress
* Calvert, Catherine

**Cassidy, George**
See Parker, Robert LeRoy

**Cassidy, James** 1861- ?    [WWL]
Author
* Story, E. M.

**Cassidy, James J.** 1869-1928    [SC]
American actor
* Cassady, James

**Cassidy, John L.**    [PA]
Author
* Larkin

**Cassidy, Red**
See Cassidy, William

**Cassidy, William** ?-1929    [BLB]
American underworld figure
* Cassidy, Red

**Cassill, R. V.**
See Cassill, Ronald Verlin

**Cassill, Ronald Verlin** 1919-
[CA, DLE]
American author and educator
* Aherne, Owen
* Cassill, R. V.
* Webster, Jesse

**Cassils, Peter**
See Keele, Kenneth D[avid]

**Cassin, Billie**
See Le Sueur, Lucille

**Cassini**
See Gardiner, James H.

**Cassini, Igor** 20th c.
Publicist
* Knickerbocker, Cholly

**Cassini, Jack Dempsey** 1919-    [BE]
American baseball player
* Cassini, Scat

**Cassini, Oleg**
See Lolewski-Cassini, Oleg

**Cassini, Scat**
See Cassini, Jack Dempsey

**Cassius**
See Foot, Michael Mackintosh

**Cassius X**
See   Clay, Cassius Marcellus, Jr.

**Cassius Longinus, Caius** 1st c. BC
[FFF, RH, SN]
*Roman general*
* [The] Last of the Romans

**Casson, Frederick Ronald
Christopher** 1910-   [AW]
*British psychiatrist and author*
* Beatty, Baden

**Cassotto, Walden Robert**
1936-1973   [FC, IPA]
*American singer*
* Darin, Bobby

**Cassou, Jean**
See   Hoffman, Josef

**Cassou, Jean** 1897-   [EWL]
*French author and art critic*
* Noir, Jean

**Castagna, Giovanni Battista**
1521-1590 [CAL]
*Pope*
* Urban VII

**Castagno, Andrea del** 1423-1457
[WBD]
*Florentine painter*
* Andreino degl'Impiccati

**Castaldo, Lee** 1915-
[EJ, PMJ, WWJ]
*American jazz musician*
* Castle, Lee

**Castanon, Roberto** 20th c.
*Spanish boxer*
* [El] Conquistador

**Castara**
See   Herbert, Lucy

**Castel, Charles Irenee** 1658-1743
[WBD]
*French author*
* Saint Pierre, Abbe de

**Castel Chiuso, Giorgione di**
See   Bayley, Peter

**Castelfranco Giorgione da**
See   Barbarelli, Giorgio

**Castell**   [RH]
*British shoemaker*
* [The] Cock of Westminster

**Castellano, Franco**
See   Sgarlato, Nico

**Castellari, E. G.**
See   Girolami, Enzo

**Castello, Giovanni Battista**
1509?-1569   [WBD]
*Italian painter and architect*
* [Il] Bergamasco

**Castellotti, Eugene** 20th c.
*Auto racer*
* [The] Beautiful One

**Castelluccio, Frank** 1936-
*American singer*
* Valli, Frankie

**Castenius, Sigrid**
See   Thyselius, Thorborg Elin
Tryggvesdotter

**Caster, Francois** 1515-1559   [PA]
*Author*
* Malleus Hereticorum

**Caster, Richard** 1949-   [IBW]
*American football player*
* Ol' Cement Hands

**Castiglia, Francesco** 1891?-1973
*American underworld figure*
* Costello, Frank
* [The] Politician
* [The] Prime Minister

**Castigliola, Angelo J.** 1924-   [NOJ]
*American jazz musician*
* Castigliola, Bubby

**Castigliola, Bubby**
See   Castigliola, Angelo J.

**Castiglione, Giovanni Benedetto**
1616-1670   [WBD]
*Italian painter and etcher*
* [Il] Grechetto

**Castiglioni, Francesco Saverio**
1761-1830   [CAL]
*Pope*
* Pius VIII

**Castiglioni, Goffredo**   ?-1241
[CAL]
*Pope*
* Celestine IV

**Castil-Blaze**
See   Blaze, Francois Henri Joseph

**Castile, Lynn** 1898-1975   [SC]
*American actress and singer*
* Canter, Lynn

**Castillo**
See   Canovas del Castillo, Antonio

**Castillo, Chuchu**
See   Castillo Aguillera, Jesus

**Castillo, Prisciliano** 20th c.   [RBE]
*Boxer*
* Castillo, Zip

**Castillo, Zip**
See   Castillo, Prisciliano

**Castillo Aguillera, Jesus** 1944-
[BX, RBE]
*Mexican boxer*
* Castillo, Chuchu

**Castillo Velasquez, Luis Alberto**
1928-   [IAW]
*Peruvian author*
* Alba, Patricio

**Castle, Damon**
See   Smith, Richard Rein

**Castle, Eva** 1922-   [ART]
*Danish-born sculptor, designer,
potter*
* E. C.

**Castle, Frances**
See   Leader, [Evelyn] Barbara
[Blackburn]

**Castle, Henry Lee** ?-1971   [BWW]
*American musician*
* Too Tight Henry

**Castle, Irene**
See   Foote, Irene

**Castle, Joyce**
See   Malicky, Lillian Joyce

**Castle, Lee**
See   Castaldo, Lee

**Castle, Lee** [joint pseudonym with
Margaret E. (Nettles) Ogan]
See   Ogan, George F.

**Castle, Lee** [joint pseudonym with
George F. Ogan]
See   Ogan, Margaret E. [Nettles]

**Castle, Margery Sharp** 1905-
[TBJ]
*Maltese-born author*
* Sharp, Margery

**Castle, Nan**
See   Castleberry, Nancy Louise

**Castle, Peggy**
See   Blair, Peggy

**Castle, Robert**
See   Hamilton, Edmond [Moore]

**Castle, Vernon**
See   Blythe, Vernon Castle

**Castle, William**
See   Schloss, William

**Castleberry, Nancy Louise** 1941-
[CWG]
*American country-western performer*
* Castle, Nan

**Castleman, Clydell** 1913-   [BE]
*American baseball player*
* Castleman, Slick

**Castleman, Slick**
See   Castleman, Clydell

**Castleman, Virginia Carter** 1864- ?
[NAA]
*American librarian and writer*
* Dixie

**Castlemon, Harry**
See   Fosdick, Charles Austin

**Castlen, Eppie Bowden**   [PA]
*Author*
* Chiquita

**Castles, Henry Neil** 1934?-
[B10, EAR]
*American auto racer*
* Castles, Soapy

**Castles, Soapy**
See   Castles, Henry Neil

**Castleton, Kate**
See   Phillips, Mrs. Henry

**Castleton, Virginia** 1925-   [CA]
*American educator and author*
* Thomas, Virginia Castleton

**Castner, Lefty**
See   Castner, Paul Henry

**Castner, Paul Henry** 1897-   [BE]
*American baseball player*
* Castner, Lefty

**Caston, Leonard** 1917-
[B10, BWW]
*American jazz musician*
* Baby Doo
* Baby Duke

**Castor [or Castorius]**
See   Beaver, John

**Castor, James Walter, Jr. [Jimmy]**
[IBW]
*American jazz musician*
* [The] E Man

**Castor, Pere**
See   Faucher, Paul

**Castorim**
See   Zobbau, M.

**Castriot [or Castriota?], George**
1403-1467   [RH]
*Prince of Albania*
* [The] Albanian Alexander
* [The] Athlete of Christendom
* Iskander Beg
* Scanderbeg
* [The] White Devil of Wallachia

**Castro, Antonio** 1946-   [WYA]
*Author*
* Castro, Tony

**Castro, Bill**
See   Castro, Williams Radhomes

**Castro, Checo**
See   Castro, Williams Radhomes

**Castro, Jose Maria** 1818-1893
[WBD]
*President of Costa Rica*
* [The] Founder of the Republic

**Castro, Jud**
See   Castro, Louis M.

**Castro, Louis M.** 1877- ?   [BE]
*Colombian-born baseball player*
* Castro, Jud

**Castro, Thomas**
See   Orton, Arthur

**Castro, Tony**
See   Castro, Antonio

**Castro, Williams Radhomes** 1953-
[BE, SMG]
*Dominican-born baseball player*
* Castro, Bill
* Castro, Checo

**Castro Novo, Hugh de**   ?-1310
[HN]
*British scholar*
* Scolasticus, Doctor

**Castro Sandoval, Luis** 1912-   [GS]
*Mexican bullfighter*
* [El] Soldado [The Soldier]

**Castulo**
See   Urena de Mendoza, Nicolas

**Castweazle, Eleanor**
See   Raynes, Frederica Rozelle
Ridgway

**Caswall, Edward** 19th c.   [SAT]
*British author*
* E. C.
* Quiz

**Caswell, Anne**
See   Denham, Mary Orr

**Caswell, Wilbur Larremore** 1883-
[NAA]
*American clergyman, playwright,
editor*
* Malone, Percy Sylvester

**[The] Cat**
See   Brecheen, Harry David

**[The] Cat**
See   Carre, Mathilde [Belard]

[The] Cat
See Coke, [Sir] Edward

[The] Cat
See Francis, Emile Percy

[The] Cat
See Macomber, George

[The] Cat
See Mantilla, Felix Lamela

[The] Cat
See Minson, Roland

[The] Cat
See Yamaguchi, Gogen

Cat Eye Clayton
See Clayton, Wilbur

Cat-Iron
See Carradine, William

Catala, Victor
See Albert i Paradis, Catalina

Catalani, Angelica 1782?-1849
[DEP, DNNS, RH]
Italian singer
* [The] Italian Nightingale
* [The] Queen of Song

Catalano, Angelo 20th c. [BLB]
American underworld figure
* Catalano, Julie

Catalano, Julie
See Catalano, Angelo

[The] Catalina Kid
See Young, George

Catamaran
See Bing, Jon

Catania, Joseph ?-1931
[BLB, PHM]
American underworld figure
* Joe the Baker

Catarino, Launcelot-Polite [PA]
Author
* Ambroise

Catay
See Mendoza Romero, Maria
Luisa

Catchpole, Margaret
See Cobbold, Richard

Catchpole, William Leslie 1900?-
[MBF]
British author
* Clifford, Martin [house
pseudonym]
* Conquest, Owen [house
pseudonym]
* Hawkins, John
* Howard, Roland
* Hunter, Rowland
* Richards, Frank [house
pseudonym]

Catena, Gerardo Vito 1902-
[BLB, PHM]
American underworld figure
* Catena, Jerry

Catena, Jerry
See Catena, Gerardo Vito

Cates, Gilbert
See Katz, Gilbert

Cates, Joseph
See Katz, Joseph

[El] Cateto [The Yokel]
See Puga, Ricardo

[The] Catharine de Medici of Africa
See Sophonisba

Cathcart, Mary
See Myers, Mary Cathcart

Cather, Willa
See Sibert, Willa

Catherall, Arthur 1906-
[CA, SAT, TCC]
British author
* Baltimore, J.
* Channel, A. R.
* Corby, Dan
* Hallard, Peter
* Maine, Trevor
* Peters, Linda
* Ruthin, Margaret

Catherine II 1729-1796
[DEP, DHA, HN]
Empress of Russia
* [The] Great
* [The] Messalina of the North
* [The] Modern Messalina
* [The] Northern Semiramis
* [The] Russian Messalina
* [The] Semiramis of the North

Catherwood, Mrs. M. H. [PA]
Author
* Hartwell, Mary

Cathey, Abner
See Cathey, Hardin

Cathey, Hardin 1919- [BE]
American baseball player
* Cathey, Abner

Cathey, Jim
See Cathey, Willis

Cathey, Willis 20th c. [OBW]
American baseball player
* Cathey, Jim

Cathode Ray
See Scroggie, Marcus Graham

[The] Catholic
See Alfonso I [Alonzo or
Alphonso]

[The] Catholic
See Ferdinand V [or Ferdinand II
of Aragon]

[The] Catholic
See Isabella I [or Isabel]

[The] Catholic Bishop of Bantry
See Decker, T.

Catholicos
See John VI [or Jean]

Catholicus
See Newman, John Henry

[La] Catin du Nord
See Elizabeth Petrovna

Catinat, Nicholas 1637-1712
[DEP, DNNS, SN]
French army officer
* Father Thoughtful
* [Le] Pere de la Pensee
* [The] Thoughtful Father

Catjuice Charley
See Hicks, Charlie

Catlett, Big Sid
See Catlett, Sidney

Catlett, Buddy
See Catlett, George James

Catlett, George James 1933-
[DAM, EJ]
American jazz musician
* Catlett, Buddy

Catlett, Sid L. 20th c. [IBW]
American basketball player
* [El] Sid

Catlett, Sidney 1910-1951
[DAM, EJ, PMJ]
American jazz musician
* Catlett, Big Sid

Catlin, George L. [PA]
Author
* Oates, Felix

Catlow, Joanna
See Lowry, Joan [Catlow]

Cato
See Burgess, George

Cato [joint pseudonym with Peter
D(unsmore) Howard and Frank
Owen]
See Foote, Michael

Cato [joint pseudonym with Frank
Owen and Michael Foote]
See Howard, Peter D[unsmore]

Cato [joint pseudonym with Peter
D(unsmore) Howard and Michael
Foote]
See Owen, Frank

Cato
See Trenchard, John

Cato, Marcus Porcius 2nd c. BC
[DNNS, WBD]
Roman statesman, general, writer
* [The] Censor
* [The] Elder

Cato, Marcus Porcius 1st c. BC
[WBD]
Roman philosopher
* Uticensis
* [The] Younger

[The] Cato of Anjou
See Pineau, Gabriel du

[The] Cato of the Age
See Prynne, William

Cato the Younger
See Barnard, [Sir] John

[La] Catolica
See Isabella I [or Isabel]

Caton, Buster
See Caton, James Howard

Caton, James Howard 1896-1948
[BE]
American baseball player
* Caton, Buster

Cats' Eyes Cunningham
See Cunningham, John

Cats, Father
See Cats, Jakob

Cats, Jakob 1577-1660 [DNNS]
Dutch poet
* Cats, Father

Catsos, Nicholas A. 1912- [ASC]
American composer
* Romero, Gary

Cattaui, Georges 1896-1974 [CAP]
French author and poet
* Francis, Michel

Catto, Max 1909- [AW]
British author
* Kent, Simon

Catto, P. Z.
See Hathaway, Ronald F.

Catullus, Caius Valerius 1st c. BC
[SN]
Roman poet
* Doctus

Catz, Max
See Glaser, Milton

Caucus, King
See Stilwell, Silas Moore

Caudle, James Robert 1933-
[CWG]
American country-western performer
* Roberts, Jim

Caudle, [Mrs.] Margaret
See Jerrold, Douglas William

Caudwell, Christopher
See Sprigg, C[hristopher] St. John

Cauldwell, Frank
See King, Francis H[enry]

Cauldwell, H. T. 20th c. [MBF]
British editor and illustrator
* Cauldwell, Jimmy

Cauldwell, Ike Reid 19th c. [FFF]
American writer
* Reid, Ike

Cauldwell, Jimmy
See Cauldwell, H. T.

Cauley, Terry
See Cauley, Troy Jesse

Cauley, Troy Jesse 1902- [CA]
American economist and writer
* Cauley, Terry

Caulfield, Jake
See Caulfield, John Joseph

Caulfield, John Joseph 1918- [BE]
American baseball player
* Caulfield, Jake

Caulfield, Malachy Francis 1915-
[CA]
Irish author
* Caulfield, Max
* McCoy, Malachy

Caulfield, Max
See Caulfield, Malachy Francis

Cauliflower, Sebastian
See Seldes, Gilbert [Vivian]

Caumery
See Languereau, Maurice

Causeur
See Hovey, William Alfred

Causey, Cecil Algernon 1893-1960
[BE]
American baseball player
* Causey, Red

Causey, Red
See Causey, Cecil Algernon

Causse, Charles 1862-1904 [SFL]
Author
* Mael, Peter [joint pseudonym
with Charles Vincent]

**Caustic, Christopher**
See Fessenden, Thomas Green

**Cauthen, Steve** 1960-
*American jockey* ·
* [The] Kid
* Wonder, Little Stevie

**[The] Cautious Tyrant**
See Du Plessis, Armand Jean

**Cauynge, William**
See Chatterton, Thomas

**Cavafy, C. P.**
See Kavaphes, Konstantinos

**Cavalcanti, Alberto**
See De Almeida-Cavalcanti,
Alberto

**Cavalcanti, Guido** 1250?-1300
[SN]
*Italian scholar and poet*
* [The] Other Eye of Florence

**[The] Cavalier**
See Breydel, Charles

**[The] Cavalier**
See Cairo, Francesco

**[The] Cavalier**
See Eon de Beaumont, Charles
Genevieve Louis Auguste Andre
Timothee d'

**[The] Cavalier**
See Le Clerc, Jean

**[The] Cavalier**
See Marini, Jean Baptiste

**[The] Cavalier**
See Nerone, Giuseppe

**[The] Cavalier**
See Ramsay, Andrew Michael

**Cavalier, Alain**
See Fraisse, Alain

**Cavalier, Jean** 1679?-1740 [FFF]
*French military leader*
* [The] Baker's Boy of Anduze

**[The] Cavalier of Song**
See Peers, Donald

**[The] Cavalier Poet**
See Cleveland, John

**[Il] Cavaliere Aretino**
See Leoni, Leone

**[Il] Cavaliere Calabrese**
See Preti, Mattia

**Cavaliere Tempesta**
See Mulier, Pieter

**Cavallaro, Ann [Abelson]** 1918-
[CA]
*American author*
* Abelson, Ann

**Cavallaro, Carmen** 1913-
*American musician and bandleader*
* [The] Poet of the Piano

**Cavalli, Francesco**
See Caletti-Bruni, Pietro Francesco

**Cavallin, Fritzie**
See Cavallin, Roy

**Cavallin, Roy** 20th c. [BBH, CSH]
*Canadian lacrosse player*
* Cavallin, Fritzie

**Cavan, Marie**
See Cawein, Mary Edith

**Cavanagh, Paul**
See Vene-Cavanagh, Paul

**Cavanaugh, Cav**
See Cavanaugh, Francis W.
[Frank]

**Cavanaugh, Francis W. [Frank]**
1866-1933 [FB]
*American football coach*
* Cavanaugh, Cav
* [The] Iron Major

**Cavanaugh, Michael J.** 1890-
[BX, RBE]
*American boxer*
* Glover, Mike

**Cavanna, Elizabeth Allen [Betty]**
1909- [CA, MJA, SAT]
*American author*
* Allen, Betsy
* Headley, Elizabeth

**[Il] Cavazzola [or Cavazzuola]**
See Morando, Paolo

**Cave, Edward** 1691-1754 [PA]
*Author*
* Urban, Sylvanus, Gent.

**Cave, Hugh B[arnett]** 1910-
[HFF, NAA, WGT]
*British-born American writer*
* Beck, Allen
* Case, Justin
* Vace, Geoffrey

**Cave, Roderick [George James
Munro]** 1935- [CA]
*British librarian and editor*
* Munro, James

**Caveat Emptor**
See Stephens, George

**Cavell, F. Margaret Strutt** 1889-
[WWL]
*British author and journalist*
* Carroll, Margot

**Cavell, Stanley L.**
See Goldstein, Stanley L.

**[The] Caveman**
See Christie, Bob

**Cavender, C. H.** 19th c. [PA]
*Author*
* Decanver, H. C.

**Cavendish**
See Jones, Henry

**Cavendish, Ada**
See Marshall, Mrs. Frank

**Cavendish, Peter**
See Horler, Sydney

**Cavendish, Richard** 1930- [CA]
*British author*
* Cornwall, Martin

**Caveney, Ike**
See Caveney, James Christopher

**Caveney, James Christopher**
1896-1949 [BE]
*American baseball player*
* Caveney, Ike

**Caverhill, Nicholas**
See Kirk-Greene, Anthony
[Hamilton Millard]

**Caverhill, William Melville** 1910-
[BEW, CC, WW]
*British author, playwright, actor*
* Melville, Alan

**Caverley, Charles S.** [PA]
*Author*
* C. S. C.

**Cavet, Pug**
See Cavet, Tiller H.

**Cavet, Tiller H.** 1889-1966 [BE]
*American baseball player*
* Cavet, Pug

**Cavill, Arthur** 20th c. [BBH]
*Stunt swimmer*
* Cavill, Tums

**Cavill, Dick** ?-1938 [BBH]
*Swimmer*
* Cavill, Playboy Dick
* Neptune, Father

**Cavill, Fred** 20th c. [BBH]
*Swimmer*
* [The] Professor

**Cavill, Playboy Dick**
See Cavill, Dick

**Cavill, Tums**
See Cavill, Arthur

**Cawdle, Chloe** 1899- [THR]
*British director*
* Gibson, Chloe

**Cawein, Mary Edith** 1889- [BBD]
*American opera singer*
* Cavan, Marie

**Cawley, Rex**
See Cawley, Warren

**Cawley, Warren** 1940- [TF]
*American track and field athlete*
* Cawley, Rex

**Cawston, Frederick Gordon** 1885-
[LAO]
*British physician and writer*
* Juvenis

**Cawston, Mervyn** 1952- [AES]
*British soccer player*
* [The] Magician

**Cawthorn, James** 1929- [ESF]
*British author, illustrator, critic*
* James, Philip

**Caxton**
See Rhodes, W. H.

**Caxton, Laura**
See Comins, Lizzie B.

**Caxton, Pisistratus**
See Bulwer-Lytton, Edward
George Earle Lytton

**Caxton, Timothy**
See Close, John

**Caxton, William** 1422?-1491
[DEP, DNNS, SN]
*British printer*
* [The] Father of English Printing
* [The] Father of the British Press

**Caylor, O. P.**
See Caylor, Oliver Perry

**Caylor, Oliver Perry** 1849-1897
[BE]
*American baseball manager*
* Caylor, O. P.

**Caynazzo, Jean** ?-1621 [PA]
*Author*
* Tabiensis

**Cayron, C. A. J.** [PA]
*Author*
* Noriac, Jules

**Cazalis, Henry** 1840-1909 [WBD]
*French physician and poet*
* Caselli, Jean
* Lahor, Jean

**Cazauran, Augustus R.** [PA]
*Author*
* Carey, Matthew
* Moray, John S.

**Cazden, Robert E.**
See Cohen, Robert E.

**Cazenave, [or Cacenabe], Pierre**
1863-1916 [GS]
*French bullfighter*
* Robert, Felix

**[The] Cean Poet**
See Simonides

**Cebulash, Mel** 1937-
[CA, IAW, SAT]
*American author*
* Carmendolla, Anthony
* Farrell, Ben
* Harlan, Glen
* Jansen, Jared
* Mara, Jeanette

**Ceccarelli, Arthur Edward** 1930-
[BE]
*American baseball player*
* Ceccarelli, Chic

**Ceccarelli, Chic**
See Ceccarelli, Arthur Edward

**Ceccarelli, Puccio** 20th c. [WF]
*Italian actor*
* Cechar, Chick

**Cecchi, Emilio** 1884-1966 [EWL]
*Italian poet, author, critic*
* [Il] Tarlo

**Cecchi D'Amico, Giovanna** 1914-
[OCF]
*Italian scriptwriter*
* Cecchi D'Amico, Suso

**Cecchi D'Amico, Suso**
See Cecchi D'Amico, Giovanna

**Cecco d'Ascoli**
See Degli Stabili, Francesco

**Ceccon, Silvius Petrus Claudius**
1937- [WEC]
*Brazilian cartoonist*
* Claudius

**Cechar, Chick**
See Ceccarelli, Puccio

**Ceciarelli, Maria Luisa** 1931?-
[BDF, FC, OCF]
*Italian actress*
* Vitti, Monica

**Cecil**
See Apperley, Charles James

**Cecil**
See Hone, William

**Cecil**
See Tongue, Cornelius

**Cecil, Devenant**
See Coleridge, Derwent

**Cecil, Henry**
See   Keller, David H[enry]

**Cecil, Henry**
See   Leon, Henry Cecil

**Cecil, R. H.**
See   Hewitt, Cecil Rolph

**Cecil, Robert [First Earl of Salisbury]**
1563?-1612   [WBD]
*British statesman*
* [The] Crooked Backed Earl

**Cecil, Robert Arthur Talbot [Third Marquis of Salisbury]** 1830-1903
[DEP]
*British statesman*
* [A] Lathe Painted to Look Like Iron

**Cecil, William**
See   Nares, Edward

**Cecil, William [First Baron Burleigh]**
1520-1598   [SN]
*British statesman*
* [The] Eremite of Tibbals
* Eremite, Sir
* [The] Little Beagle
* [The] Weasel

**Cecilio y Villanueva, Juan**
1886-1945   [GS]
*Spanish bullfighter*
* Punteret [Sharpshooter]

**Cecily, [Mother]** 20th c.   [CAT]
*Irish-born author*
* Merrick, M. M.

**Cedarholne, Jan**
See   Jeppson, Janet O.

**Ceder, Georgiana Dorcas** 20th c.
[CA, SAT]
*American author*
* Dor, Ana

**Cedric, Eugene** 1907-   [MY]
*American jazz musician*
* Cedric, Honey Bear

**Cedric, Honey Bear**
See   Cedric, Eugene

**Ceiriog**
See   Hughes, John Ceiriog

**Ceitho, Dewi**
See   Jones, Evan David

**Cela, Camilo Jose** 1916-   [CA]
*Spanish author*
* Don Camilo
* Verdu, Matilde

**Cela y Vileito, Alfonso** 1887-1932
[GS]
*Spanish bullfighter*
* Celita [Little Cela]

**Celan, Paul**
See   Antschel, Paul

**Celeste**
See   Brown, Mrs. George C.

**[The] Celestial Talleyrand**
See   Tseng Chi-tse

**Celestin, Jack**
See   Donohue, John Daniel
Marie-Celestin

**Celestin, Oscar** 1884-1954
[DAM, EJ, WWJ]
*American jazz musician*
* Celestin, Papa
* Celestin, Sonny

**Celestin, Papa**
See   Celestin, Oscar

**Celestin, Sonny**
See   Celestin, Oscar

**Celestine II**
See   Guido

**Celestine III**
See   Bobone, Giacinto

**Celestine IV**
See   Castiglioni, Goffredo

**Celestine V**
See   Di Murrone [or Morone],
Pietro

**Celia**
See   Burleigh, Mrs. C. M.

**Celine, Louis Ferdinand**
See   Destouches, Louis-Ferdinand

**Celita [Little Cela]**
See   Cela y Vileito, Alfonso

**Cellach [or Caillech]** 550?- 645?
[HN, WBD]
*Saint*
* [The] Apostle of the Allemanian Nations
* Gall [or Gallus]

**Cellarius**
See   Keller, Jacob

**Cellarius, Martin** 1499-1564   [PA]
*Author*
* Barrheus

**Cellini, Cal**
See   Sellers, Connie Leslie, Jr.

**[The] Cellini of Printing**
See   Plantin, Christopher

**Celsus, Aulus Cornelius** 1st c.   [HN]
*Roman writer*
* [The] Roman Hippocrates

**[The] Celt**
See   Davis, Thomas

**[The] Celtic Homer**
See   Ossian

**[The] Celtic Leonard Bernstein**
See   Davis, Colin

**Celtis [or Celtes], Conradus**
See   Pickel, Konrad

**Cement Head Malone**
See   Malone, John F.

**Cemetery John**
See   Hauptmann, Bruno Richard

**Cenci, Beatrice** 1577-1599
[DNNF, FF, SN]
*Roman murderer*
* [The] Beautiful Parricide
* [La] Belle Parricide

**Cendrars, Blaise**
See   Sauser-Hall, Frederic

**Cenni di Pepo** 1240?-1302?
[DNNF, DNNS, WBD]
*Italian painter*
* Cimabue, Giovanni
* [The] Father of Modern Painting

**Censor**
See   Bunce, Oliver Bell

**[The] Censor**
See   Cato, Marcus Porcius

**[The] Censor of the Age**
See   Carlyle, Thomas

**[The] Censor of the World**
See   Aretino, Pietro

**Centaur**
See   Sass, Charles

**[El] Centauro Potosino [The Centaur from San Luis Potosi]**
See   Santos Pue, Gaston

**Cente, H. F.**
See   Rocklin, Ross Louis

**[The] Centennial President**
See   Harrison, Benjamin

**Center, Marvin Earl** 1912-   [BE]
*American baseball player*
* Center, Pete

**Center, Pete**
See   Center, Marvin Earl

**Cento**
See   Cobbing, Bob

**Cento**
See   Millington, Philip

**Centobie, Boojie**
See   Centobie, Leonard

**Centobie, Leonard** 1915-   [NOJ]
*American jazz musician*
* Centobie, Boojie

**Centurion**
See   Bower, [Sir] Graham John

**Cepeda, Cha-Cha**
See   Cepeda, Orlando Manuel

**Cepeda, Orlando Manuel** 1937-
[BE, PB]
*Puerto Rican-born baseball player*
* [The] Baby Bull
* Cepeda, Cha-Cha

**Cephas**
See   Simon

**Cepronimus [or Copronymus]**
See   Constantine V [or Constantinus]

**Ceragioli, Peter A.** 1932-   [EJ]
*American jazz musician*
* Jolly, Pete

**Ceram, C. W.**
See   Marek, Kurt W[illi]

**Cerati, Carla**
See   Tironi, Carla

**Cerberus**
See   Dole, Haskell Nathan

**[The] Cerberus of Literature**
See   Johnson, Samuel

**[The] Cerberus of the Muses**
See   Lucian

**Cerchio, Fernando** 1914-   [FDG]
*Italian director*
* Ringoold, Fred

**Cerdan, Marcel** 1922-1949   [RBE]
*Algerian-born boxer*
* [The] Casablanca Clouter

**[The] Ceremonious**
See   Pedro IV [or Peter]

**Ceres**
See   Littlewood, Alan

**Cerioni, Giorgio** 20th c.   [WF]
*Italian actor*
* Greenwood, George

**Cerito, Ada**
See   Brown, Ada

**Cerkez, Vladimir** 1923-   [IAW]
*Yugoslav author and poet*
* Cez

**Cermack, Anton** 20th c.
*American politician*
* Cermack, Pushcart Tony

**Cermack, Pushcart Tony**
See   Cermack, Anton

**Cerminova, Marie** 1902-   [CAR]
*French artist*
* Toyen

**Cernick, Al** 1925-   [FC]
*American singer*
* Mitchell, Guy

**Cerny, Berthe**
See   De Choudens, Berthe

**Cerny, Frederick**
See   Guthrie, Frederick

**Cerone, John Philip** 1914-
*American underworld figure*
* Jackie the Lackey

**Cerquozzi, Michael Angelo**
1600-1660   [DEP, FFF, SN]
*Italian painter*
* [The] Michael Angelo of Battle Scenes

**Cerri, Lawrence J.** 1923-   [CA]
*American author*
* Cortesi, Lawrence

**Ceruti, Giacomo** 18th c.
*Italian painter*
* [Il] Pitocchetto [The Beggar]

**Cerutti, Maria Antonietta** 1932-
[CA]
*Italian educator and author*
* Cerutti, Toni

**Cerutti, Toni**
See   Cerutti, Maria Antonietta

**Cervantes, Jose** 1953-   [RBE]
*Colombian boxer*
* Pambelecito

**Cervantes Saavedra, Miguel de**
1547-1616   [WBD]
*Spanish author*
* [El] Manco de Lapanto

**Cervati, Giovanni** 1898-   [BX, RBE]
*Italian-born boxer*
* Sharkey, Jack
* Sharkey, Little Jackie

**Cervetto**
See   Bassevi, Giacomo

**Cervini, Marcello** 1501-1555
[CAL]
*Pope*
* Marcellus II

**Cervon, Jacqueline**
See   Moussard, Jacqueline

**Cervus, G. I.**
See   Roe, William J[ames]

**Cesar**
See   Baldiccini, Cesar

**Cesari, Giuseppe** [Cavalier d'Arpino] 1568?-1640 [WBD]
*Italian painter*
* [Il] Giuseppino

**Cesarini, Giuliano** 1398-1444 [WBD]
*Italian prelate and diplomat*
* Julian, Cardinal

**Cesarion**
See Ptolemy XV [XIV or XVI]

**Cesena, Sebastian Gayet** 1815- ? [PA]
*Author*
* Rheal

**Cestone, Michael** 1904- [GF]
*American golfer*
* [The] Montclair Mailman

**Cey, Francois Arsene** 1806- ? [PA]
*Author*
* De Cahagne, Chaise

**Cey, Ronald Charles** 1948- [SMG]
*American baseball player*
* [The] Penguin

**Cez**
See Cerkez, Vladimir

**Chabania, Jacinto** 1908-1961? [PMJ, WWJ]
*American jazz musician*
* Blake, Jerry

**Chaber, M. E.**
See Crossen, Ken[dell Foster]

**Chacon, Alfonso** 1510-1599 [PA]
*Author*
* Ciaconicus

**Chad**
See Chadwick, Henry

**Chadband, J. C.**
See Chadband, James Craig

**Chadband, James Craig** [SMG]
*American football player*
* Chadband, J. C.

**Chadbourne, Chester James** 1884-1943 [BE]
*American baseball player*
* Chadbourne, Pop

**Chadbourne, Pop**
See Chadbourne, Chester James

**Chadd, Archie** 1905- [BBH]
*American basketball player and coach*
* Little Napoleon

**Chadler, C. Adolpho**
See Da Costa, Cicero Adolpho Victorio

**Chadwick, A. Burton** [FFF]
*Entertainer*
* Burton, Charles

**Chadwick, Cassie**
See Chadwick, Elizabeth [Bigley]

**Chadwick, Charles** 1874- ? [NAA]
*American author*
* Devlin, Owen
* Life, John
* Steele, Daniel

**Chadwick, Elizabeth** [Bigley] 1857-1907 [B10]
*American swindler*
* Chadwick, Cassie

**Chadwick, Enid M.** 1902- [ART]
*British artist*
* E. M. C.

**Chadwick, Father**
See Chadwick, Henry

**Chadwick, Henry** 1824-1908 [BAB, FFF, PB]
*British-born American sportswriter*
* Chad
* Chadwick, Father
* [The] Father of Baseball
* [The] Father of the Box Score
* Old Chalk

**Chadwick, Lester** [house pseudonym] [Stratemeyer Syndicate]
See Stratemeyer, Edward L.

**Chadwick, Maurice** 20th c. [BBH]
*American basketball player*
* Chadwick, Shang

**Chadwick, Paul** [EMD]
*Author*
* House, Brant

**Chadwick, Shang**
See Chadwick, Maurice

**Chadwick, William L.** [Bill] 1915- [FHE, HK]
*American hockey referee*
* [The] Big Whistle

**Chaff, Gumbo**
See Howe, Elias, Jr.

**Chaffee, Allen**
See Gurney, Antoinette

**Chaffin, Lillie D.** 20th c. [IAW]
*American author*
* Chaffin, Randall
* Day, Lila
* Winston, Lena

**Chaffin, Randall**
See Chaffin, Lillie D.

**Chagall, Marc**
See Segal, Marc

**Chagnon, Leon Wilbur** 1902-1953 [BE]
*American baseball player*
* Chagnon, Shag

**Chagnon, Shag**
See Chagnon, Leon Wilbur

**Chagra, Jamiel** 1943?-
*American gambler*
* Chagra, Jimmy

**Chagra, Jimmy**
See Chagra, Jamiel

**Chaij, Fernando** 1909- [CA]
*Argentinian-born author*
* Alcalde, E. L.

**Chaillie, Jean Humphrey** 1925- [IAW]
*American poet and playwright*
* Sagglehorne, Sadie

**Chailness**
See Mendis, Judith

**Chain, Julian**
See Dikty, Julian Chain May

**[The] Chairman of the Board**
See Ford, Edward Charles

**[The] Chairman of the Board**
See Sinatra, Francis Albert [Frank]

**Chaitanya, Krishna**
See Nair, Krishnapillai Krishnan

**Chajug, Jehuda** 11th c. [WBD]
*Hebrew grammarian*
* [The] Prince of Hebrew Grammarians

**Chaka** 1787-1828 [IBW]
*African Zulu chieftain*
* [The] Zulu Queen

**Chakales, Chick**
See Chakales, Robert Edward

**Chakales, Robert Edward** 1927- [BE]
*American baseball player*
* Chakales, Chick

**Chakrin, Jack** 1923- [ITA]
*American actor*
* Carter, Jack

**Chalcenterus**
See Didymus

**Chalfaut, May**
See Niemeyer, Mrs.

**Chalfont, Peter**
See Sellar, Robert James Batchen

**Chalke, Herbert Davis** 1897- [WD]
*British writer*
* Blacker, Hereth

**Chalkhill, John**
See Walton, Izaak

**Challans, Mary** 1905- [AW, B10, LC]
*British author*
* Renault, Mary

**Challice, Kenneth**
See Hutchin, Kenneth Charles

**Challis, George**
See Faust, Frederick [Schiller]

**Challoner, Dorothy** 1893- [THR]
*American actress*
* Dalton, Dorothy

**Challoner, H. K.**
See Mills, Janet Melanie Ailsa

**Chalmers, Allen**
See Upward, Edward Falaise

**Chalmers, Chick**
See Chalmers, William

**Chalmers, Dut**
See Chalmers, George W.

**Chalmers, Floyd S**[herman] 1898- [CAP]
*American-born writer*
* Duke, John

**Chalmers, George** 1742-1825 [FFF]
*Scottish author*
* Oldys, Francis

**Chalmers, George W.** 1888-1960 [BE]
*Scottish-born baseball player*
* Chalmers, Dut

**Chalmers, Isaac** 20th c. [WWL]
*British author*
* Hale, Forbes

**Chalmers, William** 1934- [CEI]
*Canadian-born hockey player*
* Chalmers, Chick

**Chalom, John**
See Wallace, Henry

**Chalon, Jon**
See Chaloner, John Seymour

**Chaloner, John Seymour** 1924- [AW]
*British author*
* Chalon, Jon

**Chalupec, Apolonia** 1894?- [F1, F2, FC]
*Polish-born actress*
* Negri, Pola

**Cham**
See Noe, Amedee de

**Cham, Aliph**
See Yeldam, Walter S.

**Chamaco** [The Kid]
See Borrero Morano, Antonio

**Chamanan, Kriangsak** 20th c.
*Thai prime minister*
* Sweet Eyes

**Chamault**
See Colin, Pierre Gilbert

**Chamber**
See Chang, Mitchell

**Chamberlain, Dipper**
See Chamberlain, Wilt[on]

**Chamberlain, Elton P.** 1867-1929 [AS, BE]
*American baseball player*
* Chamberlain, Ice Box

**Chamberlain, Erwin Groves** 1915- [CEI, HK]
*Canadian-born hockey player*
* Chamberlain, Murph

**Chamberlain, Ice Box**
See Chamberlain, Elton P.

**Chamberlain, Joseph** 1836-1914 [DNNS]
*British statesman*
* Pushful Joe

**Chamberlain, Mary Booth** 19th c. [FFF]
*American poet*
* Carlton, Carrie

**Chamberlain, Mrs. John** [FFF]
*Entertainer*
* Jordan, Emily

**Chamberlain, Mrs. R. B.** [FFF]
*Entertainer*
* Willey, Abby

**Chamberlain, Murph**
See Chamberlain, Erwin Groves

**Chamberlain, Nathan Henry** [FFF]
*American clergyman and writer*
* [The] Listener
* Shawmut

**Chamberlain, Samuel** 1895-1975 [CAP]
*American author, photographer, artist*
* Beck, Phineas

**Chamberlain, Sidney Joseph**
See Hirsch, Willi

**Chamberlain, Theodore**
See Johnson, Ronald

**Chamberlain, Wilson** [joint pseudonym with Wilson McCarty]
*See* Crandall, Norma

**Chamberlain, Wilson** [joint pseudonym with Norma Crandall]
*See* McCarty, Wilson

**Chamberlain, Wilt[on]** 1936-
[BB, IPA]
*American basketball player*
* Chamberlain, Dipper
* [The] Stilt
* Wilt the Stilt

**Chamberlin, Berlin Guy**
*See* Chamberlin, Guy

**Chamberlin, Guy** 1894-1967 [AS]
*American football player*
* Chamberlin, Berlin Guy

**Chambers, Aidan** 1934- [AW]
*British author*
* Blacklin, Malcolm

**Chambers, Augusta** [PA]
*Author*
* Gussie

**Chambers, Clifford Day** 1922-
[BE]
*American baseball player*
* Chambers, Lefty

**Chambers, Dana**
*See* Leffingwell, Albert

**Chambers, Derek Hyde** 20th c.
[MBF]
*British author*
* Hyde, D. Herbert

**Chambers, E. K.**
*See* Chambers, [Sir] Edmund Kerchever

**Chambers, [Sir] Edmund Kerchever**
1866-1954 [LC]
*British author and educator*
* Chambers, E. K.

**Chambers, Howard V.**
*See* Lowenkopf, Shelly A[lan]

**Chambers, J. D.** 1801- ? [PA]
*Author*
* [A] Layman

**Chambers, James** 1909- [IBW]
*American soccer team organizer and coach*
* Chambers, Ted
* [The] Grand Old Man of Sport

**Chambers, James** 1948- [RO2]
*Jamaican singer and composer*
* Cliff, Jimmy

**Chambers, Jessie Ralph** 1864-1944
[BEW, FC]
*American actress*
* Ralph, Jessie

**Chambers, Lefty**
*See* Chambers, Clifford Day

**Chambers, Linda** 1949- [EJ7]
*American singer*
* Sharrock, Linda

**Chambers, Maria Cristina** 20th c.
[CAT]
*Mexican-born author*
* Mena, Maria Cristina

**Chambers, Peter**
*See* Phillips, Dennis John Andrew

**Chambers, Philip** 1936- [MBF]
*British author*
* Williams, Richard [house pseudonym]

**Chambers, R. W.**
*See* Chambers, Raymond Wilson

**Chambers, R. W.**
*See* Chambers, Robert William

**Chambers, Raymond Wilson**
1874-1942 [LC]
*British author and educator*
* Chambers, R. W.

**Chambers, Robert William**
1865-1933 [LC]
*American author*
* Chambers, R. W.

**Chambers, Stephen A.** 1940- [IBW]
*American composer*
* Hakim, Talib Rasul

**Chambers, Ted**
*See* Chambers, James

**Chambers, Wallace** 1951- [SMG]
*American football player*
* Mr. C

**Chambers, [Sir] William**
1726-1796 [PA]
*Author*
* W. C.

**Chambers, Yodie**
*See* Chambers, Yolande Hargrove

**Chambers, Yolande Hargrove**
1929- [IBW]
*American attorney and business executive*
* Chambers, Yodie

**Chambertin, Ilya** [joint pseudonym with Sylvia Von Block]
*See* Von Block, Bela

**Chambertin, Ilya** [joint pseudonym with Bela Von Block]
*See* Von Block, Sylvia

**Chambliss, John** 20th c. [SFP]
*Author*
* Carter, Nick [house pseudonym]
* Keith, Harrison [joint pseudonym with Philip Clark]

**Chambord, Comte de**
*See* D'Artois, Henri Charles Ferdinand Marie

**Chamier, Captain**
*See* James, William

**Chamisso, Adelbert von**
*See* De Chamisso, Louis Charles Adelaide

**Chamlee, Mario**
*See* Cholmondeley, Archer

**Chamonal, Marie** 1869- ? [THR]
*French actress*
* Megard, Andree

**Champ**
*See* Champney, James Wells

**Champagne, Champ**
*See* Champagne, Giles Maurice Herve

**Champagne, Giles Maurice Herve**
1929- [IWM]
*Canadian composer*
* Champagne, Champ

**[The] Champagne Lady**
*See* Lon, Alice

**Champagne Peter Revson**
*See* Revson, Peter Jeffrey

**Champagne, Philippe de**
1602-1674 [SN]
*Belgian-born painter*
* [The] Painter of Jansenism

**Champagne Tony Lema**
*See* Lema, Anthony David

**Champfleury**
*See* Fleury-Husson [or Husson], Jules

**[The] Champion**
*See* Grace, William Gilbert

**Champion, D. L.** 20th c. [SFP]
*Author*
* D'Arcy, Jack
* Jones, G. Wayman [house pseudonym]
* Wallace, Robert

**Champion, Edme** 1764-1853
[HN, SN]
*French philanthropist*
* [The] Little Blue-Cloak
* [Le] Petit Manteau Bleu

**Champion Jack Dupree**
*See* Dupree, William Thomas

**[The] Champion of the Cross**
*See* Edward I

**Champion of the Virgin**
*See* Cyril

**Champlin**
*See* Mason, George C.

**Champlin, E. R.** [PA]
*Author*
* Gossip, John

**Champlin, Virginia**
*See* Lord, Grace V.

**Champmesle**
*See* Chevillet, Charles

**Champney, James Wells**
1843-1903 [FFF]
*American painter and illustrator*
* Champ

**Champollion, Jean Jacques**
1778-1867 [WBD]
*French archaeologist*
* Champollion-Figeac, Jean Jacques

**Champollion-Figeac, Jean Jacques**
*See* Champollion, Jean Jacques

**Chamson, Andre J[ules] L[ouis]**
1900- [CA]
*French author*
* Lauter

**Chanaidh, Fear**
*See* Campbell, John Lorne

**Chanakya**
*See* Panikkar, K[avalam] Madhava

**Chanan, Ben**
*See* Yaffe, Richard

**Chance, Frank Leroy** 1877-1924
[AS, BE, PB]
*American baseball player and manager*
* Chance, Husk
* [The] Peerless Leader

**Chance, George**
*See* Fleming-Roberts, G. T.

**Chance, Husk**
*See* Chance, Frank Leroy

**Chance, John Newton** 1911-
[CA, ESF, MBF]
*British author*
* Chance, Jonathan
* Drummond, John
* Lymington, John
* Newton, David C.
* Reid, Desmond [house pseudonym]

**Chance, Jonathan**
*See* Chance, John Newton

**Chance, Larry**
*See* Figueiredo, Larry

**Chance, Stephen**
*See* Turner, Philip [William]

**Chancel, Joseph** 1677-1758 [WBD]
*French playwright*
* Lagrange-Chancel, Joseph de

**[Le] Chancelier du Parnasse**
*See* Alembert, Jean Le Rond d'

**[The] Chancellor**
*See* Holmes, Robert D.

**Chancellor, John**
*See* Rideaux, Charles De Balzac

**Chancellor, Richard**
*See* Courtney, Anthony Tosswill

**Chancler, Leon** 1952- [EJ7]
*American jazz musician*
* Ndugu

**Chandler, Albert Benjamin** 1898-
[PB]
*American politician and baseball commissioner*
* Chandler, Happy

**Chandler, Arthur Bertram** 1912-
[AW, CA]
*British-born author*
* Dunstan, Andrew
* Whitley, George

**Chandler, Babe**
*See* Chandler, Donald G.

**Chandler, Bessie**
*See* Parker, Elizabeth [Chandler]

**Chandler, Bryan** 1938- [RO2]
*British musician*
* Chandler, Chas

**Chandler, Chas**
*See* Chandler, Bryan

**Chandler, Donald G.** 1934- [FB]
*American football player*
* Chandler, Babe

**Chandler, Frank**
*See* Harknett, Terry

**Chandler, Gene**
*See* Dixon, Eugene

**Chandler, Happy**
*See* Chandler, Albert Benjamin

**Chandler, Jeff**
*See* Grossel, Ira

**Chandler, Lawrence**
*See* Browne, Howard

**Chandler, Marjorie** 1926?-
[IPA, PMJ]
*Canadian singer*
* Collins, Dorothy

**Chandler, Spud**
*See* Chandler, Spurgeon Ferdinand

**Chandler, Spurgeon Ferdinand**
1909- [B10, BE, PB]
*American baseball player*
* Chandler, Spud

**Chandler, Zachariah** 1813-1879
[SN]
*American politician*
* Honest Old Zach

**Chandos, Dane** [joint pseudonym
with N. Stansbury-Millett, later with
A. Stansfeld]
*See* Lilley, Peter

**Chandos, Dane** [joint pseudonym
with Peter Lilley]
*See* Stansbury-Millett, Nigel

**Chandos, Dane** [joint pseudonym
with Peter Lilley]
*See* Stansfeld, Anthony

**Chandos, Fay**
*See* Swatridge, Irene Maude
[Mossop]

**Chandos, Herbert**
*See* Maitland, T. G. Dowling

**Chandos, John**
*See* McConnell, John Lithgow
Chandos

**Chandra, Bankim**
*See* Chatterji, Bankim Chandra

**Chandravati**
*See* Sur, Atul Krishna

**Chandu the Magician**
*See* Hunter, Clarence

**Chanel, Coco**
*See* Chanel, Gabrielle

**Chanel, Gabrielle** 1882-1971 [B10]
*French fashion designer and
perfumer*
* Chanel, Coco

**Chaney, Alonso** 1886-1930 [BDF]
*American actor*
* Chaney, Lon
* [The] Man of a Thousand Faces

**Chaney, Andy**
*See* Kwasnick, Andrew

**Chaney, Chubby**
*See* Chaney, Norman

**Chaney, Creighton Tull** 1906-1973
[FC]
*American actor*
* Chaney, Lon, Jr.

**Chaney, Darrel Lee** 1948- [SMG]
*American baseball player*
* Chaney, Nort

**Chaney, Frances**
*See* Bush, Frances Cleveland

**Chaney, George** 1893-1958
[AS, BX, RBE]
*American boxer*
* Chaney, K. O. [or Kayo]
* [The] Modern K. O. King

**Chaney, K. O. [or Kayo]**
*See* Chaney, George

**Chaney, Lon**
*See* Chaney, Alonso

**Chaney, Lon, Jr.**
*See* Chaney, Creighton Tull

**Chaney, Norman** 1918-1936 [SC]
*American actor*
* Chaney, Chubby

**Chaney, Nort**
*See* Chaney, Darrel Lee

**Chaney, Wild Willie**
*See* Chaney, Willie

**Chaney, Willie** 20th c. [RBE]
*American boxer*
* Chaney, Wild Willie

**Chanfrau, Mrs. H. T.** [FFF]
*Entertainer*
* Trenchard, Sarah

**Chang Ai-ling** 1920- [WOA]
*Chinese author*
* Chang, Eileen

**Chang Chun**
*See* Ch'iu Ch'u-chi

**Chang Chung-Ch'ang** 1880?-1935?
[BL]
*Chinese warlord*
* Chang, 72 Cannon
* [The] Dog Meat General

**Chang, Eileen**
*See* Chang Ai-ling

**Chang Hsueh-liang** 1898- [WBD]
*Chinese army officer*
* [The] Young Marshal

**Chang, Mitchell** 1880- ? [LAO]
*Chinese publisher*
* Chamber

**Chang, 72 Cannon**
*See* Chang Chung-Ch'ang

**Chang, T. K.**
*See* Fee, Benjamin J.

**Changer, Hugh**
*See* Dyer, Kenneth

**Channel, A. R.**
*See* Catherall, Arthur

**Channel 32**
*See* Fuentes, Rigoberto

**Channell, Dude**
*See* Channell, Lester Clark

**Channell, Lester Clark** 1886-1954
[BE]
*American baseball player*
* Channell, Dude

**Channing, L. T.**
*See* Channing, Leslie Thomas

**Channing, Leslie Thomas** 1916-
[ART]
*British painter and architect*
* Channing, L. T.

**Channing, Stockard**
*See* Stockard, Susan

**Channing, William Ellery**
1780-1842 [FFF, WBD]
*American clergyman*
* [The] Apostle of Unitarianism

**Channing-Renton, Ernest Matthews**
1895- [LAO]
*British army officer and author*
* Bohemian

**Channing-Renton, Ernest Matthews**
(Continued)
* Matthews, Channing

**[El] Chano [The Slow One]**
*See* Chaves, Sebastian

**Chanorrier, Antoine** ?-1570 [PA]
*Author*
* Merauges

**Chanslor, Marjorie Torrey [Hood]**
1899- [MJA, WW]
*American author and illustrator*
* Bevans, Torre
* Torrey, Marjorie

**Chansonetti, Claude**
*See* Cantiuncula, M.

**Chant, Eileen Joyce** 1945- [CA]
*British librarian and writer*
* Chant, Joy

**Chant, Joy**
*See* Chant, Eileen Joyce

**Chantal, Baronne de**
*See* Fremiot, Jeanne Francoise

**Chantal, Sainte**
*See* Fremiot, Jeanne Francoise

**Chantecler**
*See* Garland, A. P.

**Chantier, P.**
*See* Gaida-Gaidamavicius, Pranas

**Chao Fa Maha Vajiravudh**
1881-1925 [WBD]
*King of Siam*
* Rama VI

**Chao Kuang-yin** ?- 976 [WBD]
*Chinese emperor*
* Kao Tsu

**Chao kung, Abbot**
*See* Trebitsch, Isaac

**Chao P'ya Chakri** 18th c. [WBD]
*King of Siam*
* Rama I

**Chapdelaine, Ovila** 1900-1948
[BX, RBE, WBC]
*Canadian boxer*
* Delaney, Bright Eyes
* Delaney, Jack
* [The] Rapier of the North

**Chapelle, Mrs. Charles** [FFF]
*Entertainer*
* Beaumont, Lottie

**Chapin, Alonzo Bowen** [FFF]
*Clergyman and writer*
* Juris Consultus

**Chapin, Katherine G[arrison]**
*See* Biddle, Katherine Garrison
Chapin

**Chapin, Paul**
*See* Farmer, Philip Jose

**Chaplin, Bert Edgar**
*See* Chapman, Bert Edgar

**Chaplin, Chappy**
*See* Chapman, Bert Edgar

**Chaplin, Charles Spencer** 1889-1977
*British-born actor*
* [The] Little Tramp

**Chaplin, James Bailey** 1905-1939
[BE]
*American baseball player*
* Chaplin, Tiny

**[The] Chaplin of the Trapeze**
*See* Rivels, Charles

**Chaplin, Tiny**
*See* Chaplin, James Bailey

**Chapman, Allen** [house pseudonym]
[Stratemeyer Syndicate]
*See* Stratemeyer, Edward L.

**Chapman, [William] Ben[jamin]**
1908- [BN]
*American baseball player*
* Chapman, Blazin' Ben

**Chapman, Bert Edgar** 1893- [BE]
*American baseball player*
* Chaplin, Bert Edgar
* Chaplin, Chappy

**Chapman, Blazin' Ben**
*See* Chapman, [William]
Ben[jamin]

**Chapman, Chappie**
*See* Chapman [William] Fred

**Chapman, D. W.** [PA]
*Author*
* Marlay

**Chapman, Edwin O.** [PA]
*Author*
* Uncle John

**Chapman [William] Fred** 1916-
[BE]
*American baseball player*
* Chapman, Chappie

**Chapman, George**
*See* Klosowski, Severin

**Chapman, George** 1559?-1634
[SN]
*British poet and playwright*
* Chapman, Silver Whiskered

**Chapman, George Warren Vernon**
1925- [CA, WW]
*British-born author*
* Warren, Vernon

**Chapman, Glenn Justice** 1906-
[BE]
*American baseball player*
* Chapman, Pete

**Chapman, J. Dudley** 1928- [CA]
*American physician and writer*
* Dudley, Jay

**Chapman, James [Keith]** 1919-
[CA]
*American historian and author*
* Keith, Hamish

**Chapman, Jay** 1879-1969 [THR]
*British actor*
* Laurier, Jay

**Chapman, John**
*See* Wyman, Walter Forestus

**Chapman, John** 1774-1845 [WBD]
*American pioneer*
* Appleseed, Johnny

**Chapman, John Stanton Higham**
1891- [ANT, TC]
*British-born American author*
* Chapman, Maristan [joint
pseudonym with Mary Hamilton
(Ilsley) Chapman]

**Chapman, Maristan** [joint
pseudonym with Mary Hamilton
(Ilsley) Chapman]
*See* Chapman, John Stanton
Higham

**Chapman, Maristan** [joint
pseudonym with John Stanton
Higham Chapman]
*See* Chapman, Mary Hamilton
[Ilsley]

**Chapman, Mary Hamilton** [Ilsley]
1895- [ANT, NAA, TC]
*American author*
* Chapman, Maristan [joint
pseudonym with John Stanton
Higham Chapman]

**Chapman, Nathaniel** 1780-1853
[FFF]
*American physician and author*
* Falkland

**Chapman, Oscar L.** 1897?-1978
*American politician*
* [The] Gentle Crusader

**Chapman, Pete**
*See* Chapman, Glenn Justice

**Chapman, R. W.**
*See* Chapman, Robert William

**Chapman, Raymond** 1924-
[AW, CA, CC]
*Welsh-born author*
* Nash, Simon

**Chapman, Robert William**
1881-1960 [LC]
*Scottish-born scholar*
* Chapman, R. W.

**Chapman, Silver Whiskered**
*See* Chapman, George

**Chapman, Stepan** 20th c. [CA]
*American author*
* Chapman, Steven

**Chapman, Steven**
*See* Chapman, Stepan

**Chapman, Vera** 1898- [CA]
*British author*
* Took, Belladonna

**Chapman, Walker**
*See* Silverberg, Robert

**Chapman-Huston, D. M.** 1884-
[WWL]
*British author, playwright, poet*
* Mountjoy, Desmond

**Chapman-Mortimer, William Charles**
1907- [CA, IAW, WD]
*Scottish-born author*
* Mortimer, Chapman
* Mortimer, Charles

**Chapnick, Norris**
*See* Ackerman, Forrest J[ames]

**Chappell, George S.** 20th c. [CAA]
*American author*
* Traprock, Walter E.

**Chappell, Jeannette**
*See* Kalt, Jeannette Chappell

**Chappelle, Big Bill**
*See* Chappelle, William Hogan
[Bill]

**Chappelle, William Hogan** [Bill]
1884-1944 [BE]
*American baseball player*
* Chappelle, Big Bill

**Chapuis, Andre** 1884- ? [OCF, SC]
*French actor*
* Cretinetti
* Deed, Andre

**Char, Yum**
*See* Barrett, Dean

**Charan, Sakthi**
*See* Nallaperumal,
Ravanasamudram Subbiah

**Charboneau, Joe** 20th c.
*American baseball player*
* Super Joe

**Charbonneau, Louis** [Henry] 1924-
[CA, ESF, SFL]
*American author*
* Young, Carter Travis

**Charby, Jay**
*See* Ellison, Harlan [Jay]

**Chard, Baldy**
*See* Chard, Howard

**Chard, Howard** [BBH]
*Boxer*
* Chard, Baldy

**Chard, Judy** 1916- [CA]
*British author*
* Gordon, Doreen

**Chardonne, Jacques**
*See* Boutelleau, Jacques

**Chares, Henry**
*See* Harris, Marion Rose [Young]

**Chargin' Charlie Beckwith**
*See* Beckwith, Charles

**Charisse, Cyd**
*See* Finklea, Tula Ellice

**Charity**
*See* Destry, Diane

**Charivaria**
*See* Emanuel, Walter Lewis

**Charlap, Moose**
*See* Charlap, Morris

**Charlap, Morris** 1928-1974
[ASC, BEW, TR]
*American composer*
* Charlap, Moose

**Charlebois, Chuck**
*See* Charlebois, Robert Richard

**Charlebois, Robert Richard** 1944-
[CEI, HR]
*Canadian-born hockey player*
* Charlebois, Chuck

**Charlemagne**
*See* Charles I [or Karl]

**[The] Charlemagne of the East**
*See* Aurungzebe [Aurangzeb or
Aurungzeb]

**Charles**
*See* Drage, Charles Hardinge

**Charles** [or Karl] 689?- 741
[HN, RH, SN]
*Frankish ruler of Austrasia*
* [The] Hammer
* Martel, Charles

**Charles** 1083?-1127 [RH, WBD]
*Count of Flanders*
* [The] Good

**Charles** 1433-1477 [HN, RH, SN]
*Fourth Duke of Burgundy*
* [The] Audacious
* [The] Bold
* [Le] Temeraire

**Charles, Chappy**
*See* Aschenbach, Charles S.

**Charles, David**
*See* Mondey, David [Charles]

**Charles Edward**
*See* Stuart, Charles Edward Louis
Philip Casimir

**Charles, Edwin Douglas** 1935- [BE]
*American baseball player*
* [The] Glider

**Charles, Emily Thornton** [PA]
*Author*
* Hawthorne, Emily

**Charles Emmanuel I** 1562-1630
[DNNS, FFF, SN]
*Duke of Savoy*
* [The] Great

**Charles, Ezzard** 1921-1975
[IBW, WBC]
*American boxer*
* Charles, Snooks
* [The] Quiet Tiger

**Charles, Franklin**
*See* Adams, Cleve F[ranklin]

**Charles, Frederick**
*See* Tomlinson, Frederick Charles

**Charles, Gerda**
*See* Lipson, Gertrude

**Charles, Henry**
*See* Brown, Henry

**Charles, J. C.**
*See* Charles, John C.

**Charles, John C.** 1944- [FB]
*American football player*
* Charles, J. C.

**Charles, Louis**
*See* Stratemeyer, Edward L.

**Charles, Mark**
*See* Bickers, Richard Leslie
Townshend

**Charles, Monsieur**
*See* Chop, Max

**Charles, Neil** [house pseudonym,
Curtis Warren]
*See* Holloway, Brian

**Charles, Neil** [house pseudonym,
Curtis Warren]
*See* Hughes, Den[n]is [Talbot]

**Charles, Neil** [house pseudonym,
Curtis Warren]
*See* Jennison, John W[illiam]

**Charles, Nicholas**
*See* Kuskin, Karla Seidman

**Charles of Bavaria**
*See* Charles VII [or Karl Albrecht]

**Charles of Durazzo**
*See* Charles III

**Charles of Luxembourg**
*See* Charles IV [or Karl]

**Charles, Pamela**
*See* Foster, Pamela

**Charles, Ray**
*See* Robinson, Ray Charles

**Charles, Raymond**
*See* Aschenbach, Charles S.

**Charles, Richard**
*See* Awdry, Richard Charles

**Charles, Riff**
*See* Embree, Charles, Jr.

**Charles, Robert**
*See* Smith, Robert Charles

**Charles, Snooks**
*See* Charles, Ezzard

**Charles, Teddy**
*See* Cohen, Theodore Charles
[Teddy]

**Charles, Theresa** [joint pseudonym
with Irene Maude (Mossop)
Swatridge]
*See* Swatridge, Charles

**Charles, Theresa** [joint pseudonym
with Charles Swatridge]
*See* Swatridge, Irene Maude
[Mossop]

**Charles 37X**
*See* Morris, Charles

**Charles, Will**
*See* Willeford, Charles [Ray, III]

**Charles I** [or Karl] 742- 814
[FFF, HN, WBD]
*King of the Franks and Emperor of
the West*
* Carolus Magnus
* Charlemagne
* [The] Great

**Charles I** 823- 877
[DNNS, FFF, SN]
*King of France and Holy Roman
emperor [as Charles II]*
* [The] Bald
* [Le] Chauve
* [The] Most Christian King

**Charles I** 1600-1649
[HN, RH, SN]
*King of England*
* [The] Ahab of the Nation
* Baby Charles
* [The] Last Man
* [The] Man of Blood
* [The] Martyr King
* [The] Royal Martyr
* [The] White King

**Charles II** 839?- 888
[FFF, RH, SN]
*King of France and Holy Roman
emperor [as Charles III]*
* [The] Fat
* [Le] Gros

**Charles II** 1246-1309 [DNNS, SN]
*King of Naples*
* [The] Cripple of Jerusalem
* [The] Lame

**Charles II** 1332-1387
[FFF, HN, SN]
*King of Navarre*
* [The] Bad
* [The] Navarrais

**Charles II** 1365-1431 [WBD]
*Duke of Lorraine*
* [The] Bold

**Charles II** 1630-1685
[DNNS, RH, SN]
*King of England*
* Bonny Black Boy
* [The] Merry Monarch
* [The] Mutton Eating King
* Old Rowley
* [The] Satyr
* [The] Son of the Last Man

**Charles II** 1661-1700
[DNNF, DNNS, RH]
*King of Spain*
* Strutt, Lord

**Charles II** 1804-1874?   [FFF]
*Duke of Brunswick*
* [The] Diamond Duke

**Charles III** 879- 929
[FFF, RH, SN]
*King of France*
* [The] Simple

**Charles III** 1345-1386   [WBD]
*King of Naples and Hungary [as Charles II]*
* Charles of Durazzo

**Charles III** 1361-1425
[FFF, RH, SN]
*King of Navarre*
* [The] Noble

**Charles III** 1543-1608
[FFF, SN, WBD]
*Duke of Lorraine*
* [The] Great

**Charles III** 1716-1788   [WBD]
*King of Spain*
* [Don] Carlos of Bourbon

**Charles IV** 1294-1328
[DNNS, FFF, SN]
*King of France*
* [Le] Bel
* [The] Fair

**Charles IV [or Karl]** 1316-1378
[DNNS, SN, WBD]
*King of Germany and Holy Roman emperor*
* Charles of Luxemburg
* [The] Parson's Emperor
* [Der] Pfaffen Kaiser
* [The] Pope's Kaiser

**Charles IX** 1550-1574   [RH]
*King of France*
* [The] Glutton

**Charles V** 1337-1380
[DEP, DNNS, FFF]
*King of France*
* [Le] Sage
* [The] Solomon of France
* [The] Wise

**Charles V** 1500-1558
[DEP, HN, SN]
*Holy Roman emperor and King of Spain [as Charles I]*
* [A] Discrowned Glutton
* [The] Harlequin
* [The] Second Charlemagne

**Charles VI** 1368-1422
[FFF, HN, RH]
*King of France*
* [Le] Bien Aime
* [The] Well Beloved

**Charles VII** 1403-1461
[DNNS, HN, SN]
*King of France*
* [Le] Bien Servi [The Well Served]

**Charles VII (Continued)**
* [The] King of Bourges
* [The] King of Kings
* [The] Mark Tapley of Kings
* [Le] Petit Roi de Bourges
* [The] Victorious

**Charles VII [or Karl Albrecht]**
1697-1745   [WBD]
*Holy Roman emperor*
* Charles of Bavaria

**Charles VIII** 1408?-1470   [WBD]
*King of Sweden and Norway*
* Karl Knutsson

**Charles VIII** 1470-1498   [HN, SN]
*King of France*
* [L']Affable
* Flagellum Dei
* [The] King of the Beggars
* [The] Scourge of God

**Charles X** 1622-1660
*King of Sweden*
* [The] Aggressor

**Charles X** 1757-1836   [SN]
*King of France*
* [The] First Gentleman of Europe

**Charles XII** 1682-1718
[DHA, FFF, HN]
*King of Sweden*
* [The] Alexander of the North
* [The] Brilliant Madman
* [The] Madman of the North
* [The] Quixote of the North
* [The] Warlike

**Charles XIV John**
*See* Bernadotte, Jean Baptiste Jules

**Charleston, Charlie**
*See* Charleston, Oscar McKinley

**Charleston, Oscar McKinley**
1896-1954   [MK]
*American baseball player*
* Charleston, Charlie

**Charlie O**
*See* Finley, Charles O.

**Charlier, Jean** 1363-1429
[HN, RH, WBD]
*French theologian*
* Christianissimus, Doctor
* Gerson, Jean de
* Kempis, Thomas a
* [The] Most Christian Doctor

**Charlier, Roger H[enri]** 1921-
[CA, IAW]
*Belgian-born American author and educator*
* Rochard, Henri
* Scott, Marco
* Wallace, Roger

**Charlotte**
*See* Vanhoutte, Marie-Leonie

**Charlotte** 1601-1664   [HN, SN]
*Countess of Derby*
* [The] Warrior Lady of Latham

**Charlotte** 20th c.
*Princess of Monaco*
* [The] Madcap Princess of Monaco

**Charlotte-Elizabeth**
*See* Tonna, Charlotte Elizabeth

**Charlson, David**
*See* Holmes, David Charles

**Charlton, Andrew** 1907?-1975
[B10, OCS]
*Australian swimmer*
* Charlton, Boy

**Charlton, Boy**
*See* Charlton, Andrew

**Charlton, H. B.**
*See* Charlton, Henry Buckley

**Charlton, Henry Buckley**
1890-1961   [LC]
*British author and educator*
* Charlton, H. B.

**Charlton, James**
*See* Hilder, John Chapman

**Charlton, John**
*See* Woodhouse, Martin

**Charlton, Walter** 1619-1707   [FFF]
*British author*
* Carleton

**Charmante Gabrielle**
*See* Estrees, Gabrielle d'

**[The] Charmer**
*See* Zettlein, George

**Charmes, Francis**
*See* Charmes, Marie Julien Joseph Francois

**Charmes, Marie Julien Joseph**
**Francois** 1848-1916   [WBD]
*French journalist*
* Charmes, Francis

**[The] Charming Vocalist**
*See* Oliver, Melvin James

**Charnance, L. P.**
*See* Hannaway, Patricia H[inman] [Patti]

**Charnet, Paul**
*See* De Leoni, Paul

**Charnock, Joan Paget** 1903-
[CAP, WD]
*British author*
* Thomson, Joan

**Charnwood, Godfrey Rathbone**
**Benson** 1864-1945   [TC]
*British author*
* Benson, Godfrey

**Charny, Carmi** 1925-   [CA]
*American-born Israeli poet, editor, translator*
* Carmi, T.

**Charondas**
*See* Le Caron

**Charpentier, Suzanne** 1909-
[F2, FC, WEF]
*French actress*
* Annabella

**Charques, Dorothy [Taylor]**
1899-1976   [CA]
*British author*
* Dorothy, R. D.

**Charriere, Henri** 1907?-1973   [BL]
*French convicted murderer and prison escapee*
* Papillon

**Charriere, Isabelle de** 1740-1805
[WBD]
*Dutch-born author*
* Abbe de La Tour
* Zelide

**[El] Charro [The Horseman]**
*See* Baz, Irineo

**[El] Charro [The Horseman]**
*See* Gomez Lopez, Rliseo

**Chartak, Michael George**
1916-1967   [BE]
*American baseball player*
* Chartak, Shotgun

**Chartak, Shotgun**
*See* Chartak, Michael George

**Charteris, Leslie**
*See* Yin, Leslie Charles Bowyer

**Chartier**
*See* Chartier, Emile-Auguste

**Chartier, Alain** 1386-1458
[HN, SN]
*French author and poet*
* [The] Father of French Eloquence

**Chartier, Emile-Auguste**
1868-1951   [CD, EWL]
*French author, educator, philosopher*
* Alain
* Chartier

**Chartier, Emilio**
*See* Estenssoro, Hugo

**[The] Chartist**
*See* Cooper, Thomas

**[The] Chartist Clergyman**
*See* Kingsley, Charles

**[The] Chartist Parson**
*See* Kingsley, Charles

**Charton, Frank Lane** 1942-   [BE]
*American baseball player*
* Charton, Pete

**Charton, Louis**   [SN]
*French politician*
* [Le] President Je Dis Ca

**Charton, Pete**
*See* Charton, Frank Lane

**Chase, Adam** [joint pseudonym with Milton Lesser]
*See* Fairman, Paul W.

**Chase, Adam** [joint pseudonym with Paul W. Fairman]
*See* Lesser, Milton

**Chase, Adam**
*See* Thomson, James C[utting]

**Chase, Alice**
*See* McHargue, Georgess

**Chase, Anya Seton** 1916-   [LC]
*American author*
* Seton, Anya

**Chase, Beatrice**
*See* Parr, Olive Katharine

**Chase, Borden**
*See* Fowler, Frank

**Chase, Charles [Charley]**
1893-1940   [FIR]
*American actor and director*
* Parrott, Charles
* Parrott, Paul?

**Chase, Chevy**
*See* Chase, Cornelius Crane

Chase, Chris 20th c.
*American actress, singer, author*
* Kane, Irene

Chase, Cleveland B.
*See* Bedford-Jones, Henry [James O'Brien]

Chase, Cornelius Crane 1943-
[B10]
*American actor*
* Chase, Chevy

Chase, Harold Harris [Hal]
1883-1947 [BE, BN, PB]
*American baseball player*
* Chase, Peerless Hal
* Prince Hal

Chase, James [Jimmy] 1892-1939
[FIR]
*American actor and director*
* Parrott, James [Jimmy]

Chase, James Hadley
*See* Raymond, Rene

Chase, Kendall Fay 1913- [BE]
*American baseball player*
* Chase, Lefty

Chase, Lefty
*See* Chase, Kendall Fay

Chase, Mrs. C. W. [FFF]
*Entertainer*
* Bernard, Hattie

Chase, Pauline
*See* Bliss, Pauline

Chase, Peerless Hal
*See* Chase, Harold Harris [Hal]

Chase, Virginia Lowell
*See* Perkins, Virginia Chase

Chaskell
*See* Markell, Charles Frederick

Chassagne, Micheline 1922-
[BDF, FC, ITA]
*French actress*
* Presle, Micheline

Chasse, General
*See* Dixon, Henry Hall

[The] Chaste
*See* Alfonso II [or Alphonso]

[The] Chaste
*See* Boleslav V

Chastlebars, Pierre de Boscaselde
*See* Ireland, William Henry

Chat-Huant
*See* Pigott, E. F. S.

Chatelet, Marquise du
*See* Le Tonnelier de Breteuil, Gabrielle Emilie

Chater, Corporal
*See* Chater, Kerry

Chater, Geoffrey
*See* Robinson, Geoffrey

Chater, Kerry 1945- [RO2]
*Canadian-born musician*
* Chater, Corporal

Chatfield, Caroline
*See* McGeachy, Irving Harding

Chatfield, Edward [FFF]
*Writer*
* Echion

Chatfield, Paul, M.D.
*See* Smith, Horatio

Chatham, Buster
*See* Chatham, Charles L.

Chatham, Charles L. 1901-1975
[BE]
*American baseball player*
* Chatham, Buster

Chatham, Frank
*See* Rochester, George Ernest

Chatham, Larry
*See* Bingley, David Ernest

Chatman, Bo
*See* Chatmon, Armenter

Chatman, John Len 1915- [BWW]
*American singer*
* Chatman, Peter
* Leroy
* Memphis Slim

Chatman, Peter
*See* Chatman, John Len

Chatman, Sam
*See* Chatmon, Sam

Chatmon, Armenter 1893-1964
[BWW]
*American singer*
* Carter, Bo
* Chatman, Bo
* Chatmon, Bo

Chatmon, Bo
*See* Chatmon, Armenter

Chatmon, Sam 1897- [BWW]
*American singer*
* Chatman, Sam

Chatmon, Sam, Jr. 20th c.
[BWW, NBB]
*American musician*
* Chatmon, Singing Sam

Chatmon, Singing Sam
*See* Chatmon, Sam, Jr.

Chatrian, Alexander 1826-1890
[WBD]
*French author*
* Erckmann Chatrian [joint pseudonym with Emile Erckmann]

Chattan, Robert
*See* Smith, Robert

Chatterji, Bankim Chandra
1838-1894 [WBD]
*Indian author*
* Chandra, Bankim

Chatterton, John 1855?-1914
[BEW, FFF]
*British-born actor*
* Perugini, Signor

Chatterton, Thomas 1752-1770
[DEP, DNNF, PA]
*British poet*
* [The] Bristol Boy
* Cauynge, William
* De Bergham, John
* [The] Marvellous Boy
* Rowley, Thomas

Chatto, William Andrew 1805- ?
[FFF, PA]
*British author*
* Fisher, P., Esq.
* Fume, Joseph
* Oliver, Stephen

Chatton, Stacy
*See* Hoisington, May Folwell

Chatton, Sydney 1918-1966 [SC]
*British-born actor*
* [The] Man of One Thousand Voices

Chattoram, Paul 1940?- [CW]
*Guyanese playwright and author*
* Smith, Walter O.

Chaucer, Daniel
*See* Hueffer, Ford Madox

Chaucer, Geoffrey 1340-1400
[DEP, RH, SN]
*British poet*
* [The] Bard of Woodstock
* [The] British Homer
* [The] Father of English Poetry
* [The] Flower of Poets
* [The] Morning Star of Song
* Tityrus
* [The] Well of English Undefiled

[The] Chaucer of Artists
*See* Duerer, Albrecht [or Albert]

[The] Chaucer of France
*See* Marot, Clement

[The] Chaucer of Painting
*See* Duerer, Albrecht [or Albert]

[The] Chaucer of Scotland
*See* Dunbar, William

Chauchoin, Lily 1905-
[BEW, F2, TR]
*French-born actress*
* Colbert, Claudette

Chaudhari, Raghuveer 1938-
[IAW]
*Indian author*
* Lokayat, Suri

Chaulet, George 20th c. [WECO]
*Belgian cartoonist*
* Georges, Francois

Chaulieu, Abbe de
*See* Amfrye, Guillaume

Chauncy, Nan
*See* Chauncy, Nancen Beryl Masterman

Chauncy, Nancen Beryl Masterman
1900-1970 [TCC]
*British author*
* Chauncy, Nan

Chaundler, Christine 1887-1972
[AW, CAP, SAT]
*British author*
* Martin, Peter

Chausable, Archdeacon
*See* Marshall, T. W.

[Le] Chauve
*See* Charles I

Chauvin [or Caulvin?], Jean
1509-1564 [DEP, PA, WBD]
*French theologian and religious reformer*
* [The] Accusative
* Alcium
* Asse, Jack
* Calvin, John
* [The] Democritus of the Sixteenth Century
* [An] Imposter
* [The] Pope of Geneva
* [The] Pope of the Reformation
* [The] Reform Pope

Chaval
*See* Le Louarn, Yvan

Chavalo [Young Lad]
*See* Ciscar, Guillermo

Chavarri, Emperatriz 1927- [BBD]
*Peruvian-born American singer*
* Sumac, Yma

Chavarria, Ossie
*See* Chavarria, Osvaldo Quijano

Chavarria, Osvaldo Quijano 1940-
[BE]
*Panamanian-born baseball player*
* Chavarria, Ossie

Chaverton, Bruce
*See* Cook, Fred Gordon

Chaves, Elias 1895- [GS]
*Peruvian bullfighter*
* Arequipeno [Man from Arequipa]

Chaves, Sebastian ?-1908 [GS]
*Spanish bullfighter*
* [El] Chano [The Slow One]

Chavigny, Theodore 1687-1771
[PA]
*Author*
* Clavignard

Chavis, Boozoo
*See* Chavis, Wilson

Chavis, Wilson 1930- [NBB]
*American singer*
* Chavis, Boozoo

Chayefsky, Paddy
*See* Chayefsky, Sidney

Chayefsky, Sidney 1923-1981
[BEW, IPA, OCF]
*American playwright, producer, director*
* Aaron, Sidney
* Chayefsky, Paddy

Chazel, Prosper
*See* Le Reboullet, A.

Che-Tsou ?-1295? [FFF, RH, SN]
*Emperor of China*
* [The] Wise

[The] Cheapside Knight
*See* Blackmore, [Sir] Richard

Cheatham, Adolphus Anthony
1905- [B10, PMJ, WWJ]
*American jazz musician*
* Cheatham, Doc

Cheatham, Catherine Smiley Bugge
1865?-1946 [BEW]
*American actress*
* Cheatham, Kitty

Cheatham, Doc
*See* Cheatham, Adolphus Anthony

Cheatham, K[aryn] Follis 1943-
[CA]
*American author*
* Long Neck Woman

Cheatham, Kitty
*See* Cheatham, Catherine Smiley Bugge

Cheatle, Cheat
*See* Cheatle, Robert Giles Lenthell

**Cheatle, Robert Giles Lenthell**
1953- [DC]
*British cricketer*
* Cheatle, Cheat

**Checker, Chubby**
See Evans, Ernest

**[The] Chee Chee Girl**
See Murphy, Rose

**Cheech**
See Marin, Richard

**Cheech, Don**
See Scalice, Frank

**[The] Cheeky Chappie**
See Sargent, Thomas Henry

**Cheerful Charles Hickman**
See Hickman, Charles Taylor

**Cheerful, [Mrs.] Mary**
See Northcroft, E. Florence

**Cheerio**
See Field, Charles K.

**Cheesborough, Essie B.** [FFF]
*Author*
* Delmer, Ide
* Hall, Motte
* South, Elma

**Cheeseboro, Warren Robert** 1946-
[EJ7]
*American jazz musician*
* Jamal, Khan

**Cheeseborough, Chandra** 1959-
*American track and field athlete*
* Cheeseborough, Cheese

**Cheeseborough, Cheese**
See Cheeseborough, Chandra

**Cheesman, Patrick** 1926-1970
[FC]
*British actor*
* Wymark, Patrick

**Cheetham, Leonard M.** 1884-1965
[FC]
*British actor*
* Mudie, Leonard

**Cheever, Henry P.** [PA]
*Author*
* Don Carlos
* Slokumb, Si

**Cheever, Henry T.** 1814- ? [PA]
*Author*
* Marble, Major

**Cheevers, Cheesy**
See Cheevers, Gerald Michael

**Cheevers, Gerald Michael** 1940-
[HK]
*Canadian-born hockey player*
* Cheevers, Cheesy

**Cheeves, Chief**
See Cheeves, Virgil Earl

**Cheeves, Virgil Earl** 1901- [BE]
*American baseball player*
* Cheeves, Chief

**Cheirel, Jeanne**
See Leriche, Jeanne

**Cheiro**
See Hamon, [Count] Louis

**Chekhonte, Antosha**
See Chekhov, Anton [Pavlovich]

**Chekhov, Anton [Pavlovich]**
1860-1904 [TLC]
*Russian playwright and author*
* Chekhonte, Antosha
* [A] Man without a Spleen
* My Brother's Brother

**Chelini, Italo Vincent** 1914-1972
[BE]
*American baseball player*
* Chelini, Lefty

**Chelini, Lefty**
See Chelini, Italo Vincent

**Chelsea**
See Nelson, Charles A.

**[The] Chelsea Philosopher**
See Carlyle, Thomas

**Cheltnam, C. Smith** [PA]
*Author*
* Shandon, Captain

**Chelton, John**
See Durst, Paul

**Chelwood, Tufton Victor Hamilton**
1917- [CA]
*British politician and author*
* Beamish, Tufton Victor Hamilton

**Chemnitz, Bogislaw Philipp von**
1605-1678 [WBD]
*German historian*
* Hippolytus a Lapide

**Chen, Aloysius**
See Guarghias, Aloysius George

**Chen, Eugene**
See Chen Yu-jen

**Chen Hwei**
See Stevenson, William

**Chen, Jack**
See Acham, Bernard Ivan Felix

**Chen Jo-hsi**
See Tuann, Lucy H[siu-mei]
C[hen]

**Chen Yu-jen** 1878-1944 [WBD]
*Chinese politician*
* Chen, Eugene

**Chenal, Pierre**
See Cohen, Pierre

**Chenault, Nell**
See Smith, Linell Nash

**Chenel y Albaldejo, Antonio** 1954-
[GS]
*Spanish bullfighter*
* Antonete [Big Antonio]

**Cheney, Peter**
See Southouse-Cheney, Reginald
Evelyn Peter

**Cheng, James K[uo] C[hiang]** 1936-
[CA, WD]
*Chinese-born author and translator*
* Cheng Yi

**Cheng Yi**
See Cheng, James K[uo] C[hiang]

**Chenier, Andre Marie de**
1762-1794 [SN]
*French poet*
* [The] Young Swan

**Chenier, Big**
See Chenier, Morris

**Chenier, Clifton** 1925- [BWW]
*American singer*
* King of the South
* King of the Zydeco

**Chenier, Morris** 1929?- [NBB]
*American singer*
* Chenier, Big

**Chenin, Emile**
See Moselly, Emile

**Chennault, Claire Lee** 1890-1958
[WWW]
*American air force officer*
* Old Leatherface

**Chenneviere, Daniel** 1895-
[BBD, CA]
*French-born American composer,
author, poet*
* Rudhyar, Dane

**Chentres, Federico** 20th c. [WF]
*Italian director*
* Owens, Richard

**Cheo-tsin** [FFF, RH]
*Emperor of China*
* [The] Sardanapalus of China

**Cheque, Pierre** ?-1542 [PA]
*Author*
* Bretagne

**Cher**
See LaPierre, Cherilyn Sakisian

**Cher, Marie**
See Scherr, Marie

**Cherbuliez, Victor** 1829-1899
[WBD]
*Swiss-born author and critic*
* Valbert, G.

**Cherer, Madame T.** [PA]
*Author*
* Hughes, E.

**Chereshkova, Valentina Vladimirovna**
20th c. [CND]
*Russian cosmonaut*
* Sea Gull

**Cheret, Jules**
*French artist*
* [The] Father of the Poster

**Cherith**
See Surtees, Fanny

**Cherkose, Eddie** 1912- [ASC]
*American composer and scriptwriter*
* Maxwell, Eddie

**Chernoff, Dorothy A.**
See Ernst, [Lyman] John

**Cherny, Sasha**
See Glueckberg, Alexander

**Cherock, Clarence Francis** 1915-
[EJ, PMJ, WWJ]
*American jazz musician*
* Sherock, Shorty

**Cherokee Bill**
See Goldsby, Crawford

**[The] Cherokee Cowboy**
See Price, Ray Noble

**[The] Cherokee Kid**
See Rogers, Will[iam Penn Adair]

**Cherokee Sue**
See Graham, Hattie

**[The] Cheronean Sage**
See Plutarch

**Cherrill, Jack**
See Paxton, John

**Cherry, Carolyn Janice** 1942-
[ESF]
*American author*
* Cherryh, C. J.

**Cherry Nose Gioe**
See Gioe, Charles

**Cherryh, C. J.**
See Cherry, Carolyn Janice

**Cherryholmes, Anne**
See Price, Olive

**[The] Cherub**
See Gerard, John

**Cherubini, Maria Luigi Carlo
Zenobio Salvatore** 1760-1842
[DEP, RH]
*Italian composer*
* [The] Italian Mozart

**Cheruit**
See Cheruit, Madeleine

**Cheruit, Madeleine** 20th c. [WFA]
*French fashion designer*
* Cheruit

**Chesbro, Happy Jack**
See Chesbro, John Dwight

**Chesbro, John Dwight** 1874-1931
[AS, DGS, PB]
*American baseball player*
* Chesbro, Happy Jack

**Chesham, Henry**
See Bingley, David Ernest

**Cheshire, Harry V.** 1892-1968
[SC]
*Actor*
* Cheshire, Pappy

**Cheshire, Pappy**
See Cheshire, Harry V.

**Chesimard, Joanne** 1947?-1979
[IBW]
*American political activist*
* Shakur, Assata
* [The] Soul of the Black
Liberation Army

**Chesley, Harry Stephen** 1906-1972
[BE]
*American baseball player*
* Child, Harry Stephen

**Chesley, Mrs. J. G.** [FFF]
*Entertainer*
* Barry, Eleanor

**Chesnan, Nicolas** 1521-1581 [PA]
*Author*
* Querculus

**Chesne-Dauphine, Isabella** 1930-
[IAW]
*Italian author*
* Stewart, Isabella

**Chesney, Esther**
See Durgan, Clara V.

**Chesney, Weatherby**
See Hyne, Charles John Cutcliffe
Wright

**Chess, Stanley** 1947?- [B10]
*American columnist*
* Marshall, Chester Alan

**Chessel**
See Caselius, Johann

**Chesser, Eustace** 1902-1973 [CA]
*Scottish-born author and psychologist*
* Hilton, Alec [joint pseudonym with Alexander Fullerton]

**Chesser, Omer Lee** 1922- [CWG]
*American country-western performer*
* Chesser, Shorty

**Chesser, Shorty**
See Chesser, Omer Lee

**Chessman, Caryl** 1921-1960
[BLB, CEC]
*American robber and rapist*
* [The] Red Light Bandit

**Chester**
See Broome, William

**Chester**
See Gorshkov, Captain

**Chester, Betty**
See Grundtvig, Betty

**Chester, Earl of**
See Hugh d'Avranches

**Chester, Elizabeth S.**
See Smith, Elizabeth A.

**Chester, Gilbert**
See Gibbons, Harry Hornaby Clifford

**Chester, John**
See Mitchell, John

**Chester, Joseph Lemuel** 1821- ?
[PA]
*Author*
* Cramer, Julian

**Chester, Lord**
See Teed, Cyrus Reed

**Chester, Peter**
See Phillips, Dennis John Andrew

**Chester, Rollin**
See Chester, Thomas Morris

**Chester, Thomas Morris**
1834-1892 [IBW]
*Editor, publisher, barrister*
* Chester, Rollin

**Chesterfield, Earl of**
See Stanhope, Philip

**Chesterfield, Fourth Earl of**
See Stanhope, Philip Dormer

**Chesterman, Jean** 1920- [WD]
*British poet and drama critic*
* Kenward, Jean

**Chesterton, Ada Elizabeth Jones**
1870-1962 [LC]
*British writer*
* Jones, Sheridan

**Chesterton, G. K.**
See Chesterton, Gilbert Keith

**Chesterton, Gilbert Keith**
1874-1936 [LAO, LC, WWS]
*British author*
* Chesterton, G. K.
* G. K. C.

**[The] Chesterton of Ceylon**
See De Fonseka, Joseph Peter

**Chestnut, Robert**
See Cooper, Clarence L., Jr.

**Chestnutt, Edgar B.** 1906- [NAA]
*American writer*
* Scott, Walter

**Chestor, Rui**
See Courtier, Sidney Hobson

**Chesty Joie Ray**
See Ray, Joie

**Chet, [Father]**
See Ball, Charles Chester Everett

**Chetham-Strode, Warren** 1896-
[CAP]
*British author*
* Hamilton, Michael

**Chetwyn, Robert**
See Suckling, Robert

**Chetwynd, Berry**
See Rayner, Claire

**Chetwynd-Hayes, Ronald Henry Glynn** 1919- [CA]
*British author*
* Campbell, Angus

**Chevaillier, Faith** 20th c. [NAA]
*American writer and welfare worker*
* Knight, Faith

**[Le] Chevalier**
See Breydel, Charles

**Chevalier**
See Hart, M. C.

**[Le] Chevalier**
See Le Clerc, Jean

**Chevalier, Albert Onesime Britannicus Gwathveoyd Louis**
1862-1923 [BMH]
*British comedian*
* [The] Coster Laureate
* [The] Kipling of the Halls
* Knight, Albert

**Chevalier, August** 1863?-1940
[BEW]
*British composer*
* Ingle, Charles

**[The] Chevalier Bayard of Our History**
See Sidney, [Sir] Philip

**[The] Chevalier de St. George**
See Stuart, James Francis Edward

**[Le] Chevalier d'Eon**
See Eon de Beaumont, Charles Genevieve Louis Auguste Andre Timothee d'

**[Le] Chevalier Sans Peur et Sans Reproche**
See Terrail, Pierre du

**Chevalier sans Reproche**
See Barbazan, Arnaud Guillaume [or Arnauld Guilhelm]

**Chevalier sans Reproche**
See Tremoille, [Vicomte] de Thouars [Prince de Talmont]

**Chevalier, Sulpice Guillaume**
1804-1866 [RH, SN, WBD]
*French illustrator and caricaturist*
* Gavarni

**[El] Chevaliere del Cairo**
See Cairo, Francesco

**Cheves, Langdon** 1776-1857
[PA, WBD]
*American banker*
* [The] Hercules of the United States Bank
* Say

**Chevigny, Hector**
See De La Chevrotiere, Hector Chevigny

**Chevillet, Charles** 1645-1701
[WBD]
*French comedian and playwright*
* Champmesle

**Cheviot**
See Parker, Eric

**Chew, Ruth** 1920- [CA, SAT]
*American author and illustrator*
* Silver, Ruth

**Chew Tobacco Ryan**
See Ryan, Frank

**Chewing Gum O'Brien**
See O'Brien, John J.

**Cheyne, [Sir] Joseph Lister Watson**
1914- [AW]
*British author and diplomat*
* Munroe, R.

**Cheyney, Peter**
See Cheyney, Reginald Southouse

**Cheyney, Reginald Southouse**
?-1951 [MBF]
*British author*
* Cheyney, Peter

**Chi, Richard Hu See-Yee** 1918-
[CA]
*Chinese-born educator and author*
* Chuan Chin
* Moncrieff, Ernest

**Chi-wei**
See Shu, Austin Chi-wei

**Chiabrera, Gabriello** 1552-1637
[DNNS, FFF, SN]
*Italian poet*
* [The] Italian Pindar
* [The] Pindar of Italy

**Chiang Chung-cheng** 1887-
*Taiwanese president*
* Chiang Kai-shek

**Chiang Kai-shek**
See Chiang Chung-cheng

**Chiang Kai-shek, Madame**
See Soong, Mei-ling [or Mayling]

**Chiang Yee** 1903- [LC, TC1]
*Chinese artist and author*
* Silent Traveller
* Yahsin-che [Dumb Walking Man]

**Chiaramonti, Luigi Barnaba**
1742-1823 [WBD]
*Pope*
* Pius VII

**Chiari, Walter**
See Annichiarico, Walter

**Chiariglione, Andrew** 1879-1935
[BX, RBE, SG]
*American boxer*
* Flynn, Fireman Jim
* Flynn, Jim
* Haymes, Andrew

**Chibnall, Marjorie [McCallum]**
1915- [CA, WD]
*British historian*
* Morgan, Marjorie

**Chicago Bill**
See Broonzy, William Lee Conley

**Chicago Bob Nelson**
See Nelson, Bob

**[The] Chicago Carpet King**
See Woods, Lawrence J.

**Chicago Cyclone**
See Hegamin, Lucille

**Chicago, Judy**
See Cohen, Judy

**Chicago May**
See Churchill, Beatrice [Desmond]

**Chicago Red**
See Sanford, John Elroy

**[The] Chicago Spider**
See Coulon, Johnny

**Chicago Sunny Boy**
See Hill, Lester

**Chicago's Kojak**
See DiLeonardi, Joseph

**Chichester, F. R.** [PA]
*Author*
* B.

**Chichester, George Forrest, Jr.**
1915- [BEW, EMT]
*American composer and lyricist*
* Forrest, Chet
* Forrest, George

**Chichester, Jane**
See Longrigg, Jane Chichester

**[The] Chicken**
See Taylor, Michael Angelo

**[El] Chico [The Little]**
See Abu Abdallah [or Abdullah]

**[El] Chico de la Blusa [The Boy of the Blouse]**
See Pastor y Duran, Vicente

**Chico the Cat**
See Hamilton, Foreststorn

**Chicorro [Husky Young Man]**
See Lara, Jose

**Chicot** 1553-1591 [HN]
*French court jester*
* King Henri's King

**[The] Chicoutimi Cucumber**
See Vezina, Georges

**Chicuelin [Youngster]**
See Jimenez Gonzalez, Manuel

**Chicuelo [Young Man]**
See Jimenez Vera, Manuel

**[The] Chief**
See Armstrong, George Edward

**[The] Chief**
See Bender, Charles Albert

**[The] Chief**
See Hoover, Herbert Clark

**[The] Chief**
See King, Wayne

**[The] Chief**
See Leach, Reginald Joseph

**[The] Chief**
*See* Litwack, Harry

**[The] Chief**
*See* Neilson, James Anthony

**Chief of Chiefs**
*See* Banda, Hastings Kamuzu

**Chief Wahoo**
*See* McDaniel, Ed

**Chiesa, Giacomo della** 1854-1922
[CBS, WBD]
*Pope*
* Benedict XV

**Chigi, Fabio** 1599-1667 [WBD]
*Pope*
* Alexander VII

**Chignon, Niles**
*See* Lingeman, Richard R[oberts]

**Chikamatsu Monzaemon**
1653-1724? [WBD]
*Japanese playwright*
* [The] Shakespeare of Japan

**[The] Child**
*See* Arnim, Bettina Brentano von

**[The] Child**
*See* Henry I

**[The] Child**
*See* Louis III [or Ludwig]

**[The] Child**
*See* Otto

**[The] Child Athlete**
*See* Purtell, William Patrick [Billy]

**Child, Charles B.**
*See* Frost, C. Vernon

**Child, H. H.**
*See* Child, Harold Hannyngton

**Child, Harold Hannyngton**
1869-1945 [LC]
*British journalist, critic, librettist*
* Child, H. H.

**Child, Harry Stephen**
*See* Chesley, Harry Stephen

**Child, Herbert** 20th c. [WWL]
*British author*
* More, Atherton

**[The] Child of Fancy**
*See* Spenser, Edmund

**[The] Child of Fortune**
*See* Massena, Andre

**[The] Child of Hale**
*See* Middleton, John

**[The] Child of Nature**
*See* Goldsmith, Oliver

**[The] Child of the Ausonian Muse**
*See* Spenser, Edmund

**Childe Harold**
*See* Field, Edward Salisbury, Jr.

**Childe Harold Janvrin**
*See* Janvrin, Harold Chandler

**Childers, Buddy**
*See* Childers, Marion

**Childers, Marion** 1926- [DAM, EJ]
*American jazz musician*
* Childers, Buddy

**Childre, Lew** 1901-1961
[CM, ECM]
*American entertainer*
* [The] Boy from Alabam
* Doctor Lew

**[The] Children's Bishop**
*See* Healy, James Augustine

**[The] Children's Friend**
*See* Berquin, Arnaud

**[The] Children's Gibson**
*See* Birch, Reginald Bathurst

**Childress, Edmund Howard** 1873-
? [NAA]
*American editor and publisher*
* Frastick, Perry

**Childs, C. Sand**
*See* Childs, Maryanna

**Childs, Clarence Algernon**
1868-1912 [AS, BE, DGS]
*American baseball player*
* Childs, Cupid

**Childs, Cupid**
*See* Childs, Clarence Algernon

**Childs, Edmund Burton** 1887-
[MBF, SFL, WGT]
*Irish-born author*
* Aynsworth, Cecil
* Blake, Royston
* Burton, Edmund

**Childs, Maryanna** 1910- [CA]
*American author and poet*
* Childs, C. Sand
* Maryanna, [Sister]

**Childs, Monroe**
*See* Rothschild, J. Monroe

**Chiles, Lawton** 20th c.
*American politician*
* Chiles, Walkin' Lawton

**Chiles, Pearce Nuget** 1867- ? [BE]
*American baseball player*
* What's the Use

**Chiles, Walkin' Lawton**
*See* Chiles, Lawton

**Chimaera**
*See* Farjeon, Eleanor

**[The] Chin**
*See* Gigante, Vincent

**Chin, Frank [Chew, Jr.]** 1940- [CA]
*American author*
* De Menton, Francisco

**Chin-tsou-jin** 1653?-1722?
[HN, RH]
*Chinese emperor*
* [The] Father and Mother of His
  People
* Kang he [or hi]
* [The] Saint

**China**
*See* Mendoza Romero, Maria
Luisa

**[The] China Clipper**
*See* Kwong, Normie

**[The] China Wall**
*See* Bower, John William

**Chincapin**
*See* Barber, W. R.

**[The] Chinese Caesar**
*See* Kao hoang-ti

**[The] Chinese Philosopher**
*See* Goldsmith, Oliver

**Chinese Tommy West**
*See* West, Thomas

**Chinito**
*See* Diaz, Hector

**Chinko the Boy Juggler**
*See* Knox, Teddy

**Chinks**
*See* Stedman, Charles Ellery

**Chinmoy, Sri**
*See* Ghose, Sri Chinmoy Kumar

**Chinualumogu, Albert** 1930-
[WOA]
*Nigerian author*
* Achebe, Chinua

**Chinwell, Walter**
*See* Ackerman, Forrest J[ames]

**Chionoi, Chartchai** 1942-
[BX, RBE]
*Thai boxer*
* Chionoi, Laemfapha

**Chionoi, Laemfapha**
*See* Chionoi, Chartchai

**Chiozza, Dino Joseph** 1914-1972
[BE]
*American baseball player*
* Chiozza, Dynamo

**Chiozza, Dynamo**
*See* Chiozza, Dino Joseph

**Chip**
*See* Bellew, Frank P. W.

**Chip, George**
*See* Chipulonis, George

**Chipman, Robert Howard**
1918-1973 [BE]
*American baseball player*
* Chips, Mr.

**Chipperfield, Joseph E[ugene]**
1912- [AW, CA, SAT]
*British author*
* Craig, John Eland

**Chipperfield, Robert Orr**
*See* Ostrander, Isabel [Egenton]

**Chipple, Walt[er John]**
*See* Chlipala, Walter John

**Chips, Mr.**
*See* Chipman, Robert Howard

**Chipulonis, George** 1888-1960
[BX, RBE]
*American boxer*
* Chip, George

**Chiquita**
*See* Castlen, Eppie Bowden

**Chiquito de Begona [Little Fellow
from Begona]**
*See* San Vicente y Navarro, Rufino

**Chiquito de Cambo**
*See* Apesteguy, Joseph

**Chiquito de la Audiencia**
*See* Martin Caro Cases, Juan

**Chiquito D'Eibar [Little Fellow from
Eibar]**
*See* Sarasqueta, Indalecio

**Chiranjib**
*See* Biswas, Chittaranjan

**Chirello, George** 1897-1968 [SC]
*American actor*
* Chirello, Shorty

**Chirello, Shorty**
*See* Chirello, George

**Chirgwin, George H.** 1854-1922
[BMH, THR]
*British comedian*
* [The] White Eyed Kaffir
* [The] White Eyed Musical Moke

**Chisholm, Alexander** 1915- [CEI]
*Canadian-born hockey player*
* Chisholm, Lex

**Chisholm, Lex**
*See* Chisholm, Alexander

**Chisholm, Lilian Mary** 1906- [AW]
*British author*
* Lorraine, Anne

**Chisholm, Matt**
*See* Watts, Peter Christopher

**Chisholm, Walter** [FFF]
*Author*
* Wattie

**Chism, Elijah** 1916- [MK]
*American baseball player*
* Chism, Little Chis

**Chism, Little Chis**
*See* Chism, Elijah

**Chisom, Sarah**
*See* Filer, Thomas Hanford

**Chissell, Kid**
*See* Chissell, Noble

**Chissell, Noble** 1910- [ITA]
*American actor*
* Chissell, Kid

**Chittenden, L. E.** [PA]
*Author*
* Adirondack

**Chitty, Edward** 1807?-1863 [FFF]
*British legal reporter*
* South, Theophilus

**Chitty, [Sir] Thomas Willes** 1926-
[B10, CA, WD]
*British author*
* Hinde, Thomas

**Ch'iu Ch'u-chi** 1148-1227 [WBD]
*Chinese Taoist monk and traveler*
* Chang Chun

**[The] Chivalrous Madman**
*See* James IV

**Chivers, Amos**
*See* Chivers, Howard

**Chivers, Howard** 20th c. [BBH]
*American skier*
* Chivers, Amos

**Chivers, Warren** 20th c. [BBH]
*American skier*
* Chivers, Winger

**Chivers, Winger**
*See* Chivers, Warren

**Chlamyda, Jehudiil**
*See* Peshkov [or Pyeshkoff], Alexei
Maximovich

**Chlipala, Walter John** 1918- [BE]
*American baseball player*
* Chipple, Walt[er John]

**Chlorus** [The Pale]
See Constantius I [Flavius Valerius Constantius]

**Cho Densu**
See Mincho

**Cho, Shinta**
See Suzuki, Shuji

**Choate, Gwen Peterson** 1922- [CA]
*American author*
* Choate, R. G.

**Choate, Lowell**
See Hopkins, Alice K[imball]

**Choate, R. G.**
See Choate, Gwen Peterson

**Choate, T. E.** 20th c. [GW]
*American rodeo performer*
* Choate, Tuck

**Choate, Tuck**
See Choate, T. E.

**Chobil**
See Leito, Arturo

**Chochlik**
See Radwanski, Pierre A[rthur]

**[The] Chocolate Chip Cookie King**
See Amos, Wally

**[The] Chocolate Coloured Coon**
See Elliott, George Henry

**Chocolate, Kid**
See Dorsey, Lee

**Chocolate, Kid**
See Henry, Travis

**Chocolate, Kid**
See Sardinias, Eligio

**Chocolate Thunder**
See Dawkins, Darryl

**Chodziesner, Gertrud** 1894- [EWL]
*German poet*
* Kolmar, Gertrud

**[The] Choir Boy**
See Viana, Nicholas

**Choiseul, [Duc] Etienne Francois de**
1719-1785 [DNNF, RH, SN]
*French statesman*
* [Le] Cocher de l'Europe
* [The] Driver of Europe

**Chokin' Kind**
See Simon, Joe

**[A] Choleric Herault**
See Brooke, Ralph

**Chollet**
See Furniss, Louise E.

**Cholly Mac McClendon**
See McClendon, Charles Y.

**Cholmondeley, Alice**
See Beauchamp, Mary Annette

**Cholmondeley, Archer** 1892- [BBD]
*American opera singer*
* Chamlee, Mario

**Cholmondeley, Mary** 1859-1925
[LC, RH, WBD]
*British author*
* [The] Bold Lady of Cheshire
* Pax

**Cholo**
See Duran, Roberto

**Cholodenko, Toby** 1916- [BEW]
*American talent and literary representative*
* Cole, Toby

**Chomette, Rene** 1898-
[BDF, FC, FD]
*French director*
* Clair, Rene

**Chomyszak, Chomy**
See Chomyszak, Steve

**Chomyszak, Steve** 1944- [SMG]
*American football player*
* Chomyszak, Chomy

**Chong**
See Chong, Thomas

**Chong, Kyong-Jo**
See Chung, Kyung Cho

**Chong, Thomas** 1940- [RO2]
*Canadian-born entertainer*
* Chong

**[EL] Choni**
See Marco Gomez, Jaime

**Choo, Tiger**
See Choo Young Bok

**Choo Young Bok** 20th c.
*South Korean politician*
* Choo, Tiger

**Choong, David**
See Choong Ewe Leong

**Choong, Eddy**
See Choong Ewe Beng

**Choong Ewe Beng** 1930- [OCS]
*Malayan badminton player*
* Choong, Eddy

**Choong Ewe Leong** 20th c. [OCS]
*Malayan badminton player*
* Choong, David

**Chop, Max** 1862-1929 [BBD]
*German writer and editor*
* Charles, Monsieur

**Chorao, Ann McKay Sproat** 1937-
[FBJ, ICB]
*American author and illustrator*
* Chorao, Kay

**Chorao, Kay**
See Chorao, Ann McKay Sproat

**Choricius** 6th c. [WBD]
*Greek sophist and rhetorician*
* Choricius of Gaza

**Choricius of Gaza**
See Choricius

**Choromokos, Robert** 1938- [TR]
*American actor and director*
* Drivas, Robert

**Chou Ch'o**
See Chou Shu-jen

**Chou, Eric** 1915- [IAW]
*Chinese-born journalist and author*
* Sung Chiao

**Chou Kung** [WBD]
*Chinese author and statesman*
* [The] Duke of Chou

**Chou Shu-jen** 1881-1936
[TLC, WOA]
*Chinese author, critic, translator*
* Chou Ch'o
* Lu Hsun

**[Le] Chouan** [The Owl]
See Cottereau, Jean

**Chouneau, Chief**
See Cadreau, William

**Chouneau, William**
See Cadreau, William

**Chowdhury, Bhaskar Roy** 1930-
[BEW]
*Indian actor, dancer, singer*
* Bhaskar

**Choynski, Chrysanthemum Joe**
See Choynski, Joe

**Choynski, Joe** 1886- [EJS]
*American boxer*
* Choynski, Chrysanthemum Joe

**Chrisley, Barbra O'Neil** 1931- [BE]
*American baseball player*
* Chrisley, Neil

**Chrisley, Neil**
See Chrisley, Barbra O'Neil

**Chrissie, Mrs. Edward** [FFF]
*Entertainer*
* Pease, Lillie

**Christ, Robert Balthasar** 1904-
[IAW]
*Swiss author and journalist*
* Brandmuller, Johannes
* Fridolin
* Glopfhaischt

**Christ, Ronald John** 1936- [IAW]
*American author*
* Patrick, John

**Christenbury, Lloyd Reid**
1893-1944 [BE]
*American baseball player*
* Christenbury, Low

**Christenbury, Low**
See Christenbury, Lloyd Reid

**Christensen, Chris**
See Christensen, George W.

**Christensen, Cuckoo**
See Christensen, Walter Neils

**Christensen, George W.** 1909-1968
[AS]
*American football player*
* Christensen, Chris

**Christensen, Jo Ippolito**
See Christensen, Yolanda Maria Ippolito

**Christensen, Seacap**
See Christensen, Walter Neils

**Christensen, Walter Neils** 1899-
*American baseball player*
* Christensen, Cuckoo
* Christensen, Seacap

**Christensen, Yolanda Maria Ippolito**
1943- [CA]
*American author and educator*
* Christensen, Jo Ippolito

**Christian, A. B.**
See Yabes, Leopoldo Y[abes]

**Christian, Al**
See Christiani, Aldo

**[The] Christian Atticus**
See Heber, Reginald

**Christian, Buddy**
See Christian, Narcisse J.

**[The] Christian Cicero**
See Lactantius, Lucius Coelius

**Christian, Frederick**
See Gehman, Richard Boyd

**[The] Christian General**
See Feng Yu-hsiang

**Christian, George**
See Grove, Helen Harriet

**Christian Jaque**
See Maudet, Christian

**Christian, Jill**
See Dilcock, Noreen

**Christian, John**
See Dixon, Roger

**Christian, Kit** [joint pseudonym with Sara Winfree Thorson]
See Thorson, Delos Russell

**Christian, Kit** [joint pseudonym with Delos Russell Thorson]
See Thorson, Sara Winfree

**Christian, Lester** 20th c. [RO2]
*American singer and songwriter*
* Dyke

**Christian, Linda**
See Welter, Blanca Rosa

**Christian, Louise**
See Grill, Nannette L.

**Christian, Narcisse J.**
1895?-1958? [WWJ]
*American jazz musician*
* Christian, Buddy

**Christian of Brunswick** 1599-1626
[WBD]
*German army officer*
* [The] Madman of Halberstadt

**Christian, Paul**
See Hubschmid, Paul

**Christian, Peter**
See Steinbrunner, Peter Christian

**[The] Christian Philosopher**
See Dick, Thomas

**[The] Christian Seneca**
See Hall, Joseph

**[The] Christian Virgil**
See Sannazaro, Jacopo [or Giacomo]

**[The] Christian Virgil**
See Vida, Marco Girolamo

**Christian II** 1480?-1559
[DEP, FFF, WBD]
*King of Denmark, Norway, and Sweden*
* [The] Cruel
* [The] Nero of the North

**Christian III** 1502?-1559
[DNNS, FFF, SN]
*King of Denmark and Norway*
* [The] Father of the People

**Christiani, Aldo** 20th c. [WF]
*Italian author*
* Christian, Al

**Christianissimus, Doctor**
See Charlier, Jean

**Christianissimus, Doctor**
See De Cusa, Nicholas

**Christianissimus Rex**
See   Louis XI

**Christians, Mady**
See   Christians, Margarethe Marie

**Christians, Margarethe Marie**
1900-1951   [BEW, FC]
*Austrian-born actress*
* Christians, Mady

**Christiansen, Chris**
See   Christiansen, Jack L.

**Christiansen, Jack L.** 1928-   [FB]
*American football player*
* Christiansen, Chris

**Christiansen, Ticho Parly Frederik**
1928-   [OP]
*Danish-born opera singer*
* Parly, Ticho

**Christiansen, Williard** 20th c.
[BLB]
*American robber*
* Warner, Matt

**Christianus Demokritus**
See   Dippel, Johann Konrad

**Christie, Agatha [Mary Clarissa]**
1890?-1976   [CA, EMD, MBF]
*British author and playwright*
* Mallowan, A[gatha] C[hristie]
* [The] Queen of Crime
* [The] Queen of Thriller Writers
* Westmacott, Mary

**Christie, Agnes Stevenson** 1948-
[OP]
*Scottish opera singer*
* Christie, Nan

**Christie, Ann Philippa Pearce**
1920-   [CA, TBJ, WD]
*British author*
* Pearce, A[nn] Philippa

**Christie, Bob** 20th c.
*Auto racer*
* [The] Caveman

**Christie, Donna**
See   Micheli, Ornella

**Christie, Douglas** 1894-   [WW]
*Author*
* Campbell, Colin
* Durie, Lynn

**Christie, Ernest** 20th c.   [WWL]
*British author*
* Clay, Weald

**Christie, Hugh**
See   Christie-Murray, David [Hugh
Arthur]

**Christie, Keith**
See   Haynes, Alfred H[enry]

**Christie, Lou**
See   Sacco, Lugee

**Christie, Lyn**
See   Christie, Lyndon Van

**Christie, Lyndon Van** 1928-
[EJ7, IWM]
*Australian-born jazz musician*
* Christie, Lyn

**Christie, Nan**
See   Christie, Agnes Stevenson

**Christie, Stephen**
See   Kuruppu, D. S. C.

**Christie, William H.** 20th c.   [SFP]
*Author*
* White, Cecil B.

**Christie-Murray, David [Hugh
Arthur]** 1913-   [CA]
*British author*
* Arthur, Hugh
* Christie, Hugh

**Christina** 1626-1689
[DHA, HN, SN]
*Queen of Sweden*
* [The] Heavenly Heroine
* [The] Miracle of Nature
* [The] Snow Queen
* [The] Swedish Amazon
* [The] Tenth Muse

**Christman, Mark**
See   Christman, Marquette Joseph

**Christman, Marquette Joseph**
1913-   [BE]
*American baseball player*
* Christman, Mark

**Christman, Paul C.** 1918-1970
[FB]
*American football player*
* Christman, Pitchin' Paul
* [The] Merry Magician

**Christman, Pitchin' Paul**
See   Christman, Paul C.

**Christmas**
See   Fearn, Henry Noel

**Christo**
See   Javacheff, Christo

**Christoforidis, Anton** 1918-   [WBC]
*Greek-born American boxer*
* [The] Golden Greek

**Christophe**
See   Colomb, Georges

**Christopher, Ann** 1947-   [ART]
*British sculptor*
* A. C.

**Christopher, Daddy**
See   Christopher, Russ[ell Ormand]

**Christopher, Feather**
See   Christopher, Russ[ell Ormand]

**Christopher, John**
See   Youd, Christopher Samuel

**Christopher, Louise**
See   Hale, Arlene

**Christopher, Matt[hew F.]** 1917-
[SAT, WD]
*American author*
* Martin, Fredric

**Christopher of Bavaria**
See   Christopher III

**Christopher Royston, George Ellis**
1941-   [DLE]
*British poet*
* Ellis, Royston

**Christopher, Russ[ell Ormand]**
1917-1954   [BN]
*American baseball player*
* Christopher, Daddy
* Christopher, Feather

**Christopher, [Dr.] T. Hudson**
See   Elmer, Robert P.

**Christopher III** 1418-1448
[DEP, DNNF, WBD]
*King of Denmark, Sweden, and
Norway*
* Christopher of Bavaria
* [The] King of Bark

**Christy, Ann**
See   Cronin, Gladys

**Christy, June**
See   Luster, Shirley

**Chrobry [The Mighty]**
See   Boleslav I [or Boleslas]

**[The] Chronicler of Canada**
See   Birney, [Alfred] Earle

**[The] Chronicler of the Indies**
See   Davila y Padilla, Agustin

**Chroniquense**
See   Logan, Olive

**Chrononhotonthologos**
See   Burgoyne, John

**Chrysanthea**
See   Harris, Lilly C.

**Chrysanthemum Joe Choynski**
See   Choynski, Joe

**Chrysantheus**
See   Harris, Thomas Lake

**Chrysippus** 3rd c. BC   [FFF, SN]
*Greek philosopher*
* [The] Knife of Academic Knots

**Chrysologus**
See   Peter [or Pietro]

**Chrysorrhoas**
See   John of Damascus [or
Johannes Damascenus]

**Chrysostom**
See   John

**[The] Chrysostom of Christ's College**
See   More, Henry

**Chrysostomus [or Chrysostom]**
See   Dion

**Chryst, Dorothea**
See   Schueler, Dorli-Maria

**Chrystal, Thomas B.**   [PA]
*Author*
* Bernadino

**Chu, Arthur [T. S.]**
See   Chu, Tsung Shou

**Chu Ch'an**
See   Blofeld, John [Eaton
Calthorpe]

**Chu Chung-yu**
See   Hsu, Benedict [Pei-Hsiung]

**Chu Feng**
See   Blofeld, John [Eaton
Calthorpe]

**Chu, Tsung Shou** 1916-   [CA]
*Chinese-born author*
* Chu, Arthur [T. S.]
* Chu, W. R.

**Chu, W. R.**
See   Chu, Tsung Shou

**Chu Yuan-chang** 1328-1398
[WBD]
*Chinese emperor*
* Hung Wu

**Chuan Chin**
See   Chi, Richard Hu See-Yee

**Chubb, Elmer**
See   Masters, Edgar Lee

**Chubbuck, Emily C.** 1817-1854
[DEL, PA]
*American author*
* Forrester, Fanny

**Chubby Cheeks Soares**
See   Soares, Mario

**Chuckin' Charley O'Rourke**
See   O'Rourke, Charles C.

**Chudleigh, Arthur**
See   Lillies, Arthur

**Chudnick, Robert** 1927-   [EJ, PMJ]
*American jazz musician*
* Rodney, Red

**Chukovsky, Kornei**
See   Korneichuk, Nikolai Ivanovich

**Chumy-Chumez**
See   Gonzalez Castrillo, Jose Maria

**Chun, Jinsie K[yung] S[hien]** 1902-
[CA]
*Chinese-born author*
* Sung, P. M.

**Chung, Henry**
See   DeYoung, Henry C.

**Chung, Kyung Cho** 1921-   [CA]
*Korean-born author*
* Chong, Kyong-Jo

**Chung Shan**
See   Sun Yat-sen

**Church, Benjamin** 1734-1780   [PA]
*Author*
* Thumb, Thomas, Esq.

**Church, Bubba**
See   Church, Emory Nicholas

**Church, Eliza Rodman** 1831- ?
[FFF]
*American poet*
* Rodman, Ella

**Church, Emory Nicholas** 1924-
[BE]
*American baseball player*
* Church, Bubba

**Church, Granville**
See   People, Granville Church

**Church, Jeffrey**
See   Kirk, Richard [Edmund]

**Church, Peter**
See   Nuttall, Jeff

**Church, R. J. Harrison**
See   Harrison-Church, Ronald
James

**Church, Ruth Ellen [Lovrien]** 20th
c.   [CA]
*American home economist and
author*
* Meade, Mary

**Churchill, Beatrice [Desmond]**
1876?-1929   [B10]
*British criminal*
* Chicago May

**Churchill, Charles** 1731-1764   [SN]
*British author and poet*
* [The] Clumsy Curate of Clapham

**Churchill, Elizabeth**
See   Hough, Richard [Alexander]

**Churchill, Frank**
See   Lewes, George Henry

**Churchill, John [First Duke of Marlborough]** 1650-1722
[DEP, DNNS, FFF]
*British army officer*
* [Le] Bel Anglais
* Corporal John
* [The] Handsome Englishman
* Queen Anne's Great Captain
* [The] Silly Duke
* [The] Tory Terrier

**Churchill, Joyce**
See   Harrison, M[ichael] John

**Churchill, Peter** 1909-1972
[BDW, WWW]
*British intelligence agent*
* Michel
* Raoul [code name used during World War II]

**Churchill, R. C.**
See   Churchill, Reginald Charles

**Churchill, Reginald Charles** 1916-
[SFL]
*British author*
* Churchill, R. C.

**Churchill, Sarah Jennings**
1660-1744   [DEP, FFF, SN]
*Duchess of Marlborough*
* Atossa
* Freeman, Mrs.
* Old Sarah
* Queen Sarah
* [The] Viceroy
* [The] Wise Duchess

**Churchill, Winnie**
See   Churchill, Winston S.

**Churchill, Winston S.** 1874-1965
[CND, NN]
*British statesman and prime minister*
* Churchill, Winnie
* Former Naval Person [code name used during World War II]
* Warden, Colonel [code name used during World War II]

**[The] Church's Wet Nurse**
See   Anne

**Churn, Chuck**
See   Churn, Clarence Nottingham

**Churn, Clarence Nottingham** 1930-
[BE]
*American baseball player*
* Churn, Chuck

**Churne, William**
See   Paget, Francis Edward

**Churton, Henry**
See   Tourgee, Albion W[inegar]

**Chute, B. J.**
See   Chute, Beatrice Joy

**Chute, Beatrice Joy** 1913-
[IAW, WYA]
*American author*
* Chute, B. J.

**Chute, M. G.**
See   Chute, Mary Grace

**Chute, Mary Grace** 20th c.
*American author*
* Chute, M. G.

**Chute, Mrs. L. J. R.**   [FFF]
*Journalist*
* Clare, Ida

**Chute, Rupert**
See   Cleveland, Philip Jerome

**Chwatt, Aaron** 1919-
[IPA, ITA, SW]
*American actor*
* Buttons, Red

**Chweig, B.**
See   Kinoy, Ernest

**Ciaconicus**
See   Cason, Pedro

**Ciaconicus**
See   Chacon, Alfonso

**Ciaffone, Lawrence Thomas [Larry]**
1924-   [BE]
*American baseball player*
* Ciaffone, Symphony

**Ciaffone, Symphony**
See   Ciaffone, Lawrence Thomas [Larry]

**Cialente, Fausta**
See   Terni, Fausta Cialente

**Cianci, Buddy**
See   Cianci, Vincent, Jr.

**Cianci, Vincent, Jr.** 1941?-
*American politician*
* Cianci, Buddy

**Cianfriglia, Giovanni** 20th c.   [WF]
*Italian actor*
* Wood, Ken

**Ciannelli, Eduardo** 1888-1969
[HCA]
*Italian-born actor*
* Ciannelli, Edward

**Ciannelli, Edward**
See   Ciannelli, Eduardo

**Ciardi, John** 1916-   [WGT]
*American author*
* Anthony, John

**Cibber, Colley** 1671-1757
[DEP, FFF, SN]
*British actor and playwright*
* King Coll [or Colley]
* [The] King of Dullness

**Cibo, Giovanni Battista** 1432-1492
[WBD]
*Pope*
* Innocent VIII

**Cica**
See   Pinto, Cecilia

**Ciccio, Frank** 1891-1962
[PMJ, SC]
*American actor and singer*
* Parker, Frank
* Parker, Pinky

**Cicero** [code name used during World War II]
See   Bazna, Elyesa

**Cicero, Dode**
See   Cicero, Joseph Francis [Joe]

**Cicero, Joseph Francis [Joe]** 1910-
[BE]
*American baseball player*
* Cicero, Dode

**Cicero, Marcus Tullius** 1st c. BC
[DEP, DNNS, SN]
*Roman orator, statesman, philosopher*
* [The] Father of His Country
* [The] Father of Roman Philosophy
* [A] Fire Kindler
* [The] God of All Philosophers
* Tully

**[The] Cicero of France**
See   Massillon, Jean Baptiste

**[The] Cicero of Germany**
See   John III [or Johann]

**[The] Cicero of Germany**
See   Sturm, Johann Christoph

**[The] Cicero of Latin Christianity**
See   Augustine

**[The] Cicero of the British Senate**
See   Canning, George

**Cicero's Mouth**
See   Pot, Philippe

**[El] Ciclon Mexicano [The Mexican Cyclone]**
See   Ruiz Camino, Carlos

**Cicotte, Alva Warren** 1929-   [BE]
*American baseball player*
* Cicotte, Bozo

**Cicotte, Bozo**
See   Cicotte, Alva Warren

**Cicotte, Edward Victor** 1884-1969
[DGS, PB]
*American baseball player*
* Cicotte, Knuckles

**Cicotte, Knuckles**
See   Cicotte, Edward Victor

**[The] Cid [Master]**
See   Diaz de Vivar, Rodrigo

**[The] Cid of Portugal**
See   Pereira, Nunez Alvarez

**Cidie**
See   Sarfatti, Margherita

**[Il] Cieco [The Blind]**
See   Bello, Francesco

**[Il] Cieco [The Blind]**
See   Groto, Luigi

**Ciego [Blind Man]**
See   Cornblit, Joey

**Cielius**
See   Rhodiginenus, Lingi Richiere

**Cielo, Astra**
See   Goldsmith, Milton

**Cieslak, Ted**
See   Cieslak, Thaddeus Walter

**Cieslak, Thaddeus Walter** 1916-
[BE]
*American baseball player*
* Cieslak, Ted

**[The] Cigar**
See   Galante, Carmine

**Cignus de Corde Benignus**
See   Thomas of Woodstock

**Cihocki, Cy**
See   Cihocki, Ed[ward Joseph]

**Cihocki, Ed[ward Joseph]** 1907-
[BE]
*American baseball player*
* Cihocki, Cy

**Cilento, Phyllis Dorothy** 1894-
[IAW]
*Australian author*
* Counsellor
* Dr. Phyl
* Hygeiea
* Marama
* Medical Mother
* Mother MD

**Cillie, Hester Francina** 1885-
[IAW]
*South African author*
* Cillie En Estelle, Hettie

**Cillie En Estelle, Hettie**
See   Cillie, Hester Francina

**Cima da Conegliano**
See   Cima, Giovanni Battista

**Cima, Giovanni Battista**
1459?-1517?   [WBD]
*Venetian painter*
* Cima da Conegliano

**Cimabue, Giovanni**
See   Cenni di Pepo

**Cimber, Matt**
See   Ottaviano, Thomas

**Cincinnatus**
See   Plumer, William

**[The] Cincinnatus of the Americas**
See   Washington, George

**[The] Cincinnatus of the West**
See   Harrison, William Henry

**[The] Cincinnatus of the West**
See   Washington, George

**Cincovillas [Five Villas]**
See   Peropadre, Miguel

**[The] Cinderella Girl of Country Music**
See   Smith, Constance [Connie]

**Cinderella in Sneakers**
See   Evert, Chris[tine Marie]

**[The] Cinderella Man**
See   Braddock, James Joseph [Jim]

**[The] Cinderella Man**
See   Pearson, Preston

**Cini, Alfred** 1927-   [PRS, RO1]
*American singer and actor*
* Martino, Al

**Cinna**
See   Sullivan, Robert Baldwin

**Cino da Pistoia**
See   De Sinibaldi, Guittoncino

**Cinquevalli, Paul**
See   Kestner, Paul

**Cinthio [or Cintio]**
See   Giraldi, Giovanni Battista

**Ciocchi del Monte, Giammaria**
1487-1555   [WBD]
*Pope*
* Julius III

**Ciorciolini, Marcello** 20th c.   [WF]
*Italian director*
* Reed, Frank

**Cipolla, Joan Bagnel**
See Bagnel, Joan

**[The] Circe of the Revolution**
See Roland de La Platiere, Jeanne
Manon

**Circuit Breaker**
See Baker, John Clifford Yorke

**Circus, Jim**
See Rosevear, John

**Circus Solly Hofman**
See Hofman, Arthur Frederick

**Cire**
See Hayden, Eric W[illiam]

**Cireni, Giuseppe** ?-1956 [BEW]
Clown
* Giacomino

**Ciriaco de Pizzicolli** 1391- ?
[WBD]
Italian humanist and antiquarian
* Cyriacus of Ancona

**Cirillo, Wallace Joseph** 1927-
[EJ7]
American jazz musician
* Cirillo, Wally

**Cirillo, Wally**
See Cirillo, Wallace Joseph

**Cirofici, Dago Frank**
See Cirofici, Frank

**Cirofici, Frank** 20th c. [BLB]
American underworld figure
* Cirofici, Dago Frank

**Ciscar, Guillermo** 20th c. [GS]
Spanish bullfighter
* Chavalo [Young Lad]

**[The] Cisco Kid**
See Rizzo, Frank Lazarro

**Cisinge, Johann** 1434-1472 [PA]
Author
* Panonius, Janus

**Cisney, Marcella**
See Abels, Marcella Ruth

**[The] Citizen King**
See Louis Philippe

**[The] Citizen of Geneva**
See Rousseau, Jean-Jacques

**[A] Citizen of Massachusetts**
See Lowell, John

**[A] Citizen of New England**
See Lowell, John

**[A] Citizen of the United States**
See Everett, Alexander Hill

**[A] Citizen of the World**
See Goldsmith, Oliver

**Citovich, Enid Sarah Kortright**
1902- [AW, WD]
British author
* Baldry, Enid

**Citrouillard, Joseph**
See Connerson, M. Jean L.
Auguste

**Cittadella, Alfonso** 1487-1537
[WBD]
Italian sculptor
* Lombardi, Alfonso

**Cittafino, Ricardo**
See Bickers, Richard Leslie
Townshend

**[The] City Builder**
See Sancho I

**City, Fred**
See Bedford, Harry

**[The] City Laureate**
See Settle, Elkanah

**Ciummei, Alfredo** 1867-1921
[BBD]
Turkish-born composer
* Donizetti, Alfredo

**Civella, Carl**
American underworld figure
* Civella, Cork

**Civella, Cork**
See Civella, Carl

**Civil Rights, Mr.**
See Marshall, Thoroughgood

**Civil Rights Number 1, Mr.**
See Houston, Charles Hamilton

**Civilis, Julius** 1st c. [HN]
Germanic military leader
* [The] Hannibal of Batavia

**Civis**
See Coles, John

**Civis**
See Deems, James Harry

**Civis**
See Peterkin, Alexander

**Civis**
See Stowell, Baron

**Civis**
See Thompson, George

**Claassen, Harold** 1905- [CAP]
American author and editor
* Pomeroy, Hub[bard]

**Clabaugh, John William** 1901-
[BE]
American baseball player
* Clabaugh, Moose

**Clabaugh, Moose**
See Clabaugh, John William

**Clack, Gentlemanly Bobby**
See Clack, Robert S. [Bobby]

**Clack, Robert S. [Bobby]**
1851-1933 [BE]
American baseball player
* Clack, Gentlemanly Bobby

**Clackson, Kim**
See Clackson, Kimbel Gerald

**Clackson, Kimbel Gerald** 1955-
[HR, SMG]
Canadian-born hockey player
* Clackson, Kim

**Clacy, Ellen** [PA]
Author
* [A] Clergyman's Daughter
* Cycla

**Cladpole, Tim**
See Lower, Richard

**Claessen, George** 1909- [ART]
British artist
* G. C.

**Clagett, Manning** 1913- [ITA]
American executive
* Clagett, Tim

**Clagett, Tim**
See Clagett, Manning

**Claiborne, Robert [Watson, Jr.]**
1919- [CA]
British-born American author
* McKenney, R. Armstrong

**[The] Claimant**
See Cleveland, [Stephen] Grover

**Clair, John, Jr.** 1908- ? [BBH]
American skiing club founder and
officer
* Ski, Mr.

**Clair, Mavis**
See Tunnell, Mavis

**Clair, Rene**
See Chomette, Rene

**Clair Stanislaus, [Brother]**
See Battersby, William J[ohn]

**Claire**
See Ritson, Claire

**Claire, Bernice**
See Jahnigan, Bernice

**Claire, Danny**
See Claire, David Matthew

**Claire, David Matthew** 1897-1929
[BE]
American baseball player
* Claire, Danny

**Claire, Ethlyne**
See Williams, Ethlyne

**Claire, Ina**
See Fagan, Ina

**Claire, Keith** [joint pseudonym with
Keith Andrews]
See Andrews, Claire

**Claire, Keith** [joint pseudonym with
Claire Andrews]
See Andrews, Keith

**Claire, Ludi**
See Bailhe, Edilou

**Clairon, Claire Josephe Hippolyte de
la Tude**
See Leris, Claire Josephe

**Clairon, Laura**
See Lehnhoff, Laura

**Clairville, Louis Francois**
See Nicolaie, Louis Francois

**Clajus, Johannes**
See Klaj, Johannes

**Clamp, Helen Mary Elizabeth** 20th
c. [AW]
British author and artist
* Leigh, Olivia

**Clancy, Bud**
See Clancy, John William

**Clancy, Francis Michael** 1903-
[CEI, FHE, HK]
Canadian-born hockey player
* Clancy, King

**Clancy, Holling Allison** 1900-
[SAT]
American author and illustrator
* Holling, Holling C[lancy]

**Clancy, John William** 1900-1968
[BE]
American baseball player
* Clancy, Bud

**Clancy, King**
See Clancy, Francis Michael

**Clancy, Louise Breitenbach** 20th c.
[NAA]
American author
* Jerrold, Louise

**Clancy, Young**
See Latzo, Pete

**Clandon, Henrietta**
See Vahey, John George Haslette

**Clanricarde, First Marquis and Fifth
Earl of**
See De Burgh, Ulick

**Clanton, Eucal Curt** 1898-1960
[BE]
American baseball player
* Clanton, Uke

**Clanton, Uke**
See Clanton, Eucal Curt

**Clapham, Leonard** 1882-1963
[BEW, F2]
Actor
* London, Tom

**Clapp, Charles** 1899-1962
[ASC, BEW]
American composer, conductor,
musician
* Clapp, Sunny

**Clapp, Eric Patrick** 1945- [RO2]
British singer
* Clapton, Eric

**Clapp, George Alfred** 1856-1924
[CED]
American entertainer
* Dockstader, Lew

**Clapp, Henry, Jr.** [FFF, PA]
Writer
* Figaro

**Clapp, Sunny**
See Clapp, Charles

**Clappe, Louise Amelia Knapp [Smith]**
1819-1906 [B10]
American pioneer and author
* Dame Shirley

**Clapper, Aubrey Victor** 1907-1978
[FHE, HK, SMG]
Canadian-born hockey player
* Clapper, Dit

**Clapper, Dit**
See Clapper, Aubrey Victor

**Clapsaddle, Hilda R.** 20th c.
American actress
* Lane, Laurie

**Clapton, Eric**
See Clapp, Eric Patrick

**Clara**
See Cole, Clara

**Clara**
See Sinclair, Carrie Bell

**Clara Belle**
See Thompson, Mrs. William

**Clarance, Mrs. Edward** [FFF]
Entertainer
* Warner, Jessie

**Clare, Ada**
See McElhinney, Jane

**Clare, Austin**
See James, Wilhelmina Martha

**Clare, Elizabeth**
See Cook, Dorothy Mary

**Clare, Francis D.**
See Aschmann,

**Clare, Gilbert de** ?-1149? [HN]
*First Earl of Pembroke and Strigul*
* Strongbow

**Clare, Gilbert de** 1243-1295
[FFF, SN]
*Eighth Earl of Gloucester*
* Rufus [The Red]

**Clare, Gladys Anna** 1900?-1954
[F2, FC]
*American actress*
* George, Gladys

**Clare, Helen**
See Hunter Blair, Pauline Clarke

**Clare, Ida**
See Chute, Mrs. L. J. R.

**Clare, John** 1793-1864
[DEL, WBD]
*British poet*
* [The] Northamptonshire Peasant
  Poet
* [The] Northamptonshire Poet
* [The] Peasant Poet of
  Northamptonshire

**Clare Lucille, [Sister]**
See Hutchinson, Lucie M.

**Clare, Margaret**
See Maison, Margaret M[ary
Bowles]

**Clare, Marguerite**
See Heppell, Mary

**Clare, Mary Frances**
See Cusack, Mary Frances

**Clare, Patrick**
See Fanning, David Christopher
Patrick St. John

**Clare, Richard de** ?-1176
[DNNS, HN, SN]
*Second Earl of Pembroke and
Stirgul*
* Strongbow

**Clarence, Fitzroy**
See Thackeray, William
Makepeace

**Clarens, Angel** 1867?- ? [CW]
*Cuban playwright*
* Acacia

**Claretie, Arsene Arnaud**
1840-1913 [FFF, WBD]
*French journalist and author*
* Candide
* Claretie, Jules

**Claretie, Jules**
See Claretie, Arsene Arnaud

**Claribel**
See Barnard, Caroline

**Clarin**
See Alas, Leopold

**Clarinda**
See Maclehose, Agnes

**Clark, Abraham** 1726-1794
[FFF, WBD]
*American politician*
* Congress Abraham
* [The] Father of Paper Currency

**Clark, Alfred Alexander Gordon**
1900-1958 [CC, EMD, LC]
*British jurist and author*
* Hare, Cyril

**Clark, Algeria Junius** 1900?-1963
[DAM, EJ, WWJ]
*American jazz musician*
* Clark, June

**Clark, Archie**
See Clark, Arthur Franklin

**Clark, Arthur Franklin** 1865- ?
[BE]
*American baseball player*
* Clark, Archie

**Clark, Babe**
See Clark, Charles

**Clark, Boobie**
See Clark, Charles

**Clark, Buddy**
See Clark, Walter, Jr.

**Clark, Buddy**
See Goldberg, Samuel

**Clark, Cap**
See Clark, John Carroll

**Clark, Car**
See Clark, James

**Clark, Catherine**
See Uniacke, Evelyn Catherine

**Clark, Champ**
See Clark, James Beauchamp

**Clark, Charles** 1806-1880
[DEL, PA]
*Author*
* Drydog, Doggrel
* Merryfellow, Malthus
* Queerfellow, Quintin

**Clark, Charles** 1950- [FB]
*American football player*
* Clark, Boobie

**Clark, Charles** 20th c. [RBE]
*American boxer*
* Clark, Babe

**Clark, Charles Heber** 1841-1915
[SFL, WGT, WWL]
*American author*
* Adeler, Max

**Clark, Charlotte Moon** 1829-1895
[PA]
*American author*
* C. M. C.
* Clay, Charles M.

**Clark, Conrad Yeatis** 1931-1963
[DAM, EJ]
*American jazz musician*
* Clark, Sonny

**Clark, Coyote Eyes**
See Clark, Mel

**Clark, Curt**
See Westlake, Donald E[dwin]

**Clark, Dale**
See Kayser, Ronal.

**Clark, Dana Board** [FFF]
* Mysterious Bachelor

**Clark, Dane**
See Zanville, Bernard

**Clark, David**
See Hardcastle, Michael

**Clark, David Allen**
See Ernst, [Lyman] John

**Clark, Dee**
See Clark, Delectus

**Clark, Delectus** 1938- [RO1]
*American singer*
* Clark, Dee

**Clark, Dick**
See Clay, Dick

**Clark, Dorothy [Park]** 1899-
[ANT, CA, WW]
*American author*
* McMeekin, Clark [joint
  pseudonym with Isabel
  (McLennan) McMeekin]

**Clark, Dutch**
See Clark, Earl Harry

**Clark, Earl Harry** 1906-1978
[FB, OCS, SMG]
*American football player and coach*
* Clark, Dutch

**Clark, Ethel**
See Schneider, Ethel

**Clark, Frederick Stephen** 1908-
[CA, WD]
*British author*
* Dalton, Clive

**Clark, G. N.**
See Clark, [Sir] George Norman

**Clark, Gail** 1944- [CA]
*American author*
* MacKeever, Maggie
* South, Grace

**Clark, Garel** [joint pseudonym with
Ethel McCullough Scott]
See Garelick, May

**Clark, Garel** [joint pseudonym with
May Garelick]
See Scott, Ethel McCullough

**Clark, George** ?-1972 [FB, SMG]
*American football coach*
* Clark, Potsy

**Clark, [Sir] George Norman** 1890-
[LC]
*British historian and author*
* Clark, G. N.

**Clark, Ginger**
See Clark, Harvey Daniel

**Clark, Greg** 1892-1977
*Canadian journalist*
* Canada's Eddie Guest

**Clark, Gretta Palmer** 1905- [NAA]
*American journalist*
* Palmer, Gretta

**Clark, Gwen** 1927- [BF]
*British actress*
* Hylton, Jane

**Clark, H. A.** [PA]
*Author*
* Boggs, Robert

**Clark, Harry** 1883-1965 [BE]
*American baseball player*
* Clark, Pep

**Clark, Harvey Daniel** 1879-1943
[BE]
*American baseball player*
* Clark, Ginger

**Clark, Howard**
See Haskin, Dorothy C[lark]

**Clark, Hungry**
See Clark, Maynard

**Clark, Irene Haas** 1929- [TBJ]
*American illustrator*
* Haas, Irene

**Clark, J. P.**
See Clark, John Pepper

**Clark, James [Jim]**
See Petrosky, James

**Clark, James** ?-1929 [PHM]
*American underworld figure*
* Clark, Car

**Clark, James [Jimmy]** ?-1968
*Scottish auto racer*
* [The] Flying Scott

**Clark, James Bayard** 1869- ?
[NAA]
*American physician and author*
* Bay, James

**Clark, James Beauchamp**
1850-1921 [WBD]
*American politician*
* Clark, Champ

**Clark, Jeremiah Simpson** 1872- ?
[NAA]
*Canadian physician and author*
* Sea Shell

**Clark, Jerome L.**
See Rapaport, Jerome L.

**Clark, Jim** 20th c. [BLB]
*American criminal*
* Clark, Oklahoma Jack

**Clark, Joe** 20th c.
*Photographer*
* [The] Hillbilly Snapshooter

**Clark, John Carroll** 1909-1957
[BE]
*American baseball player*
* Clark, Cap

**Clark, John Pepper** 1935-
*Nigerian poet*
* Clark, J. P.

**Clark, Johnson** 1886- [BMH]
*British ventriloquist*
* [The] Sportsman Ventriloquist
* [The] Squire

**Clark, Johnson** 1891-1948 [BEW]
*British-born actor*
* Bryan, Hal

**Clark, Joseph** 1894-1960 [NOJ]
*American jazz musician*
* Clark, Red

**Clark, [Charles] Joseph [Joe]** 1939-
*Canadian prime minister*
* Joe Who

**Clark, June**
See Clark, Algeria Junius

**Clark, Kay** 1910-1957 [SC]
*American actress*
* Terry, Sheila

**Clark, Lefty**
See Bischoff, William G.

**Clark, M.**
See  Runkle, Janice

**Clark, Mabel Margaret [Cowie]**
1903-1975  [CA]
*British author, playwright,
screenwriter*
* Storm, Lesley

**Clark, Manuel D., Jr.** 1922-
[CWG]
*American country-western performer*
* Clark, Old Joe

**Clark, Margery** [joint pseudonym
with Margery Quigley]
See  Clark, Mary E.

**Clark, Margery** [joint pseudonym
with Mary E. Clark]
See  Quigley, Margery

**Clark, Marie Catherine Audrey**
[IAW]
*British author*
* Curling, Audrey

**Clark, Marjorie** 20th c.  [LAO]
*Australian writer*
* Rivers, Georgia

**Clark, Mark Wayne** 1896-
[BDW, WWW]
*American army officer*
* [The] American Eagle
* [The] Eagle

**Clark, Mary E.** 1887-
*American author*
* Clark, Margery [joint pseudonym
  with Margery Quigley]

**Clark, Mary L.**  [PA]
*Author*
* Mada

**Clark, Mavis Thorpe** 20th c.
[CA, SAT]
*Australian author*
* Latham, Mavis

**Clark, Maynard** 20th c.  [EAR]
*American motorcycle racer*
* Clark, Hungry

**Clark, Mel** 20th c.  [GW]
*American rodeo performer*
* Clark, Coyote Eyes

**Clark, Merle**
See  Gessner, Lynne

**Clark, Mike** 20th c.
*American football player*
* Clark, Onside

**Clark, Mrs. Henry**  [FFF]
*Entertainer*
* Temple, Mattie

**Clark, Mrs. J. P.**  [FFF]
*Entertainer*
* Whittle, Emma

**Clark, Mrs. W. H.**  [FFF]
*Entertainer*
* Toussaint, Gertrude

**Clark, Nan**
*Comedienne*
* Rae, Nan

**Clark, Neil McCullough** 1890-
[IAW]
*American author*
* Clarke, P. H.
* McCullough, James H.

**Clark, Norman**
See  Capponi, Pier Paolo

**Clark, Oklahoma Jack**
See  Clark, Jim

**Clark, Old Joe**
See  Clark, Manuel D., Jr.

**Clark, Onside**
See  Clark, Mike

**Clark, Owen F.** 1867-1892  [BE]
*American baseball player*
* Clark, Spider

**Clark, P. L.** 20th c.  [BMH]
*British comedian*
* Auntie
* [The] Original Tramp Cyclist

**Clark, Parlin**
See  Trigg, Harry Davis

**Clark, Pep**
See  Clark, Harry

**Clark, Pepper**
See  Clark, Royal Elliott

**Clark, Pet**
See  Clark, Petula

**Clark, Petula** 1933-  [RO2]
*British singer*
* Clark, Pet

**Clark, Philip** 20th c.  [SFP]
*Author*
* Carter, Nick [house pseudonym]
* Keith, Harrison [joint pseudonym
  with John Chambliss]

**Clark, Potsy**
See  Clark, George

**Clark, Raymond Le Roy** 1917-
[CWG, DAM]
*American country-western performer*
* Clark, Yodeling Slim

**Clark, Red**
See  Clark, Joseph

**Clark, Robert Henry Hardy** 1917-
[IAW]
*British author*
* Hardy, Robert

**Clark, Royal Elliott** 1874-1925
[BE]
*American baseball player*
* Clark, Pepper

**Clark, Ruth C[ampbell]** 1920-  [CA]
*American author and educator*
* Porter, Alan

**Clark, Saville**  [PA]
*Author*
* Row, Saville

**Clark, Scott** 1958-  [RBE]
*American boxer*
* [The] Golden Boy

**Clark, Sonny**
See  Clark, Conrad Yeatis

**Clark, Spider**
See  Clark, Owen F.

**Clark, Susie Champney** 1856- ?
[SFL]
*Author*
* St. Clair, Cecil

**Clark, Sylvia** 1931-  [IBW]
*American nun*
* Mary Lucille, [Sister]

**Clark, [The Rev.] T.**
See  Galt, John

**Clark, T. H.**
See  Clark, Thomas Humphrey

**Clark, Thomas** 18th c.  [RH]
*Friend of British banker, Abraham
Newland*
* [The] King of Exeter Change

**Clark, Thomas Humphrey** 1921-
[ART]
*British artist*
* Clark, T. H.

**Clark, Virginia**
See  Gray, Patricia [Clark]

**Clark, Walter, Jr.** 1929-  [EJ]
*American jazz musician*
* Clark, Buddy

**Clark, Watty**
See  Clark, William Watson

**Clark, Wee Willie**
See  Clark, William Otis

**Clark, William Otis** 1872-1932
[BE]
*American baseball player*
* Clark, Wee Willie

**Clark, William Watson** 1902-1972
[BE]
*American baseball player*
* Clark, Watty

**Clark, William Winfield [Bill]**
1875-1959  [BE]
*American baseball player*
* Clark, Win

**Clark, Willis Gaylord** 1810-1841
[PA]
*Author*
* Ollapod

**Clark, Win**
See  Clark, William Winfield [Bill]

**Clark, Winifred** 1909-  [WW]
*Author*
* Finley, Scott

**Clark, Yodeling Slim**
See  Clark, Raymond Le Roy

**Clarke, Alan Thomas** 1896-  [BE]
*American baseball player*
* Clarke, Lefty

**Clarke, Arthur** 20th c.
*American jazz musician*
* Clarke, Babe

**Clarke, Arthur C[harles]** 1917-
[ESF, WGT]
*British author*
* O'Brien, E. G.
* Willis, Charles

**Clarke, Austin Chesterfield** 1934-
[CW]
*Barbadian author and playwright*
* Clarke, Tom

**Clarke, Babe**
See  Clarke, Arthur

**Clarke, Betty Ross**
See  Ross, Betty

**Clarke, Boileryard**
See  Clarke, William Jones

**Clarke, Brenda Margaret Lilian**
1926-  [AW, CA, WD]
*British author*
* Honeyman, Brenda

**Clarke, [Rev.] C. C.**
See  Phillips, [Sir] Richard

**Clarke, Cap**
See  Clarke, Fred Clifford

**Clarke, Cecil** 1848- ?  [WWL]
*British author*
* Old Bird

**Clarke, Charles Baron** 1832- ?
[WWL]
*British author*
* C. C.

**Clarke, Charlotte** 18th c.  [SN]
*Daughter of British actor and
playwright, Colley Cibber*
* [The] English D'Eon

**Clarke, Covington**
See  Venable, Clark

**Clarke, Cromwell**
See  Dailley, Richard

**Clarke, D[avid] Waldo** 1907-  [CA]
*Welsh-born author*
* Waldo, Dave

**Clarke, Dad**
See  Clarke, William H.

**Clarke, Derrick Harry** 1919-
[IAW]
*British author*
* Clarke, Nobby

**Clarke, Dora** 20th c.  [ART]
*British sculptor*
* D. C.

**Clarke, Dorothy Clotelle**
See  Shadi, Dorothy Clotelle Clarke

**Clarke, Frank** 1911-  [WWJ]
*American jazz musician*
* Clarke, Pete

**Clarke, Fred Clifford** 1872-1960
[BE]
*American baseball player and
manager*
* Clarke, Cap

**Clarke, George**
See  Broome, George

**Clarke, George Sydenham**
1848-1933  [SFL, WGT]
*British author*
* Seaforth, A. Nelson

**Clarke, Gertrude**
See  Paine, A. G. Amye

**Clarke, Gordon Luke** 1945-  [WFA]
*New Zealand-born fashion designer*
* Luke

**Clarke, H. M.**
See  Clarke, Hilda Margery

**Clarke, Harry** 20th c.  [ITA]
*American playwright*
* Clork, Harry

**Clarke, Henry Charles** 1899-  [CA]
*British author and editor*
* Clarke, Hockley

**Clarke, Hilda Margery** 1926-
[ART]
*British painter and designer*
* Clarke, H. M.

**Clarke, Hockley**
See Clarke, Henry Charles

**Clarke, Horace Meredith** 1940-
[PB]
*American baseball player*
* Clarke, Hoss

**Clarke, Hoss**
See Clarke, Horace Meredith

**Clarke, I. F.**
See Clarke, Ignatius Frederic

**Clarke, Ignatius Frederic** 1918-
[SF]
*Educator and author*
* Clarke, I. F.

**Clarke, J. Calvitt** 1888- [WW]
*Author*
* Addison, Carol
* Grant, Richard

**Clarke, [Captain] Jafah**
See Nesmith, Robert I.

**Clarke, Jay Justin** 1882-1949 [BE]
*Canadian-born baseball player*
* Clarke, Nig

**Clarke, John**
See Cromwell, Richard

**Clarke, John**
See Horner, T. H.

**Clarke, John**
See Laughlin, Virginia Carli

**Clarke, John**
See Sontup, Dan[iel]

**Clarke, John** 1609-1676 [FFF]
*British-born clergyman and physician*
* [The] Father of Rhode Island and of American Baptists

**Clarke, John [Campbell]** 1913- ?
[CAP]
*British author*
* Cleland, Hugh

**Clarke, John Theobald** 1926-
[FC, OCF]
*British actor, scriptwriter, director*
* Forbes, Bryan

**Clarke, [Lady] Josephine Fitzgerald [Moylan]** 20th c. [WW]
*Author*
* Fitzgerald, Erroll

**Clarke, Joshua Baldwin** 1879-1962
[BE]
*American baseball player*
* Clarke, Pepper

**Clarke, Kamylla**
See Cox, Charles Roy

**Clarke, Kenneth Spearman [Kenny]**
1914- [EJ, PMJ]
*American jazz musician*
* Clarke, Klook
* Salaam, Liaqat Ali

**Clarke, Klook**
See Clarke, Kenneth Spearman [Kenny]

**Clarke, Lefty**
See Clarke, Alan Thomas

**Clarke, Louis Albert** 1901- [EJS]
*American track and field athlete*
* Clarke, Pinky

**Clarke, Mary Bayard Devereux**
1827-1886 [FFF, PA]
*American poet*
* Leigh, Stuart
* Tenella

**Clarke, [Captain] Maurice**
See Hook, Samuel Clarke

**Clarke [or Clark?], McDonald**
1798-1842 [DNNF, FFF, SN]
*American poet*
* [The] Mad Poet

**Clarke, Michael**
See Newlon, Clarke

**Clarke, N. B.** [PA]
*Author*
* Belden, N. H.

**Clarke, Nig**
See Clarke, Jay Justin

**Clarke, Nobby**
See Clarke, Derrick Harry

**Clarke, Noisy**
See Clarke, Richard Grey [Dick]

**Clarke, P. H.**
See Clark, Neil McCullough

**Clarke, P. J.**
See Clarke, Peter John

**Clarke, Pauline**
See Hunter Blair, Pauline Clarke

**Clarke, Pepper**
See Clarke, Joshua Baldwin

**Clarke, Percy A.** 20th c. [MBF]
*British author*
* Frazer, Martin
* Lander, Dane
* Lytton, Jane
* Neilson, Vernon
* Rogers, Steve
* Watson, St. John
* Wentworth, Charles [house pseudonym]

**Clarke, Pete**
See Clarke, Frank

**Clarke, Peter John** 1927- [ART]
*British painter*
* Clarke, P. J.

**Clarke, Pinky**
See Clarke, Louis Albert

**Clarke, Rebecca** 1833-1906
[DNNF, FFF, WBD]
*American author*
* May, Sophie

**Clarke, Richard Grey [Dick]** 1912-
[BE]
*American baseball player*
* Clarke, Noisy

**Clarke, Richard W.** 1845-1930
[WBD]
*American frontiersman*
* Deadwood Dick

**Clarke, Rufe**
See Clarke, Rufus Rivers

**Clarke, Rufus Rivers** 1900- [BE]
*American baseball player*
* Clarke, Rufe

**Clarke, S. Dacre** 20th c. [MBF]
*British author and publisher*
* Rayner, Guy

**Clarke, Samuel** 1675-1729 [SN]
*British philosopher and clergyman*
* Suck All Cream

**Clarke, Tom**
See Clarke, Austin Chesterfield

**Clarke, Vibert Ernesto** 1928- [BE]
*Panamanian-born baseball player*
* Clarke, Webbo

**Clarke, Walter Irving** 1868- ?
[NAA]
*American publicist and writer*
* Fairfield, Ward

**Clarke, Webbo**
See Clarke, Vibert Ernesto

**Clarke, William A.** [PA]
*Author*
* Anicetus

**Clarke, William H.** 1865-1911
[BE]
*American baseball player*
* Clarke, Dad

**Clarke, William James** 1872- ?
[WW]
*Author*
* Monkshood, G. F.

**Clarke, William Jones** 1868-1959
[AS, BE]
*American baseball player*
* Clarke, Boileryard

**Clarke-Ward, Carrie** 1862-1926
[SC]
*American actress*
* Ward, Carrie

**Clarkson, Anthony** 1905- [IAW]
*British author*
* S. S.

**Clarkson, Arthur Hamilton**
1866-1911 [BE]
*American baseball player*
* Clarkson, Dad

**Clarkson, Blackie**
See Clarkson, William Henry [Bill]

**Clarkson, Buzz**
See Clarkson, James B.

**Clarkson, Dad**
See Clarkson, Arthur Hamilton

**Clarkson, Helen**
See McCloy, Helen [Worrell Clarkson]

**Clarkson, J. F.**
See Tubb, Edwin Charles

**Clarkson, James B.** 1918- [BE]
*American baseball player*
* Clarkson, Buzz

**Clarkson, L.**
See Whitelock, Louise [Clarkson]

**Clarkson, Orman**
See Richardson, Gladwell

**Clarkson, William Henry [Bill]**
1898- [BE]
*American baseball player*
* Clarkson, Blackie

**Clary, Cat**
See Clary, Ellis

**Clary, Ellis** 1916- [BE]
*American baseball player*
* Clary, Cat

**Clary, Robert**
See Widerman, Robert

**Claset, Gowell Sylvester** 1907-
[BE]
*American baseball player*
* Claset, Lefty

**Claset, Lefty**
See Claset, Gowell Sylvester

**Clasico [Classic One]**
See Coloma Sanjuan, Andres

**Classy Cleo Littleton**
See Littleton, Cleophus

**Classy Freddie Blassey**
See Blassey, Frederick

**Clatten, Lilian** 1882-1951 [BEW]
*American actress and playwright*
* Mayo, Margaret

**Claude**
See Carbet, Claude

**Claude** 1499-1524
[DNNS, RH, SN]
*Queen of France*
* [La] Bonne Reine
* [The] Good Queen of France

**Claude, Jean** 1619-1687 [HN]
*French clergyman*
* [The] Man of Sedition

**Claudia**
See Dargan, Clara V.

**Claudia, Susan**
See Johnston, William

**Claudius**
See Ceccon, Silvius Petrus
Claudius

**Claudius, Appius** 5th c. BC [WBD]
*Roman politician*
* Crassus

**Claudius, Appius** 4th c. BC [WBD]
*Roman politician*
* Caecus

**Claudius, Appius** 1st c. BC [WBD]
*Roman politician*
* Pulcher

**Claudius, Matthias** 1743?-1815
[FFF, WBD]
*German author and poet*
* Asmus
* [The] Messenger of Wandsbeck

**Claudius, Publius** 3rd c. BC [WBD]
*Roman politician*
* Pulcher

**Claudius II [Marcus Aurelius Claudius]** 215?- 270
[HN, RH, WBD]
*Roman emperor*
* Gothicus
* [The] Second Trajan

**Claughton, John Alan** 1956- [DC]
*British cricketer*
* Claughton, Trapper

**Claughton, Trapper**
See Claughton, John Alan

**Claughton-James, James**
See Bentley, James William Benedict

**Clausen, A. W.**
See Clausen, Alden Winship

**Clausen, Alden Winship** 1923?-
*American banker*
* Clausen, A. W.

**Clausen, Frederick William**
1869-1960 [BE]
*American baseball player*
* Clausen, Fritz

**Clausen, Fritz**
*See* Clausen, Frederick William

**Clauss, Al[bert Stanley]** 1891-1952
[BE]
*American baseball player*
* Clauss, Lefty

**Clauss, Lefty**
*See* Clauss, Al[bert Stanley]

**Claussen, Raelene** 1939- [ASC]
*American singer and composer*
* Raney, Sue

**Clavell, Stauffer**
*See* Nagele, Anton

**Clavers, [Mrs.] Mary**
*See* Kirkland, Caroline Matilda

**Claverse, Bloody**
*See* Graham, John [First Viscount of Dundee]

**Clavignard**
*See* Chavigny, Theodore

**Clavius, Christopher** 1537-1612
[SN]
*German astronomer and mathematician*
* [The] Euclid of His Age

**Clawson, John** 1885-1942 [BEW]
*American actor and playwright*
* Willard, John

**Claxton, John G.**
*See* Beaumont, Donna Brooks

**Claxton, Kate**
*See* Stevenson, Mrs. Charles

**Clay, Bertha M.**
*See* Braeme, Charlotte Monica

**Clay, Bertha M.**
*See* Coryell, John Russell

**Clay, Bertha M.**
*See* Dey, Frederic Van Rensselaer

**Clay, Bill**
*See* Clay, Frederick C.

**Clay, Cassius Marcellus, Jr.** 1942-
[BX, IPA, OCS]
*American boxer*
* Ali, Muhammad
* Cassius X
* [The] Louisville Lip

**Clay, Charles M.**
*See* Clark, Charlotte Moon

**Clay, Dain Elmer** 1919- [BE]
*American baseball player*
* Clay, Ding-a-ling

**Clay, Dick**
*American entertainer*
* Clark, Dick

**Clay, Ding-a-ling**
*See* Clay, Dain Elmer

**Clay, Duncan**
*See* Diehl, William Wells

**Clay, Frederick C.** 1875-1917 [BE]
*American baseball player*
* Clay, Bill

**Clay, Henry** 1777-1852
[DHA, HN, SN]
*American statesman*
* [The] Apostle of Liberty
* [The] Great Commoner
* [The] Great Pacificator
* Harry of the West
* [The] Judas of the West
* [The] Mill Boy of the Slashes
* Old Chief
* [The] President Maker
* [The] Second Washington

**Clay, James** [PA]
*Author*
* J. C.

**Clay, Marcel**
*See* Jones, Freddie

**Clay, Mrs. Cecil** [FFF]
*Entertainer*
* Vokes, Rosina

**[The] Clay Pigeon of the Underworld**
*See* Noland, John T.

**Clay, Rita**
*See* Estrada, Rita

**Clay, Rudolph Valentino** 1943-
[IBW]
*American boxer*
* Ali, Rahaman

**Clay, Sonny**
*See* Clay, William Rogers Campbell

**Clay, Weald**
*See* Christie, Ernest

**Clay, William Rogers Campbell**
1899- [EJ, WWJ]
*American jazz musician*
* Clay, Sonny

**Claybrook, Joan** 1937?-
*American consumer advocate*
* [The] Dragon Lady

**Clayburgh, Isabella** [FFF]
*Entertainer*
* Kemble, Frankie

**Clayburgh, Mrs. Edward** [FFF]
*Entertainer*
* Spencer, Lillian

**Claymore, Tod**
*See* Clevely, Hugh

**Clayton, Baby Sister**
*See* Clayton, Merry

**Clayton, Barbara**
*See* Pluff, Barbara Littlefield

**Clayton, Buck**
*See* Clayton, Edward Taylor

**Clayton, Buck**
*See* Clayton, Wilbur

**Clayton, Cat Eye**
*See* Clayton, Wilbur

**Clayton, Cyril James** 1900- [WWL]
*British author*
* Fairplay
* James, C.
* Lew

**Clayton, Doc**
*See* Clayton, Peter Joe

**Clayton, Doctor**
*See* Clayton, Peter Joe

**Clayton, Edward Taylor**
1921-1966 [IBW]
*American author and editor*
* Clayton, Buck

**Clayton, Estelle**
*See* Cooper, Mrs. S. E.

**Clayton, James** 1902-1963 [NOJ]
*American jazz musician*
* Clayton, Kid

**Clayton, Jan**
*See* Clayton, Jane Byral

**Clayton, Jane Byral** 1917- [BEW]
*American actress and singer*
* Clayton, Jan

**Clayton, John**
*See* Beevers, John [Leonard]

**Clayton, Kid**
*See* Clayton, James

**Clayton, Lou**
*See* Finkelstein, Louis

**Clayton, May**
*See* Wilson, Mamie

**Clayton, Merry** 20th c. [SSS]
*American singer*
* Clayton, Baby Sister

**Clayton, Mrs. Albert** [FFF]
*Entertainer*
* Tucker, Mary

**Clayton, Mrs. John** [FFF]
*Entertainer*
* Boucicault, Eva

**Clayton, Peter Joe** 1898-1947
[BWW]
*American singer*
* [The] Blues Doctor
* Clayton, Doc
* Clayton, Doctor
* Cleighton, Peter

**Clayton, Richard Henry Michael**
1907- [CA, CC, EMD]
*British civil servant and author*
* Haggard, William

**Clayton, Susan**
*See* Bailey, Alfred Goldsworthy

**Clayton, Wilbur** 1911?-
[DAM, EJ, NP]
*American jazz musician*
* Clayton, Buck
* Clayton, Cat Eye

**Cleage, Albert Buford, Jr.** 1913-
[IBW]
*American clergyman, author, community organizer*
* Agyeman, Jaramogi Abebe

**Cleage, Evangeline** 1929- [IBW]
*American fashion designer*
* Cleage, Van

**Cleage, Van**
*See* Cleage, Evangeline

**Cleamons, Clem**
*See* Cleamons, Jim

**Cleamons, Jim** 1949- [SMG]
*American basketball player*
* Cleamons, Clem

**Clean Gene McCarthy**
*See* McCarthy, Eugene Joseph

**Clean, Mr.**
*See* Flanagan, Ed

**Clean, Mr.**
*See* Miller, Al

**Clean, Mr.**
*See* Parrish, Larry

**Clean, Mrs.**
*See* Pfeiffer, Jane Cahill

**Cleanhead**
*See* James, Elmore

**Cleanhead, Mr.**
*See* Vinson, Eddie

**Clear, Claudius**
*See* Nicoll, [Sir] William Robertson

**Clearwater, Eddy**
*See* Harrington, Eddy

**Cleary, Fire**
*See* Cleary, Joseph Christopher [Joe]

**Cleary, Joseph Christopher [Joe]**
1920- [BE]
*Irish-born baseball player*
* Cleary, Fire

**Cleaveland, Kate**
*See* Nichols, Rebecca S. Reed

**Cleaver, Hylton Reginald**
1891-1961 [CA]
*British author and playwright*
* Crunden, Reginald

**Cleaver, Nancy**
*See* Mathews, Evelyn Craw

**Cleburne, Patrick Ronayne**
1828-1864 [WBD]
*American army officer*
* [The] Stonewall of the West

**Clegg, Alec**
*See* Clegg, Alexander Bradshaw

**Clegg, Alexander Bradshaw** 1909-
[CA]
*British educator and author*
* Clegg, Alec

**Clegg, W. Paul** 1936- [AW]
*British author*
* Vale, Keith

**Cleghorn, King**
*See* Cleghorn, Sprague

**Cleghorn, Odie**
*See* Cleghorn, Ogilvie

**Cleghorn, Ogilvie** 1891-1956
[CEI, FHE]
*Canadian-born hockey player*
* Cleghorn, Odie

**Cleghorn, Sprague** 1890-1956
[BBH]
*Canadian-born hockey player*
* Cleghorn, King

**Cleighton, Peter**
*See* Clayton, Peter Joe

**Cleishbotham, Jedediah**
*See* Scott, [Sir] Walter

**Cleland, Hugh**
*See* Clarke, John [Campbell]

**Cleland, Mabel**
*See* Widdemer, Mabel Cleland

**Cleland, Morton**
See Rennie, James Alan

**Cleland, William** 1660?-1689
[FFF]
*Scottish poet*
* Honeycomb, Will

**Clemastone**
See Bocciardo, Clement

**Clemenceau, Georges** 1841-1929
[CBS, NN, WBD]
*French premier*
* [The] Tiger

**Clemenges, Matthieu Nicholas de**
1360-1440 [FFF]
*French theologian*
* Theologicus, Doctor

**Clemens, Albert?**
See Lofton, Clarence

**Clemens, Brian Horace** 1931-
[AW]
*British writer and producer*
* O'Grady, Tony

**Clemens, Clem**
See Ulatowski, Clement Lambert

**Clemens, Clement Lambert**
See Ulatowski, Clement Lambert

**Clemens Non Papa [Clement not Pope]**
See Clement, Jacques

**Clemens Romanus**
See Clement I

**Clemens, Samuel Langhorne**
1835-1910 [CC, EWL, WGT]
*American author*
* Ab Originee
* De Conte, [Sieur] Louis
* Finn, Huck
* Lycurgus, Solon
* Slocum, Hi
* Swain, Mark
* Twain, Mark

**Clemens, Titus Flavius** 150?- 220?
[WBD]
*Greek theologian*
* Clement of Alexandria

**Clement**
See Willibrord

**Clement, Frank** 1886-1970 [EAR]
*British auto racer*
* [The] Governor

**Clement, George H.** 1909- [CA]
*Canadian author*
* Henri, G.

**Clement, Hal**
See Stubbs, Harry C[lement]

**Clement, Jack** 1932- [ECM]
*American musician, songwriter, record producer*
* [The] Cowboy

**Clement, Jacques** 16th c.
[SN, WBD]
*Flemish composer*
* Clemens Non Papa [Clement not Pope]

**Clement, Kay**
See Peddell, Maud Clement

**Clement, Lewis** [PA]
*Author*
* [The] Wildflower of the Linden Field

**Clement of Alexandria**
See Clemens, Titus Flavius

**Clement Scott, Joan**
See Footman, Joan

**Clement I** 30?- 100? [WBD]
*Pope*
* Clemens Romanus

**Clement II**
See Suitger

**Clement III**
See Guibert of Ravenna

**Clement III**
See Scolari, Paolo

**Clement IV**
See Foulques, Guy [or Le Gros, Guido]

**Clement IX**
See Rospigliosi, Giulio

**Clement V**
See De Got, Bertrand

**Clement VI**
See Roger, Pierre

**Clement VII**
See Medici, Giulio de

**Clement VII**
See Robert of Geneva

**Clement VIII**
See Aldobrandini, Ippolito

**Clement VIII**
See Sanchez Munoz, Gil

**Clement X**
See Altieri, Emilio

**Clement XI**
See Albani, Giovanni Francesco

**Clement XII**
See Corsini, Lorenzo

**Clement XIII**
See Della Torre Rezzonico, Carlo

**Clement XIV**
See Ganganelli, Giovanni Vincenzo Antonio

**Clement XV, [Pope]**
See Collin, Michel

**[La] Clemente**
See Elizabeth Petrovna

**Clemente, Bob**
See Clemente, Roberto Walker

**Clemente, Roberto Walker**
1934-1972 [BE]
*Puerto Rican-born baseball player*
* Clemente, Bob

**Clementia**
See Feehan, Agnes M.

**Clements, E. H.**
See Hunter, Eileen Helen

**Clements, Foots**
See Clements, W. W.

**Clements, George** 1876-1970
[NAD]
*Author*
* Hotema, Hilton

**Clements, Joy**
See Albrecht, Joyce Marie

**Clements, Vassar** 1928- [ECM]
*American country-western performer*
* Superbow

**Clements, W. W.** 1915?-
*American business executive*
* Clements, Foots

**Clements, Zeke** 1911- [ECM]
*American country-western performer*
* [The] Alabama Cowboy

**Clemons, Craig Lynn** 1949- [SMG]
*American football player*
* Clemons, Sugar Bear

**Clemons, Elizabeth**
See Nowell, Elizabeth Cameron

**Clemons, Fats**
See Clemons, Verne James

**Clemons, Sugar Bear**
See Clemons, Craig Lynn

**Clemons, Verne James** 1891-1959
[BE]
*American baseball player*
* Clemons, Fats

**Clempson, Clem**
See Clempson, David

**Clempson, David** 1949- [RM, RO2]
*British musician*
* Clempson, Clem

**Cleomenes** 6th c. BC [HN]
*King of Sparta*
* [The] Mad King of Lacedaemon

**Cleopatra** 1st c. BC [HN, RH, SN]
*Queen of Egypt*
* [The] Queen of Queens
* [The] Serpent of Old Nile
* [The] Young Isis

**Cleopatra the Egyptian Sorceress**
See Herrmann, Adelaide

**Cleophil**
See Congreve, William

**Clerc, Charles** 1879- ? [BBD]
*French composer*
* Borel-Clerc, Charles

**[A] Clergyman of the Church of Scotland**
See Peebles, William

**[A] Clergyman's Daughter**
See Clacy, Ellen

**[A] Clergyman's Daughter**
See Loyd, E. P.

**[A] Clergyman's Daughter**
See Smith, Elizabeth A.

**[A] Clergyman's Wife**
See Mapleton, S. E.

**Clericus**
See Cartwright, William

**[El] Clerigo**
See Roelas [Ruelas], Juan de las

**Clerihew, E.**
See Bentley, Edmund Clerihew

**Clerk, N. W.**
See Lewis, Clive Staples

**Clery, [Reginald] Val[entine]** 1924-
[CA]
*Canadian author and columnist*
* Janus

**Clery, William Edward**
[SFL, WGT]
*British author*
* Fryers, Austin

**Cless, George** 1907- [MY]
*American jazz musician*
* Cless, Rod

**Cless, Rod**
See Cless, George

**Cleugh, Sophia** 1887?- [TC]
*British author*
* Keene, Ursula

**Cleve, Janita**
See Rowland, D[onald] S[ydney]

**Cleve, John**
See Offutt, Andrew Jefferson

**Clevedon, John**
See Plumley, Ernest Frederick

**Cleveland, Duke**
See Cleveland, Howard

**Cleveland, Frank**
See Shaw, Frank H.

**Cleveland, Ginger**
See Cleveland, Odessa

**Cleveland, Grover**
See Cleveland, Reginald Leslie

**Cleveland, [Stephen] Grover**
1837-1908 [DNNS, FAP, FFF]
*American president*
* [The] Buffalo Hangman
* [The] Buffalo Sheriff
* [The] Claimant
* [The] Dumb Prophet
* Grover the Good
* [The] Hangman of Buffalo
* [The] Man of Destiny
* Old Grover
* Old Veto
* [The] People's President
* [The] Perpetual Candidate
* [The] Pretender
* [The] Reform Governor
* [The] Sage of Princeton
* Stubborn Old Grover
* [The] Stuffed Prophet
* Uncle Jumbo
* [The] Veto Governor
* [The] Veto Mayor
* [The] Veto President

**Cleveland, Howard** 20th c. [OBW]
*American baseball player*
* Cleveland, Duke

**Cleveland, James** 1931- [IBW]
*American musician*
* [The] King of Gospel

**Cleveland, John**
See McElfresh, [Elizabeth] Adeline

**Cleveland, John** 1613-1658 [SN]
*British poet*
* [The] Cavalier Poet

**Cleveland, Mr.**
See Seltzer, Louis B[enson]

**Cleveland, Odessa** 20th c.   [IBW]
*American actress*
* Cleveland, Ginger

**Cleveland, Philip Jerome** 1903-
[CA]
*American clergyman, author, poet*
* Adams, A. Don
* Chute, Rupert
* Frend, A.
* Lewes, Lettie
* Phillips, Jerome C.

**Cleveland, Reginald Leslie** 1948-
[PB]
*Canadian-born baseball player*
* Cleveland, Grover

**[The] Cleveland Rubber Man**
*See* Risko, Johnny

**Clevely, Hugh**   [CC, MBF, WW]
*British author*
* Claymore, Tod

**Cleven, Cathrine**
*See* Cleven, Kathryn Seward

**Cleven, Kathryn Seward** 20th c.
[CA, SAT]
*American author*
* Cleven, Cathrine

**Clevenger, Clev**
*See* Clevenger, Zora

**Clevenger, Ernest Allen, Jr.** 1929-
[CA]
*American author, educator,
columnist*
* Rovin, Ben

**Clevenger, Tex**
*See* Clevenger, Truman Eugene

**Clevenger, Truman Eugene** 1932-
[BE]
*American baseball player*
* Clevenger, Tex

**Clevenger, Zora** 1881- ?   [FB]
*American football coach and
athletic director*
* Clevenger, Clev

**Clewe, Belle Ragnar Parsons** 1878-
?   [NAA]
*American educator and writer*
* Ismar, Mademoiselle
* Tirzah, Mademoiselle

**Clewes, Jeremy**
*See* Bowskill, Derek

**Cliburn, Harvey Lavan, Jr.** 1934-
[BBD, DAM, IPA]
*American pianist*
* Cliburn, Van

**Cliburn, Van**
*See* Cliburn, Harvey Lavan, Jr.

**Cliff, Daisy**
*See* McCoy, Viola

**Cliff, Jimmy**
*See* Chambers, James

**Cliff, Laddie**
*See* Perry, Clifford Albyn

**Cliffe, Alice** 1870?-1943   [BEW]
*British-born actress*
* Belmore, Alice

**Cliffe, H. Cooper**
*See* Cooper, H. Clifford

**Clifford, Buzz**
*See* Clifford, Reese Francis, III

**Clifford, Charles**
*See* Ireland, William Henry

**Clifford, Christopher Craven** 1942-
[DC]
*British cricketer*
* Wef [Wild Eyed Fellow]

**Clifford, Clare** 1894-   [ART]
*British painter*
* Ogilvie, Clare M.

**Clifford, Eth**
*See* Rosenberg, Ethel [Clifford]

**Clifford, Francis**
*See* Thompson, Arthur Leonard
Bell

**Clifford, Geraldine Joncich** 1931-
[CA]
*American educator, author, editor*
* Joncich, Geraldine

**Clifford, Guy**
*See* Roberts, Arthur Guy

**Clifford, Harold B[urton]** 1893-
[CAP, SAT]
*American author*
* Farnham, Burt

**Clifford, Henry de** 1455-1523
[DNNF, HN, RH]
*Tenth Baron of Westmorland*
* [The] Shepherd Earl of
Cumberland
* [The] Shepherd Lord

**Clifford, Jack**
*See* Montani, Virgil

**Clifford, John**
*See* Bayliss, John Clifford

**Clifford, John de** 1435?-1461
[FFF, HN, RH]
*Ninth Baron of Westmorland*
* [The] Black Clifford
* [The] Butcher

**Clifford, Lilian**
*See* Fitzgerald, Eileen

**Clifford, Margaret Cort [Peggy]**
1929-   [CA, SAT]
*American author*
* Cort, M. C.

**Clifford, Martin** [house pseudonym]
*See* Austin, Stanley E.

**Clifford, Martin** [house pseudonym]
*See* Barnard, Alfred J.

**Clifford, Martin** [house pseudonym]
*See* Brooks, Edwy Searles

**Clifford, Martin** [house pseudonym]
*See* Carlton, G. E. L.

**Clifford, Martin** [house pseudonym]
*See* Catchpole, William Leslie

**Clifford, Martin** [house pseudonym]
*See* Cook, Fred Gordon

**Clifford, Martin** [house pseudonym]
*See* Down, C. Maurice

**Clifford, Martin** [house pseudonym]
*See* Eves, Reginald T.

**Clifford, Martin** [house pseudonym]
*See* Griffith, Percy

**Clifford, Martin**
*See* Hamilton, Charles Harold St.
John

**Clifford, Martin** [house pseudonym]
*See* Harper, Harry

**Clifford, Martin** [house pseudonym]
*See* Herman, Julius

**Clifford, Martin** [house pseudonym]
*See* Hinton, Herbert Allan

**Clifford, Martin** [house pseudonym]
*See* Hook, H. Clarke

**Clifford, Martin** [house pseudonym]
*See* Hutt, Hector

**Clifford, Martin** [house pseudonym]
*See* Kirkham, Reginald S.

**Clifford, Martin** [house pseudonym]
*See* Lowe, Claud D.

**Clifford, Martin** [house pseudonym]
*See* Newman, Kenneth E.

**Clifford, Martin** [house pseudonym]
*See* O'Mant, Hedley Percival
Angelo

**Clifford, Martin** [house pseudonym]
*See* Orme, K.

**Clifford, Martin** [house pseudonym]
*See* Pentelow, John Nix

**Clifford, Martin** [house pseudonym]
*See* Ransome, L. E.

**Clifford, Martin** [house pseudonym]
*See* Russell, C.

**Clifford, Martin** [house pseudonym]
*See* Samways, George Richmond

**Clifford, Martin** [house pseudonym]
*See* Warwick, Francis Alister

**Clifford, Martin** [house pseudonym]
*See* Wood-Smith, Noel

**Clifford, Martin** 1910-   [CA]
*American engineer and technical
writer*
* Kenian, Paul Roger

**Clifford, Maude**
*See* Sinclair, Mrs. E. V.

**Clifford, Reese Francis, III** 1942-
[RO1]
*American country-western performer*
* Clifford, Buzz

**Clifford, Rosamond de** ?-1176?
[DNNF, DNNS, RH]
*Mistress of King Henry II of
England*
* Fair Rosamond

**Clifford, Theodore**
*See* Von Block, Sylvia

**Cliffton, Katherine Potter**
*See* Bryant, Katherine Cliffton

**Clift, Betty**
*See* Devery, Elizabeth Coleman

**Clift, Darkie**
*See* Clift, Harlond Benton

**Clift, Harlond Benton** 1912-   [BE]
*American baseball player*
* Clift, Darkie

**Clift, Paddy**
*See* Clift, Patrick Bernard

**Clift, Patrick Bernard** 1953-   [DC]
*Rhodesian-born cricketer*
* Clift, Paddy

**Clift, William**   [PA]
*Author*
* Bunker, Tim

**Clifton, Flea**
*See* Clifton, Herman Earl

**Clifton Fourth**
*See* Morse, H[enry] Clifton, IV

**Clifton, Harry**
*See* Hamilton, Charles Harold St.
John

**Clifton, Herman Earl** 1909-   [BE]
*American baseball player*
* Clifton, Flea

**Clifton, Lewis**
*See* Linedecker, Clifford L.

**Clifton, Mabel**   [PA]
*Author*
* Brierwood, Frank

**Clifton, Nat[han]** 1922-   [BB, IBW]
*American basketball player*
* Clifton, Sweetwater

**Clifton, Oliver Lee**
*See* Rathborne, St. George

**Clifton, Sam** 1898-   [BMH]
*British entertainer*
* Linfield, Sam

**Clifton, Sweetwater**
*See* Clifton, Nat[han]

**Clifton, Zena**
*See* Messenger, Lilian T. R.

**Cline, Donald Biff** 20th c.   [RBE]
*American boxer*
* [The] Terror

**Cline, Eileen Peck** 1892-   [NAA]
*American poet*
* Peck, Eileen

**Cline, Frank**
*See* Rio, Frank

**Cline, Joan**
*See* Hamilton, Joan Lesley

**Cline, John** 20th c.   [BE]
*American baseball player*
* Cline, Monk

**Cline, Monk**
*See* Cline, John

**Cline, Patsy**
*See* Hensley, Virginia

**Clinton, Big Jim**
*See* Clinton, James Lawrence

**Clinton, De Witt** 1769-1828
[FFF, PA]
*American statesman and author*
* Hibernicus

**Clinton, Dirk**
*See* Silverberg, Robert

**Clinton, Edwin M.** 1926-
[SFL, WGT]
*Author*
* More, Anthony

**Clinton, George** 1942-   [IBW]
*American musician*
* [The] Godfather of Funk

**Clinton, Iris A. [Corbin]** 1901-
[CAP]
*British author*
* Corbin, Iris

**Clinton, James Lawrence**
1850-1921 [BE]
*American baseball player*
* Clinton, Big Jim

**Clinton, Jeff**
*See* Bickham, Jack M[iles]

**Clinton, Jon**
*See* Prince, Jack Harvey

**Clinton, Rupert**
*See* Bulmer, [Henry] Kenneth

**Clinton, Walter**
*See* Adams, W. H. D.

**Clio**
*See* Addison, Joseph

**Clio**
*See* Reilly, Edwin J.

**Clionas**
*See* Nicolas, [Sir] Nicholas Harris

**Cliophile**
*See* Octavio, Francesco

**Cliquot**
*See* Frederick William IV

**Clisson, Olivier de** 1320?-1407
[DNNS, HN]
*Constable of France*
* [The] Butcher
* [The] Conqueror

**Clistier, Adeline**
*See* Denenholz, Alma

**Clithero, Myrtle E[ly]** 1906- [CAP]
*American author and educator*
* Clithero, Sally

**Clithero, Sally**
*See* Clithero, Myrtle E[ly]

**Clitus** 4th c. BC [WBD]
*Macedonian army officer*
* [The] Black

**Clitus** 4th c. BC [WBD]
*Macedonian army officer*
* [The] White

**Clive**
*See* Evans, John Quentin

**Clive, Arthur**
*See* O'Grady, Standish James

**Clive, Clifford**
*See* Hamilton, Charles Harold St. John

**Clive, Clifford**
*See* Home-Gall, Edward Reginald

**Clive, Colin**
*See* Clive-Greig, Colin

**Clive, Dennis**
*See* Fearn, John Russell

**Clive, Mrs. Archer** 1711-1785 [PA]
*Author*
* V.

**Clive, Robert [Baron Clive of Plassey]**
1725-1774 [SN]
*British army officer*
* [The] Heaven Born Hero
* Sabut Jung [The Daring in War]

**Clive, William**
*See* Bassett, Ronald Leslie

**Clive-Greig, Colin** 1900-1937
[BEW]
*British actor*
* Clive, Colin

**Cloberry, Elizabeth**
*See* Savery, Constance Winifred

**Clod**
*See* Frankenstein, George L.

**Clodagh**
*See* Aubry, Clodagh

**Clodia** 1st c. BC [DNNF]
*Mistress of Roman poet, Gaius Valerius Catullus*
* Lesbia

**Clodion**
*See* Michel, Claude

**Clodius [or Claudius], Publius** 1st c.
BC [WBD]
*Roman politician*
* Pulcher

**Clolo, Carlos** 1885?-1943 [AS, BE]
*American baseball player*
* Hall, Charles Louis
* Hall, Sea Lion

**Clonblough, G. Butler**
*See* Von Seyffertitz, Gustav

**Clones, Nicholas J.** 20th c. [CA]
*American author*
* Klonis, N. I.

**Clootz, Anacharsis**
*See* Du Val-de-Grace, Jean [or Johann] Baptiste

**Clootz, Baron von**
*See* Du Val-de-Grace, Jean [or Johann] Baptiste

**Clopet, Lilane M. C.**
*See* Bethune, Mary

**Clopinel**
*See* Jean [or Jehan] de Meung

**Clork, Harry**
*See* Clarke, Harry

**Close, John** [PA]
*Author*
* Caxton, Timothy
* Dowell, Samuel
* Whitewell, A. M.

**Close, Upton**
*See* Hall, Josef Washington

**Closs, Elizabeth**
*See* Traugott, Elizabeth Closs

**Closson, Ernest** 1870-1950 [BBD]
*Belgian musician, critic, musicologist*
* Antoine, Paul

**Clot, Antoine Barthelemy**
1793-1868 [WBD]
*French physician*
* Clot Bey

**Clot Bey**
*See* Clot, Antoine Barthelemy

**[The] Clothier of England**
*See* Winchcomb, John

**Cloud, Patricia**
*See* Wallace, Pat

**Cloud, Yvonne**
*See* Kapp, Yvonne

**Clough, Arthur Hugh** 1819-1861
[FFF]
*British poet*
* Adam

**Clough, Colin**
*See* Clough, Thomas Collingwood

**Clough, Ed[gar George]** 1905-1944
[BE]
*American baseball player*
* Clough, Spec

**Clough, Spec**
*See* Clough, Ed[gar George]

**Clough, Thomas Collingwood** 20th
c. [ART]
*Welsh-born painter*
* Clough, Colin

**Cloukey, Charles**
*See* Cloutier, Charles

**Clout, Colin**
*See* Spenser, Edmund

**Cloutier, Buddy**
*See* Cloutier, Real

**Cloutier, Cecile** 1930- [CA]
*Canadian poet and writer*
* De Lantagne, Cecile

**Cloutier, Charles** 20th c. [WGT]
*Author*
* Cloukey, Charles

**Cloutier, Real** 1956- [HR]
*Canadian-born hockey player*
* Cloutier, Buddy

**Cloutman, Barbara** 1909-
*Canadian-born actress*
* Kent, Barbara

**Clover, Sam**
*See* Robinson, Nugent

**Clovis I** 465?- 511 [HN, SN]
*King of the Franks*
* [The] Constantine of Gaul
* [The] Eldest Son of the Church
* [The] Great

**Clowes, [Sir] William Laird**
1856-1905 [WBD]
*British author*
* Nauticus

**[The] Clown Prince of Auto Racing**
*See* Sachs, Edward Julius

**[The] Clown Prince of Baseball**
*See* Schacht, Al[exander]

**[The] Clown Prince of Basketball**
*See* Lemon, Meadow George, III

**[The] Clown Prince of Basketball**
*See* Tatum, Reece

**[The] Clown Prince of Rock and Roll**
*See* Hawkins, Jalacy J.

**Clowney, David Cortez** 1939-
[RO1]
*American singer*
* Cortez, Dave Baby

**Clucher, E. B.**
*See* Barboni, Enzo

**[The] Clumsy Curate of Clapham**
*See* Churchill, Charles

**Clun, Arthur**
*See* Polsby, Nelson W[oolf]

**[The] Clutch**
*See* Bednarik, Chuck

**Clutch, Mr.**
*See* Piper, Scott

**Clutch, Mr.**
*See* West, Jerry

**[The] Clutching Hand**
*See* Morello, Piddu

**Clutha, Janet Paterson Frame**
1924- [CA]
*New Zealand author*
* Frame, Janet

**Clutterbuck, [Captain] Cuthbert**
*See* Scott, [Sir] Walter

**Clutterbuck, Richard** 1917- [CA]
*British author*
* Jocelyn, Richard

**Cluzette, Jennie**
*See* Cooke, Mrs. Henry H.

**Clyde, Alton**
*See* Jeffreys, Sarah Anne

**Clyde Cool Frazier**
*See* Frazier, Walt[er]

**Clyde, Dorothy Hammerton**
1894?-1973 [TR]
*British-born actress*
* Holden, Fay

**Clyde, Kate**
*See* Thanie, C. G.

**Clyde, Kit?**
*See* Senarens, Luis Philip

**Clyde, Leonard Worswick** 1906-
[WW]
*Author*
* Baron, Peter

**Clymer, Derby Day**
*See* Clymer, William Johnston
[Bill]

**Clymer, Eleanor** 1906-
[CA, SAT, WD]
*American author*
* Bell, Janet
* Kinsey, Elizabeth

**Clymer, William Johnston [Bill]**
1873-1936 [BE]
*American baseball player*
* Clymer, Derby Day

**Clynder, Monica**
*See* Muir, Marie Agnes

**Clyne, Douglas George Wilson**
1912- [WD]
*British physician and author*
* Sinclair, Alasdair

**Clyne, Terence**
*See* Blatty, William Peter

**Clytus, John** 1929- [CA]
*American author*
* Monongo

**[The] Coach of Champions**
*See* Yancey, Joseph J., Jr. [Joe]

**[The] Coach of Coaches**
*See* Tobey, David

**Coachman, Alice** 1926- [IBW]
*American track and field athlete*
* [The] Black Pearl of the 1960 Olympiad

**Coad, Frederick Roy** 1925-
[AW, WD]
*British writer*
* Sosthenes
* Sutton, I. M.

**Coad, J.** 19th c. [PA]
*Author*
* Greendrake, Gregory, Esq.

**Coakley, Andrew James** 1882-1963
[BE]
*American baseball player*
* McAllister, Jack

**[The] Coal Burner**
*See* Edmund

**[The] Coal Heaver Preacher**
*See* Huntington, William

**Coal Oil Johnny**
*See* Steele, John

**Coal Oil Payne**
*See* Payne, Henry B.

**Coalyard Mike Handiboe**
*See* Handiboe, Aloysius James

**Coan, Leander S.** [PA]
*Author*
* Old Corporal

**Coaster Joe Connolly**
*See* Connolly, Joseph George [Joe]

**Coates, Diamond**
*See* Coates, Robert

**Coates, Robert** 19th c. [SN]
*British fashion leader*
* Coates, Diamond
* Coates, Romeo

**Coates, Romeo**
*See* Coates, Robert

**Coates, Walter John** 1880- ?
[NAA]
*American editor and clergyman*
* Whitford, Lee

**Coatman, Maureen Margaret**
1919- [ART]
*British sculptor*
* M. M. C.
* Mmcoatman

**Cobalt, Martin**
*See* Mayne, William [James Carter]

**Cobb, Arnett Cleophus**
*See* Cobbs, Arnette

**Cobb, Fat**
*See* Cobb, Joe

**Cobb, J. Storer** 1842- ? [PA]
*Author*
* Eckob, Jay
* White, Hubert

**Cobb, Jack** 1905-1966 [BB]
*American basketball player*
* Spratt, Jack

**Cobb, Jane**
*See* Berry, Jane Cobb

**Cobb, Joe** 1917- [F2]
*Actor*
* Cobb, Fat

**Cobb, Joseph Stanley [Joe]**
*See* Serafin, Joseph Stanley

**Cobb, Junie**
*See* Cobb, Junius C.

**Cobb, Junius C.** 1896?- [WWJ]
*American jazz musician*
* Cobb, Junie

**Cobb, Lee J.**
*See* Jacoby, Leo

**Cobb, Michael**
*See* Wintle, Alfred Daniel

**Cobb, Ned** 1885-1973 [NAD]
*American storyteller and tenant farmer*
* Shaw, Nate

**Cobb, Ty**
*See* Cobb, Tyrus Raymond

**Cobb, Ty, Jr.**
*See* Youngs, Ross Middlebrook

**Cobb, Tyrus Raymond** 1886-1961
[BE, IPA, PB]
*American baseball player*
* Cobb, Ty
* [The] Georgia Peach

**Cobb, William J.** 20th c. [BBH]
*Wrestler*
* Humphrey, Happy

**Cobbe, Frances Power** 1822-1904
[SFL, WGT]
*British author*
* Nostradamus, Merlin

**Cobbett**
*See* Ludovici, Anthony M[ario]

**Cobbett, Boney**
*See* Cobbett, William

**[The] Cobbett of His Day**
*See* Needham, Marchamont

**Cobbett, Richard**
*See* Pluckrose, Henry [Arthur]

**Cobbett, William** 1762-1835
[DEL, PA, SN]
*British author, journalist, politician*
* Cobbett, Boney
* Porcupine, Peter

**Cobbing, Bob** 1920- [CA]
*British poet*
* Cento

**Cobbleigh, Tom**
*See* Raymond, Walter

**[The] Cobbler Poet**
*See* Sachs, Hans

**Cobbold, Richard** 1797- ? [PA]
*Author*
* Catchpole, Margaret

**Cobbs, Arnette** 1918- [IBW, WWJ]
*American jazz musician*
* Cobb, Arnett Cleophus
* [The] World's Wildest Tenor Man

**Cobbs, Willie** 1940- [BWW]
*American singer*
* Willie C

**Cobden, Guy**
*See* Davis, Howard Charles

**Cobden, Richard** 1804-1865
[DHA, DNNF, PA]
*British statesman and political economist*
* [The] Apostle of Free Trade
* [A] Manchester Manufacturer

**Cobden-Sanderson, T. J.**
*See* Cobden-Sanderson, Thomas James

**Cobden-Sanderson, Thomas James**
1840-1922 [LC]
*British bookbinder and publisher*
* Cobden-Sanderson, T. J.

**Cobham, [Sir] Alan**
*See* Hamilton, Charles Harold St. John

**Coborn, Charlie**
*See* McCallum, Colin Whitton

**[The] Cobra**
*See* Aubrey, James T.

**Cobra Joe Frazier**
*See* Frazier, Joseph Filmore [Joe]

**Coburn, Charles F.** 1858- ? [PA]
*Author*
* Autograph

**Coburn, Doddie**
*See* Coburn, Dorothy

**Coburn, Dorothy** 1905?-1978
[FIR]
*Actress and stunt performer*
* Coburn, Doddie

**Coca Cola**
*See* Melendez Melendez, Gabriel

**Cocagnac, Augustin Maurice-Jean**
1924- [CA, SAT]
*French author and clergyman*
* Warbler, J. M.

**Cocambo**
*See* Burain, Paul

**Coccaius [or Coccaio], Merlinus**
*See* Folengo, Teofilo

**Cocceianus**
*See* Dio [or Dion] Cassius

**Cocceius [or Coccejus], Johannes**
*See* Koch, Johannes

**Coch-y-Bonddhu**
*See* Arnold, Richard

**[Le] Cocher de l'Europe**
*See* Choiseul, [Duc] Etienne Francois de

**Cocherito [The Little Coachman]**
*See* Jaureguibeitia e Ibarra, Castor

**Cochlaeus, Johannes**
*See* Dobenek [or Dobneck], Johann

**Cochran, Alvin Jackson** 1891-1947
[BE]
*American baseball player*
* Cochran, Goat

**Cochran, Goat**
*See* Cochran, Alvin Jackson

**Cochran, Jeff**
*See* Durst, Paul

**Cochran, John** 20th c. [SMG]
*American football scout*
* Cochran, Red

**Cochran, Red**
*See* Cochran, John

**Cochran, Rice E.**
*See* Monroe, Keith

**Cochran, Robert Alexander**
1917-1965 [BEW, FC, WEF]
*American actor, director, producer*
* Cochran, Steve

**Cochran, Steve**
*See* Cochran, Robert Alexander

**Cochran, Todd** 1951- [EJ7]
*American jazz musician*
* Bayete

**Cochrane, Black Mike**
*See* Cochrane, Gordon Stanley

**Cochrane, Clark B.** 1817-1867
[FFF]
*American attorney and politician*
* [The] Great Pacificator

**Cochrane, Corinna**
*See* Peterson, Corinna

**Cochrane, Cornelius** 20th c. [AES]
*American soccer coach*
* Cochrane, Mickey

**Cochrane, Freddie** 1915-
[BX, RBE]
*American boxer*
* Cochrane, Red

**Cochrane, Gordon Stanley**
1903-1962 [BE, BN, PB]
*American baseball player*
* Cochrane, Black Mike
* Cochrane, Kid
* Cochrane, Mickey
* King, Frank

**Cochrane, Kid**
*See* Cochrane, Gordon Stanley

**Cochrane, Martha J.** [FFF]
*Author*
* Dare, Sydney

**Cochrane, Mickey**
*See* Cochrane, Cornelius

**Cochrane, Mickey**
*See* Cochrane, Gordon Stanley

**Cochrane, Mrs.** [PA]
*Author*
* Dayre, Sydney

**Cochrane, Red**
*See* Cochrane, Freddie

**Cochrane, William E.** 1926- [CA]
*American author*
* Boult, S. Kye
* Paige, Leo

**Cochrane De Alencar, Gertrude
Emanuela Luise** 1906- [AW, CA]
*Austrian-born author*
* Von Schwarzenfeld, Gertrude

**[The] Cock Lane Ghost**
*See* Parsons, Elizabeth

**[The] Cock of the North**
*See* Gordon, George [Fifth Duke of Gordon]

**[The] Cock of Westminster**
*See* Castell

**Cockburn, Catherine** 1679-1749
[DNNS, HN, RH]
*Scottish playwright*
* [The] Scotch Sappho

**Cockburn, [Francis] Claud** 1904-
[SFL, WGT, WOA]
*Scottish journalist and author*
* Helvick, James
* Pitcairn, Frank

Cocker, Joe
See Cocker, John Robert

Cocker, John Robert 1944-
[PRS, RO2]
British singer
* Cocker, Joe

Cockeye
See Butler, Benjamin Franklin

Cockin, Joan
See Macintosh, Edith Joan
[Burbridge]

Cockloft, Pindar
See Irving, William

[The] Cockney Queen
See Carney, Kate

Cockrell, Amanda
See Crowe, Amanda Cockrell

[The] Cocoa Kid
See Hardwick, Louis

Cocozza, Alfredo Arnold
1921-1959 [BBD, BEW, FC]
American singer
* Lanza, Mario

Codian, Michael 1915- [ASC]
American composer
* Codian, Mickey

Codian, Mickey
See Codian, Michael

Codinus, George ?-1443 [PA]
Author
* Curopolates

Codman, John [PA]
Author
* J. C.
* Ringbolt

Codner, John 1913- [ART]
British painter
* Whitlock, John

Codner, S. M.
See Codner, Stephen Milton

Codner, Stephen Milton 1952-
[ART]
British painter, etcher, sculptor
* Codner, S. M.

Codomannus
See Darius III

Codrescu, Andrei 1946- [CA]
Rumanian-born American writer
* Laredo, Betty
* Tzara, Tristan
* Urmuz

Cody, Al
See Joscelyn, Archie Lynn

Cody, C. S.
See Waller, Leslie

Cody, Captain
See Cody, William Frederick

Cody, Commander
See Fayne, George

Cody, Ethel
See Sack, Ethel

Cody, Harry
See Covington, Van Doak

Cody, Iron Eyes
See Little Eagle

Cody, James R.
See Rohrbach, Peter Thomas

Cody, John
See Repp, Ed[ward] Earl

Cody, Lew
See Cote, Louis Joseph, Jr.

Cody, S. F.
See Cody, Samuel Franklin

Cody, Samuel Franklin 1862-1913
[LC]
American-born British aviator and
inventor
* Cody, S. F.

Cody, Stone
See Landsborough, G. H.

Cody, Walt
See Norwood, Victor G[eorge]
C[harles]

Cody, William Frederick
1846-1917 [IPA, LC, OCF]
American frontier scout and
entertainer
* Buffalo Bill
* Cody, Captain

Coe, Charles Francis 1890- [WWL]
American author
* Trent, Roy

Coe, David Allan 20th c. [ECM]
American musician and songwriter
* [The] Mysterious Rhinestone
Cowboy

Coe, Douglas [joint pseudonym with
Samuel Epstein]
See Epstein, Beryl [Williams]

Coe, Douglas [joint pseudonym with
Beryl (Williams) Epstein]
See Epstein, Samuel

Coe, Edna Reilly 1888- [NAA]
American journalist
* E. R. C.

Coe, Tucker
See Westlake, Donald E[dwin]

Coehorn, Menno van 1641-1704
[DNNF]
Dutch engineer and army officer
* [The] Dutch Vauban

Coekelberghs, Amand Joseph Richard
1922- [IAW]
Belgian author
* Camand, Richard

Coelho, Humberto 1951- [AES]
Portuguese soccer player
* Humberto

Coelho Da Rocha, Adolfo 1907-
[TCL]
Portuguese author, poet, playwright
* Torga, Miguel

Coelicus
See Petit, Adrien

Coerr, Eleanor [Beatrice] 1922-
[CA, SAT, WD]
American author
* Hicks, Eleanor B.
* Page, Eleanor

Coertse, Maria Sophia 1934- [OP]
South African opera singer
* Coertse, Mimi

Coertse, Mimi
See Coertse, Maria Sophia

Coesius
See Von Zesen, Philipp

[Le] Coeur Bas [The Base Heart]
See Lully, Jean Baptiste

Coeur de Lion [Lion-Hearted]
See Boleslav I [or Boleslas]

Coeur de Lion [Lion-Hearted]
See Louis VIII

Coeur de Lion
See Richard I

Coeur, Pierre
See D'Ambre, Anne Caroline de V.

Coeuroy, Andre
See Belime, Jean

[The] Coffee House Muse
See Bourette, Charlotte

Coffey, Brian
See Koontz, Dean R[ay]

Coffey, Coff
See Coffey, Paul

Coffey, Edward Hope, Jr.
1896-1958 [SFL]
Author
* Hope, Edward

Coffey, Jim 1891-1959 [BX, RBE]
Irish boxer
* [The] Roscommon Giant

Coffey, John Joseph 1893- [BE]
American baseball player
* Smith, John Joseph [Jack]

Coffey, Paul 1961- [SMG]
Canadian-born hockey player
* Coffey, Coff

Coffin, Charles Carleton
1823-1896 [DNNF, PA]
American author and journalist
* Carleton

Coffin, Geoffrey
See Mason, F[rancis] Van Wyck

Coffin, Joshua
See Longfellow, Henry Wadsworth

Coffin, N. W. [FFF]
American writer
* Thanelian

Coffin, Peter
See Latimer, Jonathan [Wyatt]

Coffin, Robert 1797-1857
[DEL, DNNF, FFF]
American author and poet
* [The] Boston Bard
* Gray, Barry

Coffin, Roland F. 1826?-1888
[FFF, PA]
American author
* Howard
* Nemo
* Old Sailor
* Sea

Coffin, Ruth Maynard 1913-
[BEW]
American actress and music teacher
* Maynard, Ruth

Coffman, George David 1910- [BE]
American baseball player
* Coffman, Slick

Coffman, Ramon Peyton 1896-
[CAP, SAT]
American author, columnist, editor
* Uncle Ray

Coffman, Slick
See Coffman, George David

Coffman, Virginia [Edith] 1914-
[CA]
American author
* Cross, Victor
* DuVaul, Virginia C.

Coffroth, James W. [Jimmy]
1872?-1949 [B10, BX]
American boxing promoter
* Coffroth, Sunny Jim

Coffroth, Sunny Jim
See Coffroth, James W. [Jimmy]

Cogan, Fanny Hay 1866-1929 [SC]
American actress and opera singer
* [The] Mother of the Movies

Cogan, John [PA]
Author
* C.

Cogan, Thomas ?-1607 [PA]
Author
* [A] Layman

Cogane, Gerald
See Fonarow, Jerry

Cogdill, Cougar
See Cogdill, Gail R.

Cogdill, Cougs
See Cogdill, Gail R.

Cogdill, Gail R. 1937- [FB]
American football player
* Cogdill, Cougar
* Cogdill, Cougs

Coggeshall, John Allen ?-1963
[BEW]
American theatrical performer
* Tower, Allen

Coggins, Frank[lin] 1944- [BE]
American baseball player
* Coggins, Swish

Coggins, Swish
See Coggins, Frank[lin]

Coggs, Dr.
See Giberga, Ovidio

Coghlan, Cockie
See Coghlan, Eamonn

Coghlan, Eamonn 1953?-
Irish track and field athlete
* Coghlan, Cockie

Coghlan, Frank, Jr. 1917- [F2]
Actor
* Coghlan, Junior

Coghlan, Junior
See Coghlan, Frank, Jr.

Coghlan, Rose
See Edgerly, Mrs. Clinton

Cogswell, Coralie [Norris] 1930-
[CA]
American author and educator
* Howard, Coralie

Cohalan, Cornelius 1906-1967
[BB]
American basketball player
* Cohalan, Neil

**Cohalan, Neil**
*See* Cohalan, Cornelius

**Cohen, Alfred** 1924- [CA]
*American author*
* Kern, Alfred

**Cohen, Alfred J.** 1861-1928
[B10, BEW]
*American playwright and critic*
* Dale, Alan

**Cohen, Alta Albert** 1910- [EJS]
*American baseball player*
* Cohen, Schoolboy

**Cohen, Carl E.** 1847-1931 [JL]
*Danish government official*
* Brandes, Carl E.

**Cohen, Chester** 20th c.
[SFP, WGT]
*Author*
* Conanight [joint pseudonym with
  Damon F(rancis) Knight]
* Conant, Chester B.

**Cohen, David** 20th c. [LRR]
*Singer and songwriter*
* Blue, David

**Cohen, Dorothy** ?-1918 [SC]
*American actress*
* Randolph, Dorothy

**Cohen, Elie** ?-1965 [EE]
*Israeli intelligence agent*
* Taabes, Kamil Amin

**Cohen, Elizabeth** 1916?-
[FC, OCF, TR]
*American lyricist and screenwriter*
* Comden, Betty

**Cohen, Ellen Naomi** 1943-1974
[RO2]
*American singer*
* Elliott, Cass[andra]
* Mama Cass

**Cohen, Emanuel Hirsch** 1915-
[BEW]
*American actor, playwright,
producer*
* Randolph, John

**Cohen, Gerald Bruce** 1940- [BEW]
*American theatrical production
associate and casting director*
* Cohen, Kip

**Cohen, Harry** 1883-1932 [EJS]
*American baseball player*
* Kane, Harry
* Kane, Klondike

**Cohen, Harry** 1910- [SAT]
*American author, educator, artist*
* Helfman, Harry

**Cohen, Howard** 1929- [IPA]
*American sportscaster*
* Cosell, Howard

**Cohen, Isidore** 1858-1935 [BBD]
*British composer*
* De Lara, Isidore

**Cohen, Jacob** 1922?- [CA]
*American comedian and author*
* Dangerfield, Rodney
* Roy, Jack

**Cohen, Joseph** 1918- [ASC]
*American composer*
* Cowen, Joseph

**Cohen, Judy** 1939- [CA]
*American artist and author*
* Chicago, Judy

**Cohen, Kip**
*See* Cohen, Gerald Bruce

**Cohen, Lorna** 20th c. [EE]
*Intelligence agent for Russia*
* Kroger, Helen

**Cohen, Martin A.** 20th c. [CA]
*Author*
* Albran, Kehlog [joint pseudonym
  with Sheldon R(ubin) Shacket]

**Cohen, Max**
*See* Cohen, Nessim

**Cohen, Michael** 1900-1968 [SC]
*British actor and composer*
* Carr, Michael

**Cohen, Mickey** 20th c. [PHM]
*American underworld figure*
* [The] Louse

**Cohen, Mike**
*See* Cohen, Morris

**Cohen, Morris** 1842-1927 [JL]
*Danish literary critic*
* Brandes, Georg

**Cohen, Morris** 1912- [CA]
*American author*
* Cohen, Mike

**Cohen, Morris** 20th c. [EE]
*Intelligence agent for Russia*
* Kroger, Peter

**Cohen, Morris A.** 1887-1970 [JL]
*British-born soldier of fortune*
* Cohen, Two Gun

**Cohen, Morton N[orton]** 1921-
[CA, WD]
*American author and critic*
* Moreton, John

**Cohen, Nessim** 1941- [BX, RBE]
*Moroccan-born boxer*
* Cohen, Max

**Cohen, Philip** 1886- [EJS]
*American baseball player*
* Cooney, Philip

**Cohen, Pierre** 1903- [FC]
*French director*
* Chenal, Pierre

**Cohen, Reuben** 1899-1970
[BE, EJS]
*American baseball player*
* Ewing, Reuben

**Cohen, Robert E.** 1930- [CA]
*American author*
* Cazden, Robert E.

**Cohen, Robin Harry Salaman**
1906- [BEW]
*British actor*
* Craven, Robin

**Cohen, Rosalyn**
*See* Higgins, Rosalyn [Cohen]

**Cohen, Samuel** 1913- [EMT]
*American lyricist*
* Cahn, Sammy

**Cohen, Samuel Arthur** 1896-
[BE, EJS]
*American baseball player*
* Bohne, Sammy

**Cohen, Schoolboy**
*See* Cohen, Alta Albert

**Cohen, Seymour** 1920- [EJS]
*American javelin thrower*
* Seymour, Stephen Andrew

**Cohen, Sidney** 1930-1961 [EJS]
*American jockey*
* Cole, Sidney

**Cohen, Sol B.** 1891- [ASC]
*American musician*
* Vaneuf, Andre

**Cohen, Stanley Irving** 1928- [IAW]
*American author*
* Nolamo, Stanley

**Cohen, Susan** 1938- [CA]
*American author*
* St. Clair, Elizabeth

**Cohen, Theodore Charles [Teddy]**
1928- [EJ, PMJ]
*American jazz musician*
* Charles, Teddy

**Cohen, Two Gun**
*See* Cohen, Morris A.

**Cohen, Victor** 1896-1951 [WWJ]
*American jazz musician*
* Berton, Vic

**Cohl, Emile**
*See* Courtet, Emile

**Cohn, Dutz**
*See* Cohn, Julius

**Cohn, Emil** 1881-1948 [BEW]
*German-born author and playwright*
* Ludwig, Emil

**Cohn, George Thomas** 1925-
[DAM]
*American jazz musician*
* Cohn, Sonny

**Cohn, Heinrich** 1848-1909 [BBD]
*Austrian operatic impresario*
* Conried, Heinrich

**Cohn, Helen Desfosses**
*See* Desfosses, Helen

**Cohn, Julius** 1886-1954 [EJS]
*American football player*
* Cohn, Dutz

**Cohn, Norman** 1907- [JL]
*American fencing champion*
* Armitage, Norman C.

**Cohn, Phil**
*See* Kovolick, Philip

**Cohn, Sonny**
*See* Cohn, George Thomas

**Cohn, Vera** 1907- [CA]
*Russian-born author*
* Broido, Vera

**Cohn-Bendit, Daniel** 1944-
*German anarchist*
* Danny the Red

**Cohnan, R. W.**
*See* Hogg, James

**Cohon, Barry**
*See* Cohon, Baruch J[oseph]

**Cohon, Baruch J[oseph]** 1926- [CA]
*American composer and scriptwriter*
* Cohon, Barry

**Cohrone, Lenore** 1900- [BBD]
*American opera singer*
* Corona, Leonora

**Coiffier, Antoine** 1581-1632
[WBD]
*French diplomat and soldier*
* Effiat, Marquis d'
* Ruze

**Coignet, Giles** 1530-1600 [RH]
*Flemish painter*
* Giles of Antwerp

**[The] Coiner of Weasel Words**
*See* Wilson, [Thomas] Woodrow

**Coke, Desmond** 1879- ? [MBF]
*British author*
* Blinders, Belinda

**Coke, [Sir] Edward** 1549?-1634
[HN, SN]
*British jurist*
* [The] Cat
* [The] Oracle of Law

**Coke, Edward** 1879-1951 [THR]
*British actor*
* Rigby, Edward

**Coker, Charles Mitchell** 1927-
[DAM]
*American pianist*
* Coker, Dolo

**Coker, Dolo**
*See* Coker, Charles Mitchell

**Coker, Richard** [PA]
*Author*
* Della Rosa, Signor

**Col**
*See* Bower, George Collier

**Colaabavala, Firooze Darashaw**
1924- [IAW]
*Indian journalist and author*
* [The] Captain
* Darashaw, F.
* Firooze, Frank

**Colan, Eugene** 1926- [WECO]
*American cartoonist*
* Austin, Adam

**Colar, George** 1908- [NOJ]
*American jazz musician*
* Sheik, Kid

**Colas Iglesias, Roberto** 1905-1972
[SC]
*Chilean-born actor*
* Rey, Roberto

**Colavito, Rocco Domenico** 1933-
[DGS, IPA, SMG]
*American baseball player*
* Colavito, Rocky

**Colavito, Rocky**
*See* Colavito, Rocco Domenico

**Colbath, Jeremiah Jones**
1812-1875 [FFF, PA, WBD]
*American politician*
* [The] Natick Cobbler
* Wilson, Henry

**Colberg, Walter**
*See* Bojorski, Walter

**Colbert, Claudette**
*See* Chauchoin, Lily

**Colbert, Jean Baptiste de**
1619-1683 [SN, WBD]
*French statesman*
* [Le] Nord
* [The] North Wind

**Colbin, Rod**
See Lichenstein, Irving Herbert

**Colborne, Cam**
See Colborne, Robert Cameron

**Colborne, Robert Cameron** 1954-
[HR]
*Canadian-born hockey player*
* Colborne, Cam

**Colbron, Grace Isabel** 1869-1948
[NAA, WW]
*American author*
* Marchant, R[omano Isabel]

**Colburn, Claudia Jean** 1941- [OP]
*American opera singer*
* Cummings, Claudia

**Colburn, Frona Eunice Wait**
1859-1946 [SFL]
*Author*
* Wait, Frona Eunice

**Colburn, Zerah** 1804-1840 [SN]
*American mathematical prodigy*
* [The] Calculator

**Colby, C. B.**
See Colby, Carroll Burleigh

**Colby, Carroll Burleigh** 1904-
[WYA]
*Author*
* Colby, C. B.

**Colby Jack Coombs**
See Coombs, John Wesley

**Colcroft, Henry Roeve**
See Schoolcraft, Henry R.

**Colcroft, James**
See Cole, J. W.

**[The] Cold War Witch**
See Thatcher, Margaret Hilda
[Roberts]

**Colder, Ben**
See Wooley, Shelby F.

**Coldwater Jim Hughey**
See Hughey, James Ulysses

**Cole, A. B.**
See Cole, Arthur Bertram, Jr.

**Cole, Adrian Christopher Synnot**
1949- [HFF]
*British author*
* Bryant, Adrian [joint pseudonym]

**Cole, Ann Kilborn**
See Callahan, Claire Wallis

**Cole, Annette** [joint pseudonym with
Barbara A(nnette) Steiner]
See Phillips, Kathleen

**Cole, Annette** [joint pseudonym with
Kathleen Phillips]
See Steiner, Barbara A[nnette]

**Cole, Arthur Bertram, Jr.** 1920-
[ART]
*British industrial designer*
* Cole, A. B.

**Cole, Bert** 1898-
*American baseball player*
* Cole, King

**Cole, Buddy**
See Cole, Edwin Le Mar

**Cole, Burt**
See Dixon, Thomas

**Cole, Cannon**
See Cook, Arlene Ethel

**Cole, Carole** 1945- [IBW]
*American singer and actress*
* Cole, Cookie

**Cole, Catherine**
See Field, Martha Reinhard

**Cole, Clara** [PA]
*Author*
* Clara

**Cole, Comyns** [FFF]
*British writer*
* Bras de Fer

**Cole, Cookie**
See Cole, Carole

**Cole, Cozy**
See Cole, William Randolph

**Cole, Davis**
See Elting, Mary

**Cole, Ed[ward William]**
See Kisleauskas, Edward William

**Cole, Edwin Le Mar** 1916-1964
[DAM, EJ, PMJ]
*American musician*
* Cole, Buddy

**Cole, Elizabeth** 1939- [TR]
*American actress*
* Ashley, Elizabeth

**Cole, G. D. H.**
See Cole, George Douglas Howard

**Cole, George Douglas Howard**
1889-1958 [LC]
*British author and educator*
* Cole, G. D. H.

**Cole, [Sir] Henry** 1808-1882
[DEL, PA]
*British author*
* Summerly, Felix

**Cole, J. W.** ?-1872 [PA]
*Author*
* Colcroft, James

**Cole, Jack**
See Stewart, John [William]

**Cole, Jack** 1918-1958 [WECO]
*American cartoonist and editor*
* Johns, Ralph

**Cole, Jackson**
See Schisgal, Oscar

**Cole, Janet** 1922- [BEW, CA, FC]
*American actress*
* Hunter, Kim

**Cole, Jay**
See Cole, Reuben

**Cole, King**
See Cole, Bert

**Cole, King**
See Cole, Leonard Leslie

**Cole, King**
See Coles, Nathaniel Adams

**Cole, Larry** 20th c.
*American football player*
* Cole, Lurch

**Cole, Leonard Leslie** 1886-1916
[AS, BE]
*American baseball player*
* Cole, King

**Cole, Les[ter]** 20th c. [WGT]
*Author*
* Sturgis, Colin [joint pseudonym
with Mel(vin) Sturgis]

**Cole, Lois Dwight** 20th c.
[CA, SAT]
*American author*
* Arnett, Caroline
* Avery, Lynn
* Dudley, Nancy
* Dwight, Allan
* Eliot, Anne

**Cole, Lurch**
See Cole, Larry

**Cole, Margaret Alice** 20th c. [CA]
*British author*
* Manning, Rosemary
* Renton, Julia
* Saunders, Ione

**Cole, Marian Fairman** 1812- ?
[FFF]
*British author*
* Summerly, Mrs. Felix

**Cole, Mary**
See Hanna, Mary T.

**Cole, Nat King**
See Coles, Nathaniel Adams

**Cole, Natalie Maria** 1950- [IBW]
*American singer*
* Cole, Sweetie

**Cole, Punjab**
See Cole, Ralph

**Cole, Ralph** 20th c. [OBW]
*American baseball player*
* Cole, Punjab

**Cole, Reuben** 1915-1975 [IBW]
*American jazz musician*
* Cole, Jay

**Cole, Sidney**
See Cohen, Sidney

**Cole, Stark**
See Filer, Thomas Hanford

**Cole, Stephen**
See Webbe, Gale D[udley]

**Cole, Sweetie**
See Cole, Natalie Maria

**Cole, Toby**
See Cholodenko, Toby

**Cole, William Morse** 1866- ?
[ALY]
*American author*
* Craigie, Christopher

**Cole, William Randolph** 1909-1981
[DAM, EJ, PMJ]
*American jazz musician*
* Cole, Cozy

**Coleborn, Maud** ?-1911 [WWL]
*British author*
* Coleborn, Morris

**Coleborn, Morris**
See Coleborn, Maud

**Coleman, Burl C.** 1896-1950
[BWW, NBB]
*American singer*
* Coleman, Jaybird

**Coleman, Burl C.** (Continued)
* Williams, Rabbit's Foot

**Coleman, Carole**
See Huneycutt, Betty

**Coleman, Choo Choo**
See Coleman, Clarence

**Coleman, Clarence** 1937- [BE]
*American baseball player*
* Coleman, Choo Choo

**Coleman, Clayton W[ebster]** 1901-
[CA]
*American author*
* Smith, Webster

**Coleman, Cy**
See Kaufman, Seymour

**Coleman, David Lee** 1950- [SMG]
*American baseball player*
* Coleman, Moe

**Coleman, E[velyn] S[cherabon]**
See Firchow, Evelyn Scherabon

**Coleman, Emmett**
See Reed, Ishmael

**Coleman, Irene** 1890- [THR]
*American actress*
* Murdock, Ann

**Coleman, James L.** 1889-1960
[IBW]
*American army officer*
* Coleman, Pappa
* [The] Pride of the Phillipines

**Coleman, Jaybird**
See Coleman, Burl C.

**Coleman, John Winston, Jr.** 1898-
[IAW]
*American author and historian*
* Squire

**Coleman, Kitty**
See McCarthy, Mrs. Daniel

**Coleman, Kitty**
See Walsh, Mrs. John

**Coleman, Lee**
See Lapidus, Elaine

**Coleman, Moe**
See Coleman, David Lee

**Coleman, Nelly**
See Wilson, Lena

**Coleman, Pappa**
See Coleman, James L.

**Coleman, Percy**
See Coleman, Pierce D.

**Coleman, Pierce D.** 19th c. [BE]
*American baseball player*
* Coleman, Percy

**Coleman, Rip**
See Coleman, Walter Gary

**Coleman, Robert William Alfred**
1916- [CA]
*British author and clergyman*
* Insight, James

**Coleman, Vernon** 1946- [CA]
*British author*
* Vernon, Edward

**Coleman, Walter Gary** 1931-
[BE, SMG]
*American baseball player*
* Coleman, Rip

**Coleridge, Derwent** 1800-1883
[DEL]
*British author and clergyman*
* Cecil, Devenant

**Coleridge, Ethel**
*See* Coleridge-Tucker, Ethel

**Coleridge, Henry Nelson**
1800-1843 [DEL, PA]
*British author*
* Haller, Joseph
* Hunter, Joseph

**Coleridge, John** [joint pseudonym
with Otto O(scar) Binder]
*See* Binder, Earl Andrew

**Coleridge, John** [joint pseudonym
with Earl Andrew Binder]
*See* Binder, Otto O[scar]

**Coleridge, Samuel Taylor**
1772-1834 [DEP, DNNF, DNNS]
*British poet, philosopher, critic*
* [The] Alnaschar of Modern
  Literature
* [The] Old Man Eloquent
* S. T. C.

**Coleridge-Tucker, Ethel** 1883-
[THR]
*British actress*
* Coleridge, Ethel

**Coles, Charles** 20th c. [IBW]
*American actor, dancer, theatre
manager*
* Coles, Honi

**Coles, Charles Ernest** 1876- ?
[NAA]
*British-born clergyman and author*
* Justus

**Coles, Cyril Henry** 1899?-1965
[CAP, CC, EMD]
*British author*
* Coles, Manning [joint pseudonym
  with Adelaide Frances Oke
  Manning]
* Gaite, Francis [joint pseudonym
  with Adelaide Frances Oke
  Manning]

**Coles, Detective Inspector**
*See* Sempill, Ernest

**Coles, Honi**
*See* Coles, Charles

**Coles, John** [PA]
*Author*
* Civis

**Coles, Manning** [joint pseudonym
with Adelaide Frances Oke
Manning]
*See* Coles, Cyril Henry

**Coles, Manning** [joint pseudonym
with Cyril Henry Coles]
*See* Manning, Adelaide Frances
Oke

**Coles, Nathaniel Adams**
1917?-1965 [ASC, B10, BBD]
*American singer and pianist*
* Cole, King
* Cole, Nat King

**Colette**
*See* Colette, Sidonie Gabrielle

**Colette, Sidonie Gabrielle**
1873-1954 [B10, CD, LC]
*French author*
* Colette
* Willy, Colette

**Coley, Rex** 1898- [AW]
*British author*
* Ragged Staff

**Coley, Robert**
*See* Wandrei, Howard Elmer

**Colibri**
*See* Vieux, Marie

**Colimon, Marie-Therese** 1918-
[CW]
*Haitian poet, author, playwright*
* Bec, Marie

**Colin, Jean**
*See* Bell, Joyce

**Colin, Pierre Gilbert** ?-1555 [PA]
*Author*
* Chamault

**Colinski, A. J.** 20th c. [MBF]
*British author*
* McPherson, [Captain] Angus
* Scott, [Captain] Angus

**Colizzi, Gioacchino** 1894- [WEC]
*Italian cartoonist*
* Attalo

**Coll, Mad Dog**
*See* Coll, Vincent

**Coll, Vincent** 1909-1932 [BLB]
*American underworld figure*
* Coll, Mad Dog

**Collacon**
*See* Day, E. P.

**Collans, Dev**
*See* Winchell, Prentice

**Collard, Earl Clinton** 1898-1968
[BE]
*American baseball player*
* Collard, Hap

**Collard, Hap**
*See* Collard, Earl Clinton

**Collard, John** 1769-1810 [FFF]
*British author*
* Dralloc, John

**Collazo, Bobby**
*See* Collazo Pena, Roberto

**Collazo Pena, Roberto** 1916-
[ASC]
*Cuban musician*
* Collazo, Bobby

**Colle, Raffaello dal** 1490?-1540?
[WBD]
*Tuscan painter*
* Raffaellino

**Colleano, Bonar, Jr.**
*See* Sullivan, Bonar

**Colleano, Bonar, Sr.**
*See* Sullivan, Edgar James

**Collectivus, Doctor**
*See* Caraccioli, Lardolpho

**Colledge** 17th c. [HN]
*British citizen, accused of treason*
* [The] Protestant Joiner

**Colleen** [code name used during
World War II]
*See* King, Ernest Joseph

**Collen, Neil**
*See* Lee, Lincoln

**Collerye, Roger de** 1470?-1540
[WBD]
*French poet*
* Bontemps, Roger

**Collet, Stephen**
*See* Byerley, Thomas

**Collett, Beryl Bishop** 20th c.
[NAA]
*American clergywoman and writer*
* Boswell, Clementine

**Collette, Buddy**
*See* Collette, William Marcell

**Collette, William Marcell** 1921-
[ASC, DAM, EJ]
*American jazz musician*
* Collette, Buddy

**Colleville, Anne Hyacinthe**
1761-1824 [PA]
*Author*
* De Saint Ledger, Geille

**Colley, Iain** 1940- [CA]
*British author*
* Ransome-Davies, Basil

**Collie, Biff**
*See* Collie, Hiram Abiff

**Collie, Hiram Abiff** 1926- [FCW]
*American country-western
performer, disk jockey, promoter*
* Collie, Biff

**Collie, Ruth** 20th c. [LC]
*Author*
* Stitch, Wilhelmina

**Collier, Buster**
*See* Collier, William, Jr.

**Collier, Constance**
*See* Hardie, Laura Constance

**Collier, Douglas**
*See* Fellowes-Gordon, Ian
[Douglas]

**Collier, Frank** ?-1879 [PA]
*Author*
* Leslie, Frank

**Collier, Harry**
*See* Walton, Harry

**Collier, James L[incoln]** 1928-
[CA, SAT]
*American author*
* Williams, Charles

**Collier, Jane**
*See* Shumsky, Zena Feldman

**Collier, John** 1708-1786 [PA]
*British poet*
* Bobbin, Tim

**Collier, John** 1850-1934 [SN]
*British painter*
* [The] Lancashire Hogarth

**Collier, John Payne** 1789-1883
[PA]
*British journalist and critic*
* Amicus Curiae

**Collier, Joy**
*See* Millar, Minna Henrietta Joy

**Collier, Lucille Ann** 1919-
[ITA, PMJ, SW]
*American actress and dancer*
* Miller, Ann

**Collier, Margaret**
*See* Taylor, Margaret Stewart

**Collier, Norman**
*See* Bennett, C. N.

**Collier, Old Cap**
*See* Harbaugh, Thomas Chalmers

**Collier, Old Cap**
*See* James W. I.

**Collier, Old Cap**
*See* Wayde, Bernard

**Collier, Patience**
*See* Ritcher, Rene

**Collier, William, Jr.** 1900?-
[F1, F2]
*American actor*
* Collier, Buster

**Collier, Zena**
*See* Shumsky, Zena Feldman

**Colligan, Mrs. George W.** ?-1886
[FFF]
*Entertainer*
* Larkelle, Nellie

**Collin, Jacques Albin Simon**
1794-1881 [PA]
*Author*
* Beranger, Paul
* Brindamour
* Byron and Moore
* Collin de Plancy, Jacques Albin
  Simon
* Ensanada
* Glananville
* Mullner
* Nilense, Baron
* [Le] Noven de mon Oncle
* Saint Albin
* Videlbias, Johannes

**Collin, Michel** 1905- [B10]
*Former French priest, not actually a
pope*
* Clement XV, [Pope]

**Collin de Plancy, Jacques Albin
Simon**
*See* Collin, Jacques Albin Simon

**Collin Du Bocage, Louis Jacques
Marie** 1893-1952 [MWD]
*French actor, director, playwright*
* Verneuil, Louis

**Collin-Dufresne, Isabelle** 20th c.
[SW]
*French actress*
* Violet, Ultra

**Colline**
*See* De Angelis, Alberto

**Collinge, Eileen Cecilia** 1894-
[BEW]
*Irish actress and writer*
* Collinge, Patricia

**Collinge, Patricia**
*See* Collinge, Eileen Cecilia

**Collingham, G. G.**
*See* White, Mary Helen

**Collings, Dodger**
*See* Collings, Norman

**Collings, Edwin Geoffrey** 1913-
[AW, WD]
*British author*
* Blackwell, John

**Collings, I. J.** [WD]
*British author*
* Collings, Jillie

**Collings, Jillie**
See Collings, I. J.

**Collings, Norman** 20th c. [CEI]
Canadian-born hockey player
* Collings, Dodger

**Collingswood [M.D.], Frederick**
See Lakritz, Esther

**Collingwood, Harry**
See Lancaster, William Joseph Cosens

**Collingwood, R. G.**
See Collingwood, Robin George

**Collingwood, Robin George**
1889-1943 [LC]
British author and scholar
* Collingwood, R. G.

**Collingwood, W. G.**
See Collingwood, William Gershom

**Collingwood, William Gershom**
1854-1932 [LC]
British author, artist, antiquarian
* Collingwood, W. G.

**Collins**
See Stevens, George

**Collins, Alan**
See Pigozzi, Luciano

**Collins, Barbara Ines** 20th c.
[CND]
American pro-Castro propagandist
* Beardless Barbara

**Collins, Big Tom**
See Dupree, William Thomas

**Collins, Big Tom**
See McGhee, Walter Brown

**Collins, Bootsy**
See Collins, William

**Collins, Buck**
See Collins, Orth Stein

**Collins, Burt**
See Collins, Burton I.

**Collins, Burton I.** 1931- [EJ]
American jazz musician
* Collins, Burt

**Collins, C. J.** [PA]
Author
* Priam

**Collins, Carlton Palmer** 1893- ?
[BBH]
American lacrosse player
* Collins, Collie

**Collins, Casey**
See Collins, Kevin Michael

**Collins, Charles** 1862-1914 [BE]
Canadian-born baseball player
* Collins, Chub

**Collins, Chub**
See Collins, Charles

**Collins, Cindy**
See Smith, Richard Rein

**Collins, Clark**
See Reynolds, Dallas McCord

**Collins, Cocky**
See Collins, Edward Trowbridge, Sr. [Eddie]

**Collins, Colin**
See Merland, Oliver

**Collins, Collie**
See Collins, Carlton Palmer

**Collins, Cryin' Sam**
See Collins, Samuel

**Collins, D.**
See Bulleid, Henry Anthony Vaughan

**Collins, Dapper Don**
See Tourbillon, Robert Arthur

**Collins, Dennis** 20th c. [WECO]
British cartoonist
* Kol

**Collins, Dorothy**
See Chandler, Marjorie

**Collins, Edward Trowbridge, Sr.**
[Eddie] 1887-1951 [AS, BE, DGS]
American baseball player
* Collins, Cocky
* Sullivan, Eddie

**Collins, Fidgety Phil**
See Collins, Philip Eugene

**Collins, Freda**
See Collins, Frederica Joan Hale

**Collins, Frederica Joan Hale** 1904-
[CAP]
British author and playwright
* Collins, Freda

**Collins, Geoffrey**
See Jefferies, Greg

**Collins, George M.** 20th c. [BBH]
Scottish-born soccer player and organization officer
* Collins, Old Stonewall

**Collins, Harry C.**
See Becker, Max O[ctavious]

**Collins, Harry Warren** 1896-1968
[AS, BE, FB]
American baseball player and football player
* Collins, Rip
* Collins, Two Gun

**Collins, Heidi**
See Collins, Hyacinth

**Collins, Hunt**
See Lombino, Salvatore A.

**Collins, Hyacinth** 1949- [IBW]
American attorney and legislative assistant
* Collins, Heidi

**Collins, J. L.** 19th c. [PA]
Author
* Jonquil

**Collins, James Anthony**
1904?-1970 [AS, BE, PB]
American baseball player
* Collins, Rip [or Ripper]

**Collins, James H.** 1873- ? [NAA]
American author
* Mappelbeck, John

**Collins, Joe**
See Kollonige, Joseph Edward

**Collins, John** 1624?-1683
[DEP, DNNF, DNNS]
British mathematician and physicist
* [The] English Mersenne

**Collins, John Edgar** 1892- [BE]
American baseball player
* Collins, Zip

**Collins, John Francis** 1885-1955
[AS, BE]
American baseball player
* Collins, Shano

**Collins, Joseph Lawton** 1896-1963
[BDW, WWW]
American army officer
* Collins, Lightnin' Joe
* [The] GI's General

**Collins, June**
See Weatherstone, June Irene

**Collins, Kevin Michael** 1946- [BE]
American baseball player
* Collins, Casey

**Collins, L. M.**
See Collins, Leslie Morgan

**Collins, Lawrencine May** 1942-
[CWG, DAM]
American country-western performer
* Collins, Lorrie

**Collins, Leslie Morgan** 1914-
[IBW]
American poet
* Collins, L. M.

**Collins, Lester Rallingston** 1910-
[EJ, PMJ, WWJ]
American jazz musician
* Collins, Shad

**Collins, Lightnin' Joe**
See Collins, Joseph Lawton

**Collins, Lorrie**
See Collins, Lawrencine May

**Collins, Lottie** 1866-1910 [BMH]
British entertainer
* [The] Kate Vaughan of the Music Halls

**Collins, Louis Bo** 1932-
[BWW, NBB]
American singer
* Mr. Bo

**Collins, Lucretia** 1940- [IBW]
American civil rights activist
* [The] Spirit of Nashville

**Collins, Mabel**
See Cook, Mabel Collins

**Collins, Margaret [Brandon James]**
1909- [CA]
American playwright
* Welsh, Susan

**Collins, Mary Cathleen** 1956?-
American actress
* Derek, Bo

**Collins, Michael**
See Lynds, Dennis

**Collins, Mortimer** 1827-1876 [PA]
British author and poet
* Colton, R. T.
* Colton, Robert Turner

**Collins, Old Stonewall**
See Collins, George M.

**Collins, Orth Stein** 1880-1949 [BE]
American baseball player
* Collins, Buck

**Collins, Pat**
See Allan, Patricia Colinaka

**Collins, Philip Eugene** 1900-1948
[BE]
American baseball player
* Collins, Fidgety Phil

**Collins, Rip**
See Collins, Harry Warren

**Collins, Rip [or Ripper]**
See Collins, James Anthony

**Collins, Sam**
See Vegg, Samuel

**Collins, Samuel** 1887-1949 [BWW]
American singer
* Carter, Bunny
* Collins, Cryin' Sam
* Foster, Jim
* Salty Dog Sam
* Woods, Big Boy

**Collins, Shad**
See Collins, Lester Rallingston

**Collins, Shano**
See Collins, John Francis

**Collins, Thomas Hightower** 1910-
[CA]
American author and columnist
* Hightower, Paul

**Collins, Tommy**
See Sipes, Leonard Raymond

**Collins, Two Gun**
See Collins, Harry Warren

**Collins, Virginia E. V.** 20th c.
[IBW]
American political organizer
* Abubakari, Dara

**Collins, Will**
See Corley, Edwin

**Collins, William** 1953- [IBW]
American musician
* Collins, Bootsy

**Collins, Winnie**
See Leopold, Winnie

**Collins, Zip**
See Collins, John Edgar

**Collinson, Owen?**
See Owen, [Harry] Collinson

**Collinson, Peter**
See Hammett, [Samuel] Dashiell

**Collison, Wilson** 1893- [WW]
Author
* Kent, Willis

**Collodi, Carlo**
See Lorenzini, Carlo

**Collodion** [code name used during World War II]
See Stettinius, Edward Reilley, Jr.

**Colloms, Brenda** 1919- [AW, WD]
British author
* Cross, Brenda
* Hughes, Brenda

**Colloway, Ray**
See Colucci, Mario

**Collyer, Bud**
See Collyer, Clayton

**Collyer, Clayton**
Radio and television announcer
* Collyer, Bud

**Collyer, Doric**
See Hunt, Dorothy Alice

**Collyer, June**
See Heermance, Dorothy

**Collyer, Sam**
See Jamieson, Walter

**Collymore, Colly**
See Collymore, Frank A.

**Collymore, Frank A.** 1893- [CW]
*Barbadian poet, educator, actor*
* Collymore, Colly

**Colman, George**
See Glassco, John [Stinson]

**Colman, Hila** 20th c. [SAT]
*American author*
* Crayder, Teresa

**Colman, Julia** 19th c. [PA]
*Author*
* Aunt Julia

**Colman, L.**
See Savona, Leopoldo

**Colman, Robert Wringham**
See Hogg, James

**Colmer, Graham John** 1887- [THR]
*British playwright and lyricist*
* John, Graham

**Colmolyn**
See Sotheran, Charles

**Colmore, G[eorge]**
See Weaver, Gertrude Renton

**Colom, M. J.**
See Colom, Maria Josefa

**Colom, Maria Josefa** 1926- [ART]
*Spanish painter and engraver*
* Colom, M. J.

**Coloma Sanjuan, Andres**
1907-1964 [GS]
*Spanish bullfighter*
* Clasico [Classic One]

**Coloman** 1070-1114
[FFF, RH, SN]
*King of Hungary*
* [The] Learned

**Colomb, Georges** 1856-1945
[WECO]
*French artist, writer, educator*
* Christophe

**Colombat, Claire** 1925- [FC]
*French actress*
* Laage, Barbara

**Colombo**
See Gomez, Raul

**Colombo, Dale**
See Monroe, Keith

**Colombrito, Philip** 1915-
[ASC, PMJ]
*American singer*
* Brito, Phil

**[The] Colonel**
See Combs, Earle Bryan

**Colonel Bill Williams**
See Williams, William [Bill]

**Colonna, Ottone [or Oddone]**
1368-1431 [WBD]
*Pope*
* Martin V

**Colonne, Edouard**
See Colonne, Judas

**Colonne, Judas** 1838-1910 [BBD]
*French conductor and violinist*
* Colonne, Edouard

**Colorado, Antonio J.**
See Colorado Capella, Antonio
Julio

**Colorado Capella, Antonio Julio**
1903- [CA]
*Puerto Rican author*
* Colorado, Antonio J.

**[The] Colored James Dean**
See Alexander, John M., Jr.

**[The] Colored Sophie Tucker**
See McDaniel, Hattie

**Colosimo, Big Jim**
See Colosimo, James

**Colosimo, James** 1877-1920
*American underworld figure*
* Colosimo, Big Jim

**[A] Colossus**
See Du Plessis, Armand Jean

**[The] Colossus of Danish Literature**
See Holberg, Louis [or Ludvig]

**[The] Colossus of Debate**
See Adams, John

**[The] Colossus of English Philology**
See Johnson, Samuel

**[The] Colossus of Independence**
See Adams, John

**[A] Colossus of Literature**
See Warburton, William

**[The] Colossus of the Nineteenth Century**
See Bonaparte, Napoleon

**[The] Colossus of Yiddish Literature**
See Peretz, Yitskhok Leybush

**Colpet, Max**
See Kolpe, Max

**Colson**
See Bellicour, Gillis

**Colson**
See Orton, Thora Margaret

**Colson, Bill**
See Athanas, William Verne

**Colson, Dorothea**
See Phillifent, John Thomas

**Colson, Ethel M.**
See Brazelton, Ethel M. Colson

**Colson, Frederick**
See Geis, Richard E[rwin]

**Colston-Baynes, Dorothy Julia** 20th c. [LC]
*Author*
* Creston, Dormer

**Colt, Clem**
See Nye, Nelson C[oral]

**Colt, Martin**
See Epstein, Samuel

**Colt, Winchester Remington**
See Hubbard, Lafayette Ronald

**Colteli**
See Procope-Couteau, Michael

**Colter** [code name used during
World War II]
See Arnold, Henry Harley

**Colter, Cyrus J.** 1910- [IBW]
*American author*
* Grandfather, Dr.

**Colter, Eli**
See Colter, Elizabeth

**Colter, Elizabeth** 20th c. [SFP]
*Author*
* Colter, Eli

**Colter, Jessi**
See Johnson, Miriam

**Colter, Shayne**
See Norwood, Victor G[eorge]
C[harles]

**Coltman, Ernest Vivian**
See Coltman-Allen, Ernest

**Coltman, Will**
See Bingley, David Ernest

**Coltman-Allen, Ernest** 1908- [CA]
*British author*
* Coltman, Ernest Vivian
* Dudley, Ernest

**Colton, A. J.**
See Hook, Alfred Samuel

**Colton, Anita** 1920?-
*American singer*
* O'Day, Anita

**Colton, Calvin** 1789-1857 [PA]
*Author*
* [An] American in London

**Colton, James**
See Hansen, Joseph

**Colton, Mel** 20th c. [WW]
*Author*
* Trask, Merrill

**Colton, R. T.**
See Collins, Mortimer

**Colton, Robert Turner**
See Collins, Mortimer

**Coltrane, James**
See Wohl, James P[aul]

**Coltrane, John William** 1926-1967
[IBW]
*American jazz musician*
* Coltrane, Trane

**Coltrane, Trane**
See Coltrane, John William

**Colucci, Mario** 20th c. [WF]
*Italian screenwriter*
* Colloway, Ray

**Colucci, Michel** 1944?-
*French comedian*
* Coluche

**Coluche**
See Colucci, Michel

**Columba**
See Coster, Jean

**Columba** 521- 597
[DNNF, DNNS, FFF]
*Saint*
* [The] Apostle of Caledonia
* [The] Apostle of the Highlanders

**Columbia George Smith**
See Smith, George Allen

**Columbia Lou Gehrig**
See Gehrig, [Henry] Lou[is]

**Columbo, Ruggiero De Rudolpho**
1908-1934 [CED, F2, FC]
*American singer, composer, violinist*
* Columbo, Russ

**Columbo, Russ**
See Columbo, Ruggiero De
Rudolpho

**Columbus, Chris**
See Morris, Joseph Christopher
Columbus

**Columbus, Christopher**
1447?-1506 [DEP, FFF, SN]
*Italian-born navigator*
* Iberia's Pilot
* [The] Old Admiral

**[The] Columella of New England**
See Lowell, John

**Colver, Alice Mary [Ross]** 1892-
[CA]
*American author*
* Randall, Mary

**Colver, Anne** 1908-
[B10, CA, SAT]
*American author*
* Graff, Polly Anne Colver
* Harris, Colver

**Colvett, Latayne**
See Scott, Latayne Colvett

**Colvig, Pinto**
See Colvig, Vance D.

**Colvig, Vance D.** 1892-1967 [SC]
*American actor and songwriter*
* Colvig, Pinto
* [The] Dean of Hollywood Voice
Men

**Colvil, Edward**
See Putnam, Mary Lowell

**Colvil, Samuel** [SN]
*Scottish author*
* [The] Scottish Hudibras

**Colvill, Helen Hester** 20th c.
[WWL]
*British author*
* Wylde, Katharine

**Colville, Mac**
See Colville, Matthew Lamont

**Colville, Matthew Lamont** 1916-
[CEI, FHE]
*Canadian-born hockey player*
* Colville, Mac

**Colville, Violetta**
See Andrews, Mrs. C. R.

**Colvin, Douglas** 20th c.
*American musician*
* Ramone, Dee Dee

**Colvin, Fred Herbert** 1867- ?
[NAA]
*American editor and mechanical
engineer*
* Godfrey, John R.
* Hudson, Frank C.
* Roper, Loring

**Colvin, Jack** 20th c. [BBH]
*American basketball player*
* Colvin, Tex

**Colvin, James**
See Moorcock, Michael John

**Colvin, Tex**
See  Colvin, Jack

**Colwell, Stephen** 1800-1871    [FFF]
*American author*
* Penn, Mr.
* Wise, Jonathan B.

**Comanche, Laurence** 1908-1932
[SC]
*American actor*
* Comanche, Tex

**Comanche, Tex**
See  Comanche, Laurence

**Combe, Count**
See  Combe [or Coombe], William

**Combe, Duke**
See  Combe [or Coombe], William

**Combe [or Coombe], William**
1741-1823   [DEL, SN, WBD]
*British author and adventurer*
* Combe, Count
* Combe, Duke
* Syntax, Dr.

**Comber, Bobbie**
See  Comber, Edmund

**Comber, Edmund** 1886-1942
[THR]
*British actor*
* Comber, Bobbie

**Comber, Elizabeth** 1917-   [B10]
*Chinese physician and author*
* Han Suyin

**Comber, Lillian** 1916-   [CA]
*British author*
* Beckwith, Lillian

**Combs, A.** 20th c.   [OBW]
*American baseball player*
* Combs, Jack

**Combs, Earle Bryan** 1899-1976
[BAB, BE, PB]
*American baseball player*
* [The] Colonel
* [The] Kentucky Colonel

**Combs, Glen** 1946-   [BB]
*American basketball player*
* [The] Kentucky Rifle

**Combs, Jack**
See  Combs, A.

**Combs, Robert**
See  Murray, John F[rancis]

**Comden, Betty**
See  Cohen, Elizabeth

**Comeau, Rey**
See  Comeau, Reynald Xavier

**Comeau, Reynald Xavier** 1948-
[HR]
*Canadian-born hockey player*
* Comeau, Rey

**[The] Comedy Prince of Magic**
See  Ali, [Sheik] Ben

**Comellas, Jorge** 1917-   [BE]
*Cuban-born baseball player*
* Comellas, Pancho

**Comellas, Pancho**
See  Comellas, Jorge

**[El] Comendador Griego**
See  Nunez de Guzman, Fernan [or
Fernando]

**Comer, Cornelia Atwood** 20th c.
[ESF]
*Author*
* Pratt, Cornelia Atwood

**Comer, Ralph**
See  Sanders, John

**Comer, Terry** 1949-   [RO2]
*British musician*
* Comer, Tex

**Comer, Tex**
See  Comer, Terry

**Comerford, Harry** 1877- ?   [THR]
*British comedian*
* Ford, Harry

**Comes**
See  Von Redlich, Marcellus
Donald A. R.

**Comestor, Peter [or Petrus]**
?-1198   [DEP, DNNF, SN]
*French theologian*
* [The] Great Eater
* Helluo
* [The] Master of History
* [The] Master of Stories

**Comfort, Jane Levington**
See  Sturtzel, Jane Levington

**Comfort, Lance**
See  Comfort, Lancelot Foster

**Comfort, Lancelot Foster**
1908-1966   [FDG]
*British director*
* Comfort, Lance

**Comfort, Montgomery**
See  Campbell, John Ramsey

**[The] Comic of the Day**
See  McCallum, Colin Whitton

**[El] Comico**
See  Martin Piaz, Ysabel Ponciana
Chris-Pin

**Comidas, Chinas**
See  Genser, Cynthia

**Comines [or Commines], Philippe de**
1445?-1509?   [RH, SN]
*French politician and historian*
* [The] Booted Head
* Tete Bottee

**Comingore, Dorothy**
See  Winters, Linda

**Comini, Raiberto** 1907-   [ASC]
*Italian composer*
* Comini, Tino

**Comini, Tino**
See  Comini, Raiberto

**Comins, Lizzie B.**   [PA]
*Author*
* Caxton, Laura

**Comiskey, Charles Albert**
1859-1931   [AS, BAB, PB]
*American baseball player, manager,
executive*
* Comiskey, Commy
* [The] Noblest Roman of the
National Baseball Field
* [The] Old Roman

**Comiskey, Commy**
See  Comiskey, Charles Albert

**Comley, Mrs.**   [FFF]
*Entertainer*
* Harold, Lizzie

**Command, Igor**
See  Command, James Dalton
[Jim]

**Command, James Dalton [Jim]**
1928-   [BE]
*American baseball player*
* Command, Igor

**Commander, Colin** 1906-   [BBH]
*British-born soccer player*
* [The] Father of Ohio Soccer

**[The] Commander of the Faithful**
See  Omar I

**Comment, Cuthbert**
See  Tucker, Abraham

**Commentator**
See  Allward, Maurice Frank

**[The] Commentator**
See  Averroes [or Averrhoes]

**[The] Commerce Comet**
See  Mantle, Mickey Charles

**Commissioner, Lord**
See  McCoy, John

**[The] Commodore**
See  Pond, Myron

**Commodus, Lucius Aelius** 161-
192   [DEP, FFF, HN]
*Roman emperor*
* Hercules Secundus
* [The] Roman Hercules

**Commodus, Lucius Ceionius** 130-
169   [WBD]
*Roman emperor*
* Verus, Lucius Aurelius

**[The] Commoner**
See  Bryan, William Jennings

**[The] Commons' King**
See  Servius Tullius

**Communipaw**
See  Miles, Pliny

**Communis, Doctor**
See  Aquinas, Thomas [Thomas of
Aquino]

**Como, Franca**
See  Como, Francesca

**Como, Francesca** 1937-   [OP]
*Italian opera singer*
* Como, Franca

**Como, Perry**
See  Como, Pierino

**Como, Pierino** 1913-   [IPA]
*American singer*
* Como, Perry

**Compere, Mickie**
See  Davidson, Margaret

**[The] Competitor**
See  Bruce, Robert VI

**[Il] Compirito**
See  Orsini, Giovanni Gaetano

**[The] Complete Seaman**
See  Hawkins, [Sir] Richard

**Compost** [code name used during
World War II]
See  Eden, [Sir] [Robert] Anthony

**Comptom, Jemima**
See  Gladstone, Jemima Compton

**Compton, Ann**
See  Prebble, Marjorie Mary Curtis

**Compton, Bash**
See  Compton, Peter Sebastian

**Compton, Betty**
See  Compton, Violet Halling

**Compton, D. G.**
See  Compton, David Guy

**Compton, David Guy** 1930-
[CA, SFL, WGT]
*British author*
* Compton, D. G.
* Lynch, Frances

**Compton, Edward**
See  Mackenzie, Edward

**Compton, [Sir] Edward Montagu**
1883-1973   [EWL, TC, WWS]
*British author, critic, playwright*
* Mackenzie, Compton

**Compton, Francis**
See  Mackenzie, Francis Sidney

**Compton, Francis** 20th c.   [BBH]
*American aviator*
* Compton, Fritz

**Compton, Fritz**
See  Compton, Francis

**Compton, Harry Leroy** 1882- ?
[BE]
*American baseball player*
* Compton, Jack

**Compton, Jack**
See  Compton, Harry Leroy

**Compton, Joyce**
See  Hunt, Eleanor

**Compton, Peter Sebastian** 1889-
[BE]
*American baseball player*
* Compton, Bash

**Compton, Violet Halling**
1907?-1944   [BEW]
*British-born theatrical performer*
* Compton, Betty

**Compton-Bennett, Robert** 1900-
[FDG]
*British director*
* Bennett, Compton

**Compton-Burnett, I.**
See  Burnett, Ivy Compton

**Comrade, Robert W.**
See  Brooks, Edwy Searles

**Comstock, Commy**
See  Comstock, Ralph Remick

**Comstock, Hark**
See  Kellogg, P. C.

**Comstock, Ralph Remick**
1890-1966   [BE]
*American baseball player*
* Comstock, Commy

**[Le] Comte d'I**
See  Gay, Mrs. Jules

**[The] Comus of Poetry**
See  Byron, George Gordon Noel

**Comyn, [Sir] John** ?-1306
[FFF, HN, SN]
*Scottish aristocrat*
* [The] Red Comyn

**Comyns, Barbara**
See  Comyns-Carr, Barbara Irene
Veronica

**Comyns-Carr, Barbara Irene
Veronica** 1912-   [CA]
*British author*
* Comyns, Barbara

**Conacher, Charles William, Jr.**
1932-   [CEI, FHE]
*Canadian-born hockey player*
* Conacher, Pete

**Conacher, Lionel Pretoria**
1901-1954   [CSH, FHE]
*Canadian-born hockey player*
* [The] Big Train
* [The] Travelling Netminder

**Conacher, Pete**
See  Conacher, Charles William, Jr.

**Conanight** [joint pseudonym with
Damon F(rancis) Knight]
See  Cohen, Chester

**Conanight** [joint pseudonym with
Chester Cohen]
See  Knight, Damon F[rancis]

**Conant, Chester B.**
See  Cohen, Chester

**Conant, Silliman S.**   [PA]
*Author*
* S. S. C.

**Conant, William C.** 19th c.   [FFF]
*American journalist*
* Vidi

**Conarty, Edward Lee** 20th c.   [SG]
*Boxer*
* Murphy, Irish Bob

**Conatser, Clint[on Astor]** 1921-
[BE]
*American baseball player*
* Conatser, Connie

**Conatser, Connie**
See  Conatser, Clint[on Astor]

**Conaughy, Louis** 1889-1936
[BEW]
*American-born actor*
* Kimball, Louis

**Concannon, Thomas** 20th c.
[WWL]
*Irish author*
* O Concheanainn, Tomas

**Conchita**
See  Serafina Bacigalupi, Maria De
La Concepcion Conchita

**[El] Conde Duque de Olivares**
See  De Guzman, Gaspar [Duque
de Sanlucar]

**Conde, Maria**
See  Beyer, Ernestine Cobern

**Conde, Ramon Luis** 1934-   [BE]
*Puerto Rican-born baseball player*
* Conde, Wito

**Conde, Wito**
See  Conde, Ramon Luis

**Conde Abellan, Carmen** 1907-
[IAW]
*Spanish author and poet*
* Del Mar, Florentina
* Noguera, Magdalena

**Conder, Eustace R.**   [PA]
*Author*
* E. R. C.

**Condolmieri [or Condulmer], Gabriele**
1383-1447   [WBD]
*Pope*
* Eugenius IV

**Condon, John** 20th c.   [BLB]
*American underworld figure*
* Johnny Fix-'Em

**Condor, Gladyn**
See  Davison, Gladys Patton

**Condorcanqui, Jose Gabriel**
1742-1781   [WBD]
*Peruvian revolutionist*
* [The] Last of the Incas
* Tupac Amaru

**Condray, Bruno**
See  Humphrys, Leslie George

**Cone, Fairfax M.** 1903?-1977
*American advertising executive*
* Cone, Fax

**Cone, Fax**
See  Cone, Fairfax M.

**Cone, Mike** 1910-1969   [SC]
*American actor and musician*
* Cone, Zets

**Cone, Molly [Lamken]** 1918-
[CA, SAT, TBJ]
*American author*
* More, Caroline [joint pseudonym
   with Margaret Pitcairn Strachan]

**Cone, Mrs.**   [FFF]
*Entertainer*
* Morgan, Maggie

**Cone, Zets**
See  Cone, Mike

**Conejito [Little Rabbit]**
See  De Dios y Moreno, Antonio

**Conejo Grande [Big Rabbit]**
See  Aguirre Garcia, Antonio

**Conesa, Manuel R.** 1894-1959
[SC]
*American actor*
* Paris, Manuel

**[The] Coney Island Fakir**
See  Flosso, Al

**[The] Confessor**
See  Edward [or Eadward]

**[The] Confessor**
See  Ernest [or Ernst]

**[The] Confessor**
See  Maximus

**[The] Confessor**
See  Theophanes

**[The] Confidant**
See  Goethe, Johann Wolfgang von

**Confrey, Edward Elzear**
1895-1971?   [ASC, DAM, PMJ]
*American composer and pianist*
* Confrey, Zez

**Confrey, Zez**
See  Confrey, Edward Elzear

**Confucius**
See  Lund, Philip R[eginald]

**Confucius [or K'ung Fu-tzu]** 6th c.
BC   [DEP, DNNS, SN]
*Chinese philosopher*
* Little Hillock
* [The] Moral Censor of China
* [The] Philosopher of China

**Congalton, Bunk**
See  Congalton, William Millar

**Congalton, William Millar**
1875-1937   [BE]
*Canadian-born baseball player*
* Congalton, Bunk

**Conger, Lesley**
See  Suttles, Shirley [Smith]

**Congress Abraham**
See  Clark, Abraham

**Congreve, William** 1670-1729
[DEP, FFF, SN]
*British playwright*
* Cleophil
* [The] Last of the Romans
* Ultimus Romanorum

**Conigliaro, Anthony Richard** 1945-
*American baseball player*
* Tony C.

**Coningham, [Sir] Arthur**
1895-1948   [BDW, WWW]
*British air force officer*
* Coningham, Maori

**Coningham, Maori**
See  Coningham, [Sir] Arthur

**Coningsby, Thomas** 1656?-1729
[HN]
*British statesman*
* Atterbury's Pad

**Coniston, Ed**
See  Bingley, David Ernest

**Conkle, E. P.**
See  Conkle, Ellsworth Prouty

**Conkle, Ellsworth Prouty** 1899-
[BEW]
*American playwright and educator*
* Conkle, E. P.

**Conklin, Charles** 1880-1959   [SC]
*American actor*
* Conklin, Heinie

**Conklin, Chester**
See  Cowles, Jules

**Conklin, Edward Groff** 1904-1968
[WGT]
*Author*
* DeGraeff, W. B.

**Conklin, Heinie**
See  Conklin, Charles

**Conklin, Mrs. Nathaniel**   [PA]
*Author*
* Drinkwater, Jennie M.

**Conkling, Charles**
See  Ames, Charles

**Conkright, Red**
See  Conkright, William

**Conkright, William** 20th c.   [SMG]
*American football coach*
* Conkright, Red

**Conkwright, Allen Howard** 1896-
[BE]
*American baseball player*
* Conkwright, Red

**Conkwright, Red**
See  Conkwright, Allen Howard

**Conlan, Jocko**
See  Conlan, John Bertrand

**Conlan, John Bertrand** 1899-
[BAB, BE, PB]
*American baseball umpire*
* Conlan, Jocko

**Conley, Bing**
See  Conley, William

**Conley, Dick**
See  Glen, Richard

**Conley, Frankie**
See  Conte, Francesco

**Conley, James Patrick** 1894-   [BE]
*American baseball player*
* Conley, Snipe

**Conley, Nellie** 1873-1959   [SC]
*American actress*
* Wan, [Mme.] Sul Te

**Conley, Snipe**
See  Conley, James Patrick

**Conley, William** ?-1962   [SC]
*Actor*
* Conley, Bing

**Conlin, Bernard** 1831-1891   [WBD]
*American comedian*
* Florence, William Jermyn

**Conlin, Ray, Sr.**
See  O'Connor, William

**Conlin, William J.**   [FFF]
*Entertainer*
* Florence, Billy

**Conlon, Art[hur Joseph]** 1897-   [BE]
*American baseball player*
* Conlon, Jocko

**Conlon, Jocko**
See  Conlon, Art[hur Joseph]

**Conlon, John Daly** ?-1934   [BEW]
*Irish-born actor*
* Murphy, John Daly

**Conly, Mrs. Edward**   [FFF]
*Entertainer*
* Francis, Laura

**Conly, Robert Leslie** 1918?-1973
[CA]
*American author and editor*
* O'Brien, Robert C.

**Conn, Alan**
See  Connell, Alan

**Conn, Billy** 1917-   [BX, RBE]
*American boxer*
* [The] Pittsburgh Kid

**Conn, Canary Denise** 1949-   [CA]
*American author and songwriter*
* Canary

**Conn, Catharine** 1915-   [BEW]
*American actress and singer*
* Carlisle, Kitty

**Conn, Maitland** 1908-   [CEI]
*Canadian-born hockey player*
* Conn, Red

**Conn, Red**
See  Conn, Maitland

**Connally, Big John**
See  Connally, John Bowden, Jr.

**Connally, Bud**
See Connally, Mervin Thomas

**Connally, George Walter** 1898-
[BE, BN]
American baseball player
* Connally, Lope
* Connally, Sarge

**Connally, Idanell [Brill]** 20th c.
[B10]
Wife of American politician John
Connally
* Connally, Nellie

**Connally, John Bowden, Jr.** 1917?-
American politician
* Connally, Big John

**Connally, Lope**
See Connally, George Walter

**Connally, Mervin Thomas**
1901-1964 [BE]
American baseball player
* Connally, Bud
* Connally, Mike

**Connally, Mike**
See Connally, Mervin Thomas

**Connally, Nellie**
See Connally, Idanell [Brill]

**Connally, Sarge**
See Connally, George Walter

**Connatser, Broadus Milburn**
1902-1971 [BE]
American baseball player
* Connatser, Bruce

**Connatser, Bruce**
See Connatser, Broadus Milburn

**Connaughton, Sam**
See Sellers, Connie Leslie, Jr.

**Connell, Alan** 20th c. [WGT]
Author
* Conn, Alan

**Connell, F. Norreys**
See O'Riordan, Conal O'Connell

**Connell, John**
See Robertson, John Henry

**Connell, Russell H.** [PA]
Author
* Russell

**Connelly, John H.** 1840- ? [PA]
Author
* J. H. C.

**Connelly, John M.** 1857-1896 [BE]
American baseball player
* Connelly, Red

**Connelly, Marc**
See Connelly, Marcus Cook

**Connelly, Marcus Cook** 1890-1980
[BEW, LC, TC]
American playwright, director, actor
* Connelly, Marc

**Connelly, Mike** 20th c.
American football player
* Connelly, Worm

**Connelly, Red**
See Connelly, John M.

**Connelly, Wild Bill**
See Connelly, William Wirt [Bill]

**Connelly, William Wirt [Bill]** 1925-
[BE]
American baseball player
* Connelly, Wild Bill

**Connelly, Worm**
See Connelly, Mike

**Conner, Dennis** 1943?-
American sailboat racer
* [The] Menace

**Conner, Henry**
See Gilbert, H.

**Conner, Mrs. J. W.** [FFF]
Entertainer
* Wilson, Cora

**Conner, [Patrick] Reardon** 1907-
[CA, LC, WD]
Irish-born author
* Malin, Peter

**Conners, Gene** 1930- [EJ7]
American jazz musician
* Conners, Mighty Flea

**Conners, Mighty Flea**
See Conners, Gene

**Conners, Selwyn**
See Sellers, Connie Leslie, Jr.

**Connerson, M. Jean L. Auguste**
?-1878 [PA]
Author
* Citrouillard, Joseph

**Connery, Sean**
See Connery, Thomas

**Connery, Thomas** 1930- [FC]
Scottish-born actor
* Connery, Sean

**Connett, Eugene Virginius, III**
1891-1969 [CAP, NAA]
American author
* Virginius

**[The] Connie Mack of Pro Basketball**
See Morganweck, Frank

**Conniff, James C[lifford] G[regory]**
1920- [CA]
American author
* Anthropophagus Minor
* Coolwater, John

**Connington, J[ohn] J[ervis]**
See Stewart, Alfred Walter

**Conniston, Sam**
See Sellers, Connie Leslie, Jr.

**Connolly, Blackie**
See Connolly, Thomas Francis
[Tom]

**Connolly, Charles M.** [PA]
Author
* Slater, Nic

**Connolly, Coaster Joe**
See Connolly, Joseph George [Joe]

**Connolly, Cyril [Vernon]**
1903-1974 [CAP, EWL, LC]
British author and critic
* Palinurus

**Connolly, James H.** 1840- ? [PA]
Author
* Don

**Connolly, Joseph George [Joe]**
1896-1960 [BE]
American baseball player
* Connolly, Coaster Joe

**Connolly, Little Mo**
See Connolly, Maureen

**Connolly, Maureen** 1934-1969
[AS, NN, OET]
American tennis player
* Connolly, Little Mo
* Mighty Little Mo

**Connolly, Paul**
See Wicker, Thomas Grey

**Connolly, Robert D[uggan, Jr.]**
1917- [CA]
American writer
* Duggans, Pat

**Connolly, Thomas Francis [Tom]**
1892- [BN]
American baseball player
* Boston Blackie
* Connolly, Blackie

**Connolly, Vivian** 1925- [CA]
American author
* Harris, Andrea
* Rosse, Susanna

**Connon, William John** 1929-
[ART]
Scottish painter
* Wjconnon

**Connor, Cam**
See Connor, Cameron Duncan

**Connor, Cameron Duncan** 1954-
[HR]
Canadian-born hockey player
* Connor, Cam

**Connor, Cecil** 1946-1973 [ECM]
American singer and songwriter
* Parsons, Gram

**Connor, George** 20th c.
American football player
* Connor, Moose

**Connor, James Matthew [Jim]**
See O'Connor, James Matthew

**Connor, Joseph P.** 1895-1952
[ASC]
American composer and priest
* Connor, Pierre Norman

**Connor, Joyce Mary** 1929-
[CA, WD]
British author and actress
* Marlow, Joyce

**Connor, Moose**
See Connor, George

**Connor, Mrs. E. A.** [FFF]
American editor
* Orchard, Eliza

**Connor, Norman, Jr.** 1947- [EJ7]
American jazz musician
* Connors, Norman

**Connor, Pierre Norman**
See Connor, Joseph P.

**Connor, Ralph**
See Gordon, Charles William

**Connor, Roger** 1857-1931 [BAB]
American baseball player
* [The] Oak

**Connor, Tony** 1930- [DLE]
British poet
* Anthony, John

**Connor, [Sir] William Neil**
1909-1967 [BL, LC]
British journalist
* Cassandra

**Connors, Bruton**
See Rohen, Edward

**Connors, Chuck**
See Connors, Kevin Joseph

**Connors, James Scott [Jimmy]**
1952- [B10]
American tennis player
* Connors, Jimbo

**Connors, Jimbo**
See Connors, James Scott [Jimmy]

**Connors, Kevin Joseph** 1921?-
[ITA, PB, SW]
American actor
* Connors, Chuck

**Connors, Michael**
See Ohanian, Krekor

**Connors, Norman**
See Connor, Norman, Jr.

**Conolly, Charles M.** [FFF]
Author
* Quencher, Mark

**Conolly, Mrs. Edward J.** [FFF]
Entertainer
* Ross, Virginia

**Conor, Glen**
See Cooney, Michael

**Conover, Elizabeth**
See Dugin, Miss

**[The] Conquering Invader**
See Resta, Dario

**[The] Conqueror**
See Alfonso I [Affonso or
Alphonso]

**[The] Conqueror**
See Aurungzebe [Aurangzeb or
Aurungzeb]

**[The] Conqueror**
See Clisson, Olivier de

**[The] Conqueror**
See De Bonne, Francois

**[The] Conqueror**
See Guesclin, Bertrand du

**[The] Conqueror**
See James I

**[The] Conqueror**
See Mohammed II [or Mahomet]

**[The] Conqueror**
See Montmorency, Anne de

**[The] Conqueror**
See Osman I [or Othman]

**[The] Conqueror**
See Pizarro, Francisco

**[The] Conqueror**
See Suleiman II [or Soliman]

**[The] Conqueror**
See William I

**[The] Conqueror of the Danes**
See Brian Boru

**[The] Conqueror of the World**
See Alexander III

**Conquest, Edwin Parker, Jr.** 1931-
[CA, WD]
*American author*
* Conquest, Ned

**Conquest, Ida**
*See* Moriner, Ida

**Conquest, Joan**
*See* Cooke, Joan Conquest

**Conquest, Ned**
*See* Conquest, Edwin Parker, Jr.

**Conquest, Owen** [house pseudonym]
*See* Austin, Stanley E.

**Conquest, Owen** [house pseudonym]
*See* Catchpole, William Leslie

**Conquest, Owen** [house pseudonym]
*See* Down, C. Maurice

**Conquest, Owen** [house pseudonym]
*See* Eves, Reginald T.

**Conquest, Owen**
*See* Hamilton, Charles Harold St. John

**Conquest, Owen** [house pseudonym]
*See* Newman, Kenneth E.

**Conquest, Owen** [house pseudonym]
*See* O'Mant, Hedley Percival Angelo

**Conquest, Owen** [house pseudonym]
*See* Pike, William Ernest

**Conquest, Owen** [house pseudonym]
*See* Samways, George Richmond

**Conquest, Owen** [house pseudonym]
*See* Wood-Smith, Noel

**Conquest, [George] Robert [Acworth]**
1917- [CA, DLE]
*British author and editor*
* Arden, J. E. M.

**[El] Conquistador**
*See* Castanon, Roberto

**[El] Conquistador**
*See* James I

**Conquistador**
*See* Pizarro, Francisco

**Conrad**
*See* Bunn, Alfred

**Conrad** ?- 955 [WBD]
*Duke of Lorraine*
* [The] Red

**Conrad, Andree** 1945- [CA]
*American author and translator*
* Conrad, L. K.

**Conrad, Big Tank**
*See* Conrad, Thomas

**Conrad, Brenda**
*See* Brown, Zenith [Jones]

**Conrad, C.**
*See* Benjamin, Walter

**Conrad, Charles** 1930- [B10]
*American astronaut*
* Conrad, Pete

**Conrad, Clive**
*See* King, Frank

**Conrad, Con**
*See* Dober, Conrad K.

**Conrad, Gregg**
*See* Graham, Roger Phillips

**Conrad, Hugh**
*See* Schoenfeld, William C.

**Conrad, Joseph**
*See* Korzeniowski, Teodor Jozef Konrad Nalecz

**Conrad, Kenneth**
*See* Lottich, Kenneth V[erne]

**Conrad, L. K.**
*See* Conrad, Andree

**Conrad, M.**
*See* Halls, Christopher Peter John

**Conrad, Marcus**
*See* Halls, Christopher Peter John

**Conrad, Max** 1903?-1979
*American aviator*
* [The] Flying Grandfather

**Conrad, Paul**
*See* King, Albert

**Conrad, Pete**
*See* Conrad, Charles

**Conrad, Robert**
*See* Falk, Conrad Robert

**Conrad, Thomas** 20th c. [IBW]
*American football player*
* Conrad, Big Tank

**Conrad, Tod**
*See* Wilkes-Hunter, Richard

**Conrad II** 990?-1039
[DNNS, SN, WBD]
*King of Germany and Holy Roman emperor*
* [The] Salian
* [The] Salic

**Conried, Heinrich**
*See* Cohn, Heinrich

**Conrow, Herbert** 1874- ? [SFL]
*Author*
* Orb, Clay

**Conroy, Ashton**
*See* Savoy, Ashton

**Conroy, John** ?-1948 [SC]
*American actor*
* Westley, John

**Conroy, John Wesley [Jack]** 1899-
[CA, IAW]
*American author*
* Brennan, Tim
* Morine, Hoder
* Norcross, John
* [The] Sage of Moberly

**Conroy, Patrick** 20th c. [WWL]
*Irish author*
* O Conaire, Padraic

**Conroy, Pep**
*See* Conroy, William Frederick

**Conroy, Robert**
*See* Goldston, Robert Conroy

**Conroy, Wid**
*See* Conroy, William Edward

**Conroy, William Edward**
1877-1959 [AS, BE]
*American baseball player*
* Conroy, Wid

**Conroy, William Frederick** 1899-
[BE]
*American baseball player*
* Conroy, Pep

**Conscience, Hendrick** 1812-1883?
[DNNS, RH, SN]
*Flemish author*
* [The] Walter Scott of Belgium

**[The] Conscience of the Senate**
*See* Hart, Philip A.

**Conscience Tranquelle**
*See* Bonaparte, Charles Louis Napoleon

**Conservative, Mr.**
*See* Diefenbaker, John George

**Conshankin, Bishop**
*See* Brown, Eugene

**Consistency, Mr.**
*See* Fest, Howard

**Constable de Bourbon**
*See* Du Bourbonnais, [Duc] Charles

**Constable, Jimmy Lee** 1933- [BE]
*American baseball player*
* [The] Sheriff

**Constable, Trevor James** 1925-
[CA]
*New Zealand-born American author*
* James, Trevor

**Constance**
*See* Williams, Mrs. B. W. J.

**Constanduros, Mabel**
*See* Tilling, Mabel

**[The] Constant**
*See* John [or Johann]

**Constant, Alphonse Louis** [PA]
*Author*
* Levi, Eliphas

**Constant, Benjamin**
*See* Botelho de Magalhaes, Benjamin Constant

**[The] Constant Prince**
*See* Ferdinand

**Constant, W.**
*See* Wurzbach, Constant

**Constant, Yvonne**
*See* Coronakis, Yvonne

**Constantelos, Demetrios J.** 1927-
[CA]
*Greek-born American author*
* Stachys, Dimitris

**Constantia**
*See* Sargent, Judith

**Constantine** 827- 869?
[FFF, SN, WBD]
*Saint*
* [The] Apostle of the Slavs
* Cyril

**Constantine, Learie Nicholas**
1902-1971 [EC]
*West Indian cricketer*
* Electric Heels

**Constantine, Michael**
*See* Efstration, Michael

**[The] Constantine of Gaul**
*See* Clovis I

**Constantine I [Flavius Valerius Aurelius Constantinus]** 272?- 337
[DNNS, SN, WBD]
*Roman emperor*
* [The] Great

**Constantine IV** 648- 685
[DNNS, HN, RH]
*Byzantine emperor*
* [The] Bearded
* Pogonatus

**Constantine IX** 1000?-1055 [WBD]
*Byzantine emperor*
* Monomachus [Who Fights in Single Combat]

**Constantine V [or Constantinus]** 719-
775 [SN, WBD]
*Byzantine emperor*
* Cepronimus [or Copronymus]

**Constantine VII** 905- 959
[DNNS, HN, WBD]
*Byzantine emperor*
* Porphyrogenitus [Born in the Purple]

**Constantine XI Palaeologus**
1404-1453 [WBD]
*Byzantine emperor*
* Dragases

**Constantius I [Flavius Valerius Constantius]** 250?- 306 [WBD]
*Roman emperor*
* Chlorus [The Pale]

**Constellano, Illion**
*See* Lewis, Julius Warren

**Consuegra, Sandalio Simeon Castellon** 1920- [BE]
*Cuban-born baseball player*
* Consuegra, Sandy

**Consuegra, Sandy**
*See* Consuegra, Sandalio Simeon Castellon

**Contandin, Fernand Joseph Desire**
1903-1971 [FC, IPA, OCF]
*French comedian and actor*
* Fernandel

**Contarini, Marc Antoine** ?-1550
[PA]
*Author*
* Philosopher

**Conte, Charles**
*See* MacKinnon, Charles Roy

**Conte, Francesco** 1890-1952
[BX, RBE]
*Italian-born boxer*
* Conley, Frankie

**Conte, Maria Pia** 20th c. [WF]
*Italian actress*
* Count, Marie P.

**Conte, Nicholas** 1914-1975
[FC, SC]
*American actor*
* Conte, Richard

**Conte, Richard**
*See* Conte, Nicholas

**[Le] Contemplateur**
*See* Poquelin, Jean Baptiste

**Conti, Albert**
*See* De Conti Cadassamare, Albert

**Conti, Gilda** 1887- [THR]
*Italian-born actress*
* Varesi, Gilda

**Conti, Giovanni-Francesca**
1486-1557 [PA]
*Author*
* Quinzano

**Conti, Gregorio** 12th c. [WBD]
*Antipope*
* Victor IV

**Conti, Michelangelo** 1655-1724
[WBD]
*Pope*
* Innocent XIII

**Conti, Oscar** 1914- [GA, WECO]
*Argentinian-born cartoonist*
* Oski

**Conti, Rinaldo** ?-1261 [WBD]
*Pope*
* Alexander IV

**[The] Continental Magician**
*See* Vander Linden, Anthony

**[The] Continental Wizard**
*See* Samek, Viktor Oliver

**Contino, Michael** 20th c.
*American underworld figure*
* Contino, Mustache Mike

**Contino, Mustache Mike**
*See* Contino, Michael

**[The] Continuator of Fordun**
*See* Bower [or Bowmaker?],
Robert

**Contius**
*See* Leconte, Antoine

**Contractor, Dorab Dadiba** 1929-
[ART]
*Indian-born sculptor*
* Dorab

**Contucci, Andrea** 1460-1529
[WBD]
*Italian sculptor and architect*
* Sansovino, Andrea

**Converse, Anita Marie [Stewart]**
1901- [WW]
*Author*
* Stewart, Anita

**Converse, Charles Crozat**
1834?-1918 [FFF, PA]
*American author and musician*
* Nevers, C. O.
* Reden, Karl
* Revons, E. C.

**Conversi, Spartaco** 20th c. [WF]
*Italian actor*
* Convery, Sean

**[The] Converter**
*See* Galen, Bernard de

**Convertible Conn McCreary**
*See* McCreary, Conn

**Convertisseur**
*See* Pellisson-Fontanier, Paul

**Convery, Sean**
*See* Conversi, Spartaco

**Convey, Cowboy**
*See* Convey, Edward [Eddie]

**Convey, Edward [Eddie]** 20th c.
[FHE]
*Canadian-born hockey player*
* Convey, Cowboy

**[The] Convict Writer**
*See* Torok, Lou

**Convy, Bernard Whalen** 1936-
[BEW]
*American actor*
* Convy, Bert

**Convy, Bert**
*See* Convy, Bernard Whalen

**Conway, Arlington B.**
*See* Burns, Eedson Louis Millard

**Conway, Bowen**
*See* Michel, John B.

**Conway, Denise**
*See* Prebble, Marjorie Mary Curtis

**Conway, E. Carolyn**
*See* Kermond, Evelyn Carolyn
Conway

**Conway, Faulkner**
*See* Price, Frank J.

**Conway, Gary**
*See* Carmody, Gareth

**Conway, Gerard F.** 20th c.
[ESF, WGT]
*American author*
* Moore, Wallace

**Conway, Gordon**
*See* Hamilton, Charles Harold St.
John

**Conway, H. Derwent**
*See* Inglis, Henry David

**Conway, Hugh**
*See* Fargus, Frederick J.

**Conway, Hugh Ryan** 1887-1952
[FD]
*American director*
* Conway, Jack

**Conway, J.?**
*See* Burt, [Sir] Cyril

**Conway, Jack**
*See* Conway, Hugh Ryan

**Conway, Laura**
*See* Ansle, Dorothy Phoebe

**Conway, Lillian**
*See* Camblos, Lillian

**Conway, Mai**
*See* Ryan, Mrs. Thomas

**Conway, Mark**
*See* Cahill, Frank

**Conway, Minnie**
*See* Tearle, Minnie

**Conway, Peter**
*See* Milkomane, George Alexis
Milkomanovich

**Conway, Richard Daniel** 1896-
[BE]
*American baseball player*
* Conway, Rip

**Conway, Rip**
*See* Conway, Richard Daniel

**Conway, Ritter**
*See* Knight, Damon F[rancis]

**Conway, Shirl**
*See* Crosman, Shirley Elizabeth

**Conway, Thomas Daniel** 1933-
[SW]
*American actor*
* Conway, Tim

**Conway, Tim**
*See* Conway, Thomas Daniel

**Conway, Tom**
*See* Sanders, Thomas

**Conway, Troy** [house pseudonym,
Paperback Library]
*See* Avallone, Michael [Angelo],
Jr.

**Conway, Ward**
*See* Westmoreland, Reg[inald]
[Conway]

**Conwell, Ed[ward James]** 1890-
[BE]
*American baseball player*
* Conwell, Irish

**Conwell, Irish**
*See* Conwell, Ed[ward James]

**Conwright, Samuel Cron** 1863- ?
[WWL]
*South African author*
* Conwright-Sehreiner, S. C.

**Conwright-Sehreiner, S. C.**
*See* Conwright, Samuel Cron

**Conybeare, Charles Augustus**
*See* Eliot, Thomas Stearns

**Conyers, Latham**
*See* Zagat, Arthur Leo

**Conynghame, Kate**
*See* Ingraham, Joseph Holt

**Coo-Ee**
*See* Walker, William Sylvester

**Coody, Abimelech**
*See* Verplanck, Gulian Crommalin

**Cook, Alex** 1907- [CEI]
*Canadian-born hockey player*
* Cook, Bud

**Cook, Arlene Ethel** 1936- [CA]
*American author*
* Cole, Cannon

**Cook, Bud**
*See* Cook, Alex

**Cook, Bun**
*See* Cook, Frederick Joseph

**Cook, Charles C.** 20th c. [IBW]
*American football coach*
* [The] Father of Sports at Howard

**Cook, Charles Henry** 1858- ?
[LAO]
*British barrister and author*
* Bickerdyke, John

**Cook, David** 1947- [RO2]
*British entertainer*
* Essex, David

**Cook, Doc**
*See* Cook, Luther A.

**Cook, Dorothy Mary** 20th c. [WD]
*British author*
* Cameron, D. Y.
* Clare, Elizabeth

**Cook, Enoch** 1953- [IBW]
*American circus performer*
* Pancho

**Cook, Flavius Josephus** 1838-1901
[FFF, WBD]
*American lecturer*
* Cook, Joseph
* Monday Boanerges

**Cook, [Sir] Francis Ferdinand
Maurice** 1907- [ART]
*British artist*
* F. M. C. 69

**Cook, Fred Gordon** 1900- [MBF]
*British author*
* Carew, Burleigh
* Chaverton, Bruce
* Clifford, Martin [house
pseudonym]
* Foy, Peter
* Owen, Vincent
* Richards, Frank [house
pseudonym]
* Smeaton, Fred

**Cook, Frederick Joseph** 1903-
[CEI, FHE, HK]
*Canadian-born hockey player*
* Cook, Bun

**Cook, Frederick Russell** 1882- ?
[BE]
*American baseball player*
* Winchell, Fred[erick Russell]

**Cook, Gabrielle** 1883- [THR]
*British actress and dancer*
* Ray, Gabrielle

**Cook, George Cram** 1873-1924
[MWD]
*American producer and playwright*
* Cook, Jig

**Cook, Gladys Hanson** ?-1973 [TR]
*Actress*
* Hanson, Gladys

**Cook, Gregory L.** 1946- [FB]
*American football player*
* [The] Blond Bomber

**Cook, Herman** 1934- [DAM, EJ]
*American jazz musician*
* Cook, Junior

**Cook, Jennifer** 1947- [ART]
*British textile designer and
illustrator*
* J. C.

**Cook, Jig**
*See* Cook, George Cram

**Cook, Joe**
*See* Lopez, Joseph

**Cook, Joe** [RO1, RO2]
*American singer and songwriter*
* Little Joe

**Cook, John** 1923- [DAM, EJ]
*American jazz musician*
* Cook, Willie

**Cook, John Estes**
*See* Baum, L[yman] Frank

**Cook, Joseph**
*See* Cook, Flavius Josephus

**Cook, Junior**
*See* Cook, Herman

**Cook, Justin Lord** 1947- [IBW]
*American musician*
* Lord, Justin

**Cook, Luther A.** 1889-1973 [BE]
*American baseball player*
* Cook, Doc

**Cook, Lyn**
*See* Waddell, Evelyn Margaret

**Cook, Mabel Collins** 1851-1927
[SFL, WGT]
*Author*
* Collins, Mabel

**Cook, Marc E.** [PA]
*Author*
* Brown, Vandyke

**Cook, Mary** 20th c. [ITA]
*American actress*
* Sinclair, Mary

**Cook, Patricia** 1911-1943 [SC]
*American actress and dancer*
* McCarthy, Pat

**Cook, Petronelle Marguerite Mary**
1925- [CA]
*British-born American author*
* Arnold, Margot

**Cook, Ramona Graham** 20th c.
[CA]
*American author*
* Graham, Ramona

**Cook, Robert William Arthur**
1931- [AW, CA]
*British author*
* Cook, Robin

**Cook, Robin**
*See* Cook, Robert William Arthur

**Cook, Roger** 1940- [RO2]
*British singer and songwriter*
* Jonathan

**Cook, Roy Francis** 1903- [THR]
*British actor*
* Brandt, Ivan

**Cook, Theodore P.** [PA]
*Author*
* MacArno, Mat

**Cook, Will Marion** 1869-1944
[IBW]
*American musician*
* [The] Original Genius

**Cook, William Everett** 1921- [IA]
*American author*
* Everett, Wade
* Keene, James
* Peace, Frank
* Riordan, Dan

**Cook, William Wallace** 1867-1933
[EMD]
*Author*
* Carter, Nicholas?

**Cook, Willie**
*See* Cook, John

**Cooke, Allen Lindsey** 1907-
[BE, PB]
*American baseball player, trainer,
manager*
* Cooke, Dusty

**Cooke, Anthony R.** 1933- [ART]
*British painter*
* A. R. C.

**Cooke, Arthur** [joint pseudonym with
C. Kornbluth, R. Lowndes, J.
Michel, D Wollheim]
*See* Balter, Elsie

**Cooke, Arthur** [joint pseudonym with
E. Balter, R. Lowndes, J. Michel, D.
Wollheim]
*See* Kornbluth, Cyril M.

**Cooke, Arthur** [joint pseudonym with
E. Balter, C. Kornbluth, J. Michel,
D. Wollheim]
*See* Lowndes, Robert Augustine
Ward

**Cooke, Arthur** [joint pseudonym with
C. Kornbluth, R. Lowndes, E. Balter,
D. Wollheim]
*See* Michel, John B.

**Cooke, Arthur** [joint pseudonym with
C. Kornbluth, R. Lowndes, J.
Michel, E. Balter]
*See* Wollheim, Donald A[llen]

**Cooke, Barbara**
*See* Alexander, Anna B[arbara
Cooke]

**Cooke, C. W. R.** [PA]
*Author*
* Gushington, Angelina

**Cooke, Charles L.** 1891-1958
[WWJ]
*American jazz musician*
* Cooke, Doc

**Cooke, Conversation**
*See* Cooke, William

**Cooke, Doc**
*See* Cooke, Charles L.

**Cooke, Dusty**
*See* Cooke, Allen Lindsey

**Cooke, Helen M.** [PA]
*Author*
* Linwood, Lottie

**Cooke, Hesiod**
*See* Cooke, Thomas

**Cooke, Joan Conquest** 20th c.
[WGT]
*Author*
* Conquest, Joan

**Cooke, John Esten** 1830- ? [PA]
*Author*
* Effingham, C., Esq.

**Cooke, Margaret**
*See* Creasey, John

**Cooke, Millen** 20th c. [SFP]
*Author*
* Blade, Alexander [house
pseudonym, Ziff-Davis]

**Cooke, Mrs. Henry H.** [FFF]
*Entertainer*
* Cluzette, Jennie

**Cooke, Percival**
*See* Bishop, Percy Cook

**Cooke, Rose Terry** 1827-1892
[FFF]
*American author and poet*
* Terry, Rose

**Cooke, Terry**
*See* Biggs, Ronald Arthur

**Cooke, Thomas** 1703-1756
[DNNS, WBD]
*British author and journalist*
* Cooke, Hesiod

**Cooke, William** ?-1824 [SN]
*British author, poet, journalist*
* Cooke, Conversation

**Cooker, John Lee**
*See* Hooker, John Lee

**Cookman, A. V.**
*See* Cookman, Anthony Victor

**Cookman, Anthony Victor**
1894-1962 [LC]
*British drama critic*
* Cookman, A. V.

**Cookridge, E. H.**
*See* Spiro, Edward

**Cooksley, Margaret Elizabeth** 20th
c. [OP]
*British opera company
administrator*
* Moreland, Margaret Elizabeth

**Cooksley, S[idney] Bert** 1903-
[NAA]
*British-born author and poet*
* Gray, Donald
* O'Donald, Donald

**Cookson, Catherine Ann [McMullen]**
1906- [AW, CA, SAT]
*British author*
* Fawcett, C.
* Marchant, Catherine
* McMullen, Catherine

**Cool Papa**
*See* Sadler, Haskell Robert

**Cool Papa Bell**
*See* Bell, James Thomas

**Coole, W. W.**
*See* Kulski, Wladyslaw W[szebor]

**Cooley, Adelaide J.** [FFF]
*Author*
* Addie

**Cooley, Charles**
*See* Cali, Charles

**Cooley, Donnell C.** 1910-1969
[BBD, CME, CWG]
*American country-western performer*
* Cooley, Spade
* [The] King of Western Swing

**Cooley, Duff C.** 1873-1937 [BE]
*American baseball player*
* Sir Richard

**Cooley, Spade**
*See* Cooley, Donnell C.

**Coolidge, [John] Calvin** 1872-1933
[FAP]
*American president*
* Coolidge, Red
* Coolidge, Silent Cal

**Coolidge, Red**
*See* Coolidge, [John] Calvin

**Coolidge, Rita** 1944- [ECM]
*American singer*
* [The] Delta Lady

**Coolidge, Silent Cal**
*See* Coolidge, [John] Calvin

**Coolidge, Susan**
*See* Woolsey, Sarah Chauncey

**Coolus, Romain**
*See* Weill, Rene

**Coolwater, John**
*See* Conniff, James C[lifford]
G[regory]

**Coomans, Joanna** [SN]
*Danish author*
* [The] Pearl of Zealand

**Coombe, Carol**
*See* Coombe, Gwendoline Alice

**Coombe, Gwendoline Alice**
1911-1966 [THR]
*Australian-born actress*
* Coombe, Carol

**Coomber, Mabel** 1890- [THR]
*British actress and singer*
* Green, Mabel

**Coombs, Bobby**
*See* Coombs, Raymond Franklin

**Coombs, Charles I[ra]** 1914-
[CA, SAT]
*American author*
* Coombs, Chick

**Coombs, Chick**
*See* Coombs, Charles I[ra]

**Coombs, Colby Jack**
*See* Coombs, John Wesley

**Coombs, John Wesley** 1882-1957
[BE]
*American baseball player and
manager*
* Coombs, Colby Jack

**Coombs, Joyce** 1906- [AW]
*British author*
* Hales, Joyce

**Coombs, Murdo**
*See* Davis, Frederick Clyde

**Coombs, Raymond Franklin** 1908-
[BE]
*American baseball player*
* Coombs, Bobby

**Coon, Spencer Wallace** [PA]
*Author*
* [The] Growler

**Cooner, Wayne**
*See* Eisfeld, Rainer

**Cooney, Dennis** 20th c. [BLB]
*American underworld figure*
* Cooney, Duke

**Cooney, Duke**
*See* Cooney, Dennis

**Cooney, Gentleman Gerry**
*See* Cooney, Gerry

**Cooney, Gerry** 1957?-
*Boxer*
* Cooney, Gentleman Gerry

**Cooney, James Edward** 1894- [BE]
*American baseball player*
* Cooney, Scoops

**Cooney, Laurette** 1884-1946
[BEW, F2, FC]
*American actress*
* Taylor, Laurette

**Cooney, Michael** 1921- [CA]
*Irish author*
* Conor, Glen

**Cooney, Philip**
*See* Cohen, Philip

**Cooney, Scoops**
*See* Cooney, James Edward

**Coonradt, Paul Talbot** 1897-
[NAA]
*American author*
* McCloud, David

**Coop**
See   Cooper, Frank James

**Cooper, Alfred** 20th c.   [OBW]
*American baseball player*
* Cooper, Army

**Cooper, Alfred Benjamin** 1863- ?
[LAO]
*British author*
* Preston, Paul

**Cooper, Alfred Morton** 1890-
[CAP]
*American author*
* Cooper, Morley

**Cooper, Algernon Johnson** 1944-
[IBW]
*American attorney and politician*
* Cooper, Jay

**Cooper, Alice**
See   Furnier, Vincent Damon

**Cooper, Andy** 20th c.   [OBW]
*American baseball player*
* Cooper, Lefty

**Cooper, Anthony Ashley**
1801-1885   [DEP, FFF]
*British philanthropist*
* [The] Coster's Friend
* [The] Good Earl
* Shaftesbury, Seventh Earl of

**Cooper, Army**
See   Cooper, Alfred

**Cooper, Buster**
See   Cooper, George

**Cooper, C. Everett**
See   Burgess, Michael Roy

**Cooper, Cecil Celester** 1949-
*American baseball player*
* Cooper, Flash

**Cooper, Charles**
See   Lock, Arnold Charles Cooper

**Cooper, Charles** 1908?-
[B10, MEB]
*American basketball player*
* Cooper, Tarzan

**Cooper, Charles Henry St. John**
1869-1926   [MBF]
*British author*
* Holme, Gordon
* Hoskin, Clifford
* Lefevre, [Lieut.] Paul
* St. John, Henry
* St. John, Mabel

**Cooper, Clarence L., Jr.** 20th c.
[IBW]
*American author*
* Chestnut, Robert

**Cooper, Colin Symons** 1926-   [CA]
*British author and playwright*
* Benson, Daniel

**Cooper, Coop**
See   Cooper, Everett

**Cooper, Dale T.** 1918-1977   [ECM]
*American country-western performer*
* Cooper, Stoney

**Cooper, E. A.** 1904-   [FC]
*British actor*
* Ashley, Edward

**Cooper, Edith Emma** 1862-1913
[LC]
*British author and poet*
* Field, Michael [joint pseudonym
  with Katherine Harris Bradley]

**Cooper, Edmund** 1926-   [SF]
*British author*
* Avery, Richard

**Cooper, Elizabeth** 1877- ?   [NAA]
*American author*
* Goodnow, Elizabeth

**Cooper, Emil**
See   Kuper, Emil

**Cooper, Emmanuel** 1940-   [CA]
*British potter and writer*
* Sidney, Jonathan

**Cooper, Ernest Read** 1865- ?
[WWL]
*British author*
* Suffolk Coast

**Cooper, Esther**
See   Kellner, Esther

**Cooper, Evan** 20th c.   [SFP]
*Author*
* Duhring, Nathan

**Cooper, Everett** 1915-   [IBW]
*American detective*
* Cooper, Coop

**Cooper, Flash**
See   Cooper, Cecil Celester

**Cooper, Frank**
See   Simms, William Gilmore

**Cooper, Frank James** 1901-1961
[BDF, BEW, F2]
*American actor*
* Coop
* Cooper, Gary

**Cooper, Frederick** 1866?-1939
[BEW]
*Actor*
* Renad, Frederick

**Cooper, Freemont**
See   Steffens, Arthur

**Cooper, Gary**
See   Cooper, Frank James

**Cooper, George** 1929-   [DAM, EJ]
*American jazz musician*
* Cooper, Buster

**Cooper, George William Noel**
1896-   [WD]
*American poet, historian,
genealogist*
* Noel-Cooper, George W.

**Cooper, Guy Evans** 1893-1951
[BE]
*American baseball player*
* Cooper, Rebel

**Cooper, H. Clifford** 1862-1939
[BEW]
*British-born actor*
* Cliffe, H. Cooper

**Cooper, Harry E.** 1904-   [EG, GF]
*American golfer*
* Cooper, Light Horse Harry

**Cooper, Henry**
See   Cooper, Kevin Edwin

**Cooper, Henry St. John**
See   Creasey, John

**Cooper, Hughes**
See   Leonard, George H.

**Cooper, James A.**
See   Stratemeyer, Edward L.

**Cooper, James Fenimore**
1789-1851   [PA, SN]
*American author*
* [An] American
* [The] Scott of the Sea
* [A] Traveling Bachelor

**Cooper, Janie**
See   Haill, Robert Godfrey

**Cooper, Jay**
See   Cooper, Algernon Johnson

**Cooper, Jeff** 1920-   [CA]
*American handgun expert and
author*
* Cooper, John Dean

**Cooper, Jefferson**
See   Fox, Gardner Francis

**Cooper, John C.**
See   Croydon, John

**Cooper, John Dean**
See   Cooper, Jeff

**Cooper, John Gilbert** 1723-1769
[FFF]
*British author*
* Philaretes

**Cooper, John Murray** 1908-   [WW]
*Author*
* Sutherland, William

**Cooper, John R.** [house pseudonym]
[Stratemeyer Syndicate]
See   Stratemeyer, Edward L.

**Cooper, Kevin Edwin** 1957-   [DC]
*British cricketer*
* Cooper, Henry

**Cooper, Lefty**
See   Cooper, Andy

**Cooper, Leonard** 1916-   [CA]
*American author*
* De Graffe, Richard
* St. Clair, Leonard

**Cooper, Light Horse Harry**
See   Cooper, Harry E.

**Cooper, Mae [Klein]** 20th c.   [CA]
*American author and playwright*
* Cooper-Klein, Nina
* Farewell, Nina [joint pseudonym
  with Grace Klein]

**Cooper, Mary** 1911-   [ART]
*British artist*
* M. C.

**Cooper, Mattie Lula**
See   Britton, Mattie Lula Cooper

**Cooper, Morley**
See   Cooper, Alfred Morton

**Cooper, Mrs. Fred**   [FFF]
*Entertainer*
* Woodthorpe, Georgie

**Cooper, Mrs. S. E.**   [FFF]
*Entertainer*
* Clayton, Estelle

**Cooper, Myles** 1735-1785   [PA]
*Author*
* [A] Native of the South

**Cooper, Orge Patterson** 1917-   [BE]
*American baseball player*
* Cooper, Pat

**Cooper, Pat**
See   Cooper, Orge Patterson

**Cooper, Pete B.** 1914-   [GF]
*American golfer*
* [The] King of the Caribbean

**Cooper, Rebel**
See   Cooper, Guy Evans

**Cooper, Richard**
See   Wright-Cooper, Richard

**Cooper, Richard** 1730?-1806?
[DEP, DNNS, FFF]
*British painter*
* [The] British Poussin
* [The] English Poussin
* [The] Poussin of England

**Cooper, Robert Andrew** 1926-
[IAW]
*British author*
* Andrew, [Dr.] Robert
* Hayes, Alexander
* Hayes, Robert
* Matlock, Alec
* Pheasant, [Dr.] Lundy
* Robertson, Amy
* [A] West Country Doctor

**Cooper, Samuel** 1609-1672
[HN, RH]
*British painter*
* [The] Apelles of His Age

**Cooper, Saul** 1934-   [CA]
*American author*
* Benson, Richard
* Milner, Michael

**Cooper, Stoney**
See   Cooper, Dale T.

**Cooper, Susan Fenimore**
1813-1894   [DEL]
*American author*
* [A] Lady

**Cooper, Sylvia** 1903-   [CAP]
*American author*
* Jerman, Sylvia Paul

**Cooper, Tarzan**
See   Cooper, Charles

**Cooper, Thomas** 1805-1892
[DEL, SN]
*British author and poet*
* [The] Chartist
* Hornbook, Adam

**Cooper, [Rev] W.**
See   Bertram, J. G.

**Cooper, Wilhelmina [Behmenburg]**
1939?-1980   [CA]
*Dutch-born fashion model, author,
model agency president*
* Wilhelmina

**Cooper, William**
See   Hoff, Harry Summerfield

**Cooper, William** 1885-
[PA, WWL]
*British author*
* Vanderdecken

**Cooper, William G.** 1877-1958
[BE]
*American baseball player*
* Nance, Doc
* Nance, Kid
* Nance, William G.

**Cooper-Klein, Nina**
See Cooper, Mae [Klein]

**Coover, James B[urrell]** 1925- [CA]
American author and educator
* James, C. B.

**Coover, Melanchthon** 1861- ?
[NAA]
American educator and writer
* Coover, Melanthane

**Coover, Melanthane**
See Coover, Melanchthon

**Coowescoowe [or Kooweskoowe]**
1790-1866 [WBD]
American Indian chieftain
* Ross, John

**[The] Cooz**
See Cousy, Robert J. [Bob]

**Copas, Cowboy**
See Copas, Lloyd Estel

**Copas, Lloyd Estel** 1913-1963
[CME, CWG, DAM]
American country-western performer
* Copas, Cowboy

**Cope**
See Copeland, William

**Cope, Alan Campbell** 1908- [IAW]
British author
* Douglas, Percy

**Cope, Geoffrey Alan** 1947- [DC]
British cricketer
* Cope, Todge

**Cope, Jack**
See Cope, Robert Knox

**Cope, Robert Knox** 1913- [CA]
South African author
* Cope, Jack

**Cope, Robert L.** 19th c. [PA]
Author
* Arrelsee

**Cope, Todge**
See Cope, Geoffrey Alan

**Cope, [Vincent] Zachary** 1881-
[CAP]
British physician and author
* Zeta

**Copeland, Joan**
See Miller, Joan Maxine

**Copeland, Kenny** 20th c. [RO2]
American musician
* Gold, Captain

**Copeland, Margaret Scott**
See Northe, Margaret Scott
Copeland

**Copeland, William** 1843-1883
[FFF]
American journalist
* Cope

**Copelon, Allan** 1924-1973 [CA]
American entertainer, television
producer, comedy writer
* Sherman, Allan

**[A] Copernicus**
See Dyer, George

**Copernicus, Nicolaus** 1473-1543
[SN]
Polish astronomer
* [The] Reformer of Astronomy

**Copetillo [Little Copote]**
See Copote, Jose

**Copi**
See Damonte Toborda, Raul

**Copley, Robert** 1175-1253 [HN]
British clergyman
* Grostete [Great-Head]

**Copley, William Nelson** 1919-
[CAR]
American painter
* Cply

**Copote, Jose** 20th c. [GS]
Spanish bullfighter
* Copetillo [Little Copote]

**Coppard, A. E.**
See Coppard, Alfred Edgar

**Coppard, Alfred Edgar** 1878-1957
[LC, TC]
British author
* Coppard, A. E.

**Coppe, Abiezer**
See Taylor, John [Alfred]

**Coppel, Alfred**
See De Marini y Coppel, Alfredo
Jose

**[The] Copper Farthing Dean**
See Swift, Jonathan

**Copper John, II**
See Panzram, Carl

**Copperfield, David**
See Kotkin, David

**Coppernose**
See Henry VIII

**[The] Coppersmith**
See Hamilton, Alexander

**Coppersmith, Barbara Carole**
1925- [EJ, PMJ]
American jazz musician
* Carroll, Barbara

**Coppi, Fausto** 1919-1960 [OCS]
Italian cyclist
* Campionissimo [Champion of
Champions]

**Copplestone, Bennet**
See Kitchin, Frederick Harcourt

**Coppola, Michael** 1904-1966
[BLB, PHM]
American underworld figure
* Coppola, Trigger Mike

**Coppola, Trigger Mike**
See Coppola, Michael

**Coppola, Vito** 1912-1973 [SC]
American actor
* Van, Billy

**Copway, George** 1820- ? [PA]
Author
* Kah-ge-gwa-ge-bow

**Coquelin Aine**
See Coquelin, Benoit Constant

**Coquelin, Benoit Constant**
1841-1909 [WBD]
French actor
* Coquelin Aine

**Coquelin Cadet**
See Coquelin, Ernest

**Coquelin, Ernest** 1848-1909 [WBD]
French comedian
* Coquelin Cadet

**[Un] Coquin Tenebreux [A Dark
Knave]**
See Lully, Jean Baptiste

**Coquina**
See Shields, G. O.

**Corallo, Antonio** 1913-
American underworld figure
* Corallo, Tony Ducks

**Corallo, Tony Ducks**
See Corallo, Antonio

**Coram**
See Whitaker, Thomas

**Coram, Christopher**
See Walker, Peter Norman

**Corben, Gore**
See Corben, Richard Vance

**Corben, Richard Vance** 1940-
[WECO]
American cartoonist
* Corben, Gore

**Corbett, Arleigh Jean** 20th c.
[NAA]
Canadian writer
* Barry, Nancy Rosamond

**Corbett, Chan**
See Schachner, Nat[han]

**Corbett, E. B.**
See Corbett, Elizabeth B[urgoyne]

**Corbett, Elizabeth B[urgoyne]** 1846-
? [WGT]
British author
* Corbett, E. B.
* Corbett, G.

**Corbett, G.**
See Corbett, Elizabeth B[urgoyne]

**Corbett, Gentleman Jim**
See Corbett, James John

**Corbett, James John** 1866-1933
[AS, BX, RBE]
American boxer
* Corbett, Gentleman Jim
* Dillon, Jim

**Corbett, John** [FFF]
British politician and salt-works
owner
* [The] Salt King

**Corbett, Stanley**
See Corbucci, Sergio

**Corbett, Thalberg** 1865?-1947
[BEW]
British-born actor
* Thalberg, T. B.

**Corbett, Young**
See Rothwell, William H.

**Corbett, Young, III**
See Giordano, Ralph Capabianca

**Corbiere, Edouard Joachim**
1845-1875 [WBD]
French poet
* Corbiere, Tristan

**Corbiere, Tristan**
See Corbiere, Edouard Joachim

**Corbin, Iris**
See Clinton, Iris A. [Corbin]

**Corbin, Michael**
See Cartmill, Cleve

**Corbin, Pa**
See Corbin, William H.

**Corbin, Sabra Lee**
See Malvern, Gladys

**Corbin, William**
See McGraw, William Corbin

**Corbin, William H.** 1864-1943
[AS, FB]
American football player
* Corbin, Pa

**Corbucci, Sergio** 1927- [FDG]
Italian director
* Corbett, Stanley

**Corby, Dan**
See Catherall, Arthur

**Corby, Ellen**
See Hansen, Ellen

**Corby, Jane** 1899- [WW]
Author
* Carew, Jean
* Holden, Joanne

**Corby, M.**
See Louis Philippe

**Corchaito [Little Cork]**
See Munoz y Gonzalez, Fermin

**Corcito [Little Corzo]**
See Corzo, Jose

**Corcoran, Barbara** 1911-
[CA, WD]
American author
* Dixon, Paige
* Hamilton, Gail

**Corcoran, Catherine**
See Herne, Mrs. J. A.

**Corcoran, Corky**
See Corcoran, Eugene Patrick

**Corcoran, Eugene Patrick** 1924-
[DAM, EJ, PMJ]
American jazz musician
* Corcoran, Corky

**Corcoran, Hugh Gallagher**
1890-1935 [BMH]
Scottish comedian
* Lorne, Tommy

**Corcoran, Thomas G.** 1901-1981
Advisor to American president,
Franklin Roosevelt
* Tommy the Cork

**Cord, Alex**
See Viespi, Alexander

**Cord, Barry**
See Germano, Peter B.

**Corday, Mara**
See Watts, Marilyn

**Corday, Paula** 1924- [FC]
Anglo-Swiss actress
* Corday, Rita
* Croset, Paule

**Corday, Rita**
See Corday, Paula

**Corday d'Armont, [Marie Anne]
Charlotte** 1768-1793 [SN]
French patriot
* [The] Angel of Assassination

**Cordeiro, Calisto** 1877-1957
[WEC]
*Brazilian cartoonist and painter*
* Klixto

**Cordelier, Jean**
See Giraudoux, Jean [Hippolyte]

**Cordelier, Maurice**
See Giraudoux, Jean [Hippolyte]

**Cordell, Alexander**
See Graber, Alexander

**Cordell, Cathleen**
See Kelly, Cathleen

**Cordiani, Antonio** 1483?-1546
[WBD]
*Italian architect and engineer*
* Sangallo, Antonio Picconi da

**Cordiaux, Raymond** 1898-1956
[FC, SC]
*French actor*
* Cordy, Raymond

**Cordier, Gilbert**
See Scherer, Jean Marie Maurice

**Cordis, Lonny**
See Donson, Cyril

**[El] Cordobes [The Cordovan]**
See Benitez Perez, Manuel

**Cordy, Henry**
See Korn, Henry

**Cordy, Raymond**
See Cordiaux, Raymond

**Corea, Armando Anthony** 1941-
[DAM]
*American jazz musician*
* Corea, Chick

**Corea, Chick**
See Corea, Armando Anthony

**Corea, Gena**
See Corea, Genoveffa

**Corea, Genoveffa** 1946- [CA]
*American author*
* Corea, Gena

**Corelli, Marie**
See Mackay, Mary

**Corenanda, A. L. A.**
See Numano, Allen Stanislaus
Motoyuki

**Corenne, Renee**
See Cornester, Renee

**Corey, Frank** [FFF]
*American writer*
* Winwood, Rett

**Corey, Jill**
See Speranza, Norma Jean

**Corey, Joseph**
See Martorano, Joseph

**Corfield, A. J.**
See Corfield, Alfred James

**Corfield, Alfred James** 1904-
[ART]
*British painter and textile machinery
designer*
* Corfield, A. J.

**Corfield, Charles Collingwood** 20th
c. [ART]
*British painter*
* Corfield, Colin

**Corfield, Colin**
See Corfield, Charles Collingwood

**Corfield, Wilmot** 20th c. [WWL]
*British author*
* Dak

**Corhan, Irish**
See Corhan, Roy George

**Corhan, Roy George** 1887-1958
[BE]
*American baseball player*
* Corhan, Irish

**Coria Garcia, Raul** 1932- [GS]
*Mexican bullfighter*
* [El] Gato [The Cat]

**Corilanus**
See Furius, Fredrice

**Corinna**
See Thomas, Elizabeth

**Corinna** 5th c. BC [DNNF]
*Greek poet*
* [The] Lyric Muse

**Corinne**
See De Briou, Corinne Belle

**Corinne**
See Stael, Anne Louise Germaine
de

**Corinth's Pedagogue**
See Dionysius the Younger

**Coriolanus**
See McMillan, James

**Corisande**
See Smith, Mrs. Adolphe Jerrold

**Cork, Barry Joynson** 20th c. [MBF]
*British author*
* Joynson, Barry

**Corkhill, John Stewart** 1858-1921
[AS, BE]
*American baseball player*
* Corkhill, Pop

**Corkhill, Pop**
See Corkhill, John Stewart

**Corkrey, Kathleen** 1923- [FC]
*British actress*
* Raye, Carol

**[The] Corkscrew Kid**
See Selby, Norman

**Corlett, John** [FFF, PA]
*British writer*
* Vigilant
* Wizard

**Corley, Edwin** 1931- [CA]
*American author*
* Buchanan, Patrick
* Collins, Will
* Harper, David
* Judson, William

**Corley, Ernest**
See Bulmer, [Henry] Kenneth

**Corley, J. E.**
See Corley, John Elmer

**Corley, John Elmer** 1950- [ART]
*British artist*
* Corley, J. E.

**Cormack, Alexander James Ross**
1942- [CA]
*Scottish firearms expert and writer*
* Cormack, Sandy

**Cormack, Sandy**
See Cormack, Alexander James
Ross

**Corman, Cid**
See Corman, Sidney

**Corman, Sidney** 1924- [CA, CLC]
*American poet and translator*
* Corman, Cid

**Cormier, Robert Edmund** 1925-
[SAT]
*American author*
* Fitch, John, IV

**Cormon**
See Piestre, Fernand Anne

**Corn, Alfred Jacob** 1919-
[BEW, TR]
*American actor and director*
* Ryder, Alfred

**[The] Corn Bread Man**
See Bernich, Ken

**[The] Corn Law Rhymer**
See Elliott, Ebenezer

**Cornalba, Mlle.**
See Morelli, Mme.

**Cornarus, John** [SN]
*Scientist*
* [The] Mad Cornarus

**Cornblit, Joey** 1956?-
*American jai-alai player*
* Ciego [Blind Man]

**Corneille**
See Van Beverloo, Cornelis
Guillaume

**[The] Corneille of Germany**
See Greif [Griphius or Gryphius],
Andreas

**[The] Corneille of the Boulevards**
See Pixerecourt, Rene Charles
Guilbert de

**Corneille, Pierre** 1606-1684
[DNNS, HN, SN]
*French playwright*
* [The] Creator of French
Dramatic Art
* [The] Father of French Tragedy
* [Le] Grand Corneille
* [The] Homer of the French
Drama
* [The] Shakespeare of France

**Cornelia** 2nd c. BC [DNNF, HN]
*Roman matron*
* [The] Mother of the Gracchi

**Cornelison, Ernest Eli** 1916-
[CWG]
*American country-western performer*
* Lee, Ernie

**Cornelisz, Cornelis** 1562-1638
[WBD]
*Dutch painter*
* Cornelisz van Haarlem

**Cornelisz, Jakob** 16th c. [WBD]
*Dutch painter*
* Cornelisz van Amsterdam
* Van Oostsanen, Jakob

**Cornelisz van Amsterdam**
See Cornelisz, Jakob

**Cornelisz van Haarlem**
See Cornelisz, Cornelis

**corneliszavandenheuvel**
See Van Den Heuvel, Cornelisz A.

**Cornelius, Corky**
See Cornelius, Edward

**Cornelius, Cosper** 20th c. [WECO]
*Danish cartoonist*
* Moco [joint pseudonym with
Jorgen Morgenson]

**Cornelius, Edward** 1914-1943
[WWJ]
*American jazz musician*
* Cornelius, Corky

**Cornelius, Ellanor Frances** 1869?-
? [NAA]
*American poet and writer*
* E. F. C.

**Cornelius, Siegfried** 1911- [WEC]
*Danish cartoonist*
* Cosper

**Cornelius, Sug**
See Cornelius, William

**Cornelius, William** 1907- [B10]
*American baseball player*
* Cornelius, Sug

**Cornell, J.**
See Cornell, Jeffrey

**Cornell, Jeffrey** 1945- [SAT]
*American illustrator*
* Cornell, J.

**Cornell, Mrs. E. J.** [FFF]
*Entertainer*
* Venn, Topsy

**Corner Memory Thompson**
See Thompson, John

**Cornerback, Mr.**
See Jones, Bob

**Corners, George F.**
See Viereck, George Sylvester

**Cornester, Renee** 1937- [OP]
*Rumanian-born opera singer*
* Corenne, Renee

**Cornett, Banjo Bill**
See Cornett, Bill

**Cornett, Bill** 1890- [FFA]
*American singer*
* Cornett, Banjo Bill

**Corney, Louis Dominique**
1738-1790 [PA]
*Author*
* D'Ethis

**Cornford, F. M.**
See Cornford, Francis Macdonald

**Cornford, Francis Macdonald**
1874-1943 [LC]
*British scholar and author*
* Cornford, F. M.

**Corning, Kyle**
See Gardner, Erle Stanley

**Cornish, [Doris] Mary** 1897- [AW]
*Australian author*
* Lisle, Mary

**[The] Cornish Poet**
See Harris, John

**Cornish, Samuel E.** 1790-1859
[IBW]
*American journalist and clergyman*
* [The] Father of Afro-American
Newspapers

**[The] Cornish Wonder**
*See* Opie, John

**Cornu, Mrs. Louis J.** [FFF]
*Entertainer*
* Blankenhorn, Lulu

**Cornwall, Barry**
*See* Proctor, Bryan Waller

**Cornwall, C. M.**
*See* Roe, Mary A.

**Cornwall, G.**
*See* George IV

**Cornwall, Jim**
*See* Rikhoff, James C.

**Cornwall, Martin**
*See* Cavendish, Richard

**Cornwall-Walker, Thomas James
Raglan** 1901-1961 [BEW]
*British actor*
* Raglan, James

**Cornwell, David [John Moore]**
1931- [AW, B10, CA]
*British author*
* Le Carre, John

**Cornwell, Smith**
*See* Smith, David [Jeddie] [Dave]

**Cornyn, John Hubert** 1875- ?
[NAA]
*Canadian journalist and author*
* Rey, Pepe

**Corona, Leonora**
*See* Cohrone, Lenore

**Coronakis, Yvonne** 1935- [BEW]
*French actress, singer, dancer*
* Constant, Yvonne

**[The] Coroner**
*See* Grace, Edward Mills

**[A] Coroner's Clerk**
*See* Neale, Erskine

**Corporal John**
*See* Churchill, John [First Duke of
Marlborough]

**Corporal Violet**
*See* Bonaparte, Napoleon

**Corrado** ?-1154 [CAL]
*Pope*
* Anastasius IV

**Corral de Villa, Luz** 1892?-1981
*Widow of Mexican revolutionary
leader, Pancho Villa*
* Dona Lucha

**Corrall, Alice Enid** 1916- [CA]
*British author and columnist*
* Glass, Justine C.

**Corrara, Joseph** 1893-1965
[BX, RBE]
*Italian-born boxer*
* Dundee, Johnny
* [The] Scotch Wop

**Corrario [or Correr], Angelo**
1327?-1417 [WBD]
*Pope*
* Gregory XII

**Correa**
*See* Galbraith, Jean

**Correa, Mailto** 1943- [EJ7]
*Brazilian jazz musician*
* Mayuto

**Correa, William** 1934- [DAM]
*American jazz musician*
* Bobo, Willie

**Correa da Silva, Joaquim Belford**
1908- [SFL]
*Author*
* Paco d'Arcos, J.

**Correa Garcao, Pedro Antonio
Joaquim** 1724-1772 [WBD]
*Portuguese poet*
* Erimantheo, Corydon

**[The] Corrector**
*See* Cruden, Alexander

**Correggio**
*See* Allegri da Correggio, Antonio

**Correggio?**
*See* Francis, [Sir] Philip

**[The] Correggio of Sculptors**
*See* Goujon, Jean

**[The] Correggio of the Violin**
*See* Rode, [Jacques] Pierre
[Joseph]

**Correll, Bird Dog**
*See* Correll, Victor Crosby

**Correll, Midget**
*See* Correll, Victor Crosby

**Correll, Stumpy**
*See* Correll, Victor Crosby

**Correll, Victor Crosby** 1946-
[SMG]
*American baseball player*
* Correll, Bird Dog
* Correll, Midget
* Correll, Stumpy
* 10 4
* Vic the Stick

**Corren, Grace**
*See* Hoskins, Robert

**Corretjer, Juan Antonio** 1908-
[IAW]
*Puerto Rican author and poet*
* Aracelis, Gabriel
* Montes, Emeterio

**Correy, Lee**
*See* Stine, G[eorge] Harry

**Corri, Adrienne**
*See* Riccoboni, Adrienne

**Corriden, John Michael, Sr.**
1887-1959 [BE]
*American baseball player and
manager*
* Corriden, Red

**Corriden, Red**
*See* Corriden, John Michael, Sr.

**Corridon, Fiddler**
*See* Corridon, Frank J.

**Corridon, Frank J.** 1880-1941
[AS, BE]
*American baseball player*
* Corridon, Fiddler

**Corrigan, Crash**
*See* Benard, Ray

**Corrigan, Emmett**
*See* Zilles, Antoine

**Corrigan, Mark**
*See* Lee, Norman

**Corrigan, Ray**
*See* Benard, Ray

**Corsair**
*See* Davidson, James Wood

**Corsaro, Francesco Andrea** 1924-
[CA]
*American director, actor, author*
* Corsaro, Frank

**Corsaro, Frank**
*See* Corsaro, Francesco Andrea

**Corsee, Jean Baptiste** 1760-1815
[PA]
*Author*
* Labenette

**Corsen, Yolanda** 1918-1969 [CW]
*Curacaon poet*
* Blinder, Oda

**Corsi, Gian Franco** 1927- [OP]
*Italian producer*
* Zeffirelli, Franco

**[The] Corsican**
*See* Bonaparte, Napoleon

**[The] Corsican General**
*See* Bonaparte, Napoleon

**[The] Corsican Ogre**
*See* Bonaparte, Napoleon

**[The] Corsican Sesostris**
*See* Bonaparte, Napoleon

**Corsini, Lorenzo** 1652-1740 [CAL]
*Pope*
* Clement XII

**Corson, Charlotte Catherine**
1740-1813 [PA]
*Author*
* [La] Crissoniere

**Corson, Geoffrey**
*See* Sholl, Anna McClure

**Cort, M. C.**
*See* Clifford, Margaret Cort
[Peggy]

**Cortazar, Julio** 1914- [CA]
*Belgian-born author*
* Denis, Julio

**Cortazzo, John Francis** 1904-1963
[BE]
*American baseball player*
* Cortazzo, Shine

**Cortazzo, Shine**
*See* Cortazzo, John Francis

**Corteen, Wes**
*See* Norwood, Victor G[eorge]
C[harles]

**Cortellini, Camillo** 17th c. [SN]
*Italian composer*
* [Il] Violino

**Cortelyou, Elizabeth A.** [FFF]
*Entertainer*
* Guion, Netta

**Cortes, Hernando** 1485-1547 [SN]
*Spanish explorer*
* [The] Great Marquis

**Cortesa, Valentina**
*See* Cortese, Valentina

**Cortese, Valentina** 1925- [WEF]
*Italian-born actress*
* Cortesa, Valentina

**Cortesi, Lawrence**
*See* Cerri, Lawrence J.

**Cortez, Dave Baby**
*See* Clowney, David Cortez

**Cortez, Jack** [house pseudonym]
*See* Fine, Louis

**[The] Cortez of Africa**
*See* Rowlands, John

**Cortez, Ricardo**
*See* Krantz [or Kranz?], Jacob
[Jake]

**Cortez, Stanley**
*See* Krantz [or Kranz?], Stanley

**Corti, Matteo** 1475-1542 [PA]
*Author*
* Curtius

**Cortis, Diana**
*See* Ashton, Winifred

**Cortona, Pietro da**
*See* Berrettini, Pietro

**Coruelio, Memo** 20th c. [RBE]
*Mexican boxer*
* Vega, Memo

**Corvais, Anthony**
*See* Bradbury, Ray [Douglas]

**Corvin, Eugen Alban**
*See* Gatterman, Eugen Ludwig

**Corvino, Ettore** 1926-1975 [SC]
*American-born actor and dancer*
* Patterson, Troy

**Corvinus [Little Raven]**
*See* Hunyadi, Janos [or Huniades,
John]

**Corvinus, Jakob**
*See* Raabe, Wilhelm

**Corvo, Baron**
*See* Rolfe, Frederick William
[Serafino Austin Lewis Mary]

**Corwin, Al**
*See* Corwin, Elmer Nathan

**Corwin, Cecil**
*See* Kornbluth, Cyril M.

**Corwin, Elmer Nathan** 1926- [BE]
*American baseball player*
* Corwin, Al

**Corwin, Thomas** 1794-1865
[DNNF, SN]
*American statesman and orator*
* [The] Wagon Boy

**Cory, Adela Florence** 1865-1904
[LC, TC]
*British poet*
* Hope, Laurence

**Cory, Corrine**
*See* Cory, Irene E.

**Cory, Desmond**
*See* McCarthy, Shaun [Lloyd]

**Cory, Howard L.** [joint pseudonym
with Julie Anne Jardine]
*See* Jardine, Jack Owen

**Cory, Howard L.** [joint pseudonym
with Jack Owen Jardine]
*See* Jardine, Julie Ann

**Cory, Irene E.** 1910-   [CA]
*American writer*
* Cory, Corrine
* Corya, I. E.

**Cory, Matilda Winifred Muriel [Graham]** 20th c.   [WGT]
*Author*
* Graham, Winifred

**Cory, Ray**
See   Marshall, Mel[vin]

**Cory, Vivian** 20th c.   [SFL, WGT]
*British author*
* Cross, Victoria

**Cory, William Johnson**
See   Johnson, William

**Corya, I. E.**
See   Cory, Irene E.

**Coryat, Thomas** 1577-1617
[HN, RH]
*British author and traveler*
* [The] Odcombian Legstretcher

**Coryell, John Russell** 1848-1924
[WGT, WW]
*American author*
* Carter, Nicholas
* Carter, Nick [joint pseudonym with Ormond G. Smith] [house pseudonym]
* Clay, Bertha M.
* Edwards, Julia
* Fleming, Geraldine
* Grant, Margaret
* Ryan, Sgt.

**Coryell, Russell Miers** 1891-
[NAA]
*American writer*
* Holt, Franklin

**Coryot Junior**
See   Paterson, Samuel

**[The] Coryphaeus of Bookbinders**
See   Payne, Roger

**[The] Coryphaeus of Deism**
See   Arouet, Francois Marie

**[The] Coryphaeus of German Literature**
See   Goethe, Johann Wolfgang von

**[The] Coryphaeus of Grammarians**
See   Aristarchus

**[The] Coryphaeus of his Day**
See   Viau, Theophile de

**[That] Coryphaeus of Learning**
See   Porson, Richard

**[The] Coryphaeus of Letter-Founders**
See   Caslon, William

**[The] Coryphaeus of Mathematicians**
See   Allen, Thomas

**[The] Coryphaeus of Modern Literature**
See   Gifford, William

**[The] Coryphaeus of Northern Lore**
See   Werl, Olaf

**[The] Coryphaeus of Our Elder Dramatists**
See   Jonson, Ben[jamin]

**[The] Coryphaeus of the Interpreters of Law**
See   Bartoli [or Bartolus]

**Corzo, Jose** 1890-   [GS]
*Spanish bullfighter*
* Corcito [Little Corzo]

**Cosby, Bogart**
See   Cosby, William Henry, Jr. [Bill]

**Cosby, William Henry, Jr. [Bill]** 1937-   [IBW]
*American actor and comedian*
* Cosby, Bogart

**Cosby, Yvonne Shepard** 1886?-1980   [CA]
*French-born author*
* Young, Everett

**Coscia, Silvio** 1899-   [IWM]
*Italian-born musician*
* Sylvius, C.

**Cosell, Howard**
See   Cohen, Howard

**Cosgrove, Judy** ?-1974   [SC]
*American actress*
* Somers, Carole

**Cosgrove, Rachel**
See   Payes, Rachel C[osgrove]

**Cosgrove, Stephen E[dward]** 1945-
[CA]
*American author*
* Stevens, Edward

**Cosimo the Elder**
See   Medici, Cosmo [or Cosimo] de

**Cosio Tesero, Alberto** 1926-   [GS]
*Mexican bullfighter*
* Patatero [Potato Seller]

**Cosmano, Sunny Jim**
See   Cosmano, Vincenzo

**Cosmano, Vincenzo** 20th c.   [BLB]
*American underworld figure*
* Cosmano, Sunny Jim

**Cosmas** 6th c.   [WBD]
*Egyptian traveler*
* Indicopleustes

**Cosmo, Crazy Cue**
See   Cosmo, Tom

**[The] Cosmo de Medici of Hungary**
See   Matthias Corvinus

**Cosmo, Tom** 1915?-1978   [FIR]
*Billiard player and actor*
* Cosmo, Crazy Cue

**Cosmopolite**
See   Dix, John A.

**Cosmopolite**
See   Lawson, Jahun

**Cosper**
See   Cornelius, Siegfried

**Cossart, Theophilus**
See   Glass, Montague Marsden

**Cosseboom, Kathy Groehn**
See   El Messidi, Kathy[anne] Groehn

**Cost, March**
See   Morrison, Margaret Mackie

**Costa, A.**
See   Capone, Al[phonse]

**Costa, Frank**
See   Musica, Philip

**Costa-Gavras, Henri**
See   Gavras, Konstantinos

**Costadoni, Giovanni Domenico** 1741-1785   [PA]
*Author*
* Dom Anselmo

**Costanza, Margaret** 1932-
*Administrative aide to American president Jimmy Carter*
* Costanza, Midge

**Costanza, Midge**
See   Costanza, Margaret

**Costanza, Senora**
See   Long, Gabrielle Margaret Vere [Campbell]

**Costeau**
See   Richard, Jacques

**Costello, Dan[iel Francis]** 1895-1936   [BE]
*American baseball player*
* Costello, Dashing Dan

**Costello, Dashing Dan**
See   Costello, Dan[iel Francis]

**Costello, Elvis**
See   McManus, Declan Patrick

**Costello, Frank**
See   Castiglia, Francesco

**Costello, Lou**
See   Cristillo, Louis Francis

**Costello, Maurice**
See   Blythe, Herbert

**Costello, Michael**
See   Detzer, Karl

**Costello, P. F.** [house pseudonym, Ziff-Davis]
See   Geier, Chester S.

**Costello, P. F.** [house pseudonym, Ziff-Davis]
See   Graham, Roger Phillips

**Costello, Pierre**
See   Hosken, Ernest Charles Heath

**Coster, Arthur Vennell** 1864- ?
[WWL]
*British author*
* Arveco

**Coster, F[rank] Donald**
See   Musica, Philip

**Coster, Jean** 1515-1559   [PA]
*Author*
* Columba

**[The] Coster King**
See   Hurley, Alec

**[The] Coster Laureate**
See   Chevalier, Albert Onesime Britannicus Gwathveoyd Louis

**Coster, Robert**
See   Barltrop, Robert

**[The] Coster's Friend**
See   Cooper, Anthony Ashley

**Costi y Erro, Candido** 1862?- ?
[CW]
*Cuban playwright*
* Sicto, C.

**Costinescu, Tristan**
See   Gross, Terence

**Cote, Louis Joseph, Jr.** 1884-1934
[BEW, FI, FC]
*American actor*
* Cody, Lew

**Cote, Regent** 1939-   [SMG]
*Canadian-born hockey player*
* Cote, Roger

**Cote, Roger**
See   Cote, Regent

**Cotes, Peter**
See   Boulting, Sydney

**Cotin, Charles** 1604-1682
[FFF, PA, SN]
*French clergyman*
* [The] Father of French Enigma
* [The] Father of Riddles
* [The] Father of the French Riddle
* Trissotin

**Cotler, Gordon** 1923-   [CA]
*American author*
* Gordon, Alex

**Cotrim, Alvaro** 1904-   [WEC]
*Brazilian cartoonist*
* Alvarus

**Cotten, Elizabeth** 1893-   [DAM]
*American singer*
* Cotten, Libba

**Cotten, Libba**
See   Cotten, Elizabeth

**Cotter, Harvey Louis** 1900-1955
[BE]
*American baseball player*
* Cotter, Hooks

**Cotter, Hooks**
See   Cotter, Harvey Louis

**Cotter, Jane** 1923?-   [BEW, SW]
*American actress*
* Meadows, Jayne

**Cottereau, Jean** 1757-1794   [SN]
*Leader of French insurrection*
* [Le] Chouan [The Owl]

**Cotterell, Brian**
See   Dingle, Aylward Edward

**Cotterell, [Sir] Charles** 1631-1664
[DEL, PA]
*British scholar*
* Poliarchus

**Cottin, Sophie** 1773-1807   [PA]
*Author*
* Ristaud

**Cottingham, Henry**
See   Pond, Wilf Pocklington

**Cottle, Charles**
See   Anderson, Robert C[harles]

**Cottle, Josephine** 1922-
[FC, ITA, SW]
*American actress*
* Storm, Gale

**Cotton, Baldy**
See   Cotton, Harold

**Cotton, Billy**
See   Andrews, Allen

**Cotton Ed Smith**
See   Smith, Ellison DuRant

**Cotton, Harold** 1902-
[CEI, FHE, HK]
*Canadian-born hockey player*
* Cotton, Baldy

**Cotton, James [Jimmy]** 1935-
[BWW]
*American singer*
* Denim, Joe

**Cotton, Jerri**
*See* Sellers, Connie Leslie, Jr.

**Cotton, John**
*See* Wellman, Manly Wade

**Cotton, John** 1584?-1652
[DNNS, WBD]
*British-born clergyman*
* [The] Patriarch of New England

**[The] Cotton King**
*See* Boussac, Marcel

**Cotton, Lily Elsie** 1886-1962
[EMT]
*British actress and singer*
* Elsie, Lily

**Cotton, Lucy**
*See* Magraw, Lucy Cotton

**Cottrell, John** 20th c.   [SMG]
*American baseball scout*
* Cottrell, Paddy

**Cottrell, Morganna Roberts** 20th c.
*American entertainer*
* [The] Kissing Bandit
* [The] Wild One

**Cottrell, Paddy**
*See* Cottrell, John

**Cottrelly, Mathilde**
*See* Meyer, Mathilde

**Cotts, Campbell**
*See* Mitchell-Cotts, [Sir] William
Campbell

**Coty, Francois**
*See* Spoturno, Francesco Giuseppe

**Couch, Helen F[ox]** 1907-   [CAP]
*American author*
* Fox, V. Helen

**Couch, Lizzie**   [FFF]
*Entertainer*
* Meredith, Lucille

**Couch, Osma Palmer**
*See* Tod, Osma Gallinger

**Coudreux, Alfred**
*See* Balzac, Honore de

**Couet, Yvonne** 1893-   [NAA]
*Canadian author*
* Arlesienne

**Coughlin, Bill** 1877-1943
*American baseball player*
* Coughlin, Cap
* Coughlin, Rowdy Bill

**Coughlin, Cap**
*See* Coughlin, Bill

**Coughlin, John** 20th c.
*American underworld figure*
* [The] Bathhouse
* Bathhouse John

**Coughlin, John D.**   [PA]
*Author*
* Cousin Torrence

**Coughlin, Roscoe**
*See* Coughlin, William E.

**Coughlin, Rowdy Bill**
*See* Coughlin, Bill

**Coughlin, William E.** 1866-1951
[BE]
*American baseball player*
* Coughlin, Roscoe

**Coughran, Larry C.** 1925-   [CA]
*American author*
* Craig, Larry

**Coulet Du Gard, Rene** 1919-   [CA]
*Algerian-born American author*
* Algery, Andre
* Anduze-Dufy, Raphael

**Coulevain, Augustine Favre de**
1838-1913   [WBD]
*French author*
* Coulevain, Pierre de

**Coulevain, Pierre de**
*See* Coulevain, Augustine Favre de

**Coulon, Eddie**
*See* Francois, Edgar

**Coulon, Johnny** 1889-1973
[BBH, BX]
*Canadian-born boxer*
* [The] Chicago Spider

**Coulsdon, John**
*See* Hincks, Cyril Malcolm

**Coulson, Felicity Winifred Carter**
1906-   [AW, CA, CC]
*British author*
* Bonett, Emery

**Coulson, John H[ubert] A[rthur]**
1906-   [AW, CA, CC]
*British author*
* Bonett, John

**Coulson, Juanita Ruth Wellons**
1933-   [WGT]
*American author*
* Wells, John Jay [joint pseudonym
with Marion Zimmer Bradley]

**Coulson, Robert [Stratton]** 1928-
[CA, WD]
*American author*
* Black, Roberta [joint pseudonym
with Sandra Miesel]
* Stratton, Thomas [joint
pseudonym with Eugene
DeWeese]

**Coulter, Art[hur Edmund]** 1909-
[FHE]
*Canadian-born hockey player*
* Coulter, Trapper

**Coulter, Mrs. Frazer**   [FFF]
*Entertainer*
* Thorne, Grace

**Coulter, Stephen** 1914-   [WWS]
*British author*
* Mayo, James

**Coulter, Trapper**
*See* Coulter, Art[hur Edmund]

**Coulter, Ursula** 1901-   [THR]
*British actress*
* Millard, Ursula

**Coulton, G. G.**
*See* Coulton, George Gordon

**Coulton, George Gordon**
1858-1947   [LC]
*British educator and author*
* Coulton, G. G.

**Coulton, James**
*See* Hansen, Joseph

**Coulton, Mary Rose** 20th c.   [SFL]
*Author*
* Campion, Sarah

**Coumbe, Frederick Nicholas** 1889-
[BE]
*American baseball player*
* Coumbe, Fritz

**Coumbe, Fritz**
*See* Coumbe, Frederick Nicholas

**Council, Dipper Boy**
*See* Council, Floyd

**Council, Floyd** 1911-1976   [BWW]
*American singer*
* Blind Boy Fuller's Buddy
* Council, Dipper Boy
* Devil's Daddy-in-Law

**Counsellor**
*See* Cilento, Phyllis Dorothy

**Counsilman, Doc**
*See* Counsilman, James

**Counsilman, James** 1922?-
*American swimmer and swimming
coach*
* Counsilman, Doc

**[The] Count**
*See* DeMarco, Albert Thomas, Jr.

**[The] Count**
*See* Fuqua, John

**[The] Count**
*See* Gratton, Gilles

**[The] Count**
*See* McMacken, Bill

**[The] Count**
*See* Montefusco, John Joseph, Jr.

**[The] Count**
*See* Moules, Peter

**Count, Marie P.**
*See* Conte, Maria Pia

**Count, Noah**
*See* Trafton, Edwin H.

**[The] Count of Luxemburg**
*See* Meine, Henry William

**Count Rockin' Sydney**
*See* Semien, Sidney

**Count Tony Mullane**
*See* Mullane, Anthony John

**Countess**
*See* Gilchrist, Connie

**Country Charley Pride**
*See* Pride, Charley

**[A] Country Clergyman**
*See* Cunningham, J. W.

**[The] Country Clergyman of the
Eighteenth Century**
*See* Twining, Thomas

**[A] Country Curate**
*See* Neale, Erskine

**Country Joe**
*See* McDonald, Joe

**[A] Country Parson**
*See* Boyd, Andrew Kennedy
Hutchinson

**[A] Country Parson**
*See* Moule, H.

**[A] Country Pastor**
*See* Whately, Richard

**Country Paul**
*See* Harris, Ed[ward P.]

**[The] Country Preacher**
*See* Jackson, Jesse Louis

**Country Rock, Mr.**
*See* Craddock, Billy

**Country Slim**
*See* Lewis, Ernest

**[The] Country Sunshine**
*See* West, Dorothy Marie [Dottie]

**Country Willie Nelson**
*See* Nelson, Willie

**[The] Countryman**
*See* Whitlock, Ralph

**Counts, Mel** 20th c.
*American basketball player*
* [The] Goose

**Couperin, Francois** 1631-1701?
[SN]
*French musician*
* [Le] Grand

**Coupling, J. J.**
*See* Pierce, John Robinson

**Cour, T. E.**
*See* Barter, W. G. T.

**Courage, John**
*See* Goyne, Richard

**Courance, Edgar** 1903-1969
[WWJ]
*American jazz musician*
* Courance, Spider

**Courance, Spider**
*See* Courance, Edgar

**Courcel, Nicole**
*See* Andrieux, Nicole

**Cournos, Helen Kestner
Satterthwaite** 20th c.   [CAP]
*Author*
* Hawk, John
* Norton, Sybil

**Cournos, John** 1881-1966
[CAP, WW]
*Russian-born author, poet,
playwright*
* Courtney, John
* Gault, Mark

**Cournoyer, Yvan Serge** 1943-
[FHE]
*Canadian-born hockey player*
* Roadrunner

**Course, Pamela Mary** 20th c.
[AW]
*British author*
* Becket, Lavinia
* Mansbridge, Pamela

**Courson**
*See* De Lamoignon, Urbain
Guillaume

**Court, Antoine** 1696-1760 [HN]
*French clergyman*
* [The] Restorer of the
  Protestantism of France

**Court, Don** 1903?- [F2, FC, IPA]
*American actor*
* Murray, Ken

**Court, Fancy**
See Court, Helen

**Court, Florence** 1899-1937 [SC]
*American actress*
* Miles, Lotta

**Court, Helen** 20th c. [RO2]
*British singer*
* Court, Fancy

**[The] Court Historian**
See Beresford, John Claudius

**[The] Court Jester**
See Mubarak, Hosni

**[The] Court Magician and
Ventriloquist**
See Prince, Arthur

**Court, Sharon**
See Rowland, D[onald] S[ydney]

**Courteline, Georges**
See Moinaux, Georges-Victor
Marcel

**Courtenay, Peregrine**
See Praed, Winthrop Mackworth

**[The] Courteous**
See Morgan Mwynvawr

**Courtet, Emile** 1857-1938
[FC, WEF]
*French cartoonist*
* Cohl, Emile

**Courthope, W. J.**
See Courthope, William John

**Courthope, William John**
1842-1917 [LC]
*British author*
* Courthope, W. J.

**Courtier, P. L.** 19th c. [PA]
*Author*
* Onesimus

**Courtier, Sidney Hobson**
1904-1974 [CAP, CC, EMD]
*Australian author*
* Chestor, Rui

**Courtine, Robert** 1910- [CA]
*French author*
* La Reyniere
* Savarin

**Courtland, Grace** [PA]
*Author*
* Gypsy

**Courtland, Roberta**
See Dern, Peggy Gaddis

**[The] Courtly**
See Leopold II

**Courtney, Anthony Tosswill** 1908-
[IAW]
*British writer*
* Chancellor, Richard

**Courtney, Charles E.** 20th c. [BBH]
*American rowing coach*
* Courtney, Pop

**Courtney, Clinton Dawson** 1927-
[BE, PB]
*American baseball player*
* Courtney, Scrap Iron
* [The] Toy Bull Dog

**Courtney, Edward** ?-1553 [RH]
*Earl of Devon*
* [The] White Rose of York

**Courtney, John**
See Cournos, John

**Courtney, John**
See Judd, Frederick Charles

**Courtney, Marie** ?-1967 [BMH]
*British entertainer*
* Lloyd, Marie, Jr.

**Courtney, Pop**
See Courtney, Charles E.

**Courtney, Robert**
See Ellison, Harlan [Jay]

**Courtney, Robert**
See King, Charles Daly

**Courtney, Robert**
See Robinson, Frank M[alcolm]

**Courtney, Scrap Iron**
See Courtney, Clinton Dawson

**Courtney, Thomas [Tom]** 1929-
[BWW]
*American singer*
* Courtney, Tomcat

**Courtney, Tomcat**
See Courtney, Thomas [Tom]

**Courtois, Jacques** 1621-1676
[WBD]
*French painter*
* [Le] Bourguignon

**Courtright, William** 1848-1933
[SC]
*American actor*
* Uncle Billy

**Cousans, S. W.**
See Pond, Wilf Pocklington

**Cousin Alice**
See Haven, Alice B.

**Cousin Ann**
See Lilly, Isabella Purvis

**Cousin Beedie**
See Carter, Hugh

**Cousin, Charles Yves** 1769-1840
*Author*
* Cousin d'Avallon

**Cousin Cheap**
See Carter, Hugh, Jr.

**Cousin Clara**
See Wise, Daniel

**Cousin d'Avallon**
See Cousin, Charles Yves

**Cousin Ed**
See Barrow, Edward Grant

**Cousin Egbert**
See Barrow, Edward Grant

**Cousin Gene**
See Sallaway, Myrtle May

**Cousin Herb**
See Henson, Herbert Lester

**Cousin Hot**
See Carter, James Earl, Jr.
[Jimmy]

**Cousin Jacques**
See Beffroy de Reigny, Louis Abel

**Cousin, Jean** 1500?-1590
[DEP, DNNS, HN]
*French painter, engraver, sculptor*
* [The] Michael Angelo of France
* [Le] Michel Ange Francais

**Cousin Jody**
See Summey, James C.

**Cousin Joe**
See Joseph, Pleasant

**Cousin Joseph**
See Joseph, Pleasant

**Cousin Kate**
See Bell, Catherine D.

**Cousin Kate**
See Cozans, Kate M. T.

**Cousin Kate**
See Edwards, Catherine M.

**Cousin Kate**
See McIntosh, Maria Jane

**Cousin Nourma**
See Nagle, J. E.

**Cousin Sue**
See Wright, S. A.

**Cousin Torrence**
See Coughlin, John D.

**Cousin Virginia**
See Johnson, Virginia W.

**Cousin Virginia**
See Townsend, Virginia Frances

**Cousineau, Cus**
See Cousineau, Robert Patrick

**Cousineau, Dee**
See Cousineau, Edward Thomas

**Cousineau, Edward Thomas**
1898-1951 [BE]
*American baseball player*
* Cousineau, Dee

**Cousineau, Robert Patrick** 1923-
[EJ]
*American jazz musician*
* Cousineau, Cus

**Cousins, Margaret** 1905-
[CA, SAT, WD]
*American author*
* Johns, Avery
* Masters, William
* Parrish, Mary

**Cousteau, Jacques-Yves** 1910?-
*French naval officer and marine
explorer*
* J. Y. C.

**Cousy, Robert J. [Bob]** 1928-
[MEB, SMG]
*American basketball player*
* Basketball, Mr.
* [The] Cooz
* [The] Houdini of the Hardwood
* [The] Mobile Magician

**Couthony, Marion**
See Smith, Marion C.

**Couton, Robert** ?-1371 [PA]
*Author*
* Amoenus, Doctor

**Coutts, Connie**
See Ediss, Connie

**Coutts, Francis**
See Money-Coutts, Francis

**Coutts, Hubert**
See Tucker, Hubert Coutts

**Coutu, Ovide** 1932- [OP]
*Canadian opera singer*
* Duval, Pierre

**Couture, Coutu**
See Couture, William [Billy]

**Couture, Lolo**
See Couture, Rosario

**Couture, Rosario** 1905- [CEI]
*Canadian-born hockey player*
* Couture, Lolo

**Couture, William [Billy]** 20th c.
[FHE]
*Canadian-born hockey player*
* Couture, Coutu

**Couturier, Louis [Joseph]** 1910-
[CA]
*French author*
* Carrouges, Michel

**Covay, Don** 20th c. [RO1]
*American singer*
* Pretty Boy

**Cove, Joseph Walter** 1891-
[ESF, SFL, WGT]
*British author*
* Gibbs, Lewis

**Coveleskie, Harry Frank**
See Kowalewskie, Harry Frank

**Coveleskie, Stan[ley Anthony]**
See Kowalewskie, Stanislaus

**Covell, Julia Faye** 1896-
*American actress*
* Faye, Julia

**Coventry Antiquary**
See Sharp, Thomas

**Coventry, F. H.**
See Coventry, Frederick Halford

**Coventry, Frederick Halford** 20th
c. [ART]
*British artist*
* Coventry, F. H.

**Coventry, Henry** ?-1752 [SN]
*British scholar*
* Plato

**Coverack, Gilbert**
See Warren, John Russell

**Covington, Ben** 1900?-1935?
[BWW]
*American singer*
* Covington, Blind Ben
* Covington, Bogus Ben

**Covington, Blind Ben**
See Covington, Ben

**Covington, Bogus Ben**
See Covington, Ben

**Covington, Chester**
See Van Horn, Dale R.

**Covington, Chester Rogers [Chet]**
1910-  [BE]
*American baseball player*
* Covington, Chesty

**Covington, Chesty**
See Covington, Chester Rogers [Chet]

**Covington, Clarence Otto**
1892-1963  [BE]
*American baseball player*
* Covington, Sam
* Covington, Tex

**Covington, Sam**
See Covington, Clarence Otto

**Covington, Tex**
See Covington, Clarence Otto

**Covington, Tex**
See Covington, William Wilkes [Bill]

**Covington, Van Doak** 1896-1956
[SC]
*American actor*
* Cody, Harry

**Covington, William Wilkes [Bill]**
1887-1931  [BE]
*American baseball player*
* Covington, Tex

**Cowan, Alan**
See Gilchrist, Alan W.

**Cowan, Claude** 1879?-1955  [FC]
*British comedian*
* Dampier, Claude

**Cowan, L. D.** 1930?-  [B10]
*British personnel manager*
* Cowan, Nick

**Cowan, Marcus** 1874?-1955
[BEW]
*British-born actor and writer*
* Thurston, Harry

**Cowan, Nick**
See Cowan, L. D.

**Cowan, Odessa** 1914?-
[PMJ, WWJ]
*American bandleader and singer*
* [The] Blonde Bombshell of
  Rhythm
* Hutton, Ina Ray

**Cowan, Rosalia** 1886-  [CAT]
*Irish-born author*
* Cowan, [Sister] St. Michael

**Cowan, [Sister] St. Michael**
See Cowan, Rosalia

**Cowan, Samuel** 1881-1938
[BMH, THR]
*British comedian*
* [The] Immobile One
* Mayo, Sam

**Coward, [Sir] Noel [Pierce]**
1899-1973  [CAP]
*British playwright, composer, actor,
author*
* Whittlebot, Hernia

**Coward, William C.** 1656-1725
[PA]
*Author*
* W. C. C.

**[The] Cowboy**
See Alterie, Leland Verain

**[The] Cowboy**
See Bryan, Jimmy

**[The] Cowboy**
See Clement, Jack

**[The] Cowboy**
See Flett, William Mayer [Bill]

**[The] Cowboy Auctioneer**
See Taylor, Joe Carl

**Cowboy Jack Kaenel**
See Kaenel, Jack

**Cowboy Jess Willard**
See Willard, Jess

**[The] Cowboy Rambler**
See Boyd, William [Bill]

**Cowdrey, Christopher Stuart** 1957-
[DC]
*British cricketer*
* Cowdrey, Cow

**Cowdrey, Cow**
See Cowdrey, Christopher Stuart

**Cowell, John** 1554-1611  [SN]
*British jurist*
* Cowheel, Doctor

**Cowell, Sam** 1820-1864  [BMH]
*British entertainer*
* [The] Young American Roscius

**Cowell, Sidney**
See Holmes, Mrs. Raymond

**Cowen, Eve**
See Werner, Herma

**Cowen, Frances**
See Munthe, Frances

**Cowen, Joseph**
See Cohen, Joseph

**Cowen, Laurence** 20th c.  [WWL]
*British author*
* Lesser, Columbus

**Cowen, Samuella Mardis**  [FFF]
*Journalist*
* Le Clerc

**Cowens, Herbert** 1904-  [WWJ]
*American jazz musician*
* Cowens, Kat

**Cowens, Kat**
See Cowens, Herbert

**Cowern, R. T.**
See Cowern, Raymond Teague

**Cowern, Raymond Teague** 1913-
[ART]
*British artist*
* Cowern, R. T.

**Cowheel, Doctor**
See Cowell, John

**[The] Cowkiller**
See Sagoyewatha

**Cowl, Jane**
See Cowles, Jane

**Cowles, Frederick I.** 1900-  [WWL]
*British author*
* Elliott, Graham

**Cowles, Jane** 1884-1950  [WBD]
*American actress*
* Cowl, Jane

**Cowles, Jules** 1888-1971  [FC]
*American actor*
* Conklin, Chester

**Cowles, Osborne** 1899-  [BB]
*American basketball player*
* Cowles, Ozzie

**Cowles, Ozzie**
See Cowles, Osborne

**Cowles, T. Z. C.**  [PA]
*Author*
* Buttons

**Cowley, Abraham** 1618-1667
[DEP, FFF, SN]
*British poet*
* [The] English Pindar
* [The] Horace of England
* [The] Melancholy
* [The] Pindar, Horace, and Virgil
  of England
* [The] Pindar of England

**Cowley, Frank**
See Birkenhead, Frank

**Cowley, Hannah** 1743-1809  [WBD]
*British playwright and poet*
* Matilda, Anna

**Cowley, Ramsay**
See Watterson, John William

**Cowley, William**  [PA]
*Author*
* W. C.

**Cowlin, Dorothy**
See Whalley, Dorothy

**Cowlishaw, Ranson** 1894-
[AW, CA]
*British author*
* Wash, R.
* Woodrook, R. A.

**Cowper, Francis Henry** 1906-
[AW]
*British barrister and author*
* Roe, Richard

**Cowper, Frank** 1849- ?  [LAO]
*British author*
* Diogenes Senior
* Jack All Alone

**Cowper, Richard**
See Middleton-Murry, Colin

**Cowper, William** 1731-1800
[DEP, DNNF, FFF]
*British poet*
* [The] Bard of Olney
* [The] Domestic Poet
* England's Domestic Poet

**Cowton, Robert**  [PA]
*Author*
* Stanley, Reginald Fitz-Roy

**Cox, A. B.**
See Cox, Anthony Berkeley

**Cox, Anne**  [WGT]
*British author*
* Gray, Annabel

**Cox, Anthony Berkeley**
1893-1970?  [CC, EMD, LC]
*British author*
* Berkeley, Anthony
* Cox, A. B.
* Iles, Francis

**Cox, Arthur Jean** 20th c.
[SFP, WGT]
*Author*
* Carghill, Ralph
* Cross, Gene

**Cox, Charles Roy** 1892-  [NAA]
*American writer*
* Clarke, Kamylla
* Poste, Denver

**Cox, Dick**
See Cox, Elmer Joseph

**Cox, Dorothy Isobel** 1906-1964
[BEW, FC]
*British actress*
* Wynyard, Diana

**Cox, Douglas**
See Cox, H. D.

**Cox, Edith Muriel** 20th c.
[AW, CA, WD]
*British author*
* Goaman, Muriel

**Cox, Elmer**
See Cox, Ernest Thompson [Ernie]

**Cox, Elmer Joseph** 1897-  [BE]
*American baseball player*
* Cox, Dick

**Cox, Ernest Thompson [Ernie]**
1894-  [BE]
*American baseball player*
* Cox, Elmer

**Cox, Euphrasia** 20th c.  [WWL]
*British author*
* Cox, Lewis

**Cox, Forrest** 1907-1962  [BB]
*American basketball player*
* Cox, Frosty

**Cox, Frank Bernhardt** 1858-1928
[BE]
*American baseball player*
* Cox, Runt

**Cox, Frosty**
See Cox, Forrest

**Cox, G. F. M.**
See Cox, Gertrude Florence Mary

**Cox, Gertrude Florence Mary** 20th
c.  [ART]
*British painter and etcher*
* Cox, G. F. M.

**Cox, Glenn Melvin** 1931-  [BE]
*American baseball player*
* Cox, Jingles

**Cox, H. D.** 20th c.  [MBF]
*British author*
* Cox, Douglas

**Cox, Ida** 1896-1967  [BWW]
*American singer*
* Bradley, Velma
* Lewis, Kate
* Powers, Julia
* Powers, Julius
* [The] Sepia Mae West
* Smith, Jane
* [The] Uncrowned Queen of the
  Blues

**Cox, Jingles**
See Cox, Glenn Melvin

**Cox, John** 1913-  [FC]
*American actor*
* Howard, John

**Cox, John Roberts [Jack]** 1915-
[CA, SAT]
*British author*
* Havenhand, John
* Roberts, David

**Cox, Lewis**
*See* Cox, Euphrasia

**Cox, Mrs. S. B. Hughes** [FFF]
*Writer*
* Beverley

**Cox, Mrs. William N.** 19th c. [PA]
*Author*
* Curtiss, Percy

**Cox, Nathan** 1910?-
[FC, ITA, SW]
*Canadian actor*
* Cameron, Rod

**Cox, P[atrick] Brian**
*See* Wesander, Bjoern Kenneth

**Cox, Plateau Rex** 1895- [BE]
*American baseball player*
* Cox, Red

**Cox, Red**
*See* Cox, Plateau Rex

**Cox, Richard** 1933- [SW]
*American actor*
* Sargent, Richard

**Cox, Runt**
*See* Cox, Frank Bernhardt

**Cox, Samuel Sullivan** 1824-1889
[DNNS, FFF, SN]
*American attorney, author,
politician*
* Buckeye
* Cox, Sunset

**Cox, Stephen Bernard** 1950- [ART]
*British artist*
* Nevetz
* Stephen

**Cox, Sunset**
*See* Cox, Samuel Sullivan

**Cox, W.** 1747-1828 [PA]
*Author*
* [An] Amateur

**Cox, Wiffy**
*See* Cox, Wilfred H.

**Cox, Wilfred H.** 1897-1969 [GF]
*American golfer*
* Cox, Wiffy

**Cox, William R[obert]** 1901- [CA]
*American author*
* Reeve, Joel

**Cox, William Trevor** 1928-
[B10, CA, WD]
*Irish author and playwright*
* Trevor, William

**Cox-George, Noah Arthur William**
1915- [IAW]
*Nigerian-born economist and author*
* Nijsni, K. M.
* Seminola

**Cox-Johnson, Ann**
*See* Saunders, Ann Loreille

**[The] Coxcomb**
*See* Henry III [or Henri]

**[The] Coxcomb**
*See* Richard II

**[The] Coxcomb Bird**
*See* Euxenus

**Coxe, Arthur Cleveland** 1818- ?
[PA]
*Author*
* C.

**Coxe, Kathleen Buddington** [joint
pseudonym with Edna McHugh]
*See* Long, Amelia Reynolds

**Coxe, Kathleen Buddington** [joint
pseudonym with Amelia Reynolds
Long]
*See* McHugh, Edna

**Coxe, Richard S.** 19th c. [PA]
*American author*
* [An] American Gentleman

**Coxer, Sarah** [PA]
*Author*
* Anderson, Sarah

**Coxie**
*See* Baumgardtner, Claude
Chalmers

**Coxon, Muriel [Hine]** 20th c.
[WGT]
*British author*
* Hine, Muriel

**Coycault, Ernest** 1890?- [NOJ]
*American jazz musician*
* Coycault, Nenny

**Coycault, Jerome** 1895?-1928
[NOJ]
*American jazz musician*
* Coycault, Pill

**Coycault, Nenny**
*See* Coycault, Ernest

**Coycault, Pill**
*See* Coycault, Jerome

**Coyle, Frank** 20th c. [BBH]
*American handball player*
* Coyle, Lefty

**Coyle, Lee**
*See* Coyle, Leo [Perry]

**Coyle, Lefty**
*See* Coyle, Frank

**Coyle, Leo [Perry]** 1925- [CA]
*American filmmaker and author*
* Coyle, Lee

**Coyne, Joseph E.** 1918- [CA]
*American author*
* Berch, William O.

**Coyote Eyes Clark**
*See* Clark, Mel

**Coypeau, Charles [Sieur d'Assouci]**
[SN]
*Author and translator*
* [The] Ape of Scarron
* Our Mock Ovid

**Coysevox, Antoine** 1640-1720
[DNNF, FFF, RH]
*French sculptor*
* [The] Vandyck of Sculpture

**Cozad, Robert Henry** 1865-1929
[CAR]
*American artist*
* Henri, Robert

**Cozanet, Albert** 1870-1938 [BBD]
*French writer on music*
* D'Udine, Jean

**Cozans, Kate M. T.** [FFF]
*American author*
* Cousin Kate

**Cozinski, Mary**
*See* Steinhauer, H. A.

**Cozzens, Frederick Swartwout**
1818-1869 [FFF, PA, WBD]
*American author*
* Hayward, Richard
* Haywarde, Richard
* Sparrowgrass, Mr.

**Cply**
*See* Copley, William Nelson

**[The] Crab**
*See* Burkett, Jesse Cail

**[The] Crab**
*See* Evers, John Joseph

**Crab, Roger** ?-1680 [RH]
*British indigent*
* [The] English Hermit

**[The] Crabapple Comet**
*See* Rucker, John Joel

**Crabb, Buster**
*See* Crabb, Lionel

**Crabb, Lionel** 1910- [BDW]
*British naval officer*
* Crabb, Buster

**Crabbe, Buster**
*See* Crabbe, Clarence Linden

**Crabbe, Clarence Linden** 1907?-
[FC, IPA, ITA]
*American actor*
* Crabbe, Buster
* Crabbe, Larry

**Crabbe, George** 1754-1832
[DEL, SN]
*British clergyman and poet*
* [The] Poet of the Poor
* [The] Pope in Worsted Stockings

**Crabbe, Larry**
*See* Crabbe, Clarence Linden

**Crabtree, Carlotta** 1847-1924
[BEW]
*American-born actress*
* Lotta, Charlotte

**Crabtree, Charles C.** 1891-1943
[BE]
*American baseball player*
* McDonald, Charles E.
* McDonald, Tex

**Crabtree, Crabby**
*See* Crabtree, Estel Crayton

**Crabtree, Eric** 1944- [SMG]
*American football player*
* Crabtree, Tree

**Crabtree, Estel Crayton** 1903-1967
[BE]
*American baseball player*
* Crabtree, Crabby

**Crabtree, Tree**
*See* Crabtree, Eric

**Cracken, Jael**
*See* Aldiss, Brian W[ilson]

**Craddock, Billy** 1939-
[CME, ECM]
*American country-western performer*
* Country Rock, Mr.
* Craddock, Billy Crash

**Craddock, Billy Crash**
*See* Craddock, Billy

**Craddock, Charles Egbert**
*See* Murfree, Mary Noailles

**Craddock, Olive** ?-1926 [BEW]
*Indian-born dancer*
* Roshanara

**Craddock, Vincent Eugene**
1935-1971 [PRS, RO1]
*American singer and songwriter*
* Vincent, Gene

**Craddock, William J[ames]** 1946-
[CA]
*American author*
* James, William

**Craenhals, Francois** 1926- [WECO]
*Belgian cartoonist*
* Hals, F.

**Craft, Maurice Montague** 1895-
[BE]
*American baseball player*
* Craft, Molly

**Craft, Molly**
*See* Craft, Maurice Montague

**Craft, Zachary**
*See* Kelsall, Charles

**Crafts, W. F.** [PA]
*Author*
* Uncle Will, V. M.

**Cragg, Mary** 1870-1951 [F2, FC]
*British actress*
* Ault, Marie

**Craghead, Howard Oliver**
1908-1962 [BE]
*American baseball player*
* Craghead, Judge

**Craghead, Judge**
*See* Craghead, Howard Oliver

**Cragin, Louisa T.** [PA]
*Author*
* Gray, Ellis

**Cragin, Mary A.** [PA]
*Author*
* Allison, Joy

**Craig, A. A.**
*See* Anderson, Poul [William]

**Craig, Alexander George [Alec]**
1897- [CAP]
*British author*
* Craik, Arthur

**Craig, Brian** [joint pseudonym with
Brian M[ichael] Stableford]
*See* Mackintosh, Craig M.

**Craig, Brian** [joint pseudonym with
Craig M. Mackintosh]
*See* Stableford, Brian M[ichael]

**Craig, Colin**
*See* Booth, Henry Spencer

**Craig, David**
*See* Krangel, David

**Craig, David**
*See* Tucker, [Allan] James

**Craig, Denys**
*See* Stoll, Dennis G[ray]

**Craig, Edith**
*See* Wardell, Edith

**Craig, Edward Anthony** 1905-
[AW, CA, WD]
*British author and film art-director*
* Carrick, Edward

**Craig, Edward Gordon**
*See* Wardell, Henry Edward
Gordon Godwin

**Craig, George McCarthy**
1887-1911   [BE]
*American baseball player*
* Craig, Lefty

**Craig, Georgia**
*See* Dern, Peggy Gaddis

**Craig, Gordon**
*See* Terry, Edward Gordon

**Craig, Husky**
*See* Craig, Ross Brown

**Craig, James**
*See* Meador, James H.

**Craig, Jennifer**
*See* Brambleby, Ailsa

**Craig, John Eland**
*See* Chipperfield, Joseph E[ugene]

**Craig, Jonathan**
*See* Posner, Richard

**Craig, Larry**
*See* Coughran, Larry C.

**Craig, Lee**
*See* Sands, Leo G[eorge]

**Craig, Lefty**
*See* Craig, George McCarthy

**Craig, Mary Francis** 1923-
[CA, SAT, TBJ]
*American author*
* Shura, Mary Francis

**Craig, Michael**
*See* Gregson, Michael

**Craig, Peggy**
*See* Kreig, Margaret B. [Baltzell]

**Craig, Peter**
*See* MacClure, Victor

**Craig, Randolph**
*See* Page, Norvell W.

**Craig, Ross Brown** 1884-
[BBH, CFH]
*Canadian football player*
* Craig, Husky

**Craig, Vera**
*See* Rowland, D[onald] S[ydney]

**Craig, Webster**
*See* Russell, Eric Frank

**Craig-Knox, Isa** 1831- ?
[DEL, PA]
*British poet*
* Isa

**Craigie, Christopher**
*See* Cole, William Morse

**Craigie, David**
*See* Craigie, Dorothy M.

**Craigie, Dorothy M.** 20th c.
[SFL, WGT]
*British author*
* Craigie, David

**Craigie, Pearl Mary Teresa Richards**
1867-1906   [LC, WBD]
*American-born British author and
playwright*
* Hobbes, John Oliver

**Craigie, W. A.**
*See* Craigie, [Sir] William
Alexander

**Craigie, [Sir] William Alexander**
1867-1957   [LC]
*Scottish author*
* Craigie, W. A.

**Craik, Arthur**
*See* Craig, Alexander George
[Alec]

**Craik, Mrs. George Lillie** 1826- ?
[PA]
*Author*
* Mulock, Miss

**Craille, Wesley**
*See* Rowland, D[onald] S[ydney]

**Crain, Ben** 1910-   [BBH]
*American softball player*
* [The] Iron Man

**Crain, Jeff**
*See* Meneses, Enrique

**Craine, John** 1889-   [WWL]
*British author and journalist*
* Crane, Mannin

**Cram, Bill**
*See* Cram, L D

**Cram, L D** 1898-   [ICB]
*American illustrator*
* Cram, Bill

**Cramb, John Adam** 1862-1913
[SFL]
*Author*
* Revermort, J. A.

**Cramer, Doc**
*See* Cramer, Roger Maxwell

**Cramer, Flit**
*See* Cramer, Roger Maxwell

**Cramer, Julian**
*See* Chester, Joseph Lemuel

**Cramer, Kathryn** 1943-   [CA]
*American author*
* Terzian, Kathryn

**Cramer, Roger Maxwell** 1905?-
[B10, BE, PB]
*American baseball player*
* Cramer, Doc
* Cramer, Flit

**Crampton, Bruce** 1935-
[BWG, GF]
*Australian golfer*
* [The] Iron Man

**Crampton, C[harles] Ward** 1877- ?
[NAA]
*American physician, educator,
author*
* [The] Health Doctor

**Crampton, Georgia Ronan** 1925-
[CA]
*American author and poet*
* Ronan, Georgia

**Crampton, Sean** 1918-   [ART]
*British sculptor*
* S. C.

**Cramton, Ray** 1936-   [SW]
*American actor*
* Everett, Chad

**Cranborne, Janus Emilius W. E.**
1821-1865   [PA]
*Author*
* Blind Traveler

**Cranbrook, James L.**
*See* Edwards, William B[ennett]

**Crandall, Del**
*See* Crandall, Delmar Wesley

**Crandall, Delmar Wesley** 1930-
[BR]
*American baseball player and
manager*
* Crandall, Del

**Crandall, Doc**
*See* Crandall, James Otis

**Crandall, James Otis** 1887-1951
[AS, BE]
*American baseball player*
* Crandall, Doc

**Crandall, Joy**
*See* Martin, Joy

**Crandall, Norma** 1907-   [CA]
*American writer and translator*
* Chamberlain, Wilson [joint
pseudonym with Wilson
McCarty]
* McCarty, Norma

**Crandon, Mina [Stinson]**
1888-1941   [B10]
*American medium*
* Margery

**Crane, Alex**
*See* Wilkes-Hunter, Richard

**Crane, Berkeley**
*See* Marshall, Arthur C.

**Crane, Cannonball**
*See* Crane, Edward Nicholas

**Crane, Denis**
*See* Cranfield, W. T.

**Crane, Edna Temple** [house
pseudonym, Dell Publishing Co.
Inc.]
*See* Eicher, [Ethel] Elizabeth

**Crane, Edward Nicholas**
1862-1896   [AS, BE]
*American baseball player*
* Crane, Cannonball

**Crane, Eric**
*See* Setterburg, Gabriel

**Crane, Irving** 20th c.
*American billiard player*
* [The] Deacon

**Crane, John** 18th c.   [PA]
*Author*
* Jacia

**Crane, M. A.**
*See* Wartski, Maureen [Ann
Crane]

**Crane, Mannin**
*See* Craine, John

**Crane, Norma**
*See* Zuckerman, Norma Anna
Bella

**Crane, Randolph** 1903-
[BDF, F2, FC]
*American actor*
* Scott, Randolph

**Crane, Red**
*See* Crane, Samuel Byren

**Crane, Robert**
*See* Glemser, Bernard

**Crane, Robert**
*See* Robertson, Frank C[hester]

**Crane, Robert**
*See* Sellers, Connie Leslie, Jr.

**Crane, Roy**
*See* Crane, Royston Campbell

**Crane, Royston Campbell**
1901-1977   [SAT]
*American cartoonist*
* Crane, Roy

**Crane, Samuel Byren** 1894-1955
[BE]
*American baseball player*
* Crane, Red

**Cranfield, W. T.** 20th c.   [WWL]
*British author*
* Crane, Denis

**Cranmer, Thomas** 1489-1556   [HN]
*Archbishop of Canterbury*
* [The] Luther of England

**Cranny, Titus** 1921-   [CA]
*American clergyman and author*
* Francis, Daniel

**Cranshaw, Bob**
*See* Cranshaw, Melbourne R.

**Cranshaw, Melbourne R.** 1932-
[DAM]
*American jazz musician*
* Cranshaw, Bob

**Cranston, Edward**
*See* Fairchild, William

**Cranston, Mechthild** 20th c.   [CA]
*German-born American author*
* Delorme, Michele

**Cranston, Ruth** 20th c.   [WGT]
*Author*
* Warwick, Anne

**Crary, J. M.**   [SN]
*American poet*
* [The] Sidewalk Poet

**Crassus**
*See* Claudius, Appius

**Crassus, Marcus Licinius** 1st c. BC
[WBD]
*Roman financier and politician*
* Dives [The Rich]

**Crause, Clarence** 1856-1931   [BE]
*American baseball player*
* Cross, Clarence

**[Une] Cravate Blanche**
*See* Esudier, Marie

**Cravath, Cactus**
*See* Cravath, Clifford Carlton

**Cravath, Clifford Carlton**
1881-1963   [AS, BE, PB]
*American baseball player*
* Cravath, Cactus
* Cravath, Gavvy

**Cravath, Gavvy**
See Cravath, Clifford Carlton

**Craven**
See Carleton, Captain

**Craven, Arthur Scott**
See Harvey-James, A. K.

**Craven, Elise**
See Barrett, Elise Barbara Alleyne

**Craven, Hawes**
See Green, Henry Hawes Craven

**Craven, Mrs.**
See La Forrounnays, Mlle.

**Craven, Robin**
See Cohen, Robin Harry Salaman

**Craveri, Sebastiano** 1899-1973
[WECO]
*Italian cartoonist*
* Pin-Tin

**Crawells, Carl**
See Herm, Gerhard Otto

**Crawford, A. W.**
See Lindsay, Lord

**Crawford, Anne**
See Crawford, Imelda

**Crawford, Benny Ross, Jr.** 1934-
[DAM]
*American jazz musician*
* Crawford, Hank

**Crawford, Big**
See Crawford, Harry

**Crawford, Caroline**
See McLean, Caroline Crawford

**Crawford, Char** 1935- [CA]
*American author*
* Johnson, Charlene

**Crawford, Charles Lowrie** 1914-
[BE]
*American baseball player*
* Crawford, Larry

**Crawford, Clifford Rankin** 1902-
[BE]
*American baseball player*
* Crawford, Pat

**Crawford, E. M.** [PA]
*Author*
* Genesee

**Crawford, Francis Marion**
1854-1909 [FFF]
*American author*
* [The] Lightning Story-Writer

**Crawford, Gene**
See Everett, Kenneth Neil

**Crawford, George G.** 1898- [NAA]
*American journalist*
* Gee

**Crawford, Glenn Martin**
1913-1972 [BE]
*American baseball player*
* Crawford, Shorty

**Crawford, Hank**
See Crawford, Benny Ross, Jr.

**Crawford, Harry** 20th c. [EG]
*Scottish golf caddie*
* Crawford, Big

**Crawford, Holland R.** 1924-
[DAM]
*American jazz musician*
* Crawford, Ray

**Crawford, Imelda** 1920-1956
[BEW, FC]
*British actress*
* Crawford, Anne

**Crawford, J. W.** 19th c. [FFF]
*American poet*
* Captain Jack
* [The] Poet Scout

**Crawford, Jake**
See Crawford, Rufus

**Crawford, James** 20th c. [SMG]
*American football player*
* Crawford, Mush

**Crawford, Jesse** 1895-1962
*American musician*
* [The] Poet of the Organ

**Crawford, Joan**
See Le Sueur, Lucille

**Crawford, John Richard** 1932-
[WD]
*American author*
* Walker, J.

**Crawford, Joseph** 1887-1931
[NOJ]
*American jazz musician*
* Petit, Buddy

**Crawford, Larry**
See Crawford, Charles Lowrie

**Crawford, Margaret** 20th c. [WGT]
*American author*
* Ford, Garret [joint pseudonym
    with William L. Crawford,
    Forrest J. Ackerman, etc.]

**Crawford, Michael**
See Dumble-Smith, Michael

**Crawford, Mimi**
See Pigott, Mimi

**Crawford, Murph**
See Crawford, Willie Murphy

**Crawford, Mush**
See Crawford, James

**Crawford, Oliver**
See Kaufman, Oliver

**Crawford, Pat**
See Crawford, Clifford Rankin

**Crawford, Phyllis** 1899- [SAT]
*American author*
* Turner, Josie

**Crawford, Ray**
See Crawford, Holland R.

**Crawford, Robert**
See Rae, Hugh C[rauford]

**Crawford, Robert H.** 20th c. [BBH]
*American jockey*
* Crawford, Specs

**Crawford, Rufus** 1928- [BE]
*American baseball player*
* Crawford, Jake

**Crawford, Rusty**
See Crawford, Samuel Russell

**Crawford, Sallie Wallace Brown**
1915- [AW]
*Scottish-born author*
* Trotter, Sallie

**Crawford, Samuel Earl** 1880-1968
[AS, DGS, PB]
*American baseball player*
* Crawford, Wahoo Sam
* [The] Wahoo Barber

**Crawford, Samuel Russell**
1884?-1971 [BBH, FHE]
*Canadian-born hockey player*
* Crawford, Rusty

**Crawford, Samuel W.** 1829- ? [SN]
*American army officer and surgeon*
* Physics

**Crawford, Shorty**
See Crawford, Glenn Martin

**Crawford, Specs**
See Crawford, Robert H.

**Crawford, Wahoo Sam**
See Crawford, Samuel Earl

**Crawford, William [Elbert]** 1929-
[CA]
*American author*
* Brandt, Roger
* Logan, Don
* Peterson, Jim
* Rawford, W. C.
* Ross, Paul
* Scott, Steve
* Williams, Bill

**Crawford, William L.** 20th c.
[WGT]
*American author*
* Ford, Garret [joint pseudonym
    with Margaret Crawford, Forrest
    J. Ackerman, etc.]

**Crawford, Willie Murphy** 1946-
[SMG]
*American baseball player*
* Crawford, Murph
* Willie C.

**Crawfurd, Oswald John Frederick**
1834-1909 [DEL, FFF, WWL]
*British author and poet*
* Brett, George Ira
* Dangerfield, John
* Latouche, John
* Sandys, George Windle
* Strange, Joseph

**Crawley, [Captain] Rawdon**
See Pardon, George Frederick

**Cray, Edward** 1933- [IAW]
*American author*
* Skald

**Crayder, Teresa**
See Colman, Hila

**Crayon, Diedrick, Jr.**
See Bruce, Kenneth

**Crayon, Geoffrey**
See Irving, Washington

**Craythorne, James** [FFF]
*Entertainer*
* Russell, James

**Craythorne, Mrs. James** [FFF]
*Entertainer*
* Thorne, Alice

**Crayton, Connie Curtis** 1914-
[BWW]
*American singer*
* Crayton, Pee Wee
* Homer the Great

**Crayton, Pee Wee**
See Crayton, Connie Curtis

**Crazy Corky Booze**
See Booze, Courtland

**Crazy Cue Cosmo**
See Cosmo, Tom

**Crazy Eyes Grimsley**
See Grimsley, Ross Albert, III

**Crazy Fingers Hopkins**
See Hopkins, Claude D.

**Crazy Horse**
See Tashunca-Uitco

**Crazy Horse Foli**
See Foli, Timothy John

**Crazy Horse Moss**
See Moss, Robert

**Crazy Horse Nanchoff**
See Nanchoff, George

**Crazy Jane**
See Juana [Joanna or Jane]

**Crazy Joey Gallo**
See Gallo, Joseph

**[The] Crazy Poet**
See Lee, Nathaniel

**Creach, John** 1917- [EJ7, IBW]
*American jazz musician*
* Creach, Papa John
* [The] Grandfather of Rock

**Creach, Papa John**
See Creach, John

**Creacy, A. D.** 20th c. [OBW]
*American baseball player*
* Creacy, Dewey

**Creacy, Dewey**
See Creacy, A. D.

**Creager, Eunice Whayne**
1883-1948 [IA]
*American author*
* Emerson, Alice B.
* Hope, Laura Lee

**Creagh, Patrick**
See Brasier-Creagh, Patrick

**Cream, Arnold Raymond** 1914-
[BX, RBE, WBC]
*American boxer*
* [The] Praying Puncher
* Walcott, Jersey Joe

**Creamer, George W.**
See Triebel, George W.

**Crean, Mary Walsingham** [FFF]
*American writer*
* Rie, May

**Creasey, John** 1908-1973
[CA, EMD, WGT]
*British author*
* Ashe, Gordon
* Cooke, Margaret
* Cooper, Henry St. John
* Deane, Norman
* Fecamps, Elise
* Frazer, Robert Caine
* Gill, Patrick
* Halliday, Michael

**Creasey, John** (Continued)
* Hogarth, Charles
* Hope, Brian
* Hughes, Colin
* Hunt, Kyle
* Mann, Abel
* Manton, Peter
* Marric, J. J.
* Marsden, James
* Martin, Richard
* Matheson, Rodney
* Morton, Anthony
* Ranger, Ken
* Reilly, William K.
* Riley, Tex
* St. John, Henry
* Wilde, Jimmy
* York, Jeremy

**[The] Creator of Biblical Epic Poetry**
*See* Klopstock, Friedrich Gottlieb

**[The] Creator of French Dramatic Art**
*See* Corneille, Pierre

**[The] Creator of Modern Polish Drama**
*See* Wyspianski, Stanislaw

**Creator of the New Comedy**
*See* Menander

**Crebillon**
*See* Jolyot, Prosper [Sieur de Crais-Billon]

**Crechales, Anthony George** 1926-
[CA]
*American author*
* Kent, Tony
* Trelos, Tony

**Crecy, Jeanne**
*See* Williams, Jeanne

**Cree, Alexander**
*See* Downing, George

**Cree, Birdie**
*See* Cree, William Franklin

**Cree, William Franklin** 1882-1942
[BE]
*American baseball player*
* Cree, Birdie

**Creed, Clara** [FFF]
*Author*
* Pym, T.

**Creed, David**
*See* Guthrie, James Shields

**Creeden, Pat[rick Francis]** 1906-
[BE]
*American baseball player*
* Creeden, Whoops

**Creeden, Whoops**
*See* Creeden, Pat[rick Francis]

**Creel, Jack Dalton** 1916- [BE]
*American baseball player*
* Creel, Tex

**Creel, Stephen Melville** 1938- [CA]
*American psychiatrist and author*
* Sachem, E. B.

**Creel, Tex**
*See* Creel, Jack Dalton

**[The] Creeper**
*See* Stroud, Edwin Marvin

**Creepy, Anthony**
*See* Zeglio, Primo

**Creese, Irene** 1912- [F2, FC]
*British actress*
* Ray, Rene

**Creevey, Lucy E.** 1940- [CA]
*American educator and author*
* Behrman, Lucy Creevey

**Cregan, Peekskill Pete**
*See* Cregan, Pete[r James]

**Cregan, Pete[r James]** 1875-1945
[BE]
*American baseball player*
* Cregan, Peekskill Pete

**Crehan, Ada** 1860-1916
[BEW, FFF]
*Irish-born actress*
* Rehan, Ada

**Crehan, Joseph**
*See* Wilson, Charles

**Creighton, Cleva**
*See* Bush, Frances Cleveland

**Creighton, Don**
*See* Drury, Maxine Cole

**Creighton, Jesse**
*See* Howe, Frank William

**Creighton, Rob**
*See* Mitchell, R. C.

**Cremer, Samuel**
*See* Meeus, Marcel

**Cremieux, Adolphe**
*See* Moise, Isaac

**Cremins, Lefty**
*See* Cremins, Robert Anthony [Bob]

**Cremins, Robert Anthony [Bob]**
1906- [BE]
*American baseball player*
* Cremins, Lefty

**Crenshaw, Ben** 1952-
*American golfer*
* Crenshaw, Gentle Ben

**Crenshaw, Gentle Ben**
*See* Crenshaw, Ben

**Creole George Guesnon**
*See* Guesnon, George

**[The] Creole Nightingale**
*See* Lenoir, Lucie

**Creole Pete Robertson**
*See* Robertson, Peter

**[The] Creole Songbird**
*See* Bigeou, Esther

**[The] Creole Songbird**
*See* Landreaux, Elizabeth Mary

**Crepin**
*See* Balestier, Charles Wolcott

**Crescentius, Johannes [or John]** ?-
998 [WBD]
*Roman aristocrat*
* Nomentanus

**Crespi, Creepy**
*See* Crespi, Frank Angelo Joseph

**Crespi, Frank Angelo Joseph** 1918-
[BE]
*American baseball player*
* Crespi, Creepy

**Crespi, Giuseppe Maria** 1665-1747
[WBD]
*Italian painter*
* [Lo] Spagnuolo

**Crespo, Alejandro** 1915- [MK]
*American baseball player*
* Crespo, Homerun

**Crespo, Homerun**
*See* Crespo, Alejandro

**Crespo y Borbon, Bartolome Jose**
1811-1871 [CW]
*Spanish-born playwright and poet*
* [El] Anfibio
* Ganga, Creto

**Cress, Foots**
*See* Cress, Walker James

**Cress, Walker James** 1917- [BE]
*American baseball player*
* Cress, Foots

**Creston**
*See* Lane-Jackson, Nicholas

**Creston, Dormer**
*See* Colston-Baynes, Dorothy Julia

**Creston, Paul**
*See* Guttoveggio, Joseph

**Creswell, H. B.**
*See* Creswell, Harry Bulkeley

**Creswell, Harry Bulkeley**
1869-1960 [LC, WWL]
*British author and architect*
* Creswell, H. B.
* Karshish

**Creswell, John** [FFF]
*Writer*
* Onghill

**Creticus**
*See* Metellus, Quintus Caecilius

**Cretinetti**
*See* Chapuis, Andre

**Crevecoeur, Michel Guillaume Jean
de** 1735-1813 [WBD]
*French-born author*
* St. John, J. Hector

**[The] Crew**
*See* Gerald, Roderic

**Creyton, Paul**
*See* Trowbridge, John Townsend

**Cribb, Tom**
*See* Moore, Thomas

**Criblecoblis, Otis**
*See* Dukinfield, William Claude

**Crichton, Douglas** 20th c.
[CA, WD]
*American author*
* Douglas, Michael [joint pseudonym with (John) Michael Crichton]

**Crichton, Eleanor Moyra [McGavin]**
20th c. [AW]
*Scottish-born author and social worker*
* McGavin, Moyra

**Crichton, Jack**
*See* Miln, H. Crichton

**Crichton, James** 1560-1583
[DEL, DEP, DNNF]
*Scottish scholar*
* [The] Admirable Crichton

**Crichton, Kyle Samuel** 1896-1960
[AW, TC]
*American journalist*
* Forsythe, Robert

**Crichton, [John] Michael** 1942-
[AW, CA, SAT]
*American author and screenwriter*
* Douglas, Michael [joint pseudonym with Douglas Crichton]
* Hudson, Jeffery
* Lange, John

**Cricket**
*See* Abbott, Wenonah Stevens

**[The] Cricket**
*See* Rigney, William Joseph

**Crickmore, Henry G.** [FFF]
*American editor*
* Krik

**Criden, Joseph** 1916- [CA]
*American-born author*
* Criden, Yosef

**Criden, Yosef**
*See* Criden, Joseph

**Crile, Barney**
*See* Crile, George, Jr.

**Crile, George, Jr.** 1907- [CA]
*American physician and author*
* Crile, Barney

**Crile, Helga Sandburg** 1918- [TBJ]
*American author*
* Sandburg, Helga

**Crim, Keith R[enn]** 1924- [CA]
*American writer and translator*
* Renn, Casey

**Crimmins, Dan[iel]**
*See* Lyons, Alexander M.

**Crimmins, General**
*See* Krzyminski, John

**Crimmins, John**
*See* Krzyminski, John

**Crinkle, Nym**
*See* Wheeler, Andrew Carpenter

**Crippen, Catherine [Katie]**
1895-1929 [BWW]
*American singer*
* Crippen, Little Katie
* White, Ella

**Crippen, Little Katie**
*See* Crippen, Catherine [Katie]

**Cripple Clarence Lofton**
*See* Lofton, Clarence

**[The] Cripple of Jerusalem**
*See* Charles II

**Cripps, L. L.**
*See* Cripps, Louise Lilian

**Cripps, Louise Lilian** 1914- [CA]
*British-born author*
* Cripps, L. L.
* Samoiloff, Louise Cripps

**Criqui, Eugene** 1893- [BX]
*French boxer*
* [The] Wounded Wonder

**Crisler, Fritz**
*See* Crisler, Herbert O.

**Crisler, Herbert O.** 1899- [FB]
*American football coach and athletic director*
* Crisler, Fritz

**Crisp, Anthony Thomas [Tony]**
1937?- [CA, WD]
*British psychotherapist and author*
* Western, Mark

**Crisp, S. E.** 1906- [AW]
*British journalist*
* Crispie

**Crispie**
*See* Crisp, S. E.

**Crispin Cataline**
*See* Epremesnil, Jean Jacques Duval d'

**Crispin, Edmund**
*See* Montgomery, Robert Bruce

**Crispinus**
*See* Marston, John Westland

**Crispus**
*See* Wheeler, C. C.

**Criss, Sonny**
*See* Criss, William

**Criss, William** 1927-1978
[DAM, EJ, PMJ]
*American jazz musician*
* Criss, Sonny

**[La] Crissoniere**
*See* Corson, Charlotte Catherine

**Crist, Chester Arthur** 1882-1957
[BE]
*American baseball player*
* Crist, Squack

**Crist, Squack**
*See* Crist, Chester Arthur

**Cristabel**
*See* Abrahamsen, Christine Elizabeth

**Cristadoro, Andrew** [PA]
*Author*
* [A] Reader Therein

**Cristal, Linda**
*See* Maya [or Moya?], Victoria

**Cristall, Lefty**
*See* Cristall, William Arthur [Bill]

**Cristall, William Arthur [Bill]**
1878-1939 [BE]
*American baseball player*
* Cristall, Lefty

**Cristillo, Louis Francis** 1906-1959
[FC, OCF, WEF]
*American comic actor*
* Costello, Lou

**Cristy, R. J.**
*See* DeCristoforo, Romeo John

**Criswell, Jeron**
*See* King, Charles Criswell

**Criswell, Mrs. Croller H.** [PA]
*Author*
* Di Vernon

**Criswell, Robert W.** [PA]
*Author*
* Lickshingle, Grandfather

**Critchett, Richard Claude**
1856-1928 [THR, WBD]
*British actor and playwright*
* Carton, Richard Claude

**Critchfield, Russ** 1946- [BB]
*American basketball player*
* Critchfield, Rusty

**Critchfield, Rusty**
*See* Critchfield, Russ

**Critchie, Estil**
*See* Burks, Arthur J.

**Critchley, Alfred Cecil** 1890-1964
[OCS]
*British greyhound promoter*
* [The] Father of Greyhound Racing

**Critchley, Julian [Michael Gordon]**
1930- [CA]
*British politician and author*
* Beaufitz, William

**Critchlow, Dorothy** 1904- [AW]
*British journalist*
* Dawson, Jane

**[The] Critic**
*See* Dennis, John

**Critic**
*See* Martin, [Basil] Kingsley

**Criticus**
*See* Barnes, Thomas

**Criticus**
*See* Harcourt, Melville

**Criticus**
*See* Roe, F[rederic] Gordon

**Critique**
*See* Sheahan, D. B.

**Crito**
*See* Brown, Samuel

**Crito**
*See* Duncombe, John

**Crito?**
*See* Francis, [Sir] Philip

**Crittenden, Doris** 20th c. [OP]
*American opera singer*
* Jung, Doris

**Crivelli, Uberto** ?-1187 [CAL]
*Pope*
* Urban III

**Crnjanski, Milos** 1893- [CAP]
*Hungarian-born British author*
* Mill, C. R.

**Croaker**
*See* Drake, Joseph Rodman

**Croaker and Co.**
*See* Halleck, Fitz Greene

**Croal, Frances A.** 20th c. [WWL]
*Scottish author*
* Hammond, Frances

**Croall, John Alfred Louden** 1898-
[F2, FC]
*British actor*
* Stuart, John

**Crocchiola, Francis Stanley** 1908-
[CAT]
*American author and clergyman*
* Stanley, Francis

**Crocetti, Dino** 1917-
[BDF, FC, HT]
*American actor and singer*
* Martin, Dean

**Crochon, Jean-Pierre** 1932- [WEF]
*French actor*
* Cassel, Jean-Pierre

**Crocker, Bosworth**
*See* Crocker, Mary Arnold

**Crocker, Mary Arnold** 20th c.
[NAA]
*British-born American playwright*
* Crocker, Bosworth

**Crocker, Samuel** 1845-1921
[WGT]
*American author*
* Islet, Theodore Oceanic

**Crockett, Daniel Solomon**
1875-1961 [BE]
*American baseball player*
* Crockett, Davey

**Crockett, Davey**
*See* Crockett, Daniel Solomon

**Crockett, David [Davy]** 1786-1836
[DNNS, SN]
*American pioneer, hunter, politician*
* [The] Muenchausen of the West

**Crockett, James** [joint pseudonym
with Cornelia Warriner]
*See* MacPhail, James A.

**Crockett, James** [joint pseudonym
with James A. MacPhail]
*See* Warriner, Cornelia

**Crockett, S. R.**
*See* Crockett, Samuel Rutherford

**Crockett, Samuel Rutherford**
1860-1914 [LC]
*British author*
* Crockett, S. R.

**[The] Crocodile**
*See* Harriman, W[illiam] Averell

**[The] Crocodile**
*See* Lacoste, Jean-Rene

**Crocombe, Leonard Cecil** 20th c.
[WWL]
*British writer and editor*
* Hammersley, Cecil

**Croffut, William A.** [PA]
*Author*
* Wales, Peleg

**Croft, Nita**
*See* Pycroft, Nita

**Croft, Roy**
*See* Calvert, William Robinson

**Croft, Sutton**
*See* Lunn, Arnold [Henry Moore]

**Croft, Taylor**
*See* Croft-Cooke, Rupert

**Croft-Cooke, Rupert** 1903-1979
[CA, CC, WW]
*British author*
* Bruce, Leo
* Croft, Taylor

**Croftangry, Chrystal**
*See* Scott, [Sir] Walter

**Crofton-Croker, T. F. Dillon**
1831-1912 [THR]
*British journalist and archaeologist*
* Croker, T. F. Dillon

**Crofts, James**
*See* Scott, James

**Croise, Jacques**
*See* Schakovskoy, [Princess] Zinaida

**Croisset, Francis de**
*See* Wiener, Francis de [or Franz]

**Croix-Rouge**
*See* Grant, Charles

**Croizette, Sophie**
*See* Stern, Baroness

**Croker, Boss**
*See* Croker, Richard

**Croker, John Wilson** 1780-1857
[DEL, PA]
*British author*
* C.
* T. J., Esq.
* Waverley, Edward Bradwardine

**Croker, Richard** 1841-1922 [WBD]
*American politician*
* Croker, Boss

**Croker, T. F. Dillon**
*See* Crofton-Croker, T. F. Dillon

**Croker, Thomas Crofton**
1798-1854 [SN]
*Irish author*
* [The] King of the Fairies

**Croll, Philip Columbus** 1852- ?
[NAA]
*American clergyman and author*
* Kolumbo, Kristofer

**Croly, David Goodman** 1829-1889
[FFF]
*American editor*
* Goodman, David

**Croly, Elizabeth**
*See* Farwell, Janet

**Croly, George** 1780-1860 [PA, SN]
*Irish author and clergyman*
* Croly, Saint Bernard
* Salathiel

**Croly, Herbert David** 1869-1930
[WGT]
*American author*
* Herbert, William?

**Croly, Jane Cunningham**
1829?-1901 [DEL, DNNF, FFF]
*American author*
* June, Jennie
* Veni Vidi

**Croly, Saint Bernard**
*See* Croly, George

**Crom a Boo**
*See* Bodkin, Matthias McDonnell

**Croman, Dorothy Young**
*See* Picard, Dorothy Young

**Cromarhe, Hew B. D.**
*See* Fraser, Alexander

**Cromartie, Cro**
*See* Cromartie, Warren Livingston

**Cromartie, Warren Livingston**
1953-  [SMG]
*American baseball player*
* Cromartie, Cro

**Crome, John** 1768-1821
[DNNS, FFF, SN]
*British painter*
* [The] English Hobbema
* [The] Hobbema of England

**Crome, John Bernay** 1794-1842
[WBD]
*British painter*
* Crome, Young

**Crome, Young**
*See* Crome, John Bernay

**Cromie, Alice Hamilton** 1914-
[CA]
*American author and lecturer*
* Hamilton, Alice
* Mort, Vivian

**Crompton, Herb[ert Bryan]** 1911-
[BE]
*American baseball player*
* Crompton, Workhorse

**Crompton, John**
*See* Lamburn, John Battersby Crompton

**Crompton, Margaret [Norah Mair]**
1901-  [CAP, WD]
*British author*
* Mair, Margaret

**Crompton, Richmal**
*See* Lamburn, Richmal Crompton

**Crompton, Workhorse**
*See* Crompton, Herb[ert Bryan]

**Cromwell, Cecil**
*See* Pym, Beatrice Angela Carrington

**Cromwell, Dean** 1879-1962
[BBH, TF]
*American track and field coach*
* [The] Dean
* [The] Maker of Champions

**Cromwell, Elsie**
*See* Lee, Elsie

**[The] Cromwell of France**
*See* Robespierre, Maximilien

**[The] Cromwell of New England**
*See* Adams, Samuel

**[The] Cromwell of the Jews**
*See* Judas Asmonaeus

**Cromwell, Oliver** 1599-1658
[DEP, FFF, SN]
*Lord Protector of England*
* [The] Almighty Nose
* [The] English Attila
* [The] Hammer of Kings and Thrones
* King Oliver
* [The] Man of Sin
* Old Noll
* [The] Protector
* [The] Saviour of the Nation

**Cromwell, Richard**
*See* Radebaugh, Roy

**Cromwell, Richard** 1626-1712
[FFF, HN, WBD]
*Lord Protector of England*
* Clarke, John
* Indolent Dick
* Queen Dick

**Cromwell, Richard** (Continued)
* Tumble-Down Dick

**Cromwell, Thomas [Earl of Essex]**
1490?-1540  [DEP, DNNS, SN]
*British statesman*
* [The] Hammer of Monasteries
* [The] Hammer of the Monks
* Malleus Monachorum
* [The] Maul of Monks
* [The] Vicar of Hell

**Cromwell, Victor**
*See* Bull, Albert E.

**Cromwell's Mad Chaplain**
*See* Peters [or Peter?], Hugh

**[Il] Cronaca [The Chronicler]**
*See* Pollaiuolo, Simone

**Croney, Roz** 20th c.  [IBW]
*Grenada-born dancer*
* [The] Queen of Limbo

**Cronieckschrijver**
*See* Le Feber, David

**Cronin, A. J.**
*See* Cronin, Archibald Joseph

**Cronin, Archibald Joseph**
1896-1981  [IPA, LC]
*Scottish author*
* Cronin, A. J.

**Cronin, Bernard [Charles]** 1884-
[WW]
*Author*
* Adair, Dennis
* Dixon, Wallace
* North, Eric

**Cronin, Brendon Leo** 20th c.  [WW]
*Author*
* Cronin, Michael

**Cronin, Crunchy**
*See* Cronin, William Patrick [Bill]

**Cronin, Gladys** 20th c.
*American actress*
* Christy, Ann

**Cronin, Michael**
*See* Cronin, Brendon Leo

**Cronin, William Patrick [Bill]**
1902-  [BE]
*American baseball player*
* Cronin, Crunchy

**Cronk, Claire Viola** 1897-1972
[F2]
*American actress*
* Windsor, Claire

**Cronkite, Walter** 1916-
*American television journalist*
* Old Iron Pants

**Cronmiller, George, Jr.**  [PA]
*Author*
* Marcellus, P. H.

**Cronmire, Sidney Herbert** 1866?- ?
[HN]
*Swindler*
* [The] Infant Stockbroker

**Cronus, Diodorus**
*See* Taylor, Richard

**Cronyn, Hume**
*See* Blake, Hume

**Crook, Bette [Jean]** 1921-  [CA]
*American poet and columnist*
* Leslie, San

**Crook, Compton N.** 20th c.
[ESF, WGT]
*American author*
* Tall, Stephen

**Crook, Joel**  [PA]
*Author*
* J. C.

**Crookall, Dot**
*See* Crookall, John

**Crookall, John** 20th c.  [BBH, CSH]
*Canadian lacrosse player*
* Crookall, Dot

**Crooke, Venuta Rose** 1911?-
[BEW, TR]
*American actress*
* Venuta, Benay

**[The] Crooked Backed Earl**
*See* Cecil, Robert [First Earl of Salisbury]

**Crooks, Barbara Gwendolen Anne**
1904-  [ART]
*British painter*
* B. G. A.

**Crooks, Marion**
*See* Ireland, Marion Isabel

**Crooning Andy**
*See* Razafinkeriefo, Andreamenentania Paul

**Crooning Joe Cascarella**
*See* Cascarella, Joseph Thomas

**Cropper, Mrs.**  [PA]
*Author*
* Redaxela

**Croquis, Alfred**
*See* Maclise, Daniel

**Crosbie, Flush**
*See* Crosbie, William

**Crosbie, [Hugh] Provan** 1912-
[AW, CA]
*Scottish author*
* Carrick, John

**Crosbie, Sylvia Kowitt** 1938-  [CA]
*American educator and writer*
* Kowitt, Sylvia

**Crosbie, William** 1948-  [AES]
*British soccer player*
* Crosbie, Flush

**Crosby, Bing**
*See* Crosby, Harry Lillis

**Crosby, Bob**
*See* Crosby, George W.

**Crosby, Bob** 1897-1947  [GW]
*American rodeo performer*
* Crosby, Wild Horse

**Crosby, Dixie Lee**
*See* Wyatt, Wilma Winifred

**Crosby, Edward Carlton** 1949-
[PB]
*American baseball player*
* Crosby, Spider

**Crosby, Fanny**
*See* Crosby, Frances J.

**Crosby, Frances J.** 1820-1915
[DAM]
*American lyricist and hymnist*
* Crosby, Fanny

**Crosby, George W.** 1913-  [MY]
*American singer and bandleader*
* Crosby, Bob

**Crosby, Harry C.** 20th c.  [SF]
*American author*
* Anvil, Christopher

**Crosby, Harry Lillis** 1901?-1977
[ASC, BDF, NN]
*American singer and actor*
* [Der] Bingle
* Crosby, Bing
* [The] Groaner
* Old Dad
* Old Groaner

**Crosby, Hazel**
*See* Brown, Hazel Crosby

**Crosby, Jeremiah**
*See* Crosby, Michael

**Crosby, Lee**
*See* Torrey, Ware

**Crosby, Michael** 1940-  [CA]
*American clergyman and author*
* Crosby, Jeremiah

**Crosby, R. A.**
*See* Crosby, Robert Alexander

**Crosby, Robert Alexander** 1895-
[IBW]
*American mink ranch owner*
* Crosby, R. A.

**Crosby, Ronald** 1942-  [RO2]
*American singer*
* Walker, Jerry Jeff

**Crosby, Spider**
*See* Crosby, Edward Carlton

**Crosby, Tobacco Bill**
*See* Crosby, William R.

**Crosby, Wild Horse**
*See* Crosby, Bob

**Crosby, William R.** 1866-1939
[AS]
*American trapshooter*
* Crosby, Tobacco Bill

**Croset, Paule**
*See* Corday, Paula

**Crosetti, Frank Peter Joseph** 1910-
[BE, PB]
*American baseball player*
* [The] Crow

**Crosher, Geoffry Robins** 1911-
[CA, SAT]
*British author*
* Kesteven, G. R.

**Crosland, Mrs. C.** 1812- ?  [PA]
*Author*
* Toulman, C.

**Crosman, Shirley Elizabeth** 1916-
[BEW]
*American actress*
* Conway, Shirl

**Crosneau, Maurice Arnold**
1861-1933  [WBD]
*French singer*
* Renaud

**Cross, Amanda**
*See* Heilbrun, Carolyn G[old]

**Cross, Brenda**
*See* Colloms, Brenda

**Cross, Clarence**
See  Crause, Clarence

**Cross, Colin [John]** 1928-    [CA]
*Welsh-born journalist*
* Weir, John

**Cross, Dennis**
See  Gibbons, William

**Cross, Edward Ephram** 1832-1863
[FFF]
*American author and poet*
* Everett, Richard

**Cross, Frank Atwell** 1873-1932
[BE]
*American baseball player*
* Cross, Mickey

**Cross, Gene**
See  Cox, Arthur Jean

**Cross, George Lewis** 1872-1929
[BE]
*American baseball player*
* Cross, Lem

**Cross, Henri Edmond**
See  Delacroix, Henri Edmond

**Cross, James**
See  Parry, Hugh J[ones]

**Cross, Jeff**
See  Cross, Joffre James

**Cross, Joffre James** 1918-    [BE]
*American baseball player*
* Cross, Jeff

**Cross, John Keir** 1914-1967
[CA, WW]
*Scottish-born author*
* MacFarlane, Stephen
* Morley, Susan

**Cross, Kate**    [FFF]
*Writer*
* De Kalb

**Cross, Lafayette Napoleon**
1867-1927    [BE, DGS]
*American baseball player*
* Cross, Lave

**Cross, Lave**
See  Cross, Lafayette Napoleon

**Cross, Leach**
See  Wallach, [Dr.] Louis C.

**Cross, Lem**
See  Cross, George Lewis

**Cross, Mark**
See  Pechey, Archibald Thomas

**Cross, Mickey**
See  Cross, Frank Atwell

**Cross, Milton** 1897-1975    [SC]
*American radio commentator,
singer, actor*
* [The] Voice of the Metropolitan

**Cross, Monte**
See  Cross, Montford Montgomery

**Cross, Montford Montgomery**
1869-1934    [BE]
*American baseball player*
* Cross, Monte

**Cross, Mrs. Edward J.**    [FFF]
*Entertainer*
* Bertram, Minnie

**Cross, Polton**
See  Fearn, John Russell

**Cross, T. T.**
See  Da Cruz, Daniel, Jr.

**Cross, Thomson**
See  Wood, Samuel Andrew

**Cross, Victor**
See  Coffman, Virginia [Edith]

**Cross, Victoria**
See  Cory, Vivian

**Cross, Zora Bernice May** 1890-
[LAO]
*Australian author and poet*
* May, Bernice

**Crossan, Darryl**
See  Smith, Richard Rein

**Crosscountry**
See  Campbell, Thomas F.

**Crosse, Elaine**
See  Trent, Ann

**Crosse, Launcelot**
See  Carr, M. Frank

**Crossen, Ken[dell Foster]** 1910-
[CA, SF, WGT]
*American author and journalist*
* Barlay, Bennett
* Chaber, M. E.
* Foster, Richard
* Lorac, H. R. C.?
* Monig, Christopher
* Richard, Kent?
* Richards, Clay

**Crossey, J. S.**    [PA]
*Author*
* Stewart, J. C.

**Crossley, Mrs. M. L. R.**    [FFF]
*Author*
* Rena

**Crossman, Henrietta**
See  Brown, Mrs. Sedley

**[The] Crossover King**
See  Washington, Grover, Jr.

**Crosthwaite, Ivy**
See  Barrett, Rice

**Croteau, Crow**
See  Croteau, Gary Paul

**Croteau, Gary Paul** 1946-    [SMG]
*Canadian-born hockey player*
* Croteau, Crow

**Crothers, Jessie F[rances]** 1913-
[CA]
*American puppeteer, poet, author*
* Wright, Frances J.

**Crothers, Scat Man**
See  Crothers, [Benjamin] Sherman
[Louis]

**Crothers, [Benjamin] Sherman [Louis]**
1910-    [ASC, IBW]
*American jazz musician*
* Crothers, Scat Man

**Crothers, William [Bill]** 1940-
[CSH]
*Canadian track and field athlete*
* [The] Crusader

**Crotona's Sage**
See  Pythagoras

**Crotus Rubianus**
See  Jaeger, Johannes

**Crouch, Andrae** 1950-    [IBW]
*American singer*
* Gospel's International
  Ambassador

**Crouch, Charles Alban**
See  Pallant, Norman C.

**Crouch, Jack Albert** 1903-    [BE]
*American baseball player*
* Crouch, Roxy

**Crouch, Jackie Jean** 1927?-
*American singer*
* Holt, Georgia

**Crouch, Nathaniel** 1681-1736
[FFF, PA]
*British author*
* Burton, Robert

**Crouch, Roxy**
See  Crouch, Jack Albert

**Crouch, Skip**
See  Crouch, William Henry [Bill]

**Crouch, William Henry [Bill]**
1886-1945    [BE]
*American baseball player*
* Crouch, Skip

**Crouchback**
See  Plantagenet, Edmund

**Crouchback**
See  Richard III

**[The] Croucher**
See  Jessop, Gilbert Laird

**Croucher, Dingle**
See  Croucher, Frank Donald

**Croucher, Frank Donald** 1914-
[BE]
*American baseball player*
* Croucher, Dingle

**Croudace, Glynn** 1917-    [AW, CA]
*British-born South African author
and journalist*
* Monnow, Peter

**Crouse, Buck**
See  Crouse, Clyde Elsworth

**Crouse, Clyde Elsworth** 1897-    [BE]
*American baseball player*
* Crouse, Buck

**Crouse, Mrs. Charles E.**    [FFF]
*Entertainer*
* Pease, Alfa

**Croves, Hal?**
See  Marut, Ret

**[The] Crow**
See  Aitken, Mrs.

**[The] Crow**
See  Crosetti, Frank Peter Joseph

**[The] Crow Bar Governor**
See  Bulkeley, Morgan Gardner

**Crow, Francis Luther [Frank]**
1905-1980    [CA, PMJ]
*American singer and songwriter*
* Luther, Frank

**Crow Jane Hendrix**
See  Hendrix, George

**Crow, Jim**
See  Cuff, Jim

**Crow, Levi**
See  Wellman, Manly Wade

**Crowbate, Ophelia Mae**
See  Smith, C. U.

**Crowbuck, Robert**
See  Parsons [or Persons?], Robert

**Crowcroft, Jane**
See  Crowcroft, Peter

**Crowcroft, Peter** 1923-    [CA]
*British-born author and actor*
* Crowcroft, Jane
* Muntz, James
* Orloff, Max

**Crowden, Roy** 1899-    [THR]
*British actor*
* Royston, Roy

**Crowder, Alvin Floyd** 1899-1972
[BE, PB]
*American baseball player*
* Crowder, General

**Crowder, General**
See  Crowder, Alvin Floyd

**Crowder, Jack** 1939-    [SW]
*American actor*
* Rasulala, Thalmus

**Crowder, Little Sax**
See  Crowder, Robert Henry [Bob]

**Crowder, Randy** 1953-    [SMG]
*American football player*
* Crowder, Sugar Bear

**Crowder, Robert Henry [Bob]**
1912-    [WWJ]
*American jazz musician*
* Crowder, Little Sax

**Crowder, Sugar Bear**
See  Crowder, Randy

**[The] Crowe**
See  Hobbes, Thomas

**Crowe, Amanda Cockrell** 1948-
[CA]
*American author*
* Cockrell, Amanda

**Crowe, [Lady] Bettina [Lum]** 1911-
[AW, B10, CA]
*American author*
* Lum, Peter

**Crowe, Big Daddy**
See  Crowe, George

**Crowe, F. J.**
See  Johnston, Jill

**Crowe, George** 1923-    [IBW]
*American baseball player*
* Crowe, Big Daddy

**Crowe, George D.** 20th c.    [BBH]
*American basketball player*
* Big G

**Crowe, John**
See  Lynds, Dennis

**Crowe, Maida** 1915-    [ART]
*British sculptor*
* Maida

**Crowell, Burt**
See  Crowley, Walter J.

**Crowell, Cap**
See  Crowell, Minot Joy

**Crowell, Minot Joy** 1892-1962
[BE]
*American baseball player*
* Crowell, Cap

**Crowfield, Christopher**
See Stowe, Harriet Beecher

**Crowley, Aleister**
See Crowley, Edward Alexander

**Crowley, Edward Alexander**
1875-1947 [BL, LC]
*British author, mystic, cult figure*
* [The] Beast
* Crowley, Aleister
* [The] King of Depravity
* [The] Messiah
* [The] Wickedest Man in the
  World

**Crowley, Francis** 1911-1931 [BLB]
*American murderer and bank robber*
* Crowley, Two Gun

**Crowley, J. C.**
See Crowley, John Charles

**Crowley, James H.** 1902- [FB]
*American football player*
* Crowley, Sleepy Jim

**Crowley, John Charles** 20th c.
[RO2]
*American musician*
* Crowley, J. C.

**Crowley, Ruth** ?-1955
*American columnist*
* Landers, Ann

**Crowley, Sleepy Jim**
See Crowley, James H.

**Crowley, Two Gun**
See Crowley, Francis

**Crowley, Walter J.** 1873-1946 [SC]
*American actor*
* Crowell, Burt

**Crown, Peter J.** 20th c.
[SFL, WGT]
*Author*
* Lewis, Pete

**[The] Crown Prince of Public
Relations**
See Kendrix, Moss Hyles

**Crowne, John** 1640?-1703? [SN]
*British playwright*
* Starch Johnny

**[The] Crowned Sancho**
See Louis XVI

**Crowninshield, Francis Welch**
1872-1947 [WBD]
*American editor*
* Bruce, Authur Loring

**Crowquill, Alfred**
See Forrester, Alfred Henry

**Crowson, Thomas Woodrow**
1918-1947 [BE]
*American baseball player*
* Crowson, Woody

**Crowson, Woody**
See Crowson, Thomas Woodrow

**Crowther, Wilma** 1918- [CA]
*British biologist and author*
* George, Wilma

**Croydon, John** 20th c. [SFL]
*Author*
* Cooper, John C.

**Croyland, William**
See Dulley, William

**Crozetti, Ruth G. Warner [Lora]**
1913?- [IAW, SFL]
*American author*
* Loring, J. M.
* O'Mahoney, Rich
* Warner-Crozetti, R.

**Crozier, Kathleen Muriel [Eyles]**
1913- [WW]
*Author*
* Eyles, Merle
* Tennant, Catherine

**Cruden, Alexander** 1701-1770
[DNNS, SN]
*Scottish bookseller and author*
* [The] Corrector

**Crudup, Arthur** 1905-1974
[BWW, PRS]
*American singer*
* Crudup, Big Boy
* Crudup, Percy Lee
* Crudux, Art
* Crump, Arthur
* [The] Father of Rock 'n Roll
* James, Elmer

**Crudup, Big Boy**
See Crudup, Arthur

**Crudup, Percy Lee**
See Crudup, Arthur

**Crudux, Art**
See Crudup, Arthur

**Crue, Martin** 20th c. [OBW]
*American baseball player*
* Crue, Matty

**Crue, Matty**
See Crue, Martin

**[The] Cruel**
See Christian II

**[The] Cruel**
See Henry VI [or Heinrich]

**[The] Cruel**
See Pedro

**Cruewell, Johanne Sophie Charlotte**
1826-1907 [WBD]
*German-Italian opera singer*
* Cruvelli, Johanne Sophie
  Charlotte

**Cruger, Paul** 1894- [WWL]
*American author*
* Worth, Dan

**Cruickshank, Bobby** 1894-1975
[BWG, GF]
*Scottish-born golfer*
* Cruickshank, Wee Bobby
* [The] Wee Scot

**Cruickshank, Harold F.** 1893-
[WWL]
*Canadian author*
* Fraser, Bert

**Cruickshank, Wee Bobby**
See Cruickshank, Bobby

**Cruikshank, George** 1792-1878
[SN]
*British caricaturist and illustrator*
* [The] Modern Hogarth

**Cruise O'Brien, Conor**
See O'Brien, Conor Cruise

**Cruiser, Benedict, M. M.**
See Sala, George Augustus

**Crum, Simon**
See Husky, Ferlin

**Crumbaker, Alice** 1911- [CA]
*American author*
* Baker, Allison

**Crump, Arthur**
See Crudup, Arthur

**Crump, Arthur Elliott** 1901- [BE]
*American baseball player*
* Crump, Buddy

**Crump, Buddy**
See Crump, Arthur Elliott

**Crump, Jesse** 1906- [EJ]
*American jazz musician*
* Crump, Tiny

**Crump, Spencer** 1923- [IAW]
*American author and editor*
* Arnold, Ian

**Crump, Tiny**
See Crump, Jesse

**Crumpet, Peter**
See Buckley, Fergus Reid

**Crunch, Captain**
See Draper, John

**Crunch, Captain**
See Kolen, Mike

**Crunch, Captain**
See Marotte, Jean Gilles

**Crunch, Captain**
See Quinn, Pat

**Crunch, Captain**
See Talbert, Diron

**Crunden, Reginald**
See Cleaver, Hylton Reginald

**Crus [or Cruscello]**
See Lentulus, Lucius Cornelius

**[The] Crusader**
See Crothers, William [Bill]

**Crusader**
See Saleeby, Caleb Williams

**[The] Crusader**
See Sigurd I

**Crust, Christie**
See Dennison, Eliza Freeman

**Cruster, Aud**
See Olsen, Cruster Aud

**Crusty Christopher**
See Wilson, John

**Crutchfield, Jimmie**
See Crutchfield, John W.

**Crutchfield, John W.** 1910- [MK]
*American baseball player*
* Crutchfield, Jimmie

**Crutchfield, Nels**
See Crutchfield, Nelson

**Crutchfield, Nelson** 1911- [FHE]
*Canadian-born hockey player*
* Crutchfield, Nels

**Crute, Sally**
See Kirby, Sally C.

**Cruthers, Charles Preston** 1890-
[BE]
*American baseball player*
* Cruthers, Press

**Cruthers, Press**
See Cruthers, Charles Preston

**Cruvelli, Johanne Sophie Charlotte**
See Cruewell, Johanne Sophie
Charlotte

**Cruz, Carlos** 1937-1970 [WBC]
*Dominican boxer*
* Cruz, Teo

**Cruz, Cirilio Dilan** 1951- [SMG]
*Puerto Rican-born baseball player*
* Cruz, Tommy

**Cruz, Hector Dilan** 1953- [SMG]
*Puerto Rican-born baseball player*
* Cruz, Heity

**Cruz, Heity**
See Cruz, Hector Dilan

**Cruz, Teo**
See Cruz, Carlos

**Cruz, Tommy**
See Cruz, Cirilio Dilan

**Cruz y Fernandez, Manuel de la**
1861-1896 [CW]
*Cuban author and journalist*
* Isais

**Cruze, James**
See Bosen, Jens Cruz

**Cry Baby Anson**
See Anson, Adrian Constantine

**Cryer, Neville Barker** 1924- [AW]
*British clergyman and author*
* Fern, Edwin

**Cryin' Red**
See Minter, Iverson

**Cryin' Sam Collins**
See Collins, Samuel

**Cryptonymus**
See Mackenzie, K. R. H.

**Csoma de Koros**
See Korosi Csoma, Sandor

**Csonka, Lawrence R. [Larry]** 1946-
[FB]
*American football player*
* Csonka, Zonk
* [The] Sundance Kid

**Csonka, Zonk**
See Csonka, Lawrence R. [Larry]

**Cuatro Dedos [Four Fingers]**
See Prieto Barrera, Diego

**Cub, Mr.**
See Banks, Ernest [Ernie]

**[The] Cuban Bon Bon**
See Sardinias, Eligio

**[The] Cuban Cat**
See Fuentes, Rigoberto

**[The] Cuban Comet**
See Minoso, Saturnino Orestes
Arrieta Armas

**Cubas, Braz**
See Dawes, Robyn M[ason]

**Cubieres, Michael** 1752-1820 [PA]
*Author*
* Palmezeaux

**Cubitt, Sonia Rosemary** 1900-
[IAW]
*British author*
* Keppel, Sonia

[El] Cucalambe
See Napoles Fajardo, Juan Cristobal

Cucare, Constance Jean 20th c. [OP]
American opera singer
* Cuccaro, Costanza

Cuccaro, Costanza
See Cucare, Constance Jean

Cuccinello, Anthony Francis 1907- [BE]
American baseball player
* Cuccinello, Chick

Cuccinello, Chick
See Cuccinello, Anthony Francis

Cuccurullo, Arthur Joseph 1918- [BE]
American baseball player
* Cuccurullo, Cookie

Cuccurullo, Cookie
See Cuccurullo, Arthur Joseph

[El] Cuchara [The Shovel]
See Lloyd, John Henry

Cucinotta, Salvatore 1946?-
American attorney
* Cucinotta, Sam

Cucinotta, Sam
See Cucinotta, Salvatore

Cude, Wilfred 1910-1968 [FHE]
Welsh-born hockey player
* Wilfred, Wilf

Cudlip, Annie Thomas 1838- ?
British author
* A. T.
* Thomas, Annie

Cudlipp, Edythe 1929- [CA]
American editor and author
* Alcott, Julia
* Horatio, Jane
* Roberts, Rinalda
* Van Zandt, E. F.

Cue
See Summers, A. Leonard

Cue Ball Kelly
See Zingale, Carl

Cuellar, Charlie
See Cuellar, Jesus Patracis

Cuellar, Jesus Patracis 1917- [BE]
American baseball player
* Cuellar, Charlie

Cuellar, Miguel Santana 1937- [BE, SMG]
Cuban-born baseball player
* Cuellar, Mike

Cuellar, Mike
See Cuellar, Miguel Santana

Cueto, Berto
See Cueto, Dagoberto Concepcion

Cueto, Dagoberto Concepcion 1937- [BE]
Cuban-born baseball player
* Cueto, Berto

Cueva, Francoise
See Perus, Francoise

Cuevas, Clara 1933- [CA]
Puerto Rican author and poet
* De Rivel, Isa

Cuevas Roger, Victoriano 1933- [GS]
Spanish bullfighter
* Valencia

Cuff, Barry
See Koste, Robert Francis

Cuff, Jim [DNNF]
American slave
* Crow, Jim

Cuffee, Ed[ward Emerson] 1902-1959 [WWJ]
American jazz musician
* Davidson, Cuffee

Cuidano, P.
See Burgess, Paul

Cuiringione, Tommy ?-1925 [BLB]
American underworld figure
* Rossi, Tommy

Cujacius
See Cujas, Jacques

Cujas, Jacques 1522-1590 [WBD]
French jurist
* Cujacius

Cukoschay [or Zukauskas], Joseph Paul 1902- [BX, RBE, WBC]
American boxer
* Big Skee
* [The] Fighting Fool
* Sharkey, Jack

Culex
See Stanier, Maida Euphemia Kerr

Cullaz, Albert 1941- [EJ7]
French jazz musician
* Cullaz, Alby

Cullaz, Alby
See Cullaz, Albert

Cullen, Barry
See Cullen, Charles Francis

Cullen, Charles Francis 1935- [CEI, FHE]
Canadian-born hockey player
* Cullen, Barry

Cullen, Courteous
See Cullen, [Lord] Robert

Cullen, Peta
See Pyle, Hilary

Cullen, [Lord] Robert 18th c. [SN]
Scottish jurist and writer
* Cullen, Courteous

Culler, Annette Lorena
See Penney, Annette Culler

Culliford, Pierre 1928- [WECO]
Belgian cartoonist
* Peyo

Cullingford, Guy
See Taylor, Constance Lindsay

Cullison, Edwin
See Flynn, Clarence Edwin

Cullop, Henry 1900- [BE]
American baseball player
* Cullop, Nick
* Cullop, Tomato Face

Cullop, Nick
See Cullop, Henry

Cullop, Nick
See Cullop, Norman Andrew

Cullop, Norman Andrew 1887-1961 [AS, BE]
American baseball player
* Cullop, Nick

Cullop, Tomato Face
See Cullop, Henry

Culloton, Bernard Aloysius 1896- [BE]
American baseball player
* Culloton, Bud

Culloton, Bud
See Culloton, Bernard Aloysius

Culmer, Richard [SN]
British iconoclast
* Blue Dick of Thanet

Culo di Ferro [Iron Bottom]
See Berlinguer, Enrico

Culp, Benjamin Baldy [Benny] 1914- [BN]
American baseball player
* Culp, Nitro

Culp, Nitro
See Culp, Benjamin Baldy [Benny]

Culpeper, Martin
See Pullen, George Frederick

Culver, Kathryn
See Dresser, Davis

Culver, Timothy J.
See Westlake, Donald E[dwin]

Culverwell, Charles 1837-1919 [WBD]
British actor and theatre manager
* Wyndham, [Sir] Charles

[The] Cuman
See Ladislas IV

Cumberland, Cass
See Richardson, Harold Edward

Cumberland, Gerald
See Kenyon, C. F.

Cumberland, Marten 1892-1972 [CAP, CC, WW]
British author and journalist
* Bevis, James [joint pseudonym with B. V. Shann]
* Laugier, R.
* O'Hara, Kevin

[The] Cumberland Poet
See Wordsworth, William

Cumberland, Richard 1732-1811 [DEL, DEP, DNNS]
British author and playwright
* [The] English Terence
* [The] Man without a Skin
* [The] Terence of England

Cumbermere, [Lord] Claudius Hastings
See Assollant, Jean-Baptiste-Alfred

Cumbes, Cumbesie
See Cumbes, James

Cumbes, James 1944- [DC]
British cricketer
* Cumbes, Cumbesie

[The] Cumbrian Poet
See Anderson, Robert

Cumes, James William Crawford 1922- [CA]
Australian diplomat and author
* James, C. W.

Cuming, Edward William Dirom 1862- ? [WWL]
British author
* Tempest, Evelyn

Cumming, [Sir] Alexander ?-1775 [SN]
British explorer
* [The] King of the Cherokees

Cumming, John 1810- ? [PA]
Author
* [The] Times Bee-Master

Cumming, M. I. [PA]
Author
* Carnes, Captain

Cumming, Robert Dalziel 1871- ? [NAA]
Scottish-born journalist and author
* Skookum Chuck

Cumming, Roualeyn George Gordon 1820-1866 [DNNS]
Scottish sportsman
* [The] Lion Hunter

Cumming-Skinner, Dugald Matheson 1902- ? [MBF]
Scottish-born author
* Cummings, Ken
* Dane, Donald
* De Beauregard, Henri
* Dundee, Douglas
* Moray, Dugald

Cummings, Albert Arratoon Runciman 1936- [ART]
Scottish painter and illustrator
* Runciman, A., pinx

Cummings, Amos Jay [PA]
Author
* Ziska

Cummings, Bill ?-1938
Auto racer
* Cummings, Wild Bill

Cummings, Bruce Frederick 1889-1919 [B10, LC, TC]
British author and biologist
* Barbellion, W. N. P.

Cummings, Candy
See Cummings, William Arthur

Cummings, Chance
See Cummings, Napoleon

Cummings, Claudia
See Colburn, Claudia Jean

Cummings, Constance
See Halverstadt, Constance

Cummings, Duke
See Cummings, James

cummings, e. e.
See Cummings, Edward Estlin

Cummings, Edward Estlin 1894-1962 [IPA, LC, TC]
American poet
* cummings, e. e.

Cummings, Florence
See Bonime, Florence

Cummings, James 20th c. [RBE]
American boxing manager
* Cummings, Duke

**Cummings, Johnny** 20th c.
*American musician*
* Ramone, Johnny

**Cummings, Josiah D.** [PA]
*Author*
* [The] Peasant Bard

**Cummings, Ken**
See  Cumming-Skinner, Dugald
Matheson

**Cummings, M. A.**
See  Cummings, Monette A.

**Cummings, Monette A.** 20th c.
[WGT]
*Author*
* Cummings, M. A.

**Cummings, Napoleon** 1892-   [MK]
*American baseball player*
* Cummings, Chance

**Cummings, Richard**
See  Orth, Richard

**Cummings, Wild Bill**
See  Cummings, Bill

**Cummings, William Arthur**
1848-1924  [AS, DGS, PB]
*American baseball player*
* Cummings, Candy

**Cummins, John Thomas Benedict**
1880- ?  [CAT]
*American author and clergyman*
* Patrick, [Father]

**Cummins, Mary Warmington**
1923-  [AW]
*Scottish-born author*
* Melville, Jean

**Cunard, Grace**
See  Jefferies, Harriet Mildred

**Cunati, Caroline** 1907-
[FC, OCF, WEF]
*French actress*
* Feuillere, Edwige
* Lynn, Cora

**Cunctator**
See  Fabius Maximus Verrucosus,
Quintus

**Cundy, C. B.**
See  Cundy, Clifford Benjamin

**Cundy, Clifford Benjamin** 1925-
[ART]
*British sculptor and painter*
* Cundy, C. B.

**Cuningham, Philip**
See  Boosey, Philip Harold

**Cunliffe, Barrington Windsor**
1939-  [CA]
*British archaeologist and author*
* Cunliffe, Barry

**Cunliffe, Barry**
See  Cunliffe, Barrington Windsor

**Cunliffe, Dave** 1941-  [IAW]
*British author*
* Alexander, David
* Ferkinshaw, Albert

**[The] Cunning**
See  Robert I

**Cunningham, Albert Benjamin**
1888-1962  [ANT, CC, WW]
*American author*
* Dale, Estil
* Hale, Garth

**Cunningham, Allan** 1784-1842
[DEL, FFF, SN]
*British author and poet*
* Hid-Allan
* Honest Allan
* Macrabin, Mark

**Cunningham, Baby**
See  Cunningham, Harry

**Cunningham, Bam**
See  Cunningham, Sam[uel Lewis,
Jr.]

**Cunningham, Bert**
See  Cunningham, Ellsworth Elmer

**Cunningham, Billy** 1943-  [BB]
*American basketball player*
* [The] Kangaroo Kid

**Cunningham, Cathy**
See  Cunningham, Chet

**Cunningham, Cats' Eyes**
See  Cunningham, John

**Cunningham, Cecil Claybourne**
See  Bradbury, Ray [Douglas]

**Cunningham, Chet** 1928-  [CA]
*American writer and publisher*
* Cunningham, Cathy
* Derrick, Lionel [joint pseudonym
with Mark Roberts]

**Cunningham, Daddy**
See  Cunningham, Marion

**Cunningham, E.**
See  Bradbury, Ray [Douglas]

**Cunningham, E. V.**
See  Fast, Howard [Melvin]

**Cunningham, Ellsworth Elmer**
1865-1952  [AS, BE]
*American baseball player*
* Cunningham, Bert

**Cunningham, [Captain] Frank**
See  Glick, Carl [Cannon]

**Cunningham, Glenn** 1909-  [TF]
*American track and field athlete*
* [The] Kansas Ironman

**Cunningham, Harry** 20th c.  [OBW]
*American baseball player*
* Cunningham, Baby

**Cunningham, J. Morgan**
See  Westlake, Donald E[dwin]

**Cunningham, J. W.** 19th c.  [PA]
*Author*
* [A] Country Clergyman

**Cunningham, John** 1917-
[BDW, WWW]
*British fighter pilot*
* Cunningham, Cats' Eyes

**Cunningham, Margaret Isobel**
1933-  [IAW]
*Scottish journalist*
* Silver Snaffle III

**Cunningham, Marion** 20th c.
[OBW]
*American baseball player*
* Cunningham, Daddy

**Cunningham, Mike**
See  Cunningham, Rudolph

**Cunningham, Rudolph** 20th c.  [BE]
*American baseball player*
* Cunningham, Mike

**Cunningham, Sam[uel Lewis, Jr.]**
1950-  [FB, SMG]
*American football player*
* Cunningham, Bam
* Cunningham, Sam Bam
* [The] Diving Dervish

**Cunningham, Sam Bam**
See  Cunningham, Sam[uel Lewis,
Jr.]

**Cunninghame Graham, R[obert]
B[ontine]**
See  Bontine, Robert

**Cunninghame-Graham, Robert**
See  Graham, Robert

**Cunnington, Charles Leslie** 1895-
[WWL]
*Australian author*
* C. L. C.
* [The] Old Dog
* Rustyface

**Cunynghame, Francis J. de M.**
1884-  [WWL]
*British author*
* Kingstead, Julian

**Cuppini, Gil**
See  Cuppini, Gilberto

**Cuppini, Gilberto** 1924-  [EJ]
*Italian jazz musician*
* Cuppini, Gil

**Cuppy, George Joseph**
See  Koppe, George Maceo

**Cuppy, Nig**
See  Koppe, George Maceo

**Cuq, Pierre** 1925-  [FC]
*French actor*
* Mondy, Pierre

**Curcio, Renato** 1942?-
*Italian terrorist*
* Toulouse Lautrec

**[The] Cure of Ars**
See  Vianney, Jean Baptiste Marie

**Curillo**
See  Nunez, Francisco

**Curl, James Stevens** 1937-  [CA]
*Irish-born architect and writer*
* Adytum
* Keeling, E. B.
* Parsifal

**Curle, Adam**
See  Curle, Charles T. W.

**Curle, Charles T. W.** 1916-  [CA]
*French-born educator and author*
* Curle, Adam

**Curle, M. O.** 1889-  [WWL]
*British author*
* Ormiston, Margaret

**Curler, [Mary] Bernice** 1915-  [CA]
*American author*
* Davis, Mary Bernice

**Curless, Richard [Dick]** 1932-
[ECM, FCW]
*American country-western performer*
* [The] Rice Paddy Ranger
* [The] Tumbleweed Kid

**Curley, Doc**
See  Curley, Walter James

**Curley, Dorothy Nyren** 1927-  [CA]
*American writer, editor, poet*
* Nyren, Dorothy

**Curley, Kid**
See  Hernandez, Juan G.

**Curley Top Richards**
See  Richards, Ruby

**Curley, Walter James** 1874-1920
[BE]
*American baseball player*
* Curley, Doc

**Curling, Audrey**
See  Clark, Marie Catherine
Audrey

**Curling, Bryan William Richard**
1911-  [AW, CA]
*British journalist and author*
* Hotspur
* Julius

**Curman, Billy**
See  Curmano, Billy

**Curmano, Billy** 1949-  [ART]
*American artist*
* Curman, Billy

**Curnow, [Thomas] Allen [Munro]**
1911-  [WD]
*New Zealand playwright and poet*
* Whim Wham

**Curopolates**
See  Codinus, George

**Curran, Jan Goldberg** 1937-  [CA]
*American author and columnist*
* Goldberg, Jan

**Curran, John**
See  Reile, Louis Anthony

**Curran, Mona [Elisa]** 20th c.  [CA]
*British journalist, lecturer, author*
* Merton, Giles
* Murray, Adrian
* Thomas, Mervyn

**Curran, Sam**
See  Curran, Simon Francis

**Curran, Simon Francis** 1874-1936
[BE]
*American baseball player*
* Curran, Sam

**Currie, Daniel** 1935-  [FB]
*American football player*
* Currie, Dapper Dan

**Currie, Dapper Dan**
See  Currie, Daniel

**Currie, David**
See  Allen, Sydney [Earl], Jr.

**Currie, Finlay**
See  Jefferson, Finlay

**Currie, Mary Montgomerie**
1843-1905  [WBD]
*British author*
* Fane, Violet

**Currie, Thomas Stewart**
See  Richardson, Anthony

**Currier, Jay L.**
See  Henderson, James Leal

**Curro Caro [Dear Little Curro]**
See  Martin Caro Cases, Francisco

**Curry, Avon**
See  Bowden, Jean

**Curry, Big Nose**
See  Parrott, George

**Curry, Busher**
See Curry, Floyd James

**Curry, Flat Nose**
See Parrott, George

**Curry, Floyd James** 1925-
[CEI, FHE]
*Canadian-born hockey player*
* Curry, Busher

**Curry, George James** 1888-1963
[BE]
*American baseball player*
* Curry, Soldier Boy

**Curry, George L.**
See Parrott, George

**Curry, Gladys J.**
See Washington, Gladys J[oseph]

**Curry, Goose**
See Curry, Homer

**Curry, Homer** ?-1974 [MK]
*American baseball player*
* Curry, Goose

**Curry, Kid**
See Logan, Harvey

**Curry, Otway** [FFF]
*American journalist*
* Abdallah

**Curry, Soldier Boy**
See Curry, George James

**Curry-Lindahl, Kai** 1917- [IAW]
*Swedish zoologist and author*
* K. C. L.

**Curson, Stanley**
See Merwin, [W.] Sam[uel], Jr.

**Cursor**
See Papirius, Lucius

**Curt-Hose [Short-Shanks]**
See Robert II

**Curtice, Cactus Jack**
See Curtice, Jack C.

**Curtice, Jack C.** 20th c. [BBH]
*American collegiate athletic director*
* Curtice, Cactus Jack

**Curtis, Alan**
See Ueberroth, Harry

**Curtis, Andy** 20th c. [GW]
*American rodeo performer*
* Curtis, Gump

**Curtis, Animal**
See Curtis, J. Michael

**Curtis, Beatrice**
See White, Beatrice

**Curtis, Caroline G.** 1827- ? [PA]
*American author*
* Winchester, Carroll

**Curtis, Dal**
See Dallis, Nicholas Peter

**Curtis, Ed** 1908-1965 [GW]
*American rodeo performer*
* Curtis, Ug

**Curtis, Eddie** 1927- [ASC]
*American composer and singer*
* Curtis, Tex

**Curtis, George William** 1824-1892
[FFF, PA, SN]
*American author*
* [The] American Charles Lamb

**Curtis, George William** (Continued)
* Easy Chair
* Howadji
* Lounger
* Old Bachelor
* Potiphar

**Curtis, Gump**
See Curtis, Andy

**Curtis, J. Michael** 1943- [FB]
*American football player*
* Curtis, Animal

**Curtis, James** 1912-1970 [BWW]
*American singer*
* Curtis, Peck

**Curtis, Jean-Louis**
See Lafitte, Louis

**Curtis, John**
See Prebble, John Edward Curtis

**Curtis, John Duffield** 1948- [SMG]
*American baseball player*
* J. C.

**Curtis, Ken**
See Gates, Curtis

**Curtis, King**
See Ousley, Curtis

**Curtis, Mann**
See Kurtz, Manny

**Curtis, Marjorie**
See Prebble, Marjorie Mary Curtis

**Curtis, Paul**
See Czura, Roman Peter

**Curtis, Peck**
See Curtis, James

**Curtis, Peter**
See Lofts, Norah [Robinson]

**Curtis, Price**
See Ellison, Harlan [Jay]

**Curtis, Tex**
See Curtis, Eddie

**Curtis, Tom**
See Pendower, Jacques

**Curtis, Tony**
See Schwartz, Bernard

**Curtis, Turk**
See Curtis Vern[on Eugene]

**Curtis, Ug**
See Curtis, Ed

**Curtis Vern[on Eugene]** 1920- [BE]
*American baseball player*
* Curtis, Turk

**Curtis, Wade**
See Pournelle, Jerry [Eugene]

**Curtis, Will**
See Nunn, William Curtis

**Curtis, William B.** 1837-1900
[BBH]
*American athlete*
* [The] Father of American
Amateurism
* [The] Father of American
Rowing

**Curtiss, A. A.** [FFF]
*American author*
* Nillo

**Curtiss, Irv[in Duane]** 1861-1945
[BE]
*American baseball player*
* Curtiss, Tacks

**Curtiss, Mina**
See Kirstein, Mina

**Curtiss, Percy**
See Cox, Mrs. William N.

**Curtiss, Tacks**
See Curtiss, Irv[in Duane]

**Curtius**
See Corti, Matteo

**Curtiz, Michael**
See Kertesz, Mihaly

**Curtmantle**
See Henry II

**Curval, Philippe**
See Tronche, Philippe

**[The] Curveless Wonder**
See Orth, Albert Lewis

**Curzon, Charles**
See Whittington-Egan, Richard

**Curzon, Christopher Colin** 1958-
[DC]
*British cricketer*
* Curzon, Pukey

**Curzon, Daniel**
See Brown, Daniel Russell

**Curzon, Frank**
See Deeley, Francis Arthur

**Curzon, Lucia**
See Stevenson, Florence

**Curzon, Pukey**
See Curzon, Christopher Colin

**Curzon, Sam**
See Krasney, Samuel A.

**Curzon, Virginia**
See Hawton, Hector

**Curzon-Herrick, Maud Kathleen
Cairnes Plantagenet Hastings**
1893-1965 [SFL, WGT]
*British author*
* Cairnes, Maud

**Cusack, Mary Frances** [FFF]
* Clare, Mary Frances

**Cusack, Michael J[oseph]** 1928-
[CA]
*Irish-born American author*
* O'Gorman, Samuel F.

**Cushenan, Crash**
See Cushenan, Ian Robertson

**Cushenan, Ian Robertson** 1933-
[FHE]
*Canadian-born hockey player*
* Cushenan, Crash

**Cushing, Charles C. Strong**
1879-1941 [BEW]
*American playwright*
* Cushing, Tom

**Cushing, Tom**
See Cushing, Charles C. Strong

**Cushman, Clara**
See Bradley, Emily

**Cushman, Evelyn**
See Milner, Florence Cushman

**Cushman, Josephine**
See Tetley, Mrs. William

**Cushman, Lilla N.**
See Rossiter, Anna M. S.

**Cushnie, Parke** 1907?-1962 [BEW]
*Actor*
* McGregor, Parke

**Cusseaux, Zulema** 1947- [IBW]
*American entertainer*
* Miss Z

**Custer, Bob**
See Glenn, Raymond Anthony

**Custer, Claude**
See Goddard, Norman Molyneux

**Custer, George Armstrong**
1839-1876 [FFF, PA, SN]
*American army officer*
* Long Hair
* Nomad
* Ringlets

**Cutchen, Billye Walker** 1930-
[CA, SAT]
*American author*
* Brown, Billye Walker

**Cutforth, John Ashlin** 1911- [CA]
*British educator and author*
* Ashlin, John

**Cuthbert, [Father]**
See Hess, Lawrence Anthony

**Cuthbert** 741- 758 [HN]
*Archbishop of Canterbury*
* [The] Apostle of the Lowlands

**Cuthbert, Estella Y.** 20th c. [SFL]
*Author*
* Yerex, Cuthbert

**Cuthbert, Ian Holm** 1931- [TR]
*British actor*
* Holm, Ian

**Cuthbert, Mary**
See Hellwig, Monika Konrad

**Cutler, Ivor** 1923- [CA]
*British composer, author, cartoonist*
* Knifesmith

**Cutler, Samuel**
See Folsom, Franklin [Brewster]

**Cutner, Solomon** 1902- [BBD]
*British pianist*
* Solomon

**Cutpurse, Moll**
See Frith, Mary

**Cutruzzula, Al** 20th c. [BBH]
*American softball player*
* Cutruzzula, Cotti

**Cutruzzula, Cotti**
See Cutruzzula, Al

**Cutsforth, Gloria** 1938- [OP]
*American opera singer*
* Marinacci, Gloria

**Cutshall, Cutty**
See Cutshall, Robert Dewees

**Cutshall, Robert Dewees**
1911-1968 [DAM, EJ, PMJ]
*American jazz musician*
* Cutshall, Cutty

**Cutshaw, Clancy**
See Cutshaw, George William

**Cutshaw, George William** 1887-
[BE]
*American baseball player*
* Cutshaw, Clancy

**Cutter, Bloodgood H.** [PA]
*American poet*
* [The] Long Island Farmer Poet

**Cutting, Pierce**
*See* Webb, Charles Hull

**Cuttriss, Frank** [joint pseudonym
with R. Cuttriss Hinkins]
*See* Hinkins, Frank R.

**Cuttriss, Frank** [joint pseudonym
with Frank R. Hinkins]
*See* Hinkins, R. Cuttriss

**Cutts, Mary** [PA]
*Author*
* Idamore

**Cutts, Patricia** 1926-1974 [SC]
*British actress*
* Wayne, Patricia

**Cuvier, Georges Leopold Chretien
Frederic Dagobert** 1769-1832
[DEP, HN, SN]
*French naturalist*
* [The] Aristotle of the Nineteenth
Century

**Cuyler, Cuy**
*See* Cuyler, Hazen Shirley

**Cuyler, Hazen Shirley** 1899-1950
[AS, BAB, PB]
*American baseball player*
* Cuyler, Cuy
* Cuyler, Kiki

**Cuyler, Kiki**
*See* Cuyler, Hazen Shirley

**Cuyler, Stephen**
*See* Bates, Barbara S[nedeker]

**Cy the Second**
*See* Young, Irving Melrose

**Cy the Third**
*See* Young, Harley E.

**Cybo of Genoa** [SN]
*Italian painter and illustrator*
* [The] Monk of the Golden Islands

**Cycla**
*See* Clacy, Ellen

**Cyclone Jim Duryea**
*See* Duryea, James Whitney

**Cyclone Louis Lewis**
*See* Lewis, Vach

**Cyclops**
*See* Antigonus I

**Cyclops**
*See* Day, John Robert

**Cyganiewicz, Stanislaus** ?-1967
[BL]
*Polish-born wrestler*
* Zbyszko, Stanislaus

**Cymbal, Johnny** 20th c. [RO2]
*American singer*
* Derek

**Cymon**
*See* Somerby, Frederick

**Cynan**
*See* Evans-Jones, Albert

**[The] Cynic**
*See* Diogenes

**Cynicus**
*See* Anderson, Martin

**Cynonfardd**
*See* Edwards, Thomas C.

**Cynthia**
*See* King, Florence

**Cynthia**
*See* Seymour, Marjorie F.

**Cynthius**
*See* Giraldi, Giovanni Battista

**Cypraeus**
*See* Kupperschmidt, Paul

**Cypress, J., Jr.**
*See* Hawes, William Post

**Cyprien, Anatole**
*See* Dambreville, Claude

**Cyr, Louis** 1863-1912 [CSH]
*Canadian weightlifter*
* [The] Strongest Man in the
World
* [The] Strongest Man Who Ever
Lived

**Cyrano**
*See* Orlando, Emanuels

**Cyriacus of Ancona**
*See* Ciriaco de Pizzicolli

**Cyril**
*See* Constantine

**Cyril** 376- 444 [DNNF, FFF, RH]
*Saint*
* Champion of the Virgin
* Doctor of the Incarnation

**Cyrille**
*See* D'Avril, [Baron] Adolph

**Cyrus**
*See* Teed, Cyrus Reed

**Cyrus** 6th c. BC
[DEP, DNNS, WBD]
*King of Persia*
* [The] Elder
* [The] Great
* [The] Persian King

**Cyrus the Gray**
*See* Vance, Cyrus Roberts

**Cyzicenus**
*See* Antiochus IX

**Czacki, Thaddeus** 1765-1813
[DNNF, FFF, SN]
*Polish statesman and writer*
* [The] Franklin of Poland
* [The] Polish Franklin

**Czaczkes, Shmuel Yosef** 1888-
[EWL]
*Israeli author*
* Agnon, S[hmuel] Y[osef]
* Ironi
* Mazal Tov

**Czajkowski, Michal** 1808-1886
[WBD]
*Polish revolutionist and author*
* Sadyk Pasha

**[The] Czar**
*See* Zanders, Roosevelt Smith

**Czarobski, Ziggie**
*See* Czarobski, Zygmont

**Czarobski, Zygmont** 20th c.
*American football player*
* Czarobski, Ziggie

**Czeniawski, Romain** 20th c. [EE]
*Intelligence agent*
* Armand [code name used during
World War II]

**Czernohorsky, Elisabeth** 1933-
[OP]
*Austrian opera singer*
* Schwarzenberg, Elisabeth

**Czerny Djordje**
*See* Petrovitsch [or Petrovic],
George

**Czjewski, Frank** 20th c. [SG]
*Boxer*
* Oma, Lee

**Czukor, Barbara Brantingham**
1920-1980 [FC, ITA]
*American actress*
* Britton, Barbara

**Czura, R. P.**
*See* Czura, Roman Peter

**Czura, Roman Peter** 1913- [CA]
*American author*
* Curtis, Paul
* Czura, R. P.
* Dale, Roman

# D

**D.**
See Brown, Diana Elizabeth

**D.**
See Delius, Nikolaus

**D.**
See Harle, Dennis F.

**D. A.**
See Brown, Diana Elizabeth

**D. B.**
See Baxter, Denis Charles Trevor

**D. B.**
See Brown, Diana Elizabeth

**D. B.**
See Bryant, Dena

**D. B.**
See Burpee, David

**D. C.**
See Clarke, Dora

**D. C. L.**
See Hope, Alexander James Beresford

**D. D.**
See Berolzheimer, Daniel Deronda

**D. D.**
See Davies, Antoni Douglas

**D. D.**
See Donne, Leonard David

**D. F. M.**
See Maclagan, Dorothea F.

**D. F. W.**
See Fairweather-Walker, Dorothy

**D. G.**
See Daniel, George

**D. H.**
See Hill, Derek

**D. J. B-H.**
See Berry-Hart, David James

**D. M. A.**
See Armfield, Diana M.

**D. M. S.**
See Browne, Dorothy Margaret Stuart

**D. O. N.**
See O'Neill, Daniel

**D. P. H.**
See Hanly, Daithi Patrick

**D. R.**
See Rockefeller, David

**D. Y.**
See Quincy, Edmund

**Da**
See Second element of name for further listings

**Da Bayola, Ugo**
See Bolay, Karl H.

**Da Bologna, Pellegrino**
See Tibaldi, Pellegrino

**Da Correggio, Claudio**
See Merlotti, Claudio

**Da Costa, Cicero Adolpho Victorio**
20th c.   [WF]
Director and actor
* Chadler, C. Adolpho

**Da Costa, Morton**
See Tecosky, Morton

**Da Costa, Uriel**
See Acosta, Gabriel

**Da Costa Ricci, Lewis Anselmo**
1886-1967   [LAO, LC]
British naval officer and author
* Bartimeus
* Ritchie, [Sir] Lewis

**Da Cruz, Daniel, Jr.** 1921-   [CA]
American author
* Ballantine, John
* Cross, T. T.

**Da Cunha, Maria Do Carmo**
1913?-1955   [FC, IPA, WEF]
Portuguese-born singer and actress
* [The] Brazilian Bombshell
* Miranda, Carmen

**Da Fano, Dorothea Natalie Sophia**
?-1941   [DBA]
British painter and sculptor
* Landau, Dorothea

**Da Gaeta, Giovanni** 12th c.   [WBD]
Pope
* Gelasius II

**Da Imola, Innocenzo**
See Francucci, Innocenzo di Pietro

**Da Mara**
See Delamarre, Guillaume

**Da Murano, Bartolommeo**
1432-1491?   [WBD]
Venetian painter
* Vivarini, Bartolommeo

**Da Pontedera, Andrea**
See Pisano, Andrea

**Da Silva, Howard**
See Silverblatt, Howard

**Da Silva, Leonidas** 1913-   [OCS]
Soccer player
* Leonidas

**Da Veiga Fontoura, Uriel** 1940-
[AES]
Brazilian soccer player
* Uriel

**Da Vinci, Leonardo** 1452-1519
[SN]
Florentine painter, sculptor, architect
* [The] Diviner
* [The] Father of Modern Painting
* [The] Wizard of the Italian Renaissance

**D'Abegnac, Marquis** 18th c.   [FFF]
French aristocrat who became a noted chef in England
* [The] Fashionable Salad-Maker

**D'Aboville, Gerard** 1945?-
French oarsman
* [The] Lindbergh of the Sea

**Dabrowsky, Iwan** 1881-1961
[CAR]
Russian-born painter
* Graham, John

**D'Abruzzo, Alphonso** 1936-
[BEW, TR]
American actor
* Alda, Alan

**D'Abruzzo, Alphonso Giovanni Giusseppi Roberto** 1914-
[BEW, FC, ITA]
American actor
* Alda, Robert

**D'Ache, Caran**
See Poire, Emmanuel

**Dachs, David** 1922-   [CA]
American author
* Stanley, Dave

**Dacre, Charlotte**
See Byrne, Charlotte Dacre

**Dacre, Mrs. Arthur**   [FFF]
Entertainer
* Roselle, Amy

**Dacre, [Captain] Stanley**
See Hyatt, Stanley Portal

**Dacres, Desmond** 1942-
[PRS, RO2]
Jamaican-born singer, songwriter, bandleader
* Dekker, Desmond
* King of the Blue Beat

**Dacus, Smokey**
See Dacus, William Eschol

**Dacus, William Eschol** 1911-
[CWG]
American country-western performer
* Dacus, Smokey

**Dadd, B.**
See Williams, John H.

**Daddy Deep Throat**
See Cain, Perry

**Daddy Dewdrop**
See Monda, Richard

**Daddy Hooves**
See Gerard, Gus

**[The] Daddy of the Baby**
See Johnson, Andrew

**[The] Daddy of the Blues**
See Walker, Aaron Thibeaux

**[The] Daddy of Western Swing**
See Wills, Bob

**Daddy Stovepipe**
See Watson, Johnny

**Daddy Wags Wagner**
See Wagner, Leon Lamar

**Dade, Robert E.** 1915-   [EJ]
American jazz musician
* Astor, Bob

**Dado**
See Djuric, Miodrag

**Daffan, Ted**
See Daffan, Theron Eugene

**Daffan, Theron Eugene** 1912-
[CWG, ECM, FCW]
American country-western performer
* Brown, Frankie
* Daffan, Ted

**D'Affry, Adele** 19th c.
Sculptor
* Marcello

**Dagan, Avigdor**
See Fischl, Viktor

**Daggett, Mike** 1845?-1911?   [B10]
American Indian leader
* Shoshone Mike

**Daghofer, Lillitts**
See Liletts [or Liletta], Marta Maria

**Dagmar**
See Cameron, Lou

**Dagmar**
See Egnor, Virginia Ruth

**D'Agnolo [or D'Angelo], Donato** 1444-1514 [WBD]
*Italian architect*
* Bramante
* Lazzari

**D'Agnolo di Francesco, Andrea Domenico** 1486-1531 [DNNS, RH, WBD]
*Florentine painter*
* [The] Faultless Painter
* Sarto, Andrea del

**Dago Frank Cirofici**
See Cirofici, Frank

**Dago Lawrence Mangano**
See Mangano, Lawrence

**Dagobert, Chrysotome**
See Led'huy, Jean Baptiste Alphonse

**Dagonet**
See Sims, George Robert

**Dagover, Lil**
See Liletts [or Liletta], Marta Maria

**Dagres, Angelo George** 1934- [BE]
*American baseball player*
* Dagres, Angie
* Dagres, Junior

**Dagres, Angie**
See Dagres, Angelo George

**Dagres, Junior**
See Dagres, Angelo George

**Daguesseau, Henri Francois** 1668-1751 [WBD]
*French jurist*
* Aguesseau, Henri Francois d'

**Dahl, John**
See Remar, Frits

**Dahl, Vladimir Ivanovitch** 1802?-1872 [FFF]
*Russian author*
* Luganski, Kosak

**Dahlander, Bert**
See Dahlander, Nils-Bertil

**Dahlander, Nils-Bertil** 1928- [EJ]
*Swedish-born jazz musician*
* Dahlander, Bert

**Dahlberg [or Dahlbergh], Erik Jonsson** 1625-1703 [WBD]
*Swedish engineer*
* [The] Vauban of Sweden

**Dahlen, Bad Bill**
See Dahlen, William Frederick

**Dahlen, William Frederick** 1870?-1950 [AS, DGS, PB]
*American baseball player*
* Dahlen, Bad Bill

**Dahlgren, Babe**
See Dahlgren, Ellsworth Tenney

**Dahlgren, Ellsworth Tenney** 1912- [BE, PB]
*American baseball player*
* Dahlgren, Babe

**Dahlgren, John Adolphus Bernard** 1809-1870 [FFF]
*American naval officer and author*
* Blue Jacket

**Dahlke, Jerome Alex [Jerry]** 1930- [BE]
*American baseball player*
* Dahlke, Joe

**Dahlke, Joe**
See Dahlke, Jerome Alex [Jerry]

**Dahlstierna, Gunno**
See Eurelius, Gunno

**Dahlstrom, Carl** 1913- [CEI, FHE, HK]
*American hockey player*
* Dahlstrom, Cully

**Dahlstrom, Cully**
See Dahlstrom, Carl

**Daigle, Jane Johnson** 1914- [IAW]
*American-born author*
* Johnson, Jane

**Dailey, Catherine** 1915- [FC, PMJ]
*American comedienne and singer*
* Daley, Cass

**Dailley, Richard** 1852- ? [WWL]
*British author*
* Clarke, Cromwell

**Daily, Con**
See Daily, Cornelius F.

**Daily, Cornelius F.** 1864-1928 [BE]
*American baseball player*
* Daily, Con

**Daily, Harold W.** 1902- [FCW]
*American record producer and music executive*
* Daily, Pappy

**Daily, Hugh Ignatius** 1857- ? [AS, BE]
*American baseball player*
* Daily, One Arm

**Daily, One Arm**
See Daily, Hugh Ignatius

**Daily, Pappy**
See Daily, Harold W.

**Dain, Alex**
See Lukeman, Alex

**Dainton, Marie**
See Sharlach, Marie

**Daintrey, Adrian Maurice** 1902- [ART]
*British painter*
* A. D.
* A. M. D.

**Daisies, Anthony**
See Margheriti, Antonio

**Daisne, Johan**
See Thiery, Herman

**Daisy**
See Margrethe II

**Daix, Daisy**
See Cariveac, Denis

**Daixel, William Wolf** 1919- [BEW]
*American actor, dancer, choreographer*
* Valentine, Paul

**Dak**
See Corfield, Wilmot

**Dake, Seymour R.** [PA]
*Author*
* [A] Southerner

**Dakers, Elaine Kidner** 1905-1978 [CA]
*British author*
* Lane, Jane

**Dakoske, Doc**
See Dakoske, Edwin P.

**Dakoske, Edwin P.** 1940-
*American baseball player*
* Dakoske, Doc
* [The] Terror of the Infield

**Dakotan**
See Winsted, Huldah Lucile

**Dal Canton, John Bruce** 1942- [SMG]
*American baseball player*
* Dal Canton, Prof

**Dal Canton, Prof**
See Dal Canton, John Bruce

**D'Alaux, Gustave**
See Raybaud, Maxime

**D'Albano, Montreal** ?-1354 [HN]
*Mercenary soldier*
* Moriale, [Fra]

**D'Albans, Vicompte**
See Ratazzi, Mme.

**D'Albon, Claude Camille Francois** 18th c. [SN]
*French author and physician*
* His Thinker

**Dalburgius**
See Von Dalberg, Johann Kamera

**Dalby, B. J.**
See Maples, Evelyn Lucille [Palmer]

**Dale, Adam** [house pseudonym, Curtis Warren]
See Holloway, Brian

**Dale, Adrian**
See Fuller, Edith Jean

**Dale, Alan**
See Cohen, Alfred J.

**Dale, Austin**
See Calvert, William Robinson

**Dale, Charlie**
See Marks, Charlie

**Dale, Darley**
See Steele, Francesca Maria

**Dale, Dash**
See Rathborne, St. George

**Dale, Edwin**
See Home-Gall, Edward Reginald

**Dale, Ellis**
See Mackenzie, G. A.

**Dale, Estil**
See Cunningham, Albert Benjamin

**Dale, Flora**
See Brown, Ida G.

**Dale, Flora**
See Henderson, Rosa [Rose]

**Dale, George E.**
See Asimov, Isaac

**Dale, Glen**
See Garforth, Glenn

**Dale, Grover**
See Aitken, Grover Robert

**Dale, Jack**
See Holliday, Joseph [Joe]

**Dale, Jean**
See Diestelhorst, H. Jean

**Dale, Jim**
See Smith, James

**Dale, Margaret**
See Bolam, Margaret

**Dale, Margaret J[essy] Miller** 1911- [AW, CA]
*Scottish-born author*
* Miller, Margaret J.

**Dale, Norman**
See Tubb, Edwin Charles

**Dale, Peggy**
See Dudley, Margaret Dale

**Dale, Robin**
See Hadfield, Alan

**Dale, Roman**
See Czura, Roman Peter

**Dale, Salvia**
See Dalsheimer, Alice

**Dale, V. R.**
See Van Horn, Dale R.

**Dale, Vernon**
See Slaughter, Marion T.

**Daley, Bill**
See Appleman, John Alan

**Daley, Buddy**
See Daley, Leavitt Leo

**Daley, Cass**
See Dailey, Catherine

**Daley, Leavitt Leo** 1932- [BE]
*American baseball player*
* Daley, Buddy

**Daley, Pete**
See Daley, Thomas Francis [Tom]

**Daley, Thomas Francis [Tom]** 1884-1934 [BE]
*American baseball player*
* Daley, Pete

**Dalgetty, Dugald**
See Tulloch, [Sir] A. M.

**Dalhart, Vernon**
See Slaughter, Marion T.

**D'Alibi, Cardinal** ?-1418 [HN]
*Prelate*
* [The] Devil of Arras

**Dalio, Marcel**
See Blauschild, Marcel Benoit

**Dalis, Irene**
See Dalis, Yvonne Patricia

**Dalis, Yvonne Patricia** 1930- [OP]
*American opera singer*
* Dalis, Irene

**Dalitz, Moe** 20th c.    [BLB, PHM]
*American underworld figure*
* Davis, Moe

**Dall, Ian**
*See*  Higgins, Charles S.

**Dall, John**
*See*  Thompson, John Dall

**Dallamano, Massimo** 1917-    [FDG]
*Italian director*
* Dillmann, Max

**Dallard, Eggie**
*See*  Dallard, William

**D'Allard, Hunter**
*See*  Ballard, [Willis] Todhunter

**Dallard, William** 20th c.    [OBW]
*American baseball player*
* Dallard, Eggie

**Dallas, Athena Gianakas**
*See*  Dallas-Damis, Athena
G[ianakas]

**Dallas, Francis Dominic Joseph**
1931-    [EJ]
*American jazz musician*
* Dallas, Sonny

**Dallas, Isabelle Gearns** 1823-1889
[FFF]
*British actress*
* Glyn, Miss

**Dallas, Letitia Marion**  ?-1917
[BEW]
*Actress*
* Darragh, Miss

**Dallas, Sandra**
*See*  Atchison, Sandra Dallas

**Dallas, Sonny**
*See*  Dallas, Francis Dominic
Joseph

**Dallas, Vincent**
*See*  Werner, Victor Emile

**Dallas-Damis, Athena G[ianakas]**
1925-    [CA]
*American author*
* Dallas, Athena Gianakas

**D'Allenger, Hugh**
*See*  Kershaw, John Hugh
D'Allenger

**Dallessandro, Dim Dom**
*See*  Dallessandro, Nicholas
Dominic

**Dallessandro, Nicholas Dominic**
1913-    [BE]
*American baseball player*
* Dallessandro, Dim Dom

**Dallis, Nicholas Peter** 1911-    [B10]
*American psychiatrist and cartoonist*
* Curtis, Dal
* Nichols, Paul

**Dallwitz-Wegner, Richard Von** 1873-
?    [LAO]
*German physicist and author*
* Weda [or Wegner], Richard

**Dally, Ann Gwendolen Mullins**
1926-    [AW, CA]
*British physician and author*
* Mullins, Ann

**Dalmas, John**
*See*  Mandel, Leon

**Dalmatoff, B.**
*See*  Lutschitsch-Dalmatoff, B.

**Dalmocand**
*See*  Macdonald, George

**Dalroy, Harry** 1879-1954    [SC]
*American actor*
* Dalroy, Rube
* [The] Mayor of Gower Gulch

**Dalroy, Rube**
*See*  Dalroy, Harry

**Dalrymple-Hay, Barbara** 20th c.
[AW]
*Australian author*
* Hay, John [joint pseudonym with
John Dalrymple-Hay]

**Dalrymple-Hay, John** 1928-    [AW]
*Australian author*
* Hay, John [joint pseudonym with
Barbara Dalrymple-Hay]

**Dalsace, Lionel** 20th c.    [SFL]
*Author*
* Blech, Aimee

**Dalsheimer, Alice** 1845-1880    [FFF]
*American poet*
* Dale, Salvia

**Dalton, Claire**
*See*  Burns, Alma

**Dalton, Clive**
*See*  Clark, Frederick Stephen

**Dalton, Dorothy**
*See*  Challoner, Dorothy

**Dalton, Dorothy** 1915-    [CA]
*American poet*
* Kuehn, Dorothy Dalton

**Dalton, Gilbert** 20th c.    [MBF]
*British author*
* Carstairs, Rod
* Norton, Victor

**Dalton, Howard**
*See*  Van Horn, Dale R.

**Dalton, Jack**
*See*  Dalton, Talbot Percy

**Dalton, John P. [Jack]** 1889-1919
[FB]
*American football player*
* Three to Nothing Jack

**Dalton, Lacy J.**
*See*  Byrem, Jill

**Dalton, Priscilla**
*See*  Avallone, Michael [Angelo],
Jr.

**Dalton, Talbot Percy** 1885-    [PB]
*American baseball player*
* Dalton, Jack

**Dalton, William Julian** 1882-1941
[BEW, F1, FC]
*American actor and female
impersonator*
* Eltinge, Julian

**D'Altra, Marie** 1848?-1932    [BEW]
*Actress*
* Rignold, Marie

**Daly, Augustin**    [PA]
*Author*
* [Le] Perin

**Daly, Dixie**
*See*  Francis, Rosie

**Daly, Dutch**
*See*  Daly, William James

**Daly, George Joseph** 1887-1957
[BE]
*American baseball player*
* Daly, Pecks

**Daly, Hamlin**
*See*  Price, Edgar Hoffman

**Daly, James J.** 1865-1938    [BE]
*American baseball player*
* Daly, Sun

**Daly, Jim**
*See*  Stratemeyer, Edward L.

**Daly, John**
*See*  Besemeres, John

**Daly, Joseph** 1886-1926
[BX, RBE]
*American boxer*
* Thomas, Joe

**Daly, Mark**
*See*  Hobson, Mark

**Daly, [Sister] Mary Virgene**
*See*  Daly, Mary Virginia

**Daly, Mary Virginia** 1925-    [CA]
*American author*
* Daly, [Sister] Mary Virgene

**Daly, Maureen**
*See*  McGivern, Maureen Daly

**Daly, Pat**
*See*  Munger, Gordon C.

**Daly, Pauline** 20th c.    [SC]
*American opera singer and actress*
* Mansfield, Mary Lou

**Daly, Pecks**
*See*  Daly, George Joseph

**Daly, Sun**
*See*  Daly, James J.

**Daly, Thomas Peter** 1866-1939
[BE]
*American baseball player*
* Daly, Tido

**Daly, Tido**
*See*  Daly, Thomas Peter

**Daly, William James** 1848- ?
[THR]
*British comedian*
* Daly, Dutch

**Dalyell [or Dalzell], Thomas**
1599?-1685    [WBD]
*Scottish soldier*
* [The] Muscovy General

**Dalzel, Peter**
*See*  Dalzel Job, P[atrick]

**Dalzel Job, P[atrick]** 1913-    [CA]
*British writer*
* Dalzel, Peter

**Dalzell, Allan C.**
*See*  Pfeifer, Allan Cameron

**Dalziell, Denis** 1943-    [RO2]
*British musician*
* D'Ell, Denis

**Dam, Arbie**
*See*  Dam, Elbridge Rust

**Dam, Bill**
*See*  Dam, Elbridge Rust

**Dam, Elbridge Rust** 1885-1930
[BN]
*American baseball player*
* Dam, Arbie
* Dam, Bill

**Damas, Leon Gontran** 1912-1978
[CW]
*West Indian poet*
* Cabassou, Lionel George Andre

**Damaso De Alonso, Luis Antonio**
1905-    [F2, FC, ITA]
*Mexican-born actor*
* Roland, Gilbert

**Damasus II**
*See*  Poppo

**Damaszek, Marvin** 1925-    [BEW]
*American actor, comedian, writer*
* Deems, Mickey

**D'Amato, Elinor Barbara**    [IWM]
*American musician*
* Amati, Orlanda

**D'Amato, Maria Grazia Rosa
Domenica** 1942-    [EJ7]
*American singer*
* Muldaur, Maria

**D'Amboise, Jacques**
*See*  Ahearn, Jacques

**D'Ambre, Anne Caroline de V.**
[PA]
*Author*
* Coeur, Pierre

**Dambreville, Claude** 1932?-    [CW]
*Haitian author*
* Cyprien, Anatole

**D'Ambrosio, Charles A.** 1932-
[CA]
*American educator and author*
* Dollar Investor

**D'Ambrosio, Luigi** 1913-
[BBH, BX, RBE]
*American boxer*
* Ambers, Lou
* [The] Herkimer Hurricane

**Dame, Aurelia N.** 20th c.    [CEI]
*Canadian-born hockey player*
* Dame, Bunny

**Dame, Bunny**
*See*  Dame, Aurelia N.

**[La] Dame de Beaute**
*See*  Sorel, Agnes

**Dame, Lawrence** 1898-    [CAP]
*American author*
* Pomfret, Baron

**Dame Shirley**
*See*  Clappe, Louise Amelia Knapp
[Smith]

**Damelowicz** 13th c.    [FFF, SN]
*Prince of Halicz*
* [The] Lion

**Dameron, Tadd**
*See*  Dameron, Tadley Ewing

**Dameron, Tadley Ewing**
1917-1965    [ASC, EJ, PMJ]
*American jazz musician*
* Dameron, Tadd

**D'Ami, Rinaldo** 20th c.    [WECO]
*Italian cartoonist*
* D'Amy, Roy

**Damia**
See Damien, Marie Louise

**Damiano, Laila**
See Rosenkrantz, Linda

**Damien, Marie Louise** 1890?-1978
[FIR]
*French singer*
* Damia

**Damiens, Robert Francois**
1714?-1757 [DNNF, FFF, RH]
*Attempted to assassinate King Louis XV*
* [Le] Diable
* Robert the Devil

**Damita Jo**
See DuBlanc, Damita Jo

**Damita, Lili**
See Carre, Lilliane

**Damman, Wee Willie**
See Damman, William Henry [Bill]

**Damman, William Henry [Bill]**
1872-1948 [BE]
*American baseball player*
* Damman, Wee Willie

**Damne, Konrad**
See Jean, Eddy Arnold

**Damocles**
See Browne, Hablot Knight

**Damon, Carl**
See Demmon, Calvin W.

**Damon, Stuart**
See Zonis, Stuart Michael

**Damone, Vic**
See Farinola, Vito

**Damonte Toborda, Raul** 1939-
[WECO]
*Argentinian cartoonist*
* Copi

**Damor, Hakji**
See Lesser, Roger Harold

**Dampier, Claude**
See Cowan, Claude

**Dampier, [Sir] William Cecil**
See Whetham, William Cecil Dampier

**Damrosch, Helen Therese**
See Tee-Van, Helen Damrosch

**[The] Damsel of Brittany**
See Eleanor

**D'Amy, Roy**
See D'Ami, Rinaldo

**Dan, Fyodor I.**
See Gurvich, Fyodor I.

**Dana, Bill** 1924- [ASC]
*American comedian*
* Jimenez, Jose

**Dana, Mrs. J. M.** [FFF]
*American author*
* Aunt Adna

**Dana, Rose**
See Ross, William Edward Daniel

**Dana, Viola**
See Flugrath, Violet

**Danaher, Kevin** 1913- [CA]
*Irish educator and author*
* O Danachair, Caoimhin

**[The] Danburian**
See MacGeachy, Charles E. A.

**[The] Danbury Newsman**
See Bailey, James Montgomery

**Danby, Frank**
See Frankau, Julia [Davis]

**Danby, Mary**
See Calvert, Mary

**[The] Dancing Bear**
See McDole, Ron

**[The] Dancing Chancellor**
See Hatton, [Sir] Christopher

**[The] Dancing Chancellor**
See Nompar de Caumont, Antonin

**[The] Dancing Doll of the South**
See Wynn, Roberta Lee

**[The] Dancing Evangelist**
See Becton, George W.

**[The] Dancing Fool**
See Stanford, Jack

**Dancourt**
See Racot, Adolph

**Dancourt, Florent Carton**
1661-1725? [DEP, DNNS, RH]
*French playwright and comedian*
* [The] Teniers of Comedy

**Dancourt, Marie Anne Carton**
1685-1780 [PA]
*Author*
* Mimi

**Dancy, M. M.**
See McClendon, Marie Millicent Dancy

**Dancyger, Irene** 1926- [IAW]
*British author*
* Bridgeman, Irene
* James, Rachel

**Dandhu Panth** 1825?-1860?
[WBD]
*Leader of the Sepoy mutiny*
* Nana Sahib

**Dandilo, Kwame**
See Van P. Polanen

**D'Andouins, Diane** 1554-1620
[DNNS, RH, SN]
*Countess of Guiche and Grammont*
* [The] Beautiful Corisande
* [La] Belle Corisande

**D'Andrea, Kate** [joint pseudonym with Barbara A(nnette) Steiner]
See Phillips, Kathleen

**D'Andrea, Kate** [joint pseudonym with Kathleen Phillips]
See Steiner, Barbara A[nnette]

**Dandridge, Bobby** 1947- [IBW]
*American basketball player and coach*
* Dandridge, Pick

**Dandridge, Hooks**
See Dandridge, Raymond Emmett

**Dandridge, Louis** 1900?-1946
[PMJ, WWJ]
*American jazz musician*
* Dandridge, Putney

**Dandridge, Pick**
See Dandridge, Bobby

**Dandridge, Putney**
See Dandridge, Louis

**Dandridge, Raymond Emmett**
1913- [MK]
*American baseball player*
* Dandridge, Hooks

**Dandurand, Joseph Viateur**
1889-1964 [FHE, HK]
*American hockey team owner*
* Dandurand, Leo

**Dandurand, Leo**
See Dandurand, Joseph Viateur

**[The] Dandy Coloured Coon**
See Ruhlmann, Eugene Augustus

**Dandy Don Meredith**
See Meredith, Joe Don

**Dandy, Jess**
See Danzig, Jesse A.

**[The] Dandy Killer**
See Brummel, George Bryan

**[The] Dandy King**
See Murat, Joachim

**Dandy Phil Kastel**
See Kastel, Philip

**Dandy Sandy Saddler**
See Saddler, Joseph

**Dane, Barbara**
See Spillman, Barbara

**Dane, Carl**
See Adams, F[rank] Ramsay

**Dane, Clemence**
See Ashton, Winifred

**Dane, Donald**
See Cumming-Skinner, Dugald Matheson

**Dane, Joel Y.**
See Delany, Joseph Francis

**Dane, Karl**
See Gottlieb, Rasmus Karl Thekelsen

**Dane, Mark**
See Avallone, Michael [Angelo], Jr.

**Dane, Mary**
See Morland, Nigel

**Dane, W. N.?**
See Ackerman, Wendayne

**Dane, Zel**
See Timms, Edward Vivian

**Daneel, Sylvia**
See Lakomska, Sylvia Jadviga

**Danei, Paolo Francesco** 1694-1775
[FFF, SN, WBD]
*Saint*
* Paul of the Cross

**Danesford, Earle**
See Symonds, Francis Addington

**Daney, Art**
See Daney, Lee

**Daney, Lee** 1905- [BE]
*American baseball player*
* Daney, Art
* Daney, Whitehorn

**Daney, Lee** (Continued)
* Whitehorn, Arthur Lee

**Daney, Whitehorn**
See Daney, Lee

**Danforth, Dauntless Dave**
See Danforth, David Charles

**Danforth, David Charles**
1890-1970 [BE, PB]
*American baseball player*
* Danforth, Dauntless Dave

**Danforth, Ethel M.** 1908- [CA]
*American author*
* Hagar, George
* Maria Del Rey, [Sister]
* Victoria, [Sister] M.

**Danforth, Paul M.**
See Allen, John E[lliston]

**D'Angelo, Lou**
See D'Angelo, Luciano

**D'Angelo, Luciano** 1932- [CA]
*American author*
* D'Angelo, Lou

**Danger**
See Latude, Jean Henry

**Dangerfield, Balfour**
See McCloskey, [John] Robert

**Dangerfield, Captain**
See Anderson, G. J. B.

**Dangerfield, Clint**
See Norwood, Victor G[eorge] C[harles]

**Dangerfield, Harlan**
See Padgett, Ron

**Dangerfield, Harry**
See Patten, William George

**Dangerfield, John**
See Crawfurd, Oswald John Frederick

**Dangerfield, Rodney**
See Cohen, Jacob

**Dangerous Dan Newman**
See Newman, Kenneth Daniel

**Dangle**
See Thompson, Alexander Mattock

**Danican, Francois Andre**
1726?-1795 [DNNS, PA]
*French composer and chess player*
* Philidor

**Daniel** 12th c. [WBD]
*Russian ecclesiastic*
* [The] Pilgrim

**Daniel, Anita** 1893?-1978 [SAT]
*Rumanian-born author*
* Anita

**Daniel, Anne**
See Steiner, Barbara A[nnette]

**Daniel, Arnaud [Arnaut or Arnault]**
12th c. [DNNS, WBD]
*French troubadour*
* [The] Great Master of Love

**Daniel, Billy**
See Baker, William

**[The] Daniel Boone of Southern Kentucky**
See Lynn, Benjamin

**Daniel, Dan**
See Daniel, W. C.

**Daniel, Diamond**
See Daniel, Wayne Wendell

**Daniel, Elna Worrell**
See Stone, Elna

**Daniel, George** 1790-1864 [PA]
*Author*
* D. G.

**Daniel, Glyn [Edmund]** 1914-
[CA, CC, EMD]
*British archaeologist, educator, author*
* Rees, Dilwyn

**Daniel, Julii [or Yuli]** 1925?- [B10]
*Russian author*
* Arzhak, Nikolai

**Daniel, Laurent**
See Blick, Elsa

**Daniel, Mrs. Mackenzie**
See Pickering, Ellen

**Daniel Rops**
See Petiot, Henry Jules

**Daniel, Samuel** 1562-1619
[FFF, SN]
*British poet*
* Daniel, Well Languaged
* Musus

**Daniel, W. C.** 20th c. [IPA]
*American politician*
* Daniel, Dan

**Daniel, Wayne Wendell** 1956-
[DC]
*West Indian cricketer*
* Daniel, Diamond

**Daniel, Well Languaged**
See Daniel, Samuel

**Danielewski, Tad**
See Danielewski, Tadeusz Zbigniew

**Danielewski, Tadeusz Zbigniew**
1921- [BEW]
*Polish-born American director, producer, scenarist*
* Danielewski, Tad

**Daniell, Albert Scott** 1906-1965
[CA]
*British author*
* Bowood, Richard
* Daniell, David Scott
* Lewesdon, John

**Daniell, Charles Addison** 19th c.
[PA]
*Author*
* Addison, D. C.

**Daniell, David Scott**
See Daniell, Albert Scott

**Daniels, Bebe**
See Daniels, Virginia

**Daniels, Bernard Elmer** 1882-1958
[BE]
*American baseball player*
* Daniels, Bert

**Daniels, Bert**
See Daniels, Bernard Elmer

**Daniels, Bo**
See Daniels, Clemon

**Daniels, Charles N.** 1878-1943
[ASC, PMJ]
*American composer*
* Moret, Neil

**Daniels, Clemon** 1937- [FB]
*American football player*
* Daniels, Bo

**Daniels, Coralin** [PA]
*Author*
* Lucrece

**Daniels, Danny**
See Giagni, Danny

**Daniels, Dellareese** 1960- [IBW]
*American fashion model*
* Daniels, Dumpsy

**Daniels, Dorothy** 1915- [CA]
*American author*
* Dorsett, Danielle
* Gray, Angela
* Kavanaugh, Cynthia
* Ross, Helaine
* Somers, Suzanne
* Thayer, Geraldine
* Weston, Helen Gray

**Daniels, Dumpsy**
See Daniels, Dellareese

**Daniels, Fred Clinton** 1924- [BE]
*American baseball player*
* Daniels, Tony

**Daniels, Frederick Edward** 1908-
[AW]
*British editor*
* Friars, Austin

**Daniels, [Harold] Jack** 1927- [BE]
*American baseball player*
* Daniels, Sour Mash

**Daniels, John S.**
See Overholser, Wayne D.

**Daniels, Law**
See Daniels, Lawrence Long

**Daniels, Lawrence Long**
1862-1929 [BE]
*American baseball player*
* Daniels, Law

**Daniels, Leon** 20th c. [OBW]
*American baseball player*
* Daniels, Pepper

**Daniels, Louis G.**
See Galouye, Daniel F[rancis]

**Daniels, Mrs.** [FFF]
*Entertainer*
* Raymond, Louise

**Daniels, Norman [A.]** 20th c.
[CA, SFL, SFP]
*American author*
* Benton, John
* Brady, Peter
* Brooker, Wallace
* Jones, G. Wayman [house pseudonym]
* Judd, Harrison
* Robeson, Kenneth [house pseudonym, Street & Smith]

**Daniels, Pepper**
See Daniels, Leon

**Daniels, Shouri**
See Ramanujan, Molly

**Daniels, Sour Mash**
See Daniels, [Harold] Jack

**Daniels, Tony**
See Daniels, Fred Clinton

**Daniels, Victor** 1899?-1955
[FC, ITA]
*American actor*
* Thundercloud, Chief

**Daniels, Virginia** 1901-1971
[BDF, FC, PMJ]
*American actress*
* Daniels, Bebe

**Danielson, J. D.**
See James, M. R.

**Danilo, Don**
See Dewey, Elmer

**Danilowitz, Abraham Phineas** 20th
c. [EJS]
*South African lawn bowler*
* Danilowitz, Pinky

**Danilowitz, Pinky**
See Danilowitz, Abraham Phineas

**[The] Danish Butler**
See Holberg, Louis [or Ludvig]

**[The] Danish Lafontaine**
See Andersen, Hans Christian

**[The] Danish Luther**
See Tausen, Hans

**[The] Danish Moliere**
See Holberg, Louis [or Ludvig]

**[The] Danish Nelson**
See Wessel, Peder

**[The] Danish Perry Como**
See Fabric, Bent

**[The] Danish Plautus**
See Holberg, Louis [or Ludvig]

**[The] Danish Viking**
See Pipgras, George

**Dank, David**
See Zweibelsharf, David

**D'Anka, Cornelie**
See Ingram, Mrs.

**Dannay, Frederic**
See Nathan, Daniel

**Dannecker, John Heinrich**
1758-1841 [HN]
*German sculptor*
* [The] Nestor of German Sculptors

**Dannenberg, George** [PA]
*Author*
* Raimund, Golo

**Danner, Buck**
See Danner, Henry Frederick

**Danner, Henry Frederick**
1891-1949 [BE]
*American baseball player*
* Danner, Buck

**Danning, Harry** 1911-
[BE, EJS, PB]
*American baseball player*
* Harry the Horse
* [The] Horse

**Danning, Melrod**
See Gluck, Sinclair

**D'Annunzio, Gabriele** 1863-1938
[EWL, TC, WBD]
*Italian poet, author, military leader*
* Duca Minimo [The Least of the Dukes]
* Rapagnetto-D'Annunzio, Gabriele [original family surname?]

**Danny the Red**
See Cohn-Bendit, Daniel

**Dano, Tony**
See Soldano, Anthony

**Danoff, Kathy** 1944- [RO2]
*American singer*
* Danoff, Taffy

**Danoff, Taffy**
See Danoff, Kathy

**Danrit, Captain**
See Driant, Emile A[ugustin Cyprien]

**Danry, Jean**
See Latude, Jean Henry

**Dansey, Herbert**
See Tassinari, Berte Danyell

**Dante**
See Alighieri, Durante

**Dante**
See Jansen, Harry August

**Dante, Michael**
See Vitti, Ralph

**[The] Dante of Philosophy**
See Pico, John Baptist

**D'Antibes, Germain**
See Simenon, Georges [Joseph Christian]

**Dantin, Louis**
See Seers, Eugene

**Dantley, Adrian** 20th c. [IBW]
*American basketball player*
* A. D.

**Danton, Georges Jacques**
1759-1794 [DEP, HN, SN]
*French revolutionary leader*
* [The] Mirabeau of the Markets
* [The] Mirabeau of the Mob
* [The] Mirabeau of the Sans Culottes
* [The] Strong Arm

**Danton, Jean Pierre** 1800-1869
[WBD]
*French sculptor*
* [The] Younger

**[The] Danton of Modern Poetry**
See Browning, Robert

**[The] Danton of the Cevennes**
See Seguier, Pierre

**[The] Danton of the Gironde**
See Isnard, Maximin

**Danton, Rebecca**
See Roberts, Janet Louise

**Dantonio, Fats**
See Dantonio, John James

**Dantonio, John James** 1919- [BE]
*American baseball player*
* Dantonio, Fats

**Dantzler, Louise** 1908-    [FC]
*American actress*
* Brian, Mary

**D'Anvers, Caleb**
See   Amherst, Nicholas

**Danvers, Jack**
See   Caseleyr, Cam[ille Auguste Marie]

**Dany**
See   Henrotin, Daniel

**Danzell, George**
See   Bond, Nelson S[lade]

**Danzig, Babe**
See   Danzig, Harold P.

**Danzig, Harold P.** 1887-    [BE]
*American baseball player*
* Danzig, Babe

**Danzig, Jesse A.** 1871-1923    [SC]
*American actor*
* Dandy, Jess

**Danziger, Adolphe**
See   De Castro, Gustaf Adolf Danziger

**Danziger, Gustav A.**
See   De Castro, Gustaf Adolf Danziger

**D'Apery, Helen [Burrell]** 1842-1915    [WW]
*Author*
* Harper, Olive

**Daphne**
See   Davenant, [Sir] William

**Dapper Dan Currie**
See   Currie, Daniel

**Dapper Dan Flood**
See   Flood, Daniel J.

**Dapper Dan Howley**
See   Howley, Daniel Philip

**Dapper Don Collins**
See   Tourbillon, Robert Arthur

**Daquin, Felicity**
See   Deakin, Phyllis A.

**D'Aquino, Iva Ikuko [Toguri]** 1916-
*Japanese-American propagandist during World War II*
* Orphan Annie
* Tokyo Rose?

**Darashaw, F.**
See   Colaabavala, Firooze Darashaw

**Darby, Big Ike**
See   Darby, Ike

**Darby, Blind Blues**
See   Darby, Theodore [Teddy]

**Darby, Catherine**
See   Peters, Maureen

**Darby, Christopher Lovett** 20th c.    [SFL]
*Author*
* Oudeis

**Darby, George**    [PA]
*Author*
* G. D.

**Darby, Ike** 1933-    [BWW]
*American singer*
* Darby, Big Ike

**Darby, J. N.**
See   Govan, [Mary] Christine Noble

**Darby, John**
See   Garretson, J. E.

**Darby, Ken**
See   Lorin, Kenneth

**Darby, Kim**
See   Zerby, Deborah [or Derby?]

**Darby, Teddy Roosevelt**
See   Darby, Theodore [Teddy]

**Darby, Theodore [Teddy]** 1906-    [BWW]
*American singer*
* Darby, Blind Blues
* Darby, Teddy Roosevelt
* Turner, Blind Squire

**Darcel, Denise**
See   Billecard, Denise

**Darcy**
See   Cadry, Jean Baptiste

**D'Arcy, Alex**
See   Sarruf, Alexander

**D'Arcy, Colin** 1912-    [ASC]
*American musician*
* Young, Billy

**Darcy [or D'Arcy], Don**
See   Arcesi, John

**D'Arcy, Jack**
See   Champion, D. L.

**Darcy, James Leslie** 1895-1917    [BX]
*Australian boxer*
* Darcy, Les

**Darcy, Jean**
See   Lepley, Jean Elizabeth

**Darcy, Les**
See   Darcy, James Leslie

**D'Arcy, Roy**
See   Guisti, Roy F.

**D'Arcy, Ruth** 20th c.    [B10]
*American columnist and editor*
* Lee, Jane

**D'Arcy, Sheila**
See   Heffner, Rebecca

**D'Arcy-Orga, Ates** 1944-    [WD]
*British author*
* Orga, Ates

**Darden, Thomas** 20th c.    [BBH]
*American sailboat racer*
* Darden, Toby

**Darden, Toby**
See   Darden, Thomas

**Dare, Alan**
See   Goodchild, George

**DaRe, Aldo** 1926-    [BDF, FC, ITA]
*American actor*
* Ray, Aldo

**Dare, Captain**
See   Shaw, Stanley Gordon

**Dare, Dorris**
See   Prince, Dorris

**Dare, Evelyn**
See   Everett-Green, Evelyn

**Dare, Howard**
See   Byrne, Stuart J[ames]

**Dare, M. P.**
See   Dare, Marcus Paul

**Dare, Marcus Paul** 1902-1962    [HFF]
*British author*
* Dare, M. P.

**Dare, Mrs. T. S.**    [FFF]
*Entertainer*
* Hall, Ada

**Dare, Phyllis**
See   Dones, Phyllis

**Dare, Roland**
See   Morris, Charles Smith

**Dare, Shirley**
See   Power, Susan C. Dunning

**Dare, Simon**
See   Huxtable, Marjorie

**Dare, Sydney**
See   Cochrane, Martha J.

**Dare, Zena**
See   Dones, Zena

**Dareff, Hal** 1920-    [CA]
*American author*
* Foley, Scott

**Dargan, Clara V.** 19th c.    [FFF]
*American writer*
* Claudia

**Dargan, Olive [Tilford]** 20th c.    [ANT, TC]
*American author and poet*
* Burke, Fielding

**Dargon, Augusta**
See   Piercy, Mrs.

**D'Argyre, Gilles**
See   Klein, Gerard

**Darian**
See   Dingle, Adrian

**Darien, Peter**
See   Bassett, William B. K.

**Darin, Bobby**
See   Cassotto, Walden Robert

**Daring, Victor**
See   Gannon, E. J.

**Daringer, Cliff[ord Clarence]** 1885-    [BE]
*American baseball player*
* Daringer, Shanty

**Daringer, Shanty**
See   Daringer, Cliff[ord Clarence]

**Dario, Ruben**
See   Garcia y Sarmiento, Felix Ruben

**Darius I** 6th c. BC    [DNNS, SN, WBD]
*King of Persia*
* Ahasuerus [Lion-Hearted]
* [The] Great
* [The] Huckster
* Hystaspis [Son of Hystaspes]

**Darius II**
See   Ochus

**Darius III** 4th c. BC    [WBD]
*King of Persia*
* Codomannus

**Dark, Alvin Ralph** 1922-    [BE]
*American baseball player and manager*
* Dark, Blackie

**Dark Angel of the Violin**
See   South, Eddie

**Dark, Blackie**
See   Dark, Alvin Ralph

**[The] Dark Horse President**
See   Hayes, Rutherford Birchard

**Dark, James**
See   Workman, James

**Dark, Johnny**
See   Norwood, Victor G[eorge] C[harles]

**[The] Dark Lantern Man**
See   St. John, Oliver

**[The] Dark Priest**
See   Mouskos, Mikhail

**Darkcloud, Beulah**
See   Filson, Beulah T.

**D'Arlhac, M.**    [PA]
*Author*
* Gerald

**[The] Darling**
See   Booth, Amos Smith

**Darling Amos Booth**
See   Booth, Amos Smith

**Darling, Bernard** 20th c.    [SMG]
*American football player*
* Darling, Boob

**Darling, Bessie**
See   Berry, Mrs. Charles

**Darling, Boob**
See   Darling, Bernard

**Darling, Candy**
See   Slattery, James

**Darling, Ding**
See   Darling, Jay Norwood

**Darling, Hope**
See   Johnson, Anna M.

**Darling, Jay Norwood** 1876-1962    [NAA, WA, WEC]
*American cartoonist and author*
* Darling, Ding
* Ding

**Darling, Jean**
See   LeVake, Dorothy Jean

**Darling, John** 1936-    [OP]
*British opera singer*
* Wakefield, John

**Darling, Joseph Robinson** 1872- ?    [NAA]
*American civil engineer and author*
* Don Jose

**[The] Darling of European Swimming**
See   Den Ouden, Willy

**[The] Darling of Mankind**
See   Sabinus Vespasianus, Titus Flavius

**[The] Darling of Mankind**
See   Vespasian, Titus Flavius Sabinus

**[The] Darling of the Graces**
See   Aristophanes

[The] Darling of the Graces
See Heine, Harry

[The] Darling of the Nine
See Manning, Thomas

Darlington, W. A.
See Darlington, William Aubrey

Darlington, William Aubrey 1890-
[BEW, LC]
British drama critic and playwright
* Darlington, W. A.

Darlouze, Rene 1876-1938 [CW]
Haitian poet, playwright, author
* Moravia, Charles

Darlton, Clark
See Ernsting, Walter

D'Arnal, Etienne 1733-1801 [PA]
Author
* Scipion

Darnel, Bill
See Darnell, Bill

Darnell, Bill 1920- [PMJ]
American singer
* Darnel, Bill

Darnell, Linda
See Darnell, Marietta Eloisa

Darnell, Marietta Eloisa
1921?-1965 [BDF, FC]
American actress
* Darnell, Linda

Darnley, Herbert
See McCarthy, Herbert

Darppil
See Lippard, George

Darragh, Darrach
See Moriarty, W[illia]m Daniel

Darragh, Miss
See Dallas, Letitia Marion

Darran, Mark
See Goddard, Norman Molyneux

Darrell, Maisie
See Hardie, Maisie

Darrell, Walter
See Burrage, Edwin Harcourt

Darren, James
See Ercolani, James

Darrich, Sybah
See Di Prima, Diane

Darrid, William
See Blum, William David

Darrington, Hugh 1940- [SFL]
British author
* Ross, James [joint pseudonym
   with Tony Halliwell]

Darro, Frankie
See Johnson, Frank

Darroch, Sandra Jobson 1942-
[CA]
Australian-born author
* Jobson, Sandra

Darrow, Alice Vicki 20th c.
Suspected embezzler
* Smith, Barbara Newman

Darrow, Jack
See Kornoelje, Clifford

Dart, Rufus, II
See Kline, Burton

D'Artois, Henri Charles Ferdinand
Marie 1820-1883
[DNNF, FF, FFF]
Claimant to French throne
* Chambord, Comte de
* Dieu-Donne [God-Given]
* [The] Miraculous Child

D'Artois, Louis [FFF, RH]
French aristocrat
* [The] First Gentleman of Europe

Darvi, Bella
See Wegier, Bayla

Darwell, Jane
See Woodward, Patti

Darwin, M. B.
See McDavid, Raven I[oor], Jr.

Daryl, Phillipe
See Grousset, Paschal

Daryl, Sydney
See Straight, Douglas

Das, Kamala 1934- [WD]
Indian poet and author
* Madhavikutty

Das, Prafulla Chandra 1927- [AW]
Indian author
* Subhadra-Nandan

Dash, Comtesse
See De St. Mars, Vicomtesse

Dash, Pauly
See Dashiff, Paul Walter

Dashaway, Kate
See Ward, Mabella Ann

Dashiff, Paul Walter 1918-1974
[SC]
American actor
* Dash, Pauly

Dashing Dan Costello
See Costello, Dan[iel Francis]

Dashmore, Frank
See Downing, Fanny Murdaugh

Dashner, Lee Claire 1887-1959
[BE]
American baseball player
* Dashner, Lefty

Dashner, Lefty
See Dashner, Lee Claire

Dashwood, Robert Julian 1899-
[CAP]
British author
* Hillas, Julian

DaSilva, Leon
See Wallmann, Jeffrey M[iner]

Daskam, Josephine Dodge
See Bacon, Josephine Dodge
[Daskam]

Dass, Petter 1647-1708 [WBD]
Norwegian clergyman and poet
* [The] Father of Modern
   Norwegian Poetry

Dassault, Darius P.
See Bloch, Darius P.

Dassault, Marcel
See Bloch, Marcel

Dassler, Adi
See Dassler, Adolf

Dassler, Adolf 1901?-1978
American business executive
* Dassler, Adi

Dastagir, Sabu 1924-1963
[B10, BEW, CED]
Indian actor
* Sabu

Datas
See Bottle, J. M.

Dati, Carlo Roberto 1619-1675
[SN]
Italian scholar and author
* [The] Bewildered
* Smarrito

Daub, Daniel William 1868-1951
[BE]
American baseball player
* Daub, Mickey

Daub, Mickey
See Daub, Daniel William

Dauban, M. L.
See Dauban, May Lilian

Dauban, May Lilian 1907- [ART]
British painter
* Dauban, M. L.

Daube, Belle 1888-1959 [SC]
British-born actress
* Daube, Harda

Daube, Harda
See Daube, Belle

D'Aubigne, Francoise 1635-1719
[DNNS, FF, SN]
Wife of King Louis XIV of France
* [La] Belle Indienne
* Maintenon, Marquise de
* Solidity, Madame
* Votre Solidite

Daudet, Alphonse 1840-1897
[DNNS, FFF]
French author
* [The] French Dickens
* Froissart, Jean

Daudet, Ernest [PA]
Author
* Reymond, Louis

Daudet, Julie Rosalie Celeste
1847-1940 [FFF]
French author and poet
* Sterne, Karl

Daufel, Andre
See Van Offel, David

Dauferius 1027-1087 [WBD]
Pope
* Desiderius
* Victor III

Daugherty, Doc
See Daugherty, Harold Ray

Daugherty, Duffy
See Daugherty, Hugh

Daugherty, Harold Ray 1927- [BE]
American baseball player
* Daugherty, Doc

Daugherty, Hugh 1915- [FB]
American football coach
* Daugherty, Duffy

[The] Daughter of the Confederacy
See Davis, Varina Anne Jefferson

Daughter of the Nile
See Kalthoum, Um

Daughters, Red
See Daughters, Robert Francis
[Bob]

Daughters, Robert Francis [Bob]
1914- [BE]
American baseball player
* Daughters, Red

Daughtry, Bird
See Daughtry, Eugene

Daughtry, Eugene 20th c. [RO2]
American singer
* Daughtry, Bird

Daukes, Sidney Herbert 1879- ?
[WGT]
Author
* Fairway, Sidney

Daumer, Georg Friedrich
1800-1875 [WBD]
German author and poet
* Eusebius Emmeran

Daumier, Honore Victorin
1818?-1879 [FFF]
French caricaturist
* [The] Aristophanes of Caricature

Daun, [Count] Leopold von
1705-1766 [HN]
Austrian army officer
* [The] Fabius of Austria

D'Aunet, Leonie
See Baird, Madame

Daunt, Atherley
See Evans, Frank Howel

Daunt, William
See Busteed, William

Daunt, William Joseph O'Neill
1807-1894 [PA]
Author
* [An] Ex M. P.
* Moriarty, Denis Ignatius

Dauntless Dave Danforth
See Danforth, David Charles

[Le] Dauphin
See Guy VIII

Dauphin, Claude
See LeGrand, Claude Maria
Eugent

Daurat, Jean 1507-1588 [PA]
Author
* Auratus

Daurignac, J. M. S.
See Orliac, Mme. J. M. S.

Dauss, George August 1889-1963
[AS, BE, PB]
American baseball player
* Dauss, Hooks

Dauss, Hooks
See Dauss, George August

D'Autremont, Roy 20th c. [BLB]
American train robber and murderer
* Elliott, William

Davalillo, Pompeyo Antonio 1931-
[BE]
Venezuelan-born baseball player
* Davalillo, Yo-Yo

Davalillo, Yo-Yo
See Davalillo, Pompeyo Antonio

**Davaux, Jean Baptiste** ?-1822
[DNNF, FFF, SN]
*French composer*
* [The] Father of the Rondo
* [Le] Pere aux Rondeaux

**Dave Baby Cortez**
See Clowney, David Cortez

**Dave, Shyam** [joint pseudonym with Hugh Gantzer]
See Gantzer, Colleen

**Dave, Shyam** [joint pseudonym with Colleen Gantzer]
See Gantzer, Hugh

**Davenant, [Sir] William** 1606-1668
[SN]
*British poet and playwright*
* Daphne
* Jeered Will
* Old Daph
* [A] Poetical Rochefoucault

**Davenport, Arthur Rankin** 1900-1947
*American actor*
* Rankin, Arthur

**Davenport, Bear Man**
See Davenport, Lloyd

**Davenport, Burnu** 1920- [FC]
*American actress*
* Acquanetta

**Davenport, Charles [Edward]**
1894?-1955 [BWW, DAM, EJ]
*American jazz musician*
* Bat the Hummingbird
* Davenport, Cow Cow
* Georgia Grinder
* Hamilton, George
* Memphis Slim

**Davenport, Christopher** 1598-1680
[FFF]
*British clergyman*
* Sancta Clara

**Davenport, Cow Cow**
See Davenport, Charles [Edward]

**Davenport, Elizabeth** [HN]
*Actress*
* Lord Oxford's Miss
* Roxalana

**Davenport, Fanny**
See Price, Mrs. E. H.

**Davenport, Francine**
See Tate, Velma

**Davenport, Gertrude Mary** ?-1972
[LC]
*British writer and translator*
* Paul, Cedar

**Davenport, Guy [Mattison], Jr.**
1927- [CA]
*American educator, author, poet*
* Montgomery, Max

**Davenport, James Houston** 1933-
[SMG]
*American baseball coach*
* Davenport, Peanut

**Davenport, Lloyd** 20th c. [OBW]
*American baseball player*
* Davenport, Bear Man

**Davenport, Louise**
See Sheridan, Mrs. W. H.

**Davenport, May**
See Seymour, Mrs. William

**Davenport, Peanut**
See Davenport, James Houston

**Davenport, Spencer**
See Stratemeyer, Edward L.

**Davenport, Tex**
See Tiltman, Hugh Hessell

**Davenson, Henri**
See Marrou, Henri Irenee

**Davertige**
See Denis, Villard

**Davey, Frank**
See Davey, Frankland Wilmot

**Davey, Frankland Wilmot** 1940-
[CA]
*Canadian poet*
* Davey, Frank

**Davey, Jocelyn**
See Raphael, Chaim

**Davey, John**
See Richey, David

**Davey, Mary Augusta** 1865-1932
[BEW]
*American actress, director, producer*
* Fiske, Minnie Maddern

**Davey, Nuna**
See Symonds, Margaret

**Daviault, Pierre** 1899- [NAA]
*Canadian journalist and author*
* Hartex, Pierre

**David**
See Abraham, David

**David**
See Greenway, Roger

**David** [HN]
*Irish aristocrat*
* [The] Harp of Ireland

**David** 520?- 589? [FFF]
*Saint*
* [The] Apostle of Wales

**David, Emily** [joint pseudonym with Emily Alman]
See Alman, David

**David, Emily** [joint pseudonym with David Alman]
See Alman, Emily

**David, Ernst**
See Eichler, Ernst

**[The] David Harum of Hockey**
See Smythe, Constantine Falkland Kerrys

**David, Jacques Louis** 1748-1825
[HN, SN]
*French painter*
* [The] Artist of the Revolution

**David, Jay**
See Adler, William [Bill]

**David, Jonathan**
See Ames, Lee J[udah]

**David, K.**
See Robertson, Alice Alberthe

**David, Moses**
See Berg, David Brandt

**David, Mrs. Frank** [FFF]
*Entertainer*
* Bartine, Jennie

**David, Nicholas**
See Morgan, Thomas Bruce

**David, Paul**
See Robison, David Victor

**David, Vincent**
See Di Biase, Edoardo J.

**David, William**
See Sandman, Peter M[ark]

**David I** 1084-1153 [WBD]
*King of Scotland*
* [The] Scotch Justinian

**Davidge, Mrs. William, Jr.** [FFF]
*Entertainer*
* Harold, Maggie

**Davidoff, Abraham** 20th c.
[EJS, SG]
*American boxer*
* Davis, Al
* Davis, Bummy

**Davidor, Robert** 1886?-1956
[THR]
*Russian-born producer and director*
* Milton, Robert

**Davidov [or Davidoff], Denis**
**Vassilievitch** 1784-1839
[DNNS, RH]
*Russian army officer and poet*
* [The] Black Captain
* [Le] Capitaine Noir

**Davids, Charles**
See Wingham, Charles Wing

**Davids, John**
See Dixwell, John

**Davidsohn, Hans** 1887-1942 [TCL]
*German poet*
* Van Hoddis, Jakob

**Davidson, Allan M.** 1892- ?
[FHE, HK]
*Canadian-born hockey player*
* Davidson, Scotty

**Davidson, Big John**
See Davidson, John Arthur

**Davidson, Bing**
See Davidson, James B.

**Davidson, Clarissa Start**
See Lippert, Clarissa Start

**Davidson, Claude Boucher**
1896-1956 [BE]
*American baseball player*
* Davidson, Davey

**Davidson, Cuffee**
See Cuffee, Ed[ward Emerson]

**Davidson, Davey**
See Davidson, Claude Boucher

**Davidson, David** 20th c.
*American television scriptwriter*
* Sanders, Albert

**Davidson, David Leroy** 1935-
[NLG]
*American baseball umpire*
* Davidson, Satch

**Davidson, Divvy**
See Davidson, Homer Hurd

**Davidson, Dora** [FFF]
*Entertainer*
* Austin, Ramie

**Davidson, Gene A.**
See Lesperance, David

**Davidson, Gladys** 20th c. [WWL]
*British author*
* G. D.

**Davidson, Hilda Roderick Ellis**
1914- [CA]
*British educator and author*
* Ellis, Hilda Roderick

**Davidson, Homer Hurd** 1884-1948
[BE]
*American baseball player*
* Davidson, Divvy

**Davidson, Hugh**
See Hamilton, Edmond [Moore]

**Davidson, Ian Stuart** 1936- [ART]
*British sculptor*
* I. D.

**Davidson, Israel**
See Movshovitz, Israel

**Davidson, James B.** 1939-1965
[SC]
*American actor*
* Davidson, Bing

**Davidson, James Wood** [FFF]
*Journalist*
* Corsair

**Davidson, Jennie** 1900-1973 [MS]
*Russian-born opera singer*
* Tourel, Jennie

**Davidson, John**
See Reid, Charles [Stuart]

**Davidson, John Arthur** 1953-
[SMG]
*Canadian-born hockey player*
* Davidson, Big John
* J. D.

**Davidson, Lawrence H.**
See Lawrence, David Herbert

**Davidson, Margaret** 1936- [CA]
*American author*
* Compere, Mickie
* Davidson, Mickie

**Davidson, Marion**
See Garis, Howard Roger

**Davidson, Michael**
See Rorvik, David M[ichael]

**Davidson, Mickie**
See Davidson, Margaret

**Davidson, Rufus Eldon** 20th c.
[CWG]
*American country-western performer*
* Davis, Rufe

**Davidson, Satch**
See Davidson, David Leroy

**Davidson, Scotty**
See Davidson, Allan M.

**Davidson, Ted**
See Davidson, Thomas Eugene

**Davidson, Thomas Eugene** 1939-
[BE]
*American baseball player*
* Davidson, Ted

**Davidson, Virginia E.** [FFF]
*American writer*
* Virginia

**Davidson, Wilder Bristol**
See   Patterson, Arthur W.

**Davie, Pinkle**
See   Davie, Robert H.

**Davie, Robert H.** 1912-    [CEI]
*Canadian-born hockey player*
* Davie, Pinkle

**Davie, Robert Worthington** 1897-
[NAA]
*American poet and technical writer*
* Hunt, Robert Lile

**Davie-Martin, Hugh**
See   McCutcheon, Hugh
Davie-Martin

**Davied, Camille**
See   Rose, Camille Davied

**Davies, Antoni Douglas** 1946-
[ART]
*Scottish potter*
* D. D.

**Davies, Betty Evelyn** 20th c.    [WW]
*Author*
* Warwick, Pauline

**Davies, Blodwen** 1897-    [NAA]
*Canadian author*
* Abbott, Brook

**Davies, Buck**
See   Davies, Kenneth George

**Davies, Cecilia**    [SN]
*British singer*
* [L']Inglesina

**Davies, Charles** 1900-    [BB]
*American basketball coach*
* Davies, Chick

**Davies, Chick**
See   Davies, Charles

**Davies, Chick**
See   Davies, Lloyd Garrison

**Davies, Christie**
See   Davies, John Christopher
Hughes

**Davies, Colin**
See   Elliot, Ian

**Davies, David Ivor** 1893-1951
[EMT, FC, WBD]
*Welsh-born composer, playwright,
actor*
* Novello, Ivor

**Davies, David Margerison** 1923-
[AW, CA]
*Welsh-born physician and author*
* Margerson, David

**Davies, Eileen Winifred** 1910-
[CAP]
*British author*
* Elias, Eileen

**Davies, Ernest** 1873- ?    [WW]
*Author*
* Martin, Oliver

**Davies, Frances** 1883-1952    [BBD]
*New Zealand-born opera singer*
* Alda, Frances

**Davies, Fredric** [joint pseudonym
with Steve Tolliver]
See   Ellik, Ron[ald C.]

**Davies, Fredric** [joint pseudonym
with Ron(ald C.) Ellik]
See   Tolliver, Steve

**Davies, Gwen**
See   Levy, Estelle

**Davies, Howell** 20th c.
[ESF, SFL, WGT]
*British author*
* Marvell, Andrew

**Davies, Jasper** 20th c.    [WD]
*British author, screenwriter,
playwright*
* Mather, Berkely

**Davies, Joan Howard** 20th c.
[AW, WD]
*British author*
* Drake, Joan

**Davies, John Christopher Hughes**
1941-    [CA, IAW]
*British sociologist and author*
* Davies, Christie

**Davies, Kenneth George** 1922-
[CEI]
*Canadian-born hockey player*
* Davies, Buck

**Davies, Leslie Purnell** 1914-
[CA, WD]
*British author*
* Berne, Leo
* Blake, Robert
* Bridgeman, Richard
* Evans, Morgan
* Jefferson, Ian
* Peters, Lawrence
* Philips, Thomas
* Thomas, G. K.
* Vardre, Leslie
* Welch, Rowland

**Davies, Lloyd Garrison** 1892-    [BE]
*American baseball player*
* Davies, Chick

**Davies, Louise**
See   Golding, Louise Sarah

**Davies, Lucian**
See   Beeston, L. J.

**Davies, M. C.**
See   Davies, Mary Catherine

**Davies, Marion**
See   Douras, Marion Cecilia

**Davies, Mary Catherine** 20th c.
[WGT]
*Author*
* Davies, M. C.

**Davies, Mrs. Christian**    [RH, SN]
*British soldier*
* [A] Female Soldier
* Ross, Mother

**Davies, Naunton** 1901-1970    [THR]
*Welsh-born actor*
* Wayne, Naunton

**Davies, Noel**
See   Hicklin, Noel Anthony

**Davies, O. T.**    [RBE]
*Boxer*
* Davis, O. T.

**Davies, Ramona**
See   Myers, Ramona

**Davies, Robert** 1770-1836    [SN]
*Welsh author*
* Bard Nantglyn

**Davies, Robert E. [Bob]** 1920-
[BB, BBH]
*American basketball player*
* [The] Harrisburg Houdini

**Davies, Robertson** 1913-
[CLC, DLE]
*Canadian author, playwright, critic*
* Marchbanks, Samuel

**Davies, Trevor** 20th c.    [RM]
*Musician*
* Dozy

**Davies, W. H.**
See   Davies, William Henry

**Davies, Walter C.**
See   Kornbluth, Cyril M.

**Davies, William** 1771-1824    [PA]
*Author*
* Goff, Elijir

**Davies, William Henry** 1871-1940
[LC]
*British poet*
* Davies, W. H.

**Daviess, Jo**
See   Daviess, Joseph Hamilton

**Daviess, Joseph Hamilton** ?-1811
[FFF]
*American attorney and author*
* Daviess, Jo

**Davila Garibi, Jose Ignacio** 1888-
[NAA]
*Mexican attorney and author*
* Motolinicafoutli

**Davila-Jimeno, Raul** 20th c.
*Colombian underworld figure*
* [The] Black Tuna

**Davila y Padilla, Agustin**
1562-1604    [WBD]
*Mexican historian*
* [The] Chronicler of the Indies

**Davin, Nicholas Francis Flood**
[PA]
*Author*
* E.
* Templeton, Tristram

**Davino**
See   Kotkin, David

**Daviot, Gordon**
See   Mackintosh, Elizabeth

**Davis, A. W.** 1943-    [BB]
*American basketball player*
* [The] Man with the Golden Arm

**Davis, A. W.** 20th c.    [MBF]
*British author*
* Richards, Frank [house
pseudonym]

**Davis, [Daisie] Adelle** 1904-1974
[CA]
*American nutritionist and author*
* Dunlap, Jane

**Davis, Al**
See   Davidoff, Abraham

**Davis, Al** 1917-    [MY]
*American jazz musician*
* Davis, Slim

**Davis, Alabam**
See   Davis, Bob

**Davis, Alfonzo DeFord** 1875-1919
[BE]
*American baseball player*
* Davis, Lefty

**Davis, Andrea**
See   Riperton, Minnie

**Davis, Andrew Jackson** 1826- ?
[DNNS, RH]
*American spiritualist*
* [The] Poughkeepsie Seer

**Davis, Arthur Willard** 1942-    [BE]
*American baseball player*
* Davis, Bill

**Davis, Babe**
See   Davis, Spencer

**Davis, Babe**
See   Davis, Woodrow Wilson

**Davis, Bee Jay**
See   Davis, Betty Jack

**Davis, Betty Jack** 20th c.    [RO1]
*American country-western performer*
* Davis, Bee Jay

**Davis, Bill**
See   Davis, Arthur Willard

**Davis, Blind Gary**
See   Davis, Gary

**Davis, Blind John**
See   Davis, John Henry

**Davis, Bob** 1910-1971    [SC]
*American actor*
* Davis, Alabam

**Davis, Brandy**
See   Davis, Robert Brandon

**Davis, Brock**
See   Davis, Bryshear Barnett

**Davis, Bryshear Barnett** 1943-
[BE, PB]
*American baseball player*
* Davis, Brock

**Davis, Bud**
See   Davis, John Wilbur

**Davis, Bummy**
See   Davidoff, Abraham

**Davis, Burton** 1893-    [WW]
*Author*
* Saunders, Lawrence [joint
pseudonym with Clarisy
Musadore (Ogden) Davis]

**Davis, Buster**
See   Davis, Carl Estes, Jr.

**Davis, Butch**
See   Davis, Robert Brandon

**Davis, Carl Estes, Jr.** 1920-    [BEW]
*American vocal arranger*
* Davis, Buster

**Davis, Catfish**
See   Davis, Roy

**Davis, Chan**
See   Davis, Horace Chandler

**Davis, Charles Augustus**
1795-1867    [PA]
*American writer*
* Downing, J., major
* Scriber, Peter

**Davis, Charlie** 20th c.    [BWW]
*American musician*
* Papa Charlie

**Davis, Clare [Ogden]**
See  Davis, Clarisy Musadore [Ogden]

**Davis, Clarisy Musadore [Ogden]** 1892-  [WW]
*Author*
* Davis, Clare [Ogden]
* Saunders, Lawrence [joint pseudonym with Burton Davis]

**Davis, Cliff**
See  Smith, Richard Rein

**Davis, Clifford** 1887-1941  [BEW]
*British-born librettist and lyricist*
* Grey, Clifford

**Davis, Clifton** 1895?-1976 [IBW, WWL]
*American jazz musician*
* Davis, Pike

**Davis, Colin** 1927-  [MS]
*British conductor*
* [The] Celtic Leonard Bernstein

**Davis, Comet**
See  Davis, William Henry [Willie]

**Davis, Coonskin**
See  Davis, Curt[is Benton]

**Davis, Country**
See  Davis, John Wilbur

**Davis, Crash**
See  Davis, Lawrence Columbus

**Davis, Curt[is Benton]** 1903-1965 [BE, BN, PB]
*American baseball player*
* Boone, Dan'l
* Davis, Coonskin
* Davis, Old Coonskin

**Davis, Daisy**
See  Davis, John A.

**Davis, Dan** 1881- ?  [THR]
*British actor*
* Agar, Dan

**Davis, Danny**
See  Nowlan, George

**Davis, Darrel** 1932?-
*American football coach*
* Davis, Mouse

**Davis, David Paget, III** 1896-1941 [FD]
*American director*
* Howard, David

**Davis, David Thomas** 1855-1918 [BBD]
*British singer*
* Ffrangcon-Davies, David Thomas

**Davis, Dixie**
See  Davis, Frank Talmadge

**Davis, Dixie**
See  Davis, Hilton

**Davis, Dixie**
See  Davis, J. Richard

**Davis, Don**
See  Dresser, Davis

**Davis, Dutch**
See  Davis, Grenville

**Davis, Dwight** 1949-  [BB]
*American basketball player*
* Double D

**Davis, Eddie** 1921-  [EJ, PMJ]
*American jazz musician*
* Davis, Lockjaw

**Davis, Edith Vezolles** 1889-  [NAA]
*American author*
* Vezelay, Edith

**Davis, Edward A. [Eddie]** 20th c. [OBW]
*American baseball player*
* Davis, Peanuts

**Davis, Elisabeth Switzer** 1886- [NAA]
*American writer*
* Joy, Elisabeth

**Davis, Elizabeth**
See  Davis, Lou Ellen

**Davis, Frank Allen** 1909-  [PMJ]
*American jazz musician*
* Davis, Pat

**Davis, Frank Talmadge** 1890-1944 [AS, BE]
*American baseball player*
* Davis, Dixie

**Davis, Frederick Clyde** 1902- [WW]
*Author*
* Coombs, Murdo
* Ransome, Stephen

**Davis, Frederick William** 1858-1933  [EMD, WW]
*Author*
* Campbell, Scott
* Carter, Nicholas

**Davis, Freeman** 1903-1974  [SC]
*American entertainer*
* Brother Bones

**Davis, Gary** 1896-1972  [BWW]
*American singer*
* Davis, Blind Gary

**Davis, George Allen** 1890-1961 [BE]
*American baseball player*
* Davis, Iron

**Davis, George Willis** 1902-  [BE]
*American baseball player*
* Davis, Kiddo

**Davis, Gil**
See  Gilmore, Don

**Davis, Glen Vincent**
See  Musolino, Vincenzo

**Davis, Glenn Ashby** 1934-  [BBH]
*American track and field athlete*
* Davis, Jeep

**Davis, Glenn W.** 1924-  [FB]
*American football player*
* Outside, Mr.

**Davis, Gordon**
See  Dietrich, Robert S[alisbury]

**Davis, Gordon**
See  Hunt, E[verette] Howard, Jr.

**Davis, Grania** 1943-  [CA]
*American author*
* Mama G.

**Davis, Grenville** 20th c. [BBH, CSH]
*Canadian lacrosse player*
* Davis, Dutch

**Davis, Gwen** 1936-  [CA]
*American author and screenwriter*
* Fink, Brat

**Davis, Ham**
See  Davis, Leonard

**Davis, Hammie** 1908-  [BWW]
*American singer*
* Nickerson, Hammie
* Nixon, Hammie

**Davis, Harold Eugene** 1902-  [IAW]
*American historian and author*
* Hed

**Davis, Harry**
See  Hill, Roberta

**Davis, Harry H.** 1873-1947 [AS, BE]
*American baseball player*
* Davis, Jasper

**Davis, Henry** 19th c.  [PA]
*Author*
* H. D. of Cheltenham

**Davis, Herbert** 1896- ?  [BF]
*Canadian-born director*
* Davis, Redd

**Davis, Hilton**
*American lobbyist*
* Davis, Dixie

**Davis, Horace Chandler** 1926- [WGT]
*American author*
* Davis, Chan

**Davis, Howard Charles** 1909- [IAW]
*British author*
* Cobden, Guy

**Davis, Howard, Jr.** 1956-  [IBW]
*American boxer*
* [The] Kayo Kid

**Davis, Ike**
See  Davis, Isaac Marion

**Davis, [J] Ira** 1870-1942  [BE]
*American baseball player*
* Davis, Slats

**Davis, Iron**
See  Davis, George Allen

**Davis, Isaac Marion** 1895-  [BE]
*American baseball player*
* Davis, Ike

**Davis, Ivan** 20th c.  [BBH, CSH]
*Canadian lacrosse promoter*
* Davis, Turk

**Davis, J. Richard** 20th c.  [MM]
*American attorney with underworld ties*
* Davis, Dixie

**Davis, Jackie**
See  Davis, Jackson

**Davis, Jackson** 1920-  [EJ]
*American jazz musician*
* Davis, Jackie

**Davis, James [Jimmy]**
See  Thomas, Charles

**Davis, James** 1853-1907 [BEW, EMT]
*Irish-born librettist, lyricist, playwright*
* Hall, Owen

**Davis, James D.** 19th c.  [PA]
*American author*
* Old Times

**Davis, James J.** ?-1921  [BE]
*American baseball player*
* Davis, Jumbo

**Davis, Jasper**
See  Davis, Harry H.

**Davis, Jeep**
See  Davis, Glenn Ashby

**Davis, Jeff**
See  Davis, Jefferson

**Davis, Jeff**
See  Panzram, Carl

**Davis, Jefferson** 1884-1968  [SC]
*American actor*
* Davis, Jeff

**Davis, Jim**
See  Smith, Richard Rein

**Davis, Jimmy** 20th c.  [RO2]
*American musician*
* J. D.

**Davis, Joan**
See  Davis, Madonna Josephine

**Davis, John**  [PA]
*Author*
* De la Salle, John

**Davis, John** 1787-1854  [WBD]
*American politician*
* Honest John

**Davis, John** 1920-  [IBW]
*American weightlifter*
* [The] Brown Giant

**Davis, John A.** 1858- ?  [BE]
*American baseball player*
* Davis, Daisy

**Davis, John Gus** 1915?-  [PMJ]
*American singer*
* Davis, Scat

**Davis, John Henry** 1913-  [BWW]
*American singer*
* Davis, Blind John

**Davis, John Humphrey** 1916-  [B10]
*American baseball player*
* Davis, Red

**Davis, John Wilbur** 1889-1967 [BE]
*American baseball player*
* Davis, Bud
* Davis, Country

**Davis, Julia**
See  Marsh, John

**Davis, Julia** 1904?- [CA, SAT, WD]
*American author and playwright*
* Draco, F.

**Davis, Jumbo**
See  Davis, James J.

**Davis, K. M.**
See  Davis, Kenneth Morton

**Davis, Karl** 1908?-1977  [FIR]
*American actor and wrestler*
* Davis, Killer

**Davis, Kay**
See  Wimp, Kathryn Elizabeth

**Davis, Kenneth Morton** 1939-
[ART]
*American artist*
* Davis, K. M.

**Davis, Kiddo**
*See* Davis, George Willis

**Davis, Killer**
*See* Davis, Karl

**Davis, Larry** 1936-   [BWW]
*American singer*
* Davis, Totsy

**Davis, Lavinia [Riker]** 1909-1961
[WW]
*Author*
* Farmer, Wendell

**Davis, Lawrence Columbus** 1919-
[BE]
*American baseball player*
* Davis, Crash

**Davis, Lefty**
*See* Davis, Alfonzo DeFord

**Davis, Leonard** 1905-1957   [WWJ]
*American jazz musician*
* Davis, Ham

**Davis, Lily May** 20th c.   [CA]
*British author*
* Davis, Rosemary L. [joint
    pseudonym with Rosemary Davis]

**Davis, Lockjaw**
*See* Davis, Eddie

**Davis, Lois Carlile** 1921-   [CA]
*British author*
* Lamplugh, Lois

**Davis, Lorenzo** 1917-   [MK]
*American baseball player*
* Davis, Piper

**Davis, Lou Ellen** 1936-   [CA, SFL]
*American author*
* Bannister, Pat
* Davis, Elizabeth

**Davis, Madonna Josephine**
1913?-1961   [BEW]
*American actress*
* Davis, Joan

**Davis, Mama**
*See* Davis, Mary Lee

**Davis, Maralee G.**
*See* Gibson, Maralee G.

**Davis, Marcus** 18th c.   [PA]
*Author*
* M. D.

**Davis, Martha [Wirt]**   [WW]
*Author*
* Van Arsdale, Wirt

**Davis, Mary Bernice**
*See* Curler, [Mary] Bernice

**Davis, Mary Lee** 20th c.   [BWW]
*American songwriter*
* Davis, Mama

**Davis, Mary Octavia** 1901-
[B10, CAP, SAT]
*American educator, author,
illustrator*
* Dutz

**Davis, Matthew Livingston**
1773-1850   [FFF, PA]
*American author and journalist*
* [The] Genevese Traveller
* Marcus

**Davis, Matthew Livingston**
(Continued)
* Spy in Washington

**Davis, Maxine**
*See* McHugh, Maxine Davis

**Davis, Mercurial Miles**
*See* Davis, Miles Dewey, Jr.

**Davis, Mickey** 1950-   [SMG]
*American basketball player*
* [The] Spirit

**Davis, Miles Dewey, Jr.** 1926-
[IBW]
*American jazz musician*
* Davis, Mercurial Miles

**Davis, Moe**
*See* Dalitz, Moe

**Davis, Mouse**
*See* Davis, Darrel

**Davis, Nathan**   [PA]
*Author*
* E. H. C. M.

**Davis, Norman**
*See* Lucas, Christopher Norman

**Davis, O. T.**
*See* Davies, O. T.

**Davis, Old Coonskin**
*See* Davis, Curt[is Benton]

**Davis, Otis Allen** 1920-   [BE]
*American baseball player*
* Davis, Scat

**Davis, Pat**
*See* Davis, Frank Allen

**Davis, Pat**
*See* Pattee, David E.

**Davis, Patti**
*See* Reagan, Patricia

**Davis, Peaches**
*See* Davis, Ray Thomas

**Davis, Peanuts**
*See* Davis, Edward A. [Eddie]

**Davis, Phebe**
*See* Grismer, Mrs. Joseph R.

**Davis, Pike**
*See* Davis, Clifton

**Davis, Piper**
*See* Davis, Lorenzo

**Davis, Rareback**
*See* Davis, Saul Henry

**Davis, Ray Thomas** 1905-   [BE]
*American baseball player*
* Davis, Peaches

**Davis, Red**
*See* Davis, John Humphrey

**Davis, Redd**
*See* Davis, Herbert

**Davis, Redtop**
*See* Cain, Murray

**Davis, Richard Bingham**   [FFF]
*American writer*
* Martlet

**Davis, Robert Brandon** 1928-
[BE, OBW]
*American baseball player*
* Davis, Brandy
* Davis, Butch

**Davis, Robert Hart** 20th c.   [SFP]
*Author*
* Grant, Maxwell [house
    pseudonym]

**Davis, Robert Prunier** 1929-
[CA, WD]
*American author and screenwriter*
* Brandon, Joe

**Davis, Robert S.** 19th c.   [PA]
*Author*
* Trebor

**Davis, Rosemary**   [CA]
*British author*
* Davis, Rosemary L. [joint
    pseudonym with Lily May Davis]

**Davis, Rosemary L.** [joint
pseudonym with Rosemary Davis]
*See* Davis, Lily May

**Davis, Rosemary L.** [joint
pseudonym with Lily May Davis]
*See* Davis, Rosemary

**Davis, Roy**   [GW]
*American rodeo performer*
* Davis, Catfish

**Davis, Rufe**
*See* Davidson, Rufus Eldon

**Davis, Saul Henry** 1901-   [MK]
*American baseball player*
* Davis, Rareback

**Davis, Scat**
*See* Davis, John Gus

**Davis, Scat**
*See* Davis, Otis Allen

**Davis, Shawn**   [GW]
*American rodeo performer*
* [The] Bishop

**Davis, Skeeter**
*See* Penick, Mary Frances

**Davis, Slats**
*See* Davis, [J] Ira

**Davis, Slim**
*See* Davis, Al

**Davis, Spencer** 20th c.   [OBW]
*American baseball player*
* Davis, Babe

**Davis, Spud**
*See* Davis, Virgil Lawrence

**Davis, Steel Arm**
*See* Davis, Walter

**Davis, Stratford**
*See* Bolton, Maisie Sharman

**Davis, Suzanne**
*See* Sugar, Bert Randolph

**Davis, Sydney Charles Houghton**
1887-   [CA]
*British author*
* Casque, Sammy

**Davis, Ted**
*See* Cain, Murray

**Davis, Thomas**   [PA]
*Author*
* [The] Celt

**Davis, Thomas Oscar** 1924-   [BE]
*American baseball player*
* Davis, Tod

**Davis, Timothy Francis Tothill**
1941-   [CA]
*British author*
* Cashman, John

**Davis, Tod**
*See* Davis, Thomas Oscar

**Davis, Totsy**
*See* Davis, Larry

**Davis, Turk**
*See* Davis, Ivan

**Davis, Varina Anne Jefferson**
1864-1898   [WBD]
*American author*
* [The] Daughter of the
    Confederacy

**Davis, Virgil Lawrence** 1904-
[BE, DGS, PB]
*American baseball player*
* Davis, Spud

**Davis, Walter** 1902?-1935   [MK]
*American baseball player*
* Davis, Steel Arm

**Davis, Walter** 1912-1963?   [BWW]
*American singer*
* Hooker Joe

**Davis, Walter** 1955-   [IBW]
*American basketball player, track
and field athlete*
* Sir Walter

**Davis, Wild Bill**
*See* Davis, William Strethen

**Davis, William Henry [Willie]**
1940-   [PB, SMG]
*American baseball player*
* Davis, Comet
* [The] 3 Dog

**Davis, William Strethen** 1918-
[DAM, EJ, PMJ]
*American jazz musician*
* Davis, Wild Bill

**Davis, Woodrow Wilson** 1913-
[BE]
*American baseball player*
* Davis, Babe
* Davis, Woody

**Davis, Woody**
*See* Davis, Woodrow Wilson

**Davison, Anna Lutz** 1891?-1977
[FIR]
*Film editor*
* Davison, Millie

**Davison, Brian Fettes** 1946-   [DC]
*Rhodesian-born cricketer*
* Davison, Davo

**Davison, Davo**
*See* Davison, Brian Fettes

**Davison, Dwight** 20th c.
*American boxer*
* Davison, Dynamite

**Davison, Dynamite**
*See* Davison, Dwight

**Davison, Gertrude** 1870?-1961
[BEW]
*Actress and producer*
* Mouillot, Gertrude

**Davison, Gladys Patton** 1905-
[CAP]
*American writer*
* Condor, Gladyn

Davison, Millie
See Davison, Anna Lutz

Davison, Wild Bill
See Davison, William

Davison, William 1906-
[DAM, EJ, PMJ]
American jazz musician
* Davison, Wild Bill

D'Avoi, Paul
See Erie, Paul

D'Avril, [Baron] Adolph [PA]
Author
* Cyrille

Davy, Charles William [PA]
Author
* Agogas

Davy, G. M. O.
See Davy, George Mark Oswald

Davy, George Mark Oswald 1898-
[ART]
British painter and sculptor
* Davy, G. M. O.

Davy, [Sir] Humphrey 1778-1829
[PA]
Author
* [An] Angler

Davy de La Pailleterie, Alexandre
1762-1806 [DNNS, HN, WBD]
French army officer
* Dumas, Alexandre
* [The] Horatius Cocles of the
Tyrol

Davys, Sarah
See Manning, Rosemary Joy

Dawdle, Dolly
See Painter, Mary C.

Dawe, Robert Shaen 1910?- [FC]
American actor
* Shayne, Robert

Dawes, Angela Kathleen 1911-
[NAA]
Canadian poet
* Nichevo

Dawes, Edmund 1909?-1974 [FIR]
Radio and television performer
* Dawes, Skipper

Dawes, Robyn M[ason] 1936- [CA]
American psychologist and author
* Cubas, Braz

Dawes, Skipper
See Dawes, Edmund

Dawkins, Darryl 1957?-
American basketball player
* Chocolate Thunder
* Sham, Sir
* Slam, Sir

Dawkins, Fast Fingers
See Dawkins, James Henry
[Jimmy]

Dawkins, James Henry [Jimmy]
1936- [BWW]
American singer
* Dawkins, Fast Fingers

Dawkins, Whit M. 1925- [IBW]
American veterinarian
* [The] Tuskegee Cowboy

Dawley, Thomas Robinson, Jr. 1862-
? [NAA]
American author and publicist
* Marler, Walt A.

Dawlish, Peter
See Kerr, James Lennox

Dawn, Dolly
See Stabile, Theresa Maria

Dawn, Hazel
See Tout, Hazel Dawn

Dawn, Marpessa
See Menor, Gypsy Marpessa Dawn

Dawson, A. M. E.
See Dawson, Alva Mary Elizabeth

Dawson, Alva Mary Elizabeth
1915- [ART]
British painter
* Dawson, A. M. E.

Dawson, Anthony
See Margheriti, Antonio

Dawson, Bart
See Rose, Fred

Dawson, Buck
See Dawson, William Forrest

Dawson, Charles Kenneth 1888-
[WWL]
British author
* West Country

Dawson, Edward Walter [FFF]
American author
* Benedict

Dawson, Eli
See Marks, Elias J.

Dawson, Elizabeth
See Geach, Christine

Dawson, Elmer A. [house
pseudonym] [Stratemeyer
Syndicate]
See Stratemeyer, Edward L.

Dawson, Ernest 20th c. [WWL]
British author
* Athos

Dawson, Florence 1905?-
[EMT, FC]
British actress, singer, dancer
* Desmond, Florence

Dawson, Geoffrey
See Robinson, George Geoffrey

Dawson, Jane
See Critchlow, Dorothy

Dawson, Joe
See Dawson, Ralph Fenton

Dawson, Peter
See Faust, Frederick [Schiller]

Dawson, Ralph Fenton 1898- [BE]
American baseball player
* Dawson, Joe

Dawson, Sheila 1929- [EJ7]
American singer
* Jordan, Sheila

Dawson, William Forrest 20th c.
[B10]
American sports promoter and civic
leader
* Dawson, Buck

Dawud, Talib Ahmad
See Barrymore, Al

Dax, Anthony
See Hunter, [Alfred] John

Day, A. Grove 1904- [NAA]
American author
* Saxon, Carl

Day, Beth [Feagles] 1924- [CA]
American author
* Feagles, Elizabeth

Day, Bobby
See Byrd, Robert

Day, Boots
See Day, Charles Frederick

Day, Charles Frederick 1947-
[BE, PB]
American baseball player
* Day, Boots

Day, Chauncey Addison 1907-
[WEC]
American cartoonist
* Day, Chon

Day, Chon
See Day, Chauncey Addison

Day, Clarence Henry 1901-
[CEI, FHE, HK]
Canadian-born hockey player
* Day, Hap [or Happy]

Day, Clyde Henry 1899-1934 [PB]
American baseball player
* Day, Pea Ridge

Day, Connie
See Day, Wilson C.

Day, Dennis
See McNulty, Eugene Dennis

Day, Donald
See Harding, Donald Edward

Day, Doris
See Kappelhoff, Doris

Day, Dorothy
See Ettlinger, Dorothy

Day, E. P. [PA]
Author
* Collacon

Day, Frances
See Schenk, Frances Victoria

Day, George 20th c. [MBF]
British author
* Howard, Bruce

Day, George Harold 1900-
[AW, CAP]
British physician and author
* Quince, Peter

Day, Hap [or Happy]
See Day, Clarence Henry

Day, Irene
See Orme, Eve

Day, Jim 1911-1959 [CWG]
American country-western performer
* Day, Lazy Jim

Day, John Robert 1917- [IAW]
British author
* Cyclops

Day, Lady
See McKay, Eleanor Gough

Day, Laraine
See Johnson, Laraine

Day, Lazy Jim
See Day, Jim

Day, Lila
See Chaffin, Lillie D.

Day, Lionel
See Black, Ladbroke Lionel Day

Day, Margaret 1916- [FC, WEF]
British actress
* Lockwood, Margaret

Day, Max
See Cassiday, Bruce [Bingham]

Day, Michael
See Dempewolff, Richard
F[rederic]

Day, Ned 20th c. [GSH]
Bowler
* [The] Gentleman Bowler

Day, Pea Ridge
See Day, Clyde Henry

Day, Thomas Franklin 1852- ?
[NAA]
American clergyman and author
* McPherrin, Jones

Day, Wilson C. 20th c. [OBW]
American baseball player
* Day, Connie

Day-Lewis, C[ecil] 1904-1972
[AW, CA, CC]
British author, poet, critic
* Blake, Nicholas

Dayle, Malcolm
See Hincks, Cyril Malcolm

Daylie, Daddy-O
See Daylie, Holmes

Daylie, Holmes 20th c. [IBW]
American disc jockey and television
performer
* Daylie, Daddy-O

Daymore, Reginald Leigh
1891-1967 [F1, F2, FC]
British actor
* Denny, Reginald

Dayre, Sydney
See Cochrane, Mrs.

Dayton, Mrs. Peter [FFF]
Entertainer
* McNeil, Minnie

Dayton, [Captain] Will
See Burleigh, Cecil

Daza ?- 314 [WBD]
Roman emperor
* Maximinus, Galerius Valerius

Daza, Hilarion
See Grosole, Hilarion

Dazai, Osamu
See Tsushima, Shuji

Dazey, Agnes J[ohnston] 20th c.
[CAP, SAT]
American screenwriter
* Johnston, Agnes Christine

Dazey, Mrs. Charles T. [FFF]
Entertainer
* Harding, Edith

Dazie, Mademoiselle
See Peterkin, Daisy

[The] Dazzler
See Vance, Clarence Arthur

**D'Carnoux, C. Albert** 19th c. [PA]
*Author*
* Bertall

**De**
*See* Second element of name for
further listings

**De Abreu, Pamplona** 1936- [WFA]
*Brazilian fashion designer*
* Dener

**De Acosta, Donald Barry** 1912-
[FC, ITA, SW]
*American actor*
* Barry, Don

**De Almeida-Cavalcanti, Alberto**
1897- [BDF, WEF]
*Brazilian director and producer*
* Cavalcanti, Alberto

**De' Alq, Louise**
*See* Ebhardt, Olga

**De Andrada, Djalma** 1928- [EJ7]
*Brazilian-born jazz musician*
* Sete, Bola

**De Angelis, Alberto** 1885- [LAO]
*Italian journalist*
* Colline

**De Arizonac, Baron**
*See* Reavis, James Addison

**De Arona, Juan**
*See* Paz-Soldan y Unanue, Pedro

**De Assis Pacheco, Armando** 1914-
[OP]
*Brazilian opera singer*
* Pacheco, Assis

**De Aubry, Diane**
*See* Rubini, Diane

**De Azambuya**
*See* Oleastro, Hieronimo

**De Balbe de Crillon, Louis**
1541-1615 [DEP, DNNS, WBD]
*French soldier*
* [Le] Brave des Braves
* [The] Bravest of the Brave
* [L']Homme sans Peur

**De Balker, Habakuk, II**
*See* Ter Balkt, Herman Hendrik

**De Banzie, Eric** 1894- [WW]
*Author*
* Baxter, Gregory [joint pseudonym
with John Sellar Matheson
Ressich]

**De Barcena [or Barzena], Alonso**
1528-1598 [DEP, DNNS]
*Spanish Jesuit*
* [The] Apostle of Peru

**De Bary, Anna** 20th c. [WWL]
*British author*
* Bunston, Anna

**De Bary, Brett**
*See* Nee, Brett de Bary

**De' Beauclerk, Lady**
*See* De Vere, [Lady] D.

**De Beaufort, Pierre Roger**
1331-1378 [WBD]
*Pope*
* Gregory XI

**De Beaumarchais, Pierre Augustin**
**Caron**
*See* Caron, Pierre Augustin

**De Beauregard, Henri**
*See* Cumming-Skinner, Dugald
Matheson

**De Beausobre, Julia Mikhailovna**
*See* Namier, Julia

**De Bekker, Jay**
*See* Winchell, Prentice

**De Bellemare, Eugene Louis Gabriel**
1809-1852 [WBD]
*French author*
* Ferry, Gabriel

**De Bellemare, Gabriel** 1846- ?
[WBD]
*French author and playwright*
* Ferry, Gabriel

**De Bellet, Liane** 20th c. [AW]
*Italian-born author*
* De Facci, Liane

**De Belser, Reimond Karel Maria**
1929- [CLC]
*Dutch author and poet*
* Ruyslinck, Ward

**De Belsunce, Henri Francois Xavier**
1671-1755 [FFF, HN, RH]
*Bishop of Marseilles*
* [The] Good Bishop of Marseilles
* Marseilles' Good Bishop

**De Bensaude, Mrs.** [FFF]
*Entertainer*
* Cameron, Violet

**De Bergham, John**
*See* Chatterton, Thomas

**De Bermans, A.** [PA]
*Author*
* Dubrony, A.

**De Bernhard, Charles**
*See* Barnard, Charles

**De Bettignies, Louise** ?-1918 [EE]
*French intelligence agent*
* Dubois, Alice

**De Biere, Victor Huge** 1891-1943
[SC]
*American actor*
* Brooke, Tyler

**De Biraben, Alfredo** 1905?-1956
[BEW]
*Argentinian-born actor*
* Norton, Barry

**De Blacam, Hugh [Aodh]**
1890?-1951 [CAT]
*Irish author and columnist*
* Roddy the Rover

**De Blowitz, Henri**
*See* Opper, Adolf

**De Boccage, Pierre-Jean**
1700-1767 [PA]
*Author*
* Ficquat

**De Bois, Helma**
*See* De Bois, Wilhelmina J. E.

**De Bois, Wilhelmina J. E.** 1923-
[CA]
*Dutch-born author*
* De Bois, Helma

**De Bois-Hebert, Guy** 1860- ?
[WBD]
*French author*
* Bovet, Marie Anne de

**De Boisjolin,**
**Jacques-Francois-Marie Vieilh**
1761-1841 [SN]
*French poet*
* [The] French Erasmus Darwin

**De Boissy, Marquese T.** [PA]
*Author*
* Guiccioli, [Countess] T.

**De Bologne, Michele** [PA]
*Author*
* Sygrianus

**De Bonne, Francois** 1543-1626
[HN]
*French soldier*
* [The] Conqueror
* Lesdiguieres, Duc de

**De Born, Edith**
*See* Bisch, Edith

**De Bouhelier-Lepelletier, Georges**
1876-1947 [WBD]
*French author, poet, playwright*
* Bouhelier, Saint-Georges de

**De Bourdeille, Pierre** 1535?-1614
[SN]
*French author*
* [The] Grammont of His Age
* [The] Pepys of His Age

**De Bourgogne, Antoine** 1421-1504
[DNNF, DNNS, SN]
*Son of Philip the Good, Duke of
Burgundy*
* [Le] Grand Batard
* [The] Great Bastard

**De Bourgogne, Louis** 1682-1712
[DNNF, FFF, RH]
*Grandson of King Louis XIV of
France*
* [The] Little Dauphin

**De Bow, J. D. B.** 1820- ? [PA]
*Author*
* J. D.

**De Braganca, Miguel Maria Evaristo**
1802-1866 [WBD]
*Aspirant to Portuguese throne*
* Dom Miguel

**De Brampton, William** 19th c. [PA]
*Author*
* Fleta

**De Brant, Cyr**
*See* Higginson, Joseph Vincent

**De Bray, Henry**
*See* Narino, Henry

**De Brest, James [Jimmy]**
1937-1973 [EJ, EJ7]
*American jazz musician*
* De Brest, Spanky

**De Brest, Spanky**
*See* De Brest, James [Jimmy]

**De Breteuil, Gilberte**
*See* Ronet, E.

**De Breval, John Durant**
1661?-1789 [FFF, HN]
*British soldier and author*
* Gay, Joseph

**De Breville**
*See* Desnoyers, Edward

**De Brie, Simon** 1210?-1285 [WBD]
*Pope*
* Martin IV

**De Briou, Corinne Belle** 1873-1937
[BEW]
*American-born theatrical performer*
* Corinne

**De Brissac, Malcolm**
*See* Dickinson, Peter

**De Brives, Martial** ?-1581 [PA]
*Author*
* Dumas, Frere

**De Bruges, Louis** 1422-1492 [PA]
*Author*
* Gruthuyse

**De Brunne, Robert**
*See* Mannyng, Robert

**De Bueil, Honorat** 1589-1670 [SN]
*French poet*
* [A] Heretic in Verse
* Racan, Marquis de

**De Bulhoes, Fernando** 1195-1231
[HN, SN]
*Saint*
* Anthony of Padua
* Optimus, Doctor
* [The] Thaumaturgus of His Age

**De Bully, Edouard Roger**
1809-1866 [WBD]
*French poet, playwright, author*
* Beauvoir, Roger de

**De Burgh, A.**
*See* Alborough, Edward Morgan

**De Burgh, Ulick** 1604-1657?
[WBD]
*Irish aristocrat*
* Clanricarde, First Marquis and
Fifth Earl of
* [The] Great Earl

**De Bury, F. Blaze** 20th c.
[SFL, WGT]
*Author*
* Dickberry, F.

**De Bus, Caesar** 1544-1607
[DEP, FFF, SN]
*French ecclesiastic*
* [The] Founder of the Fathers of
Christian Doctrine

**De Cahagne, Chaise**
*See* Cey, Francois Arsene

**De Caire, Edwin**
*See* Williams, Edwin Alfred

**De Camille**
*See* Lebrun, Pauline Guyot

**De Camp, L[yon] Sprague** 1907-
[CA, SAT]
*American author*
* Lyon, Lyman R.
* Wells, J. Wellington

**De Campos, Alvaro**
*See* Pessoa, Fernando [Antonio
Nogueira]

**De Campos, Henrique**
*See* De Oliveira Campos, Henrique
Xavier

**De Campos, Luis** 20th c. [WF]
*Author*
* Gold, Frank

**De Campus, Eddie** 1893-1919
[BX, RBE]
*American boxer*
* Campi, Eddie

**De Cappet, Theodosia**
See Goodman, Theodosia

**De Cardo, Passidonio** 1901?-1964
[BEW]
*Portuguese-born theatrical performer*
* De Carmo, Pussy

**De Carlo, Yvonne**
See Middleton, Peggy Yvonne

**De Carmo, Pussy**
See De Cardo, Passidonio

**De Casalis, Jeanne**
See Casalis De Pury, Jeanne

**De Cassamajor, Marquis** ?-1878
[PA]
*Author*
* Rene, Jules

**De Castro, Gustaf Adolf Danziger**
1859?-1959 [WGT]
*American author*
* Danziger, Adolphe
* Danziger, Gustav A.

**De Cavagnac, G.** [PA]
*Author*
* [Un] Rural

**De Chair, Somerset [Struben]**
1911- [CA]
*British author*
* Honourable Member for X

**De Chamisso, Louis Charles Adelaide**
1781-1838 [WBD]
*German author*
* Chamisso, Adelbert von

**De Chandeneux, Claire**
See Beranger, Emily

**De Chatellerault, Victor**
See Beaudoin, Kenneth Lawrence

**De Cheux, Georges** 1894-1969
[SC]
*French-born actor and director*
* Renavent, George

**De Chevette, J.**
See Aronstam, Noah E.

**De Choudens, Berthe** 20th c.
[THR]
*French actress*
* Cerny, Berthe

**De Colange, Leo** 19th c. [PA]
*Author*
* Doctor Leo

**De Collibus, Nicholas** 1913- [ASC]
*American musician*
* Nicholas, Don

**De Commines, Philippe**
See Bercoff, Andre

**De Comyne, Alexander**
See Browne, Charles Thomas

**De Conde, Syn**
See Mariano de Aguiar, Sinesio

**De Conte, [Sieur] Louis**
See Clemens, Samuel Langhorne

**De Conti Cadassamare, Albert**
1887-1967 [SC]
*Austrian-born actor*
* Conti, Albert

**De Conti, Giovanni Lotario**
1161-1216 [WBD]
*Pope*
* Innocent III

**De Cordova, Arturo**
See Garcia, Arturo

**De Cormenin, Viscount** [PA]
*Author*
* Timon

**De Costa, Benjamin Franklin** 19th
c. [FFF]
*American journalist*
* Bunker Hill
* Hickling, William

**De Costa, Morris**
See Miller, Morris

**De Coteau, Delano** 1940-1974
[CW]
*Trinidadian poet*
* Malik, Abdul

**De Courchamps, Comte** 19th c.
[HN]
*Literary forger*
* [The] Cagliostro of Literature

**De Courcy, Kate**
See Armstrong, Catherine

**De Cranki, Lunatico**
See Harris, Edward

**De Crayencour, Marguerite** 1903-
[B10, EWL]
*French author*
* Yourcenar, Marguerite

**De Crespigny, [Capt.] Charles** [joint
pseudonym with Charles Norris
Williamson]
See Williamson, Alice Muriel
[Livingston]

**De Crespigny, [Capt.] Charles** [joint
pseudonym with Alice Muriel L.
Williamson]
See Williamson, Charles Norris

**De Culwen, Dorothea**
See Hines, Dorothea

**De Curnieu, Georges** 1860-1926
[BEW]
*Playwright*
* Ancey, Georges

**De Curtis-Gagliardi, Antonio Furst**
1897?-1967 [FC, WEF]
*Italian comedian and actor*
* Toto

**De Cusa, Nicholas** 1401-1464
[DEP, FFF, HN]
*German prelate and philosopher*
* Christianissimus, Doctor
* [The] Most Christian Doctor

**De Dienes, Andre**
See Dienes, Andre

**De Dios y Moreno, Antonio**
1871-1931 [GS]
*Spanish bullfighter*
* Conejito [Little Rabbit]

**De Elzaburu, Manuel** 1852-1892
[CW]
*Puerto Rican critic, poet, journalist*
* Amador, Americo
* Montes, Fabian

**De Extramuros, Quixote**
See Espino, Federico [Licsi, Jr.]

**De Facci, Liane**
See De Bellet, Liane

**De Faut, Volly**
See De Faut, Voltaire

**De Faut, Voltaire** 1904-1973
[EJ, EJ7, WWJ]
*American jazz musician*
* De Faut, Volly

**De Ferrare, Baptiste** ?-1490 [PA]
*Author*
* Panaetius

**De Ferriers**
See Raoul, M.

**De Feure, Georges**
See Van Sluijters, Georges Joseph

**De Field, Edward**
See Casey, John E.

**De Fieschi, Sinibaldo** ?-1254
[WBD]
*Pope*
* Innocent IV

**De Filippi, Amedeo** 1900- [ASC]
*Italian-born musician*
* Weston, Philip

**De Filippo, Eduardo**
See Passarelli, Eduardo

**De Filippo, Giuseppo** 1903- [IAW]
*Italian playwright, actor, producer*
* De Filippo, Peppino

**De Filippo, Peppino**
See De Filippo, Giuseppo

**De Firmount, Monsieur**
See Edgeworth, Henry Essex

**De Flavigny, Marie Catherine Sophie**
1800- ? [DNNF, FFF, WBD]
*French author*
* Agoult, Comtesse d'
* Stern, Daniel

**De Fletin, P.**
See Fielden, Thomas Perceval

**De Foigny, Gabriel** 20th c. [SFP]
*Author*
* Sadeur, James

**De Fonseka, Joseph Peter**
1897-1948 [CAT]
*Ceylonese author*
* [The] Chesterton of Ceylon

**De Forciglioni, Antonio**
See Pierozzi, Antonio

**De Ford, Miriam Allen**
See Shipley, Miriam Allen De Ford

**De Forest, Hal**
See De Sylva, Aloysius J.

**De Forest, Lee** 1873-1961 [WBD]
*American inventor*
* [The] Father of Radio

**De Francia**
See Muris, Johannes [or Julianus]
de

**De Franco, Boniface Ferdinand
Leonardo** 1923- [EJ7]
*American jazz musician*
* De Franco, Buddy

**De Franco, Buddy**
See De Franco, Boniface
Ferdinand Leonardo

**De Freitas, Michael** 1932- [IBW]
*British political activist*
* Malik, Michael Abdul
* Michael X

**De Gamez, Tana**
See Alba De Gamez, Cielo
Cayetana

**De Garmo, Mrs. Charles** [FFF]
*Entertainer*
* Stanley, Alma Stuart

**De Garnerin, Maximilian Joseph**
1759-1838 [WBD]
*Bavarian statesman*
* Montgelas, Maximilian Joseph
von

**De Gaulle, Yvonne** 1900?-1979
*Widow of French president, Charles
De Gaulle*
* Aunt Yvonne

**De Ghelderode, Michel**
See Martens,
Adolphe-Adhemar-Louis-Michel

**De Ghesquiere, Joseph Jean**
1731-1802 [PA]
*Author*
* Raemsdonck

**De Glouvet, Jules**
See Quesnay de Beaurepaire, Jules

**De Goede, Jules**
See De Goede, Julien Maximilien

**De Goede, Julien Maximilien** 1937-
[ART]
*Dutch-born painter*
* De Goede, Jules

**De Gontaut, Armand** 1524?-1592
[WBD]
*Marshal of France*
* Biron, Baron de
* [Le] Boiteux

**De Gontaut, Charles** 1562-1602
[WBD]
*French army officer*
* Biron, Duc de
* [The] Thunderbolt of France

**De Gostrie, Roland** 1890-1946
[FC, FD]
*Irish-born director*
* Neill, Roy William

**De Got, Bertrand** 1264-1314
[WBD]
*Pope*
* Clement V

**De Gournay, Marie Lejars**
1566-1645 [DEP, RH, SN]
*French author and poet*
* [The] Tenth Muse

**De Graeff, Allen**
See Blaustein, Albert P[aul]

**De Graffe, Richard**
See Cooper, Leonard

**De Gramont, Sanche** 1932- [CA]
*Swiss-born American author and
journalist*
* Morgan, Ted

**De Grantmesnil, Yvo** 12th c. [HN]
*Soldier*
* [The] Rope Dancer

**De Grasse, Will**
See Furniss, William

**De Grazia, Ettore** 1909-   [CA]
*American author and illustrator*
* De Grazia, Ted

**De Grazia, Ted**
*See*   De Grazia, Ettore

**De Gresac, Fredeique Rosine** 20th
c.   [THR]
*French playwright*
* Gresac, [Madame] Fred

**De Grimoard, Guillaume**
1310-1370   [WBD]
*Pope*
* Urban V

**De Groot, Edward Stanley** 20th c.
[BMH]
*British musician and comedian*
* Stanelli

**De Guiche, Dorothy** 1898-1968
[F1, FC, WEF]
*American actress*
* Gish, Dorothy

**De Guiche, Lillian** 1896-
[BDF, F1, FC]
*American actress*
* Gish, Lillian

**De Guillet, Leblanc** 1730-1799
[PA]
*Author*
* Blanc, Antonio

**De Guy Latteur**
*See*   Mouligneau, Michel

**De Guzman, Gaspar [Duque de
Sanlucar]** 1587-1645   [WBD]
*Spanish statesman*
* [El] Conde Duque de Olivares
* Olivares, Conde de

**De Haan, Margaret**
*See*   Freed, Margaret De Haan

**De Hamel, Felix John**
*See*   Hamel, Felix John

**De Harcourt, Henri** 1601-1666
[SN]
*French general*
* Cadet la Perle [The Pearl Son]

**De Hartog, Jan** 1914-   [CA]
*Dutch playwright and author*
* Eckmar, F. R.

**De Havilland, Joan De Beauvoir**
1917-   [BDF, BEW, FC]
*British-born actress*
* Fontaine, Joan

**De Heredia, Marie Louise Antoinette**
1875- ?   [CD]
*French poet and author*
* D'Houville, Gerard

**De Hondt, Joos** 1563-1611   [WBD]
*Flemish-born engraver*
* Hondius, Jodocus

**De Hondt, Pieter** 1521-1597
[WBD]
*Saint*
* Canisius, Peter

**De Hory, Elmyr**
*See*   Hoffman, Josef

**De Hubbenet, Lydia** 1874-1921
[THR]
*Russian-born actress*
* Yavorska, Lydia

**De Jacques, Eallallean [or Eulallean?]**
1892-1955   [CED, EMT, PMJ]
*American actress and singer*
* Lorraine, Lillian

**De Jaegher, Raymond-Joseph**
1905-1980   [CA, CAP]
*Belgian-born missionary and author*
* Lei Chen Yuan

**De Jeremie**
*See*   Gottschel, Albert Bitzius

**De Jesus, Ivan** 1953-   [BE]
*Puerto Rican baseball player*
* Alvarez, Ivan

**De Joncieres, Victorin**
*See*   Rossignol, Felix Ludger

**De Jong-Keesing, Elisabeth**
*See*   Van Tricht, Elisabeth Emmy

**De Jong Van Hage, T. P. Merkrid**
*See*   Rempt, Jan Dirk

**De Jouy, Victor Joseph Etienne**
*See*   Jouy, Victor Joseph Etienne

**De Juanes [or Joanes], Juan**
*See*   Macip, Vicente Juan

**De Kalb**
*See*   Cross, Kate

**De Kay, James E.** 19th c.   [PA]
*Author*
* [An] Amateur

**De Kiriline, Louise**
*See*   Lawrence, Louise De Kiriline

**De Kowa, Viktor**
*See*   Kowarzik, Viktor

**De Kremer, Jean Raymond**
1887-1964   [B10]
*Belgian author*
* Flanders, John
* Ray, Jean

**De L. G.**
*See*   Henry, Captain

**De la Boderie, Gui Lefevre**
1541-1598   [PA]
*Author*
* Boderianus, Fabricus

**De la Boe, Franz** 1614-1672
[WBD]
*Prussian-born physician and
anatomist*
* Sylvius, Franciscus

**De La Chevrotiere, Hector Chevigny**
1904-   [NAA]
*American writer and radio dramatist*
* Chevigny, Hector

**De la Compassion, Marie Augustine**
*See*   Jamet, Marie

**De La Condamine, Robert**
1877-1966   [THR]
*British actor*
* Farquharson, Robert

**De La Cruz, Joe**
*See*   De La Cruz, Jose

**De La Cruz, Jose** 1892-1961   [SC]
*Actor*
* De La Cruz, Joe

**De La Cruz, Juana Ines** 1651-1695
[FFF]
*Spanish nun and poet*
* [The] Tenth Muse

**De La Flechere, John William**
1729-1785   [WBD]
*British clergyman*
* Fletcher, John William

**De La Flor, Serafin**
*See*   Torres y Feria, Manuel de

**De La Fonte, Jeanne** 1898-1933
[BDF, F2, WEF]
*French-born actress*
* Adoree, Renee

**De La Garza, E.**
*American politician*
* De La Garza, Kika

**De La Garza, Kika**
*See*   De La Garza, E.

**De La Glannege, Roger-Maxe**
*See*   Legman, George Alexander

**De La Guard, Theodore**
*See*   Ward, Nathaniel

**De La Haba, Antonio** 1922-1965
[GS]
*Spanish bullfighter*
* Zurito [Little Wild Dove]

**De La Haba Vargas, Gabriel** 1945-
[GS]
*Spanish bullfighter*
* Zurito [LIttle Wild Dove]

**De La Hoz, Miguel Angel** 1939-
[BE]
*Cuban-born baseball player*
* De La Hoz, Mike

**De La Hoz, Mike**
*See*   De La Hoz, Miguel Angel

**De La Llana, Pedro** 1895-   [NAA]
*Filipino journalist*
* Lopana

**De La Maraja, Xeres**
*See*   Begovic, Milan

**De La Marck, Comte**
*See*   Arenberg, Auguste Marie
Raymond d'

**De La Mare, Walter [John]**
1873-1956   [EWL, LC, WGT]
*British poet and author*
* Ramal, Walter
* W. J. D.

**De la Moote, Col.**   [PA]
*Author*
* [An] Antiquary

**De La Pasture, Edmee Elizabeth
Monica** 1890-1943   [BEW, LC]
*British author and playwright*
* Delafield, E. M.

**De la Pierre, Jean**
*See*   Heynlin, Johann

**De La Ramee, [Marie] Louise**
*See*   Rame, Marie Louise

**De La Rosa, Frank**
*See*   Estaban, Francisco, Jr.

**De la Salle, John**
*See*   Davis, John

**De La Torre, Bertrand**   [HN]
*Medieval scholar*
* Famosus, Doctor

**De La Torre, Lillian**
*See*   McCue, Lillian Bueno

**De La Torre-Bueno, Lillian**
*See*   McCue, Lillian Bueno

**De la Touche, Janet** 19th c.   [PA]
*Author*
* Isalin

**De la Ville, Bernard Germain Etienne**
1756-1825   [DEP, DNNS, SN]
*French naturalist*
* [The] King of Reptiles
* Lacepede, Comte de
* [Le] Roi des Reptiles

**De La Warr, Third Baron**
*See*   West, Thomas

**De Lacretille, Jean C. Dominique**
1766-1855   [PA]
*Author*
* Jeune

**De Laffemas, Isaac** 17th c.   [SN]
*Public executioner*
* [The] Cardinal's Hangman

**De Lamoignon, Urbain Guillaume**
1674-1742   [WBD]
*French politician*
* Courson

**De Lantagne, Cecile**
*See*   Cloutier, Cecile

**De Lanty, Virginia** 1907-   [BEW]
*American playwright*
* Powys, Stephen

**De Lara, Isidore**
*See*   Cohen, Isidore

**De Las Cuevas, Ramon**
*See*   Harrington, Mark Raymond

**De Lasseran-Massencome, Blaise**
1502?-1527   [DNNF, FFF, SN]
*French army officer*
* Montluc, Seigneur de
* [The] Royalist Butcher

**De l'Aude**
*See*   Fabre, Jean Pierre

**De Launay, [Vicomte] Charles**
*See*   Gay, Delphine

**De Lausanne, Laurent-Jean**
?-1876   [PA]
*Author*
* Jan, Laurent

**De Lavalette, Nichault**
*See*   Gay, Maria Frances Sophie

**De Leath, Vaughn** 1896-1943
[BWW]
*American singer*
* Green, Sadie
* [The] Original Radio Girl

**De Leeuw, Cateau Wilhelmina**
1903-   [AW, CA]
*American author and illustrator*
* Hamilton, Kay
* Lyon, Jessica

**De Leighbur, Don**
*See*   Burley, Daniel Gardner

**De Leon, Antonio** 1590?-1660?
[WBD]
*Spanish jurist and historian*
* Pinelo

**De Leon, Stuart**
*See*   Lyman, G. H.

**De Leoni, Paul**   [PA]
*Author*
* Charnet, Paul

**De l'Epine, Francesca Margherita**
18th c.   [SN]
*Singer*
* Greber's Peg
* Hecate

**De l'Espagne, Jean** 1591-1659
[SN]
*French theologian*
* Belle Lumiere des Pasteurs

**De Lestres, Alonie**
*See* Grenly, Lionel

**De Lima, Clara Rosa** 1922-   [CA]
*West Indian author and poet*
* Driftwood, Penelope

**De Lima, Sigrid**
*See* Greene, Sigrid

**De Lima Gil, Manuel Heraldo y Hugo**
*See* Hidalgo, Miguel A.

**De Lisieux, Zacharie** 1582-1660
[FFF]
*Medieval writer*
* Firmianus, Petrus

**De Lisle, Ferdinand**
*See* De Maune, Edward

**De Loi, Raimon**
*See* Jameson, Raymond Deloy

**De Lolme, John Louis** 1740-1806
[SN]
*Swiss jurist and author*
* [The] English Montesquieu

**De Londres, Henry** 13th c.
[DNNF, HN, RH]
*Archbishop of Dublin*
* Burnbill

**De Longueil, Christophe**
1490-1522   [PA]
*Author*
* Longalius

**De Lora, Joann S.**
*See* Sandlin, Joann S[chepers] De
Lora

**De Lorenzo, Salvatore** 1899-1962
[SC]
*American actor*
* Hogan, Society Kid

**De Los Angeles, Victoria**
*See* Gomez Cima, Victoria

**De Los Colorados, Caballero**
*See* Reavis, James Addison

**De Lovetot, J.**   [PA]
*Author*
* Fleta

**De Lubano, M.**
*See* Ghnassia, Maurice
[Jean-Henri]

**De Luc**
*See* Caligny, Jean Antenor Huede

**De Luce, Virginia**
*See* Wilson, Virginia De Luce

**De Lugo, Paula** 1916-   [BEW, TR]
*American actress and singer*
* Laurence, Paula

**De Luna, Pedro** 1328?-1423?
[WBD]
*Antipope*
* Benedict XIII

**De Mairone, Francois** ?-1327
[HN]
*French author*
* Illuminated Doctor
* Illuminatus et Acutus, Doctor
* Magister Abstractionum

**De Mar, Esmeralda**
*See* Mellen, Ida M[ay]

**De Mar, Paul**
*See* Foley, Pearl

**De Marets, Samuel** 1599-1663
[DEP, FFF, SN]
*French religious reformer*
* [The] Little Preacher

**De Marguetel de Saint-Denis,
Charles** 1610?-1703   [SN]
*French courtier and author*
* [The] Old Satyr
* Saint Evremond, Seigneur de

**De Marini y Coppel, Alfredo Jose**
1921-   [CA, ESF, SFL]
*American author*
* Coppel, Alfred
* Galaxan, Sol
* Gilman, Robert Cham
* Leppoc, Derfla
* Marin, A. C.
* Marin, Alfred

**De Marsalle, L.**
*See* Kirchner, Ernst Ludwig

**De Marval, Gerard** 1808-1856
[PA]
*Author*
* Lebrunie, Gerard

**De Masi, Francesco** 20th c.   [WF]
*Italian composer*
* Mason, Frank

**De Maune, Edward** ?-1880   [PA]
*Author*
* A. D. S.
* Barteville, Alexis
* De Lisle, Ferdinand
* Dupri
* Novel, Edward

**De Mejo, Carlo** 20th c.   [WF]
*Italian actor*
* May, Stewart

**De Melvin, Henri** 19th c.   [BMH]
*Female impersonator*
* [The] London Star
* [The] Wonderful Baritone
* [The] Wonderful Soprano

**De Mendelssohn, Hilde Maria**
1911-   [AW]
*Austrian-born author*
* Spiel, Hilde

**De Menton, Francisco**
*See* Chin, Frank [Chew, Jr.]

**De Mesne, Eugene [Frederick]** 20th
c.   [CA]
*British-born author and editor*
* Ocean, Julian

**De Meyer, Adolf** 1868-1949   [B10]
*French-American photographer*
* De Meyer, Gayne

**De Meyer, Gayne**
*See* De Meyer, Adolf

**De Michele, Angelo** 1890-1952
[SC]
*American actor*
* Ward, Harry

**De Migliorati, Cosimo** 1336?-1406
[WBD]
*Pope*
* Innocent VII

**De Mille, Agnes**
*See* Prude, Agnes George

**De Mille, Katherine**
*See* Lester, Katherine

**De Mille, Richard** 1922-   [CA]
*American author*
* Dimrecken, B. Grayer

**De Modrone, Luchino Visconti**
1906-   [FC]
*Italian writer and director*
* Visconti, Luchino

**De Molina, Tirso**
*See* Tellez, Gabriel

**De Montfort, Guy**
*See* Johnson, Donald McI[ntosh]

**De Montreuil, Gaetane**
*See* Belanger-Gill, Georgiana

**De Mora, James Vincenzo**
1904-1936   [BLB, PHM]
*American underworld figure*
* Gebardi, Vincent
* Machine Gun Jack
* McGurn, Jack

**De Morny, Peter**
*See* Wynne-Tyson, Esme

**De Morra, Alberto** ?-1187   [CAL]
*Pope*
* Gregory VIII

**De Moss, Bingo**
*See* De Moss, Elwood

**De Moss, Elwood** 1899-   [IBW]
*American baseball player*
* De Moss, Bingo

**De Mouchy, Antoine** 1494-1574
[PA]
*Author*
* Demochares

**De Mourant, George Souli**
*See* Bedford-Jones, Henry [James
O'Brien]

**De Muenck, Carlotta Patti**   [FFF]
* Patti, Carlotta

**De Muldor, Carl**
*See* Miller, Charles Henry

**De Munoz Marin, Muna Lee** 1895-
[WW]
*Author*
* Gayle, Newton [joint pseudonym
with Maurice C. Guinness]

**De Musi, Agostino** 1490?-1540?
[WBD]
*Italian engraver*
* Veneziano, Agostino

**De Narni, Erasmo**
*See* Gattamelata, Erasmo

**De Navarrete, Manuel Maria**
1768-1809   [FFF]
*Mexican author*
* Anfriso

**De Navery, Raoul**
*See* Fullerton, Georgiana

**De Neergaard, Beatrice**
*See* Flood, Beatrice

**De Neufchateau, Francois**
*See* Francois, Nicolas Louis

**De Nyse, Mrs. Edward**   [FFF]
*Entertainer*
* Prior, Lulu

**De Oliveira Campos, Henrique Xavier**
1909-   [FDG]
*Director*
* De Campos, Henrique

**De Oliveira Sayao, Balduina** 1902-
[MS]
*Brazilian opera singer*
* Sayao, Bidu

**De Osorno, Marques**
*See* Higgins, Ambrose

**De Pablo, Juan Carlos** 1943-
[IAW]
*Argentinian economist and author*
* De Padua, Antonio

**De Padua, Antonio**
*See* De Pablo, Juan Carlos

**De Paoli, Giuditta** 1944-   [OP]
*Italian-born opera singer*
* DePaul, Judith

**De Paor, Risteard**
*See* Power, Richard

**De Partibus**
*See* Despars, Jacques

**De Paul, Lynsey**
*See* Ruben, Lynsey

**De Pembroke, Morgan**
*See* Evans, Morgan

**De Pesmes, Francois Louis**
1668-1737   [PA]
*Author*
* Saint Saphorin

**De Petrus**
*See* Borel, Pierre Bord d'Hautoine

**De Peyster, John Watts** 1821-1873
[FFF, PA]
*American author*
* Anchor
* [A] Layman

**De Piano, Freddie** 1924-1958   [SC]
*American actor*
* Dee, Freddie

**De Piccolomini, Enea Silvio**
1405-1464   [WBD]
*Pope*
* Pius II
* Silvius [or Sylvius], Aeneas

**De Pietro, Albert** 1913-   [IAW]
*American author*
* Lorel, Phil

**De Plata, Manitas**
*See* Ballardo, Ricardo

**De Poliakoff-Baidaroff, Marina**
1937?-   [BDF, FC, WEF]
*French actress*
* Vlady, Marina

**De Poliakoff-Baidaroff, Militza**
1930-   [FC]
*French actress*
* Versois, Odile

**De Polman, Willem**
*See* Nichols, Dale [William]

**De Portu**
*See* O'Fihely, Maurice

**De Pow, Johnny** 20th c. [BLB]
*American politician*
* Powers, Johnny

**De Pre, Jean-Anne**
*See* Avallone, Michael [Angelo],
Jr.

**De Quincey, Thomas** 1785-1859
[DEL, PA, SN]
*British author*
* [The] English Opium-Eater
* Plato
* X. Y. Z.

**De Rambouillet, Mme.** 1588- ?
[PA]
*Author*
* Arthenice

**De Ransart, Robert**
*See* Goffart, Francis-Leo

**De Ravenne, Arthur** 1910?-1962
[BEW]
*French-born actor*
* Dulac, Arthur

**De Regniers, Beatrice Schenk
Freedman** 1914- [IA]
*American author*
* Kitt, Tamara

**De Reneville, Mary Margaret Motley
Sheridan** 1912- [CA, WD]
*British-born French author*
* Motley, Mary

**De Reszke, Jan Mieczislaw**
1850-1925 [BBD]
*Polish-born opera singer*
* De Reszke, Jean
* Di Reschi, Giovanni

**De Reszke, Jean**
*See* De Reszke, Jan Mieczislaw

**De Reyna, Diane Detzer** 1930-
[ESF, SFL, WGT]
*American author*
* De Reyna, Jorge
* Detzer, Diane
* Lukens, Adam

**De Reyna, Jorge**
*See* De Reyna, Diane Detzer

**De Riallo, J. Girard** 19th c. [PA]
*Author*
* Stephanowitch, Dantri

**De Ribeaupierre, Claude** 20th c.
[WECO]
*Swiss cartoonist*
* Derib

**De Ridder, Alfons** 1882-1960
[CD, EWL, TCL]
*Flemish author and poet*
* Elsschot, Willem

**De Riso, Arpad** 20th c. [WF]
*Italian screenwriter*
* Keaton, Robert

**De Rivel, Isa**
*See* Cuevas, Clara

**De Rochbrune, Jean** 1934- [FC]
*French actor*
* Sorel, Jean

**De Roche, Charles**
*See* De Rochefort, Charles

**De Rochechouart-Mortemart, Marie
Clementine** 1847-1933 [WBD]
*French sculptor and author*
* Manuela

**De Rochechouart-Mortemart, Marie
Clementine** (Continued)
* Uzes, Duchesse d'

**De Rochefort, Charles** 1886- [CU]
*French-born actor*
* De Roche, Charles

**De Rosa, Peter** 20th c.
*Author*
* Boyd, Neil

**De Rossi, Francesco** 1510-1563
[WBD]
*Italian painter*
* Salviati, Cecco di

**De Rossi, Giovanni Battista**
1494-1540 [WBD]
*Florentine painter*
* [Il] Rosso Fiorentino

**De Rothschild, [Baron] Henri**
1872?-1947 [BEW]
*Playwright and producer*
* Pascal, Andre

**De Roussy De Sales, Raoul**
1896-1942 [CAT]
*French-born author and journalist*
* Fransales, Jacques

**De Rouvigny, Rachel** [HN]
* [La] Belle et Vertueuse
  Huguenotte

**De Ryke, DeLores** 1929- [IWM]
*American musician*
* De Ryke, Fiddling De

**De Ryke, Fiddling De**
*See* De Ryke, DeLores

**De Sabe, Aristide**
*See* Denis, Lorimer

**De Sacchi, Giovanni Antonio**
1483-1539 [WBD]
*Venetian painter*
* Pordenone, Giovanni Antonio da
* Regillo

**De Saint Amand, Gabriel Randon**
1867-1933 [WBD]
*French poet*
* Rictus, Jehan

**De Saint Ange, Ange Francois**
1747-1810 [PA]
*Author*
* Farian

**De St. Balman, Madam**
*See* D'Ernecourt, Barre

**De Saint Cricq, Lorenzo** [PA]
*Author*
* Marcoy, Paul

**De St Hilaire, Marco**
*See* Hillaire, Emile Marc

**De Saint Ledger, Geille**
*See* Colleville, Anne Hyacinthe

**De Saint Luc, Jean**
*See* Glassco, John [Stinson]

**De St. Mars, Vicomtesse**
1779-1847 [PA]
*Author*
* Dash, Comtesse

**De Salignac, Charles**
*See* Hasson, James

**De Salluste [or Salustius?], Guillaume**
1544-1590 [SN]
*French poet*
* Bartas, Seigneur de

**De Salluste [or Salustius?], Guillaume**
(Continued)
* [A] Gascon Moses
* Some French Angel

**De Saulieu, Thierry** 1947- [IAW]
*French journalist*
* Remerond

**De Savallo, Teresa [Marquesa
d'Alpens]**
*See* Williamson, Alice Muriel
[Livingston]

**De Schanschieff, Juliet Dymoke**
1919- [WD]
*British author*
* Dymoke, Juliet

**De Scoraille de Roussilles, Marie
Angelique** 1661-1681 [SN]
*Mistress of King Louis XIV*
* Fontanges, Brilliant
* Fontanges, Duchesse de

**De Serment, Louise Anastasie** [SN]
*French poet*
* [The] Philosopher

**De Serres, Jean** 1540-1598 [PA]
*Author*
* Serranus

**De Silva, Angelita Helena**
1868-1949 [BEW]
*Actress*
* De Silva, Nina

**De Silva, David** 1887- [WWL]
*Author*
* Parasara

**De Silva, Nina**
*See* De Silva, Angelita Helena

**De Simone [or Desimons?], Giovanni
Alfredo** 1920?- [ITA, PMJ]
*American singer*
* Desmond, Johnny

**De Sinibaldi, Guittoncino**
1270-1336 [WBD]
*Italian jurist and poet*
* Cino da Pistoia

**De Smet, Pierre Jean** 1801-1873
[WBD]
*Belgian-born missionary*
* Blackrobe

**De Sola, John**
*See* Morland, Nigel

**De Souza, Joao Jose Pereira** 1934-
[EJ7]
*Brazilian jazz musician*
* De Souza, Raul

**De Souza, Raul**
*See* De Souza, Joao Jose Pereira

**De Speciosa Villa**
*See* Gayton, Edmund

**De Sponde, Jean** 1557-1595 [PA]
*Author*
* Spondanus

**De Steuch, Harriet Henry**
1897?-1974 [CA]
*American author*
* Henry, Harriet

**De Stolz, Madam**
*See* Begon, F.

**De Stratton, Adam** [PA]
*Author*
* Fleta

**De Sylva, Aloysius J.** 1862-1938
[SC]
*American actor and director*
* De Forest, Hal

**De Sylva, Buddy**
*See* De Sylva, George Gard

**De Sylva, George Gard** 1895-1950
[EPM]
*American lyricist, composer,
librettist, producer*
* De Sylva, Buddy

**De Tarde, Gabriel** 1843-1904 [CD]
*French sociologist and philosopher*
* Tarde, Gabriel

**De Teffe, Antonio** 20th c. [WF]
*Italian actor*
* Steffen, Anthony

**De Tessier, Emilie** 20th c. [WECO]
*French cartoonist*
* Duval, Marie

**De Themuseuil, Chevalier**
*See* Saint Hyacinthe, Cardonner

**De Tirtoff, Romain** 1892-
[B10, CA]
*Russian-born French fashion
designer*
* Erte

**De Todany, James**
*See* Beaudoin, Kenneth Lawrence

**De Tolnay, Charles Erich** 1899-
[CA]
*Hungarian-born American author*
* Tolnai, Karoly
* Tolnai, Vagujhelyi Karoly

**De Toth, Andre**
*See* Toth, Andreas

**De Traz, Georges** 1881- ? [CC]
*Author and art historian*
* Fosca, Francois

**De Treville, Yvonne**
*See* La Gierse, Edyth

**De Valera, Dev**
*See* De Valera, Eamon

**De Valera, Eamon** 1883-1975
[NN]
*Irish statesman and military leader*
* De Valera, Dev
* [The] Father of the Irish
  Republic

**De Valois, [Dame] Ninette**
*See* Stannus, Edris

**De Varona, Donna** 1947- [SWI]
*American swimmer*
* Dee, Donna

**De Vaux, Baron** [PA]
*Author*
* Martin, Eugene

**De Vera, Cris**
*See* Masilongan, Christobal

**De Vere, Clementine Duchene**
*See* Wood De Vere, Clementine
Duchene

**De Vere, [Lady] D.** [PA]
*Author*
* De' Beauclerk, Lady

**De Vere, Jane**
*See* Watson, Julia

**De Vermond, Louis**
*See* Enault, Louis

**De Viellerge, M.**
*See* Balzac, Honore de

**De Vignerot du Plessis, Louis Francois Armand** 1696-1788 [SN]
*French army officer and diplomat*
* Marauder, Father
* Richelieu, Duc de

**De Villedieu, Mme.** 1640?-1683 [WBD]
*French author*
* Desjardins, Marie Catherine

**De Villiers, Cosm** 1680-1758 [PA]
*Author*
* Saint Etienne

**De Villiers, Ryno B.**
*See* Nienaber, Petrus Johannes

**De Villiers, Victor**
*See* Hugo, Leon Hargreaves

**De Vio, Tommaso** 1469-1534 [WBD]
*Italian cardinal*
* Cajetan, Cardinal

**De Virigens**
*See* Winterfield, Carl Georg August

**De Vivelle, Jean**
*See* Cannirt, Charles

**De Viviers, Cardinal**
*See* Allarmet [or D'Alouzier], Jean

**De Voisons, [Countess] Gilbert**
*See* Taglioni, Maria

**De Voraggio, Giacomo** 1230-1298 [PA]
*Author*
* De Voragine, Jacques

**De Voragine, Jacques**
*See* De Voraggio, Giacomo

**De Voto, Bernard [Augustine]** 1897-1955 [ANT, B10, EWL]
*American author and critic*
* August, John
* Hewes, Cady

**De Voy, Albert** 1870- ? [THR]
*British entertainer*
* Le Fre, Albert

**De Waal, Violet Mary** 20th c. [NAA]
*Canadian-born author*
* Irwin, Violet

**De Warville**
*See* Brissot, Jean-Pierre

**De Wavrin, Andre** 20th c. [BDW]
*French intelligence agent*
* Passy, Colonel

**De Weyland, Thomas** [PA]
*Author*
* Fleta

**De Willigen, Elisabeth** 1905- [IAW]
*Dutch author*
* Vuyk, Beb

**De Winton, Alice**
*See* Wilson, Alice

**De Wit [or de Witte], Pieter** 1548?-1628 [WBD]
*Flemish painter*
* Candido, Pietro

**De Witt, Denise**
*See* Schoeb, Erika

**De Wohl, Louis**
*See* Von Wohl, Ludwig

**De Wolfe, Billy**
*See* Jones, William Andrew

**De Wolfe, Margaret** 1884-1956 [THR]
*British actress*
* Wycherly, Margaret

**De Wreder, Paul**
*See* Heming, John [Winton]

**De Wyzewa, Theodore**
*See* Wyzewski, Theodore

**De Yepis y Alvarez, Juan** 1542-1591 [WBD]
*Saint*
* John of the Cross

**De Younge, A.**
*See* Watson, A.

**De Zamacois y Quintana, Eduardo** 20th c. [TC]
*Spanish author and playwright*
* Zamacois, Eduardo

**De Ziel, Henri Frans** 1916- [CW]
*Surinamese poet and author*
* Trefossa

**Deacon**
*See* Calkins, Hiram

**Deacon [Secret Service code name]**
*See* Carter, James Earl, Jr. [Jimmy]

**[The] Deacon**
*See* Crane, Irving

**[The] Deacon**
*See* Henry of Lausanne

**Deacon Bill McKechnie**
*See* McKechnie, William Boyd

**Deacon Dan Reeves**
*See* Reeves, Daniel E.

**Deacon Dan Towler**
*See* Towler, Daniel L.

**Deacon Danny MacFayden**
*See* MacFayden, Daniel Knowles

**Deacon, Richard**
*See* McCormick, [George] Donald [King]

**Dead Beat**
*See* Howard, Joseph

**Dead Eye Norris**
*See* Norris, William James

**[The] Deadly Austrian**
*See* Maria Louisa

**Deadmarsh, Butch**
*See* Deadmarsh, Ernest Charles

**Deadmarsh, Ernest Charles** 1950- [CEI, HR]
*Canadian-born hockey player*
* Deadmarsh, Butch

**Deadwood Dick**
*See* Clarke, Richard W.

**Deadwood Dick**
*See* Dickey, Robert

**Deaf Charley Hank**
*See* Hanks, O. C.

**Deagle, Lorenzo Burroughs** 1858-1937 [BE]
*American baseball player*
* Deagle, Ren

**Deagle, Ren**
*See* Deagle, Lorenzo Burroughs

**Deagon, Lyda** 1869?-1912 [BEW, CED]
*American singer*
* Gilson, Lottie
* [The] Little Magnet

**Deak, Andras** 1941- [AES]
*Hungarian-born American soccer player*
* Deak, Andy

**Deak, Andy**
*See* Deak, Andras

**Deakin, Phyllis A.** 20th c. [IAW]
*British author and journalist*
* Daquin, Felicity

**Deakins, Cyril Edward** 1916- [ART]
*British artist*
* C. D.

**Deal, Borden** 1922- [AW, CA, WD]
*American author*
* Borden, Lee [or Leigh]

**Deal, Cot**
*See* Deal, Ellis Fergason

**Deal, Ellis Fergason** 1923- [SMG]
*American baseball coach*
* Deal, Cot

**Deal, John Wesley** 1879-1944 [BE]
*American baseball player*
* Deal, Snake

**Deal, Mason**
*See* Eliot, Henry Ware

**Deal, Snake**
*See* Deal, John Wesley

**Deale, Kenneth Edwin Lee** 1907- [CA]
*Irish barrister and author*
* Martin, Paul

**Deamer, Dulcie**
*See* Goldie, Mary Elizabeth Kathleen Dulcie

**[The] Dean**
*See* Cromwell, Dean

**[The] Dean**
*See* Herder, Johann Gottfried von

**Dean**
*See* Young, Welton

**Dean, Abner**
*See* Epstein, Abner

**Dean, Alfred Lovill** 1916-1970 [BE, PB]
*American baseball player*
* Dean, Chubby

**Dean, Charles Wilson** 1852-1935 [BE]
*American baseball player*
* Dean, Dory

**Dean, Chubby**
*See* Dean, Alfred Lovill

**Dean, Daffy**
*See* Dean, Paul Dee

**Dean, Dizzy**
*See* Dean, Jay Hanna

**Dean, Donald**
*See* Hope, William Edward Stanton

**Dean, Dory**
*See* Dean, Charles Wilson

**Dean, Dudley**
*See* McGaughy, Dudley Dean

**Dean, Eddie**
*See* Glosup, Edward Dean

**Dean, Erica**
*See* Gillooly, Edna Rae

**Dean, Gregory**
*See* Posner, Jacob D.

**Dean, Ida**
*See* Grae, Ida

**Dean, Isabel**
*See* Hodgkinson, Isabel

**Dean, James**
*See* Byron, James

**Dean, Jay Hanna** 1911-1974 [BAB, DGS, PB]
*American baseball player*
* Dean, Dizzy
* Dean, Jerome Herman

**Dean, Jerome Herman**
*See* Dean, Jay Hanna

**Dean, Jimmy**
*See* Ward, Seth

**Dean, John Edwin** 1940- [CA]
*American author, journalist, attorney*
* Bumppo, Nathaniel John Balthazar
* Bumppo, Natty

**Dean, Laura**
*See* Fredericks, Mrs. William

**Dean, Maggie**
*See* Bland, Mrs. Lionel E.

**Dean, Man Mountain**
*See* Leavitt, Frank S.

**Dean, Marguerite Mooers Marshall** 1887- [NAA]
*American author*
* Marshall, Marguerite Mooers

**[The] Dean Martin of Country Music**
*See* Reeves, [Franklin] Delano

**Dean, Mary** 1923- [AW]
*British author*
* Mee, Mary

**Dean, Max**
*See* Righi, Massimo

**Dean, Nell Marr** 1910- [CA]
*American author*
* Roberts, Virginia

**Dean, Nelson**
*See* Whipple, Nelson S.

**[The] Dean of Afro-American Composers**
*See* Still, William Grant

[The] Dean of American Animal
Artists
See Bransom, Paul

[The] Dean of American Fashion
Designers
See Levinson, Norman

[The] Dean of American Inventors
See Woods, Granville T.

[The] Dean of American Playwrights
See Thomas, Augustus

[The] Dean of Black American
Designers
See Lowe, Anne

[The] Dean of Black Hucksters
See Jackson, James Albert

[The] Dean of Black Industrial
Scientists
See Hall, Lloyd Augustus

[The] Dean of Black Photographers
See Vander Zee, James

[The] Dean of Black Racing
See Scott, Wendell, Sr.

[The] Dean of Black Research
Bibliographers
See Porter, Dorothy Louise Burnett

[The] Dean of Black Sports Writers
See Lacy, Sam

[The] Dean of Black Sportswriters
See Young, Frank A.

[The] Dean of California Journalists
See Bass, Charlotta A.

[The] Dean of Chicago Gunmen
See Stevens, Walter

[The] Dean of Colored Motion
Pictures
See Foster, William

[The] Dean of Hollywood Voice Men
See Colvig, Vance D.

[The] Dean of Polish Dramatists
See Szaniawski, Jerzy

[The] Dean of Referees
See Walder, Jimmy

[The] Dean of Russian Literature
See Kheraskov, Mikhail
Matveevich

[The] Dean of St. Patrick's
See Swift, Jonathan

[The] Dean of Show Biz
See Allen, Shepard

[The] Dean of the Folk Singers
See Kincaid, Bradley

[The] Dean of TV Art Directors
See Olden, Georg

[The] Dean of Western Singers
See Duncan, Tommy

Dean, Paul Dee 1913-1981
[BE, PB]
American baseball player
* Dean, Daffy

Dean, Robert George 20th c. [WW]
Author
* Griswold, George

Dean, Spencer
See Winchell, Prentice

Dean, Tommy
See Overstreet, Tommy

Dean, Vinnie
See DiVittorio, Vincent

[La] Deana
See Aybar o Rodriguez, Manuela

Deane, Charles
See Saunders, Edward

Deane, Dee Shirley
See Brass, Dee Shirley

Deane, Elisabeth
See Beilenson, Edna

Deane, Kenner
See Smith, Charlotte

Deane, Lorna
See Wilkinson, Lorna Hilda
Kathleen

Deane, Margery
See Pitman, Margaret J.

Deane, Martha 1908-1973 [B10]
American radio commentator
* Young, Marian

Deane, Norman
See Creasey, John

Deane, Sonia
See Soutar, Gwendoline Amy

Deane, Vesey
See Murray, Andrew Nicholas

Deane-Turner, William Cunningham
1877-1922 [FD]
Irish director
* Taylor, William Desmond

DeAngelis, Nancy
See Angelo, Nancy Carolyn
Harrison

Deans, Jennie
See Swisshelm, Jane Grey

Dear Abby
See Phillips, Pauline Esther
[Friedman]

Dear, Basil 1911-1971 [BF]
British director
* Dearden, Basil

Dear, Buddy
See Dear, Paul Stanford

[A] Dear Liberty Boy
See Hollis, Thomas

Dear, Paul Stanford 1905- [BE]
American baseball player
* Dear, Buddy

Dear, Peter 1912- [THR]
British actor and director
* Dearing, Peter

[The] Dear Saxon
See Handel, Georg Friedrich

Dearbon, Benjamin 1755-1838
[PA]
Author
* [The] Friend of Industry

Dearborn, Laura
See Picton, Nina

Dearden, Basil
See Dear, Basil

Dearing, Peter
See Dear, Peter

DeArmond, Charles Hommer
[Charlie] 1877-1933 [BE]
American baseball player
* DeArmond, Hummer

DeArmond, Hummer
See DeArmond, Charles Hommer
[Charlie]

Dearth, Kathleen 1907- [CWG]
American country-western performer
* Dee, Kathy

Deas, James Alvin 1895-1972
[MK]
American baseball player
* Deas, Yank

Deas, Yank
See Deas, James Alvin

Dease, Bobby
See McCahan, Robert C.

Deasley, Pat
See Deasley, Thomas H.

Deasley, Thomas H. 1857-1943
[BE]
American baseball player
* Deasley, Pat

Deason, Muriel Ellen 1919-
[CME, ECM, FCW]
American country-western performer
* [The] Queen of Country Music
* Wells, Kitty

Deast, Basil
See Butler, William Huxford [Bill]

D'Easum, Cedric [Godfrey] 1907-
[CA]
American author and columnist
* D'Easum, Dick

D'Easum, Dick
See D'Easum, Cedric [Godfrey]

Death, Dr.
See Grigson, James

Death, Mr.
See Whitehead, John L., Jr.

Death to Flying Things
See Ferguson, Robert V.

Death Valley Jim
See Scott, James

Death Valley Scotty
See Scott, Walter

Deauville, Max
See Duwez, Maurice

DeBakey, Michael 1908-
American surgeon
* [The] Texas Tornado

DeBeaubien, Philip Francis
1913-1979 [CA]
American publisher and columnist
* Holiday, Homer

Debella, George 1931- [EJ]
American jazz musician
* Devens, George

Debenedet, Flavio Nelson 1947-
[HR]
Italian-born hockey player
* Debenedet, Nels

Debenedet, Nels
See Debenedet, Flavio Nelson

Debenham, Cicely
See Debnam, Cicely

DeBernardi, De
See DeBernardi, Forrest S.

DeBernardi, Forrest S. 1899-1970
[AS, BB, BBH]
American basketball player
* DeBernardi, De
* DeBernardi, Red

DeBernardi, Red
See DeBernardi, Forrest S.

DeBerry, Hank
See DeBerry, John Herman

DeBerry, John Herman 1893-1951
[BE]
American baseball player
* DeBerry, Hank

DeBlasio, Gene 1940-1971 [SC]
American actor
* Savage, Houston
* Savoy, Houston

Debnam, Cicely 1891-1955 [THR]
British actress and singer
* Debenham, Cicely

[Le] Debonnaire
See Baldwin V

[Le] Debonnaire
See Louis I

Deborin, Abram M.
See Joffe, Abram

DeBozoky, Barbara
See Springer, Barbara

Debrah, Ebenezer Moses 1928-
[IBW]
Ghanaian diplomat
* Debrah, Tojo

Debrah, Tojo
See Debrah, Ebenezer Moses

Debrett, Hal [joint pseudonym with
Kathleen Rollins]
See Dresser, Davis

Debrett, Hal [joint pseudonym with
Davis Dresser]
See Rollins, Kathleen

Debrot, Cola
See Debrot, Nicolaas

Debrot, Nicolaas 1902- [IAW]
Dutch author, poet, politician
* Debrot, Cola

[The] Decalogist
See Dod, John

Decanus
See Hoare, Edward Mavenham

Decanver, H. C.
See Cavender, C. H.

DeCapite, Andrea Lee 1946- [RO1]
American singer
* Carroll, Andrea

DeCarlo, Angelo 20th c.
American underworld figure
* [The] Gyp

Decaux, Lucile
See Bibesco, Marthe-Lucile
[Lahovary]

DeCavalcante, Simone Rizzo 20th
c. [PHM]
American underworld figure
* [The] Plumber
* Sam the Plumber

**December, William, Jr.** 1940-
[IBW]
*American actor*
* Williams, Billy Dee

**Dechet, Hippolyte Louis Alexandre**
1801-1830   [WBD]
*French comedian and poet*
* Jenneval

**Decius**
*See*  Gardner, Samuel Jackson

**Decker, Duane** 1910-1964
[CA, SAT]
*American author*
* Wayne, Richard

**Decker, Frank** 1848-1919  [WBD]
*American painter, sculptor, etcher*
* Duveneck, Frank

**Decker, George Henry** 1947-  [BE]
*American baseball player*
* Decker, Joe

**Decker, Joe**
*See*  Decker, George Henry

**Decker, Mrs. Nelson**   [FFF]
*Entertainer*
* Almayne, Nard

**Decker, T.** ?-1639  [PA]
*Author*
* [The] Catholic Bishop of Bantry
* [The] Man of Business

**Deckers, Jeannine** 1933?-
[B10, RO1]
*Belgian singer and former nun*
* Luc Gabrielle, [Sister]
* [The] Singing Nun
* Soeur Sourire [Sister Smile]

**Declan, Peter**
*See*  Francoeur, Robert Thomas

**Declercq, Aime** 1898-  [IAW]
*Belgian theatre director, poet,
playwright*
* Dundee, Alex

**Decles, Jon**
*See*  Studebaker, Don

**Decolta, Ramon**
*See*  Whitfield, Raoul

**DeCosta, Joan** 1930-  [EJ]
*American singer and songwriter*
* Shaw, Joan

**DeCoverley, Roger**
*See*  Hathaway, Ronald F.

**DeCristoforo, Romeo John** 1917-
[CA]
*American writer on manual arts*
* Cristy, R. J.
* Williams, Cris

**DeCurtis, Dolls**
*See*  DeCurtis, Guido

**DeCurtis, Guido**  ?-1977
*American underworld figure*
* DeCurtis, Dolls

**DeCurtis, Julia A.** 1942-  [OP]
*American opera singer*
* Barrera, Giulia

**Dedeaux, Rauol** 1915-  [BBH, BE]
*American baseball player and coach*
* Dedeaux, Rod

**Dedeaux, Rod**
*See*  Dedeaux, Rauol

**Dedrick, Lyle F.** 1918-   [EJ, PMJ]
*American jazz musician*
* Dedrick, Rusty

**Dedrick, Rusty**
*See*  Dedrick, Lyle F.

**Dee, Bobby**
*See*  Bender, D. C.

**Dee, Dare**
*See*  Steffens, Arthur

**Dee, Dave**
*See*  Harmon, David

**Dee, Donna**
*See*  De Varona, Donna

**Dee, Frances**
*See*  Dee, Jean

**Dee, Frankie**
*See*  Brown, Frankie Dee

**Dee, Freddie**
*See*  De Piano, Freddie

**Dee, Henry**
*See*  Torbett, Harvey Douglas Louis

**Dee, Jean** 1907-  [FC]
*American actress*
* Dee, Frances

**Dee, Joey**
*See*  Di Nicola, Joseph

**Dee, John**
*See*  Fanning, David Christopher
Patrick St. John

**Dee, John** 1527-1608  [HN, SN]
*Welsh astrologer and mathematician*
* [The] English Faust
* Nobilis Mathematicus
* Praestantissimus Mathematicus

**Dee, Johnny**
*See*  Loudermilk, John D.

**Dee, Kathy**
*See*  Dearth, Kathleen

**Dee, Kiki**
*See*  Matthews, Pauline

**Dee, Maurice F.** 1891-  [BE]
*Canadian-born baseball player*
* Dee, Shorty

**Dee, Mercy**
*See*  Walton, Mercy Dee

**Dee, Merri**
*See*  Dorham, Mary

**Dee, Nicholas**
*See*  Aiken, Joan Delano

**Dee, Papa**
*See*  Allen, Thomas Sylvester

**Dee, Roger**
*See*  Aycock, Roger Dee

**Dee, Ruby**
*See*  Wallace, Ruby Ann

**Dee, Sandra**
*See*  Zuck, Alexandra

**Dee, Shorty**
*See*  Dee, Maurice F.

**Dee, Sylvia**
*See*  Proffitt, Josephine Moore

**Dee Tee**
*See*  Thomas, Dennis

**Deed, Andre**
*See*  Chapuis, Andre

**[The] Deed Door**
*See*  Edmund I [or Eadmund]

**Deeds, Cameron Scott** 20th c.
[BBH]
*American collegiate athletic director*
* Deeds, Scotty

**Deeds, Scotty**
*See*  Deeds, Cameron Scott

**Deegan, Dummy**
*See*  Deegan, W. John

**Deegan, Jon J.** [house pseudonym,
Hamilton]
*See*  Campbell, Herbert J.

**Deegan, Jon J.** [house pseudonym,
Hamilton]
*See*  Sharp, Robert [George]

**Deegan, W. John** 20th c.  [BE]
*American baseball player*
* Deegan, Dummy

**Deeks, Barbara** 1937-  [FC, TR]
*British actress*
* Windsor, Barbara

**Deeley, Ben**
*See*  Deeley, J. Bernard

**Deeley, Francis Arthur** 1868-1927
[BEW]
*British-born producer and actor*
* Curzon, Frank

**Deeley, J. Bernard** 1878-1924  [SC]
*American actor*
* Deeley, Ben

**Deeming, Richard**
*See*  Deming, Richard

**Deems, Charles Force** 1820- ?   [PA]
*Author*
* C. F. D.

**Deems, James Harry** 1848- ?
[ALY]
*American author and musician*
* Civis

**Deems, Mickey**
*See*  Damaszek, Marvin

**Deen, Elizabeth Ann**  ?-1975  [SC]
*American actress*
* Deen, Nedra

**Deen, Nedra**
*See*  Deen, Elizabeth Ann

**Deep, Charlie**
*See*  Sanders, Charlie

**Deeping, George Warwick** 1877- ?
[WWL]
*British author*
* Warwick, George

**Deer, M. J.** [joint pseudonym with
Mary J. Deer Smith]
*See*  Smith, George H[enry]

**Deer, M. J.** [joint pseudonym with
George H(enry) Smith]
*See*  Smith, Mary J. Deer

**Deering, [Sir] Edward**   [SN]
*British politician*
* [The] Silver Trumpet of the
House

**Deery, Joan** 20th c.   [BEW]
*Australian-born actress*
* Wetmore, Joan

**Dees, Rick**
*See*  Dees, Rigdon Osmond, III

**Dees, Rigdon Osmond, III** 1950-
[RO2]
*American singer and songwriter*
* Dees, Rick

**DeFate, Clyde** 1898-1963   [BE]
*American baseball player*
* DeFate, Tony

**DeFate, Tony**
*See*  DeFate, Clyde

**Defender and Baron of the Holy
Sepulchre**
*See*  Godfrey of Bouillon

**[The] Defender of German
Independence**
*See*  Henry II [or Henri]

**Defender of the Faith**
*See*  Henry VIII

**Defender of the Faith**
*See*  Torquemada, Juan de [or
John]

**Defender of the Faith of God**
*See*  Abd-er-Rahman III

**[The] Defender of Thermopylae**
*See*  Leonidas

**Defense, Mr.**
*See*  Vinson, Carl

**Deficit, Madame**
*See*  [Josephe Jeanne] Marie
Antoinette

**Defillo De Casals, Pau Carlos
Salvador** 1876-1973  [CA]
*Spanish-born cellist, composer,
conductor*
* Casals, Pablo

**Defoe, Daniel**
*See*  Foe, Daniel

**DeFranco, Boniface Ferdinand
Leonardo** 1923-  [ASC, DAM, EJ]
*American jazz musician*
* DeFranco, Buddy

**DeFranco, Buddy**
*See*  DeFranco, Boniface Ferdinand
Leonardo

**DeFrees, Madeline** 1919-
[CA, WD]
*American educator, author, poet*
* Mary Gilbert, [Sister]

**Dege, Lin**
*See*  Grimard, Luc

**Degee, Olivier** 1890-1944  [CD]
*Belgian author*
* Tousseul, Jean

**Degener, Claire S.**
*See*  Sweeney, Claire Cynthia

**Deghy, Guy [Stephen]** 1912-
[AW, CAP, WD]
*British author and playwright*
* Froy, Herald [joint pseudonym
with Keith (Spencer)
Waterhouse]
* Gibb, Lee [joint pseudonym with
Keith (Spencer) Waterhouse]

**Degler, Claude** 20th c.   [SFP]
*Author*
* Rogers, Don

**Degli Stabili, Francesco**
1257?-1327   [WBD]
*Italian poet and philosopher*
* Cecco d'Ascoli

**Degni, Lou** 1933-   [FC, SW]
*American gymnast and actor*
* Forest, Mark

**DeGraeff, W. B.**
*See*   Conklin, Edward Groff

**DeGroff, Edward Arthur**
1879-1955   [BE]
*American baseball player*
* DeGroff, Rube

**DeGroff, Rube**
*See*   DeGroff, Edward Arthur

**DeGros, J. H.**
*See*   Villiard, Paul

**Dehan, Richard**
*See*   Graves, Clotilda Inez Mary

**Dehner, John**
*See*   Forkum, John

**Dehner, Louis** 1914-   [BB]
*American basketball player*
* Dehner, Pick

**Dehner, Pick**
*See*   Dehner, Louis

**Dehnert, Dutch**
*See*   Dehnert, Henry

**Dehnert, Henry** 1898-   [BB]
*American basketball player*
* Dehnert, Dutch

**Dei Filipepi, Alessandro di Mariano**
1444?-1510   [WBD]
*Italian painter*
* Botticelli, Sandro

**Dei Guardati, Tommaso** 15th c.
[WBD]
*Italian author*
* Masuccio di Salerno

**Deihl, Edna Groff** 1881- ?   [NAA]
*American author*
* Aunt Este
* Forge, Andre

**Deindorfer, Robert Greene** 1922-
[CA]
*American author*
* Bender, Jay
* Dender, Jay
* Greene, Robert

**Deininger, Otto Charles** 1877-1950
[BE]
*German-born baseball player*
* Deininger, Pep

**Deininger, Pep**
*See*   Deininger, Otto Charles

**Deisel, Edward** 1875-1948   [BE]
*American baseball player*
* Deisel, Pat

**Deisel, Pat**
*See*   Deisel, Edward

**DeJong, David C[ornel]** 1905-1967
[CA, SAT]
*Dutch-born American author*
* Breda, Tjalmar

**DeKalb, Lorimer**
*See*   Knorr, Marian L[ockwood]

**Dekemel, Matthew Antoine Desire**
1900?-1967   [NOJ]
*American jazz musician*
* Buglin Sam, the Waffle Man

**Dekker, Albert**
*See*   Van Dekker, Albert

**Dekker, Carl**
*See*   Laffin, John [Alfred Charles]

**Dekker, Desmond**
*See*   Dacres, Desmond

**Dekker, Eduard Douwes**
1820-1887   [WBD]
*Dutch author*
* Multatuli

**Dekkers, Ad**
*See*   Dekkers, Adrian

**Dekkers, Adrian** 1938-   [CAR]
*Dutch painter*
* Dekkers, Ad

**DeKnight, Jimmy**
*See*   Myers, James E.

**Dekobra, Maurice**
*See*   Tessier, Ernest Maurice

**Del Barco, Lucy Salamanca**   [CA]
*British-born author and artist*
* Salamanca, Lucy

**Del Campo y Alvarez, Domingo**
1873-1900?   [GS, OCS]
*Spanish bullfighter*
* Dominguin [Little Domingo]

**Del Mar, Claire**
*See*   Mohr, Clare Eloise

**Del Mar, Florentina**
*See*   Conde Abellan, Carmen

**Del Martia, Astron** [house
pseudonym, Gaywood Press]
*See*   Fawcett, F[rank] Dubrez

**Del Martia, Astron** [house
pseudonym, Gaywood Press]
*See*   Fearn, John Russell

**Del Monte, Felix Maria** 1819-1899
[CW]
*Dominican poet, playwright,
journalist*
* Delio

**Del Monte y Aponte, Domingo**
1804-1853   [CW]
*Cuban poet and author*
* Almadovar, Sanchez de
* Sanchez de Almodovar, Bachiller
Toribo

**Del Norte, Scott**
*See*   Smith, Raymond Harley

**Del Pozo y Jimenez, Manuel** 1906-
[GS]
*Spanish bullfighter*
* Rayito [Little Flash]

**Del Rey, Lester** [joint pseudonym
with Paul W. Fairman]
*See*   Alvarez Del Rey, Ramon
Felipe San Juan Mario Silvio Enrico

**Del Rey, Lester** [joint pseudonym
with Ramon Felipe San Juan Mario
Alvarez Del Rey]
*See*   Fairman, Paul W.

**Del Riego, Philip** 1883-   [THR]
*British actor*
* Desborough, Philip

**Del Rio, Dolores**
*See*   Asunsolo De Martinez, Lolita
Dolores

**Del Rio, Eduardo** 1934-   [WEC]
*Mexican cartoonist*
* Rius

**Del Rio, James Cohen** 1924-   [IBW]
*American politician and jurist*
* Ash Can Joe

**Del Tolveno, Arricha**
*See*   Hollaender, Viktor

**Del Val, Jean**
*See*   Gautier, Jean

**Del Vecchio, Gabriel** 1923-   [TR]
*West Indian-born actor*
* Dell, Gabriel

**Delacroix, Ferdinand Victor Eugene**
1798-1863   [SN]
*French painter*
* [The] Rubens of France
* [The] Veronese of France
* [The] Victor Hugo of Painting

**Delacroix, Henri Edmond**
1856-1910   [WBD]
*French painter*
* Cross, Henri Edmond

**DeLacy, Louise**
*See*   Hickey, Madelyn Eastlund

**Delafield, E. M.**
*See*   De La Pasture, Edmee
Elizabeth Monica

**Delahanty, Big Ed**
*See*   Delahanty, Edward James

**Delahanty, Del**
*See*   Delahanty, Edward James

**Delahanty, Edward James**
1867-1903   [AS, BAB, PB]
*American baseball player*
* Delahanty, Big Ed
* Delahanty, Del

**Delahanty, Frank George**
1885-1966   [BE]
*American baseball player*
* Delahanty, Pudgie

**Delahanty, Pudgie**
*See*   Delahanty, Frank George

**Delaisne, Jean**
*See*   Soreil, [Joseph] Arsene

**Delamarre, Guillaume** 1470-1550
[PA]
*Author*
* Da Mara

**Delamarre, Victor** 1888-1955
[CSH]
*Canadian strongman*
* [The] Man with no Master but
God
* [The] New Samson

**DeLamarter, Jeanne**
*See*   Bonnette, Jeanne

**DeLamotte, Roy Carroll** 1917-
[CA]
*American clergyman, educator,
author*
* Wilson, Gregory

**DeLand, Tracy**
*See*   Leete, Frederick De Land

**Delaney, Art[hur D.]**
*See*   Helenius, Arthur D.

**Delaney, Bright Eyes**
*See*   Chapdelaine, Ovila

**Delaney, Bud**
*See*   Delaney, Francis, Jr.

**Delaney, Denis**
*See*   Green, Peter [Morris]

**Delaney, Francis, Jr.** 1931-   [CA]
*American author*
* Delaney, Bud

**Delaney, Franey**
*See*   O'Hara, John [Henry]

**Delaney, Frederick George**
1856-1940   [BMH]
*British entertainer*
* Griffiths, Fred

**Delaney, Jack**
*See*   Chapdelaine, Ovila

**Delaney, Jack J[ames]** 1921-   [CA]
*American librarian and author*
* Stone, Richard

**Delaney, James** 20th c.   [SG]
*Boxer*
* Doyle, Jimmy

**Delaney, Marshall**
*See*   Fulford, Robert

**Delaney, Mary Murray** 1913-
[CA, WD]
*American writer*
* Lane, Mary D.

**Delany, Chip**
*See*   Delany, Samuel R[ay]

**Delany, Joseph Francis** 1905-
[WW]
*Author*
* Dane, Joel Y.

**Delany, Samuel R[ay]** 1942-   [SF]
*American author*
* Delany, Chip

**Delaporte, Theophile**
*See*   Green, Julien [Hartridge]

**Delattre [or de Lattre], Roland**
1532?-1594   [WBD]
*Belgian-born composer*
* Lasso, Orlando di
* Lassus, Orlandus [or Roland] de

**DeLaube**
*See*   Cardena, Clement

**Delaware, Lord**
*See*   West, Thomas

**Delay, Claude**
*See*   Delay-Tubiana, Claude

**Delay-Baillen, Claude** 1934-   [CA]
*French psychoanalyst and writer*
* Baillen, Claude

**Delay-Tubiana, Claude** 1934-   [CA]
*French psychoanalyst and author*
* Delay, Claude

**[The] Delayer**
*See*   Fabius Maximus Verrucosus,
Quintus

**Delf, Juliet** 1888?-1962   [BEW]
*Theatrical performer*
* Miss Juliet

**Delf, Thomas**  [PA]
*Author*
* Martell, Charles

**Delfano, M. M.**
*See*  Flammonde, Paris

**Delfont, Bernard**
*See*  Winogradsky, Barnet

**Delgado, Adelaida** 1923-  [FC, ITA]
*American dancer and actress*
* Mara, Adele

**Delharpe [or Delaharpe], Jean
Francois** 1739-1803  [WBD]
*French poet and critic*
* Laharpe, Jean Francois de

**Delhi, Flame**
*See*  Delhi, Lee William

**Delhi, Lee William** 1890-1966
[BE]
*American baseball player*
* Delhi, Flame

**Deliberate Pedant**
*See*  Eliot, Thomas Stearns

**Delibes, Miguel**
*See*  Delibes Setien, Miguel

**Delibes Setien, Miguel** 1920-  [CA]
*Spanish author*
* Delibes, Miguel

**[The] Delicious**
*See*  Browne, Charles Farrar

**[The] Delight of Mankind**
*See*  Maximilian II

**[The] Delight of Mankind**
*See*  Sabinus Vespasianus, Titus
Flavius

**[The] Delightful**
*See*  William

**Deligne y Figueroa, Rafael Alfredo**
1863-1902  [CW]
*Dominican poet, playwright, author*
* Candido, Pepe

**Deligny, Louis**
*See*  Maurault, Olivier

**Delio**
*See*  Del Monte, Felix Maria

**Delio**
*See*  Iturrondo, Francisco

**DeLisle, Louis**
*See*  Nelson, Louis Delisle

**Delius, Frederick**
*See*  Delius, Fritz Albert Theodor

**Delius, Fritz Albert Theodor**
1862-1934  [BBD]
*British composer*
* Delius, Frederick

**Delius, Nikolaus**  [PA]
*Author*
* D.

**[The] Deliverer of America**
*See*  Washington, George

**Delk, Robert Carlton** 1920-  [CA]
*Canadian-born American author and
educator*
* Carlton, Alva
* Tenness, George

**Dell, Belinda**
*See*  Bowden, Jean

**Dell, Claudia**
*See*  Smith, Claudia Dell

**D'Ell, Denis**
*See*  Dalziell, Denis

**Dell, Dorothy**
*See*  Goff, Dorothy

**Dell, Draycot Montagu** 1888- ?
[MBF]
*British author*
* Anson, Piers
* Thompson, Stephen

**Dell, Dudley**
*See*  Gold, Horace Leonard

**Dell, Gabriel**
*See*  Del Vecchio, Gabriel

**Dell, Paul**
*See*  Blaisdell, Paul

**Dell, Wheezer**
*See*  Dell, William George

**Dell, William George** 1887-1966
[BE]
*American baseball player*
* Dell, Wheezer

**Della**
*See*  Hollow, Della

**Della Caravauna**
*See*  Caravane, Pietro

**Della Crusca**
*See*  Merry, Robert

**Della Genga, Annibale Francesco**
1760-1829  [WBD]
*Pope*
* Leo XII

**Della Pieve, Pier**
*See*  Vannucci, Pietro

**Della Rosa, Signor**
*See*  Coker, Richard

**Della Rovere, Francesco**
1414-1484  [WBD]
*Pope*
* Sixtus IV

**Della Rovere, Giuliano** 1443-1513
[SN, WBD]
*Pope*
* Julius II
* [A] Second Mars

**Della Tiorba**
*See*  Ferrari, Benedetto

**Della Torre Rezzonico, Carlo**
1693-1769  [WBD]
*Pope*
* Clement XIII

**Della Viola**
*See*  Alessandro, Romano

**Della Vite, Giovanni**
*See*  Miel [or Meel], Jan

**Dellacroce, Aniello** 1915-
*American underworld figure*
* O'Neill, Father

**Dellbridge, John** 1887-
[WW, WWL]
*British author*
* Plummy

**Delle Ape [Of the Bees]**
*See*  Bracciolini, Francis

**Dellinger, Allan Miles** 1929-
[BEW]
*American dance notator and teacher*
* Miles, Allan

**Delmaine, Lottie**
*See*  Allen, Mrs. George W.

**Delmar, Alexander** 1836- ?  [PA]
*Author*
* Kwang Chang Ling

**Delmar, Eddie**
*See*  Frandsen, Robert

**Delmar, Ethel**
*See*  Osborne, Alma

**Delmar, Roy**
*See*  Wexler, Jerome [LeRoy]

**Delmas, Delphin**  [BLB]
*American attorney*
* [The] Little Napoleon of the
West Coast Bar

**Delmer, Ide**
*See*  Cheesborough, Essie B.

**Delmere, Bella**
*See*  Wood, Matilda Alice Victoria

**Delminio**
*See*  Camillo, Giulio

**Delmonico, Andrea**
*See*  Morrison, Eula Atwood

**Delmont, Al**
*See*  Delmonti, Alfredo

**Delmonte, Armand Romeo** 1927-
[CEI, SMG]
*Canadian-born hockey player*
* Delmonte, Dutch

**Delmonte, Dutch**
*See*  Delmonte, Armand Romeo

**Delmonti, Alfredo** 1885-  [BX]
*Italian-born boxer*
* Delmont, Al

**Delna, Marie**
*See*  Ledan, Marie

**Delock, Ike**
*See*  Delock, Ivan Martin

**Delock, Ivan Martin** 1929-  [BE]
*American baseball player*
* Delock, Ike

**Deloire, Pierre**
*See*  Peguy, Charles Pierre

**DeLone, Ruth**
*See*  Rankin, Ruth [DeLone]
I[rvine]

**Delores**
*See*  Rose, Kathleen Mary

**Delorm, Tad**
*See*  Delorm, Thomas Andrew

**Delorm, Thomas Andrew** 1955-
*American soccer player*
* Delorm, Tad

**Delorme, Daniele**
*See*  Girard, Gabrielle

**Delorme, Michele**
*See*  Cranston, Mechthild

**DeLorme, Mrs. Henry**  [FFF]
*Entertainer*
* Hynes, Adeline

**Delorme, Reve**  [PA]
*Author*
* Haus, Ladovie

**Deloughery, Grace L.** 1933-  [WD]
*American educator and author*
* Wiest, Grace L.

**Delp, Buddy**
*See*  Delp, Grover

**Delp, Grover** 20th c.
*American horse trainer*
* Delp, Buddy

**D'Elpeux, Ravin**  [FFF]
* Murio-Celli, Mme.

**Delphi**
*See*  Hodson, Arnold Wienholt

**Delphin**
*See*  Sirveaux, Jules

**Delphine**
*See*  Baker, P.

**Delroy, Irene**
*See*  Sanders, Josephine

**Delta**
*See*  Denham, Edward

**Delta**
*See*  Dennett, Herbert Victor

**Delta**
*See*  Disraeli, Benjamin

**Delta**
*See*  Domett, Henry W.

**Delta**
*See*  Harvey, Moses

**Delta**
*See*  Moir, David Macbeth

**Delta**
*See*  Turnbull, Dora Amy Elles
Dillon

**Delta Joe**
*See*  Luandrew, Albert

**Delta John**
*See*  Hooker, John Lee

**[The] Delta Lady**
*See*  Coolidge, Rita

**DeLucia, Anthony**
*See*  DeLucia, Felice

**DeLucia, Felice** 1897-1972
[BLB, MM, PHM]
*Italian-born American underworld
figure*
* Barstow, Paul
* DeLucia, Anthony
* Maglio, Paul
* [The] Porter
* Ricca, Mops
* Ricca, Paul
* Salvi, Paul
* Viela, Paul
* Villa, Paul
* [The] Waiter

**Deluna, Carl** 20th c.
*American underworld figure*
* Deluna, Tuffy

**Deluna, Tuffy**
*See*  Deluna, Carl

**DeLunatico, F.**
*See*  James, George

**Delvecchio, Alex Peter** 1931-
[FHE]
*Canadian-born hockey player*
* Delvecchio, Fats

**Delvecchio, Fats**
*See* Delvecchio, Alex Peter

**Delving, Michael**
*See* Williams, Jay

**Delysia, Alice**
*See* Lapize, Alice

**DeMaestri, Joseph Paul** 1928-
[BE]
*American baseball player*
* DeMaestri, Oats

**DeMaestri, Oats**
*See* DeMaestri, Joseph Paul

**DeMaggio, Giuseppe Paolo, Jr.**
1914- [BAB, SR]
*American baseball player*
* Di, Joe
* DiMaggio, Joltin Joe
* DiMaggio, Joseph Paul [Joe]
* [The] Yankee Clipper

**DeMain, Gordon** 1897-1967 [SC]
*Actor*
* Wood, Gordon D.

**Demaine, Don**
*See* Drinkall, Gordon [Don]

**DeMange, Big Frenchy**
*See* DeMange, George

**DeMange, George** 20th c. [BLB]
*American underworld figure*
* DeMange, Big Frenchy

**Demar, Carmen**
*See* Porrata Dorio de Aponte,
Carmen

**Demara, Ferdinand Waldo, Jr.**
1921- [BL]
*American impersonator*
* Demara, Fred
* [The] Great Imposter

**Demara, Fred**
*See* Demara, Ferdinand Waldo, Jr.

**DeMarco, Ab**
*See* DeMarco, Albert Thomas, Jr.

**DeMarco, Ab**
*See* DeMarco, Albert Thomas, Sr.

**DeMarco, Albert Thomas, Jr.**
1949- [CEI, FHE, HK]
*American-born hockey player*
* [The] Count
* DeMarco, Ab

**DeMarco, Albert Thomas, Sr.**
1916- [CEI, FHE]
*Canadian-born hockey player*
* DeMarco, Ab

**DeMarco, Billygoat**
*See* DeMarco, Pat

**DeMarco, Paddy**
*See* DeMarco, Pat

**DeMarco, Pat** 1928-
[BX, RBE, WBC]
*American boxer*
* [The] Brooklyn Billygoat
* DeMarco, Billygoat
* DeMarco, Paddy

**Demarco, Tony**
*See* Liotta, Leonardo

**Demaree, Frank**
*See* Dimaria, Joseph Franklin

**Demarest, Ann**
*See* Bond, Florence Demarest
[Foos]

**Demarest, Doug**
*See* Barker, Will

**Demaris, Ovid**
*See* Desmarais, Ovide E.

**DeMars, Kid**
*See* DeMars, William Lester
[Billy]

**DeMars, William Lester [Billy]**
1925- [BE]
*American baseball player*
* DeMars, Kid

**DeMartin, Imelda**
*See* DeMartin Di Fabbro, Imelda
Italia

**DeMartin Di Fabbro, Imelda Italia**
1936- [BEW]
*Italian actress, dancer, singer*
* DeMartin, Imelda

**DeMayo, Chee Chee**
*See* DeMayo, Frank

**DeMayo, Frank** 20th c. [BLB]
*American underworld figure*
* DeMayo, Chee Chee

**Demelikoff, Jodi** 20th c. [SFP]
*Author*
* McCarter, Jody [joint pseudonym
with Vermille McCarter]

**Demento, Dr.**
*See* Hansen, Barry

**DeMerit, John Stephen** 1936- [BE]
*American baseball player*
* DeMerit, Thumper

**DeMerit, Thumper**
*See* DeMerit, John Stephen

**Demetrius I** 4th c. BC
[HN, RH, WBD]
*King of Macedonia*
* [The] Besieger
* Poliorcetes

**Demetrius I** 2nd c. BC [WBD]
*King of Syria*
* Soter [Preserver]

**Demetrius I** ?-1606 [WBD]
*Russian ruler*
* Pseudo Demetrius

**Demetrius II** 2nd c. BC [WBD]
*King of Syria*
* Nicator

**Demetrius III** 1st c. BC [WBD]
*King of Syria*
* Eukairos
* Philometor

**Demijohn**
*See* Pratt, F. Alcott

**Demijohn, Thom** [joint pseudonym
with John Sladek]
*See* Disch, Thomas M.

**Demijohn, Thom** [joint pseudonym
with Thomas M. Disch]
*See* Sladek, John T[homas]

**Demikov, Jules**
*See* Demikovosky, Jevel

**Demikovosky, Jevel** 1922- [CAR]
*American painter*
* Demikov, Jules
* Olitski, Jules

**Deming, Richard** 1915-
[CA, WD, WGT]
*American author*
* Deeming, Richard
* Franklin, Max

**Demling, Arthur** 1948- [AES]
*American soccer player*
* Demling, Buzz

**Demling, Buzz**
*See* Demling, Arthur

**Demme, Hermann Christoph
Gottfried** 1760-1822 [FFF, WBD]
*German author and poet*
* Stille, Karl

**Demmon, Calvin W.** 20th c. [SFP]
*Author*
* Damon, Carl

**Demochares**
*See* De Mouchy, Antoine

**Democritus**
*See* Potter, Henry Glasford

**Democritus** 5th c. BC
[DNNF, FF, SN]
*Greek philosopher*
* [The] Abderite
* [The] Derider
* [The] Laughing Philosopher

**Democritus Junior**
*See* Burton, Robert

**[The] Democritus of the Sixteenth
Century**
*See* Chauvin [or Caulvin?], Jean

**Demoisey, Frenchy**
*See* Demoisey, John

**Demoisey, John** 1912- [BB]
*American basketball player*
* Demoisey, Frenchy

**DeMola, Donald John** 1952-
[SMG]
*American baseball player*
* DeMola, Mole

**DeMola, Mole**
*See* DeMola, Donald John

**Demoliere, M. Hippolyte Jules**
?-1878 [PA]
*Author*
* Moleri

**[The] Demon Bowler**
*See* Spofforth, Frederick Robert

**[The] Demon of Frome**
*See* Dredge, Colin Herbert
[Herbie]

**[The] Demon of Rebellions**
*See* La Tour d'Auvergne, Henri de
[Duc de Bouillon]

**[The] Demon of the South**
*See* Philip II

**Demont, Gene**
*See* DeMontreville, Eugene
Napoleon

**DeMontreville, Eugene Napoleon**
1874-1935 [BE]
*American baseball player*
* Demont, Gene

**Demos, Erik**
*See* Ross, Chuck

**DeMoss, Bingo**
*See* DeMoss, Elwood

**DeMoss, Elwood** 1889-1965
[AS, MK]
*American baseball player*
* DeMoss, Bingo

**Demosthenes** 4th c. BC
[DNNS, SN]
*Athenian orator*
* [The] Prince of Orators

**[The] Demosthenes of America**
*See* Webster, Daniel

**[The] Demosthenes of France**
*See* Riquetti, Honore Gabriel
Victor

**[The] Demosthenes of the Pulpit**
*See* Rennell, Thomas

**DeMott, Ben**
*See* DeMott, Benyew Harrison

**DeMott, Benyew Harrison**
1889-1963 [BE]
*American baseball player*
* DeMott, Ben

**Dempewolff, Richard F[rederic]**
1914- [CA]
*American editor and author*
* Day, Michael
* Frederick, Dick
* Wolf, Frederick

**Dempsey, Con**
*See* Dempsey, Cornelius Francis

**Dempsey, Cornelius Francis** 1923-
[BE]
*American baseball player*
* Dempsey, Con

**Dempsey, Henry** 1925-
[ESF, SFL, WGT]
*American author*
* Boyd, Felix
* Hall, Cameron [joint pseudonym
with Ramon Felipe San Juan
Mario Felipe San Juan
Mario Alvarez Del Rey]
* Harrison, Harry Maxwell
* Kaempfert, Wade [house
pseudonym, Space Publications]

**Dempsey, Jack**
*See* Dempsey, William Harrison

**Dempsey, Jack**
*See* Kelly, John

**Dempsey, James Clifford** 1937-
[CWG, DAM]
*American country-western performer*
* Dempsey, Little Jimmy

**Dempsey, James E.** 1876-1918
[ASC]
*American composer and singer*
* Ford, Powell I.
* Grayson, Paul

**Dempsey, John Rikard** 1949-
[BE, SMG]
*American baseball player*
* Dempsey, Rick

**Dempsey, Little Jimmy**
*See* Dempsey, James Clifford

**Dempsey, Rick**
*See* Dempsey, John Rikard

**Dempsey, William Harrison** 1895-
[BX, RBE, WBC]
*American boxer*
* Blackie, Kid
* Dempsey, Jack
* [The] Manassa Mauler

**Demsky, Issur Danielovich** 1916-
[BDF, FC, HT]
*American actor*
* Douglas, Kirk

**Den Ouden, Willy** 1918?-   [BBH]
*Swimmer*
* [The] Darling of European
  Swimming

**Den, Petr**
*See* Radimsky, Ladislaw

**Dena**
*See* Bryant, Dena

**Denali, Peter**
*See* Holm, Don[ald Raymond]

**Denard, Robert [Bob]** 1928?-
*French mercenary soldier*
* Mouhadjou [or Mahdjou], [Said]
  Moustapha
* Robin

**Denarius**
*See* Penny, William

**Denarius Philosophorum**
*See* Thornborough, Bishop

**DeNaut, George Matthews** 1915-
[ASC]
*American musician*
* DeNaut, Jud

**DeNaut, Jud**
*See* DeNaut, George Matthews

**Denbie, Roger** [joint pseudonym with
Alan (Baer) Green]
*See* Brodie, Julian Paul

**Denbie, Roger** [joint pseudonym with
Julian Paul Brodie]
*See* Green, Alan [Baer]

**Denbigh, Maurice**
*See* Nutbrown, Maurice

**Denbry, R. Emmet?**
*See* Murfree, Mary Noailles

**Dendel, Esther [Sietmann Warner]**
1910-   [CA]
*American author*
* Warner, Esther S.

**Dender, Jay**
*See* Deindorfer, Robert Greene

**Dene, Alan**
*See* Wignall, Trevor

**Dene, Hampton**
*See* Hook, Samuel Clarke

**Denenberg, Herbert S[idney]** 1929-
[CA]
*American attorney, educator, writer*
* Dumpty, Humpty S.

**Denenholz, Alma** 1912-   [CA]
*American author*
* Clistier, Adeline
* Denny, Alma

**Dener**
*See* De Abreu, Pamplona

**Deneuve, Catherine**
*See* Dorleac, Catherine

**Dengyo Daishi**
*See* Saicho

**Denham, Edward**   [FFF]
*American writer*
* Delta
* Epsilon

**Denham, [Sir] John** 1615-1669
[SN]
*British poet*
* That Limping Old Bard

**Denham, June Catherine Church**
1909-   [THR]
*Scottish-born actress and singer*
* St. Denis, Teddie

**Denham, Mary Orr** 1918-   [CA]
*American author and actress*
* Caswell, Anne
* Orr, Mary

**Denham, Sully**
*See* Budd, Mavis

**Denholm, David** 1924-   [WD]
*Australian author*
* Forrest, David

**Denholm, Mark**
*See* Fearn, John Russell

**Denholm, Therese Mary Zita White**
1933-   [CA]
*Australian author*
* White, Zita

**Deni**
*See* Denisov, Viktor Nikolayevich

**Denim, Joe**
*See* Cotton, James [Jimmy]

**Denis [or Denys]** ?-272
[FF, HN, SN]
*Saint*
* [The] Apostle of the French
* [The] Apostle of the Gauls

**Denis, Barbara J.** 1940-   [CA]
*American author*
* Carroll, Anne Kristin

**Denis, Jean Paul** 1924-   [CEI]
*Canadian-born hockey player*
* Denis, Johnny

**Denis, Johnny**
*See* Denis, Jean Paul

**Denis, Julio**
*See* Cortazar, Julio

**Denis le Flamand**
*See* Calvaert [or Calvart], Denis

**Denis, Lorimer** 1904-1957   [CW]
*Haitian critic and educator*
* De Sabe, Aristide

**Denis, Louis Gilbert** 1928-   [CEI]
*Canadian-born hockey player*
* Denis, Lulu

**Denis, Lulu**
*See* Denis, Louis Gilbert

**Denis P.**
*See* Peploe, Denis Frederic Neil

**Denis, Villard** 1940-   [CW]
*Haitian poet and painter*
* Davertige

**Denison, Corrie**
*See* Partridge, Eric Honeywood

**Denison, Mary Andrews**   [PA]
*Author*
* M. A. D.
* Vance, Clara

**Denison, Mrs.**   [FFF]
*Entertainer*
* Madison, Matilda

**Denisov, Viktor Nikolayevich**
1893-1946   [WEC]
*Russian cartoonist*
* Deni

**Denman**
*See* Denman-Jones, Gladys

**Denman-Jones, Gladys** 1900-
[DBA]
*British painter*
* Denman

**Denmark, Harrison**
*See* Zelazny, Roger [Joseph]

**Dennehy, Thomas Francis** 1899-
[BE]
*American baseball player*
* Dennehy, Tod

**Dennehy, Tod**
*See* Dennehy, Thomas Francis

**D'Ennery, Adolph**
*See* Dennery, Eugene Phillip

**Dennery, Eugene Phillip** 1812- ?
[PA]
*Author*
* D'Ennery, Adolph

**Denness, Haggis**
*See* Denness, Michael Henry
[Mike]

**Denness, Michael Henry [Mike]**
1940-   [DC]
*British cricketer*
* Denness, Haggis

**Dennett, Herbert Victor** 1893-
[CA]
*British author*
* Delta
* Syntax, John
* Tent, Ned

**Dennie, Joseph** 1768-1812
[DEL, PA, SN]
*American author*
* [The] Addison of America
* [The] American Addison
* [The] Farrago
* [The] Lay Preacher
* Oldschool, Oliver

**Denning, Dasher**
*See* Denning, Peter William

**Denning, Dutch**
*See* Denning, Otto George

**Denning, Laurence**
*See* Sellers, Connie Leslie, Jr.

**Denning, Melita**
*See* Godfrey, Vivian

**Denning, Otto George** 1912-   [BE]
*American baseball player*
* Denning, Dutch

**Denning, Patricia**
*See* Willis, Corinne Denneny

**Denning, Peter William** 1949-
[DC]
*British cricketer*
* Denning, Dasher

**Denning, Richard**
*See* Denninger, Louis A.

**Denninger, Louis A.** 1914-   [FC]
*American actor*
* Denning, Richard

**Dennis, Amanda E.** 19th c.   [FFF]
*Writer*
* Amanda
* [The] Poet of Wicomisco

**Dennis, Arthur**
*See* Edmonds, Arthur Denis

**Dennis, Bruce**
*See* O'Brien, David Wright

**Dennis, Denny**
*See* Dennis, Stanley

**Dennis, Eve**
*See* Wornum, Miriam

**Dennis, John** 1657-1734
[FFF, RH, SN]
*British critic and playwright*
* [The] Best Abused Man in
  England
* [The] Critic
* Python
* [The] Royal Midas
* Tremendous, Sir
* Young Zoilus
* Zoilus

**[The] Dennis of His Day**
*See* Gacon, Francois

**Dennis, Patrick**
*See* Tanner, Edward Everett, III

**Dennis, Ruth** 1878-1968
[SC, WBD]
*American dancer and teacher of
dancing*
* St. Denis, Ruth

**Dennis, Stanley** 1906-   [MY]
*American jazz musician*
* Dennis, Denny

**Dennis, Walter L.** 20th c.
[ESF, WGT]
*American author*
* McDermott, Dennis [joint
  pseudonym with P. Schuyler
  Miller and Aubrey McDermott]

**Dennis-Jones, H[arold]** 1915-
[AW, CA, WD]
*British translator and author*
* Hamilton, Paul
* Hessing, Dennis

**Dennison, Aaron Lufkin**
1812-1895   [WBD]
*American watch manufacturer*
* [The] Father of American
  Watchmaking

**Dennison, Charles W.** 19th c.
[FFF, PA]
*American author*
* Penniman, Major

**Dennison, Dorothy**
*See* Golden, Dorothy

**Dennison, Eliza Freeman**   [PA]
*Author*
* Crust, Christie

**Denniston, Elinore** 1900-1978
[CA, CC, WW]
*American author*
* Allan, Dennis
* Foley, Rae

**Denny, Alma**
See Denenholz, Alma

**Denny, Brian**
See Doughty, Bradford

**Denny, Jerry**
See Eldridge, Jeremiah Dennis

**Denny, John Thomas** [FFF]
*British writer*
* Free Lance
* Leigh, Hart
* Winwood, Brent

**Denny, Reginald**
See Daymore, Reginald Leigh

**Denny, William Henry**
See Dugmore, William Henry

**Densel, Mary**
See McCobb, Mary Selden

**Denslow, Martin Van Buren** [PA]
*Author*
* O'Quill, Maurice

**Denslow, W. W.**
See Denslow, William Wallace

**Denslow, William Wallace**
1856-1915 [FBJ]
*American author and illustrator*
* Denslow, W. W.

**Dent, Anthony Austen** 1915-
[AW, CA]
*British author*
* Amplegirth, Anthony
* [El] Bundukhari
* Garthwaite, Malaby
* Lampton, Austen

**Dent, Bucky**
See Dent, Russell Earl

**Dent, C. H.** 20th c. [MBF]
*British author*
* Fanshaw, Cecil
* Hudleston, John
* Hudleston, Robert

**Dent de Fer**
See Frederick II

**Dent, Denis**
See Williams, Graeme

**Dent, Eddie**
See Dent, Elliott Estill

**Dent, Elliott Estill** 1887- [BE]
*American baseball player*
* Dent, Eddie

**Dent, J. M.**
See Dent, Joseph Mallaby

**Dent, Joseph Mallaby** 1849-1926
[LC]
*British publisher*
* Dent, J. M.

**Dent, Lester** 1905?-1959
[ESF, SFL, WGT]
*American author*
* Grant, Maxwell [house
    pseudonym]
* Roberts, Kenneth
* Robeson, Kenneth [house
    pseudonym, Street & Smith]
* Ryan, Tim

**Dent, Richard** 1902- [ART]
*British artist*
* Richard D.

**Dent, Russell Earl** 1951-
[SMG, WWB]
*American baseball player*
* Dent, Bucky

**Dentatus, Sicinius** 5th c. BC
[FFF, RH, SN]
*Roman tribune*
* [The] Achilles of Rome
* [The] Roman Achilles
* [The] Roman Roland
* [The] Second Achilles

**Dente, Blackie**
See Dente, Samuel Joseph

**Dente, Samuel Joseph** 1922- [BE]
*American baseball player*
* Dente, Blackie

**Dentinger, Stephen**
See Hoch, Edward D.

**Denton, James**
See Hughes, Robert J.

**Denver, Boone**
See Rennie, James Alan

**Denver, Bruce**
See Hope, William Edward
Stanton

**Denver, Drake C.**
See Nye, Nelson C[oral]

**Denver, John**
See Deutschendorf, Henry John,
Jr.

**Denver, Rod**
See Edson, John Thomas

**Denvers, Jake**
See Edgar, Alfred

**Denys** ?- 95 [HN]
*Saint*
* [The] Apostle of France
* Dionysius the Areopagite

**Denzer, Ann Wiseman**
See Wiseman, Ann [Sayre]

**Denzer, Peaceful Valley**
See Denzer, Roger

**Denzer, Roger** 1871-1949 [BE]
*American baseball player*
* Denzer, Peaceful Valley

**Deodato**
See Deodato, Eumir

**Deodato, Eumir** 20th c. [RO2]
*Brazilian-born singer*
* Deodato

**Deodato, Ruggero** 20th c. [WF]
*Italian director*
* Rockfeller, Roger

**DePaolo, Peter**
*Auto racer*
* [The] Golden Man of the
    Speedways

**DePaul, Judith**
See De Paoli, Giuditta

**Deplazes, Gion** 1918- [IAW]
*Swiss author*
* Vial, Gion

**Depond, Moise** 1917- [WEC]
*French cartoonist*
* Mose

**[The] Deputy Governor**
See Gorst, Gilpin

**DeQuatro, Dominick** 20th c.
[PHM]
*American underworld figure*
* Dom the Sailor

**Der**
See Second element of name

**Derba, Mimi**
See Perez de Leon, Hermina

**Derby Day Clymer**
See Clymer, William Johnston
[Bill]

**Derby Dick Thompson**
See Thompson, Herbert John

**Derby, Elias Haskett** 1739-1799
[FFF]
*American merchant and author*
* Massachusetts

**Derby, 14th Earl of**
See Stanley, Edward George
Geoffrey Smith

**Derby, George Horatio** 1823-1861
[DEL, PA, WBD]
*American author*
* Phoenix, John, Gentleman
* Squibob

**Derby, Mark**
See Wilcox, Harry

**Derbyshire, Jane**
See Green, Madge

**Derbyshire, John Henry** 1878-1938
[SWI]
*British swimmer*
* Derbyshire, Rob

**Derbyshire, Rob**
See Derbyshire, John Henry

**DeRego, Anthony** 1897- [BE]
*American baseball player*
* Rego, Anthony [Tony]

**Derek**
See Cymbal, Johnny

**Derek, Bo**
See Collins, Mary Cathleen

**Derek, John**
See Harris, Derek

**Dereme, Tristan**
See Huc, Philippe

**Derib**
See De Ribeaupierre, Claude

**DeRidder, Lucille** 1921- [EJ]
*American singer*
* Reed, Lucy

**[The] Derider**
See Democritus

**Dering, Cini Willoughby**
See Buddicom, Jacintha Laura
May

**Dering, Ross George**
See Balfour, Frederic H[enry]

**[The] Deritend Martyr**
See Rogers, John

**Derleth, August [William]**
1909-1971 [CA, CC, WGT]
*American author and poet*
* Grendon, Stephen
* Heath, Eldon
* Holmes, Kenyon
* Mason, Tally

**Derleth, August [William]**
(Continued)
* West, Michael

**Dermitius**
See O'Meara, Dermand

**Dermot, Gertrude** 1874-1950
[THR]
*American actress*
* Elliott, Gertrude

**Dermot, Jessie** 1868?-1940
*American actress*
* Elliott, Maxine

**Dermott, Stephen**
See Bradbury, Parnell

**Dermott, Vern**
See Frye, Vern D.

**Dern, Peggy Gaddis** 1895-1966
[CA, NAA]
*American author*
* Courtland, Roberta
* Craig, Georgia
* Gaddis, Peggy
* Jordan, Gail
* Lee, Caroline
* Lindsay, Perry
* Sherman, Gail
* Sherman, Joan

**D'Ernecourt, Barre** ?-1660 [PA]
*Author*
* De St. Balman, Madam

**DeRocher, L. E.**
See DeRocher, Lawrence Edwin

**DeRocher, Lawrence Edwin** 1912-
[BEW]
*Canadian-born theatre manager*
* DeRocher, L. E.

**DeRoin, Nancy** 1934- [CA]
*American writer, editor, translator*
* Ross, Nancy

**Derounian, Avodis Arthur** 1909-
[TC1]
*American journalist*
* Carlson, John Roy

**D'Erquar, Mar. Jozon**
See Querard, Joseph-Maria

**Derrick, Claud Lester** 1886-1974
[BE]
*American baseball player*
* Derrick, Deek

**Derrick, Deek**
See Derrick, Claud Lester

**Derrick, Frances**
See Motley, Mrs.

**Derrick, Lionel** [joint pseudonym
with Mark Roberts]
See Cunningham, Chet

**Derrick, Lionel** [joint pseudonym
with Chet Cunningham]
See Roberts, Mark

**Derrick, Samuel** 1724?-1769 [PA]
*Author*
* Wilkes, Thomas

**Derringer, Duke**
See Derringer, Paul

**Derringer, Oom Paul**
See Derringer, Paul

**Derringer, Paul** 1906-
[BE, DGS, PB]
*American baseball player*
* Derringer, Duke
* Derringer, Oom Paul

**Derringer, Rick**
*See* Zehringer, Richard

**Derrington, Blackie**
*See* Derrington, Charles James
[Jim]

**Derrington, Charles James [Jim]**
1939-  [BE]
*American baseball player*
* Derrington, Blackie

**[The] Derrydown Triangle**
*See* Stewart, Robert [Viscount
Castlereagh]

**Dersonnes, Jacques**
*See* Simenon, Georges [Joseph
Christian]

**Derventio**
*See* Hughes, Walter Dudley

**Dery, George** 20th c.  [SMG]
*American baseball scout*
* Dery, Pat

**Dery, Pat**
*See* Dery, George

**Des**
*See* Asmussen, Andreas

**Des Essaut, M. Davrelle**  [PA]
*Author*
* Maitre

**Des Freux, Andre** ?-1556  [PA]
*Author*
* Frusius

**Des Houx, Henri**
*See* Durand-Morimbau, Henri

**Des Ormes, Renee**
*See* Turgeon, [Madame] Leonida
F.

**Des Pres, Josquin** 1450?-1521
[SN]
*Flemish composer*
* [The] Father of Modern
Harmony

**Des Reaux, Gedeon Tallemant**
[SN]
*French author*
* [The] Calomniographe of His
Age

**Des Roches, Francis** 1895-  [NAA]
*Canadian author*
* Frandere

**DeSalvo, Albert** 1932-1973
*American murderer*
* [The] Boston Strangler

**Desana, Dorothy**
*See* Trent, Ann

**Desautels, Eugene Abraham** 1907-
[BE]
*American baseball player*
* Desautels, Red

**Desautels, Red**
*See* Desautels, Eugene Abraham

**Desbillons, Francois Joseph Terasse**
1751?-1789  [DEP, DNNF, FFF]
*French scholar*
* [The] Last of the Romans

**Desborough, Philip**
*See* Del Riego, Philip

**Deschamps, Emile** 1791-1871  [PA]
*Author*
* [Le] Jeune Moraliste

**Deschamps, Eugenio** 1861-1919
[CW]
*Dominican poet and journalist*
* [El] Tribuno Popular

**Deschamps, Eustache** 1320-1402
[PA]
*Author*
* Morel

**Deschamps, M. Pierre**  [PA]
*Author*
* Poche

**Deschamps, Marguerite**
*See* Lafontant-Medard, Michaelle

**Deserres, Gaston**  [PA]
*Author*
* Vatel

**[The] Desert Fox**
*See* Rommel, Erwin

**Desforges, Evariste Desire [Chevalier
de Parny]** 1753-1814
[DNNF, HN, SN]
*French poet*
* [The] French Tibullus
* [The] Tibullus of France

**Desfosses, Helen** 1945-  [CA]
*American author*
* Cohn, Helen Desfosses

**Deshoulieres, Antoinette du Ligier de
la Garde** 1633?-1694
[DEP, DNNS, RH]
*French poet*
* Amaryllis
* [The] French Calliope
* [The] Tenth Muse

**Desiderius**
*See* Dauferius

**Desiderius, [Father]**
*See* Lenz, Peter

**[Le] Desire**
*See* Louis XVI

**[Le] Desire**
*See* Louis XVIII

**DesJardien, Paul R.** 1893-1956
[AS, FB]
*American football player*
* DesJardien, Shorty

**DesJardien, Shorty**
*See* DesJardien, Paul R.

**Desjardins, Marie Catherine**
*See* De Villedieu, Mme.

**Desjardins, Martin**
*See* Van den Bogaert, Martin

**Desjardins, Pete[r]** 1907-  [SWI]
*American swimmer*
* [The] Little Bronze Statue from
Florida

**Deslandes, Celie-Diaquoi**
*See* Diaquoi-Deslandes, Celie

**Deslandes, [Baroness] M.** 20th c.
[WWL]
*French author*
* Ossit

**Deslys, Gabrielle** 1884-1920
[BEW]
*French theatrical performer*
* Deslys, Gaby

**Deslys, Gaby**
*See* Deslys, Gabrielle

**Desmarais, Barbara G.**
*See* Taylor, Barbara G.

**Desmarais, Ovide E.** 1919-  [CA]
*American author*
* Demaris, Ovid

**Desmarettes**
*See* Le Brun, Jean Baptiste

**Desmaretz, Jean** ?-1524  [WBD]
*French poet*
* Marot, Jean

**Desmasures, Louis** 1510-1580  [PA]
*Author*
* Masurius

**D'Esme, Jean**
*See* D'Esmenard, Jean

**D'Esmenard, Jean** 1893-1966
[SFL, WGT]
*French author*
* D'Esme, Jean

**Desmond, Florence**
*See* Dawson, Florence

**Desmond, Johnny**
*See* De Simone [or Desimons?],
Giovanni Alfredo

**Desmond, Paul**
*See* Breitenfeld, Paul Emile

**Desmonde, Jerry**
*See* Sadler, James Robert

**Desmoulins, [Lucie Simplice] Camille
[Benoit]** 1762?-1794
[DEP, HN, WBD]
*French revolutionary leader*
* [The] Aristophanes of the
Revolution
* [The] Attorney General of the
Lantern
* Procureur de la Lanterne

**Desnoyers, Edward** 1814- ?  [PA]
*Author*
* De Breville

**Despard, Leslie**
*See* Howitt, John Leslie Despard

**Despars, Jacques** 1380-1458  [PA]
*Author*
* De Partibus

**D'Espence, Charles** 1511-1571
[PA]
*Author*
* Expencoeus

**Desperate Dan Dillinger**
*See* Dillinger, John Herbert

**Desplaines, [Baroness] Julie**
*See* Jennings, Leslie Nelson

**Desportes, Philippe** 1546?-1606
[DNNF]
*French poet*
* [The] French Tibullus

**Desrosiers, Marie Antoinette Tardif**
1895-  [NAA]
*Canadian author*
* Le Normand, Michelle

**Desroussels, Felix**
*See* Dorismond, Jean-Baptiste

**Dessaix**
*See* Hairdet, M.

**Dessaix, Joseph Marie** 1764-1834
[WBD]
*French army officer*
* [L']Intrepide

**Dessau, Frank Rolland** 1883-1952
[BE]
*American baseball player*
* Dessau, Rube

**Dessau, Rube**
*See* Dessau, Frank Rolland

**Dessaur, Catherine Irma** 1931-
[IAW]
*Dutch author*
* Burnier, Andreas

**Desses, Jean**
*See* Verginie, Jean Dimitre

**Deste, Luli**
*See* Von Hohenberg, Luli

**Destinn, Emmy**
*See* Kittl, Ema

**Destiny, Archibald**
*See* Shaw, Lawrence Taylor
[Larry]

**Destouches, Louis-Ferdinand**
1894-1961  [CD, EWL, LC]
*French author*
* Celine, Louis Ferdinand

**Destouches, Philippe**
*See* Nericault, Philippe

**[The] Destroyer**
*See* Attles, Alvin J., Jr.

**[The] Destroyer of Heresy**
*See* Louis XIV

**[The] Destroying Prince**
*See* Timur [or Timour]

**Destry, Diane** 20th c.  [RO2]
*Singer*
* Charity

**Destry, Vince**
*See* Norwood, Victor G[eorge]
C[harles]

**Desval**
*See* Valdes Machuca, Ignacio

**DeSylva, B. G.**
*See* DeSylva, George Gard

**DeSylva, Buddy**
*See* DeSylva, George Gard

**DeSylva, George Gard** 1895?-1950
[ASC, B10, BEW]
*American songwriter and producer*
* DeSylva, B. G.
* DeSylva, Buddy

**Detached Badger**
*See* Walford, J. H.

**[A] Detective**
*See* Beal, Andrew Edward

**Detective's Daughter**
*See* Porter, Mrs. Robert P.

**Detering-Nathan, Patricia** 1910-
[BF]
*Chinese-born actress*
* Maritza, Sari

**D'Ethis**
See   Corney, Louis Dominique

**Detine, Padre** [joint pseudonym with Ib Spang Olsen]
See   Frederiksen, Erik E.

**Detine, Padre** [joint pseudonym with Erik E. Frederiksen]
See   Olsen, Ib Spang

**Detlef, Karl**
See   Bauer, Klara

**Detroit Jr.**
See   Williams, Emery H.

**Detroit, Karl** 1827-1878   [WBD]
*German-born Turkish army officer*
* Mehemet Ali Pasha

**Detroit Red**
See   Little, Malcolm

**Detroit Red**
See   Perryman, Rufus G.

**Detroit's Black Angel**
See   Waddles, Charleszetta Campbell

**Detweiler, Ducky**
See   Detweiler, Robert Sterling

**Detweiler, Robert Sterling** 1919-
[BE]
*American baseball player*
* Detweiler, Ducky

**Detzer, Diane**
See   De Reyna, Diane Detzer

**Detzer, Karl** 1891-   [CAP]
*American author*
* Costello, Michael

**Deubler, Konrad** 1814-1884   [WBD]
*Austrian philosopher*
* [The] Peasant Philosopher

**[The] Deuce**
See   Ford, Henry, II

**Deuch, Brother**
See   Kaing Kech Ieu

**Deuchar, Maude** 20th c.   [WWL]
*British author*
* Tremaine, Herbert

**Deuel, Peter** 1940-1971   [FC]
*American actor*
* Duel, Pete

**Deufer, Johann Heinrich** ?-1770
[PA]
*Author*
* Jansen

**Deus Philosophorum [God of Philosophers]**
See   Aristocles

**Deusdedit** 7th c.   [WBD]
*Pope*
* Adeodatus I

**D'Euse, Jacques** 1249-1334   [WBD]
*Pope*
* John XXII

**Deuster, Joseph Anthony** 1912-
[BEW, FC, FD]
*American actor, director, playwright*
* Anthony, Joseph

**Deutsch, Dutch**
See   Deutsch, M. A.

**Deutsch, Friedrich** 1902-   [BBD]
*Austrian-born musicologist*
* Dorian, Frederick

**Deutsch, Kurt** 1911-   [CA]
*Austrian-born American author and editor*
* Singer, Kurt D[eutsch]

**Deutsch, M. A.** 20th c.   [SMG]
*American baseball scout*
* Deutsch, Dutch

**Deutsch, Nikolaus**
See   Manuel, Nikolaus

**Deutsch, Roszika** 1892-1970
[EMT, PMJ, F1]
*Hungarian-born actress and dancer*
* Dolly, Rosie

**Deutsch, Yansci [or Janszieka]**
1892-1941   [BEW, EMT, PMJ]
*Hungarian-born actress and dancer*
* Dolly, Jenny

**[Der] Deutsche Michael**
See   Obertraut, Johann Michael

**Deutschendorf, Henry John, Jr.**
1943-   [IPA]
*American singer*
* Denver, John

**Deutscher, Isaac** 1907-1967   [CA]
*Polish-born author and journalist*
* Peregrine

**Deutzman, Lawrence F[rederick]**
1880- ?   [NAA]
*American author and editor*
* [The] Rambler
* Travis, Lawrence

**Deux, Emilienne** 1874- ?   [THR]
*French actress*
* Dux, Emilienne

**Devajee, Ved**
See   Gool, Reshard

**Deval, Jacques**
See   Boularan, Jacques

**Devala**
See   Banerjee [or Bandyopadhyay], Abani Mohan

**Devant, David**
See   Wighton, David

**D'Evelyn, Rose**
See   Broemel, Rose

**Devens, George**
See   Debella, George

**Devere, Francesca** 1891-1952   [SC]
*American actress*
* Devere, Frisco

**Devere, Frisco**
See   Devere, Francesca

**Devereux, Penelope** 1562?-1607
[DNNF, FFF, SN]
*Daughter of Walter, First Earl of Essex*
* Stella

**Devereux, Robert [Second Earl of Essex]** 1566-1601   [HHF, SN]
*British army officer*
* Boots, Bonny
* [The] English Achilles

**Devereux, Robert [Third Earl of Essex]** 1591-1646   [SN]
*British army officer*
* Old Robin

**Devereux, Roy**
See   Pember-Devereux, Margaret R[ose Roy McAdam]

**Devery, Elizabeth Coleman** 20th c.
[NAA]
*American writer*
* Clift, Betty

**Devi, Nila**
See   Woody, Regina Jones

**[The] Devil**
See   Genna, Michael

**[The] Devil**
See   Hunyadi, Janos [or Huniades, John]

**[The] Devil**
See   Ledain, Olivier

**[The] Devil**
See   Medici, Giovanni de

**[The] Devil**
See   Paganini, Nicolo

**[The] Devil**
See   Robert I

**Devil Dick**
See   Porson, Richard

**[The] Devil Doll**
See   Franco, Edmund

**Devil May Kaer**
See   Kaer, Morton A.

**[The] Devil of Arras**
See   D'Alibi, Cardinal

**[The] Devil of Vendee**
See   Rossignol, Jean Antoine

**[The] Devil on Two Sticks**
See   Morton, Oliver [Hazard] Perry [Throck]

**DeVilbiss, Philip**
See   Mebane, John [Harrison]

**Devil's Daddy-in-Law**
See   Council, Floyd

**[The] Devil's Football**
See   Austin, Henry Willard

**[The] Devil's Missionary**
See   Arouet, Francois Marie

**[The] Devil's Son-in-Law**
See   Bunch, William

**Devin, Marius**
See   Landau, Edwin Maria

**Devin, Thomas C.**   [SN]
*Army officer*
* Old Tommy
* Old War-Horse

**Devine**
See   Tennyson, Joe

**Devine, Bing**
See   Devine, Paul Adrian

**Devine, Bing**
See   Devine, Vaughan P.

**Devine, D. M.**
See   Devine, David McDonald

**Devine, David McDonald** 1920-
[CA, EMD, WD]
*Scottish author*
* Devine, D. M.
* Devine, Dominic
* Munro, David

**Devine, Dominic**
See   Devine, David McDonald

**Devine, Mickey**
See   Devine, William Patrick

**Devine, Paul Adrian** 1951-   [SMG]
*American baseball player*
* Devine, Bing

**Devine, Vaughan P.** 1917-   [PB]
*American baseball executive*
* Devine, Bing

**Devine, William M.** 20th c.   [BEW]
*American theatrical performer*
* Armstrong, William [Billy]

**Devine, William Patrick**
1892-1937   [BE]
*American baseball player*
* Devine, Mickey

**DeVita, Teddy** 1963?-1980
*American victim of bone marrow disease*
* [The] Boy in the Glass Cage

**Devlan, Eugene** 1890-1960
[BEW, TC]
*American author, playwright, journalist*
* Fowler, Gene

**Devlin, Blubber**
See   Devlin, Frank

**Devlin, Frank** ?-1929   [BLB]
*American underworld figure*
* Devlin, Blubber

**Devlin, Owen**
See   Chadwick, Charles

**Devon, John Anthony**
See   Payne, [Pierre Stephen] Robert

**Devon, Nicholas**
See   Dolphin, Reginald Charles [Rex]

**Devon, Nicola**
See   Dolphin, Reginald Charles [Rex]

**Devon, Sarah**
See   Walker, Emily Kathleen

**[The] Devonshire Poet**
See   Jones, Owen

**DeVries, Con**
See   Sellers, Connie Leslie, Jr.

**DeWalt, Autrey, Jr.** 1942-   [RO2]
*American musician*
* Walker, Junior

**Dewar, Ted Royal** 1904-   [BEW]
*American composer, orchestrator, arranger*
* Royal, Ted

**Dewart, Leslie**
See   Gonzalez, Gonzalo

**Dewdney, Peter**
See   Brock, Alan St. Hill

**DeWeese, Eugene** 1934-
[CA, WD, WGT]
*American author*
* DeWeese, Jean
* Stratton, Thomas [joint pseudonym with Robert (Stratton) Coulson]

**DeWeese, Jean**
See   DeWeese, Eugene

**Dewes, Simon**
See  Muriel, John Saint Clair

**Dewey, Ariane** 1937-  [CA, SAT]
*American illustrator*
* Aruego, Ariane

**Dewey, Elmer** 1884-1954  [SC]
*American actor*
* Danilo, Don

**Dewey, James**
See  McNeilly, Mildred Masterson

**Dewey, Thomas B[lanchard]** 1915-
[CA, CC, EMD]
*American author*
* Brandt, Tom
* Wainer, Cord

**DeWitt, James**
See  Lewis, Mildred D.

**DeWolf, Carnelis** 20th c.  [AES]
*Dutch soccer player*
* DeWolf, Cees

**DeWolf, Cees**
See  DeWolf, Carnelis

**Dexter, Al**
See  Poindexter, Albert

**Dexter, Anthony**
See  Fleischmann, Walter Reinhold
Alfred

**Dexter, Aubrey**
See  Jonas, Douglas Peter

**Dexter, Edwin?**
See  Shaver, Richard S[harpe]

**Dexter, J. B.**
See  Glasby, John [Stephen]

**Dexter, Martin**
See  Faust, Frederick [Schiller]

**Dexter, Peter**
See  Shaver, Richard S[harpe]

**Dexter, Roy Evatt** 1955-  [DC]
*British cricketer*
* Lord Ted

**Dexter, Timothy** 1747-1806  [PA]
*Author*
* Lord Timothy

**Dexter, William**
See  Pritchard, William Thomas

**Dey, Frederic Van Rensselaer**
1861-1922  [EMD, WW]
*Author*
* Beckman, Ross
* Burr, Aaron Ainsworth
* Carter, Nicholas
* Clay, Bertha M.
* Dey, Marmaduke
* Gilmore, Marian
* Ormond, Frederic
* Van Doren, Dirck
* Vanardy, Varick

**Dey, John William** 1915?-  [B10]
*American artist*
* Uncle Jack

**Dey, Joseph C., Jr.** 1907-  [GF]
*American golfer*
* Golf, Mr.

**Dey, Larry**
See  Deybrook, L. M.

**Dey, Marjorie**
See  Sandford, Marjorie

**Dey, Marmaduke**
See  Dey, Frederic Van Rensselaer

**[The] Dey of Algiers**
See  Ballantyne, John

**Deybrook, L. M.** 1910-  [ASC]
*American composer*
* Dey, Larry

**DeYoung, Henry C.** 1890-  [NAA]
*Korean-born American author*
* Chung, Henry

**Deyssel, Lodewijk Van**
See  Alberdingk Thijm, Karel Joan
Lodewijk

**Dezsery, Andras**
See  Dezsery, Endre Istvan

**Dezsery, Endre Istvan** 1920-  [IAW]
*Hungarian-born author*
* Dezsery, Andras

**Dheeran**
See  Naa Parthasarathy,
Naarayana-Parthasarathy

**Dheere, Ching**
See  Dheere, Marcel Albert

**Dheere, Marcel Albert** 1920-  [CEI]
*Canadian-born hockey player*
* Dheere, Ching

**D'hele**
See  Hales, Thomas

**D'Hervilly, Ernest**  [PA]
*Author*
* [Un] Passant

**Dhery, Robert**
See  Fourrey, Robert

**D'Heylli, Georges**
See  Poinsot, Austin Edward

**Dhorme, Edouard** 1881- ?  [WBD]
*French monk and scholar*
* Paul, [Father]

**D'Houville, Gerard**
See  De Heredia, Marie Louise
Antoinette

**D'Hugues, Varnac**
See  Prevost, Alain

**Di**
See      Second element of name for
further listings

**Di Bassetto, Corno**
See  Shaw, George Bernard

**Di Biase, Edoardo J.** 1924-  [ASC]
*American musician*
* David, Vincent

**Di Borgo, Luca**
See  Pacioli [or Paccioli], Luca

**Di Camerino, Giuliana** 1920-
[WFA]
*Italian fashion designer*
* Di Camerino, Roberta
* Roberta of Venice

**Di Camerino, Roberta**
See  Di Camerino, Giuliana

**Di Castel, Guido**  [SN]
*Provided refuge for the oppressed*
* [The] Simple Lombard

**Di Cesaro, Simonetta** 20th c.
[WFA]
*Italian fashion designer*
* Simonetta

**Di Cione, Andrea** 1308?-1368?
[WBD]
*Florentine painter, sculptor,
architect*
* Orcagna

**Di Cione di Ser Buonaccorso,
Lorenzo** 1378-1455  [WBD]
*Florentine goldsmith, painter,
sculptor*
* Ghiberti, Lorenzo

**Di Cristina, Paul**
See  Marchese, Paul

**Di Cristofano Bigi, Francesco**
1482?-1525  [WBD]
*Florentine painter*
* Franciabigio

**Di Dono, Paolo** 1397-1475  [WBD]
*Florentine painter*
* Uccello, Paolo

**Di Ferra, Count**
See  Flumiani, Carlo Maria

**Di Fidanza, Giovanni** 1221-1274
[DEP, SN, WBD]
*Saint*
* Bonaventura
* [The] Seraphic Doctor
* Seraphicus, Doctor

**Di Francavilla, Caterina** 1929-
[FC]
*Italian-British television performer*
* Boyle, Catherine

**Di Giovanni, Domenico** 1404-1449
[SN, WBD]
*Florentine poet*
* [Il] Burchiello
* Burchiello, Domenico
* [The] Rhyming Barber

**Di Guisa, Giano**
See  Praz, Mario

**Di, Joe**
See  DeMaggio, Giuseppe Paolo, Jr.

**Di Lese di Sandro, Benozzo**
1420-1498  [WBD]
*Florentine painter*
* Gozzoli, Benozzo

**Di Lorenzo, Ambrogio**
See  Lorenzetti, Ambrogio

**Di Lutero, Battista**  ?-1548?
[WBD]
*Italian painter*
* Dossi, Battista

**Di Lutero, Giovanni** 1479?-1542
[WBD]
*Italian painter*
* Dosso Dossi

**Di Marco di Giacomo Raibolini,
Francesco** 1450?-1517?  [WBD]
*Italian painter and goldsmith*
* Francia

**Di Michele Cione, Andrea**
1435-1488  [WBD]
*Florentine sculptor and painter*
* Verrocchio [or Verocchio],
Andrea del

**Di Murrone [or Morone], Pietro**
1215-1296  [WBD]
*Pope*
* Celestine V

**Di Murska, Ilma**
See  Hill, Mrs. J. T.

**Di Napoli, Mario** 1914-  [ASC]
*American musician*
* Di Napoli, Mike

**Di Napoli, Mike**
See  Di Napoli, Mario

**Di Niccolo di Betto Bardi, Donato**
1386?-1466  [WBD]
*Italian sculptor*
* Donatello

**Di Nicola, Joseph** 1940-  [SW]
*American singer*
* Dee, Joey

**Di Pace, Domenico** 1486-1551
[WBD]
*Italian painter and sculptor*
* Beccafumi, Domenico
* [Il] Meccherino

**Di Pagolo del Fattorino,
Bartolommeo** 1475-1517  [WBD]
*Florentine painter*
* Baccio della Porta
* Bartolommeo, [Fra]
* [Il] Frate

**Di Paola Levin, Jorge Alberto**
1940-  [IAW]
*Argentinian author*
* Dipi

**Di Pietro, Giovanni** 16th c.  [WBD]
*Italian painter*
* [Lo] Spagna

**Di Pietro, Guido** 1387-1455  [WBD]
*Italian friar and painter*
* Angelico, [Fra]
* Fiesole, Giovanni da

**Di Pietro Averlino [or Averulino]**
1400?-1470?  [WBD]
*Florentine architect and sculptor*
* Filarete

**Di Porca, Peter**
See  Hogsmouth, Peter

**Di Prima, Diane** 1934-  [WD]
*American author, poet, playwright*
* Darrich, Sybah

**Di Reschi, Giovanni**
See  De Reszke, Jan Mieczislaw

**Di Savuto, Baroness**
See  La Spina, Greye Bragg

**Di Stefano, Francesco** 1422?-1457
[WBD]
*Florentine painter*
* [Il] Pesellino

**Di Tommaso Bigordi, Domenico**
1449-1494  [WBD]
*Florentine painter*
* Ghirlandajo [or Ghirlandaio]

**Di Vernon**
See  Criswell, Mrs. Croller H.

**[Le] Diable**
See  Damiens, Robert Francois

**[Le] Diable**
See  Ledain, Olivier

**[Le] Diable**
See  Robert I

**Diablo Cojuelo [Limping Devil]** [joint
pseudonym with Serafin Alvarez
Quintero]
See  Alvarez Quintero, Joaquin

**Diablo Cojuelo [Limping Devil]** [joint pseudonym with Joaquin Alvarez Quintero]
*See* Alvarez Quintero, Serafin

**Diabolus**
*See* Howard, Joseph

**[El] Diacono [The Deacon]**
*See* Bermudo I

**Diagoras** 5th c. BC [WBD]
*Greek poet*
* [The] Atheist

**Dial, Joan** 1937- [CA]
*British-born American author*
* Kent, Katherine
* York, Amanda

**Diamant, Lincoln** 1923-
[CA, IAW]
*American author*
* Goya, Fred
* Klopfinger, Herman, III
* McDougal, Stan

**Diamante Negro [Black Diamond]**
*See* Sanchez Olivares, Luis

**Diamond, Do Boy**
*See* Diamond, William

**[The] Diamond Duke**
*See* Charles II

**Diamond, Frank**
*See* Maritote, Frank

**Diamond, Graham** 1945- [CA]
*British-born American author*
* Leslie, Rochelle

**Diamond, I[sadore] A. L.**
*See* Dommnici, Itek

**Diamond Jim Brady**
*See* Brady, James Buchanan [Jim]

**Diamond Jim Brady**
*See* Brady, James Joseph [Jim]

**Diamond Jim Gentile**
*See* Gentile, James Edward

**Diamond Joe**
*See* Reynolds, Joseph

**Diamond Joe Esposito**
*See* Esposito, Joseph

**Diamond Joe Rickert**
*See* Rickert, Joseph Francis [Joe]

**Diamond, John**
*See* Bayley, Barrington J[ohn]

**Diamond, John Thomas [Jack]**
*See* Noland, John T.

**Diamond, Legs**
*See* Noland, John T.

**Diamond, Lillian**
*See* Patrick, Lilian

**[The] Diamond Man**
*See* Rosenzweig, Harry

**Diamond Tooth Lil**
*See* Ornstein, Honora

**Diamond, William** 1913?- [BWW]
*American singer*
* Diamond, Do Boy

**Diana**
*See* Adams, Abigail Smith

**Diana** 1961?-
*Princess of Wales*
* Lady Di
* Shy Di
* Spencer, Diana

**[The] Diana of the Stage**
*See* Bracegirdle, Anne

**Diaquoi-Deslandes, Celie** 1907-
[CW]
*Haitian poet*
* Deslandes, Celie-Diaquoi

**Diarist**
*See* Thayer, Alexander Wheelock

**Dia's Naomi Andrea**
*See* Donaldson, Mary E. Muir

**Dias, Patrick Walter** 1918- [IAW]
*Indian poet and author*
* Jalap

**Diavolo, [Fra]**
*See* Pezza, Michele

**Diaz, Baudilio Jose** 1953- [SMG]
*Venezuelan-born baseball player*
* Diaz, Bo

**Diaz, Bo**
*See* Diaz, Baudilio Jose

**Diaz, E.** 20th c. [OBW]
*American baseball player*
* Diaz, Yoyo

**Diaz, Hector** 20th c. [RBE]
*Dominican boxer*
* Chinito

**Diaz, Juan Martin** 1775-1825
[HN, WBD]
*Spanish patriot*
* [El] Empecinado

**Diaz, Manny**
*See* Diaz, Pedro

**Diaz, Pedro** 20th c. [OBW]
*American baseball player*
* Diaz, Manny

**Diaz, Yoyo**
*See* Diaz, E.

**Diaz Cordero, Luis** 1907- [GS]
*Spanish bullfighter*
* Madrilenito [Little Fellow from Madrid]

**Diaz de Vivar, Rodrigo**
1040?-1099 [DEP, DNNS, RH]
*Spanish soldier*
* Campeador [Champion]
* [The] Cid [Master]

**Diaz Del Busto, Severiano**
1887-1920 [GS]
*Spanish bullfighter*
* Praderito [Little Meadow]

**Diaz Ordonez, Virgilio** 1895-1968
[CW]
*Dominican poet and author*
* Vizardi, Ligio

**Diaz Pavia, Domingo** 1902-1961
[SC]
*Mexican actor*
* Soler, Domingo

**Diaz y Perez, Francisco** 1897-1967
[GS]
*Spanish bullfighter*
* Pacorro

**Dibbets, Gerardus Johannes Maria**
1941- [CAR]
*Dutch artist*
* Dibbets, Jan

**Dibbets, Jan**
*See* Dibbets, Gerardus Johannes Maria

**Dibdin, Charles** 1745-1814 [SN]
*British playwright, actor, composer*
* [The] Bard of the British Navy
* [The] Tyrtaeus of the British Navy

**Dibdin, Thomas Frognall**
1776?-1847 [FFF, PA, WBD]
*British bibliographer*
* [The] Beau Brummel of Living Authors
* Bibliophobia
* Mercurius Rusticus
* [A] Pastor
* [The] Prince of Bibliomaniacal Writers
* Wolfe, Reginald

**D'Iberville, Berthe**
*See* Boissonnault, Marie D.

**Dibos, Corinne** 1925-
[FC, ITA, SW]
*French actress*
* Calvet, Corinne

**Dice, Maralin Fae** [OP]
*American opera singer*
* Niska, Maralin Fae

**Dick, Alexandra**
*See* Erikson, [Cicely] Sibyl Alexandra

**Dick, Kay** 20th c. [SFL]
*Author*
* Scott, Jeremy

**Dick of Aberdaron**
*See* Jones, Richard Robert

**Dick, Philip K[indred]** 1928- [CA]
*American author*
* Phillips, Richard

**Dick, R. A.**
*See* Leslie, Josephine Aimee Campbell

**Dick, Robert** [SN]
*Scottish geologist and botanist*
* [The] Thurso Baker

**Dick the Bruiser**
*See* Afflis, Richard

**Dick, Thomas** 1772-1857 [SN]
*Scottish author*
* [The] Christian Philosopher

**[The] Dick Turpin of France**
*See* Bourguignon, Louis Dominique

**Dick, William Brisbane** 1828- ?
[PA]
*Author*
* Jinks, Joshua Jedediah
* Trumps

**Dick-Lauder, [Sir] George Andrew**
1917- [AW, WD]
*Scottish author*
* Lauder, George [Dick]

**Dickberry, F.**
*See* De Bury, F. Blaze

**Dicke [or Duke?], Willis** [PA]
*Author*
* Wyseman, Demetrius

**Dickens, Charles** 1812-1870
[DEL, HN, PA]
*British author*
* Boz
* Quiz
* Sparks, Timothy
* Uncommercial Traveler

**Dicken's Dutchman**
*See* Langheimer, Charles

**Dickens, Jimmy** 1925- [CME]
*American country-western performer*
* Dickens, Little Jimmy

**Dickens, Little Jimmy**
*See* Dickens, Jimmy

**Dickens, Norman**
*See* Eisenberg, Lawrence B[enjamin]

**Dickerson, B. B.**
*See* Dickerson, Morris DeWayne

**Dickerson, Buttercup**
*See* Dickerson, Louis Pessano

**Dickerson, Louis Pessano**
1858-1920 [BE]
*American baseball player*
* Dickerson, Buttercup

**Dickerson, Mary A.**
*See* Donahey, Mary Dickerson

**Dickerson, Morris DeWayne** 1949-
[PRS]
*American musician*
* Dickerson, B. B.

**Dickerson, Thais** 1916-1945 [SC]
*American actress*
* Dickson, Gloria

**Dickerson-Watkins, L.**
*See* Rourke, Louise Musgrave

**Dickey, George Willard** 1915- [BE]
*American baseball player*
* Dickey, Skeets

**Dickey, Gwen** 20th c. [RO2]
*American singer*
* Dickey, Rose

**Dickey, Lee**
*See* Bremyer, Jayne Dickey

**Dickey, R. P.**
*See* Dickey, Robert Preston

**Dickey, Robert** 1840-1912 [HHF]
*American scout, marshal, trapper*
* Deadwood Dick

**Dickey, Robert Preston** 1936-
[IAW]
*American author*
* Dickey, R. P.

**Dickey, Rose**
*See* Dickey, Gwen

**Dickey, Skeets**
*See* Dickey, George Willard

**Dickinson, Angie**
*See* Brown, Angeline

**Dickinson, Anne Hepple** 1877- ?
[WWL]
*British author*
* Hepple, Anne

**Dickinson, Bo**
*See* Dickinson, Richard L.

**Dickinson, Charles M.**    [PA]
*Author*
* [The] Village Schoolmaster
* [The] Village Shoemaker

**Dickinson, Hal** 1913-    [MY]
*American singer*
* Dickinson, Spook

**Dickinson, Hester A.** 19th c.    [PA]
*Author*
* Benedict, Hester A.

**Dickinson, John** 1732-1808
[DNNS, FFF, WBD]
*American statesman and author*
* Fabius
* [The] Pennsylvania Farmer

**Dickinson, Margaret**
*See* Muggeson, Margaret
Elizabeth

**Dickinson, Martha Gilbert**
*See* Bianchi, Martha Dickinson

**Dickinson, Peter** 1927-    [CA]
*British author*
* De Brissac, Malcolm

**Dickinson, Richard L.** 20th c.
[SMG]
*American football player*
* Dickinson, Bo

**Dickinson, Spook**
*See* Dickinson, Hal

**Dickinson, Susan E.**    [PA]
*Author*
* Vernon, Ada

**[The] Dickon of the Broom**
*See* Richard I

**Dickshot, John Oscar**
*See* Dicksus, John Oscar

**Dickson, Carr**
*See* Carr, John Dickson

**Dickson, Carter**
*See* Carr, John Dickson

**Dickson, E. M.**
*See* Dickson, Evangeline Mary
Lambart

**Dickson, Ellen** 1819-1873    [FFF]
*British composer*
* Dolores

**Dickson, Evangeline Mary Lambart**
1922-    [ART]
*British artist*
* Dickson, E. M.

**Dickson, Gloria**
*See* Dickerson, Thais

**Dickson, Helen**
*See* Reynolds, Helen Mary
Greenwood Campbell

**Dickson, Hickory**
*See* Dickson, Walter R.

**Dickson, James Grierson** 20th c.
[MBF]
*British author*
* King, Hilary

**Dickson, Naida** 1916-    [CA, SAT]
*American author and illustrator*
* Richardson, Grace Lee

**Dickson, Olive**    [FFF]
*Entertainer*
* Berkely, Olive

**Dickson, Samuel Henry** 1798-1872
[PA]
*Author*
* [A] Physician

**Dickson, Walter R.** 1883-1918
[BE]
*American baseball player*
* Dickson, Hickory

**Dickson, Willa** 1941-    [IBW]
*American astrologer*
* Queen Willa

**Dicksus, John Oscar** 1910-    [BE]
*American baseball player*
* Dickshot, John Oscar

**[The] Dictator of a Day**
*See* Pavia y Alburquerque, Manuel

**[The] Dictator of Letters**
*See* Arouet, Francois Marie

**Diddley, Bo**
*See* Bates, Otha Ellas

**Didelot, Marie**
*See* Ford, Marie Elizabeth

**Diderot, Denis** 1713-1784    [WBD]
*French philosopher and author*
* Diderot, Pantophile

**Diderot, Pantophile**
*See* Diderot, Denis

**Didius [Salvius] Julianus** 133- 193
[WBD]
*Roman emperor*
* Didius Severus Julianus, Marcus

**Didius Severus Julianus, Marcus**
*See* Didius [Salvius] Julianus

**[The] Didot of America**
*See* Thomas, Isaiah

**Didrikson, Babe**
*See* Zaharias, Mildred Didrikson

**Didymus** ?- 10    [WBD]
*Greek scholar*
* Chalcenterus

**Didymus** 308?- 394?
[DNNS, WBD]
*Alexandrian scholar and theologian*
* [The] Blind

**Die**
*See*    Second element of name

**Dief the Chief**
*See* Diefenbaker, John George

**Diefenbaker, John George** 1895-1979
*Canadian prime minister*
* Conservative, Mr.
* Dief the Chief

**Diegel, Eagle**
*See* Diegel, Leo

**Diegel, Leo** 1899-1951
[BBH, GME]
*American golfer*
* Diegel, Eagle
* Diegel, Third Round

**Diegel, Third Round**
*See* Diegel, Leo

**Diehl, William Wells** 1916-    [CA]
*American writer and columnist*
* Clay, Duncan

**Diehm, Lorain F.** 1926-    [BBH]
*American collegiate athletic trainer*
* Diehm, Tow

**Diehm, Tow**
*See* Diehm, Lorain F.

**Diehnel, Ellie Tatum**
*See* Diehnel, Tabitha Ellen

**Diehnel, Tabitha Ellen** 1878- ?
[NAA]
*American writer*
* Diehnel, Ellie Tatum

**Dienes, Andre** 1913-    [IAW]
*Hungarian-born artist,
photographer, author*
* De Dienes, Andre

**Dienes, Zoltan Paul** 1916-    [AW]
*Hungarian-born educator and
author*
* Zed

**Diestelhorst, H. Jean** 1904-    [ASC]
*American singer, composer, music
publisher*
* Dale, Jean

**Dieterle, Wilhelm** 1893-1972
[FD, FDG, OCF]
*German director and actor*
* Dieterle, William

**Dieterle, William**
*See* Dieterle, Wilhelm

**Dietrich, Adam** 1711-1782    [WBD]
*German botanist*
* [The] Botanist of Ziegenhain

**Dietrich, Bullfrog**
*See* Dietrich, William John

**Dietrich, Marie Magdalene** 1901-
*German-born actress and singer*
* Dietrich, Marlene
* Von Losch, Marie Magdalene

**Dietrich, Marlene**
*See* Dietrich, Marie Magdalene

**Dietrich, Richard V[incent]** 1924-
[CA]
*American geologist and author*
* Dirk, R.

**Dietrich, Robert**
*See* Hunt, E[verette] Howard, Jr.

**Dietrich, Robert S[alisbury]** 1928-
[CA]
*American author*
* Davis, Gordon

**Dietrich von Bern [Theodoric of
Verona]**
*See* Theodoric

**Dietrich, William John** 1910-    [BE]
*American baseball player*
* Dietrich, Bullfrog

**Dietz, Dutch**
*See* Dietz, Lloyd Arthur

**Dietz, Gertrud** 1912-    [B10, EWL]
*German author, poet, playwright*
* Fussenegger, Gertrud

**Dietz, Lloyd Arthur** 1912-1972
[BE]
*American baseball player*
* Dietz, Dutch

**Dietz, Lone Star**
*See* Dietz, William

**Dietz, William** 1886?-1964
[AS, FB]
*American football coach*
* Dietz, Lone Star

**Dietzel, Ad**
*See* Dietzel, Adolf

**Dietzel, Adolf** 1910-    [BB]
*American basketball player*
* Dietzel, Ad

**Dietzel, Leroy Louis** 1931-    [BE]
*American baseball player*
* Dietzel, Roy

**Dietzel, Roy**
*See* Dietzel, Leroy Louis

**Dietzenschmidt**
*See* Schmidt, Anton Franz

**Dieu-Donne [God-Given]**
*See* D'Artois, Henri Charles
Ferdinand Marie

**Dieu-Donne [God-Given]**
*See* Louis XIV

**Diez, Francisco** 1840-1910    [GS]
*Spanish bullfighter*
* Paco De Oro [Paco the Golden
One]

**Diez, Mrs. M. A.**    [PA]
*Author*
* Henry, William

**Difani, Clarence Joseph** 1923-    [BE]
*American baseball player*
* Difani, Jay

**Difani, Jay**
*See* Difani, Clarence Joseph

**Difficilis, Doctor**
*See* John of Ripatransone

**Diffin, Charles W[illard]** 20th c.
[ESF, WGT]
*American author*
* Willard, C. D.

**DiFiglia, Michael Bennett** 1943-
[EMT]
*American director, choreographer,
dancer*
* Bennett, Michael

**Digby, [Sir] Henry** 1770?-1843
[HN]
*British naval officer*
* [The] Silver Captain

**Digby, [Sir] Kenelm** 1603-1665
[SN]
*British author, naval officer,
diplomat*
* [The] Mirandola of His Age

**Digby-Worsley, Bruce** 1899-
[THR]
*British theatrical manager*
* Worsley, Bruce

**DiGennara, Frank** 1901-
[BX, RBE]
*American boxer*
* Genaro, Frankie

**Digges, Jeremiah**
*See* Berger, Josef

**Diggs, Diggsy**
*See* Diggs, Reese Wilson

**Diggs, Reese Wilson** 1915-    [BE]
*American baseball player*
* Diggs, Diggsy

**DiGiovanni, Joseph** 1888- [BLB]
*Italian-born American underworld figure*
* DiGiovanni, Scarface

**DiGiovanni, Peter** 20th c. [BLB]
*Italian-born American underworld figure*
* DiGiovanni, Sugarhouse Pete

**DiGiovanni, Scarface**
See DiGiovanni, Joseph

**DiGiovanni, Sugarhouse Pete**
See DiGiovanni, Peter

**DiGregorio, Ernie** 1951- [BB]
*American basketball player*
* Ernie D.

**DiGregorio, Gasper**
See DiGregorio, Gasperino

**DiGregorio, Gasperino** 1905-
[PHM]
*Italian-born American underworld figure*
* DiGregorio, Gasper

**Dihogo, Martin** 1905-1971 [MK]
*American baseball player*
* [El] Maestro [The Master]

**Dikty, Julian Chain May** 1931-
[WGT]
*American author*
* Chain, Julian
* May, J. C.
* May, Julian [C.]

**Dikty, T. E.**
See Dikty, Thaddeus Eugene

**Dikty, Thaddeus Eugene** 1920-
[SF]
*American editor*
* Dikty, T. E.

**Dil, Zakhmi**
See Hilton, Richard

**Dilcock, Noreen** 1907- [AW, WD]
*British author*
* Christian, Jill
* Ford, Norrey
* Walford, Christian

**DiLeonardi, Joseph** 1932?-
*American police official*
* Chicago's Kojak
* Joe D.

**Dilion, Paul**
See Bourde, Paul

**Dilks, John M.** [PA]
*Author*
* La Thorne, Jean
* [A] Traveling Showman

**Dill, Carlton** 1943- [AES]
*Bermudan soccer player*
* Dill, Pepe

**Dill, J. M.** [PA]
*Author*
* Moralisto

**Dill, James Reid** [PA]
*Author*
* J. R. D.

**Dill, Pepe**
See Dill, Carlton

**Dillard, Bones**
See Dillard, Harrison

**Dillard, Harrison** 1923- [IBW]
*American track and field athlete*
* Dillard, Bones

**Dillard, Pat**
See Dillard, Robert Lee

**Dillard, Robert Lee** 1874-1907
[BE]
*American baseball player*
* Dillard, Pat

**Diller, Phyllis**
See Driver, Phyllis

**Dilley, Dill**
See Dilley, Graham Roy

**Dilley, Graham Roy** 1959- [DC]
*British cricketer*
* Dilley, Dill
* Dilley, Picca

**Dilley, Picca**
See Dilley, Graham Roy

**Dillhoefer, Pickles**
See Dillhoefer, William Martin

**Dillhoefer, William Martin**
1894-1922 [BE]
*American baseball player*
* Dillhoefer, Pickles

**Dilli, Rick**
See Sellers, Connie Leslie, Jr.

**Dilling, Judith**
See Rhoades, Judith G[rubman]

**Dillinger, Desperate Dan**
See Dillinger, John Herbert

**Dillinger, Harley Hugh** 1894-1959
[BE]
*American baseball player*
* Dillinger, Hoke
* Dillinger, Lefty

**Dillinger, Hoke**
See Dillinger, Harley Hugh

**Dillinger, John Herbert** 1903- ?
[BLB]
*American bank robber*
* Dillinger, Desperate Dan
* Donovan, John
* Hall, John
* Harris, Joseph
* Hellman, Carl
* Sullivan, Frank

**Dillinger, Lefty**
See Dillinger, Harley Hugh

**Dillingham**
See Foulke, William Dudley

**Dillmann, Max**
See Dallamano, Massimo

**Dillon, Cec**
See Dillon, Cecil Graham

**Dillon, Cecil Graham** 1908- [FHE]
*American hockey player*
* Dillon, Cec

**Dillon, Dick**
See Bowstead, Kenneth

**Dillon, Eilis**
See O'Cuilleanain, Eilis Dillon

**Dillon, Fannie**
See Parker, Mrs. Richard E.

**Dillon, Frank Edward** 1873-1931
[BE]
*American baseball player*
* Dillon, Pop

**Dillon, George** 1888-1965 [SC]
*American actor*
* Dillon, Tim

**Dillon, Hook**
See Dillon, John

**Dillon, Jack**
See Price, Ernest Cutler

**Dillon, Jim**
See Corbett, James John

**Dillon, John** 1924- [BB]
*American basketball player*
* Dillon, Hook

**Dillon, John M[yles]** 1939- [CA]
*American author and columnist*
* [The] Western Spy

**Dillon, Leo**
See Dillon, Lionel J.

**Dillon, Lionel J.** 1933- [ICB]
*American illustrator*
* Dillon, Leo

**Dillon, Packard Andrew** ?-1890
[BE]
*American baseball player*
* Dillon, Packy

**Dillon, Packy**
See Dillon, Packard Andrew

**Dillon, Pop**
See Dillon, Frank Edward

**Dillon, Tim**
See Dillon, George

**Dilman, Hugh**
See McGoughy, Hugh Dilman

**Dilone, Miguel Angel** 1954- [BE]
*Dominican-born baseball player*
* Reyes, Miguel Angel

**Dilweg, Laverne** 20th c. [BBH]
*American football player*
* Dilweg, Lavvie

**Dilweg, Lavvie**
See Dilweg, Laverne

**Dim Dom Dallessandro**
See Dallessandro, Nicholas Dominic

**DiMaggio, Dominic Paul** 1918-
[BE, PB]
*American baseball player*
* [The] Little Professor

**DiMaggio, Joltin Joe**
See DeMaggio, Giuseppe Paolo, Jr.

**DiMaggio, Joseph Paul [Joe]**
See DeMaggio, Giuseppe Paolo, Jr.

**Dimancheff, Babe**
See Dimancheff, Boris

**Dimancheff, Boris** 20th c. [SMG]
*Football player*
* Dimancheff, Babe

**Dimaria, Joseph Franklin**
1910-1958 [BE]
*American baseball player*
* Demaree, Frank

**Dimelfi, Giuseppe** 1897-
[BX, RBE]
*Italian-born boxer*
* [The] Young Zulu Kid

**Diminutive Peter**
See Robinson, Patrick

**Dimitrihoff, Dimitri Ivanovich**
1891-1957 [BE]
*Russian-born baseball player*
* Schauer, Alexander
* Schauer, Rube

**Dimitrijevic, Dragutin** 1876-1917
[WBD]
*Serbian soldier*
* Apis

**Dimitry, Alexander** 1805-1883
[FFF]
*Author*
* Guarnerius, Tobias

**Dimitry, Charles Patton** 1837- ?
[FFF]
*Author*
* Field, Braddock
* Guarnerius, Tobias, Jr.

**Dimont, Penelope**
See Mortimer, Penelope [Ruth]

**Dimrecken, B. Grayer**
See De Mille, Richard

**Dimson, Wendy**
See Baron, [Ora] Wendy

**Dimt, Christine** 1915- [B10, EWL]
*Austrian poet*
* Busta, Christine

**DiMucci, Dion** 1939- [RO1]
*American singer and songwriter*
* Dion

**Din, Dulce** 1936?-1975 [FIR]
*Entertainer*
* Asia's Queen of Jazz

**Din, Salima** 20th c.
*American hotel manager*
* Westgate, Lady

**Dinesen, Isak**
See Blixen, Karen [Christentze Dinesen]

**Ding**
See Darling, Jay Norwood

**Dinges, George**
See Dinges, Vance

**Dinges, John [Charles]** 1941- [CA]
*American author and journalist*
* Marsano, Ramon

**Dinges, Vance** 1915- [BE]
*American baseball player*
* Dinges, George

**Dingle, Adrian** 1912-1974 [WECO]
*Canadian cartoonist*
* Darian

**Dingle, Aylward Edward**
1874-1947 [MBF, SFL, WGT]
*British author*
* Cotterell, Brian
* Dingle, Capt.
* Sinbad

**Dingle, Capt.**
See Dingle, Aylward Edward

**Dingleberry, Mr.**
See Dinsdale, Timothy Kay

**Dingus**
See James, Jesse Woodson

**Dingwall, Peter**
See Forsythe, Robin

**Dinhofer, Alfred** 1929- [CA]
*American author and photographer*
* Dino

**Diniz** 1261-1325 [WBD]
*King of Portugal*
* Re Lavrador [Farmer or Laborer
King]

**Diniz da Cruz e Silva, Antonio**
1731-1799 [WBD]
*Portuguese poet*
* [The] Portuguese Pindar

**Dinks**
See Peel, [Captain] Jonathan

**Dinneen, Big Bill**
See Dinneen, William Henry

**Dinneen, Patrick Stephen** 20th c.
[WWL]
*Irish author and playwright*
* O Duinnin, Padraig

**Dinneen, William Henry**
1876-1955 [BE, PB]
*American baseball player*
* Dinneen, Big Bill

**[The] Dinner Bell**
See Burke, Edmund

**Dinner, William** 20th c. [AW]
*British author and playwright*
* Smith, Surrey [joint pseudonym
with William Morum]

**Dinnies, Anna Peyre** 19th c. [FFF]
*American poet*
* Moina

**Dino**
See Dinhofer, Alfred

**Dinsdale, Timothy Kay** 1924-
[IAW]
*Welsh-born author*
* Dingleberry, Mr.

**Dinsmoor, Robert** 1757-1836 [PA]
*Author*
* [The] Rustic Bard

**Dinsmore, Charles** 1903- [CEI]
*Canadian-born hockey player*
* Dinsmore, Dinny

**Dinsmore, Dinny**
See Dinsmore, Charles

**Dinsmore, Duke**
See Dinsmore, J. Carlyle

**Dinsmore, J. Carlyle** 1913- [EAR]
*American auto racer*
* Dinsmore, Duke

**Dinwiddie, Faye Velma Love** 20th
c. [IAW]
*American author*
* Foster, Faye Love

**Dio [or Dion] Cassius** 155?- ?
[WBD]
*Roman politician and historian*
* Cocceianus

**[Il] Dio dell'Opera Buffa**
See Logroscino [or Lo Groscino],
Nicola

**Dio, Johnny**
See Dioguardi, John

**Diocletian [Gaius Aurelius Valerius
Diocletianus]** 245- 313 [WBD]
*Roman emperor*
* Jovius

**Diogenes**
See McEvoy, Bernard

**Diogenes**
See Romanus IV

**Diogenes**
See Salola, Eeero

**Diogenes**
See Trenchard, John

**Diogenes** 4th c. BC
[DEP, DNNF, RH]
*Greek philosopher*
* [The] Cynic
* [The] Dog
* [The] Mad Socrates

**Diogenes Jr.**
See Brougham, John

**Diogenes Senior**
See Cowper, Frank

**Dioguardi, John** 20th c.
[CEC, PHM]
*American underworld figure*
* Dio, Johnny

**Diomede, John K.**
See Effinger, George Alec

**Dion**
See DiMucci, Dion

**Dion**
See Tillinghast, Joseph Leonard

**Dion** 90?- 117? [HN, WBD]
*Greek scholar*
* Chrysostomus [or Chrysostom]
* [The] Golden Mouth

**Dion, [Sister] Anita** 1918- [CA]
*American educator and author*
* Raymond de Jesus, [Mother]

**Dion, Clarence J. H.** 1903-1932
[SC]
*American actor, director,
screenwriter*
* O'Neill, Mickey

**Dion-Levesque, Rosaire**
See Levesque, Leo A.

**Dionne, Beaver**
See Dionne, Marcel Elphege

**Dionne, Lou**
See Dionne, Marcel Elphege

**Dionne, Marcel Elphege** 1951-
[SMG]
*Canadian-born hockey player*
* Dionne, Beaver
* Dionne, Lou

**[A] Dionysiac Singing Woman**
See Hortensius, Quintus

**Dionysius** ?- 265 [DNNS]
*Saint*
* [The] Great
* [The] Teacher of the Catholic
Church

**Dionysius Exiguus** 6th c. [SN]
*Roman monk*
* [The] Little

**Dionysius the Areopagite**
See Denys

**Dionysius the Younger** 4th c. BC
[FFF]
*Tyrant of Syracuse*
* Corinth's Pedagogue

**Dionysus**
See Antiochus XII

**Dionysus**
See Fordham, Peta

**Diotima**
See Wynne-Tyson, Esme

**Dipalermo, Joseph** 20th c. [PHM]
*American underworld figure*
* Beck, Joe

**Dipi**
See Di Paola Levin, Jorge Alberto

**Diplomat**
See Carter, John Franklin

**Diplomat**
See Von Redlich, Marcellus
Donald A. R.

**Dippel, Johann Konrad** 1673-1734
[WBD]
*German theologian, physician,
alchemist*
* Christianus Demokritus

**Dipper Boy Council**
See Council, Floyd

**[The] Dircaean Swan**
See Pindar

**Dirceu**
See Gonzaga, Tomaz Antonio

**[The] Director of Studies**
See Friend, John

**Dirk, R.**
See Dietrich, Richard V[incent]

**Dirty Al Gallagher**
See Gallagher, Alan Mitchell
Edward George

**Dirty Jack Doyle**
See Doyle, John Joseph

**Dirty Red**
See Wilborn, Nelson

**[The] Disbanded Volunteer**
See Barber, Joseph

**Disch, Thomas M.** 1940-
[CA, DLE, ESF]
*American author*
* Demijohn, Thom [joint
pseudonym with John Sladek]
* Hargrave, Leonie
* Knye, Cassandra [joint
pseudonym with John Sladek]
* Thorpe, Dobbin

**Discipulus**
See Pearce, Ethel Katherine

**Discipulus Aldi**
See Pickering, William

**[The] Disco Diva**
See Jones, Grace

**[The] Disco Kid**
See McCoy, Van Allen

**[A] Discrowned Glutton**
See Charles V

**D'Isly, Georges**
See Simenon, Georges [Joseph
Christian]

**[The] Dismal**
See Finch, Heneage [First Earl of
Nottingham]

**Dismukes, Dizzy**
See Dismukes, William

**Dismukes, William** 20th c.
[IBW, OBW]
*American baseball player, manager,
coach*
* Dismukes, Dizzy

**Disraeli, Benjamin** 1804-1881
[DEL, DEP, FFF]
*British prime minister and author*
* Delta
* Dizzy
* [The] Primrose Sphynx
* Runnymede

**Disraeli, Isaac** 1766-1848 [DEL]
*British author*
* Tag, Rag, and Bobtail, Messrs.

**Disrobeson, Kin I.**
See Stivers, Mark

**Disston, Harry** 1899- [CA]
*American author and columnist*
* Hill, H. D. N.

**Distel, Dutch**
See Distel, George Adam

**Distel, George Adam** 1896-1967
[BE]
*American baseball player*
* Distel, Dutch

**Distich, Dick**
See Pope, Alexander

**[The] Distressed Statesman**
See Pitt, William [Earl of
Chatham]

**D'Istria, Dora**
See Massalsky, Helen Koltzoff

**Ditka, Hammer**
See Ditka, Michael K.

**Ditka, Michael K.** 1939- [FB]
*American football player*
* Ditka, Hammer
* Ditka, Monk

**Ditka, Monk**
See Ditka, Michael K.

**Ditmas, Francis Ivan Leslie** [LAO]
*British engineer and technical writer*
* Rosedale, Ivan

**Dito und Idem** [joint pseudonym with
Marie Kremnitz]
See Elizabeth, [Queen]

**Dito und Idem** [joint pseudonym with
Elizabeth, Queen of Rumania]
See Kremnitz, Marie

**Ditson, Dick**
See Saley, M. L.

**Ditta, Lolita** 20th c. [RO1]
*Austrian singer*
* Lolita

**Ditzen, [Wilhelm Friedrich] Rudolf**
1893-1947 [EWL, LC, TC]
*German author*
* Fallada, Hans

**DiVarco, Joseph Vincent** 1911-
[BLB]
*American underworld figure*
* Little Caesar

**Diver, James Francis**
See   Dwyer, James Francis

**Diver, Maud**
See   Marshall, Katherine Helen Maud

**Dives [The Rich]**
See   Crassus, Marcus Licinius

**[La] Divina**
See   Gustafsson, Greta Lovisa

**[La] Divina**
See   Kalogeropoulos, Maria Anna Sofia Cecilia

**[The] Divine**
See   Ariosto, Lodovico

**Divine, [Father]**
See   Baker, George

**[The] Divine**
See   Herrera, Ferdinand [or Fernando] de

**[The] Divine**
See   John

**[The] Divine**
See   Morales, Luis de

**[The] Divine**
See   Santi [or Sanzio?], Raffaello

**Divine, Arthur Durham** 1904-
[WW]
*Author*
* Divine, David
* Rame, David

**Divine, David**
See   Divine, Arthur Durham

**[The] Divine Doctor**
See   Ruysbroek, Jean de

**[The] Divine Emilie**
See   Le Tonnelier de Breteuil, Gabrielle Emilie

**[The] Divine Madman**
See   Buonarroti, Michelangelo [or Michael Angelo]

**Divine Majesty**
See   Medici, Giovanni de

**[The] Divine Miss M**
See   Midler, Bette

**[The] Divine One**
See   Vaughan, Sarah [Lois]

**[The] Divine Pagan**
See   Hypatia

**[The] Divine Sarah**
See   Bernard, [Henriette] Rosine

**[The] Divine Sarah**
See   Vaughan, Sarah [Lois]

**[The] Divine Speaker**
See   Tyrtamos

**[The] Diviner**
See   Da Vinci, Leonardo

**[The] Diving Dervish**
See   Cunningham, Sam[uel Lewis, Jr.]

**[The] Diving Venus**
See   Kellerman, Annette

**[Il] Divino**
See   Aretino, Pietro

**[El] Divino Calvo [The Divine Bald-Headed One]**
See   Gomez Ortega, Rafael

**Divinus, Doctor**
See   Ruysbroek, Jean de

**DiVittorio, Vincent** 1929-   [EJ]
*American jazz musician*
* Dean, Vinnie

**[Il] Divoratore de Libri [The Devourer of Books]**
See   Magliabecchi, Antonio [or Anthony]

**Dix, Billy**
See   Dixon, William H.

**Dix, Digger**
See   Dix, Jim

**Dix, Dorothy**
See   Gilmer, Elizabeth [Meriwether]

**Dix, J. R.**
See   Phillips, George Spencer

**Dix, Jim** 20th c.   [GW]
*American rodeo performer*
* Dix, Digger

**Dix, John A.** 1798-1880   [PA]
*Author*
* Cosmopolite
* J. D.

**Dix, Richard**
See   Brimmer, Ernest Carlton

**Dixelius, Hildur**
See   Dixelius-Brettner, Hildur

**Dixelius-Brettner, Hildur** 1879- ?
[TC]
*Swedish author*
* Dixelius, Hildur

**Dixey, Marmaduke**
See   Howard, Geoffrey

**Dixey, Mrs. Henry E.**   [FFF]
*Entertainer*
* Glover, Ida

**Dixie**
See   Castleman, Virginia Carter

**Dixie**
See   Doyle, J. Dixie

**[The] Dixie Derrick**
See   Anderson, Paul

**[The] Dixie Dew Drop**
See   Macon, David Harrison

**[The] Dixie Kid**
See   Brown, Aaron L.

**[The] Dixie Nightingale**
See   Gibbons, Irene

**[The] Dixie Thrush**
See   Nicklin, Samuel Strang

**Dixie's Dainty Dewdrop**
See   Withers, Jane

**Dixon**
See   Masson, Mme. Clemence Harding

**Dixon**
See   Roberts, Will

**Dixon, Alan** 1954-   [SMG]
*American football player*
* Dixon, Snake

**Dixon, Andrew**   [PA]
*Author*
* Sackett, Harry

**Dixon, Arthur** 1921-   [AW]
*British author*
* Whye, Felix

**Dixon, Big Willie**
See   Dixon, Willie James

**Dixon, Bingham**
See   Borland, William Armstrong

**Dixon, Denver** 1890-1972   [FD]
*American director*
* Adamson, Victor

**Dixon, Don**
See   Stein, J. H.

**Dixon, Dwayne** 20th c.   [BBH]
*American athletic director*
* Dixon, Spike

**Dixon, Eugene** 1937-   [PRS, RO1]
*American singer and record producer*
* Chandler, Gene

**Dixon, Floyd** 1929-   [BWW]
*American singer*
* Dixon, Skeet

**Dixon, Franklin W.** [house pseudonym] [Stratemeyer Syndicate]
See   Adams, Harriet S[tratemeyer]

**Dixon, Franklin W.** [house pseudonym] [Stratemeyer Syndicate]
See   Stratemeyer, Edward L.

**Dixon, Franklin W.** [house pseudonym] [Stratemeyer Syndicate]
See   Svenson, Andrew E.

**Dixon, George** 1870-1909
[BX, OCS, RBE]
*Canadian-born boxer*
* Little Chocolate

**Dixon, Helena**
See   Story, Adeline E.

**Dixon, Henry Hall** 1822-1870
[PA, RH, WBD]
*British author*
* Chasse, General
* [The] Druid

**Dixon, Herbert Albert** 1902-1945
[MK]
*American baseball player*
* Dixon, Rap

**Dixon, Hewritt F.** 1940-   [FB]
*American football player*
* Dixon, Tank

**Dixon, Howard Francis**
See   Evergood, Philip

**Dixon, James** 20th c.   [B10]
*American composer and bandleader*
* Dixon, Willie

**Dixon, Jean**
See   Jacques, Marie

**Dixon, Jeane**
See   Pinckert, Jeane

**Dixon, John Craig** 1924-   [BE]
*American baseball player*
* Dixon, Sonny

**Dixon, Marjorie [Mack]** 1887-
[CAP]
*British author*
* Mack, Marjorie

**Dixon, Mrs.**   [FFF]
*Author*
* Leslie, Emma

**Dixon, Paige**
See   Corcoran, Barbara

**Dixon, Paul**
See   Schleier, Gregory

**Dixon, Rap**
See   Dixon, Herbert Albert

**Dixon, Rex**
See   Martin, Reginald Alec

**Dixon, Richard**
See   Walker, Clifton Reginald

**Dixon, Robert W.**
See   Bullivant, Cecil Henry

**Dixon, Roger** 1930-   [CA, WD]
*British author*
* Christian, John
* Lewis, Charles

**Dixon, Rosie**
See   Wood, Christopher [Hovelle]

**Dixon, Ruth**
See   Barrows, [Ruth] Marjorie

**Dixon, Skeet**
See   Dixon, Floyd

**Dixon, Snake**
See   Dixon, Alan

**Dixon, Sonny**
See   Dixon, John Craig

**Dixon, Spike**
See   Dixon, Dwayne

**Dixon, Tank**
See   Dixon, Hewritt F.

**Dixon, Thomas** 1930-   [ESF]
*American author*
* Cole, Burt

**Dixon, Wallace**
See   Cronin, Bernard [Charles]

**Dixon, William H.** 1911-1973   [SC]
*American actor and rodeo performer*
* Dix, Billy

**Dixon, William Hepworth**
1821-1879   [FFF]
*British author*
* Yorke, Onslow

**Dixon, Willie**
See   Dixon, James

**Dixon, Willie James** 1915-   [BWW]
*American singer*
* Dixon, Big Willie

**Dixwell, John** 1607?-1689   [FFF]
*Participated in the trial and execution of King Charles I of England*
* Davids, John

**Diz**
See   Ardizzone, Edward

**Dizzy**
See   Disraeli, Benjamin

**Djalski, Ksaver Sandor**
See   Babic, Ljubomir

**Djang, Yuan Shan** 1892-    [LAO]
*Chinese editor*
* Wise

**Djezzar**
*See* Ahmed [or Achmed] Pasha

**Djordjevich, Voya George**
1895-1951  [SC]
*American actor*
* George, Voya

**Djuric, Miodrag** 1933-    [CAR]
*Yugoslav painter*
* Dado

**Djuricic, Uladen St.** 1889-    [IAW]
*Yugoslav author and poet*
* Drincic, Sava
* Mlad-Miltijad

**Dlugosz, Jean** 1415-1480  [PA]
*Author*
* Longinus

**DM-92**
*See* Ackerman, Forrest J[ames]

**Dneprov, Anatoly**
*See* Mitskevich, A. P.

**Do Boy Diamond**
*See* Diamond, William

**Doak**
*See* Rankin, Hugh Doak

**Doak, Doakie**
*See* Doak, Gary Walter

**Doak, Gary Walter** 1946-    [SMG]
*Canadian-born hockey player*
* Doak, Doakie

**Doak, Spittin' Bill**
*See* Doak, William Leopold

**Doak, William Leopold** 1891-1954
[BE, PB]
*American baseball player*
* Doak, Spittin' Bill

**Doane, Dinger**
*See* Doane, Erling

**Doane, Erling** 1897-1949  [AS]
*American football player*
* Doane, Dinger

**Doane, Jerry**
*See* Morse, Katharine Duncan

**Doane, Marion S.**
*See* Woodward, Grace Steele

**Dobb, John Kenneth** 1901-    [BE]
*American baseball player*
* Dobb, Lefty

**Dobb, Lefty**
*See* Dobb, John Kenneth

**Dobell, Isabel Marian Barclay**
1909-  [CAP, SAT]
*Canadian author*
* Barclay, Isabel

**Dobell, Sydney** 1824-1874  [DEL]
*British poet*
* Yendys, Sydney

**Dobenek [or Dobneck], Johann**
1479-1552  [WBD]
*German theologian*
* Cochlaeus, Johannes

**Dobens, Lefty**
*See* Dobens, Ray[mond Joseph]

**Dobens, Ray[mond Joseph]** 1906-
[BE]
*American baseball player*
* Dobens, Lefty

**Dober, Conrad K.** 1891-1938
[ASC, BEW, PMJ]
*American composer, pianist, music
publisher*
* Conrad, Con

**Dobernic, Andrew Joseph** 1917-
[BE]
*American baseball player*
* Dobernic, Jess

**Dobernic, Jess**
*See* Dobernic, Andrew Joseph

**Dobie, Gilmour** 1879-1948
[AS, FB]
*American football coach*
* Dobie, Gloomy Gil

**Dobie, Gloomy Gil**
*See* Dobie, Gilmour

**Dobie, William** 1897-1960  [SC]
*American actor*
* Marr, William

**Dobinson, Eric Arthur** 1927-
[ART]
*British furniture designer and
illustrator*
* E. A. D.

**Doblado, Don Lucadio**
*See* White, James Blanco

**Dobner, Maeva Park** 1918-    [CA]
*American writer*
* Park, Maeva

**Dobnievski, David** 1892-    [IPA]
*Polish-born American labor leader*
* Dubinsky, David

**Dobraczynski, Jan** 1910-    [CAP]
*Polish author*
* Hozjusz
* Kurowski, Eugeniusz

**Dobru, R.**
*See* Ravales, Robin

**Dobson, Burrhead**
*See* Dobson, Joseph Gordon

**Dobson, Cleon** 1888?-1976  [B10]
*American blacksmith*
* Dobson, Tinker

**Dobson, Joseph Gordon** 1917-    [BE]
*American baseball player*
* Dobson, Burrhead

**Dobson, Mrs. Frank**    [FFF]
*Entertainer*
* Wallace, Jennie

**Dobson, Tinker**
*See* Dobson, Cleon

**Dobson, William** 1610-1646
[DEP, DNNS, FFF]
*British painter*
* [The] English Tintoretto
* [The] English Vandyck
* [The] Tintoretto of England
* [The] Vandyck of England

**Doc**
*See* Yap, Diosdado M.

**Doc O**
*See* Odom, Herbert

**Docherty, James L.**
*See* Raymond, Rene

**[The] Dockers' K. C.**
*See* Bevin, Ernest

**Dockins, George Woodrow** 1917-
[BE]
*American baseball player*
* Dockins, Lefty

**Dockins, Lefty**
*See* Dockins, George Woodrow

**Dockstader, Lew**
*See* Clapp, George Alfred

**Dockweiler, Joseph Harold**
1920?-1948?  [ESF, WGT]
*American author*
* Lavond, Paul Dennis [joint
pseudonym with F. Pohl, R.
Lowndes, C. Kornbluth] [house
pseudonym]
* Wylie, Dirk [joint pseudonym
with C. Kornbluth, F. Kummer,
F. Pohl]

**[The] Doctor**
*See* Addington, Henry [First
Viscount Sidmouth]

**[The] Doctor**
*See* Gehlen, Reinhard

**[The] Doctor**
*See* Lenkaitis, William Edward

**[The] Doctor**
*See* Watson, James

**Dr. A**
*See* Asimov, Isaac

**Dr. A**
*See* Silverstein, Alvin

**Doctor Clayton's Buddy**
*See* Luandrew, Albert

**Dr. Edith**
*See* Summerskill, Edith

**Doctor H.**
*See* Jolderland, Hother

**Dr. J**
*See* Erving, Julius

**Dr. Joe**
*See* Martinez de Hoz, Jose Alfredo

**Dr. John, the Night Tripper**
*See* Rebennack, Malcolm John

**Dr. K**
*See* Kenon, Larry

**Doctor Leo**
*See* De Colange, Leo

**Doctor Lew**
*See* Childre, Lew

**Doctor of Asia**
*See* Polycarp

**[The] Doctor of Dancing**
*See* Beauchamps

**Dr. of Determination**
*See* Jessye, Eva Alberta

**[The] Doctor of Grace**
*See* Augustine

**Doctor of Mimeography**
*See* Kan Tse-kao

**Doctor of the Holy Church of Smyrna**
*See* Polycarp

**Doctor of the Incarnation**
*See* Cyril

**Dr. Pfalzgraf**
*See* Marwedi, Friedrich Carl

**Dr. Phyl**
*See* Cilento, Phyllis Dorothy

**[The] Doctor with Good Foundations**
*See* Aegidius [or Giles] of Colonna

**Dr. X**
*See* Jascalevich, Mario E.

**Dr. X**
*See* Nourse, Alan E[dward]

**Doctorow, E. L.**
*See* Doctorow, Edgar Laurence

**Doctorow, Edgar Laurence** 1931-
[SFL]
*American author*
* Doctorow, E. L.

**Doctorum, Doctor**
*See* Alexander of Hales

**Doctus**
*See* Catullus, Caius Valerius

**Dod, Charlotte** 1871?-1962
[EG, OET]
*British tennis player and golfer*
* Dod, Lottie

**Dod, John** 1549?-1645  [DEP]
*British clergyman*
* [The] Decalogist

**Dod, Lottie**
*See* Dod, Charlotte

**Dodd, Allen Robert** 1887-    [SFL]
*Author*
* Allen, Robert

**Dodd, Charles**
*See* Tootell, Hugh

**Dodd, Derrick**
*See* Gassaway, Frank

**Dodd, Douglas**
*See* Fearn, John Russell

**Dodd, E. A.** 1875?- ?    [CW]
*Jamaican author*
* Snod, E.

**Dodd, Edward Howard, Jr.** 1905-
[CA]
*American publisher and author*
* Hill, W. M.

**Dodd, Marguerite** 1911-    [CA]
*American business executive and
author*
* Braymer, Marguerite

**Dodd, Neal** 1878-1966  [SC]
*American actor and director*
* [The] Padre of Hollywood

**Dodd, Wayne [Donald]** 1930-
[CA, WD]
*American author and poet*
* Wayne, Donald

**Dodds, Baby**
*See* Dodds, Warren

**Dodds, Johnny** 1892-1940  [DAM]
*American jazz musician*
* Dodds, Joliet

**Dodds, Joliet**
*See* Dodds, Johnny

**Dodds, Warren** 1898-1959
[BBD, EJ, PMJ]
*American jazz musician*
* Dodds, Baby

**Dodge, Elizabeth C.** [PA]
*Author*
* Stedman

**Dodge, Frederick** 1859-1937
[BEW, FFF]
*American actor and author*
* Paulding, Frederick

**Dodge, Fremont**
*See* Grimes, Lee

**Dodge, Langdon**
*See* Wolfson, Victor

**Dodge, Mary Abigail** 1830?-1896
[DEL, PA, WBD]
*American author*
* Hamilton, Gail

**Dodge, Mary Mapes** [PA]
*Author*
* M. M. D.

**Dodge, Mary Thurston**
*See* Le Feuvre, Amy

**Dodge, Ossian E.** [PA]
*Author*
* Ort, Ivan

**Dodge, Steve**
*See* Becker, Stephen [David]

**Dodge, Wendell Phillips** 1883-
[NAA]
*American author and playwright*
* Fletcher, Richard
* Phillips, W.

**Dodger**
*See* Thompson, Peter

**Dodgion, Dottie**
*See* Giaimo, Dorothy

**Dodgson, Charles Lutwidge**
1832-1898 [DEL]
*British author*
* Carroll, Lewis

**Dodick, John** 1899-1945
[BX, EJS, RBE]
*American boxer*
* Bernstein, Jack

**Dods, Jeanie**
*See* Mackay, Miss

**Dods, Meg**
*See* Johnston, Mrs.

**Dodsley, Robert** 1703-1764 [SN]
*British author, editor, publisher*
* [The] Livery Muse

**Doe, Al[fred George]** 1864-1938
[BE]
*American baseball player*
* Doe, Count

**Doe, Charles Henry** 1838- ? [FFF]
*American author and journalist*
* Blotter, Samuel

**Doe, Count**
*See* Doe, Al[fred George]

**Doe, Deadrick**
*See* Caldwell, Mack M.

**Doe, Dorothy**
*See* Anderson, Mrs. Galusha

**Doe, John**
*See* Thayer, Tiffany Ellsworth

**Doe, John James**
*See* O'Nuallain, Brian

**Doeblin, Alfred** 1878-1957
[EWL, TC]
*German author, playwright, poet*
* Linke Poot

**D'Oefelse, Andreas Felix**
1706-1780 [PA]
*Author*
* Evelius

**Doeg**
*See* Settle, Elkanah

**Doehring, Bull**
*See* Doehring, John

**Doehring, John** 20th c. [SMG]
*American football player*
* Doehring, Bull

**Doely, Sarah Bentley**
*See* Bentley, Sarah

**Doenim, Susan**
*See* Effinger, George Alec

**Doerffler, Alfred** 1884- [CA]
*American clergyman and author*
* Dunn, Harris
* Ford, Fred
* Thomas, Carl H.

**Doerkes, Ruth-Margret** 1932- [OP]
*German opera singer*
* Puetz, Ruth-Margret

**Doermann, Felix**
*See* Biedermann, Felix

**Doerner, Gus**
*See* Doerner, Wilfred

**Doerner, Wilfred** 1922- [BB]
*American basketball player*
* Doerner, Gus

**Doesticks, Q. K. Philander**
*See* Thomson, Mortimer

**[The] Dog**
*See* Diogenes

**[The] Dog Meat General**
*See* Chang Chung-Ch'ang

**Dog Whip**
*See* Smith, L. D.

**Dogbolt, Barnaby**
*See* Silvette, Herbert

**Dohen, Dorothy** 1923- [CAT]
*American writer*
* Williams, Elizabeth

**Doherty, Big Do**
*See* Doherty, Reginald Frank

**Doherty, Frank** [SG]
*Boxer*
* Jerome, Frankie

**Doherty, G. D.**
*See* Doherty, Geoffrey Donald

**Doherty, Geoffrey Donald** 1927-
[SF]
*British educator and author*
* Doherty, G. D.

**Doherty, Hugh Lawrence**
1876-1919 [OCS, OET]
*British lawn tennis player*
* Doherty, Laurie
* Doherty, Little Do

**Doherty, Ivy R. Duffy** 1922- [CA]
*Australian-born American author*
* Hardwick, Sylvia

**Doherty, Laurie**
*See* Doherty, Hugh Lawrence

**Doherty, Little Do**
*See* Doherty, Hugh Lawrence

**Doherty, Reginald Frank**
1874-1910 [OCS, OET]
*British lawn tennis player*
* Doherty, Big Do

**Doherty, Robert R.** [FFF]
*American author and editor*
* Yonge, Remington

**Dohrn, Bernardine** 1942?-
*American political organizer*
* Douglas, Lou

**Doihara, Kenji** 20th c. [EE]
*Japanese intelligence chief*
* Soma, Ito

**Dokes, Dynamite**
*See* Dokes, Michael

**Dokes, Michael** 20th c.
*American boxer*
* Dokes, Dynamite

**Dolan, Alvin James**
*See* Alberts, James

**Dolan, Ann** 1912-1966 [SC]
*American actress*
* Nagel, Anne

**Dolan, Cozy**
*See* Alberts, James

**Dolan, Cozy**
*See* Dolan, Patrick Henry

**Dolan, Patrick Henry** 1872-1907
[BE]
*American baseball player*
* Dolan, Cozy

**D'Olanda, Luca**
*See* Hugensz, Lucas

**Dolaro, Selina**
*See* Belasco, Mrs. Isaac

**Dolberg, Alexander** 1933- [AW]
*Russian-born British author and translator*
* Burg, David

**Dolbokov** [joint pseudonym with
Boris Dolgov]
*See* Bok, Hannes Vajn

**Dolbokov** [joint pseudonym with
Hannes Vajn Bok]
*See* Dolgov, Boris

**Dolby, Doctor** [PA]
*Author*
* Leatherstocking

**Dolcebono, Giacomo** [SN]
*Italian architect and sculptor*
* [The] Master of Stone-Cutting

**Dole, Charles Minot** 1899-1976
[BBH]
*American skiing organization founder*
* Dole, Minnie
* [The] Father of the National Ski
  Patrol System
* [The] Father of the Tenth
  Mountain Division

**Dole, Haskell Nathan** 1852-1935
[FFF]
*American author, poet, critic*
* Cerberus

**Dole, Minnie**
*See* Dole, Charles Minot

**Dolega-Kamienski**
*See* Kamienski, Lucian

**Doleman, Robert**
*See* Parsons [or Persons?], Robert

**Dolent, Jean**
*See* Fournier, Antoine

**Dolenzai, Julien A.** 1896-1947 [SC]
*American actress*
* Beaubien, Julien

**Dolgoff, Sam** 1902- [CA]
*American author*
* Wiener, Sam

**Dolgoruki [or Dolgorukov], Vasili
Mikhailovich** 1722-1782 [WBD]
*Russian soldier*
* Krymski

**Dolgov, Boris** 20th c. [HFF]
*Artist*
* Dolbokov [joint pseudonym with
  Hannes Vajn Bok]

**Dolin, Anton**
*See* Kay, Patrick Healey

**Dolinsky, Meyer** 1923- [CA]
*American author and television
scriptwriter*
* Dolinsky, Mike

**Dolinsky, Mike**
*See* Dolinsky, Meyer

**D'Oliveira, Basil Lewis** 1931- [DC]
*South African-born cricketer*
* D'Oliveira, Dolly

**D'Oliveira, Dolly**
*See* D'Oliveira, Basil Lewis

**D'Oliviera, Severino** 1930- [EJ7]
*Brazilian jazz musician*
* Sivuca

**Doll, Art[hur James]** 1913- [BE]
*American baseball player*
* Doll, Moose

**Doll, Moose**
*See* Doll, Art[hur James]

**Dolland, George** 1774-1852 [PA]
*Author*
* Huggins

**Dollar Bill Bradley**
*See* Bradley, William [Bill]

**Dollar Investor**
*See* D'Ambrosio, Charles A.

**Dollen, Charles Joseph** 1926- [CA]
*American clergyman, librarian,
author*
* Benedict, Joseph

**Dolley, Marcus, J.**
*See* Watney, Bernard Martyn

**Dolling, Father**
*See* Dolling, Robert William
Radclyffe

**Dolling, Richard Radclyffe**
1851-1902 [DNNS]
*British clergyman*
* [The] Poor Man's Priest

**Dolling, Robert William Radclyffe**
1851-1902 [WBD]
*British social reformer*
* Dolling, Father

**Dollinger, Johann Joseph I.**
1799-1890 [PA]
*Author*
* [An] Englishman
* Janus

**Dolly, Jenny**
See Deutsch, Yansci [or Janszieka]

**Dolly, Rosie**
See Deutsch, Roszika

**Dolman, Frederick William** 1895-
[THR]
*British actor*
* Dolman, Richard

**Dolman, Richard**
See Dolman, Frederick William

**Dolmatch, Theodore B[ieley]** 1924-
[CA]
*American publisher and author*
* Josephs, Stephen

**Dolnansky, Herman** 1928- [CA]
*American clergyman and author*
* Donin, Hayim Halevy

**Dolores**
See Dickson, Ellen

**Dolphin, Reginald Charles [Rex]**
1915- [IAW, MBF]
*British author*
* Devon, Nicholas
* Devon, Nicola
* Reid, Desmond [house
  pseudonym]
* Williams, Richard [house
  pseudonym]

**Dolson, Hildegarde**
See Lockridge, Hildegarde
[Dolson]

**Dom Anselmo**
See Costadoni, Giovanni Domenico

**Dom Helder**
See Camara, Helder Pessoa

**Dom Maur**
See Jourdain, Francois Claude

**Dom Miguel**
See De Braganca, Miguel Maria
Evaristo

**Dom the Sailor**
See DeQuatro, Dominick

**Doman, June**
See Beveridge, Meryle Secrest

**Domaninska, Libuse**
See Klobaskova, Libuse

**Domanska, Janina**
See Laskowski, Janina Domanska

**Domb, Leiba**
See Trepper, Leopold

**Dombrowski, Katrina**
See Von Dombrowski zu Papros
und Krusvic, Kathe

**Domenichino**
See Zampieri, Domenico

**Domenico Fiorentino**
See Barbiere, Domenico del

**Domergue, Maurice** 1907- [CA]
*French technical writer*
* Dunoyer, Maurice

**[The] Domestic Poet**
See Cowper, William

**Domett, Henry W.** [FFF]
*American journalist*
* Delta

**Domina Anglorum**
See Matilda [or Maud]

**Domingo, Pedro** 20th c. [SFP]
*Author*
* Santos, Domingo

**Dominguez, Joe**
See Dominguez, Jose J.

**Dominguez, Jose J.** 1894-1970
[SC]
*Mexican-born actor*
* Dominguez, Joe

**Dominguez, Ruben**
See Dominguez Perez, Aurelio

**Dominguez Aragones, Edmundo**
1938- [IAW]
*Spanish-born journalist and author*
* Acal, Luis Jacobo
* O'Henry, Henry

**Dominguez Perez, Aurelio** 1940-
[OP]
*Venezuelan opera singer*
* Dominguez, Ruben

**Dominguin [Little Domingo]**
See Del Campo y Alvarez,
Domingo

**Dominguin [Little Domingo]**
See Gonzalez Lucas, Luis Miguel

**Domini, Jon**
See LaRusso, Dominic A[nthony]

**Domini, Rey**
See Lorde, Audre

**Dominic, R. B.** [joint pseudonym
with Mary J. Latis]
See Henissart, Martha

**Dominic, R. B.** [joint pseudonym
with Martha Hennissart]
See Latsis, Mary J.

**[The] Dominican Dandy**
See Marichal, Juan Antonio
Sanchez

**[The] Dominie**
See Hughes, William Jesse

**[The] Dominie Sampson of Germany**
See Jung, Heinrich

**Dominique, Albert** 1908?-
[PMJ, WWJ]
*American jazz musician*
* Albert, Don

**Dominique, Anatie** 1896-
[DAM, EJ, WWJ]
*American jazz musician*
* Dominique, Natty

**Dominique, Natty**
See Dominique, Anatie

**Domino**
See Valter, M.

**Domino, Antoine** 1928-
[B10, DAM, EJ]
*American singer, pianist, songwriter*
* Domino, Fats

**Domino, Fats**
See Domino, Antoine

**Domino, John**
See Averill, Esther [Holden]

**Domitian?**
See Francis, [Sir] Philip

**Domitius Ahenobarbus, Lucius** 37-
68 [SN, WBD]
*Roman emperor*
* Mero, Caldius Biberius
* Nero [Claudius Caesar Drusus
  Germanicus]

**Dommnici, Itek** 1920- [WEF]
*Rumanian-born scriptwriter*
* Diamond, I[sadore] A. L.

**Dompo, Kwesi**
See Parkes, Frank Kobina

**Domsaitis, Adelheid Agathe Marie**
1900- [IWM]
*German-born singer*
* Armhold, Adelheid

**Don**
See Arora, Ramesh Chandra

**Don**
See Connolly, James H.

**[A] Don**
See Stephen, [Sir] Leslie

**Don**
See Trone, Roland

**Don Benito**
See Nielsen, Bent Rosenkilde

**Don Camilo**
See Cela, Camilo Jose

**Don Carlos**
See Cheever, Henry P.

**Don Chick Gambino**
See Gambino, Frank

**Don John**
See Ingelow, Jean

**Don Jose**
See Darling, Joseph Robinson

**Don Juan**
See Matus, Juan

**Don, Laura**
See Fox, Mrs.

**Don Quixote**
See Erskine, Gladys [Shaw]

**[The] Don Quixote of New Jersey**
See Livingston, William

**Don Roberto**
See Bontine, Robert

**Don Santiago**
See Carrillo, Santiago

**Don Vitone**
See Genovese, Vito

**Dona Lucha**
See Corral de Villa, Luz

**Donahey, Mary Dickerson** 1876- ?
[NAA]
*American author*
* Dickerson, Mary A.
* Halloway, Jane

**Donahue, Charles Michael**
1877-1947 [BE]
*American baseball player*
* Donahue, She

**Donahue, Deacon**
See Donahue, John Stephen
Michael

**Donahue, Francis Rostell**
1873-1913 [AS, BE]
*American baseball player*
* Donahue, Red

**Donahue, Hal** 1884?-1931 [BEW]
*American screenwriter and
playwright*
* Barry, Tom

**Donahue, Jean** 20th c. [HCA]
*American actress*
* Willes, Jean

**Donahue, Jiggs**
See Donahue, John Augustus

**Donahue, Jiggs**
See Donahue, John Frederick

**Donahue, John Augustus**
1879-1913 [BE]
*American baseball player*
* Donahue, Jiggs

**Donahue, John Frederick**
1894-1949 [BE]
*American baseball player*
* Donahue, Jiggs

**Donahue, John Stephen Michael**
1922- [BE]
*American baseball player*
* Donahue, Deacon

**Donahue, Red**
See Donahue, Francis Rostell

**Donahue, She**
See Donahue, Charles Michael

**Donahue, Troy**
See Johnson, Merle, Jr.

**Donald** 14th c. [DNNF, FFF, RH]
*Chief of Islay*
* Lord of the Isles

**Donald, Charles Hiliard** 1873- ?
[WWL]
*British author*
* Exile

**Donald, Jean Margaret Davenport**
1829-1903 [BEW]
*British-born actress*
* Lander, Jean Margaret
  Davenport

**Donald, R. V.**
See Floren, Lee

**Donald, Richard Atley** 1910- [BE]
*American baseball player*
* Donald, Swampy

**Donald, Robin**
See Smith, Donald Robin

**Donald, Swampy**
See Donald, Richard Atley

**Donald, Vivian**
See MacKinnon, Charles Roy

**Donalda, Pauline**
See Lightstone, Pauline

**Donalds, Ed[ward Alexander]**
1885-1950 [BE]
*American baseball player*
* Donalds, Skipper

**Donalds, Gordon**
See Shirreffs, Gordon D[onald]

**Donalds, Skipper**
See Donalds, Ed[ward Alexander]

**Donaldson, Bo**
See Donaldson, Robert

**Donaldson, Dan**
Radio announcer
* Warrren, Charlie

**Donaldson, Donella Lightfoot**
1910- [BEW]
American actress
* Haydon, Julie

**Donaldson, Jack** 20th c. [SMG]
American football coach
* J. D.

**Donaldson, Mary E. Muir** 1876- ?
[WWL]
Scottish author
* Dia's Naomi Andrea

**Donaldson, Robert** 1954- [RO2]
American musician
* Donaldson, Bo

**Donaldson, Stephen R.** 1947- [CA]
American author
* Stephens, Reed

**Donaldus**
See Von Redlich, Marcellus
Donald A. R.

**Donan, J. Lee**
See Loy, Mino

**Donart, Arthur C[harles]** 1936-
[CA]
American educator and author
* Donat, Anton

**Donat, Anton**
See Donart, Arthur C[harles]

**Donatello**
See Burleigh, F. J. Le Moyne

**Donatello**
See Di Niccolo di Betto Bardi,
Donato

**Donati, Corso** ?-1308 [HN]
Florentine political leader
* Malefammi, Baron

**Donatus** 4th c. [DNNS]
Bishop of Carthage
* [The] Great

**Donavan, John**
See Morland, Nigel

**Donavan, Wild Bill**
See Donavan, William

**Donavan, William** 20th c. [GW]
American rodeo performer
* Donavan, Wild Bill

**Donday, Auguste Marie** [PA]
Author
* O'Neddy, Philothie

**Dondero, Leonard Peter [Len]**
1903- [BE]
American baseball player
* Dondero, Mike

**Dondero, Mike**
See Dondero, Leonard Peter [Len]

**Doneau, Hughues** 1527-1591 [PA]
Author
* Donellius

**Donegan, Anthony James** 1931-
[RO1]
Scottish-born singer
* Donegan, Lonnie

**Donegan, Lonnie**
See Donegan, Anthony James

**Donelli, Aldo** 1907- [FB, SMG]
American football player and coach
* Donelli, Buff

**Donelli, Buff**
See Donelli, Aldo

**Donellius**
See Doneau, Hughues

**Dones, Phyllis** 1890-1975 [EMT]
British actress and singer
* Dare, Phyllis

**Dones, Zena** 1887- [THR]
British actress
* Dare, Zena

**Donez, Ian** 1891- [ASC]
American composer, singer,
producer
* Inez, Dolly

**Dongados, Jean Francois** 1763- ?
[PA]
Author
* Venance, Father

**Donicht, Mark Allen** 1946- [CA]
American author and publisher
* Allen, Marcus
* Allen, Mark

**Donin, Hayim Halevy**
See Dolnansky, Herman

**Donisthorpe, Ida Margaret Loder**
1873- ? [LC, WWL]
British author
* Pansy

**Donizetti, Alfredo**
See Ciummei, Alfredo

**Donkey, John**
See English, Thomas Dunn

**Donleavy, J. P.**
See Donleavy, James Patrick

**Donleavy, James Patrick** 1926-
[WYA]
American author
* Donleavy, J. P.

**Donlevy, Brian**
See Donlevy, Waldo Bruce

**Donlevy, Waldo Bruce** 1901-1972
Irish-born actor
* Donlevy, Brian

**Donley, Doug** 20th c.
American football player
* White Lightning

**Donlin, Michael Joseph** 1878-1933
[BE, DGS, PB]
American baseball player
* Donlin, Turkey Mike

**Donlin, Turkey Mike**
See Donlin, Michael Joseph

**Donn-Byrne, Brian Oswald**
1889-1928 [LC, NAA, TC]
American author
* Byrne, Donn
* O'Beirne, Brian

**Donnadieu, Marguerite** 1914-
[FDG, TCL]
French author, playwright, director
* Duras, Marguerite

**Donne, Jack**
See Bloom, Jack Don

**Donne, Leonard David** 1926-
[ART]
British painter
* D. D.

**Donne, Maxim**
See Duke, Madelaine [Elizabeth]

**Donnell, Jean** 1921- [SW]
American actress
* Donnell, Jeff

**Donnell, Jeff**
See Donnell, Jean

**Donnelly, A.**
See Aitken, A. Donnelly

**Donnelly, Antoinette** ?-1964 [B10]
Columnist
* Blake, Doris

**Donnelly, Augustine Stanislaus**
1923- [AW, WD]
Australian accountant and writer
* Bear, Bullen

**Donnelly, Blix**
See Donnelly, Sylvester Urban

**Donnelly, Ignatius [Loyola]**
1831-1901 [ESF, SFL, WGT]
American author and politician
* Boisgilbert, Edmund

**Donnelly, Mrs. John F.** [FFF]
Entertainer
* Hanley, Josie

**Donnelly, Muttonleg**
See Donnelly, Theodore

**Donnelly, Sylvester Urban**
1914-1976 [B10, BE]
American baseball player
* Donnelly, Blix

**Donnelly, Theodore** 1912-1958
[WWJ]
American jazz musician
* Donnelly, Muttonleg

**Donnelly, Thomas F.** [FFF, PA]
American author
* Bookworm
* Pomeroy, Eugene

**Donner, Grove**
See Harvey, Florence

**Donnet, [Baron] Michael Gabriel
Libert Marie** 1917- [IAW]
British-born aviator and author
* Mike

**Donoher, Don** 1932- [BB]
American basketball coach
* Donoher, Mickey

**Donoher, Mickey**
See Donoher, Don

**Donohue, Dorothy Howell** 1916-
[BEW]
American actress and artists
representative
* Parrish, Judy

**Donohue, John Daniel Marie-Celestin**
1894- [THR]
Irish playwright
* Celestin, Jack

**Donosti, Mario**
See Luciolli, Mario

**Donovan**
See Leitch, Donovan P.

**Donovan, Bonita R.** 1947- [CA]
American author and educator
* Donovan, Bonnie

**Donovan, Bonnie**
See Donovan, Bonita R.

**Donovan, Dick**
See Preston-Muddock, Joyce
Emmerson

**Donovan, Hobart**
Radio director and scriptwriter
* Donovan, Hobe

**Donovan, Hobe**
See Donovan, Hobart

**Donovan, Hugh**
See Melvin, G. S.

**Donovan, John**
See Dillinger, John Herbert

**Donovan, Laurence** 20th c. [SFP]
Author
* Robeson, Kenneth [house
pseudonym, Street & Smith]

**Donovan, Lawrence William** 1934-
American baseball player
* Donovan, Red

**Donovan, Mike** 1847-1918 [BX]
American boxer
* Donovan, Professor

**Donovan, Patrick Joseph**
1865-1953 [AS, BE, DGS]
Irish-born baseball player and
manager
* Donovan, Patsy

**Donovan, Patsy**
See Donovan, Patrick Joseph

**Donovan, Professor**
See Donovan, Mike

**Donovan, Red**
See Donovan, Lawrence William

**Donovan, Smiling Bill**
See Donovan, William Edward

**Donovan, Tony** 1884- [IBW]
Entertainer
* [The] Man with a Thousand
Songs

**Donovan, Wild Bill**
See Donovan, William Edward

**Donovan, Wild Bill**
See Donovan, William Joseph

**Donovan, William**
See Berkebile, Fred D[onovan]

**Donovan, William Edward**
1876-1923 [AS, BE, DGS]
American baseball player
* Donovan, Smiling Bill
* Donovan, Wild Bill

**Donovan, William Joseph**
1883-1959 [BDW, EE, WWW]
American intelligence chief
* Donovan, Wild Bill

**Donson, Cyril** 1919- [CA, SFL]
British author
* Cordis, Lonny
* Hartford, Via
* Kidd, Russ
* Mackin, Anita

**Donson, Don**
See Scarpa, Salvatore

**Doo, Dickey**
See Granahan, Gerry

**Doog, K. Caj**
See Good, I[rving] John

**Doogin, Skinny**
See Vawter, L. P.

**Dooin, Charles Sebastian**
1879-1952 [AS, BE]
*American baseball player and manager*
* Dooin, Red

**Dooin, Red**
See Dooin, Charles Sebastian

**Dool, John D.** 1887-1928 [SC]
*Scottish-born actor*
* Dooley, Johnny

**Doolan, Mickey**
See Doolittle, Michael Joseph

**Dooley, Anita Donna** 1889?-1961
[FI, FC, IPA]
*Italian-American actress*
* Naldi, Nita

**Dooley, Blind Simmie**
See Dooley, Simmie

**Dooley, Dan de le**
See Burke, James

**Dooley, Ebon**
See Dooley, Thomas

**Dooley, Johnny**
See Dool, John D.

**Dooley, Mr.**
See Dunne, Finley Peter

**Dooley, Rachel Rice** 1896-
[BEW, THR]
*Scottish-born actress, comedienne, dancer*
* Dooley, Rae

**Dooley, Rae**
See Dooley, Rachel Rice

**Dooley, Simmie** 1881-1961 [BWW]
*American singer*
* Dooley, Blind Simmie

**Dooley, Thomas** 1942- [IBW]
*American poet*
* Dooley, Ebon

**Doolittle, Hilda** 1886-1961
[CA, EWL, LC]
*American poet*
* H. D.
* Helforth, John

**Doolittle, Michael Joseph**
1880-1951 [BE]
*American baseball player*
* Doolan, Mickey

**Doom, Dr.**
See Kaufman, Henry

**Dooms, Harry E.** ?-1899 [BE]
*American baseball player*
* Dooms, Jack

**Dooms, Jack**
See Dooms, Harry E.

**Doone, Jice**
See Marshall, James Vance

**Dor, Ana**
See Ceder, Georgiana Dorcas

**Dora d'Istria**
See Ghica, Helene

**Dorab**
See Contractor, Dorab Dadiba

**Dorais, Charles E.** 1891?-1954
[AS, FB, SMG]
*American football coach*
* Dorais, Gus

**Dorais, Gus**
See Dorais, Charles E.

**Doraiswajy, Trivandrum Krishna Iyer**
1922- [IAW]
*Indian author*
* Nakulan
* Nayar, S.

**Doran, John Michael** 1911- [CEI]
*Canadian-born hockey player*
* Doran, Red

**Doran, Mary**
See Arnot, Florence

**Doran, Red**
See Doran, John Michael

**Dorant, Gene**
See Lent, D[ora] Geneva

**Dorat, Jean** 1504?-1588
[DEP, FFF, SN]
*French poet*
* [The] French Lycophron
* [The] French Pindar
* [The] Golden
* [The] Pindar of France

**Dorchato, Jean**
See Bentein, Jean-Marie Georges Joseph

**Dorcy, Mary Jean** 1914- [CA]
*American author and illustrator*
* Bennett, Jean Frances
* Mary Jean, [Sister]

**Dore, Abba**
See Dore, David M.

**Dore, Claire [Morin]** 1934- [CA]
*Canadian author*
* France, Claire
* Morin, Claire

**Dore, David M.** 1955- [IBW]
*American clergyman*
* Dore, Abba

**Dore, Gabriel**
See Psenka, R. Jaromir

**Dore, Pierre** 1500-1599 [PA]
*Author*
* Auratus, Petrus

**Dorey, Flipper**
See Dorey, Robert James [Jim]

**Dorey, Robert James [Jim]** 1947-
[FHE]
*Canadian-born hockey player*
* Dorey, Flipper

**Dorgan, Thomas Aloysius**
1877-1929 [WEC]
*American cartoonist*
* Tad

**Dorge, Jeanne Emilie Marie** 20th
c. [IAW]
*French missionary and author*
* Du Sacre-Coeur, [Sister] Marie-Andre

**Dorgeles, Roland**
See Lecavele, Roland

**Dorham, Kenny**
See Dorham, McKinley Howard

**Dorham, Mary** 1938- [IBW]
*American disc jockey and newscaster*
* Dee, Merri

**Dorham, McKinley Howard**
1924-1972 [DAM, EJ, PMJ]
*American jazz musician*
* Dorham, Kenny

**Doria, Andrea** 1468-1560
[DNNS, HN, WBD]
*Genoese statesman and naval officer*
* [The] Father of His Country
* [The] Father of Peace
* [The] Liberator of Genoa

**Doria, Clara**
See Rogers, Clara Kathleen

**Dorian, Angela** 1944- [FC]
*Australian actress*
* Vetri, Victoria

**Dorian, Frederick**
See Deutsch, Friedrich

**Dorian, Harry**
See Hamilton, Charles Harold St. John

**Doricha** 6th c. BC [WBD]
*Greek courtesan*
* Rhodopis

**Doris, Mrs. John B.** [FFF]
* Stokes, Ella

**Dorish, Fritz**
See Dorish, Harry

**Dorish, Harry** 1921- [BE]
*American baseball player*
* Dorish, Fritz

**Dorismond, Jean-Baptiste** 1891?-
[CW]
*Haitian poet and journalist*
* Desroussels, Felix

**Dorji, Paljore**
*Bhutanese jurist*
* C. J.

**Dorleac, Catherine** 1943-
[BDF, FC]
*French actress*
* Deneuve, Catherine

**Dorliae, Peter Gondro** 1935- [CA]
*Liberian author*
* Dorliae, Saint

**Dorliae, Saint**
See Dorliae, Peter Gondro

**Dorling, Henry Taprell** 1883-1968
[LC, WWS]
*Scottish-born author*
* Taffrail

**Dorman, Charlie**
See Dorman, Dwight Dexter

**Dorman, Dwight Dexter** 1903-
[BE]
*American baseball player*
* Dorman, Charlie
* Dorman, Red

**Dorman, Kathleen**
See Ellwood, Marjorie Barker

**Dorman, Luke**
See Bingley, David Ernest

**Dorman, Red**
See Dorman, Dwight Dexter

**Dorman-Smith, Chink**
See Dorman-Smith, [Sir] Eric

**Dorman-Smith, [Sir] Eric**
1895-1969 [WWW]
*British army officer*
* Dorman-Smith, Chink

**D'Orme, Aileen**
See Burke, Aileen

**Dorn, Dean M.** 20th c. [WW]
*Author*
* Morgan, Michael [joint pseudonym with C. E. Carle]

**Dorn, Dolores**
See Dorn-Heft, Dolores

**Dorn, Philip**
See Van Dungen, Fritz

**Dorn, William S.** 1928- [CA]
*American computer expert and author*
* Earlson, Ian Malcolm

**Dorn-Heft, Dolores** 1935-
[BEW, FC]
*American actress*
* Dorn, Dolores

**Dornhoefer, Gary**
See Dornhoefer, Gerhardt Otto

**Dornhoefer, Gerhardt Otto** 1943-
[CEI, FHE, HK]
*Canadian-born hockey player*
* Dornhoefer, Gary

**Dornya, Maria**
See Hankla, Donna Maria

**Doro, Marie**
See Stewart, Marie Kathryn

**Dorot, Peter?**
See Shaver, Richard S[harpe]

**Dorothy, R. D.**
See Charques, Dorothy [Taylor]

**Dorr, Mrs. J. C.** [PA]
*Author*
* Ripley, Julia C.

**Dorrance, Gordon** 1890- [NAA]
*American publisher and author*
* Gordon, John

**Dorree, Babette** 1906-1974 [SC]
*Austrian-born actress and figure skater*
* Dorree, Bobbie

**Dorree, Bobbie**
See Dorree, Babette

**Dors, Diana**
See Fluck, Daisy

**Dorsainvil, J. C.**
See Dorsainvil, Justin Chrysostome

**Dorsainvil, Justin Chrysostome**
1880-1942 [CW]
*Haitian author*
* Dorsainvil, J. C.

**Dorsan, Luc**
See Simenon, Georges [Joseph Christian]

**Dorsange, Jean**
See Simenon, Georges [Joseph Christian]

**D'Orsay, Fifi**
See Lussier, Yvonne

**D'Orsay, Lawrence**
See Lawrence, Dorset William

**Dorset, Richard**
See  Shaver, Richard S[harpe]

**Dorset, Ruth**
See  Ross, William Edward Daniel

**Dorsett, Cal[vin Leavell]** 1916-
[BE]
*American baseball player*
* Dorsett, Preacher

**Dorsett, Danielle**
See  Daniels, Dorothy

**Dorsett, Preacher**
See  Dorsett, Cal[vin Leavell]

**Dorsey, Arnold [Gerry]** 1936-
[IPA, LRR]
*British-born singer*
* Humperdinck, Engelbert

**Dorsey, Big Yellow**
See  Dorsey, Bob

**Dorsey, Bob** 1915-   [MY]
*American jazz musician*
* Dorsey, Big Yellow

**Dorsey, Dino**
See  Dorsey, Larry

**Dorsey, Larry** 1953-   [SMG]
*American football player*
* Dorsey, Dino

**Dorsey, Lee** 20th c.   [RO1]
*American singer and boxer*
* Chocolate, Kid

**Dorsey, Sarah Anne** 1829-1879
[FFF]
*American author*
* Filia Ecclesiae

**Dorsey, Thomas A[ndrew]** 1899-
[BWW, IBW]
*American jazz musician*
* Barrelhouse Tommy
* [The] Father of Modern Gospel
  Music
* Georgia Tom
* Memphis Jim
* Memphis Mose
* Railroad Bill
* Ramsey, George?
* Smokehouse Charley
* Texas Tommy

**Dorst, Jean [Pierre]** 1924-   [CA]
*French museum director,
ornithologist, author*
* D'Urstelle, Pierre

**Dorworth, Alice Grey** 20th c.
[IAW]
*American author*
* Lynch, Grey

**Dory-Boutin, Elmyr**
See  Hoffman, Josef

**Dorziat, Gabrielle**
See  Moppert, Gabrielle

**Dos Reis Machado, Manuel** 20th c.
[IBW]
*Brazilian athlete*
* Bimbi, Meste

**Dos Reis Pereira, Jose Maria**
1901-1969   [EWL]
*Portuguese poet, playwright, author*
* Regio, Jose

**Dos Santos, Manoel Francisco**
1933-   [OCS]
*Brazilian soccer player*
* Garrincha

**Dos Santos, Zemaria** 1939-   [AES]
*Brazilian soccer player*
* Zemaria

**Dosa, Marta Leszlei** 20th c.   [CA]
*Hungarian-born author and
librarian*
* Leszlei, Marta

**Dosch, Audrey Ann**  ?-1955   [SC]
*American actress*
* Russell, Ann

**Doscher, Herm**
See  Doscher, John Henry, Sr.

**Doscher, John Henry, Sr.**
1852-1934   [BE]
*American baseball player*
* Doscher, Herm

**Dosh**
See  Gardosh, Kariel

**Dositheus**
See  Obradovic, Dimitrije

**Dossage, Jean**
See  Simenon, Georges [Joseph
Christian]

**Dossi, Battista**
See  Di Lutero, Battista

**Dosso Dossi**
See  Di Lutero, Giovanni

**D'Ostie, Cardinal**
See  Allarmet [or D'Alouzier], Jean

**Dot, Marcel**
See  Morris, Michael

**Doto, Giuseppe** 1902-1972
[BLB, MM]
*Italian-born American underworld
figure*
* Adone, Joe
* Adonis, Joe
* Joey A

**Dotson, Clarence** 1881-1954   [IBW]
*American dancer*
* Dotson, One Eye

**Dotson, One Eye**
See  Dotson, Clarence

**Dotterer, Dutch**
See  Dotterer, Henry John

**Dotterer, Henry John** 1931-   [BE]
*American baseball player*
* Dotterer, Dutch

**Dottley, John**   [SMG]
*American football player*
* Dottley, Kayo

**Dottley, Kayo**
See  Dottley, John

**Dottore, Charles A.** 1895-   [F2]
*Actor*
* La Torre, Charles A.

**Dottsy**
See  Brodt, Dottsy

**Doty, Babe**
See  Doty, Elmer L.

**Doty, Elmer L.** 1867-1929   [BE]
*American baseball player*
* Doty, Babe

**Doty, Gladys** 1908-   [CA]
*American educator and author*
* Douglass, Marcia Kent

**Doty, Jean Slaughter** 1929-   [CA]
*American author and horsewoman*
* Slaughter, Jean

**Dotzenko, Grisha**   [IBY]
*Russian-born illustrator*
* Grisha

**[Le] Douanier**
See  Rousseau, Henri

**Double D**
See  Davis, Dwight

**Double D**
See  Drysdale, Donald Scott

**Double Duty Radcliffe**
See  Radcliffe, Theodore [Ted]

**Double Joe Dwyer**
See  Dwyer, Joseph Michael

**Double No-Hit**
See  Vander Meer, John Samuel

**Double No-No**
See  Foster, Alan Benton

**Double O**
See  Bristol, James David

**Double O**
See  McBean, Alvin O'Neal

**Double X**
See  Foxx, James Emory

**Doubled, Victor**   [PA]
*Author*
* Peccadille

**Doubleday, Neltje de Graff**
1865-1918   [WBD]
*American author*
* Blanchan, Neltje

**Doubleday, Roman**
See  Long, Lily Augusta

**Doubleday, Thomas**   [PA]
*Author*
* [The] North Country Angler

**[A] Doubtful Gentleman**
See  Paulding, James Kirke

**Douce, Francis** 1757-1834
[PA, SN]
*British scholar*
* [The] Porson of Old English and
  French Literature
* Prospero

**Doud, Oliver B.**   [FFF]
*Entertainer*
* Byron, Oliver Doud

**Doudna, Edgar G.** 1877- ?   [NAA]
*American educator and author*
* Schoolmaster, John

**Doudney, Henry Eric John** 1905-
[ART]
*British industrial designer and
sculptor*
* E. J. D.

**Doudy, Reginald** 1902-   [FC]
*British actor*
* Garrick, John

**Dougherty, Betty** 1922-   [CA]
*British graphic designer and author*
* Mount, Elisabeth

**Dougherty, Charles** 1879-1940
[IBW, OBW]
*American baseball player*
* Dougherty, Pat

**Dougherty, Edward** 20th c.   [GW]
*American rodeo performer*
* Dougherty, Red Dog

**Dougherty, Genevieve** 1888-   [ASC]
*American composer*
* Dougherty, Jennie

**Dougherty, Jennie**
See  Dougherty, Genevieve

**Dougherty, Joanna Foster**
See  Foster, Joanna

**Dougherty, Nathan W.** 1886-   [FB]
*American football player and
athletic director*
* [The] Big One

**Dougherty, Pat**
See  Dougherty, Charles

**Dougherty, Patrick Henry**
1876-1940   [AS, BE]
*American baseball player*
* Dougherty, Patsy

**Dougherty, Patsy**
See  Dougherty, Patrick Henry

**Dougherty, Red Dog**
See  Dougherty, Edward

**Dougherty, Sugar Boy**
See  Dougherty, Thomas James
[Tom]

**Dougherty, Thomas James [Tom]**
1881-1953   [BE]
*American baseball player*
* Dougherty, Sugar Boy

**Dougherty, Walter Hampden**
1879-1955   [BEW, F1, FC]
*American actor*
* Hampden, Walter

**Doughnut Bill Carrick**
See  Carrick, William Martin

**Doughty, Bradford** 1921-   [CA]
*American author*
* Denny, Brian

**Doughty, C. M.**
See  Doughty, Charles Montagu

**Doughty, Charles Montagu**
1843-1926   [LC]
*British author*
* Doughty, C. M.

**Doughty, Francis W.** 20th c.
[EMD]
*American author*
* [A] N. Y. Detective

**Doughty, Frank?**
See  Senarens, Luis Philip

**Doughty, Nigel**
See  Whittington-Egan, Richard

**Douglas, Aaron** 1900?-1979
*American artist*
* [The] Father of Black American
  Art

**Douglas, Albert**
See  Armstrong, Douglas Albert

**Douglas, Ann C.**
See  Welch, Ann Courtenay
Edmonds

**Douglas, Archibald** 1328?-1400?
[WBD]
*Third Earl of Douglas*
* [The] Black Douglas
* [The] Grim

**Douglas, Archibald** 1372-1424
[DNNF, HN, RH]
*Fourth Earl of Douglas*
* Tineman [or Tyneman]

**Douglas, Archibald** 1450?-1514
[DHA, DNNF, RH]
*Fifth Earl of Angus*
* Bell the Cat
* [The] Great Earl

**Douglas, Archibald** 1489?-1557
[SN]
*Sixth Earl of Angus*
* Gray Steel

**Douglas, Archibald** 1555-1588
[DNNF, DNNS, RH]
*Eighth Earl of Angus*
* [The] Good Earl

**Douglas, Arthur**
See  Moreton, Douglas Arthur

**Douglas, Brain**
See  Burne, Philip Lauraine

**Douglas, C. H.**
See  Grieve, Christopher Murray

**Douglas, Catherine** 15th c.  [HHF]
*Attempted to save life of King James
I of Scotland*
* Barlass, Kate

**Douglas, Charles William** 1935-
[BE]
*American baseball player*
* Douglas, Whammy

**Douglas, Donald**
See  Kinleyside, Douglas

**Douglas, Drake**
See  Zimmermann, Werner

**Douglas, Edith**
See  Burnham, Clara Louise [Root]

**Douglas, Ellen**
See  Haxton, Josephine A.

**Douglas, Ellen**
See  Williamson, Ellen Douglas

**Douglas, Emory** 1943-  [IBW]
*American cartoonist*
* [The] People's Artist

**Douglas, Felicity**
See  Tomlin, Felicity

**Douglas, Frank**
See  Langley, F. E.

**Douglas, Fred** 1817- ?  [PA]
*Author*
* Bailey

**Douglas, George**
See  Brown, George Douglas

**Douglas, George**
See  Fisher, Douglas George

**Douglas, George Norman**
1868-1952  [LC, TC, WGT]
*British author*
* Normyx

**Douglas, Glenn**
See  Duckett, Alfred

**Douglas, Helen Bee**
See  Bee, Helen L.

**Douglas, Helen Gahagan**
1900-1980  [CA]
*American politician and author*
* Gahagan, Helen

**Douglas, Hudson**
See  Aitken, Robert

**Douglas, [Sir] James** 1286-1330
[FFF, SN, WBD]
*Lord of Douglas*
* [The] Black Douglas
* [The] Good

**Douglas, James** 1371?-1443
[SN, WBD]
*Seventh Earl of Douglas*
* [The] Fat
* [The] Gross

**Douglas, James McM.**
See  Butterworth, William
Edmund, III

**Douglas, Jeff** [joint pseudonym with
Andrew Jefferson Offutt]
See  Berry, Douglas Bruce

**Douglas, Jeff** [joint pseudonym with
Douglas Bruce Berry]
See  Offutt, Andrew Jefferson

**Douglas, John** 1721-1807  [PA]
*Author*
* Roe, Leonard

**Douglas, John Lee** 1943-  [NAD]
*Religious leader*
* Yukteswar Sri Babajhan, [Yogi]

**Douglas, Joyce**
See  Moreton, Douglas Arthur

**Douglas, Kathryn**
See  Ewing, Kathryn

**Douglas, Keith** 1915-1973  [FC]
*American actor*
* Kennedy, Douglas

**Douglas, Kenneth**
See  Savory, Kenneth

**Douglas, Kent**
See  Montgomery, Robert Douglass

**Douglas, Kid**
See  Douglas, Lizzie

**Douglas, Kim**
See  Woodford, [Irene] Cecile

**Douglas, Kirk**
See  Demsky, Issur Danielovich

**Douglas, Klondike**
See  Douglas, William B.

**Douglas, Leon** 1954-
*American basketball player*
* Number 1

**Douglas, Leonard**
See  Bradbury, Ray [Douglas]

**Douglas, Lizzie** 1897-1973  [BWW]
*American singer*
* Douglas, Kid
* Douglas, Minnie
* Gospel Minnie
* McCoy, Minnie
* Memphis Minnie
* Texas Tessie

**Douglas, Lou**
See  Dohrn, Bernardine

**Douglas, Malcolm**
See  Sanderson, [Ronald] Douglas

**Douglas, Margaret** 15th c.
[DNNS, FFF, HN]
*Daughter of Archibald, Fifth Earl of
Douglas*
* [The] Fair Maid of Galloway

**Douglas, Marguerite France** 1918-
[ART]
*British painter*
* M. F. D.

**Douglas, Marian**
See  Robinson, Annie Douglas

**Douglas, Melvyn**
See  Hesselberg, Melvyn E.

**Douglas, Michael**
See  Bright, Robert

**Douglas, Michael** [joint pseudonym
with Douglas Crichton]
See  Crichton, [John] Michael

**Douglas, Michael** [joint pseudonym
with (John) Michael Crichton]
See  Crichton, Douglas

**Douglas, Mike**
See  Dowd, Michael Delaney, Jr.

**Douglas, Minnie**
See  Douglas, Lizzie

**Douglas, Mrs. John**  [FFF]
*Entertainer*
* Steinberg, Amy

**Douglas, Myrtle R.** 20th c.  [SFP]
*Author*
* Morojo

**Douglas, Nigel**
See  Leigh-Pemberton, Nigel
Douglas

**Douglas, Percy**
See  Cope, Alan Campbell

**Douglas, Philips Brooks**
1890-1952  [AS, BE, PB]
*American baseball player*
* Douglas, Shufflin' Phil

**Douglas, R. M.**
See  Mason, Douglas R[ankine]

**Douglas, Robert**
See  Andrews, [Charles] Robert
D[ouglas Hardy]

**Douglas, Robert**
See  Finlayson, Robert Douglas

**Douglas, Shane**
See  Wilkes-Hunter, Richard

**Douglas, Shufflin' Phil**
See  Douglas, Philips Brooks

**Douglas, Stephen Arnold**
1813-1861  [DEP, DNNF, DNNS]
*American statesman*
* [The] Little Giant

**Douglas, Syble G.** 1942?-  [CW]
*Guyanese poet, artist, educator*
* Sylvia

**Douglas, Thorne**
See  Haas, Ben[jamin] L[eopold]

**Douglas, Tom**
See  Lee-Doolan, Tom

**Douglas, Wally**
See  Froes, Walter J.

**Douglas, Whammy**
See  Douglas, Charles William

**Douglas, Wild Bill**
See  Douglas, William Orville

**Douglas, [Sir] William**  ?-1298
[FFF, SN, WBD]
*First Lord of Douglas*
* [The] Hardy

**Douglas, [Sir] William** 1300?-1353
[DNNF, DNNS, HN]
*Lord of Liddesdale*
* [The] Flower of Chivalry
* [The] Knight of Liddesdale

**Douglas, William** 1637-1695  [SN]
*First Duke of Queensberry*
* [The] Proto Rebel

**Douglas, William** 1691-1752  [PA]
*Author*
* Nader, William, S. X. Q.

**Douglas, William** 1724-1810
[FFF, SN, WBD]
*Earl of March and Duke of
Queensberry*
* Old Q

**Douglas, William B.** 1872-1953
[BE]
*American baseball player*
* Douglas, Klondike

**Douglas, William Orville** 1896-1980
*American Supreme Court Justice*
* Douglas, Wild Bill

**Douglas-Home, Alec**
See  Home, Alexander Frederick

**Douglass, Amanda Hart**
See  Wallmann, Jeffrey M[iner]

**Douglass, Ellsworth** 20th c.  [WGT]
*British author*
* Werner, Isaiah

**Douglass, Frederick**
See  Bailey, Frederick Augustus
Washington

**Douglass, Marcia Kent**
See  Doty, Gladys

**Douglass, Marian**
See  Greene, Anne D.

**Douglass, Miss**  [PA]
*Author*
* Bell, Douglas

**Douglass, Stephen**
See  Fitch, Stephen

**Dounamus, Georgius**
See  Downame, George

**Doune, Ercil**
See  Drysdale, Janey C.

**[The] Dour Scot**
See  Sutherland, John Bain

**Douras, Marion Cecilia** 1897-1961
[BDF, BEW, F1]
*American actress*
* Davies, Marion

**Douri, Fremin** 1512-1578  [PA]
*Author*
* Durius, Firminius

**Dourlein, Pieter** 20th c.  [EE]
*Dutch intelligence agent*
* Paul [code name used during
World War II]

**Douse, Anthony** 20th c.  [MBF]
*British author*
* Reid, Desmond [house
pseudonym]

**Douthit, Taylor Lee** 1901-    [PB]
*American baseball player*
* [The] Ball Hawk

**Douthitt, Wilfred** 1888-    [BBD]
*British singer*
* Graveure, Louis

**D'Outremer**
*See* Louis IV

**Doux [Gentle]**
*See* Durelle, Yvon

**[The] Dove**
*See* Bohney, Lillian

**Dove, Billie**
*See* Bohney, Lillian

**Doveglion**
*See* Villa, Jose Garcia

**Dover, Derry**
*See* Khaury, Herbert

**Dover, Fostoria**
*See* Mulcahy, A. E.

**[The] Doves**
*See* Aiuppa, Joseph John [Joe]

**Dovgolenko, Maria Karnilovich**
1920-    [EMT]
*American actress, dancer, singer*
* Karnilova, Maria

**Dovima**
*See* Horan, Dorothy

**Dovlos, Jay**
*See* Joyce, Jon L[oyd]

**Dow Jr.**
*See* Paige, Elbridge Gerry

**Dow, Neal** 1804-1897    [SN, WBD]
*American temperance advocate*
* [The] Father of the Maine Law
* [The] Kossuth of the Temperance
  Revolution

**Dow, Peggy**
*See* Varnadow, Peggy

**Dowd, Buttermilk Tommy**
*See* Dowd, Thomas Jefferson

**Dowd, James Joseph** 1889-1960
[BE]
*American baseball player*
* Dowd, Skip

**Dowd, Maxine E.**
*See* Jensen, Maxine Dowd

**Dowd, Michael Delaney, Jr.** 1925-
[IPA, ITA, PMJ]
*American television performer*
* Douglas, Mike

**Dowd, Raymond Bernard**
1897-1962    [BE]
*American baseball player*
* Dowd, Snooks

**Dowd, Skip**
*See* Dowd, James Joseph

**Dowd, Snooks**
*See* Dowd, Raymond Bernard

**Dowd, Thomas Jefferson**
1869-1933    [AS, BE]
*American baseball player*
* Dowd, Buttermilk Tommy

**Dowden, Anne Ophelia [Todd]**
1907-    [CA, SAT]
*American author and illustrator*
* Todd, Anne Ophelia

**Dowding, A. L.** 20th c.
[SFL, WGT, WWL]
*British author*
* Ramsden, Lewis

**Dowding, [Sir] Hugh C. T.**
1882-1970    [BDW, WWW]
*British air force officer*
* Dowding, Stuffy

**Dowding, Stuffy**
*See* Dowding, [Sir] Hugh C. T.

**Dowdy, [Mrs.] Regera**
*See* Gorey, Edward [St. John]

**Dowell, Duck**
*See* Dowell, Robert

**Dowell, Horace Kirby** 1904-
[ASC, PMJ, WWJ]
*American jazz musician*
* Dowell, Saxie

**Dowell, Robert** 1912-    [BB]
*American basketball player*
* Dowell, Duck

**Dowell, Samuel**
*See* Close, John

**Dowell, Saxie**
*See* Dowell, Horace Kirby

**Dowell, Susan Irene** 1944-    [OP]
*American opera singer*
* Marsee, Susanne

**Dower, Penn**
*See* Pendower, Jacques

**Dowley, D. M.**
*See* Marrison, Leslie William

**Dowling, Allen** 1900-    [CA]
*American author*
* King, Jack

**Dowling, Dutch**
*See* Dowling, Elmer Sylvester

**Dowling, Eddie**
*See* Goucher, Joseph Nelson

**Dowling, Elmer Sylvester** 20th c.
[BLB]
*American underworld figure*
* Dowling, Dutch

**Dowling, Levi H.** 1844-1911
[NAD]
*Preacher and physician*
* Levi

**Dowling, Lois Darlington** 1909-
[F2]
*Actress*
* Moran, Lois

**Dowling, Rodney J.** 1868-1944
[BE]
*American baseball player*
* Glenalvin, Robert J. [Bob]

**Dowling, Vincent** ?-1852
[DNNS, FFF, SN]
*British sportsman*
* [The] Long Scribe

**Down, Avril** 1900-    [ART]
*British painter*
* A. D.

**Down, C. Maurice** 20th c.    [MBF]
*British author*
* Clifford, Martin [house
  pseudonym]
* Conquest, Owen [house
  pseudonym]

**Down, C. Maurice** (Continued)
* Howard, Prosper [house
  pseudonym]
* Richards, Frank [house
  pseudonym]

**Downame, George** ?-1634    [FFF]
*British theologian and author*
* Dounamus, Georgius

**Downes, Andrew** 1550-1627    [PA]
*Author*
* Dunoeus

**Downes, Quentin**
*See* Harrison, Michael

**Downey, Alexander Cummings**
1889-1949    [BE]
*American baseball player*
* Downey, Red

**Downey, Edmund** 1856-1937
[LAO, SFL, WWL]
*Irish author and editor*
* Allen, F. M.

**Downey, Raymond Joseph** 1914-
[ASC]
*American composer*
* Wells, Roy

**Downey, Red**
*See* Downey, Alexander Cummings

**Downie, Mary Alice** 1934-
[CA, SAT]
*American-born poet and writer*
* Hunter, Dawe

**Downing, Ace**
*See* Downing, Alphonso Erwin

**Downing, Alphonso Erwin** 1941-
[BE, SMG]
*American baseball player*
* Downing, Ace
* Downing, Gentleman Al

**Downing, Fanny Murdaugh** 1835?-
?    [FFF, PA]
*American poet*
* Dashmore, Frank
* Viola

**Downing, Gentleman Al**
*See* Downing, Alphonso Erwin

**Downing, George** 20th c.    [EE]
*American intelligence agent*
* Cree, Alexander
* Rawlings, Harry

**Downing, J., major**
*See* Davis, Charles Augustus

**Downing, [Major] Jack**
*See* Smith, Seba

**Downs, Bill**
*See* Sellers, Connie Leslie, Jr.

**Downs, Bunny**
*See* Downs, McKinley

**Downs, Jerome Willis** 1883-1939
[BE]
*American baseball player*
* Downs, Red

**Downs, McKinley** 20th c.    [OBW]
*American baseball player*
* Downs, Bunny

**Downs, Red**
*See* Downs, Jerome Willis

**Downs, T. Nelson** 20th c.    [BS]
*Magician*
* [The] King of Koins

**Downton, Nobby**
*See* Downton, Paul Rupert

**Downton, Paul Rupert** 1957-    [DC]
*British cricketer*
* Downton, Nobby

**Dowse, Thomas** 1772-1856    [FFF]
*American book collector*
* [The] Literary Leather-Dresser

**Dowsett, Joseph Morewood** 1864-
?    [LAO]
*British author*
* Teswod
* Traveller

**Dowsey, Rose Walker** 1907-1951
[SC]
*American actress*
* Walker, Rose

**Dowty, A. A.**    [PA]
*Author*
* Smiff, O. P. Q. Philander
* [The] Young and Happy
  Husband

**Doyle, Bobby**
*See* Santucci, Girolamo

**Doyle, Charles [Desmond]** 1928-
[CA]
*British-born Canadian poet and
  educator*
* Doyle, Mike

**Doyle, Conny**
*See* Doyle, Cornelius J.

**Doyle, Cornelius J.** 1858-1927
[BE]
*American baseball player*
* Doyle, Conny

**Doyle, Danny**
*See* Doyle, Howard James

**Doyle, David**
*See* Carter, David C[harles]

**Doyle, Dirty Jack**
*See* Doyle, John Joseph

**Doyle, Donovan**
*See* Boegehold, Betty [Doyle]

**Doyle, Gene**
*See* Taubenhaus, Eugene

**Doyle, H. B.** 19th c.
[DNNF, PA, RH]
*British artist*
* H. B.

**Doyle, Howard James** 1917-    [BE]
*American baseball player*
* Doyle, Danny

**Doyle, J. Dixie**    [FFF]
*American journalist*
* Dixie

**Doyle, James J.** 20th c.    [WWL]
*Irish author*
* O Dubhghaill, Seamus

**Doyle, James Kildare Leighlin**
1786?-1834    [HN]
*Irish clergyman*
* J. K. L.

**Doyle, James Warren** 1834- ?    [PA]
*Author*
* Irish Catholic

**Doyle, Jefferson E. P.** 1837- ?
[FFF]
*American writer*
* Joslyn, [Major] Jep
* Modoc

**Doyle, Jefferson E. P.** (Continued)
* Vidette

**Doyle, Jimmy**
See Delaney, James

**Doyle, John**
See Ellison, Harlan [Jay]

**Doyle, John**
See Graves, Robert Von Ranke

**Doyle, John Joseph** 1869-1958
[BE, PB]
Irish-born baseball player
* Doyle, Dirty Jack

**Doyle, Judd Bruce** 1881-1947 [BE]
American baseball player
* Doyle, Slow Joe

**Doyle, Laughing Larry**
See Doyle, Lawrence Joseph

**Doyle, Lawrence Joseph** 1886-
[BE, PB]
American baseball player
* Doyle, Laughing Larry

**Doyle, Little Patsy**
See Doyle, Patrick

**Doyle, Lynn**
See Montgomery, Leslie Alexander

**Doyle, Martin**
See Hickey, William

**Doyle, Mike**
See Doyle, Charles [Desmond]

**Doyle, Moya** 1888- [THR]
British actress and singer
* Mannering, Moya

**Doyle, Mugsy**
See Doyle, Robert Dennis [Denny]

**Doyle, Patrick** ?-1914 [BLB]
American gangster
* Doyle, Little Patsy

**Doyle, Richard** 1826- ? [PA]
Author
* Brown, Jones, and Robinson

**Doyle, Richard A.** 20th c. [SMG]
American football player
* Doyle, Skip

**Doyle, Robert Dennis [Denny]** 1944-
American baseball player
* Doyle, Mugsy

**Doyle, Rosina [Wheeler]** [FFF]
Author
* Alciphron

**Doyle, Skip**
See Doyle, Richard A.

**Doyle, Slow Joe**
See Doyle, Judd Bruce

**Dozier, Buzz**
See Dozier, William Joseph

**Dozier, William Joseph** 1927- [BE]
American baseball player
* Dozier, Buzz

**Dozo, Monique** 1931- [EJ7]
Monacan-born singer
* Aldebert, Monique

**Dozy**
See Davies, Trevor

**Drabkin, Yakov Davidovich**
1874-1933 [TC]
Author
* Gusev, Sergey Ivanovich

**Drabowsky, Moe**
See Drabowsky, Myron Walter

**Drabowsky, Myron Walter** 1935-
[BE, EJS]
Polish-born American baseball
player
* Drabowsky, Moe

**Drachman, Julian M[oses]** 1894-
[CA]
American author, poet, educator
* Adam, Ben
* Goodall, Melanie
* Octopus

**Drackett, Phil[ip Arthur]** 1922-
[AW, CA, WD]
British author
* King, Paul

**Draco, F.**
See Davis, Julia

**Draeger, Siegfried**
See Stashynsky, Bogdan

**Dragases**
See Constantine XI Palaeologus

**Drage, Charles Hardinge** 1897-
[IAW]
British author
* Charles

**Dragna, Jack** 20th c. [PHM]
Italian-born American underworld
figure
* [The] Al Capone of Los Angeles
* Rizzoti, Antonio

**Drago, Harry Sinclair** 1888-1979
[CA, WYA]
American author
* Ermine, Will
* Lomax, Bliss

**Dragomanoff, Michael** 1841-1895
[FFF]
Russian historian and author
* Stepniak

**Dragon, Carolyn**
See DuBreuil, Elizabeth Lorinda

**Dragon, Daryl** 20th c.
American musician
* [The] Captain

**[The] Dragon Lady**
See Cannon, Noel

**[The] Dragon Lady**
See Claybrook, Joan

**Dragpmet, edward**
See Williamson, Thames Ross

**Drahlegne**
See Englehardt, Frederick J.

**Draig Glas**
See Johnson, Arthur Tysilio

**Draitser, Emil** 1937- [CA]
Russian-born American author
* Abramov, Emil

**Drake, Alfred**
See Capurro, Alfred

**Drake, Charles**
See Ruppert, Charles

**Drake, Charlie**
See Springall, Charles

**Drake, Dona**
See Novella, Rita

**Drake, Douglas**
See Lamy, Douglas N.

**Drake, Ducky**
See Drake, Elvin

**Drake, Elvin** 20th c. [BBH]
American athletic trainer
* Drake, Ducky

**Drake, Fabia**
See McGlinchy, Fabia Drake

**Drake, Frank**
See Hamilton, Charles Harold St.
John

**Drake, Harry** 1915- [BBH]
American archer
* Flight, Mr.

**Drake, Jimmy** 20th c. [RO1]
American singer and songwriter
* Norvus, Nervous

**Drake, Joan**
See Davies, Joan Howard

**Drake, Joseph Rodman** 1795-1820
[FFF, PA]
American poet
* Croaker

**Drake, Kimbal**
See Gallagher, Rachel

**Drake, Lisl**
See Beer, Eloise C. S.

**Drake, Morgan**
See Berry, Douglas Bruce

**Drake, Plunk**
See Drake, William

**Drake, Rupert**
See Belfield, Harry Wedgwood

**Drake, Steve**
See Fink, Dale Laurence

**Drake, Tom**
See Alderdice, Alfred

**Drake, William** 1895- [MK]
American baseball player
* Drake, Plunk

**Dralloc, John**
See Collard, John

**Drand, Georg** 1573-1635 [PA]
Author
* Drandius

**Drandius**
See Drand, Georg

**Dranmor**
See Von Schmidt, Ferdinand

**Dransfield, Michael [John] Pender**
1948- [CA]
Australian poet and editor
* Tate, Edward

**Draper, Ben** 20th c. [MBF]
British author
* Roberts, Holt

**Draper, Blanche A.**
See Webb, Blanche A.

**Draper, Canyon**
See Harrison, Hank

**Draper, Farrell** 20th c. [CWG]
American country-western performer
* Draper, Rusty

**Draper, Hastings**
See Jeffries, Roderic [Graeme]

**Draper, John** 20th c.
American convicted of fraud
* Crunch, Captain

**Draper, Old Colonel**
See Draper, T. Waln-Morgan

**Draper, Rusty**
See Draper, Farrell

**Draper, T. Waln-Morgan**
1855?-1915 [SC]
Actor
* Draper, Old Colonel

**Draper, Warwick Herbert** 1873- ?
[WGT]
Author
* Watchman

**Draper, [Sir] William** 1721-1787
[FFF]
British army officer
* Modestus

**Draper, William Henry** 1801-1874
[FFF]
Canadian jurist
* Sweet William

**Drapier, M. B.**
See Swift, Jonathan

**Drasin, Tamara Swann** 1907-1943
[BEW, EMT]
Russian-born actress and singer
* Tamara

**Draskau, Jennifer** 1940- [IAW]
British author
* Kewley, Jennifer

**Drauer**
See Renard, Jules

**Draw, Thom**
See Ward, Thomas

**Drawcansir, [Sir] Alexander**
See Fielding, Henry

**Drax, Peter**
See Addis, Eric Elrington

**Drayne, George**
See McCulley, Johnston

**Drayson, A. W.**
See Warwick, Sidney

**Drayton, Alfred**
See Varick, Alfred

**Drayton, Michael** 1563-1631
[HN, SN]
British poet
* [The] Golden Mouthed
* [The] Ovid of the English Nation

**Drayton, William Henry**
1742-1779 [PA]
Author
* Freeman

**[The] Dreadful Woman**
See Caroline

**Dreadstone, Carl** [house pseudonym]
See Campbell, John Ramsey

**[The] Dream**
See Meminger, Dean

[The] Dream Backup
See Fox, Jim

[The] Dream King
See Louis II [or Ludwig]

[The] Dream Singer
See Kirbery, Ralph

[A] Dreamer
See Lowell, Amy

[The] Dreamer
See Moscherosch [or Mosenrosh], Johann Michael

[The] Dreamer of Whitby
See Caedmon

Dreck [Dirt]
See Mayer, Johann

Drecoll
See Drecoll, Christopher

Drecoll, Christopher 20th c. [WFA]
Belgian-born fashion designer
* Drecoll

Dredge, Colin Herbert [Herbie] 1954- [DC]
British cricketer
* [The] Demon of Frome

Dreeke, Frederick Ludwig 1895-1946 [SC]
American actor
* Woods, Al

Dreisell, Charles 1931- [BB]
American basketball player
* Dreisell, Lefty

Dreisell, Lefty
See Dreisell, Charles

Dreiser, Paul 1857-1906 [BEW, PMJ]
American songwriter and vaudevillian
* Dresser, Paul

Dreisewerd, Clement John 1916- [BE]
American baseball player
* Dreisewerd, Steamboat

Dreisewerd, Steamboat
See Dreisewerd, Clement John

Drelincourt, Charles 1595-1669 [HN]
French clergyman
* [The] Scourge of the Propagators of the Faith

Drella
See Warhol, Andy

Dremann, Janis 1921- [FC]
American actress
* Carter, Janis

Drescher, Dutch
See Drescher, William Clayton [Bill]

Drescher, Moose
See Drescher, William Clayton [Bill]

Drescher, William Clayton [Bill] 1921-1968 [BE]
American baseball player
* Drescher, Dutch
* Drescher, Moose

Dresdel, Sonia
See Obee, Lois

Dress, Sue 1949-
American actress
* Skirt, Buckley

Dressel, De Witt Ewing
See Ewing, Dressel De Witt

Dressel, Patricia 1945- [SW]
American actress
* Van Devere, Trish

Dresser, Davis 1904-1977 [B10, CC, EMD]
American author
* Baker, Asa
* Blood, Matthew
* Carson, Sylvia
* Culver, Kathryn
* Davis, Don
* Debrett, Hal [joint pseudonym with Kathleen Rollins]
* Halliday, Brett
* Scott, Anthony
* Shelley, Peter
* Wayne, Anderson

Dresser, Louise
See Kerlin, Louise

Dresser, Mary 20th c. [SFL]
Author
* Savage, Mary

Dresser, Paul
See Dreiser, Paul

Dressler, Marie
See Koerber, Leila Marie

Drew, Allan 20th c. [IBW]
American comedian
* [The] Black Milton Berle

Drew, Big Red
See Drew, Charles Richard

Drew, Charles Richard 1904-1950 [IBW]
American physician
* Drew, Big Red

Drew, Ellen
See Ray, Terry

Drew, Georgie
See Barrymore, Georgiana Emma

Drew, John
See Stein, Jacob

Drew, May Niblo
See Hanley, Mrs. Phillips

Drew, Mona [PA]
Author
* M. B.

Drew, Morgan
See Price, Robert

Drew, Mrs. Sidney
See McVey, Lucille

Drew, Reginald
See Home-Gall, William Benjamin

Drew, Sheridan
See Fearn, John Russell

Drew, Sidney
See Murray, Edgar Joyce

Drew, Sidney
See White, Sidney

Drewery, Mary
See Smith, Mary

Drewitt, G. C.
See Drewitt, Geoffrey Crellin

Drewitt, Geoffrey Crellin 1921- [ART]
British painter
* Drewitt, G. C.

Drexel, Jay B.
See Bixby, Jerome Lewis

Drexel, Nancy
See Kitchen, Dorothy

Drexler, Rosalyn 1926- [CA]
American author and playwright
* Sorel, Julia

Dreyfus, Fred
See Rosenblatt, Fred

Dreyfus, Jean-Paul 1909- [FC, OCF, WEF]
French director
* Le Chanois, Jean-Paul

Driant, Emile A[ugustin Cyprien] 1855- ? [WGT]
French author
* Danrit, Captain

Dridzo, Solomon Abramovich 1878-1952 [B10]
Russian government official
* Lozovskii, Aleksandr

Drift-Wood
See Longfellow, Henry Wadsworth

Driftin' Slim
See Mickle, Elmon

Driftwood, Penelope
See De Lima, Clara Rosa

Driggs, Alyce 20th c. [PMJ]
American singer
* King, Alyce

Driggs, Donna 20th c. [PMJ]
American singer
* King, Donna

Driggs, Louise 20th c. [PMJ]
American singer
* King, Louise

Driggs, Yvonne 20th c. [PMJ]
American singer
* King, Yvonne

Drille, Hearton
See Gray, Jennie H.

Drinan, Adam
See Macleod, Joseph [Todd Gordon]

Drincic, Sava
See Djuricic, Uladen St.

Dring, Nathaniel
See McBroom, R. Curtis

Drinkall, Gordon [Don] 1927- [CA]
British editor and author
* Demaine, Don

Drinker, Anna 1830- ? [FFF, PA]
American poet
* May, Edith

Drinkrow, John
See Hardwick, [John] Michael [Drinkrow]

Drinkwater, Jennie M.
See Conklin, Mrs. Nathaniel

Driscoll, Annette Sophia 1857- ? [NAA]
American writer
* Stephens, Francis H.

Driscoll, Denny
See Driscoll, John F.

Driscoll, Drisk
See Driscoll, Peter

Driscoll, John F. 1855-1886 [BE]
American baseball player
* Driscoll, Denny

Driscoll, John Leo 1896-1968 [AS, FB, SMG]
American football player
* Driscoll, Paddy

Driscoll, Paddy
See Driscoll, John Leo

Driscoll, Peter 1954- [SMG]
Canadian-born hockey player
* Driscoll, Drisk

Drivas, Robert
See Choromokos, Robert

Driver, C. C.
See Lovin, Roger Robert

Driver, Christopher Prout 1932- [AW]
British journalist
* Archestratus

Driver, Edward
See Gritt, Brian Edward

[The] Driver of Europe
See Choiseul, [Duc] Etienne Francois de

Driver, Phyllis 1917- [IPA]
American comedienne
* Diller, Phyllis

[The] Driving Force
See Roosevelt, Theodore [Teddy]

Driving Hawk, Virginia
See Sneve, Virginia Driving Hawk

Drizin, Chuck
See Drizin, Herman

Drizin, Herman 20th c. [EJS]
American basketball player
* Drizin, Chuck

Droch
See Bridges, Robert

Drohan, David 1883-1955 [BE]
American baseball player
* Rowan, David [Dave]

Drolet, Annie 1865?-1947 [BEW]
American actress
* Ashley, Annie

[The] Droll
See Brueghel [or Bruegel], Pieter

[The] Drone
See Kissinger, Henry Alfred

Drootin, Benjamin 1920?- [EJ]
Russian-born American jazz musician
* Drootin, Buzzy

Drootin, Buzzy
See Drootin, Benjamin

Drop Shot
See Cable, George Washington

Dropo, Mauler
See Dropo, Walter

Dropo, Moose [or Moosup]
See Dropo, Walter

**Dropo, Walter** 1923-   [BE, PB]
*American baseball player*
* Dropo, Mauler
* Dropo, Moose [or Moosup]

**Dropper, H.**
*See* Jennings, Louis J.

**Dropper, Kid**
*See* Kaplan, Nathan

**Dror, Yehezkel**
*See* Freeman, Yehezkel

**Drotning, Phillip T[homas]** 1920-
[CA]
*American author and business
executive*
* Phillips, Tom

**Drott, Hummer**
*See* Drott, Richard Fred

**Drott, Richard Fred** 1936-   [BE]
*American baseball player*
* Drott, Hummer

**Drouin, Paul Emile** 1916-   [CEI]
*Canadian-born hockey player*
* Drouin, Polly

**Drouin, Polly**
*See* Drouin, Paul Emile

**Drouineau, Francois** 1917-   [FC]
*French actor*
* Villard, Frank

**Drower, Ethel Stefana May**
1879-1972   [CAP]
*British author*
* Stevens, E. S.

**Drower, M. S.**
*See* Hackforth-Jones, Margaret
Stefana

**Drozdov, Vasili Mikhailovich**
1782-1867   [WBD]
*Metropolitan of Moscow*
* Philaret

**Dru, Joanne**
*See* La Cock, Joanne Letitia

**Drucci, Vincent** 1885-1927
[BLB, PHM]
*American underworld figure*
* [The] Schemer
* [The] Shootin' Fool

**Druce, Christopher**
*See* Pulling, Christopher Robert
Druce

**[The] Druid**
*See* Dixon, Henry Hall

**Druid**
*See* Flint, Henry M.

**Druid**
*See* Witherspoon, John

**Druit, Henry**
*See* Flint, William

**Drukker, J.**
*See* Presser, [Gerrit] Jacob

**Drummond, Anthony**
*See* Hunter, [Alfred] John

**Drummond, Charles**
*See* Giles, Kenneth

**Drummond, Dolores**
*See* Green, Dolores

**Drummond, Edith Marie Dulce
Carman** 1883-1970   [AW, CAP]
*British-born author, journalist, poet*
* Carman, Dulce

**Drummond, Humphrey** 1922-
[AW]
*British author*
* Ap Evans, Humphrey

**Drummond, Ivor**
*See* Longrigg, Roger [Erskine]

**Drummond, Jack** 1923?-1978   [CA]
*American author*
* Redder, George

**Drummond, John**
*See* Chance, John Newton

**Drummond, John Peter**
*See* Mullen, Stanley [B.]

**Drummond, Patrick Hamilton** 1857-
?   [LAO]
*Irish-born author*
* Shaw, Barton

**Drummond, V. H.**
*See* Swetenham, Violet Hilda

**Drummond, Walter**
*See* Silverberg, Robert

**Drummond, William** 1585-1649
[SN]
*Scottish poet*
* Bo-Peep
* [The] Scotian Petrarch

**[The] Drunkard**
*See* Michael III

**[The] Drunkard**
*See* Wenceslaus [or Wenceslas]

**Drunken Barnaby**
*See* Braithwaite, Richard

**Drury, Clare Marie**
*See* Hoskyns-Abrahall, Clare
[Constance Drury]

**Drury, Maxine Cole** 1914-   [CA]
*American author*
* Creighton, Don

**Drussai, Garen** 20th c.   [WGT]
*Author*
* Kirkman, Milo

**Drusus Caesar** ?- 23   [WBD]
*Roman politician*
* Drusus Junior

**Drusus Germanicus, Nero Claudius**
1st c. BC   [WBD]
*Roman general*
* Drusus Senior

**Drusus Junior**
*See* Drusus Caesar

**Drusus Senior**
*See* Drusus Germanicus, Nero
Claudius

**Drutel, Marcelle Louise Marie**
1897-   [IAW]
*French author*
* L'Aubanelenco

**Dryander**
*See* Enzinas, Francisco de

**Dryasdust?**
*See* Heron-Allen, Edward

**Dryasdust, [The] Rev. Dr.**
*See* Scott, [Sir] Walter

**Dryden, John**
*See* Rowland, D[onald] S[ydney]

**Dryden, John** 1631-1700?
[DNNS, HN, SN]
*British poet*
* [The] Bacon of the Rhyming
Crew
* Glorious John
* [The] Poet Squab
* Reverend Levi
* [The] Squab Poet

**Dryden, Lennox**
*See* Steen, Marguerite

**Dryden, Leo**
*See* Wheeler, George Dryden

**[The] Dryden of Germany**
*See* Opitz, Martin

**Drydog, Doggrel**
*See* Clark, Charles

**Dryhurst, Edward**
*See* Roberts, Edward

**Drysdale, Donald Scott** 1936-
[BE, DGS, PB]
*American baseball player*
* Airdale
* Big D
* [The] Big Warrior
* Double D

**Drysdale, Janey C.** 20th c.   [WWL]
*Scottish writer and lyricist*
* Doune, Ercil

**Drzewiecki, Henryk**
*See* Rosenbaum, Hercel

**Du**
*See*   Second element of name for
further listings

**Du Barry, Camille** 20th c.   [NAA]
*American actress and poet*
* Wood, Carole

**Du Barry, Comtesse**
*See* Becu, Marie Jeanne

**Du Blane, Daphne**
*See* Groom, Arthur William

**Du Bois, Shirley Graham**
1906-1977   [CA, WD]
*American-born author and
playwright*
* Graham, Shirley

**Du Bois, W. E. B.**
*See* Du Bois, William Edward
Burghardt

**Du Bois, William Edward Burghardt**
1868-1963   [LC]
*American educator and author*
* Du Bois, W. E. B.

**Du Bourbonnais, [Duc] Charles**
1489?-1527   [DNNF, SN]
*French military leader*
* Constable de Bourbon

**Du Cental**
*See* Richard, A.

**Du Chatel, Pierre** ?-1552   [PA]
*Author*
* Castellanus

**Du Jow, Francois** 1545-1602   [PA]
*Author*
* Junius

**Du Jura**
*See* Germain, Jean Francois

**Du Maurier, Daphne**
*See* Browning, Daphne Du Maurier

**Du Mort, Reuben**
*See* Burton, Edward

**Du Motier, Marie Joseph Paul Yves
Roch Gilbert** 1754?-1834
[DNNF, FFF, HN]
*French statesman and army officer*
* Grandison Cromwell
* Lafayette, Marquis de

**Du Perry, Jean**
*See* Simenon, Georges [Joseph
Christian]

**Du Plessis, Armand Jean**
1585-1642   [DEP, DNNS, SN]
*French statesman and cardinal*
* [The] Cardinal of Atheists
* [The] Cardinal of Huguenots
* [The] Cardinal of La Rochelle
* [The] Cautious Tyrant
* [A] Colossus
* [L']Eminence Rouge
* [The] Great Cardinal
* [The] King of the King
* [The] Lovelace of His Time
* [The] Mayor of the Palace
* [The] New Luther
* [The] Pontiff of Calvinists
* [The] Pope of the Huguenots
* Richelieu, Cardinal de
* [Le] Roi du Roi

**Du Plessis, Johannes** 1944-   [IAW]
*South African author*
* Du Plessis, Phil

**Du Plessis, Phil**
*See* Du Plessis, Johannes

**Du Pont, Pete**
*See* Du Pont, Pierre S., IV

**Du Pont, Pierre S., IV** 1935?-
*American politician*
* Du Pont, Pete

**Du Sacre-Coeur, [Sister]
Marie-Andre**
*See* Dorge, Jeanne Emilie Marie

**Du Solle, John S.**   [PA]
*Author*
* Knickerbocker

**Du Tertre, Jacques** 1610-1687
[PA]
*Author*
* Baptiste, Jean

**Du Val-de-Grace, Jean [or Johann]
Baptiste** 1755-1794
[RH, SN, WBD]
*French revolutionary leader*
* Clootz, Anacharsis
* Clootz, Baron von
* Gier-Ber, Ali
* [The] Orator of the Human Race

**Du Var**
*See* Gautier, Isadore M. B.

**Duane, Andrew**
*See* Briney, Robert E[dward]

**Duane, Carl**
*See* Yacconetti, Carlo

**Duane, Frank**
*See* Rosengren, Frank Duane

**Duane, Jack**
*See* Padjan, Jack

**Duane, Jim**
*See* Hurley, Vic

**Duane, Toby?**
See Ganley, W. Paul

**Duane, W. N.** 19th c. [FFF]
*American author*
* Camp, Phineas

**Duarte, Anselmo**
See Duarte Bento, Anselmo

**Duarte, Jose Napoleon** 1927?-
*Salvadoran president*
* Duarte, Napo

**Duarte, Napo**
See Duarte, Jose Napoleon

**Duarte Bento, Anselmo** 1920-
[WEF]
*Brazilian director and screenwriter*
* Duarte, Anselmo

**Dubenion, Duby**
See Dubenion, Elbert

**Dubenion, Elbert** 1933- [FB, SMG]
*American football player*
* Dubenion, Duby
* Dubenion, Golden Wheels

**Dubenion, Golden Wheels**
See Dubenion, Elbert

**Dubensky, Herbert** 1931- [CA]
*Russian-born author*
* Aldouby, Zwy H[erbert]

**Dubey, Matt**
See Dubinsky, Matthew David

**Dubiel, Monk**
See Dubiel, Walter John

**Dubiel, Walter John** 1919-1969
[BE]
*American baseball player*
* Dubiel, Monk

**Dubillard, Roland** 1923- [MWD]
*French actor and playwright*
* Gregoire

**Dubinsky, David**
See Dobnievski, David

**Dubinsky, Matthew David** 1928-
[BEW]
*American lyricist*
* Dubey, Matt

**DuBlanc, Damita Jo** 1940- [RO1]
*American singer*
* Damita Jo

**Dublin, Conrad Padraic**
See Kidd, Walter Evans

**Duboc, Edouard** 1822-1910 [WBD]
*German author*
* Waldmueller, Robert

**Dubofsky, Maurice** 20th c. [EJS]
*American football player*
* Dubofsky, Mush

**Dubofsky, Mush**
See Dubofsky, Maurice

**Dubois, Alan**
See Wood, Clement

**Dubois, Alfred**
See Bowes, James Stuart

**Dubois, Alice**
See De Bettignies, Louise

**DuBois, Dick**
See Wood, Richard Kennedy
[Dick]

**Dubois, Jean** ?-1626 [PA]
*Author*
* Bosco, Joannes A.

**Dubois, M.**
See Kent, Arthur [William Charles]

**DuBose, Catherine A. [Richards]**
[FFF]
*Author*
* Cameron, Leila

**Dubov, Gwen Bagni** 20th c. [CA]
*American author and screenwriter*
* Bagni, Gwen
* Gielgud, Gwen Bagni

**DuBreuil, Elizabeth Lorinda** 1924-
[SFL]
*American author*
* Brown, L. J.
* Browning, L. J.
* Cameron, Kate
* Carewe, S. C.
* Dragon, Carolyn
* DuBreuil, Linda
* Evans, Ellen
* Evans, Emerald
* Lindner, D. Berry
* Marshall, Catherine
* Royal, D.
* Seattle Frank
* Todd, Eric

**DuBreuil, Linda**
See DuBreuil, Elizabeth Lorinda

**Dubrony, A.**
See De Bermans, A.

**Dubs, Adolph** ?-1979
*American diplomat*
* Dubs, Spike

**Dubs, Spike**
See Dubs, Adolph

**Dubuc, Chauncey**
See Dubuc, Jean Arthur

**Dubuc, Jean Arthur** 1888-1958
[BE]
*American baseball player*
* Dubuc, Chauncey

**Duca Minimo [The Least of the Dukes]**
See D'Annunzio, Gabriele

**Ducaigne, R. E.**
See Heath, W. McKendee

**Ducander, Sten Carl** 1923- [IWM]
*Finnish composer*
* Kosta, Ensio

**Ducas**
See Eudosia, Makrembolitissa

**Ducas Mourtzuphlos**
See Alexius V

**Ducasse, Isidore Lucien** 1846-1870
[WBD]
*Uruguayan-born poet*
* Lautreamont, le Comte de

**Ducdame**
See Hooper, Henry

**[Il] Duce**
See Mussolini, Benito

**Ducette, Vince** 20th c. [SFL]
*Author*
* Kullinger, J. L.

**Duchacek, Ivo Maria Rudolf** 1913-
[SFL, WD]
*American author and educator*
* Duka, Ivo

**Duchamp, Gaston** 1875-1963
[WEC]
*French painter, engraver, cartoonist*
* Villon, Jacques

**Duchatelet**
See Paine, Thomas

**Duchenne de Boulogne**
See Duchenne, Guillaume Benjamin Amand

**Duchenne, Guillaume Benjamin Amand** 1806-1875 [WBD]
*French physician*
* Duchenne de Boulogne

**Duchesne, Albert** [PA]
*Author*
* Jacques

**Duchesne, Andre** 1584-1640
[DNNF, DNNS, SN]
*French historian*
* [The] Father of French History
* [Le] Pere de l'Histoire de France

**Duchesne, Father**
See Hebert, Jacques Rene

**Duchesne, Jacques**
See Saint Denis, Michel Jacques

**[The] Duchess**
See Argles, Margaret

**[The] Duchess**
See Hay, Mary Cecil

**[The] Duchess**
See Hungerford, Margaret Wolfe

**[The] Duchess of Dimples**
See Spencer, Georgiana

**Duchess Olga**
See Liminana, Eva

**Duchi, Jacob** [PA]
*Author*
* Tamor, Caspipini

**Duck, Captain**
See Pinkwater, Daniel Manus

**Duck, Donald**
See Bailey, Donald Orlando

**Duck, Stephen** ?-1756 [SN]
*British poet*
* [The] Wiltshire Bard

**Duckert, Mary** 1929- [CA]
*American author and educator*
* Hall, Ann

**Duckett, Alfred** 1917- [CA]
*American poet and journalist*
* Douglas, Glenn

**Duckpin [code name used during World War II]**
See Eisenhower, David Dwight

**Duckworth, Dodenius**
See Greene, Asa

**Duckworth, Leslie Blakey** 1904-
[IAW]
*British author*
* Blake, Leslie
* Leslie, Blake

**Ducornet, Erica** 1943- [CA]
*American author and illustrator*
* Rikki

**Ducrot, Frank**
See Fritz, T. Francis

**Dudden, Arthur P[ower]** 1921-
[CA]
*American author and historian*
* Power, Arthur

**[The] Dude**
See May, Rudolph, Jr.

**[The] Dude President**
See Arthur, Chester Alan

**Dudek, Gerd**
See Dudek, Gerhard Rochus

**Dudek, Gerhard Rochus** 1938-
[EJ7]
*German jazz musician*
* Dudek, Gerd

**Dudeney, Wilfred** 1911- [ART]
*British sculptor*
* W. D.

**Duder, J. Douglas** 1910?-1961
[BEW]
*Canadian-born actor and artist*
* Walton, Douglas

**Dudet, Alphonse** 1800- ? [PA]
*Author*
* Gaston, Maria

**Dudevant, Amandine Lucille Aurore Dupin** 1804-1876
[DEL, DNNF, FFF]
*French author*
* Sand, George

**Dudevant, Maurice** 1823-1889
[PA, WBD]
*French painter and author*
* Sand, Maurice

**D'Udine, Jean**
See Cozanet, Albert

**Dudlah, David**
See Kelly, David Wiliford

**Dudlestone, Barry** 1945- [DC]
*British cricketer*
* Dudlestone, Danny

**Dudlestone, Danny**
See Dudlestone, Barry

**Dudley, Arthur**
See Campbell, Charlotte [Countess of Bury]

**Dudley, Barbara Hudson** 1921-
[CA]
*American author and educator*
* Powers, Barbara Hudson

**Dudley, Bide**
See Dudley, Walter Bronson

**Dudley, Bullet Bill**
See Dudley, William M.

**Dudley, Charles** 1950- [SMG]
*American basketball player*
* Dudley, Hopper

**Dudley, Dud**
See Lee, Ernest Dudley

**Dudley, Duds**
See Dudley, Rick

**Dudley, Ernest**
See Coltman-Allen, Ernest

**Dudley, Frank**
See  Greene, Ward

**Dudley, [Sir] Henry Bate**
1745-1824  [SN]
*British clergyman, magistrate,*
*journalist*
* Bate, Parson

**Dudley, Hopper**
See  Dudley, Charles

**Dudley, Jay**
See  Chapman, J. Dudley

**Dudley, Margaret Dale** 1903-1967
[SC]
*American actress*
* Dale, Peggy

**Dudley, Nancy**
See  Cole, Lois Dwight

**Dudley, Perle**
See  Wilkinson, Mrs. Arthur P.

**Dudley, Rick** 1949-  [SMG]
*Canadian-born hockey player*
* Dudley, Duds

**Dudley, Robert** 1532-1588  [HN]
*First Earl of Leicester*
* [The] Gipsy

**Dudley, Walter Bronson**
1877-1944  [BEW, NAA]
*American author, playwright, critic*
* Dudley, Bide

**Dudley, William M.** 1921-
[BBH, FB]
*American football player*
* Dudley, Bullet Bill

**Dudley-Smith, Trevor** 1920-
[AW, CA, DLE]
*British author*
* Black, Mansell
* Burgess, Trevor
* Fitzalan, Peter
* Fitzalan, Roger
* Hall, Adam
* North, Howard
* Rattray, Simon
* Scott, Warwick
* Smith, Caesar
* Smith, T. D.
* Trevor, Elleston

**Dudu**
See  Fletcher, Julia Constance

**[The] Duel Fighter**
See  Jackson, Andrew

**Duel, Pete**
See  Deuel, Peter

**[The] Duellist**
See  Bagenal, Beauchamp

**[The] Duellist**
See  Martin, Samuel

**Duerer, Albrecht [or Albert]**
1471-1528  [DEP, HN, SN]
*German painter*
* [The] Chaucer of Artists
* [The] Chaucer of Painting
* [The] Father of the German
  School
* [The] Prince of Artists

**[The] Duesseldorf Vampire**
See  Kuerten, Peter

**Dufault, Joseph Ernest Nephtali**
1892-1942  [TCC]
*Canadian author*
* James, Will

**Duff, Arleigh Elton** 1924-
[CWG, DAM]
*American singer and songwriter*
* Duff, Arlie

**Duff, Arlie**
See  Duff, Arleigh Elton

**Duff, Cecil Elba** 1896-  [BE]
*American baseball player*
* Duff, Larry

**Duff, Charles [St. Lawrence]**
1894-1966  [CA]
*Irish-born author and translator*
* O Dubh, Cathal

**Duff, Douglas Valder** 1901-  [CAT]
*Argentinian-born author*
* Savage, Leslie
* Stanhope, Douglas
* Wickloe, Peter

**Duff, Larry**
See  Duff, Cecil Elba

**Duff, Mary Ann**  [SN]
*American actress*
* [The] Queen of the American
  Stage
* [The] Siddons of America

**Duffee, Charles Edward** 1866-1894
[BE]
*American baseball player*
* Duffee, Home Run

**Duffee, Home Run**
See  Duffee, Charles Edward

**Duffee, Mary Gordon** 1840- ?
[FFF]
*American author*
* Gordon, Mary Duff

**Duffell, Anne** 19th c.  [FFF, PA]
*Author*
* McKenzie, Christian

**Duffle**
See  Galt, John

**Duffmeier**
See  Duffy, Hugh

**Duffus, Louis George** 1904-  [IAW]
*Australian-born author*
* Vagrant

**Duffy, Antonia Susan** 1936-  [IAW]
*British author*
* Byatt, A. S.

**Duffy, Beatrice** 20th c.  [BF]
*British actress*
* Adair, Janice

**Duffy, Ben**
See  Duffy, Bernard C.

**Duffy, Bernard C.** 1902-1972  [CA]
*American advertising executive and*
*writer*
* Duffy, Ben

**Duffy, Big Bill**
See  Duffy, William J.

**Duffy, Emlyn Arthur Joseph** 1916-
[ART]
*British painter*
* Dy

**Duffy, F. X.** 20th c.  [BBH]
*American boxer*
* Duffy, Pat

**Duffy, Hugh** 1866-1954  [BAB]
*American baseball player*
* Duffmeier

**Duffy, Kate** 1872-1943
*Irish-born actress*
* Price, Kate

**Duffy, Michael Francis** 1906-
[MBF]
*British author*
* Richards, Frank [house
  pseudonym]

**Duffy, Olive** 1898-1920  [F1, F2]
*Actress*
* Thomas, Olive

**Duffy, Pat**
See  Duffy, F. X.

**Duffy, Thomas** ?-1926  [PHM]
*American underworld figure*
* [The] Goat

**Duffy, William J.** 20th c.  [BLB]
*American underworld figure*
* Duffy, Big Bill

**Dufour, Pierre**
See  Lacroix, Paul

**Dufourquet**
See  Bastide, Jenny

**Dugan, Joseph Anthony** 1897-
[BE, PB]
*American baseball player*
* Dugan, Jumping Joe

**Dugan, Jumping Joe**
See  Dugan, Joseph Anthony

**Dugazon, Jean Baptiste Henri**
See  Gourgaud, Jean Baptiste Henri

**Duggan, Denise Valerie** 20th c.
[AW]
*British author*
* Egerton, Denise

**Duggan, Tom**
See  Goss, Thomas Duggan

**Duggans, Pat**
See  Connolly, Robert D[uggan,
Jr.]

**Duggleby, Frosty Bill**
See  Duggleby, William James

**Duggleby, William James**
1874-1944  [BE]
*American baseball player*
* Duggleby, Frosty Bill

**Dughet, Gaspar** 1613-1675
[FFF, RH, WBD]
*French painter*
* [Le] Guaspre
* Poussin, Gaspar
* [The] Poussin of France

**Dugin, Miss**  [PA]
*Author*
* Conover, Elizabeth

**Dugmore, William Henry**
1853-1915  [THR]
*British actor*
* Denny, William Henry

**Dugout Doug**
See  MacArthur, Douglas

**Duguid, Robert**
See  Pring-Mill, Robert D[uguid]
F[orrest]

**Duhamel, Georges** 1884-1966
[CD, EWL, TC]
*French poet, playwright, author*
* Thevenin, Denis

**Duhring, Nathan**
See  Cooper, Evan

**Dujardin, Benigne** 1722- ?  [PA]
*Author*
* Boispreaux

**Duka, Ivo**
See  Duchacek, Ivo Maria Rudolf

**Dukakis, Michael** 1934?-
*American politician*
* [The] Duke

**Dukanfield, William Claude**
1887-1953  [CU]
*Scottish-born actor*
* Finlayson, Jimmy

**[The] Duke** [code name used during
World War II]
See  Borch-Johansen, Eigil

**[The] Duke**
See  Bresnahan, Roger Philip

**[The] Duke**
See  Dukakis, Michael

**[The] Duke**
See  Ellington, Edward Kennedy

**[The] Duke**
See  Morrison, Marion Michael

**[The] Duke**
See  Snider, Edwin Donald

**Duke, Anita** 20th c.  [WD]
*British author*
* Hewett, Anita

**Duke, Anna Marie** 1946-  [IPA]
*American actress*
* Duke, Patty

**Duke, Billy**
See  Tesone, William N.

**Duke, Derek**
See  Phillips, Horace

**Duke, Donald Norman** 1929-  [CA]
*American author and publisher*
* Valentine, Roger

**Duke, John**
See  Chalmers, Floyd S[herman]

**Duke, Madelaine [Elizabeth]** 1925-
[AW, CA, WD]
*Swiss-born British author and critic*
* Donne, Maxim
* Duncan, Alex

**[The] Duke of Braintree**
See  Adams, John

**[The] Duke of Chou**
See  Chou Kung

**[The] Duke of Darnick**
See  Scott, [Sir] Walter

**[The] Duke of Del Rey**
See  Klosterman, Donald

**[The] Duke of Langosta [Locust]**
See  Amadeus

**[The] Duke of Luxembourg**
See  Lewis, Meade Anderson

[The] Duke of Milwaukee
See Szymanski, Aloysius Harry

[The] Duke of Paducah
See Ford, Benjamin Francis
[Benny]

[The] Duke of Thunder
See Nelson, Horatio

[The] Duke of Tralee
See Bresnahan, Roger Philip

[The] Duke of Uganda
See Bruce, John Edward

[The] Duke of Wonsan
See Smith, Allan E.

Duke of Xensi
See Holm, Frits

Duke, Patty
See Duke, Anna Marie

Duke, Raoul
See Thompson, Hunter S[tockton]

Duke, Vernon
See Dukelsky, Vladimir

Duke, Will
See Gault, William Campbell

Dukelsky, Vladimir 1903-1969
[BBD, BEW, CA]
Russian-born American composer
and author
* Duke, Vernon

Dukes, Charles W. [FFF]
Entertainer
* Wilford, Charles

Dukes, Laura 1907- [BWW]
American singer
* Dukes, Little Laura

Dukes, Little Laura
See Dukes, Laura

Dukes, Philip
See Bickers, Richard Leslie
Townshend

Dukinfield, William Claude
1879-1946 [BDF, EMT, WEF]
American comic actor and
screenwriter
* Bogle, Charles
* Criblecoblis, Otis
* Fields, W. C.
* Jeeves, Mahatma Kane

Dulac, Arthur
See De Ravenne, Arthur

Dulac, Germaine
See Saisset-Schneider, Charlotte
Elisabeth Germaine

[The] Dulcifluous Doctor
See Andreas, Antonio [or
Anthony]

Duleepsinhji, Kumar Shri
1905-1959 [EC]
Indian prince and cricketer
* Smith, Mr.

Dulieu, Jean
See Van Oort, Jan

Duling, Vincent 20th c. [BWW]
American musician
* Guitar Red

Dulley, Clarice 1886-1966 [THR]
British actress and singer
* Mayne, Clarice

Dulley, William 1879- ? [WWL]
British author
* Croyland, William

Duloup, Victor
See Volkoff, Vladimir

Dum Dum
See Kendall, John Kaye

Dumarchais, Pierre MacOrlan
1882-1970 [CA, CD, EWL]
French poet and author
* MacOrlan, Pierre

Dumart, Porky
See Dumart, Woodrow Wilson
Clarence

Dumart, Woodrow Wilson Clarence
1916- [CEI, FHE, HK]
Canadian-born hockey player
* Dumart, Porky
* Dumart, Woody

Dumart, Woody
See Dumart, Woodrow Wilson
Clarence

Dumas, Alexandre
See Davy de La Pailleterie,
Alexandre

Dumas, Alexandre 1802-1870
[WBD]
French author and playwright
* Dumas pere
* [The] King of Romance

Dumas, Alexandre 1824-1895
[WBD]
French author and playwright
* Dumas fils

Dumas, Claire
See Van Weddingen, Marthe

Dumas, Duke
See Dumas, James Madison

Dumas fils
See Dumas, Alexandre

Dumas, Frere
See De Brives, Martial

Dumas, Jacques 1904- [WECO]
French cartoonist, writer, editor
* Marijac

Dumas, James Madison 1941-
[CWG, DAM]
American singer and bandleader
* Dumas, Duke

Dumas, Jean Baptiste Andre
1800-1884 [FFF]
French chemist
* [The] Poet of Hygiene

Dumas pere
See Dumas, Alexandre

[The] Dumb Captain
See Bourbon, Louis I de [Prince de
Conde]

[The] Dumb Ox
See Aquinas, Thomas [Thomas of
Aquino]

[The] Dumb Prophet
See Cleveland, [Stephen] Grover

Dumbarton, A.
See Macauley, Robie [Mayhew]

Dumble-Smith, Michael 1942-
[FC]
British actor
* Crawford, Michael

Dumesnil, Marie Francoise
See Marchand, Marie Francoise

Dumler, Counselor
See Dumler, Doug

Dumler, Doug 1950- [SMG]
American football player
* Dumler, Counselor

Dumm, Frances Edwina 1893-
[WECO]
American cartoonist
* Edwina

Dumont, George Henry 1895-1956
[BE]
American baseball player
* Dumont, Pea Soup

Dumont, Jean 1700-1781
[FFF, RH, SN]
French painter
* [Le] Romain
* [The] Roman

[The] Dumont of Letters
See Hazlitt, William

Dumont, Pea Soup
See Dumont, George Henry

DuMoulin, Seppi
See DuMoulin, Septimus Stuart

DuMoulin, Septimus Stuart 20th c.
[BBH, CSH]
Canadian football player
* DuMoulin, Seppi

Dumpty, Humpty S.
See Denenberg, Herbert S[idney]

Duna, Steffi
See Berindey, Stephanie

Dunbar, Agnes 1312?-1369
[HN, WBD]
Countess of Dunbar and March
* Black Agnes

Dunbar, Allen 1949- [IBW]
American football player
* Dunbar, Jubilee

Dunbar, George 1774-1851 [PA]
Author
* G. D.

Dunbar, Jubilee
See Dunbar, Allen

Dunbar, Noel
See Ingraham, Prentiss

Dunbar, Paul Laurence 1872-1906
[IBW]
American poet, author, playwright
* [The] Poet Genius of His People

Dunbar, William 1465-1530 [HN]
Scottish poet
* [The] Chaucer of Scotland

Dunboyne, [Lord] 1917- [WD]
British jurist and author
* Butler, Patrick

Duncan, Actea 1913- [WW]
Author
* Thomas, Carolyn

Duncan, Albert 1886-1961
[F2, SC]
American actor
* Duncan, Bud

Duncan, Alex
See Duke, Madelaine [Elizabeth]

Duncan, Blanche
See Heath-Miller, Mavis Blanche

Duncan, Bruce
See Greenfield, Irving A.

Duncan, Bud
See Duncan, Albert

Duncan, David Edwin 1945- [PB]
American baseball player
* Duncan, Dunk

Duncan, Duke
See Rathborne, St. George

Duncan, Dunk
See Duncan, David Edwin

Duncan, Frances
See Manning, Frances Duncan

Duncan, Gregory
See McClintock, Marshall

Duncan, J. 1720-1808 [PA]
Author
* Brick, Richard
* Brighte, John

Duncan, James
See Hadath, John Edward Gunby

Duncan, Jane
See Cameron, Elizabeth Jane

Duncan, Julia K. [house pseudonym]
[Stratemeyer Syndicate]
See Karig, Walter

Duncan, Julia K. [house pseudonym]
[Stratemeyer Syndicate]
See Stratemeyer, Edward L.

Duncan, Kathleen Mary 1907-
[AW]
British author
* Simmons, Catherine
* Simmons, Kim

Duncan, Keene
See MacLachlan, Kenneth D.

Duncan, Kunigunde 1886-
[CA, NAA]
American author
* Isely, Flora Kunigunde Duncan

Duncan, Leslie H. 1942- [FB]
American football player
* Duncan, Speedy

Duncan, Lois
See Arquette, Lois S[teinmetz]

Duncan, Louis Baird 1893-1960
[BE, PB]
American baseball player
* Duncan, Pat

Duncan, Malcolm 1945- [RO2]
Scottish-born musician
* Duncan, Mollie

Duncan, Mollie
See Duncan, Malcolm

Duncan, Pat
See Duncan, Louis Baird

Duncan, Professor
See Patterson, John

**Duncan, Renault Renaldo**
1904-1980   [FC]
*American actor and artist*
* Renaldo, Duncan

**Duncan, Robert Gordon** 1895-1971
[SC]
*American actor*
* Gordon, Robert

**Duncan, Robert Lipscomb** 1927-
[SFL]
*Author*
* Roberts, James Hall

**Duncan, Ronald [Frederick Henry]**
1914-   [WD]
*British author, playwright, poet*
* Marsland, Bishop of
* Marsland, Maj. Gen.

**Duncan, Speedy**
See   Duncan, Leslie H.

**Duncan, Terence Edward** 1947-
[ART]
*British painter*
* Terry

**Duncan, Tommy** 1911-1968   [CM]
*American country-western performer*
* [The] Dean of Western Singers

**Duncan, W[illiam] Murdoch** 1909-
[CA, WW]
*Scottish author*
* Cassells, John
* Graham, Neill
* Locke, Martin
* Malloch, Peter
* Marshall, Lovat

**Dunckley, Henry** 19th c.   [PA]
*Author*
* Verax

**Duncombe, John** 1730-1785   [FFF]
*British author*
* Crito

**Dundas, D. R.**
See   Dundas, Douglas Roberts

**Dundas, Douglas Roberts** 1900-
[ART]
*Australian painter*
* Dundas, D. R.

**Dundas, Henry** 1742-1811
[DNNF, DNNS, FFF]
*First Lord Melville*
* Dundas, Starvation

**Dundas, Starvation**
See   Dundas, Henry

**Dundee, Alex**
See   Declercq, Aime

**Dundee, Bonny**
See   Graham, John [First Viscount
of Dundee]

**Dundee, Douglas**
See   Cumming-Skinner, Dugald
Matheson

**Dundee, Joe**
See   Lazzaro, Samuel

**Dundee, Johnny**
See   Corrara, Joseph

**Dundee, Mike**
See   Posateri, Mike

**Dundee, Robert**
See   Kirsch, Robert R.

**Dundee, Vince**
See   Lazzaro, Vincent

**Dundon, Dummy**
See   Dundon, Ed[ward Joseph]

**Dundon, Ed[ward Joseph]**
1859-1893   [BE]
*American baseball player*
* Dundon, Dummy

**Dundreary, Lord**
See   Kingsley, Charles

**Dunham, By**
See   Dunham, William D.

**Dunham, Elmer Lewis** 1914-
[EJ, PMJ, WWJ]
*American jazz musician*
* Dunham, Sonny

**Dunham, Katherine** 1910-   [CA]
*American author and dancer*
* Dunn, Kaye

**Dunham, Mrs. E. B. S.**   [FFF]
*American writer*
* Leoline

**Dunham, Robert [Bob]** 1931-   [CA]
*American author and journalist*
* Yuma, Dan

**Dunham, Sonny**
See   Dunham, Elmer Lewis

**Dunham, William D.** 1910-   [ASC]
*American composer and scriptwriter*
* Dunham, By

**Dunheved**
See   Robbins, Alfred Farthing

**Dunhill, Lawrence** 1953-   [RO2]
*American musician*
* Dunn, Larry

**Dunk, Dr.**
See   Griffith, Darrell

**Dunk, Dr.**
See   Hillman, Darnell

**Dunk, Dr.**
See   Wilkins, Dominique

**Dunkenstein, Dr.**
See   Griffith, Darrell

**Dunker** [code name used during
World War II]
See   Skryabin, Vyacheslav
Mikhailovich

**Dunkerley, Elsie Jeanette** ?-1960
[TCC]
*British author*
* Oxenham, Elsie

**Dunkerley, William Arthur**
1852-1941   [LC, TC, WW]
*British author and poet*
* Oxenham, John

**Dunkle, Davey**
See   Dunkle, Edward Perks

**Dunkle, Edward Perks** 1872-1941
[BE]
*American baseball player*
* Dunkle, Davey

**Dunlap, A. J.**   [PA]
*Author*
* Express

**Dunlap, Frederick C.** 1859-1902
[BE]
*American baseball player*
* Dunlap, Sure Shot

**Dunlap, Grant Lester** 1923-   [BE]
*American baseball player*
* Dunlap, Snap

**Dunlap, Jane**
See   Davis, [Daisie] Adelle

**Dunlap, Lon**
See   McCormick, Wilfred

**Dunlap, M. L.**   [PA]
*Author*
* Rural

**Dunlap, Snap**
See   Dunlap, Grant Lester

**Dunlap, Sure Shot**
See   Dunlap, Frederick C.

**Dunlap, William** 1766-1839
*American theatre manager and
playwright*
* [The] Father of the American
Stage

**Dunleavy, Janet Egleson** 1928-
[CA]
*American author*
* Egleson, Janet F.
* Frank, Janet

**Dunlop, Agnes M. R.** 20th c.
[AW, CA, MJA]
*Scottish author*
* Kyle, Elisabeth
* Ralston, Jan

**Dunlop, Bobby** 20th c.   [BMH]
*American entertainer*
* [The] American Fat Man

**Dunlop, William**   [FFF]
*Author*
* Ballantyne, Colin, R.N.

**Dunn, Aiken**
See   Latto, Thomas C.

**Dunn, Alphonse** 20th c.   [OBW]
*American baseball player*
* Dunn, Blue

**Dunn, Blue**
See   Dunn, Alphonse

**Dunn, Caleb** 1834- ?   [PA]
*Author*
* My Pen
* Poningoe
* Shingle, Solon

**Dunn, Deborah**
See   Stockton, Mrs. Frank R.

**Dunn, Donald** 1941-   [SSS]
*American musician*
* Dunn, Duck

**Dunn, Dorothy**
See   Brandon, Dorothy

**Dunn, Duck**
See   Dunn, Donald

**Dunn, Eliza**
See   Norton, Edith Eliza Ames

**Dunn, Gertrude**
See   Weaver, Gertrude Renton

**Dunn, Harris**
See   Doerffler, Alfred

**Dunn, James**
See   Wilkes-Hunter, Richard

**Dunn, Joseph** 20th c.   [SMG]
*American football player*
* Dunn, Red

**Dunn, Judith F.**
See   Bernal, Judith F.

**Dunn, Judy**
See   Spangenberg, Judith [Dunn]

**Dunn, Kaye**
See   Dunham, Katherine

**Dunn, Larry**
See   Dunhill, Lawrence

**Dunn, Marie Bickford** 1898-1937
[F1, F2, FC]
*Canadian-born actress*
* Prevost, Marie

**Dunn, Mary Alice** 1897-   [AW]
*Scottish author*
* Faid, Mary

**Dunn, Michael**
See   Miller, Gary Neil

**Dunn, Nell**
See   Sandford, Nell Mary

**Dunn, Philip Hart** 1891-   [BEW]
*American playwright, producer,
director*
* Dunning, Philip Hart

**Dunn, Philip M.** 1946-   [ESF]
*British author and publisher*
* Dunn, Saul

**Dunn, R. G.**
See   Dunn, Reginald George

**Dunn, Red**
See   Dunn, Joseph

**Dunn, Reginald George** 1907-
[ART]
*British painter*
* Dunn, R. G.

**Dunn, Sara** 1884-1955   [BWW]
*American singer*
* [The] Blues Sensation from the
West
* Johnson, Margaret
* Martin, Sara
* [The] Queen of the Blues
* Roberts, Sally

**Dunn, Saul**
See   Dunn, Philip M.

**Dunn, Willie** 1870-1952   [EG]
*Scottish golfer*
* Dunn, Young Willie

**Dunn, Young Willie**
See   Dunn, Willie

**Dunne, Berthold** 1924-   [ART]
*Irish painter*
* Berthold

**Dunne, Charles**
See   Hilts, Edward Leonard [Len]

**Dunne, Desmond**
See   Lee-Richardson, James

**Dunne, Finley Peter** 1867-1936
[LC, TC]
*American satirist*
* Dooley, Mr.

**Dunne, J. W.**
See   Dunne, John William

**Dunne, John T.**
See Lovecraft, Howard Phillips

**Dunne, John William** 1875-1949
[LC]
*British author*
* Dunne, J. W.

**Dunne, Mary Collins** 1914-
[CA, SAT]
*Irish-born American author*
* Moore, Regina

**Dunnell, Duke Foster** 1889-1948
[SC]
*American actor*
* Murphy, Robert [Bob]

**Dunnell, Edgar G.** [PA]
*Author*
* E. G. D.

**Dunner, Joseph** 1908- [CA]
*German-born American author*
* Germanicus
* Roth, Alexander

**Dunnett, Alastair MacTavish**
1908- [IAW]
*Scottish author*
* Sinclair, Duncan
* Tavis, Alec

**Dunnett, Dorothy** 20th c. [WD]
*Scottish author*
* Halliday, Dorothy

**Dunnie-Wassail**
See Campbell, Alexander

**Dunnigan, Belle** [FFF]
*Entertainer*
* Gold, Beatrice

**Dunning, Alice**
See Lingard, Mrs. William

**Dunning, Harriet Sarah** 1850- ?
[FFF, PA]
*Author*
* Lingard, Dickey

**Dunning, M. O. B.** [PA]
*Author*
* Lorimer, Mary

**Dunning, Mrs. A. K.** [PA]
*Author*
* Grahame, Nellie

**Dunning, Philip Hart**
See Dunn, Philip Hart

**Dunoeus**
See Downes, Andrew

**Dunois, Jean** 1403-1468
[DNNS, HN, SN]
*French army officer*
* [The] Bastard of Orleans
* Batard d'Orleans

**Dunoyer, Maurice**
See Domergue, Maurice

**Duns Scotus**
See Scott, [Sir] Walter

**Duns Scotus, Johannes** 1265-1308
[DNNF, HN, SN]
*Scottish theologian*
* Marianus, Doctor
* Subtilis, Doctor
* Subtilissimus, Doctor
* [The] Subtle Doctor
* [The] Wise

**Dunshunner, Augustus**
See Aytoun, William Edmonstoune

**Dunstable, John**
See Dunstaple, John

**Dunstan** 925- 988 [HN]
*Saint*
* [The] Father of the English
Benedictines

**Dunstan, Andrew**
See Chandler, Arthur Bertram

**Dunstan, Bernard** 1920- [ART]
*British painter*
* B. D.

**Dunstan, Gregory**
See Rowe, John Gabriel

**Dunstan, [Sir] Jeffrey** [SN]
*British politician*
* Old Wigs

**Dunstaple, John** 1370?-1453
[WBD]
*British mathematician and composer*
* Dunstable, John

**Dunstone, Max**
See Dunstone, Maxwell Frederick

**Dunstone, Maxwell Frederick**
1915- [IAW]
*British author*
* Dunstone, Max

**Dunton, Edith Kellogg** 1875- ?
[NAA]
*American author*
* Warde, Margaret

**Duparc, Elizabeth** 18th c. [SN]
*French singer*
* [La] Francesina

**Dupee, George Washington** 1826-
? [IBW]
*American clergyman*
* Dupee, Pappy

**Dupee, Pappy**
See Dupee, George Washington

**Duperier, Charles** 1620-1692 [HN]
*French poet*
* [The] Prince of Lyric Poets

**Dupin, August Dupont**
See Taylor, John [Alfred]

**Dupin, Paul** 1865-1949 [BBD]
*French composer*
* Lothar, Louis

**Duplessis [or De Prins], Armand**
1883-1924 [FDG]
*Belgian director*
* Duplessy, Armand

**Duplessis Mornay**
See Mornay, Philippe de [Seigneur
du Plessis-Marly]

**Duplessis, Yves**
See Jaurand, Yvonne

**Duplessy, Armand**
See Duplessis [or De Prins],
Armand

**Duplex** [joint pseudonym with N. F.
Hallows]
See Bradley, Ian [Roberts
Ambrose]

**Duplex** [joint pseudonym with Ian
(Roberts Ambrose) Bradley]
See Hallows, N. F.

**Dupont, Adley**
See Stoltz, Adley

**Dupont, Andre** 1949- [FHE, SMG]
*Canadian-born hockey player*
* Dupont, Moose

**Dupont, Dennis** 1505- ? [PA]
*Author*
* Pontanus

**Dupont, E. A.**
See Dupont, Ewald Andre

**Dupont, Ewald Andre** 1891-1956
[FC, FDG]
*German director*
* Dupont, E. A.

**Dupont, Kurt**
See Ruellan, Andre

**Dupont, Moose**
See Dupont, Andre

**Dupont, Paul**
See Frewin, Leslie Ronald

**Duprean, Gabriel** 1511-1588 [PA]
*Author*
* Prateolus

**DuPree, B. J.**
See DuPree, Billy Joe

**DuPree, Billy Joe** 1950- [SMG]
*American football player*
* DuPree, B. J.

**Dupree, Champion Jack**
See Dupree, William Thomas

**Dupree, Morrison**
See Gass, Sherlock Bronson

**Dupree, William Thomas** 1910-
[BWW]
*American singer*
* Brother Blues
* Collins, Big Tom
* Dupree, Champion Jack
* Johnson, Blind Boy
* Johnson, Meathead
* Jordan, Willie
* Lightnin' Jr.

**Dupres, Henri**
See Fawcett, F[rank] Dubrez

**Duprey de la Ruffiniere, Pierre**
1911- [CW]
*West Indian author and journalist*
* Textu

**Dupri**
See De Maune, Edward

**Dupuy**
See Acton, Thomas

**Duquesnoy, Francois** 1594?-1642
[WBD]
*Belgian sculptor*
* Flamand, Francois

**[The] Durable Dane**
See Nielson, Oscar M.

**Durable Mike Malloy**
See Malloy, Mike

**Durac, Jack**
See Rachman, Stanley Jack

**Duran, Carolus**
See Durand, Charles Auguste
Emile

**Duran, Roberto** 1951?-
*Panamanian boxer*
* [The] Animal
* Cholo

**Duran, Roberto** (Continued)
* Manos de Piedra [Hands of
Stone]

**Durand, Alice Marie Celeste Fleury**
1842-1902 [FFF, WBD]
*French author*
* Greville, Henry

**Durand, Charles**
See Springmeyer, Charles E., Jr.

**Durand, Charles Auguste Emile**
1837-1917 [WBD]
*French painter*
* Duran, Carolus

**Durand, Francois** 1880-1959 [SFL]
*Author*
* Miomandre, Francis de

**Durand, J. P.** 19th c. [PA]
*Author*
* Phillips, [Doctor] J. P.

**Durand, Nicholas** 1510-1571
[FF, FFF]
*French admiral*
* [The] Cain of America
* Villegaignon, Chevalier de

**Durand de St. Pourcain, Guillaume**
1267-1332 [DNNS, FFF, HN]
*French scholastic philosopher*
* [The] Most Resolute Doctor
* Resolutissimus, Doctor

**Durand-Morimbau, Henri**
1848?-1911 [WWL]
*French journalist and author*
* Des Houx, Henri

**Durango, Francisco** 1950- [RBE]
*Colombian boxer*
* Durango, Yata

**Durango Kid**
See Seale, Johnny Ray

**Durango, Yata**
See Durango, Francisco

**Durant, Ariel**
See Durant, Ida Kaufman

**Durant, Henry Fowle**
See Smith, Henry Welles

**Durant, Horato** 1910- [WWJ]
*Panamanian-born jazz musician*
* Durant, Ray

**Durant, Ida Kaufman** 1898?-1981
*American historian and author*
* Durant, Ariel

**Durant, Joseph** 20th c.
*American jurist*
* Let-'em-Go Joe

**Durant, Ray**
See Durant, Horato

**Durante, James Francis [Jimmy]**
1893-1980 [FC, PMJ]
*American comedian*
* Durante, Ragtime Jimmy
* [The] Schnoz
* Schnozzle
* Schnozzola

**Durante, Ragtime Jimmy**
See Durante, James Francis
[Jimmy]

**Duranty, Charles Henry** 1918-
[ART]
*British painter*
* C. H. D.

**Duras, Marguerite**
See Donnadieu, Marguerite

**Duray, Leon** 20th c.
*French auto racer*
* [The] Flying Frenchman
* [The] Frenchman

**Durben, Wolfgang Johannes Maria**
1933- [IAW]
*German poet, author, artist*
* Pasdeloup, Jean-Marie
* Wendolin
* Willibald, Graf

**Durbin, Blaine A.** 1886- [BE]
*American baseball player*
* Durbin, Kid

**Durbin, Deanna**
See Durbin, Edna Mae

**Durbin, Edna Mae** 1921?-
[BDF, CED, FC]
*Canadian-born actress*
* Durbin, Deanna

**Durbin, Kid**
See Durbin, Blaine A.

**Durbridge, Francis** 1912-
[EMD, WW]
*British author, playwright,
screenwriter*
* Temple, Paul [joint pseudonym
  with James Douglas Rutherford
  McConnell]

**Durcie, John** [PA]
*Author*
* Touchstone

**Durelle, Yvon** 20th c.
*Canadian boxer*
* Doux [Gentle]

**Duren, Clarence Edward** 1950-
[SMG]
*American football player*
* Duren, Jason

**Duren, Jason**
See Duren, Clarence Edward

**Duren, Rinold George** 1929- [BE]
*American baseball player*
* Duren, Ryne

**Duren, Ryne**
See Duren, Rinold George

**Durfort de Duras, Louis de**
1640?-1709 [SN]
*French-born British diplomat and
army officer*
* Feversham, Earl of
* [The] King Dowager

**Durgan, Clara V.** [FFF]
*Writer*
* Chesney, Esther

**Durgin, Francis Timothy** 1922?-
[FC, ITA, SW]
*American actor*
* Calhoun, Rory

**Durgnat, Raymond [Eric]** 1932-
[CA]
*British educator and author*
* Green, O. O.

**Durham, Anne**
See Walker, Emily Kathleen

**Durham, Bull**
See Durham, Don[ald Gary]

**Durham, Bull**
See Durham, Edward Fant

**Durham, Bull**
See Durham, Louis G.

**Durham, David**
See Vickers, Roy

**Durham, Don[ald Gary]** 1949- [BE]
*American baseball player*
* Durham, Bull

**Durham, Edward Fant** 1907- [BE]
*American baseball player*
* Durham, Bull

**Durham, Edward Lee** 1915-
[BWW]
*American singer*
* Mr. Buddy

**Durham, Joseph Vann [Joe]** 1931-
[BE]
*American baseball player*
* Durham, Pop

**Durham, Louis G.** 1881- ? [BE]
*American baseball player*
* Durham, Bull

**Durham, Mae**
See Roger, Mae Durham

**Durham, Pop**
See Durham, Joseph Vann [Joe]

**Duri Durani [Pearl of Pearls]**
See Ahmed Shah

**Durie, Lynn**
See Christie, Douglas

**Durieux, Tilla**
See Godeffroy, Ottilie

**Durius, Firminius**
See Douri, Fremin

**Durivage, Francis Alexander**
1814-1880 [FFF, PA]
*Author*
* Old 'Un

**Durkee, John** 1728-1782 [FFF]
*American Indian-fighter*
* Bold Bean-Hiller

**Durkin, Junior**
See Durkin, Trent

**Durkin, Trent** 1915-1935 [FC]
*American actor*
* Durkin, Junior

**Durley, Alexander** 20th c. [BBH]
*American collegiate athletic director*
* Durley, Chips

**Durley, Chips**
See Durley, Alexander

**Durnbaugh, Robert Eugene [Bobby]**
1933- [BE]
*American baseball player*
* Durnbaugh, Scroggy

**Durnbaugh, Scroggy**
See Durnbaugh, Robert Eugene
[Bobby]

**Durocher, Leo Ernest** 1905-
[BE, PB, SR]
*American baseball player and
manager*
* [The] All American Out
* Durocher, Lippy
* Durocher, Screechy
* [The] Lip

**Durocher, Lippy**
See Durocher, Leo Ernest

**Durocher, Screechy**
See Durocher, Leo Ernest

**Duroeus**
See Dury, Jean

**Durrant, Theo** [joint pseudonym]
See Offord, Lenore Glen

**Durrell, Jane**
See Fulks, Sarah Jane

**Durrell, Lawrence [George]** 1912-
[CA, LC, TC]
*British author and poet*
* Norden, Charles
* Peeslake, Gaffer

**Durrett, Elmer Charles** 1921- [BE]
*American baseball player*
* Durrett, Red

**Durrett, Red**
See Durrett, Elmer Charles

**Durst, Paul** 1921- [CA, WW]
*American author*
* Bannon, Peter
* Chelton, John
* Cochran, Jeff
* Shane, John

**D'Urstelle, Pierre**
See Dorst, Jean [Pierre]

**Durtain, Luc**
See Nepveu, Andre

**Dury, Jean** ?-1637 [PA]
*Author*
* Duroeus

**Duryea, Charles Edgar** 1861-1938
[WBD]
*American inventor and
manufacturer*
* [The] Father of the Automobile

**Duryea, Cyclone Jim**
See Duryea, James Whitney

**Duryea, George** 1896?-1963
[BEW, F2, FC]
*American actor*
* Keene, Tom
* Powers, Richard

**Duryea, James Whitney** 1862-1942
[AS, BE]
*American baseball player*
* Duryea, Cyclone Jim
* Duryea, Jesse

**Duryea, Jesse**
See Duryea, James Whitney

**Dusak, Ervin Frank** 1920- [BE]
*American baseball player*
* Dusak, Four Sack

**Dusak, Four Sack**
See Dusak, Ervin Frank

**Dusenberry, V. Hugo**
See Bunner, Henry Cuyler

**Dusenbury, Winifred Loesch**
See Frazer, Winifred [Loesch]
Dusenbury

**Dushnitzky-Shner, Sara** 1913-
[CA]
*Polish-born Israeli author*
* Neshamith, Sara

**Dusiak [or Dusick?], Michele Lee**
1942- [BEW, FC, SW]
*American actress, singer, dancer*
* Lee, Michele

**Dusic, Stanko**
See Begovic, Milan

**[The] Dusky Queen**
See Henderson, May

**Dussaud, Angele** 1850- ? [FFF]
*French author*
* Vincent, Jacques

**Dusty**
See Nash, Willard G.

**Dusty, Slim**
See Kirkpatrick, David Gordon

**[The] Dutch Augustus**
See Carausius, Marcus Aurelius
Valerius

**[The] Dutch Demon**
See Taral, Fred

**[The] Dutch Hesiod**
See Poot, Huibert Cornelisz[oon]

**[The] Dutch Hogarth**
See Zoffani, John

**[The] Dutch Master**
See Vander Meer, John Samuel

**[The] Dutch Sappho**
See Lescaille, Catherine

**[A] Dutch Sappho**
See Roemers, Anna

**[The] Dutch Vauban**
See Coehorn, Menno van

**[The] Dutchman**
See Flegenheimer, Arthur

**[The] Dutchman**
See Van Brocklin, Norm[an]

**[The] Dutchman**
See Wolgust, Adolphus

**Dutchman, Kalamu**
See Roskam, Karel Lodewijk

**Dutchy**
See Sigel, Franz

**Duthus**
See Innes, Alexander Taylor

**Dutkowski, Duke**
See Dutkowski, Laudes

**Dutkowski, Laudes** 1902- [CEI]
*Canadian-born hockey player*
* Dutkowski, Duke

**Dutschke, Red Rudi**
See Dutschke, Rudi

**Dutschke, Rudi** 1941?-1979
*German political activist*
* Dutschke, Red Rudi

**Dutt, Shosher Chunder** [PA]
*Author*
* Barton, J. A. G.

**Dutta, Reginald** 1914- [CA]
*British author*
* Dutta, Rex

**Dutta, Rex**
See Dutta, Reginald

**Dutton, John** 1951- [FB]
*American football player*
* Dutton, Lurch

**Dutton, Lurch**
See Dutton, John

**Dutton, Margaret Payne**
See Baker, Elizabeth W.

**Dutton, Mervyn A.** 1898-
[CEI, FHE, HK]
*Canadian-born hockey player and league executive*
* Dutton, Red

**Dutton, Red**
See Dutton, Mervyn A.

**Dutz**
See Davis, Mary Octavia

**Duval, Claude** 1643-1670 [HN]
*French highwayman*
* [The] Gentleman Highwayman

**Duval, Colette** 1898- [FBJ]
*French author*
* Vivier, Colette

**Duval, D. Z.**
See Duval, Dorothy Zinaida

**Duval, Dorothy Zinaida** 1917-
[ART]
*British painter*
* Duval, D. Z.

**Duval, Georges** [PA]
*Author*
* Tabarin

**DuVal, Joe**
See DuVal, Jose

**DuVal, Jose** 1907-1966 [SC]
*Actor*
* DuVal, Joe

**Duval, Margaret**
See Robinson, Patricia Colbert

**Duval, Marie**
See De Tessier, Emilie

**Duval, Paul** 1850?-1906 [B10]
*French author*
* Lorrain, Jean

**Duval, Pierre**
See Coutu, Ovide

**Duvalier, Francois** 1907-1971
[CW]
*Haitian president and author*
* Abderrahman
* Papa Doc

**Duvalier, Jean-Claude** 1951-
*Haitian president*
* Baby Doc

**Duvalles**
See Duvalles, Frederic

**Duvalles, Frederic** 1895-1971 [SC]
*French actor*
* Duvalles

**DuVaul, Virginia C.**
See Coffman, Virginia [Edith]

**Duveneck, Frank**
See Decker, Frank

**Duveyrier, Anne Honore Joseph**
1787-1865 [WBD]
*French playwright*
* Melesville

**Duviella**
See Basko, Maurice P. Duviella

**Duvoisin, Louise** 20th c. [IAW]
*Swiss-born author*
* Fatio, Louise

**Duwez, Maurice** 1881- ? [CD]
*Belgian author and playwright*
* Deauville, Max

**Dux, Emilienne**
See Deux, Emilienne

**Duyckinck, Evert Augustus**
1816-1878 [FFF]
*American author and critic*
* Merry, Felix

**Duyn, Willem** 1942- [RO2]
*Dutch singer*
* Mouth

**Dvorak, Ann**
See McKim, Ann

**Dvorak, Antonin** 1841-1904
*Czech composer*
* Old Borax

**Dvorsky**
See Hofmann, Josef Casimir

**Dwan, Allan**
See Dwan, Joseph Aloysius

**Dwan, Dorothy**
See Smith, Dorothy

**Dwan, Joseph Aloysius** 1885-
[BDF, FD]
*Canadian-born director*
* Dwan, Allan

**Dwig**
See Dwiggins, Clare Victor

**Dwiggins, Clare Victor** 1874-1959
[WECO]
*American cartoonist*
* Dwig

**Dwight, Allan**
See Cole, Lois Dwight

**Dwight, James** 1862-1948
[AS, BBH, OET]
*American tennis player*
* [The] Father of American Tennis

**Dwight, Phoebe**
See Hannah, Persis Dwight

**Dwight, Reginald Kenneth** 1947-
[IPA]
*British singer and pianist*
* John, Elton

**D'Wolf, William** 1858-1935 [PMJ]
*American actor and singer*
* Hopper, DeWolf

**Dwrocher, Leon**
See Reybaud, Marie Roch Louis

**Dwyer, Big Bill**
See Dwyer, William Vincent

**Dwyer, Double Joe**
See Dwyer, Joseph Michael

**Dwyer, James Francis** 1874-1952
[SFL]
*Author*
* Diver, James Francis

**Dwyer, Joseph Michael** 1904- [BE]
*American baseball player*
* Dwyer, Double Joe

**Dwyer, K. M.**
See Koontz, Dean R[ay]

**Dwyer, William Vincent** 20th c.
[BLB, MM]
*American underworld figure*
* Dwyer, Big Bill

**Dwyer, Winifred**
See Grover, Winifred Powell

**Dy**
See Duffy, Emlyn Arthur Joseph

**Dyce, Gilbert**
See Fitzgerald, Percy Hetherington

**Dyck [or Dijk], Philip van**
1680?-1752 [WBD]
*Dutch painter*
* [The] Little Van Dyck

**Dye, Anne G.**
See Phillips, Anne G[arvey]

**Dye, Babe**
See Dye, Cecil Henry

**Dye, Cecil Henry** 1898-1962
[CEI, FHE, HK]
*Canadian-born hockey player*
* Dye, Babe

**Dye, Charles**
See MacLean, Katherine

**Dye, Paul, Jr.** 1925- [GF]
*American golf course architect*
* Dye, Pete

**Dye, Pete**
See Dye, Paul, Jr.

**Dye, Tippy**
See Dye, William

**Dye, William** 1915- [BB]
*American basketball coach*
* Dye, Tippy

**Dyer, Brian** [joint pseudonym with Brian Rothery]
See Petrocelli, Orlando R[alph]

**Dyer, Brian** [joint pseudonym with Orlando R(alph) Petrocelli]
See Rothery, Brian

**Dyer, Charles [Raymond]** 1928-
[CA, WD]
*British author and playwright*
* Kraselchik, R.
* Stretton, Charles
* Stretton, Renshaw

**Dyer, Donald Robert** 1945-
[BE, SMG, WWB]
*American baseball player*
* Dyer, Duffy

**Dyer, Duffy**
See Dyer, Donald Robert

**Dyer, George** 1755-1841 [SN]
*British author*
* [An] Archimagus
* [An] Archimedes
* [A] Copernicus
* [A] Tycho Brahe

**Dyer, John Lewis** 1812-1901
[BBH]
*American clergyman*
* [The] Snowshoe Itinerant

**Dyer, Ken** 1946- [SMG]
*American football player*
* [The] Blade

**Dyer, Kenneth** 1899- [WWL]
*British author*
* Changer, Hugh

**Dyer, Minnie Theresa** [FFF]
*Author*
* Myrtle, Minnie

**Dyer, Sabine**
See Talbot, Mary Lee Keister

**Dyer, Skip** 1942- [IBW]
*Jamaican-born baseball player*
* Kali, Omar

**Dyer, Walter Alden** 1878- ? [ALY]
*American author*
* Fearing, Alden

**Dyer-Bennet, Richard** 1913-
[FCW]
*British-born American musician*
* [The] Twentieth Century Minstrel

**Dygert, James Henry** 1884-1936
[BE]
*American baseball player*
* Dygert, Sunny Jim

**Dygert, Sunny Jim**
See Dygert, James Henry

**Dyke**
See Christian, Lester

**Dykeman, Wilma**
See Stokely, Wilma Dykeman

**Dykes, Jack**
See Owen, Jack

**Dykes, James Joseph [Jimmy]**
1896- [BN]
*American baseball player and manager*
* [The] Oakmont Orator

**Dylan, Bob**
See Zimmerman, Robert

**Dylan, Ellie**
See Hellman, Elinor Angel

**Dymoke, Juliet**
See De Schanschieff, Juliet Dymoke

**Dymond, John** 20th c. [RM]
*Musician*
* Beaky

**Dymond, Rosalind**
See Cartwright, Rosalind Dymond

**Dynamita, Kid**
See Morales, Jorge

**Dynamite Eddie James**
See James, Eddie

**Dynamite Gus Sonnenberg**
See Sonnenberg, Gustave

**Dynamite, Mr.**
See Brown, James

**[The] Dynamo**
See Califano, Joseph Anthony, Jr.

**[The] Dynamo of Power**
See Roosevelt, Theodore [Teddy]

**Dyomin, Mikhail**
See Trifonov, Georgy

**Dyscolus [The Crabbed]**
See Appollonius of Alexandria

**Dyson, Geoffrey Harry George**
1914- [IAW]
*British-born author*
* Geoff

**Dyson, Timothy J.** [FFF, PA]
*American writer*
* Quiver

**Dzedzeji, Jerry** 1944- [SMG]
*American football player and scout*
* Shay, Jerry

**Dzhin-Dzhikh-Shivil**
*See* Tyshler, Alexandr Grigorievich

**Dzhugashvili, Iosif Vissarionovich**
1879-1953 [CND, IPA, NN]
*Russian premier*
* Glyptic [code name used during
    World War II]
* Stalin, Joseph
* Uncle Joe

**Dzidzornu, Kwasi** 20th c. [SSS]
*Musician*
* Dzidzornu, Rocki

**Dzidzornu, Rocki**
*See* Dzidzornu, Kwasi

**Dzierzak, Bob** 1952- [SMG]
*American football player*
* Dzierzak, Butch

**Dzierzak, Butch**
*See* Dzierzak, Bob

**Dzyubin [or Dzhubin], Eduard**
**Georgievich** 1895-1934 [CD, EWL]
*Russian poet*
* Bagritsky [or Bagritzky], Eduard

# E

**E.**
*See* Davin, Nicholas Francis Flood

**E. A.**
*See* Alexander, Eleanor Jane

**E. A.**
*See* Anati, Emmanuel

**E. A.**
*See* Ardizzone, Edward

**E. A. B.**
*See* Baker, Ernest A.

**E. A. B.**
*See* Baughan, Edward Algernon

**E. A. D.**
*See* Dobinson, Eric Arthur

**E. A. M.**
*See* Maddock, Mrs. E. A.

**E. B.**
*See* Beers, Ethelinda Elliot

**E. B.**
*See* Brooks, Erastus

**E. C.**
*See* Castle, Eva

**E. C.**
*See* Caswall, Edward

**E. C. A.**
*See* Agnew, Emily C.

**E. C. B.**
*See* Burton, Claude Edward
Cole-Hamilton

**E. C. M.**
*See* McBride, Peter

**E. D. E. N.**
*See* Southworth, Emma Dorothy
Eliza [Nevitte]

**E. D. G.**
*See* Garman, Evelyn Daphne

**E. F. C.**
*See* Cornelius, Ellanor Frances

**E. F. L.**
*See* Floyd, Mr.

**E. G.**
*See* Gledstanes, Elsie

**E. G. D.**
*See* Dunnell, Edgar G.

**E. H. C. M.**
*See* Davis, Nathan

**E. H. R.**
*See* Mitchell, Elizabeth Harcourt

**E. H. S.**
*See* Stanley, Edward H. Smith

**E. H. W. M.**
*See* Meyerstein, Edward Harry
William

**E. J.**
*See* Jones, Edgar

**E. J. D.**
*See* Doudney, Henry Eric John

**E. K.**
*See* Kirke, Edward

**E. K.**
*See* Korsmo, Emil

**E. L.**
*See* Lord, Elaezar

**E. M.**
*See* Magrath, E.

**E. M.**
*See* Malmquist, Eve Theodor

**E. M. B.**
*See* Gellie, Mrs. William

**E. M. C.**
*See* Chadwick, Enid M.

**E. M. E.**
*See* Millard, E. E.

**E. M. H.**
*See* Heaton, Edwin Maria

**[The] E Man**
*See* Castor, James Walter, Jr.
[Jimmy]

**E. P.**
*See* Perry, Ernest Thomas

**E. P.**
*See* Pound, Ezra [Loomis]

**E. Q. A. B.**
*See* Bull, Mrs.

**E. Q. B.**
*See* Banchard, E. Quentin

**E. R. B.**
*See* Burroughs, Edgar Rice

**E. R. C.**
*See* Coe, Edna Reilly

**E. R. C.**
*See* Conder, Eustace R.

**E. R. Z.**
*See* Ziar, Elizabeth Rosemary

**E. S.**
*See* Seymour, Edward

**E. S.**
*See* Sonntag, Erik Nicholas

**E. S. A.**
*See* Appleyard, Ernst Sylvanus

**E. S. L.**
*See* Law, Elizabeth Susan

**E. U.**
*See* Uncles, Ewart Charles

**E. V. B.**
*See* Boyle, Eleanor Vere

**E. V. L.**
*See* Lucas, Edward Verrall

**E. W. A.**
*See* Allderdice, Eliza Winslow

**E. W. M.**
*See* Marwick, Ernest Walker

**E. Y.**
*See* Young, Eileen

**Eade, Charles** 1903-1964    [SFL]
*Author*
* Prole, Lozania [joint pseudonym
with Ursula (Harvey) Bloom]

**Eady, Mary Aline** 1912-    [SFL]
*British author*
* Wesley, Mary

**Eagan, Bad Bill**
*See* Eagan, William

**Eagan, Charles Eugene** 1877-1949
[BE]
*American baseball player*
* Eagan, Truck

**Eagan, Truck**
*See* Eagan, Charles Eugene

**Eagan, William** 1869-1905    [BE]
*American baseball player*
* Eagan, Bad Bill

**Eagar, Richard Michael Cardwell**
1919-    [ART]
*British artist*
* R. M. C. E.

**Eager, Jimmy**
*See* Woodbridge, Hudson

**Eager, Johnney**
*See* Tanner, John

**Eager, Mary Ann** 20th c.    [ASC]
*Irish-born composer*
* Eager, Molly

**Eager, Molly**
*See* Eager, Mary Ann

**Eager, Phoebe** 1896-    [THR]
*American actress*
* Foster, Phoebe

**[The] Eagle**
*See* Baldelli, Ecola

**[The] Eagle**
*See* Clark, Mark Wayne

**[The] Eagle**
*See* Ferrari, Gaudenzio

**Eagle Eye**
*See* Beckley, Jacob Peter [Jake]

**Eagle Eye**
*See* Hemphill, Charles Judson

**[The] Eagle of Brittany**
*See* Guesclin, Bertrand du

**[The] Eagle of Divines**
*See* Aquinas, Thomas [Thomas of
Aquino]

**[The] Eagle of France**
*See* Ailly, Pierre d'

**[The] Eagle of Lille**
*See* Immelmann, Max

**[The] Eagle of Meaux**
*See* Bossuet, Jacques Benigne

**[The] Eagle of the Doctors of France**
*See* Ailly, Pierre d'

**[The] Eagle of the North**
*See* Oxenstierna, Axel Gustafsson

**[The] Eagle of Toledo**
*See* Bahamontes, Federico

**[The] Eagle Orator of Tennessee**
*See* Henry, Gustavus Adolphus

**Eagle, Solomon**
*See* Squire, John Collings

**Eagleburger, Lawrence** 1931-
*American diplomat*
* Larry of Macedonia

**Eagles, John** 1784-1855    [FFF, PA]
*British author and artist*
* Penrose, Llewellyn
* Themaninthemoon

**Eaglesfield, Francis**
*See* Guirdham, Arthur

**Eaglin, Blind Snooks**
See   Eaglin, Fird

**Eaglin, Fird** 1936-   [BWW]
*American singer*
* Eaglin, Blind Snooks
* Eaglin, Ford
* Eaglin, Snooks

**Eaglin, Ford**
See   Eaglin, Fird

**Eaglin, Snooks**
See   Eaglin, Fird

**Eakin, Mary Blair** 1895?-1947
[BEW]
*American actress*
* Blair, Mary

**Ealham, Alan George Ernest** 1944-
[DC]
*British cricketer*
* Ealham, Clogger
* Ealham, Ealy

**Ealham, Clogger**
See   Ealham, Alan George Ernest

**Ealham, Ealy**
See   Ealham, Alan George Ernest

**Ealhwine**
See   Alcuin [or Albinus]

**Eames, Juanita** 20th c.   [ASC]
*American musician*
* Masters, Juan

**Eanes, Homer Robert, Jr.** 1923-
[CWG, DAM]
*American country-western performer*
* Eanes, Jim

**Eanes, Jim**
See   Eanes, Homer Robert, Jr.

**Eardley-Wilmot, [Sir] Sydney Marow**
1847-1929   [SFL]
*Author*
* Searchlight

**Earhart, Amelia** 1899-1937?
*American aviatrix*
* A. E.
* Lady Lindy

**Earl, Mary**
See   Keiser, Robert

**[The] Earl of Flint**
See   Jeffreys, George [First Baron
Jeffreys of Wem]

**Earl of Grant**
See   Grant, Earl

**[The] Earl of Milton's Comus**
See   Egerton, John [First Earl of
Bridgewater]

**[The] Earl of Pleasure Bay**
See   Hastings, Hugh J.

**[The] Earl of Snohomish**
See   Averill, [Howard] Earl

**[The] Earl of Snohomish**
See   Torgeson, [Clifford] Earl

**Earle, Ambrose**
See   Jones, J. G.

**Earle, Blanche** 1883-1952   [SC]
*American actress*
* Earle, Bonnie

**Earle, Bonnie**
See   Earle, Blanche

**Earle, D. M.**
See   Earle, Donald Maurice

**Earle, Donald Maurice** 1928-
[ART]
*British painter*
* Earle, D. M.

**Earle, Jack**
See   Ehrlich, Jacob

**Earle, Josephine**
See   McEwan, Josephine

**Earle, M. A.**   [PA]
*Author*
* Carlton, [Cousin] May

**Earle, Marilee**
See   Zdenek, Marilee

**Earle, W. J.?**
See   Senarens, Luis Philip

**Earle, William**
See   Johns, [Captain] William
Earle

**Earle, William Moffat** 1867-1946
[BE]
*American baseball player*
* [The] Little Globetrotter

**Earley, Martha**
See   Westwater, [Sister] Agnes
Martha

**Earley, Robert**
See   Sharples, Robert

**Earll, Tony**
See   Buckland, Raymond

**Earlson, Ian Malcolm**
See   Dorn, William S.

**Early, Deloreese Patricia** 1932-
[IPA]
*American singer*
* Ferro, Della
* Reese, Della

**Early, Jubal Anderson** 1816-1894
[DNNS, FFF, SN]
*American army officer*
* [The] Bad Old Man

**Earlywine, Hargis**
See   Kinnaird, Clark

**Earnshaw, Catharine**
See   Pool, Maria L.

**Earnshaw, George Livingston**
1900-   [BE, PB]
*American baseball player*
* Earnshaw, Moose

**Earnshaw, Moose**
See   Earnshaw, George Livingston

**Earnshaw, Patricia** 1922-   [AW]
*British biologist and author*
* Mann, Patricia

**Earp [or Earpe?], Francis**
1897-1969   [AS, BBH]
*American football player*
* Earp, Jug
* [The] Man Mountain of
  Professional Ball

**Earp, James William** 1888-   [NAA]
*American writer*
* Girouard, Jacques

**Earp, Jug**
See   Earp [or Earpe?], Francis

**Earp, Virgil**
See   Keevill, Henry J[ohn]

**Earrol, Paul**
See   Gustafson, Paul

**Eason, B. Reeves** 1886-1956   [FD]
*American actor*
* Eason, Breezy

**Eason, Breezy**
See   Eason, B. Reeves

**Eason, Breezy, Jr.**
See   Eason, Reeves

**Eason, Kid**
See   Eason, Malcolm Wayne

**Eason, Malcolm Wayne** 1879-1970
[BE]
*American baseball player*
* Eason, Kid

**Eason, Reeves** 1913-1921   [SC]
*American actor*
* Eason, Breezy, Jr.

**[An] East Anglien**
See   Feist, Charles

**East, Easty**
See   East, Raymond Eric

**East, Michael**
See   West, Morris L[anglo]

**East, Raymond Eric** 1947-   [DC]
*British cricketer*
* East, Easty
* East, Spindle

**East, Roger**
See   Burford, Roger D'Este

**[The] East Side Assassin**
See   Agati, James

**East, Spindle**
See   East, Raymond Eric

**Eastaway, Edward**
See   Thomas, [Philip] Edward

**Easter, Ebber D[arnell]** 1882-1961
[AS, BBH]
*American bowler*
* Easter, Ed
* Easter, Sarge

**Easter, Ed**
See   Easter, Ebber D[arnell]

**Easter, Luke**
See   Easter, Luscious

**Easter, Luscious** 1916?-1979
*American baseball player*
* Easter, Luke

**Easter, Sarge**
See   Easter, Ebber D[arnell]

**Easterley, Robert and Wilbraham,
John**
See   Potter, Robert

**Easterling, Narena** 20th c.   [WW]
*Author*
* Easterling, Rene

**Easterling, Rene**
See   Easterling, Narena

**Easterly, James Morris** 1953-
*American baseball player*
* Easterly, Rat

**Easterly, Rat**
See   Easterly, James Morris

**Easterwood, Roy Charles** 1915-
[BE]
*American baseball player*
* Easterwood, Shag

**Easterwood, Shag**
See   Easterwood, Roy Charles

**Eastham, Thomas** 1923-   [CA]
*American journalist*
* Harling, Thomas

**Eastlund, Madelyn**
See   Hickey, Madelyn Eastlund

**Eastman, Alexander F.**
See   Fraser, Alexander

**Eastman, Ann Heidbreder** 1933-
[CA]
*American author*
* Heidbreder, Margaret Ann

**Eastman, Ben** 20th c.
*Track and field athlete*
* Eastman, Blazing Ben

**Eastman, Blazing Ben**
See   Eastman, Ben

**Eastman, Charles A[lexander]**
1858-1939   [YAB]
*American author*
* Ohiyesa

**Eastman, Edward Monk**
See   Osterman, Edward Monk

**Eastman, Fred** 1886-   [NAA]
*American educator, author,
playwright*
* Morse, Richard

**Eastman, G. Don**
See   Oosterman, Gordon

**Eastman, Jack**
See   Abbott, Jack Henry

**Eastman, P. D.**
See   Eastman, Philip Dey

**Eastman, Philip Dey** 1909-   [ICB]
*American author and illustrator*
* Eastman, P. D.

**Easton, Amos** 1905-   [BWW]
*American singer*
* Armstrong, Shelley
* Bumble Bee Slim

**[The] Easton Assassin**
See   Holmes, Larry

**Easton, Bill**
See   Easton, Millard E.

**Easton, Carol D.** 20th c.   [IBW]
*American author*
* Laini, Safisha

**Easton, Dale** 1918-   [FC]
*American actor*
* McClure, Greg

**Easton, Edward**
See   Malerich, Edward P.

**Easton, Goose**
See   Easton, John David

**Easton, John David** 1933-   [BE]
*American baseball player*
* Easton, Goose

**Easton, Millard E.** 1906-
[BBH, TF]
*American track coach*
* Easton, Bill

**Eastwick, Rawlins Jackson, III**
1950- [BR]
*American baseball player*
* Eastwick, Rawly

**Eastwick, Rawly**
See Eastwick, Rawlins Jackson, III

**Eastwood, C[harles] Cyril** 1916-
[CA]
*British clergyman and author*
* Hale, Philip

**Eastwood, Francis**
See Knevals, Mrs. D. C.

**Eastwood, Helen** 1892- [AW, WW]
*British author*
* Baxter, Olive
* Ramsay, Fay

**Eastwood, Irene Frances** 1910-
[THR]
*British actress and singer*
* Ziegler, Anne

**Easy Chair**
See Curtis, George William

**Easy Ed Macauley**
See Macauley, Edward C.

**Easy Papa Johnson**
See Sykes, Roosevelt

**Eatmon, Narvell** 20th c. [NBB]
*American entertainer*
* Cadillac Baby

**Eaton, David H.** 1854- ? [PA]
*Author*
* Ortyx
* Umbellus, T.

**Eaton, George B.** [PA]
*Author*
* Jacobstaff

**Eaton, George L.**
See Montayne, Harold B.

**Eaton, George L.**
See Verral, Charles Spain

**Eaton, James**
See Latessa, James

**Eaton, Red**
See Eaton, Zebulon Vance

**Eaton, Zeb**
See Eaton, Zebulon Vance

**Eaton, Zebulon Vance** 1920- [BE]
*American baseball player*
* Eaton, Red
* Eaton, Zeb

**Eaves, Chief**
See Eaves, Vallie Ennis

**Eaves, Vallie Ennis** 1911-1960
[BE]
*American baseball player*
* Eaves, Chief

**Eban, Abba**
See Solomon, Abba

**Eban, Aubrey**
See Solomon, Abba

**Ebbett, Frances Eva** 1925- [IAW]
*British author*
* Burfield, Eva

**Ebel, Henry** 1938- [IAW]
*German-born author*
* Batstein, William
* Moses the Son of Jehoshar

**Ebel, Suzanne**
See Goodwin, Suzanne

**Eben-ezer**
See Aldred, Eben

**Eberhard, Al** 1952-
*American basketball player*
* Eberhard, Country

**Eberhard, Country**
See Eberhard, Al

**Eberhard, E. H.**
See Eberhard, Ernst Hans

**Eberhard, Ernst Hans** 1866- ?
[LAO]
*German author*
* Eberhard, E. H.

**Eberhardt, John J.** 1869- ? [NAA]
*American poet*
* [The] Poet 'o the Plains
* [The] Poet of Childhood

**Eberhardt, Peter**
See Adams, Robert [Franklin]

**Eberhart, Ebbie**
See Eberhart, Elder J.

**Eberhart, Elder J.** 20th c. [BBH]
*American basketball coach*
* Eberhart, Ebbie

**Eberle, Irmengarde** 1898-1979
[CA, SAT]
*American author*
* Allen, Allyn
* Carter, Phyllis Ann

**Eberle, Josef** 1901- [EWL]
*German poet, critic, editor*
* Blau, Sebastian

**Eberle, Robert** 1916- [PMJ]
*American singer*
* Eberly, Bob

**Eberly, Bob**
See Eberle, Robert

**Ebert, Arthur Frank** 1902-
[CA, CC, WW]
*British author and playwright*
* Arthur, Frank

**Ebhardt, C.** 19th c. [PA]
*Author*
* Justus

**Ebhardt, Olga** [PA]
*Author*
* De' Alq, Louise

**Ebigwei, Patricia** 20th c. [IBW]
*Nigerian-born actress*
* Ebigwei, Yum-Yum

**Ebigwei, Yum-Yum**
See Ebigwei, Patricia

**Eblis, J. Philip**
See Phillips, James W.

**Ebn El-Nil**
See Abdel-Malek, Anouar

**Ebner, Jeannie**
See Ebner-Allinger, Jeannie

**Ebner-Allinger, Jeannie** 1918-
[IAW]
*Austrian author*
* Ebner, Jeannie

**Eboli, Thomas** ?-1972
[BLB, PHM]
*American underworld figure*
* Ryan, Tommy

**[The] Ebon Eagle**
See Levister, Wendell W.

**Ebony**
See Blackwood, William

**[The] Ebony Antelope**
See Owens, James Cleveland

**[The] Ebony Nora Bayes**
See Waters, Ethel

**Eboracensis, Joannes**
See Belmeys, John

**Eboracus**
See Broom, W. W.

**Eboue, Fe-Fe**
See Eboue, [Adolphe] Felix
[Sylvestre]

**Eboue, [Adolphe] Felix [Sylvestre]**
1884-1944 [CW]
*West Indian statesman, historian,
folklorist*
* Eboue, Fe-Fe

**[L']Ebreo**
See Rossi, Salomone

**Ebright, Buck**
See Ebright, Hiram C.

**Ebright, Carroll F.** 20th c. [BBH]
*American rowing coach*
* Ebright, Ky

**Ebright, Hiram C.** 1859-1916 [BE]
*American baseball player*
* Ebright, Buck

**Ebright, Ky**
See Ebright, Carroll F.

**Ebsen, Buddy**
See Ebsen, Christian Rudolf, Jr.

**Ebsen, Christian Rudolf, Jr.** 1908-
[ASC, EMT, FC]
*American actor and dancer*
* Ebsen, Buddy

**Eby, Lois Christine** 1908- [IA]
*American author*
* Lawson, Patrick

**Eccard, Johann Georg von**
1664-1730 [WBD]
*German historian*
* Eckhart, Johann Georg von

**Ecce Homo**
See Seeley, John Robert

**Eccles**
See Williams, Ferelith Eccles

**Eccles, Buggs**
See Eccles, Harry Josiah

**Eccles, Charlotte O'Conor** 20th c.
[WGT]
*British author*
* Godfrey, Hal

**Eccles, George Clinton** 1916-
[BEW]
*American actor, producer, theatre
owner*
* Terrell, St. John

**Eccles, Harry Josiah** 1893-1955
[BE]
*American baseball player*
* Eccles, Buggs

**Ecclesiasticus**
See Gammie, Alexander

**Eccleston, H. N.**
See Eccleston, Harry Norman

**Eccleston, Harry Norman** 1923-
[ART]
*British painter and engraver*
* Eccleston, H. N.

**Echion**
See Chatfield, Edward

**Echo Club**
See Taylor, Bayard

**Echo, Oliver**
See Forbes, Seloftus D.

**Echols, Anita** 1924- [IBW]
*American comedienne*
* [The] Atomic Bombshell

**Ecir**
See Rice, Isaac L.

**Eck, Johann**
See Mayer, Johann

**Ecke, Betty Tseng Yu-ho** 1923-
[TCA]
*Chinese-born artist, educator,
author*
* Tseng Yu-ho

**Eckels, Jon** 20th c. [LBA]
*American author*
* Akhnaton, Askia

**Eckert, Al[bert George]** 1906- [BE]
*American baseball player*
* Eckert, Obbie

**Eckert, Anne Seymour** 1909-
[BEW]
*American actress*
* Seymour, Anne

**Eckert, Buzz**
See Eckert, Charles William
[Charlie]

**Eckert, Charles William [Charlie]**
1898- [BE]
*American baseball player*
* Eckert, Buzz

**Eckert, Horst** 1931- [CA, SAT]
*Polish-born German author and
illustrator*
* Janosch

**Eckert, Johanna** 20th c.
[BEW, EMT, TR]
*German-born choreographer and
director*
* Holm, Hanya

**Eckert, Obbie**
See Eckert, Al[bert George]

**Eckert, Powder Face**
See Eckert, Tom

**Eckert, Tom** 20th c. [GW]
*American rodeo performer*
* Eckert, Powder Face

**Eckhardt, Oscar George**
1901-1951 [BE]
*American baseball player*
* Eckhardt, Ox

**Eckhardt, Ox**
See Eckhardt, Oscar George

**Eckhart, Johann Georg von**
See Eccard, Johann Georg von

**Eckhart [Eckart or Eckardt], Johannes** 1260-1329 [FFF, WBD]
*German theologian*
* Eckhart, Meister
* [The] Father of Modern Pantheism

**Eckhart, Meister**
See Eckhart [Eckart or Eckardt], Johannes

**Eckman, J. Forester**
See Ackerman, Forrest J[ames]

**Eckmar, F. R.**
See De Hartog, Jan

**Eckob, Jay**
See Cobb, J. Storer

**Eckstein, William Clarence** 1914- [DAM, PMJ]
*American singer and bandleader*
* Eckstine, Billy
* Mr. B

**Eckstine, Billy**
See Eckstein, William Clarence

**Eclair, Lyden**
See Flash, Henry Lyden

**Eclov, Shirley**
See Pfoutz, Shirley Eclov

**Economo, Constantin** 1876- ? [LAO]
*Austrian physician and technical writer*
* Von Economo, C.

**[The] Ecstatic Doctor**
See Ruysbroek, Jean de

**Ecstaticus, Doctor**
See Ruysbroek, Jean de

**Ed**
See Teneyck, Edward

**Eddie**
See Jones, Eddie

**Eddison, E. R.**
See Eddison, Eric Ruecker

**Eddison, Eric Ruecker** 1882-1945 [HFF]
*British author*
* Eddison, E. R.

**Eddleman, Dike**
See Eddleman, Dwight

**Eddleman, Dwight** 1923- [BB]
*American basketball player*
* Eddleman, Dike

**Eddy, Charles**
See Rose, Charles E.

**Eddy, Everett** 20th c. [IBW]
*American martial arts expert*
* [The] Monster Man

**Eddy, Miriam**
See Johnson, Miriam

**Eddy, Teddy Jack**
See Busey, Gary

**Eddya, Borhan** [PA]
*Author*
* Zernoudjy

**Edele, Bud**
See Edele, Durand J.

**Edele, Durand J.** 20th c. [ITA]
*American film executive*
* Edele, Bud

**Edelen, Doc**
See Edelen, Ed[ward Joseph]

**Edelen, Ed[ward Joseph]** 1912- [BE]
*American baseball player*
* Edelen, Doc

**Edelstein, Gertrude** 1899-1966 [FC]
*American actress*
* Berg, Gertrude

**Edelstein, Hyman** 1889-1957
*Irish-born Canadian author and poet*
* Synge, Don

**Edelstein, Samson Iosifovich** 1921- [WEF]
*Russian actor*
* Samsonov, Samson

**Edelstein, Scott** 20th c. [SFP]
*Author*
* Bronson, Donna

**Edelsten, Anita** 1898- [THR]
*British actress*
* Elson, Anita

**Eden, Ann** 1918?-1975 [FIR]
*Actress*
* [The] Most Beautiful Girl on Radio

**Eden, [Sir] [Robert] Anthony** 1897-1977 [CND]
*British prime minister*
* Compost [code name used during World War II]

**Eden, Barbara**
See Huffman, Barbara

**Eden, Dorothy Enid** 1912-
*Author*
* Paradise, Mary

**Eden, Eleanor** [PA]
*Author*
* L. E.

**Eden, John Lancelot** 1885- [WWL]
*British author*
* Artax

**Eden, Rob** [joint pseudonym with Robert Ferdinand Burkhardt]
See Burkhardt, Eve

**Eden, Rob** [joint pseudonym with Eve Burkhardt]
See Burkhardt, Robert Ferdinand

**Eden, William** [FFF]
*Entertainer*
* Herbert, William

**Edeveain, Templer Edward** 1866-1935 [BEW]
*British-born actor*
* Saxe, Templer

**Edgar [or Eadgar]** 944- 975 [DNNS, WBD]
*King of England*
* [The] Peaceful
* [The] Red Fox

**Edgar [or Eadgar]** 1050?-1130? [WBD]
*British prince*
* [The] Aetheling

**Edgar, Alfred** 1896- [MBF, SFL, WGT]
*British-born playwright*
* Denvers, Jake
* Fowey, Roger
* Gregory, Hylton [house pseudonym]
* Lyndon, Barre?
* Rogers, Tom
* Ryder, Steven
* Sansom, John [joint pseudonym with Jimmy Sangster]
* Sayers, Edgar
* Steele, Howard [house pseudonym]

**[The] Edgar Allan Poe of Russian Literature**
See Andreyev, Leonid [Nikolaevich]

**Edgar, Frank Terrell Rhoades** 1932- [CA]
*American historian and author*
* Ritchie, Bill

**Edgar, Icarus Walter**
See Bishop, Stanley Walter Edgar

**Edgar, [Sir] John**
See Steele, [Sir] Richard

**Edgar, Josephine**
See Mussi, Mary

**Edgar, Mrs. R.** [FFF]
*Entertainer*
* Marriott, Alice

**Edgar, Peter**
See King-Scott, Peter

**Edgcumbe, Ursula** 1900- [ART]
*British sculptor and painter*
* U. E.

**Edge, Butch**
See Edge, Claude L.

**Edge, Claude L.** 1956- [ALR]
*American baseball player*
* Edge, Butch

**Edge, Jack**
See Haylon, Jack

**Edgehill, Champ**
See Edgehill, John W.

**Edgehill, John W.** 1922- [IBW]
*American boxer*
* Edgehill, Champ

**Edgerly, Mrs. Clinton** [FFF]
*Entertainer*
* Coghlan, Rose

**Edgerly, Webster** 1852- ? [NAA]
*American author*
* Shaftsbury, Edmund

**Edgerton, Sarah S. G.** 1819-1848 [PA]
*Author*
* Garret, Edward

**Edgerton, Wild**
See McVicker, Brock

**Edgewood, Henry**
See Sturgill, Virgil Leon

**Edgeworth, Henry Essex** 1745-1807 [RH]
*Irish attendant to King Louis XVI*
* De Firmount, Monsieur

**Edgley, Leslie** 1912- [WW]
*Author*
* Bloomfield, Robert
* Hastings, Brook [joint pseudonym with Mary Edgley]

**Edgley, Mary** 20th c. [WW]
*Author*
* Hastings, Brook [joint pseudonym with Leslie Edgley]

**Edgun**
See Wulff, Edgun Valdemar

**Edianez, Anna**
See Fluiriot, Zenaide Marie Ann

**Edilog**
See Ilogu, Edmund Christopher Onyedum

**Edinboro, Arlington** 1924- [IBW]
*American basketball coach*
* Edinboro, Ollie
* [The] Pied Piper of Harlem

**Edinboro, Ollie**
See Edinboro, Arlington

**Edington, Arlo Channing** 1890- [NAA]
*American author*
* [The] Edingtons [joint pseudonym with Carmen Bullen Edington]

**Edington, Carmen Bullen** 20th c. [NAA]
*American author*
* [The] Edingtons [joint pseudonym with Arlo Channing Edington]

**Edington, Jacob Frank** 1891- [BE]
*American baseball player*
* Edington, Stump

**Edington, Stump**
See Edington, Jacob Frank

**[The] Edingtons** [joint pseudonym with Carmen Bullen Edington]
See Edington, Arlo Channing

**[The] Edingtons** [joint pseudonym with Arlo Channing Edington]
See Edington, Carmen Bullen

**Edison, Harry** 1915- [ASC, DAM, EJ]
*American jazz musician*
* Edison, Sweets

**Edison, Judith**
See Paul, Judith Edison

**Edison, Sweets**
See Edison, Harry

**Edison, Theodore?**
See Stratemeyer, Edward L.

**Edison, Thomas Alva** 1847-1931
*American inventor*
* [The] Wizard of Menlo Park

**Ediss, Connie** 1871-1934 [THR]
*British actress*
* Coutts, Connie

**Editors Drawer**
See Seaver, W. A.

**Edlin, Henry** 1882-  [THR]
*British actor*
* Edlin, Tubby

**Edlin, John Bruce** 1945-  [IAW]
*New Zealand-born journalist*
* Hudd, John

**Edlin, Tubby**
See  Edlin, Henry

**Edmeades, Robert Thomas**
1902?-1962  [BEW]
*American theatrical performer*
* Roberts, Jimmy

**Edmiston, Helen Jean Mary** 1913-
[AW, CC, WW]
*British author*
* Robertson, Helen

**Edmond, Jay**
See  Jones, Jack

**Edmonds, Alan**
See  Edmonds, Arthur Denis

**Edmonds, Ann C.**
See  Welch, Ann Courtenay
Edmonds

**Edmonds, Arthur Denis** 1932-  [CA]
*British-born author*
* Arthur, Alan
* Dennis, Arthur
* Edmonds, Alan
* Graham, Elizabeth

**Edmonds, Charles**
See  Carrington, Charles Edmund

**Edmonds, Goat**
See  Edmonds, Phillippe Henri

**Edmonds, Helen [Woods]**
1904-1968  [CA, WGT, WOA]
*British author*
* Ferguson, Helen
* Kavan, Anna

**Edmonds, Henry**
See  Edmonds, Phillippe Henri

**Edmonds, Ivy Gordon** 1917-  [CA]
*American author*
* Gordon, Gary

**Edmonds, Margaret Hammett** 20th
c.  [CA]
*American author*
* Edmonds, Margot

**Edmonds, Margot**
See  Edmonds, Margaret Hammett

**Edmonds, Paul**
See  Kuttner, Henry

**Edmonds, Phillippe Henri** 1951-
[DC]
*Zambian-born cricketer*
* Edmonds, Goat
* Edmonds, Henry

**Edmonds, Robert Humphrey Gordon**
1920-  [CA]
*British diplomat and author*
* Edmonds, Robin

**Edmonds, Robin**
See  Edmonds, Robert Humphrey
Gordon

**Edmondson, G. C.**
See  Edmondson y Cotton, Jose
Mario Garry Ordonez

**Edmondson, James** 1911?-1976
[B10]
*American radio performer*
* Backwards, Professor

**Edmondson, Keith** 20th c.
*American basketball player*
* [The] Ice Man

**Edmondson, Sybil [Armstrong]**
1898-  [AW]
*British author*
* Armstrong, Sybil

**Edmondson, Wallace**
See  Ellison, Harlan [Jay]

**Edmondson y Cotton, Jose Mario
Garry Ordonez** 1922-  [ESF, SF]
*American author*
* Edmondson, G. C.
* Gast, Kelly P.

**Edmonson, Axel**
See  Edmonson, Edward Earl
[Eddie]

**Edmonson, Edward Earl [Eddie]**
1889-1971  [BE]
*American baseball player*
* Edmonson, Axel

**Edmonton, Dennis** 20th c.  [RM]
*Musician*
* Bonfire, Mars

**Edmund [or Eadmund]** 841?- 870
[DEP, WBD]
*King of East Anglia and Saint*
* [The] English St. Sebastian
* [The] Martyr

**Edmund** 1026-1051  [HN]
*King of Sweden*
* [The] Coal Burner

**Edmund, Sean**
See  Pringle, Laurence P.

**Edmund I [or Eadmund]** 922?- 946
[DNNS, WBD]
*King of the West Saxons and
Mercians*
* [The] Deed Door
* [The] Magnificent

**Edmund II** 989-1017
[DHA, HN, RH]
*King of the Anglo-Saxons*
* Ironside

**Edmunds, George Franklin**
1828-1919  [FFF]
*American politician*
* Saint Jerome

**Edmundson, Clarence** 1886-1964
[BB]
*American basketball coach*
* Edmundson, Hec

**Edmundson, Duke**
See  Edmundson, Garry

**Edmundson, Garry** 20th c.  [SMG]
*Hockey player*
* Edmundson, Duke

**Edmundson, Hec**
See  Edmundson, Clarence

**Edouin, Willie**
See  Boyer, William Frederick

**Edschmid, Kasimir**
See  Schmid, Eduard

**Edson, George Alden**
See  Ernst, Paul Frederick

**Edson, Harold**
See  Hall, Asa Zadel

**Edson, John Thomas** 1928-  [CA]
*British author*
* Denver, Rod
* Nolan, Chuck

**Edson, Merritt Austin** 1897-1955
[WWW]
*American military leader*
* Edson, Red Mike

**Edson, Red Mike**
See  Edson, Merritt Austin

**Edstrom, Katherine** 1901-1973
[FIR, SC]
*American actress*
* Queen of the Alligator Wrestlers

**Eduardi, Guillermo**
See  Edwards, William B[ennett]

**Edur, Tom**
See  Edur, Toomas

**Edur, Toomas** 1954-  [HR]
*Canadian-born hockey player*
* Edur, Tom

**Edward**  [HN, SN]
*Father of Queen Margaret of
Scotland*
* [The] Outlaw

**Edward [Eadward or Eadweard]**
870?- 924  [HN, WBD]
*King of the Angles and Saxons*
* [The] Elder

**Edward [or Eadward]** 963?- 978
[DNNS, HN, WBD]
*King of the West Saxons*
* [The] Martyr

**Edward [or Eadward]** 1002?-1066
[DNNS, HN, WBD]
*King of the West Saxons*
* [The] Confessor

**Edward** 1330-1376  [HN, WBD]
*Prince of Wales*
* [The] Black Prince

**Edward I** 1239-1307
[FFF, HN, RH]
*King of England*
* [The] Champion of the Cross
* [The] English Justinian
* [The] Hammer of Scotland
* [The] Justinian of England
* Longshanks
* Malleus Scotorum
* [The] Scourge of Scotland
* [The] Scourge of Wales

**Edward III** 1312-1377  [HN]
*King of England*
* [The] Father of English
Commerce
* [The] King of the Sea

**Edward IV** 1441?-1483
[DNNS, FFF, SN]
*King of England*
* [The] Robber

**Edward VI** 1537-1553
[DNNS, HN, SN]
*King of England*
* [The] Josiah of England
* [The] Josiah of his Country
* [The] Pious
* [The] Saint

**Edward VII** 1841-1910  [WBD]
*King of England*
* [The] Peacemaker

**Edwardes, Allen**
See  Kinsley, Daniel Allan

**Edwardes, George**
See  Edwards, George

**Edwardes, Pauline**
See  Bowskill, Derek

**Edwards**
See  Eisler, Gerhard

**Edwards, A. C.**
See  Edwards, Aubrey Carroll

**Edwards, Agnes**
See  Pratt, Agnes Rothery

**Edwards, Al**
See  Nourse, Alan E[dward]

**Edwards, Albert**
See  Bullard, Arthur

**Edwards, Albert Glen** 1907-1973
[FB, SMG]
*American football player*
* Edwards, Turk

**Edwards, Alexander**
See  Fleischer, Leonore

**Edwards, Aubrey Carroll** 1909-
[BEW]
*American educator and publisher*
* Edwards, A. C.

**Edwards, Bass**
See  Edwards, Henry

**Edwards, Bertram**
See  Edwards, Herbert Charles

**Edwards, Big Bill**
See  Edwards, William H.

**Edwards, Big Sonny**
See  Edwards, Robert

**Edwards, Blake**
See  McEdwards, William Blake

**Edwards, Bobby**
See  Moncrief, Robert

**Edwards, Bronwen Elizabeth**
See  Rose, Wendy

**Edwards, Bull**
See  Edwards, Charles Bruce

**Edwards, Butterbeans**
See  Edwards, Jodie [or Jody]

**Edwards, Carl J.** 1914-  [ART]
*British artist*
* C. E.

**Edwards, Catherine M.**  [FFF]
* Cousin Kate

**Edwards, Chancellor** 20th c.
[OBW]
*American baseball player*
* Edwards, Jack

**Edwards, Charles** 1933-  [BWW]
*American singer*
* Good Rockin' Charles

**Edwards, Charles Bruce** 1923-1975
[BE]
*American baseball player*
* Edwards, Bull

**Edwards, Charman**
See  Edwards, Frederick Anthony

**Edwards, Cliff** 1895-1971
[F2, PMJ, TR]
*American singer, ukelele player,
actor*
* Ukelele Ike

**Edwards, Daddy**
See　Edwards, Eddie

**Edwards, Darlene**
See　Stafford, Jo

**Edwards, Dave** 20th c.
*American football player*
* Edwards, Fuzzy

**Edwards, David** 1915-
[BWW, NBB]
*American singer*
* Edwards, Honeyboy
* Honey Eddie
* Honey, Mr.

**Edwards, Doc**
See　Edwards, Howard Rodney

**Edwards, Dolton**
See　Laissing, W. K.

**Edwards, Donald Earl**
See　Harding, Donald Edward

**Edwards, Eddie**
See　Edwards, Foster Hamilton

**Edwards, Eddie** 1891-1963　[NOJ]
*American jazz musician*
* Edwards, Daddy

**Edwards, Elizabeth**
See　Inderlied, Mary Elizabeth

**Edwards, Elwyn Hartley** 1927-
[CA]
*British horseman, journalist, author*
* Leyhart, Edward

**Edwards, Ethelbert** 1882-1952
[BF]
*British actor and director*
* Edwards, Henry

**Edwards, F. E.**
See　Nolan, William F[rancis]

**Edwards, Flossie**
See　Byrnes, Mrs. J. H. W.

**Edwards, Foster Hamilton** 1903-
[BE]
*American baseball player*
* Edwards, Eddie

**Edwards, Frederick Anthony** 1896-
[WW]
*British author*
* Edwards, Charman
* Van Dyke, J.

**Edwards, Fuzzy**
See　Edwards, Dave

**Edwards, G. W.**
See　Miner, William

**Edwards, Gary William** 1947-
[SMG]
*Canadian-born hockey player*
* Edwards, Scoop

**Edwards, Gawain**
See　Pendray, G[eorge] Edwards

**Edwards, George** 1693-1773
[DNNF, DNNS, FFF]
*British naturalist*
* [The] Father of Ornithologists

**Edwards, George** 1855-1915
[EMT, NN]
*British theatre manager*
* Edwardes, George
* [The] Gov'nor

**Edwards, George Graveley** 1896-
[AW]
*American-born author*
* Graveley, George

**Edwards, Glen** 1947-　[SMG]
*American football player*
* Edwards, Pine

**Edwards, Gus**
See　Simon, Gus

**Edwards, Hamm?**
See　Evans, Thelma D. Hamm

**Edwards, Hartley** 1895?-1978
*American army bugler during World
War I*
* Edwards, Hot Lips

**Edwards, Henry**
See　Edwards, Ethelbert

**Edwards, Henry** 1898-1965　[WWJ]
*American jazz musician*
* Edwards, Bass

**Edwards, Herbert Charles** 1912-
[CA, SAT]
*British author*
* Edwards, Bertram

**Edwards, Honeyboy**
See　Edwards, David

**Edwards, Hot Lips**
See　Edwards, Hartley

**Edwards, Howard Rodney** 1937-
[BE, SMG]
*American baseball player and coach*
* Edwards, Doc

**Edwards, Jack**
See　Allen, John Edward

**Edwards, Jack**
See　Edwards, Chancellor

**Edwards, James** 18th c.　[SN]
*British bookseller*
* [The] Exotic Bookseller

**Edwards, James Corbette**
1894-1965　[BE]
*American baseball player*
* Edwards, Jim Joe

**Edwards, James G.**
See　MacQueen, James William

**Edwards, Jane Campbell** 1932-
[CA, SAT]
*American author*
* Campbell, Jane

**Edwards, Jim Joe**
See　Edwards, James Corbette

**Edwards, Jimmy**
See　O'Neill, James Keith

**Edwards, Jodie [or Jody]** 1897-
[BWW, IBW]
*American entertainer*
* Edwards, Butterbeans

**Edwards, John** 1806-1887　[FFF]
*Welsh-born author*
* [The] Nightingale of the Twrch

**Edwards, John H.**
See　Haynes, John Edward

**Edwards, John Milton**
See　Jenks, George Charles

**Edwards, Johnson**
See　Shute, Walter

**Edwards, Jonathan**
See　Wetstein, Paul

**Edwards, Joseph**　[PA]
*Author*
* Agrikler

**Edwards, Julia**
See　Coryell, John Russell

**Edwards, Julie**
See　Stratemeyer, Edward L.

**Edwards, Julie**
See　Wells, Julia Elizabeth

**Edwards, June**
See　Bhatia, Jamunadevi

**Edwards, Leon**
See　Calhoun, Alfred R.

**Edwards, Leonard**
See　Wild, Reginald Leonard

**Edwards, Lillie** 1877- ?　[THR]
*British comedienne*
* Langtry, Baby
* Langtry, Lillie

**Edwards, Lionel Dalhousie Robertson**
1878- ?　[WWL]
*British author*
* Anniseed

**Edwards, Margaret Marie** 1902-
[NAA]
*American journalist and poet*
* Porter, Alice

**Edwards, Max**
See　Pohlman, Max Edward

**Edwards, Michael**
See　Slowitzky, Michael

**Edwards, Mill**
See　Edwards, Millard

**Edwards, Millard** 20th c.
*American singer*
* Edwards, Mill

**Edwards, Mrs.**　[PA]
*Author*
* L. E.

**Edwards, Neely**
See　Limbach, Cornelius

**Edwards, Norman** [joint pseudonym
with Theodore Edwin White]
See　Carr, Terry [Gene]

**Edwards, Norman** [joint pseudonym
with Terry (Gene) Carr]
See　White, Theodore Edwin [Ted]

**Edwards, Pine**
See　Edwards, Glen

**Edwards, R. M.**
See　Edwards, Roselyn

**Edwards, Robert** 20th c.　[RO2]
*American singer*
* Edwards, Big Sonny

**Edwards, Robert Hamilton**
1872-1932　[MBF]
*British author and editor*
* Grant, E. Gordon
* Sapte, W.

**Edwards, Roselyn** 1929-　[CA]
*American author*
* Alexander, Marge
* Edwards, R. M.

**Edwards, Samuel**
See　Gerson, Noel Bertram

**Edwards, Scoop**
See　Edwards, Gary William

**Edwards, Shallow**
See　Edwards, Thomas

**Edwards, Stephen**
See　Palestrant, Simon S.

**Edwards, Susie** 1896-1963　[BWW]
*American singer*
* [The] Queen of the Blues

**Edwards, Ted**
See　Barrell, M. E.

**Edwards, Thomas** ?-1647　[SN]
*British theologian and author*
* Edwards, Shallow
* [The] Presbyterian Paul-Pry

**Edwards, Thomas C.** 1848- ?
[ALY]
*Welsh-born author*
* Cynonfardd

**Edwards, Tryon** 1809- ?　[FFF]
*American theologian and author*
* Berkeley, Everard

**Edwards, Turk**
See　Edwards, Albert Glen

**Edwards, Vince**
See　Zorio, Vincent Edward

**Edwards, Walter**
See　Shute, Walter

**Edwards, Ward**
See　Rathborne, St. George

**Edwards, William B[ennett]** 1927-
[CA]
*American firearms authority and
author*
* Benet, Edouard
* Brandt, Harvey
* Cranbrook, James L.
* Eduardi, Guillermo
* Johnson, Charles S.
* Jones, [Captain] Wilbur
* Thompson, William C. L.

**Edwards, William Earle**
See　Erb, William E.

**Edwards, William H.** 1887-1943
[FB]
*American football player*
* Edwards, Big Bill

**Edwin**
See　Vaughn, Thomas

**Edwina**
See　Dumm, Frances Edwina

**Edwy [or Eadwig]** ?- 959
[DNNS, WBD]
*King of Wessex*
* [The] Fair

**Edy-Legrand**
See　Edy-Legrand, Edouard Leon
Louis

**Edy-Legrand, Edouard Leon Louis**
1893-　[ICB]
*French illustrator*
* Edy-Legrand

**Ee-Yah**
See Jennings, Hugh Ambrose

**Eeee**
See Ackerman, Forrest J[ames]

**[The] Eel**
See Henry, Camille

**Eerfeld, B.**
See Le Feber, David

**Efendi, Mohammed Esaad** 1790- ?
[PA]
*Author*
* Sahafzadeh

**Eff**
See Ferguson, Roy Young

**Effel, Jean**
See Lejeune, Francois

**Effiat, Marquis d'**
See Coiffier, Antoine

**Effinger, George Alec** 1947-    [ESF]
*American author*
* Diomede, John K.
* Doenim, Susan

**Effingham, C., Esq.**
See Cooke, John Esten

**Efjay**
See Ackerman, Forrest J[ames]

**Efkay, Jay**
See Krakauer, Jay Frank

**Efros, Israel [Isaac]** 1891-    [CA]
*Polish-born Israeli author*
* Efrot

**Efrot**
See Efros, Israel [Isaac]

**Efstration, Michael** 1927-    [BEW]
*American actor*
* Constantine, Michael

**Egalite, Monsieur**
See Orleans, Louis Philippe Joseph
d'

**Egalite, Philippe**
See Orleans, Louis Philippe Joseph
d'

**Egan, Aloysius Jerome** 1881-1951
[BE]
*American baseball player*
* Egan, Wish

**Egan, Arthur Augustus** 1883-1968
[BE]
*American baseball player*
* Egan, Ben

**Egan, Ben**
See Egan, Arthur Augustus

**Egan, Boxcar**
See Egan, Martin Joseph

**Egan, Edward Welstead** 1922-
[CA]
*American author and translator*
* MacAedhagan, Eamon

**Egan, John Joseph** 1871-1950    [BE]
*American baseball player*
* Egan, Rip

**Egan, Lesley**
See Linington, Elizabeth

**Egan, Martin Joseph** 1918-
[CEI, FHE, HK]
*Canadian-born hockey player*
* Egan, Boxcar

**Egan, Martin Joseph** (Continued)
* Egan, Pat

**Egan, Pat**
See Egan, Martin Joseph

**Egan, Pierce** 1772-1849
[DEL, RH]
*British sportswriter*
* [An] Amateur

**Egan, Rip**
See Egan, John Joseph

**Egan, Shorty**
See Egan, William

**Egan, William** 20th c.    [BLB]
*American underworld figure*
* Egan, Shorty

**Egan, Wish**
See Egan, Aloysius Jerome

**Egbert, H. M.**
See Emanuel, Victor Rousseau

**Egbert, Virginia Wylie**
See Kilborne, Virginia Wylie

**Egede, Hans** 1686-1758    [DNNS]
*Norwegian missionary*
* [The] Apostle of Greenland

**Egerton, Denise**
See Duggan, Denise Valerie

**Egerton, Francis** 1736-1803
[DEP, HN, SN]
*Third Duke of Bridgewater*
* [The] Father of British Inland
   Navigation
* [The] Parent of Canal Navigation

**Egerton, George**
See Bright, Mary Chavelita
[Dunne]

**Egerton, J. K.** 20th c.    [SFP]
*Author*
* Metcalfe, Francis

**Egerton, John [First Earl of
Bridgewater]** 1579-1649    [SN]
*British politician*
* [The] Earl of Milton's Comus

**Egerton, Lucy**
See Malleson, Lucy Beatrice

**Egerton, Randolph**
See Beswick, Harry

**Egestorff, Georg**
See Ompteda, [Baron] Georg von

**Egg, Maria** 1910-    [CA]
*Hungarian-born Swiss educator and
author*
* Egg-Benes, Maria

**Egg-Benes, Maria**
See Egg, Maria

**Egge, Ray**
See Agee, Ray[mond Clinton]

**Egger, Ellen**
See Mirus, Ludmilla

**Eggert, Elmer Albert** 1902-1971
[BE]
*American baseball player*
* Eggert, Mose

**Eggert, Mose**
See Eggert, Elmer Albert

**Eggleston, Edward** 1837-1902
[FFF, PA]
*American author*
* Penholder

**Eggleston, Egg**
See Eggleston, Macajah Machand

**Eggleston, Estelle** 1936-    [SW]
*American actress*
* Stevens, Stella

**Eggleston, George Cary**    [PA]
*Author*
* [A] Rebel

**Eggleston, Macajah Machand**
1896-    [MK]
*American baseball player*
* Eggleston, Egg
* Eggleston, Mack

**Eggleston, Mack**
See Eggleston, Macajah Machand

**Egleson, Janet F.**
See Dunleavy, Janet Egleson

**Eglin**
See Goetz, Raphael

**Eglinton, John**
See Magee, William Kirkpatrick

**Egnatzik, Joseph** 1920-    [ASC]
*American composer and musician*
* Nelson, Sandy

**Egnor, Virginia Ruth** 1927-    [B10]
*American television performer*
* Dagmar

**Ego-Queque**
See Zenea, Juan Clemente

**Egomet, Demens**
See Williams, Thomas

**Egorova, Evgeniia Nikolaevna**
?-1937?    [B10]
*Latvian revolutionist*
* Lepin, Ella-Marta

**Egremont, Michael**
See Harrison, Michael

**Egstrom, Norma Dolores** 1920-
[FC, ITA, OCF]
*American singer, composer, actress*
* Lee, Peggy

**[The] Egyptian Enigma**
See Ali, Hadji

**[The] Egyptian Solomon**
See Ramses III [or Rameses]

**Egyptus**
See Thompson, Joseph Parrish

**Ehlers, Friedrich Robert** 1858- ?
[LAO]
*German philosopher, physiologist,
author*
* Robert, Friedrich

**Ehmke, Bob**
See Ehmke, Howard Jonathan

**Ehmke, Howard Jonathan**
1894-1959    [BE]
*American baseball player*
* Ehmke, Bob

**Ehrenberg, Geoffrey Rudolph**
1921-    [LC]
*German-born educator and author*
* Elton, G[eoffrey] R[udolph]

**Ehrenfried, Georg** 1893-1959
[WEC]
*German cartoonist and painter*
* Grosz, George

**Ehrenreich, Dan**
*Radio and television producer and
director*
* Enright, Dan

**Ehrenzweig, Robert** 1904-    [CA]
*Austrian-born author and
playwright*
* Lucas, Robert

**Ehret, Philip Sydney** 1868-1940
[AS, BE]
*American baseball player*
* Ehret, Red

**Ehret, Red**
See Ehret, Philip Sydney

**Ehrhardt, Rube**
See Ehrhardt, Welton Claude

**Ehrhardt, Welton Claude** 1894-
[BE]
*American baseball player*
* Ehrhardt, Rube

**Ehrlich, Bettina [Bauer]** 1903-
[CAP, MJA, SAT]
*Austrian-born author and illustrator*
* Bettina

**Ehrlich, Jacob** 1906-1952    [SC]
*American actor and circus performer*
* Earle, Jack

**Ehrlich, Martha** 1900-1923    [SC]
*American actress*
* Mansfield, Martha

**Ehrmann, Joe** 1949-    [SMG]
*American football player*
* Ehrmann, Rookie

**Ehrmann, Rookie**
See Ehrmann, Joe

**Eibel, Hack**
See Eibel, Henry H.

**Eibel, Henry H.** 1893-1945    [BE]
*American baseball player*
* Eibel, Hack

**Eich, Guenter** 1907-1971    [CA]
*German poet and playwright*
* Guenter, Erich

**Eichberger, Wilhelm [Willy]** 1905-
[FC, THR]
*Austrian actor*
* Esmond, Carl

**Eichelbaum, Albert** 1884-1967
[WBD]
*American producer and film studio
executive*
* Warner, Albert

**Eichelbaum, Harry Morris**
1881-1958    [WBD]
*American producer and film studio
executive*
* Warner, Harry Morris

**Eichelbaum, Jack L.** 1892-    [WBD]
*American producer and film studio
executive*
* Warner, Jack L.

**Eichelbaum, Samuel Louis**
1887-1927    [WBD]
*American producer and film studio
executive*
* Warner, Samuel Louis

**Eichelberger, Thomas W.** [PA]
*Author*
* Berger, Ike L.

**Eicher, [Ethel] Elizabeth** 20th c.
[CA]
*American author*
* Crane, Edna Temple [house
  pseudonym, Dell Publishing Co.
  Inc.]
* Paul, Emily
* Paul, William

**Eichhorn, Wilhelm** 20th c.   [FDG]
*Dutch-born director*
* Winar, Ernst

**Eichler, Ernst** 1932-   [IAW]
*Austrian poet and author*
* David, Ernst

**Eichner, Maura** 1915-   [CA]
*American poet*
* Maura, [Sister]

**Eichrodt, Fred[erick George]**
1903-1965   [BE]
*American baseball player*
* Eichrodt, Ike

**Eichrodt, Ike**
*See*  Eichrodt, Fred[erick George]

**Eichrodt, Ludwig** 1827-1892
[WBD]
*German poet and jurist*
* Rodt, Rudolf

**Eide, Edith** 20th c.   [WGT]
*Author*
* Tigrina

**Eiermann, Edward** 1894?-1971
[NOJ]
*American jazz musician*
* Eiermann, Lefty

**Eiermann, Lefty**
*See*  Eiermann, Edward

**[The] Eight**
*See*  Motassem, Al-

**Eiker, Mathilde** 1893-   [CC, WW]
*Author*
* Evermay, March

**Eikerenkoetter, Frederick J.**
1935?-   [B10]
*American evangelist*
* Reverend Ike

**Eilshemus, Louis Michael**
1864-1941   [SFL]
*Author*
* Elshemus, Louis M.

**Einem, Karl von** 1853-1934   [WBD]
*German army officer*
* Rothmaler, Karl von

**Einselen, Anne F.** 20th c.   [ANT]
*American author*
* Paterson, Anne

**Einstein, Harry** 1904-1958   [FC]
*American comedian*
* Parke, Harry
* Parkyakarkus

**[The] Einstein of Jazz**
*See*  Armstrong, [Daniel] Louis

**[Der] Einzige**
*See*  Richter, Jean Paul Friedrich

**Eirelin, Glenn**
*See*  Evans, Glen

**Eisbein, Adrienne** 1873-1951
[BBD]
*American opera singer*
* Osborne, Adrienne

**Eisele, Mark** 20th c.   [GW]
*American rodeo performer*
* Eisele, Stretch

**Eisele, Stretch**
*See*  Eisele, Mark

**Eisen, Carol G.**
*See*  Rinzler, Carol Eisen

**Eisenberg, Ben** 1916-   [ITA, WEF]
*American screenwriter*
* Roberts, Ben

**Eisenberg, Lawrence B[enjamin]** 20th
c.   [CA]
*American author*
* Dickens, Norman

**Eisendrath, Blanche Goodman** 1878-
?   [NAA]
*American writer*
* Goodman, Blanche

**Eisenhower, David Dwight**
1890-1969   [BBH, CND, FAP]
*American president and military
leader*
* Duckpin [code name used during
  World War II]
* Eisenhower, Dwight David
* General Ike
* Ike
* [The] Kansas Cyclone

**Eisenhower, Dwight David**
*See*  Eisenhower, David Dwight

**Eisenstat, Jane Sperry** 1920-   [CA]
*American author and illustrator*
* Sperry, J. E.

**Eisfeld, Rainer** 20th c.   [SFP]
*Author*
* Caine, Jeff
* Cooner, Wayne
* Reed, Allan
* Rohl, Wolf Detlef

**Eisler, Gerhard** 20th c.   [EE]
*German-born intelligence agent for
Russia*
* Berger, Hans
* Edwards

**Eisner, Betty** 1925-   [BEW]
*American dancer, singer, comedienne*
* Bruce, Betty

**Eisner, Betty Grover** 1915-   [CA]
*American psychologist, author,
lyricist*
* Rev. B

**Eisner, Simon**
*See*  Kornbluth, Cyril M.

**Eisner, Will[iam Erwin]** 1917-
[WECO]
*American cartoonist*
* Erwin, Will
* Rensie, Willis

**Eisumenger, Samuel** 1534-1585
[PA]
*Author*
* Siderocrates

**Eklund, Gordon** 1945-   [ESF]
*American author*
* Stewart, Wendall

**Eklund, Jane Mary**
*See*  Ball, Jane Eklund

**Ekwensi, C. O. D.**
*See*  Ekwensi, Cyprian [O. D.]

**Ekwensi, Cyprian [O. D.]** 1921-
[CA]
*Nigerian author*
* Ekwensi, C. O. D.

**El**
*See*     Second element of name for
further listings

**El Limac, Nassour**
*See*  Camille, Roussan

**El Melenas [The Long-Haired One]**
*See*  Rojas, Jose

**El Messidi, Kathy[anne] Groehn**
1946-   [CA]
*American writer*
* Cosseboom, Kathy Groehn

**El Michelle, Niccolaiih**
*See*  Flemming, Herb

**El Panzon [The Belly]**
*See*  Soto, Roberto

**El Shabazz, El-Hajj Malik**
*See*  Little, Malcolm

**El Shati, Bent**
*See*  Abdel-Rahmen, Aisha

**El y**
*See*  Asnyk, Adam

**Elaine**
*See*  Leverson, Ada

**Elam, Shelby S.** 1878- ?   [NAA]
*American writer and editor*
* Johnson, Ruie

**Elberfeld, Brownie**
*See*  Elberfeld, Norman Arthur

**Elberfeld, Kid**
*See*  Elberfeld, Norman Arthur

**Elberfeld, Norman Arthur**
1875-1944   [AS, BE, BN]
*American baseball player*
* Elberfeld, Brownie
* Elberfeld, Kid
* [The] Tabasco Kid

**Elbertus, [Fra]**
*See*  Hubbard, Elbert

**Elbogen, Paul** 1894-   [IAW]
*Austrian-born author*
* Schotte, Paulus

**Elbrown**
*See*  Thomas, Lillian

**Elclair, Mollie?**
*See*  Shaver, Richard S[harpe]

**[The] Elder**
*See*  Cato, Marcus Porcius

**[The] Elder**
*See*  Cyrus

**[The] Elder**
*See*  Edward [Eadward or
Eadweard]

**[The] Elder**
*See*  Justin I

**[The] Elder**
*See*  Medici, Lorenzo de

**[The] Elder**
*See*  Pepin

**[The] Elder**
*See*  Pliny [Gaius Plinius Secundus]

**[The] Elder**
*See*  Scipio Africanus, Publius
Cornelius

**[The] Elder**
*See*  Strozzi, Filippo

**[The] Elder**
*See*  Teniers, David

**Elder, Art**
*See*  Montgomery, Rutherford
George

**Elder, Evelyn**
*See*  Burge, Milward Rodon
Kennedy

**Elder, Heinie**
*See*  Elder, Henry Knox

**Elder, Henry Knox** 1890-   [BE]
*American baseball player*
* Elder, Heinie

**Elder, Leon**
*See*  Young, Noel

**Elder, Marc**
*See*  Tendron, Marcel

**[The] Elder Pitt**
*See*  Pitt, William [Earl of
Chatham]

**Elder Statesman Number One**
*See*  Baruch, Bernard Mannes

**[The] Elder Statesman of Jazz**
*See*  Carter, Bennett Lester

**Elder, Suicide**
*See*  Elder, Ted

**Elder, Susan Blanchard** 1835- ?
[FFF]
*American writer*
* Hermine

**Elder, Ted** 20th c.   [GW]
*American rodeo performer*
* Elder, Suicide

**Elderise, Phil**
*See*  Alderisio, Felix Anthony

**Eldershaw, Flora Sydney Patricia**
1897-   [SFL, WGT]
*Author*
* Eldershaw, M. Barnard [joint
  pseudonym with Marjorie Faith
  Barnard]

**Eldershaw, M. Barnard** [joint
pseudonym with Marjorie Faith
Barnard]
*See*  Barnard, Marjorie Faith

**Eldershaw, M. Barnard** [joint
pseudonym with Marjorie Faith
Barnard]
*See*  Eldershaw, Flora Sydney
Patricia

**[The] Eldest Son of the Church**
*See*  Clovis I

**Eldon, Cleo**
*See*  Wilcox, Don

**Eldon, Earl of**
*See*  Scott, John

**Eldred, Brian**
*See*  Bradbury, Ray [Douglas]

**Eldridge, Florence**
*See*  McKechnie, Florence

**Eldridge, Jeremiah Dennis**
1859-1927 [AS, BE]
*American baseball player*
* Denny, Jerry

**Eldridge, Little Jazz**
See Eldridge, [David] Roy

**Eldridge, [David] Roy** 1911-
[DAM, EJ, PMJ]
*American jazz musician*
* Eldridge, Little Jazz
* Elliott, Roy

**Eleanor, [Mother]**
See Brosnahan, Katherine Mary

**Eleanor** ?-1241 [DNNS, HN, RH]
*Niece of King John of England*
* [La] Belle Bretonne
* [The] Damsel of Brittany
* [The] Maid of Brittany
* [The] Pearl of Brittany

**Electric Charlie Wilson**
See Wilson, Charles Edward

**Electric Heels**
See Constantine, Learie Nicholas

**Elegant Arthur**
See Arthur, Chester Alan

**Elen, Ernest Augustus** 1862- ?
[THR]
*British entertainer*
* Elen, Gus

**Elen, Gus**
See Elen, Ernest Augustus

**[The] Elephant Man**
See Merrick, John

**Eleuter**
See Iwaszkiewicz, Jaroslaw

**[The] Eleven Thousand Dollar Beauty**
See Marquard, Richard William

**[The] Eleven Thousand Dollar Lemon**
See Marquard, Richard William

**[The] Eleven Thousand Dollar Wonder**
See Marquard, Richard William

**[The] Elf**
See McDonald, Tommy

**Elgar, Avril**
See Williams, Avril

**Elia**
See Lamb, Charles

**Eliacin**
See Hervieu, Paul Ernest

**Eliades, David** 20th c. [SFL]
*Author*
* Forrest, David [joint pseudonym with Robert Forrest-Webb]

**Elias, Eileen**
See Davies, Eileen Winifred

**[The] Elias of Guatemala**
See Victoria, Tomas

**Eliav, Arie L[ova]** 1921- [CA]
*Israeli government official and author*
* Ben Ami

**Elie, Abel** 1841-1876 [CW]
*Haitian poet*
* Franck

**Elies i Bracons, Feliu** 1878-1948
[WEC]
*Spanish cartoonist*
* Apa

**Elik, Bo**
See Elik, Boris

**Elik, Boris** 1929- [CEI]
*Canadian-born hockey player*
* Elik, Bo

**Elin Pelin**
See Jotov, Dimitur Ivanov

**Eline, Marie** [FIR]
*American actress*
* [The] Thanhouser Kid

**Eliot, Alice**
See Jewett, Sarah Orne

**Eliot, Anne**
See Cole, Lois Dwight

**Eliot, Annie M. D.** [FFF]
*American writer*
* Eliot, Max

**Eliot, G. F.** [SFP]
*Author*
* Scanlon, C. K. M.

**Eliot, George**
See Evans, Marian

**Eliot, Henry Ware** 1879- ? [WW]
*Author*
* Deal, Mason

**Eliot, John** 1604-1690
[DEP, DNNS, SN]
*British-born missionary*
* [The] Apostle of the Indians
* [The] Indian Apostle

**Eliot, Marvin** 1926- [CA]
*American weather broadcaster*
* Eliot, Sonny

**Eliot, Max**
See Eliot, Annie M. D.

**Eliot, Sonny**
See Eliot, Marvin

**Eliot, T. S.**
See Eliot, Thomas Stearns

**Eliot, Thomas Stearns** 1888-1965
[CA]
*American-born British poet and playwright*
* Aged Eagle
* Conybeare, Charles Augustus
* Deliberate Pedant
* Eliot, T. S.
* Grimble, [Reverend] Charles James
* Krutzch, Gus
* Old Possum
* Schwartz, Muriel A.
* Spence, J. A. D.
* Trundlett, Helen B.

**Eliott, E. C.**
See Martin, Reginald Alec

**Elis, Islwyn Ffowc**
See Ellis, Islwyn Foulkes

**Elisa**
See Voiart, Anne E. Petitpain

**Elisabeth Katharina Christine**
1718-1746 [WBD]
*Regent of Russia during reign of her infant son*
* Anna Karlovna

**Elisabeth Katharina Christine**
(Continued)
* Anna Leopoldovna

**Eliza**
See Carter, Elizabeth

**Eliza**
See Nicholson, Eliza Jane Poitevent

**Elizabeth**
See Beauchamp, Mary Annette

**Elizabeth**
See Russell, Elizabeth Mary

**Elizabeth** 1207-1231 [FFF]
*Saint*
* [The] Patron Saint of Queens

**Elizabeth** 1465-1503 [HN]
*Wife of King Henry VII of England*
* [The] Rose of York
* [The] White Rose

**Elizabeth** 1596-1662
[DEP, HN, RH]
*Queen of Bohemia*
* Palsgrave, Goody
* [The] Queen of Hearts
* [The] Snow Queen
* [The] Winter Queen

**Elizabeth, [Queen]** 1843-1916
[LC, WBD]
*Queen of Rumania and author*
* Dito und Idem [joint pseudonym with Marie Kremnitz]
* Sylva, Carmen

**Elizabeth Petrovna** 1709-1762
[DNNS, FFF, SN]
*Empress of Russia*
* [La] Catin du Nord
* [La] Clemente
* [L']Infame Catin du Nord
* [The] Infamous
* [The] Northern Harlot

**Elizabeth I** 1533-1603
[DEP, RH, SN]
*Queen of England*
* Bloody Queen Bess
* [The] English Diana
* Fortune's Empress
* Gloriana
* Good Queen Bess
* [The] Maiden Queen
* Nature's Glory
* Oriana
* Queen Bess
* [The] Queen of Shepherds
* [The] Queen of the Northern Seas
* [The] Queen of Virgins
* [The] Virgin Queen
* [The] World's Wonder

**Elkan, Sophie** 1853-1921 [WBD]
*Swedish author*
* Roest, Rust

**Elkins, Edward B.** 1880?-1945
[BEW]
*American actor*
* Fielding, Edward

**Elkins, Elk**
See Elkins, Lawrence C.

**Elkins, Ella Ruth** 1929- [CA]
*American educator and author*
* Beddoe, Ellaruth
* Wren, Ellaruth

**Elkins, Lawrence C.** 1943- [FB]
*American football player*
* Elkins, Elk

**Elko, Peter** 1918- [BE]
*American baseball player*
* Elko, Piccolo Pete

**Elko, Piccolo Pete**
See Elko, Peter

**Elkon, Juliette**
See Elkon-Hamelecourt, Juliette

**Elkon-Hamelecourt, Juliette** 1912-
[CA]
*Belgian-born author*
* Elkon, Juliette

**Ellacott, S. E.**
See Ellacott, Samuel Ernest

**Ellacott, Samuel Ernest** 1911-
[WYA]
*Author*
* Ellacott, S. E.

**Ellam, Roy** 1886-1948 [BE]
*American baseball player*
* Ellam, Slippery
* Ellam, Whitey

**Ellam, Slippery**
See Ellam, Roy

**Ellam, Whitey**
See Ellam, Roy

**Ellanbee, Boyd** [joint pseudonym with William C(louser) Boyd]
See Boyd, Lyle G[ifford]

**Ellanbee, Boyd** [joint pseudonym with Lyle G(ifford) Boyd]
See Boyd, William C[louser]

**Ellanby, Boyd** [joint pseudonym with William C(louser) Boyd]
See Boyd, Lyle G[ifford]

**Ellanby, Boyd** [joint pseudonym with Lyle G(ifford) Boyd]
See Boyd, William C[louser]

**Ellen**
See Nichols, Rebecca S. Reed

**Ellen, Henry**
See Hope, James Barron

**Ellen Louise**
See Moulton, Ellen Louise Chandler

**Ellen, Robert**
See Shad, Bob

**Ellenby, Rose** [ART]
*British painter and illustrator*
* Carruthers, Rose

**Ellenwood, Henry S.** [FFF]
* [The] Cape Cod Bard

**Eller, Carl** 1942- [FB]
*American football player*
* Eller, Moose

**Eller, Hod**
See Eller, Horace Owen

**Eller, Horace Owen** 1894-1961
[AS, BE]
*American baseball player*
* Eller, Hod

**Eller, Moose**
See Eller, Carl

**Ellerbe, Francis Rogers** 1895-   [BE]
*American baseball player*
* Ellerbe, Governor

**Ellerbe, Governor**
See  Ellerbe, Francis Rogers

**Ellerbeck, Rosemary** 20th c.
*Author*
* L'Estrange, Anna

**Ellerman, Annie Winifred** 1894-
[LC]
*British author*
* Bryher, Winifred

**Ellerman, Gene**
See  Wells, Basil

**Ellerre**
See  Russi, Luciano

**Ellers, Marjii**
See  Ellersieck, Marjorie

**Ellersieck, Marjorie**   [SFP]
*Author*
* Ellers, Marjii

**Ellerthorpe, John**   [SN]
*British workman*
* [The] Hero of the Humber

**Ellet, Charles** 1810-1862   [WBD]
*American engineer*
* [The] Brunel of America

**Ellett, Harold Pincton** 1882-   [WW]
*Author*
* Burnaby, Nigel

**Ellice, Edward** 1786?-1863   [SN]
*British politician*
* [The] Nestor of the House of
Commons

**Ellice, Lucy**
See  Moriarty, Ellen

**Ellik, Ron[ald C.]** 1938-1968
[ESF, WGT]
*American author*
* Davies, Fredric [joint pseudonym
with Steve Tolliver]

**Ellin, E. M.**
See  Ellin, Elizabeth Muriel

**Ellin, Elizabeth Muriel** 1905-
[TCC]
*New Zealand author*
* Ellin, E. M.

**Ellingford, Herbert Frederick** 20th
c.   [LAO]
*British musician, composer, author*
* Winter, Herbert

**Ellingsen, H. Bruce** 1949-   [SMG]
*American baseball player*
* Ellingsen, Little Pod

**Ellingsen, Little Pod**
See  Ellingsen, H. Bruce

**Ellington, Duke**
See  Ellington, Edward Kennedy

**Ellington, Edward Kennedy**
1899-1974   [ASC, BBD, CA]
*American jazz musician*
* [The] Aristocrat of Swing
* [The] Duke
* Ellington, Duke
* [The] King of Jazz

**Elliot, Bump**
See  Elliot, Chalmers W.

**Elliot, C. S.**
See  Sellers, Connie Leslie, Jr.

**Elliot, Chalmers W.** 1925-   [FB]
*American football coach*
* Elliot, Bump

**Elliot, Daniel**
See  Feldman, Leonard

**Elliot, Edith**
See  Howard, Anna H. C.

**Elliot, Frank** 20th c.   [BLB]
*American bank robber*
* Elliot, Peg Leg

**Elliot, Gangster**
See  Elliot, Jimmy

**Elliot, Geraldine**
See  Bingham, Evangeline
M[arguerite] L[adys] [Elliot]

**Elliot, Ian** 1925-   [CA]
*American author*
* Davies, Colin

**Elliot, James F.** 1915-1981   [TF]
*American track coach*
* Elliot, Jumbo

**Elliot, Jimmy** 20th c.
*American football player*
* Elliot, Gangster

**Elliot, Jumbo**
See  Elliot, James F.

**Elliot, Lee** [house pseudonym, Curtis
Warren]
See  Bird, William Henry Fleming

**Elliot, Lee** [house pseudonym, Curtis
Warren]
See  Hughes, Den[n]is [Talbot]

**Elliot, Madge**
See  Eytinge, Margaret

**Elliot, Peg Leg**
See  Elliot, Frank

**Elliot, Ruth**
See  Peck, Lillie

**Elliott, Ace**
See  Elliott, Allen Clifford

**Elliott, Ace**
See  Elliott, Harold William [Hal]

**Elliott, Allen Clifford** 1897-   [BE]
*American baseball player*
* Elliott, Ace

**Elliott, Alonzo** 1891-1964
[ASC, BEW, DAM]
*American composer and lyricist*
* Elliott, Zo

**Elliott, Bruce** [Walter Gardner Lively
Stacy] 1915?-1973   [CA, SFP]
*American publisher, editor, author*
* Grant, Maxwell [house
pseudonym]
* Lively, Walter
* Stacy, Bruce
* Stacy, Walter

**Elliott, Buck**
See  Adnopoz, Elliott Charles

**Elliott, C. W.**   [PA]
*Author*
* Whyte, [Mr.] Thomas

**Elliott, Cass[andra]**
See  Cohen, Ellen Naomi

**Elliott, Chaucer**
See  Elliott, Edwin S.

**Elliott, Chip**
See  Elliott, Escalus Emmert, III

**Elliott, Don**
See  Helfman, Donald Elliott

**Elliott, Don**
See  Silverberg, Robert

**Elliott, Ebenezer** 1781-1849
[DNNS, FFF, HN]
*British poet*
* [The] Corn Law Rhymer

**Elliott, Edwin S.** 1879-1913   [HK]
*Canadian hockey referee*
* Elliott, Chaucer

**Elliott, Elinor**
See  Sargent, Ella S.

**Elliott, Ernest** 1898?-   [WWJ]
*American jazz musician*
* Elliott, Sticky

**Elliott, Escalus Emmert, III** 1945-
[CA]
*American author*
* Elliott, Chip

**Elliott, G. R.**
See  Elliott, George Roy

**Elliott, George Henry** 1884-1962
[BMH, THR]
*British entertainer*
* [The] Chocolate Coloured Coon

**Elliott, George Roy** 1883-   [WWL]
*American author*
* Elliott, G. R.

**Elliott, Gertrude**
See  Dermot, Gertrude

**Elliott, [Herbert] Glenn** 1919-1969
[BE]
*American baseball player*
* Elliott, Lefty

**Elliott, Gordon** 1906-1965
[F2, FC]
*American actor*
* Elliott, Wild Bill
* Elliott, William

**Elliott, Graham**
See  Cowles, Frederick I.

**Elliott, Harold H.** 1890-1934   [BE]
*American baseball player*
* Elliott, Rowdy

**Elliott, Harold William [Hal]**
1899-1963   [BE]
*American baseball player*
* Elliott, Ace

**Elliott, J. J.**   [FFF]
*American writer*
* Vidette

**Elliott, Jack**
See  Adnopoz, Elliott Charles

**Elliott, James Thomas** 1900-1970
[AS, BE]
*American baseball player*
* Elliott, Jumbo Jim

**Elliott, John B.** 1907-   [ASC]
*American composer and recording
executive*
* Moon, Jack

**Elliott, Jumbo Jim**
See  Elliott, James Thomas

**Elliott, Lefty**
See  Elliott, [Herbert] Glenn

**Elliott, Lesley** 1905-   [CA]
*British author*
* Gordon, Lesley,

**Elliott, Malissa Childs** 1929?-1979
[CA]
*American author and editor*
* Redfield, Malissa

**Elliott, Maud Howe** 1854- ?
[NAA]
*American author and lecturer*
* Howe, Maud

**Elliott, Maxine**
See  Dermot, Jessie

**Elliott, Milton** 1896-1920   [SC]
*American actor and stunt performer*
* Elliott, Skeets

**Elliott, Ramblin' Jack**
See  Adnopoz, Elliott Charles

**Elliott, Robert**
See  Garfinkel, Bernard

**Elliott, Rowdy**
See  Elliott, Harold H.

**Elliott, Roy**
See  Eldridge, [David] Roy

**Elliott, Sam** 1912?-   [BBH]
*American softball player*
* Elliott, Sambo

**Elliott, Sambo**
See  Elliott, Sam

**Elliott, Seamus** 1934-1971   [OCS]
*Irish cyclist*
* Elliott, Shay

**Elliott, Shay**
See  Elliott, Seamus

**Elliott, Skeets**
See  Elliott, Milton

**Elliott, Sticky**
See  Elliott, Ernest

**Elliott, Sumner Locke** 1917-   [CA]
*Australian-born American actor,
author, playwright*
* Locke-Elliott, Sumner

**Elliott, Wild Bill**
See  Elliott, Gordon

**Elliott, William**
See  Bradbury, Ray [Douglas]

**Elliott, William**
See  D'Autremont, Roy

**Elliott, William**
See  Elliott, Gordon

**Elliott, William** 1788-1863
[FFF, PA]
*American author*
* Agricola
* Fiesco

**Elliott, Zo**
See  Elliott, Alonzo

**Elliott-Cannon, Arthur Elliott**
1919-   [AW]
*British author*
* Forde, Nicholas
* Martyn, Myles

**Ellis, Alex** 20th c.   [MEB]
*American basketball player*
* Ellis, Boo

**Ellis, Allan Delon** 1951-   [SMG]
*American football player*
* Ellis, Fast

**Ellis, Audrey**
*See*   Gelhar, Audrey Pearl Alford

**Ellis, Big Boy**
*See*   Ellis, Wilbert Thirkield

**Ellis, Big Chief**
*See*   Ellis, Wilbert Thirkield

**Ellis, Boo**
*See*   Ellis, Alex

**Ellis, Craig** [house pseudonym]
*See*   Rogow, Lee

**Ellis, Craig** [house pseudonym]
*See*   Vern, David

**Ellis, Dellie Madeline [or Magdalen?]**
1926?-   [BEW, FC]
*American actress*
* Lorring, Joan

**Ellis, Dick**
*See*   Blackwell, Richard

**Ellis, Dick**
*See*   Elsenpeter, Richard William

**Ellis, Dock Phillip, Jr.** 1945-   [IBW]
*American baseball player*
* [The] Ali of Baseball

**Ellis, E. T.** 1893-   [WWL]
*British author*
* [A] Book Collector
* Bookworm
* F. R. H. S.

**Ellis, Edward S[ylvester]**
1840-1916   [YAB]
*American author*
* Belknap, B. H.
* Bethune, J. G.
* Carleton, [Captain] L. C.
* Gordon, [Colonel] H. R.
* Hawthorne, [Captain] R. M.
* Jayne, [Lieutenant] R. H.
* Lassalle, C. E.
* Lisle, Seward D.
* Muller, Billex
* Randolph, [Lieutenant] J. H.
* Robins, Seelin
* Rodman, Emerson
* Wheeler, Captain

**Ellis, Elmo I[srael]**
*See*   Israel, Elmo

**Ellis, Fast**
*See*   Ellis, Allan Delon

**Ellis, Florence Hawley** 1906-   [CA]
*American anthropologist and author*
* Hawley, Florence M.
* Senter, Florence H.

**Ellis, George** 1745-1815   [DEL, PA]
*British author*
* Gander, [Sir] Gregory

**Ellis, George William** 1885-1938
[BE]
*American baseball player*
* Ellis, Rube

**Ellis, Glyn Geoffrey** 1945-   [PRS]
*British singer*
* Fontana, Wayne

**Ellis, Gracie** 1875?-1950   [BEW]
*Actress*
* Leigh, Gracie

**Ellis, Hilda Roderick**
*See*   Davidson, Hilda Roderick Ellis

**Ellis, Islwyn Foulkes** 1924-   [CA]
*Welsh author*
* Elis, Islwyn Ffowc

**Ellis, John**
*See*   McKibbon, J. E.

**Ellis, Julian**
*See*   O'Mahony, C. K.

**Ellis, Killer**
*See*   Ellis, Tommy

**Ellis, Landon**
*See*   Ellison, Harlan [Jay]

**Ellis, Louise**
*See*   Walker, Emily Kathleen

**Ellis, Luke**
*See*   Hopps, John Page

**Ellis, Mary**
*See*   Elsas, Mary

**Ellis, Michael**
*See*   Abrahamson, Mayer Ellis

**Ellis, Molly** 1908-   [FC]
*British actress*
* Napier, Diana

**Ellis, Mrs.** 1812- ?   [PA]
*Author*
* Stickney, Sarah

**Ellis, Oliver C. De C.** 1889-   [AW]
*British author and poet*
* Briony, Henry

**Ellis, Olivia**
*See*   Wintle, Anne

**Ellis, Patricia**
*See*   O'Brien, Patria Gene

**Ellis, Peter Berresford** 1943-
[CA, IAW]
*British author*
* Tremayne, Peter

**Ellis, R. S.**   [PA]
*Author*
* Anglicanus

**Ellis, Royston**
*See*   Christopher Royston, George
Ellis

**Ellis, Rube**
*See*   Ellis, George William

**Ellis, Toby**
*See*   Elsenpeter, Richard William

**Ellis, Tommy** 20th c.   [RBE]
*American boxer*
* Ellis, Killer

**Ellis, Vep**
*See*   Ellis, Vesphew Benton

**Ellis, Vesphew Benton** 1917-
*American clergyman and songwriter*
* Ellis, Vep

**Ellis, Welbore** 18th c.   [HN]
*British politician*
* Grildig
* [The] Manikin

**Ellis, Wilbert Thirkield** 1914-1977
[BWW]
*American singer*
* Ellis, Big Boy
* Ellis, Big Chief

**Ellis, William Donohue** 1918-
[IAW]
*American author*
* Garth, Jackson

**Ellis-Morris, Esther** 20th c.
[WWL]
*British author*
* Estelle

**Ellison, Babe**
*See*   Ellison, Herbert Spencer

**Ellison, Biff**
*See*   Ellison, James

**Ellison, Ellis**
*See*   Snell, E. L.

**Ellison, Glenn** 1911-   [CA]
*American football coach and author*
* Ellison, Tiger

**Ellison, Harlan [Jay]** 1934-
[ESF, WGT]
*American author*
* Archer, Lee [house pseudonym,
   Ziff-Davis]
* Beldon, Phil Cheech
* Bird, C[ordwainer]
* Charby, Jay
* Courtney, Robert
* Curtis, Price
* Doyle, John
* Edmondson, Wallace
* Ellis, Landon
* Ellson, Hal?
* Harson, Sley [joint pseudonym
   with Henry Slesar]
* Hart, Ellis
* Jarvis, E. K. [house pseudonym,
   Ziff-Davis]
* Jorgensen, Ivar [house
   pseudonym, Ziff-Davis]
* Maddern, Al
* Magnus, John
* Merchant, Paul
* Mitchell, Clyde [house
   pseudonym, Ziff-Davis]
* Nosille, Nalrah
* Parker, Bert
* Robertson, Ellis [joint pseudonym
   with Robert Silverberg]
* Roeder, Pat
* Solo, Jay
* Tiger, Derry

**Ellison, Herbert Spencer**
1896-1955   [BE]
*American baseball player*
* Ellison, Babe

**Ellison, James**
*See*   Smith, James Ellison

**Ellison, James** 20th c.   [PHM]
*Irish-born American underworld
figure*
* Ellison, Biff

**Ellison, James E.** 1927-   [CA]
*American author*
* Flavius, [Brother]

**Ellison, Jerome** 1907-   [CA]
*American author*
* Emorey, N.

**Ellison, Joan Audrey [Anderson]**
1928-   [AW, WD]
*British writer*
* Robertson, Elspeth

**Ellison, Tiger**
*See*   Ellison, Glenn

**Ellison, Virginia Howell** 1910-
[CA, SAT, WD]
*American author*
* Howell, Virginia Tier
* Leong, Gor Yun
* Mapes, Mary A.
* Mussey, Virginia T. H.
* Soskin, V. H.

**Elliston, Grace**
*See*   Rutter, Grace

**Elliston, Robert William**
1774-1831   [DEP, FFF, RH]
*British actor*
* [The] Napoleon of the Drama

**Elliston, Valerie Mae [Watkinson]**
1929-   [CA]
*Australian author*
* Watkinson, Valerie

**Ellsen, Ellis**
*See*   Snell, E. L.

**Ellsler, Effie**
*See*   Ellsler, Euphemia Murray

**Ellsler, Euphemia Murray**
1823-1918   [BEW]
*American actress*
* Ellsler, Effie

**Ellson, Hal?**
*See*   Ellison, Harlan [Jay]

**Ellsworth**
*See*   Wadman, Elmer E.

**Ellsworth, Elmer, Jr.**
*See*   Thayer, Tiffany Ellsworth

**Ellsworth, Henry Leavitt**
1791-1858   [WBD]
*American government official*
* [The] Father of the Department
   of Agriculture

**Ellsworth, O.**   [PA]
*Author*
* Thistle, Timothy

**Ellsworth, Paul**
*See*   Triem, Paul Ellsworth

**Ellsworth, Sallie Bingham** 1937-
[CA]
*American author*
* Bingham, Sallie

**Ellwood, Ella**
*See*   Shade, Ellen

**Ellwood, Gracia-Fay** 1938-   [CA]
*American author*
* Linwood, Lucy-Anne

**Ellwood, Marjorie Barker** 1904-
[NAA]
*Canadian writer*
* Dorman, Kathleen

**Elmakyn, George** 1223-1273   [PA]
*Author*
* Ibn-Abid

**Elman, Harry**
*See*   Finkelman, Harry

**Elman, Richard** 1934-   [CA]
*American writer and poet*
* Pearl, Eric

**Elman, Ziggy**
*See*   Finkelman, Harry

**Elmer, Billy**
*See*   Johns, William E.

**Elmer, Doc**
See Elmer, Raymond S.

**Elmer, Raymond S.** ?-1947 [BBH]
*American skiing official and organization founder*
* Elmer, Doc

**Elmer, Robert P.** 1877- ? [NAA]
*American physician and author*
* Christopher, [Dr.] T. Hudson

**Elmer the Great**
See Beck, Walter William

**Elmer the Great**
See McDuffie, Terris

**Elmo**
See Handford, Thomas W.

**Elmore, Bruce**
See Kennedy, Alfred G.

**Elmore, Carol**
See Lucy, Thomas Elmore

**Elmore, Emily W.**
See Greeley, Emily Elmore

**Elmwood, Eluathan, Esq.**
See Green, Assa

**Eloi [or Eligius]** 588- 659 [HN]
*Saint*
* [The] Patron Saint of Smiths and Artists

**[The] Eloquent Doctor**
See Aureolus, Peter

**Elorde, Flash**
See Elorde, Gabriel

**Elorde, Gabriel** 1935- [BX, RBE]
*Filipino boxer*
* Elorde, Flash

**Elorrieta, Jose Maria** 1922?-1974 [WF]
*Spanish director*
* Lacy, Joe

**Elphick, Jeanette** 1935- [FC]
*Australian actress*
* Shaw, Victoria

**Elphinstone, Francis**
See Powell-Smith, Vincent [Walter Francis]

**Elphinstone, Murgatroyd**
See Kahler, Hugh [Torbert] MacNair

**Elpidon**
See Balucki, Michal

**Elron**
See Hubbard, Lafayette Ronald

**Elroy, Mrs. Edwin** [FFF]
*Entertainer*
* Brent, Marion

**Elsas, Mary** 1900- [BEW, EMT, FC]
*American actress and singer*
* Ellis, Mary

**Elsasser, Pauline** 1862- ? [FFF]
*American opera singer*
* L'Allemand, Pauline

**Elsenpeter, Richard William** 1927- [CWG]
*American country-western performer*
* Ellis, Dick
* Ellis, Toby

**Elsensohn, Edith M.** 1897- [CAT]
*American author*
* Mary Alfreda, [Sister]

**Elsheimer, Adam** 1578-1610 [WBD]
*German painter and etcher*
* [Il] Tedesco

**Elshemus, Louis M.**
See Eilshemus, Louis Michael

**Elsie, Lily**
See Cotton, Lily Elsie

**Elskwatawa**
See Lalawethika

**Elsna, Hebe**
See Ansle, Dorothy Phoebe

**Elsom, Isobel**
See Reed, Isabella

**Elson, Anita**
See Edelsten, Anita

**Elson, R. N.**
See Nelson, Radell Faraday

**Elspeth**
See Bragdon, Elspeth [MacDuffie]

**Elsschot, Willem**
See De Ridder, Alfons

**Elstar, Dow**
See Gallun, Raymond Z[inke]

**Elston, Natalie** 1940?- [BWW]
*American singer*
* Lamb, Natalie

**Elting, Mary** 1906- [CA, MJA, SAT]
*American author*
* Brewster, Benjamin [joint pseudonym with Franklin (Brewster) Folsom]
* Cole, Davis
* Gorham, Michael [joint pseudonym with Franklin (Brewster) Folsom]
* Tatham, Campbell

**Eltinge, Julian**
See Dalton, William Julian

**Elton, G[eoffrey] R[udolph]**
See Ehrenberg, Geoffrey Rudolph

**Elton, John**
See Marsh, John

**Elton, Max**
See Fearn, John Russell

**Eluard, Paul**
See Grindel, Eugene

**Elvestad, Sven** 1884-1934 [WBD]
*Norwegian author*
* Riverton, Stein

**Elvey, Maurice**
See Folkard, William Seward

**Elvin, Anne Katharine Stevenson** 1933- [CA]
*British-born poet*
* Stevenson, Anne

**Elvin, Drake**
See Beha, Ernest

**Elvin, Joe**
See Keegan, Joe

**Elvin, Little**
See Keegan, Joe

**Elvis the Pelvis**
See Presley, Elvis Aaron

**Elward, James [Joseph]** 1928- [CA]
*American author and playwright*
* James, R.

**Ely, Bones**
See Ely, Frederick William

**Ely, Bones**
See Marion, Martin Whiteford

**Ely, David**
See Lilienthal, David E.

**Ely, Frederick William** 1863-1952 [AS, BE]
*American baseball player*
* Ely, Bones

**Ely, George Herbert** 1866-1958 [LC]
*Author*
* Strang, Herbert [joint pseudonym with Charles James L'Estrange]

**Ely, Ron**
See Pierce, Ronald

**Ely, the Carpenter's Son**
See Hall, Ellis

**Elysio, Filinto**
See Nascimento, Francisco Manoel do

**Elytis, Odysseus**
See Alepoudelis, Odysseus

**Elzinga, Kenneth G[erald]** 1941- [CA]
*American author*
* Jevons, Marshall [joint pseudonym with William (Leo) Breit]

**[The] Emancipator of the Platter**
See Jacobs, Hirsch

**Emanuel, V. R.**
See Emanuel, Victor Rousseau

**Emanuel, Victor Rousseau** 1879-1951 [SF, WGT]
*British-born American author*
* Egbert, H. M.
* Emanuel, V. R.
* Rousseau, Victor
* Trent, Clive?

**Emanuel, Walter Lewis** 1869-1915 [WWL]
*British author*
* Charivaria

**Emanuel I [Manuel or Manoel]** 1469-1521 [DNNS, SN, WBD]
*King of Portugal*
* [The] Fortunate
* [The] Great
* [The] Happy
* [The] Portuguese Maecenas of Arts and Sciences

**[The] Emathian Conqueror**
See Alexander III

**Embey, Philip**
See Philipp, Elliot Elias

**Emblen, Donald Lewis** 1918- [CA]
*American educator and author*
* Reynolds, Bart

**Embree, Charles, Jr.** 1919- [ASC]
*American composer and music publisher*
* Charles, Riff

**Embree, Charles Willard** 1917- [BE]
*American baseball player*
* Embree, Red

**Embree, Red**
See Embree, Charles Willard

**Embro, Gump**
See Embro, Raymond

**Embro, Raymond** 1939- [SMG]
*Hockey team trainer*
* Embro, Gump

**Embry, Cap**
See Embry, William R.

**Embry, Charles Akin** 1901-1947 [BE]
*American baseball player*
* Embry, Slim

**Embry, Slim**
See Embry, Charles Akin

**Embry, William R.** 1878- ? [IBW]
*American baseball player and official*
* Embry, Cap

**Emburey, Embers**
See Emburey, John Ernest [Ernie]

**Emburey, John Ernest [Ernie]** 1952- [DC]
*British cricketer*
* Emburey, Embers

**Embury, Emma Catherine Manley** 1806?-1863 [DEL, FFF]
*American author*
* Ianthe

**Emeff**
See Flagg, Mary

**Emel**
See Lane, Mary Louisa

**Emerson**
See Tennent, [Sir] James Emerson

**Emerson, Alice B.**
See Creager, Eunice Whayne

**Emerson, Alice B.** [house pseudonym] [Stratemeyer Syndicate]
See Stratemeyer, Edward L.

**Emerson, Anne** 1816- ? [PA]
*Author*
* Uncle Jerry

**Emerson, Chester Arthur** 1889-1971 [BE]
*American baseball player*
* Emerson, Chuck

**Emerson, Chuck**
See Emerson, Chester Arthur

**Emerson, Eddie K.** 1892- [BBH, CFH]
*American football player*
* [The] Iron Man

**Emerson, Henry Oliver** 1893- [CAP]
*British author*
* Gordon, Oliver

**Emerson, John**
See Paden, Clifton

**Emerson, Marion Winslow** 1886- [NAA]
*American journalist*
* Burncoat, Nancy

**Emerson, Mary Lee**
See   Kennedy, Mary

**Emerson, Pee Wee**
See   Emerson, Robert

**Emerson, Ralph Waldo** 1803-1882
[DNNF, FF, RH]
*American author and poet*
* [The] American Montaigne
* [The] Sage of Concord

**Emerson, Robert** 20th c.   [RBE]
*American boxer*
* Emerson, Pee Wee

**Emerson, Ronald**
See   Scotland, James

**Emerson, William Robert** 1929-
[BWW, NBB]
*American singer*
* Billy the Kid
* [The] Kid

**Emerton, Hugh Fitzray** 1892-1944
[BEW]
*British-born actor*
* Emerton, Roy

**Emerton, Roy**
See   Emerton, Hugh Fitzray

**Emery, Gilbert**
See   Pottle, Gilbert Emery Bensley

**Emery, Herrick Smith** 1898-   [BE]
*American baseball player*
* Emery, Spoke

**Emery, Spoke**
See   Emery, Herrick Smith

**Emilia**
See   Vinning, Pamelia S.

**Emin Pasha, Mehmed**
See   Schnitzer, Eduard

**[L']Eminence Grise**
See   Leclerc du Tremblay, Francois

**[L']Eminence Rouge**
See   Du Plessis, Armand Jean

**Emm, Andrew** 1886?-1938   [BEW]
*Producer, director, actor, playwright*
* Melville, Andrew

**Emma** ?-1052   [HN, RH, WBD]
*Daughter of Richard I, Duke of Normandy*
* Aelfgifu
* [The] Gem of Normandy
* [The] Pearl of Normandy

**Emma** 12th c.   [RH]
*Wife of David, King of North Wales*
* [The] Saxon

**Emmanuel**
See   Anati, Emmanuel

**Emmanuel, Pierre**
See   Mathieu, Noel

**Emmbe**
See   Berte, Marie

**Emmerich [or Emmerick], Anna Katharina** 1774-1824   [WBD]
*German nun*
* [The] Nun of Duelmen

**Emmerich, Slim**
See   Emmerich, William Peter

**Emmerich, William Peter** 1919-
[BE]
*American baseball player*
* Emmerich, Slim

**Emmerson, Beaver Felt**
See   Emmerson, Bruce

**Emmerson, Bruce** 20th c.   [GW]
*American rodeo performer*
* Emmerson, Beaver Felt

**Emmett, Mrs. Charles E.**   [FFF]
*Entertainer*
* Placide, Alice
* Sydell, Rose

**Emmons, Elise**
See   Emmons, Elizabeth Wales

**Emmons, Elizabeth Wales** 1867- ?
[WWL]
*British author*
* Emmons, Elise

**Emmrich, Curt [or Kurt]**
1897-1975   [CAP, EWL]
*German author and critic*
* Bamm, Peter

**Emms, Hap [or Happy]**
See   Emms, Leighton

**Emms, Leighton** 1905-
[CEI, HK, SMG]
*Canadian-born hockey player*
* Emms, Hap [or Happy]

**Emmwood**
See   Musgrave-Wood, John

**Emo, E. W.**
See   Wojtek, Emerich Josef

**Emorey, N.**
See   Ellison, Jerome

**Emory, Alan [Steuer]**
See   Epstein, Alan [Steuer]

**[El] Empecinado**
See   Diaz, Juan Martin

**[El] Emperador [The Emperor]**
See   Alfonso VII [Alphonso or Alonso]

**[The] Emperor of Believers**
See   Omar I

**[The] Emperor of Bowlers**
See   Shaw, Alfred

**[The] Emperor of Elba**
See   Bonaparte, Napoleon

**[The] Emperor of the German Kingdoms**
See   William I [Wilhelm Friedrich Ludwig]

**[The] Emperor of the Mountains**
See   Peter

**[The] Emperor of the West**
See   Murray, John

**[El] Emplazado**
See   Ferdinand IV

**Employee X**
See   Fautsko, Timothy F[rank]

**[The] Empress**
See   Jiang Qing

**Empress of India**
See   Victoria

**[The] Empress of the Blues**
See   Smith, Bessie

**Empty Barrel**
See   Hancock, John

**Empty Face**
See   Mubarak, Hosni

**Empy, Cleo** 1897?-1954   [BEW]
*Actress*
* Mayfield, Cleo

**Emrich, Duncan [Black Macdonald]**
1908-   [CA, SAT]
*American author and folklorist*
* Macdonald, Blackie

**Emsh**
See   Emshwiller, Ed[mund Alexander]

**Emshwiller, Ed[mund Alexander]**
1925-   [ESF, SF, WGT]
*American author, illustrator, filmmaker*
* Alexander, Ed?
* Emsh
* Emsler?
* Gars, Henry
* Willer?

**Emsler?**
See   Emshwiller, Ed[mund Alexander]

**Emsley, Clare**
See   Plummer, Clare [Emsley]

**Emslie, M. L.**
See   Simpson, Myrtle L[illias]

**Enacryos**
See   Boex, Joseph-Henri Honore

**Enault, Louis** 1824- ?   [PA]
*Author*
* De Vermond, Louis

**Encausse, Gerard** 1865-1917
[NAD]
*French cabalist*
* Papus

**[The] Enchanter**
See   Van Buren, Martin

**Endacott, Endy**
See   Endacott, Paul

**Endacott, Paul** 1902-
*American basketball player*
* Endacott, Endy

**Endfield, Cy**
See   Endfield, Cyril Raker

**Endfield, Cyril Raker** 1914-
[BDF, FD, FDG]
*South African director*
* Endfield, Cy
* Raker, Hugh
* Roach, Jonathan

**Endo, Shusaku** 1923?-
*Japanese author and actor*
* Horafuki [Teller of Tall Tales]

**Enesco, Georges**
See   Enescu, Georges

**Enescu, Georges** 1881-1955   [MS]
*Rumanian composer*
* Enesco, Georges

**[L']Enfant Cheri de la Victorie**
See   Massena, Andre

**[L']Enfant de la Fortune**
See   Massena, Andre

**[L']Enfant de Miracle**
See   Bonaparte, Napoleon

**[L']Enfant du Miracle**
See   Bourbon, Charles Ferdinand de

**[L']enfant Paganini**
See   Rodes, Alfred

**[L']Enfant Sublime**
See   Hugo, Victor Marie

**Enfantin, Barthelemy Prosper**
1796-1864   [HN, WBD]
*French Socialist leader*
* Enfantin, Pere
* [Le] Pere Enfantin

**Enfantin, Pere**
See   Enfantin, Barthelemy Prosper

**Enfield, Harold Hugh** 1907-1949
[BEW]
*American actor*
* Reynolds, Craig

**Enfield, Hugh**
See   Hughes, Fielden

**[The] Enforcer**
See   Nitti, Frank

**Engel, David Georg** 1924-   [CA]
*Austrian-born American author*
* Gil, David G[eorg]

**Engel, Lyle Kenyon** 20th c.   [ESF]
*American author and editor*
* Lord, Jeffrey [house pseudonym]

**Engelberg, Bugsy**
See   Engelberg, Lewis

**Engelberg, Lewis** 20th c.   [SMG]
*American football coach*
* Engelberg, Bugsy

**Engelhardt, Frederick**
See   Hubbard, Lafayette Ronald

**Engell, Dee**
See   Van Horn, Dale R.

**Engels, Christiaan J. H.** 1907-
[CW]
*Dutch-born poet and author*
* Tournier, Luc

**Engh, Bjorg Larsen** 1945-   [IAW]
*Norwegian journalist*
* Bjornstad, Marianne
* Minus

**Engh, Rohn** 1938-   [CA]
*American photographer and writer*
* White, H. T.

**Engine Charlie Wilson**
See   Wilson, Charles Erwin

**Enginger, Bernard** 1923-   [CA]
*French-born author*
* Satprem

**Englaender, Richard** 1859-1919
[B10, CD, EWL]
*Austrian author*
* Altenberg, Peter

**England Dan**
See   Seals, Danny

**England, E. M.**
See   Anders, Edith [Mary] England

**England, E Squires**
See   Ball, Sylvia Patricia

**England, Edith**
See   Anders, Edith [Mary] England

**England, John** 1786-1842 [WBD]
*Irish-born prelate*
* [The] Founder of the Catholic
  Church in Australia

**England, Norman**
*See* Webb, Godfrey Edward
Charles

**England, Paul**
*See* Janes, Paul

**England's Darling**
*See* Hereward

**England's Domestic Poet**
*See* Cowper, William

**England's Pride and Westminster's
Glory**
*See* Burdett, [Sir] Francis

**Engle, Arthur Clyde** 1884-1939
[BE]
*American baseball player*
* Engle, Hack

**Engle, Charles A.** 1906- [FB]
*American football coach*
* Engle, Rip

**Engle, Hack**
*See* Engle, Arthur Clyde

**Engle, John D[avid], Jr.** 1922- [CA]
*American poet and playwright*
* Johnn, David

**Engle, Peter King** 1916-1972 [FC]
*American actor*
* Whitney, Peter

**Engle, Rip**
*See* Engle, Charles A.

**Englehardt, Charles Harold** 20th c.
[BBH]
*American basketball player and
coach*
* Englehardt, Shrimp

**Englehardt, Frederick J.** [FFF, PA]
*Author*
* Drahlegne
* Gray Eagle

**Englehardt, Shrimp**
*See* Englehardt, Charles Harold

**Engler, William George** ?-1961
[BEW]
*Theatrical performer*
* Rand, Bill

**Englise, Charles Carmen** 1914-
[BLB]
*American underworld figure*
* English, Charles Carmen

**[The] English Achilles**
*See* Devereux, Robert [Second Earl
of Essex]

**[The] English Achilles**
*See* Talbot, John

**[The] English Achilles**
*See* Wellesley, Arthur

**English, Alex** 1954- [SMG]
*American basketball player*
* English, Flick
* English, Slim

**[The] English Alexander**
*See* Henry V

**[The] English Anacreon**
*See* Brome, Alexander

**[The] English Aristides**
*See* Pym, John

**[The] English Aristophanes**
*See* Foote, Samuel

**English, Arnold**
*See* Hershman, Morris

**[The] English Athanasius**
*See* Milner, John

**[The] English Atticus**
*See* Addison, Joseph

**[The] English Attila**
*See* Cromwell, Oliver

**[The] English Bach**
*See* Bach, Johann Christian

**English, Brenda H.**
*See* Riddolls, Brenda Harks

**English, Charles**
*See* Nuetzel, Charles [Alexander]

**English, Charles Carmen**
*See* Englise, Charles Carmen

**[The] English Chrysostom**
*See* Taylor, Jeremy

**[The] English Claude**
*See* Gainsborough, Thomas

**[The] English Claude**
*See* Wilson, Richard

**[An] English Critic**
*See* Townsend, George Henry

**English, David** 1942- [RO2]
*American singer*
* Franklin, Melvin

**[The] English Demosthenes**
*See* Baxter, Richard

**[The] English D'Eon**
*See* Clarke, Charlotte

**[The] English Diana**
*See* Elizabeth I

**English, Don**
*See* Owen, D. E.

**English, Elwood George** 1907- [BE]
*American baseball player*
* English, Woody

**[The] English Ennius**
*See* Layamon

**[The] English Eusebius**
*See* Burnet, Gilbert

**[The] English Faust**
*See* Dee, John

**English, Flick**
*See* English, Alex

**[The] English Francoise Sagan**
*See* Hill, Susan [Elizabeth]

**[The] English Hermit**
*See* Crab, Roger

**[The] English Hippocrates**
*See* Sydenham, Thomas

**[The] English Hobbema**
*See* Crome, John

**[The] English Hobbema**
*See* Nasmyth, Patrick [or Peter?]

**[The] English Horace**
*See* Jonson, Ben[jamin]

**[The] English Horace**
*See* Pope, Alexander

**English, Jessie Millard** [NAA]
*American educator and author*
* Jarvys, Gayne

**[The] English Joan of Arc**
*See* Ambree, Mary

**[The] English Justinian**
*See* Edward I

**[The] English Juvenal**
*See* Hall, Joseph

**[The] English Juvenal**
*See* Oldham, John

**[The] English Lysippus**
*See* Gibbons, Grinling

**[The] English Marivaux**
*See* Richardson, Samuel

**[The] English Merlin**
*See* Lilly, William

**[The] English Mersenne**
*See* Collins, John

**English, Michael**
*See* Hilts, Edward Leonard [Len]

**[The] English Milo**
*See* Topham, Thomas

**[The] English Montesquieu**
*See* De Lolme, John Louis

**[The] English Mozart**
*See* Bishop, [Sir] Henry

**[The] English Opium-Eater**
*See* De Quincey, Thomas

**[The] English Palestrina**
*See* Gibbons, Orlando

**[The] English Palladio**
*See* Jones, Inigo

**[The] English Persius**
*See* Hall, Joseph

**[The] English Petrarch**
*See* Sidney, [Sir] Philip

**[The] English Pindar**
*See* Cowley, Abraham

**[The] English Pindar**
*See* Gray, Thomas

**[The] English Plato**
*See* Norris, John

**[An] English Play-Goer**
*See* Oxenford, John

**[The] English Pope**
*See* Breakspear, Nicholas

**[The] English Poussin**
*See* Cooper, Richard

**[The] English Rabelais**
*See* Amory, Thomas

**[The] English Rabelais**
*See* Sterne, Laurence

**[The] English Rabelais**
*See* Swift, Jonathan

**[The] English Raphael**
*See* Stothard, Thomas

**English, Richard**
*See* Shaver, Richard S[harpe]

**[The] English Roscius**
*See* Burbage, Richard

**[The] English Roscius**
*See* Garrick, David

**[The] English Roscius**
*See* Tarlton, Richard

**[The] English St. Sebastian**
*See* Edmund [or Eadmund]

**[The] English Salvator Rosa**
*See* Mortimer, John Hamilton

**[The] English Sappho**
*See* Robinson, Mary Darby

**[The] English Scarron**
*See* Oldys, Alexander

**[The] English Seneca**
*See* Hall, Joseph

**[The] English Seneca**
*See* Sterne, Laurence

**English, Slim**
*See* English, Alex

**[The] English Socrates**
*See* Johnson, Samuel

**[The] English Solomon**
*See* Henry VII

**[The] English Solomon**
*See* James I

**[The] English Strabo**
*See* Camden, William

**[The] English Teniers**
*See* Morland, George

**[The] English Terence**
*See* Cumberland, Richard

**English, Thomas Dunn** [PA]
*Author*
* Donkey, John

**[The] English Thoreau**
*See* Jefferies, Richard

**[The] English Tintoretto**
*See* Dobson, William

**[The] English Tyrtaeos**
*See* Minot, Laurence

**[The] English Vandyck**
*See* Dobson, William

**[The] English Virgil**
*See* Tennyson, Alfred [First Baron
Tennyson]

**[The] English Vitruvius**
*See* Jones, Inigo

**English, Woody**
*See* English, Elwood George

**[An] Englishman**
*See* Dollinger, Johann Joseph I.

**[An] Englishman**
*See* Gough, John

**[An] Englishman**
*See* Hobhouse, John Cave

**[An] Englishman**
*See* Holland, Lord

**[An] Englishman Abroad**
*See* Gregory, Alexander Tighe

**[An] Englishwoman**
*See* Wright, Frances

**Engotti, Samuel** 1915- [BX, RBE]
*American boxer*
* Angott, Sammy

**Engren, Edith** [joint pseudonym with Robert Jesse McCaig]
*See* McCaig, Edith

**Engren, Edith** [joint pseudonym with Edith McCaig]
*See* McCaig, Robert Jesse

**Engressia, Joe** 1950?-
*American convicted of fraud*
* [The] Whistler

**Engstroem, Arthur Hamilton** 1873?-1958 [BEW]
*Actor*
* Revelle, Arthur Hamilton

**Enid**
*See* Banks, Elizabeth

**Enke, Elizabeth Edith** 1929?- [BEW, FC, SW]
*American actress and singer*
* Adams, Edie

**[The] Enlightened Doctor**
*See* Lully, Raymond

**Ennis, Hack**
*See* Ennis, Russ[ell Elwood]

**Ennis, Robert** 1909-1963 [PMJ, WWJ]
*American jazz musician*
* Ennis, Skinnay

**Ennis, Russ[ell Elwood]** 1897-1949 [BE]
*American baseball player*
* Ennis, Hack

**Ennis, Skinnay**
*See* Ennis, Robert

**[The] Ennius of France**
*See* Jean [or Jehan] de Meung

**Ennius, Quintus** 3rd c. BC [DEP, SN]
*Roman poet*
* [The] Father of the Latin Poets
* [The] Rhodian Master
* [The] Roman Chaucer

**[An] Ennuyee**
*See* Murphey, Anna

**Enoch, Pierre** ?-1590 [PA]
*Author*
* [La] Meschinerie

**Enos, William Berkeley** 1895- [BDF, EMT, FC]
*American choreographer, director, actor*
* Berkeley, Busby

**Enotrio Romano**
*See* Carducci, Giosue

**Enrico** ?-1147 [HN]
*Italian hermit*
* [The] False Hermit

**Enright, D. J.**
*See* Enright, Dennis Joseph

**Enright, Dan**
*See* Ehrenreich, Dan

**Enright, Dennis Joseph** 1920- [LC]
*British author, poet, critic*
* Enright, D. J.

**Enright, Maurice** ?-1920 [BLB, PHM]
*American gangster*
* Enright, Mossy

**Enright, Mossy**
*See* Enright, Maurice

**Enriquez de Paz, Antonio** 1602-1662? [WBD]
*Spanish author*
* Enriquez Gomez, Antonio

**Enriquez Gomez, Antonio**
*See* Enriquez de Paz, Antonio

**Ens, Anton** 1884-1950 [BE]
*American baseball player*
* Ens, Mutz

**Ens, Cotton**
*See* Ens, Jewel Willoughby

**Ens, Jewel Willoughby** 1889-1950 [BN]
*American baseball player, manager, coach*
* Ens, Cotton

**Ens, Mutz**
*See* Ens, Anton

**Ensanada**
*See* Collin, Jacques Albin Simon

**Ensign, Thomas** 1940- [CA]
*American author, attorney, political organizer*
* Ensign, Tod

**Ensign, Tod**
*See* Ensign, Thomas

**Ensley, Wilma Evangeline** 1907- [IA]
*American author*
* Walton, Evangeline

**Ensor, Alick Charles Davidson** 1906- [IAW]
*British politician and author*
* Ensor, David

**Ensor, David**
*See* Ensor, Alick Charles Davidson

**Ensor, R. C. K.**
*See* Ensor, [Sir] Robert Charles

**Ensor, [Sir] Robert Charles** 1877-1958 [LC]
*British educator, journalist, poet*
* Ensor, R. C. K.
* Scrutator

**Enthoven, R. E.**
*See* Enthoven, Roderick Eustace

**Enthoven, Roderick Eustace** 1900- [ART]
*British architect*
* Enthoven, R. E.

**Enton, Harry** 1855- ? [FFF, PA, SFP]
*American writer*
* Haines, Henry Harrison
* Noname [house pseudonym]
* Versatile, Val

**Entratta, Charles** 20th c. [BLB]
*American underworld figure*
* Green, Charlie

**Entwistle, Lillian Millicent** 1908-1932 [BEW, SC]
*British-born actress*
* Entwistle, Peg

**Entwistle, Peg**
*See* Entwistle, Lillian Millicent

**Enver Bey** 1881?-1922 [WBD]
*Turkish soldier*
* Enver Pasha

**Enver Pasha**
*See* Enver Bey

**[The] Envoy of the Messiah**
*See* Martins de Miranda, David

**Enzenroth, Clarence Herman** 1885-1944 [BE]
*American baseball player*
* Enzenroth, Jack

**Enzenroth, Jack**
*See* Enzenroth, Clarence Herman

**Enzinas, Francisco de** 1520?-1552? [WBD]
*Spanish theologian*
* Dryander

**Eolopoesis**
*See* Bigelow, Jacob

**Eon de Beaumont, Charles Genevieve Louis Auguste Andre Timothee d'** 1728-1810 [RH, SN, WBD]
*French soldier*
* [The] Cavalier
* [Le] Chevalier d'Eon

**Epafrodito**
*See* Wagner, C[harles] Peter

**Epaminondas**
*See* Granger, Gideon

**Epernay, Mark**
*See* Galbraith, John Kenneth

**Epernon, Duc d'**
*See* Nogaret de la Valette, Jean Louis de

**Ephemera**
*See* Fitzgibbon, Henry

**Ephesian**
*See* Roberts, [Carl Eric] Bechhofer

**[The] Ephesian Poet**
*See* Hipponax

**Ephraem** 308?- 373? [DNNF, FFF, WBD]
*Saint*
* Ephraem Syrus [The Syrian]
* [The] Prophet of the Syrians

**Ephraem Syrus [The Syrian]**
*See* Ephraem

**[An] Epicure**
*See* Saunders, Frederick

**[The] Epicurus of China**
*See* Tao-tse

**Epicurus Rotundus**
*See* Brooks, Shirley

**Epiphanes [The Illustrious]**
*See* Antiochus IV

**Epiphanes**
*See* Nicomedes II

**Epiphanes**
*See* Ptolemy V

**Epiphanes Dionysus**
*See* Antiochus VI

**Epiphanes Nicator**
*See* Seleucus VI

**Epiphanes Philadelphus**
*See* Antiochus XI

**Epiphanius** 6th c. [HN, RH, SN]
*Italian scholar*
* [The] Scholastic

**Episcopus, Simon** 1583-1643 [PA]
*Author*
* Bischop

**Epistographas**
*See* Carr, Governor

**Epp, Margaret A[gnes]** 20th c. [CA]
*Canadian author*
* Goossen, Agnes

**Eppa Jeptha Rixey**
*See* Rixey, Eppa P.

**Epperly, Al[bert Paul]** 1918- [BE]
*American baseball player*
* Epperly, Pard

**Epperly, Pard**
*See* Epperly, Al[bert Paul]

**Eppie**
*See* Naismith, Helen

**Eppinoff, Ivan**
*Orchestra leader*
* Scott, Ivan

**Epps, Aubrey Lee** 1912- [BE]
*American baseball player*
* Epps, Yo-Yo

**Epps, Clarence Bradley** 1913- [BEW]
*American choreographer, director, producer*
* Bradley, Buddy

**Epps, Ernestine** 1918- [BEW]
*American actress and artists representative*
* McClendon, Ernestine

**Epps, Eugene** 20th c.
*American football player*
* Epps, Pitt Lips

**Epps, Pitt Lips**
*See* Epps, Eugene

**Epps, Yo-Yo**
*See* Epps, Aubrey Lee

**Epremesnil, Francoise Augustine d'** 1754-1794 [WBD]
*Wife of French politician, Jean Jacques Duval d'Epremesnil*
* Mere des Pauvres [Mother of the Poor]

**Epremesnil, Jean Jacques Duval d'** 1746-1794 [DNNS]
*French jurist and politician*
* Crispin Cataline

**Epsilon**
*See* Betjeman, [Sir] John

**Epsilon**
*See* Denham, Edward

**Epstein, Abner** 1910- [WEC]
*American cartoonist*
* Dean, Abner

**Epstein, Alan [Steuer]** 1922- [CA]
*American journalist*
* Emory, Alan [Steuer]

**Epstein, Beryl [Williams]** 1910-
[CA, SAT]
*American author*
* Allen, Adam [joint pseudonym
  with Samuel Epstein]
* Coe, Douglas [joint pseudonym
  with Samuel Epstein]
* Williams, Beryl

**Epstein, Charlotte** 1885-1938
[EJS]
*American swimming coach*
* Epstein, Eppie

**Epstein, Eppie**
See  Epstein, Charlotte

**Epstein, Judith Sue** 1947-  [CA]
*American poet and songwriter*
* Judy Sue

**Epstein, Michael Peter** 1943-  [BE]
*American baseball player*
* Superjew

**Epstein, Samuel** 1909-
[CA, MJA, SAT]
*American author*
* Allen, Adam [joint pseudonym
  with Beryl (Williams) Epstein]
* Campbell, Bruce
* Coe, Douglas [joint pseudonym
  with Beryl (Williams) Epstein]
* Colt, Martin
* Strong, Charles

**Equiano, Olaudah** 1745-1801
[IBW]
*Nigerian-born abolitionist*
* Vassa, Gustavus

**[The] Era of Good Feeling President**
See  Monroe, James

**Erao**
See  Brooks, Erastus

**Erasmus**
See  Gilder, Jeannette L.

**Erasmus, Desiderius**
See  Gerhards, Gerhard [or Geert]

**Erasmus, M. Nott**
See  Stuber, Stanley I[rving]

**Erastus, Thomas**
See  Lieber [or Liebler], Thomas

**Erato**
See  Gallagher, William D.

**Erautt, Joseph Michael [Joe]** 1921-
[BE]
*Canadian-born baseball player*
* Erautt, Stubby

**Erautt, Stubby**
See  Erautt, Joseph Michael [Joe]

**Erb, William E.** 1903?-1974  [B10]
*American author and copywriter*
* Edwards, William Earle

**Erby, John J.** 1902-  [BWW]
*American singer*
* Seymour, George
* [The] Singing Pianist
* Smith, Guy
* Suddoth, J. Guy

**Erceldoune**
See  Bocock, Willis H.

**Erckmann Chatrian** [joint
pseudonym with Emile Erckmann]
See  Chatrian, Alexander

**Erckmann Chatrian** [joint
pseudonym with Alexander
Chatrian]
See  Erckmann, Emile

**Erckmann, Emile** 1822-1899
[WBD]
*French author*
* Erckmann Chatrian [joint
  pseudonym with Alexander
  Chatrian]

**Ercolani, James** 1936-  [FC]
*American actor*
* Darren, James

**Erdan, Alexander**
See  Jacob, Andre Alexander

**Erdelyi, Tommy** 20th c.
*American musician*
* Ramone, Tommy

**Erdstelulov**
See  Ackerman, Forrest J[ames]

**Eremita**
See  L'Ermite, Daniel

**[The] Eremite of Tibbals**
See  Cecil, William [First Baron
Burleigh]

**Eremite, Sir**
See  Cecil, William [First Baron
Burleigh]

**[The] Eretrian Bull**
See  Menedemos

**Ergo, Gabriel**
See  Harvey, Gabriel

**Erha**
See  Hamaoui, Ernest

**Erhard, Werner**
See  Rosenberg, John Paul [Jack]

**Erholm, Ester** 1906-  [IAW]
*Finnish author*
* Erhomaa, Ester

**Erhomaa, Ester**
See  Erholm, Ester

**Eric**
See  Erickson, Carl

**Eric, Kenneth**
See  Henley, Arthur

**Eric Magnusson**
See  Eric II

**Eric the Red**
See  Tipton, Eric Gordon

**Eric I** 1056-1103  [WBD]
*King of Denmark*
* Evergood

**Eric II** ?-1137  [WBD]
*King of Denmark*
* [The] Memorable

**Eric II** 1268-1299  [WBD]
*King of Norway*
* Eric Magnusson
* Priest Hater

**Eric III** ?-1147  [WBD]
*King of Denmark*
* [The] Lamb

**Eric IV [or VI]** 1216-1250  [WBD]
*King of Denmark*
* Ploughpenny

**Eric IX** ?-1161?  [FFF, RH, WBD]
*King of Sweden*
* [The] Pious
* [The] Saint

**Eric V [or VII]** 1249?-1286
[HN, WBD]
*King of Denmark*
* Glipping [or Klipping]

**Eric VI [or VIII]** 1274-1319  [WBD]
*King of Denmark*
* Moendved [or Menved]

**Eric XI** ?-1250  [WBD]
*King of Sweden*
* [The] Lame
* [The] Lisping

**Erick, Fred**
See  Allsopp, Fred W.

**Erickson, Buck**
See  Erickson, E. O.

**Erickson, Carl** 1891-1958  [WFA]
*American fashion artist*
* Eric

**Erickson, E. O.** 20th c.  [BBH]
*American sports editor and ski
jumping promoter*
* Erickson, Buck

**Erickson, Henry Nels [Hank]**
1907-1964  [BE]
*American baseball player*
* Erickson, Popeye

**Erickson, John Morris** 1886-1969
[SC]
*American actor*
* Morris, Johnnie

**Erickson, Leif**
See  Anderson, William Wycliffe

**Erickson, Paul Walford** 1916-  [BE]
*American baseball player*
* Li'l Abner

**Erickson, Popeye**
See  Erickson, Henry Nels [Hank]

**Erickson, Sabra Rollins** 1912-
[CA]
*American author*
* Holbrook, Sabra

**Ericson, Frank**
See  Eyck, Ulrich Franz Joseph
[Frank]

**Ericson, John**
See  Meibes, Joseph

**Ericson, Walter**
See  Fast, Howard [Melvin]

**Erie, Paul** 20th c.  [WGT]
*French author*
* D'Avoi, Paul

**Erigena [The Irishman]**
See  Scotus, Johannes [or John]

**Erikson, Charlotte**
See  Erikson, [Cicely] Sibyl
Alexandra

**Erikson, Erik H[omburger]** 1902-
[CA]
*German-born American
psychoanalyst and author*
* Homburger, Erik

**Erikson, [Cicely] Sibyl Alexandra**
20th c.  [WW]
*Author*
* Dick, Alexandra

**Erikson, [Cicely] Sibyl Alexandra**
(Continued)
* Erikson, Charlotte
* Hay, Frances

**Eriksson, Buntel**
See  Bergman, [Ernst] Ingmar

**Eriksson, Li**
See  Eriksson, Lillemor

**Eriksson, Lillemor**  [IWM]
*Swedish musician*
* Eriksson, Li

**Erimantheo, Corydon**
See  Correa Garcao, Pedro Antonio
Joaquim

**Eris, Hermann**
See  Brantsch, Ingmar

**Erith, Lynn**
See  Fox, Edward

**Erlanger, Baba**
See  Trahey, Jane

**Erlanger, Baroness**  [FFF]
*Entertainer*
* Sessi, Mathilde

**Erman, Jack**
See  Ackerman, Forrest J[ames]

**Erman, Jacques deForest**
See  Ackerman, Forrest J[ames]

**Ermanaric** 4th c.  [WBD]
*King of the Ostrogoths*
* [The] Gothic Alexander

**Ermayne, Laurajean**
See  Ackerman, Forrest J[ames]

**Ermelli, Claudio**
See  Foa, Ettore

**Ermengem, Frederic van** 1881- ?
[WBD]
*Belgian author*
* Hellens, Franz

**Ermine, Will**
See  Drago, Harry Sinclair

**Ermite**
See  Moriarty, Patrick Eugene

**Erne, Vincent**
See  Gill, Vincent

**Ernest, [Brother]**
See  Ryan, Ernest

**Ernest**  [SN]
*Duke of Austria*
* [The] Iron Handed

**Ernest [or Ernst]** 1497-1546
[HN, WBD]
*Duke of Brunswick-Luneburg*
* [The] Confessor

**Ernest, William**
See  Berkebile, Fred D[onovan]

**Ernest I [or Ernst]** 1601-1675
[FFF, SN, WBD]
*Duke of Saxe-Weimar and Saxe-
Gotha*
* [Der] Fromme
* [The] Pious

**Ernie D.**
See  DiGregorio, Ernie

**Ernst, Clara**
See  Barnes, Clara Ernst

**Ernst, [Lyman] John** 1940-  [CA]
*American publishing executive and author*
* Chernoff, Dorothy A.
* Clark, David Allen

**Ernst, Otto**
See  Schmidt, Otto Ernst

**Ernst, Paul Frederick** 1902-
[ESF, SF, WGT]
*American writer*
* Edson, George Alden
* Robeson, Kenneth [house pseudonym, Street & Smith]
* Stern, Paul Frederick

**Ernsting, Walter** 1920-
[CA, ESF, SF]
*German author and translator*
* Darlton, Clark
* MacPatterson, F.

**Ero**
See  Rhinewine, Abraham

**Erodore**
See  Abbott, Jacob

**Erpenius**
See  Van Erpe, Thomas

**Errans Mus**
See  Gerhards, Gerhard [or Geert]

**Erratic Enrique**
See  Lukens, Henry Clay

**[The] Erratic Star**
See  Giornovichi, Giovanni Mane

**Errickson, Lief**
See  Errickson, Richard Merriwell

**Errickson, Richard Merriwell**
1914-  [BE]
*American baseball player*
* Errickson, Lief

**Errico, Con**
See  Errico, Consolato

**Errico, Consolato** 1921?-
*American jockey*
* Errico, Con
* Errico, Scamp

**Errico, Greg** 1946-  [SSS]
*Musician*
* Errico, Hand Feet

**Errico, Hand Feet**
See  Errico, Greg

**Errico, Scamp**
See  Errico, Consolato

**Errisson, King**
See  Johnson, Errisson Pallman

**Erro**
See  Gudmundsson, Gudmundur

**Errol, Leon**
See  Sims-Errol, Leon

**Errym, Malcolm J.**
See  Merry, Malcolm James

**Erskine, Carl Daniel** 1926-  [BE]
*American baseball player*
* Erskine, Oisk

**Erskine, Douglas**
See  Buchan, John

**Erskine, Firth** [joint pseudonym with Ivan Eustace Firth]
See  Erskine, Gladys [Shaw]

**Erskine, Firth** [joint pseudonym with Gladys (Shaw) Erskine]
See  Firth, Ivan Eustace

**Erskine, Gladys [Shaw]** 1895-
[NAA, WW]
*American author and poet*
* Antonia
* Don Quixote
* Erskine, Firth [joint pseudonym with Ivan Eustace Firth]

**Erskine, James** 1891-1957
[AS, BE, EJS]
*American baseball player*
* Mayer, Erskine
* Mayer, Scissors

**Erskine, John** 1675-1732
[DHA, FFF, SN]
*11th Earl of Mar*
* Bobbing John
* [A] Rogue of a Scot

**Erskine, Margaret**
See  Williams, [Margaret] Wetherby

**Erskine, Oisk**
See  Erskine, Carl Daniel

**Erskine, Rosalind**
See  Longrigg, Roger [Erskine]

**Erskine, Ruth** 1880-1961  [THR]
*British actress*
* Maitland, Ruth

**Erskine, Samuel Frankel**
1893-1962  [BE]
*American baseball player*
* Mayer, Sam[uel Frankel]

**Erskine, Thomas**  [SN]
* Tonans, Jupiter

**Ert, Dan** 1937?-
*Danish-born Israeli intelligence agent*
* Aerbel, Dan

**Erte**
See  De Tirtoff, Romain

**Erteszek, Olga** 20th c.  [WFA]
*Polish-born fashion designer*
* Olga

**Ertle, Johnny** 1896-  [BX, RBE]
*Austrian-born boxer*
* Ertle, Kewpie

**Ertle, Kewpie**
See  Ertle, Johnny

**Ervie**
See  Pearson, Emily C.

**Ervin, Patrick**
See  Howard, Robert Ervin

**Ervin, Susan**
See  Ervin-Tripp, Susan Moore

**Ervin-Tripp, Susan Moore** 1927-
[CA]
*American educator and writer*
* Ervin, Susan

**Erving, Julius** 1950-
[BB, IPA, SMG]
*American basketball player*
* Dr. J

**Erwen, Keith**
See  Urwin, Ranald Keith

**Erwin** 1244?-1318  [WBD]
*German architect*
* Erwin von Steinbach

**Erwin, Annabel**
See  Barron, Ann Forman

**Erwin, George** 1913-
[ASC, DAM, EJ]
*American jazz musician*
* Erwin, Pee Wee

**Erwin, Howard W.**
See  Ingraham, Prentiss

**Erwin, LeRoy Franklin** 1925-1958
[SC]
*American actor and screenwriter*
* Erwin, Roy

**Erwin, Mike**
See  Erwin, Ross Emil

**Erwin, Pee Wee**
See  Erwin, George

**Erwin, Ross Emil** 1885-1953
[BE, BN]
*American baseball player*
* Erwin, Mike
* Erwin, Tex

**Erwin, Roy**
See  Erwin, LeRoy Franklin

**Erwin, Tex**
See  Erwin, Ross Emil

**Erwin von Steinbach**
See  Erwin

**Erwin, Will**
See  Eisner, Will[iam Erwin]

**Erythroeus, James Ficias**
See  Rosio, Giovanni Vittorio

**Erz-Philister**
See  Nicolai, Christopher Friedrich

**Escalera, Nino**
See  Escalera, Saturnino Cuadrado

**Escalera, Saturnino Cuadrado**
1929-  [BE]
*Puerto Rican-born baseball player*
* Escalera, Nino

**Eschenbach, Christoph**
See  Ringmann, Christoph

**Escherich, Elsa Falk** 1888-  [CA]
*American author*
* Falk, Elsa

**[El] Esclavo [The Slave]**
See  Pareja, Juan de

**Escobar y Mellado, Antonio**
1867-1912  [GS]
*Spanish bullfighter*
* [El] Boto [The Dull One]

**Escoffer, Tremim M.**  [PA]
*Author*
* Temothie

**Escolar, Carlos** 20th c.  [GS]
*Spanish bullfighter*
* Frascuelo [after the famous Frascuelo]

**Escott, Jonathan** 1922-  [CA]
*British author and entertainer*
* Scott, Jack S.

**Escovedo, Coke**
See  Escovedo, Pete

**Escovedo, Pete** 20th c.  [RM]
*Musician*
* Escovedo, Coke

**Escudero, Rafael** 1898-1970
[WWJ]
*Puerto Rican jazz musician*
* Escudero, Ralph

**Escudero, Ralph**
See  Escudero, Rafael

**Eseki, Bruno**
See  Mphahlele, Ezekiel

**Esenin, Sergei Aleksandrovich**
1895-1925  [WBD]
*Russian poet*
* [The] Poet Laureate of the Revolution

**Eseoghene**
See  Barrett, C. Lindsay

**Eskadale, Evan**
See  Fraser, Alexander

**Eskdale Tam**
See  Telford, Thomas

**Eskew, Jim** 20th c.  [GW]
*American rodeo performer*
* Eskew, Junior

**Eskew, Junior**
See  Eskew, Jim

**Esmeralda, Aurora**
See  Mighels, Ella Sterling Cummins

**Esmond, Carl**
See  Eichberger, Wilhelm [Willy]

**Esmond, Harriet**
See  Burke, John [Frederick]

**Esmond, Henry Vernon**
See  Jack, Henry Vernon

**Espadas, Guty**
See  Espadas Cruz, Gustavo Hernan

**Espadas Cruz, Gustavo Hernan**
1954-  [RBE]
*Mexican boxer*
* Espadas, Guty

**Esper, Charles H.** 1868-1910
[AS, BE]
*American baseball player*
* Esper, Duke

**Esper, Duke**
See  Esper, Charles H.

**Esperanto, Dr.**
See  Zamenhof, Lazarus Ludwig

**Espinasse, Albert** 1903?-1972
[BDF, CA, WEF]
*French actor and playwright*
* Brasseur, Pierre

**Espinda, David** 1914?-1975  [FIR]
*Hawaiian television performer*
* Espinda, Lippy

**Espinda, Lippy**
See  Espinda, David

**Espino, Federico [Licsi, Jr.]** 1939-
[CA]
*Philippine poet and author*
* De Extramuros, Quixote

**Espinosa, Arnulfo Acevedo** 1953-
[SMG]
*Dominican-born baseball player*
* Espinosa, Nino

**Espinosa, Juan** 1804-1871   [FFF]
*South American army officer*
* [The] Soldier of the Andes

**Espinosa, Nino**
*See* Espinosa, Arnulfo Acevedo

**Espinosa, Rudy**
*See* Espinoza, Rudolph Louis

**Espinosa de los Monteros, Armando**
1912-1957   [SC]
*Mexican actor*
* Periquin

**Espinosa Saucedo, Fermin** 1911-
[GS, OCS]
*Mexican bullfighter*
* Armillita Chico [Little Armillita]

**Espinoza, Rudolph Louis** 1933-
[CA]
*American author and educator*
* Espinosa, Rudy

**Esposito, Diamond Joe**
*See* Esposito, Joseph

**Esposito, Joseph** 1872-1928
[BLB, PHM]
*Italian-born American underworld
figure*
* Esposito, Diamond Joe

**Espriella, Manuel Alvarez**
*See* Southey, Robert

**Espronceda, Jose de** 1808-1842
[WBD]
*Spanish poet*
* [The] Spanish Byron

**Espy, James Pollard** 1785-1860
[FFF, WBD]
*American meteorologist*
* [The] Storm King

**Espy, Willard Richardson** 1910-
[IAW]
*American author*
* Wede

**Esquin, Mamertus** 1826-1883
[FFF]
*South American clergyman*
* [The] Lacordaire of America

**Esrom, D. A.**
*See* Morse, Theodora

**Ess, Johann Heinrich van**
1772-1847   [WBD]
*German theologian and monk*
* Ess, Leander van

**Ess, Leander van**
*See* Ess, Johann Heinrich van

**Essay Kaigh**
*See* Kenner, Scipio A.

**[The] Essence of Eccentricity**
*See* Liddy, Eleanor Jane

**Essington, R. W.**   [PA]
*Author*
* Kingsman

**Esser, Hans**
*See* Wallraff, Guenter

**Essex, Captain**
*See* Starr, Richard Harry

**Essex, David**
*See* Cook, David

**Essex, Frank**
*See* Simmonds, Michael Charles
[Mike]

**Essex, Frederick** 1875?-1951
[BEW]
*Composer and theatrical performer*
* Whitlock, Billy

**Essex, Jon**
*See* Watford, Joel Albert

**Essex, Lewis**
*See* Isaacs, Levi

**Essex, Mary**
*See* Bloom, Ursula [Harvey]

**Essex, Richard**
*See* Starr, Richard Harry

**Essick, Vinegar Bill**
*See* Essick, William Earl [Bill]

**Essick, William Earl [Bill]**
1881-1951   [BE]
*American baseball player*
* Essick, Vinegar Bill

**Esslin, Martin**
*See* Pereszlenyi, Martin

**Esslinger, Pat M.**
*See* Carr, Pat M[oore]

**Essoe, Gabe**
*See* Essoe, Gabor Attila

**Essoe, Gabor Attila** 1944-   [SFL]
*Hungarian-born author*
* Essoe, Gabe

**Esson, [Thomas] Louis [Buvelot]**
1879-1943   [MWD]
*Australian playwright*
* [The] Father of Australian
  Drama

**Est**
*See* Scott-Taggart, Elizabeth Mary
Josephine

**Est-il-Possible**
*See* George

**Estaban, Francisco, Jr.** 1933-   [EJ7]
*American jazz musician*
* De La Rosa, Frank

**Estalella, Bobby**
*See* Estalella, Roberto Mendez

**Estalella, Roberto Mendez** 1911-
[BE]
*Cuban-born baseball player*
* Estalella, Bobby

**Estang, Luc**
*See* Bastard, Lucien

**Esteban**
*See* Matison, Steven Martin

**Estebanez Calderon, Serafin**
1779-1867   [WBD]
*Spanish author, poet, political
leader*
* [El] Solitario

**Estelle**
*See* Bogart, Elizabeth

**Estelle**
*See* Ellis-Morris, Esther

**Estelle**
*See* Harris, Emily Marion

**Estenssoro, Hugo** 1946-   [CA]
*Bolivian-born photographer and
writer*
* Chartier, Emilio

**Estep, Harold** 20th c.   [SC]
*Actor*
* Sawyer, Buddy

**Esterbrook, Dude**
*See* Esterbrook, Thomas Jefferson

**Esterbrook, Thomas Jefferson**
1860-1901   [BE]
*American baseball player*
* Esterbrook, Dude

**Esterbrook, Tom** [house pseudonym]
*See* Hubbard, Lafayette Ronald

**Esterel**
*See* Martin, Charles

**Esterre, Neville D'**
*See* Lee, Archibald Edward John

**Estes, Baby Huey**
*See* Estes, Wayne

**Estes, Elliott Marantette** 1916-
*American automobile executive*
* Estes, Pete

**Estes, John Adams** 1899?-1977
[BWW, DAM, IBW]
*American singer and guitarist*
* Estes, Sleepy John

**Estes, Pete**
*See* Estes, Elliott Marantette

**Estes, Sleepy John**
*See* Estes, John Adams

**Estes, Wayne** 1943-1965   [BB]
*American basketball player*
* Estes, Baby Huey

**Estevao, Carlos**
*See* Souza, Carlos Estevao de

**Esteven, John**
*See* Shellabarger, Samuel

**Esteves, Jose, Jr.** 1921-   [EJ]
*American jazz musician*
* Loco, Joe

**Estevez, Ramon** 1940-
[ITA, SW, TR]
*American actor*
* Sheen, Martin

**Esther**
*See* Buchan, A. W.

**Estival**
*See* Estival, Ivan Leon

**Estival, Ivan Leon** 20th c.   [WGT]
*Author*
* Estival

**Estoril, Jean**
*See* Allan, Mabel Esther

**Estrada, Rita** 20th c.
*American author*
* Clay, Rita

**[De L']Estrapade**
*See* Tardieu, Antoine Francois

**Estrees, Antoine d'** ?-1530   [WBD]
*French aristocrat*
* [Le] Jeune

**Estrees, Gabrielle d'** 1573-1599
[FFF, HN, RH]
*Mistress of King Henry IV of France*
* [The] Beautiful Gardener
* [La] Belle Gabrielle
* [La] Belle Jardiniere
* Charmante Gabrielle

**Estridge, Robin** 20th c.   [CC]
*Author*
* Loraine, Philip

**Estrithson**
*See* Sweyn II

**[El] Estudiante [The Student]**
*See* Gomez Calleja, Luis

**Esudier, Marie**   [PA]
*Author*
* [Une] Cravate Blanche

**Etan, Raymond**
*See* Melhorn, Nathan R.

**Etchebarren, Andrew Auguste**
1943-   [SMG]
*American baseball player and coach*
* Etchebarren, Etch

**Etchebarren, Etch**
*See* Etchebarren, Andrew Auguste

**Etcheverry, Pierre** 1937-   [OP]
*French opera singer*
* Garazzi, Peyo

**Etcheverry, Sam** 20th c.   [CFH]
*American-born football player*
* [The] Rifle

**Etchison, Buck**
*See* Etchison, Clarence Hampton

**Etchison, Clarence Hampton** 1915-
[BE]
*American baseball player*
* Etchison, Buck

**Ethardo** 1835-1911   [BMH]
*Italian acrobat*
* [The] Spiral Ascensionist

**Ethel, Agnes**
*See* Tracy, Mrs.

**Ethelflaeda** ?-918   [HN]
*Daughter of King Alfred of England*
* [The] Lady of Mercia

**Ethelred II** 968-1016
[DNNS, RH, SN]
*King of England*
* [The] Unready

**Ethelwold** 908?-984
[DNNF, DNNS, FFF]
*Saint*
* [The] Father of Monks

**Etherege, [Sir] George**
1635?-1691?   [SN]
*British playwright*
* Medley?

**Etheridge, Bobby Lamar** 1943-
[BE]
*American baseball player*
* Etheridge, Luke

**Etheridge, Kelsic**
*See* Smith, W. B.

**Etheridge, Luke**
*See* Etheridge, Bobby Lamar

**Etherington, Mary Susan**
1864-1942   [BEW, EMT, FC]
*British singer and actress*
* Tempest, [Dame] Marie

**Etienne**
*See* Jouy, Victor Joseph Etienne

**Etienne**
*See* King-Hall, [William] Stephen
[Richard]

**Etienne, Franck** 1936- [CW]
*Haitian poet, author, playwright*
* Franketienne

**Etincelle**
See Peyronney, Vicomtesse de

**Etiquette, Madame**
See Noailles, Duchesse de

**Eton, Robert**
See Meynell, Laurence [Walter]

**Etonensis**
See Gladstone, William Ewart

**Etri, Anthony** 1917- [MY]
*American musician*
* Etri, Bus

**Etri, Bus**
See Etri, Anthony

**Etrulia, Claire** 1876-1954 [BEW]
*American-born theatrical performer*
* Shattuck, Truly

**Etteilla**
See Alliette

**Ettel, Elizabeth** 1898- [FC]
*German actress*
* Bergner, Elisabeth

**Ettlinger, Dorothy** 1898- [BEW]
*American actress, critic, playwright*
* Day, Dorothy

**[The] Ettrick Shepherd**
See Hogg, James

**Eubank, Honest John**
See Eubank, John Franklin

**Eubank, John Franklin** 1872-1958
[BE]
*American baseball player*
* Eubank, Honest John

**Eubanks, Poss**
See Eubanks, Uel Melvin

**Eubanks, Uel Melvin** 1902-1954
[BE]
*American baseball player*
* Eubanks, Poss

**Euclid** 4th c. BC [SN]
*Greek mathematician*
* [The] Sage of Alexandria

**[The] Euclid of His Age**
See Clavius, Christopher

**Eudocia**
See Athenais

**Eudosia, Makrembolitissa** ?-1096
[PA]
*Author*
* Ducas

**Euergetes**
See Antiochus VII

**Euergetes [Benefactor]**
See Ptolemy III

**Euergetes II**
See Ptolemy VIII [or VII]

**[The] Eugene O'Neill of the French
Stage**
See Lenormand, Henri-Rene

**Eugenius III**
See Paganelli [or Pignatelli],
Bernardo

**Eugenius IV**
See Condolmieri [or Condulmer],
Gabriele

**Eukairos**
See Demetrius III

**Eulenspiegel, Alexander**
See Shea, Robert [Joseph]

**Eunick, Ferd**
See Eunick, Fernandas Bowen

**Eunick, Fernandas Bowen**
1896-1959 [BE]
*American baseball player*
* Eunick, Ferd

**Eunson, Joan** 1934- [FC]
*American actress*
* Evans, Joan

**[The] Eunuch**
See Eutropius

**Eupator [Of a Good Father]**
See Antiochus V

**Euphan**
See Todd, Barbara Euphan

**Euphemides, Aristes**
See Von Koerber, Hans Nordewin

**Euphrosyne**
See Graves, Richard

**[The] Euphuist**
See Lilly, John

**Eurelius, Gunno** 1661-1709 [WBD]
*Swedish author*
* Dahlstierna, Gunno

**Euripides** 5th c. BC [SN]
*Greek playwright*
* [The] Philosophic Bard

**[The] Euripides of Italian Opera**
See Verdi, Giuseppe

**European**
See Mosley, [Sir] Oswald [Ernald]

**Europe's Liberator**
See Wellesley, Arthur

**Eusebes [The Pious]**
See Antiochus X

**Eusebia**
See Somerset, Frances Thynne
[Countess of Hertford]

**Eusebio**
See Ferreira, Eusebio

**Eusebius**
See Prime, Edward Dorr Griffith

**Eusebius Emmeran**
See Daumer, Georg Friedrich

**Eusebius of Caesarea** 265?-338?
[DNNS, HN, SN]
*Theologian and historian*
* [The] Father of Church History
* [The] Father of Ecclesiastical
History
* Pamphili

**Eustace, Alice**
See Thomas, Mary Alice

**Eustace, Robert**
See Barton, [Dr.] Eustace Robert

**Eustathius [or Eumathius]** 12th c.
[WBD]
*Byzantine author*
* Macrembolites

**Eustis, Laurette**
See Murdock, Laurette P.

**Eustis, Mrs. Frederick J.** [FFF]
*Entertainer*
* Bell, Ida

**Eutropius** 4th c. [DNNS]
*Byzantine statesman*
* [The] Eunuch

**Euxenus** [SN]
*Tutor of Apollonius*
* [The] Coxcomb Bird

**Eva**
See Kelly, Mary Eva

**Eva, Marion** 1723-1822 [PA]
*Author*
* Violetti

**Evagrius** 536?-600? [WBD]
*Byzantine historian*
* Scholasticus

**Evan, Carol**
See Goldsmith, Carol Evan

**Evan, Evin**
See Faust, Frederick [Schiller]

**[The] Evangelic Doctor**
See Wycliffe [or Wyclif], John

**[The] Evangelical Prophet**
See Isaiah

**Evangelicus, Doctor**
See Wycliffe [or Wyclif], John

**Evangeline**
See Moriarty, Ellen

**[The] Evangelist**
See John

**[The] Evangelist**
See Philip

**[The] Evangelist**
See Sunday, William Ashley
[Billy]

**Evangelist Mary Flowers**
See Miles, Josephine [Josie]

**[The] Evangelist of Economy**
See Goethe, Johann Wolfgang von

**[The] Evangelist of Rhythm**
See Robison, Willard

**Evans, Alan**
See Stoker, Alan

**Evans, Augusta**
See Wilson, Mrs. A. J.

**Evans, Bennett**
See Berger, Ivan [Bennett]

**Evans, Bloody Jake**
See Evans, Jacob

**Evans, Caleb** 1737-1791 [PA]
*Author*
* Americanus

**Evans, Caradoc**
See Evans, David

**Evans, Charles Franklin** 1889-1916
[BE]
*American baseball player*
* Evans, Chick

**Evans, Charles, Jr.** 1890-1979
[BWG, EG, GF]
*American golfer*
* Evans, Chick

**Evans, Chick**
See Evans, Charles Franklin

**Evans, Chick**
See Evans, Charles, Jr.

**Evans, Chin**
See Evans, Felix

**Evans, Constance May** 1890-
[CA, WD]
*Canadian author*
* Gray, Jane
* O'Nair, Mairi

**Evans, Dale**
See Smith, Frances

**Evans, Dardanella Lister** 1921-
[IAW]
*American author and poet*
* Evans, Dee

**Evans, David** 1878-1945
[LC, TCL]
*Welsh author*
* Evans, Caradoc

**Evans, Dee**
See Evans, Dardanella Lister

**Evans, Dewey**
See Evans, Dwight Michael

**Evans, Dixie** 20th c. [FIR]
*American entertainer*
* [The] Marilyn Monroe of
Burlesque

**Evans, Doc**
See Evans, Joseph Patton

**Evans, Doc**
See Evans, Paul Wesley

**Evans, Dwight Michael** 1951-
[SMG]
*American baseball player*
* Evans, Dewey

**Evans, E. Everett** 1893-1958
[WGT]
*American author*
* Gardener, Henry
* Verett, E.
* Verett, H. E. [joint pseudonym
with Thelma D. Hamm Evans]

**Evans, Eastwick** [PA]
*Author*
* Belarius of Cymbeline

**Evans, Elizabeth** 1887-1958 [FC]
*British actress*
* Risdon, Elizabeth

**Evans, Ellen**
See DuBreuil, Elizabeth Lorinda

**Evans, Emerald**
See DuBreuil, Elizabeth Lorinda

**Evans, Ernest** 1941-
[ASC, FC, LRR]
*American singer and dancer*
* Checker, Chubby

**Evans, Evan**
See Faust, Frederick [Schiller]

**Evans, F. M. G.**
See Higham, Florence May Greir

**Evans, Fanny Wentworth Osborn
Porteus** 1849?-1934 [BEW]
*American actress*
* Wentworth, Fanny

**Evans, Felix** 20th c. [OBW]
*American baseball player*
* Evans, Chin

**Evans, Fighting Bob**
See Evans, Robley Dunglison

**Evans, Frances Monet Carter**
See Carter, Frances Monet

**Evans, Frank**
See Slaughter, Marion T.

**Evans, Frank Howel** 20th c. [MBF]
*British author*
* Daunt, Atherley
* Payne, Crutchley

**Evans, George** 1870-1915
[BEW, PMJ]
*Welsh-born comedian*
* Evans, Honey Boy

**Evans, George Bird** 1906-
[CA, WW]
*American author*
* Bird, Brandon [joint pseudonym
  with Kay Harris Evans]
* Evans, Harris [joint pseudonym
  with Kay Harris Evans]

**Evans, Gil**
See Green, Ian Ernest Gilmore

**Evans, Glen** 1921- [CA]
*American author*
* Eirelin, Glenn

**Evans, Gwnfil Arthur** 1899-1938
[MBF]
*Welsh-born author*
* Evans, Gwyn
* Gwynne, Arthur
* Western, Barry

**Evans, Gwyn**
See Evans, Gwnfil Arthur

**Evans, Hap [or Happy]**
See Evans, William Demont, II

**Evans, Harris** [joint pseudonym with
Kay Harris Evans]
See Evans, George Bird

**Evans, Harris** [joint pseudonym with
George Bird Evans]
See Evans, Kay Harris

**Evans, Herschel** 20th c. [NP]
*American jazz musician*
* Evans, Tex

**Evans, Hilary** 1929- [CA]
*British author*
* Agard, H. E.

**Evans, Honey Boy**
See Evans, George

**Evans, Hugh Austin** 20th c. [WW]
*Author*
* Austin, Hugh

**Evans, I. O.**
See Evans, Idrisyn Oliver

**Evans, Idrisyn Oliver** 1894- [SF]
*British author*
* Evans, I. O.

**Evans, Jack**
See Evans, William John

**Evans, Jacob** ?-1907 [BE]
*American baseball player*
* Evans, Bloody Jake

**Evans, James Carmichael, Jr.**
1941- [IBW]
*American government official*
* Evans, Mike

**Evans, Jean** 1939- [CA]
*British author*
* Graham, Ruth

**Evans, Jean Bell Shaw** 1910- [AW]
*Scottish-born author*
* Shaw, Jane

**Evans, Jean Lorna** 20th c. [IAW]
*British writer*
* Jacoby, Jean

**Evans, Joan**
See Eunson, Joan

**Evans, John**
See Browne, Howard

**Evans, John** 1879- ? [BMH]
*British entertainer*
* Riskit, Jack

**Evans, John** 19th c. [FFF]
*British author*
* [The] Poet Laureate of the Bees

**Evans, John** 20th c. [BAB]
*American baseball player*
* Evans, Shane

**Evans, John Quentin** 1933- [WFA]
*British fashion designer*
* Clive

**Evans, Joseph Patton** 1895-1953
[BE]
*American baseball player*
* Evans, Doc

**Evans, Julia [Rendel]** 1913-
[AW, CA, WD]
*British author*
* Hobson, Polly

**Evans, Kay Harris** 1906- [CA]
*American author*
* Bird, Brandon [joint pseudonym
  with George Bird Evans]
* Evans, Harris [joint pseudonym
  with George Bird Evans]

**Evans, Lawrence Watt** 1954- [CA]
*American author*
* Watt-Evans, Lawrence

**Evans, Leo C.** [FFF]
*Writer*
* Grin

**Evans, Louis** 1912- [ASC]
*American composer, musician,
recording executive*
* Evans, Redd

**Evans, Louis Richard** 1885-1943
[BE]
*American baseball player*
* Evans, Steve

**Evans, Madge**
See Evans, Margherita

**Evans, Margherita** 1909- [BEW]
*American actress*
* Evans, Madge

**Evans, Marguerite Florence Helene
Jervis** 1894- [WGT]
*British author*
* Barcynska, Countess
* Sandys, Oliver

**Evans, Marian** 1819-1880 [DEL]
*British author*
* Eliot, George

**Evans, Mike**
See Evans, James Carmichael, Jr.

**Evans, Moon**
See Evans, William Wilbur

**Evans, Morgan**
See Davies, Leslie Purnell

**Evans, Morgan** [PA]
*Author*
* De Pembroke, Morgan

**Evans, Oliver** 1755-1819 [WBD]
*American inventor*
* [The] Watt of America

**Evans, Pamela** 1933?- [DIL]
*Irish author*
* Wykham, Helen

**Evans, Patricia Healy**
See Carpenter, Patricia [Healy
Evans]

**Evans, Paul Wesley** 1907-1977
[EJ, PMJ, WWJ]
*American jazz musician*
* Evans, Doc

**Evans, Red**
See Evans, Russell Earl

**Evans, Redd**
See Evans, Louis

**Evans, Richard**
See Kunitz, Richard E.

**Evans, Robley Dunglison**
1846-1912 [WBD]
*American naval officer*
* Evans, Fighting Bob

**Evans, Russell Earl** 1906- [BE]
*American baseball player*
* Evans, Red

**Evans, Samuel** [PA]
*Author*
* Bede, Seth

**Evans, Shane**
See Evans, John

**Evans, Steve**
See Evans, Louis Richard

**Evans, Tabor**
See Cameron, Lou

**Evans, Tex**
See Evans, Herschel

**Evans, Tex**
See Evans, William John

**Evans, Thelma D. Hamm** 20th c.
[WGT]
*Author*
* Edwards, Hamm?
* Hamm, T. D.
* Hamm, Thelma D.
* Verett, H. E. [joint pseudonym
  with E. Everett Evans]

**Evans, William** 1895- [IAW]
*Welsh cardiologist and author*
* Amnon III

**Evans, William** 1921- [EJ]
*American jazz musician*
* Lateef, Yusef

**Evans, William Demont, II** 1899-
[MK]
*American baseball player*
* Evans, Hap [or Happy]
* [The] Grey Ghost

**Evans, William John** 1928-
[CEI, FHE, SMG]
*Welsh-born hockey player*
* Evans, Jack
* Evans, Tex

**Evans, William Wilbur** 1907- ?
[BBH]
*American lacrosse player*
* Evans, Moon

**Evans-Jones, Albert** 1895- [CA]
*Welsh poet and playwright*
* Cynan

**Evanti, [Madame] Lillian**
See Tibbs, Lillian Evans

**Evarts, Esther**
See Benson, Sara Mahala Redway
[Smith]

**Evarts, Jeremiah** 1781-1831
[FFF, PA]
*American editor*
* Penn, William
* William

**Evarts, William H.**
See Hentz, William

**Evarts, William Maxwell**
1818-1901 [FFF]
*American attorney and statesman*
* Our Own Evarts

**Evashevski, Evy**
See Evashevski, Forest

**Evashevski, Forest** 1918- [FB]
*American football coach*
* Evashevski, Evy

**Eve**
See Maillot, Antoine Francois

**Eve, Barbara**
See Reiss, Barbara Eve

**Eveleigh, Mary** 1904-1943 [BEW]
*British-born actress*
* Leigh, Mary

**Evelius**
See D'Oefelse, Andreas Felix

**Evelyn, A. W.**
See Wilkes, W.

**Evelyn, Anthony**
See Ward Thomas, Evelyn Bridget
Patricia

**Evelyn, Clara**
See Smith, Clara Evelyn

**Evelyn, Janet**
See Sothern, Janet Evelyn

**Evelyn, John** 1620-1706 [SN]
*British author*
* Evelyn, Sylva

**Evelyn, Judith**
See Allen, Judith Evelyn

**Evelyn, [John] Michael** 1916-
[CA, CC, WW]
*British barrister and author*
* Underwood, Michael

**Evelyn, Sylva**
See Evelyn, John

[The] Evening Star of Stepney
See Greenhill, William

Evens, Glyn Kinnaird   [WW]
Author
* Raq

[The] Ever Memorable
See Hales, John

Everaerts, Jan Nicolai 1511-1536
[WBD]
Dutch poet
* Secundus, Johannes

Everard, Maurice
See Bullivant, Cecil Henry

Everard, Walter
See Garrish, Harold J.

Everest, Hope
See James, Wilhelmina Martha

Everett, Alexander Hill 1792-1847
[PA]
Author
* [A] Citizen of the United States

Everett, Bill 1917-1973   [WECO]
American cartoonist
* Blake, Everett
* Blake, William

Everett, Chad
See Cramton, Ray

Everett, David 1770-1813   [FFF]
American writer
* Junius Americanus

Everett, Elizabeth Abbey 20th c.
[NAA]
American writer
* Everett, Eza
* Fairbanks, Sabrina

Everett, Eza
See Everett, Elizabeth Abbey

Everett, Gail
See Hale, Arlene

Everett, Gifo G.
See Viett, George Frederic

Everett, Katherine Calmes 1883-
[NAA]
American writer
* Calmes, Neville

Everett, Kenneth Neil 1930-
[CWG]
American country-western performer
* Crawford, Gene

Everett, Laura Bell 20th c.   [NAA]
American writer
* Battelle, Adah Fairbanks

Everett, Marshall
See Neil, [Judge] Henry

Everett, Mary
See Krey, Laura Lettie [Smith]

Everett, Paul
See Lovejoy, Cornelia

Everett, Richard
See Cross, Edward Ephram

Everett, Ronald McKinley 1942- ?
[B10]
American Black Muslim leader
* Karenga, Ron

Everett, Thomas Arthur 1938-
[BEW]
American actor, dancer, director
* Everett, Timmy

Everett, Timmy
See Everett, Thomas Arthur

Everett, Wade
See Cook, William Everett

Everett-Green, Evelyn 1856-1932
[TCC]
British author
* Adair, Cecil
* Dare, Evelyn
* H. F. E.

Evergood
See Eric I

Evergood, Philip 1901-1973   [CA]
American artist
* Dixon, Howard Francis

Evergreen
See Irving, Washington

Evergreen Pam
See Temple, Henry John

Evermay, March
See Eiker, Mathilde

Everpoint
See Field, Joseph M.

Evers, Hoot
See Evers, Walter Arthur

Evers, John Joseph 1881-1947
[BE, DGS, PB]
American baseball player
* [The] Crab
* [The] Trojan

Evers, Walter Arthur 1921-
[BE, SMG]
American baseball player
* Evers, Hoot

Eversdyk-Smulders, Emilie Caroline
Henriette 1903-   [IAW]
Dutch author
* Eversdyk-Smulders, Lily

Eversdyk-Smulders, Lily
See Eversdyk-Smulders, Emilie
Caroline Henriette

Eversley, David Edward Charles
1921-   [CA]
German-born British author and
educator
* Small, William

Everson, Carol 1933?-1964   [BEW]
Actress
* Shreve, Tiffany

Everson, Lottie
See Beaman, Lottie Kimbrough

Everson, William [Oliver] 1912-
[B10, CA, WD]
American poet and literary critic
* Antoninus, [Brother]

Evert, Chris[tine Marie] 1954-
[NN]
American tennis player
* Cinderella in Sneakers
* Evert, Little Chrissie
* Evert Lloyd, Chris
* Frigidaire, Miss

Evert, Little Chrissie
See Evert, Chris[tine Marie]

Evert Lloyd, Chris
See Evert, Chris[tine Marie]

Everton, Francis
See Stokes, Francis William

Everts, Henry   [FFF]
Entertainer
* Messell, Hank

Every, Philip Cochrane
See Burnford, Sheila [Philip
Cochrane Every]

Everything, Mr.
See Baylor, Elgin

Everything, Mr.
See Hawkins, Connie

Everything, Mr.
See Kazmaier, Richard W., Jr.

Eves, Reginald T. 20th c.   [MBF]
British author and editor
* Britton, Herbert
* Clifford, Martin [house
pseudonym]
* Conquest, Owen [house
pseudonym]

Evetts, L. C.
See Evetts, Leonard Charles

Evetts, Leonard Charles 1909-
[ART]
British artist
* Evetts, L. C.

Evoe
See Knox, Edmund George Valpy

Ewan Dhu
See Cameron, [Sir] Evan

Ewart, Ernest Andrew 1878- ?
[LAO]
British author, journalist,
screenwriter
* Cable, Boyd

Ewart, Stephen T.
See Stewart, Stephen

Ewbank, T. 1792-1870   [PA]
Author
* Westman, Hab'k O.

Ewbank, Weeb
See Ewbank, Wilbur

Ewbank, Wilbur 1907-
[B10, FB, OCS]
American football coach
* Ewbank, Weeb

Ewell, Barney
See Ewell, Norwood

Ewell, Doc
See Ewell, James

Ewell, James 20th c.   [SMG]
American baseball trainer
* Ewell, Doc

Ewell, Norwood 1918-   [TF]
American track and field athlete
* Ewell, Barney

Ewell, Tom
See Tompkins, Yewell

Ewen, Mary Cecilia 1836-1866
[FFF]
American actress
* Our Mary

Ewens, Gwendoline Wilson 20th c.
[WD]
Australian historian and author
* Ashley, Gladys
* Wilson, Gwendoline

Ewer, Gus
See Ewer, Raymond Crawford

Ewer, Raymond Crawford 20th c.
[WECO]
Cartoonist
* Ewer, Gus

Ewing, Aileen 1907-   [F2]
Actress
* Grey, Anne

Ewing, Bob
See Ewing, George Lemuel

Ewing, Buck
See Ewing, William

Ewing, Dressel De Witt 1883-
[NAA]
American electrical engineer and
author
* Dressel, De Witt Ewing

Ewing, Frederick R.
See Waldo, Edward Hamilton

Ewing, George Lemuel 1873-1947
[AS, BE]
American baseball player
* Ewing, Bob
* Ewing, Long Bob

Ewing, John 1917-   [WWJ]
American jazz musician
* Ewing, Streamline

Ewing, Juliana Horatia   [PA]
Author
* Overtheway, Mrs.

Ewing, Kathryn 1921-   [CA]
American author
* Douglas, Kathryn

Ewing, Long Bob
See Ewing, George Lemuel

Ewing, Reuben
See Cohen, Reuben

Ewing, Samuel   [FFF]
Writer
* Jacques

Ewing, Streamline
See Ewing, John

Ewing, William 1859-1906
[AS, DGS, PB]
American baseball player
* Ewing, Buck

Ewoldt, Art[hur Lee] 1892-   [BE]
American baseball player
* Ewoldt, Sheriff

Ewoldt, Sheriff
See Ewoldt, Art[hur Lee]

Ex Barber Fribbleton
See Greene, Asa

[An] Ex Editor
See Picton, Thomas

[An] Ex M. P.
See Daunt, William Joseph O'Neill

Ex Officio Jemmy
See Scarlett, [Sir] James [First
Baron Abinger]

**Ex Private X**
*See* Burrage, Alfred McLelland

**Ex-R.S.M.**
*See* Lindsay, Harold Arthur

**Exall, Barry**
*See* Nugent, John Peer

**Excellent, Matilda**
*See* Farson, Daniel Negley

**Exile**
*See* Donald, Charles Hiliard

**[The] Exile of Erin**
*See* Newman, M. W.

**[The] Existentialist Pass Defender**
*See* Saimes, George

**[The] Exotic Bookseller**
*See* Edwards, James

**Expencoeus**
*See* D'Espence, Charles

**Expertus**
*See* MacColl, Malcolm

**[The] Expositor**
*See* Averroes [or Averrhoes]

**[The] Expounder of the Constitution**
*See* Marshall, John

**[The] Expounder of the Constitution**
*See* Webster, Daniel

**Express**
*See* Dunlap, A. J.

**[The] Express**
*See* Ryan, [Lynn] Nolan

**[The] Exterminator**
*See* Montbars

**[The] Extinguished Exile**
*See* Reid, T. W.

**Exton, Winifred** 1872- ? [THR]
*British actress*
\* Fraser, Winifred

**Extra Billy**
*See* Smith, William

**Eyck, Ulrich Franz Joseph [Frank]**
1921- [IAW]
*German-born author*
\* Ericson, Frank

**Eyen, Jerome**
*See* Eyen, Tom

**Eyen, Tom** 20th c. [CA]
*American playwright*
\* Eyen, Jerome
\* Short, Roger, Jr.

**Eyerly, Jeannette Hyde** 1908-
[CA, SAT]
*American author*
\* Griffith, Jeannette [joint
pseudonym with Valeria Winkler
Griffith]

**Eyesbright, Daisy**
*See* Johnson, Mrs. S. O.

**Eyler, Emile**
*See* Osten, M.

**Eyles, Merle**
*See* Crozier, Kathleen Muriel
[Eyles]

**Eyre, Annette**
*See* Worboys, Annette Isobel

**Eyre, Gerald**
*See* Ryan, Gerald

**Eyre, Sophie**
*See* Lonsdale, Mrs.

**Eyster, William Reynolds**
1841-1918 [WW]
*Author*
\* Wilby, R. Hunt

**Eythe, Dutch**
*See* Eythe, Howard

**Eythe, Howard** 20th c. [FIR]
*American football player*
\* Eythe, Dutch

**Eytinge, Margaret** [PA]
*American author*
\* Elliot, Madge

**Eytinge, Mrs. Walter** [FFF]
*Entertainer*
\* Bailey, Josephine

**Eytinge, Rose**
*See* Searle, Mrs. Cyril

**Eyvind Finnson** 10th c. [WBD]
*Norwegian government advisor and
author*
\* Skaldaspillir

**Ezami, Henri**
*See* Lutoslawski, Wincenty

**Ezekiel the Great**
*See* Robinson, Ezekial R.

**Ezinicki, Wild Bill**
*See* Ezinicki, William

**Ezinicki, William** 1924-
[FHE, HK]
*Canadian-born hockey player*
\* Ezinicki, Wild Bill

**Ezzelino IV** 1194-1259
[FFF, HN, RH]
*Chief of the Ghibellines and
Governor of Vicenza*
\* [The] Son of the Devil

# F

**F.**
See Fenton, Katherine

**F.**
See Fryer, Stan

**F. A.**
See Arnold, Frederick

**F. B.**
See Burton, [Sir] Richard Francis

**F. C. G.**
See Gould, [Sir] Francis
Carruthers

**F. D. R.**
See Roosevelt, Franklin Delano

**F. E. H. H.**
See Haines, F. E. H.

**F. E. P.**
See Paget, Francis Edward

**F. F.**
See Fysh, Frederick

**F. F. of the Cedars**
See Herbert, Henry William

**F. G.**
See Gaume, Francois

**F. G. R.**
See Roe, F[rederic] Gordon

**F. K.**
See Kinwelmersh, Francis

**F. L. M.**
See Moore, F. L.

**F. M.**
See Lockard, Francis Marion
[Frank]

**F. M.**
See Madden, [Sir] Frederick

**F. M.**
See Marshall, Francis

**F. M. C. 69**
See Cook, [Sir] Francis Ferdinand
Maurice

**F. M. P.**
See Peard, F. M.

**F. O. O.**
See Street, Cecil John Charles

**F. P. A.**
See Adams, Franklin Pierce

**F. Q. T.**
See Funkquist, Herman Peter
Anton

**F. R.**
See Richards, Frances

**F. R. H. S.**
See Ellis, E. T.

**F. T.**
See Topolski, Feliks

**F. W. R.**
See Rankin, Fannie W.

**Fa Presto**
See Giordano, Luca

**Fabares, Michele** 1944- [RO1]
American singer and actress
* Fabares, Shelly

**Fabares, Ruby Bernadette Nanette
Theresa** 1920?- [BEW, EMT, F2]
American actress and singer
* Fabray, Nanette

**Fabares, Shelly**
See Fabares, Michele

**Fabens, J. W.** [PA]
Author
* [A] Resident of San Domingo

**Faber**
See Lefevre, Francois Antoine

**Faber, Hermann**
See Goldschmidt, Hermann

**Faber, John [or Johannes]**
See Heigerlin, Johannes

**Faber, Red**
See Faber, Urban Charles

**Faber, Urban Charles** 1888-1976
[DGS, PB, SMG]
American baseball player
* Faber, Red

**Fabian**
See Forte, Fabian Anthony

**Fabian, Madge**
See Wilks, Madge

**Fabian, Ruth**
See Quigley, Aileen

**Fabian, Warner**
See Adams, Samuel Hopkins

**Fabius**
See Dickinson, John

**[The] Fabius of America**
See Washington, George

**[The] Fabius of Austria**
See Daun, [Count] Leopold von

**[The] Fabius of France**
See Montmorency, Anne de

**Fabius Maximus, Quintus** 4th c.
BC [WBD]
Roman politician
* Rullianus

**Fabius Maximus Verrucosus, Quintus**
?- 203 [FFF, HN, RH]
Roman military and political leader
* Cunctator
* [The] Delayer
* [The] Lingerer
* [The] Shield of Rome

**Fabray, Nanette**
See Fabares, Ruby Bernadette
Nanette Theresa

**Fabre d'Eglantine**
See Fabre, Philippe Francois
Nazaire

**Fabre, Jean Pierre** 1755-1832 [PA]
Author
* De l'Aude

**Fabre, Philippe Francois Nazaire**
1750-1794 [WBD]
French playwright and politician
* Fabre d'Eglantine

**Fabric, Bent** 1927- [RO1]
Danish musician
* [The] Danish Perry Como

**Fabricius** 3rd c. BC [HN, RH]
Roman military leader and
statesman
* [The] Incorruptible

**Fabricius, Georg**
See Goldschmied, Georg

**Fabricius, John Albert** 1668-1736
[HN]
German scholar
* [The] Librarian of the Republic
of Letters

**Fabricius, Sara** 1880-1974
[AW, TCL]
Norwegian author
* Sandel, Cora

**Fabricus, Wilhelm** 1560-1634 [PA]
Author
* Hildanus

**Fabrilo [Workman]**
See Aparici y Pascual,

**Fabrique, Albert LaVerne**
1887-1960 [BE]
American baseball player
* Fabrique, Bunny

**Fabrique, Bunny**
See Fabrique, Albert LaVerne

**Fabrizius, Peter** [joint pseudonym
with Max Knight]
See Fabry, Joseph B[enedikt]

**Fabrizius, Peter** [joint pseudonym
with Joseph B[enedikt] Fabry]
See Knight, Max

**Fabry, Claude**
See Bonhomme, Arthur

**Fabry, Joseph B[enedikt]** 1909-
[CA, WD]
American author, editor, translator
* Fabrizius, Peter [joint pseudonym
with Max Knight]

**[El] Fabulista Principiante**
See Nunes de Caceres, Jose

**Fac et Spera**
See Harding, William

**Facchinetti, Giovanni Antonio**
1519-1591 [CAL]
Pope
* Innocent IX

**Faccio, Rina** 1879- ? [CD]
Italian author and poet
* Aleramo, Sibilla

**Facciuto, Eugene Louis** 20th c.
American dance instructor
* Luigi

**Face, Elroy Leon** 1928- [BE]
American baseball player
* Face, Roy

**Face, Roy**
See Face, Elroy Leon

**Fachion, Frances**
See Ferguson, Bessie Gowan

**Fack, Caroline** 1846- ? [LAO]
German author
* Fack, Lina

**Fack, Lina**
See Fack, Caroline

**Factor, John** 20th c. [BLB]
American underworld figure
* Gest, J.
* Jake the Barber
* Spencer, Norman D.
* Wise, Harry

[The] Factory King
See Oastler, Richard

Facultades [Abilities]
See Peralta Seleron, Francisco

Faddis, William L. [PA]
Author
* Toxophilus

Fadette
See Reeves, Marian Calhoun Legare

Fadeyev, Alexander [Alexandrovich]
See Bulyga

Fadiman, Edwin, Jr. 1925- [CA]
American author
* Mark, Edwina

Fag, Frederick
See Johnson, James Weldon

Fagan, Clinkers
See Fagan, William A. [Bill]

Fagan, Ina 1892?-
[BEW, EMT, FC]
American actress
* Claire, Ina

Fagan, Nutsy
See Reeve, Edward H. [Ted]

Fagan, William A. [Bill] 19th c.
[BE]
American baseball player
* Fagan, Clinkers

Fagerman
See Bartholomew, Annie E.

Fagerstrom, Stan 1923- [CA]
American writer
* Scott, Stanley

Fagius, Paul 1504-1550 [PA]
Author
* Bucheim

Fago, Giovanni 20th c. [WF]
Italian director
* Lean, Sidney

Fagri, Anders 1948- [AES]
Norwegian soccer player
* Fagri, Nobby

Fagri, Nobby
See Fagri, Anders

Fagus
See Faillet, Georges Eugene

Fagyas, Maria 20th c. [CA]
Hungarian-born author and playwright
* Fay, Mary Helen

Fahey, Cap
See Fahey, Howard Simpson

Fahey, Howard Simpson
1892-1971 [BE]
American baseball player
* Fahey, Cap
* Fahey, Kid

Fahey, Kid
See Fahey, Howard Simpson

Fahr, Gerald Warren 1924- [BE]
American baseball player
* Fahr, Red

Fahr, Red
See Fahr, Gerald Warren

Fahrenkopf, Anne 20th c. [WW]
Author
* Irving, Alexander [joint pseudonym with Ruth Fox]

Fahrer, Clarence Willie 1890-1967
[BE]
American baseball player
* Fahrer, Pete

Fahrer, Pete
See Fahrer, Clarence Willie

Faico
See Gonzalez, Francisco

Faid, Mary
See Dunn, Mary Alice

Faillet, Georges Eugene 1872-1933
[CD]
French poet
* Fagus

Fain, Burrhead
See Fain, Ferris Roy

Fain, Ferris Roy 1922- [BE, PB]
American baseball player
* Fain, Burrhead

Fain, Michael 20th c.
American author
* Michael, Judith [joint pseudonym with Judith Barnard]

Fain, Sammy
See Feinberg, Samuel

[Le] Faineant
See Louis V

Fainzilber, Ilya Arnoldovich
1897-1937 [CD]
Russian author and journalist
* Ilf, Ilya Arnoldovich

[The] Fair
See Albert I [or Albrecht]

[The] Fair
See Charles IV

[The] Fair
See Edwy [or Eadwig]

[The] Fair
See Frederick III

[The] Fair
See Philip IV [or Philippe]

Fair, A. A.
See Gardner, Erle Stanley

Fair, Adrah
See Brunner, Adrah

[The] Fair Geraldine
See Fitzgerald, Elizabeth

[The] Fair Haired
See Macintyre, Duncan

Fair, J. Murray
See Hoisington, May Folwell

[The] Fair Maid of Anjou
See Plantagenet, Edith

[The] Fair Maid of Galloway
See Douglas, Margaret

[The] Fair Maid of Kent
See Joan

[The] Fair Maid of Norway
See Margaret

[The] Fair One
See Lenska, Rula

[The] Fair Perdita
See Robinson, Mary Darby

[The] Fair Quakeress
See Lightfoot, Hannah

Fair Rosamond
See Clifford, Rosamond de

Fair, W. B.
See Fair, William Burnham

Fair, William Burnham 1850-1901
[BMH]
British comedian and singer
* Fair, W. B.

Fairbairn, Ann
See Tait, Dorothy

Fairbairn, Helen
See Southard, Helen Fairbairn

Fairbairn, Roger
See Carr, John Dickson

Fairbairn, [Sir] Thomas 1823- ?
[DEL]
British author
* Amicus

Fairbank, James Lee [Jim]
1881-1955 [BE]
American baseball player
* Fairbank, Smoky

Fairbank, Smoky
See Fairbank, James Lee [Jim]

Fairbanks, Carol 1935- [CA]
American author and educator
* Myers, C. F.
* Myers, Carol Fairbanks

Fairbanks, Charles Bullard 19th c.
[FFF]
American writer
* Aguecheek

Fairbanks, Douglas, Sr.
See Ulman, Douglas Elton

Fairbanks, Mrs. A. W. [FFF]
American journalist
* Myra

Fairbanks, Nat
See Pearce, Charles Louis St. John

Fairbanks, Sabrina
See Everett, Elizabeth Abbey

Fairbrother, Sydney
See Tapping, Sydney

Fairburn, A. R. D.
See Fairburn, Arthur Rex Dugard

Fairburn, Arthur Rex Dugard
1904-1957 [LC]
New Zealand author
* Fairburn, A. R. D.

Fairburn, Eleanor 1928-
[AW, CA, WD]
British author
* Carfax, Catherine

Fairburn, Werly 20th c. [CWG]
American country-western performer
* [The] Singing Barber

Fairchild, Cooky
See Fairchild, Edgar

Fairchild, Edgar 1914?-1975 [FIR]
Orchestra leader
* Fairchild, Cooky

Fairchild, William 20th c. [CA]
British director, screenwriter, playwright
* Cranston, Edward

Faircloth, Charlie Raiford 1927-
[CWG, DAM]
American country-western performer
* Faircloth, Peanuts

Faircloth, James Lamar 1892-
[BE]
American baseball player
* Faircloth, Rags

Faircloth, Peanuts
See Faircloth, Charlie Raiford

Faircloth, Rags
See Faircloth, James Lamar

Faire, Virginia Brown
See LaBuna, Virginia

Faire, Zabrina
See Stevenson, Florence

Fairer, F. P.
See Fairer, Frederick Park

Fairer, Frederick Park 1910-
[ART]
British painter
* Fairer, F. P.

Fairfax, Beatrice
See Manning, Marie

Fairfax, Beatrice
See McCarroll, Marion C[lyde]

Fairfax, Beatrice
See Wolfe, Lilian Lauferty

Fairfax, Edward ?-1635 [SN]
Scottish poet and translator
* [The] Poetical Father of Waller

Fairfax, Marion
See Neiswanger, Marion

Fairfax, Ruth
See Stibbes, Agnes Jean

Fairfax, Thomas [Third Baron
Fairfax] 1612-1671 [SN]
Commander of the Parliamentary Army
* Fiery Young Tom

Fairfax-Blakeborough, John
1883-1978? [CA, LAO]
British author and journalist
* Hambletonian

Fairfield, Cecily Isabel 1892-
[CA, EWL, IPA]
British author, critic, journalist
* Lynx
* West, Rebecca

Fairfield, John
See Livingstone, Harrison Edward

Fairfield, Richard Ivan 1937-
[IAW]
American author
* Rich

Fairfield, Ward
See Clarke, Walter Irving

Fairford, Alan
See Kent, John

[The] Fairhaired
See Harold I

**Fairholt, F. W.** 19th c.  [PA]
*Author*
* [A] Literary Antiquary

**Fairie, Fanny**
*See* Waggamon, Mary T.

**Fairleigh, Christopher**
*See* Parcell, Norman H[owe]

**Fairleigh, Frank**
*See* Smedley, Francis Edward
[Frank]

**Fairless, Michael**
*See* Barber, Margaret Fairless

**Fairley, Alisdair**
*See* Aird, Alisdair

**Fairman, Austin**
*See* Fehrman, Austin

**Fairman, Paul W.** 1916-1977
[ESF, SF, SFL]
*American author and editor*
* Chase, Adam [joint pseudonym
  with Milton Lesser]
* Del Rey, Lester [joint pseudonym
  with Ramon Felipe San Juan
  Mario Alvarez Del Rey]
* Garson, Clee [house pseudonym,
  Ziff-Davis]
* Jarvis, E. K. [house pseudonym,
  Ziff-Davis]
* Jorgensen, Ivar [house
  pseudonym]
* Lee, Robert
* Lohrman, Paul [house
  pseudonym, Ziff-Davis]
* Paul, F. W.
* Storm, Mallory

**Fairman, Virgil B.**
*See* Klarmann, Andrew F.

**Fairmont, Ethel**
*See* Beebe, Ethel Fairmont

**Fairplay**
*See* Clayton, Cyril James

**Fairplay, Roger**
*See* Phillips, Michael Joseph

**Fairs, John** 1844-1921
[THR, WBD]
*British actor and theatre manager*
* Hare, [Sir] John

**Fairway, Sidney**
*See* Daukes, Sidney Herbert

**Fairweather-Walker, Dorothy**
1915-  [ART]
*British painter*
* D. F. W.

**Faison, Tree**
*See* Faison, William E.

**Faison, William E.** 1939-  [FB]
*American football player*
* Faison, Tree

**Faith**
*See* Hillard, Brenda

**Faith, Adam**
*See* Neilhams, Terence

**Faithful Monitor?**
*See* Francis, [Sir] Philip

**[The] Faithful Norman**
*See* Prendergast

**Faithful, Gail** 1936-  [CA, SAT]
*American author*
* Keller, Gail Faithfull

**Faithfull, Joan Margaret Caldwell**
1923-  [ART]
*Scottish potter*
* J. F.

**Fakir, Abdul**  [RO2]
*American singer*
* Fakir, Duke

**Fakir, Duke**
*See* Fakir, Abdul

**Falana, Lola**
*See* Falana, Loletha Elaine

**Falana, Loletha Elaine** 1945-
[IBW]
*American singer, dancer, actress*
* Falana, Lola

**Falaschi, Flash**
*See* Falaschi, Nello D.

**Falaschi, Nello D.** 20th c.  [FB]
*American football player*
* Falaschi, Flash

**Falca, Pietro** 1702-1785  [WBD]
*Venetian painter*
* Longhi, Pietro

**Falcandus, Hugo** 12th c.  [SN]
*Sicilian historian*
* [The] Tacitus of Sicily

**Falcaro, Chesty**
*See* Falcaro, Joseph Lawrence

**Falcaro, Joseph Lawrence**
1896-1951  [BBH]
*American bowler*
* Falcaro, Chesty

**Falck, Dorothy** 1891-  [F1]
*British actress*
* Bellew, Dorothy

**Falck, Kyrle** 1887-  [THR]
*British actress*
* Bellew, Kyrle

**Falco, Gian**
*See* Papini, Giovanni

**Falcon**
*See* Nestle, John Francis

**Falcon**
*See* Smith, Soule

**Falcon, Richard**
*See* Shapiro, Samuel

**Falconbridge**
*See* Kelly, Jonathan F.

**Falcone, Aniello** 1600-1665  [WBD]
*Italian painter*
* [L']Oracolo delle Battaglie

**Falconer, Edmund**
*See* O'Rourke, Edmund

**Falconer, Frank**
*See* Carvalho, E. N.

**Falconer, James**
*See* Kirkup, James

**Falconer, Kenneth**
*See* Kornbluth, Cyril M.

**Falconer, Lanoe**
*See* Hawker, Mary Elizabeth

**Falconer, William** 1730-1769  [PA]
*Author*
* Arion
* [A] Layman

**Fales, Fanny**
*See* Smith, Frances Elizabeth

**Falik, Fernando** 1924-  [JL]
*Argentinian sculptor*
* Kosice, Gyula

**Falk, Bibb August** 1899-
[BE, DGS, PB]
*American baseball player*
* Falk, Jockey

**Falk, Chester Emanuel** [Chet]
1905-  [BE]
*American baseball player*
* Falk, Spot

**Falk, Conrad Robert** 1935-
[FC, ITA]
*American actor*
* Conrad, Robert

**Falk, Elsa**
*See* Escherich, Elsa Falk

**Falk, Jockey**
*See* Falk, Bibb August

**Falk, Richard**
*See* Shirach, Baldur von

**Falk, Spot**
*See* Falk, Chester Emanuel [Chet]

**Falk, Sybil** 1923-  [IPA]
*British astrologer*
* Leek, Sybil

**Falkberget, Johan** [Petter]
*See* Lillebakken, J. P.

**Falke, Konrad** 1880-1942  [WBD]
*Swiss author, playwright, poet*
* Frey, Karl

**Falkenberg, Cy**
*See* Falkenberg, Frederick Peter

**Falkenberg, Frederick Peter**
1880-1961  [AS, BE]
*American baseball player*
* Falkenberg, Cy

**Falkenburg, Eugenia** 1919-  [FC]
*American model and actress*
* Falkenburg, Jinx

**Falkenburg, Jinx**
*See* Falkenburg, Eugenia

**Falkirk, Richard**
*See* Lambert, Derek

**Falkland**
*See* Chapman, Nathaniel

**Falkland, Frank**
*See* Wilson, G. L.

**Falkland, Samuel**
*See* Heijermans, Herman

**Falkner, Annemy** 1921-  [IAW]
*German journalist and author*
* Bellman, Erik Maria

**Falkner, John**
*See* Gale, E. F.

**Falkner, William** [Cuthbert]
1897-1962  [CA]
*American author*
* Faulkner, William [Cuthbert]

**Fall, Thomas**
*See* Snow, Donald Clifford

**Falla, Frank W.** 1911-  [AW]
*British journalist*
* Sarnian

**Fallada, Hans**
*See* Ditzen, [Wilhelm Friedrich]
Rudolf

**Fallen, Mrs. Frederick**  [FFF]
*Entertainer*
* Hart, Enid

**Fallenstin, Ed[ward Joseph]**
*See* Valestin, Edward Joseph

**Fallenstin, Jack**
*See* Valestin, Edward Joseph

**Fallere, Felicia**
*See* Knist, F[rances] Emma

**Fallon, Charles**
*See* Von Der Belin, Charles

**Fallon, Flash**
*See* Fallon, George Decatur

**Fallon, George**
*See* Bingley, David Ernest

**Fallon, George Decatur** 1916-  [BE]
*American baseball player*
* Fallon, Flash

**Fallon, Martin**
*See* Patterson, Harry

**Falls, Fred** ?-1963  [BEW]
*American theatrical performer*
* Binder, Fred

**Fallshaw, Keith George** 1946-
[ART]
*British painter and sculptor*
* K. F.

**Falorp, Nelson P.**
*See* Jones, Stephen [Phillip]

**[The] False Coiner**
*See* Philip III [or Philippe]

**[The] False Hermit**
*See* Enrico

**[The] False Prophet**
*See* Mohammed Ahmed

**[The] False Smerdis**
*See* Gaumata

**Falzone, Salvatore Joseph** 1933-
[EJ7]
*American jazz musician*
* Falzone, Sam

**Falzone, Sam**
*See* Falzone, Salvatore Joseph

**Fame, Georgie**
*See* Powell, Clive

**Fame, Herb**
*See* Feemster, Herbert

**[A] Family Doctor**
*See* Hutchin, Kenneth Charles

**Famosissimus, Doctor**
*See* Peter of Tarentaise [Pietro di
Tarantasia]

**Famosus, Doctor**
*See* De La Torre, Bertrand

**Famous Barnaby**
*See* Braithwaite, Richard

**Fan Fan**
*See* Blackburn, Victoria Grace

**Fanchon**
*See* Sanford, Laura

**Fanchon**
See  Starr, Laura B.

**Fane, Bron**
See  Fanthorpe, R[obert] Lionel

**Fane, Julian Charles Henry**
1827-1870   [DEL, PA]
*British author and poet*
* Temple, Neville
* Trevor, Edward

**Fane, Violet**
See  Currie, Mary Montgomerie

**Fanfan**
See  Smith, Mrs. F. B.

**Fangareggi, Ugo** 20th c.   [WF]
*Italian actor*
* Smith, Hugh Fangar

**Fangio, Juan Manuel** 1911-
*Italian auto racer*
* [The] Bowlegged One
* [The] Old Man

**Fannin, Clifford Bryson** 1924-1966
[BE]
*American baseball player*
* Fannin, Mule

**Fannin, Mule**
See  Fannin, Clifford Bryson

**Fanning, David Christopher Patrick
St. John** 1940-   [IAW]
*Irish-born author*
* Clare, Patrick
* Dee, John
* Lane, Gerald

**Fanok, Harry Michael** 1940-   [BE]
*American baseball player*
* [The] Flame Thrower

**Fanovich, Frank Joseph** 1922-   [BE]
*American baseball player*
* Fanovich, Lefty

**Fanovich, Lefty**
See  Fanovich, Frank Joseph

**Fanshaw, Cecil**
See  Dent, C. H.

**Fant, Eli**
See  Underhill, Edward Bean

**[El] Fantasma [The Ghost]**
See  Olguin Rangel, Eduardo

**Fanthorpe, R[obert] Lionel** 1935-
[CA, SF, WGT]
*British author*
* Balfort, Neil
* Baron, Othello
* Barton, Erle
* Barton, Lee
* Bell, Thornton
* Bertram, Noel
* Brett, Leo
* Fane, Bron
* Hobel, Phil
* Jay, Mel
* Johns, Marston
* La Salle, Victor [house
   pseudonym, John Spencer]
* Lerteth, Oban
* Lionel, Robert
* Muller, John E. [house
   pseudonym]
* Neef, Elton T.
* Nobel, Phil
* O'Flinn, Peter
* O'Flynn, Peter
* Roberts, Lionel
* Rolant, Rene

**Fanthorpe, R[obert] Lionel**
(Continued)
* Spartacus, Deutero
* Tate, Robin
* Thanet, Neil
* Thorpe, Trebor
* Thorpe, Trevor
* Torro, Pel
* Trent, Olaf
* Zeigfreid, Karl

**Farabi, Abu Nasr Mohammed al-**
[SN]
*Arabic physician and composer*
* [The] Orpheus of Arabia

**Faradge, Aboul** 1226-1286   [PA]
*Author*
* Barhebroeus

**Faragalli, Alfred Joseph** 1911-
[BBH]
*American bowler*
* Faragalli, Lindy

**Faragalli, Lindy**
See  Faragalli, Alfred Joseph

**Farago**
See  Szelenyi, Laszlo

**Farah, Jameel** 20th c.
*American actor*
* Farr, Jamie

**Faralla, Dana**
See  Faralla, Dorothy W.

**Faralla, Dorothy W.** 1909-
[CA, SAT]
*American author and poet*
* Faralla, Dana
* Wilma, Dana

**Farazdaq, al-**
See  Hammam

**Farbrick, Jonathan**
See  Holbrook, Silas Pinckney

**[The] Farceur**
See  Beolco, Angelo

**Fardin, Dieudonne**
See  Pierre Benoit, Louis Marie

**Fardon, Don**
See  Maughn, Donald

**Farel, Conrad**
See  Bardens, Dennis [Conrad]

**Farely, Alison**
See  Poland, Dorothy Elizabeth
Hayward

**Farenthold, Frances** 1926-
*American politician and college
administrator*
* Farenthold, Sissy

**Farenthold, Sissy**
See  Farenthold, Frances

**Farewell, Nina** [joint pseudonym
with Grace Klein]
See  Cooper, Mae [Klein]

**Farewell, Nina** [joint pseudonym
with Mae (Klein) Cooper]
See  Klein, Grace

**Farfariello**
See  Migliaccio, Edward

**Fargo, Donna**
See  Vaughan, Yvonne

**Fargo, Doone**
See  Norwood, Victor G[eorge]
C[harles]

**[The] Fargo Express**
See  Petrolle, Billy

**Fargo, Joe**
See  Rikhoff, James C.

**Fargo the Boy Wizard**
See  Weintrop, Reuben

**Fargus, Frederick J.** 1847-1885
[DNNF, FF]
*British author*
* Conway, Hugh

**Farian**
See  De Saint Ange, Ange Francois

**Farid ud-din Attar**
See  Mohammed ibn-Ibrahim

**Faridi, S. N.**
See  Faridi, Shah Nasiruddin
Mohammad

**Faridi, Shah Nasiruddin Mohammad**
1929-   [CA]
*Indian author and economist*
* Faridi, S. N.
* Jareed

**Farigoule, Louis** 1885-1972
[B10, CA, CD]
*French author, playwright, poet*
* Romains, Jules

**Farina**
See  Hoskins, Alan Clay, Jr.

**Farina, Salvatore** 1846-1918
[WBD]
*Italian author*
* [The] Italian Dickens

**Farinacci, Frankie** 1903-1953   [SC]
*American actor*
* Farr, Frankie

**Farinelli, Carlo**
See  Broschi, Carlo

**Farini, Gilarmi A.** 1839-1929
[WBD]
*Tightrope walker*
* Farini the Great

**Farini the Great**
See  Farini, Gilarmi A.

**Farinola, Vito** 1928?-
[FC, IPA, ITA]
*American singer and actor*
* Damone, Vic

**Faris, Will S.**   [PA]
*Author*
* Howard, Harvey

**Farjeon, [Eve] Annabel** 1919-
[AW, CA, SAT]
*British ballet critic and author*
* Jefferson, Sarah

**Farjeon, Eleanor** 1881-1965
[CAP, SAT]
*British author, poet, playwright*
* Chimaera
* Tomfool

**Farjeon, J[oseph] Jefferson**
1883-1955   [CC, MBF, TC1]
*British author*
* Swift, Anthony
* White, Leonard

**Farkas, Andre** 1915-   [CA, WEC]
*French cartoonist*
* Francois, Andre

**Farlane, Jason**
See  Munro, [Macfarlane] Hugh

**Farleigh, Elsie** 1900-   [ART]
*British painter*
* Neville, Anne

**Farley, Albert**
See  Farnese, Alberto

**Farley, Carol** 1936-   [SAT]
*American author*
* McDole, Carol

**Farley, Helen H.**   [PA]
*Author*
* Gilmore, Ernest

**Farley, Ralph Milne**
See  Hoar, Roger Sherman

**Farlow, Tal**
See  Farlow, Talmadge Holt

**Farlow, Talmadge Holt** 1921-
[DAM, EJ]
*American jazz musician*
* Farlow, Tal

**Farmacevten**
See  Holm, Sven [Aage]

**Farman, Ella**   [PA]
*Author*
* Shephard, Dorothea Alice

**[The] Farmer**
See  Bell, George Glenn

**Farmer, A. W.**
See  Wilkins, Isaac

**Farmer, Arthur**
See  Jardine, Jack Owen

**Farmer, Bernard J[ames]** 1902-
[CA, CC, WW]
*British author*
* Fox, Owen

**Farmer, Bess** 1919-   [CWG, DAM]
*American country-western performer*
* Miss Bess

**Farmer, Floyd Haskell** 1892-1970
[BE]
*American baseball player*
* Farmer, Jack

**Farmer George**
See  George III

**Farmer, Henry** 20th c.   [MBF]
*British author*
* Wright, Franklin

**Farmer, Jack**
See  Farmer, Floyd Haskell

**[The] Farmer King**
See  George III

**Farmer, Minnie Elizabeth** 1884-
[WWL]
*British author*
* Harrington, Elizabeth

**Farmer, Philip Jose** 1918-
[ESF, IAW, WGT]
*American author*
* Chapin, Paul
* Greystoke, Lord
* Keen, Rod
* Manders, Harry
* Somers, Jonathan Swift, III
* Tincrowdor, Leo Queequeg

**Farmer, Philip Jose** (Continued)
* Trout, Kilgore
* Watson, John H., MD

**[The] Farmer President**
*See* Harrison, William Henry

**[The] Farmer President**
*See* Washington, George

**Farmer, R. L.**
*See* Lamont, Rosette C[lementine]

**Farmer, Wendell**
*See* Davis, Lavinia [Riker]

**Farmers, Eileen Elizabeth**
**[Honeyman]** 1918-    [AW]
*Australian author*
* Lane, Elizabeth

**Farmington, Stone T.**
*See* Ackerman, Forrest J[ames]

**Farnash, Hugh**
*See* Luff, Stanley George Anthony

**Farnborough**
*See* Pearce, Brian Leonard

**Farndale, John**
*See* Harvey, John Wilfred

**Farnese, A.** 20th c.    [WGT]
*Author*
* Franchezzo

**Farnese, Alberto** 20th c.    [WF]
*Italian actor*
* Farley, Albert

**Farnese, Alessandro** 1468-1549
[WBD]
*Pope*
* Paul III

**Farnham, Burt**
*See* Clifford, Harold B[urton]

**Farnill, Barrie** 1923-    [WD]
*British author and journalist*
* Wellington, John

**Farningham, Marianne**
*See* Hearn, Mary Ann

**Farnsworth, Duncan**
*See* O'Brien, David Wright

**Farnsworth, James**
*See* Pohle, Robert W[arren], Jr.

**Farnum, Franklyn**
*See* Smith, William

**Farnum, K. T.**
*See* Rips, Ervine M[ilton]

**Farnum, Smiling Frank**
*See* Smith, William

**Farolito [Little Lighthouse]**
*See* Marron Eufrasio, Alejandro

**Farquar, Agnes Stephens** 1892-
[NAA]
*American writer*
* O'Hara, Joy

**Farquhar, George** 1678-1707
[DEP, FFF, RH]
*British playwright*
* [The] Fielding of the Drama
* [The] Smollett of the Stage

**Farquhar, Milton** 1945-    [IBW]
*American fashion designer*
* Farquhar, Pockets

**Farquhar, Pockets**
*See* Farquhar, Milton

**Farquharson, Martha**
*See* Finley, Martha Farquharson

**Farquharson, Robert**
*See* De La Condamine, Robert

**Farr, Diana Pullein-Thompson**
[CA]
*British author*
* Pullein-Thompson, Diana

**Farr, Douglas**
*See* Gilford, Charles Bernard

**Farr, Fiona**
*See* Lewis, Judith Mary
[Berrisford]

**Farr, Florence** 20th c.    [WWL]
*British author and actress*
* S. S. D. D.

**Farr, Frankie**
*See* Farinacci, Frankie

**Farr, Jamie**
*See* Farah, Jameel

**Farr, John**
*See* Webb, Jack

**Farr, Norman Richard** 1947-    [CEI]
*Canadian-born hockey player*
* Farr, Rocky

**Farr, Rocky**
*See* Farr, Norman Richard

**Farr, Sebastian**
*See* Blom, Eric Walter

**Farra, [Madame] E.**
*See* Fawcett, F[rank] Dubrez

**[The] Farrago**
*See* Dennie, Joseph

**Farrakhan, Louis**
*See* Walcott, Louis Gene

**Farrant, Walter** 1913-    [CEI]
*Canadian-born hockey player*
* Farrant, Whitey

**Farrant, Whitey**
*See* Farrant, Walter

**Farrar, Doctor**    [PA]
*Author*
* Hope, F. T. L.

**Farrar, John C[hipman]** 1896-1974
[CA]
*American playwright and poet*
* Prosper, John [joint pseudonym
  with Prosper Buranelli]

**Farrell, Ben**
*See* Cebulash, Mel

**Farrell, Bill**
*See* Fiorelli, William

**Farrell, Catharine**
*See* O'Connor, [Sister] Mary
Catharine

**Farrell, Charles**
*See* Fielder, Charles Farrell

**Farrell, Charles Andrew** 1866-1925
[AS, BE]
*American baseball player*
* Farrell, Duke

**Farrell, David**
*See* Smith, Frederick E[screet]

**Farrell, Desmond**
*See* Organ, John

**Farrell, Doc**
*See* Farrell, Edward Stephen

**Farrell, Duke**
*See* Farrell, Charles Andrew

**Farrell, Edward Stephen**
1901-1966    [BE]
*American baseball player*
* Farrell, Doc

**Farrell, Fred**
*See* Varelli, Alfredo

**Farrell, Gilbert Hastings**
1845-1901    [BEW, BMH]
*British actor, playwright, singer*
* [The] Great Macdermott
* Hastings, Gilbert
* Macdermott, G. H.

**Farrell, Hartford Jack**
*See* Farrell, John

**Farrell, James T[homas]**
1904-1979    [CA, WD]
*American author, poet, critic*
* Fogarty, Jonathan Titulescu, Esq.

**Farrell, Joe**
*See* Firrantello, Joseph Carl

**Farrell, John** ?-1916    [BE]
*American baseball player*
* Farrell, Hartford Jack

**Farrell, John A.** 1857-1914    [BE]
*American baseball player*
* Farrell, Moose

**Farrell, John Wade** [house
pseudonym]
*See* MacDonald, John D[ann]

**Farrell, M. J.**
*See* Keane, Molly

**Farrell, M. J.**
*See* Skrine, Mary Nesta

**Farrell, Moose**
*See* Farrell, John A.

**Farrell, Patricia**
*See* Zelver, Patricia [Farrell]

**Farrell, Richard Joseph** 1934-1977
[BE]
*American baseball player*
* Farrell, Turk

**Farrell, Skip**
*See* Fielder, Charles Farrell

**Farrell, Suzanne**
*See* Ficker, Roberta Sue

**Farrell, Turk**
*See* Farrell, Richard Joseph

**Farren, Babs**
*See* Farren, Clara Bianca Rouhan

**Farren, Clara Bianca Rouhan**
1904-    [THR]
*British actress*
* Farren, Babs

**Farren, David**
*See* McFerran, Douglass David

**Farren, Ellen** 1848-1904    [WBD]
*British actress*
* Farren, Nellie

**Farren, Nellie**
*See* Farren, Ellen

**Farren, Richard J.**
*See* Betjeman, [Sir] John

**Farren, Robert** 1909-    [CAT, DIL]
*Irish poet and critic*
* O Farachain, Roibeard

**Farrere, Claude**
*See* Bargone, [Frederic] Charles
[Pierre Edouard]

**Farrington, Bo**
*See* Farrington, John R.

**Farrington, John R.** 1936-1964
[AS, SMG]
*American football player*
* Farrington, Bo

**Farrington, Maude**
*See* Hickey, Madelyn Eastlund

**Farrow, J.**
*See* Fonarow, Jerry

**Farrow, James S.**
*See* Tubb, Edwin Charles

**Farrow, R.** 1920-    [AW]
*British physician and author*
* Vincent, John

**Farson, Daniel Negley** 1927-    [CA]
*British author*
* Excellent, Matilda

**Farthing Jamie**
*See* Lowther, [Sir] James

**[The] Farthing Poet**
*See* Horne, Richard Hengist

**Farwell, Janet** 1897-    [WWL]
*British author*
* Croly, Elizabeth

**Farwest**
*See* Ackerman, Forrest J[ames]

**Fasano [or Phasianus], Leo** ?-1009
[CAL]
*Pope*
* John XVIII [or XIX]

**[The] Fashionable Salad-Maker**
*See* D'Abegnac, Marquis

**Fassbinder, Carlton J.**
*See* Yerke, Theodore Bruce

**Fast Black Brown**
*See* Brown, Percy

**Fast Eddie Sachs**
*See* Sachs, Edward Julius

**Fast Fingers Dawkins**
*See* Dawkins, James Henry
[Jimmy]

**Fast, Howard [Melvin]** 1914-
[B10, CA, WD]
*American author*
* Cunningham, E. V.
* Ericson, Walter

**Fast, Julius** 1919-    [CA]
*American author*
* Barnett, Adam

**[The] Fastest Kid in the World**
*See* Goldsmith, Willie E., Jr.

**[The] Fastest Man in North America**
*See* Gorman, Charles

**[The] Fasting Woman of Tutbury**
*See* Moore, Ann

**Fastlife**
*See* Grogan, Emmett

**Faszholz, John Edward [Jack]**
1927-    [BE]
*American baseball player*
* Faszholz, Preacher

**Faszholz, Preacher**
*See*  Faszholz, John Edward [Jack]

**[The] Fat**
*See*  Alfonso II [Affonso, Alonzo or Alphonso]

**[The] Fat**
*See*  Charles II

**[The] Fat**
*See*  Douglas, James

**[The] Fat**
*See*  Henry I

**[The] Fat**
*See*  Lambert, David

**[The] Fat**
*See*  Louis VI

**[The] Fat**
*See*  Olaf II [or Olaus]

**[The] Fat Adonis of Forty [or Fifty]**
*See*  George IV

**Fat Alburt**
*See*  Norman, William

**Fat Charley Makley**
*See*  Makley, Charles

**Fat Contributor**
*See*  Griswold, A. Miner

**[The] Fat Contributor**
*See*  Thackeray, William Makepeace

**Fat Freddie**
*See*  McGregor, Charles

**Fat Freddie Fitzsimmons**
*See*  Fitzsimmons, Frederick Landis

**Fat Jack Fisher**
*See*  Fisher, John Howard

**[The] Fat Man**
*See*  Campo, John [Johnny]

**[The] Fat One**
*See*  Goering, Hermann

**Fat Tony Salerno**
*See*  Salerno, Anthony

**Father Abraham**
*See*  Franklin, Benjamin

**Father Abraham**
*See*  Lincoln, Abraham

**Father Ambrose**
*See*  Barker, Matthew Henry

**[The] Father Among Philological English Antiquaries**
*See*  Honywood, Michael

**[The] Father and Mother of His People**
*See*  Chin-tsou-jin

**Father Bill**
*See*  Schmeisser, William C. [Bill]

**Father Fritz**
*See*  Frederick II

**[The] Father of African Education**
*See*  Aggrey, James Emman Kodwo Mensa Humanfunsam Kwegyir

**[The] Father of African Socialism**
*See*  Nyerere, Julius Kambarage

**[The] Father of Afro-American Newspapers**
*See*  Cornish, Samuel E.

**[The] Father of Age-Group Swimming**
*See*  Bauer, Carl Otto

**[The] Father of Algebra**
*See*  Viete [or Vieta], Francois

**[The] Father of all Dancing-Masters**
*See*  Beauchamps

**[The] Father of America**
*See*  Adams, Samuel

**[The] Father of American Amateurism**
*See*  Curtis, William B.

**[The] Father of American Anthropology**
*See*  Morgan, Lewis Henry

**[The] Father of American Football**
*See*  Camp, Walter Chauncey

**[The] Father of American Geography**
*See*  Morse, Jedediah

**[The] Father of American Geology**
*See*  Maclure, William

**[The] Father of American Grape Culture**
*See*  Longworth, Nicholas

**[The] Father of American Independence**
*See*  Adams, John

**[The] Father of American Map Making**
*See*  Gannett, Henry

**[The] Father of American Minstrelsy**
*See*  Rice, Thomas Dartmouth

**[The] Father of American Organized Skiing**
*See*  Tellefsen, Carl

**[The] Father of American Rowing**
*See*  Curtis, William B.

**[The] Father of American Shipbuilding**
*See*  Roche, John

**[The] Father of American Surgery**
*See*  Physick, Philip Syng

**[The] Father of American Tennis**
*See*  Dwight, James

**[The] Father of American Watchmaking**
*See*  Dennison, Aaron Lufkin

**[The] Father of Angling**
*See*  Walton, Izaak

**[The] Father of Arabic Literature**
*See*  Mamoun, al-

**[The] Father of Australian Drama**
*See*  Esson, [Thomas] Louis [Buvelot]

**[The] Father of Baseball**
*See*  Chadwick, Henry

**[The] Father of Believers**
*See*  Mohammed [or Mahomet]

**[The] Father of Biblical Criticism**
*See*  Origen

**[The] Father of Black American Art**
*See*  Douglas, Aaron

**[The] Father of Black Letter Collectors**
*See*  Moore, John

**[The] Father of Black Letter Lore**
*See*  Pepys, Samuel

**[The] Father of Bluegrass Music**
*See*  Monroe, William [Bill]

**[The] Father of Botany**
*See*  Brunfels, Otto

**[The] Father of Botany**
*See*  Tournefort, Joseph Pittou de

**[The] Father of British Blues**
*See*  Mayall, John

**[The] Father of British Inland Navigation**
*See*  Egerton, Francis

**[The] Father of Broadcast Journalism**
*See*  Klauber, Edward

**[The] Father of Burlesque Poetry**
*See*  Hipponax

**[The] Father of Business Efficiency**
*See*  Taylor, Frederick Winslow

**[The] Father of Card Counting**
*See*  Thorp, Edward

**[The] Father of Chautauqua County**
*See*  Foote, Elial Todd

**[The] Father of Chemistry**
*See*  Arnaud de Villeneuve

**[The] Father of Choral Epode**
*See*  Stesichorus

**[The] Father of Chronology**
*See*  Scaliger, Josephus Justus

**[The] Father of Church History**
*See*  Eusebius of Caesarea

**[The] Father of Clock-Making**
*See*  Tompion, Thomas

**[The] Father of Colonization in America**
*See*  Gorges, [Sir] Ferdinando

**[The] Father of Comedy**
*See*  Aristophanes

**[The] Father of Commercial Hillbilly Music**
*See*  Rodgers, James Charles [Jimmie]

**[The] Father of Congo Independence**
*See*  Kasavubu, Joseph

**[The] Father of Country Music**
*See*  Rodgers, James Charles [Jimmie]

**[The] Father of Cruelty**
*See*  Hakim I [or Hakam] al-

**[The] Father of Curtesie**
*See*  Beauchamp, Richard de

**[The] Father of Cybernetics**
*See*  Wiener, Norbert

**[The] Father of Democracy in Virginia**
*See*  Ritchie, Thomas

**[The] Father of Dietetics**
*See*  Funk, Casimir

**[The] Father of Dithyrambic Poetry**
*See*  Arion

**[The] Father of Dixieland Drums**
*See*  Stephens, Mike

**[The] Father of Dutch Poetry**
*See*  Maerlant, Jakob

**[The] Father of Ecclesiastical History**
*See*  Bede [Baeda, or Beda]

**[The] Father of Ecclesiastical History**
*See*  Eusebius of Caesarea

**[The] Father of Ecclesiastical History**
*See*  Polygnotus

**[The] Father of Electric Traction**
*See*  Sprague, Frank Julian

**[The] Father of Electricity**
*See*  Gilbert, William

**[The] Father of English Botany**
*See*  Turner, William

**[The] Father of English Cathedral Music**
*See*  Tallis [or Tallys], Thomas

**[The] Father of English Commerce**
*See*  Edward III

**[The] Father of English Deism**
*See*  Herbert, Edward

**[The] Father of English Dramatic Poetry**
*See*  Marlowe, Christopher

**[The] Father of English General Baptists**
*See*  Smith [or Smyth?], John

**[The] Father of English Geology**
*See*  Smith, William

**[The] Father of English Golf**
*See*  Balfour, Arthur James

**[The] Father of English Grammar**
*See*  Murray, Lindley

**[The] Father of English Learning**
*See*  Bede [Baeda, or Beda]

**[The] Father of English Natural History**
*See*  Wray, John

**[The] Father of English Numbers**
*See*  Waller, Edmund

**[The] Father of English Poetry**
*See*  Chaucer, Geoffrey

**[The] Father of English Pottery**
*See*  Wedgwood, Josiah

**[The] Father of English Printing**
*See*  Caxton, William

**[The] Father of English Prose**
*See*  Ascham, Roger

**[The] Father of English Prose**
*See*  Wycliffe [or Wyclif], John

**[The] Father of English Song**
*See*  Caedmon

**[The] Father of English Surgery**
*See*  Wiseman, Richard

**[The] Father of English Unitarianism**
*See*  Biddle, John

**[The] Father of English Watchmaking**
*See*  Tompion, Thomas

**[The] Father of Epic Poetry**
*See* Homer

**[The] Father of Equity**
*See* Finch, Heneage [First Earl of Nottingham]

**[The] Father of Esperanto**
*See* Zamenhof, Lazarus Ludwig

**[The] Father of Europe**
*See* Monnet, Jean

**[The] Father of Field Theory**
*See* Lewin, Kurt Z.

**[The] Father of Flemish Poets**
*See* Maerlant, Jakob

**[The] Father of Foreign Mission Work**
*See* Mills, Samuel John

**[The] Father of Frankish History**
*See* Florentius, Georgius

**[The] Father of French Burlesque**
*See* Scarron, Paul

**[The] Father of French Chemistry**
*See* Arnaud de Villeneuve

**[The] Father of French Comedy**
*See* Poquelin, Jean Baptiste

**[The] Father of French Eloquence**
*See* Chartier, Alain

**[The] Father of French Enigma**
*See* Cotin, Charles

**[The] Father of French History**
*See* Brial, Michel-Jean-Joseph

**[The] Father of French History**
*See* Duchesne, Andre

**[The] Father of French History**
*See* Joinville, Jean de

**[The] Father of French History**
*See* Villehardouin, Geoffroi de

**[The] Father of French Philosophy**
*See* Alembert, Jean Le Rond d'

**[The] Father of French Poetry**
*See* Thibaut IV

**[The] Father of French Prose**
*See* Villehardouin, Geoffroi de

**[The] Father of French Satire**
*See* Regnier, Mathurin

**[The] Father of French Sculpture**
*See* Goujon, Jean

**[The] Father of French Sculpture**
*See* Pilon, Germain

**[The] Father of French Surgery**
*See* Pare, Ambroise

**[The] Father of French Tragedy**
*See* Corneille, Pierre

**[The] Father of French Tragedy**
*See* Garnier, Robert

**[The] Father of Geology**
*See* Avicenna [or Abou-ibn-Sina]

**[The] Father of German Exegesis**
*See* Simon, Richard

**[The] Father of German Literature**
*See* Lessing, Gotthold Ephraim

**[The] Father of German Minstrelsy**
*See* Henry of Veldig

**[The] Father of German Music**
*See* Schutz, Heinrich

**[The] Father of German Rationalism**
*See* Semler, Johann Salomo

**[The] Father of Good Works**
*See* Mohammed II [or Mahomet]

**[The] Father of Grace and Elegance**
*See* Bellay, Joachim du

**[The] Father of Grain Inspection**
*See* Rumsey, Julian Sidney

**[The] Father of Greek Didactic Poetry**
*See* Hesiod

**[The] Father of Greek Drama**
*See* Aeschylus

**[The] Father of Greek Music**
*See* Terpander

**[The] Father of Greek Philosophy**
*See* Aristotle

**[The] Father of Greek Prose**
*See* Herodotus

**[The] Father of Greek Tragedy**
*See* Aeschylus

**[The] Father of Greek Tragedy**
*See* Thespis

**[The] Father of Greenbacks**
*See* Spaulding, Elbridge Gerry

**[The] Father of Greyhound Racing**
*See* Critchley, Alfred Cecil

**[The] Father of Gymnastics**
*See* Jahn, Friedrich Ludwig

**[The] Father of Harlequins**
*See* Rich, John

**[The] Father of High School Wrestling**
*See* Martin, George Alfred

**[The] Father of High School Wrestling**
*See* Tomaras, William [Bill]

**[The] Father of His Country**
*See* Andronicus II Palaeologus

**[The] Father of His Country**
*See* Caesar, [Gaius] Julius

**[The] Father of His Country**
*See* Cicero, Marcus Tullius

**[The] Father of His Country**
*See* Doria, Andrea

**[The] Father of His Country**
*See* Frederick I [or Friedrich]

**[The] Father of His Country**
*See* Henry I [or Heinrich]

**[The] Father of His Country**
*See* Louis XVIII

**[The] Father of His Country**
*See* Medici, Cosmo [or Cosimo] de

**[The] Father of His Country**
*See* O'Toole, Laurence

**[The] Father of His Country**
*See* Octavius, Gaius

**[The] Father of His Country**
*See* Sancho I

**[The] Father of His Country**
*See* Sobhuza II

**[The] Father of His Country**
*See* Suger

**[The] Father of His Country**
*See* Washington, George

**[The] Father of Historic Painting**
*See* Polygnotus

**[The] Father of Historical Societies**
*See* Pintard, Lewis

**[The] Father of History**
*See* Herodotus

**[The] Father of Hockey**
*See* Sutherland, James T.

**[The] Father of Holography**
*See* Gabor, Dennis

**[The] Father of Iambic Verse**
*See* Archilochus

**[The] Father of Indian Nationalism**
*See* Naoroji, Dadabhai

**[The] Father of Inductive Philosophy**
*See* Bacon, Francis [First Baron Verulam]

**[The] Father of International Law**
*See* Grotius, Hugo

**[The] Father of Iron Bridges**
*See* Whipple, Squire

**[The] Father of Iron Shipbuilding in America**
*See* Roche, John

**[The] Father of Italian Novelists**
*See* Boccaccio, Giovanni

**[The] Father of Italian Prose**
*See* Boccaccio, Giovanni

**[The] Father of Jests**
*See* Miller, Joseph [Joe]

**[The] Father of Jurisprudence**
*See* Glanville, Ranulph de

**[The] Father of Kansas Relays**
*See* Outland, John H.

**[The] Father of Lacrosse**
*See* Beers, William George

**[The] Father of Landscape Gardening**
*See* Lenotre, Andre

**[The] Father of Lebanon Skiing**
*See* Heistad, Erling

**[The] Father of Legal-Reserve Life Insurance**
*See* Wright, Elizur

**[The] Father of Letters**
*See* Francis I or [Francois]

**[The] Father of Letters**
*See* Louis XII

**[The] Father of Letters**
*See* Medici, Lorenzo de

**[The] Father of Lies**
*See* Herodotus

**[The] Father of Logical Semantics**
*See* Tarski, Alfred

**[The] Father of London**
*See* Barnard, [Sir] John

**[The] Father of Medicine**
*See* Aretaeos of Cappadocia

**[The] Father of Medicine**
*See* Hippocrates

**[The] Father of Mesmerism**
*See* Mesmer, Friedrich Anton

**[The] Father of Method Acting**
*See* Strasberg, Lee

**[The] Father of Modern American Gangsterdom**
*See* Torrio, John [Johnny]

**[The] Father of Modern Art**
*See* Guidi, Tommaso

**[The] Father of Modern Astronomy**
*See* Kepler, Johannes [or John]

**[The] Father of Modern Baseball**
*See* Cartwright, Alexander Joy, Jr.

**[The] Father of Modern Black History**
*See* Woodson, Carter Godwin

**[The] Father of Modern Chinese Poetry**
*See* Mei Sheng

**[The] Father of Modern Commentators**
*See* Grey, Zachary

**[The] Father of Modern Diving**
*See* Brandsten, Ernst

**[The] Father of Modern Drama**
*See* Ibsen, Henrik [Johan]

**[The] Father of Modern French Literature**
*See* Seyssel, Claude de

**[The] Father of Modern French Poetry**
*See* Malherbe, Francois de

**[The] Father of Modern French Song**
*See* Panard, Charles-Francois

**[The] Father of Modern German Poetry**
*See* Opitz, Martin

**[The] Father of Modern Gospel Music**
*See* Dorsey, Thomas A[ndrew]

**[The] Father of Modern Harmony**
*See* Des Pres, Josquin

**[The] Father of Modern Harness Racing**
*See* Levy, George Morton

**[The] Father of Modern Hydraulic Engineering**
*See* Francis, James Bicheno

**[The] Father of Modern Japanese Poetry**
*See* Hagiwara, Sakutaro

**[The] Father of Modern Jazz**
*See* Young, Lester Willis

**[The] Father of Modern Lawn Tennis**
*See* Renshaw, William Charles

**[The] Father of Modern Magnetism**
*See* Van Vleck, John

**[The] Father of Modern Mental Magic**
*See* Squires, Theodore

**[The] Father of Modern Music**
*See* Mozart, Johannes Chrysostom Wolfgangus Theophilus

**[The] Father of Modern Neurophysiology**
*See* Bernstein, Julius

**[The] Father of Modern Nigerian Nationalism**
*See* Azikiwe, Nnamdi

**[The] Father of Modern Norwegian Poetry**
*See* Dass, Petter

**[The] Father of Modern Oil Painting**
*See* Van Eyck, Jan [or John]

**[The] Father of Modern Painting**
*See* Cenni di Pepo

**[The] Father of Modern Painting**
*See* Da Vinci, Leonardo

**[The] Father of Modern Pantheism**
*See* Eckhart [Eckart or Eckardt], Johannes

**[The] Father of Modern Piano Music**
*See* Bach, Johann Sebastian

**[The] Father of Modern Practice in Medicine**
*See* Sydenham, Thomas

**[The] Father of Modern Prose Fiction**
*See* Foe, Daniel

**[The] Father of Modern Scepticism**
*See* Bayle, Pierre

**[The] Father of Modern Skiing**
*See* Schneider, Hannes

**[The] Father of Modern Swedish Poetry**
*See* Olai, Georgius

**[The] Father of Modern Swimming**
*See* Handy, H. Jamison

**[The] Father of Modern Toryism**
*See* Murray, William [First Earl of Mansfield]

**[The] Father of Modern Volleyball**
*See* Idell, A. Provost

**[The] Father of Monks**
*See* Ethelwold

**[The] Father of Moral Philosophy**
*See* Aquinas, Thomas [Thomas of Aquino]

**[The] Father of Music**
*See* Palestrina, Giovanni

**[The] Father of Navigation**
*See* Henry [or Don Henrique]

**[The] Father of Negro Songs**
*See* Graupner, Johann Christian Gotlieb

**[The] Father of New Spain**
*See* Velasco, Luis de

**[The] Father of Obstetric Surgery**
*See* Paulus Aeginela

**[The] Father of Ohio Soccer**
*See* Commander, Colin

**[The] Father of One Wall Handball**
*See* O'Connell, Charles J.

**[The] Father of Oregon Track**
*See* Hayward, William

**[The] Father of Organized Baseball**
*See* Cartwright, Alexander Joy, Jr.

**[The] Father of Ornithologists**
*See* Edwards, George

**[The] Father of Orthodoxy**
*See* Athanasius

**[The] Father of Paper Currency**
*See* Clark, Abraham

**[The] Father of Parody**
*See* Hipponax

**[The] Father of Pastoral Romance**
*See* Urfe, Honore d'

**[The] Father of Peace**
*See* Doria, Andrea

**[The] Father of Philosophy**
*See* Bacon, Roger

**[The] Father of Philosophy**
*See* Haller, Albrecht von

**[The] Father of Physical Geography**
*See* Humboldt, [Friedrich Heinrich] Alexander von

**[The] Father of Physiognomy**
*See* Lavater, Johann Caspar

**[The] Father of Physiology**
*See* Haller, Albrecht von

**[The] Father of Pittsburgh**
*See* Washington, George

**[The] Father of Poetical Taste**
*See* Percy, Thomas

**[The] Father of Poetry**
*See* Homer

**[The] Father of Poland**
*See* Boleslav I [or Boleslas]

**[The] Father of Political Dissenters**
*See* Oldcastle, [Sir] John

**[The] Father of Power Politics**
*See* Morgenthau, Hans J.

**[The] Father of Presbyterianism in New York**
*See* McNish, George

**[The] Father of Presbyterianism in Virginia**
*See* Morris, Samuel

**[The] Father of Professional Baseball**
*See* Wright, William Henry

**[The] Father of Public Television**
*See* Killian, James R.

**[The] Father of Radio**
*See* De Forest, Lee

**[The] Father of Reclamation**
*See* Warren, Francis Emroy

**[The] Father of Reform**
*See* Cartwright, John

**[The] Father of Rhode Island and of American Baptists**
*See* Clarke, John

**[The] Father of Riddles**
*See* Cotin, Charles

**[The] Father of Ridicule**
*See* Rabelais, Francois

**[The] Father of Rifle Practice**
*See* Wingate, George Wood

**[The] Father of Rock 'n Roll**
*See* Crudup, Arthur

**[The] Father of Rock 'n' Roll**
*See* Haley, Bill

**[The] Father of Rock 'n Roll**
*See* Presley, Elvis Aaron

**[The] Father of Roman Philosophy**
*See* Cicero, Marcus Tullius

**[The] Father of Roman Satire**
*See* Lucilius, Caius

**[The] Father of Russian Diplomacy**
*See* Kurakin, Boris Ivanovich

**[The] Father of Russian Graphic Art**
*See* Favorsky, Vladimir Andreyevich

**[The] Father of Russian History**
*See* Nestor

**[The] Father of Russian Literature**
*See* Pushkin, Alexander Sergeivitch

**[The] Father of Satire**
*See* Archilochus

**[The] Father of Scandinavian Poetry**
*See* Arrebo, Anders Christensen

**[The] Father of Science Fiction**
*See* Gernsback, Hugo

**[The] Father of Scotch Landscape Painting**
*See* Thomson, John

**[The] Father of Scottish Landscape Art**
*See* Nasmyth, Alexander

**[The] Father of Sentiment**
*See* Rousseau, Jean-Jacques

**[The] Father of Sickle Cell Anemia Research**
*See* Scott, Roland B.

**[The] Father of Skiing**
*See* Harris, Fred

**[The] Father of Song**
*See* Homer

**[The] Father of Space Opera**
*See* Smith, Edward Elmer

**[The] Father of Spanish History**
*See* Mariana, Juan de [or John]

**[The] Father of Sports at Howard**
*See* Cook, Charles C.

**[The] Father of Statics**
*See* Archimedes

**[The] Father of Swedish Eloquence**
*See* Nordenhjelm

**[The] Father of Swedish Mechanics**
*See* Polhem, Christopher

**[The] Father of Swedish Music**
*See* Roman, Johan Helmich

**[The] Father of Swiss History**
*See* Tschudi, Aegidius [or Gilg von]

**[The] Father of Symphony**
*See* Haydn, [Franz] Joseph

**[The] Father of the A-Bomb**
*See* Oppenheimer, J[ulius] Robert

**[The] Father of the American Labor Movement**
*See* Gompers, Samuel

**[The] Father of the American Navy**
*See* Adams, John

**[The] Father of the American Navy**
*See* Humphreys [or Humphries], Joshua

**[The] Father of the American Navy**
*See* Tracy, Benjamin Franklin

**[The] Father of the American Stage**
*See* Dunlap, William

**[The] Father of the Atomic Submarine**
*See* Rickover, Hyman

**[The] Father of the Australian Ballot**
*See* Nicholson, William

**[The] Father of the Automobile**
*See* Duryea, Charles Edgar

**[The] Father of the Barge Canal**
*See* Symons, Thomas William

**[The] Father of the Blues**
*See* Handy, William Christopher

**[The] Father of the Box Score**
*See* Chadwick, Henry

**[The] Father of the British Blues Revival**
*See* Korner, Alexis

**[The] Father of the British Press**
*See* Caxton, William

**[The] Father of the Church**
*See* Bossuet, Jacques Benigne

**[The] Father of the Church in Islam**
*See* Ghazzali [or Ghazali], al-

**[The] Father of the Connecticut School Fund**
*See* Granger, Gideon

**[The] Father of the Constitution**
*See* Madison, James

**[The] Father of the Constitution**
*See* Senghor, Leopold Sedar

**[The] Father of the Declaration of Independence**
*See* Jefferson, Thomas

**[The] Father of the Department of Agriculture**
*See* Ellsworth, Henry Leavitt

**[The] Father of the Dutch Reformed Church in America**
*See* Livingston, John Henry

**[The] Father of the Engineers**
*See* Graves, Ernest

**[The] Father of the English Benedictines**
*See* Dunstan

**[The] Father of the English Novel**
*See* Fielding, Henry

**[The] Father of the European Community**
*See* Monnet, Jean

**[The] Father of the French Drama**
*See* Jodelle, Etienne

**[The] Father of the French Drama**
*See* Rotrou, Jean de

**[The] Father of the French Riddle**
*See* Cotin, Charles

**[The] Father of the Game of Whist**
*See* Hoyle, Edmond

**[The] Father of the German Landsknechte**
*See* Frundsberg [or Frondsberg], Georg von

[The] Father of the German School
See  Duerer, Albrecht [or Albert]

[The] Father of the Greek Drama
See  Thespis

[The] Father of the Halls
See  Morton, Charles

[The] Father of the Homestead Act
See  Johnson, Andrew

[The] Father of the Hotel System of
the United States
See  Boyden, Simeon

[The] Father of the House
See  Arap Moi, Daniel Torotich

[The] Father of the House
See  Kelley, William Darrah

[The] Father of the House of
Commons
See  O'Connor, Thomas Power

[The] Father of the House of Lords
See  Mount Cashel, Earl of

[The] Father of the Hydrogen Bomb
See  Teller, Edward

[The] Father of the Indian Army
See  Lawrence, Stringer

[The] Father of the Irish Republic
See  De Valera, Eamon

[The] Father of the Jurisprudence of
Louisiana
See  Martin, Francois Xavier

[The] Father of the Latin Poets
See  Ennius, Quintus

[The] Father of the Locomotive
See  Trevethick, Richard

[The] Father of the Maine Law
See  Dow, Neal

[The] Father of the Military Academy
See  Thayer, Sylvanus

[The] Father of the Modern German
Drama
See  Greif [Griphius or Gryphius],
Andreas

[The] Father of the Modern Soviet
Army
See  Ogarkov, Nikolai

[The] Father of the Modern
T-Formation
See  Shaughnessy, Clark D.

[The] Father of the Monitors
See  Smith, Joseph

[The] Father of the Monks
See  Otto of Bamberg

[The] Father of the National Ski
Patrol System
See  Dole, Charles Minot

[The] Father of the NCAA Hockey
Tournament
See  Tutt, William Thayer

[The] Father of the New York Bar
See  Jones, Samuel

[The] Father of the New York Bar
See  Van Vechten, Abraham

[The] Father of the North Carolina
Bar
See  Moore, Bartholomew Figures

[The] Father of the Oratorio
See  Animuccia, Giovanni

[The] Father of the People
See  Christian III

[The] Father of the People
See  Henry IV [or Henri]

[The] Father of the People
See  Louis XII

[The] Father of the People
See  Louis XVIII

[The] Father of the People
See  Pineau, Gabriel du

[The] Father of the Poets
See  Spenser, Edmund

[The] Father of the Poor
See  Gilpin, Bernard

[The] Father of the Poster
See  Cheret, Jules

[The] Father of the Potteries
See  Wedgwood, Josiah

[The] Father of the Profession
See  McCallum, Colin Whitton

[The] Father of the Profession
See  Parnell, Thomas Frederick

[The] Father of the Public School
System of Pennsylvania
See  Wolf, George

[The] Father of the Revolution
See  Sun Yat-sen

[The] Father of the Rocky Mountain
National Park
See  Mills, Enos Abijah

[The] Father of the Rondo
See  Davaux, Jean Baptiste

[The] Father of the Spanish Drama
See  Vega Carpio, Lope Felix de

[The] Father of the Telegraph
See  Morse, Samuel Finley Breese

[The] Father of the Tenth Mountain
Division
See  Dole, Charles Minot

[The] Father of the Turf
See  Vernon, Richard

[The] Father of the Twentieth
Amendment
See  Norris, George William

[The] Father of the University of
Virginia
See  Jefferson, Thomas

[The] Father of the Vaudeville
See  Basselin, Olivier

[The] Father of the Virgin
See  Abou Bekr

[The] Father of Tragedy
See  Aeschylus

[The] Father of Transactional
Analysis
See  Bernstein, Eric [Lennard]

[The] Father of Tropical Medicine
See  Manson, [Sir] Patrick

[The] Father of Tuscan Poetry
See  Tasso, Torquato

[The] Father of Universalism in
America
See  Murray, John

[The] Father of Vaudeville
See  Pastor, Antonio [Tony]

[The] Father of Vertu in England
See  Howard, Thomas [14th Earl of
Arundel]

[The] Father of War Correspondents
See  Richardson, William

[The] Father of Water Color Painting
See  Nicholson, Francis

[The] Father of Watercolor Art
See  Sandby, Paul

[The] Father of Wisconsin Basketball
See  Steinmetz, Christian

[The] Father of Yiddish Literature
See  Peretz, Yitskhok Leybush

[The] Father of Your Country
See  Vincent de Paul

Father Thoughtful
See  Catinat, Nicholas

Father Violet
See  Bonaparte, Napoleon

Fatio, Louis 1880-1895  [IBW]
American adventurer
* Pacheco, Luis

Fatio, Louise
See  Duvoisin, Louise

Fatiziece, Undine 1927-  [IAW]
Latvian author
* Indrane, Ilze

Fatso Marco Marcella
See  Marcella, Marco

[Il] Fattore [The Steward]
See  Penni, Giovanni Francesco

Fatty George
See  Pressler, Franz

Faucher, Paul 1898-1969  [B10]
French author, editor, publisher
* Castor, Pere

Fauconberg [or Falconberg], Thomas
?-1471  [WBD]
British soldier
* Thomas the Bastard

Fauley, Wilbur Finley 1872-1942
[SFL]
Author
* Fawley, Wilbur

Faulk, Odie B. 1933-  [WD]
American author
* Professor X

Faulkner, Anne Irvin 1906-  [CA]
American author
* Faulkner, Nancy

Faulkner, Dorothea M. 20th c.
[WGT]
Author
* Magill, Rory

Faulkner, George 1700-1775
[DNNS, FFF, SN]
Irish printer and author
* [The] Irish Atticus
* Paragraph, Peter

Faulkner, Georgene 1873- ?  [NAA]
American writer and radio
personality
* [The] Story Lady

Faulkner, James LeRoy [Jim]
1899-1962  [BE]
American baseball player
* Faulkner, Lefty

Faulkner, Lefty
See  Faulkner, James LeRoy [Jim]

Faulkner, Nancy
See  Faulkner, Anne Irvin

Faulkner, Robert Trevor 1929-
[ART]
British sculptor
* T. F.

Faulkner, Walt 20th c.
Auto racer
* [The] Little Dynamo

Faulkner, William [Cuthbert]
See  Falkner, William [Cuthbert]

Faulknor, Cliff[ord Vernon] 1913-
[CA]
Canadian author and columnist
* Williams, Pete

[The] Faultless Painter
See  D'Agnolo di Francesco,
Andrea Domenico

Faure, Edgar 1908-  [B10]
French politician
* Sanday, Edgar

Fausett, Buck
See  Fausett, Robert Shaw

Fausett, Leaky
See  Fausett, Robert Shaw

Fausett, Robert Shaw 1908-  [BE]
American baseball player
* Fausett, Buck
* Fausett, Leaky

Faust, Alexander
See  Altshuler, Harry

Faust, Camille 1872-1945  [WBD]
French author
* Mauclair, Camille

Faust, Charles Victor [Charlie]
1880-1915  [PB]
American baseball player
* Faust, Victory

Faust, Frederick [Schiller]
1892-1944  [EMD, LC, WGT]
American author
* Austin, Frank
* Baxter, George Owen
* Bolt, Lee
* Brand, Max
* Butler, Walter C.
* Challis, George
* Dawson, Peter
* Dexter, Martin
* Evan, Evin
* Evans, Evan
* Frederick, John
* Frost, Frederick
* [The] King of the Pulp Writers
* Lawton, Dennis
* M. B.
* Manning, David
* Morland, Peter Henry
* Owen, Hugh
* Silver, Nicholas
* Uriel, Henry
* Ward, Peter

**Faust, Mrs. A. J.**　[FFF]
*Entertainer*
* Montrose, Kate

**Faust, Ray** 1902?-1964　[BEW]
*Actor and stuntman*
* Spiker, Ray

**Faust, Victory**
*See* Faust, Charles Victor
[Charlie]

**Faustina, John Marcellus** 1920-
[IBW]
*American musician and educator*
* Faustina, Ted

**Faustina, Ted**
*See* Faustina, John Marcellus

**Faustman, Erik** 1919-1961　[SC]
*Swedish actor, director, screenwriter*
* Faustman, Hampe

**Faustman, Hampe**
*See* Faustman, Erik

**Fautsko, Timothy F[rank]** 1945-
[CA]
*American author*
* Employee X

**Fauver, Cayt**
*See* Fauver, Clayton King

**Fauver, Clayton King** 1872-1942
[BE]
*American baseball player*
* Fauver, Cayt
* Fauver, Pop

**Fauver, Pop**
*See* Fauver, Clayton King

**Favonius**
*See* West, Richard

**Favor, Mrs. Edward M.**　[FFF]
*Entertainer*
* Sinclair, Edith

**[The] Favored Child of Victory**
*See* Massena, Andre

**[The] Favorite Disciple of Coleridge**
*See* Allsop, Thomas

**Favorsky, Vladimir Andreyevich**
1886-　[GA]
*Russian graphic artist*
* [The] Father of Russian Graphic
Art

**Fawcett, C.**
*See* Cookson, Catherine Ann
[McMullen]

**Fawcett, Eric**
*See* Burbidge, Eric

**Fawcett, F[rank] Dubrez**
1891-1968　[CAP, ESF]
*British author*
* Del Martia, Astron [house
pseudonym, Gaywood Press]
* Dupres, Henri
* Farra, [Madame] E.
* Glen, Eugene
* Griff [house pseudonym?]
* McCann, Coolidge
* Saks, Elmer Eliot
* Sarto, Ben
* Stokes, Simpson

**Fawcett, James** 20th c.　[BLB]
*American underworld figure*
* Fawcett, Red

**Fawcett, Marion**
*See* Campbell, Katherine Roger

**Fawcett, Marion**
*See* Sanderson, Sabina W[arren]

**Fawcett, Red**
*See* Fawcett, James

**Fawcette, Wyliaume**
*See* Willcox, J. K. Hamilton

**Fawcitt, Helen**
*See* Martin, Lady Theodore

**Fawkes, Frank Attfield** 20th c.
[WGT]
*Author*
* X

**Fawkes, Guy**
*See* James, Edward

**Fawkes, Guy** 1577?-1606　[RH]
*British conspirator*
* Johnstone, John

**Fawkes, Walter Ernest** 1924-
[WEC]
*British cartoonist*
* Trog

**Fawley, Wilbur**
*See* Fauley, Wilbur Finley

**Fawn, James**
*See* Simmons, James

**Fawssett**
*See* Atkin, Ann

**Faxon, Henry W.**　[PA]
*Author*
* Parin, A. P. L.

**Faxon, Lavinia**
*See* Russ, Lavinia

**Fay**
*See* Smead, Mrs.

**Fay, Dorothy**
*See* Lindholm, Anna Chandler

**Fay, Gerda**
*See* Gemmer, Caroline M.

**Fay, Lottie**
*See* Woodson, Mrs. W. L.

**Fay, Mary Helen**
*See* Fagyas, Maria

**Fay, Nicholas**
*See* Sherren, Wilkinson

**Fay, Stanley**
*See* Stanley, Fay Grissom
[Shulman]

**Faye, Alice**
*See* Leppert, Alice Jeanne

**Faye, Joey**
*See* Palladino, Joseph Anthony

**Faye, Julia**
*See* Covell, Julia Faye

**Faye, Rita**
*See* Sinks, Rita Faye

**Faylen, Frank**
*See* Ruf, Frank

**Fayne, George** 20th c.　[RO2]
*American singer*
* Cody, Commander

**Fayre, Eleanor**
*See* Smith-Thomas, Eleanor Mary
Tydfil

**Fazio, Basil** 1908-　[BBH]
*American bowler*
* Fazio, Buzz

**Fazio, Buzz**
*See* Fazio, Basil

**Fazola, Faz**
*See* Prestopnik, Irving Henry

**Fazola, Irving Henry**
*See* Prestopnik, Irving Henry

**Fazy, James**
*See* Fazy, Jean Jacques

**Fazy, Jean Jacques** 1794-1878
[WBD]
*Swiss statesman, journalist, author*
* Fazy, James

**Fazzano, Joseph E.** 1929-　[CA]
*American attorney and author*
* Fitzgerald, John

**Feagles, Anita MacRae** 1926-
[CA, SAT, WW]
*American author*
* MacRae, Travis

**Feagles, Elizabeth**
*See* Day, Beth [Feagles]

**Fear, A. H.** 1901-　[CFH]
*British-born football player*
* Fear, Cap

**Fear, Cap**
*See* Fear, A. H.

**Fear, Luvern Carl** 1924-　[BE]
*American baseball player*
* Fear, Vern

**Fear, Vern**
*See* Fear, Luvern Carl

**Fearing, Alden**
*See* Dyer, Walter Alden

**Fearing, Kenneth [Flexner]**
1902-1961　[CA, WGT]
*American poet and author*
* Bedford, Donald F. [joint
pseudonym with Donald Friede
and Henry Bedford-Jones]

**[The] Fearless**
*See* John [or Jean]

**[The] Fearless**
*See* Moran, Owen

**[The] Fearless**
*See* Richard I

**Fearless Lil Jackson**
*See* Jackson, Lillie Mae Carroll

**Fearn, C. Eaton** 20th c.　[MBF]
*British author and editor*
* Lang, Peter
* Macrae, Herbert
* Merrick, Jim

**Fearn, Henry Noel** 1811- ?　[PA]
*Author*
* Christmas

**Fearn, John Russell** 1908-1960
[ESF, SF, SFL]
*British author*
* Armstrong, Geoffrey
* Ayre, Thorton
* Blayn, Hugo
* Boyce, Morton

**Fearn, John Russell** (Continued)
* Clive, Dennis
* Cross, Polton
* Del Martia, Astron [house
pseudonym, Gaywood Press]
* Denholm, Mark
* Dodd, Douglas
* Drew, Sheridan
* Elton, Max
* Firth, N. Wesley
* Gordon, Spike
* Gridban, Volsted [house
pseudonym, Scion]
* Griff [house pseudonym, Modern
Publications]
* Hartley, Malcolm
* Hayes, Timothy
* Holt, Conrad G.
* Jones, Frank
* Kayne, Marvin
* Lloyd, Herbert
* Lorraine, Paul [house pseudonym,
Curtis Warren]
* Passante, Dom
* Rose, Francis [Frank]
* Rose, Laurence F.
* Ross, Ward
* Russell, John
* Sclanders, Doorn
* Seagar, Joan
* Shaw, Brian [house pseudonym,
Curtis Warren]
* Slate, John
* Statten, Vargo
* Tarne, Rosina
* Thomas, K.
* Titan, Earl
* Waterhouse, Arthur
* Werheim, John
* Winiki, Ephriam

**Fearnley, John**
*See* Schiott, Johannes

**Fearon, George Edward**
*See* Margoliouth, George Edward

**Fearon, Percy Arthur** 1874-1948
[WEC]
*British cartoonist*
* Poy

**Feathers, Big Chief**
*See* Feathers, William B.

**Feathers, William B.** 1908-　[FB]
*American football player*
* Feathers, Big Chief

**Featherston, Vane**
*See* Featherstonhaugh, Vane

**Featherstone, D.**
*See* Warren, David

**Featherstone, Eddie**
*See* Fetherston, Eddie

**Featherstone, Norman George**
1949-　[DC]
*Rhodesian-born cricketer*
* Featherstone, Smokey

**Featherstone, Smokey**
*See* Featherstone, Norman George

**Featherstonehaugh, Francis**
*See* MacGregor, Alasdair Alpin
[Douglas]

**Featherstonhaugh, Buddy**
*See* Featherstonhaugh, Rupert
Edward Lee

**Featherstonhaugh, Constance**
*See* Samwell, Gertrude Constance

**Featherstonhaugh, Rupert Edward Lee** 1909- [EJ, PMJ]
*French-born jazz musician*
* Featherstonhaugh, Buddy

**Featherstonhaugh, Vane** 1864-1948 [BEW]
*British-born actress*
* Featherston, Vane

**Febiger, Christian** 1746-1796 [FFF]
*Danish-born soldier*
* Old Denmark

**Febronius, Justinus**
See Hontheim, Johann Nikolaus [or John Nicholas] von

**Fecamps, Elise**
See Creasey, John

**Fecher, Constance** 1911- [B10, CA, SAT]
*British actress and author*
* Heaven, Constance

**Fechner, Gustav Theodor** 1801-1887 [WBD]
*German physicist, philosopher, psychologist*
* Mises, Dr.

**Feckenham, John de**
See Howman, John

**Fedden, Henry [Romilly]** 1908- [CA]
*British author*
* Fedden, Robin

**Fedden, Robin**
See Fedden, Henry [Romilly]

**Feddersen, Bill** 20th c. [GW]
*American rodeo performer*
* Feddersen, Good Time

**Feddersen, Don** 20th c. [GW]
*American rodeo performer*
* Feddersen, Heavy Duty

**Feddersen, Good Time**
See Feddersen, Bill

**Feddersen, Heavy Duty**
See Feddersen, Don

**Feder, George** 1901-1951 [SC]
*American actor, cameraman, director*
* Raymond, Jack

**Feder, Robert Arthur** 1909-1969 [FC, WGT]
*American author and producer*
* Arthur, Robert

**Federoff, Al[fred]** 1924- [BE]
*American baseball player*
* Federoff, Whitey

**Federoff, Whitey**
See Federoff, Al[fred]

**Fedorovich, Nicholas** 1908- [IAW]
*Ukranian-born clergyman and author*
* Verkhovynetz, M.

**Fee, Benjamin J.** 1909- [IAW]
*Chinese-born writer and poet*
* Chang, T. K.
* Yun, Mu

**Feehan, Agnes M.** 1878- ? [CAT]
*American author*
* Clementia
* Mary Edward, [Sister]

**Feelgood, Doctor**
See Perryman, William Lee [Willie]

**Feemster, Herbert** 1942- [IBW]
*American singer*
* Fame, Herb

**Feeney, Charles Stoneham** 1921- [PB]
*American baseball executive*
* Feeney, Chub

**Feeney, Chub**
See Feeney, Charles Stoneham

**Feeney, Franklin** 1898-1950 [SC]
*American actor*
* Stevens, Lynn

**Feeney, Gerard Martin** 1927- [BEW]
*American educator*
* Patrick, [Brother] Benilde

**Feeney, Katharine Scully** 1928- [FC]
*American actress*
* Forrest, Sally

**Feher, Tibor**
See Szacsvay-Feher, Tibor

**Fehrenbach, Theodore Reed** 1925- [WD]
*American author*
* Freeman, Thomas

**Fehring, Dutch**
See Fehring, William Paul [Bill]

**Fehring, William Paul [Bill]** 1912- [BBH, BE]
*American baseball player and coach*
* Fehring, Dutch

**Fehrman, Austin** 1892-1964 [THR]
*British-born actor*
* Fairman, Austin

**Fehrman, Minny** 1856-1925 [BBD]
*British opera singer*
* Brema, Marie

**Feigenbaum, Harold** 1926- [CA, SAT]
*American author and book designer*
* Franklin, Harold

**Feikema, Feike**
See Feikema, Frederick

**Feikema, Frederick** 1912- [CA, TC, WD]
*American author*
* Feikema, Feike
* Manfred, Frederick Feikema

**Feilding, Beau**
See Feilding, Robert

**Feilding, Dorothy** 1884- [LC, TC, WW]
*British author*
* Fielding, A.

**Feilding, Handsome**
See Feilding, Robert

**Feilding, Robert** 1651?-1712 [DNNS, WBD]
*British army officer and politician*
* Feilding, Beau
* Feilding, Handsome

**Feilen, John**
See May, Julian

**Feinberg, Bea** 20th c. [CA]
*American author*
* Freeman, Cynthia

**Feinberg, Edward [Eddie]** 1918- [BE]
*American baseball player*
* Feinberg, Itzy

**Feinberg, Itzy**
See Feinberg, Edward [Eddie]

**Feinberg, Samuel** 1902- [BEW, EMT]
*American composer*
* Fain, Sammy

**Feinblum**
See Feinstein, Dianne

**Feininger, Charles Leonell** 1871-1956 [CAR]
*American painter*
* Feininger, Lyonel

**Feininger, Lyonel**
See Feininger, Charles Leonell

**Feinstein, Dianne** 1934?- 
*American politician*
* Feinblum

**Feinstein, Irving** ?-1940 [PHM]
*American underworld figure*
* Feinstein, Puggy

**Feinstein, Puggy**
See Feinstein, Irving

**Feinstone, Ezra Chaim** 1917- [BEW]
*American director, actor, producer*
* Stone, Ezra

**Feist, Charles** 19th c. [PA]
*Author*
* [An] East Anglien

**Feist, Henry Mort** [FFF, PA]
*British sportswriter*
* Augur
* Hotspur

**Feistkorn, W.** [FFF]
*German writer*
* Hilarius

**Felber, Rudolph** 1891- [IAW]
*Czech-born composer, author, playwright*
* Fuerb, Raoul

**Feld**
See Rosenfeld, Friedrich

**Feld, Marc** 1948- [RO2]
*British musician*
* Bolan, Marc

**Felder, Benny**
See Felder, William

**Felder, Paul**
See Wellen, Edward [Paul]

**Felder, William** 20th c. [OBW]
*American baseball player*
* Felder, Benny

**Feldman, Anatole** 20th c. [SFP]
*Author*
* Jones, G. Wayman [house pseudonym]

**Feldman, Andrea**
See Whips, Andrea

**Feldman, Charles K.**
See Gould, Charles

**Feldman, Cocky**
See Feldman, Harry

**Feldman, Ellen [Bette]** 1941- [CA]
*American author*
* Russell, Amanda
* Villars, Elizabeth

**Feldman, Harry** 1915-1950 [EJS]
*South African jockey*
* Feldman, Cocky

**Feldman, Herbert [H. S.]** 1910- [CA]
*British barrister and author*
* McLeod, Ross

**Feldman, Joshua** 1922-1980 [EJ, PMJ]
*American arranger and composer*
* Fielding, Jerry

**Feldman, Leonard** 1927- [CA]
*American author*
* Elliot, Daniel

**Feldman, Scott** 1923- [JL]
*American literary agent*
* Meredith, Scott

**Feldman, Sophie** 1930?-1978
*American comedienne*
* Fields, Totie

**Feldon, Barbara**
See Hall, Barbara

**Feldstein, Sandy**
See Feldstein, Saul

**Feldstein, Saul** 1940- [ASC]
*American composer and teacher*
* Feldstein, Sandy

**Felhauser, George** 20th c. [EJS]
*American jockey*
* Fields, George

**Felicita, Maria** 1867-1955 [BBD]
*Italian violinist*
* Maria Di Gesu, [Sister]
* Tua, Teresina

**Felious, Odetta**
See Holmes, Odetta

**Felipe, Alfredo** 1931-1958 [SC]
*Portuguese actor*
* [The] Portuguese Fernandel

**Felix**
See Martin, Bon Louis Henri

**Felix**
See Sulla, Lucius Cornelius

**Felix, August Guenther** 1895-1960 [BE]
*American baseball player*
* Felix, Gus

**Felix, Elisa** 1820-1858 [WBD]
*French actress*
* Rachel, Mlle.

**Felix, Gus**
See Felix, August Guenther

**Felix, M.**
See Wanostrocht, Nicholas

**Felix, Minutius**
See Hardinge, George

**Felix the Fixer**
See Rohatyn, Felix

**Felix V**
See Amadeus

**Felkin, Alfred Laurence** 1856- ?
[LAO]
*British author*
* St. Laurence, A.

**Felkin, Ellen Thorneycroft**
1860-1929   [LAO]
*British author*
* Fowler, Ellen Thorneycroft

**Fell, Archie**
See   Capron, M. J.

**Fell, Barry**
See   Fell, H[oward] Barraclough

**Fell, H[oward] Barraclough** 1917-
[CA]
*British-born zoologist and author*
* Fell, Barry

**Fell, William Richmond** 1897-
[WD]
*New Zealand author*
* Richmond, William

**Feller, Happy**
See   Feller, James P.

**Feller, James P.** 1949-   [FB]
*American football player*
* Feller, Happy

**Feller, Rapid Robert**
See   Feller, Robert William
Andrew

**Feller, Robert William Andrew**
1918-   [BE, GSH]
*American baseball player*
* Feller, Rapid Robert

**Fellig, Arthur** 1899-1968   [B10]
*American photographer*
* Weegee

**Fellinge, H. L.**
See   Fellinge, Harry Lee

**Fellinge, Harry Lee** 1888-   [NAA]
*American author and musician*
* Fellinge, H. L.
* Fellings, Henry
* Fielding, Harry Lee
* Lee, Harry

**Fellings, Henry**
See   Fellinge, Harry Lee

**Fellini, Federico** 1920-
*Italian director*
* [Il] Maestro

**Felloes**
See   Fellows, Laurence

**Fellowes, Anne**
See   Mantle, Winifred Langford

**Fellowes, G. W.**   [FFF]
*Author*
* Romeo

**Fellowes, Robert** 1770-1847   [DEL]
*British author*
* [The] Spirit of Hampden

**Fellowes-Gordon, Ian [Douglas]**
1921-   [AW, CA, WW]
*American-born British journalist*
* Collier, Douglas
* Gordon, Ian

**Fellowes-Robinson, Dora**
See   Robinson, Dora

**Fellows, Laurence** 1885-1964
[WEC]
*American cartoonist*
* Felloes

**Fellows, Robert** 19th c.   [PA]
*Author*
* Philalethes

**Fells, George**
See   Flevitsky, George

**Felsch, Happy**
See   Felsch, Oscar Emil

**Felsch, Oscar Emil** 1891-1964
[AS, BE]
*American baseball player*
* Felsch, Happy

**Felsen, Henry Gregor** 1916-
[CA, SAT]
*American author*
* Vicar, Henry
* Vicker, Angus

**Felsenstein, Peter** 1930-   [OP]
*Austrian operatic stage director and
producer*
* Brenner, Peter

**Felstein, Ivor** 1933-
[AW, CA, IAW]
*Scottish-born physician and medical
journalist*
* McCann, Philip
* Steen, Frank

**Felton, Eve**
See   Simpson, Edith Eva

**Felton, Francis J., Jr.** 1908-1964
[SC]
*American actor*
* Felton, Happy

**Felton, Frederick A.** 20th c.   [MBF]
*British author*
* Armstrong, Jack

**Felton, Happy**
See   Felton, Francis J., Jr.

**Felton, John** 1595?-1628   [SN]
*British army officer who
assassinated the Duke of
Buckingham*
* Honest Jack
* Little David

**Felton, Ronald Oliver** 1909-
[AW, CA, SAT]
*Welsh-born author*
* Welch, Ronald

**[The] Female Ali**
See   Tonawanda, Jackie

**[The] Female Bert Williams**
See   McDaniel, Hattie

**[A] Female Fontenelle**
See   Geoffrin, Marie Therese

**[The] Female Freemason**
See   St. Leger, Elizabeth

**[The] Female Howard**
See   Fry, Elizabeth

**[The] Female Maecenas**
See   Montagu, Mary Wortley

**[The] Female Marine**
See   Snell, Hannah

**[A] Female Soldier**
See   Davies, Mrs. Christian

**Fendell, Bob** 1925-   [CA]
*American writer*
* Roberts, Dell

**Fender, Freddy**
See   Huerta, Baldemar

**Fendt, Rene** 1948-   [ART]
*Swiss-born painter*
* R. F.

**Fenelon, Fania**
See   Goldstein, Fania

**Fenelon, Francois de Salignac de la
Mothe** 1651-1715   [DEP, FFF, SN]
*French prelate and author*
* [The] Swan of Cambray

**[The] Fenelon of Germany**
See   Herder, Johann Gottfried von

**[The] Fenelon of Germany**
See   Lavater, Johann Caspar

**[The] Fenelon of Scotland**
See   Leighton, Robert

**[The] Fenelon of the Reformation**
See   Arnd [or Arndt], Johann

**Feng Yu-hsiang** 1880-1948   [WBD]
*Chinese army officer*
* [The] Christian General

**Fengler, Harlan**
*Auto racer*
* [The] Wonder Boy of the
Speedways

**Fenimore, Ford**
See   Hoft, Ford Fenimore

**Fenimore, Robert** 1925-   [FB]
*American football player*
* [The] Blond Blizzard

**[El] Fenix de Espana**
See   Vega Carpio, Lope Felix de

**Fenkell, Doc**
See   Fenkell, Neal K.

**Fenkell, Neal K.** 20th c.   [SMG]
*American baseball team staff
member*
* Fenkell, Doc

**Fenn, Caroline K.** 20th c.   [WW]
*Author*
* McGrew, Fenn [joint pseudonym
with Julia McGrew]

**Fenn, Dorothy Francis** 20th c.
[BEW]
*American actress*
* Fenn, Peggy

**Fenn, Eleanor** 1744-1813
[FFF, PA, RH]
*British author*
* Lovechild, Mrs.
* Teachwell, Mrs.

**Fenn, George Manville** 1831-1909
[MBF]
*British author*
* Manville, George

**Fenn, Peggy**
See   Fenn, Dorothy Francis

**Fenner, Carol**
See   Williams, Carol

**Fenner, Hod**
See   Fenner, Horace Alfred

**Fenner, Horace Alfred** 1897-1954
[BE]
*American baseball player*
* Fenner, Hod

**Fenner, James R.**
See   Tubb, Edwin Charles

**Fenollosa, Mary McNeil** 20th c.
[NAA]
*American author*
* McCall, Sidney

**[El] Fenomeno de Triana [The
Phenomenon of Triana]**
See   Belmonte y Garcia, Juan

**Fensch, Thomas** 1943-   [CA]
*American author*
* Moore, Lander

**Fenton, Doc**
See   Fenton, G. E.

**Fenton, Frank**
See   Fenton-Morgan, Frank

**Fenton, Freda**
See   Rowland, D[onald] S[ydney]

**Fenton, G. E.** 1887-1968   [FB]
*American football player*
* Fenton, Doc

**Fenton, Katherine** 20th c.   [ART]
*British painter*
* F.
* K. F.

**Fenton, Mabel**
See   Towne, Ada

**Fenton, Mrs. Charles**   [FFF]
*Entertainer*
* Parker, Caroline

**Fenton-Morgan, Frank** 1906-1957
[SC]
*American actor and screenwriter*
* Fenton, Frank

**Fenwick, Bloop**
See   Fenwick, Robert Richard
[Bobby]

**Fenwick, Irene**
See   Frizzel, Irene

**Fenwick, Kay**
See   Bean, Keith F[enwick]

**Fenwick, Mrs. I.** 19th c.   [SN]
* I. F.

**Fenwick, Peter**
See   Holmes, Peter Fenwick

**Fenwick, Robert Richard [Bobby]**
1946-   [BE]
*Japanese-born baseball player*
* Fenwick, Bloop

**Fenwick, Thomas**   [FFF]
*Canadian clergyman and author*
* Blue Bonnet
* Hydrophilus

**Fenwick-Owen, Roderic Franklin
Rawnsley** 1921-   [AW]
*British author*
* Owen, Roderic

**Fenwood, Harry**
See   Walsh, William W.

**Feraco, Dizzy**
See   Feraco, Jimmy

**Feraco, Jimmy** ?-1940?   [PHM]
*American underworld figure*
* Feraco, Dizzy

**Ferdinand**
See   Vonnegut, Kurt, Jr.

**Ferdinand** 1402-1443   [WBD]
*Portuguese prince*
* [The] Constant Prince

**Ferdinand, Roger** 1898-1967
[MWD]
*French playwright*
* Roger Ferdinand

**Ferdinand, Val** 1947- [IBW]
*American author, playwright, poet*
* Salaam, Kalamu Ya

**Ferdinand I** ?-1065
[DNNS, SN, WBD]
*King of Castile and Leon*
* [The] Great
* [EL] Magno

**Ferdinand I** 1345-1383 [WBD]
*King of Portugal*
* [The] Handsome

**Ferdinand I** 1373?-1416
[FFF, RH, SN]
*King of Aragon*
* [The] Just

**Ferdinand II** 1810-1859
[DEP, HN, SN]
*King of Naples and Sicily*
* Bomba
* King Bomba

**Ferdinand III** 1199-1252
[DNNS, WBD]
*King of Castile and Leon*
* [The] Saint
* [El] Santo

**Ferdinand IV** 1285?-1312
[HN, WBD]
*King of Castile and Leon*
* [El] Emplazado
* [The] Summoned

**Ferdinand V [or Ferdinand II of
Aragon]** 1452-1516 [FFF, RH, SN]
*King of Aragon and Castile*
* [The] Catholic
* [The] Wily

**Ferdinand VI** 1713-1759 [WBD]
*King of Spain*
* [El] Sabio

**Ferenczi, Sandor**
*See* Fraenkel, Sandor

**Ferens, Lefty**
*See* Ferens, Stan[ley]

**Ferens, Stan[ley]** 1915- [BE]
*American baseball player*
* Ferens, Lefty

**Ferguson, Bessie Gowan** 20th c.
[NAA]
*Canadian journalist*
* Fachion, Frances
* Gowan, Elizabeth

**Ferguson, Bob**
*See* Miller, Bob

**Ferguson, Charles W.** 1901- [CA]
*American author*
* Gregory, Hilton

**Ferguson, Elmer W.** 1885-1972
[CSH]
*Canadian journalist*
* Ferguson, Fergy

**Ferguson, Evelyn** 1910- [WD]
*American author*
* Nevin, Evelyn C.

**Ferguson, Fergie**
*See* Ferguson, Joe Vance

**Ferguson, Fergy**
*See* Ferguson, Elmer W.

**Ferguson, Helen**
*See* Edmonds, Helen [Woods]

**Ferguson, Hilda**
*See* Gibbons, Hildegarde

**Ferguson, J. E.** [FFF]
*American journalist*
* Josslyn, Jeff

**Ferguson, James** 1710-1776
[DEP, DNNS, RH]
*Scottish astronomer*
* [The] Peasant Boy Philosopher

**Ferguson, Jock**
*See* Ferguson, John

**Ferguson, Joe Vance** 1946- [SMG]
*American baseball player*
* Ferguson, Fergie
* Ferguson, Tarzan

**Ferguson, John** 20th c. [BBH]
*Scottish soccer player*
* Ferguson, Jock

**Ferguson, Ma**
*See* Ferguson, Miriam A. Wallace

**Ferguson, Marilyn** 1938- [CA]
*American poet*
* Renzelman, Marilyn

**Ferguson, Miriam A. Wallace**
1875-1961 [WBD]
*Wife of American politician, James
Edward Ferguson*
* Ferguson, Ma

**Ferguson, R. Y.**
*See* Ferguson, Roy Young

**Ferguson, Rachel** 1893- [WWL]
*British author*
* Rachel

**Ferguson, Richard** ?-1800
[DNNS, FFF, RH]
*British highwayman*
* Galloping Dick

**Ferguson, Road Runner**
*See* Ferguson, Rufus

**Ferguson, Robert** ?-1714
[DNNS, SN, WBD]
*Scottish conspirator and political
pamphleteer*
* [The] Plotter

**Ferguson, Robert B.** 1927- [CWG]
*American country-western performer*
* Possumtrot, Eli

**Ferguson, Robert V.** 1845-1894
[BE]
*American baseball player and
manager*
* Death to Flying Things

**Ferguson, Roy Young** 1907- [ART]
*Scottish artist*
* Eff
* Ferguson, R. Y.

**Ferguson, Rufus** 20th c. [IBW]
*American football player*
* Ferguson, Road Runner

**Ferguson, Tarzan**
*See* Ferguson, Joe Vance

**Ferguson, William Blair Morton**
1882- [WW]
*Author*
* Morton, William

**Fergusson Hannay, [Lady]**
[AW, CA, WD]
*British author*
* Leslie, Doris

**Ferin, Agostino** 1928- [OP]
*Italian opera singer*
* Ferrin, Agostino

**Ferkinshaw, Albert**
*See* Cunliffe, Dave

**Ferland, Paul-Henri**
*See* Friedlander, Saul

**Ferling, Lawrence**
*See* Ferlinghetti, Lawrence
[Monsanto]

**Ferlinghetti, Lawrence [Monsanto]**
1919?- [CA]
*American poet*
* Ferling, Lawrence

**Fermor, Arabella** [PA]
*Author*
* Belinda

**Fern, Edwin**
*See* Cryer, Neville Barker

**Fern, Fanny**
*See* Parton, Sara Payson Willis

**Fern, Sable**
*See* Steward, Sable

**Fernandel**
*See* Contandin, Fernand Joseph
Desire

**Fernandes, Millor** 1924- [WEC]
*Brazilian cartoonist and playwright*
* Millor
* Vao Gogo, Emmanuel

**Fernandes/Oates**
*See* Oates, Joyce Carol

**Fernandez, Antonio** 1838-1912
[GS]
*Spanish bullfighter*
* [El] Barrero [The Potter]

**Fernandez, Armand** 1928- [CAR]
*French-born American artist*
* Arman

**Fernandez, Armando** 20th c.
*Chilean army officer*
* Romeral

**Fernandez, Chico**
*See* Fernandez, Humberto Perez

**Fernandez, Chico**
*See* Fernandez, Lorenzo Marto

**Fernandez, Cirilo** 1943- [AES]
*Uruguayan soccer player*
* Fernandez, Pepe

**Fernandez, Froilan** 1918- [BE]
*American baseball player*
* Fernandez, Nanny

**Fernandez, Humberto Perez** 1932-
[BE, SMG]
*Cuban-born baseball player*
* Fernandez, Chico

**Fernandez, Lorenzo Marto** 1939-
[BE]
*Cuban-born baseball player*
* Fernandez, Chico

**Fernandez, Manuel Felix**
1789-1843 [WBD]
*President of Mexico*
* Victoria, Guadalupe

**Fernandez, Mildred**
*See* Thomas, Lillian

**Fernandez, Nanny**
*See* Fernandez, Froilan

**Fernandez, Pepe**
*See* Fernandez, Cirilo

**Fernandez Bernabe, Vicente** 1940-
[GS]
*Spanish bullfighter*
* [El] Caracol [The Snail]

**Fernandez Coronel, Maria**
1602-1665 [WBD]
*Spanish nun*
* Agreda, Maria de
* Maria de Jesus

**Fernandez De Ibarbourou, Juana**
*See* Fernandez Morales, J.

**Fernandez Morales, J.** 1895-
[EWL]
*Uruguayan poet*
* Fernandez De Ibarbourou, Juana

**Fernandez Navarrete, Juan**
1526-1575 [WBD]
*Spanish painter*
* [El] Mudo [The Mute]

**Fernandez Perez, Angel** 1840-1915
[GS]
*Spanish bullfighter*
* Valdemoro

**Fernandez Sanchez, Angel** 1903-
[CW]
*Puerto Rican poet*
* Ariel, Guido de

**Fernandez y Pedraza, Angel**
1893-1931 [GS]
*Spanish bullfighter*
* Angelete [Big Angel]

**Fernando** 15th c. [SN]
*Captured city of Anteguera from the
Moors*
* [El] Infante de Anteguera

**Fernel, Jean** 1497-1558 [WBD]
*French physician, astronomer,
mathematician*
* [The] Modern Galen

**Ferney, Manuel**
*See* Wellman, Manly Wade

**Ferneyhough, Roger Edmund**
1941- [IAW]
*British author*
* Hart, R. W.

**Ferns, Jim** 1874-1952
[AS, BX, RBE]
*American boxer*
* Ferns, Rube
* [The] Kansas Rube

**Ferns, Rube**
*See* Ferns, Jim

**[The] Ferocious Beast of Ausonia**
*See* Bassianus

**Ferocious Fred Mills**
*See* Mills, Freddie

**Ferragus**
*See* Ulbach, Louis

**Ferrand, Eula Pearl** ?-1970 [SC]
*American actress*
* Pearl, Eula

**Ferrante, Don**
*See* Gerbi, Antonello

**Ferrar, Gul**
See Smith, William Joseph Thomas

**Ferrara, Alfred John** 1939- [BE]
*American baseball player*
* [The] Bull

**Ferrara, Romano** 20th c. [WF]
*Italian director*
* Williams, Mike

**[Il] Ferrarese**
See Mazzoli [or Mazzuoli], Lodovico

**Ferrarese del Bene**
See Gabrielli, Francesca

**Ferrarese, Donald Hugh** 1929-
[BE]
*American baseball player*
* Ferrarese, Midget

**Ferrarese, Midget**
See Ferrarese, Donald Hugh

**Ferrari, Antoine** 1444-1516 [PA]
*Author*
* Galateo

**Ferrari, Benedetto** 1597-1681 [SN]
*Italian musician and composer*
* Della Tiorba

**Ferrari, Gaudenzio** 1484?-1546
[SN]
*Italian painter*
* [The] Eagle

**Ferrari, Raquel** 1953?-1978 [FIR]
*Actress and fashion model*
* Mak, Marii

**Ferraro, Piermiranda**
See Ferraro, Pietro Silvio

**Ferraro, Pietro Silvio** 1924- [OP]
*Italian opera singer*
* Ferraro, Piermiranda

**Ferraro, Sam**
See Ferrigno, Steven

**Ferrars, E. X.**
See Brown, Morna Doris
[MacTaggart]

**Ferrars, Elizabeth**
See Brown, Morna Doris
[MacTaggart]

**Ferreira, Anthonie Michal** 1955-
[DC]
*South African-born cricketer*
* Ferreira, Anton
* Ferreira, Yogi

**Ferreira, Anton**
See Ferreira, Anthonie Michal

**Ferreira, Antonio** 1528-1569
[DEP, DNNS, RH]
*Portuguese poet*
* [The] Horace of Portugal
* [The] Portuguese Horace

**Ferreira, Eusebio** 1942- [AES]
*Portuguese soccer player*
* Eusebio

**Ferreira, Yogi**
See Ferreira, Anthonie Michal

**Ferrell, Red**
See Ferrell, Willie

**Ferrell, Willie** 20th c. [OBW]
*American baseball player*
* Ferrell, Red

**Ferreol, Marcel Auguste**
1899-1974 [CA]
*French playwright*
* Achard, Marcel

**Ferrer, Cucho**
See Ferrer, Sergio

**Ferrer, Edward Harry** 1894- [NOJ]
*American jazz musician*
* Ferrer, Mose

**Ferrer, Jose**
See Ferrer y Cintron, Jose Vicente

**Ferrer, Mel**
See Ferrer, Melchor Gaston

**Ferrer, Melchor Gaston** 1917-
[BDF, BEW, FD]
*American actor, director, producer*
* Ferrer, Mel

**Ferrer, Mose**
See Ferrer, Edward Harry

**Ferrer, Sergio** 1951- [SMG]
*Puerto Rican-born baseball player*
* Ferrer, Cucho

**Ferrer-Peralta, Magda** 1931-
[ART]
*Spanish painter*
* Magda F.

**Ferrer y Cintron, Jose Vicente**
1909?- [BDF, FD, WEF]
*Puerto Rican-born actor and director*
* Ferrer, Jose

**Ferrer y Rodriguez, Francisco**
1884-1927 [GS]
*Algerian-born bullfighter*
* Pastoret [Shepherd]

**Ferrick, Swede**
See Ferrick, Thomas Jerome
[Tom]

**Ferrick, Thomas Jerome** [Tom]
1915- [BN]
*American baseball player*
* Ferrick, Swede

**Ferrier, Janet Mackay** 1919- [CA]
*Scottish-born educator and author*
* Love, Janet

**Ferrier, Lucy**
See Penzler, Otto

**Ferrigni, Pietro C.** 19th c. [PA]
*Author*
* Yorick

**Ferrigno, Steven** ?-1930 [BLB]
*American underworld figure*
* Ferraro, Sam

**Ferrin, Agostino**
See Ferin, Agostino

**Ferris, Albert Sayles** 1877-1938
[AS, BE]
*American baseball player*
* Ferris, Hobe

**Ferris, Arthur**
See Rowe, John Gabriel

**Ferris, Canada Kid**
See Ferris, Lee

**Ferris, Cora**
See Gruen, Mrs. Herman

**Ferris, Hobe**
See Ferris, Albert Sayles

**Ferris, James Cody** [house pseudonym] [Stratemeyer Syndicate]
See Karig, Walter

**Ferris, James Cody** [house pseudonym] [Stratemeyer Syndicate]
See Stratemeyer, Edward L.

**Ferris, Lee** 20th c. [GW]
*Canadian rodeo performer*
* Ferris, Canada Kid

**Ferris, Tom**
See Walker, Peter Norman

**Ferriss, Boo**
See Ferriss, David Meadow

**Ferriss, David Meadow** 1921-
[BE, PB]
*American baseball player*
* Ferriss, Boo

**Ferro, Della**
See Early, Deloreese Patricia

**Ferroni, Giorgio** 1908- [FDG]
*Italian director*
* Padget, Calvin Jackson

**Ferry, Alfred Joseph** 1878-1938
[BE]
*American baseball player*
* Ferry, Cy

**Ferry, Cornelius** ?-1925 [BLB]
*American underworld figure*
* Ferry, Needles

**Ferry, Cy**
See Ferry, Alfred Joseph

**Ferry, Gabriel**
See De Bellemare, Eugene Louis
Gabriel

**Ferry, Gabriel**
See De Bellemare, Gabriel

**Ferry, Jules Francois Camille**
1832-1893 [DEP, DHA]
*French statesman*
* [Le] Tonkinois

**Ferry, Needles**
See Ferry, Cornelius

**Ferson, Alex[ander]** 1866- ? [BE]
*American baseball player*
* Ferson, Colonel

**Ferson, Colonel**
See Ferson, Alex[ander]

**Ferster, Marilyn B.**
See Gilbert, Marilyn B[ender]

**Fertilis, Doctor**
See Francis of Candia

**Ferus**
See Wild, Johann

**Ferval, Paul**
See Bedford-Jones, Henry [James O'Brien]

**Ferzetti, Gabriele**
See Ferzetti, Pasquale

**Ferzetti, Pasquale** 1925-
[FC, OCF, WEF]
*Italian actor*
* Ferzetti, Gabriele

**Fessenden, Beverly** 1926- [FC]
*American actress*
* Garland, Beverly

**Fessenden, Thomas Green**
1771-1837 [DEL, FFF, PA]
*American poet and editor*
* Caustic, Christopher
* Pepperbox, Peter

**Fest, Howard** 1946- [SMG]
*American football player*
* Consistency, Mr.

**Fet, Afansi Afanasievich**
See Foeth, Afanasi Afanasievich

**Fetherston, Eddie** ?-1965 [SC]
*American actor*
* Featherstone, Eddie

**Fetherston, Patrick**
See Fetherstonhaugh, Patrick
William Edward

**Fetherstonhaugh, Patrick William
Edward** 1928- [AW, WD]
*British author and poet*
* Fetherston, Patrick

**Fetrazzini, Eva**
See Campanini, Cleofonte

**Fettamen, Ann**
See Hoffman, Anita

**Fetter, Elizabeth Head** 1904-1973
[CA, WW]
*American author*
* Lees, Hannah

**Feuchtwanger, Lion** 1884-1958
[B10, CD, TC]
*German author and playwright*
* Wetcheek, J. L.

**Feuchtwanger, Walter** 1894-1968
[BDF, FC]
*American producer*
* Wanger, Walter

**Feuillere, Edwige**
See Cunati, Caroline

**Feuillet, Octave** 1821-1890
[FFF, PA]
*French author and playwright*
* Hazard, Desire

**Feur, D. Cy**
See Stahl, Fred Alan

**Feval, Paul Henri** 1817-1887 [FFF]
*French author*
* [The] New Alexandre Dumas
* Troloppe, Francis

**Feveril, Hubert**
See Murray, A. C.

**Feversham, Earl of**
See Durfort de Duras, Louis de

**Fewell, Laura R.** [FFF]
*Writer*
* Richards, Parke

**Fewster, Chick**
See Fewster, Wilson Lloyd

**Fewster, Wilson Lloyd** 1895-1945
[BE]
*American baseball player*
* Fewster, Chick

**Fey, Valentin Ludwig** 1882-1948
[B10]
*German comedian*
* Valentin, Karl

**Feyder, Jacques**
See Frederix, Jacques

**Feyjoo [or Feijoo] y Montenegro, Frey Benito** 1701?-1764
[DNNF, DNNS]
*Spanish monk, critic, scholar*
* [The] Spanish Addison

**Ff**
See  Ffolkes, Michael [Brian Davis]

**Ffolkes, Michael [Brian Davis]**
1925-   [ART]
*British illustrator and cartoonist*
* Ff

**Ffrangcon-Davies, David Thomas**
See  Davis, David Thomas

**Fiacc, Padraic**
See  O'Connor, Patrick Joseph

**Fiammingo, Pietro**
See  Verschaffelt, Pierre Antoine

**Fiarotta, Phyllis**
See  Ficarotta, Phyllis

**Fiber [or Fiberius]**
See  Beaver, John

**Fibonacci, Leonardo** 1180?-1250?
[WBD]
*Italian mathematician*
* Leonardo da Pisa
* Pisano, Leonardo

**Ficarotta, Phyllis** 1942-   [SAT]
*American author and illustrator*
* Fiarotta, Phyllis

**Fichter, George S.** 1922-   [CA]
*American author*
* Warner, Matt

**Fichtner, Rocky**
See  Fichtner, Ross

**Fichtner, Ross** 1938-   [SMG]
*American football player and coach*
* Fichtner, Rocky

**Ficke, Arthur Davison** 20th c.   [TC]
*American author*
* Knish, Anne

**Ficker, Roberta Sue** 20th c.
*American ballerina*
* Farrell, Suzanne

**Fickling, G. G.**
See  Fickling, Skip Forrest

**Fickling, Skip Forrest** 1925-   [CA]
*American author*
* Fickling, G. G.

**Ficquat**
See  De Boccage, Pierre-Jean

**Fiddler**
See  Beers, Robert Harlan

**Fiddler Bill McGee**
See  McGee, William Henry

**Fiddler Joss**
See  Poole, Joseph

**Fiddler, Mrs.**
See  Beers, Evelyne Christine Sauer

**Fiddlin' Arthur Smith**
See  Smith, Arthur

**Fiddlin' Joe Martin**
See  Martin, Joe

**Fiddlin' John Carson**
See  Carson, John

**Fiddlin' Kate Warren**
See  Warren, Margie Ann

**Fiddlin' Sid Harkreader**
See  Harkreader, Sid

**Fiddling De De Ryke**
See  De Ryke, DeLores

**Fidelio**
See  Hunt, Edgar H[ubert]

**Fidelsberger, Heinz** 1920-   [IAW]
*Austrian physician and author*
* Hillmann, [Dr.] Heinz

**Fidgety Phil Collins**
See  Collins, Philip Eugene

**Fidler, Kathleen**
See  Goldie, Kathleen Annie

**Fidrych, Mark Steven** 1954-
[SMG]
*American baseball player*
* [The] Bird

**Fidus Achates**
See  Ballantyne, John

**Fieber, Clarence Thomas** 1913-
[BE]
*American baseball player*
* Fieber, Lefty

**Fieber, Lefty**
See  Fieber, Clarence Thomas

**Fiedler, Arthur** 1894-1979
*American conductor*
* Pops, Mr.

**Field, Allan**
See  Wallack, John Johnstone

**Field, Braddock**
See  Dimitry, Charles Patton

**Field, Cap**
See  Field, Walter

**Field, Charles**
See  Rowland, D[onald] S[ydney]

**Field, Charles K.**
*Radio performer*
* Cheerio

**Field, Edward Salisbury, Jr.**
1878-1936   [IA]
*American author*
* Childe Harold

**Field, Frances Fox** 1913?-1977
[CA]
*American dancer, artist, author*
* Fox, Frances Margaret

**Field, Frank Chester**
See  Robertson, Frank C[hester]

**Field, Frederick** 1952?-
*American business executive*
* Field, Teddy

**Field, Gans T.**
See  Wellman, Manly Wade

**Field, Gladys**
See  O'Brien, Gladys

**Field, Joan** 1921-   [BF, TR]
*British actress*
* Carr, Jean
* Kent, Jean

**Field, Joanna**
See  Milner, Marion [Blackett]

**Field, John** 1782-1837   [SN]
*British composer*
* Field, Russian

**Field, Joseph M.** 1810-1856
[FFF, PA]
*American actor and journalist*
* Everpoint
* Old Straws
* Straws

**Field, Julian Osgood** 1849-1925
[CC, WGT, WW]
*British author*
* Sigma
* X. L.

**Field, Kate**   [PA]
*Author*
* Strauss, Jr.

**Field, Leslie A.**
See  Sheinfeld, Leslie A.

**Field, Lila**
See  Scholefield, Lillia

**Field, M. J.** 20th c.   [AW]
*British anthropologist and author*
* Freshfield, Mark

**Field, Margaret Cynthia** 1917-
[FC, ITA]
*British-born actress*
* Field, Virginia

**Field, Martha Reinhard** 1855-1898
[FFF]
*American journalist*
* Cole, Catherine

**Field, Mary Katherine Keemle [Kate]**
1838-1896   [FFF]
*American journalist, actress, author*
* Straws, Jr.

**Field, Matthew C.** 1812-1844
[FFF, PA]
*American poet*
* Phazma

**Field, Medora**
See  Perkerson, Medora [Field]

**Field, Michael** [joint pseudonym with Edith Emma Cooper]
See  Bradley, Katharine Harris

**Field, Michael** [joint pseudonym with Katherine Harris Bradley]
See  Cooper, Edith Emma

**Field, Mrs. E. B.**   [PA]
*Author*
* Blanche

**Field, Munsell B.** 1822-1875   [PA]
*Author*
* Old Stager

**Field Officer**
See  Madden, T. E.

**Field, Penelope**
See  Giberson, Dorothy [Dodds]

**Field, Peter**
See  Mines, Samuel

**Field, Peter**
See  Repp, Ed[ward] Earl

**Field, Peter** 1935-   [CA]
*Hungarian-born American psychologist and author*
* Suedfeld, Peter

**Field, Reshad**
See  Field, Richard Timothy

**Field, Richard Timothy** 1934-   [CA]
*British-born author*
* Field, Reshad

**Field, Robert**
See  Rounesville, Robert

**Field, Russian**
See  Field, John

**Field, Sara Bard**
See  Wood, Sara Bard Field

**Field, Sylvia**
See  Johnson, Harriet Louisa

**Field, Teddy**
See  Field, Frederick

**Field, Virginia**
See  Field, Margaret Cynthia

**Field, Walter** 1872?- ?   [B10]
*American actor*
* Field, Cap

**Fielden, Thomas Perceval** 1882-
[CA]
*British educator and author*
* De Fletin, P.
* Flint, E. de P.

**Fielder, Charles Farrell** 1919-1962
[SC]
*American actor and singer*
* Farrell, Charles
* Farrell, Skip

**Fielders, Mrs. Frank M.**   [FFF]
*Entertainer*
* Purcell, Estelle

**Fielding, A.**
See  Feilding, Dorothy

**Fielding, A. D.**
See  Ash, Edward Cecil

**Fielding, A. W.**
See  Wallace, Alexander Fielding

**[A] Fielding Among Painters**
See  Hogarth, William

**Fielding, Ann**
See  Wakenshaw, Janet Mackie

**Fielding, Barbara** 1908-1940   [SC]
*American actress*
* McLeod, Barbara

**Fielding, Beau**
See  Fielding, Henry

**Fielding, Edward**
See  Elkins, Edward B.

**Fielding, Fanny**
See  Upshur, Mary J. S.

**Fielding, Gabriel**
See  Barnsley, Alan Gabriel

**Fielding, Harry Lee**
See  Fellinge, Harry Lee

**Fielding, Henry** 1707-1754
[DEL, DNNS, FFF]
*British author and playwright*
* Drawcansir, [Sir] Alexander
* [The] Father of the English Novel
* Fielding, Beau
* [The] Hogarth of Novelists
* [The] Prince of Novelists
* [The] Prose Homer of Human Nature

**Fielding, Howard**
See  Anderson, G. J. B.

**Fielding, Howard**
See  Hooke, Charles Witherle

**Fielding, Hubert**
See  Schonfield, Hugh J[oseph]

**Fielding, Jerry**
See Feldman, Joshua

**Fielding, [Sir] John** ?-1780 [RH]
*British jurist*
* [The] Blind Beak

**Fielding, May**
See Scovel, Mrs.

**Fielding, Michael**
See Sciapiro, Michel

**Fielding, Minnie**
See Flynn, Minnie

**[The] Fielding of the Drama**
See Farquhar, George

**Fielding, Xan**
See Wallace, Alexander Fielding

**Fieldmouse, Timon**
See Rands, William Brightly

**Fields, Arthur B.** 1889-1965 [ASC]
*Austrian-born composer*
* Fields, Buddy

**Fields, Benny**
See Geisenfeld, Benjamin

**Fields, Buddy**
See Fields, Arthur B.

**Fields, Carl Donnell** 1915-
[DAM, EJ, PMJ]
*American jazz musician*
* Fields, Kansas

**Fields, Fanny** 1884-1961 [BMH]
*American comedienne*
* Fields, Happy Fanny
* [The] Happy Little Dutch Girl

**Fields, Geechie**
See Fields, Julius

**Fields, George**
See Felhauser, George

**Fields, Gracie**
See Stansfield, Grace

**Fields, Happy Fanny**
See Fields, Fanny

**Fields, J. M.** ?-1856 [PA]
*Author*
* Straus

**Fields, Jackie**
See Finkelstein, Jacob

**Fields, Jocko**
See Fields, John Joseph

**Fields, Joe** 20th c. [SMG]
*American football player*
* Fields, W. C.

**Fields, John Joseph** 1864-1950
[BE]
*Irish-born baseball player*
* Fields, Jocko

**Fields, Julius** 1903?- [WWJ]
*American jazz musician*
* Fields, Geechie

**Fields, Kansas**
See Fields, Carl Donnell

**Fields, Lew**
See Schanfield, Lewis Maurice

**Fields, Marguerite** 1883-1968 [SC]
*American actress*
* Meade, Claire

**Fields, Red**
See Fields, Wilmer

**Fields, Ross Eugene** 1943-
*American boxing promoter and suspected embezzler*
* [The] Black Jesse James
* Smith, Harold J.

**Fields, Stanley**
See Agnew, Walter L.

**Fields, Tommy**
See Stansfield, Thomas

**Fields, Totie**
See Feldman, Sophie

**Fields, W. C.**
See Dukinfield, William Claude

**Fields, W. C.**
See Fields, Joe

**Fields, Wilmer** 1922- [MK]
*American baseball player*
* Fields, Red
* [The] Great

**Fielhauer, Otto Magnus** 1929-
[IAW]
*Austrian author*
* Glasbrenner
* Habakuk

**Fiene, Big Finn**
See Fiene, Lou[is Henry]

**Fiene, Lou[is Henry]** 1884-1964
[BE]
*American baseball player*
* Fiene, Big Finn

**Fiennes, Nathaniel** 1608?-1669
[SN]
*British politician*
* Young Subtlety

**Fiennes, Ranulph**
See Twistleton-Wykeham-Fiennes,
[Sir] Ranulph

**Fiennes, Richard**
See Twistleton-Wykeham-Fiennes,
Richard Nathaniel

**Fiennes, William [First Viscount
Saye and Sele]** 1582-1662 [SN]
*British politician*
* Old Subtlety

**Fiennes-Foster**
See Otley, Barbara Kathleen

**Fierabrace**
See Guillaume d'Orange

**[The] Fierce**
See Alexander I

**[The] Fierce**
See Alfonso IV [Affonso, Alfonzo,
or Alphonso]

**Fiersohn, Reba** 1884-1938 [BBD]
*American opera singer*
* Gluck, Alma

**Fiery**
See Carey, John

**[The] Fiery Face**
See James II

**Fiery Young Tom**
See Fairfax, Thomas [Third Baron
Fairfax]

**Fieschi, Ottobono** ?-1276 [CAL]
*Pope*
* Adrian V

**Fiesco**
See Elliott, William

**Fiesole, Giovanni da**
See Di Pietro, Guido

**[The] Fifth Doctor of the Church**
See Aquinas, Thomas [Thomas of
Aquino]

**5029**
See Winkworth, Derek William

**Figaro**
See Clapp, Henry, Jr.

**Figaro**
See Larra, Mariano Jose de

**[The] Figaro of His Age**
See Caron, Pierre Augustin

**Figgins, Jane** [TR]
*British actress*
* Wenham, Jane

**Figgis, [M.] Darrell** 1882-1925
[SFL, WGT]
*Irish author*
* Ireland, Michael

**[The] Fighter**
See Alfonso I [or Alphonso]

**[A] Fighter Pilot**
See Johnston, Hugh Anthony
Stephen

**Fighting Bob Evans**
See Evans, Robley Dunglison

**Fighting Bob Martin**
See Martin, Bob

**[The] Fighting Chaplain**
See Nowel, Samuel

**Fighting Dick**
See Richardson, Israel Bush

**[The] Fighting Fool**
See Cukoschay [or Zukauskas],
Joseph Paul

**Fighting Harry Wolverton**
See Wolverton, Harry

**[The] Fighting Irishman of South
Boston**
See McCormack, John W.

**Fighting Joe Henriquez**
See Henriquez, Joseph Stephen

**Fighting Joe Hooker**
See Hooker, Joseph

**[The] Fighting Marine**
See Tunney, James Joseph

**Fighting Nat**
See FitzRandolph, Nathaniel

**[The] Fighting Parson**
See Brownlow, William Gannaway

**[The] Fighting Parson**
See Moody, Granville

**Fighting Phil**
See Kearny, Philip

**[The] Fighting Pope**
See Pacelli, Eugenio Maria
Giovanni

**[The] Fighting Prelate**
See Spencer, Henry

**Fighton, George Z.**
See Winteler de Weindeck, U. M.
C.

**Figlia, Giorgio** 1924-
[EJ, IEJ, PMJ]
*American jazz musician*
* Wallington, George
* Wallington, Lord

**Figueiredo, Larry** 1940- [RO1]
*American singer*
* Chance, Larry

**Figueras, Fermin** 20th c. [GS]
*Venezuelan bullfighter*
* [El] Boris

**Figueras Alvarez, Rafael Antonio**
1931- [GS]
*Venezuelan bullfighter*
* Armillita de Venezuela [Armillita
from Venezuela]

**Figueres, Jose** 20th c.
*Costa Rican politician*
* Figueres, Pepe

**Figueres, Pepe**
See Figueres, Jose

**Figueroa, Eduardo** 1948- [BE]
*Puerto Rican-born baseball player*
* Padilla, Eduardo

**Figueroa, Loida**
See Figueroa-Mercado, Loida

**Figueroa Del Rivero, Dolores
Conchita** 1933- [BEW, EMT, TR]
*American actress, singer, dancer*
* Rivera, Chita

**Figueroa-Mercado, Loida** 1917-
[CA]
*Puerto Rican author and poet*
* Figueroa, Loida

**Fikso, Eunice Cleland** 1927- [CA]
*American author and artist*
* Griffin, C. F.

**Filanovsky, Alexander** 1873- ?
[SFL]
*Author*
* Findlay, Alexander [Tobias]

**Filarete**
See Di Pietro Averlino [or
Averulino]

**File, Charles E.** 1843- ? [FFF, PA]
*American writer*
* Brick, Titus A.
* C. F.

**Filer, Thomas Hanford** 1925-
[IAW, SFL]
*American author*
* Buck, Doug
* Chisom, Sarah
* Cole, Stark

**Filia Dolorosa [Grieving Daughter]**
See Bourbon, Marie Therese
Charlotte de

**Filia Ecclesiae**
See Dorsey, Sarah Anne

**Filipelli, Joseph Edward** 1915-
[IEJ]
*American jazz musician*
* Phillips, Flip

**Filipowicz, Flip**
See Filipowicz, Stephen Charles [Steve]

**Filipowicz, Stephen Charles [Steve]** 1921-1975 [BE]
*American baseball player*
* Filipowicz, Flip

**Filippo del Carmine**
See Lippi, [Fra] Filippo

**Filippo II**
See Strozzi, Giambattista

**Filkins, Grace**
See Sweetman, Grace

**Fillmore, Millard** 1800-1874 [FAP]
*American president*
* [The] Accidental President
* [The] American Louis Philippe
* His Accidency
* [The] Wool Carder President

**Film**
See Laudet, Fernand Charles

**Filmonster, Mr.**
See Ackerman, Forrest J[ames]

**Filolezes**
See Luz y Caballero, Jose Cipriano de la

**Filomena**
See Miller, Florence Fenwick

**Filomena, Saint**
See Nightingale, Florence

**Filsinger, Sara Teasdale** 1884- [WWL]
*American author*
* Teasdale, Sara Filsinger

**Filson, Beulah T.** ?-1946 [SC]
*American actress*
* Darkcloud, Beulah

**Fin-Bec**
See Jerrold, William Blanchard

**Finality John**
See Russell, [Lord] John Earl

**Finan, Fines**
See Finan, Nicholas Hugh

**Finan, Nicholas Hugh** 1954- [DC]
*British cricketer*
* Finan, Fines

**Finbar, Owen**
See Smith, A. De Herries

**Finch, Charles** 20th c.
*American politician*
* Finch, Cliff

**Finch, Cliff**
See Finch, Charles

**Finch, Daniel [Second Earl of Nottingham]** 1647-1730 [HN]
*British statesman*
* [The] Silver Tongue

**Finch, Gloria Stuart** 1909- [FC]
*American actress*
* Stuart, Gloria

**Finch, Heneage [First Earl of Nottingham]** 1621-1682 [DEP, DNNF, SN]
*British jurist and statesman*
* [The] Dismal
* [The] Father of Equity

**Finch, Matthew**
See Fink, Merton

**Finch, Merton**
See Fink, Merton

**Finch, Peter**
See Mitchell, William

**Finch, W. R.**
See Finch, William Robert

**Finch, William Robert** 1905- [ART]
*British artist*
* Finch, W. R.

**Finchy**
See Mitchell, William

**Findlater, Richard**
See Bain, Kenneth Bruce Findlater

**Findlay, Alexander [Tobias]**
See Filanovsky, Alexander

**Findlay, J. Dawson** [PA]
*Author*
* Marvel, Scott

**Findlay, Muriel Angelus** 1909- [FC]
*British actress*
* Angelus, Muriel

**Findley, Ferguson**
See Frey, Charles Weiser

**Fine, David** 1952?- [B10]
*American revolutionist*
* Lewes, William James

**Fine, Estelle**
See Jelinek, Estelle C.

**Fine, Larry**
See Fineburg, Laurence

**Fine, Louis** 1914-1971 [WECO]
*American cartoonist*
* Berold, Basil [house pseudonym]
* Cortez, Jack [house pseudonym]
* Lectron, E.

**Fine, Peter** 20th c. [SFL]
*American author*
* Heath, Peter

**Fineburg, Laurence** 1911-1975 [SC]
*American actor*
* Fine, Larry

**Fineman, Irving** 1893- [CA]
*American author*
* Joseph, Jonathan

**Fingers, Roland Glen** 1946- [SMG]
*American baseball player*
* Fingers, Rollie

**Fingers, Rollie**
See Fingers, Roland Glen

**Finian**
See Ryan, Frederick

**Finiguerra, Maso**
See Finiguerra, Tommaso di Antonio

**Finiguerra, Tommaso di Antonio** 1426-1464 [WBD]
*Florentine goldsmith, niellist, engraver*
* Finiguerra, Maso

**Fink, Brat**
See Davis, Gwen

**Fink, Dale Laurence** 1923-1948 [SC]
*American actor*
* Drake, Steve

**Fink, Janis** 1951?- [JL, RO2]
*American singer and songwriter*
* Ian, Janis

**Fink, Merton** 1921- [AW, CA, WD]
*British dental surgeon and author*
* Finch, Matthew
* Finch, Merton

**Fink, Stevanne Auerbach**
See Auerbach, Stevanne

**Finkel, George [Irvine]** 1909-1975 [AW, CAP, SAT]
*British-born author*
* Pennage, E. M.

**Finkelman, Harry** 1914-1968 [EJ, SC, WWJ]
*American jazz musician*
* Elman, Harry
* Elman, Ziggy

**Finkelstein, Arnold Lawrence** 1938- [EJ7, JL]
*American jazz musician*
* Lawrence, Arnie

**Finkelstein, Jacob** 1907- [BX, EJS, RBE]
*American boxer*
* Fields, Jackie

**Finkelstein, Leonid Vladimirovitch** 1924- [CA]
*Russian-born editor, journalist, author*
* Vladimirov, Leonid

**Finkelstein, Louis** 1887-1950 [SC]
*American actor*
* Clayton, Lou

**Finkelstein, Mark** 1922- [CA]
*American author*
* Atkins, Jack
* Harris, Mark
* Ingram, Willis J.
* Martha, Henry
* Washington, Alex
* Wiggen, Henry J.
* Wright, Jack R.

**Finklea, Tula Ellice** 1921?- [BDF, FC, IPA]
*American dancer and actress*
* Charisse, Cyd

**Finlay, Fiona**
See Stuart, Vivian [Finlay]

**Finlay, Michael**
See Roberts, Edna

**Finlay, Robert [Bob]**
See Bush, Robert Finlay

**Finlay, William**
See Mackay, James [Alexander]

**Finlayson, Jimmy**
See Dukanfield, William Claude

**Finlayson, Robert Douglas** 1909?- [BEW, FC]
*British actor, director, producer*
* Douglas, Robert

**Finley, Annette** 1892?-1962 [BEW]
*Actress*
* Roberts, Nancy

**Finley, Charles O.** 1918-
*American baseball club owner*
* Charlie O

**Finley, Frank** 20th c. [GW]
*American rodeo performer*
* Finley, Squarehead

**Finley, Glenna**
See Witte, Glenna Finley

**Finley, Larry** 20th c. [GW]
*American rodeo performer*
* Finley, Prairie Dog

**Finley, Martha Farquharson** 1828-1909 [PA, WBD]
*American author*
* Farquharson, Martha

**Finley, Prairie Dog**
See Finley, Larry

**Finley, Scott**
See Clark, Winifred

**Finley, Squarehead**
See Finley, Frank

**Finn**
See Godecke, Peter Auguste

**Finn, Anna E.**
See Hoopes, Mary Howard

**Finn, Cornelius Francis** 1902-1933 [BE]
*American baseball player*
* Finn, Mickey

**Finn, Huck**
See Clemens, Samuel Langhorne

**Finn, Huck**
See Wirtanen, Atos Kasimir

**Finn, Huckleberry**
See Schoendienst, Albert Fred

**Finn, Julio**
See Arnold, Augustus [Gus]

**Finn, Mickey**
See Finn, Cornelius Francis

**Finn, R. L.**
See Finn, Ralph Leslie

**Finn, R[eginald Patrick Arthur] Welldon** 1900- [CA]
*British author*
* Finn, Rex Welldon

**Finn, Ralph Leslie** 1912- [SFL]
*British author*
* Finn, R. L.

**Finn, Rex Welldon**
See Finn, R[eginald Patrick Arthur] Welldon

**Finnegan, Honeyboy**
See Finnegan, Richard G.

**Finnegan, Richard G.** 1902- [BX]
*American boxer*
* Finnegan, Honeyboy

**Finnegan, Robert**
See Ryan, Paul William

**Finnegan, Ruth H.**
See Murray, Ruth Hilary

**Finnegan, Terry**
See McCarroll, James

**Finnell, Carrie**
See Morris, Carrie Finnell

**Finneran, Happy**
See Finneran, Joseph Ignatius

**Finneran, Joseph Ignatius**
1891-1942 [BE]
*American baseball player*
* Finneran, Happy
* Finneran, Smokey Joe

**Finneran, Smokey Joe**
See Finneran, Joseph Ignatius

**Finnerty, Adam Daniel** 1944- [CA]
*American author*
* McKenna, A. Daniel

**Finney, Humphrey S.** 1902- [CA]
*British-born author, horse breeder
and judge*
* Nothing Venture

**Finney, Jack**
See Finney, Walter Braden

**Finney, Mark**
See Muir, Kenneth [Arthur]

**Finney, Walter Braden** 1911-
[SF, WGT]
*American author*
* Braden, Walter
* Finney, Jack

**Finnigan, Joan**
See MacKenzie, Joan

**Finucane, Brendan** 1920-1942
[BDW]
*Irish fighter pilot*
* Finucane, Paddy

**Finucane, Paddy**
See Finucane, Brendan

**Fiore della Neve**
See Loghem, Martinus Gesinus
Lambert van

**Fiore, Lefty**
See Fiore, Michael Garry Joseph

**Fiore, Michael Garry Joseph** 1944-
[BE]
*American baseball player*
* Fiore, Lefty

**Fiorelli, William** 1926?- [PMJ]
*American singer*
* Farrell, Bill

**Fioun**
See Whyte, Henry

**Fips, Socrates**
See Gernsback, Hugo

**Firbank, Butch**
See Firbank, Louis

**Firbank, Louis** 1944- [PRS, RO2]
*American singer and songwriter*
* Firbank, Butch
* [The] King Freak of New York
* [The] King of Decadence
* [The] Prince of Darkness
* Reed, Lou

**Firchow, E. S.**
See Firchow, Evelyn Scherabon

**Firchow, Evelyn Scherabon** 1932-
[CA]
*Austrian-born American author*
* Coleman, E[velyn] S[cherabon]
* Firchow, E. S.

**Firdusi [or Firdausi]**
See Mansur [or Hasan?], Abul
Qasim

**[A] Fire Kindler**
See Cicero, Marcus Tullius

**Fireball Frankie Sinkwich**
See Sinkwich, Frank

**[The] Firebrand of France**
See John of Lancaster

**[The] Firebrand of the Universe**
See Timur [or Timour]

**Fireman, A.**
See Izbitsky [or Ishbitsky], Samuel

**Fireman Jim Flynn**
See Chiariglione, Andrew

**Firestone, Tom**
See Newcomb, Duane G[raham]

**Firko, Vivia** 1921- [BEW]
*American actress*
* Nathan, Vivian

**Firmani, Eddie** 1933- [AES]
*Italian soccer player*
* [The] Golden Turkey

**Firmianus, Petrus**
See De Lisieux, Zacharie

**Firooze, Frank**
See Colaabavala, Firooze
Darashaw

**Firpo, Luis Angel** 1896-1960
[BX, RBE]
*Argentinian boxer*
* [The] Wild Bull of the Pampas

**Firrantello, Joseph Carl** 1937-
[EJ7]
*American jazz musician*
* Farrell, Joe

**[The] First Dark Horse**
See Polk, James Knox

**[The] First English Martyr**
See Sawtre, William

**[The] First Gentleman of Europe**
See Charles X

**[The] First Gentleman of Europe**
See D'Artois, Louis

**[The] First Gentleman of Europe**
See George IV

**[The] First Gentleman of the Land**
See Arthur, Chester Alan

**[The] First Grenadier of France**
See La Tour [or Latour]
d'Auvergne, Theophile Malo Corret
de

**[The] First Lady of Disco**
See Gaines, Donna

**[The] First Lady of Doowah**
See Holt, Patricia

**[The] First Lady of Song**
See Fitzgerald, Ella

**[The] First Lady of Sydney Radio**
See Reeve, Goodie

**[The] First Lady of the Air**
See Young, Gladys

**[The] First Lady of the American
Stage**
See Brown, Helen Hayes

**[The] First Martyr of Liberty**
See Snider, Christopher

**[The] First of Philosophers**
See Leibnitz [or Leibniz],
Gottfried Wilhelm von

**[The] First of the British Periodical
Essayists**
See Steele, [Sir] Richard

**[The] First of the Knickerbockers**
See Myers, P. Hamilton

**[The] First of the Scholastics**
See Leontius of Byzantium

**[The] First Poet of the Screen**
See Mayer, Carl

**[The] First Scotch Reformer**
See Hamilton, Patrick

**Firth, Ivan Eustace** 1891- [WW]
*Author*
* Erskine, Firth [joint pseudonym
with Gladys (Shaw) Erskine]

**Firth, N. Wesley**
See Fearn, John Russell

**Firth, Violet Mary** 1890-1946
[SFL, WGT]
*British author*
* Fortune, Dion

**Firuz Shah II** ?-1295 [WBD]
*King of Delhi*
* Jalal-ud-din

**Firuz I** 1st c. [WBD]
*King of Persia*
* Arsaces XXIV

**Fisch, Harold** 1923- [CA]
*British-born author*
* Harel-Fisch, Aharon

**Fischart, Johann** 1545?-1614?
[DEP, DNNS, RH]
*German author and poet*
* Mentzer
* [The] Rabelais of Germany

**Fischer, Albert Dietrich** 1925-
[MS]
*German opera singer*
* Fischer-Dieskau, Dietrich

**Fischer, Alice**
See Harcourt, Alice

**Fischer, Axel** 20th c. [WF]
*German actor*
* Burn, Cly

**Fischer, Bruno** 1908- [CA]
*German-born American author*
* Gray, Russell

**Fischer, Bulldog**
See Fischer, Henry William

**Fischer, Carl**
See Fischer, Charles William

**Fischer, Charles William**
1905-1963 [BE]
*American baseball player*
* Fischer, Carl

**Fischer, Henry William** 1940- [BE]
*American baseball player*
* Fischer, Bulldog

**Fischer, Jakob**
See Morentz, Ethel Irene

**Fischer, Johnny**
See Phillips, John Henry, Sr.

**Fischer, Larry** 20th c. [RM]
*American singer and songwriter*
* Fischer, Wild Man

**Fischer, Leopold** 1923- [CA]
*Austrian-born American educator
and author*
* Bharati, Agehananda

**Fischer, Margaret Ann Peterson**
1883-1933 [WGT]
*British author*
* Green, Glint
* Peterson, Margaret

**Fischer, Margarita** 1893- [F2]
*Actress*
* Fisher, Margarita

**Fischer, Marie Louise** 1922- [IAW]
*German-born author*
* Holm, Katja
* Lindstroem, Kirsten

**Fischer, Pat** 20th c.
*American football player*
* Fischer, Sparky

**Fischer, Reuben Walter** 1916- [BE]
*American baseball player*
* Fischer, Rube

**Fischer, Rube**
See Fischer, Reuben Walter

**Fischer, Ruth**
See Fishbein, Ruth

**Fischer, Sparky**
See Fischer, Pat

**Fischer, Vera Kistiakowsky**
See Kistiakowsky, Vera

**Fischer, Wild Man**
See Fischer, Larry

**Fischer-Dieskau, Dietrich**
See Fischer, Albert Dietrich

**Fischl, Viktor** 1912- [CA]
*Czech-born Israeli diplomat and
author*
* Dagan, Avigdor

**Fischman, Harve** 1930- [ITA]
*American producer*
* Bennett, Harve

**Fischtrom, Harvey** 1933-1974
[CAP, TBJ]
*American author and educator*
* Zemach, Harve

**Fischtrom, Margot Zemach** 1931-
[TBJ]
*American author and illustrator*
* Zemach, Margot

**[The] Fish**
See Hunter, James Augustus [Jim]

**[The] Fish**
See Melton, Barry

**Fish, Albert**
See Fish, Hamilton

**Fish Bait Miller**
See Miller, William Mosley

**Fish, Billy**
See Robinson, Wilbert

**Fish, Everett** 1905- [BB]
*American basketball player*
* Fish, Gus

**Fish, Gus**
See Fish, Everett

**Fish, Hamilton** 1870-1936
[BLB, CEC]
*American kidnapper*
* Fish, Albert
* Hayden, Robert
* Howard, Frank
* [The] Moon Maniac
* Pell, John W.
* Sprague, Thomas A.

**Fish Hook Stout**
See   Stout, Allyn McClelland

**Fish, Horace** 1885-   [NAA]
*American author*
* Xavier, Francis

**Fish, Julian**
See   Campbell, Blanche

**Fish, Michael** 20th c.   [WFA]
*British fashion designer*
* Fish, Mr.

**Fish, Mr.**
See   Fish, Michael

**Fish, Mr.**
See   Suzuki, Zenko

**Fish, Mrs. M. J.**   [FFF]
*Entertainer*
* Benson, Jennie

**Fish, Robert L.** 1912-1981
[AW, CA, EMD]
*American author*
* Lamprey, A. C.
* Pike, Robert L.

**Fishbein, Ruth** 1895-   [BEW]
*Rumanian-born press representative*
* Fischer, Ruth

**Fisher, A. E.**
See   Fisher, Edward

**Fisher, Allan Forest** 1889-1941
[SC]
*American actor*
* Forrest, Alan

**Fisher, Ambrose** 17th c.   [HN]
*Scholar*
* [The] Blind Scholar

**Fisher, Arthur Stanley Theodore**
1906-   [CA, IAW]
*British author*
* Scarrott, Michael

**Fisher, Audrey** 20th c.   [THR]
*British actress*
* Ford, Audrey

**Fisher, Brock** 1927-   [BEW]
*American actor and singer*
* Peters, Brock

**Fisher, Bud**
See   Fisher, Harry Conway

**Fisher, Chauncey Burr** 1872-1939
[BE]
*American baseball player*
* Fisher, Peach

**Fisher, Cherokee**
See   Fisher, William Charles

**Fisher, Clay**
See   Allen, Henry Wilson

**Fisher, Cyrus T.**
See   Teilhet, Darwin L[e Ora]

**Fisher, Dorothea [Frances] Canfield**
1879-1958   [NAA, TC, YAB]
*American author*
* Canfield, Dorothy

**Fisher, Douglas George** 1902-
[AW]
*British author*
* Douglas, George

**Fisher, Edward** 1902-   [WD]
*American author*
* Fisher, A. E.

**Fisher, Eliza M. A.** 19th c.   [FFF]
*American writer*
* Mason, Ida

**Fisher, Fat Jack**
See   Fisher, John Howard

**Fisher, Fish**
See   Fisher, Paul Bernard

**Fisher, Frances C.**   [PA]
*Author*
* Reid, Christian

**Fisher, Freddie** 1904-1967
[PMJ, SC]
*American bandleader*
* Fisher, Schnicklefritz

**Fisher, Frederick Brown** 1941-
[BE]
*American baseball player*
* Fisher, Fritz

**Fisher, Fritz**
See   Fisher, Frederick Brown

**Fisher, G. C.**   [FFF]
*Author*
* Hornes

**Fisher, Gene L[ouis]** 1947-
[CA, ESF, SFL]
*American author*
* Lancour, Gene

**Fisher, George**
See   Fisher, Graham

**Fisher, George Aloys** 1899-   [BE]
*American baseball player*
* Fisher, Showboat

**Fisher, George Clinton** 1907-
[CWG, ECM]
*American country-western performer*
* Fisher, Shug

**Fisher, Graham** 1920-   [IAW]
*British author*
* Fisher, George

**Fisher, H. A. L.**
See   Fisher, Herbert Albert
Laurens

**Fisher, Harry Conway** 20th c.
[WECO]
*Cartoonist*
* Fisher, Bud

**Fisher, Herbert Albert Laurens**
1865-1940   [LC]
*British legislator and author*
* Fisher, H. A. L.

**Fisher, John [Oswald Hamilton]**
1909-   [AW]
*British author*
* Piper, Roger

**Fisher, John Gus** 1887-1940   [BE]
*American baseball player*
* Fisher, Red

**Fisher, John Howard** 1939-   [BE]
*American baseball player*
* Fisher, Fat Jack

**Fisher, Joseph E.** 1856- ?   [PA]
*Author*
* Mohican

**Fisher, Laine**
See   Howard, James A[rch]

**Fisher, M. F. K.**
See   Fisher, Mary Frances Kennedy

**Fisher, Margaret Trusler** 1901-
[IA]
*American poet*
* Benedict, Margaret
* Trusler, Margaret

**Fisher, Margarita**
See   Fischer, Margarita

**Fisher, Mary**   [FFF]
*Entertainer*
* Milforde, Marie

**Fisher, Mary Frances Kennedy**
1908-   [CA]
*American author*
* Fisher, M. F. K.
* Parrish, Mary Frances

**Fisher, Meyer** 1904-1963
[BB, EJS]
*American basketball coach*
* Fisher, Mickey

**Fisher, Mickey**
See   Fisher, Meyer

**Fisher, Mrs. Frederick**   [FFF]
*Entertainer*
* Holloway, Maggie

**Fisher, Myrta** 1917-   [ART]
*British artist*
* M. F.

**Fisher, Orpheus** 1900-   [IBW]
*American architect*
* Fisher, Razz

**Fisher, P., Esq.**
See   Chatto, William Andrew

**Fisher, Paul Bernard** 1954-   [DC]
*British cricketer*
* Fisher, Fish

**Fisher, Payne** 1614-1693   [FFF]
*British poet*
* Piscator, Paganus

**Fisher, Peach**
See   Fisher, Chauncey Burr

**Fisher, Razz**
See   Fisher, Orpheus

**Fisher, Red**
See   Fisher, John Gus

**Fisher, Red**
See   Fisher, Thomas Chalmers
[Tom]

**Fisher, Reuben** 1923-   [ASC]
*American composer and writer*
* Fisher, Ruby

**Fisher, Ruby**
See   Fisher, Reuben

**Fisher, Schnicklefritz**
See   Fisher, Freddie

**Fisher, Showboat**
See   Fisher, George Aloys

**Fisher, Shug**
See   Fisher, George Clinton

**Fisher, Sidney George** 1856-1927
[FFF]
*American author*
* Kent

**Fisher, Stephen Gould** 1912-
[EMD, WW]
*American author*
* Gould, Stephen
* Lane, Grant

**Fisher, Thomas Chalmers [Tom]**
1880-1972   [BE]
*American baseball player*
* Fisher, Red

**Fisher, Wade**
See   Norwood, Victor G[eorge]
C[harles]

**Fisher, William Charles** 1845-1912
[BE]
*American baseball player*
* Fisher, Cherokee

**Fishkin, Arnold**
See   Fishkind, Arnold

**Fishkind, Arnold** 1919-   [EJ]
*American jazz musician*
* Fishkin, Arnold

**Fishman, Jack** 20th c.   [CA]
*Author*
* Gilman, J. D. [joint pseudonym
with Douglas Orgill]

**Fishman, Joseph** 1897-   [CA]
*Russian-born American publisher
and author*
* Gaer, Joseph [or Yossef]

**Fisk, Carlton Ernest** 1947-
[PB, SMG]
*American baseball player*
* Fisk, Pudge

**Fisk, Pudge**
See   Fisk, Carlton Ernest

**Fiske, Estelle Louise** ?-1958   [SC]
*American actress*
* Butler, Louise

**Fiske, John**
See   Green, Edmund Fisk

**Fiske, Marion**
See   Martin, Mrs. T. J.

**Fiske, Marjorie**
See   Lowenthal, Marjorie Fiske

**Fiske, Mary Hewins**   [FFF]
*Journalist*
* Belle, Clara
* Giddy Gusher

**Fiske, Minnie Maddern**
See   Davey, Mary Augusta

**Fiske, Mrs. Stephen**   [PA]
*Author*
* M. H. T.

**Fiske, Nathan** 1733-1799
[FFF, PA]
*American writer*
* General Observer
* [The] Worcester Speculator

**Fiske, Richard**
See   Potts, Thomas Richard

**Fiske, Samuel** ?-1864   [PA]
*Author*
* Brown, Dunn

**Fiske, Stephen R.**   [PA]
*Author*
* Ariel

**Fiske, Tarleton**
See   Bloch, Robert [Albert]

**Fitch, Clarke**
See   Sinclair, Upton [Beall]

**Fitch, John, IV**
See   Cormier, Robert Edmund

**Fitch, Stephen** 1921-   [TR]
*American actor and singer*
* Douglass, Stephen

**Fitch, William Edward** 1867- ?
[NAA]
*American physician, historian, author*
* Tifew, H. C.

**Fitchett, William Henry** 20th c.
[WWL]
*Australian author*
* Vedette

**Fite, Mack**
See   Schneck, Stephen

**Fitt, Mary**
See   Freeman, Kathleen

**Fittipaldi, Emerson** 20th c.   [EAR]
*Brazilian auto racer*
* Rato [Rat]

**Fitts, Harry** 1866- ?   [THR]
*Australian-born entertainer*
* Atkinson, Harry
* [The] Australian Orpheus

**Fitz**
See   Fitzpatrick, Daniel Robert

**Fitz Empress**
See   Henry II

**Fitz, Mr.**
See   Fitzsimmons, James

**Fitzalan, Peter**
See   Dudley-Smith, Trevor

**Fitzalan, Roger**
See   Dudley-Smith, Trevor

**Fitzalan-Howard, Edmund Bernard**
1855-1947   [WBD]
*Viceroy of Ireland*
* Talbot, Edmund Bernard

**Fitzball, Edward**
See   Ball, Edward

**Fitzberger, Charles Caspar [Charlie]**
1904-1965   [BE]
*American baseball player*
* Fitzberger, Hon

**Fitzberger, Hon**
See   Fitzberger, Charles Caspar
[Charlie]

**Fitzboodle, George**
See   Thackeray, William
Makepeace

**Fitzerburtus, Nic**
See   Fitzherbert, Nicholas

**FitzGerald**
See   Baro, Bonaventura

**Fitzgerald, Ara** 1894?-1957   [BEW]
*Australian-born actress and opera singer*
* Gerald, Ara

**Fitzgerald, Arlene J.** 20th c.   [CA]
*American author*
* Heath, Monica

**Fitzgerald, Barbara**
See   Newman, Mona Alice Jean

**Fitzgerald, Barry**
See   Shields, William Joseph

**Fitzgerald, C. P.**
See   Fitzgerald, Charles Patrick

**Fitzgerald, Charles Patrick** 1902-
[WYA]
*Author*
* Fitzgerald, C. P.

**Fitzgerald, Edwin** 1854?-1928
[BEW, EMT, PMJ]
*American actor, dancer, comedian*
* Foy, Eddie

**Fitzgerald, Edwin, Jr.** 1905-   [EMT]
*American actor*
* Foy, Eddie, Jr.

**Fitzgerald, Eileen** 20th c.   [WWL]
*British author*
* Clifford, Lilian

**Fitzgerald, Elizabeth** 1528?-1589
[DNNS, SN, WBD]
*Daughter of Gerald Fitzgerald, ninth Earl of Kildare*
* [The] Fair Geraldine

**Fitzgerald, Ella** 1918-
[EPM, IBW, SSS]
*American singer*
* [La] Bella Ella
* [The] First Lady of Song
* [The] Hemingway of Singers

**Fitzgerald, Ena**
See   Macmillan, Georgina
Fitzgerald

**Fitzgerald, Erroll**
See   Clarke, [Lady] Josephine
Fitzgerald [Moylan]

**Fitzgerald, Fighting**
See   Fitzgerald, George Robert

**Fitzgerald, Fitz**
See   Fitzgerald, John

**Fitzgerald, Frederick**
See   Foxcroft, Frank

**Fitzgerald, George Robert** 18th c.
[SN]
*British swordsman and gambler*
* Fitzgerald, Fighting

**Fitzgerald, Gerald**
See   Green, Gerald B.

**Fitzgerald, Gerald** ?-1513   [WBD]
*Eighth Earl of Kildare*
* More the Great

**Fitzgerald, Gerald M.** 1894-   [CAT]
*American author and clergyman*
* [A] Page on Father Page

**Fitzgerald, Hal**
See   Johnson, Joseph E[arl]

**Fitzgerald, Howard Chumney**
[Howie] 1902-1959   [BE]
*American baseball player*
* Fitzgerald, Lefty

**Fitzgerald, [Captain] Hugh**
See   Baum, L[yman] Frank

**Fitzgerald, Jack**
See   Shea, John Gerald

**Fitzgerald, James** 1570?-1601
[WBD]
*16th Earl of Desmond*
* [The] Queen's Earl of Desmond
* [The] Tower Earl

**Fitzgerald, John**
See   Fazzano, Joseph E.

**Fitzgerald, John** 1948-   [SMG]
*American football player*
* Fitzgerald, Fitz

**Fitzgerald, John F.** 1863-1950
*American politician*
* Honey Fitz

**Fitzgerald, Julia**
See   Watson, Julia

**Fitzgerald, Justin Howard**
1890-1945   [BE]
*American baseball player*
* Fitzgerald, Mike

**FitzGerald, Lady** ?-1831   [PA]
*Author*
* Pamela

**Fitzgerald, Lawrence P[ennybaker]**
1906-1976   [CA]
*American author*
* Lawrence, Jack

**Fitzgerald, Lefty**
See   Fitzgerald, Howard Chumney
[Howie]

**Fitzgerald, Mike**
See   Fitzgerald, Justin Howard

**Fitzgerald, Patrick** 1882-1965
[F2, FC]
*Irish-born actor*
* Hale, Creighton

**Fitzgerald, Percy Hetherington**
1834-1925   [WW]
*Author*
* Dyce, Gilbert

**Fitzgerald, Robert Allan**   [PA]
*Author*
* Quid

**Fitzgerald, Roy**
See   Scherer, Roy Harold, Jr.

**Fitzgerald, Thomas** 1513-1536?
[HN, WBD]
*Vice-deputy of Ireland*
* [The] Silken Lord
* Silken Thomas

**Fitzgerald, Walter**
See   Bond, Walter

**Fitzgerald, William**
See   Jenkins, Will[iam]
F[itzgerald]

**Fitzgerald, William** 1814-1883
[PA]
*Author and clergyman*
* Newlight, [Rev] Aristarchus

**Fitzgerald, William Thomas**
1759-1829   [DEL]
*British poet*
* [The] Small Beer Poet

**Fitzgibbon, Catherine** 1823-1896
[WBD]
*American nun*
* Irene, [Sister]

**Fitzgibbon, Henry**   [PA]
*Author*
* Ephemera

**FitzGibbon, Paul Thomas** 1930-
[BEW]
*American educator, director, editor*
* Gray, Paul

**Fitzgibbons, Patrick**
See   McDonnell, John W.

**Fitzgig**
See   Fitzpatrick

**Fitzhardinge, Joan Margaret** 1912-
[AW, CA, SAT]
*Australian author*
* Phipson, Joan

**Fitzharris, Edward** 1890-1974   [SC]
*British-born actor and costume designer*
* Fitzharris, Fitz

**Fitzharris, Fitz**
See   Fitzharris, Edward

**Fitzherbert, Nicholas** 1550-1612?
[FFF]
*British author*
* Fitzerburtus, Nic

**Fitzhugh, Percy Keese** 1876- ?
[NAA]
*American author*
* Lloyd, Hugh

**Fitzhugh, William Henry**
1792-1830   [FFF]
*American author*
* Opimius

**Fitzke, Bob**
See   Fitzke, Paul Frederick Herman

**Fitzke, Paul Frederick Herman**
1900-1950   [BE]
*American baseball player*
* Fitzke, Bob

**Fitzmaurice, Michael T.**
See   Fitzmaurice-Kelly, Michael

**Fitzmaurice-Kelly, Michael**
1908-1967   [SC]
*American actor*
* Fitzmaurice, Michael T.

**Fitznoodle, Francis**
See   Valentine, Benjamin Bennaton

**FitzOsbert, William** ?-1199?   [HN]
* King of the Poor
* Longbeard
* [The] Saviour of the People

**Fitzosborne, [Sir] Thomas**
See   Melmoth, William

**Fitzpatrick**   [SN]
*Actor*
* Fitzgig

**Fitzpatrick, Alexander Stewart**
1944-   [CEI]
*Scottish-born hockey player*
* Fitzpatrick, Sandy

**Fitzpatrick, Daniel Robert**
1891-1969   [WEC]
*American cartoonist*
* Fitz

**Fitzpatrick, Ernest Hugh** 20th c.
[SFL, WGT]
*Author*
* Barnaby, Hugo

**Fitzpatrick, Margaret** 1911-1980
[FC]
*American actress*
* Patrick, Gail

**Fitzpatrick, Marjorie Seymour**
1899?-1956    [BEW]
*Canadian-born actress*
* Seymour, Jane

**Fitzpatrick, Mrs. M. J.**    [FFF]
*Entertainer*
* Beebe, Ella

**Fitzpatrick, Sandy**
See  Fitzpatrick, Alexander Stewart

**Fitzpatrick, William John** 1890- ?
[PA]
*Author*
* W. J. F.

**FitzRandolph, Nathaniel** 18th c.
[DNNS, FFF]
*American soldier*
* Fighting Nat

**Fitzroy, James**
See  Scott, James

**Fitzsimmons, Cotton**
See  Fitzsimmons, Lowell

**Fitzsimmons, Fat Freddie**
See  Fitzsimmons, Frederick Landis

**Fitzsimmons, Freckled Bob**
See  Fitzsimmons, Robert [Bob]

**Fitzsimmons, Frederick Landis**
1901-1979    [BE]
*American baseball player and manager*
* Fitzsimmons, Fat Freddie

**Fitzsimmons, James** 1874-1966
[AS, BBH]
*American horse trainer*
* Fitz, Mr.
* Fitzsimmons, Sunny Jim

**Fitzsimmons, Lowell** 1931-
[BB, SMG]
*American basketball coach*
* Fitzsimmons, Cotton

**Fitzsimmons [or Fitzsimons?], Maureen** 1920?-    [BDF, FC, IPA]
*Irish-born actress*
* O'Hara, Maureen

**Fitzsimmons, Robert [Bob]**
1862-1917    [B10, BX, RBE]
*British-born boxer*
* Fitzsimmons, Freckled Bob
* Fitzsimmons, Ruby Robert
* [The] Lanky Cornishman

**Fitzsimmons, Ruby Robert**
See  Fitzsimmons, Robert [Bob]

**Fitzsimmons, Sunny Jim**
See  Fitzsimmons, James

**FitzWalter, Robert** ?-1235
[HN, SN]
*Led the English barons against King John*
* [The] Marshal of the Army of God and Holy Church

**Fitzwilliam, Michael**
See  Lyons, J. B.

**Five By Five, Mr.**
See  Rushing, James Andrew [Jimmy]

**500 Per Cent More Man**
See  Bates, Otha Ellas

**Five of Clubs**
See  Proctor, Richard A.

**[The] Five P's**
See  Oxberry, William

**Fix It, Mr.**
See  Pelham, Alfred Montgomery

**Fix, Marie** 1895-    [THR]
*British actress*
* Ney, Marie

**Fix, Paul**
See  Morrison, Paul Fix

**Fix, Ress**
See  Fix, Ressie Mae

**Fix, Ressie Mae** 1893-1975    [SC]
*American actress*
* Fix, Ress

**Fixit, Mr.**
See  Rohatyn, Felix

**Fjeld, Erling**
See  Sonsteby, Gunnar

**Flaccus**
See  Alcuin [or Albinus]

**Flaccus**
See  Levy, Newman

**Flaccus**
See  Ward, Thomas

**Flaccus**
See  Waters, John

**Flachsenhaar, Martin** 1924-    [EJ]
*American jazz musician*
* Flax, Marty

**Flacius Illyricus, Matthias**
1520-1575    [WBD]
*German theologian*
* Frankovic Ilir, Matija
* Vlacic Ilir, Matija

**Flack, Captain**    [DEL, PA]
*Author*
* [The] Ranger

**Flack, Isaac Harvey** 1912-1966
[SFL, WGT]
*British author*
* Graham, Harvey

**Flack, Naomi John White** 20th c.
[CA]
*American author*
* Sellers, Naomi

**Flacon, Joseph Henry** 1781-1834
[PA]
*Author*
* Rochelle

**Flagellum Dei**
See  Charles VIII

**Flagg, Elizabeth**    [PA]
*Author*
* BLoomfield, Robert

**Flagg, Francis**
See  Weiss, Henry George

**Flagg, John**
See  Gearon, John

**Flagg, Kenneth**
See  Ayvazian, L. Fred

**Flagg, Mary**    [PA]
*Author*
* Emeff

**Flaggare, Madam**
See  Carlin, Emelia F.

**Flagstead, Ira James** 1893-1940
[AS, BE, PB]
*American baseball player*
* Flagstead, Pete

**Flagstead, Pete**
See  Flagstead, Ira James

**Flaharty, W. E.** 19th c.    [PA]
*Author*
* W. E. F.

**Flaherty, Patrick Joseph**
1876-1968    [AS, BE]
*American baseball player*
* Flaherty, Patsy

**Flaherty, Patsy**
See  Flaherty, Patrick Joseph

**Flaherty, Ray** 20th c.
*American football coach*
* Flaherty, Red

**Flaherty, Red**
See  Flaherty, Ray

**Flair, Al[bert Dell]** 1916-    [BE]
*American baseball player*
* Flair, Broadway

**Flair, Broadway**
See  Flair, Al[bert Dell]

**Flake, Otto**
See  Kotta, Leo F.

**Flaman, Ferdinand Charles** 1927-
[CEI, FHE, HK]
*Canadian-born hockey player*
* Flaman, Fernie

**Flaman, Fernie**
See  Flaman, Ferdinand Charles

**Flamand, Francois**
See  Duquesnoy, Francois

**Flambeau**
See  Vail, Floyd

**Flame, Lord**
See  Johnson, Samuel

**[The] Flame Thrower**
See  Fanok, Harry Michael

**[The] Flamethrower**
See  Riccardo, John

**Flammia, Michael** 20th c.    [SG]
*Boxer*
* [The] Zula Kid

**Flammonde, Paris** 20th c.    [CA]
*American author, poet, critic*
* Delfano, M. M.

**Flanagan, Ann** ?-1975    [SC]
*British comedienne and dancer*
* Flanagan, Curley

**Flanagan, Bud**
See  Flanagan, Edward Vanes, Jr.

**Flanagan, Bud**
See  Weintrop, Reuben

**Flanagan, Curley**
See  Flanagan, Ann

**Flanagan, Ed**
*American football player*
* Clean, Mr.

**Flanagan, Edward Vanes, Jr.**
1908-1968    [FC, SC]
*American actor, director, screenwriter*
* Flanagan, Bud
* O'Keefe, Dennis

**Flanagan, Edward Vanes, Jr.**
(Continued)
* Ricks, Jonathan

**Flanagan, Florence** 1876-1940
[BMH]
*Australian-born comedienne and singer*
* [The] Australian Marie Lloyd
* Forde, Florrie

**Flanagan, James Paul** 1881-1947
[BE]
*American baseball player*
* Flanagan, Steamer

**Flanagan, Joseph David Stanislaus**
1903-    [CA]
*American author*
* Raymond, [Father] M.

**Flanagan, Steamer**
See  Flanagan, James Paul

**Flanders, John**
See  De Kremer, Jean Raymond

**[A] Flanders Mare**
See  Anne of Cleves

**Flaneur**
See  Benjamin, Park

**Flaneur**
See  Greene, Charles Gordon

**Flaneur**
See  Hall, Blakely

**Flaneur**
See  Philp, Kenward

**Flaneur**
See  Yates, Edmund Hodgson

**Flannam, Richard** 1896-    [THR]
*British actor*
* Gray, Richard

**Flannelfoot**
See  Vicars, Henry Edward

**Flanner, Abbe**    [PA]
*Author*
* Campbell, Ellen A. F.

**Flanner, Janet** 1892-1978
[B10, CA]
*American journalist and author*
* Genet

**Flannery, Thomas** 20th c.    [WWL]
*Irish author and poet*
* O Flannghaile, Tomas

**Flash, Henry Lyden** 1835- ?    [FFF]
*American poet*
* Eclair, Lyden

**Flaskamper, Flash**
See  Flaskamper, Ray Harold

**Flaskamper, Ray Harold** 1901-
[BE]
*American baseball player*
* Flaskamper, Flash

**Flat Jack Simmons**
See  Simmons, Jack

**Flat Nose Curry**
See  Parrott, George

**[The] Flatboat Man**
See  Lincoln, Abraham

**Flatow, Robert** 1929-    [SFL]
*American playwright*
* Thom, Robert

[The] Flatterer
See Vitellius, Aulus

[The] Flatterer of Louis XIV
See Boileau-Despreaux, Nicolas

Flavell, Carol Willsey Bell 1939-
[CA]
*American genealogist and writer*
* Bell, Carol

Flavius, [Brother]
See Ellison, James E.

Flavius
See Heron-Allen, Edward

Flavius, Gnaus
See Kantorowicz, Hermann

Flax
See Palacio, Lino

Flax, Marty
See Flachsenhaar, Martin

Flaxman, E. 20th c. [MBF]
*British author*
* Grey, Gordon

Flaxman, Traudl 1942- [CA]
*German-born American educator
and author*
* Traudl

[The] Flayed Fox
See Fuchs, Leonhard

[The] Flea
See Bell, Ed

[The] Flea
See Patek, Freddie Joe

[The] Flea
See Roberts, Walt

Fleagle, Brick
See Fleagle, Jacob Roger

Fleagle, Jacob Roger 1906-
[EJ, WWJ]
*American jazz musician*
* Fleagle, Brick

Flechier, [Valentin] Esprit
1632-1710 [DNNS, FFF, SN]
*French bishop and orator*
* [The] French Isocrates
* [The] Isocrates of France

Flecker, Herman Elroy 1884-1915
[LC]
*British poet*
* Flecker, James Elroy

Flecker, James Elroy
See Flecker, Herman Elroy

Flecknor, Richard
See Adcock, [Arthur] St. John

Fleet, George Rutland 1853-1922
[BEW, THR]
*Actor and author*
* Barrington, Rutland

Fleet, Gordon 1945- [RO2]
*Australian musician*
* Fleet, Snowy

Fleet, Snowy
See Fleet, Gordon

Fleet, Thomas 1685-1758 [PA]
*Author*
* Mother Goose

Fleetwood, Frances
See Buss, Frances

Fleetwood, Frank
See Buss, Frances

Fleg, Edmond
See Flegenheimer, Edmond

Flegenheimer, Arthur 1900?-1935
[B10]
*American underworld figure*
* [The] Dutchman
* Schultz, Dutch

Flegenheimer, Edmond 1874-1963
[JL]
*French poet and playwright*
* Fleg, Edmond

Flegg, Harry 1878-1960 [OCS]
*Australian rugby player*
* Flegg, Jersey

Flegg, Jersey
See Flegg, Harry

Fleischer, Anthony Charles 1928-
[AW]
*South African author*
* Hofmeyer, Hans

Fleischer, Leonore 1933-
*American author*
* Cary, Webster
* Edwards, Alexander
* Roote, Mike
* Williams, Booker

Fleischer, Nat[haniel Stanley]
1887-1972 [BX]
*American sportswriter and editor*
* Boxing, Mr.

Fleischmann, Arthur John 1896-
[ART]
*Czech-born sculptor*
* A. F.

Fleischmann, Walter Reinhold Alfred
1919- [FC, SW]
*American actor*
* Dexter, Anthony

Fleisser, Marieluise
See Haindl, Marieluise

Fleitman, Alex O. 1924- [ASC]
*American musician*
* Foster, Al

Fleming, Bill
See Fleming, Leslie Fletchard

Fleming, Bryant
See Barr, Byron Ellsworth

Fleming, George
See Fletcher, Julia Constance

Fleming, Geraldine
See Coryell, John Russell

Fleming, Guy
See Masur, Harold Q.

Fleming, Harry
See Bird, William Henry Fleming

Fleming, Hugh
See Hague, Frances Dorothy

Fleming, Ian
See Macfarlane, Ian

Fleming, Ian [Lancaster]
1908-1964 [CA, SAT]
*British author*
* Atticus

Fleming, John Morris 1918-
[CWG]
*American country-western performer*
* Fleming, Sonny

Fleming, Leslie Fletchard 1913-
[BE]
*American baseball player*
* Fleming, Bill

Fleming, Leslie Harvey 1915- [BE]
*American baseball player*
* Fleming, Moe

Fleming, Macklin
See Stainback, Macklin

Fleming, Marion
See Mordaunt, Mrs. F. S.

Fleming, May Agnes [FFF]
*Author*
* Carleton, Cousin May

Fleming, Moe
See Fleming, Leslie Harvey

Fleming, Nellie [FFF]
*Entertainer*
* Rand, Ellen

Fleming, Oliver [joint pseudonym
with Ronald MacDonald]
See MacDonald, Philip

Fleming, Oliver [joint pseudonym
with Philip MacDonald]
See MacDonald, Ronald

Fleming [or Flemming], Paul
1609-1640 [HN, SN]
*German poet*
* [The] Anacreon of Germany
* [The] German Herrick
* [The] Herrick of Germany

Fleming, [Robert] Peter 1907-1971
[TC, WW]
*British author*
* Moth
* Strix

Fleming, Rhonda
See Louis, Marilyn

Fleming, Sleuth
See Fleming, Thomas Vincent
[Tom]

Fleming, Sonny
See Fleming, John Morris

Fleming, Stuart
See Knight, Damon F[rancis]

Fleming, Thomas J[ames] 1927-
[CA, SAT]
*American author*
* Cain, Christopher
* James, T. F.
* Thomas, J. F.

Fleming, Thomas Vincent [Tom]
1873-1957 [BE]
*American baseball player*
* Fleming, Sleuth

Fleming, Waldo
See Williamson, Thames Ross

Fleming-Roberts, G. T. 20th c.
[SFP]
*Author*
* Chance, George

[The] Flemish Raphael
See Vriendt, Frans de

Flemming
See Sorenson, Flemming

Flemming, Harford
See Hare, Harriet

Flemming, Herb 1904- [EJ]
*American jazz musician*
* El Michelle, Niccolaiih

Flemming, Nicholas Coit 1936-
[CA]
*British oceanographer and author*
* James, Stanton

Flers, P. L.
See Pujol, Pierre Leon

Fleta
See De Brampton, William

Fleta
See De Lovetot, J.

Fleta
See De Stratton, Adam

Fleta
See De Weyland, Thomas

Fleta
See Hamilton, Kate W.

Fleta, Pierre
See Burro-Fleta, Anatole

Fletcher, A. [PA]
*Author*
* Sheelah

Fletcher, Adam
See Flexner, Stuart Berg

Fletcher, Adele [Whitely] 1898-
[CAP]
*American author*
* Ormiston, Roberta

Fletcher, Alfred Vanoide 1924-
[BE]
*American baseball player*
* Fletcher, Van

Fletcher, Black Jack
See Fletcher, Frank

Fletcher, C. R. L.
See Fletcher, Charles Robert Leslie

Fletcher, Charles Robert Leslie
1857-1934 [LC]
*British author*
* Fletcher, C. R. L.

Fletcher, Charlie May Hogue
1897- [CA, SAT]
*American author*
* Simon, Charlie May

Fletcher, Christopher David Bryan
1957- [DC]
*British cricketer*
* Fletcher, Fletch
* Fletcher, Godber

Fletcher, David
See Barber, Dulan F.

Fletcher, Elbie
See Fletcher, Elburt Preston

Fletcher, Elburt Preston 1916-
[BE]
*American baseball player*
* Fletcher, Elbie

Fletcher, Fletch
See Fletcher, Christopher David
Bryan

Fletcher, Frances 1894- [WWL]
*American author*
* Woodbridge, Anne

Fletcher, Frank 1885-1973
[WWW]
*American naval officer*
* Fletcher, Black Jack

Fletcher, George 1914-1957   [GW]
*American rodeo performer*
* Fletcher, Kid

Fletcher, George U.
See  Pratt, [Murray] Fletcher

Fletcher, Gnome
See  Fletcher, Keith William
Robert

Fletcher, Godber
See  Fletcher, Christopher David
Bryan

Fletcher, Harry Lutf Verne 1902-
[AW, CA, WW]
*British author*
* Garden, John
* Hereford, John

Fletcher, Helen Jill 1911-
[CA, SAT]
*American author*
* Lee, Carol
* Morey, Charles

Fletcher, John Arthur 1906-
[WWL]
*British author*
* Tempest, J. Fletcher

Fletcher, John Walter James 1937-
[IAW]
*British author*
* Fune, Jonathan

Fletcher, John William
See  De La Flechere, John William

Fletcher, Joseph Smith 1863-1935
[EMD, TC]
*British author*
* Son of the Soil

Fletcher, Julia Constance
1858-1938   [BEW, FFF, PA]
*American author*
* Dudu
* Fleming, George

Fletcher, Keith William Robert
1944-   [DC]
*British cricketer*
* Fletcher, Gnome

Fletcher, Kid
See  Fletcher, George

Fletcher, Lucille
See  Wallop, Lucille Fletcher

Fletcher, [Sir] Norton   [HN]
*British politician*
* Bullface Doubleface, Sir

Fletcher, Richard
See  Dodge, Wendell Phillips

Fletcher, Robert
See  Wyckoff, Robert Fletcher

Fletcher, Robert James 1877- ?
[WW]
*Author*
* Asterisk

Fletcher, Scott
See  Pfeiffer, C. Boyd

Fletcher, Tex   [CWG]
*American country-western performer*
* Benner, Bill
* [The] Lonely Cowboy

Fletcher, Tex (Continued)
* Render, Bill

Fletcher, Van
See  Fletcher, Alfred Vanoide

Flett, Cowboy
See  Flett, William Mayer [Bill]

Flett, William Mayer [Bill] 1943-
[CEI, FHE, SMG]
*Canadian-born hockey player*
* [The] Cowboy
* Flett, Cowboy

Fleur, Anne 20th c.   [IBY, ICB]
*American author and illustrator*
* Sari

Fleur de Lys
See  Birch, Percival Lea

Fleur, Paul
See  Pohl, Frederik

Fleur, William
See  Gosling, William Flower

Fleuranges, Seigneur de
See  La Marck, Robert III de

Fleuridas, Ellie Rae
See  Sherman, Eleanor Rae

Fleury, Alice   [PA]
*Author*
* Greville, Henry

Fleury, Delphine 20th c.   [CA]
*American psychologist and author*
* Amatora, [Sister] Mary

Fleury, Jean ?-1469   [PA]
*Author*
* Floridas

Fleury, Joseph Nicolas Robert
1797-1890   [WBD]
*French painter*
* Robert Fleury

Fleury-Battier, Alcibiade
See  Battier, Alcibiade Fleury

Fleury-Husson [or Husson], Jules
1821-1889   [WBD]
*French author*
* Champfleury

Flevitsky, George 1902-1960   [SC]
*American actor and screenwriter*
* Fells, George

Flexner, Stuart Berg 1928-   [CA]
*American editor and author*
* Fletcher, Adam
* Mees, Steve
* Santee, Collier

Flic
See  Hensman, Howard

Flick, Friedrich Christian 20th c.
*German industrialist*
* Flick, Mick

Flick, Gert-Rudolf 20th c.
*German industrialist*
* Flick, Muck

Flick, Mick
See  Flick, Friedrich Christian

Flick, Muck
See  Flick, Gert-Rudolf

Fliegel, Hellmuth 1913-   [MGL]
*German author*
* Heym, Stefan

Flight
See  Bruno, Harry A.

Flight Archer, Mr.
See  Powell, Ruben

Flight, Mr.
See  Drake, Harry

Flinders, Karl
See  Milton, Saul

Flindt, Homer Eon ?-1924   [SFL]
*Author*
* Flint, Homer Eon

Flinn, William H. 1853-1902
[BEW]
*American minstrel*
* West, William H.

Flint, E. de P.
See  Fielden, Thomas Perceval

Flint, F. S.
See  Flint, Frank Stewart

Flint, Frank Stewart 1885-1960
[LC, TC]
*British poet, translator, civil servant*
* Flint, F. S.

Flint, Frank Sylvester 1855-1892
[BE]
*American baseball player*
* Flint, Silver

Flint, Henry M. ?-1868   [FFF, PA]
*American writer*
* Druid

Flint, Homer Eon
See  Flindt, Homer Eon

Flint Jack
See  Simpson, Edward

Flint, Silver
See  Flint, Frank Sylvester

Flint, William   [PA]
*Author*
* Druit, Henry

Flip
See  Paxton, Gary

Flitcraft, Hildreth Milton 1923-
[BE]
*American baseball player*
* Flitcraft, Hilly

Flitcraft, Hilly
See  Flitcraft, Hildreth Milton

[The] Flo Ziegfeld of Country Music
See  Frank, Joe L.

Flock, Fonty
See  Flock, Truman Fontella

Flock, Truman Fontella 1921-1972
[EAR]
*American auto racer*
* Flock, Fonty

Flohr, Dutch
See  Flohr, Moritz Herman

Flohr, Moritz Herman 1911-   [BE]
*American baseball player*
* Flohr, Dutch
* Flohr, Mort

Flohr, Mort
See  Flohr, Moritz Herman

Flood, Beatrice 1908-   [BEW]
*American actress*
* De Neergaard, Beatrice

Flood, Curtis Charles 1938-   [IBW]
*American baseball player*
* [The] Abe Lincoln of Baseball
* Flood, Rembrandt

Flood, Daniel J. 1904?-
*American politician*
* Flood, Dapper Dan

Flood, Dapper Dan
See  Flood, Daniel J.

Flood, Flash
See  Robinson, Jan M.

Flood, Pauline 1915-1917   [SC]
*American actress*
* Sunshine, Baby
* [The] Tiniest Star in Films

Flood, Rembrandt
See  Flood, Curtis Charles

Flood-Murphy, Pip
See  Flood-Murphy, William
Frederick

Flood-Murphy, William Frederick
1933-   [OP]
*British opera technical director*
* Flood-Murphy, Pip

Floor Show Nance
See  Nance, Willis

Florelle [or Florette?]
See  Rousseau, Odette

Floren, Lee 1910-   [CA, WD]
*American author*
* Austin, Brett
* Donald, R. V.
* Hall, Claudia
* Hamilton, Wade
* Harding, Matthew Whiteman
  [Matt]
* Horton, Feliz Lee
* Jason, Stuart
* Kirby, Mark
* Lang, Grace
* Nelson, Marguerite
* Smith, Lew
* Sterling, [Maria] Sandra
* Thomas, Lee
* Turner, Len
* Watson, Will
* Wilson, Dave

Florence
See  Osgood, Frances Sargent
Locke

Florence
See  Tyng, Florence

Florence
See  Wabbes, Maria

Florence, Billy
See  Conlin, William J.

Florence, Evangeline
See  Houghton, Evangeline

Florence, Paul Robert 1900-   [BE]
*American baseball player*
* Florence, Pep

Florence, Pep
See  Florence, Paul Robert

Florence, William Jermyn
See  Conlin, Bernard

Florensz, Adrian 1459-1523   [CAL]
*Pope*
* Adrian VI

**Florentius, Georgius** 538?- 593
[SN, WBD]
*Saint*
* [The] Father of Frankish History
* Gregory of Tours
* [The] Herodotus of Barbarism

**Flores, Gil**
*See* Flores, Gilberto Garcia

**Flores, Gilberto Garcia** 1952-
[SMG]
*Puerto Rican-born baseball player*
* Flores, Gil

**Florian, Flor**
*See* Florian, Jerry John

**Florian, Jerry John** 1915- [MY]
*American jazz musician*
* Florian, Flor

**Floridas**
*See* Fleury, Jean

**Floridor**
*See* Soulas, Josias de [Sieur de Primefosse]

**Floridus, Francisco** 1500-1547
[PA]
*Author*
* Sabinus

**Florinda** 8th c. [SN]
*Daughter of Count Julian, governor of Ceuta*
* [The] Helen of Spain

**Florio**
*See* Brooks, James Gordon

**Florio, Caryl**
*See* Robjohn, William James

**Florio, Dan**
*See* Florio, Dominick

**Florio, Dominick** 1896?-1965 [AS]
*American boxing manager-trainer*
* Florio, Dan

**Florio, John** 1545?-1625
[DNNF, RH, SN]
*British philologist*
* [The] Resolute

**Floris, Frans**
*See* Vriendt, Frans de

**Florizel**
*See* George IV

**Florry**
*See* Kernan, J. Frank

**Flory, Med**
*See* Flory, Meredith Irwin

**Flory, Meredith Irwin** 1926- [EJ]
*American jazz musician*
* Flory, Med

**Flory, Regine**
*See* Arlaz, Regine

**Flosso, Al** 1895-1976 [BS]
*American magician*
* [The] Coney Island Fakir

**Flotsam**
*See* Hilliam, B. C.

**[The] Flower**
*See* LaFleur, Guy Damien

**[The] Flower of Chivalry**
*See* Douglas, [Sir] William

**[The] Flower of Chivalry**
*See* Sidney, [Sir] Philip

**[The] Flower of Chivalry**
*See* Terrail, Pierre du

**[The] Flower of French Chivalry**
*See* Guesclin, Bertrand du

**[The] Flower of Kings**
*See* Arthur

**[The] Flower of Poets**
*See* Chaucer, Geoffrey

**[The] Flower of Strathearn**
*See* Oliphant, Carolina [Baroness Nairne]

**[The] Flower of the Forest**
*See* Washington, George

**[The] Flower of Yarrow**
*See* Scott, Mary

**Flowerdew, Phyllis**
*See* Kingsbury, Phyllis May

**Flowers, Allen R.** 1899- [FB]
*American football player*
* Flowers, Buck

**Flowers, Buck**
*See* Flowers, Allen R.

**Flowers, D'Arcy Raymond**
1902-1962 [BE]
*American baseball player*
* Flowers, Jake

**Flowers, Dino**
*See* Flowers, Roderick

**Flowers, Evangelist Mary**
*See* Miles, Josephine [Josie]

**Flowers, Jake**
*See* Flowers, D'Arcy Raymond

**Flowers, Roderick** 1955- [IBW]
*American fashion designer*
* Flowers, Dino

**Flowers, Theodore** 1895-1927
[AS, BX, RBE]
*American boxer*
* Flowers, Tiger
* [The] Georgia Deacon

**Flowers, Tiger**
*See* Flowers, Theodore

**Floyd, Bubba**
*See* Floyd, Leslie Roe

**Floyd, Charles Arthur** 1901-1934
[BLB]
*American bank robber and murderer*
* Floyd, Pretty Boy
* Hamilton, Jack
* [The] Robin Hood of the Cookson Hills

**Floyd, Cornelia** [PA]
*Author*
* Forrest, Neil

**Floyd, Frank** 1908- [BWW]
*American singer*
* Floyd, Rambling King
* Harmonica Frank
* [The] Silly Kid

**Floyd, Gilbert** 20th c. [MBF]
*British author*
* Grenfell, John
* Revel, Harry
* Shand, Captain
* Storm, Duncan

**Floyd, Leslie Roe** 1917- [BE]
*American baseball player*
* Floyd, Bubba

**Floyd, Mr.** [PA]
*Author*
* E. F. L.

**Floyd, Pretty Boy**
*See* Floyd, Charles Arthur

**Floyd, Rambling King**
*See* Floyd, Frank

**Fluck, Daisy** 1931- [FC]
*British actress*
* Dors, Diana

**Fludd, Robert** 1574-1637
[DNNF, FFF, SN]
*British physician and philosopher*
* [The] Searcher

**Fluellen, Bad Ike**
*See* Fluellen, Ike

**Fluellen, Ike** 20th c. [RBE]
*American boxer*
* Fluellen, Bad Ike

**Flugrath, Leona** 1900-
[CED, F1, FC]
*American actress*
* Mason, Shirley

**Flugrath, Violet** 1897- [F1, FC]
*American actress*
* Dana, Viola

**Fluhrer, John L.** 1893-1946 [BE]
*American baseball player*
* Morris, William

**Fluiriot, Zenaide Marie Ann** [PA]
*Author*
* Edianez, Anna

**Flumiani, Carlo Maria** 1902-
[NAA]
*Italian-born author*
* Di Ferra, Count

**Flurie, Edward Cletus** 1943- [RO2]
*American singer and songwriter*
* Rambeau, Eddie

**[The] Fly**
*See* Rozelle, Richard

**[The] Flying Deacon**
*See* Carroll, Julian

**[The] Flying Dutchman**
*See* Kitzmiller, John

**[The] Flying Dutchman**
*See* Wagner, John Peter

**[The] Flying Dutchman**
*See* Willebrands, Johannes

**[The] Flying Dutchman**
*See* Willman, Tony

**[The] Flying Eagle**
*See* Ross, Charles Isaiah

**[The] Flying Finn**
*See* Nurmi, Paavo

**[The] Flying Fish**
*See* Furuhashi, Hironashin

**[The] Flying Frenchman**
*See* Duray, Leon

**[The] Flying Grandfather**
*See* Conrad, Max

**[The] Flying Highwayman**
*See* Harrow, William

**[The] Flying Highwayman**
*See* Turpin, Richard [Dick]

**[The] Flying Hussar**
*See* Voss, Werner

**[The] Flying Mantuan**
*See* Nuvolari, Tazio

**Flying Officer X**
*See* Bates, Herbert Ernest

**[The] Flying Peacemaker**
*See* Kissinger, Henry Alfred

**[The] Flying Policeman**
*See* Keino, Hezekiah Kipchoge

**[The] Flying Scot**
*See* Guild, Alex

**[The] Flying Scot**
*See* Stewart, Jackie

**[The] Flying Scot**
*See* Thomson, Robert Brown [Bobby]

**[The] Flying Scott**
*See* Clark, James [Jimmy]

**[The] Flying Terror**
*See* Grange, Harold E.

**[The] Flying Yankee**
*See* Zimmerman, Arthur A.

**Flynn, Carney**
*See* Flynn, Cornelius Francis Xavier

**Flynn, Clarence Edwin** 1886-
[NAA]
*American clergyman and writer*
* Cullison, Edwin

**Flynn, Clipper**
*See* Flynn, William

**Flynn, Cornelius Francis Xavier**
1875-1947 [BE]
*American baseball player*
* Flynn, Carney

**Flynn, Dibby**
*See* Flynn, George A.

**Flynn, Fireman Jim**
*See* Chiariglione, Andrew

**Flynn, Flynnegan**
*See* Flynn, James William

**Flynn, George A.** 1870-1901 [BE]
*American baseball player*
* Flynn, Dibby

**Flynn, [Sir] J. Albert** 1863- ?
[WWL]
*British author*
* Oliver, Owen

**Flynn, Jackson**
*See* Shirreffs, Gordon D[onald]

**Flynn, James William** 1948-
[SMG]
*American baseball player*
* Flynn, Flynnegan

**Flynn, Janet** 1909-1963 [FC]
*American actress*
* Malo, Gina

**Flynn, Jim**
*See* Chiariglione, Andrew

**Flynn, Jocko**
*See* Flynn, John A.

**Flynn, John A.** 1864-1907 [BE]
*American baseball player*
* Flynn, Jocko

**Flynn, Kerri**
See Gillooly, Edna Rae

**Flynn, Lefty**
See Flynn, Maurice B.

**Flynn, Mary Margaret** 1915-    [AW]
*Australian author*
* Livingstone, Margaret

**Flynn, Maurice B.** 1893-1959    [SC]
*Actor*
* Flynn, Lefty

**Flynn, Minnie** 1871-1936    [SC]
*Actress*
* Fielding, Minnie

**Flynn, Thomas W.** 1875?-1961
[BEW]
*Irish-born actor*
* Tracey, Thomas F.

**Flynn, William** 1850-1881    [BE]
*American baseball player*
* Flynn, Clipper

**Flynt, Josiah**
See Willard, Josiah Flynt

**F'Murr**
See Peyzaret, Richard

**Foa, Ettore** 1892-1964    [SC]
*Italian actor*
* Ermelli, Claudio

**Foakes-Jackson, Frederick John**
See Jackson, Frederick John

**Foat, Foaty**
See Foat, James Clive [Jim]

**Foat, James Clive [Jim]** 1952-    [DC]
*British cricketer*
* Foat, Foaty

**Foch, Dirk**
See Fock, Dirk

**Foch, Nina**
See Fock, Nina Consuelo Maud

**Fock, Dirk** 1886-    [BBD]
*Dutch composer and conductor*
* Foch, Dirk

**Fock, Gorch**
See Kinau, Johann

**Fock, Nina Consuelo Maud** 1924-
[BEW]
*Dutch-born actress*
* Foch, Nina

**Focke, Ernest Paul Walter** 1896-
[AW]
*British-born author*
* Paul, Ernest

**Foda, Aun**
See Foxe, Arthur N[orman]

**Fodge, [Eu]gene [Arlan]** 1931-    [BE]
*American baseball player*
* Fodge, Suds

**Fodge, Suds**
See Fodge, [Eu]gene [Arlan]

**Fodor, Ladislaus** 1898-    [THR]
*Hungarian-born playwright*
* Vulpius, Paul

**Fodor, Nandor?**
See Carrington, Hereward Hubert
Lavington

**Foe, Daniel** 1663?-1731
[DEP, DNNS, WBD]
*British author*
* Defoe, Daniel
* [The] Father of Modern Prose
Fiction
* Moreton, Andrew
* [The] Sunday Gentleman

**Foeldi, Andras Harry** 1926-    [OP]
*Hungarian-born opera singer*
* Foldi, Andrew Harry

**Foeng, J. A. Chin A.** 1941?-    [CW]
*Surinamese poet*
* Juanchi

**Foerder, Heinz** 1909-    [JL]
*Israeli chess player*
* Porat, Yosef

**Foerster, Lotte B[rand]** 1910-    [CA]
*American art historian and author*
* Philip, Lotte Brand

**Foerster-Nietzsche, Elisabeth**
See Lamb, Antonia

**Foeth, Afanasi Afanasievich**
1820?-1892    [WBD]
*Russian poet*
* Fet, Afansi Afanasievich
* Shenshin, Afanasi Afanasievich

**Foff, Arthur R[aymond]** 1925-1973
[CAP]
*American educator and author*
* Lawrence, A. R.
* Lawrence, Karl

**[The] Fog**
See Pioche de la Vergne, Marie
Madeleine

**Fogarty, Jonathan Titulescu, Esq.**
See Farrell, James T[homas]

**Fogel, Daniel Mark** 1948-    [CA]
*American author and poet*
* Kahn-Fogel, Daniel [Mark]

**Fogel, Maurice** 1911-    [BMH]
*British entertainer*
* [The] Amazing Fogel

**Fogelberg, Ola** 1894-1952    [WEC]
*Finnish cartoonist*
* Fogeli

**Fogeli**
See Fogelberg, Ola

**Fogerty, John** 20th c.    [PRS]
*Musician*
* Blue Ridge Rangers

**Foghammar, Stig Sverker** 20th c.
[IAW]
*Swedish author*
* Sverkers, Stig

**Fogolin, Fogey**
See Fogolin, Lee

**Fogolin, Lee**
See Fogolin, Lidio John

**Fogolin, Lee** 1955-    [SMG]
*American-born hockey player*
* Fogolin, Fogey

**Fogolin, Lidio John** 1926-    [CEI]
*Canadian-born hockey player*
* Fogolin, Lee

**Foix, Gaston de [Duc de Nemours]**
1489-1512    [DHA, DNNF, FFF]
*French army officer*
* [The] Thunderbolt of Italy

**Fojak**
See Ackerman, Forrest J[ames]

**Folard, Jean Charles de** 1669-1752
[HN]
*French soldier*
* [The] French Vegetius

**Foldi, Andrew Harry**
See Foeldi, Andras Harry

**Folengo, Teofilo** 1496?-1544
[WBD]
*Italian poet*
* Coccaius [or Coccaio], Merlinus

**Foley, Charles Joseph** 1856-1898
[BE]
*Irish-born American baseball player*
* Foley, Curry

**Foley, Clyde Julian** 1910-1968
[CME, CWG, DAM]
*American country-western performer*
* Foley, Red

**Foley, Curry**
See Foley, Charles Joseph

**Foley, Dave** 20th c.
[ESF, SFL, WGT]
*American author*
* Hatch, Gerald

**Foley, Gilbert Anthony** 1945-    [CEI]
*Canadian-born hockey player*
* Foley, Rick

**Foley, Helen**
See Fowler, Helen Rosa [Huxley]

**Foley, Jack** 1940-    [BB]
*American basketball player*
* [The] Shot

**Foley, John** ?-1925    [BLB, PHM]
*American bootlegger*
* Foley, Mitters

**Foley, [Cedric] John** 1917-1974
[CA]
*British army officer and author*
* Sawyer, John
* Sinclair, Ian

**Foley, Mitters**
See Foley, John

**Foley, Pat**
See Greene, Patrick Joseph

**Foley, Pearl** 20th c.    [WW]
*Canadian author*
* De Mar, Paul

**Foley, Rae**
See Denniston, Elinore

**Foley, Red**
See Foley, Clyde Julian

**Foley, Rick**
See Foley, Gilbert Anthony

**Foley, Scott**
See Dareff, Hal

**Foli, Crazy Horse**
See Foli, Timothy John

**Foli, Timothy John** 1950-    [PB]
*American baseball player*
* Foli, Crazy Horse

**Folio, Tom**
See Babson, Joseph E.

**Folio, Tom**
See Rawlinson, Thomas

**Folkard, William Seward**
1887-1967    [F1, FC, FDG]
*British director*
* Elvey, Maurice

**Folke, Will** [house pseudonym]
See Bloch, Robert [Albert]

**Folkins, Lee** 20th c.
*American football player*
* Folkins, Snake

**Folkins, Snake**
See Folkins, Lee

**Follen, Adolf Ludwig**
See Follen, August

**Follen, August** 1794-1855    [WBD]
*German poet and politician*
* Follen, Adolf Ludwig

**Follett, Kenneth Martin** 1949-
[WWS]
*British author*
* Myles, Symon

**Follis, Charles W.** 1879- ?    [IBW]
*American football player*
* [The] Black Cyclone from
Wooster

**[The] Follower in the Footsteps**
See Van Buren, Martin

**Folsom, Franklin [Brewster]** 1907-
[CA, SAT]
*American author*
* Brewster, Benjamin [joint
pseudonym with Mary Elting]
* Cutler, Samuel
* Gorham, Michael [joint
pseudonym with Mary Elting]
* Hopkins, Lyman
* Nesbit, Troy

**Folsom, James E.** 1908-
*American politician*
* Folsom, Kissing Jim

**Folsom, Jim** 1949?-
*American politician*
* Folsom, Little Jim

**Folsom, Kissing Jim**
See Folsom, James E.

**Folsom, Little Jim**
See Folsom, Jim

**Folupa, Frank**
See Sidis, William James

**Fonarow, Jerry** 1935-    [CA]
*American author*
* Cogane, Gerald
* Farrow, J.

**Fondane, Benjamin**
See Fundoianu, Benjamin

**Fonnerean, Thomas George**    [PA]
*Author*
* H. E. O.

**Fons Vitae**
See Alexander of Hales

**Fontaine, Joan**
See De Havilland, Joan De
Beauvoir

**Fontana, Jean Pierre** 20th c.    [SFP]
*Author*
* Scovel, Juy

**Fontana, Nicola** 1500?-1557
[WBD]
*Italian mathematician*
* Tartaglia, Niccolo

**Fontana, Wayne**
See Ellis, Glyn Geoffrey

**Fontanges, Brilliant**
See De Scoraille de Roussilles, Marie Angelique

**Fontanges, Duchesse de**
See De Scoraille de Roussilles, Marie Angelique

**Fontanne, Lillie Louise** 20th c. [BEW]
*British actress*
* Fontanne, Lynn

**Fontanne, Lynn**
See Fontanne, Lillie Louise

**Fontcreuse, Marquis De**
See Jaeger, Cyril Karel Stuart

**Fontenelle, Bernard Le Bovier de** 1657-1757 [SN]
*French author*
* Fontenelle, Centenary

**Fontenelle, Centenary**
See Fontenelle, Bernard Le Bovier de

**[The] Fontenelle of His Generation**
See La Harpe, Jean Francois de

**Fonteyn, Margot**
See Hookham, Margaret

**Fonteyne, Val**
See Fonteyne, Valere Ronald

**Fonteyne, Valere Ronald** 1933- [HK]
*Canadian-born hockey player*
* Fonteyne, Val

**Fonti, Bartholomew** 1445-1513 [PA]
*Author*
* Fontius

**Fontius**
See Fonti, Bartholomew

**Foo, Chung Ling**
See Robinson, William Ellsworth

**Fook, Monte**
See Mong, Yuk

**[The] Foolish**
See Louis VII

**Foot, Michael Mackintosh** 1913- [SFL, WGT]
*British author*
* Cassius

**Foot, Victorine Anne** 1920- [ART]
*British painter*
* V. F.

**Football, Mr.**
See Robinson, Eddie

**Foote, Alexander** 1905- ? [EE]
*British-born intelligence agent for Russia*
* Granatov, Major

**Foote, Elial Todd** 1796-1877 [FFF]
*Physician*
* [The] Father of Chautauqua County

**Foote, Irene** 1893-1969 [EMT, F2, FC]
*American actress and dancer*
* Castle, Irene

**Foote, Michael** 20th c. [CA]
*Author*
* Cato [joint pseudonym with Peter D(unsmore) Howard and Frank Owen]

**Foote, Samuel** 1722-1777 [DEP, DNNF, SN]
*British comedian and playwright*
* [A] Beau Nasty
* [The] English Aristophanes
* [The] Modern Aristophanes

**Footman, Joan** 1907-1969 [THR]
*British actress*
* Clement Scott, Joan

**Foran, Dick**
See Foran, Nicholas [Nick]

**Foran, Nicholas [Nick]** 1910?- [CWG, FC]
*American actor and singer*
* Foran, Dick

**Foran, [Capt.] William Robert** 20th c. [WGT]
*British author*
* Bedrod-Foran, Capt. [joint pseudonym with Henry Bedford-Jones]

**Foray, Verge**
See Myers, Howard L.

**Forberg, Ati**
See Forberg, Beate Gropius

**Forberg, Beate Gropius** 1925- [FBJ]
*German-born illustrator*
* Forberg, Ati

**Forbes**
See Forbes-Dalrymple, Arthur Ewan

**Forbes, Aleck**
See Rathborne, St. George

**Forbes, Alexander P.** 19th c. [PA]
*Author*
* A. P. F.

**Forbes, Athol**
See Phillips, Alexander Forbes

**Forbes, Brenda**
See Taylor, Brenda Forbes

**Forbes, Bryan**
See Clarke, John Theobald

**Forbes, Cabot L.**
See Hoyt, Edwin P[almer], Jr.

**Forbes, Cabot L[owell]** 1943- [CA]
*American-born author*
* Smith, Christopher Martin

**Forbes, Daniel**
See Kenyon, Michael

**Forbes, De [or Dee?]**
See Forbes, DeLoris [Florine] Stanton

**Forbes, DeLoris [Florine] Stanton** 1923- [CA, CC, EMD]
*American author*
* Forbes, De [or Dee?]
* Forbes, Stanton
* Rydell, Forbes [joint pseudonym with Helen B. Rydell]
* Wells, Tobias

**Forbes, Dick** 1894?-1949 [BEW]
*Playwright*
* O'Daly, Cormac

**Forbes, Frances** 20th c. [THR]
*Scottish-born actress*
* Ivor, Frances

**Forbes, Glacier**
See Forbes, James David

**Forbes, Graham B.** [house pseudonym] [Stratemeyer Syndicate]
See Stratemeyer, Edward L.

**Forbes, Henry** 1851- ? [LAO]
*British biologist and author*
* Viator

**Forbes, J. H.** 19th c. [PA]
*Author*
* Locker, Arthur

**Forbes, Jake**
See Forbes, Vernon

**Forbes, James David** 1809-1868 [PA]
*Author*
* Forbes, Glacier

**Forbes, John** 1710-1759 [FFF]
*British army officer*
* [The] Head of Iron

**Forbes, Kathryn**
See McLean, Kathryn [Anderson]

**Forbes, Meriel**
See Forbes-Robertson, Meriel

**Forbes, Mrs. Simelde** [PA]
*Author*
* June, Jessie

**Forbes, Norman**
See Forbes-Robertson, Norman

**Forbes, Ralph**
See Taylor, Ralph

**Forbes, Rosita**
See Torr, Joan Rosita

**Forbes, Seloftus D.** [FFF, PA]
*Author*
* Echo, Oliver
* [The] Sylvan Scribe

**Forbes, Stanton**
See Forbes, DeLoris [Florine] Stanton

**Forbes, Vernon** 20th c. [CEI]
*Canadian-born hockey player*
* Forbes, Jake

**Forbes-Dalrymple, Arthur Ewan** 1912- [DBA]
*British painter*
* Forbes

**Forbes-Dennis, Phyllis** 1884-1963 [CA]
*British author*
* Bottome, Phyllis

**Forbes-Robertson, Eric** 1865?-1935 [BEW]
*Actor*
* Kelt, John

**Forbes-Robertson, Ian** 1858-1936 [BEW, THR]
*British-born actor and stage manager*
* Franke, Ian
* Robertson, Ian

**Forbes-Robertson, [Sir] Johnston** 1853-1937 [LC]
*British actor*
* Robertson, Forbes

**Forbes-Robertson, Meriel** 1913- [BEW, FC]
*British actress*
* Forbes, Meriel

**Forbes-Robertson, Norman** 1858-1932 [THR]
*British actor*
* Forbes, Norman

**[The] Forces' Sweetheart**
See Lynn, Vera

**Ford, Albert Lee**
See Stratemeyer, Edward L.

**Ford, Aleck** 1899-1965 [BWW]
*American singer*
* King of the Harmonica
* Little Boy Blue
* Miller, Alex
* Miller, Rice
* Miller, Willie
* Sib
* Williams, Willie
* Williamson, Sonny Boy
* Williamson, Willie

**Ford, Alfred** [PA]
*Author*
* Balloonist

**Ford, Antoinette** 1945- [IBW]
*American oceanographer*
* Ford, Toni

**Ford, Audrey**
See Fisher, Audrey

**Ford, Barry**
See Whitford, Joan

**Ford, Benjamin Francis [Benny]** 1901- [CME, CWG, DAM]
*American country-western performer*
* [The] Duke of Paducah
* Ford, Whitey

**Ford, Bugs Bunny**
See Ford, Phil

**Ford, Chris** 1949-
*American basketball player*
* Ford, Count

**Ford, Consuelo Urisarri** 1903- [SFL]
*Author*
* Urn, Althea

**Ford, Corey** 1902- [CC, NAA, WW]
*American author*
* Riddell, John

**Ford, Count**
See Ford, Chris

**Ford, D. M.**
See Northcroft, Dorothea M.

**Ford, Dan**
See Ford, Darnell Glenn, Sr.

**Ford, Darnell Glenn, Sr.** 1952- [SMG]
*American baseball player*
* Ford, Dan

**Ford, David**
See Harknett, Terry

**Ford, Edward Charles** 1928- [BE, IPA, PB]
*American baseball player*
* [The] Chairman of the Board
* Ford, Whitey

**Ford, Elbur**
See Hibbert, Eleanor Alice
[Burford]

**Ford, Elizabeth**
See Bidwell, Marjory Elizabeth
Sarah

**Ford, Ernest Jennings** 1919-
[ASC, CWG, DAM]
*American composer and singer*
* Ford, Tennesse Ernie

**Ford, Fenton** 1878-1938 [SC]
*American actor and playwright*
* Forrest, Belford

**Ford, Ford Madox**
See Hueffer, Ford Madox

**Ford, Francis [Frank]**
See O'Feeney, Francis

**Ford, Fred**
See Doerffler, Alfred

**Ford, Garret** [joint pseudonym with
Margaret Crawford, William L.
Crawford, etc.]
See Ackerman, Forrest J[ames]

**Ford, Garret** [joint pseudonym with
William L. Crawford, Forrest J.
Ackerman, etc.]
See Crawford, Margaret

**Ford, Garret** [joint pseudonym with
Margaret Crawford, Forrest J.
Ackerman, etc.]
See Crawford, William L.

**Ford, Gerald Rudolph [Jerry]**
See King, Leslie Lynch, Jr.

**Ford, Gib**
See Ford, Gilbert

**Ford, Gilbert** 1931- [BB]
*American basketball player*
* Ford, Gib

**Ford, Glenn**
See Ford, Gwyllin [or Gwyllyn]
Samuel Newton

**Ford, Gwyllin [or Gwyllyn] Samuel
Newton** 1916- [BDF, FC, SW]
*Canadian-born actor*
* Ford, Glenn

**Ford, Harry**
See Comerford, Harry

**Ford, Helen**
See Barnett, Helen Isabel

**Ford, Henry, II** 1917-
*American industrialist*
* [The] Deuce
* Hank the Deuce
* Henry the Deuce

**Ford, Hilary**
See Youd, Christopher Samuel

**Ford, Hildegarde**
See Morrison, Velma Ford

**Ford, Hod**
See Ford, Horace Hills

**Ford, Horace Hills** 1897- [BE]
*American baseball player*
* Ford, Hod

**Ford, J. Massingberd**
See Ford, Josephine Massyngberde

**Ford, John**
See O'Feeney, Sean

**Ford, Josephine Massyngberde**
[CA]
*British-born educator and author*
* Ford, J. Massingberd

**Ford, Junie**
See King, Leslie Lynch, Jr.

**Ford, Kirk**
See Spence, William John Duncan

**Ford, Leslie**
See Brown, Zenith [Jones]

**Ford, Lewis B.**
See Patten, Lewis B[yford]

**Ford, Marcia**
See Radford, Ruby L[orraine]

**Ford, Marie Elizabeth** 1903-
[NAA]
*American writer*
* Didelot, Marie

**Ford, Mary**
See Summers, Colleen

**Ford, Mary** 1874?-1944 [BS]
*British magician*
* [The] Queen of Coins
* Talma, Mercedes

**Ford, Mary Anne McMullen**
1841-1876 [PA]
*Author*
* Una

**Ford, Mike**
See Braun, Thomas Eugene

**Ford, Montgomery**
See Halsey, Brett

**Ford, Norrey**
See Dilcock, Noreen

**Ford, Nox**
See Bradford, William

**Ford, Pappy**
See O'Feeney, Sean

**Ford, Paul**
See Weaver, Paul Ford

**Ford, Percival Edmund Wentworth**
1946- [BE]
*Bahamian-born baseball player*
* Ford, Wenty

**Ford, Phil** 1956- [IBW]
*American basketball player*
* Ford, Bugs Bunny

**Ford, Powell I.**
See Dempsey, James E.

**Ford, Quinton**
See Pothecary, Raymond

**Ford, T[homas] Murray** 1854- ?
[MBF, SFL, WWL]
*British author and editor*
* Le Breton, Thomas

**Ford, Tennesse Ernie**
See Ford, Ernest Jennings

**Ford, Thelma Booth** 1907-
[BEW, EMT, FC]
*American actress*
* Booth, Shirley

**Ford, Toni**
See Ford, Antoinette

**Ford, Wallace**
See Jones, Samuel

**Ford, Webster**
See Masters, Edgar Lee

**Ford, Wenty**
See Ford, Percival Edmund
Wentworth

**Ford, Whitey**
See Ford, Benjamin Francis
[Benny]

**Ford, Whitey**
See Ford, Edward Charles

**Ford, Williston Merrick** 1886-
[SFL]
*Author*
* Merrick, Williston

**Forde, A. N.** 1923- [CW]
*Barbadian poet, playwright, author*
* Forde, Freddie

**Forde, Feodora** 1909- [FC]
*British actress*
* Baxter, Jane

**Forde, Florrie**
See Flanagan, Florence

**Forde, Freddie**
See Forde, A. N.

**Forde, Nicholas**
See Elliott-Cannon, Arthur Elliott

**Forde, Walter**
See Seymour, Thomas

**Forden, James**
See Barlow, James Henry Stanley

**[The] Fordham Flash**
See Frisch, Frank Francis

**Fordham Johnny Murphy**
See Murphy, John Joseph

**Fordham, Peta** 20th c. [IAW]
*British author and journalist*
* Dionysus

**Fordwych, Jack**
See Garrish, Harold J.

**Fordwych, John Edmund**
See Garrish, Harold J.

**Fordyce, Alexander** 19th c. [SN]
*British financier*
* [The] Shark of the Exchange

**[The] Foreign Invader**
See Resta, Dario

**[The] Foreigner**
See Louis IV

**[The] Foreigners' Friend**
See MacMurrough, Dermot

**Foreiro, Francisco** 1523-1587 [PA]
*Author*
* Forerius

**Foreman, August** 1897-1953 [BE]
*American baseball player*
* Foreman, Happy

**Foreman, Brownie**
See Foreman, John Davis

**Foreman, Chuck**
See Foreman, Walter E.

**Foreman, F.** 20th c. [OBW]
*American baseball player*
* Foreman, Hooks

**Foreman, George** 1949- [WBC]
*American boxer*
* Lightning Destroyer

**Foreman, Happy**
See Foreman, August

**Foreman, Hooks**
See Foreman, F.

**Foreman, John Davis** 1875-1926
[BE]
*American baseball player*
* Foreman, Brownie

**Foreman, Walter E.** 1950- [FB]
*American football player*
* Foreman, Chuck

**Forerius**
See Foreiro, Francisco

**Forest, Felix C.**
See Linebarger, Paul M[yron]
A[nthony]

**Forest, Frank**
See Hayek, Frank

**Forest, John**
See Brice, Douglas Francis
Aloysius

**Forest, Mark**
See Degni, Lou

**Forest, Salambo**
See Bellini, Tina

**Forester, C. S.**
See Forester, Cecil Scott

**Forester, Cecil Scott** 1899-1966
[LC]
*British author*
* Forester, C. S.

**Forester, Elspeth Lascelles** 20th c.
[WWL]
*British author*
* His Mother

**Forester, Fanny**
See Judson, Emily Chubbuck

**Forester, Frank**
See Herbert, Henry William

**Forestier, Antoine,** [PA]
*Author*
* Sylviolus

**Foresto, Franco**
See Hayek, Frank

**Forey, Conley Michael** 1950-
[SMG]
*Canadian-born hockey player*
* Forey, Connie

**Forey, Connie**
See Forey, Conley Michael

**Forez**
See Mauriac, Francois [Charles]

**Forge, Andre**
See Deihl, Edna Groff

**Forge, John**
See Twyman, Harold William

**Forgeron, Charles**
See Kovarovic, Karel

**Forgues, Paul Emile Durand** 1813-
? [PA]
*Author*
* Old Nick

**Forijay**
See  Ackerman, Forrest J[ames]

**Forio, Robert**
See  Weiss, Irving J.

**Forkbeard**
See  Sweyn I [or Sueno]

**Forkum, John** 1915-    [HCA]
*American actor*
* Dehner, John

**Forlano, Jiggs**
See  Forlano, Nicholas

**Forlano, Nicholas** 20th c.    [PHM]
*American underworld figure*
* Forlano, Jiggs

**Forlorn Hope**
See  Bailey, Matilda A.

**Form, Tom**
See  O'Keefe, Lester

**Forman, Joan** 20th c.    [CA]
*British author and playwright*
* Greene, Pamela

**Forman, William Henry**    [FFF]
*Author*
* Ashton, Alfred

**Formby, George, Jr.**
See  Booth, George Hoy

**Formby, George, Sr.**
See  Booth, James

**Former Naval Person** [code name used during World War II]
See  Churchill, Winston S.

**[A] Former Resident of the Hub**
See  Bachelder, John

**Fornaris y Joaquin, lorenzo Luaces**
See  Luaces, Joaquin Lorenzo

**Forneau, Leon** 20th c.    [BMH]
*Songwriter*
* Xanrof, Leon

**Forney, John W.** 1817- ?    [PA]
*Author*
* Occasional

**Fornieles, Jose Miguel Torres**
1932-    [BE]
*Cuban-born baseball player*
* Fornieles, Mike

**Fornieles, Mike**
See  Fornieles, Jose Miguel Torres

**Forrest, Alan**
See  Fisher, Allan Forest

**Forrest, Belford**
See  Ford, Fenton

**Forrest, Caleb**
See  Telfer, Dariel

**Forrest, Chet**
See  Chichester, George Forrest, Jr.

**Forrest City Joe**
See  Pugh, Joe Bennie

**Forrest, David**
See  Denholm, David

**Forrest, David** [joint pseudonym with Robert Forrest-Webb]
See  Eliades, David

**Forrest, David** [joint pseudonym with David Eliades]
See  Forrest-Webb, Robert

**Forrest, Gail**
See  Barton, Mrs. Charles

**Forrest, George**
See  Chichester, George Forrest, Jr.

**Forrest, George**
See  Wood, John George

**Forrest, Mark**
See  Morton, Guy Mainwaring

**Forrest, Neil**
See  Floyd, Cornelia

**Forrest, Norman**
See  Morland, Nigel

**Forrest, Sally**
See  Feeney, Katharine Scully

**Forrest, Steve**
See  Andrews, William Forrest

**Forrest, Sybil**
See  Markun, Patricia Maloney

**Forrest, William Mentzel** 1868- ?
[NAA]
*American educator and author*
* Mansfield, Lawrence

**Forrest-Webb, Robert** 1929-
[CA, IAW, SFL]
*British journalist and editor*
* Forrest, David [joint pseudonym with David Eliades]
* Tremayne, Jonathan
* Trevelyan, Robert
* Webb, Forrest
* Webb, Robert Forrest

**Forrester, Alfred Henry** 1805-1872
[DEL]
*British author*
* Crowquill, Alfred

**Forrester, Fanny**
See  Chubbuck, Emily C.

**Forrester, Francis, Esq.**
See  Wise, Daniel

**Forrester, Gilbert**
See  Braddon, [Sir] Henry Yule

**Forrester, Helen**
See  Bhatia, Jamunadevi

**Forrester, Howard Wilson** 1922-
[CWG, DAM]
*American country-western performer*
* Forrester, Howdy

**Forrester, Howdy**
See  Forrester, Howard Wilson

**Forrester, Mary**
See  Humphries, Elsie Mary

**Forrestier, James** 16th c.    [PA]
*Author*
* Hester, John, the Spagericke

**Forristall, Frosty**
See  Forristall, John

**Forristall, John** 20th c.    [SMG]
*American hockey trainer*
* Forristall, Frosty

**Fors, Olga Dmitrievna** 1873-1961
[EWL]
*Russian author*
* Terek, A.

**Forsey, Peter Q.**
See  Garbutt, John L.

**Forshaw, Charles Frederick** 1863-
?    [WWL]
*British author*
* Sinclair, Clarence

**Forsith, Nat**
See  Stainforth, Frank

**Forsman, Georg Zachris**
1830-1903    [WBD]
*Finnish historian*
* Yrjo-Koskinen, Yrjo Sakari

**Forst, Willi**
See  Frohs, Wilhelm

**Forster, Bobbie Hughes** 1913-
[NAA]
*American journalist*
* Benedict, I.

**Forster, E. M.**
See  Forster, Edward Morgan

**Forster, Edward Morgan**
1879-1970    [LC]
*British author*
* Forster, E. M.

**Forster, Emily Rachel** 1896-
[THR]
*British actress*
* Hinton, Mary

**Forster, Robert**
See  Foster, Robert, Jr.

**Forsyth, Bruce**
See  Johnson, Bruce Forsyth

**Forsythe, Charles**
See  Vocalis, Lambros Charles

**Forsythe, Helen**
See  Bagge, Mrs. Henry

**Forsythe, Irene**
See  Hanson, Irene [Forsythe]

**Forsythe, James** 20th c.    [BLB]
*American underworld figure*
* Forsythe, Red

**Forsythe, John**
See  Freund, John Lincoln

**Forsythe, Mimi**
See  Armstrong, Marie G.

**Forsythe, Red**
See  Forsythe, James

**Forsythe, Robert**
See  Crichton, Kyle Samuel

**Forsythe, Robin** 1879- ?    [WW]
*Author*
* Dingwall, Peter

**Forsythe, Ronald**
See  Teal, G. Donn

**Fort, Eleanor H.** 1914-    [ASC]
*American composer and singer*
* Fort, Hank

**Fort, Hank**
See  Fort, Eleanor H.

**Forte, Dan** 1935-    [CA]
*American educator and author*
* Fortebraccia, Donato

**Forte, Donald Ray** 1954-    [SMG]
*American football player*
* Forte, Ike

**Forte, Fabian Anthony** 1940?-
[IPA, LRR, SW]
*American singer*
* Fabian

**Forte, Ike**
See  Forte, Donald Ray

**Fortebraccia, Donato**
See  Forte, Dan

**Forteguerri [or Fortiguerra], Niccolo**
1674-1735    [WBD]
*Italian prelate and poet*
* Carteromaco

**Fortescue, Chichester Samuel**
1823-1898    [WBD]
*British political administrator*
* Parkinson-Fortescue, Chichester
  Samuel

**Fortescue, John Henry** 1923-1976
[BWW]
*American singer*
* Guitar Shorty
* Kearney, David William

**Fortescue, Mabel** 1894-1930
[FI, FC, OCF]
*American actress*
* Fortescue, Muriel
* Normand, Mabel

**Fortescue, Muriel**
See  Fortescue, Mabel

**Fortier, Bronson**
See  Fortier, David Edward

**Fortier, David Edward** 1951-
[SMG]
*Canadian-born hockey player*
* Fortier, Bronson

**Fortin, Marie Des Neiges** 1898-
[NAA]
*Canadian writer*
* Odette

**Fortina, Martha**
See  Laffeaty, Christina

**Fortis, Giovanni Battista**
1741-1803    [PA]
*Author*
* Albert

**Fortnum, Peggy**
See  Nuttall-Smith, Margaret
Emily Noel

**Fortuna [Fortune]**
See  Mazquiaran y Torrontegui,
Diego

**[The] Fortunate**
See  Emanuel I [Manuel or
Manoel]

**[The] Fortunate**
See  John IV

**[The] Fortunate**
See  Philip VI [or Philippe]

**Fortune, Dion**
See  Firth, Violet Mary

**Fortune, Garrett Reese** 1894-1955
[BE]
*American baseball player*
* Fortune, Gary

**Fortune, Gary**
See  Fortune, Garrett Reese

**Fortune's Empress**
See  Elizabeth I

**Fortunio, P. N.**
See  Niboyet, Pauline Fortunio

**Fortuny**
See  Fortuny y Madrazo, Mariano

**Fortuny y Madrazo, Mariano**
1871-1949   [WFA]
*Spanish-born painter, architect,*
*fashion designer*
* Fortuny

**Forty, Cecil Heber** 20th c.   [WWL]
*British author*
* Sniper

**[The] 44-Caliber Killer**
See   Berkowitz, David R.

**Forward, Luke**
See   Patrick, Johnstone G[illespie]

**[The] Forward Pass King**
See   Merillat, Louis A., Jr.

**Forwards, Marshal**
See   Bluecher, Gebhard Leberecht
von

**Fosca, Francois**
See   De Traz, Georges

**Fosco, Piero**
See   Pastrone, Giovanni

**Fosco, Placide** 1509-1574   [PA]
*Author*
* Prognostes

**Foscolo, Niccolo** 1778-1827
[WBD]
*Italian author and poet*
* Foscolo, Ugo

**Foscolo, Ugo**
See   Foscolo, Niccolo

**Fosdick, Charles Austin** 1842-1915
[DNNF, WBD]
*American author*
* Castlemon, Harry

**Foss, Charles J.** 1857-1938   [BEW]
*Actor*
* Fulton, Charles J.

**Foss, Deeby**
See   Foss, George Dueward

**Foss, Edward** 1787-1870
[DEL, FFF, RH]
*British barrister and author*
* Gifford, John

**Foss, George Dueward** 1898-1969
[BE]
*American baseball player*
* Foss, Deeby

**Foss, John**
See   Gordon, James

**Foss, Lukas**
See   Fuchs, Lukas

**Fosse, Alfred**
See   Jelly, George Oliver

**Fosse, Harold C.**
See   Gold, Horace Leonard

**Fosse, Mule**
See   Fosse, Ray[mond Earl]

**Fosse, Ray[mond Earl]** 1947-   [PB]
*American baseball player*
* Fosse, Mule

**Foster, Abbey** 1900-1962   [NOJ]
*American jazz musician*
* Foster, Chinee

**Foster, Al**
See   Fleitman, Alex O.

**Foster, Alan Benton** 1946-   [SMG]
*American baseball player*
* Double No-No

**Foster, Albert**   [OBW]
*American baseball player*
* Foster, Red

**Foster, Andrew** 1879-1930
[AS, MK]
*American baseball player*
* Foster, Rube

**Foster, Bud**
See   Foster, Harold

**Foster, Calico**
See   Foster, Charles

**Foster, Charles** 1828-1904   [FFF]
*American politician*
* Foster, Calico

**Foster, Charles J.** 1820-1883   [FFF]
*American author*
* Privateer

**Foster, Chinee**
See   Foster, Abbey

**Foster, Clarence Francis**
1878-1944   [BE]
*American baseball player*
* Foster, Pop

**Foster, Dianne**
See   Laruska, Dianne

**Foster, Don[ald]** 1948-   [CA, WD]
*American poet*
* Saint Eden, Dennis

**Foster, E. C.**
See   Foster, Elizabeth Connell

**Foster, Edward Cunningham**
1888-1937   [AS, BE]
*American baseball player*
* Foster, Kid

**Foster, Elizabeth**   [PA]
*Author*
* Mother Goose

**Foster, Elizabeth Connell** 1902-
[IAW]
*American author*
* Foster, E. C.

**[The] Foster Father of Our Language**
See   Bembo, Pietro

**Foster, Faye Love**
See   Dinwiddie, Faye Velma Love

**Foster, Frederick**
See   Godwin, John [Frederick]

**Foster, George**
See   Haswell, Chetwynd John
Drake

**Foster, George** 1889-   [BE]
*American baseball player*
* Foster, Rube

**Foster, George Cecil** 1893-   [WW]
*Author*
* Seaforth

**Foster, George Murphy** 1892-1969
[DAM, EJ, PMJ]
*American jazz musician*
* Foster, Pops

**Foster, Grant**
See   Garrish, Harold J.

**Foster, Harold** 1906-   [BB]
*American basketball player and*
*coach*
* Foster, Bud

**Foster, Harry** 20th c.   [CFH]
*Canadian football player*
* Foster, Red

**Foster, Harry C.** 1907-
[CEI, SMG]
*Canadian-born hockey player*
* Foster, Yip

**Foster, Iris**
See   Posner, Richard

**Foster, Jim**
See   Collins, Samuel

**Foster, Joanna** 1928-   [CA]
*American author*
* Dougherty, Joanna Foster

**Foster, John** 1812- ?   [PA]
*Author*
* J. F.

**Foster, Kid**
See   Foster, Edward Cunningham

**Foster, Leroy** 1923-1958
[BWW, NBB]
*American singer*
* Baby Face
* Baby Face Leroy

**Foster, Leroy A.** 1872-1934   [IA]
*American author*
* O'Tyne, Nicholas

**Foster, Little Willie**
See   Foster, Willie [or Willy]

**Foster, Margery Land May** 20th c.
[NAA]
*American author*
* May, Margery Land

**Foster, Marian Curtis** 1909-1978
[CA, TBJ]
*American author and illustrator*
* Mariana

**Foster, Mary A.**   [FFF]
*American columnist*
* Neville, Mary

**Foster, Mary F.**   [FFF, PA]
*Author*
* Cactus

**Foster, Mrs. Frank**   [FFF]
*Entertainer*
* Booth, Polly

**Foster, Mrs. Laurence** 1909-
[WBD]
*British author*
* Godden, Rumer

**Foster, Norman**
See   Hoeffer, Norman

**Foster, Oscar E.** 1867-1908   [BE]
*American baseball player*
* Foster, Reddy

**Foster, Pamela** 1932-   [TR]
*British actress and singer*
* Charles, Pamela

**Foster, Phoebe**
See   Eager, Phoebe

**Foster, Pop**
See   Foster, Clarence Francis

**Foster, Pops**
See   Foster, George Murphy

**Foster, Red**
See   Foster, Albert

**Foster, Red**
See   Foster, Harry

**Foster, Reddy**
See   Foster, Oscar E.

**Foster, Richard**
See   Crossen, Ken[dell Foster]

**Foster, Robert, Jr.** 1941-   [SW]
*American actor*
* Forster, Robert

**Foster, Rube**
See   Foster, Andrew

**Foster, Rube**
See   Foster, George

**Foster, Simon**
See   Glen, Duncan Munro

**Foster, Susanna**
See   Larsen, Suzan

**Foster, Theodore** 19th c.   [PA]
*American author*
* Summerfield, Charles

**Foster, W. Bert** 1869-1929   [EMD]
*Author*
* Carter, Nicholas?

**Foster, William** 20th c.   [IBW]
*American producer*
* [The] Dean of Colored Motion
Pictures

**Foster, Willie [or Willy]** 1922-
[BWW]
*American singer*
* Foster, Little Willie

**Foster, Yip**
See   Foster, Harry C.

**Fothergill, Fats [or Fatty]**
See   Fothergill, Robert Roy [Bob]

**Fothergill, Robert Roy [Bob]**
1897-1938   [AS, DGS, PB]
*American baseball player*
* Fothergill, Fats [or Fatty]

**Fotiu, Nicholas Evlampios** 1952-
[SMG]
*American hockey player*
* Fotiu, Nickey

**Fotiu, Nickey**
See   Fotiu, Nicholas Evlampios

**Fouche, Sam** 20th c.   [BWW]
*American entertainer*
* [The] Sepia Mae West

**Fougasse**
See   Bird, [Cyril] Kenneth

**Fougner, Baron**
See   Fougner, G. Selmer

**Fougner, G. Selmer** 1884-   [NAA]
*American journalist*
* Fougner, Baron

**Foul Weather Jack**
See   Byron, John

**Foul Weather Jack**
See   Norris, [Sir] John

**Fould, Wilhelmine Josephine**
**Simonin**   [FFF]
*Author*
* Valerie

**Foulds, E. V.**
See Foulds, Elfrida Vipont

**Foulds, Elfrida Vipont** 1902-
[CA, TCC, WD]
*British author*
* Foulds, E. V.
* Vipont, Charles
* Vipont, Elfrida

**Foulds, Pal**
See Foulds, Proveso A. L.

**Foulds, Proveso A. L.** 20th c.
[BBH]
*American soccer official*
* Foulds, Pal

**Foulis, Hugh**
See Munro, Neil

**Foulke, Fatty**
See Foulke, William J.

**Foulke, William Dudley** 1848- ?
[ALY]
*American author*
* Dillingham

**Foulke, William J.** 20th c.    [SR]
*British soccer player*
* Foulke, Fatty

**Foulques, Guy [or Le Gros, Guido]**
?-1268    [WBD]
*Pope*
* Clement IV

**Found Dead**
See Payn, James

**[The] Founder of Chemistry**
See Geber

**[The] Founder of Chivalry in Germany**
See Henry I [or Heinrich]

**[The] Founder of Christian Eloquence**
See Bourdaloue, Louis

**[The] Founder of Modern Mycology**
See Tulasne, Louis Rene

**Founder of Peace**
See Benedict

**[The] Founder of Physiognomy**
See Lavater, Johann Caspar

**[The] Founder of Polish Modernism**
See Przybyszewski, Stanislaw

**[The] Founder of Rome**
See Camillus, Marcus Furius

**[The] Founder of the Catholic Church in Australia**
See England, John

**[The] Founder of the English Domestic Novel**
See Richardson, Samuel

**[The] Founder of the Fathers of Christian Doctrine**
See De Bus, Caesar

**[The] Founder of the French Theatre**
See Rotrou, Jean de

**[The] Founder of the Greek Drama**
See Aeschylus

**[The] Founder of the Republic**
See Castro, Jose Maria

**Fountain, Lucy**
See Hilliard, Kate

**[The] Fountain of Life**
See Alexander of Hales

**4 e**
See Ackerman, Forrest J[ames]

**Four Eyed George**
See Meade, George Gordon

**Four Eyes**
See Roosevelt, Theodore [Teddy]

**Four Sack Dusak**
See Dusak, Ervin Frank

**4 sJ**
See Ackerman, Forrest J[ames]

**Four, Yer**
See Woo, Chun Hoi

**Fourcade, Simon**
See Saslavsky, Luis

**Fourest, Michel**
See Wynne-Tyson, [Timothy] Jon
[Lyden]

**Fourfold** [code name used during World War II]
See Marshall, George Catlett

**Fournet, Victor** 1801-1869    [PA]
*Author*
* Bernadillo

**Fournier, Alain**
See Fournier, Henri Alban

**Fournier, Antoine**    [PA]
*Author*
* Dolent, Jean

**Fournier, Claude** 1745-1823    [PA]
*Author*
* [The] American

**Fournier, Frenchy**
See Fournier, [F.] Henry

**Fournier, Henri Alban** 1886-1914
[CD, EWL, TC]
*French author and poet*
* Alain-Fournier
* Fournier, Alain

**Fournier, [F.] Henry** 19th c.    [BE]
*American baseball player*
* Fournier, Frenchy

**Fournier, Jacques**
See Fournier, John Frank

**Fournier, Jacques** ?-1342    [CAL]
*Pope*
* Benedict XII

**Fournier, John Frank** 1892-1973
[BE, DGS]
*American baseball player*
* Fournier, Jacques

**Fournier, Pierre** 1916-    [B10, EWL]
*French journalist and author*
* Gascar, Pierre

**Fourquet**
See Laisne, Jeanne

**Fourrey, Robert** 1921-    [BEW]
*French actor, writer, director*
* Dhery, Robert

**[The] Fourth Brother**
See Aung, [Maung] Htin

**Fouts, Edward Lee** 1902-    [WW]
*Author*
* Lee, Edward

**Fouts, Tom C.** 1918-    [CWG, DAM]
*American country-western performer*
* Stubby, Captain

**Foutz, David Luther** 1856-1897
[AS]
*American baseball player*
* Foutz, Scissors

**Foutz, Scissors**
See Foutz, David Luther

**Fowey, Roger**
See Edgar, Alfred

**Fowke, Gerard**
See Smith, Charles Mitchell

**[The] Fowler**
See Henry I [or Heinrich]

**Fowler, Boob**
See Fowler, Joseph Chester

**Fowler, Bud**
See Jackson, John

**Fowler, Clara Ann** 1927-
[FC, IPA, ITA]
*American singer*
* Page, Patti

**Fowler, Craig Hill** 1926-    [FIR]
*American actor*
* Hill, Craig

**Fowler, Ellen Thorneycroft**
See Felkin, Ellen Thorneycroft

**Fowler, Ethelia** 1881-1955    [EMT]
*American actress, singer, dancer*
* Levey, Ethel

**Fowler, Frank** 1900-1971    [WEF]
*American author and screenwriter*
* Chase, Borden

**Fowler, Gene**
See Devlan, Eugene

**Fowler, H. W.**
See Fowler, Henry Watson

**Fowler, Hec**
See Fowler, Norman

**Fowler, Helen Rosa [Huxley]** 1917-
[AW, CAP]
*British author*
* Foley, Helen

**Fowler, Henry Watson** 1858-1933
[LC]
*British author*
* Fowler, H. W.

**Fowler, Irving**    [CA]
*American actor*
* Brooks, Alan

**Fowler, Jesse** 1898-1973    [BE]
*American baseball player*
* Fowler, Pete

**Fowler, John W.**
See Jackson, John

**Fowler, Joseph Chester** 1900-    [BE]
*American baseball player*
* Fowler, Boob

**Fowler, Kenneth A[brams]** 1900-
[AW, CA, WD]
*American author*
* Brooker, Clark

**Fowler, Mary Jane**
See Wheeler, Mary Jane

**Fowler, Norman** 20th c.    [CEI]
*Hockey player*
* Fowler, Hec

**Fowler, Pete**
See Fowler, Jesse

**Fowler, Sydney**
See Wright, Sydney Fowler

**Fowler, Walter** 1860-1930    [DBA]
*British painter*
* Burroughs-Fowler, Walter John

**Fowler, William**    [PA]
*Author*
* [The] Butcher

**Fowlkes, Bryan** 1897-    [CA]
*American author*
* Fulks, Bryan

**[The] Fox**
See Friedhofer, Hugo Wilhelm

**[The] Fox**
See Hickman, Edward

**[The] Fox**
See Jones, John Raymond

**[The] Fox**
See Repo, Seppo

**[The] Fox**
See Snowden, Fred

**[The] Fox**
See Torrio, John [Johnny]

**[The] Fox**
See Van Buren, Martin

**[The] Fox**
See Whittaker, Norman

**[The] Fox**
See Williams, George Dale

**Fox, Arnim LeRoy** 1910-    [ECM]
*American country-western performer*
* Fox, Curly

**Fox, Brian**
See Ballard, [Willis] Todhunter

**Fox, Charles** 1921-    [AW]
*British writer and critic*
* Jeremy, Richard

**Fox, Charles Francis** 1921-
[BE, PB]
*American baseball manager*
* Fox, Irish

**Fox, Charles James** 1749-1806
[DNNF, FFF, SN]
*British statesman*
* Khan, Carlo
* [The] Last of the Romans
* [The] Man of the People
* Niger
* [The] Young Cub

**Fox, Curly**
See Fox, Arnim LeRoy

**Fox, David**
See Ostrander, Isabel [Egenton]

**Fox, Edward**    [PA]
*Author*
* Erith, Lynn

**Fox, Eleanor**
See St. John, Wylly Folk

**Fox, Eleanor Byrne** 1905-1967
[THR]
*American actress*
* Allenby, Peggy

**Fox, Emily** 19th c.    [PA]
*Author*
* King, Toler

Fox, Ervin 1909-1966 [AS, BE]
American baseball player
* Fox, Pete

Fox, Foxy
See Fox, Jim

Fox, Frances Margaret
See Field, Frances Fox

Fox, [Sir] Frank 1874- ? [WWL]
British author
* G. S. O.

Fox, Freeman
See Hamilton, Charles Harold St. John

Fox, G. F.
See Fox, Gardner Francis

Fox, Gardner Francis 1911-
[CA, ESF, SFL]
American author
* Cooper, Jefferson
* Fox, G. F.
* Gardner, Jeffrey
* Kendricks, James
* Majors, Simon
* Matthews, Kevin
* Somers, Bart

Fox, George 1624-1691 [FFF, SN]
British religious leader
* [The] Boehme of England
* [The] Man with the Leather Breeches

Fox, George 20th c. [BE]
American baseball player
* Fox, Paddy

Fox, Gilbert T[heodore] 1915- [CA]
American cartoonist
* Fox, Gill
* Fox, Ted

Fox, Gill
See Fox, Gilbert T[heodore]

Fox, Harry
See Carringford, Arthur

Fox, Henry [First Baron Holland]
1705-1774 [SN]
British statesman
* [The] Sly Fox

Fox, Hugh [Bernard, Jr.] 1932-
[CA]
American educator and author
* Magnetica, Electra

Fox, Irish
See Fox, Charles Francis

Fox, Irwin 20th c. [ET]
American television executive
* Fox, Sonny

Fox, Jacob Nelson 1927-1975
[B10, IPA, SMG]
American baseball player
* Fox, Nellie

Fox, James M.
See Knipscheer, James M. W.

Fox, Jay J. 1883-1940 [SC]
American actor, director, producer
* Carewe, Edwin

Fox, Jim 1943- [SMG]
American basketball player
* [The] Dream Backup
* Fox, Foxy

Fox, John
See Todd, John M[urray]

Fox, John Linwood 1907-1954
[BX]
American boxer
* Fox, Tiger Jack

Fox, Karrell 20th c. [BS]
American magician
* Milky the Clown
* Mix-Up, Professor
* Wow the Wizard

Fox, Marion
See Ward, Marion Inez Douglas

Fox, Mona Alexis [Brand] 1915-
[AW, WD]
Australian poet, author, playwright
* Brand, Mona

Fox, Mrs. [FFF]
Entertainer
* Don, Laura

Fox, Mrs. Charles F. [FFF]
Entertainer
* Wilson, Julia

Fox, Myron [PA]
Author
* Reynard

Fox, Nellie
See Fox, Jacob Nelson

Fox, Owen
See Farmer, Bernard J[ames]

Fox, Paddy
See Fox, George

Fox, Pete
See Fox, Ervin

Fox, Petronella
See Balogh, Penelope

Fox, Phil 20th c. [EJS]
American discus thrower
* Levy, Phil

Fox, Ruby Owens 1910-1963
[CWG]
American country-western performer
* Ruby, Texas

Fox, Ruth 20th c. [WW]
Author
* Irving, Alexander [joint pseudonym with Anne Fahrenkopf]

Fox, Sebastian
See Bullett, Gerald [William]

Fox, Sonny
See Fox, Irwin

Fox, Stella
See Boyle, Mrs. Charles H.

Fox, Ted
See Fox, Gilbert T[heodore]

Fox, Tiger Jack
See Fox, John Linwood

Fox, V. Helen
See Couch, Helen F[ox]

Fox, [Colonel] Victor J.
See Winston, Robert Alexander

Fox, Will H. 1858- ? [THR]
American entertainer
* Paddywhiski

Fox, William
See Friedman, William

Fox, William Johnson 1786-1864
[FFF, PA]
British politician and author
* [The] Norwich Weaver Boy
* Publicola

Fox-Davies, Arthur Charles
1871-1928 [WW, WWL]
British author
* Temple Bar
* X

Fox-Sheinwold, Patricia 20th c.
[CA]
American author
* Sheinwold, Patricia

Foxcar, Nicias
See Jacox, Francis

Foxcroft, Frank [PA]
Author
* Reynard

Foxcroft, Frank 1892- [NAA]
British-born American editor
* Fitzgerald, Frederick

Foxcroft, George A. 19th c.
[FFF, PA]
American writer
* Sass, Job

Foxe, Arthur N[orman] 1902- [CA]
American psychiatrist and author
* Foda, Aun

Foxe, Fanne
See Battistella, Annabella

Foxglove, Judas K.
See Khaury, Herbert

Foxton, E.
See Palfrey, Sarah G.

Foxx, Jack
See Pronzini, Bill

Foxx, James Emory 1907-1967
[AS, BE, PB]
American baseball player
* [The] Beast
* Double X

Foxx, Redd
See Sanford, John Elroy

Foxy GGM [Great-Grandmother]
See Brown, Olive

Foxy Grandpa Bannon
See Bannon, James Henry
[Jimmy]

Foy, Bryan 1897-1977
American producer
* [The] King of the B's

Foy, Eddie
See Fitzgerald, Edwin

Foy, Eddie, Jr.
See Fitzgerald, Edwin, Jr.

Foy, Kenneth R[ussell] 1922- [CA]
American educator and author
* Franklin, Keith

Foy, Louis Andre 1912- [IAW]
French journalist
* Tellier, Jacques

Foy, Peter
See Cook, Fred Gordon

Foy, Tom 1879-1917 [BMH]
British comedian
* [The] Yorkshire Lad

Foyal, Jean
See Achard, Marcel

Foyle, W. A.
See Foyle, William Alfred

Foyle, William Alfred 1885-1963
[LC]
British bookseller
* Foyle, W. A.

Foyt, A. J.
See Foyt, Anthony Joseph, Jr.

Foyt, Anthony Joseph, Jr. 1935-
[EAR]
American auto racer
* Foyt, A. J.
* Foyt, Tough Tony
* Super Tex
* [The] Texas Tornado

Foyt, Tough Tony
See Foyt, Anthony Joseph, Jr.

Fra
See Second element of name for further listings

[The] Fra Angelico of Equador
See Bedon, Peter

Frackman, Nathaline 1903?-1977
[CA]
American author and socialite
* Lee, Nata

Fraddle, Farragut
See Mearns, David Chambers

Fraeniel
See Paillere, Madeleine Dominique

Fraenkel, Heinrich 1897-
[AW, CA, WD]
German-born British author
* Assiac

Fraenkel, Karl 1861-1916 [WBD]
German bacteriologist
* Fraenken, Karl

Fraenkel, Sandor 1873-1933 [JL]
Hungarian-born psychologist
* Ferenczi, Sandor

Fraenken, Karl
See Fraenkel, Karl

Frafuso, Pasqualino 20th c.
Italian underworld figure
* Seven Beauties

Fragson, Harry
See Pott, Leon Vince Philip

Frahm, Herbert Ernst Karl 1913-
[CA]
West German chancellor and author
* Brandt, Willy

Frahse, Mary Jane 1918?-
[FC, PMJ]
American singer and actress
* Frazee, Jane

Fraisse, Alain 1931- [WEF]
French director
* Cavalier, Alain

Fraknoi, Vilmos
See Frankl, Wilhelm

Fraleck, Edison Baldwin 1841- ?
[NAA]
Canadian jurist and writer
* Publicus
* Triboniam

**Frame, Janet**
See   Clutha, Janet Paterson Frame

**Frampton, Doctor**
See   Gilman, William

**Francasi [or Francasci], Amelia**
See   Marchena de Leyba, Amelia
Francisco

**Francavilla, Joe** 20th c.    [RO1]
*American singer and songwriter*
* Villa, Joe

**France, Alexis**
See   McFarlane, Alexis

**France, Anatole**
See   Thibault,
Jacques-Anatole-Francois

**France, Claire**
See   Dore, Claire [Morin]

**France, Evangeline**
See   France-Hayhurst, Evangeline
[Chaworth-Musters]

**France, Osman B.** 1859-1947    [BE]
*American baseball player*
* France, Ossie

**France, Ossie**
See   France, Osman B.

**France, Richard**
See   Schweizer, Richard Gene

**France, Thelma Edith Minnie**
1907-    [IAW]
*New Zealand author*
* Berg, Rilla

**France, Victor**
See   Jordan, Philip [Furneaux]

**France-Hayhurst, Evangeline**
[Chaworth-Musters] 1904-
[AW, CAP]
*British author*
* France, Evangeline

**Frances Mary Theresa, [Mother]**
See   Ball, Frances

**Frances of Rome**
See   Bussa di Leoni, Francesca

**Frances, Stephen D.** 20th c.
[ESF, SFP]
*Author and publisher*
* Janson, Hank

**Francesca, Piero della**
See   Franceschi, Piero dei

**Francesca, Rosina**
See   Brookman, Rosina Francesca

**Francescatti, Rene** 1902-    [MS]
*French musician*
* Francescatti, Zino

**Francescatti, Zino**
See   Francescatti, Rene

**Franceschi, Piero dei** 1420?-1492
[WBD]
*Italian painter*
* Francesca, Piero della

**Franceschini, Baldassare**
1611-1689    [WBD]
*Florentine painter*
* [Il] Volterrano

**Francesco Cieco**
See   Landino, Francesco

**Francesco degli Organi**
See   Landino, Francesco

**Francesconi, Anselmo** 1921-    [ART]
*Italian-born painter and sculptor*
* Anselmo

**[La] Francesina**
See   Duparc, Elizabeth

**Franchezzo**
See   Farnese, A.

**Franchi, Antonio**
See   Bonavino, Francesco

**Franchi, Ausonio**
See   Bonavino, Cristoforo

**[The] Franchise**
See   Seaver, George Thomas [Tom]

**Francia**
See   Di Marco di Giacomo
Raibolini, Francesco

**Franciabigio**
See   Di Cristofano Bigi, Francesco

**Franciosa, Anthony [Tony]**
See   Papaleo, Anthony

**Francis, Ann Margaret** 1931-
[BEW]
*American actress*
* Hillary, Ann

**Francis, Anne**
See   Bird, Florence [Bayard]

**Francis, Anne**
See   Wintle, Anne

**Francis, Arlene**
See   Kazanjian, Arlene Francis

**Francis, Basil [Hoskins]** 1906-
[CAP, WW]
*British author and playwright*
* Rhode, Austen

**Francis, Bevo**
See   Francis, Clarence

**Francis, C. D. E.**
See   Howarth, Patrick John
Fielding

**Francis, Charles**
See   Parker, Francis James

**Francis, Clarence** 1932-    [BB]
*American basketball player*
* Francis, Bevo

**Francis, Connie**
See   Franconero, Constance

**Francis, Daniel**
See   Cranny, Titus

**Francis d'Assisi**
See   Bernardone, Giovanni
Francesco

**Francis, David Albert** 1918-
[B10, EJ, WWJ]
*American jazz musician*
* Francis, Panama

**Francis de Paule** 1416-1507    [DEP]
*Saint*
* [A] Bonhomme

**Francis, Dee**
See   Haas, Dorothy F.

**Francis, Doris**
See   Akast, Doris

**Francis, Emile Percy** 1926-
[CEI, FHE, HK]
*Canadian-born hockey player and
coach*
* [The] Cat

**Francis, Gregory** [joint pseudonym
with Frank Parnell]
See   MacGregor, James [Murdoch]

**Francis, Gregory** [joint pseudonym
with James (Murdoch) MacGregor]
See   Parnell, Frank

**Francis, Harrison** 20th c.    [BBH]
*American football player*
* Francis, Sam

**Francis, Hayward**
See   Shewring, Walter

**Francis, Illinois Jimmy**
See   Francis, James

**Francis, James** 20th c.    [BLB]
*American train robber*
* Francis, Illinois Jimmy

**Francis, James Bicheno** 1815-1892
[WBD]
*British-born engineer*
* [The] Father of Modern
Hydraulic Engineering

**Francis, Kay**
See   Gibbs, Katherine Edwina

**Francis, Laura**
See   Conly, Mrs. Edward

**Francis, Lee** [house pseudonym]
See   Browne, Howard

**Francis, M. E.**
See   Sweetman, M. E.

**Francis, Marvin A.** 20th c.    [BBH]
*American sports information
director*
* Francis, Skeeter

**Francis, Michel**
See   Cattaui, Georges

**Francis of Candia**    [HN]
*Scholar*
* Fertilis, Doctor

**Francis, Panama**
See   Francis, David Albert

**Francis, Philip**
See   Lockyer, Roger Walter

**Francis, [Sir] Philip** 1740-1818
[DEL, DNNF, FFF]
*British government official and
author*
* Amicus Curiae?
* Atticus?
* Augur?
* Bifrons?
* Correggio?
* Crito?
* Domitian?
* Faithful Monitor?
* Junius?
* Moderator?
* Nemesis?
* Phalaris?
* Pomona?
* Poplicola?
* Testis?
* Valerius?
* Vindex?

**Francis, Rosie** 1897?-1963    [BEW]
*Theatrical performer*
* Daly, Dixie

**Francis, Sam**
See   Francis, Harrison

**Francis, Skeeter**
See   Francis, Marvin A.

**Francis, Stephen D.** 20th c.    [MBF]
*British author*
* Reid, Desmond [house
pseudonym]
* Williams, Richard [house
pseudonym]

**Francis, Victor**
See   Hammond, Lawrence Victor
Francis

**Francis, Virginia**
See   Bateman, Virginia F.

**Francis, William**
See   Urell, William Francis

**Francis Williams, Lord**
See   Williams, Edward Francis

**Francis Fytton, Charles Farid Bassili**
1928-    [AW]
*British writer*
* Fytton, Francis

**Francis I or [Francois]** 1494-1547
[DEP, HN, SN]
*King of France*
* [The] Father of Letters
* [Le] Grand
* [The] Maecenas of France
* [Le] Pere des Lettres

**Francis II** 1836-1894
[DEP, HN, RH]
*King of the Two Sicilies*
* Bomba II
* Bombalino

**Francisque**
See   Millet [or Mile], Jean Francois

**Francius, Peter** 1645-1703    [PA]
*Author*
* Franz

**Franck**
See   Elie, Abel

**Franck, Dr.**
See   Ortea, Francisco Carlos

**Franck, Frederick Sigfred** 1909-
[AW, CA, WD]
*Dutch-born American author*
* Fredericks, [Dr.] Frank

**Franck, Sebastian**
See   Jacoby, Henry

**Franck [or Frank], Sebastian**
1499-1543?    [WBD]
*German religious reformer and
author*
* Franck von Woerd

**Franck von Woerd**
See   Franck [or Frank], Sebastian

**Francks, Hawley**
See   Kewstub, F.

**Franco, Battista** 1510-1561    [WBD]
*Italian painter*
* [Il] Semolei

**Franco, Edmund** 20th c.    [FB]
*American football player*
* [The] Devil Doll

**Franco, Fulvia** 20th c.    [WF]
*Italian actress*
* Larsen, Lola

**Franco, Harry**
See Briggs, Charles Frederick

**Franco, Jess**
See Manera, Jesus Franco

**Francoeur, Ida Shaw** 1852-1941
[SC]
*American actress*
* Waterman, Ida

**Francoeur, Robert Thomas** 1931-
[IAW]
*American author*
* Declan, Peter
* Leclerc, Thomas

**Francois, Andre**
See Farkas, Andre

**Francois, Edgar** [SG]
*Boxer*
* Coulon, Eddie

**Francois, Nicolas Louis** 1750-1828
[WBD]
*French statesman*
* De Neufchateau, Francois

**Francoise**
See Seignobosc, Francoise

**Francona, John Patsy** 1933- [BE]
*American baseball player*
* Francona, Tito

**Francona, Tito**
See Francona, John Patsy

**Franconero, Constance** 1938-
[ASC, FC, ITA]
*American singer and actress*
* Francis, Connie

**Franconi, King**
See Murat, Joachim

**Francucci, Innocenzo di Pietro**
1494-1550? [WBD]
*Bolognese painter*
* Da Imola, Innocenzo

**Francy, Paul**
See Gilson, Paul

**Frandere**
See Des Roches, Francis

**Frandsen, Robert** 1886-1944 [SC]
*American actor*
* Delmar, Eddie

**Franes, S. O.** 20th c. [MBF]
*British author*
* Williams, Richard [house
pseudonym]

**Frangipani, Lando dei** 12th c.
[WBD]
*Antipope*
* Innocent III

**Frank**
See Pedder, James

**Frank?**
See Stratemeyer, Edward L.

**Frank, Bab**
See Frank, Gilbert

**Frank, Gilbert** 1870?-1933 [NOJ]
*American jazz musician*
* Frank, Bab

**Frank, Jacob**
See Leibowicz, Jankiew

**Frank, Janet**
See Dunleavy, Janet Egleson

**Frank, Joe L.** 1900-1952 [ECM]
*American country music promoter*
* [The] Flo Ziegfeld of Country
Music

**Frank, Johnny**
See Sellers, John

**Frank, Lee**
See Griffin, Arthur J.

**Frank, Pat**
See Hart, Harry

**Frank, R., Jr.**
See Ross, Frank [Xavier], Jr.

**[The] Frank Sinatra of Latin Music**
See Rodriguez, Tito

**Frank, T. C.**
See Laughlin, Tom

**Frank, Theodore**
See Gardiner, Dorothea Frances

**Frank, Waldo David** 1889-1967
[CA, TC, WW]
*American author*
* Search Light

**Frankau, Aline** 1881-1955 [BEW]
*American stage designer and writer*
* Bernstein, Aline

**Frankau, Julia [Davis]** 1864-1916
[LC, WW]
*British author*
* Danby, Frank

**Frankau, Mary Evelyn Atkinson**
1899- [CAP, SAT]
*British playwright and author*
* Atkinson, M. E.

**Frankau, Pamela** 1908-
[CC, LC, TC1]
*British author*
* Naylor, Eliot

**Frankau, Ronald** 1894-1951 [THR]
*British actor and entertainer*
* Ronalds, Danby

**Franke, H. F.** [PA]
*Author*
* Rausse

**Franke, Ian**
See Forbes-Robertson, Ian

**Frankel, Bernice** 1926?-
[BEW, EMT, IPA]
*American actress*
* Arthur, Beatrice

**Frankel, Harry** ?-1948 [PMJ]
*American singer*
* [The] Barbasol Man
* Singin' Sam

**Franken, Rose** 1898- [TC]
*American playwright, author,
director*
* Grant, Margaret [joint
pseudonym with William Brown
Meloney]
* Meloney, Franken [joint
pseudonym with William Brown
Meloney]

**Frankenberg, Joyce Penelope
Wilhimena** 20th c.
*American actress*
* Seymour, Jane

**Frankenburg, Charis Ursula** 1892-
[WWL]
*British author*
* Barnett, Charis

**Frankenburger, Paul** 1897- [BBD]
*Israeli composer*
* Ben-Haim, Paul

**Frankenstein, George L.** [PA]
*Author*
* Clod
* O. H. I. O.
* Wait

**Franketienne**
See Etienne, Franck

**Frankhouse, Fred[rick Meloy]**
1904- [BN]
*American baseball player*
* Frankhouse, Jughandle Freddie

**Frankhouse, Jughandle Freddie**
See Frankhouse, Fred[rick Meloy]

**Frankian, Ike**
See Frankian, Malcolm

**Frankian, Malcolm** 1907?-1963
[AS]
*American football player*
* Frankian, Ike

**Frankiewicz, Casey**
See Frankiewicz, Kazimir

**Frankiewicz, Kazimir** 1939- [AES]
*Polish soccer player*
* Frankiewicz, Casey

**Frankl, Wilhelm** 1843-1924 [WBD]
*Hungarian historian and prelate*
* Fraknoi, Vilmos

**Franklin, A.**
See Arnold, Adlai F[ranklin]

**Franklin, Aretha** 1942- [IBW, SSS]
*American singer*
* [The] Queen of Soul
* Soul, Lady

**Franklin, Benjamin** 1706-1790
[DNNS, FFF, SN]
*American statesman, philosopher,
diplomat*
* [The] American Socrates
* Father Abraham
* [The] Liberator of the New
World
* [The] Nestor of America
* Poor Richard
* Saunders, Richard

**Franklin, Careful**
See Franklin, Henry

**Franklin, Charles**
See Usher, Frank Hugh

**Franklin, Cynthia** 20th c. [WW]
*Author*
* Neville, C. J.

**Franklin, Edgar**
See Stearns, Edgar Franklin

**Franklin, Edward Lamonte**
1928-1975 [BWW]
*American singer*
* Franklin, Pete
* Guitar Pete

**Franklin, Elizabeth**
See Campbell, Hannah

**Franklin, Eugene**
See Bandy, Eugene Franklin, Jr.

**Franklin, George** 1887- [BMH]
*British comedian*
* [The] Great Herman

**Franklin, Harold**
See Feigenbaum, Harold

**Franklin, Harold L[eroy]** 1934-
[CA]
*American author and illustrator*
* Alimayo, Chikuyo

**Franklin, Henry** 1903-1969 [NOJ]
*American jazz musician*
* Franklin, Careful

**Franklin, Jack**
See Franklin, James Wilford

**Franklin, James Wilford** 1919-
[BE]
*American baseball player*
* Franklin, Jack

**Franklin, Jay**
See Carter, John Franklin

**Franklin, Joseph Paul**
See Vaughn, James Clayton, Jr.

**Franklin, Keith**
See Foy, Kenneth R[ussell]

**Franklin, Madeleine**
See Camp, Madeleine L'Engle

**Franklin, Matthew** 20th c.
*American boxer*
* Muhammad, Matthew Saad

**Franklin, Max**
See Deming, Richard

**Franklin, Melvin**
See English, David

**Franklin, Moe**
See Franklin, Murray Asher

**Franklin, Murray Asher** 1914-
[EJS]
*American baseball player*
* Franklin, Moe

**Franklin, Nat**
See Bauer, Erwin A.

**[The] Franklin of Germany**
See Moeser, Justus

**[The] Franklin of Poland**
See Czacki, Thaddeus

**[The] Franklin of Theology**
See Fuller, Andrew

**Franklin, Paul**
See Walton, Bryce

**Franklin, Pete**
See Franklin, Edward Lamonte

**Franklin, Sidney**
See Frumkin, Sidney

**Franklin, Steve**
See Stevens, Franklin

**Frankovic Ilir, Matija**
See Flacius Illyricus, Matthias

**Franks, Tom** 1869- ? [BMH]
*Irish-born ventriloquist*
* O'Reilly, Navan

**Fransales, Jacques**
See De Roussy De Sales, Raoul

**Fransen, Piet Frans** 1913- [IAW]
*Belgian author*
* Van Doornik, Piet

**Frantic Fay Thomas**
See　Thomas, Fannie Crawford

**Frantic Frankie Lane**
See　Lane, Frank C.

**Franz**
See　Francius, Peter

**Franz, J. H.**
See　Hochberg, Bolko von

**Franz, Robert**
See　Knauth, Robert

**Franzese, John** 20th c.　[PHM]
*American underworld figure*
* Franzese, Sonny

**Franzese, Sonny**
See　Franzese, John

**Frapan-Akunian, Ilse**
See　Levien, Ilse

**Frapolli, Madame**　[FFF]
*Entertainer*
* Pisani, Carmen

**[Il] Frare**
See　Bianchi-Ferrari, Francesco

**Frasca, Mary** ?-1973　[SC]
*American actress and singer*
* [La] Sorrentina

**Frascatoro, Gerald**
See　Hornback, Bert G[erald]

**Frascella, Peter** 1886-1963　[RBE]
*American boxer*
* Murphy, Kid

**Frascuelo [after the famous Frascuelo]**
See　Escolar, Carlos

**Fraser, Agnes Maude** 1859- ?
[LAO]
*British author*
* McNab, Frances

**Fraser, Alec**
See　Fraser-Smith, Alec

**Fraser, Alex**
See　Brinton, Henry

**Fraser, Alexander** 1860- ?　[ALY]
*Scottish-born author*
* Cromarhe, Hew B. D.
* Eastman, Alexander F.
* Eskadale, Evan

**Fraser, Anthea** 20th c.　[CA]
*British author*
* Graham, Vanessa

**Fraser, Augusta Zelia** 20th c.
[WWL]
*British author*
* Spinner, Alice

**Fraser, Bert**
See　Cruickshank, Harold F.

**Fraser, Bruce** 1888?-1981
*British naval officer*
* Fraser, Tubby

**Fraser, Charles Carrolton**
1871-1940　[AS, DGS]
*American baseball player*
* Fraser, Chick

**Fraser, Chick**
See　Fraser, Charles Carrolton

**Fraser, Dorothy May** 1903?-1980
[CA]
*British author*
* Fraser, Maxwell

**Fraser, Douglas Jamieson** 1910-
[IAW]
*Scottish poet*
* Hope, David

**Fraser, Elizabeth**
See　Grant, Maude Margaret

**Fraser, Elizabeth Bertha [Liz]**
1914-　[ART]
*British sculptor*
* Scott-Fraser, Elizabeth

**Fraser, G. S.**
See　Fraser, George Sutherland

**Fraser, George MacDonald** 1925-
[CA]
*British author and journalist*
* MacNeill, Dand

**Fraser, George Sutherland** 1915-
[MBL, WOA]
*Scottish critic and poet*
* Fraser, G. S.

**Fraser, Harold** 1886-1962
[F1, F2, FC]
*Australian comedian*
* Pollard, Snub

**Fraser, James**
See　White, Alan

**Fraser, Jane**
See　Pilcher, Rosamunde

**Fraser, Jefferson?**
See　Wilding, Philip

**Fraser, John A.** 20th c.　[WW]
*Author*
* Hawkshaw

**Fraser, Maxwell**
See　Fraser, Dorothy May

**Fraser, Rev. Dr.** ?-1885　[FFF]
*Bishop of Manchester*
* Bishop of all the Denominations

**Fraser, Ronald**
See　Tiltman, Ronald Frank

**Fraser, Shelagh** 20th c.　[IAW]
*British actress, playwright, author*
* Gyles, Sheila
* Sydney, Carol

**Fraser, Tubby**
See　Fraser, Bruce

**Fraser, Waller Brown** 1905-　[CAP]
*American author*
* Waller, Brown

**Fraser, [Sir] William A.** 1816-1898
[FFF]
*British author*
* Morar

**Fraser, Winifred**
See　Exton, Winifred

**Fraser-Simson, Harold**
See　Simson, Harold

**Fraser-Smith, Alec** 1884-　[THR]
*British actor and singer*
* Fraser, Alec

**Frastick, Perry**
See　Childress, Edmund Howard

**[Il] Frate**
See　Di Pagolo del Fattorino,
Bartolommeo

**Frater Georgius**
See　Martinuzzi, George

**Fratianno, James [Jimmy]** 1911?-
*American underworld figure*
* [The] Weasel

**[The] Fraud President**
See　Hayes, Rutherford Birchard

**Frauenlob [Praise of Women]**
See　Heinrich von Meissen

**Fray Gerundio**
See　Lafuente [or La Fuente],
Modesto

**Frayne, June** 1924-　[CA]
*Canadian author*
* Callwood, June

**Frazaer, Mary**　[PA]
*Author*
* Hayden, Sarah Marshall

**Frazee, Charles S[tephen]** 1909-
[WGT]
*American author*
* Jennings, Dean

**Frazee, Jane**
See　Frahse, Mary Jane

**Frazer, Allison**
See　Rochester, George Ernest

**Frazer, Andrew**
See　Lesser, Milton

**Frazer, Fred**
See　Avallone, Michael [Angelo],
Jr.

**Frazer, J. G.**
See　Frazer, [Sir] James George

**Frazer, [Sir] James George**
1854-1941　[LC]
*Scottish-born anthropologist and author*
* Frazer, J. G.

**Frazer, James Ian Arbuthnot** 1912-
[SFL, WWL]
*British author*
* Frazer, Shamus

**Frazer, Lawrence**
See　Abbott, Lawrence Fraser

**Frazer, Martin**
See　Clarke, Percy A.

**Frazer, Robert Caine**
See　Creasey, John

**Frazer, Shamus**
See　Frazer, James Ian Arbuthnot

**Frazer, Winifred [Loesch] Dusenbury**
1916-　[CA]
*American author*
* Dusenbury, Winifred Loesch

**Frazier, Arthur**
See　Bulmer, [Henry] Kenneth

**Frazier, Buckwheat**
See　Frazier, James

**Frazier, Cie**
See　Frazier, Josiah H.

**Frazier, Clyde**
See　Frazier, Walt[er]

**Frazier, Clyde Cool**
See　Frazier, Walt[er]

**Frazier, Cobra Joe**
See　Frazier, Joseph Filmore [Joe]

**Frazier, Corinne Reid** 20th c.
[NAA]
*American writer*
* French, Caroline
* Manning, Catharine

**Frazier, Evelyn McDaniel**
See　Bryan, Evelyn McDaniel
Frazier

**Frazier, James** 20th c.　[IBW]
*American actor*
* Frazier, Buckwheat

**Frazier, Joe** 1943-　[RO1]
*American singer*
* Frazier, Speedo

**Frazier, Joseph [Joe]** 1944-　[IBW]
*American boxer*
* Frazier, Smokin' Joe

**Frazier, Joseph Filmore [Joe]**
1922-　[BE]
*American baseball player*
* Frazier, Cobra Joe

**Frazier, Josiah H.** 1904-
*American jazz musician*
* Frazier, Cie

**Frazier, S. M.**
See　Morris, Charles Smith

**Frazier, Sarah**
See　Wirt, Winola Wells

**Frazier, Smokin' Joe**
See　Frazier, Joseph [Joe]

**Frazier, Speedo**
See　Frazier, Joe

**Frazier, Walt[er]** 1945-　[BB, IBW]
*American basketball player*
* Frazier, Clyde
* Frazier, Clyde Cool

**Freak Man Porter**
See　Porter, George

**Freckled Bob Fitzsimmons**
See　Fitzsimmons, Robert [Bob]

**Fred**
See　Aristides, Othon

**Freda, Riccardo** 1909-　[FDG]
*Italian director*
* Hampton, Robert
* Lincoln, George

**Frederic IV**　[SN]
*Austrian prince*
* [The] Pennyless

**Frederici, Blanche**
See　Campbell, Blanche Friderici

**Frederick**
See　Vahrer, M.

**Frederick** ?-1058　[CAL]
*Pope*
* Stephen IX [or X]

**Frederick** 1332-1381　[WBD]
*Margrave of Meissen*
* [The] Stern

**Frederick Augustus** 1763-1827
[DNNF, DNNS, FFF]
*Son of King George III of England*
* [The] Soldiers' Friend

**Frederick Augustus** (Continued)
* York and Albany, Duke of

**Frederick Augustus I** 1750-1827
[DNNS, WBD]
*King of Saxony*
* [The] Just

**Frederick Charles** 1828-1885
[DHA, DNNS, FFF]
*Prussian army officer*
* Always in Front, Prince
* [The] Red Prince

**Frederick, Dick**
*See* Dempewolff, Richard
F[rederic]

**Frederick, Jane** 1952-
*American Olympic athlete*
* [The] Horse

**Frederick, John**
*See* Faust, Frederick [Schiller]

**Frederick, Lee**
*See* Nussbaum, Al[bert F.]

**Frederick Louis** 1707-1751
[DNNS, HN]
*Prince of Wales*
* Titi, Prince

**Frederick of Austria**
*See* Frederick III

**Frederick, Orlin**
*See* Tremaine, F[rederick] Orlin

**Frederick, Oswald**
*See* Snelling, Oswald Frederick

**Frederick, Pauline**
*See* Libbey, Pauline

**[The] Frederick the Great of Thought**
*See* Lessing, Gotthold Ephraim

**Frederick, Walter**
*See* Handschin, Charles Hart

**Frederick William** 1620-1688
[DNNF, HN, RH]
*Elector of Brandenburg*
* [The] Great Elector

**Frederick William** 1831-1888
[DEP, DHA, DNNS]
*Emperor of Germany*
* [The] Noble
* Our Fritz
* Unser Fritz

**Frederick William I** 1688-1740
[DEP]
*King of Prussia*
* [The] Caporal King

**Frederick William IV** 1795-1861
[FFF, HN, RH]
*King of Prussia*
* Cliquot

**Frederick I [or Friedrich]**
1121?-1190    [FFF, HN, SN]
*Emperor of Germany*
* Barbarossa
* [The] Father of His Country
* Red Beard

**Frederick I** 1370-1428
[DNNS, WBD]
*Elector of Saxony*
* [The] Warlike

**Frederick I** 1425-1476
[DNNS, SN, WBD]
*Elector of the Palatinate*
* [The] Victorious

**Frederick II** 1194-1250
[DEP, RH, SN]
*Emperor of Germany*
* [The] Caesar of Caesars
* [The] Law Giver
* [A] Second Aristotle
* This Phoenix Among Kings
* [The] Wonder of the World

**Frederick II** 1411?-1464
[DNNS, WBD]
*Elector of Saxony*
* [The] Gentle
* [The] Meek
* [The] Mild

**Frederick II** 1413-1471
[FFF, RH, SN]
*Elector of Brandenburg*
* Dent de Fer
* [The] Iron Tooth

**Frederick II** 1482-1556
[DNNS, WBD]
*Elector of the Palatinate*
* [The] Wise

**Frederick II** 1712-1786
[DNNF, DNNS, SN]
*King of Prussia*
* Alaric Cottin
* [Der] Alte Fritz
* Father Fritz
* Fritz der Einzige
* [The] Great
* Luc [Luke]
* [Le] Marquis de Brandenbourg
* Old Fritz
* [The] Philosopher of Sans Souci
* [The] Philosopher Prince
* [The] Protestant Hero
* [Le] Sablonnier [The Sand-Dealer]

**Frederick III** 1286-1330
[DNNS, HN, WBD]
*King of Germany*
* [The] Fair
* Frederick of Austria
* [The] Handsome

**Frederick III** 1341-1377   [WBD]
*King of Sicily*
* [The] Simple

**Frederick III** 1415-1493
[DNNS, FFF, SN]
*Holy Roman emperor and King of Germany [as Frederick IV]*
* [The] Indolent
* [The] Pacific

**Frederick III** 1463-1525
[DNNS, RH, SN]
*Elector of Saxony*
* [The] Wise

**Frederick III** 1515-1576
[DNNS, WBD]
*Elector of the Palatinate*
* [The] Pious

**Frederick IV** 1574-1610    [WBD]
*Elector of the Palatinate*
* [The] Upright

**Frederick V** 1596-1632
[FFF, RH, SN]
*Elector of the Palatinate*
* Palsgrave, Goodman
* [The] Snow King
* [The] Winter King

**Fredericks, Arnold**
*See* Kummer, Frederic Arnold

**Fredericks, [Dr.] Frank**
*See* Franck, Frederick Sigfred

**Fredericks, Frohm**
*See* Kerner, Fred

**Fredericks, Jimmy**
*See* Frederico, Jimmy

**Fredericks, Mrs. William**    [FFF]
*Entertainer*
* Dean, Laura

**Fredericks, Vic** [house pseudonym]
*See* Majeski, William [Bill]

**Frederickson, Ivan C.** 1943-    [FB]
*American football player*
* Frederickson, Tucker

**Frederickson, Tucker**
*See* Frederickson, Ivan C.

**Frederico, Jimmy** 20th c.    [BLB]
*American underworld figure*
* Fredericks, Jimmy

**Frederika** 1917-
*Queen of Greece*
* [The] Iron Queen

**Frederiksen, Erik E.** 20th c.    [CA]
*Author*
* Detine, Padre [joint pseudonym with Ib Spang Olsen]

**Frederix, Jacques** 1887?-1948
[BDF, FC, OCF]
*French director*
* Feyder, Jacques

**Fredianelli, Renaldo** 20th c.
*American entertainer*
* Gaylord, Ron

**Fredol**
*See* Tandon, Horace B. A. Moquin

**Fredricks, Henry Sainte Claire**
1940-    [BWW]
*American singer*
* Mahal, Taj

**Fredrik, Burry**
*See* Gerber, Erna Helene

**Fredro, Alexander** 1793-1876
[WBD]
*Polish playwright*
* [The] Polish Moliere

**Free**
*See* Hoffman, Abbie

**Free, Harry B.**
*See* Boynton, Harry F.

**Free Lance**
*See* Denny, John Thomas

**Free, Lloyd** 20th c.    [SMG]
*American basketball player*
* All World

**[The] Free Press Man**
*See* Lewis, Charles Bertrand

**Freeborn John**
*See* Lilburne, John

**Freed, Arthur**
*See* Grossman, Arthur

**Freed, Barry**
*See* Hoffman, Abbie

**Freed, Margaret De Haan** 1917-
[CA]
*American author and educator*
* De Haan, Margaret

**Freedgood, Morton** 1912?-
[B10, EMD, WW]
*American author*
* Godey, John

**Freedland, Nat[haniel]**
*See* Friedland, Nathaniel

**Freedlin, Harry** 1911-
*American bandleader*
* Barron, Blue

**Freedman, James Dillet** 1912-
[CA]
*American author*
* Freeman, James Dillet
* Mann, D. J.

**Freedom, Mr.**
*See* Roberts, Tommy

**Freeland, Beverly**
*Singer*
* Beverly

**Freeland, Jay**
*See* McLeod, John F[reeland]

**Freeland, Kathleen** 1878-1961    [SC]
*British-born actress*
* Kinsella, Kathleen

**Freeling, Nicolas** 1927-
[CA, CC, WD]
*British author*
* Nicolas, F. R. E.

**[A] Freeman**
*See* Blanc, Jean Joseph Louis

**Freeman**
*See* Drayton, William Henry

**Freeman, Alexander Vernon** 1896-
[BE]
*American baseball player*
* Freeman, Buck

**Freeman, Alfred Percy** 1888-1965
[OCS]
*British cricketer*
* Freeman, Tich

**Freeman, Anne Frances** 1936-    [CA]
*American author*
* Huether, Anne Frances

**Freeman, Anthony**
*See* Novelli, Mario

**Freeman, Buck**
*See* Freeman, Alexander Vernon

**Freeman, Buck**
*See* Freeman, James

**Freeman, Buck**
*See* Freeman, John Edward

**Freeman, Buck**
*See* Freeman, John Frank

**Freeman, Bud**
*See* Freeman, Lawrence

**Freeman, Buster**
*See* Freeman, Hershell Baskin

**Freeman, Cynthia**
*See* Feinberg, Bea

**Freeman, E.** 20th c.    [MBF]
*British author*
* Freeman, Jack

**Freeman, Earl Lavon** 1922-    [EJ7]
*American jazz musician*
* Freeman, Von

**Freeman, Frank**
*See* Smithson, Noble

**Freeman, Gillian** 1929-   [WD]
*British author and screenwriter*
* George, Eliot

**Freeman, Graydon La Verne** 1904-
[CA]
*American author*
* Freeman, Larry
* Thompson, James H.
* Wood, Serry

**Freeman, H. W.**
*See* Freeman, Harold Webber

**Freeman, Harold Webber** 1899-
[LC]
*British author*
* Freeman, H. W.

**Freeman, Hershell Baskin** 1928-
[BE]
*American baseball player*
* Freeman, Buster

**Freeman, Ida**
*See* Brydges, Mrs. Castel

**Freeman, Jack**
*See* Freeman, E.

**Freeman, James** 1904-   [BB]
*American basketball player*
* Freeman, Buck

**Freeman, James Dillet**
*See* Freedman, James Dillet

**Freeman, Jean Todd** 1929-   [IAW]
*American author*
* Morgan, Justina
* Todd, Sarah Manning

**Freeman, John Crosby** 1941-   [CA]
*American author and editor*
* Guthrie, Hugh
* McDowell, Crosby

**Freeman, John Edward** 1901-1958
[BE]
*American baseball player*
* Freeman, Buck

**Freeman, John Frank** 1871-1949
[AS, BE, PB]
*American baseball player*
* Freeman, Buck

**Freeman, John Henry Gordon**
1903-   [MBF]
*British author*
* Merry Andrew

**Freeman, Kathleen** 1897-1959
[CC, LC, WW]
*British author*
* Fitt, Mary

**Freeman, Larry**
*See* Freeman, Graydon La Verne

**Freeman, Lawrence** 1906-
[ASC, DAM, EJ]
*American jazz musician*
* Freeman, Bud

**Freeman, Leonard** 1921-1974   [SC]
*American actor and producer*
* Roberts, Glen

**Freeman, M. E.**
*See* Freeman, Mary Eleanor
Wilkins

**Freeman, Mary Eleanor Wilkins**
1852-1930   [ALY, LC]
*American author*
* Freeman, M. E.
* Wilkins, Mary E.

**Freeman, Mona**
*See* Freeman, Monica

**Freeman, Monica** 1926-   [FC]
*American actress*
* Freeman, Mona

**Freeman, Mrs.**
*See* Churchill, Sarah Jennings

**Freeman, Mrs. E. W.**   [FFF]
*Entertainer*
* Sidnal, Emma

**Freeman, Peggy Anne Donyale
Aragonea Pegeon** 1945-1979
[IBW]
*American fashion model and actress*
* Luna, Donyale

**Freeman, R. Austin**
*See* Freeman, Richard

**Freeman, Raoul**
*See* Freeman, Reuel Silvan

**Freeman, Reuel Silvan** 1894-1971
[SC]
*American actor*
* Freeman, Raoul

**Freeman, Richard [Dick]**
*See* Wallace, Walter

**Freeman, Richard** 1862-1943
[CC, EMD, WGT]
*British physician and author*
* Ashdown, Clifford [joint
   pseudonym with John James
   Pitcairn]
* Freeman, R. Austin
* Piers, Ashdown [joint pseudonym
   with John James Pitcairn]

**Freeman, Thomas**
*See* Fehrenbach, Theodore Reed

**Freeman, Tich**
*See* Freeman, Alfred Percy

**Freeman, Tommy** 1904-   [WBC]
*American boxer*
* [The] Arkansas Razorback

**Freeman, Von**
*See* Freeman, Earl Lavon

**Freeman, Yehezkel** 1928-   [JL]
*Austrian-born political scientist and
author*
* Dror, Yehezkel

**Freer, Martha Agnes** 20th c.
[ALY]
*American author and poet*
* Lee, Agnes

**Freese, Augie**
*See* Freese, Eugene Lewis

**Freese, Bud**
*See* Freese, George Walter

**Freese, Eugene Lewis** 1934-   [BE]
*American baseball player*
* Freese, Augie

**Freese, George Walter** 1926-   [BE]
*American baseball player*
* Freese, Bud

**Freeth, John** 1730-1808
[DNNS, FFF, SN]
*British poet and songwriter*
* [The] Birmingham Poet

**Freeze, Carl Alexander** 1900-   [BE]
*American baseball player*
* Freeze, Jake

**Freeze, Jake**
*See* Freeze, Carl Alexander

**Fregni, Mirella** 1935-   [OP]
*Italian opera singer*
* Freni, Mirella

**Frei, Bruno**
*See* Freistadt, Benedikt

**Freier, Gustav**
*See* Lafontaine, August Heinrich
Julius

**Freigau, Howard Earl** 1902-1932
[BE]
*American baseball player*
* Freigau, Ty

**Freigau, Ty**
*See* Freigau, Howard Earl

**Freihofer, Lois Diane** 1933-   [CA]
*American author*
* Barth, Lois

**Freinshemius**
*See* Freinshiem, Johann

**Freinshiem, Johann** 1608-1660
[PA]
*Author*
* Freinshemius

**Freistadt, Benedikt** 1897-   [IAW]
*Czech-born author and historian*
* Frei, Bruno

**Freitas, Antonio** 1908-   [BE]
*American baseball player*
* Freitas, Tony

**Freitas, Rock [or Rocky]**
*See* Freitas, Rockne Crowningburg

**Freitas, Rockne Crowningburg**
1945-   [SMG]
*American football player*
* Freitas, Rock [or Rocky]

**Freitas, Tony**
*See* Freitas, Antonio

**Freleng, Friz**
*See* Freleng, Isadore

**Freleng, Isadore** 1905?-   [WEC]
*American animator and producer*
* Freleng, Friz

**Fremault, Anita Louise**
1915?-1970   [F2, FC]
*American actress*
* Louise, Anita

**Fremiot, Jeanne Francoise**
1572-1641   [WBD]
*Saint*
* Chantal, Baronne de
* Chantal, Sainte

**Fremlin, Celia**
*See* Goller, Celia [Fremlin]

**Fremlin, Victor**
*See* Philips, George Norman

**Fremont, John Charles** 1813-1890
[FFF, DNNF, SN]
*American army officer and explorer*
* [The] Pathfinder

**Fremont, W. B.**
*See* Bowers, Warner Fremont

**Fremstad, Olive**
*See* Rundquist, Anna Olivia

**Freeze, Jake**
*See* Freeze, Carl Alexander

**French, Albert** 1911?-1977   [FIR]
*American jazz musician*
* French, Papa

**French, Alice** 1850-1934   [LC]
*American author*
* Thanet, Octave

**[The] French Anacreon**
*See* Laujon, Pierre

**[The] French Anacreon**
*See* Thiard, Pontus de

**[The] French Aristides**
*See* Grevy, Albert

**[The] French Aristophanes**
*See* Poquelin, Jean Baptiste

**French, Ashley**
*See* Robins, Denise [Naomi]

**[The] French Boehme**
*See* Saint Martin, Louis Claude de

**French, Bruce Nicholas** 1959-   [DC]
*British cricketer*
* French, Kermit

**[The] French Burns**
*See* Beranger, Pierre Jean de

**[The] French Byron**
*See* Musset, [Louis Charles]
Alfred de

**[The] French Calliope**
*See* Deshoulieres, Antoinette du
Ligier de la Garde

**French, Caroline**
*See* Frazier, Corinne Reid

**French, Charles K.**
*See* Krauss, Charles E.

**[The] French Chaucer**
*See* Marot, Clement

**[The] French Chaucer**
*See* Ronsard, Pierre de

**[The] French Chrysostom**
*See* Auger, Edmond

**[The] French Defoe**
*See* Restif, Nicolas Edme

**[The] French Devil**
*See* Bart [or Barth?], Jean

**[The] French Dick Turpin**
*See* Bourguignon, Louis
Dominique

**[The] French Dickens**
*See* Daudet, Alphonse

**French, Don**
*See* Thody, Philip Malcolm Waller

**French, Doris**
*See* Shackleton, Doris [Cavell]

**[The] French Ennius**
*See* Guillaume de Lorris

**[The] French Ennius**
*See* Jean [or Jehan] de Meung

**[The] French Erasmus Darwin**
*See* De Boisjolin,
Jacques-Francois-Marie Vieilh

**[The] French Fabius**
*See* Montmorency, Anne de

**French, Fitz**
*See* French, Walter Edward

French, Frank Alexander
1893-1969    [BE]
*American baseball player*
* French, Pat

[The] French Garrick
See   Boyron, Michel [or Michael]

[The] French Germanicus
See   Louis

French, Helen
See   Krauss, Helen

French, Hermene
See   Camelinat, Hermine

[The] French Homer
See   La Fontaine, Jean de

[The] French Horace
See   Beranger, Pierre Jean de

[The] French Horace
See   Macrinus [or Salmon?], Jean

[The] French Iliad
See   Guillaume de Lorris

[The] French Isocrates
See   Flechier, [Valentin] Esprit

[The] French Justinian
See   Remi, Philippe de

French, Kathryn
See   Mosesson, Gloria R[ubin]

French, Kermit
See   French, Bruce Nicholas

French, L. Virginia 1830-1881
[FFF, PA]
*American author*
* [L']Inconnue

[The] French Lope da Vega
See   Hardi, Alexandre

[The] French Lycophron
See   Dorat, Jean

[The] French Maccabaeus
See   Montford, Simon de

[The] French Mansfield
See   Gerbier, Pierre Jean Baptiste

French, Marilyn 1929-   [CA]
*American author*
* Solwoska, Mara

[The] French Ovid
See   Bellay, Joachim du

French, Papa
See   French, Albert

French, Pat
See   French, Frank Alexander

French, Paul
See   Asimov, Isaac

[The] French Phidias
See   Goujon, Jean

[The] French Phidias
See   Pigalle, Jean Baptiste

[The] French Pindar
See   Dorat, Jean

[The] French Pindar
See   Lebrun, Ponce Denis
Ecouchard

[The] French Poet
See   Ronsard, Pierre de

French Politician
See   Scherer, Edmond

[The] French Propertius
See   Bertin, Antoine

[The] French Quintilian
See   La Harpe, Jean Francois de

[The] French Raphael
See   Boucher, Francois

[The] French Raphael
See   Le Sueur [or Lesueur],
Eustache

[The] French Ritson
See   Rive, Jean Joseph

[The] French Roscius
See   Boyron, Michel [or Michael]

[The] French Roscius
See   Talma, Francois Joseph

[The] French Sappho
See   Scuderi, Magdalen [or
Madeleine] de

[The] French Tiberius
See   Louis XI

[The] French Tibullus
See   Desforges, Evariste Desire
[Chevalier de Parny]

[The] French Tibullus
See   Desportes, Philippe

[The] French Titian
See   Blanchard, Jacques

French, Valerie
See   Harrison, Valerie

[The] French Van Dyck
See   Rigau y Ros, Hyacinthe
Francois Honorat Mathias Pierre
Martyr Andre

[The] French Vegetius
See   Folard, Jean Charles de

[The] French Virgil
See   Arouet, Francois Marie

French, Walter Edward 1899-   [BE]
*American baseball player*
* French, Fitz

[The] Frenchman
See   Duray, Leon

Frend, A.
See   Cleveland, Philip Jerome

Frend, William Hugh Clifford
1916-   [IAW]
*British author*
* Philo

Freneau, Philip Morin 1752-1832
[PA, WBD]
*American poet*
* [The] Poet of the American
  Revolution
* Slender, Robert

Freni, Mirella
See   Fregni, Mirella

Frenk, Mariana
See   Frenk-Westheim, Mariana

Frenk-Westheim, Mariana   [IAW]
*German-born author and translator*
* Frenk, Mariana

Frenkel, Theodorus 1871-1956
[BF]
*Dutch actor and director*
* Bouwmeester, Theo

Frere, John Hookham 1769-1846
[DEL, DNNF, FFF]
*British author and statesman*
* Whistlecraft, William and Robert

Freron, Elie-Catherine 1719-1776
[SN]
*French journalist*
* [The] Poor Devil

Frese, Dolores Warwick 1936-
[CA]
*American poet*
* Warwick, Dolores

[The] Freshest Man on Earth
See   Latham, Walter Arlington

Freshfield, Mark
See   Field, M. J.

Fresnay, Pierre
See   Laudenbach, Pierre Jules
Louis

[The] Fresno Flash
See   Vucerovich, William

Freud, Clay
See   Freud, Clement Raphael

Freud, Clement Raphael 1924-
[B10]
*British author, legislator,
broadcaster*
* Freud, Clay

Freugon, Ruby
See   Ashby, Rubie Constance

Freund, Edward 20th c.   [WF]
*Cinematographer*
* Tokarski, E. F.

Freund, John Lincoln 1918-
[BEW, FC, TR]
*American actor*
* Forsythe, John

Freund, Joki
See   Freund, Walter Jakob

Freund, Walter Jakob 1926-   [EJ7]
*German jazz musician*
* Freund, Joki

Frewin, Leslie Ronald 1917?-
[CA, WD]
*British author and editor*
* Dupont, Paul

Frey, A. R. 1856- ?   [PA]
*Author*
* [The] Raven

Frey, Charles Weiser 1910-   [WW]
*Author*
* Findley, Ferguson

Frey, Junior
See   Frey, Linus Reinhard

Frey, Karl
See   Falke, Konrad

Frey, Linus Reinhard 1910-   [BE]
*American baseball player*
* Frey, Junior
* Frey, Lonny

Frey, Lonny
See   Frey, Linus Reinhard

Freybe, Heidi Huberta 1911?-
[CA, CC, EMD]
*German-born American author*
* Albrand, Martha
* Holland, Katrin
* Lambert, Christine

Freyer, Erick
See   Shroyer, Frederick

Freyer, Frederic
See   Ballinger, William Sanborn
[Bill]

[The] Friar
See   Bacon, Phanuel

Friars, Austin
See   Daniels, Frederick Edward

Frias, Pepe
See   Frias Andujar, Jesus Maria

Frias Andujar, Jesus Maria 1948-
[SMG, WWB]
*Dominican-born baseball player*
* Frias, Pepe

Fribbleton, George
See   Greene, Asa

Friberg, Augustaf Bernhardt
1899-1958   [BE]
*American baseball player*
* Friberg, Barney

Friberg, Barney
See   Friberg, Augustaf Bernhardt

Frick, C. H.
See   Irwin, Constance Frick

Frick, Constance
See   Irwin, Constance Frick

Fricken, Anthony ?-1903   [BE]
*American baseball player*
* Fricken, Hon

Fricken, Hon
See   Fricken, Anthony

Frida, Emil 1853-1912
[CD, EWL, WBD]
*Czech poet, playwright, translator*
* Vrchlicky, Jaroslav

Friday, Grier William 1896-1962
[BE]
*American baseball player*
* Friday, Skipper

Friday, Peter
See   Harris, Herbert

Friday, Skipper
See   Friday, Grier William

Friderici, Blanche
See   Campbell, B. F.

Fridley, Big Jim
See   Fridley, James Riley [Jim]

Fridley, James Riley [Jim] 1924-
[BE]
*American baseball player*
* Fridley, Big Jim

Fridolin
See   Christ, Robert Balthasar

Fridolin, Major
See   Pasha, Khalil Sheriff

Fridzeri, Marie Antoine 1741-1800
[PA]
*Author*
* Frixer

Fried, Arthur Edwin 1897-   [BE]
*American baseball player*
* Fried, Cy

Fried, Cy
See   Fried, Arthur Edwin

**Fried, Emanuel** 1913- [CA]
*American actor and playwright*
* Mann, Edward

**Fried, Pat**
*See* Fried, Waldemar H.

**Fried, Waldemar H.** 1889- [BBH]
*American lacrosse player and official*
* Fried, Pat

**Friedan, Betty**
*See* Goldstein, Betty Naomi

**Friede, Donald** 20th c. [CA, WGT]
*Author*
* Bedford, Donald F. [joint pseudonym with Henry Bedford-Jones and Kenneth Fearing]

**Friedhofer, Hugo Wilhelm** ?-1981 [FIR]
*American composer*
* [The] Boss
* [The] Fox
* [The] Man

**Friedkin, Bernie** 20th c. [EJS]
*American boxer*
* Friedkin, Schoolboy

**Friedkin, Schoolboy**
*See* Friedkin, Bernie

**Friedland, Nathaniel** 1936- [CA]
*American author and journalist*
* Freedland, Nat[haniel]
* Kenyon, Paul

**Friedland, Ronald Lloyd** 1937-1975 [CAP]
*American author*
* Lloyd, Ronald

**Friedland, Valentin** 1490-1556 [WBD]
*German educator*
* Trotzendorf, Valentin

**Friedland, Lewis** 1901-1962 [FC, FD]
*American director*
* Landers, Lew

**Friedlander, Norma** 1911- [EJ]
*American jazz musician*
* Teagarden, Norma Louise

**Friedlander, Saul** 1933?-
*Israeli historian*
* Ferland, Paul-Henri
* Friedlander, Shaul

**Friedlander, Shaul**
*See* Friedlander, Saul

**Friedlander, Walter A[ndreas]** 1891- [CA]
*German-born educator and author*
* Kraft, Walter Andreas

**Friedli, Emilie Ida** 1889- [SFL]
*Author*
* Van Ith, Lily

**Friedman, Bus**
*See* Friedman, M.

**Friedman, Elias**
*See* Friedman, Jacob Horace

**Friedman, Eve Rosemary** 1929- [AW, CA, WD]
*British author*
* Tibber, Robert
* Tibber, Rosemary

**Friedman, Irving** 1903- [PMJ, WWJ]
*American jazz musician*
* Friedman, Izzy

**Friedman, Izzy**
*See* Friedman, Irving

**Friedman, Jacob Horace** 1916- [WD]
*South African author, poet, translator, clergyman*
* Friedman, Elias
* Friedman, John
* Pater, Elias

**Friedman, Jake**
*See* Goodman, Jake

**Friedman, Jerrold David** 1944- [CA, SFL, WGT]
*American author*
* Gerrold, David

**Friedman, John**
*See* Friedman, Jacob Horace

**Friedman, Josephine Troth** 1928- [CA]
*American author and illustrator*
* Friedman, Joy Troth

**Friedman, Joy Troth**
*See* Friedman, Josephine Troth

**Friedman, Kinky**
*See* Friedman, Richard

**Friedman, M.** 20th c. [EJS]
*American football player*
* Friedman, Bus

**Friedman, Marty**
*See* Friedman, Max

**Friedman, Max** 1889- [BB]
*American basketball player*
* Friedman, Marty

**Friedman, Max Motel** 1908- [BLB]
*American safecracker and robber*
* Manion, Red
* Rudensky, Morris
* Rudensky, Red

**Friedman, Phil**
*See* Friedman, Philburn

**Friedman, Philburn** 1921- [BEW]
*American stage manager*
* Friedman, Phil

**Friedman, Richard** 1944- [CME]
*American country-western performer*
* Friedman, Kinky

**Friedman, Theodore Leopold** 1892-1971 [ASC, EJ, PMJ]
*American bandleader*
* [The] High Hat Tragedian of Song
* Lewis, Ted

**Friedman, William** 1879-1952 [FC]
*Hungarian-American film executive*
* Fox, William

**Friedman, William Frederic** 1891-1969 [WWW]
*American cryptographer*
* [The] Man Who Broke Purple

**Friedmann, Andrei** 1913-1954 [JL]
*Hungarian-born photographer*
* Capa, Robert

**Friedrich, Robert** 1890-1966 [AS, BL]
*American wrestler*
* Lewis, Ed
* Lewis, Strangler

**Friedrich Wilhelm** 20th c. [NN]
*German crown prince*
* Little Willie

**Friedrichs, Frederick** 1926- [BEW]
*German-born actor and director*
* Rolf, Frederick

**Friedwalt, A.**
*See* Messer, August

**Friend, Ed**
*See* Wormser, Richard [Edward]

**Friend, Florence** 1876-1953 [BEW]
*British-born actress*
* Mannering, Mary

**Friend, John** [SN]
* [The] Director of Studies

**[The] Friend of Helpless Children**
*See* Hoover, Herbert Clark

**[The] Friend of Industry**
*See* Dearbon, Benjamin

**[The] Friend of Man**
*See* Riquetti, Victor

**[The] Friend of Man**
*See* Wilberforce, William

**[A] Friend of the Family**
*See* Ayrton, William Edward

**[The] Friend of the Jews**
*See* Grant, Robert

**[The] Friend of the People**
*See* Marat, Jean Paul

**Friend, Oscar J[erome]** 1897-1963 [NAA, SFP, WW]
*American author*
* Jerome, Owen Fox
* Saturn, Sergeant [house pseudonym]
* Smith, Ford

**Friend, Owen Lacey** 1927- [BE]
*American baseball player*
* Friend, Red

**Friend, Red**
*See* Friend, Owen Lacey

**Friend, Robert Bartmess** 1930- [BE]
*American baseball player*
* [The] Warrior

**[A] Friend to Peace**
*See* Lowell, John

**Friendly, Aunt**
*See* Baker, Sarah S. Tuthill

**Friendly, Fred W.**
*See* Wachenheimer, Fred

**Frierson, Buck**
*See* Frierson, Robert Lawrence

**Frierson, Revoyda** 1934- [DAM]
*American singer*
* Lester, Ketty

**Frierson, Robert Lawrence** 1917- [BE]
*American baseball player*
* Frierson, Buck

**Fries, William [Bill]** 1928- [RO2]
*American singer and advertising executive*
* McCall, C. W.
* [The] Rubber Duck

**Friese, [Dr.] Edzard**
*See* Budde, Gerhard August

**Friese-Greene, William**
*See* Green, William Edward

**Friesell, Red**
*See* Friesell, William H.

**Friesell, William H.** 1894?-1974 [B10]
*American football referee*
* Friesell, Red

**Friesen, Samile Diane** 1938- [FC, SW]
*American actress*
* Cannon, Dyan

**Friganza, Trixie**
*See* O'Callaghan, Brigid

**Frigerio, Elvezio** 1930- [OP]
*Italian scenic and costume designer*
* Frigerio, Ezio

**Frigerio, Ezio**
*See* Frigerio, Elvezio

**Frigidaire, Miss**
*See* Evert, Chris[tine Marie]

**Friis, Babbis**
*See* Friis-Baastad, Babbis Ellinor

**Friis-Baastad, Babbis Ellinor** 1921-1970 [CA, SAT, TBJ]
*Norwegian author*
* Baastad, Babbis Friis
* Babbis, Eleanor
* Friis, Babbis

**Frijsh, Povla**
*See* Frisch, Paula

**Frikell, Samri**
*See* Oursler, [Charles] Fulton

**Frimbo, E[rnest] M[alcolm]**
*See* Whitaker, Rogers Ernest Malcolm

**Frimel, Rudolf** 1879-1972 [BBD]
*Czech-born composer*
* Friml, Rudolf

**Friml, Rudolf**
*See* Frimel, Rudolf

**Frings, Katherine Hartley** 1920?-1981 [BEW]
*American author and playwright*
* Frings, Ketti

**Frings, Ketti**
*See* Frings, Katherine Hartley

**Frinton, Freddie**
*See* Hargate, Frederick [Freddie]

**Frisbee, Bunt**
*See* Frisbee, Charles Augustus [Charlie]

**Frisbee, Charles Augustus [Charlie]** 1874-1954 [BE]
*American baseball player*
* Frisbee, Bunt

**Frisch, Frank Francis** 1898-1973 [BE, BN, FB]
*American baseball and football player*
* [The] Fordham Flash

**Frisch, Frank Francis** (Continued)
* Onkel Franz

**Frisch, Paula** 1881-1960 [MS]
*Danish singer*
* Frijsh, Povla

**Frisco**
See Bingham, Jocelyn

**Frisco, Joe**
See Joseph, Louis Wilson

**Frisella, Bear**
See Frisella, Daniel Vincent

**Frisella, Daniel Vincent** 1946- [BE]
*American baseball player*
* Frisella, Bear

**Frisius**
See Gamma, Regnier

**Friskey, Margaret Richards** 1901-
[CA, SAT]
*American author and editor*
* Sherman, Elizabeth

**Friso, Charles Henry** 1711-1751
[WBD]
*Stadholder of Holland*
* William IV

**Friswell, J. Hain** 1827- ?
[FFF, PA]
*Author*
* Jaques

**Frith, John** 1503-1553? [FFF]
*British clergyman and religious reformer*
* Brightwell, Richard

**Frith, Mary** 1589?-1664?
[DEP, RH, WBD]
*British pickpocket*
* Cutpurse, Moll

**Fritschel, Geo[rge] John** 1867- ?
[NAA]
*American author*
* Gaus, Geo. J.

**Fritz**
See Mosher, Frederick C.

**Fritz**
See Whitehall, Harold

**Fritz der Einzige**
See Frederick II

**Fritz, Dutchman**
See Fritz, Harry Koch

**Fritz, Harry Koch** 1890-1974 [BE]
*American baseball player*
* Fritz, Dutchman

**Fritz, T. Francis** ?-1938 [BS]
*American magician, editor, publisher*
* Ducrot, Frank

**Frixer**
See Fridzeri, Marie Antoine

**Frizzel, Irene** 1887-1936 [BEW]
*American actress*
* Fenwick, Irene

**Frizzell, Lefty**
See Frizzell, William Orville

**Frizzell, William Orville**
1928-1975 [CME, CWG, DAM]
*American country-western performer*
* Frizzell, Lefty

**Froelich, Ben**
See Froelich, William Palmer

**Froelich, William Palmer**
1887-1916 [BE]
*American baseball player*
* Froelich, Ben

**Froes, Froggie**
See Froes, Walter J.

**Froes, Walter J.** 1922-1958 [SC]
*American actor*
* Douglas, Wally
* Froes, Froggie

**Frohlich, Caroline Lili Bume** 1886-
[ART]
*Austrian-born author*
* Frohlich-Bume, Lili

**Frohlich-Bume, Lili**
See Frohlich, Caroline Lili Bume

**Frohman, Charles** 1860-1915
[WBD]
*American theatrical manager*
* [The] Napoleon of the Drama

**Frohs, Wilhelm** 1903- [FDG, OCF]
*Austrian director and actor*
* Forst, Willi

**Froissart, Jean**
See Daudet, Alphonse

**Froissart, Jean** 1337?-1410?
[DNNS, SN]
*French chronicler and poet*
* [Le] Valet des Princes
* [The] Walter Scott of the Middle Ages

**Frome, David**
See Brown, Zenith [Jones]

**Froment, Mathilde** [PA]
*Author*
* Bourdon, Madam

**Fromm, Erika** 1910- [IAW]
*German-born psychologist and author*
* Oppenheimer, Erika

**Frommann, Friedrich Johannes**
[SN]
*German bookseller*
* [The] Nestor of the German Book Trade

**[Der] Fromme**
See Ernest I [or Ernst]

**Fromme, Lynette Alice** 1949?-
[B10]
*American who attempted assassination of President Gerald Ford*
* Fromme, Squeaky

**Fromme, Squeaky**
See Fromme, Lynette Alice

**Fronabarger, David Poole** 1912-1969
*American actor*
* Barclay, David
* O'Brien, Dave

**Frost, C. Vernon** 1903- [EMD]
*British writer*
* Child, Charles B.

**Frost, Erica**
See Supraner, Robyn

**Frost, Frank Otis** 1936- [BWW]
*American singer*
* [The] Rhythm and Blues King

**Frost, Frederick**
See Faust, Frederick [Schiller]

**Frost, Harold G.** 1893-1959 [ASC]
*American composer*
* Frost, Jack

**Frost, Helen** 1898- [CAP]
*American author and poet*
* Nichols, Dave

**Frost, Jack**
See Frost, Harold G.

**Frost, Jack**
See Frost, R. B.

**Frost, Jack**
See Frost, Russell E.

**Frost, Morgan**
See Huntington, Thomas Waterman

**Frost, R. B.** 20th c. [BBH]
*American collegiate athletic director*
* Frost, Jack

**Frost, Russell E.** 1900- [NAA]
*American author and editor*
* Frost, Jack

**Frost, Sarah Frances** 1866-1950
[BEW, IPA, THR]
*Scottish-born actress*
* Brough, Fanny
* Marlowe, Julia

**Frosty Bill Duggleby**
See Duggleby, William James

**Frothingham, Washington** 1832- ?
[FFF, PA]
*American author and clergyman*
* Hermit of New York
* Macaulay
* Martel
* Rosicrucian

**[The] Frothy General**
See Santerre, Antoine Joseph

**Froude, James Anthony** 1818- ?
[PA]
*Author*
* Zeta

**Frowick, Roy Halston** 1932-
[WFA]
*American fashion designer*
* Halston

**Froy, Herald** [joint pseudonym with Keith (Spencer) Waterhouse]
See Deghy, Guy [Stephen]

**Froy, Herald** [joint pseudonym with Guy (Stephen) Deghy]
See Waterhouse, Keith [Spencer]

**Frueauff, Elaine Storrs** 1921-
[BEW]
*American actress, producer, director*
* Perry, Elaine

**Frueauff, Margaret Hall** 1913-
[BEW]
*American actress, director, playwright*
* Perry, Margaret

**Frugi**
See Calpurnius Piso, Lucius

**Frumentius** ?- 360?
[DNNF, HN, WBD]
*Saint*
* Abba Salamah [Father of Peace]
* Abuna [Our Father]

**Frumentius** (Continued)
* [The] Apostle of Ethiopia
* [The] Apostle of the Abyssinians

**Frumkin, Sidney** 1905- [EJS]
*American bullfighter*
* Franklin, Sidney

**Frundsberg [or Frondsberg], Georg von** 1473-1528 [WBD]
*German army officer*
* [The] Father of the German Landsknechte

**Frusius**
See Des Freux, Andre

**Fry, Barbara** 1932- [CA]
*American author*
* Greco, Margaret

**Fry, Bob** 20th c.
*American football player*
* [The] Old Man

**Fry, Caroline**
See Wilson, Mrs.

**Fry, Christopher**
See Harris, Christopher Fry

**Fry, David**
See Roper, William L[eon]

**Fry, Elizabeth** 1780-1844
[DEP, DNNS, SN]
*British philanthropist*
* [The] Female Howard

**Fry, James William** 1910- [ART]
*British painter*
* J. F.

**Fry, Jay**
See Fry, Johnson

**Fry, Johnson** 1901-1959 [BE]
*American baseball player*
* Fry, Jay

**Fry, Mrs.**
See Gurney, Elizabeth

**Fry, Pete**
See King, [James] Clifford

**Fryatt, Fanny** [PA]
*Author*
* Sepia

**Frydman, Szajko** 1911- [CA]
*Polish-born author*
* Szajkowski, Zosa

**Frye, Leslie** 1897- [THR]
*British actor and singer*
* Sarony, Leslie

**Frye, Marie** 1923-1965 [FC]
*American actress*
* [The] Body
* McDonald, Marie

**Frye, Vern D.** 1931- [SFL]
*Author*
* Dermott, Vern

**Fryer, Donald S[idney, Jr.]** 1934-
[CA]
*American poet and performer*
* Sidney-Fryer, Donald

**Fryer, Stan** 1906- [ART]
*British artist*
* F.

**Fryers, Austin**
See Clery, William Edward

**Frykberg, August**
See Sunesson, Lambert

**Fryman, Woodie**
See Fryman, Woodrow Thompson

**Fryman, Woodrow Thompson**
1940-   [SMG]
*American baseball player*
* Fryman, Woodie

**Ftorek, Fitzy**
See Ftorek, Robert Brian

**Ftorek, Robert Brian** 1952-   [SMG]
*American hockey player*
* Ftorek, Fitzy

**Fuad I**
See Ahmed Fuad Pasha

**Fuber, Mrs. Edward**   [FFF]
*Entertainer*
* Pfeiffer, Tillie

**Fuchs, Emil Edwin** 1878-1961   [PB]
*German-born baseball team owner*
* Fuchs, Judge

**Fuchs, Judge**
See Fuchs, Emil Edwin

**Fuchs, Leonhard** 1501-1566   [SN]
*German botanist*
* [The] Flayed Fox

**Fuchs, Lukas** 1922-   [BBD]
*German-born pianist and composer*
* Foss, Lukas

**Fuchs, Sonia Husid** 1906-   [AW]
*Russian-born author*
* Seedo, Sonia

**Fucini, Renato** 1843-1921
[CD, PA, WBD]
*Italian poet and author*
* Neri Tanfucio

**[The] Fudge Family**
See Moore, Thomas

**Fuechsel, Franz** 1927-   [WEC]
*Danish cartoonist*
* Skaerbaek

**Fuentes, Martha Ayers** 1923-   [CA]
*American playwright*
* Lorimer, Scat

**Fuentes, Mickey**
See Fuentes, Miguel

**Fuentes, Miguel** 1949-1970   [BE]
*Puerto Rican baseball player*
* Fuentes, Mickey

**Fuentes, Rigoberto** 1944-
[PB, SMG, WWB]
*Cuban-born baseball player*
* Channel 32
* [The] Cuban Cat
* Fuentes, Tito
* [The] Hot Dog
* [The] Parakeet

**Fuentes, Tito**
See Fuentes, Rigoberto

**Fuerb, Raoul**
See Felber, Rudolph

**[El] Fuerte**
See Sancho II

**[El] Fuerte [The Strong]**
See Sancho VII

**Fufuka, Karama**
See Morgan, Sharon A[ntonia]

**Fugazy, Humbert J.** 1889-1964
[BX]
*American boxing promoter*
* Fugazy, Jack

**Fugazy, Jack**
See Fugazy, Humbert J.

**Fugger, Jakob, II** 1459-1525
[WBD]
*Bavarian financier*
* [The] Rich

**Fuhrman, Alfred J.** 1896-1969
[BE]
*American baseball player*
* Fuhrman, Ollie

**Fuhrman, Ollie**
See Fuhrman, Alfred J.

**Fuiks, Lewis J.** 1893?-1962   [BEW]
*American conductor*
* Arden, Victor

**Fujiwara, Michiko** 1946-
[CA, SAT]
*Japanese author and illustrator*
* Saito, Michiko

**Fulford, Robert** 1932-   [CA]
*Canadian author*
* Delaney, Marshall

**Fulgentius, Fabius Claudius
Gordianus** 464?- 533   [HN]
*Saint*
* [The] Augustine of his Age

**Fulghum, Dot**
See Fulghum, James Lavoisier

**Fulghum, James Lavoisier**
1900-1967   [BE]
*American baseball player*
* Fulghum, Dot

**Fulginas**
See Gentle, Gentili

**Fulk I** 888?- 938   [WBD]
*Count of Anjou*
* [The] Red

**Fulk IV** 11th c.   [WBD]
*Count of Anjou*
* [Le] Rechin

**Fulk V** 11th c.   [WBD]
*Count of Anjou*
* [The] Young

**Fulke, Commissioner**
See Lomax, W. J.

**Fulks, Bryan**
See Fowlkes, Bryan

**Fulks, Joe** 1921-   [BB]
*American basketball player*
* Fulks, Jumping Joe

**Fulks, Jumping Joe**
See Fulks, Joe

**Fulks, Sarah Jane** 1914-
[AM, BDF, ITA]
*American actress*
* Durrell, Jane
* Wyman, Jane

**Full Pack Stanhouse**
See Stanhouse, Don[ald Joseph]

**Fullam, Everett** 1930?-
*American clergyman*
* Fullam, Terry

**Fullam, Maureen Nina** 1934-   [OP]
*British opera singer*
* Morelle, Maureen

**Fullam, Terry**
See Fullam, Everett

**Fullard-Leo, Ellen** ?-1974   [BBH]
*South African-born swimming club
organizer*
* Leo, Ma

**Fuller, Andrew** 1754-1815
[DEL, DNNS, SN]
*British clergyman*
* [The] Franklin of Theology

**Fuller, Beverley Bozeman** 1927-
[CA]
*American actress, producer,
choreographer*
* Bozeman, Beverley

**Fuller, Blind Boy**
See Allen, Fulton

**Fuller, Blind Boy, 2**
See McGhee, Walter Brown

**Fuller, Charles F.** 20th c.   [BE]
*American baseball player*
* Fuller, Nig

**Fuller, Dorothy Mason** 1898-   [CA]
*American author*
* Thorne, Sterling

**Fuller, Edith Jean** 20th c.   [NAA]
*American author*
* Dale, Adrian

**Fuller, Edmund [Maybank]** 1914-
[CA]
*American author and editor*
* Amicus Curiae

**Fuller, Frank Edward** 1893-1965
[BE]
*American baseball player*
* Fuller, Rabbit

**Fuller, Henry Blake** 1857-1929
[TC]
*American author and critic*
* Page, Stanton

**Fuller, Hiram** 19th c.   [FFF, PA]
*Author*
* Brittan, Belle

**Fuller, Howard** 20th c.   [IBW]
*American political organizer*
* Sadaukai, Owusu

**Fuller, Hoyt [William]** 1927-   [CA]
*American author and editor*
* Barrow, William

**Fuller, Iola**
See McCoy, Iola Fuller

**Fuller, Irene**
See Goodall, Irene

**Fuller, James Franklin** 1835- ?
[PA, WWL]
*Irish author*
* Ignotus

**Fuller, Jesse** 1896?-1976
[B10, DAM]
*American songwriter, singer,
guitarist*
* Fuller, Lone Cat

**Fuller, Little Boy**
See Trice, Rich[ard]

**Fuller, Lone Cat**
See Fuller, Jesse

**Fuller, Margaret Sarah** 1810-1850
[PA]
*Author*
* Ossoli

**Fuller, Nig**
See Fuller, Charles F.

**Fuller, Playboy**
See Minter, Iverson

**Fuller, Rabbit**
See Fuller, Frank Edward

**Fuller, Rene**
See Goodall, Irene

**Fuller, Richard Lee**
See Minter, Iverson

**Fuller, Rocky**
See Minter, Iverson

**Fuller, Roger**
See Tracy, Don[ald Fiske]

**Fuller, Rosetta**
See Fuller, Walter

**Fuller, Shorty**
See Fuller, William Benjamin

**Fuller, Walter** 1910-   [DAM, EJ]
*American jazz musician*
* Fuller, Rosetta

**Fuller, William Benjamin**
1867-1904   [BE]
*American baseball player*
* Fuller, Shorty

**Fullerton, Alexander** 20th c.   [CA]
*Author*
* Hilton, Alec [joint pseudonym
with Eustace Chesser]

**Fullerton, Gail Putney** 1927-
[CA, WD]
*American sociologist and author*
* Putney, Gail J.

**Fullerton, George H.** 19th c.   [PA]
*Author*
* Rambler

**Fullerton, Georgiana**   [PA]
*Author*
* De Navery, Raoul

**Fullerton, J. M.** 1911-   [FC]
*American actress*
* Muir, Jean

**Fullerton, Mrs. Alexander G.** 1812-
?   [PA]
*Author*
* Gower, Georgiana

**Fullilove, Mrs. E. J.**   [FFF]
*American writer*
* Warwick, Elsie

**Fullis, Charles Philip** 1904-1946
[BE]
*American baseball player*
* Fullis, Chick

**Fullis, Chick**
See Fullis, Charles Philip

**Fulljames, Henry J.** 20th c.   [WWL]
*British author*
* Avicus

**Fullonius**
See Le Toulon, Guillaume

**Fulmer, Charles John** 1851-1940
[BE]
*American baseball player and manager*
* Fulmer, Chick

**Fulmer, Chick**
See Fulmer, Charles John

**Fulsom, Lowell**
See Fulson, Lowell

**Fulson, Lowell** 1921- [BWW]
*American singer*
* Fulsom, Lowell
* Tulsa Red

**Fulton**
See Lazarus, Mel

**Fulton, Charles J.**
See Foss, Charles J.

**Fulton, Eileen**
See McLarty, Margaret Elizabeth

**Fulton, Joan** 1929- [FC]
*American comedienne*
* Shawlee, Joan

**Fulwood, Ramon** 20th c. [RO2]
*American musician*
* Fulwood, Tiki

**Fulwood, Tiki**
See Fulwood, Ramon

**Fum the Fourth**
See George IV

**Fume, Joseph**
See Chatto, William Andrew

**Fumoleau, Blanche** 1897-1964
[BEW, F1, FC]
*French actress*
* Morlay, Gaby

**Funchess, John** 1931- [BWW]
*American singer*
* Littlejohn, John

**Fundatissimus, Doctor**
See Aegidius [or Giles] of Colonna

**Fundatus, Doctor**
See Varro, William

**Fundatus et Copiosus, Doctor**
See Middleton, Richard

**Fundi, Ibibio**
See Austin, Jo

**Fundoianu, Benjamin** 1898-1944
[JL]
*Rumanian-born poet*
* Fondane, Benjamin

**Fune, Jonathan**
See Fletcher, John Walter James

**Fune no Kabashima [Kabashima of the Ships]**
See Kabashima, Katsuichi

**Funicello, Annette** 1942- [RO1]
*American singer and actress*
* Annette

**Funk, Casimir** 1884-1967 [JL]
*Polish biochemist*
* [The] Father of Dietetics

**Funk, Elias Calvin** 1904-1968 [BE]
*American baseball player*
* Funk, Liz

**Funk, Liz**
See Funk, Elias Calvin

**Funk, Thompson** 1911- [CA, SAT]
*American illustrator*
* Funk, Tom

**Funk, Tom**
See Funk, Thompson

**Funkhouser, Leonidas Pyrrhus** 1860-1912 [BE]
*American baseball player*
* Lee, Leonidas Pyrrhus

**Funkquist, Herman Peter Anton** 1870- ? [LAO]
*Swedish educator and author*
* F.Q.T.

**Funny Face**
See Pleon, Alec

**[The] Funny Man of the Times**
See Alden, William L.

**Funny, Mr.**
See Williams, Berl

**Funny Papa Smith**
See Smith, John T.

**Fuqua, Frenchy**
See Fuqua, John

**Fuqua, John** 1946- [IBW, SMG]
*American football player*
* [The] Count
* Fuqua, Frenchy

**Fuqua, Richard** 1950- [BB]
*American basketball player*
* [The] Mad Bomber

**Fuqua, Robert**
See Tillotson, Joe W.

**Fureteur, Jean Le**
See Magloire, Auguste

**Furey, Michael**
See Ward, Arthur Henry

**Furgerson, Samuel** [PA]
*Author*
* Hefferman, Michael

**Furgurson, Ernest B[aker, Jr.]** 1929- [CA]
*American journalist*
* Furgurson, Pat

**Furgurson, Pat**
See Furgurson, Ernest B[aker, Jr.]

**Furibondo**
See Albicante, Giovanni Alberto

**Furillo, Carl Anthony** 1922- [BE, PB]
*American baseball player*
* Furillo, Skoonj
* [The] Reading Rifle

**Furillo, Skoonj**
See Furillo, Carl Anthony

**[Il] Furioso**
See Robusti, Jacopo

**[The] Furious**
See John

**Furius, Fredrice** 1510-1592 [PA]
*Author*
* Corilanus

**Furlong, Vivienne Carole** 1941- [IAW]
*British author*
* Welburn, Vivienne

**Furnier, Vincent Damon** 1948- [IPA]
*American singer*
* Cooper, Alice
* [The] Queen of Rock 'n Rouge

**Furniss, Louise E.** [FFF]
*American writer*
* Chollet

**Furniss, William** 19th c. [PA]
*Author*
* De Grasse, Will

**Furnivall, F. J.**
See Furnivall, Frederick James

**Furnivall, Frederick James** 1825-1910 [LC]
*British educator and editor*
* Furnivall, F. J.

**Furnley, Maurice**
See Wilmot, Frank Leslie Thomson

**Furry, Elda** 1890?-1966 [F1, FC, WEF]
*American columnist and actress*
* Hopper, Hedda

**Fursch-Madi, Mme.**
See Verle, Emy

**Furth, Carleton**
See Gibson, Joe

**Furth, Happy**
See Furth, Solomon

**Furth, Solomon** 1907- [EJS]
*American track and field athlete*
* Furth, Happy

**Furthman, Jules**
See Furthmann, Jules Grinnel

**Furthmann, Jules Grinnel** 1888-1966 [FD, WEF]
*American director and screenwriter*
* Furthman, Jules

**Furuhashi, Hironashin** 1928- [SWI]
*Japanese swimmer*
* [The] Flying Fish

**Furukawa, Toshi** 1924- [CA]
*Japanese author*
* Kanzawa, Toshiko

**Fury, Nick**
See Parry, Michel Patrick

**[The] Fury of the Gironde**
See Terwagne, Anne Joseph

**Furze, Barton**
See Rochester, George Ernest

**Fusbos**
See Plunkett, Henry

**Fuseli, Johann Kaspar** 1706?-1781? [HN]
*Swiss painter*
* [The] Milton of Painting

**Fuss, Martin** 1921- [FC, ITA, WEF]
*American producer*
* Hunter, Ross

**Fussell, Fred[erick Morris]** 1895-1966 [BE]
*American baseball player*
* Fussell, Moonlight Ace

**Fussell, Moonlight Ace**
See Fussell, Fred[erick Morris]

**Fussenegger, Gertrud**
See Dietz, Gertrud

**Fuzuli**
See Mehmet Suleiman

**Fuzzy Guzzy**
See Burleigh, William Henry

**Fyfe, H. B.**
See Fyfe, Horace Brown

**Fyfe, Horace Brown** 1918- [SF, WGT]
*American author*
* Fyfe, H. B.
* MacDuff, Andrew

**Fysh, Frederick** [PA]
*Author*
* F. F.

**Fyson, J. G.**
See Fyson, Jenny Grace [Harrison]

**Fyson, Jenny Grace [Harrison]** 1904- [AW]
*British author*
* Fyson, J. G.

**Fytton, Francis**
See Francis Fytton, Charles Farid Bassili

# G

**G.**
*See* Gent, L. C.

**G. A. G. B.**
*See* Brooke, Geoffrey Arthur George

**G. A. S.**
*See* Sala, George Augustus

**G. B.**
*See* Boas, Guy [Herman Sidney]

**G. B. S.**
*See* Shaw, George Bernard

**G. C. [Gnome Club]**
*See* Atkin, Ann

**G. C.**
*See* Claessen, George

**G. D.**
*See* Darby, George

**G. D.**
*See* Davidson, Gladys

**G. D.**
*See* Dunbar, George

**G. E. P.**
*See* Packard, Gilian E.

**G. E. W.**
*See* Wickham, Geoffrey Earle

**G. F. P.**
*See* Pardon, George Frederick

**G. H. P.**
*See* Putnam, George H[aven]

**G. H. R.**
*See* Rhoades, Geoffrey H.

**G. K. C.**
*See* Chesterton, Gilbert Keith

**G. L. M.**
*See* Meason, Gilbert Laing

**G. M.**
*See* Mackie, George

**G. M.**
*See* Markham, Gervasse

**G. M.**
*See* Meistermann, Georg

**G. M., Mrs.**
*See* McIver, Tennie Stewart

**G. O. M.**
*See* Gladstone, William Ewart

**[The] G. O. M. of Athens**
*See* Pericles

**G. P. C.**
*See* Panconcelli-Calzia, Giulio

**G. R. W.**
*See* Wyllie, George Ralston

**G. S.**
*See* Slater, George

**G. S. O.**
*See* Fox, [Sir] Frank

**G. W.**
*See* Wales, Geoffrey

**G. W. B.**
*See* Blunt, George W.

**G. W. M.**
*See* Meadley, George Wilson

**G. W. M.**
*See* Melcher, Gilbert W[ayne]

**G. W. P.**
*See* Pettes, George W.

**G. W. S.**
*See* Smalley, George W.

**G. W. W.**
*See* Williams, George W.

**Gaal, Franceska**
*See* Zilveritch, Fanny

**Gaathon, A[ryeh] L[udwig]**
*See* Gruenbaum, Ludwig

**Gabbler Gridiron**
*See* Haslewood, Joseph

**Gabel, Joseph** 1912- [CA]
*Hungarian-born author and sociologist*
* Geroely, Kalman
* Gombossy, Zoltan
* Martin, Lucien

**Gabi**
*See* Arnao, Gabriel

**Gabin, Jean**
*See* Moncorge, Jean-Alexis

**Gable, Clark** 1901-1960 [CU]
*American actor*
* [The] King

**Gable, J. Harris**
*See* Gable, Jacob Henry, Jr.

**Gable, Jacob Henry, Jr.** 1902-
[NAA]
*American librarian and author*
* Gable, J. Harris

**Gable, Mary** 1899- [CAT]
*American author and poet*
* Mariella, [Sister]

**Gable, Rufe**
*See* Livingston, Don Leslie

**Gabler, Frank Harold** 1911-1967
[BE]
*American baseball player*
* [The] Great Gabbo

**Gabler, Gabe**
*See* Gabler, John Richard

**Gabler, Gabe**
*See* Gabler, William Louis [Bill]

**Gabler, John Richard** 1930- [BE]
*American baseball player*
* Gabler, Gabe

**Gabler, William Louis [Bill]** 1930-
[BE]
*American baseball player*
* Gabler, Gabe

**Gabo, Naum**
*See* Pevsner, Naum Neemia

**Gabor, Dennis** 1900- [JL]
*British physicist*
* [The] Father of Holography

**Gabor, Sari** 1919?- [FC, ITA, SW]
*Hungarian-born actress*
* Gabor, Zsa Zsa

**Gabor, Zsa Zsa**
*See* Gabor, Sari

**Gabriel, Gabe**
*See* Gabriel, Roman

**Gabriel, John**
*See* Rowe, John Gabriel

**Gabriel, Roman** 1940- [FB]
*American football player*
* Gabriel, Gabe

**Gabriel, Tex**
*See* Gabriel, Wayne

**Gabriel, Virginia**
*See* Marsh, Constance Crane

**Gabriel, Wayne** 20th c. [RM, RO2]
*American musician*
* Gabriel, Tex

**Gabrielli, Domenico** 17th c. [SN]
*Italian composer and musician*
* [Il] Menghino del Violoncello

**Gabrielli, Francesca** 18th c. [SN]
*Italian singer*
* Ferrarese del Bene

**Gabrielli, Trifone** [SN]
*Venetian scholar*
* [The] Socrates of His Age

**Gabrielson, Gabe**
*See* Gabrielson, Leonard Gary

**Gabrielson, Leonard Gary** 1940-
[SMG]
*American baseball player*
* Gabrielson, Gabe

**Gabrini, Niccolo** 1313-1354
[DEP, RH, WBD]
*Italian patriot*
* [The] Last of the Romans
* [The] Last of the Tribunes
* Rienzi, Cola di
* Tribune of Liberty, Peace, and Justice

**Gachet, Alice**
*See* Gachet De La Fourniere, Alice Mary

**Gachet, Paul Ferdinand** 1828-1909
[B10]
*French physician and artist*
* Van Ryssel, Paul

**Gachet De La Fourniere, Alice Mary**
?-1960 [BEW]
*Actress, director, educator*
* Gachet, Alice

**Gackle, Kathleen** 1950-
*American actress*
* Lloyd, Kathleen

**Gacon, Francois** 1667-1725 [SN]
*French poet*
* [The] Dennis of His Day

**Gadd, David Bernard Hallard**
1935- [IAW]
*New Zealand author*
* Werata, Tota

**Gadd, Paul** 1944- [RO2]
*British singer*
* Glitter, Gary
* Monday, Paul

**Gaddes, Peter**
*See* Sheldon, Peter

**Gaddis, Peggy**
*See* Dern, Peggy Gaddis

**Gaddy, John Wilson** 1914-1966
[BE]
*American baseball player*
* Gaddy, Sheriff

**Gaddy, Sheriff**
*See* Gaddy, John Wilson

**Gade, Henry** [house pseudonym]
See  Palmer, Raymond A[rthur]

**Gaechter, Bad Actor**
See  Gaechter, Mike

**Gaechter, Mike** 20th c.
*American football player*
* Gaechter, Bad Actor

**[The] Gaelic Homer**
See  Ossian

**Gaer, Joseph** [or Yossef]
See  Fishman, Joseph

**Gaess, William C., Jr.** 1911?-1978
*American billboard designer*
* [The] Man Who Lit Up
    Broadway

**Gaetano, Aleardo** 1812-1878
[WBD]
*Italian poet and painter*
* Aleardi, Aleardo

**Gaetano, Antonio G.** 1885-1951
[WEF]
*Italian-born cinematographer*
* Gaudio, Tony

**Gaetano** [or Caetani], **Benedetto**
1235?-1303   [SN, WBD]
*Pope*
* Boniface VIII
* [The] Prince of the New
    Pharisees

**Gafa, Al**
See  Gafa, Alexander

**Gafa, Alexander** 1941-   [EJ7]
*American jazz musician*
* Gafa, Al

**Gaffney, Honest John**
See  Gaffney, John H.

**Gaffney, John H.** 1855-1913   [BE]
*American baseball manager*
* Gaffney, Honest John
* King of the Umpires

**Gage, Frances Dana Barker**
1808-1884   [FFF]
*American author*
* Aunt Fanny

**Gage, Nicholas**
See  Ngagoyeanes, Nicholas

**Gage, Walter**
See  Inge, William

**Gage, Wilson**
See  Steele, Mary Q[uintard
Govan]

**Gagliano, Gaetano** ?-1953   [PHM]
*American underworld figure*
* Gagliano, Joseph

**Gagliano, Joseph**
See  Gagliano, Gaetano

**Gagliardo, Ruth Garver** 1896?-1980
*American librarian*
* [The] Kansas Book Lady

**Gagnon, Black Cat**
See  Gagnon, John

**Gagnon, Chick**
See  Gagnon, Harold Dennis

**Gagnon, Harold Dennis** 1897-1970
[BE]
*American baseball player*
* Gagnon, Chick

**Gagnon, John** 1905-
[B10, CEI, FHE]
*Canadian-born hockey player*
* Gagnon, Black Cat

**Gahagan, Helen**
See  Douglas, Helen Gahagan

**Gaida-Gaidamavicius, Pranas**
1914-   [IAW]
*Lithuanian-born author*
* Chantier, P.
* Zaidys, Pranas

**Gaidi, Brother**
See  Henry, Milton

**Gaige, Truman**
See  Ruhland, Stanley

**Gail, Zoe**
See  Stapleton, Zoe Margaret

**Gaillard, Angier** 1530-1593   [PA]
*Author*
* [Le] Rondie

**Gaillard, Bulee** 1916-
[ASC, EJ, PMJ]
*American jazz musician*
* Gaillard, Slim

**Gaillard, Slim**
See  Gaillard, Bulee

**Gaines, Big House**
See  Gaines, Clarence

**Gaines, Clarence** 1923-   [BB]
*American basketball player*
* Gaines, Big House

**Gaines, Clark**   [SMG]
*American football player*
* Gaines, Super

**Gaines, Donna** 1949?-   [IBW]
*American singer*
* [The] First Lady of Disco
* [The] Queen of Disco
* Summer, Donna

**Gaines, Joel Dennis** 1943-   [CA]
*American author and backgammon
expert*
* Kansil, Joli

**Gaines, Jonas** 20th c.   [IBW]
*American-born baseball player*
* Gaines, Lefty

**Gaines, Joseph** 1874-1910
[BX, RBE, SG]
*American boxer*
* Gans, Joe
* [The] Old Master

**Gaines, Lefty**
See  Gaines, Jonas

**Gaines, Nemo**
See  Gaines, Willard Roland

**Gaines, Robert**
See  Summersales, Rowland

**Gaines, Roy** 20th c.   [BWW]
*American entertainer*
* Little T Bone

**Gaines, Super**
See  Gaines, Clark

**Gaines, Willard Roland** 1897-   [BE]
*American baseball player*
* Gaines, Nemo

**Gainham, Sarah**
See  Ames, Rachel

**Gainor, Delos Charles** 1886-1947
[BE]
*American baseball player*
* Gainor, Sheriff

**Gainor, Dutch**
See  Gainor, Norman

**Gainor, Laura** 1906-
[BDF, F2, WEF]  ·
*American actress*
* Gaynor, Janet

**Gainor, Norman** 1904-   [CEI, SMG]
*Canadian-born hockey player*
* Gainor, Dutch

**Gainor, Sheriff**
See  Gainor, Delos Charles

**Gainsborough, Thomas** 1727-1788
[HN]
*British painter*
* [The] English Claude

**Gaite, Francis** [joint pseudonym with
Adelaide Frances Oke Manning]
See  Coles, Cyril Henry

**Gaite, Francis** [joint pseudonym with
Cyril Henry Coles]
See  Manning, Adelaide Frances
Oke

**Gaither, Alonzo S.** 1905-
[FB, IBW]
*American football coach*
* Gaither, Jake

**Gaither, Barry**
See  Gaither, Edmund B.

**Gaither, Bill** 20th c.
*American singer*
* Leroy's Buddy

**Gaither, Edmund B.** 1925-   [IBW]
*American art historian and museum
curator*
* Gaither, Barry

**Gaither, Jake**
See  Gaither, Alonzo S.

**Gaius Caesar** 12- 41   [WBD]
*Roman emperor*
* Caligula

**Gajdusek, Robert Elemer** 1925-
[CA]
*American author and poet*
* Gajdusek, Robin

**Gajdusek, Robin**
See  Gajdusek, Robert Elemer

**Galan, Alfonso** 20th c.   [GS]
*Spanish bullfighter*
* [El] Galan del Toreo [The
    Gallant of Bullfighting]

**[El] Galan del Toreo [The Gallant of
Bullfighting]**
See  Galan, Alfonso

**Galanos, James**
See  Gorgoliatos, James

**Galantara, Gabriele** 1865-1937
[WEC]
*Italian cartoonist*
* Rata-Langa

**Galante, Carmine** 1910-1979
*American underworld figure*
* [The] Cigar
* Lillo

**Galateo**
See  Ferrari, Antoine

**Galaxan, Sol**
See  De Marini y Coppel, Alfredo
Jose

**Galazewski, Stanley Joseph** 1919-
[BE]
*American baseball player*
* Galle, Stan[ley Joseph]

**Galbraith, Georgie Starbuck**
1909-1980   [CAP]
*American author and poet*
* Page, G. S.
* Patrice, Ann
* Pennington, Penny
* Pennington, Stuart

**Galbraith, Jean** 1906-   [CA]
*Australian author and botanist*
* Correa
* Green, Judith

**Galbraith, John Kenneth** 1908-
[CA]
*Canadian-born American economist*
* Epernay, Mark
* McLandress, Herschel

**Galbraith, Percival** 1899-
[CEI, SMG]
*Canadian-born hockey player*
* Galbraith, Perk

**Galbraith, Perk**
See  Galbraith, Percival

**Galbreath, Frank** 1913-   [MY]
*American jazz musician*
* Galbreath, Gabbus

**Galbreath, Gabbus**
See  Galbreath, Frank

**Galcai, Lalauga Malana Au Faoa
Taupou O. Tuffle Tuimanua** 1958-
[IBW]
*Samoan princess*
* Rasmussen, Juliana

**Gale, Alan**
See  Sempill, Ernest

**Gale, E. F.** 20th c.   [SFL]
*British author*
* Falkner, John

**Gale, Ethel**
See  Smith, Helen E.

**Gale, H. Winter**
See  Maitland, T. G. Dowling

**Gale, John**
See  Gaze, Richard

**Gale, John**
See  Openshaw, G. H.

**Gale, Laddie**
See  Gale, Lauren

**Gale, Lauren** 1916-   [BB]
*American basketball player*
* Gale, Laddie

**Gale, Linn A. E.** 1892-   [WWL]
*American author*
* Allen, Adams
* Weston, Warren

**Gale, William**   [PA]
*Author*
* Aura

**Gale, William C.**
See  Giles, Carl H[oward]

**Galecki, Tadeusz** 1873-1937   [CD]
*Polish author*
* Strug, Andrzej

**Galen, Bernard de** 1606-1678   [SN]
*German prelate*
* [The] Converter

**Galen, Graf Clemens von** 1878- ?
[BDW]
*German clergyman*
* [The] Lion of Munster

**Galen, Philipp**
*See*  Lange, Ernst Philipp Karl

**[The] Galena Tanner**
*See*  Grant, Hiram Ulysses

**Galento, Tony** 1910-1979
[BX, RBE]
*American boxer*
* Galento, Two Ton Tony

**Galento, Two Ton Tony**
*See*  Galento, Tony

**Galgario, [Fra]**
*See*  Ghislandi, [Fra] Vittore

**Galiani, Ferdinand** 1728-1787   [SN]
*Italian political economist*
* [A] Little Machiavelli

**[The] Galilaean**
*See*  Jesus Christ

**[The] Galilean**
*See*  Judas

**Galindo, Beatrix** 1475-1535   [PA]
*Author*
* [The] Latine

**Galindo, P.**
*See*  Hinojosa, Rolando

**Galitz, Sandra Ester** 1937-   [RO1]
*American singer*
* Stewart, Sandy

**Galitzin, Vasili** 1633?-1713?
[DNNS]
*Russian army officer and politician*
* [The] Great

**Gall [or Gallus]**
*See*  Cellach [or Caillech]

**Gall, George** 1885-1939   [THR]
*American actor*
* Gaul, George

**Gallager, Gale**
*See*  Oursler, Will[iam Charles]

**Gallagher, Alan Mitchell Edward
George** 1945-   [BE]
*American baseball player*
* Gallagher, Dirty Al
* Gallagher, Patrick Henry

**Gallagher, Dirty Al**
*See*  Gallagher, Alan Mitchell
Edward George

**Gallagher, Ed[ward Michael]** 1910-
[BE]
*American baseball player*
* Gallagher, Lefty

**Gallagher, Frank** 1893-1962   [DIL]
*Irish journalist, historian, author*
* Hogan, David

**Gallagher, George Gately** 1928-
[WEC]
*American cartoonist*
* Gately, George

**Gallagher, Gil**
*See*  Gallagher, Lawrence Kirby

**Gallagher, John** 1904-   [BB]
*American basketball coach*
* Gallagher, Taps

**Gallagher, Joseph Emmett [Joe]**
1914-   [BE]
*American baseball player*
* Gallagher, Muscles

**Gallagher, Lawrence Kirby**
1896-1957   [BE]
*American baseball player*
* Gallagher, Gil

**Gallagher, Lefty**
*See*  Gallagher, Ed[ward Michael]

**Gallagher, Mary Dominic** 1917-
[CA]
*Canadian-born educator and author*
* Mary Dominic, [Sister]

**Gallagher, Muscles**
*See*  Gallagher, Joseph Emmett
[Joe]

**Gallagher, Patrick Henry**
*See*  Gallagher, Alan Mitchell
Edward George

**Gallagher, Rachel** 20th c.   [CA]
*American author*
* Drake, Kimbal

**Gallagher, Richard** 1891-1955
[F2, FC]
*American actor*
* Gallagher, Skeets

**Gallagher, Skeets**
*See*  Gallagher, Richard

**Gallagher, Taps**
*See*  Gallagher, John

**Gallagher, William D.** 1808- ?
[PA]
*Author*
* Erato

**[The] Gallant**
*See*  Pelham, John

**[The] Gallant King**
*See*  Victor Emmanuel II

**Gallatin, Harry** 1928-   [BB]
*American basketball player and
coach*
* [The] Horse

**[The] Gallatin Squash**
*See*  Perdue, Hubbard E.

**Galle, Stan[ley Joseph]**
*See*  Galazewski, Stanley Joseph

**Gallego Mateo, Jose** 1883-1910
[GS]
*Spanish bullfighter*
* Pepete [Big Joe]

**Gallello, Al**   [RBE]
*American boxing historian*
* Gallello, Scoop

**Gallello, Scoop**
*See*  Gallello, Al

**Gallenga, Antonio Carlo Napoleone**
1810-1895   [WBD]
*Italian educator, journalist,
politician*
* Mariotti, Luigi

**[The] Gallerite**
*See*  Bason, Fred[erick Thomas]

**Galli, Amelita** 1882-1963   [MS]
*Italian opera singer*
* Galli-Curci, Amelita

**Galli, Giovanni Giuseppe Gilberto**
1940-   [EAR]
*Italian auto racer*
* Galli, Nanni

**Galli, Ida** 20th c.   [WF]
*Italian actress*
* Stewart, Evelyn

**Galli, Nanni**
*See*  Galli, Giovanni Giuseppe
Gilberto

**Galli-Curci, Amelita**
*See*  Galli, Amelita

**Gallia, Bert**
*See*  Gallia, Melvin Allys

**Gallia, Melvin Allys** 1891-   [BE]
*American baseball player*
* Gallia, Bert

**[The] Galliard**
*See*  Johnstone, William

**[The] Gallic Bully**
*See*  William III

**[The] Gallic Caesar**
*See*  Bonaparte, Napoleon

**Gallichan, Walter M.** 1861- ?
[LAO]
*British author*
* Blount, Anna
* Mortimer, January

**Gallieni, Joseph Simon** 1849-1916
[WBD]
*French army officer*
* [The] Savior of Paris

**Galliher, Marvelous Marv**
*See*  Galliher, Marvin Gene

**Galliher, Marvin Gene** 1947-
[SMG]
*American baseball player*
* Galliher, Marvelous Marv

**Gallimore, Catherine**
*See*  Anderson, Catherine

**Gallinger, Osma Couch**
*See*  Tod, Osma Gallinger

**Gallio**
*See*  Annaeus Novatus, Marcus

**Gallister, Michael**
*See*  Bedford-Jones, Henry [James
O'Brien]

**Gallito [Little Rooster]**
*See*  Gomez Ortega, Jose

**Gallito de Zafra [Little Rooster from
Zafra]**
*See*  Ortiz, J. M.

**Gallitzin, Demetrius Augustine**
1770-1840   [WBD]
*Dutch-born clergyman and
missionary*
* Smith [or Schmet], Augustine

**[El] Gallo [The Rooster]**
*See*  Gomez Ortega, Rafael

**Gallo, Albert** 20th c.   [BLB]
*American underworld figure*
* Blast, Kid

**Gallo, Crazy Joey**
*See*  Gallo, Joseph

**Gallo, Joseph** 1929-1972
*American underworld figure*
* Gallo, Crazy Joey

**Gallo, Larry** 20th c.   [BLB]
*American underworld figure*
* [The] Blond

**Gallois, Marcelle** 1888?-   [B10]
*French etcher*
* Genevieve, [Mother]

**Galloping Dick**
*See*  Ferguson, Richard

**[The] Galloping Ghost**
*See*  Grange, Harold E.

**[The] Galloping Ghost**
*See*  Wheatley, William [Bill]

**Galloway, Bad News**
*See*  Galloway, James Cato

**Galloway, Charles** 1865?-1914
[DAM, NOJ]
*American jazz musician*
* Galloway, Happy
* Galloway, Sweet Lovin

**Galloway, Chick**
*See*  Galloway, Clarence Edward

**Galloway, Clarence Edward**
1896-1969   [AS, BE]
*American baseball player*
* Galloway, Chick

**Galloway, Dicey**
*See*  Galloway, William [Bill]

**Galloway, Happy**
*See*  Galloway, Charles

**Galloway, James Cato** 1887-1950
[BE]
*American baseball player*
* Galloway, Bad News

**Galloway, James M.** 20th c.   [WGT]
*Author*
* Moore, Anon

**[The] Galloway Poet**
*See*  Nicholson, William

**Galloway, Sweet Lovin**
*See*  Galloway, Charles

**Galloway, Sylvia** 1901-   [THR]
*British actress and singer*
* Welling, Sylvia

**Galloway, William [Bill]**   [RO1]
*American singer*
* Galloway, Dicey

**Gallun, Raymond Z[inke]** 1911-
[CA, ESF, SFL]
*American author*
* Allport, Arthur
* Callahan, John
* Callahan, William
* Elstar, Dow
* Raymond, E. V.

**Gallus, Jacobus**
*See*  Handl [or Haendl], Jakob

**Galoot**
*See*  Kendall, Edward P.

**Galouye, Daniel F[rancis]** 1920-
[WGT]
*American author*
* Daniels, Louis G.

**Galpin, J. A.** 20th c.   [SFL]
*Author*
* Blackstone, Valerius D.

**Galsworthy, John** 1867-1933
[EWL, LC, TC]
*British author, playwright, critic*
* A. R. P. - M.
* Sinjohn, John

**Galt, Eric S.**
*See* Ray, James Earl

**Galt, John** 1779-1839 [DEL, PA]
*British author*
* Balwhidder, [Rev] Micah
* Clark, [The Rev.] T.
* Duffle
* Prior, Samuel

**Galt, William Hamilton** 1856- ?
[PA]
*Author*
* Nitgenockle
* Ulrich, Charles, Jr.

**Galub, Jack** 1915- [CA]
*American author*
* Gant, Chuck

**Galuppi, Baldassare** 1706-1785
[SN, WBD]
*Italian composer*
* [Il] Buranello

**Galvani, Dino**
*See* Galvanoni, Dino

**Galvanoni, Dino** 1890-1960 [THR]
*Italian-born actor*
* Galvani, Dino

**Galvany, Marisa**
*See* Genis, Myra Beth

**[The] Galveston Giant**
*See* Johnson, John Arthur [Jack]

**Galvez De Montalvo, Luis**
*See* Avalle-Arce, Juan Bautista

**Galvin, Gentle Jeems**
*See* Galvin, James Francis

**Galvin, George** 1860-1904
[BEW, BMH]
*British comedian*
* [The] King's Jester
* Leno, Dan

**Galvin, James Francis** 1855?-1902
[AS, BE, PB]
*American baseball player*
* Galvin, Gentle Jeems
* Galvin, Pud
* [The] Little Steam Engine

**Galvin, Pud**
*See* Galvin, James Francis

**Galvin, Sydney Paul** 1892?-1962
[BEW]
*Theatrical performer and writer*
* Leno, Dan, Jr.

**Galway, Herbert**
*See* Teague, George Herbert

**Gam, Rita**
*See* Mackay, Rita Eleanore

**Gama, Gulam Mohammed** [BL]
*Indian wrestler*
* [The] Great Gama

**Gambier, Kenyon**
*See* Lathrop, Lorin Andrews

**Gambino, Don Chick**
*See* Gambino, Frank

**Gambino, Frank** 20th c. [BLB]
*American underworld figure*
* Gambino, Don Chick

**Gambino, Vincenzo** 1939- [EJ7]
*American jazz musician*
* Wallace, Vince

**Gamble, Elizabeth Washington**
1784-1857 [PA]
*Author*
* [A] Lady

**Gamble, Fred**
*See* Gambold, Frederick Alvin

**Gamble, Judy** 1916- [FC]
*British actress*
* Campbell, Judy

**Gambold, Frederick Alvin**
1868-1939 [SC]
*American actor*
* Gamble, Fred

**[The] Game Chicken**
*See* Pearce

**Gamelle**
*See* Orleans, Louis Philippe Joseph
d'

**Gamelyn**
*See* Parrish, [Emma] Kenyon

**Gamma**
*See* Booth, Andrew Donald

**Gamma**
*See* Osborne, John D.

**Gamma, Regnier** 1508-1555 [PA]
*Author*
* Frisius

**Gammell, Susanna Valentine Mitchell**
1897?-1979 [CA]
*American poet, author, playwright*
* Mitchell, S. Valentine

**Gammie, Alexander** 1870- ?
[WWL]
*Scottish author*
* Ecclesiasticus

**Gammon, D. J.** 20th c. [MBF]
*British author*
* Robins, Fenton

**Gammon, John Francis** 1864-1952
[BE]
*American baseball player*
* Smith, John Francis
* Smith, Phenomenal

**Gammon, Robert William** 1867- ?
[NAA]
*American clergyman and editor*
* R. W. G.

**Gammon, Von**
*See* Gammon, William A.

**Gammon, William A.** 1905-1974
[NOJ]
*American jazz musician*
* Gammon, Von

**Gammons, Daff**
*See* Gammons, John Ashley

**Gammons, John Ashley** 1876-1963
[BE]
*American baseball player*
* Gammons, Daff

**Gan, Benjamin** 1913- [RBE, SG]
*Filipino-born boxer*
* Montana, Small

**Gan Index**
*See* Williams, David Rhys

**Gancev, Stojan** 1929- [OP]
*Bulgarian opera singer*
* Stojanov, Stojan

**Gancs, Edith** 1927- [OP]
*German opera singer*
* Kertesz-Gabry, Edith

**Gandalac, Lennard**
*See* Bernstein, Eric [Lennard]

**Gander, [Sir] Gregory**
*See* Ellis, George

**Gander, Leonard Marsland** 1902-
[IAW]
*British author and journalist*
* Meabey, Leonard

**Gandhi, Indira Nehru** 1917-
*Indian prime minister*
* Behnji [Honored Sister]

**Gandhi, Mahatma [Great-Souled]**
*See* Gandhi, Mohandas
Karamchand

**Gandhi, Mohandas Karamchand**
1869-1948 [IPA, NAD]
*Indian head of state and spiritual
leader*
* Bapu
* Gandhi, Mahatma
 [Great-Souled]

**Gandil, Charles Arnold** 1888-1970
[AS, BE, PB]
*American baseball player*
* Gandil, Chick

**Gandil, Chick**
*See* Gandil, Charles Arnold

**Gandley, Kenneth Royce** 1920-
[CA, WWS]
*British author*
* Jacks, Oliver
* Royce, Kenneth

**Gandy, Mabel** 20th c. [WWL]
*British author*
* Soderland, M.

**Ganga, Creto**
*See* Crespo y Borbon, Bartolome
Jose

**Ganganelli, Giovanni Vincenzo
Antonio** 1705-1774
[DNNF, FFF, WBD]
*Pope*
* Clement XIV
* [The] Protestant Pope

**[The] Ganger [or Walker]**
*See* Rollo [Rolf or Hrolf]

**Gangoly, O. C.**
*See* Gangoly, Orun Coomar

**Gangoly, Orun Coomar** 1920- [GA]
*Indian graphic artist*
* Gangoly, O. C.

**Ganley, W. Paul** 20th c.
[SFL, WGT]
*Author*
* Duane, Toby?

**Ganly, Rosaleen Brigid** 1909-
[ART]
*Irish artist*
* R. B. G.

**Gannett, Henry** 1846-1914 [WBD]
*American cartographer*
* [The] Father of American Map
 Making

**Gannold, John**
*See* Langdon, John [Franklin
Coasten]

**Gannon, E. J.** 20th c. [MBF]
*British author*
* Daring, Victor
* Kent, Beverley

**Gannon, Gussie**
*See* Gannon, James Edward

**Gannon, James Edward** 1873-1966
[BE]
*American baseball player*
* Gannon, Gussie

**Gannon, James Kimball** 1900-1974
[ASC, PMJ]
*American lyricist*
* Gannon, Kim

**Gannon, Kim**
*See* Gannon, James Kimball

**Ganpat**
*See* Gompertz, Martin Louis Alan

**Gans, Bird**
*See* Stein, Bird

**Gans, Italian Joe**
*See* Camerlengo, Anthony

**Gans, Joe**
*See* Gaines, Joseph

**Gans, Jude**
*See* Gans, Robert Edward

**Gans, Robert Edward** 20th c.
[OBW]
*American baseball player*
* Gans, Jude

**Gant, Cecil** 1913-1951 [BWW]
*American singer*
* Carr, Gunter Lee
* [The] GI Sing-Sation

**Gant, Chuck**
*See* Galub, Jack

**Gant, Jonathan**
*See* Adams, Clifton

**Gantenbein, Joseph Steven [Joe]**
1916- [BE]
*American baseball player*
* Gantenbein, Sep

**Gantenbein, Sep**
*See* Gantenbein, Joseph Steven
[Joe]

**Gantner, Neilma** 1922- [AW, WD]
*Australian author*
* Sidney, Neilma

**Gantry, Susan Nadler** 1947- [CA]
*American author*
* Nadler, Susan

**Gantzer, Colleen** 20th c. [CA]
*Author*
* Dave, Shyam [joint pseudonym
 with Hugh Gantzer]

**Gantzer, Hugh** 1931- [CA]
*Indian author*
* Dave, Shyam [joint pseudonym
 with Colleen Gantzer]
* Kale, Arvind and Shanta

**Ganzel, Babe**
*See* Ganzel, Foster Pirie

**Ganzel, Foster Pirie** 1901- [BE]
*American baseball player*
* Ganzel, Babe

[A] Gaol Chaplain
See Neale, Erskine

Gaon Elijah of Wilna
See Wilna, Elijah [or Elias]

Gaona y Jimenez, Rodolfo
1866-1975 [GS]
Mexican bullfighter
* [El] Califa de Leon [The Caliph of Leon]
* [El] Indio Grande [The Great Indian]
* [El] Petronio de los Toreros [The Petronio of the Bullfighters]

Gaonita [Little Gaona]
See Ramirez, Jose

[The] Gap
See Petrilli, Dominick

GaPersono, Stran
See Ackerman, Forrest J[ames]

Gar
See Garczynski, J.

Garabedian, Garabed Hagop Robutlay 1909- [CA]
American attorney and author
* Garry, Charles R.

Garate Echenique, Enrique
1870-1929 [GS]
Peruvian bullfighter
* Limeno [From Lima]

Garate y Hernandez, Jose
1895-1921 [GS]
Spanish bullfighter
* Limeno [From Lima]

Garavani, Valentino 1932- [IPA]
Italian fashion designer
* Valentino

Garazzi, Peyo
See Etcheverry, Pierre

Garbach, Michael Nathaniel 1916-
[BE]
American baseball player
* Garbark, Michael Nathaniel [Mike]

Garbach, Robert Michael 1909-
[BE]
American baseball player
* Garbark, Robert Michael

Garbark, Michael Nathaniel [Mike]
See Garbach, Michael Nathaniel

Garbark, Robert Michael
See Garbach, Robert Michael

Garber, Jan 1897-
American bandleader
* [The] Idol of the Airlanes

Garbo, Greta
See Gustafsson, Greta Lovisa

Garbutt, John L. 20th c. [MBF]
British author
* Allen, John
* Brearley, John
* Cameron, Clifford
* Forsey, Peter Q.
* Templar, John

Garcia, Alfonso Rafael 1953-
[SMG, WWB]
American baseball player
* Garcia, Kiko

Garcia, Andres 1901-1954 [SC]
Argentinian actor
* Roldan, Enrique

Garcia, Antonio 20th c. [GS]
Spanish bullfighter
* Utrerito [Little Fellow from Utrera]

Garcia, Arturo 1908-1973 [FC]
Mexican actor
* De Cordova, Arturo

Garcia, Cannibal
See Garcia, Frankie

Garcia, Chico
See Garcia, Vinicio Uzcanga

Garcia, Chucho 20th c. [RBE]
Mexican boxer
* Garcia, Jessie

Garcia, E.
See Garcia Sanchez, Jesus

Garcia, Edward Miguel 1923-
[BE, BTB]
American baseball player
* [The] Big Bear
* Garcia, Mike

Garcia, Francisco 1876- ? [GS]
Spanish bullfighter
* Pedrucho [Big Pedro]

Garcia, Frank 1927- [BS]
American magician
* [The] Man with the Million Dollar Hands

Garcia, Frankie 20th c. [RO2]
American musician
* Garcia, Cannibal

Garcia, Jerry 1943-
American musician
* Trips, Captain

Garcia, Jessie
See Garcia, Chucho

Garcia, Julio 1900- [GS]
Spanish bullfighter
* Palmeno [Man from Palma Del Rio]

Garcia, Kiko
See Garcia, Alfonso Rafael

Garcia, King
See Garcia, Louis K.

Garcia, Louis K. 1905- [WWJ]
Puerto Rican-born jazz musician
* Garcia, King

Garcia, Manuel 1938- [GS]
Spanish bullfighter
* Palmeno [Man from Palma Del Rio]

Garcia, Mike
See Garcia, Edward Miguel

Garcia, Nellie
See Garcia, Nelson Jose

Garcia, Nelson Jose 1950- [SMG]
Venezuelan-born baseball player
* Garcia, Nellie

Garcia, Peter
See Garcia, Prudencio

Garcia, Prudencio 20th c. [BBH]
Spanish-born soccer player and official
* Garcia, Peter

Garcia, Vinicio Uzcanga 1924-
[BE]
Mexican-born baseball player
* Garcia, Chico

Garcia De La Flor, Angel
1872-1913 [GS]
Spanish bullfighter
* Padilla [Small Oven]

Garcia de Paredes, Diego
1466-1530 [DNNF]
Spanish army officer
* [The] Spanish Bayard

Garcia Jimenez, Juan 1934- [GS]
Spanish bullfighter
* Mondeno [The Clean One]

Garcia-Junceda i Supervia, Joan
1881-1948 [WEC]
Spanish cartoonist
* Junceda

Garcia Lopez, Ricardo 20th c.
[WECO]
Spanish cartoonist
* K-Hito

Garcia Reverte, Manuel 1882-1924
[GS]
Spanish bullfighter
* Revertito [Little Reverte]

Garcia Rodriguez, Jose 1891-1964
[GS]
Spanish bullfighter
* Alcalareno [Man from Alcala]

Garcia Sanchez, Jesus 1945-
[IAW]
Spanish author and editor
* Garcia, E.
* Pascual

Garcia y Diaz, Agustin 1886-1920
[GS]
Spanish bullfighter
* Malla

Garcia y Lopez, Manuel
1896-1924 [GS]
Spanish bullfighter
* Maera

Garcia y Rodriguez, Jose
1875-1947 [GS]
Spanish bullfighter
* [El] Algabeno [The Man from La Algaba]

Garcia y Sarmiento, Felix Ruben
1867-1916 [EWL, TC, TCL]
Nicaraguan poet and author
* Dario, Ruben

Garcilaso de la Vega 1503-1536
[DNNF, RH, SN]
Spanish poet
* [The] Petrarch of Spain
* [The] Prince of Castilian Poets
* [The] Prince of Spanish Poetry
* [The] Spanish Petrarch

Garcilaso de la Vega 1539?-1616
[RH]
Peruvian historian
* [The] Inca

Garczynski, J. [FFF, PA]
American writer
* Gar

Gard, Gardy
See Gard, Trevor

Gard, Janice
See Latham, Jean Lee

Gard, Joyce 1911- [CA]
British author
* Reeves, Joyce

Gard, Trevor 1957- [DC]
British cricketer
* Gard, Gardy

Gardel, Carlos
See Gardes, Charles Romuald

Gardella, Daniel Louis [Danny]
1920- [PB]
American baseball player
* Gardella, Tarzan

Gardella, Tarzan
See Gardella, Daniel Louis [Danny]

Gardella, Tess ?-1950 [CED]
American vaudevillian
* Aunt Jemima

Garden, Bruce
See Mackay, James [Alexander]

Garden, John
See Fletcher, Harry Lutf Verne

Gardener, Henry
See Evans, E. Everett

Gardener, Hilde
See Schaefer, Hildegard

Gardenia, Vincent
See Scognamiglio, Vincenzio

Gardes, Charles Romuald
1890?-1935 [FIR, SC]
French-born singer and actor
* Gardel, Carlos
* [El] Mago [The Magician]
* [El] Morocho del Abasto [The Brown-Haired Man from the Market]
* [El] Zorzal Crillo [The Native Thrush]

Gardiner, A. G.
See Gardiner, Alfred George

Gardiner, Alfred George
1865-1946 [LAO, LC]
British journalist
* Alpha of the Plough
* Gardiner, A. G.

Gardiner, Bert
See Gardiner, Wilbert

Gardiner, Clarke
See Adams, William Edward

Gardiner, Dorothea Frances 20th c. [WW]
Author
* Frank, Theodore

Gardiner, James H. [PA]
Author
* Cassini

Gardiner, Toni 20th c.
British-born Jordanian princess
* Muna el Hussein [Desire of Hussein]

Gardiner, Wilbert 1913- [CEI]
Canadian-born hockey player
* Gardiner, Bert

Gardini, Mrs. [FFF]
Entertainer
* Gerster, Etelka

Gardner, Adam
See Gelbtrunk, Adam

**Gardner, Andrew Lee** 1917-　[IBW]
*American jazz musician*
* Gardner, Goon

**Gardner, Anne**
*See* Shultz, Gladys Denny

**Gardner, Ava**
*See* Johnson, Lucy

**Gardner, Calvin Pearly** 1924-
[FHE]
*Canadian-born hockey player*
* Gardner, Ginger

**Gardner, Chappy**
*See* Gardner, Eustace

**Gardner, Dave**
*See* Weingarten, David

**Gardner, E. D.** 20th c.　[WGT]
*Author*
* Schire

**Gardner, Ed**
*See* Poggenburg, Edward Francis

**Gardner, Erle Stanley** 1889-1970
[CA, CC, EMD]
*American author*
* Corning, Kyle
* Fair, A. A.
* Green, Charles M.
* Kendrake, Carleton
* Kenny, Charles J.
* Parr, Robert
* Tillray, Les

**Gardner, Eustace** 20th c.　[IBW]
*American journalist*
* Gardner, Chappy

**Gardner, Floyd** 1895-1977
[IBW, MK]
*American baseball player*
* Gardner, Jelly

**Gardner, Francis Henry** 1903-1957
[WWJ]
*American jazz musician*
* Gardner, Jack
* Gardner, Jumbo Jack

**Gardner, Frank** 20th c.　[BBH]
*American wrestling coach*
* Gardner, Sprig

**Gardner, Franklin W.** 1859-1914
[BE]
*American baseball player*
* Gardner, Gid

**Gardner, Gerald Brosseau** 1884-
[SFL]
*Author*
* Scrire. O. T. O. 4-7

**Gardner, Gid**
*See* Gardner, Franklin W.

**Gardner, Ginger**
*See* Gardner, Calvin Pearly

**Gardner, Goon**
*See* Gardner, Andrew Lee

**Gardner, Jack**
*See* Gardner, Francis Henry

**Gardner, Jeffrey**
*See* Fox, Gardner Francis

**Gardner, Jelly**
*See* Gardner, Floyd

**Gardner, Jim**
*See* Goldman, Jim

**Gardner, Julian** 1870-1946　[BEW]
*British-born actor*
* Royce, Julian

**Gardner, Jumbo Jack**
*See* Gardner, Francis Henry

**Gardner, Lawrence**
*See* Brannon, William T.

**Gardner, Maurice** 1909-　[ASC]
*American composer, conductor, arranger*
* Norman, Robert
* Pollock, Martin
* Tolmage, Gerald

**Gardner, Nancy Bruff** 1909?-
[CA, WD]
*American author and poet*
* Bruff, Nancy

**Gardner, Noel**
*See* Kuttner, Henry

**Gardner, Pardner**
*See* Gardner, Robert Gene

**Gardner, Peter** 1921-　[ART]
*British painter*
* P. G.

**Gardner, Richard [or Dic]**
*See* Orth, Richard

**Gardner, Richard Frank** 1944-
[BE]
*American baseball player*
* Gardner, Rob

**Gardner, Rob**
*See* Gardner, Richard Frank

**Gardner, Robert Gene** 1923-
[CWG]
*American disc jockey*
* Gardner, Pardner

**Gardner, Samuel Jackson**　[FFF]
*American editor*
* Decius

**Gardner, Shotgun**
*See* Gardner, William Frederick

**Gardner, Sprig**
*See* Gardner, Frank

**Gardner, William Frederick** 1927-
[BE]
*American baseball player*
* Gardner, Shotgun

**Gardner, William Henry** 1865- ?
[ALY]
*American author*
* Aiken, Henry

**Gardner-Ballinger, Bruce**
1905-1970　[THR]
*British actor and singer*
* Carfax, Bruce

**Gardons, S. S.**
*See* Snodgrass, William DeWitt

**Gardosh, Kariel** 1921-　[WEC]
*Israeli cartoonist*
* Dosh

**Garelick, May** 1910-　[CA]
*Russian-born American author and editor*
* Clark, Garel [joint pseudonym with Ethel McCullough Scott]

**Garfield, Brian [Francis] Wynne**
1939-　[CA, WD, WWS]
*American author*
* Garland, Bennett

**Garfield, Brian [Francis] Wynne**
(Continued)
* Hawk, Alex
* O'Brian, Frank
* Ward, Jonas
* Wynne, Brian
* Wynne, Frank

**[The] Garfield Gunner**
*See* Pilleteri, Tony

**Garfield, James Abram** 1831-1881
[DEP, FAP]
*American president*
* [The] Canal Boy
* [The] Martyr President
* [The] Preacher President
* [The] Teacher President

**Garfield, John**
*See* Garfinkle, Julius

**Garfield, Jules**
*See* Garfinkle, Julius

**Garfinkel, Bernard** 1929-　[CA]
*American author*
* Allen, Robert
* Elliott, Robert
* Martin, Janet

**Garfinkel, Dutch**
*See* Garfinkel, Jack

**Garfinkel, Jack** 1920-　[EJS]
*American basketball player*
* Garfinkel, Dutch

**Garfinkle, Julius** 1913-1952
[BDF, FC, OCF]
*American actor*
* Garfield, John
* Garfield, Jules

**Garforth, Glenn** 1943-　[RO2]
*British musician*
* Dale, Glen

**Garfunkel, Art** 1942-　[RO1]
*American singer and songwriter*
* Tom

**Garfunkel, Sid** 1901?-1973　[PMJ]
*Singer*
* Garry [or Gary], Sid

**Gari, Ralph**
*See* Garofalo, Ralph

**Garibaldi, Giuseppe** 1807-1882
[FFF, DNNF, DNNS]
*Italian statesman*
* [Il] Capitano del Popolo
* [The] Hero of Modern Italy
* [The] Liberator of Italy
* [The] People's Captain
* [The] Warrior of Freedom

**Garibaldi, Giuseppe** 1879-1950
[WBD]
*Australian-born soldier*
* Garibaldi, Peppino

**Garibaldi, Peppino**
*See* Garibaldi, Giuseppe

**Garis, Howard Roger** 1873-1962
[CA, ESF, WGT]
*American author and journalist*
* Appleton, Victor [house pseudonym] [Stratemeyer Syndicate]
* Davidson, Marion

**Garko, Gianni** 20th c.　[WF]
*Italian actor*
* Garko, John

**Garko, John**
*See* Garko, Gianni

**Garland, A. P.** 20th c.　[WWL]
*British author and journalist*
* Chantecler

**Garland, Bennett**
*See* Garfield, Brian [Francis] Wynne

**Garland, Beverly**
*See* Fessenden, Beverly

**Garland, David John** 1864- ?
[LAO]
*Irish-born clergyman and writer*
* Mede, Joseph

**Garland, Edward B.** 1895-
[EJ, WWJ]
*American jazz musician*
* Garland, Montudie

**Garland, George**
*See* Roark, Garland

**Garland, [Mary] Isabel** 1903-
[WW]
*Author*
* Lord, Garland [joint pseudonym with Mindret Lord]

**Garland, John**
*See* Lee, Alice Louise

**Garland, Judy**
*See* Gumm, Frances

**Garland, Mary Magdalene**
1880-1960　[ECM, FCW]
*American country-western performer*
* Jackson, Aunt Mollie

**Garland, Montudie**
*See* Garland, Edward B.

**Garland, Red**
*See* Garland, William M.

**Garland, William M.** 1923-　[EJ]
*American jazz musician*
* Garland, Red

**Garlic, Parson**
*See* Tucker, Josiah [or Joseph?]

**Garlington, John** 1946-　[SMG]
*American football player*
* Garlington, Junior

**Garlington, Junior**
*See* Garlington, John

**Garlits, Big Daddy**
*See* Garlits, Donald Glenn

**Garlits, Donald Glenn** 20th c.
[EAR]
*Auto racer*
* Garlits, Big Daddy
* Garlits, Swamp Rat

**Garlits, Swamp Rat**
*See* Garlits, Donald Glenn

**Garlow, Bon Ton**
*See* Garlow, Clarence Joseph

**Garlow, Clarence Joseph** 1911-
[BWW]
*American singer*
* Garlow, Bon Ton
* Parran

**Garman, Douglas Mavin** 20th c.
[CA]
*Author*
* Mavin, John [joint pseudonym with (John) Edgell Rickword]

**Garman, Evelyn Daphne** 1912-
[ART]
*British sculptor*
* E. D. G.

**Garne, Gaston?**
See Senarens, Luis Philip

**Garner, Big Bird**
See Garner, Joel

**Garner, Cactus Jack**
See Garner, John Nance

**Garner, E. M.**
See Lee-Hankey, Edith Mary

**Garner, Gary** 20th c. [GW]
*American rodeo performer*
* Garner, Mad Dog

**Garner, Graham**
See Rowland, D[onald] S[ydney]

**Garner, Hammer**
See Garner, Henry

**Garner, Henry** 20th c. [RO2]
*American musician*
* Garner, Hammer

**Garner, Hugh** 1913- [CA]
*Canadian author*
* Warwick, Jarvis

**Garner, James**
See Baumgarner, James

**Garner, Joel** 1952- [DC]
*West Indian cricketer*
* Garner, Big Bird

**Garner, John Nance** 1868?-1967
*American vice president*
* Garner, Cactus Jack

**Garner, Katherine Minta** 1882- ?
[WWL]
*British playwright*
* Touchwood

**Garner, Mad Dog**
See Garner, Gary

**Garner, Roberta** 1943- [CA]
*American sociologist and author*
* Ash, Roberta

**Garner, Rolf**
See Berry, Bryan

**Garnet, G.**
See Ashkenazy, Irwin

**Garnett, David** 1891?-
[CA, TC, WD]
*British author and publisher*
* Burke, Leda

**Garnett, Edward William** 20th c.
[LC]
*Playwright*
* Byrne, James

**Garnett, [Captain] Mayn Clew**
See Hains, Thornton Jenkins

**Garnett, Roger**
See Morland, Nigel

**Garnett, Tay**
See Garnett, William Taylor

**Garnett, William Taylor** 1905-
[FD]
*American director*
* Garnett, Tay

**Garney, Faith**
See Whitney, Mrs. A. T.

**Garnier, Francis**
See Garnier, Marie Joseph
Francois

**Garnier, Jean Joseph** 1816- ? [PA]
*Author*
* Jules

**Garnier, Marie Joseph Francois**
1839-1873 [WBD]
*French explorer*
* Garnier, Francis

**Garnier, Pierre**
See Maurras,
Charles-Marie-Photius

**Garnier, Robert** 1534-1590
[DEP, FFF, SN]
*French playwright*
* [The] Father of French Tragedy

**Garofalo, Benvenuto da**
See Tisi [or Tisio], Benvenuto

**Garofalo, Ralph** 1927- [EJ]
*American jazz musician*
* Gari, Ralph

**Garofalo, Reebee**
See Garofalo, Robert L.

**Garofalo, Robert L.** 1944- [CA]
*American author*
* Garofalo, Reebee

**Garonva, Camlan**
See Williams, Rowland

**Garr, Ralph Allen** 1945-
[PB, SMG]
*American baseball player*
* Road Runner

**Garrard, Christopher**
See Milton, John R.

**Garrard, Gene**
See Garrard, Jeanne Sue

**Garrard, Jackie**
See Naylor, Jerry

**Garrard, Jeanne Sue** 20th c. [CA]
*American author*
* Garrard, Gene

**Garrard, Peter John** 1929- [ART]
*British painter*
* P. J. G.

**Garratt, Alfred Charles** 1896-
[AW]
*British-born author*
* Garratt, Teddie

**Garratt, J. G.**
See Garratt, John Geoffrey

**Garratt, John Geoffrey** 1914-
[ART]
*British artist*
* Garratt, J. G.

**Garratt, Teddie**
See Garratt, Alfred Charles

**Garret, Edward**
See Edgerton, Sarah S. G.

**Garret, Mac**
See Goldstein, Max

**Garret, Maxwell Robert**
See Goldstein, Max

**Garretson, J. E.** [PA]
*Author*
* Darby, John

**Garrett, A. C.**
See Garrett, Albert Charles

**Garrett, Albert Charles** 1915-
[ART]
*British painter and engraver*
* Garrett, A. C.

**Garrett, Clara Maud** 1880?- ?
[CW]
*Jamaican author and poet*
* C. M. G.

**Garrett, Clarence Raymond** 1891-
[BE]
*American baseball player*
* Garrett, Laz

**Garrett, Dudley** 1924- [CEI]
*Canadian-born hockey player*
* Garrett, Red

**Garrett, Edward**
See Mayo, Isabella Fyvie

**Garrett, Edward Peter** 1878-1954
[TC, WBD]
*American journalist, economist,
publicist*
* Garrett, Garet

**Garrett, Eileen J[eanette]**
1893-1970 [CAP]
*Irish-born parapsychologist and
author*
* Lyttle, Jean

**Garrett, Garet**
See Garrett, Edward Peter

**Garrett, Irving** 20th c. [IBW]
*Yoruban religious leader*
* Ogunseye, Obalumi

**Garrett, Laz**
See Garrett, Clarence Raymond

**Garrett, Myron H.**
See August, Garry J.

**Garrett, Pauline** 1860-1919 [SC]
*American actress and opera singer*
* Kimball, Pauline

**Garrett, [Gordon] Randall [Philip
David]** 1927- [ESF, SF, WGT]
*American author*
* Aghill, Gordon [joint pseudonym
with Robert Silverberg]
* Barretton, Grandall
* Blade, Alexander [joint
pseudonym with Robert
Silverberg] [house pseudonym,
Ziff-Davis]
* Bupp, Walter
* Burke, Ralph [joint pseudonym
with Robert Silverberg]
* Gordon, David
* Greer, Richard [joint pseudonym
with Robert Silverberg] [house
pseudonym, Ziff-Davis]
* Jorgensen, Ivar [joint pseudonym
with Robert Silverberg] [house
pseudonym, Ziff-Davis]
* Langart, Darrel T.
* Mitchell, Clyde [joint pseudonym
with Robert Silverberg] [house
pseudonym, Ziff-Davis]
* Phillips, Mark [joint pseudonym
with Laurence M(ark) Janifer]
* Randall, Robert [joint pseudonym
with Robert Silverberg]
* Spencer, Leonard G. [joint
pseudonym with Robert
Silverberg] [house pseudonym,
Ziff-Davis]

**Garrett, [Gordon] Randall [Philip
David]** (Continued)
* Tenneshaw, S. M. [joint
pseudonym with Robert
Silverberg] [house pseudonym,
Ziff-Davis]
* Vance, Gerald [joint pseudonym
with Robert Silverberg] [house
pseudonym, Ziff-Davis]

**Garrett, Red**
See Garrett, Dudley

**Garrett, Ruth**
See Mayo, Isabella Fyvie

**Garrett, Sam** 20th c. [WF]
*Actor*
* West, Adam

**Garrett, Truman**
See Judd, Margaret Haddican

**Garrick, David** 1716-1779
[DEP, DNNF, RH]
*British actor*
* [The] British Roscius
* [The] English Roscius
* Roscius Britannicus
* [The] Roscius of England
* [The] Whitfield of the Stage

**Garrick, John**
See Doudy, Reginald

**Garrigan, John Frederic** 1920-
[CA]
*American poet*
* Bennett, John [Frederic]

**Garrincha**
See Dos Santos, Manoel Francisco

**Garriott, Rabbit**
See Garriott, Virgil Cecil

**Garriott, Virgil Cecil** 1916- [BE]
*American baseball player*
* Garriott, Rabbit

**Garrish, Harold J.** ?-1956 [MBF]
*British author and editor*
* Belbin, Harry
* Everard, Walter
* Fordwych, Jack
* Fordwych, John Edmund
* Foster, Grant
* Gerrish, George
* Morrell, Wallace

**Garrison, Anet**
See Woodward, Tena Garrison

**Garrison, Arv**
See Garrison, Arvin Charles

**Garrison, Arvin Charles** 1922-1960
[EJ]
*American jazz musician*
* Garrison, Arv

**Garrison, Charles M.** 20th c.
[SFL, WGT]
*Author*
* MacDaniel, Charles

**Garrison, Edward** 1868-1930?
[AS, BBH]
*American jockey*
* Garrison, Snapper
* Garrison, Snapper Jack

**Garrison, [Robert] Ford** 1915- [BE]
*American baseball player*
* Garrison, Rocky
* Garrison, Snapper

**Garrison, Frederick**
See Sinclair, Upton [Beall]

**Garrison, Gary L.** 1944-
[FB, SMG]
*American football player*
* Garrison, Ghost

**Garrison, Ghost**
*See* Garrison, Gary L.

**Garrison, Joan**
*See* Neubauer, William Arthur

**Garrison, Maude**
*See* Neal, Jennie

**Garrison, Rocky**
*See* Garrison, [Robert] Ford

**Garrison, Snapper**
*See* Garrison, [Robert] Ford

**Garrison, Snapper**
*See* Garrison, Edward

**Garrison, Snapper Jack**
*See* Garrison, Edward

**Garrison, Webb B[lack]** 1919-   [CA]
*American clergyman and author*
* Webster, Gary

**Garrity**
*See* Gerrity, David James

**Garrity, Francis Joseph** 1908-1962
[BE]
*American baseball player*
* Garrity, Hank

**Garrity, Hank**
*See* Garrity, Francis Joseph

**Garrity, Joan Theresa** 1940-
[B10, CA]
*American author and publicist*
* Garrity, Terry
* J.

**Garrity, Terry**
*See* Garrity, Joan Theresa

**Garrod, V. N.**
*See* Garrod, Violet Nellie

**Garrod, Violet Nellie** 1898-   [ART]
*British artist*
* Garrod, V. N.
* V. N. G.

**Garron, Robert A.**
*See* Wandrei, Howard Elmer

**Garrow**
*See* Trollope, Mrs. Thomas
Adolphus

**Garroway, Henry Stephenson**
1871-1956   [BEW, FC]
*British actor*
* Stephenson, Henry

**Garrulous, George**
*See* Arnold, George

**Garry, Charles R.**
*See* Garabedian, Garabed Hagop
Robutlay

**Garry [or Gary], Sid**
*See* Garfunkel, Sid

**Gars, Henry**
*See* Emshwiller, Ed[mund
Alexander]

**Garskof, Michele Hoffnung**
*See* Hoffnung, Michele

**Garson, Clee** [house pseudonym,
Ziff-Davis]
*See* Fairman, Paul W.

**Garson, Clee** [house pseudonym,
Ziff-Davis]
*See* O'Brien, David Wright

**Garson, Vaseleos**
*See* Garson, William J.

**Garson, William J.**   [SFL]
*Author*
* Garson, Vaseleos

**Garstang, Basil**
*See* Brereton, John Le Gay

**Garstang, Jack**
*See* Garstang, James Gordon

**Garstang, James Gordon** 1927-
[CA]
*British-born author*
* Garstang, Jack

**Garstin, A.** 20th c.   [MBF]
*British author*
* Reid, Desmond [house
pseudonym]

**Garstin, Daisy** 1874-1954   [SC]
*British-born actress*
* Belmore, Daisy

**Garten, H. F.**
*See* Koenigsgarten, Hugo F.

**Garth, Cecil**
*See* Carlton, Grace [Greenwood]

**Garth, Jackson**
*See* Ellis, William Donohue

**Garth, Samuel** 1661-1719   [SN]
*British poet*
* [The] Kit-Kat Poet

**Garth, Will** [house pseudonym]
*See* Binder, Otto O[scar]

**Garth, Will** [house pseudonym]
*See* Hamilton, Edmond [Moore]

**Garth, Will** [house pseudonym]
*See* Kuttner, Henry

**Garth, Will** [house pseudonym]
*See* Weisinger, Mort[imer]

**Garth, Will** [house pseudonym]
*See* Wellman, Manly Wade

**Garthwaite, Malaby**
*See* Dent, Anthony Austen

**Gartmann, Heinz** 1917-1960
[WGT]
*German author*
* Wehr, Werner

**Garton, Durham Keith** 20th c.
[SFP]
*Author*
* Keys, Durham

**Gartside, Thomas Henry**
1837-1910   [BEW]
*Actor and producer*
* Neville, [Thomas] Henry

**Garve, Andrew**
*See* Winterton, Paul

**Garvey, A.** 20th c.   [SMG]
*American football player*
* Garvey, Hec

**Garvey, Hec**
*See* Garvey, A.

**Garvin, Amelia Warnock** 1878- ?
[WWL]
*Canadian author*
* Hale, Katherine

**Garvin, J. L.**
*See* Garvin, James Louis

**Garvin, James Louis** 1868-1947
[LC]
*British journalist and author*
* Garvin, J. L.

**Garvin, Jerry**
*See* Garvin, Theodore Jared

**Garvin, Ned**
*See* Garvin, Virgil Lee

**Garvin, Theodore Jared** 1955-
[ALR]
*American baseball player*
* Garvin, Jerry

**Garvin, Virgil Lee** 1874-1908
[AS, BE]
*American baseball player*
* Garvin, Ned

**Garwood, Humble**
*See* Garwood, Rod

**Garwood, Rod** 20th c.   [RO2]
*British musician*
* Garwood, Humble

**Gary, Romain**
*See* Kacew, Romain

**Garza Arrambide, Lorenzo** 1908-
[GS]
*Mexican bullfighter*
* Lorenzo, El Magnifico [Lorenzo
the Magnificent]

**[The] Gas House Tartar**
*See* Samperi, Anthony

**Gasca, Louis Angel** 1940-   [EJ7]
*American jazz musician*
* Gasca, Luis

**Gasca, Luis**
*See* Gasca, Louis Angel

**Gascar, Pierre**
*See* Fournier, Pierre

**Gascard, Gilbert** 1931-   [WECO]
*Belgian cartoonist*
* Tibet

**Gascoigne, [Sir] Bernard**
*See* Guasconi, Bernardo [or
Bernardino]

**Gascoigne, Eric**
*See* Mowbray, W. J.

**Gascoigne, Mrs. C. L.** 1813- ?   [PA]
*Author*
* Smith, C. L.

**[The] Gascon**
*See* Miller, Frederick [Walter
Gascoyne]

**[A] Gascon Moses**
*See* De Salluste [or Salustius?],
Guillaume

**Gash, Jonathan**
*See* Grant, John

**Gash, Sondra Lee** 1930-   [BEW]
*American actress and dancer*
* Lee, Sondra

**Gashbuck, Greno**
*See* Gernsback, Hugo

**[The] Gashed**
*See* Lorraine, Henry I [or Henri]
de

**Gaskell, Elizabeth Cleghorn**
1812-1865   [PA]
*Author*
* Stevenson

**Gaskell, Jane**
*See* Gaskell Denvil, Jane

**Gaskell Denvil, Jane** 1941-   [AW]
*British author*
* Gaskell, Jane

**Gasko, Gordon** 20th c.   [WGT]
*Author*
* Gordon, Nathaniel

**Gaskoin, Charles Jacinth Bellairs**
20th c.   [LAO]
*British historian and author*
* Merridew, Arthur

**Gaspard, Nelson Octave** 1870?- ?
[NOJ]
*American jazz musician*
* Gaspard, Oak

**Gaspard, Oak**
*See* Gaspard, Nelson Octave

**Gasparotti, Elizabeth Seifert** 1897-
[AW, CA]
*American author*
* Seifert, Elizabeth

**Gass, Sherlock Bronson** 1878- ?
[NAA]
*American educator and author*
* Dupree, Morrison

**Gassaway, Charles Cason [Charlie]**
1918-   [BE]
*American baseball player*
* Gassaway, Sheriff

**Gassaway, Frank**   [PA]
*Author*
* Dodd, Derrick

**Gassaway, Sheriff**
*See* Gassaway, Charles Cason
[Charlie]

**Gassion, Edith Giovanna**
1915-1963   [BEW, IPA]
*French singer*
* [The] Little Sparrow
* Piaf, Edith
* Sparrow, Kid

**Gassion, Jean de** 1609-1647   [SN]
*French army officer*
* [La] Guerre

**Gassner, Jeno Waldhorn** 1903-
[BEW]
*Hungarian-born playwright, critic,
producer*
* Gassner, John

**Gassner, Johann Joseph** 1727-1779
[RH]
*German clergyman*
* Thaumaturgus

**Gassner, John**
*See* Gassner, Jeno Waldhorn

**Gast, Kelly P.**
*See* Edmondson y Cotton, Jose
Mario Garry Ordonez

**Gast, Peter**
*See* Koeselitz, Heinrich

**Gastoldi, Ernesto** 20th c.   [SFP]
*Author*
* Berry, Julian

**Gaston, Cito**
See  Gaston, Clarence Edwin

**Gaston, Clarence Edwin** 1944-
[PB, SMG, WWB]
American baseball player
* Gaston, Cito

**Gaston, Maria**
See  Dudet, Alphonse

**Gaston Marin, Gheorghe**
See  Grossman, Gheorghe

**Gaston, Rab Roy**
See  Gaston, Robert

**Gaston, Robert** 20th c.   [OBW]
American baseball player
* Gaston, Rab Roy

**Gaston, William James [Bill]** 1927-
[WD]
British author
* Bannatyne, Jack

**Gaston III** 1331-1391
[DNNS, HN, RH]
Comte de Foix
* Phoebus

**Gastreich, Henry Carl** 1865-1937
[BE]
American baseball player
* Gastright, Henry Carl

**Gastright, Henry Carl**
See  Gastreich, Henry Carl

**Gatehouse, Frank** 1898-1953
[THR]
British actor
* Allenby, Frank

**Gately, George**
See  Gallagher, George Gately

**Gates, Bet-You-A-Million**
See  Gates, John Wayne

**Gates, Curtis** 20th c.   [PMJ]
Actor and singer
* Curtis, Ken

**Gates, Helen** ?-1950  [BE]
Playwright, author, poet
* Granville-Barker, Helen

**Gates, John Wayne** 1855-1911
[WBD]
American promoter, speculator,
gambler
* Gates, Bet-You-A-Million

**Gates, Michael**
See  Machuisdean, Hamish

**Gates, Mother**
See  Grigaitis, Walter

**Gates, Pearl Ann** 1957?-
German-born singer
* Gates, Pearl E.
* Harbour, Pearl

**Gates, Pearl E.**
See  Gates, Pearl Ann

**Gates, Pearson** 1888-1966  [BE]
American actress
* Gates, Ruth

**Gates, Ruth**
See  Gates, Pearson

**Gath**
See  Townsend, George Alfred

**Gathings, Ezekiel C.** 1904?-1979
American politician
* Gathings, Took

**Gathings, Took**
See  Gathings, Ezekiel C.

**Gatley, Alfred** 1816-1863   [HN]
British sculptor
* [The] Landseer of Sculpture

**Gatley, Dorothy Walton**
1902-1981   [BEW, F2, FC]
American actress
* Harding, Ann

**[El] Gato [The Cat]**
See  Coria Garcia, Raul

**Gato, J. A.**
See  Keller, John E[sten]

**Gato, Phil**
See  Alderisio, Felix Anthony

**Gattamelata, Erasmo** 1370?-1443
[WBD]
Italian mercenary soldier
* De Narni, Erasmo

**Gatterman, Eugen Ludwig** 1886-
[LAO]
German author and composer
* Corvin, Eugen Alban
* Renner, A. M.

**Gatti, Arthur Gerard** 1942-   [CA]
American author
* Gerard, Andrew
* Katz, Basho
* Lane, Charles

**Gatti, Bernardino** 1495?-1575
[WBD]
Italian painter
* [Il] Soiaro

**Gatting, Gat**
See  Gatting, Michael William

**Gatting, Michael William** 1957-
[DC]
British cricketer
* Gatting, Gat

**Gattoni, Paul Steven** 1924-   [BEW]
American actor
* Stevens, Paul

**Gatty, Mrs. Alfred** 19th c.   [PA]
Author
* Aunt Judy

**Gaudio, Jennie**
See  Wilkinson, Jennie Gaudio

**Gaudio, Tony**
See  Gaetano, Antonio G.

**Gaul, George**
See  Gall, George

**Gaulden, Ray** 1914-   [CA]
American author
* Ray, Wesley

**Gaule, Beatrice**
See  O'Neill, [Sister] Mary Agatha

**Gaulli, Giovanni Battista**
1639-1709   [WBD]
Italian painter
* [Il] Baciccio

**Gault, Henry** 1929-   [BX, RBE]
American boxer
* Gault, Pappy

**Gault, Mark**
See  Cournos, John

**Gault, Pappy**
See  Gault, Henry

**Gault, William Campbell** 1910-
[CA]
American author
* Duke, Will
* Scott, Roney

**Gaultier, Bon** [joint pseudonym with
(Sir) Theodore Martin]
See  Aytoun, William Edmonstoune

**Gaultier, Bon** [joint pseudonym with
William Edmonstoune Aytoun]
See  Martin, [Sir] Theodore

**Gaumata** 6th c. BC   [WBD]
Magian priest from Media
* [The] False Smerdis

**Gaume, Francois** 19th c.   [PA]
Author
* F. G.

**Gaunt, Bernice** 1909?-1975
[FC, PMJ, SC]
American singer and actress
* Ross, Shirley

**Gaunt, Jeffrey**
See  Rochester, George Ernest

**Gaunt, Michael**
See  Robertshaw, [James] Denis

**Gauntier, Gene**
See  Liggett, Genevieve Gauntier

**Gaus, Geo. J.**
See  Fritschel, Geo[rge] John

**[The] Gause Ghost**
See  Moore, Joe Gregg

**Gautama Buddha**
See  Siddhartha

**Gauthier, Fern**
See  Gauthier, Rene Fernand

**Gauthier, Jerry H.** 1933-   [CA]
American educator and author
* Gill, Jerry H.

**Gauthier, Rene Fernand** 1919-
[CEI]
Canadian-born hockey player
* Gauthier, Fern

**Gauthier-Villars, Henri** 1859-1931
[BBD, BEW, LC]
French music critic and playwright
* [L']Ouvreuse du Cirque
* Willy

**Gautier, Isadore M. B.** 1769-1824
[PA]
Author
* Du Var

**Gautier, Jean** 1892?-1975   [SW]
French-born actor
* Del Val, Jean

**Gautisolo, Miguel**
See  Moncho y Gilabert, Antonio

**Gautreau, Doc**
See  Gautreau, Walter Paul

**Gautreau, Walter Paul** 1904-1970
[BE]
American baseball player
* Gautreau, Doc

**Gautreaux, Pudge**
See  Gautreaux, Sid[ney Allen]

**Gautreaux, Sid[ney Allen]** 1912-
[BE]
American baseball player
* Gautreaux, Pudge

**Gautsch, Francoise Annette** 1931-
[BDF, FC, ITA]
French actress
* Arnoul, Francoise

**Gavarni**
See  Chevalier, Sulpice Guillaume

**Gaver, Claude H.** 1906-1974
[BEW, CA]
American drama editor and critic
* Gaver, Jack

**Gaver, Jack**
See  Gaver, Claude H.

**Gavilan, Kid**
See  Gonzalez, Gerardo

**Gavilan, Peak**
See  Pope, Henry

**Gavira**
See  Cano e Iriborne, Enrique

**Gavit, Daniel E.**   [PA]
Author
* Tivag

**Gavras, Konstantinos** 1933-
[FDG, IPA]
Greek director
* Costa-Gavras, Henri

**Gaw, Chippy**
See  Gaw, George Joseph

**Gaw, George Joseph** 1892-1968
[BE]
American baseball player
* Gaw, Chippy

**Gawain**
See  Newton, Henry Chance

**Gawaine, John**
See  Hamilton-Hill, Donald

**Gawkey, Lord**
See  Grenville, Richard Temple
[First Earl Temple]

**Gawsworth, John**
See  Armstrong, Terence Ian Fytton

**Gawsworth, John**
See  Bates, Herbert Ernest

**Gawthorne-Briggs, Hedley**
1907-1968   [THR]
British actor, producer, designer,
dancer
* Briggs, Hedley

**Gaxiola, Arturo Antonio**
1893-1963   [BEW, EMT, F2]
American actor and singer
* Gaxton, William

**Gaxton, William**
See  Gaxiola, Arturo Antonio

**Gay, Amelia**
See  Hogarth, Grace Weston

**Gay, Bernard** 1921-   [ART]
British painter and designer
* B. G.

**[The] Gay Blade**
See  McBean, Alvin O'Neal

**Gay, Caster Abney, Jr.** 1921-1959
[SC]
*American actor*
* Cass, Guy

**[The] Gay Castillion**
*See* Gomez, Vernon Louis

**[The] Gay Deceiver**
*See* Kissinger, Henry Alfred

**Gay, Delphine** 1804-1855
[DNNS, RH, WBD]
*French author and playwright*
* De Launay, [Vicomte] Charles
* [La] Muse de la Patrie [The
    Country's Muse]
* [The] Tenth Muse

**Gay, Francis**
*See* Gee, Herbert Leslie

**Gay, Getty**
*See* Bennett, Mrs. William

**Gay, Greer**
*See* Payne, Hazel Belle
[Saulisberry]

**Gay, J. Drew**
*See* Welch, Edgar L[uderne]

**Gay, John** 1688?-1732
[DEP, DNNF, DNNS]
*British poet and playwright*
* [The] Aesop of England
* [The] Orpheus of Highwaymen

**Gay, Joseph**
*See* De Breval, John Durant

**Gay, Lettie**
*See* Carson, Lettie Gay

**Gay, Maisie**
*See* Munro-Noble, Maisie

**Gay, Maria Frances Sophie**
1776-1852  [PA]
*Author*
* De Lavalette, Nichault

**Gay, Mrs. Jules**  [PA]
*Author*
* [Le] Comte d'I

**Gay, Noel**
*See* Armitage, Reginald Moxon

**Gay, Ramon**
*See* Gaytan, Ramon

**[The] Gay Reliever**
*See* Page, Joseph Francis [Joe]

**Gaye, Carol**
*See* Shann, Renee

**Gayle, Crystal**
*See* Webb, Brenda Gail

**Gayle, Harold** 1910-  [ESF]
*Canadian author*
* Gayle, Henry K.

**Gayle, Henry K.**
*See* Gayle, Harold

**Gayle, Newton** [joint pseudonym
with Maurice C. Guinness]
*See* De Munoz Marin, Muna Lee

**Gayle, Newton** [joint pseudonym
with Muna Lee De Munoz Marin]
*See* Guinness, Maurice C.

**Gaylor, Grace** ?-1955  [SC]
*American actress and singer*
* Lair, Grace

**Gaylord, Glance**
*See* Bradley, Warren S.

**Gaylord, Ron**
*See* Fredianelli, Renaldo

**Gaynes, George**
*See* Jongejans, George

**Gayno, Creole**
*See* Guesnon, George

**Gaynor, Gloria** 1949-  [RO2]
*American singer*
* [The] Queen of the Discotheques

**Gaynor, Janet**
*See* Gainor, Laura

**Gaynor, Mitzi**
*See* Von Gerber, Francesca Mitzi
Marlene

**Gayre, George Robert** 1907-  [CA]
*Irish-born author and editor*
* Gayre of Gayre and Nigg, Robert
* Gayre of Gayre, R.

**Gayre of Gayre and Nigg, Robert**
*See* Gayre, George Robert

**Gayre of Gayre, R.**
*See* Gayre, George Robert

**Gaytan, Ramon** 1917-1960  [SC]
*Mexican actor*
* Gay, Ramon

**Gayton, Edmund** 1609-1666  [FFF]
*British author*
* De Speciosa Villa

**Gayton, Mrs. Edmund** 17th c.  [PA]
*Author*
* Albert, Bessie

**Gazdanov, Gaito**
*See* Gazdanov, Georgii

**Gazdanov, Georgii** 1903-  [SFL]
*Author*
* Gazdanov, Gaito

**Gaze, Richard** 1917-
[AW, CA, CC]
*British author*
* Gale, John

**[The] Gazelle**
*See* Gravelle, Joseph Gerard Leo

**[La] Gazelle**
*See* Rudolph, Wilma Glodean
Ward

**Gazzara, Ben**
*See* Gazzara, Biago Anthony

**Gazzara, Biago Anthony** 1930-
[BDF, BEW, IPA]
*American actor*
* Gazzara, Ben

**Gdanski, Marek**
*See* Thee, Marek

**Geach, Christine** 1930-
[AW, CA, WD]
*British author*
* Dawson, Elizabeth
* Lowing, Anne
* Wilson, Christine

**Gearhart, Gary**
*See* Gearhart, Lloyd William

**Gearhart, Lloyd William** 1923-
[BE]
*American baseball player*
* Gearhart, Gary

**Gearin, Dennis John** 1897-1959
[BE]
*American baseball player*
* Gearin, Dinty

**Gearin, Dinty**
*See* Gearin, Dennis John

**Gearing-Thomas, G.**
*See* Norwood, Victor G[eorge]
C[harles]

**Gearon, John**  [CC]
*Author*
* Flagg, John

**Gears, Harold** 20th c.  [BBH]
*American softball player*
* Gears, Shifty

**Gears, Shifty**
*See* Gears, Harold

**Geary, Bud**
*See* Geary, S. Maine

**Geary, Eugene Francis Joseph**
1917-  [BE]
*American baseball player*
* Geary, Huck

**Geary, Huck**
*See* Geary, Eugene Francis Joseph

**Geary, Robert Norton [Bob]** 1891-
[BE]
*American baseball player*
* Geary, Speed

**Geary, S. Maine** 1899-1946  [SC]
*American actor*
* Geary, Bud

**Geary, Speed**
*See* Geary, Robert Norton [Bob]

**Gebardi, Vincent**
*See* De Mora, James Vincenzo

**Gebe**
*See* Blondeau, Georges

**Geber** 9th c.  [SN]
*Arab scholar*
* [The] Founder of Chemistry

**Gebhard** 1018-1057  [WBD]
*Pope*
* Victor II

**Gebhart, Charles Frederick**
1889?-1942  [OCF]
*American actor*
* Jones, Buck

**Gebhart, Fred J.** 20th c.  [SFL]
*Author*
* Wise, Robert A.

**[The] Gebir**
*See* Landor, Walter Savage

**Gebrian, Gabe**
*See* Gebrian, Peter

**Gebrian, Peter** 1923-  [BE]
*American baseball player*
* Gebrian, Gabe

**Gedda, Nicolai**
*See* Ustinov, Nicolai

**Geddes, Barbara** 1922-
[BEW, FC, ITA]
*American actress*
* Bel Geddes, Barbara

**Geddie, John** 1937-  [CA]
*American journalist*
* Shannon, M.

**Gedney, Alfred W.** 1849-1922  [BE]
*American baseball player*
* Gedney, Count

**Gedney, Count**
*See* Gedney, Alfred W.

**Gedzikova, Ivona** 1944-  [OP]
*Czech opera singer*
* Valentova, Ivona

**Gee**
*See* Crawford, George G.

**Gee Double You**
*See* Hinkley, G. W.

**Gee, Herbert Leslie** 1901-
[IAW, WWL]
*British author and journalist*
* Armicus
* Gay, Francis

**Gee, John Alexander** 1915-  [BE]
*American baseball player*
* Gee, Whiz

**Gee, Osman**
*See* Hincks, Cyril Malcolm

**Gee, Whiz**
*See* Gee, John Alexander

**Geen, Clifford** 1891-  [AW]
*British author*
* Berkley, Tom

**Geerlink, Will**
*See* Hofdorp, Pim [William]

**Geers, Edward F.** 1851?-1924  [AS]
*American harness racer*
* Geers, Pop

**Geers, Pop**
*See* Geers, Edward F.

**Geeves-Booth, James** 1933-  [TR]
*British actor*
* Booth, James

**Geffin, Aaron** 20th c.  [EJS]
*South African rugby player*
* [The] Boot
* Geffin, Okey
* [The] Rand Goal Mine

**Geffin, Okey**
*See* Geffin, Aaron

**Gehlen, Reinhard** 20th c.  [EE]
*German intelligence chief*
* [The] Doctor
* Number 30

**Gehman, Betsy Holland** 1932-
[CA]
*American author and editor*
* Klainikite, Anne

**Gehman, Richard Boyd** 1921-1972
[CA]
*American author*
* Christian, Frederick
* Scott, Martin

**Gehrig, Biscuit Pants**
*See* Gehrig, [Henry] Lou[is]

**Gehrig, Buster**
*See* Gehrig, [Henry] Lou[is]

**Gehrig, Columbia Lou**
*See* Gehrig, [Henry] Lou[is]

**Gehrig, Larrupin' Lou**
*See* Gehrig, [Henry] Lou[is]

**Gehrig, Little Joe**
*See* Gehrig, [Henry] Lou[is]

**Gehrig, [Henry] Lou[is]** 1903-1941
[BAB, BE, PB]
*American baseball player*
* Gehrig, Biscuit Pants
* Gehrig, Buster
* Gehrig, Columbia Lou
* Gehrig, Larrupin' Lou
* Gehrig, Little Joe
* [The] Iron Horse
* Lewis, Henry
* [The] Pride of the Yankees

**Gehringer, Charles Leonard** 1903-
[DGS]
*American baseball player*
* [The] Mechanical Man
* [The] Silent Man

**Gehrman, Dutch**
*See* Gehrman, Paul Arthur

**Gehrman, Paul Arthur** 1912-   [BE]
*American baseball player*
* Gehrman, Dutch

**Geibel, Adam** 1855- ?   [ALY]
*German-born composer and author*
* Linders, Carl
* Taylor, Walter G.

**Geier, Chester S.** 1921-
[ESF, WGT]
*American author and editor*
* Archette, Guy
* Blade, Alexander [house
   pseudonym, Ziff-Davis]
* Costello, P. F. [house pseudonym,
   Ziff-Davis]
* Kastel, Warren [house
   pseudonym, Ziff-Davis]
* Tenneshaw, S. M. [house
   pseudonym, Ziff-Davis]
* Vance, Gerald [house pseudonym,
   Ziff-Davis]
* Worth, Peter [house pseudonym,
   Ziff-Davis]

**Geier, Little Phil**
*See* Geier, Louis Phillip

**Geier, Louis Phillip** 1875-1967
[BE]
*American baseball player*
* Geier, Little Phil

**Geiger, Herman B.** 1907-   [OP]
*German-born producer, director,
actor*
* Geiger-Torel, Herman B.

**Geiger, Karin Hallberg** 1920-
[WFA]
*Swedish fashion designer*
* Katja of Sweden

**Geiger-Torel, Herman B.**
*See* Geiger, Herman B.

**Geiringer, Hilde** 1917-   [MS]
*Austrian opera singer*
* Gueden, Hilde

**Geis, Bernard** 20th c.   [CA, SAT]
*American author*
* Stevens, Peter [joint pseudonym
   with Darlene (Stern) Geis]

**Geis, Darlene [Stern]** 20th c.
[CA, SAT]
*American author and editor*
* Kelly, Ralph
* London, Jane
* Stevens, Peter [joint pseudonym
   with Bernard Geis]

**Geis, Richard E[rwin]** 1927-
[CA, SFL, SFP]
*American author*
* Colson, Frederick
* Jackson, Albina
* Kunzur, Sheela
* Owen, Robert N. [Bob]
* Radway, Ann
* Swann, Peggy
* Swenson, Peggy

**Geise, [Dr.] Otto** 1857- ?   [LAO]
*German author*
* Von Homberg, Otto

**Geisel, Theodor Seuss** 1904-
[ASC, B10, CA]
*American author and illustrator*
* Le Sieg, Theo
* Seuss, Dr.

**Geisenfeld, Benjamin** 1894-1959
[SC]
*American actor*
* Fields, Benny

**Geiser, Robert L[ee]** 1931-   [CA]
*American author and psychologist*
* Peters, Steven

**Geishuesler, Oswald** 1488-1552
[WBD]
*Swiss clergyman*
* Myconius [or Mykonius], Oswald

**Geisler, Horst** 20th c.   [RBE]
*Canadian boxer*
* Him

**Geisman, Ella** 1917-
[BDF, FC, ITA]
*American actress*
* Allyson, June

**Geistweit, Carole Christine** 1936-
[OP]
*American opera singer*
* Bogard, Carole Christine

**Gelasius II**
*See* Da Gaeta, Giovanni

**Gelaste**
*See* Poquelin, Jean Baptiste

**Gelber, Melo**
*See* Gelber, Sammy

**Gelber, Sammy** 20th c.   [EJS]
*American boxer*
* Gelber, Melo

**Gelberg, George** 1922-   [CA]
*American marketing executive,
photographer, author*
* Gilbert, George
* Jordan, Gil
* Stevens, Pam

**Gelbtrunk, Adam**
*Musician*
* Gardner, Adam

**[Der] Gelehrte [The Scholar]**
*See* Moritz

**Gelfman, Judith S[chlein]** 1937-
[CA]
*American author and television
script writer*
* Starr, Judy

**Gelhar, Audrey Pearl Alford** 20th
c.   [IAW]
*British author*
* Ellis, Audrey

**Gelien, Art[hur Andrew]** 1931-
[FC, IPA]
*American actor*
* Hunter, Tab

**Gell, Frank**
*See* Kowet, Don

**Gellee [or Gelee], Claude**
1600-1682   [FF, WBD]
*French painter and engraver*
* Lorrain [or Lorraine], Claude

**Gellers, Irving** 1907-   [ASC]
*American musician*
* Carroll, Irv

**Gellert**
*See* Walsh, William W.

**Gellert, Lew**
*See* Wellen, Edward [Paul]

**Gellie, Mrs. William**   [PA]
*Author*
* E. M. B.

**Gellinek, Janis Little**
*See* Solomon, Janis Little

**Gellis, Roberta L[eah Jacobs]**
1927-   [CA]
*American author and editor*
* Jacobs, Leah

**Gellman, Jacob** 1913-
[BEW, EMT, TR]
*American actor*
* Gilford, Jack

**[The] Gem of Normandy**
*See* Emma

**Gemel**
*See* Manuel, George

**Gemmer, Caroline M.**   [PA]
*Author*
* Fay, Gerda

**Genaro, Frankie**
*See* DiGennara, Frank

**Gendre, Louis** 1919?-
[BEW, FC, IPA]
*French actor*
* Jourdan, Louis

**Gendron, Jean Guy** 1934-
[CEI, FHE, HK]
*Canadian-born hockey player*
* Gendron, Smitty

**Gendron, Smitty**
*See* Gendron, Jean Guy

**Gene the Machine**
*See* Littler, [Eu]gene [Alex]

**[The] General**
*See* Lloyd, Joe

**[Le] General Entrepreneur**
*See* Bonaparte, Napoleon

**General Idea, Miss**
*See* Morris, Michael

**General Ike**
*See* Eisenhower, David Dwight

**General Observer**
*See* Fiske, Nathan

**[The] General Undertaker**
*See* Bonaparte, Napoleon

**General X**
*See* Hoar, Roger Sherman

**Genero, Joseph** 20th c.   [PHM]
*American underworld figure*
* Genero, Peppy

**Genero, Peppy**
*See* Genero, Joseph

**Generoso, Marc-Antoine**
*See* Schweizer, Marc

**Genesee**
*See* Crawford, E. M.

**Genesee**
*See* Gilmore, J. H.

**Genesius, Josephus** 10th c.   [WBD]
*Byzantine historian*
* Byzantinus, Josephus

**Genet**
*See* Flanner, Janet

**Genet, Eliazar** 16th c.   [SN]
*Composer*
* [Il] Carpentrasso

**[The] Geneva Bull**
*See* Marshall, Stephen

**Geneve, Pierre**
*See* Schweizer, Marc

**[The] Genevese Traveller**
*See* Davis, Matthew Livingston

**Genevieve**
*See* Auger, Ginette Marguerite

**Genevieve, [Mother]**
*See* Gallois, Marcelle

**Genghis Khan**
*See* Temujin [or Temuchin]

**Genia**
*See* Wennerstrom, Genia
Katherine

**[The] Genial Militant**
*See* Giri, Varahagiri Venkata

**Geniat, Marcelle**
*See* Martin, Eugenie

**Genins, [C.] Frank** 1866-1922   [BE]
*American baseball player*
* Genins, Frenchy

**Genins, Frenchy**
*See* Genins, [C.] Frank

**Genis, Myra Beth** 1936-   [OP]
*American opera singer*
* Galvany, Marisa

**[The] Genius**
*See* Robinson, Ray Charles

**Genn, Calder**
*See* Gillie, Christopher

**Genna, Angelo** ?-1926   [BLB]
*Italian-born American underworld
figure*
* Genna, Bloody Angelo

**Genna, Antonio** ?-1925   [BLB]
*Italian-born American underworld
figure*
* Tony the Gentleman

**Genna, Bloody Angelo**
*See* Genna, Angelo

**Genna, Jim**
*See* Genna, Vincenzo

**Genna, Michael** ?-1925 [BLB]
*Italian-born American underworld figure*
* [The] Devil

**Genna, Vincenzo** 20th c. [BLB]
*Italian-born American underworld figure*
* Genna, Jim

**Gennadius II**
See Scholarios, Georgios

**Genone, Hudor**
See Roe, William J[ames]

**Genoud, Antoine Eugene**
1792-1849 [WBD]
*French journalist*
* Genoude

**Genoude**
See Genoud, Antoine Eugene

**Genovese, James** 1915?- [PMJ]
*American singer*
* Ray, Jimmy

**Genovese, Vito** 1897-1969 [BLB]
*American underworld figure*
* Don Vitone

**[The] Genre Poet of Germany**
See Uhland, Johann Ludwig

**Genser, Cynthia** 1950- [CA]
*American poet*
* Comidas, Chinas

**Genseric** ?- 477 [FFF, HN, RH]
*King of the Vandals*
* [The] Scourge of God
* Virga Dei

**[The] Gent**
See Burke, James [Jimmy]

**Gent, Isaac Tompkins**
See Brougham, Lord

**Gent, L. C.** [PA]
*Author*
* G.

**Genter, Harry**
See Von Stackelberg-Treutlein, Freda Fanny Erica

**Genth, Frederick Augustus**
See Genth, Friedrich August Ludwig Karl Wilhelm

**Genth, Friedrich August Ludwig Karl Wilhelm** 1820-1893 [WBD]
*German-born chemist*
* Genth, Frederick Augustus

**[Le] Gentil Belleau**
See Belleau, Remi

**[Le] Gentil Bernard**
See Bernard, Pierre Joseph

**Gentile, Culicchia**
See Gentile, Nicola

**Gentile da Fabriano**
See Massi, Gentile

**Gentile, Diamond Jim**
See Gentile, James Edward

**Gentile, James Edward** 1934-
[BE, PB]
*American baseball player*
* Gentile, Diamond Jim

**Gentile, Nicola** 20th c. [BLB, MM]
*Italian-born American underworld figure*
* Gentile, Culicchia
* Uncle Cola

**[Le] Gentilhomme de la Peinture**
See Rubens, Peter Paul

**Gentilini, Maria Teresa** 20th c.
[WF]
*Italian actress*
* Loy, Barbara

**[The] Gentle**
See Frederick II

**[The] Gentle**
See Walton, Izaak

**Gentle Ben Crenshaw**
See Crenshaw, Ben

**[The] Gentle Crusader**
See Chapman, Oscar L.

**Gentle, Gentili** ?-1348 [PA]
*Author*
* Fulginas

**[The] Gentle Giant**
See Hubbard, Robert Cal

**[The] Gentle Grafter**
See Remus, George

**Gentle Jeems Galvin**
See Galvin, James Francis

**[The] Gentle Lochiel**
See Cameron, Donald

**[The] Gentle Shepherd**
See Grenville, George

**Gentle Willie Murphy**
See Murphy, William N. [Willie]

**[The] Gentleman**
See Sedgman, Frank

**Gentleman Al Downing**
See Downing, Alphonso Erwin

**[The] Gentleman Bowler**
See Day, Ned

**Gentleman Dave Malarcher**
See Malarcher, David Julius

**[The] Gentleman from North Carolina**
See Joyner, Andrew Jackson

**Gentleman George**
See Barrett, George Hooker

**Gentleman George**
See George IV

**Gentleman George**
See Pendleton, George Hunt

**Gentleman George Carpentier**
See Carpentier, Georges

**Gentleman George Haddock**
See Haddock, George Silas

**Gentleman Gerry Cooney**
See Cooney, Gerry

**[The] Gentleman Highwayman**
See Duval, Claude

**[The] Gentleman Highwayman**
See King, Tom

**Gentleman Jack Lynch**
See Lynch, John

**Gentleman Jim Corbett**
See Corbett, James John

**Gentleman Jim Lonborg**
See Lonborg, James Reynold

**Gentleman Jim Reeves**
See Reeves, James Travis [Jim]

**[The] Gentleman Painter**
See Rubens, Peter Paul

**[A] Gentleman who has Left his Lodgings**
See Russell, [Lord] John Earl

**[A] Gentleman with a Duster**
See Begbie, [Edward] Harold

**Gentlemanly Bobby Clack**
See Clack, Robert S. [Bobby]

**Gentner, Joan Diana** 1936-1977
[BEW]
*American actress*
* Hyland, Diana

**Gentry, Arthur**
See Sellers, Connie Leslie, Jr.

**Gentry, Bobbie**
See Street, Bobbie Lee

**Gentry, Chief**
See Gentry, John

**Gentry, James Ruffus** 1918- [BE]
*American baseball player*
* Gentry, Rufe

**Gentry, John** 20th c. [SMG]
*American basketball team staff member*
* Gentry, Chief

**Gentry, Peter** [joint pseudonym with Frank Schaefer]
See Newcomb, Kerry

**Gentry, Peter** [joint pseudonym with Kerry Newcomb]
See Schaefer, Frank

**Gentry, Rufe**
See Gentry, James Ruffus

**Geoff**
See Dyson, Geoffrey Harry George

**Geoffrey [or Geoffroy?]**
[FFF, RH, SN]
*Crusader*
* [The] Bearded

**Geoffrey, Charles**
See Muller, Charles G[eorge]

**Geoffrey, Theodate**
See Wayman, Dorothy [Godfrey]

**Geoffrey IV** 1113-1151
[HN, WBD]
*Count of Anjou*
* Grisognel the Grey Cloak
* [The] Handsome
* Plantagenet

**Geoffrin, Marie Therese**
1699-1777 [SN]
*French patron of literature*
* [A] Female Fontenelle

**Geoffrion, Bernard** 1931-
[CEI, FHE, HK]
*Canadian-born hockey player*
* [The] Boomer
* Geoffrion, Boom-Boom

**Geoffrion, Boom-Boom**
See Geoffrion, Bernard

**George** ?- 303? [DNNS, FFF]
*Saint*
* [The] Apostle of the English
* [The] Red Cross Knight

**George** 9th c. [WBD]
*Byzantine ecclesiastic and historian*
* Syncellus

**George** 1471-1539 [DNNS, WBD]
*Duke of Saxony*
* [The] Bearded
* [The] Rich

**George** 1653-1708
[DNNF, DNNS, SN]
*Prince of Denmark*
* Est-il-Possible

**George, Amara**
See Kaufmann, Mathilde Binder

**George, Charles Peter** 1912-1975
[BE]
*American baseball player*
* George, Greek

**George, [Chief] Dan**
See Slaholt, Geswanouth

**George, Daniel**
See Bunting, Daniel George

**George, David**
See Vogenitz, David George

**George, Eliot**
See Freeman, Gillian

**George, Florence**
See Guthrie, Catherine

**George, G. C.**
See George, Grace Courtenay

**George, Gladys**
See Clare, Gladys Anna

**George, Grace Courtenay** 1909-
[ART]
*British artist*
* George, G. C.

**George, Greek**
See George, Charles Peter

**George, H. R.** 20th c. [IBW]
*American investor*
* [The] Black Wolf of Wall Street

**George, Henry Stephen**
See Tomlison, Henry

**George, Jonathan** [joint pseudonym with George Theiner]
See Burke, John [Frederick]

**George, Jonathan** [joint pseudonym with John (Frederick) Burke]
See Theiner, George

**George, Lefty**
See George, Thomas Edward

**George, Lloyd** 1924- [ECM]
*American country-western performer*
* Lonzo
* Marvin, Ken

**George, Marion E.**
See Pohlman, Max Edward

**George, Mlle.**
See Weimer, Marguerite Josephine

**George, Peter [Bryan]** 1924-1966
[SF, WW]
*Welsh-born author*
* Bryant, Peter
* Peters, Bryan

**George, Robert Esmonde Gordon**
1890-1969 [CAP]
*New Zealand-born author*
* Sencourt, Robert [Esmonde]

**George, S. C.**
See George, Sidney Charles

**George, Sidney Charles** 1898-
[SFL]
*British author*
* George, S. C.

**George the Lesser**
See Brummel, George Bryan

**George, Thomas Edward**
1886-1955 [BE]
*American baseball player*
* George, Lefty

**George, Vernon**
See Vernon, George S[hirra]
G[ibb]

**George, Voya**
See Djordjevich, Voya George

**George, W. L.**
See George, Walter Lionel

**George, Walter Lionel** 1882-1926
[LC, TC]
*British author*
* George, W. L.

**George, Wilma**
See Crowther, Wilma

**George I** 1660-1727
[DNNF, FFF, RH]
*King of England*
* [The] Turnip-Hoer

**George II** 1605-1661 [WBD]
*Landgrave of Hesse-Darmstadt*
* [The] Learned

**George II** 1683-1760 [HN]
*King of England*
* [The] Guardian and Lieutenant
of the Realm
* [The] Little Captain
* Tite, Prince

**George III** 1738-1820
[HN, RH, SN]
*King of England*
* Farmer George
* [The] Farmer King
* [The] Patriot King
* [The] Solomon of Great Britain
* Ulysses
* [A] Whig of the Revolution

**George IV** 1762-1830
[FFF, HN, PA]
*King of England*
* [The] Beau of Princes
* Carleton, [Admiral] George
* Cornwall, G.
* [The] Fat Adonis of Forty [or
Fifty]
* [The] First Gentleman of Europe
* Florizel
* Fum the Fourth
* Gentleman George
* [The] Greater
* Handsome Al Raschid
* [The] Magnificent
* [The] Mere Dandini

**Georges, Francois**
See Chaulet, George

**Georges, Georges Martin**
See Simenon, Georges [Joseph
Christian]

**Georges, Jean**
See Bentein, Jean-Marie Georges
Joseph

**Georgia Bill**
See McTell, Willie Samuel

**Georgia Boy**
See Boyd, George

**Georgia Boy Johnson**
See Johnson, Lucius Brinson

**[The] Georgia Deacon**
See Flowers, Theodore

**Georgia Grinder**
See Davenport, Charles [Edward]

**[The] Georgia Peach**
See Cobb, Tyrus Raymond

**Georgia Peach**
See Hegamin, Lucille

**[The] Georgia Peach**
See Stribling, William Lawrence

**Georgia Pine**
See Harris, Ed[ward P.]

**Georgia Pine Boy**
See McCoy, Joe

**[The] Georgia Rabbit**
See Ball, George W.

**Georgia Slim**
See Seward, Alexander T. [Alec]

**Georgia Tom**
See Dorsey, Thomas A[ndrew]

**Georgian, Carolyn Ann** 20th c.
[BBH]
*American swimmer*
* Georgian, Papsie

**[The] Georgian Laureate**
See Abercrombie, Lascelles

**Georgian, Papsie**
See Georgian, Carolyn Ann

**Georgiana, [Sister]**
See Terstegge, Mabel Alice

**Georgiou, Stephen Demetre** 1948-
[B10]
*British singer and songwriter*
* Islam, Yusef
* Stevens, Cat

**Geraci, Angelo** 1903-
[BX, RBE, SA]
*Italian-born boxer*
* Graham, Bushy

**Geraghty, Leslie March** 1902- [FC]
*British actor*
* Marsh, Garry

**Gerahty, Digby George** [WW]
*Author*
* Standish, Robert

**Geraint**
See McHale, Frank

**Gerald**
See D'Arlhac, M.

**Gerald, Ara**
See Fitzgerald, Ara

**Gerald, Frank**
See Pearson, Francis Gates

**Gerald, Jim**
See Guenod, Jacques

**Gerald, Louise**
See Lacoste, Mathilde de

**Gerald, Roderic** 1957- [IBW]
*American football player*
* [The] Crew

**Gerald, Ziggy**
See Zeigerman, Gerald

**Geraldo**
See Bright, Gerald

**Geraldy, Paul**
See Le Fevre, Paul

**Geran, George Pierce** 1896- [CEI]
*American baseball player*
* Geran, Jerry

**Geran, Jerry**
See Geran, George Pierce

**Gerard** 12th c. [WBD]
*Clergyman*
* [The] Blessed

**Gerard, Andrew**
See Gatti, Arthur Gerard

**Gerard, David Frederick** 1936-
[BE]
*American baseball player*
* Gerard, Jug

**Gerard, Gaston**
See Ostergaard, Geoffrey Nielsen

**Gerard, Gus** 1953- [SMG]
*American basketball player*
* Hooves, Daddy

**Gerard, Jean Ignace Isidore**
1803-1847 [WBD]
*French illustrator and caricaturist*
* Grandville

**Gerard, John** 20th c. [MBF]
*British author*
* [The] Cherub

**Gerard, Jug**
See Gerard, David Frederick

**Gerard, Jules** 1817-1864
[FFF, SN]
*French army officer and hunter*
* [The] Lion Killer

**Gerard, Lillie** 1872-1943 [THR]
*British actress and singer*
* Leighton, Lillie
* Leighton, Queenie

**Gerard, Marie**
See Grimard, Luc

**Gerard, Morice**
See Teague, John Jessop

**Gerard of Burgundy** 980?-1061
[WBD]
*Pope*
* Nicholas II

**Gerard, Paul Emile** 1850- ? [THR]
*French playwright and librettist*
* Sylvane, Andre

**Gerard, Philippe** 1930- [CAR]
*French painter*
* Benrath, Frederic

**Gerard, Pierre S.** [PA]
*Author*
* Piccadilly

**Gerard, Richard**
See Husch, Richard J.

**Gerard, Rosemonde**
See Rostand, Louise Rose
Etiennette

**Gerard, Teddie**
See Cabre, Teresa

**Gerard-Libois, Jules C.** 1923- [CA]
*Belgian political scientist and author*
* Heinz, G.

**Geraud, [Charles Joseph] Andre**
1882-1974 [B10, CA, LC]
*French journalist and author*
* Pertinax

**Gerault, Charles** 1878- ? [LC]
*French journalist*
* Pertinax

**Geray, Steve**
See Gyergyay, Stefan

**Gerber, Erna Helene** 1925- [BEW]
*American producer, stage manager,
director*
* Fredrik, Burry

**Gerber, Fireball**
See Gerber, Warren

**Gerber, Israel J[oshua]** 1918- [CA]
*American author*
* Mordechai, Ben

**Gerber, Mr.**
See Namath, Joseph W.

**Gerber, Spooks**
See Gerber, Walter H. [Wally]

**Gerber, Walter H. [Wally]**
1891-1951 [AS, BE, PB]
*American baseball player*
* Gerber, Spooks

**Gerber, Warren** 20th c. [BBH]
*American softball player*
* Gerber, Fireball

**Gerbert** 930?-1003 [RH, WBD]
*Pope*
* Sylvester II
* [The] Wonder of the World

**Gerbi, Antonello** 1904-1976 [CA]
*Italian author*
* Ferrante, Don

**Gerbier, Pierre Jean Baptiste**
1725-1788 [SN]
*French attorney and orator*
* [The] French Mansfield

**Gercke, Charlotte** 1936- [BEW]
*American actress*
* Oliver, Susan

**Gergen, David R.** 1942?-
*American presidential aide*
* Gergen, Voodoo

**Gergen, Voodoo**
See Gergen, David R.

**Gerguson, Harry** 1890-1972
[FC, SC]
*American restaurateur and actor*
* Obolenski, [Prince] Dimitri
Romanoff
* Romanoff, Mike

**Gerhard, Karl**
See Johnson, Karl Gerhard

**Gerhardi, William Alexander**
1895-1977 [CA]
*Russian-born British author*
* Gerhardie, William Alexander

**Gerhardie, William Alexander**
See   Gerhardi, William Alexander

**Gerhards, Gerhard [or Geert]**
1466?-1536   [SN, WBD]
*Dutch scholar*
* [The] Batavian Buffoon
* Erasmus, Desiderius
* Errans Mus
* [The] Voltaire of the Sixteenth
  Century

**Gerhardt, Allen Russell** 1950-
[SMG]
*American baseball player*
* Gerhardt, Rusty

**Gerhardt, Dagobert von** 1831-1910
[WBD]
*German author*
* Von Amyntor, Gerhard

**Gerhardt, John Joseph** 1855-1922
[BE]
*American baseball player*
* Move Up Joe

**Gerhardt, Rusty**
See   Gerhardt, Allen Russell

**Gerheauser, Albert** 1917-1972   [BE]
*American baseball player*
* Gerheauser, Lefty

**Gerheauser, Lefty**
See   Gerheauser, Albert

**Gerhold, German**
See   Schmidt, Willy

**Gerik**
See   Schjelderup, Gerik

**Geris, Tom Erwin**
See   Weisinger, Mort[imer]

**Gerken, George Herbert** 1903-
[BE]
*American baseball player*
* Gerken, Pickles

**Gerken, Pickles**
See   Gerken, George Herbert

**Gerkin, Splinter**
See   Gerkin, Stephen Paul [Steve]

**Gerkin, Stephen Paul [Steve]** 1915-
[BE]
*American baseball player*
* Gerkin, Splinter

**Gerlac, Peterson** 1378-1411   [PA]
*Author*
* Petri, Gerlacus

**Gerlache, Adrien de** 1866-1934
[WBD]
*Belgian naval officer and explorer*
* Gerlache de Gomery

**Gerlache de Gomery**
See   Gerlache, Adrien de

**Germain, Germaine** 1913-   [B10]
*French model*
* Manouche

**Germain, Jean Francois** 1762-1825
[PA]
*Author*
* Du Jura

**[The] German**
See   Louis II [or Ludwig]

**German Barber**
See   Ralph, Julian E.

**[The] German Cicero**
See   Sturm, Johann Christoph

**[The] German Cid**
See   Arminius [or Armin]

**German, Daniel** 1918-   [WOA]
*Russian author*
* Granin, Daniel [Alexandrovich]

**[The] German Dickens**
See   Hacklaender, Friedrich
Wilhelm

**German, [Sir] Edward**
See   Jones, Edward German

**[The] German Herrick**
See   Fleming [or Flemming], Paul

**[The] German Horace**
See   Ramler, Charles William

**[The] German Mary Pickford**
See   Staglich, Oswalda

**[The] German Milton**
See   Klopstock, Friedrich Gottlieb

**[A] German Mithridates**
See   Maximilian II

**[The] German Nestor of Philosophy**
See   Platner, Ernst

**[The] German Paul**
See   Luther, Martin

**[The] German Peabody**
See   Schroeder, John Henry

**[The] German Plato**
See   Jacobi, Friedrich Heinrich

**[The] German Pliny**
See   Gesner, Konrad von

**[The] German Princess**
See   Carlton, Mary

**[The] German Proteus**
See   Schwarzert, Philipp

**[The] German Sappho**
See   Karsch [or Karschin], Anna
Luise

**[The] German Shakespeare**
See   Greif [Griphius or Gryphius],
Andreas

**[The] German Socrates**
See   Mendelssohn, Moses

**[The] German Strabo**
See   Muenster, Sebastian

**[The] German Trimegistus**
See   Rudolf II [or Rudolph]

**[The] German Voltaire**
See   Goethe, Johann Wolfgang von

**[The] German Voltaire**
See   Wieland, Christoph Martin

**Germanicus**
See   Dunner, Joseph

**Germanicus, Claudius Tiberius** 41-
55   [WBD]
*Son of Roman emperor, Claudius*
* Britannicus

**Germano, Margaret** 20th c.   [PMJ]
*American singer*
* Mann, Peggy

**Germano, Peter B.** 20th c.
[SFL, WGT]
*Author*
* Bertin, Jack [house pseudonym]
* Cord, Barry
* Kane, Jim

**Germany's Satchmo**
See   Joachim, Peter Mico

**Gerner, Ed[win Frederick]** 1897-
[BE]
*American baseball player*
* Gerner, Lefty

**Gerner, Lefty**
See   Gerner, Ed[win Frederick]

**Gernsback, Hugo** 1884-1967
[ESF, SFP, WGT]
*American author*
* Banshuck, Grego
* [The] Father of Science Fiction
* Fips, Socrates
* Gashbuck, Greno
* Habergock, Gus N.
* Munchausen, Baron
* Ulysses, Mohammed

**Gerobulus**
See   Oudraadt, Jean

**Geroely, Kalman**
See   Gabel, Joseph

**Geronimo**
See   Goyathlay

**Gerosa, Guido** 1933-   [CA]
*Italian-born author*
* Guado, Sergio

**Gerowski, John**
See   Girowski, John

**Gerrard, Douglas**
See   McMurrogh-Kavanagh,
Douglas Gerrard

**Gerrard, Gene**
See   O'Sullivan, Eugene

**Gerrard, Kenner**
See   Nolan, S. E.

**Gerrard, Teddie**
See   Cabrie, Therese Theodora
Gerard

**Gerrare, Wirt**
See   Greener, William Oliver

**Gerrish, George**
See   Garrish, Harold J.

**Gerrish, T.**   [FFF]
*American author*
* Old Private

**Gerrity, David James** 1923-   [CA]
*American author*
* Garrity
* Goran, Calli
* Hardin, Mitch

**Gerrold, David**
See   Friedman, Jerrold David

**Gerron, Kurt**
See   Gerson, Kurt

**Gerry**
See   Marsden, Gerrard

**Gerry, Ebby**
See   Gerry, Elbridge Thomas

**Gerry, Elbridge Thomas** 1908-
[BBH]
*American harness racing
organization officer*
* Gerry, Ebby

**Gersbach, Carl Robert** 1947-
[SMG]
*American football player*
* Gersbach, Otto

**Gersbach, Otto**
See   Gersbach, Carl Robert

**Gersh, Squire**
See   Girsback, William

**Gershon, Karen**
See   Tripp, Karen

**Gershvin, Israel** 1896-   [EMT]
*American lyricist*
* Gershwin, Ira

**Gershvin, Jacob** 1898-1937
[BBD, BEW, EMT]
*American composer*
* Gershwin, George

**Gershwin, George**
See   Gershvin, Jacob

**Gershwin, Ira**
See   Gershvin, Israel

**Gerson, Jean de**
See   Charlier, Jean

**Gerson, Kurt** ?-1944   [SC]
*German actor and director*
* Gerron, Kurt

**Gerson, Noel Bertram** 1914-   [CA]
*American author*
* Burgess, Ann Marie
* Burgess, Michael
* Edwards, Samuel
* Lewis, Paul
* Phillips, Leon
* Vaughan, Carter A.

**Gerson, Vassily Vassilijevich** 20th
c.   [EE]
*Russian intelligence agent*
* St. Innocence, [Sister]

**Gersoni, Diane** 1947-   [CA]
*American author and editor*
* Gersoni-Stavn, Diane

**Gersoni-Stavn, Diane**
See   Gersoni, Diane

**Gersonides**
See   Levi ben Gershon [or Gerson]

**Gerstad, John**
See   Gjerstad, John Leif

**Gerster, Etelka**
See   Gardini, Mrs.

**Gerstner, Karl** 1930-   [CAR]
*Swiss artist*
* Klarer, Streng

**Gert, Valeska**
See   Anderson, Gertrud

**Gertrude**
See   Bell, Jane

**Gertrude**
See   Simpson, Jane [Cross]

**Gertrude** 1256-1311
[DNNS, WBD]
*Saint*
* [The] Great

**Gerun, Tom**
See Gerunovitch, Thomas

**Gerunovitch, Thomas** 20th c. [PMJ]
*American bandleader*
* Gerun, Tom

**Gervais, C. H.**
See Gervais, Charles Henry

**Gervais, Charles Henry** 1946- [CA]
*Canadian author, poet, playwright*
* Gervais, C. H.
* Gervais, Marty

**Gervais, Lefty**
See Gervais, Lucien Edward

**Gervais, Lucien Edward** 1890- [BE]
*American baseball player*
* Gervais, Lefty

**Gervais, Marty**
See Gervais, Charles Henry

**Gervas, Thaurr**
See Canfield, Arthur Graves

**Gervin, George** 20th c.
*American basketball player*
* [The] Iceman

**Gervis, Burt** 1945- [SW]
*American actor*
* Ward, Burt

**Gesling, Henry L.** 1840- ? [PA]
*Author*
* Laurent, Henry

**Gesner, Konrad von** 1516-1565
[DEP, DNNS, SN]
*Swiss naturalist*
* [The] German Pliny
* [The] Modern Pliny

**Gessler, Doc**
See Gessler, Harry Homer

**Gessler, Harry Homer** 1880-1924
[BE]
*American baseball player*
* Gessler, Doc

**Gessner, Lynne** 1919- [WD]
*American author*
* Clark, Merle

**Gest, J.**
See Factor, John

**Geszler, George**
See Geszler, Gyorgy

**Geszler, Gyorgy** 1913- [IWM]
*Hungarian musician*
* Geszler, George

**Get**
See Getterman, Orla

**Getterman, Orla** 1913- [WEC]
*Danish cartoonist*
* Get

**Gettig, Charles H. [Charlie]**
See Gettinger, Charles H.

**Gettinger, Charles H.** 1875- ? [BE]
*American baseball player*
* Gettig, Charles H. [Charlie]

**Gettinger, William A.** 1889-1966
[SC]
*American actor and stunt performer*
* Steele, William [Bill]

**Gettleman, Susan**
See Braiman, Susan

**Gettman, Leslie** 1922- [FC]
*American actress*
* Brooks, Leslie

**Getty, J[ean] Paul, III** 1956?-
*American oil heir and kidnap victim*
* [The] Golden Hippie

**Gettysburg Eddie Plank**
See Plank, Edward Stewart

**Getz, Gee-Gee**
See Getz, Gustave

**Getz, Gustave** 1889-1969 [BE]
*American baseball player*
* Getz, Gee-Gee

**Getzein, Charles H.** 1864-1932
[AS, BE]
*American baseball player*
* Getzein, Pretzels

**Getzein, Pretzels**
See Getzein, Charles H.

**Geva, Tamara**
See Gevergeva, Sheversheieva

**Gevergeva, Sheversheieva** 1907-
[BEW, EMT]
*Russian actress and dancer*
* Geva, Tamara

**Geyer, Forest P.** 1890-1932 [FB]
*American football player*
* Geyer, Spot

**Geyer, Jacob Bowman** 1885- [BE]
*American baseball player*
* Geyer, Rube

**Geyer, Rube**
See Geyer, Jacob Bowman

**Geyer, Spot**
See Geyer, Forest P.

**Geygan, Chappie**
See Geygan, James Edward

**Geygan, James Edward** 1903-1966
[BE]
*American baseball player*
* Geygan, Chappie

**Geyler, Johann** 1445-1510 [SN]
*Swiss clergyman*
* [The] Herald of the Reformation

**Gezi, Kalil I.** 1930- [CA]
*Iraqi-born educator and author*
* Kal

**Gharrity, Edward Patrick**
1892-1966 [BE]
*American baseball player*
* Gharrity, Patsy

**Gharrity, Patsy**
See Gharrity, Edward Patrick

**Ghastly**
See Ingels, Graham

**Ghazi, al- [The Conqueror]**
See Osman Nuri Pasha

**Ghazi, al-**
See Osman I [or Othman]

**Ghazlo, Arvin L.** 1912- [IBW]
*Puerto Rican-born martial arts
instructor*
* Ghazlo, Tony

**Ghazlo, Tony**
See Ghazlo, Arvin L.

**Ghazzali [or Ghazali], al-**
1058-1111 [WBD]
*Arab philosopher*
* [The] Father of the Church in
Islam

**Ghengis Khan**
See Timur [or Timour]

**Gheon, Henri**
See Vanglon, Henri

**Gherardesca, Ugolino della [Conte di
Donoratico]** 1220?-1289 [WBD]
*Italian conspirator*
* Ugolino da Pisa

**Gherardini, Lisa di Anton Maria** 15th
c. [WBD]
*Florentine aristocrat and subject of
a Leonardo da Vinci painting*
* [La] Gioconda
* Mona Lisa

**Gherea-Dobrogeanu, Constantin**
See Katz, Solomon

**[The] Ghetto Wizard**
See Leiner, Benjamin

**Ghibbes [or Gibbes?], James Alban**
[SN]
*Poet*
* [The] Horace of His Age

**Ghiberti, Lorenzo**
See Di Cione di Ser Buonaccorso,
Lorenzo

**Ghica, Helene** 1828-1888 [WBD]
*Rumanian author*
* Dora d'Istria

**Ghirlandajo [or Ghirlandaio]**
See Di Tommaso Bigordi,
Domenico

**Ghislandi, [Fra] Vittore** 1655-1743
[WBD]
*Italian painter and Franciscan monk*
* Galgario, [Fra]
* Paolotto, [Fra]

**Ghislieri, Michele** 1504-1572
[WBD]
*Pope*
* Pius V

**Ghiuselev, Nicola**
See Guzelev, Nikola Nikolaev

**Ghiyath ibn-Harith** 640?- 710?
[WBD]
*Arabic poet*
* Akhtal, al-

**Ghnassia, Maurice [Jean-Henri]**
1920- [CA, IAW]
*French-born author, producer,
director*
* De Lubano, M.
* Malpott, Virgule
* Morriss, J. H.
* Picou, Alphonse

**Ghose, Aurobindo** 1872-1950
[WOA]
*Indian poet, philosopher, mystic*
* Sri Aurobindo

**Ghose, Sri Chinmoy Kumar** 1931-
[CA]
*Indian lecturer and author*
* Chinmoy, Sri

**[The] Ghost Breaker**
See Rucker, Henry

**[The] Ghost of the Ghetto**
See Terris, Sid

**[The] Ghost with a Hammer in His
Hand**
See Wilde, James [Jimmy]

**[The] Ghostess with the Mostest**
See Nixon, Marni

**Ghylichkhani, Parviz** 1948- [AES]
*Iranian soccer player*
* Parviz

**[The] GI Sing-Sation**
See Gant, Cecil

**Giacalone, Billy Jack**
See Giacalone, Vito

**Giacalone, Vito** 20th c.
*American underworld figure*
* Giacalone, Billy Jack

**Giacomino**
See Cireni, Giuseppe

**Giagni, Danny** 1924- [BEW]
*American choreographer, dancer,
director*
* Daniels, Danny

**Giaimo, Dorothy** 1929- [EJ7]
*American jazz musician*
* Dodgion, Dottie

**Gialong**
See Nguyen-Anh

**Giamberti, Giuliano** 1445-1516
[WBD]
*Florentine architect, sculptor,
engineer*
* Sangallo, Giuliano da

**Gian**
See Bosco, Gianfabio

**Gian, Paolo** 20th c. [WF]
*Italian director*
* Maxwell, Paul

**Giancana, Momo**
See Giancana, Salvatore

**Giancana, Salvatore** 1908-1975
[B10]
*American underworld figure*
* Giancana, Momo
* Giancana, Sam
* Mooney, Sam

**Giancana, Sam**
See Giancana, Salvatore

**Gianelli, John** 1950- [BB]
*American basketball player*
* Big G

**Giannone, Maude Allen** ?-1956
[SC]
*American actress*
* Allen, Maude

**Giannone, Saverio** 1881-1939
[BX, RBE, SG]
*Italian-born boxer*
* Grim, Joe
* [The] Human Punching Bag
* [The] Iron Man

**Giannoulakos, Wassilios** 1933-
[OP]
*Greek opera singer*
* Janulako, Wassili

**Gianpaolo**
See Luciani, Albino

**[The] Giant from Minnesota**
See McEwan, John J.

**[The] Giant Killer**
See Kowalewskie, Harry Frank

**[The] Giant Killer**
See McDonald, Webster

**[The] Giant of Literature**
See Johnson, Samuel

**Giard, Joseph Oscar [Joe]**
1898-1956 [BE]
American baseball player
* Giard, Peco

**Giard, Peco**
See Giard, Joseph Oscar [Joe]

**Giardello, Joey**
See Tilelli, Carmine Orlando

**Giarraputo, Lucas Thomas Aco**
1922- [BEW]
American actor, director,
choreographer
* Aco, Lucas
* Lucas, Jonathan

**Gibb, Barbara** 1912- [THR]
British actress
* Waring, Barbara

**Gibb, Lee** [joint pseudonym with
Keith (Spencer) Waterhouse]
See Deghy, Guy [Stephen]

**Gibb, Lee** [joint pseudonym with Guy
(Stephen) Deghy]
See Waterhouse, Keith [Spencer]

**Gibbes, Frances Guignard**
See Keith, Frances Guignard
Gibbes

**Gibbon, Lewis Grassic**
See Mitchell, James Leslie

**Gibbons, Fredda**
See Lipson, Fredda

**Gibbons, Gib**
See Gibbons, James E.

**Gibbons, Grinling** 1648-1721 [HN]
British woodcarver and sculptor
* [The] English Lysippus

**Gibbons, Harry Hornaby Clifford**
1888-1958 [MBF]
British author
* Chester, Gilbert
* Kempster, Bert

**Gibbons, Helen**
See Gibbons, William

**Gibbons, Hildegarde** 1903-1933
[SC]
American actress
* Ferguson, Hilda

**Gibbons, Irene** 1895-1977
[BWW, PMJ, WWJ]
American singer
* [The] Dixie Nightingale
* Henderson, Catherine
* [The] Queen of the Moaners
* Taylor, Eva
* Williams, Irene

**Gibbons, Irene** 1907-1962 [WFA]
American fashion designer
* Irene

**Gibbons, James E.** 1936- [FB]
American football player
* Gibbons, Gib

**Gibbons, John** 1907- [BB]
American basketball player
* Gibbons, Tex

**Gibbons, Mike** 1887-1956
[BX, RBE]
American boxer
* [The] St. Paul Phantom
* [The] Wizard

**Gibbons, Orlando** 1583-1625
[FFF, SN, WBD]
British musician and composer
* [The] English Palestrina

**Gibbons, Tex**
See Gibbons, John

**Gibbons, William** 1781- ? [PA]
Author
* Vindex

**Gibbons, William** 1900- [MBF]
British author
* Cross, Dennis
* Gibbons, Helen
* Richards, Frank [house
pseudonym]

**Gibbs, Barry** 1948- [SMG]
Canadian-born hockey player
* Gibbs, Gibby

**Gibbs, Betty** 1920- [BEW]
American publisher and editor
* Blake, Betty

**Gibbs, Cosmo** 1872?-1942
[BEW, LC]
British author and playwright
* Hamilton, Cosmo

**Gibbs, Georgia**
See Lipson, Fredda

**Gibbs, Gibby**
See Gibbs, Barry

**Gibbs, Henry**
See Rumbold-Gibbs, Henry St.
John Clair

**Gibbs, Jake**
See Gibbs, Jerry Dean

**Gibbs, Jerry Dean** 1938-
[BE, FB, PB]
American baseball and football
player
* Gibbs, Jake

**Gibbs, Katherine Edwina**
1899?-1968 [BDF, F2, FC]
American actress
* Francis, Kay

**Gibbs, Lewis**
See Cove, Joseph Walter

**Gibbs, Mary Ann**
See Bidwell, Marjory Elizabeth
Sarah

**Gibbs, Montgomery** [PA]
Author
* Mortimer, Gilbert

**Gibbs, Oliver** [PA]
Author
* Oliver

**Gibbs, T. F.**
See Gibbs, Timothy Francis

**Gibbs, Terry**
See Gubenko, Julius

**Gibbs, Timothy Francis** 1923-
[ART]
British painter
* Gibbs, T. F.

**Gibbs, Tony**
See Gibbs, Wolcott, Jr.

**Gibbs, Wolcott, Jr.** 1935- [CA]
American author
* Gibbs, Tony

**Gibbs-Smith, Charles Harvard**
1909- [CA]
British author
* Harvard, Charles

**Giberga, Ovidio** 20th c. [SFL]
Author
* Coggs, Dr.

**Giberson, Dorothy [Dodds]** [CA]
American author
* Field, Penelope

**Gibson, Amanda Melvina Thorley**
20th c. [WGT]
Author
* Mathieson, Una Cooper

**Gibson, Bullet**
See Gibson, Robert

**Gibson, Charles Hammond** 1874- ?
[NAA]
American author
* Sudbury, Richard

**Gibson, Chloe**
See Cawdle, Chloe

**Gibson, Clifford** 1901-1963
[BWW]
American singer
* Gibson, Grandpappy
* Sluefoot Joe

**Gibson, Edmund Richard**
1892-1960 [BEW, OCF]
American actor
* Gibson, Hoot
* [The] Hooter

**Gibson, Edward** 1856?-1920
[BEW]
Actor
* Lyle, Lyston

**Gibson, Floyd**
See King, Albert

**Gibson, Fredda [or Freddie]**
See Lipson, Fredda

**Gibson, George** 1880-1967
[BE, BN, PB]
Canadian baseball player and
manager
* Gibson, Gibby
* Gibson, Hack
* Gibson, Moon [or Mooney]

**Gibson, Gib**
See Gibson, Kirk Harold

**Gibson, Gibby**
See Gibson, George

**Gibson, Grandpappy**
See Gibson, Clifford

**Gibson, Hack**
See Gibson, George

**Gibson, Harry**
Comedian
* Harry the Hipster

**Gibson, Harry** 20th c. [IEJ]
American jazz musician
* [The] Hipster

**Gibson, Harry Clark**
See Hubler, Richard Gibson

**Gibson, Harvey** 1935- [IBW]
American pilot
* Gibson, Hoot

**Gibson, Helen**
See Wenger, Rose August

**Gibson, Hoot**
See Gibson, Edmund Richard

**Gibson, Hoot**
See Gibson, Harvey

**Gibson, Hoot**
See Gibson, Joshua

**Gibson, Hoot**
See Gibson, Robert

**Gibson, Joe** 20th c. [SFP, WGT]
Author
* Bridger, John
* Furth, Carleton
* Gibson, John

**Gibson, John**
See Gibson, Joe

**Gibson, Josephine** [joint pseudonym
with Sesyle Joslin Hine]
See Hine, Al[fred Blakelee]

**Gibson, Josephine** [joint pseudonym
with Al(fred Blakelee) Hine]
See Hine, Sesyle Joslin

**Gibson, Joshua** 1911-1947
[AS, IBW, MK]
American baseball player
* [The] Black Babe Ruth
* [The] Brown Bambino
* Gibson, Hoot

**Gibson, Katharine**
See Wicks, Katharine Gibson

**Gibson, Kirk Harold** 1957- [SMG]
American baseball player
* Gibson, Gib

**Gibson, Lee**
See Gibson, Leighton B.

**Gibson, Leighton B.** 1866- ? [BE]
American baseball player
* Gibson, Lee

**Gibson, Ma**
See Gibson, Marie

**Gibson, Madeline**
See Stride, Madeline

**Gibson, Maralee G.** 1924- [CA]
American poet
* Davis, Maralee G.

**Gibson, Margaret**
See Palmer, Patricia

**Gibson, Marice Louise** 1884-
[SFL, WGT]
American author
* Goetchius, Marie Louise
* Rutledge, Maryse
* Van Saanen, Marie Louise

**Gibson, Marie** 20th c. [GW]
American rodeo performer
* Gibson, Ma

**Gibson, Mary Frances**  [PA]
*Author*
* Winnefred

**Gibson, Mary W. Stanely**  [PA]
*Author*
* Woodfern, Winnie

**Gibson, Moon [or Mooney]**
*See*  Gibson, George

**Gibson, Robert** 1935-
[BE, IBW, PB]
*American baseball player*
* Gibson, Bullet
* Gibson, Hoot

**Gibson, Rosemary**
*See*  Newell, Rosemary

**Gibson, Russell** 20th c.  [BLB]
*American underworld figure*
* Gibson, Slim Gray

**Gibson, Slim Gray**
*See*  Gibson, Russell

**Gibson, W. W.**
*See*  Gibson, Wilfrid Wilson

**Gibson, Walter B[rown]** 1897-
[EMD, SFL, WGT]
*American magician and author*
* Grant, Maxwell [house
  pseudonym]
* Thurston, Howard

**Gibson, Wilfrid Wilson** 1878-1962
[LC]
*British poet*
* Gibson, W. W.

**Gibson, William** 1914-  [CA]
*American author and playwright*
* Mass, William

**Gibson, Winifred** 1905-  [BEW]
*American actress*
* Gibson, Wynne

**Gibson, Wynne**
*See*  Gibson, Winifred

**Gichermann, Mordechai** 1922-
[CA]
*German-born Israeli archaeologist
and author*
* Gichon, Mordechai

**Gicheru, Samuel Mwangi** 1947-
[IAW]
*Kenyan writer*
* Skeleton
* Slim

**Gichon, Mordechai**
*See*  Gichermann, Mordechai

**Giddings, Joshua Reed** 1795-1864
[PA]
*Author*
* Pacificus

**Giddy, Eric Cawood Gwyddn** 1895-
[WGT]
*Author*
* Knight, [W.] Kobold

**Giddy Gusher**
*See*  Fiske, Mary Hewins

**Gielgud, Gwen Bagni**
*See*  Dubov, Gwen Bagni

**Giello, Larry** 20th c.  [RBE]
*American boxer*
* Gillio, Larry

**Gier-Ber, Ali**
*See*  Du Val-de-Grace, Jean [or
  Johann] Baptiste

**Giergielewicz, Mieczyslaw** 20th c.
[CAP]
*Polish-born educator and author*
* Bielski, Feliks
* M. G.

**Giersch, Julius**
*See*  Arnade, Charles W[olfgang]

**Giesebrecht, Gus**
*See*  Giesebrecht, Roy

**Giesebrecht, Roy** 1918-  [CEI]
*Canadian-born hockey player*
* Giesebrecht, Gus

**Giesler, Harold Lee** 1887?-1962
[BEW]
*American theatrical attorney*
* Giesler, Jerry

**Giesler, Jerry**
*See*  Giesler, Harold Lee

**Giffard, Hardinge Goulburn** 1880-
?  [WGT]
*British author*
* Bath, Oliver

**Giffin, Frank**
*See*  Carter, Ernest Frank

**Gifford, F. O.**  [PA]
*Author*
* Tracts, Hartley Wintney

**Gifford, John**
*See*  Foss, Edward

**Gifford, John**
*See*  Green, John Richards

**Gifford, John, Esq.**
*See*  Whellier, Alexander

**Gifford, Norman** 1940-  [DC]
*British cricketer*
* Gifford, 'Oss

**Gifford, 'Oss**
*See*  Gifford, Norman

**Gifford, Sharkey**
*See*  Gifford, Tom

**Gifford, Tom** 20th c.  [BBH, CSH]
*Canadian lacrosse player*
* Gifford, Sharkey

**Gifford, William** 1756-1826  [SN]
*British critic and poet*
* [The] Coryphaeus of Modern
  Literature

**Gifford-Jones, W.**
*See*  Walker, Kenneth Francis

**[The] Gift of God**
*See*  Philip II [or Philippe]

**Gift, Theo**
*See*  Boulger, Theodora Henrietta
[Havers]

**Gigante, Vincent** 20th c.
*American underworld figure*
* [The] Chin

**Giggal, Kenneth** 1927-  [IAW]
*British author*
* Marlin, Henry
* Ross, Angus
* Savage, Ian

**Giggle, Philip** 1949-  [ART]
*British painter, illustrator,
photographer*
* P. G.

**Gigliucci, Countess**
*See*  Novello, Clara A.

**Gijsen, Marnix**
*See*  Goris, Jan-Albert

**Gil**
*See*  Lenoir, Carlos

**Gil, Antonio** 1823-1902  [GS]
*Spanish bullfighter*
* Gil, Don

**Gil, David G[eorg]**
*See*  Engel, David Georg

**Gil, Don**
*See*  Gil, Antonio

**Gil, Gus**
*See*  Gil, Tomas Gustavo

**Gil the Brain**
*See*  Beckley, Gilbert Lee

**Gil, Tomas Gustavo** 1940-  [BE]
*Venezuelan-born baseball player*
* Gil, Gus

**Gilbert**
*See*  Robinson, William Stevens

**Gilbert, Alfred** 1887-1957  [SC]
*American actor*
* La Mont, Harry

**Gilbert, Anthony**
*See*  Malleson, Lucy Beatrice

**Gilbert, Ben W.**
*See*  Goldberg, Ben W.

**Gilbert, Bennett Harold Rochefort**
1896-  [BE]
*American baseball player*
* Rochefort, Bennett Harold

**Gilbert, Billy**
*See*  Barron, William Gilbert

**Gilbert, Billy**
*See*  Campbell, William V.

**Gilbert, Buddy**
*See*  Gilbert, Drew Edward

**Gilbert, C. L.** 1941-  [GF]
*American golfer*
* Gilbert, Gibby

**Gilbert, Daniel A.** 20th c.  [BLB]
*American police officer with
underworld ties*
* Gilbert, Tubbo
* [The] World's Richest Cop

**Gilbert, Drew Edward** 1935-  [BE]
*American baseball player*
* Gilbert, Buddy

**Gilbert, Fred** ?-1927  [BBH]
*American trapshooter*
* [The] Wizard of Spirit Lake

**Gilbert, Frederic** 19th c.  [PA]
*Author*
* Rambaud, Yveling

**Gilbert, George**
*See*  Gelberg, George

**Gilbert, Gibby**
*See*  Gilbert, C. L.

**Gilbert, H.** 20th c.  [MBF]
*British author*
* Conner, Henry

**Gilbert, Harold Joseph** 1929-1967
[BE]
*American baseball player*
* Gilbert, Tookie

**Gilbert, Jackrabbit**
*See*  Gilbert, John Robert [Jack]

**Gilbert, Jean**
*See*  Winterfeld, Max

**Gilbert, Jean** 20th c.  [WWL]
*British author*
* Wanderer

**Gilbert, [Agnes] Joan [Sewell]**
1931-  [CA]
*American author*
* Baer, Jill

**Gilbert, John**
*See*  Pringle, John

**Gilbert, John Robert [Jack]**
1875-1941  [BE]
*American baseball player*
* Gilbert, Jackrabbit

**Gilbert, Lou**
*See*  Gitlitz, Louis

**Gilbert, Manu**
*See*  West, Joyce [Tarlton]

**Gilbert, Marie Dolores Eliza
Rosanna** 1818?-1861  [FC, WBD]
*British dancer*
* Montez, Lola

**Gilbert, Marilyn B[ender]** 1926-
[CA]
*American writer and editor*
* Ferster, Marilyn B.

**Gilbert, Miriam**
*See*  Presberg, Miriam Goldstein

**Gilbert, Mrs. R. L.**  [PA]
*Author*
* Knight, Charles D.

**Gilbert, Nan**
*See*  Gilbertson, Mildred [Geiger]

**Gilbert, Paul**
*See*  MacMahon, Paul

**Gilbert, Rocky**
*See*  Gilbert, Rodrigue Gabriel

**Gilbert, Rod**
*See*  Gilbert, Rodrigue Gabriel

**Gilbert, Rodrigue Gabriel** 1941-
[FHE, HK, SMG]
*Canadian-born hockey player*
* Gilbert, Rocky
* Gilbert, Rod

**Gilbert, Ruth Gallard Ainsworth**
1908-  [AW, CA]
*British author*
* Ainsworth, Ruth

**Gilbert, Tookie**
*See*  Gilbert, Harold Joseph

**Gilbert, Tubbo**
*See*  Gilbert, Daniel A.

**Gilbert, William** 1540-1603  [WBD]
*British physician and physicist*
* [The] Father of Electricity

**Gilbert, [Sir] William Schwenck**
1836-1911 [TLC, WW, WWL]
*British librettist, playwright, poet*
* Bab
* La Tour, Tomline
* Tomline, F.

**Gilbert, Willie**
See Gomberg, William Gilbert

**Gilbertson, Mildred [Geiger]** 1908-
[CA, SAT, WD]
*American author*
* Gilbert, Nan
* Mendel, Jo [house pseudonym,
Albert Whitman & Co.]

**Gilboa, Yehoshua**
See Globerman, Yehoshua A.

**Gilchrist, Alan W.** 1913- [CA]
*British author*
* Cowan, Alan

**Gilchrist, Carlton C.** 1935- [FB]
*American football player*
* Gilchrist, Cookie

**Gilchrist, Connie** 1922- [FIR]
*American actress*
* [The] Big Blonde
* Big Girl
* Countess

**Gilchrist, Cookie**
See Gilchrist, Carlton C.

**Gilchrist, J. A.** 20th c. [BBH]
*Canadian swimmer*
* Gilchrist, Sandy

**Gilchrist, Sandy**
See Gilchrist, J. A.

**Gilda**
See Rickert, Shirley Jean

**Gildas [or Gildus]** 516- 570
[RH, SN, WBD]
*British author*
* [The] British Jeremiah
* Saint Gildas the Wise
* Sapiens
* [The] Wise

**Gilday, Mrs. Charles** [FFF]
*Entertainer*
* Beane, Fannie

**Gilden, Bert** 1915?-1971 [CA]
*American author*
* Gilden, K. B. [joint pseudonym
with Katya Gilden]

**Gilden, K. B.** [joint pseudonym with
Katya Gilden]
See Gilden, Bert

**Gilden, K. B.** [joint pseudonym with
Bert Gilden]
See Gilden, Katya

**Gilden, Katya** 20th c. [CA]
*American author*
* Gilden, K. B. [joint pseudonym
with Bert Gilden]

**Gilder, Jeannette L.** 1849-1916
[FFF]
*American journalist*
* Erasmus

**Gilder, Joseph B.** [FFF]
*American writer*
* [The] Lounger

**Gilder, Richard Watson** 1844-1909
[FFF, PA]
*American poet and editor*
* Old Cabinet

**Gilderoy, Roland**
See Rowley, Charles, Jr.

**[Un] Gildista**
See Por, Odon

**Gile, Bear**
See Gile, Don[ald Loren]

**Gile, Don[ald Loren]** 1935- [BE]
*American baseball player*
* Gile, Bear

**Giles, Carl H[oward]** 1935- [CA]
*American educator and author*
* Gale, William C.

**Giles, Elizabeth**
See Holt, John [Robert]

**Giles, Geoffrey** [joint pseudonym
with Walter Gillings]
See Ackerman, Forrest J[ames]

**Giles, Geoffrey** [joint pseudonym
with Forrest J[ames] Ackerman]
See Gillings, Walter

**Giles, Gordon A.** [joint pseudonym
with Otto O(scar) Binder]
See Binder, Earl Andrew

**Giles, Gordon A.** [joint pseudonym
with Earl Andrew Binder]
See Binder, Otto O[scar]

**Giles, Joanna Elder** 20th c. [LAO]
*British author*
* Magill, Marcus [joint pseudonym
with Brian (Merrikin) Hill?]

**Giles, Johnny**
See Mellenbruch, Giles Edward

**Giles, Kenneth** 20th c. [CC]
*Author*
* Drummond, Charles
* McGirr, Edmund

**Giles, Kris**
See Nielsen, Helen Berniece

**Giles, Lester**
See Gillis, Lester

**Giles, Marvin, III** 1943- [EG, GF]
*American golfer*
* Giles, Vinny

**Giles of Antwerp**
See Coignet, Giles

**Giles, Paul Kirk**
See Gyles, Paul Kirk

**Giles, R. A.** 20th c. [WGT]
*Author*
* Barry, B. X.

**Giles, Raymond**
See Holt, John [Robert]

**Giles, Vinny**
See Giles, Marvin, III

**Gilford, Charles Bernard** 1920-
[CA]
*American playwright*
* Campbell, Donald
* Farr, Douglas
* Gregory, Elizabeth

**Gilford, Jack**
See Gellman, Jacob

**Gilhooley, Flash**
See Gilhooley, Frank Patrick

**Gilhooley, Frank Patrick**
1892-1959 [BE]
*American baseball player*
* Gilhooley, Flash

**Gilhooley, Lord**
See Seymour, Frederick H[enri]

**Gilje, Goose**
See Gilje, Theodore Michael

**Gilje, Theodore Michael** 1950-
[SMG]
*American baseball player*
* Gilje, Goose

**Gilkyson, Hamilton Henry** 1919?-
[DAM]
*American singer, guitarist,
songwriter*
* Gilkyson, Terry

**Gilkyson, Terry**
See Gilkyson, Hamilton Henry

**Gill, Alan**
See Gillespie, Alfred

**Gill, Amory T.** 1901-1966
[AS, BB]
*American basketball coach*
* Gill, Slats

**Gill, Andre**
See Gosset de Guines, Louis
Alexandre

**Gill, Bartholomew**
See McGarrity, Mark

**Gill, Dudley Arthur** 1901?-1973
[B10]
*Australian veterinarian*
* Gill, Jim

**Gill, Haddie**
See Gill, Harold Edmund

**Gill, Harold Edmund** 1899-1932
[BE]
*American baseball player*
* Gill, Haddie

**Gill, Hugh**
See Hugill, Robert

**Gill, Jerry H.**
See Gauthier, Jerry H.

**Gill, Jim**
See Gill, Dudley Arthur

**Gill, John** 1697-1771 [SN]
*British clergyman and scholar*
* [The] Learned Dr. Gill

**Gill, John Wesley** 1905- [BE]
*American baseball player*
* Gill, Patcheye

**Gill, Lilly K. E.** 1922- [ART]
*German-born sculptor*
* L. G.

**Gill, Patcheye**
See Gill, John Wesley

**Gill, Patrick**
See Creasey, John

**Gill, Paul**
See Snow, Gilbert Wilson

**Gill, Ralph** 1919- [ASC]
*American composer and singer*
* Gill, Rusty

**Gill, Rusty**
See Gill, Ralph

**Gill, S. H.**
See Gill, Stanley Herbert

**Gill, Slats**
See Gill, Amory T.

**Gill, Stanley Herbert** 1912- [ART]
*British artist*
* Gill, S. H.

**Gill, Traviss** 1891- [CAP]
*British author*
* Odell, Gill [joint pseudonym with
Carol Odell]

**Gill, Vincent** 1884- [THR]
*British actor*
* Erne, Vincent

**Gillain, Joseph** 1914- [WECO]
*Belgian cartoonist and illustrator*
* Jije

**Gillaizeau, Genevieve** 1946- [FC]
*French actress*
* Gilles, Genevieve

**Gillars, Mildred Elizabeth** 1901?-
[CND]
*American pro-Nazi propagandist*
* Axis Sally

**Gillease, Elizabeth Ellen** 1934-
[BEW, FC, TR]
*American actress and singer*
* Allen, Elizabeth

**Gilleland, Samuel** 1870-1905 [BE]
*American baseball player*
* Gillen, Sam[uel]

**Gillen, Sam[uel]**
See Gilleland, Samuel

**Gilles, Albert S[imeon], Sr.** 1888-
[CA]
*American author and poet*
* Oklahoma Peddler

**Gilles, Genevieve**
See Gillaizeau, Genevieve

**Gillese, John Patrick** 1920-
[CA, IAW]
*Irish-born Canadian author*
* O'Hara, Dale
* Shark, Gill
* Starr, John A.

**Gillespie, Alfred** 1924- [CA]
*American author*
* Gill, Alan

**Gillespie, Bunch**
See Gillespie, Robert William
[Bob]

**Gillespie, Dizzy**
See Gillespie, John Birks

**Gillespie, Iris Sylvia** 1923- [CA]
*British author*
* Andreski, Iris

**Gillespie, John Birks** 1917-
[ASC, BBD, DAM]
*American jazz musician*
* Gillespie, Dizzy

**Gillespie, John Patrick** 1900-1954
[BE]
*American baseball player*
* Gillespie, Silent John

**Gillespie, Lefty**
See Gillespie, Murray

**Gillespie, Murray** 20th c. [OBW]
*American baseball player*
* Gillespie, Lefty

**Gillespie, Nan**
*See* Buranelli, Agnes Wallace

**Gillespie, Robert William [Bob]**
1918- [BE]
*American baseball player*
* Gillespie, Bunch

**Gillespie, Silent John**
*See* Gillespie, John Patrick

**Gillespie, Susan**
*See* Turton-Jones, Edith Constance
[Bradshaw]

**Gillespie, William Houyman** [PA]
*Author*
* Tisanthrope, Ter

**Gillet, Stanislaus** 1875-1951 [CAT]
*French author and clergyman*
* Martin, [Frater]

**Gillett, H. M.**
*See* Gillett, Henry Martin

**Gillett, Henry Martin** 1902- [CAT]
*British author*
* Gillett, H. M.

**Gillette, A. S.**
*See* Gillette, Arnold Simpson

**Gillette, Arnold Simpson** 1904-
[BEW]
*American educator and scenic
designer*
* Gillette, A. S.

**Gillette, Bob**
*See* Shaw, Bynum G[illette]

**Gillette, Leland J.** 1912- [ASC]
*American composer, musician,
singer, producer*
* Bergdahl, Enid

**Gillette, Virginia M[ary]** 1920-
[CA]
*American author*
* McLean, J. Sloan [joint
pseudonym with Josephine M.
Wunsch]

**Gillham, Art** 1895-1961 [CED]
*American musician and composer*
* [The] Whispering Pianist

**Gilliam, Holly** 1944- [SW]
*American singer and actress*
* Phillips, Michelle

**Gilliam, James William** 1928-1978
[BE, PB]
*American baseball player*
* Gilliam, Junior

**Gilliam, Joe, Jr.** 1952- [IBW]
*American football player and coach*
* Jefferson Street Joe

**Gilliam, John R.** 1945- [FB]
*American football player*
* Gilliam, Tally

**Gilliam, Junior**
*See* Gilliam, James William

**Gilliam, Tally**
*See* Gilliam, John R.

**Gillian, Kay**
*See* Smith, Kay Nolte

**Gillie, Christopher** 1914- [CA]
*British author*
* Genn, Calder

**Gillie, Mary E.** [PA]
*Author*
* M. E. B.

**Gillies, Clark** 1954- [SMG]
*Canadian-born hockey player*
* Gillies, Jethro

**Gillies, Jethro**
*See* Gillies, Clark

**Gillies, Mary** [PA]
*Author*
* Myrtle, Harriet

**Gillies, Robert Pierce** 19th c.
[DEL, SN]
*Scottish author*
* Kempferhausen

**Gilliford, Gorilla**
*See* Gilliford, Paul Gant

**Gilliford, Paul Gant** 1945- [BE]
*American baseball player*
* Gilliford, Gorilla

**Gilliland, Charles**
*See* Muller, Charles G[eorge]

**Gillings, David** 1864-1947 [BMH]
*British comedian*
* Mozart, George

**Gillings, Walter** 1912- [ESF, WGT]
*British journalist and editor*
* Giles, Geoffrey [joint pseudonym
with Forrest J(ames) Ackerman]
* Sheridan, Thomas

**Gillio, Larry**
*See* Giello, Larry

**Gillis, Alex**
*See* Gillis, Lester

**Gillis, Ann**
*See* O'Connor, Alma Mabel

**Gillis, Lester** 1908-1934 [BLB]
*American underworld figure*
* Giles, Lester
* Gillis, Alex
* Nelson, Baby Face
* Nelson, Big George
* Nelson, George
* Nelson, Jimmie

**Gillison, Margaret** 1916- [ART]
*British painter and illustrator*
* M.
* M. G.

**Gillman, Margaret C.** 1908-1969
*American journalist*
* Beege

**Gillmore, Inez Haynes**
*See* Irwin, Inez Haynes

**Gillmore, Parker** [DEL, FFF, PA]
*American author*
* Ubique

**Gillooly, Edna Rae** 1932- [SW]
*American actress*
* Burstyn, Ellen
* Dean, Erica
* Flynn, Kerri
* McRae, Ellen

**Gillum, Jazz**
*See* Gillum, William McKinley
[Bill]

**Gillum, William McKinley [Bill]**
1904-1966 [BWW]
*American singer*
* Gillum, Jazz
* McKinley, Bill

**Gilman, Ada**
*See* Richardson, Mrs. Leander

**Gilman, Dorothy**
*See* Butters, Dorothy Gilman

**Gilman, George G.**
*See* Harknett, Terry

**Gilman, J. D.** [joint pseudonym with
Douglas Orgill]
*See* Fishman, Jack

**Gilman, J. D.** [joint pseudonym with
Jack Fishman]
*See* Orgill, Douglas

**Gilman, James**
*See* Gilmore, Joseph L[ee]

**Gilman, [Mrs.] Maria**
*See* Barnard, C. F., Jr.

**Gilman, Mrs.**
*See* Ballou, Hosea

**Gilman, Pit**
*See* Gilman, Pitkin Clark

**Gilman, Pitkin Clark** 1864-1950
[BE]
*American baseball player*
* Gilman, Pit

**Gilman, Robert Cham**
*See* De Marini y Coppel, Alfredo
Jose

**Gilman, William** 1724-1804 [PA]
*Author*
* Frampton, Doctor

**Gilmer, Ann**
*See* Ross, William Edward Daniel

**Gilmer, Elizabeth [Meriwether]**
1861?-1951 [B10, NAA]
*American journalist*
* Dix, Dorothy

**Gilmore, Anthony** [joint pseudonym
with Desmond W. Hall]
*See* Bates, Harry Arthur

**Gilmore, Anthony** [joint pseudonym
with Harry Arthur Bates]
*See* Hall, Desmond Winter

**Gilmore, Artis** 20th c. [IBW]
*American basketball and football
player*
* Gilmore, Franchise

**Gilmore, Christopher Cook** 1940-
[CA]
*American author*
* Pary, C. C.

**Gilmore, Don** 1930- [CA]
*American author*
* Davis, Gil

**Gilmore, Ernest**
*See* Farley, Helen H.

**Gilmore, Eugene, Airman** 1932-
[IBW]
*American-born bullfighter*
* Morenito de Seville, Gino

**Gilmore, Franchise**
*See* Gilmore, Artis

**Gilmore, J. H.** [FFF, PA]
*American writer*
* Genesee

**Gilmore, James Roberts** 1822-1903
[DEL, DNNF, FFF]
*American author*
* Kirke, Edmund

**Gilmore, Janette**
*See* Maloney, Janette

**Gilmore, John**
*See* Hirsch, Willi

**Gilmore, Joseph L[ee]** 1929- [CA]
*American author*
* Bennett, Daniel
* Gilman, James

**Gilmore, Leonard Preston [Len]**
1917- [BE]
*American baseball player*
* Gilmore, Meow

**Gilmore, Marian**
*See* Dey, Frederic Van Rensselaer

**Gilmore, Meow**
*See* Gilmore, Leonard Preston
[Len]

**Gilmore, Patrick Sarsfield**
1829-1892 [WBD]
*American bandleader and songwriter*
* Lambert, Louis

**Gilmore, Virginia**
*See* Poole, Virginia Sherman

**Gilmour, Billy**
*See* Gilmour, Hamilton
Livingstone

**Gilmour, G. F.**
*See* Gilmour, George Fisher

**Gilmour, George Fisher** 20th c.
[ART]
*British painter*
* Gilmour, G. F.

**Gilmour, Hamilton Livingstone**
1885-1959 [HK]
*Canadian-born hockey player*
* Gilmour, Billy

**Gilner, Elias**
*See* Ginsburg, Elihu

**Gilpatrick**
*See* Patrick, Gilbert

**Gilpin, Bernard** 1517-1583
[DNNF, DNNS, SN]
*British clergyman*
* [The] Apostle of the North
* [The] Father of the Poor

**[The] Gilroy Cowboy**
*See* Archer, George B.

**Gilson, Harold [Hal]** 1942- [BE]
*American baseball player*
* Gilson, Lefty

**Gilson, Hibbart**
*See* Hibbart-Gilson, M. M. T.

**Gilson, Jef**
*See* Quievreux, Jean-Francois

**Gilson, Lefty**
*See* Gilson, Harold [Hal]

**Gilson, Lottie**
*See* Deagon, Lyda

**Gilson, Paul** 1927- [OP]
*Belgian opera company administrator*
* Francy, Paul

**Gilzean, Elizabeth Houghton Blanchet** 1913- [AW, CA]
*Canadian-born author*
* Houghton, Elizabeth
* Hunton, Mary

**Gim, H. W.**
See Gim, Hom Wing

**Gim, Hom Wing** 1908-1973 [SC]
*Chinese-born actor*
* Gim, H. W.

**Gimbel, Sophie** 20th c. [WFA]
*American fashion designer*
* Sophie

**Gimel**
See Andrews, Elisha Benjamin

**Ginder, Richard** 1914- [CA]
*American author and composer*
* McGlynn, Christopher
* Monday, Michael

**Ginez de Sepulveda, Juan** 1490-1572 [HN]
*Spanish theologian and historian*
* [The] Livy of Spain

**Giniva, Alaska Jack**
See Giniva, John

**Giniva, John** 1868-1936 [SC]
*American actor*
* Giniva, Alaska Jack

**Ginn, Bo**
See Ginn, Ronald

**Ginn, Hubert** 1947- [SMG]
*American football player*
* Ginn, Wizard

**Ginn, Ronald** 20th c. [CBS]
*American politician*
* Ginn, Bo

**Ginn, Wizard**
See Ginn, Hubert

**Ginnes, Abram S.**
See Hershel, Abram Samuel

**Ginnes, Judith S.** 20th c. [CA]
*American author*
* Mitchell, Paige

**Ginnings, Harriett Wilcoxen** 1905- [CA]
*American author and illustrator*
* Harriett

**Ginsberg, Joe**
See Ginsberg, Myron Nathan

**Ginsberg, Myron Nathan** 1926- [BE, EJS]
*American baseball player*
* Ginsberg, Joe

**Ginsberg, Sol** 1885-1963 [ASC, BEW]
*Russian-born composer and musician*
* Violinsky, Solly

**Ginsburg, Elihu** 1888?-1976 [B10]
*American author*
* Gilner, Elias

**Gintzburger, Pierre** 1901- [JL]
*French political figure*
* Villon, Pierre

**Ginzberg, Asher** 1856-1927 [WBD]
*Russian author*
* Achad Haam

**Ginzburg, Natalia** 1916- [CA]
*Italian author and playwright*
* Tournimparte, Alessandra

**[La] Gioconda**
See Gherardini, Lisa di Anton Maria

**Gioe, Charles** ?-1954 [BLB, PHM]
*American underworld figure*
* Gioe, Cherry Nose

**Gioe, Cherry Nose**
See Gioe, Charles

**Giordano, Luca** 1632-1705 [WBD]
*Neapolitan painter*
* Fa Presto

**Giordano, Ralph Capabianca** 1905- [BX, RBE]
*Italian-born boxer*
* Corbett, Young, III

**Giordano, T-Bone**
See Giordano, Thomas Arthur [Tommy]

**Giordano, Thomas Arthur [Tommy]** 1925- [BE]
*American baseball player*
* Giordano, T-Bone

**Giorelli, Joseph** 20th c. [PHM]
*American underworld figure*
* Jelly, Joe

**[Il] Giorgione**
See Barbarelli, Giorgio

**Giornovichi, Giovanni Mane** 1745?-1804 [SN, WBD]
*Italian musician and composer*
* [The] Erratic Star
* Jarnowick

**[Il] Giovane [The Younger]**
See Palma, Jacopo

**Giovannetti, P. L.**
See Giovannetti, Pericle Luigi

**Giovannetti, Pericle Luigi** 1916- [GA]
*Italian cartoonist, illustrator, painter*
* Giovannetti, P. L.

**Giovanni delle Bande Nere [John of the Black Bands]**
See Medici, Giovanni de

**Giovanni, Nikki**
See Giovanni, Yolande Cornelia, Jr.

**Giovanni, Yolande Cornelia, Jr.** 1943- [CA, IBW]
*American poet, author, lecturer*
* Giovanni, Nikki
* [The] Princess of Black Poetry

**Giovannone, Anthony J.** 1923- [ASC]
*American musician*
* Johnson, Chatta

**Gipp, George** 1895-1920 [AS, FB]
*American football player*
* [The] Gipper

**[The] Gipper**
See Gipp, George

**Gippius, Zinaida Nikolaievna** 1869-1945 [B10]
*Russian author and poet*
* Krainy, Anton

**Gipson, Alvin** 20th c. [OBW]
*American baseball player*
* Gipson, Bubber

**Gipson, Bubber**
See Gipson, Alvin

**Gipstein, Yaacov** 1928- [JL]
*Israeli artist*
* Agam, Yaacov

**[The] Gipsy**
See Dudley, Robert

**Gir**
See Giraud, Jean

**Giraldez, Jose** 1837-1902 [GS]
*Spanish bullfighter*
* Jaqueta [Jacket]

**Giraldi, Giovanni Battista** 1504-1573 [DNNS, WBD]
*Italian author and poet*
* Cinthio [or Cintio]
* Cynthius

**Giraldus Cambrensis**
See Giraldus [or Gerald] de Barri

**Giraldus [or Gerald] de Barri** 1147-1222 [HN, RH, WBD]
*Welsh scholar, geographer, historian*
* Giraldus Cambrensis

**Girard, Earl** 20th c. [SMG]
*American football player*
* Girard, Jug

**Girard, Florence**
See Abbey, Mrs. Henry E.

**Girard, Gabrielle** 1926- [FC, OCF]
*French actress*
* Delorme, Daniele

**Girard, Jean Baptiste** 1765-1850 [WBD]
*Swiss educator*
* Gregoire, [Le Pere]

**Girard, Joe** 20th c.
*American author*
* [The] World's Greatest Salesman

**Girard, Jug**
See Girard, Earl

**Girardin, Dr.** 19th c. [FFF]
*Author*
* Alfred

**Girardin, Marc** 1801-1873 [WBD]
*French politician and author*
* Saint Marc Girardin, Francois Auguste

**Giraud, Albert**
See Kayenbergh, Marie Emile Albert

**Giraud, Henri** 1879-1949 [WWW]
*French army officer*
* King Pin [code name used during World War II]

**Giraud, Jean** 1938- [ESF]
*French cartoonist*
* Gir
* Moebius

**Giraudoux, Jean [Hippolyte]** 1882-1944 [EWL, TLC]
*French playwright and author*
* Andouard

**Giraudoux, Jean [Hippolyte]** (Continued)
* Cordelier, Jean
* Cordelier, Maurice
* Maniere, J. E.

**Girdansky, Gid**
See Girdansky, Joseph

**Girdansky, Joseph** 1890-1952 [EJS]
*American basketball player*
* Girdansky, Gid

**Giri, Varahagiri Venkata** 1895?-1980
*Indian president*
* [The] Genial Militant

**[The] Girl in the Red Velvet Swing**
See Thaw, Evelyn Nesbit

**[The] Girl in White**
See Henie, Sonja

**[The] Girl of Smiles**
See Moore, Monette

**[The] Girl with a Thousand Voices**
See Turner, Joan

**[The] Girl with Green Hair**
See Rhodes, Zandra Lindsey

**[The] Girl with the Golden Throat**
See Carr, Marie Louise

**[The] Girl with the Million Dollar Legs**
See Walters, Frankie

**[The] Girl with the Million Dollar Smile**
See Bigeou, Esther

**Girling, Zoe** 20th c. [WBD]
*Irish-born author*
* Hare, Martin

**Girodet de Roucy, Anne Louis** 1767-1824 [WBD]
*French painter*
* Girodet-Trioson

**Girodet-Trioson**
See Girodet de Roucy, Anne Louis

**Girolami, Enzo** 20th c. [FDG, WF]
*Italian actor and director*
* Castellari, E. G.
* Moore, Thomas
* Rowland, E. G.

**Girolami, Marino** 20th c. [FDG]
*Italian director*
* Wilson, Fred

**Giron, Curro**
See Giron Diaz, Francisco

**Giron Diaz, Francisco** 1938- [GS]
*Venezuelan bullfighter*
* Giron, Curro

**Gironella, Jose Maria**
See Gironella Pous, Jose Maria

**Gironella Pous, Jose Maria** 1917- [TC1]
*Spanish author*
* Gironella, Jose Maria

**Girotti, Mario** 1941- [SW, WF]
*Italian actor*
* Hill, Terence

**Girouard, Jacques**
See Earp, James William

Giroux, Colette 1935-    [OP]
*Canadian opera singer*
* Boky, Colette

Girowski, John 20th c.    [RBE]
*American boxer*
* Gerowski, John

Girsback, William 1913-    [EJ]
*American jazz musician*
* Gersh, Squire

Girty, Simon 1741-1818    [WBD]
*American soldier*
* [The] Great Renegade

[The] GI's General
See  Bradley, Omar Nelson

[The] GI's General
See  Collins, Joseph Lawton

Gisander
See  Schnabel, Johann Gottfried

Giscard, Monsieur
See  Carrillo, Santiago

Giscard d'Estaing, Valery 1926-
*French president*
* [The] Monarch

Gisentaner, Lefty
See  Gisentaner, Willie

Gisentaner, Willie 20th c.    [OBW]
*American baseball player*
* Gisentaner, Lefty

Gish, Dorothy
See  De Guiche, Dorothy

Gish, Lillian
See  De Guiche, Lillian

Gislingham, William Philip
1873-1958    [FC]
*British circus clown and acrobat*
* Kellino, Will P.

Gist, Kenneth, Jr. 20th c.    [RO2]
*American singer and songwriter*
* O'Dell, Kenny

Gistl, Johannes N. Franz Xavier
[PA]
*Author*
* Tilesius, G.

Gitana, Gertie
See  Astbury, Gertrude Mary

Gitanillo [Little Gypsy]
See  Lausin y Lopez, Braulio

Gitanillo de Triana [Little Gypsy
from Triana]
See  Vega De Los Reyes, Francisco

Gite
See  Turgeon, Jean

Gitfiddle Jim
See  Arnold, James

Gitlitz, Louis 1909-1978
[BEW, TR]
*American actor*
* Gilbert, Lou

Gittings, Jo [Grenville] Manton
1919-    [AW, CA, SAT]
*British author*
* Manton, Jo

Gittler, Morris 1905?-1959    [BEW]
*Polish-born lyricist and theatrical
performer*
* Gordon, Mack

Giudici, Ann Couper 1929-    [CA]
*American author*
* Tucker, Ann
* Tucker-Fettner, Ann

Giuliani, Angelo John 1912-    [BE]
*American baseball player*
* Giuliani, Tony

Giuliani, Tony
See  Giuliani, Angelo John

Giulio Romano
See  Caccini, Giulio

Giunta, Giuseppe 1907-1929
[BLB, PHM]
*Italian-born American underworld
figure*
* Giunta, Hop Toad
* Giunta, Joseph

Giunta, Hop Toad
See  Giunta, Giuseppe

Giunta, Joseph
See  Giunta, Giuseppe

Giunta, Pierre 1540?-1612?
[WBD]
*French playwright and translator*
* Larivey, Pierre de

Giuri, Adele
See  Pizzarno, Madame

Giuri, Marie
See  Rizzotti, Madame

Giurlani, Aldo 1885-1974
[CA, EWL, TCL]
*Italian poet and author*
* Palazzeschi, Aldo

[Il] Giuseppino
See  Cesari, Giuseppe [Cavalier
d'Arpino]

Give 'Em Hell Harry
See  Truman, Harry

Give-'em-Hell Mary
See  Buchanan, Mary Estill

Givenchy
See  Givenchy, Hubert de

Givenchy, Hubert de 1927-    [WFA]
*French fashion designer*
* Givenchy

Givot, George
*Comedian*
* [The] Greek Ambassador of
Goodwill

Gizoni, Anthony 20th c.    [BBH]
*American wrestler*
* Gizoni, Vic

Gizoni, Vic
See  Gizoni, Anthony

Gizycka, Eleanor M.
See  Patterson, Eleanor Medill

Gjerstad, John Leif 1924-
[BEW, TR]
*American actor, producer, director,
playwright*
* Gerstad, John

[The] Glacier Priest
See  Hubbard, Bernard Rosecrans

Gladden, E[dgar] Norman 1897-
[CA, WD]
*British civil servant and author*
* Mansfield, Norman

Gladding, Bear
See  Gladding, Fred Earl

Gladding, Fred Earl 1936-
[PB, SMG]
*American baseball player*
* Gladding, Bear

[The] Gladiator
See  Browning, Louis Rogers

Gladman, Buck
See  Gladman, John H.

Gladman, John H. 1864- ?    [BE]
*American baseball player*
* Gladman, Buck

Gladstone, Arthur 1861- ?    [LAO]
*British poet and author*
* Stone, Arthur

Gladstone, Arthur M. 1921-    [CA]
*American author*
* Gladstone, Maggie
* Norcross, Elizabeth
* Sebastian, Margaret
* Whitmore, Cilla

Gladstone, Jemima Compton    [FFF]
*Author*
* Comptom, Jemima

Gladstone, Josephine 1938-    [CA]
*British-born author and illustrator*
* Marquand, Josephine

Gladstone, Maggie
See  Gladstone, Arthur M.

[The] Gladstone of America
See  Blaine, James Gillespie

[The] Gladstone of America
See  Thurman, Allen Granbery

Gladstone, William Ewart
1809-1898    [DEP, FFF, PA]
*British statesman*
* [The] Atticus of Midlothian
* Bouverie, Bartholomew
* Etonensis
* G. O. M.
* [The] Grand Old Man
* [The] Grand Old Muddler
* [The] Great Commoner
* [The] Napoleon of Oratory
* [The] Old Man Eloquent
* [The] People's William

Gladwyn, Edward
See  Porter, David John

Glaisbrunner, Adolph 1810- ?    [PA]
*Author*
* Brunglas, Adolph

Glaiser, Bert
See  Glaiser, John Burke

Glaiser, Cukoo
See  Glaiser, John Burke

Glaiser, John Burke 1894-1959
[BN]
*American baseball player*
* Glaiser, Bert
* Glaiser, Cukoo

Glamack, George 1918-    [BB]
*American basketball player*
* [The] Blind Bomber

Glamis, Walter
See  Schachner, Nat[han]

Glamone, Pietro 1676-1748    [PA]
*Author*
* Jannonius

Glananville
See  Collin, Jacques Albin Simon

Glanville, Ranulph de  ?-1190
[DEP, SN]
*British statesman, jurist, author*
* [The] Father of Jurisprudence

Glanz, Lew
See  Glanzman, Louis

Glanz, Sarah 1877-1954    [SC]
*American actress*
* Berle, Sandra

Glanzman, Louis 20th c.    [SFP]
*Author*
* Glanz, Lew

Glareanus, Henricus
See  Loris, Heinrich

Glasbrenner
See  Fielhauer, Otto Magnus

Glasby, John [Stephen] 1928-    [SFL]
*British author*
* Cameron, Berl [joint pseudonym
with Arthur O. Roberts] [house
pseudonym, Curtis Warren]
* Dexter, J. B.
* La Salle, Victor [house
pseudonym]
* Le Page, Rand [joint pseudonym
with Arthur O. Roberts] [house
pseudonym, Curtis Warren]
* Lorraine, Paul [joint pseudonym
with Arthur O. Roberts] [house
pseudonym, Curtis Warren]
* Merak, A. J.
* Powers, J. L.

Glascock, Crystal
See  Glascock, David Albert

Glascock, David Albert 20th c.
[BBH]
*American basketball coach*
* Glascock, Crystal

Glaser, Comstock
See  Glaser, Kurt

Glaser, Eleanor Dorothy
See  Zonik, Eleanor Dorothy

Glaser, Karl Georg Hermann 1928-
[IAW]
*German author*
* Baier, Eric

Glaser, Kurt 1914-    [WD]
*American educator and author*
* Glaser, Comstock

Glaser, Milton 1929-    [CA, SAT]
*American author and illustrator*
* Catz, Max

Glaskin, Gerald Marcus 1923-
[AW, CA, WD]
*Australian author and playwright*
* Jackson, Neville

Glass Arm Eddie Brown
See  Brown, Edward William

Glass, Edgar 1879-1944    [FB]
*American football player*
* Glass, Ned

Glass, Frank 1884-1965    [FHE]
*Canadian-born hockey player*
* Glass, Pud

Glass, Justine C.
See  Corrall, Alice Enid

**Glass, Montague Marsden**
1877-1934   [TC]
*American author and playwright*
* Cossart, Theophilus

**Glass, Ned**
See  Glass, Edgar

**Glass, Pud**
See  Glass, Frank

**Glass, Sandra**
See  Shea, Robert [Joseph]

**Glass, Ted**
See  Golascu, Eduard

**Glass, Theodore** 1896-   [SFL]
*Author*
* Theodamus

**Glassbrenner, Adolf** 1810-1876
[WBD]
*German author*
* Brennglas, Adolf

**Glassco, John [Stinson]** 1909-
[AW, CA, CLC]
*Canadian poet and author*
* Bayer, Sylvia
* Colman, George
* De Saint Luc, Jean
* Gooch, Silas N.
* Okada, Hideki
* Underwood, Miles

**Glasscock, Amnesia**
See  Steinbeck, John [Ernst]

**Glasscock, Anne Bonner** 1924-
[CA]
*American author*
* Bonner, Michael

**Glasscock, John Wesley**
1859-1947   [AS, BE, BN]
*American baseball player*
* Glasscock, Pebbles
* Glasscock, Pebbly Jack

**Glasscock, Pebbles**
See  Glasscock, John Wesley

**Glasscock, Pebbly Jack**
See  Glasscock, John Wesley

**Glasse, Mrs.**
See  Hill, [Sir] John

**Glasser, Allen** 20th c.   [SFP]
*Author*
* Langell, Sears
* Zambock, George

**Glassford, James** 19th c.   [PA]
*Author*
* J. G.

**Glassford, Kate**
See  Burnett, Mrs. John

**Glassford, Wilfred**
See  McNeilly, Wilfred Glassford

**Glassmire, Augustin J.** 1879-1946
[SC]
*American actor*
* Glassmire, Gus

**Glassmire, Gus**
See  Glassmire, Augustin J.

**Glassock, W. D.** 1886?-1964
[BEW]
*Performer and theatre operator*
* Leon, W. D.

**Glatz, Herta** 1908-   [MS]
*Austrian opera singer*
* Glaz, Herta

**Glatzle, Mary** 1943-
*American police officer*
* Muggable Mary

**Glaviano, Rabbit**
See  Glaviano, Thomas Giatano

**Glaviano, Thomas Giatano** 1923-
[BE]
*American baseball player*
* Glaviano, Rabbit

**Glaz, Herta**
See  Glatz, Herta

**Glaze, Red Hot Willie**
See  McTell, Willie Samuel

**Glazer, Joe** 1918-   [FFA]
*American singer*
* Labor's Troubadour
* [The] Political Minstrel

**Glazer, Nona Y.**
See  Glazer-Malbin, Nona

**Glazer-Malbin, Nona** 1932-   [CA]
*American sociologist and author*
* Glazer, Nona Y.

**Glazner, Charles Franklin** 1893-
[BE]
*American baseball player*
* Glazner, Whitey

**Glazner, Whitey**
See  Glazner, Charles Franklin

**Gleadow, Rupert Seeley** 1909-
[AW, CA]
*British author*
* Case, Justin

**Gleaner**
See  Bowditch, Nathaniel Ingersoll

**Gleason, Kid**
See  Gleason, William J.

**Gleason, Lucille**
See  Webster, Lucille

**Gleason, William J.** 1866-1933
[AS, BE, PB]
*American baseball player and
manager*
* Gleason, Kid

**Glebov, Igor**
See  Asafiev, Boris Vladimirovitch

**Gledstanes, Elsie** 20th c.   [ART]
*British painter*
* E. G.

**Gleeson, Gee Gee**
See  Gleeson, James Joseph

**Gleeson, James Joseph** 1912-   [BE]
*American baseball player*
* Gleeson, Gee Gee

**Gleich, Frank Elmer** 1894-1949
[BE]
*American baseball player*
* Gleich, Inch

**Gleich, Inch**
See  Gleich, Frank Elmer

**Gleig, George Robert** 1796- ?   [PA]
*Author*
* [An] Officer

**Glemser, Bernard** 1908-
[ESF, SFL, WGT]
*British author*
* Crane, Robert
* Napier, Geoffrey
* Napier, Geraldine

**Glen, Duncan Munro** 1933-
[AW, WD]
*British poet, author, critic*
* Foster, Simon
* Munro, Ronald Eadie

**Glen, Eugene**
See  Fawcett, F[rank] Dubrez

**Glen, Richard** 1920-   [ITA]
*American business executive*
* Conley, Dick

**Glenalvin, Robert J. [Bob]**
See  Dowling, Rodney J.

**Glendinning, Sally**
See  Glendinning, Sara W[ilson]

**Glendinning, Sara W[ilson]** 1913-
[CA]
*American journalist*
* Glendinning, Sally

**Glendower, Owen** 1350?-1415?
[HN]
*Welsh rebel*
* [The] Wallace of Wales

**Glengarry**
See  Macdonald of Glengarry

**Glenmore, Addie**
See  Griffin, Alice McClure

**Glenn, Bob**
See  Glenn, Burdette

**Glenn, Burdette** 1894-   [BE]
*American baseball player*
* Glenn, Bob

**Glenn, Country**
See  Glenn, Hubert

**Glenn, Evans Tyree** 1912-   [MY]
*American jazz musician*
* Glenn, Fats

**Glenn, Fats**
See  Glenn, Evans Tyree

**Glenn, Gabber**
See  Gurzensky, Joseph Charles

**Glenn, Gertrude**
See  Ware, Mary Harris

**Glenn, Howdy**
See  Glenn, Morris

**Glenn, Hubert** 20th c.   [OBW]
*American baseball player*
* Glenn, Country

**Glenn, Ida**
See  Perley, Mrs. Frank

**Glenn, Joseph Charles**
See  Gurzensky, Joseph Charles

**Glenn, Morris** 1953-   [IBW]
*American country-western performer*
* Glenn, Howdy

**Glenn, Raymond Anthony** 1898-
[F2]
*Actor*
* Custer, Bob

**Gliatto, Sal**
See  Gliatto, Salvador Michael

**Gliatto, Salvador Michael** 1902-
[BE]
*American baseball player*
* Gliatto, Sal

**Glicenstein, Emanuel** 1904-   [WBD]
*Italian-born painter*
* Romano, Emanuel

**Glick, Bear**
See  Glick, Frederick C.

**Glick, Carl [Cannon]** 1890-1971
[CA, SAT]
*American author, playwright,
screenwriter*
* Cunningham, [Captain] Frank
* Holbrook, Peter

**Glick, Frederick C.** 1937-   [FB]
*American football player*
* Glick, Bear

**Glick, Virginia Kirkus** 1893-1980
[CAP]
*American author*
* Kirkus, Virginia

**Glidden, Frederick D[illey]**
1908-1975   [B10, CAP]
*American author*
* Short, Luke

**[The] Glider**
See  Charles, Edwin Douglas

**Gliewe, Unada [Grace]** 1927-
[CA, SAT, WD]
*American author and illustrator*
* Unada

**Gligor, Jovan**
See  Gligorijevic, Jovan

**Gligorijevic, Jovan** 1914-   [OP]
*Yugoslav opera singer*
* Gligor, Jovan

**Gline, Frank**
See  Rio, Frank

**Glipping [or Klipping]**
See  Eric V [or VII]

**Glitter, Gary**
See  Gadd, Paul

**Gloan**
See  Logan, Thomas A.

**Globerman, Yehoshua A.** 1918-
[CA]
*Polish-born Israeli journalist and
author*
* Gilboa, Yehoshua

**[The] Globetrotter**
See  Jeffords, Jerome

**Gloom, Dr.**
See  Wojnilower, Albert

**[The] Gloomy Dean**
See  Inge, William Ralph

**Gloomy Gil Dobie**
See  Dobie, Gilmour

**Gloomy Gus**
See  Nixon, Richard Milhous

**Gloomy Gus Henderson**
See  Henderson, Elmer C.

**Gloomy Gus Williams**
See  Williams, August

**[The] Gloomy Scribe**
See  Snaith, John Collis

**Glopfhaischt**
See  Christ, Robert Balthasar

**Gloriana**
See  Elizabeth I

**[The] Glorious**
See  Athelstan

**Glorious John**
See Dryden, John

**[The] Glorious Preacher**
See John

**[Der] Glorreiche [The Glorious]**
See Leopold VI

**[The] Glory and Reproach of Scotland**
See Burns, Robert

**[The] Glory of Italy**
See Battistini, Mattia

**[The] Glossator**
See Aldred

**Glossop, Maria Elizabeth** [FFF]
*Entertainer*
* Harris, Maria

**Glosup, Edward Dean** 1907?-
[ECM, FC]
*American actor and singer*
* Dean, Eddie

**Glosz, Marie**
See Golz, Rosemary

**Gloux, Olivier** 1818-1883 [WBD]
*French author*
* Aimard, Gustave

**Glovatski, Alexander**
See Glowacki, Aleksander

**Glover, Caroline H.** 1823- ? [FFF]
*American author*
* Howard, Caroline

**Glover, Denis [James Matthews]**
1912-1980 [CA]
*New Zealand author and poet*
* Kettle, Peter

**Glover, Frederick Austin [Freddie]**
1928- [FHE]
*Canadian-born hockey player*
* Glover, No Kid

**Glover, G. Clabon** ?-1934? [MBF]
*British author*
* Glover, Mark

**Glover, Ida**
See Dixey, Mrs. Henry E.

**Glover, Lefty**
See Glover, Thomas

**Glover, Leonides**
See Glover, Richard

**Glover, Lilian** 20th c. [BWW]
*American singer*
* Rainey, Memphis Ma

**Glover, Mark**
See Glover, G. Clabon

**Glover, Mike**
See Cavanaugh, Michael J.

**Glover, Modwena** 1916- [AW]
*British author and actress*
* Sedgwick, Modwena

**Glover, Mrs. Eliot** [FFF]
*American writer*
* Vey, Elinor

**Glover, No Kid**
See Glover, Frederick Austin
[Freddie]

**Glover, Richard** 1712-1785 [SN]
*British poet*
* Glover, Leonides

**Glover, Thomas** 1920- [IBW]
*American jazz musician*
* Josue, [Brother]

**Glover, Thomas** 20th c. [OBW]
*American baseball player*
* Glover, Lefty

**Glow-Worm**
See Baldwin, John Loraine

**Glowacki, Aleksander** 1847-1912
[CD, SFL]
*Polish journalist and author*
* Glovatski, Alexander
* Prus, Boleslaw

**Glubok, Shirley**
See Tamarin, Shirley Astor Glubok

**Gluchen, Freidrich Wilhelm**
1717-1783 [PA]
*Author*
* Russworm

**Gluck**
See Gluckstein, Hannah

**Gluck, Alma**
See Fiersohn, Reba

**Gluck, Arnold Jack** 1903?-1962
[BEW]
*Theatrical performer*
* Arnold, Jack

**Gluck, Christoph Willibald**
1714-1787 [DNNS, FFF, HN]
*German composer*
* [The] Hercules of Music
* [The] Michael Angelo of Music

**Gluck, Sinclair** 1887- [WW]
*Author*
* Danning, Melrod

**Gluckstein, Hannah** 1895- [CAR]
*British painter*
* Gluck

**Glud, Don**
See Glut, Donald F[rank]

**Glue Fingers Lavelli**
See Lavelli, Dante

**Glueck, Barbara Elisabeth**
1814-1894 [WBD]
*Austrian poet and author*
* Paoli, Betty

**Glueckberg, Alexander** 1880-1932
[JL]
*Russian poet*
* Cherny, Sasha

**Glut, Donald F[rank]** 1944-
[CA, WD]
*American author*
* Glud, Don
* Grant, Don
* Jason, Johnny
* Morrison, Victor
* Richmond, Rod
* Rogers, Mick
* Spektor, [Dr.] Adam
* Steele, Dale
* Thorne, Bradley D.

**[The] Glutton**
See Apicius, [Marcus] Gavius

**[The] Glutton**
See Charles IX

**[The] Glutton**
See Vitellius, Aulus

**Glyn, Harrison**
See Steffens, Arthur

**Glyn, Miss**
See Dallas, Isabelle Gearns

**Glyn, Neva Carr** ?-1975 [FIR]
*Australian actress*
* [The] Grand Old Lady of
Australian Theatre

**Glyndon, Howard**
See Searing, Laura C. Redden

**Glynn, A. A.**
See Glynn, Anthony Arthur

**Glynn, Anthony Arthur** 1929-
[SFL, SFP]
*Author*
* Glynn, A. A.
* Martin, Anthony
* Muller, John E. [house
pseudonym]

**Glynn, Bill**
See Moore, Muriel Sarah

**Glynn-Ward, H.**
See Howard, Hilda Glynn

**Glynne, Angela**
See West, Angela

**Glynne, Mary**
See Aitken, Mary

**Glyptic** [code name used during
World War II]
See Dzhugashvili, Iosif
Vissarionovich

**Gnaegy, Charles** 1938- [CA]
*American author*
* Grange, Chris
* Gregory, Chuck

**Gnass, Friedrich** 1892-1958 [SC]
*German actor*
* Gnass, Fritz

**Gnass, Fritz**
See Gnass, Friedrich

**Gniffke, Rudolf** 1937- [OP]
*German opera singer*
* Hartmann, Rudolf

**Gnoli, Domenico** 1838-1915 [CD]
*Italian poet and critic*
* Orsini, Giulio

**Gnosticus**
See Weschcke, Carl L[ouis]

**Goalie, Mr.**
See Hall, Glenn Henry

**Goaman, Muriel**
See Cox, Edith Muriel

**Goar, Joshua Mercer** 1870-1947
[BE]
*American baseball player*
* Goar, Jot

**Goar, Jot**
See Goar, Joshua Mercer

**[The] Goat**
See Duffy, Thomas

**[Il] Gobbo [The Hunchback]**
See Bonzi, Peter Paul

**[Il] Gobbo [The Hunchback]**
See Lonati

**[Il] Gobbo [The Hunchback]**
See Solari [or Solario], Christoforo

**[Del] Gobbo**
See Solari, Andrea

**[Il] Gobbo di Pisa**
See Amelunghi, Geronimo
[Girolamo]

**Gobel, George Leslie** 1919- [CWG]
*American comedian and actor*
* Gobel, Little Georgie
* [The] Little Cowboy
* Lonesome George

**Gobel, Little Georgie**
See Gobel, George Leslie

**[The] God of All Philosophers**
See Aristocles

**[The] God of All Philosophers**
See Cicero, Marcus Tullius

**[The] God of Dancing**
See Vestris, Gaetano Apollino
Balthazar

**[The] God of Flowers**
See Varelst, Simon

**[The] God of Hell Fire**
See Wilton, Arthur

**Godard, Jean-Luc** 1930- [CA]
*French screenwriter and director*
* Lucas, Hans

**Goddard, Alfred**
See Harper, Carol Ely

**Goddard, Ernest Hope** 1879-1939
[MBF]
*British editor*
* Hamilton, Ernest

**Goddard, Josephine Lawrence**
1930- [ITA]
*American actress*
* Lawrence, Jody

**Goddard, Norman Molyneux**
1881-1917 [MBF]
*British author*
* Barr, Nat
* Cannon, J. R.
* Custer, Claude
* Darran, Mark
* Haviland, [Captain] Fergus
* Pergarth, Peter
* Rich, Henry K.

**Goddard, Paulette**
See Levee, Pauline Marion
Goddard

**Godden, Rumer**
See Foster, Mrs. Laurence

**Godden, Rumer**
See Haynes Dixon, Margaret
Rumer

**[The] Goddess of Liberty**
See Malliard, Mlle.

**Gode, Alexander**
See Gode Von Aesch, Alexander
[Gottfried Friedrich]

**Gode Von Aesch, Alexander**
[Gottfried Friedrich] 1906-1970
[CAP]
*German-born American author*
* Gode, Alexander

**Godeau, Antoine** [SN]
*Author and poet*
* Julia's Dwarf

**Godebska, Marie Sophie Olga Zenaide** 1872-1950
*Russian-born patron of the Arts*
* Sert, Misia

**Godecke, Peter Auguste** [FFF]
*Swedish author and editor*
* Finn

**Godeffroy, Ottilie** 1881-1971 [SC]
*Austrian-born actress*
* Durieux, Tilla

**Goderic**
See Henry I

**Goderich, Goosey**
See Robinson, Frederick John [Viscount Goderich and Earl of Ripon]

**Godey, John**
See Freedgood, Morton

**[The] Godfather**
See Sandoval Alarcon, Mario

**[The] Godfather of Funk**
See Clinton, George

**[The] Godfather of Soul**
See Brown, James

**Godfrey, Charles**
See Lacey, Paul

**Godfrey, Charles**
See Webb, Godfrey Edward Charles

**Godfrey, [Sir] Edmundbury** 1621-1678 [DEP]
*British jurist*
* [The] Protestant Martyr

**Godfrey, George**
See Williams, Feab. S.

**Godfrey, Hal**
See Eccles, Charlotte O'Conor

**Godfrey, Jane**
See Bowden, Joan Chase

**Godfrey, John R.**
See Colvin, Fred Herbert

**Godfrey, Lionel Robert Holcombe** 1932- [AW, WD]
*British author*
* Kennedy, Elliot
* Mitchell, Scott

**Godfrey, Marcel**
See Isaacs, Marcel Godfrey

**Godfrey of Bouillon** 1061?-1100 [HN]
*Leader of First Crusade*
* Baron of the Holy Sepulchre
* Defender and Baron of the Holy Sepulchre

**Godfrey, R. H.**
See Tubb, Edwin Charles

**Godfrey, Rocky**
See Godfrey, Warren Edward

**Godfrey, Vivian** 1921- [CA]
*British author*
* Denning, Melita

**Godfrey, Warren Edward** 1931- [CEI, FHE, HK]
*Canadian-born hockey player*
* Godfrey, Rocky

**Godfrey, William**
See Youd, Christopher Samuel

**Godfrey-Turner, L.**
See Turner, Leopold McClintock

**Godithe [or Godiva]**
See Matilda [or Maud]

**Godley, John**
See Kilbracken, John [Raymond Godley]

**Godley, Robert** 1908- [WW]
*Author*
* James, Franklin

**Godly, J. P.**
See Plawin, Paul

**[The] Godmother of the Israeli Fashion Image**
See Leitersdorf, Fini

**Godolphin, Sidney** 1645-1712 [SN]
*British statesman*
* Volpone

**Godoy, Manuel de** 1767-1851 [DHA, DNNF, DNNS]
*Spanish statesman*
* [The] Prince of the Peace
* Principe de la Paz

**Godoy Alcayaga, Lucila** 1889-1957 [B10, EWL]
*Chilean poet and educator*
* Mistral, Gabriela

**God's Fool**
See Van Wagener, Isabelle

**God's Pamphleteer**
See Munoz Marin, Luis

**Godwin, Frank**
See Starr, Richard Harry

**Godwin, John [Frederick]** 1922- [CA]
*British author*
* Foster, Frederick

**Godwin, John** 1929- [CA]
*Australian-born author*
* Stark, John

**Godwin, Mary** 1759-1797 [PA]
*Author*
* Wollstoncroft

**Godwin, William** 1756-1836 [DEL, FFF, PA]
*British author and philosopher*
* Baldwin, [Rev.] Edward
* Marcliffe, Theophilus
* [The] Sage of Skinner Street
* Verax

**Goebel, Dutch**
See Goebel, William A.

**Goebel, William A.** 1887-1960 [FB]
*American football player*
* Goebel, Dutch

**Goedeke, Karl** 1814-1887 [WBD]
*German scholar*
* Stahl, Karl

**Goedicke, Patricia [McKenna]** 1931- [CA]
*American poet and educator*
* McKenna, Patricia

**Goering, Helga**
See Wallmann, Jeffrey M[iner]

**Goering, Hermann** 1893-1946 [BDW]
*German Nazi leader*
* [The] Fat One

**Goes, Clifford T.** 20th c. [BBH]
*American rowboat racer*
* Rowing U.S.A., Mr.

**Goetchius, Marie Louise**
See Gibson, Marice Louise

**Goetgheluck Le Rouge Taillard Des Acres De Presfontaines, Jean Rene** 1907- [OCF, WEF]
*French director and critic*
* Mitry, Jean

**Goethals, Henry** 1227-1293 [DNNF, DNNS, SN]
*Scholar*
* Henry of Ghent
* [The] Illustrious Doctor
* [The] Solemn Doctor
* Solemnis, Doctor

**Goethe, Johann Wolfgang von** 1749-1832 [DNNS, FFF, SN]
*German poet*
* [The] Confidant
* [The] Coryphaeus of German Literature
* [The] Evangelist of Economy
* [The] German Voltaire
* [The] Great Heathen
* [The] Honest Goetz von Berlichingen
* [The] Master
* [Der] Meister
* [The] Prince of Poets
* [The] Voltaire of Germany
* [The] Wanderer

**Goethe, Katharina Elizabeth** 18th c. [SN]
*Mother of German poet, Johann Wolfgang von Goethe*
* Aja, Frau

**Goethe-Tischbein**
See Tischbein, Johann Heinrich Wilhelm

**Goetsch-Trevelyan, Katharine**
See Trevelyan, Katharine

**Goetten, L. J.** 20th c. [ITA]
*American producer and director*
* Marlowe, Louis J.

**Goetz, Fred** 20th c. [BLB]
*American underworld figure*
* Ziegler, Shotgun

**Goetz, George** 1900-1940 [TC]
*American critic and editor*
* Calverton, Victor Francis

**Goetz, Raphael** 1559-1662 [PA]
*Author*
* Eglin

**Goetz with the Iron Hand**
See Berlichingen, Goetz [or Gottfried] von

**Goff, Dorothy** 1915-1934 [SC]
*American actress*
* Dell, Dorothy

**Goff, Elijir**
See Davies, William

**Goffage, John** 1909-1971 [FC, OCF]
*Australian actor*
* Rafferty, Chips

**Goffart, Francis-Leo** 1903- [IAW]
*Belgian-born author*
* De Ransart, Robert

**Goffstein, M. B.**
See Schaaf, Marilyn Brooke Goffstein

**Gog**
See Hogg, Gordon

**Goggan, John Patrick** 1906?- [TC1]
*American playwright*
* Patrick, John

**Gogisgi**
See Arnett, Carroll

**Goheen, Francis Xavier** 1894- [BBH, WA]
*American hockey player*
* Goheen, Moose

**Goheen, Moose**
See Goheen, Francis Xavier

**Gohm, D. C.**
See Van De Gohm, Richard

**Gohm, Douglas**
See Van De Gohm, Richard

**Gohman, Fred Joseph** 1918- [CA]
*American author and illustrator*
* Webb, Spider

**Goimbault, Odette** 1901- [F2, FC]
*French actress*
* Odette, Mary

**Goins, Nellie Louise** 1940- [IBW]
*American auto racer*
* Goins, Nitro Nellie

**Goins, Nitro Nellie**
See Goins, Nellie Louise

**Gojawiczynska, Apolonia** 1896- [CD]
*Polish author*
* Gojawiczynska, Pola

**Gojawiczynska, Pola**
See Gojawiczynska, Apolonia

**Gojkovic, Dusan** 1931- [EJ]
*Yugoslav-born jazz musician*
* Gojkovic, Dusko

**Gojkovic, Dusko**
See Gojkovic, Dusan

**Gokceli, Yashar Kemal** 1922- [B10, CA]
*Turkish author and journalist*
* Kemal, Yashar

**Golab, Tony** 20th c. [CFH]
*Canadian football player*
* [The] Golden Boy

**Golan, Matti**
See Goldwasser, Matti

**Golascu, Eduard** 1892- [CAR]
*American artist*
* Glass, Ted

**Golaw, Salomon von**
See Logau, Friedrich von

**Golay, Alice** 20th c. [IAW]
*Swiss author*
* Rivaz, Alice

**Gold, Alan R[obert]** 1948- [CA]
*American optometrist and writer*
* Simmons, David

**Gold, Beatrice**
See Dunnigan, Belle

**Gold, Captain**
See Copeland, Kenny

[The] Gold Chain Troubador
See Tubb, Ernest Dale

Gold Ela Krzesinska
See Krzesinska, Elzbieta

Gold, Ernest
See Goldner, Ernest Siegmund

Gold, Evelyn Paige 20th c. [WGT]
American author
* Paige, Evelyn

Gold, Frank
See De Campos, Luis

Gold, H. L.
See Gold, Horace Leonard

Gold, Hal
See Goldberg, Harry

Gold, Harry
See Golodnotzky, Harry

Gold, Horace Leonard 1914-
[ESF, SF, WGT]
Canadian-born author and editor
* Campbell, Clyde Crane
* Dell, Dudley
* Fosse, Harold C.
* Gold, H. L.
* Graey, Julian
* Keith, Leigh
* Story, Richard

Gold, Jack
See Gold, Jacob

Gold, Jacob 1921- [ASC]
American composer, singer,
recording executive
* Gold, Jack

Gold, Michael
See Granich, Irving

Gold Mine Jimmy
See Carrigio, Jimmy

Gold, Phyllis
See Goldberg, Phyllis

Goldast, Melchior 1578-1635
[WBD]
German jurist and historian
* Goldast von Haimensfeld

Goldast von Haimensfeld
See Goldast, Melchior

Goldberg, Arthur 1923- [JL]
Austrian-born poet
* Gregor, Arthur

Goldberg, Ben W. 1918- [JL]
American journalist
* Gilbert, Ben W.

Goldberg, Biggie
See Goldberg, Marshall

Goldberg, Doc
See Goldberg, Edward

Goldberg, Dora 1880-1928
[EMT, FC, PMJ]
American singer and actress
* Bayes, Nora

Goldberg, Edward 1913- [MY]
American jazz musician
* Goldberg, Doc

Goldberg, Harry 1912- [ASC]
American musician
* Gold, Hal

Goldberg, Jan
See Curran, Jan Goldberg

Goldberg, Louis T[heodore] 1943-
[CA]
American educator and author
* Grant, Louis T[heodore]
* Magister, Joseph

Goldberg, Mad Marshall
See Goldberg, Marshall

Goldberg, Marshall 1917?-
[EJS, FB]
American football player
* Goldberg, Biggie
* Goldberg, Mad Marshall

Goldberg, Milton M. 1918- [JL]
American sociologist and author
* Gordon, Milton M.

Goldberg, Phyllis 1941- [CA]
American author
* Gold, Phyllis

Goldberg, Reuben Lucius
1883-1970 [ASC, SC]
American cartoonist and author
* Goldberg, Rube

Goldberg, Rube
See Goldberg, Reuben Lucius

Goldberg, Samuel 1911?-1949
[BEW, PMJ]
American singer
* Clark, Buddy

Goldberger, Marvin 1922?-
American physicist
* Goldberger, Murph

Goldberger, Murph
See Goldberger, Marvin

Goldblatt, Charles 1929- [TR]
Irish-born actor, director, producer
* Vance, Charles

Goldblatt, Emanuel 1904- [EJS]
American basketball player
* Goldblatt, Menchy

Goldblatt, Menchy
See Goldblatt, Emanuel

Goldblatt, Mose 1869-1941 [EJS]
American horse trainer and owner
* Uncle Mose

Goldbogen [or Goldenborgen], Avrom
1907-1958 [BEW, EMT, FC]
American producer
* Todd, Michael

Goldemberg, Rose Leiman 20th c.
[CA]
American author and playwright
* Schiller, Rose Leiman
* Traven, Beatrice

[The] Golden
See Dorat, Jean

[The] Golden Arm
See Brkovich, Mike

[The] Golden Ball
See Hughes, Ball

[The] Golden Bear
See Nicklaus, Jack William

[The] Golden Boy
See Brown, Robert William

[The] Golden Boy
See Clark, Scott

[The] Golden Boy
See Golab, Tony

Golden Boy Hornung
See Hornung, Paul

Golden, Doc
See Golden, Edward

Golden, Dorothy 20th c. [AW]
British author
* Dennison, Dorothy

Golden Eagle
See Popovich, Pavel

Golden, Edward 1887?-1972 [FIR]
Producer
* Golden, Doc

Golden Girl
See Booker, Mease

[The] Golden Girl
See Hollins, Marion

[The] Golden Gorf
See Guindon, Robert

[The] Golden Greek
See Agganis, Harry

[The] Golden Greek
See Christoforidis, Anton

[The] Golden Greek
See Grammas, Alexander Peter

[The] Golden Greek
See Londos, Jim

[The] Golden Greek
See Pappas, Milt[on Steven]

Golden, Harry
See Goldhurst, Harry

[The] Golden Hippie
See Getty, J[ean] Paul, III

[The] Golden Jet
See Hull, Robert Marvin [Bobby]

[The] Golden Man of the Speedways
See DePaolo, Peter

Golden, Max T.
See Marryshow, Theophilus Albert

Golden Mouth
See Anderton, Laurence

[The] Golden Mouth
See Dion

Golden Mouth
See John

[The] Golden Mouthed
See Drayton, Michael

[The] Golden Necklace of the Blues
See Rainey, Gertrude Malissa Nix
[Pridgett]

Golden Nose
See Brahe, Tycho

Golden Rule Jones
See Jones, Samuel Milton

Golden Silver
See Storm, Hyemeyohsts

Golden Speech
See Peter [or Pietro]

[The] Golden Stream
See John of Damascus [or
Johannes Damascenus]

[The] Golden Tongued
See Menot, Michael

[The] Golden Tongued
See Peter [or Pietro]

[The] Golden Torpedo
See Hveger, Ragnhild

[The] Golden Turkey
See Firmani, Eddie

[The] Golden Voice of the North
See Balewa, [Sir] Alhaji Abukakar
Tafewa

Golden Wheels Dubenion
See Dubenion, Elbert

Goldenberg, Buckets
See Goldenberg, Charles R.

Goldenberg, Charles R. 1911-
[EJS, SMG]
American football player
* Goldenberg, Buckets

Goldenberg, Emanuel 1893-1973
[BEW, F2, FC]
Rumanian-born American actor
* Robinson, Edward G.

Goldenthal, Allan Benarria 1920-
[CA]
American author
* Benarria, Allan

Goldfeder, [Anne] Cheryl Suzanne
1949- [CA, SAT]
American author and illustrator
* Pahz, [Anne] Cheryl Suzanne
* Paz, Zan

Goldfeder, [Kenneth] James 1943-
[CA, SAT]
American educator and author
* Pahz, James Alon
* Paz, A.

Goldfield, Donald Elliott 1930-
[EJ]
American jazz musician
* Goldie, Don

Goldfinger
See Vaughan, Jack

Goldfish, Samuel 1882?-1974
[BDF, FC, IPA]
Polish-born American producer
* Goldwyn, Samuel

Goldfrank, Helen [Colodny] 1912-
[B10, CA, SAT]
American author
* Kay, Helen

Goldfrap, John Henry 1879-1917
[SFL]
Author
* Lawton, [Capt.] Wilbur

Goldfus, Emil R.
See Abel, Rudolf Ivanovich

Goldgraber, Kenneth 1909- [CAT]
American author
* Raphael, [Father] M.
* Simon, Kenneth

Goldhurst, Harry 1902-1981 [IPA]
American author
* Golden, Harry

Goldie, Don
See Goldfield, Donald Elliott

Goldie, Kathleen Annie 20th c.
[AW]
British author
* Fidler, Kathleen

**Goldie, Mary Elizabeth Kathleen Dulcie** 1890- [WWL]
*Australian author*
* Deamer, Dulcie

**Goldin, Miriam** 1898- [BEW]
*Russian-born actress and director*
* Goldina, Miriam

**Goldin, Stephen** 1947- [CA]
*American author*
* Stephens, Charles

**Goldina, Miriam**
See Goldin, Miriam

**Golding, Louise Sarah** 1923- [AW]
*British author and nutritionist*
* Davies, Louise

**Golding, Morton J[ay]** 1925- [CA]
*American author*
* Lloyd, Stephanie
* Martin, Jay
* Michaeles, M. M.
* Morton, Patricia

**Goldlace**
See Banning, E. P.

**Goldman, Harry**
See Stacher, Joseph

**Goldman, Harry** 1857-1941 [EJS]
*American financier*
* Goldman, Judge

**Goldman, Jim** 20th c.
*American television journalist*
* Gardner, Jim

**Goldman, Judge**
See Goldman, Harry

**Goldman, Theodore** 1924- [TR]
*American producer and director*
* Mann, Theodore

**Goldman, William W.** 1931-
[CA, WD]
*American author, playwright, screenwriter*
* Longbaugh, Harry

**Goldmann, Max** 1873-1943
[BEW, IPA, LC]
*Austrian producer and director*
* Reinhardt, Max

**Goldmark, Aaron** 1911?-1977
[FIR]
*Musician*
* Goldmark, Goldie

**Goldmark, Goldie**
See Goldmark, Aaron

**Goldner, Ernest Siegmund** 1921-
[PAC]
*Austrian-born American composer*
* Gold, Ernest

**Goldney, Kate** 1856-1931 [BEW]
*British actress*
* Phillips, Kate

**Goldoni, Carlo** 1707-1793
[DEP, DNNF, FFF]
*Italian playwright*
* [The] Italian Moliere
* [The] Moliere of Italy

**Goldring, Douglas** 1887- [LAO]
*British author and poet*
* Willoughby, George

**Goldsberry, Alonzo E.** 20th c.
[BBH]
*American basketball player and coach*
* Goldsberry, Goldie
* Goldsberry, Lon

**Goldsberry, Goldie**
See Goldsberry, Alonzo E.

**Goldsberry, Lon**
See Goldsberry, Alonzo E.

**Goldsby, Crawford** 1876-1896
[IBW]
*American Indian scout*
* Cherokee Bill

**Goldschmidt, [Dr.] Hans** 1893-
[NAA]
*German-born American tool designer and engineer*
* Smith, H. W.

**Goldschmidt, Hermann** 1860- ?
[LAO]
*German author and playwright*
* Faber, Hermann
* Goldschmidt-Faber, Hermann

**Goldschmidt, M. A.** [PA]
*Author*
* Meyer, Adolph

**Goldschmidt-Faber, Hermann**
See Goldschmidt, Hermann

**Goldschmied, Georg** 1516-1571
[WBD]
*German scholar, philologist, poet*
* Fabricius, Georg

**Goldsmith, Carol Evan** 1930- [CA]
*American author*
* Evan, Carol

**Goldsmith, Cele**
See Lalli, Cele G[oldsmith]

**Goldsmith, Christabel**
See Smith, Fannie N.

**Goldsmith, Edith** 1913- [BEW, TR]
*American author and drama critic*
* Oliver, Edith

**Goldsmith, Hilliard Oliver Claude**
1918- [BEW]
*American songwriter, producer, publisher*
* Hilliard, Bob

**Goldsmith, Howard** 1943- [CA]
*American author*
* Smith, Ward

**Goldsmith, [Rev.] J.**
See Phillips, [Sir] Richard

**Goldsmith, Jay Carlton** [FFF, PA]
*Author*
* Carlton, Jay

**Goldsmith, John Herman Thorburn**
1903- [IAW]
*British author*
* Thorburn, John

**Goldsmith, Milton** 1861- ? [NAA]
*American author, playwright, poet*
* Cielo, Astra

**[The] Goldsmith of America**
See Taylor, Benjamin Franklin

**[The] Goldsmith of the Bar**
See Burrowes, Peter

**Goldsmith, Oliver** 1728-1774
[DEP, DNNF, PA]
*British author, poet, playwright*
* [The] Child of Nature
* [The] Chinese Philosopher
* [A] Citizen of the World
* Goldy
* [The] Impenetrable Goodman Dull
* [The] Inspired Idiot

**Goldsmith, Peter**
See Priestley, John Boynton

**Goldsmith, Willie E., Jr.** 1964-
[IBW]
*American track and field athlete*
* [The] Fastest Kid in the World

**Goldstandt, Edit** 1895-1971 [SC]
*German-born actress*
* Angold, Edit

**Goldstein, Ann Brody** 1884-1944
[SC]
*Polish-born actress*
* Brody, Ann

**Goldstein, Betty Naomi** 1921-
[IPA]
*American feminist author*
* Friedan, Betty

**Goldstein, Braham** 1943- [TR]
*British director*
* Murray, Braham

**Goldstein, Elliott** 1938-
[BEW, EMT, FC]
*American actor*
* Gould, Elliott

**Goldstein, Ervine Max** ?-1928
[EJS]
*American football player*
* Goldstein, Goldy

**Goldstein, Fania** 1918- [CA]
*French author and musician*
* Fenelon, Fania

**Goldstein, Goldie**
See Goldstein, Hyman

**Goldstein, Goldy**
See Goldstein, Ervine Max

**Goldstein, Hyman** 1892- [EJS]
*American football player*
* Goldstein, Goldie

**Goldstein, Little Lou**
See Goldstein, Lou

**Goldstein, Lou** 20th c. [MEB]
*American basketball player*
* Goldstein, Little Lou

**Goldstein, Max** 1917- [EJS]
*American fencing coach*
* Garret, Mac
* Garret, Maxwell Robert

**Goldstein, Michael** 20th c. [FIR]
*American actor*
* Gorrin, Michael

**Goldstein, Moisei Markovich**
1891-1918 [B10]
*Russian revolutionist*
* Volodarsky

**Goldstein, Reuben** 1907-
[BX, EJS, RBE]
*American boxer*
* Goldstein, Ruby
* [The] Jewel of the Ghetto

**Goldstein, Ruby**
See Goldstein, Reuben

**Goldstein, Stanley L.** 1926- [JL]
*American philosopher*
* Cavell, Stanley L.

**Goldstein, William Isaac** 1932-
[CA]
*American author*
* Lode, Rex

**Goldstick, Cecil** 20th c. [SMG]
*Sportscaster*
* Goldstick, Tiger

**Goldstick, Tiger**
See Goldstick, Cecil

**Goldston, Black Happy**
See Goldston, Christopher

**Goldston, Christopher** 1894-1968
[NOJ]
*American jazz musician*
* Goldston, Black Happy

**Goldston, Robert Conroy** 1927-
[AW, B10, CA]
*American author*
* Conroy, Robert
* Stark, James

**Goldstone, Aline Lewis** 20th c.
[NAA]
*American poet*
* Lewis, May

**Goldstone, Lawrence Arthur** 1903-
[CA, CC, WW]
*American author*
* Treat, Lawrence

**Goldsworthy, Goldy**
See Goldsworthy, William Alfred

**Goldsworthy, William Alfred** 1944-
[SMG]
*Canadian-born hockey player*
* Goldsworthy, Goldy

**Goldszmit, Henryk** 1878-1942
[B10]
*Polish poet, psychologist, educator*
* Korczak, Janusz

**Goldwasser, Alexander Jacob**
1932- [CA]
*Polish-born American political scientist and author*
* Groth, Alexander J[acob]

**Goldwasser, Matti** 1936- [CA]
*Israeli author*
* Golan, Matti

**Goldwater, Barry [Morris]** 1909-
*American politician*
* Au H2O
* Old Goldy

**Goldwyn, Samuel**
See Goldfish, Samuel

**Goldy**
See Goldsmith, Oliver

**Goldy, Purn**
See Goldy, Purnal William

**Goldy, Purnal William** 1937-
[SMG]
*American baseball player*
* Goldy, Purn

**Golf Bag Hunt**
See Hunt, Samuel McPherson

**Golf, Loyal Eugene** 1926-  [CA]
*American clergyman and author*
* Golv, Loyal E[ugene]

**Golf, Mr.**
*See* Dey, Joseph C., Jr.

**Goliard, Roy**
*See* Shipley, Joseph Twaddell

**Golitsa**
*See* Bulgakov, Mikhail Ivanovich

**Goll, Iwan [or Yvan]**
*See* Lang, Isaac

**Goller, Celia [Fremlin]** 1914-  [CA]
*British author*
* Fremlin, Celia

**Golodnotzky, Harry** 20th c.  [JL]
*Swiss-born intelligence agent*
* Gold, Harry

**Golon, Anne** 20th c.  [SFL]
*Author*
* Golon, Sergeanne [joint
   pseudonym with Serge Golon]

**Golon, Serge** 1903-1972  [SFL]
*Author*
* Golon, Sergeanne [joint
   pseudonym with Anne Golon]

**Golon, Sergeanne** [joint pseudonym
with Serge Golon]
*See* Golon, Anne

**Golon, Sergeanne** [joint pseudonym
with Anne Golon]
*See* Golon, Serge

**Golsworthy, Arnold** 1864- ?
[WWL]
*British author*
* Holcombe, Arnold
* Jingle

**Golv, Loyal E[ugene]**
*See* Golf, Loyal Eugene

**Golz, Rosemary** 1880-1963  [SC]
*Actress and opera singer*
* Glosz, Marie

**Gomarus, Franciscus**
*See* Gommer, Franciscus

**Gombell, Minna** 1900-1973
[F2, FC]
*American actress*
* Carter, Nancy
* Lee, Winifred

**Gomberg, Vladimir Germanovich**
1894-  [TC]
*Russian author*
* Lidin, Vladimir

**Gomberg, William Gilbert** 1916-
[BEW, CA]
*American playwright and
screenwriter*
* Bensol, Oscar
* Gilbert, Willie
* Mareth, Glenville [joint
   pseudonym with Jack Weinstock]

**Gombossy, Zoltan**
*See* Gabel, Joseph

**Gomez, Adriesue** 1942?-  [B10]
*American truck driver*
* Gomez, Bitzi

**Gomez, Alfredo**  [GS]
*Mexican bullfighter*
* [El] Brilliantino [The Little Shiny
  One]

**Gomez, Augie**
*See* Gomez, Augustine Whitecloud

**Gomez, Augustine Whitecloud**
1891-1966  [SC]
*American actor*
* Gomez, Augie

**Gomez, Bitzi**
*See* Gomez, Adriesue

**Gomez, Chile**
*See* Gomez, Jose Luis Rodriguez

**Gomez, Goofy**
*See* Gomez, Vernon Louis

**Gomez, Jose**  [GS]
*Spanish bullfighter*
* [El] Alba [The Dawn]

**Gomez, Jose Luis Rodriguez** 1909-
[BE]
*Mexican-born baseball player*
* Gomez, Chile

**Gomez, Lefty**
*See* Gomez, Vernon Louis

**Gomez, Melchior**
*See* Gonzales, Louis Jean
Emmanuel

**Gomez, Preston**
*See* Gomez Martinez, Pedro

**Gomez, Raul** 20th c.  [GS]
*Colombian bullfighter*
* Colombo

**Gomez, Vernon Louis** 1909-
[BE, DGS, PB]
*American baseball player*
* [The] Gay Castillion
* Gomez, Goofy
* Gomez, Lefty

**Gomez Calleja, Luis** 1911-  [GS]
*Spanish bullfighter*
* [El] Estudiante [The Student]

**Gomez Cima, Victoria** 1923-
[BBD]
*Spanish opera singer*
* De Los Angeles, Victoria

**Gomez De Baquero, Eduardo**
1866-1929  [CD]
*Spanish journalist and critic*
* Andrenio

**Gomez de la Serna, Ramon** 1891-
[TC, WBD]
*Spanish author and poet*
* Ramon

**Gomez Leon, Diego** 1911-1962
[GS]
*Spanish bullfighter*
* Laine

**Gomez Lopez, Rliseo** 1932-  [GS]
*Mexican bullfighter*
* [El] Charro [The Horseman]

**Gomez Martinez, Pedro** 1923-
[BE, PB, SMG]
*Cuban-born baseball coach and
manager*
* Gomez, Preston

**Gomez Ortega, Jose** 1895-1920
[GS, OCS, SA]
*Spanish bullfighter*
* Gallito [Little Rooster]
* Joselito [Little Joe]

**Gomez Ortega, Rafael** 1882-1960?
[GS, OCS]
*Spanish bullfighter*
* [El] Divino Calvo [The Divine
  Bald-Headed One]
* [El] Gallo [The Rooster]

**Gomez y Canete, Julio** 1886-1947
[GS]
*Spanish bullfighter*
* Relampaguito [Little Lightning
  Flash]

**Gommer, Franciscus** 1563-1641
[WBD]
*Dutch theologian*
* Gomarus, Franciscus

**Gompers, Samuel** 1850-1924  [JL]
*British-born labor leader*
* [The] Father of the American
  Labor Movement

**Gompertz, [Major] M. L. A.**
*See* Gompertz, Martin Louis Alan

**Gompertz, Martin Louis Alan**
1886-1951  [CAT, WW, WGT]
*British author*
* Ganpat
* Gompertz, [Major] M. L. A.

**Gondelin, Peter** 1550-1619  [PA]
*Author*
* Gudelinus

**Gondi, Jean Francois Paul de**
1614-1679  [FFF, HN, SN]
*French prelate and politician*
* Monsieur le Coadjuteur
* Retz, Cardinal de
* Retz, Catiline

**Gonelli, Giovanni** 1610-1664  [HN]
*Italian sculptor*
* [The] Blind Man of Cambassi
* [The] Blind Sculptor

**Goneril, Ramon**
*See* Gonzales, Louis Jean
Emmanuel

**Gongora y Argote, Luis de**
1561-1627  [SN]
*Spanish poet*
* [The] Wonderful

**Gonsalves, Bill** 1908-  [BBH]
*American soccer player*
* Soccer, Mr.

**Gonsalves, John P.** 1925-  [ASC]
*American composer, singer,
recording executive*
* Gonsalves, Joli

**Gonsalves, Joli**
*See* Gonsalves, John P.

**Gonsalves, Mex**
*See* Gonsalves, Paul

**Gonsalves, Paul** 1920-1974  [EJ7]
*American jazz musician*
* Gonsalves, Mex

**Gonsoulin, Austin** 1938-
[FB, SMG]
*American football player*
* Gonsoulin, Goose

**Gonsoulin, Goose**
*See* Gonsoulin, Austin

**Gonthier de Biran, Marie Francois
Pierre** 1766-1824  [WBD]
*French philosopher*
* Maine de Biran

**Gonzaga, Tomaz Antonio**
1744-1807  [WBD]
*Portuguese poet*
* Dirceu

**Gonzales, Bli** ?-1756
[DNNF, DNNS, FFF]
*Spanish felon*
* Spanish Jack
* Symmonds, John

**Gonzales, Joe**
*See* Gonzales, Jose Madrid

**Gonzales, John**
*See* Terrall, Robert

**Gonzales, Jose Madrid** 1915-  [BE]
*American baseball player*
* Gonzales, Joe

**Gonzales, Louis Jean Emmanuel**
1815-1887  [FFF]
*French journalist*
* Caliban
* Gomez, Melchior
* Goneril, Ramon

**Gonzales, Pancho**
*See* Gonzales, Richard Alonzo

**Gonzales, Richard Alonzo** 1928-
[B10, OCS, OET]
*American tennis player*
* Gonzales, Pancho

**Gonzales, Valentin** 1909?-  [CBS]
*Spanish Republican soldier during
1936-39 civil war*
* [El] Campesino

**Gonzales, Vince**
*See* Gonzales, Wenceslao O'Reilly

**Gonzales, Wenceslao O'Reilly**
1925-  [BE]
*Cuban-born baseball player*
* Gonzales, Vince

**Gonzalez, Andres Antonio** 1936-
[BE]
*Cuban-born baseball player*
* Gonzalez, Tony

**Gonzalez, Argentina Mercedes Maria**
20th c.  [BEW]
*Dominican-born singer and actress*
* Boyar, Monica

**Gonzalez, Arky**
*See* Gonzalez, Arturo Francis, Jr.

**Gonzalez, Arturo Francis, Jr.**
1928-  [AW]
*American writer*
* Gonzalez, Arky

**Gonzalez, Carmen Pagliaro**
*See* Vallejo Gonzalez, Carmen

**Gonzalez, Francisco** 1872-1933
[GS]
*Spanish bullfighter*
* Faico

**Gonzalez, Froilan** 20th c.
*Auto racer*
* [The] Wild Bull of the Pampas

**Gonzalez, Gerardo** 1926-
[BX, RBE, SA]
*Cuban-born boxer*
* Gavilan, Kid
* [The] Hawk

**Gonzalez, Gonzalo** 1922-  [CA]
*Spanish-born author and educator*
* Dewart, Leslie
* Philomythes

**Gonzalez, Gonzalo** (Continued)
* Ross, William

**Gonzalez, Jaime** 20th c. [GS]
*Colombian bullfighter*
* [El] Puno

**Gonzalez, Jose Victoriano**
1887-1927 [WEC]
*Spanish painter, sculptor, cartoonist*
* Gris, Juan

**Gonzalez, Luis** 1920-1970 [SC]
*Spanish-born actor and singer*
* Mariano, Luis

**Gonzalez, Manuel** 1820?-1893
[FFF]
*Mexican army officer and political leader*
* Pacificator of the Occident

**Gonzalez, Miguel Angel Cordero**
1890- [BE]
*Cuban-born baseball player and manager*
* Gonzalez, Mike

**Gonzalez, Mike**
*See* Gonzalez, Miguel Angel Cordero

**Gonzalez, Nilda**
*See* Gonzalez Monclova, Nilda

**Gonzalez, Pedro** 20th c. [GS]
*Venezuelan bullfighter*
* [El] Venezolano [The Man from Venezuela]

**Gonzalez, Tony**
*See* Gonzalez, Andres Antonio

**Gonzalez Buzon, Manuel**
1880-1961 [GS]
*Spanish bullfighter*
* Rerre

**Gonzalez Castrillo, Jose Maria**
1930- [WEC]
*Spanish cartoonist*
* Chumy-Chumez

**Gonzalez de Mendoza, Pedro**
1428-1495 [DNNF]
*Spanish statesman and prelate*
* [The] Great Cardinal

**Gonzalez de Riancho, Lucrecia Borja**
1887-1960 [BBD, WBD]
*Spanish opera singer*
* Bori, Lucrezia

**Gonzalez Lopez, Jose** 1907-1947
[GS, OCS]
*Mexican bullfighter*
* Carnicerito de Mejico [Little Butcher from Mexico]

**Gonzalez Lucas, Luis Miguel**
1926- [GS]
*Spanish bullfighter*
* Dominguin [Little Domingo]

**Gonzalez Marin, Francisco**
1863-1897 [CW]
*Puerto Rican poet, author, playwright*
* Pachin Marin

**Gonzalez Monclova, Nilda** 1929-
[BEW]
*Puerto Rican educator*
* Gonzalez, Nilda

**Gonzalez y Delgado, Hilario**
1883-1908 [GS]
*Spanish bullfighter*
* Serranito [Little Fellow from the Mountain]

**Gonzalez y Madrid, Rafael**
1880-1955 [GS]
*Spanish bullfighter*
* Machaquito [Little Strong One]

**Gonzalez y Mazon, Angel**
1881-1959 [GS]
*Spanish bullfighter*
* Angelillo [Little Angel]

**Gonzalez y Saus, Pascual**
1871-1936 [GS]
*Spanish bullfighter*
* Almanseno [Man from Almansa]

**Gonzalvo di Cordova, Hernandez**
1453-1515 [FFF, HN, RH]
*Spanish soldier*
* [El] Gran Capitan
* [The] Great Captain
* [The] Prince of the Youth

**Goobalathaldin** [tribal name]
*See* Roughsey, Dick

**[The] Goober Genius**
*See* Carver, George Washington

**Gooch, G. P.**
*See* Gooch, George Peabody

**Gooch, George Peabody** 1873-1968
[LC]
*British author*
* Gooch, G. P.

**Gooch, Graham Alan** 1953- [DC]
*British cricketer*
* Gooch, Zap

**Gooch, Silas N.**
*See* Glassco, John [Stinson]

**Gooch, Zap**
*See* Gooch, Graham Alan

**[The] Good**
*See* Albert Francis Charles Augustus Emmanuel of Saxe-Coburg-Gotha

**[The] Good**
*See* Alfonso IV [or Alphonso]

**[The] Good**
*See* Alfonso VIII [or Alphonso]

**[The] Good**
*See* Beauchamp, Richard de

**[The] Good**
*See* Charles

**[The] Good**
*See* Douglas, [Sir] James

**[The] Good**
*See* Haakon I [Hakon or Haco]

**[The] Good**
*See* John II [or Jean]

**[The] Good**
*See* John III [or Jean]

**[The] Good**
*See* John V [or Jean]

**[The] Good**
*See* Magnus I

**[The] Good**
*See* Matilda [or Maud]

**[The] Good**
*See* Philip [or Philippe]

**[The] Good**
*See* Rene I

**[The] Good**
*See* Richard II

**[The] Good**
*See* William II

**[The] Good Bishop of Marseilles**
*See* De Belsunce, Henri Francois Xavier

**Good, Charles H.**
*See* Goodrich, Charles [H.]

**Good, Dolly**
*See* Good, Dorothy Laverne

**Good, Dorothy Laverne** 1915-1967
[CWG]
*American country-western performer*
* Good, Dolly

**[The] Good Duke**
*See* Seymour, Edward

**[The] Good Duke Humphrey**
*See* Humphrey [Duke of Gloucester and Earl of Pembroke]

**[The] Good Duke of Argyll**
*See* Campbell, John

**[The] Good Duke of Gloucester**
*See* Humphrey [Duke of Gloucester and Earl of Pembroke]

**[The] Good Earl**
*See* Cooper, Anthony Ashley

**[The] Good Earl**
*See* Douglas, Archibald

**Good Friend**
*See* Bonaparte, Charles Louis Napoleon

**[The] Good Gray Poet**
*See* Whitman, Walt[er]

**Good, I[rving] John** 1916- [CA]
*British mathematician and author*
* Doog, K. Caj

**[The] Good Judge**
*See* Paston, [Sir] William

**Good Kid Susce**
*See* Susce, George Cyril Methodius

**Good King Rene**
*See* Anjou, Rene d'

**[The] Good King Rene**
*See* Rene I

**[The] Good Knight Without Fear and Without Reproach**
*See* Terrail, Pierre du

**Good, Lefty**
*See* Good, Wilbur David

**[The] Good Lord Cobham**
*See* Oldcastle, [Sir] John

**[The] Good Marquis**
*See* Graham, James

**Good, Morris Edward** 20th c.
*British author, antique dealer, sculptor*
* Oved, Mosheh

**Good News Barnes**
*See* Barnes, Marvin

**Good Old Smitty**
*See* Smith, Ian

**Good Queen Anne**
*See* Anne of Bohemia

**Good Queen Bess**
*See* Elizabeth I

**Good Queen Maud**
*See* Matilda [or Maud]

**[The] Good Queen of France**
*See* Claude

**[The] Good Regent**
*See* Stewart [or Stuart], James

**Good Rockin Brown**
*See* Brown, Roy James

**Good Rockin' Charles**
*See* Edwards, Charles

**Good Rockin' Robinson**
*See* Robinson, Louis Charles

**Good Rocking Sam**
*See* Maghett, Sam[uel]

**[The] Good Samaritan of London**
*See* Todd, Silas

**[The] Good Shoemaker**
*See* Sacco, Nicolo

**[The] Good Swordsman**
*See* Murat, Joachim

**Good Time Bill**
*See* Lamar, William Harmong

**Good Time Feddersen**
*See* Feddersen, Bill

**Good, Wilbur David** 1885-1963
[BE]
*American baseball player*
* Good, Lefty

**Good, Will B.**
*See* Arbuckle, Roscoe Conklin

**Goodale, Mary Green** [FFF]
*American poet*
* Alston, Edith

**Goodall, Irene** ?-1927 [SC]
*American actress*
* Fuller, Irene
* Fuller, Rene
* Lygo, Mary

**Goodall, J. S.**
*See* Goodall, John Strickland

**Goodall, Jane**
*See* Van Lawick-Goodall, Jane

**Goodall, John Strickland** 1908-
[ART]
*British artist*
* Goodall, J. S.

**Goodall, Melanie**
*See* Drachman, Julian M[oses]

**Goodall, Vanne Morris**
*See* Morris-Goodall, Vanne

**Goodbody, Buzz**
*See* Goodbody, Mary Ann

**Goodbody, Mary Ann** 1946?-1975
[B10]
*British director*
* Goodbody, Buzz

**Goodchild, George** 1888-
[CC, WGT, WW]
*British author*
* Dare, Alan
* Reid, Wallace Q.
* Templeton, Jesse

**Goodchild, Harry** 1889-1972
[BMH]
*British comedian*
* Mooney, Harry

**Goode, Arthur Russell** 1889-
[SFL, SFP]
*Author*
* Russell, Arthur

**Goode, Don** 1951- [SMG]
*American football player*
* Goode, Sugar

**Goode, Gerald** 20th c. [CA]
*American author*
* Rainer, Jerome

**Goode, Jack**
*See* Whittridge, Irwin Thomas

**Goode, Joe**
*See* Bueno, Jose

**Goode, Ruth** 1905- [CA]
*American author*
* Rainer, Julia
* Seinfel, Ruth

**Goode, Sugar**
*See* Goode, Don

**Goode, Uncle Abner**
*See* Vawter, L. P.

**Goodell, John Henry William**
1907- [BE]
*American baseball player*
* Goodell, Lefty

**Goodell, Lefty**
*See* Goodell, John Henry William

**Gooden, Ernest** 20th c. [OBW]
*American baseball player*
* Gooden, Pud

**Gooden, Pud**
*See* Gooden, Ernest

**Goodenough, Evelyn**
*See* Pitcher, Evelyn G[oodenough]

**Goodenough, Izzy**
*See* Goodenough, Larry

**Goodenough, Larry** 1953- [SMG]
*Canadian-born hockey player*
* Goodenough, Izzy

**Goodfellow, Ebbie**
*See* Goodfellow, Ebenezer Ralston

**Goodfellow, Ebenezer Ralston**
1907- [CEI, FHE, HK]
*Canadian-born hockey player*
* Goodfellow, Ebbie

**Goodhouse, Grace**
*See* Hedley, Evalena Fryer

**Goodliffe the Magician**
*See* Neale, C. Goodliffe

**Goodman, Alfred**
*See* Guttmann, Alfred

**Goodman, Benjamin David [Benny]**
1909-
*American jazz musician*
* [The] King of Swing

**Goodman, Blanche**
*See* Eisendrath, Blanche Goodman

**Goodman, Bud**
*See* Goodman, James E.

**Goodman, David**
*See* Croly, David Goodman

**Goodman, George J[erome] W[aldo]**
1930- [CA]
*American author and editor*
* Smith, Adam

**Goodman, Goodie**
*See* Goodman, Ival Richard

**Goodman, Harry** 20th c. [EJS]
*British boxing trainer*
* Goodman, Spitzel

**Goodman, Ival Richard** 1908- [BE]
*American baseball player*
* Goodman, Goodie

**Goodman, J. H.**
*See* Zuta, Jack

**Goodman, Jake** 1867- ? [THR]
*British comedian*
* Friedman, Jake

**Goodman, James E.** 20th c.
*American automobile executive*
* Goodman, Bud

**[The] Goodman of Ballengeich**
*See* James V

**Goodman, Rebecca Gruver** 1931-
[CA]
*American historian and author*
* Gruver, Rebecca

**Goodman, Sonya**
*See* Arcone, Sonya

**Goodman, Spitzel**
*See* Goodman, Harry

**Goodman, Theodosia** 1890-1955
[BDF, BEW, F1]
*American actress*
* Bara, Theda
* De Cappet, Theodosia

**Goodman, Wimberley Calvin, Jr.**
1918?-1975 [SW]
*American actor*
* Calvin, Henry

**Goodnow, Elizabeth**
*See* Cooper, Elizabeth

**Goodrich, Charles [H.]** 20th c.
[SFL]
*Author*
* Good, Charles H.

**Goodrich, Edna**
*See* Stephens, Edna

**Goodrich, Frank Boott** 1826- ?
[DEL, PA]
*American author*
* Tinto, Dick

**Goodrich, Gail** 1943- [BB, SMG]
*American basketball player*
* Goodrich, Stumpy

**Goodrich, Jimmy**
*See* Moran, James Edward

**Goodrich, Louis**
*See* Abbot-Anderson, Louis

**Goodrich, Samuel G.** [PA]
*Author*
* Lilly, Lambert

**Goodrich, Samuel Griswold**
1793-1860 [DEL, FFF, RH]
*American author and editor*
* Parley, Peter

**Goodrich, Sandra** 1947- [RO2]
*British singer*
* Shaw, Sandie

**Goodrich, Stumpy**
*See* Goodrich, Gail

**Goodrich, William**
*See* Arbuckle, Roscoe Conklin

**Goodrich-Freer, Adela M.** ?-1931
[CC, SFL]
*Psychical researcher and author*
* Miss X

**Goodridge Roberts, Theodore**
*See* Roberts, George Edward
Theodore

**Goodson, Goody**
*See* Goodson, James Edward

**Goodson, James Edward** 1948-
[SMG]
*American baseball player*
* Goodson, Goody

**Goodson, Wilhelmina Madison**
1907-1974 [BWW]
*American singer*
* Pierce, Billie

**Goodspeed, Marjorie** 1921- [FC]
*American actress*
* Reynolds, Marjorie

**Goodspeed, Mildred K.**
*See* Keefe, Mildred Jones

**Goodwin, Budd**
*See* Goodwin, L. B.

**Goodwin, Claire Vernon** 1894-
[BE]
*American baseball player*
* Goodwin, Pep

**Goodwin, Estelle** 1883- [FC]
*British actress*
* Winwood, Estelle

**Goodwin, Eugene D.**
*See* Kaye, Marvin [Nathan]

**Goodwin, Francis**
*See* Mullaly, Charles J.

**Goodwin, George B.** [PA]
*Author*
* Muldoon, Dennis

**Goodwin, Goody**
*See* Goodwin, J. T.

**Goodwin, Harold Leland [Hal]**
1914- [CA, SAT]
*American author*
* Blaine, John [joint pseudonym
with Philip Harkins]
* Gordon, Hal
* Savage, Blake

**Goodwin, J. T.** ?-1913 [AS]
*American rowing champion*
* Goodwin, Goody

**Goodwin, John**
*See* Gowing, Sidney Floyd

**Goodwin [or Goodwyn], John**
1593-1665? [RH, SN]
*British clergyman*
* [The] Great Red Dragon of
Coleman Street

**Goodwin [or Goodwyn], John**
(Continued)
* [The] Windmill with a
Weathercock Atop

**Goodwin, L. B.** 20th c. [BBH]
*American swimmer*
* Goodwin, Budd

**Goodwin, Mark**
*See* Matthews, Stanley G[oodwin]

**Goodwin, Maude**
*See* Richards, Mrs. George

**Goodwin, Mrs. Nat C.** [FFF]
*Entertainer*
* Weathersby, Eliza

**Goodwin, Pep**
*See* Goodwin, Claire Vernon

**Goodwin, Suzanne** 20th c. [CA]
*British author*
* Ebel, Suzanne
* Shelbourne, Cecily

**Goodyear, Stephen Frederick**
1915- [AW]
*British writer*
* Taylor, Sam

**Gool, Reshard** 1931- [CA]
*British-born author, poet, editor*
* Devajee, Ved

**Goolsby, Ox**
*See* Goolsby, Ray[mond Daniel]

**Goolsby, Ray[mond Daniel]** 1919-
[BE]
*American baseball player*
* Goolsby, Ox

**[The] Goose**
*See* Counts, Mel

**Gooseneck Bill McDonald**
*See* McDonald, William

**Goosequill, Gregory**
*See* Tullock, W. W.

**Goossen, Agnes**
*See* Epp, Margaret A[gnes]

**Gopher**
*See* Pentz, Jacob

**Gor [Wild Ass]**
*See* Bahram V

**Goran, Calli**
*See* Gerrity, David James

**Gorczyca, John Joseph Perry**
1915- [BE]
*American baseball player*
* Gorsica, John Joseph Perry

**Gordet, Allen** 1905?-1954 [NOJ]
*American jazz musician*
* Gordet, Hunter

**Gordet, Hunter**
*See* Gordet, Allen

**Gordianus Pius**
*See* Gordianus III, Marcus
Antonius

**Gordianus I, Marcus Antonius** 158-
238 [WBD]
*Roman emperor*
* Africanus

**Gordianus III, Marcus Antonius**
224?- 244   [WBD]
*Roman emperor*
* Gordianus Pius

**Gordigiani, Luigi** 19th c.   [SN]
*Italian composer*
* [The] Italian Schubert

**Gordin, Morris** 1893-   [NAA]
*Russian-born lecturer and author*
* Novomirsky

**Gordito [Little Fat One]**
*See* Carmona, Antonio

**Gordito [Little Fat One]**
*See* Carmona y Garcia, Jose

**[O] Gordo**
*See* Alfonso II [Affonso, Alonzo or Alphonso]

**Gordon**
*See* Gordon-Montagnon, Rosemary Adrienne Anna

**Gordon, Alex**
*See* Cotler, Gordon

**Gordon, Alexander** 1692?-1754?
[WBD]
*Scottish antiquary*
* Singing Sandie

**Gordon, Archibald F.**   [PA]
*Author*
* [The] Referee
* Syntax, Doctor

**Gordon, Bert** 1898-1974   [FIR, SC]
*American actor*
* [The] Mad Russian

**Gordon, C. Henry**
*See* Racke, Henry

**Gordon, [Lady] Catherine** 16th c.
[HN]
*Daughter of George, Second Earl of Huntly*
* [The] White Rose of Scotland

**Gordon, Charles George** 1833-1885
[DEP, SN, WBD]
*British army officer*
* Gordon, Chinese
* Gordon of Khartoum
* Gordon Pasha
* [The] Uncrowned King

**Gordon, Charles William**
1860-1937   [LC, NAA, TC]
*Canadian author*
* Connor, Ralph

**Gordon, Chinese**
*See* Gordon, Charles George

**Gordon, Constance**
*See* Blades, Kitty

**Gordon, [Sir] Cosmo**
*See* Brydges, [Sir] Edgerton

**Gordon, David**
*See* Garrett, [Gordon] Randall
[Philip David]

**Gordon, Don** 1915?-1978   [FIR]
*Radio performer*
* Gordon, Knuckles

**Gordon, Donald**
*See* Payne, Donald Gordon

**Gordon, Doreen**
*See* Chard, Judy

**Gordon, Flash**
*See* Gordon, Joseph Lowell

**Gordon, Frederick** [house pseudonym] [Stratemeyer Syndicate]
*See* Stratemeyer, Edward L.

**Gordon, Fritz** [joint pseudonym with Robert F. Van Beever]
*See* Jarvis, Fred[erick] G[ordon], Jr.

**Gordon, Fritz** [joint pseudonym with Fred(erick) G(ordon) Jarvis, Jr.]
*See* Van Beever, Robert F.

**Gordon, Gale**
*See* Aldrich, Charles T., Jr.

**Gordon, Gary**
*See* Edmonds, Ivy Gordon

**Gordon, Gavin**
*See* Brown, Gavin

**Gordon, Geoffrey**
*See* Jones, J. G.

**Gordon, George**
*See* Hasford, [Jerry] Gustav

**Gordon, George**   [FFF, PA]
*Author*
* Honeycomb, Will

**Gordon, George [Fifth Duke of Gordon]** 1770-1836
[DNNF, DNNS, FFF]
*Scottish army officer*
* [The] Cock of the North

**Gordon, George Hamilton [Fourth Earl of Aberdeen]** 1784-1860
[FFF, SN]
*British statesman*
* [The] Athenian Aberdeen

**Gordon, Giles [Alexander Esme]**
1940-   [CA]
*Scottish-born author and poet*
* Boswell

**Gordon, Glenda**
*See* Beadle, Gwyneth Gordon

**Gordon, Gordon** 1912-   [CA]
*American author*
* [The] Gordons [joint pseudonym with Mildred Gordon]

**Gordon, [Colonel] H. R.**
*See* Ellis, Edward S[ylvester]

**Gordon, Hal**
*See* Goodwin, Harold Leland [Hal]

**Gordon, Harry**
*See* Gordon, Henry Alfred

**Gordon, Hayes**
*See* Gordon, Haymes

**Gordon, Haymes** 1920-   [BEW]
*American director and producer*
* Gordon, Hayes

**Gordon, Henry Alfred** 1925-   [CA]
*Australian journalist and author*
* Gordon, Harry

**Gordon, Hew**
*See* Stoker, Hew Gordon Dacre

**Gordon, Horatio**
*See* Hutchinson, Horace Gordon

**Gordon, Ian**
*See* Fellowes-Gordon, Ian [Douglas]

**Gordon, James**   [PA]
*Author*
* Pious Jeems

**Gordon, James** 1912-   [WW]
*Author*
* Foss, John

**Gordon, Jan** 1882-1944   [WW]
*Author*
* Gore, William

**Gordon, Jane**
*See* Lee, Elsie

**Gordon, Janet**
*See* Woodham-Smith, Cecil Blanche [Fitzgerald]

**Gordon, Jean**
*See* Wickham, Jean

**Gordon, Jehuda Leb**
*See* Ben Asher, Judah Loeb

**Gordon, Jimmy** 20th c.   [BWW]
*American singer*
* Peetie Wheatstraw's Brother

**Gordon, John**
*See* Dorrance, Gordon

**Gordon, Joseph Lowell** 1915-1978
[BE, PB]
*American baseball player and manager*
* Gordon, Flash

**Gordon, Kathleen** 20th c.   [THR]
*British actress*
* Gordon-Lee, Kathleen

**Gordon, Keith**
*See* Bailey, Gordon

**Gordon, Kitty**
*See* Blades, Kitty

**Gordon, Knuckles**
*See* Gordon, Don

**Gordon, Kurtz**
*See* Kurtz, C[larence] Gordon

**Gordon, Leon**
*See* Lilly, Leon

**Gordon, Lesley,**
*See* Elliott, Lesley

**Gordon, Lew**
*See* Baldwin, Gordon C.

**Gordon, Mack**
*See* Gittler, Morris

**Gordon, Marjorie**
*See* Kettlewell, Marjorie

**Gordon, Mary Duff**
*See* Duffee, Mary Gordon

**Gordon, Max**
*See* Salpeter, Mechel

**Gordon, Mildred** 1912-1979   [CA]
*American author*
* [The] Gordons [joint pseudonym with Gordon Gordon]

**Gordon, Millard Verne**
*See* Wollheim, Donald A[llen]

**Gordon, Milton M.**
*See* Goldberg, Milton M.

**Gordon, Nancy**
*See* Heinl, Nancy G[ordon]

**Gordon, Nathaniel**
*See* Gasko, Gordon

**Gordon, Neil**
*See* Macdonell, Archibald Gordon

**Gordon of Khartoum**
*See* Gordon, Charles George

**Gordon, Oliver**
*See* Emerson, Henry Oliver

**Gordon Pasha**
*See* Gordon, Charles George

**Gordon, Paul**
*See* Achelis, Thomas

**Gordon, Peter**
*See* Wilkes-Hunter, Richard

**Gordon, Ralph**
*See* Utley, Fred Burton

**Gordon, Ray**
*See* Wainwright, Gordon Ray

**Gordon, Rex**
*See* Hough, Stanley Bennett

**Gordon, Richard**
*See* Murray, Adrian

**Gordon, Richard**
*See* Ostlere, Gordon

**Gordon, Robert**
*See* Duncan, Robert Gordon

**Gordon, Ruth**
*See* Jones, Ruth Gordon

**Gordon, S. S.**
*See* Shaw, Stanley Gordon

**Gordon, Selma**
*See* Lanes, Selma Gordon

**Gordon, Slim**
*See* Weaver, Curley James

**Gordon, Spike**
*See* Fearn, John Russell

**Gordon, Stanley**
*See* Shaw, Stanley Gordon

**Gordon, Stewart**
*See* Shirreffs, Gordon D[onald]

**Gordon, Stuart**
*See* Stuart, Richard Gordon

**Gordon, Susan** 1942-   [ART]
*British sculptor*
* S. G.

**Gordon, Tom**
*See* Thomas, Gordon

**Gordon, Waxey**
*See* Wexler, Irving

**Gordon, William** 1801?-1849
[DEP, DNNS, FFF]
*British philanthropist*
* [The] People's Friend

**Gordon, William Murray**
*See* Graydon, William Murray

**Gordon-Lee, Kathleen**
*See* Gordon, Kathleen

**Gordon-Lennox, Cosmo Charles**
1869-1921   [THR]
*British actor and playwright*
* Stuart, Cosmo

**Gordon-Montagnon, Rosemary**
**Adrienne Anna** 1928-   [IAW]
*British psychologist and author*
* Gordon

[The] Gordons [joint pseudonym with Mildred Gordon]
See Gordon, Gordon

[The] Gordons [joint pseudonym with Gordon Gordon]
See Gordon, Mildred

Gordox
See Pike, Noah W.

Gordy, Bear
See Gordy, John

Gordy, John 20th c.
American football player
* Gordy, Bear

Gordy, Robert 20th c. [RO1]
American singer, actor, music publisher
* Kayli, Bob

Gore, George F. 1857-1933 [DGS]
American baseball player
* Gore, Piano Legs

Gore, Piano Legs
See Gore, George F.

Gore, William
See Gordon, Jan

Goreed, Joseph 1918-
[BWW, EJ, PMJ]
American singer
* Williams, Joe
* Williams, Jumpin' Joe

Gorenko, Anna Andreyevna
1888?-1966 [CD, EWL, LC]
Russian poet
* Akhmatova, Anna

Gorete [Little Cap]
See Nieto, Manuel

Gorey, Edward [St. John] 1925-
[CA]
American illustrator and writer
* Blutig, Eduard
* Dowdy, [Mrs.] Regera
* Grode, Redway
* Mude, O.
* Weary, Ogdred
* Wodge, Dreary

Gorgeous George
See Wagner, George Raymond

Gorgeous George Sisler
See Sisler, George Harold

Gorgeous Weed
See Phelps, Arthur

Gorges, [Sir] Ferdinando
1565-1647 [FFF]
British proprietor in America
* [The] Father of Colonization in America

Gorgoliatos, James 1929- [WFA]
American fashion designer
* Galanos, James

Gorham, Elsie
See Carter, Mrs.

Gorham, Maurice Anthony Coneys
1902- [CA]
British-born author and editor
* Rault, Walter

Gorham, Michael [joint pseudonym with Franklin (Brewster) Folsom]
See Elting, Mary

Gorham, Michael [joint pseudonym with Mary Elting]
See Folsom, Franklin [Brewster]

Gorin, George 1853-1889 [BMH]
British entertainer
* Letine

Goring, Butch
See Goring, Robert Thomas

Goring, Robert Thomas 1949-
[CEI, HK, HR]
Canadian-born hockey player
* Goring, Butch

Gorinski, Igor
See Gorinski, Robert John

Gorinski, Robert John 1952-
[SMG]
American baseball player
* Gorinski, Igor

Goris, Jan-Albert 1899- [CD]
Flemish poet and author
* Gijsen, Marnix

Gorky, Arshile
See Adoian, Vosdanik

Gorky, Maxim
See Peshkov [or Pyeshkoff], Alexei Maximovich

Gorlitz, Jeannette 1894?-1936
[BEW]
Actress
* Sherwin, Jeannette

Gorm 860?- 935? [DNNS, WBD]
King of Denmark
* [The] Old

Gorman, Big Tom
See Gorman, Thomas David [Tom]

Gorman, Charles 1897-1940 [CSH]
Canadian skater
* [The] Fastest Man in North America

Gorman, Ginny
See Zachary, Hugh

Gorman, Howard Paul [Howie]
1913- [BE]
American baseball player
* Gorman, Lefty

Gorman, John F. [Jack] ?-1889
[BE]
American baseball player
* Gorman, Stooping Jack

Gorman, Lefty
See Gorman, Howard Paul [Howie]

Gorman, Stooping Jack
See Gorman, John F. [Jack]

Gorman, Terry
See Powers, Richard M.

Gorman, Thomas David [Tom]
1916- [BE]
American baseball player
* Gorman, Big Tom

Gorn-Old, Walter 1864-1929
[NAD]
British astrologer
* Sepharial

Gornetzky, Jay 1896- [BEW]
Russian-born composer, writer, director
* Gorney, Jay

Gorney, Jay
See Gornetzky, Jay

Gornicki, Frank Ted 1911- [BE]
American baseball player
* Gornicki, Hank

Gornicki, Hank
See Gornicki, Frank Ted

Gorovitz, Vladimir 1904- [MS]
Russian-born pianist
* Horowitz, Vladimir
* [The] Thunderer

Gorraez Arcante, Francisco 1908-
[GS]
Mexican bullfighter
* Cachorro [The Cub]

Gorria, Tobio
See Boito, Arrigo

Gorrin, Michael
See Goldstein, Michael

Gorshkov, Captain 20th c. [EE]
Russian intelligence agent
* Chester

Gorsica, John Joseph Perry
See Gorczyca, John Joseph Perry

Gorst, Gilpin [PA]
Author
* [The] Deputy Governor

Gorsuch, Anne M. 20th c.
American government official
* [The] Ice Queen

Goryan, Sirak
See Saroyan, William

Gose, Carl Chester 1915-
[BEW, TR]
American actor
* McKay, Scott

Gosebett, Paul
See Lever, Charles James

Gosfield, C. Heddingham
See Brooks, Edwy Searles

Gosfield, Reuben 20th c. [ECM]
American country-western performer
* Oceans, Lucky

[The] Goshen Schoolmaster
See Leever, Samuel

Goslin, Goose
See Goslin, Leon Allen

Goslin, Leon Allen 1900-1971
[BE, DGS, PB]
American baseball player
* Goslin, Goose

Gosling, Veronica 1931- [AW]
British author
* Henriques, Veronica

Gosling, William Flower 1901-
[WD]
British writer
* Fleur, William

Goslovich, Marianne
See Brown, Morris Cecil

[The] Gospel Doctor
See Wycliffe [or Wyclif], John

Gospel Minnie
See Douglas, Lizzie

Gospel's International Ambassador
See Crouch, Andrae

Goss, Thomas Duggan 1915-1969
[SC]
American actor and newscaster
* Duggan, Tom

Gossaert [Gossart], Jan
1478?-1533? [WBD]
Flemish painter
* Mabuse [or Malbodius]

Gossage, Goose
See Gossage, Rich[ard Michael]

Gossage, Rich[ard Michael] 1951-
[SMG]
American baseball player
* Gossage, Goose

Gosset de Guines, Louis Alexandre
1840-1885 [WBD]
French painter, illustrator, caricaturist
* Gill, Andre

Gossett, Dick
See Gossett, John Star

Gossett, John Star 1891-1962 [BE]
American baseball player
* Gossett, Dick

Gossip, John
See Champlin, E. R.

Gosting, Richard 1941- [ASC]
American singer and songwriter
* St. John, Dick

Gotama, Ramta Yogi
See Bissoondoyal, Basdeo

Gotescalc 806- 868 [HN]
German monk
* [The] Second Effulgence

Gotham
See Wheatley, Richard

Gothamite
See Picton, Thomas

[The] Gothic Alexander
See Ermanaric

Gothicus
See Claudius II [Marcus Aurelius Claudius]

Gothofredus
See Abelin, Johann Philipp

Gotshalk, Len 20th c.
American football player
* [The] Mortician

Gott, K. D.
See Gott, Kenneth Davidson

Gott, Kenneth Davidson 1923-
[CA]
Australian author
* Gott, K. D.
* Hogbotel, Sebastian

Gott, Strafer
See Gott, William

Gott, William 1897-1942 [WWW]
British army officer
* Gott, Strafer

Gottesman, S. D. [joint pseudonym with Robert Augustine Lowndes and Frederik Pohl]
See Kornbluth, Cyril M.

Gottesman, S. D. [joint pseudonym with Cyril M. Kornbluth and Frederik Pohl]
See Lowndes, Robert Augustine Ward

Gottesman, S. D. [joint pseudonym with Cyril M. Kornbluth and Robert Lowndes]
See Pohl, Frederik

Gottfried, Johann Ludwig
See Abelin, Johann Philipp

Gottfried, Theodore Mark 1928-
[CA]
American author
* Behan, Leslie
* Gregory, Harry
* Marco, Lou
* Mark, Ted
* Tobias, Katherine

Gotthelf, Geremias
See Britzius, Albert

Gotthelf, Jeremias
See Bitzius, Albert

Gottlieb, Edward 1898-
Ukrainian-born American basketball executive
* Gottlieb, Gotty

Gottlieb, Elaine 20th c. [CA]
American author
* Hemley, Elaine Gottlieb

Gottlieb, Gotty
See Gottlieb, Edward

Gottlieb, Joseph Abraham 1918-
[FC, IPA, SW]
American comedian
* Bishop, Joey

Gottlieb, Rasmus Karl Thekelsen 1887-1934 [BEW]
Danish-born actor
* Dane, Karl

Gottliebsen, Ralph Joseph 1910-
[AW]
Australian author
* Scott, O. R.

Gottsacker, H. L. 1903-1964 [SC]
American actor
* Leonardo, Harry

Gottschalk, Laura Riding
See Reichenthal, Laura

Gottschalk, Louis M. 1829-1869
[PA]
Author
* [A] Pianist

Gottsched, Johann Christoph 1700-1766 [SN]
German scholar
* [Der] Tadler [The Fault-Finder]

Gottsched, Louisa A. Victoria 1713-1762 [PA]
Author
* Kulmus

Gottschel, Albert Bitzius 1797- ?
[PA]
Author
* De Jeremie

Gottshall, Franklin Henry 1902-
[CA]
American author and educator
* Borneman, H.

Goucher, Joseph Nelson 1894-1976
[BEW, CED, EMT]
American actor, director, producer, playwright
* Dowling, Eddie

Goud, Anne 1917- [CA]
French author
* Anne Mariel
* Karina

Goudie, Big Boy
See Goudie, Frank

Goudie, Frank 1899-1964 [WWJ]
American jazz musician
* Goudie, Big Boy

Gouffe, Armand 1775-1845
[HN, RH]
French songwriter
* Bandy Legged
* [The] Panard of the 19th Century

Gouge, Orson
See Larner, Jeremy

Gough, Irene
See Hall, Irene

Gough, John 18th c. [PA]
British author
* [An] Englishman

Gough, Kathleen
See Aberle, Kathleen Gough

Gough, Richard 1735-1809 [FFF]
British historian
* [The] Camden of the Eighteenth Century

Gougov, Nikola Delchev 1914-
[CA]
Bulgarian author
* Vezhinov, Pavel

Goujaud, Aime Jacques Alexandre 1773-1858 [WBD]
French naturalist
* Bonpland, Aime Jacques Alexandre

Goujon, Jean 1510?-1572
[DEP, DNNF, SN]
French sculptor
* [The] Correggio of Sculptors
* [The] Father of French Sculpture
* [The] French Phidias

Goulait, Snooze
See Goulait, Theodore Lee [Ted]

Goulait, Theodore Lee [Ted] 1889-1936 [BE]
American baseball player
* Goulait, Snooze

Goulart, Frances Sheridan 1938-
[CA]
American author
* Johnson, C. F.

Goulart, Ron[ald Joseph] 1933-
[CA]
American author
* Lee, Howard
* Robeson, Kenneth [house pseudonym, Street & Smith]
* Shawn, Frank S.
* Steffanson, Con [house pseudonym]

Gould, Al[bert Frank] 1893- [BE]
American baseball player
* Gould, Pudgy

Gould, Alan
See Canning, Victor

Gould, Arthur Lee
See Lee, Arthur Stanley Gould

Gould, Avery H. 1907- [BBH]
American lacrosse player
* Gould, Red

Gould, Benjamin F. [PA]
Author
* Spicer, Seth

Gould, Bernard
See Partridge, [Sir] Bernard

Gould, Charles 1904-1968
[FC, WEF]
American talent agent and producer
* Feldman, Charles K.

Gould, Edward Sherman 1808-1885 [FFF]
American author
* Man in Claret

Gould, Elliott
See Goldstein, Elliott

Gould, [Sir] Francis Carruthers 1844-1925 [WEC]
British cartoonist
* F. C. G.

Gould, Gouldy
See Gould, Ian James

Gould, Gypsy
See Vaughn, Vivian

Gould, Ian James 1957- [DC]
British cricketer
* Gould, Gouldy

Gould, Jason 1836-1892 [SN]
American financier
* Gould, Jay
* [The] Railway King

Gould, Jay
See Gould, Jason

Gould, Joy
See Boyum, Joy Gould

Gould, Michael
See Ayrton, Michael

Gould, Pudgy
See Gould, Al[bert Frank]

Gould, Red
See Gould, Avery H.

Gould, Stephen
See Fisher, Stephen Gould

Goulder, Grace
See Izant, Grace Goulder

Goulding, Edmund 1891-1959
British-born American director
* [The] Lion Tamer

Gouled, Vivian G[loria] 1911- [CA]
American author and poet
* Peters, Marcia

Goupille, Clifford 1915- [CEI]
Canadian-born hockey player
* Goupille, Red

Goupille, Red
See Goupille, Clifford

Gourdine, Anthony 1941- [SSS]
American singer
* Little Anthony

Gourdine, Flash
See Gourdine, Meredith C.

Gourdine, Meredith C. 1929-
[IBW]
American physicist, track and field athlete
* Gourdine, Flash

Gourgaud, Jean Baptiste Henri 1746-1809 [WBD]
French comedian
* Dugazon, Jean Baptiste Henri

Gourlay, Mary P. 1898- [EG]
Golfer
* Gourlay, Molly

Gourlay, Molly
See Gourlay, Mary P.

Gourley, A. S.
See Gourley, Alan Stenhouse

Gourley, Alan Stenhouse 1909-
[ART]
Scottish painter
* Gourley, A. S.

Gourley, Lorraine 1924-1968 [SC]
American actress
* Andrews, Lois

Gourre
See Isabella of Bavaria

Gourron, Albert 1861-1933
[BBD, BEW]
French opera singer
* Alvarez, Albert Raymond

Goursat, Georges 1863-1934
[WEC]
French caricaturist and author
* Sem

Gousev, Lieutenant 20th c. [EE]
Russian intelligence agent
* Henry

[The] Gouty
See Medici, Piero de

Gouye, Jean 1933- [B10]
French producer, author, actor
* Yanne, Jean

Gouzenko, Igor 1919- [EE]
Russian intelligence agent
* Klark

Govan, [Mary] Christine Noble 1897?- [CA, SAT, WD]
American author
* Allerton, Mary
* Darby, J. N.
* Morton, Patience

Gove, William Hazeltine 1817-1876 [FFF]
American orator
* [The] Silver Tongued Orator of New Hampshire

Gover, [John] Robert 1929- [CN]
American author
* Govi, O.

Gover, William C. [PA]
Author
* [The] Captain

[The] Governor
See Clement, Frank

[The] Governor
See Morford, Henry

[The] Governor General
See Macartney, Charles George

Govi, O.
See Gover, [John] Robert

**Govier, Edward** 1925-  [BX, RBE]
*British boxer*
* Allen, Terry

**Govinda, Anagarika** 1898-  [IAW]
*Indian author*
* Wangchuk, Anangavajra
  Khamsum

**[The] Gov'nor**
*See* Edwards, George

**[The] Gov'nor**
*See* Sinatra, Francis Albert
[Frank]

**Gow, Lucienne** 20th c.  [DBA]
*British painter and etcher*
* Lugow

**Gow, Neil** 1727-1807  [SN]
*Scottish musician and composer*
* [The] King of Scotch Fiddlers

**Gowan, Elizabeth**
*See* Ferguson, Bessie Gowan

**Gowans, Elsa**
*See* Watt, Elsie Gowans

**Gowans, Kip**
*See* Gowans, William

**Gowans, William** 20th c.
*British director*
* Gowans, Kip

**Gowdy, Hank**
*See* Gowdy, Harry

**Gowdy, Harry** 1889-1966  [AS]
*American baseball player*
* Gowdy, Hank

**Gower, Craven**
*See* Hosken, Ernest Charles Heath

**Gower, David Ivon** 1957-  [DC]
*British cricketer*
* Gower, Lulu

**Gower, Georgiana**
*See* Fullerton, Mrs. Alexander G.

**Gower, John** 1320-1402
[DNNS, FFF, RH]
*British poet*
* [The] Moral Gower

**Gower, Lulu**
*See* Gower, David Ivon

**Gowing, Sidney Floyd** 1878- ?
[MBF, WW, WWL]
*British author*
* Goodwin, John
* Tregellis, John

**Gowon, Jack**
*See* Gowon, Yakubu

**Gowon, Yakubu** 1934-
*Nigerian army officer and former
head of state*
* Gowon, Jack

**Goy, Philip**
*See* Goy, Philippe

**Goy, Philippe** 1941-  [ESF]
*French author*
* Goy, Philip

**Goya, Fred**
*See* Diamant, Lincoln

**Goyathlay** 1829-1909  [IPA]
*American Indian chieftain*
* Geronimo

**Goyau, [Pierre Louis Theophile]
Georges** 1869-1939  [WBD]
*French historian*
* Gregoire, Leon

**Goyder, Margot** 1903-  [CC, WW]
*Author*
* Neville, Margot [joint pseudonym
  with Neville (Goyder) Joske]

**Goyeneche, Gabriel**
*See* Avalle-Arce, Juan Bautista

**Goyette, Joseph Georges Philippe**
1933-  [FHE, HK]
*Canadian-born hockey player*
* Goyette, Phil

**Goyette, Phil**
*See* Goyette, Joseph Georges
Philippe

**Goyne, Richard** 1902-1957
[MBF, WW]
*British author*
* Blair, David
* Courage, John
* Renin, Paul
* Standish, Richard

**Gozzi, Gaspare** 1713-1786  [DEP]
*Italian author*
* [The] Venetian Addison

**Gozzoli, Benozzo**
*See* Di Lese di Sandro, Benozzo

**Graa**
*See* Bruhn, Carl

**Graaf, Peter**
*See* Youd, Christopher Samuel

**Graat, Heinrich**
*See* Wolk, George

**Grabarkewitz, Bill Cordell** 1946-
[SMG]
*American baseball player*
* Billy G.
* Grabarkewitz, Grabby

**Grabarkewitz, Grabby**
*See* Grabarkewitz, Bill Cordell

**Graber, Alexander** 1914-
[CA, SAT]
*Welsh author*
* Cordell, Alexander

**Grabiner, Jew Kid**
*See* Grabiner, Joseph

**Grabiner, Joseph** 20th c.
[BLB, PHM]
*American underworld figure*
* Grabiner, Jew Kid

**Grabiner, June Dorothea** 20th c.
*Actress*
* Travis, June

**Grable, Betty**
*See* Grasle, Elizabeth

**Grabowski, Al**
*See* Grabowski, Alfons Francis

**Grabowski, Alfons Francis**
1901-1966  [BE]
*American baseball player*
* Grabowski, Al
* Grabowski, Hook

**Grabowski, Grabo**
*See* Grabowski, James S.

**Grabowski, Hook**
*See* Grabowski, Alfons Francis

**Grabowski, James S.** 1944-  [FB]
*American football player*
* Grabowski, Grabo

**Grabowski, John Patrick**
1900-1946  [BE]
*American baseball player*
* Grabowski, Nig

**Grabowski, Nig**
*See* Grabowski, John Patrick

**Grabowski, Ronald David** 1938-
[EJ]
*American jazz musician*
* Greb, Ronnie

**Grabowski, Z[bigniew] Anthony**
1903-  [CA]
*Polish-born author, editor,
translator*
* Heyst, Axel

**Gracchus**
*See* Thompson, John

**Gracchus, Caius**
*See* Babeuf, Francois Noel

**Grace, Carol**
*See* Marcus, Carol

**Grace, Catherine Frances**
1799-1861  [PA]
*Author*
* C. F. G.

**Grace, Charles Manuel** 1882-1960
[IBW]
*Founder of religious cult*
* Grace, Sweet Daddy

**[The] Grace Darling of America**
*See* Lewis, Ida

**Grace, Dinah**
*See* Schmidt, Ilse

**Grace, Edward Mills** 1841-1911
[EC]
*British cricketer*
* [The] Coroner

**Grace, Eliza**
*See* Thomson, Katherine Byerley

**Grace, Joseph**
*See* Hornby, John [Wilkinson]

**Grace, Sweet Daddy**
*See* Grace, Charles Manuel

**Grace, William Gilbert** 1848-1915
[EC]
*British cricketer*
* [The] Champion
* [The] Grand Old Man of English
  Cricket
* [The] Old Man

**Gracia Vidal de Santo Silas, Maria
Africa Antonia** 1920-1951  [FIR]
*Dominican-born actress*
* Montez, Maria

**Gracian, Baltasar** 1601-1658
[WBD]
*Spanish author*
* Gracian, Lorenzo

**Gracian, Lorenzo**
*See* Gracian, Baltasar

**Gracie, Sally**
*See* Gracie, Sarah Ellen

**Gracie, Sarah Ellen** 20th c.  [BEW]
*American actress*
* Gracie, Sally

**[The] Gracious**
*See* Nerses

**Gracq, Julien**
*See* Poirier, Louis

**Grade, [Sir] Lew**
*See* Winogradsky, Lew

**[A] Graduate of Oxford**
*See* Ruskin, John

**Gradus, Iosif Moiseevich** 1900-
[THR]
*Russian director*
* Raevsky, Iosif Moiseevich

**Grady, Ronan Calistus, Jr.** 1921-
[CA]
*American army officer and author*
* Murphy, John

**Grady, Tex**
*See* Webb, Jack

**Grae, Ida** 1918-  [CA]
*American author and weaving
instructor*
* Dean, Ida

**Graeme, Bruce**
*See* Jeffries, Graham Montague

**Graeme, David**
*See* Jeffries, Graham Montague

**Graeme, Roderic**
*See* Jeffries, Roderic [Graeme]

**Graeve [or Greffe], Johann Georg**
1632-1703  [WBD]
*German philologist*
* Graevius, Johann Georg

**Graevius, Johann Georg**
*See* Graeve [or Greffe], Johann
Georg

**Graey, Julian**
*See* Gold, Horace Leonard

**Graf, Ike**
*See* Graf, Irwin

**Graf, Irwin** 20th c.  [MEB]
*American basketball player*
* Graf, Ike

**Graf Wickenburg, Erik** 1903-
[IAW]
*Austrian author*
* Von Den Steinen, Robert

**Graff, John Franklin**  [PA]
*Author*
* Graybeard

**Graff, Polly Anne Colver**
*See* Colver, Anne

**Graff, Wilton**
*See* Ratcliffe, Wilton Calvert

**Grafton, Ann**
*See* Owens, Thelma

**Grah, Bill**
*See* Grah, Wilhelm Josef

**Grah, Wilhelm Josef** 1928-  [EJ]
*German-born jazz musician*
* Grah, Bill

**Graham, [Brother]**
*See* Jeffery, Graham

**Graham, Alexis**
*See* Brown, G. W.

**Graham, Alice Walworth** 1905-
[NAA]
*American author*
* Walworth, Alice

**Graham, Angus A.** 1867- ?   [NAA]
*Canadian clergyman and writer*
* Maharg, S. A.

**Graham, Archibald Wright**
1879-1965
*American baseball player*
* Graham, Moonlight

**Graham, Arthur William**
1909-1967   [BE]
*American baseball player*
* Graham, Skinny

**Graham, Automatic Otto**
See   Graham, Otto

**Graham, Bill**
See   Grajonca, Wolfgang

**Graham, Bonnie** 1914-   [BB]
*American basketball player*
* Graham, Country

**Graham, Bushy**
See   Geraci, Angelo

**Graham, Carlotta**
See   Wallmann, Jeffrey M[iner]

**Graham, Charles S.**
See   Tubb, Edwin Charles

**Graham, Charlotte**
See   Bowden, Joan Chase

**Graham, Chele** 1936-
*American actress*
* Spelvin, Georgina

**Graham, Colin**
See   Graham-Bonnalie, Colin

**Graham, Country**
See   Graham, Bonnie

**Graham, Dante**
See   Graham, Donald L.

**Graham, Daphne** 1903-   [THR]
*British actress*
* Sheridan, Mary

**Graham, Dawson Frank** 1892-1962
[BE]
*American baseball player*
* Graham, Tiny

**Graham, Donald L.** 1944-1971
[IBW]
*American poet, artist, musician*
* Graham, Dante

**Graham, Elizabeth**
See   Edmonds, Arthur Denis

**Graham, Ennis**
See   Molesworth, Mary Louisa
Stewart

**Graham, Eve**
See   Beatson, Evelyn May

**Graham, Felix**
See   Brown, Fredric

**Graham, Frank** 1915-1950   [SC]
*American radio announcer and film
narrator*
* [The] Man with a Thousand
Voices

**Graham, George** 1673-1751   [SN]
*British watch-maker and inventor*
* Honest George

**Graham, George Frederick**
1880-1939   [BE]
*American baseball player*
* Graham, Peaches

**Graham, George I.**   [PA]
*Author*
* Langdale, Launcelot

**Graham, Grace**
See   Titterington, Mrs. S. B.

**Graham, Harvey**
See   Flack, Isaac Harvey

**Graham, Hattie** 1922-1967   [CWG]
*American country-western performer*
* Cherokee Sue

**Graham, Homer**
See   Little, George A.

**Graham, Howard**
See   Wandrei, Howard Elmer

**Graham, Hugh**
See   Barrows, [Ruth] Marjorie

**Graham, Irvin**
See   Abraham, Irvin

**Graham, James**
See   Patterson, Harry

**Graham, James** 1612-1650
[DNNF, HN, RH]
*Lord lieutenant and captain general
of Scotland*
* [The] Great Marquis
* Montrose, First Marquis of

**Graham, James** 1631?-1669
[DNNS, WBD]
*Scottish aristocrat and soldier*
* [The] Good Marquis
* Montrose, Second Marquis of

**Graham, Janet**
See   Rance, Janet Mary

**Graham, John**
See   Dabrowsky, Iwan

**Graham, John [First Viscount of
Dundee]** 1649?-1689   [SN, WBD]
*Scottish army officer*
* Claverse, Bloody
* Dundee, Bonny

**Graham, Johnston**
See   Smith, David [Larmer]

**Graham, Katharine** 20th c.
*American publisher*
* Graham, Krusty Kay

**Graham, Kennon**
See   Harrison, David L[ee]

**Graham, Kenny**
See   Skingle, Kenneth Thomas

**Graham, Krusty Kay**
See   Graham, Katharine

**Graham, Lady**
See   Callcott, Maria

**Graham, Lloyd M.** 1889-   [CA]
*Canadian-born author, composer,
painter*
* Krypton

**Graham, Moonlight**
See   Graham, Archibald Wright

**Graham, Neill**
See   Duncan, W[illiam] Murdoch

**Graham, Otto** 1921-   [FB]
*American football player*
* Graham, Automatic Otto

**Graham, Peaches**
See   Graham, George Frederick

**Graham, [Lieut.] Preston**
See   Ingraham, Prentiss

**Graham, Ramona**
See   Cook, Ramona Graham

**Graham, Robert**
See   Haldeman, Joe [William]

**Graham, Robert** ?-1797?   [WBD]
*Scottish poet*
* Cunninghame-Graham, Robert

**Graham, Roger Phillips** 1909-1965
[ESF, SF, WGT]
*American author*
* Ames, Clinton
* Arnette, Robert [house
pseudonym, Ziff-Davis]
* Bahl, Franklin
* Blade, Alexander [house
pseudonym, Ziff-Davis]
* Browning, Craig
* Conrad, Gregg
* Costello, P. F. [house pseudonym,
Ziff-Davis]
* Kumara, Sanandana
* Lee, Charles
* Mann, Charles
* Mann, Milton
* McGowan, Inez
* Phillips, Rog
* Rogers, Melva
* Ruppert, Chester
* Sawtelle, William Carter
* Steber, A. R. [house pseudonym,
Ziff-Davis]
* Vance, Gerald [house pseudonym,
Ziff-Davis]
* Wiley, John
* Worth, Peter [house pseudonym,
Ziff-Davis]

**Graham, Rosa**
See   Post, Sarah L.

**Graham, Ruth**
See   Evans, Jean

**Graham, Shirley**
See   Du Bois, Shirley Graham

**Graham, Skinny**
See   Graham, Arthur William

**Graham, [Maude Fitzgerald] Susan**
1912-   [CA]
*New Zealand journalist*
* Susan

**Graham, Tiny**
See   Graham, Dawson Frank

**Graham, Tom**
See   Lewis, [Harry] Sinclair

**Graham, Vanessa**
See   Fraser, Anthea

**Graham, Virginia**
See   Guttenberg, Virginia

**Graham, W. S.**
See   Graham, William Sydney

**Graham, William Sydney** 1918-
[MBL, WOA]
*Scottish poet*
* Graham, W. S.

**Graham, Winifred**
See   Cory, Matilda Winifred
Muriel [Graham]

**Graham-Bonnalie, Colin** 1931-
[OP]
*British producer and set designer*
* Graham, Colin

**Grahame, Allen**
See   Arnold, George

**Grahame, Bert**
See   Stanford, R. A. S.

**Grahame, Gloria**
See   Hallward, Gloria Grahame

**Grahame, James** 1765-1811   [SN]
*Scottish poet*
* Grahame, Sepulchral
* [A] Poetical Spagnoletto

**Grahame, Nellie**
See   Dunning, Mrs. A. K.

**Grahame, Sepulchral**
See   Grahame, James

**Grahame-Thomson, Leslie** 1896-
[DBA]
*Scottish architect*
* MacDougall, Leslie Grahame

**Grainger, B. M.**
See   Grainger, Bernard Montague

**Grainger, Bernard Montague** 1907-
[ART]
*British artist*
* Grainger, B. M.

**Grainger, Francis Edward**
1857-1924   [EMD, WW]
*British author*
* Hill, Headon

**Grainger, Ike**
See   Grainger, Isaac B.

**Grainger, Isaac B.** 1895-   [GF]
*United States Golf Association
official*
* Grainger, Ike

**Grajonca, Wolfgang** 1931-   [PRS]
*German-born recording executive,
promoter, booking agent*
* Graham, Bill

**Grambach, Donald** 1927-   [MS]
*American opera singer*
* Gramm, Donald

**Gramm, Donald**
See   Grambach, Donald

**[The] Grammarian**
See   Starkey, Geoffrey

**Grammas, Alexander Peter** 1926-
[SMG]
*American baseball manager and
coach*
* [The] Golden Greek

**[The] Grammatical Cur**
See   Gronovius, James

**[The] Grammatical Cynic**
See   Scioppius, Gaspar

**Grammaticorum Princeps**
See   Appollonius of Alexandria

**Grammaticus**
See   Aelfric

**Grammaticus**
See   Benedict V

**Grammaticus**
See Blaiklock, Edward Musgrave

**Grammaticus**
See Musaeus

**Grammaticus, Caius**
See Scioppius, Gaspar

**[The] Grammont of His Age**
See De Bourdeille, Pierre

**Gramsch, Walter** 20th c. [EE]
*German intelligence agent*
* Brutus

**[El] Gran Capitan**
See Gonzalvo di Cordova, Hernandez

**[Il] Gran Diavolo**
See Medici, Giovanni de

**Granada, Cecil**
See Prentice, Cecil

**Granada, Manuel**
See Ingenito, Benjamin

**[El] Granadino**
See Cano, Alonso [or Alonzo]

**Granados, Paul**
See Kent, Arthur [William Charles]

**Granahan, Gerry** 1939- [RO1]
*American singer*
* Doo, Dickey

**Granatov, Major**
See Foote, Alexander

**Granbeck, Marilyn** 1927- [CA]
*American author*
* Carter, Nick [house pseudonym]
* Grant, Ben
* Hamilton, Adam
* Moore, Clayton
* Saxon, Van

**Granby, Milton**
See Wallmann, Jeffrey M[iner]

**[Le] Grand**
See Bonaparte, Napoleon

**[Le] Grand**
See Couperin, Francois

**[Le] Grand**
See Francis I or [Francois]

**[Le] Grand Batard**
See De Bourgogne, Antoine

**[Le] Grand Carnot**
See Carnot, Lazare-Nicolas-Marquerite

**[The] Grand Chef**
See Trepper, Leopold

**Grand Comnenus**
See Alexius I

**[Le] Grand Corneille**
See Corneille, Pierre

**[The] Grand Corrupter**
See Walpole, [Sir] Robert [First Earl of Orford]

**[Le] Grand Dauphin**
See Louis

**[Le] Grand David**
See Bull, David

**[Le] Grand Epistolier de France**
See Balzac, Jean Louis Guez de

**[Le] Grand Frederic**
See Lemaitre, Antoine Louis Prosper

**[The] Grand Hetman of the Crown**
See Rzewuski, Stanislaw

**[Le] Grand Monarque**
See Louis XIV

**[Le] Grand Nash**
See Nash, Richard

**[The] Grand Old Lady of Australian Theatre**
See Glyn, Neva Carr

**[The] Grand Old Man**
See Gladstone, William Ewart

**[The] Grand Old Man**
See Hoover, Herbert Clark

**[The] Grand Old Man**
See Levine, Ben

**[The] Grand Old Man**
See Macon, David Harrison

**[The] Grand Old Man**
See Rooney, Arthur J.

**[The] Grand Old Man of Baseball**
See Anson, Adrian Constantine

**[The] Grand Old Man of Black Liberation**
See Randolph, Asa Philip

**[The] Grand Old Man of English Cricket**
See Grace, William Gilbert

**[The] Grand Old Man of Football**
See Stagg, Amos Alonzo

**[The] Grand Old Man of India**
See Naoroji, Dadabhai

**[The] Grand Old Man of Sport**
See Chambers, James

**[The] Grand Old Man of the Fringe**
See Velikovsky, Immanuel

**[The] Grand Old Man of the Midway**
See Stagg, Amos Alonzo

**[The] Grand Old Muddler**
See Gladstone, William Ewart

**[Le] Grand Orange**
See Staub, Daniel Joseph

**[Le] Grand Pan**
See Arouet, Francois Marie

**Grand, Sarah**
See McFall, Frances Elizabeth [Clark]

**[The] Grand Slam Champion**
See McCulloch, Ernie

**[The] Grand Slammer**
See Jones, Robert Tyre, Jr.

**[The] Grand Wrestler**
See Lincoln, Abraham

**Granda, Michael** 1951- [RO2]
*American musician*
* Granda, Supe

**Granda, Supe**
See Granda, Michael

**Grandais, Susanne** ?-1920 [SC]
*French actress*
* [The] Mary Pickford of France

**[The] Granddaddy of the Hillbillies**
See Robison, Carson J.

**Grande, Juan** 1546-1600 [HN]
* [The] Preacher

**[La] Grande Mademoiselle**
See Orleans, Anne Marie Louise d'

**Grandfather**
See St. John, Sergius

**Grandfather, Dr.**
See Colter, Cyrus J.

**[The] Grandfather of British Rhythm and Blues**
See Korner, Alexis

**[The] Grandfather of British Rock**
See Mayall, John

**[The] Grandfather of Rock**
See Creach, John

**[The] Grandfather of Yiddish Literature**
See Abromowitz, Sholem Yakob

**Grandfather's Hat**
See Harrison, Benjamin

**Grandison Cromwell**
See Du Motier, Marie Joseph Paul Yves Roch Gilbert

**Grandlien, Doctor**
See Lavaden, Leon

**[The] Grandmother of the Russian Revolution**
See Breshkovsky, Catherine

**Grandower, Elissa**
See Waugh, Hillary Baldwin

**Grandpa's Grandson**
See Harrison, Benjamin

**Grandstaff, Olive** 1933- [FC, SW]
*American actress*
* Grant, Kathryn

**Grandval, Gilbert**
See Hirsch-Ollendorf, Gilbert

**Grandville**
See Gerard, Jean Ignace Isidore

**Granella, Victor**
See Tardieu, J. R.

**Granfeldt, Taivo** 1923- [CA]
*Estonian-born American oceanographer and author*
* Laevastu, Taivo

**Grange, Chris**
See Gnaegy, Charles

**Grange, Cyril** 1900- [CAP]
*British author and illustrator*
* Onlooker
* Quill

**Grange, Gardie**
See Grange, Garland

**Grange, Garland** 20th c. [SMG]
*American football player*
* Grange, Gardie

**Grange, Harold E.** 1903-
[FB, OCS, SR]
*American football player*
* [The] Flying Terror
* [The] Galloping Ghost
* Grange, Red
* Old 77
* [The] Wheaton Ice Man

**Grange, Peter**
See Nicole, Christopher Robin

**Grange, Pierre Eugene** 1810- ?
[PA]
*Author*
* Baste

**Grange, Red**
See Grange, Harold E.

**Granger, D. J.**
See Lesser, Milton

**Granger, Gideon** 1767-1822
[FFF, PA]
*American statesman and author*
* Epaminondas
* [The] Father of the Connecticut School Fund
* Senectus
* Sidney, Algernon

**Granger, Maude**
See Baxter, Mrs. William R.

**Granger, Stewart**
See Stewart, James L.

**Granich, Irving** 1893?-1967
[CA, TC]
*American author, playwright, journalist*
* Gold, Michael

**Granick, Harry** 1898- [CA]
*Russian-born American playwright*
* Taylor, Harry

**Granin, Daniel [Alexandrovich]**
See German, Daniel

**Granite, Tony**
See Politella, Dario

**Granlund, Nils Thor** 1892?-1957
[BEW]
*Swedish-born producer*
* N. T. G.

**Granovsky, Alexander**
See Azarch, Abraham

**Grant**
See Zabotin, Colonel

**Grant, [Major] A. F.**
See Harbaugh, Thomas Chalmers

**Grant, Alan**
See Kennington, [Gilbert] Alan

**Grant, Allan**
See Wilson, William

**Grant, Ambrose**
See Raymond, Rene

**Grant, Anne** 1755-1838 [WBD]
*Scottish author*
* Grant of Laggan, Mrs.

**Grant, B. Donald** 20th c. [ET]
*American television executive*
* Grant, Bud

**Grant, Barney**
See Younger, John Leo

**Grant, Ben**
See Granbeck, Marilyn

**Grant, Big Back**
See Grant, Ike

**Grant, Bitsy**
See Grant, Bryan

**Grant, Bryan** 20th c. [OET, SR]
*American tennis player*
* Grant, Bitsy

**Grant, Bryan** (Continued)
* [The] Mighty Atom

**Grant, Bud**
See Grant, B. Donald

**Grant, Bud**
See Grant, Harold P.

**Grant, Butcher**
See Grant, Hiram Ulysses

**Grant, C. B. S.**
See Haga, Enoch John

**Grant, Cary**
See Leach, Archibald Alexander

**Grant, Charles**
See Lengel, William Charles

**Grant, Charles** ?-1932 [IBW]
*American baseball player*
* Tokohama, Charlie

**Grant, Charles** 20th c. [WWL]
*British author*
* Croix-Rouge
* Red Cross

**Grant, Coot**
See Pettigrew, Leola B.

**Grant, Don**
See Glut, Donald F[rank]

**Grant, Douglas**
See Merland, Oliver

**Grant, Douglas**
See Ostrander, Isabel [Egenton]

**Grant, E. Gordon**
See Edwards, Robert Hamilton

**Grant, Earl** 1931-1970 [IBW]
*American musician*
* Earl of Grant

**Grant, Edward Leslie** 1883-1918
[BE, PB]
*American baseball player*
* Grant, Harvard Eddie

**Grant, Ethel Watts Mumford** 1878-
? [NAA]
*American author and playwright*
* Mumford, Ethel Watts

**Grant, Francis**
See Makgill, [Sir] George

**Grant, Frank** 1867- ? [MK]
*American baseball player*
* [The] Black Dunlap

**Grant, Gogi**
See Brown, Audrey

**Grant, Harold P.** 1927- [FB]
*American football coach*
* Grant, Bud

**Grant, Harvard Eddie**
See Grant, Edward Leslie

**Grant, Hilda Kay** 1910- [CA]
*Canadian author*
* Hilliard, Jan

**Grant, Hiram Ulysses** 1822-1885
[DNNS, FFF, FAP]
*American president*
* [The] American Caesar
* [The] Butcher from Galena
* [The] Galena Tanner
* Grant, Butcher
* Grant, Texas
* Grant, U. S.
* Grant, Ulysses Simpson

**Grant, Hiram Ulysses** (Continued)
* Grant, Uncle Sam
* Grant, Unconditional Surrender
* Grant, Union Safeguard
* Grant, United States
* Grant, United We Stand
* Grant, Unprecedented Strategist
* Grant, Unquestionably Skilled
* Grant, Useless
* [The] Great Hammerer
* [The] Great Peacemaker
* [The] Hero of Appomattox
* [The] Hero of Fort Donelson
* Old Three Stars
* Old United States
* [The] Silent Man
* [The] Tanner President

**Grant, Howard**
See Wright, W. George

**Grant, Ike** 20th c. [SMG]
*American football player*
* Grant, Big Back

**Grant, James** 1806- ? [PA]
*Author*
* One of No Party

**Grant, James Miller** 1853- ?
[NAA]
*Scottish-born author*
* Balfour, Grant

**Grant, James Timothy** 1935-
[BE, PB, SMG]
*American baseball player*
* Grant, Mudcat

**Grant, Jane**
See Leader, [Evelyn] Barbara
[Blackburn]

**Grant, Joan**
See Kelsey, Joan Marshall

**Grant, John** 1933- [CA]
*British author*
* Gash, Jonathan

**Grant, K. F.**
See Grant, Keith Frederick

**Grant, Kathryn**
See Grandstaff, Olive

**Grant, Keith Frederick** 1930-
[ART]
*British painter*
* Grant, K. F.

**Grant, Kirby**
See Horn, Kirby Grant

**Grant, Landon**
See Gribble, Leonard R[eginald]

**Grant, Lee**
See Rosenthal, Lyova Haskell

**Grant, Leola B.**
See Pettigrew, Leola B.

**Grant, Louis T[heodore]**
See Goldberg, Louis T[heodore]

**Grant, Margaret**
See Coryell, John Russell

**Grant, Margaret** [joint pseudonym
with William Brown Meloney]
See Franken, Rose

**Grant, Margaret** [joint pseudonym
with Rose Franken]
See Meloney, William Brown

**Grant, Matthew G.**
See May, Julian

**Grant, Maude Margaret** 20th c.
[NAA]
*American educator and author*
* Fraser, Elizabeth
* Patterson, Margaret
* Stanley, Alixe Russell

**Grant, Maurice Harold** 1872- ?
[WWL]
*British author*
* Linesman

**Grant, Maxwell** [house pseudonym]
See Davis, Robert Hart

**Grant, Maxwell** [house pseudonym]
See Dent, Lester

**Grant, Maxwell** [house pseudonym]
See Elliott, Bruce [Walter Gardner
Lively Stacy]

**Grant, Maxwell** [house pseudonym]
See Gibson, Walter B[rown]

**Grant, Maxwell** [house pseudonym]
See Lynds, Dennis

**Grant, Maxwell** [house pseudonym]
See Richardson, Gladwell

**Grant, Maxwell** [house pseudonym]
See Tinsley, Theodore

**Grant, Mudcat**
See Grant, James Timothy

**Grant, Neil** 1938- [CA]
*British author*
* Mountfield, David

**Grant of Laggan, Mrs.**
See Grant, Anne

**Grant, Pappy**
See Grant, Ray

**Grant, Ray**
*Singer*
* Grant, Pappy

**Grant, Richard**
See Clarke, J. Calvitt

**Grant, Robert** [SN]
*British politician*
* [The] Friend of the Jews

**Grant, Seafield** 1909- [FC]
*South African-born actor*
* Hayward, Louis

**Grant, Texas**
See Grant, Hiram Ulysses

**Grant, U. S.**
See Grant, Hiram Ulysses

**Grant, Ulysses Simpson**
See Grant, Hiram Ulysses

**Grant, Uncle Sam**
See Grant, Hiram Ulysses

**Grant, Unconditional Surrender**
See Grant, Hiram Ulysses

**Grant, Union Safeguard**
See Grant, Hiram Ulysses

**Grant, United States**
See Grant, Hiram Ulysses

**Grant, United We Stand**
See Grant, Hiram Ulysses

**Grant, Unprecedented Strategist**
See Grant, Hiram Ulysses

**Grant, Unquestionably Skilled**
See Grant, Hiram Ulysses

**Grant, Useless**
See Grant, Hiram Ulysses

**Grant, Venzo**
See Stansberger, Richard

**Grant, Whitney**
See Keif, Aubrey

**Grantham, Boots**
See Grantham, George Farley

**Grantham, George Farley**
1900-1954 [AS, DGS, PB]
*American baseball player*
* Grantham, Boots

**Grantham, Gerald**
See Wallace, John

**Grantland, Keith**
See Nutt, Charles

**Granville, Augustus Bozzi** [PA]
*Author*
* A. B. G.

**Granville, Charlotte**
See Stuart, Charlotte

**Granville, Christine**
See Skarbek, Krystyne

**Granville, Clive** [EE]
*British intelligence agent*
* Special Duty Agent Three-Three

**Granville-Barker, Harley**
See Barker, H[arley] Granville

**Granville-Barker, Helen**
See Gates, Helen

**Grape, Oliver**
See Wood, Christopher [Hovelle]

**Grapheus**
See Schryver, Corneilise

**Grapho**
See Oakley, Eric Gilbert

**Grappelli, Stephane**
See Grappelly, Stephane

**Grappelly, Stephane** 1908- [IEJ]
*French-born jazz musician*
* Grappelli, Stephane

**Grasdorf, Reginald** 1896-1953
[FC]
*British actor*
* Purdell, Reginald

**Grasle, Elizabeth** 1916-1973
[BDF, FIR, WEF]
*American actress*
* Grable, Betty
* Haig, Ruth

**[The] Grasshopper**
See Callimides

**Grasshopper Jim Whitney**
See Whitney, James E.

**Grassman, Dan** 1853-1929 [SC]
*American actor*
* Mason, Dan

**Grasso, Arnold** 20th c. [ALR]
*American baseball player*
* Grasso, Mickey

**Grasso, Mickey**
See Grasso, Arnold

**Gratacap**
See Cap, Paul Antoine

**Grate, Buckeye**
See   Grate, Don[ald]

**Grate, Don[ald]** 1923-    [BE]
*American baseball player*
* Grate, Buckeye

**Grath, Mrs. J. W.**    [FFF]
*Entertainer*
* Boshell, Ada

**Grathmer, Ingahild**
See   Margrethe II

**Gratiant, Gilbert** 1895-    [CW]
*West Indian poet and author*
* Nous-Terre, Jean
* Nous-Tous, Jean

**Gratianus, Johannes**   ?-1048?
[WBD]
*Pope*
* Gregory VI

**Grattan, Henry** 1746?-1820
[DNNS, RH]
*Irish orator and statesman*
* [The] Patriot of Humanity

**Grattan, Thomas Colley** 1796-1864
[DEL, PA]
*British author, playwright, poet*
* [A] Walking Gentleman

**Gratton, Fred**
See   Wilkinson, Fred

**Gratton, Gilles** 1952-    [SMG]
*Canadian-born hockey player*
* [The] Count

**Gratton, Norm**
See   Gratton, Normand Lionel

**Gratton, Normand Lionel** 1950-
[CEI, HR]
*Canadian-born hockey player*
* Gratton, Norm

**Gratz, Barbara Jeannette** 1937-
[BEW]
*American actress*
* Lord, Barbara

**Grauaug, Colette** 20th c.    [OP]
*Swiss opera singer*
* Lorand, Colette

**Graupner, Johann Christian Gotlieb**
18th c.    [IBW]
*American singer*
* [The] Father of Negro Songs

**Grautoff, Ferdinand [Heinrich]**
1871-1935    [SFL, WGT]
*German author*
* Parabellum
* Seestern

**Gravel, Fern**
See   Hall, James Norman

**Gravel, George** 20th c.    [SR]
*Hockey official*
* Gravel, Gertie

**Gravel, Gertie**
See   Gravel, George

**Gravelet, Jean Francois** 1824-1897
[WBD]
*French tightrope walker*
* Blondin, Charles

**Graveley, George**
See   Edwards, George Graveley

**Gravelle, Joseph Gerard Leo** 1925-
[FHE]
*Canadian-born hockey player*
* [The] Gazelle
* Gravelle, Tiger

**Gravelle, Tiger**
See   Gravelle, Joseph Gerard Leo

**Gravelot, Hubert Francois**
See   Bourguignon, Hubert Francois

**Graveney, David Anthony** 1953-
[DC]
*British cricketer*
* Graveney, Gravity

**Graveney, Gravity**
See   Graveney, David Anthony

**Graves, A. P.**
See   Graves, Alfred Percival

**Graves, Alexander** 1936-    [RO1]
*American singer*
* Graves, Pete

**Graves, Alfred Percival** 1846-1931
[LC]
*Irish music publisher*
* Graves, A. P.

**Graves, Charles Parlin** 1911-1972
[CA, SAT]
*American author*
* Parlin, John

**Graves, Clotilda Inez Mary**
1863-1932    [LC, WW]
*Irish author and playwright*
* Dehan, Richard

**Graves, David Marion** 1861?-1934
[BEW]
*American actor, playwright,
manager*
* Marion, Dave

**Graves, Ernest** 1880-1953    [FB]
*American football coach*
* [The] Father of the Engineers
* Graves, Pot

**Graves, Kid**
See   Graves, Perry Ivia

**Graves, Perry Ivia** 1892-
[BX, RBE]
*American boxer*
* Graves, Kid

**Graves, Pete**
See   Graves, Alexander

**Graves, Peter**
See   Aurness, Peter

**Graves, Pot**
See   Graves, Ernest

**Graves, Richard** 1715-1804
[FFF, PA]
*British clergyman and author*
* Euphrosyne
* Pomfret, Peter

**Graves, Robert Von Ranke** 1895-
[CN, TC]
*British author and poet*
* Boyle, Paul
* Doyle, John

**Graves, [Samuel] Sid[ney]** 1901-
[BE]
*American baseball player*
* Graves, Whitey

**Graves, Susan B[ernard]** 1933-
[CA, CN]
*American writer*
* Bernard, Marley
* Rich, Barbara [joint pseudonym
  with Laura Reichenthal]

**Graves, Whitey**
See   Graves, [Samuel] Sid[ney]

**Gravet, Fernand**
See   Martens, Fernand

**Graveure, Louis**
See   Douthitt, Wilfred

**Graveyard, Aloysius**
See   Thody, Philip Malcolm Waller

**Graviere, Caroline**
See   Rueleus, Mme. C.

**Graw, William P.**    [FFF]
*Entertainer*
* Welser, Albert

**Gray, Ada**
See   Watkins, Mrs. Charles A.

**Gray, Andrew**
See   Murray, A. C.

**Gray, Angela**
See   Daniels, Dorothy

**Gray, Annabel**
See   Cox, Anne

**Gray, Arthur** 1852-1940
[SFL, WWL]
*British author*
* Ingulphus

**Gray, Arvella** 1906-    [BWW]
*American singer*
* Gray, Blind Arvella

**Gray, Barry**
See   Coffin, Robert

**Gray, Barry**
See   Yaroslaw, Bernard

**Gray, Barton**
See   Sass, George H.

**Gray, Beata**
See   Pederson, Lily

**Gray, Berkeley**
See   Brooks, Edwy Searles

**Gray, Betty**
See   Pederson, Lily

**Gray, Big Dog**
See   Gray, Leon

**Gray, Blind Arvella**
See   Gray, Arvella

**Gray, Charles**
See   Tubb, Edwin Charles

**Gray, Charles D.**
See   Gray, Donald Marshall

**Gray, Cheryl** 1953-    [RO2]
*Australian singer*
* Sang, Samantha

**Gray, Chummy**
See   Gray, George Edward

**Gray, Claude** 1932-    [FCW]
*American country-western performer*
* [The] Tall Texan

**Gray, Coleen**
See   Jensen, Doris

**Gray, Dobie**
See   Ainsworth, Leonard Victor, Jr.

**Gray Dog**
See   Gray, John Gordon

**Gray, Dolly**
See   Gray, Stan[ley Oscar]

**Gray, Dolly**
See   Gray, William Denton

**Gray, Don**
See   Graydon, Robert Murray

**Gray, Donald**
See   Cooksley, S[idney] Bert

**Gray, Donald Marshall** 1928-
[BEW, FC, TR]
*British actor*
* Gray, Charles D.

**Gray, Dorothy Kate** 1918-
[AW, WD]
*British author*
* Haynes, Dorothy K.

**Gray, Dulcie**
See   Bailey, Dulcie

**Gray Eagle**
See   Englehardt, Frederick J.

**[The] Gray Eagle**
See   Speaker, Tristram E.

**Gray, Elizabeth Janet**
See   Vining, Elizabeth Gray

**Gray, Ellington**
See   Jacob, Naomi Ellington

**Gray, Ellis**
See   Cragin, Louisa T.

**Gray, Esca**
See   Adamson, Frances A.

**[The] Gray Fox of Long Island Sound**
See   Shields, Cornelius

**Gray, Gene** 1899-1950    [SC]
*American actor*
* Silver King of the Cowboys

**Gray, Genevieve S[tuck]** 1920-
[CA, SAT]
*American educator and writer*
* Gray, Jenny

**Gray, Geoffrey**
See   Murray, C. Geoffrey

**Gray, George Edward** 1873-1913
[BE]
*American baseball player*
* Gray, Chummy

**Gray, George Hugh** 1922-    [CA]
*Irish-born author*
* Gray, Tony

**[The] Gray Ghost**
See   Yost, Charles W.

**[The] Gray Ghost of Gonzaga**
See   Canadeo, Anthony [Tony]

**Gray, Gilda**
See   Michalska, Marianna

**Gray, Glen**
See   Knoblaugh, Glen Gray

**Gray, Harriet**
See   Robins, Denise [Naomi]

**Gray, Henry** 1925-    [BWW]
*American singer*
* Little Henry

**Gray, James D.** 20th c.   [BE]
*American baseball player*
* Gray, Reddy

**Gray, Jane**
See   Evans, Constance May

**Gray, Jennie H.**   [PA]
*Author*
* Drille, Hearton

**Gray, Jennifer**
See   Skinner, Jennifer

**Gray, Jenny**
See   Gray, Genevieve S[tuck]

**Gray, Jerry**
See   Graziano, Jerry

**Gray, John**
See   Raffety, Gordon Edward

**Gray, John Baker** 20th c.   [BEW]
*American writer, theatrical
performer, director*
* Gray, Timothy

**Gray, John Gordon** 1949-   [SMG]
*Canadian-born hockey player*
* Gray Dog

**Gray, Jonathan**
See   Adams, Herbert

**Gray, Jonathan**
See   Taylor, Jack

**Gray, Leon** 1951-   [SMG]
*American football player*
* Gray, Big Dog

**Gray, Lorna** 20th c.   [FIR]
*American actress*
* Booth, Adrian

**Gray, Louisa M.** 19th c.   [PA]
*Author*
* Thorne, Kate

**Gray, Marian**
See   Pierce, Edith Gray

**Gray, Marion** 1885-1975   [SC]
*American actress*
* McIntyre, Marion

**Gray, Maxwell**
See   Tuttiett, Mary Gleed

**Gray, Minnie Oscar**
See   Stephens, Mrs. W. T.

**Gray, Nadia**
See   Kujnir-Herescu, Nadia

**Gray, Old Billy**
See   Gray, William

**Gray, Oswald** 1866-1942   [BEW]
*Australian-born theatre proprietor
and producer*
* Stoll, [Sir] Oswald

**Gray, Patricia [Clark]** 20th c.
[CA, SAT, SFP]
*American author*
* Clark, Virginia
* Gray, Patsey
* Pogo

**Gray, Patsey**
See   Gray, Patricia [Clark]

**Gray, Paul**
See   FitzGibbon, Paul Thomas

**Gray, Pete**
See   Wyshner, Peter J.

**Gray, Philip**
See   Perlman, Jess

**Gray, R. E.** 20th c.   [MBF]
*British author*
* Grayling, Ronald

**Gray, Reddy**
See   Gray, James D.

**Gray, Richard**
See   Flannam, Richard

**Gray, Russell**
See   Fischer, Bruno

**Gray, Sad Sam**
See   Gray, Samuel David

**Gray, Sally**
See   Stevens, Constance

**Gray, Samuel David** 1897-1953
[AS, BE]
*American baseball player*
* Gray, Sad Sam

**Gray, Simon** 1936-   [CA, WD]
*British author and playwright*
* Holliday, James
* Reade, Hamish

**Gray Skin**
See   Harold II

**Gray, Spike**
See   Knoblaugh, Glen Gray

**Gray, Stan[ley Oscar]** 1888-1964
[BE]
*American baseball player*
* Gray, Dolly

**Gray Steel**
See   Douglas, Archibald

**Gray, Thomas** 1716-1771
[DEP, HN, SN]
*British poet*
* [The] British Pindar
* [The] English Pindar
* Orosmades
* [The] Pindar of England
* [The] Sweet Lyrist of Peter
  House
* [The] Torre of Poetry

**Gray, Thomas B.** 1905?-   [WWJ]
*American jazz musician*
* Gray, Tick

**Gray, Tick**
See   Gray, Thomas B.

**Gray, Timothy**
See   Gray, John Baker

**Gray, Tony**
See   Gray, George Hugh

**Gray, Vanessa**
See   Aeby, Jacquelyn

**Gray, Whitley** 1887-   [NAA]
*American poet, editor, publisher*
* Armenheim, Gregory
* Shawn, Semas

**Gray, Widett**
See   Ray, De Witt Grinnell

**Gray, William**
See   Kolb, John W.

**Gray, William** 19th c.   [SN]
*American merchant*
* Gray, Old Billy

**Gray, William Denton** 1878-1956
[BE]
*American baseball player*
* Gray, Dolly

**Gray Wolf**
See   Hofsinde, Robert

**Gray, Woody**
See   Rapuzzi, G. L.

**Graybeard**
See   Graff, John Franklin

**Graybille, But**
See   Graybille, Durwood

**Graybille, Durwood** 1910?-1978
[FIR]
*Photographer*
* Graybille, But

**Graydon, Mark**
See   Graydon, Robert Murray

**Graydon, Robert Murray**  ?-1937
[MBF, WGT]
*American-born British author*
* Gray, Don
* Graydon, Mark
* Hamilton, Murray [joint
  pseudonym with George Heber
  Teed]
* Murray, Robert
* O'Flynn, Jimmy
* Roberts, Murray

**Graydon, William Murray**
1864-1946   [MBF]
*American-born author*
* Armitage, Alfred
* Gordon, William Murray
* Murray, William
* Olliver, Tom

**Grayfell**
See   Harold II

**Grayland, Valerie Merle [Spanner]**
[B10, CA, WD]
*New Zealand author*
* Belvedere, Lee
* Spanner, Valerie
* Subond, Valerie

**Grayling, Ronald**
See   Gray, R. E.

**Graysmith, Robert**
See   Smith, Robert Gray

**Grayson, Alice Barr**
See   Grossman, Jean Schick

**Grayson, Bette**
See   Lipper, Bette

**Grayson, Betty Evans** 20th c.
[BBH]
*American softball player*
* [The] Blonde Bomber
* Grayson, Bullet

**Grayson, Bullet**
See   Grayson, Betty Evans

**Grayson, David**
See   Baker, Ray Stannard

**Grayson, Eldred**
See   Hare, Robert

**Grayson, [Capt.] J. J.**
See   Wright, Elsie N.

**Grayson, Kathryn**
See   Hedrick, Zelma Kathryn

**Grayson, Laura**
See   Wilson, Barbara

**Grayson, Paul**
See   Dempsey, James E.

**Grayson, Richard**
See   Grindal, Richard

**Grayson, Richard**
See   Rosenblatt, Richard Andrew

**Graystark, Chon**
See   Ackerman, Forrest J[ames]

**Graystone, Lynn**
See   Brennan, Joseph L[omas]

**[The] Graystone Sage**
See   Tilden, Samuel Jones

**Graziano, Jerry** 1915-   [PMJ]
*American arranger and bandleader*
* Gray, Jerry

**Graziano, Rocky**
See   Barbella, Rocco

**Graziati, Aldo** 1902?-1953
[FC, OCF, WEF]
*Italian cinematographer*
* Aldo, G. R.

**Grazzini, Antonio Francesco [or
Antonfrancesco]** 1503-1584
[SN, WBD]
*Italian author*
* [Il] Lasca [The Roach]

**Grealey, Thomas Louis** 1916-   [CA]
*British author*
* Southworth, Louis

**Greason, Booster**
See   Greason, William Henry [Bill]

**Greason, William Henry [Bill]**
1924-   [BE]
*American baseball player*
* Greason, Booster

**Greasy Thumb Guzik**
See   Guzik, Jake

**[The] Great**
See   Abbas I

**[The] Great**
See   Akbar

**[The] Great**
See   Albert [or Albrecht]

**[The] Great**
See   Albert [Count of Bollstadt]

**[The] Great**
See   Albuquerque, Alfonso [or
Affonso] de

**[The] Great**
See   Alexander, Archie Alphonso

**[The] Great**
See   Alexander III

**[The] Great**
See   Alfonso III [or Alphonso]

**[The] Great**
See   Alfred

**[The] Great**
See   Amadeus V

**[The] Great**
See   Antiochus III

**[The] Great**
See   Asoka [or Acoka]

**[The] Great**
See   Athanasius

**[The] Great**
See Aurungzebe [Aurangzeb or Aurungzeb]

**[The] Great**
See Basil [or Basilius]

**[The] Great**
See Bernard, Roger

**[The] Great**
See Bonaparte, Napoleon

**[The] Great**
See Bruno I [or Brun]

**[The] Great**
See Camoens, Luis de

**[The] Great**
See Canute II

**[The] Great**
See Casimir III

**[The] Great**
See Catherine II

**[The] Great**
See Charles Emmanuel I

**[The] Great**
See Charles I [or Karl]

**[The] Great**
See Charles III

**[The] Great**
See Clovis I

**[The] Great**
See Constantine I [Flavius Valerius Aurelius Constantinus]

**[The] Great**
See Cyrus

**[The] Great**
See Darius I

**[The] Great**
See Dionysius

**[The] Great**
See Donatus

**[The] Great**
See Emanuel I [Manuel or Manoel]

**[The] Great**
See Ferdinand I

**[The] Great**
See Fields, Wilmer

**[The] Great**
See Frederick II

**[The] Great**
See Galitzin, Vasili

**[The] Great**
See Gertrude

**[The] Great**
See Gregory I

**[The] Great**
See Gustavus Adolphus

**[The] Great**
See Hanno

**[The] Great**
See Henry IV [or Henri]

**[The] Great**
See Herod

**[The] Great**
See Herod Agrippa I [or Julius Agrippa I]

**[The] Great**
See Hiao-wen-tee

**[The] Great**
See Hugh [or Hugo] of Cluny

**[The] Great**
See Hugh [or Hugues]

**[The] Great**
See Hurtado de Mendoza, Diego

**[The] Great**
See Ivan III Vasilievich

**[The] Great**
See James II

**[The] Great**
See John I [or Joao]

**[The] Great**
See John II

**[The] Great**
See Justinian I [Flavius Anicius Justinianus]

**[The] Great**
See Khosru I [or Chosroes]

**[The] Great**
See Leo I

**[The] Great**
See Leo I

**[The] Great**
See Leopold I

**[The] Great**
See Llewelyn ab Iorwerth

**[The] Great**
See Louis

**[The] Great**
See Louis I

**[The] Great**
See Louis XIV

**[The] Great**
See Mahmud

**[The] Great**
See Mails, John Walter

**[The] Great**
See Matthias Corvinus

**[The] Great**
See Maximilian I

**[The] Great**
See Medici, Cosmo [or Cosimo] de

**[The] Great**
See Mircea

**[The] Great**
See Mithridates II

**[The] Great**
See Mithridates VI Eupator

**[The] Great**
See Mohammed II [or Mahomet]

**[The] Great**
See Nerses

**[The] Great**
See Nicholas I

**[The] Great**
See Niall

**[The] Great**
See Otto I [or Otho]

**[The] Great**
See Ottokar II

**[The] Great**
See Pedro III [or Peter]

**[The] Great**
See Peter I [Petr Alekseevich]

**[The] Great**
See Pompey [or Pompeius], Cneius

**[The] Great**
See Procop [or Procopius], Andrew

**[The] Great**
See Sancho III

**[The] Great**
See Sforza, James

**[The] Great**
See Shapur II [or Sapor]

**[The] Great**
See Sigismund I

**[The] Great**
See Stephen of Moldavia

**[The] Great**
See Theodoric

**[The] Great**
See Theodosius I

**[The] Great**
See Tigranes

**[The] Great**
See Tiridates III

**[The] Great**
See Visconti, Matteo

**[The] Great**
See Vladimir I

**[The] Great**
See Waldemar [or Valdemar]

**[The] Great**
See Waldemar I

**[The] Great**
See William V

**[The] Great**
See Xerxes I

**[The] Great Agnostic**
See Ingersoll, Robert Green

**[The] Great American Condenser**
See Wood, John B.

**[The] Great American Doctor**
See Ricord, Philippe

**[The] Great American Traveller**
See Pratt, Daniel

**[The] Great American Trouper**
See Baker, Phil

**[The] Great Apostle of the French**
See Remi [or Remigius]

**[The] Great Arnauld**
See Arnauld, Antoine

**[The] Great Astrologer**
See Kindi, al- [Abu Yusef al-Kindi]

**[The] Great Baron**
See Von Brandenburg, Hugo

**[The] Great Bastard**
See De Bourgogne, Antoine

**[The] Great Bear**
See Johnson, Samuel

**[The] Great Blackstone**
See Bouton, Harry

**[The] Great Border Minstrel**
See Scott, [Sir] Walter

**[The] Great Bullet-Head**
See Cadoudal, Georges

**[The] Great Captain**
See Gonzalvo di Cordova, Hernandez

**[The] Great Captain**
See Manuel I Comnenus

**[The] Great Cardinal**
See Du Plessis, Armand Jean

**[The] Great Cardinal**
See Gonzalez de Mendoza, Pedro

**[The] Great Cardinal of Spain**
See Hurtado de Mendoza, Diego

**[The] Great Carini**
See Leach, Archibald Alexander

**[The] Great Carlton**
See Philps, Arthur Carlton

**[The] Great Carter**
See Carter, Charles J.

**[The] Great Cham of Literature**
See Johnson, Samuel

**[The] Great Commoner**
See Barnard, [Sir] John

**[The] Great Commoner**
See Clay, Henry

**[The] Great Commoner**
See Gladstone, William Ewart

**[The] Great Commoner**
See Pitt, William [Earl of Chatham]

**[The] Great Commoner**
See Stevens, Thaddeus

**[The] Great Communicator**
See Reagan, Ronald Wilson

**[The] Great Comte**
See Hawkesworth, Eric

**[The] Great Conde**
See Bourbon, Louis II de [Prince de Conde]

**[The] Great Coram**
See Whitaker, Thomas

**[The] Great Count**
See Roger I

**[The] Great Countess**
See Matilda of Tuscany

**[The] Great Crocodile**
See Sobhuza II

**[The] Great Dane**
See Rasmussen, Harold Ralph

**[The] Great Dauphin**
See Louis

**[The] Great Duke**
See Wellesley, Arthur

**[The] Great Duke of the West**
See Philip [or Philippe]

[The] Great Eagle
See Adler, Jacob Pavlovitch

[The] Great Eagle
See Maimonides [or Moses ben Maimon]

[The] Great Earl
See De Burgh, Ulick

[The] Great Earl
See Douglas, Archibald

[The] Great Earl
See O'Brien, Donough [Baron of Ibrickan]

[The] Great Earl of Cork
See Boyle, Richard [First Earl of Cork]

[The] Great Eater
See Comestor, Peter [or Petrus]

[The] Great Elector
See Frederick William

[The] Great Eltchi [or Elchi]
See Canning, [Sir] Stratford [First Viscount Stratford de Redcliffe]

[The] Great Emancipator
See Lincoln, Abraham

[The] Great Excavator
See Guilford, Jesse P.

[The] Great Fontonelle
See Sutton, William

[The] Great Gabbo
See Gabler, Frank Harold

[The] Great Gama
See Gama, Gulam Mohammed

[The] Great Goose
See Ligon, Jim

[The] Great Gretzky
See Gretzky, Wayne

[The] Great Hammerer
See Grant, Hiram Ulysses

Great Head
See Malcolm III

[The] Great Healer
See Bodie, Sam

[The] Great Heathen
See Goethe, Johann Wolfgang von

[The] Great Helmsman
See Mao Tse-tung

[The] Great Herman
See Franklin, George

[The] Great Iconoclast
See Luther, Martin

[The] Great Imposter
See Demara, Ferdinand Waldo, Jr.

[The] Great Jesuit of the West
See Picquet, Francois

[The] Great Lafayette
See Neuberger, Sigmund

[The] Great Letter-Writer
See Voiture, Vincent

[The] Great Light [Llever Mawr]
See Linus

[The] Great Little Mackney
See Relph, Harry

[The] Great Little Robson
See Brownbill, Thomas Robson

[The] Great Little Tilley
See Powles, Matilda Alice

[The] Great Loyalist
See Paulet, John

[The] Great Lyle
See Lyle, Cecil

[The] Great Macdermott
See Farrell, Gilbert Hastings

[The] Great Magician of the North
See Scott, [Sir] Walter

[The] Great Marquis
See Carvalho e Mello, Sebastiao Jose de

[The] Great Marquis
See Cortes, Hernando

[The] Great Marquis
See Graham, James

[The] Great Master of Love
See Daniel, Arnaud [Arnaut or Arnault]

[The] Great Merlini
See Rawson, Clayton

[The] Great Milton
See Milton, Tommy

[The] Great Moralist
See Johnson, Samuel

[The] Great Mountain
See Sobhuza II

[The] Great O
See O'Connell, Daniel

[The] Great Objector
See Holman, William Steele

[The] Great Obstructionist
See Allen, James Browning

[The] Great One
See Sethunsa, Khotso

[The] Great Pacificator
See Clay, Henry

[The] Great Pacificator
See Cochrane, Clark B.

[The] Great Pan
See Arouet, Francois Marie

[The] Great Peacemaker
See Grant, Hiram Ulysses

[The] Great Ponzi
See Ponzi, Charles

Great Profile
See Blythe, John

[The] Great Red Dragon of Coleman Street
See Goodwin [or Goodwyn], John

[The] Great Renegade
See Girty, Simon

[The] Great Sante
See Tucker, Samuel

[The] Great Seer
See Johnson, Samuel

[The] Great Sopper [Gros Soupier]
See Beda, Noel

[The] Great Sow
See Isabella of Bavaria

[The] Great Stone Face
See Keaton, Joseph Francis

[The] Great Teacher of Gardening
See Abercrombie, John

[The] Great Tentmaker
See Omar Khayyam

[The] Great Tinclarian Doctor
See Mitchell, William

[The] Great Train Robber
See Biggs, Ronald Arthur

[The] Great Unbowlable
See Woodfull, William Maldon

[The] Great Unknown
See Scott, [Sir] Walter

[The] Great Vance
See Stevens, Alfred Peck

[The] Great Verulam
See Bacon, Francis [First Baron Verulam]

[The] Great White Chief
See Roosevelt, Theodore [Teddy]

[The] Great Witch of Balwery
See Aiken, Margaret

[The] Greater
See George IV

[The] Greater
See James

[The] Greatest Comedian on the American Stage
See Williams, Egbert Austin

[The] Greatest Cub
See Banks, Ernest [Ernie]

[The] Greatest of the Herrmanns
See Herrmann, Adelaide

Greathead
See Grosseteste, Robert

Greatrex, Charles 19th c. [SAT]
British author
* Meadows, Lindon

Greaves, Clotilda [FFF]
American playwright
* Stannus, Austin

Greaves, Horace 1880-? [THR]
British comedian
* Lane, Horace

Greaves, Norman
See Brooks, Edwy Searles

Greaves, R. B.
See Greaves, Robert Bertram Aloysius, III

Greaves, Richard
See McCutcheon, George Barr

Greaves, Robert Bertram Aloysius, III 1944- [RO2]
American singer
* Greaves, R. B.

Greb, Edward Henry 1894-1926 [AS, BX, RBE]
American boxer
* Greb, Harry
* [The] Human Windmill
* [The] Pittsburgh Windmill

Greb, Harry
See Greb, Edward Henry

Greb, Mel 20th c. [EJS]
American boxing promoter
* Greb, Red

Greb, Red
See Greb, Mel

Greb, Ronnie
See Grabowski, Ronald David

Greber's Peg
See De l'Epine, Francesca Margherita

[Il] Grechetto
See Castiglione, Giovanni Benedetto

[El] Greco [The Greek]
See Agudo, Angel

[El] Greco
See Theotokopoulos, Domenikos

Greco, Armando 1926- [ASC, DAM, EJ]
American singer
* Greco, Buddy

Greco, Buddy
See Greco, Armando

Greco, Costanzo 1918- [CA]
Italian-born American dancer, choreographer, actor
* Greco, Jose

Greco, Jose
See Greco, Costanzo

Greco, Margaret
See Fry, Barbara

[The] Greek
See Alvarez, Manuel

[The] Greek Ambassador of Goodwill
See Givot, George

[The] Greek Commentator
See Nunez de Guzman, Fernan [or Fernando]

[The] Greek Livy
See Joseph ben Matthias

Greeley, Emily Elmore 1886- [NAA]
American writer
* Elmore, Emily W.

Greeley, Horace 1811-1872 [DEP, SN]
American politician and journalist
* [The] Napoleon of Essayists
* [The] Prince of Paragraphists
* [The] Sage of Chappaqua

Greely, Robert H. [PA]
Author
* O'Gotham, Bob

Green, Adam
See Weisgard, Leonard [Joseph]

Green, Alan [Baer] 1906-1975 [CA, CC, WW]
American author and advertising executive
* Alan, Jack
* Burne, Glen [joint pseudonym with Gladys Elizabeth (Blun) Green]
* Denbie, Roger [joint pseudonym with Julian Paul Brodie]

Green, Anna
See Schneider-Green, Ann

**Green, Anna Katharine**
See Rohlfs, Anna Katharine
[Green]

**Green, Assa** [PA]
*Author*
* Elmwood, Eluathan, Esq.

**Green Bar Bill**
See Bjerregaard-Jensen, Wilhelm
Hans

**Green, Benny**
See Green, Bernard

**Green, Bernard** 1927- [CA]
*British jazz musician and author*
* Green, Benny

**Green, Big**
See Green, Charlie

**Green, Boy**
See Green, Dave

**Green, Bunky**
See Green, Vernice, Jr.

**Green, Candy**
See Green, Clarence

**Green, Charles** 1902-
[BX, EJS, RBE]
*American boxer*
* Rosenberg, Charley Phil

**Green, Charles** 20th c. [OBW]
*American baseball manager*
* Green, Joe

**Green, Charles M.**
See Gardner, Erle Stanley

**Green, Charlie**
See Entratta, Charles

**Green, Charlie** 1900-1935 [DAM]
*American jazz musician*
* Green, Big

**Green, Chin**
See Green, Leslie

**Green, Clarence** 1929- [BWW]
*American singer*
* Green, Candy
* Green, Galveston

**Green, Cornelius** 1928-
[BWW, NBB]
*American singer*
* Lonesome Sundown

**Green, Cornell** 20th c.
*American football player*
* Green, Greeny

**[The] Green Count**
See Amadeus VI

**Green, D.**
See Casewit, Curtis

**Green, Danny**
See Green, Edward

**Green, Dave** 20th c. [RBE]
*British boxer*
* Green, Boy

**Green, David** 1886-1973 [IPA]
*Israeli prime minister*
* Ben Gurion, David
* [The] Little Giant

**Green, Dolores** 1834-1926 [BEW]
*British-born actress*
* Drummond, Dolores

**Green, Dorothy** 1915- [AW]
*Australian author*
* Auchterlonie, Dorothy

**Green, Dudley E.** 1912- [GF]
*American golf writer*
* Green, Waxo

**Green, E. Helen**
See Beale, Elizabeth Helen

**Green, Edmund Fisk** 1842-1901
[WBD]
*American philosopher and historian*
* Fiske, John

**Green, Edward** 1876-1914 [BE]
*American baseball player*
* Green, Danny

**Green, Elijah Jerry** 1933- [BE]
*American baseball player*
* Green, Pumpsie

**Green, Elisabeth Sara** 1940- [WD]
*British author*
* Tresilian, Liz

**Green, Ethel Victoria** 1914- [BEW]
*British actress and playwright*
* Green, Janet

**Green, F. L.**
See Green, Frederick Lawrence

**Green, Frederick Lawrence**
1902-1953 [LC]
*British author*
* Green, F. L.

**Green, Galveston**
See Green, Clarence

**Green, Gerald B.** 20th c. [MBF]
*British author*
* Fitzgerald, Gerald

**Green, Gladys Elizabeth [Blun]**
1908- [WW]
*American author*
* Burne, Glen [joint pseudonym
   with Alan (Baer) Green]

**Green, Glint**
See Fischer, Margaret Ann
Peterson

**[The] Green Goddess**
See Brundtland, Gro Harlem

**Green, Greeny**
See Green, Cornell

**Green, Hannah**
See Greenberg, Joanne Goldenberg

**Green, Harry**
See Blitzer, Harry

**Green, Henrietta Howland [Robinson]**
1834-1916 [WA]
*American financier*
* Green, Hetty

**Green, Henry**
See Yorke, Henry Vincent

**Green, Henry Hawes Craven**
1837-1910 [BEW]
*Theatrical scene painter*
* Craven, Hawes

**Green, Hetty**
See Green, Henrietta Howland
[Robinson]

**Green, Hubert Unsworth** 1886-
[NAA]
*British-born naturalist and writer*
* Lascelles, Tony

**Green, I. G.**
See Greenblatt, Ira

**Green, Ian Ernest Gilmore** 1912-
[EJ, PMJ]
*Canadian-born jazz musician*
* Evans, Gil

**Green, J. C. R.**
See Green, James

**Green, James** 1949- [IAW]
*Scottish author and publisher*
* Green, J. C. R.

**Green, Janet**
See Green, Ethel Victoria

**Green, Joan Elizabeth** 1951- [CA]
*American poet*
* Whitebird, J[oanie]

**Green, Joe**
See Green, Charles

**Green, John**
See Townsend, George Henry

**Green, John** 1933- [BB]
*American basketball player*
* Green, Jumpin' Johnny

**Green, John Richards** 1758-1818
[DEL]
*British author and publisher*
* Gifford, John

**Green, Joseph Henry [Joe]** 1897-
[BE]
*American baseball player*
* Green, Tilly

**Green, Judith**
See Galbraith, Jean

**Green, Julien [Hartridge]** 1900-
[CA]
*French-born American author*
* Delaporte, Theophile
* Ireland, David

**Green, Jumpin' Johnny**
See Green, John

**Green, L. Dunton**
See Grein, Louis John Herman

**Green, Lee** 20th c. [BWW]
*American musician*
* Pork Chop Lee

**Green, Leslie** 20th c. [OBW]
*American baseball player*
* Green, Chin

**Green, Mabel**
See Coomber, Mabel

**[The] Green Machine**
See O'Grady, Sean

**Green, Madge** 1927- [IAW]
*British author and journalist*
* Derbyshire, Jane
* Haddon, Sarah

**Green, Mae** 1915?- [FC, SW]
*American actress*
* Parker, Jean

**Green, Martyn**
See Martyn-Green, William

**Green, Maxwell Revenell** 1929-
[AW]
*British author*
* Cabby with Camera

**Green, Mitzi**
See Keno, Elizabeth

**[The] Green Mountain Boy**
See Haynes, Lemuel B.

**Green, Norman G.** 1907-1975
[BWW]
*American singer*
* Green, Slim
* Guitar Slim

**Green, O. O.**
See Durgnat, Raymond [Eric]

**Green, Peter**
See Bulmer, [Henry] Kenneth

**Green, Peter [Morris]** 1924-
[CA, WD, WW]
*British author, translator, editor*
* Delaney, Denis

**Green, Peter** 20th c. [LAO]
*British clergyman and author*
* Artifex

**Green, Pumpsie**
See Green, Elijah Jerry

**Green, Red**
See Green, Redvers

**Green, Redvers** 20th c. [SMG]
*Hockey player*
* Green, Red

**Green, Richard** 20th c. [B10]
*American author*
* Richards, Leslie

**Green, Robert**
See Smith, Richard Rein

**Green, Roland [James]** 1944-
[SFL, WGT]
*American author*
* Lord, Jeffrey [house pseudonym]

**Green, Rosa**
See Henderson, Rosa [Rose]

**Green, Sadie**
See Brown, Bessie

**Green, Sadie**
See De Leath, Vaughn

**Green, Sheila Ellen** 1934-
[CA, SAT]
*American author and illustrator*
* Greenwald, Sheila

**Green, Shorty**
See Green, Wilfred

**Green, Si**
See Green, Sihugo

**Green, Sihugo** 1934- [BB]
*American basketball player*
* Green, Si

**Green, Slim**
See Green, Norman G.

**Green, Tilly**
See Green, Joseph Henry [Joe]

**Green, Urban Clifford** 1926-
[ASC, DAM, EJ]
*American jazz musician*
* Green, Urbie

**Green, Urbie**
See Green, Urban Clifford

**Green, Vernice, Jr.** 1935- [DAM]
*American jazz musician*
* Green, Bunky

**Green, Violet**
See Smith, Clara

**Green, Waxo**
See   Green, Dudley E.

**Green, Wilfred** 1896-1960
[CEI, FHE, HK]
*Canadian-born hockey player*
* Green, Shorty

**Green, William Edward** 1855-1921
[OCF, WEF]
*British photographer and inventor*
* Friese-Greene, William

**Green, William M[ark]** 1929-    [CA]
*American author and actor*
* Iden, William

**Green, Woodrow, Jr.** 1952-    [FB]
*American football player*
* Green, Woody

**Green, Woody**
See   Green, Woodrow, Jr.

**Green-Wanstall, Kenneth** 1918-
[CA]
*British journalist and author*
* Wanstall, Ken

**Greenall, Jack** 20th c.    [WEC]
*British cartoonist*
* Maddocks

**Greenaway, Gladys** 1901-    [CA]
*British author*
* Manners, Julia

**Greenbank, Anthony Hunt** 1933-
[CA]
*British author*
* Hunt, Nigel

**Greenbaum, Mutz** 1896-1968    [FC]
*German-born cinematographer*
* Greene, Max

**Greenberg, Big Greenie**
See   Greenberg, Harry

**Greenberg, Big Maxey**
See   Greenberg, Max

**Greenberg, Edward** 1916-1974
*American actor and singer*
* Platt, Edward

**Greenberg, Hammerin' Hank**
See   Greenberg, Henry Benjamin

**Greenberg, Harry**  ?-1939?
[BLB, PHM]
*American underworld figure*
* Greenberg, Big Greenie

**Greenberg, Henry Benjamin** 1911-
[BE, EJS]
*American baseball player*
* Greenberg, Hammerin' Hank

**Greenberg, Ivan** 1908-1973   [CA]
*Russian-born editor and author*
* Rahv, Philip

**Greenberg, Joanne Goldenberg**
1932-   [CLC, WYA]
*American author*
* Green, Hannah

**Greenberg, Max**  ?-1928   [MM]
*American underworld figure*
* Greenberg, Big Maxey

**Greenberg, Uri Zvi** 1898-   [WOA]
*Austrian-born Yiddish poet*
* Tur-Malka

**Greenbie, Marjorie Barstow** 1891-
[NAA]
*American author*
* Latta, Marguerite

**Greenblatt, Ira** 20th c.    [SFL]
*American author*
* Green, I. G.

**Greenburgh, Gilbert Adrian**
1903-1959    [WFA]
*American fashion designer*
* Adrian

**Greenbury, Judith Pamela** 1924-
[ART]
*British painter*
* J. G.

**Greendrake, Gregory, Esq.**
See   Coad, J.

**Greene, Adam**
See   Scott, Peter Dale

**Greene, Albert Gorton** 1802-1868
[PA]
*Author*
* Old Grimes

**Greene, Alvin Carl** 1923-    [CA]
*American author and editor*
* Randolph, Arthur C.
* Weaver, Mateman

**Greene, Anne D.**    [PA]
*Author*
* Douglass, Marian

**Greene, Asa** 1788-1837    [PA]
*Author*
* Duckworth, Dodenius
* Ex Barber Fribbleton
* Fribbleton, George

**Greene, Bert**
See   Greene, Charles Herbert

**Greene, Burton** 1937-    [EJ7]
*American jazz musician*
* Greene, Narada

**Greene, Charles Edward** 1946-
[B10, FB]
*American football player*
* Greene, Joe
* Greene, Mean Joe

**Greene, Charles Gordon** 1804-1886
[FFF]
*American journalist*
* Flaneur

**Greene, Charles Herbert** 1944-
[BWG]
*American golfer*
* Greene, Bert

**Greene, Cornelius** 20th c.    [IBW]
*American football player*
* Greene, Flam

**Greene, Dennis**
See   Greene, Frederick

**Greene, Edith Elizabeth** 1876-1917
[THR]
*British actress*
* Greene, Evie

**Greene, Eustace**
See   Monar, Motilall Rooplalln

**Greene, Evie**
See   Greene, Edith Elizabeth

**Greene, Flam**
See   Greene, Cornelius

**Greene, Fred**
See   Cadet, John

**Greene, Freddie** 20th c.    [NP]
*American jazz musician*
* Greene, Pep

**Greene, Frederick** 1949-    [RO2]
*American singer*
* Greene, Dennis

**Greene, Gene** 1877-1930    [CED]
*American singer*
* [The] Ragtime King

**Greene, Gladys Georgianna** 1905?-
[BDF, BEW, F2]
*American actress*
* Arthur, Jean

**Greene, Hiram**
See   Wilkins, William A.

**Greene, Jack** 1930-    [ECM]
*American country-western performer*
* Jolly Giant

**Greene, James** 1912-    [IBW]
*American baseball player*
* Greene, Joe

**Greene, Joe**
See   Greene, Charles Edward

**Greene, Joe**
See   Greene, James

**Greene, L. Patrick**
See   Greene, Louis Montague

**Greene, Lefty**
See   Greene, Nelson George

**Greene, Linda** 20th c.    [IBW]
*American singer*
* Peaches

**Greene, Louis Montague** 20th c.
[WW]
*Author*
* Greene, L. Patrick

**Greene, Mabel**
See   Bean, Mabel Greene

**Greene, Max**
See   Greenbaum, Mutz

**Greene, Mean Joe**
See   Greene, Charles Edward

**Greene, Nancy** 1944-    [CSH]
*Canadian skier*
* Greene, Tiger

**Greene, Narada**
See   Greene, Burton

**Greene, Nelson George** 1900-    [BE]
*American baseball player*
* Greene, Lefty

**Greene, Pamela**
See   Forman, Joan

**Greene, Patrick Joseph** 1875-1934
[BE]
*American baseball player*
* Foley, Pat
* Greene, Willie

**Greene, Pep**
See   Greene, Freddie

**Greene, Robert**
See   Deindorfer, Robert Greene

**Greene, Robert** 1560?-1592    [SN]
*British author, playwright, poet*
* [The] Ape of Euphues
* [The] King of the Paper Stage
* [The] Patriarch of Shifters
* [The] Scrivener of Crosbiters

**Greene, Sigrid** 1921-    [WD]
*American author*
* De Lima, Sigrid

**Greene, Thomas**  ?-1684    [PA]
*Author*
* [A] Lover of Literature

**Greene, Tiger**
See   Greene, Nancy

**Greene, Ward** 1892-1956
[ANT, TC, WW]
*American author*
* Dudley, Frank

**Greene, Willie**
See   Greene, Patrick Joseph

**Greenege, Slicker**
See   Greenege, Victor

**Greenege, Victor** 20th c.    [OBW]
*American baseball player*
* Greenege, Slicker

**Greener, William Oliver** 1862- ?
[WW]
*Author*
* Gerrare, Wirt

**Greenfield, Darby**
See   Ward, Philip

**Greenfield, Elizabeth Taylor**
1809-1876    [IBW]
*American singer*
* [The] Black Swan

**Greenfield, Irving A.** 1928-    [SFL]
*American author*
* Duncan, Bruce

**Greenfield, Sammy** 1878-1945
[F2, FC]
*American actor*
* Sidney, George

**Greengroin, Artie**
See   Brown, Harry [Peter McNab]

**Greenhalgh, Fred** 1872-1927
[BMH]
*British trapeze performer*
* Rolo

**Greenhalgh, Mary** 1919-    [THR]
*British actress*
* Martlew, Mary

**Greenhill, William** 17th c.    [SN]
*British clergyman and author*
* [The] Evening Star of Stepney

**Greenhood, [Clarence] David** 1895-
[CA]
*American author and poet*
* Sawyer, Mark

**Greenhorn**
See   Thompson, George

**Greenhough, Terence [Terry]** 1944-
[ESF]
*British author*
* Lester, Andrew

**Greenig, John A.** 19th c.    [BE]
*American baseball player*
* Greening, John A.

**Greening, Hamilton**
See   Hamilton, Charles Harold St.
John

**Greening, John A.**
See   Greenig, John A.

**Greenland, William Kingscote** 1868-
?   [WWL]
*British author and journalist*
* King, W. Scott

**Greenleaf, Lawrence N.**    [PA]
*Author*
* Punever, Peter

**Greenlee, Gus**
*See* Greenlee, W. A.

**Greenlee, W. A.** 20th c.    [OBW]
*American baseball player*
* Greenlee, Gus

**Greenman, Ethel** 1890?-1963
[BEW]
*Theatrical performer*
* Shattuck, Ethel

**Greenough, A. J.**
*See* Avery, Jane G.

**Greenough, Thurkle** 20th c.    [GW]
*American rodeo performer*
* Greenough, Turk

**Greenough, Turk**
*See* Greenough, Thurkle

**Greenspun, Hank**
*See* Greenspun, Herman Milton

**Greenspun, Herman Milton** 1909-
[B10, CAP]
*American journalist*
* Greenspun, Hank

**Greenstein, Joseph L.** 1893-1977
*Polish-born strong man*
* [The] Mighty Atom

**Greenwald, Milton** 1919-
[BEW, EMT, TR]
*American choreographer and director*
* Kidd, Michael

**Greenwald, Sheila**
*See* Green, Sheila Ellen

**Greenway, Roger** 1942-    [RO2]
*British singer and songwriter*
* David

**Greenwich, Larry**
*See* Greenwich, Lorenzo Keith, Jr.

**Greenwich, Lorenzo Keith, Jr.**
1936-    [IWM]
*American musician*
* Greenwich, Larry

**Greenwood, George**
*See* Cerioni, Giorgio

**Greenwood, George Arthur** 1893-
[WWL]
*British author*
* Howley, Mark

**Greenwood, Grace**
*See* Lippincott, Sara Jane [Clarke]

**Greenwood, Greenie**
*See* Greenwood, Robert Chandler [Bob]

**Greenwood, James** 1690- ?
[DNNS, FFF, PA]
*British author and journalist*
* [The] Amateur Casual

**Greenwood, Julia Eileen Courtney**
1910-    [CAP, WD]
*British author*
* Askham, Francis

**Greenwood, Monty**
*See* Poli, Maurice

**Greenwood, Robert Chandler [Bob]**
1928-    [BE]
*Mexican-born baseball player*
* Greenwood, Greenie

**Greenwood, Thomas** 20th c.    [WD]
*Author*
* Verval, Alain [joint pseudonym with Lawrence Montague Lande]

**Greer, Bettyjane** 1924-    [FC]
*American actress*
* Greer, Jane

**Greer, Hal** 1937-    [IBW]
*American basketball player*
* Greer, Sage

**Greer, Jane**
*See* Greer, Bettyjane

**Greer, Mrs. S. D.**    [PA]
*Author*
* [An] Irish Lady

**Greer, Richard** [joint pseudonym with Robert Silverberg] [house pseudonym, Ziff-Davis]
*See* Garrett, [Gordon] Randall [Philip David]

**Greer, Richard** [joint pseudonym with Randall Garrett] [house pseudonym, Ziff-Davis]
*See* Silverberg, Robert

**Greer, Sage**
*See* Greer, Hal

**Greer, Sonny**
*See* Greer, William Alexander

**Greer, William Alexander** 1903-
[DAM, EJ, PMJ]
*American jazz musician*
* Greer, Sonny

**Greet, Ben**
*See* Barling, Philip

**Greet, [Sir] Philip**
*See* Barling, Philip

**Greeven, Alice Augusta** 1894-1944
[THR]
*British playwright and producer*
* Orme, Michael

**Greg**
*See* Regnier, Michel

**Greg, William Rathburn**
1809-1881    [PA]
*Author*
* W. R. G.

**Gregg, Andrew K.** 1929-    [CA]
*American author*
* Hearn, Sneed
* Vinegar, Tom

**Gregg, David Charles [Dave]**
1891-1965    [BE]
*American baseball player*
* Gregg, Highpockets

**Gregg, Highpockets**
*See* Gregg, David Charles [Dave]

**Gregg, Hilda Caroline** 1868-1933
[SFL]
*Author*
* Grier, Sydney C.

**Gregg, Martin**
*See* McNeilly, Wilfred Glassford

**Gregg, Sylveanus Augustus**
1885-1964    [BE]
*American baseball player*
* Gregg, Vean

**Gregg, Vean**
*See* Gregg, Sylveanus Augustus

**Gregoire**
*See* Dubillard, Roland

**Gregoire, [Le Pere]**
*See* Girard, Jean Baptiste

**Gregoire, Leon**
*See* Goyau, [Pierre Louis Theophile] Georges

**Gregor, Arthur**
*See* Goldberg, Arthur

**Gregor, Lee** [joint pseudonym with Milton A. Rothman]
*See* Pohl, Frederik

**Gregor, Lee** [joint pseudonym with Frederik Pohl]
*See* Rothman, Milton A.

**Gregori, Mercia**
*See* McLaughlin, Mercia

**Gregori, Primo Giovanni** 1924-
[IWM]
*British composer, conductor, arranger*
* Gregory, John

**Gregorian, Vartan** 1935-    [CA]
*Iranian-born author and editor*
* Herian, V.

**Gregorios, Paulos Mar**
*See* Verghese, Paul

**Gregory** 257?- 332?
[DNNF, DNNS, FFF]
*Saint*
* [The] Apostle of the Armenians
* [The] Illuminator

**Gregory, Alexander Tighe**    [PA]
*Author*
* [An] Englishman Abroad

**Gregory, Chuck**
*See* Gnaegy, Charles

**Gregory, Dave**
*See* Taylor, W. T.

**Gregory, Edmund** 1925-    [EJ, PMJ]
*American jazz musician*
* Shihab, Sahib

**Gregory, Edna**
*See* Steinberg, Edna

**Gregory, Elizabeth**
*See* Gilford, Charles Bernard

**Gregory, Grover LeRoy** 1938-    [BE]
*American baseball player*
* Gregory, Lee

**Gregory, Harry**
*See* Gottfried, Theodore Mark

**Gregory, Hilton**
*See* Ferguson, Charles W.

**Gregory, Hylton** [house pseudonym]
*See* Edgar, Alfred

**Gregory, Hylton** [house pseudonym]
*See* Hill, Harry Egbert

**Gregory, [Lady] Isabella Augusta Persse** 1852-1932    [TLC]
*Irish playwright, producer, poet*
* [The] Mother of the Irish Drama

**Gregory, James** 1638-1675    [PA]
*Author*
* Seaworthy, [Captain] Gregory

**Gregory, John**
*See* Gregori, Primo Giovanni

**Gregory, Julian R.**
*See* Knowles, Leo

**Gregory, Kate**
*See* Carrell, Lenore Kathrin Cary Gregory

**Gregory, Lee**
*See* Gregory, Grover LeRoy

**Gregory, Lisa**
*See* Camp, Candace P[auline]

**Gregory, Malcolm** 1934-    [ART]
*British painter*
* MacGregory

**Gregory, Mason** [joint pseudonym with Doris Meek]
*See* Jones, Adrienne

**Gregory, Mason** [joint pseudonym with Adrienne Jones]
*See* Meek, Doris

**Gregory, Milton Nathaniel** 20th c.
[IBW]
*American musician*
* Gregory, Sir

**Gregory of Fonts**    [HN]
*Scholar*
* Venerandus, Doctor

**Gregory of Nazianzus** 329?- 390?
[DNNS, HN, WBD]
*Saint*
* [The] Theologian
* Theologus

**Gregory of Neocaesarea** 213?-
270?    [DNNF, FFF, RH]
*Saint*
* Thaumaturgus
* [The] Wonder Worker

**Gregory of Nyssa** 332?- 395?
[FFF, RH]
*Saint*
* Pater Patrum

**Gregory of Rimini**  ?-1357?
[DNNF, HN, SN]
*Medieval scholar*
* [The] Authentic Doctor
* Authenticus, Doctor

**Gregory of Tours**
*See* Florentius, Georgius

**Gregory, Paul**
*See* Lenhart, Jason Gregory

**Gregory, Paul Edwin** 1908-    [BE]
*American baseball player*
* Gregory, Pop

**Gregory, Pop**
*See* Gregory, Paul Edwin

**Gregory, Sean**
*See* Hossent, Harry

**Gregory, Sir**
*See* Gregory, Milton Nathaniel

**Gregory, Stephan**
*See* Pendleton, Don[ald Eugene]

**Gregory, Stephen**
*See* Penzler, Otto

**Gregory, T. S.**
See  Gregory, Theophilus Stephen

**Gregory, Theophilus Stephen** 1897-
[CAT]
*British author*
* Gregory, T. S.

**Gregory, W. A.**
See  Gregory, William Alfred, Jr.

**Gregory, William Alfred, Jr.** 1923-
[BEW]
*American producer and director*
* Gregory, W. A.

**Gregory I** 544- 604
[DNNF, FFF, HN]
*Pope*
* [The] Apostle of the English
* [The] Great
* [The] Servant of the Servants of
God
* Servus Servorum Dei

**Gregory IX**
See  Ugolino [Count of Segni]

**Gregory V**
See  Bruno of Carinthia

**Gregory VI**
See  Gratianus, Johannes

**Gregory VII**
See  Hildebrand

**Gregory VIII**
See  Bourdin, Maurice

**Gregory VIII**
See  De Morra, Alberto

**Gregory X**
See  Visconti, Teobaldo

**Gregory XI**
See  De Beaufort, Pierre Roger

**Gregory XII**
See  Corrario [or Correr], Angelo

**Gregory XIII**
See  Buoncompagni, Ugo

**Gregory XIV**
See  Sfondrati, Niccolo

**Gregory XV**
See  Ludovisi, Alessandro

**Gregory XVI**
See  Cappellari, Bartolommeo
Alberto

**Gregr, Eduard**
See  Groeger, Eduard

**Gregson, Michael** 1928-    [FC, TR]
*British actor*
* Craig, Michael

**Gregson, Paul**
See  Oakley, Eric Gilbert

**Greif [Griphius or Gryphius], Andreas**
1616-1664    [HN, SN, WBD]
*German poet and playwright*
* [The] Corneille of Germany
* [The] Father of the Modern
German Drama
* [The] German Shakespeare
* [The] Prince of Silesian Poets

**Greig, Maysie** 1901?-1971
[AW, LC, WW]
*Australian-born author*
* Ames, Jennifer
* Barclay, Ann
* Thompson, Madeline

**Greig, Maysie** (Continued)
* Warren, Mary Douglas

**Grein, J. T.**
See  Grein, Jacob Thomas

**Grein, Jacob Thomas** 1862-1935
[LC]
*Dutch-born British drama critic*
* Grein, J. T.

**Grein, Louis John Herman** 1872- ?
[LAO]
*Dutch-born music critic*
* Green, L. Dunton

**Grellet du Mobillier, Etienne de**
1773-1855    [WBD]
*French-born missionary*
* Grellet, Stephen

**Grellet, Stephen**
See  Grellet du Mobillier, Etienne
de

**[The] Gremlin**
See  Tunnell, Emlen

**Gremminger, Battleship**
See  Gremminger, [Lorenzo]
Ed[ward]

**Gremminger, [Lorenzo] Ed[ward]**
1874-1942    [BE]
*American baseball player*
* Gremminger, Battleship

**Gremp, Buddy**
See  Gremp, Louis Edward

**Gremp, Louis Edward** 1919-    [BE]
*American baseball player*
* Gremp, Buddy

**Grendon, Edward**
See  LeShan, Lawrence L[ee]

**Grendon, Stephen**
See  Derleth, August [William]

**Grenelle, Lisa**
See  Munroe, Elizabeth L[ee]

**Grenfell, John**
See  Floyd, Gilbert

**Grenfell, Joyce**
See  Phipps, Joyce Irene

**Grenly, Lionel** 20th c.    [NAA]
*Canadian historian and author*
* De Lestres, Alonie

**Grennell, Dean A.** 20th c.    [WGT]
*Author*
* Wesley, Art

**Grensted, L. W.**
See  Grensted, Laurence William

**Grensted, Laurence William**
1884-1964    [LC]
*British theologian and author*
* Grensted, L. W.

**Grenvil, William**
See  Martyn, Wyndham

**Grenville, George** 1712-1770
[DEP, DNNF, RH]
*British statesman*
* [The] Gentle Shepherd

**Grenville, George N.** 1788-1850
[PA]
*Author*
* Hampden, John

**Grenville, Pelham**
See  Wodehouse, Pelham Grenville

**Grenville, Richard Temple [First Earl
Temple]** 1711-1770?
[DNNF, FFF, HN]
*British politician*
* Gawkey, Lord
* Tiddy Doll

**Gres, Mme.**
See  Barton, Alix Gres

**Gresac, [Madame] Fred**
See  De Gresac, Fredeique Rosine

**Greschner, Gresch**
See  Greschner, Ronald John

**Greschner, Ronald John** 1954-
[SMG]
*Canadian-born hockey player*
* Greschner, Gresch

**Gresham, Claude Hamilton, Jr.**
1922-    [CA]
*American writer, photographer,
columnist*
* Gresham, Grits

**Gresham, Elizabeth [Fenner]** 1904-
[CA, WW]
*American author and playwright*
* Grey, Robin

**Gresham, Grits**
See  Gresham, Claude Hamilton,
Jr.

**Gresser, Seymour** 1926-    [CA]
*American sculptor, author, poet*
* Gresser, Sy

**Gresser, Sy**
See  Gresser, Seymour

**Gretry, Andre Ernest Modeste**
1741-1813    [SN]
*French composer*
* [The] Moliere of Music

**Gretzky, Gretz**
See  Gretzky, Wayne

**Gretzky, Wayne** 1961-    [SMG]
*Canadian-born hockey player*
* [The] Great Gretzky
* Gretzky, Gretz

**Greve, Felix Paul** 1879-1948    [ESF]
*German-born Canadian author*
* Grove, Frederick Philip

**Greville, Henry**
See  Durand, Alice Marie Celeste
Fleury

**Greville, Henry**
See  Fleury, Alice

**Greville, Robert Fulke** 1554-1628
[PA]
*Author*
* [An] Invalid

**Grevy, Albert** 1813-1891
[DEP, HN]
*French president*
* [The] French Aristides

**Grew, William**
See  O'Farrell, William

**Grex, Leo**
See  Gribble, Leonard R[eginald]

**Grey, A. F.**
See  Neal, Adeline Phyllis

**Grey, Anne**
See  Ewing, Aileen

**Grey, Anthony**
See  Schiller, Henry Carl

**Grey, Beryl**
See  Groom, Beryl

**Grey, Brenda**
See  Mackinlay, Leila Antoinette
Sterling

**Grey, Carlton**
See  Bullivant, Cecil Henry

**Grey, Carol**
See  Lowndes, Robert Augustine
Ward

**Grey, Charles [First Earl Grey]**
1729-1807    [FFF, SN, WBD]
*British soldier*
* Grey, No Flint

**Grey, Clifford**
See  Davis, Clifford

**Grey, Donald**
See  Thomas, Eugene

**Grey, Elizabeth**
See  Hogg, Beth [Tootill]

**Grey, Fannie**
See  Hundley, Mrs. E. D.

**[The] Grey Ghost**
See  Evans, William Demont, II

**Grey, Gilbert**
See  Margerison, John S.

**Grey, Gordon**
See  Flaxman, E.

**Grey, Heraclitus**
See  Marshall, Charles

**Grey, James**
See  Snell, Hannah

**Grey, Jane**
See  Tyrrell, Mary E.

**Grey, Joel**
See  Katz, Joel

**Grey, Judson** [joint pseudonym with
Ron Haydock]
See  Harmon, Jim

**Grey, Judson** [joint pseudonym with
Jim Harmon]
See  Haydock, Ron

**Grey, Katherine**
See  Best, Katherine

**Grey, Lita**
See  McMurry, Lolita

**Grey, Louis**
See  Gribble, Leonard R[eginald]

**Grey, Mary**
See  Bryant, Ada Bevan ap Rees

**Grey, Nan**
See  Miller, Eschal

**Grey, No Flint**
See  Grey, Charles [First Earl
Grey]

**Grey, Olga**
See  Zachak, Anna

**Grey Owl**
See  Belaney, Archibald Stansfeld

**Grey Owl**
See  Wa-Sha-Quon-Asin

**Grey, Reddy**
See Grey, William Tobin [Bill]

**Grey, Robertson**
See Raymond, Rossiter Worthington

**Grey, Robin**
See Gresham, Elizabeth [Fenner]

**Grey, Rowland**
See Brown, Lilian Rowland

**[The] Grey Sister of Hearts**
See Wittinghoff, Julienne

**Grey, William Tobin [Bill]**
1871-1932 [BN]
*American baseball player*
* Grey, Reddy
* Grey, Zaza

**Grey, Zachary** 1687-1766 [SN]
*British clergyman and editor*
* [The] Father of Modern Commentators

**Grey, Zaza**
See Grey, William Tobin [Bill]

**Greybeard, Father**
See Hewlet, William

**[The] Greyhound**
See Sobchuk, Dennis

**Greylock, Godfrey**
See Smith, Joseph Edwards Adams

**Greyson, R. E. H.**
See Rogers, Henry

**Greysteel**
See Montgomerie, Alexander

**Greysteil**
See Ruthven, Lord

**Greystoke, Lord**
See Farmer, Philip Jose

**Greysun, Doriac**
See Bertin, Eddy C[harly]

**Gribaldi, Matteo** 1520-1564 [PA]
*Author*
* Mosa

**Gribbin, Katherina Houston** 1902-
[FC]
*British vaudevillian*
* Houston, Renee

**Gribbin, L. B.**
See Gribbin, Lancelot Benedict

**Gribbin, Lancelot Benedict** 1927-
[ART]
*British painter and photographer*
* Gribbin, L. B.

**Gribbin, Lenore S.** 1922- [CA]
*American author and librarian*
* Worblefister, Petunia

**Gribble, Leonard R[eginald]** 1908-
[CC, EMD, WW]
*British author*
* Browning, Sterry
* Grant, Landon
* Grex, Leo
* Grey, Louis
* Muir, Dexter

**Gribbon, William Lancaster**
1879-1940 [ESF, SFL, WGT]
*British-born American author*
* Mundy, Talbot

**Gridban, Volsted** [house pseudonym, Scion]
See Fearn, John Russell

**Gridban, Volsted** [house pseudonym, Scion Publications]
See Tubb, Edwin Charles

**Gridiron, Gabble**
See Haselwood, Joseph

**Grieco, Sergio** 1917- [FDG]
*Italian director*
* Hathaway, Terence

**[El] Griego**
See Alvarez, Manuel

**Grien [or Gruen], Hans**
See Baldung, Hans

**Grier, Claude** 20th c. [OBW]
*American baseball player*
* Grier, Red

**Grier, Red**
See Grier, Claude

**Grier, Roosevelt** 1932- [FB]
*American football player*
* Grier, Rosey

**Grier, Rosey**
See Grier, Roosevelt

**Grier, Sydney C.**
See Gregg, Hilda Caroline

**Grierson, Edward** 1914- [WD]
*British author*
* Stevenson, John P.

**Grierson, Francis**
See Shepard, Benjamin Henry Jesse Francis

**Grierson, Jane**
See Woodward, Edward [Emberlin]

**Grierson, [Sir] Robert** [SN]
*Persecuted the Covenanters*
* [The] Laird of Lag

**Grieve, Christopher Murray**
1892-1978 [CA, CLC, WD]
*Scottish poet and author*
* Douglas, C. H.
* Guthrie, Isobel
* Laidlaw, A. K.
* Leslie, Arthur
* Mac A'Ghreidhir, Gillechriosd
* MacDiarmid, Hugh
* MacLaren, James
* [The] Modern Burns
* Pteleon

**Griff** [house pseudonym?]
See Fawcett, F[rank] Dubrez

**Griff** [house pseudonym, Modern Publications]
See Fearn, John Russell

**Griff**
See Griffiths, Harry Hadden

**Griff** [house pseudonym?]
See McKeag, Ernest L[ionel]

**Griff, Alan**
See Suddaby, [William] Donald

**Griffen, Clarence J.** 1888-1973
[BBH]
*American tennis player*
* Griffen, Peck

**Griffen, Peck**
See Griffen, Clarence J.

**Griffenhoof, Anthony**
See Parry, John Humphreys

**Griffenhoof, Arthur**
See Mathews, J. Brander

**Griffey, Ken** 1949- [IBW]
*American baseball player*
* [The] Human Blur

**Griffies, Ethel**
See Woods, Ethel

**Griffin, Alice McClure** [FFF]
*American poet*
* Glenmore, Addie
* Tell, Muni

**Griffin, Anne J.**
See Griffin, Arthur J.

**Griffin, Anthony Jerome**
1866-1935 [WGT]
*Author*
* Altair

**Griffin, Arthur J.** 1921- [CA]
*American author*
* Frank, Lee
* Griffin, Anne J.
* James, Susan

**Griffin, Bessie**
See Broil, Arlette B.

**Griffin, C. F.**
See Fikso, Eunice Cleland

**Griffin, Chris**
See Griffin, Gordon

**Griffin, Clarence J.** 1888- [OET]
*Tennis player*
* Griffin, Peck

**Griffin, David**
See Maugham, Robert Cecil Romer

**Griffin, Debralee** 1933-
[BDF, FC, ITA]
*American actress*
* Paget, Debra

**Griffin, Douglas Lee, Jr.** 1947-
[SMG]
*American baseball player*
* Griffin, Dude

**Griffin, Dude**
See Griffin, Douglas Lee, Jr.

**Griffin, Francis Arthur** 1896-1951
[BE]
*American baseball player*
* Griffin, Pug

**Griffin, Frank** 1911- [AW]
*British author*
* Atkin, Charles
* Noble, John

**Griffin, Gordon** 1915- [PMJ, WWJ]
*American jazz musician*
* Griffin, Chris

**Griffin, Gregory**
See Canning, George

**Griffin, Hank**
See Griffin, John Linton

**Griffin, James** 20th c. [RO1]
*American singer*
* Griffin, Sonny

**Griffin, James** 20th c. [RO2]
*American musician and songwriter*
* James, Arthur

**Griffin, John Linton** 1886- [BE]
*American baseball player*
* Griffin, Hank

**Griffin, Little Brother**
See Griffin, Roosevelt

**Griffin, Peck**
See Griffin, Clarence J.

**Griffin, Pug**
See Griffin, Francis Arthur

**Griffin, Roosevelt** 1933- [NBB]
*American musician*
* Griffin, Little Brother

**Griffin, Sandy**
See Griffin, Tobias Charles

**Griffin, Sonny**
See Griffin, James

**Griffin, Tobias Charles** 1858-1926
[BE]
*American baseball player and manager*
* Griffin, Sandy

**Griffis, Si**
See Griffis, Silas Seth

**Griffis, Silas Seth** 1883-1950
[CEI, FHE, HK]
*American hockey player*
* Griffis, Si
* Griffis, Sox

**Griffis, Sox**
See Griffis, Silas Seth

**Griffith**
See Alford, Michael

**Griffith, Clark Calvin** 1869-1955
[BE, BBH, PB]
*American baseball player and manager*
* Griffith, Dago
* Griffith, Griff
* [The] Old Fox

**Griffith, Corinne** 1898?-1979
*American actress*
* [The] Orchid of the Screen

**Griffith, D. W.**
See Griffith, David Wark

**Griffith, Dago**
See Griffith, Clark Calvin

**Griffith, Darrell** 1959?-
*American basketball player*
* Dunk, Dr.
* Dunkenstein, Dr.
* [The] Louisville Legend

**Griffith, David Wark** 1874?-1948
[FI, FC]
*American producer and director*
* Griffith, D. W.

**Griffith, E. G.** 20th c. [WW]
*Author*
* Griffith, Jason [joint pseudonym with Mrs. E. G. Griffith]

**Griffith, George Chetwynd**
See Griffith-Jones, George Chetwynd

**Griffith, Griff**
See Griffith, Clark Calvin

**Griffith, Jason** [joint pseudonym with Mrs. E. G. Griffith]
See Griffith, E. G.

**Griffith, Jason** [joint pseudonym with E. G. Griffith]
See   Griffith, Mrs. E. G.

**Griffith, Jeannette** [joint pseudonym with Valeria Winkler Griffith]
See   Eyerly, Jeannette Hyde

**Griffith, Jeannette** [joint pseudonym with Jeannette Hyde Eyerly]
See   Griffith, Valeria Winkler

**Griffith, Lawrence Rector** 20th c.
[NAA]
*American poet, editor, publisher*
* Griffo the Gripper
* L. R. G.
* [The] Philosopher of Sunshine and Rain

**Griffith, Maria Aline** 1921-    [CA]
*American-born author*
* Quintanilla, Maria Aline Griffith y Dexter, Condesa De
* Romanones, Countess of

**Griffith, Mrs. E. G.** 20th c.    [WW]
*Author*
* Griffith, Jason [joint pseudonym with E. G. Griffith]

**Griffith, Percy** 20th c.    [MBF]
*British author and editor*
* Clifford, Martin [house pseudonym]

**Griffith, Valeria Winkler** 20th c.
[CA, SAT]
*Author*
* Griffith, Jeannette [joint pseudonym with Jeannette Hyde Eyerly]

**Griffith-Jones, George Chetwynd** 1857-1906  [ESF, SF, WW]
*British author*
* Carnac, Levin
* Griffith, George Chetwynd
* Lara
* Morich, Stanton

**Griffith-Shaw, Grace Kellogg** 20th c.    [NAA]
*American author*
* Kellogg, Grace

**Griffiths, Aileen Esther** 20th c.
[AW, WD]
*British author*
* Passmore, Aileen Esther

**Griffiths, Albert** 1871-1927
[BX, RBE]
*Australian-born boxer*
* Griffo, Young

**Griffiths, Annie** 1835-1912    [BEW]
*British-born actress*
* Yeamans, Annie

**Griffiths, Captain** 19th c.
[FFF, RH]
*British naval officer*
* Griffiths, Honor and Glory

**Griffiths, Charles Tom Watson** 1919-    [AW, WD]
*British author*
* Bold, Ralph

**Griffiths, David Arthur** 20th c.
[SFL]
*Author*
* Hunt, Gill [house pseudonym, Curtis Warren]
* Lang, King [house pseudonym, Curtis Warren]
* Shaw, Brian [house pseudonym, Curtis Warren]
* Shaw, David

**Griffiths, Edgar H.**
*American business executive*
* Bottom Line Ed

**Griffiths, Fred**
See   Delaney, Frederick George

**Griffiths, G. D.**
See   Griffiths, Gordon Douglas

**Griffiths, Gordon Douglas** 1910-1973  [TCC, WYA]
*British author*
* Griffiths, G. D.

**Griffiths, Harry Hadden**  ?-1945
[BMH]
*British juggler and comedian*
* Griff

**Griffiths, Helen**
See   Santos, Helen

**Griffiths, Honor and Glory**
See   Griffiths, Captain

**Griffiths, Maurice**
See   Lowe, Claud D.

**Griffiths, Robert L., III**
See   Pauker, John

**Griffo the Gripper**
See   Griffith, Lawrence Rector

**Griffo, Young**
See   Griffiths, Albert

**Grigaitis, Walter** 1912?-1977
[FIR]
*Musician*
* Gates, Mother

**Griggs, Barbara**
See   Van Der Zee, Barbara Blanche

**Griggs, Hal**
See   Griggs, Haldane A.

**Griggs, Haldane A.** 20th c.    [BBH]
*American basketball, football and baseball player*
* Griggs, Hal

**Griggs, Mary** 1853-1927    [SC]
*American actress*
* Hilforde, Mary

**Grigsby, Alcanoan O.** 20th c.
[SFL, WGT]
*Author*
* Adams, Jack

**Grigson, James** 1933?-
*American psychiatrist*
* Death, Dr.

**Grildig**
See   Ellis, Welbore

**Grile, Dod**
See   Bierce, Ambrose [Gwinett]

**Grill, Nannette L.** 1935-    [CA]
*American author*
* Christian, Louise

**Grill, Sebastian**
See   Groll, Gunter

**Grillo, Frank** 1912-    [EJ]
*American jazz musician*
* Machito

**[The] Grim**
See   Douglas, Archibald

**Grim, Anthony**
See   Linecar, Arthur

**Grim, Joe**
See   Giannone, Saverio

**Grimaldi, [Princess] Caroline [Louise Marguerite]** 1957-
*Princess of Monaco*
* Grimaldi, Grimmy

**Grimaldi, Giovanni Francesco** 1606-1680  [WBD]
*Italian painter*
* [Il] Bolognese

**Grimaldi, Grimmy**
See   Grimaldi, [Princess] Caroline [Louise Marguerite]

**Grimaldo, Benjamin**
See   Torre Lopez, Fernando

**Grimani, Julia C.**    [PA]
*Author*
* J. C. G.

**Grimard, Luc** 1866-1954    [CW]
*Haitian poet, journalist, educator*
* Dege, Lin
* Gerard, Marie

**Grimaud**
See   Sylvestri, Armaud

**Grimble, [Reverend] Charles James**
See   Eliot, Thomas Stearns

**Grimbosh, Herman**
See   Mackey, Charles

**Grimes, Burleigh Arland** 1893-
[BE, BN, PB]
*American baseball player*
* Grimes, Old Stubblebeard
* Grimes, Senator
* Grimes, Wirewhiskers

**Grimes, Katharine A.** 1877- ?
[NAA]
*American author and editor*
* Stephen, Mary

**Grimes, Lee** 1920-    [CA]
*American author*
* Dodge, Fremont

**Grimes, Lloyd** 1916?-
[EJ, PMJ, WWJ]
*American jazz musician*
* Grimes, Tiny

**Grimes, Old Stubblebeard**
See   Grimes, Burleigh Arland

**Grimes, Senator**
See   Grimes, Burleigh Arland

**Grimes, Tiny**
See   Grimes, Lloyd

**Grimes, Wirewhiskers**
See   Grimes, Burleigh Arland

**Grimke, Francis James** 1850-1937
[IBW]
*American clergyman*
* [The] Black Puritan

**Grimm**
See   Achard, Louis Amede Eugene

**Grimm, Baron**
See   Millaird, M. Albert

**Grimm, Charles John** 1899-
[BE, DGS, PB]
*American baseball player and manager*
* Grimm, Jolly Cholly

**Grimm, Cherry Barbara** 1930-
[CA]
*New Zealand-born author*
* Wilder, Cherry

**Grimm, Friedrich Melchior von** 1723-1807  [HN]
*German journalist and critic*
* Tyran de Blanc

**Grimm, Jolly Cholly**
See   Grimm, Charles John

**Grimm, Richard**    [FFF]
* Ryder, [Prof.] G. W.

**Grimshaw, Ivan Gerould** 1900-
[NAA]
*British-born educator and author*
* Saca Bona

**Grimshaw, Mark**
See   Belfield, Harry Wedgwood

**Grimshaw, Mark**
See   McKeag, Ernest L[ionel]

**Grimshaw, Moose**
See   Grimshaw, Myron Frederick

**Grimshaw, Myron Frederick** 1875-1936  [BE]
*American baseball player*
* Grimshaw, Moose

**Grimshaw, Roland William Wrigley** 1880- ?  [WWL]
*British author*
* Parthian

**Grimsley, Crazy Eyes**
See   Grimsley, Ross Albert, III

**Grimsley, Gordon**
See   Groom, Arthur William

**Grimsley, Lefty**
See   Grimsley, Ross Albert

**Grimsley, Ross Albert** 1922-    [BE]
*American baseball player*
* Grimsley, Lefty

**Grimsley, Ross Albert, III** 1950-
[PB]
*American baseball player*
* Grimsley, Crazy Eyes
* Grimsley, Scuz

**Grimsley, Scuz**
See   Grimsley, Ross Albert, III

**Grimston, Dorothy May**
See   Kendal, Dorothy May

**Grimston, William Hunter** 1843-1917  [BEW, WBD]
*British-born actor and producer*
* Kendal, William Hunter

**Grin**
See   Evans, Leo C.

**Grindal, Richard** 20th c.    [WW]
*Author*
* Grayson, Richard

**Grinde, Harry A.** 1894-    [FD]
*American director*
* Grinde, Nicholas [Nick]

**Grinde, Nicholas [Nick]**
See Grinde, Harry A.

**Grindel, Eugene** 1895-1952
[EWL, TCL]
*French poet*
* Eluard, Paul

**Grinder**
See Marks, Harry H.

**Grindle, Carleton**
See Page, Gerald W[ilburn]

**Griner, Dan**
See Griner, Donald Dexter

**Griner, Donald Dexter** 1888-1950
[BE]
*American baseball player*
* Griner, Dan
* Griner, Rusty

**Griner, Rusty**
See Griner, Donald Dexter

**Gringhuis, Dirk**
See Gringhuis, Richard H.

**Gringhuis, Richard H.** 1918-
[B10, CA, SAT]
*American author and illustrator*
* Gringhuis, Dirk

**Gringo, Harry**
See Wise, Henry Augustus

**Gringoire**
See Irving, Noel

**Grinling, Antony Gibbons** 1896-
[ART]
*British sculptor*
* A. G. G.

**Grinnell, David**
See Wollheim, Donald A[llen]

**Grip**
See Welch, Edgar L[uderne]

**Grip Fast**
See Baker, Frank Leslie

**Gripus, Judge**
See Yorke, Philip [First Earl of Hardwicke]

**Gris, Juan**
See Gonzalez, Jose Victoriano

**Grise, Jeanne** 1902- [NAA]
*Canadian poet and journalist*
* Regis

**Grise, Jeannette**
See Thomas, Jeannette Grise

**Grisha**
See Dotzenko, Grisha

**Grishaver, Arnold Buddy** 1926-
[EJ]
*American jazz musician*
* Arnold, Buddy

**Grismer, Mrs. Joseph R.** [FFF]
*Entertainer*
* Davis, Phebe

**Grisognel the Grey Cloak**
See Geoffrey IV

**Grissom, Gus**
See Grissom, Virgil

**Grissom, Lee Theo** 1907- [BE]
*American baseball player*
* Grissom, Lefty

**Grissom, Lefty**
See Grissom, Lee Theo

**Grissom, Virgil** 1926-1967
*American astronaut*
* Grissom, Gus

**Griswold, A. Miner** 1834-1891
[FFF, PA]
*American author*
* Fat Contributor

**Griswold, George**
See Dean, Robert George

**Griswold, Grace**
See Hall, Grace

**Griswold, William McCrillis** [FFF]
*American writer*
* Venner, Arthur

**Grit**
See Bruce, John Edward

**Gritt, Brian Edward** 1938- [AW]
*British social worker and writer*
* Driver, Edward

**Gritz, Bo**
See Gritz, James

**Gritz, James** 1939?-
*American army officer*
* Gritz, Bo

**Grizzly Bear Jeffries**
See Jeffries, James Jackson

**[The] Groaner**
See Crosby, Harry Lillis

**Grob, Connie**
See Grob, Conrad George

**Grob, Conrad George** 1932- [BE]
*American baseball player*
* Grob, Connie

**[The] Grocer**
See Heath, Edward R[ichard] G[eorge]

**[The] Grocer's Daughter**
See Thatcher, Margaret Hilda [Roberts]

**Grock**
See Wettach, Adrien

**Grode, Redway**
See Gorey, Edward [St. John]

**Grodzicki, Grod**
See Grodzicki, John

**Grodzicki, John** 1917- [SMG]
*American baseball player and coach*
* Grodzicki, Grod

**Groeger, Eduard** 1829-1907
[WBD]
*Czech politician*
* Gregr, Eduard

**Grofalo, Blasio** 1677-1762 [PA]
*Author*
* Caryophilus

**Grofe, Ferde**
See Von Grofe, Ferdinand Rudolph

**Grogan, Emmett** 1942-1978 [CA]
*American author*
* Fastlife
* Wisdom, Kenny

**Grogan, Joanne** 1938- [EJ7]
*American jazz musician*
* Brackeen, Joanne

**Grogg, Colonel**
See Scott, [Sir] Walter

**Groh, Heinie**
See Groh, Henry Knight

**Groh, Henry Knight** 1889-1968
[BE]
*American baseball player*
* Groh, Heinie

**Groh, Lew[is Carl]** 1883-1960 [BE]
*American baseball player*
* Groh, Silver

**Groh, Silver**
See Groh, Lew[is Carl]

**Grolier, Jean** 1479-1565 [SN]
*French patron of literature*
* [The] Maecenas of Book-Lovers

**Groll, Gunter** 1914- [IAW]
*German author*
* Grill, Sebastian

**Gronovius, James** [SN]
*Dutch antiquary*
* [The] Grammatical Cur

**Groom, Alison** 1875-1952 [FC]
*British actress*
* Skipworth, Alison

**Groom, Arthur William** 1898-1964
[CA, SAT]
*British author*
* Adamson, Graham
* Anderson, George
* Du Blane, Daphne
* Grimsley, Gordon
* Pembury, Bill
* Stanstead, John
* Templar, Maurice
* Toonder, Martin

**Groom, Beryl** 1927- [THR]
*British dancer*
* Grey, Beryl

**Grooms, Charles Roger** 1937-
[B10]
*American artist and filmmaker*
* Grooms, Red

**Grooms, Red**
See Grooms, Charles Roger

**Grooms, Red**
See Grooms, W. J.

**Grooms, W. J.** 20th c. [BLB]
*American detective*
* Grooms, Red

**[Le] Gros**
See Charles II

**[Le] Gros**
See Louis VI

**[Le] Gros Bill**
See Beliveau, Jean

**Grosbec**
See Bonaparte, Charles Louis Napoleon

**Grosofsky, Leslie**
See Gross, Leslie

**Grosole, Hilarion** 1840-1894
[WBD]
*President of Bolivia*
* Daza, Hilarion

**[The] Gross**
See Douglas, James

**Gross, Ewell** 1896-1936 [BE]
*American baseball player*
* Gross, Turkey

**Gross, Jesse**
See Gross, Joshua

**Gross, Joshua** 1929- [BEW]
*American theatre reporter*
* Gross, Jesse

**Gross, Leon T.** 1912-1973 [BWW]
*American singer*
* Archibald
* Archie Boy

**Gross, Leslie** 1927- [CA]
*American writer*
* Grosofsky, Leslie

**Gross, Michael [Robert]** 1952-
[CA]
*American author*
* Alexander, Robert

**Gross, Natan** 1919- [IAW]
*Israeli director, journalist, author*
* Hagrizi, Natan

**Gross, Sheldon H.** 1921-
[BEW, CA]
*American producer and author*
* Gross, Shelly

**Gross, Shelly**
See Gross, Sheldon H.

**Gross, Terence** 1947- [CA]
*American author and translator*
* Costinescu, Tristan

**Gross, Turkey**
See Gross, Ewell

**Grossberg, Irving** 1923-
*American artist*
* Rivers, Larry

**Grossel, Ira** 1918-1961
[ASC, BDF, BEW]
*American actor*
* Chandler, Jeff

**Grosseteste, Robert** 1174-1253
[HN, WBD]
*British theologian and scholar*
* Greathead
* Magister Contradictionis
* Magister Scolarum

**Grossi, Lodovico** 1564-1627
[WBD]
*Italian composer*
* Viadana, Lodovico

**Grosskloss, Howard Hoffman** 1908-
*American baseball player*
* Grosskloss, Howdie

**Grosskloss, Howdie**
See Grosskloss, Howard Hoffman

**Grossman, Arthur** 1894-1973
[BDF, OCF]
*American producer*
* Freed, Arthur

**Grossman, David** 1927- [CA]
*British-born educator and author*
* Vital, David

**Grossman, Gheorghe** 1919- [JL]
*Rumanian government official*
* Gaston Marin, Gheorghe

**Grossman, Jean Schick** 1894-1972
[CA]
*American educator and author*
* Grayson, Alice Barr

**Grossman, Josephine Judith** 1923-
[B10, CA]
*American author and editor*
* Hamilton, Ernest
* Judd, Cyril [joint pseudonym with Cyril M. Kornbluth]
* Merril, Judith
* Sharon, Rose
* Thorstein, Eric

**Grossmann, Gustavus Frederick William** 1744-1796   [SN]
*German playwright and actor*
* [The] Shakespeare of Germany

**Grosso, Count**
See   Grosso, Donald

**Grosso, Donald** 1915-   [CEI]
*Canadian-born hockey player*
* Grosso, Count

**Grostete [Great-Head]**
See   Copley, Robert

**Grosvenor, Luther** 20th c.   [RM]
*Musician*
* Bender, Ariel

**Grosz, George**
See   Ehrenfried, Georg

**Groszewski, Antocz Franziszek** 1884-   [FC]
*Polish-born art director*
* Grot, Anton

**Grot, Anton**
See   Groszewski, Antocz Franziszek

**Groth, Alexander J[acob]**
See   Goldwasser, Alexander Jacob

**Grotius, Hugo** 1583-1645
[DEP, HN, SN]
*Dutch jurist*
* [The] Father of International Law
* [The] Oracle of Delft
* [The] Phoenix of Literature

**Groto, Luigi** 1541-1585   [SN]
*Italian poet*
* [Il] Cieco [The Blind]

**Groues, Henri Antoine** 1910-   [B10]
*French priest*
* Pierre, [Abbe]

**Groupe, Darryl R.**
See   Bunch, David R.

**Grousset, Paschal** 1845?-1909
[ESF, SFL, WGT]
*French politician and author*
* Daryl, Phillipe
* Laurie, Andre

**Grove, Fred**
See   Palmer, Fred

**Grove, Frederick Philip**
See   Greve, Felix Paul

**Grove, Helen Harriet** 1917-   [IA]
*American author*
* Christian, George

**Grove, Henriette** 1922-   [IAW]
*South African author*
* Joubert, Linda

**Grove, Lefty**
See   Grove, Robert Moses

**Grove, Marguerite** 1895-   [CA]
*American author*
* Modak, Manorama Ramkrishna

**Grove, Mose**
See   Grove, Robert Moses

**Grove, Old Mose**
See   Grove, Robert Moses

**Grove, Robert Moses** 1900-1975
[BE, BN, PB]
*American baseball player*
* Grove, Lefty
* Grove, Mose
* Grove, Old Mose

**Grove, Sybil**
See   Wingrove, Sybil Westmacott

**Grove, Will O.**
See   Brister, Richard

**Grover, Albert** 19th c.   [PA]
*Author*
* Revorg, Trebla

**Grover, Arthur** 1918-   [ASC]
*American musician*
* Grover, Buddy

**Grover, Buddy**
See   Grover, Arthur

**Grover, Bugs**
See   Grover, Charles Bert [Charlie]

**Grover, Charles Bert [Charlie]** 1891-1971   [BE]
*American baseball player*
* Grover, Bugs

**Grover, Stanley**
See   Nienstedt, Stanley Grover

**Grover the Good**
See   Cleveland, [Stephen] Grover

**Grover, William** ?-1943   [EAR]
*British auto racer*
* Williams

**Grover, Winifred Powell** 20th c.
[SFL]
*Author*
* Dwyer, Winifred

**Groves, Georgina**
See   Symons, [Dorothy] Geraldine

**Groves, J. W.**
See   Groves, John William

**Groves, John William** 1910-   [SFL]
*British author*
* Groves, J. W.

**Groves, William E.** 20th c.   [MBF]
*British author*
* Scott, Ernest

**Groves-Raines, George Percy** 1872-1962   [BEW]
*Theatrical performer*
* Percy, George

**[The] Growler**
See   Coon, Spencer Wallace

**Groza, Louis** 1924-   [FB]
*American football player*
* [The] Toe

**Grubb, Lillie**
See   Hayman, Mrs. David

**Grubbs, Judge**
See   Grubbs, Thomas Dillard [Tom]

**Grubbs, Maude**   [FFF]
*Entertainer*
* Stuart, Maude

**Grubbs, Thomas Dillard [Tom]** 1894-   [BE]
*American baseball player*
* Grubbs, Judge

**Grube, Franklin Thomas** 1905-1945   [BE]
*American baseball player*
* Grube, Hans

**Grube, Hans**
See   Grube, Franklin Thomas

**Grubendol**
See   Oldham, John

**Gruber, Frank** 1904-1969
[CAP, EMD, SFP]
*American author and screenwriter*
* Acre, Stephen
* Boston, Charles K.
* Gunn, Tom [house pseudonym]
* Scanlon, C. K. M. [house pseudonym]
* Stockbridge, Grant [house pseudonym]
* Vedder, John K.

**Gruber, Ruth**   [CA]
*American author*
* Michaels, Ruth Gruber

**Gruen, Anastasius**
See   Auersperg, Anton Alexander von

**Gruen, Mrs. Herman**   [FFF]
*Entertainer*
* Ferris, Cora

**Gruenbaum, Ludwig** 1898-   [CA]
*German-born Israeli economist and writer*
* Gaathon, A[ryeh] L[udwig]

**Gruenig, Ace**
See   Gruenig, Robert F.

**Gruenig, Robert F.** 1913-1958
[AS, BB]
*American basketball player*
* Gruenig, Ace

**Gruenthal, Joseph** 1910-   [BBD]
*Israeli composer*
* Tal, Joseph

**Grumbach, Jean-Pierre** 1917-1973
[FDG, OCF, WEF]
*French director and producer*
* Melville, Jean-Pierre

**Grundtvig, Betty** 1895-1943   [THR]
*British actress*
* Chester, Betty

**Grundtvig, Nikolai Frederik Saverni** 1783-1872   [SN]
*Danish poet*
* [The] Younger Brother of Oehlenschlaeger

**Grundy, Miss**
See   Snead, Austine

**Grundy, Wilfred Walker** 1884-
[LAO]
*British educator and writer*
* Aber

**Grunt, Blindboy**
See   Zimmerman, Robert

**Grunting Jim Shaw**
See   Shaw, James Aloysius

**Grunwald, Al[fred Henry]** 1930-
[BE]
*American baseball player*
* Grunwald, Stretch

**Grunwald, Helen Mary** 1925-
[ART]
*Austrian-born painter, designer, illustrator*
* Helen

**Grunwald, Stefan** 1933-   [CA]
*German-born educator, editor, author*
* Ludwig, Eric
* Ludwig, Frederic

**Grunwald, Stretch**
See   Grunwald, Al[fred Henry]

**Grusenberg, Mikhail Markovich** 1884-1953   [WBD]
*Russian diplomat*
* Borodin, Mikhail Markovich

**Gruthuyse**
See   De Bruges, Louis

**Grutz, Mariellen Procopio** 1946-
[CA]
*American author*
* Procopio, Mariellen

**Gruver, Rebecca**
See   Goodman, Rebecca Gruver

**Grypus [Hooked Nose]**
See   Antiochus VIII

**Gstrein, Heinz** 1941-   [IAW]
*Austrian journalist and author*
* H. G.

**Guado, Sergio**
See   Gerosa, Guido

**Guaff**
See   Victor Emmanuel II

**Gualandi, Anselmo**
See   Guerrazzi, Francesco Domenico

**Guaragna, Salvatore** 1893-1981
[OCF]
*American songwriter*
* Warren, Harry

**Guard, Kit**
See   Klitgaard, Christen

**[The] Guardian and Lieutenant of the Realm**
See   George II

**[The] Guardian Angel of France**
See   [Josephe Jeanne] Marie Antoinette

**Guardino, Johnny** 20th c.   [BLB]
*American underworld figure*
* Guardino, Two Gun

**Guardino, Two Gun**
See   Guardino, Johnny

**Guardiola, Santos** 1812?-1862
[DNNS, FFF, WBD]
*President of Honduras*
* [The] Tiger of Central America
* [The] Tiger of Honduras

**Guarghias, Aloysius George** 1933-
[IAW]
*Indonesian-born journalist and translator*
* Chen, Aloysius
* Ibrahim, Ischak
* Irghen, George

**Guarghias, Aloysius George**
(Continued)
* Kwan, George
* Ribeiro, Antonio

**Guarnerius, Tobias**
See Dimitry, Alexander

**Guarnerius, Tobias, Jr.**
See Dimitry, Charles Patton

**Guasconi, Bernardo [or Bernardino]**
1614-1687 [WBD]
Italian-born soldier and diplomat
* Gascoigne, [Sir] Bernard

**[Le] Guaspre**
See Dughet, Gaspar

**Gubbins, Nathaniel**
See Mott, Edward Spencer

**Gubelman, Yemelyan** 1878-1943
[JL]
Russian government official
* Yaroslavsky, Yemelyan

**Gubenko, Julius** 1924-
[ASC, EJ, PMJ]
American jazz musician
* Gibbs, Terry

**Gubitosi, Michael** 1933?-
[FC, IPA, SW]
American actor
* Blake, Robert

**Gubner, Gary** 20th c. [BBH]
American weightlifter
* [The] World's Strongest
Teen-Ager

**Guckenheimer, [Dr.] Fritz**
See Gump, Richard

**Gudabutsu**
See Natsume, Kinnosuke

**Gudelinus**
See Gondelin, Peter

**Gudiol, Jose**
See Gudiol i Ricart, Josep

**Gudiol i Ricart, Josep** 1904- [CA]
Spanish art historian and author
* Gudiol, Jose
* Gudiol Ricart, Jose M.
* Gudiol Ricart, Josep

**Gudiol Ricart, Jose M.**
See Gudiol i Ricart, Josep

**Gudiol Ricart, Josep**
See Gudiol i Ricart, Josep

**Gudjonsson, Halldor Kiljan** 1902-
[EWL, TC1]
Icelandic author, playwright, poet
* Laxness, Halldor Kiljan

**Gudmundsson, Gudmundur** 1932-
[CAR]
Icelandic painter
* Erro

**Gueden, Hilde**
See Geiringer, Hilde

**Guehenne, Jean** 1890- [IAW]
French journalist and author
* Guehenno, Marcel

**Guehenno, Marcel**
See Guehenne, Jean

**Guenczler, Josephine** 1885- [THR]
Hungarian-born actress
* Victor, Josephine

**Guenod, Jacques** 1889-1958
[F1, FC]
French actor
* Gerald, Jim

**Guenter, Erich**
See Eich, Guenter

**Guercino**
See Barbieri, Giovanni [or Gian]
Francesco

**Guerisse, Albert** 1911-
[BDW, WWW]
Belgian physician and undercover
agent
* O'Leary, Pat

**Guernsey, H. W.**
See Wandrei, Howard Elmer

**Guernsey, Minerva**
See King, Mrs. O. A.

**Guero Alvirez [Blonde Alvirez]**
See Alvirez, Pablos Alfonso

**Guero Guadalupe [Blonde Guadalupe]**
See Rodriguez Sanchez,
Guadalupe

**Guerra, Alberto** 20th c. [RBE]
Mexican boxer
* Guerra, Pelon

**Guerra, Fermin Romero** 1912- [BE]
Cuban-born baseball player
* Guerra, Mike

**Guerra, Mike**
See Guerra, Fermin Romero

**Guerra, Pelon**
See Guerra, Alberto

**Guerra y Bejarano, Rafael**
1862-1941 [GS, OCS]
Spanish bullfighter
* Guerrita [Little Guerra]

**Guerrazzi, Francesco Domenico**
1804-1873 [WBD]
Italian statesman and author
* Gualandi, Anselmo

**[La] Guerre**
See Gassion, Jean de

**Guerrerito [Little Warrior]**
See Guerrero y Roman, Antonio

**Guerrero y Roman, Antonio**
1871-1933 [GS]
Spanish bullfighter
* Guerrerito [Little Warrior]

**Guerrini, Olindo** 1845-1916 [WBD]
Italian poet
* Stecchetti, Lorenzo

**Guerrita [Little Guerra]**
See Guerra y Bejarano, Rafael

**Guertin, Raphaelle-Berthe** 1909-
[NAA]
Canadian poet
* Raphaelle

**Guesclin, Bertrand du** 1320-1380
[FFF, HN, SN]
Constable of France
* [The] Conqueror
* [The] Eagle of Brittany
* [The] Flower of French Chivalry

**Guesde, Jules**
See Basile, Mathieu

**Guese, Theodore** 1873-1951 [BE]
American baseball player
* Guese, Whitey

**Guese, Whitey**
See Guese, Theodore

**Guesnon, Creole George**
See Guesnon, George

**Guesnon, Curly**
See Guesnon, George

**Guesnon, George** 1907-1968
[BWW]
American singer
* [The] Banjo King of the
Southland
* Gayno, Creole
* Guesnon, Creole George
* Guesnon, Curly

**Guess, Edward Preston** 1925- [CA]
American author and editor
* Preston, Edward

**Guess, George**
See Sequoya [or Sequoyah]

**Guest, Francis Narold** 1901- [WW]
Author
* Spenser, James

**Guest, Genia Pauline Hindes** 1921-
[BEW]
American theatre executive
* Guest, Jean H.

**Guest, Harry**
See Guest, Henry Bayly

**Guest, Henry Bayly** 1932- [CA]
Welsh-born educator and poet
* Guest, Harry

**Guest, Jean H.**
See Guest, Genia Pauline Hindes

**Guest, Val**
See Guest, Valmond

**Guest, Valmond** 1921- [BF]
British screenwriter, director,
producer
* Guest, Val

**Guetary, Georges**
See Worloou, Lambros

**Guetersloh, Albert Paris**
See Kiehtreiber, Albert Konrad

**Guevara, Che**
See Guevara, Ernesto

**Guevara, Ernesto** 1928-1967 [B10]
Argentinian-born revolutionary
leader
* Guevara, Che

**Guevremont, Jocelyn Marcel** 1951-
[HK, HR]
Canadian-born hockey player
* Guevremont, Josh

**Guevremont, Josh**
See Guevremont, Jocelyn Marcel

**Gueye, Fatou**
See Harvey, Shirley

**Guggenheimer, Ernest** 1886-1960
[SC]
German actor
* Stahl-Nachbaur, Ernest

**Guggisberg, [Sir] F. G.** 20th c.
[WWL]
British author
* Ubique

**Guese, Theodore** 1873-1951 [BE]
American baseball player
* Guese, Whitey

**Guglielmi, Goog**
See Guglielmi, Ralph V.

**Guglielmi, Ralph V.** 20th c. [FB]
American football player
* Guglielmi, Goog

**Guglielmi Di Valentina
D'Antonguolla, Rodolpho Alfonso
Raffaelo P.** 1895-1926
[BDF, BEW, F1]
Italian-born American actor
* [The] Pink Powder Puff
* Valentino, Rudolph

**Guibert of Ravenna** 1030?-1100
[WBD]
Antipope
* Clement III

**Guiccioli, [Countess] T.**
See De Boissy, Marquese T.

**Guichard [or Guischard], Karl
Gottlieb** 1724-1775 [WBD]
German soldier and author
* Quintus Icilius

**Guichardan, Roger Jean-Baptiste**
1906- [IAW]
French clergyman, journalist, author
* Ouvard, Jacques

**[Le] Guide**
See Mobutu, Joseph Desire

**[The] Guide and Master of Our
Tongue**
See Bembo, Pietro

**Guidi, Carlo Alessandro** 1650-1712
[SN]
Italian poet
* [The] Italian Gray

**Guidi, Philipert** 1535-1595 [PA]
Author
* Hegemon

**Guidi, Tommaso** 1401-1428 [WBD]
Italian painter
* [The] Father of Modern Art
* Masaccio

**Guido** ?-1144 [CAL]
Pope
* Celestine II

**Guido d'Arezzo [or Aretino]**
995?-1050? [WBD]
Monk and musical theorist
* Guittone, [Fra]

**Guido, [Cecily] Margaret** 1912-
[CA]
British archaeologist and author
* Piggott, C. M.

**Guido of Crema** ?-1168 [WBD]
Antipope
* Paschal III

**Guido of Vienne [or Burgundy]**
?-1124 [WBD]
Pope
* Calixtus II

**Guidolin, Armand** 1925-
[CEI, FHE, HK]
Canadian-born hockey player and
coach
* Guidolin, Bep

**Guidolin, Bep**
See Guidolin, Armand

**Guidry, Ron[ald Ames]** 1950-
American baseball player
* [The] Cajun Whip

**Guidry, Ron[ald Ames]** (Continued)
* Louisiana Lightning
* [The] Ragin' Cajun

**Guiffi, Ignacius Pasquale** 1914-
[BX, RBE]
*American boxer*
* Jeffra, Harry

**Guigo, Ernest Philip** 20th c. [WW]
*Author*
* Holt, E. Carleton

**Guilbeau, Cajun Gib**
See Guilbeau, Gib

**Guilbeau, Gib** 20th c. [ECM]
*American country-western performer*
* Guilbeau, Cajun Gib

**Guilbert, Yvette** 1865-1944 [BMH]
*French-born entertainer*
* [The] Sarah Bernhardt of the
    Cafe Concert

**Guild, Alex** 20th c. [AES]
*American soccer player*
* [The] Flying Scot

**Guild, Leo** 20th c. [SFL]
*Author*
* Scram, Arthur N.

**Guild, Mr.** 19th c. [FFF]
*American author*
* Bulletin

**Guildford, John**
See Hunter, Bluebell Matilda

**Guilford, Jesse P.** 1894-
[CSH, EG]
*American golfer*
* [The] Boston Siege Gun
* [The] Great Excavator
* Guilford, Siege Gun

**Guilford, Lady** [HN]
*Governess to Mary, sister of Henry
VIII*
* Guilford, Mother

**Guilford, Mother**
See Guilford, Lady

**Guilford, Siege Gun**
See Guilford, Jesse P.

**Guillaume [or William]** ?-1046
[HN, SN]
*First Count of Apulia*
* Iron Arm

**Guillaume d'Auvergne**
See Guillaume de Paris

**Guillaume de Lorris** 1235-1265
[HN, SN]
*French author*
* [The] French Ennius
* [The] French Iliad

**Guillaume de Paris** 1180?-1249
[WBD]
*French prelate and philosopher*
* Guillaume d'Auvergne

**Guillaume d'Orange** ?- 812 [WBD]
*French soldier*
* Fierabrace
* Marquis au Courtnez
* St. Guillaume de Gellone

**Guillaume, Ferdinando** 1887?-1977
[FIR]
*Italian actor*
* Polidor

**Guillaume, Robert**
See Sneddon, Robert W[illiam]

**Guillaume, Robert**
See Williams, Robert

**Guilledo, Francisco** 1901-1925
[AS, BX, RBE]
*Filipino-born boxer*
* Villa, Pancho

**Guillermo**
See Calderon, Fernando Juan
Iglesias

**Guillevic**
See Guillevic, Eugene

**Guillevic, Eugene** 1907- [CA]
*French poet*
* Guillevic
* Serpieres

**Guillory, Martin** 20th c. [IBW]
*American golfer*
* Guillory, Tex

**Guillory, Tex**
See Guillory, Martin

**Guillot, Olga** 1925- [IBW]
*Cuban-born singer*
* Queen of the Radio

**Guilty, Joseph**
See Van Eijk, Kees

**Guimaraens, Manoel Pedro** 1868-
? [WWL]
*Author*
* Romayne, Leicester

**Guimard, [Marie] Madeleine**
1743-1816 [SN]
*French dancer*
* [La] Squelette des Graces

**Guimorva Moreira, Airto** 1941-
[EJ7]
*Brazilian-born jazz musician*
* Airto

**Guin, Francois** 1938- [EJ7]
*French jazz musician*
* Guin, Frick

**Guin, Frick**
See Guin, Francois

**Guin, Wyman [Woods]** 1915-
[ESF, WGT]
*American author*
* Menasco, Norman

**Guinan, Mary Louise Cecelia**
1888?-1933 [F1, F2, PMJ]
*American actress and singer*
* Guinan, Texas

**Guinan, Texas**
See Guinan, Mary Louise Cecelia

**Guindon, Robert** 1950- [SMG]
*Canadian-born hockey player*
* [The] Golden Gorf

**Guinn, Drannon Eugene** 1944- [BE]
*American baseball player*
* Guinn, Skip

**Guinn, Pat**
See Patton, Fred

**Guinn, Skip**
See Guinn, Drannon Eugene

**Guinness, Bryan**
See Moyne, Bryan Walter
Guinness

**Guinness, Maurice C.** 1897-
[AW, WW]
*Irish-born author*
* Brewer, Mike
* Gayle, Newton [joint pseudonym
    with Muna Lee De Munoz Marin]

**Guion, Netta**
See Cortelyou, Elizabeth A.

**Guion, Raymond** 1908-
[BEW, CED, FC]
*American actor*
* Raymond, Gene

**Guirdham, Arthur** 1905- [WD]
*British author*
* Eaglesfield, Francis

**Guiscard**
See Robert I

**Guise, Duc de**
See Lorraine, Henry II [or Henri]
de

**Guise, Lefty**
See Guise, Witt Orison

**Guise, 3rd Duc de**
See Lorraine, Henry I [or Henri]
de

**Guise, 2nd Duc de**
See Lorraine, Francois de

**Guise, Witt Orison** 1908-1968 [BE]
*American baseball player*
* Guise, Lefty

**Guisti, Roy F.** 1894-1969 [F1, F2]
*Actor*
* D'Arcy, Roy

**Guitar Boogie Smith**
See Smith, Arthur

**Guitar Eddy**
See Harrington, Eddy

**Guitar Jr.**
See Baker, Lee, Jr.

**Guitar Jr.**
See Johnson, Luther, Jr.

**Guitar Nubbitt**
See Hankerson, Alvin

**Guitar Papa**
See Barnes, Bill

**Guitar Pete**
See Franklin, Edward Lamonte

**Guitar Red**
See Duling, Vincent

**Guitar Red**
See Johnson, Paul

**Guitar Red**
See Minter, Iverson

**Guitar Shorty**
See Fortescue, John Henry

**Guitar Slim**
See Green, Norman G.

**Guitar Slim**
See Jones, Eddie

**Guitar Slim**
See Seward, Alexander T. [Alec]

**[The] Guitar Wizard**
See Woodbridge, Hudson

**Guitry, Alexandre** 1895-1957 [IPA]
*Russian actor and director*
* Guitry, Sacha

**Guitry, Sacha**
See Guitry, Alexandre

**Guittone, [Fra]**
See Guido d'Arezzo [or Aretino]

**Guizar, Frederick** 1910?- [AM]
*Mexican singer*
* Guizar, Tito

**Guizar, Tito**
See Guizar, Frederick

**Guizot, Francois Pierre Guillaume**
1787, 1874 [SN]
*French historian and statesman*
* [The] Historian Philosopher

**Guizot, M.** 19th c. [HN]
*French royalist*
* [The] Man of Ghent

**Gulick, Bill**
See Gulick, Grover C.

**Gulick, Grover C.** 1916- [CA]
*American author*
* Gulick, Bill

**Gulick, Merle A.** 1906- [FB]
*American football player*
* [The] Hobart Hurricane

**Gull, Cyril Arthur Edward Ranger**
1876-1923 [ESF, WGT, SFL]
*British author and journalist*
* Ingleby, Leonard Cresswell
* Thorne, Guy

**Gulliver in a Baseball Suit**
See Howard, Frank Oliver

**Gulliver, Lemuel**
See Hastings, Macdonald

**Gulliver, Lemuel**
See Swift, Jonathan

**Gulotta, Peter** 1896-1973
[BX, RBE]
*American boxer*
* Herman, Pete

**Gum-Shoe Bill**
See Stone, William Joel

**Gumbert, Ad**
See Gumbert, Addison Courtney

**Gumbert, Addison Courtney**
1868-1925 [BE]
*American baseball player*
* Gumbert, Ad

**Gumbert, Gunboat**
See Gumbert, Harry Edward

**Gumbert, Harry Edward** 1909-
[BE]
*American baseball player*
* Gumbert, Gunboat

**Gumm, Albert** 1878-1956
[BEW, PMJ]
*American composer*
* Von Tilzer, Albert

**Gumm, Frances** 1922-1969
[BDF, FC, IPA]
*American actress and singer*
* Garland, Judy

**Gumm, Harry** 1872-1946
[BEW, PMJ]
*American composer*
* Von Tilzer, Harry

**Gumm, Mary Jane** 1916?-1964
[BEW]
*Theatrical performer*
* Gumm, Suzanne

**Gumm, Suzanne**
*See* Gumm, Mary Jane

**Gump, Richard** 1906- [ASC]
*American musician*
* Guckenheimer, [Dr.] Fritz

**[The] Gumper**
*See* Worsley, Lorne John

**Gundel, Vilem** 1912- [IWM]
*Yugoslav-born composer*
* Gunovsky, Vilem

**Gundelfinger, Friedrich** 1880-1931
[JL]
*German scholar*
* Gundolf, Friedrich

**Gunder the Wonder**
*See* Haig, Gunder

**Gundolf, Friedrich**
*See* Gundelfinger, Friedrich

**Gunkel, Red**
*See* Gunkel, Woodward William

**Gunkel, Woodward William**
1894-1954 [BE]
*American baseball player*
* Gunkel, Red

**Gunn, Gladys** 1897- [FC]
*Irish actress*
* Henson, Gladys

**Gunn, James E[dwin]** 1923- [CA]
*American author*
* James, Edwin

**Gunn, Judy**
*See* Winfindale, Judy

**Gunn, Mrs. Michael** [FFF]
*Entertainer*
* Sudlow, Bessie

**Gunn, Thom**
*See* Gunn, Thomson William

**Gunn, Thomson William** 1929-
[LC]
*British-born poet*
* Gunn, Thom

**Gunn, Tom** [house pseudonym]
*See* Gruber, Frank

**Gunn, Victor**
*See* Brooks, Edwy Searles

**Gunness, Belle** 1859-1908? [CEC]
*Norwegian-born murderer*
* Belle of Indiana

**Gunovsky, Vilem**
*See* Gundel, Vilem

**Gunston, Norman**
*See* McDonald, Garry

**Gunter, Addison Yancey, III** 1936-
[IAW]
*American author*
* Gunter, Pete

**Gunter, Al** 20th c. [BWW]
*American musician*
* Gunter, Little Al

**Gunter, Archibald Clavering**
1847-1907 [WW]
*Author*
* Warneford, Lieut.

**Gunter, Hardrock**
*See* Gunter, Sidney Louie, Jr.

**Gunter, Little Al**
*See* Gunter, Al

**Gunter, Pete**
*See* Gunter, Addison Yancey, III

**Gunter, Sidney Louie, Jr.** 1925-
[CWG, DAM]
*American singer and songwriter*
* Gunter, Hardrock

**Gunther, Gerald**
*See* Gutenstein, Gerald

**Gunther, William**
*See* Sprecher, William Gunther

**Gupta, Rajendra Prasad** 1940-
[IAW]
*Indian poet and playwright*
* Sanjay, Rajendra

**Gupta, Ram Chandra** 1927- [CA]
*Indian writer*
* Rama

**Gupta, Sushil Kumar** 1927- [CA]
*Indian-born physician and author*
* Placere, Morris N.

**Gurbrand, John** [PA]
*Author*
* Herks

**Gurdin, Natasha** 1938-1981
[BDF, FC, HT]
*American actress*
* Wood, Natalie

**Gurie, Sigrid**
*See* Haukelid, Sigrid Gurie

**Gurino, Socko**
*See* Gurino, Vito

**Gurino, Vito** 20th c. [BLB, PHM]
*American underworld figure*
* Gurino, Socko

**Gurney, A. R.**
*See* Gurney, Albert Ramsdell, Jr.

**Gurney, Albert Ramsdell, Jr.** 1930-
[CA]
*American author and playwright*
* Gurney, A. R.
* Gurney, Pete

**Gurney, Antoinette** 1884-
[NAA, WD]
*American author*
* Chaffee, Allen

**Gurney, David**
*See* Bair, Patrick

**Gurney, Dennis**
*See* Jacks, Dennis Alexander

**Gurney, Elizabeth** 1780-1845 [PA]
*Author*
* Fry, Mrs.

**Gurney, Hudson** 18th c. [PA]
*Author*
* H. G.

**Gurney, Pete**
*See* Gurney, Albert Ramsdell, Jr.

**Gurster, Eugen** 1895- [IAW]
*German author*
* Lepel, H.
* Steinhausen, H.

**Guru [Teacher]**
*See* Nanak

**[The] Guru of Cambridge**
*See* Richards, Ivor Armstrong

**[The] Guru of Chaos**
*See* Venturi, Robert

**Gurvich, Fyodor I.** 1871-1947 [JL]
*Russian government official*
* Dan, Fyodor I.

**Gurvish, Alexander G.** 1874-1954
[JL]
*Russian biochemist*
* Gurwitsch, Alexander G.

**Gurwitsch, Alexander G.**
*See* Gurvish, Alexander G.

**Gurzensky, Joseph Charles** 1908-
[BE]
*American baseball player*
* Glenn, Gabber
* Glenn, Joseph Charles

**Gusev, Sergey Ivanovich**
*See* Drabkin, Yakov Davidovich

**Gusev, Sergey Ivanovich** 1867- ?
[TC]
*Russian author*
* Gusev-Orenburgsky [or
　Gussiev-Orenburgsky], Sergey
　Ivanovich
* Orenburgsky, Sergey Ivanovich

**Gusev-Orenburgsky [or
Gussiev-Orenburgsky], Sergey
Ivanovich**
*See* Gusev, Sergey Ivanovich

**Gushington, Angelina**
*See* Cooke, C. W. R.

**Gushington, Angelina**
*See* Sheridan, Helen Selina
[Countess of Dufferin]

**Gushington, Impulsia**
*See* Sheridan, Helen Selina
[Countess of Dufferin]

**Gussie**
*See* Chambers, Augusta

**Gustaf**
*See* Gustavus V

**Gustafson, Howard Joseph** 1915-
[BEW]
*American composer and lyricist*
* Howard, Bart

**Gustafson, Paul** 1916- [WECO]
*American cartoonist*
* Earrol, Paul

**Gustafson, Sarah R.**
*See* Riedman, Sarah R[egal]

**Gustafsson, Greta Lovisa** 1905-
[BDF, F2, FC]
*Swedish-born actress*
* [La] Divina
* Garbo, Greta
* [The] Norma Shearer of Sweden
* [The] Sphinx

**Gustavino [Little Gustave]**
*See* Rosso, Gustavo

**Gustavus Adolphus** 1594-1632
[DEP, DNNS, SN]
*King of Sweden*
* [The] Great
* [The] Lion of the North
* [The] Northern Victor
* [The] Savior of Protestantism
* [The] Snow King
* [The] Star of the North

**Gustavus Adolphus** (Continued)
* [The] Swedish Maccabaeus

**Gustavus Eriksson**
*See* Gustavus I

**Gustavus Vasa**
*See* Gustavus I

**Gustavus I** 1496-1560 [WBD]
*King of Sweden*
* Gustavus Eriksson
* Gustavus Vasa

**Gustavus V** 1858-1950 [WBD]
*King of Sweden*
* Gustaf

**Gut, Gom**
*See* Simenon, Georges [Joseph
Christian]

**Gutchee, Gene**
*See* Gutsche, Romeo E.

**Gutcheon, Beth R[ichardson]** 1945-
[CA]
*American author*
* Richardson, Beth

**Gutenko, John** 1893-1963
[AS, BX, RBE]
*Danish-born boxer*
* Williams, Kid

**Gutenstein, Gerald** 1927- [CA]
*German-born American legal
scholar and author*
* Gunther, Gerald

**Guterrez, Laura**
*See* Bunke, Haydee Tamara

**Guterson, Vladimar** ?-1964 [BEW]
*Conductor*
* Guterson, Wally

**Guterson, Wally**
*See* Guterson, Vladimar

**Gutesha, Bobby**
*See* Gutesha, Mladen

**Gutesha, Mladen** 1923- [EJ]
*Yugoslav-born jazz musician*
* Gutesha, Bobby

**Guth, Bucky**
*See* Guth, Charles Henry

**Guth, Charles Henry** 1947- [BE]
*American baseball player*
* Guth, Bucky

**Guthrie, A. B., Jr.**
*See* Guthrie, Alfred Bertram, Jr.

**Guthrie, Alan**
*See* Tubb, Edwin Charles

**Guthrie, Alfred Bertram, Jr.** 1901-
[WYA]
*American author*
* Guthrie, A. B., Jr.

**Guthrie, Archibald**
*See* Shaw, Frank H.

**Guthrie, Catherine** 1915-
*American singer*
* George, Florence

**Guthrie, David**
*See* Allen, Hubert Raymond

**Guthrie, Frederick** 1833-1886
[WBD]
*British physicist, author, poet*
* Cerny, Frederick

**Guthrie, Hugh**
See Freeman, John Crosby

**Guthrie, Isobel**
See Grieve, Christopher Murray

**Guthrie, Jack**
See Guthrie, Leon

**Guthrie, James Shields** 1931- [CA]
*British author*
* Creed, David

**Guthrie, Leon** 1915-1948 [ECM]
*American country-western performer*
* Guthrie, Jack

**Guthrie, Ramsay**
See Bowran, John George

**Guthrie, Thomas** 1803-1873
[WBD]
*Scottish clergyman and philanthropist*
* [The] Apostle of Ragged Schools

**Guthrie, Thomas Anstey**
1856-1934 [BEW, FC, LC]
*British author and playwright*
* Anstey, F.

**Guthrie, Tommie Lee** 1937- [CWG]
*American country-western performer*
* Tall, Tom

**Guthrie, Woodrow Wilson**
1912-1967 [CME]
*American singer and songwriter*
* Guthrie, Woody

**Guthrie, Woody**
See Guthrie, Woodrow Wilson

**Gutierrez, Cesar Dario** 1943-
[PB, SMG]
*Venezuelan-born baseball player*
* Gutierrez, Cocoa

**Gutierrez, Cocoa**
See Gutierrez, Cesar Dario

**Gutmann, Jean** 1923- [JL]
*French dancer*
* Babilee, Jean

**Gutsche, Romeo E.** 1907- [BBD]
*German-born American composer*
* Gutchee, Gene

**Guttenberg, Virginia** 1914- [CA]
*American author*
* Graham, Virginia

**Guttero, Lee** 1912- [BB]
*American basketball player*
* Guttero, Rubberlegs

**Guttero, Rubberlegs**
See Guttero, Lee

**Guttmann, Alfred** 1920- [BBD]
*German-born American composer*
* Goodman, Alfred

**Guttmann, Arnold** 1878-1955
[SWI]
*Hungarian swimmer*
* Hajos, Alfred

**Guttoveggio, Joseph** 1906- [BBD]
*American composer*
* Creston, Paul

**[The] Guv'nor**
See Abel, Robert

**[The] Guv'nor**
See Korner, Alexis

**Guy, Buddy**
See Guy, George

**Guy, Buzz**
See Guy, Melwood N.

**Guy, George** 1936- [BWW, NBB]
*American singer*
* Buddy Boy
* Guy, Buddy

**Guy, Jean** 1900-1966 [SC]
*American actress*
* Harvey, Jean

**Guy, L.** 20th c. [WGT]
*Author*
* [A] Patriot

**Guy, Melwood N.** 20th c. [SMG]
*American football player*
* Guy, Buzz

**Guy the Gorilla**
See Botham, Ian Terrance

**Guy, William Augustus** 1810- ?
[PA]
*British author*
* [The] London Physician

**Guy VIII** [FF]
*Count of Vienne*
* [Le] Dauphin

**Guyard, Marie** 1599-1672 [WBD]
*French-born nun and educator*
* Mary of the Incarnation

**Guyon**
See Young, R.

**Guyon, Indian Joe**
See Guyon, Joseph [Joe]

**Guyon, Joc**
See Guyon, Joseph [Joe]

**Guyon, Joseph [Joe]** 1892-1971
[BBH]
*American football player*
* Guyon, Indian Joe
* Guyon, Joc

**Guyonnet, Jacques** 20th c. [WF]
*Composer*
* Olivier, Jacques

**Guyonvarch, Irene Cecilia** 1915-
[AW]
*British author*
* Pearl, Irene

**Guzelev, Nikola Nikolaev** 1936-
[OP]
*Bulgarian opera singer*
* Ghiuselev, Nicola

**Guzik, Greasy Thumb**
See Guzik, Jake

**Guzik, Jake** 1886-1956
[BLB, MM, PHM]
*American underworld figure*
* Guzik, Greasy Thumb

**Guzman, Francisco** 1946- [OET]
*Ecuadorian tennis player*
* Guzman, Pancho

**Guzman, Pancho**
See Guzman, Francisco

**Gwalia, Alfred**
See Thomas, Alfred

**Gwendolyn**
See Bennett, [Enoch] Arnold

**Gwenwyn** 12th c. [HN]
*Prince of Powysland*
* [The] Torch of Pengwern
* [The] Wolf of Plinlimmon

**Gwinn, Christine Margaret** 1900-
[WD]
*British writer on gardening*
* Kelway, Christine

**Gwinn, William R.** 20th c. [WW]
*Author*
* Randall, William

**Gwyn [or Gwynne], Eleanor**
See Symcott, Margaret

**Gwyn [or Gwynne], Nell**
See Symcott, Margaret

**Gwynn, Audrey Jean** 20th c. [AW]
*British author*
* Thomson, Audrey

**Gwynn, Ursula Grace** 1886-
[WWL]
*British author*
* Leigh, Ursula

**Gwynne, A. C.** 20th c. [BBH]
*American athletic trainer*
* Gwynne, Whitey

**Gwynne, Anne**
See Trice, Marguerite Gwynne

**Gwynne, Arthur**
See Evans, Gwnfil Arthur

**Gwynne, Horace** 1913-
[BBH, CSH]
*Canadian boxer*
* Gwynne, Lefty

**Gwynne, Lefty**
See Gwynne, Horace

**Gwynne, Paul**
See Slater, Ernest

**Gwynne, Whitey**
See Gwynne, A. C.

**Gwynne-Jones, Allan** 1892- [ART]
*British painter and etcher*
* A. G. J.

**Gyamtso, Choskyi** 1939- [NAD]
*Tibetan Buddhist teacher*
* Trungpa, Chogyam

**Gyau, Joseph** 20th c. [AES]
*Ghanaian soccer player*
* Gyau, Nana

**Gyau, Nana**
See Gyau, Joseph

**Gyergyay, Stefan** 1904- [FC]
*Hungarian-born actor*
* Geray, Steve

**Gyles, Paul Kirk** 1895- [BEW]
*American actor and union executive*
* Giles, Paul Kirk

**Gyles, Sheila**
See Fraser, Shelagh

**Gyllenhammar, Pehr** 1936?-
*Swedish business executive*
* P. G.

**Gynt, Greta**
See Woxholt, Greta

**[The] Gyp**
See DeCarlo, Angelo

**Gyp**
See Riquetti de Mirabeau, Sibylle
Gabrielle Marie Antoinette

**Gyp the Blood**
See Horowitz, Harry

**Gypsey**
See Courtland, Grace

**[The] Gypsy**
See Solario, Antonio

**[The] Gypsy Goalie**
See Pelletier, Marcel

**Gypsy Joe Harris**
See Harris, Joe Louis

# H

**H.**
*See* Herbert, Henry William

**H.**
*See* Hewison, William

**H. A. L., The Old Shekarry**
*See* Leveson, Henry Astbury

**H. A. M.**
*See* Mulligan, Hugh A.

**H. B.**
*See* Beals, Helen Raymond Abbott

**H. B.**
*See* Busby, Hamilton

**H. B.**
*See* Doyle, H. B.

**H. B. B.**
*See* Boycott-Brown, Hugh

**H. B. M.**
*See* Bartlett-Merriman, Horace

**H. C.**
*See* Carroll, Howard

**H. C., Esq.**
*See* Ireland, William Henry

**H. C. L.**
*See* Leonard, H. C.

**H. D.**
*See* Doolittle, Hilda

**H. D. of Cheltenham**
*See* Davis, Henry

**H. E. M.**
*See* Manning, Henry E.

**H. E. O.**
*See* Fonnerean, Thomas George

**H. E. P.**
*See* Phillimon, Harriet Eleanor

**H. F. B.**
*See* Bantock, [Lady] Helen Francesca

**H. F. E.**
*See* Everett-Green, Evelyn

**H. F. P.**
*See* Parker, Helen F.

**H. G.**
*See* Gstrein, Heinz

**H. G.**
*See* Gurney, Hudson

**H. H.**
*See* Jackson, Helen Maria Hunt

**H. H. H.**
*See* Humphrey, Hubert Horatio

**H. K.**
*See* Kynaston, Herbert

**H. L. W.**
*See* Woodward, Henry Lovett

**H. M.**
*See* Martineau, Harriet

**H. M. J. K.**
*See* Klein, Harry Martin John

**H. M. K.**
*See* Mackenzie, H. Millicent

**H. M. K.**
*See* Mackenzie, Henry

**H. M. M.**
*See* Moggridge, Helen

**H. M. S.**
*See* Stephens, Harriet Marion

**H. M. W.**
*See* Wang, Hui-Ming

**H. R. H.**
*See* Hoopes, Helen Rhoda

**H. S. T.**
*See* Truman, Harry

**H. T.**
*See* Tucker, Herbert

**H. T. P.**
*See* Parker, Henry Taylor

**H. W.**
*See* Weinberger, Harry

**H. W.**
*See* Williams, Herbert

**H. W. H.**
*See* Herbert, Henry William

**Ha-Kadosh**
*See* Judah I [or Jehudah]

**Ha-Nasi**
*See* Judah I [or Jehudah]

**Haakon I [Hakon or Haco]** 920?-961  [DNNS, WBD]
*King of Norway*
* [The] Good

**Haakon II** 1147-1162  [WBD]
*King of Norway*
* Herdebred [Broadshouldered]

**Haakon IV Haakonsson** 1204-1263  [WBD]
*King of Norway*
* [The] Old

**Haakon VII**
*See* Carl

**Haarer, Alec Ernest** 1894-  [CA]
*British author*
* Shanwa

**Haas, Ben[jamin] L[eopold]** 1926-1977  [CA]
*American author*
* Benteen, John
* Douglas, Thorne
* Meade, Richard

**Haas, Boon**
*See* Haas, Bruno Philip

**Haas, Bruno Philip** 1891-1952 [BE]
*American baseball player*
* Haas, Boon

**Haas, Bryan Edmund** 1956-  [SMG]
*American baseball player*
* Haas, Moose

**Haas, Claramae** 1920-  [BEW, OP]
*American singer and actress*
* Turner, Claramae

**Haas, Dolly**
*See* Haas, Dorothy Clara Louise

**Haas, Dorothy Clara Louise** 1910- [BEW]
*German-born actress*
* Haas, Dolly

**Haas, Dorothy F.** 20th c.  [CA]
*American author and editor*
* Francis, Dee

**Haas, Edward** 1880-1915  [THR]
*American actor*
* Robins, Edward H.

**Haas, George William** 1903-1974 [B10, BE, BTB]
*American baseball player*
* Haas, Mule

**Haas, Irene**
*See* Clark, Irene Haas

**Haas, Moose**
*See* Haas, Bryan Edmund

**Haas, Mule**
*See* Haas, George William

**Haase, Ann Marie Bernazza** 1942- [CA]
*American author and educator*
* Bernazza, Ann Marie

**Habakuk**
*See* Fielhauer, Otto Magnus

**Habbacknee**
*See* Bowie, Edith Charlotte [Habback]

**Habbema, Koos**
*See* Heijermans, Herman

**Habberton, John**  [PA]
*Author*
* Burton, H. A.

**Habe, Hans**
*See* Bekessy, Jean

**Habenicht, Hobby**
*See* Habenicht, Robert Julius [Bob]

**Habenicht, Robert Julius [Bob]** 1926-  [BE]
*American baseball player*
* Habenicht, Hobby

**Habenton, Hebbie**
*See* Hebenton, Andrew Clayton

**Haberdasher Harry**
*See* Truman, Harry

**Habergock, Gus N.**
*See* Gernsback, Hugo

**Haberkom, Mrs. Emil**  [FFF]
*Entertainer*
* Mather, Margaret

**Habernig, Christine** 1915-  [B10]
*Austrian author*
* Lavant, Christine

**Habersham, Elizabeth** [joint pseudonym with Madeline Porter]
*See* Harper, Shannon

**Habersham, Elizabeth** [joint pseudonym with Shannon Harper]
*See* Porter, Madeline

**Habershon, Keith**
*See* McComb, Frederick Wilson Henry

**Haberstitch, Samuel**  [FFF]
*German author*
* Bitter, Arthur

**Habington, William** 1605-1654
[RH]
*British poet*
* Araphil [or Araphill]

**Hacek, Harry** 20th c.
*American horse racing agent*
* [The] Hat

**Hach, Irv[in]** 1873-1936    [BE]
*American baseball player*
* Hach, Major

**Hach, Major**
*See*   Hach, Irv[in]

**Hachette, Jeanne**
*See*   Laisne, Jeanne

**Hack, Charles** 1947-    [IBW]
*American film studio executive*
* Hack, Cheer

**Hack, Cheer**
*See*   Hack, Charles

**Hack, Smiling Stan**
*See*   Hack, Stanley Camfield

**Hack, Stanley Camfield** 1909-
[BE]
*American baseball player*
* Hack, Smiling Stan

**Hackenschmidt, George** 20th c.
[BMH]
*Entertainer*
* [The] Russian Lion

**Hackenschmied, Alexander** 1910?-
[FC]
*German-born filmmaker*
* Hammid, Alexander

**[The] Hacker**
*See*   Wilson, Lewis Robert

**Hacker, Leonard** 1924-
[BEW, IPA, SW]
*American comedian*
* Hackett, Buddy

**Hacket, William** ?-1592   [HN]
*British imposter*
* King Jesus

**Hackett, Buddy**
*See*   Hacker, Leonard

**Hackett, James Joseph [Jim]**
1877-1961   [BE]
*American baseball player*
* Hackett, Sunny Jim

**Hackett, Mert**
*See*   Hackett, Mortimer Martin

**Hackett, Mortimer Martin**
1859-1938   [BE]
*American baseball player*
* Hackett, Mert

**Hackett, Sunny Jim**
*See*   Hackett, James Joseph [Jim]

**Hackforth-Jones, Margaret Stefana**
1911-   [IAW]
*British author*
* Drower, M. S.

**Hacklaender, Friedrich Wilhelm**
1816-1877   [SN]
*German author*
* [The] German Dickens

**Hackle, B.**
*See*   Monheimer, A.

**Hackle, Palmer**
*See*   Blakely, Robert

**Hackleman, Wauneta** 1915-   [WD]
*American author*
* Mason, Val

**Hadath, John Edward Gunby**
?-1954   [MBF]
*British author*
* Duncan, James
* Mowbray, John
* O'Grady, Felix
* Pearson, Shepperd

**Haddi**
*See*   Hidayatuliah, Mohammad

**Haddix, Cecille**
*See*   Haddix-Kontos, Cecille P.

**Haddix, Harvey, Jr.** 1925-
[BE, PB, SMG]
*American baseball player*
* [The] Kitten

**Haddix-Kontos, Cecille P.** 1937-
[CA]
*American author*
* Haddix, Cecille
* Kontos, Cecille

**Haddo, Oliver**
*See*   Puechner, Ray

**Haddock, Albert**
*See*   Herbert, [Sir] Alan Patrick

**Haddock, Gentleman George**
*See*   Haddock, George Silas

**Haddock, George Silas** 1866-1926
[BE]
*American baseball player*
* Haddock, Gentleman George

**Haddon, Christopher**
*See*   Palmer, John Leslie

**Haddon, Peter**
*See*   Tildsley, Peter

**Haddon, Sarah**
*See*   Green, Madge

**Haddow, John Falcnor** 1890-   [BE]
*American baseball player*
* Black, John Falcnor

**Haderman, Jeanette**
*See*   Walworth, Mrs.

**Hades, Micky** 20th c.   [BS]
*Canadian publisher and author*
* Hades, Professor
* Micky the Magician

**Hades, Professor**
*See*   Hades, Micky

**Hadfield, Alan** 1904-   [AW]
*British author*
* Dale, Robin

**Hadfield, [Ellis] Charles [Raymond]**
1909-   [CA]
*South African-born author*
* Alexander, Charles
* Hadfield, E. C. R.

**Hadfield, E. C. R.**
*See*   Hadfield, [Ellis] Charles
[Raymond]

**Hadfield, Miles** 1903-   [ART]
*British author and illustrator*
* M. H.

**Hadham, John**
*See*   Parkes, James William

**Hadi, Shafi**
*See*   Porter, Curtis

**Hading, Jane**
*See*   Koenig, Madame Victor

**Hading, Jane**
*See*   Trefouret, Jeanne Alfredine

**Hadley, Bump**
*See*   Hadley, Irving Darius

**Hadley, Franklin**
*See*   Winterbotham, Russell Robert

**Hadley, Irving Darius** 1904-1963
[AS, BE, PB]
*American baseball player*
* Hadley, Bump

**Hadley, Lee** 1934-   [CA]
*American author*
* Irwin, Hadley [joint pseudonym
  with Ann(abelle Bowen) Irwin]

**Hadley, Reed**
*See*   Herring, Reed

**Haefeli, Charles** 1889-1955   [SC]
*American actor*
* Haefeli, Jockey

**Haefeli, Jockey**
*See*   Haefeli, Charles

**Haefner, Mickey Mouse**
*See*   Haefner, Milton Arnold

**Haefner, Milton Arnold** 1912-
[BN]
*American baseball player*
* Haefner, Mickey Mouse

**Haeselbairth, A. C.**   [PA]
*Author*
* A. C. H.

**Hafey, Bud**
*See*   Hafey, Daniel Albert

**Hafey, Charles James** 1903?-1973
[B10, DGS, PB]
*American baseball player*
* Hafey, Chick

**Hafey, Chick**
*See*   Hafey, Charles James

**Hafey, Daniel Albert** 1912-   [BE]
*American baseball player*
* Hafey, Bud

**Hafey, Thomas Francis [Tom]**
1913-   [BE]
*American baseball player*
* [The] Arm

**Hafiz**
*See*   Stott, Mr.

**Hafiz, Mohammed** ?-1388?
[DNNF, HN, SN]
*Persian poet*
* [The] Anacreon of Persia
* [The] Persian Anacreon
* Sugar Lip
* Tschegerleb

**[The] Hag**
*See*   Cash, John R. [Johnny]

**Haga, Enoch John** 1931-   [IAW]
*American author*
* Grant, C. B. S.

**Hagan, Cliff** 1931-   [BB]
*American basketball player*
* Lil Abner

**Hagan, Patricia**
*See*   Howell, Patricia Hagan

**Hagar, George**
*See*   Danforth, Ethel M.

**Hagberg, Nancy** 1939-   [CA]
*American playwright*
* Holmgren, Norah
* Walter, Nancy

**Hagberg, Rudolph** 1907-1960   [AS]
*American football player*
* Hagberg, Swede

**Hagberg, Swede**
*See*   Hagberg, Rudolph

**Hageman, Casey**
*See*   Hageman, Kurt Moritz

**Hageman, Kurt Moritz** 1887-1964
[BE]
*American baseball player*
* Hageman, Casey

**Hagen, Christopher**
*See*   Stammel, Heinz-Josef

**Hagen, Festus**
*See*   Hagen, Martin

**Hagen, Jean**
*See*   Verhagen, Jean

**Hagen, John Milton** 1902-   [CA]
*American author, playwright,
songwriter*
* Sherwin, Sterling

**Hagen, Joseph F.** 1878-1942
[AS, BX, RBE]
*American boxer*
* O'Brien, Jack
* O'Brien, Philadelphia Jack

**Hagen, Martin** 20th c.
*American biathlete*
* Hagen, Festus

**Hagen, Martin S.**
*See*   Pahlow, Mannfried Otto
Siegfried

**Hagen, Peter** 1569-1620   [PA]
*Author*
* Hagius

**Hagen, Walter Charles** 1892-1969
[EG, GME, SA]
*American golfer*
* [The] Haig

**Hagen-William, Louis**
*See*   Williams, Louis

**Hager, Jean** 1932-   [CA]
*American author*
* Kyle, Marlaine
* McAllister, Amanda
* North, Sara
* Stephens, Jeanne

**Hager, N. W.** 20th c.   [RBE]
*Boxing agent*
* Hager, Tex

**Hager, Tex**
*See*   Hager, N. W.

**Hagerman, Rip**
*See*   Hagerman, Zeriah Zequiel

**Hagerman, Zeriah Zequiel**
1889-1930   [BE]
*American baseball player*
* Hagerman, Rip

**Haggard, [Captain] Edward Arthur**
*See*   Amyand, Arthur

**Haggard, J. Harvey** 20th c.    [WGT]
*Author*
* [The] Planet Prince

**Haggard, Paul**
*See* Longstreet, [Henry] Stephen
[Weiner]

**Haggard, William**
*See* Clayton, Richard Henry
Michael

**Haggerty, Horace** 20th c.    [MEB]
*American basketball player*
* Haggerty, Horse

**Haggerty, Horse**
*See* Haggerty, Horace

**Hagius**
*See* Hagen, Peter

**Hagiwara, Sakutaro** 1886-1942
[WOA]
*Japanese poet*
* [The] Father of Modern Japanese
  Poetry

**Hagler, Marvelous Marvin**
*See* Hagler, Marvin

**Hagler, Marvin** 20th c.
*American boxer*
* Hagler, Marvelous Marvin

**Hagman, Hakki**
*See* Hagman, Matti

**Hagman, Matti** 1955-    [SMG]
*Finnish-born hockey player*
* Hagman, Hakki

**Hagon, Priscilla**
*See* Allan, Mabel Esther

**Hagrizi, Natan**
*See* Gross, Natan

**Hague, Frances Dorothy** 1882- ?
[WWL]
*British author and poet*
* Fleming, Hugh

**Hague, William L. [Bill]**
*See* Haug, William L.

**Hagy, Ruth Geri**
*See* Brod, Ruth Hagy

**Hahn, Frank George** 1879-1960
[AS, BE, PB]
*American baseball player*
* Hahn, Noodles

**Hahn, George R.** 20th c.    [WGT]
*Author*
* Mand, Cyril [joint pseudonym
  with Richard Levin]

**Hahn, Noodles**
*See* Hahn, Frank George

**Hahnemann, [Christian Friedrich]
Samuel** 1755-1843
[DEP, FFF, SN]
*German physician*
* [The] Prodigy of Learning

**[The] Haig**
*See* Hagen, Walter Charles

**Haig, Alexander Meigs** 1924-
*American military leader and
diplomat*
* [The] Vicar

**Haig, Fenil**
*See* Hueffer, Ford Madox

**Haig, Gunder** 20th c.
*Track and field athlete*
* Gunder the Wonder

**Haig, Ruth**
*See* Grasle, Elizabeth

**Haik, J. Michael** 1946-    [FB]
*American football player*
* Haik, Mac

**Haik, Mac**
*See* Haik, J. Michael

**Haile Selassie**
*See* Makonnen, Ras Tafari

**Haill, Robert Godfrey** 1938-    [IAW]
*British-born author*
* Cooper, Janie
* Satane, Paul

**Hailsham of St. Marylebone, Lord**
*See* Hogg, Quintin McGarel

**Haime, Agnes Irvine Constance
[Adams]** 1884-    [CAP]
*British author*
* Persis

**Haindl, Marieluise** 1901-1974
[CA]
*German author and playwright*
* Fleisser, Marieluise

**Haines, Charles Glidden**
1793-1825    [PA]
*Author*
* Tacitus

**Haines, Connie**
*See* Jamais, Yvonne Marie

**Haines, E[dwin] Irvine** 1877- ?
[NAA]
*American journalist*
* I. R. V.
* Mandeville, John

**Haines, F. E. H.** 19th c.    [PA]
*Author*
* F. E. H. H.

**Haines, Henry Harrison**
*See* Enton, Harry

**Haines, Henry Luther** 1898-    [BE]
*American baseball player*
* Haines, Hinkey

**Haines, Hinkey**
*See* Haines, Henry Luther

**Haines, Jesse Joseph** 1893-1978
[BE, DGS, PB]
*American baseball player*
* Haines, Pop

**Haines, John**
*See* Richardson, Gladwell

**Haines, Nat Burden** 1887?-1962
[BEW]
*American actor*
* Burns, Nat

**Haines, Pop**
*See* Haines, Jesse Joseph

**Haines, Ronald**
*See* Hutchinson, W.

**Hains, Thornton Jenkins** 1866- ?
[WW]
*Author*
* Garnett, [Captain] Mayn Clew

**Hainstock, Elizabeth**
*See* Andrews, Elizabeth

**Hairbrain, Timothy**
*See* Anderson, James

**Hairbreadth Harry Hamilton**
*See* Hamilton, Jack Edwin

**Hairdet, M.**    [PA]
*Author*
* Dessaix

**Hairston, Gene** 1930-    [IBW]
*American boxer*
* Hairston, Silent Gene

**Hairston, George** 1894-    [IBW]
*American billiard player*
* Rotation Slim

**Hairston, Happy**
*See* Hairston, Harold

**Hairston, Harold** 1942-    [BB]
*American basketball player*
* Hairston, Happy

**Hairston, Silent Gene**
*See* Hairston, Gene

**Hajdu, Emeric** 1911-    [WEC]
*French animated cartoon director
and producer*
* Image, Jean

**Hajime, Kijima**
*See* Kojima, Shozo

**Hajji Baba of Ispahan**
*See* Morier, James Justinian

**Hajji Khalfah [Assessor Who Has
Made the Pilgrimage]**
*See* Mustafa ibn-Abdallah

**Hajmassy, Ilona** 1912-    [FC, PMJ]
*Hungarian-born actress*
* Massey, Ilona

**Hajos, Alfred**
*See* Guttmann, Arnold

**Hajos, Magdalena [or Marishka]**
1891-    [CED, PMJ]
*Hungarian-born actress and singer*
* Hajos, Mitzi
* [The] Wonder Child

**Hajos, Mitzi**
*See* Hajos, Magdalena [or
Marishka]

**Hakim, al-** 985-1021    [WBD]
*Fatimid caliph*
* [The] Mad Caliph

**Hakim ben Allah** 8th c.    [SN, WBD]
*Founder of Arabic religious sect*
* Mokanna, al-
* Mokanna the Veiled
* [The] Veiled Prophet of
  Khorassan

**Hakim, Sadik**
*See* Thornton, Argonne Dense

**Hakim, Talib Rasul**
*See* Chambers, Stephen A.

**Hakim I [or Hakam] al-** ?- 822
[HN]
*Emir of Cordoba*
* [The] Father of Cruelty
* He of the Suburbs

**Hal a Dacotah**
*See* Sibley, Henry H.

**Hal, Dane**
*See* MacFall, Haldane

**Halaby, Elizabeth** 1952?-
*American-born Queen of Jordan*
* Nur el Hussein [Light of
  Hussein]
* Nur, Queen

**Halacy, D. S.**
*See* Halacy, Daniel Stephen, Jr.

**Halacy, Daniel Stephen, Jr.** 1919-
[SFL]
*American author*
* Halacy, D. S.

**Halas, George S.** 1895-    [FB, SA]
*American football player and coach*
* Halas, Papa Bear
* Pro Football, Mr.

**Halas, Papa Bear**
*See* Halas, George S.

**Halasz, Gyula** 1899-    [B10]
*French photographer*
* Brassai

**Halberg, Arvo** 1911-
*American Communist party leader*
* Halbert, Arvie
* Hall, Gus
* Howell, John

**Halbert, Arvie**
*See* Halberg, Arvo

**Halbrook, Swede**
*See* Halbrook, Wade

**Halbrook, Wade** 1933-    [BB]
*American basketball player*
* Halbrook, Swede

**Halcro, Claud**
*See* Breckinridge, John

**Haldane, J. B. S.**
*See* Haldane, John Burdon
Sanderson

**Haldane, John Burdon Sanderson**
1892-1964    [LC, TC]
*British biologist and author*
* Haldane, J. B. S.

**Haldane, Robert** 1764-1842
[DEP, DNNS]
*Scottish philanthropist and author*
* [The] Scottish Boanerges

**Haldane-Stevenson, James Patrick**
*See* Stevenson, James Patrick

**Haldeman, Bob**
*See* Haldeman, Harry Robbins

**Haldeman, H. R.**
*See* Haldeman, Harry Robbins

**Haldeman, Harry Robbins** 1926-
*Administrative aide to American
president Richard Nixon*
* Haldeman, Bob
* Haldeman, H. R.

**Haldeman, Joe [William]** 1943-
[CA]
*American author*
* Graham, Robert

**Haldeman, Samuel Stehman**
1812-1880    [FFF, PA]
*American naturalist, philologist,
author*
* Ago, Felix

**Haldeman-Julius, Emanuel**
*See* Julius, Emanuel

**Halderson, Harold** 1900-  [CEI]
*Canadian-born hockey player*
* Halderson, Slim

**Halderson, Slim**
*See* Halderson, Harold

**Haldimand**
*See* Marcet, Mary

**Haldorson, B. E.** 1934-  [BB]
*American basketball player*
* Haldorson, Burdie

**Haldorson, Burdie**
*See* Haldorson, B. E.

**Hale, Alan**
*See* McKahan, Rufus Alan

**Hale, Allison**
*See* Blackledge, Ethel H.

**Hale and Hearty**
*See* Hales, A. G.

**Hale, Arlene** 1924-  [CA]
*American author*
* Christopher, Louise
* Everett, Gail
* Kirkland, Will
* Tate, Mary Anne
* Williams, Lynn

**Hale, Arvel Odell** 1908-  [BE]
*American baseball player*
* Hale, Bad News

**Hale, Bad News**
*See* Hale, Arvel Odell

**Hale, Binnie**
*See* Hale-Monro, Beatrice Mary

**Hale, Christopher**
*See* Stevens, Frances Moyer [Ross]

**Hale, Clement**
*See* Steffens, Arthur

**Hale, Corky**
*See* Hecht, Merrilyn Cecelia

**Hale, Creighton**
*See* Fitzgerald, Patrick

**Hale, Dad**
*See* Hale, Ray L.

**Hale, Edith** 19th c.  [PA]
*Author*
* Talmon, Thrace

**Hale, Edward Everett** 1822-1909
[SAT, SFL, WGT]
*American clergyman, author, poet*
* Ingham, [Colonel] Frederic

**Hale, Edwin** 20th c.
*American football player*
* Hale, Goat

**Hale, Eugenia**
*See* Woolsey, Maryhale

**Hale, Forbes**
*See* Chalmers, Isaac

**Hale, Garth**
*See* Cunningham, Albert Benjamin

**Hale, George Ellery** 20th c.
*American astronomer and
cosmologist*
* Hale, Thinker

**Hale, Goat**
*See* Hale, Edwin

**Hale, Helen**
*See* Mulcahy, Lucille Burnett

**Hale, Innis**
*See* Hook, Samuel Clarke

**Hale, J. Robert**
*See* Hale-Monro, J. Robert

**Hale, Jonathan**
*See* Hatley, Jonathan

**Hale, Julian A[nthony] S[tuart]**
1940-  [CA]
*Welsh-born author*
* Stuart, Anthony

**Hale, Katherine**
*See* Garvin, Amelia Warnock

**Hale, Kathleen** 20th c.  [AW]
*Scottish-born author*
* McClean, Kathleen

**Hale, Little**
*See* Hale, Teddy

**Hale, Margaret**
*See* Higonnet, Margaret Randolph

**Hale, Martin**
*See* Rochester, George Ernest

**Hale, Mary**
*See* Woolsey, Maryhale

**Hale, Michael**
*See* Bullock, Michael [Hale]

**Hale, Philip**
*See* Eastwood, C[harles] Cyril

**Hale, Ray L.** 1880-1946  [BE]
*American baseball player*
* Hale, Dad

**Hale, Sonnie**
*See* Hale-Monro, John Robert

**Hale, Teddy** 1924-  [IBW]
*American dancer*
* Hale, Little

**Hale, Thinker**
*See* Hale, George Ellery

**Hale, William Harlan** 1910-1974
[B10]
*American editor*
* Thomas, Harlan C.

**Hale-Monro, Beatrice Mary** 1899-
[EMT]
*British actress, singer, dancer*
* Hale, Binnie

**Hale-Monro, J. Robert** 1874-1940
*British actor*
* Hale, J. Robert

**Hale-Monro, John Robert**
1902-1959  [F2, FC]
*British actor, singer, director*
* Hale, Sonnie
* Munro, Robert

**Hales, A. G.** 1870- ?  [MBF]
*British author and editor*
* Hale and Hearty
* Hales, Smiler

**Hales, John** 1584-1656
[DEL, RH, SN]
*British clergyman*
* [The] Ever Memorable
* Hales, Little
* [A] Walking Library

**Hales, Joyce**
*See* Coombs, Joyce

**Hales, Little**
*See* Hales, John

**Hales, Smiler**
*See* Hales, A. G.

**Hales, Thomas** 1740-1780  [PA]
*Author*
* D'hele

**Halevi, Zev Ben Shimon**
*See* Kenton, Warren

**Halevy**
*See* Levy, Jacques Fromental Elie

**Haley, Bill** 1926?-1981
*American musician*
* [The] Father of Rock 'n' Roll

**Haley, Gail E.**
*See* Arnold, Gail Einhart Haley

**Half Pint Jaxon**
*See* Jaxon, Frankie

**Half-Mast Mel**
*See* Thomson, Meldrim

**Halfenstein, Ernest**
*See* Oakes, Elizabeth

**Halfpenny, Peter** 1899-1973  [SC]
*Actor*
* Martin, Pete

**Haliburton, Hugh**
*See* Robertson, James Logie

**Haliburton, Thomas Chandler**
1796-1865  [FFF, RH, WBD]
*Canadian jurist and author*
* Slick, Samuel

**Halibut, Edward**
*See* Wilson, Richard

**Halicki, Edward Louis** 1950-
[SMG]
*American baseball player*
* Halicki, Ho-Ho

**Halicki, H. G.** 1941-
*American motion picture executive*
* Halicki, Toby

**Halicki, Ho-Ho**
*See* Halicki, Edward Louis

**Halicki, Toby**
*See* Halicki, H. G.

**Halidom, M. Y.?**
*See* Heron-Allen, Edward

**Halifax, [Dr.] Clifford**
*See* Beaumont, Edgar

**Hall, Abraham Oakey** 1826-1898
[FFF]
*American politician and author*
* Yorkel, Hans

**Hall, Ada**
*See* Dare, Mrs. T. S.

**Hall, Adam**
*See* Dudley-Smith, Trevor

**Hall, Al**
*See* Hall, Archibald W.

**Hall, Alfred** 1895-1946
[DAM, EJ, WWJ]
*American jazz musician*
* Hall, Tubby

**Hall, Amanda Benjamin**
*See* Brownell, Amanda Benjamin
Hall

**Hall, Anmer**
*See* Horne, Alderson Burrell

**Hall, Ann**
*See* Duckert, Mary

**Hall, Archibald W.** ?-1885  [BE]
*American baseball player*
* Hall, Al

**Hall, Archie** 1909-  [EJ, WWJ]
*American jazz musician*
* Hall, Skip

**Hall, Asa Zadel** 1875-1965  [CA]
*American author*
* Edson, Harold

**Hall, Aylmer**
*See* Hall, Norah E. L.

**Hall, B. K.**
*See* Mosser, Ann J.

**Hall, Bad Joe**
*See* Hall, Joseph Henry

**Hall, Barbara** 1941-  [SW]
*American actress*
* Feldon, Barbara

**Hall, Barnard R.**  [PA]
*Author*
* Carlton, Robert

**Hall, Basil** 1788-1844  [SN]
*British naval officer and author*
* [A] Literary Sinbad

**Hall, Bennie Caroline [Humble]** 20th
c.  [CA]
*American author and editor*
* Bennett, Hall
* Marshall, Emily

**Hall, Blakely**  [FFF]
*American writer*
* Flaneur

**Hall, Bush**
*See* Hall, Sam

**Hall, Cameron** [joint pseudonym
with Henry Dempsey]
*See* Alvarez Del Rey, Ramon
Felipe San Juan Mario Silvio Enrico

**Hall, Cameron** [joint pseudonym
with Ramon Felipe San Juan Mario
Alvarez Del Rey]
*See* Dempsey, Henry

**Hall, Charles Louis**
*See* Clolo, Carlos

**Hall, Charles W. [Charlie]** 20th c.
[BE]
*American baseball player*
* Hall, Doc

**Hall, Claudia**
*See* Floren, Lee

**Hall, D. W.**
*See* Hall, Desmond Winter

**Hall, Dale** 1924-  [BB]
*American basketball player*
* Hall, Smiley

**Hall, Del Allison** 1949-  [SMG]
*Canadian-born hockey player*
* Hall, Reddy

**Hall, Desmond Winter** 20th c.
[ESF, WGT]
*American author and editor*
* Gilmore, Anthony [joint
  pseudonym with Harry Arthur
  Bates]
* Hall, D. W.
* Winter, H. G. [joint pseudonym
  with Harry Arthur Bates]

Hall, Diane 1946- [SW]
*American actress*
* Keaton, Diane

Hall, Doc
*See* Hall, Charles W. [Charlie]

Hall, Elizabeth Wason 1912- [CA]
*American author*
* Wason, Betty

Hall, Ellis 16th c. [SN]
*Considered himself to be a prophet*
* Ely, the Carpenter's Son
* [The] Manchester Prophet

Hall, Evan
*See* Halleran, Eugene E[dward]

Hall, Evelyn 1895-1958 [BEW]
*American actress*
* Varden, Evelyn

Hall, Frank Richards 1900- [IA]
*American author*
* Naber, Charles R.

Hall, Gertrude
*See* Brownell, Anna Gertrude
[Hall]

Hall, Gertrude 1912- [ASC]
*American composer*
* Hall, Sugar

Hall, Glenn Henry 1931- [FHE]
*Canadian-born hockey player*
* Goalie, Mr.

Hall, Gordon Langley 1937- [CA]
*Author*
* Simmons, Dawn Langley

Hall, Grace 1872?-1927 [BEW]
*American actress and playwright*
* Griswold, Grace

Hall, Gus
*See* Halberg, Arvo

Hall, H. W.
*See* Hall, Halbert Weldon

Hall, Halbert Weldon 1941- [SFL]
*American author*
* Hall, H. W.

Hall, Haywood 1898- [CA]
*American author and political
organizer*
* Haywood, Harry

Hall, Helen 20th c. [ASC]
*American composer and singer*
* Hall, Teddy

Hall, Henry 1920- [FC]
*American actor*
* Hall, Huntz

Hall, Holworthy
*See* Porter, Harold Everett

Hall, Huntz
*See* Hall, Henry

Hall, Ian 1940- [IBW]
*Guyanese-born musician*
* [The] Proud African

Hall, Irene 20th c. [AW]
*Australian author and poet*
* Gough, Irene

Hall, J. De P.
*See* McKelway, St. Clair

Hall, James
*See* Brown, James

Hall, James
*See* Kuttner, Henry

Hall, James [FFF]
*American editor and journalist*
* Orlando

Hall, James Norman 1887-1951
[SAT]
*American-born author*
* Gravel, Fern

Hall, Jarvis
*See* Bagg, Helen

Hall, Jay C.
*See* Hall, John C.

Hall, Jesse
*See* Boesen, Victor

Hall, Joe
*See* Hall, Nelson Howard

Hall, John
*See* Braughal, Michael

Hall, John
*See* Dillinger, John Herbert

Hall, John 1718-1785
[FFF, SN, WBD]
*British poet*
* [The] Lord of Crazy Castle
* Stevenson, John Hall

Hall, John C. 1915- [CA]
*American writer, editor, publisher*
* Hall, Jay C.

Hall, John Ryder
*See* Rotsler, William

Hall, Jon
*See* Locher, Charles

Hall, Josef Washington 1894-1960
[NAA, TC]
*American author and lecturer*
* Close, Upton

Hall, Joseph 1574-1656
[DNNF, HN, SN]
*British prelate*
* [The] Christian Seneca
* [The] English Juvenal
* [The] English Persius
* [The] English Seneca

Hall, Joseph 1943- [RO1]
*American singer*
* Little Joey

Hall, Joseph Henry 1882-1919
[FHE]
*British-born hockey player*
* Hall, Bad Joe

Hall, Juanita
*See* Long, Juanita

Hall, Kendall
*See* Heath, Harry E[ugene], Jr.

Hall, Laura Nelson
*See* Barnhurst, Laura Nelson

Hall, Lloyd Augustus 1894-1971
[IBW]
*American chemist*
* [The] Dean of Black Industrial
Scientists

Hall, Marcia
*See* Sellers, Connie Leslie, Jr.

Hall, Margaret [PA]
*Author*
* Markham, Pauline

Hall, Marie Boas 1919- [CA]
*American science historian and
author*
* Boas, Marie

Hall, Marjory
*See* Yeakley, Marjory Hall

Hall, Mark W.
*See* Hallowitz, Mark W.

Hall, Mary Bowen 1932- [CA]
*American writer*
* Bowen, Mary

Hall, Minor 1897-1959
[DAM, EJ, WWJ]
*American jazz musician*
* Hall, Ram

Hall, Motte
*See* Cheesborough, Essie B.

Hall, Nelson Howard 1906- [MY]
*Canadian-born musician*
* Hall, Joe

Hall, Norah E. L. 1914- [TCC]
*British author*
* Hall, Aylmer

Hall, O. M.
*See* Hall, Oakley [Maxwell]

Hall, Oakley [Maxwell] 1920-
[CA, WW]
*American author*
* Hall, O. M.
* Manor, Jason

Hall, Owen
*See* Davis, James

Hall, Pauline
*See* White, Mrs. Frank

Hall, Pauline [FFF]
*Entertainer*
* Brand, Pauline

Hall, Penelope C[oker] 1933- [CA]
*American author*
* Wilson, Penelope Coker

Hall, Ram
*See* Hall, Minor

Hall, Reddy
*See* Hall, Del Allison

Hall, Richard
*See* Holton, Walter H.

Hall, Robert
*See* Vien, Charles

Hall, Robert G. [FFF]
*Entertainer*
* Burton, Robert G.

Hall, Rupert
*See* Home-Gall, Edward Reginald

Hall, Sam 1904?-1934 [NOJ]
*American jazz musician*
* Hall, Bush

Hall, Sea Lion
*See* Clolo, Carlos

Hall, Sell
*See* Hall, Sellers McKee

Hall, Sellers McKee 20th c. [OBW]
*American baseball player*
* Hall, Sell

Hall, Skip
*See* Hall, Archie

Hall, Smiley
*See* Hall, Dale

Hall, Spencer T. [HN, PA]
*Author*
* S. H.
* [The] Sherwood Forester

Hall, Steve 20th c. [WGT]
*Author*
* Markham, Russ

Hall, Sugar
*See* Hall, Gertrude

Hall, Teddy
*See* Hall, Helen

Hall, Tom Edward 1947-
[PB, SMG]
*American baseball player*
* [The] Blade

Hall, Tom T. 1936- [ECM]
*American country-western performer*
* [The] Mark Twain of Country
Music

Hall, [Midshipman] Tom W.
*See* Ingraham, Prentiss

Hall, Tubby
*See* Hall, Alfred

Hall, Valerie 1939- [IAW]
*British author*
* Pitt, Valerie

Hall, Vera 1906?-1964 [BWW]
*American singer*
* Reed, Nora
* Ward, Vera Hall

Hall, Wendell 1896-1969
[CED, ECM]
*American singer*
* [The] Red Headed Music Maker

Hall, Whyte
*See* Rayner, Augustus Alfred

Hall, William Otterburn 1935-
[IAW]
*British columnist, director, producer*
* Judge, Philip

Halla, R. C.
*See* Halla, Robert Christian

Halla, Robert Christian 1949-
[CA]
*American poet and editor*
* Billings, Ezra
* Halla, R. C.

Hallahan, Hully
*See* Hallahan, John

Hallahan, John 1927- [SMG]
*American baseball team equipment
manager*
* Hallahan, Hully

Hallahan, Wild Bill
*See* Hallahan, William Anthony

Hallahan, William Anthony 1902-
[BE, PB]
*American baseball player*
* Hallahan, Wild Bill

Hallam
*See* Hughes, William Jesse

Hallam, Basil
*See* Hallam-Radford, Basil

Hallam, Jay
*See* Rice, Joan Odette

**Hallam-Radford, Basil** 1889-1916
[THR]
*British actor and singer*
* Hallam, Basil

**Hallard, Peter**
*See* Catherall, Arthur

**Hallard, Ruth**
*See* Tetzner, Ruth

**Hallas, Richard**
*See* Knight, Eric [Mowbray]

**Hallbing, Kjell Kare** 1934- [IAW]
*Norwegian author*
* Cameron, Ward
* Manning, Leo
* Masterson, Louis
* Morgan, Lee

**[The] Halle Bach**
*See* Bach, Wilhelm Friedemann

**Halle, [Sir] Charles**
*See* Halle, Karl

**Halle, Karl** 1819-1895 [WBD]
*German-born musician and
conductor*
* Halle, [Sir] Charles

**Halleck, Fitz Greene** 1795-1867
[PA]
*Author*
* Croaker and Co.

**Halleck, Henry Wager** 1815-1872
[FFF, SN]
*American army officer*
* Old Brains

**Hallelujah Joe**
*See* McCoy, Joe

**Haller, Albrecht von** 1708-1777
[FFF, HN, RH]
*Swiss physician*
* [The] Father of Philosophy
* [The] Father of Physiology

**Haller, Bill**
*See* Bechko, Peggy Anne

**Haller, Fox**
*See* Haller, William Edward

**Haller, Gustave**
*See* Simonim, Wilhelmina
Josephine

**Haller, Hatch**
*See* Haller, Thomas Frank

**Haller, Joseph**
*See* Coleridge, Henry Nelson

**Haller, Thomas Frank** 1937-
[SMG]
*American baseball player*
* Haller, Hatch

**Haller, William Edward** 1935- [PB]
*American baseball umpire*
* Haller, Fox

**Halleran, Eugene E[dward]** 1905-
[CA]
*American author*
* Broward, Donn
* Hall, Evan

**Hallgarten, Fritz**
*See* Hallgarten, Siegfried Solomon

**Hallgarten, S. F.**
*See* Hallgarten, Siegfried Solomon

**Hallgarten, Siegfried Solomon**
1902- [IAW]
*German-born author*
* Hallgarten, Fritz
* Hallgarten, S. F.

**Hallgrimson, Jansson** 1888-1945
[EWL]
*Icelandic playwright and author*
* Kamban, Guomundur

**Halliday, Ben**
*See* Manning, William Henry

**Halliday, Brett**
*See* Dresser, Davis

**Halliday, Brett**
*See* Terrall, Robert

**Halliday, Charlotte Mary Irvine**
1935- [ART]
*British artist*
* C. M. I. H.

**Halliday, Dorothy**
*See* Dunnett, Dorothy

**Halliday, Hugh** 20th c. [RO2]
*British musician*
* Halliday, Pigmy

**Halliday, James**
*See* Symington, David

**Halliday, Michael**
*See* Creasey, John

**Halliday, Pigmy**
*See* Halliday, Hugh

**Halliday, Shirley**
*See* Bobin, Donald E. M.

**Halliday, T. S.**
*See* Halliday, Thomas Symington

**Halliday, Thomas Symington**
1902- [ART]
*Scottish artist*
* Halliday, T. S.

**Hallidie, Andrew Smith**
*See* Smith, Andrew

**Halligan, Jocko**
*See* Halligan, William E.

**Halligan, William E.** 1867-1945
[BE]
*American baseball player*
* Halligan, Jocko

**Halliwell, David [William]** 1936-
[CA]
*British playwright, actor, director*
* Arms, Johnson

**Halliwell, James Orchard**
1820-1889 [WBD]
*British librarian and scholar*
* Halliwell-Phillipps, James
Orchard

**Halliwell, Tony** 20th c. [SFL]
*Author*
* Ross, James [joint pseudonym
with Hugh Darrington]

**Halliwell-Phillipps, James Orchard**
*See* Halliwell, James Orchard

**Hallock, Charles** [PA]
*Author*
* Penman

**Halloway, Jane**
*See* Donahey, Mary Dickerson

**Halloway, Vance** 1916- [CA]
*British-born author, playwright,
poet*
* Van Woeart, Alpheus

**Hallowell, Russell F.** 1897-1965
[ASC]
*American composer*
* Stewart, Gene

**Hallowitz, Mark W.** 1943- [CA]
*American author*
* Hall, Mark W.

**Hallows, N. F.** 20th c. [WD]
*British writer*
* Duplex [joint pseudonym with Ian
(Roberts Ambrose) Bradley]

**Halls, Christopher Peter John**
1930- [IAW]
*Australian author*
* Conrad, M.
* Conrad, Marcus

**Hallstrom, Carl** 20th c. [SFP]
*Author*
* Sedolin, Sture

**Hallus, Tak**
*See* Robinett, Stephen [Allen]

**Hallward, Gloria Grahame**
1925?-1981 [BDF, FC, ITA]
*American actress*
* Grahame, Gloria

**Halm**
*See* Lovell, Mrs.

**Halm, Friedrich**
*See* Von Muench-Bellinghausen,
Eligius

**Haloander, Gregor**
*See* Meltzer, Gregor

**Halper, Leivick** 1888-1962 [EWL]
*Russian-born Yiddish poet and
playwright*
* Leivick, H.

**Halpern, Gertrude** 1927?-1978
[FIR]
*Singer and comedienne*
* Lawrence, Trudy

**Halpern, Oscar Saul** 1912- [CA]
*American author, playwright,
screenwriter*
* Saul, Oscar

**Halpine, Charles Graham**
1829-1868 [DEL, DNNF, FFF]
*American author and poet*
* Broadbent, Charles
* O'Reilly, [Private] Miles

**Hals, F.**
*See* Craenhals, Francois

**Halse, G.** 19th c. [SAT]
*British author*
* Rattlebrain

**Halsey, Brett** 20th c. [WF]
*Actor*
* Ford, Montgomery

**Halsey, Bull**
*See* Halsey, William F.

**Halsey, Harlan Page** 1837-1898
[FFF, PA]
*Author*
* Old Sleuth

**Halsey, Harlan Page** (Continued)
* Pastor, Tony

**Halsey, William F.** 1882-1959
[WWW]
*American naval officer*
* Halsey, Bull

**Halsham, John**
*See* Scott, G. Forrester

**Halstan, Margaret**
*See* Hertz, Margaret

**Halstead, E. Sinclair**
*See* Brooks, Edwy Searles

**Halstead, Robert**
*See* Henry [Earl of Peterborough]

**Halstead, S. B.**
*See* Brooks, Edwy Searles

**Halston**
*See* Frowick, Roy Halston

**Halt, Robert**
*See* Vieu, M.

**Halverson, Leslie Eugene**
1904-1953 [SC]
*American actor, dancer, ice skater*
* Leslie, Gene

**Halverstadt, Constance** 1910-
[BEW, FC]
*American actress*
* Cummings, Constance

**Ham Gravy**
*See* Brown, Robert

**Ham Hocks Hannah**
*See* Hannah, John Allen

**Hamadhani, al-** 969-1007 [WBD]
*Moslem poet*
* Badi al-Zaman [Wonder of the
Age]

**Hamann, Doc**
*See* Hamann, Elmer Joseph

**Hamann, Elmer Joseph** 1900- [BE]
*American baseball player*
* Hamann, Doc

**Hamann, Johann Georg** 1730-1788
[DNNF, FFF, SN]
*German author*
* [The] Magician of the North
* Magus aus dem Norden
* Magus of the North

**Hamaoui, Ernest** 1916- [IAW]
*Egyptian-born author*
* Erha

**Hamas, Hurricane**
*See* Hamas, Steve

**Hamas, Steve** 1909-1974 [B10, SG]
*American boxer*
* Hamas, Hurricane

**Hambden**
*See* Orr, Isaac

**Hambidge, Edward John**
1867-1924 [WBD]
*Canadian-born artist*
* Hambidge, Jay

**Hambidge, Jay**
*See* Hambidge, Edward John

**Hambledon, Phyllis**
*See* MacVean, Phyllis

**Hambleton, Ham**
*See* Hambleton, Iceal E.

**Hambleton, Iceal E.** 1919?-
*American air force officer*
* Hambleton, Ham

**Hambletonian**
See  Fairfax-Blakeborough, John

**Hambrick, Charles H.** 1863- ?
[BE]
*American baseball player*
* Hamburg, Charles H. [Charlie]

**[The] Hamburg Bach**
See  Bach, Karl Philipp Emanuel

**Hamburg, Charles H. [Charlie]**
See  Hambrick, Charles H.

**Hamburger, Anne Ellen** 1929-
[IAW]
*British author*
* Beresford

**Hamburger, Ursula-Maria** 20th c.
[EE]
*Russian intelligence agent*
* Sonia

**Hamby, Cracker**
See  Hamby, James Sanford [Jim]

**Hamby, James Sanford [Jim]** 1900-
[BE]
*American baseball player*
* Hamby, Cracker

**Hamel, Felix John** 20th c.　[WW]
*Author*
* De Hamel, Felix John
* Hexham, Lionel J. F.

**Hamel, Hap**
See  Hamel, Herbert

**Hamel, Herbert** 20th c.　[CEI]
*Hockey player*
* Hamel, Hap

**Hamer, Murray** 1885-1941　[THR]
*British actor*
* Carrington, Murray

**Hamerik, Asger**
See  Hammerich, Asger

**Hamerling, Robert**
See  Hammerling, Rupert

**Hamerstrom, Frances** 1907-　[CA]
*American author*
* Windsor, Claire

**Hamfoot Ham**
See  McCoy, Joe

**Hamidi bin Muhammad**
1837?-1905　[WBD]
*Trader and slave merchant in Africa*
* Tipoo Tib [or Tip]

**Hamilcar** 3rd c. BC　[SN]
*Carthaginian general*
* Barca
* Lightning

**Hamill, Ethel**
See  Webb, Jean Francis

**Hamill, Red**
See  Hamill, Robert George

**Hamill, Robert George** 1917-
[CEI, SMG]
*Canadian-born hockey player*
* Hamill, Red

**Hamilton**
See  Watson, William Robinson

**Hamilton, Adam**
See  Granbeck, Marilyn

**Hamilton, Alex** 20th c.　[AW]
*British author*
* Pooter

**Hamilton, Alexander** 1757-1804
[DEL, FFF, PA]
*American statesman*
* Camillus
* [The] Coppersmith
* [The] King of the Feds
* Pacificus
* Phocian
* Publius

**Hamilton, Alice**
See  Cromie, Alice Hamilton

**Hamilton, Alice King** 1869-1970
[FFF]
*American author*
* King, Alice

**Hamilton, Bones**
See  Hamilton, Robert A.

**Hamilton, Bugs**
See  Hamilton, John

**Hamilton, Buzz**
See  Hemming, Roy

**Hamilton, C. G.**　[PA]
*Author*
* C. G. H.

**Hamilton, Charles**
See  Hamilton-Groves, Charles
Antony Bennett

**Hamilton, Charles Harold St. John**
1875-1961　[CA, LC, SAT]
*British author*
* Clifford, Martin
* Clifton, Harry
* Clive, Clifford
* Cobham, [Sir] Alan
* Conquest, Owen
* Conway, Gordon
* Dorian, Harry
* Drake, Frank
* Fox, Freeman
* Greening, Hamilton
* Herbert, Cecil
* Howard, Prosper
* Jennings, Robert
* Jones, Gillingham
* Llewelyn, T. Harcourt
* Owen, Clifford
* Redway, Ralph
* Redway, Ridley
* Richards, Frank
* Richards, Hilda
* Robbins, Raleigh
* Rogers, Robert
* Stanhope, Eric
* Stanley, Robert
* Wallace, Nigel
* Wynyard, Talbot

**Hamilton, Chico**
See  Hamilton, Foreststorn

**Hamilton, Chico**
See  Hamilton, Ian

**Hamilton, Cicely**
See  Hammill, Cicely Mary

**Hamilton, Clare**
See  Lawless, Bettyclare Hamilton

**Hamilton, Clive**
See  Lewis, Clive Staples

**Hamilton, Cosmo**
See  Gibbs, Cosmo

**Hamilton, Dave**
See  Troyer, Byron L[eRoy]

**Hamilton, Dorothy**
See  Jones, Dorothy

**Hamilton, Ed**
See  Hamilton, J. C.

**Hamilton, Edmond [Moore]**
1904-1977　[ESF, SF, SFL]
*American author*
* Blade, Alexander [house
pseudonym, Ziff-Davis]
* Castle, Robert
* Davidson, Hugh
* Garth, Will [house pseudonym]
* Hamilton, World Saver
* Sterling, Brett [house pseudonym,
Standard Magazines]
* Tenneshaw, S. M. [house
pseudonym, Ziff-Davis]
* Wentworth, Robert
* World Destroyer
* [The] World Wrecker

**Hamilton, Ernest**
See  Goddard, Ernest Hope

**Hamilton, Ernest**
See  Grossman, Josephine Judith

**Hamilton, Floyd** 1921-　[BB]
*American basketball player*
* Hamilton, Scotty

**Hamilton, Foreststorn** 1921-
[DAM, EJ, IBW]
*American jazz musician*
* Chico the Cat
* Hamilton, Chico

**Hamilton, Gail**
See  Corcoran, Barbara

**Hamilton, Gail**
See  Dodge, Mary Abigail

**Hamilton, George**
See  Davenport, Charles [Edward]

**Hamilton, George**
See  Teed, George Heber Hamilton

**Hamilton, George** 1888-　[NOJ]
*American jazz musician*
* Hamilton, Pop

**Hamilton, George** 1901-1957
[ASC]
*American composer and conductor*
* Hamilton, Spike

**Hamilton, George Rostrevor** 1888-
[WWL]
*British author and poet*
* Rostrevor, George

**Hamilton, Hairbreadth Harry**
See  Hamilton, Jack Edwin

**Hamilton, Ham**
See  Hamilton, Thomas Ball [Tom]

**Hamilton, Ian** 1950-　[AES]
*British soccer player*
* Hamilton, Chico

**Hamilton, J. C.** 20th c.　[OBW]
*American baseball player*
* Hamilton, Ed

**Hamilton, Jack**
See  Brannon, William T.

**Hamilton, Jack**
See  Floyd, Charles Arthur

**Hamilton, Jack Edwin** 1938-　[BE]
*American baseball player*
* Hamilton, Hairbreadth Harry

**Hamilton, Janet**　[SN]
*Scottish poet*
* [The] Peasant Poetess

**Hamilton, Joan Lesley** 1942-　[CA]
*British author*
* Cline, Joan

**Hamilton, John** 1911-1947　[WWJ]
*American jazz musician*
* Hamilton, Bugs

**Hamilton, John** 1916-
[BDF, FC, SW]
*American actor*
* Hayden, Sterling

**Hamilton, John** 20th c.　[BLB]
*American bank robber*
* Three Fingered Jack

**Hamilton, John H. [Jack]**
1879?-1925　[SC]
*American actor*
* Hamilton, Shorty

**Hamilton, Julia**
See  Watson, Julia

**Hamilton, Kate W.**　[FFF, PA]
*American author*
* Fleta

**Hamilton, Kay**
See  De Leeuw, Cateau Wilhelmina

**Hamilton, Leigh Brackett Douglass**
1915-1978　[WGT]
*American author*
* Brackett, Leigh

**Hamilton, Mary Agnes [Adamson]**
1883?-1966　[LC, TC, WW]
*Scottish author*
* Iconoclast

**Hamilton, Max**
See  Hammill, Cicely Mary

**Hamilton, May**
See  Tilt, Julia

**Hamilton, Michael**
See  Chetham-Strode, Warren

**Hamilton, Mollie**
See  Kaye, Mary Margaret [Mollie]

**Hamilton, Mrs.** 1730-1788　[RH]
*British actress*
* Tripe

**Hamilton, Murray** [joint pseudonym
with George Heber Teed]
See  Graydon, Robert Murray

**Hamilton, Murray** [joint pseudonym
with Robert Murray Graydon]
See  Teed, George Heber Hamilton

**Hamilton, Patrick** 1504?-1528?
[DNNF, DNNS, SN]
*Scottish religious reformer*
* [The] First Scotch Reformer

**Hamilton, Paul**
See  Dennis-Jones, H[arold]

**Hamilton, Pop**
See  Hamilton, George

**Hamilton, Raymond Lee** 1951-
[SMG]
*American football player*
* Hamilton, Sugar Bear

**Hamilton, Robert A.** 20th c.    [FB]
*American football player*
* Hamilton, Bones

**Hamilton, Robert Douglas**    [FFF]
*Canadian author*
* Pollock, Guy

**Hamilton, Robert W.**
See   Stratemeyer, Edward L.

**Hamilton, Scotty**
See   Hamilton, Floyd

**Hamilton, Shorty**
See   Hamilton, John H. [Jack]

**Hamilton, Single Speech**
See   Hamilton, William Gerard

**Hamilton, Sliding Billy**
See   Hamilton, William Robert

**Hamilton, Spike**
See   Hamilton, George

**Hamilton, Sugar Bear**
See   Hamilton, Raymond Lee

**Hamilton, [Sir] Thomas**   ?-1563
[DNNF, FFF, SN]
*Scottish barrister*
* Tam of the Cowgate

**Hamilton, [Capt.] Thomas**
1789-1842    [PA]
*Author*
* T. H.
* Thornton, Cyril

**Hamilton, Thomas Ball [Tom]**
1925-1973    [BE]
*American baseball player*
* Hamilton, Ham

**Hamilton, Wade**
See   Floren, Lee

**Hamilton, William**
See   Canaway, William Hamilton
[Bill]

**Hamilton, William Gerard**
1729-1796    [DNNS, RH, SN]
*British politician*
* Hamilton, Single Speech

**Hamilton, William Robert**
1866-1940    [AS, BE]
*American baseball player*
* Hamilton, Sliding Billy

**Hamilton, World Saver**
See   Hamilton, Edmond [Moore]

**Hamilton-Groves, Charles Antony
Bennett** 1941-    [OP]
*British producer, set designer, actor*
* Hamilton, Charles

**Hamilton-Hill, Donald** 1915-
[IAW]
*Canadian-born author*
* Gawaine, John

**Hamilton-Wilkes, Edwin Montague**
1914-    [AW]
*British author*
* Hamilton-Wilkes, Monty
* Uncle Monty

**Hamilton-Wilkes, Monty**
See   Hamilton-Wilkes, Edwin
Montague

**Hamlen, Georgia**    [FFF, PA]
*Author*
* Our Tender
* Stephenson, Valentine

**Hamlet, Ham**
See   Hamlet, L. Alton

**Hamlet, L. Alton** 1903-    [NAA]
*American journalist*
* Hamlet, Ham

**[The] Hamlet of the Halls**
See   Williams, Bransby

**Hamlet, Ova**
See   Lupoff, Richard Allen [Dick]

**Hamlin, Hot Potato**
See   Hamlin, Luke Daniel

**Hamlin, Luke Daniel** 1906-    [BE]
*American baseball player*
* Hamlin, Hot Potato

**Hamlin, Mrs. Paul**    [FFF]
*Entertainer*
* Newcomb, Ada

**Hamm, Marie Roberson** 1917-
[CA]
*American author*
* Roberson, Marie

**Hamm, T. D.**
See   Evans, Thelma D. Hamm

**Hamm, Thelma D.**
See   Evans, Thelma D. Hamm

**Hammack, Robert Dean Michael**
1944-    [IAW]
*American author and poet*
* Atlee, Phil
* Romack, D. M.

**Hammaersbough, Olga** 1899-
[BEW]
*American talent representative*
* Lee, Olga

**Hammam** 640?- 732?    [WBD]
*Arabic poet*
* Farazdaq, al-

**Hammarskjold, Lars** 1785-1827
[WBD]
*Swedish scholar*
* Hammarskjold, Lorenzo

**Hammarskjold, Lorenzo**
See   Hammarskjold, Lars

**[The] Hammer**
See   Aaron, Henry Louis [Hank]

**[The] Hammer**
See   Burrell, Stanley

**[The] Hammer**
See   Charles [or Karl]

**[The] Hammer**
See   Judas Asmonaeus

**[The] Hammer**
See   Schultz, David [Dave]

**[The] Hammer**
See   Williamson, Fred R.

**[The] Hammer and Scourge of
England**
See   Wallace, [Sir] William

**[The] Hammer of Heresies [or
Heretics]**
See   Augustine

**[The] Hammer of Heretics**
See   Ailly, Pierre d'

**[The] Hammer of Heretics**
See   Heigerlin, Johannes

**[The] Hammer of Kings and Thrones**
See   Cromwell, Oliver

**[The] Hammer of Monasteries**
See   Cromwell, Thomas [Earl of
Essex]

**[The] Hammer of Scotland**
See   Edward I

**[The] Hammer of the Arians**
See   Hilary

**[The] Hammer of the Monks**
See   Cromwell, Thomas [Earl of
Essex]

**Hammerbeck, Nick**
See   Browne, Nicholas Simon
Fitz-Gerald

**Hammergafferstein, Hans**
See   Longfellow, Henry Wadsworth

**Hammerich, Asger** 1843-1923
[BBD]
*Danish composer*
* Hamerik, Asger

**Hammerich, Bodil** 1878-1942
*Danish-born actress*
* Rosing, Bodil

**Hammerin' Hank Armstrong**
See   Jackson, Henry

**Hammerin' Hank Greenberg**
See   Greenberg, Henry Benjamin

**Hammerin' Henry [or Hank] Aaron**
See   Aaron, Henry Louis [Hank]

**Hammerken, Thomas** 1380-1471
[PA]
*Author*
* Kempis, Thomas A.

**Hammerlein, Felix**    [PA]
*Author*
* Malleolus

**Hammerling, Rupert** 1830-1889
[WBD]
*Austrian poet*
* Hamerling, Robert

**Hammersley, Cecil**
See   Crocombe, Leonard Cecil

**Hammerton, Grenville**
See   Shaw, Frank H.

**Hammerton, [Sir] John Alexander**
1871- ?    [WWL]
*British author*
* Orion

**Hammett, [Samuel] Dashiell**
1894-1961    [CC, EMD, WW]
*American author*
* Collinson, Peter

**Hammid, Alexander**
See   Hackenschmied, Alexander

**Hammill, Cicely Mary** 1872-1952
[BEW, MBF]
*British playwright, actress, writer*
* Hamilton, Cicely
* Hamilton, Max
* Rae, Scott

**Hammond, Anthony** 1668-1738
[DNNF, FFF]
*British poet*
* [The] Silver Tongued

**Hammond, Dorothy**
See   Plaskitt, Dorothy

**Hammond, Frances**
See   Croal, Frances A.

**Hammond, J. L.**
See   Hammond, John Lawrence Le
Breton

**Hammond, Jack**
See   Hammond, Walter Charles

**Hammond, James Henry**
1807-1864    [FFF]
*American statesman*
* Hammond, Mudsill

**Hammond, Jane**
See   Poland, Dorothy Elizabeth
Hayward

**Hammond, John Lawrence Le Breton**
1872-1949    [LC]
*British author and journalist*
* Hammond, J. L.

**Hammond, Johnny**
See   Smith, John Robert

**Hammond, Kate**
See   Kauffman, Helen Reed

**Hammond, Kay**
See   Standing, Dorothy

**Hammond, Keith** [joint pseudonym
with Catherine Lucile Moore]
See   Kuttner, Henry

**Hammond, Keith** [joint pseudonym
with Henry Kuttner]
See   Moore, Catherine Lucile

**Hammond, Lawrence Victor Francis**
1925-    [AW]
*British author and journalist*
* Francis, Victor

**Hammond, Mary Hope** 1877- ?
[NAA]
*American editor and writer*
* Harvey, Hope

**Hammond, Mrs.** 1847- ?    [PA]
*Author*
* Capsadell, Louise

**Hammond, Mudsill**
See   Hammond, James Henry

**Hammond, Orpha**
See   Turner, Orpha

**Hammond, Ralph**
See   Hammond Innes, Ralph

**Hammond, W. C.**
See   Hammond, William Charles

**Hammond, Wally**
See   Bolton, F. T.

**Hammond, Walter Charles**
1892-1942    [BE]
*American baseball player*
* Hammond, Jack

**Hammond, William Charles** 1890-
?    [BF]
*British director*
* Hammond, W. C.

**Hammond Innes, Ralph** 1913-
[B10, CA, WD]
*British author*
* Hammond, Ralph
* Innes, Hammond

**Hamner, Bruz**
See   Hamner, Ralph Conant

**Hamner, Granny**
See Hamner, Granville Wilbur

**Hamner, Granville Wilbur** 1927-
[BE]
*American baseball player*
* Hamner, Granny

**Hamner, Ralph Conant** 1916- [BE]
*American baseball player*
* Hamner, Bruz

**Hamon, [Count] Louis** 1866-1939
[NAD, SFL]
*Irish occultist*
* Cheiro
* Hamong, [Count] Leigh de

**Hamong, [Count] Leigh de**
See Hamon, [Count] Louis

**Hamp, Pierre**
See Bourillon, Pierre

**Hampden**
See Hooper, William

**Hampden, John**
See Grenville, George N.

**Hampden, John** 1898- [AW]
*British author*
* Montagu, Robert

**Hampden, Walter**
See Dougherty, Walter Hampden

**Hampshire, Hamps**
See Hampshire, John Harry

**Hampshire, John Harry** 1941-
[DC]
*British cricketer*
* Hampshire, Hamps

**Hampson, John**
See Simpson, John Hampson

**Hampton, Crow**
See Hampton, Rick

**Hampton, Ike**
See Hampton, Isaac Bernard

**Hampton, Isaac Bernard** 1951-
[SMG]
*American baseball player*
* Hampton, Ike

**Hampton, Kathleen** 1923- [CA]
*American author and journalist*
* Street, Lee

**Hampton, Locksley Wellington**
1932- [DAM, EJ]
*American jazz musician*
* Hampton, Slide

**Hampton, Mark**
See Norwood, Victor G[eorge]
C[harles]

**Hampton, Rick** 1956- [SMG]
*Canadian-born hockey player*
* Hampton, Crow

**Hampton, Robert**
See Freda, Riccardo

**Hampton, Slide**
See Hampton, Locksley Wellington

**Hamst, Olphar**
See Thomas, Ralph

**Hamsun, Knut**
See Pedersen, Knut

**Hamza** [HN, RH]
*Uncle of Mohammed, the Islamic
prophet*
* [The] Lion of God and His
Prophet

**Han Suyin**
See Comber, Elizabeth

**Han, Ulrich** ?-1478 [WBD]
*Austrian-born printer*
* Barbatus

**Han Wen-kung**
See Han Yu

**Han Yu** 768- 824 [WBD]
*Chinese poet, author, philosopher*
* Han Wen-kung
* [The] Prince of Literature

**Hanania, Stella** 20th c. [WFA]
*Lebanese-born fashion designer*
* Stella

**Hanauer, John Arno** 1929- [ART]
*German-born artist*
* J. A. H.

**Hanburger, Chris[tian]** 20th c.
*American football player*
* Hanburger, Grumpy

**Hanburger, Grumpy**
See Hanburger, Chris[tian]

**Hance, Margaret** 1924?-
*American politician*
* [The] Mother of the Mountains

**Hancken, Buddy**
See Hancken, Morris Medlock

**Hancken, Morris Medlock** 1914-
[SMG]
*American baseball player*
* Hancken, Buddy

**Hancock, Bill** 20th c. [GW]
*American rodeo performer*
* Hancock, Wild Bill

**Hancock, Frances**
See McNaught, Rosamond
Livingstone

**Hancock, Hazel**
See Mattox, Hazel

**Hancock, Herbert Jeffrey [Herbie]**
1940- [EJ7]
*American jazz musician*
* Mwandishi [Composer]

**Hancock, John** 1737-1793 [SN]
*American statesman*
* Empty Barrel
* Hancock, Old Mother

**Hancock, Malcolm** 1936- [CA]
*American cartoonist*
* Mal

**Hancock, Marty**
See Hancock, Myrtle J.

**Hancock, Myrtle J.** 1883?-1948
[BEW]
*American minstrel*
* Hancock, Marty

**Hancock, Old Mother**
See Hancock, John

**Hancock, Wild Bill**
See Hancock, Bill

**Hancock, Winfield Scott**
1824-1886 [DNNS, FFF, SN]
*American army officer and
politician*
* [The] Superb

**Hand Feet Errico**
See Errico, Greg

**Hand, Geoffrey Joseph Philip
Macaulay** 1931- [CA]
*Irish historian and author*
* Sweeney, Barry

**Hand, [Andrus] Jackson** 1913-
[CA]
*American author and editor*
* Carpenter, Fred

**Hand, John**
See Pierson, John H[erman]
G[roesbeck]

**Hand, John Raymond** 1886-1967
[IA]
*American author*
* [The] Hoosier Schoolmaster

**[The] Handcuff King**
See Brindmour, George

**[The] Handcuff King**
See Weiss, Ehrich

**Handel, Georg Friedrich**
1685-1759 [DEP, FFF, SN]
*German composer*
* Bold Briareus
* [The] Briareus of Music
* [The] Dear Saxon
* [The] Monarch of the Musical
Kingdom
* [The] Orpheus of the Eighteenth
Century
* [The] Saxon Giant
* [The] Thunderbolt

**Handford, Thomas W.** [FFF]
*American author*
* Elmo

**Handiboe, Aloysius James**
1887-1953 [BE]
*American baseball player*
* Handiboe, Coalyard Mike
* Handiboe, Mike

**Handiboe, Coalyard Mike**
See Handiboe, Aloysius James

**Handiboe, Mike**
See Handiboe, Aloysius James

**Handl [or Haendl], Jakob**
1550-1591 [WBD]
*German composer*
* Gallus, Jacobus

**Handler, Motsy**
See Handler, Philip Jacob

**Handler, Philip Jacob** 1908- [EJS]
*American football player*
* Handler, Motsy

**Handley, Jeep**
See Handley, Lee Elmer

**Handley, Lee Elmer** 1913-1970
[BE, BTB]
*American baseball player*
* Handley, Jeep

**Handschin, Charles Hart** 1873- ?
[ALY]
*American author*
* Frederick, Walter

**[The] Handsome**
See Albert I [or Albrecht]

**[The] Handsome**
See Ferdinand I

**[The] Handsome**
See Frederick III

**[The] Handsome**
See Geoffrey IV

**[The] Handsome**
See Philip I

**Handsome Al Raschid**
See George IV

**Handsome Beard**
See Baldwin IV

**[The] Handsome Englishman**
See Churchill, John [First Duke of
Marlborough]

**Handsome Frank**
See Pierce, Franklin

**Handsome Harry Howell**
See Howell, Harry

**Handsome Harry Taylor**
See Taylor, Harry Warren

**Handsome Henry Boyle**
See Boyle, Henry J.

**Handsome Hugh McQuillan**
See McQuillan, Hugh A.

**Handsome Jack Carney**
See Carney, John Joseph [Jack]

**Handsome Ransom Jackson**
See Jackson, Ransom Joseph

**[The] Handsome Swordsman**
See Murat, Joachim

**Handy Andy High**
See High, Andrew Aird

**Handy Andy Pafko**
See Pafko, Andrew

**Handy, Captain John**
See Handy, John

**Handy, George**
See Hendleman, George Joseph

**Handy, H. Jamison** 20th c. [BBH]
*American swimmer and contributor
of new swimming techniques*
* [The] Father of Modern
Swimming
* Handy, Jam

**Handy, Jam**
See Handy, H. Jamison

**Handy, John** 1900-1971 [WWJ]
*American jazz musician*
* Handy, Captain John

**Handy, W. C.**
See Handy, William Christopher

**Handy, William Christopher**
1873-1958 [ASC, PMJ]
*American composer*
* [The] Father of the Blues
* Handy, W. C.

**Handysides, Mrs. Clarence** [FFF]
*Entertainer*
* Baker, Katie

**Haney, Fred Girard** 1898-1977
[BE, PB]
*American baseball player, manager, sportscaster*
* Haney, Pudge

**Haney, J. Francis**
*See* Haney, Will J.

**Haney, Pudge**
*See* Haney, Fred Girard

**Haney, Will J.** ?-1964 [BEW]
*Theatrical performer*
* Haney, J. Francis

**[The] Hanging Judge**
*See* Khalkhali, [Ayatollah] Sadegh

**[The] Hanging Judge**
*See* Norbury, Earl of

**[The] Hanging Judge**
*See* Page, [Sir] Francis

**[The] Hanging Judge**
*See* Parker, Isaac

**[The] Hanging Judge**
*See* Toler, John [Earl of Norbury]

**[The] Hangman**
*See* Cantonwine, Howard

**[The] Hangman**
*See* Heydrich, Reinhard

**[The] Hangman of Buffalo**
*See* Cleveland, [Stephen] Grover

**[The] Hangman of Hilversum**
*See* Stender, Jan

**[The] Hangman of Lithuania**
*See* Mouravieff, Nicholas

**[The] Hangman of the Ardeatine Caves**
*See* Kappler, Herbert

**[The] Hangman of the East**
*See* Balcys, Wilhelm

**Hangsleben, Alan** 1953- [SMG]
*American hockey player*
* Hangsleben, Fonzie

**Hangsleben, Fonzie**
*See* Hangsleben, Alan

**Hanif Mohammad** 1934- [EC]
*Pakistani cricketer*
* Little Tich

**Hanifin, J.** 20th c. [SFP]
*Author*
* Phineas

**Hank, Deaf Charley**
*See* Hanks, O. C.

**Hank the Deuce**
*See* Ford, Henry, II

**Hank the Drifter**
*See* Andrade, Daniel Ray

**Hankerson, Alvin** 1923-
[BWW, NBB]
*American singer*
* Guitar Nubbitt

**Hankey, Rosalie A.**
*See* Wax, Rosalie [Amelia] H.

**Hankins, Arthur Preston** 1880- ?
[NAA, WW]
*American author*
* Arthur, H. Preston
* Kinsburn, Emart
* Preston, Arthur

**Hankins, Clabe**
*See* McDonald, Erwin L[awrence]

**Hankins, Paul** 1937- [NBB]
*American musician*
* Hankins, Tall Paul

**Hankins, Tall Paul**
*See* Hankins, Paul

**Hankinson, Charles James** 1866- ?
[LAO]
*British author*
* Holland, Clive

**Hankla, Donna Maria** 20th c. [OP]
*American opera singer*
* Dornya, Maria

**Hanks, Camilla**
*See* Hanks, O. C.

**Hanks, O. C.** [BLB]
*American train robber*
* Hank, Deaf Charley
* Hanks, Camilla
* Jones, Charley

**Hanks, Robert Lowery** 1916-1971
[FC]
*American actor*
* Lowery, Robert

**Hanlan, Edward [Ned]** 1855-1908
[CSH]
*Canadian rowboat racer*
* [The] Boy in Blue

**Hanley, Clifford** 1922-
[AW, CA, CC]
*Scottish author and journalist*
* Calvin, Henry

**Hanley, Emma**
*See* Allen, Louise

**Hanley, Hugh**
*See* Price, Emerson Field

**Hanley, James** 1901- [CA, WD]
*Irish-born author and playwright*
* Shone, Patric

**Hanley, Josie**
*See* Donnelly, Mrs. John F.

**Hanley, Mrs. Phillips** [FFF]
*Entertainer*
* Drew, May Niblo

**Hanlon, Big Bill**
*See* Hanlon, William [Bill]

**Hanlon, John**
*See* Mitchell, John Hanlon

**Hanlon, William [Bill]** 20th c. [BE]
*American baseball player*
* Hanlon, Big Bill

**Hanly, D. P.**
*See* Hanly, Daithi Patrick

**Hanly, Daithi Patrick** 1917- [ART]
*Irish architect, landscape designer, sculptor*
* D. P. H.
* Hanly, D. P.

**Hann, Roma** 1902-1947 [SC]
*American actress*
* Roma, Clarice

**Hanna, Frances [Nichols]** 20th c.
[WW]
*Author*
* Nichols, Fan

**Hanna, Jake**
*See* Hanna, John

**Hanna, John** 1931- [EJ7]
*American jazz musician*
* Hanna, Jake

**Hanna, Mary T.** 1935- [CA]
*American author*
* Cole, Mary

**Hannah, Ham Hocks**
*See* Hannah, John Allen

**Hannah, James Harrison** 1891-
[BE]
*American baseball player*
* Hannah, Truck

**Hannah, John Allen** 1951- [SMG]
*American football player*
* Hannah, Ham Hocks

**Hannah, Persis Dwight** 20th c.
[B10]
*American journalist*
* Dwight, Phoebe

**Hannah, Truck**
*See* Hannah, James Harrison

**Hannam, Edna** 1908-1957 [SC]
*American actress*
* Marion, Edna

**Hannaway, Patricia H[inman] [Patti]**
1929- [CA]
*American writer*
* Charnance, L. P.

**Hannay, James Owen** 1865-1950
[BEW, LAO, LC]
*Irish-born playwright and author*
* Birmingham, George A.

**Hannays, Kitty** 1930?- [CW]
*Trinidadian author and journalist*
* Macaw

**Hanneford, Edwin** [F2]
*Actor*
* Hanneford, Poodles

**Hanneford, Poodles**
*See* Hanneford, Edwin

**Hannegan, Dennis** [PA]
*Author*
* Robinson, Doctor

**Hannen, Athene** 1889- [SW]
*British actress*
* Seyler, Athene

**Hannet, John** [PA]
*Author*
* Arnet

**Hannibal**
*See* Alexander, Stanley Walter

**Hannibal**
*See* Peterson, Marvin

**Hannibal**
*See* Silliman, George Joseph L. W.

**Hannibal** 3rd c. BC
[DEP, DNNS, FF]
*Carthaginian general*
* [The] Carthaginian Lion
* [The] Mall of Italy

**Hannibal, Julius Caesar**
*See* Levison, J.

**[The] Hannibal of Batavia**
*See* Civilis, Julius

**Hanno** 3rd c. BC [DNNS, WBD]
*Carthaginian politician*
* [The] Great

**Hannoch, Leonard John** 20th c.
[BEW]
*American talent representative, director, producer*
* Lenny, Jack

**[The] Hannotin of Flanders**
*See* John [or Jean]

**Hans of Cuestrin**
*See* John

**Hansell, Antonina**
*See* Looker, Antonina [Hansell]

**Hansen, Andrew Viggo** 1924- [BE]
*American baseball player*
* Hansen, Swede

**Hansen, Anton** 1878-1940 [EWL]
*Estonian author and playwright*
* Tammsaare, A. H.

**Hansen, Asgar** 1926-
*American oilwell troubleshooter*
* Hansen, Boots

**Hansen, Barry** 1941-
*American disc jockey*
* Demento, Dr.

**Hansen, Boots**
*See* Hansen, Asgar

**Hansen, Ellen** 1913?- [FC, SW]
*American actress*
* Corby, Ellen

**Hansen, Emil** 1867-1956 [CAR]
*German painter*
* Nolde, Emil

**Hansen, Henry Olaf** 1887-1960
[SC]
*Norwegian-born actor*
* Tenbrook, Harry

**Hansen, Joseph** 1923- [CA]
*American author*
* Brock, Rose
* Colton, James
* Coulton, James

**Hansen, Jurij** 1938- [CA]
*Danish author and composer*
* Moskvitin, Jurij

**Hansen, Kaja Andrea Karoline Eide**
1884-1968 [DAM]
*Norwegian opera singer*
* Norena, Eide

**Hansen, L. Taylor**
*See* Hansen, Louis Ingvald

**Hansen, Louis Ingvald** 1904-
[WGT]
*Author*
* Hansen, L. Taylor

**Hansen, Mike**
*See* Rifkin, Stanley Mark

**Hansen, Roy Emil** 1907- [BE]
*American baseball player*
* Hansen, Snipe

**Hansen, Snipe**
*See* Hansen, Roy Emil

**Hansen, Swede**
*See* Hansen, Andrew Viggo

**Hanshew, Hazel Phillips** [joint pseudonym with Thomas W. Hanshew]
*See* Hanshew, Mary E.

**Hanshew, Hazel Phillips** [joint pseudonym with Mary E. Hanshew]
*See* Hanshew, Thomas W.

**Hanshew, Mary E.** 20th c. [WW]
*Author*
* Hanshew, Hazel Phillips [joint pseudonym with Thomas W. Hanshew]
* Kingsley, Anna [joint pseudonym with Thomas W. Hanshew]

**Hanshew, Thomas W.** 1857-1914 [CC, EMD, WW]
*Author*
* Carter, Nicholas?
* Hanshew, Hazel Phillips [joint pseudonym with Mary E. Hanshew]
* Kingsley, Anna [joint pseudonym with Mary E. Hanshew]
* Kingsley, Charlotte May

**Hansi**
*See* Hirschmann, Maria Anne

**Hansi**
*See* Waltz, J. Jacques

**Hanski, Don[ald Thomas]**
*See* Hanyzewski, Donald Thomas

**Hanson, Earl Sylvester** 1896- [BE]
*American baseball player*
* Hanson, Ollie

**Hanson, Eddy**
*See* Hanson, Ethwell

**Hanson, Ethwell** 20th c. [ASC]
*American composer and musician*
* Hanson, Eddy

**Hanson, Gladys**
*See* Cook, Gladys Hanson

**Hanson, Irene [Forsythe]** 1898- [CA]
*American missionary and author*
* Forsythe, Irene

**Hanson, John**
*See* Watts, John

**Hanson, Michael** 1936- [IAW]
*British author*
* Heman, Nicholas

**Hanson, Ollie**
*See* Hanson, Earl Sylvester

**Hanson, Raymond W.** 20th c. [BBH]
*American coach and collegiate athletic director*
* Hanson, Rock

**Hanson, Rock**
*See* Hanson, Raymond W.

**Hanson, V. J.** 20th c. [MBF]
*British author*
* Reid, Desmond [house pseudonym]

**Hanson, Winifred** 1901-1971 [EMT, F2, FC]
*American actress, singer, dancer*
* Lightner, Winnie

**Hansraj Bhatia**
*See* Oak, Purushottam Nagesh

**Hansson, Laura** 1854-1928 [WBD]
*Swedish author*
* Marholm, Laura

**Hanussen, Eric**
*See* Steinschneider, Hermann

**Hanyzewski, Donald Thomas** 1916-1957 [BE]
*American baseball player*
* Hanski, Don[ald Thomas]

**Haozous, Bob**
*See* Houser, Robert Lee

**Hapi**
*See* Jack, Alex

**[The] Happy**
*See* Emanuel I [Manuel or Manoel]

**Happy Fanny Fields**
*See* Fields, Fanny

**Happy Jack Chesbro**
*See* Chesbro, John Dwight

**Happy Jack Hawn**
*See* Hawn, John

**Happy Jack Stivetts**
*See* Stivetts, John Elmer

**Happy John**
*See* Roberts, Edwin F.

**Happy, John**
*See* Roberts, J. P.

**[The] Happy Little Dutch Girl**
*See* Fields, Fanny

**[The] Happy Philosopher**
*See* Campbell, Bill

**[The] Happy Tramp**
*See* McGregor, Edward

**[The] Happy Warrior**
*See* Humphrey, Hubert Horatio

**[The] Happy Warrior**
*See* Roosevelt, Theodore [Teddy]

**[The] Happy Warrior**
*See* Smith, Al[fred Emanuel]

**Hara, Nobuo**
*See* Tsukahara, Nobuo

**Harada, Fighting**
*See* Harada, Masahiko

**Harada, Katsuhiro**
*See* Harada, Ushiwakamaru

**Harada, Masahiko** 1943- [BX, RBE]
*Japanese boxer*
* Harada, Fighting

**Harada, Ushiwakamaru** 1947- [RBE]
*Japanese boxer*
* Harada, Katsuhiro

**Harald, Eric**
*See* Boesen, Victor

**Harbach, Otto**
*See* Hauerbach, Otto Abels

**Harbage, Alfred B[ennett]** 1901- [CA, CC, EMD]
*American educator and author*
* Kyd, Thomas

**Harbaugh, Thomas Chalmers** 1849-1924 [EMD, WW]
*Author*
* Carter, Nicholas?
* Collier, Old Cap
* Grant, [Major] A. F.
* Holmes, [Capt.] Howard
* Howard, Charles
* Inman, Robert Randolph?
* Lincoln, Howard

**Harbaugh, Thomas Chalmers** (Continued)
* Scott, [Major] S. S.

**Harbert, Chick**
*See* Harbert, Melvin R.

**Harbert, Melvin R.** 1915- [EG, GF, GME]
*American golfer*
* Harbert, Chick

**Harbin, Robert**
*See* Williams, Ned

**Harbinson, A. Marshall** 1896- [NAA]
*American journalist*
* Howard, Paul

**Harbinson, Robert**
*See* Bryans, Robert Harbinson [Robin]

**Harbinson, William Allen** 1941- [CA]
*Irish-born editor and author*
* Howarth, John

**Harbour, Pearl**
*See* Gates, Pearl Ann

**Harburg, E. Y.**
*See* Harburg, Edgar Yipsel

**Harburg, Edgar Yipsel** 1898-1981 [ASC, DAM, TR]
*American lyricist and librettist*
* Harburg, E. Y.
* Harburg, Yip

**Harburg, Yip**
*See* Harburg, Edgar Yipsel

**Harcourt, Alice** 1869?-1947 [BEW]
*American actress*
* Fischer, Alice

**Harcourt, Edward**
*See* Vernon, Edward

**Harcourt, James**
*See* Hudson, James

**Harcourt, Melville** 1909- [CA]
*British-born clergyman and author*
* Criticus

**Harcourt, Mrs. William** [FFF]
*Entertainer*
* Balfe, Louise

**Harcourt, Thomas A.** 20th c. [WGT]
*Author*
* Herman, William [joint pseudonym with Ambrose (Gwinett) Bierce]

**Harcourt, [Sir] William Vernon** 1827-? [DEL]
*British author*
* Historicus

**Hard Cider**
*See* Harrison, William Henry

**Hard, Edward W[ilhelm], Jr.** 1939- [CA]
*American author*
* Hard, T. W.

**Hard, Francis**
*See* Wright, Farnsworth

**Hard Guy Bedwell**
*See* Bedwell, Harvey Guy

**[The] Hard Luck Girl**
*See* Robertson, Mary Imogene

**Hard Luck Hank**
*See* Bruder, Hank

**Hard Pan**
*See* Bonner, Geraldine

**[The] Hard Rock from Down Under**
*See* Heeney, Tom

**Hard Ruler**
*See* Harold III

**Hard, T. W.**
*See* Hard, Edward W[ilhelm], Jr.

**Hardcastle, Daniel**
*See* Page, Richard

**Hardcastle, Ephraim**
*See* Pyne, William Henry

**Hardcastle, Michael** 1933- [CA, WD]
*British author*
* Clark, David

**Hardeen**
*See* Weiss, Theo

**Harden, Maximilian**
*See* Witkowski, Maximilian

**Harden-Hickey, James** [PA]
*Author*
* Saint Patrice

**Hardenberg, Friedrich von** 1772-1801 [DNNF, FFF, HN]
*German poet*
* Novalis
* [The] Pascal of Germany

**Harder, Chief**
*See* Harder, Melvin Le Roy

**Harder, Marlin** 1922- [FB]
*American football player*
* Harder, Pat

**Harder, Melvin Le Roy** 1909- [BE, PB]
*American baseball player*
* Harder, Chief
* Harder, Wimpy

**Harder, Pat**
*See* Harder, Marlin

**Harder, Wimpy**
*See* Harder, Melvin Le Roy

**Hardforth, Carrie**
*See* Becker, Max O[ctavius]

**Hardge, Johnny** [BWW]
*American entertainer*
* Hodges, Johnny

**Hardham, John** [SN]
*British merchant*
* [The] Maecenas of Embryo Players

**[Le] Hardi**
*See* Philip [or Philippe]

**[Le] Hardi**
*See* Philip III [or Philippe]

**Hardi, Alexandre** 17th c. [SN]
*French playwright and actor*
* [The] French Lope da Vega
* [A] Shakespeare Without Genius

**Hardie, A. M.**
*See* Hardie, Alexander Merrie

**Hardie, Alexander Merrie** 1910-
[ART]
*British painter*
* Hardie, A. M.

**Hardie, Brian Ross** 1950- [DC]
*British cricketer*
* Hardie, Lager

**Hardie, David**
*See* McLean, John David Ruari

**Hardie, [James] Keir** 1856-1915
[NN]
*British politician*
* Hardie, Queer

**Hardie, Lager**
*See* Hardie, Brian Ross

**Hardie, Laura Constance**
1878-1955 [F1, F2, FC]
*British actress*
* Collier, Constance

**Hardie, Maisie** 1901- [THR]
*British actress*
* Darrell, Maisie

**Hardie, Queer**
*See* Hardie, [James] Keir

**Hardie, Robert** [PA]
*Author*
* Reid, Hartlaw
* Trebor, Eidrah

**Hardin**
*See* Weiss, Theo

**Hardin, Bud**
*See* Hardin, William Edgar

**Hardin, Clement**
*See* Newton, Dwight Bennett

**Hardin, Glenn** 1910?-1975 [B10]
*American track and field athlete*
* Hardin, Slats

**Hardin, L. S.** 1840- ? [PA]
*Author*
* Nibrah

**Hardin, Louis Thomas** 1916- [EJ]
*American jazz musician*
* Moondog

**Hardin, Mitch**
*See* Gerrity, David James

**Hardin, Peter**
*See* Vaczek, Louis Charles

**Hardin, Slats**
*See* Hardin, Glenn

**Hardin, Tom**
*See* Bauer, Erwin A.

**Hardin, Ty**
*See* Hungerford, Orton [or Orison]
Whipple, II

**Hardin, Wes**
*See* Keevill, Henry J[ohn]

**Hardin, William Edgar** 1922- [BE]
*American baseball player*
* Hardin, Bud

**Harding, Ann**
*See* Gatley, Dorothy Walton

**Harding, Bertita**
*See* Radetzky Von Radetz,
[Countess] Berta Leonarz De
Harding

**Harding, Buster**
*See* Harding, Lavere

**Harding, Carl B.**
*See* Barker, Elver A.

**Harding, Charles H. [Charlie]**
1891- [BE]
*American baseball player*
* Harding, Slim

**Harding, David Llewellyn**
1867-1952 [BEW, FC]
*British actor*
* Harding, Lyn

**Harding, Donald Edward** 1916-
[CA]
*American author, poet, playwright*
* Day, Donald
* Edwards, Donald Earl
* Parrish, Eugene

**Harding, Edith**
*See* Dazey, Mrs. Charles T.

**Harding, George**
*See* Raubenheimer, George
Harding

**Harding, Jumbo**
*See* Harding, Lou[is Edward]

**Harding, Lavere** 1917-1965
[DAM, EJ, PMJ]
*American jazz musician*
* Harding, Buster

**Harding, Lee** 1937- [ESF]
*Australian author*
* Nye, Harold G.

**Harding, Lou[is Edward]** 20th c.
[BE]
*American baseball player*
* Harding, Jumbo

**Harding, Lyn**
*See* Harding, David Llewellyn

**Harding, Matthew Whiteman [Matt]**
*See* Floren, Lee

**Harding, Mrs. Roger** [FFF]
*Entertainer*
* Oakley, Daisy

**Harding, Muriel** 1886- [F1, FC]
*British-born actress*
* Petrova, Olga

**Harding, Slim**
*See* Harding, Charles H. [Charlie]

**Harding, William** [FFF]
*American writer*
* Bashibazouk
* Fac et Spera

**Hardinge, Belle Boyd** 1843-1900
[FFF]
*American Confederate spy*
* Boyd, Belle

**Hardinge, Charles Wrexe** 1904-
[MBF]
*British author*
* Hardinge, Rex
* Quintin, Rex
* Wrexe, Charles

**Hardinge, George** 1744-1816 [PA]
*Author*
* Felix, Minutius

**Hardinge, George Edward Charles**
1921- [LC, WW]
*British author*
* Milner, George

**Hardinge, Rex**
*See* Hardinge, Charles Wrexe

**Hardinge, Thomas** 1512-1572 [PA]
*Author*
* [A] Layman

**Hardison, Osborne B.** 1928- [WD]
*American author, critic, poet*
* Bennett, H. O.

**Hardman, Richards Lynden** 1924-
[CA]
*American producer and author*
* Howitzer, Bronson

**Hardt, Richard** 1907- [ASC]
*American composer and musician*
* Kapp, Paul

**Hardwick, Archer** 1918- [ASC]
*American composer and musician*
* Archer, George

**Hardwick, Cathy**
*See* Shura, Kashina

**Hardwick, Homer**
*See* Rogers, Paul [Patrick]

**Hardwick, Huntington R.**
1892-1949 [AS, FB]
*American football player*
* Hardwick, Tack

**Hardwick, Louis** [SG]
*Boxer*
* [The] Cocoa Kid

**Hardwick, [John] Michael [Drinkrow]**
1924- [CA, WD]
*British author and playwright*
* Drinkrow, John

**Hardwick, Mollie** 20th c. [CA]
*British author and playwright*
* Atkinson, Mary

**Hardwick, Otto** 1904-1970
[EJ, PMJ, WWJ]
*American jazz musician*
* Hardwick, Toby

**Hardwick, Richard Holmes, Jr.**
1923- [CA, SAT]
*American author*
* Holmes, Rick

**Hardwick, Sylvia**
*See* Doherty, Ivy R. Duffy

**Hardwick, Tack**
*See* Hardwick, Huntington R.

**Hardwick, Toby**
*See* Hardwick, Otto

**Hardwicke, Cecil Webster**
1893-1964 [BF, SC]
*British actor, director, producer*
* Hardwicke, [Sir] Cedric

**Hardwicke, [Sir] Cedric**
*See* Hardwicke, Cecil Webster

**[The] Hardy**
*See* Douglas, [Sir] William

**Hardy, Adam**
*See* Bulmer, [Henry] Kenneth

**Hardy, Alice Dale** [house
pseudonym] [Stratemeyer
Syndicate]
*See* Stratemeyer, Edward L.

**Hardy, Arthur S.**
*See* Steffens, Arthur

**Hardy, Babe**
*See* Hardy, Norvell

**Hardy, Bobbie**
*See* Hardy, Marjorie Enid

**Hardy, C. Colburn** 1910- [CA]
*American public relations executive
and author*
* Blake, Jonas
* Munn, Hart
* Peck, Leonard

**Hardy, Douglas**
*See* Andrews, [Charles] Robert
D[ouglas Hardy]

**Hardy, Florence Deric**
*See* Small, Florence

**Hardy, Francis Joseph** 1923- [BE]
*American baseball player*
* Hardy, Red

**Hardy, Jason**
*See* Oxley, William

**Hardy, Jocelyn** 1945- [CEI]
*Canadian-born hockey player*
* Hardy, Joe

**Hardy, Joe**
*See* Hardy, Jocelyn

**Hardy, Marjorie Enid** 1913-
[AW, WD]
*Australian author*
* Hardy, Bobbie

**Hardy, Mark**
*See* May, Herbert Richard
Duffield

**Hardy, Norvell** 1892-1957
[BDF, WEF]
*American comic actor*
* Hardy, Babe
* Hardy, Oliver

**Hardy, Oliver**
*See* Hardy, Norvell

**Hardy, Phillip**
*See* Lowe, Claud D.

**Hardy, Red**
*See* Hardy, Francis Joseph

**Hardy, Robert**
*See* Clark, Robert Henry Hardy

**Hardy, Russ**
*See* Snow, Charles Horace

**Hardy, Sam**
*See* Hayes, Samuel Stewart

**Hardy, Stuart**
*See* Schisgal, Oscar

**Hardy, W. G.**
*See* Hardy, William George

**Hardy, Walter** 1904- [WEF]
*British photographer and designer*
* Beaton, Cecil

**Hardy, William George** 1895-
[SFL]
*Canadian author*
* Hardy, W. G.

**Hare, Auburn** 1930- [NBB]
*American musician*
* Hare, Pat

**Hare, Cyril**
*See* Clark, Alfred Alexander
Gordon

**Hare, Emily**
*See* Winthrop, Laura

**Hare, Harriet**   [PA]
*Author*
* Flemming, Harford

**Hare, [Sir] John**
*See* Fairs, John

**Hare, Martin**
*See* Girling, Zoe

**Hare, Pat**
*See* Hare, Auburn

**Hare, Robert**
*See* Hutchinson, Robert Hare

**Hare, Robert** 1781-1858   [FFF]
*American chemist and writer*
* Grayson, Eldred

**Hare, T. Truxton** 1878-1956
[BBH]
*American football player*
* Hare, Trux

**Hare, Trux**
*See* Hare, T. Truxton

**Hare, William Hobart** 1838-1909
[WBD]
*American prelate*
* [The] Apostle to the Sioux

**Hareen, Malcolm** 1937-
*Canadian dancer*
* Blisterfeet

**Harefoot**
*See* Harold I

**Harel-Fisch, Aharon**
*See* Fisch, Harold

**Harford, Henry**
*See* Hudson, William Henry

**Harford, John** 1938?-
*American musician*
* Hartford, John

**Hargate, Frederick [Freddie]**
1911?-1968   [BMH, SC]
*British comedian and actor*
* Frinton, Freddie

**Harge, Ira** 20th c.   [MEB]
*American basketball player*
* Harge, Large

**Harge, Large**
*See* Harge, Ira

**Hargo, Chocolate**
*See* Hargo, Duane

**Hargo, Duane** 1961-   [IBW]
*American rodeo bullfighter*
* Hargo, Chocolate

**Hargrave, Bubbles**
*See* Hargrave, Eugene Franklin

**Hargrave, Eugene Franklin**
1892-1969   [BE, DGS, PB]
*American baseball player*
* Hargrave, Bubbles

**Hargrave, John** 1894-   [WWL]
*British author*
* White Fox

**Hargrave, Leoni?**
*See* Vidal, Eugene Luther, Jr.

**Hargrave, Leonie**
*See* Disch, Thomas M.

**Hargrave, Pinky**
*See* Hargrave, William McKinley

**Hargrave, William McKinley**
1896-1942   [BE]
*American baseball player*
* Hargrave, Pinky

**Hargreaves, Reginald [Charles]**
1888-   [CAP, SFP]
*British author*
* Aiguillette
* Melville, Lewis [joint pseudonym
   with Lewis Saul Benjamin]

**Hargreaves-Mawdsley, W[illiam]**
**Norman** 1921-   [CA]
*British-born historian and author*
* Mawdsley, Norman

**Hari Kari**
*See* Carr, Elias F.

**Haring, G. W. H.**   [PA]
*Author*
* W. S.

**Haring, John**   [HN]
*Defended Diemerdyke against the*
*Spaniards*
* Horatius Cocles of the Horn

**Haring [or Haering], Wilhelm**
1798-1871   [FFF, WBD]
*German author*
* Alexis, Wilibald

**Hark, Mildred**
*See* McQueen, Mildred Hark

**Harkavy, Zvi** 1908-   [IAW]
*Israeli author*
* Yerushalmi, Gershon
* Zvi, H.

**Harkaway**
*See* Marshall, Charles

**Harkaway, Hal**
*See* Stratemeyer, Edward L.

**Harkaway, Jack**
*See* Hemynge, Bracebridge

**Harkins, John Joseph** 1859-1940
[BE]
*American baseball player*
* Harkins, Pa

**Harkins, Pa**
*See* Harkins, John Joseph

**Harkins, Philip** 1912-
[B10, CA, SAT]
*American author*
* Blaine, John [joint pseudonym
   with Harold Leland Goodwin]

**Harkness, Edith Myrtella** 20th c.
[NAA]
*American author and poet*
* Southerland, Myrtella

**Harkness, Frederick Harvey**
1887-1952   [BE]
*American baseball player*
* Harkness, Specs

**Harkness, Specs**
*See* Harkness, Frederick Harvey

**Harkness, Thomas William** 1937-
[BE]
*Canadian-born baseball player*
* Harkness, Tim

**Harkness, Tim**
*See* Harkness, Thomas William

**Harknett, Terry** 1936-   [CA]
*British author*
* Chandler, Frank

**Harknett, Terry** (Continued)
* Ford, David
* Gilman, George G.
* Harman, Jane
* Hedges, Joseph
* James, William M. [joint
   pseudonym with Laurence James]
* Pike, Charles R.
* Pine, William
* Russell, James
* Stone, Thomas H.
* Terry, William

**Harkreader, Fiddlin' Sid**
*See* Harkreader, Sid

**Harkreader, Sid** 1898-   [CWG]
*American country-western performer*
* Harkreader, Fiddlin' Sid

**Harkshaw, Mrs.** 19th c.   [FFF]
*British author*
* Aunt Effie

**Harkwood**
*See* Acuto, John

**Harlan**
*See* Shaw, William Harlan

**Harlan, Glen**
*See* Cebulash, Mel

**Harland, Ada**
*See* Mathews, Mrs. Brander

**Harland, Henry** 1861-1905
[FFF, LC, WBD]
*Russian-born American author*
* Luska, Sidney

**Harland, Marion**
*See* Terhune, Mary Virginia
[Hawes]

**Harle, Dennis F.** 1920-   [ART]
*British painter*
* D.

**Harle, Elizabeth**
*See* Roberts, Irene M.

**[The] Harlem Hitler**
*See* Jordan, Robert Obadiah

**[The] Harlem Hotshot**
*See* Smith, Walker

**[The] Harlem Hurricane**
*See* Smith, Walker

**Harlem Joe Kiefer**
*See* Kiefer, Joseph William [Joe]

**[The] Harlem Spider**
*See* Kelly, Tommy

**Harlem Tommy Kelly**
*See* Kelly, Tommy

**Harlem Tommy Murphy**
*See* Murphy, Tommy

**Harlem's Favorite**
*See* Hegamin, Lucille

**Harlem's Mae West**
*See* Sylvester, Hannah

**Harlem's Son of Fun**
*See* Russell, Nipsey

**[The] Harlequin**
*See* Charles V

**Harlequin**
*See* Harley, Robert [First Earl of
Oxford]

**Harlequin**
*See* Reed, Alexander Wyclif

**Harley, Charles W.** 1893?-1974
[B10, FB, SMG]
*American football player*
* Harley, Chic

**Harley, [Lady] Charlotte** 1809- ?
[SN]
*Friend of British poet, Lord Byron*
* Ianthe

**Harley, Chic**
*See* Harley, Charles W.

**Harley, Dick**
*See* Harley, Henry Risk

**Harley, Henry Risk** 1874-1961
[BE]
*American baseball player*
* Harley, Dick

**Harley, John**
*See* Marsh, John

**Harley, Mark** 1860-1937   [THR]
*British playwright*
* Ambient, Mark

**Harley, Robert [First Earl of Oxford]**
1661-1724   [FFF, HN, SN]
*British statesman*
* Bold, Roger
* Harlequin
* Hermodactyl
* [The] King of Book-Collectors

**Harling, Thomas**
*See* Eastham, Thomas

**Harlock, K. W.**   [PA]
*Author*
* Scrutator

**Harlow, Jean**
*See* Carpenter [or Carpentier?],
Harlean

**Harman, Jane**
*See* Harknett, Terry

**Harmensen [or Hermansz], Jacob**
1560-1609   [WBD]
*Dutch theologian*
* Arminius, Jacobus

**Harmer, Anthony**
*See* Wharton, Henry

**Harmer, Ruth Mulvey** 1919-   [CA]
*American author and journalist*
* Mulvey, Ruth Watt

**Harmon, Big Ed**
*See* Harmon, Ed

**Harmon, David** 20th c.   [RM]
*Musician*
* Dee, Dave

**Harmon, Ed** 1946-   [SMG]
*American football player*
* Harmon, Big Ed

**Harmon, Ernest Nason** 1894-1979
*American army officer*
* Old Gravel Voice

**Harmon, H. H.**
*See* Williams, Robert Moore

**Harmon, Hickory Bob**
*See* Harmon, Robert Greene

**Harmon, Jack**
*See* Boring, Wayne

**Harmon, Jim** 20th c.   [SFP]
*Author*
* Grey, Judson [joint pseudonym
   with Ron Haydock]

**Harmon, Jim** (Continued)
* Newton, Clark

**Harmon, Nancy** 20th c.   [WD]
*Author*
* St. John, Leonie [joint pseudonym
  with William Bayer]

**Harmon, Robert Greene** 1887-1961
[BE]
*American baseball player*
* Harmon, Hickory Bob

**Harmon, Thomas D.** 1919-   [FB]
*American football player*
* Old 98

**Harmonica Frank**
*See* Floyd, Frank

**Harmonica Harry**
*See* Mickle, Elmon

**Harmonica King**
*See* Smith, George

**Harmonica Slim**
*See* Blaylock, Travis L.

**Harmonica Slim**
*See* Moore, James

**Harms, Valerie**
*See* Sheehan, Valerie Harms

**Harmston, Olivia**
*See* Weber, Nancy

**Harnack, F. B.**
*See* Harnack, Frederick Bertrand

**Harnack, Fid**
*See* Harnack, Frederick Bertrand

**Harnack, Frederick Bertrand**
1897-   [ART, DBA]
*British painter and engraver*
* Harnack, F. B.
* Harnack, Fid

**Harnan, Terry** 1920-   [CA, SAT]
*American author*
* Hull, Eric Traviss

**Harnott, Happy**
*See* Harnott, Walter

**Harnott, Walter** 1912-   [CEI, SMG]
*Canadian-born hockey player*
* Harnott, Happy

**Harold**
*See* Jaffe, Harold

**Harold** ?-985?   [DNNS, HN]
*King of Denmark*
* Blue Tooth

**Harold Hen [The Gentle]** ?-1080
[WBD]
*King of Denmark*
* Harold Sweynson

**Harold, Lizzie**
*See* Comley, Mrs.

**Harold, Maggie**
*See* Davidge, Mrs. William, Jr.

**Harold Sweynson**
*See* Harold Hen [The Gentle]

**Harold I** ?-1040   [DNNS, RH, SN]
*King of the English*
* Harefoot

**Harold I** 850?- 933   [DNNS, WBD]
*King of Norway*
* [The] Fairhaired

**Harold II** 930?- 977?
[DNNS, WBD]
*King of Norway*
* Gray Skin
* Grayfell

**Harold II** 1022?-1066
[DNNS, SN]
*King of the English*
* [The] Last of the Saxons

**Harold III** 1015-1066
[DNNS, WBD]
*King of Norway*
* Hard Ruler
* [The] Stern

**Harolde, Ralf**
*See* Wigger, Ralf Harolde

**Haroun al Raschid** 765?- 808?
[FFF, RH, SN]
*Abbasside caliph*
* [The] Just

**Harp, John** 1927-   [ITA]
*American actor*
* Sands, Johnny

**[The] Harp of Ireland**
*See* David

**Harper, Blue Sleeve**
*See* Harper, William Homer [Bill]

**Harper, Bull**
*See* Harper, Roland

**Harper, Carol Ely** 20th c.   [CA]
*American author and editor*
* Ben, Ilke
* Goddard, Alfred

**Harper, Charles William**
1878-1950   [AS, BE]
*American baseball player*
* Harper, Jack

**Harper, Daniel**
*See* Brossard, Chandler

**Harper, David**
*See* Corley, Edwin

**Harper, Frances Ellen Watkins**
[FFF]
*Author*
* Afton, Effie

**Harper, Gillis**
*See* Miln, H. Crichton

**Harper, Harry** 20th c.   [MBF]
*British author and journalist*
* Clifford, Martin [house
  pseudonym]

**Harper, Jack**
*See* Harper, Charles William

**Harper, James**
*See* Tiroff, James [Jim]

**Harper, John**   [PA]
*Author*
* Hautboy

**Harper, Lucius Clinton** 1895-1952
[IBW]
*American editor*
* [The] Walking Morgue

**Harper, M. C.** 1903-   [CWG, DAM]
*American singer and songwriter*
* Harper, Redd

**Harper, Mabel Herbert** 20th c.
[ALY]
*American author*
* Urner, Mabel Herbert

**Harper, Olive**
*See* D'Apery, Helen [Burrell]

**Harper, Redd**
*See* Harper, M. C.

**Harper, Roland** 1953-   [SMG]
*American football player*
* Harper, Bull

**Harper, Shannon** 20th c.
*American author*
* Habersham, Elizabeth [joint
  pseudonym with Madeline Porter]
* James, Anna [joint pseudonym
  with Madeline Porter]

**Harper, William Homer [Bill]**
1889-1951   [BE]
*American baseball player*
* Harper, Blue Sleeve

**Harpo, Slim**
*See* Moore, James

**Harrah, Charles Clayton**
1900-1969   [B10]
*American manufacturer*
* Harrah, Duke

**Harrah, Colbert Dale** 1948-
[BE, SMG, WWB]
*American baseball player*
* Harrah, Toby

**Harrah, Dennis** 20th c.
*American football player*
* Harrah, Herk

**Harrah, Duke**
*See* Harrah, Charles Clayton

**Harrah, Herk**
*See* Harrah, Dennis

**Harrah, Toby**
*See* Harrah, Colbert Dale

**Harranth, Wolf** 1941-   [IAW]
*Austrian author*
* Ney, Wolfgang

**Harraway, Charley** 20th c.
*American football player*
* Harraway, Rev

**Harraway, Rev**
*See* Harraway, Charley

**Harrell, Cowboy**
*See* Harrell, Raymond James

**Harrell, Irene B[urk]** 1927-   [CA]
*American author*
* Amor, Amos
* Waylan, Mildred

**Harrell, Oscar Martin** 1890-1971
[BE]
*American baseball player*
* Harrell, Slim

**Harrell, Raymond James** 1912-
[BE]
*American baseball player*
* Harrell, Cowboy

**Harrell, Slim**
*See* Harrell, Oscar Martin

**Harrelson, Bud**
*See* Harrelson, Derrel McKinley

**Harrelson, Derrel McKinley** 1944-
[B10, PB, SMG]
*American baseball player*
* Harrelson, Bud
* Harrelson, Twiggy

**Harrelson, Kenneth Smith** 1941-
[BE, PB]
*American baseball player*
* [The] Hawk

**Harrelson, Twiggy**
*See* Harrelson, Derrel McKinley

**Harriet Annie**
*See* Wilkins, H. A.

**Harriett**
*See* Ginnings, Harriett Wilcoxen

**Harriford, Daphne**
*See* Harris, Marion Rose [Young]

**Harrigan, Grace** 1902-   [THR]
*American actress*
* Harrigan, Nedda

**Harrigan, Jon Lucien** 1942-   [EJ7]
*West Indian jazz musician*
* Lucien, Jon

**Harrigan, Nedda**
*See* Harrigan, Grace

**Harriman, Blanche Avicestill**
*See* Verbeck, Blanche Avicestill
Harriman

**Harriman, W[illiam] Averell** 1891-
*American industrialist, banker,
diplomat*
* [The] Crocodile

**Harring, Harro**
*See* Szymanski, Ignatius S.

**Harrington, Carey Bell** 1936-
[BWW]
*American singer*
* Bell, Carey

**Harrington, Eddy** 1935-   [BWW]
*American singer*
* Clearwater, Eddy
* Guitar Eddy

**Harrington, Elizabeth**
*See* Farmer, Minnie Elizabeth

**Harrington, Hago**
*See* Harrington, Leland

**Harrington, John A.**   [PA]
*Author*
* Carboy, John

**Harrington, K.**
*See* Bean, Keith F[enwick]

**Harrington, Lee**
*See* Barker, Reginald Charles

**Harrington, Leland** 20th c.
[CEI, SMG]
*American hockey player*
* Harrington, Hago

**Harrington, Mark Raymond**
1882-1971   [CAP]
*American author*
* De Las Cuevas, Ramon
* Jiskogo
* Tonashi

**Harriot, Thomas** 1560-1621   [SN]
*British mathematician*
* [The] Universal Philosopher

**Harriott, Arthurlin** 1928-1973
[DAM, EJ, EJ7]
*Jamaican-born jazz musician*
* Harriott, Joe

**Harriott, Joe**
*See* Harriott, Arthurlin

**Harris, Ace**
See Harris, Asa

**Harris, Addie** 1940- [RO1]
*American singer*
* Harris, Micky

**Harris, Alf[red]** 1928- [CA, SFL]
*Canadian-born author*
* Addison, Gwen
* Moore, Harris [joint pseudonym with Arthur Moore]

**Harris, Alonzo** 1947- [BE]
*American baseball player*
* Harris, Candy

**Harris, Amanda Bartlett** 19th c.
[FFF, PA]
*Author*
* A. B. H.
* Kirkland

**Harris, Andrea**
See Connolly, Vivian

**Harris, Andrew**
See Poole, Frederick King

**Harris, [Sir] Arthur** 1892-
[BDW, WWW]
*British air force officer*
* Harris, Bomber

**Harris, Arthur** 1952- [IBW]
*American boxer*
* Harris, Tap City

**Harris, Asa** 1910-1964 [SC]
*American actor and singer*
* Harris, Ace

**Harris, Barbara**
See Markowitz, Sandra

**Harris, Beaver**
See Harris, William Godvin

**Harris, Benjamin** 1919- [DAM, EJ]
*American jazz musician*
* Harris, Little Benny

**Harris, Bill**
See Harris, Willard Palmer

**Harris, Black Charlie**
See Harris, Charlie

**Harris, Bomber**
See Harris, [Sir] Arthur

**Harris, Bubba**
See Harris, Charles [Charlie]

**Harris, Bucky**
See Harris, Stanley Raymond

**Harris, Buddy**
See Harris, Walter Francis, Jr.

**Harris, C. L.** [PA]
*Author*
* Ledyard, Hope

**Harris, Candy**
See Harris, Alonzo

**Harris, Carrol Wayne** 1938- [BBH]
*American-born football player*
* [The] Thumper

**Harris, Chalmer Luman** 1915-
[BE]
*American baseball player and manager*
* Harris, Lum

**Harris, Charles [Charlie]** 1926-
[BE]
*American baseball player*
* Harris, Bubba

**Harris, Charles A.** 1887?-1962
[BEW]
*Theatrical performer*
* Harris, Honey

**Harris, Charles H.** [PA]
*Author*
* Pretzel, Karl

**Harris, Charles T.** [PA]
*Author*
* Bermudas

**Harris, Charlie** 20th c. [BLB]
*American underworld figure*
* Harris, Black Charlie

**Harris, Christopher Fry** 1907-
[BEW, CA, LC]
*British playwright, translator, author*
* Fry, Christopher

**Harris, Cliff** 20th c.
*American football player*
* Harris, Snowstorm

**Harris, Colver**
See Colver, Anne

**Harris, David Stanley** 1900-1973
[BE]
*American baseball player*
* Harris, Sheriff

**Harris, De Long** 20th c. [IBW]
*American attorney*
* [The] Black Clarence Darrow

**Harris, Derek** 1926- [FC, WEF]
*American actor and director*
* Derek, John

**Harris, Doc**
See Stacher, Joseph

**Harris, Don** 1938-
[BWW, RM, RO1]
*American singer and songwriter*
* Harris, Sugarcane

**Harris, Duke**
See Harris, George Francis

**Harris, Ed[ward P.]** 1923-1953
[BWW]
*American singer*
* Carolina Slim
* Country Paul
* Georgia Pine
* Jammin' Jim
* Lazy Slim Jim

**Harris, Edna Edith** 1893- [WWL]
*British author*
* Mansfield, Estrith

**Harris, Edward** 19th c. [FFF]
*British author*
* De Cranki, Lunatico

**Harris, Emily Marion** 19th c. [PA]
*Author*
* Estelle

**Harris, F[rank] Brayton** 1932-
[CA]
*American author*
* West, Kirkpatrick

**Harris, Frank**
See Harris, James Thomas

**Harris, Fred** 1887- ? [BBH]
*American skiing club founder*
* [The] Father of Skiing

**Harris, George Francis** 1942-
[CEI]
*Canadian-born hockey player*
* Harris, Duke

**Harris, George W.** 1805-1869 [PA]
*Author*
* Lovingood, Sut

**Harris, Gypsy Joe**
See Harris, Joe Louis

**Harris, Harry**
See Slaughter, Marion T.

**Harris, Harry** 1880-1959
[BX, EJS, RBE]
*American boxer*
* [The] Human Hairpin
* [The] Human Scissors

**Harris, Henry** 20th c. [CEI]
*Hockey player*
* Harris, Smokey

**Harris, Herbert** 1911- [IAW]
*British author*
* Bury, Frank
* Friday, Peter
* Moore, Michael

**Harris, Hi Tide**
See Boyd [or Gitry?], Willie

**Harris, Hinky**
See Harris, William Edward

**Harris, Homer William** 1909-
[CWG]
*American country-western performer*
* [The] Seven Foot Cowboy

**Harris, Honey**
See Harris, Charles A.

**Harris, Ike**
See Harris, Isiah, Jr.

**Harris, Integrity Jean**
See Harris, Jean Struven

**Harris, Isiah, Jr.** 1952- [SMG]
*American football player*
* Harris, Ike

**Harris, J. P.**
See Stacher, Joseph

**Harris, James D. [Jimmie]** 1921-
[BWW, NBB]
*American singer*
* Cadillac Jake
* Shakey Jake

**Harris, James Thomas** 1856-1931
[LC, TCL]
*Welsh author, journalist, editor*
* Harris, Frank

**Harris, Jean Struven** 1923?-
*American educator, convicted of murder*
* Harris, Integrity Jean

**Harris, Jed**
See Horowitz, Jacob

**Harris, Joe Louis** 1946- [IBW]
*American boxer*
* Harris, Gypsy Joe

**Harris, Joel Chandler** 1848-1906
[WWL]
*American author and editor*
* Uncle Remus

**Harris, John** 13th c. [SN]
*British poet*
* [The] Cornish Poet

**Harris, John** 1802-1856 [PA]
*Author*
* Kuhlos

**Harris, John** 1916- [CA, WD]
*British author*
* Hebden, Mark
* Hennessy, Max

**Harris, John [Wyndham Parkes Lucas] Beynon** 1903-1969
[ESF, SF, WW]
*British author*
* Beynon, John
* Harris, Johnson
* Parkes, Lucas
* Parkes, Wyndham
* Wyndham, John

**Harris, Johnson**
See Harris, John [Wyndham Parkes Lucas] Beynon

**Harris, Joseph**
See Dillinger, John Herbert

**Harris, Joseph** 1891-1959
[AS, DGS, PB]
*American baseball player*
* Harris, Moon

**Harris, Joseph Upper** 1891-
[WWL]
*American author*
* Upper, Joseph

**Harris, Josephine** 20th c. [ART]
*British artist*
* J. H.

**Harris, Kathleen**
See Humphries, Adelaide M.

**Harris, Kathryn [Beatrice] Gibbs**
1930- [CA]
*American poet*
* Hayes, Wilson

**Harris, Larry M[ark]** 1933-
[CA, ESF, WGT]
*American author*
* Beach, Tom
* Blake, Alfred
* Blake, Andrew
* Janifer, Laurence M[ark]
* Logan, William
* Phillips, Mark [joint pseudonym with Randall Garrett]
* Wilson, Barbara

**Harris, Lee O.** [PA]
*Author*
* O'Hannegan, Larry

**Harris, Lilly C.** [PA]
*Author*
* Chrysanthea

**Harris, Little Benny**
See Harris, Benjamin

**Harris, Lucy**
See Harris, Lusia

**Harris, Lum**
See Harris, Chalmer Luman

**Harris, Lusia** 1956- [IBW]
*American basketball player*
* [The] Cage Queen
* Harris, Lucy

**Harris, MacDonald**
See Heiney, Donald [William]

**Harris, Mae**
See Henderson, Rosa [Rose]

**Harris, Mamie**
See Henderson, Rosa [Rose]

**Harris, Maria**
See Glossop, Maria Elizabeth

**Harris, Marilyn**
See Springer, Marilyn Harris

**Harris, Marion Rose [Young]**
1925- [CAP, WD]
*British writer*
* Chares, Henry
* Harriford, Daphne
* Rogers, Keith
* Young, Rose

**Harris, Mark**
See Finkelstein, Mark

**Harris, Maurice Charles** 1917-
[BE]
*American baseball player*
* Harris, Mickey

**Harris, Mickey**
See Harris, Maurice Charles

**Harris, Micky**
See Harris, Addie

**Harris, Middleton A.** ?-1977
[IBW]
*American author and historian*
* Harris, Spike

**Harris, Moon**
See Harris, Joseph

**Harris, Pearl**
See Miles, Josephine [Josie]

**Harris, Peppermint**
See Nelson, Harrison

**Harris, Richard** 17th c. [PA]
*Author*
* Cardrac, Verdillo
* Whipem, Benedick

**Harris, Robert P.** 1878-1936
[THR]
*British playwright, lyricist, composer*
* Weston, Robert P.

**Harris, Roger**
See Wilson, Roger Harris Lebus

**Harris, Roy** 1898?-1979
*American composer*
* [The] Walt Whitman of American Music

**Harris, Samuel** 1724- ?
[DNNF, SN]
*American clergyman*
* [The] Apostle of Virginia

**Harris, Sara Lee**
See Stadelman, Sara Lee

**Harris, Sheriff**
See Harris, David Stanley

**Harris, Smokey**
See Harris, Henry

**Harris, Snowstorm**
See Harris, Cliff

**Harris, Spike**
See Harris, Middleton A.

**Harris, Stanley Raymond**
1896-1977 [BE, PB, SMG]
*American baseball manager and scout*
* [The] Boy Manager
* Harris, Bucky

**Harris, Sugarcane**
See Harris, Don

**Harris, Tap City**
See Harris, Arthur

**Harris, Thistle Y.**
See Stead, Thistle Yolette

**Harris, Thomas Lake** 1823- ? [PA]
*Author*
* Chrysantheus

**Harris, Walter Francis, Jr.** 1948-
[BE]
*American baseball player*
* Harris, Buddy

**Harris, Willard Palmer** 1916-1973
[EJ, EJ7, WWJ]
*American jazz musician*
* Harris, Bill

**Harris, William Bevan** 1887-1957
[F2, FC, OCF]
*Australian-born actor*
* Bevan, Billy

**Harris, William Bliss** 1901?-1981
*American editor, horticulturist, writer*
* Pettingill, Amos

**Harris, William Edward** 1935-
[FHE]
*Canadian-born hockey player*
* Harris, Hinky

**Harris, William Edward** 1952-
[SMG]
*Canadian-born hockey player*
* Harry O

**Harris, William Godvin** 1936-
[EJ7]
*American jazz musician*
* Harris, Beaver

**Harris, William Torrey** 1835-1909
[FFF]
*American philosopher, educator, author*
* Hermes

**Harris, [Theodore] Wilson** 1921-
[CW]
*Guyanese author, critic, poet*
* Kona Woruk

**Harris, Wynonie** 1915-1969
[BWW]
*American singer*
* Blues, Mr.
* [The] Mississippi Mockingbird
* Peppermint Cane

**Harris-Burland, J. B.**
See Harris-Burland, John Burland

**Harris-Burland, John Burland**
1870-1926 [SFL, WGT]
*British author*
* Burland, Harris
* Harris-Burland, J. B.

**[The] Harrisburg Houdini**
See Davies, Robert E. [Bob]

**Harrison, Alice**
See Metz, Alice

**Harrison, Ben**
See Harrison, Leo J.

**Harrison, Benjamin** 1833-1901
[FAP, FFF]
*American president*
* [The] Centennial President
* Grandfather's Hat
* Grandpa's Grandson
* Harrison, Chinese
* Harrison, Kid Gloves
* Little Ben
* [The] Son of His Grandfather

**Harrison, Bruce**
See Pangborn, Edgar

**Harrison, Byron Patton** 1881-1941
[WBD]
*American politician*
* Harrison, Pat

**Harrison, Carey**
See Reppeteau, Carey Harrison

**Harrison, Chinese**
See Harrison, Benjamin

**Harrison, Constance Cary**
1843-1920 [FFF]
*American author*
* Refugitta

**Harrison, David L[ee]** 1937- [CA]
*American author*
* Graham, Kennon

**Harrison, Dutch**
See Harrison, Ernest Joseph

**Harrison, Edwin**
See Ballard, Eric Alan

**Harrison, Ernest Joseph** 1910-
[BWG, EG, GF]
*American golfer*
* [The] Arkansas Traveler
* Harrison, Dutch

**Harrison, Flash**
See Harrison, Kenny

**Harrison, Frieda** 1943?- [FC]
*British actress*
* Kendall, Suzy

**Harrison, G. B.**
See Harrison, George Bagshawe

**Harrison, G. D.**
See Honey, Philip

**Harrison, George Bagshawe** 1894-
[LC]
*British-born educator and author*
* Harrison, G. B.

**Harrison, George Robert** 1874- ?
[NAA]
*American journalist and poet*
* Johnson, Jonathan

**Harrison, Hank** 1940- [CA]
*American psychologist and writer*
* Draper, Canyon
* McGluphy

**Harrison, Harry Maxwell**
See Dempsey, Henry

**Harrison, Henry Sydnor**
1880-1930 [TC]
*American author*
* Second, Henry

**Harrison, J. C.**
See Harrison, John Cyril

**Harrison, Jay**
See Smolens, Jay

**Harrison, John Cyril** 1898- [ART]
*British painter*
* Harrison, J. C.

**Harrison, Kenny** 1953- [SMG]
*American football player*
* Harrison, Flash

**Harrison, Kid Gloves**
See Harrison, Benjamin

**Harrison, Leo J.** 20th c. [BE]
*American baseball player*
* Harrison, Ben

**Harrison, Log Cabin**
See Harrison, William Henry

**Harrison, Louis**
See Metz, Louis

**Harrison, Louise** [FFF]
*Entertainer*
* Schutz, Emma

**Harrison, M[ichael] John** 1945-
[CA]
*British author*
* Churchill, Joyce

**Harrison, Mary Bennett** 1877- ?
[NAA]
*American author*
* Warden, Francis

**Harrison, Mary Kent** 1915- [ART]
*British painter*
* Kent, Mary

**Harrison, Mary St. Leger [Kingsley]**
1852-1931 [LAO, LC, TC]
*British author and playwright*
* Malet, Lucas

**Harrison, Michael** 1907-
[EMD, WW]
*British author*
* Downes, Quentin
* Egremont, Michael

**Harrison, Pat**
See Harrison, Byron Patton

**Harrison, Peter Basil** 1913- [TR]
*British actor*
* Markham, David

**Harrison, Phyllis** 1892- [THR]
*British actress and dancer*
* Monkman, Phyllis

**Harrison, Reginald Carey** 1908-
*British actor*
* Harrison, Rex
* Sexy Rexy

**Harrison, Rex**
See Harrison, Reginald Carey

**Harrison, Richard [Motte]** 1901-
[CC, WW]
*Author*
* Motte, Peter

**Harrison, Valerie** 1932- [TR]
*British actress*
* French, Valerie

**Harrison, Vernon** 1925- [BWW]
*American singer*
* Boogie Woogie Red
* Piano Red

**Harrison, Whit**
See Whittington, Harry

**Harrison, William Henry**
1773-1841 [DNNF, FAP, FFF]
*American president*
* [The] Cincinnatus of the West

**Harrison, William Henry**
(Continued)
* [The] Farmer President
* Hard Cider
* Harrison, Log Cabin
* [The] Hero of Tippecanoe
* [The] Log Cabin President
* Old Granny
* Old Tip
* Old Tippecanoe
* Tippecanoe
* [The] Washington of the West

**Harrison-Church, Ronald James**
1915-    [IAW]
*British geographer and author*
* Church, R. J. Harrison

**Harriss, Slim**
*See* Harriss, William Jennings
Bryan

**Harriss, William Jennings Bryan**
1896-1963    [AS, BE]
*American baseball player*
* Harriss, Slim

**Harrist, Earl** 1919-    [BE]
*American baseball player*
* Harrist, Irish

**Harrist, Irish**
*See* Harrist, Earl

**Harroun, Ray** 20th c.
*Auto racer*
* [The] Sheik

**[A] Harrow Tutor**
*See* Holmes, Cecil Frederick

**Harrow, William** ?-1763
[DNNF, DNNS, FFF]
*British highway robber*
* [The] Flying Highwayman

**Harry O**
*See* Harris, William Edward

**Harry of the West**
*See* Clay, Henry

**Harry the Hipster**
*See* Gibson, Harry

**Harry the Horse**
*See* Danning, Harry

**Harry the Horse**
*See* Heilmann, Harry Edwin

**Harshman, Marv**
*See* Harshman, Marvel

**Harshman, Marvel** 1918-    [BB]
*American basketball coach*
* Harshman, Marv

**Harson, Sley** [joint pseudonym with
Henry Slesar]
*See* Ellison, Harlan [Jay]

**Harson, Sley** [joint pseudonym with
Harlan (Jay) Ellison]
*See* Slesar, Henry

**Hart, Barry**
*See* Bloom, Herman Irving

**Hart, Billy**
*See* Lenhart, William

**Hart, [Senator] Bob**
*See* Sutherland, Robert

**Hart, Bob**
*See* Trace, Al[bert J.]

**Hart, Charles B.**    [PA]
*Author*
* Benjamins, Mr.

**Hart, Connie**
*See* Hart, Mary Conaleeta

**Hart, Cornelius A., Jr.** 1879-1949
[F1, F2, SC]
*American actor and director*
* Hart, Neal

**Hart, Cyril Charles** 1901-    [WWL]
*British writer*
* Max, Raymond

**Hart, Dolores**
*See* Hicks, Dolores

**Hart, E. J.**
*See* Hart, Edward J.

**Hart, Edward J.** 1887-1956    [FB]
*American football player*
* Hart, E. J.

**Hart, Ellis**
*See* Ellison, Harlan [Jay]

**Hart, Enid**
*See* Fallen, Mrs. Frederick

**Hart, Gerald**
*See* Irving, Thomas J.

**Hart, Gerald William** 1948-    [SMG]
*Canadian-born hockey player*
* Hart, Hartie

**Hart, Gizzy**
*See* Hart, Wilfred

**Hart, Harry** 1907-    [SF]
*American author*
* Frank, Pat

**Hart, Hartie**
*See* Hart, Gerald William

**Hart, Hub**
*See* Hart, James Henry

**Hart, Indian Jack**
*See* Hart, Jack

**Hart, J. E. T.**
*See* Wright, James Richard

**Hart, Jack** 1872-1974    [SC]
*American actor and rodeo performer*
* Hart, Indian Jack

**Hart, James**
*See* Higgins, James Hart

**Hart, James Henry** 1878-1960
[BE]
*American baseball player*
* Hart, Hub

**Hart, John**
*See* Hedges, Frank Hinckley

**Hart, John**
*See* Noland, John T.

**Hart, Leonard**
*See* Barnard, Alfred J.

**Hart, M. C.**    [PA]
*Author*
* Chevalier

**Hart, Mary Conaleeta** 1950-
[IWM]
*American musician*
* Hart, Connie

**Hart, Mrs.**    [PA]
*Author*
* Jerningham, Mrs.

**Hart, Neal**
*See* Hart, Cornelius A., Jr.

**Hart, Peter**
*See* Honey, Philip

**Hart, Philip A.** 1912-1976
*American politician*
* [The] Conscience of the Senate

**Hart, Pop**
*See* Hart, William V.

**Hart, R. W.**
*See* Ferneyhough, Roger Edmund

**Hart, Robert Alton** 1897?-1957
[BEW, EMT, FC]
*American choreographer*
* Alton, Robert

**Hart, Susanne**
*See* Harthoorn, Susanne [Widrich]

**Hart, Sylvan Ambrose** 1906-    [B10]
*American recluse*
* Buckskin Bill

**Hart, Tony**
*See* Cannon, Anthony J.

**Hart, True Gun**
*See* Hart, William Woodrow [Bill]

**Hart, Wilfred** 1902-    [CEI]
*Canadian-born hockey player*
* Hart, Gizzy

**Hart, William Sterling** 1917-
[FC, ITA, SW]
*American actor*
* Sterling, Robert

**Hart, William V.** 1867-1925    [SC]
*American actor*
* Hart, Pop

**Hart, William Woodrow [Bill]**
1913-1968    [BN]
*American baseball player*
* Hart, True Gun

**Harte, Betty**
*See* Light, Daisy Mae

**Harte, Marjorie**
*See* McEvoy, Marjorie Harte

**Harte, Oliver**
*See* Stagg, J. R.

**Hartenstein, Charles Oscar** 1942-
[BE]
*American baseball player*
* Hartenstein, Twiggy

**Hartenstein, Twiggy**
*See* Hartenstein, Charles Oscar

**Harter, Chief**
*See* Harter, Franklin Pierce

**Harter, Franklin Pierce** 1886-1959
[BE]
*American baseball player*
* Harter, Chief

**Hartex, Pierre**
*See* Daviault, Pierre

**Hartford Jack Farrell**
*See* Farrell, John

**Hartford, John**
*See* Harford, John

**Hartford, Via**
*See* Donson, Cyril

**Harthoorn, Susanne [Widrich]**
1927-    [AW]
*Austrian-born veterinarian and
author*
* Hart, Susanne

**Hartley, Chick**
*See* Hartley, Walter Scott

**Hartley, Christine**
*See* Thomson, Christine Campbell

**Hartley, Ellen R[aphael]** 1915-
[WD]
*American author*
* Knauff, Ellen Raphael

**Hartley, Grover Allen** 1888-1964
[BE]
*American baseball player*
* Hartley, Slick

**Hartley, Hare**
*See* Hartley, Stuart Neil

**Hartley, L. P.**
*See* Hartley, Leslie Poles

**Hartley, Leslie Poles** 1895-1972
[LC]
*British author*
* Hartley, L. P.

**Hartley, Malcolm**
*See* Fearn, John Russell

**Hartley, Slick**
*See* Hartley, Grover Allen

**Hartley, Stuart Neil** 1956-    [DC]
*British cricketer*
* Hartley, Hare

**Hartley, Vivian Mary** 1913-1967
[BDF, BEW, EMT]
*British actress*
* Leigh, Vivien

**Hartley, Walter Scott** 1880-1948
[BE]
*American baseball player*
* Hartley, Chick

**Hartman, Darlene** 1934-
[SFL, WGT]
*American author*
* Lang, Simon

**Hartman, Don**
*See* Hartman, Samuel

**Hartman, Dutch**
*See* Hartman, Frederick Orrin

**Hartman, Frederick Orrin**
1868-1938    [BE]
*American baseball player*
* Hartman, Dutch

**Hartman, Grace**
*See* Abbott, Grace Barrett
Hartman

**Hartman, John** 20th c.    [RM, RO2]
*American musician*
* Hartman, Little John

**Hartman, Jonathan William**
1872-1965    [SC]
*American actor*
* Hartman, Pop

**Hartman, Little John**
*See* Hartman, John

**Hartman, Patience**
*See* Zawadsky, Patience

**Hartman, Pop**
*See* Hartman, Jonathan William

**Hartman, Roger**
See  Mehta, Rustam Jehangir

**Hartman, Samuel** 1901-1958  [FC]
*American screenwriter*
* Hartman, Don

**Hartmann, Franz** 1838-1912
[WGT]
*Author*
* [A] Student of Occultism

**Hartmann, Helmut Henry** 1931-
[WD, WW]
*German-born British author*
* Seymour, Henry

**Hartmann, Pater**
See  Von An Der Lan-Hochbrunn,
Paul Eugen Josef

**Hartmann, Rudolf**
See  Gniffke, Rudolf

**Hartnett, Charles Leo** 1900-1972
[B10, DGS, PB]
*American baseball player*
* Hartnett, Gabby
* Old Tomato Face

**Hartnett, Gabby**
See  Hartnett, Charles Leo

**Hartnett, Happy**
See  Hartnett, Pat[rick J.]

**Hartnett, Pat[rick J.]** 1863-1935
[BE]
*American baseball player*
* Hartnett, Happy

**Hartocollis, Peter** 1922-  [CA]
*Greek-born psychiatrist and author*
* Mandrepelias, Loizos
* Palli, Pitsa

**Hartree, Charles** 1914-
*British actor*
* Hawtrey, Charles

**Hartsel, Topsy**
See  Hartsel, Tully Frederick

**Hartsel, Tully Frederick**
1874-1944  [AS, BE]
*American baseball player*
* Hartsel, Topsy

**Hartsfield, Mousey**
See  Hartsfield, Roy Thomas

**Hartsfield, Roy Thomas** 1925-
[PB]
*American baseball player*
* Hartsfield, Mousey

**Hartung, Clinton Clarence** 1922-
[BE, PB]
*American baseball player*
* Baseball's Paul Bunyan
* Hartung, Floppy
* [The] Hondo Hurricane
* Superman

**Hartung, Floppy**
See  Hartung, Clinton Clarence

**Hartwell, Alice Booth** 20th c.
[NAA]
*American editor and writer*
* Booth, Alice

**Hartwell, Mary**
See  Catherwood, Mrs. M. H.

**Hartwell, Nancy**
See  Callahan, Claire Wallis

**Hartwig, Eva Brigitta** 1917-
[BEW, EMT, FC]
*German-born dancer and actress*
* Zorina, Vera

**Harty, [Sir] Hamilton** 1879-1941
[MS]
*Irish conductor*
* [The] Prince of Accompanists

**Haruki, Shimazaki** 1872-1943
[TCL]
*Japanese author and poet*
* Toson, Shimazaki

**Harvard, Charles**
See  Gibbs-Smith, Charles Harvard

**Harvard Eddie Grant**
See  Grant, Edward Leslie

**Harvard Senior**
See  Ward, H. D.

**Harvel, Luther Raymond** 1905-
[BE]
*American baseball player*
* Harvel, Red

**Harvel, Red**
See  Harvel, Luther Raymond

**Harvester, Simon**
See  Rumbold-Gibbs, Henry St.
John Clair

**Harvey, Bud**
See  Harvey, Glynn

**Harvey, Buster**
See  Harvey, Frederick John
Charles

**Harvey, Buzz**
See  Harvey, Charles

**Harvey, Charles** 1885?-  [NOJ]
*American jazz musician*
* Harvey, Buzz

**Harvey, Coin**
See  Harvey, William Hope

**Harvey, Erwin K.** 1878- ?  [BN]
*American baseball player*
* Harvey, Silent
* Harvey, Zaza

**Harvey, Florence** 20th c.  [SFL]
*Author*
* Donner, Grove

**Harvey, Frederick John Charles**
1950-  [CEI, HR, SMG]
*Canadian-born hockey player*
* Harvey, Buster

**Harvey, Gabriel** 1545?-1630?  [SN]
*British poet*
* [The] Aristarchus of his Day
* Ergo, Garbriel
* Howliglasse, Gabriel
* Our Talatamtana
* This Mud Born Bubble
* This Ropemaker

**Harvey, Glynn** 1912-  [GF]
*American journalist*
* Harvey, Bud

**Harvey, Hank**
See  Heacker, Herman

**Harvey, Harry** 1907-  [OCS]
*Dog trainer*
* Harvey, Jack

**Harvey, Hope**
See  Hammond, Mary Hope

**Harvey, Irene** 1875- ?  [WWL]
*British author*
* Osgood, Irene

**Harvey, Jack**
See  Harvey, Harry

**Harvey, Jean**
See  Guy, Jean

**Harvey, John**
See  Johnson, J. Harvey, Jr.

**Harvey, John Wilfred** 20th c.
[WW]
*Author*
* Farndale, John

**Harvey, Laurence**
See  Skikne, Larushka Mischa

**Harvey, Moses**  [FFF]
*Canadian journalist*
* Delta

**Harvey, Nigel** 1916-  [CA, WD]
*British author*
* Willoughby, Hugh

**Harvey, Pat**
See  Yallup, Pat

**Harvey, Paul**
See  Aurandt, Paul Harvey

**Harvey, Rachel**
See  Bloom, Ursula [Harvey]

**Harvey, Richard**  [SN]
*British astronomer and astrologer*
* [The] Almanack Maker
* Astrological Richard
* Io Paean Dick
* Pierian Dick

**Harvey, Ross**
See  Hook, H. Clarke

**Harvey, Shirley** 20th c.  [IBW]
*American-born social worker and
jewelry designer*
* Gueye, Fatou

**Harvey, Silent**
See  Harvey, Erwin K.

**Harvey, W. F.**
See  Harvey, William Fryer

**Harvey, William** 1808- ?  [PA]
*Author*
* Aleph

**Harvey, William Fryer** 1885-1937
[HFF]
*British author*
* Harvey, W. F.

**Harvey, William Hope** 1851-1936
[WBD]
*American economist*
* Harvey, Coin

**Harvey, William King**  ?-1976
*American intelligence agent*
* [The] Pear

**Harvey, Zaza**
See  Harvey, Erwin K.

**Harvey-James, A. K.**  ?-1917
[BEW]
*Actor and playwright*
* Craven, Arthur Scott

**Harvuot, Inez** 1917?-  [BEW, FC]
*American actress and singer*
* Manning, Irene

**Harwick, B. L.**
See  Keller, Beverly [Lou]

**Harwin, Brian**
See  Henderson, LeGrand

**Harwood, Gina**
See  Battiscombe, E[sther]
Georgina [Harwood]

**Harwood, Isabella** 1840?-1888
[FFF]
*American author and playwright*
* Neil, Ross

**Harwood, John**
See  Miner, Charles

**Hasan Ali Shah** 1800-1881  [WBD]
*Moslem religious leader*
* Aga Khan I

**Hasan ibn-Hani, al-** 756?- 810?
[WBD]
*Arabic poet*
* Abu Nuwas

**Hasbrook, Robert Lyndon** 1893-
[BE]
*American baseball player*
* Hasbrook, Ziggy

**Hasbrook, Ziggy**
See  Hasbrook, Robert Lyndon

**Hasbrouck, Louise Seymour**
See  Zimm, Louise Hasbrouck

**Hasekidis, Lolos**
See  Hasekidis, Theodore

**Hasekidis, Theodore** 1940-  [AES]
*Greek soccer player*
* Hasekidis, Lolos

**Haselfoot, Edward**
See  Walker, William Sidney

**Haseltine, W. H. H.**  [PA]
*Author*
* W. H. H.

**Haselwood, Joseph** 1769-1833
[PA]
*Author*
* Gridiron, Gabble

**Hasford, [Jerry] Gustav** 1947-  [CA]
*American author*
* Gordon, George

**Hashashian, Arousiak** 1890-1973
[SC]
*Turkish-born actor*
* Abrahamian, Arousiak

**Haskin, Dorothy C[lark]** 1905-
[CA]
*American writer*
* Clark, Howard

**Haskins, Barbara**
See  Stone, Barbara Haskins

**Haskins, Big Daddy**
See  Haskins, Clem

**Haskins, Clarence** 20th c.  [RO2]
*American singer*
* Haskins, Fuzzy

**Haskins, Clem** 1944-  [SMG]
*American basketball player*
* Haskins, Big Daddy

**Haskins, Dick**
See  Andrade, A.

**Haskins, Fuzzy**
See  Haskins, Clarence

**Haslam, Mrs. Charles A.**   [FFF]
*Entertainer*
* Sherwood, Alice

**Haslette, John**
See  Vahey, John George Haslette

**Haslewood, Joseph** 1769-1833
[DEL, FFF]
*British bibliographer*
* Gabbler Gridiron
* Valdarfer, Christopher

**Hasolle, James**
See  Ashmole, Elias

**Hasoutra**
See  Simpson, Ryllis Barnes

**Haspinian, Jean** 1515-1575   [PA]
*Author*
* Wirth

**Hassamaer, Roaring Bill**
See  Hassamaer, William Louis
[Bill]

**Hassamaer, William Louis [Bill]**
1864-1910   [BE]
*American baseball player*
* Hassamaer, Roaring Bill

**Hassan-ben-Sabah** ?-1124   [SN]
*Founder of religious sect*
* [The] Old Man of the Mountain

**Hasse, Henry L.**   [ESF, WGT]
*American author*
* Pine, Theodore [joint pseudonym
  with Emil (Theodore) Petaja]

**Hasse, Johann Adolf** 1699-1783
[SN]
*German composer*
* [Il] Caro Sassone

**Hassel, Sven**
See  Pedersen, Sven

**Hasselgard, Ake** 1922-1948
[EJ, PMJ]
*Swedish jazz musician*
* Hasselgard, Stan

**Hasselgard, Stan**
See  Hasselgard, Ake

**Hassen, Silaki Ali**
See  Mihilakis, Ulysses George

**Hassett, Buddy**
See  Hassett, John Aloysius

**Hassett, John Aloysius** 1911-   [BE]
*American baseball player*
* Hassett, Buddy

**Hasso, Signe**
See  Larsson, Signe

**Hasson, James** 1892-   [AW]
*Egyptian-born author*
* De Salignac, Charles

**Hastings, Alan**
See  Williamson, Geoffrey

**Hastings, Brook** [joint pseudonym
with Mary Edgley]
See  Edgley, Leslie

**Hastings, Brook** [joint pseudonym
with Leslie Edgley]
See  Edgley, Mary

**Hastings, Elizabeth**
See  McKenzie, Grace E.

**Hastings, Gilbert**
See  Farrell, Gilbert Hastings

**Hastings, Gorilla**
See  Hastings, Mike

**Hastings, Graham**
See  Jeffries, Roderic [Graeme]

**Hastings, Harrington**
See  Marsh, John

**Hastings, Hudson** [joint pseudonym
with Catherine Lucile Moore]
See  Kuttner, Henry

**Hastings, Hudson** [joint pseudonym
with Henry Kuttner]
See  Moore, Catherine Lucile

**Hastings, Hugh J.** 1820-1883
[FFF]
*American journalist*
* [The] Earl of Pleasure Bay

**Hastings, Jonathan** 18th c.   [SN]
*British farmer*
* Yankee Jonathan

**Hastings, Louis Royer** 20th c.
[WFA]
*American-born fashion designer*
* Royer

**Hastings, Macdonald** 1909-
[CA, WD]
*British author*
* Gulliver, Lemuel

**Hastings, Mike** 1892-1965   [GW]
*American rodeo performer*
* Hastings, Gorilla

**Hastings, Phyllis Dora Hodge** 20th
c.   [CA]
*British author*
* Bedford, John
* Hodge, E. Chatterton
* Land, Rosina
* Mayfield, Julia

**Haswell, Chetwynd John Drake**
1919-   [AW, CA, WD]
*British author*
* Foster, George
* Haswell, Jock

**Haswell, Jock**
See  Haswell, Chetwynd John
Drake

**[The] Hat**
See  Hacek, Harry

**[The] Hat**
See  Walker, Harry William

**Hatar, Gyozo Victor John** 1914-
[AW]
*Hungarian-born author*
* Medveczky

**Hatch, David Patterson** 1846-1912
[SFL, WGT]
*Author*
* Karishka, Paul

**Hatch, Gerald**
See  Foley, Dave

**Hatch, Ike**
See  Hatch, Isaac Flower

**Hatch, Isaac Flower** 1892?-1961
[BEW]
*American-born theatrical performer*
* Hatch, Ike

**Hatcher, Charles** 1942-   [RO2]
*American singer*
* Starr, Edwin

**Hatcher, John E.**   [PA]
*Author*
* Brick, George Washington

**[The] Hatchet**
See  Navarro, Ruben

**Hatfield, Frank**
See  Stevens, John

**Hatfield, Mrs.**   [FFF]
*Entertainer*
* Worrell, Jennie

**Hatfield, Penelope** 20th c.   [TR]
*British actress*
* Keith, Penelope

**Hatfield, Richard**
See  Hinckley, Robert

**Hathaway, Alan** 20th c.   [SFL]
*Author*
* Robeson, Kenneth [house
  pseudonym, Street & Smith]

**Hathaway, Donny** 1945-
[PRS, RO2]
*American musician*
* Pitts, Donny

**Hathaway, J.**
See  Bossard, Frank Clifton

**Hathaway, Jan**
See  Neubauer, William Arthur

**Hathaway, Louise**
See  Metlova, Maria

**Hathaway, Mavis**
See  Avery, Ira

**Hathaway, Ronald F.** 1937-   [IAW]
*American author*
* Catto, P. Z.
* DeCoverley, Roger

**Hathaway, Terence**
See  Grieco, Sergio

**Hathcock, Lloyd** 20th c.   [IBW]
*American fighter pilot and camera
designer*
* Hathcock, Scotty

**Hathcock, Scotty**
See  Hathcock, Lloyd

**Hatherway, Cyril**
See  Burrage, Alfred Sherrington

**Hathi**
See  Smith, [Edgar] Dennis

**Hatley, Jonathan** 1892-1966   [FC]
*American actor*
* Hale, Jonathan

**Hatteberg, Richard** 1938-
*American oilwell troubleshooter*
* Hatteberg, Toots

**Hatteberg, Toots**
See  Hatteberg, Richard

**[The] Hatted King**
See  Joseph II

**Hatter, Clyde Melno** 1908-1937
[BE]
*American baseball player*
* Hatter, Mad

**Hatter, Mad**
See  Hatter, Clyde Melno

**Hatteras, Owen** [joint pseudonym
with George Jean Nathan]
See  Mencken, Henry Louis

**Hatteras, Owen** [joint pseudonym
with Henry Louis Mencken]
See  Nathan, George Jean

**Hatteras, Owen, III**
See  McDavid, Raven I[oor], Jr.

**Hatton, [Sir] Christopher**
1540-1591   [DNNS, RH, SN]
*British statesman*
* [The] Dancing Chancellor

**Hatton, Joshua**   [DEL]
*Author*
* Roslyn, Guy

**Hatuey**
See  Henriquez Urena, Max

**Hatzidakis, Nicholas** 1872- ?
[LAO]
*German mathematician and author*
* Vradinnos, Zefiros

**Hauck, Leo Florian** 1888-1950
[BX, RBE]
*American boxer*
* Houck, Leo

**Hauck, Louise [Platt]** 1883-1943
[NAA, WW]
*American author*
* Archer, Lane
* Ash, Peter
* Landon, Louise

**Hauck, Mignon** 1851-1929   [BBD]
*American opera singer*
* Hauk, Minnie

**Hauer, Tris**
See  Hauer, Tristan C.

**Hauer, Tristan C.** 1921-   [MY]
*American jazz musician*
* Hauer, Tris

**Hauerbach, Otto Abels** 1873-1963
[EMT]
*American librettist and lyricist*
* Harbach, Otto

**Haug, William L.** 1852- ?   [BE]
*American baseball player*
* Hague, William L. [Bill]

**Haughey, Bud**
See  Haughey, Chris[topher
Francis]

**Haughey, Chris[topher Francis]**
1925-   [BE]
*American baseball player*
* Haughey, Bud

**Hauk, Maung**
See  Hobbs, Cecil [Carlton]

**Hauk, Minnie**
See  Hauck, Mignon

**Hauk, Minnie**
See  Hesse-Wartegg, Minnie von

**Haukelid, Sigrid Gurie** 1911-1969
[FC]
*American-Norwegian actress*
* Gurie, Sigrid

**Hauptmann, Bruno Richard**
1899-1936   [BLB]
*German-born murderer and
kidnapper*
* Cemetery John

**Haus, Ladovie**
See  Delorme, Reve

**Hauser, Arnold J.** 1888-    [BE]
*American baseball player*
* Hauser, Pee Wee

**Hauser, Carl**    [FFF]
*Author*
* Schnake

**Hauser, Heinrich** 1901-1955
[WGT]
*German author*
* Blade, Alexander [house
    pseudonym, Ziff-Davis]

**Hauser, Joseph John** 1899-
[BE, BN]
*American baseball player*
* Hauser, Unser Choe
* Hauser, Zip

**Hauser, Margaret L[ouise]** 1909-
[CAP, SAT]
*American author*
* Head, Gay

**Hauser, Pee Wee**
See   Hauser, Arnold J.

**Hauser, Unser Choe**
See   Hauser, Joseph John

**Hauser, Zip**
See   Hauser, Joseph John

**Hausman, Martin** 1925-    [EJ]
*American jazz musician*
* Holmes, Marty

**Hauss, Len** 20th c.
*American football player*
* Hauss, Zeke
* Maddox, Lester

**Hauss, Zeke**
See   Hauss, Len

**Haussmann, Jacques** 1902-
[BDF, BEW, FC]
*Rumanian-born American producer*
* Houseman, John

**Hautboy**
See   Harper, John

**Hautzig, Esther Rudomin** 1930-
[CA, SAT, WD]
*Polish-born American author*
* Rudomin, Esther

**[The] Havelock of the War**
See   Howard, Oliver Otis

**Haven, Alice B.** 1825-1863    [FFF]
*American author*
* Cousin Alice

**Haven, Charna**
See   Kichaven, Charna E.

**Havenhand, John**
See   Cox, John Roberts [Jack]

**Havens, Stewart**
See   Lee, Wayne Cyril

**Haver, June**
See   Stovenour, June

**Haverhoek, Hendrik** 1947-    [EJ7]
*Dutch jazz musician*
* Haverhoek, Henk

**Haverhoek, Henk**
See   Haverhoek, Hendrik

**Haverschmidt, Francois** 1835-1894
[WBD]
*Dutch clergyman and author*
* Paaltjens, Piet

**Haverstock, Nathan Alfred** 1931-
[CA]
*American author and columnist*
* Alfred, Richard [joint pseudonym
    with Richard C. Schroeder]

**Havil, Anthony**
See   Philipp, Elliot Elias

**Haviland, [Captain] Fergus**
See   Goddard, Norman Molyneux

**Havinden, Ashley Eldrid** 1903-
[GA]
*British graphic artist*
* Ashley

**Havlicek, Hondo**
See   Havlicek, John

**Havlicek, John** 1940-    [BB, SMG]
*American basketball player*
* Havlicek, Hondo
* Havlicek, Spider

**Havlicek, Karel** 1821-1856    [WBD]
*Czech journalist*
* Borovsky, Havel

**Havlicek, Spider**
See   Havlicek, John

**Havoc, June**
See   Hovick, June

**Haw Haw, Lord**
See   Joyce, William

**[The] Hawaiian Guitar Wizard**
See   Weldon, Will

**Haweis, Stephen** 1878-1968?    [CW]
*British-born poet, author, painter*
* Hawys, Stephen

**Hawes, Baldwin** 1919-    [DAM]
*American musician*
* Hawes, Butch

**Hawes, Butch**
See   Hawes, Baldwin

**Hawes, John** 20th c.    [FCW]
*American musician*
* Hawes, Pete[r]

**Hawes, Pete[r]**
See   Hawes, John

**Hawes, William Post** 1821-1842
[FFF, PA]
*American author*
* Cypress, J., Jr.

**Hawk** [code name]
See   Bykovsky, Valery Feodorovich

**[The] Hawk**
See   Gonzalez, Gerardo

**[The] Hawk**
See   Harrelson, Kenneth Smith

**[The] Hawk**
See   Hawkins, Coleman

**[The] Hawk**
See   Hawkins, Connie

**[The] Hawk**
See   Hawkins, Harold F.

**[The] Hawk**
See   Hogan, Benjamin William

**[The] Hawk**
See   Hutto, Joseph Benjamin

**[The] Hawk**
See   Rupolo, Ernest

**Hawk, Alex**
See   Garfield, Brian [Francis]
Wynne

**Hawk, Alex**
See   Kelton, Elmer

**Hawk, Jack**
See   Sellers, Connie Leslie, Jr.

**Hawk, John**
See   Cournos, Helen Kestner
Satterthwaite

**Hawke, Dick**
See   Hawke, William Victor [Bill]

**Hawke, Nancy**
See   Nugent, Nancy

**Hawke, [Captain] Robert**
See   Bowman, Gerald

**Hawke, [Captain] Robert**
See   O'Mant, Hedley Percival
Angelo

**Hawke, William Victor [Bill]**
1870-1902    [BE]
*American baseball player*
* Hawke, Dick

**Hawken, Henry** 1888-1962    [THR]
*British actor*
* Caine, Henry

**Hawker, J.**
See   Heesch, David W.

**Hawker, Mary Elizabeth**
1848?-1908    [SFL, WGT, WWL]
*British author*
* Falconer, Lanoe
* L. F.

**Hawker, Robert** 1753-1827    [PA]
*Author*
* R. H.

**Hawkes, Chip**
See   Hawkes, Len

**Hawkes, Len** 1946-    [RO2]
*British musician*
* Hawkes, Chip

**Hawkes, Thorndike Proctor**
1852-1929    [BE]
*American baseball player*
* Hawkes, Thorny

**Hawkes, Thorny**
See   Hawkes, Thorndike Proctor

**Hawkesworth, Eric** 1921-
[CA, SAT]
*British author*
* [The] Great Comte

**Hawkeye**
See   Carlisle, R. H.

**Hawkeye Man**
See   Burdette, Robert J.

**Hawkin, Martin**
See   Hawkins, Martin

**Hawkins, [Sir] Anthony Hope**
1863-1933    [FC, LC, TC]
*British author*
* Hope, Anthony

**Hawkins, Augustus Freeman** 1907-
[IBW]
*American politician*
* Hawkins, Gus

**Hawkins, Bean**
See   Hawkins, Coleman

**Hawkins, Benjamin C.** 1944-    [FB]
*American football player*
* Hawkins, Hawk

**Hawkins, Bubbles**
See   Hawkins, Robert

**Hawkins, Charles Ashton**    [PA]
*Author*
* Vidocq

**Hawkins, Coleman** 1904-1969
[EJ, PMJ]
*American jazz musician*
* [The] Hawk
* Hawkins, Bean

**Hawkins, Connie** 1942-    [BB, IBW]
*American basketball player*
* Everything, Mr.
* [The] Hawk

**Hawkins, Erskine Ramsey** 1914-
[IBW]
*American jazz musician*
* [The] Twentieth Century Gabriel

**Hawkins, Etta James** 1938-    [RO1]
*American singer*
* James, Etta

**Hawkins, Gus**
See   Hawkins, Augustus Freeman

**Hawkins, Hanging**
See   Hawkins, [Sir] Henry [Baron
Brampton]

**Hawkins, Harold F.** 1921-1963
[CM, CME, CWG]
*American country-western performer*
* [The] Hawk
* Hawkins, Hawkshaw

**Hawkins, Hawk**
See   Hawkins, Benjamin C.

**Hawkins, Hawk**
See   Hawkins, Lemuel

**Hawkins, Hawk**
See   Hawkins, Wynn Firth

**Hawkins, Hawkshaw**
See   Hawkins, Harold F.

**Hawkins, [Sir] Henry [Baron
Brampton]** 1817-1907    [WBD]
*British jurist*
* Hawkins, Hanging

**Hawkins, Jalacy J.** 1929-
[BWW, IBW]
*American singer and musician*
* [The] Clown Prince of Rock and
    Roll
* Hawkins, Jay
* Hawkins, Screamin' Jay

**Hawkins, Jay**
See   Hawkins, Jalacy J.

**Hawkins, John**
See   Catchpole, William Leslie

**Hawkins, Lemuel** 20th c.    [OBW]
*American baseball player*
* Hawkins, Hawk

**Hawkins, Martin** 20th c.
[ESF, SFL]
*British author*
* Hawkin, Martin

**Hawkins, Peter** 1926-    [IAW, SFL]
*British author*
* Maras, Karl [house pseudonym]
* Ramon, Boris

**Hawkins, [Sir] Richard** 1562-1622
[DEP]
*British naval officer*
* [The] Complete Seaman

**Hawkins, Robert** 1954- [SMG]
*American basketball player*
* Hawkins, Bubbles

**Hawkins, Screamin' Jay**
*See* Hawkins, Jalacy J.

**Hawkins, Sekatary**
*See* Schulkers, Robert Franc

**Hawkins, Tom**
*See* Buckley, Theodore William
Alois

**Hawkins, William**
*See* Caiano, Mario

**Hawkins, Wynn Firth** 1936- [BE]
*American baseball player*
* Hawkins, Hawk

**Hawks, Chicken**
*See* Hawks, Nelson Louis

**Hawks, Francis Lister** 1798-1866
[FFF]
*American clergyman and author*
* Uncle Philip

**Hawks, Nelson Louis** 1896- [BE]
*American baseball player*
* Hawks, Chicken

**Hawkshaw**
*See* Fraser, John A.

**Hawkwood, Allan**
*See* Bedford-Jones, Henry [James
O'Brien]

**Hawley, Blue**
*See* Hawley, Marvin

**Hawley, Emerson P.** 1872-1938
[AS, BE]
*American baseball player*
* Hawley, Pink

**Hawley, Florence M.**
*See* Ellis, Florence Hawley

**Hawley, Henrietta Ripperger**
1890?-1974 [CA]
*American author*
* Ripperger, Henrietta

**Hawley, James** 1966-
*Japanese-American karate expert*
* Holly, Jimmy Lee

**Hawley, Mabel C.** [house
pseudonym] [Stratemeyer
Syndicate]
*See* Stratemeyer, Edward L.

**Hawley, Marvin** 20th c. [BN]
*American baseball player*
* Hawley, Blue

**Hawley, Mrs. D. R.** [FFF]
*Entertainer*
* Oswald, Maude

**Hawley, Pink**
*See* Hawley, Emerson P.

**Hawn, Happy Jack**
*See* Hawn, John

**Hawn, John** 1883-1964 [SC]
*American actor and stunt performer*
* Hawn, Happy Jack

**Haworth, Martha** 1922- [ITA, SW]
*American actress*
* Stewart, Martha

**Haworth, Mary**
*See* Young, Mary Elizabeth

**Haws, Duncan** 1921- [CA]
*British author and illustrator*
* Pertinax

**Hawtayne, G. H.** 1854?- ? [CW]
*Guyanese folklorist*
* Beke, X.

**Hawthorne, Alice**
*See* Winner, Septimus

**Hawthorne, Emily**
*See* Charles, Emily Thornton

**Hawthorne, Grace**
*See* Murray, Mrs. John

**Hawthorne, Julian** 1846-1934 [TC]
*American author*
* Hollinshed, Judith

**Hawthorne, Kate**
*See* Lacey, Mrs. Henry

**Hawthorne, [Captain] R. M.**
*See* Ellis, Edward S[ylvester]

**Hawthorne, Rainey**
*See* Riddell, Charlotte Eliza
Lawson [Cowan]

**Hawthorne, Rose** 1851-1926
[WBD]
*Founder of American religious order*
* Alphonsa, [Mother]

**Hawton, Hector** 1901-
[CA, MBF, WW]
*British author*
* Curzon, Virginia
* Sylvester, John

**Hawtrey, Charles**
*See* Hartree, Charles

**Hawy, Valentine** 18th c. [FFF]
*Invented printing with raised letters*
* [The] Apostle to the Blind

**Hawys, Stephen**
*See* Haweis, Stephen

**Haxall, James T.** 1860-1939 [FB]
*American football player*
* Haxall, Jerry

**Haxall, Jerry**
*See* Haxall, James T.

**Haxton, Josephine A.** 1921- [IAW]
*American author*
* Douglas, Ellen

**Hay, Elzey**
*See* Andrews, Eliza Frances
[Fanny]

**Hay, Frances**
*See* Erikson, [Cicely] Sibyl
Alexandra

**Hay, George** ?-1830 [PA]
*Author*
* Hortentius

**Hay, George** 1922- [ESF]
*British author and editor*
* Lang, King [house pseudonym,
Curtis Warren]

**Hay, George Dewey** 1895-1968
[ECM, FCW]
*American radio station executive
and founder of the Grand Ole Opry*
* [The] Solemn Old Judge

**Hay, Gyula** 1900-1975 [WOA]
*Hungarian playwright*
* Hay, Julius

**Hay, Helen** 1874-1957 [F2, FC]
*British actress*
* Haye, Helen

**Hay, Ian**
*See* Beith, [Sir] John Hay

**Hay, Jacob** 1920- [CA]
*American author*
* Terme, Hilary

**Hay, James Alexander** 1931- [CEI]
*Canadian-born hockey player*
* Hay, Red Eye

**Hay, John** [joint pseudonym with
John Dalrymple-Hay]
*See* Dalrymple-Hay, Barbara

**Hay, John** [joint pseudonym with
Barbara Dalrymple-Hay]
*See* Dalrymple-Hay, John

**Hay, Julius**
*See* Hay, Gyula

**Hay, Mary**
*See* Caldwell, Mary

**Hay, Mary Cecil** 1840?-1886 [PA]
*Author*
* [The] Duchess
* Markham, Howard

**Hay, Nigel**
*See* Nagle-Healy, James Anthony

**Hay, Red**
*See* Hay, William Charles

**Hay, Red Eye**
*See* Hay, James Alexander

**Hay, Timothy**
*See* Brown, Margaret Wise

**Hay, Valerie**
*See* Hay-Austin, Valerie

**Hay, Will** 1888-1949 [BMH]
*British comedian*
* [The] Schoolmaster Comedian

**Hay, William Charles** 1935-
[CEI, FHE, HK]
*Canadian-born hockey player*
* Hay, Red

**Hay-Austin, Valerie** 1910- [THR]
*British actress and singer*
* Hay, Valerie

**Hay-Plumb, Edward** 1883-1960
[BF]
*British actor and director*
* Plumb, Hay

**Hayakawa, Kintaro** 1889-1973
[SC]
*Japanese actor, producer, author*
* Hayakawa, Sessue

**Hayakawa, Samuel Ichiye** 1906-
*American politician and former
college president*
* Hayakewa, S. I.
* [The] Sominex Kid

**Hayakawa, Sessue**
*See* Hayakawa, Kintaro

**Hayakewa, S. I.**
*See* Hayakawa, Samuel Ichiye

**Hayashi, Takashi** 20th c. [SFP]
*Author*
* Kigi, Takataro

**Haycroft, Pendleton**
*See* Hayward, Percy Roy

**Haydel, Richard** 1927-1949 [SC]
*American actor*
* Jordan, Ricky

**Hayden, Buddy**
*See* Hayden, N. S.

**Hayden, C[harles] Gervin** 1938-
[CA]
*American writer*
* Wicker, Randolfe Hayden

**Hayden, Eric W[illiam]** 1919- [CA]
*British clergyman and author*
* Cire

**Hayden, [Eu]gene [Franklin]** 1935-
[BE]
*American baseball player*
* Hayden, Lefty

**Hayden, Lefty**
*See* Hayden, [Eu]gene [Franklin]

**Hayden, Lucky**
*See* Lucid, Pate

**Hayden, Melissa**
*See* Herman, Mildred

**Hayden, N. S.** 20th c.
*American newspaper publisher*
* Hayden, Buddy

**Hayden, Robert**
*See* Fish, Hamilton

**Hayden, Russell**
*See* Lucid, Pate

**Hayden, Sarah Marshall**
*See* Frazaer, Mary

**Hayden, Sterling**
*See* Hamilton, John

**Haydn, [Franz] Joseph** 1732-1809
[DEP, DNNS, SN]
*Austrian composer*
* [The] Father of Symphony
* Haydn, Papa

**Haydn, Papa**
*See* Haydn, [Franz] Joseph

**Haydock, Ron** 1940?-1977
[FIR, SFP]
*Author*
* Grey, Judson [joint pseudonym
with Jim Harmon]
* Lord, Lonnie
* Saxon, Vin

**Haydon, Adrianne Shirley** 1938-
[OCS]
*British tennis player*
* Haydon, Ann

**Haydon, Ann**
*See* Haydon, Adrianne Shirley

**Haydon, Julie**
*See* Donaldson, Donella Lightfoot

**Haydon, Monty**
*See* Haydon, Percy Montague

**Haydon, N. G.** 20th c. [MBF]
*British author*
* Pembury, Grosvenor

**Haydon, Percy Montague** 1895-
[MBF]
*British author*
* Haydon, Monty

**Haye, Helen**
*See* Hay, Helen

**Hayek, F. A.**
*See* Hayek, Friedrich August Von

**Hayek, Frank** 1896-1976 [SC]
*American actor and opera singer*
* Forest, Frank
* Foresto, Franco

**Hayek, Friedrich August Von**
1899- [LC]
*Austrian-born economist and author*
* Hayek, F. A.

**Hayes, Alexander**
*See* Cooper, Robert Andrew

**Hayes, Allison**
*See* Hayes, Mary Jane

**Hayes, Blimp**
*See* Hayes, Franklin Witman

**Hayes, Bullet Bob**
*See* Hayes, Robert L.

**Hayes, Bun**
*See* Hayes, Burnalle James

**Hayes, Burnalle James** 1903-1969
[MK]
*American baseball player*
* Hayes, Bun

**Hayes, Catherine** 1820?-1861
[FFF]
*Irish-born singer*
* [The] Irish Nightingale

**Hayes, Clancy**
*See* Hayes, Clarence Leonard

**Hayes, Clarence Leonard**
1908-1972 [DAM, PMJ]
*American singer and musician*
* Hayes, Clancy

**Hayes, Doc**
*See* Hayes, Elmore

**Hayes, Edgar Junius** 1904- [IBW]
*American musician*
* [The] Man with a Thousand
  Fingers

**Hayes, Edward Brian** 1935-1973
[EJ, EJ7]
*British jazz musician*
* Hayes, Tubby

**Hayes, Elmore** 1906-1973 [BB]
*American basketball coach*
* Hayes, Doc

**Hayes, Elvin** 1945- [BB]
*American basketball player*
* [The] Big E

**Hayes, Evelyn**
*See* Bethell, Mary Ursula

**Hayes, Frances X.** ?-1978 [FIR]
*Entertainer*
* Hayes, Jack

**Hayes, Franklin Witman**
1914-1955 [BE]
*American baseball player*
* Hayes, Blimp

**Hayes, Gabby**
*See* Hayes, George Francis

**Hayes, George Francis** 1885-1969
[F2, FC, OCF]
*American actor*
* Hayes, Gabby

**Hayes, Granny**
*See* Hayes, Rutherford Birchard

**Hayes, Helen**
*See* Brown, Helen Hayes

**Hayes, Henry**
*See* Kirk, Ellen Warner Olney

**Hayes, Isaac** 1942- [IBW, SSS]
*American musician*
* [The] Black Moses
* Hayes, Sack

**Hayes, Ivor**
*See* Ransome, L. E.

**Hayes, Jack**
*See* Hayes, Frances X.

**Hayes, Jackie**
*See* Hayes, Minter Carney

**Hayes, John Essix** 1904- [MK]
*American baseball player*
* Hayes, Pap

**Hayes, Joseph [Arnold]** 1918-
[CA, WD]
*American author, playwright,
screenwriter*
* Arnold, Joseph H.

**Hayes, Kiffin Ayres** 1917- [CA]
*American author and editor*
* Rockwell, Kiffin Ayres

**Hayes, Larry Ray** 1940- [ASC]
*American composer*
* Ray, Larry

**Hayes, Lawrence** 1853- ? [BE]
*American baseball player*
* Hayes, Mike

**Hayes, M.** [PA]
*Author*
* Bishop, Thomas

**Hayes, Maggie**
*See* Ottenheimer, Florette Regina

**Hayes, Mary Jane** 1930- [FC]
*American actress*
* Hayes, Allison

**Hayes, Mike**
*See* Hayes, Lawrence

**Hayes, Minter Carney** 1906- [BE]
*American baseball player*
* Hayes, Jackie

**Hayes, Pap**
*See* Hayes, John Essix

**Hayes, Percival** 1889-1943
*New Zealand-born actor, director,
screenwriter*
* Julian, Rupert

**Hayes, Peter Lind**
*See* Lind, Joseph Conrad

**Hayes, Ralph E[ugene]** 1927- [CA]
*American author*
* Carter, Nick

**Hayes, Robert**
*See* Cooper, Robert Andrew

**Hayes, Robert L.** 1942- [FB, TF]
*American football player and track
athlete*
* Hayes, Bullet Bob

**Hayes, Robert L.** (Continued)
* Hayes, Speedo

**Hayes, Rutherford Birchard**
1822-1893 [FAP]
*American president*
* [The] Dark Horse President
* [The] Fraud President
* Hayes, Granny
* [The] Hero of '77
* His Fraudulency
* Old Eight to Seven
* President De Facto

**Hayes, Sack**
*See* Hayes, Isaac

**Hayes, Samuel Stewart** 1905-1958
[SC]
*American actor and radio announcer*
* Hardy, Sam

**Hayes, Speedo**
*See* Hayes, Robert L.

**Hayes, Thomas** 20th c. [WWL]
*Irish author and playwright*
* O hAodha, Tomas

**Hayes, Timothy**
*See* Fearn, John Russell

**Hayes, Tubby**
*See* Hayes, Edward Brian

**Hayes, Wayne Woodrow** 1913-
[B10, FB]
*American football coach*
* Hayes, Woody

**Hayes, Wilson**
*See* Harris, Kathryn [Beatrice]
Gibbs

**Hayes, Woody**
*See* Hayes, Wayne Woodrow

**Hayley, William** 1745-1820 [RH]
*British poet*
* Hermit

**Hayley Bell, Mary** 20th c. [CA]
*British playwright*
* Bell, Mary Hayley

**Haylon, Jack** 1891- [BMH]
*British comedian*
* Edge, Jack

**Hayman**
*See* Peel, Hazel Mary [Wallis]

**Hayman, Bugs**
*See* Hayman, Charles

**Hayman, Charles** 20th c. [OBW]
*American baseball player*
* Hayman, Bugs

**Hayman, Mrs. David** [FFF]
*Entertainer*
* Grubb, Lillie

**Hayman, Robert** 17th c. [PA]
*Author*
* Quodlibets

**Haymen, Helen Violet Carolyn**
1918- [THR]
*British actress and singer*
* Lynne, Carole

**Haymes, Andrew**
*See* Chiariglione, Andrew

**Haymond, Alvin H.** 1942- [FB]
*American football player*
* Haymond, Juggie

**Haymond, Juggie**
*See* Haymond, Alvin H.

**Haynau, Julius Jakob von**
1786-1853 [DNNS, HN, SN]
*Austrian army officer*
* [The] Austrian Hyena
* [The] Hyena of Brescia
* [The] Woman Flogger

**Hayne, Paul Hamilton** 1830-1886
[FFF]
*American poet*
* [The] Laureate of the South
* [The] Longfellow of the South

**Haynes, Abner** 1937- [FB]
*American football player*
* Haynes, Butch

**Haynes, Alfred H[enry]** 1910- [CA]
*British author*
* Christie, Keith

**Haynes, Anne**
*See* Madlee, Dorothy [Haynes]

**Haynes, Bill**
*See* Haynes, H. J.

**Haynes, Brian Arthur** 1944- [RO2]
*British musician*
* Laine, Denny

**Haynes, Butch**
*See* Haynes, Abner

**Haynes, Dorothy K.**
*See* Gray, Dorothy Kate

**Haynes, George** 1907- [EJ]
*American jazz musician*
* Haynes, Tiger

**Haynes, H. J.** 1925- [B10]
*American petroleum executive*
* Haynes, Bill

**Haynes, Henry D.** 1918?-1971
[CME, CWG, DAM]
*American country-western performer*
* Homer

**Haynes, John Edward** 1825- ? [PA]
*Author*
* Edwards, John H.

**Haynes, John Robert**
*See* Wilding, Philip

**Haynes, Lemuel B.** 1753-1833
[IBW]
*American clergyman*
* [The] Green Mountain Boy

**Haynes, Leroy H.** 1915- [IBW]
*American football player*
* Haynes, Rough House

**Haynes, Linda**
*See* Swinford, Betty [June Wells]

**Haynes, Marques Oreole** 1925-
[IBW]
*American basketball player*
* [The] World's Greatest Dribbler

**Haynes, Pat**
*See* McKeag, Ernest L[ionel]

**Haynes, Race Horse**
*See* Haynes, Richard

**Haynes, Richard** 20th c.
*American attorney*
* Haynes, Race Horse

**Haynes, Rough House**
*See* Haynes, Leroy H.

**Haynes, Tiger**
See  Haynes, George

**Haynes Dixon, Margaret Rumer**
1907-  [IAW]
*British author*
* Godden, Rumer

**Hays, Elinor Rice** 20th c.  [CA]
*American author*
* Rice, Elinor

**Hays, Harold** 20th c.
*American football player*
* Hays, Hurricane

**Hays, Hurricane**
See  Hays, Harold

**Hays, Janice Nicholson** 1929-
[WD]
*American poet*
* Loonie, Janice Hays

**Hayter, Cecil Goodenough**
1871-1922  [MBF]
*British author*
* Bird, Lewis
* Steel, Howard

**Hayter, S. W.**
See  Hayter, Stanley William

**Hayter, Stanley William** 1901-
[ART]
*British-born painter, engraver,
etcher*
* Hayter, S. W.

**Haythorne, Joan**
See  Haythornthwaite, Joan

**Haythornthwaite, Joan** 1915-  [FC]
*British actress*
* Haythorne, Joan

**Hayton, Richard Neil** 1916-  [CA]
*American author*
* Starling, Thomas

**Hayward, Dagney**
See  Major, J. D.

**Hayward, Louis**
See  Grant, Seafield

**Hayward, Mrs. Louis**  [FFF]
*Entertainer*
* Robinson, Josie

**Hayward, Percy Roy** 1884-  [NAA]
*Canadian-born educator and author*
* Haycroft, Pendleton
* Percival, Hayward

**Hayward, Richard**
See  Cozzens, Frederick Swartwout

**Hayward, Richard**
See  Kendrick, Baynard
H[ardwick]

**Hayward, Susan**
See  Marriner, Edythe

**Hayward, Thomas**
See  Oldys, William

**Hayward, William** 1868-1949
[BBH]
*Canadian-born track and field coach*
* [The] Father of Oregon Track

**Haywarde, Richard**
See  Cozzens, Frederick Swartwout

**Haywire Mac**
See  McClintock, Harry Kirby

**Haywood, Albert** 20th c.  [OBW]
*American baseball player*
* Haywood, Buster

**Haywood, Buster**
See  Haywood, Albert

**Haywood, Cedric** 1916?-  [MY]
*American jazz musician*
* Haywood, Yardbird

**Haywood, Harry**
See  Hall, Haywood

**Haywood, Spencer** 1949?-
*American basketball player*
* [The] Moor of Venice

**Haywood, Yardbird**
See  Haywood, Cedric

**Hayworth, Myron Claude** 1915-
[BE]
*American baseball player*
* Hayworth, Red

**Hayworth, Red**
See  Hayworth, Myron Claude

**Hayworth, Rita**
See  Cansino, Margarita Carmen

**Hazard, Desire**
See  Feuillet, Octave

**Hazard, Harry**
See  Badger, Joseph E.

**Hazard, Jack**
See  Booth, Edwin

**Hazel, Arthur** 1903-1968
[EJ, PMJ, WWJ]
*American jazz musician*
* Hazel, Monk

**Hazel, Harry**
See  Jones, Justin

**Hazel, Homer H.** 1895-1968  [FB]
*American football player*
* Hazel, Pop

**Hazel, Monk**
See  Hazel, Arthur

**Hazel, Pop**
See  Hazel, Homer H.

**Hazel, William?**
See  St. Clair, Margaret

**Hazell, Hy**
See  O'Higgins, Hyacinth Hazel

**Hazeltine, Horace**
See  Wayne, Charles Stokes

**Hazeltine, Mayo H.**  [PA]
*Author*
* M. W. H.

**Hazeltine, Miron J.**  [PA]
*Author*
* Miron

**Hazelton, Alexander**
See  Armstrong, William
A[lexander]

**Hazelton, Mabel**
See  Reed, C. H.

**Hazelwood, Adelaide** 20th c.
[CWG]
*American country-western performer*
* Wood, Del

**Hazen, M. P.**  [PA]
*Author*
* Mabel

**Hazinski, Stanley Frank** 1913-
[BE]
*American baseball player*
* Rogers, Packy
* Rogers, Stanley Frank

**Hazle, Hurricane**
See  Hazle, Robert Sidney [Bob]

**Hazle, Robert Sidney [Bob]** 1930-
[BE]
*American baseball player*
* Hazle, Hurricane

**Hazleton, Doc**
See  Hazleton, Willard Carpenter

**Hazleton, Mrs. J. H.**  [FFF]
*Entertainer*
* Melville, Ada

**Hazleton, Willard Carpenter**
1876-1941  [BE]
*American baseball player*
* Hazleton, Doc

**Hazlett, William** 1875-1948  [SC]
*American actor and rodeo performer*
* Many Treaties, Chief

**Hazlitt, Joseph**
See  Strage, Mark

**Hazlitt, Pygmalion**
See  Hazlitt, William

**Hazlitt, William** 1778-1830
[FFF, SN]
*British author*
* [The] Dumont of Letters
* Hazlitt, Pygmalion
* Phantastes
* Search, Edward

**Hazzard, Walt** 1942-  [BB, SMG]
*American basketball player*
* Abdul-Rahman, Mahdi

**Hazzard, Wilton**
See  St. Clair, Margaret

**Hazziez, Yusef**
See  Arrington, Joseph, Jr.

**He of the Suburbs**
See  Hakim I [or Hakam] al-

**Heacker, Herman** ?-1929  [SC]
*American actor*
* Harvey, Hank

**Head, Ann**
See  Morse, Anne Christensen

**Head, Archibald**
See  Turner, John M.

**Head, Eddy**
See  Head, Timothy John

**Head, [Sir] Francis Bond**
1793-1875  [FFF, RH]
*British traveller and author*
* Head, Galloping
* [An] Old Man

**Head, Galloping**
See  Head, [Sir] Francis Bond

**Head, Gay**
See  Hauser, Margaret L[ouise]

**Head, Matthew**
See  Canaday, John [Edwin]

**[The] Head of Iron**
See  Forbes, John

**Head, Richard** 1637?-1678?  [FFF]
*Irish playwright*
* Careless, Franck

**Head, Timothy John** 1957-  [DC]
*British cricketer*
* Head, Eddy

**Headen, John**
See  Thompson, John H.

**Headlam, James Wycliffe**
1863-1929  [WBD]
*British historian*
* Headlam-Morley, [Sir] James
  Wycliffe

**Headlam-Morley, [Sir] James
Wycliffe**
See  Headlam, James Wycliffe

**Headley, Elizabeth**
See  Cavanna, Elizabeth Allen
[Betty]

**Headley, George Alphonso** 1909-
[EC]
*Jamaican cricketer*
* [The] Bradman of the Caribbeans

**Headley-Neave, Alice** 1903-  [ART]
*British painter*
* Neave, A. H.

**Headon, Nicky** 1956?-
*British musician*
* Headon, Topper

**Headon, Topper**
See  Headon, Nicky

**Heagerty, Travers John** 1874-1965
[FC]
*British actor*
* Travers, Henry

**Heal, Edith** 1903-  [B10, CA, SAT]
*American author*
* Berrien, Edith Heal
* Page, Eileen
* Page, Mary
* Powers, Margaret

**Heald, Hazel**
See  Bishop, Zealia Brown Reed

**Heald, Leslie V.** 20th c.  [SFP]
*Author*
* Walsby, Charnock

**Healey, B. J.**
See  Healey, Benjamin James

**Healey, Benjamin James** 1908-
[CA, IAW]
*British author*
* Healey, B. J.
* Jeffreys, J. G.
* Sturrock, Jeremy

**Healey, Brooks**
See  Albert, Burton Jr.

**[The] Health Doctor**
See  Crampton, C[harles] Ward

**Healy, Egyptian**
See  Healy, John J.

**Healy, James Augustine**
1830-1900  [IBW]
*American clergyman*
* [The] Children's Bishop

**Healy, James N.**
See  Nagle-Healy, James Anthony

**Healy, John** 1854-1926  [BEW]
*Irish-born theatrical performer*
* Le Hay, John

**Healy, John J.** 1866-1899 [AS]
*American baseball player*
* Healy, Egyptian

**Healy, Patrick Francis** 1834-1882
[IBW]
*American clergyman and educator*
* [The] Spaniard

**Heanley, John** 1912- [THR]
*British actor and dancer*
* Byron, John

**Heard, Eugene M.** 1923- [EJ]
*American jazz musician*
* Heard, Fats

**Heard, Fats**
See Heard, Eugene M.

**Heard, Gerald**
See Heard, Henry Fitzgerald

**Heard, H. F.**
See Heard, Henry Fitzgerald

**Heard, Henry Fitzgerald**
1889-1971 [AW, CAP, CC]
*British-born philosopher, educator,*
*author*
* Heard, Gerald
* Heard, H. F.

**Heard, J. C.**
See Heard, James Charles

**Heard, J[oseph] Norman** 1922-
[CA]
*American author*
* Norman, Joe

**Heard, James Charles** 1917-
[DAM, EJ, PMJ]
*American jazz musician*
* Heard, J. C.

**Heard, Jay**
See Heard, Jehosie

**Heard, Jehosie** 1925- [BE]
*American baseball player*
* Heard, Jay

**Hearden, Red**
See Hearden, Thomas F.

**Hearden, Thomas F.** 1904?-1964
[AS]
*American football player*
* Hearden, Red

**Hearn, Bunn** 1891-1959 [BE]
*American baseball player*
* Hearn, Bunny

**Hearn, Bunny**
See Hearn, Bunn

**Hearn, Bunny**
See Hearn, Elmer Lafayette

**Hearn, Elmer Lafayette** 1904- [BE]
*American baseball player*
* Hearn, Bunny

**Hearn, John** 1920- [CA]
*British-born author, poet,*
*playwright*
* Pentecost, Martin

**Hearn, [Patricios] Lafcadio [Tessima**
**Carlos]** 1850-1904 [WGT]
*Greek-born author*
* Yakumo, Koizumi

**Hearn, Mary Ann** 1834-1909
[SFL, WGT]
*British author*
* Farningham, Marianne

**Hearn, Sneed**
See Gregg, Andrew K.

**Hearnden, Beryl** 20th c. [WW]
*Author*
* Balfour, Hearnden [joint
pseudonym with Eva Balfour]

**Hearne, Eddie**
*Auto racer*
* Hearne, Grandpa

**Hearne, George Richard Mant**
[MBF]
*British author*
* Mant, Richard

**Hearne, Grandpa**
See Hearne, Eddie

**Hearne, John** 1926- [B10, WD]
*British author and playwright*
* Morris, John [joint pseudonym
with Morris Cargill]

**Hearne, John William** 1891-1965
[EC]
*British cricketer*
* Hearne, Young Jack

**Hearne, Mrs. George** [FFF]
*Entertainer*
* Bell, Caroline

**Hearne, Richard** 1909- [BF]
*British actor*
* Pastry, Mr.

**Hearne, Young Jack**
See Hearne, John William

**Hearns, Thomas** 1959?-
*American boxer*
* [The] Hit Man
* [The] Motor City Cobra

**Hearst, Patricia Campbell [Patty]**
1954- [B10]
*American newspaper heiress and*
*kidnap victim*
* Tania

**Hearst, William Randolph** 1863-1951
*American newspaper publisher*
* W. R. H.

**Heartfield, John**
See Herzfelde, Helmut

**Heartman, Harold**
See Mebane, John [Harrison]

**Heaslip, Mark Patrick** 1951-
[SMG]
*American hockey player*
* M. P. H.

**Heath, Albert** 1935- [DAM, EJ7]
*American musician*
* Heath, Kuumba
* Heath, Tootie

**Heath, Bernard**
See Smith, Bernard

**Heath, Edward R[ichard] G[eorge]**
1916- [NN]
*British prime minister*
* [The] Grocer

**Heath, Eldon**
See Derleth, August [William]

**Heath, Elizabeth Alden**
See Holton, Edith Austin

**Heath, Harry E[ugene], Jr.** 1919-
[CA]
*American author and poet*
* Hall, Kendall

**Heath, Hy**
See Heath, Walter Henry

**Heath, James Edward [Jimmy]**
1926- [IBW]
*American jazz musician*
* Little Bird

**Heath, Kuumba**
See Heath, Albert

**Heath, Maggie E.** [FFF]
*Writer*
* Miriam
* Neale, Nettie

**Heath, Marie**
See Ashley, Mrs. Warren

**Heath, Mickey**
See Heath, Minor Wilson

**Heath, Minor Wilson** 1904- [BE]
*American baseball player*
* Heath, Mickey

**Heath, Monica**
See Fitzgerald, Arlene J.

**Heath, Nita**
See Kelly, Gwen Nita

**Heath, Peter**
See Fine, Peter

**Heath, Royston**
See Wallis, George C.

**Heath, Sandra**
See Wilson, Sandra

**Heath, Tootie**
See Heath, Albert

**Heath, Veronica**
See Blackett, Veronica Heath
Stuart [Tegner]

**Heath, W. McKendee** [PA]
*Author*
* Ducaigne, R. E.

**Heath, W. Shaw**
See Williamson, William Henry

**Heath, Walter Henry** 1890-1965
[ASC]
*American composer*
* Heath, Hy

**Heath-Miller, Mavis Blanche**
1914- [IAW]
*British author*
* Duncan, Blanche

**Heathcote, Claud**
See Panting, James Harwood

**Heathcott, Mary**
See Keegan, Mary Heathcott

**Heatherbell**
See Smith, Eleanor

**Heatherley, Clifford**
See Lamb, Clifford

**Heaton, Edwin Maria** [PA]
*Author*
* E. M. H.

**Heaton, Eva** [FFF]
*Entertainer*
* Wardell, Etelka

**[The] Heaven Born Hero**
See Clive, Robert [Baron Clive of
Plassey]

**Heaven, Constance**
See Fecher, Constance

**[The] Heaven-Sent Minister**
See Pitt, William

**[The] Heavenly Heroine**
See Christina

**Heaverlo, David Wallace** 1950-
[SMG]
*American baseball player*
* Heaverlo, Kojak
* Heaverlo, Tuna

**Heaverlo, Kojak**
See Heaverlo, David Wallace

**Heaverlo, Tuna**
See Heaverlo, David Wallace

**Heavy Duty Feddersen**
See Feddersen, Don

**Hebbard, William Wallace**
1621-1704 [PA]
*Author*
* Searcher, Leland

**Hebblethwaite, Peter** 1930- [CA]
*British author and television critic*
* Myddleton, Robert

**Hebden, Mark**
See Harris, John

**Hebenton, Andrew Clayton** 1953-
[SMG]
*Canadian-born hockey player*
* Habenton, Hebbie

**Heber, Austin**
See Poole, Reginald Heber

**Heber, Reginald**
See Poole, Reginald Heber

**Heber, Reginald** 1783-1826
[DNNS, FFF, SN]
*British prelate and hymn-writer*
* [The] Christian Atticus

**Heber, Richard** 1773-1833
[PA, SN]
*British book collector and author*
* Atticus
* [The] Magnificent Heber
* Parans, Cato

**Heberden, Mary Violet** 1906-
[CC, WW]
*Author*
* Leonard, Charles L.

**Hebert, Jacques Rene** 1755-1794
[DNNF, RH, SN]
*French journalist and politician*
* Duchesne, Father
* [Le] Pere Duchesne

**Hebert, Preacher**
See Hebert, Wallace Andrew
[Wally]

**Hebert, Wallace Andrew [Wally]**
1907- [BE]
*American baseball player*
* Hebert, Preacher

**Hecate**
See De l'Epine, Francesca
Margherita

**Hecht, Ben** 1893-1964 [SFL]
*American journalist, author,*
*playwright*
* Long, Peter

**Hecht, Clinton James** 1906-1937
[SC]
*American actor*
* Nixon, Clint

**Hecht, Friedrich** 1903- [WGT]
*German author*
* Langrenus, Manfred

**Hecht, Henri Joseph** 1922-
[CA, SAT]
*French illustrator and author*
* Maik, Henri

**Hecht, Merrilyn Cecelia** 1931- [EJ]
*American jazz musician*
* Hale, Corky

**Hecht, Ted**
See Hekt, Theodore

**Heckelmann, Charles N[ewman]**
1913- [CA]
*American author*
* Lawton, Charles

**Heclawa**
See Himmelwright, Abraham
Lincoln

**Hector, Annie [French]** 1825-1902
[LC]
*British author*
* Alexander, Mrs.

**[The] Hector of Germany**
See Joachim II

**Hed**
See Davis, Harold Eugene

**Hedayat, Dashiell**
See Leger, Jack-Alain

**Hedberg, Anders** 1951- [SMG]
*Swedish-born hockey player*
* [The] Swedish Express

**Hedden, Worth Tuttle** 1896- [CAP]
*American author*
* Woodley, Winifred

**Hedenstierna, Alfred** 1852-1906
[WBD]
*Swedish author*
* Sigurd

**Hedges, Bonny** [FFF]
*Entertainer*
* Bliss, Louise

**Hedges, Frank Hinckley** 1895-
[NAA]
*American journalist*
* Hart, John

**Hedges, Joseph**
See Harknett, Terry

**Hedison, Al**
See Heditsian, Ara

**Hedison, David**
See Heditsian, Ara

**Heditsian, Ara** 1928- [FC]
*American actor*
* Hedison, Al
* Hedison, David

**Hedley, Evalena Fryer** 20th c.
[NAA]
*American writer*
* Goodhouse, Grace

**Hedlund, Michael David** 1946-
[BE]
*American baseball player*
* Hedlund, Red

**Hedlund, Red**
See Hedlund, Michael David

**Hedrick, Zelma Kathryn** 1922?-
[FC, IPA, PMJ]
*American singer and actress*
* Grayson, Kathryn

**Heenan, John C.** 19th c.
[DNNS, FF, FFF]
*American boxer*
* [The] Benicia Boy

**Heenan, Mrs. John C.** 19th c.
[FFF]
*Entertainer*
* Stevens, Sarah

**Heeney, Tom** 1898- [BX]
*New Zealand-born American boxer*
* [The] Hard Rock from Down
Under

**Heerdt, Alfred** 1881-1958 [BB]
*American basketball player*
* Heerdt, Allie

**Heerdt, Allie**
See Heerdt, Alfred

**Heeresma, Heere** 1932- [CA]
*Dutch author*
* Heeresma Inc. [joint pseudonym]

**Heeresma Inc.** [joint pseudonym]
See Heeresma, Heere

**Heerkens, Ad**
See Heerkens, Adrianus Ludovicus
Cornelis Donatus

**Heerkens, Adrianus Ludovicus
Cornelis Donatus** 1913- [IWM]
*Dutch educator and author*
* Heerkens, Ad

**Heermance, Dorothy** 1907-1968
[F2, FC]
*American actress*
* Collyer, June

**Heesch, David W.** 1940?- [B10]
*American truck driver and
extortionist*
* Hawker, J.

**Heffelfinger, Heff**
See Heffelfinger, William Walter

**Heffelfinger, Pudge**
See Heffelfinger, William Walter

**Heffelfinger, William Walter**
1867-1954 [AS, B10, FB]
*American football player*
* Heffelfinger, Heff
* Heffelfinger, Pudge

**Hefferman, Michael**
See Furgerson, Samuel

**Heffner, Butch**
See Heffner, Robert Frederic

**Heffner, Donald Henry** 1911- [BE]
*American baseball player and
manager*
* Heffner, Jeep

**Heffner, Jeep**
See Heffner, Donald Henry

**Heffner, Rebecca** 20th c. [SC]
*Actress*
* D'Arcy, Sheila

**Heffner, Robert Frederic** 1938-
[BE]
*American baseball player*
* Heffner, Butch

**Heflin, Donald**
See Wallmann, Jeffrey M[iner]

**Heflin, Emmett Evan, Jr.**
1910-1971 [BDF, BEW, FC]
*American actor*
* Heflin, Van

**Heflin, Van**
See Heflin, Emmett Evan, Jr.

**Hefner, Hugh**
See Hefner, Larry Douglas

**Hefner, Larry Douglas** 1948-
[SMG]
*American football player*
* Hefner, Hugh

**Hegamin, Lucille** 1894-1970
[BWW]
*American singer*
* Baker, Fanny
* [The] Blues Singer Supreme
* [The] Cameo Girl
* Chicago Cyclone
* Georgia Peach
* Harlem's Favorite

**Hegarty, Ellen** 1918- [CA]
*American author*
* Hegarty, [Sister] M[ary] Loyola

**Hegarty, [Sister] M[ary] Loyola**
See Hegarty, Ellen

**Hegeler, Sten** 1923- [IAW]
*Danish psychologist and author*
* Borel, Helene
* Stein, Jan

**Hegeman, Mary** 1907- [CA, WD]
*American educator and author*
* Mary Theodore, [Sister]

**Hegemon**
See Guidi, Philipert

**Hegesippus**
See Schonfield, Hugh J[oseph]

**Heidbreder, Margaret Ann**
See Eastman, Ann Heidbreder

**Heide, Florence Parry** 1919- [CA]
*American author*
* Allen, Alex B.
* McDonald, Jamie

**Heidemann, Paul** 1886-1968 [SC]
*German actor*
* Heidemann, Paulchen

**Heidemann, Paulchen**
See Heidemann, Paul

**Heidendberg, Johannes** 1462-1516
[WBD]
*German scholar*
* Tritheim, Johannes

**Heidrick, John Emmett** 1876-1916
[BE]
*American baseball player*
* Heidrick, Snags

**Heidrick, Snags**
See Heidrick, John Emmett

**Heifer, Frank[lin]** 1854-1893 [BE]
*American baseball player*
* Heifer, Heck

**Heifer, Heck**
See Heifer, Frank[lin]

**Heigerlin, Johannes** 1478-1541
[DNNS, SN, WBD]
*German clergyman*
* Faber, John [or Johannes]
* [The] Hammer of Heretics
* Malleus Hereticorum

**Heigh-Ho**
See Norris, Henry

**Heigius, Alexander** 1440?-1498
[HN]
*German scholar*
* [The] Restorer of Letters

**Heijermans, Herman** 1864-1924
[BEW, EWL]
*Dutch author and playwright*
* Falkland, Samuel
* Habbema, Koos
* Jelakowitch, Iwan

**Heikel, Karin Alice** 1901-1944
[EWL]
*Finnish poet*
* Vala, Katri Wadenstroem

**Heikes, Pop**
See Heikes, Rolla O.

**Heikes, Rolla O.** 1856-1934 [BBH]
*American trapshooter*
* Heikes, Pop

**Heilbrun, Carolyn G[old]** 1926-
[CA, CC]
*American educator and author*
* Cross, Amanda

**Heileman, Chink**
See Heileman, John George

**Heileman, John George** 1872-1940
[BE]
*American baseball player*
* Heileman, Chink

**Heilmann, Harry Edwin** 1894-1951
[BAB, BE, PB]
*American baseball player*
* Harry the Horse
* Heilmann, Slug

**Heilmann, Slug**
See Heilmann, Harry Edwin

**Heimach, Fred Amos** 1901-1973
[BE]
*American baseball player*
* Heimach, Lefty

**Heimach, Lefty**
See Heimach, Fred Amos

**Heimberg, Marilyn Markham**
See Ross, Marilyn Heimberg

**Heimberger, Edward Albert** 1908-
[BEW, EMT, FC]
*American actor*
* Albert, Eddie

**Hein, Mel** 20th c.
*American football player and coach*
* Hein, Old Indestructible

**Hein, Old Indestructible**
See Hein, Mel

**Hein, Piet** 1905- [CA]
*Danish scientist, inventor, author*
* Kumbel

**Heinberg, Alexander** 1883-1935
[SC]
*German-born actor*
* Schultz, Harry

**Heindel, Max**
See Van Grasshoff, Carl Louis

**Heine, Bud**
See Heine, William Henry

**Heine, Harry** 1797-1856
[DEP, WBD]
*German poet*
* [The] Darling of the Graces
* Heine, Heinrich

**Heine, Heinrich**
*See* Heine, Harry

**Heine, William Henry** 1900- [BE]
*American baseball player*
* Heine, Bud

**Heinecken, Christian Heinrich**
1721-1725 [FFF, HN, SN]
*German child prodigy*
* [The] Infant of Luebeck

**Heinemann, Katherine** 1918- [CA]
*American writer and poet*
* Kaki

**Heiney, Donald [William]** 1921-
[CA]
*American author*
* Harris, MacDonald

**Heinke, Terry** [RBE]
*American boxer*
* Hinke, Terry

**Heinkel, Stanford**
*See* Hennel, Stanford

**Heinl, Nancy G[ordon]** 1916- [CA]
*British-born author and columnist*
* Gordon, Nancy

**Heinlein, Robert A[nson]** 1907-
[CA, SF, WGT]
*American author*
* MacDonald, Anson
* Monroe, Lyle
* Riverside, John
* Saunders, Caleb
* York, Simon

**Heinlen, Howard Atlee** 1926-
[BEW]
*American press representative*
* Atlee, Howard

**Heino, Kyllikki**
*See* Polviander, Anni Kyllikki

**Heinrich, Edward Oscar** 20th c.
[BLB]
*American criminologist*
* [The] Wizard of Berkeley

**Heinrich von Meissen** 1250?-1318
[WBD]
*German poet*
* Frauenlob [Praise of Women]

**Heinrich von Moelk** [SN]
*German satirist*
* [The] Juvenal of Chivalry

**Heinz, Bob** 1947- [SMG]
*American football player*
* Heinz, Policeman

**Heinz, G.**
*See* Gerard-Libois, Jules C.

**Heinz, Gerard**
*See* Hinze, Gerard

**Heinz, H. John, III** 1939-
*American politician*
* Heinz, Pickles

**Heinz, Jerome** 1921-
[BBD, IPA, OP]
*American opera singer*
* Hines, Jerome

**Heinz, Pickles**
*See* Heinz, H. John, III

**Heinz, Policeman**
*See* Heinz, Bob

**[The] Heir of the Republic**
*See* Bonaparte, Napoleon

**Heirens, William** 1929- [BLB]
*American murderer and burglar*
* Murman, George

**Heise, Clarence Edward** 1907-
[BE]
*American baseball player*
* Heise, Lefty

**Heise, Lefty**
*See* Heise, Clarence Edward

**Heiser, Leroy Barton** 1942- [BE]
*American baseball player*
* Heiser, Roy

**Heiser, Roy**
*See* Heiser, Leroy Barton

**Heismann, Christian Ernest**
1880-1951 [BE]
*American baseball player*
* Heismann, Crese

**Heismann, Crese**
*See* Heismann, Christian Ernest

**Heiss, John Strange** 1871-1936
[EMT]
*Australian-born entertainer*
* Asche, Oscar

**Heistad, Erling** 1897-1967 [BBH]
*Norwegian-born skiing coach*
* [The] Father of Lebanon Skiing

**Heiter, Amalie**
*See* Amalie Marie Friederike
Auguste [Duchess of Saxony]

**Heitler, Michael** ?-1931
[BLB, PHM]
*American underworld figure*
* Mike the Pike

**Heitmuller, Heinie**
*See* Heitmuller, William Frederick

**Heitmuller, William Frederick**
1883-1912 [BE]
*American baseball player*
* Heitmuller, Heinie

**Heitner, Iris** 20th c. [WW]
*Author*
* James, Robert

**Heitzmann, W[illia]m Ray** 1948-
[CA]
*American author and educator*
* Vincent, William R.

**Hejmadi, Padma** 20th c. [DLE]
*Indian author*
* Perera, Padma

**Hekt, Theodore** 1908-1969 [SC]
*American actor*
* Hecht, Ted

**Helassie, Saile** 20th c. [IBW]
*Ethiopian wrestler*
* [The] Human Concrete Mixer

**Held, Bud**
*See* Held, Franklin

**Held, Country**
*See* Held, Mel[vin Nicholas]

**Held, Franklin** 1927- [TF]
*American javelin thrower*
* Held, Bud

**Held, Mel[vin Nicholas]** 1929- [BE]
*American baseball player*
* Held, Country

**Held, Peter**
*See* Carroll-Held, Peter

**Held, Woodie**
*See* Held, Woodson George

**Held, Woodson George** 1932- [BE]
*American baseball player*
* Held, Woodie

**Helders, Major**
*See* Knauss, Robert

**Helding, Clair**
*See* Ackerman, Forrest J[ames]

**Helen**
*See* Burrough, Helen Mary

**Helen**
*See* Grunwald, Helen Mary

**Helen**
*See* Whitman, Sarah Helen Power

**[The] Helen of Spain**
*See* Florinda

**Helenius, Arthur D.** 1897-1970
[BE]
*American baseball player*
* Delaney, Art[hur D.]

**Helfer, Al**
*See* Helfer, George

**Helfer, George** 1911?-1975 [B10]
*American sportscaster*
* Helfer, Al

**Helfman, Donald Elliott** 1926-
[BEW, EJ, PMJ]
*American jazz musician*
* Elliott, Don

**Helfman, Harry**
*See* Cohen, Harry

**Helforth, John**
*See* Doolittle, Hilda

**Helfrich, Emory Wilbur**
1890-1955 [BE]
*American baseball player*
* Helfrich, Ty

**Helfrich, Ty**
*See* Helfrich, Emory Wilbur

**Heliogabalus [or Elagabalus]**
*See* Avitus Bassianus, Varius

**Hell, Theodore**
*See* Winkler, C. G. T.

**Hellar, Gloria**
*See* Sheridan, Clara Lou

**Hellens, Franz**
*See* Ermengem, Frederic van

**Heller**
*See* Iranek-Osmecki, Kazimierz

**Heller, Ehrhardt Henry** 1910-
[CEI, FHE, HK]
*Canadian-born hockey player*
* Heller, Ott

**Heller, Frank**
*See* Serner, Martin G[unnar]

**Heller, Ott**
*See* Heller, Ehrhardt Henry

**Heller, Robert**
*See* Palmer, William Henry

**Helley, Denis**
*See* Allen, Hubert Raymond

**Hellinga, Gerben Wytzes** 1937-
[IAW]
*Swiss-born author and playwright*
* Hellinger

**Hellinger**
*See* Hellinga, Gerben Wytzes

**Hellman, Carl**
*See* Dillinger, John Herbert

**Hellman, Elinor Angel** 1953-
*American disc jockey*
* Dylan, Ellie

**Hellmuth the Taciturn**
*See* Moltke, Hellmuth Karl
Bernhard von

**Hello, Mme. Ernst** 19th c. [PA]
*Author*
* Lander, Jean

**Helluo**
*See* Comestor, Peter [or Petrus]

**Helluo**
*See* Magliabecchi, Antonio [or
Anthony]

**Hellwig, Monika Konrad** 1929-
[CA]
*German-born educator and author*
* Cuthbert, Mary

**Helm, Breeze**
*See* Helm, Louis

**Helm, Brigette**
*See* Schittenhelm, Gisele Eve

**Helm, Louis** 20th c.
*American football player*
* Helm, Breeze

**Helman, Albert**
*See* Lichtveld, [Dr.] L. A. M.

**Helmer, William J[oseph]** 1936-
[CA]
*American editor and author*
* Naismith, Horace

**Helmericks, Bud**
*See* Helmericks, Harmon R.

**Helmericks, Harmon R.** 1917-
[CA]
*American author*
* Helmericks, Bud

**Helmi, Jack**
*See* Sands, Leo G[eorge]

**Helner, Edward**
*See* Koch, Ernest

**Heloise**
*See* Marchelle, Ponce Kiah

**Heloise**
*See* Reese, Heloise [Bowles]

**Helphingstine, Mary J[ane]** [NAA]
*American missionary and writer*
* Wroughtwell, Faith

**Heltzel, Heinie**
*See* Heltzel, William Wade

**Heltzel, William Wade** 1913-   [BE]
*American baseball player*
* Heltzel, Heinie

**Helvick, James**
*See* Cockburn, [Francis] Claud

**Hely, Elizabeth**
*See* Younger, Elizabeth

**Helyot, Pierre** 1660-1716   [WBD]
*French monk and historian*
* Hippolyte, [Le Pere]

**Heman, Nicholas**
*See* Hanson, Michael

**Hemans, Felicia Dorothea**
1794-1835   [PA]
*Author*
* Balfour, Clara

**[The] Hemans of America**
*See* Sigourney, Lydia Howard

**Hembling, Nina [Clark]** 1875- ?
[NAA]
*American writer*
* [The] Ink Dabbler
* Siebert, Eloise McElroy

**Heming, Frederick** 1865-1936   [SC]
*British-born actor*
* Walton, Fred

**Heming, John [Winton]** 1900-1953
[ESF, SFL, SFP]
*Australian author*
* De Wreder, Paul

**Hemingway, Chas.**
*See* Smith, Leonard B.

**Hemingway, Ed**
*See* Hemingway, Edson M.

**Hemingway, Edson M.** 1893-   [BE]
*American baseball player*
* Hemingway, Ed

**Hemingway, Ernest** 1899-1961
*American author*
* Hemingway, Papa

**Hemingway, Joan** 1950-
*American author*
* Hemingway, Muffet

**Hemingway, Muffet**
*See* Hemingway, Joan

**[The] Hemingway of Singers**
*See* Fitzgerald, Ella

**Hemingway, Papa**
*See* Hemingway, Ernest

**Hemingway, Taylor**
*See* Rywell, Martin

**Hemley, Elaine Gottlieb**
*See* Gottlieb, Elaine

**Hemmerling, E. C.** 1914-   [CEI]
*Canadian-born hockey player*
* Hemmerling, Tony

**Hemmerling, Tony**
*See* Hemmerling, E. C.

**Hemming, N. K.**
*See* Hemming, Nora Kathleen

**Hemming, Nora Kathleen**
1927-1960   [WGT]
*British author*
* Hemming, N. K.

**Hemming, Roy** 1928-   [CA]
*American author and editor*
* Hamilton, Buzz

**Hemmings, Edward Ernest [Eddie]**
1949-   [DC]
*British cricketer*
* [The] Whale

**Hemp, Ducky**
*See* Hemp, William H.

**Hemp, William H.** 1867-1923   [BE]
*American baseball player*
* Hemp, Ducky

**Hempel, George** 1859-1921   [WBD]
*American philologist*
* Hempl, George

**Hemphill, Charles Judson**
1876-1953   [AS, BE]
*American baseball player*
* Eagle Eye

**Hemphill, Scad**
*See* Hemphill, Shelton

**Hemphill, Shelton** 1906-1959
[WWJ]
*American jazz musician*
* Hemphill, Scad

**Hempl, George**
*See* Hempel, George

**Hempton, Paul Andrew Keates**
1946-   [ART]
*British artist*
* P. H.

**Hemric, Dick**
*See* Hemric, Dixon

**Hemric, Dixon** 1933-   [BB, SMG]
*American basketball player*
* Hemric, Dick

**Hemsley, Ralston Burdett**
1907-1972   [BE, PB]
*American baseball player*
* Hemsley, Rollie

**Hemsley, Rollie**
*See* Hemsley, Ralston Burdett

**Hemus, Solly**
*See* Hemus, Solomon Joseph

**Hemus, Solomon Joseph** 1923-
[BE]
*American baseball player and
manager*
* Hemus, Solly

**Hemynge, Bracebridge**   [FFF]
*Author*
* Harkaway, Jack

**Henaghan, Jim** 1919-   [CA]
*British-born author*
* O'Neill, Archie

**Henderley, Brooks** [house
pseudonym] [Stratemeyer
Syndicate]
*See* Stratemeyer, Edward L.

**Henderson, Alfred**
*See* Bryan, Ralph Burgess

**Henderson, Archibald** 1877-1963
[TC]
*American mathematician, historian,
author*
* Steele, Erskine

**Henderson, Arthur Chauncy** 1897-
[MK]
*American baseball player*
* Henderson, Rats

**Henderson, Barnyard**
*See* Henderson, Bernard D.
[Bernie]

**Henderson, Bernard D. [Bernie]**
1899-1966   [BE]
*American baseball player*
* Henderson, Barnyard

**Henderson, Big Joe**
*See* Henderson, Joe

**Henderson, Bill**
*See* Henderson, R. E.

**Henderson, Bill** 1941-   [CA]
*American author and editor*
* Walton, Luke

**Henderson, Catherine**
*See* Gibbons, Irene

**Henderson, De-Wayne**
*See* Henderson, Wayne David

**Henderson, Del**
*See* Henderson, George Delbert

**Henderson, Donald Landels** 1905-
[WW]
*Author*
* Landels, D. H.

**Henderson, Douglas** ?-1928
[BWW]
*American comedian*
* Henderson, Slim

**Henderson, Elmer C.** 1889-1965
[FB]
*American football coach*
* Henderson, Gloomy Gus

**Henderson, George** 1944-
*American cheerleader*
* Henderson, Krazy George

**Henderson, George Delbert**
1883-1956   [FD]
*Canadian-born director*
* Henderson, Del

**Henderson, Gloomy Gus**
*See* Henderson, Elmer C.

**Henderson, H.** 20th c.   [OBW]
*American baseball player*
* Henderson, Long

**Henderson, Hardie**
*See* Henderson, James Harding

**Henderson, Henrietta**   [PA]
*Author*
* [The] Man in the Front-Row

**Henderson, Hollywood**
*See* Henderson, Tom

**Henderson, James Fletcher**
1897?-1952   [DAM, EJ, WWJ]
*American jazz musician*
* Henderson, Smack

**Henderson, James Harding**
1862-1903   [AS]
*American baseball player*
* Henderson, Hardie

**Henderson, James Leal** 1913-
[WW]
*Author*
* Currier, Jay L.

**Henderson, James Woolfolk**
1876?-1951   [BBH]
*American trapshooter*
* Henderson, Woolly

**Henderson, Joe** 20th c.   [RO1]
*American singer*
* Henderson, Big Joe

**Henderson, John** 1747-1785   [SN]
*British actor*
* [The] Bath Roscius

**Henderson, John** 1757-1788
[DEL, RH, SN]
*Irish poet and author*
* [The] Irish Crichton

**Henderson, John Duncan** 1933-
[CEI]
*Canadian-born hockey player*
* Henderson, Long John

**Henderson, John Murray** 1921-
[CEI]
*Canadian-born hockey player*
* Henderson, Moe

**Henderson, John William** 1910-
[BWW, NBB]
*American singer*
* Homesick James
* Jick
* Williamson, James
* Williamson, John A.

**Henderson, Kenneth Joseph** 1946-
[SMG]
*American baseball player*
* Henderson, Skitch

**Henderson, Krazy George**
*See* Henderson, George

**Henderson, LeGrand** 1901-1965
[CA, SAT]
*American author and illustrator*
* Harwin, Brian
* LeGrand

**Henderson, Lisle** 1904-   [FC, SW]
*American actor*
* Hollywood, Lysle
* Talbot, Lyle

**Henderson, Long**
*See* Henderson, H.

**Henderson, Long John**
*See* Henderson, John Duncan

**Henderson, Lyle Russell Cedric**
1918-   [DAM, IPA, ITA]
*American bandleader*
* Henderson, Skitch

**Henderson, Mary**
*See* Mavor, Osborne Henry

**Henderson, May** 1884-1937
[BMH, THR]
*British comedienne*
* [The] Dusky Queen

**Henderson, Moe**
*See* Henderson, John Murray

**Henderson, Mrs. Alexander**   [FFF]
*Entertainer*
* Thompson, Lydia

**Henderson, N. J.**   [PA]
*Author*
* Tricotrin

**Henderson, R. E.** 20th c.   [BBH]
*American coach and collegiate
athletic director*
* Henderson, Bill

**Henderson, Rats**
*See* Henderson, Arthur Chauncy

**Henderson, Ray**
See Brost, Raymond

**Henderson, Robert Bolden [Bobby]**
1910-1969 [EJ, EJ7]
*American jazz musician*
* Bolden, Jody

**Henderson, Rosa [Rose]** 1896-1968
[BWW]
*American singer*
* Dale, Flora
* Green, Rosa
* Harris, Mae
* Harris, Mamie
* Johnson, Sara
* Ritz, Sally
* Thomas, Josephine
* White, Gladys
* Williams, Bessie

**Henderson, Skitch**
See Henderson, Kenneth Joseph

**Henderson, Skitch**
See Henderson, Lyle Russell
Cedric

**Henderson, Slim**
See Henderson, Douglas

**Henderson, Smack**
See Henderson, James Fletcher

**Henderson, Sylvia** 1908- [CA, LC]
*New Zealand educator and author*
* Ashton-Warner, Sylvia
[Constance]
* Sylvia

**Henderson, Thomas Louis** 1949-
[CA]
*American poet*
* Mberi, Antar Sudan Katara

**Henderson, Thulia Susannah** [PA]
*Author*
* T. S. H.

**Henderson, Tom** 20th c.
*American football player*
* Henderson, Hollywood

**Henderson, Wayne David** 1927-
[CWG]
*American country-western performer*
* Henderson, De-Wayne

**Henderson, Woolly**
See Henderson, James Woolfolk

**Henderson-Howart, Gerald**
See Howat, Gerald Malcolm David

**Hendie, Paul** [PA]
*Author*
* Pangloss
* Spavento

**Hendleman, George Joseph** 1920-
[EJ, PMJ]
*American composer and arranger*
* Handy, George

**Hendren, Elias Henry** 1889-1962
[EC]
*British cricketer*
* Hendren, Patsy

**Hendren, Patsy**
See Hendren, Elias Henry

**Hendrick, Gink**
See Hendrick, Harvey Lee

**Hendrick, Harvey Lee** 1897-1941
[BE]
*American baseball player*
* Hendrick, Gink

**Hendrick, Hendo**
See Hendrick, Michael

**Hendrick, Michael** 1948- [DC]
*British cricketer*
* Hendrick, Hendo

**Hendricks, A. L.** 1922- [CW]
*Jamaican poet, journalist,
broadcaster*
* Hendriks, Micky

**Hendricks, Ace**
See Hendricks, Horace

**Hendricks, Big Ed**
See Hendricks Ed[ward]

**Hendricks Ed[ward]** 1886-1930
[BE]
*American baseball player*
* Hendricks, Big Ed

**Hendricks, Ellie**
See Hendricks, Elrod Jerome

**Hendricks, Elrod Jerome** 1940-
[BE]
*American baseball player*
* Hendricks, Ellie

**Hendricks, Frederick Wilmoth**
1901-1973 [ASC, IBW]
*West Indian-born composer and
singer*
* Houdini, King
* Houdini, Wilmoth

**Hendricks, Horace**
*American football player*
* Hendricks, Ace

**Hendricks, John Carl** 1921- [IBW]
*American jazz musician*
* [The] Poet Laureate of Modern
Jazz

**Hendricks, Ted** 1947- [FB]
*Guatemalan-born football player*
* [The] Mad Stork
* [The] Stork

**Hendrickson, Al**
See Hendrickson, Alton Reynolds

**Hendrickson, Alton Reynolds**
1920- [DAM, PMJ]
*American jazz musician and singer*
* Hendrickson, Al

**Hendriks, Micky**
See Hendricks, A. L.

**Hendriks, P. G.**
See Pistorius, Pieter

**Hendrix, Crow Jane**
See Hendrix, George

**Hendrix, George** 20th c. [BWW]
*American musician*
* Hendrix, Crow Jane

**Hendrix, James Marshall [Jimi]**
1942-1970 [BWW, IBW]
*American singer*
* James, Jimmy
* [The] Wild Man of Pop

**Hendrix, N. E.** ?-1973 [FIR, SC]
*Actor*
* Hendrix, Shorty

**Hendrix, Shorty**
See Hendrix, N. E.

**Hendrix, Sonny**
See Barkan, Stanley Howard

**Hendry, Eugene** 1940- [ALR]
*American baseball umpire*
* Hendry, Ted

**Hendry, J. F.**
See Hendry, James Findlay

**Hendry, James Findlay** 1912-
[WYA]
*Author*
* Hendry, J. F.

**Hendry, Ted**
See Hendry, Eugene

**Hengle, Emory J.** 1858- ? [BE]
*American baseball player*
* Hengle, Moxie

**Hengle, Moxie**
See Hengle, Emory J.

**Henham, Ernest George** 1870- ?
[LAO]
*British author*
* Trevena, John

**Henie, Sonja** 1912-1969 [BBH]
*Norwegian-born ice skater*
* [The] Girl in White
* [The] Norwegian Doll
* [The] Queen of the Ice

**Henisch, Heinz K.** 1922- [CA]
*German-born physicist and writer*
* Spear, Benjamin

**Henissart, Martha** 1930?-
[CC, EMD, WD]
*American economist and author*
* Dominic, R. B. [joint pseudonym
with Mary J. Latis]
* Lathen, Emma [joint pseudonym
with Mary J. Latis]

**Henkel, Barbara Osborn** 1921-
[CA]
*American nursing instructor and
author*
* Osborn, Barbara M.

**Henkle, Henrietta** 1909- [B10, CA]
*American author*
* Buckmaster, Henrietta

**Henley, Arthur** 1921- [CA]
*American author*
* Eric, Kenneth
* Jones, Webb

**Henley, Gail**
See Olsheski, Gail

**Henley, George**
See Rankin, Arthur McKee

**Henley, Georgina** 1858?-1937
[BEW]
*British actress*
* Wright, Georgie

**Henley, John** 1692-1756
[DNNS, HN, SN]
*British clergyman*
* [The] Cain of Literature
* Henley, Orator
* [The] Zany of His Age

**Henley, John Lee** 1919- [BWW]
*American singer*
* Lee, John

**Henley, Orator**
See Henley, John

**Henley, P. A.**
See Protheroe, Ernest

**Henley, W. E.**
See Henley, William Ernest

**Henley, William Ernest** 1849-1903
[LC]
*Playwright and poet*
* Henley, W. E.

**Henline, Butch**
See Henline, Walter John

**Henline, Walter John** 1894-1957
[AS, BE]
*American baseball player*
* Henline, Butch

**Henneberg, Charles** [joint
pseudonym with N. Henneberg zu
Irmelshausen Wasungen]
See Henneberg zu Irmelshausen
Wasungen, Charles

**Henneberg, Charles** [joint
pseudonym with C. Henneberg zu
Irmelshausen Wasungen]
See Henneberg zu Irmelshausen
Wasungen, Nathalie

**Henneberg, Nathalie-Charles**
See Henneberg zu Irmelshausen
Wasungen, Nathalie

**Henneberg zu Irmelshausen
Wasungen, Charles** 1899-1959
[ESF]
*German-French author*
* Henneberg, Charles [joint
pseudonym with N. Henneberg zu
Irmelshausen Wasungen]

**Henneberg zu Irmelshausen
Wasungen, Nathalie** 1917-1977
[ESF]
*Russian-French author*
* Henneberg, Charles [joint
pseudonym with C. Henneberg zu
Irmelshausen Wasungen]
* Henneberg, Nathalie-Charles

**Hennel, Stanford** 20th c. [SFP]
*Author*
* Heinkel, Stanford

**Hennepin, Johannes** 1640-1701?
[WBD]
*Flemish-born explorer and author*
* Hennepin, Louis

**Hennepin, Louis**
See Hennepin, Johannes

**Hennessey, Caroline**
See Von Block, Sylvia

**Hennessey, George** 1910- [BE]
*American baseball player*
* Hennessey, Three Star

**Hennessey, Three Star**
See Hennessey, George

**Hennessy, John C.** [PA]
*Author*
* Irraghiconnor

**Hennessy, Max**
See Harris, John

**Hennessy, Mrs. Augustus** [FFF]
*Entertainer*
* Ames, Amy

**Hennessy, James Albert** 1863- ?
[NAA]
*American editor and author*
* Thane, Francois

**Henning, Cotton**
See Henning, Harry

**Henning, Doug[las James]** 1947-
[BS]
*Canadian magician*
* [The] Kid in Tennis Shoes

**Henning, Harry**    [BBH]
*American race car mechanic and owner*
* Henning, Cotton

**Henning, Katja**
*See* Weber, Annemarie

**Henning, Lorne Edward** 1952-
[SMG]
*Canadian-born hockey player*
* Henning, Scoop

**Henning, Roslyn Brogue** 1919-
[IWM]
*American musician*
* Brogue, Roslyn

**Henning, Scoop**
*See* Henning, Lorne Edward

**Henningsson, Rik**
*See* Sommer, Richard Jerome

**Henot, Georges** 1848-1918    [SFL]
*Author*
* Ohnet, Georges

**Henreid, Paul**
*See* Von Hernreid, Paul George Julius

**Henrey, Madeleine** 1906-    [CA]
*French author*
* Henrey, Robert

**Henrey, Robert**
*See* Henrey, Madeleine

**Henri, Colonel**
*See* Bleicher, Hugo

**Henri, Florette** 1908-    [CA]
*American author and playwright*
* Winters, Marjorie

**Henri, G.**
*See* Clement, George H.

**Henri, Robert**
*See* Cozad, Robert Henry

**Henrich, Thomas David** 1913-
[BE, BTB]
*American baseball player*
* Old Reliable

**Henricks, Kaw**
*See* Wolfe, Charles Keith

**Henrietta Maria** 1609-1669    [HN]
*Wife of King Charles I of England*
* Queen Henry
* [The] She Majesty Generalissimo

**Henriksen, Olaf** 1888-1962    [BE]
*Danish-born baseball player*
* Henriksen, Swede

**Henriksen, Swede**
*See* Henriksen, Olaf

**Henrion, F. H. K.**
*See* Henrion, Frederick Henri Kay

**Henrion, Frederick Henri Kay**
1914-    [GA]
*British graphic artist*
* Henrion, F. H. K.

**Henriot, Emile**
*See* Maigrot, Emile

**Henrioud, Charles** 1926-    [OP]
*Swiss scenic and costume designer*
* Matias

**Henriques, R. D.**
*See* Henriques, Robert David Quixano

**Henriques, Robert David Quixano**
1905-1967    [LC]
*British army officer and author*
* Henriques, R. D.

**Henriques, Veronica**
*See* Gosling, Veronica

**Henriquez, Fighting Joe**
*See* Henriquez, Joseph Stephen

**Henriquez, Joseph Stephen** 1933-
[IBW]
*American naval officer*
* Henriquez, Fighting Joe

**Henriquez, Rafael Americo**
1899-1968    [CW]
*Dominican poet*
* Puchungo

**Henriquez Urena, Max** 1885-1968
[CW]
*Dominican author, poet, playwright*
* Hatuey

**Henriquez y Alfau, Enrique**
1859-1940    [CW]
*Dominican poet and journalist*
* Razonador, Amable

**Henrotin, Daniel** 20th c.    [WECO]
*Belgian cartoonist*
* Dany

**Henry**
*See* Gousev, Lieutenant

**Henry**    [SN]
*Prince of Wales*
* Our English Marcellus

**Henry [Earl of Peterborough]**    [PA]
*Author*
* Halstead, Robert

**Henry** ?-1613    [RH]
*Son of King James I*
* Maliades

**Henry** 1129-1195
[DNNS, FFF, SN]
*Duke of Saxony and Bavaria*
* [The] Lion

**Henry** 1215?-1288    [WBD]
*Margrave of Meissen*
* [The] Illustrious

**Henry [or Don Henrique]**
1394-1460    [DEP, DNNS, SN]
*Prince of Portugal*
* [The] Father of Navigation
* [The] Navigator

**Henry** 1473-1541    [WBD]
*Duke of Saxony*
* [The] Pious

**Henry, Ainsley E. T.** 1911-    [CW]
*Jamaican columnist*
* A. E. T.

**Henry, Arthur**
*See* Anderson, Arthur Henry

**Henry, Bessie Walker** 1921-    [CA]
*British educator and author*
* Walker, Bessie

**Henry, Big Bill**
*See* Henry, Bill

**Henry, Bill** 1924-    [BB]
*American basketball player*
* Henry, Big Bill

**Henry, Buck**
*See* Zuckerman, Buck Henry

**Henry, Bunky**
*See* Henry, George W.

**Henry, Buzz**
*See* Henry, Robert

**Henry, Caleb Sprague** 1804- ?
[PA]
*American author*
* Oldham of Greystones, Dr.

**Henry, Camille** 1933-
[CEI, FHE, HK]
*Canadian-born hockey player*
* [The] Eel

**Henry, Captain**    [PA]
*Author*
* De L. G.

**Henry, Charles** 1885-1960    [NOJ]
*American jazz musician*
* Henry, Sunny

**Henry, Chicken**
*See* Henry, Oscar

**Henry, Clarence** 1937-    [PRS, RO1]
*American musician*
* Henry, Frogman

**Henry, Daniel**
*See* Kahnweiler, Daniel Henry

**Henry, Dutch**
*See* Henry, Frank John

**Henry, Earl Clifford** 1917-    [BE]
*American baseball player*
* Henry, Hook

**Henry, Edgar**
*See* Tourgee, Albion W[inegar]

**Henry, Fats**
*See* Henry, Wilbur F.

**Henry, Frank** 1909-    [B10, WWJ]
*American jazz musician*
* Henry, Haywood

**Henry, Frank John** 1902-1968
[AS, BE]
*American baseball player*
* Henry, Dutch

**Henry, Frederick Marshall** 1895-
[BE]
*American baseball player*
* Henry, Snake

**Henry, Fredericks** 1942-    [IBW]
*African-born singer, bandleader, musician*
* Taj Mahal

**Henry, Frogman**
*See* Henry, Clarence

**Henry, George W.** 1944-    [GF]
*American golfer*
* Henry, Bunky

**Henry, Gig**
*See* Rosenfeld, Henry

**Henry, Gordon David** 1926-
[CEI, SMG]
*Canadian-born hockey player*
* Henry, Red

**Henry, Gustavus Adolphus**
1804-1880    [FFF]
*American orator*
* [The] Eagle Orator of Tennessee

**Henry, Harriet**
*See* De Steuch, Harriet Henry

**Henry, Haywood**
*See* Henry, Frank

**Henry, Hi**
*See* Henry, Hiram

**Henry, Hiram** 1845?-1920    [BEW]
*Minstrel*
* Henry, Hi

**Henry, Hook**
*See* Henry, Earl Clifford

**Henry, John Patrick** 20th c.
[WWL]
*Irish author*
* MacEnri, Seaghan

**Henry, Josiah F.** 1896-    [IBW]
*American attorney*
* Two, Mr.

**Henry, Leo** 20th c.    [OBW]
*American baseball player*
* Henry, Preacher

**Henry, Marion**
*See* Alvarez Del Rey, Ramon Felipe San Juan Mario Silvio Enrico

**Henry, Mary H.**    [PA]
*Author*
* Benning, Howe

**Henry, Milton** 1920-    [IBW]
*American political organizer*
* Gaidi, Brother

**Henry, Mrs. I. M. P.**    [FFF]
*Writer*
* Hope, Ethel

**Henry, O.**
*See* Porter, William Sydney

**Henry of Bruys**
*See* Henry of Lausanne

**Henry of Cluny**
*See* Henry of Lausanne

**Henry of Ghent**
*See* Goethals, Henry

**Henry of Lancaster**
*See* Henry IV

**Henry of Lausanne** 12th c.    [WBD]
*French leader of religious sect*
* [The] Deacon
* Henry of Bruys
* Henry of Cluny
* Henry of Toulouse

**Henry of Luxemburg**
*See* Henry VII

**Henry of Navarre**
*See* Henry IV [or Henri]

**Henry of Toulouse**
*See* Henry of Lausanne

**Henry of Veldig** 12th c.    [SN]
*Poet*
* [The] Father of German Minstrelsy

**Henry, Oliver**
*See* Porter, William Sydney

**Henry, Oscar** 1888-   [NOJ]
*American jazz musician*
* Henry, Chicken

**Henry, Patrick** 1736-1799   [HN]
*American revolutionary leader*
* [The] Orator of Nature

**Henry, Pete**
*See* Henry, Wilbur F.

**Henry, Preacher**
*See* Henry, Leo

**Henry, Red**
*See* Henry, Gordon David

**Henry, Richard** 20th c.   [IBW]
*American author*
* Obadele, Imari Abubakaru, I

**Henry, Robert** [house pseudonym]
*See* MacDonald, John D[ann]

**Henry, Robert** 1931-1971   [SC]
*American actor, stuntman, rodeo performer*
* Henry, Buzz

**Henry, Samuel James** 1920-
[CEI, FHE, HK]
*Canadian-born hockey player*
* Henry, Sugar Jim

**Henry, Snake**
*See* Henry, Frederick Marshall

**Henry, Sugar Jim**
*See* Henry, Samuel James

**Henry, Sunny**
*See* Henry, Charles

**Henry the Deuce**
*See* Ford, Henry, II

**Henry the K**
*See* Kissinger, Henry Alfred

**Henry the Mistrel** 15th c.
[HN, WBD]
*Scottish poet*
* Blind Harry

**Henry the Morgue**
*See* Morgenthau, Henry J.

**Henry, Travis** 20th c.   [IBW]
*American boxer*
* Chocolate, Kid

**Henry, Wilbur F.** 1897-1952
[AS, FB]
*American football player*
* Henry, Fats
* Henry, Pete

**Henry, Will**
*See* Allen, Henry Wilson

**Henry, William**
*See* Diez, Mrs. M. A.

**Henry I [or Heinrich]** 876- 936
[DNNS, HN, SN]
*King of Germany*
* [The] Father of His Country
* [The] Founder of Chivalry in Germany
* [The] Fowler
* [The] Iron Duke
* [The] Romulus of Brandenburg
* [The] Saxon

**Henry I** 1068-1135
[DNNF, FF, HN]
*King of England*
* Beauclerc [Good Scholar]
* Goderic
* [The] Lion of Justice

**Henry I** 1210?-1274   [WBD]
*King of Navarre*
* [The] Fat

**Henry I** 1244-1308   [WBD]
*Landgrave of Hesse*
* [The] Child

**Henry II** 951- 995   [WBD]
*Duke of Bavaria*
* [The] Quarrelsome
* [The] Wrangler

**Henry II [or Heinrich]** 972?-1024
[DNNS, HN, SN]
*King of Germany and Holy Roman emperor*
* [The] Lame
* [The] Saint

**Henry II** 1133-1189   [HN, WBD]
*King of England*
* Curtmantle
* Fitz Empress
* Longsword

**Henry II [or Henri]** 1519-1559
[HN, SN]
*King of France*
* [Le] Belliqueux
* [The] Defender of German Independence
* [The] Popinjay
* [The] Warlike

**Henry III [or Heinrich]** 1017-1056
[HN]
*Holy Roman emperor*
* [The] Black King

**Henry III** 1207-1272   [HN]
*King of England*
* Winchester

**Henry III** 1379-1406   [DNNS]
*King of Castile*
* [The] Sickly

**Henry III [or Henri]** 1551-1589
[DNNS, FFF, HN]
*King of France*
* [The] Coxcomb
* [The] Man Milliner
* [Le] Mignon

**Henry IV** 1367-1413
[FFF, SN, WBD]
*King of England*
* Bolingbroke
* Henry of Lancaster

**Henry IV** 1425-1474   [DNNS]
*King of Castile*
* [The] Impotent

**Henry IV [or Henri]** 1553-1610
[DEP, FFF, SN]
*King of France*
* [The] Bearnais
* [The] Father of the People
* [The] Great
* Henry of Navarre
* [The] King of Brave Men
* Mon Soldat [My Soldier]
* [Le] Roi des Braves
* Vert Gallant [Devoted Admirer]

**Henry IX**
*See* Stuart, Henry Benedict Maria Clemens

**Henry IX** ?-1126   [WBD]
*Duke of Bavaria*
* [The] Black

**Henry V [or Heinrich]** 1081-1125
[HN, SN]
*King of Germany and Holy Roman emperor*
* [The] Parricide

**Henry V** 1387-1422
[DNNS, HN, RH]
*King of England*
* [The] English Alexander
* Monmouth
* [The] Prince of Priests

**Henry VI [or Heinrich]** 1165-1197
[HN, SN]
*King of Germany and Holy Roman emperor*
* [The] Cruel

**Henry VI** 1421-1471
[DNNS, HN, RH]
*King of England*
* [The] Martyr King
* Windsor

**Henry VII** 1275?-1318   [WBD]
*King of Germany and Holy Roman emperor*
* Henry of Luxemburg

**Henry VII** 1457-1509
[DEP, DNNF, RH]
*King of England*
* [The] English Solomon
* [The] Second Solomon
* [The] Solomon of England

**[The] Henry VII of Japan**
*See* Iyeasu

**Henry VIII** 1457-1509
[FF, FFF, SN]
*King of England*
* Bluff King Hal
* Burly King Harry
* Coppernose
* Defender of the Faith
* Old Harry
* [The] Royal Butcher
* Stout Harry
* Walter

**Henry X** 1108?-1139   [WBD]
*Duke of Bavaria*
* [The] Proud

**Henschke, Alfred** 1890-1928
[CD, EWL, WBD]
*German author, playwright, poet*
* Klabund

**Hensel, Fanny Cecile** 1805-1847
[SN]
*Sister of German composer, Felix Mendelssohn*
* [The] Cantor

**Hensel, Octavia**
*See* Seymour, Alice

**Hensel, Walther**
*See* Janiczek, Julius

**Hensen, Herwig**
*See* Mielants, Florent Constant Albert

**Henshall, James A.**   [PA]
*Author*
* Oconomowoc

**Henshaw, Kid**
*See* Henshaw, Roy K.

**Henshaw, Mrs.**   [PA]
*Author*
* Aunt Maggie

**Henshaw, Roy K.** 1911-   [BN]
*American baseball player*
* Henshaw, Kid

**Hensiek, Phil[ip Frank]** 1901-1972
[BE]
*American baseball player*
* Hensiek, Sid

**Hensiek, Sid**
*See* Hensiek, Phil[ip Frank]

**Hensley, J. L.**
*See* Hensley, Joe Louis

**Hensley, Joe Louis** 1926-   [ESF]
*American author*
* Adams, Louis J. A. [joint pseudonym with Alexei Panshin]
* Hensley, J. L.

**Hensley, Virginia** 1932-1963
[CME, CWG]
*American country-western performer*
* Cline, Patsy

**Hensley, William Paden** 1909-
[BWW]
*American singer*
* Washboard Willie

**Hensman, Howard** ?-1916   [WWL]
*British journalist*
* Flic
* Vedette

**Henson, Charles** 20th c.   [GW]
*American rodeo performer*
* Henson, Heavy

**Henson, Gladys**
*See* Gunn, Gladys

**Henson, Hawkeye**
*See* Henson, Monty

**Henson, Heavy**
*See* Henson, Charles

**Henson, Herbert Lester** 1925- ?
[CWG, DAM]
*American singer and songwriter*
* Cousin Herb

**Henson, Josiah** 1789-1883   [IBW]
*American clergyman and abolitionist orator*
* Henson, Si

**Henson, Monty** 20th c.   [GW]
*American rodeo performer*
* Henson, Hawkeye

**Henson, Si**
*See* Henson, Josiah

**Henton, Collett**
*See* Batchelor, Richard A. C.

**Henty, G. A.**
*See* Henty, George Alfred

**Henty, George Alfred** 1832-1902
[LC]
*British author*
* Henty, G. A.

**Hentz, Caroline Lee** 1800-1856
[PA]
*Author*
* Aunt Patty

**Hentz, William** 1867?-1940   [BEW]
*American actor*
* Evarts, William H.

**Hepburn, Audrey**
*See* Hepburn-Ruston, Audrey

**Hepburn, Thomas Nicoll** 1861- ?
[WWL]
*Scottish author*
* Setoun, Gabriel

**Hepburn-Ruston, Audrey** 1929-
[BEW, FC]
*Belgian-born actress*
* Hepburn, Audrey

**Hepenstall, Edward** 19th c.    [FFF]
*British police officer*
* [The] Walking Gallows

**Hepenstall, Hazel** 1913-    [THR]
*South African-born actress*
* Hughes, Hazel

**Heppell, Mary** 20th c.    [WW]
*Author*
* Clare, Marguerite

**Hepple, Anne**
See   Dickinson, Anne Hepple

**Hepworth, Mrs. George H.**    [PA]
*Author*
* Savin, Una

**Her, Erich**
See   Paetel, Erich

**Her Nibs**
See   Lipson, Fredda

**Her Temperance**
See   Pakington, [Sir] John

**Heraclitos [or Heraclitus]** 6th c.
BC    [DNNF, HN, RH]
*Greek philosopher*
* [The] Obscure Philosopher
* [The] Weeping Philosopher

**Herald, Kathleen**
See   Peyton, Kathleen Wendy
[Herald]

**[The] Herald of the Reformation**
See   Geyler, Johann

**Herbe, Michele**
See   Herbe-Fouan, Michele

**Herbe-Fouan, Michele** 1940-    [OP]
*French opera singer*
* Herbe, Michele

**Herber, Arnold** 1910-1969    [FB]
*American football player*
* Herber, Champ
* Herber, Flash

**Herber, Champ**
See   Herber, Arnold

**Herber, Flash**
See   Herber, Arnold

**Herber, Lewis**
See   Bookchin, Murray

**Herbert, A. P.**
See   Herbert, [Sir] Alan Patrick

**Herbert, [Sir] Alan Patrick**
1890-1971    [LC, TC, WBD]
*British author*
* A. P. H.
* Haddock, Albert
* Herbert, A. P.

**Herbert, Arthur**
See   Shappiro, Thomas [Arthur]

**Herbert, Cecil**
See   Hamilton, Charles Harold St.
John

**Herbert, Don** 1917-    [CA, SAT]
*American television performer and
author*
* Wizard, Mr.

**Herbert, Edward**
See   Reynolds, John Hamilton

**Herbert, Edward** 1583-1648
[WBD]
*British philosopher and diplomat*
* [The] Father of English Deism

**Herbert, Ernie Albert** 1887-1968
[BE]
*American baseball player*
* Herbert, Tex

**Herbert, Evelyn**
See   Houstellier, Evelyn

**Herbert, Francis**
See   Bryant, William Cullen

**Herbert, Francis**
See   Verplanck, Gulian Crommalin

**Herbert, Francis, Esq.**
See   Sands, Robert Charles

**Herbert, Fred[erick]**
See   Kemman, Herbert Frederick

**Herbert, George** 1593-1633
[DNNF, DNNS, FFF]
*British poet*
* [The] Sweet Singer of the Temple

**Herbert, Henry** 1693-1751    [WBD]
*Ninth Earl of Pembroke*
* [The] Architect Earl

**Herbert, Henry William**
1807-1858    [DEL, PA]
*British-born author*
* F. F. of the Cedars
* Forester, Frank
* H.
* H. W. H.
* [The] Old Yorkshire Turfman
* Sponge, Mr.

**Herbert, Holmes**
See   Sanger, Edward

**Herbert, John**
See   Brundage, John Herbert

**Herbert, Lucy** 17th c.    [RH]
*Friend of British poet, William
Habington*
* Castara

**Herbert, Mort**
See   Pelovitz, Morton Herbert

**Herbert, S. A. F.** 19th c.    [PA]
*Author*
* Newbury, Herbert

**Herbert, Tex**
See   Herbert, Ernie Albert

**Herbert, Walter**
See   Seligman, Walter Herbert

**Herbert, William?**
See   Croly, Herbert David

**Herbert, William**
See   Eden, William

**Herbert, William** 1580-1630    [PA]
*Author*
* W. H.

**Herbertson, John Anthony**
1901?-1962    [BEW]
*Scottish theatrical performer*
* Anthony, Jack

**Herbie the Herbalist**
See   Ushewokunze, Herbert

**Herblock**
See   Block, Herbert Lawrence

**Herbst, Josephine**
See   Herrmann, Josephine Herbst

**Herchenroeder, Nicholas**
1867-1894    [BE]
*American baseball player*
* Reeder, Nicholas [Nick]

**Herco**
See   Owain, Owain

**[The] Hercules of Music**
See   Gluck, Christoph Willibald

**[The] Hercules of the Jews**
See   Samson

**[The] Hercules of the Screen**
See   Bonomo, Joe

**[The] Hercules of the United States
Bank**
See   Cheves, Langdon

**Hercules Secundus**
See   Commodus, Lucius Aelius

**Herculius**
See   Maximian

**Herd, Alexander** 1868-1944
[EG, GF, OCS]
*Scottish-born golfer*
* Herd, Sandy

**Herd, David** 1930-    [THR]
*British actor*
* O'Brien, David

**Herd, Henry** 1886-    [F2]
*Actor*
* Lorraine, Harry

**Herd, Sandy**
See   Herd, Alexander

**Herdebred [Broadshouldered]**
See   Haakon II

**Herder, Johann Gottfried von**
1744-1803    [SN]
*German philosopher*
* [The] Dean
* [The] Fenelon of Germany
* [The] Plato of the Christian
World

**Hereford, John**
See   Fletcher, Harry Lutf Verne

**[A] Heretic in Verse**
See   De Bueil, Honorat

**Hereward** ?-1072?
[DEP, DNNS, HN]
*British outlaw and patriot*
* England's Darling
* [The] Last of the English
* [The] Wake

**Herfurt, Arthur** 1911-
[PMJ, WWJ]
*American jazz musician*
* Herfurt, Skeets

**Herfurt, Skeets**
See   Herfurt, Arthur

**Herge**
See   Remi [or Remy], Georges

**Herget, John L.** 1868-1945
[AS, RBE]
*American boxer*
* Mitchell, Young

**Herian, V.**
See   Gregorian, Vartan

**Heriat, Philippe**
See   Payelle, Raymond-Gerard

**Hericault, Charles d'**
See   Ricault, Charles Joseph de

**Heritage, A. J.**
See   Addis, Hazel Iris Wilson

**Heritage, John**
See   Shaw, Stanley Gordon

**Heritage, Martin**
See   Horler, Sydney

**Herkes, Max**
See   Herkes, Robert

**Herkes, Robert** 1957-    [DC]
*British cricketer*
* Herkes, Max

**[The] Herkimer Hurricane**
See   D'Ambrosio, Luigi

**Herks**
See   Gurbrand, John

**Herle, Nicolae** 1927-    [OP]
*Rumanian opera singer*
* Herlea, Nicolae

**Herlea, Nicolae**
See   Herle, Nicolae

**Herlie, Eileen**
See   O'Herlihy, Eileen

**Herm, Gerhard Otto** 1931-    [IAW]
*German author*
* Crawells, Carl

**Herman**
See   Noone, Peter Blair Denis
Bernard

**Herman, Aladore** 1870-1951
[BEW]
*Hungarian-born producer and
playwright*
* Woods, A. H.
* Woods, Albert Herman

**Herman, Alan** 1916?-    [CA, WD]
*Canadian author and playwright*
* Allan, Ted
* Maxwell, Edward

**Herman, Babe**
See   Herman, Floyd Caves

**Herman, Floyd Caves** 1903-
[BE, DGS, PB]
*American baseball player*
* Herman, Babe
* [The] Incredible Herman

**Herman, Julius** 1894-1955    [MBF]
*South African-born author*
* Clifford, Martin [house
pseudonym]
* Richards, Frank [house
pseudonym]

**Herman, Lasser** ?-1961    [BEW]
*Journalist and screenwriter*
* Lania, Leon

**Herman, Lewis** 20th c.
*Actor, producer, author*
* Morris, Hugh

**Herman, Louis**
See Sellers, Connie Leslie, Jr.

**Herman, Mildred** 1928- [JL]
*Canadian-born dancer*
* Hayden, Melissa

**Herman, Pete**
See Gulotta, Peter

**Herman, William** [joint pseudonym with Thomas A. Harcourt]
See Bierce, Ambrose [Gwinett]

**Herman, William** [joint pseudonym with Ambrose (Gwinett) Bierce]
See Harcourt, Thomas A.

**Herman, Woodrow Wilson** 1913-
[ASC, IEJ]
*American bandleader*
* [The] Boy Wonder of the Clarinet
* Herman, Woody

**Herman, Woody**
See Herman, Woodrow Wilson

**Hermann**
See Arminius [or Armin]

**Hermann**
See Huppen, Hermann

**Hermann, Cone**
See Hermann, Cornelius

**Hermann, Cornelius** 1903-1957
[BBH]
*American bowler*
* Hermann, Cone

**Hermann, Emily**
See Luders, Catherine

**Hermann, Frank** 1928-1971 [SC]
*American-born actor*
* Wolff, Frank

**Hermann, Georg** 1871- ? [BBD]
*German singer and voice teacher*
* Armin, Georg

**Hermann von Reichenau**
1013-1054 [DNNS, WBD]
*German monk, historian, poet*
* Hermanus Contractus
* [Der] Lahme
* [The] Lame

**Hermanns, Peter**
See Brannon, William T.

**Hermanus Contractus**
See Hermann von Reichenau

**Hermeling, Pigpen**
See Hermeling, Terry

**Hermeling, Terry** 20th c.
*American football player*
* Hermeling, Pigpen

**Hermes**
See Canaway, William Hamilton [Bill]

**Hermes**
See Harris, William Torrey

**Hermes**
See Lumley, B.

**Hermes** [FFF]
*Egyptian philosopher*
* Trismegistus [Thrice Greatest]

**Hermes, Paul**
See Thayer, William Roscoe

**[The] Hermes Trismegistus of Germany**
See Rudolf II [or Rudolph]

**Hermine**
See Elder, Susan Blanchard

**Herminia**
See Urena de Henriquez, Salome

**Hermippus** 5th c. BC [WBD]
*Athenian author and politician*
* [The] One Eyed

**Hermit**
See Hayley, William

**[The] Hermit**
See Paul of Thebes

**[The] Hermit**
See Peter of Amiens

**[The] Hermit Author of Palo Alto**
See Hoover, Herbert Clark

**[The] Hermit of Grub Street**
See Welby, Henry

**[The] Hermit of Hampole**
See Rolle, Richard

**[The] Hermit of La Ripaille**
See Amadeus VIII

**[The] Hermit of Lathom**
See Swarsbrick, Robert

**[The] Hermit of Literature**
See Baker, Thomas

**Hermit of New York**
See Frothingham, Washington

**[The] Hermit of Newfane**
See Brown, David

**Hermlin, Stephan**
See Leder, Rudolf

**Hermodactyl**
See Harley, Robert [First Earl of Oxford]

**Hermolaus**
See Albrizzi, Almoro

**Hermon-Hodge, Harry Baldwin**
1885- [WWL]
*British author*
* Langa-Langa

**Hermoso, Angel Remigio** 1946-
[BE]
*Venezuelan-born baseball player*
* Hermoso, Remy

**Hermoso, Remy**
See Hermoso, Angel Remigio

**Hermsen, Clarence** 20th c. [SMG]
*American basketball player*
* Hermsen, Kleggie

**Hermsen, Kleggie**
See Hermsen, Clarence

**Hern, [George] Anthony** 1916-
[AW, CA]
*British author*
* Hope, Andrew
* Potiphar [joint pseudonym with J. F. Marrack]

**Hern, Riley**
See Hern, William Milton

**Hern, William Milton** 1880-1929
[HK]
*Canadian-born hockey player*
* Hern, Riley

**Hernaiz, Jesus Rafael** 1948- [BE]
*Puerto Rican-born baseball player*
* Rodriguez, Jesus Rafael

**Hernandez, Arturo** [RBE]
*Boxing agent*
* Hernandez, Cuyo

**Hernandez, Chico**
See Hernandez, Ricardo

**Hernandez, Chico**
See Hernandez, Salvador Jose Ramos

**Hernandez, Cuyo**
See Hernandez, Arthuro

**Hernandez, Guillermo** 1955-
[SMG]
*Puerto Rican-born baseball player*
* Hernandez, Willie

**Hernandez, Jacinto Zulueta** 1940-
[BE]
*Cuban-born baseball player*
* Hernandez, Jackie

**Hernandez, Jackie**
See Hernandez, Jacinto Zulueta

**Hernandez, Jose P. H.** 1892-1922
[CW]
*Puerto Rican poet*
* Peache

**Hernandez, Juan G.** 1896-1970
[IBW, SC]
*Puerto Rican-born actor, director, boxer*
* Curley, Kid
* Hernandez, Juano

**Hernandez, Juano**
See Hernandez, Juan G.

**Hernandez, Ricardo** 20th c. [OBW]
*American baseball player*
* Hernandez, Chico

**Hernandez, Rodolfo** 1952-
[BE, SMG]
*Mexican-born baseball player*
* Acosta, Rodolfo
* Hernandez, Rudy

**Hernandez, Rudy**
See Hernandez, Rodolfo

**Hernandez, Salvador Jose Ramos**
1916- [BE]
*Cuban-born baseball player*
* Hernandez, Chico

**Hernandez, Victor P.**
See Raphaela, Cornelius [Nechi]

**Hernandez, Willie**
See Hernandez, Guillermo

**Hernandez y Castro, Joaquin**
1873-1941 [GS]
*Spanish bullfighter*
* Parrao [Spreading]

**Herndon, Agnes**
See Jessel, Mrs. Joseph A.

**Herne, Huxley**
See Brooker, Bertram

**Herne, James A.**
See Ahearn, James A.

**Herne, Mrs. J. A.** [FFF]
*Entertainer*
* Corcoran, Catherine

**Herne, Thomas**
See Stewart-Cockerton, Josephine

**Hernhuter, Albert** 20th c. [WGT]
*Author*
* Ahearne, Burt
* Jarvis, Lee

**[The] Hero of a Hundred Fights**
See Nelson, Horatio

**[The] Hero of a Hundred Fights**
See Wellesley, Arthur

**[The] Hero of Appomattox**
See Grant, Hiram Ulysses

**[The] Hero of Austerlitz**
See Bonaparte, Napoleon

**[The] Hero of Debt**
See Sheridan

**[The] Hero of Fable**
See Lorraine, Henry II [or Henri] de

**[The] Hero of Fort Donelson**
See Grant, Hiram Ulysses

**[The] Hero of Modern Italy**
See Garibaldi, Giuseppe

**[The] Hero of New Orleans**
See Jackson, Andrew

**[The] Hero of Palestro**
See Victor Emmanuel II

**[The] Hero of Rora**
See Janavel, Joshua

**[The] Hero of San Juan Hill**
See Roosevelt, Theodore [Teddy]

**[The] Hero of '77**
See Hayes, Rutherford Birchard

**Hero of the Crater**
See Mahone, William

**[The] Hero of the Crossing**
See Sadat, Anwar

**[The] Hero of the Humber**
See Ellerthorpe, John

**[The] Hero of the Nile**
See Nelson, Horatio

**[The] Hero of the Nine Hostages**
See Niall

**[The] Hero of the Peninsula**
See Wellesley, Arthur

**[The] Hero of Tippecanoe**
See Harrison, William Henry

**[The] Hero of Upper Canada**
See Brock, [Sir] Isaac

**Herod** 1st c. BC [DNNS]
*King of Judea*
* [The] Great

**Herod Agrippa I [or Julius Agrippa I]**
?- 44 [FFF, WBD]
*King of Judea*
* Agrippa
* [The] Great

**Herod Antipas**
See Antipas

**Herod Archelaus**
See Archelaus

**Herod Philip**
See Philip

**Herodotus** 5th c. BC
[DEP, DNNF, SN]
*Greek historian*
* [The] Father of Greek Prose
* [The] Father of History
* [The] Father of Lies
* [The] Homer of History

**[The] Herodotus of Barbarism**
See   Florentius, Georgius

**[The] Herodotus of China**
See   Sse-ma-Thsian

**[The] Herodotus of Old London**
See   Stow, John

**Heroet, Antoine** ?-1568   [WBD]
*French clergyman and poet*
* [La] Maisonneuve

**Heron, Bijou**
See   Miller, Mrs. Henry

**Heron, Bijou**
See   Stoepel, Helene

**Heron, E.**
See   Prichard, Kate O'Brien
Hesketh

**Heron, H.**
See   Prichard, Hesketh Vernon
Hesketh

**Heron, Matilda**
See   Stoepfel, Mrs. Robert

**Heron, Robert**
See   Pinkerton, John

**Heron-Allen, Edward** 1861-1943
[ESF, HFF, SFL]
*British author*
* Blayre, Christopher
* Dryasdust?
* Flavius
* Halidom, M. Y.?

**Heroux, George L.** 1869-1946   [BE]
*American baseball player*
* Wheeler, George L.

**Herpin, Clara Adele Luce**
1845-1914   [WBD]
*French author*
* Perey, Lucien

**Herrera, Antonio de** 1559-1625
[SN]
*Spanish historian*
* [The] Prince of Historians

**Herrera, Bobby**
See   Herrera, Procopio Rodriguez

**Herrera, Ferdinand [or Fernando] de**
1534?-1597   [FFF, RH, WBD]
*Spanish poet*
* [The] Divine

**Herrera, Francisco de** 1576-1656
[WBD]
*Spanish painter*
* [El] Viejo

**Herrera, Francisco de** 1622-1685
[WBD]
*Spanish painter*
* [El] Mozo
* [Lo] Spagnuolo dei Pesci

**Herrera, Jose Concepcion** 1942-
[BE]
*Venezuelan-born baseball player*
* Herrera, Loco

**Herrera, Juan Francisco** 1934-
[BE]
*Cuban-born baseball player*
* Herrera, Pancho

**Herrera, Loco**
See   Herrera, Jose Concepcion

**Herrera, Mike**
See   Herrera, Ramon

**Herrera, Pancho**
See   Herrera, Juan Francisco

**Herrera, Procopio Rodriguez**
1926-   [BE]
*Mexican-born baseball player*
* Herrera, Bobby
* Herrera, Tito

**Herrera, Rafael** 20th c.   [BX]
*Mexican boxer*
* Herrera, Raul

**Herrera, Ramon** 1897-   [BE]
*Cuban-born baseball player*
* Herrera, Mike

**Herrera, Raul**
See   Herrera, Rafael

**Herrera, Tito**
See   Herrera, Procopio Rodriguez

**Herrerita [Little Blacksmith]**
See   Alonso, Manuel

**Herriage, Dutch**
See   Herriage, [William] Troy

**Herriage, [William] Troy** 1930-
[BE]
*American baseball player*
* Herriage, Dutch

**Herrick, Jean Mellin**
See   Mellin, Jeanne

**Herrick, Marvin Theodore**
1899-1966   [CA]
*American educator and author*
* Smith, John [joint pseudonym
with Hoyt Hudson]

**[The] Herrick of Germany**
See   Fleming [or Flemming], Paul

**Herrick, Robert** 1591-1674
[DNNF, FFF]
*British poet and clergyman*
* Poor Robin

**Herrick, Thornecliff [house
pseudonym]**
See   Bixby, Jerome Lewis

**Herrigan, Jackie**
See   McDonald, Paula

**Herrigan, Jeff**
See   McDonald, Richard C.

**Herrin, Caller**
See   Smith, Annie

**Herring, Arthur L.** 1907-   [BE]
*American baseball player*
* Herring, Sandy

**Herring, Lefty**
See   Herring, Silas Clarke

**Herring, Paul** 20th c.   [MBF]
*British author*
* Raeburn, David

**Herring, Reed** 1911-   [FC]
*American actor*
* Hadley, Reed

**Herring, Sandy**
See   Herring, Arthur L.

**Herring, Silas Clarke** 1880- ?   [BE]
*American baseball player*
* Herring, Lefty

**Herring, Smoke**
See   Herring, William Francis
[Bill]

**Herring, William Francis [Bill]**
1893-1962   [BE]
*American baseball player*
* Herring, Smoke

**Herriot, James**
See   Wight, James Alfred

**Herrmann, Adelaide** 1853?-1932
[BS]
*British-born American magician*
* Cleopatra the Egyptian Sorceress
* [The] Greatest of the Herrmanns

**Herrmann, Alexander** ?-1896   [BS]
*American magician*
* Herrmann the Great

**Herrmann, August** 1859-1931
[PB, SMG]
*American baseball executive*
* Herrmann, Garry

**Herrmann, Edward Martin** 1946-
[SMG]
*American baseball player*
* Herrmann, Fort
* Herrmann, Sup

**Herrmann, Fort**
See   Herrmann, Edward Martin

**Herrmann, Garry**
See   Herrmann, August

**Herrmann, Josephine Herbst** 1897-
[NAA]
*American author*
* Herbst, Josephine

**Herrmann, Sup**
See   Herrmann, Edward Martin

**Herrmann the Great**
See   Herrmann, Alexander

**Herrnstein, Barbara**
See   Smith, Barbara Herrnstein

**Herrod, Walter**
See   Light, Walter Herrod

**Herron, Edna** 1904-   [WGT]
*Author*
* Aronin, Ben

**Herron, Mrs. Henry** 19th c.   [PA]
*Author*
* Australie

**Herschberger, Ruth [Margaret]**
1917-   [CA]
*American poet and playwright*
* Langstaff, Josephine

**Herschel, Friedrich Wilhelm**
1738-1822   [WBD]
*British astronomer*
* Herschel, [Sir] William

**Herschel, [Sir] William**
See   Herschel, Friedrich Wilhelm

**Herschman, Charles L.** 1887-
[EJS]
*American football player*
* Herschman, Heff

**Herschman, Heff**
See   Herschman, Charles L.

**Herscovitz, Moe**
See   Herscovitz, Montgomery

**Herscovitz, Montgomery** 20th c.
[EJS]
*Canadian boxer*
* Herscovitz, Moe

**Hersey, Frances Lester Warner**
1888-   [NAA]
*American author*
* Warner, Frances Lester

**Hersey, Harold** 1892-   [WGT]
*Author*
* Buxton, C.
* Kemp, H.
* Kennedy, P.
* Kiproy, C.?
* Le Moyne, Roy
* Le Moyne, Seymour
* Lerrovitch
* Owens, A.
* Tyson, A.
* Vernon, V.

**Hersh, Carl** 20th c.
*American television cameraman*
* [El] Iman [The Magnet]

**Hershberger, Hazel Kuhns** 20th c.
[CA]
*American author*
* Allen, Hazel

**Hershberger, L. L.**
See   Hershberger, Leander Leonard

**Hershberger, Leander Leonard**
1890-1950   [IA]
*American poet*
* Ander, Lee
* Hershberger, L. L.

**Hershel, Abram Samuel** 1914-
[BEW]
*American playwright*
* Ginnes, Abram S.

**Hershey, Barbara**
See   Herzstein, Barbara

**Hershfield, Harry**
See   Kabible, Abe

**Hershman, Morris** 1920-   [CA]
*American author*
* Bond, Evelyn
* English, Arnold
* Webb, Lionel
* Wilcox, Jess

**[A] Hertfordshire Incumbent**
See   Blakesley, Joseph Williams

**Hertz, Carl**
See   Morganstern, Carl

**Hertz, George**
See   Hirst, George Stanley

**Hertz, Grete Janus** 1915-
[CA, SAT]
*Danish author and translator*
* Janus, Grete

**Hertz, Henrik**
See   Heymannn, Henrik

**Hertz, Margaret** 1879- ?   [THR]
*British actress*
* Halstan, Margaret

**Hertz, Solange [Strong]** 1920-   [CA]
*American author*
* Strong, Solange

**Hertzberg, Nancy Florence** [Keesing]
1923-   [AW]
*Australian author and poet*
* Keesing, Nancy

**Hertzberg, Sidney** 1922-
[EJS, SMG]
*American basketball player*
* Hertzberg, Sonny

**Hertzberg, Sonny**
*See* Hertzberg, Sidney

**Hertzler, Edith DeVilliers** 1878- ?
[NAA]
*American writer*
* Sarazen, Dolores

**Herve**
*See* Ronge [or Ronger], Florimond

**Herve, Aime Marie Edouard**
1835-1899   [WBD]
*French journalist*
* Valnay, Raoul

**Herve, Jean-Luc**
*See* Humbaraci, D[emir] Arslan

**Herve-Bazin, Jean Pierre** 1911-
[B10]
*French author*
* Bazin, Herve

**Hervey, E. L.** 1811- ?   [PA]
*Author*
* Montague, E. L.

**Hervey, Hedley** 20th c.   [MBF]
*British author*
* Strong, James

**Hervey, Irene**
*See* Herwick, Irene

**Hervey, Jane**
*See* McGaw, Naomi Blanche
Thoburn

**Hervey, John** [Baron Hervey of
Ickworth] 1696-1743
[DNNF, DNNS, FFF]
*British author and politician*
* Lord Fanny
* Sporus

**Hervey, Thomas Kibble** 1804-1859
[PA]
*Author*
* Ketch, Jack

**Hervieu, Paul Ernest** 1857-1915
[WBD]
*French author and playwright*
* Eliacin

**Herwick, Irene** 1916?-   [FC]
*American actress*
* Hervey, Irene

**Herz, Jerome Spencer** [Jerry]   [CA]
*American author*
* Spencer

**Herz, Peggy** 1936-   [CA]
*American author*
* Hudson, Peggy

**Herzen** [or Hertzen], **Aleksandr
Ivanovich**
*See* Yakovlev, Aleksandr Ivanovich

**Herzfelde, Helmut** 1891-1968
[CAR, GA]
*German artist*
* Heartfield, John

**Herzog, Buck**
*See* Herzog, Charles Lincoln

**Herzog, Charles Lincoln**
1885-1953   [AS, BE]
*American baseball player and
manager*
* Herzog, Buck

**Herzog, Dorrel Norman Elvert**
1931-   [BR, PB, SMG]
*American baseball player and
manager*
* Herzog, Relly
* Herzog, Whitey

**Herzog, Emile** [Salomon Wilhelm]
1885-1967   [CD, EWL, IPA]
*French author*
* Maurois, Andre

**Herzog, Eric** 1926-   [CA]
*Hungarian-born American author*
* Roman, Eric

**Herzog, Guy** 1923-   [WECO]
*Belgian cartoonist*
* Bara

**Herzog, Relly**
*See* Herzog, Dorrel Norman Elvert

**Herzog, Robert** 1937-   [CA]
*Hungarian-born linguist and author*
* Hetzron, Robert

**Herzog, Werner**
*See* Stipetic, Werner H.

**Herzog, Whitey**
*See* Herzog, Dorrel Norman Elvert

**Herzstein, Barbara** 1948-   [SW]
*American actress*
* Hershey, Barbara
* Seagull

**Heseltine, Philip** 1894-1930
[BBD, HDM]
*British composer and writer*
* Warlock, Peter

**Hesiod** 8th c. BC
[DNNS, SN, WBD]
*Greek poet*
* [The] Ascraean Poet
* [The] Ascraean Sage
* [The] Father of Greek Didactic
Poetry
* [The] Old Ascraean

**Heslin, Red Ted**
*See* Heslin, Ted

**Heslin, Ted**
*British politician*
* Heslin, Red Ted

**Heslin, Thomas** 1875-1945   [BE]
*American baseball player*
* Hess, Thomas [Tom]

**Heslop, F.**
*See* Park, Fanny

**Hespro, Herbert**
*See* Robinson, Herbert Spencer

**Hess, Lawrence Anthony**
1866-1939   [CAT]
*British author and clergyman*
* Cuthbert, [Father]

**Hess, Rudolf** 1894?-   [NN]
*German Nazi leader*
* [The] Prisoner of Spandau

**Hess, Thomas** [Tom]
*See* Heslin, Thomas

**Hesse, Hermann** 1877-1962   [CAP]
*German-born author*
* Lauscher, Hermann
* Sinclair, Emil

**Hesse-Wartegg, Minnie von**
1852?-1929   [FFF]
*American opera singer*
* Hauk, Minnie

**Hesselberg, Melvyn E.** 1901-1981
[BDF, FC, OCF]
*American actor*
* Douglas, Melvyn

**Hessell, Henry**
*See* Tiltman, Hugh Hessell

**Hessing, Dennis**
*See* Dennis-Jones, H[arold]

**Hessling, Catherine**
*See* Heuschling, Andree

**Hessus, Helius Eobanus**
*See* Koch, Helius Eobanus

**Hester, John, the Spagericke**
*See* Forrestier, James

**Heston, Charlton**
*See* Carter, Charlton

**Hesychius** 6th c.   [DNNS]
*Greek historian and author*
* [The] Illustrious

**Hetherington, John Rowland** 1899-
[IAW]
*British author*
* Attaboy

**Hettinger, John** 1880- ?
[SFL, WGT]
*Author*
* Johnhett

**Hetzel, Pierre Jules** 1814-1886
[PA, WBD]
*French publisher and author*
* Stahl, P. J.
* Stahl, Pierre Jules

**Hetzron, Robert**
*See* Herzog, Robert

**Heuman, William** 1912-1971
[CA, SAT]
*American author*
* Kramer, George

**Heuschling, Andree** 20th c.   [OCF]
*French actress*
* Hessling, Catherine

**Heusser, Edward Burleton**
1909-1956   [BE]
*American baseball player*
* [The] Wild Elk of the Wasatch

**Heussgen** [or Huessgen], **Johannes**
1482-1531   [WBD]
*German theologian*
* Oecolampadius, Johannes

**Hevelin, James** 20th c.   [SFP]
*Author*
* Barron, Rusty

**Hevelius, Johannes**
*See* Hewel [Hewelcke or
Hoewelcke], Johannes

**Hevesi, Ludwig** 1843-1910   [WBD]
*Hungarian-born Austrian journalist*
* Onkel Tom

**Hewel** [Hewelcke or Hoewelcke],
**Johannes** 1611-1687   [WBD]
*Astronomer*
* Hevelius, Johannes

**Hewelcke, Geoffrey** 20th c.   [WGT]
*Author*
* Jeffries, Hugh

**Hewes, Cady**
*See* De Voto, Bernard [Augustine]

**Hewett, Anita**
*See* Duke, Anita

**Hewison, William** 1925-   [ART]
*British artist*
* H.

**Hewit, Augustine Francis**
*See* Hewit, Nathaniel Augustus

**Hewit, Nathaniel Augustus**
1820-1897   [WBD]
*American clergyman*
* Hewit, Augustine Francis

**Hewitt, Agnes**
*See* Sothern, Mrs. Lytton

**Hewitt, Ben**
*See* Mitchell, Adrian

**Hewitt, Cecil Rolph** 1901-
[AW, B10, CA]
*British author, editor, penologist*
* Cecil, R. H.
* Milton, Oliver
* Rolph, C. H.

**Hewitt, Frederic M.** 1916-   [BBH]
*American lacrosse player and coach*
* Hewitt, Rip

**Hewitt, Harry S.** 1856- ?   [PA]
*Author*
* Keld

**Hewitt, Kathleen Douglas** 1893-
[WW]
*Author*
* Martin, Dorothea

**Hewitt, Martin**
*See* Morrison, Arthur

**Hewitt, Mary Elizabeth** 1808- ?
[FFF]
*American poet*
* Ione

**Hewitt, Rip**
*See* Hewitt, Frederic M.

**Hewlet, William** 17th c.   [SN]
*British regicide*
* Greybeard, Father

**Hewlett, J.** 19th c.   [PA]
*Author*
* Priggins, Peter

**Hewson, Charles**
*See* Cameron, Ludovick Charles
Richard

**Hewson, Irene Dale** 20th c.   [SFL]
*Author*
* Ross, Jean

**Hewson, John** 17th c.   [FFF, SN]
*British army officer*
* Hewson the Cobbler
* Old Hewson the Cobbler

**Hewson the Cobbler**
*See* Hewson, John

**Hexham, Lionel J. F.**
*See* Hamel, Felix John

**Heximer, Obs**
See Heximer, Orville Russell

**Heximer, Orville Russell** 1910-
[CEI]
*Canadian-born hockey player*
* Heximer, Obs

**Hext, Harrington**
See Phillpotts, Eden

**Hextall, David**
See Phillips-Birt, Douglas

**Heydon, J. K.**
See Heydon, Joseph Kentigern

**Heydon, Joseph Kentigern** [WGT]
*Author*
* Heydon, J. K.
* Trevarthen, Hal P.

**Heydrich, Reinhard** 1904-1942
[CBS]
*German Nazi police official*
* [The] Butcher of Prague
* [The] Hangman

**Heyer, Georgette** 1902-1974
[CA, LC, WW]
*British author*
* Martin, Stella

**Heyliger**
See Pieters, Eddie

**Heyliger, William** 1884-1955
[CAT, YAB]
*American author*
* [The] Horatio Alger of Today
* Williams, Hawley

**Heym, Stefan**
See Fliegel, Hellmuth

**Heymannn, Henrik** 1797-1870
[WBD]
*Danish author, poet, playwright*
* Hertz, Henrik

**Heyne, Christian Gottlob**
1729-1812 [SN]
*German scholar*
* [The] King of Critics

**Heynlin, Johann** ?-1496 [WBD]
*Theologian*
* De la Pierre, Jean

**Heyst, Axel**
See Grabowski, Z[bigniew]
Anthony

**Heywood, Anne**
See Pretty, Violet

**Hi Hat Hattie**
See McDaniel, Hattie

**Hi Ski Hi**
See Norton, Caroline Elizabeth
Sarah

**Hi Test Testerman**
See Testerman, Don

**Hi Tide Harris**
See Boyd [or Gitry?], Willie

**Hiao-wen-tee** 2nd c. BC [FFF]
*Emperor of China*
* [The] Great

**Hiat, Elchik**
See Katz, Menke

**Hiatt, Ruth**
See Redfern, Ruth

**Hibbard, Carrie S.** [FFF]
*American writer*
* St. Clair, Mabel

**Hibbart-Gilson, M. M. T.** 1899-
[WWL]
*Irish poet*
* Gilson, Hibbart

**Hibbert, Eleanor Alice [Burford]**
1906- [CA, EMD, WW]
*British author*
* Burford, Eleanor
* Carr, Philippa
* Ford, Elbur
* Holt, Victoria
* Kellow, Kathleen
* Plaidy, Jean
* Tate, Ellalice

**Hibbler, Albert George** 1915-
[IBW]
*American musician*
* [The] Nibbler

**Hibbs, John Alfred Blyth** 1925-
[AW, WD]
*British author and poet*
* Blyth, John

**Hibe, Henry** 1915?-1978 [FIR]
*Entertainer*
* [The] World's Tallest Man

**[The] Hibernian Hebe**
See Loftus, Marie

**[The] Hibernian Roscius**
See Brooke, Gustavus Vaughan

**Hibernicus**
See Clinton, De Witt

**Hicken, Una** 20th c. [SFL]
*Author*
* Kindler, Asta

**Hickenlooper, Lucie Mary Olga
Agnes** 1882-1948 [MS]
*American musician*
* Samaroff, Olga

**Hickey, Donna Lee** 1930-
[ITA, SW]
*American actress*
* Wynn, May

**Hickey, H. B.**
See Livingston, Berkeley

**Hickey, H. B.**
See Livingston, Herb

**Hickey, Hitch**
See Hickey, Patrick Joseph

**Hickey, Howard** 20th c. [SMG]
*American football coach*
* Hickey, Red

**Hickey, James Robert [Jim]** 1920-
[BE]
*American baseball player*
* Hickey, Sid

**Hickey, Madelyn Eastlund** 20th c.
[WD]
*American author and poet*
* Bailey, Betty
* DeLacy, Louise
* Eastlund, Madelyn
* Farrington, Maude
* Sullivan, Eric Harrison

**Hickey, Patrick Joseph** 1953-
[SMG]
*Canadian-born hockey player*
* Hickey, Hitch
* Hickey, Wheels

**Hickey, Red**
See Hickey, Howard

**Hickey, Sid**
See Hickey, James Robert [Jim]

**Hickey, Wheels**
See Hickey, Patrick Joseph

**Hickey, William** [PA]
*Author*
* Doyle, Martin

**Hicklin, Noel Anthony** 1945- [OP]
*British conductor*
* Davies, Noel

**Hickling, E. A.**
See Hickling, Edward Albert

**Hickling, Edward Albert** 1913-
[ART]
*British painter*
* Hickling, E. A.

**Hickling, William**
See De Costa, Benjamin Franklin

**Hickman, Bernard** 1911- [BB]
*American basketball player*
* Hickman, Peck

**Hickman, Charles Taylor**
1876-1934 [AS, BE, BN]
*American baseball player*
* Hickman, Cheerful Charles
* Hickman, Piano Legs

**Hickman, Cheerful Charles**
See Hickman, Charles Taylor

**Hickman, Edward** 1907-1928
[BLB]
*American kidnapper and murderer*
* [The] Fox

**Hickman, Herman M., Jr.**
1911-1958 [FB]
*American football player and
wrestler*
* [The] Poet Laureate of the Little
  Smokies
* [The] Tennessee Terror

**Hickman, Lynn** 20th c. [SFP]
*Author*
* Jones, Plato

**Hickman, Myrthas Helen** 1929-
[FC, ITA]
*American actress*
* Westcott, Helen

**Hickman, Peck**
See Hickman, Bernard

**Hickman, Piano Legs**
See Hickman, Charles Taylor

**Hickok, Hick**
See Hickok, Lorena

**Hickok, James Butler** 1837-1876
[WBD]
*American frontier scout and U.S.
marshal*
* Hickok, Wild Bill

**Hickok, Lorena** ?-1968
*American journalist*
* Hickok, Hick

**Hickok, Wild Bill**
See Hickok, James Butler

**Hickok, Wild Bill**
See Hickok, William O.

**Hickok, William O.** 1874-1933
[FB]
*American football player*
* Hickok, Wild Bill

**Hickory**
See Jackson, Thomas W.

**Hickory Bob Harmon**
See Harmon, Robert Greene

**Hicks, Buddy**
See Hicks, Clarence Walter

**Hicks, Campbell U.** 1903-1974
[SC]
*American actor*
* Page, Paul

**Hicks, Charlie** 1900-1963 [BWW]
*American singer*
* Catjuice Charley
* Laughing Charley
* Lincoln, Charlie

**Hicks, Clarence Walter** 1927- [BE]
*American baseball player*
* Hicks, Buddy

**Hicks, Dolores** 1938- [FC]
*American actress*
* Hart, Dolores

**Hicks, Don T.** ?-1964 [SC]
*American actor*
* Hix, Don

**Hicks, Doug** 1955- [SMG]
*Canadian-born hockey player*
* Hicks, Hicksy

**Hicks, Edna** 1895-1925 [BWW]
*American singer*
* Alix, Mae
* Vivian, Lila

**Hicks, Eleanor B.**
See Coerr, Eleanor [Beatrice]

**Hicks, Harvey**
See Stratemeyer, Edward L.

**Hicks, Hicksy**
See Hicks, Doug

**Hicks, Jennie E.** [FFF, PA]
*Author*
* Sparkle, Sophie

**Hicks, Otis V.** 1913-1974 [BWW]
*American singer*
* Lightnin' Slim

**Hicks Pasha**
See Hicks, William

**Hicks, R. W.**
See Hicks, Richard

**Hicks, Reginald Ernest** 1915-
[WECO]
*Australian cartoonist*
* Hix

**Hicks, Richard** 1951- [SMG]
*American football player*
* Hicks, R. W.

**Hicks, Robert [Bob]** 1902-1931
[BWW]
*American singer*
* Barbecue Bob

**Hicks, Stanley** 1879- ? [THR]
*British actor*
* Brett, Stanley

**Hicks, Thomas** 1936-
[BMH, FC, LRR]
*British actor and singer*
* Broadway's Cockney Star
* Steele, Tommy

**Hicks, W. K.**
*See* Hicks, Wilmer Kenzie

**Hicks, William** 1830-1883 [WBD]
*British army officer*
* Hicks Pasha

**Hicks, Wilmer Kenzie** 1942-
[FB, SMG]
*American football player*
* Hicks, W. K.

**Hid-Allan**
*See* Cunningham, Allan

**Hidalgo, Miguel A.** 1896- [NAA]
*Mexican author and poet*
* De Lima Gil, Manuel Heraldo y
  Hugo

**Hidayatuliah, Mohammad** 1905-
[IAW]
*Indian author*
* Haddi

**Hidden, Norman Frederick** 20th c.
[IAW]
*British author and poet*
* Kryptos

**Hiebel, Henriette Margarethe**
1905-1940 [SC]
*German actress and dancer*
* [La] Jana

**Hieover, Harry**
*See* Brindley, Charles

**Hierophilos**
*See* McHale, John

**Hierophilos**
*See* Moriarty, Patrick Eugene

**Hiersingius**
*See* Sparre, Nicolas

**Higdon, Hal** 1931- [SAT]
*American writer*
* Smith, Lafayette

**Higgenbotham, Robert** 1933-
[BWW]
*American singer*
* Tucker, Tee
* Tucker, Tommy

**Higgin, John Chippendall
Montesquieu** 1823-1874 [WBD]
*British clergyman*
* Bellew, John Chippendall
  Montesquieu

**Higginbotham, Higgy**
*See* Higginbotham, Jack

**Higginbotham, J. C.**
*See* Higginbotham, Jack

**Higginbotham, Jack** 1906-1973
[DAM, EJ, MY]
*American jazz musician*
* Higginbotham, Higgy
* Higginbotham, J. C.
* Higginbotham, Jay C.

**Higginbotham, Jay C.**
*See* Higginbotham, Jack

**Higgins, Ambrose** 1720?-1801
[WBD]
*Irish-born army officer and
government official in South
America*
* De Osorno, Marques
* O'Higgins, [Don] Ambrosio

**Higgins, Charles** 20th c. [BLB]
*American underworld figure*
* Higgins, Vannie

**Higgins, Charles Eli** 20th c. [SFL]
*Author*
* Muelier

**Higgins, Charles S.** 1893-
[ART, DBA]
*Argentinian-born author and painter*
* Dall, Ian
* Pic

**Higgins, Eddie**
*See* Higgins, Haydn

**Higgins, Haydn** 1932- [DAM]
*American musician*
* Higgins, Eddie

**Higgins, Henry** 1945?-1978 [FIR]
*British bullfighter*
* Canadas, Enrique

**Higgins, Ink**
*See* Weiss, Morris S[amuel]

**Higgins, Jack**
*See* Patterson, Harry

**Higgins, James Hart** 1911- [MBF]
*British author*
* Hart, James

**Higgins, John**
*See* Noland, John T.

**Higgins, Martyn**
*See* Sellers, Connie Leslie, Jr.

**Higgins, Matthew James**
1815-1868 [DEL, FFF, RH]
*British author*
* J. O.
* Omnium, Jacob

**Higgins, Michael Franklin**
1909-1969 [AS, BE, PB]
*American baseball player and
manager*
* Higgins, Pinky

**Higgins, Pinky**
*See* Higgins, Michael Franklin

**Higgins, Rosalyn [Cohen]** 1937-
[CA]
*British barrister and author*
* Cohen, Rosalyn

**Higgins, Vannie**
*See* Higgins, Charles

**Higginson, Francis L.** 20th c.
[BBH]
*American rowboat racer*
* Higginson, Peter

**Higginson, Joseph Vincent** 1896-
[ASC]
*American musician and educator*
* De Brant, Cyr

**Higginson, Peter**
*See* Higginson, Francis L.

**Higginson, Stephen** 18th c. [SN]
*American merchant and university
steward*
* [The] Man of Ross

**Higgs, Alec Stansbury** 1890-
[WWL]
*British author*
* Stansbury, Alec

**Higgs, Blake** 20th c. [BWW]
*Bahamian singer*
* Blind Blake

**Higgs, Higgy**
*See* Higgs, Kenneth

**Higgs, Kenneth** 1937- [DC]
*British cricketer*
* Higgs, Higgy

**High, Andrew Aird** 1897- [BE]
*American baseball player*
* High, Handy Andy

**[The] High Born Demosthenes**
*See* William I

**High, Bunny**
*See* High, Hugh Jenken

**High, Ed[ward]** 20th c. [BE]
*American baseball player*
* High, Lefty

**High, Handy Andy**
*See* High, Andrew Aird

**[The] High Hat Tragedian of Song**
*See* Friedman, Theodore Leopold

**High, Hugh Jenken** 1887-1962
[BE]
*American baseball player*
* High, Bunny
* High, Lefty

**High, Lefty**
*See* High, Ed[ward]

**High, Lefty**
*See* High, Hugh Jenken

**High Mettled Harry**
*See* St. John, Henry

**High Pockets Johnson**
*See* Johnson, Paul Vincent

**High Pockets Kelly**
*See* Kelly, George Lange

**[The] High Priest of Bebop**
*See* Monk, Thelonious Sphere

**[The] High Priest of Fashion in
Motion**
*See* Munkacsi, Martin

**[The] High Priest of Music**
*See* Sowande, Fela

**[The] High Priestess of Soul**
*See* Waymon, Eunice Kathleen

**[The] High Sheriff from Hell**
*See* Bunch, William

**High Tax Harry**
*See* Truman, Harry

**High-Smith, Domini** 1942- [CA]
*British author*
* Van Hassen, Amy
* Wiles, Domini
* Williams, Tina

**Higham, Florence May Greir**
1896-1980 [CA, WD]
*British historian and author*
* Evans, F. M. G.

**Highet, Helen**
*See* MacInnes, Helen

**[The] Highgate Prophet**
*See* Powell, William

**Highland, Dora**
*See* Avallone, Michael [Angelo],
Jr.

**[The] Highland Laddie**
*See* Stuart, Charles Edward Louis
Philip Casimir

**Highland, Lawrence**
*See* Linfield, Mary Barrow

**Highland Mary**
*See* Campbell, Mary

**Highsmith, [Mary] Patricia** 1921-
[CC, WD, WW]
*American author*
* Morgan, Claire

**Hightower, Donna** 20th c. [IBW]
*American-born singer*
* [The] Queen of Soul

**Hightower, Paul**
*See* Collins, Thomas Hightower

**Highwater, Jamake** 1942- [CA]
*American author*
* Marks, J

**Higinbotham, John D.** 1864- ?
[NAA]
*Canadian writer*
* Polo, Articum

**Hignell, Alastair James** 1955- [DC]
*British cricketer*
* Hignell, Higgy

**Hignell, Higgy**
*See* Hignell, Alastair James

**Higon, Albert**
*See* Jeury, Michel

**Higonnet, Margaret Randolph**
1941- [CA]
*American educator and author*
* Hale, Margaret

**Higson, Philip John Willoughby**
*See* Willoughby-Higson, Philip
John

**Higuchi, Chako**
*See* Higuchi, Hisako Matsui

**Higuchi, Hisako Matsui** 1945-
[GF]
*Japanese golfer*
* Higuchi, Chako

**[La] Hija del Caribe**
*See* Padilla de Sanz, Trina

**[El] Hijo del Damuji**
*See* Hurtado del Valle, Antonio

**Hilaire, Emile Marc** 1790?-1887
[FF, DNNF, WBD]
*French author*
* St. Hilaire, Marco de

**Hilarius**
*See* Feistkorn, W.

**Hilary**
*See* Wickham, Hilary Judith

**Hilary** 300- 367? [DEP, FFF, SN]
*Saint*
* [The] Hammer of the Arians
* Malleus Arianorum
* [The] Rhone of Christian
  Eloquence
* [The] Rhone of Latin Eloquence

**Hilcher, Walter Frank** 1909-1962
[BE]
*American baseball player*
* Hilcher, Whitey

**Hilcher, Whitey**
*See* Hilcher, Walter Frank

**Hild, H.** 20th c. [MBF]
*British author*
* Brand, Dudley

**Hilda**
*See* Abel, Mrs. Peter E.

**Hilda**
*See* Siller, Hilda

**Hildanus**
*See* Fabricus, Wilhelm

**Hildebert** 1055-1133 [HN]
*French prelate*
* Venerabilis, Doctor

**Hildebrand**
*See* Beets, Nikolaas

**Hildebrand** 1020?-1085
[RH, WBD]
*Pope*
* Gregory VII
* Turk Gregory

**Hildebrand, Bunny**
*See* Hildebrand, Jane Cullum

**Hildebrand, Hall**
*See* Birdsall, A. F.

**Hildebrand, Jane Cullum** 1913-
[MY]
*American jazz musician*
* Hildebrand, Bunny

**Hildebrand, Palmer Marion**
1884-1960 [BE]
*American baseball player*
* Hildebrand, Pete

**Hildebrand, Pete**
*See* Hildebrand, Palmer Marion

**Hildebrand, Ray** 1940- [PRS, RO1]
*American singer*
* Paul

**Hildegarde**
*See* Hoskins, Josephine R.

**Hildegarde**
*See* Sell, Hildegarde Loretta

**Hilder, John Chapman** 1892-
[NAA]
*British-born writer*
* Charlton, James

**Hildick, E. W.**
*See* Hildick, [Edmund] Wallace

**Hildick, [Edmund] Wallace** 1925-
[CA, SAT]
*British author*
* Hildick, E. W.

**Hildreth, Sarah**
*See* Butler, Mrs. Benjamin

**Hildyard, James** 1809- ? [PA]
*Author*
* Ingoldsby

**Hiles, Bartram**
*See* Hiles, Frederick John

**Hiles, Frederick John** 1872-1927
[DBA]
*British painter*
* Hiles, Bartram

**Hilforde, Mary**
*See* Griggs, Mary

**Hilgard, [Ferdinand] Heinrich
[Gustav]** 1835-1900 [FFF]
*American journalist, financier,
business executive*
* Villard, Henry

**Hilgenberg, Sheep**
*See* Hilgenberg, Wally

**Hilgenberg, Wally** 20th c.
*American football player*
* Hilgenberg, Sheep

**Hilgerink, William Edward**
1887-1953 [BE]
*American baseball player*
* Hilly, William Edward [Bill]

**[The] Hill**
*See* McGill, Bill

**Hill, Agnes Isabel Aston** 1887-
[NAA]
*British poet and editor*
* Aunt Marian

**Hill, Alan** 1950- [DC]
*British cricketer*
* Hill, Bud

**Hill, Anthony** 1930- [CAR]
*British artist*
* Redo
* Rem Doxfud

**Hill, Arthur**
*See* Tullock, W. W.

**Hill, Bass**
*See* Hill, Ernest

**Hill, Bennett** 20th c.
*Auto racer*
* Little Nemo

**Hill, Bertha** 1900?-1950
[DAM, EJ, PMJ]
*American singer*
* Hill, Chippie

**Hill, Bev[erly Jean]** 1938-1978
[BWW]
*American singer*
* Big Mama Bev

**Hill, Billie**
*See* Leonard, Billie

**Hill, Boot**
*See* Hill, Marc Kevin

**Hill, Brian [Merrikin]** 1896-
[AW, CAP, LAO]
*British author*
* Magill, Marcus [joint pseudonym
with Joanna Elder Giles?]

**Hill, Buck**
*See* Hill, Roger

**Hill, Bud**
*See* Hill, Alan

**Hill, Bunker**
*See* Hill, Carmen Proctor

**Hill, Calvin** 20th c.
*American football player*
* Hill, Reuben

**Hill, Carmen Proctor** 1895- [BE]
*American baseball player*
* Hill, Bunker
* Hill, Specs

**Hill, Caroline**
*See* Kelcey, Mrs. Herbert

**Hill, Chippie**
*See* Hill, Bertha

**Hill, [John Edward] Christopher**
1912- [CA, WD]
*British historian and author*
* Holme, K. E.

**Hill, Clarence** 20th c. [BBH]
*American skier*
* Hill, Coy

**Hill, Clifford J.** 1894-1938 [BE]
*American baseball player*
* Hill, Red

**Hill, Coleman**
*See* Bernd, Aaron Blum

**Hill, Coy**
*See* Hill, Clarence

**Hill, Craig**
*See* Fowler, Craig Hill

**Hill, Dan W.** [FB]
*American football player*
* Hill, Tiger

**Hill, David** 1929?-
*American religious cult leader*
* Washington, Edward Emmanuel

**Hill, Dee**
*See* Zucker, Dolores Mae Bolton

**Hill, Derek** 1916- [ART]
*British painter and stage designer*
* D. H.

**Hill, Devra**
*See* Zucker, Dolores Mae Bolton

**Hill, Douglas [Arthur]** 1935-
[AW, CA]
*Canadian-born author*
* Hillman, Martin

**Hill, Elleen**
*See* Stack, Nicolete Meredith

**Hill, Ellen Wise** 1942- [CA]
*American author and poet*
* Hill, Nellie

**Hill, Ernest** 1900-1964 [WWJ]
*American jazz musician*
* Hill, Bass

**Hill, Fiona**
*See* Pall, Ellen Jane

**Hill, G. C.** [PA]
*Author*
* Lackland, Thomas

**Hill, George** 1796- ? [PA]
*Author*
* [The] Peasant Bard
* [A] Voyager

**Hill, George Handel** 1809-1849
[FFF, SN]
*American actor*
* Hill, Yankee

**Hill, Grace [Livingston]** 1865-1947
[TC]
*American author*
* MacDonald, Marcia

**Hill, Grace Brooks** [house
pseudonym] [Stratemeyer
Syndicate]
*See* Stratemeyer, Edward L.

**Hill, H. D. N.**
*See* Disston, Harry

**Hill, H. Gregory**
*See* Hill, Harry Egbert

**Hill, H. Haverstock**
*See* Walsh, James Morgan

**Hill, Harry Egbert** 20th c. [MBF]
*British author*
* Gregory, Hylton [house
pseudonym]
* Hill, H. Gregory

**Hill, Headon**
*See* Grainger, Francis Edward

**Hill, Helen**
*See* Miller, Helen Hill

**Hill, Hyacinthe**
*See* Anderson, Virginia [R.
Cronin]

**Hill, J. Preston** 1880-1951 [MK]
*American baseball player*
* Hill, Pete

**Hill, Jack**
*See* Keefe, Cornelius

**Hill, James**
*See* Jameson, [Margaret] Storm

**Hill, Jenny** 1851-1896 [BMH]
*British entertainer*
* [The] Vital Spark

**Hill, Jimmy** 20th c. [OBW]
*American baseball player*
* Hill, Lefty

**Hill, [Sir] John** 1716-1775
[FFF, SN]
*British author*
* [The] Cain of Literature
* Glasse, Mrs.
* [A] Janus Faced Critic
* [A] Literary Proteus
* [A] Paltry Dunghill

**Hill, John Melvin** 1914-
[CEI, FHE]
*Canadian-born hockey player*
* Hill, Sudden Death

**Hill, John S[tanley]** 1929- [CA]
*American educator and author*
* Wiley, Stan

**Hill, Kathleen Louise** 1917- [CA]
*Nova Scotian-born author,
playwright, television journalist*
* Hill, Kay

**Hill, Kathryn**
*See* Carver, Kathryn

**Hill, Kay**
*See* Hill, Kathleen Louise

**Hill, King**
*See* Robertson, Frank C[hester]

**Hill, King Solomon**
*See* Holmes, Joe

**Hill, King Solomon**
*See* Williams, Joe

**Hill, Lefty**
*See* Hill, Jimmy

**Hill, Lester** 1921-1957 [BWW]
*American singer*
* Chicago Sunny Boy
* Lewis, Johnny
* Little Joe
* Louis, Joe Hill

**Hill, Lucienne**
*See* Palmer, Lucienne

**Hill, Marc Kevin** 1952-  [SMG]
*American baseball player*
* Hill, Boot
* Hill, Musky

**Hill, Margaret [Ohler]** 1915-  [CA]
*American author*
* Bennett, Rachel
* Thomas, Andrea

**Hill, Margaret Shirley** 1930-
[IWM]
*Australian composer*
* Mildred, [Sister] M.

**Hill, Mary Raymond** 1923-  [CA]
*American author*
* Raymond, Lee

**Hill, Monica**
*See* Watson, Jane Werner

**Hill, Mrs. J. T.** 1836-1889  [FFF]
*Yugoslav-born opera singer and actress*
* Di Murska, Ilma

**Hill, Murray**
*See* Holliday, Robert Cortes

**Hill, Musky**
*See* Hill, Marc Kevin

**Hill, Nellie**
*See* Hill, Ellen Wise

**Hill, Pete**
*See* Hill, J. Preston

**Hill, Philip Toll** 1927-  [EAR]
*American auto racer*
* [El] Battalador [The Battler]

**Hill, Polly**
*See* Humphreys, Mary Eglantyne Hill

**Hill, Prudence**
*See* Maxfield, Prudence M.

**Hill, Red**
*See* Hill, Clifford J.

**Hill, Reginald [Charles]** 1936-
[CA, WD]
*British author*
* Morland, Dick
* Ruell, Patrick
* Underhill, Charles

**Hill, Reuben**
*See* Hill, Calvin

**Hill, Robert**  [SN]
*Mastered several foreign languages while working as a tailor*
* [The] Learned Tailor

**Hill, Roberta**  [WW]
*Author*
* Davis, Harry

**Hill, Roger** 1928-  [EJ]
*American jazz musician*
* Hill, Buck

**Hill, Rosa**
*See* Renaud, Mme. Rene

**Hill, Rosa Lee** 1910-1968  [BWW]
*American singer*
* Hill, Rosalie

**Hill, Rosalie**
*See* Hill, Rosa Lee

**Hill, Rowland [First Viscount Hill]**
1772-1842  [DNNS, SN]
*British army officer*
* [The] Waterloo Hero

**Hill, Roy Leeuwenhoek Aloysius**
1929-  [IAW]
*American author and poet*
* Bashiri, Chungulia Kwakwa
* Windisch, Gerard Roland

**Hill, Ruth A.**
*See* Viguers, Ruth Hill

**Hill, Ruth Livingston**
*See* Munce, Ruth Hill

**Hill, Sinclair**
*See* Sinclair-Hill, Gerard Arthur

**Hill, Sonny**
*See* Hill, William Randolph

**Hill, Specs**
*See* Hill, Carmen Proctor

**Hill, Steven**
*See* Berg, Solomon

**Hill, Still Bill**
*See* Hill, William C.

**Hill, Sudden Death**
*See* Hill, John Melvin

**Hill, Susan [Elizabeth]** 1942-
[WOA]
*British author and playwright*
* [The] English Francoise Sagan

**Hill, Terence**
*See* Girotti, Mario

**Hill, Thelma**
*See* Hillerman, Thelma

**Hill, Tiger**
*See* Hill, Dan W.

**Hill, Tom**
*See* Wolfgang, Otto

**Hill, W. M.**
*See* Dodd, Edward Howard, Jr.

**Hill, Warren**
*See* Norman, Harold Christopher Francis

**Hill, Weldon**
*See* Scott, William R[alph]

**Hill, William C.** 1874-1938  [BE]
*American baseball player*
* Hill, Still Bill

**Hill, William Randolph** 20th c.
[IBW]
*American basketball league founder*
* Hill, Sonny

**Hill, Yankee**
*See* Hill, George Handel

**Hillaire, Emile Marc** 1790- ?  [PA]
*Author*
* De St Hilaire, Marco

**Hillard, Brenda** 20th c.  [RO2]
*Singer*
* Faith

**Hillary, Ann**
*See* Francis, Ann Margaret

**Hillas, Julian**
*See* Dashwood, Robert Julian

**[The] Hillbilly Cat**
*See* Presley, Elvis Aaron

**[The] Hillbilly Shakespeare**
*See* Williams, Hiram King

**[The] Hillbilly Snapshooter**
*See* Clark, Joe

**[The] Hillbilly Waltz King**
*See* Moody, Clyde

**Hillcourt, William**
*See* Bjerregaard-Jensen, Wilhelm Hans

**Hillebrand, A. R. T.** ?-1941  [FB]
*American football player*
* Hillebrand, Doc

**Hillebrand, Doc**
*See* Hillebrand, A. R. T.

**Hiller, Charles Joseph** 1935-  [BE]
*American baseball player*
* Hiller, Iron Hands

**Hiller, Doris**
*See* Nussbaum, Al[bert F.]

**Hiller, Dutch**
*See* Hiller, Frank Walter

**Hiller, Dutch**
*See* Hiller, Wilbert Carl

**Hiller, Frank Walter** 1920-  [BE]
*American baseball player*
* Hiller, Dutch

**Hiller, Harvey Max** 1893-1956
[BE]
*American baseball player*
* Hiller, Hob

**Hiller, Hob**
*See* Hiller, Harvey Max

**Hiller, Iron Hands**
*See* Hiller, Charles Joseph

**Hiller, John Frederick** 1943-
[SMG]
*Canadian-born baseball player*
* Hiller, Ratso

**Hiller, Ratso**
*See* Hiller, John Frederick

**Hiller, Wilbert Carl** 1915-
[CEI, FHE, SMG]
*Canadian-born hockey player*
* Hiller, Dutch

**Hillerman, Thelma** 1906-1938
*American actress*
* Hill, Thelma

**Hillers, Herman William** 1925-
[CA]
*American author*
* Hillus, Wilhelm

**Hillersberg, Alexander** 1900-
[BBD]
*Polish-born conductor*
* Hilsberg, Alexander

**Hilley, Ed[ward Garfield]**
1879-1956  [BE]
*American baseball player*
* Hilley, Whitey

**Hilley, Whitey**
*See* Hilley, Ed[ward Garfield]

**Hilliam, B. C.** 1890-  [BMH]
*British entertainer*
* Flotsam
* Holland, Lloyd

**Hilliard, Bob**
*See* Goldsmith, Hilliard Oliver Claude

**Hilliard, Jan**
*See* Grant, Hilda Kay

**Hilliard, Kate**  [FFF, PA]
*Poet and author*
* Fountain, Lucy

**Hilliard, Kathlyn**
*See* Miller, Kathlyn

**Hilliard, Patricia**
*See* Penn-Gaskell, Patricia

**Hilliers, Ashton**
*See* Wallis, Henry Marriage

**Hillis, Mack**
*See* Hillis, Malcolm David

**Hillis, Malcolm David** 1901-1961
[BE]
*American baseball player*
* Hillis, Mack

**Hillman, Darius Dutton** 1927-  [BE]
*American baseball player*
* Hillman, Dave

**Hillman, Darnell** 20th c.  [IBW]
*American basketball player*
* Dunk, Dr.

**Hillman, Dave**
*See* Hillman, Darius Dutton

**Hillman, Martin**
*See* Hill, Douglas [Arthur]

**Hillman, Sergius**
*See* Montanari, Sergio

**Hillmann, [Dr.] Heinz**
*See* Fidelsberger, Heinz

**Hills, Baldwin**
*See* Wohl, Burton

**Hills, Frances Elizabeth** 1934-
[WD]
*British author*
* Mercer, Frances

**Hills, Hillbilly**
*See* Hills, Richard William

**Hills, Richard William** 1951-  [DC]
*British cricketer*
* Hills, Hillbilly
* Hills, Vicar

**Hills, Vicar**
*See* Hills, Richard William

**Hillus, Wilhelm**
*See* Hillers, Herman William

**Hilly, William Edward [Bill]**
*See* Hilgerink, William Edward

**Hillyer, Richard**
*See* Stranks, Charles James

**Hilsberg, Alexander**
*See* Hillersberg, Alexander

**Hilton, Alec** [joint pseudonym with Alexander Fullerton]
*See* Chesser, Eustace

**Hilton, Alec** [joint pseudonym with Eustace Chesser]
*See* Fullerton, Alexander

**Hilton, James** 1900-1954
[CC, EMD, LC]
*British author*
* Trevor, Glen

**Hilton, John Buxton** 1921-
[AW, CA, WD]
*British author*
* Stanley, Warwick

**Hilton, Josephine**
*See* Roberts, Edna

**Hilton, Richard** 1894- [CAP]
*British author*
* Dil, Zakhmi

**Hilts, Edward Leonard [Len]** 1922-
[IAW]
*American author*
* Dunne, Charles
* English, Michael

**Hilyard, Robert** ?-1469 [HN]
*British insurgent*
* Robin of Redesdale

**Him**
*See* Geisler, Horst

**Himel, Coco**
*See* Himel, Otto

**Himel, Otto** 1904?- [NOJ]
*American jazz musician*
* Himel, Coco

**Himery, Paul**
*See* Millaud, M. Albert

**Himmebrand, Abraham** 1900-1946
[BMH]
*American-born musician*
* Brown, Teddy

**Himmelwright, Abraham Lincoln**
1865- ? [ALY]
*American author*
* Heclawa

**Himsl, Avitus Bernard** 1917- [BE]
*American baseball manager*
* Himsl, Vedie

**Himsl, Vedie**
*See* Himsl, Avitus Bernard

**Hin me Geong**
*See* Armitage, John

**Hinckley, Helen**
*See* Jones, Helen Hinckley

**Hinckley, Robert** 1853- ? [ALY]
*American author*
* Hatfield, Richard

**Hincks, Cyril Malcolm** 1881-1954
[MBF]
*British author*
* Coulsdon, John
* Dayle, Malcolm
* Gee, Osman
* Howard, John M.
* Malcolm, Charles

**Hinde, Alfred** 20th c. [SFP]
*Author*
* Rochdale, Thomas

**Hinde, Thomas**
*See* Chitty, [Sir] Thomas Willes

**Hindi**
*See* Mustafavi, Ruhollah

**Hindin, Nathan**
*See* Bloch, Robert [Albert]

**Hinds, E. M.**
*See* Hinds, [Evelyn] Margery

**Hinds, [Evelyn] Margery** [CA]
*Canadian author*
* Hinds, E. M.

**Hine, Al[fred Blakelee]** 1915- [CA]
*American author*
* Gibson, Josephine [joint
pseudonym with Sesyle Joslin
Hine]
* Kirtland, G. B. [joint pseudonym
with Sesyle Joslin Hine]

**Hine, Muriel**
*See* Coxon, Muriel [Hine]

**Hine, Sesyle Joslin** 1929- [CA]
*American author*
* Gibson, Josephine [joint
pseudonym with Al(fred Blakelee)
Hine]
* Joslin, Sesyle
* Kirtland, G. B. [joint pseudonym
with Al(fred Blakelee) Hine]

**Hines, Dorothea** 20th c. [AW]
*British author*
* De Culwen, Dorothea

**Hines, Earl Kenneth** 1905-1978
[ASC, DAM, IPA]
*American jazz musician*
* Hines, Fatha

**Hines, Fatha**
*See* Hines, Earl Kenneth

**Hines, Henry F.** 1870-1928 [BE]
*American baseball player*
* Hines, Hunkey

**Hines, Hunkey**
*See* Hines, Henry F.

**Hines, Jerome**
*See* Heinz, Jerome

**Hines, Milton** 1926- [FC]
*American entertainer*
* Sales, Soupy

**Hingle, Martin Patterson** 1924-
[BEW]
*American actor*
* Hingle, Pat

**Hingle, Pat**
*See* Hingle, Martin Patterson

**Hinke, Terry**
*See* Heinke, Terry

**Hinkey, Frank A.** 1871-1925 [FB]
*American football player*
* Hinkey, Silent Frank

**Hinkey, Silent Frank**
*See* Hinkey, Frank A.

**Hinkins, Frank R.** 20th c. [WWL]
*British author*
* Cuttriss, Frank [joint pseudonym
with R. Cuttriss Hinkins]

**Hinkins, R. Cuttriss** 20th c.
[WWL]
*British author*
* Cuttriss, Frank [joint pseudonym
with Frank R. Hinkins]

**Hinkle, Agnes** 1896-1940
[F1, F2, FC]
*American actress*
* Ayres, Agnes

**Hinkle, Paul** 1899- [BB]
*American basketball coach*
* Hinkle, Tony

**Hinkle, Tony**
*See* Hinkle, Paul

**Hinkley, G. W.** 1853- ? [NAA]
*American educator and author*
* Gee Double You

**Hinkson, Katherine Tynan** 20th c.
[WWL]
*Author*
* Tynan, Katharine

**Hinky Dink Kenna**
*See* Kenna, Michael

**Hinmaton-Yalaktit** 1840?-1904
[FFF, WBD]
*American Indian chieftain*
* Joseph
* [The] Napoleon of the Indian
Race

**Hino, Ashihei**
*See* Tamai, Katsunori

**Hinojosa, Rolando** 1929- [IAW]
*American author*
* Galindo, P.

**Hinrichs, Dutch**
*See* Hinrichs, William Louis

**Hinrichs, Herky**
*See* Hinrichs, Paul Edwin

**Hinrichs, Herman** 1880?-1956
[BEW, CED]
*American entertainer*
* Oakland, Will

**Hinrichs, Paul Edwin** 1925-1972
[BE]
*American baseball player*
* Hinrichs, Herky

**Hinrichs, William Louis** 1889-
[BE]
*American baseball player*
* Hinrichs, Dutch

**Hinshaw, John E.** 1862- ? [NAA]
*American author and poet*
* J. E. H.

**Hinton, Henry L.** [PA]
*Author*
* Morely, Ralph

**Hinton, Herbert Allan** 1888-1945
[MBF]
*British author and editor*
* Clifford, Martin [house
pseudonym]
* Howard, Prosper [house
pseudonym]
* Richards, Frank [house
pseudonym]

**Hinton, Judge**
*See* Hinton, Milt[on John]

**Hinton, Mary**
*See* Forster, Emily Rachel

**Hinton, Milt[on John]** 1910- [EJ7]
*American jazz musician*
* Hinton, Judge

**Hinton, Richard W.**
*See* Angoff, Charles

**Hinton, S. E.**
*See* Inhofe, Susan Eloise Hinton

**Hintz, Loren E.** 1917- [NAA]
*American author*
* Baum, Loren

**Hinze, Gerard** 1904- [THR]
*German-born actor*
* Heinz, Gerard

**Hip Cat**
*See* Smith, George

**Hip Pocket Harry**
*See* Blackmun, Harry A.

**Hipkins, Charles Hammond** 1893-
[WW]
*Author*
* Talbot, Carl

**Hipolito**
*See* Sanchez Rodriguez, Jose

**Hipp, George**
*See* Abrams, George J[oseph]

**Hippius**
*See* Merezhkovskaya, Zinaida
Nikolaevna

**Hipple, Hugh Herbert** 1911?-
[BEW, FC, ITA]
*American actor*
* Marlowe, Hugh

**Hippocrates** 5th c. BC
[DNNF, DNNS, FFF]
*Greek physician*
* [The] Father of Medicine

**Hippocrates, Dr.**
*See* Schoenfield, Eugene

**[The] Hippocrates of the Arabs**
*See* Avicenna [or Abou-ibn-Sina]

**Hippolyte, [Le Pere]**
*See* Helyot, Pierre

**Hippolyte, Dominique** 1889-1967
[CW]
*Haitian poet, playwright, author*
* Breville, Pierre

**Hippolytus a Lapide**
*See* Chemnitz, Bogislaw Philipp
von

**Hipponax** 6th c. BC
[DNNS, FFF, SN]
*Greek poet*
* [The] Ephesian Poet
* [The] Father of Burlesque Poetry
* [The] Father of Parody

**Hippopotamus, Eugene H.**
*See* Kraus, Robert

**Hipps, Juanita Redmond**
1913?-1979 [CA]
*American army nurse and author*
* Redmond, Juanita

**Hipsch [or Huebsch] Martin**
*See* Schongauer, Martin

**[The] Hipster**
*See* Gibson, Harry

**Hirai, Taro** 1894- [CC, SFL]
*Author*
* Rampo, Edogawa

**Hiraoka, Kimitake** 1925-1970
[B10, CA]
*Japanese author*
* Mishima, Yukio

**Hirashima, Chick**
*See* Hirashima, Takeo

**Hirashima, Takeo** [EAR]
*Japanese-American auto racer*
* Hirashima, Chick

**[La] Hire [The Growler]**
*See* Vignoles, Etienne

**Hirenbach, Karl** 20th c.   [WF]
*Actor*
* Lawrence, Peter Lee

**Hirsch, Crazylegs**
*See*   Hirsch, Elroy L.

**Hirsch, Elroy L.** 1923-   [FB]
*American football player*
* Hirsch, Crazylegs

**Hirsch, Heinrich Theodor** 1926-
[BEW]
*German-born actor and director*
* Hurst, David

**Hirsch, Paul** 1926-   [CA]
*British author and publisher*
* Peel, Norman Lemon

**Hirsch, Phil** 1926-   [CA]
*American author and publisher*
* Vlasic, Bob

**Hirsch, Willi** 1908-1961   [EE]
*German-born intelligence agent for
Russia*
* Chamberlain, Sidney Joseph
* Gilmore, John

**Hirsch, William Randolph** [joint
pseudonym with Richard Lingeman
and Victor Navasky]
*See*   Kitman, Marvin

**Hirsch, William Randolph** [joint
pseudonym with Marvin Kitman and
Victor S. Navasky]
*See*   Lingeman, Richard R[oberts]

**Hirsch, William Randolph** [joint
pseudonym with Marvin Kitman and
R. Lingeman]
*See*   Navasky, Victor S.

**Hirsch-Ollendorf, Gilbert** 1904-
[JL]
*French government official*
* Grandval, Gilbert

**Hirschmann, Maria Anne** 20th c.
[CA]
*Czech-born American author*
* Hansi

**Hirshfield, Henry I.** 20th c.   [SFP]
*Author*
* Mayfield, M. I. [joint pseudonym
   with G. M. Mateyko]

**Hirst, George Stanley** 1923-   [IAW]
*British author*
* Hertz, George

**Hirst, Gillian Jose Charlotte** 1938-
[AW]
*British author*
* Baxter, Gillian

**Hirt, Al**
*See*   Hirt, Alois Maxwell

**Hirt, Alois Maxwell** 1922-
[DAM, PMJ]
*American jazz musician*
* Hirt, Al

**Hirt, Gerald** 20th c.   [NOJ]
*American jazz musician*
* Hirt, Slick

**Hirt, Slick**
*See*   Hirt, Gerald

**His Accidency**
*See*   Arthur, Chester Alan

**His Accidency**
*See*   Fillmore, Millard

**His Accidency**
*See*   Johnson, Andrew

**His Accidency**
*See*   Tyler, John

**His Fraudulency**
*See*   Hayes, Rutherford Birchard

**His Majesty**
*See*   Hubbard, Robert Cal

**His Mother**
*See*   Forester, Elspeth Lascelles

**His Mother**
*See*   Rolls, M. M.

**His, Mrs. Albert**   [FFF]
*Entertainer*
* Turner, Carrie

**His Rotundity**
*See*   Adams, John

**His Thinker**
*See*   D'Albon, Claude Camille
Francois

**Hisamatsu, Shin'ichi** 1889-   [IAW]
*Japanese author*
* Hoseki

**Hiscock, Leslie** 1902-   [WW]
*Author*
* Marsh, Patrick

**Hiscocks, Richard** 1907-   [IAW]
*British author*
* Seymour, Edward

**Hiskey, Babe**
*See*   Hiskey, Bryant

**Hiskey, Bryant** 1938-   [GF]
*American golfer*
* Hiskey, Babe

**Hispanus, Petrus** ?-1277   [WBD]
*Pope*
* John XXI

**Historian**
*See*   Marley, Frank Elsworth

**[The] Historian of the Long
Parliament**
*See*   May, Thomas

**[The] Historian Philosopher**
*See*   Guizot, Francois Pierre
Guillaume

**Historicus**
*See*   Harcourt, [Sir] William
Vernon

**[L']Historien Trop Paye**
*See*   Racine, Jean Baptiste

**[The] Hit Man**
*See*   Hearns, Thomas

**Hitch, Clove**
*See*   Briscoe, Arthur John Trevor

**Hitchcock, Alfred** 1899-1980   [CA]
*British-born director*
* Hitchcock, Hitch
* [The] Master of Suspense

**Hitchcock, Francis**   [PA]
*Author*
* Murdoch, Frank

**Hitchcock, Hitch**
*See*   Hitchcock, Alfred

**Hitchcock, Keith**
*See*   Kenneth, Keith

**Hitchcock, Reginald Ingram
Montgomery** 1892?-1950
[BDF, FC, FD]
*Irish-born director*
* Ingram, Rex

**Hitchens, Dolores** [Birk] 1907-
[CC]
*Author*
* Birkley, Dolan
* Burke, Noel
* Olsen, D. B.

**Hitchin, Martin Mewburn** 1917-
[AW, CA]
*British author*
* Mewburn, Martin

**Hite, Matie** [or **Mattie**]
1890?-1935?   [BWW]
*American singer*
* Hite, Nellie?

**Hite, Nellie?**
*See*   Hite, Matie [or Mattie]

**Hite, Robert, Jr.** 1943?-1981   [RM]
*American singer*
* [The] Bear

**Hitherley, W.**   [PA]
*Author*
* [A] Layman

**Hitotsubashi** 1837-1902   [WBD]
*Japanese shogun*
* Keiki
* [The] Last of the Tycoons
* Yoshinobu

**Hitt, Rhino**
*See*   Hitt, Roy Wesley

**Hitt, Roy Wesley** 1884-1956   [BE]
*American baseball player*
* Hitt, Rhino

**Hittle, Lloyd Eldon** 1924-   [BE]
*American baseball player*
* Hittle, Red

**Hittle, Red**
*See*   Hittle, Lloyd Eldon

**Hivnor, Robert** 1916-   [CA]
*American playwright*
* Askew, Jack
* Pismire, Osbert

**Hix**
*See*   Hicks, Reginald Ernest

**Hix, Don**
*See*   Hicks, Don T.

**Hlinka, Vojtech** 1817-1904   [WBD]
*Czech author*
* Pravda, Frantisek

**Hlojzy, Nagel** 1930-   [IAW]
*Polish author*
* Jozk, Wickov
* Mulkor, Pioter

**Hlybinny, Vladimir**
*See*   Seduro, Vladimir

**Ho Chi Mihn** 1890-1969   [CBS]
*Vietnamese Communist leader*
* Uncle Ho

**Hoadley, Bungalow**
*See*   Hoadley, Simon Peter

**Hoadley, H. O[rlo]** 20th c.   [WGT]
*Author*
* Mitchell, Gene

**Hoadley, Hoaders**
*See*   Hoadley, Simon Peter

**Hoadley, Irene Braden** 1938-   [CA]
*American librarian and author*
* Braden, Irene A.

**Hoadley, Sid**
*See*   Hoadley, Simon Peter

**Hoadley, Simon Peter** 1956-   [DC]
*British cricketer*
* Hoadley, Bungalow
* Hoadley, Hoaders
* Hoadley, Sid

**Hoak, Donald Albert** 1928-1969
[AS, BE, PB]
*American baseball player*
* Hoak, Tiger

**Hoak, Tiger**
*See*   Hoak, Donald Albert

**Hoar, Peter** 1912-   [AW, WD]
*British author and playwright*
* Amberley, Simon

**Hoar, Roger Sherman** 1887-1963
[SF, WGT]
*American author*
* Farley, Ralph Milne
* General X
* Orth, Bennington
* Pease, [Lt.] John

**Hoar-Stevens, Thomas Terry**
1911-   [FC, IPA, ITA]
*British actor*
* Terry Thomas

**Hoard, Cactus**
*See*   Hoard, John

**Hoard, John** 20th c.   [IBW]
*American entertainer*
* Hoard, Cactus

**Hoare, Edward Mavenham**   [PA]
*Author*
* Decanus

**Hoare, P.** 1755-1834   [PA]
*Author*
* [A] Layman

**Hoare, [Sir] Richard Colt**
1758-1838   [PA]
*Author*
* R. C. H.

**[The] Hoary Bard of Night**
*See*   Young, Edward

**Hob** [or **Hobbe**]**, King**
*See*   Robert I

**Hobart, Alice Nourse** 1882-1967
[CA]
*American author*
* Hobart, Alice Tisdale

**Hobart, Alice Tisdale**
*See*   Hobart, Alice Nourse

**Hobart, Augustus C.** 1822- ?   [PA]
*Author*
* Roberts, Captain

**[The] Hobart Hurricane**
*See*   Gulick, Merle A.

**Hobart Pasha**
*See*   Hobart-Hampden, Augustus
Charles

**Hobart, Rose**
*See*   Kefer, Rose

**Hobart-Hampden, Augustus Charles**
1822-1886   [WBD]
*British naval officer*
* Hobart Pasha

**Hobbema, Minderhout** 1638-1709
[SN]
*Dutch painter*
* [The] Painter of Coolness

**[The] Hobbema of England**
*See* Crome, John

**[The] Hobbema of Scotland**
*See* Nasmyth, Patrick [or Peter?]

**Hobbes, John Oliver**
*See* Craigie, Pearl Mary Teresa
Richards

**Hobbes, Thomas** 1588-1679
[DEL, DNNF, SN]
*British philosopher*
* [The] Atheist
* [The] Bear
* [The] Crowe
* [The] Mighty Leviathan
* [The] Philosopher of Malmesbury

**[The] Hobbler**
*See* Jean [or Jehan] de Meung

**[The] Hobbler**
*See* Tyrtaeus

**Hobbs, Cecil [Carlton]** 1907- [CA]
*American clergyman and author*
* Hauk, Maung

**Hobbs, Colt**
*See* Hobbs, Robin Nicholas Stuart

**Hobbs, Jack**
*See* Horler, Sydney

**Hobbs, [Sir] John Berry** 1882-1963
[OCS]
*British cricketer*
* [The] Master

**Hobbs, Leonard** 1897?-1977
*American aviation engineer*
* Hobbs, Luke

**Hobbs, Luke**
*See* Hobbs, Leonard

**Hobbs, Perry**
*See* Blackmur, Richard Palmer

**Hobbs, Robin Nicholas Stuart**
1942- [DC]
*British-born cricketer*
* Hobbs, Colt

**Hobel, Phil**
*See* Fanthorpe, R[obert] Lionel

**Hobgood, Freddie** 20th c. [OBW]
*American baseball player*
* Hobgood, Lefty

**Hobgood, Lefty**
*See* Hobgood, Freddie

**Hobhouse, John Cave** 1786- ? [PA]
*Author*
* [An] Englishman

**Hobin, Hobie**
*See* Hobin, Michael Patrick

**Hobin, Michael Patrick** 1954-
[SMG]
*Canadian-born hockey player*
* Hobin, Hobie

**Hobman, Joseph Burton** 1872- ?
[LAO]
*British journalist*
* [The] Man from the North

**Hobsbawm, Eric J[ohn Ernest]**
1917- [CA, WD]
*British historian and writer*
* Newton, Francis

**Hobson, Butch**
*See* Hobson, Clell Lavern, Jr.

**Hobson, Clell Lavern, Jr.** 1951-
[SMG, WWB]
*American baseball player*
* Hobson, Butch

**Hobson, Coralie [Von Werner]**
1891- [WW]
*Author*
* Salt, Sarah

**Hobson, Hank**
*See* Hobson, Harry

**Hobson, Harold**
*See* Hobson, Thorpe Hesley

**Hobson, Harry** 1908-
[CAP, CC, WW]
*British author*
* Hobson, Hank
* Janson, Hank [house
pseudonym?]

**Hobson, Hobby**
*See* Hobson, Howard A.

**Hobson, Howard A.** 1903-
*American basketball coach*
* Hobson, Hobby

**Hobson, Laura Z.**
*See* Zametkin, Laura K.

**Hobson, Mark** 1887-1957 [THR]
*Scottish-born actor*
* Daly, Mark

**Hobson, Polly**
*See* Evans, Julia [Rendel]

**Hobson, Robert** [PA]
*Author*
* R. H.

**Hobson, Thorpe Hesley** 1904-
[BEW]
*British drama critic*
* Hobson, Harold

**Hoch, Cyrus** 1880-1911 [BE]
*American baseball player*
* Hooker, Cy
* Hooker, William E.

**Hoch, Edward D.** 1930- [CA]
*American author*
* Booth, Irwin
* Dentinger, Stephen
* McMahon, Pat
* Mr. X
* Stephens, R. L.

**Hochberg, Bolko von** 1843-1926
[BBD]
*German composer*
* Franz, J. H.

**Hoche, [Louis] Lazarus** 1768-1797
[HN]
*French army officer*
* [Le] Pacificateur de la Vendee

**Hochheimer, Albert** 1900- [IAW]
*German-born author*
* Jurat, Bert

**Hochstein, Peter** 1939- [SFL]
*American author*
* Short, Jackson

**Hockaby, Stephen**
*See* Mitchell, Gladys [Maude
Winifred]

**Hockenberry, Hope**
*See* Newell, Hope Hockenberry

**Hockette, George Edward** 1908-
[BE]
*American baseball player*
* Hockette, Lefty

**Hockette, Lefty**
*See* Hockette, George Edward

**Hockey Bob Lamey**
*See* Lamey, Bob

**Hockey, Mr.**
*See* Howe, Gordon [Gordie]

**Hockey, Mr.**
*See* Patrick, Lester

**Hockey, Mr.**
*See* Turner, Lloyd

**Hocking, Anne**
*See* Messer, Mona Naomi Anne
[Hocking]

**Hockley, Lewis**
*See* Longhurst, Percy William

**[The] Hocuspocus**
*See* Laud, William

**Hodder, Alfred** 1866-1907
[EMD, WW]
*Author*
* Walton, Francis

**Hodder, Edwin** 1837- ?
[DEL, FFF, WWL]
*British author*
* Old Merry

**Hodder-Williams, John Christopher
Glazebrook** 1927?-
[DLE, ESF, WGT]
*British author and songwriter*
* Brogan, James

**[La] Hode**
*See* La Mothe, N. Pere

**Hodemart, Peter**
*See* Audemars, Pierre

**Hodge, Clarence Clement**
1893-1967 [BE]
*American baseball player*
* Hodge, Shovel

**Hodge, E. Chatterton**
*See* Hastings, Phyllis Dora Hodge

**Hodge, Gomer**
*See* Hodge, Harold Morris

**Hodge, Harold Morris** 1944- [BE]
*American baseball player*
* Hodge, Gomer

**Hodge, Horace Emerton**
1904-1958 [BEW]
*New Zealand-born playwright*
* Hodge, [Dr.] Merton

**Hodge, [Dr.] Merton**
*See* Hodge, Horace Emerton

**Hodge, Shovel**
*See* Hodge, Clarence Clement

**Hodge, T. Shirby**
*See* Tracy, Roger Sherman

**Hodge, Toby**
*See* McIlvaine, Charles

**Hodges, Barbara K. [Webber]**
1893-1949 [LC, TC, TC1]
*British author*
* Cambridge, Elizabeth

**Hodges, Donald Clark** 1923-
[IAW]
*American author*
* Blake, Justin

**Hodges, Doris Marjorie** 1915-
[AW, CA, WD]
*British author*
* Hunt, Charlotte

**Hodges, John Cornelius [Johnny]**
1906-1970 [EJ, WWJ]
*American jazz musician*
* Hodges, Rabbit

**Hodges, Johnny**
*See* Hardge, Johnny

**Hodges, Rabbit**
*See* Hodges, John Cornelius
[Johnny]

**Hodges, Turner**
*See* Morehead, Albert H[odges]

**Hodges, Will** 20th c. [BWW]
*American entertainer*
* Hogg, Smokey

**Hodgkin, Robert Allason** 1916-
[CA]
*British author*
* Hodgkin, Robin A.

**Hodgkin, Robin A.**
*See* Hodgkin, Robert Allason

**Hodgkins, David C.**
*See* Budrys, Algirdas Jonas

**Hodgkinson, Conway Loveridge**
1879- ? [CC]
*Author*
* Solicitor

**Hodgkinson, Isabel** 1918- [FC]
*British actress*
* Dean, Isabel

**Hodgkinson, W. P.**
*See* Hodgkinson, Wilfred Philip

**Hodgkinson, Wilfred Philip** 1912-
[ART]
*British artist*
* Hodgkinson, W. P.
* W. P. H.

**Hodgson, Alan** 1951- [DC]
*British cricketer*
* Hodgson, Hodge

**Hodgson, Alfred** 1870-1951 [THR]
*British actor and theatrical manager*
* Paumier, Alfred

**Hodgson, David**
*See* Lewis, David

**Hodgson, Ethelyn**
*See* McCoy, Mrs. U. E.

**Hodgson, Hodge**
*See* Hodgson, Alan

**Hodgson, M. A.** [PA]
*Author*
* Aunt Mary

**Hodgson, Margaret**
*See* Ballinger, [Violet] Margaret
[Livingstone]

**Hodgson, Norma**
*See* Russell, Norma Hull Lewis

**Hodgson, Ralph** 20th c. [WECO]
*British cartoonist*
* Yorick

**Hodgson, W. H.**
See Hodgson, William Hope

**Hodgson, William Archer** 1887-
[LAO]
*British dental surgeon and author*
* Thearcher

**Hodgson, William Hope**
1877-1918 [SF]
*Author*
* Hodgson, W. H.

**Hodkey, Aloysius Joseph** 1917-
[BE]
*American baseball player*
* Hodkey, Eli

**Hodkey, Eli**
See Hodkey, Aloysius Joseph

**Hodson, Arnold Wienholt** 20th c.
[LAO]
*British politician and author*
* Delphi

**Hoeffer, Norman** 1900-
[BDF, F2, WEF]
*American director and actor*
* Foster, Norman

**Hoellriegel, Arnold**
See Bermann, Richard Arnold

**Hoelskoetter, Art[hur H.]**
1882-1954 [BE]
*American baseball player*
* Hostetter, Art

**Hoene, Jozef Maria** 1778-1853
[WBD]
*Polish mathematician and
philosopher*
* Hoene-Wronski, Jozef Maria
* Wronski, Jozef Maria

**Hoene-Wronski, Jozef Maria**
See Hoene, Jozef Maria

**Hoerberg, Peter** 1746-1814
[HN, RH]
*Swedish painter*
* [The] Peasant Painter of Sweden

**Hoernschemeyer, Hunch**
See Hoernschemeyer, Robert

**Hoernschemeyer, Leopold
Christopher** 1889-1966 [AS, BE]
*American baseball player*
* Magee, Lee
* Magee, Leo Christopher

**Hoernschemeyer, Robert** 1925-
[FB]
*American football player*
* Hoernschemeyer, Hunch

**Hoerst, Francis Joseph** 1917- [BE]
*American baseball player*
* Hoerst, Lefty

**Hoerst, Lefty**
See Hoerst, Francis Joseph

**Hoey, Dennis**
See Hyams, Samuel David

**Hofdorp, Pim [William]** 1912-
[AW]
*Dutch author*
* Geerlink, Will

**Hofer, Andreas** 1767-1810
[DNNS, HN, SN]
*Tyrolese patriot*
* [The] Wallace of Switzerland
* [The] William Tell of the Tyrol

**Hofer, Peter**
See Kortner, Peter

**Hoff**
See Hoff, Syd

**Hoff, Bobby** 20th c.
*American poker player*
* [The] Wizard

**Hoff, Boo Boo**
See Hoff, Max

**Hoff, Carl**
See Hoffmayr, Carl

**Hoff, Chester Cornelius** 1891- [BE]
*American baseball player*
* Hoff, Red

**Hoff, Harry Summerfield** 1910-
[B10, CA, LC]
*British author and playwright*
* Cooper, William

**Hoff, Max** 20th c. [BLB]
*American underworld figure*
* Hoff, Boo Boo

**Hoff, Red**
See Hoff, Chester Cornelius

**Hoff, Syd** 1912- [AW]
*American cartoonist*
* Hoff

**Hoffe, Barbara**
See Hylton, Barbara

**Hoffe, Monckton**
See Hoffe-Miles, Reaney
Monckton

**Hoffe-Miles, Reaney Monckton**
1880?-1951 [BEW, LC]
*Irish-born playwright and actor*
* Hoffe, Monckton

**Hoffenberg, Mason** 20th c.
[CA, WD]
*Author*
* Kenton, Maxwell [joint
   pseudonym with Terry Southern]

**Hoffer, F. P.**
See Hoffer, Franz Peter Bernard

**Hoffer, Franz Peter Bernard** 1924-
[ART]
*German-born architect and painter*
* Hoffer, F. P.

**Hoffer, William Leopold**
1870-1959 [BE]
*American baseball player*
* Hoffer, Wizard

**Hoffer, Wizard**
See Hoffer, William Leopold

**Hoffman, Abbie** 1936- [CA]
*American political activist*
* Free
* Freed, Barry
* Igloo, Spiro
* Metesky, George
* Samuels, Howie

**Hoffman, Anita** 1942- [CA]
*American author*
* Fettamen, Ann

**Hoffman, Bear**
See Hoffman, Paul J.

**Hoffman, Bill**
See Hoffman, Elwood C.

**Hoffman, Charles** 1856-1915 [BE]
*American baseball player*
* Hoffman, Mickey

**Hoffman, Clarence Casper**
1904-1962 [BE]
*American baseball player*
* Hoffman, Dutch

**Hoffman, D. T.**
See Tennow, Dorothy

**Hoffman, Dutch**
See Hoffman, Clarence Casper

**Hoffman, Edward H.** 1893-1947
[BE]
*American baseball player*
* Hoffman, Tex

**Hoffman, Elwood C.** 1918?-1962
[BEW]
*American playwright and writer*
* Hoffman, Bill

**Hoffman, Frank J.** 19th c. [BE]
*American baseball player*
* [The] Texas Wonder

**Hoffman, Gertrude**
See Anderson, Gertrude

**Hoffman, Goldie** 1925- [OP]
*American opera singer*
* Hoffman, Grace

**Hoffman, Grace**
See Hoffman, Goldie

**Hoffman, Harry C.** 1875-1942
[BE]
*American baseball player*
* Hoffman, Izzy

**Hoffman, Izzy**
See Hoffman, Harry C.

**Hoffman, John Edward** 1943- [BE]
*American baseball player*
* Hoffman, Pork Chop

**Hoffman, Josef** 1906-1976 [BL]
*Hungarian-born art forger*
* Cassou, Jean
* De Hory, Elmyr
* Dory-Boutin, Elmyr
* Raynal, Louis

**Hoffman, Lee**
See Hoffman, Shirley Bell

**Hoffman, Lisa** 1919- [CA]
*German-born author*
* Candida

**Hoffman, Mickey**
See Hoffman, Charles

**Hoffman, Mrs.** [FFF]
* Bonfanti, Mlle.

**Hoffman, Paul J.** 20th c. [BBH]
*American basketball player*
* Hoffman, Bear

**Hoffman, Pork Chop**
See Hoffman, John Edward

**Hoffman, Richard**
See Andrews, Richard

**Hoffman, Shirley Bell** 1932- [SFL]
*American author*
* Hoffman, Lee

**Hoffman, Tex**
See Hoffman, Edward H.

**Hoffman, Wilhelmus Adrianus
Franciscus Xaverius** 1908- [IAW]
*Dutch author and playwright*
* Hoogland, Marianne

**Hoffmann, August Heinrich**
1798-1874 [WBD]
*German poet, philologist, historian*
* Hoffmann von Fallersleben

**Hoffmann, Donald** 1933- [IAW]
*American author and critic*
* Allured, Lloyd

**Hoffmann, E. L.** 1899-1950 [MGL]
*German poet*
* Langgaesser, Elisabeth

**Hoffmann, Ede** 1830-1898 [WBD]
*Hungarian musician*
* Remenyi, Ede

**Hoffmann, Lothar** 20th c. [EE]
*Russian intelligence agent*
* Sanger, Herbert

**Hoffmann, [Professor] Louis**
See Lewis, Angelo J.

**Hoffmann, Phil** 1868- ? [NAA]
*American journalist*
* Roustabout

**Hoffmann von Fallersleben**
See Hoffmann, August Heinrich

**Hoffmayr, Carl** 1905?- [PMJ]
*American bandleader*
* Hoff, Carl

**Hoffnung, Michele** 1944- [CA]
*American author and educator*
* Garskof, Michele Hoffnung

**Hoffstadt, John Alvin** 1917- [ITA]
*American actor*
* Alvin, John

**Hofman, Anton**
See Hollo, Anselm

**Hofman, Arthur Frederick**
1882-1956 [AS, BE]
*American baseball player*
* Hofman, Circus Solly

**Hofman, Circus Solly**
See Hofman, Arthur Frederick

**Hofmann, Bootnose**
See Hofmann, Fred

**Hofmann, Fred** 1894-1964 [BE]
*American baseball player*
* Hofmann, Bootnose

**Hofmann, Josef Casimir**
1876-1957 [WBD]
*Polish musician and composer*
* Dvorsky

**Hofmannsthal, Hugo Hofmann, Edler
Von** 1874-1929 [TC]
*Austrian poet and playwright*
* Loris
* Morren, Theophil

**Hofmeyer, Hans**
See Fleischer, Anthony Charles

**Hofner, Adolph** 20th c. [ECM]
*American country-western performer*
* Hofner, Dub

**Hofner, Dub**
See Hofner, Adolph

**Hofsinde, Robert** 1902-1973
[B10, TBJ]
*Danish-born author, illustrator,*
*folklorist*
* Gray Wolf

**Hofstede, Geert H[endrik]** 1928-
[CA]
*Dutch-born author*
* Hofstede, Gerard

**Hofstede, Gerard**
*See* Hofstede, Geert H[endrik]

**Hoft, Ford Fenimore** ?-1941   [SC]
*American actor*
* Fenimore, Ford

**Hogan, Babette Hilda** 1905-   [THR]
*British actress and singer*
* Warren, Betty

**Hogan, Bantam Ben**
*See* Hogan, Benjamin William

**Hogan, Benjamin William** 1912-
[BWG, EG]
*American golfer*
* [The] Hawk
* Hogan, Bantam Ben
* [The] Wee Iceman

**Hogan, David**
*See* Gallagher, Frank

**Hogan, Earl**
*See* Traynor, Earl Richard

**Hogan, G. T.**
*See* Hogan, Granville T.

**Hogan, Granville T.** 1929-   [EJ]
*American jazz musician*
* Hogan, G. T.

**Hogan, Hap**
*See* Traynor, Earl Richard

**Hogan, Happy**
*See* Hogan, William Henry

**Hogan, James Francis** 1906-1967
[AS, BE, PB]
*American baseball player*
* Hogan, Shanty

**Hogan, James J.** 1876-1910   [FB]
*Irish-born football player*
* Hogan, Yale

**Hogan, Mary Alice**   [FFF]
*Entertainer*
* Atherton, Alice

**Hogan, [Robert] Ray** 1908?-
[AW, CA]
*American author*
* Ringold, Clay

**Hogan, Shanty**
*See* Hogan, James Francis

**Hogan, Society Kid**
*See* De Lorenzo, Salvatore

**Hogan, William Henry** 1884-1974
[BE]
*American baseball player*
* Hogan, Happy

**Hogan, Yale**
*See* Hogan, James J.

**Hoganson, Dale Gordon** 1949-
[CEI, HR]
*Canadian-born hockey player*
* Hoganson, Red

**Hoganson, Hogy**
*See* Hoganson, Paul

**Hoganson, Paul** 1949-   [SMG]
*Canadian-born hockey player*
* Hoganson, Hogy

**Hoganson, Red**
*See* Hoganson, Dale Gordon

**Hogarth, Arthur Paul** 1917-   [ART]
*British illustrator*
* P. H.

**Hogarth, Charles**
*See* Creasey, John

**Hogarth, Douglas**
*See* Phillips-Birt, Douglas

**Hogarth, Emmett** [joint pseudonym
with Mitchell A. Wilson]
*See* Polonsky, Abraham

**Hogarth, Emmett** [joint pseudonym
with Abraham Polonsky]
*See* Wilson, Mitchell A.

**Hogarth, Grace Weston** 1905-
[AW, TCC, WW]
*American author*
* Allen, Grace
* Gay, Amelia
* Weston, Allen [joint pseudonym
with Alice Mary Norton]

**[The] Hogarth of Novelists**
*See* Fielding, Henry

**Hogarth, William** 1697-1764
[FFF, RH, SN]
*British painter and engraver*
* [The] Beautifyer
* [A] Fielding Among Painters
* [The] Juvenal of Painters
* [A] Lillo Among Painters
* Painter Pug
* [The] Painting Moralist
* [The] Pensioned Dauber

**Hogarth, William, Jr.**
*See* Kent, Rockwell

**Hogben, Lancelot Thomas**
1895-1975   [B10]
*British scientist*
* Page, Kenneth Calvin

**Hogbotel, Sebastian**
*See* Gott, Kenneth Davidson

**Hoge, Phyllis** 1926-   [CA]
*American poet*
* Rose, Phyllis
* Thompson, Phyllis Hoge

**Hogg, Andrew** 1914-1960
[BWW, NBB]
*American singer*
* Hogg, Smokey
* Wheatstraw, Little Peetie

**Hogg, Bert**
*See* Hogg, Wilbert George

**Hogg, Beth [Tootill]** 1917-   [CA]
*British author*
* Grey, Elizabeth

**Hogg, Buffalo Bill**
*See* Hogg, William [Bill]

**Hogg, Cervantes**
*See* Barret, E. S.

**Hogg, Curly**
*See* Hogg, Jack

**Hogg, Gordon** 20th c.   [WECO]
*British cartoonist*
* Gog

**Hogg, Hoggie**
*See* Hogg, William

**Hogg, Jack** 1917?-1974   [B10, SC]
*American actor and singer*
* Hogg, Curly
* King of the Banjoes

**Hogg, James** 1770-1835
[DEL, PA]
*British author and poet*
* Cohnan, R. W.
* Colman, Robert Wringham
* [The] Ettrick Shepherd
* [A] Justified Sinner

**Hogg, Nathan**
*See* Baird, Henry

**Hogg, [Brig.] O. F. G.**
*See* Hogg, Oliver Frederick Gillian

**Hogg, Oliver Frederick Gillian**
1887-   [WD]
*British writer*
* Hogg, [Brig.] O. F. G.

**Hogg, Quintin McGarel** 1907-
[CAP]
*British author*
* Hailsham of St. Marylebone,
Lord

**Hogg, Smokey**
*See* Hodges, Will

**Hogg, Smokey**
*See* Hogg, Andrew

**Hogg, Smokey**
*See* Hogg, Willie Anderson

**Hogg, Wilbert George** 1913-   [BE]
*American baseball player*
* Hogg, Bert

**Hogg, William [Bill]** 1880-1909
[BE]
*American baseball player*
* Hogg, Buffalo Bill

**Hogg, William** 1955-   [DC]
*British cricketer*
* Hogg, Hoggie

**Hogg, Willie Anderson** 1908-
[BWW]
*American singer*
* Hogg, Smokey

**[The] Hogge**
*See* Richard III

**Hogrogian, Nonny**
*See* Kherdian, Nonny Hogrogian

**Hogsett, Chief**
*See* Hogsett, Elon Chester

**Hogsett, Elon Chester** 1903-   [BE]
*American baseball player*
* Hogsett, Chief

**Hogsmouth, Peter** ?- 847   [RH]
*Pope*
* Di Porca, Peter
* Sergius II

**Hogue, Dock**
*See* Hogue, Wilbur Owings

**Hogue, Duke**
*See* Hogue, Paul

**Hogue, Paul** 1940-   [BB]
*American basketball player*
* Hogue, Duke

**Hogue, Wilbur Owings** 20th c.
[WW]
*Author*
* Hogue, Dock
* Shannon, Carl

**[The] Hohenwald Flash**
*See* Brasfield, Rodney Leon

**Hohoff, Tay**
*See* Torrey, Therese Von Hohoff

**Hoisington, May Folwell** 1874- ?
[NAA]
*American author and poet*
* Chatton, Stacy
* Fair, J. Murray

**Hoke, Helen L.** 1903-   [CA]
*British author and editor*
* Sterling, Helen

**Holbeach, Henry**
*See* Rands, William Brightly

**Holbeche, Philippa [Jack]** 1919-
[AW, CAP]
*British author*
* Shore, Philippa

**Holberg, Louis [or Ludvig]**
1684?-1754   [HN, SN]
*Danish author*
* [The] Colossus of Danish
Literature
* [The] Danish Butler
* [The] Danish Moliere
* [The] Danish Plautus

**[The] Holberg of Norway**
*See* Wergeland, Henrik Arnold

**Holbrook, James Marbury** 1910-
[BE]
*American baseball player*
* Holbrook, Sammy

**Holbrook, John**
*See* Vance, John Holbrook [Jack]

**Holbrook, Peter**
*See* Glick, Carl [Cannon]

**Holbrook, Sabra**
*See* Erickson, Sabra Rollins

**Holbrook, Sammy**
*See* Holbrook, James Marbury

**Holbrook, Silas Pinckney**
1796-1835   [FFF, PA]
*American author*
* Farbrick, Jonathan

**Holcombe, Arnold**
*See* Golsworthy, Arnold

**Holcroft, M. H.**
*See* Holcroft, Montague Harry

**Holcroft, Montague Harry** 1902-
[LC]
*New Zealand author*
* Holcroft, M. H.

**Holdaway, Neville Aldridge** 1894-
[CC, WW]
*Author*
* Temple-Ellis, N. A.

**Holden, David [Shipley]** 1924-1977
[CA]
*British journalist*
* Shipley, David

**Holden, Donald** 1931-   [CA]
*American author and editor*
* Blake, Wendon

**Holden, Fay**
See　Clyde, Dorothy Hammerton

**Holden, Genevieve**
See　Pou, Genevieve [Long]

**Holden, J. G. P.**　[PA]
*Author*
* Redwood, Ralph

**Holden, Jan**
See　Wilkinson, Jan

**Holden, Joanne**
See　Corby, Jane

**Holden, Joseph Francis [Joe]** 1913-
[BE]
*American baseball player*
* Holden, Socks

**Holden, Luther L.**　[PA]
*Author*
* Rambler

**Holden, Maria**　[PA]
*Author*
* Myrtle, May

**Holden, Raymond [Peckham]**
1894-1972　[CA, TC, WW]
*American author, editor, poet*
* Peckham, Richard

**Holden, Socks**
See　Holden, Joseph Francis [Joe]

**Holden, Viola**
See　Martinelli, Viola

**Holden, William**
See　Beedle, William Franklin, Jr.

**Holder, John Wesley** 1939?-
[BWW]
*American singer*
* Holder, Ram John

**Holder, Ram John**
See　Holder, John Wesley

**Holding, Ephraim**
See　Mogridge, George

**Holding, James [Clark Carlisle, Jr.]**
1907-　[CA, SAT]
*American author*
* Carlisle, Clark
* Queen, Ellery, Jr.

**Holdstock, Robert P.** 1948-　[ESF]
*British author*
* Black, Robert
* Carlsen, Chris

**Holdsworth, James [Jim]** 19th c.
[BE]
*American baseball player*
* Holdsworth, Long Jim

**Holdsworth, Long Jim**
See　Holdsworth, James [Jim]

**Hole, E. M.** 20th c.　[BBH]
*American basketball coach and
collegiate athletic director*
* Hole, Mose

**Hole, Mose**
See　Hole, E. M.

**Holiday, Bert**
See　Bonaldi, Bert

**Holiday, Billie**
See　McKay, Eleanor Gough

**Holiday, Homer**
See　DeBeaubien, Philip Francis

**Holiday, Joe**
See　Befumo, Joseph A.

**Holke, Union Man**
See　Holke, Walter Henry

**Holke, Walter Henry** 1892-1954
[AS, BE]
*American baseball player*
* Holke, Union Man

**Hollaender, Frederick** 1896-
[WEF]
*British-born composer*
* Hollander, Frederick

**Hollaender, Viktor** 1866-1940
[BBD]
*German composer*
* Del Tolveno, Arricha

**Holland, Brud**
See　Holland, Jerome H.

**Holland, Clive**
See　Hankinson, Charles James

**Holland, Dutch**
See　Holland, Robert Clyde

**Holland, E. M.**
See　Holland, Edmund Milton

**Holland, Edith** 1898-　[WWL]
*British author*
* Holland, Ruth

**Holland, Edmund Milton**
1848-1913　[BEW]
*Theatrical performer*
* Holland, E. M.

**Holland, Herbert Lee** 1910-
[EJ, PMJ, WWJ]
*American jazz musician*
* Holland, Peanuts

**Holland, Howard Arthur**
1903-1969　[BE]
*American baseball player*
* Holland, Mul

**Holland, Isabelle** 1920-　[TCC]
*American author*
* Hunt, Francesca

**Holland, James R.** 1944-　[CA]
*American film producer and author*
* Rand, J. H.

**Holland, Jerome H.** 1916-
[FB, IBW]
*American football player*
* Holland, Brud

**Holland, Josiah Gilbert** 1819-1881
[DEL, DNNS, FFF]
*American author and poet*
* [The] American Tupper
* Mannering, Max
* Titcomb, Timothy

**Holland, Katrin**
See　Freybe, Heidi Huberta

**Holland, Kel**
See　Whittington, Harry

**Holland, Lloyd**
See　Hilliam, B. C.

**Holland, Lord** 1788-1873　[PA]
*British author*
* [An] Englishman

**Holland, Mul**
See　Holland, Howard Arthur

**Holland, Peanuts**
See　Holland, Herbert Lee

**Holland, Philemon** 1552-1637
[DNNF, DNNS, FFF]
*British translator*
* Translator General

**Holland, R. V.**
See　Holland, Reginald V.

**Holland, Reginald V.** 1916-　[BEW]
*American educator*
* Holland, R. V.

**Holland, Robert Clyde** 1903-　[BE]
*American baseball player*
* Holland, Dutch

**Holland, Ruth**
See　Holland, Edith

**Holland, Sheila** 1937-　[CA]
*British author*
* Lamb, Charlotte
* Lancaster, Sheila

**Holland, Vyvyan [Beresford]**
See　Wilde, Vyvyan Beresford

**Hollander, Frederick**
See　Hollaender, Frederick

**Hollander, Zander** 1923-　[CA]
*American author*
* Peters, Alexander

**Hollandersky, Abraham** 1888-
[EJS, SG]
*American boxer*
* Abe the Newsboy

**Hollenback, Big Bill**
See　Hollenback, William M.

**Hollenback, William M.**
1886-1968　[AS, FB]
*American football player*
* Hollenback, Big Bill

**Hollenbeck, Webb Parmelee**
1893?-1966　[BDF, EMT, F2]
*American actor*
* Webb, Clifton

**Hollerbochen**
See　Bradbury, Ray [Douglas]

**Hollett, Flash**
See　Hollett, William

**Hollett, William** 1912-
[CEI, FHE, HK]
*Canadian-born hockey player*
* Hollett, Flash

**Holley, Charles Hardin** 1938-1959
[DAM, ECM, LRR]
*American singer*
* Holly, Buddy

**Holley, Major Quincy, Jr.** 1924-
[DAM]
*American jazz musician*
* Holley, Mule

**Holley, Marietta** 1836-1926
[NAA, WBD]
*American author*
* Josiah Allen's Wife

**Holley, Mule**
See　Holley, Major Quincy, Jr.

**Holliday, Bug**
See　Holliday, James Wear

**Holliday, Doc**
See　Holliday, John Henry

**Holliday, James**
See　Gray, Simon

**Holliday, James Wear** 1867-1910
[AS, BE, DGS]
*American baseball player*
* Holliday, Bug

**Holliday, John Henry** 1852-1887
*American gunfighter*
* Holliday, Doc

**Holliday, Joseph [Joe]** 1910-
[AW, CAP, SAT]
*Canadian author*
* Bosco, Jack
* Dale, Jack

**Holliday, Judy**
See　Tuvim, Judith

**Holliday, Marjorie**
See　St. Angel, Marjorie

**Holliday, Robert Cortes** 1880-1946
[TC]
*American author and editor*
* Hill, Murray

**Holliman, Earl**
See　Numkena, Anthony

**Holling, Holling C[lancy]**
See　Clancy, Holling Allison

**Hollingbery, Babe**
See　Hollingbery, Orin E.

**Hollingbery, Orin E.** 1893-1974
[B10, FB]
*American football coach*
* Hollingbery, Babe

**Hollingshead, Holly**
See　Hollingshead, John Samuel

**Hollingshead, John Samuel**
1853-1926　[BE]
*American baseball manager*
* Hollingshead, Holly

**Hollingshead, Maidie** 1881-1937
[THR]
*British actress*
* Hope, Maidie

**Hollingsworth, Albert Wayne**
1908-　[BE, PB]
*American baseball player*
* Hollingsworth, Boots

**Hollingsworth, Bonnie**
See　Hollingsworth, John Burnett

**Hollingsworth, Boots**
See　Hollingsworth, Albert Wayne

**Hollingsworth, Herbert Barrington**
1872-1933　[SC]
*American actor*
* Barrington, Herbert

**Hollingsworth, John Burnett** 1895-
[BE]
*American baseball player*
* Hollingsworth, Bonnie

**Hollingworth, Bucky**
See　Hollingworth, Gordon

**Hollingworth, Gordon** 1933-　[CEI]
*Canadian-born hockey player*
* Hollingworth, Bucky

**Hollins, Lionel** 20th c.
*American basketball player*
* Hollins, Train

**Hollins, Marion** 1892-1944　[GF]
*American golfer*
* [The] Golden Girl

**Hollins, Train**
See Hollins, Lionel

**Hollinshed, Judith**
See Hawthorne, Julian

**Hollis, H. H.**
See Ramey, Ben N.

**Hollis, Jim** [joint pseudonym with Louis P(reston) Trimble]
See Summers, Hollis [Spurgeon, Jr.]

**Hollis, Jim** [joint pseudonym with Hollis (Spurgeon) Summers]
See Trimble, Louis P[reston]

**Hollis, Thomas** ?-1804 [SN]
*British philanthropist*
* [A] Dear Liberty Boy
* Ultimus Romanorum [Last of the Romans]

**Hollis, Wilburn** 1930- [IBW]
*American football player*
* [The] Wizard of the Winged-T

**Hollmig, Hondo**
See Hollmig, Stan[ley Ernest]

**Hollmig, Stan[ley Ernest]** 1926- [BE]
*American baseball player*
* Hollmig, Hondo

**Hollo, Anselm** 1934- [CA]
*Finnish-born author*
* Bielyi, Sergei
* Hofman, Anton

**Holloman, Alva Lee** 1924- [PB]
*American baseball player*
* Holloman, Bobo

**Holloman, Bobo**
See Holloman, Alva Lee

**Holloman, John Lawrence Sullivan, Jr.** 1920- [IBW]
*American physician*
* Holloman, Mike

**Holloman, Mike**
See Holloman, John Lawrence Sullivan, Jr.

**Hollow, Della** 1922- [ART]
*British artist*
* Della

**Holloway, Arthur Thomas** 1870- ? [DBA]
*British artist*
* Long-Holloway, A.

**Holloway, Brenda W[ilmar]** 1908- [CAP]
*British author*
* Verney, Sarah

**Holloway, Brian** 20th c. [SFL]
*Author*
* Cameron, Berl [house pseudonym, Curtis Warren]
* Charles, Neil [house pseudonym, Curtis Warren]
* Dale, Adam [house pseudonym, Curtis Warren]
* Lang, King [house pseudonym, Curtis Warren]
* Le Page, Rand [house pseudonym, Curtis Warren]
* Storm, Brian [house pseudonym, Curtis Warren]

**Holloway, Christopher Columbus** 1896-1972 [MK]
*American baseball player*
* Holloway, Crush

**Holloway, Crush**
See Holloway, Christopher Columbus

**Holloway, Ernest A.** 1919- [DBA]
*British painter*
* Noble, James

**Holloway, George**
See Capitani, Giorgio

**Holloway, James** 1897-1975 [BMH, TR]
*British entertainer*
* Nervo, Jimmy

**Holloway, James L.** 1927- [DAM]
*American jazz musician*
* Holloway, Red

**Holloway, Maggie**
See Fisher, Mrs. Frederick

**Holloway, Red**
See Holloway, James L.

**Holloway, Teresa [Bragunier]** 1906- [CA]
*American author*
* Beatty, Elizabeth
* McLeod, Margaret Vail

**Holly, Buddy**
See Holley, Charles Hardin

**Holly, J. Hunter**
See Holly, Joan C[arol]

**Holly, Jimmy Lee**
See Hawley, James

**Holly, Joan C[arol]** 1932- [CA, SF]
*American author*
* Holly, J. Hunter

**Hollywood, Lysle**
See Henderson, Lisle

**Hollywood, Mr.**
See Rudolph, Marvin

**Hollywood, Rock**
See Sorey, Revie Cee, Jr.

**Holm, Don[ald Raymond]** 1918- [CA]
*American author*
* Denali, Peter

**Holm, Frits** 1881- ? [WWL]
*Author*
* Duke of Xensi

**Holm, Hanya**
See Eckert, Johanna

**Holm, Ian**
See Cuthbert, Ian Holm

**Holm, Katja**
See Fischer, Marie Louise

**Holm, Klaus**
See Kuntze, Klaus

**Holm, Roscoe Albert** 1901-1950 [BE]
*American baseball player*
* Holm, Wattie

**Holm, Saxe**
See Jackson, Helen Maria Hunt

**Holm, Sven [Aage]** 1902- [CAP]
*Danish author*
* Farmacevten

**Holm, Wattie**
See Holm, Roscoe Albert

**Holman, Bill**
See Holman, Willis

**Holman, G. A.**
See Holman, George Alfred

**Holman, George Alfred** 1911- [ART]
*British artist*
* Holman, G. A.

**Holman, [Clarence] Hugh** 1914- [WW]
*Author*
* Hunt, Clarence

**Holman, James** 1787-1857 [DEL, PA]
*British author*
* [The] Blind Traveller

**Holman, Libby**
See Holtzman, Elizabeth

**Holman, Mrs. H. S.** [FFF]
*Entertainer*
* Barry, Helen

**Holman, Nat** 1896- [BB, EJS]
*American basketball player and coach*
* Basketball, Mr.

**Holman, William Steele** 1822-1897 [FFF, WBD]
*American politician*
* [The] Great Objector
* [The] Watch Dog of the Treasury

**Holman, Willis** 1927- [EJ7]
*American composer*
* Holman, Bill

**Holmberg, John-Henri** 20th c. [SFP]
*Author*
* Brandon, Carl, Jr.

**Holme, Gordon**
See Cooper, Charles Henry St. John

**Holme, K. E.**
See Hill, [John Edward] Christopher

**Holme-Sumner, Patrick** 1897-1974 [THR]
*British actor*
* Somerset, Patrick

**Holmes, A. R.**
See Bates, Harry Arthur

**Holmes, Alvin** 1913- [RO1]
*American musician*
* Holmes, Leroy

**Holmes, Cecil Frederick** [PA]
*Author*
* [A] Harrow Tutor

**Holmes, Charles**
See Nordhoff, Charles

**Holmes, Charles Henry** 20th c. [IBW]
*American author*
* Adams, Clayton

**Holmes, David Charles** 1919- [CA]
*American author*
* Charlson, David

**Holmes, Ducky**
See Holmes, Howard Elbert

**Holmes, Ducky**
See Holmes, James William

**Holmes, Ernie** 1948?-
*American football player*
* Holmes, Fats

**Holmes, Fats**
See Holmes, Ernie

**Holmes, Floyd** 1910- [CWG]
*American country-western performer*
* Holmes, Salty

**Holmes, Geoffrey Andrew** 1926- [IAW]
*British accountant and writer*
* Millbank, F. T.
* Mycroft

**Holmes, Gordon** [joint pseudonym with Louis Tracy]
See Shiel, Matthew Phipps

**Holmes, Gordon** [joint pseudonym with Matthew Phipps Shiel]
See Tracy, Louis

**Holmes, Grant**
See Knipscheer, James M. W.

**Holmes, Groove**
See Holmes, Richard Arnold

**Holmes, H. H.**
See White, William A[nthony] P[arker]

**Holmes, Hap**
See Holmes, Harold

**Holmes, Harold** 1889-1941 [CEI, HK]
*Canadian-born hockey player*
* Holmes, Hap

**Holmes, [Capt.] Howard**
See Harbaugh, Thomas Chalmers

**Holmes, Howard Elbert** 1883-1945 [BE]
*American baseball player*
* Holmes, Ducky

**Holmes, Isaac Edward** 1796-1815 [PA]
*Author*
* Telltale, George

**Holmes, Jack D[avid] L[azarus]**
See Lazarus, Jack David

**Holmes, James William** 1869-1932 [AS, BE]
*American baseball player*
* Holmes, Ducky

**Holmes, Jay**
See Holmes, Joseph Everett

**Holmes, Joe** 1897-1949 [BWW]
*American singer*
* Blind Lemon's Buddy
* Hill, King Solomon

**Holmes, John**
See Souster, Raymond

**Holmes, Joseph Everett** 1922- [CA, WD]
*American author*
* Holmes, Jay

**Holmes, Kelly**
See Holmes, Thomas Francis

**Holmes, Kenyon**
See Derleth, August [William]

Holmes, Larry 1950-  [IBW]
*American boxer*
* [The] Easton Assassin

Holmes, Leroy
See  Holmes, Alvin

Holmes, Leroy 20th c.  [OBW]
*American baseball player*
* Holmes, Phillie

Holmes, Lucky
See  Holmes, Samuel

Holmes, Margaret
See  Bates, Mrs. M. V.

Holmes, Marty
See  Hausman, Martin

Holmes, Marvin 20th c.  [GW]
*American rodeo performer*
* Holmes, Pick

Holmes, Mrs. Raymond  [FFF]
*Entertainer*
* Cowell, Sidney

Holmes, Odetta 1930-  [FCW]
*American singer*
* Felious, Odetta
* Odetta

Holmes, Oliver Wendell 1809-1894
[DNNF, FF, PA]
*American author*
* [The] Autocrat
* [The] Autocrat of the Breakfast
  Table
* [The] Poet at the Breakfast Table
* [The] Professor at the Breakfast
  Table

Holmes, Peter Fenwick 1932-
[AW]
*British author*
* Fenwick, Peter

Holmes, Phillie
See  Holmes, Leroy

Holmes, Pick
See  Holmes, Marvin

Holmes, Raymond
See  Souster, Raymond

Holmes, Richard Arnold 1931-
[DAM]
*American musician*
* Holmes, Groove

Holmes, Rick
See  Hardwick, Richard Holmes,
Jr.

Holmes, Robert 1945-  [SMG]
*American football player*
* Holmes, Tank

Holmes, Robert D.  [PA]
*Author*
* [The] Chancellor

Holmes, Salty
See  Holmes, Floyd

Holmes, Samuel 1945-  [IBW]
*American basketball player*
* Holmes, Lucky

Holmes, Tank
See  Holmes, Robert

Holmes, Thomas Francis 1917-
[BE]
*American baseball player*
* Holmes, Kelly

Holmes, Wilfred Jay 1900-  [CA]
*American author*
* Hudson, Alec

Holmes, William Kersley 1882-
[CAP]
*British author*
* Serrifile, F. O. O.

Holmgren, [Sister] George Ellen
See  Holmgren, Helen Jean

Holmgren, Helen Jean 1930-  [CA]
*American author, artist, illustrator*
* Holmgren, [Sister] George Ellen

Holmgren, Norah
See  Hagberg, Nancy

Holmquist, Anders 1933-  [CA]
*Swedish photographer and author*
* Ostrowsky

Holmvik, Oyvind 1914-  [CA]
*Norwegian editor and author*
* Oy-vik
* Paprika
* Sepia

Holroyd, Sam
See  Burton, Samuel Holroyd

Holst, Gustav Theodore
See  Von Holst, Gustavus Theodore

Holt, Andrew
See  Anhalt, Edward

Holt, Conrad G.
See  Fearn, John Russell

Holt, E. Carleton
See  Guigo, Ernest Philip

Holt, E. S.
See  Holt, Eric Stace

Holt, Elise
See  Wall, Mrs. Henry

Holt, Eric Stace 1944-  [ART]
*British painter*
* Holt, E. S.

Holt, Franklin
See  Coryell, Russell Miers

Holt, Gareth Ray 1952-  [HR]
*Canadian-born hockey player*
* Holt, Gary

Holt, Gary
See  Holt, Gareth Ray

Holt, Gavin
See  Rodda, Charles

Holt, George
See  Tubb, Edwin Charles

Holt, Georgia
See  Crouch, Jackie Jean

Holt, Isaac 1932-  [DAM, EJ]
*American jazz musician*
* Holt, Red

Holt, James 1923-1971
[BDF, FDG]
*Palestinian-born director*
* Holt, Seth

Holt, James Emmett Madison
1894-1961  [BE]
*American baseball player*
* Holt, Red

Holt, John [Robert] 1926-  [CA]
*American author*
* Arre, John
* Giles, Elizabeth

Holt, John [Robert] (Continued)
* Giles, Raymond

Holt, John Charles, III 1919-1973
[SC]
*American actor*
* Holt, Tim

Holt, Marie 1894-  [FC]
*British actress*
* Burke, Marie

Holt, Morris 1937-  [BWW]
*American singer*
* Magic Slim

Holt, Patricia 1944-  [IBW, RO2]
*American singer*
* [The] First Lady of Doowah
* LaBelle, Patti

Holt, Patrick
See  Parsons, Patrick

Holt, Red
See  Holt, Isaac

Holt, Red
See  Holt, James Emmett Madison

Holt, Richard
See  Holton, Walter H.

Holt, Robert R[utherford]
See  Watson, Robert R[utherford]

Holt, Seth
See  Holt, James

Holt, Stephen
See  Thompson, Harlan Howard

Holt, Tex
See  Joscelyn, Archie Lynn

Holt, Tim
See  Holt, John Charles, III

Holt, Victoria
See  Hibbert, Eleanor Alice
[Burford]

Holtgrave, Lavern George 1942-
[BE, SMG]
*American baseball player*
* Holtgrave, Vern
* Holtgrave, Woody

Holtgrave, Vern
See  Holtgrave, Lavern George

Holtgrave, Woody
See  Holtgrave, Lavern George

Holton, Edith Austin 1881- ?
[WW]
*Author*
* Heath, Elizabeth Alden

Holton, H. B.
See  Hossent, Harry

Holton, Leonard
See  Wibberley, Leonard [Patrick
O'Connor]

Holton, Mary Ward 20th c.  [BEW]
*American actress and press
representative*
* Ward, Mary

Holton, Walter H. 20th c.  [MBF]
*British author*
* Hall, Richard
* Holt, Richard

Holtz, Curly
See  Holtz, Hyman

Holtz, Hyman 20th c.  [BLB]
*American underworld figure*
* Holtz, Curly

Holtzman, Elizabeth 1906-1971
[EMT]
*American actress and singer*
* Holman, Libby

Holtzmann, Wilhelm 1532-1576
[WBD]
*German scholar and philologist*
* Xylander, Wilhelm

Holwey, Albert R. 1902-  [CEI]
*Canadian-born hockey player*
* Holwey, Toots

Holwey, Toots
See  Holwey, Albert R.

[The] Holy
See  Judah I [or Jehudah]

[A] Holy Autolycus
See  Tetzel, John [or Johann]

Holy Cross Bill
See  Camgan, Bill

[The] Holy Maid
See  Joan of Arc [or Jeanne d'Arc]

[The] Holy Maid of Kent
See  Barton, Elizabeth

[The] Holy Maid of Kent
See  Baxter, Elizabeth

[The] Holy Main
See  Basie, William

[The] Holy Satyr
See  Rasputin, Grigori Efimovich

Holyer, Erna Maria 1925-
[CA, WD]
*German-born American author*
* Holyer, Ernie

Holyer, Ernie
See  Holyer, Erna Maria

Holz, Detlev
See  Benjamin, Walter

Holzapfel, Rudolf Patrick [Rudi]
1938-  [CAP]
*French-born author and poet*
* hurkey, rooan
* Ward, R. Patrick

Holzman, Red
See  Holzman, William

Holzman, William 1920-  [BB, EJS]
*American basketball player*
* Holzman, Red

Holzner, Joseph 1875-1947  [CAT]
*German clergyman and author*
* Hylander, Franz Josef

Homa, Harry 20th c.  [SMG]
*American baseball team
photographer*
* Homa, Lens

Homa, Lens
See  Homa, Harry

Homan, Samuel H. 1842- ?  [PA]
*Author*
* Homer
* Roy, Luxymon

Homburger, Erik
See  Erikson, Erik H[omburger]

**Home, Alexander Frederick** 1903-
[CA]
*British author and politician*
* Douglas-Home, Alec

**Home, Michael**
*See* Bush, Charlie Christmas

**Home Run Baker**
*See* Baker, Howard

**Home Run Johnson**
*See* Johnson, Charles Cleveland
[Charlie]

**Home, T.**
*See* Home-Gall, William Benjamin

**Home-Gall, Edward Reginald**
1899- [MBF]
*British author*
* Clive, Clifford
* Dale, Edwin
* Hall, Rupert

**Home-Gall, William Benjamin**
1861-1936 [MBF, SFL, WGT]
*British author*
* Drew, Reginald
* Home, T.
* Wray, Reginald

**Home-Gall, William Bolinbroke**
1894- [MBF]
*British author*
* Bolinbroke, William
* Young, Will

**Homeier, George Vincent** 1930-
[ITA, SW]
*American actor*
* Homeier, Skip

**Homeier, Skip**
*See* Homeier, George Vincent

**Homer**
*See* Haynes, Henry D.

**Homer**
*See* Homan, Samuel H.

**Homer** [DNNF, FFF, SN]
*Greek poet*
* [The] Blind Bard
* [The] Blind Old Man of Scio's
  Rocky Isle
* [The] Father of Epic Poetry
* [The] Father of Poetry
* [The] Father of Song
* [The] Maeonian Poet
* [The] Maeonian Swan
* Maeonides
* [The] Man of Chios
* Melesigenes
* Scio's Blind Old Bard
* [The] Swan of the Meander
* [The] Thunderer

**[The] Homer and Virgil of Portugal**
*See* Camoens, Luis de

**[The] Homer of Britain**
*See* Milton, John

**[The] Homer of Dramatic Poets**
*See* Shakespeare, William

**[The] Homer of Ferrara**
*See* Ariosto, Lodovico

**[The] Homer of Geometry**
*See* Archimedes

**[The] Homer of His Age**
*See* Angilbert

**[The] Homer of History**
*See* Herodotus

**[The] Homer of Khorasan**
*See* Mansur [or Hasan?], Abul
Qasim

**[The] Homer of Modern Days**
*See* Scott, [Sir] Walter

**[The] Homer of Orators**
*See* John

**[The] Homer of Persia**
*See* Mansur [or Hasan?], Abul
Qasim

**[The] Homer of Philosophers**
*See* Aristocles

**[The] Homer of Portugal**
*See* Camoens, Luis de

**[The] Homer of Scotland**
*See* Wilkie, William

**[The] Homer of the Celts**
*See* Ossian

**[The] Homer of the Franks**
*See* Angilbert

**[The] Homer of the French Drama**
*See* Corneille, Pierre

**Homer the Great**
*See* Crayton, Connie Curtis

**Homer the Younger**
*See* Philiscos

**[A] Homeric Ajax**
*See* Saxe, [Hermann] Maurice de

**Homeromastix**
*See* Zoilus [or Zoilos]

**Homer's Scourge**
*See* Zoilus [or Zoilos]

**Homersham, Basil Henry** 1902-
[WW]
*Author*
* Manningham, Basil

**Homes, Geoffrey**
*See* Mainwaring, Daniel

**Homes, Geoffrey**
*See* Woolrich, Daniel

**Homes, Mary Sophie Shaw** 1830?-
? [FFF]
*American author*
* Mayfield, Millie

**Homesick James**
*See* Henderson, John William

**Homespun, Sophia**
*See* Monmouth, Elizabeth H.

**Homicide Hank Armstrong**
*See* Jackson, Henry

**[L']Homme de Decembre**
*See* Bonaparte, Charles Louis
Napoleon

**[L']Homme du Lit de Fer**
*See* Orleans, Henri Eugene
Philippe Louis d'

**[L']Homme Qui-Let**
*See* Poignart, J.

**[L']Homme sans Peur**
*See* De Balbe de Crillon, Louis

**Homo**
*See* Parkyn, Walter A.

**Homo**
*See* Westcott, Charles S.

**Homo, [Dr.] Ali**
*See* Hompf, Alois

**Homoras**
*See* Nuttall, Jeff

**Hompf, Alois** 20th c. [WGT]
*Author*
* Homo, [Dr.] Ali

**Honda, Takashi** 1945- [EJ7]
*Japanese jazz musician*
* Honda, Takehiro

**Honda, Takehiro**
*See* Honda, Takashi

**Hondius, Jodocus**
*See* De Hondt, Joos

**[The] Hondo Hurricane**
*See* Hartung, Clinton Clarence

**Hone, William** 1779?-1842 [PA]
*British author*
* Cecil

**Honest Abe**
*See* Lincoln, Abraham

**Honest Abe Martin**
*See* Martin, Othol H.

**Honest Allan**
*See* Cunningham, Allan

**Honest Ben Jonson**
*See* Jonson, Ben[jamin]

**[The] Honest Broker**
*See* Bismarck, Otto Eduard
Leopold von

**Honest Eddie Murphy**
*See* Murphy, John Edward

**Honest George**
*See* Graham, George

**Honest George**
*See* Monk, George [Duke of
Albemarle]

**[The] Honest Goetz von Berlichingen**
*See* Goethe, Johann Wolfgang von

**Honest Jack**
*See* Felton, John

**Honest Jack**
*See* Lawless, John

**Honest Jack Boyle**
*See* Boyle, John Anthony

**Honest John**
*See* Davis, John

**Honest John**
*See* Sherman, John

**Honest John [or Jack]**
*See* Spencer, John Charles [Lord
Althorp]

**Honest John Anderson**
*See* Anderson, John Joseph

**Honest John Eubank**
*See* Eubank, John Franklin

**Honest John Gaffney**
*See* Gaffney, John H.

**Honest John Kelly**
*See* Kelly, John

**Honest John McCloskey**
*See* McCloskey, John

**Honest John Morrill**
*See* Morrill, John Francis

**[The] Honest Lawyer**
*See* Trelawny, Edward

**Honest Man King**
*See* Victor Emmanuel II

**Honest Old Zach**
*See* Chandler, Zachariah

**Honest Tom**
*See* Warton, Thomas

**Honest Tom Niland**
*See* Niland, Thomas James [Tom]

**Honestus**
*See* Austin, Benjamin

**Honey Bear Cedric**
*See* Cedric, Eugene

**Honey Bear Lanier**
*See* Lanier, Willie E.

**Honey Bear Sedric**
*See* Sedric, [Eu]gene

**Honey Bee**
*See* Smith, Elizabeth A.

**Honey Boy Evans**
*See* Evans, George

**Honey Boy Shaw**
*See* Shaw, Albert

**Honey Boy Smith**
*See* Woodbridge, Hudson

**Honey Bunny Boo**
*See* Rushing, James Andrew
[Jimmy]

**Honey Eddie**
*See* Edwards, David

**Honey Fitz**
*See* Fitzgerald, John F.

**Honey, Mr.**
*See* Edwards, David

**Honey, Philip** 20th c. [WD]
*British author and journalist*
* Harrison, G. D.
* Hart, Peter
* Phillips, H. C.
* Taurus

**Honeyboy**
*See* Patt, Frank

**Honeycomb, Will**
*See* Cleland, William

**Honeycomb, Will**
*See* Gordon, George

**[The] Honeydripper**
*See* Liggins, Joe

**[The] Honeydripper**
*See* Sykes, Roosevelt

**[The] Honeyed Teacher**
*See* Bernard of Clairvaux

**Honeyman, Brenda**
*See* Clarke, Brenda Margaret
Lilian

**Honeyman, Walter MacDonald**
1899- [TR]
*Scottish director and manager*
* MacDonald, Murray

**Honeyman, William C.** 20th c.
[WW]
*Author*
* M'Govan, James

**Honeysuckle, Philip**
See Neagu, Paul

**Honeywell, E. L.** 20th c. [WW]
*Author*
* Stanley, Olin

**Hong, Jane Fay** 1954- [CA]
*American author*
* Sheridan, Adora [joint pseudonym with Evelyn Marie Pavlik]

**Hongo, Francis Secardi** 17th c. [SN]
*Venetian consul*
* Huppazoli

**Honigfeld, Gilbert** 1934- [CA]
*American medical writer*
* Howard, Gilbert

**Honkanen, Hilja Loviisa Valkeapaa** 1912- [IAW]
*Finnish author*
* Anni, Makituvan
* Kare, Kaarina
* Outi
* Pelkonen, Elina
* Ursula, Sanna

**Honnor, Sylvia Crofts** 1933- [IAW]
*British author*
* Redstone, Sylvia

**Honolulu Johnny Williams**
See Williams, John Brodie [Johnny]

**Honor and Glory Griffiths**
See Griffiths, Captain

**Honoria**
See Power, Marguerite A.

**Honorius II**
See Cadalous, Pietro

**Honorius II**
See Scannabecchi, Lamberto

**Honorius III**
See Savelli, Cencio

**Honorius IV**
See Savelli, Giacomo

**Honourable Member for X**
See De Chair, Somerset [Struben]

**Honri, Percy**
See Thompson, Percy Henry

**Hontheim, Johann Nikolaus [or John Nicholas] von** 1701-1790 [HN, WBD]
*German prelate*
* Febronius, Justinus

**Honywood, Michael** 17th c. [SN]
*British clergyman and book collector*
* [The] Father Among Philological English Antiquaries

**Hood, Abe**
See Hood, Aubrey Lincoln

**Hood, Aldine Robin**
See Burrage, Alfred Sherrington

**Hood, Archer Leslie** 1869?-1944 [SFL, WGT]
*Author*
* Leslie, Lilian [joint pseudonym with Violet Lilian Perkins]

**Hood, Aubrey Lincoln** 1903- [BE]
*American baseball player*
* Hood, Abe

**Hood, Jack**
See Hood-Phillips, J. H.

**Hood, James** 1907- [BB]
*American basketball player*
* Hood, Lindy

**Hood, Lindy**
See Hood, James

**Hood, Sarah**
See Killough, [Karen] Lee

**Hood, Stephen**
See Lewis, Jack

**Hood, Sydney Paxton** 1860-1930 [BEW]
*British-born actor and producer*
* Paxton, Sydney

**Hood-Phillips, J. H.** 1902- [WWL]
*British author*
* Hood, Jack

**Hoogland, Marianne**
See Hoffman, Wilhelmus Adrianus Franciscus Xaverius

**Hooi, Richard** 1944?- [CW]
*Surinamese poet*
* Seku, Yerba

**[The] Hook**
See Aleman, Harry

**[The] Hook**
See Sawyer, Ray

**Hook, Alfred Samuel** 20th c. [WW]
*Author*
* Colton, A. J.

**Hook, Captain**
See Sigel, Mike

**Hook, Dr.**
See Sawyer, Ray

**Hook, H. Clarke** 20th c. [MBF]
*British author*
* Clifford, Martin [house pseudonym]
* Harvey, Ross
* Paine, Hammond
* Richards, Frank [house pseudonym]

**Hook, Samuel Clarke** 20th c. [MBF]
*British author*
* Clarke, [Captain] Maurice
* Dene, Hampton
* Hale, Innis
* Hope, Edgar
* Lancaster, Captain
* Merriman, Maurice
* Monteith, Owen

**Hook, Sandy**
See Jones, Alexander

**Hook, Theodore Edward** 1788-1841 [DEL, FFF, WBD]
*British author*
* Blenkinsop, Vicesimus
* Jones, Richard
* Ramsbottom, Mrs.

**Hook, W. F.** 1778-1841 [PA]
*Author*
* [A] Layman

**Hooke, Charles Witherle** 1861-1929 [WGT, WW]
*American author*
* Fielding, Howard

**Hooker, Cy**
See Hoch, Cyrus

**Hooker, Fanny** [FFF]
*Author*
* Hoven, Ernest

**Hooker, Fighting Joe**
See Hooker, Joseph

**Hooker, Hook**
See Hooker, Orville J.

**Hooker Joe**
See Davis, Walter

**Hooker, John Lee** 1917- [BWW, FCW]
*American singer*
* Birmingham Sam
* Boogie Man
* Booker, John Lee
* Cooker, John Lee
* Delta John
* Lee, Johnny
* Texas Slim
* Williams, Johnny

**Hooker, Joseph** 1814-1879 [DNNF, DNNS, SN]
*American army officer*
* Hooker, Fighting Joe

**Hooker, Lois** 1927- [FC]
*Canadian-born actress*
* Maxwell, Lois

**Hooker, Orville J.** 20th c. [BBH]
*American basketball player and coach*
* Hooker, Hook

**Hooker, Richard**
See Hornberger, H. Richard

**Hooker, Richard** 1553?-1600 [DNNS, FFF, SN]
*British clergyman*
* [The] Judicious Hooker

**Hooker, William E.**
See Hoch, Cyrus

**Hookham, Margaret** 1919- [IPA]
*British ballerina*
* Fonteyn, Margot

**Hooper, Bett**
See Hooper, Elizabeth Edna

**Hooper, Byrd**
See St. Clair, Byrd Hooper

**Hooper, Elizabeth Edna** 1906- [NAA]
*American author*
* Hooper, Bett

**Hooper, Henry** [PA]
*Author*
* Ducdame

**Hooper, Johnson J.** [PA]
*Author*
* Suggs, Simon

**Hooper, Lucy** 1816-1841 [PA]
*Author*
* L. H.

**Hooper, Nesbert** 1938- [DAM]
*American jazz musician*
* Hooper, Stix

**Hooper, Stanley** 20th c. [MBF]
*British author*
* Brandon, Roy

**Hooper, Stix**
See Hooper, Nesbert

**Hooper, William** 1742-1790 [FFF]
*American revolutionary leader*
* Hampden

**Hoopes, Helen Rhoda** 1879- ? [NAA]
*American author and columnist*
* H. R. H.

**Hoopes, Mary Howard** 20th c. [NAA]
*American author*
* Finn, Anna E.
* Peterson, Maud Howard

**Hoopii, Sol**
See Kaaiai, Sol Hoopii

**Hoopington, Ambrose**
See Binney, Cecil

**Hoopman, Harold D.** 1920?-
*American business executive*
* Hoopman, Hoop

**Hoopman, Hoop**
See Hoopman, Harold D.

**Hoosier**
See Morris, Samuel V.

**Hoosier Hank**
See Miner, Virginia Scott

**Hoosier Hannah**
See Miner, Virginia Scott

**[The] Hoosier Poet**
See Riley, James Whitcomb

**[The] Hoosier Schoolmaster**
See Aldridge, Victor Eddington

**[The] Hoosier Schoolmaster**
See Hand, John Raymond

**[The] Hoosier Thunderbolt**
See Rusie, Amos Wilson

**Hoosman, Al**
See Hoosman, Alston

**Hoosman, Alston** 1921- [IBW]
*American actor and boxer*
* Hoosman, Al

**Hoot Man Huth**
See Huth, Gerry

**Hooten, David** 20th c. [CME]
*American country-western performer*
* Lonzo

**[The] Hooter**
See Gibson, Edmund Richard

**Hooton, Burt Carlton** 1950- [SMG]
*American baseball player*
* Hooton, Happy
* [The] Owl

**Hooton, Charles**
See Rowe, Vivian C[laud]

**Hooton, Happy**
See Hooton, Burt Carlton

**Hoover, Buster**
See Hoover, William J.

**Hoover, Helen [Drusilla Blackburn]** 1910- [CA, SAT, WD]
*American author*
* Price, Jennifer

**Hoover, Herbert Clark** 1874-1964 [FAP]
*American president*
* [The] Chief
* [The] Friend of Helpless Children
* [The] Grand Old Man

**Hoover, Herbert Clark** (Continued)
* [The] Hermit Author of Palo Alto
* [The] Man of Great Heart

**Hoover, William J.** 1863- ?    [BE]
*American baseball player*
* Hoover, Buster

**Hooves, Daddy**
*See* Gerard, Gus

**Hop Toad Giunta**
*See* Giunta, Giuseppe

**Hope**
*See* Bailey, Albert

**Hope, Alexander James Beresford**
1820- ?    [PA]
*Author*
* D. C. L.

**Hope, Amanda**
*See* Lewis, Judith Mary
[Berrisford]

**Hope, Andrew**
*See* Hern, [George] Anthony

**Hope, Anthony**
*See* Hawkins, [Sir] Anthony Hope

**Hope, Ascott R.**
*See* Moncrieff, Robert Hope

**Hope, Bob**
*See* Hope, Leslie Townes

**Hope, Brian**
*See* Creasey, John

**Hope, Camilla**
*See* Thompson, Grace E.

**Hope, Cecil**
*See* Spero, Leopold

**Hope, David**
*See* Fraser, Douglas Jamieson

**Hope, Edgar**
*See* Hook, Samuel Clarke

**Hope, Edward**
*See* Coffey, Edward Hope, Jr.

**Hope, Elizabeth**
*See* Mance, Elizabeth Hope

**Hope, [Frances] Essex [Theodora]**
20th c.    [WW]
*Author*
* Smith, Essex

**Hope, Ethel**
*See* Henry, Mrs. I. M. P.

**Hope, F. T. L.**
*See* Farrar, Doctor

**Hope, Felix**
*See* Williamson, Claude C[harles]
H.

**Hope, James Barron** 1827- ?    [FFF]
*American poet*
* Ellen, Henry

**Hope, Laura Lee** [house pseudonym]
[Stratemeyer Syndicate]
*See* Adams, Harriet S[tratemeyer]

**Hope, Laura Lee**
*See* Creager, Eunice Whayne

**Hope, Laura Lee** [house pseudonym]
[Stratemeyer Syndicate]
*See* Stratemeyer, Edward L.

**Hope, Laurence**
*See* Cory, Adela Florence

**Hope, Leslie Townes** 1903-
[BEW, EMT, HT]
*British-born American comedian and
actor*
* Hope, Bob

**Hope, Maidie**
*See* Hollingshead, Maidie

**Hope, Marion**
*See* Parker, Marion Dominica
Hope

**Hope, Mark**
*See* Murray, Eustace Clare
Grenville

**Hope, Mr.** [code name used during
World War II]
*See* Peresitch, [Colonel]

**Hope, Walter**
*See* Phillips, Horace

**Hope, William Edward Stanton**
1889-1961    [MBF]
*British author*
* Dean, Donald
* Denver, Bruce
* Richards, Frank [house
    pseudonym]
* Stanton, William

**Hopf, Alice L[ightner]** 1904-
[CA, SAT]
*American author*
* Lightner, A. M.

**Hopkins, A. T.**
*See* Turngren, Annette

**Hopkins, Alice K[imball]** 1839- ?
[SFL, WGT]
*Author*
* A. K. H.
* Choate, Lowell

**Hopkins, Allen** 20th c.
*American billiard player*
* Hopkins, Hoppe

**Hopkins, Alphonso A.**    [PA]
*Author*
* Linton, A. H.

**Hopkins, B.** 20th c.    [MBF]
*British author*
* Williams, Richard [house
    pseudonym]

**Hopkins, [Frances] Betty** 1915-
[IAW]
*British translator*
* John, Miriam

**Hopkins, Claude D.** 1903-    [IBW]
*American jazz musician*
* Hopkins, Crazy Fingers

**Hopkins, Crazy Fingers**
*See* Hopkins, Claude D.

**Hopkins, David Charles** 1957-
[DC]
*British cricketer*
* Hopkins, Hoppy

**Hopkins, Doc**
*See* Hopkins, Doctor Howard

**Hopkins, Doctor Howard** 1899-
[CWG]
*American country-western performer*
* Hopkins, Doc

**Hopkins, Ellen** 1902-1972    [OCF]
*American actress*
* Hopkins, Miriam

**Hopkins, Gail** 20th c.    [SMG]
*American baseball player*
* Hopkins, Hoppy

**Hopkins, Hoppe**
*See* Hopkins, Allen

**Hopkins, Hoppy**
*See* Hopkins, David Charles

**Hopkins, Hoppy**
*See* Hopkins, Gail

**Hopkins, Joel** 1904-1975    [BWW]
*American singer*
* Hopkins, Squatty

**Hopkins, John** ?-1732    [RH, SN]
*British merchant*
* Hopkins, Vulture

**Hopkins, John Winston** 1883-1929
[BE]
*American baseball player*
* Hopkins, Sis

**Hopkins, Kenneth** 1914-    [CA]
*British author*
* Adams, Christopher
* Burney, Anton
* Mannon, Warwick
* Marsh, Paul
* Marshall, Edmund
* Meredith, Arnold

**Hopkins, Lightnin'**
*See* Hopkins, Sam

**Hopkins, Lyman**
*See* Folsom, Franklin [Brewster]

**Hopkins, Margaret Briscoe** 1864-
?    [NAA]
*American author*
* Briscoe, Margaret Sutton

**Hopkins, Marty**
*See* Hopkins, Meredith Hilliard

**Hopkins, Matthew** 17th c.
[FFF, RH, SN]
*British eccentric*
* [The] Witchfinder

**Hopkins, Meredith Hilliard**
1907-1963    [BE]
*American baseball player*
* Hopkins, Marty

**Hopkins, Miriam**
*See* Hopkins, Ellen

**Hopkins, Omar**
*See* Zeglio, Primo

**Hopkins, Pauline Mackie** 1874- ?
[NAA]
*American author*
* Mackie, Pauline Bradford

**Hopkins, Prynce [C.]** 1885-1970
[CAP]
*American psychologist and author*
* Hopkins, Pryns

**Hopkins, Pryns**
*See* Hopkins, Prynce [C.]

**Hopkins, Robert**    [WWS]
*American author*
* Rostand, Robert

**Hopkins, Sam** 1912-1982
[DAM, EJ, LRR]
*American singer and guitarist*
* Hopkins, Lightnin'

**Hopkins, Sis**
*See* Hopkins, John Winston

**Hopkins, Squatty**
*See* Hopkins, Joel

**Hopkins, Viola**
*See* Winner, Viola Hopkins

**Hopkins, Vulture**
*See* Hopkins, John

**Hopkinson, Henry Thomas [Tom]**
1905-    [WD]
*British author*
* Pembroke, Thomas
* Vindicator

**Hopley, George**
*See* Hopley-Woolrich, Cornell
George

**Hopley-Woolrich, Cornell George**
1903?-1968    [CAP, CC, EMD]
*American author*
* Hopley, George
* Irish, William
* Woolrich, Cornell

**Hopp, Hippity**
*See* Hopp, John Leonard

**Hopp, John Leonard** 1916-    [BE]
*American baseball player*
* Hopp, Hippity

**Hopp, Signe Marie** 1905-    [AW]
*Norwegian author*
* Zinken

**Hoppe, William**    [FFF]
*Entertainer*
* Mestayer, William

**Hoppe, Willie** 1888?-    [BBH]
*American billiards player*
* Billiards, Mr.

**Hoppen, Harriet**
*See* Hoppen-Ram, Henderika
Wilhelmina Christina

**Hoppen-Ram, Henderika Wilhelmina
Christina** 1919-    [IAW]
*Dutch author*
* Hoppen, Harriet
* Wijnstroom, Christy

**Hopper, Bird Dog**
*See* Hoppper, William Booth [Bill]

**Hopper, C. F.** 19th c.    [BE]
*American baseball player*
* Hopper, Lefty

**Hopper, DeWolf**
*See* D'Wolf, William

**Hopper, Hedda**
*See* Furry, Elda

**Hopper, Lefty**
*See* Hopper, C. F.

**Hoppper, William Booth [Bill]**
1890-1965    [BE]
*American baseball player*
* Hopper, Bird Dog

**Hopps, John Page** 1834-1911
[WWL]
*British clergyman and author*
* Ellis, Luke

**Hopson, Janet L[ouise]** 1950-    [CA]
*American author*
* Weinberg, Janet Hopson

**Horace in Cincinnati**
*See* Pierce, Thomas

**[The] Horace of England**
*See* Cowley, Abraham

[The] Horace of England
See Jonson, Ben[jamin]

[The] Horace of France
See Amfrye, Guillaume

[The] Horace of France
See Beranger, Pierre Jean de

[The] Horace of France
See Macrinus [or Salmon?], Jean

[The] Horace of France
See Ronsard, Pierre de

[The] Horace of His Age
See Ghibbes [or Gibbes?], James
Alban

[The] Horace of Portugal
See Ferreira, Antonio

[The] Horace of Spain
See Argensola, Bartolome
Leonardo de

[The] Horace of Spain
See Argensola, Lupercio Leonardo
de

Horafuki [Teller of Tall Tales]
See Endo, Shusaku

Horai, Julius 20th c.   [SMG]
American football team staff
member
* Horai, Whitey

Horai, Whitey
See Horai, Julius

Horan, Dorothy 20th c.
American fashion model
* Dovima

Horan, Joseph Patrick 1894-1968
[BE]
American baseball player
* Horan, Shags

Horan, Shags
See Horan, Joseph Patrick

[The] Horatio Alger of Today
See Heyliger, William

Horatio, Jane
See Cudlipp, Edythe

Horatius Cocles of the Horn
See Haring, John

[The] Horatius Cocles of the Tyrol
See Davy de La Pailleterie,
Alexandre

Horazdovsky, Albert W.
1886-1956   [BE]
American baseball player
* Nelson, Albert Francis
* Nelson, Red

Hori
See Ackerman, Forrest J[ames]

Horlen, Joe
See Horlen, Joel Edward

Horlen, Joel Edward 1937-   [BE]
American baseball player
* Horlen, Joe

Horler, Sydney 1888-1954
[EMD, MBF, WW]
British author
* Cavendish, Peter
* Heritage, Martin
* Hobbs, Jack
* Standish, J. O.

Horn, Alfred Aloysius
See Smith, Alfred Aloysius

Horn, Emily 1887?-1955   [BEW]
American theatrical performer
* Abbott, Dolly

Horn, Holloway 1886-   [WW]
Author
* Waghorn, H. L.

Horn, Kirby Grant 1914-   [FC]
American actor
* Grant, Kirby

Horn, Maurice 1931-   [CA]
French-born American author
* Sauvage, Franck

Horn, Miriam Burns 1904-1951
[GF]
American golfer
* Horn, Tyson

Horn, Peter [house pseudonym,
Ziff-Davis]
See Kuttner, Henry

Horn, Peter [house pseudonym,
Ziff-Davis]
See Vern, David

Horn, Ted
See Von Horn, Eylard Theodore

Horn, Trader
See Smith, Alfred Aloysius

Horn, Tyson
See Horn, Miriam Burns

Hornback, Bert G[erald] 1935-
[CA]
American author and playwright
* Frascatoro, Gerald
* Plumm, Norman D.

Hornberger, H. Richard 20th c.
[B10]
American physician and author
* Hooker, Richard

Hornbook, Adam
See Cooper, Thomas

Hornbrook, Charles 1874-1937
[SC]
American actor
* Hornbrook, Gus

Hornbrook, Gus
See Hornbrook, Charles

Hornby, John [Wilkinson] 1913-
[AW, CA]
British author and historian
* Brent, Calvin
* Grace, Joseph
* Summers, Gordon

Hornby, Lesley 1949-
[B10, IPA, NN]
British fashion model
* Twiggy

Horne, Alderson Burrell 1863-1953
[BEW]
British-born director, producer,
actor
* Hall, Anmer

Horne, Berlyn Dale 1899-   [BE]
American baseball player
* Horne, Sonny
* Horne, Trader

Horne, Cynthia Miriam 1939-
[CA]
British author
* Pilkington, Cynthia

Horne, Geoffrey 1916-
[AW, CA, CC]
British author
* North, Gil

Horne, George 20th c.   [CEI]
Hockey player
* Horne, Shorty

Horne, Howard
See Payne, [Pierre Stephen]
Robert

Horne, Hugh Robert 1915-   [CA]
American author and columnist
* Madison, Jane

Horne, John 1736-1812   [DNNS]
British politician and philologist
* [The] Philosopher of Wimbledon
* Tooke, Horne

Horne, Reg
See Horne, Reginald W.

Horne, Reginald W. 1908-   [EG]
British golfer
* Horne, Reg

Horne, Richard Hengist 1803-1884
[FFF]
British author and poet
* [The] Farthing Poet

Horne, Shorty
See Horne, George

Horne, Sonny
See Horne, Berlyn Dale

Horne, Thomas Hartwell
1780-1862?   [PA, RH]
British clergyman and author
* [A] Lincolnshire Grazier

Horne, Trader
See Horne, Berlyn Dale

Horne-Wishin, S. 1905-   [BF]
British actress
* Wilshin, Sunday [or Sundae]

Horneck, Catharine [Kate] 1750?-
?   [DNNF, FFF, SN]
Friend of British author, Oliver
Goldsmith
* Little Comedy

Horneck, Charles 17th c.   [SN]
Friend of British author, Oliver
Goldsmith
* [The] Captain in Lace

Horneck, Mary 18th c.
[DNNF, SN]
Friend of British author, Oliver
Goldsmith
* [The] Jessamy Bride

Hornem, Horace
See Byron, George Gordon Noel

Horner, George Reginald 1909-
[CEI, FHE, HK]
Canadian-born hockey player
* Horner, Red

Horner, Jack
See Horner, William Frank

Horner, Jed
See Horner, Jedediah Edward

Horner, Jedediah Edward 1922-
[BEW]
American director
* Horner, Jed

Horner, Red
See Horner, George Reginald

Horner, T. H.   [PA]
Author
* Clarke, John

Horner, William Frank 1863-1910
[BE]
American baseball player
* Horner, Jack

Hornes
See Fisher, G. C.

Hornig, Charles D. 1916-
[ESF, WGT]
American editor
* Lesser, Derwin

Horniman, A. E. F.
See Horniman, Annie Elizabeth
Fredericka

Horniman, Annie Elizabeth
Fredericka 1860-1937   [LC]
British theatrical backer
* Horniman, A. E. F.

Hornsby, Rogers 1896-1963
[AS, DGS, PB]
American baseball player and
manager
* [The] Rajah

Hornung, E. W.
See Hornung, Ernest William

Hornung, Ernest William
1866-1921   [LC]
British author
* Hornung, E. W.

Hornung, Golden Boy
See Hornung, Paul

Hornung, Michael Joseph
1857-1931   [AS, BE]
American baseball player
* Hornung, Ubbo Ubbo

Hornung, Paul 1935-   [BBH]
American football player
* Hornung, Golden Boy

Hornung, Ubbo Ubbo
See Hornung, Michael Joseph

Horowitz, Al
See Horowitz, Israel A.

Horowitz, Harry 20th c.   [BLB]
American underworld figure
* Gyp the Blood

Horowitz, Israel A. 1907-1973
[CA]
American chess writer and champion
* Horowitz, Al

Horowitz, Jacob 1900-1979   [BEW]
Austrian-born producer and director
* Harris, Jed

Horowitz, Vladimir
See Gorovitz, Vladimir

Horrell, Babe
See Horrell, Edwin C.

Horrell, Edwin C. 1902-   [FB]
American football player
* Horrell, Babe

Horrocks, Frank 1924- [EJ]
*British jazz musician*
* Horrox, Frank

Horrocks, Peter 1926- [FC]
*British actor*
* Reynolds, Peter

Horrox, Frank
See Horrocks, Frank

[The] Horse
See Ameche, Alan D.

[The] Horse
See Danning, Harry

[The] Horse
See Frederick, Jane

[The] Horse
See Gallatin, Harry

[The] Horse
See Howard, Frank Oliver

[The] Horse
See Stautner, Ernie

Horse Belly Sargent
See Sargent, Joseph Alexander
[Joe]

Horsely, David
See Bingley, David Ernest

Horsely, Ramsbottom
See Bernstein, Eric [Lennard]

[The] Horseman
See Prusias II

Horsman, Edward 1807-1876 [HN]
*British politician*
* [The] Superior Person

Horstmann, Rosemary
See Waters, Rosemary Elizabeth

Hortensius, Quintus 1st c. BC
[DNNF, FFF, SN]
*Roman tribune and orator*
* [A] Dionysiac Singing Woman
* [The] King of the Courts

Hortentius
See Hay, George

Horter, Kristin
See Lahany, Kristin Elaine
Eggleston

Horton, Boozie
See Horton, Willie Wattison

Horton, Elmer E. 1869- ? [BE]
*American baseball player*
* Horton, Herky Jerky

Horton, Feliz Lee
See Floren, Lee

Horton, Herky Jerky
See Horton, Elmer E.

Horton, Joanne Barbara 1932-
[BWW]
*British-born singer*
* Horton, Pug

Horton, Johnny 1929-1960 [CWG]
*American country-western performer*
* [The] Singing Fisherman

Horton, Juanita 1898?-
[BEW, F1, FC]
*American actress*
* Love, Bessie

Horton, Mead Howard 1924- [FC]
*American actor*
* Horton, Robert

Horton, Miles Gilbert 1930-1974
[B10, CEI, FHE]
*Canadian-born hockey player*
* Horton, Tim

Horton, Pug
See Horton, Joanne Barbara

Horton, [Sir] R. J. W. [PA]
*Author*
* Philalethes

Horton, Robert
See Horton, Mead Howard

Horton, Shakey
See Horton, Walter

Horton, Tim
See Horton, Miles Gilbert

Horton, Walter 1917-
[BWW, NBB, RM]
*American singer*
* Big Walter
* Horton, Shakey
* Mumbles
* Tangle Eye

Horton, Willie Wattison 1942-
[PB]
*American baseball player*
* Horton, Boozie

Horush [Arouj, Horuc or Koruk]
1473?-1518 [HN, WBD]
*Sultan of Algiers*
* Barbarossa I
* Red Beard

Horvath, Bronco
See Horvath, Joseph

Horvath, Joseph 1930- [FHE]
*Canadian-born hockey player*
* Horvath, Bronco

Horwich, Frances R[appaport]
1908- [CAP, SAT]
*American educator, author,
television performer*
* Miss Frances

Hoseki
See Hisamatsu, Shin'ichi

Hosemann, Andreas 1498-1552
[WBD]
*German theologian*
* Osiander, Andreas

Hosenfeldt, Vera 1910-1967 [SC]
*German-born actress*
* Krupp, Vera

Hosier, Helen Kooiman 1928- [CA]
*American author*
* Kooiman, Helen W.

Hosken, Alice Cecil Seymour 1877-
? [LAO]
*British author*
* Stanton, Coralie

Hosken, Clifford James Wheeler
1882- [CC, LAO, WW]
*British author and journalist*
* Keverne, Richard

Hosken, Ernest Charles Heath 1875-
? [LAO, MBF]
*British author*
* Costello, Pierre
* Gower, Craven

Hoskin, Clifford
See Cooper, Charles Henry St.
John

Hoskin, Cyril Henry 1911-
[B10, NAD]
*British-born Tibetan monk*
* Lobsang Rampa, Tuesday

Hoskins, Alan Clay, Jr.
*Actor*
* Farina

Hoskins, Dave 20th c. [IBW]
*American baseball player*
* Savior of the Texas League

Hoskins, John 1566-1638 [SN]
*British author*
* [The] Universal Aristarchus

Hoskins, Josephine R. [FFF]
*Writer*
* Hildegarde

Hoskins, Robert 1933- [CA]
*American author and editor*
* Corren, Grace
* Jennifer, Susan
* Redfield, Jennifer

Hoskyns-Abrahall, Clare [Constance
Drury] [CA, SAT]
*British author*
* Abrahall, C. H.
* Abrahall, Clare Hoskyns
* Drury, Clare Marie

Hosmer, Harriet 1831- ? [PA]
*Author*
* Kilosa

Hossent, Harry 1916-
[CAP, IAW, WD]
*British author*
* Gregory, Sean
* Holton, H. B.
* O'Malley, Kevin
* Savage, David

Host, [Eu]gene [Earl] 1933- [BE]
*American baseball player*
* Host, Slick
* Host, Twinkles

Host, Slick
See Host, [Eu]gene [Earl]

Host, Twinkles
See Host, [Eu]gene [Earl]

Hostetter, Art
See Hoelskoetter, Art[hur H.]

Hostetter, Iris Adrian 1913-
[FC, ITA, SW]
*American actress*
* Adrian, Iris

[The] Hot Dog
See Fuentes, Rigoberto

[The] Hot Gospeller
See Barnes, Robert

[The] Hot Gospeller
See Underhill, Edward

Hot Lips Edwards
See Edwards, Hartley

Hot Lips Levine
See Levine, Henry

Hot Lips Page
See Page, Elizabeth Lawson

Hot Lips Page
See Page, Oran Thaddeus

Hot Potato Hamlin
See Hamlin, Luke Daniel

Hot Rod Hulbert
See Hulbert, Maurice

Hot Rod Hundley
See Hundley, Rod

Hot Rod Kanehl
See Kanehl, Rod[erick Edwin]

Hot Rod McDonald
See McDonald, James LeRoy

Hot Rod Red
See Polfus, Lester

Hot Shot Willie
See McTell, Willie Samuel

Hot Stove Jimmy
See Quinn, Jimmy

Hotaling, Monkey
See Hotaling, Peter James

Hotaling, Peter James 1856-1928
[BE]
*American baseball player*
* Hotaling, Monkey

Hotema, Hilton
See Clements, George

Hotspur
See Buck, Henry

Hotspur
See Curling, Bryan William
Richard

Hotspur
See Feist, Henry Mort

Hotspur
See Percy, Henry

[The] Hotspur of Debate
See Stanley, Edward George
Geoffrey Smith

Hotspur, Paul
See Bidston, Lester

Hotten, John Camden 1832-1873
[PA, RH]
*British author*
* Brick, Titus A.
* J. C. H.
* [A] London Antiquary
* Rowlands, Cadwallader
* Sylvester, Joshua
* Taylor, Theodore

Hou, Fu-Wu
See Houn, Franklin W.

Houck, Byron Simon 1887- [BE]
*American baseball player*
* Houck, Duke

Houck, Duke
See Houck, Byron Simon

Houck, Leo
See Hauck, Leo Florian

Houck, Sadie
See Houck, Stephen Arnold
Douglas

Houck, Stephen Arnold Douglas
1856- ? [BE]
*American baseball player*
* Houck, Sadie

Houdar de La Motte, Antoine
1672-1731 [WBD]
*French poet and critic*
* Lamotte-Houdar

**Houdini?**
See Lovecraft, Howard Phillips

**Houdini, Harry**
See Weiss, Ehrich

**[The] Houdini in the White House**
See Roosevelt, Franklin Delano

**Houdini, King**
See Hendricks, Frederick Wilmoth

**Houdini, [Prof.] Merlin X.**
See Borgmann, Dmitri A[lfred]

**[The] Houdini of the Hardwood**
See Cousy, Robert J. [Bob]

**[The] Houdini of the Hardwood**
See Townsend, John

**Houdini, Wilmouth**
See Hendricks, Frederick Wilmoth

**Hough No**
See Wolsey, Thomas

**Hough, Richard [Alexander]** 1922-
[CA, TCC]
*British author and editor*
* Carter, Bruce
* Churchill, Elizabeth
* Strong, Pat

**Hough, Stanley Bennett** 1917-
[CA, CC, SF]
*British author*
* Gordon, Rex
* Stanley, Bennett

**Houghston, Walter** 1884-1950
[BDF, EMT, F2]
*Canadian-born actor*
* Huston, Walter

**Houghton, Claude**
See Oldfield, Claude Houghton

**Houghton, Elizabeth**
See Gilzean, Elizabeth Houghton
Blanchet

**Houghton, Evangeline** 1873-1928
[BBD]
*American opera singer*
* Florence, Evangeline

**Houghton, William** 1873-1941
[SC]
*American actor*
* Bennett, Red

**Houk, Ralph George** 1919- [BE]
*American baseball player and manager*
* [The] Major

**Houn**
See Ohara, Yutaka

**Houn, Franklin W.** 1920- [CA]
*Chinese-born author*
* Hou, Fu-Wu

**[The] Hound**
See Kelly, Robert James

**[The] Hound**
See McClain, Ted

**Hound Dog Taylor**
See Taylor, Theodore

**Hounsfield, Thirza M.**
See Bruce, Rose Evelyn

**Hountha, John Philip** 1891-1962
[NOJ]
*American jazz musician*
* Stein, Johnny

**Houpe, Sanford** 20th c. [RBE]
*American boxer*
* Houpe, Young Sanford

**Houpe, Young Sanford**
See Houpe, Sanford

**Hours, Madeleine** 1915- [CA]
*French curator and author*
* Hours-Miedan, Madeleine [or
Magdeleine]

**Hours-Miedan, Madeleine [or
Magdeleine]**
See Hours, Madeleine

**House, Anne W.**
See McCauley, Elfrieda B[abnick]

**House, Brant**
See Chadwick, Paul

**House, Eddie James, Jr.** 1902-
[DAM, IBW]
*American singer*
* House, Son
* [The] Tractor King

**House, [Henry] Frank[lin]** 1930-
[BE, BTB]
*American baseball player*
* House, Pig

**House, Fred**
See House, Wilfred E.

**House, Pig**
See House, [Henry] Frank[lin]

**House, Son**
See House, Eddie James, Jr.

**House, Wilfred E.** 1891- [BE]
*American baseball player*
* House, Fred

**Houseman, John**
See Haussmann, Jacques

**Houser, John** 1900?-1964 [BEW]
*American actor*
* Knight, John

**Houser, Robert Lee** 1943- [B10]
*American sculptor*
* Haozous, Bob

**Housman, A. E.**
See Housman, Alfred Edward

**Housman, Alfred Edward**
1859-1936 [LC]
*British poet*
* Housman, A. E.

**Houssaye, Arsene**
See Housset, Arsene

**Housset, Arsene** 1815-1896
[PA, WBD]
*French author and poet*
* Houssaye, Arsene
* L'Estoilo, Pierre

**Houstellier, Evelyn** 1898- [EMT]
*American actress and singer*
* Herbert, Evelyn

**Houston, Bee**
See Houston, Edward Wilson

**Houston, Charles Hamilton**
1895-1950 [IBW]
*American attorney and civil rights activist*
* Civil Rights Number 1, Mr.

**Houston, Chub**
See Houston, Ken

**Houston, Cisco**
See Houston, Gil[bert Vandine]

**Houston, Cissy**
See Houston, Emily Drinkard

**Houston, Edward Wilson** 1938-
[BWW]
*American singer*
* Houston, Bee

**Houston, Emily Drinkard** 20th c.
[RO2]
*American singer*
* Houston, Cissy

**Houston, Eugene A.** [PA]
*Author*
* Useless, Ipecac, M.D.

**Houston, Fats**
See Houston, Matthew

**Houston, Gil[bert Vandine]**
1918-1961 [DAM, FFA]
*American singer*
* Houston, Cisco

**Houston, Ken** 1953- [SMG]
*Canadian-born hockey player*
* Houston, Chub

**Houston, Matthew** 1910- [NOJ]
*American jazz musician*
* Houston, Fats

**Houston, R. B.**
See Rae, Hugh C[rauford]

**Houston, Renee**
See Gribbin, Katherina Houston

**Houtz, Fred** 1875-1959 [BE]
*American baseball player*
* Houtz, Lefty

**Houtz, Lefty**
See Houtz, Fred

**Houy, Clint** 20th c.
*American football team trainer*
* Houy, Pee Wee

**Houy, Pee Wee**
See Houy, Clint

**Hove, Edna** 1900-1974 [SC]
*British-born actress*
* Best, Edna

**Hoven, Ernest**
See Hooker, Fanny

**Hoven, J.**
See Vesque von Puettlingen,
Johann

**Hovey, Sonya Levien** 1886-1960
[AM]
*Russian-born screenwriter*
* Levien, Sonya

**Hovey, Wayne**
See Johnson, George William

**Hovey, William Alfred** 19th c.
[FFF]
*American writer*
* Causeur

**Hovick, June** 1916-
[BEW, FC, IPA]
*American actress*
* Havoc, June

**Hovick, Rose Louise** 1914-1970
[BEW, CC, EMT]
*American entertainer*
* Lee, Gypsy Rose

**Hovorre, M. Auburre**
See Howard, Albert Waldo

**Hovsepian, Vanig** 1918- [EJ]
*American jazz musician*
* Van Lake, Turk

**How, Cappy**
See Knight, Robert Cedric

**Howadji**
See Curtis, George William

**Howard**
See Coffin, Roland F.

**Howard**
See Noah, Mordecai Manuel

**Howard, Albert Waldo** 20th c.
[WGT]
*Author*
* Hovorre, M. Auburre

**Howard, Ann**
See Swadling, Ann Pauline

**Howard, Anna H. C.** [FFF]
*American writer*
* Elliot, Edith
* Lux Dux

**Howard, Assunta**
See Salter, Edith A.

**Howard, Avery** 1908-1966
[DAM, WWJ]
*American jazz musician*
* Howard, Kid

**Howard, Bart**
See Gustafson, Howard Joseph

**Howard, Bob**
See Joyner, Howard

**Howard, Bruce**
See Day, George

**Howard, Capt.?**
See Senarens, Luis Philip

**Howard, Carleton**
See Howe, Charles H[orace]

**Howard, Caroline**
See Glover, Caroline H.

**Howard, Caroline K.** 1794-1858
[PA]
*American author*
* Jervis, Mrs.
* [A] New England Housekeeper
* [A] Southern Matron

**Howard, Cecil**
See Smith, Cecil [Howard, III]

**Howard, Charles**
See Harbaugh, Thomas Chalmers

**Howard, Coralie**
See Cogswell, Coralie [Norris]

**Howard, Cordelia**
See Macdonald, Mrs. Edmond

**Howard, Corrie**
See Jardine, Julie Ann

**Howard, Curly**
See　Howard, Jerome [Jerry]

**Howard, Daisy**
See　McCrum, Myra Daisy

**Howard, David**
See　Davis, David Paget, III

**Howard, David Austin [Dave]**
1889-1956　[BE]
*American baseball player*
* Howard, Del

**Howard, Del**
See　Howard, David Austin [Dave]

**Howard, Del**
See　Howard, George Elmer

**Howard, Del**
See　Howard, Paul Joseph

**Howard, Dewey**
See　Howard, Duane

**Howard, Dorothy Gray** 1902-　[CA]
*American author*
* Mills, Dorothy

**Howard, Duane** 20th c.　[GW]
*American rodeo performer*
* Howard, Dewey

**Howard, Edwin** 1924-　[CA]
*American author and journalist*
* Lott, Monroe

**Howard, Elizabeth**
See　Mizner, Elizabeth Howard

**Howard, Ellie**
See　Howard, Elston Gene

**Howard, Elston Gene** 1929-　[BE]
*American baseball player*
* Howard, Ellie

**Howard, Ernest**
See　Ladd, Ernest

**Howard, Eugene**
See　Levkowitz, Isidore

**Howard, Francis** 1921-　[FC, TR]
*British actor*
* Howerd, Frankie

**Howard, Francis L.** 1919-
[EJ, PMJ]
*American jazz musician*
* Howard, Joe

**Howard, Frank**
See　Fish, Hamilton

**Howard, Frank J.** 1909-　[FB]
*American football coach*
* [The] Little Giant

**Howard, Frank Oliver** 1936-
[BE, PB, SMG]
*American baseball player*
* [The] Capital Punisher
* Gulliver in a Baseball Suit
* [The] Horse
* Howard, Hondo
* [The] Monster

**Howard, Gene**
See　Johnston, Gene Howard

**Howard, Geoffrey** 1889-1973
[SFL]
*Author*
* Dixey, Marmaduke

**Howard, George Elmer** 1877-1956
[BE]
*American baseball player*
* Howard, Del

**Howard, George, Esq.**
See　Laird, Francis C.

**Howard, Gilbert**
See　Honigfeld, Gilbert

**Howard, H. L.**
See　Wells, Charles Jeremiah

**Howard, Harlan** 1929-　[ECM]
*American songwriter*
* [The] King of Country
　Songwriters

**Howard, Harry** 20th c.　[SMG]
*American football player*
* Howard, Stones

**Howard, Hartley**
See　Ognall, Leopold Horace

**Howard, Harvey**
See　Faris, Will S.

**Howard, Henrietta [Countess of
Suffolk]** 1681-1767　[HN]
*Mistress of King George II of
England*
* Howard, Sister

**Howard, Herbert Edmund** 1900-
[WW]
*Author*
* Philmore, R.

**Howard, Herman** 20th c.　[OBW]
*American baseball player*
* Howard, Red

**Howard, Hilda Glynn** 1887-
[WWL]
*British author*
* Glynn-Ward, H.

**Howard, Hondo**
See　Howard, Frank Oliver

**Howard, J. C.**
See　Howard, James Campbell

**Howard, Jack**
See　Rathborne, St. George

**Howard, James** 1626-1701　[PA]
*Author*
* [A] London Physician

**Howard, James A[rch]** 1922-　[CA]
*American author*
* Fisher, Laine

**Howard, James Audra** 1908-
[CWG]
*American country-western performer*
* Kentucky Slim

**Howard, James Campbell** 1906-
[ART]
*British painter*
* Howard, J. C.

**Howard, Jean**
See　MacGibbon, Jean

**Howard, Jerome [Jerry]** 1906-1952
[B10, SC]
*American comic actor*
* Howard, Curly

**Howard, Jessica**
See　Schere, Monroe

**Howard, Jill**
See　Jaffe, Susanne

**Howard, Joe**
See　Howard, Francis L.

**Howard, Joe, Jr.**　[PA]
*Author*
* Howard of the Times

**Howard, John**
See　Cox, John

**Howard, [Sir] John [First Duke of
Norfolk]** 1430?-1485
[DHA, HN, WBD]
*British army officer and diplomat*
* Jack of Norfolk
* [The] Jockey of Norfolk

**Howard, John** 1726-1790
[RH, SN]
*British prison reformer*
* [The] Philanthropist

**Howard, John M.**
See　Hincks, Cyril Malcolm

**Howard, Joseph** ?-1924?　[BLB]
*American underworld figure*
* Howard, Ragtime Joe

**Howard, Joseph** 1842- ?　[FFF, PA]
*American journalist*
* Dead Beat
* Diabolus
* Jug, M. T.
* Monsieur X

**Howard, Katherine**
See　Black, Margaret K[atherine]

**Howard, Keble**
See　Bell, John Keble

**Howard, Kid**
See　Howard, Avery

**Howard, Kid**
See　Howard, Richard

**Howard, Leigh** 20th c.　[WW]
*Author*
* Krislov, Alexander

**Howard, Leslie**
See　Stainer, Leslie Howard

**Howard, Lillian**
See　White, Mrs. Charles O.

**Howard, Margaret?**
See　Burt, [Sir] Cyril

**Howard, Mark**
See　Rigsby, Howard

**Howard, Mary**
See　Mussi, Mary

**Howard, Maurice** 1954-　[SMG]
*American basketball player*
* Howard, Mo

**Howard, Mo**
See　Howard, Maurice

**Howard, Mrs. A. W. M.**　[FFF]
*Author*
* Von Vohning

**Howard, Mrs. L.**　[FFF]
*Entertainer*
* Pomeroy, Iola

**Howard, Munroe** 1913-1974　[CAP]
*American author*
* St. Clair, Philip

**Howard, Nick**
See　Nostro, Nick

**Howard, Nona**
See　Luxton, Leonora Kathrine

**[The] Howard of Russia**
See　Venning, John

**Howard of the Times**
See　Howard, Joe, Jr.

**Howard, Oliver Otis** 1830-1909
[SN]
*American army officer*
* [The] Havelock of the War

**Howard, Patrick**
See　Howard, Robert Ervin

**Howard, Paul**
See　Harbinson, A. Marshall

**Howard, Paul Joseph** 1884-　[BE]
*American baseball player*
* Howard, Del

**Howard, Peter**
See　Weiss, Howard Peter

**Howard, Peter** 1878-1969　[SC]
*Irish-born actor*
* Pete the Hermit

**Howard, Peter D[unsmore]**
1908-1965　[CAP]
*British author*
* Cato [joint pseudonym with
　Frank Owen and Michael Foote]

**Howard, Prosper** [house pseudonym]
See　Down, C. Maurice

**Howard, Prosper**
See　Hamilton, Charles Harold St.
John

**Howard, Prosper** [house pseudonym]
See　Hinton, Herbert Allan

**Howard, Ragtime Joe**
See　Howard, Joseph

**Howard, Ralph**
See　Peterson, Ralph Howard

**Howard, Red**
See　Howard, Herman

**Howard, Richard** 1928-
[BBH, CSH]
*Canadian boxer*
* Howard, Kid

**Howard, Robert Ervin** 1906-1936
[HFF, NAA, WGT]
*American writer*
* Ervin, Patrick
* Howard, Patrick
* Taveral, John
* Walser, Sam
* Ward, Robert

**Howard, Robert West** 1908-
[CA, SAT]
*American author*
* Case, Michael

**Howard, Roland**
See　Catchpole, William Leslie

**Howard, Ronnalie Roper**
See　Roper, Ronnalie J.

**Howard, Rosetta** 1914?-1974
[BWW]
*American singer*
* [The] Viper Girl

**Howard, Samuel** 1891-1955　[B10]
*American comic actor*
* Howard, Shemp

**Howard, Shemp**
See　Howard, Samuel

**Howard, Sister**
See   Howard, Henrietta [Countess of Suffolk]

**Howard, Stones**
See   Howard, Harry

**Howard, Thomas**
See   James, Jesse Woodson

**Howard, Thomas [14th Earl of Arundel]** 1585?-1646   [SN]
British patron of arts
* [The] Father of Vertu in England

**Howard, Tom**
See   Black, Tom

**Howard, Troy**
See   Paine, Lauran [Bosworth]

**Howard, Vechel**
See   Rigsby, Howard

**Howard, Warren F.**
See   Pohl, Frederik

**Howard, Wendy**
See   Black, Wendy

**Howard, [Lord] William**
1563-1640   [DNNF, HN, WBD]
British scholar
* Bauld Willie
* Belted Will

**Howard, Willie**
See   Levkowitz, Wilhelm

**Howard-Ellis, Charles** 1895-
[WWL]
Author
* Austral

**Howard-Jones, Ray** 1903-
[ART, DBA]
British artist and poet
* Ray

**Howarth, Jocelyn** 1915-1963   [SC]
Australian-born actress
* Worth, Constance

**Howarth, John**
See   Harbinson, William Allen

**Howarth, Pamela** 1954-   [CA]
British author
* Barrow, Pamela

**Howarth, Patrick John Fielding**
1916-   [AW, WW]
British author
* Francis, C. D. E.

**Howat, Gerald Malcolm David**
1928-   [WD]
British historian and writer
* Henderson-Howart, Gerald

**Howatt, Garry Robert Charles**
1952-   [SMG]
Canadian-born hockey player
* Howatt, Howie
* Howatt, Hurricane
* [The] Toy Tiger

**Howatt, Howie**
See   Howatt, Garry Robert Charles

**Howatt, Hurricane**
See   Howatt, Garry Robert Charles

**Howe, Blinky**
See   Howe, Gordon [Gordie]

**Howe, Charles H[orace]** 1912-
[CA]
American poet
* Howard, Carleton

**Howe, Doris Kathleen** 20th c.
[CA, WD]
British author
* Munro, Mary
* Nash, Newlyn [joint pseudonym with Muriel Howe]
* Stewart, Kaye

**Howe, Elias, Jr.** 1842- ?   [PA]
Author
* Chaff, Gumbo

**Howe, Frank William** 1865- ?
[NAA]
American educator and author
* Creighton, Jesse

**Howe, Gordon [Gordie]** 1928-
[BBH, SR]
Canadian-born hockey player
* Hockey, Mr.
* Howe, Blinky
* Howe, Old Blinky

**Howe, James Wong**
See   Wong Tung Jim

**Howe, John** 1630-1706?
[FFF, HN, SN]
British clergyman
* [The] Plato of the Puritans
* [The] Platonic Puritan
* [The] Puritan Plato

**Howe, John** 20th c.   [BE]
American baseball player
* Howe, Shorty

**Howe, Julia Ward** 1819-1910   [PA]
American author and composer
* [A] Lady

**Howe Les[ter Curtis]** 1895-   [BE]
American baseball player
* Howe, Lucky

**Howe, Lucky**
See   Howe Les[ter Curtis]

**Howe, Lyman** 19th c.   [SN]
American innkeeper
* [The] Squire

**Howe, M. A. De Wolfe**
See   Howe, Mark Antony De Wolfe

**Howe, Mark Antony De Wolfe**
1864-1960   [TC]
American author and editor
* Howe, M. A. De Wolfe

**Howe, Maud**
See   Elliott, Maud Howe

**Howe, Muriel** 20th c.   [WD]
British author
* Nash, Newlyn [joint pseudonym with Doris Kathleen Howe]
* Redmayne, Barbara

**Howe, Old Blinky**
See   Howe, Gordon [Gordie]

**Howe, Shorty**
See   Howe, John

**Howell, Billiken**
See   Howell, Roland Boatner

**Howell, Dixie**
See   Howell, Homer Elliott

**Howell, Dixie**
See   Howell, Millard Fillmore

**Howell, Dixie**
See   Howell, Millard Filmore

**Howell, Handsome Harry**
See   Howell, Harry

**Howell, Harry**
See   Howell, Henry Vernon

**Howell, Harry** 1876-1956
[AS, BE]
American baseball player
* Howell, Handsome Harry

**Howell, Henry** 20th c.
American politician
* Howell, Howlin' Henry

**Howell, Henry Vernon** 1932-
[CEI, HK]
Canadian-born hockey player
* Howell, Harry

**Howell, Homer Elliott** 1919-   [BE]
American baseball player
* Howell, Dixie

**Howell, Howlin' Henry**
See   Howell, Henry

**Howell, Jane L.**   [PA]
Author
* Vane, Volet

**Howell, John**
See   Halberg, Arvo

**Howell, Joshua Barnes** 1888-1966
[BWW]
American singer
* Howell, Peg Leg

**Howell, Mike** 20th c.
American football player
* Howell, Trackdown

**Howell, Millard Fillmore**
1920-1960   [BE]
American baseball player
* Howell, Dixie

**Howell, Millard Filmore**  ?-1971
[FB]
American football player
* Howell, Dixie

**Howell, Murray Donald** 1909-1950
[BE]
American baseball player
* Howell, Porky
* Howell, Red

**Howell, Patricia Hagan** 1939-
[CA]
American author
* Hagan, Patricia

**Howell, Peg Leg**
See   Howell, Joshua Barnes

**Howell, Porky**
See   Howell, Murray Donald

**Howell, Red**
See   Howell, Murray Donald

**Howell, Roland Boatner** 1892-
[BE]
American baseball player
* Howell, Billiken

**Howell, S.**
See   Styles, Frank Showell

**Howell, Scott**
See   King, Albert

**Howell, Trackdown**
See   Howell, Mike

**Howell, Virginia Tier**
See   Ellison, Virginia Howell

**Howells, Annie T.**   [FFF]
American author
* Aitiaiche

**Howerd, Frankie**
See   Howard, Francis

**Howerton, Clarence** 1913?-1975
[FIR]
American actor and circus performer
* Major Mite

**Howerton, Hopalong**
See   Howerton, William Ray [Bill]

**Howerton, William Ray [Bill]**
1921-   [BE]
American baseball player
* Howerton, Hopalong

**Howes, George W.**   [FFF]
American writer
* Strix

**Howes, Jane**
See   Shiras, Wilmar H.

**Howgrave-Graham, Robert P.** 1880-
?   [WWL]
British author
* R. P. H. G.

**Howith, Harry** 1934-   [CA, WD]
Canadian poet and playwright
* Wyman, Marc

**Howitt, John Leslie Despard** 20th
c.   [WW]
Author
* Despard, Leslie
* Leslie, John

**Howitzer, Bronson**
See   Hardman, Richards Lynden

**Howk, Joseph, Jr.** 1939-   [BLB]
American murderer
* Abdullah, Mohammed

**Howland, Frances Louise** 1855- ?
[NAA]
American author
* West, Kenyon

**Howland, Olin** 1896-1959   [FC]
American actor
* Howlin, Olin

**Howlett, John**
See   Parsons [or Persons?], Robert

**Howley, Daniel Philip** 1885-1944
[BE]
American baseball manager
* Howley, Dapper Dan

**Howley, Dapper Dan**
See   Howley, Daniel Philip

**Howley, Mark**
See   Greenwood, George Arthur

**Howliglasse, Gabriel**
See   Harvey, Gabriel

**Howlin' Henry Howell**
See   Howell, Henry

**Howlin' Mad Smith**
See   Smith, Holland Metyeire

**Howlin, Olin**
See   Howland, Olin

**Howlin' Wolf**
See   Burnett, Chester Arthur

**Howlin' Wolf**
See   Smith, John T.

**Howman, John** 1518?-1585   [WBD]
British clergyman
* Feckenham, John de

**Howorth, M. K.**
See Black, Margaret K[atherine]

**Howorth, Margaret**
See Black, Margaret K[atherine]

**Howroyd, Frank** 1882- ? [THR]
*British actor*
* Royde, Frank

**Hoy, Dummy**
See Hoy, William Ellsworth

**Hoy, George**
See Booth, George Hoy

**Hoy Ping Pong**
See Tucker, [Arthur] Wilson

**Hoy, William Ellsworth**
1862?-1961 [AS, B10, PB]
*American baseball player*
* Hoy, Dummy

**Hoyer, Mildred N.** 20th c. [IAW]
*American author and poet*
* Merritt, Si

**Hoyle, Edmond** 1672-1769 [RH]
*British author*
* [The] Father of the Game of
   Whist

**Hoyle, Martha Byrd**
See Byrd, Martha

**Hoyle, Roland Edison** 1921- [BE]
*American baseball player*
* Hoyle, Tex

**Hoyle, Tex**
See Hoyle, Roland Edison

**Hoyt, Edward Jonathan** 1840-1918
*American frontiersman*
* Buckskin Joe

**Hoyt, Edwin P[almer], Jr.** 1923-
[CA]
*American author*
* Forbes, Cabot L.
* Martin, Christopher
* Smith, C. Pritchard
* Stuart, David

**Hoyt, George H.** 1883-1962
*American basketball official*
* Basketball, Mr.

**Hoyt, Helen**
See Lyman, Helen Hoyt

**Hoyt, Mrs. Charles H.** [FFF]
*Entertainer*
* Walsh, Flora

**Hoyt, Schoolboy**
See Hoyt, Waite Charles

**Hoyt, Waite Charles** 1899-
[BAB, BE, PB]
*American baseball player*
* [The] Brooklyn Schoolboy
* Hoyt, Schoolboy
* [The] Merry Mortician

**Hozjusz**
See Dobraczynski, Jan

**Hrabosky, Alan Thomas** 1949-
[SMG]
*American baseball player*
* [The] Mad Hungarian

**Hrechkosy, David John** 1951-
[SMG]
*Canadian-born hockey player*
* [The] Wrecker

**Hribar, Bartholomew J.**
See Hribar, Erneytsck

**Hribar, Erneytsck** 1881-
*Yugoslav-born boxer*
* Hribar, Bartholomew J.
* Murphy, Mike

**Hrubec [or Hubacek], Charles**
?-1927 [BLB, PHM]
*American underworld figure*
* Big Hayes

**Hrunek, Patricia Betsy** 1929-
[BEW, TR]
*American actress*
* Palmer, Betsy

**Hruza, Lubomir** 1933- [OP]
*Czech scenic and costume designer*
* Hruza, Lubos

**Hruza, Lubos**
See Hruza, Lubomir

**Hsia Hsiao**
See Liu, Wu-chi

**Hsien Feng** 1831-1861 [WBD]
*Chinese emperor*
* I Chu

**Hsu, Benedict [Pei-Hsiung]** 1933-
[CA]
*Chinese-born American journalist*
* Chu Chung-yu

**Hsu, C. M.**
See Hsu, Chung-Ming

**Hsu, Chung-Ming** 1914- [ART]
*Indonesian artist*
* Hsu, C. M.

**Hsuan Chu**
See Shen Yen-ping

**Hsuan T'ung** 1906-1967 [WBD]
*Chinese emperor*
* Kang Te [or Kang Teh] [Exalted
   Virtue]
* P'u-yi, Henry

**Hua Kuo-feng**
See Su Kuo-feng

**Huai-nan Tzu**
See Liu An

**Huang Hsin Chao**
See Wong, Hin

**Huard, Emile** 1912- [BEW]
*American actor and singer*
* Brooks, Lawrence

**[The] Hub**
See Hubbell, Carl Owen

**Hubay, Jeno** 1858-1937 [WBD]
*Hungarian musician and composer*
* Hubay von Szalatna

**Hubay von Szalatna**
See Hubay, Jeno

**Hubbard, Al[len]** 1860-1930 [BE]
*American baseball player*
* West, Al

**Hubbard, Bernard Rosecrans**
1888- [CAT]
*American author and clergyman*
* [The] Glacier Priest

**Hubbard, Elbert** 1856-1915
[B10, TC]
*American author, editor, printer*
* Elbertus, [Fra]

**Hubbard, Frank McKinney**
1868-1930 [NAA, TC, WBD]
*American journalist and caricaturist*
* Hubbard, Kin
* Martin, Abe

**Hubbard, Hub**
See Hubbard, Phil

**Hubbard, Jerry Reed** 1937-
[ECM, RO1]
*American singer and songwriter*
* Reed, Jerry

**Hubbard, Jesse** 1895- [IBW, OBW]
*American baseball player*
* Hubbard, Mountain

**Hubbard, Kin**
See Hubbard, Frank McKinney

**Hubbard, Lafayette Ronald** 1911-
[ESF, HFF, SF]
*American author and founder of
Scientology*
* Colt, Winchester Remington
* Elron
* Engelhardt, Frederick
* Esterbrook, Tom [house
   pseudonym]
* Lafayette, Rene
* Northrup, [Capt.] B. A.
* Von Rachen, Kurt

**Hubbard, Margaret Ann**
See Priley, Margaret Hubbard

**Hubbard, Mountain**
See Hubbard, Jesse

**Hubbard, Phil** 1956-
*American basketball player*
* Hubbard, Hub

**Hubbard, Richard** 20th c. [SFL]
*Author*
* Stratton, Chris

**Hubbard, Robert Cal** 1900-
[BAB, BBH]
*American football player and
baseball official*
* [The] Gentle Giant
* His Majesty

**Hubbell, Carl Owen** 1903-
[BE, DGS, PB]
*American baseball player*
* [The] Hub
* Hubbell, Old Soupbone
* King Carl
* [The] Meal Ticket

**Hubbell, Martha Stone** 1814-1856
[PA]
*Author*
* [A] Pastor's Wife

**Hubbell, Myron**
See McElroy, William E.

**Hubbell, Old Soupbone**
See Hubbell, Carl Owen

**Hubel, Eduard** 1879- ? [LAO]
*Estonian author*
* Metsanurk, Mait

**Hubelaire, Jacubus?**
See Keller, David H[enry]

**Huber**
See Rogoz, Viorica-Georgina

**Huber, Billie**
See Huber, Juanita

**Huber, Clarence Bill** 1897-1965
[BE]
*American baseball player*
* Huber, Gilly

**Huber, Florence M.**
See Huber, Mary Florence

**Huber, George** 1947?-
*American poker player*
* Huber, Mustache George

**Huber, Gilly**
See Huber, Clarence Bill

**Huber, Johann [or John] Rudolphe**
1658?-1748 [DNNS, RH]
*Swiss painter*
* [The] Tintoretto of Switzerland

**Huber, Juanita** 1905-1965 [SC]
*American actress and dancer*
* Huber, Billie

**Huber, Mary Florence** 20th c.
[NAA]
*American writer and poet*
* Huber, Florence M.

**Huber, Mrs. Fred J.** [FFF]
*Entertainer*
* Allyne, Kitty

**Huber, Mustache George**
See Huber, George

**Hubert**
See Bland, John O. P.

**Hubert** 656- 730?
[DEP, FFF, HN]
*Saint*
* [The] Apostle of the Ardennes

**Hubert, Allison T. S.** [FB]
*American football player*
* Hubert, Pooley

**Hubert, Bubber**
See Hubert, Willie

**Hubert, Frank**
See Shaw, Frank H.

**Hubert, Pooley**
See Hubert, Allison T. S.

**Hubert, Willie** [OBW]
*American baseball player*
* Hubert, Bubber

**Hubler, Richard Gibson** 1912-
[CA]
*American author*
* Gibson, Harry Clark

**Hubschmid, Paul** 1917- [FC]
*German-Swiss actor*
* Christian, Paul

**Huc, Philippe** 1889-1941 [WBD]
*French poet*
* Dereme, Tristan

**Huch, Ricarda** 1864-1947 [EWL]
*German poet, author, historian*
* Hugo, Richard

**Huchet, Claire**
See Bishop, Claire Huchet

**Huckle, Paul**
See Sullivan, John Florence

**Hucko, Michael Andrew** 1918-
[DAM, EJ, PMJ]
*American jazz musician*
* Hucko, Peanuts

**Hucko, Peanuts**
See Hucko, Michael Andrew

**[The] Huckster**
See Darius I

**Hudd, John**
See Edlin, John Bruce

**Huddleston, Clarence** 20th c.
[SMG]
*American football and basketball player*
* Huddleston, Hud

**Huddleston, Dee**
See Huddleston, Walter D.

**Huddleston, Hud**
See Huddleston, Clarence

**Huddleston, Sisley** 1883- [LAO]
*British author and journalist*
* Vernon, Peter

**Huddleston, Walter D.**
*American politician*
* Huddleston, Dee

**Hudgens, A[lice] Gayle** 1941- [CA]
*American author*
* Watson, Gayle Hudgens

**Hudgins, Elmore** 20th c. [BBH]
*American sports information director*
* Hudgins, Scoop

**Hudgins, Scoop**
See Hudgins, Elmore

**Hudkins, Ace** 1905-1973
[BX, RBE]
*American boxer*
* [The] Nebraska Wildcat

**Hudleston, Gilbert Roger**
1874-1936 [WGT]
*British author*
* Pater, [Philip] Roger

**Hudleston, John**
See Dent, C. H.

**Hudleston, Robert**
See Dent, C. H.

**Hudlin, Ace**
See Hudlin, George Willis

**Hudlin, George Willis** 1906-
[BE, PB]
*American baseball player*
* Hudlin, Ace

**Hudnut, Winifred**
See Shaunessy, Winifred

**Hudson, Alec**
See Holmes, Wilfred Jay

**Hudson, Billy Jack**
See Hudson, Rex Haughton

**Hudson, Frank**
See Kimball, George

**Hudson, Frank C.**
See Colvin, Fred Herbert

**Hudson, Gabrielle** 1912- [THR]
*British actress and singer*
* Brune, Gabrielle

**Hudson, George** 1800-1871
[DNNS, HN, RH]
*British speculator*
* [The] Railway King

**Hudson, H. Lindsay** 20th c.
[WWL]
*British author and journalist*
* Lindsay, Harry

**Hudson, Hal Campbell** 1927- [BE]
*American baseball player*
* Hudson, Lefty

**Hudson, Harry**
See Hunter, Henry

**Hudson, Hoyt** 20th c. [CA]
*Author*
* Smith, John [joint pseudonym with Marvin Theodore Herrick]

**Hudson, James** 1873-1951 [THR]
*British actor*
* Harcourt, James

**Hudson, James** 1934- [RO1]
*American singer*
* Hudson, Pookie

**Hudson, Jan**
See Smith, George H[enry]

**Hudson, Jeffery**
See Crichton, [John] Michael

**Hudson, Jeffrey** 1619-1682 [SN]
*British dwarf*
* Minimus, Lord

**Hudson, Lefty**
See Hudson, Hal Campbell

**Hudson, Lou** 1944-
*American basketball player*
* Hudson, SuperLou

**Hudson, Meg**
See Koehler, Margaret [Hudson]

**Hudson, Peggy**
See Herz, Peggy

**Hudson, Pookie**
See Hudson, James

**Hudson, Rex Haughton** 1953-
[SMG]
*American baseball player*
* Hudson, Billy Jack

**Hudson, Robert**
See Mantell, Robert Bruce

**Hudson, Rock**
See Scherer, Roy Harold, Jr.

**Hudson, Stephen**
See Schiff, Sydney

**Hudson, SuperLou**
See Hudson, Lou

**Hudson, W. H.**
See Hudson, William Henry

**Hudson, W. H.**
See Hudson, William Henry

**Hudson, William Cadwalader**
1843-1915 [WW]
*Author*
* North, Barclay

**Hudson, William Henry** 1841-1922
[LC, TC]
*British author*
* Harford, Henry
* Hudson, W. H.

**Hudson, William Henry** 1862-1918
[LC]
*British author*
* Hudson, W. H.

**Hudspeth, Highpockets**
See Hudspeth, Robert

**Hudspeth, Robert** 20th c. [OBW]
*American baseball player*
* Hudspeth, Highpockets

**Hueffer, Ford Madox** 1873-1939
[EWL, LC, TC]
*British author and critic*
* Chaucer, Daniel
* Ford, Ford Madox
* Haig, Fenil

**Hueffer, Francis**
See Hueffer, Franz

**Hueffer, Franz** 1845-1889 [WBD]
*German-born music critic and author*
* Hueffer, Francis

**Hueffer, Oliver Madox** 1879- ?
[WWL]
*Author and playwright*
* Wardle, Jane

**Huerlimann, Bettina**
See Huerlimann-Kiepenheuer, Bettina

**Huerlimann-Kiepenheuer, Bettina**
1909- [TBJ]
*German-born author*
* Huerlimann, Bettina

**Huerta, Baldemar** 1937-
*American singer*
* Fender, Freddy

**Huerta Rivera, Jose** 1934- [GS]
*Mexican bullfighter*
* [El] Indio de Tetela [The Indian from Tetela]
* Joselito [Little Joe]

**Hues, Mrs. Frank** [FFF]
*Entertainer*
* Miller, May

**[El] Hueso [The Bone]**
See Videla, Jorge Rafael

**Hueston, Billy** 1896-1957 [ASC]
*American composer, publisher, producer*
* Morgan, Bruce

**Huet, Jean** 20th c. [WECO]
*French cartoonist*
* Ache, Jean

**Huether, Anne Frances**
See Freeman, Anne Frances

**Huey Piano Smith**
See Smith, Huey

**Huff, Jack**
See Kirkhuff, John

**Huff, Robert Lee** 1934- [FB, IPA]
*American football player*
* Huff, Sam

**Huff, Sam**
See Huff, Robert Lee

**Huff, Tom Elmer** 1938?-
*American author*
* Marlow, Edwina
* Parker, Beatrice
* St. Clair, Katherine
* Wilde, Jennifer

**Huffman, Barbara** 1934- [FC]
*American actress*
* Eden, Barbara

**Hufschmid, Maynard Michael**
1912- [CA]
*American writer*
* Hufschmidt, Maynard Michael

**Hufschmidt, Maynard Michael**
See Hufschmid, Maynard Michael

**Hugensz, Lucas** 1494-1533 [WBD]
*Dutch painter and engraver*
* D'Olanda, Luca
* Jacobsz, Lucas
* Lucas van Leyden

**Huggins**
See Dolland, George

**Huggins, Hug**
See Huggins, Miller James

**Huggins, Jeremy** 1935- [FC, TR]
*British actor*
* Brett, Jeremy

**Huggins, Miller James** 1879-1929
[AS, BAB, BE]
*American baseball player and manager*
* Huggins, Hug
* Little Mr. Everywhere
* [The] Mighty Manager
* [The] Mighty Mite
* [The] Mite Manager
* Proctor, Miller
* [The] Rabbit

**Huggins, Ruth Mabel**
See Arthur, Ruth M.

**Huggins, William** 1820-1884
[DEP, DNNS, HN]
*British painter*
* [The] Liverpool Landseer

**Hugh [or Hugues]** ?- 956
[DNNS, WBD]
*Count of Paris and Duke of France*
* [The] Great
* [The] White

**Hugh d'Avranches** ?-1101 [HN]
*Anglo-Norman leader*
* Chester, Earl of
* Hugh Wolf [Hugh Lupus]

**Hugh [or Hugo] of Cluny**
1024-1109 [WBD]
*Saint*
* [The] Great

**Hugh Wolf [Hugh Lupus]**
See Hugh d'Avranches

**Hugh II** 12th c. [WBD]
*Duke of Burgundy*
* Borel

**Hughes, Annie**
See Hughes-Gass, Annie

**Hughes, Ball** 19th c. [DEP]
*British dandy*
* [The] Golden Ball

**Hughes, Billy**
See Hughes, Wilfred Perry

**Hughes, Brenda**
See Colloms, Brenda

**Hughes, Brent**
See Hughes, Brenton Alexander

**Hughes, Brenton Alexander** 1943-
[HK, HR]
*Canadian-born hockey player*
* Hughes, Brent

**Hughes, Colin**
See Creasey, John

**Hughes, David**
See Blees, David Hughes

**Hughes de St. Victor** 1096?-1140?
[HN]
*Theologian and philosopher*
* [The] Second St. Augustine

**Hughes, Den[n]is [Talbot]** 20th c.
[SFL]
*British author*
* Barry, Ray
* Cameron, Berl [house pseudonym, Curtis Warren]
* Carter, Dee
* Charles, Neil [house pseudonym, Curtis Warren]
* Elliot, Lee [house pseudonym, Curtis Warren]
* Hunt, Gill [house pseudonym, Curtis Warren]
* Kent, Brad [house pseudonym, Curtis Warren]
* Lane, John [house pseudonym, Curtis Warren]
* Reed, Van [house pseudonym, Curtis Warren]
* Rey, Russell [house pseudonym, Curtis Warren]

**Hughes, E.**
See Cherer, Madame T.

**Hughes, Eden**
See Butterworth, William Edmund, III

**Hughes, Fielden** 20th c. [SFL]
*British author*
* Enfield, Hugh

**Hughes, Hazel**
See Hepenstall, Hazel

**Hughes, J.** 20th c. [CEI]
*Hockey player*
* Hughes, Rusty

**Hughes, Jeep**
See Hughes, Roy John

**Hughes, John** 1798-1864 [PA]
*Author*
* Buller of Brazenose

**Hughes, John Ceiriog** 1832-1887
[WBD]
*Welsh poet*
* Ceiriog

**Hughes, Johnnie Lee** 20th c. [IBW]
*American politician*
* Hughes, Pete

**Hughes, [James] Langston**
1902-1967 [CLC, MWD]
*American poet, author, playwright*
* [The] Poet Laureate of Harlem

**Hughes, Lefty**
See Hughes, Vern[on Alexander]

**Hughes, Leroy** 20th c. [SMG]
*American football player*
* Hughes, Mini Tank

**Hughes, Long Tom**
See Hughes, Thomas J.

**Hughes, M. Alison**
See Steed, Mabel A.

**Hughes, Mary** [PA]
*Author*
* Aunt Mary

**Hughes, Matilda**
See MacLeod, Charlotte [Matilda Hughes]

**Hughes, Mini Tank**
See Hughes, Leroy

**Hughes, Patrick C.** 1908-
[EJ, PMJ]
*British jazz musician and critic*
* Hughes, Spike
* Mike

**Hughes, Pete**
See Hughes, Johnnie Lee

**Hughes, Philip**
See Phillips, Hugh

**Hughes, Robert J.** 1916- [ASC]
*Canadian-born musician*
* Denton, James
* Moffatt, James

**Hughes, Roy John** 1911- [BE, BN]
*American baseball player*
* Hughes, Jeep
* Hughes, Sage
* Hughes, Whispering Roy

**Hughes, Rush**
See Hughes, Russell Sheldon

**Hughes, Russell Sheldon**
1910-1958 [SC]
*American actor and screenwriter*
* Hughes, Rush

**Hughes, Rusty**
See Hughes, J.

**Hughes, Sage**
See Hughes, Roy John

**Hughes, Sam**
See Wilks, Brian

**Hughes, Spike**
See Hughes, Patrick C.

**Hughes, Thomas** 1823- ? [PA]
*Author*
* Brown, Tom
* Old Boy
* Viator, Vacuus

**Hughes, Thomas J.** 1878-1956
[AS, BE]
*American baseball player*
* Hughes, Long Tom

**Hughes, Vern[on Alexander]**
1893-1961 [BE]
*American baseball player*
* Hughes, Lefty

**Hughes, Virginia**
See Wallis, Geraldine McDonald

**Hughes, Walter Dudley** 1918-
[AW]
*British educator and author*
* Derventio

**Hughes, Walter Llewellyn** 1910-
[ESF, SFL, WGT]
*British author*
* Walters, Hugh

**Hughes, Whispering Roy**
See Hughes, Roy John

**Hughes, Wilfred Perry** 20th c.
[BBH]
*Canadian football coach*
* Hughes, Billy

**Hughes, William Jesse** 1912-
[AW, WD]
*British author*
* [The] Dominie
* Hallam
* Northerner

**Hughes, Zach**
See Zachary, Hugh

**Hughes-Gass, Annie** 1869-1954
[THR]
*British actress*
* Hughes, Annie

**Hughey, Coldwater Jim**
See Hughey, James Ulysses

**Hughey, James Ulysses** 1869-1945
[BE]
*American baseball player*
* Hughey, Coldwater Jim

**Hughson, Cecil Carlton** 1916- [BE]
*American baseball player*
* Hughson, Tex

**Hughson, Tex**
See Hughson, Cecil Carlton

**Hugi, Maurice Gaspard** 20th c.
[SFL]
*Author*
* Kent, Brad [house pseudonym, Curtis Warren]

**Hugill, Robert** 20th c. [WD]
*British author*
* Gill, Hugh

**Hugo, Etienne**
See Hugo, Leon Hargreaves

**Hugo, Leon Hargreaves** 1931-
[IAW]
*South African author*
* De Villiers, Victor
* Hugo, Etienne

**Hugo, Richard**
See Huch, Ricarda

**Hugo, Victor Marie** 1802-1885
[SN]
*French author*
* [L']Enfant Sublime
* [The] Michael Angelo of Modern Literature
* [The] Sublime Child

**[The] Huguenot Pope**
See Mornay, Philippe de [Seigneur du Plessis-Marly]

**Huguet**
See Armand, Francais

**Huhn, Emil Hugo** 1892-1925 [BE]
*American baseball player*
* Huhn, Hap

**Huhn, Hap**
See Huhn, Emil Hugo

**Hulanicki, Barbara** 20th c. [WFA]
*British fashion designer*
* Biba

**Hulbert, Hot Rod**
See Hulbert, Maurice

**Hulbert, Joan Margery** 1911-
[AW, IAW]
*British writer*
* Rostron, P. R.
* Rostron, Primrose

**Hulbert, Lloyd**
See Pope, F. W.

**Hulbert, Maurice** 1922- [IBW]
*American dancer and disc jockey*
* Hulbert, Hot Rod

**Hulburd, Bud**
See Hulburd, H. L.

**Hulburd, H. L.** ?-1973 [SC]
*American actor and stunt performer*
* Hulburd, Bud

**Huley, Pete** 1893-1973 [SC]
*Austrian-born actor and gold prospector*
* Klondike Pete

**Hull, E. Mayne**
See Van Vogt, Edna Mayne Hull

**Hull, Eric Traviss**
See Harnan, Terry

**Hull, H. Braxton**
See Jacobs, Helen Hull

**Hull, Henry**
See Vaughan, Henry

**Hull, James** [PA]
*Author*
* Restless, Jimmy

**Hull, Josephine**
See Sherwood, Josephine

**Hull, Opal**
See Lehnus, Opal [Hull]

**Hull, Richard**
See Sampson, Richard Henry

**Hull, Robert Marvin [Bobby]** 1939-
[FHE, HK]
*Canadian-born hockey player*
* [The] Golden Jet

**Hull, Samuel** [FFF]
*Author*
* Abdiel

**Hullah, Mrs.** [PA]
*Author*
* M. H.

**Hulme, T. E.**
See Hulme, Thomas Ernest

**Hulme, Thomas Ernest** 1883-1917
[LC]
*British writer and translator*
* Hulme, T. E.

**Hulme Beaman, S. G.**
See Hulme Beaman, Sydney George

**Hulme Beaman, Sydney George**
1886-1932 [TCC]
*British author*
* Hulme Beaman, S. G.

**Hulsebos, Jan** 1925- [FDG]
*Dutch director*
* Vrijman, Jan

**Hulvey, Hank**
See Hulvey, James Hensel

**Hulvey, James Hensel** 1897- [BE]
*American baseball player*
* Hulvey, Hank

**[The] Human Beast**
See Wagner, Gustav Franz

[The] Human Billiard Table
See Kestner, Paul

[The] Human Blur
See Griffey, Ken

[The] Human Bowling Ball
See Nottingham, Don

[The] Human Canary
See Khaury, Herbert

[The] Human Computer
See Magriel, Paul

[The] Human Concrete Mixer
See Helassie, Saile

[The] Human Eraser
See Webster, Marvin

[The] Human Flea
See Bonner, Frank J.

[The] Human Fly
See Rojatt, Rick

[The] Human Hairpin
See Harris, Harry

[The] Human Hairpin
See Philps, Arthur Carlton

[The] Human Mosquito
See Slagle, James Franklin

[The] Human Polar Bear
See Brickner, Gustave

[The] Human Punching Bag
See Giannone, Saverio

[The] Human Scissors
See Harris, Harry

[The] Human Whipcord
See Savidge, Ralph Austin

[The] Human Windmill
See Greb, Edward Henry

[The] Humanitarian Prince
See Talal bin Abdul Azziz al-Saud

Humbaraci, D[emir] Arslan 1923-
[CA]
Turkish-born British journalist
* Abdallah, Omar
* Herve, Jean-Luc

Humberger, William ?-1978 [FIR]
Actor
* Murdock, William

Humberto
See Coelho, Humberto

Humble and Heavenly-Minded
See Sibbes, Richard

Humboldt, [Friedrich Heinrich]
Alexander von 1769-1859 [HN]
German naturalist and statesman
* [The] Father of Physical
Geography

Hume, Abraham 19th c. [DEL]
British author
* [A] Lancashire Incumbent

Hume, Adversity
See Hume, Joseph

Hume, David
See Turner, John Victor

Hume, David 1711-1776 [PA]
Author
* Waitford, Hannah

Hume, Fergus
See Hume, Ferguson Wright

Hume, Ferguson Wright
1859-1932 [LC, TC, WW]
British-born author
* Hume, Fergus

Hume, Frances
See Buckland-Wright, Mary
Elizabeth

Hume, Joseph 1777-1855 [WBD]
British politician
* Hume, Adversity

Hume, Mickey
See Bevard, Camille

Humes, Helen 20th c. [NP]
American jazz musician
* Humes, Homey

Humes, Homey
See Humes, Helen

Humfrey, C.
See Osborne, Charles Humfrey
Caulfeild

Hummel, John Edwin 1883-1959
[BE]
American baseball player
* Hummel, Silent John

Hummel, Silent John
See Hummel, John Edwin

[The] Hump
See Humphrey, Hubert Horatio

Humpage, Farsley
See Humpage, Geoffrey William

Humpage, Geoffrey William 1954-
[DC]
British cricketer
* Humpage, Farsley
* Humpage, Humpty

Humpage, Humpty
See Humpage, Geoffrey William

[The] Humpback
See Amelunghi, Geronimo
[Girolamo]

[The] Humpback
See Solari, Andrea

Humperdinck, Engelbert
See Dorsey, Arnold [Gerry]

Humperdink, Engelbert 1854-1921
[DNNS]
German composer
* [The] Modern Wagner

Humphrey [Duke of Gloucester and
Earl of Pembroke] 1391-1447
[DNNF, DNNS, HN]
Lord protector of England
* [The] Good Duke Humphrey
* [The] Good Duke of Gloucester

Humphrey, Barbara Ann 1950-
[EJ7]
American jazz musician
* Humphrey, Bobbi

Humphrey, Bobbi
See Humphrey, Barbara Ann

Humphrey, Happy
See Cobb, William J.

Humphrey, Hubert Horatio
1911-1978
American legislator and vice
president
* H. H. H.
* [The] Happy Warrior
* [The] Hump

Humphrey, Hubert Horatio, III 20th
c.
American politician
* Humphrey, Skip

Humphrey, L. J. 20th c. [WWL]
British writer
* R. H. L.

Humphrey, Skip
See Humphrey, Hubert Horatio,
III

Humphrey, Terry
See Humphrey, Terryal Gene

Humphrey, Terryal Gene 1949-
[BR]
American baseball player
* Humphrey, Terry

Humphreys, Andrew Atkinson
1810-1883 [FFF, SN]
American army officer
* Old Mathematics

Humphreys, Arthur L. 1865- ?
[WWL]
British author
* Pendenys, Arthur

Humphreys, B. V.
See Schneider, Betty Vance
Humphreys

Humphreys, John
See Owain, Owain

Humphreys [or Humphries], Joshua
1751-1838 [FFF]
American shipbuilder
* [The] Father of the American
Navy

Humphreys, Mary Eglantyne Hill
1914- [CA]
British economist and author
* Hill, Polly

Humphreys [or Humphries],
Murray [BLB, PHM]
American underworld figure
* [The] Camel

Humphreys, Violet 1914- [THR]
British actress
* Loxley, Violet

Humphreys Booth, Eliza Margaret J.
[Gollan] ?-1938 [LAO, LC, WW]
Scottish author
* Rita

Humphries, Adelaide M. 1898-
[CAP, WW]
American author
* Harris, Kathleen
* Way, Wayne
* West, Token

Humphries, David John 1953- [DC]
British cricketer
* Humphries, Humpty

Humphries, Elsie Mary 1905-
[AW, CA, WD]
British author
* Forrester, Mary

Humphries, Humpty
See Humphries, David John

Humphries, Jack
See Kelly, Jonathan F.

Humphries, Sydney Vernon 1907-
[WD]
British author
* Vane, Michael

Humphrys, Geoffrey
See Humphrys, Leslie George

Humphrys, Leslie George 1921-
[AW, SFL, WD]
British author
* Brack, Vektis [house pseudonym,
Gannet Press]
* Condray, Bruno
* Humphrys, Geoffrey

Humpty-Dumpty
See King, William

Hundertwasser, Fritz
See Stowasser, Friedrich

Hundley, Hot Rod
See Hundley, Rod

Hundley, Mrs. E. D. [PA]
Author
* Grey, Fannie

Hundley, Rod 1934- [BB, SMG]
American basketball player and
sportscaster
* Hundley, Hot Rod

Huneycutt, Betty 1922?-1964
[BEW]
American theatrical performer
* Coleman, Carole

Hung Hsiu-ch'uan 1812-1864
[WBD]
Leader of rebellion in China
* T'ien-wang [Heavenly Prince]

Hung Long Tom
See Owen, Frank

Hung Wu
See Chu Yuan-chang

[The] Hungarian Rhapsody
See Baulsy, Banky Vilma

[The] Hungarian Rhapsody
See Medwick, Joseph Michael

Hunger
See Olaf I

Hungerford, Margaret Wolfe
1855?-1897 [WBD]
Irish author
* [The] Duchess

Hungerford, Orton [or Orison]
Whipple, II 1930- [FC, SW]
American actor
* Hardin, Ty

Hungerford, Pixie
See Brinsmead, Hesba Fay

Hungling, Bernard Herman [Bernie]
1896-1968 [BE]
American baseball player
* Hungling, Bud

Hungling, Bud
See Hungling, Bernard Herman
[Bernie]

Hunkins, Lee
See Hunkins, Leecynth

Hunkins, Leecynth 1930- [IBW]
American playwright
* Hunkins, Lee

**Hunnefield, Wild Bill**
See Hunnefield, William Fenton

**Hunnefield, William Fenton** 1899-
[BE]
*American baseball player*
* Hunnefield, Wild Bill

**Hunold, Christian Friedrich**
1680-1721 [WBD]
*German author*
* Menantes

**Hunsecker, Ralph Uriah** 1914-
[BEW, EMT]
*American composer, lyricist, singer*
* Blane, Ralph

**Hunt, Barbara** 1907- [SFL]
*American author*
* Watters, Barbara H.

**Hunt, Ben[jamin Franklin]** 1888-
[BE]
*American baseball player*
* Hunt, Highpockets

**Hunt, Bernice Kohn** 1920- [IAW]
*American author*
* Kohn, Bernice

**Hunt, Charlotte**
See Hodges, Doris Marjorie

**Hunt, Clarence**
See Holman, [Clarence] Hugh

**Hunt, Diana** 1897-1937 [BEW]
*British-born actress*
* Wilson, Diana

**Hunt, Dorothy Alice** 1896- [AW]
*British author*
* Collyer, Doric

**Hunt, E[verette] Howard, Jr.** 1918-
[CA, EMD, WW]
*American intelligence agent and
author*
* Baxter, John
* Davis, Gordon
* Dietrich, Robert
* St. John, David

**Hunt, Earthquake**
See Hunt, Jim L.

**Hunt, Edgar H[ubert]** 1909- [CAP]
*British author and music teacher*
* Fidelio

**Hunt, Eleanor** 1907- [F2, FC]
*American actress*
* Compton, Joyce

**Hunt, Francesca**
See Holland, Isabelle

**Hunt, Francis** [house pseudonym]
[Stratemeyer Syndicate]
See Stratemeyer, Edward L.

**Hunt, Frazier** 1885-1967 [WA]
*American journalist*
* Hunt, Spike

**Hunt, Frederick Knight** 1814-1854
[PA]
*Author*
* [A] Student of Law

**Hunt, George Wylie Paul**
1859-1934 [SC]
*American politician and actor*
* Hunt, W. P.

**Hunt, Gill** [house pseudonym, Curtis
Warren]
See Brunner, John [Kilian
Houston]

**Hunt, Gill** [house pseudonym, Curtis
Warren]
See Griffiths, David Arthur

**Hunt, Gill** [house pseudonym, Curtis
Warren]
See Hughes, Den[n]is [Talbot]

**Hunt, Gill** [house pseudonym, Curtis
Warren]
See Jennison, John W[illiam]

**Hunt, Gill** [house pseudonym, Curtis
Warren]
See Tubb, Edwin Charles

**Hunt, Golf Bag**
See Hunt, Samuel McPherson

**Hunt, H. L.**
See Hunt, Haroldson Lafayette

**Hunt, Haroldson Lafayette**
1889?-1974
*American industrialist*
* Hunt, H. L.

**Hunt, Harrison**
See Ballard, [Willis] Todhunter

**Hunt, Henry** 1773-1835
[DNNS, RH]
*British politician*
* Hunt, Orator

**Hunt, Highpockets**
·See Hunt, Ben[jamin Franklin]

**Hunt, Hurricane**
See Hunt, Robert [Bobby]

**Hunt, James** 1948-
*British auto racer*
* [The] Shunt

**Hunt, Jim L.** 1937?-1975 [B10]
*American football player and coach*
* Hunt, Earthquake

**Hunt, Jodie**
See Hunt, [Oliver] Joel

**Hunt, [Oliver] Joel** 1905- [BE]
*American baseball player*
* Hunt, Jodie

**Hunt, Katherine Chandler** 20th c.
[WW]
*Author*
* Nash, Chandler

**Hunt, Kyle**
See Creasey, John

**Hunt, [James Henry] Leigh**
1784-1859 [SN]
*British author and poet*
* [The] Jove of the Modern Critical
Olympus
* Lord Mayor of the Theatric Sky

**Hunt, Marcia** 1917- [FC]
*American actress*
* Hunt, Marsha

**Hunt, Marsha**
See Hunt, Marcia

**Hunt, Maurice**
See Parsons, B.

**Hunt, Nigel**
See Greenbank, Anthony Hunt

**Hunt, Orator**
See Hunt, Henry

**Hunt, Pee Wee**
See Hunt, Walter

**Hunt, Penelope**
See Napier, Priscilla

**Hunt, Peter** [joint pseudonym with
George Worthing Yates]
See Marshall, Charles Hunt

**Hunt, Peter** [joint pseudonym with
Charles Hunt Marshall]
See Yates, George Worthing

**Hunt, Robert [Bobby]** 20th c.
[IBW]
*American wrestler*
* Hunt, Hurricane

**Hunt, Robert Lile**
See Davie, Robert Worthington

**Hunt, Ronald Kenneth** 1941- [PB]
*American baseball player*
* Hunt, Zeke

**Hunt, Samuel McPherson** ?-1955
[BLB, PHM]
*American underworld figure*
* Hunt, Golf Bag

**Hunt, Spike**
See Hunt, Frazier

**Hunt, W. P.**
See Hunt, George Wylie Paul

**Hunt, Walter** 1907-1979
[EJ, PMJ, WWJ]
*American jazz musician*
* Hunt, Pee Wee

**Hunt, Zeke**
See Hunt, Ronald Kenneth

**[The] Hunter**
See Philibert I

**Hunter, Alberta** 1895- [BWW]
*American singer*
* Alix, May
* America's Foremost Brown Blues
Singer
* Beatty, Josephine
* Marian Anderson of the Blues
* Roberts, Helen

**Hunter, Alison**
See Hunter-Blair, Norma

**Hunter, Anson**
See Orrmont, Arthur

**Hunter, Big Game**
See Hunter, Les

**Hunter, Bluebell Matilda** 1887-
[WGT, WW]
*Author*
* Guildford, John
* Lancing, George

**Hunter, Buddy**
See Hunter, Harold James

**Hunter, Cat**
See Hunter, James Augustus [Jim]

**Hunter, Catfish**
See Hunter, James Augustus [Jim]

**Hunter, Christine**
See Hunter, Maud L[ily]

**Hunter, Clarence** 1923- [IBW]
*American entertainer*
* Chandu the Magician

**Hunter, Clementine**
See Keynes, Helen Mary

**Hunter, Dave** 1958- [SMG]
*Canadian-born hockey player*
* Hunter, Hunts

**Hunter, Dawe**
See Downie, Mary Alice

**Hunter, Deacon**
See Hunter, Steve

**Hunter, E. Waldo**
See Waldo, Edward Hamilton

**Hunter, Eileen Helen** 1905- [AW]
*British author*
* Clements, E. H.

**Hunter, Evan**
See Lombino, Salvatore A.

**Hunter, Frederick Creighton**
1880-1963 [BE]
*American baseball player*
* Hunter, Newt

**Hunter, Gernie**
See Rellihan, Gernie Floss Hunter

**Hunter, Goldfish**
See Hunter, James Augustus [Jim]

**Hunter, Harold James** 1947- [BE]
*American baseball player*
* Hunter, Buddy

**Hunter, Henry**
See Jacobson, Arthur

**Hunter, Henry** [PA]
*Author*
* Hudson, Harry

**Hunter, Henry MacGregor** 1929-
[GF]
*American golfer*
* Hunter, Mac

**Hunter, Hunts**
See Hunter, Dave

**Hunter, Ivory Joe**
See Hunter, Joseph

**Hunter, James Augustus [Jim]**
1946- [IPA, PB, WWB]
*American baseball player*
* [The] Fish
* Hunter, Cat
* Hunter, Catfish
* Hunter, Goldfish

**Hunter, Jean**
See Hunter, [Alfred] John

**Hunter, Jeffrey**
See McKinnies, Henry H.

**Hunter, Joe**
See McNeilly, Wilfred Glassford

**Hunter, John**
See Ballard, [Willis] Todhunter

**Hunter, John**
See Hunter, Maud L[ily]

**Hunter, [Alfred] John** 1891-1961
[MBF, WW, WWL]
*British author*
* Addiscombe, John
* Brenning, L. H.
* Brent, Francis
* Dax, Anthony
* Drummond, Anthony
* Hunter, Jean
* Meriton, Peter

**Hunter, John Kelso** [SN]
*Scottish painter*
* J. K.
* Kobbler, John

**Hunter, Joseph**
See Coleridge, Henry Nelson

**Hunter, Joseph** 1911-1974
[DAM, IBW]
*American singer and songwriter*
* Hunter, Ivory Joe

**Hunter, Kim**
See Cole, Janet

**Hunter, Leah** 1892- [THR]
*British actress*
* Bateman, Leah

**Hunter, Lem**
See Hunter, Robert Lemuel

**Hunter, Les** 1942- [BB]
*American basketball player*
* Hunter, Big Game

**Hunter, Lois**
See Nowedonah

**Hunter, Mac**
See Hunter, Henry MacGregor

**Hunter, Maud L[ily]** 1910-
[CA, IAW]
*British author*
* Hunter, Christine
* Hunter, John
* Steer, Charlotte

**Hunter, Mollie**
See McIlwraith, Maureen Mollie
Hunter

**Hunter, Mrs. Henry** [FFF]
*Entertainer*
* Searle, Louise

**Hunter, Newt**
See Hunter, Frederick Creighton

**Hunter, Patsy**
See Pettigrew, Leola B.

**Hunter, Paul**
See Weaver, Bertrand

**[The] Hunter Preacher**
See Lynn, Benjamin

**Hunter, Robert Lemuel** 1863-1956
[BE]
*American baseball player*
* Hunter, Lem

**Hunter, Ross**
See Fuss, Martin

**Hunter, Rowland**
See Catchpole, William Leslie

**Hunter, Seymour** 20th c. [SMG]
*Hockey team official*
* Hunter, Sonny

**Hunter, Slim**
See Broonzy, William Lee Conley

**Hunter, Sonny**
See Hunter, Seymour

**Hunter, Steve** 20th c. [RM]
*Musician*
* Hunter, Deacon

**Hunter, Tab**
See Gelien, Art[hur Andrew]

**Hunter, William F.** 1901- [NAA]
*American author*
* Retnuh X

**Hunter-Blair, Norma** 1932- [AW]
*British author*
* Hunter, Alison

**Hunter Blair, Pauline Clarke** 1921-
[AW, CA, SAT]
*British author*
* Clare, Helen
* Clarke, Pauline

**Hunter Blair, Peter** 1912- [AW]
*British author*
* Blair, Peter

**Hunting, M. E.** 20th c. [WWL]
*Poet*
* Lucia

**Hunting, Sylvia**
See Mannix, Mary Walsh

**Huntingdon, Harry**
See Pentelow, John Nix

**Huntingdon, John**
See Phillips, Gerald William

**Huntingdon, John** 16th c. [FFF]
*British author*
* Pantolabus, Ponce

**Huntington, H. S.**
See Smith, Herbert Huntington

**Huntington, Mrs. Wright** [FFF]
*Entertainer*
* Periere, Inez

**Huntington, Thomas Waterman**
1893- [WWL]
*Author*
* Frost, Morgan

**Huntington, William** 1744-1813
[DEL, SN]
*British clergyman*
* [The] Coal Heaver Preacher
* Sinner Saved

**Huntley, G. P., Jr.** 1904-
*American-born actor*
* Huntley, Timothy

**Huntley, Mrs. J. H.** [FFF]
*Entertainer*
* Kennedy, Florence

**Huntley, Timothy**
See Huntley, G. P., Jr.

**Huntly, Frances E.**
See Mayne, Ethel Colburn

**Huntly, Stanley** 1846- ? [PA]
*Author*
* Spoopendyke

**Hunton, Mary**
See Gilzean, Elizabeth Houghton
Blanchet

**Huntsman**
See Berkeley, F. Grantley

**Huntzinger, Shakes**
See Huntzinger, Walter Henry

**Huntzinger, Walter Henry** 1899-
[BE]
*American baseball player*
* Huntzinger, Shakes

**Hunyadi, Janos** [or Huniades, John]
1400-1456 [HN, RH, SN]
*Governor of Hungary*
* Corvinus [Little Raven]
* [The] Devil
* Jancus Lain [The Wicked]
* [The] Raven Knight
* [The] White Knight

**Hunzicker, Beatrice Plumb** 1886-
[CA]
*British-born American author*
* Plumb, Beatrice

**Huppazoli**
See Hongo, Francis Secardi

**Huppen, Hermann** 1938- [WECO]
*Belgian cartoonist*
* Hermann

**Hurd, Edith** [Thacher] 1910-
[CA, SAT]
*American author*
* Sage, Juniper [joint pseudonym
with Margaret Wise Brown]

**Hurd, Jud**
See Hurd, Justin

**Hurd, Justin** 1912- [WEC]
*American cartoonist and publisher*
* Hurd, Jud

**Hurd, Percy Angier** [LAO]
*British journalist*
* Windermere

**Hurd, Richard** 1720-1808 [SN]
*British prelate and author*
* [A] Literary Sycophant

**Hurd, Thomas Carr** [Tom] 1924-
[BE]
*American baseball player*
* Hurd, Whitey

**Hurd, Whitey**
See Hurd, Thomas Carr [Tom]

**hurkey, rooan**
See Holzapfel, Rudolf Patrick
[Rudi]

**Hurkos, Peter**
See Van Der Hurk, Peter

**Hurlburt, William Henry** 1827- ?
[PA]
*Author*
* Raimond

**Hurley, Alec** 1871-1913 [BMH]
*British comedian*
* [The] Coster King

**Hurley, Dick**
See Hurley, William F.

**Hurley, Doran** 1900-1964 [CA]
*American author*
* McGregor

**Hurley, Ruby** 1910?-1980
*American civil rights activist and
attorney*
* [The] Queen of Civil Rights

**Hurley, Vic** 1898- [CA]
*American author*
* Duane, Jim
* Richards, Duane

**Hurley, William F.** 1847- ? [BE]
*American baseball player*
* Hurley, Dick

**Hurlock, Elizabeth B.**
See Beckman, Elizabeth Hurlock

**Hurnscot, Loran**
See Taylor, Gay Stuart

**Hurren, Bernard John** 1907- [AW]
*British author*
* Nott, Barry

**[The] Hurricane**
See Riquetti, Honore Gabriel
Victor

**Hurricane Hec Kilrea**
See Kilrea, Hector J.

**Hurricane Henry Armstrong**
See Jackson, Henry

**Hurry Up Yost**
See Yost, Fielding H.

**Hurst, Ardath Frances**
See Mayhar, Ardath F[rances]

**Hurst, Brian**
See Sellers, Connie Leslie, Jr.

**Hurst, David**
See Hirsch, Heinrich Theodor

**Hurst, Don**
See Hurst, Frank O'Donnell

**Hurst, Frank O'Donnell** 1905-1952
[AS, BE]
*American baseball player*
* Hurst, Don

**Hurst, Lulu**
See Atkinson, Mrs. Paul

**Hurst, Virginia Radcliffe**
1914?-1976 [CA]
*American author*
* Radcliffe, Virginia

**Hurt, Charles Gilbert** 1901-1967
[CWG]
*American country-western performer*
* Hurt, Chick

**Hurt, Chick**
See Hurt, Charles Gilbert

**Hurt, Edward Paisley** [Eddie]
1900- [IBW]
*American college athletic director
and coach*
* [The] Little Giant

**Hurt, Helen** 1879?-1954 [BEW]
*Actress and writer*
* Ashley, Helen

**Hurt, John** 1892-1966
[DAM, LRR]
*American singer*
* Hurt, Mississippi John

**Hurt, Mississippi John**
See Hurt, John

**Hurtado, Alfredo** 20th c. [FIR]
*Actor, screenwriter, technician*
* Pitusin

**Hurtado de Mendoza, Diego**
1503?-1575 [SN]
*Spanish statesman and scholar*
* [The] Great
* [The] Great Cardinal of Spain

**Hurtado del Valle, Antonio**
1842-1875 [CW]
*Cuban poet*
* [El] Hijo del Damuji

**Hurtubise, Hercules**
See Hurtubise, Jim

**Hurtubise, Jacques** 1950- [WECO]
*Canadian cartoonist*
* Zyx

**Hurtubise, Jim**
*Auto racer*
* Hurtubise, Hercules

**Hurvitz, Yigal** 1919?-
*Israeli government official*
* Yigal the Printer

**Hurwitz, Jerome** 1920- [EJ]
*American jazz musician*
* Lloyd, Jerome [Jerry]

**Hurwitz, Shari** 1934- [IPA]
*American puppeteer*
* Lewis, Shari

**Hurwood, Bernhardt J[ackson]**
1926- [CA, SAT, SFL]
*American author*
* Knight, Mallory T.
* Wilde, D. Gunther
* Xavier, [Father]

**Hus Desforges, Pierre Louis**
1773-1838 [WBD]
*Italian musician and composer*
* Jarnowick

**Husayn Ali** 1817-1892 [WBD]
*Persian religious leader*
* Bahaullah [Splendor of God]

**Husband of the Church**
See Medici, Giovanni de

**[The] Husbandman**
See Tusser, Thomas

**Husch, Richard J.** 1876?-1948
[BEW]
*American lyricist*
* Gerard, Richard

**Huskinson, Richard King** 1879- ?
[WWL]
*British author*
* King, Richard

**Husky, Ferlin** 1927- [CME, CWG]
*American country-western performer*
* Crum, Simon
* Preston, Terry

**[The] Hussar of Krefeld**
See Voss, Werner

**Hussein** 1935-
*King of Jordan*
* P. L. K. [Plucky Little King]

**Hussein, Saddam** 1936?-
*Iraqi president*
* [The] Butcher of Baghdad

**Hussey, H. J.**
See Hussey, Henry James

**Hussey, Harry**
See Tourbillon, Robert Arthur

**Hussey, Henry James** 1913- [ART]
*British sculptor and stonemason*
* Hussey, H. J.

**Hussey, Leonard**
See Pearce, Brian Leonard

**Hussey, Ruth**
See O'Rourke, Ruth Carol

**Hussingtree, Martin**
See Baldwin, Oliver Ridsdale

**Husta, Carl Lawrence** 1902-1951
[MEB]
*American basketball player*
* Husta, Sox

**Husta, Sox**
See Husta, Carl Lawrence

**Husted, James William** 1833- ?
[FFF]
*American politician*
* [The] Bald Eagle of Westchester

**Husting, Bert**
See Husting, Berthold Juneau

**Husting, Berthold Juneau**
1878-1948 [BE]
*American baseball player*
* Husting, Bert
* Husting, Pete

**Husting, Pete**
See Husting, Berthold Juneau

**Hustle, Charlie**
See Rose, Pete[r Edward]

**Hustling Dan O'Leary**
See O'Leary, Daniel

**Hustling Horace Phillips**
See Phillips, Horace

**Huston, Fran**
See Miller, R. S.

**Huston, Henry Augustus** 1858- ?
[NAA]
*American agricultural chemist and
writer*
* Spang Gipe

**Huston, Ronald Earle** 1945- [SMG]
*Canadian-born hockey player*
* Huston, Spike

**Huston, Spike**
See Huston, Ronald Earle

**Huston, Walter**
See Houghston, Walter

**Hutchcroft, Vera** 1923- [CA]
*American author*
* Richter, Vernon

**Hutchenrider, Clarence** 1908-
[MY]
*American jazz musician*
* Hutchenrider, Hutch

**Hutchenrider, Hutch**
See Hutchenrider, Clarence

**Hutcheson, Joseph Johnson [Joe]**
1905- [BE]
*American baseball player*
* Hutcheson, Poodles

**Hutcheson, Poodles**
See Hutcheson, Joseph Johnson
[Joe]

**Hutchin, Kenneth Charles** 1908-
[IAW, WD]
*British physician and author*
* Challice, Kenneth
* [A] Family Doctor
* Travers, Kenneth

**Hutchings, Monica**
See Baber, Monica Mary

**Hutchins, Bobby**
*Actor*
* Wheezer

**Hutchins, Francis Gilman** 1939-
[CA, WD]
*American author and historian*
* Madison, Frank

**Hutchinson, A. S. M.**
See Hutchinson, Arthur
Stuart-Menteth

**Hutchinson, Ace**
See Hutchinson, Willie

**Hutchinson, Ann** [SN]
*Founder of religious sect in New
England*
* [The] Non Such

**Hutchinson, Arthur Stuart-Menteth**
1879-1971 [LC]
*British author*
* Hutchinson, A. S. M.

**Hutchinson, Benjamin Peters**
1829-1899 [WBD]
*American speculator*
* Old Hutch

**Hutchinson, Big Bear**
See Hutchinson, Frederick Charles

**Hutchinson, Charles** 20th c. [SC]
*American actor and director*
* Hutchinson, Lightning Hutch

**Hutchinson, Frederick Charles**
1919-1964 [OBW, PB]
*American baseball player*
* Hutchinson, Big Bear
* Hutchinson, Hutch

**Hutchinson, Gladys** 20th c.
[F1, F2]
*Actress*
* Hyland, Peggy

**Hutchinson, Horace Gordon**
1859-1932? [CC]
*Author*
* Gordon, Horatio

**Hutchinson, Hutch**
See Hutchinson, Frederick Charles

**Hutchinson, John** 1830?-1916
[WWL]
*British author and poet*
* Ladylift

**Hutchinson, Lightning Hutch**
See Hutchinson, Charles

**Hutchinson, Lucie M.** 1919-
[IWM]
*American musician*
* Clare Lucille, [Sister]

**Hutchinson, R. C.**
See Hutchinson, Ray Coryton

**Hutchinson, Ray Coryton** 1907-
[LC, TC]
*British author*
* Hutchinson, R. C.

**Hutchinson, Robert Hare** 1887-
[WW]
*Author*
* Hare, Robert

**Hutchinson, W.** 1901- [BF]
*British director*
* Haines, Ronald

**Hutchinson, William** [FFF]
*American writer*
* Sands, John

**Hutchinson, Willie** 20th c. [OBW]
*American baseball player*
* Hutchinson, Ace

**Hutchinson Scott, Jay**
See Scott, Jay

**Hutchison, David Joseph** 1952-
[SMG]
*Canadian-born hockey player*
* Hutchison, Hutch

**Hutchison, Graham Seton** 1890-
[WW]
*Author*
* Seton, Graham

**Hutchison, Hutch**
See Hutchison, David Joseph

**Hutchison, Ronald** 1902- [BMH]
*British comedian*
* Tate, Harry, Jr.

**Hutchison, Ronald Macdonald**
1872-1940 [BEW, BMH]
*Scottish-born theatrical performer*
* Tate, Henry [or Harry]

**Hutchison, Wild Bill**
See Hutchison, William Forrest

**Hutchison, William Forrest**
1859-1926 [AS, BE]
*American baseball player*
* Hutchison, Wild Bill

**Huth, Gerry** 20th c.
*American football player*
* Huth, Hoot Man

**Huth, Hoot Man**
See Huth, Gerry

**[Le] Hutin**
See Louis X

**Hutson, Donald M.** 1913- [FB]
*American football player*
* [The] Alabama Antelope

**Hutt, Hector** 20th c. [MBF]
*British writer*
* Clifford, Martin [house
pseudonym]

**Hutto, J. B.**
See Hutto, Joseph Benjamin

**Hutto, Joseph Benjamin** 1926-
[BWW, NBB]
*American singer*
* [The] Hawk
* Hutto, J. B.

**Hutton, Barbara** 1913?-1979
*American heiress*
* Poor Little Rich Girl

**Hutton, Betty**
See Thornburg, Elizabeth June

**Hutton, Bouse**
See Hutton, John Bower

**Hutton, Butch**
See Thornburg, Marion

**Hutton, Clarke** 1898- [ART]
*British artist*
* C. H.

**Hutton, Ginger**
See Hutton, Virginia Carol

**Hutton, Ina Ray**
See Cowan, Odessa

**Hutton, John Bower** 1877-1962
[FHE, HK]
*Hockey player*
* Hutton, Bouse

**Hutton, Lauren**
See Hutton, Mary

**Hutton, Marion**
See Thornburg, Marion

**Hutton, Mary** 1943- [SW]
*American actress*
* Hutton, Lauren

**Hutton, Nedinia** 1925?- [ITA, SW]
*American actress*
* Merrill, Dina

**Hutton, Ralph W.** 1948-
[BBH, SWI]
*Canadian swimmer*
* [The] Iron Man

**Hutton, Robert**
See Winne, Robert Bruce

**Hutton, Silver**
See Hutton, Thomas George

**Hutton, Thomas George** 1946-
[SMG]
*American baseball player*
* Hutton, Silver

**Hutton, Virginia Carol** 1940- [CA]
*American author*
* Hutton, Ginger

**Huxley, Herbert H[enry]** 1916-
[CA]
*British author and educator*
* Stenus

**Huxley, Julian [Sorell]** 1887-1975
[CA]
*British biologist, philosopher,*
*author*
* Balbus

**Huxley, Rena** 1935- [IAW]
*Australian author*
* Briand, Rena

**Huxtable, Marjorie** 20th c. [LC]
*Author*
* Dare, Simon

**Huygh-De Keuster, Maria-Frieda**
1924- [IAW]
*Belgian author*
* Van Goeree, Irina

**Huyke, Elwood Bernard** 1937-
[B10]
*Puerto Rican baseball player*
* Huyke, Woody

**Huyke, Woody**
See Huyke, Elwood Bernard

**Huysman [or Huysmann], Roelof**
1443-1485 [WBD]
*Dutch scholar, painter, musician*
* Agricola, Rodolphus

**Huysmans, Charles Marie Georges**
1848-1907 [CD]
*French author*
* Huysmans, Joris Karl

**Huysmans, Joris Karl**
See Huysmans, Charles Marie
Georges

**Huzard, Antoinette** 1874-1953
[WBD]
*French author*
* Yver, Colette

**Hveger, Ragnhild** 1920- [SWI]
*Danish swimmer*
* [The] Golden Torpedo

**Hviezdoslav**
See Orszagh, Pavol

**Hwfa Mon**
See Williams, Rowland

**Hyacinth** 1185?-1257 [WBD]
*Saint*
* [The] Apostle of the North

**Hyacinthe, Pere**
See Loyson, Charles Jean Marie

**Hyams, Samuel David** 1893-1960
[BEW, FC]
*British actor*
* Hoey, Dennis

**Hyatt, Ham**
See Hyatt, Robert Hamilton

**Hyatt, Robert Hamilton**
1884-1963 [BE]
*American baseball player*
* Hyatt, Ham

**Hyatt, Stanley Portal** 1877-1914
[MBF]
*British author*
* Dacre, [Captain] Stanley

**Hybrida, Antonius**
See Antonius, Gaius

**Hyde, Bubber**
See Hyde, Cowan

**Hyde, Cowan** 20th c. [OBW]
*American baseball player*
* Hyde, Bubber

**Hyde, D. Herbert**
See Chambers, Derek Hyde

**Hyde, Dayton O[gden]** 20th c.
[CA, SAT]
*American author*
* Hyde, Hawk

**Hyde, Douglas** 1860-1949 [TC]
*Irish president and author*
* An Craoibhin Aoibhinn
   [Delightful Little Branch]

**Hyde, E. A. Watson**
See Hyde, Elizabeth A[dshead]

**Hyde, Eleanor**
See Munthe, Frances

**Hyde, Elizabeth A[dshead]** 1876- ?
[NAA]
*British-born author*
* Hyde, E. A. Watson

**Hyde, Hawk**
See Hyde, Dayton O[gden]

**Hyde, Robin**
See Wilkinson, Iris Guiver

**Hyde, Sidney**
See Pike, Mary Caroline

**Hyde, Tracy Elliot**
See Venning, Corey

**Hyde-White, Wilfrid**
See White, Wilfrid

**Hyder, Doc**
See Hyder, George

**Hyder, George** 20th c. [BWW]
*American entertainer*
* Hyder, Doc

**Hyder, John** 1912- [BB]
*American basketball player*
* Hyder, Whack

**Hyder, Whack**
See Hyder, John

**Hydrant Chuck**
See Martin, J. F.

**Hydrophilus**
See Fenwick, Thomas

**[The] Hyena of Brescia**
See Haynau, Julius Jakob von

**Hygeiea**
See Cilento, Phyllis Dorothy

**Hyland, Ann** 1936- [WD]
*British writer*
* Ross, Laurence
* Trailrider

**Hyland, Diana**
See Gentner, Joan Diana

**Hyland, M. E. F.** 20th c.
[SFL, WWL]
*British author*
* Wylwynne, Kythe

**Hyland, Peggy**
See Hutchinson, Gladys

**Hyland, [Dr.] Robert F.** 1886-1950
[PB]
*American physician*
* [The] Surgeon General of
   Baseball

**Hylander, Franz Josef**
See Holzner, Joseph

**Hylton, Barbara** [THR]
*British actress*
* Hoffe, Barbara

**Hylton, Jane**
See Clark, Gwen

**Hymack, Mr.**
See Macpherson, Quinton

**Hyman, Grace Lloyd** 1875?-1961
[BEW]
*Theatrical performer*
* Lloyd, Grace

**Hyman, Jeffrey** 20th c.
*American musician*
* Ramone, Joey

**Hyman, John Wigginton** 1899-
[ASC, EJ, WWJ]
*American jazz musician*
* Wiggs, Johnny

**Hyman, Shirley Jackson**
1919-1965 [WGT]
*American author*
* Jackson, Shirley

**Hymie the Polack**
See Wajcieckowski, Earl

**Hynam, John Charles** 1915-1974
[ESF, SFL, WGT]
*British author*
* Kippax, John

**Hynd, Lavinia Leitch** 20th c.
[SFL, WGT]
*Author*
* Leitch, Lavinia

**Hyndman, Jane Andrews [Lee]**
1912-1978 [CA, SAT]
*Russian-born American author*
* Wyndham, Lee

**Hyndman, Robert Utley**
1906?-1973 [CA, SAT]
*American author*
* Wyndham, Robert

**Hyne, C. J. Cutcliffe**
See Hyne, Charles John Cutcliffe
Wright

**Hyne, Charles John Cutcliffe Wright**
1865-1944 [LC, WW]
*British author*
* Chesney, Weatherby
* Hyne, C. J. Cutcliffe

**Hynes, Adeline**
See DeLorme, Mrs. Henry

**Hypatia** ?- 415 [DEP]
*Philosopher*
* [The] Divine Pagan

**Hyperion**
See Quincy, Josiah

**[L']Hypochondre**
See Poquelin, Jean Baptiste

**[The] Hypocrite**
See Lobb, Stephen

**[L']Hypocrite Rimeur**
See Racine, Jean Baptiste

**Hyson, Dorothy**
See Hyson, Peggy

**Hyson, Peggy** 1915- [BF]
*American-born actress*
* Hyson, Dorothy

**Hystaspis [Son of Hystaspes]**
See Darius I

# I

**I. B.**
*See* Black, Ian

**I Chu**
*See* Hsien Feng

**I. D.**
*See* Davidson, Ian Stuart

**[The] I Don't Care Girl**
*See* Tanguay, Eva

**I. F.**
*See* Fenwick, Mrs. I.

**I Hsin [or Yi Hshin]**
*See* Kung

**I. R. V.**
*See* Haines, E[dwin] Irvine

**I. S.**
*See* Schneider, Isidor

**I Sabbah, Hassan**
*See* Butler, William Huxford [Bill]

**Iacocca, Lee**
*See* Iacocca, Lido Anthony

**Iacocca, Lido Anthony** 1924-
*American automobile executive*
* Iacocca, Lee

**Iams, Jack**
*See* Iams, Samuel H.

**Iams, Samuel H.** 1910-   [CC, EMD]
*American author*
* Iams, Jack

**Ian, Janis**
*See* Fink, Janis

**Iannone, Jeanne [Koppel]** 1912-
[B10, CA, SAT]
*American author*
* Balzano, Jeanne [Koppel]
* Bell, Gina
* Bell-Zano, Gina

**Ianthe**
*See* Embury, Emma Catherine
Manley

**Ianthe**
*See* Harley, [Lady] Charlotte

**Iasigi, Mrs. A. D.**   [FFF]
*Entertainer*
* Stembler, May

**Iba, Henry [Hank]** 1904-   [BB]
*American basketball coach*
* [The] Iron Duke

**Ibarra, Crisostomo**
*See* Yabes, Leopoldo Y[abes]

**Ibarruri, Dolores** 1895-   [CBS]
*Spanish revolutionist*
* [La] Pasionaria

**Iberia's Pilot**
*See* Columbus, Christopher

**Ibn-Abid**
*See* Elmakyn, George

**Ibn-al-Saigh**
*See* Avempace [or Avenpace]

**Ibn-Bajjah**
*See* Avempace [or Avenpace]

**Ibn-Buhaina, Abdullah**
*See* Blakey, Art

**Ibn-Maat**
*See* Zavavi, Aboul-Halcon

**Ibn-Muhammed, Zakarija**
1200-1283   [FFF, HN, SN]
*Scholar*
* Kazwini
* [The] Pliny of the East

**Ibn-Rushd**
*See* Averroes [or Averrhoes]

**Ibn-Zuhr [or Ibn-Zohr]**
*See* Avenzoar [or Abumeron]

**Ibrahim, Abdul Rahim**
*See* Carn, Doug

**Ibrahim, Abdullah**
*See* Brand, Adolph Johannes

**Ibrahim, Ischak**
*See* Guarghias, Aloysius George

**Ibsen, Henrik [Johan]** 1828-1906
[MWD, TLC]
*Norwegian playwright and poet*
* Bjarme, Brynjolf
* [The] Father of Modern Drama

**Iburg, Ham**
*See* Iburg, Herman Edward

**Iburg, Herman Edward** 1878-1945
[EJS]
*American baseball player*
* Iburg, Ham

**Ice Box Chamberlain**
*See* Chamberlain, Elton P.

**[The] Ice Man**
*See* Edmondson, Keith

**[The] Ice Man**
*See* Wilson, Edwin P.

**[The] Ice Queen**
*See* Gorsuch, Anne M.

**Iceberg Slim**
*See* Beck, Robert

**Iceblink [code name used during
World War II]**
*See* Byrnes, James F.

**[The] Iceman**
*See* Butler, Jerry

**[The] Iceman**
*See* Gervin, George

**[The] Iceman**
*See* Woolf, George

**Iconoclast**
*See* Bradlaugh, Charles

**Iconoclast**
*See* Hamilton, Mary Agnes
[Adamson]

**Idal, Sveinn**
*See* Indridason, Indridi

**Idamore**
*See* Cutts, Mary

**[The] Idea Man of French
Ready-to-Wear**
*See* Takada, Kenzo

**Idea, Marcel**
*See* Morris, Michael

**Idell, A. Provost** 1889-1965   [AS]
*American volleyball player, coach,
official*
* [The] Father of Modern
  Volleyball
* Idell, Pop

**Idell, Albert E.** 1901-   [ANT]
*American author*
* Rogers, Phillips

**Idell, Pop**
*See* Idell, A. Provost

**Iden, William**
*See* Green, William M[ark]

**Idestone**
*See* Pierce, Thomas

**Idle Albert Thorogood**
*See* Thorogood, Albert

**[The] Idol of Ohio**
*See* McKinley, William

**[The] Idol of the Airlanes**
*See* Garber, Jan

**[The] Idol Smasher**
*See* Mahmud

**Idole du Temple [Idol of the Temple]**
*See* Marie Charlotte

**Idris**
*See* Mee, Arthur

**[The] Idumaean**
*See* Antipater

**Iffy the Dopester**
*See* Bingay, Malcolm

**Igaya, Chick**
*See* Igaya, Chiharu

**Igaya, Chiharu** 1935-   [BBH]
*Japanese-born skier*
* Igaya, Chick

**Iger, Jerry**
*See* Iger, Samuel Maxwell

**Iger, Samuel Maxwell** 1903-
[WECO]
*American cartoonist and editor*
* Iger, Jerry

**Iglehart, Alfredda** 20th c.   [BBH]
*American soccer coach*
* Iglehart, Missa

**Iglehart, Missa**
*See* Iglehart, Alfredda

**Igloo, Spiro**
*See* Hoffman, Abbie

**Ignasiak, Gary Raymond** 1949-
[SMG]
*American baseball player*
* Ignasiak, Iggy

**Ignasiak, Iggy**
*See* Ignasiak, Gary Raymond

**Ignatiev, Pauline** 1893-1966   [SC]
*American actress*
* Russ, Paula

**Ignatius, [Father]**
*See* Lyne, Joseph Leycester

**Ignatius, [Father]**
*See* Spencer, George

**Ignatius** 2nd c.   [WBD]
*Saint*
* Theophorus

**Ignatius** 799?- 878   [WBD]
*Saint*
* Nicetas

**Ignoto**
*See* Barnfield, Richard

**Ignotus**
*See* Adams, Henry Joseph

**Ignotus**
See Fuller, James Franklin

**Ignotus**
See Mueller-Guttenbrunn, Adam

**Ignotus**
See Platel, Felix

**Ignotus**
See Veigelsberg, Hugo

**Ignotus, Miles**
See Luttwak, Edward Nicolae

**Igoe, Owen Joseph** 1923-    [EJ]
*American jazz musician*
* Igoe, Sonny

**Igoe, Sonny**
See Igoe, Owen Joseph

**Ihetu, Richard** 1929-1971
[IBW, RBE, WBC]
*Nigerian boxer*
* Tiger, Dick

**Ihle, Charlotte Elizabeth**
1878?-1964    [THR]
*British actress*
* Inescort, Elaine

**Ii Kamon no kami**
See Ii Naosuke

**Ii Naosuke** 1815-1860    [WBD]
*Japanese statesman*
* Ii Kamon no kami

**Iijima, Takao** 1931-    [CAR]
*Japanese artist*
* Ay-O

**Ijames, Mary Tunstall** 1894-1963
[ASC, BEW]
*American composer, actress, singer*
* Sunshine, Marion

**Ike**
See Eisenhower, David Dwight

**Ike**
See Lane, Katharine A.

**Ikhnaton [or Akhenaten]**    [WBD]
*King of Egypt*
* Amenhotep IV
* [The] Religious Revolutionary

**Il**
See    Second element of name

**Ildefonso, [Father]**
See Tettemer, John Moynihan

**Ilderim [or Yilderim] [Lightning]**
See Bajazet I [Bayazid or Bajasid]

**Iles, Bert**
See Ross, Zola Helen

**Iles, Francis**
See Cox, Anthony Berkeley

**Ilf, Ilya Arnoldovich**
See Fainzilber, Ilya Arnoldovich

**Ill-Used Candidate**
See Caley, J. C.

**Illes, Doris**
See Illes, Theodora

**Illes, Theodora** 1946-    [SFL]
*German-born bibliographer*
* Illes, Doris

**Illibatus, Doctor**
See Alemanicus, Alexander

**Illington, Margaret**
See Light, Maud

**Illington, Marie**
See Inman, Marie

**Illingworth, Prunella** 1932-    [TR]
*British actress*
* Scales, Prunella

**[The] Illinois Baboon**
See Lincoln, Abraham

**Illinois Jimmy Francis**
See Francis, James

**[The] Illinois Thunderbolt**
See Papke, William Herman
[Billy]

**Illuminated Doctor**
See De Mairone, Francois

**[The] Illuminated Doctor**
See Lully, Raymond

**[The] Illuminated Doctor**
See Tauler, Johann

**[The] Illuminator**
See Gregory

**Illuminatus, Doctor**
See Lully, Raymond

**Illuminatus, Doctor**
See Tauler, Johann

**Illuminatus et Acutus, Doctor**
See De Mairone, Francois

**Illustratus, Doctor**
See Marca, Francois de

**[The] Illustrious**
See Albert V [or Albrecht]

**[The] Illustrious**
See Henry

**[The] Illustrious**
See Hesychius

**[The] Illustrious**
See Jam-Sheid

**[The] Illustrious**
See Kien-Long

**[The] Illustrious**
See Nicomedes II

**[The] Illustrious**
See Otto II

**[The] Illustrious**
See Ptolemy V

**[The] Illustrious Doctor**
See Goethals, Henry

**[The] Illustrious Infidel**
See Ingersoll, Robert Green

**Ilogu, Edmund Christopher Onyedum**
1920-    [IAW]
*Nigerian author*
* Edilog

**Ilyin, Mikhail Andreyevich**
1878-1942    [CD]
*Russian author and journalist*
* Osorgin, Mikhail Andreyevich

**Image, Jean**
See Hajdu, Emeric

**[The] Imam**
See Mustafavi, Ruhollah

**Iman**
See Abdulmajid, Iman Mohamed

**[El] Iman [The Magnet]**
See Hersh, Carl

**[The] Imbecile**
See Juana [Joanna or Jane]

**Imbert-Terry, [Sir] Henry Machu**
1854-1938    [WW]
*Author*
* Terry, Henry Machu

**Imhoff, Darrall** 1938-    [BB]
*American basketball player*
* Big D

**Imlach, George** 1918-
[FHE, HK, SMG]
*Canadian-born hockey coach and
manager*
* Imlach, Punch

**Imlach, Punch**
See Imlach, George

**Imlay, Doc**
See Imlay, Harry Miller

**Imlay, Harry Miller** 1889-1948
[BE]
*American baseball player*
* Imlay, Doc

**Immelmann, Max** 1890-1916
*German fighter pilot*
* [The] Eagle of Lille

**[The] Immobile One**
See Cowan, Samuel

**[The] Immortal**
See Yong-Tching

**[The] Immortal Azcue**
See Azcue, Jose Joaquin

**[The] Immortal Dreamer**
See Bunyan, John

**Immortal Pindar's Foe**
See Perrault, Charles

**[The] Immortal Tinker**
See Bunyan, John

**[The] Imp Girl**
See Lawrence, Florence

**[The] Impeccable One**
See Jones, Hank

**[The] Impenetrable Goodman Dull**
See Goldsmith, Oliver

**[The] Imperial Machiavelli**
See Nero Caesar, Tiberius
Claudius

**[The] Impertinent**
See Lowry, Henry Dawson

**Imported Sparrow**
See Rhys, Horton

**Impossible, Mr.**
See Robinson, Brooks [Calbert,
Jr.]

**[The] Imposter**
See Aswad, al-

**[An] Imposter**
See Chauvin [or Caulvin?], Jean

**[The] Impotent**
See Henry IV

**[The] Impudent**
See Phipps, [Sir] Constantine

**Imson, Mrs.**    [FFF]
*Entertainer*
* Burt, Bessie

**Inabnett, Marvin** 1938-    [ASC]
*American singer*
* Ingram, Marvin

**Inbar, Joseph**
See Burstein, Joseph

**[The] Inca**
See Garcilaso de la Vega

**Ince, Alexander**
See Incze, Sandor

**Inchfawn, Fay**
See Ward, Elizabeth Rebecca

**Incledon, Philip**
See Worner, Philip Arthur
Incledon

**[El] Inclusero [The Foundling]**
See Tebar Perez, Gregorio

**Incogniteau, Jean-Louis**
See Kerouac, Jean-Louis Lebrid
De

**[The] Incomparable Orinda**
See Philips, Katherine

**[The] Incomprehensible Holofernes**
See Johnson, Samuel

**[L']Inconnue**
See French, L. Virginia

**[The] Incorruptible**
See Fabricius

**[The] Incorruptible**
See Marvell, Andrew

**[The] Incorruptible**
See Robespierre, Maximilien

**[The] Incorruptible**
See Shippen, William

**[The] Incorruptible Lucas**
See Lucas, Charles

**[The] Incredible Herman**
See Herman, Floyd Caves

**[The] Incredible Hulk**
See Siltanen, Risto

**Incrocci, Agenore**    [WF]
*Screenwriter*
* Age

**Incze, Sandor** 1892-    [BEW]
*Hungarian-born producer and
publisher*
* Ince, Alexander

**Ind, Allison** 1903-1974    [CAP]
*American author*
* Stanley, Phil
* Wallace, Richard

**[An] Independent**
See Quincy, Josiah

**Inderlied, Mary Elizabeth** 1945-
[CA]
*American author*
* Edwards, Elizabeth

**[The] India Rubber Man**
See Wooden, John

**[The] Indian**
See Benitez, Gaspar

**Indian Agent**
See Bowles, William Augustus

[The] Indian Apostle
See Eliot, John

[The] Indian Apostle
See Las Casas, Bartolome de

Indian Bob Johnson
See Johnson, Robert Lee [Bob]

[The] Indian Bradman
See Nayudu, Cottari Kanakayia

[The] Indian Fighter
See Talcott, John

[The] Indian Hercules
See Naidu, [Rama] Murti

Indian Jack Hart
See Hart, Jack

Indian Jack Jacobs
See Jacobs, Jack

Indian Joe Guyon
See Guyon, Joseph [Joe]

[The] Indian Princess
See Thomas, Lillian

[The] Indiana Kid
See Weygand, James Lamar

Indicator
See Poynter, James William

Indicopleustes
See Cosmas

Indicus
See Bell, Evans

[The] Indignant Bard
See Alcaeus

[El] Indio [The Indian]
See Larios Alvarez, Jose

[El] Indio de Tetela [The Indian from Tetela]
See Huerta Rivera, Jose

[El] Indio Grande [The Great Indian]
See Gaona y Jimenez, Rodolfo

[The] Indolent
See Frederick III

[The] Indolent
See Louis V

Indolent Dick
See Cromwell, Richard

Indrane, Ilze
See Fatiziece, Undine

Indridason, Indridi 1908-    [IAW]
Icelandic author
* Idal, Sveinn
* Sveinsson, Aslakur

Indrikis, Vecais
See Kikauka, Talis Talivaldis Tully

Inescort, Elaine
See Ihle, Charlotte Elizabeth

Inescort, Frieda
See Wightman, Frieda

[The] Inexplicable
See Sobhuza II

Inez, Dolly
See Donez, Ian

Infallible
See Pelagius II

[L']Infame Catin du Nord
See Elizabeth Petrovna

[The] Infamous
See Elizabeth Petrovna

[The] Infant
See Louis III [or Ludwig]

[The] Infant of Luebeck
See Heinecken, Christian Heinrich

[The] Infant Roscius
See Betty, William Henry West

[The] Infant Stockbroker
See Cronmire, Sidney Herbert

[El] Infante de Anteguera
See Fernando

Infarinato
See Salviati, Leonardo

Infascelli, Roberto 20th c.    [WF]
Italian director
* Raymond, Bob

Infield, Glenn [Berton] 1920-    [CA]
American author
* Powers, George
* Rodgers, Frank
* Tolby, Arthur

Information Please
See Kieran, John

Ingber, Lou    [EJS]
American boxing gym owner
* Stillman, Lou

Inge, W. R.
See Inge, William Ralph

Inge, William 1913-1973    [SC]
American playwright, screenwriter, actor
* Gage, Walter

Inge, William Ralph 1860-1954
[LC]
British author and clergyman
* [The] Gloomy Dean
* Inge, W. R.

Ingelow, Jean 1830-1881    [PA]
Author
* Don John

Ingels, Graham 1915-    [WECO]
American cartoonist
* Ghastly

Ingenito, Benjamin 20th c.    [FIR]
Actor and screenwriter
* Granada, Manuel

Inger, Nan
See Oestman, Nan Inger

Ingersley, R. M.
See Markland, Russell

Ingersoll, Charles Jared 1782-1862
[PA]
Author
* [A] Northern Man

Ingersoll, Drake
See Bowerman, Paul

Ingersoll, L. D.    [PA]
Author
* Linkensale

Ingersoll, Ralph Isaacs 1788-1872
[FFF]
American politician
* Young Hotspur

Ingersoll, Robert Green 1833-1899
[DNNS, SN]
American attorney and politician
* [The] Great Agnostic
* [The] Illustrious Infidel

Ingerton, Scotty
See Ingerton, William John

Ingerton, William John 1886-1956
[BE]
American baseball player
* Ingerton, Scotty

Ingham, Daniel
See Lambot, Isobel Mary

Ingham, [Colonel] Frederic
See Hale, Edward Everett

Ingham, Peter Geoffrey 1956-
[DC]
British cricketer
* Ingham, Ping

Ingham, Ping
See Ingham, Peter Geoffrey

Inghirami, Tommaso 1470-1516
[SN]
Italian actor
* Phaedra

Ingle, Charles
See Chevalier, August

Ingleby, Leonard Cresswell
See Gull, Cyril Arthur Edward Ranger

Inglesby, Mona
See Vredenburg, Mona

[L']Inglesina
See Davies, Cecilia

Inglis, Henry David 1795-1835
[PA]
Author
* Conway, H. Derwent

Inglis, J. 19th c.    [PA]
Author
* Maore

Ingoldsby
See Hildyard, James

Ingoldsby, Thomas
See Barham, Richard Harris

Ingolia, Concetta Ann 1938-
[FC, ITA, SW]
American actress
* Stevens, Connie

Ingpen, Joan
See Williams, Joan Mary Eileen

Ingraham, Joseph Holt 1809-1860
[FFF, PA]
American clergyman and author
* Conynghame, Kate
* [A] Yankee

Ingraham, Prentiss 1843-1904
[WW]
Author
* Burr, Dangerfield
* Dunbar, Noel
* Erwin, Howard W.
* Graham, [Lieut.] Preston
* Hall, [Midshipman] Tom W.
* Inman, Robert Randolph?
* King, T. W.
* Lafitte, [Colonel] Leon
* Perry, Harry Dennies
* Powell, Frank
* Stoddard, [Major] Henry B.

Ingraham, Prentiss (Continued)
* Taylor, [Capt.] Alfred B.

Ingram, Forrest L[eo] 1938-    [CA]
American author and educator
* Van Rijn, Ignatius

Ingram, John H. 1849-1916
[WWL]
Author
* Salamanca, D. F. Se

Ingram, Lancelot Albert 1925-
[OP]
Australian-born opera singer
* Lance, Albert

Ingram, Marvin
See Inabnett, Marvin

Ingram, Mrs.    [FFF]
Entertainer
* D'Anka, Cornelie

Ingram, Red
See Ingram, Robert

Ingram, Rex
See Hitchcock, Reginald Ingram Montgomery

Ingram, Robert 20th c.    [NBB]
American musician
* Ingram, Red

Ingram, Thomas Theodore Scott
1927-    [IAW]
Scottish physician and writer
* Scott, Titus

Ingram, Willis J.
See Finkelstein, Mark

Ingrams, Richard 20th c.    [CA]
Author
* Reid, Philip [joint pseudonym with Andrew Philip Kingsford Osmond]

Ingulphus
See Gray, Arthur

Inhofe, Susan Eloise Hinton 1949-
[FBJ]
American author
* Hinton, S. E.

[The] Ink Dabbler
See Hembling, Nina [Clark]

Inkiow, [Janakiev] Dimiter 1932-
[CA]
Bulgarian-born author and playwright
* Verin, Velko

Inkpot, Doctor
See Standish, John

Inman, Marie 1856?-1927    [THR]
British actress
* Illington, Marie

Inman, Robert Randolph?
See Harbaugh, Thomas Chalmers

Inman, Robert Randolph?
See Ingraham, Prentiss

Inman, Robert Randolph?
See Manning, William Henry

Inman, Robert Randolph?
See Morris, Charles Smith

Inman, Will
See McGirt, William Archibald

Innes, Alan
See Tubb, Edwin Charles

**Innes, Alexander Taylor** [FFF]
*Author*
* Duthus

**Innes, Brian** 20th c. [IAW]
*British author*
* Powell, Neil

**Innes, Hammond**
See Hammond Innes, Ralph

**Innes, Jean**
See Saunders, Jean

**Innes, Michael**
See Stewart, John Innes
Mackintosh

**Innes, Rosemary E[lizabeth Jackson]**
20th c. [CA]
*Scottish author*
* Jackson, R. E.

**Innocent II**
See Papareschi, Gregorio

**Innocent III**
See De Conti, Giovanni Lotario

**Innocent III**
See Frangipani, Lando dei

**Innocent IV**
See De Fieschi, Sinibaldo

**Innocent IX**
See Facchinetti, Giovanni Antonio

**Innocent V**
See Peter of Tarentaise [Pietro di
Tarantasia]

**Innocent VI**
See Aubert, Etienne

**Innocent VII**
See De Migliorati, Cosimo

**Innocent VIII**
See Cibo, Giovanni Battista

**Innocent X**
See Pamfili, Giovanni Battista

**Innocent XI**
See Odescalchi, Benedetto

**Innocent XII**
See Pignatelli, Antonio

**Innocent XIII**
See Conti, Michelangelo

**Inonu, Ismet**
See Ismet Pasa

**Inoue, Yukitoshi** 1945- [CA]
*Japanese poet and illustrator*
* Yuki

**[The] Inquisitor of Atheists**
See Naigeon, Jacques Andre

**Inside, Mr.**
See Bates, Mickey

**Inside, Mr.**
See Blanchard, Felix Anthony

**Insight, James**
See Coleman, Robert William
Alfred

**[The] Insolent**
See Majorano, Gaetano

**Inspector F.**
See Russell, William

**[El] Inspirado [The Inspired One]**
See Munguia, Miguel

**[The] Inspired Idiot**
See Goldsmith, Oliver

**[The] Inspired Tinker**
See Bunyan, John

**Insulaneus**
See Menaptus, Wilhelm

**Integrity Jean Harris**
See Harris, Jean Struven

**[The] Intellectual Artist**
See Poussin, Nicolas

**[An] Intellectual Epicure**
See More, Henry

**Intelligence Officer**
See James, Lionel

**Intendente de Fortificazione**
See Acontius, Jacobus

**[The] International Entertainer**
See White, Princess

**[The] Interpreter of the Renaissance**
See Buonarroti, Michelangelo [or
Michael Angelo]

**[The] Intimidator**
See Wilcox, David

**[The] Intrepid**
See Boleslav I [or Boleslas]

**Intrepid** [code name]
See Stephenson, [Sir] William
Samuel

**[L']Intrepide**
See Dessaix, Joseph Marie

**[An] Invalid**
See Greville, Robert Fulke

**[An] Invalid**
See Martineau, Harriet

**[The] Invalid Laureate**
See Scarron, Paul

**[The] Inventive Skelton**
See Skelton, John

**Invincibilis, Doctor**
See Occam [or Ockham], William
of

**[The] Invincible**
See Medici, Cosmo [or Cosimo] de

**[The] Invincible**
See Suvorov [or Suwarof],
Aleksandr Vasilievich

**[The] Invincible Doctor**
See Occam [or Ockham], William
of

**[The] Invisible Commander**
See Somerset, Fitzroy James
Henry

**[The] Invisible Prince**
See Bentinck, William John
Cavendish Scott

**Inwall** [code name used during
World War II]
See Stilwell, Joseph W.

**Inyart, Gene**
See Namovicz, Gene Inyart

**Io Paean Dick**
See Harvey, Richard

**Ioffe, Adolf Abramovich**
1883-1927 [B10]
*Russian communist leader and
pamphleteer*
* Krymskii, Victor

**Iolo Morgannwg**
See Williams, Edward

**Ion, Fred J.** 1886-1944 [HK]
*Canadian-born hockey referee*
* Ion, Mickey

**Ion, Mickey**
See Ion, Fred J.

**Iona, Andy**
See Long, Andy Iona

**Ione**
See Hewitt, Mary Elizabeth

**Ione**
See Moore, Jane L.

**Ionel**
See Ronn, Yuval

**Ionicus**
See Armitage, Joshua Charles

**Iota**
See Caffyn, Kathleen Mannington

**Iota**
See Waller, John Francis

**Iott, Clarence Eugene** 1919- [BE]
*American baseball player*
* Iott, Hooks

**Iott, Happy**
See Iott, John

**Iott, Hooks**
See Iott, Clarence Eugene

**Iott, John** 20th c. [BE]
*American baseball player*
* Iott, Happy

**Ippoliti, Silvano** 20th c. [WF]
*Italian cinematographer*
* Wallace, Sylvan

**Ippolitov-Ivanov, Mikhail
Mikhailovitch**
See Ivanov, Mikhail Mikhailovitch

**Iranek-Osmecki, Kazimierz** 1897-
[CA]
*Polish-born author and journalist*
* Antoni
* Heller
* Makary

**Irani, Merwan S.** 1894-1969
[NAD]
*Indian-born prophet*
* Meher, [Baba]

**Irani, Ray**
See Irani, Riyad

**Irani, Riyad** 1935- [B10]
*American chemist*
* Irani, Ray

**Irbe, A. G.**
See Irbe, Gunars

**Irbe, Andrejs**
See Irbe, Gunars

**Irbe, Gunars** 1924- [IAW]
*Latvian-born sociologist and author*
* Irbe, A. G.
* Irbe, Andrejs

**Iredale, John**
See Valentine, Benjamin Bennaton

**Irelan, Grump**
See Irelan, Harold [Hal]

**Irelan, Harold [Hal]** 1890-1944
[BE]
*American baseball player*
* Irelan, Grump

**Ireland, David**
See Green, Julien [Hartridge]

**Ireland, Doreen**
See Lord, Douglas

**Ireland, G. Tom**
See Ireland, George Thomas

**Ireland, George Thomas**
1865-1963 [DAM]
*American jazz musician*
* Ireland, G. Tom

**Ireland, John** ?-1808 [SN]
*British author*
* [The] Linnaeus of Hogarth

**Ireland, M. J.** 20th c. [WGT]
*Author*
* Maxwell, Joslyn

**Ireland, Marion Isabel** 1941-
[IAW]
*Australian author*
* Crooks, Marion

**Ireland, Maude**
See Thompson, Jane Maude
Evelyn De Gourey Ireland

**Ireland, Michael**
See Figgis, [M.] Darrell

**Ireland, William Henry** 1777-1835
[PA]
*Author*
* Chastlebars, Pierre de Boscaselde
* Clifford, Charles
* H. C., Esq.

**Irenaeus**
See Prime, Samuel Irenaeus

**Irenaeus** 130?- 208?
[DNNF, DNNS, SN]
*Saint*
* [The] Apostle of the Gauls

**Irenaeus, Philopater**
See Beling, Richard

**Irene, [Sister]**
See Fitzgibbon, Catherine

**Irene**
See Gibbons, Irene

**Irghen, George**
See Guarghias, Aloysius George

**Irial**
See Ryan, Frederick

**[The] Irish Agitator**
See O'Connell, Daniel

**[The] Irish Anacreon**
See O'Carolan, Turloch

**[The] Irish Atticus**
See Faulkner, George

**Irish Bob Murphy**
See Conarty, Edward Lee

**Irish Catholic**
See Doyle, James Warren

**[The] Irish Crichton**
See Henderson, John

[The] Irish De Stael
See   Morgan, Sydney

[The] Irish Judas
See   Blood, Thomas

[An] Irish Lady
See   Greer, Mrs. S. D.

[The] Irish Lady
See   Thatcher, Evelyn

[An] Irish Man
See   Moore, Thomas

[The] Irish Nightingale
See   Hayes, Catherine

[The] Irish Plato
See   Berkeley, George

Irish Priest
See   O'Farrell, M. J.

[The] Irish Roscius
See   Barry, Spranger

[The] Irish Smollett
See   Lever, Charles James

Irish Whiskey Drinker
See   Sheehan, John

Irish, William
See   Hopley-Woolrich, Cornell
George

[An] Irish Woman
See   Perrier, Anna

Irner
See   Martin, Bon Louis Henri

Irnerius 1050?-1130?   [FFF, SN]
Jurist
* [The] Lamp of the Law

Iron Arm
See   Guillaume [or William]

Iron Arm
See   Lanoue, Francois de

[The] Iron Butterfly
See   Marcos, Imelda

[The] Iron Calvinist of Rosny
See   Bethune, Maximilien de [Duc
de Sully]

[The] Iron Chancellor
See   Bismarck, Otto Eduard
Leopold von

[The] Iron Duke
See   Bethune, Maximilien de [Duc
de Sully]

[The] Iron Duke
See   Henry I [or Heinrich]

[The] Iron Duke
See   Iba, Henry [Hank]

[The] Iron Duke
See   Stiller, Mosche [or Mowscha]

[The] Iron Duke
See   Wellesley, Arthur

[The] Iron Emperor
See   Nicholas I [Nikolai Pavlovich]

Iron Eyes Cody
See   Little Eagle

[The] Iron Glove
See   Stuart, Richard Lee

Iron Hand
See   Berlichingen, Goetz [or
Gottfried] von

[The] Iron Hand
See   Tonti, Henri de

[The] Iron Handed
See   Ernest

Iron Hands Hiller
See   Hiller, Charles Joseph

[The] Iron Horse
See   Gehrig, [Henry] Lou[is]

Iron, John
See   Carlile, John Charles

[The] Iron Lady of British Politics
See   Thatcher, Margaret Hilda
[Roberts]

[The] Iron Maiden
See   Navratilova, Martina

[The] Iron Maiden
See   Thatcher, Margaret Hilda
[Roberts]

[The] Iron Major
See   Cavanaugh, Francis W.
[Frank]

[The] Iron Man
See   Crain, Ben

[The] Iron Man
See   Crampton, Bruce

[The] Iron Man
See   Emerson, Eddie K.

[The] Iron Man
See   Giannone, Saverio

[The] Iron Man
See   Hutton, Ralph W.

[The] Iron Man
See   McGinnity, Joseph Jerome

[The] Iron Man
See   Satre, Magnus

Iron Man Brown
See   Brown, Larry

Iron Man Ian
See   Smith, Ian

Iron Man Johnson
See   Johnson, John

Iron Man Mueller
See   Mueller, Ray Coleman

Iron Man Piatt
See   Piatt, Wiley Harold

Iron Man Starr
See   Starr, Raymond Francis

[The] Iron Master
See   Wright, Edward H.

Iron Mike Marshall
See   Marshall, Michael Grant

Iron Mike Michalske
See   Michalske, August

Iron Mike O'Daniel
See   O'Daniel, John Wilson

[The] Iron Ogli
See   Ozdemir

Iron Pants Semyonov
See   Semyonov, Vladimir

[The] Iron Poet
See   Mayakovsky, Vladimir
Vladimirovich

[The] Iron Queen
See   Frederika

Iron, Ralph
See   Schreiner, Olive [Emily
Albertina]

[The] Iron Stomach
See   Kissinger, Henry Alfred

[The] Iron Tooth
See   Frederick II

Irondequoit
See   Buckland, Francis Trevelyan

Ironi
See   Czaczkes, Shmuel Yosef

Ironimus
See   Peichl, Gustav

Ironmaster, Maximus
See   Wilkinson, John [Donald]

Ironquill
See   Ware, Eugene Fitch

Ironside
See   Edmund II

Ironside, John
See   Tait, Euphemia Margaret

Ironside, Matthew
See   Bobin, John William [Jack]

Ironside, Nestor
See   Steele, [Sir] Richard

Irraghiconnor
See   Hennessy, John C.

Irrefragabilis, Doctor
See   Alexander of Hales

[The] Irrefragable Doctor
See   Alexander of Hales

Irurzun, Hugo 20th c.
Alleged assassin of Nicaraguan
dictator, Anastasio Somoza
* Santiago, Captain

Irvin, Dick
See   Irvin, James Dickinson

Irvin, James Dickinson 1892-1957
[CEI, FHE, HK]
Canadian-born hockey player and
coach
* Irvin, Dick

Irvin, Monford Merrill 1919-
[BAB, MK, PB]
American baseball player
* Irvin, Monte
* Nelson, Jimmy

Irvin, Monte
See   Irvin, Monford Merrill

Irvine, Douglas 1943-   [OET]
Rhodesian tennis player
* Irvine, Hank

Irvine, Edward James 1896-
[WWL]
American author
* Ray, Violet

Irvine, George 1948-   [SMG]
American basketball player
* Irvine, Hawkeye

Irvine, Hank
See   Irvine, Douglas

Irvine, Hawkeye
See   Irvine, George

Irving, Alexander [joint pseudonym
with Ruth Fox]
See   Fahrenkopf, Anne

Irving, Alexander [joint pseudonym
with Anne Fahrenkopf]
See   Fox, Ruth

Irving, Ben
See   Silverstein, Benjamin Irving

Irving, Clifford Michael 1930-
[CA]
American author
* Anderson, Clifford [joint
pseudonym with Robert Anderson
and Richard Gardner]
* Luckless, John [joint pseudonym
with Herbert Burkholz]

Irving, Clive
See   Bates, Clive

Irving, Compton
See   Carter, John L[ouis Justin]

Irving, Edward 1792-1834
[FFF, RH, SN]
Scottish clergyman
* [A] Son of Thunder
* Squintum, Doctor

Irving, George S.
See   Shelasky, George Irving

Irving, H. B.
See   Irving, John Henry Brodribb

Irving, Henry
See   Kanter, Hal

Irving, Isabel
See   Washington, Isabel

Irving, John Henry Brodribb
1870-1919   [THR]
British actor and author
* Irving, H. B.

Irving, John Treat 1804?-1838
[FFF, PA]
American author
* Quod, John

Irving, Jules
See   Israel, Jules

Irving, Lawrence
See   Brodribb, Sydney

Irving, Miles
See   Walden, Walter

Irving, Noel 1872- ?   [WWL]
British author
* Gringoire

Irving, Robert
See   Adler, Irving

Irving, Theodore 1809-1880   [PA]
Author
* [A] Layman

Irving, Thomas J.   [PA]
Author
* Hart, Gerald

Irving, Washington 1783-1859
[DEL, FFF]
American author
* Agapida, [Friar] Antonio
* Crayon, Geoffrey
* Evergreen
* Knickerbocker, Diedrich
* Langstaff, Launcelot [joint
pseudonym with William Irving
and James Kirke Paulding]
* Oldstyle, Jonathan

**Irving, William** 1766-1821
[DEL, FFF]
*American author*
* Cockloft, Pindar
* Langstaff, Launcelot [joint pseudonym with Washington Irving and James Kirke Paulding]

**Irwin, Ann[abelle Bowen]** 1915-
[CA]
*American author*
* Irwin, Hadley [joint pseudonym with Lee Hadley]

**Irwin, Big Dee**
See Irwin, Dee

**Irwin, Charles** 20th c. [GW]
*American rodeo performer*
* Irwin, Sharkey

**Irwin, Constance Frick** 1913-
[CA, SAT, WD]
*American author, historian, critic*
* Frick, C. H.
* Frick, Constance

**Irwin, Cynthia C.** 1936- [CA]
*American anthropologist and author*
* Irwin-Williams, Cynthia [Cora]

**Irwin, Dee** 20th c. [RO1]
*American singer*
* Irwin, Big Dee

**Irwin, Dink**
See Irwin, George

**Irwin, Fenelon Arroyo Seco** 20th c.
[CEC]
*American murderer*
* Irwin, Robert

**Irwin, Flo**
See Campbell, Flora

**Irwin, G. H.**
See Palmer, Raymond A[rthur]

**Irwin, G. H.** [house pseudonym]
See Shaver, Richard S[harpe]

**Irwin, George** 20th c. [MEB]
*American basketball player*
* Irwin, Dink

**Irwin, H. C.** 20th c. [SFL]
*Author*
* Time, Mark

**Irwin, Hadley** [joint pseudonym with Ann(abelle Bowen) Irwin]
See Hadley, Lee

**Irwin, Hadley** [joint pseudonym with Lee Hadley]
See Irwin, Ann[abelle Bowen]

**Irwin, Inez Haynes** 1873-1970
[SFL, WGT]
*American author*
* Gillmore, Inez Haynes

**Irwin, Ivan Duane** 1927- [FHE]
*American hockey player*
* Ivan the Terrible

**Irwin, John T[homas]** 1940- [CA]
*American author and poet*
* Bricuth, John

**Irwin, Lightning**
See Irwin, Walt[er Kingsley]

**Irwin, Margaret E.**
See Monsell, Margaret E[mma Irwin]

**Irwin, May**
See Campbell, Ada

**Irwin, P. K.**
See Page, Patricia Kathleen

**Irwin, Phil**
See Irwin, William Franklin [Bill]

**Irwin, Robert**
See Irwin, Fenelon Arroyo Seco

**Irwin, Sharkey**
See Irwin, Charles

**Irwin, Violet**
See De Waal, Violet Mary

**Irwin, Wallace Admah** 1875-1959
[TC]
*American author*
* Togo, Hashimura

**Irwin, Walt[er Kingsley]** 1897-
[BE]
*American baseball player*
* Irwin, Lightning

**Irwin, William Franklin [Bill]**
1859-1933 [BE]
*American baseball player*
* Irwin, Phil

**Irwin-Williams, Cynthia [Cora]**
See Irwin, Cynthia C.

**Is-Orval**
See Ordonez, Valeriano

**Isa**
See Craig-Knox, Isa

**Isaacs, Adelaide Mary** 1874-1966
[BMH]
*British comedienne*
* Reeve, Ada

**Isaacs, Alan** 1925- [WD]
*British author*
* Valentine, Alec

**Isaacs, Arnold** 1931- [IPA]
*Canadian-born fashion designer*
* Scaasi, Arnold

**Isaacs, Barnett** 1852-1897
[DNNS, WBD]
*British speculator*
* Barnato, Barnett [Barney]
* [The] Kaffir King

**Isaacs, Charles Edward** 1923- [EJ]
*American jazz musician*
* Isaacs, Ike

**Isaacs, Edith J. R.**
See Rich, Edith J. R.

**Isaacs, Ike**
See Isaacs, Charles Edward

**Isaacs, Ike**
See Isaacs, Isadore

**Isaacs, Isadore** 1901-1957 [SC]
*American actor*
* Isaacs, Ike

**Isaacs, Jacob**
See Kranzler, George G[ershon]

**Isaacs, Levi** 20th c. [MBF]
*British author*
* Essex, Lewis

**Isaacs, Marcel Godfrey** 1893-
[WWL]
*British author*
* Godfrey, Marcel
* Lofty

**Isabel**
See Ogden, Anna Cora

**Isabel**
See Simms, William Gilmore

**Isabel [or Elizabeth]** 1271-1336
[WBD]
*Queen of Portugal and Saint*
* [The] Peacemaker

**Isabella of Bavaria** 1370-1435
[DNNS, FFF, SN]
*Wife of King Charles VI of France*
* Gourre
* [The] Great Sow

**Isabella of France** 1292-1358
[DEP, DNNS, SN]
*Wife of King Edward II of England*
* [The] She Wolf of France

**Isabella of Valois** 1389-1409
[DNNS, FFF, RH]
*Queen of England*
* [The] Little Queen

**Isabella I [or Isabel]** 1451-1504
[DNNS, FFF, WBD]
*Queen of Castile*
* [The] Catholic
* [La] Catolica

**Isacson, Betty Ann** 1925- [BEW]
*American actress*
* Isacson, Lenke
* Peterson, Lenka

**Isacson, Lenke**
See Isacson, Betty Ann

**Isaiah** 8th c. BC [HN]
*Hebrew prophet*
* [The] Evangelical Prophet

**Isais**
See Cruz y Fernandez, Manuel de la

**Isalin**
See De la Touche, Janet

**Isambard**
See Williams, Jac Lewis

**Isaure, Clemence** 1463?-1513?
[DNNF, DNNS, SN]
*French poet*
* [The] Sappho of Toulouse

**[The] Isaurian**
See Leo III

**Isban [or Izban], Samuel**
See Izbitsky [or Ishbitsky], Samuel

**Isbell, William Frank** 1875-1941
[BE]
*American baseball player*
* Bald Eagle

**Isbister, Clair**
See Isbister, Jean Sinclair

**Isbister, Jean Sinclair** 1915- [CA]
*Australian physician and author*
* Isbister, Clair

**Isely, Flora Kunigunde Duncan**
See Duncan, Kunigunde

**Ish Kabibble**
See Bogue, Merwyn

**Ishitsuji, Keiichi** 1927- [EJ]
*Japanese jazz musician*
* Kawabe, Kinichi

**Isidore [or Isidro]** ?-1130 [DNNS]
*Saint*
* [The] Ploughman of Madrid

**Isidore of Alexandria** 370-440?
[RH]
*Saint*
* Thaumaturgus

**Isidore of Seville** 570?-636 [HN]
*Saint*
* [The] Theologian

**Isis**
See Torbett, Harvey Douglas Louis

**Iskander**
See Yakovlev, Aleksandr Ivanovich

**Iskander Beg**
See Castriot [or Castriota?], George

**Iskowitz, Edward Israel** 1892-1964
[BEW, FC, PMJ]
*American actor, singer, comedian*
* Banjo Eyes
* Cantor, Eddie

**Islam, Kazi Nazrul** 1899?-1976
[CA]
*Bangladesh poet*
* [The] Rebel Poet

**Islam, Yusef**
See Georgiou, Stephen Demetre

**Islay, Nicholas**
See Murray, Andrew Nicholas

**Isler, Ursula** 1923- [IAW]
*Swiss author*
* Jucker, Iwan

**Islet, Theodore Oceanic**
See Crocker, Samuel

**Isley, Phylis Lee** 1919-
[BDF, BEW, FC]
*American actress*
* Jones, Jennifer

**Ismail Pasha**
See Kmety, Gyoergy

**Ismar, Mademoiselle**
See Clewe, Belle Ragnar Parsons

**Ismay, [Sir] Hastings** 1887-1965
[BDW, WWW]
*British army officer*
* Ismay, Pug

**Ismay, Pug**
See Ismay, [Sir] Hastings

**Ismet Pasa** 1884- ? [WBD]
*Turkish statesman*
* Inonu, Ismet

**Isnard, Maximin** 1755-1825 [HN]
*French politician*
* [The] Danton of the Gironde

**Isocrates** 4th c. BC
[DNNS, FFF, RH]
*Athenian orator*
* [The] Old Man Eloquent

**[The] Isocrates of France**
See Flechier, [Valentin] Esprit

**Isogai, Hiroshi** 1940- [CA]
*Japanese illustrator and photographer*
* Ko, Kanzein

**Isouard, Nicolas** 1775-1818 [WBD]
*Franco-Italian musician and composer*
* Niccolo

**Israel, Elmo** 1918- [CA]
*American writer and poet*
* Ellis, Elmo I[srael]

**Israel, Jules** 1925- [TR]
*American director and producer*
* Irving, Jules

**Israel, Melvin** 1913- [EJS]
*American sportscaster*
* Allen, Mel

**Issachar**
See Stanford, John Keith

**[The] It Girl**
See Bow, Clara

**It Matters Not Who**
See Nares, Edward

**[The] Italian Callimachus**
See Buonaccorsi, Filippo

**[The] Italian Dickens**
See Farina, Salvatore

**[The] Italian Froebel**
See Rosmini-Serbati, Antonio

**[The] Italian Gray**
See Guidi, Carlo Alessandro

**[The] Italian Gray**
See Pindemonte, Ippolito

**Italian Joe Gans**
See Camerlengo, Anthony

**[The] Italian Moliere**
See Goldoni, Carlo

**[The] Italian Mozart**
See Cherubini, Maria Luigi Carlo
Zenobio Salvatore

**[The] Italian Nightingale**
See Catalani, Angelica

**[The] Italian Pindar**
See Chiabrera, Gabriello

**[The] Italian Samson**
See Milo

**[The] Italian Schubert**
See Gordigiani, Luigi

**[The] Italian Sex Bomb**
See Rivelli, Francesca

**[The] Italian Stallion**
See Musso, John, Jr.

**Italiano, Anna Maria Luisa** 1931-
[BDF, BEW, FIR]
*American actress*
* Bancroft, Anne
* Marno, Anne
* St. Raymond, Anne
* Tulane, Anne

**Italiski**
See Suvorov [or Suwarof],
Aleksandr Vasilievich

**[The] Itinerant Dey of New Jersey**
See Livingston, William

**Iturbide, Agusto** 1784?-1824
[DNNF, FFF, SN]
*Emperor of Mexico*
* [The] Napoleon of Mexico

**Iturrondo, Francisco** 1800-1868
[CW]
*Cuban poet*
* Delio

**Itzmunsh**
See Avigador, Ben Moise

**Ivan**
See Allison, Jerry

**Ivan, Gustave E.** 20th c. [CAP]
*Author*
* Tavo, Gus [joint pseudonym with
Martha Miller Pfaff Ivan]

**Ivan Kalita [Moneybag]**
See Ivan I

**Ivan Krasny [The Red]**
See Ivan II

**Ivan, Martha Miller Pfaff** 1909-
[CAP]
*American author*
* Miller, Martha
* Tavo, Gus [joint pseudonym with
Gustave E. Ivan]

**Ivan the Terrible**
See Irwin, Ivan Duane

**Ivan the Terrible**
See Serov, Ivan A.

**Ivan I** ?-1341 [WBD]
*Grand duke of Russia*
* Ivan Kalita [Moneybag]

**Ivan II** 1326-1359 [WBD]
*Grand duke of Russia*
* Ivan Krasny [The Red]

**Ivan III Vasilievich** 1440-1505
[DNNS, WBD]
*Duke of Moscow*
* [The] Great

**Ivan IV Vasilievich** 1530?-1584
[DNNS, FFF, HN]
*Czar of Russia*
* [The] Terrible
* [The] Tyrant Basilides

**Ivanichevitch, Paul** 1900- [ITA]
*French-born cinematographer*
* Ivano, Paul

**Ivano, Paul**
See Ivanichevitch, Paul

**Ivanov, Mikhail Mikhailovitch**
1859-1935 [BBD]
*Russian composer*
* Ippolitov-Ivanov, Mikhail
Mikhailovitch

**Ivarius, Alice** 1876-1943 [THR]
*American opera singer*
* Nielsen, Alice

**Ivens, Georg Henri Anton** 1898-
[FDG]
*Dutch director*
* Ivens, Joris

**Ivens, Joris**
See Ivens, Georg Henri Anton

**Ivens, Michael William** 1924-
[IAW]
*British author and poet*
* Yorick

**Ivers, Hardinge Furenzo** [PA]
*Author*
* Alithinas

**Ives, Edward D[awson]** 1925- [CA]
*American author, folklorist,
folksinger*
* Ives, Sandy

**Ives, Laurel** [GW]
*American rodeo performer*
* Ives, Lum

**Ives, Lawrence**
See Woods, Frederick

**Ives, Lum**
See Ives, Laurel

**Ives, Mary Alice** [PA]
*Author*
* Octavia

**Ives, Sandy**
See Ives, Edward D[awson]

**Ivison, Elizabeth** 1931- [AW]
*Australian author*
* Towers, Tricia
* Wilson, Elizabeth

**Ivo, T. V.**
See Ivo, Tommy

**Ivo, Tommy** [EAR]
*Auto racer*
* Ivo, T. V.

**Ivoguen, Maria**
See Von Gunther, Ilse [or Inge?]

**Ivor, Frances**
See Forbes, Frances

**Ivory, Beryl** 1926- [FC]
*British actress*
* Baxter, Beryl

**Ivory, Buster**
See Ivory, Raymond

**Ivory Joe Hunter**
See Hunter, Joseph

**Ivory Lee Semien**
See Semien, Lee

**Ivory, Raymond** 20th c. [GW]
*American rodeo performer*
* Ivory, Buster

**Ivy, Frank** 20th c. [CFH, SMG]
*Canadian football coach*
* Ivy, Pop

**Ivy, Pop**
See Ivy, Frank

**Iwamatsu, Jun Atsushi** 1908- [CA]
*Japanese-born author and
illustrator*
* Yashima, Taro

**Iwaszkiewicz, Jaroslaw** 1894-
[CD, EWL]
*Polish poet, author, playwright*
* Eleuter

**Iwerks, Ub**
See Iwerks, Ubbe

**Iwerks, Ubbe** 1901-1971 [WEC]
*American cartoonist and animator*
* Iwerks, Ub

**Ixion**
See Johnson, Llewellyn H.

**Ixion**
See Salmon, Leon N.

**Iyeasu** 1542-1616 [HN]
*Japanese general and statesman*
* [The] Henry VII of Japan

**Izant, Grace Goulder** 1893- [CAP]
*American author*
* Goulder, Grace

**Izax, Ickabod**
See Stebbins, G. S.

**Izbitsky [or Ishbitsky], Samuel**
1905- [CA, IAW]
*Polish-born author and journalist*
* Fireman, A.
* Isban [or Izban], Samuel
* Krantz, D.
* Laks, S.

**Izis**
See Bidermanas, Israel

**Izquierdo, Enrique Roberto** 1931-
[BE]
*Cuban-born baseball player*
* Izquierdo, Hank

**Izquierdo, Hank**
See Izquierdo, Enrique Roberto

**Izquierdo, Mitzou** 20th c. [WFA]
*Spanish fashion designer*
* Mitzou

# J

**J.**
*See* Garrity, Joan Theresa

**J.**
*See* Jerrold, Douglas William

**J. A.**
*See* Ayling, Joan

**J. A. B.**
*See* Beringer, Joseph August

**J. A. H.**
*See* Hanauer, John Arno

**J. A. S.**
*See* Shepherd, William James Affleck

**J. A. W.**
*See* Watts, Joan Alwyn

**J. B.**
*See* Barr, James Leland

**J. B. T.**
*See* Taylor, Joyce Barbara

**J. C.**
*See* Agajanian, Joshua James

**J. C.**
*See* Carlyon, John

**J. C.**
*See* Clay, James

**J. C.**
*See* Codman, John

**J. C.**
*See* Cook, Jennifer

**J. C.**
*See* Crook, Joel

**J. C.**
*See* Curtis, John Duffield

**J. C. B.**
*See* Boyce, John Coxe

**J. C. G.**
*See* Grimani, Julia C.

**J. C. H.**
*See* Hotten, John Camden

**J. C. S.**
*See* Stone, John Christopher

**J. D.**
*See* Davidson, John Arthur

**J. D.**
*See* Davis, Jimmy

**J. D.**
*See* De Bow, J. D. B.

**J. D.**
*See* Dix, John A.

**J. D.**
*See* Donaldson, Jack

**J. D. R. 3**
*See* Rockefeller, John Davison, III

**J. E. H.**
*See* Hinshaw, John E.

**J. E. M.**
*See* Milne, John Erskine

**J. E. W.**
*See* Whitly, Jonas E.

**J. F.**
*See* Faithfull, Joan Margaret Caldwell

**J. F.**
*See* Foster, John

**J. F.**
*See* Fry, James William

**J. F. K.**
*See* Kennedy, John Fitzgerald [Jack]

**J. F. N.**
*See* Noll, John Francis

**J. F. W.**
*See* Waller, John Francis

**J. G.**
*See* Glassford, James

**J. G.**
*See* Greenbury, Judith Pamela

**J. H.**
*See* Harris, Josephine

**J. H.**
*See* McCarthy, Denis Florence

**J. H. C.**
*See* Connelly, John H.

**J. H. K.**
*See* Kocman, Jiri Hynek

**J. H. N.**
*See* Newman, John Henry

**J. J.**
*See* Jennings, James H.

**J. J.**
*See* Joyce, John

**J. J.**
*See* Judkins, Jeff

**J. J.**
*See* Rousseau, Jean-Jacques

**J. J. R.**
*See* Rouel, Joseph Jules

**J. K.**
*See* Hunter, John Kelso

**J. K.**
*See* Knoblock, Joan

**J. K.**
*See* Lamptey, Jonathan Kwesi

**J. K. L.**
*See* Doyle, James Kildare Leighlin

**J. K. S.**
*See* Stephen, James Kenneth

**J. M.**
*See* Martin, John

**J. M.**
*See* Milner, J.

**J. M.**
*See* Morley, John

**J. M.**
*See* Muir, John

**J. M. B.**
*See* Bulloch, John Malcolm

**J. M. B.**
*See* Butterworth, John Malcolm

**J. M. R.**
*See* Ramsey, Joseph McCray

**J. O.**
*See* Higgins, Matthew James

**J. P.**
*See* Narayan, Jayaprakash

**J. P.**
*See* Parker, John

**J. R.**
*See* Roche, James

**J. R. D.**
*See* Dill, James Reid

**J. R. M.**
*See* McCulloch, Hugh

**[The] J. R. of the National Party**
*See* Botha, Pieter

**J. R. R. T.**
*See* Tolkien, John Ronald Reuel

**J. S.**
*See* Stoddart, [Sir] John

**J. S. K.**
*See* Kirkwood, John Sutherland

**J. S. of Dale**
*See* Stimson, Frederic Jesup

**J. S. T.**
*See* Taylor, James Spencer

**J. S. W.**
*See* Scrymgeour Wedderburn, Janet

**J. T.**
*See* Bell, Eric Temple

**J. T.**
*See* Taylor, James Spencer

**J. T.**
*See* Tonks, John

**J. T.**
*See* Torrio, John [Johnny]

**J. V. Z.**
*See* Veazie, Joseph

**J. W.**
*See* Wade, John

**J. W.**
*See* Warburton, Joan

**J. W.**
*See* Wilson, John

**J. W.**
*See* Woodcock, John

**J. W.**
*See* Wroughton, Julia

**J. W. H. M.**
*See* Molyneaux, John William Henry

**J. W. L.**
*See* Lethaby, John W.

**J. W. L.**
*See* Whitaker, Rogers Ernest Malcolm

**J. Y. A.**
*See* Akerman, John Yonge

**J. Y. C.**
*See* Cousteau, Jacques-Yves

**J. Z.**
*See* Zulawski, Juliusz

**Jabali, Warren**
*See* Armstrong, Warren

**Jabet, George S.** [PA]
*Author*
* Warwick, Eden

**Jabez**
See Nicol, Eric [Patrick]

**Jablonowski, Peter William** 1904-
[BE, PB]
*American baseball player*
* Appleton, Jake
* Appleton, Peter William

**Jablonski, Jabbo**
See Jablonski, Raymond Leo

**Jablonski, Raymond Leo** 1926-
[BE, BTB]
*American baseball player*
* Jablonski, Jabbo

**Jabusch, Reinhold** 20th c. [AES]
*American soccer player and coach*
* Jabusch, Ron

**Jabusch, Ron**
See Jabusch, Reinhold

**Jac**
See Jacovitti, Benito

**Jacia**
See Crane, John

**Jack?**
See Stratemeyer, Edward L.

**Jack, Alex** 1945- [NAD]
*American author*
* Hapi

**Jack All Alone**
See Cowper, Frank

**Jack Amend-All**
See Cade, John [Jack]

**Jack, Bud**
See Jack, James R.

**[The] Jack Cade of France**
See Caillet, Guillaume

**[The] Jack Frost Lady**
See Thompson, Jean M.

**Jack, Henry Vernon** 1869-1922
[BEW]
*British-born theatrical performer
and playwright*
* Esmond, Henry Vernon

**Jack, James R.** 20th c. [BBH]
*American collegiate athletic director*
* Jack, Bud

**Jack of Clubs**
See Sheridan, Philip Henry

**Jack of Newbury**
See Winchcomb, John

**Jack of Norfolk**
See Howard, [Sir] John [First
Duke of Norfolk]

**Jack of Spades**
See Logan, John Alexander

**Jack Rabbit Smith-Johannsen**
See Smith-Johannsen, Herman

**Jack the Dropper**
See Kaplan, Nathan

**Jack the Giant Killer**
See Pfiestenberger, John Theodore
Joseph [Jack]

**Jack the Giant Killer**
See Price, Ernest Cutler

**Jack the Giant-Killer**
See Randolph, John

**Jack the Painter**
See Aitken, James

**[The] Jackal**
See Ramirez-Sanchez, Ilyich

**Jackboot John Vorster**
See Vorster, Balthazar Johannes

**Jackie O**
See Onassis, Jacqueline Lee
[Bouvier] [Kennedy]

**[The] Jackie Robinson of
Broadcasting**
See White, William [Bill]

**Jackie the Lackey**
See Cerone, John Philip

**Jackman, Cannonball**
See Jackman, William

**Jackman, Jackers**
See Jackman, Robin David

**Jackman, Robin David** 1945- [DC]
*British cricketer*
* Jackman, Jackers

**Jackman, William** 1897-1972
[MK]
*American baseball player*
* Jackman, Cannonball

**Jackmon, Marvin X.** 1944- [CA]
*American poet, playwright, lecturer*
* [El] Muhajir

**Jacks, Dennis Alexander** 1897-
[BEW]
*British actor and director*
* Gurney, Dennis

**Jacks, L. P.**
See Jacks, Lawrence Pearsall

**Jacks, Lawrence Pearsall**
1860-1955 [LC]
*British author and clergyman*
* Jacks, L. P.

**Jacks, M. L.**
See Jacks, Maurice Leonard

**Jacks, Maurice Leonard**
1894-1964 [LC]
*British author and educator*
* Jacks, M. L.

**Jacks, Oliver**
See Gandley, Kenneth Royce

**Jackson, Albert** 1898?-1978
[FIR, NOJ]
*American jazz musician*
* Jackson, Loochie [or Luchie]

**Jackson, Albina**
See Geis, Richard E[rwin]

**Jackson, Alex**
See Jackson, Alexandra Elizabeth

**Jackson, Alexandra Elizabeth**
1952- [SWI]
*British swimmer*
* Jackson, Alex

**Jackson, Alvin Neil** 1935- [BR]
*American baseball player and
manager*
* Jackson, Jack

**Jackson, Andrew** 1767-1845
[FAP, FFF, HN]
*American president*
* Big Knife
* [The] Duel Fighter
* [The] Hero of New Orleans

**Jackson, Andrew** (Continued)
* King Andrew the First
* [The] Land Hero of 1812
* Mischievous Andy
* [The] Old Hero
* Old Hickory
* [The] People's President
* Pointed Arrow
* [The] Sage of the Hermitage
* Sharp Knife

**Jackson, Arthur** 1911-1977
[BWW]
*American singer*
* Jackson, Sam
* Peg Leg Sam
* Peg Pete

**Jackson, Ashes**
See Jackson, William

**Jackson, Aunt Mollie**
See Garland, Mary Magdalene

**Jackson, Bags**
See Jackson, Milt[on]

**Jackson, Barbara Ann Garvey
Seagrave** 1929- [WD]
*American musicologist and author*
* Seagrave, Barbara Ann Garvey

**Jackson, Benjamin Clarence** 1919-
[EJ]
*American jazz musician*
* Jackson, Bull Moose

**Jackson, Bessie**
See Bogan, Lucille

**Jackson, Billboard**
See Jackson, James Albert

**Jackson, Buck**
See Jackson, Grant Dwight

**Jackson, Buddha**
See Jackson, Noah Dale

**Jackson, Bull Moose**
See Jackson, Benjamin Clarence

**Jackson, Bunny**
See Jackson, Burnella Jane Hayes
Burke

**Jackson, Burnella Jane Hayes Burke**
20th c. [IBW]
*American public relations firm
founder*
* Jackson, Bunny

**Jackson, Busher**
See Jackson, Harvey

**Jackson, Butter**
See Jackson, Quentin Leonard

**Jackson, C. D.**
See Jackson, Charles Douglas

**Jackson, C[aary] Paul** 1902-
[CA, SAT]
*American author*
* Jackson, O. B.
* Lochlons, Colin
* Paulson, Jack

**Jackson, Carol** 1911- [CAT]
*American author*
* Michaels, Peter

**Jackson, Charles Douglas** 1902-
[BEW]
*American publishing executive*
* Jackson, C. D.

**Jackson, Charles Herbert [Charlie]**
1894-1968 [BE]
*American baseball player*
* Jackson, Lefty

**Jackson, Charles Melvin** 1950-
[EJ7]
*American jazz musician*
* Jackson, Chip

**Jackson, Charlie** ?-1938 [BWW]
*American singer*
* Carter, Charlie
* Jackson, Papa Charlie

**Jackson, Chip**
See Jackson, Charles Melvin

**Jackson, Chubby**
See Jackson, Greig Stewart

**Jackson, Chumly**
See Jackson, Noah Dale

**Jackson, Clarence** 20th c. [SMG]
*American football player*
* Jackson, Jazz

**Jackson, Clarence J. L.**
See Bulliet, Richard W[illiams]

**Jackson, Cliff**
See Jackson, Clifton Luther

**Jackson, Clifton Luther** 1902-1970
[EJ7]
*American jazz musician*
* Jackson, Cliff

**Jackson, Consequential**
See Jackson, William

**Jackson, Cubby** 20th c. [RBE]
*American boxer*
* Jackson, Top Cat

**Jackson, Duff Clark** 1953- [EJ7]
*American jazz musician*
* Jackson, Duffy

**Jackson, Duffy**
See Jackson, Duff Clark

**Jackson, E. F.**
See Tubb, Edwin Charles

**Jackson, Elmer Martin, Jr.** 1906-
[NAA]
*American journalist and author*
* Jackson, Jay

**Jackson, Emory O.** 1908-1975
[IBW]
*American journalist*
* Black Moses of the Black Press

**Jackson, Ethel** 1884-1952 [SC]
*American actress*
* Kent, Ethel

**Jackson, Ethel Shannon** 1898-1951
[SC]
*American actress*
* Shannon, Ethel

**Jackson, Everatt**
See Muggeson, Margaret
Elizabeth

**Jackson, Fats**
See Jackson, Lester

**Jackson, Fearless Lil**
See Jackson, Lillie Mae Carroll

**Jackson, Flora Mae King**
1930-1965 [BL]
*Entertainer*
* Baby Flo

**Jackson, Franklin Jefferson**
See Watkins, Mel

**Jackson, Frederick John**
1855-1941 [WBD]
*British theologian*
* Foakes-Jackson, Frederick John

**Jackson, [Sir] Frederick Stanley**
1870-1947 [EC]
*British cricketer*
* Jackson, Jacker

**Jackson, G. W.**
See Jackson, George William

**Jackson, Gator**
See Jackson, Willis

**Jackson, George Christopher**
1882-1972 [BE]
*American baseball player*
* Jackson, Hickory

**Jackson, George William** 1914-
[ART]
*British artist*
* Jackson, G. W.

**Jackson, Giles**
See Leffingwell, Albert

**Jackson, Grant Dwight** 1942-
[BE, SMG]
*American baseball player*
* Jackson, Buck

**Jackson, Greig Stewart** 1918-
[ASC, DAM, EJ]
*American jazz musician*
* Jackson, Chubby

**Jackson, Handsome Ransom**
See Jackson, Ransom Joseph

**Jackson, Harvey** 1911-1966
[CEI, FHE, HK]
*Canadian-born hockey player*
* Jackson, Busher

**Jackson, Helen Maria Hunt**
1830-1885 [DNNF, FFF, WBD]
*American author*
* H. H.
* Holm, Saxe

**Jackson, Henry** 1912-
[BX, RBE, SG]
*American boxer*
* Armstrong, Hammerin' Hank
* Armstrong, Henry
* Armstrong, Homicide Hank
* Armstrong, Hurricane Henry
* Jackson, Melody
* Perpetual Motion

**Jackson, Henry Martin** 1912-
[B10]
*American politician*
* Jackson, Scoop

**Jackson, Hickory**
See Jackson, George Christopher

**Jackson, Howard**
See McGraw, J. H.

**Jackson, Howard** 1952- [IBW]
*American martial arts expert*
* Jackson, Karate

**Jackson, Hurricane**
See Jackson, Thomas [Tommy]

**Jackson, Jack**
See Jackson, Alvin Neil

**Jackson, Jacker**
See Jackson, [Sir] Frederick
Stanley

**Jackson, Jackie**
See Jackson, Sigmund Esco

**Jackson, James Albert** 1878- ?
[IBW]
*American public relations officer,
marketing and advertising specialist*
* [The] Dean of Black Hucksters
* Jackson, Billboard

**Jackson, Jay**
See Jackson, Elmer Martin, Jr.

**Jackson, Jazz**
See Jackson, Clarence

**Jackson, Jelly**
See Jackson, Norman

**Jackson, Jesse Louis** 1942- [IBW]
*American clergyman and political
organizer*
* [The] Country Preacher

**Jackson, Jill** 1942- [PRS, RO1]
*American singer*
* Paula

**Jackson, Joe**
See Jiranek, Joseph Francis

**Jackson, John** 1847?-1908? [MK]
*American baseball player*
* Fowler, Bud
* Fowler, John W.

**Jackson, John H.** 1924- [BWW]
*American singer*
* Jackson, Mississippi John

**Jackson, John William, Jr.** 1945-
[SFL, WGT]
*American author*
* Silent, William T.

**Jackson, Joseph [Francis Ambrose]**
1867- ? [NAA]
*American author and editor*
* Scott, Churchill

**Jackson, Joseph Jefferson**
1887?-1951 [AS, DGS, PB]
*American baseball player*
* Jackson, Shoeless Joe

**Jackson, Josephine**
See Whitehead, Mrs. C. B.

**Jackson, Julian**
See Wilson, John Park

**Jackson, Karate**
See Jackson, Howard

**Jackson, Laura [Riding]**
See Reichenthal, Laura

**Jackson, Lawrence** 1921-1974
[SC]
*American actor and dancer*
* Baby Laurence

**Jackson, Lee** 1907- [BWW]
*American singer*
* Lee, Warren

**Jackson, Lefty**
See Jackson, Charles Herbert
[Charlie]

**Jackson, Lester** 20th c. [BWW]
*American entertainer*
* Jackson, Fats

**Jackson, Lewis**
See Lewis, Jack

**Jackson, Lil Son**
See Jackson, Melvin

**Jackson, Lillie Mae Carroll**
1889-1975 [IBW]
*American civil rights activist*
* Jackson, Fearless Lil

**Jackson, Loochie [or Luchie]**
See Jackson, Albert

**Jackson, Lucille**
See Strauss, [Mary] Lucille
Jackson

**Jackson, Lucious** 1941- [BB]
*American basketball player*
* Jackson, Luke

**Jackson, Luke**
See Jackson, Lucious

**Jackson, Mahalia** 1911-1972
[IBW]
*American singer*
* [The] World's Greatest Gospel
Singer

**Jackson, Mary Hilliard** 20th c.
*American painter*
* Mary

**Jackson, Melody**
See Jackson, Henry

**Jackson, Melvin** 1915-1976
[BWW, NBB]
*American singer*
* Jackson, Lil Son

**Jackson, Michael Joseph** 1958-
[IBW]
*American singer*
* [The] Little Prince of Soul

**Jackson, Milt[on]** 1923-
[DAM, EJ, PMJ]
*American jazz musician*
* Jackson, Bags

**Jackson, Mississippi John**
See Jackson, John H.

**Jackson, Mrs. T. J.** [FFF]
*Entertainer*
* Newcomb, Theresa

**Jackson, Neville**
See Glaskin, Gerald Marcus

**Jackson, Noah Dale** 1951- [SMG]
*American football player*
* Jackson, Buddha
* Jackson, Chumly

**Jackson, Nora**
See Tennant, Nora Jackson

**Jackson, Norman** 20th c. [OBW]
*American baseball player*
* Jackson, Jelly

**Jackson, O. B.**
See Jackson, C[aary] Paul

**Jackson of Exeter**
See Jackson, William

**Jackson, Oliver, Jr.** 1934- [EJ]
*American jazz musician*
* Bops Junior

**Jackson, Papa Charlie**
See Jackson, Charlie

**Jackson, Peter**
See Brice, Douglas Francis
Aloysius

**Jackson, Peter** 1861-1901 [IBW]
*West Indian-born boxer*
* [The] Black Prince of the Ring

**Jackson, Philander**
See Burrage, Alfred Sherrington

**Jackson, Preston**
See McDonald, James Preston

**Jackson, Quentin Leonard**
1909-1976 [EJ, PMJ, WWJ]
*American jazz musician*
* Jackson, Butter

**Jackson, R. E.**
See Innes, Rosemary E[lizabeth
Jackson]

**Jackson, Randy**
See Jackson, Ransom Joseph

**Jackson, Ransom Joseph** 1926-
[BE]
*American baseball player*
* Jackson, Handsome Ransom
* Jackson, Randy

**Jackson, Raymond** 1927- [WEC]
*British cartoonist*
* Jak

**Jackson, Red**
See Jackson, Walter

**Jackson, Reginald [Reggie]** 1946-
[IBW]
*American baseball player*
* Muscles, Mr.
* October, Mr.

**Jackson, Rich[ard] S.** 1941- [FB]
*American football player*
* Jackson, Tombstone

**Jackson, Robert** 1918?-1978 [FIR]
*Musician*
* Jackson, Squeezebox

**Jackson, Robert R.** 1870-1942
[IBW]
*American politician and civic leader*
* [The] Major

**Jackson, Roland Thomas** 1944-
[BE, PB]
*American baseball player*
* Jackson, Sonny

**Jackson, Rufus** 20th c. [OBW]
*American baseball player*
* Jackson, Sonnyman

**Jackson, Sally**
See Kellogg, Jean [Defrees]

**Jackson, Sam**
See Jackson, Arthur

**Jackson, Sam**
See Trumbo, Dalton

**Jackson, Scoop**
See Jackson, Henry Martin

**Jackson, Shirley**
See Hyman, Shirley Jackson

**Jackson, Shoeless Joe**
See Jackson, Joseph Jefferson

**Jackson, Sigmund Esco** 1951-
[RO2, SSS]
*American singer*
* Jackson, Jackie

**Jackson, Sonny**
See Jackson, Roland Thomas

**Jackson, Sonnyman**
See Jackson, Rufus

**Jackson, Squeezebox**
See Jackson, Robert

**Jackson, Stephen**
See Stevenson, John

**Jackson, Stonewall**
See Jackson, Thomas Jonathan

**Jackson, Stonewall**
See Jackson, Travis Calvin

**Jackson, Thomas** 1810- ? [PA]
*Author*
* Maritzburg, Pieter

**Jackson, Thomas [Tommy]**
1931-1982 [BX]
*American boxer*
* Jackson, Hurricane

**Jackson, Thomas Gregory** 1947-
[RO2]
*American singer*
* James, Tommy

**Jackson, Thomas Jonathan**
1824-1863 [DNNF, FFF, SN]
*American army officer*
* Jackson, Stonewall
* Old Jack

**Jackson, Thomas W.** [FFF]
*American writer*
* Hickory

**Jackson, Tito**
See Jackson, Toriano

**Jackson, Tombstone**
See Jackson, Rich[ard] S.

**Jackson, Top Cat**
See Jackson, Cubby

**Jackson, Toriano** 1953- [SSS]
*American singer*
* Jackson, Tito

**Jackson, Travis Calvin** 1903-
[BE, BTB]
*American baseball player*
* [The] Arkansas Traveler
* Jackson, Stonewall

**Jackson, Wallace**
See Budd, William John

**Jackson, Walter** 20th c. [CEI]
*Canadian-born hockey player*
* Jackson, Red

**Jackson, William** 1730-1803
[WBD]
*British composer*
* Jackson of Exeter

**Jackson, William** 1750-1815 [SN]
*British clergyman*
* Jackson, Consequential
* Poor Con

**Jackson, William** 20th c. [OBW]
*American baseball player*
* Jackson, Ashes

**Jackson, Willie**
See Tobler, Oscar

**Jackson, Willis** 1932- [EJ7]
*American jazz musician*
* Jackson, Gator

**Jackspur**
See Lawrence, Christopher George
Holman

**Jacob, Andre Alexander** [PA]
*Author*
* Erdan, Alexander

**Jacob, Giles** 1686-1744 [DNNS]
*British author*
* [The] Scourge of Grammar

**Jacob, Naomi Ellington** 1889-1964
[WBD]
*British author*
* Gray, Ellington

**Jacob, P. L., Bibliophile**
See Lacroix, Paul

**Jacob, Pierre** 1905- [CAR]
*French painter*
* Tal-Coat, Pierre

**Jacob, Piers A[nthony] D[illingham]**
1934- [CA, SF, WD]
*British-born American author*
* Anthony, Piers

**Jacob the Silent**
See Pincus, Jacob

**Jacobi, Friedrich Heinrich**
1743-1819 [DNNF, FFF, SN]
*German philosopher*
* [The] German Plato
* [The] Plato of Germany

**Jacobi, Lou**
See Jacobovitch, Lou

**Jacobovitch, Lou** 1913- [JL]
*Canadian-born comic actor*
* Jacobi, Lou

**Jacobs, Allen S.**
See Jacobs, Alma Sylvia

**Jacobs, Alma Sylvia** 20th c. [NAA]
*American writer and columnist*
* Blair, Sylvia
* Jacobs, Allen S.

**Jacobs, Amos** 1914-
[FC, IPA, ITA]
*American entertainer*
* Thomas, Danny

**Jacobs, Austin Lewis** 1907-1972
[BEW]
*American actor*
* Parker, Lew

**Jacobs, Bucky**
See Jacobs, Newton Smith

**Jacobs, Doc**
See Jacobs, George W.

**Jacobs, Edward** 1899-1952?
[WWJ]
*American jazz musician*
* Jacobs, Pete

**Jacobs, Forrest Vandergrift** 1925-
[BE]
*American baseball player*
* Jacobs, Spook

**Jacobs, Francis** 1907- [THR]
*British actor*
* James, Francis

**Jacobs, George Herman** 1889-1952
[SC]
*American actor*
* Ward, Sam

**Jacobs, George W.** 1900?-1968
[BBH]
*American coach and collegiate
athletic director*
* Jacobs, Doc

**Jacobs, Harriet** [FFF]
*American author*
* Brent, Linda

**Jacobs, Helen Hull** 1908-
[CA, SAT]
*American tennis player and author*
* Hull, H. Braxton

**Jacobs, Hirsch** 1904- [EJS]
*American horse trainer and breeder*
* [The] Emancipator of the Platter

**Jacobs, Howard** 1908- [CA]
*American author, columnist, poet*
* [The] Bard of Avondale

**Jacobs, Indian Jack**
See Jacobs, Jack

**Jacobs, Irving**
See Amendola, Mario

**Jacobs, Jack** 1921- [BBH, CFH]
*American-born football player*
* Jacobs, Indian Jack

**Jacobs, Jake**
See Jacobs, Lamar Gary

**Jacobs, Jill** 1942- [CA]
*American-born author, editor, poet*
* Bharti, Ma Satya
* Safian, Jill

**Jacobs, Joe** 1896-1940 [AS, EJS]
*American boxing manager*
* Yussel the Muscle

**Jacobs, Lamar Gary** 1937- [BE]
*American baseball player*
* Jacobs, Jake

**Jacobs, Leah**
See Gellis, Roberta L[eah Jacobs]

**Jacobs, Linda C.** 1943- [CA]
*American author*
* Austin, Tom
* Blackburn, Claire

**Jacobs, Margaret** 1937-
*American actress*
* Thomas, Marlo

**Jacobs, Marion Walter** 1930-1968
[BWW, NBB]
*American singer*
* Little Walter
* Little Walter J

**Jacobs, Marita** 20th c. [OP]
*South African-born opera singer*
* Napier, Marita

**Jacobs, Matthew** 1929?- [BWW]
*American singer*
* Boogie Jake

**Jacobs, Mike**
See Jacobs, Morris Elmore

**Jacobs, Morris Elmore** 20th c.
[BE]
*American baseball player*
* Jacobs, Mike

**Jacobs, Newton P.** 1900- [ITA]
*American film executive*
* Jacobs, Red

**Jacobs, Newton Smith** 1913- [BE]
*American baseball player*
* Jacobs, Bucky

**Jacobs, Pete**
See Jacobs, Edward

**Jacobs, Pim**
See Jacobs, Willem Bernard

**Jacobs, Red**
See Jacobs, Newton P.

**Jacobs, Rosetta** 1932-
[FC, ITA, SW]
*American actress*
* Laurie, Piper

**Jacobs, Ruth Harriet** 1924- [CA]
*American sociologist and author*
* Miller, Ruth

**Jacobs, Spook**
See Jacobs, Forrest Vandergrift

**Jacobs, Steven**
See Sellers, Connie Leslie, Jr.

**Jacobs, T[homas] C[urtis] H[icks]**
See Pendower, Jacques

**Jacobs, W. W.**
See Jacobs, William Wymark

**Jacobs, Walter**
See Vinson, Walter Jacobs

**Jacobs, Walter Darnell** 1922- [CA]
*American author and educator*
* Oboe, Peter

**Jacobs, Willem Bernard** 1934- [EJ]
*Dutch jazz musician*
* Jacobs, Pim

**Jacobs, William Wymark**
1863-1943 [LC, TC]
*British author*
* Jacobs, W. W.

**Jacobson, Adolph R.** 1890-1953
[BBH]
*American bicycle racer and official*
* Jacobson, Jake

**Jacobson, Albert L.** 1881-1933
[BE]
*American baseball player*
* Jacobson, Beany

**Jacobson, Arthur**
*Actor*
* Hunter, Henry

**Jacobson, Baby Doll**
See Jacobson, William Chester

**Jacobson, Beany**
See Jacobson, Albert L.

**Jacobson, Bud**
See Jacobson, Orville Kenneth

**Jacobson, Buddy**
See Jacobson, Howard

**Jacobson, Howard** 1931- [EJS]
*American horse trainer*
* Jacobson, Buddy

**Jacobson, Irving** 20th c. [SMG]
*American baseball scout*
* Jacobson, Rabbit

**Jacobson, Jake**
See Jacobson, Adolph R.

**Jacobson, Jake**
See Jacobson, Larry Paul

**Jacobson, Jake**
See Jacobson, Merwin John
William

**Jacobson, Larry Paul** 1949- [SMG]
*American football player*
* Jacobson, Jake

**Jacobson, Marcus A. I.** 1921-
[IAW]
*German-born engineer and writer*
* Maj, M. A.

**Jacobson, Merwin John William**
1894- [BE]
*American baseball player*
* Jacobson, Jake

**Jacobson, Orville Kenneth**
1906-1960 [WWJ]
*American jazz musician*
* Jacobson, Bud

**Jacobson, Rabbit**
*See* Jacobson, Irving

**Jacobson, Richard** 20th c.
*American actor*
* Jason, Rick

**Jacobson, Robert Navra** 1912-
[BEW]
*American production associate and stage manager*
* Linden, Robert

**Jacobson, William Chester** 1890-
[BE, DGS, PB]
*American baseball player*
* Jacobson, Baby Doll

**Jacobsson, P.** 20th c. [WW]
*Author*
* Oldfeld, Peter, [joint pseudonym with Vernon Bartlett]

**Jacobstaff**
*See* Eaton, George B.

**Jacobsz, Lucas**
*See* Hugensz, Lucas

**Jacobus** 4th c. [HN]
*Saint*
* [The] Moses of Mesopotamia

**Jacobus de Ascoli** [HN]
*Medieval scholar*
* Profundus, Doctor

**Jacobus, Larry**
*See* Jacobus, Stuart Louis

**Jacobus, Stuart Louis** 1893-1965
[BE]
*American baseball player*
* Jacobus, Larry

**Jacoby, Glenn J.** 1907-1972 [BBH]
*American collegiate athletic director*
* Jacoby, Red

**Jacoby, Henry** 1905- [CA]
*German-born author*
* Franck, Sebastian
* Martin, Andre

**Jacoby, Jean**
*See* Evans, Jean Lorna

**Jacoby, Leo** 1911- [FIR]
*American actor*
* Cobb, Lee J.

**Jacoby, Red**
*See* Jacoby, Glenn J.

**Jacot, B. L.**
*See* Jacot De Boinod, Bernard Louis

**Jacot De Boinod, Bernard Louis**
1898-1977 [CA]
*British author*
* Jacot, B. L.

**Jacovitti, Benito** 1923- [WECO]
*Italian cartoonist*
* Jac

**Jacox, Francis** [FFF, PA]
*British writer and clergyman*
* Foxcar, Nicias
* Parson Frank

**Jacques**
*See* Duchesne, Albert

**Jacques**
*See* Ewing, Samuel

**Jacques, Hattie**
*See* Jacques, Josephine Edwina

**Jacques, Josephine Edwina** 1924-
[TR]
*British actress*
* Jacques, Hattie

**Jacques, Marie** 1896- [BEW]
*American actress*
* Dixon, Jean

**Jacquet, Illinois**
*See* Jacquet, Jean Baptiste

**Jacquet, Jean Baptiste** 1922-
[DAM]
*American jazz musician*
* Jacquet, Illinois

**Jacquier**
*See* Skinner, I. G. M.

**Jacquot, Charles Jean Baptiste**
1812-1880 [WBD]
*French journalist*
* Mirecourt, Eugene de

**Jaded Observer**
*See* Zolf, Larry

**Jaden, Donna Mae** 1922-
[BEW, EMT, FC]
*American actress and singer*
* Paige, Janis

**Jaeckel, Jake**
*See* Jaeckel, Paul Henry

**Jaeckel, Paul Henry** 1942- [BE]
*American baseball player*
* Jaeckel, Jake

**Jaeckel, R. Hanley** 1926- [FIR]
*American actor*
* Jaeckel, Richard

**Jaeckel, Richard**
*See* Jaeckel, R. Hanley

**Jaeger, C. K.**
*See* Jaeger, Cyril Karel Stuart

**Jaeger, Cyril Karel Stuart** 1912-
[IAW, SFL]
*British author*
* Fontcreuse, Marquis De
* Jaeger, C. K.

**Jaeger, Johannes** 1480?- ? [WBD]
*German humanist*
* Crotus Rubianus

**Jaffa, George**
*See* Wallace-Clarke, George

**Jaffe, Charles**
*See* Yaffe, Kadish

**Jaffe, Elsa**
*See* Bartlett, Elsa Jaffe

**Jaffe, Gabriel Vivian** 1923- [AW]
*British physician and writer*
* Poole, Vivian

**Jaffe, Harold** 1922- [ART]
*American artist*
* Harold

**Jaffe, Hosea** 1921- [IAW]
*South African-born author*
* Nxeleafrika, Mnguni

**Jaffe, Hyman** 1882- [WGT]
*Author*
* Alterego

**Jaffe, Susanne** 20th c.
*Author*
* Howard, Jill

**Jaffee, Mary L.**
*See* Lindsley, Mary F[lora]

**Jagade, Chick**
*See* Jagade, Harry

**Jagade, Harry** 1928-1968 [AS]
*American football player*
* Jagade, Chick

**Jagelka, Charles** 1923- [EJ, PMJ]
*American jazz musician*
* Wayne, Chuck

**Jagendorf, M.** 1888- [NAA]
*Austrian-born playwright*
* Adair, Towle
* Relonde, Maurice

**Jagger, Dean**
*See* Jeffries, Dean

**Jagger, Michael Philip** 1943-
[IPA, RO2]
*British singer*
* Jagger, Mick

**Jagger, Mick**
*See* Jagger, Michael Philip

**Jaguar**
*See* Jaguaribe, Sergio de Magalhaes Gomes

**Jaguar Jon Arnett**
*See* Arnett, Jon D.

**Jaguaribe, Sergio de Magalhaes Gomes** 1932- [WEC]
*Brazilian cartoonist*
* Jaguar

**Jahiz, al-** [The Goggle-Eyed]
*See* Amr ibn-Bahr

**Jahn, Friedrich Ludwig** 1778-1852
[PA, WBD]
*Prussian gymnastic director*
* [The] Father of Gymnastics
* Jahn, Vater

**Jahn, Vater**
*See* Jahn, Friedrich Ludwig

**Jahnigan, Bernice** 1909- [F2]
*American actress*
* Claire, Bernice

**Jahr, Adolf** 1894-1964 [SC]
*Swedish actor and opera singer*
* [The] Swedish Douglas Fairbanks

**Jak**
*See* Jackson, Raymond

**Jake the Barber**
*See* Factor, John

**Jake the Snake**
*See* Plante, [Joseph] Jacques

**Jakes, John W[illiam]** 1932- [CA]
*American author*
* Payne, Alan

**Jakes, John W[illiam]** (Continued)
* Scotland, Jay

**Jakobson, Roman [Osipovich]**
1896- [WOA]
*Russian-born linguist and literary historian*
* Alyagrov

**Jakucki, Jack**
*See* Jakucki, Sigmund

**Jakucki, Sigmund** 1909- [BE]
*American baseball player*
* Jakucki, Jack

**Jalal-al-Din [Majesty of Religion]**
*See* Malik Shah

**Jalal-ud-din**
*See* Firuz Shah II

**Jalap**
*See* Dias, Patrick Walter

**Jalas, Jussi**
*See* Blomstedt, Jussi

**Jam-Sheid** 8th c. BC [FFF, SN]
*King of Persia*
* [The] Illustrious

**Jamais, Yvonne Marie** 1922- [PMJ]
*American singer*
* Haines, Connie

**Jamal, Ahmad**
*See* Jones, Fritz

**Jamal, Khan**
*See* Cheeseboro, Warren Robert

**Jamblichus** 4th c. [RH]
*Philosopher*
* Thaumaturgus

**Jambon, Jean**
*See* Macdonald, J. Hay

**Jamerson, Charles Dewey [Charlie]**
1900- [BE]
*American baseball player*
* Jamerson, Lefty

**Jamerson, Lefty**
*See* Jamerson, Charles Dewey [Charlie]

**James** ?- 44 [FFF, WBD]
*Saint*
* [The] Apostle of Spain
* [The] Greater
* St. James of Compostela

**James** ?- 62? [SN]
*Saint*
* [The] Just
* [The] Lesser
* [The] Younger

**James, Alfred**
*See* Andriola, Alfred

**James, Allen**
*See* Allen, James L[ovic], Jr. [Jim]

**James, Allen**
*See* Lorenz, Ellen Jane

**James, Andrew**
*See* Kirkup, James

**James, Anna** [joint pseudonym with Madeline Porter]
*See* Harper, Shannon

**James, Anna** [joint pseudonym with Shannon Harper]
*See* Porter, Madeline

**James, Arthur**
See Griffin, James

**James, Ben**
See Solomon, James B.

**James, Bernie**
See James, Robert Byrne

**James, Berton Hulon** 1886- [BE]
*American baseball player*
* James, Bob

**James, Big Bill**
See James, William Henry

**James, Billy**
See Phelps, Arthur

**James, Bob**
See James, Berton Hulon

**James, Brian**
See Tierney, John Lawrence

**James, [David] Burnett [Stephen]**
1919- [CA]
*British author, critic, editor*
* Vizard, Stephen

**James, C.**
See Clayton, Cyril James

**James, C. B.**
See Coover, James B[urrell]

**James, C. L. R.**
See James, Cyril Lionel Robert

**James, C. W.**
See Cumes, James William
Crawford

**James, Chappie**
See James, Daniel, Jr.

**James, Cornelius** 1927- [DAM]
*American singer*
* James, Pinocchio

**James, Cy**
See Watts, Peter Christopher

**James, Cyril Lionel Robert** 1901-
[CW]
*Trinidadian author, critic, political
theorist*
* James, C. L. R.

**James, Daisy** ?-1940 [BMH, THR]
*British comedienne*
* Martin, Daisy

**James, Daniel, III** 20th c. [IBW]
*American air force pilot*
* James, Spike

**James, Daniel, Jr.** 1920-1978
[IBW]
*American air force officer*
* [The] Black Panther
* James, Chappie

**James, Dempsey**
See James, William

**James, Dynamite Eddie**
See James, Eddie

**James, Dynely** [joint pseudonym with
William (James Carter) Mayne]
See Caesar, R. D.

**James, Dynely** [joint pseudonym with
R. D. Caesar]
See Mayne, William [James
Carter]

**James, Eddie** 20th c. [BBH, CFH]
*Canadian football player*
* James, Dynamite Eddie

**James, Edward**
See Masur, Harold Q.

**James Edward**
See Stuart, James Francis Edward

**James, Edward** [PA]
*Author*
* Fawkes, Guy

**James, Edwin**
See Gunn, James E[dwin]

**James, Elmer**
See Crudup, Arthur

**James, Elmo**
See James, Elmore

**James, Elmore** 1918-1963 [BWW]
*American singer*
* Cleanhead
* James, Elmo
* James, Joe Willie

**James, Elmore, Jr.**
See Minter, Iverson

**James, Ernest**
See Pike, William Ernest

**James, Etta**
See Hawkins, Etta James

**James, Florence Alice [Price]**
1857-1929 [FFF, WW]
*Author and entertainer*
* Warden, Florence

**James, Fob**
See James, Forrest Hood, Jr.

**James, Forrest Hood, Jr.** 1935?-
*American politician*
* James, Fob

**James, Francis**
See Jacobs, Francis

**James, Franklin**
See Godley, Robert

**James, Freddie**
See Sullivan, John Florence

**James, Freddy**
See Paolella, Alfred

**James, George** 19th c. [SAT]
*British author*
* DeLunatico, F.

**James, Godfrey Warden** 1888-
[CC, WW, WWL]
*British author*
* Broome, Adam

**James, [Lady] Heather** 1914-
[CA, WD]
*British author*
* Jenner, Heather

**James, Henry**
See Kellenberger, L. C.

**James, Herbert Wentworth** 20th c.
[MBF]
*British author*
* Wentworth, Herbert

**James, James**
See Adams, Arthur Henry

**James, James McCutchen**
1873-1901 [AS, BE]
*American baseball player*
* McJames, Doc
* McJames, James McCutchen

**James, Jeff[rey Lynn]** 1941- [BE]
*American baseball player*
* James, Jesse

**James, Jesse**
See James, Jeff[rey Lynn]

**James, Jesse Woodson** 1847-1882
*American gunfighter*
* Dingus
* Howard, Thomas

**James, Jimmy**
See Casey, James

**James, Jimmy**
See Hendrix, James Marshall
[Jimi]

**James, Joe Willie**
See James, Elmore

**James, John** 20th c.
*American football player*
* James, Skunk

**James, Joni**
See Babbo, Joan Carmello

**James, Josephine** [joint pseudonym
with Emma Gelders Sterne]
See Lindsay, Barbara

**James, Josephine** [joint pseudonym
with Barbara Lindsay]
See Sterne, Emma Gelders

**James, Judith**
See Jennings, Leslie Nelson

**James, Kristin**
See Camp, Candace P[auline]

**James, Laurence** 20th c. [CA]
*Author*
* James, William M. [joint
pseudonym with Terry Harknett]

**James, Lefty**
See James, William A.

**James, Lionel** 1868- ? [WWL]
*British author*
* Intelligence Officer
* O.

**James, M. R.**
See James, Montague Rhodes

**James, M. R.** 1940- [CA]
*American author and publisher*
* Danielson, J. D.

**James, Marlise Ann** 1945- [CA]
*American author and editor*
* Wabun [East Wind]

**James, Matthew**
See Lucey, James D[ennis]

**James, Michael** 1936- [TR]
*British actor*
* Jayston, Michael

**James, Montague Rhodes**
1862-1936 [HFF]
*British author*
* James, M. R.

**James, Mrs. Louis** [FFF]
*Entertainer*
* Wainwright, Marie

**James, Nehemiah** 1902-1969
[DAM]
*American singer*
* James, Skip

**James of the Iron Belt**
See James IV

**James, P. D.**
See White, Phyllis [James]

**James, Paul**
See Warburg, James Paul

**James, Peregrine**
See Shepherd, William James

**James, Peter** 1925- [THR]
*British actor*
* Murray, Peter

**James, Philip** [joint pseudonym with
James H. Beard]
See Alvarez Del Rey, Ramon
Felipe San Juan Mario Silvio Enrico

**James, Philip** [joint pseudonym with
Ramon Felipe San Juan Mario
Alvarez Del Rey]
See Beard, James H.

**James, Philip**
See Cawthorn, James

**James, Philip Robert** 1949- [SMG]
*American baseball player*
* James, Skip

**James, Pinocchio**
See James, Cornelius

**James, Po**
See James, Ron[ald]

**James, R.**
See Elward, James [Joseph]

**James, Rachel**
See Dancyger, Irene

**James, Robert**
See Heitner, Iris

**James, Robert Byrne** 1905- [BE]
*American baseball player*
* James, Bernie

**James, Ron[ald]** 1949- [FB]
*American football player*
* James, Po

**James, Ronald**
See Preston, James

**James, Seattle Bill**
See James, William Lawrence

**James, Simon**
See Kunen, James Simon

**James, Skip**
See James, Nehemiah

**James, Skip**
See James, Philip Robert

**James, Skunk**
See James, John

**James, Sonny**
See Loden, James [Jimmie]

**James, Spike**
See James, Daniel, III

**James, Stanton**
See Flemming, Nicholas Coit

**James, Susan**
See Griffin, Arthur J.

**James, T. F.**
See Fleming, Thomas J[ames]

**James, Thomas N.**
See Neal, James T[homas]

**James, Tommy**
See Jackson, Thomas Gregory

**James, Trevor**
*See* Constable, Trevor James

**James, Vernon**
*See* Bridges, Victor

**James W. I.** 20th c. [WW]
*Author*
* Baxter, Young
* Collier, Old Cap

**James, Walter S.**
*See* Sheldon, Walt[er J.]

**James, Westbrook**
*See* Weygand, James Lamar

**James, Wilhelmina Martha** 20th c.
[WWL]
*British author*
* Clare, Austin
* Everest, Hope

**James, Will**
*See* Dufault, Joseph Ernest
Nephtali

**James, William**
*See* Craddock, William J[ames]

**James, William** [PA]
*Author*
* Chamier, Captain

**James, William** 20th c. [RO1]
*American singer*
* James, Dempsey

**James, William A.** 1889-1933 [BE]
*American baseball player*
* James, Lefty

**James, William Henry** 1888-1942
[AS, BE]
*American baseball player*
* James, Big Bill

**James, William Lawrence**
1892-1971 [BE, PB]
*American baseball player*
* James, Seattle Bill

**James, William M.** [joint pseudonym
with Laurence James]
*See* Harknett, Terry

**James, William M.** [joint pseudonym
with Terry Harknett]
*See* James, Laurence

**James, William Milbourne** 1881- ?
[CAP]
*British author*
* T. B. D.

**James I** 1206?-1276
[DNNS, RH, WBD]
*King of Aragon*
* [The] Conqueror
* [El] Conquistador

**James I** 1394-1437 [SN]
*King of Scotland*
* [The] Orpheus of Scotland

**James I** 1566-1625
[DEP, FFF, SN]
*King of England and Scotland [as
James VI]*
* [The] English Solomon
* [The] Most Learned Fool in
Christendom
* Royal 'Prentice in the Art of
Poesy
* [The] Scottish Heliogabalus
* [The] Scottish Solomon
* [The] Second Solomon
* [The] Solomon of England
* [The] Wise

**James I** (Continued)
* [The] Wisest Fool in Christendom

**James II** 1261?-1327
[DNNS, FFF, SN]
*King of Aragon*
* [The] Great
* [The] Just

**James II** 1430-1460 [SN]
*King of Scotland*
* [The] Fiery Face

**James II** 1633-1701 [DEP, SN]
*King of England*
* [The] King Over the Water
* [The] Popish Duke
* [A] Sant'ring Bully

**James III**
*See* Stuart, James Francis Edward

**James IV** 1473-1513 [HN]
*King of Scotland*
* [The] Chivalrous Madman
* James of the Iron Belt

**James V** 1512-1542 [HN, RH, SN]
*King of Scotland*
* [The] Goodman of Ballengeich
* [The] King of the Commons

**Jameson, Anna Murphy** 1797-1860
[DEL]
*British author and critic*
* [A] Lady

**Jameson, Annie Edith** 1868-1931
[LAO, WGT]
*British author*
* Buckrose, J. E.

**Jameson, Eric**
*See* Trimmer, Eric James

**Jameson, Malcolm** 1891-1945
[SFP, WGT]
*American author*
* Keith, Colin
* MacGregor, Mary

**Jameson, Raymond Deloy** 1896-
[NAA]
*American author and educator*
* De Loi, Raimon

**Jameson, Robert** 20th c. [MBF]
*British author*
* Jameson, Roland

**Jameson, Roland**
*See* Jameson, Robert

**Jameson, [Margaret] Storm** 1891-
[WD]
*British author*
* Hill, James
* Lamb, William

**Jameson, Twiggs**
*See* Twiggs, James

**Jamesone, George** 1586?-1644
[HN, SN]
*Scottish painter*
* [The] Caledonian Vandyck
* [The] Scottish Vandyke

**Jamet, Marie** 1820-1893 [WBD]
*Founder of French religious order*
* De la Compassion, Marie
Augustine

**Jamieson, Charles Devine**
1893-1969 [DGS]
*American baseball player*
* Jamieson, Jamie

**Jamieson, Jamie**
*See* Jamieson, Charles Devine

**Jamieson, Leland Shattuck** 1904-
[NAA]
*American airline pilot and writer*
* Beehan, Jack Rogers
* Shrewsbury, Ralph

**Jamieson, Rex** 20th c. [BMH]
*British comedian*
* Shufflewick, Mrs.

**Jamieson, Walter** 1842-1904
[AS, RBE]
*British-born American boxer*
* Collyer, Sam

**Jamison, Bud**
*See* Jamison, William

**Jamison, Jane**
*See* Trachsel, Myrtle Jamison

**Jamison, William** 1894-1943
[F1, F2, SC]
*American actor*
* Jamison, Bud

**Jammin' Jim**
*See* Harris, Ed[ward P.]

**Jan**
*See* Noble, John [Appelbe]

**Jan, Emerson**
*See* Bixby, Jerome Lewis

**Jan, Laurent**
*See* De Lausanne, Laurent-Jean

**[La] Jana**
*See* Hiebel, Henriette Margarethe

**Janardan**
*See* Bhatt, Janardan T.

**Janauschek, Fanny**
*See* Janauschek, Franziska
Magdalena Romance

**Janauschek, Franziska Magdalena
Romance** 1830-1904 [WBD]
*Bohemian actress*
* Janauschek, Fanny

**Janavel, Joshua** 17th c. [HN]
*Defeated a troop of Irishmen*
* [The] Hero of Rora

**Jancus Lain** [The Wicked]
*See* Hunyadi, Janos [or Huniades,
John]

**Jane I** 1325-1382 [DNNS]
*Queen of Naples*
* [The] Mary Stuart of Italy

**Janenz, Theodor Friedrich Emil**
1884-1950 [BDF, FC]
*Swiss-born actor*
* Jannings, Emil

**Janes, Paul** 1893-1968 [THR]
*British actor and singer*
* England, Paul

**Janet, Lillian** [joint pseudonym with
Lillian Ressler]
*See* O'Daniel, Janet

**Janet, Lillian** [joint pseudonym with
Janet O'Daniel]
*See* Ressler, Lillian

**Janice**
*See* Brustlein, Janice Tworkov

**Janiczek, Julius** 1887-1956 [BBD]
*German music educator*
* Hensel, Walther

**Janifer, Laurence M[ark]**
*See* Harris, Larry M[ark]

**Janin, Jules Gabriel** 1804-1874
[DNNF, FFF, PA]
*French journalist*
* [The] King of Feuilletons
* [A] Married Critic
* [Le] Prince de la Critique
* [Le] Roi des Feuilletons

**Janis, Byron**
*See* Yanks, Byron

**Janis, Elsie**
*See* Bierbower [or Bierbauer],
Elsie

**Janner, Greville Ewan** 1928- [CA]
*British author*
* Mitchell, Ewan

**Janney, Leon**
*See* Ramon, Laon

**Jannings, Emil**
*See* Janenz, Theodor Friedrich
Emil

**Jannonius**
*See* Glamone, Pietro

**Janosch**
*See* Eckert, Horst

**Jans, Zephyr**
*See* Zekowski, Arlene

**Jansen**
*See* Deufer, Johann Heinrich

**Jansen, Harry August** 1883-1955
[BEW]
*Danish-born magician*
* Dante

**Jansen, Jared**
*See* Cebulash, Mel

**Jansen, Marie**
*See* Key, Mrs. Barton

**Jansen, Michel**
*See* Van Herp, Jacques

**Janson, Hank**
*See* Frances, Stephen D.

**Janson, Hank** [house pseudonym?]
*See* Hobson, Harry

**Janson, Hank** [house pseudonym?]
*See* Norwood, Victor G[eorge]
C[harles]

**Janssen, David**
*See* Meyer, David

**Janssens, Abraham** 1575?-1632
[WBD]
*Flemish painter*
* Janssens van Nuyssen

**Janssens van Nuyssen**
*See* Janssens, Abraham

**Jantzen, Heinie**
*See* Jantzen, Walter C.

**Jantzen, Walter C.** 1890- [BE]
*American baseball player*
* Jantzen, Heinie

**Janulako, Wassili**
*See* Giannoulakos, Wassilios

**Janus**
*See* Buchanan, Robert Angus

**Janus**
*See* Clery, [Reginald] Val[entine]

**Janus**
*See* Dollinger, Johann Joseph I.

**[A] Janus Faced Critic**
*See* Hill, [Sir] John

**Janus, Grete**
*See* Hertz, Grete Janus

**Janvier**
*See* Woodward, Joseph Janvier

**Janvier, Ivan**
*See* Budrys, Algirdas Jonas

**Janvier, Margaret Thomson**
1844-1913   [WBD]
*American author*
* Vandegrift, Margaret

**Janvier, Paul**
*See* Budrys, Algirdas Jonas

**Janvrin, Childe Harold**
*See* Janvrin, Harold Chandler

**Janvrin, Harold Chandler**
1892-1962   [BE]
*American baseball player*
* Janvrin, Childe Harold

**Jaques**
*See* Friswell, J. Hain

**Jaqueta [Jacket]**
*See* Giraldez, Jose

**Jaramillo, Joe**   [RO2]
*American musician*
* Jaramillo, Yo-Yo

**Jaramillo, Rabbit**
*See* Jaramillo, Robert

**Jaramillo, Robert** 20th c.   [RO2]
*American musician*
* Jaramillo, Rabbit

**Jaramillo, Yo-Yo**
*See* Jaramillo, Joe

**Jarana [Merrymaker]**
*See* Arana Carmona, Antonio

**Jarbeau, Vernona**
*See* Bernstein, Mrs. Jefferson F.

**Jarber, E.**
*See* Jarnes Bergua, Enrique

**Jardim, Arsenio** 1949-   [AES]
*Angolan soccer player*
* Seninho

**Jardin, Rex** [joint pseudonym with
Robert Ferdinand Burkhardt]
*See* Burkhardt, Eve

**Jardin, Rex** [joint pseudonym with
Eve Burkhardt]
*See* Burkhardt, Robert Ferdinand

**Jardine, Jack Owen** 1931-
[CA, ESF, SFL]
*American author*
* Cory, Howard L. [joint
   pseudonym with Julie Anne
   Jardine]
* Farmer, Arthur
* Maddock, Larry

**Jardine, Julie Ann** 1926-
[SFL, WGT]
*American author*
* Cory, Howard L. [joint
   pseudonym with Jack Owen
   Jardine]
* Howard, Corrie

**Jardine, Warwick** [house
pseudonym]
*See* Bayfield, William John

**Jardine, Warwick** [house
pseudonym]
*See* Warwick, Francis Alister

**Jareed**
*See* Faridi, Shah Nasiruddin
Mohammad

**Jarnes Bergua, Enrique** 1919-
[IAW]
*Spanish author*
* Jarber, E.

**Jarnowick**
*See* Giornovichi, Giovanni Mane

**Jarnowick**
*See* Hus Desforges, Pierre Louis

**Jarrett, Cora [Hardy]** 1877- ?
[EMD, TC, WW]
*American author*
* Keene, Faraday

**Jarrin' Jawn Kimbrough**
*See* Kimbrough, John

**Jarring Jim Bausch**
*See* Bausch, James

**Jarvie, Nichol**
*See* Wood, William McDonald

**Jarvis, Bud**
*See* Jarvis, James

**Jarvis, E. K.** [house pseudonym,
Ziff-Davis]
*See* Bloch, Robert [Albert]

**Jarvis, E. K.** [house pseudonym,
Ziff-Davis]
*See* Ellison, Harlan [Jay]

**Jarvis, E. K.** [house pseudonym,
Ziff-Davis]
*See* Fairman, Paul W.

**Jarvis, E. K.** [house pseudonym,
Ziff-Davis]
*See* Silverberg, Robert

**Jarvis, E. K.** [house pseudonym,
Ziff-Davis]
*See* Williams, Robert Moore

**Jarvis, Fred[erick] G[ordon], Jr.**
1930-   [SFL]
*American author*
* Gordon, Fritz [joint pseudonym
   with Robert F. Van Beever]

**Jarvis, James** 1907-   [CEI]
*Canadian-born hockey player*
* Jarvis, Bud

**Jarvis, Jarvo**
*See* Jarvis, Kevin Bartram Sidney

**Jarvis, Kevin Bartram Sidney**
1953-   [DC]
*British cricketer*
* Jarvis, Jarvo
* K. J.

**Jarvis, Lee**
*See* Hernhuter, Albert

**Jarvis, Leon Raeminton** 1949-
[SMG]
*American football player*
* Jarvis, Ray

**Jarvis, LeRoy Gilbert** 1926-   [BE]
*American baseball player*
* Jarvis, Roy

**Jarvis, Ray**
*See* Jarvis, Leon Raeminton

**Jarvis, Roy**
*See* Jarvis, LeRoy Gilbert

**Jarvys, Gayne**
*See* English, Jessie Millard

**Jascalevich, Mario E.** 1926?-   [B10]
*American physician*
* Dr. X

**Jasienski, Bruno**
*See* Zyskind, Bruno

**Jaskulek, Byron** 20th c.   [BBH]
*American editor*
* Jaskulek, Jake

**Jaskulek, Jake**
*See* Jaskulek, Byron

**Jasmin d'Agen**
*See* Boe, Jacques

**Jasmin, Jacques**
*See* Boe, Jacques

**Jasnorzewska, Marja**
*See* Pawlikowska, Marja [Kossak]

**Jason**
*See* Munro, [Macfarlane] Hugh

**Jason**
*See* Stannus, [James] Gordon
[Dawson]

**Jason, Jerry**
*See* Smith, George H[enry]

**Jason, Johnny**
*See* Glut, Donald F[rank]

**Jason, Rick**
*See* Jacobson, Richard

**Jason, Stuart**
*See* Avallone, Michael [Angelo],
Jr.

**Jason, Stuart**
*See* Floren, Lee

**Jason, Wm.**
*See* Machlin, Milton Robert

**Jasper, Harry W.** 1887-1937   [BE]
*American baseball player*
* Jasper, Hi

**Jasper, Hi**
*See* Jasper, Harry W.

**Jastrow, Marcus** 1829-1903
[WBD]
*Polish-born clergyman and author*
* Jastrow, Morris

**Jastrow, Morris**
*See* Jastrow, Marcus

**Jastrun, Mieczyslaw**
*See* Agatstein, Mieczyslaw

**Jaudenes, Jose Alvares** 1891-1967
[SC]
*Spanish actor*
* Jaudenes, Lepe

**Jaudenes, Lepe**
*See* Jaudenes, Jose Alvares

**Jaunot**
*See* Lemaire, M.

**Jaunt, Jeremy**
*See* Mogridge, George

**[The] Jaunting Carr**
*See* Carr, [Sir] John

**Jaurand, Yvonne** 1912-   [CA]
*French author*
* Duplessis, Yves

**Jaureguibeitia e Ibarra, Castor**
1876-1928   [GS]
*Spanish bullfighter*
* Cocherito [The Little Coachman]

**Javacheff, Christo** 1935-   [B10]
*Bulgarian-born American sculptor*
* Christo

**Javal, Camille** 1934-   [BDF, WEF]
*French actress*
* Bardot, Brigitte

**Javali**
*See* Beadnell, Charles Marsh

**Javeau, Claude A.** 1940-   [IAW]
*Belgian sociologist and author*
* Remacle, Stephane

**Javery, Alva William** 1918-   [BE]
*American baseball player*
* Javery, Bear Tracks

**Javery, Bear Tracks**
*See* Javery, Alva William

**Javier, Al**
*See* Javier, Ignacio

**Javier, Hoolie**
*See* Javier, [Manuel] Julian
Liranzo

**Javier, Ignacio** 1954-   [SMG]
*Dominican-born baseball player*
* Javier, Al

**Javier, [Manuel] Julian Liranzo**
1936-   [BE, PB]
*Dominican-born baseball player*
* Javier, Hoolie
* [The] Phantom

**Jawbone, Sir**
*See* Bowen, [Sir] George Ferguson

**Jaworski, Ron**
*American football player*
* [The] Polish Rifle

**Jaxon, Frankie** 1895-
[BWW, PMJ, WWJ]
*American jazz musician*
* Jaxon, Half Pint
* Thomas, Cotton

**Jaxon, Half Pint**
*See* Jaxon, Frankie

**Jaxon, Milt**
*See* Kimbro, John M.

**Jay**
*See* Steele, [Sir] Richard

**Jay, Charlotte**
*See* Jay, Geraldine Mary

**Jay, Donald**
*See* Meyer, Charles R[obert]

**Jay, Ernest**
*See* Alberge, Ernest

**Jay, Geraldine Mary** 1919-
[CC, WW]
*Author*
* Jay, Charlotte

**Jay, Harriet** 1863-1932 [BEW]
*British actress, playwright, author*
* Marlowe, Charles

**Jay, Marion**
See Spalding, Ruth

**Jay, Mel**
See Fanthorpe, R[obert] Lionel

**Jay, Morty**
See Saroff, Morton

**Jay, Ruth I[ngrid]** 1920- [CA]
*American author*
* Johnson, Ruth I.

**Jay, Simon**
See Alexander, Colin James

**Jay, Thomas**
See Kendall, Stephen

**Jay, W. L. M.**
See Woodruff, Julia Louisa
Matilda

**Jayhawker**
See Woodard, J. H.

**Jayne, Edward** 20th c.
*American government official*
* Jayne, Randy

**Jayne, Faith**
See Powley, Faith Hinckley

**Jayne, [Lieutenant] R. H.**
See Ellis, Edward S[ylvester]

**Jayne, Randy**
See Jayne, Edward

**Jaynes, Clare** [joint pseudonym with
Clara Gatzert Spiegel]
See Mayer, Jane Rothschild

**Jaynes, Clare** [joint pseudonym with
Jane Rothschild Mayer]
See Spiegel, Clara Gatzert

**Jayston, Michael**
See James, Michael

**Jazz Organ, Mr.**
See Smith, James Oscar [Jimmy]

**[The] Jazzbo Syncopator**
See Thomas, Lillian

**Jazzie Jeanie**
See Kittrell, Jean

**Jazz's Angry Man**
See Mingus, Charles [Charlie]

**Jeacock, Caleb** ?-1786 [DEL, SN]
*British author*
* [The] Literary Baker

**Jeake, Samuel, Jr.**
See Aiken, Conrad [Potter]

**Jeames**
See Thackeray, William
Makepeace

**Jean**
See Jones, Brenda Lee

**Jean** 16th c. [RH]
*Celebrated chef*
* Careme, Jean de

**Jean [or Jehan] de Meung**
1260-1320 [DNNS, HN, SN]
*French poet*
* Clopinel
* [The] Ennius of France
* [The] French Ennius
* [The] Hobbler
* [The] Lame
* [The] Lydgate of His Day
* Pere de l'Eloquence

**Jean De Milan, [Sister]**
See Jean, Gabrielle [Lucille]

**Jean d'Epee [John with the Sword]**
See Bonaparte, Napoleon

**Jean, Eddy Arnold** 1952- [CW]
*Haitian poet and critic*
* Damne, Konrad

**Jean, Gabrielle [Lucille]** 1924-
[CA]
*American educator and author*
* Jean De Milan, [Sister]

**Jean, Gloria**
See Schoonover, Gloria Jean

**Jean Louis**
See Kerouac, Jean-Louis Lebrid
De

**Jean, Monsieur**
See Bleicher, Hugo

**Jean-Louis, Victor** 1915?- [CW]
*West Indian author and poet*
* Baghio'o, Jean-Louis

**Jeanes, Ernest Lee** 1900-1973 [BE]
*American baseball player*
* Jeanes, Tex

**Jeanes, Tex**
See Jeanes, Ernest Lee

**Jeanette, Buddy**
See Jeanette, Harry

**Jeanette, Harry** 1917- [BB]
*American basketball player*
* Jeanette, Buddy

**Jeanettei, Joseph** 1879-1958 [BX]
*American boxer*
* Jennette, Joe

**Jeanmaire, Renee** 1924- [BEW]
*French dancer, singer, actress*
* Jeanmaire, Zizi

**Jeanmaire, Zizi**
See Jeanmaire, Renee

**Jeanneret-Gris, Charles Edouard**
1887-1965 [B10, LC, TC1]
*Swiss architect, artist, author*
* Le Corbusier

**Jeans, Angela**
See Watt, Esme Violet

**Jeans, Barbara**
See Tufty, Barbara Jean

**Jeans, Herbert** 1876- ? [WWL]
*British author*
* Maddox, Max

**Jeans, Ursula**
See McMinn, Ursula

**Jebaltowsky, Morris Benjamin**
1907- [BX, EJS, RBE]
*American boxer*
* Jeby, Ben

**Jebavy, Vaclav Ignac** 1868-1929
[B10, CD, EWL]
*Czech poet*
* Brezina, Otokar

**Jeby, Ben**
See Jebaltowsky, Morris Benjamin

**Jedlitzka, Mizzi** 1887- [BBD]
*Czech-born opera singer*
* Jeritza, Maria

**Jedor**
See Latude, Jean Henry

**Jedteles, Itzig** 1815-1857 [PA]
*Author*
* Seidlitz, Julius

**Jeered Will**
See Davenant, [Sir] William

**Jeeves, Mahatma Kane**
See Dukinfield, William Claude

**Jeffcoate, [Sir] [Thomas] Norman
[Arthur]** 1907- [WD]
*British physician and writer*
* Jeffcoate, T. N. A.

**Jeffcoate, T. N. A.**
See Jeffcoate, [Sir] [Thomas]
Norman [Arthur]

**Jefferies, Greg** 1938- [AW]
*British author*
* Collins, Geoffrey

**Jefferies, Harriet Mildred**
1893-1967 [SC]
*American actress*
* Cunard, Grace

**Jefferies, Richard** 1848-1887
[FFF]
*British author and naturalist*
* [The] English Thoreau

**Jeffers, Jo**
See Johnson, Joan Helen

**Jefferson, Arthur Stanley**
1890-1965 [BDF, F1, FC]
*British-born comic actor*
* Laurel, Stan

**Jefferson, Blind Lemon**
See Jefferson, Lemon

**Jefferson, Finlay** 1878-1968 [FC]
*Scottish actor*
* Currie, Finlay

**Jefferson, Henry Lee**
See Cabell, James Branch

**Jefferson, Ian**
See Davies, Leslie Purnell

**Jefferson, Lemon** 1897-1930
[BWW, EJ]
*American jazz musician*
* Bates, [Deacon] L. J.
* Brown, [Elder] J. C.
* Jefferson, Blind Lemon

**Jefferson, Little Tom**
See Jefferson, Thomas

**Jefferson, Omar Xavier**
See Jefferson, Xavier T[homas]

**Jefferson, Roland Parris** 1926-
[EJ]
*American jazz musician*
* Jefferson, Ron

**Jefferson, Ron**
See Jefferson, Roland Parris

**Jefferson, Roy** 20th c.
*American football player*
* Jefferson, Sweet Pea

**Jefferson, Sarah**
See Farjeon, [Eve] Annabel

**Jefferson Street Joe**
See Gilliam, Joe, Jr.

**Jefferson, Sweet Pea**
See Jefferson, Roy

**Jefferson, Thomas** 1743-1826
[FAP, FFF, HN]
*American president*
* [The] Apostle of Liberty
* [The] Father of the Declaration
of Independence
* [The] Father of the University of
Virginia
* Long Tom
* [The] Man of the People
* [The] Pen of the Revolution
* [The] Philosopher of Democracy
* [The] Red Fox
* [The] Sage of Monticello
* [The] Scribe of the Revolution

**Jefferson, Thomas** 1920- [EJ]
*American jazz musician*
* Jefferson, Little Tom

**Jefferson, Xavier T[homas]** 1952-
[CA]
*American author and playwright*
* Jefferson, Omar Xavier

**Jeffery, Graham** 1935- [WD]
*British author and cartoonist*
* Graham, [Brother]

**Jeffery, Grant** 1924- [CA]
*Canadian-born author*
* Turner, Peter Paul

**Jeffery, Jeffery E.**
See Marston, [Major] Jeffery
Eardley

**Jefferys, William Hamilton** 1871-
? [ALY, NAA]
*American author, surgeon,
missionary*
* Latissioner, John
* Z

**Jefford, Bat**
See Bingley, David Ernest

**Jeffords, Jerome** 1891-1962
[AS, BX, RBE]
*American boxer*
* [The] Globetrotter
* Smith, Jeff

**Jeffra, Harry**
See Guiffi, Ignacius Pasquale

**Jeffrey, Christopher**
See Leach, Michael

**Jeffrey, Ellen**
See Wangner, Ellen D.

**Jeffrey, Francis** 1773-1850 [SN]
*Scottish critic and jurist*
* [The] Aristarchus of the
Edinburgh Review

**Jeffrey, Rosa Vertner** [FFF, PA]
*British author*
* Rosa

**Jeffrey, Ruth**
See Bell, Louise Price

**Jeffrey-Smith, May Thornton**
1882- [AW]
*Jamaican writer*
* Aunt Maysie
* Thornton, Maimee

**Jeffreys, Anne**
*See* Carmichael, Anne Jeffreys

**Jeffreys, George [First Baron Jeffreys of Wem]** 1640?-1689 [HN, SN]
*British jurist*
* [The] Earl of Flint
* [The] Western Hangman

**Jeffreys, J. G.**
*See* Healey, Benjamin James

**Jeffreys, Sarah Anne** [PA]
*Author*
* Clyde, Alton

**Jeffries, Dean** 1903- [F2, FC]
*American actor*
* Jagger, Dean

**Jeffries, Graham Montague** 1900-
[CC, EMD, WWS]
*British author*
* Bourne, Peter
* Graeme, Bruce
* Graeme, David

**Jeffries, Grizzly Bear**
*See* Jeffries, James Jackson

**Jeffries, Herb[ert Jeffrey]** 1917-
[IBW]
*American singer, actor, songwriter*
* [The] Bronze Buckaroo

**Jeffries, Hugh**
*See* Hewelcke, Geoffrey

**Jeffries, James Jackson** 1875-1953
[RBE, SG, WBC]
*American boxer*
* [The] Beast
* [The] Boilermaker
* [The] California Grizzly
* Jeffries, Grizzly Bear

**Jeffries, Jeff**
*See* Boatfield, Jeffrey Montagu

**Jeffries, Richard** 19th c. [PA]
*Author*
* R. J.

**Jeffries, Roderic [Graeme]** 1926-
[CA, CC, EMD]
*British author*
* Alding, Peter
* Ashford, Jeffrey
* Draper, Hastings
* Graeme, Roderic
* Hastings, Graham

**Jeffs, Rae**
*See* Sebley, Frances Rae

**Jehan, Jean** 20th c.
*French narcotics smuggler*
* [The] Silver Fox

**Jehan, Noor**
*See* Rattray, Henrietta Barbara

**Jehu**
*See* Louis XVIII

**Jeier, Thomas** 1947- [IAW]
*German author*
* Thomas, M. L.

**Jelakowitch, Iwan**
*See* Heijermans, Herman

**Jelincich, Frank Anthony** 1919-
[BE]
*American baseball player*
* Jelincich, Jelly

**Jelincich, Jelly**
*See* Jelincich, Frank Anthony

**Jelinek, Estelle C.** 1935- [CA]
*American author and editor*
* Fine, Estelle

**Jellinek, Frances** 1903-1959
[BEW, EMT, PMJ]
*American actress and singer*
* Williams, Frances

**Jellings-Blow, Sidney** 1878-1961
[BEW]
*British-born playwright and actor*
* Blow, Sidney

**Jelly, George Oliver** 1909- [WD]
*British author and poet*
* Fosse, Alfred

**Jelly, Joe**
*See* Giorelli, Joseph

**Jelly, Louise Isabel** 1910- [BEW]
*American actress*
* Kirtland, Louise

**Jelly Roll Morton**
*See* La Menthe, Ferdinand Joseph

**Jemison, David Victor** 1873- ?
[IBW]
*American clergyman*
* [The] Saint of Selma

**Jemmy**
*See* Wordsdale, James

**Jenatzy, Camille**
*Auto racer*
* [The] Red Devil

**Jenings, Elizabeth Janet** 19th c.
[DNNF, FFF]
*Author*
* Lane, Wickliffe

**Jenkins**
*See* Wilson, Wesley

**Jenkins, Allen**
*See* McGonegal, Alfred

**Jenkins, Bill** 1921?- [B10]
*American auto racer*
* Jenkins, Grumpy

**Jenkins, Bobo**
*See* Jenkins, John Pickens

**Jenkins, Butch**
*See* Jenkins, Jackie

**Jenkins, Clarence** 1903-1968 [MK]
*American baseball player*
* Jenkins, Fats

**Jenkins, Clarence** 20th c. [MEB]
*American basketball player*
* Jenkins, Fat

**Jenkins, Fat**
*See* Jenkins, Clarence

**Jenkins, Fats**
*See* Jenkins, Clarence

**Jenkins, Fergie**
*See* Jenkins, Ferguson Arthur

**Jenkins, Ferguson Arthur** 1943-
[BR]
*Canadian-born baseball player*
* Jenkins, Fergie

**Jenkins, Floyd**
*See* Rose, Fred

**Jenkins, Frederic Douglass [Freddy]**
1906- [DAM, EJ, WWJ]
*American jazz musician*
* Jenkins, Posey

**Jenkins, Grumpy**
*See* Jenkins, Bill

**Jenkins, Gus** 1931- [BWW]
*American singer*
* Jinkins, Gus
* Little Temple
* Pharoah, Jaarone
* [The] Young Wolf

**Jenkins, Harold** 1933-
[CME, LRR]
*American singer*
* Twitty, Conway

**Jenkins, Howard** 1876-1970 [SC]
*American actor and circus performer*
* Jenks, Si

**Jenkins, Jack**
*See* Jenkins, Warren Washington

**Jenkins, Jackie** 1938- [FC]
*American actor*
* Jenkins, Butch

**Jenkins, James** 20th c. [OBW]
*American baseball player*
* Jenkins, PeeWee

**Jenkins, John Pickens** 1916-
[BWW]
*American singer*
* Jenkins, Bobo

**Jenkins, Lew**
*See* Jenks, Verlin

**Jenkins, MacGregor** 1869- ?
[NAA]
*American author*
* Rusticus

**Jenkins, Marie M[agdalen]** 1909-
[CA, SAT]
*American author and columnist*
* Markins, W. S.
* Mary Scholastica, [Sister]

**Jenkins, Norman** 1910- [IAW]
*British author*
* Brown, George

**Jenkins, Pat**
*See* Jenkins, Sidney

**Jenkins, PeeWee**
*See* Jenkins, James

**Jenkins, Phyllis**
*See* Schwalberg, Carol[yn Ernestine Stein]

**Jenkins, Posey**
*See* Jenkins, Frederic Douglass [Freddy]

**Jenkins, Richard Walter, Jr.** 1925-
[BDF, BEW, FC]
*Welsh-born actor*
* Burton, Richard

**Jenkins, S. Joshua**
*See* Taylor, E. D.

**Jenkins, Sidney** 1914- [WWJ]
*American jazz musician*
* Jenkins, Pat

**Jenkins, Thomas Griffin** 1898-
[BE]
*American baseball player*
* Jenkins, Tut

**Jenkins, Tut**
*See* Jenkins, Thomas Griffin

**Jenkins, Warren Washington**
1943- [SMG]
*American baseball player*
* Jenkins, Jack

**Jenkins, Wendy** 1912- [FC]
*British-born actress*
* Barrie, Wendy

**Jenkins, Will[iam] F[itzgerald]**
1896-1975 [CA, ESF, NAA]
*American author*
* Fitzgerald, William
* Lee, Louisa Carter
* Leinster, Murray

**Jenks, George Charles** 1850-1929
[WW, WGT]
*British-born American author*
* Carter, Nicholas
* Edwards, John Milton
* Lawson, W. B.

**Jenks, Si**
*See* Jenkins, Howard

**Jenks, Verlin** 1916- [BX, RBE]
*American boxer*
* Jenkins, Lew
* [The] Sweetwater Swatter

**Jennens, Charles** ?-1773 [RH, SN]
*British librettist*
* Soliman the Magnificent

**Jenner, Caryl**
*See* Ripman, Penelope

**Jenner, Heather**
*See* James, [Lady] Heather

**Jennette, Joe**
*See* Jeanettei, Joseph

**Jenneval**
*See* Dechet, Hippolyte Louis Alexandre

**Jenney, Jack**
*See* Jenney, Truman Elliott

**Jenney, Truman Elliott** 1910-1945
[PMJ, WWJ]
*American jazz musician*
* Jenney, Jack

**Jennifer, Susan**
*See* Hoskins, Robert

**Jennings, Alamazoo**
*See* Jennings, Alfred

**Jennings, Alfred** 1851-1894 [BE]
*American baseball player*
* Jennings, Alamazoo

**Jennings, Bo**
*See* Jennings, Burl

**Jennings, Burl** 20th c. [BBH]
*American wrestler*
* Jennings, Bo

**Jennings, Cowboy**
*See* Jennings, Henry Alexander

**Jennings, Cut**
*See* Jennings, Merle

**Jennings, Dean**
*See* Frazee, Charles S[tephen]

**Jennings, Dog**
See Jennings, Henry Constantine

**Jennings, Frances** 17th c. [SN]
*Sister of Sarah Jennings, Duchess of Marlborough*
* [The] White Milliner

**Jennings, Henry Alexander** 1892-
[IBW]
*American horse trainer*
* Jennings, Cowboy

**Jennings, Henry Constantine**
1731-1819 [SN]
*British antiquary*
* Jennings, Dog

**Jennings, Hugh Ambrose**
1870-1928 [BE, DGS, PB]
*American baseball player and manager*
* Ee-Yah

**Jennings, James H.** 1952- [FB]
*American football player*
* J. J.

**Jennings, Jenks**
See Jennings, Keith Francis

**Jennings, John [Edward, Jr.]**
1906-1973 [B10, CA, CAP]
*American author*
* Baldwin, Bates
* Williams, Joel

**Jennings, John J.** [FFF]
*American writer*
* Magoogin

**Jennings, Keith Francis** 1953- [DC]
*British cricketer*
* Jennings, Jenks

**Jennings, Leslie Nelson** 1890-1972
[CAP]
*American author, poet, editor*
* Brooke, A. B.
* Carfagne, Cyril
* Cartwright, James McGregor
* Desplaines, [Baroness] Julie
* James, Judith
* Rayson, Paul

**Jennings, Louis J.** [PA]
*Author*
* Dropper, H.

**Jennings, Merle** 20th c. [BBH]
*American wrestler*
* Jennings, Cut

**Jennings, Michael** 1931- [CA]
*American author*
* Brazos, Waco
* Kinkaid, Wyatt E.

**Jennings, Robert**
See Hamilton, Charles Harold St. John

**Jennings, S. M.**
See Meyer, Jerome Sydney

**Jennings, Waylon** 1937-
*American country-western performer*
* [The] Outlaw

**Jennison, C. S.**
See Starbird, Kaye

**Jennison, John W[illiam]** 20th c.
[SFL]
*Author*
* Charles, Neil [house pseudonym, Curtis Warren]
* Hunt, Gill [house pseudonym, Curtis Warren]

**Jennison, John W[illiam]** (Continued)
* Lang, King [house pseudonym, Curtis Warren]

**Jenoure, Aida**
See Ullithorne, Aida

**Jensen, Doris** 1922- [FC, ITA, SW]
*American actress*
* Gray, Coleen

**Jensen, Forrest Docenus** 1907-
[BE]
*American baseball player*
* Jensen, Woody

**Jensen, Jens Arnold Diederich**
1849-1936 [WBD]
*Danish naval officer*
* Bildsoe, J. A. D. J.

**Jensen, Jeppe** 1866-1930 [EWL]
*Danish poet and author*
* Aakjaer, Jeppe

**Jensen, Jo**
See Pelton, Beverly Jo

**Jensen, Julie**
See McDonald, Julie

**Jensen, Maxine Dowd** 1919- [CA]
*American writer*
* Dowd, Maxine E.

**Jensen, Pauline Marie [Long]**
1900- [CAP]
*American author*
* Long, Ann Marie

**Jensen, Peter**
See Wallmann, Jeffrey M[iner]

**Jensen, Woody**
See Jensen, Forrest Docenus

**Jensi, Muganwa Nsiku**
See Shorter, Aylward

**[The] Jenson of His Day**
See Baskerville, John

**Jeppson, Janet O.** 1926- [WD]
*American physician and author*
* Cedarholne, Jan

**Jepson, Ring**
See Latham, Henry Jepson

**Jepson-Turner, Gladys** 1924- [FC]
*British ice skater and actress*
* Belita

**Jerchower, Jerome Victor** 1908-
[BEW]
*American stage manager and production supervisor*
* Whyte, Jerome

**Jerdau, William** 1782-1854 [PA]
*Author*
* Teutha

**Jeremy, Richard**
See Fox, Charles

**Jerezano [Man from Jerez]**
See Lara y Reyes, Manuel

**[El] Jerezano [The Man from Jerez]**
See Parra, Luis

**Jeritza, Maria**
See Jedlitzka, Mizzi

**Jerkin, Hannibal**
See Jordan, [William] Hamilton

**Jerky Jake Northrop**
See Northrop, George Howard

**Jerman, Sylvia Paul**
See Cooper, Sylvia

**Jermyn, Dud**
See Benjamin, Walter Romeyn

**Jerningham, Edward** 1727-1812
[PA]
*Author*
* [The] Bard

**Jerningham, Mrs.**
See Hart, Mrs.

**Jerome, Daisy**
See Witkowski, Daisy

**Jerome, Ferris**
See Jones, Alice Ilgenfritz

**Jerome, Frankie**
See Doherty, Frank

**Jerome, George**
See Joyal, George

**Jerome, Mark**
See Appleman, Mark J[erome]

**Jerome, Owen Fox**
See Friend, Oscar J[erome]

**Jerome, Sadie**
See Witkowski, Sadie

**Jerram, Charles** 1770-1853 [PA]
*Author*
* Scrutator

**Jerrel, Broc**
See Jerrel, Bryan Leigh

**Jerrel, Bryan Leigh** 20th c. [BBH]
*American basketball player*
* Jerrel, Broc

**Jerret, Nick**
See Bertocci, Nicholas

**Jerrold, Douglas William**
1803-1857 [FFF, PA, SAT]
*British author and playwright*
* Brownrigg, Henry
* Caudle, [Mrs.] Margaret
* J.
* Prendergast, Paul
* Whitefeather, [Captain] Barabbas

**Jerrold, Ianthe** 1897- [WD]
*British author, playwright, poet*
* Bridgman, Geraldine

**Jerrold, Louise**
See Clancy, Louise Breitenbach

**Jerrold, Mary**
See Allen, Mary

**Jerrold, William Blanchard** 1826-
? [DEL, PA]
*British author*
* Fin-Bec

**[The] Jersey Bobcat**
See Shugrue, Joe

**Jersey Joe Stripp**
See Stripp, Joseph Valentine

**Jersey Joe Walcott**
See Cream, Arnold Raymond

**[The] Jersey Lily**
See Le Breton, Emilie Charlotte

**Jervis, John** 1734-1823 [HN]
*British naval officer*
* Blue, Billy

**Jervis, Mrs.**
See Howard, Caroline K.

**Jeskins, Richard**
See Story, Rosamond Mary

**Jessamine, James**
See Proctor, Bryan Waller

**[The] Jessamy Bride**
See Horneck, Mary

**Jesse, Michael**
See Baldwin, Michael

**Jessel, George** 1898-1981
*American comedian and singer*
* America's Toastmaster General
* [The] Toastmaster General of the United States

**Jessel, John**
See Weinbaum, Stanley G[rauman]

**Jessel, Mrs. Joseph A.** [FFF]
*Entertainer*
* Herndon, Agnes

**Jessen, M.** 20th c. [BF]
*Danish actress*
* Blanche, Margaret

**Jessey, Cornelia**
See Sussman, Cornelia Silver

**Jessop, Gilbert Laird** 1874-1955
[OCS]
*British cricketer*
* [The] Croucher

**Jessup, Frances**
See Van Briggle, Margaret F[rances] Jessup

**Jessye, Eva Alberta** 1897- [IBW]
*American composer, musician, poet, journalist*
* Dr. of Determination

**[The] Jester**
See Lincoln, Abraham

**Jesty, Jets**
See Jesty, Trevor Edward

**Jesty, Trevor Edward** 1948- [DC]
*British cricketer*
* Jesty, Jets

**Jesus Christ** ?- 29?
[DEP, DNNF, RH]
*Founder of Christianity*
* [The] Galilaean
* Jesus of Nazareth
* [The] Lamb of God
* [The] Light of the World
* [The] Prince of Light
* [The] Prince of Princes

**Jesus of Nazareth**
See Jesus Christ

**[The] Jet**
See Jeter, John

**[The] Jet**
See Jethroe, Samuel

**[The] Jet**
See Walker, Chet

**[The] Jet Man**
See Locas, Jacques

**Jeter, John** 1944- [SMG]
*American baseball player*
* [The] Jet

**Jethro**
See Burns, Kenneth C.

**Jethroe, Samuel** 1922- [IBW, MK]
*American baseball player*
* [The] Jet

**Jetsam**
See McEachern, Malcolm

**Jeune**
See De Lacretille, Jean C.
Dominique

**[Le] Jeune**
See Estrees, Antoine d'

**[Le] Jeune**
See Louis VII

**[Le] Jeune Aventureux**
See La Marck, Robert III de

**[Le] Jeune Damoisel Richart**
See Richard II

**[Le] Jeune Moraliste**
See Deschamps, Emile

**Jeury, Michel** 1934- [ESF]
*French author*
* Higon, Albert

**Jevons, Marshall** [joint pseudonym
with K. G. Elzinga]
See Breit, William [Leo]

**Jevons, Marshall** [joint pseudonym
with William (Leo) Breit]
See Elzinga, Kenneth G[erald]

**Jew Kid Grabiner**
See Grabiner, Joseph

**[The] Jew of Tewkesbury**
See Salomon

**[The] Jewel**
See Roscius, Quintus

**Jewel, John** 1522-1571 [SN]
*British prelate*
* [The] Jewel of Bishops

**[The] Jewel of Bishops**
See Jewel, John

**[The] Jewel of the Ghetto**
See Goldstein, Reuben

**Jewett, Eleanor**
See Lundberg, Eleanor Jewett

**Jewett, Sarah Orne** 1849-1909
[FFF]
*American author*
* Eliot, Alice

**[The] Jewish Billy Graham**
See Jungreis, Esther

**[The] Jewish Hercules**
See Samson

**[The] Jewish Jack La Lanne**
See Baer, Walter

**[The] Jewish Mark Twain**
See Rabinowitz, Solomon J.

**[The] Jewish Plato**
See Philo Judaeus

**[The] Jewish Pompadour**
See Lupescu, Elena

**[The] Jewish Socrates**
See Mendelssohn, Moses

**[The] Jewish Soul on Fire**
See Jungreis, Esther

**Jez, Teodor Tomasz**
See Milkowski, Zygmunt

**Jiang Qing** 1914?-
*Widow of Chinese leader, Mao Tse-
tung*
* [The] Empress
* Lan Ping [Blue Apple]

**Jick**
See Henderson, John William

**Jig-Saw**
See Milnes, Thomas Wray

**Jije**
See Gillain, Joseph

**Jill**
See Lynne, Glenys

**Jim Crow Rice**
See Rice, Thomas Dartmouth

**Jim Daddy Walker**
See Walker, James

**Jimenez, B.** 20th c. [OBW]
*American baseball player*
* Jimenez, Hooks

**Jimenez, Baba**
See Jimenez, Nestor

**Jimenez, Cha Cha**
See Jimenez, Jose

**Jimenez, Francisco Javier**
See Barrios, Francisco Javier

**Jimenez, Hooks**
See Jimenez, B.

**Jimenez, Jose**
See Dana, Bill

**Jimenez, Jose** 1949- [B10]
*American revolutionist*
* Jimenez, Cha Cha

**Jimenez, Nestor** 1947- [RBE]
*Colombian boxer*
* Jimenez, Baba

**Jimenez Gonzalez, Manuel** 1923-
[GS]
*Mexican bullfighter*
* Chicuelin [Youngster]

**Jimenez Sola, Enrique** 1911- [CW]
*Puerto Rican poet*
* A. R.?

**Jimenez Vera, Manuel** 1879-1907
[GS]
*Spanish bullfighter*
* Chicuelo [Young Man]

**Jimenez y Najar, Bartolome**
1867-1923 [GS]
*Spanish bullfighter*
* Murcia [From Murcia]

**Jiminez, Marcos** 1952- [RBE]
*Spanish boxer*
* Paperito

**Jimmy Blue Eyes**
See Alo, Vincent

**Jimmy the Greek**
See Synodinos, Dimitrios

**Jimmy Three Sticks**
See Robinson, James D., III

**Jingle**
See Golsworthy, Arnold

**Jingle Joints Sellers**
See Sellers, Ron

**Jinkins, Gus**
See Jenkins, Gus

**Jinks, Joshua Jedediah**
See Dick, William Brisbane

**Jiranek, Joseph Francis**
1880?-1942 [BEW]
*Austrian-born comedian*
* Jackson, Joe

**Jiskogo**
See Harrington, Mark Raymond

**Jittery Joe Berry**
See Berry, Jonas Arthur

**Jix**
See Joynson-Hicks, William

**Joachim** 1145?-1202? [FFF, SN]
*Abbot of Fiore*
* [The] Prophet

**Joachim, Al** 1901-1965 [F1, IPA]
*American actor*
* Ritz, Al

**Joachim, Andrew** 20th c. [RO2]
*Canadian-born singer*
* Kim, Andy

**Joachim, Peter Mico** 1923- [IBW]
*West Indian-born musician*
* Germany's Satchmo
* Mo, Billy

**Joachim II** 1505-1571
[DEP, DNNF, SN]
*Elector of Brandenburg*
* [The] Hector of Germany

**Joad, C. E. M.**
See Joad, Cyril Edwin Mitchinson

**Joad, Cyril Edwin Mitchinson**
1891-1953 [LC, TC]
*British philosopher*
* Joad, C. E. M.

**Joan** 1321-1362 [DNNS, WBD]
*Queen of Scotland*
* Joan of the Tower
* Makepeace, Joan

**Joan** 1328-1385
[DHA, DNNF, HN]
*Countess of Salisbury*
* [The] Fair Maid of Kent

**Joan, Mary**
See Picken, Mary Brooks

**Joan of Arc** [or Jeanne d'Arc]
1412-1431 [DNNF, HN, SN]
*Saint*
* [The] Holy Maid
* [The] Maid of Orleans
* [La] Pucelle
* [The] Wondrous Maid

**[The] Joan of Arc of Peace**
See Krudener, Julia de Weitinghoff

**Joan of Art**
See Mondale, Joan

**Joan of Kent**
See Bocher, Joan

**Joan of the Tower**
See Joan

**Joanette, Kit**
See Joanette, Rosario

**Joanette, Rosario** 1915- [CEI]
*Canadian-born hockey player*
* Joanette, Kit

**Joannes, Count**
See Jones, George

**Joans, Ted**
See Jones, Theodore

**Job**
See Bass, Josef

**Job**
See Onfroy de Breville, Jacques

**Job, Edwin** [FFF]
*Entertainer*
* Arnott, Edwin

**Jobb, Jamie** 1945- [CA]
*American journalist and author*
* Kabibble, Osh

**Jobe, Duke**
See Jobe, Lequeint

**Jobe, Lequeint** [RO2]
*American musician*
* Jobe, Duke

**Jobson, Sandra**
See Darroch, Sandra Jobson

**Jocelyn, Richard**
See Clutterbuck, Richard

**[The] Jock Presbyter**
See Jones, [Sir] William

**[The] Jockey of Norfolk**
See Howard, [Sir] John [First
Duke of Norfolk]

**Jocund Johnny**
See Ballantyne, John

**Jodelle, Etienne** 1532-1573
[DEP, DNNS, SN]
*French dramatic poet*
* [The] Father of the French
Drama

**Joe**
See Burgess, Joseph

**Joe Boy Washington**
See Washington, Joe

**Joe D.**
See DiLeonardi, Joseph

**Joe E.**
See Tucker, Thurman Lowell

**Joe Fingers Carr**
See Bush, Louis F.

**Joe the Baker**
See Catania, Joseph

**Joe the Jet**
See Perry, Fletcher

**Joe Who**
See Clark, [Charles] Joseph [Joe]

**Joel, Billy** 1949- [RO2]
*American singer*
* Martin, Bill

**Joel, Jack Bernato** 1862-1940
[EJS]
*British horse owner and breeder*
* Uncle Jack

**Joel, Lydia**
See Tarnower, Lydia

**Joergensen, Johannes** 1866-1956
[CAT]
*Danish author*
* Unicus [Alone]

**Joey A**
See  Doto, Giuseppe

**Joffe, Abram** 1881-1963    [JL]
*Russian philosopher*
* Deborin, Abram M.

**Joffrey, Robert**
See  Khan, Abdullah Jaffa Bey

**Johannes**
See  Van Shaick, John

**Johannes Eremita**
See  Cassianus, Johannes

**Johannes fac Totum [Jack of All Trades]**
See  Shakespeare, William

**Johannes Hagustaldensis** 12th c.
[RH]
*Chronicler*
* John of Hexham

**Johannes Hispalensis** 12th c.
[WBD]
*Spanish scholar*
* John of Seville

**Johannes Leo**
See  Leo Africanus

**Johannes Massiliensis**
See  Cassianus, Johannes

**Johannes, R.**
See  Moss, Rose

**Johannes von Goch**
See  Pupper, Johann

**Johannesson, Olof**
See  Alfven, Hannes O[lof]
G[oesta]

**Johanson, Elisabeth**
See  Verwer, Johanna Elisabeth

**Johanson, Jai Johnny** 1944-    [RO2]
*American musician*
* Johanson, Jaimoe

**Johanson, Jaimoe**
See  Johanson, Jai Johnny

**Johansson, Tor** 1903-1971    [SC]
*Swedish-born actor and wrestler*
* Johnson, Tor

**John**
See  Beach, John Wesley

**John** 6?- 104?    [DNNF, RH, WBD]
*Saint*
* [The] Beloved Disciple
* [The] Divine
* [The] Evangelist

**John** 347?- 407    [DNNS, FFF, RH]
*Saint*
* [The] Almoner
* Chrysostom
* [The] Glorious Preacher
* Golden Mouth
* [The] Homer of Orators
* [The] Thirteenth Apostle

**John** 11th c.    [CAL]
*Pope*
* Sylvester III

**John** 1167?-1216
[DHA, DNNS, HN]
*King of England*
* Lackland [or Sans Terre]

**John** 12th c.    [HN]
*Norwegian chieftain*
* [The] Furious

**John [or Johann]** 1296?-1346
[DNNS]
*King of Bohemia*
* [The] Blind

**John [or Jean]** 1371-1419
[DNNS, HN, SN]
*Duke of Burgundy*
* [The] Fearless
* [The] Hannotin of Flanders
* Sans Peur

**John [or Johann]** 1468?-1532
[DNNS, HN, SN]
*Elector of Saxony*
* [The] Constant
* [The] Second Parent of the
   Reformed Church

**John** 1513-1571    [WBD]
*Margrave of Brandenburg-Cuestrin*
* Hans of Cuestrin

**John** 16th c.    [HN]
*Son of King Ferdinand V, of Castile
and Aragon*
* [The] Marcellus of Spain

**John, B.**
See  John, Elizabeth Beaman

**John, Betty**
See  John, Elizabeth Beaman

**John Bull's Girl**
See  Monks, Victoria

**John, Dane**
See  Major, Alan P[ercival]

**John de Montfort** ?-1345    [WBD]
*Duke of Brittany*
* John IV

**John, Elizabeth Beaman** 1907-
[CA, IAW]
*American author*
* John, B.
* John, Betty
* St. John, Beth
* Sinjun

**John, Elton**
See  Dwight, Reginald Kenneth

**John, Eugenie** 1825-1887    [WBD]
*German author*
* Marlitt, E.

**John, Evan**
See  Simpson, Evan

**John Frederick** 1503-1554
[DNNS, WBD]
*Elector of Saxony*
* [The] Magnanimous

**John, Graham**
See  Colmer, Graham John

**John, Isaac Johnny** 1865-1967
[SC]
*American actor*
* Big Tree, [Chief] John

**John, Jasper**
See  Muspratt, Rosalie Helen

**John, John Pico** 1906-    [WFA]
*German-born fashion designer*
* John, Mr.

**John, Miriam**
See  Hopkins, [Frances] Betty

**John, Mr.**
See  John, John Pico

**John [or Johann] Nepomuk Maria
Joseph** 1801-1873    [FFF, WBD]
*King of Saxony*
* Philalethes

**John Nepomuk Salvator** 1852-1891
[WBD]
*Archduke of Austria and Prince of
Tuscany*
* Orth, Johann

**John of Antioch**
See  John II

**John of Bruges**
See  Van Eyck, Jan [or John]

**John of Damascus [or Johannes
Damascenus]** 700?- 754?
[DNNS, WBD]
*Saint*
* Chrysorrhoas
* [The] Golden Stream

**John of Gaunt** 1340-1399    [SN]
*Duke of Lancaster*
* Lancaster, Time Honored

**John of God**
See  Juan Ciudad

**John of Hexham**
See  Johannes Hagustaldensis

**John of Kronshtadt [or Cronstadt]**
See  Sergiev, Ioann

**John of Lancaster** 1389-1435
[DHA, FFF, RH]
*Duke of Bedford*
* [The] Firebrand of France
* John with the Leaden Sword

**John of Leyden**
See  Becold [Boccold, or
Bockholdt], John

**John of Manchester**
See  Bosworth, John

**John of Ripatransone**    [HN]
*Medieval scholar*
* Difficilis, Doctor

**John of Salisbury** 1110?-1180?
[DNNS, HN]
*British prelate, scholar, author*
* [The] Little
* [The] Little Deacon

**John of Seville**
See  Johannes Hispalensis

**John [or Johannes] of Swabia**
1290-1313?    [DNNS, SN]
*German prince*
* [The] Parricide

**John of the Cross**
See  De Yepis y Alvarez, Juan

**John of Wesel**
See  Ruchrath [or Ruchrad],
Johannes

**John of York**
See  Tobin, John H.

**John Paul I**
See  Luciani, Albino

**John Paul II**
See  Wojtyla, Karol

**John, Robert**
See  Pedrick, Robert, Jr.

**John, Rosamund**
See  Jones, Nora

**John the Prophet**
See  Pittman, Jack

**John, Thomas Edward** 1943-
[SMG]
*American baseball player*
* T. J.

**John with the Leaden Sword**
See  John of Lancaster

**John I [or Joao]** 1357-1433
[DNNS, WBD]
*King of Portugal*
* [The] Bastard
* [The] Great

**John II**
See  Mercurius

**John II** ?- 577    [HN]
*Patriarch of Constantincple*
* John of Antioch
* Scolasticus

**John II [or Jean]** 1319-1364
[DNNS, FFF, SN]
*King of France*
* [Le] Bon
* [The] Good

**John II** 1455-1495
[DNNS, FFF, SN]
*King of Portugal*
* [The] Great
* [The] Perfect

**John II Casimir** 1609-1672    [WBD]
*King of Poland*
* Casimir V

**John II Comnenus** 1088-1143    [HN]
*Byzantine emperor*
* Calojoannes [Handsome]
* [The] Marcus Aurelius of the
   Base Empire

**John III [or Jean]** 1286-1341
[DNNS, FFF, WBD]
*Duke of Brittany*
* [Le] Bon
* [The] Good

**John III [or Johann]** 1455-1499
[DEP, DNNS, SN]
*Elector of Brandenburg*
* [The] Cicero of Germany

**John III Sobieski** 1624-1696
[DHA, SN]
*King of Poland*
* [The] Wizard

**John IV**
See  John de Montfort

**John IV [or Jean]** 1338-1399
[FFF, RH, SN]
*Duke of Brittany*
* [The] Valiant

**John IV** 1605-1656    [DNNS, WBD]
*King of Portugal*
* [The] Fortunate

**John V [or Jean]** 1389-1442
[FFF, SN, WBD]
*Duke of Brittany*
* [The] Good
* [Le] Sage
* [The] Wise

**John V** 1689-1750
[DNNF, FFF, SN]
*King of Portugal*
* Most Faithful Majesty

**John VI [or Jean]** 9th c.    [SN]
*Patriarch of Armenia*
* Catholicos

**John VIII** 820?- 882    [HN]
*Pope*
* Pope Joan

**John XII**
*See* Octavius

**John XII** 938?- 964    [WBD]
*Pope*
* [The] Boy Pope

**John XIV**
*See* Campanora, Peter

**John XVI**
*See* Philagathus

**John XVII [or XVIII]**
*See* Siccone

**John XVIII [or XIX]**
*See* Fasano [or Phasianus], Leo

**John XXI**
*See* Hispanus, Petrus

**John XXII**
*See* D'Euse, Jacques

**John XXIII**
*See* Roncalli, Angelo Giuseppe

**Johnhett**
*See* Hettinger, John

**Johnn, David**
*See* Engle, John D[avid], Jr.

**Johnness**
*See* You, Dominique

**Johnny Fix-'Em**
*See* Condon, John

**Johnny O**
*See* Omohundro, John

**Johnny U**
*See* Unitas, Johnny

**Johns, Augie**
*See* Johns, Augustus Francis

**Johns, Augustus Francis** 1899-
[BE]
*American baseball player*
* Johns, Augie
* Johns, Lefty

**Johns, Avery**
*See* Cousins, Margaret

**Johns, C. Mitchell** 1952-    [SMG]
*American football player*
* Johns, Earthquake
* Johns, Skip

**Johns, Earthquake**
*See* Johns, C. Mitchell

**Johns, Foster**
*See* Seldes, Gilbert [Vivian]

**Johns, Geoffrey**
*See* Warner, [George] Geoffrey
John

**Johns, Gilbert**
*See* Stagg, James

**Johns, Jap**
*See* Johns, Jasper

**Johns, Jasper** 1930?-
*American artist*
* Johns, Jap

**Johns, June**
*See* Johns Smith, June

**Johns, Kenneth** [joint pseudonym
with John Newman]
*See* Bulmer, [Henry] Kenneth

**Johns, Kenneth** [joint pseudonym
with (Henry) Kenneth Bulmer]
*See* Newman, John

**Johns, Lefty**
*See* Johns, Augustus Francis

**Johns, Marston**
*See* Fanthorpe, R[obert] Lionel

**Johns, Pete**
*See* Johns, William R.

**Johns, Ralph**
*See* Cole, Jack

**Johns, Skip**
*See* Johns, C. Mitchell

**Johns, Thompson**
*See* Thompson, John H.

**Johns, W. E.**
*See* Johns, [Captain] William
Earle

**Johns, Whitey**
*See* White, John I[rwin]

**Johns, William E.** 1870-1945    [SC]
*American actor*
* Elmer, Billy

**Johns, [Captain] William Earle**
1893-1968    [CA, LC]
*British author and journalist*
* Earle, William
* Johns, W. E.

**Johns, William R.** 1889-1964    [BE]
*American baseball player*
* Johns, Pete

**Johns, Willy**
*See* Meeker, W. Johns

**Johns Smith, June** 1925-    [AW]
*British author*
* Johns, June

**Johnson, A.**
*See* Johnson, Annabell Jones

**Johnson, A. E.** [joint pseudonym with
Edgar Raymond Johnson]
*See* Johnson, Annabell Jones

**Johnson, A. E.** [joint pseudonym with
Annabell Jones Johnson]
*See* Johnson, Edgar Raymond

**Johnson, Abbie**
*See* Johnson, Albert J.

**Johnson, Adam Rankin, Sr.**
1888-1972    [BE]
*American baseball player*
* Johnson, Tex

**Johnson, Airplane**
*See* Johnson, Dennis

**Johnson, Alan**
*See* Phillifent, John Thomas

**Johnson, Albert A.** 20th c.    [BBH]
*American postmaster*
* [The] Snowshoe Expressman

**Johnson, Albert J.** 1910-
[DAM, PMJ, WWJ]
*American jazz musician*
* Johnson, Budd

**Johnson, Albert J.** 20th c.    [BE]
*American baseball player*
* Johnson, Abbie

**Johnson, Alex** 20th c.    [BBH]
*Canadian lacrosse player*
* Johnson, Buck

**Johnson, Alonzo** 1889-1970
[BWW, PMJ]
*American singer*
* Johnson, Lonnie
* Jordan, Jimmy
* Jordan, Tom
* [The] World's Greatest Blues
Singer

**Johnson, Anderson Sidney** 1952-
[SMG]
*American football player*
* A. J.
* Johnson, Andy

**Johnson, Andrew** 1808-1875    [FAP]
*American president*
* [The] Daddy of the Baby
* [The] Father of the Homestead
Act
* His Accidency
* King Andy the First
* Old Andy
* Old Veto
* Sir Veto
* [The] Tennessee Tailor
* [The] Veto President

**Johnson, Andy**
*See* Johnson, Anderson Sidney

**Johnson, Anna C.** 1832-1883
[DEL, DNNF, PA]
*American author*
* Myrtle, Minnie

**Johnson, Anna M.** 1860- ?    [ALY]
*American author*
* Darling, Hope

**Johnson, Annabell Jones** 1921-
[CA, SAT]
*American author*
* Johnson, A.
* Johnson, A. E. [joint pseudonym
with Edgar Raymond Johnson]

**Johnson, Art[hur Henry]** 1916-
[BE]
*American baseball player*
* Johnson, Lefty

**Johnson, Arthur Tysilio** 1873- ?
[WWL]
*Welsh author*
* Draig Glas

**Johnson, Ban**
*See* Johnson, Byron Bancroft

**Johnson, Barney**
*See* Johnson, Walter Perry

**Johnson, Bart**
*See* Johnson, Clair Barth

**Johnson, Benjamin F., of Boone**
*See* Riley, James Whitcomb

**Johnson, Big Bill**
*See* Broonzy, William Lee Conley

**Johnson, Big Hands**
*See* Johnson, Gary

**Johnson, Big John**
*See* Johnson, John Henry

**Johnson, Bill**    [SMG]
*American football coach*
* Johnson, Tiger

**Johnson, Billy** 1952-    [SMG]
*American football player*
* Johnson, White Shoes

**Johnson, Bizz**
*See* Johnson, Harold

**Johnson, Blind Boy**
*See* Dupree, William Thomas

**Johnson, Blind Willie**
*See* Johnson, Willie

**Johnson, Blues**
*See* Carr, Leroy

**Johnson, Bruce Forsyth** 1928-
[BMH, TR]
*British comedian*
* Boy Bruce, the Mighty Atom
* Forsyth, Bruce

**Johnson, Brummagem**
*See* Parr, Samuel

**Johnson, Buck**
*See* Johnson, Alex

**Johnson, Budd**
*See* Johnson, Albert J.

**Johnson, Buddy**
*See* Johnson, Woodrow Wilson

**Johnson, Bull**
*See* Johnson, William Russell

**Johnson, Bumpy**
*See* Johnson, Ellsworth Raymond

**Johnson, Bunk**
*See* Johnson, William Geary

**Johnson, Burdetta Fay Beebe**
1920-    [IAW]
*American author*
* Beebe, B. F.

**Johnson, Byron Bancroft**
1864-1931    [DGS]
*American baseball executive*
* Johnson, Ban

**Johnson, C.** 20th c.    [OBW]
*American baseball player*
* Johnson, Sess

**Johnson, C. F.**
*See* Goulart, Frances Sheridan

**Johnson, Cactus**
*See* Johnson, Fred[erick Edward]

**Johnson, Caleb**
*See* Stockbridge, Frank Parker

**Johnson, Carlos**
*See* Johnson, Charles William

**Johnson, Carol Diahann** 1935-
[EMT, IPA, SW]
*American actress and singer*
* Carroll, Diahann

**Johnson, Chappie**
*See* Johnson, George

**Johnson, Charlene**
*See* Crawford, Char

**Johnson, Charles** 1949-    [SMG]
*American basketball player*
* Johnson, Jack

**Johnson, Charles Cleveland [Charlie]**
1885-1940    [BE]
*American baseball player*
* Johnson, Home Run

**Johnson, Charles E.** 1872- ? [IBW]
*American entertainer*
* [The] Cakewalk King

**Johnson, Charles LaVere** 1910-
[WWJ]
*American jazz musician*
* LaVere, Charles

**Johnson, Charles Randolph**
1903-1974 [SC]
*American actor and columnist*
* Johnson, Chubby

**Johnson, Charles S.**
*See* Edwards, William B[ennett]

**Johnson, Charles William** 1943-
[IAW]
*American-born author*
* Johnson, Carlos

**Johnson, Chatta**
*See* Giovannone, Anthony J.

**Johnson, Cherokee**
*See* Johnson, Robert Lee [Bob]

**Johnson, Chick**
*See* Johnson, Harold

**Johnson, Chief**
*See* Johnson, George Murphy

**Johnson, Ching**
*See* Johnson, Ivan Wilfred

**Johnson, Christopher** 1931- [CA]
*British economist and author*
* McIntosh, Louis

**Johnson, Chubby**
*See* Johnson, Charles Randolph

**Johnson, Clair Barth** 1950- [SMG]
*American baseball player*
* Johnson, Bart

**Johnson, Clara** [FFF]
*Entertainer*
* Bernetta, [Mlle.] Clara

**Johnson, Clarence L.** 1910?-
*American aircraft designer*
* Johnson, Kelly

**Johnson, Claude** 20th c. [RO1]
*American singer*
* Johnson, Sonny

**Johnson, Claude** 20th c. [OBW]
*American baseball player*
* Johnson, Hooks

**Johnson, Claudia Alta [Taylor]**
1912- [B10]
*Wife of American president Lyndon Johnson*
* Johnson, Lady Bird

**Johnson, Clifford** 1922- [BE]
*American baseball player*
* Johnson, Connie

**Johnson, Connie**
*See* Johnson, Clifford

**Johnson, Corinthian** 20th c. [RO1]
*American singer*
* Johnson, Kripp

**Johnson, Crockett**
*See* Leisk, David Johnson

**Johnson, Curley**
*See* Johnson, John

**Johnson, Curt[is Lee]** 1928- [CA]
*American editor and author*
* Wallek, Lee

**Johnson, Curt[is Lee]** (Continued)
* Whiz, Walter

**Johnson, Dan** 20th c. [OBW]
*American baseball player*
* Johnson, Shang

**Johnson, Daniel** 1629-1675 [FFF]
*British buccaneer*
* [The] Terror

**Johnson, Deacon**
*See* Johnson, Lem[uel Charles]

**Johnson, Dennis** 1954- [SMG]
*American basketball player*
* Johnson, Airplane

**Johnson, Dibo**
*See* Johnson, George

**Johnson, Dicta**
*See* Johnson, Louis

**Johnson, Dink**
*See* Johnson, Oliver [Ollie]

**Johnson, Donald McI[ntosh]** 1903-
[CA]
*British physician and author*
* De Montfort, Guy

**Johnson, Donald Spore** 1911- [BE]
*American baseball player*
* Johnson, Pep

**Johnson, Dudley Vaughan** 20th c.
[MBF]
*British author*
* Vaughan, Dudley

**Johnson, E. Ned**
*See* Johnson, Enid

**Johnson, Earl Douglas** 1919- [BE]
*American baseball player*
* Johnson, Lefty

**Johnson, Earvin** 1959- [IBW]
*American basketball player*
* Johnson, Magic

**Johnson, Easy Papa**
*See* Sykes, Roosevelt

**Johnson, Edgar Raymond** 1912-
[CA, SAT]
*American author*
* Johnson, A. E. [joint pseudonym with Annabell Jones Johnson]

**Johnson, Edith North** 1905?-
[BWW]
*American singer*
* Allen, Maybelle
* North, Hattie

**Johnson, Eleanor**
*See* Seymour, Dorothy Jane Z[ander]

**Johnson, Elinore** 1902- [F2, ITA]
*British actress*
* Swinburne, Nora

**Johnson, Ellsworth Raymond** 20th
c. [IBW]
*American gambler*
* [The] Black Robin Hood of Harlem
* Johnson, Bumpy

**Johnson, Elmer Ellsworth**
1884-1966 [BE]
*American baseball player*
* Johnson, Hickory

**Johnson, Enid** 1892- [CA]
*American author*
* Johnson, E. Ned

**Johnson, Enoch J.** 20th c.
[BLB, PHM]
*American underworld figure*
* Johnson, Nucky

**Johnson, Eppa**
*See* Johnson, Lloyd William

**Johnson, Ernest [Ernie]** 1886-1963
[FHE, HK]
*Canadian-born hockey player*
* Johnson, Moose

**Johnson, Ernest** 20th c. [BWW]
*American musician*
* Johnson, 44

**Johnson, Errisson Pallman** 1941-
[EJ7]
*Bahamian jazz musician*
* Errisson, King

**Johnson, Essex** 1946- [SMG]
*American football player*
* Big Play, Mr.

**Johnson, Esther** 1681-1728
[DEL, DNNF]
*Wife of British author, Jonathan Swift*
* Stella

**Johnson, Evelyn Kimball** 19th c.
[FFF]
*American editor*
* McFlimsey, Flora

**Johnson, Fannie**
*See* McCoy, Viola

**Johnson, Footer**
*See* Johnson, Richard Allan [Dick]

**Johnson, Forrest B.** 1935- [SFL]
*Author*
* Johnson, Frosty

**Johnson, 44**
*See* Johnson, Ernest

**Johnson, Frank** 1917- [FC]
*American actor*
* Darro, Frankie

**Johnson, Fred[erick Edward]**
1897-1973 [BE]
*American baseball player*
* Johnson, Cactus

**Johnson, Frederic H.** 1908-1967
[EJ, PMJ, WWJ]
*American jazz musician*
* Johnson, Keg

**Johnson, Frederick** 20th c. [RO1]
*American entertainer*
* Johnson, Money

**Johnson, Frederick Ayres**
1876-1926 [BBD]
*American composer*
* Ayres, Frederic

**Johnson, Frosty**
*See* Johnson, Forrest B.

**Johnson, Gary** 1952- [SMG]
*American football player*
* Johnson, Big Hands

**Johnson, General**
*See* Johnson, Norman

**Johnson, George**
*See* Leopold, Nathan F.

**Johnson, George**
*See* Loeb, Richard A.

**Johnson, George** 20th c. [OBW]
*American baseball player*
* Johnson, Dibo

**Johnson, George** 20th c.
[IBW, OBW]
*American baseball player*
* Johnson, Chappie

**Johnson, George Metcalf** 1885-
[NAA]
*American author*
* Metcalf, George

**Johnson, George Murphy**
1887-1922 [BE]
*American baseball player*
* Johnson, Chief

**Johnson, George William** [FFF]
*Author*
* Hovey, Wayne

**Johnson, Georgia Boy**
*See* Johnson, Lucius Brinson

**Johnson, Gilbert H.** ?-1972 [IBW]
*American military officer*
* Johnson, Hashmark

**Johnson, Gladys**
*See* McCoy, Viola

**Johnson, Grant** 1874- ? [MK]
*American baseball player*
* Johnson, Homerun

**Johnson, Gus**
*See* Alex, Gus

**Johnson, Gus** 1939- [IBW]
*American basketball player*
* Johnson, Honeycomb

**Johnson, H. B.**
*See* Wyman, Walter Forestus

**Johnson, Harold** 1891-1962
[EMT, WEF]
*American comic actor and producer*
* Johnson, Chick

**Johnson, Harold** 1908?-
*American politician*
* Johnson, Bizz

**Johnson, Harold** 1918- [WWJ]
*American jazz musician*
* Johnson, Money

**Johnson, Harold** 20th c. [BAB]
*American sportswriter*
* Johnson, Speed

**Johnson, Harriet Laight C.** 1862- ?
[NAA]
*Canadian writer*
* Strafford

**Johnson, Harriet Louisa** 1901-
[BEW]
*American actress*
* Field, Sylvia

**Johnson, Hashmark**
*See* Johnson, Gilbert H.

**Johnson, Heavy**
*See* Johnson, Oscar

**Johnson, Henry**
*See* McGhee, Walter Brown

**Johnson, Henry** 1908-1974 [BWW]
*American singer*
* Johnson, Rufe

**Johnson, Henry** 20th c. [SG]
*Boxer*
* Towne, Artie

**Johnson, Henry T.** 1858-1930
[MBF]
*British author*
* Thomson, Neil

**Johnson, Herbert Fisk** 1899?-1978
*American executive*
* Johnson, Hib

**Johnson, Hewlett** 1874-1965    [NN]
*British ecclesiastic*
* [The] Red Dean

**Johnson, Hib**
See  Johnson, Herbert Fisk

**Johnson, Hickory**
See  Johnson, Elmer Ellsworth

**Johnson, High Pockets**
See  Johnson, Paul Vincent

**Johnson, Home Run**
See  Johnson, Charles Cleveland
[Charlie]

**Johnson, Homerun**
See  Johnson, Grant

**Johnson, Honeycomb**
See  Johnson, Gus

**Johnson, Hooks**
See  Johnson, Claude

**Johnson, Hooks**
See  Johnson, Kenneth Carstensen

**Johnson, Hopson** 20th c.    [BWW]
*American singer*
* Johnson, Hotbox

**Johnson, Hotbox**
See  Johnson, Hopson

**Johnson, Howard W.** 1910-1945
[AS]
*American football player*
* Johnson, Smiley

**Johnson, Howard William** 1908-
[B10, WWJ]
*American jazz musician*
* Johnson, Swan

**Johnson, Indian Bob**
See  Johnson, Robert Lee [Bob]

**Johnson, Iron Man**
See  Johnson, John

**Johnson, Ivan Wilfred** 1897-
[CEI, FHE, HK]
*Canadian-born hockey player*
* Johnson, Ching

**Johnson, J. Harvey, Jr.** 1917-
[BEW]
*American talent representative*
* Harvey, John

**Johnson, J. J. [or Jay Jay]**
See  Johnson, James Louis

**Johnson, Jack**
See  Johnson, Charles

**Johnson, Jack** 20th c.    [AES]
*American soccer player*
* Johnson, Offside

**Johnson, James** 1905?-1972?
[BWW]
*American singer*
* Johnson, Stump
* Little Man
* Roberts, Snitcher
* Shorty George

**Johnson, James** 1916-
[BDW, WWW]
*British air force officer*
* Johnson, Johnnie

**Johnson, James** 20th c.
*American jazz musician*
* Johnson, Steady Roll

**Johnson, James Arthur** 1930?-
[FC, FD, SW]
*American actor*
* St. Jacques, Raymond

**Johnson, James C.** 20th c.    [SMG]
*American baseball team staff
member*
* Johnson, Slick

**Johnson, James Louis** 1924-
[DAM, EJ, PMJ]
*American jazz musician*
* Johnson, J. J. [or Jay Jay]

**Johnson, James Weldon** 1871- ?
[DEL, WWL]
*American author and poet*
* Fag, Frederick

**Johnson, Jane**
See  Daigle, Jane Johnson

**Johnson, Jeep**
See  Johnson, Jimmy

**Johnson, Jerry Mack** 1927-    [CA]
*American author*
* Mack, Jerry

**Johnson, Jimmy** 20th c.    [OBW]
*American baseball player*
* Johnson, Jeep

**Johnson, Jimmy** 20th c.
*American baseball player*
* Johnson, Slim

**Johnson, Jing**
See  Johnson, Russell Conwell

**Johnson, Jinna**
See  Johnson, Virginia

**Johnson, Joan Helen** 1931-    [CA]
*American author*
* Jeffers, Jo

**Johnson, John**    [BBH]
*American sled dog racer*
* Johnson, Iron Man

**Johnson, John** 20th c.    [SMG]
*American football player*
* Johnson, Curley

**Johnson, John Arthur [Jack]**
1878-1946    [BX, SR, WBC]
*American boxer*
* Big Smoke
* [The] Black Avenger
* [The] Galveston Giant
* Johnson, Little Artha

**Johnson, John Clifford [Johnny]**
1914-    [BE]
*American baseball player*
* Johnson, Swede

**Johnson, John Henry** 1929-    [FB]
*American football player*
* Johnson, Big John

**Johnson, John Louis**
See  Mercer, John Louis

**Johnson, John Ralph** 1860- ?    [BE]
*American baseball player*
* Johnson, Spud

**Johnson, Johnnie**
See  Johnson, James

**Johnson, Johnny**
See  Johnson, Malcolm

**Johnson, Jonathan**
See  Harrison, George Robert

**Johnson, Joseph** 20th c.    [IBW]
*American dancer, choreographer,
producer*
* Johnson, Ziggy

**Johnson, Joseph E[arl]** 1946-    [CA]
*American author*
* Fitzgerald, Hal

**Johnson, Judy**
See  Johnson, William Julius

**Johnson, Junior**
See  Johnson, Robert Glenn

**Johnson, Karl Gerhard** 1891?-1964
[BEW]
*Actor and songwriter*
* Gerhard, Karl

**Johnson, Keg**
See  Johnson, Frederic H.

**Johnson, Kelly**
See  Johnson, Clarence L.

**Johnson, Kenneth Carstensen**
1923-    [BE]
*American baseball player*
* Johnson, Hooks

**Johnson, Kripp**
See  Johnson, Corinthian

**Johnson, Lady Bird**
See  Johnson, Claudia Alta
[Taylor]

**Johnson, Lamar** 1950-    [SMG]
*American baseball player*
* Johnson, Lee

**Johnson, Landslide Lyndon**
See  Johnson, Lyndon Baines

**Johnson, Laraine** 1917?-
[FC, ITA, SW]
*American actress*
* Day, Laraine

**Johnson, Laurence Bernard** 1908-
[BEW, FC, TR]
*British actor*
* Naismith, Laurence

**Johnson, Lee**
See  Johnson, Lamar

**Johnson, Lefty**
See  Johnson, Art[hur Henry]

**Johnson, Lefty**
See  Johnson, Earl Douglas

**Johnson, Lem[uel Charles]** 1909-
[WWJ]
*American jazz musician*
* Johnson, Deacon

**Johnson, Leslie** 1933-
[BWW, NBB]
*American singer*
* Lazy Lester
* Thomas, Henry

**Johnson, Light Bulb**
See  Johnson, Lyndon Baines

**Johnson, Lilian Clara** 1895-    [THR]
*British actress and singer*
* St. John, Lily

**Johnson, Linda** 1884-1949    [F1]
*Actress*
* Arvidson, Linda

**Johnson, Little Artha**
See  Johnson, John Arthur [Jack]

**Johnson, Little Willie**
See  Johnson, William Edward John

**Johnson, Llewellyn H.**    [FFF]
*American bicycle racer*
* Ixion

**Johnson, Lloyd William** 1910-    [BE]
*American baseball player*
* Johnson, Eppa

**Johnson, Lonnie**
See  Johnson, Alonzo

**Johnson, Louis** 20th c.    [OBW]
*American baseball player*
* Johnson, Dicta

**Johnson, Louis Brown** 1934-    [BE]
*American baseball player*
* Johnson, Slick
* Johnson, Sweet Lou

**Johnson, Lucius Brinson**
1934-1976    [BWW]
*American singer*
* Johnson, Georgia Boy
* Johnson, Luther
* Johnson, Snake
* King, Luther
* Little Luther

**Johnson, Lucy** 1922-    [BDF, FC]
*American actress*
* Gardner, Ava

**Johnson, Luther**
See  Johnson, Lucius Brinson

**Johnson, Luther, Jr.** 1939-    [BWW]
*American singer*
* Black Jr.
* Guitar Jr.
* Little Jr.

**Johnson, Lyndon Baines**
1908-1973    [FAP]
*American president*
* Johnson, Landslide Lyndon
* Johnson, Light Bulb
* L. B. J.

**Johnson, Magic**
See  Johnson, Earvin

**Johnson, Malcolm** 1902?-    [PMJ]
*American bandleader*
* Johnson, Johnny

**Johnson, Margaret**
See  Dunn, Sara

**Johnson, Marguerita** 1928-    [CLC]
*American author, poet, playwright*
* Angelou, Maya

**Johnson, Marilue Carolyn** 1931-
[CA]
*American author and illustrator*
* Marilue

**Johnson, Marilyn Jeanne** 1927-
[BEW]
*American singer and actress*
* Johnson, Susan

**Johnson, Marion Georgina [Wikeley]**
1912-1980    [AW, CA]
*British author*
* Masson, Georgina

**Johnson, Martha**
See   Beaman, Lottie Kimbrough

**Johnson, Mary** 1900?-   [BWW]
*American singer*
* Johnson, Signifyin' Mary

**Johnson, Mary Louise**
See   King, Mary Louise

**Johnson, Maud Lalita** 1875- ?
[SFL]
*Author*
* Lalita

**Johnson, Meathead**
See   Dupree, William Thomas

**Johnson, Merle Allison** 1934-   [CA]
*American clergyman and author*
* Pastor X

**Johnson, Merle, Jr.** 1936?-
[FC, ITA, SW]
*American actor*
* Donahue, Troy

**Johnson, Mickey**
See   Johnson, Wallace

**Johnson, Mike**
See   Sharkey, John Michael

**Johnson, Miriam** 1947-
[ECM, RO2]
*American singer and songwriter*
* Colter, Jessi
* Eddy, Miriam

**Johnson, Money**
See   Johnson, Frederick

**Johnson, Money**
See   Johnson, Harold

**Johnson, Moose**
See   Johnson, Ernest [Ernie]

**Johnson, Morrison** 20th c.   [BWW]
*American musician*
* Johnson, Red

**Johnson, Mrs. S. O.** 19th c.   [FFF]
*Author*
* Eyesbright, Daisy

**Johnson, Norman** 20th c.   [RO2]
*American singer*
* Johnson, General

**Johnson, Nucky**
See   Johnson, Enoch J.

**Johnson, Offside**
See   Johnson, Jack

**Johnson, Oliver [Ollie]** 1892-1954
[DAM, EJ, WWJ]
*American jazz musician*
* Johnson, Dink

**Johnson, Ornamental**
See   Brower, Roy

**Johnson, Oscar** 20th c.   [OBW]
*American baseball player*
* Johnson, Heavy

**Johnson, Pamela Hansford**
1912-1981   [CA, WD, WW]
*British author, playwright, poet*
* Lombard, Nap [joint pseudonym
  with Neil Stewart]

**Johnson, Pamela P.** 1958-   [IBW]
*American actress*
* P. J.

**Johnson, Paul** 20th c.   [BWW]
*American musician*
* Guitar Red

**Johnson, Paul Vincent** 1947-
[SMG]
*American baseball player*
* Johnson, High Pockets

**Johnson, Pep**
See   Johnson, Donald Spore

**Johnson, Pussyfoot**
See   Johnson, William Eugene

**Johnson, Red**
See   Johnson, Morrison

**Johnson, Richard**
See   Richey, David

**Johnson, Richard Allan [Dick]**
1932-   [BE]
*American baseball player*
* Johnson, Footer
* Johnson, Treads

**Johnson, Robert** 1898-1937   [IBW]
*American singer*
* [The] King of Delta Blues Singers

**Johnson, Robert** 1953-   [RO2]
*American musician*
* Johnson, Shotgun

**Johnson, Robert Glenn** 1931?-
[B10]
*American auto racer*
* Johnson, Junior

**Johnson, Robert Lee [Bob]** 1906-
[BE, PB]
*American baseball player*
* Johnson, Cherokee
* Johnson, Indian Bob

**Johnson, Robert Walter, Sr.**
1899-1971   [IBW]
*American tennis and football player*
* Johnson, Whirlwind

**Johnson, Ronald** 1935-   [DLE]
*American poet*
* Chamberlain, Theodore

**Johnson, Roy** 20th c.   [BBH]
*American coach and collegiate
athletic director*
* Old Iron Head

**Johnson, Ruby Kelley** 1928-   [CA]
*American linguist and author*
* Kelley, Ruby M.

**Johnson, Rufe**
See   Johnson, Henry

**Johnson, Ruie**
See   Elam, Shelby S.

**Johnson, Russell Conwell**
1894-1950   [BE]
*American baseball player*
* Johnson, Jing

**Johnson, Ruth I.**
See   Jay, Ruth I[ngrid]

**Johnson, Sam** 20th c.   [NBB]
*American singer*
* Johnson, Suitcase

**Johnson, Samuel** 1705-1773   [RH]
*British playwright*
* Flame, Lord

**Johnson, Samuel** 1709-1784
[FFF, HN, SN]
*British lexicographer*
* Blinking Sam

**Johnson, Samuel** (Continued)
* [The] Bolt Court Philosopher
* [The] Cerberus of Literature
* [The] Colossus of English
  Philology
* [The] English Socrates
* [The] Giant of Literature
* [The] Great Bear
* [The] Great Cham of Literature
* [The] Great Moralist
* [The] Great Seer
* [The] Incomprehensible
  Holofernes
* [The] Leviathan of Literature
* [The] Literary Anvil
* [The] Literary Castor
* [The] Literary Colossus
* Malakoff
* [The] Polyphemus of Literature
* Ultimus Romanorum
* Ursa Major

**Johnson, Sara**
See   Henderson, Rosa [Rose]

**Johnson, Sarge**
See   Johnson, Thomas

**Johnson, Sess**
See   Johnson, C.

**Johnson, Shang**
See   Johnson, Dan

**Johnson, Shotgun**
See   Johnson, Robert

**Johnson, Si**
See   Johnson, Silas Kenneth

**Johnson, Sidney Richard** 1905-
[BS]
*British-born Canadian magician*
* Lorraine, Sid

**Johnson, Signifyin' Mary**
See   Johnson, Mary

**Johnson, Silas Kenneth** 1906-   [BE]
*American baseball player*
* Johnson, Si

**Johnson, Sivert Bertil** 1930-   [EJ7]
*American jazz musician*
* Johnson, Sy

**Johnson, Skinny**
See   Johnson, William C.

**Johnson, Sleepy Bill**
See   Johnson, William T.

**Johnson, Slick**
See   Johnson, James C.

**Johnson, Slick**
See   Johnson, Louis Brown

**Johnson, Slick**
See   Johnson, Timothy E.

**Johnson, Slim**
See   Johnson, Jimmy

**Johnson, Smiley**
See   Johnson, Howard W.

**Johnson, Snake**
See   Johnson, Lucius Brinson

**Johnson, Sonny**
See   Johnson, Claude

**Johnson, Speed**
See   Johnson, Harold

**Johnson, Spud**
See   Johnson, John Ralph

**Johnson, Steady Roll**
See   Johnson, James

**Johnson, Stump**
See   Johnson, James

**Johnson, Suitcase**
See   Johnson, Sam

**Johnson, Susan**
See   Johnson, Marilyn Jeanne

**Johnson, Swan**
See   Johnson, Howard William

**Johnson, Swede**
See   Johnson, John Clifford
[Johnny]

**Johnson, Sweet Lou**
See   Johnson, Louis Brown

**Johnson, Sy**
See   Johnson, Sivert Bertil

**Johnson, Syl**
See   Johnson, Sylvester W.

**Johnson, Syl**
See   Thompson, Sylvester

**Johnson, Sylvester W.** 1900-   [BE]
*American baseball player*
* Johnson, Syl

**Johnson, Tex**
See   Johnson, Adam Rankin, Sr.

**Johnson, Thomas** 1922?-1980
*American boxing coach*
* Johnson, Sarge

**Johnson, Tiger**
See   Johnson, Bill

**Johnson, Timothy E.** 1949-   [SMG]
*American baseball player*
* Johnson, Slick

**Johnson, Tor**
See   Johansson, Tor

**Johnson, Treads**
See   Johnson, Richard Allan [Dick]

**Johnson, Victor Hugo** 1912-   [AW]
*American author*
* Bell, John

**Johnson, Virginia** 1914-1975
[CA, CAP]
*American poet*
* Johnson, Jinna

**Johnson, Virginia W.**   [FFF, PA]
*American author*
* Cousin Virginia

**Johnson, W. Bolingbroke**
See   Bishop, Morris Gilbert

**Johnson, W. F.**   [FFF]
*American writer*
* Malakoff

**Johnson, W. Ryerson** 20th c.
*Author*
* Robeson, Kenneth [house
  pseudonym, Street & Smith]

**Johnson, Wallace**
*American business executive*
* [The] Praying Millionaire

**Johnson, Wallace** 1952-   [NBA]
*American basketball player*
* Johnson, Mickey

**Johnson, Walter Perry** 1887-1946
[BE, DGS, PB]
*American baseball player and manager*
* [The] Big Train
* Johnson, Barney

**Johnson, Warren** 1938-
*American artist*
* Blue Sky

**Johnson, Whirlwind**
*See* Johnson, Robert Walter, Sr.

**Johnson, White Shoes**
*See* Johnson, Billy

**Johnson, William** 1823-1892
[WBD]
*British poet*
* Cory, William Johnson

**Johnson, William B.** 1856- ?    [IBW]
*Canadian-born clergyman*
* [The] Quill Man

**Johnson, William C.** 1911-    [BBH]
*American basketball player*
* Johnson, Skinny

**Johnson, William Edward John**
?-1968    [IBW]
*American singer*
* Johnson, Little Willie

**Johnson, William Eugene**
1862-1945    [WBD]
*American journalist and social reformer*
* Johnson, Pussyfoot

**Johnson, William Geary**
1879-1949    [BBD, DAM, EJ]
*American jazz musician*
* Johnson, Bunk

**Johnson, William Julius** 1899-
[BAB, CBS, MK]
*American baseball player*
* [The] Black Pie Traynor
* Johnson, Judy

**Johnson, William O.**    [CA]
*Author*
* Nicholas, William [joint pseudonym with Nicholas Palen (Nick) Thimmesch]

**Johnson, William Russell** 1918-
[BE]
*American baseball player*
* Johnson, Bull

**Johnson, William T.** ?-1921    [BE]
*American baseball player*
* Johnson, Sleepy Bill

**Johnson, Willie** 1902-1949    [DAM]
*American singer*
* Johnson, Blind Willie

**Johnson, Woodrow Wilson**
1915-1977    [ASC, EJ, PMJ]
*American jazz musician*
* Johnson, Buddy

**Johnson, Youngy**
*See* Mercer, John Louis

**Johnson, Ziggy**
*See* Johnson, Joseph

**Johnson's Spitting-Pot**
*See* Boswell, James

**Johnston, Agnes Christine**
*See* Dazey, Agnes J[ohnston]

**Johnston, Alma Calder** 19th c.
[FFF]
*American author*
* Calder, Alma

**Johnston, Anna Isabel** 1866-1902
[DIL]
*Irish poet*
* Carbery, Ethna

**Johnston, Brenda** 1930-    [ART]
*British artist*
* B. J.

**Johnston, Charles Haven Ladd** 1877-
?    [NAA]
*American author*
* Uncle Charles

**Johnston, D. S. B.**    [PA]
*Author*
* Seab, Lenial

**Johnston, David Claypole**    [SN]
*American caricaturist*
* Our American Cruikshank

**Johnston, Doc**
*See* Johnston, Wheeler Roger

**Johnston, E. J.**
*See* Johnston, Edward Joseph

**Johnston, Edward Joseph** 1936-
[SMG]
*Canadian-born hockey player*
* Johnston, E. J.

**Johnston, Fred**
*See* Johnston, Wilfred Ivy

**Johnston, Gene Howard** 1920-
[MY]
*American singer*
* Howard, Gene

**Johnston, George Henry**
1912-1970    [DLE]
*American author*
* Martin, Shane

**Johnston, George Joseph** 1920-
[CEI]
*Canadian-born hockey player*
* Johnston, Wingy

**Johnston, Gerald McIntosh**
?-1944    [SC]
*Canadian-born actor*
* Kent, Gerald

**Johnston, Grace L. Keith** 20th c.
[WWL]
*Scottish author*
* Keith, Leslie

**Johnston, H. H.**
*See* Johnston, [Sir] Harry Hamilton

**Johnston, Harrison R.** 1896-1969
[GF]
*American golfer*
* Johnston, Jimmy

**Johnston, [Sir] Harry Hamilton**
1858-1927    [LC]
*British author*
* Johnston, H. H.

**Johnston, Hugh** 1916-    [BBH]
*Irish-born softball player*
* Johnston, Lefty

**Johnston, Hugh Anthony Stephen**
1913-1967    [CAP]
*Irish-born author*
* [A] Fighter Pilot
* Sturton, Hugh

**Johnston, Jill** 1929-    [CA]
*British-born author*
* Crowe, F. J.

**Johnston, Jimmy**
*See* Johnston, Harrison R.

**Johnston, Lefty**
*See* Johnston, Hugh

**Johnston, Little Bill**
*See* Johnston, William M.

**Johnston, Mabel**    [FFF]
*Entertainer*
* Bert, Mabel

**Johnston, Mrs.** 19th c.    [PA]
*Author*
* Dods, Meg

**Johnston, Mrs. R. J.**    [FFF]
*Entertainer*
* Atkinson, Maude

**Johnston, Portia**
*See* Takakjian, Portia

**Johnston, Randolph**
*See* Rasley, John M.

**Johnston, Red Top**
*See* Johnston, Wilfred Ivy

**Johnston, Richard Malcolm**
1822-1898    [FFF]
*American author*
* Perch, Philemon

**Johnston, Susan T.** 1942-    [CA]
*American author*
* Johnston, Tony

**Johnston, Tony**
*See* Johnston, Susan T.

**Johnston, Velma B.** 1912?-1977
[CA]
*American author and lobbyist*
* Wild Horse Annie

**Johnston, Wheeler Roger**
1887-1961    [AS, BE]
*American baseball player*
* Johnston, Doc

**Johnston, Wilfred Ivy** 1901-    [BE]
*American baseball player*
* Johnston, Fred
* Johnston, Red Top

**Johnston, William** 1924-    [CA]
*American author*
* Claudia, Susan
* Sinclair, Heather

**Johnston, William M.** 1894-1946
[BBH, OET]
*American tennis player*
* Johnston, Little Bill

**Johnston, Wingy**
*See* Johnston, George Joseph

**Johnstone, Jay**
*See* Johnstone, John William

**Johnstone, John**
*See* Fawkes, Guy

**Johnstone, John William** 1946-
[SMG]
*American baseball player*
* Johnstone, Jay

**Johnstone, Ted**
*See* McDaniel, David [Edward]

**Johnstone, William**    [SN]
*Scottish freebooter*
* [The] Galliard

**Johnstone-Wilson, Angus Frank**
1913-    [TC1]
*British author*
* Wilson, Angus

**Joiner, Pop**
*See* Joiner, Roy Merrill

**Joiner, Roy Merrill** 1906-    [BE]
*American baseball player*
* Joiner, Pop

**Joines, Zuleika Angel** ?-1976
[B10]
*Brazilian dress designer*
* Angel, Zuzu

**Joinville, Jean de** 1224?-1317    [SN]
*French historian*
* [The] Father of French History

**Jok**
*See* Whittet, George Sorley

**Jok, Stan[ley Edward]** 1926-1972
[BE]
*American baseball player*
* Jok, Tucker

**Jok, Tucker**
*See* Jok, Stan[ley Edward]

**Jokai, Maurus**
*See* Jokai, Mor

**Jokai, Mor** 1825-1904    [SFL]
*Hungarian author*
* Jokai, Maurus

**Jolderland, Hother**    [PA]
*Author*
* Doctor H.

**Joli-Ox**
*See* Manyase, Lenchman Thozamile

**Joliat, Aurel Emile** 1901-    [BBH]
*Canadian-born hockey player*
* [The] Little Giant
* [The] Mighty Atom

**Joliat, Bobby**
*See* Joliat, Rene

**Joliat, Rene** 20th c.    [CEI]
*Hockey player*
* Joliat, Bobby

**Joliot, Frederic** 1900-1958    [WBD]
*French physicist*
* Joliot-Curie, Frederic

**Joliot-Curie, Frederic**
*See* Joliot, Frederic

**Jolley, Smead Powell** 1902-    [BE]
*American baseball player*
* Jolley, Smudge

**Jolley, Smudge**
*See* Jolley, Smead Powell

**Jolling, Jack**
*See* Judd, Alfred

**Jolly Cholly Grimm**
*See* Grimm, Charles John

**Jolly Clara Smith**
*See* Smith, Clara

**Jolly, David** 1924-1963    [BE]
*American baseball player*
* Jolly, Gabby

**Jolly, Gabby**
See Jolly, David

**Jolly Giant**
See Greene, Jack

**[The] Jolly Green Giant**
See Unseld, Westley

**Jolly John Nash**
See Nash, John

**Jolly, Pete**
See Ceragioli, Peter A.

**Jolly, Pete**
See Jolly, Raymond

**Jolly, Raymond** 20th c. [BBH]
*American basketball coach*
* Jolly, Pete

**Jolly Roger Bradfield**
See Bradfield, Roger

**Jolson, Al**
See Yoelson, Asa

**Joltin Joe DiMaggio**
See DeMaggio, Giuseppe Paolo, Jr.

**Jolting Joe Perry**
See Perry, Fletcher

**Jolyot, Prosper [Sieur de Crais-Billon]** 1674-1762 [WBD]
*French poet*
* Crebillon

**Jolyot de Crebillon, Claude Prosper** 1707-1777 [SN]
*French author*
* [The] Petronius of France

**Jon**
See Kingman, E.

**Jon, B.**
See Jonson, Ben[jamin]

**Jonah** 990?-1050? [WBD]
*Spanish clergyman and scholar*
* Marinus, R.

**Jonas, Doris F[rances]** 1916- [CA]
*British author*
* Klein, Doris F.

**Jonas, Douglas Peter** 1898-1958 [BEW]
*British-born actor*
* Dexter, Aubrey

**Jonas, Johanna** 1914- [IAW]
*Austrian author and poet*
* Jonas-Lichtenwallner, Johanna

**Jonas-Lichtenwallner, Johanna**
See Jonas, Johanna

**Jonasova, Jana**
See Ruzkova, Jana

**Jonathan, [Brother]**
See Blewitt, Octavius

**Jonathan**
See Cook, Roger

**Jonathan Wild the Second**
See Bonaparte, Napoleon

**Joncich, Geraldine**
See Clifford, Geraldine Joncich

**Joncures, Victoria** [PA]
*Author*
* Keunius

**Jones, Adrienne** 20th c. [WW]
*Author*
* Gregory, Mason [joint pseudonym with Doris Meek]
* Mason, Gregory [joint pseudonym with Doris Meek]

**Jones, Alan** 1938- [DC]
*Welsh cricketer*
* Jones, Sam

**Jones, Alan Lewis** 1957- [DC]
*Welsh cricketer*
* Jones, Jonah
* Jones, Posh

**Jones, Alan Philip** 1935- [OP]
*British opera singer*
* Van Allan, Richard

**Jones, Albert Edward** 1874-1958 [BE]
*American baseball player*
* Jones, Bronco
* Jones, Cowboy

**Jones, Alexander** [FFF]
*American author*
* Hook, Sandy

**Jones, Alice Ilgenfritz** ?-1906 [SFL, WGT]
*Author*
* Jerome, Ferris
* Two Women of the West [joint pseudonym with Ella Marchant]

**Jones, Allan Arthur** 1947- [DC]
*British cricketer*
* Jones, Jonah

**Jones, Alvin Bernard** 1919- [CEI]
*Canadian-born hockey player*
* Jones, Buck

**Jones, Angel Sleeves**
See Jones, Ryerson L.

**Jones, Annabel**
See Lewis, Mary Christianna [Milne]

**Jones, Arthur Barclay** 1869-1943 [BBD]
*British conductor*
* Barclay, Arthur

**Jones, Arthur Llewellyn** 1863-1947 [HFF, WGT]
*Welsh author*
* Machen, Arthur
* Perrot, Gervase
* Siluriensis, Leolinus

**Jones, Arthur Owen** 1872-1914 [EC]
*British cricketer*
* Jones, Jonah

**Jones, Augusta**
See Miles, Josephine [Josie]

**Jones, Available**
See Jones, Sheldon Leslie

**Jones, B. B.**
See Nichols, Alvin

**Jones, Ba**
See Jones, Barry John Richardson

**Jones, Baldy**
See Jones, Henry M.

**Jones, Barry John Richardson** 1955- [DC]
*British cricketer*
* Jones, Ba
* Jones, Jonah

**Jones, Biff**
See Jones, Lawrence McCeney

**Jones, Binky**
See Jones, John Joseph

**Jones, Birmingham**
See Birmingham, Wright

**Jones, Bob** 1951- [SMG]
*American football player*
* Cornerback, Mr.

**Jones, Booker T.** 1944- [RM, RO1]
*American musician*
* Booker T.

**Jones, Brenda Lee** 20th c. [RO1]
*American singer and songwriter*
* Jean

**Jones, Broadway**
See Jones, Jesse F.

**Jones, Broadway**
See Jones, Ken[neth Frederick]

**Jones, Bronco**
See Jones, Albert Edward

**Jones, Buck**
See Gebhart, Charles Frederick

**Jones, Buck**
See Jones, Alvin Bernard

**Jones, Bud**
See Jones, Herbert Ingham

**Jones, Buddy**
See Jones, Burgher William

**Jones, Bull Faced**
See Jones, [Sir] William

**Jones, Bumpus**
See Jones, Charles Leander

**Jones, Burgher William** 1924- [EJ]
*American jazz musician*
* Jones, Buddy

**Jones, Calico**
See Richardson, Gladwell

**Jones, Carol** 1942- [SW]
*American actress*
* Lynley, Carol

**Jones, Carroll Elmer** 1893-1952 [BE]
*American baseball player*
* Jones, Deacon

**Jones, Casey**
See Jones, Charles C.

**Jones, Casey**
See Jones, Clinton

**Jones, Casey**
See Jones, Frederick McKinley

**Jones, Casey**
See Jones, John Luther

**Jones, Charles C.** 1876-1947 [BE]
*American baseball player*
* Jones, Casey

**Jones, Charles Leander** 1870-1938 [BE]
*American baseball player*
* Jones, Bumpus

**Jones, Charles Wesley**
See Rippay, Benjamin Wesley

**Jones, Charley**
See Hanks, O. C.

**Jones, Clara**
See Baldwin, Dorothy Anne Clare

**Jones, Clifford** 1900?-1947 [EJ, WWJ]
*American jazz musician*
* Jones, Snags

**Jones, Clifford** 20th c. [IBW]
*American clergyman*
* Rasheed, [Rev.] Hakeem

**Jones, Clinton** 20th c. [OBW]
*American baseball player*
* Jones, Casey

**Jones, Cobe**
See Jones, Coburn Dyas

**Jones, Coburn Dyas** 1907-1969 [BE]
*American baseball player*
* Jones, Cobe

**Jones, Codel**
See Jones, James R. [Jim]

**Jones, Cowboy**
See Jones, Albert Edward

**Jones, D. F.**
See Jones, Dennis Feltham

**Jones, Dale Eldon** 1918- [BE]
*American baseball player*
* Jones, Nubs

**Jones, Daniel Albion** 1860-1936 [BE]
*American baseball player*
* Jones, Jumping Jack

**Jones, David** 1938?- [B10, FB, IPA]
*American football player*
* Jones, Deacon

**Jones, David Jefferson** 1880- ? [BE, PB]
*American baseball player*
* Jones, Kangaroo

**Jones, David Robert Hayward** 1947- [RM, RO2, WYA]
*British singer and songwriter*
* Bowie, David

**Jones, Davy**
See Molinar, Demostines

**Jones, Deacon**
See Jones, Carroll Elmer

**Jones, Deacon**
See Jones, David

**Jones, Deacon**
See Jones, Grover William, Jr.

**Jones, Decatur Poindexter** 1902- [BE]
*American baseball player*
* Jones, Dick

**Jones, Dennis Feltham** 20th c. [SF]
*British author*
* Jones, D. F.

**Jones, Diana Wynne**
See Burrow, Diana Wynne

**Jones, Dick**
See Jones, Decatur Poindexter

**Jones, Dill**
See Jones, Dillwyn Owen

**Jones, Dillwyn Owen** 1923- [EJ7]
*Welsh-born jazz musician*
* Jones, Dill

**Jones, Dorothy** 1897- [THR]
*British actress*
* Hamilton, Dorothy

**Jones, Dorothy Holder** 20th c.
[CA]
*American author*
* Jones, Duane

**Jones, Duane**
See Jones, Dorothy Holder

**Jones, Dub**
See Jones, Will

**Jones, Dub**
See Jones, William

**Jones, Ducky**
See Jones, Robert Walter

**Jones, E. B. C.**
See Jones, Emily Beatrix
Coursolles

**Jones, E. D.**
See Jones, Evan David

**Jones, Earl Leslie** 1919- [BE]
*American baseball player*
* Jones, Lefty

**Jones, Ed** 1951- [FB, SMG]
*American football player*
* Jones, Too Tall

**Jones, Eddie** 1926-1959
[BWW, EJ]
*American singer and guitarist*
* Guitar Slim

**Jones, Eddie** 20th c. [SFP]
*Author*
* Eddie

**Jones, Edgar** 1956-
*American basketball player*
* E. J.

**Jones, Edward [Eddie]** 1929- [EJ]
*American jazz musician*
* Jones, Jonesy

**Jones, Edward Coley** 1833-1898
[WBD]
*British painter and designer*
* Burne-Jones, [Sir] Edward Coley

**Jones, Edward German** 1862-1936
[BBD, WBD]
*British conductor and composer*
* German, [Sir] Edward

**Jones, Elizabeth** ?-1952 [SC]
*American actress*
* Jones, Tiny

**Jones, Elizabeth B[rown]** 1907-
[CA]
*American author*
* Brown, Betty

**Jones, Elizabeth Myfanwy** 1938-
[OP]
*British opera singer*
* Vaughan, Elizabeth

**Jones, Ellen** ?-1961 [THR]
*Irish-born actress*
* O'Malley, Ellen

**Jones, Emily** [PA]
*Author*
* Melville, Emily

**Jones, Emily Beatrix Coursolles**
1893-1966 [LAO, LC]
*Author and critic*
* Jones, E. B. C.
* Lucas, Emily Beatrix Coursolles

**Jones, Emperor**
See Jones, Robert Tyre, Jr.

**Jones, Ernest Mahlon** 1908-
*American singer*
* Baker, Jack
* [The] Louisiana Lark

**Jones, Esther Mae** 1935?-
[BWW, EJ7]
*American singer*
* Little Esther
* Phillips, Esther

**Jones, Evan David** 1903- [IAW]
*Welsh author*
* Ceitho, Dewi
* Jones, E. D.
* Rhydderch, Ieuan

**Jones, Fewlass** 1866-1941 [THR]
*British actor, producer, playwright*
* Llewellyn, Fewlass

**Jones, Flip Flap**
See Jones, Oscar Winfield

**Jones, Fox**
See Jones, William

**Jones, Francis** [WGT]
*Author*
* Peril, Milton R.

**Jones, Frank**
See Fearn, John Russell

**Jones, Frank H.** 1899- [AW]
*British accountant and writer*
* Mentor

**Jones, Franklin** 1939- [NAD, WD]
*American author and spiritual
teacher*
* Bubba Free John

**Jones, Freddie** 20th c. [RBE]
*American boxer*
* Clay, Marcel

**Jones, Frederick McKinley**
1892-1961 [IBW]
*American inventor*
* Jones, Casey

**Jones, Fritz** 1931- [IBW]
*American jazz musician*
* Jamal, Ahmad

**Jones, Fuzzy Q.**
See St. John, Al

**Jones, G. Wayman** [house
pseudonym]
See Burkhilder, Edwin

**Jones, G. Wayman** [house
pseudonym]
See Champion, D. L.

**Jones, G. Wayman** [house
pseudonym]
See Daniels, Norman [A.]

**Jones, G. Wayman** [house
pseudonym]
See Feldman, Anatole

**Jones, George** 1791-1879 [PA]
*Author*
* Joannes, Count

**Jones, George** 1931- [ECM]
*American country-western performer*
* [The] Rolls Royce of Country
Singers

**Jones, George Warren** 1921-
[BEW]
*American actor, singer, director*
* Warren, Jeff

**Jones, Giles** 19th c. [PA]
*Author*
* Tripp, Tom

**Jones, Gillingham**
See Hamilton, Charles Harold St.
John

**Jones, Golden Rule**
See Jones, Samuel Milton

**Jones, Gonner**
See Jones, P. F. G.

**Jones, Gorilla**
See Jones, William

**Jones, Grace** 1953- [IBW]
*Jamaican-born singer and fashion
model*
* [The] Disco Diva

**Jones, Grandpa**
See Jones, Louis M.

**Jones, Grandpa**
See Jones, Marshall Louis

**Jones, Grover William, Jr.** 1934-
[SMG]
*American baseball player and scout*
* Jones, Deacon

**Jones, Hank** 1918- [IBW]
*American jazz musician*
* [The] Impeccable One

**Jones, Harold**
See Page, Gerald W[ilburn]

**Jones, Harriet**
See Marble, Harriet Clement

**Jones, Harry Austin** 1912- [AW]
*Welsh-born author*
* Jons, Hal

**Jones, Helen Hinckley** 1903-
[CA, WD]
*American author*
* Hinckley, Helen

**Jones, [Max Him] Henri** 1921-
[CA]
*French-born educator and author*
* Maxhim, Tristan

**Jones, Henry** 1831-1899
[DEL, WBD]
*British author and physician*
* Cavendish

**Jones, Henry M.** 19th c. [BE]
*American baseball player*
* Jones, Baldy

**Jones, Herbert Ingham** 1943-
[IWM]
*American-born jazz musician*
* Jones, Bud

**Jones, Homer C.** 1941- [FB]
*American football player*
* Jones, Rhino

**Jones, Hoppy**
See Jones, Orville

**Jones, Horace Allyn** 1908- [BBH]
*American horse trainer*
* Jones, Jimmy

**Jones, Inigo** 1573-1653
[DNNF, FFF, SN]
*British architect*
* [The] English Palladio
* [The] English Vitruvius
* [The] Vitruvius of England

**Jones, Isham Russell, II** 1932-
[EJ7]
*American jazz musician*
* Jones, Rusty

**Jones, J. G.** 20th c. [MBF]
*British author*
* Bloomer, Steve
* Earle, Ambrose
* Gordon, Geoffrey
* Trew, Dighton

**Jones, Jack**
See Jones, Ryerson L.

**Jones, Jack** 1924- [CA]
*American author*
* Edmond, Jay

**Jones, Jake**
See Jones, James Murrell

**Jones, James Chamberlain**
1809-1859 [FFF, SN]
*American politician*
* Bean Pole
* Jones, Lean Jimmy

**Jones, James Francis Marion**
1908-1971 [IBW]
*American evangelist*
* Jones, Prophet

**Jones, James Murrell** 1920- [BE]
*American baseball player*
* Jones, Jake

**Jones, James R. [Jim]** 1940?-
*American politician*
* Jones, Codel

**Jones, James Tilford [Jim]**
1878-1953 [BE]
*American baseball player*
* Jones, Sheriff

**Jones, Jennifer**
See Isley, Phylis Lee

**Jones, Jesse F.** 1899- [BE]
*American baseball player*
* Jones, Broadway

**Jones, Jimmy**
See Jones, Horace Allyn

**Jones, Jo**
See Jones, Jonathan

**Jones, Joanna**
See Burke, John [Frederick]

**Jones, John** 1924-1964
[BWW, NBB]
*American singer*
* Jones, Little Johnny

**Jones, John A.** 1947- [FB]
*American football player*
* Jones, Spike

**Jones, John Daniel** 1865- ? [WWL]
*British clergyman and author*
* Myrddin, Fardd

**Jones, John J.**
See Lovecraft, Howard Phillips

Jones, John Joseph 1899-1961
[BE]
*American baseball player*
* Jones, Binky

Jones, John Luther 1863-1900
[IBW]
*American railroad fireman*
* Jones, Casey

Jones, John Paul
See   Baldwin, John

Jones, John Paul
See   Paul, John

Jones, John Raymond 1899-   [IBW]
*West Indian-born politician*
* [The] Fox

Jones, John William 1901-1956
[BE]
*American baseball player*
* Jones, Skins

Jones, Johnny
See   Peil, Charles Edward

Jones, Jonah
See   Jones, Alan Lewis

Jones, Jonah
See   Jones, Allan Arthur

Jones, Jonah
See   Jones, Arthur Owen

Jones, Jonah
See   Jones, Barry John Richardson

Jones, Jonah
See   Jones, Robert Elliott

Jones, Jonathan 1911-   [NP]
*American jazz musician*
* Jones, Samson
* Jones, Jo

Jones, Jonesy
See   Jones, Edward [Eddie]

Jones, Joseph Rudolph 1923-
[DAM, EJ, PMJ]
*American jazz musician*
* Jones, Philly Joe

Jones, Jumping Jack
See   Jones, Daniel Albion

Jones, Justin   [MBF]
*British author*
* Hazel, Harry

Jones, Kangaroo
See   Jones, David Jefferson

Jones, Kathleen Eve 1944-   [CA]
*British author and art historian*
* Adler, Kathleen

Jones, Ken[neth Frederick] 1904-
[BE]
*American baseball player*
* Jones, Broadway

Jones, Kenneth Westcott 1921-
[CA]
*British author and columnist*
* Taunton, Eric
* Westcott-Jones, K[enneth]

Jones, Killer
See   Jones, Robert

Jones, Laurence Clifton 1884-1975
[IBW]
*American educator*
* [The] Little Professor of the
   Piney Woods

Jones, Lawrence McCeney 1895-
[B10, FB]
*American football coach*
* Jones, Biff

Jones, Lean Jimmy
See   Jones, James Chamberlain

Jones, Leanell 1952-   [SMG]
*American football player*
* Jones, Nell

Jones, Lefty
See   Jones, Earl Leslie

Jones, [Everett] LeRoi 1934-
[CA, TR, WD]
*American author, playwright, poet*
* Baraka, Imamu Amiri

Jones, Leroy 20th c.   [RBE]
*Boxing agent*
* Jones, Rocco

Jones, Leslie Grove 1779-1839
[PA]
*Author*
* Radical

Jones, Lewis Arthur 1927-   [CA]
*American historian and author*
* Tambs, Lewis Arthur

Jones, Lillie Mae 1930-   [EJ]
*American singer*
* Carter, Betty
* Carter, Betty Be-Bop

Jones, Lindley Armstrong
1911-1964   [ASC, BBD, PMJ]
*American bandleader*
* Jones, Spike
* [The] King of Corn

Jones, Linguist
See   Jones, [Sir] William

Jones, Little Johnny
See   Jones, John

Jones, Llewelly
See   Allen, Hubert Raymond

Jones, Louis M. 1913-   [CM]
*American country-western performer*
* Jones, Grandpa

Jones, Lucy M. 20th c.   [WW]
*Author*
* Lux

Jones, Mack 1938-   [BE]
*American baseball player*
* Mack the Knife

Jones, Maggie
See   Barnes, Fae

Jones, Major
See   Thompson, William Theodore

Jones, Mamie
See   Waters, Ethel

Jones, Margaret Elizabeth Mary
[PA]
*Author*
* M. E. M. J.

Jones, Marshall 20th c.   [RO2]
*American musician*
* Jones, Rock

Jones, Marshall Louis 1913-
[CME, CWG, DAM]
*American country-western performer*
* Jones, Grandpa

Jones, Mary [Harris] 1830-1930
[NAD]
*Irish-born labor leader*
* Jones, Mother

Jones, Mary R. 1913-   [IAW]
*American writer*
* Sterling-Jones, M.

Jones, Mary Tupper 1878?-1964
[BEW]
*American actress*
* Tupper, Mary

Jones, Maude
See   Thomas, Lillian

Jones, Maurice 20th c.   [IBW]
*American engineer*
* Jones, Tex

Jones, Maurice Morris 1914-   [BE]
*American baseball player*
* Jones, Red

Jones, Maynard Benedict
1904-1972   [CA, WW]
*American journalist, editor, author*
* Jones, Nard

Jones, Melville
See   Bander, Peter

Jones, Midget
See   Jones, William Dennis [Bill]

Jones, Miriam
See   Schuchman, Joan

Jones, Mother
See   Jones, Mary [Harris]

Jones, Nard
See   Jones, Maynard Benedict

Jones, Nell
See   Jones, Leanell

Jones, Nippy
See   Jones, Vernal Leroy

Jones, Noel 1939-   [CA]
*Irish author and playwright*
* Aalben, Patrick

Jones, Nora 1913-   [FC]
*British actress*
* John, Rosamund

Jones, Norris 1940-   [EJ7]
*American jazz musician*
* Sirone

Jones, Nubs
See   Jones, Dale Eldon

Jones, Orlando
See   Looker, Antonina [Hansell]

Jones, Orville
*Singer*
* Jones, Hoppy

Jones, Oscar Winfield 1879-1946
[BE, BN]
*American baseball player*
* Jones, Flip Flap

Jones, Owen 1740-1814   [PA]
*British poet*
* [The] Devonshire Poet

Jones, P. F. G.   [SFP]
*Author*
* Jones, Gonner

Jones, Parnelli
See   Jones, Rufus Parnell

Jones, Pat
See   Jones, Virgil Carrington

Jones, Paul
See   Pond, Paul

Jones, Perry 1888-1970   [OET]
*American tennis promoter*
* Tennis, Mr.

Jones, Phillipe
See   Roberts-Jones, Phillipe John
A. G.

Jones, Philly Joe
See   Jones, Joseph Rudolph

Jones, Plato
See   Hickman, Lynn

Jones, Posh
See   Jones, Alan Lewis

Jones, Preacher
See   Jones, Wardell

Jones, Prophet
See   Jones, James Francis Marion

Jones, Puddin' Head
See   Jones, William Edward

Jones, Quincy Delight, Jr. 1933-
[IBW]
*American jazz musician*
* Q

Jones, Ralph 1928-   [BX]
*American boxer*
* Jones, Tiger

Jones, Raymond F. 1915-
[ESF, WGT]
*American author*
* Anderson, David

Jones, Red
See   Jones, Maurice Morris

Jones, Red
See   Jones, Sam

Jones, Rhino
See   Jones, Homer C.

Jones, Richard
See   Hook, Theodore Edward

Jones, Richard Robert   [SN]
*British linguist*
* Dick of Aberdaron

Jones, Roadblock
See   Jones, Sherman Jarvis

Jones, Robert 20th c.
*American football player*
* Jones, Killer

Jones, Robert Elliott 1909?-
[DAM, EJ, PMJ]
*American jazz musician*
* Jones, Jonah

Jones, Robert Page 20th c.   [SFP]
*Author*
* Page, Thomas [joint pseudonym
   with Daniel T. Streib]

Jones, Robert Tyre, Jr. 1902-1971
[BBH]
*American golfer*
* [The] Boy Wonder
* [The] Grand Slammer
* Jones, Emperor

Jones, Robert Walter 1889-1964
[BE]
*American baseball player*
* Jones, Ducky

Jones, Rocco
*See* Jones, Leroy

Jones, Rock
*See* Jones, Marshall

Jones, Rufus 1936- [DAM]
*American jazz musician*
* Jones, Speedy

Jones, Rufus Parnell 1933-
[EAR, OCS]
*American auto racer*
* Jones, Parnelli

Jones, Rusty
*See* Jones, Isham Russell, II

Jones, Ruth [Lee] 1924-1963
[BWW, PRS]
*American singer*
* [The] Queen of the Blues
* Washington, Dinah

Jones, Ruth Gordon 1896-
[BEW, F1, FC]
*American actress and playwright*
* Gordon, Ruth

Jones, Ryerson L. 20th c. [BE]
*American baseball player*
* Jones, Angel Sleeves
* Jones, Jack

Jones, Sad Sam
*See* Jones, Samuel

Jones, Sad Sam
*See* Jones, Samuel Pond

Jones, Sadie
*See* Brown, Ida G.

Jones, Salena
*See* Shaw, Joan

Jones, Sally Roberts 1935- [CA]
*British author, poet, playwright*
* Roberts, Sally

Jones, Sam
*See* Jones, Alan

Jones, Sam[uel Porter] 1847-1906
[FFF]
*American clergyman*
* [The] Mountain Evangelist

Jones, Sam 20th c. [OBW]
*American baseball player*
* Jones, Red

Jones, Samson
*See* Jones, Jonathan

Jones, Samuel 1734-1819 [FFF]
*American attorney*
* [The] Father of the New York
　Bar

Jones, Samuel 1897?-1966 [BEW]
*British actor*
* Ford, Wallace

Jones, Samuel 1925-1971
[BE, PB, SMG]
*American baseball player*
* Jones, Sad Sam
* Jones, Toothpick Sam

Jones, Samuel Milton 1846-1904
[WBD]
*American industrialist, politician,
reformer*
* Jones, Golden Rule

Jones, Samuel Pond 1892-1966
[AS, BE, DGS]
*American baseball player*
* Jones, Sad Sam

Jones, Sanford W.
*See* Thorn, John

Jones, Sheldon Leslie 1922- [BE]
*American baseball player*
* Jones, Available

Jones, Sheridan
*See* Chesterton, Ada Elizabeth
Jones

Jones, Sheriff
*See* Jones, James Tilford [Jim]

Jones, Sherman Jarvis 1935- [BE]
*American baseball player*
* Jones, Roadblock

Jones, Skins
*See* Jones, John William

Jones, Slick
*See* Jones, Wilmore

Jones, Slim
*See* Jones, Stuart

Jones, Snags
*See* Jones, Clifford

Jones, Speedy
*See* Jones, Rufus

Jones, Spike
*See* Jones, John A.

Jones, Spike
*See* Jones, Lindley Armstrong

Jones, Stephen [Phillip] 1935- [CA]
*American author and journalist*
* Falorp, Nelson P.
* [The] Water Rat

Jones, Stephen Keith 20th c. [IBW]
*American singer*
* Keith, Stevie

Jones, Stuart 1913-1938 [MK]
*American baseball player*
* Jones, Slim

Jones, Suicide
*See* Jones, Willie

Jones, Susan Carleton 1864-1926
[WGT, WW]
*Author*
* Carleton Milecete
* Carleton, S.
* Milecete, Helen

Jones, T. C.
*See* Jones, Thomas Craig

Jones, T. Percy
*See* Aytoun, William Edmonstoune

Jones, Tad
*See* Jones, Thomas Albert Dwight

Jones, Tex
*See* Jones, Maurice

Jones, Tex
*See* Jones, William Roderick

Jones, Thad
*See* Jones, Thaddeus Joseph

Jones, Thaddeus Joseph 1923-
[EJ7]
*American jazz musician*
* Jones, Thad

Jones, Theodore 1928- [IBW]
*American poet*
* Joans, Ted

Jones, Thomas Albert Dwight
1887-1957 [AS, B10, FB]
*American football coach*
* Jones, Tad

Jones, Thomas Craig 1920-1971
[BEW, SC]
*American dancer, actor, female
impersonator*
* Jones, T. C.

Jones, Thomas W[arren] 1947-
[CA]
*American author*
* Butck, Zulie

Jones, Tiger
*See* Jones, Ralph

Jones, Tiny
*See* Jones, Elizabeth

Jones, Tom
*See* Woodward, Thomas Jones

Jones, Too Tall
*See* Jones, Ed

Jones, Toothpick Sam
*See* Jones, Samuel

Jones, Trinity
*See* Jones, William

Jones, Turk
*See* Jones, William G.

Jones, Vernal Leroy 1925- [BE]
*American baseball player*
* Jones, Nippy

Jones, Vernon 20th c. [WGT]
*Author*
* Young, Raymond A.

Jones, Virgil Carrington 1906-
[CA]
*American author*
* Jones, Pat

Jones, Virginia 1920?-
[BDF, FC, ITA]
*American actress*
* Mayo, Virginia

Jones, Volcano
*See* Mitchell, Adrian

Jones, Wah-Wah
*See* Jones, Wallace

Jones, Wali
*See* Jones, Walter [Wally]

Jones, Wallace 1926- [BB]
*American basketball player*
* Jones, Wah-Wah

Jones, Walter [Wally] 1942-
[BB, SMG]
*American basketball player*
* Jones, Wali

Jones, Walter [Wally] (Continued)
* Wonder, Wally

Jones, Wardell 1905?- [WWJ]
*American jazz musician*
* Jones, Preacher

Jones, Webb
*See* Henley, Arthur

Jones, [Captain] Wilbur
*See* Edwards, William B[ennett]

Jones, Will 20th c. [RO1]
*American musician*
* Jones, Dub

Jones, [Sir] William 17th c. [SN]
*British attorney and politician*
* [The] Jock Presbyter
* Jones, Bull Faced

Jones, William 1726-1800
[DNNF, FFF, SN]
*British clergyman and author*
* Jones, Trinity

Jones, [Sir] William 1746-1794
[SN]
*British linguist*
* Jones, Linguist

Jones, William 1906- [BX, RBE]
*American boxer*
* Jones, Gorilla

Jones, William 20th c. [OBW]
*American baseball player*
* Jones, Fox

Jones, William 20th c. [SMG]
*American football coach*
* Jones, Dub

Jones, William Andrew 1907-1974
[BEW, FC, TR]
*American actor*
* De Wolfe, Billy

Jones, William Dennis [Bill]
1887-1946 [BE]
*Canadian-born baseball player*
* Jones, Midget

Jones, William Edward 1925-
[BE, BTB]
*American baseball player*
* Jones, Puddin' Head

Jones, William G. 1905?- [B10]
*American advertising executive and
ecologist*
* Jones, Turk

Jones, William Roderick
1885-1938 [BE]
*American baseball player*
* Jones, Tex

Jones, Willie 1915- [IBW]
*American stunt performer*
* Jones, Suicide

Jones, Wilmore 1907-1969
[EJ, PMJ, WWJ]
*American jazz musician*
* Jones, Slick

Jones, Zelda
*See* Schuchman, Joan

Jones-Lewis, Curigwen 20th c.
[THR]
*Welsh-born actress*
* Lewis, Curigwen

Jones's Boswell
*See* Keeler, Oscar Baun

**Jongejans, George** 1917-
[BEW, TR]
*Finnish-born actor and singer*
* Gaynes, George

**Jongh, Edward A. de** 1923- [CW]
*Curacaon poet and author*
* Bartolome, Johan

**Jonnard, Bubber**
*See* Jonnard, Clarence James

**Jonnard, Clarence James** 1897-
[BE]
*American baseball player*
* Jonnard, Bubber

**Jonquil**
*See* Collins, J. L.

**Jons, Hal**
*See* Jones, Harry Austin

**Jonson, Ben[jamin]** 1574?-1637
[DEP, DNNF, SN]
*British playwright and poet*
* [The] Bricklayer
* [The] Coryphaeus of Our Elder
  Dramatists
* [The] English Horace
* [The] Horace of England
* Jon, B.
* Jonson, Honest Ben
* Jonson, Rare Ben
* [The] Juvenal of the English
  Drama
* [The] Virgil of Dramatic Poets
* [The] Young Horace

**Jonson, Honest Ben**
*See* Jonson, Ben[jamin]

**Jonson, Rare Ben**
*See* Jonson, Ben[jamin]

**Jonsson, Jon** 1917- [IAW]
*Icelandic author*
* Voer, Jon Ur

**[The] Joplin Ghost**
*See* Smith, Horton

**Joplin, Janis** 1943-1970 [PRS]
*American singer and lyricist*
* Pearl

**Joplin, Scott** 1868-1917 [IBW]
*American composer*
* [The] King of Ragtime
  Composers

**Joratz, Robert** 1941- [EJ7]
*American jazz musician*
* Shew, Bobby

**Jordan, Barbara Leslie**
*See* Yellott, Barbara Leslie

**Jordan, Baxter Byerly** 1907- [BE]
*American baseball player*
* Jordan, Buck

**Jordan, Buck**
*See* Jordan, Baxter Byerly

**Jordan, Charles [Charley]**
1890?-1954 [BWW]
*American singer*
* Uncle Skipper?

**Jordan, Dorothea [or Dorothy]**
*See* Bland, Dorothea

**Jordan, Duke**
*See* Jordan, Irving Sidney

**Jordan, Emily**
*See* Chamberlain, Mrs. John

**Jordan, Gail**
*See* Dern, Peggy Gaddis

**Jordan, Gil**
*See* Gelberg, George

**Jordan, H.** 20th c. [OBW]
*American baseball player*
* Jordan, Hen

**Jordan, Ham**
*See* Jordan, [William] Hamilton

**Jordan, [William] Hamilton** 1945?-
*Administrative aide to American
president, Jimmy Carter*
* Jerkin, Hannibal
* Jordan, Ham

**Jordan, Hen**
*See* Jordan, H.

**Jordan, Irving Sidney** 1922-
[DAM, EJ, PMJ]
*American jazz musician*
* Jordan, Duke

**Jordan, James** 1897- [FC, IPA]
*American radio comedian*
* McGee, Fibber

**Jordan, James** 1915- [WWJ]
*American jazz musician*
* Jordan, Taft

**Jordan, Jimmy**
*See* Johnson, Alonzo

**Jordan, June** 1936-
[CA, SAT, WD]
*American author and poet*
* Meyer, June

**Jordan, Kate**
*See* Vermilye, Kate

**Jordan, Killer**
*See* Jordan, Lee Roy

**Jordan, Lanky**
*See* Jordan, Raymond Willis

**Jordan, Lee Roy** 20th c.
*American football player*
* Jordan, Killer

**Jordan, Leroy** 1948- [PRS]
*American musician*
* Jordan, Lonnie

**Jordan, Lonnie**
*See* Jordan, Leroy

**Jordan, Louis Thomas** 1908-1975
[BWW]
*American singer*
* King of the Jukeboxes

**Jordan, Marian Driscoll** 1898-1961
*American radio comedienne*
* McGee, Molly

**Jordan, Monica**
*See* Caruba, Alan

**Jordan, Nell**
*See* Barker, Elsa [McCormick]

**Jordan, Philip [Furneaux]** 1902-
[LAO]
*British author*
* France, Victor

**Jordan, Ralph** 1911?-1980
*American football coach*
* Jordan, Shug

**Jordan, Raymond Willis**
1889-1960 [BE]
*American baseball player*
* Jordan, Lanky
* Jordan, Rip

**Jordan, Ricky**
*See* Haydel, Richard

**Jordan, Rip**
*See* Jordan, Raymond Willis

**Jordan, Robert Obadiah** 1900-
[IBW]
*Jamaican-born political organizer*
* [The] Harlem Hitler

**Jordan, Sheila**
*See* Dawson, Sheila

**Jordan, Shug**
*See* Jordan, Ralph

**Jordan, Taft**
*See* Jordan, James

**Jordan, Tom**
*See* Johnson, Alonzo

**Jordan, Vernon Eulion, Jr.** 1935-
[IBW]
*American civil rights activist*
* [The] Warrior of Today

**Jordan, W.** [PA]
*Author*
* Andre, W. J.

**Jordan, Willie**
*See* Dupree, William Thomas

**Jorgens, Arndt Ludwig** 1905- [BE]
*Norwegian-born baseball player*
* Jorgens, Art

**Jorgens, Art**
*See* Jorgens, Arndt Ludwig

**Jorgensen, Asger Oluf** 1914-1973
[CAR]
*Danish painter and sculptor*
* Jorn, Asger

**Jorgensen, Bud**
*See* Jorgensen, Carl

**Jorgensen, Carl** 1914- [BE]
*American baseball player*
* Jorgensen, Pinky

**Jorgensen, Carl** 20th c.
[BBH, SMG]
*American football team trainer*
* Jorgensen, Bud
* Jorgensen, Jurgy

**Jorgensen, Ivar** [house pseudonym,
Ziff-Davis]
*See* Ellison, Harlan [Jay]

**Jorgensen, Ivar** [house pseudonym]
*See* Fairman, Paul W.

**Jorgensen, Ivar** [joint pseudonym
with Robert Silverberg] [house
pseudonym, Ziff-Davis]
*See* Garrett, [Gordon] Randall
[Philip David]

**Jorgensen, Ivar** [joint pseudonym
with Randall Garrett] [house
pseudonym, Ziff-Davis]
*See* Silverberg, Robert

**Jorgensen, J. S.** 20th c. [SFP]
*Author*
* Storm, Jannick

**Jorgensen, John Donald** 1919-
[BE, BTB]
*American baseball player*
* Jorgensen, Spider

**Jorgensen, Jorgy**
*See* Jorgensen, Michael

**Jorgensen, Jurgy**
*See* Jorgensen, Carl

**Jorgensen, Mary Venn** 20th c.
[CA]
*American author*
* Adrian, Mary

**Jorgensen, Michael** 1948- [SMG]
*American baseball player*
* Jorgensen, Jorgy

**Jorgensen, Pinky**
*See* Jorgensen, Carl

**Jorgensen, Spider**
*See* Jorgensen, John Donald

**Jorgenson, Alf A.** 1899-
[SFL, WGT]
*Norwegian-born American author*
* Arne, Aaron

**Jorgenson, Theodore**
*See* Narvestad, Joerund

**Jorgensson, A. K.**
*See* Roach, Robert W. A.

**Joris, David** 1501?-1556 [WBD]
*Leader of Dutch religious sect*
* Van Brugge, Jan

**Jorn, Asger**
*See* Jorgensen, Asger Oluf

**Jorrocks, John**
*See* Sartees, M. Edward

**Josaphat, Israel Beer** 1816-1899
[WBD]
*German pioneer newsgatherer*
* Reuter, Paul Julius von

**Joscelyn, Archie Lynn** 1899-
[CA, WW]
*American author*
* Archer, A[rchie] A[lexander]
* Cody, Al
* Holt, Tex
* McKenna, Evelyn
* Westland, Lynn

**Jose De Guadaloupe, [Brother]**
*See* Mojica, Jose

**Jose, Ellen J.**
*See* Waye, Ellen Jeanne

**Joselito [Little Joe]**
*See* Gomez Ortega, Jose

**Joselito [Little Joe]**
*See* Huerta Rivera, Jose

**Josellilo de Colombia [Little Joe from
Colombia]**
*See* Zuniga Villquiran, Jose

**Joseph**
*See* Hinmaton-Yalaktit

**Joseph, [Father]**
*See* Leclerc du Tremblay, Francois

**Joseph ben Matthias** 37- 95?
[HN, WBD]
*Historian*
* [The] Greek Livy
* Josephus, Flavius

**Joseph, Edgar** 1906-1977 [NOJ]
*American jazz musician*
* Joseph, Sambo

**Joseph, Franz**
*See* Schnaubelt, Franz Joseph

**Joseph, Frog**
*See* Joseph, Waldren

**Joseph, James** 1814-1897 [WBD]
*British-born mathematician*
* Sylvester, James Joseph

**Joseph, James Herz** 1924- [CA]
*American author*
* Adams, Lowell

**Joseph, John** 1877-1965 [NOJ]
*American jazz musician*
* Papa John

**Joseph, Jonathan**
*See* Fineman, Irving

**Joseph, Kaiser**
*See* Joseph, Willie

**Joseph, Louis Wilson** 1890?-1958
[BEW]
*American theatrical performer*
* Frisco, Joe

**Joseph, M. K.**
*See* Joseph, Michael Kennedy

**Joseph, Michael Kennedy** 1914-
[LC]
*British-born author and poet*
* Joseph, M. K.

**Joseph, Newt**
*See* Joseph, Newton

**Joseph, Newton** 20th c. [OBW]
*American baseball player*
* Joseph, Newt

**Joseph, Pleasant** 1907- [BWW]
*American singer*
* Brother Joshua
* Cousin Joe
* Cousin Joseph
* Pleasant, Cousin Joe
* Pleasant Joe
* Smiling Joe

**Joseph, Ricardo Emelino** 1940-
[BE]
*Dominican-born baseball player*
* Joseph, Rick

**Joseph, Rick**
*See* Joseph, Ricardo Emelino

**Joseph, Sambo**
*See* Joseph, Edgar

**Joseph, Stephen M.** 1938- [CA]
*American poet*
* Waterman, Bic

**Joseph, Waldren** 1918?- [NOJ]
*American jazz musician*
* Joseph, Frog

**Joseph, Willie** 1892?-1951 [NOJ]
*American jazz musician*
* Joseph, Kaiser

**Joseph X**
*See* Arrington, Joseph, Jr.

**Joseph, Yvonne** 1925- [BF]
*British actress*
* Mitchell, Yvonne

**Joseph I** 1676?-1711 [HN, SN]
*King of Hungary and Emperor of Germany*
* [The] Victorious

**Joseph II** 1741-1790 [HN]
*King of Germany and Holy Roman emperor*
* [The] Hatted King
* [The] Kalapos King
* [The] Titus of Germany
* [The] Unfortunate

**Josephs, John** [FFF]
*Entertainer*
* Selywn, John H.

**Josephs, Ray** 1912- [CA]
*American author*
* Raphael, Jay

**Josephs, Stephen**
*See* Dolmatch, Theodore B[ieley]

**Josephson, Duane Charles** 1942-
[SMG]
*American baseball player*
* Josephson, Josie

**Josephson, Josey**
*See* Josephson, Lester

**Josephson, Josie**
*See* Josephson, Duane Charles

**Josephson, Lester** 1942- [FB]
*American football player*
* Josephson, Josey

**Josephus, Flavius**
*See* Joseph ben Matthias

**Josey, E. J.**
*See* Josey, Elonnie Junius

**Josey, Elonnie Junius** 1924- [LBA]
*American library administrator and author*
* Josey, E. J.

**Joshua, Josh**
*See* Joshua, Von Everett

**[The] Joshua of Scotland**
*See* Robert I

**Joshua, Von Everett** 1948- [SMG]
*American baseball player*
* Joshua, Josh

**Josiah Allen's Wife**
*See* Holley, Marietta

**[The] Josiah of England**
*See* Edward VI

**[The] Josiah of his Country**
*See* Edward VI

**Josika, Miklos Nicholas**
1796-1865 [FFF]
*Hungarian author*
* [The] Walter Scott of Hungary

**Joske, Neville [Goyder]** 1893-
[CC, WW]
*Author*
* Neville, Margot [joint pseudonym with Margot Goyder]

**Joslin, Sesyle**
*See* Hine, Sesyle Joslin

**Joslyn, [Major] Jep**
*See* Doyle, Jefferson E. P.

**Joss, Addie**
*See* Joss, Adrian

**Joss, Adrian** 1880-1911
[B10, BE, SMG]
*American baseball player*
* Joss, Addie

**Josslyn, Jeff**
*See* Ferguson, J. E.

**Josue, [Brother]**
*See* Glover, Thomas

**Jotov, Dimitur Ivanov** 1878-1949
[EWL]
*Bulgarian author*
* Elin Pelin

**Joubert, Dian**
*See* Joubert, Dirk Daniel

**Joubert, Dirk Daniel** 1933- [IAW]
*South African sociologist and author*
* Joubert, Dian

**Joubert, Hendrik Johannes** 1926-
[IWM]
*South African musician*
* Joubert, Hennie

**Joubert, Hennie**
*See* Joubert, Hendrik Johannes

**Joubert, Linda**
*See* Grove, Henriette

**Joubert, Petrus Jacobus** 1834-1900
[WBD]
*South African soldier and statesman*
* Joubert, Piet

**Joubert, Piet**
*See* Joubert, Petrus Jacobus

**Jouhandeau, Marcel Henri**
1888-1979 [B10, CA, CD]
*French author*
* Provence, Marcel

**Jourdain, Francois Claude**
1696-1782 [PA]
*Author*
* Dom Maur

**Jourdan, Louis**
*See* Gendre, Louis

**Jourdemain, Marjory** ?-1441
[HN]
*Accused of witchcraft*
* [The] Witch of Eye

**Journeyman Engineer**
*See* Wright, Thomas

**Journeyman Printer**
*See* Smith, C. Manby

**Jouvenet, Jean** 1647?-1707?
[DNNS, HN, SN]
*French painter*
* [The] Caracci of France

**Jouvin, B.** [PA]
*Author*
* Benedict

**Jouy, Victor Joseph Etienne**
1764-1846 [PA, WBD]
*French playwright, librettist, author*
* De Jouy, Victor Joseph Etienne
* Etienne

**Jovanovic, Jovan** 1833-1904
[WBD]
*Serbian journalist and author*
* Zmaj

**[The] Jove of Jolly Fellows**
*See* Van Buren, John

**[The] Jove of the Modern Critical Olympus**
*See* Hunt, [James Henry] Leigh

**[The] Jovial**
*See* Otto [or Otho]

**Jovial Jawn Adams**
*See* Adams, John J. [Jack]

**[The] Jovial Toper**
*See* Mapes, Walter

**Jovius**
*See* Diocletian [Gaius Aurelius Valerius Diocletianus]

**Joy, Alice**
*Singer*
* Radio's Dream Girl

**Joy, Crystal**
*See* Billouin, Crystal Joy

**Joy, Elisabeth**
*See* Davis, Elisabeth Switzer

**Joy, Jimmy**
*See* Maloney, James Monte

**Joy, Leatrice**
*See* Zeidler, Leatrice Joy

**Joy, Richard** 1675-1742 [DEP]
* [The] Kentish Samson

**Joyal, George** [RBE]
*Canadian boxer*
* Jerome, George

**Joyce, Brenda**
*See* Leabo, Betty

**Joyce, John** 1939- [NOJ]
*American jazz musician*
* J. J.

**Joyce, Jon L[oyd]** 1937- [CA]
*American clergyman and author*
* Dovlos, Jay

**Joyce, Laura**
*See* Bell, Mrs. Digby

**Joyce, Mike**
*See* O'Neill, Michael Joyce

**Joyce, Peggy Hopkins**
*See* Upton, Margaret

**Joyce, Scrappy Bill**
*See* Joyce, William Michael

**Joyce, William** 1906-1946
[CBS, CND, LC]
*Irish-born pro-Nazi propagandist*
* Haw Haw, Lord

**Joyce, William Michael** 1865-1941
[BE]
*American baseball player*
* Joyce, Scrappy Bill

**Joyeuse, Anne de** 1561?-1587 [SN]
*French army officer*
* [The] King's King

**Joyeuse, Vyvian**
*See* Praed, Winthrop Mackworth

**Joyner, Andrew Jackson**
1861-1943 [OCS]
*American horse trainer*
* [The] Gentleman from North Carolina

**Joyner, Howard** 1906-
[PMJ, WWJ]
*American jazz musician*
* Howard, Bob

**Joynson, Barry**
See Cork, Barry Joynson

**Joynson-Hicks, William**
1865-1932 [NN]
*British politician*
* Jix

**Jozk, Wickov**
See Hlojzy, Nagel

**Juan Carlos** 1938?-
*Spanish king*
* Juan Carlos the Brief

**Juan Carlos the Brief**
See Juan Carlos

**Juan Ciudad** 1495-1550 [WBD]
*Saint*
* John of God

**Juana** 1462-1530 [WBD]
*Daughter of Queen Isabella of Castile*
* [La] Beltraneja

**Juana [Joanna or Jane]** 1479-1555
[HN, SN, WBD]
*Queen of Castile*
* Crazy Jane
* [The] Imbecile
* [La] Loca
* [The] Mad Queen

**Juanchi**
See Foeng, J. A. Chin A.

**Juarez, Benito Pablo** 1807?-1872
[FFF]
*Mexican president*
* [The] Mexican Washington
* [The] Second Washington

**Juaristi Mendizabal, Mariano**
1904- [OCS]
*Spanish pelota player*
* Atano III

**Jubilee Dicky**
See Norris, Henry

**Jucker, Iwan**
See Isler, Ursula

**Juckes, Bing**
See Juckes, Winston Bryan

**Juckes, Winston Bryan** 1926-
[CEI]
*Canadian-born hockey player*
* Juckes, Bing

**Jud, Leo** 1482-1542 [WBD]
*Swiss clergyman*
* Meister Leu

**Judah**
See Aristobulus I

**Judah, Samuel Benjamin Helbert**
1804-1876
*American playwright, poet, author*
* Phlogobombos, Terentius

**Judah I [or Jehudah]** 135?- 220
[DNNS, WBD]
*Jewish scholar*
* Ha-Kadosh
* Ha-Nasi
* [The] Holy
* [The] Prince
* Rabbi

**Judas** 1st c. [DNNS]
*Leader of Jewish uprising against the Romans*
* [The] Galilean

**Judas Asmonaeus** 2nd c. BC
[DNNS, HN, SN]
*Jewish patriot*
* [The] Cromwell of the Jews
* [The] Hammer
* Maccabaeus

**[The] Judas of the West**
See Clay, Henry

**Judd, Alfred** 20th c. [MBF]
*British author*
* Jolling, Jack
* Power, Nelson

**Judd, Cyril** [joint pseudonym with Cyril M. Kornbluth]
See Grossman, Josephine Judith

**Judd, Cyril** [joint pseudonym with Josephine Judith Grossman and Frederik Pohl]
See Kornbluth, Cyril M.

**Judd, Cyril** [joint pseudonym with Cyril M. Kornbluth]
See Pohl, Frederik

**Judd, Frances K.** [house pseudonym]
[Stratemeyer Syndicate]
See Stratemeyer, Edward L.

**Judd, Frederick Charles** 1914-
[AW, CA]
*British recording executive and writer*
* Courtney, John
* Lester-Rands, A.
* Miller, G. R.

**Judd, Harrison**
See Daniels, Norman [A.]

**Judd, Margaret Haddican** 1906-
[CA, WW]
*American author*
* Garrett, Truman

**Judd, Ossie**
See Judd, Thomas William Oscar

**Judd, Thomas William Oscar**
1908- [BE]
*Canadian-born baseball player*
* Judd, Ossie

**Jude, [Father]**
See Mead, Jude

**[O] Judeu**
See Silva, Antonio Jose da

**Judge**
See Menchan, W. McKinley

**Judge Louis**
See Buchalter, Louis

**Judge, Peter** 1891-1947
[BEW, FC]
*Irish actor*
* McCormick, F. J.

**Judge, Philip**
See Hall, William Otterburn

**[The] Judicious Hooker**
See Hooker, Richard

**Judkins, Jeff** 1956-
*American basketball player*
* J. J.
* Judkins, Jud

**Judkins, Jud**
See Judkins, Jeff

**Judson, Edward Zane Carroll**
1822?-1886 [FFF, MBF, WBD]
*American author*
* Buntline, Ned

**Judson, Emily Chubbuck**
1817-1854 [FFF]
*American author*
* Forester, Fanny

**Judson, Ralph** 20th c. [WGT]
*Author*
* Stranger, Ralph

**Judson, William**
See Corley, Edwin

**Judy, Lyle LeRoy** 1913- [BE]
*American baseball player*
* Judy, Punch

**Judy, Punch**
See Judy, Lyle LeRoy

**Judy Sue**
See Epstein, Judith Sue

**Judy, Will[iam Lewis]** 1891- [CA]
*American editor, publisher, author*
* Port, Wymar

**Juelich, John Samuel** 1916-1970
[BE]
*American baseball player*
* Juelich, Red

**Juelich, Red**
See Juelich, John Samuel

**Juergen, Anna**
See Mueller-Tannewitz, Anna

**Juergensmeyer, Jane Stuart**
See Stuart, Jane

**Juesp**
See Spahr, Juerg

**Jug, M. T.**
See Howard, Joseph

**Jughandle Freddie Frankhouse**
See Frankhouse, Fred[rick Meloy]

**Jughandle Johnny Morrison**
See Morrison, John Dewey

**Juhasz, Leslie Albert** 1929- [CA]
*Hungarian-born educator and author*
* Shepard, Leslie Albert

**Juice**
See Simpson, Orenthal James

**Juke Boy Barner**
See Bonner, Weldon H. Philip

**Juke Boy Bonner**
See Bonner, Weldon H. Philip

**Jules**
See Garnier, Jean Joseph

**Jules**
See Radilovic, Julio

**[The] Jules Verne of America**
See Senarens, Luis Philip

**Julia Virginia**
See Laengsdorff, Julia Virginia

**Julian [Flavius Claudius Julianus]**
331- 363 [DNNS, FFF, SN]
*Roman emperor*
* [The] Apostate

**Julian, Alvin T.** 1901-1967
[AS, BB, SMG]
*American basketball coach*
* Julian, Doggie [or Doggy]

**Julian, Cardinal**
See Cesarini, Giuliano

**Julian, Doggie [or Doggy]**
See Julian, Alvin T.

**Julian, George W.** [SN]
* [The] Orator of Free-Dirt

**Julian, Percy Lavon** 1898-1975
[IBW]
*American chemist*
* [The] Soybean Chemist

**Julian, Rupert**
See Hayes, Percival

**Julia's Dwarf**
See Godeau, Antoine

**Julie**
See Robbins, June

**Julie of Colorado Springs**
See Robbins, June

**Julien, Frenchy**
See Julien, Joseph J.

**Julien, Joseph J.** 1907- [BBH]
*American lacrosse player and official*
* Julien, Frenchy

**Julien, Noel** 1799-1873 [WBD]
*French scholar*
* Julien, Stanislas

**Julien, Simon** 1736-1800 [HN]
*French painter*
* [The] Apostate

**Julien, Stanislas**
See Julien, Noel

**Juliet, Jean** 1880?-1964 [BEW]
*Actor*
* Moser, Hans

**Juline, Ruth Bishop**
See Ritchie, Ruth

**Julius**
See Curling, Bryan William Richard

**Julius, Emanuel** 1889-1951 [WBD]
*American publisher and author*
* Haldeman-Julius, Emanuel

**Julius II**
See Della Rovere, Giuliano

**Julius III**
See Ciocchi del Monte, Giammaria

**Julyan, Louise Elizabeth** 20th c.
[NAA]
*Canadian journalist*
* Leith, Elizabeth

**Jumbo Jack Gardner**
See Gardner, Francis Henry

**Jumbo Jim Elliott**
See Elliott, James Thomas

**Jumbo Joe Stydahar**
See Stydahar, Joseph L.

**Jumillano**
See Ortuno Duplaix, Emilio

**Jump, A.**
See Sparks, Jesse Wadlington

**Jump Steady Templeton**
See  Templeton, Garry Lewis

**Jumpin' Joe Savoldi**
See  Savoldi, Joseph A.

**Jumpin' Joe Williams**
See  Goreed, Joseph

**Jumpin' Johnny Green**
See  Green, John

**Jumpin' Johnny Wilson**
See  Wilson, John E.

**Jumping Jack Jones**
See  Jones, Daniel Albion

**Jumping Jack McCracken**
See  McCracken, John D.

**Jumping Jack Spinella**
See  Spinella, Barney

**Jumping Joe Dugan**
See  Dugan, Joseph Anthony

**Jumping Joe Fulks**
See  Fulks, Joe

**Jumping Joe Perrault**
See  Perrault, Paul Joseph

**Jumpp, Hugo**
See  MacPeek, Walter G.

**Jun, Terahata**
See  Kirkup, James

**Junceda**
See  Garcia-Junceda i Supervia, Joan

**June**
See  Tripp, June Howard

**June, Ava**
See  Wiggins, Ava June

**June, Jennie**
See  Croly, Jane Cunningham

**June, Jessie**
See  Forbes, Mrs. Simelde

**Jung, Doris**
See  Crittenden, Doris

**Jung, Heinrich** 1740-1817
[FFF, WBD]
*German author and mystic*
* [The] Dominie Sampson of Germany
* Jung-Stilling, Johann Heinrich
* Stilling, Heinrich [or John Henry]

**Jung-Stilling, Johann Heinrich**
See  Jung, Heinrich

**Jungels, Curly**
See  Jungels, Kenneth Peter

**Jungels, Kenneth Peter** 1916-1975
[BE]
*American baseball player*
* Jungels, Curly

**Jungk, Robert**
See  Baum, Robert

**Jungle Doctor**
See  White, Paul Hamilton Hume

**Jungle Jim Loscutoff**
See  Loscutoff, James

**Jungle Jim Martin**
See  Martin, James R.

**Jungle Jim Rivera**
See  Rivera, Manuel Joseph

**Jungman, Nico** 1872-1935  [DBA]
*British painter and illustrator*
* Nico

**Jungreis, Esther** 1936?-
*Jewish evangelist*
* [The] Jewish Billy Graham
* [The] Jewish Soul on Fire
* [The] Rebbetzin [Rabbi's Wife]

**Junior**
See  Baron, Hyacinthe-Theodore

**Junior Sub**
See  Beith, [Sir] John Hay

**Junius**
See  Brown, James H.

**Junius**
See  Du Jow, Francois

**Junius?**
See  Francis, [Sir] Philip

**Junius**
See  Walford, Cornelius

**Junius Americanus**
See  Everett, David

**Junius Americanus**
See  Lee, Arthur

**[The] Junk Man**
See  Lopatnyski, Edmund Walter

**Junkin, Margaret**
See  Preston, Mrs. M. J.

**Junot, Andoche** 1771-1813
[DNNF, DNNS, FFF]
*French army officer*
* [The] Tempest
* [La] Tempete

**[A] Jupiter in Sabots**
See  Millet [or Mile], Jean Francois

**Jupiter Scapin**
See  Bonaparte, Napoleon

**[The] Jupiter Tonans of His Party**
See  Van Buren, John

**Jur, Jerzy**
See  Lerski, George Jan

**Jurado, Katy**
See  Jurado Garcia, Maria Christina

**Jurado Garcia, Maria Christina**
1927-  [FC, ITA, OCF]
*Mexican actress*
* Jurado, Katy

**Jurat, Bert**
See  Hochheimer, Albert

**Jurgen, Helen Marie** 1908-1958
[BEW, F2, FC]
*American actress*
* Twelvetrees, Helen

**Jurgenson, Christian Adolph, III**
1934-  [FB]
*American football player*
* Jurgenson, Sonny

**Jurgenson, Sonny**
See  Jurgenson, Christian Adolph, III

**Jurinac, Sena**
See  Jurinac, Srebrenka

**Jurinac, Srebrenka** 1921-  [OP]
*Austrian opera singer*
* Jurinac, Sena

**Juris Consultus**
See  Chapin, Alonzo Bowen

**Jurista**
See  Acosta, Gabriel

**Jurka, Blanche** 20th c.  [BEW]
*American actress, author, director*
* Yurka, Blanche

**[The] Just**
See  Aristides [or Aristeides]

**[The] Just**
See  Casimir II

**[The] Just**
See  Ferdinand I

**[The] Just**
See  Frederick Augustus I

**[The] Just**
See  Haroun al Raschid

**[The] Just**
See  James

**[The] Just**
See  James II

**[The] Just**
See  Louis XII

**[The] Just**
See  Louis XIII

**[The] Just**
See  Moran

**[The] Just**
See  Pedro I

**[The] Just**
See  Roland de La Platiere, Jean Marie

**Just, Joseph Erwin [Joe]**
See  Juszczak, Joseph Erwin

**[The] Just King [Shah Endeb]**
See  Baharam

**[The] Just King**
See  Khosru I [or Chosroes]

**Justice, Charles Ronald** 1924-
[B10, FB]
*American football player*
* Justice, Choo Choo

**Justice, Choo Choo**
See  Justice, Charles Ronald

**Justice, William** 1913-
[FC, ITA, SW]
*American actor*
* Travis, Richard

**Justiciar**
See  Powell-Smith, Vincent [Walter Francis]

**[The] Justiciary**
See  Pedro I

**Justificus**
See  Pappas, George Stephen

**[A] Justified Sinner**
See  Hogg, James

**Justin** 100?- 163?  [DNNS, WBD]
*Saint*
* [The] Martyr
* [The] Philosopher

**Justin, Morgan**
See  Wurman, Claude Olin

**Justin I** 452- 527  [WBD]
*Byzantine emperor*
* [The] Elder

**Justin II** ?- 578  [WBD]
*Byzantine emperor*
* [The] Younger

**[The] Justinian of England**
See  Edward I

**Justinian I [Flavius Anicius
Justinianus]** 483- 565
[DNNS, FFF, SN]
*Byzantine emperor*
* [The] Great

**Justinian II** 669- 711  [WBD]
*Byzantine emperor*
* Rhinotmetus [With the Nose Cut Off]

**Justis, Smoke**
See  Justis, Walt[er]

**Justis, Walt[er]** 1883-1941  [BE]
*American baseball player*
* Justis, Smoke

**Justitia**
See  Lowe, Bennett

**Justo de Lara**
See  Armas y Cardenas, Jose de

**Justus**
See  Coles, Charles Ernest

**Justus**
See  Ebhardt, C.

**Justus**
See  Voudel, Jesse Vanden

**Juszczak, Joseph Erwin** 1916-  [BE]
*American baseball player*
* Just, Joseph Erwin [Joe]

**Juta, Jan** 1895-  [CA]
*South African-born American artist and writer*
* Juta, Rene

**Juta, Rene**
See  Juta, Jan

**Jutze, Alfred Henry** 1947-  [WWB]
*American baseball player*
* Jutze, Skip

**Jutze, Skip**
See  Jutze, Alfred Henry

**Jutzi, Phil**
See  Jutzi, Piel

**Jutzi, Piel** 1894-  [FDG]
*German director*
* Jutzi, Phil

**Juvenal [Decimus Junius Juvenalis]**
60?- 140?  [DNNS, HN, SN]
*Roman poet*
* [The] Aquinian Sage
* [The] Last Poet of Rome

**[The] Juvenal of Chivalry**
See  Heinrich von Moelk

**[The] Juvenal of England**
See  Oldham, John

**[The] Juvenal of Painters**
See  Hogarth, William

**[The] Juvenal of the English Drama**
See  Jonson, Ben[jamin]

**[The] Juvenal of the Provencals**
*See* Cardenal [or Cardinal?],
Pierre

**Juvenile**
*See* Picton, Thomas

**Juvenis**
*See* Cawston, Frederick Gordon

**Juvenon**
*See* Thuitleru, Francois Jean

**Juvinell, Uncle**
*See* Morrison, Heady

**Jyotirmoy, Ghosh Dastider**
*See* Moharaj, Soncu

# K

**K.**
*See* Kernoff, Harry

**K.**
*See* Knight, John Collyer

**K.**
*See* Russell, Kathleen Barbara

**K. A. U.**
*See* Underwood, Keith Alfred

**K. B.**
*See* Barratt, Krome

**K. C.**
*See* Casey, Harry Wayne

**K. C.**
*See* Kent, [William] Charles
[Mark]

**K. C. L.**
*See* Curry-Lindahl, Kai

**K. F.**
*See* Fallshaw, Keith George

**K. F.**
*See* Fenton, Katherine

**K. J.**
*See* Jarvis, Kevin Bartram Sidney

**K. K.**
*See* Kempshall, Hubert Kim

**K. M.**
*See* Beauchamp, Kathleen
Mansfield

**K. O. S.**
*See* Von Dombrowski zu Papros
und Krusvic, Kathe

**K. O. T. P.**
*See* Parbury, Kathleen Ophir
Theodora

**K (1)**
*See* Beith, [Sir] John Hay

**K. S. W.**
*See* White, Katharine S.

**K. W. B.**
*See* Billings, Kathleen Wyatt

**K. W. P.**
*See* William Powlett, Katherine

**K-Doe, Ernie**
*See* Kador, Ernest, Jr.

**K-Hito**
*See* Garcia Lopez, Ricardo

**Kaaiai, Sol Hoopii** 1905-1953    [SC]
*American actor and musician*
* Hoopii, Sol

**Kaaihue, Johnny** 1901-1971
[DAM]
*Hawaiian bandleader and actor*
* Ukelele, Johnny

**Kaat, James Lee [Jim]** 1938-
[PB, SMG]
*American baseball player*
* Kaat, Kitty

**Kaat, Kitty**
*See* Kaat, James Lee [Jim]

**Kabashima, Katsuichi** 1888-1965
[WECO]
*Japanese illustrator*
* Fune no Kabashima [Kabashima
of the Ships]
* Tofujin

**Kabdebo, Tamas**
*See* Kabdebo, Thomas

**Kabdebo, Thomas** 1934-
[CA, SAT]
*Hungarian-born British author*
* Kabdebo, Tamas

**Kabibble, Osh**
*See* Jobb, Jamie

**Kabible, Abe** 1885-1974    [SC]
*American actor, cartoonist,
journalist*
* Hershfield, Harry

**Kac, Isser** 1896-1958    [FC]
*Polish-born actor*
* Katch, Kurt

**Kacew, Romain** 1914-1980    [CA]
*French diplomat and author*
* Ajar, Emile
* Bogat, Shatan
* Gary, Romain
* Sinbaldi, Fosco

**Kachalov, Vasili Ivanovich**
*See* Shverubovich, Vasili Ivanovich

**Kackley, Bob**
*See* Miller, Bob

**Kaden**
*See* Bandrowski, Juljusz

**Kadish, I.**
*See* Yaffe, Kadish

**Kador, Ernest, Jr.** 20th c.    [RO1]
*American singer and songwriter*
* K-Doe, Ernie

**Kadosh, A.**
*See* Quinones, Francisco Mariano

**Kaempfert, Wade**
*See* Alvarez Del Rey, Ramon
Felipe San Juan Mario Silvio Enrico

**Kaempfert, Wade** [house pseudonym,
Space Publications]
*See* Dempsey, Henry

**Kaenel, Cowboy Jack**
*See* Kaenel, Jack

**Kaenel, Jack** 20th c.
*American jockey*
* Kaenel, Cowboy Jack

**Kaer, Devil May**
*See* Kaer, Morton A.

**Kaer, Morton A.** 1902-    [FB]
*American football player*
* Kaer, Devil May

**[The] Kaffir King**
*See* Isaacs, Barnett

**Kafora, Frank Jacob [Jake]**
1889-1928    [BE]
*American baseball player*
* Kafora, Tomatoes

**Kafora, Tomatoes**
*See* Kafora, Frank Jacob [Jake]

**Kagan, Arthur** 1927-    [OP]
*American opera singer*
* Sergi, Arturo

**Kagey, Rudolf**
*See* Steel, Rudolph Hornaday

**Kah-ge-gwa-ge-bow**
*See* Copway, George

**Kahakalau, Robert** 1922-
[EJ, PMJ]
*American jazz musician*
* Carter, Bob

**Kahana, Michael**
*See* Kahana, Mirel

**Kahana, Mirel** 1948-    [OP]
*Israeli opera singer*
* Kahana, Michael

**Kahl**
*See* Calvinus, Johann

**Kahler, George Rannels** 1889-1924
[BE]
*American baseball player*
* Kahler, Krum

**Kahler, Hugh [Torbert] MacNair**
1883-1969    [CA, CAA]
*American author*
* Elphinstone, Murgatroyd

**Kahler, Krum**
*See* Kahler, George Rannels

**Kahler, Maude** 1908-1944    [F2, SC]
*American actress*
* Kennedy, Merna

**Kahm, Harold S.** 20th c.    [CA]
*American author*
* Sackerman, Henry

**Kahn, Balthazar**
*See* Carlisle, Thomas [Fiske]

**Kahn, E. J., Jr.**
*See* Kahn, Ely Jacques, Jr.

**Kahn, Edwin Bernard [Eddie]**
1911-1945    [AS, EJS]
*American football player*
* Kahn, King Kong

**Kahn, Ely Jacques, Jr.** 1916-
[WYA]
*American author*
* Kahn, E. J., Jr.

**Kahn, Herta Hess** 1919-    [CA]
*German-born American investment
analyst and author*
* Levy, Herta Hess

**Kahn, Jack**
*See* Kahn, Owen Earle

**Kahn, King Kong**
*See* Kahn, Edwin Bernard [Eddie]

**Kahn, Norman** 1924-1953
[EJ, PMJ]
*American jazz musician*
* Kahn, Tiny

**Kahn, Owen Earle** 1905-    [BE]
*American baseball player*
* Kahn, Jack

**Kahn, Smitty**
*See* Kahn, William

**Kahn, Tiny**
*See* Kahn, Norman

**Kahn, William** 1882-1959    [SC]
*American actor*
* Kahn, Smitty

**Kahn, Yitzhak** 1908-    [IAW]
*Polish-born author*
* Ben Chaim
* Lebenson

**Kahn-Fogel, Daniel [Mark]**
*See* Fogel, Daniel Mark

**Kahnweiler, Daniel Henry**
1884-1979 [B10, CA]
*German art dealer and publisher*
* Henry, Daniel

**Kain, Cobber**
*See* Kain, Edgar

**Kain, Edgar** 1918-1940 [BDW]
*New Zealand fighter pilot*
* Kain, Cobber

**Kain, Malcolm**
*See* Oglesby, Joseph

**Kaine, George S.**
*See* Morris, Charles Smith

**Kainen, Ray**
*See* Kainulainen, Ray

**Kaing Kech Ieu** 20th c.
*Cambodian government official*
* Deuch, Brother

**Kainulainen, Ray** 20th c. [SFL]
*Author*
* Kainen, Ray
* Kalnen, Ray

**[The] Kaiser**
*See* Beckenbauer, Franz

**Kaiser, Al[fred Edward]** 1886-1969
[BE]
*American baseball player*
* Kaiser, Deerfoot

**Kaiser, Arnold** 1889-1956
[F1, F2, FC]
*American actor*
* Kerry, Norman

**Kaiser, Bill**
*See* Sumner, David [W. K.]

**Kaiser, Deerfoot**
*See* Kaiser, Al[fred Edward]

**Kaiser, [Clyde] Don[ald]** 1935- [BE]
*American baseball player*
* Kaiser, Tiger

**Kaiser, Geza** 1907?- [BEW, FC]
*Hungarian-born actor and director*
* Korvin, Charles

**Kaiser Klaes**
*See* Bonaparte, Napoleon

**Kaiser, Tiger**
*See* Kaiser, [Clyde] Don[ald]

**Kaiser William**
*See* Burnside, Ambrose Everett

**Kaiserman, Mauricio Alberto** 1952-
*Brazilian singer and composer*
* Albert, Morris

**Kajar the Magician**
*See* Bowen, Reuben Bochert

**Kajot, Jek**
*See* Kucharski, Jan Edward

**Kaki**
*See* Heinemann, Katherine

**Kal**
*See* Gezi, Kalil I.

**Kalanag**
*See* Schrieber, Helmut

**[The] Kalapos King**
*See* Joseph II

**Kalatozishvili, Mikhail** 1903-1973
[OCF, WEF]
*Russian director*
* Kalatozov, Mikhail

**Kalatozov, Mikhail**
*See* Kalatozishvili, Mikhail

**Kalau, Abraham** 1612-1686 [WBD]
*German theologian*
* Calov, Abraham

**Kalbfliesh, Jeff**
*See* Kalbfliesh, Walter

**Kalbfliesh, Walter** 1911- [CEI]
*Canadian-born hockey player*
* Kalbfliesh, Jeff

**Kale, Arvind and Shanta**
*See* Gantzer, Hugh

**Kaleem, Musa**
*See* Wright, Orlando

**[The] Kalem Girl**
*See* Liggett, Genevieve Gauntier

**Kaler, James Otis** 1848-1912
[FFF, SAT, WGT]
*American writer*
* Otis, James
* Perkins, Abigail
* Walraven

**Kaleta, Alexander** 1919-
[CEI, FHE]
*Canadian-born hockey player*
* Kaleta, Killer

**Kaleta, Killer**
*See* Kaleta, Alexander

**Kalfass, Lefty**
*See* Kalfass, William Philip [Bill]

**Kalfass, William Philip [Bill]** 1916-
[BE]
*American baseball player*
* Kalfass, Lefty

**Kali, Omar**
*See* Dyer, Skip

**Kalichmam, Claire** 1944- [IAW]
*Belgian author*
* Calliam, Selma

**Kalidasa** 5th c. [WBD]
*Indian playwright and poet*
* [The] Shakespeare of India

**Kalin, Fats**
*See* Kalinkiewicz, Frank Bruno

**Kalin, Frank Bruno**
*See* Kalinkiewicz, Frank Bruno

**Kalinkiewicz, Frank Bruno** 1917-
[BE]
*American baseball player*
* Kalin, Fats
* Kalin, Frank Bruno

**Kalionzes, Janet**
*See* Manson, Janet

**Kalish, Scheindel**
*Actress*
* Shepherd, Ann

**Kallestad, Reidar B[ernhard]** 1917-
[CA]
*Norwegian-born American author*
* Bjornard, Reidar B[ernhard]

**Kallet, Aaron Harry** 1887-1965
[EJS]
*Polish-born American football
player*
* Kallet, Fuzzy

**Kallet, Fuzzy**
*See* Kallet, Aaron Harry

**Kallicharran, Alvin Isaac** 1949-
[DC]
*Guyanese cricketer*
* Kallicharran, Kalli

**Kallicharran, Kalli**
*See* Kallicharran, Alvin Isaac

**Kallio, Sinikka**
*See* Nevanlinna, Sinikka Sisko

**Kallio-Visapaa, Sinikka**
*See* Nevanlinna, Sinikka Sisko

**Kallwitz, Seth** 1556-1615 [WBD]
*German musician*
* Calvisius, Sethus

**Kalman, Bernard** 1924- [BEW]
*American director and producer*
* Cahlman, Robert

**Kalmus, Ain**
*See* Mand [or Maend], Ewald [or
Evald]

**Kalnen, Ray**
*See* Kainulainen, Ray

**Kalogeropoulos, Maria Anna Sofia
Cecilia** 1923-1977
*American opera singer*
* Callas, Maria
* [La] Divina

**Kalpana, Mohan**
*See* Lalla, Mohan Bulchand

**Kalra, Rajinder Mohan** 1939-
[IAW]
*Indian educator and author*
* Raj

**Kalt, Jeannette Chappell**
1898?-1976 [CA]
*American poet and tennis player*
* Chappell, Jeannette

**Kaltenborn, H. V.**
*See* Kaltenborn, Hans von

**Kaltenborn, Hans von** 1878-1965
[WBD]
*American editor and radio
commentator*
* Kaltenborn, H. V.

**Kalthoum, Um** 1898-1975 [SC]
*Egyptian actress and singer*
* Daughter of the Nile

**Kalula**
*See* Ramsden, F. E.

**Kalusky, Isidor** 20th c. [BMH]
*South African-born entertainer*
* Kaye, Irving

**Kalwara, Walter** 1896-1974 [SC]
*American actor and wrestler*
* Wahl, Walter Dare

**Kamaci, Cemal** 1943- [RBE]
*Turkish boxer*
* Kamaci, Turk

**Kamaci, Turk**
*See* Kamaci, Cemal

**Kamau, Johnstone**
*See* Ngengi, Kamau wa

**Kamban, Guomundur**
*See* Hallgrimson, Jansson

**Kambu, Joseph**
*See* Amamoo, Joseph Godson

**Kamdois, Kurt**
*See* Ackerman, Forrest J[ames]

**Kamehameha I** 1758?-1819 [WBD]
*King of the Hawaiian Islands*
* Nu'i [The Great]

**Kamenev, Lev Borisovich**
*See* Rosenfeld, Lev Borisovich

**Kamerman, Sylvia E.**
*See* Burack, Sylvia

**Kamiat, Bernice** 1925- [FC, ITA]
*American comedienne*
* Williams, Cara

**Kamienski, Lucian** 1885- ? [WBD]
*Polish-born composer*
* Dolega-Kamienski

**Kamin, Nick**
*See* Antonick, Robert J.

**Kaminker, Simone** 1921-
[BDF, FC, IPA]
*French actress*
* Signoret, Simone

**Kaminsky [or Kominski?], David
Daniel** 1913- [BDF, BEW, FC]
*American entertainer*
* Kaye, Danny

**Kaminsky, Howard** 1940?-
*American author*
* Stanwood, Brooks [joint
pseudonym with Susan Stanwood
Kaminsky]

**Kaminsky, Melvin** 1928- [IPA]
*American writer, producer, director*
* Brooks, Mel

**Kaminsky, Susan Stanwood** 1937?-
*American author*
* Stanwood, Brooks [joint
pseudonym with Howard
Kaminsky]

**Kamiyama, Sojin** 1891-1954 [SC]
*Japanese actor*
* Sojin

**Kammerstein, Benjamin** 1919-
[CA]
*Israeli author and sculptor*
* Tammuz, Benjamin

**Kamp, Alphonse Francis**
1900-1955 [BE]
*American baseball player*
* Kamp, Ike

**Kamp, Ike**
*See* Kamp, Alphonse Francis

**Kampf, Abraham** 1920- [CA]
*American educator and writer*
* Kampf, Avram

**Kampf, Avram**
*See* Kampf, Abraham

**Kampf, Harold** 1916- [WW]
*Author*
* Kaye, Harold B.

**Kampman, Bingo**
*See* Kampman, Rudolph

**Kampman, Rudolph** 1914-
[CEI, FHE]
*Canadian-born hockey player*
* Kampman, Bingo

**Kan Tse-kao** 1905?-
*Chinese vice premier*
* Doctor of Mimeography
* Teng Hsiao-ping [Little Peace]

**Kanaris, Constantine** 1795?-1855?
[HN]
*Greek naval commander and prime
minister*
* [The] Themistocles of Modern
  Greece

**Kanazawa, Masakata** 1934-    [CA]
*Japanese musicologist and editor*
* Kanazawa, Roger

**Kanazawa, Roger**
*See* Kanazawa, Masakata

**Kane, Abigail** 1885-1966    [SC]
*American actress*
* Kane, Gail

**Kane, Bernie**
*See* Aquino, Frank J.

**Kane, Diana**
*See* Wilson, Roberta

**Kane, Francis** 1916-    [CA]
*American author*
* Robbins, Harold
* Rubin, Harold

**Kane, Francis Thomas [Frank]**
*See* Kiley, Francis Thomas

**Kane, Frank** 1912-1968    [CA, CC]
*American author*
* Boyd, Frank

**Kane, Gail**
*See* Kane, Abigail

**Kane, Gil**
*See* Katz, Eli

**Kane, Harry**
*See* Cohen, Harry

**Kane, Helen**
*See* Schroder, Helen

**Kane, Irene**
*See* Chase, Chris

**Kane, Jim**
*See* Germano, Peter B.

**Kane, Julia**
*See* Robins, Denise [Naomi]

**Kane, Katherine** 20th c.
*Actress*
* Kane, Sugar

**Kane, Klondike**
*See* Cohen, Harry

**Kane, Pablo**
*See* Zachary, Hugh

**Kane, Philip**
*See* Case, John Francis

**Kane, Sugar**
*See* Kane, Katherine

**Kane, Sugar**
*See* Kiley, Francis Thomas

**Kane, Thomas Joseph [Tom]** 1906-
[BE]
*American baseball player*
* Kane, Sugar

**Kane, Wilson** [house pseudonym,
Ziff-Davis]
*See* Bloch, Robert [Albert]

**Kanehl, Hot Rod**
*See* Kanehl, Rod[erick Edwin]

**Kanehl, Rod[erick Edwin]** 1934-
[BE]
*American baseball player*
* Kanehl, Hot Rod

**Kang he [or hi]**
*See* Chin-tsou-jin

**Kang Te [or Kang Teh] [Exalted
Virtue]**
*See* Hsuan T'ung

**K'ang Yu-wei** 1858-1927    [WBD]
*Chinese scholar and political
reformer*
* [The] Modern Sage
* [The] Rousseau of China

**Kang-wang** 12th c.    [FFF, SN]
*Chinese emperor*
* [The] Peaceful

**[The] Kangaroo**
*See* Smith, Don[ald A.]

**Kangaroo, Captain**
*See* Keesham, Bob

**[The] Kangaroo Kid**
*See* Cunningham, Billy

**[The] Kangaroo Kid**
*See* Pollard, Jim

**Kanitz, Ernest**
*See* Kanitz, Ernst

**Kanitz, Ernst** 1894-    [BBD]
*Austrian-born composer*
* Kanitz, Ernest

**Kannan, Lakshmi** 1943-    [IAW]
*Indian author*
* Tilly

**Kannegiesser, Sheldon Bruce** 1947-
[SMG]
*Canadian-born hockey player*
* Kannegiesser, Shelly

**Kannegiesser, Shelly**
*See* Kannegiesser, Sheldon Bruce

**Kannengiser, Henriette** 1889-1956
[WFA]
*Austrian-born fashion designer*
* Carnegie, Hattie

**Kano, Morinobu** 1602-1674    [WBD]
*Japanese painter*
* Kano, Tanyu

**Kano, Tanyu**
*See* Kano, Morinobu

**[The] Kansas Book Lady**
*See* Gagliardo, Ruth Garver

**Kansas City Bill**
*See* Weldon, Will

**[The] Kansas City Butterball**
*See* Beaman, Lottie Kimbrough

**Kansas City Red**
*See* Stephson, Arthur Lee

**[The] Kansas Cyclone**
*See* Eisenhower, David Dwight

**[The] Kansas Cyclone**
*See* Sayers, Gale E.

**[The] Kansas Ironman**
*See* Cunningham, Glenn

**Kansas Joe**
*See* McCoy, Joe

**Kansas, Rocky**
*See* Tozzo, Rocco

**[The] Kansas Rube**
*See* Ferns, Jim

**Kansil, Joli**
*See* Gaines, Joel Dennis

**Kantakarjuna**
*See* Arjunwadkar, Krishna S.

**Kanter, Hal** 1918-    [CA]
*American screenwriter*
* Irving, Henry

**Kantlehner, Erv**
*See* Kantlehner, Ervine Leslie

**Kantlehner, Ervine Leslie** 1892-
[BE]
*American baseball player*
* Kantlehner, Erv

**Kanto, Peter**
*See* Zachary, Hugh

**Kantor-Berg, Friedrich** 1908-1979
[CA, MGL]
*Austrian poet, author, translator*
* Torberg, Friedrich

**Kantorowicz, Hermann** 1877-1940
[WBD]
*German jurist*
* Flavius, Gnaus

**Kanzawa, Toshiko**
*See* Furukawa, Toshi

**Kao hoang-ti** 3rd c. BC    [HN]
*Chinese emperor*
* [The] Chinese Caesar

**Kao Tsu**
*See* Chao Kuang-yin

**Kao Tsu**
*See* Li Yuan

**Kaonohi, David** 20th c.    [ASC]
*Hawaiian composer and conductor*
* Pineapple, Johnny

**Kaplan, Anne Bernays** 1930-    [CA]
*American author*
* Bernays, Anne

**Kaplan, Barry** 20th c.    [SFL]
*Author*
* Kingsley, Bettina

**Kaplan, Boche** 1926-    [CA]
*American author*
* Roche, A. K. [joint pseudonym
  with Roslyn Kroop Abisch]

**Kaplan, Eddie** 1907?-1964    [BEW]
*Theatrical performer and talent
representative*
* Kaplan, Nuts

**Kaplan, Howard Lawrence** 1947-
[RO2]
*American singer*
* Kaylan, Howard

**Kaplan, Jean Caryl Korn** 1926-
[CA, SAT]
*American author*
* Caryl, Jean

**Kaplan, Kid**
*See* Kaplan, Louis

**Kaplan, Leigh Wright** 1937-
[IWM]
*American musician*
* Wright, Elsie

**Kaplan, Li'l Lou**
*See* Kaplan, Louis

**Kaplan, Louis** 1902-
[BX, RBE, WBC]
*Russian-born American boxer*
* Kaplan, Kid
* Kaplan, Li'l Lou
* Little Napoleon
* Miller, Benny

**Kaplan, M. M.** 20th c.    [WGT]
*Author*
* Barshofsky, Philip
* Bartel, Philip Jacques

**Kaplan, Nathan** ?-1923    [BLB]
*American underworld figure*
* Dropper, Kid
* Jack the Dropper

**Kaplan, Nuts**
*See* Kaplan, Eddie

**Kaplan, Philip** 1906-1971    [SC]
*American actor*
* Kaye, Sparky

**Kapp, Paul**
*See* Hardt, Richard

**Kapp, Yvonne** 1903-    [AW]
*British author*
* Cloud, Yvonne

**Kappel, Heinie**
*See* Kappel, Henry

**Kappel, Henry** 1892-1905    [BE]
*American baseball player*
* Kappel, Heinie

**Kappelhoff, Doris** 1924-
[BDF, FC, ITA]
*American actress and singer*
* Day, Doris

**Kappler, Herbert** 1908?-1978
*German Nazi war criminal*
* [The] Hangman of the Ardeatine
  Caves

**Kapusta, Paul**
*See* Bickers, Richard Leslie
Townshend

**Karageorge [or Karadjordje]**
*See* Petrovitsch [or Petrovic],
George

**Karageorge, Michael?**
*See* Anderson, Poul [William]

**Karamzin, Nicholas Michaelovitch**
1765-1826    [DEP, HN, RH]
*Russian historian, author, poet*
* [The] Russian Livy

**Kardec, Allan**
*See* Rivail, Leon Hippolyte
Denisart

**Kardow, Paul Otto** 1915-    [BE]
*American baseball player*
* Kardow, Tex

**Kardow, Tex**
*See* Kardow, Paul Otto

**Kare, Kaarina**
*See* Honkanen, Hilja Loviisa
Valkeapaa

**Karenga, Ron**
See   Everett, Ronald McKinley

**Karg, Sigfrid** 1877-1933
[BBD, WBD]
*German organist and composer*
* Karg-Elert, Sigfrid

**Karg-Elert, Sigfrid**
See   Karg, Sigfrid

**Kari**
See   Suomalainen, Kari Yrjana

**Karig, Walter** 1898-1956
[ANT, TC1, WW]
*American author and journalist*
* Duncan, Julia K. [house
   pseudonym] [Stratemeyer
   Syndicate]
* Ferris, James Cody [house
   pseudonym] [Stratemeyer
   Syndicate]
* Keene, Carolyn [house
   pseudonym] [Stratemeyer
   Syndicate]
* Patrick, Keats

**Karilivacz, Carl F.** 1930-1969    [AS]
*American football player*
* Karilivacz, Kava

**Karilivacz, Kava**
See   Karilivacz, Carl F.

**Karina**
See   Goud, Anne

**Karina, Anna**
See   Bayer [or Beyer?], Hanne
Karin Blarke

**Karishka, Paul**
See   Hatch, David Patterson

**Kark, Nina Mary [Mabey]** 1925-
[CA, CC, SAT]
*British author*
* Bawden, Nina

**Karkalits, Patsy Lou** 1932-    [BEW]
*American singer, dancer, actress*
* Karr, Patti

**Karl, Big Bates**
See   Karl, George

**Karl, George** ?-1925    [PHM]
*American underworld figure*
* Karl, Big Bates

**Karl Knutsson**
See   Charles VIII

**Karl, Larry** 20th c.
*American football team staff
member*
* [The] Kronic Krisis

**Karlin, George**
See   Krotkov, Yuri

**Karlin, Miriam**
See   Samuels, Miriam

**Karloff, Boris**
See   Pratt, William Henry

**Karlon, Hank**
See   Karlon, William John [Bill]

**Karlon, William John [Bill]**
1909-1964    [BE]
*American baseball player*
* Karlon, Hank

**Karlson, Phil**
See   Karlstein, Philip N.

**Karlstadt [Carlstadt or Karolstadt]**
See   Bodenstein, Andreas Rudolf

**Karlstein, Philip N.** 1908-
[BDF, FC, FD]
*American director*
* Karlson, Phil

**Karlsten, Henry**
See   Lueders, Charles Henry

**Karlweis, Oscar**
See   Karlweiss, Oskar

**Karlweiss, Oskar** 20th c.
*Actor*
* Karlweis, Oscar

**Karmi, Abdul Karim** 1907?-1980
[CA]
*Palestinian-born author and poet*
* Salma, Abu

**Karmu**
See   Warner, Edgar

**Karniewski, Janusz**
See   Wittlin, Tadeusz

**Karnilova, Maria**
See   Dovgolenko, Maria
Karnilovich

**Karno, Fred**
See   Wescott, Frederick

**Karol, Alexander**
See   Kent, Arthur [William
Charles]

**Karol, K. S.**
See   Kewes, Karol

**Karp, David** 1922-    [WD]
*American author and playwright*
* Singer, Adam
* Ware, Wallace

**Karpau, Uladzimir**
See   Karpov, Vladimir

**Karpel, Herb[ert]** 1917-    [BE]
*American baseball player*
* Karpel, Lefty

**Karpel, Lefty**
See   Karpel, Herb[ert]

**Karpeles, Jiri** 1882-1945    [JL]
*Bohemian artist*
* Kars, Jiri

**Karpis, Alvin**
See   Karpowicz, Alvin

**Karpis, Old Creepy**
See   Karpowicz, Alvin

**Karpov, Vladimir** 1912?-1977    [CA]
*Byelorussian author*
* Karpau, Uladzimir

**Karpowicz, Alvin** 1908-
[BLB, MM]
*Canadian-born American
underworld figure*
* Karpis, Alvin
* Karpis, Old Creepy

**Karr, Baldy**
See   Karr, Benjamin Joyce

**Karr, Benjamin Joyce** 1893-1968
[BE]
*American baseball player*
* Karr, Baldy

**Karr, Harold**
See   Katz, Harold H.

**Karr, Patti**
See   Karkalits, Patsy Lou

**Karras, Alex[ander G.]** 1935-    [FB]
*American football player*
* Karras, Tippy Toes
* [The] Mad Duck

**Karras, Tippy Toes**
See   Karras, Alex[ander G.]

**Karriam, Elijah**
See   Poole, Elijah

**Kars, Jiri**
See   Karpeles, Jiri

**Karsavin, Tamara** 1885- ?
[THR, WBD]
*Russian dancer*
* Karsavina, Tamara
* [La] Tamara

**Karsavina, Tamara**
See   Karsavin, Tamara

**Karsch [or Karschin], Anna Luise**
1722-1791    [WBD]
*German poet*
* [The] German Sappho

**Karshish**
See   Creswell, Harry Bulkeley

**Karson, Kit**
See   Miller, Alexander R. G.

**Karst, John Gottlieb** 1893-    [BE]
*American baseball player*
* Karst, King

**Karst, King**
See   Karst, John Gottlieb

**Karta, Nat**
See   Norwood, Victor G[eorge]
C[harles]

**Kartaetschenprinz**
See   William I [Wilhelm Friedrich
Ludwig]

**Karter, Kim**
See   Bradley, Vera Jeanne

**Karter, Kissing Kim**
See   Bradley, Vera Jeanne

**Kartheiser, Frank Clemence**
1888-1968    [BBH]
*American bowler*
* Kartheiser, Midge

**Kartheiser, Midge**
See   Kartheiser, Frank Clemence

**Karweem, Musheed**
See   Powell, Everard Stephen, Sr.

**Kasa [or Kassa]** 1818?-1868
[WBD]
*King of Abyssinia*
* Theodore

**Kasandra, John**
See   Anderson, John W.

**Kasavubu, Joseph** 1910?-1969
[IBW]
*President of the Republic of the
Congo*
* [The] Father of Congo
   Independence

**Kaschnitz, Marie Luise**
See   Von Kaschnitz-Weinberg,
Marie Luise

**Kaselman, Cy**
See   Kaselman, David

**Kaselman, David** 20th c.
*American basketball player*
* Kaselman, Cy

**Kaser, Arthur LeRoy** 1890-1956
*Author*
* Campion, Rose [joint pseudonym
   with Jean Lee Latham and Ruth
   Perry]

**Kasper**
See   Kasper, Herbert

**Kasper, Herbert** 20th c.    [WFA]
*American fashion designer*
* Kasper

**Kassil, Leo**
See   Kassil, Lev Abramovich

**Kassil, Lev Abramovich** 1905-
[SFL]
*Author*
* Kassil, Leo

**Kassman, Larry** 1942-    [RO1]
*American singer*
* Kaye, Larry

**Kasson, Helen Weinbaum** 20th c.
[WGT]
*Author*
* Weinbaum, Helen

**Kassulke, Cowboy**
See   Kassulke, Karl O.

**Kassulke, Karl O.** 1941-    [FB]
*American football player*
* Kassulke, Cowboy

**Kastel, Dandy Phil**
See   Kastel, Philip

**Kastel, Philip** 20th c.
[BLB, MM, PHM]
*American underworld figure*
* Kastel, Dandy Phil

**Kastel, Warren** [house pseudonym,
Ziff-Davis]
See   Geier, Chester S.

**Kastel, Warren** [house pseudonym,
Ziff-Davis]
See   Silverberg, Robert

**Kastle, Herbert D[avid]** 1924-    [CA]
*American author*
* Lee, Herbert d'H.

**Kastos, Emiro**
See   Toro, Fermin

**Kasznar, Kurt S.**
See   Serwischer, Kurt

**Kataev, Valentin Petrovich** 1897-
[MWD]
*Russian author and playwright*
* [The] Noel Coward of Russia

**Katayev, Yevgeni Petrovich**
1903-1942    [CD, TC]
*Russian humorist and journalist*
* Petrov, Eugene [or Yevgeni]

**Katazzi, Mme.** 1830- ?    [PA]
*Author*
* Bernard, Camille

**Katcavage, James R.** 1934-    [FB]
*American football player*
* Katcavage, Kat

**Katcavage, Kat**
See   Katcavage, James R.

**Katch, Kurt**
See   Kac, Isser

**Katcha, Vahe**
See Katchadourian, Vahe

**Katchadourian, Vahe** 1928- [CA]
*French critic, journalist, author*
* Katcha, Vahe

**Katchalski, Aharon** 1914-1972
[JL]
*Israeli chemist*
* Katzir, Aharon

**Kate**
See Barmby, Katherine R.

**[The] Kate Smith of Harlem**
See Thomas, Lillian

**Kate the Great**
See Schmidt, Kate

**[The] Kate Vaughan of the Music
Halls**
See Collins, Lottie

**Katerla, Jozef**
See Zeromski, Stefan

**[The] Katherine de Medici of China**
See Voo-chee

**Kathryn**
See Searle, Kathryn Adrienne

**Katib Chelebi [Noble Secretary]**
See Mustafa ibn-Abdallah

**Katja of Sweden**
See Geiger, Karin Hallberg

**Kato, Joe**
See Valachi, Joseph Michael

**Kato, Tomoichi** 1905-1974 [SC]
*Japanese actor*
* Sawamura, Kunitaro

**Katolique, A. DeFout**
See Ackerman, Forrest J[ames]

**Katsakis, George** 20th c. [RO1]
*American musician*
* Kaye, George

**Katt, William Henry** 1916-
[FC, ITA]
*American actor*
* Williams, Bill

**Katydid**
See McKinney, Kate Slaughter

**Katz, Basho**
See Gatti, Arthur Gerard

**Katz, Eli** 1926- [WECO]
*American cartoonist and publisher*
* Kane, Gil

**Katz, Gilbert** 1934- [BEW]
*American producer and director*
* Cates, Gilbert

**Katz, Harold H.** 1921- [BEW]
*American composer*
* Karr, Harold

**Katz, Hilda**
See Weber, Hulda

**Katz, Joel** 1932- [EMT, IPA, SW]
*American actor, singer, dancer*
* Grey, Joel

**Katz, Joseph** 1924- [BEW]
*American producer and director*
* Cates, Joseph

**Katz, Menke** 1906- [CA, IAW]
*Lithuanian-born poet*
* Badanes, Menke

**Katz, Menke** (Continued)
* Hiat, Elchik

**Katz, Mickey**
See Katz, Myron Meyer

**Katz, Myron Meyer** 1909- [CA]
*American musician, comedian,
author*
* Katz, Mickey

**Katz, Otto** 1900?-1952 [EE]
*Czech intelligence agent*
* Simone, Andre

**Katz, Solomon** 1855-1920 [JL]
*Rumanian philosopher*
* Gherea-Dobrogeanu, Constantin

**Katzenburg, Yasha** 20th c. [BLB]
*American underworld figure*
* King of the Smugglers

**Katzin, Olga** 1896- [LC]
*British author and poet*
* Sagittarius

**Katzir, Aharon**
See Katchalski, Aharon

**Katznelson-Shazar, Rachel**
1888-1975 [CA]
*Russian-born Israeli editor, labor
organizer, author*
* Shazar, Rachel

**Kauffman, Helen Reed** [ASC]
*American poet and songwriter*
* Hammond, Kate

**Kauffman, Ruth [Hammitt]** ?-1952
[WW]
*Author*
* Wright, Ruth

**Kauffmann, Stanley** 1916-
[B10, CA]
*American author and critic*
* Barry, Spranger

**Kaufman, Bob** 1925- [CA, IBW]
*American poet*
* [The] Black American Rimbaud
* Bomkauf

**Kaufman, Denis Arkadievitch**
1896-1954 [BDF, OCF, WEF]
*Russian director*
* Vertov, Dziga

**Kaufman, Henry** 20th c.
*American economist*
* Doom, Dr.

**Kaufman, Isadore** 1892-1978 [CA]
*Austrian-born journalist and author*
* Weer, William

**Kaufman, Louis** 1916- [WW]
*Author*
* Keller, Dan

**Kaufman, M.** 19th c. [PA]
*Author*
* Marchaud, Alfred

**Kaufman, Martin Ellis** 1899-
[ASC]
*American composer and conductor*
* Kaufman, Whitey

**Kaufman, Murray** 1922?-1982
[B10]
*American disc jockey*
* Murray the K

**Kaufman, Oliver** 1917- [CA]
*American screenwriter and author*
* Crawford, Oliver

**Kaufman, Seymour** 1929- [EJ]
*American jazz musician*
* Coleman, Cy

**Kaufman, Sue**
See Barondess, Sue K[aufman]

**Kaufman, Wallace** 1939- [CA]
*American author and columnist*
* Vickers

**Kaufman, Whitey**
See Kaufman, Martin Ellis

**Kaufmann, Ajax**
See Kaufmann, Bob

**Kaufmann, Bob** 1946- [BB]
*American basketball player*
* Kaufmann, Ajax

**Kaufmann, John** 1931- [CA, SAT]
*American author and illustrator*
* Swift, David

**Kaufmann, Mathilde Binder**
1835-1901 [WBD]
*German poet and author*
* George, Amara

**Kaufmann, Nicolaus** 1620?-1687
[WBD]
*German mathematician, astronomer,
engineer*
* Mercator, Nicolaus

**Kaufmann, Walter** 20th c. [WF]
*German actor*
* Mercator, John

**Kaulitz-Niedeck, R.**
See Anderson, Rosa

**Kaumeyer, Dorothy** 1914-
[BDF, CED, FC]
*American actress*
* Lamour, Dorothy

**Kaumudi, Kavita**
See Arnold, Elizabeth

**Kaur, Krishna**
See Oliver, Thelma

**Kautz, Wibs**
See Kautz, Wilbur

**Kautz, Wilbur** 1915- [BB]
*American basketball player*
* Kautz, Wibs

**Kavan, Anna**
See Edmonds, Helen [Woods]

**Kavanagh, Charles Hugh [Charlie]**
1893- [BE]
*American baseball player*
* Kavanagh, Silk

**Kavanagh, Herminie Templeton** 20th
c. [WGT]
*Author*
* Templeton, Herminie

**Kavanagh, P J.**
See Kavanagh, Patrick Joseph
Gregory

**Kavanagh, Patrick Joseph Gregory**
1931- [DLE]
*Irish poet*
* Kavanagh, P J.

**Kavanagh, Silk**
See Kavanagh, Charles Hugh
[Charlie]

**Kavanaugh, Cynthia**
See Daniels, Dorothy

**Kavaphes, Konstantinos** 1863-1933
[LC]
*Egyptian-born poet*
* Cavafy, C. P.

**Kaverin, Veniamin**
See Zilberg, Veniamin A.

**Kawabe, Kinichi**
See Ishitsuji, Keiichi

**Kawalec, W. G.**
See Kawalec, Witold Gracjan

**Kawalec, Witold Gracjan** 1922-
[ART]
*Polish-born sculptor*
* Kawalec, W. G.

**Kawamura, Korekiyo** 1854-1936
[WBD]
*Japanese financier*
* Takahashi, Korekiyo

**Kay, Barbara**
See Kelley, Ethel [May]

**Kay, Bill**
See Kay, Walter B.

**Kay, Charles**
See Piff, Charles

**Kay, Connie**
See Kirnon, Conrad Henry

**Kay, Ernest** 1915- [CA]
*British author*
* Ludlow, George
* Random, Alan

**Kay, George**
See Lambert, Eric

**Kay, Helen**
See Goldfrank, Helen [Colodny]

**Kay, John**
See Krauledat, Joachim

**Kay, Marlene**
See Ackerman, Forrest J[ames]

**Kay, Nora** 20th c. [ART]
*British artist*
* N. K.

**Kay, Patrick Healey** 1904- [THR]
*British dancer*
* Dolin, Anton

**Kay, Phoebe**
See Miner, Virginia Scott

**Kay, Tommy** 1917- [MY]
*American musician*
* Kay, Tony

**Kay, Tony**
See Kay, Tommy

**Kay, Wallace**
See Arter, Wallace E.

**Kay, Walter B.** 1878-1945 [BE]
*American baseball player*
* Kay, Bill
* King Bill

**Kay, Zell**
See Kemp, Roy Z[ell]

**Kaye, A. P.**
See Kaye, Albert Patrick

**Kaye, Albert Patrick** 1878-1946
[BEW]
*British-born actor*
* Kaye, A. P.

**Kaye, Barbara**
See Muir, Barbara K[enrick Gowing]

**Kaye, Barrington** 1924- [WD]
*British author and poet*
* Kaye, Tom

**Kaye, Carol**
See Smith, Carol Louise

**Kaye, Danny**
See Kaminsky [or Kominski?], David Daniel

**Kaye, George**
See Katsakis, George

**Kaye, H. R.**
See Knox, Hugh [Randolph]

**Kaye, Harold B.**
See Kampf, Harold

**Kaye, Irving**
See Kalusky, Isidor

**Kaye, Larry**
See Kassman, Larry

**Kaye, M. M.**
See Kaye, Mary Margaret [Mollie]

**Kaye, Marvin [Nathan]** 1938-
[CA, IAW, WD]
*American author and playwright*
* Goodwin, Eugene D.
* Lavinson, Joseph
* Terry, Saralee

**Kaye, Marx** [house pseudonym]
See Byrne, Stuart J[ames]

**Kaye, Mary Margaret [Mollie]**
1909- [CA]
*British author*
* Hamilton, Mollie
* Kaye, M. M.

**Kaye, Nora**
See Koreff, Nora

**Kaye, Peter**
See Kunatz, Peter

**Kaye, Sparky**
See Kaplan, Philip

**Kaye, Tom**
See Kaye, Barrington

**Kaye, Wilmot**
See Trent, Paul

**Kayenbergh, Marie Emile Albert**
1860-1929 [CD, WBD]
*Belgian poet*
* Giraud, Albert

**Kaylan, Howard**
See Kaplan, Howard Lawrence

**Kayli, Bob**
See Gordy, Robert

**Kayne, Marvin**
See Fearn, John Russell

**[The] Kayo Kid**
See Davis, Howard, Jr.

**Kayser, Ronal.** 20th c. [WW]
*Author*
* Clark, Dale

**Kazak, Edward Terrance**
See Tkacczuk, Edward Terrance

**Kazan, Elia**
See Kazanjoglou, Elia

**Kazanjian, Arlene Francis** 1908-
[BEW, IPA, ITA]
*American actress*
* Francis, Arlene

**Kazanjoglou, Elia** 1909-
[BDF, HT, WEF]
*American director*
* Kazan, Elia

**Kazmaier, Kaz**
See Kazmaier, Richard W., Jr.

**Kazmaier, Richard W., Jr.** 1930-
[FB]
*American football player*
* Everything, Mr.
* Kazmaier, Kaz
* [The] Nassau Nugget

**Kazwini**
See Ibn-Muhammed, Zakarija

**Ke-Kumbha, Kanya**
See McGhee, Norman L., Jr.

**Kea, Adrian Joseph** 1948- [HR]
*Dutch-born hockey player*
* Kea, Ed

**Kea, Ed**
See Kea, Adrian Joseph

**Keane, Constance**
See Ockleman, Constance Frances Marie

**Keane, Ellsworth McG.** 1927-
[CW]
*West Indian poet, musician, educator*
* Keane, Shake

**Keane, John** 1945?-
*American detective*
* Bones, Sherlock

**Keane, Molly** 20th c.
*Irish author and playwright*
* Farrell, M. J.

**Keane, Morris**
See Keane, Thomas

**Keane, Shake**
See Keane, Ellsworth McG.

**Keane, Thomas** ?-1923 [PHM]
*American underworld figure*
* Keane, Morris

**Kearney, Broadway**
See Kearney, Jim

**Kearney, David William**
See Fortescue, John Henry

**Kearney, Jim** 20th c.
*American football player*
* Kearney, Broadway

**Kearney, Ruth Elizabeth**
See Carlson, Ruth [Elizabeth] Kearney

**Kearns, Dasher**
See Kearns, Thomas J. [Tom]

**Kearns, Doc**
See McKernan, John Leo

**Kearns, Jack**
See McKernan, John Leo

**Kearns, Thomas J. [Tom]**
1859-1938 [BE]
*American baseball player*
* Kearns, Dasher

**Kearny, Philip** 1815?-1862
[DNNS, SN]
*American army officer*
* Fighting Phil
* [The] One Armed Devil
* One Armed Phil

**Kearse, Edward Paul [Eddie]**
1918-1968 [BE]
*American baseball player*
* Kearse, Truck

**Kearse, Truck**
See Kearse, Edward Paul [Eddie]

**Keating, Bern**
See Keating, Leo Bernard

**Keating, Chick**
See Keating, Walter Francis

**Keating, H. R. F.**
See Keating, Henry Raymond Fitzwilliam

**Keating, Henry Raymond Fitzwilliam**
1926- [WWS]
*British author and critic*
* Keating, H. R. F.

**Keating, John Henry** 1870-1963
[ASC]
*American composer*
* Udall, Lyn

**Keating, Katherine**
See Satz, Frances

**Keating, Lawrence A.** 1903-1966
[CA]
*American author*
* Bassett, John Keith
* Thomas, H. C.

**Keating, Leo Bernard** 1915-
[CA, SAT]
*Canadian-born American author*
* Keating, Bern

**Keating, Walter Francis**
1891-1959 [BE]
*American baseball player*
* Keating, Chick

**Keatley, Sheila Marjorie** 1912-
[AW]
*British author*
* Avon, Margaret

**Keaton, Buster**
See Keaton, Joseph Francis

**Keaton, Diane**
See Hall, Diane

**Keaton, Joseph Francis** 1895-1966
[BDF, F1, FC]
*American actor and director*
* [The] Great Stone Face
* Keaton, Buster

**Keaton, Robert**
See De Riso, Arpad

**Keats, Duke**
See Keats, Gordon Blanchard

**Keats, Gordon Blanchard**
1895-1972 [CEI, FHE, HK]
*Canadian-born hockey player*
* Keats, Duke

**Keats, Gwendoline** 20th c. [WWL]
*British author*
* Zack

**Keats, Myron**
See Strong, Charles Stanley

**Kebin, Jody**
See Lawrence, Jodi

**Keck, Cactus**
See Keck, Frank Joseph

**Keck, Edith N.** 20th c. [BEW]
*American actress*
* King, Edith

**Keck, Frank Joseph** 1899- [BE]
*American baseball player*
* Keck, Cactus

**Keck, J. Stanton** 1907-1951 [FB]
*American football player*
* Keck, Stan

**Keck, Maud** 20th c. [WW]
*Author*
* Orbison, Keck [joint pseudonym with Olive Orbison]

**Keck, Stan**
See Keck, J. Stanton

**Keddie, Henrietta** 1827-1914
[DEL, DNNF, WWL]
*British author*
* Tytler, Sarah

**Keefe, Cornelius** 1900-1972 [SC]
*American actor*
* Hill, Jack

**Keefe, Dave**
See Keefe, Davis Edwin

**Keefe, Davis Edwin** 1897- [BE]
*American baseball player*
* Keefe, Dave

**Keefe, Mildred Jones** 1896- [IAW]
*American poet*
* Goodspeed, Mildred K.

**Keefe, Timothy John** 1856-1933
[AS, BE]
*American baseball player*
* Sir Timothy

**Keefer, Catherine** [joint pseudonym with Margaret E. (Nettles) Ogan]
See Ogan, George F.

**Keefer, Catherine** [joint pseudonym with George F. Ogan]
See Ogan, Margaret E. [Nettles]

**Keefer, James Barry** 20th c. [LRR]
*American singer*
* Keith

**Keegan, Joe** 1862-1935
[BMH, THR]
*British comedian*
* Elvin, Joe
* Elvin, Little

**Keegan, Mary Heathcott** 1914-
[CA]
*British author*
* Heathcott, Mary
* Raymond, Mary

**Keegan, Robert Charles** 1920- [BE]
*American baseball player*
* Keegan, Smiley

**Keegan, Smiley**
See Keegan, Robert Charles

**Keel, Harold Clifford** 1917?-
[FC, ITA, PMJ]
*American singer and actor*
* Keel, Howard

**Keel, Howard**
See Keel, Harold Clifford

**Keel, John A.**
*See* Kiehle, John Alva

**Keele, Kenneth D[avid]** 1909- [CA]
*British author*
* Cassils, Peter

**Keeler, Bushel Basket**
*See* Keeler, William Henry

**Keeler, Ethel Hilda** 1909-
[EMT, SW]
*Canadian-born actress and dancer*
* Keeler, Ruby

**Keeler, O. B.**
*See* Keeler, Oscar Baun

**Keeler, Oscar Baun** 1882-1950
[GF]
*American journalist*
* Jones's Boswell
* Keeler, O. B.

**Keeler, Ruby**
*See* Keeler, Ethel Hilda

**Keeler, Sugar**
*See* Keeler, Willie

**Keeler, Wee Willie**
*See* Keeler, William Henry

**Keeler, William Henry** 1872-1923
[AS, BAB, PB]
*American baseball player*
* Keeler, Bushel Basket
* Keeler, Wee Willie

**Keeler, Willie** 20th c. [F2]
*Actor*
* Keeler, Sugar

**Keeling, Butch**
*See* Keeling, Melville Sidney

**Keeling, E. B.**
*See* Curl, James Stevens

**Keeling, Melville Sidney** 1905-
[CEI, FHE, HK]
*Canadian-born hockey player*
* Keeling, Butch

**Keen, Frederick Grinham**
1858-1933 [BEW, F2, FC]
*British actor and director*
* Kerr, Frederick

**Keen, Geoffrey** 1895- [BEW]
*British actor and playwright*
* Kerr, Geoffrey

**Keen, Geraldine**
*See* Norman, Geraldine [Lucia]

**Keen, John** [RM, RO2]
*British singer*
* Keen, Speedy

**Keen, Malcolm**
*See* Knee, Malcolm

**Keen, Rod**
*See* Farmer, Philip Jose

**Keen, Royal**
*See* Schrader, F. F.

**Keen, Speedy**
*See* Keen, John

**Keenan, Hank** 20th c. [GW]
*American rodeo performer*
* Keenan, Tinhorn

**Keenan, Harry Leon** 1875-1903
[BE]
*American baseball player*
* Keenan, Kid

**Keenan, James William [Jimmie]**
1889- [BE]
*American baseball player*
* Keenan, Sparkplug

**Keenan, Kid**
*See* Keenan, Harry Leon

**Keenan, Sparkplug**
*See* Keenan, James William
[Jimmie]

**Keenan, Tinhorn**
*See* Keenan, Hank

**Keene, Bob**
*See* Kuhn, Robert

**Keene, Burt**
*See* Bickers, Richard Leslie
Townshend

**Keene, Carolyn** [house pseudonym]
[Stratemeyer Syndicate]
*See* Adams, Harriet S[tratemeyer]

**Keene, Carolyn** [house pseudonym]
[Stratemeyer Syndicate]
*See* Karig, Walter

**Keene, Carolyn** [house pseudonym]
[Stratemeyer Syndicate]
*See* Stratemeyer, Edward L.

**Keene, Faraday**
*See* Jarrett, Cora [Hardy]

**Keene, James**
*See* Cook, William Everett

**Keene, Linda**
*See* McCrory, Florence

**Keene, Rebel**
*See* Keene, William Brown [Bill]

**Keene, Tom**
*See* Duryea, George

**Keene, Ursula**
*See* Cleugh, Sophia

**Keene, William Brown [Bill]** 1891-
[BE]
*American baseball player*
* Keene, Rebel

**Keener, Beans**
*See* Keener, [Joshua] Harry

**Keener, [Joshua] Harry** 1869-1912
[BE]
*American baseball player*
* Keener, Beans

**Keerl, Cap**
*See* Keerl, George Henry

**Keerl, George Henry** 1847-1923
[BE]
*American baseball player*
* Keerl, Cap

**Kees [Keys, Kay or Key], John**
1510-1573 [WBD]
*British physician*
* Caius, John

**Keese, William Linn** [PA]
*Author*
* W. L. K.

**Keesham, Bob** 1927?-
*American television performer*
* Kangaroo, Captain

**Keesing, Nancy**
*See* Hertzberg, Nancy Florence
[Keesing]

**Keevill, Henry J[ohn]** 1914- [CAP]
*British author*
* Allison, Clay
* Bonney, Bill
* Earp, Virgil
* Hardin, Wes
* McLowery, Frank
* Ringo, Johnny

**Kefer, Rose** 1906- [BEW]
*American actress*
* Hobart, Rose

**Kefferstan, Jean**
*See* Pedrick, Jean

**Keghouse**
*See* Wilkins, [Robert] Tim[othy]

**Keif, Aubrey** 20th c. [NAA]
*American editor and writer*
* Grant, Whitney

**Keifer, Katie**
*See* Keifer, Sherman C.

**Keifer, Sherman C.** 1892- [BE]
*American baseball player*
* Keifer, Katie

**Keightley, David Noel** 1932-
[ESF, SFL, WGT]
*British-born American author*
* Keyes, Noel

**Keiki**
*See* Hitotsubashi

**Keimberg, Allyn**
*See* Kimbro, John M.

**Keinath, Charles** 1886-1966 [BB]
*American basketball player*
* Keinath, Kid

**Keinath, Kid**
*See* Keinath, Charles

**Keino, Hezekiah Kipchoge** 1941-
[IBW]
*Kenyan-born track and field athlete*
* [The] Flying Policeman
* Keino, Kip

**Keino, Kip**
*See* Keino, Hezekiah Kipchoge

**Keir, Christine**
*See* Popescu, Christine

**Keiser, Robert** 1862-1932
[ASC, BEW]
*American composer*
* Earl, Mary
* King, Bobo
* King, Robert A.
* Ravenhall, Mrs.
* Wilson, R. A.

**Keister, Wagon Tongue**
*See* Keister, William Hoffman

**Keister, William Hoffman**
1874-1924 [BE]
*American baseball player*
* Keister, Wagon Tongue

**Keitel, Wilhelm** 1882-1946 [BDW]
*German army officer*
* Lakaitel [Little Lackey]

**Keith**
*See* Keefer, James Barry

**Keith, Brian**
*See* Keith, Robert, Jr.

**Keith, Byron**
*See* Schwitters, Cletus Lee

**Keith, Carlton**
*See* Robertson, Keith [Carlton]

**Keith, Colin**
*See* Jameson, Malcolm

**Keith, David**
*See* Steegmuller, Francis

**Keith, Donald** [joint pseudonym with
Keith Monroe]
*See* Monroe, Donald

**Keith, Donald** [joint pseudonym with
Donald Monroe]
*See* Monroe, Keith

**Keith, Frances Guignard Gibbes**
[NAA]
*American author and poet*
* Gibbes, Frances Guignard

**Keith, Hamish**
*See* Chapman, James [Keith]

**Keith, Harrison** [joint pseudonym
with Philip Clark]
*See* Chambliss, John

**Keith, Harrison** [joint pseudonym
with John Chambliss]
*See* Clark, Philip

**Keith, Ian**
*See* Ross, Keith

**Keith, J. Kilmeny**
*See* Malleson, Lucy Beatrice

**Keith, K. Wymand**
*See* Bowen, Leonard Claude

**Keith, Lee**
*See* Sunners, William

**Keith, Leigh**
*See* Gold, Horace Leonard

**Keith, Leslie**
*See* Johnston, Grace L. Keith

**Keith, Marion**
*See* Miller, Mary Ester

**Keith, Penelope**
*See* Hatfield, Penelope

**Keith, Robert**
*See* Applebaum, Stan

**Keith, Robert**
*See* Richey, Robert Keith

**Keith, Robert, Jr.** 1921-
[FC, WEF]
*American actor*
* Keith, Brian

**Keith, Sherwood**
*See* LaCount, Sherwood Keith

**Keith, Stevie**
*See* Jones, Stephen Keith

**Keith X**
*See* Armstrong, Keith F[rancis]
W[hitfield]

**Kel-Kun**
*See* Texier, Edward

**Kelb, George Francis** 1870-1936
[BE]
*American baseball player*
* Kelb, Lefty
* Kelb, Pugger

**Kelb, Lefty**
*See* Kelb, George Francis

**Kelb, Pugger**
See Kelb, George Francis

**Kelcey, Herbert**
See Lamb, Herbert

**Kelcey, Mrs. Herbert** [FFF]
Entertainer
* Hill, Caroline

**Keld**
See Hewitt, Harry S.

**Keler, Bela**
See Von Keller, Adalbert

**Keleti, Agnes**
See Klein, Agnes

**Keliher, Maurice Michael**
1890-1930 [BE]
American baseball player
* Keliher, Mickey

**Keliher, Mickey**
See Keliher, Maurice Michael

**Kelker, Doc**
See Kelker, Frank

**Kelker, Frank** 20th c. [IBW]
American athlete
* Kelker, Doc

**Kell, Everett Lee** 1929- [BE]
American baseball player
* Kell, Skeeter

**Kell, Joseph**
See Wilson, John [Anthony]
Burgess

**Kell, Skeeter**
See Kell, Everett Lee

**Kellard, Ralph**
See Kelly, Thomas J. J.

**Kelleher, Albert Aloysius**
1893-1947 [BE]
American baseball player
* Kelleher, Duke

**Kelleher, Duke**
See Kelleher, Albert Aloysius

**Kellenberger, L. C.** 20th c. [SFP]
Author
* James, Henry

**Keller, Asaph**
See Shamir, Moshe

**Keller, Beverly [Lou]** 20th c. [CA]
American author
* Harwick, B. L.

**Keller, Charles Ernest** 1916-
[BE, BN, PB]
American baseball player
* Keller, King Kong
* Keller, Tarzan

**Keller, Dan**
See Kaufman, Louis

**Keller, David H[enry]** 1880-1963
[WGT]
American author
* Cecil, Henry
* Hubelaire, Jacubus?
* Worth, Amy

**Keller, Gail Faithfull**
See Faithfull, Gail

**Keller, H. A.** 1894- [WWL]
American writer
* Stentor, Ivy

**Keller, Jacob** 1568-1631 [PA]
Author
* Cellarius

**Keller, John E[sten]** 1917- [CA]
American educator and author
* Gato, J. A.

**Keller, King Kong**
See Keller, Charles Ernest

**Keller, Tarzan**
See Keller, Charles Ernest

**Kellerman, Annette** 1887?-1975
[BMH, SC]
Australian-born actress, swimmer,
dancer
* [The] Diving Venus
* [The] Million Dollar Mermaid

**Kellerman, Bernard**
See Kellermann, Bernhard

**Kellermann, Bernhard** 1879-1951
[SFL]
German author
* Kellerman, Bernard

**Kellett, Donald Stafford**
1909-1970 [BE]
American baseball player
* Kellett, Red

**Kellett, Red**
See Kellett, Donald Stafford

**Kelley, Arthur** 1924- [BWW]
American singer
* Kelley, Guitar

**Kelley, Audrey**
See Roos, Audrey [Kelley]

**Kelley, Brian Lee** 1951- [SMG]
American football player
* Kelley, Ralph

**Kelley, Ethel [May]** 20th c. [NAA]
American author
* Kay, Barbara
* Whitney, Lucia

**Kelley, Francis Clement** 1870- ?
[NAA]
Canadian-born clergyman and
author
* Muredach, Myles

**Kelley, Guitar**
See Kelley, Arthur

**Kelley, Hugh** [FFF]
Writer
* Babbler

**Kelley, John** 1907- [BBH]
American hockey coach
* Kelley, Snooks

**Kelley, John Dickman** 1900?-
[EJ, PMJ, WWJ]
American jazz musician
* Kelley, Peck

**Kelley, Peck**
See Kelley, John Dickman

**Kelley, Ralph**
See Kelley, Brian Lee

**Kelley, Ray** 20th c. [BAB]
American baseball player
* Kelley, Speed

**Kelley, Ruby M.**
See Johnson, Ruby Kelley

**Kelley, Snooks**
See Kelley, John

**Kelley, Speed**
See Kelley, Ray

**Kelley, William Darrah** 1814-1890
[SN]
American politician
* [The] Father of the House

**Kelliher, Dan T.** 20th c. [WW]
Author
* Secrist, Kelliher [joint pseudonym
with W. G. Secrist]

**Kelliher, Frank Mortimer**
1899-1956 [BE]
American baseball player
* Kelliher, Yucca

**Kelliher, Yucca**
See Kelliher, Frank Mortimer

**Kellin, Mike**
See Kellin, Myron

**Kellin, Myron** 1922- [BEW]
American actor
* Kellin, Mike

**Kellino, Pamela** 1918- [SW]
British actress
* Mason, Pamela

**Kellino, Will P.**
See Gislingham, William Philip

**Kellner, Esther** [CA]
American author
* Cooper, Esther

**Kellner, Sandor** 1893-1956
Hungarian-born producer and
director
* Korda, Alexander
* Korda, Sandor

**Kellner, Zoltan** 1895-1961 [BF]
Hungarian-born director
* Korda, Zoltan

**Kellock, Archibald P.**
See Mavor, Osborne Henry

**Kellogg, Gene**
See Kellogg, Jean [Defrees]

**Kellogg, Grace**
See Griffith-Shaw, Grace Kellogg

**Kellogg, Jean [Defrees]** 1916-
[CA, SAT]
American author
* Jackson, Sally
* Kellogg, Gene

**Kellogg, P. C.** [PA]
Author
* Comstock, Hark

**Kellogg, Raymond N.** 1875- ? [BE]
American baseball player
* Nelson, Ray[mond Nelson]

**Kellogg, Vernon Lyman** 1867- ?
[NAA]
American zoologist and author
* Vernon, Max

**Kellough, Deacon**
See Kellough, Manuel

**Kellough, Manuel** 20th c. [RO2]
American musician
* Kellough, Deacon

**Kellow, Kathleen**
See Hibbert, Eleanor Alice
[Burford]

**Kellum, Win**
See Kellum, Winford Ansley

**Kellum, Winford Ansley**
1876-1951 [BE]
Canadian-born baseball player
* Kellum, Win

**Kelly, A. M.** [PA]
Author
* [The] Virginia Confederate

**Kelly, Albert Michael** 1884-1961
[BE]
American baseball player
* Kelly, Red

**Kelly, Battleship**
See Kelly, John Robert

**Kelly, Big Bill**
See Kelly, William Henry [Bill]

**Kelly, Bubbles**
See Kelly, Mary

**Kelly, Caroline E.** [PA]
Author
* C. E. K.

**Kelly, Cathleen** 1917- [BEW]
American actress
* Cordell, Cathleen

**Kelly, Charles J.** 1859-1918 [BEW]
Canadian-born actor
* Ross, Charles J.

**Kelly, Cue Ball**
See Zingale, Carl

**Kelly, David Wiliford** 1892-1947
[SC]
American actor
* Dudlah, David

**Kelly, Donald Patrick** 1924-1966
[SC]
American actor
* O'Kelly, Don

**Kelly, Eleanor Mercein** 1880- ?
[NAA]
American author
* Mercein, Eleanor

**Kelly, Father**
See Kelly, John Francis

**Kelly, George Lange** 1895-
[BE, PB]
American baseball player
* Kelly, High Pockets

**Kelly, George R.** 1897-1954 [BLB]
American bootlegger and kidnapper
* Kelly, Machine Gun
* Moore, E. W.
* Tichenor, J. C.

**Kelly, Glenn**
See McNeilly, Mildred Masterson

**Kelly, Gloria** 1915-1934 [SC]
American actress and dancer
* Warner, Gloria

**Kelly, Guy**
See Moore, Nicholas

**Kelly, Gwen Nita** 1922- [IAW]
Australian author
* Heath, Nita

**Kelly, Harlem Tommy**
See Kelly, Tommy

**Kelly, High Pockets**
See Kelly, George Lange

**Kelly, Honest John**
See Kelly, John

**Kelly, Hugo**
See  Mitchell, Ugo

**Kelly, James**
See  Borah, Leo Arthur

**Kelly, James** 1915-1964  [SC]
*American actor*
* Tiny

**Kelly, James Edward** 1855-1933
[WBD]
*American sculptor*
* [The] Sculptor of American
  History

**Kelly, James J.** 1928-  [IBW]
*American air force officer*
* [The] Master of Air Defense

**Kelly, James Plunkett** 1920-  [CA]
*Irish television executive and author*
* Plunkett, James

**Kelly, James Robert [Jim]**
See  Taggart, Robert John

**Kelly, Jeep**
See  Kelly, John-Paul

**Kelly, John** 1856-1926  [BE]
*American baseball player and
manager*
* Kelly, Honest John

**Kelly, John** 1862-1895  [RBE]
*Irish-born boxer*
* Dempsey, Jack
* [The] Nonpareil

**Kelly, John Francis** 1859- ?  [BE]
*American baseball player*
* Kelly, Father
* Kelly, Kick

**Kelly, John-Paul** 1959-  [SMG]
*Canadian-born hockey player*
* Kelly, Jeep

**Kelly, John Robert** 1946-  [FHE]
*Canadian-born hockey player*
* Kelly, Battleship

**Kelly, Jonathan F.** 1820- ?
[FFF, PA]
*American author*
* Falconbridge
* Humphries, Jack
* Stampede

**Kelly, Karen** 1935-  [CA]
*American author and columnist*
* Lee, Kay

**Kelly, Kenneth** 1943-  [RO2]
*American singer*
* Kelly, Wally

**Kelly, Kick**
See  Kelly, John Francis

**Kelly, King**
See  Kelly, Michael Joseph

**Kelly, Leonard Patrick** 1927-
[B10, CEI, FHE]
*Canadian hockey player and
member of Parliament*
* Kelly, Red

**Kelly, Luther Sage** 1849-1928
[B10]
*American scout*
* Kelly, Yellowstone

**Kelly, Machine Gun**
See  Kelly, George R.

**Kelly, Martha Mott [Patsy]** 20th c.
[CC, EMD, WW]
*Author*
* Patrick, Q. [joint pseudonym with
  Richard Wilson Webb]

**Kelly, Martha Rose** 1914-  [CA]
*American author*
* Kelly, Marty

**Kelly, Marty**
See  Kelly, Martha Rose

**Kelly, Mary** 1895-1941  [SC]
*American actress*
* Kelly, Bubbles

**Kelly, Mary Eva**  [PA]
*Author*
* Eva

**Kelly, Maurice Anthony** 1931-
[CA]
*British marine engineer and writer*
* Springfield

**Kelly, Michael Joseph** 1857-1894
[AS, BAB, PB]
*American baseball player*
* Kelly, King
* [The] Ten Thousand Dollar
  Beauty

**Kelly, Patsy**
See  Kelly, Sarah Veronica Rose

**Kelly, Paul**
See  Vaccarelli, Paolo Antonini

**Kelly, Pauline Agnes** 1936-  [CA]
*American author*
* Barrett, Raina

**Kelly, Pep**
See  Kelly, Regis J.

**Kelly, Ralph**
See  Geis, Darlene [Stern]

**Kelly, Red**
See  Kelly, Albert Michael

**Kelly, Red**
See  Kelly, Leonard Patrick

**Kelly, Red**
See  Kelly, Thomas Raymond

**Kelly, Regis J.** 1914-  [CEI]
*Canadian-born hockey player*
* Kelly, Pep

**Kelly, Ren**
See  Kelly, Reynolds Joseph

**Kelly, Reynolds Joseph** 1899-1963
[BE]
*American baseball player*
* Kelly, Ren

**Kelly, Robert Brown [Bob]**
1884-1949  [BE]
*American baseball player*
* Kelly, Speed

**Kelly, Robert James** 1950-
[FHE, SMG]
*Canadian-born hockey player*
* [The] Hound

**Kelly, Sarah Veronica Rose**
1910-1931  [EMT]
*American actress*
* Kelly, Patsy

**Kelly, Speed**
See  Kelly, Robert Brown [Bob]

**Kelly, Spider**
See  Kelly, Tommy

**Kelly, Thomas J. J.** 1884-1955
[BEW]
*American actor*
* Kellard, Ralph

**Kelly, Thomas Raymond** 1927-
[DAM, EJ]
*American jazz musician*
* Kelly, Red

**Kelly, Tim** 1937-  [WD]
*American author, playwright,
screenwriter*
* Bibolet, R. H.

**Kelly, Tommy** 1867- ?
[AS, BX, RBE]
*American boxer*
* [The] Harlem Spider
* Kelly, Harlem Tommy
* Kelly, Spider

**Kelly, Wally**
See  Kelly, Kenneth

**Kelly, Wild Bill**
See  Kelly, William

**Kelly, William** 20th c.  [FB]
*American football player*
* Kelly, Wild Bill

**Kelly, William Henry [Bill]** 1899-
[BE]
*American baseball player*
* Kelly, Big Bill

**Kelly, Willie**
See  Sykes, Roosevelt

**Kelly, Yellowstone**
See  Kelly, Luther Sage

**Keloid**
See  Burton, Leonard Lamming

**Kelsall, Charles** 19th c.  [PA]
*Author*
* Craft, Zachary

**Kelser, Greg** 1957-
*American basketball player*
* Special K

**Kelsey, Joan Marshall** 1907-  [CA]
*British author*
* Grant, Joan

**Kelt, John**
See  Forbes-Robertson, Eric

**Kelton, Aryan**
See  Kelton, Aryon Lewis

**Kelton, Aryon Lewis** 1892-  [SFL]
*Author*
* Kelton, Aryan

**Kelton, Elmer** 1926-  [CA, WD]
*American author*
* Hawk, Alex
* McElroy, Lee

**Kelty, Chief**
See  Kelty, John E. Joseph

**Kelty, John E. Joseph** 1867- ?  [BE]
*American baseball player*
* Kelty, Chief

**Kelway, Christine**
See  Gwinn, Christine Margaret

**Kemal Atatuerk**
See  Mustafa [or Mustapha],
Kemal

**Kemal Bey**
See  Mehmed Namik

**Kemal Pasha**
See  Mustafa [or Mustapha],
Kemal

**Kemal, Yashar**
See  Gokceli, Yashar Kemal

**Kemble, Frances A.** 1829- ?  [PA]
*Author*
* Butler, Mrs.

**Kemble, Frankie**
See  Clayburgh, Isabella

**Kemman, Herbert Frederick**
1887-1963  [BE]
*American baseball player*
* Herbert, Fred[erick]

**Kemmerer, Dutch**
See  Kemmerer, Russell Paul

**Kemmerer, Russell Paul** 1931-
[BE]
*American baseball player*
* Kemmerer, Dutch
* Kemmerer, Rusty

**Kemmerer, Rusty**
See  Kemmerer, Russell Paul

**Kemner, Dutch**
See  Kemner, Herman John

**Kemner, Herman John** 1899-  [BE]
*American baseball player*
* Kemner, Dutch

**Kemp, Alan** 1938-  [BMH]
*British female impersonator*
* Lana

**Kemp, Alec M.** 20th c.  [MBF]
*British author*
* Richards, Frank [house
  pseudonym]

**Kemp, H.**
See  Hersey, Harold

**Kemp, Jeremy**
See  Walker, Edmund

**Kemp, Jumbo**
See  Kemp, Nicholas John

**Kemp, Mrs. Maurice F.**  [FFF]
*Entertainer*
* Phipps, Beatrix

**Kemp, Nicholas John** 1956-  [DC]
*British cricketer*
* Kemp, Jumbo
* Kemp, Nick Nack

**Kemp, Nick Nack**
See  Kemp, Nicholas John

**Kemp, Roy Z[ell]** 1910-  [CA]
*American poet*
* Kay, Zell

**Kemp, T. C.**
See  Kemp, Thomas Charles

**Kemp, Thomas Charles** 1891-1955
[THR]
*British drama critic*
* Kemp, T. C.

**Kempadoo, Peter** 1926-  [CW]
*Guyanese author*
* Lauchmonen

**Kempener [or Kempeneer], Peter de**
1503-1580  [WBD]
*Belgian-born painter*
* Campana, Pedro de

**Kemper, Louise Brega** 1872?-1951
[BEW]
*Canadian-born actress*
* Latham, Hope

**Kempf, Edward J.** 20th c.   [BBH]
*American roller skating supporter and adviser*
* Uncle Ed

**Kempferhausen**
*See* Gillies, Robert Pierce

**Kempis, Thomas a**
*See* Charlier, Jean

**Kempis, Thomas A.**
*See* Hammerken, Thomas

**Kempner, Alfred** 1867-1948
[EWL, WBD]
*German author and critic*
* Kerr, Alfred

**Kempner, Lydia Rabinowitsch** 1871-
?   [LAO]
*Russian-born bacteriologist and author*
* Rabinowitsch, Lydia

**Kempshall, Hubert Kim** 1934-
[ART]
*British artist*
* K. K.

**Kempshall, Julia A.**   [PA]
*Author*
* Willis, Julia A.

**Kempster, Bert**
*See* Gibbons, Harry Hornaby
Clifford

**Kempton, Barney**
*See* Kempton, George

**Kempton, George** 20th c.   [BBH]
*Irish soccer player*
* Kempton, Barney

**Kempton, Jean Welch** 1914-
[CA, SAT]
*American author*
* Welch, Jean-Louise

**Kenbrovin, Jaan**
*See* Vincent, Nathaniel Hawthorne

**Kendal, Dorothy May** 20th c.
[THR]
*British actress*
* Grimston, Dorothy May

**Kendal, June**
*See* Stiff, Dorothy Aileen

**Kendal, [Dame] Madge**
*See* Robertson, Margaret

**Kendal, William Hunter**
*See* Grimston, William Hunter

**Kendall, Carlton** 1895-   [NAA]
*American author*
* Ladnek, Odlaw

**Kendall, Edward P.**   [PA]
*Author*
* Galoot

**Kendall, John**
*See* Brash, Margaret Maud

**Kendall, John Kaye** 1869- ?   [LAO]
*British poet*
* Dum Dum

**Kendall, Katherine Githa** 20th c.
[WWL]
*British playwright*
* Sowerby, Githa

**Kendall, Kay**
*See* McCarthy, Justine

**Kendall, Lace**
*See* Stoutenburg, Adrien [Pearl]

**Kendall, Marie** 1873-1964   [BMH]
*British entertainer*
* Baby Chester

**Kendall, Stephen** 20th c.   [WWL]
*British writer*
* Jay, Thomas

**Kendall, Suzy**
*See* Harrison, Frieda

**Kendall, Tony**
*See* Stella, Luciano

**Kendall, Willmoore** 1909-   [CA]
*American educator and author*
* Monk, Alan

**Kendrake, Carleton**
*See* Gardner, Erle Stanley

**Kendrick, Baynard H[ardwick]**
1894-1977   [CA]
*American author*
* Hayward, Richard

**Kendrick, Frances**   [DNNS, RH]
*Daughter of Sir William Kendrick, second baronet*
* [The] Berkshire Lady

**Kendrick, Mrs. F. M.**   [FFF]
*Entertainer*
* Bray, Adele

**Kendricks, James**
*See* Fox, Gardner Francis

**Kendrix, Moss Hyles** 1917-   [IBW]
*American public relations counselor*
* [The] Crown Prince of Public
Relations

**Kenian, Paul Roger**
*See* Clifford, Martin

**Kenley, John**
*See* Zayanskovsky, John Kremchek

**Kenna, Ed[ward Benninghaus]**
1877-1972   [BE]
*American baseball player*
* [The] Pitching Poet

**Kenna, Ed[ward Aloysious]** 1897-
[BE]
*American baseball player*
* Kenna, Scrap Iron

**Kenna, Hinky Dink**
*See* Kenna, Michael

**Kenna, Michael** 20th c.
*American underworld figure*
* Kenna, Hinky Dink

**Kenna, Scrap Iron**
*See* Kenna, Ed[ward Aloysious]

**Kennard, Jane**
*See* Lothian, Jane

**Kennedy, Albert R.** 1876-1969   [FB]
*American football coach*
* Kennedy, Doc

**Kennedy, Alfred G.** 1885-1940
[SC]
*American actor*
* Elmore, Bruce

**Kennedy, Arthur, Jr.** 1943-   [IBW]
*American speedboat racer*
* Kennedy, Butch

**Kennedy, Benjamin Hall**
1804-1889   [FFF]
*British scholar*
* [The] Nestor of English
Scholarship

**Kennedy, Beulah**
*See* Rafael, Beulah K.

**Kennedy, Bill** 1938-   [BB]
*American basketball player*
* Kennedy, Pickles

**Kennedy, Brickyard**
*See* Kennedy, William V.

**Kennedy, Butch**
*See* Kennedy, Arthur, Jr.

**Kennedy, Doc**
*See* Kennedy, Albert R.

**Kennedy, Doc**
*See* Kennedy, Michael Joseph

**Kennedy, Douglas**
*See* Douglas, Keith

**Kennedy, Elena**
*See* Ortea, Virginia Elena

**Kennedy, Elliot**
*See* Godfrey, Lionel Robert
Holcombe

**Kennedy, Florence**
*See* Huntley, Mrs. J. H.

**Kennedy, G. A. Studdert** 20th c.
[WWL]
*British author*
* Woodbine Willie

**Kennedy, Gene**
*See* Kennedy, Kenneth

**Kennedy, Gerald [Hamilton]** 1907-
[CA]
*American clergyman and author*
* Kish, G. Hobab

**Kennedy, Happiness**
*See* Kennedy, Hershall

**Kennedy, Hershall** 20th c.   [RO2]
*American musician*
* Kennedy, Happiness

**Kennedy, Howard**
*See* Woolfolk, Josiah Pitts

**Kennedy, John Edward** 1941-
*American baseball player*
* Super Sub

**Kennedy, John Fitzgerald [Jack]**
1917-1963
*American president*
* J. F. K.

**Kennedy, John Pendleton**
1795-1870   [FFF, PA, WBD]
*American politician and author*
* Littleton, Mark
* Second Thoughts, Solomon

**Kennedy, Joseph Charles** 1929-
[B10, CA]
*American poet and educator*
* Kennedy, X. J.

**Kennedy, Kenneth** 1933-   [CM]
*American radio executive*
* Kennedy, Gene

**Kennedy, Lefty**
*See* Kennedy, Montia Calvin

**Kennedy, Lefty**
*See* Kennedy, William Aulton

**Kennedy, Lena**
*See* Smith, Lena [Kennedy]

**Kennedy, Ma**
*See* Kennedy, Minnie

**Kennedy, Mary** 20th c.   [CA]
*American author, actress, playwright*
* Emerson, Mary Lee

**Kennedy, Matthew** 1908-1957   [BB]
*American basketball referee*
* Kennedy, Pat

**Kennedy, Merna**
*See* Kahler, Maude

**Kennedy, Michael Joseph**
1855-1920   [BE]
*American baseball player*
* Kennedy, Doc

**Kennedy, Milward**
*See* Burge, Milward Rodon
Kennedy

**Kennedy, Minnie** 20th c.
*Mother of evangelist Aimee Semple McPherson*
* Kennedy, Ma

**Kennedy, Monte**
*See* Kennedy, Montia Calvin

**Kennedy, Montia Calvin** 1922-
[BE]
*American baseball player*
* Kennedy, Lefty
* Kennedy, Monte

**Kennedy, Mrs. Frank**   [FFF]
*Entertainer*
* Sinclair, Lottie

**Kennedy, P.**
*See* Hersey, Harold

**Kennedy, Pat**
*See* Kennedy, Matthew

**Kennedy, Pickles**
*See* Kennedy, Bill

**Kennedy, Robert Francis [Bobby]**
1925-1968
*American politician*
* R. F. K.

**Kennedy, Sherman Montgomery**
1877-1944   [BE]
*American baseball player*
* Kennedy, Snapper

**Kennedy, Snapper**
*See* Kennedy, Sherman
Montgomery

**Kennedy, Teeder**
*See* Kennedy, Theodore S. [Ted]

**Kennedy, Theodore S. [Ted]** 1925-
[CEI, FHE, HK]
*Canadian-born hockey player*
* Kennedy, Teeder

**Kennedy, William Aulton** 1921-
[BE]
*American baseball player*
* Kennedy, Lefty

**Kennedy, William V.** 1868-1915
[AS, BE, DGS]
*American baseball player*
* Kennedy, Brickyard

**Kennedy, X. J.**
*See* Kennedy, Joseph Charles

**Kenneggy, Richard**
*See* Nettell, Richard [Geoffrey]

**Kenner, Scipio A.** 20th c. [FFF]
*American writer*
* Essay Kaigh

**Kenneth**
*See* Battelle, Kenneth

**Kenneth, Esther Sarah**
*See* Babson, Mrs. E. M.

**Kenneth, Keith** 1887-1966 [SC]
*British-born actor and author*
* Hitchcock, Keith

**Kenneth I** ?- 858 [WBD]
*King of Scotland*
* MacAlpine

**Kennett, [Houn] Jiyu**
*See* Kennett, Peggy Teresa Nancy

**Kennett, Peggy Teresa Nancy**
1924- [CA]
*British-born American author and Buddhist priest*
* Kennett, [Houn] Jiyu

**Kennie, Jessie**
*See* MacPherson, Jessie Ingram

**Kennington, [Gilbert] Alan** 1906-
[WW]
*Author*
* Grant, Alan

**Kenny, Charles J.**
*See* Gardner, Erle Stanley

**Kenny, Ellsworth Newcomb** 1909-
[CA]
*American author*
* Newcomb, Ellsworth

**Kenny, George**
*See* Whitcomb, Kenneth G.

**Kenny, Kathryn**
*See* Bowden, Joan Chase

**Kenny, Kathryn** [house pseudonym]
*See* Stack, Nicolete Meredith

**Kenny, Lee**
*See* Kenny, Leola

**Kenny, Leola** 1892-1956 [SC]
*American actress*
* Kenny, Lee

**Keno, Elizabeth** 1920-1969 [FC]
*American actress*
* Green, Mitzi

**Kenon, Larry** 1953?-
*American basketball player*
* Dr. K

**[The] Kensington Martyr**
*See* Caroline

**[The] Kensington Megaera**
*See* Caroline

**Kent**
*See* Fisher, Sidney George

**Kent, Alexander**
*See* Reeman, Douglas [Edward]

**Kent, Arden**
*See* Marion, Frieda

**Kent, Arnold**
*See* Manetti, Lido

**Kent, Arthur [William Charles]**
1925- [AW, WD]
*British author*
* Boswell, James
* Bradwell, James
* Dubois, M.
* Granados, Paul
* Karol, Alexander
* Stamper, Alex
* Vane, Bret

**Kent, Barbara**
*See* Cloutman, Barbara

**Kent, Barry**
*See* Sautereau, Barry

**Kent, [Sister] Benen**
*See* Kent, Margaret Agnes

**Kent, Beverley**
*See* Gannon, E. J.

**Kent, Brad** [house pseudonym, Curtis
Warren]
*See* Hughes, Den[n]is [Talbot]

**Kent, Brad** [house pseudonym, Curtis
Warren]
*See* Hugi, Maurice Gaspard

**Kent, [William] Charles [Mark]**
1823-1902 [DEL, PA]
*British author and poet*
* K. C.
* Oscotean
* Rochester, Mark
* Templar

**Kent, Christopher**
*See* Kjellin, Alf

**Kent, Christopher**
*See* Palmer, William Thomas

**Kent, Clark**
*See* Kosco, Andrew John

**Kent, Corita** 1919?-
*American artist*
* [The] Painting Nun

**Kent, David**
*See* Birney, [Herman] Hoffman

**Kent, Edward**
*See* Sukulov, Victor

**Kent, Elizabeth**
*See* Rochester, George Ernest

**Kent, Ethel**
*See* Jackson, Ethel

**Kent, George**
*See* Stacher, Joseph

**Kent, George** [PA]
*Author*
* Bramwahld, Theodore

**Kent, Gerald**
*See* Johnston, Gerald McIntosh

**Kent, Gordon**
*See* Tubb, Edwin Charles

**Kent, James** 1763-1847 [FFF]
*American jurist*
* [The] American Blackstone

**Kent, Jean**
*See* Field, Joan

**Kent, John** 19th c. [FFF]
*Canadian editor*
* Fairford, Alan

**Kent, Katherine**
*See* Dial, Joan

**Kent, Kelvin** [joint pseudonym with
Henry Kuttner]
*See* Barnes, Arthur K[elvin]

**Kent, Kelvin** [joint pseudonym with
Arthur K(elvin) Barnes]
*See* Kuttner, Henry

**Kent, Lena**
*See* King, Lettice A.

**Kent, Louise Andrews** 1886-1969
[ANT, CA]
*American author and columnist*
* Tempest, Theresa

**Kent, Mallory**
*See* Lowndes, Robert Augustine
Ward

**Kent, Margaret Agnes** 1917-
[IWM]
*American music instructor*
* Kent, [Sister] Benen

**Kent, Marjorie** 1919-1971 [SC]
*American actress and ballet dancer*
* Kent, Marsha

**Kent, Marsha**
*See* Kent, Marjorie

**Kent, Mary**
*See* Harrison, Mary Kent

**Kent, Michael**
*See* Brown, Beatrice Bradshaw

**Kent, Pete**
*See* Richardson, Gladwell

**Kent, Philip**
*See* Bulmer, [Henry] Kenneth

**Kent, Richard**
*See* Owen, Frank

**Kent, Robert**
*See* Blackley, Douglas

**Kent, Rockwell** 1882-1971
[CA, CAA, SAT]
*American artist and writer*
* Hogarth, William, Jr.
* R. K.

**Kent, Simon**
*See* Catto, Max

**Kent, Tony**
*See* Crechales, Anthony George

**Kent, Willis**
*See* Collison, Wilson

**[The] Kentish Moll**
*See* Carlton, Mary

**[The] Kentish Samson**
*See* Joy, Richard

**Kenton, Bernard J.**
*See* Siegel, Jerome

**Kenton, Egon F.**
*See* Kornstein, Egon F.

**Kenton, Margaret Ann Borden**
1935- [EJ]
*American singer*
* Richards, Ann

**Kenton, Maxwell** [joint pseudonym
with Terry Southern]
*See* Hoffenberg, Mason

**Kenton, Maxwell** [joint pseudonym
with Mason Hoffenberg]
*See* Southern, Terry

**Kenton, Warren** 1933- [CA, WD]
*British author*
* Halevi, Zev Ben Shimon

**[The] Kentucky Colonel**
*See* Combs, Earle Bryan

**Kentucky Colonel**
*See* Maynard, Colonel

**[The] Kentucky Folk Singer**
*See* Osborne, Jimmie

**[The] Kentucky Mountain Boy**
*See* Kincaid, Bradley

**[The] Kentucky Rifle**
*See* Combs, Glen

**[The] Kentucky Rosebud**
*See* Camnitz, Samuel Howard

**Kentucky Slim**
*See* Howard, James Audra

**[The] Kentucky Wonder**
*See* Akeman, David

**Kenward, Jean**
*See* Chesterman, Jean

**Kenworthy, Duke**
*See* Kenworthy, William Jennings

**Kenworthy, Hugh**
*See* Walker, Rowland

**Kenworthy, William Jennings**
1887-1950 [BE]
*American baseball player*
* Kenworthy, Duke

**Kenyatta, Charles**
*See* Morris, Charles

**Kenyatta, Jomo**
*See* Ngengi, Kamau wa

**Kenyon, C. F.** 1881-1926 [BBD]
*British critic and writer*
* Cumberland, Gerald

**Kenyon, [Margaret] Doris** 1897-1979
*American actress and singer*
* Taylor, Margaret

**Kenyon, John** 1784-1856 [SN]
*British poet*
* [The] Apostle of Cheerfulness

**Kenyon, Michael** 1931- [WD]
*British author*
* Forbes, Daniel

**Kenyon, Neil**
*See* McKinnon, Neil

**Kenyon, Paul**
*See* Friedland, Nathaniel

**Kenyon, Robert O.**
*See* Kuttner, Henry

**Keogh, Lilian Gilmore** 1927- [CA]
*Irish-born author and educator*
* Patrick, Lilian

**Kepac, Coil**
*See* Ackerman, Forrest J[ames]

**Kepler, Johannes [or John]**
1571-1630   [SN]
*German astronomer*
* [The] Father of Modern
Astronomy

**Keplinger, Mrs. E. M. Patterson**
[FFF]
*Poet*
* Queen of Hearts

**Keppel, Sonia**
*See*   Cubitt, Sonia Rosemary

**Ker, W. P.**
*See*   Ker, William Paton

**Ker, William Paton** 1855-1923
[LC]
*Scottish-born educator and author*
* Ker, W. P.

**Keraunos [or Ceraunus]**
*See*   Ptolemy

**Kerba, Buck**
*See*   Baker, George Cornelius

**Kerby, Susan Alice**
*See*   Burton, [Alice] Elizabeth

**Kerekes, Tibor** 1893-1969   [CAP]
*Hungarian-born historian and
author*
* Rotarius

**Kerhouel, Gaetan**
*See*   Vigne, Paul

**Keriazakos, Constantine Nicholas**
1931-   [BE]
*American baseball player*
* Keriazakos, Gus

**Keriazakos, Gus**
*See*   Keriazakos, Constantine
Nicholas

**Kerigan, Florence** 1896-
[CA, SAT]
*American author*
* Kerry, Frances

**Kerlay, Allis**
*See*   Ackerman, Forrest J[ames]

**Kerlin, Cy**
*See*   Kerlin, Orie Milton

**Kerlin, Louise** 1879?-1965
[F2, FC]
*American actress*
* Dresser, Louise

**Kerlin, Orie Milton** 1891-   [BE]
*American baseball player*
* Kerlin, Cy

**Kermond, Evelyn Carolyn Conway**
1927-   [WD]
*American author*
* Conway, E. Carolyn

**Kermoyan, Kalem Missak** 1925-
[BEW]
*American actor and singer*
* Kermoyan, Michael

**Kermoyan, Michael**
*See*   Kermoyan, Kalem Missak

**Kern, Alfred**
*See*   Cohen, Alfred

**Kern, E. R.**
*See*   Kerner, Fred

**Kern, Gregory** [house pseudonym]
*See*   Tubb, Edwin Charles

**Kernan, J. Frank**   [FFF]
*American author*
* Florry

**Kernell, Mrs. John**   [FFF]
*Entertainer*
* Vivian, Emily

**Kerner, Fred** 1921-   [CA]
*Canadian publisher and author*
* Fredericks, Frohm
* Kern, E. R.
* Kerr, Frederick
* Thaler, M. N.

**Kernoff, Harry** 1900-   [ART]
*Irish painter and engraver*
* K.

**Kerouac, Jack**
*See*   Kerouac, Jean-Louis Lebrid
De

**Kerouac, Jean-Louis Lebrid De**
1922-1969   [CA, TCL]
*American author*
* Incogniteau, Jean-Louis
* Jean Louis
* Kerouac, Jack
* Kerouac, John

**Kerouac, John**
*See*   Kerouac, Jean-Louis Lebrid
De

**Keroul, Henri**
*See*   Queyroul, Henri

**Kerpestein, Leroy** 1914-   [BEW]
*American choreographer*
* Loring, Eugene

**Kerr, Albert** 20th c.   [FHE]
*Canadian-born hockey player*
* Kerr, Dubbie

**Kerr, Alfred**
*See*   Kempner, Alfred

**Kerr, Ben**
*See*   Ard, William [Thomas]

**Kerr, Buddy**
*See*   Kerr, John Joseph

**Kerr, Deborah**
*See*   Kerr-Trimmer, Deborah Jane

**Kerr, Doc**
*See*   Kerr, John Jonas

**Kerr, Dubbie**
*See*   Kerr, Albert

**Kerr, Frederick**
*See*   Keen, Frederick Grinham

**Kerr, Frederick**
*See*   Kerner, Fred

**Kerr, Geoffrey**
*See*   Keen, Geoffrey

**Kerr, James Lennox** 1899-1963
[TCC]
*Scottish author*
* Dawlish, Peter

**Kerr, Joe**
*See*   Ackerman, Forrest J[ames]

**Kerr, John** 1932-   [BB]
*American basketball player*
* Kerr, Red

**Kerr, John Jonas** ?-1937   [BE]
*American baseball player*
* Kerr, Doc

**Kerr, John Joseph** 1922-   [BE]
*American baseball player*
* Kerr, Buddy

**Kerr, John O'Connell**
*See*   Whittet, George Sorley

**Kerr, Larry**
*See*   Kerr, Lorence

**Kerr, Lorence** ?-1968   [SC]
*Actor*
* Kerr, Larry

**Kerr, M. E.**
*See*   Meaker, Marijane

**Kerr, Norman D.**
*See*   Sieber, Sam Dixon

**Kerr, Orpheus C.**
*See*   Newell, Robert Henry

**Kerr, Red**
*See*   Kerr, John

**Kerr, Sherrill**
*See*   Magruder, Julia

**Kerr-Trimmer, Deborah Jane**
1921-   [BDF, BEW, FC]
*Scottish-born actress*
* Kerr, Deborah

**Kerry, Frances**
*See*   Kerigan, Florence

**Kerry, Lois**
*See*   Arquette, Lois S[teinmetz]

**Kerry, Norman**
*See*   Kaiser, Arnold

**Kerschner, Irvin** 1923-   [FD, WEF]
*American director*
* Kershner, Irvin

**Kershau, Beulah Sevenney** 1914-
[IAW]
*American poet and singer*
* Beulah

**Kershaw, John Hugh D'Allenger**
1931-   [AW, CA]
*British author*
* D'Allenger, Hugh

**Kershaw, Nelson** 20th c.   [ECM]
*American country-western performer*
* Kershaw, Pee Wee

**Kershaw, Pee Wee**
*See*   Kershaw, Nelson

**Kershaw, Peter**
*See*   Lucie-Smith, [John] Edward
[McKenzie]

**Kershaw, Russell Lee** 20th c.
[ECM]
*American country-western performer*
* Kershaw, Rusty

**Kershaw, Rusty**
*See*   Kershaw, Russell Lee

**Kershaw, Willette**
*See*   Mansfield, Willette

**Kershner, Irvin**
*See*   Kerschner, Irvin

**Kertesz, Mihaly** 1888-1962
[BDF, FC, FD]
*Hungarian-born director*
* Curtiz, Michael

**Kertesz-Gabry, Edith**
*See*   Gancs, Edith

**Kessel, Lipmann** 1914-   [CA]
*South African-born author*
* Paul, Daniel

**Kesselman, Judi R[osenthal]** 1934-
[CA]
*American writer*
* Turkel, Pauline

**Kessler, Henry** 1847-1900   [BE]
*American baseball player*
* Kessler, Lucky

**Kessler, Lucky**
*See*   Kessler, Henry

**Kesteloot, Lilyan** 1931-   [CA]
*Belgian-born educator and author*
* Lagneau-Kesteloot, Lilyan

**Kesteven, G. R.**
*See*   Crosher, Geoffry Robins

**Kestin, Helen**   [FFF]
*American writer*
* Vaughn, Kate

**Kestner, Paul** ?-1918   [BMH]
*Polish-born juggler*
* Cinquevalli, Paul
* [The] Human Billiard Table
* [The] Little Flying Devil

**Ketch, Jack**
*See*   Hervey, Thomas Kibble

**Ketch, Jack**
*See*   Tibbetts, John C[arter]

**Ketcham, James**   [FFF]
*American politician*
* Whispering Jimmie

**Ketchel, Cyclone**
*See*   Kiecal, Stanislaus

**Ketchel, Stanley**
*See*   Kiecal, Stanislaus

**Ketchum, Black Jack**
*See*   Ketchum, Thomas

**Ketchum, Philip** 1902-   [WW]
*Author*
* Saunders, Carl McK.

**Ketchum, Thomas** 1866-1901
[BLB]
*American murderer and train robber*
* Ketchum, Black Jack

**Ketola, Veli Pekka** 1948-   [SMG]
*Finnish-born hockey player*
* Ketola, Vello

**Ketola, Vello**
*See*   Ketola, Veli Pekka

**Kettell, Samuel** 1800-1885
[FFF, RH]
*American author and editor*
* Parley, Peter
* Peeping Tom
* Titterwell, Timothy

**Kettering, Boss**
*See*   Kettering, Charles Franklin

**Kettering, Charles Franklin**
1876-1958
*American automobile executive and
inventor*
* Kettering, Boss

**Kettle, Peter**
*See*   Glover, Denis [James
Matthews]

**Kettlewell, Marjorie** 1893-    [THR]
*British actress and singer*
* Gordon, Marjorie

**Keunius**
See  Joncures, Victoria

**Keveren, A. G.** 20th c.    [MBF]
*British author*
* Veren, Gilbert

**Kevern, Barbara**
See  Shepherd, Donald [Lee]

**Keverne, Richard**
See  Hosken, Clifford James
Wheeler

**Kevin, Jodi**
See  Lawrence, Jodi

**Kevin, Neil** 1903-    [CAT]
*Irish clergyman and author*
* Boyne, Don

**Kew, Andrew**
See  Morton, A. Q.

**Kewes, Karol** 1924-    [CA]
*Polish-born author*
* Karol, K. S.

**Kewley, Jennifer**
See  Draskau, Jennifer

**Kewstub, F.** 20th c.    [WWL]
*British playwright*
* Francks, Hawley

**Key, Ellen Karoline Sofia**
1849-1926    [WBD]
*Swedish feminist and author*
* [The] Pallas of Sweden

**Key, Julian**
See  Keymolen, Julien

**Key, Mrs. Barton**    [FFF]
*Entertainer*
* Jansen, Marie

**Key note**
See  Shepard, Nathan

**[The] Key of all the Universe**
See  Medici, Giovanni de

**Key, R. Blake**    [PA]
*Author*
* Palmer, Hackle

**Key, Samuel Whittell** 1874- ?
[WWL]
*British author*
* Key, Uel

**Key, Uel**
See  Key, Samuel Whittell

**Keyes, Noel**
See  Keightley, David Noel

**Keyes, Steve** 20th c.    [OBW]
*American baseball player*
* Keyes, Youngie

**Keyes, Youngie**
See  Keyes, Steve

**Keymolen, Julien** 1930-    [GA]
*Belgian graphic artist*
* Key, Julian

**Keyne, Gordon**
See  Bedford-Jones, Henry [James
O'Brien]

**Keynes, Helen Mary** 20th c.    [WW]
*Author*
* Hunter, Clementine

**Keynes, J. M.**
See  Keynes, John Maynard

**Keynes, John Maynard** 1883-1946
[LC]
*British economist*
* Keynes, J. M.

**Keys, Bunch**
See  Keys, Nelson

**Keys, Crash**
See  Keys, Leonard F.

**Keys, Durham**
See  Garton, Durham Keith

**Keys, John** 1910-1970    [BF]
*British director, author, painter*
* Carstairs, John Paddy

**Keys, Leonard F.** 1935-    [IBW]
*American helicopter pilot*
* Keys, Crash

**Keys, Nelson** 1886-1939    [EMT]
*British actor, singer, dancer*
* Keys, Bunch

**Keystone, Oliver**
See  Mantinband, James H.

**Khacidovitch, Tamara** 1917-
[THR]
*Russian-born dancer*
* Toumanova, Tamara

**Khair Eddin [or ed-Din]**
See  Khizr

**Khalaf, Salah** 20th c.
*Palestinian terrorist*
* Abu Iyad

**Khaled [or Khalid]** 582- 642
[HN, RH, WBD]
*Conqueror of Syria*
* [The] Scourge of Infidels
* [The] Sword of Allah
* [The] Sword of God

**[The] Khalifa [Adviser]**
See  Abdullah et Taaisha

**Khalkhali, [Ayatollah] Sadegh**
*Iranian jurist*
* [The] Hanging Judge

**Khan, Abdul**
See  Robinson, William Ellsworth

**Khan, Abdullah Jaffa Bey** 1930-
[IPA]
*American choreographer*
* Joffrey, Robert

**Khan, Carlo**
See  Fox, Charles James

**Khan, Chaka**
See  Stevens, Yvette Marie

**Khan, Inti**
See  Khan, Intikhab Alam

**Khan, Intikhab Alam** 1941-    [DC]
*Indian-born cricketer*
* Khan, Inti

**Khan, Javed Miandad** 1957-    [DC]
*Pakistani-born cricketer*
* Mummy Daddy
* Noon Ghunna

**Khan, Noor Inayat** 1914-1944
[BDW, EE, WWW]
*Russian-born intelligence agent for
Britain*
* Madeleine [code name used
   during World War II]

**Khan, Noor Inayat** (Continued)
* Regnier, Jeanne-Marie

**Khanshendel, Chiron**
See  Rose, Wendy

**Khare, Narayan Bhaskar** 1882-
[CAP]
*Indian author*
* Bapu

**Khaury, Herbert** 1933-
[IPA, LRR, RO2]
*American entertainer*
* Dover, Derry
* Foxglove, Judas K.
* [The] Human Canary
* Love, Larry
* Tiny Tim

**Khaury, Mrs. Herbert Buckingham**
20th c.
*Former wife of American
entertainer, Tiny Tim [Herbert
Khaury]*
* Miss Vicky

**Khayyam, Omar Hakim**
See  Alexander, Dave

**Khazan, Jibreel**
See  Blair, Ezell, Jr.

**[The] Khazar**
See  Leo IV

**Kheraskov, Mikhail Matveevich**
1733-1807    [WBD]
*Russian poet*
* [The] Dean of Russian Literature

**Kherdian, Nonny Hogrogian** 1932-
[TBJ]
*American author and illustrator*
* Hogrogian, Nonny

**Khizr** 1466?-1546    [HN, WBD]
*Sultan of Algiers*
* Barbarossa II
* Khair Eddin [or ed-Din]
* Red Beard

**Khlebnikov, Velimir**
See  Khlebnikov, Viktor
Vladimirovich

**Khlebnikov, Viktor Vladimirovich**
1885-1922    [CD, EWL, TCL]
*Russian poet*
* Khlebnikov, Velimir

**Khokhlov, Nicolai** 20th c.    [EE]
*Russian intelligence agent*
* Wittgenstein, Oberleutnant

**Khomeini, [Ayatollah] Ruhollah**
See  Mustafavi, Ruhollah

**Khorrum [or Khurram]** 1592-1662
[SN, WBD]
*Emperor of Hindustan*
* [The] King of the World
* Shah Jehan

**Khosru I [or Chosroes]** 531- 579
[DNNS, RH, WBD]
*King of Persia*
* Anushirvan [Having an Immortal
   Soul]
* [The] Great
* [The] Just King
* [The] Magnanimous
* [The] Magnificent
* [The] Noble Soul

**Khosru II [or Chosroes]** ?- 628
[FFF, RH, WBD]
*King of Persia*
* Parviz

**Khosru II [or Chosroes]** (Continued)
* [The] Victorious

**Khun, Bernard Daniel** 1899-1956
[BE]
*American baseball player*
* Khun, Bub

**Khun, Bub**
See  Khun, Bernard Daniel

**Ki Dost, Zamin**
See  Armstrong, Willimina Leonora

**Ki He Gha [Leader]**
See  Owens, Steve E.

**Kiam, Alexander** 1894-1954
[WFA]
*Mexican-born fashion designer*
* Kiam, Omar

**Kiam, Omar**
See  Kiam, Alexander

**Kibbie, Hod**
See  Kibbie, Horace Kent

**Kibbie, Horace Kent** 1903-    [BE]
*American baseball player*
* Kibbie, Hod

**Kibble, Happy**
See  Kibble, John Wesley [Jack]

**Kibble, John Wesley [Jack]** 1892-
[BE]
*American baseball player*
* Kibble, Happy

**Kichaven, Charna E.** 1925-1971
[SC]
*American actress and musician*
* Haven, Charna

**[The] Kid**
See  Cauthen, Steve

**[The] Kid**
See  Emerson, William Robert

**[The] Kid**
See  Maloney, David Wilfred

**[The] Kid**
See  McCarthy, Thomas Francis
Michael [Tommy]

**[The] Kid**
See  Moeller, Ron[ald Ralph]

**[The] Kid**
See  Muehfeldt, Freddie

**[The] Kid**
See  Norris, Walter Oster

**[The] Kid**
See  Williams, Theodore Samuel
[Ted]

**Kid Gloves Harrison**
See  Harrison, Benjamin

**[The] Kid in Tennis Shoes**
See  Henning, Doug[las James]

**[The] Kid with the Gauze in His Jaws**
See  Torme, Mel[vin Howard]

**Kidd, E. Culver** 1915?-
*American politician*
* [The] Silver Fox

**Kidd, J. Roby**
See  Kidd, James Robbins

**Kidd, James Robbins** 1915-    [CA]
*Canadian author and educator*
* Kidd, J. Roby

**Kidd, Kenneth** 1935?- [BWW]
*American singer*
* Prez Kenneth

**Kidd, Mary** 1900-1941 [SC]
*American actress and opera singer*
* Lewis, Mary

**Kidd, Michael**
See Greenwald, Milton

**Kidd, Mildred Virginia** 20th c.
[WGT]
*American author*
* Blish, Virginia

**Kidd, Russ**
See Donson, Cyril

**Kidd, Walter Evans** 1905?-
[CA, NAA]
*American author and poet*
* Dublin, Conrad Padraic
* Pendleton, Conrad Padraic

**Kidd, [Captain] William**
1645?-1701 [HN]
*Pirate*
* [The] Wizard of the Sea

**Kidder, Frederic** 1804-1885 [PA]
*Author*
* Orient
* Sagadahoc

**Kidder, Joseph** [PA]
*Author*
* Reddick

**Kidder, Mrs. Edward E.** [FFF]
*Entertainer*
* Raymond, Augusta

**Kiecal, Stanislaus** 1886?-1910
[AS, BX, RBE]
*American boxer*
* Ketchel, Cyclone
* Ketchel, Stanley
* [The] Michigan Assassin
* [The] Montana Wonder

**Kiefer, Adolph** 20th c. [BBH]
*American swimmer*
* Kiefer, Sonny

**Kiefer, Bill**
See Kiefer, Tillman W.

**Kiefer, Harlem Joe**
See Kiefer, Joseph William [Joe]

**Kiefer, Joseph William [Joe]** 1899-
[BE]
*American baseball player*
* Kiefer, Harlem Joe
* Kiefer, Smoke

**Kiefer, Middleton** [joint pseudonym
with Harry Middleton]
See Kiefer, Warren David

**Kiefer, Middleton** [joint pseudonym
with Warren David Kiefer]
See Middleton, Harry

**Kiefer, Smoke**
See Kiefer, Joseph William [Joe]

**Kiefer, Sonny**
See Kiefer, Adolph

**Kiefer, Tillman W.** 1898- [CA]
*American businessman and writer*
* Kiefer, Bill

**Kiefer, Warren David** 1930- [WD]
*American author and screenwriter*
* Kiefer, Middleton [joint
pseudonym with Harry
Middleton]

**Kiehle, John Alva** 20th c. [SFL]
*Author*
* Keel, John A.

**Kiehtreiber, Albert Konrad** 1887-
[EWL]
*Austrian author, poet, artist*
* Guetersloh, Albert Paris

**Kien-Long** 1711-1799 [FFF, SN]
*Chinese emperor*
* [The] Illustrious

**Kienzle, Raymond Nicholas** 1911-
[BDF, FC, FD]
*American director*
* Ray, Nicholas

**Kienzle, William X[avier]** 1928-
[CA]
*American author*
* Boyle, Mark

**Kiepper, Shirley Morgan** 1933-
[CA]
*British-born author*
* Morgan, Shirley

**Kieran, John** 1892?-1981
*American sportswriter*
* Information Please

**Kies, Margaret** 1910- [FC]
*American actress*
* Lindsay, Margaret

**Kieschner, Sidney** 1906-
[FC, LC, TC]
*American playwright*
* Kingsley, Sidney

**Kiesler, Hedwig Eva Marie** 1913?-
[F2, FC, OCF]
*Austrian-born actress*
* Kieslerova, Hedy
* Lamarr, Hedy

**Kieslerova, Hedy**
See Kiesler, Hedwig Eva Marie

**Kiffer, Raoul** 20th c. [EE]
*British intelligence agent*
* Paul [code name used during
World War II]

**Kigi, Takataro**
See Hayashi, Takashi

**Kiick, James F. [Jim]** 1946- [FB]
*American football player*
* Cassidy, Butch

**Kikauka, Talis Talivaldis Tully**
1929- [IAW]
*Latvian-born author*
* Indrikis, Vecais
* Vitols, Valdis

**Kilborne, Virginia Wylie** 1912-
[CA]
*American author*
* Egbert, Virginia Wylie

**Kilbourn, Timothy**
See Montgomery, Richmond Ames

**Kilbourne, Fannie**
See Schubart, Fannie Kilbourne

**Kilbracken, John [Raymond Godley]**
1920- [CA]
*British journalist and author*
* Godley, John

**Kilburger, C. Eyna**
See Bluthgen, Clara

**Kilburn, Henry**
See Rigg, Henry Kilburn

**Kilby, Morgan**
See Bump, Franklin E., Jr.

**Kildare, John**
See King, John Boswell

**Kildare, Maurice**
See Richardson, Gladwell

**Kiley, Francis Thomas** 1895-1962
[BE]
*American baseball player*
* Kane, Francis Thomas [Frank]
* Kane, Sugar

**Kilgallen, Milton**
See Roberts, Kenneth [Lewis]

**Kilhullen, Joseph Isadore**
1888-1922 [BE]
*American baseball player*
* Kilhullen, Pat

**Kilhullen, Pat**
See Kilhullen, Joseph Isadore

**Kilian** ?- 697 [HN]
*Saint*
* [The] Patron Saint of Wuerzburg

**Kilina, Patricia**
See Tarnawsky, Patricia W[arren]

**Kilkenny, Killer**
See Kilkenny, Michael David
[Mike]

**Kilkenny, Michael David [Mike]**
1945- [PB]
*Canadian-born baseball player*
* Kilkenny, Killer

**Kill, Don** 20th c. [BS]
*American magician*
* [The] Amazing Kildon

**Killebrew, Harmon Clayton** 1936-
[ALR, BE]
*American baseball player*
* Killebrew, Killer

**Killebrew, Killer**
See Killebrew, Harmon Clayton

**Killefer, Lollypop**
See Killefer, Wade

**Killefer, Red**
See Killefer, Wade

**Killefer, Reindeer Bill**
See Killefer, William Levier, Jr.

**Killefer, Wade** 1884-1958 [BE]
*American baseball player*
* Killefer, Lollypop
* Killefer, Red

**Killefer, William Levier, Jr.**
1888-1960 [AS, BE, PB]
*American baseball player*
* Killefer, Reindeer Bill

**Killen, Buddy**
See Killen, W. D.

**Killen, Frank Bissell** 1870-1939
[BE]
*American baseball player*
* Killen, Lefty

**Killen, Lefty**
See Killen, Frank Bissell

**Killen, W. D.** 20th c. [CM]
*American music publisher and
producer*
* Killen, Buddy

**[The] Killer**
See Lewis, Jerry Lee

**[The] Killer**
See Madden, Owen

**[The] Killer**
See Miller, Bill

**Killian, Edwin Henry** 1876-1928
[BE]
*American baseball player*
* Killian, Twilight Ed

**Killian, James R.** 20th c. [ET]
*Educator and television
commissioner*
* [The] Father of Public Television

**Killian, Larry**
See Wellen, Edward [Paul]

**Killian, Twilight Ed**
See Killian, Edwin Henry

**Killigrew, Thomas** 1612-1683 [SN]
*British playwright*
* Merry Droll

**Killingsworth, Katherine** 1928-
[EJ]
*American singer*
* Noble, Kitty

**Killingworthe, George** 16th c. [RH]
*Russian courtier*
* [The] Bearded

**Killion, John Joseph** 1859-1937
[AS, RBE]
*American boxer*
* Kilrain, Jake

**Killough, [Karen] Lee** 1942- [CA]
*American author*
* Hood, Sarah
* Leigh, Kathy

**Kilmer, Aline** 1888-1941 [CAT]
*American poet*
* Murray, Aline

**Kilmer, Billy** 20th c.
*American football player*
* Kilmer, Whiskey

**Kilmer, Whiskey**
See Kilmer, Billy

**Kilosa**
See Hosmer, Harriet

**Kilpatrick, Ben** 20th c. [BLB]
*American train robber*
* Arnold, Benjamin
* [The] Tall Texan

**Kilpatrick, [Hugh] Judson**
1836-1881 [FFF, SN]
*American army officer*
* Kilpatrick, Kill
* [The] Raider

**Kilpatrick, Kill**
See Kilpatrick, [Hugh] Judson

**Kilpatrick, Sarah**
See Underwood, Mavis Eileen

**Kilrain, Jake**
See Killion, John Joseph

**Kilrea, Hector J.** 1907- [HK]
*Canadian-born hockey player*
* Kilrea, Hurricane Hec

**Kilrea, Hurricane Hec**
See Kilrea, Hector J.

**Kilreon, Beth**
See Walker, Barbara K[erlin]

**Kilroy, Bucko**
See Kilroy, Frank

**Kilroy, Frank** 20th c.   [SMG]
*American football team staff member*
* Kilroy, Bucko

**Kilroy, Marilyn** 1927-   [IBW]
*American singer*
* Leighton, Mauri Lynn

**Kilroy, Matches**
See Kilroy, Matthew Aloysius

**Kilroy, Matthew Aloysius**
1866-1940   [BE]
*American baseball player*
* Kilroy, Matches

**Kilting** [code name used during World War II]
See Truman, Harry

**Kim**
See Simenon, Georges [Joseph Christian]

**Kim, Andre** 20th c.   [WFA]
*Korean fashion designer*
* [The] Pierre Cardin of Korea

**Kim, Andy**
See Joachim, Andrew

**Kim, C. I. Eugene**
See Kim, Chong-ik Eugene

**Kim, Chong-ik Eugene** 1930-
[IAW]
*Korean-born author*
* Kim, C. I. Eugene

**Kim, Sang Soo** 20th c.   [B10]
*Korean karate expert*
* Kim, Tiger

**Kim, Tiger**
See Kim, Sang Soo

**Kimball, Atkinson** [joint pseudonym with Richard B(owland) Kimball]
See Kimball, Grace Lucia [Atkinson]

**Kimball, Atkinson** [joint pseudonym with Grace Lucia (Atkinson) Kimball]
See Kimball, Richard B[owland]

**Kimball, George**   [PA]
*Author*
* Hudson, Frank

**Kimball, Grace Lucia** [Atkinson]
1875-1923   [WGT]
*Author*
* Kimball, Atkinson [joint pseudonym with Richard B(owland) Kimball]

**Kimball, Louis**
See Conaughy, Louis

**Kimball, Nancy**
See Upson, Norma

**Kimball, Newell W.** 1915-   [BE]
*American baseball player*
* Kimball, Newt

**Kimball, Newt**
See Kimball, Newell W.

**Kimball, Pauline**
See Garrett, Pauline

**Kimball, Richard B[owland]** 20th c.
[WGT]
*Author*
* Kimball, Atkinson [joint pseudonym with Grace Lucia (Atkinson) Kimball]

**Kimball, Thomas** 20th c.   [SMG]
*American basketball player*
* Kimball, Toby

**Kimball, Toby**
See Kimball, Thomas

**Kimber, Bobbie**
See Kimberley, Robert

**Kimberley, Earl of**
See Wodehouse, John

**Kimberley, Hugh**
See Morland, Nigel

**Kimberley, Robert** 1918-   [BMH]
*British ventriloquist and female impersonator*
* Kimber, Bobbie

**Kimberlin, Harry Lydle** 1909-   [BE]
*American baseball player*
* Kimberlin, Murphy

**Kimberlin, Murphy**
See Kimberlin, Harry Lydle

**Kimbro, Jean**
See Kimbro, John M.

**Kimbro, John M.** 1929-   [CA]
*American author, playwright, composer*
* Allyson, Kym
* Ashton, Ann
* Bramwell, Charlotte
* Jaxon, Milt
* Keimberg, Allyn
* Kimbro, Jean
* Kimbrough, Katheryn
* Lambec, Zoltan
* Milton, Jack

**Kimbrough, Jarrin' Jawn**
See Kimbrough, John

**Kimbrough, John** 20th c.   [FB]
*American football player*
* Kimbrough, Jarrin' Jawn

**Kimbrough, Katheryn**
See Kimbro, John M.

**Kimbrough, Lena**
See Beaman, Lottie Kimbrough

**Kimchi, David** 1160-1235   [WBD]
*Grammarian and Biblical scholar*
* ReDaK

**Kime, Harold Lee [Hal]** 1899-1939
[BE]
*American baseball player*
* Kime, Lefty

**Kime, Lefty**
See Kime, Harold Lee [Hal]

**Kimsey, Chad**
See Kimsey, Clyde Elias

**Kimsey, Clyde Elias** 1905-1942
[BE]
*American baseball player*
* Kimsey, Chad

**Kinahan, [Lady] Coralie** 1924-
[ART]
*British painter*
* C. I. de B. K.

**Kinard, Bruiser**
See Kinard, Frank M.

**Kinard, Frank M.** 1914-   [FB]
*American football player*
* Kinard, Bruiser

**Kinau, Johann** 1880-1916   [WBD]
*German author*
* Fock, Gorch

**Kincaid, Alan**
See Rikhoff, James C.

**Kincaid, Aron**
See Williams, Norman Neale, III

**Kincaid, Bradley** 1895-
[CME, CWG]
*American country-western performer*
* America's Foremost Folk Singer
* [The] Dean of the Folk Singers
* [The] Kentucky Mountain Boy
* [The] Original Authentic Folk Singer

**Kind, K. K.**
See Walker, Katherine C.

**Kindall, Gerald Donald** 1935-   [BE]
*American baseball player*
* Kindall, Slim

**Kindall, Slim**
See Kindall, Gerald Donald

**Kindberg, Agnes Marie** 1906-
[ART]
*British artist*
* A. K.
* Marie

**Kinder, Ellis Raymond** 1914-1968
[BE, PB]
*American baseball player*
* Kinder, Kinny
* Kinder, Old Folks
* Kinder, Old Granddad

**Kinder, Kinny**
See Kinder, Ellis Raymond

**Kinder, Old Folks**
See Kinder, Ellis Raymond

**Kinder, Old Granddad**
See Kinder, Ellis Raymond

**[The] Kinderhook Fox**
See Van Buren, Martin

**[The] Kinderhook Roarer**
See Vanderpoel, Aaron

**Kindi, al- [Abu Yusef al-Kindi]** 9th
c.   [WBD]
*Arab physician, philosopher, commentator*
* [The] Great Astrologer
* [The] Philosopher of the Arabs
* [The] Phoenix of His Age

**Kindler, Asta**
See Hicken, Una

**Kindratiw, Rostyslaw** 1945-   [AES]
*Austrian-born American soccer player*
* Kindratiw, Rusty

**Kindratiw, Rusty**
See Kindratiw, Rostyslaw

**Kiner, Ralph McPherran** 1922-
[BAB]
*American baseball player*
* Ozark Ike

**Kines, Pat Decker** 1937-
[CA, SAT]
*American author and educator*
* Tapio, Pat Decker

**[The] King**
See Brewster, Kingman, Jr.

**[The] King**
See Gable, Clark

**[The] King**
See Linderman, Bill

**[The] King**
See Petty, Richard

**[The] King**
See Presley, Elvis Aaron

**[The] King**
See Solomon, Eddie, Jr.

**King, Al**
See Smith, Alvin K.

**King, Alan**
See Kniberg, Irwin

**King, Alan** 1946-   [RM, RO2]
*British musician*
* King, Bam

**King, Albert**
See Nelson, Albert

**King, Albert** 1903-1943   [ASC]
*American musician*
* King, Jack

**King, Albert** 1924-   [ESF]
*British author and journalist*
* Bannon, Mark
* Conrad, Paul
* Gibson, Floyd
* Howell, Scott
* King, Christopher
* Muller, Paul

**King, Alice**
See Hamilton, Alice King

**King, Alison**
See Martini, Teri

**King, Alyce**
See Driggs, Alyce

**King, Andrea**
See Barry, Georgetta

**King Andrew the First**
See Jackson, Andrew

**King Andy the First**
See Johnson, Andrew

**King, Annette**
See Reid, Charlotte T.

**King, Archer**
See Klein, Archer

**King, Arthur**
See Cain, Arthur H[omer]

**King, Arthur**
See Lake, Kenneth R[obert]

**King Arthur**
See Scargill, Andy

**[The] King Arthur of the Stage**
See Macready, William Charles

**King, B. B.**
See King, Riley B.

**King, Bam**
See King, Alan

**King, Ben E.**
See Nelson, Benjamin Earl

**King Bill**
See Kay, Walter B.

**King, Bobo**
See Keiser, Robert

**King Bomba**
See Ferdinand II

**King, Bruce** 1897?-1976 [B10, CA]
American astrologer, publisher, inventor, author
* Zolar

**King, Bubbles**
See King, Evelyn

**King Carl**
See Hubbell, Carl Owen

**King Carl**
See Snavely, Carl G.

**King, Carole**
See Klein, Carole

**King, Caroline Blanche**
See Campion, Katherine

**King, Carroll E.** 1893- [NAA]
American journalist
* Asabore
* King, Worth
* Sarlo

**King, Champagne**
See King, Evelyn

**King, Charles Criswell** 20th c. [IA]
American journalist
* Criswell, Jeron

**King, Charles Daly** 1895-1963
[WGT, WW]
American author
* Courtney, Robert
* Phelan, Jeremiah

**King, Charles Frederick**
See Koenig, Charles Frederick

**King, Charles Gilbert** 1930- [BE]
American baseball player
* King, Chick

**King, Chick**
See King, Charles Gilbert

**King, Christopher**
See King, Albert

**King, [James] Clifford** 1914- [WW]
Author
* Fry, Pete

**King Coll [or Colley]**
See Cibber, Colley

**King, Country**
See King, Jim

**King David**
See Ruffin, David

**King, Dennis**
See Pratt, Dennis

**King, Dig**
See King, Lynn Paul

**King, Dolly**
See King, William

**King, Donna**
See Driggs, Donna

**[The] King Dowager**
See Durfort de Duras, Louis de

**King, Edith**
See Keck, Edith N.

**King, Edward** 1897-1968 [SC]
American actor
* Baker, Eddie

**King, Ernest** 1916?-1975 [FIR]
American country-western performer
* [The] Washboard King

**King, Ernest Joseph** 1878-1956
[CND]
American military leader
* Colleen [code name used during World War II]

**King, Evelyn** 1960?- [IBW]
American singer
* King, Bubbles
* King, Champagne

**King, Florence** 20th c. [AN]
American author
* Cynthia
* King, Veronica
* Reed, Emmett X.
* Stavros, Niko
* Winston, Mike

**King, Francis H[enry]** 1923-
[AW, CA, WD]
British author and poet
* Cauldwell, Frank

**King, Frank**
See Cochrane, Gordon Stanley

**King, Frank** 1892-1958 [WW]
Author
* Conrad, Clive

**King, Frank** 1914-
[CME, CWG, DAM]
American country-western performer
* King, Pee Wee

**King Franklin**
See Roosevelt, Franklin Delano

**[The] King Freak of New York**
See Firbank, Louis

**King, Fred**
See Slaughter, Marion T.

**King Freddie**
See Mutesa, Edward, II

**King, George** 1899-1966 [BF]
British director and producer
* King of the Quota Quickies

**King Henri's King**
See Chicot

**King, Hilary**
See Dickson, James Grierson

**King, Horace Maybray** 1901- [CA]
British politician and author
* Maybray-King, Horace

**King Ivory Lee**
See Semien, Lee

**King, Jack**
See Dowling, Allen

**King, Jack**
See King, Albert

**King James**
See Rempe, Jim

**King Jesus**
See Hacket, William

**King, Jim** 1941- [BB]
American basketball player
* King, Country

**King, John**
See Angersola, John

**King, John**
See McKeag, Ernest L[ionel]

**King, John Boswell** 20th c. [AW]
British author
* Boswell, John
* Kildare, John

**King, Kathryn** 20th c. [BBH]
American softball player
* King, Sis

**King Kevin**
See White, Kevin Hagan

**King Kong Kahn**
See Kahn, Edwin Bernard [Eddie]

**King Kong Keller**
See Keller, Charles Ernest

**King Kong Korab**
See Korab, Jerry

**King Larry**
See Lajoie, Napoleon

**King Leo**
See Massey, Harry

**King, Leslie Lynch, Jr.** 1913-
[FAP]
American president
* Ford, Gerald Rudolph [Jerry]
* Ford, Junie

**King, Lettice A.** 1888?- [CW]
Jamaican poet and author
* Kent, Lena

**King, Lewis**
See Capuano, Luigi

**King Louis**
See Narcisse, Louis H.

**King, Louisa Yeomans** [NAA]
American author
* Yeomans, Louisa

**King, Louise**
See Driggs, Louise

**King, Luther**
See Johnson, Lucius Brinson

**King, Lynn Paul** 1907-1972 [BE]
American baseball player
* King, Dig

**King, Marjorie Cameron** 1909-
[CA]
Canadian-born writer
* King, Peggy Cameron

**King, Marshal Ney** 1848-1911
[BE]
American baseball player
* King, Mart

**King, Mart**
See King, Marshal Ney

**King, Martha Bennett** 1902- [FFA]
American singer
* King, Marty

**King, Martin**
See Marks, Stan[ley]

**King, Martin Luther, Jr.**
See King, Michael Luther, Jr.

**King Martin the First**
See Van Buren, Martin

**King, Marty**
See King, Martha Bennett

**King, Mary Louise** 1911- [CA]
American author
* Johnson, Mary Louise

**King, Maxine Joyce** 1944- [B10]
American air force officer and diver
* King, Micki

**King, Michael**
See Buse, Renee

**King, Michael Luther, Jr.**
1929-1968 [IBW, SAT]
American clergyman and civil rights leader
* King, Martin Luther, Jr.
* [The] Prince of Peace

**King, Micki**
See King, Maxine Joyce

**King, Moira** 1926- [FC]
Scottish-born dancer and actress
* Shearer, Moira

**King, Moses** 1884-1956 [EJS]
American boxing coach
* King, Mosey

**King, Mosey**
See King, Moses

**King, Mrs. John J.** [FFF]
Entertainer
* Martinez, Isidora

**King, Mrs. O. A.** [FFF]
Entertainer
* Guernsey, Minerva

**King, Mule**
See King, Reggie

**King, [Miss] Nancy**
See King, William Rufus

**King, Norman A.**
See Tralins, S[andor] Robert
[Bob]

**King, Nosmo**
See Watson, Vernon

**King, O. B. Royal**
See King, Oscar Benjamin

**[The] King of Afro Beat**
See Anikulapo-Kuti, Fela

**[The] King of Arragon**
See Arrigoni, Carlo

**[The] King of Baritones**
See Battistini, Mattia

**[The] King of Bark**
See Christopher III

**[The] King of Bath**
See Nash, Richard

**[The] King of Boogie Woogie**
See Santiago, Burnell

**[The] King of Book-Collectors**
See Harley, Robert [First Earl of Oxford]

**[The] King of Bourges**
See Charles VII

**[The] King of Brave Men**
*See*   Henry IV [or Henri]

**[The] King of Burlesque**
*See*   O'Hanlon, George Samuel

**[The] King of Cards**
*See*   Morganstern, Carl

**[The] King of Cards**
*See*   Weiss, Ehrich

**[The] King of Cling**
*See*   Burrows, Stephen

**[The] King of Comedy**
*See*   Sinnott, Michael

**[The] King of Corn**
*See*   Jones, Lindley Armstrong

**[The] King of Cotswold**
*See*   Brydges, Grey

**[The] King of Country and Western Music**
*See*   Cash, John R. [Johnny]

**[The] King of Country Music**
*See*   Acuff, Roy

**[The] King of Country Songwriters**
*See*   Howard, Harlan

**[The] King of Critics**
*See*   Heyne, Christian Gottlob

**[The] King of Dance**
*See*   Vestris, Gaetano Apollino Balthazar

**[The] King of Decadence**
*See*   Firbank, Louis

**[The] King of Delta Blues Singers**
*See*   Johnson, Robert

**[The] King of Depravity**
*See*   Crowley, Edward Alexander

**[The] King of Diamonds**
*See*   Winston, Harry

**[The] King of Dullness**
*See*   Cibber, Colley

**[The] King of England's Viceroy**
*See*   Louis XVIII

**[The] King of Exeter Change**
*See*   Clark, Thomas

**[The] King of Feuilletons**
*See*   Janin, Jules Gabriel

**[The] King of Fire**
*See*   Bonaparte, Napoleon

**[The] King of Gospel**
*See*   Cleveland, James

**[The] King of Gospel Music**
*See*   Robinson, Cleophus

**[The] King of Hearts**
*See*   Talbot, Charles

**[The] King of Hi-De-Ho**
*See*   Calloway, Cabell

**[The] King of Jazz**
*See*   Ellington, Edward Kennedy

**[The] King of Jazz**
*See*   Whiteman, Paul

**[The] King of Khorassan**
*See*   Anvari

**King of Kings**
*See*   Ardashir I

**[The] King of Kings**
*See*   Charles VII

**[The] King of Koins**
*See*   Downs, T. Nelson

**[The] King of Laughter**
*See*   Williams, Egbert Austin

**King of Men**
*See*   Ardashir I

**[The] King of Painters**
*See*   Parrhasius

**[The] King of Paris**
*See*   Lorraine, Henry I [or Henri] de

**[The] King of Phrases**
*See*   Buffon, Georges Louis Leclerc de

**[The] King of Poets**
*See*   Ronsard, Pierre de

**[The] King of Preachers**
*See*   Bourdaloue, Louis

**[The] King of Ragtime Composers**
*See*   Joplin, Scott

**[The] King of Reptiles**
*See*   De la Ville, Bernard Germain Etienne

**[The] King of Roads**
*See*   Macadam, John Loudon

**[The] King of Rock 'n Roll**
*See*   Presley, Elvis Aaron

**[The] King of Romance**
*See*   Dumas, Alexandre

**[The] King of Rome**
*See*   Bernis, Francois Joachim de Pierre de

**[The] King of Rome**
*See*   Bonaparte, Francois Charles Joseph [Duc de Reichstadt]

**[The] King of Satire**
*See*   Luard, Nicholas Lambert

**[The] King of Scotch Fiddlers**
*See*   Gow, Neil

**[The] King of Sexual Delinquents**
*See*   Kuerten, Peter

**[The] King of Ships**
*See*   Carausius, Marcus Aurelius Valerius

**[The] King of Sion**
*See*   Becold [Boccold, or Bockholdt], John

**[The] King of Slops**
*See*   Louis XVIII

**[The] King of Soul Singers**
*See*   Redding, Otis

**[The] King of Swing**
*See*   Goodman, Benjamin David [Benny]

**[The] King of Terror**
*See*   Robespierre, Maximilien

**King of the Airbrush**
*See*   Schomburg, Alex

**King of the Banjo**
*See*   Bolyer, Maurice

**King of the Banjo**
*See*   Peabody, Eddy

**King of the Banjo**
*See*   Schirmer, Joe

**King of the Banjo Players**
*See*   Macon, David Harrison

**King of the Banjoes**
*See*   Hogg, Jack

**[The] King of the Barricades**
*See*   Louis Philippe

**[The] King of the Beggars**
*See*   Carew, Bamfylde Moore

**[The] King of the Beggars**
*See*   Charles VIII

**[The] King of the Black Isles**
*See*   Nicolson, John Urban

**King of the Blue Beat**
*See*   Dacres, Desmond

**King of the Blues**
*See*   King, Riley B.

**King of the Bombers**
*See*   Belcastro, James

**King of the Bootleggers**
*See*   Remus, George

**[The] King of the Border**
*See*   Scott, Adam

**[The] King of the B's**
*See*   Foy, Bryan

**King of the Candlepins**
*See*   Martel, Wilbert

**[The] King of the Canebrakes**
*See*   Stribling, William Lawrence

**[The] King of the Card Counters**
*See*   Uston, Kenneth

**[The] King of the Caribbean**
*See*   Cooper, Pete B.

**[The] King of the Cherokees**
*See*   Cumming, [Sir] Alexander

**[The] King of the Commons**
*See*   James V

**King of the Costume Novel**
*See*   Yerby, Frank Garvin

**[The] King of the Courts**
*See*   Hortensius, Quintus

**[The] King of the Cowboys**
*See*   Slye, Leonard

**[The] King of the Derbies**
*See*   Stern, Georges

**[The] King of the Fairies**
*See*   Croker, Thomas Crofton

**[The] King of the Feds**
*See*   Hamilton, Alexander

**[The] King of the Gypsies**
*See*   Carew, Bamfylde Moore

**King of the Gypsies of Europe**
*See*   Salva, Pierre

**King of the Harmonica**
*See*   Ford, Aleck

**King of the High C's**
*See*   Pavarotti, Luciano

**King of the Hillbillies**
*See*   Macon, David Harrison

**[The] King of the Hillbilly Piano Players**
*See*   Mullican, Aubrey Wilson

**[The] King of the Hills**
*See*   Vincent

**King of the Isle of Man**
*See*   Bek, Anthony

**[The] King of the Jockeys**
*See*   Stern, Georges

**King of the Jukeboxes**
*See*   Jordan, Louis Thomas

**[The] King of the King**
*See*   Du Plessis, Armand Jean

**[The] King of the Lobby**
*See*   Ward, Sam[uel]

**[The] King of the Markets**
*See*   Vendome, Francois de

**[The] King of the Midgets**
*See*   Rosen, [Captain] James

**[The] King of the Mille Miglia**
*See*   Biondetti, Clemente

**King of the Nets**
*See*   Tilden, William Tatem, II

**[The] King of the Paper Stage**
*See*   Greene, Robert

**[The] King of the Peak**
*See*   Vernon, [Sir] George

**[The] King of the Pimps**
*See*   Lucania, Salvatore

**King of the Poor**
*See*   FitzOsbert, William

**[The] King of the Pulp Writers**
*See*   Faust, Frederick [Schiller]

**[The] King of the Quakers**
*See*   Pemberton, Israel

**King of the Quota Quickies**
*See*   King, George

**King of the Robots**
*See*   Blake, Alva D.

**[The] King of the Scandinavian Singers**
*See*   Oehlenschlaeger, Adam Gottlob

**[The] King of the Sea**
*See*   Edward III

**King of the Smugglers**
*See*   Katzenburg, Yasha

**King of the South**
*See*   Chenier, Clifton

**[The] King of the Strings**
*See*   Maphis, Otis W.

**King of the Stroll**
*See*   Willis, Chuck

**[The] King of the Teign**
*See*   Baldrick

**King of the 12 String Guitar Players**
*See*   Ledbetter, Huddie [William]

**King of the Umpires**
*See*   Gaffney, John H.

**[The] King of the West**
*See*   Pyne, John

**King of the Wheel**
*See*   Zimmerman, Arthur A.

**[The] King of the World**
See   Khorrum [or Khurram]

**King of the Zydeco**
See   Chenier, Clifton

**[The] King of Thieves**
See   Scott, Adam

**[The] King of Western Country Music**
See   Williams, Hiram King

**[The] King of Western Swing**
See   Cooley, Donnell C.

**[The] King of Wisdom**
See   Omar Khayyam

**King Oliver**
See   Cromwell, Oliver

**King, Oliver**   [PA]
*Author*
* Carlton, Ethel
* O. K.

**King, Oscar Benjamin** 1889-
[NAA]
*American educator and author*
* King, O. B. Royal

**King, Oswin Kerryn** 1889-   [NAA]
*American publisher and sportswriter*
* Uncle Jake

**[The] King Over the Water**
See   James II

**[The] King Over the Water**
See   Stuart, Charles Edward Louis
Philip Casimir

**[The] King Over the Water**
See   Stuart, James Francis Edward

**King, Patricia** 1930-   [CA]
*American educator and author*
* Wilde, Kathey

**King, Paul**
See   Drackett, Phil[ip Arthur]

**King, Pee Wee**
See   King, Frank

**King, Peggy Cameron**
See   King, Marjorie Cameron

**King Penguin**
See   Peterson, Roger Tory

**King, Pep**
See   King, Wiley

**King Pin** [code name used during
World War II]
See   Giraud, Henri

**King Radio**
See   Span, Norman

**King, Reefe**
See   Barker, Albert W.

**King, Reggie**
*American basketball player*
* King, Mule

**King, Richard**
See   Huskinson, Richard King

**King Richard**
See   Lundy, Richard

**King, Riley B.** 1925-
[BWW, DAM, SSS]
*American singer and guitarist*
* [The] Beale Street Blues Boy
* [The] Blues Boy
* Bossman of the Blues
* [The] Boy from Beale Street

**King, Riley B.** (Continued)
* King, B. B.
* King of the Blues

**King, Robert A.**
See   Keiser, Robert

**King, Ruth Rodney**
See   Manley, Ruth Rodney King

**King, Sherry**
See   King, [Raymond] Sherwood

**King, [Raymond] Sherwood** 1904-
[WW]
*Author*
* King, Sherry

**King, Silver**
See   Koenig, Charles Frederick

**King, Sis**
See   King, Kathryn

**King Solomon**
See   White, Solomon

**King Solomon Hill**
See   Holmes, Joe

**King, T. W.**
See   Ingraham, Prentiss

**King, Teri**
See   Ratcliffe, Patricia

**King, Toler**
See   Fox, Emily

**King Tom**
See   Maitland, [Sir] Thomas

**King, Tom** ?-1739   [HN]
*British robber*
* [The] Gentleman Highwayman

**King Tut**
See   Tuttle, Henry

**King, Veronica**
See   King, Florence

**King, Vincent**
See   Vinson, Rex Thomas

**King, W. Scott**
See   Greenland, William Kingscote

**King, Wak**
See   King, William

**King, Walter Woolf**
See   Woolf, Walter

**King, Wayne** 1901-
*American bandleader*
* [The] Waltz King

**King, Wayne** 1951-   [SMG]
*Canadian-born hockey player*
* [The] Chief

**King, Wiley** 1885?-   [NOJ]
*American jazz musician*
* King, Pep

**King, William**   [SN]
*Author*
* Humpty-Dumpty

**King, William** 1915-   [IBW]
*American baseball, football and
basketball player*
* King, Dolly

**King, William** 1950-   [IBW]
*American musician and
choreographer*
* King, Wak

**King, William Rufus** 1786-1853
[FFF, SN]
*American politician*
* King, [Miss] Nancy

**King, Worth**
See   King, Carroll E.

**King, Yolanda** 1956?-
*American actress*
* Yoki

**King, Yvonne**
See   Driggs, Yvonne

**King-Hall, Magdalen** 1904-1971
[CAP]
*British author*
* Knox, Cleone

**King-Hall, [William] Stephen
[Richard]** 1893-1966   [CA]
*British author, naval officer,
legislator*
* Etienne

**King-Scott, Peter** 1918-
[ESF, SFL, WGT]
*British author*
* Edgar, Peter

**[The] Kingfish**
See   Long, Huey Pierce

**Kinghorn, A. M.**
See   Kinghorn, Alexander Manson

**Kinghorn, Alexander Manson**
1926-   [CA]
*British author*
* Kinghorn, A. M.
* Sharp, James

**[The] Kingmaker**
See   Neville, Richard

**Kingman, David Arthur** 1948-
[B10]
*American baseball player*
* Kingman, Kong

**Kingman, E.**   [FFF]
*American writer*
* Jon

**Kingman, Kong**
See   Kingman, David Arthur

**Kingman, Lee**
See   Natti, Mary Lee

**Kingpetch, Pone**
See   Seadoaghob, Nana

**[The] King's Convertisseur**
See   Pellisson-Fontanier, Paul

**[The] King's Jester**
See   Galvin, George

**[The] King's King**
See   Joyeuse, Anne de

**Kingsbury, Phyllis May** 20th c.
[IAW]
*British author*
* Flowerdew, Phyllis

**Kingsford, Guy**
See   Murray, C. Geoffrey

**Kingsford, Jane**
See   Barnard, C. F., Jr.

**Kingsford, William** 18th c.   [PA]
*Author*
* W. K.

**Kingsley, Anna** [joint pseudonym
with Thomas W. Hanshew]
See   Hanshew, Mary E.

**Kingsley, Anna** [joint pseudonym
with Mary E. Hanshew]
See   Hanshew, Thomas W.

**Kingsley, Bettina**
See   Kaplan, Barry

**Kingsley, Charles** 1819-1875
[DEL, DNNF, PA]
*British author and poet*
* C. K.
* [The] Chartist Clergyman
* [The] Chartist Parson
* Dundreary, Lord
* Lot, Parson
* [A] Minute Philosopher

**Kingsley, Charlotte May**
See   Hanshew, Thomas W.

**Kingsley, Hamilton**
See   Martin, W.

**Kingsley, Margaret**
See   Polkinghorne, Margaret

**Kingsley, O. A.**   [PA]
*Author*
* Quercus

**Kingsley, Sidney**
See   Kieschner, Sidney

**Kingsman**
See   Essington, R. W.

**Kingsmill, Hugh**
See   Lunn, Hugh Kingsmill

**Kingstead, Julian**
See   Cunynghame, Francis J. de M.

**Kingston, Brian**
See   Longhurst, Percy William

**Kingston, Charles**
See   O'Mahony, C. K.

**Kingston, Gertrude**
See   Konstam, Gertrude

**Kingston, John**
See   Roberts, Keith [John
Kingston]

**Kingston, May**
See   Lane, Sarah

**Kingston, Syd**
See   Bingley, David Ernest

**Kininmonth, Christopher** 1917-
[CA, WD]
*British author*
* Brennan, Christopher [joint
pseudonym with Roland Baird]

**Kinisi, Paul** 15th c.   [HN]
*Hungarian army officer*
* [The] Murat of the Magyar Army

**Kinkaid, Matt**
See   Adams, Clifton

**Kinkaid, Wyatt E.**
See   Jennings, Michael

**Kinkead, Eleanor Talbot**
See   Short, Eleanor Talbot Kinkead

**Kinkel, Madame**
See   Sheppard, Elizabeth Sara

**Kinleyside, Douglas** 1905-1945?
[F2, FC]
*American actor*
* Douglas, Donald

**Kinmont Willie**
*See* Armstrong, William

**Kinnaird, Clark** 1901-   [AW, CA]
*American columnist and editor*
* Adams, John Paul
* Earlywine, Hargis
* Norris, Edgar Poe

**Kinnear, Gunner**
*See* Kinnear, Guy

**Kinnear, Guy** 20th c.   [SMG]
*Canadian hockey team trainer*
* Kinnear, Gunner

**Kinney, Robert** 1920-   [BB]
*American basketball player*
* Bat 'em Bob

**Kinney, Thomas**
*See* Thomas, Curtis

**Kinnicutt, Susan Sibley** 1926-   [CA]
*American author*
* Shelby, Susan
* Sibley, Susan

**Kinnoch, R. G. B.**
*See* Barclay, George

**Kinnosuke, Natsume** 1867-1916
[TCL]
*Japanese author, poet, critic*
* Soseki, Natsume

**Kinor, Jehuda**
*See* Rothmuller, Aron Marko

**Kinoy, Ernest** 20th c.
*American television scriptwriter*
* Chweig, B.

**Kinross, Patrick** 1904-1976   [CA]
*British journalist and author*
* Balfour, Patrick

**Kinsayder, W.**
*See* Marston, John

**Kinsburn, Emart**
*See* Hankins, Arthur Preston

**Kinsella, Ed[ward William]** 1882- ?
[BE]
*American baseball player*
* Kinsella, Rube

**Kinsella, Kathleen**
*See* Freeland, Kathleen

**Kinsella, Linda Iris** 1914-   [ART]
*British painter*
* L. K.

**Kinsella, Rube**
*See* Kinsella, Ed[ward William]

**Kinsella, Thomas**   [PA]
*Author*
* Brooklyn

**Kinsey, Elizabeth**
*See* Clymer, Eleanor

**Kinsey-Jones, Brian**
*See* Ball, Brian N[eville]

**Kinski, Nastassja** 1961?-
*German actress*
* Kinski, Nasti

**Kinski, Nasti**
*See* Kinski, Nastassja

**Kinsley, Daniel Allan** 1939-   [CA]
*American author*
* Edwardes, Allen

**Kinver, Richard**
*See* Vogel, Harry Benjamin

**Kinwelmersh, Francis**   [DEL]
*Author and poet*
* F. K.

**Kinzy, Henry Hersel [Harry]** 1910-
[BE]
*American baseball player*
* Kinzy, Slim

**Kinzy, Slim**
*See* Kinzy, Henry Hersel [Harry]

**[The] Kipling of the Halls**
*See* Chevalier, Albert Onesime
Britannicus Gwathveoyd Louis

**Kiplinger, David**
*See* Miner, Virginia Scott

**Kippax, John**
*See* Hynam, John Charles

**Kiproy, C.?**
*See* Hersey, Harold

**Kirbery, Ralph**
*Singer*
* [The] Dream Singer

**Kirby, Arthur**
*See* MacLean, Arthur George

**Kirby, Beecher** 20th c.   [ECM]
*American country-western performer*
* Bashful Brother Oswald
* Kirby, Pete

**Kirby, Big Daddy**
*See* Kirby, George

**Kirby, Clay**
*See* Kirby, Clayton Laws, Jr.

**Kirby, Clayton Laws, Jr.** 1948-
[BR]
*American baseball player*
* Kirby, Clay

**Kirby, D. A.** 20th c.   [GW]
*American rodeo performer*
* Kirby, Swanny

**Kirby, George** 1924-   [IBW]
*American comedian, singer, dancer*
* Kirby, Big Daddy

**Kirby, Jean** [house pseudonym,
Whitman Publishing]
*See* McDonnell, Virginia
B[leecker] [Jinny]

**Kirby, Jean** [house pseudonym,
Whitman Publishing]
*See* Robinson, Chaille Howard
[Payne]

**Kirby, K. Sarah N.** 1903-   [ART]
*British painter*
* S. K.

**Kirby, Mark**
*See* Floren, Lee

**Kirby, Pete**
*See* Kirby, Beecher

**Kirby, Sally C.** 1886-1971   [SC]
*American actress*
* Crute, Sally

**Kirby, Swanny**
*See* Kirby, D. A.

**Kirchner, Ernst Ludwig** 1880-1938
[CAR]
*German painter and author*
* De Marsalle, L.

**Kireeff, O.** 19th c.   [PA]
*Author*
* O. K.

**Kirienko-Voloshin, Maximilian
Aleksandrovich** 1877-1932   [CD]
*Russian poet, critic, artist*
* Voloshin, Maximilian
Aleksandrovich

**Kirk, Alexis**
*See* Vemian, Alex Kirk

**Kirk, Eddie**
*See* Kirkland, Eddie

**Kirk, Eleanor**
*See* Ames, Eleanor Maria
[Easterbrook]

**Kirk, Ellen Warner Olney**
1842-1928   [FFF, WBD]
*American author*
* Hayes, Henry

**Kirk, Fay B.**
*See* Baker, Fay

**Kirk, Irene** 1926-   [CA]
*Manchurian-born author*
* Kirk, Irina

**Kirk, Irina**
*See* Kirk, Irene

**Kirk, Jack**
*See* Kirkhuff, John

**Kirk, James Prior** 1851-1922   [TC]
*British author*
* Prior, James

**Kirk, Jeremy**
*See* Powell, Richard [Pitts]

**Kirk, Junior**
*See* Kirk, Walton

**Kirk, Laurence**
*See* Simson, Eric Andrew

**Kirk, Michael**
*See* Knox, William [Bill]

**Kirk, Pappy**
*See* Kirkhuff, John

**Kirk, Phyllis**
*See* Kirkegaard, Phyllis

**Kirk, Rahsaan Roland**
*See* Kirk, Ronald T.

**Kirk, Richard [Edmund]** 1931-
[CA]
*American author*
* Church, Jeffrey

**Kirk, Ronald T.** 1936-   [DAM]
*American jazz musician*
* Kirk, Rahsaan Roland

**Kirk, Ted**
*See* Bank, Theodore P[aul], II
[Ted]

**Kirk, Thomas Hobson** 1899-   [CAP]
*British author*
* Thomas, K. H.

**Kirk, Walton** 1924-   [BB]
*American basketball player*
* Kirk, Junior

**Kirk, William H. F.** 1902-1971
[SC]
*American actor*
* Kirke, Donald

**Kirk-Greene, Anthony [Hamilton
Millard]** 1925-   [CA]
*British educator and author*
* Caverhill, Nicholas

**Kirkaldy, Andra**
*See* Kirkaldy, Andrew

**Kirkaldy, Andrew** 1860-1934   [EG]
*Scottish golfer*
* Kirkaldy, Andra

**Kirke, Charles D.**   [FFF, PA]
*American author*
* Se De Kay

**Kirke, Donald**
*See* Kirk, William H. F.

**Kirke, Edmund**
*See* Gilmore, James Roberts

**Kirke, Edward** 1553-1613   [WBD]
*British author*
* E. K.

**Kirke, Jay**
*See* Kirke, Judson Fabian

**Kirke, Judson Fabian** 1888-1968
[BE]
*American baseball player*
* Kirke, Jay

**Kirkeby, Ed**
*See* Kirkeby, Wallace Theodore

**Kirkeby, Wallace Theodore**
1891-1978   [ASC, WWJ]
*American jazz musician and
manager*
* Kirkeby, Ed
* Loyd, Ed
* Wallace, Ted

**Kirkegaard, Phyllis** 1926-   [FC]
*American actress*
* Kirk, Phyllis

**Kirkendall, Clyde** ?-1957   [BBH]
*American softball player*
* Kirkendall, Dizzy

**Kirkendall, Dizzy**
*See* Kirkendall, Clyde

**Kirkham, Nellie**
*See* Myatt, Nellie

**Kirkham, Reginald S.** 20th c.
[MBF]
*British author*
* Clifford, Martin [house
pseudonym]
* Richards, Frank [house
pseudonym]
* Vincent, Frank

**Kirkhuff, John** 1895-1948   [SC]
*American actor*
* Huff, Jack
* Kirk, Jack
* Kirk, Pappy

**Kirkland**
*See* Harris, Amanda Bartlett

**Kirkland, Caroline Matilda**
1801-1864   [FFF, PA, WBD]
*American author*
* Clavers, [Mrs.] Mary

**Kirkland, Eddie** 1928-   [BWW]
*Jamaican-born singer*
* [The] Blues Man
* Kirk, Eddie
* Kirkland, Little Eddie

Kirkland, Little Eddie
See Kirkland, Eddie

Kirkland, Odette 1869-1936 [THR]
American actress and playwright
* Tyler, Odette

Kirkland, Will
See Hale, Arlene

Kirkland, Winifred Margaretta 1872-
? [NAA]
American author
* Priceman, James

Kirkman, Francis
See Ratcliffe, Samuel Kirkham

Kirkman, Milo
See Drussai, Garen

Kirkman, Sidney 1886-1945
[BMH, THR]
British comedian
* Walker, Syd

Kirkpatrick, David Gordon 1927-
[ECM]
Australian singer
* Dusty, Slim

Kirkpatrick, M. Glen 1889- [NAA]
American editor
* McKay, Grif

Kirkpatrick, Oliver Austin 1921-
[CW]
Jamaican author and poet
* Canoe, John

Kirkup, James 1924?-
[AW, CA, SAT]
British author and poet
* Falconer, James
* James, Andrew
* Jun, Terahata
* Shigeru, Tsuyuki
* Summerforest, Ivy B.

Kirkus, Virginia
See Glick, Virginia Kirkus

Kirkwood, John Sutherland 1947-
[ART]
Scottish artist
* J. S. K.

Kirkwood, Pat 1921- [BMH]
British entertainer
* [The] Schoolgirl Songstress

Kirnon, Conrad Henry 1927- [EJ]
American jazz musician
* Kay, Connie

Kirsch, Robert R. 1922- [CA]
American journalist and author
* Bancroft, Robert
* Dundee, Robert

Kirschner, Fritz
See Bickers, Richard Leslie
Townshend

Kirson, Alice Atkinson 1868- ?
[ALY]
American author
* Atkinson, Alice M.

Kirstein, Mina 1896- [BBD]
American musicologist
* Curtiss, Mina

Kirsten, Kirsey
See Kirsten, Peter Noel

Kirsten, Peter Noel 1955- [DC]
South African-born cricketer
* Kirsten, Kirsey

Kirtland, Ethel Schwartz
1881-1963 [IA]
American writer
* Paddie Kak

Kirtland, G. B. [joint pseudonym
with Sesyle Joslin Hine]
See Hine, Al[fred Blakelee]

Kirtland, G. B. [joint pseudonym
with Al(fred Blakelee) Hine]
See Hine, Sesyle Joslin

Kirtland, Louise
See Jelly, Louise Isabel

Kirwan
See Murray, Nicholas

Kirwan, Molly [Morrow] 1906-
[AW, CAP]
British author
* Morrow, Charlotte

Kirwan, Thomas 1829-1911 [WGT]
Author
* Wonder, William

Kirwan-Ward, Bernard Edward
1909- [AW]
British-born journalist and author
* Ward, Kirwan

Kiser, Big Bear
See Kiser, Larry Grant

Kiser, Larry Grant 1949- [SMG]
American baseball player
* Kiser, Big Bear

Kish, G. Hobab
See Kennedy, Gerald [Hamilton]

Kisiel, Teodor Klon
See Kisielewski, Stefan

Kisielewski, Stefan 1911- [IAW]
Polish author and composer
* Kisiel, Teodor Klon

Kisleauskas, Edward William
1909- [BE]
American baseball player
* Cole, Ed[ward William]

Kismet
See Sears, Mrs. Newton

Kisner, Jack
See Kisner, Jacob

Kisner, Jacob 1926- [IAW]
American author, poet, playwright
* Kisner, Jack
* Smallwood, Jason

[The] Kisser
See Moura, Joaq

[The] Kissing Bandit
See Cottrell, Morganna Roberts

[The] Kissing Bandit
See Murray, Edna

Kissing Jim Folsom
See Folsom, James E.

Kissing Kim Karter
See Bradley, Vera Jeanne

Kissinger, Charles Samuel
1876-1941 [BE]
American baseball player
* Kissinger, Rube

Kissinger, Henry Alfred 1923-
[NN]
American scholar and diplomat
* [The] Drone

Kissinger, Henry Alfred (Continued)
* [The] Flying Peacemaker
* [The] Gay Deceiver
* Henry the K
* [The] Iron Stomach
* Super Kraut

Kissinger, Rube
See Kissinger, Charles Samuel

Kissinger, Shang
See Kissinger, William Francis
[Bill]

Kissinger, William Francis [Bill]
1871-1929 [BE]
American baseball player
* Kissinger, Shang

Kissling, Dorothy Hight [Richardson]
1904- [WGT]
American author
* Langley, Dorothy

Kissoff, Joseph F.
See Zelinsky, Joseph F.

Kistiakowsky, Vera 1928- [CA]
American author
* Fischer, Vera Kistiakowsky

Kit
See Adams, J. B.

[The] Kit-Kat Poet
See Garth, Samuel

Kitabatake, Miyo 1903- [IAW]
Japanese author
* Yaho

Kitayama, Kassy
See Kitayama, Kazuko

Kitayama, Kazuko 1947- [IBW]
American singer
* Kitayama, Kassy

Kitchen, Dorothy
Actress
* Drexel, Nancy

Kitchen, M. J.
See Kitchen, Mervyn John

[The] Kitchen Maid in Ireland
See Mountjoy, Earl

Kitchen, Mervyn John 1940- [DC]
British cricketer
* Kitchen, M. J.

Kitchin, C. H. B.
See Kitchin, Clifford Henry Benn

Kitchin, Clifford Henry Benn
1895-1967 [LC]
British author and journalist
* Kitchin, C. H. B.

Kitchin, Frederick Harcourt
1867-1932 [CC, WW, WWL]
Scottish author
* Copplestone, Bennet

[The] Kite
See Aelfric

Kite, Larry
See Schneck, Stephen

Kitman, Marvin 1929- [CA]
American author
* Hirsch, William Randolph [joint
  pseudonym with Richard
  Lingeman and Victor Navasky]

Kitt, Tamara
See De Regniers, Beatrice Schenk
Freedman

[The] Kitten
See Haddix, Harvey, Jr.

Kittl, Ema 1878-1930 [BBD]
Czech-born opera singer
* Destinn, Emmy

Kittredge, G. L.
See Kittredge, George Lyman

Kittredge, George Lyman
1860-1941 [LC]
American educator and author
* Kittredge, G. L.

Kittrell, Jean 1927- [BWW]
American singer
* Jazzie Jeanie

Kitzmiller, John 1904- [FB]
American football player
* [The] Flying Dutchman

Kivi, Alexis
See Stenvall, Alexis

Kiyomura, Koji 1926- [CA]
Japanese-born economist and author
* Taira, Koji

Kjaken
See Sonsteby, Gunnar

Kjellin, Alf 1920- [WEF]
Swedish-born actor and director
* Kent, Christopher

Klabund
See Henschke, Alfred

Klaerner, Dutch
See Klaerner, Hugo Emil

Klaerner, Hugo Emil 1908- [BE]
American baseball player
* Klaerner, Dutch

Klainer, Albert S. 20th c. [SFL]
Author
* Peters, L. T. [joint pseudonym
  with Jo-Ann Klainer]

Klainer, Jo-Ann 20th c. [SFL]
Author
* Peters, L. T. [joint pseudonym
  with Albert S. Klainer]

Klainikite, Anne
See Gehman, Betsy Holland

Klaj, Johannes 1535-1592 [WBD]
German grammarian
* Clajus, Johannes

Klarer, Streng
See Gerstner, Karl

Klark
See Gouzenko, Igor

Klarmann, Andrew F. 1866-1931
[CAT]
German-born author and clergyman
* Fairman, Virgil B.

Klasen, Gertrud Alexandra Dagmar
Lawrence 1898-1952 [EMT]
British actress, singer, dancer
* Lawrence, Gertrude

Klass, Eugene 1921-
[FC, ITA, SW]
American actor
* Barry, Gene

Klass, Philip 1920- [SF, WGT]
American author
* Putnam, Kenneth
* Tenn, William

**Klauber, Edward** ?-1954   [ET]
*Television executive*
* [The] Father of Broadcast
   Journalism

**Klaue, Lola Shelton** 1903-   [CA]
*American author*
* Shelton, Lola

**Klausman, Samuel** 1914-1975
[FC, SC]
*American actor*
* Parks, Larry

**Klavun, Waldemar Joseph** 1906-
[BEW]
*American actor and director*
* Klavun, Walter

**Klavun, Walter**
*See* Klavun, Waldemar Joseph

**Klaxon**
*See* Bower, John Graham

**Klee, Babe**
*See* Klee, Ollie Chester

**Klee, Ollie Chester** 1900-   [BE]
*American baseball player*
* Klee, Babe

**Kleifum, [Fra] Magnea**
*See* Magnusdottir, Magnea

**Klein, A. M.**
*See* Klein, Abraham Moses

**Klein, Aaron E.** 1930-   [CA]
*American editor, educator, author*
* Little, A. Edward

**Klein, Abraham Moses** 1909-
[LC, TC1]
*Canadian poet, scholar, barrister*
* Klein, A. M.

**Klein, Agnes** 1921-   [EJS]
*Hungarian-born Israeli gymnast*
* Keleti, Agnes

**Klein, Alex** 20th c.   [EJS]
*American football player*
* Klein, Shon

**Klein, Archer** 20th c.   [BEW]
*American talent representative,
producer, film distributor*
* King, Archer

**Klein, Carole** 1941?-   [JL, RO1]
*American singer and songwriter*
* King, Carole

**Klein, Dede**
*See* Klein, James Lloyd

**Klein, Doris F.**
*See* Jonas, Doris F[rances]

**Klein, Gerard** 1937-   [CA, ESF]
*French economist and author*
* D'Argyre, Gilles
* Pagery, Francois
* Starr, Mark

**Klein, Grace** 20th c.   [CA]
*American author*
* Farewell, Nina [joint pseudonym
  with Mae (Klein) Cooper]

**Klein, Harry Martin John** 1873- ?
[NAA]
*American educator and writer*
* H. M. J. K.

**Klein, James Lloyd** 1910-   [CEI]
*Canadian-born hockey player*
* Klein, Dede

**Klein, Joanne Kim** 1945?-1976
[B10]
*American model*
* Bryan, Kim

**Klein, K. K.**
*See* Turner, Robert [Harry]

**Klein, Morris** 20th c.   [PHM]
*American underworld figure*
* Klein, Snag

**Klein, Regina**
*See* Von Heine, Baroness Gustav

**Klein, Shon**
*See* Klein, Alex

**Klein, Snag**
*See* Klein, Morris

**Klein, Waldemir**
*See* Carlin, Emelia F.

**Kleinbach, Henry** 1910-   [FC]
*American actor*
* Brandon, Henry

**Kleinfield, N. R.**
*See* Kleinfield, Nathan Richard

**Kleinfield, Nathan Richard** 20th c.
*American author and journalist*
* Kleinfield, N. R.
* Kleinfield, Sonny

**Kleinfield, Sonny**
*See* Kleinfield, Nathan Richard

**Kleinke, Norbert George**
1912-1950   [BE]
*American baseball player*
* Kleinke, Nub

**Kleinke, Nub**
*See* Kleinke, Norbert George

**Kleinow, John Peter** 1879-1929
[BE]
*American baseball player*
* Kleinow, Red

**Kleinow, Pete** 20th c.   [RM]
*Musician*
* Sneaky Pete

**Kleinow, Red**
*See* Kleinow, John Peter

**Klem, Catfish**
*See* Klimm, William Joseph

**Klem, William Joseph [Bill]**
*See* Klimm, William Joseph

**Klenbort, Charlotte**
*See* Sempell, Charlotte

**Klepfer, Big Ed**
*See* Klepfer, Edward Lloyd

**Klepfer, Edward Lloyd** 1888-1950
[BE]
*American baseball player*
* Klepfer, Big Ed

**Klett, Harold**
*See* Lord, Halkett

**Klewin, W[illiam] Thomas** 1921-
[CA]
*American clergyman and writer*
* Matthews, Tom

**Klieman, Babe**
*See* Klieman, Edward Frederick

**Klieman, Edward Frederick** 1918-
[BE]
*American baseball player*
* Klieman, Babe

**Klier, Crystal**
*See* Klier, Leo

**Klier, Leo** 1923-   [BB]
*American basketball player*
* Klier, Crystal

**Klimaris, J. S.**
*See* Kubilius, Walter

**Klimentov, Andrei Platonovich**
1899-1951   [WOA]
*Russian author*
* Platonov, Andrei

**Klimm, William Joseph** 1874-1951
[BAB]
*American baseball official*
* Klem, Catfish
* Klem, William Joseph [Bill]
* [The] Old Arbitrator

**Klimo, Jake**
*See* Klimo, Vernon

**Klimo, Vernon** 1914-   [CA]
*American author*
* Klimo, Jake

**Klinckerfuss, Ingabor Katrine**
1915?-1967   [FC, SC]
*German-born actress*
* Verne, Karen
* Young, Catherine

**Kline, Burton** 20th c.   [NAA]
*American author and journalist*
* Dart, Rufus, II

**Kline, Clarence** 20th c.   [BBH]
*American baseball coach*
* Kline, Jake

**Kline, Frank**
*See* Rio, Frank

**Kline, Frank** 1925-   [FC]
*American actor*
* Latimore, Frank

**Kline, Jake**
*See* Kline, Clarence

**Kline, Junior**
*See* Kline, Robert George

**Kline, Robert George** 1909-   [BE]
*American baseball player*
* Kline, Junior

**Kling, John Gradwohl** 1875-1947
[BE, PB]
*American baseball player*
* Kling, Noisy

**Kling, Noisy**
*See* Kling, John Gradwohl

**Klingler, Paul** 20th c.   [BS]
*American magician*
* Paulo the Magic Clown

**Klingsor, Tristan**
*See* Leclere, Leon

**Klinikus**
*See* Visser, Willem Johannes
Conradie

**Klink, Al** 1915-   [MY]
*American jazz musician*
* Klink, Mose

**Klink, Mose**
*See* Klink, Al

**Klio**
*See* Berenyi, Maria

**Klitgaard, Christen** 1894-1961
[SC]
*Danish-born actor*
* Guard, Kit

**Kliun, Ivan**
*See* Kliunkow, Ivan Vasilevitsch

**Kliunkow, Ivan Vasilevitsch**
1873-1943   [CAR]
*Russian artist*
* Kliun, Ivan

**Klivecka, Ray**
*See* Klivecka, Rimantis

**Klivecka, Rimantis** 20th c.   [AES]
*American soccer player and coach*
* Klivecka, Ray

**Klixto**
*See* Cordeiro, Calisto

**Klobaskova, Libuse** 1924-   [OP]
*Czech opera singer*
* Domaninska, Libuse

**Klondike Pete**
*See* Huley, Pete

**Klonis, N. I.**
*See* Clones, Nicholas J.

**Klopfenstein, Kenneth Vladimir**
1927-   [BEW]
*American actor and dancer*
* LeRoy, Ken

**Klopfinger, Herman, III**
*See* Diamant, Lincoln

**Klopman, Vera** 1897-   [BEW]
*American actress*
* Allen, Vera

**Klopp, Betz**
*See* Klopp, Stan[ley Harold]

**Klopp, Stan[ley Harold]** 1910-   [BE]
*American baseball player*
* Klopp, Betz

**Klopstock, Friedrich Gottlieb**
1724-1803   [DEP, HN, SN]
*German poet*
* [The] Birmingham Milton
* [The] Creator of Biblical Epic
  Poetry
* [The] German Milton
* [The] Milton of Germany

**Klosowski, Severin** ?-1903   [CEC]
*Polish-born murderer*
* Chapman, George

**Klossowski De Rola, Balthasar**
1908-   [B10]
*French artist*
* Balthus

**Klosterman, Donald** 20th c.   [FB]
*American football player*
* [The] Duke of Del Rey

**Klot, Lillian Claire Laizer Getel**
1933-   [BEW, TR]
*British actress and singer*
* Brown, Georgia

**Klotz, Louis** 1920-   [BB]
*American basketball player*
* Klotz, Red

**Klotz, Red**
*See* Klotz, Louis

**Kloza, John Clarence** 1904-1962
[BE]
*American baseball player*
* Kloza, Nap

**Kloza, Nap**
See Kloza, John Clarence

**Kluszewski, Big Klu**
See Kluszewski, Theodore Bernard [Ted]

**Kluszewski, Klu**
See Kluszewski, Theodore Bernard [Ted]

**Kluszewski, Theodore Bernard [Ted]** 1924- [BE, PB, SMG]
*American baseball player*
* Kluszewski, Big Klu
* Kluszewski, Klu

**Klutts, Gene Ellis** 1954- [WWB]
*American baseball player*
* Klutts, Mickey

**Klutts, Mickey**
See Klutts, Gene Ellis

**Kmety, Gyoergy** 1810-1865 [WBD]
*Hungarian-born army officer*
* Ismail Pasha

**Knabe, Dutch**
See Knabe, Franz Otto

**Knabe, Franz Otto** 1884-1961 [BE]
*American baseball player*
* Knabe, Dutch

**Knapman, Phyllis** 1914- [THR]
*British actress, singer, dancer*
* Stanley, Phyllis

**Knapp, Chris**
See Knapp, Robert Christian

**Knapp, Robert Christian** 1953- [BR]
*American baseball player*
* Knapp, Chris

**Knapp, Samuel Lorenzo** 1784-1838 [PA]
*Author*
* Robinson, Ignatius Loyola

**Knapp, Terry** 1943- [RO2]
*American singer*
* Knight, Terry

**Knauff, Ellen Raphael**
See Hartley, Ellen R[aphael]

**Knaupp, Cotton**
See Knaupp, Henry Antone

**Knaupp, Henry Antone** 1889-1967 [BE]
*American baseball player*
* Knaupp, Cotton

**Knauss, Robert** 1892-1955 [SFL, SFP, WGT]
*German author*
* Helders, Major

**Knauth, Robert** 1815-1892 [WBD]
*German composer*
* Franz, Robert

**Kneafcy, Thomas** 1928- [OP]
*British opera singer*
* Swift, Tom

**Knee, Malcolm** 1887- [F2]
*Actor*
* Keen, Malcolm

**Kneeland, Fred J.** 1888?-1964 [BEW]
*Magician*
* Kriss, Fred

**Knef, Hildegard** 1925- [CA, DAM, FC]
*German actress, singer, author*
* Neff, Hildegarde

**Kneller, [Sir] Godfrey**
See Kniller, Gottfried

**Knelme, William J.** 1858-1921 [BE]
*German-born baseball player*
* Kuehne, Willie

**Knerr, Lou**
See Knerr, Wallace Luther

**Knerr, Wallace Luther** 1921- [BE]
*American baseball player*
* Knerr, Lou

**Kness, Richard M.**
See Kniess, Richard M.

**Knetzer, Baron**
See Knetzer, Elmer Ellsworth

**Knetzer, Elmer Ellsworth** 1885-1975 [BE]
*American baseball player*
* Knetzer, Baron

**Knevals, Mrs. D. C.** [PA]
*Author*
* Eastwood, Francis

**Kniberg, Irwin** 1927- [SW]
*American actor and comedian*
* King, Alan

**Knickerbocker**
See Du Solle, John S.

**Knickerbocker, Cholly**
See Cassini, Igor

**Knickerbocker, Diedrich**
See Irving, Washington

**Knickerbocker, Suzy**
See Mehle, Aileen

**Knickers, Mr.**
See Saraceni, Eugene

**Kniess, Richard M.** 1937- [OP]
*American opera singer*
* Kness, Richard M.

**Knievel, Evel**
See Knievel, Robert Craig

**Knievel, Robert Craig** 1938- [IPA]
*American motorcyclist*
* Knievel, Evel

**[The] Knife of Academic Knots**
See Chrysippus

**Knifesmith**
See Cutler, Ivor

**Knight, Adam**
See Rosenblum, Lawrence

**Knight, Albert**
See Chevalier, Albert Onesime Britannicus Gwathveoyd Louis

**Knight, Alonzo P.** 1853-1932 [BE]
*American baseball player and manager*
* Knight, Lon

**Knight, Arthur**
See Rosenheimer, Arthur

**Knight, Bernard** 1931- [AW, CA, WD]
*Welsh author and physician*
* Picton, Bernard

**Knight, Billy** 20th c. [IBW]
*American basketball player*
* Knight, Smooth

**Knight, Bubba**
See Knight, Merald

**Knight, Butch**
See Knight, Warren

**Knight, Charles** 1791-1873 [FFF, PA]
*British author and publisher*
* Aymar, Patterson

**Knight, Charles D.**
See Gilbert, Mrs. R. L.

**Knight, Damon F[rancis]** 1922- [ESF, SFP, WGT]
*American author and editor*
* Conanight [joint pseudonym with Chester Cohen]
* Conway, Ritter
* Fleming, Stuart
* Laverty, Donald [joint pseudonym with James (Benjamin) Blish]

**Knight, David**
See Mintz, David

**Knight, David**
See Prather, Richard S[cott]

**Knight, Elmer Russell** 1895- [BE]
*American baseball player*
* Knight, Jack

**Knight, Eric [Mowbray]** 1897-1943 [SAT, TC]
*British-born American author*
* Hallas, Richard

**Knight, Etheridge** 1931- [LBA]
*American author*
* Soa, Imamu Etheridge Knight

**Knight, Faith**
See Chevaillier, Faith

**Knight, Francis Edgar [Frank]** 1905- [CA]
*British author*
* Salter, Cedric

**Knight, Frida**
See Knight, Frideswide Frances Emma

**Knight, Frideswide Frances Emma** 1910- [IAW]
*British author*
* Knight, Frida

**Knight, Fuzzy**
See Knight, J. Forrest

**Knight, Gareth**
See Wilby, Basil Leslie

**Knight, Gene**
See O'Connor, James F. [Jim]

**Knight, George S.**
See Sloan, George

**Knight, Harry** [GW]
*American rodeo performer*
* Knight, Stormy

**Knight, J. Forrest** 1901- [FC]
*American actor and musician*
* Knight, Fuzzy

**Knight, Jack**
See Knight, Elmer Russell

**Knight, James**
See Schneck, Stephen

**Knight, Jean**
See Caliste, Jean

**Knight, Joe**
See Knight, Jonas William

**Knight, John**
See Houser, John

**Knight, John Collyer** 19th c. [PA]
*Author*
* K.

**Knight, John Wesley** 1885-1965 [BE]
*American baseball player*
* Knight, Schoolboy

**Knight, Jonas William** ?-1938 [BE]
*American baseball player*
* Knight, Joe
* Knight, Quiet Joe

**Knight, June**
See Valliquietto, Margaret Rose

**Knight, Kate Wilhelm** 1928- [WGT]
*American author*
* Wilhelm, Kate

**Knight, Kathleen Moore** 20th c. [CC, WW]
*Author*
* Amos, Alan

**Knight, Knighty**
See Knight, Roger David Verdon

**Knight, [W.] Kobold**
See Giddy, Eric Cawood Gwyddn

**Knight, Lon**
See Knight, Alonzo P.

**Knight, Mallory T.**
See Hurwood, Bernhardt J[ackson]

**Knight, Max** 1909- [CA, WD]
*Austrian-born American author*
* Fabrizius, Peter [joint pseudonym with Joseph B(enedikt) Fabry]

**Knight, Merald** 1942-
*American singer*
* Knight, Bubba

**Knight, Mrs. S. G.** [PA]
*Author*
* Manton, Kate

**[The] Knight of Innishowen**
See Sheehan, John

**[The] Knight of Kennett Square**
See Pennock, Herb[ert Jefferis]

**[The] Knight of Liddesdale**
See Douglas, [Sir] William

**[The] Knight of the Cloak**
See Raleigh, [Sir] Walter

**[The] Knight of the Post**
See Oates, Titus

**[The] Knight of the Whistle**
See Lally, Patrick Joseph

**Knight, Oliver** [PA]
*Author*
* Pontiac

**Knight, Pete**
See Knight, William

**Knight, Quiet Joe**
See Knight, Jonas William

**Knight, Red Ted**
See Knight, Ted

**Knight, Robert Cedric** 1891-
[WWL]
*British writer*
* How, Cappy

**Knight, Roger David Verdon** 1946-
[DC]
*British cricketer*
* Knight, Knighty

**Knight, Schoolboy**
See Knight, John Wesley

**Knight, Smooth**
See Knight, Billy

**Knight, Stormy**
See Knight, Harry

**Knight, Ted** 20th c.
*British politician*
* Knight, Red Ted

**Knight, Terry**
See Knapp, Terry

**Knight, Vick R[alph], Jr.** 1928-
[CA]
*American author*
* Tweed, J. H.

**Knight, Warren** 1948- [RO2]
*American musician*
* Knight, Butch

**Knight, William** 20th c. [B10]
*American aviator*
* Knight, Pete

**Knight without Reproach**
See Barbazan, Arnaud Guillaume
[or Arnauld Guilhelm]

**Knight-Adkin, James Harry** 1879-
? [LAO]
*British author*
* Adkin, Knight

**Knight-Patterson, W. M.**
See Kulski, Wladyslaw W[szebor]

**Knightley, D. G.** 20th c. [MBF]
*British author*
* Prior, Harry

**Knights, Leslie Douglas** 1914-
[AW]
*British author*
* Leslie, Val

**Kniller, Gottfried** 1646-1723
[WBD]
*German-born painter*
* Kneller, [Sir] Godfrey

**Knipe, Alden Arthur** 1870- ?
[NAA]
*American author*
* Shea, Timothy

**Knipe, Emilie Benson** 1870-1958
[NAA, WW]
*American author*
* Benson, Therese

**Knipscheer, James M. W.** 20th c.
[WW]
*Author*
* Fox, James M.
* Holmes, Grant

**Knipschield, Edward Henry**
1907?-1964 [BEW]
*Aerialist*
* Captain Eddie

**Knish, Anne**
See Ficke, Arthur Davison

**Knist, F[rances] Emma** 1948- [CA]
*American author*
* Fallere, Felicia

**[The] Knob Hill Terror**
See Attell, Monte

**Knoblauch, Edward** 1874-1945
[BEW]
*American actor and author*
* Knoblock, Edward

**Knoblaugh, Glen Gray** 1906-1963
[DAM, EJ, PMJ]
*American bandleader*
* Gray, Glen
* Gray, Spike

**Knoblock, Edward**
See Knoblauch, Edward

**Knoblock, Joan** 1917- [ART]
*British painter*
* J. K.

**Knode, Kenneth Thomson** 1895-
[BE]
*American baseball player*
* Knode, Mike

**Knode, Mike**
See Knode, Kenneth Thomson

**Knode, Ray**
See Knode, Robert Troxell [Bob]

**Knode, Robert Troxell [Bob]** 1901-
[BE]
*American baseball player*
* Knode, Ray

**Knoles, William** 20th c. [SFL]
*Author*
* Allison, Clyde
* Ames, Clyde

**Knoll, Charles Elmer** 1881-1960
[BE]
*American baseball player*
* Knoll, Punch

**Knoll, Punch**
See Knoll, Charles Elmer

**Knolls, Hub**
See Knolls, Oscar Edward

**Knolls, Oscar Edward** 1883-1946
[BE]
*American baseball player*
* Knolls, Hub

**Knollys, Hansard** 1598-1691 [FFF]
*Clergyman*
* Knowless, Mr. Absurd

**Knorr, Marian L[ockwood]** 1910-
[CA]
*American author and poet*
* DeKalb, Lorimer

**Knothe, Fritz**
See Knothe, Wilfred Edgar

**Knothe, Wilfred Edgar** 1903-1963
[BE]
*American baseball player*
* Knothe, Fritz

**Knott, Alan Philip Eric** 1946- [DC]
*British cricketer*
* Knott, Knotty

**Knott, Edward**
See Wilson, Matthias

**Knott, Knotty**
See Knott, Alan Philip Eric

**Knott, Nick**
See Knott, William Earl

**Knott, Roselle**
See Roselle, Agnes

**Knott, William Cecil, Jr. [Bill]**
1927- [CA, SAT, WD]
*American author*
* Carol, Bill J.

**Knott, William Earl** 1920- [CEI]
*Canadian-born hockey player*
* Knott, Nick

**Knotts, Raymond**
See Volk, Gordon

**Knouff, Edward** 1867-1900 [BE]
*American baseball player*
* Knouff, Fred

**Knouff, Fred**
See Knouff, Edward

**Knowall, George**
See O'Nuallain, Brian

**Knowles, Alec** 1850-1917 [BEW]
*Scottish-born journalist*
* Affable, Sir

**Knowles, David**
See Knowles, Michael Clive

**Knowles, Leo** 20th c. [SFL]
*Author*
* Gregory, Julian R.

**Knowles, Mabel Winifred**
1875-1949 [ESF, LAO, WGT]
*British author*
* Lurgan, Lester
* Wynne, May

**Knowles, Marie**
See Ringer, Ada

**Knowles, Michael Clive** 1896-1974
[B10]
*British author, lecturer, priest*
* Knowles, David

**Knowles, Patric**
See Knowles, Reginald Lawrence

**Knowles, R. G.**
See Knowles, Richard George

**Knowles, Reginald Lawrence** 1911-
[FC, ITA, SW]
*British actor*
* Knowles, Patric

**Knowles, Richard George**
1858-1919 [BMH]
*Canadian-born comedian*
* Knowles, R. G.

**Knowles, Thomas E.**
See McLure, R.

**Knowless, Mr. Absurd**
See Knollys, Hansard

**Knox, Andrew Jackson [Andy]**
1864-1940 [BE]
*American baseball player*
* Knox, Dasher

**Knox, Bud**
See Knox, Cliff[ord Hiram]

**Knox, Calvin M.**
See Silverberg, Robert

**Knox, Cleone**
See King-Hall, Magdalen

**Knox, Cliff[ord Hiram]** 1902-1965
[BE]
*American baseball player*
* Knox, Bud

**Knox, Dasher**
See Knox, Andrew Jackson [Andy]

**Knox, E. V.**
See Knox, Edmund George Valpy

**Knox, Edmund George Valpy**
1881-1971 [CA, LC, TC]
*British journalist and editor*
* Evoe
* Knox, E. V.

**Knox, Hard**
See Knox, Ronald Arbuthnott

**Knox, Hugh**
See Koch, Hugo B.

**Knox, Hugh [Randolph]** 1942-
[SFL]
*American author*
* Kaye, H. R.

**Knox, James**
See Brittain, William

**Knox, John** 1505-1572
[FFF, HN, SN]
*Scottish religious reformer and
author*
* [The] Apostle of Presbytery
* [The] Apostle of the Scottish
Reformers
* [The] Reformer of a Kingdom

**Knox, Lisbeth**
See Ward, Rose Elizabeth Knox

**Knox, Northrup R.** 20th c. [SMG]
*Hockey executive*
* Knox, Norty

**Knox, Norty**
See Knox, Northrup R.

**Knox, Ronald Arbuthnott** 1888-
[CAT]
*British author and clergyman*
* Knox, Hard

**Knox, Teddy** 1896-1974
[BF, BMH]
*British entertainer*
* Chinko the Boy Juggler

**Knox, Thomas** 18th c. [PA]
*Author*
* Walneerg

**Knox, William [Bill]** 1928-
[AW, CA, WD]
*Scottish author*
* Kirk, Michael
* MacLeod, Robert
* Webster, Noah

**Knox, Winifred Frances**
See Peck, Winifred Frances
[Knox]

**Knox-Johnston, Robin**
See Knox-Johnston, William
Robert Patrick

**Knox-Johnston, William Robert
Patrick** 1939- [CA, WD]
*British author*
* Knox-Johnston, Robin

**Knucher, Robert Watson**
1888-1965 [SC]
*American actor*
* Watson, Bobby

**Knuckles, Grafton** 20th c.    [GW]
*American rodeo performer*
* [The] Texas Kid

**Knudsen, Big Bill**
See   Knudsen, Signius Wilhelm
Paul

**Knudsen, Bunkie**
See   Knudsen, Semon E.

**Knudsen, Semon E.** 20th c.
*American business executive*
* Knudsen, Bunkie

**Knudsen, Signius Wilhelm Paul**
1879-1948   [WBD]
*Danish-born American automobile
executive*
* Knudsen, Big Bill
* Knudsen, William S.

**Knudsen, William S.**
See   Knudsen, Signius Wilhelm
Paul

**Knudson, R. R.**
See   Knudson, Rozanne Ruth

**Knudson, Rozanne Ruth** 1932-
[CA, SAT]
*American author*
* Knudson, R. R.

**Knust, Valli** 1882-1927   [BEW]
*German-born comedienne*
* Valli, Valli

**Knutt, A. P.**
See   Livandais, Augustus M. D.

**Knye, Cassandra** [joint pseudonym
with John Sladek]
See   Disch, Thomas M.

**Knye, Cassandra** [joint pseudonym
with Thomas M. Disch]
See   Sladek, John T[homas]

**Ko, Kanzein**
See   Isogai, Hiroshi

**Kobart, Ruth**
See   Kohn, Ruth Maxine

**Kobayashi, Masako Matsuno**
1935-   [CA]
*Japanese author*
* Matsuno, Masako

**Kobbler, John**
See   Hunter, John Kelso

**Kobo Daishi**
See   Kukai

**Koch, Barton** 1906-1964   [AS, FB]
*American football player*
* Koch, Botchey

**Koch, Botchey**
See   Koch, Barton

**Koch, Charlotte** 20th c.   [CA]
*American author*
* Raymond, Charles [joint
     pseudonym with Raymond Koch]

**Koch, Erich** 1875-1944   [WBD]
*German statesman and political
reformer*
* Koch-Weser, Erich

**Koch, Ernest**   [PA]
*Author*
* Helner, Edward

**Koch, Helius Eobanus** 1488-1540
[WBD]
*German poet*
* Hessus, Helius Eobanus

**Koch, Hugo B.**   ?-1926   [SC]
*American actor and director*
* Knox, Hugh

**Koch, Johannes** 1603-1669   [WBD]
*German-born theologian*
* Cocceius [or Coccejus], Johannes

**Koch, Raymond** 20th c.   [CA]
*American author*
* Raymond, Charles [joint
     pseudonym with Charlotte Koch]

**Koch-Weser, Erich**
See   Koch, Erich

**Kochanska, Praxede Marcelline**
1858-1935   [BBD]
*Polish-born opera singer*
* Sembrich, Marcella

**Kocman, Jiri Hynek** 1947-   [CAR]
*Czech artist*
* J. H. K.

**Kocsis, James C.** 1936-   [IBY]
*American painter and illustrator*
* Paul, James

**Koczan, Mor** 20th c.   [EJS]
*Hungarian javelin thrower*
* Kovacs, Mor

**Koda, Cub**
See   Koda, Michael John

**Koda, Michael John** 1948-   [RO2]
*American singer*
* Koda, Cub

**Koecher, Highpockets**
See   Koecher, Richard Finlay
[Dick]

**Koecher, Richard Finlay [Dick]**
1926-   [BE]
*American baseball player*
* Koecher, Highpockets

**Koegel, Moose**
See   Koegel, Warren

**Koegel, Warren** 20th c.   [SMG]
*American football player*
* Koegel, Moose

**Koehler, Ben**
See   Koehler, Bernard James

**Koehler, Bernard James** 1877-1961
[BE]
*German-born baseball player*
* Koehler, Ben

**Koehler, Horace Levering** 1902-
[BE]
*American baseball player*
* Koehler, Pip

**Koehler, Margaret [Hudson]** 20th
c.   [CA]
*American author*
* Hudson, Meg
* Mead, Russell

**Koehler, Pip**
See   Koehler, Horace Levering

**Koehn, Ilse**
See   Van Zwienen, Ilse Charlotte
Koehn

**Koenig, Charles Frederick**
1868-1938   [AS, BE, DGS]
*American baseball player*
* King, Charles Frederick
* King, Silver

**Koenig, Madame Victor**   [FFF]
*Entertainer*
* Hading, Jane

**Koenig, Marie Adrienne** 1889-1965
[FI, FC, IPA]
*American actress*
* Murray, Mae

**Koenigsberg, Moe**
See   Koenigsberg, Moses

**Koenigsberg, Moses** 20th c.
[WECO]
*American editor*
* Koenigsberg, Moe

**Koenigsgarten, Hugo F.** 1904-
[BEW]
*Austrian author and educator*
* Garten, H. F.

**Koepfel, Wolfgang Fabricius**
1478-1541   [WBD]
*German clergyman*
* Capito, Wolfgang Fabricius

**Koerber, Leila Marie** 1869-1934
[BDF, BEW, EMT]
*Canadian-born actress*
* Dressler, Marie

**Koerner, John** 1938-   [BWW]
*American singer*
* Koerner, Spider

**Koerner, Karl Theodor [or Carl
Theodore]** 1791-1813   [HN, SN]
*German poet and playwright*
* [The] Tyrtaeus of Germany

**Koerner, Spider**
See   Koerner, John

**Koes, Friedrich** 1684-1766   [PA]
*Author*
* Rosius

**Koeselitz, Heinrich** 1854-1918
[BBD]
*German writer and composer*
* Gast, Peter

**Koester, Frank**
See   Koester, Franz

**Koester, Franz** 1876-1927   [WBD]
*German-born engineer*
* Koester, Frank

**Koestler, Gisela Maria** 1925-
[IAW]
*Austrian author*
* Rosenberg, Gill

**Koestlin, Christian Reinhold**
1813-1856   [WBD]
*German jurist, poet, author*
* Reinhold, C.

**Koestner, Bob**
See   Koestner, Elmer Joseph

**Koestner, Elmer Joseph** 1885-1959
[BE]
*American baseball player*
* Koestner, Bob

**Koevoets, Pamela** 20th c.   [WF]
*Dutch actress*
* Rose, Pamela

**Koff, Joseph** 1887-1942   [SC]
*American actor and screenwriter*
* Watson, Joseph K.

**Koffler, Camilla**   ?-1955   [MJA]
*Austrian-born photographer and
illustrator*
* Ylla

**Kofoed, J. C.**
See   La Spina, Greye Bragg

**Koford, Helen** 1929?-
[FC, ITA, SW]
*American actress*
* Moore, Terry

**Kogan, Schmil** 20th c.   [EE]
*Russian-born intelligence agent*
* Carr, Sam

**Kohavi, Y.**
See   Stern, Jay B.

**Kohlman, Blackie**
See   Kohlman, Joseph James [Joe]

**Kohlman, Joseph James [Joe]**
1913-   [BE]
*American baseball player*
* Kohlman, Blackie

**Kohn, Bernice**
See   Hunt, Bernice Kohn

**Kohn, Fritz Nathan** 1892-1970
[FC]
*Austrian actor*
* Kortner, Fritz

**Kohn, Ruth Maxine** 1924-
[BEW, TR]
*American singer and actress*
* Kobart, Ruth

**Kohn, Zsigmond** 1879-1929   [JL]
*Hungarian government official*
* Kunfi, Zsigmond

**Kohnstamm, Anna** 1914-   [THR]
*British actress*
* Konstam, Anna

**Kohnstamm, Phyllis** 1907-   [THR]
*British actress*
* Konstam, Phyllis

**Kohut, Les**
See   Kohut, Nester C[larence]

**Kohut, Nester C[larence]** 1925-
[CA]
*Canadian-born author*
* Kohut, Les

**Koilpillai, [Jesudas] Charles** 20th c.
[CA]
*Indian-born economist and author*
* Koilpillai, Das

**Koilpillai, Das**
See   Koilpillai, [Jesudas] Charles

**Kojima, Shozo** 1928-   [CA]
*Japanese author*
* Hajime, Kijima

**Kokos, Richard Jerome**
See   Kokoszka, Richard Jerome

**Kokoszka, Richard Jerome** 1928-
[BE]
*American baseball player*
* Kokos, Richard Jerome

**Kol**
See   Collins, Dennis

**Kolb, John W.** 1860?-1943 [BEW]
*Actor and playwright*
* Gray, William

**Kolba, Tamara** 20th c. [CA, SAT]
*Russian-born American author and illustrator*
* St. Tamara

**Kole, A. K.**
See Lovingood, Alvin

**Kole, Robert**
See Kolodin, Robert

**Kolen, Mike** 1948- [SMG]
*American football player*
* Crunch, Captain

**Kolff, Roelof Coenraad** 1935-
[IAW]
*Dutch writer*
* Van Haren, Wouter

**Kollo, Rene**
See Kollodzieyski, Rene

**Kollodzieyski, Rene** 1937- [OP]
*German opera singer*
* Kollo, Rene

**Kollonige, Joseph Edward** 1922-
[BE]
*American baseball player*
* Collins, Joe

**Kollontay, Alexandra** 20th c.
[LAO]
*Russian diplomat and author*
* Schura

**Kolloway, Butch**
See Kolloway, Donald Martin

**Kolloway, Cab**
See Kolloway, Donald Martin

**Kolloway, Donald Martin** 1918-
[BE]
*American baseball player*
* Kolloway, Butch
* Kolloway, Cab

**Kolmar, Gertrud**
See Chodziesner, Gertrud

**Kolodin, Robert** 1932- [ASC]
*American composer*
* Kole, Robert

**Kolon, Nita**
See Onadipe, Nathaniel Kolawole

**Kolos-Vary**
See Kolos-Vary, Sigismond

**Kolos-Vary, Sigismond** 1899-
[CAR]
*French painter*
* Kolos-Vary

**Kolp, Jockey**
See Kolp, Raymond Carl

**Kolp, Raymond Carl** 1894-1967
[AS, BE]
*American baseball player*
* Kolp, Jockey

**Kolpe, Max**
*Lyricist*
* Colpet, Max

**Kolumbo, Kristofer**
See Croll, Philip Columbus

**Komed**
See Langer, Alfons

**Komeda, Christopher**
See Komeda-Trzcinski, Krxystof

**Komeda, K. T.**
See Komeda-Trzcinski, Krxystof

**Komeda-Trzcinski, Krxystof**
1931-1969 [EJ7, WEF]
*Polish-born composer*
* Komeda, Christopher
* Komeda, K. T.

**Komer, Blowtorch Bob**
See Komer, Robert

**Komer, Robert** 1922?-
*American government official*
* Komer, Blowtorch Bob

**Komives, Butch**
See Komives, Howard

**Komives, Howard** 1942- [BB]
*American basketball player*
* Komives, Butch

**Komlos, Aladar**
See Kredens, Aladar

**Kommers, Bugs**
See Kommers, Fred Raymond

**Kommers, Fred Raymond**
1886-1943 [BE]
*American baseball player*
* Kommers, Bugs

**Komoda, Kiyo**
See Komoda, Kiyoaki

**Komoda, Kiyoaki** 1937- [ICB]
*Japanese-born illustrator*
* Komoda, Kiyo

**Komorowski, Tadeusz** 1895-1966
[WWW]
*Polish army officer*
* Bor [code name used during World War II]

**Kona Woruk**
See Harris, [Theodore] Wilson

**Konadu, S. A.**
See Konadu, Samuel Asare

**Konadu, Samuel Asare** 1932-
[CA, IAW]
*Ghanaian author*
* Asare, Bediako
* Bediako, K. A.
* Konadu, S. A.
* Sabu, Frank

**Koncil, Frank** ?-1927 [BLB]
*American underworld figure*
* Koncil, Lefty

**Koncil, Lefty**
See Koncil, Frank

**Kondor, R. W.**
See Konecny, Robert Walter

**Kondratowicz, Ludwik Wladyslaw**
1823-1862 [WBD]
*Polish author*
* Syrokomla, Wladyslaw

**Konecny, Robert Walter** 1937-
[BEW]
*American producer and business manager*
* Kondor, R. W.

**Konetchy, Big Ed**
See Konetchy, Edward Joseph

**Konetchy, Edward Joseph**
1885-1947 [AS, BE]
*American baseball player*
* Konetchy, Big Ed
* Koney, Ed

**Koney, Ed**
See Konetchy, Edward Joseph

**Konigsberg, Allen Stewart** 1935-
[CA, FC, FD]
*American actor, director, writer*
* Allen, Heywood
* Allen, Woody

**Konigsberg, C. I.**
See Konigsberg, Isidore

**Konigsberg, Harold** 1922?-
*American underworld figure*
* Konigsberg, Kayo

**Konigsberg, Isidore** 1916- [AW]
*British author*
* Konigsberg, C. I.

**Konigsberg, Kayo**
See Konigsberg, Harold

**Konigsburg, E. L.**
See Konigsburg, Elaine Lobl

**Konigsburg, Elaine Lobl** 1930-
[TCC]
*American author*
* Konigsburg, E. L.

**Konikowski, Alex[ander James]**
1928- [BE]
*American baseball player*
* Konikowski, Whitey

**Konikowski, Whitey**
See Konikowski, Alex[ander James]

**Koning, Fred Wittop** 1921-
[BEW, TR]
*Dutch-born costume and scenic designer, dancer*
* Rey, Frederico
* Wittop, Freddy

**Koning, Hans**
See Koningsberger, Hans

**Koningsberger, Hans** 1912?-
[SAT, WD]
*Dutch-born author, playwright, screenwriter*
* Koning, Hans

**Koningsbruggen, Rob van**
See Koningsbruggen, Rudolphus Johannes Philippus van

**Koningsbruggen, Rudolphus Johannes Philippus van** 1948- [CAR]
*Dutch painter*
* Koningsbruggen, Rob van

**Konishi, Masatoshi A.** 1938-
[IAW]
*Japanese author*
* Ashok

**Kono, Tamio** 1930- [BBH]
*American weightlifter*
* Kono, Tommy

**Kono, Tommy**
See Kono, Tamio

**Konrad** 12th c. [DNNS]
*German poet*
* [The] Priest

**Konrad, George**
See Konrad, Gyoergy

**Konrad, Gyoergy** 1933- [CA, CLC]
*Hungarian-born author*
* Konrad, George

**Konstam, Anna**
See Kohnstamm, Anna

**Konstam, Gertrude** 1866-1937
[BEW]
*British actress and producer*
* Kingston, Gertrude

**Konstam, Phyllis**
See Kohnstamm, Phyllis

**Konstantinov, F. D.**
See Konstantinov, Fyodor Denisovich

**Konstantinov, Fyodor Denisovich**
1910- [GA]
*Russian graphic artist*
* Konstantinov, F. D.

**Konstantopoulou, Katina**
1900-1973 [SC, WEF]
*Greek actress*
* Paxinou, Katina

**Konte, Frank** 20th c. [RO2]
*American musician*
* Konte, Skip

**Konte, Skip**
See Konte, Frank

**Kontos, Cecille**
See Haddix-Kontos, Cecille P.

**Konx Ompax**
See Whately, Richard

**Koo, V[i] K[yuin] Wellington**
See Ku Wei-chun

**Kooiman, Helen W.**
See Hosier, Helen Kooiman

**Koomoter, Zeno**
See Marnell, Joseph

**Koontz, Annie Elizabeth Duncan**
1919- [IBW]
*American educator and government official*
* Koontz, Libby

**Koontz, Dean R[ay]** 1945-
[ESF, WGT]
*American author*
* Axton, David
* Coffey, Brian
* Dwyer, K. M.

**Koontz, Gerda** 20th c. [SFL]
*Author*
* Amber, Gracie

**Koontz, Libby**
See Koontz, Annie Elizabeth Duncan

**Koop, Katherine C.** 1923- [CA]
*American educator and author*
* LaMancusa, Katherine C.

**Kootch, Danny**
See Kortchmar, Danny

**Kopacz, George Felix** 1941- [BE]
*American baseball player*
* Kopacz, Sonny

**Kopacz, Sonny**
See Kopacz, George Felix

**Kopchia, Joseph** 1930- [BE]
*American baseball player*
* Koppe, Joe

**Kopeliovitch, Leonard** 1923- [JL]
*Russian-born sportswriter*
* Koppett, Leonard

**Koper, Bud**
*See* Koper, Herbert

**Koper, Herbert** 1942- [BB]
*American basketball player*
* Koper, Bud

**Kopf, William Lorenz** 1890-
[BE, SMG]
*American baseball player*
* Brady, Fred

**Koplinka, Charlotte**
*See* Lukas, Charlotte Koplinka

**Koppe, George Maceo** 1869-1922
[AS, BE]
*American baseball player*
* Cuppy, George Joseph
* Cuppy, Nig

**Koppe, Joe**
*See* Kopchia, Joseph

**Koppelman, Charlie** 20th c. [RO1]
*American singer*
* Cane, Charlie

**Koppett, Leonard**
*See* Kopeliovitch, Leonard

**Korab, Jerry** 1948- [SMG]
*Canadian-born hockey player*
* Korab, King Kong

**Korab, King Kong**
*See* Korab, Jerry

**Korcheck, Hoss**
*See* Korcheck, Stephen Joseph
[Steve]

**Korcheck, Stephen Joseph [Steve]**
1932- [BE]
*American baseball player*
* Korcheck, Hoss

**Korczak, Janusz**
*See* Goldszmit, Henryk

**Korda, Alexander**
*See* Kellner, Sandor

**Korda, Sandor**
*See* Kellner, Sandor

**Korda, Zoltan**
*See* Kellner, Zoltan

**Koreff, Nora** 1920- [IPA]
*American ballerina*
* Kaye, Nora

**Kores, Art[hur Emil]** 1886- [BE]
*American baseball player*
* Kores, Dutch

**Kores, Dutch**
*See* Kores, Art[hur Emil]

**Koresh**
*See* Teed, Cyrus Reed

**Korges, James** 1930-1975 [CAP]
*American writer*
* Longleigh, Peter J., Jr.

**Korince, George Eugene** 1946-
[BE]
*Canadian-born baseball player*
* Korince, Moose

**Korince, Moose**
*See* Korince, George Eugene

**Korn, Henry** 1908-1965 [SC]
*American actor and opera singer*
* Cordy, Henry

**Korn, Peggy**
*See* Liss, Peggy K[orn]

**Kornblum, Cinda** 1950- [CA]
*American writer and poet*
* Wormley, Cinda

**Kornbluth, C. M.**
*See* Kornbluth, Cyril M.

**Kornbluth, Cyril M.** 1923-1958
[ESF, SF, WGT]
*American author*
* Balons, Earl
* Barclay, Gabriel [house
  pseudonym]
* Cooke, Arthur [joint pseudonym
  with E. Balter, R. Lowndes, J.
  Michel, D. Wollheim]
* Corwin, Cecil
* Davies, Walter C.
* Eisner, Simon
* Falconer, Kenneth
* Gottesman, S. D. [joint
  pseudonym with Robert
  Augustine Lowndes and Frederik
  Pohl]
* Judd, Cyril [joint pseudonym with
  Josephine Judith Grossman and
  Frederik Pohl]
* Kornbluth, C. M.
* Lavond, Paul Dennis [joint
  pseudonym with J. H. Dockweiler,
  R. A. Lowndes, F. Pohl]
* Mariner, Scott [joint pseudonym
  with Frederik Pohl]
* Park, Jordan [joint pseudonym
  with Frederik Pohl]
* Pearson, Martin [joint pseudonym
  with Donald A(llen) Wollheim]
* Wylie, Dirk [joint pseudonym
  with Joseph Harold Dockweiler
  and Frederik Pohl]

**Korneichuk, Nikolai Ivanovich**
1882-1969 [WOA]
*Russian author*
* Chukovsky, Kornei

**Korner, Alexis** 1928- [PRS]
*French-born musician*
* [The] Father of the British Blues
  Revival
* [The] Grandfather of British
  Rhythm and Blues
* [The] Guv'nor

**Kornfeld, Ruth** 1919- [BEW, TR]
*American producer and director*
* Mitchell, Ruth

**Kornoelje, Clifford** 20th c. [SFP]
*Author*
* Darrow, Jack

**Kornstadt, Grethe Gerda**
1906-1971? [OCF, WEF]
*German actress*
* Parlo, Dita

**Kornstein, Egon F.** 1891- [BBD]
*Hungarian-born musicologist*
* Kenton, Egon F.

**Korolyova, Glafira Serafimovna**
*See* Koslova, Glafira Serafimovna

**Korosi Csoma, Sandor** 1798?-1842
[WBD]
*Hungarian philologist*
* Csoma de Koros

**Korostasheffsky, Adolphe Borisovitch**
1909- [BEW]
*American educator and author*
* Stasheff, Edward

**Korsmo, Emil** 1863- ? [LAO]
*Norwegian educator and author*
* E. K.

**Kortchmar, Danny** 20th c. [RM]
*Musician*
* Kootch, Danny

**Kortner, Fritz**
*See* Kohn, Fritz Nathan

**Kortner, Peter** 1924- [WD]
*American author and screenwriter*
* Hofer, Peter

**Kortooms, Antonius Johannes**
1916- [IAW]
*Dutch author*
* Kortooms, Toon

**Kortooms, Toon**
*See* Kortooms, Antonius Johannes

**Korvin, Charles**
*See* Kaiser, Geza

**Korwin-Piotrowska, Gabrjela**
1860-1921 [CD]
*Polish author and playwright*
* Zapolska, Gabrjela

**Korzeniowski, Teodor Jozef Konrad
Nalecz** 1857-1924
[EWL, IPA, LC]
*Polish-born British author*
* Conrad, Joseph
* Von Aschendorf, Ignatz

**Kosco, Andrew John** 1941- [SMG]
*American baseball player*
* Kent, Clark

**Koshorek, Clem[ent John]** 1926-
[BE]
*American baseball player*
* Koshorek, Scooter

**Koshorek, Scooter**
*See* Koshorek, Clem[ent John]

**Kosice, Gyula**
*See* Falik, Fernando

**Kosinski, Jerzy [Nikodem]** 1933-
[B10, CA, WD]
*Polish-born American author*
* Novak, Joseph

**Koski, T-Bone**
*See* Koski, William John [Bill]

**Koski, William John [Bill]** 1932-
[BE]
*American baseball player*
* Koski, T-Bone

**Kosleck, Martin**
*See* Yoshkin, Nicolai

**Koslo, Dave**
*See* Koslowski, George Bernard

**Koslo, George Bernard**
*See* Koslowski, George Bernard

**Koslova, Glafira Serafimovna**
1936- [OP]
*Russian opera singer*
* Korolyova, Glafira Serafimovna

**Koslowski, George Bernard**
1920-1975 [B10, BE]
*American baseball player*
* Koslo, Dave
* Koslo, George Bernard

**Kosow, Sophia** 1910-
[BEW, F2, FC]
*American actress*
* Sidney, Sylvia

**Kossack, N. E.** 20th c. [EJS]
*American football player*
* Kossack, Tully

**Kossack, Tully**
*See* Kossack, N. E.

**Kossak, Zofia**
*See* Kossak-Szczucka, Zofia

**Kossak-Szczucka, Zofia** 1890-
[TC1]
*Polish author*
* Kossak, Zofia

**[The] Kossuth of the Temperance
Revolution**
*See* Dow, Neal

**Kosta, Ensio**
*See* Ducander, Sten Carl

**Koste, Robert Francis** 1933- [CA]
*American author*
* Cuff, Barry

**Koster, Cornelius** 1905- [BEW]
*American actor, singer, director*
* Tudor, Rowan

**Koster, Fred[erick Charles]** 1905-
[BE]
*American baseball player*
* Koster, Fritz

**Koster, Fritz**
*See* Koster, Fred[erick Charles]

**Koster, Henry**
*See* Kosterlitz, Hermann

**Kosterlitz, Hermann** 1905-
[BDF, FC, FD]
*German-born director*
* Koster, Henry

**Kostia, Conde**
*See* Valdivia y Sisay, Aniceto

**Kostiuk, Hryhory** 1902-
[CA, IAW]
*Ukranian-born American author*
* Podoliak, Boris

**Kostraba, Daniel** 1924- [EJ]
*American jazz musician*
* Terry, Dan

**Kostrowitski, Wilhelm [or
Guillaume?]** 1880-1918
[EWL, LC, TC]
*French poet, author, critic*
* Apollinaire, Guillaume

**Kotey, David** 20th c. [RBE]
*African boxer*
* Poison, David

**Kotkin, David** 1956- [BS]
*American magician*
* Copperfield, David
* Davino
* Omar, the Magnificent

**Kotschnig, John Walter** 1931- [OP]
*American opera theatre technical
director*
* Priest, John

**Kotta, Leo F.** 1880-1965 [EWL]
*German author and critic*
* Flake, Otto

**Kotzebue, August Friedrich Ferdinand von** 1761-1819
[DEP, HN, SN]
*German author and playwright*
* [The] Shakespeare of Germany

**Kotzebue, Wilhelm** 1813-1887
[WBD]
*Diplomat, author, playwright*
* Augustsohn, W.

**Koues, Helen**
See Bodine, Helen Koues

**Koutoukas, H. M.**
See Rivoli, Mario

**Kouts, Hertha Pretorius** 1922-
[CA]
*American author*
* Pretorius, Hertha

**Kovacs, Laszlo** 20th c. [WF]
*Cinematographer*
* Kovaks, Leslie

**Kovacs, Mor**
See Koczan, Mor

**Kovaks, Leslie**
See Kovacs, Laszlo

**Kovarovic, Karel** 1862-1920
[WBD]
*Czech conductor and composer*
* Forgeron, Charles

**Kove, Kenneth**
See Bridgewater, John William Stevenson

**Kover, Joe**
See Ackerman, Forrest J[ames]

**Kovner, B.**
See Adler, Jacob

**Kovolick, Little Farvel**
See Kovolick, Philip

**Kovolick, Philip** 20th c.
[BLB, MM]
*American underworld figure*
* Cohn, Phil
* Kovolick, Little Farvel
* [The] Stick

**Kowalewskie, Harry Frank**
1886-1950 [BAB, BE, PB]
*American baseball player*
* Coveleskie, Harry Frank
* [The] Giant Killer

**Kowalewskie, Stanislaus** 1889-
[BAB, BE]
*American baseball player*
* Coveleskie, Stan[ley Anthony]
* [The] Silent Pole

**Kowarzik, Viktor** 1904-1973 [SC]
*German actor and director*
* De Kowa, Viktor

**Kowet, Don** 1937- [CA]
*American author*
* Gell, Frank

**Kowitt, Sylvia**
See Crosbie, Sylvia Kowitt

**Koxinga** 1623-1663 [WBD]
*Chinese general and pirate*
* [The] Pirate Patriot

**Koy, Chief**
See Koy, Ernest Anyz

**Koy, Ernest Anyz** 1909- [BE]
*American baseball player*
* Koy, Chief

**Kozak, Don** 1952- [SMG]
*Canadian-born hockey player*
* Kozak, Kozy

**Kozak, Kozy**
See Kozak, Don

**Kracher, Joseph Peter [Joe]** 1915-
[BE]
*American baseball player*
* Kracher, Jug

**Kracher, Jug**
See Kracher, Joseph Peter [Joe]

**Kraemer, Franz** 1906- [OP]
*German opera singer*
* Kraemer, Hans

**Kraemer, Hans**
See Kraemer, Franz

**Kraenzel, Margaret [Powell]** 1899-
[CA]
*American author and poet*
* Blue, Wallace

**Kraft, Big Boy**
See Kraft, Clarence Otto

**Kraft, Clarence Otto** 1887-1958
[BE]
*American baseball player*
* Kraft, Big Boy

**Kraft, Walter Andreas**
See Friedlander, Walter A[ndreas]

**Kragen, Jinx**
See Morgan, Judith A[dams]

**Krah, Marc**
See Krahmalkov, Max

**Krahmalkov, Max** 1906-1973 [SC]
*Actor*
* Krah, Marc

**Krainy, Anton**
See Gippius, Zinaida Nikolaievna

**Krakauer, Jay Frank** 1894- [WWL]
*American writer*
* Efkay, Jay

**Krake, Philip Gordon** 1943-
[CEI, HR, SMG]
*Canadian-born hockey player*
* Krake, Skip

**Krake, Skip**
See Krake, Philip Gordon

**Kraly, Lefty**
See Kraly, Steve Charles

**Kraly, Steve Charles** 1929- [BE]
*American baseball player*
* Kraly, Lefty

**Kramer, Benjamin** 1913- [EJS]
*American basketball player*
* Kramer, Red

**Kramer, Billy J.**
See Ashton, William

**Kramer, Frank**
See Parolini, Gianfranco

**Kramer, George**
See Heuman, William

**Kramer, Janet** 1939?-1978 [FIR]
*Canadian actress and producer*
* Kramer, Sue

**Kramer, Josef** 1906-1945 [BDW]
*German Nazi official*
* [The] Beast of Belsen

**Kramer, Oaf**
See Kramer, Ron

**Kramer, Red**
See Kramer, Benjamin

**Kramer, Ron** 20th c.
*American football player*
* Kramer, Oaf

**Kramer, Stanley**
See Abramson, Stanley J.

**Kramer, Sue**
See Kramer, Janet

**Kramish, Arnold** 1923- [CA]
*American author*
* Paine, J. Lincoln

**Krampe, Hugh Charles** 1928?-
[BEW, IPA, SW]
*American actor*
* O'Brian, Hugh

**Krampf, Max** 1874-1933 [SC]
*German actor*
* Adalbert, Max

**Krangel, David** 1923- [BEW]
*American lyricist and librettist*
* Craig, David

**Krantz, D.**
See Izbitsky [or Ishbitsky], Samuel

**Krantz [or Kranz?], Jacob [Jake]**
1899-1977 [F2, FC, FD]
*American actor*
* Cortez, Ricardo

**Krantz [or Kranz?], Stanley** 1908-
[FC, OCF, WEF]
*American cinematographer*
* Cortez, Stanley

**Kranzler, George G[ershon]** 1916-
[CA]
*German-born author*
* Isaacs, Jacob
* Kranzler, Gershon

**Kranzler, Gershon**
See Kranzler, George G[ershon]

**Krapiva**
See Atrakhovich, Kondrat Kondratyevich

**Krapp, [Eu]gene [H.]** 1888-1923
[BE]
*American baseball player*
* Krapp, Rubber

**Krapp, R. M.** 1915- [CA]
*American author and critic*
* Adams, Robert Martin

**Krapp, Rubber**
See Krapp, [Eu]gene [H.]

**Kraselchik, R.**
See Dyer, Charles [Raymond]

**Krasicki, Ignatius** 1774-1801
[DNNS, FFF, SN]
*Polish author and poet*
* [The] Polish Voltaire
* [The] Voltaire of Poland

**Krasko, Ivan**
See Botto, Jan

**Krasne, Betty**
See Levine, Betty K[rasne]

**Krasney, Samuel A.** 1922-
[CA, WW]
*American author*
* Curzon, Sam

**Krasnov, Petr Nikolaevich**
1869-1947 [SFL]
*Author*
* Krassnoff, Peter N.

**Krassnoff, Peter N.**
See Krasnov, Petr Nikolaevich

**Kraszewski, Jozef Ignacy**
1812-1887 [WBD]
*Polish author*
* Boleslawita

**Kratos**
See Power, Norman S[andiford]

**Krauledat, Joachim** 1944- [RO2]
*German-born musician*
* Kay, John

**Kraus, Ahuva**
See Krivitzki, Ahuva

**Kraus, Alfredo**
See Kraus Trujillo, Alfredo

**Kraus, Babe**
See Kraus, Francis Lucas

**Kraus, Cactus**
See Kraus, John William

**Kraus, Francis Lucas** 1899- ?
[BBH]
*American lacrosse player and coach*
* Kraus, Babe

**Kraus, John William** 1918-1976
[BN]
*American baseball player*
* Kraus, Cactus
* Kraus, Tex
* Kraus, Texas Jack

**Kraus, Robert** 1925- [TBJ]
*American author and illustrator*
* Hippopotamus, Eugene H.

**Kraus, Tex**
See Kraus, John William

**Kraus, Texas Jack**
See Kraus, John William

**Kraus Trujillo, Alfredo** 1927- [OP]
*Spanish opera singer*
* Kraus, Alfredo

**Krause, Edward** 1913- [BB]
*American basketball and football player, coach*
* Krause, Moose

**Krause, Ernst Ludwig** 1839-1903
[WBD]
*German author*
* Carus Sterne

**Krause, Hal**
See Krause, Harry William

**Krause, Harry William** 1887-1940
[BE]
*American baseball player*
* Krause, Hal
* Krause, Lefty

**Krause, Lefty**
See Krause, Harry William

**Krause, Moose**
See Krause, Edward

**Krauss, Charles E.** 1860-1952
*American actor*
* French, Charles K.

**Krauss, Helen** 1863-1917 [SC]
*American actress*
* French, Helen

**Krauth, Violet** 1913- [FC]
*American actress*
* Marsh, Marion

**Krautter, Elisa [Bialk]** [CA]
*American author*
* Bialk, Elisa

**Kravchinski, Sergei Mikhailovich**
1852-1895 [WBD]
*Russian author*
* Stepnyak, Sergei Mikhailovich

**Kravitz, Beak**
See Kravitz, Daniel

**Kravitz, Daniel** 1930- [BE]
*American baseball player*
* Kravitz, Beak
* Kravitz, Dusty

**Kravitz, Dusty**
See Kravitz, Daniel

**Kravitz, Louis** 20th c. [BLB]
*American underworld figure*
* Kravitz, Shadows

**Kravitz, Nathaniel [or Nathan]**
See Krivitsky, Nathaniel

**Kravitz, Shadows**
See Kravitz, Louis

**Krazy George Henderson**
See Henderson, George

**Krebs, Mary Tomlinson** 1890-1975
[FC, IPA]
*American actress*
* Main, Marjorie

**Krech, Warren William** 1895-1948
[F2, FC]
*American actor*
* William, Warren

**Kredens, Aladar** 1892- [JL]
*Hungarian literary critic*
* Komlos, Aladar

**Kreeger, Marianne** 1929- [ART]
*German-born painter*
* M. K.

**Krefetz, Ruth** 1931-1972 [CAP]
*Austrian-born author and illustrator*
* Marossi, Ruth

**Kreig, Margaret B. [Baltzell]** 1922-
[CA]
*American author*
* Craig, Peggy

**Kreis, Erna** 1899- [IAW]
*Swiss author, poet, playwright*
* Modena, Maria

**Kreitz, Ralph Wesley** 1886-1941
[BE]
*American baseball player*
* Kreitz, Red

**Kreitz, Red**
See Kreitz, Ralph Wesley

**Krejci, Jerome** 1918- [CA]
*American author*
* Taylor, Jerome

**Kremer, Ray**
See Kremer, Remy Peter

**Kremer, Remy Peter** 1893-1965
[AS, BE, PB]
*American baseball player*
* Kremer, Ray
* Kremer, Wiz

**Kremer, Wiz**
See Kremer, Remy Peter

**Kremlin**
See Robinson, William Stevens

**Kremnitz, Marie** 1852-1916
*German writer*
* Allan, George
* Dito und Idem [joint pseudonym
  with Elizabeth, Queen of
  Rumania]

**Krentel, Mildred White** 1921- [CA]
*American author*
* Miggy, Mrs.

**Krenz-Senior, Ethel Rosabelle**
1903- [IAW]
*Dutch writer*
* Miranda, Maria

**Krepps, Robert W[ilson]**
1919-1980 [CA, WGT]
*American author*
* Brandon, Beatrice
* Logan, Jake [house pseudonym,
  Playboy Press]
* St. Reynard, Geoff

**Kresge, George Joseph, Jr.** 1935-
[CA]
*American entertainer*
* [The] Amazing Kreskin
* Kreskin

**Kreskin**
See Kresge, George Joseph, Jr.

**Kress, Frederick** 1912-1961 [SC]
*American actor and screenwriter*
* Brady, Fred

**Kress, Ralph** 1907-1962 [AS, BE]
*American baseball player*
* Kress, Red

**Kress, Red**
See Kress, Ralph

**Kreuger, Ivar** 1880-1932 [CEC]
*Swedish industrialist and forger*
* [The] Match King

**Kreuter, Margot**
See Kreuter-Trankel, Margot

**Kreuter-Trankel, Margot** 1929-
[IAW]
*German author*
* Kreuter, Margot
* Stephan, Agnes
* Trankel, Margot

**Kreuzenau, Michael**
See Law, Michael Haldane

**Krevitsky, Nathan I.** 1914- [CA]
*American educator and author*
* Krevitsky, Nik

**Krevitsky, Nik**
See Krevitsky, Nathan I.

**Krey, Laura Lettie [Smith]** 1890-
[TC]
*American author*
* Everett, Mary

**Kriedt, David N.** 1922- [EJ]
*American jazz musician*
* Van Kriedt, David

**Krieger, Al**
See Kunde, Al

**Krieger, Dutch**
See Krieger, Kurt Ferdinand

**Krieger, Kurt Ferdinand**
1926-1970 [BE]
*Austrian-born baseball player*
* Krieger, Dutch

**Krieger, Maxime**
See Melamed, Samuel Max

**Krieger, William**
See Melamed, Samuel Max

**Krietner, Albert Joseph** 1922- [BE]
*American baseball player*
* Krietner, Mickey

**Krietner, Mickey**
See Krietner, Albert Joseph

**Krik**
See Crickmore, Henry G.

**Krishna**
See Sarma, Challa Radhakrishna

**Krishnamurti, Jiddu** 1895- [CA]
*Indian-born writer and lecturer*
* Alcyone

**Krislov, Alexander**
See Howard, Leigh

**Kriss, Fred**
See Kneeland, Fred J.

**Kriss Kringle [or Christ Kinkle]**
See Nicholas

**Krist, Howard Wilbur** 1916- [BE]
*American baseball player*
* Krist, Spud

**Krist, Spud**
See Krist, Howard Wilbur

**Kristian, Hans**
See Neerskov, Hans Kristian

**Kristian, Marty**
See Vanags, Martin

**Kristofferson, Kris** 1936?-
*American singer, songwriter, actor*
* Carson, Kris

**Krivitsky, Nathaniel** 1905- [CA]
*Rumanian-born American author*
* Ben Horav, Naphthali
* Kravitz, Nathaniel [or Nathan]

**Krivitzki, Ahuva** 1932- [EJS]
*Israeli high-jump champion*
* Kraus, Ahuva

**Kriyananda, [Swami]**
See Walker, J. Donald

**Kroates**
See Polk, Josiah F.

**Kroeber, Theodora [Kracaw]**
1897-1979 [CA]
*American anthropologist and author*
* Kroeber-Quinn, Theodora

**Kroeber-Quinn, Theodora**
See Kroeber, Theodora [Kracaw]

**Kroene, Karl**
*American frisbee player*
* Kroene, Mountain

**Kroene, Mountain**
See Kroene, Karl

**Kroepcke, Karol**
See Krolow, Karl [Gustav
Heinrich]

**Kroger, Helen**
See Cohen, Lorna

**Kroger, Peter**
See Cohen, Morris

**Krogh, Bud**
See Krogh, Egil

**Krogh, Egil** 1939?-
*American government official
involved in Watergate political
scandal*
* Krogh, Bud

**Kroh, Floyd Myron** 1886-1944
[BE]
*American baseball player*
* Kroh, Rube

**Kroh, Rube**
See Kroh, Floyd Myron

**Krol, Joe** 20th c. [CFH]
*Canadian football player*
* Krol, King

**Krol, King**
See Krol, Joe

**Kroll, Burt**
See Rowland, D[onald] S[ydney]

**Krolow, Karl [Gustav Heinrich]**
1915- [CA]
*German poet*
* Kroepcke, Karol

**Krome**
See Barratt, Krome

**[The] Kronic Krisis**
See Karl, Larry

**Kross, Rudy**
See Vogelland, Rico

**Krotki, Karol J[ozef]** 1922- [CA]
*Polish-born statistician and writer*
* Krzywan, Jozef

**Krotkov, Yuri** 1917-
*Russian author*
* Karlin, George

**Krsnich, Rocco Peter** 1927- [BE]
*American baseball player*
* Krsnich, Rocky

**Krsnich, Rocky**
See Krsnich, Rocco Peter

**Krudener, Julia de Weitinghoff**
1764-1824 [SN]
*Russian author and mystic*
* [The] Joan of Arc of Peace

**Krueger, Arthur William**
1876-1961 [BE]
*American baseball player*
* Krueger, Oom Paul
* Krueger, Otto

**Krueger, Bum**
See Krueger, Willy

**Krueger, Franz** 1797-1857 [WBD]
*German painter*
* Krueger, Pferde [Horse-Krueger]

**Krueger, Oom Paul**
See Krueger, Arthur William

**Krueger, Otto**
See Krueger, Arthur William

**Krueger, Pferde [Horse-Krueger]**
See Krueger, Franz

**Krueger, Willy** 1906-1971 [SC]
*German actor*
* Krueger, Bum

**Kruess, James** 1926- [CA, SAT]
*German author*
* Polder, Markus
* Ritter, Felix

**Krug, Chris**
*See* Krug, Everett Ben

**Krug, Everett Ben** 1939- [BE]
*American baseball player*
* Krug, Chris

**Krug, [Wenzel] Joseph** 1858-1915
[BBD]
*German composer and conductor*
* Krug-Waldsee, [Wenzel] Joseph

**Krug-Waldsee, [Wenzel] Joseph**
*See* Krug, [Wenzel] Joseph

**Kruger, Harold** 1897?-1965 [AS]
*American swimming champion and movie stunt man*
* Kruger, Stubby

**Kruger, Paul**
*See* Sebenthal, Roberta Elizabeth

**Kruger, Paul [or Paulus]**
1825-1904 [NN]
*President of the Transvaal republic*
* Uncle Paul

**Kruger, Stephanus Johannes**
1825-1904 [DNNS, WBD]
*South African president*
* Oom Paul

**Kruger, Stubby**
*See* Kruger, Harold

**Krull, Felix**
*See* White, Stanley

**Krumbein, Maurice** 1908- [ASC]
*American musician*
* Carter, Ray

**Krupp, D. Dudley** 1894- [ASC]
*American composer and physician*
* Manners, Dudley

**Krupp, Vera**
*See* Hosenfeldt, Vera

**Kruse, June Millichamp**
*See* Anderson, Karen

**Krusty Kay Graham**
*See* Graham, Katharine

**Krutzch, Gus**
*See* Eliot, Thomas Stearns

**Krylenko, Nikolai Vasilievich**
1885-1938? [WBD]
*Russian Communist leader*
* Abram

**Krymski**
*See* Dolgoruki [or Dolgorukov],
Vasili Mikhailovich

**Krymskii, Victor**
*See* Ioffe, Adolf Abramovich

**Krypton**
*See* Graham, Lloyd M.

**Kryptos**
*See* Hidden, Norman Frederick

**Krzesinska, Elzbieta** 1934- [TF]
*Polish track and field athlete*
* Krzesinska, Gold Ela

**Krzesinska, Gold Ela**
*See* Krzesinska, Elzbieta

**Krzyminski, John** 1895- [BBH]
*American bowler*
* Crimmins, General
* Crimmins, John

**Krzywan, Jozef**
*See* Krotki, Karol J[ozef]

**Ku Wei-chun** 1888- [CA]
*Chinese-born diplomat and author*
* Koo, V[i] K[yuin] Wellington

**Kuang Hsu [or Kwang Hsu]**
1871-1908 [WBD]
*Chinese emperor*
* Tsai T'ien [Glorious Succession]

**Kubelsky, Benjamin [Benny]**
1894-1974 [BDF, BMH, FC]
*American comedian*
* Benny, Benny K.
* Benny, Jack

**Kubie, Nora Gottheil Benjamin**
1899- [CA]
*American author*
* Benjamin, Nora

**Kubilius, Walter** 1918- [WGT]
*American author*
* Klimaris, J. S.

**Kubis, Pat** 1928- [CA]
*American author*
* Scott, Casey

**Kuchacevich Ze Schluderpacheru,
Herbert Charles Angelo** 1917- [FC]
*Czech actor*
* Lom, Herbert

**Kucharski, Jan Edward** 1914-
[IAW]
*Polish author*
* Kajot, Jek

**Kuczek, Stanislaw Leo** 1924- [BE]
*American baseball player*
* Kuczek, Steve

**Kuczek, Steve**
*See* Kuczek, Stanislaw Leo

**Kuczynski, Bernard Carl** 1920-
[BE]
*American baseball player*
* Kuczynski, Bert

**Kuczynski, Bert**
*See* Kuczynski, Bernard Carl

**Kuebler-Ross, Elizabeth** 1926-
[CA]
*Swiss-born psychiatrist and author*
* Ross, Elizabeth

**Kuechenberg, Bob** 1947- [SMG]
*American football player*
* Kuechenberg, Kooch

**Kuechenberg, Kooch**
*See* Kuechenberg, Bob

**Kuehn, Dorothy Dalton**
*See* Dalton, Dorothy

**Kuehne, August** 1829-1883 [WBD]
*German author and army officer*
* Van Dewall, Johannes

**Kuehne, John** 1942- [RO2]
*American musician*
* London, John

**Kuehne, Willie**
*See* Knelme, William J.

**Kuehnelt-Leddihn, Erik [Ritter Von]**
1909- [CA, WD]
*Austrian author*
* Campbell, Francis Stuart
* O'Leary, Chester F.
* Vitezovic, Tomislav

**Kuenstler, Morton** 1927- [SAT]
*American illustrator*
* Mutz

**Kuerschner, Konrad** 1478-1556
[WBD]
*Swiss scholar*
* Pellicanus, Konrad

**Kuerten, Peter** 1883-1931 [CEC]
*German murderer*
* [The] Duesseldorf Vampire
* [The] King of Sexual Delinquents

**Kuether, Edith Lyman** 1915- [CA]
*American author*
* Malcolm, Margaret

**Kuhar, Lovro** 1893-1950 [EWL]
*Slovene author*
* Prezihov, Voranc

**Kuhhorn, Martin** 1491-1551
[WBD]
*German religious reformer*
* Aretius Felinus
* Bucer [or Butzer], Martin

**Kuhlos**
*See* Harris, John

**Kuhn, Doggie**
*See* Kuhn, Gordon

**Kuhn, Gordon** 20th c. [CEI]
*Canadian-born hockey player*
* Kuhn, Doggie

**Kuhn, Red**
*See* Kuhn, Walt[er Charles]

**Kuhn, Robert** 1922- [EJ]
*American jazz musician*
* Keene, Bob

**Kuhn, Walt[er Charles]** 1884-1935
[BE]
*American baseball player*
* Kuhn, Red

**Kuhne, Marie [Ahnighito Peary]**
1893-1978 [CA]
*Greenland-born author*
* Peary, Marie Ahnighito

**Kujnir-Herescu, Nadia** 1923-
[FI, FC]
*Russian-Rumanian actress*
* Gray, Nadia

**Kukai** 774- 835 [WBD]
*Japanese clergyman*
* Kobo Daishi

**Kuklos**
*See* Wray, W. Fitzwater

**Kukucin, Martin**
*See* Bencur, Matej

**Kukulowicz, Adolph Frank** 1933-
[CEI]
*Canadian-born hockey player*
* Kukulowicz, Aggie

**Kukulowicz, Aggie**
*See* Kukulowicz, Adolph Frank

**Kulichev, Ignati**
*See* Radolfi, Alexander

**Kulik, Buzz**
*See* Kulik, Seymour

**Kulik, Seymour** 1922-
[FD, ITA, WEF]
*American director and producer*
* Kulik, Buzz

**Kulkavich, Bomber**
*See* Kulky, Henry [Hank]

**Kulky, Henry [Hank]** 1911-1965
[SC]
*American actor and wrestler*
* Kulkavich, Bomber

**Kullinger, J. L.**
*See* Ducette, Vince

**Kullman, Charles**
*See* Kullmann, Charles

**Kullmann, Charles** 1903- [MS]
*American opera singer*
* Kullman, Charles

**Kulmbach, Hans von**
*See* Suess, Hans

**Kulmus**
*See* Gottsched, Louisa A. Victoria

**Kulski, Władysław W[szebor]**
1903- [CA, WD]
*Polish-born political scientist and author*
* Coole, W. W.
* Knight-Patterson, W. M.
* Politicus

**Kumara, Sanandana**
*See* Graham, Roger Phillips

**Kumari, Meena**
*See* Begum, Mehzabeenara

**Kumbel**
*See* Hein, Piet

**Kummer, Clare**
*See* Bacher, Clare Rodman

**Kummer, Frederic Arnold**
1873-1943 [NAA, WGT, WW]
*American author*
* Arnold, John
* Fredericks, Arnold
* Vaeth, Martin
* Wylie, Dirk [joint pseudonym
 with Joseph Harold Dockweiler]

**Kummer, Thomas Jay** 1933-1969
[SC]
*American actor and hair stylist*
* Sebring, Jay

**Kunatz, Peter** 1918- [CWG, DAM]
*American singer*
* Kaye, Peter

**Kuncewicz, Jan** 1580-1623 [WBD]
*Saint*
* Kuncewicz, Josaphat

**Kuncewicz, Josaphat**
*See* Kuncewicz, Jan

**Kuncewicz, Maria [Szczepanska]**
1899- [CAP]
*Russian-born author*
* Kuncewiczowa, Maria

**Kuncewiczowa, Maria**
*See* Kuncewicz, Maria
[Szczepanska]

**Kunde, Al** 1888-1952 [SC]
*American actor and boxer*
* Krieger, Al

**Kunen, James Simon** 1948- [CA]
*American author*
* James, Simon

**Kunfi, Zsigmond**
See Kohn, Zsigmond

**Kung** 1833-1898 [WBD]
*Chinese statesman*
* I Hsin [or Yi Hshin]

**Kung Fu, Mr.**
See Casel, Tyari

**Kung, H. H.**
See K'ung Hsiang-hsi

**K'ung Hsiang-hsi** 1881-1967
[WBD]
*Chinese statesman*
* Kung, H. H.

**Kunitz, Richard E.** 1919- [ASC]
*American composer and banker*
* Evans, Richard

**Kunitz, Stanley [Jasspon]** 1905-
[CA, WD]
*American poet and critic*
* Tante, Dilly

**Kunjufu, Johari M. Amini**
See Latimore, Jewel C.

**Kuntze, Klaus** 1920- [BEW]
*German-born scenic and lighting
designer*
* Holm, Klaus

**Kunz, Earl Dewey** 1899-1963 [BE]
*American baseball player*
* Kunz, Pinch

**Kunz, Pinch**
See Kunz, Earl Dewey

**Kunze, Julia** 1928- [BEW]
*American actress*
* Meade, Julia

**Kunze, Rolf** 1902?-1977 [FIR]
*German author*
* Avena, Rolf

**Kunzur, Sheela**
See Geis, Richard E[rwin]

**Kuper, Emil** 1877-1960 [JL]
*American conductor*
* Cooper, Emil

**Kuper, Yuri**
See Kuperman, Yuri

**Kuperman, Yuri** 1940- [CA]
*Russian-born author and artist*
* Kuper, Yuri

**Kupferberg, Naphtali** 1923- [CA]
*American author*
* Kupferberg, Tuli

**Kupferberg, Tuli**
See Kupferberg, Naphtali

**Kupper, Christiaan Emil Marie**
1883-1931 [CAR]
*Dutch painter*
* Van Doesburg, Theo

**Kupperschmidt, Paul** 1563-1609
[PA]
*Author*
* Cypraeus

**Kuppord, Skelton**
See Adams, J.

**Kurakin, Boris Ivanovich**
1676-1727 [WBD]
*Russian diplomat*
* [The] Father of Russian
Diplomacy

**Kurdsen, Stephen**
See Noon, Brian

**Kurland, Foothills**
See Kurland, Robert A.

**Kurland, Michael** 1938- [CA]
*American author*
* Plum, Jennifer

**Kurland, Robert A.** 1924- [BBH]
*American basketball player*
* Kurland, Foothills

**Kurnitz, Harry** 1908?-1968
[CC, EMD, WW]
*American author and playwright*
* Page, Marco

**Kurowski, Eugeniusz**
See Dobraczynski, Jan

**Kurowski, George John** 1918- [BE]
*American baseball player*
* Kurowski, Whitey

**Kurowski, Whitey**
See Kurowski, George John

**Kurschner, Conrad** 1478-1556 [PA]
*Author*
* Pelican

**Kursh, Charlotte Olmsted** 1912-
[CA]
*American author*
* Olmsted, Charlotte

**Kurt, Gary David** 1947- [SMG]
*Canadian-born hockey player*
* Kurt, Kurty

**Kurt, K. S.**
See Sobotta, Kurt

**Kurt, Kurty**
See Kurt, Gary David

**Kurtsinger, Charles F. [Charlie]**
1907-1946? [BBH]
*American jockey*
* Kurtsinger, Chicken

**Kurtsinger, Chicken**
See Kurtsinger, Charles F.
[Charlie]

**Kurtz, Bud**
See Kurtz, Harold James [Hal]

**Kurtz, C[larence] Gordon** 1902-
[CA]
*American playwright*
* Gordon, Kurtz

**Kurtz, Harold James [Hal]** 1943-
[BE]
*American baseball player*
* Kurtz, Bud

**Kurtz, Manny** 1911- [ASC]
*American composer*
* Curtis, Mann

**Kuruppu, D. S. C.** 20th c. [MBF]
*Ceylonese journalist*
* Christie, Stephen

**Kurz, Artur R.**
See Scortia, Thomas N[icholas]

**Kusborski, Edward** 1912- [MY]
*American jazz musician*
* Kusby, Eddie

**Kusby, Eddie**
See Kusborski, Edward

**Kusenberg, Kurt** 1904- [IAW]
*Swedish-born author*
* Ohl, Hans

**Kushner, Renee Diane** 20th c.
[RO2]
*American singer*
* Renay, Diane

**Kuskin, Karla Seidman** 1932-
[TBJ]
*American author and illustrator*
* Charles, Nicholas

**Kustus, Joe**
See Kustus, Julius

**Kustus, Julius** 20th c. [BE]
*American baseball player*
* Kustus, Joe

**Kuttner, Eugene** 1875-1951 [BEW]
*American drama critic*
* Allen, Kelcey

**Kuttner, Henry** 1915-1958
[ESF, HFF, WGT]
*American author*
* Bellin, Edward J. [house
pseudonym]
* Edmonds, Paul
* Gardner, Noel
* Garth, Will [house pseudonym]
* Hall, James
* Hammond, Keith [joint
pseudonym with Catherine Lucile
Moore]
* Hastings, Hudson [joint
pseudonym with Catherine Lucile
Moore]
* Horn, Peter [house pseudonym,
Ziff-Davis]
* Kent, Kelvin [joint pseudonym
with Arthur K[elvin] Barnes]
* Kenyon, Robert O.
* Liddell, C. H. [joint pseudonym
with Catherine Lucile Moore]
* Maepen, Hugh
* Maepen, K. H.
* Morgan, Scott
* O'Donnell, Lawrence [joint
pseudonym with Catherine Lucile
Moore]
* Padgett, Lewis [joint pseudonym
with Catherine Lucile Moore]
* Smith, Woodrow Wilson
* Stoddard, Charles [house
pseudonym]

**Kutyna, Marion John** 1932- [BE]
*American baseball player*
* Kutyna, Marty

**Kutyna, Marty**
See Kutyna, Marion John

**Kuyumjian, Dikran** 1895-1956
[CC, TC, WW]
*Bulgarian-born British author and
playwright*
* Arlen, Michael

**Kuzava, Robert LeRoy** 1923- [BE]
*American baseball player*
* Kuzava, Sarge

**Kuzava, Sarge**
See Kuzava, Robert LeRoy

**Kuzmowycz, Olha** 1917- [IAW]
*Ukranian-born writer*
* Oka

**Kuznetsov, Anatoli** 1929-1979
[CA]
*Russian author*
* Anatol, A.

**Kvitka, Grigori Petrovich**
1778-1843 [WBD]
*Russian author*
* Osnovyanenko

**Kvitka, Laryssa Petrovna**
1781-1913 [WBD]
*Ukrainian poet*
* Ukrainka, Lesya

**Kwak, Chong Won** 1915- [IAW]
*Korean author*
* Pa, Choon

**Kwalick, Ted**
See Kwalick, Thaddeus John

**Kwalick, Thaddeus John** 1947-
[FB, IPA]
*American football player*
* Kwalick, Ted

**Kwamdela, Odimumba**
See Braithwaite, J. Ashton

**Kwan, George**
See Guarghias, Aloysius George

**Kwang Chang Ling**
See Delmar, Alexander

**Kwant, R. C.**
See Kwant, Remigius C[ornelis]

**Kwant, Remigius C[ornelis]** 1918-
[CA]
*Dutch author*
* Kwant, R. C.
* Kwant, Remy C.

**Kwant, Remy C.**
See Kwant, Remigius C[ornelis]

**Kwasnick, Andrew** 20th c. [SG]
*Boxer*
* Chaney, Andy

**Kwietniewski, Casimir Eugene**
1926- [BE]
*American baseball player*
* Michaels, Casimir Eugene
* Michaels, Cass

**Kwolek, Constance**
See Porcari, Constance Kwolek

**Kwong, King**
See Kwong, Lawrence

**Kwong, Lawrence** 1923- [CEI]
*Canadian-born hockey player*
* Kwong, King

**Kwong, Normie** 20th c. [CFH]
*Canadian football player*
* [The] China Clipper

**Kyd, Thomas**
See Harbage, Alfred B[ennett]

**Kyle, Duncan**
See Broxholme, John Franklin

**Kyle, Elisabeth**
See Dunlop, Agnes M. R.

**Kyle, Gus**
See Kyle, Walter Lawrence

**Kyle, Marlaine**
See Hager, Jean

**Kyle, Robert**
See Terrall, Robert

**Kyle, Sefton**
See Vickers, Roy

**Kyle, Walter Lawrence** 1923-
[CEI, FHE]
*Canadian-born hockey player*
* Kyle, Gus

**Kynaston, Herbert**   [PA]
*Author*
* H. K.

**Kyner, Junior Sylvester** 1932-   [EJ]
*American jazz musician*
* Kyner, Sonny Red

**Kyner, Sonny Red**
*See*   Kyner, Junior Sylvester

**Kyprianos, Iossif**
*See*   Samarakis, Antonis

**Kyrle**
*See*   Tosswill, Leonard R. Major

**Kyrle, John** 1637-1724
[DEL, HN, RH]
*British philanthropist*
* [The] Man of Ross

**Kyser, James Kern** 1906-   [MY]
*American bandleader*
* Kyser, Kay

**Kyser, Kay**
*See*   Kyser, James Kern

# L

* Indicates Assumed Name

**L.**
*See* Lennox, James

**L.**
*See* Lyons, Lady, of Strathmore

**L.**
*See* Swanwick, Catherine

**L. B. J.**
*See* Johnson, Lyndon Baines

**L. B. T.**
*See* Thomas, Lawrence Buckley

**L. C. M.**
*See* Moulton, Ellen Louise Chandler

**L. E.**
*See* Eden, Eleanor

**L. E.**
*See* Edwards, Mrs.

**L. E. L.**
*See* Landon, Letitia Elizabeth

**L. F.**
*See* Hawker, Mary Elizabeth

**L. G.**
*See* Gill, Lilly K. E.

**L. H.**
*See* Hooper, Lucy

**L. I.**
*See* Pratt, J. Loring

**L. K.**
*See* Kinsella, Linda Iris

**L. L. T.**
*See* Toynbee, Lawrence

**L. N. R.**
*See* Ranyard, Ellen Henrietta White

**L. R. G.**
*See* Griffith, Lawrence Rector

**L. W.**
*See* Whistler, Laurence

**La**
*See* Second element of name for further listings

**La Barbera, Pascel** 1944-  [EJ7]
*American jazz musician*
* La Barbera, Pat

**La Barbera, Pat**
*See* La Barbera, Pascel

**La Belle, Chemet**
*See* Lanham, Ceora B.

**La Bolina, Jack**
*See* Vacchi, Augustus Victor

**La Bruyere, Jean de** 1645-1696
[DNNS, RH]
*French author*
* [The] Theophrastus of France

**La Cock, Joanne Letitia** 1923-
[BDF, FC, WEF]
*American actress*
* Dru, Joanne
* Marshall, Joanne

**La Colere [or Lacolere], Francois**
*See* Aragon, Louis

**La Coste, Guy Robert** 20th c.
[WW]
*Author*
* Berton, Guy [joint pseudonym with Eadfrid A. Bingham]

**La Due, Hubert** 1891-  [NAA]
*American author, critic, journalist*
* Moore, Kenneth

**La Faye, Julian** 1907?-  [F2, FC]
*American actor and singer*
* Carroll, John

**La Fayette, Comtesse de**
*See* Pioche de la Vergne, Marie Madeleine

**La Flesche, Susette**
*See* Bright Eyes

**La Fontaine, Blanche**
*See* Schwalberg, Carol[yn Ernestine Stein]

**La Fontaine, Jean de** 1621-1695
[DNNF, SN]
*French poet and author*
* [The] Aesop of France
* [The] French Homer
* Polyphile

**[The] La Fontaine of the Vaudeville**
*See* Panard, Charles-Francois

**La Forrounnays, Mlle.**  [PA]
*Author*
* Craven, Mrs.

**La Fruelen, Mademoiselle**  ?-1801
[FFF]
*Daughter of Emperor Francis Joseph I of Austria*
* [The] Lady of the Haystack?

**La Gierse, Edyth** 1881-1954  [BBD]
*American opera singer*
* De Treville, Yvonne

**La Guardia, Fiorello Henry**
1882-1947
*American politician*
* [The] Little Flower

**La Harpe, Jean Francois de**
1739-1803  [DNNS, SN]
*French poet and critic*
* [The] Fontenelle of His Generation
* [The] French Quintilian

**La Hiff, Anne Veronica**
1905?-1965  [BEW, CED, F2]
*American actress*
* Carroll, Nancy

**La Marck, Guillaume [or William] de**
1446?-1485  [DNNF, FFF, WBD]
*Belgian soldier*
* Sanglier des Ardennes
* [The] Wild Boar of the Ardennes

**La Marck, Robert III de**
1491?-1537?  [WBD]
*Marshal of France*
* Bouillon, Comte de
* Fleuranges, Seigneur de
* [Le] Jeune Aventureux

**La Marr, Barbara**
*See* Watson, Reatha

**La Menthe, Ferdinand Joseph**
1885-1941  [BBD, IBW, WWJ]
*American jazz musician*
* Morton, Jelly Roll
* Morton, William Ferdinand Joseph

**La Mont, Harry**
*See* Gilbert, Alfred

**La Mothe Le Vayer, Francois de**
1583?-1672  [DEP, DNNS, RH]
*French philosopher and author*
* [The] Modern Plutarch
* [The] Plutarch of France

**La Mothe, N. Pere** 1680-1740
[PA]
*Author*
* [La] Hode

**La Motte-Fouque, Friedrich Heinrich Karl de** 1777-1843  [RH]
*German author*
* Pellegrin

**La Plante, Sandra**
*See* Lyons, Luella B.

**La Remnee, Francine** 1898-  [BEW]
*French-born actress*
* Larrimore, Francine

**La Reyniere**
*See* Courtine, Robert

**La Roca, Pete**
*See* Sims, Peter

**[The] La Rochefoucauld of England**
*See* Stanhope, Philip Dormer

**La Rocque De La Rour, Roderick**
1896?-1969  [F1, F2, FC]
*American actor*
* La Rocque, Rod

**La Rocque, Rod**
*See* La Rocque De La Rour, Roderick

**La Roque**
*See* Boyer, Louis

**La Rose, Anthony**
*See* La Rose, John A.

**La Rose, John A.** 1917-  [CW]
*Trinidadian poet, critic, publisher*
* La Rose, Anthony

**La Roy, Rita**
*See* Stuart, Ina

**La Rue, Danny**
*See* Carroll, Daniel Patrick

**La Rue, Jack**
*See* Biondolillo, Gaspare

**La Rue, Jean**
*See* Bailey, Eugene Marcus

**La Salle, Victor** [house pseudonym, John Spencer]
*See* Fanthorpe, R[obert] Lionel

**La Salle, Victor** [house pseudonym]
*See* Glasby, John [Stephen]

**La Santera [The Sanctuary Keeper]**
*See* Martin, Jose

**La Spina, Greye Bragg** 1880-1969
[HFF, NAA, SFP]
*American writer*
* Di Savuto, Baroness
* Kofoed, J. C.
* Putnam, Isra

**La Thorne, Jean**
*See* Dilks, John M.

**La Torre, Charles A.**
*See* Dottore, Charles A.

**La Torre, Giuseppe** 20th c.  [WF]
*Italian cinematographer*
* Tower, Joseph L.

**La Tour d'Auvergne, Henri de [Duc de Bouillon]** 1555-1623   [DEP]
*Marshal of France*
* [The] Demon of Rebellions

**La Tour [or Latour] d'Auvergne, Theophile Malo Corret de** 1743-1800   [DEP, DNNS, SN]
*French soldier*
* [The] First Grenadier of France
* [Le] Premier Grenadier de France
* [Le] Premier Grenadier de la Republique

**La Tour, Tomline**
*See* Gilbert, [Sir] William Schwenck

**La Valliere, Duchesse de**
*See* Baume Le Blanc, Francoise Louise de la

**La Varre, John Merton** 1901-1959 [SC]
*American actor*
* Merton, John

**La Vernie, Laura**
*See* Anderson, Laura

**La Vinder, Gracille**
*See* Mattox, Hazel

**Laage, Barbara**
*See* Colombat, Claire

**Laar [or Laer], Pieter van** 1613?-1674?   [DNNS, RH, SN]
*Dutch painter*
* [Il] Bamboccio [The Deformed]
* Michael Angelo de Kermesses
* [Le] Michel Ange des Bamboches

**Laaveg, Bronco**
*See* Laaveg, Paul

**Laaveg, Paul** 20th c.
*American football player*
* Laaveg, Bronco

**Labadie, Joseph Gilles Michel** 1932-   [CEI]
*Canadian-born hockey player*
* Labadie, Mike

**Labadie, Mike**
*See* Labadie, Joseph Gilles Michel

**Labadie, Mrs. Francis**   [FFF]
*Entertainer*
* Russell, Hattie

**Labaigt, Laurent** 1859-1942 [WBD]
*French poet and author*
* Rameau, Jean

**LaBastille, Anne** 1938-   [CA]
*American author and illustrator*
* Bowes, Anne LaBastille

**L'Abbe, Maurice Joseph** 1947- [CEI]
*Canadian-born hockey player*
* L'Abbe, Moe

**L'Abbe, Moe**
*See* L'Abbe, Maurice Joseph

**Labby**
*See* Labouchere, Henry

**Labe, Louise** 1526-1566 [DNNS, FFF, SN]
*French poet*
* [The] Aspasia of Lyons
* [The] Beautiful Ropemaker
* [La] Belle Cordiere

**Labe, Louise** (Continued)
* Captain Louisa
* Loys, Captain

**LaBelle, Patti**
*See* Holt, Patricia

**Labenette**
*See* Corsee, Jean Baptiste

**Labeo [The Thick-Lipped]**
*See* Notker

**LaBlanche, George**
*See* Blais, George

**LaBorde, Rene**
*See* Neuffer, Irene LaBorde

**Labor's Troubadour**
*See* Glazer, Joe

**Labouchere, Henry** 1831-1912 [FFF]
*British author and journalist*
* Besieged Resident
* Labby
* Our Member for Paris

**Laboy, Coco**
*See* Laboy, Jose Alberto

**Laboy, Jose Alberto** 1939-   [BE]
*Puerto Rican-born baseball player*
* Laboy, Coco

**Labraaten, Dan** 1951-   [SMG]
*Swedish-born hockey player*
* Labraaten, Rusty

**Labraaten, Rusty**
*See* Labraaten, Dan

**Labronio, G.**
*See* Marradi, Giovanni

**Labrousse, M.**   [PA]
*Author*
* Carbon

**Labrunie, Gerard** 1808-1855 [WBD]
*French author*
* Nerval, Gerard de

**Labuchin, Rassoul** 1939-   [CW]
*Haitian poet, author, playwright*
* Medard, Yves

**LaBuna, Virginia** 1905?-1980
*American actress*
* Faire, Virginia Brown

**Lacanal, Joseph** 1762-1845   [WBD]
*French educator and politician*
* Lakanal, Joseph

**Lacanza, Manuel**   [PA]
*Author*
* Ben-Ezra, Juan J.

**Lacepede, Comte de**
*See* De la Ville, Bernard Germain Etienne

**Lacey, Ginger**
*See* Lacey, J. H.

**Lacey, J. H.** 1917-   [BDW]
*British fighter pilot*
* Lacey, Ginger

**Lacey, John**
*See* Alexander, Boyd

**Lacey, Mrs. Henry**   [FFF]
*Entertainer*
* Hawthorne, Kate

**Lacey, Paul** 1851-1900   [BMH]
*British entertainer*
* Godfrey, Charles

**Lach-Szyrma, Wladislaw Somerville** 1841-1915   [SFL, WGT]
*British author*
* W. S. L. S.

**LaChance, Candy**
*See* LaChance, George Joseph

**LaChance, George Joseph** 1870-1932   [AS, BE]
*American baseball player*
* LaChance, Candy

**Lachoff, Sol** 1911-   [ASC]
*American composer*
* Lake, Sol

**Lack, B. D.**
*See* Lack, Barbara Dacia

**Lack, Barbara Dacia** 20th c. [ART]
*British artist*
* Lack, B. D.

**Lack, Pearl** 20th c.   [BEW]
*American choreographer and dancer*
* Lang, Pearl

**Lack, Simon**
*See* Macalpine, Simon

**Lackland [or Sans Terre]**
*See* John

**Lackland, Thomas**
*See* Hill, G. C.

**Lackritz, Steven** 1934-   [EJ]
*American jazz musician*
* Lacy, Steve

**Lacks, Cecilia** 1945-   [CA]
*American author and educator*
* Lacks, Cissy

**Lacks, Cissy**
*See* Lacks, Cecilia

**Lacks, Henrietta**
*Author*
* Lane, Helen

**Laclede, Pierre**
*See* Liguest, Pierre Laclede

**LaCock, Pete**
*See* LaCock, Ralph Pierre, II

**LaCock, Ralph Pierre, II** 1952- [SMG, WWB]
*American baseball player*
* LaCock, Pete

**Lacon**
*See* Watson, Edmund Henry Lacon

**[The] Lacordaire of America**
*See* Esquin, Mamertus

**LaCosta**
*See* Tucker, LaCosta

**Lacoste, Jean Amand** 1797-1885 [FFF]
*French playwright*
* Saint Amand

**Lacoste, Jean-Rene** 1905-   [BBH]
*French tennis player*
* [The] Crocodile

**Lacoste, Mathilde de**   [FFF]
*French author*
* Gerald, Louise

**Lacoume, Emile** 1885-1946   [NOJ]
*American jazz musician*
* Lacoume, Stalebread

**Lacoume, Stalebread**
*See* Lacoume, Emile

**LaCount, Sherwood Keith** 1912-1972   [SC]
*American actor*
* Keith, Sherwood

**Lacroix, Paul** 1806-1884 [FFF, PA, WBD]
*French author*
* Bibliophile Jacob
* Dufour, Pierre
* Jacob, P. L., Bibliophile

**Lacroix, Ramon**
*See* McKeag, Ernest L[ionel]

**Lactantius, Lucius Coelius** ?- 330 [DNNF, HN, SN]
*Author and religious leader*
* [The] Christian Cicero

**Lactilla**
*See* Yearsley, Ann

**Lacy, Ed**
*See* Zinberg, Leonard

**Lacy, Francis Maurice** 1725-1801 [WBD]
*Irish-born army officer*
* Lascy, Franz Moritz

**Lacy, Frank**
*See* Stocken, Frank

**Lacy, Joe**
*See* Elorrieta, Jose Maria

**Lacy, Lee**
*See* Lacy, Leondaus

**Lacy, Leondaus** 1948-   [BE, SMG]
*American baseball player*
* Lacy, Lee

**Lacy, Peter** 1678-1751   [WBD]
*Irish-born army officer*
* Lascy, Pierre

**Lacy, Rube**
*See* Lacy, Rubin

**Lacy, Rubin** 1901-1972?   [BWW]
*American singer*
* Lacy, Rube

**Lacy, Sam** 20th c.   [IBW]
*American columnist*
* [The] Dean of Black Sports Writers

**Lacy, Steve**
*See* Lackritz, Steven

**[The] Lad**
*See* Almagro, Diego de

**[The] Lad from Wigan**
*See* Booth, James

**Ladd, Alan, Jr.** 1938?-
*American film studio executive*
* Ladd, Laddie

**Ladd, Catherine Stratton** 1809- ? [FFF]
*Writer*
* Alida
* Arcturus
* Mayflower, Minnie
* Morna

**Ladd, Cheryl**
*See* Stoppelmoor, Cheryl

**Ladd, Diane**
See Ladnier, Diane

**Ladd, Ernest** 1875-1940 [SC]
*American actor*
* Howard, Ernest

**Ladd, Fred**
See Laderman, Fred

**Ladd, Joseph Brown** 1764-1786
[FFF]
*American poet*
* Arouet

**Ladd, Laddie**
See Ladd, Alan, Jr.

**Ladd, Marion Frances** 1916-1971
[SC]
*American actress*
* Robinson, Frances

**Ladd, William** 1778-1841 [PA]
*Author*
* Philanthropos

**Lade, Doyle Marion** 1921- [BE]
*American baseball player*
* Lade, Porky

**Lade, Porky**
See Lade, Doyle Marion

**Laderman, Fred** 1927- [WEC]
*American animator and producer*
* Ladd, Fred

**Ladislas Posthumus**
See Ladislas V [or VI]

**Ladislas I** 1040?-1095 [WBD]
*King of Hungary*
* [The] Saint

**Ladislas IV** 1262-1290 [WBD]
*King of Hungary*
* [The] Cuman

**Ladislas V [or VI]** 1440-1457
[WBD]
*King of Hungary*
* Ladislas Posthumus

**Ladislaus [or Lancelot]**
1379?-1414 [SN]
*King of Naples*
* [The] Victorious

**Ladnek, Odlaw**
See Kendall, Carlton

**Ladnier, Diane** 1932- [SW]
*French-born actress*
* Ladd, Diane

**LaDoux, Scott** 20th c. [RBE]
*American boxer*
* Ledoux, Scott

**Lady**
See Black, Lillian

**[A] Lady**
See Cooper, Susan Fenimore

**[A] Lady**
See Gamble, Elizabeth
Washington

**[A] Lady**
See Howe, Julia Ward

**[A] Lady**
See Jameson, Anna Murphy

**[A] Lady**
See Rundell, Mrs.

**[A] Lady**
See Sewell, Elizabeth Missing

**Lady Bird Johnson**
See Johnson, Claudia Alta
[Taylor]

**Lady Di**
See Diana

**[The] Lady Freemason**
See St. Leger, Elizabeth

**Lady Gustine**
See Weaver, Gustine Courson

**Lady Lindy**
See Earhart, Amelia

**[The] Lady Magistrate**
See Berkley, Lady

**[The] Lady of Christ College**
See Milton, John

**[The] Lady of England**
See Matilda [or Maud]

**[The] Lady of Mercia**
See Ethelflaeda

**[A] Lady of New York**
See Rogers, Sarah

**[A] Lady of Quality**
See Bagnold, Enid

**[The] Lady of the Haystack?**
See La Fruelen, Mademoiselle

**[The] Lady of the Mercians**
See Aethelflaed [Aethelfled or
Elflida]

**[The] Lady of the Sun**
See Perrers [or Pierce?], Alice

**Lady of Virginia**
See McGuire, Mrs. J. P.

**Lady Pearl**
See Mitchell, Lottie Pearl

**[The] Lady with the Lamp**
See Nightingale, Florence

**Ladylift**
See Hutchinson, John

**Laelius, Gaius** 2nd c. BC
[DEP, WBD]
*Roman general and statesman*
* [The] Roman Socrates
* Sapiens

**Laengsdorff, Julia Virginia** 1878- ?
[LAO]
*German author*
* Julia Virginia

**Laertes**
See Townsend, George Alfred

**Laertes, Joseph**
See Saltzman, Joseph [Joe]

**Laevastu, Taivo**
See Granfeldt, Taivo

**Lafargue, Philip**
See Philpot, Joseph Henry

**Lafayette, Carlos**
See Boiles, Charles Lafayette, Jr.

**Lafayette, Marquis de**
See Du Motier, Marie Joseph Paul
Yves Roch Gilbert

**Lafayette, Rene**
See Hubbard, Lafayette Ronald

**Laffan, Kevin [Barry]** 1922- [CA]
*British playwright, actor, director*
* Barry, Kevin

**Laffeaty, Christina** 1932- [AW]
*South African-born author*
* Carstens, Netta
* Fortina, Martha

**Laffer, Arthur** 20th c.
*American economist*
* Laffer, Curve

**Laffer, Curve**
See Laffer, Arthur

**Lafferty, Flip**
See Lafferty, Frank Bernard

**Lafferty, Frank Bernard**
1854-1910 [BE]
*American baseball player*
* Lafferty, Flip

**Lafferty, Kid**
See Lafferty, Louis

**Lafferty, Louis** 20th c. [BBH]
*Boxer*
* Lafferty, Kid

**Lafferty, Martha Janet** 1921-
[BEW, FC, PMJ]
*American actress, singer, dancer*
* Blair, Janet

**Lafferty, R. A.**
See Lafferty, Raphael Aloysius

**Lafferty, Raphael Aloysius** 1914-
[SF]
*American author*
* Lafferty, R. A.

**Lafferty, Wilson**
See Wilson, Gene

**Laffin, John [Alfred Charles]** 1922-
[AW, CA, WD]
*Australian-born author*
* Dekker, Carl
* Napier, Mark
* Sabre, Dirk

**Lafitte, Doc**
See Lafitte, Edward Francis

**Lafitte, Edward Francis** 1886-
[BE]
*American baseball player*
* Lafitte, Doc

**Lafitte, Jean** 1780?-1826? [DNNS]
*French pivateer and smuggler*
* [The] Pirate of the Gulf

**Lafitte, [Colonel] Leon**
See Ingraham, Prentiss

**Lafitte, Louis** 1917- [ESF]
*French writer*
* Curtis, Jean-Louis

**LaFleur, Guy Damien** 1951-
*Canadian-born hockey player*
* [The] Flower

**Lafontaine, August Heinrich Julius**
1758-1831 [WBD]
*German clergyman and author*
* Freier, Gustav
* Miltenberg
* Selchow

**Lafontant-Medard, Michaelle**
1949- [CW]
*Haitian poet and author*
* Deschamps, Marguerite

**LaForest, Byron Joseph** 1919-1947
[BE]
*Canadian-born baseball player*
* LaForest, Ty

**LaForest, Ty**
See LaForest, Byron Joseph

**Laforest-Divonne, Philomene De**
1887- [WGT]
*Author*
* Silve, Claude

**Laforet, Georg**
See Seitz, Franz

**Lafrensen, Nils** 1737-1807 [WBD]
*Swedish painter*
* Lavreince, Nicolas

**Lafrentz, Ferdinand William** 1859-
? [NAA]
*German-born poet*
* Von Fehmarn

**Lafuente [or La Fuente], Modesto**
1806-1866 [WBD]
*Spanish historian and author*
* Fray Gerundio
* Tirabeque

**Lagaboeter [Reformer of the Laws]**
See Magnus VI

**Lagartija [The Rogue]**
See Ruiz y Vargas, Juan

**Lagartijillo [Little Lizard]**
See Moreno y Fernandez, Antonio

**Lagartijillo-Chico [Tiny Lizard]**
See Moreno del Moral, Jose

**Lagartijo [Lizard]**
See Molina y Martinez, Rafael

**Lagartijo [Lizard]**
See Molina y Sanchez, Rafael

**Lagartijo Chico [Little Lizard]**
See Molina y Martinez, Rafael

**Lageniensis**
See O'Hanlon, John

**Lagerwall, Edna** 20th c. [CA]
*American editor and author*
* Traynor, Alex

**Lagevi, Bo**
See Blom, Karl Arne

**Lagevi, Bo**
See Bolinder, Jean Adolf

**Lagger, Alexander** 1942- [OP]
*Swiss opera singer*
* Malta, Alexander

**Lagneau-Kesteloot, Lilyan**
See Kesteloot, Lilyan

**Lago Severino, Francisco**
1875-1964 [SC]
*Actor*
* Salas, Paco

**Lagrange**
See Cardeilhac, Augustin

**Lagrange-Chancel, Joseph de**
See Chancel, Joseph

**LaGrone, Oliver** 20th c. [LBA]
*American sculptor and poet*
* Oliver, Clarence

**Lahany, Kristin Elaine Eggleston**
1931- [IAW]
*American author*
* Horter, Kristin

**Laharpe, Jean Francois de**
See Delharpe [or Delaharpe], Jean Francois

**[Der] Lahme**
See Hermann von Reichenau

**Lahor, Jean**
See Cazalis, Henry

**Lahoud, Duck**
See Lahoud, Joseph Michael

**Lahoud, Joseph Michael** 1947-
[BE]
*American baseball player*
* Lahoud, Duck

**Lahr, Bert**
See Lahrheim, Irving

**Lahrheim, Irving** 1895-1967
[BEW, EMT, FC]
*American actor*
* Lahr, Bert

**Lahtinen, Duke**
See Lahtinen, Warner H.

**Lahtinen, Warner H.** 1910-1968
[SC]
*American actor*
* Lahtinen, Duke

**Laicus**
See Abbott, Lyman

**Laicus, Phillipe**
See Wasserburg, Phillipp

**Laidlaw, A. K.**
See Grieve, Christopher Murray

**Laidler, Gavin Graham** 1908-1940
[WEC]
*British cartoonist*
* Pont

**Laine**
See Gomez Leon, Diego

**Laine, Alfred** 1895-1957
[NOJ, WWJ]
*American jazz musician*
* Laine, Baby
* Laine, Pantsy

**Laine, Baby**
See Laine, Alfred

**Laine, Cleo**
See Campbell, Clementina Dinah

**Laine, Denny**
See Haynes, Brian Arthur

**Laine, Digger**
See Laine, Julian

**Laine, Frankie**
See LoVecchio, Frank Paul

**Laine, George Vitelle** 1873-1966
[DAM, EJ, WWJ]
*American jazz musician*
* Papa Jack

**Laine, Jack** 1873-1966 [NOJ]
*American jazz musician*
* Laine, Papa

**Laine, Julian** 1907-1957 [NOJ]
*American jazz musician*
* Laine, Digger

**Laine, Pantsy**
See Laine, Alfred

**Laine, Papa**
See Laine, Jack

**Laing, Alexander** 1787-1857 [DEL]
*British poet*
* [The] Brechin Poet

**Laing, Anne C.**
See Schachterle, Nancy [Lange]

**Laing, Patrick**
See Long, Amelia Reynolds

**Laini, Safisha**
See Easton, Carol D.

**Lair, Clara**
See Negron Munoz, Mercedes

**Lair, Grace**
See Gaylor, Grace

**Laird, Dorothy**
See Carr, Dorothy Stevenson Laird

**Laird, Francis C.** 1794- ?
[FFF, PA]
*British author*
* Howard, George, Esq.

**Laird, G. F.** 20th c. [BBH]
*American baseball coach*
* Laird, Red

**Laird, Jean E[louise]** 1930- [CA]
*American writer*
* McKeever, Marcia
* Wakefield, Jean L.

**[The] Laird of Cockpen**
See Caross, Mark

**[The] Laird of Lag**
See Grierson, [Sir] Robert

**[The] Laird of the Halls**
See MacLennan, Harry

**Laird, Red**
See Laird, G. F.

**Laisne, Jeanne** 15th c. [WBD]
*French heroine*
* Fourquet
* Hachette, Jeanne

**Laissing, W. K.** 20th c. [SFP]
*Author*
* Edwards, Dolton

**Lait, Jack**
See Lait, Jacquin

**Lait, Jacquin** 1882-1954
[ALY, SC]
*American author*
* Lait, Jack

**Lajeunesse, Marie Louise Cecilia Emma** 1847-1930 [BBD, BEW]
*Canadian opera singer*
* Albani, Emma

**Lajoie, Larry**
See Lajoie, Napoleon

**Lajoie, Nap**
See Lajoie, Napoleon

**Lajoie, Napoleon** 1875-1959
[AS, BE, PB]
*American baseball player and manager*
* King Larry
* Lajoie, Larry
* Lajoie, Nap

**Lakaitel [Little Lackey]**
See Keitel, Wilhelm

**Lakanal, Joseph**
See Lacanal, Joseph

**Lake, Arthur**
See Silverlake, Arthur

**Lake, Claude**
See Blind, Mathilde

**Lake, Edward Erving [Eddie]** 1916-
[BN]
*American baseball player*
* Lake, Inky

**Lake, Florence**
See Silverlake, Florence

**Lake, Harriette** 1909-
[EMT, F2, FC]
*American actress and singer*
* Sothern, Ann

**Lake, Inky**
See Lake, Edward Erving [Eddie]

**Lake, Joe Barry** 20th c. [WW]
*Author*
* Barry, Joe

**Lake, John**
See Laycock, John W.

**Lake, Kenneth R[obert]** 1931-
[CA, WD]
*British writer*
* Boyer, Robert
* King, Arthur
* Roberts, Ken
* Soutter, Fred

**Lake, Mrs. W. P.** [FFF]
*Entertainer*
* Byron, Clara

**Lake, Sarah**
See Weiner, Margery Sarah

**Lake, Sol**
See Lachoff, Sol

**Lake, Veronica**
See Ockleman, Constance Frances Marie

**Lakeman, Albert Wesley** 1918-
[BE]
*American baseball player*
* Lakeman, Moose

**Lakeman, Moose**
See Lakeman, Albert Wesley

**Laker, Cecil**
See Bainbridge, Harriette Smith

**Laklan, Carli**
See Laughlin, Virginia Carli

**Lakomska, Sylvia Jadviga** 1931-
[BEW]
*Polish-born actress*
* Daneel, Sylvia

**Lakritz, Esther** 1928- [WD]
*American author*
* Collingswood [M.D.], Frederick

**Laks, S.**
See Izbitsky [or Ishbitsky], Samuel

**Lalawethika** 1768?-1834? [WBD]
*American Indian religious leader*
* Elskwatawa
* [The] Prophet
* Tenskwatawa

**Lalita**
See Johnson, Maud Lalita

**Lalla, Mohan Bulchand** 1930-
[IAW]
*Indian author*
* Kalpana, Mohan

**L'Allemand, Pauline**
See Elsasser, Pauline

**Lalli, Cele G[oldsmith]** 1933-
[WGT]
*American author*
* Goldsmith, Cele

**Lallo, Moose**
See Lallo, Morris

**Lallo, Morris** 20th c. [SMG]
*Hockey executive*
* Lallo, Moose

**Lally, Bud**
See Lally, Daniel J.

**Lally, Daniel J.** 1867-1936 [BE]
*American baseball player*
* Lally, Bud

**Lally, Patrick Joseph** 1868-1956
[CSH]
*Canadian lacrosse player*
* [The] Knight of the Whistle

**Lally, William** 1908-1956 [SC]
*American actor and film editor*
* Wallace, Bill

**Lalonde, Edouard** 1887-1970
[CEI, FHE, HK]
*Canadian-born hockey player*
* Lalonde, Newsy

**Lalonde, Newsy**
See Lalonde, Edouard

**Lalonde, Newsy**
See Lalonde, Ron

**Lalonde, Ron** 1952- [SMG]
*Canadian-born hockey player*
* Lalonde, Newsy

**LaMancusa, Katherine C.**
See Koop, Katherine C.

**LaManna, Frank** 1919- [BE]
*American baseball player*
* LaManna, Hank

**LaManna, Hank**
See LaManna, Frank

**Lamanske, Frank James**
1906-1971 [BE]
*American baseball player*
* Lamanske, Lefty

**Lamanske, Lefty**
See Lamanske, Frank James

**Lamar, Ashton**
See Sayler, Harry Lincoln

**Lamar, Bo**
See Lamar, Dwight

**Lamar, Dwight** 1951- [BB, SMG]
*American basketball player*
* Lamar, Bo

**Lamar, Pete**
See Lamar, Pierre

**Lamar, Pierre** 1874-1970 [BE]
*American baseball player*
* Lamar, Pete

**Lamar, William Harmong** 1897-
[BE]
*American baseball player*
* Good Time Bill

**Lamare, Hilton Napoleon** 1907?-
[ASC, DAM, PMJ]
*American jazz musician*
* Lamare, Nappy

**Lamare, Nappy**
See Lamare, Hilton Napoleon

**Lamarr, Hedy**
See Kiesler, Hedwig Eva Marie

**LaMarsh, Judy**
See LaMarsh, Julia Verlyn

**LaMarsh, Julia Verlyn** 1924- [CA]
*Canadian writer*
* LaMarsh, Judy

**Lamartine, Alphonse Marie Louis de Prat de** 1790-1869 [SN]
*French poet*
* [The] Narcissus of France

**[The] Lamb**
See Eric III

**[The] Lamb**
See Sampson, Edgar Melvin

**Lamb, Allan Joseph** 1954- [DC]
*South African cricketer*
* Lamb, Lambie

**Lamb, Antonia** 1943- [IAW]
*American author*
* Foerster-Nietschze, Elisabeth

**Lamb, Charles** 1775-1834 [DEL, SN]
*British author and poet*
* Elia
* [The] Mitre Courtier
* Upright Telltruth, Esq.

**Lamb, Charles Bentall** 1914- [CA]
*British author and naval officer*
* Achilles

**Lamb, Charlotte**
See Holland, Sheila

**Lamb, Clifford** 1888- [THR]
*British actor*
* Heatherley, Clifford

**Lamb, Elizabeth Searle** 1917- [CA]
*American author*
* Mitchell, K. L.

**Lamb, Geoffrey Frederick**
[CA, SAT, WD]
*British author*
* Balaam

**Lamb, Helen B.**
See Lamont, Helen Lamb

**Lamb, Herbert** 1855-1917 [BEW]
*British-born actor*
* Kelcey, Herbert

**Lamb, J.** [PA]
*Author*
* [A] Manchester Man

**Lamb, Lambie**
See Lamb, Allan Joseph

**Lamb, Mary** 1765-1847 [PA]
*Author*
* M. B.

**Lamb, Natalie**
See Elston, Natalie

**[The] Lamb of God**
See Jesus Christ

**Lamb, Ruth** 19th c. [FFF]
*American author*
* Buck, Ruth

**Lamb, William**
See Jameson, [Margaret] Storm

**Lambart, Richard**
See Leighton, Eric

**Lambe, F.** 20th c. [MBF]
*British author*
* Reid, Desmond [house pseudonym]

**Lambeau, Curly**
See Lambeau, Earl L.

**Lambeau, Earl L.** 1898-1965
[AS, FB, SMG]
*American football player and coach*
* Lambeau, Curly

**Lambec, Zoltan**
See Kimbro, John M.

**Lambecius**
See Lambeck, Peter

**Lambeck, Peter** 1628-1680 [PA]
*Author*
* Lambecius

**Lamber, Juliette**
See Adam, Juliette

**Lambert, Arthur**
See Widner, Arthur L.

**Lambert, Christine**
See Freybe, Heidi Huberta

**Lambert, David** 1770-1809 [RH]
*Weighed 739 lbs. at death*
* [The] Fat

**Lambert, Derek** 1929- [CA, WD]
*British author*
* Falkirk, Richard

**Lambert, Elisabeth**
See Ortiz, Elisabeth Lambert

**Lambert, Elizabeth [Minnie]** 1933- [CA]
*Canadian author and playwright*
* Lee, Betty

**Lambert, Eric** 1918-1966 [CAP]
*British author*
* Brennand, Frank
* Kay, George

**Lambert, F. A. Heygate** 20th c. [WWL]
*Welsh author and poet*
* Arthur, Frederick

**Lambert, Francois** 1487-1530 [PA]
*Author*
* Serranus

**Lambert, Franz** 1486?-1530 [WBD]
*Theologian*
* Lambert of Avignon

**Lambert, Harold** 1901- [PMJ]
*American singer*
* Lambert, Scrappy

**Lambert, Leslie Harrison** 1883-1940 [LC, WW]
*British author and broadcaster*
* Alan, A. J.

**Lambert, Louis**
See Gilmore, Patrick Sarsfield

**Lambert, Marion**
See Perry, Montanye

**Lambert of Avignon**
See Lambert, Franz

**Lambert, Piggy**
See Lambert, Ward L.

**Lambert, S. H.**
See Southwold, Stephen

**Lambert, Scrappy**
See Lambert, Harold

**Lambert, T. H.** 20th c. [MBF]
*British author*
* Lumberjack

**Lambert, Ward L.** 1888-1958
[AS, BB]
*American basketball coach*
* Lambert, Piggy

**Lamberti, Michael** ?-1950 [SC]
*American actor*
* Lamberti, Professor

**Lamberti, Professor**
See Lamberti, Michael

**Lambertini, Prospero** 1675-1758 [WBD]
*Pope*
* Benedict XIV

**Lambot, Isobel Mary** 1926- [AW, CA, WD]
*British author*
* Ingham, Daniel
* Rees, Meriel
* Turner, Mary

**Lambourne, John**
See Lamburn, John Battersby Crompton

**Lambton, Hedworth** 1856-1929 [WBD]
*British naval officer*
* Meux, [Sir] Hedworth

**Lamburn, John Battersby Crompton** 1893- [CAP]
*British author*
* Crompton, John
* Lambourne, John

**Lamburn, Richmal Crompton** 1890-1969 [CAP, LC, SAT]
*British author*
* Crompton, Richmal

**[The] Lame**
See Albert II

**[The] Lame**
See Charles II

**[The] Lame**
See Eric XI

**[The] Lame**
See Henry II [or Heinrich]

**[The] Lame**
See Hermann von Reichenau

**[The] Lame**
See Jean [or Jehan] de Meung

**[The] Lame**
See Prusias I

**[The] Lame**
See Tyrtaeus

**Lamey, Bob** 1939- [SMG]
*American sportscaster*
* Lamey, Hockey Bob

**Lamey, Hockey Bob**
See Lamey, Bob

**Lamline, Dutch**
See Lamline, Fred[erick Arthur]

**Lamline, Fred[erick Arthur]** 1891-1970 [BE]
*American baseball player*
* Lamline, Dutch

**Lamm, Baron**
See Lamm, Herman K.

**Lamm, Herman K.** ?-1930 [BLB]
*German-born American bank robber*
* Lamm, Baron

**Lamont, Duncan**
See Tubb, Edwin Charles

**Lamont, Gil**
See Lamont, Gilvan Derwent

**Lamont, Gilvan Derwent** 1947- [SFL]
*British-born author*
* Lamont, Gil

**Lamont, Helen Lamb** 1906?-1975 [CA]
*American economist, educator, author*
* Lamb, Helen B.

**Lamont, Jack**
See Capitola, Jack

**Lamont, Marianne**
See Rundle, Anne

**Lamont, N. B.**
See Barnitt, Nedda Lemmon

**Lamont, Nedda**
See Barnitt, Nedda Lemmon

**Lamont, Rosette C[lementine]** 20th c. [CA]
*French-born American educator and author*
* Farmer, R. L.

**Lamont, Victor**
See Maiorana, Victor E.

**LaMoore, Louis [Dearborn]** 1908- [CA, WD]
*American author and screenwriter*
* Burns, Tex
* L'Amour, Louis [Dearborn]

**LaMotta, Jacob [Jake]** 1921- [BX, RBE]
*American boxer*
* [The] Bronx Bull

**Lamotte-Houdar**
See Houdar de La Motte, Antoine

**Lamour, Dorothy**
See Kaumeyer, Dorothy

**L'Amour, Louis [Dearborn]**
See LaMoore, Louis [Dearborn]

**[The] Lamp of the Law**
See Irnerius

**Lamplugh, Lois**
See Davis, Lois Carlile

**Lampman, Evelyn Sibley** 1907-1980 [CA, MJA, SAT]
*American author*
* Bronson, Lynn

**Lamprecht** 12th c. [DNNS]
*Frankish poet*
* [The] Priest

**Lamprey, A. C.**
See Fish, Robert L.

**Lamptey, Jonathan Kwesi** 1909-
[IAW]
*Ghanaian writer*
* J. K.
* Uncle Kwesi

**Lampton, Austen**
*See* Dent, Anthony Austen

**Lampton, W. J.**    [FFF]
*American writer*
* Mary Jane
* Waxem of Wayback, Jedge

**Lamson, Frank** 1851-1938    [WBD]
*American botanist*
* Lamson-Scribner, Frank

**Lamson, Gertrude** 1874- ?    [BEW]
*American actress*
* O'Neil, Nance

**Lamson-Scribner, Frank**
*See* Lamson, Frank

**Lamy, Douglas N.** 1919-1951    [SC]
*American actor*
* Drake, Douglas
* Mitchell, John

**Lan Ping [Blue Apple]**
*See* Jiang Qing

**Lana**
*See* Kemp, Alan

**[The] Lancashire Burns**
*See* Waugh, Edwin

**[The] Lancashire Hogarth**
*See* Collier, John

**[A] Lancashire Incumbent**
*See* Hume, Abraham

**[The] Lancashire Lad**
*See* Cash, Morny

**[The] Lancashire Poet**
*See* Waugh, Edwin

**Lancashire's Own Principal Boy**
*See* Wood, Daisy

**Lancaster, Captain**
*See* Hook, Samuel Clarke

**Lancaster, Evelyn**
*See* Sizemore, Chris[tine] Costner

**Lancaster, G. B.**
*See* Lyttleton, Edith J.

**Lancaster, Jack**
*See* Burrage, Alfred McLelland

**Lancaster, Sheila**
*See* Holland, Sheila

**Lancaster, Thunderbird**
*See* Lancaster, William Byard

**Lancaster, Time Honored**
*See* John of Gaunt

**Lancaster, William**
*See* Warren, John Byrne Leicester
[Baron de Tabley]

**Lancaster, William Byard** 1942-
[EJ7]
*American jazz musician*
* Lancaster, Thunderbird

**Lancaster, William Joseph Cosens**
1851-1922    [MBF, SFL, WGT]
*British author*
* Collingwood, Harry

**Lance, Albert**
*See* Ingram, Lancelot Albert

**Lance, John**
*See* Bungay, E. Newton

**Lancelotz, Corneille** 1547-1622
[PA]
*Author*
* Lancilottus

**Lancewood, Lawrence**
*See* Wise, Daniel

**Lanchester, Elsa**
*See* Sullivan, Elizabeth

**Lancia, Joseph** 20th c.    [BLB]
*American underworld figure*
* Lancia, Jumbo

**Lancia, Jumbo**
*See* Lancia, Joseph

**Lancilottus**
*See* Lancelotz, Corneille

**Lancing, George**
*See* Hunter, Bluebell Matilda

**Lancour, Gene**
*See* Fisher, Gene L[ouis]

**Land**
*See* Landry, Robert John

**Land, Doc**
*See* Land, William Gilbert

**Land, George Thomas Lock** 1933-
[IAW]
*American author*
* Lock, Thomas

**[The] Land Hero of 1812**
*See* Jackson, Andrew

**Land, Jane and Ross** [joint
pseudonym with Helen Ross (Smith)
Speicher]
*See* Borland, Kathryn Kilby

**Land, Jane and Ross** [joint
pseudonym with Kathryn Kilby
Borland]
*See* Speicher, Helen Ross [Smith]

**Land, Rosina**
*See* Hastings, Phyllis Dora Hodge

**Land, William Gilbert** 1903-    [BE]
*American baseball player*
* Land, Doc

**Landau, Abe** 20th c.    [BLB]
*American underworld figure*
* Landau, Misfit

**Landau, Dorothea**
*See* Da Fano, Dorothea Natalie
Sophia

**Landau, Edwin Maria** 1904-    [IAW]
*German-born author*
* Devin, Marius

**Landau, Mark Aleksandrovich**
1886?-1957    [CD, EWL, TC]
*Russian author*
* Aldanov, Mark Aleksandrovich

**Landau, Misfit**
*See* Landau, Abe

**Lande, Jules**
*Musician*
* [The] Troubador of the Violin

**Lande, Lawrence Montague** 1906-
[WD]
*Canadian author and poet*
* Verval, Alain [joint pseudonym
with Thomas Greenwood]

**Landels, D. H.**
*See* Henderson, Donald Landels

**Landenberger, Ken[neth Henry]**
1928-1960    [BE]
*American baseball player*
* Landenberger, Red

**Landenberger, Red**
*See* Landenberger, Ken[neth
Henry]

**Lander, Dane**
*See* Clarke, Percy A.

**Lander, Jean**
*See* Hello, Mme. Ernst

**Lander, Jean Margaret Davenport**
*See* Donald, Jean Margaret
Davenport

**Lander, Meta**
*See* Lawrence, Margaret Woods

**Landers, Ann**
*See* Crowley, Ruth

**Landers, Ann**
*See* Lederer, Esther Pauline
[Friedman]

**Landers, Lew**
*See* Friedlander, Lewis

**Landesman, Irving Ned** 1919-
[BEW]
*American producer and playwright*
* Landesman, Jay

**Landesman, Jay**
*See* Landesman, Irving Ned

**Landesmann, Heinrich** 1821-1902
[WBD]
*German author and poet*
* Lorm, Hieronymus

**[The] Landgrave**
*See* Montague, Eleonora Louisa

**[The] Landgrave of Hesse**
*See* Rosen, Michael

**Landi, Elissa**
*See* Zanardi-Landi, Elizabeth
Marie

**Landino, Francesco** 1325?-1397
[WBD]
*Florentine muscian and composer*
* Francesco Cieco
* Francesco degli Organi

**Landis, Carole**
*See* Ridste, Frances Lillian Mary

**Landis, Doc**
*See* Landis, Samuel H.

**Landis, Jerry**
*See* Simon, Paul Frederick

**Landis, Jessie Royce**
*See* Medbury, Jessie Royse

**Landis, Samuel H.** 1854- ?    [BE]
*American baseball player*
* Landis, Doc

**Landon, Batesy**
*See* Landon, Bruce

**Landon, Bruce** 1949-    [SMG]
*American hockey player*
* Landon, Batesy

**Landon, Letitia Elizabeth**
1802-1838    [DEL]
*British author and poet*
* L. E. L.

**Landon, Louise**
*See* Hauck, Louise [Platt]

**Landon, Melville De Lancey**
1839-1910    [FFF, SFL, WGT]
*American author*
* Perkins, Eli

**Landon, Michael**
*See* Orowitz, Eugene Maurice

**Landor, Walter Savage** 1775-1864
[SN]
*British author and poet*
* [The] Gebir

**Landreaux, Elizabeth Mary**
1895-1963    [BWW, PMJ, WWJ]
*American singer*
* [The] Creole Songbird
* Miles, Lizzie
* Queen Elleezee
* [La] Rose Noire de Paris [The
Black Rose of Paris]
* Smith, Mandy

**Landrith, Hobert Neal** 1930-    [BE]
*American baseball player*
* Landrith, Hobie

**Landrith, Hobie**
*See* Landrith, Hobert Neal

**Landrum, Terry Lee** 1954-    [SMG]
*American baseball player*
* Landrum, Tito

**Landrum, Tito**
*See* Landrum, Terry Lee

**Landry, Robert John** 1903-    [CA]
*American editor and critic*
* Land

**Landsborough, G. H.** 20th c.
[MBF]
*British author*
* Cody, Stone
* M'Cracken, Mike

**[The] Landseer of Sculpture**
*See* Gatley, Alfred

**[The] Landseer of the Present**
*See* Ansdell, Richard

**Landslide Lyndon Johnson**
*See* Johnson, Lyndon Baines

**Landwirth, Heinz** 1927-    [B10]
*Austrian author*
* Lind, Jakov

**Landy, Dad**
*See* Landy, G. W.

**Landy, G. W.** ?-1930    [BLB]
*American bank robber*
* Landy, Dad

**Landy, Tonny**
*See* Nuppenau, Tonny Landy

**Lane, Allan**
*See* Albershart, Harry

**Lane, Arthur**
*See* Tremaine, F[rederick] Orlin

**Lane, Bay Bay**
*See* Lane, Calvin

**Lane, Burton**
*See* Levy, Burton

**Lane, Calvin** 1954-    [SMG]
*American football player*
* Lane, Bay Bay

**Lane, Chappy**
See  Lane, George M.

**Lane, Charles**
See  Gatti, Arthur Gerard

**Lane, Charles**
See  Lucania, Salvatore

**Lane, Dick** 20th c.
*American billiard player*
* Lane, Night Train

**Lane, Dodo**
See  Lane, [James] Hunter

**Lane, Elizabeth**
See  Farmers, Eileen Elizabeth
[Honeyman]

**Lane, Frank C.** 1896-    [PB]
*American baseball executive*
* Lane, Frantic Frankie

**Lane, Frantic Frankie**
See  Lane, Frank C.

**Lane, George M.**  ?-1896    [BE]
*American baseball player*
* Lane, Chappy

**Lane, Gerald**
See  Fanning, David Christopher
Patrick St. John

**Lane, Gloria**
See  Siet, Gloria

**Lane, Grant**
See  Fisher, Stephen Gould

**Lane, Helen**
See  Lacks, Henrietta

**Lane, Horace**
See  Greaves, Horace

**Lane, [James] Hunter** 1900-    [BE]
*American baseball player*
* Lane, Dodo

**Lane, James A.** 1924-
[BWW, NBB]
*American singer*
* Rogers, James [Jimmy]

**Lane, James Woods** 19th c.    [FFF]
*American writer*
* Cameroy

**Lane, Jane**
See  Dakers, Elaine Kidner

**Lane, Jerry**
See  Martin, Patricia Miles

**Lane, John** [house pseudonym,
Curtis Warren]
See  Hughes, Den[n]is [Talbot]

**Lane, John** [house pseudonym]
See  MacDonald, John D[ann]

**Lane, Katharine A.** 20th c.    [NAA]
*American author*
* Ike

**Lane, Kenneth Westmacott** 1893-
[WW]
*Author*
* West, Keith

**Lane, Laurie**
See  Clapsaddle, Hilda R.

**Lane, Lola**
See  Mullican, Dorothy

**Lane, Lupino**
See  Lupino, Henry George

**Lane, Mary D.**
See  Delaney, Mary Murray

**Lane, Mary Louisa** 1894-    [WWL]
*Australian writer*
* Emel
* Lee, Mariel

**Lane, Master Juba**
See  Lane, William Henry

**Lane, Night Train**
See  Lane, Dick

**Lane, Night Train**
See  Lane, Richard

**Lane, Nipper**
See  Lupino, Henry George

**Lane, Priscilla**
See  Mullican, Priscilla

**Lane, R.**
See  Vanderbilt, Cornelius, Jr.

**Lane, Ralph Norman Angell**
1872-1967    [LC, TC]
*British economist and author*
* Angell, [Sir] Norman

**Lane, Richard** 1928-    [FB]
*American football player*
* Lane, Night Train

**Lane, Rocky**
See  Albershart, Harry

**Lane, Rose Wilder** 1887-1968
[WYA]
*American author*
* Wilder, Rose

**Lane, Rosemary**
See  Mullican, Rosemary

**Lane, Sarah**    [FFF]
*Author*
* Kingston, May

**Lane, Sheena Porter** 1935-    [TBJ]
*British author*
* Porter, Sheena

**Lane, Sherry**
See  Smith, Richard Rein

**Lane, Temple**
See  Leslie, Mary Isabel

**Lane, Wallace**
See  Lupino, Wallace

**Lane, Wickliffe**
See  Jenings, Elizabeth Janet

**Lane, William Henry** 1825-1853
[IBW]
*American dancer*
* Lane, Master Juba

**Lane, Yoti** 20th c.    [CA]
*Irish-born author, director, critic*
* Mayo, Mark

**Lane Fox, Augustus Henry**
1827-1900    [WBD]
*British army officer*
* Pitt-Rivers, Augustus Henry

**Lane-Jackson, Nicholas** 1849- ?
[LAO]
*British journalist*
* Creston

**Lanes, Selma Gordon** 1929-
[CA, SAT]
*American author*
* Gordon, Selma

**Lanford, Lewis Grover** 1886-    [BE]
*American baseball player*
* Lanford, Sam

**Lanford, Sam**
See  Lanford, Lewis Grover

**Lang, Andrew** 1844-1912
[SFL, TCC, WGT]
*Scottish author and poet*
* Longway, A. Huge
* [A] Well Known Author

**Lang, Anthony**
See  Vahey, John George Haslette

**Lang, Bunny**
See  Lang, Violet Ranney

**Lang, Chip**
See  Lang, Robert David

**Lang, Eddie**
See  Massaro, Salvatore

**Lang, Frances**
See  Mantle, Winifred Langford

**Lang, Grace**
See  Floren, Lee

**Lang, Gregor**
See  Birren, Faber

**Lang, Howard**
See  Lange, Frederick

**Lang, Isaac** 1891-1950
[B10, TCL, WOA]
*French-born poet, author,
playwright*
* Goll, Iwan [or Yvan]
* Lassang, Iwan
* Thor, Johannes
* Thor, Tristan
* Torsi, Tristan

**Lang, Jim**
See  Sellers, Connie Leslie, Jr.

**Lang, June**
See  Vlasek, June

**Lang, King** [house pseudonym,
Curtis Warren]
See  Griffiths, David Arthur

**Lang, King** [house pseudonym,
Curtis Warren]
See  Hay, George

**Lang, King** [house pseudonym,
Curtis Warren]
See  Holloway, Brian

**Lang, King** [house pseudonym,
Curtis Warren]
See  Jennison, John W[illiam]

**Lang, King** [house pseudonym,
Curtis Warren]
See  Tubb, Edwin Charles

**Lang, Lefty**
See  Lang, Martin John [Marty]

**Lang, Maria**
See  Lange, Maria Dagmar

**Lang, Martin**
See  Birren, Faber

**Lang, Martin John [Marty]**
1906-1968    [BE]
*American baseball player*
* Lang, Lefty

**Lang, Maud**
See  Williams, Claerwen

**Lang, Pearl**
See  Lack, Pearl

**Lang, Peter**
See  Fearn, C. Eaton

**Lang, Rex**
See  Lyttle, Richard B[ard]

**Lang, Robert David** 1952-    [SMG]
*American baseball player*
* Lang, Chip

**Lang, Ronny**
See  Langinger, Ronald

**Lang, Simon**
See  Hartman, Darlene

**Lang, Stewart**
See  Muir, Wardrop Openshaw

**Lang, T. T.**
See  Taylor, Theodore

**Lang, Theo**
See  Langbehn, Theo

**Lang, Thomas**    [PA]
*Author*
* Mofussillite

**Lang, Violet Ranney** 1924-1956
[B10]
*American poet*
* Lang, Bunny

**Langa-Langa**
See  Hermon-Hodge, Harry
Baldwin

**Langart, Darrel T.**
See  Garrett, [Gordon] Randall
[Philip David]

**Langbehn, Theo** 20th c.    [WW]
*Author*
* Lang, Theo
* Piper, Peter

**Langdale, Launcelot**
See  Graham, George I.

**Langdon, John [Franklin Coasten]**
1913-    [IAW]
*American author*
* Gannold, John
* Russell, Rex

**Langdon, Mary**
See  Pike, Mary H. Green

**Lange, Carl Gustav Albert** 1885-
[LAO]
*German author*
* Penklub

**Lange, Ernst Philipp Karl**
1813-1899    [WBD]
*German author*
* Galen, Philipp

**Lange, Frederick** 1876?-1941
[BEW]
*Actor*
* Lang, Howard

**Lange, John**
See  Crichton, [John] Michael

**Lange, John Frederick, Jr.** 1931-
[ESF, SFL, WGT]
*American author*
* Norman, John

**Lange, Little Eva**
See  Lange, William Alexander

**Lange, Maria Dagmar** 1914-    [AW]
*Swedish-born author*
* Lang, Maria

**Lange, Ned**
See    Sheckley, Robert

**Lange, William Alexander**
1871-1950    [BE, PB]
*American baseball player*
* Lange, Little Eva

**Langel**
See    Orleans, Louis Philippe Albert
d'

**Langell, Sears**
See    Glasser, Allen

**Langenstein, Heinrich** 1320-1397
[PA]
*Author*
* Von Hassia, Henricus

**Langer, Alfons** 1859- ?    [LAO]
*German author and chemist*
* Komed
* Schultze, Paul

**Langeveld**
See    Macropedius, Georgius

**Langford, Elton** 1900-    [BE]
*American baseball player*
* Langford, Sam

**Langford, Frances**
See    Newbern, Frances

**Langford, James R[ouleau]** 1937-
[CA]
*American editor and author*
* Langford, Jerome J.

**Langford, Jane**
See    Mantle, Winifred Langford

**Langford, Jerome J.**
See    Langford, James R[ouleau]

**Langford, Sam**
See    Langford, Elton

**Langford, Sam** 1880?-1956
[AS, BX, RBE]
*Canadian-born boxer*
* [The] Boston Tar Baby

**Langgaesser, Elisabeth**
See    Hoffmann, E. L.

**Langguth, A. J.**
See    Langguth, Arthur John

**Langguth, Arthur John** 1933-
[SFL]
*American author*
* Langguth, A. J.

**Langhanke, Lucille Vasconcellos**
1906-    [BDF, BEW, CA]
*American actress*
* Astor, Mary

**Langheimer, Charles** 1806?-1883
[FFF]
*American prison inmate*
* Dicken's Dutchman

**Langholm, Neil**
See    Bulmer, [Henry] Kenneth

**Langier, Joseph Tidele** 1802- ?
[PA]
*Author*
* Le Genie, Toulounais

**Langiewicz, Marjan** 1827-1887
[WBD]
*Polish patriot*
* Langle

**Langinger, Ronald** 1927-
[EJ, PMJ]
*American jazz musician*
* Lang, Ronny

**Langland, William**
See    Muntz, [Isabelle] Hope

**Langle**
See    Langiewicz, Marjan

**Langley, Dorothy**
See    Kissling, Dorothy Hight
[Richardson]

**Langley, F. E.**    [FFF]
*Author*
* Douglas, Frank

**Langley, Frank**
See    Torrio, John [Johnny]

**Langley, Helen**
See    Rowland, D[onald] S[ydney]

**Langley, John Prentice**
See    Rathborne, St. George

**Langley, Lee**
See    Langley, Sarah

**Langley, Roger** 1930-    [CA]
*American author and journalist*
* Power, Rex

**Langley, Sarah** 20th c.    [CC]
*Author*
* Langley, Lee

**Langlin, Henry**    [FFF]
*Entertainer*
* Vokes, Harry

**Langlois, Albert** 1934-    [CEI, FHE]
*Canadian-born hockey player*
* Langlois, Junior

**Langlois, Junior**
See    Langlois, Albert

**Langmann, Claude** 1934-
[FC, FDG]
*French director*
* Berri, Claude

**Langrenus, Manfred**
See    Hecht, Friedrich

**Langsford, Robert William [Bob]**
See    Lankswert, Robert William

**Langstaff, Josephine**
See    Herschberger, Ruth
[Margaret]

**Langstaff, Launcelot** [joint
pseudonym with William Irving and
James Kirke Paulding]
See    Irving, Washington

**Langstaff, Launcelot** [joint
pseudonym with Washington Irving
and James Kirke Paulding]
See    Irving, William

**Langstaff, Launcelot** [joint
pseudonym with Washington Irving
and William Irving]
See    Paulding, James Kirke

**Langton, Basil C.**
See    Calvert-Langton, Basil

**Langtry, Baby**
See    Edwards, Lillie

**Langtry, Lillie**
See    Edwards, Lillie

**Langtry, Lily [or Lillie]**
See    Le Breton, Emilie Charlotte

**Languereau, Maurice** 20th c.
[WECO]
*French writer and publisher*
* Caumery

**Languichatte**
See    Beaubrun, Theodore

**Languid Bob Meusel**
See    Meusel, Robert William [Bob]

**Lanham, Ceora B.** 20th c.    [NAA]
*American entertainer and author*
* Bee, Betty
* La Belle, Chemet

**Lania, Leon**
See    Herman, Lasser

**Lanier, Alison Raymond** 1917-
[CA]
*American author*
* Raymond, G. Alison

**Lanier, Bob** 1948-
*American basketball player*
* Lanier, Bob-A-Dob

**Lanier, Bob-A-Dob**
See    Lanier, Bob

**Lanier, [Dr.] Clement** 1879-1967
[CW]
*Haitian author*
* Robion, Jean

**Lanier, Contact**
See    Lanier, Willie E.

**Lanier, Honey Bear**
See    Lanier, Willie E.

**Lanier, Lorenzo** 1948-    [BE]
*American baseball player*
* Lanier, Rimp

**Lanier, Rimp**
See    Lanier, Lorenzo

**Lanier, Willie E.** 1945-    [FB, IBW]
*American football player*
* Lanier, Contact
* Lanier, Honey Bear

**Lanigan, George Thomas**
1845-1886    [PA]
*Canadian author*
* Aesop, George Washington

**Lankswert, Robert William**
?-1907    [BE]
*American baseball player*
* Langsford, Robert William [Bob]

**[The] Lanky Cornishman**
See    Fitzsimmons, Robert [Bob]

**Lanna, A. August** 1914?-1976
[B10]
*American labor mediator and tennis
umpire*
* Lanna, Gus

**Lanna, Gus**
See    Lanna, A. August

**Lanne, William F.**
See    Leopold, Nathan F.

**Lanning, John Young** 1910-    [BE]
*American baseball player*
* Tobacco Chewin' Johnny

**Lanning, Les[ter Alfred]** 1895-1962
[BE]
*American baseball player*
* Lanning, Red

**Lanning, Red**
See    Lanning, Les[ter Alfred]

**Lanoe, Jacques**
See    Lanoe, Jiquel

**Lanoe, Jiquel**    [F2]
*Actor*
* Lanoe, Jacques

**Lanoue, Conrad** 1908-    [ASC]
*American musician*
* Lanoue, Tee

**Lanoue, Francois de** 1531-1591
[DNNF, RH, SN]
*French army officer*
* Bras de Fer
* Iron Arm

**Lanoue, Tee**
See    Lanoue, Conrad

**Lanphere, Gladys**  ?-1948    [SC]
*Actress*
* Banjamin, Gladys

**Lansberry, Paula Vivien** 1922-
[IAW]
*British author*
* Batchelor, Paula

**[The] Lansdowne Laureate**
See    Moore, Thomas

**Lansdowne, Marquis of**
See    Petty, [Sir] William

**Lansing, [Eu]gene [Hewitt]**
1898-1945    [BE]
*American baseball player*
* Lansing, Jigger

**Lansing, Henry**
See    Rowland, D[onald] S[ydney]

**Lansing, Jigger**
See    Lansing, [Eu]gene [Hewitt]

**Lansing, Joi**
See    Wasmansdoff, Joyce

**Lansing, Robert**
See    Brown, Robert Howell

**Lansky, Meyer**
See    Suchowljansky, Maier

**Lanson, Roy** 20th c.    [PMJ]
*American singer*
* Lanson, Snooky

**Lanson, Snooky**
See    Lanson, Roy

**Lant, Harvey**
See    Rowland, D[onald] S[ydney]

**Lantree, Ann** 1943-    [RO2]
*British musician*
* Lantree, Honey

**Lantree, Honey**
See    Lantree, Ann

**Lantry, Mike**
See    Tubb, Edwin Charles

**Lantz, Constantine P.** 1934?-
*American jurist*
* Lantz, Dick

**Lantz, Dick**
See    Lantz, Constantine P.

**Lantz, Kid**
See Lantz, Russell

**Lantz, Russell** 20th c. [BBH]
*Boxer*
* Lantz, Kid

**Lanum, Jake**
See Lanum, R.

**Lanum, R.** 20th c. [SMG]
*American football player*
* Lanum, Jake

**Lanza, Isabel** 1952?-
*Cuban-born fashion model*
* Ardigo, Isabella

**Lanza, Joseph** 20th c. [CEC, PHM]
*American underworld figure*
* Lanza, Socks

**Lanza, Mario**
See Cocozza, Alfredo Arnold

**Lanza, Silverio**
See Amoros, Juan Bautista

**Lanza, Socks**
See Lanza, Joseph

**[El] Lanzallama**
See Lopez, Aurelio Alejandro

**Lao-tzu [or Lao-tse]**
See Li Erh

**Laoide, Seosamh**
See Lloyd, Joseph H.

**[The] Lap King**
See Olaf

**Lapage**
See Boccage, Marie Anne

**LaPalme, Lefty**
See LaPalme, Paul Edmore

**LaPalme, Paul Edmore** 1923- [BE]
*American baseball player*
* LaPalme, Lefty

**Lapaquellerie, Yvon**
See Bizardel, Yvon

**Lapauze, Jeanne** 1860-1921 [WBD]
*French author*
* Lesueur, Daniel

**Lapide, Phinn E.**
See Lapide, Pinchas E.

**Lapide, Pinchas E.** 1922- [CA]
*Israeli diplomat, army officer, author*
* Lapide, Phinn E.

**Lapidus, Elaine** 1939- [CA]
*American author and television scriptwriter*
* Coleman, Lee
* Peters, Lane

**LaPierre, Cherilyn Sakisian** 1946- [IPA, RO2]
*American singer*
* Cher

**LaPietra, Mary** 1929- [CA]
*American writer*
* Patanne, Maria

**Lapihuska, Andrew [Andy]** 1922- [BE]
*American baseball player*
* Lapihuska, Apples

**Lapihuska, Apples**
See Lapihuska, Andrew [Andy]

**Lapize, Alice** 1888- [EMT]
*French-born actress and singer*
* Delysia, Alice

**Laplace, Pierre Simon de** 1749-1827 [SN]
*French astronomer*
* [The] Modern Newton

**Lapland Willie Weaver**
See Weaver, William [Bill]

**LaPlante, Violet Virginia** 20th c. [FIR]
*American actress*
* Avon, Violet

**Lapointe, Jumbo**
See Lapointe, Rick

**Lapointe, Rick** 1955- [SMG]
*Canadian-born hockey player*
* Lapointe, Jumbo

**LaPore, James**
See Marino, James

**LaPorte, Frank Breyfogle** 1880-1939 [BE]
*American baseball player*
* LaPorte, Pot

**LaPorte, Pot**
See LaPorte, Frank Breyfogle

**Lara**
See Griffith-Jones, George Chetwynd

**Lara, Jose** 1837-1902 [GS]
*Spanish bullfighter*
* Chicorro [Husky Young Man]

**Lara y Merino, Matias** 1887-1957 [GS]
*Spanish bullfighter*
* Larita [Little Lara]

**Lara y Reyes, Manuel** 1867-1912 [GS]
*Spanish bullfighter*
* Jerezano [Man from Jerez]

**Laraia, Carol Maria** 1932- [EMT, IPA, SW]
*American actress, singer, dancer*
* Lawrence, Carol

**Laramy, Grant**
See Longo, Germano

**Laraque, Paul** 1920- [CW]
*Haitian poet and author*
* Lenoir, Jacques

**Larbalestier, Philip George** 20th c. [WW]
*Author*
* Scott, Archer G.

**Lardner, Ring**
See Lardner, Ringgold Wilmer

**Lardner, Ringgold Wilmer** 1885-1933 [AS, IPA, LC]
*American author*
* Lardner, Ring

**Laredo, Betty**
See Codrescu, Andrei

**Laredo, Johnny**
See Caesar, [Eu]gene [Lee]

**Lariar, Lawrence**
See Rosenblum, Lawrence

**Larin, Yuri**
See Lurye, Mikhail

**Larios Alvarez, Jose** 1912- [GS]
*Mexican bullfighter*
* [El] Indio [The Indian]

**Larista, Pepe**
See Schweizer, Marc

**Larita [Little Lara]**
See Lara y Merino, Matias

**Larius, R. Q.**
See Arcularius, Henry W.

**Larivey, Pierre de**
See Giunta, Pierre

**Lariviere, Bimbo**
See Lariviere, Garry Joseph

**LaRiviere, Edmond** 1895-1964 [BE]
*Canadian-born baseball player*
* Wingo, Ed[mund Armand]

**Lariviere, Garry Joseph** 1954- [SMG]
*Canadian-born hockey player*
* Lariviere, Bimbo

**Lark, J. C.**
See Ackerman, Forrest J[ames]

**Lark, Jody**
See Sellers, Connie Leslie, Jr.

**Larkelle, Nellie**
See Colligan, Mrs. George W.

**Larkin**
See Cassidy, John L.

**Larkin, Frank** [BE]
*American baseball player*
* Larkin, Terry

**Larkin, Joseph A.** 1951- [SMG]
*American football player*
* Larkin, Meadow

**Larkin, Maia**
See Wojciechowska, Maia [Teresa]

**Larkin, Meadow**
See Larkin, Joseph A.

**Larkin, Milton** 1910- [WWJ]
*American jazz musician*
* Larkin, Tippy

**Larkin, R. T.**
See Larkin, Rochelle

**Larkin, Rochelle** 1935- [CA]
*American author and editor*
* Larkin, R. T.

**Larkin, Sarah**
See Loening, Sarah Larkin

**Larkin, Terry**
See Larkin, Frank

**Larkin, Tippy**
See Larkin, Milton

**Larkin, Tippy**
See Pilleteri, Tony

**Larkins, Ned**
See Larkins, Wayne

**Larkins, Wayne** 1953- [DC]
*British cricketer*
* Larkins, Ned

**Larkins, William Frederick** 1931- [AW]
*Australian author*
* Long, Gerry

**Larminie, Margaret Rivers**
See Tragett, Margaret Rivers

**Larmore, Red**
See Larmore, Robert McCahan [Bob]

**Larmore, Robert McCahan [Bob]** 1896-1964 [BE]
*American baseball player*
* Larmore, Red

**Larner, Jeremy** 1937- [CA]
*American author*
* Gouge, Orson

**Larneuil, Michel**
See Batbedat, Jean

**LaRocca, Dominick James** 1889-1961 [ASC]
*American jazz musician*
* LaRocca, Nick

**LaRocca, Nick**
See LaRocca, Dominick James

**LaRocca, Pasquale**
See Lilly, Patrick J.

**LaRocca, Patty**
See Lilly, Patrick J.

**Laroche, Rene**
See McKeag, Ernest L[ionel]

**Larocque, Bunny**
See Larocque, Michel Raymond

**Larocque, Michel Raymond** 1952- [HR, SMG]
*Canadian-born hockey player*
* Larocque, Bunny

**Larose, Claude** 1955- [SMG]
*Canadian-born hockey player*
* [The] Rocket

**LaRoss, Harry Raymond** 1891-1954 [BE]
*American baseball player*
* LaRoss, Spike

**LaRoss, Spike**
See LaRoss, Harry Raymond

**Larr, Sven**
See Lyngstad, Sverre

**Larra, Mariano Jose de** 1809-1837 [FFF, WBD]
*Spanish poet, playwright, author*
* Figaro

**Larralde, Romulo, Jr.** 1902- [BEW, FC, SW]
*Mexican actor, director, playwright*
* Brent, Romney

**Larrimore, Francine**
See La Remnee, Francine

**Larrupin' Lou Gehrig**
See Gehrig, [Henry] Lou[is]

**Larry**
See Parkes, Terence

**Larry of Macedonia**
See Eagleburger, Lawrence

**Larsen, Carl** 1934- [CA]
*American poet, author, playwright*
* Poots-Booby, Edna

**Larsen, Egon**
See Lehrburger, Egon

**Larsen, Erik** 1911- [IAW]
*Austrian-born author*
* Petronius

**Larsen, Erling** 1909-   [CA]
*American author*
* Brand, Peter

**Larsen, Erling Arthur** 1913-   [BE]
*American baseball player*
* Larsen, Swede

**Larsen, Geraldine** 20th c.   [BS]
*American magician*
* [The] Magic Lady

**Larsen, Henry Hertzberg**
1867-1922   [WBD]
*Australian author*
* Lawson, Henry Hertzberg

**Larsen, Lola**
*See* Franco, Fulvia

**Larsen, Peter**
*See* Lehrburger, Peter

**Larsen, Suzan** 1924-   [FC]
*American opera singer and actress*
* Foster, Susanna

**Larsen, Swede**
*See* Larsen, Erling Arthur

**Larsocchi, Eduard**
*See* Neagu, Paul

**Larson, Eve**
*See* St. John, Wylly Folk

**Larsson, Carl Filip** 1877- ?   [CD]
*Swedish poet and author*
* Larsson I By, Carl

**Larsson, Signe** 20th c.
*Swedish-born actress*
* Hasso, Signe

**Larsson I By, Carl**
*See* Larsson, Carl Filip

**LaRue, Dione** 1945-   [RO1]
*American singer*
* Sharp, Dee Dee

**Larusdottir, Elinborg** 1891-   [IAW]
*Icelandic author*
* Sunna

**Laruska, Dianne** 1928-   [FC]
*Canadian actress*
* Foster, Dianne

**LaRusso, Dominic A[nthony]** 1924-
[CA]
*American educator and author*
* Domini, Jon

**Larwood, Harold** 1904-   [EC]
*British cricketer*
* Larwood, Lol

**Larwood, Jacob**
*See* Sadler, L. R.

**Larwood, Lol**
*See* Larwood, Harold

**Lary, Broadway**
*See* Lary, Lynford Hobart

**Lary, Bulldog**
*See* Lary, Frank Strong

**Lary, Frank Strong** 1931-
[BE, PB, SMG]
*American baseball player*
* Lary, Bulldog
* Lary, Mule
* [The] Yankee Killer

**Lary, Lyn**
*See* Lary, Lynford Hobart

**Lary, Lynford Hobart** 1906-1973
[BE, PB]
*American baseball player*
* Lary, Broadway
* Lary, Lyn

**Lary, Mule**
*See* Lary, Frank Strong

**Las Casas, Bartolome de**
1474-1566   [DNNF, HN, SN]
*Spanish missionary*
* [The] Apostle of the Indians
* [The] Indian Apostle
* Protector of the Indians

**Las Cases, Emmanuel Augustin
Dieudonne de** 1766-1842
[FFF, RH, SN]
*French historian*
* [Le] Sage
* [The] Wise

**[Il] Lasca [The Roach]**
*See* Grazzini, Antonio Francesco
[or Antonfrancesco]

**Lascaris, Andreas Johannes [or
Janus]** 1445?-1535   [WBD]
*Greek scholar and educator*
* Rhyndacenus

**Lascelles, [Lady] Caroline**
*See* Maxwell, Mary Elizabeth
[Braddon]

**Lascelles, Emma**
*See* Queen, Mrs. Frederick E.

**Lascelles, Tony**
*See* Green, Hubert Unsworth

**Laschever, Barnett D.** 1924-   [CA]
*American journalist and author*
* Barnett, L. David

**Lascy, Franz Moritz**
*See* Lacy, Francis Maurice

**Lascy, Pierre**
*See* Lacy, Peter

**Lasell, Fen H.**
*See* Calvert, Elinor H.

**Lasha, Prince**
*See* Lasha, William B.

**Lasha, William B.** 1929-   [DAM]
*American musician*
* Lasha, Prince

**Lashwood, George** 1863-1942
[BMH]
*British comedian and singer*
* [The] Beau Brummell of the
Halls

**Laski, Marghanita** 1915-   [LC]
*British author*
* Russell, Sarah

**Laskowski, Janina Domanska** 20th
c.   [TBJ]
*Polish-born author and illustrator*
* Domanska, Janina

**Lasky, Jesse Louis, Jr.** 1910-   [AW]
*American author, poet, playwright*
* Smeed, Frances

**Laslett, Peter** 1915-   [CA]
*British author*
* Russell, Thomas

**Lasley, Bill**
*See* Lasley, Willard Almond

**Lasley, Willard Almond** 1902-   [BE]
*American baseball player*
* Lasley, Bill

**Lassalle, C. E.**
*See* Ellis, Edward S[ylvester]

**Lassang, Iwan**
*See* Lang, Isaac

**Lasser, David** 1902-   [WGT]
*American author*
* Penny, Richard

**Lassez, M.**
*See* Bedford-Jones, Henry [James
O'Brien]

**Lassiter, Luther** 20th c.   [IBW]
*American billiard player*
* Lassiter, Wimpy

**Lassiter, Wimpy**
*See* Lassiter, Luther

**Lasso, Orlando di**
*See* Delattre [or de Lattre], Roland

**Lassus, Orlandus [or Roland] de**
*See* Delattre [or de Lattre], Roland

**[The] Last Astrologer**
*See* Lilly, William

**[The] Last English Maecenas**
*See* Rogers, Samuel

**Last, Jef**
*See* Last, Josephus Carel
Franciscus

**Last, Josephus Carel Franciscus**
1898-1972   [CAP]
*Dutch poet, author, translator*
* Last, Jef

**[The] Last Man**
*See* Charles I

**[The] Last Marine**
*See* Somoza Debayle, Anastasio

**[The] Last Minstrel of the English
Stage**
*See* Shirley, James

**[The] Last of Monsters**
*See* Braschi, Giovanni Angelo

**[The] Last of the Barons**
*See* Neville, Richard

**[The] Last of the Cocked Hats**
*See* Mease, John

**[The] Last of the Cocked Hats**
*See* Monroe, James

**[The] Last of the Dandies**
*See* Orsay, Alfred Guillaume
Gabriel d'

**[The] Last of the English**
*See* Hereward

**[The] Last of the Fathers**
*See* Bernard of Clairvaux

**[The] Last of the Goths**
*See* Roderick

**[The] Last of the Greeks**
*See* Philopoemen

**[The] Last of the Incas**
*See* Atahualpa [or Atahuallpa]

**[The] Last of the Incas**
*See* Condorcanqui, Jose Gabriel

**[The] Last of the Knights**
*See* Maximilian I

**[The] Last of the Lion Comiques**
*See* Lloyd, Arthur

**[The] Last of the Medici**
*See* Medici, Anna Maria Ludovica
de

**[The] Last of the Platonists**
*See* Scotus, Johannes [or John]

**[The] Last of the Puritans**
*See* Adams, Samuel

**[The] Last of the Red Hot Mamas**
*See* Abuza, Sophie

**[The] Last of the Romans**
*See* Aetius, Flavius

**[The] Last of the Romans**
*See* Boethius, Anicius Manlius
Severinus

**[The] Last of the Romans**
*See* Bonifacius

**[The] Last of the Romans**
*See* Brutus, Marcus Junius

**[The] Last of the Romans**
*See* Cassius Longinus, Caius

**[The] Last of the Romans**
*See* Congreve, William

**[The] Last of the Romans**
*See* Desbillons, Francois Joseph
Terasse

**[The] Last of the Romans**
*See* Fox, Charles James

**[The] Last of the Romans**
*See* Gabrini, Niccolo

**[The] Last of the Romans**
*See* Stilicho, Flavius

**[The] Last of the Romans**
*See* Walpole, Horatio [Fourth Earl
of Orford]

**[The] Last of the Saxons**
*See* Harold II

**[The] Last of the Schoolmen**
*See* Biel [or Byll], Gabriel

**[The] Last of the Schoolmen**
*See* Suarez, Francisco [or
Francois]

**[The] Last of the Stuarts**
*See* Stuart, Henry Benedict Maria
Clemens

**[The] Last of the Tribunes**
*See* Gabrini, Niccolo

**[The] Last of the Troubadours**
*See* Baline, Israel

**[The] Last of the Troubadours**
*See* Boe, Jacques

**[The] Last of the Troubadours**
*See* Rene I

**[The] Last of the Tycoons**
*See* Hitotsubashi

**[The] Last Poet of Rome**
*See* Juvenal [Decimus Junius
Juvenalis]

**[The] Last True Bard of Ireland**
*See* O'Carolan, Turloch

[The] Last who Spoke Cornish
See Pentreath, Doll

Lateef, Yusef
See Evans, William

Latell, Lyle
See Zeiem, Lyle

Lateral Pass
See Stern, Bill

Latessa, James 1934-1964 [SC]
American actor
* Eaton, James

Lateur, Frank 1871- ? [CD]
Flemish author
* Streuvels, Stijn

Latham, Arlie
See Latham, Walter Arlington

Latham, Dwight
Singer
* Latham, Red

Latham, Edward Bryan 1895-
[IAW]
British author
* Bryan, E.

Latham, George Warren
1852-1914 [BE]
American baseball player
* Latham, Juice

Latham, Henry Jepson [PA]
Author
* Jepson, Ring

Latham, Hope
See Kemper, Louise Brega

Latham, Jean Lee 1902-
[CLC, TCC]
American author, poet, playwright
* Campion, Rose [joint pseudonym
  with Arthur LeRoy Kaser and
  Ruth Perry]
* Gard, Janice
* Lee, Julian

Latham, Juice
See Latham, George Warren

Latham, Mavis
See Clark, Mavis Thorpe

Latham, O'Neill
See O'Neill, Rose Cecil

Latham, Philip
See Richardson, Robert S[hirley]

Latham, Red
See Latham, Dwight

Latham, Sade 1889-1940 [SC]
British-born actress
* Carr, Sade

Latham, Walter Arlington
1859-1952 [BE]
American baseball player
* [The] Freshest Man on Earth
* Latham, Arlie

Lathbury, Mary Artemisia
1841-1913 [FFF, PA]
American author
* Aunt Mary

Lathe, Herbert William 1851- ?
[ALY]
American clergyman and author
* Nichols, Nicholas

[A] Lathe Painted to Look Like Iron
See Cecil, Robert Arthur Talbot
[Third Marquis of Salisbury]

Lathen, Emma [joint pseudonym
with Mary J. Latis]
See Henissart, Martha

Lathen, Emma [joint pseudonym
with Martha Hennissart]
See Latsis, Mary J.

Lathers, Charles Ten Eyck 1888-
[BE]
American baseball player
* Lathers, Chick

Lathers, Chick
See Lathers, Charles Ten Eyck

Lathrop, Cornelia Sterrett [Penfield]
1892-1938 [WW]
Author
* Penfield, Cornelia

Lathrop, Francis
See Leiber, Fritz

Lathrop, G. P. [PA]
Author
* [The] Masque of Poets

Lathrop, Lorin Andrews 1858- ?
[WW]
Author
* Gambier, Kenyon
* Loring, Andrew

Lathrop, Mary Torrans [FFF]
Author
* Lena

Lathy, Thomas P. 19th c. [PA]
British author
* Piscator

Lathyros
See Ptolemy IX [or VIII]

Latimer, Clifford Wesley
1875-1936 [BE]
American baseball player
* Latimer, Tacks

Latimer, Faith
See Miller, Mrs. John A.

Latimer, Hugh 1472?-1555 [HN]
British religious reformer
* [The] Apostle of England

Latimer, Jonathan [Wyatt] 1906-
[EMD]
American author
* Coffin, Peter

Latimer, Rupert
See Mills, Algernon Victor

Latimer, Tacks
See Latimer, Clifford Wesley

Latimore, Frank
See Kline, Frank

Latimore, Jewel C. 1935- [LBA]
American poet
* Amini, Johari
* Kunjufu, Johari M. Amini

[The] Latin Ulysses
See Bohemond I

[The] Latin Walt Whitman
See Reyes Basualto, [Ricardo
Eliezer] Neftali

[The] Latine
See Galindo, Beatrix

Latissioner, John
See Jefferys, William Hamilton

Latman, Arnold Barry 1936- [EJS]
American baseball player
* Latman, Shoulders

Latman, Shoulders
See Latman, Arnold Barry

Latner, Pat Wallace
See Wallace, Pat

Latonius
See Masson, Barthelemy

Latouche, John
See Crawfurd, Oswald John
Frederick

Latour, M. Chabaud
See Louis Philippe

Latsis, Mary J. 1928?-
[CC, EMD, WD]
American attorney and author
* Dominic, R. B. [joint pseudonym
  with Martha Hennissart]
* Lathen, Emma [joint pseudonym
  with Martha Hennissart]

Latta, Marguerite
See Greenbie, Marjorie Barstow

Lattas, Michael 1806-1871 [WBD]
Turkish army officer
* Omer [or Omar] Pasha

Lattimore, Sloathful Bill
See Lattimore, William Hershel
[Bill]

Lattimore, William Hershel [Bill]
1884-1920 [BE]
American baseball player
* Lattimore, Sloathful Bill

Lattin, Big Daddy
See Lattin, David

Lattin, David 1943- [BB]
American basketball player
* Lattin, Big Daddy

Latto, Thomas C. 1818- ?
[FFF, PA]
American writer
* Dunn, Aiken

Latude, Jean Henry 1725-1805
[WBD]
French army officer
* Danger
* Danry, Jean
* Jedor
* Masers d'Aubrespy
* Masers de Latude

Latzo, Pete 1902-1968 [WBC]
American boxer
* Clancy, Young

Lau, Viggo
See Tolderlund, Hother

Laub, Phoebe 1951-
American singer
* Snow, Phoebe

L'Aubanelenco
See Drutel, Marcelle Louise Marie

Laubenthal Horst R.
See Neumaier, Horst R.

Lauchlan, Isabel [FFF]
Scottish eccentric
* Mad Bell

Lauchmonen
See Kempadoo, Peter

Laud, William 1573-1645 [SN]
British prelate
* [The] Hocuspocus
* [The] Little Vermin
* Parva Laus [Little Laud]
* [The] Urchin

Laudenbach, Pierre Jules Louis
1897-1975 [BEW, FC, OCF]
French actor
* Fresnay, Pierre

Lauder, Agnes 1880- ? [DBA]
Scottish painter
* Lauder, Nancy

Lauder, George [Dick]
See Dick-Lauder, [Sir] George
Andrew

Lauder, Harry
See MacLennan, Harry

Lauder, Nancy
See Lauder, Agnes

Laudet, Fernand Charles 1860- ?
[LAO]
French author
* Film

Lauffer, Pierre
See Martes, Jose Antonio

[The] Laughing Blacksmith
See Nash, John

Laughing Charley
See Hicks, Charlie

[The] Laughing Killer
See Selz, Ralph Jerome Von Braun

Laughing Larry Doyle
See Doyle, Lawrence Joseph

[The] Laughing Philosopher
See Democritus

Laughing Sam Carey
See Carey, Sam

Laughlin, Tom 1938- [B10]
American actor and director
* Frank, T. C.

Laughlin, Virginia Carli 1907-
[B10, CA, SAT]
American author
* Clarke, John
* Laklan, Carli

Laughton, Thomas R. [PA]
Author
* Wallis, Ik

Laugier, R.
See Cumberland, Marten

Laujon, Pierre 1727-1811
[DEP, RH]
French poet
* [The] Anacreon of the French
* [The] French Anacreon

Lauler, Michael
See Osenburg, Richard

Laumer, [John] Keith 1925-
[SFL, WGT]
American author
* LeBaron, Anthony

Laumer, March 20th c.
[SFL, WGT]
Author
* Severance, Felix

**Laumer, March** (Continued)
* Xanthus, Xavier

**Launay**
See Boaistnan, Pierre

**Launay, Andrew [Joseph]** 1930-
[CA, WW]
*British author*
* Adony, Raoul
* Launay, Droo

**Launay, Droo**
See Launay, Andrew [Joseph]

**Launis, Armas Emanuel**
See Lindberg, Armas Emanuel

**Laura**
See Perdomo y Heredia, Josefa
Antonia

**Laurac, Serge**
See Schweizer, Marc

**Laurati, Pietro**
See Lorenzetti, Pietro

**[The] Laureate of the Gentle Craft**
See Sachs, Hans

**[The] Laureate of the South**
See Hayne, Paul Hamilton

**Laurel, Doy**
See Laurel, Salvador

**Laurel, Salvador** 20th c.
*Filipino politician*
* Laurel, Doy

**Laurel, Stan**
See Jefferson, Arthur Stanley

**Laurence, Clarice**
See Sadler, Clarice Laurence

**Laurence, John**
See Pritchard, John Laurence

**Laurence, Paula**
See De Lugo, Paula

**Laurence, Will**
See Smith, Willard L[aurence]

**Laurence, William Leonard**
See Siew, William Leonard

**Laurens, John** 1756?-1782 [FFF]
*American army officer*
* [The] Bayard of the Revolution

**Laurent**
See Meslin, Michael Neure

**Laurent, Emmanuel** 1899- [IAW]
*Belgian author*
* Renault

**Laurent, Henry**
See Gesling, Henry L.

**Laurent-Cely, Jacques** 1919-
[WGT]
*French author*
* Saint Laurent, Cecil

**Lauri**
See Salola, Eeero

**Lauri, Pikku**
See Salola, Eeero

**Laurie, Andre**
See Grousset, Paschal

**Laurie, Harry C.**
See Cahn, Zvi

**Laurie, Piper**
See Jacobs, Rosetta

**Laurier, Jay**
See Chapman, Jay

**Lauritsen, John [Phillip]** 1939-
[CA]
*American author*
* Red Butterfly

**Lauscher, Hermann**
See Hesse, Hermann

**Lausen, John R.** 1911-
[EJ, PMJ, WWJ]
*American jazz musician*
* Lawson, John R.
* Lawson, Yank

**Lausin y Lopez, Braulio** 1898-1967
[GS]
*Spanish bullfighter*
* Gitanillo [Little Gypsy]

**Lauter**
See Chamson, Andre J[ules]
L[ouis]

**Lautreamont, le Comte de**
See Ducasse, Isidore Lucien

**Lauzun, Duc de**
See Nompar de Caumont, Antonin

**Lavaden, Leon** [PA]
*Author*
* Grandlien, Doctor

**Lavado, Joaquin** 1932- [WECO]
*Argentinian cartoonist*
* Quino

**Lavagetto, Cookie**
See Lavagetto, Harry Arthur

**Lavagetto, Harry Arthur** 1914-
[B10, BE, PB]
*American baseball player and
manager*
* Lavagetto, Cookie

**Laval, Pierre** 1883-1945 [CND]
*French attorney and politician*
* Mossbank [code name used
during World War II]

**Lavan, Doc**
See Lavan, John Leonard

**Lavan, Henry** 1921- [EMT]
*American composer and lyricist*
* Merrill, Bob

**Lavan, John Leonard** 1890-1952
[BE]
*American baseball player*
* Lavan, Doc

**Lavant, Christine**
See Habernig, Christine

**Lavater, Johann Caspar** 1741-1801
[DNNS, HN, SN]
*Swiss poet and theologian*
* [The] Father of Physiognomy
* [The] Fenelon of Germany
* [The] Founder of Physiognomy

**Lavelle, Gary Robert** 1949- [SMG]
*American baseball player*
* Lavelle, Pudge

**Lavelle, Pudge**
See Lavelle, Gary Robert

**Lavelli, Dante** 1923- [BBH]
*American football player*
* Lavelli, Glue Fingers

**Lavelli, Glue Fingers**
See Lavelli, Dante

**Lavender, Grover C.** 1932- [CM]
*American booking agent and
musician*
* Lavender, Shorty

**Lavender, Shorty**
See Lavender, Grover C.

**Lavengro**
See Borrow, George

**Laver, James** 1899-1975 [CA]
*British fashion historian, poet,
author*
* Reval, Jacques

**LaVere, Charles**
See Johnson, Charles LaVere

**Laverne, Maud**
See Barlow, Maud

**Laverty, Donald** [joint pseudonym
with Damon F[rancis] Knight]
See Blish, James [Benjamin]

**Laverty, Donald** [joint pseudonym
with James (Benjamin) Blish]
See Knight, Damon F[rancis]

**Lavigne, George** 1869-1928?
[AS, BX, RBE]
*American boxer*
* Lavigne, Kid
* [The] Saginaw Kid

**Lavigne, Kid**
See Lavigne, George

**Lavigne, Mark**
See Leopold, Emmanuel-Flavia

**Lavine, Lewis H[erbert]** 1934- [CA]
*American historian and author*
* Carlson, Lewis H[erbert]

**Lavington, Hubert?**
See Carrington, Hereward Hubert
Lavington

**Lavinson, Joseph**
See Kaye, Marvin [Nathan]

**Laviolette, Jack**
See Laviolette, Jean Baptiste

**Laviolette, Jean Baptiste**
1879-1960 [CSH, HK]
*Canadian-born hockey player*
* Laviolette, Jack
* [The] Speed Merchant

**Lavoie, Kent** 1943- [RO2]
*American singer*
* Lobo

**Lavoix, Jean**
See Sauvageau, Juan

**Lavond, Paul Dennis** [joint
pseudonym with F. Pohl, R.
Lowndes, C. Kornbluth] [house
pseudonym]
See Dockweiler, Joseph Harold

**Lavond, Paul Dennis** [joint
pseudonym with J. H. Dockweiler, R.
A. Lowndes, F. Pohl]
See Kornbluth, Cyril M.

**Lavond, Paul Dennis** [joint
pseudonym with J. H. Dockweiler, C.
Kornbluth, F. Pohl]
See Lowndes, Robert Augustine
Ward

**Lavond, Paul Dennis** [joint
pseudonym with J. Dockweiler, C.
Kornbluth, R. Lowndes]
See Pohl, Frederik

**Lavreince, Nicolas**
See Lafrensen, Nils

**[A] Law Abiding Revolutionist**
See Wellman, Bert J.

**Law, Beau**
See Law, John

**Law, Deacon**
See Law, Vernon Sanders

**Law, Elizabeth Susan** [PA]
*Author*
* E. S. L.

**Law, George** 1806-1881 [FFF]
*American shipbuilder*
* Live Oak George

**[The] Law Giver**
See Frederick II

**[The] Law Giver**
See Suleiman II [or Soliman]

**Law, Janice**
See Trecker, Janice Law

**Law, John** 1671-1729
[DNNF, HN, SN]
*Scottish financier*
* Law, Beau
* [The] Paper King
* [The] Projector

**Law, Michael Haldane** 1925- [AW]
*British author*
* Kreuzenau, Michael

**Law, Ruth Helen** 1909- [ART]
*British painter*
* Woodbridge, Ruth

**Law, Vernon Sanders** 1930- [PB]
*American baseball player*
* Law, Deacon

**Law, Virginia W.**
See Shell, Virginia Law

**[The] Lawgiver of Parnassus**
See Boileau-Despreaux, Nicolas

**Lawing, Garland Fred** 1919- [BE]
*American baseball player*
* Lawing, Knobby

**Lawing, Knobby**
See Lawing, Garland Fred

**Lawlars, Ernest** 1900-1961 [BWW]
*American singer*
* Little Son Joe
* Son Joe

**Lawler, C. F.** 19th c. [PA]
*British author*
* Pindar, Peter?

**Lawless, Anthony**
See MacDonald, Philip

**Lawless, Bettyclare Hamilton**
1915- [CA]
*American author*
* Hamilton, Clare

**Lawless, John** 1772-1837 [SN]
*Irish agitator*
* Honest Jack

**Lawlor, Glenn** 20th c.   [BBH]
*American coach and collegiate athletic director*
* Lawlor, Jake

**Lawlor, Jake**
*See*   Lawlor, Glenn

**Lawlor, Pat[rick Anthony]** 1893-
[AW, CAP, WD]
*New Zealand author*
* Bagarag, Shibli
* Penn, Christopher

**Lawrence**
*See*   Stephens, Lawrence Sterne

**Lawrence, A. R.**
*See*   Foff, Arthur R[aymond]

**Lawrence, Andrea Mead** 20th c.
[BBH]
*American skier*
* Lawrence, Andy

**Lawrence, Andy**
*See*   Lawrence, Andrea Mead

**Lawrence, Arnie**
*See*   Finkelstein, Arnold Lawrence

**Lawrence, [Lieut.] Ashbury**
*See*   Calhoun, Alfred R.

**Lawrence, Babe**
*See*   Lawrence, William

**Lawrence, Bessie**   [PA]
*Author*
* Agatha

**Lawrence, Birdie**
*See*   Lawrence, Edith Bird

**Lawrence, Bud**
*See*   Lawrence, George H.

**Lawrence, Carol**
*See*   Laraia, Carol Maria

**Lawrence, Charlie**
*See*   Lorenzon, Livio

**Lawrence, Chester**
*See*   Campbell, Sydney G.

**Lawrence, Christopher George Holman** 1866-1950   [MBF]
*British author*
* Abbott, Lawrence
* Jackspur
* Lynn, Escott
* Metcalfe, [Captain] W. C.

**Lawrence, D. H.**
*See*   Lawrence, David Herbert

**Lawrence, David Herbert** 1885-1930   [LC]
*British author*
* Davidson, Lawrence H.
* Lawrence, D. H.

**Lawrence, Dorset William** 1853-1931   [BEW]
*British actor*
* D'Orsay, Lawrence

**Lawrence, E. S.**
*See*   Bradburne, E[lizabeth] Sutton

**Lawrence, Edith Bird** 1914-   [MY]
*American musician*
* Lawrence, Birdie

**Lawrence, Elliot**
*See*   Broza, Elliot Lawrence

**Lawrence, Florence** 1886-1939
[CU, SC]
*Canadian-born actress*
* Baby Flo
* [The] Biograph Girl
* [The] Imp Girl

**Lawrence, George H.** 20th c.
*American business executive*
* Lawrence, Bud

**Lawrence, Gertrude**
*See*   Klasen, Gertrud Alexandra Dagmar Lawrence

**Lawrence, H. L**
*See*   Lawrence, Henry Lionel

**Lawrence, Harold G.** 1928-   [IBW]
*American author, poet, editor*
* Wangara, Harun Kofi

**Lawrence, Henry Lionel** 1908-
[SFL]
*British author*
* Lawrence, H. L

**Lawrence, Irene**
*See*   Marsh, John

**Lawrence, Jack**
*See*   Fitzgerald, Lawrence P[ennybaker]

**Lawrence, Jack**
*See*   Schwartz, Jacob Lawrence

**Lawrence, James**
*See*   Tames, Richard Lawrence

**Lawrence, Jerome**
*See*   Schwartz, Jerome Lawrence

**Lawrence, Jodi** 1938-   [CA]
*American author, playwright, screenwriter*
* Kebin, Jody
* Kevin, Jodi
* Lawrence, John

**Lawrence, Jody**
*See*   Goddard, Josephine Lawrence

**Lawrence, Joe** 20th c.   [BMH]
*British comedian*
* [The] Upside Down Comedian

**Lawrence, John**
*See*   Lawrence, Jodi

**Lawrence, Joyce** 1898-   [FC, OCF]
*British actress*
* Carey, Joyce

**Lawrence, Joyce Whitsett** 1938-
[IBW]
*American poet*
* Wangara, Malaika Ayo

**Lawrence, Karl**
*See*   Foff, Arthur R[aymond]

**Lawrence, Kenneth G.**
*See*   Ringgold, Gene

**Lawrence, Larry**
*See*   Lawrence, Robert Andrew [Bob]

**Lawrence, Lesley**
*See*   Lewis, Lesley

**Lawrence, Louise**
*See*   Wintle, Elizabeth Rhoda

**Lawrence, Louise De Kiriline** 1894-   [CA, SAT]
*Canadian writer*
* De Kiriline, Louise

**Lawrence, Margaret Woods** 19th c.   [FFF]
*American author*
* Lander, Meta

**Lawrence, Michael**
*See*   Rosenblum, Lawrence

**Lawrence of Arabia**
*See*   Lawrence, Thomas Edward

**Lawrence, P.**
*See*   Tubb, Edwin Charles

**Lawrence, Peter Lee**
*See*   Hirenbach, Karl

**Lawrence, Richard**
*See*   Bartle, L. E.

**Lawrence, Richard A.**
*See*   Leopold, Nathan F.

**Lawrence, Robert**
*See*   Beum, Robert [Lawrence]

**Lawrence, Robert Andrew [Bob]** 1899-   [BE]
*American baseball player*
* Lawrence, Larry

**Lawrence, Slingsby**
*See*   Lewes, George Henry

**Lawrence, Stephen**
*See*   Stephens, Lawrence Sterne

**Lawrence, Steve**
*See*   Liebowitz, Sidney

**Lawrence, Stringer** 1697-1775
[WBD]
*British army officer*
* [The] Father of the Indian Army

**Lawrence, T. E.**
*See*   Lawrence, Thomas Edward

**Lawrence, Thomas**
*See*   Roberts, Thom[as Sacra]

**Lawrence, [Sir] Thomas** 1769-1830
[HN]
*British painter*
* [The] Wonderful Boy of Devizes

**Lawrence, Thomas Edward** 1888-1935   [CBS, IPA, LC]
*British author, soldier, adventurer*
* Lawrence of Arabia
* Lawrence, T. E.
* Shaw, Thomas Edward

**Lawrence, Trudy**
*See*   Halpern, Gertrude

**Lawrence, Ulysses Brooks** 1925-
[BE, BTB]
*American baseball player*
* [The] Bull

**Lawrence, Vesta** 1873-1951
[BEW, BMH, THR]
*British comedienne and singer*
* Baby Victoria
* Little Victoria
* Victoria, Vesta

**Lawrence, William** 1875-1953
[RBE]
*American boxer*
* McPartland, Kid

**Lawrence, William** 1896-1947
[SC]
*American actor*
* Lawrence, Babe

**Lawrence, William Beach** 1800-1880   [PA]
*American author*
* [An] American Citizen

**Lawrie, Marie McDonald McLaughlin** 1948-
[FC, LRR, RO2]
*Scottish singer*
* Lulu

**Lawry, Otis Carroll** 1893-1965
[BE]
*American baseball player*
* Lawry, Rabbit

**Lawry, Rabbit**
*See*   Lawry, Otis Carroll

**Laws, Joe** 20th c.   [BBH]
*American football player*
* Laws, Tiger

**Laws, Tiger**
*See*   Laws, Joe

**Laws, Tony** 1935-   [ART]
*British silversmith designer*
* T. L.

**Lawson, Big Jim**
*See*   Lawson, Harry

**Lawson, Chet**
*See*   Tubb, Edwin Charles

**Lawson, Edward**
*See*   Reulbach, Edward Marvin

**Lawson, Eleanor**
*See*   Smith, Eleanor

**Lawson, Harry** 1904-   [WWJ]
*American jazz musician*
* Lawson, Big Jim

**Lawson, Henry Hertzberg**
*See*   Larsen, Henry Hertzberg

**Lawson, Horace Lowe** 1900-   [CA]
*American author, journalist, educator*
* Lawson, M. C.
* Summers, John A.

**Lawson, Humanity**
*See*   Lawson, John

**Lawson, Jahun** 1779- ?   [PA]
*Author*
* Cosmopolite

**Lawson, John** 1867-1920   [BMH]
*British entertainer*
* Lawson, Humanity

**Lawson, John R.**
*See*   Lausen, John R.

**Lawson, M. C.**
*See*   Lawson, Horace Lowe

**Lawson, Michael**
*See*   Ryder, Michael Lawson

**Lawson, Patrick**
*See*   Eby, Lois Christine

**Lawson, [Dr.] Philip**
*See*   Trimmer, Eric James

**Lawson, Ruth Penelope** 1890-
[IAW]
*British author*
* [A] Member of CSMV
* [A] Religious of CSMV

**Lawson, Smirle** 20th c.   [CFH]
*Canadian football player*
* [The] Big Train

**Lawson, Steve**
See Turner, Robert [Harry]

**Lawson, Ted**
See Lehrman, Theodore H.

**Lawson, W. B.**
See Jenks, George Charles

**Lawson, W. B.**
See Rathborne, St. George

**Lawson, W. B.?**
See Stratemeyer, Edward L.

**Lawson, Warren J.**
See Bobin, Donald E. M.

**Lawson, Wilfrid**
See Worsnop, Wilfrid

**Lawson, Yank**
See Lausen, John R.

**Lawton, Charles**
See Heckelmann, Charles N[ewman]

**Lawton, Dennis**
See Faust, Frederick [Schiller]

**Lawton, Effie**
See Bell, Mrs. S. May

**Lawton, Mrs. W. H.** [FFF]
*Singer*
* Beebe, Henrietta

**Lawton, Sherman P[axton]** 1908-
[CAP]
*American author and educator*
* Paxton, Jack
* Paxton, [Dr.] John

**Lawton, [Capt.] Wilbur**
See Goldfrap, John Henry

**Laxness, Halldor Kiljan**
See Gudjonsson, Halldor Kiljan

**[The] Lay Bishop**
See Savile, [Sir] Henry

**Lay, Dilys** 1934- [TR]
*British actress*
* Laye, Dilys

**[The] Lay Preacher**
See Dennie, Joseph

**Layamon** 13th c. [DEP, FFF, SN]
*British poet*
* [The] English Ennius

**Laycock, John W.** 1904-1960 [SC]
*American actor*
* Lake, John

**Laycock, Lucky**
See Laycock, Robert E.

**Laycock, Robert E.** 1907-1968
[WWW]
*British military leader*
* Laycock, Lucky

**Laye, Dilys**
See Lay, Dilys

**[A] Layman**
See Allibone, Samuel Austin

**[A] Layman**
See Anderson, Edward Hall

**[A] Layman**
See Anderson, John Larnicourt

**[A] Layman**
See Bagley, [Sir] John

**[A] Layman**
See Bevans, J.

**[A] Layman**
See Bush, H. R.

**[A] Layman**
See Chambers, J. D.

**[A] Layman**
See Cogan, Thomas

**[A] Layman**
See De Peyster, John Watts

**[A] Layman**
See Falconer, William

**[A] Layman**
See Hardinge, Thomas

**[A] Layman**
See Hitherley, W.

**[A] Layman**
See Hoare, P.

**[A] Layman**
See Hook, W. F.

**[A] Layman**
See Irving, Theodore

**[A] Layman**
See Lowell, John

**[A] Layman**
See Milnes, Richard Monckton
[First Baron Houghton]

**[A] Layman**
See Norton, J.

**[A] Layman**
See Park, James Allen

**[A] Layman**
See Poynder, John

**[A] Layman**
See Rivington, William

**[A] Layman**
See Robinson, Solon

**[A] Layman**
See Rowland, D.

**[A] Layman**
See Sanden, Thomas

**[A] Layman**
See Scott, [Sir] Walter

**[A] Layman**
See Seeley, Robert B.

**[A] Layman**
See Skinner, J.

**[A] Layman**
See Taylor, Jeremy

**Layne, Ivoria Hillis** 1918- [BE]
*American baseball player*
* Layne, Tony

**Layne, Tony**
See Layne, Ivoria Hillis

**Layton, Andrea**
See Bancroft, Iris [Nelson]

**Layton, Dennis** 1948- [BB]
*American basketball player*
* Layton, Mo

**Layton, F. G.**
See Layton, Frank George

**Layton, Frank George** 1872-1941
[WGT, WWL]
*British author*
* Andrew, Stephen
* Layton, F. G.

**Layton, Irving**
See Lazarovitch, Irving

**Layton, Joe**
See Lichtman, Joseph

**Layton, Mo**
See Layton, Dennis

**Layton, Phil** 1917- [MY]
*American jazz musician*
* Layton, Skippy

**Layton, Skippy**
See Layton, Phil

**Lazar, Irving Paul** 1907-
*American literary representative*
* Lazar, Swifty

**Lazar, Swifty**
See Lazar, Irving Paul

**Lazarovitch, Irving** 1912- [JL]
*Canadian poet*
* Layton, Irving

**Lazarus, Arnold Leslie** 1914-
[IAW]
*American author and poet*
* Leslie, A. L.

**Lazarus, Jack David** 1930- [CA]
*American author*
* Holmes, Jack D[avid] L[azarus]

**Lazarus, Mel** 1927- [WECO]
*American cartoonist*
* Fulton
* Mell

**Lazeroff, Bernard** 1921- [PMJ]
*American musician*
* Leighton, Bernie

**Lazerowitz, Alice Ambrose** 1906-
[WD]
*American writer*
* Ambrose, Alice

**Lazy Bill Lucas**
See Lucas, William [Bill]

**Lazy Jim Day**
See Day, Jim

**Lazy Lester**
See Johnson, Leslie

**Lazy Slim Jim**
See Harris, Ed[ward P.]

**Lazzara, Bernadette** 1948- [TR]
*American actress and singer*
* Peters, Bernadette

**Lazzari**
See D'Agnolo [or D'Angelo],
Donato

**Lazzaro, Samuel** 1902- [BX, RBE]
*Italian-born American boxer*
* Dundee, Joe

**Lazzaro, Vincent** 1904-1949
[AS, BX, RBE]
*Italian-born American boxer*
* Dundee, Vince

**Lazzeri, Anthony Michael [Tony]**
1903-1946 [AS, BE, PB]
*American baseball player*
* Push 'em Up Tony

**Le**
See Second element of name for
further listings

**Le Bargy, Simone**
See Benda, Simone

**Le Baron, Marie**
See Bielby, Mrs.

**Le Bas, R. A.**
See Le Bas, Rachel Ann

**Le Bas, Rachel Ann** 1923- [ART]
*British painter and engraver*
* Le Bas, R. A.

**Le Blond, Louis Vincent Joseph**
[Comte de St. Hilaire]
[DNNF, FFF, SN]
*French army officer*
* [The] Roland of the Army

**Le Bossu, Jacques** 1546-1626 [PA]
*Author*
* Bossolus

**Le Bouvier, Gilles** 1386-1460 [PA]
*Author*
* Berry

**Le Bozec, Marcel** 1894-1947
[BEW]
*French-born director*
* Varnel, Marcel

**Le Breton, Auguste**
See Montfort, Auguste

**Le Breton, Emilie Charlotte**
1852-1929 [BEW, IPA, NN]
*British actress and courtesan*
* [The] Jersey Lily
* Langtry, Lily [or Lillie]

**Le Breton, Thomas**
See Ford, T[homas] Murray

**Le Brun, Jean Baptiste** ?-1731
[PA]
*Author*
* Desmarettes

**Le Caron** 1536-1617 [PA]
*Author*
* Charondas

**Le Caron, Henry**
See Beach, Thomas Miller

**Le Carre, John**
See Cornwell, David [John Moore]

**Le Chanois, Jean-Paul**
See Dreyfus, Jean-Paul

**Le Clerc**
See Cowen, Samuella Mardis

**Le Clerc, Jean** 1587-1633
[FFF, RH]
* [The] Cavalier
* [Le] Chevalier

**Le Clercq, Jacques George**
**Clemenceau** 1898-1972 [CA]
*Austrian-born American educator*
*and poet*
* Tanaquil, Paul

**Le Clerq, Augustus Howard**
1884-1969 [FC]
*British actor*
* McNaughton, Gus

**Le Conner, Hans Patrick**
See Bowman, J. L.

**Le Corbusier**
See Jeanneret-Gris, Charles Edouard

**Le Couteur, Brember** 1883?-1948 [THR]
*British actor*
* Wills, Brember

**Le Feber, David** 1903- [IAW]
*Dutch author*
* Cronieckschrijver
* Eerfeld, B.

**Le Feuvre, Amy** ?-1929 [TCC]
*British author*
* Dodge, Mary Thurston

**Le Fevre, Felicite**
See Smith-Masters, Margaret

**Le Fevre, Paul** 1885- [CD]
*French poet and playwright*
* Geraldy, Paul

**Le Fre, Albert**
See De Voy, Albert

**Le Gallienne, Irma Hinton** 1876?-1955 [BEW]
*Actress*
* Perry, Irma

**Le Gallienne, Richard** 1866- ? [WWL]
*Author and poet*
* Logroller

**Le Genie, Toulounais**
See Langier, Joseph Tidele

**Le Grand, Franc** 20th c. [BEW]
*French author*
* Nohain, Franc

**Le Grand, Margaret** 1896-1976 [BEW]
*Canadian actress*
* Bannerman, Margaret

**Le Hay, John**
See Healy, John

**Le Louarn, Yvan** 1915-1968 [WEC]
*French cartoonist and illustrator*
* Chaval

**Le Marchant, Jacques** 1537-1609 [PA]
*Author*
* Merchantius

**Le Meingre, Jean** ?-1368 [WBD]
*French soldier*
* Bouciquaut

**Le Moyne, Charles**
See Lemon, Charles J.

**Le Moyne, Roy**
See Hersey, Harold

**Le Moyne, Seymour**
See Hersey, Harold

**Le Moyne, W. J.**
See Le Moyne, William

**Le Moyne, William** 1831-1905 [BEW]
*Actor*
* Le Moyne, W. J.

**Le Noire, Felicia**
See Bliss, Lena Edith

**Le Normand, Michelle**
See Desrosiers, Marie Antoinette Tardif

**Le Page, Rand** [house pseudonym, Curtis Warren]
See Bird, William Henry Fleming

**Le Page, Rand** [joint pseudonym with Arthur O. Roberts] [house pseudonym, Curtis Warren]
See Glasby, John [Stephen]

**Le Page, Rand** [house pseudonym, Curtis Warren]
See Holloway, Brian

**Le Page, Rand** [house pseudonym, Curtis Warren]
See O'Brien, David

**Le Page, Rand** [house pseudonym, Curtis Warren]
See Protheroe, Cyril

**Le Page, Rand** [joint pseudonym with John (Stephen) Glasby] [house pseudonym, Curtis Warren]
See Roberts, Arthur O.

**Le Paul, Paul**
See Braden, Paul

**Le Pelley, Guernsey** 1910- [CA]
*American playwright and cartoonist*
* Norman, Kerry
* Richard, Lee

**Le Pinski, Gwendolyn** 1906-
*American actress*
* Lee, Gwen

**Le Querrec, A. Charles** 20th c. [THR]
*French playwright*
* Mirande, Yves

**Le Reboullet, A.** [PA]
*Author*
* Chazel, Prosper

**Le Roi, David [De Roche]** 1905- [CA]
*American author and journalist*
* Roche, John

**Le Roux, Henri** 1860-1925 [WBD]
*French journalist*
* Le Roux, Hughes

**Le Roux, Hughes**
See Le Roux, Henri

**Le Roux, S. P. Daniel** 1922- [TCL]
*Afrikaans author*
* Leroux, Etienne

**Le Sage, Aimard**
See Backer, Desaix

**Le Sieg, Theo**
See Geisel, Theodor Seuss

**Le Sueur [or Lesueur], Eustache** 1617-1655 [DEP, DNNF, FFF]
*French painter*
* [The] French Raphael
* [The] Raphael of France

**Le Sueur, Lucille** 1904?-1977 [BDF, FC, WEF]
*American actress*
* Cassin, Billie
* Crawford, Joan

**Le Tonnelier de Breteuil, Gabrielle Emilie** 1706-1749 [HN]
*French author*
* Chatelet, Marquise du
* [The] Divine Emilie

**Le Toulon, Guillaume** 1493-1568 [PA]
*Author*
* Fullonius

**Le Voe, Spivy** 1907-1971 [SC]
*American entertainer*
* Madame Spivy

**Lea, Alec** 1907- [SAT]
*Canadian-born author*
* Lea, Richard

**Lea, Biffy**
See Lea, Langdon

**Lea, Constance Nicholson** 1881- ? [NAA]
*British-born writer*
* Shorthouse, Rebecca

**Lea, Joan**
See Lowry, Joan [Catlow]

**Lea, Langdon** 1874-1937 [AS, FB]
*American football player*
* Lea, Biffy

**Lea, Richard**
See Lea, Alec

**Lea, Terrea** 20th c. [SFL]
*Author*
* Stacy, Terry

**Lea, Timothy**
See Wood, Christopher [Hovelle]

**Leabo, Betty** 1918- [FC]
*American actress*
* Joyce, Brenda

**Leach, Archibald Alexander** 1904- [BDF, BS, SW]
*British-born American actor*
* Grant, Cary
* [The] Great Carini

**Leach, Buddy**
See Leach, Claude

**Leach, Claude** 1935?-
*American politician*
* Leach, Buddy

**Leach, Harry Harwood** [PA]
*Author*
* [A] Sentimental Idler

**Leach, Harvey** ?-1847 [PA]
*Author*
* Nano, Hervis

**Leach, Michael** 1940- [CA]
*American author*
* Jeffrey, Christopher

**Leach, Reginald Joseph** 1950- [FHE]
*Canadian-born hockey player*
* [The] Chief

**Leach, Thomas W.** 1877-1969 [AS]
*American baseball player*
* Leach, Wee Tommy

**Leach, Wee Tommy**
See Leach, Thomas W.

**Leacroft, Eric**
See Young, Eric Brett

**Leadbeater, Barrie** 1943- [DC]
*British cricketer*
* Leadbeater, Bungalow
* Leadbeater, Leady

**Leadbeater, Bungalow**
See Leadbeater, Barrie

**Leadbeater, Leady**
See Leadbeater, Barrie

**Leadbelly**
See Ledbetter, Huddie [William]

**Leader, [Evelyn] Barbara [Blackburn]** 1898- [CA]
*British author*
* Blackburn, Barbara
* Castle, Frances
* Grant, Jane

**Leader, Benjamin Williams**
See Williams, Benjamin

**Leader, Charles**
See Smith, Robert Charles

**Leader, James**
See Tanner, James T.

**Leader Scott**
See Baxter, Lucy E.

**Leaderman, George**
See Robinson, Richard Blundell

**Leadlay, Frank R.** 20th c. [CFH]
*Canadian football player*
* Leadlay, Pep

**Leadlay, Pep**
See Leadlay, Frank R.

**Leaf, [Wilbur] Munro** 1905-1976 [CA, TC1, TCC]
*American author and illustrator*
* Calvert, John
* Mun

**Leak, C. J.**
See Leak, Curtis James

**Leak, Curtis James** 1953- [SMG]
*American football player*
* Leak, C. J.

**Leal, Orlando**
See Ramirez, Orlando

**Leal Kuri, Alfredo** 1930- [GS]
*Mexican bullfighter*
* Principe del Toreo [Prince of Bullfighting]

**Leal y Casado, Cayetano** 1865-1950 [GS]
*Spanish bullfighter*
* Pepe Hillo [Little Joe]

**Leal y Casado, Eduardo** 1875-1931 [GS]
*Spanish bullfighter*
* Llavarito

**Lean, Garth Dickinson** 1912- [CA]
*Welsh-born journalist and editor*
* Tenax

**Lean Jimmy Jones**
See Jones, James Chamberlain

**Lean, Sidney**
See Fago, Giovanni

**Leander, Richard**
See Volkmann, Richard von

**Leaping Mike Menosky**
See Menosky, Michael William

**Leapor, Mary** 1722-1746 [DEL, SN]
*British poet*
* [The] Untaught Poetess

**Lear, Charles Bernard** 1891- [BE]
*American baseball player*
* Lear, King

**Lear, Fred[rick Francis]** 1894-1955
[BE]
*American baseball player*
* Lear, King

**Lear, Hal** 1935-   [BB]
*American basketball player*
* Lear, King

**Lear, King**
*See* Lear, Charles Bernard

**Lear, King**
*See* Lear, Fred[rick Francis]

**Lear, King**
*See* Lear, Hal

**Lear, Peter**
*See* Lovesey, Peter

**Leard, Wild Bill**
*See* Leard, William Wallace [Bill]

**Leard, William Wallace [Bill]**
1885-1970   [BE]
*American baseball player*
* Leard, Wild Bill

**Learmont, Thomas** 13th c.
[DNNF, RH, SN]
*Scottish magician, prophet, poet*
* [The] Merlin of Scotland
* Thomas of Ercerldoune
* Thomas the Rhymer
* True Thomas

**[The] Learned**
*See* Coloman

**[The] Learned**
*See* George II

**[The] Learned Blacksmith**
*See* Burritt, Elihu

**[The] Learned Cabbage-Eater**
*See* Ritson, Joseph

**[The] Learned Dr. Gill**
*See* Gill, John

**[The] Learned Painter**
*See* Lebrun, Charles

**[The] Learned Printer**
*See* Bowyer, William

**[The] Learned Selden**
*See* Selden, John

**[The] Learned Tailor**
*See* Hill, Robert

**[The] Learned Tailor**
*See* Wild, Henry

**[The] Learned Weaver**
*See* Young, Joseph

**Leasley, F. W.**   [PA]
*Author*
* Almon, Caspar

**Leatham, Louis Salisbury** 1902-
[IAW]
*American author*
* Lou

**Leather, George**
*See* Swallow, Norman

**Leatherstocking**
*See* Dolby, Doctor

**Leaver, Philip** 1904-   [THR]
*British actor and playwright*
* Brandon, Philip

**Leaver, Ruth**
*See* Tomalin, Ruth

**Leavis, F. R.**
*See* Leavis, Frank Raymond

**Leavis, Frank Raymond** 1895-
[LC, TC1]
*British critic and educator*
* Leavis, F. R.

**Leavitt, Abe**
*See* Leavitt, Douglas

**Leavitt, Douglas** 1883-1960   [SC]
*American actor*
* Leavitt, Abe

**Leavitt, Frank S.** 1890-1953   [SC]
*American actor and wrestler*
* Dean, Man Mountain

**Lebar, John**
*See* Wright, Gilbert Munger

**LeBaron, Anthony**
*See* Laumer, [John] Keith

**Lebeck, Fats**
*See* Lebeck, George

**Lebeck, George**   [F1]
*Actor*
* Lebeck, Fats

**Lebenson**
*See* Kahn, Yitzhak

**Lebert, Randy**
*See* Brannon, William T.

**Lebies, Rene**
*See* Seibel, Werner

**Lebitsky, Leonard** 1911-1973   [SC]
*American entertainer*
* Leonard, Jack E.

**LeBlanc, Georgette**
*See* Maeterlinck, Georgette

**LeBlanc, J. P.**
*See* LeBlanc, Jean-Paul

**LeBlanc, Jean-Paul** 1946-   [SMG]
*Canadian-born hockey player*
* LeBlanc, J. P.

**Lebo, Deli**
*See* Lebo, Dell

**Lebo, Dell** 1922-   [IAW]
*American author and poet*
* Bell, [Prof.] Leo D.
* Lebo, Deli

**Leborgne**
*See* Boigne, Beuvit

**LeBourveau, Bevo**
*See* LeBourveau, DeWitt Wiley

**LeBourveau, DeWitt Wiley**
1896-1947   [BE]
*American baseball player*
* LeBourveau, Bevo

**Lebreo, Steward**
*See* Weiner, Stewart

**Lebreo, Stewart**
*See* Weiner, Stewart

**Lebrowitz, Barney** 1891-1949
[AS, BX, RBE]
*American boxer*
* Levinsky, Battling
* Williams, Barney

**Lebrun, Charles** 1619-1690
[DNNS, FFF, SN]
*French painter*
* [The] Learned Painter

**Lebrun, M.**
*See* Louis Philippe

**Lebrun, Pauline Guyot** 1815- ?
[PA]
*Author*
* De Camille

**Lebrun Pindare**
*See* Lebrun, Ponce Denis
Ecouchard

**Lebrun, Ponce Denis Ecouchard**
1729-1807   [DEP, FFF, WBD]
*French poet*
* [The] French Pindar
* Lebrun Pindare
* [The] Pindar of France

**Lebrunie, Gerard**
*See* De Marval, Gerard

**Lecale, Errol**
*See* McNeilly, Wilfred Glassford

**Lecavele, Roland** 1886-1973
[CD, EWL, WBD]
*French author*
* Dorgeles, Roland

**Lechon, Jan**
*See* Serafinowicz, Leszek

**Leckenby, Derek** 1945-   [RO2]
*British musician*
* Leckenby, Lek

**Leckenby, Lek**
*See* Leckenby, Derek

**Leckie, Peter Martin** 1890-
[ESF, SFL, WGT]
*British author*
* Martin, Peter

**Leckie, Robert [Hugh]** 1920-   [CA]
*American author*
* Barlow, Roger
* Porter, Mark

**Leclerc du Tremblay, Francois**
1577-1638   [DHA, SN, WBD]
*French monk and diplomat*
* Alter Ego of Richelieu
* Bras Droit du Cardinal
* [The] Cardinal's Right Arm
* [L']Eminence Grise
* Joseph, [Father]
* [A] Nero
* Patelin

**Leclerc, Renald** 1947-   [CEI, HR]
*Canadian-born hockey player*
* Leclerc, Rene

**Leclerc, Rene**
*See* Leclerc, Renald

**Leclerc, Thomas**
*See* Francoeur, Robert Thomas

**Leclere, Leon** 1874-1966   [WBD]
*French poet, painter, musician*
* Klingsor, Tristan

**Leconte, Antoine** 1526-1586   [PA]
*Author*
* Contius

**Leconte, Charles Marie** 1818-1894
[WBD]
*French poet*
* Leconte de Lisle, Charles Marie

**Leconte de Lisle, Charles Marie**
*See* Leconte, Charles Marie

**Lecoq de Boisbaudran, Francois**
*See* Lecoq de Boisbaudran, Paul
Emile

**Lecoq de Boisbaudran, Paul Emile**
1838?-1912?   [WBD]
*French chemist*
* Lecoq de Boisbaudran, Francois

**Lectron, E.**
*See* Fine, Louis

**Ledain, Olivier** ?-1484
[HN, RH, SN]
*Flemish barber*
* [The] Devil
* [Le] Diable

**Ledan, Marie** 1875-1932   [BBD]
*French opera singer*
* Delna, Marie

**Ledbetter, Huddie [William]**
1885?-1949   [BBD, BWW, FCW]
*American singer and composer*
* King of the 12 String Guitar
  Players
* Leadbelly

**Ledbetter, Ralph Overton** 1894-
[BN]
*American baseball player*
* Ledbetter, Razor
* Ledbetter, Slats

**Ledbetter, Razor**
*See* Ledbetter, Ralph Overton

**Ledbetter, Slats**
*See* Ledbetter, Ralph Overton

**Leder, Rudolf** 1915-   [MGL]
*German poet*
* Hermlin, Stephan

**Lederer, Edith Madelon**
*See* Weiner, Edith

**Lederer, Eppie**
*See* Lederer, Esther Pauline
[Friedman]

**Lederer, Esther Pauline [Friedman]**
1918-   [B10]
*American columnist*
* Landers, Ann
* Lederer, Eppie

**Lederer, Evelyn** 1907?-   [F2, FC]
*American actress*
* Carol, Sue

**Lederer, Francis**
*See* Lederer, Frantisek [or Franz]

**Lederer, Frantisek [or Franz]**
1906-   [BEW, F2]
*Czech-born actor and director*
* Lederer, Francis

**Ledesma, Gonzales** 20th c.
[WECO]
*Spanish cartoonist*
* Silver Kane

**Ledford, Minnie Lena** 1922-
[CWG]
*American country-western performer*
* Black Eyed Susan

**Led'huy, Jean Baptiste Alphonse**
[FFF]
*French author*
* Dagobert, Chrysotome

**Ledoux, John Walter** 1860-1932
[SFL]
*Author*
* Calson, Isaac

**Ledoux, Scott**
See  LaDoux, Scott

**Ledsam**
See  Savory, [Sir] Reginald Arthur

**Leduc, Albert** 1901-
[CEI, FHE, HK]
*Canadian-born hockey player*
* Leduc, Battleship

**Leduc, Battleship**
See  Leduc, Albert

**Leduc, Claudine**
See  Lindsay, Sadi

**Ledyard, Hope**
See  Harris, C. L.

**Lee, A. E. L.**  [PA]
*Author*
* A. E. L.

**Lee, A. R.**
See  Ash, Rene Lee

**Lee, Agnes**
See  Freer, Martha Agnes

**Lee, [Rev.] Albert** 1858- ?  [LAO]
*British author*
* Mason, Adrian
* Romaine, Linton

**Lee, Alexander**  [SN]
* Lord Barrymore's Tiger

**Lee, Alfred E.** 1896-1954  [SC]
*American actor*
* Powell, Lee

**Lee, Alice G.**
See  Bradley, Emily

**Lee, Alice Louise** 1868- ?  [ALY]
*American author*
* Garland, John

**Lee, Amber**
See  Baldwin, Faith

**Lee, Andrew**
See  Auchincloss, Louis Stanton

**Lee, Ann** 1736-1784
[DEP, RH, WBD]
*British-born religious leader*
* Ann the Word
* Mother Ann

**Lee, Anna**
See  Winnifrith, Joanna

**Lee, Anthony**
See  Ayers, William [Bill]

**Lee, Archibald Edward John** 1881-
?  [WWL]
*British author*
* Esterre, Neville D'

**Lee, Arthur** 1740-1792  [PA]
*Author*
* Junius Americanus

**Lee, Arthur Stanley Gould**
1894-1975  [SFL, WGT]
*Author*
* Gould, Arthur Lee

**Lee, Aura**
See  Urziceanu, Aura

**Lee, Austin** 1904-1965  [CAP, WW]
*British author*
* Austwick, John
* Callender, Julian

**Lee, Babs**
See  Lee, Marion [Van Der Veer]

**Lee, [Brother] Basil Leo** 1909-1974
[CA]
*American educator and author*
* Lee, George Leslie

**Lee, Bessie**
See  Smith, Trixie

**Lee, Betty**
See  Lambert, Elizabeth [Minnie]

**Lee, Big Bill**
See  Lee, William Crutcher

**Lee, Bill**
See  Williams, James Edwards Lee

**Lee, Bill** 20th c.  [SMG]
*American baseball player*
* Lee, Spaceman

**Lee, Billy**
See  Levise, William S., Jr. [Billy]

**Lee, Blah**
See  Lee, Blair, III

**Lee, Blair, III** 20th c.
*American politician*
* Lee, Blah

**Lee, Bob**
See  McGrath, Robert L[ee]

**Lee, Bob** 20th c.
*American football player*
* Lee, Brook Trout

**Lee, Bonafide**
See  Lee, Ron

**Lee, Brenda**
See  Tarpley, Brenda Mae

**Lee, Brook Trout**
See  Lee, Bob

**Lee, Bruce**
See  Lee Yuen Kam

**Lee, Buck**
See  Lee, Ford Washington

**Lee, C. Y.**
See  Li Chin-yang

**Lee, Canada**
See  Canegata, Leonard Lionel
Cornelius

**Lee, Carol**
See  Fletcher, Helen Jill

**Lee, Caroline**
See  Brown, Bessie

**Lee, Caroline**
See  Dern, Peggy Gaddis

**Lee, Charles**
See  Graham, Roger Phillips

**Lee, Charles**
See  Levy, Charles

**Lee, Charles H.**
See  Story, Rosamond Mary

**Lee chee-men** 597?- 626  [RH]
*Chinese emperor*
* [The] Solomon of China
* Tae-tsong I

**Lee, Chief**
See  Lee, Edward E.

**Lee, Devon**
See  Pohle, Robert W[arren], Jr.

**Lee, Dickey**
See  Lipscomb, Dickey

**Lee, Dixie**
See  Williamson, LaVerne

**Lee, Dixie**
See  Wyatt, Wilma Winifred

**Lee, Don[ald] L[uther]** 1942-
[CA, IBW]
*American poet*
* Madhubuti, Haki R.

**Lee, Dorothy**
See  Millsap, Marjorie

**Lee, Dud**
See  Lee, Ernest Dudley

**Lee, Edward**
See  Fouts, Edward Lee

**Lee, Edward**
See  Seabrooke, Edward

**Lee, Edward E.** 20th c.  [IBW]
*American politician*
* Lee, Chief

**Lee, Elsie** 1912-  [CA]
*American author*
* Cromwell, Elsie
* Gordon, Jane
* Sheridan, Lee [joint pseudonym
   with Michael Sheridan]

**Lee, Eric**
See  Page, Gerald W[ilburn]

**Lee, Ernest Dudley** 1899-1971
[BE]
*American baseball player*
* Dudley, Dud
* Lee, Dud

**Lee, Ernie**
See  Cornelison, Ernest Eli

**Lee, Ford Washington** ?-1955
[IBW]
*American entertainer*
* Lee, Buck

**Lee, Francis Nigel** 1934-  [CA]
*British-born author*
* Nik

**Lee, Franz John Tennyson** 1938-
[IAW]
*South African-born author*
* Lesizwe, Ilizwi
* Letromache, Maeng

**Lee, Gabby**
See  Woolridge, Anna Marie

**Lee, George Leslie**
See  Lee, [Brother] Basil Leo

**Lee, Griffin**
See  Randolph, Paschal Beverly

**Lee, Gwen**
See  Le Pinski, Gwendolyn

**Lee, Gypsy Rose**
See  Hovick, Rose Louise

**Lee, Harold Burnham** 1905-  [BE]
*American baseball player*
* Lee, Sheriff

**Lee, Harry**
See  Fellinge, Harry Lee

**Lee, Henry** 1756-1818
[DNNS, FFF, SN]
*American army officer*
* Legion Harry
* Light Horse Harry

**Lee, Herbert d'H.**
See  Kastle, Herbert D[avid]

**Lee, Holme**
See  Parr, Harriet

**Lee, Holsey S.** 1899-1974  [MK]
*American baseball player*
* Lee, Scrip

**Lee, Horse**
See  Lee, Jerry

**Lee, Horse**
See  Lee, Robert Dean

**Lee, Howard**
See  Goulart, Ron[ald Joseph]

**Lee, Jane**
See  D'Arcy, Ruth

**Lee, Jennie** 1846?-1930  [BEW]
*British-born actress*
* Lee, Jo

**Lee, Jerry** 1953-  [SMG]
*American football player*
* Lee, Horse

**Lee, Jimmy**
See  Robinson, Jimmy Lee

**Lee, Jo**
See  Lee, Jennie

**Lee, John**
See  Henley, John Lee

**Lee, John**
See  Li, Shu-T'ien

**Lee, John** 1953-  [SMG]
*American football player*
* Lee, Shaft

**Lee, Johnny**
See  Hooker, John Lee

**Lee, Julian**
See  Latham, Jean Lee

**Lee, Kamikaze**
See  Lee, Ron

**Lee, Kay**
See  Kelly, Karen

**Lee, Keng-Yen**
See  Li, Shu-T'ien

**Lee, Larry**
See  Levine, Lawrence

**Lee, Laura**
See  Smith, Laura Newton
Rundless

**Lee, Leapy**
See  Lee, Peter Granville

**Lee, Lefty**
See  Lee, Thornton Starr

**Lee, Leonidas Pyrrhus**
See  Funkhouser, Leonidas Pyrrhus

**Lee, Lila**
See  Appel, Augusta

**Lee, Lincoln** 1922-  [CA]
*British airline pilot and writer*
* Collen, Neil

**Lee, Lonesome**
See  Robinson, Jimmy Lee

**Lee, Louisa Carter**
See  Jenkins, Will[iam]
F[itzgerald]

**Lee, M. F.**
See Lee, Man-Fong

**Lee, Man-Fong** 1913- [ART]
*Chinese painter*
* Lee, M. F.

**Lee, Manfred B[ennington]**
See Lepofsky, Manfred

**Lee, Maria Berl** 1924- [CA]
*Austrian-born American author*
* Berl-Lee, Maria

**Lee, Mariel**
See Lane, Mary Louisa

**Lee, Marion [Van Der Veer]** 1914-
[WW]
*Author*
* Lee, Babs

**Lee, Mary Elizabeth** 1813-1849
[PA]
*Author*
* M. E. L.

**Lee, Matt**
See Merwin, [W.] Sam[uel], Jr.

**Lee, Michele**
See Dusiak [or Dusick?], Michele
Lee

**Lee, Mildred**
See Scudder, Mildred Lee

**Lee, Minnie Mary**
See Wood, Julia A.

**Lee, Moose**
See Lee, Robert Dean

**Lee, Nata**
See Frackman, Nathaline

**Lee, Nathaniel** 1657?-1690?
[DNNF, DNNS, HN]
*British playwright*
* [The] Crazy Poet
* [The] Mad Poet

**Lee, Norah**
See Barstow, Norah Lee Haymond
Bradley

**Lee, Norman** 1905- [CC, WW]
*Author*
* Armstrong, Raymond
* Corrigan, Mark

**Lee, O. H.**
See Oswald, Lee Harvey

**Lee, Olga**
See Hammaersbough, Olga

**Lee, Palmer** 1927- [FC, ITA, SW]
*American actor*
* Palmer, Gregg

**Lee, Parker**
See Turner, Robert [Harry]

**Lee, Patty**
See Carey, Alice

**Lee, Peggy**
See Egstrom, Norma Dolores

**Lee, Peter Granville** 1945- [DC]
*British cricketer*
* Lee, Leapy

**Lee, Pinky**
See Leff, Pincus

**Lee, Ranger**
See Snow, Charles Horace

**Lee, Raymond**
See Martin, E. Le Breton

**Lee, Rebecca Smith** 1894- [CA]
*American author*
* Smith, Rebecca

**Lee, Robert**
See Fairman, Paul W.

**Lee, Robert Dean** 1937- [BE]
*American baseball player*
* Lee, Horse
* Lee, Moose

**Lee, Robert Edward** 1807-1870
[DEP, SN]
*American army officer*
* [The] Bayard of the Confederate
Army
* Uncle Robert

**Lee, Roberta**
See McGrath, Robert L[ee]

**Lee, Ron** 1952-
*American basketball player*
* Lee, Kamikaze
* [The] Tasmanian Devil

**Lee, Ron** 1952- [SMG]
*American football player*
* Lee, Bonafide

**Lee, Ronny**
See Leventhal, Ronald

**Lee, Rooney**
See Lee, William Henry Fitzhugh

**Lee, Rose**
See McQuoid, Rose Lee

**Lee, Rosie**
See Aiken, Joan Delano

**Lee, Rowena**
See Bartlett, Marie [Swan]

**Lee, Ruth**
See Rhodes, Ruth

**Lee, Sammy**
See Levy, Samuel

**Lee, Scrip**
See Lee, Holsey S.

**Lee, Shaft**
See Lee, John

**Lee, Sheriff**
See Lee, Harold Burnham

**Lee, [Sir] Sidney**
See Lee, Solomon Lazarus

**Lee Siu Loong**
See Lee Yuen Kam

**Lee, Solomon Lazarus** 1859-1926
[LC]
*British editor and author*
* Lee, [Sir] Sidney

**Lee, Sondra**
See Gash, Sondra Lee

**Lee, Sonny**
See Lee, Thomas Ball

**Lee, Spaceman**
See Lee, Bill

**Lee, Stan**
See Leiber, Stanley

**Lee, Steve**
See Parry, Michel Patrick

**Lee, Stuart** 1938- [CA]
*American author*
* Woods, Stuart

**Lee, Theodis** 1946-1979 [IBW]
*American basketball player*
* Lee, Wolfman

**Lee, Thomas Ball** 1904-
[PMJ, WWJ]
*American jazz musician*
* Lee, Sonny

**Lee, Thornton Starr** 1906- [BE]
*American baseball player*
* Lee, Lefty

**Lee, Ting**
See Tingley, Richard Hoadley

**Lee, Vanessa**
See Moule, Winifred Ruby

**Lee, Vernon**
See Paget, Violet

**Lee, Veronica**
See Woodford, [Irene] Cecile

**Lee, Warren**
See Jackson, Lee

**Lee, Watty**
See Lee, Wyatt Arnold

**Lee, Wayne Cyril** 1917-
[ESF, IAW, SFL]
*American author*
* Havens, Stewart
* Sheldon, Lee

**Lee, William [or Willy]**
See Burroughs, William [Seward]

**Lee, William Crutcher** 1909- [BE]
*American baseball player*
* Lee, Big Bill

**Lee, William Henry Fitzhugh**
1837-1891 [WBD]
*American army officer*
* Lee, Rooney

**Lee, Winifred**
See Gombell, Minna

**Lee, Wolfman**
See Lee, Theodis

**Lee, Wyatt Arnold** 1879-1936 [BE]
*American baseball player*
* Lee, Watty

**Lee Yuen Kam** 1940-1973 [SC]
*American-born actor and martial
arts expert*
* Lee, Bruce
* Lee Siu Loong
* [The] Little Dragon

**Lee-Doolan, Tom** 1903- [THR]
*American actor*
* Douglas, Tom

**Lee-Hankey, Edith Mary** 1881- ?
[DBA]
*British painter*
* Garner, E. M.

**Lee-Richardson, James** 1913-
[AW]
*Irish-born author*
* Dunne, Desmond

**Leech, Margaret** 1893-1974 [CA]
*American historian and author*
* Pulitzer, Margaret Leech

**Leech, Richard**
See McClelland, Richard Leeper

**Leeds, Andrea**
See Lees, Antoinette

**Leeds, Herbert I.**
See Levy, Herbert I.

**Leef, David**
See Lefkowitz, David

**Leek, Sybil**
See Falk, Sybil

**Leemans, Alphonse E.** 20th c. [FB]
*American football player*
* Leemans, Tuffy

**Leemans, Tuffy**
See Leemans, Alphonse E.

**Leeming, Jo Ann**
See Leeming, Joseph

**Leeming, Joseph** 1897-1968 [CA]
*American author*
* Leeming, Jo Ann
* Swift, Merlin
* Zingara, Professor

**Lees, Antoinette** 1914- [FC]
*American actress*
* Leeds, Andrea

**Lees, Hannah**
See Fetter, Elizabeth Head

**Lees, James Cameron** [PA]
*Author*
* A. R. A.

**Lees, John Morton**
See Middleton, Ellis

**Lees-Craston, Eily Sophie**
1879-1961 [SC]
*British-born actress*
* Malyon, Eily

**Leete, Frederick De Land** 1866- ?
[NAA]
*American clergyman and author*
* DeLand, Tracy

**Leever, Samuel** 1871-1953 [BE]
*American baseball player*
* [The] Goshen Schoolmaster

**Leevitt, Don T. B.**
See Spence, James Mudie

**Lefaur, Andre**
See Lefaurichon, Andre

**Lefaurichon, Andre** 1879-1952
[SC]
*French actor*
* Lefaur, Andre

**Lefebure-Wely, Louis James Alfred**
See Lefebvre, Louis James Alfred

**Lefebvre, Catherine Hubscher**
[Duchess of Dantzig] 18th c.
[DEP, DHA, DNNS]
*Wife of Napoleon's marshal,
Francois Lefebvre*
* Sans Gene, Madame

**Lefebvre, Frenchy**
See Lefebvre, James Kenneth
[Jim]

**Lefebvre, Germaine** 1933?-
[FC, ITA, SW]
*French-born actress*
* Capucine

**Lefebvre, James Kenneth [Jim]**
1943- [PB, SMG]
*American baseball player*
* Lefebvre, Frenchy

LeFebvre, Lefty
See   LeFebvre, Wilfrid Henry [Bill]

Lefebvre, Louis James Alfred
1817-1870   [WBD]
French musician and composer
* Lefebure-Wely, Louis James
  Alfred

LeFebvre, Wilfrid Henry [Bill]
1915-   [BE, SMG]
American baseball player and scout
* LeFebvre, Lefty

LeFevre, Al
See   LeFevre, Alfredo Modesto

LeFevre, Alfredo Modesto 1898-
[BE]
American baseball player
* LeFevre, Al

Lefevre, Francois Antoine
1670-1737   [PA]
Author
* Faber

Lefevre, Gui
See   Bickers, Richard Leslie
Townshend

Lefevre, [Lieut.] Paul
See   Cooper, Charles Henry St.
John

Lefevre d'Etaples, Jacques
1450?-1537?   [WBD]
French scholar, theologian, religious
reformer
* Stapulensis

Leff, Pincus 20th c.   [ITA]
American entertainer
* Lee, Pinky

Leffingwell, Albert 1895-1946
[WW]
Author
* Chambers, Dana
* Jackson, Giles

Lefkowitz, David 20th c.   [B10]
American singer
* Leef, David

Lefley, Charles Thomas 1950-
[SMG]
Canadian-born hockey player
* [The] Break Away Kid

LeFlore, Flo
See   LeFlore, Ron[ald]

LeFlore, Ron[ald] 1952-   [IBW]
American baseball player
* LeFlore, Flo
* Twinkle Toes

[The] Left Bank Mother Confessor
See   Powell, Altivia Edwards

Lefty Louis Rosenberg
See   Rosenberg, Louis

Legatee, Residuary
See   Sargent, Henry Jackson

Legendre, Louis 1756?-1797
[DNNF, DNNS, SN]
French politician
* [Le] Paysan du Danube
* [The] Peasant of the Danube

Leger, [Marie-Rene] Alexis
Saint-Leger 1887-1975
[CA, EWL, TC]
French diplomat and poet
* Leger, Saintleger
* Saint-John, Perse

Leger, Jack-Alain 1949-   [IAW]
French author
* Hedayat, Dashiell

Leger, Raymond Alfred 1883-
[SFL, WGT]
Author
* McDonald, Raymond [joint
  pseudonym with Edward Richard
  McDonald]

Leger, Saintleger
See   Leger, [Marie-Rene] Alexis
Saint-Leger

Legett, Doc
See   Legett, Lou[is Alfred]

Legett, Lou[is Alfred] 1901-   [BE]
American baseball player
* Legett, Doc

Legg, W. Dorr 20th c.   [SFL]
Author
* Auctor Ignotus?

Leggatt, Albert G. 1880-1959
[BEW]
American actor
* Sterling, Richard

Legge, Alfred Owen   [PA]
Author
* Stowell, Augustus

Leggett, Eric
See   Rimel, Duane [Weldon]

Leggio, Carmelo John 1927-   [EJ]
American jazz musician
* Leggio, Carmen

Leggio, Carmen
See   Leggio, Carmelo John

Leginska, Ethel
See   Liggins, Ethel

Legion Harry
See   Lee, Henry

[The] Legislator of Parnassus
See   Boileau-Despreaux, Nicolas

Legman, G[ershon]
See   Legman, George Alexander

Legman, George Alexander 1917-
[CA, CC]
American author
* De La Glannege, Roger-Maxe
* Legman, G[ershon]

Legnon, Albert 1898?-   [NOJ]
American jazz musician
* Legnon, Red

Legnon, Red
See   Legnon, Albert

Legrady, Thomas Theodore
See   Tassy, Tamas

Legrand
See   Belleville, Henri

LeGrand
See   Henderson, LeGrand

LeGrand, Claude Maria Eugent
1903?-   [BEW, TR]
French-born actor and director
* Dauphin, Claude

Legrand, Francois
See   Antel, Franz

Legrand, Martin
See   Rice, James

Legs Larry Smith
See   Smith, Larry

Lehman, Helen Miller 1893-
[NAA]
American writer
* Mann, H. Leigh

Lehmann, R. C.
See   Lehmann, Rudolf Chambers

Lehmann, Rudolf Chambers
1856-1929   [LC]
British author
* Lehmann, R. C.

Lehner, Gulliver
See   Lehner, Paul Eugene

Lehner, Paul Eugene 1920-1967
[BE]
American baseball player
* Lehner, Gulliver

Lehnhoff, Laura   [FFF]
Entertainer
* Clairon, Laura

Lehnus, Opal [Hull] 1920-
[CA, WD]
American author
* Hull, Opal

Lehovich, Eugenie Ouroussow
See   Ouroussow, Eugenie

Lehr, Clarence Emanuel
1886-1948   [BE]
American baseball player
* Lehr, King

Lehr, King
See   Lehr, Clarence Emanuel

Lehr, King
See   Lehr, Norm[an Carl Michael]

Lehr, Norm[an Carl Michael]
1901-1968   [BE]
American baseball player
* Lehr, King

Lehrburger, Egon 20th c.   [CA]
Author
* Larsen, Egon

Lehrburger, Peter 1933-   [CA]
British-born writer and
photographer
* Larsen, Peter

Lehrman, Liza
See   Williams, Liza

Lehrman, Theodore H. 1929-
[ASC]
American composer
* Lawson, Ted

Lehrmann, Chanan
See   Lehrmann, Charles C[uno]

Lehrmann, Charles C[uno] 1905-
[CA]
Austrian-born rabbi and author
* Lehrmann, Chanan
* Lehrmann, Cuno Chanan

Lehrmann, Cuno Chanan
See   Lehrmann, Charles C[uno]

Lei Chen Yuan
See   De Jaegher, Raymond-Joseph

Leiber, Fritz 1910-   [CA, WW]
American author
* Lathrop, Francis

Leiber, Stanley 20th c.   [SF]
Author
* Lee, Stan

Leibich, Augusta   [FFF]
American writer
* March, Marjorie

Leibnitz [or Leibniz], Gottfried
Wilhelm von 1646-1716
[DEP, DNNS, SN]
German philosopher and
mathematician
* [The] First of Philosophers
* [A] Living Dictionary

Leibold, Harry Loran 1892-   [BE]
American baseball player
* Leibold, Nemo

Leibold, Nemo
See   Leibold, Harry Loran

Leibowicz, Jankiew 1726?-1791
[WBD]
Polish founder of religious sect
* Frank, Jacob

Leibowitz, Michael 1941-   [RO2]
South African-born musician
* Mann, Manfred

Leibowitz, Samuel Simon
1894?-1978
Rumanian-born American jurist
* Leibowitz, Sentencing Sam

Leibowitz, Sentencing Sam
See   Leibowitz, Samuel Simon

Leibrook, Min
See   Leibrook, Wilford F.

Leibrook, Wilford F. 1903-1943
[WWJ]
American jazz musician
* Leibrook, Min

Leidersdorf, Franz 19th c.   [PA]
Author
* Wallner, Franz

Leidhof, Charles   [PA]
Author
* Mohr, Frederick

Leifield, Albert Peter 1883-1970
[BE]
American baseball player
* Leifield, Lefty

Leifield, Lefty
See   Leifield, Albert Peter

Leigh, [Capt.] Arthur
See   Steffens, Arthur

Leigh, Carolyn
See   Rosenthal, Carolyn

Leigh, Dorma
See   Woodleigh, Dorma

Leigh, Eugene
See   Seltzer, Leon E[ugene]

Leigh, Florence
See   Wilbur, Anna T.

Leigh, Gracie
See   Ellis, Gracie

Leigh, Hart
See   Denny, John Thomas

Leigh, Janet
See   Morrison, Jeanette Helen

Leigh, Johanna
See   Sayers, Dorothy L[eigh]

**Leigh, Kathy**
See Killough, [Karen] Lee

**Leigh, Larry**
See Warner, L. T.

**Leigh, Magda**
See Shirley, Florence Henderson

**Leigh, Mary**
See Eveleigh, Mary

**Leigh, Mitch**
See Michnick, Irwin S.

**Leigh, Olivia**
See Clamp, Helen Mary Elizabeth

**Leigh, Palmer**
See Palmer, Pamela Lynn

**Leigh, Percival** [PA]
Author
* Pipps, Mr.

**Leigh, Ruth**
See Sclater, Ruth Leigh

**Leigh, Stuart**
See Clarke, Mary Bayard
Devereux

**Leigh, Ursula**
See Gwynn, Ursula Grace

**Leigh, Vivien**
See Hartley, Vivian Mary

**Leigh-Pemberton, Nigel Douglas**
1934- [OP]
British opera singer
* Douglas, Nigel

**Leighton**
See Appleton, Jesse

**Leighton, Ann**
See Smith, Isadore Leighton Luce

**Leighton, Bernie**
See Lazeroff, Bernard

**Leighton, Bert**
See Leighton, James Albert

**Leighton, Eric** ?-1924 [BEW]
Actor
* Lambart, Richard

**Leighton, F. S.** [PA]
Author
* Lernier, Luke

**Leighton, Florence**
See Pfalzgraf, Florence Leighton

**Leighton, Frederick** 1830-1896
[FFF]
British painter
* Limmer, Luke, Esq.

**Leighton, George N.**
See Leitao, George Neves

**Leighton, James Albert**
1877?-1964 [BEW]
American theatrical performer and
songwriter
* Leighton, Bert

**Leighton, John** 1822-1912
[PA, WWL]
Author and illustrator
* Limner, Luke

**Leighton, Lee**
See Overholser, Wayne D.

**Leighton, Lillie**
See Gerard, Lillie

**Leighton, Mauri Lynn**
See Kilroy, Marilyn

**Leighton, Queenie**
See Gerard, Lillie

**Leighton, Robert** 1611-1684 [SN]
Scottish prelate
* [The] Fenelon of Scotland

**Leijel, Carl F.** 1875-1925 [BEW]
British-born producer
* Leyel, Carl F.

**Leila**
See Barlow, Emma

**Leila**
See Caldwell, Ella

**Leiner, Benjamin** 1896-1947
[AS, BX, EJS]
American boxer
* [The] Ghetto Wizard
* Leonard, Benny
* [The] Mama's Boy

**Leinster, Murray**
See Jenkins, Will[iam]
F[itzgerald]

**Leipiar, Louise** 20th c. [WGT]
Author
* Reynolds, L. Major

**Leisenring, Margaret** 1904-1926
[SC]
American actress
* Stuart, Jean

**Leishman, J. B.**
See Leishman, James Blair

**Leishman, James Blair** 1902-1963
[LC]
British educator and author
* Leishman, J. B.

**Leisk, David Johnson** 1906-1975
[CA, SAT, TBJ]
American cartoonist, author,
illustrator
* Johnson, Crockett

**Leisure, Piddleton**
See Vawter, L. P.

**Leisy, James Franklin** 1927-
[CA, WD]
American song editor and writer
* Lynn, Frank

**Leitao, George Neves** 20th c.
[IBW]
American politician
* Leighton, George N.

**Leitch, Cecil**
See Leitch, [Charlotte] Cecilia

**Leitch, [Charlotte] Cecilia** 1891-
[BBH, EG]
British golfer
* Leitch, Cecil

**Leitch, Donovan P.** 1946-
[LRR, NAD]
Scottish-born singer
* Donovan

**Leitch, Lavinia**
See Hynd, Lavinia Leitch

**Leite, George Thurston** 1920-
[WW]
Author
* Scott, Thurston [joint pseudonym
with Jody Scott]

**Leitersdorf, Fini** 1906- [WFA]
Israeli fashion designer
* [The] Godmother of the Israeli
Fashion Image

**Leith, Elizabeth**
See Julyan, Louise Elizabeth

**Leith, Shady Bill**
See Leith, William [Bill]

**Leith, William [Bill]** 1874-1940
[BE]
American baseball player
* Leith, Shady Bill

**Leitner, Doc**
See Leitner, George Aloysius

**Leitner, Dummy**
See Leitner, George Michael

**Leitner, George Aloysius**
1865-1937 [BE]
American baseball player
* Leitner, Doc

**Leitner, George Michael**
1871-1960 [BE]
American baseball player
* Leitner, Dummy

**Leito, Arturo** 1910- [CW]
Curacaon author
* Chobil
* Tuyuchi

**Leitzel, Lillian**
See Pelikan, Lillian Alize Elianore

**Leivick, H.**
See Halper, Leivick

**Lejeune, Francois** 1908- [WEC]
French cartoonist and illustrator
* Effel, Jean

**LeJeune, Larry**
See LeJeune, Sheldon Aldenbury

**LeJeune, Sheldon Aldenbury**
1885-1952 [BE]
American baseball player
* LeJeune, Larry

**Lekain, Henri Louis**
See Cain, Henri Louis

**Leland, Charles Godfrey**
1824-1903 [DEL, PA]
American author and poet
* Breitmann, Hans
* Meister Karl
* Sloper, Mace

**Leland, George** 1945- [IBW]
American politician
* Leland, Mickey

**Leland, Mickey**
See Leland, George

**Lelio**
See Riccoboni, Luigi

**Lell, Jennie**
See Smith, Jane Luella Dowd

**Lelland, Frank**
See Burrage, Alfred McLelland

**Lely, [Sir] Peter**
See Van der Faes, Pieter

**Lema, Anthony David** 1934-1966
[AS, EG, GF]
American golfer
* Lema, Champagne Tony

**Lema, Champagne Tony**
See Lema, Anthony David

**Lemaire, M.** 19th c. [HN]
French diplomat
* Jaunot

**Lemaitre, Antoine Louis Prosper**
1800-1876 [SN, WBD]
French actor
* [Le] Grand Frederic
* Lemaitre, Frederic [or Frederick]
* [The] Talma of the Boulevards

**Lemaitre, Frederic [or Frederick]**
See Lemaitre, Antoine Louis
Prosper

**Lemaster, Bones**
See Lemaster, Johnnie Lee

**Lemaster, Denny**
See Lemaster, Denver Clayton

**Lemaster, Denver Clayton** 1939-
[BE]
American baseball player
* Lemaster, Denny

**Lemaster, Johnnie Lee** 1954-
[SMG]
American baseball player
* Lemaster, Bones

**Lembo, Diana L.**
See Spirt, Diana L[ouise]

**Lemesurier, Peter**
See Britton, Peter Ewart

**Lemieux, Marc** 1948- [CA]
American author
* Best, Marc

**Lemir, Andre**
See Rimel, Duane [Weldon]

**Lemire, Aubert** 1573-1640 [PA]
Author
* Miroeus

**Lemke, Henry E.**
See Tooker, Richard

**Lemm-Margadant, Simon**
1511?-1550 [WBD]
German author and poet
* Lemnius, Simon

**Lemmitz, Hans**
See Brauer-Tuchorze, Johann
Ernst

**Lemmon, Laura Elizabeth** 1917-
[WW]
Author
* Wilson, Lee

**Lemnius, Simon**
See Lemm-Margadant, Simon

**Lemoine, Adolph** 1812- ? [PA]
Author
* Montigny, L.

**Lemoine, Ernest**
See Roy, Ewell Paul

**Lemoine, Sauvelle** 1671-1701
[FFF]
Governor of Louisiana
* [The] American Prodigy

**Lemon, Charles J.** 1880-1956 [SC]
American actor
* Le Moyne, Charles

**Lemon, Lem**
See Lemon, Robert Granville
[Bob]

**Lemon, Meadow George, III** 1934-
[BB, IBW]
*American basketball player*
* [The] Clown Prince of Basketball
* Lemon, Meadowlark

**Lemon, Meadowlark**
*See* Lemon, Meadow George, III

**Lemon, Mrs. Henry W.** [FFF]
*Entertainer*
* Melrose, Julia

**Lemon, Robert Granville [Bob]**
1920- [PB]
*American baseball player and manager*
* Lemon, Lem

**LeMond, Alan** 1938- [CA]
*American author*
* Tahlaquah, David

**Lemons, Overton Amos** 1920-1966
[BWW]
*American singer*
* Lewis, Smiley
* Lewis, Smiling

**Lena**
*See* Lathrop, Mary Torrans

**Lena, Lily**
*See* Archer, Lily

**Lenanton, Carola Mary Anima Oman**
*See* Oman, Carola [Mary Anima]

**Lenarduzzi, Sam**
*See* Lenarduzzi, Silvano

**Lenarduzzi, Silvano** 1948- [AES]
*Italian-born Canadian soccer player*
* Lenarduzzi, Sam

**Lenau, Nikolaus**
*See* Niembsch von Strehlenau, Nikolaus

**L'Enclos, Anne** 1615?-1705
[HN, SN, WBD]
*French coutesan*
* [The] Aspasia of France
* [The] Aspasia of the Seventeenth Century
* Ninon de Lenclos

**Lency, C.**
*See* Train, Arthur

**Lender, Marcelle**
*See* Bastien, Marie

**Lendon, Kenneth Harry** 1928-
[CA, WD]
*Canadian-born author*
* Vaughan, Leo

**Lengel, Frances**
*See* Trocchi, Alexander

**Lengel, William Charles** 1888-
[NAA]
*American author*
* Grant, Charles
* Spencer, Warren

**L'Engle, Madeleine**
*See* Camp, Madeleine L'Engle

**Lengsfelder, Hans Jan** 1903-
[ASC]
*Austrian-born American composer, author, recording executive*
* Lenk, Harry

**Lengyel, Cornel Adam** 1915- [CA]
*American author*
* Adam, Cornel

**Lengyel, Geza** 1904- [ASC]
*Hungarian-born American composer*
* Adams, George

**Lenhardt, Donald Eugene** 1922-
[BE]
*American baseball player*
* Lenhardt, Footsie

**Lenhardt, Footsie**
*See* Lenhardt, Donald Eugene

**Lenhart, Jason Gregory** 1920?-
[BEW, FC]
*American actor, producer, talent representative*
* Gregory, Paul

**Lenhart, William** 1864-1942 [SC]
*American actor*
* Hart, Billy

**Lenihan, F. J.** [PA]
*Author*
* Romanus

**Lenin, Nicolai**
*See* Ulyanov, Vladimir Ilich

**Lenk, Harry**
*See* Lengsfelder, Hans Jan

**Lenkaitis, William Edward** 1946-
[SMG]
*American football player*
* [The] Doctor

**Lennon, Arch**
*See* Lennon, Robert Albert [Bob]

**Lennon, Florence Becker**
[Tanenbaum] 1895- [CA]
*American author and poet*
* Becker, Florence

**Lennon, Mrs. Nestor** [FFF]
*Entertainer*
* McCall, Lizzie

**Lennon, Robert Albert [Bob]** 1928-
[BE]
*American baseball player*
* Lennon, Arch

**Lennox, Edward**
*See* Nixson, Maisie Mayer

**Lennox, Eggie**
*See* Lennox, James Edgar

**Lennox, James** ?-1878 [PA]
*Author*
* L.

**Lennox, James Edgar** 1885-1939
[BE]
*American baseball player*
* Lennox, Eggie

**Lenny, Jack**
*See* Hannoch, Leonard John

**Leno, Dan**
*See* Galvin, George

**Leno, Dan, Jr.**
*See* Galvin, Sydney Paul

**Lenoir, Carlos** 1878-1906 [WEC]
*Brazilian cartoonist*
* Gil
* Vaz, Gil

**Lenoir, J. B.** 1929-1967 [BWW]
*American singer*
* Lenore, J. B.

**Lenoir, Jacques**
*See* Laraque, Paul

**Lenoir, Lucie** 1873- ? [IBW]
*American singer*
* [The] Creole Nightingale
* Walker, Rachel

**Lenon, Edmund Fitz-Maurice**
1863?-1928 [BEW]
*Actor*
* Maurice, Edmund

**Lenore, J. B.**
*See* Lenoir, J. B.

**Lenormand, Henri-Rene**
1882-1951 [MWD]
*French playwright*
* [The] Eugene O'Neill of the French Stage

**Lenormand, Marie Anne Adelaide**
1772-1843 [WBD]
*French fortune teller*
* [La] Sibylle du Faubourg Saint-Germain

**Lenotre, Andre** 1613-1700
[DEP, DNNS, FFF]
*French landscape architect*
* [The] Father of Landscape Gardening

**Lens**
*See* Saleeby, Caleb Williams

**Lenska, Rula** 1948?-
*British actress*
* [The] Fair One

**Lent, Blair** 1930- [CA, SAT, TBJ]
*American author and illustrator*
* Small, Ernest

**Lent, D[ora] Geneva** 1904- [CA]
*Canadian artist and author*
* Dorant, Gene

**Lentulus, Lucius Cornelius** 1st c.
BC [WBD]
*Roman politician*
* Crus [or Cruscello]

**Lentulus, Publius Cornelius** 1st c.
BC [WBD]
*Roman politician*
* Sura

**Lentulus, Publius Cornelius** 1st c.
BC [WBD]
*Roman politician*
* Spinther

**Lenya, Lotte**
*See* Blamauer, Karoline

**Lenz, Peter** 1832-1928 [WBD]
*German painter, architect, sculptor*
* Desiderius, [Father]

**Leo**
*See* Casey, J. K.

**Leo**
*See* Martin, Egbert

**Leo**
*See* Pemberton, Col.

**Leo** [HN]
*Army commander*
* [The] Ajax of the East

**Leo Africanus** 16th c. [WBD]
*Arab geographer*
* Johannes Leo

**Leo, Alan**
*See* Allan, Frederick William

**Leo, Bessie**
*See* Murray, Leslie

**Leo, Frank**
*See* Peers, Frank

**Leo Hebraeus**
*See* Abrabanel, Judah Leon

**Leo, Jim** 20th c.
*American football player*
* Leo, Nomad

**Leo, Juan** 1483-1522 [PA]
*Moorish geographer*
* [The] African

**Leo, Ma**
*See* Fullard-Leo, Ellen

**Leo, Nomad**
*See* Leo, Jim

**Leo I** 390?- 461 [DNNS]
*Pope*
* [The] Great

**Leo I** 400?- 474 [DNNS, WBD]
*Byzantine emperor*
* [The] Great
* Makeles [The Butcher]
* [The] Thracian

**Leo III** 680?- 741 [DNNS, WBD]
*Byzantine emperor*
* [The] Isaurian

**Leo IV** 750?- 780 [WBD]
*Byzantine emperor*
* [The] Khazar

**Leo IX**
*See* Bruno

**Leo V** ?- 820 [DNNS, WBD]
*Byzantine emperor*
* [The] Armenian

**Leo VI** 866- 912 [DNNS, HN]
*Byzantine emperor*
* [The] Philosopher
* [The] Wise

**Leo X**
*See* Medici, Giovanni de

**Leo XI**
*See* Medici, Alessandro Ottaviano de

**Leo XII**
*See* Della Genga, Annibale Francesco

**Leo XIII**
*See* Pecci, Gioacchino Vincenzo

**Leola**
*See* Rogers, Loula K.

**Leoline**
*See* Dunham, Mrs. E. B. S.

**Leon**
*See* Boitel, Leonard

**Leon**
*See* Van Roey, Leon

**Leon, Casper**
*See* Leoni, Gaspare

**Leon, Eddie**
*See* Leon, Eduardo Antonio

**Leon, Eduardo Antonio** 1946- [BE]
*American baseball player*
* Leon, Eddie

**Leon Felipe**
*See* Camino, Leon Felipe

**Leon, Frere**
*See* Sauget, J. S.

**Leon Hebreo**
See Abrabanel, Judah Leon

**Leon, Henry Cecil** 1902-1976
[CC, EMD, TR]
*British author and playwright*
* Cecil, Henry

**Leon, John** 1934- [TR]
*British actor*
* Standing, John

**Leon, Max**
See Leon, Maximino Molina

**Leon, Maximino Molina** 1950-
[SMG]
*Mexican-born baseball player*
* Leon, Max

**Leon, W. D.**
See Glassock, W. D.

**Leona**
See Button, Margaret Helen

**Leonard**
See Lewis, Leonard

**Leonard, A. B.**
See Aldrich, Earl Augustus

**Leonard, Agnes**
See Bangs, Mrs. F. C.

**Leonard, Benny**
See Leiner, Benjamin

**Leonard, Billie** 20th c. [THR]
*British actress and singer*
* Hill, Billie

**Leonard, Bob** 1932- [BB]
*American basketball player*
* Leonard, Slick

**Leonard, Buck**
See Leonard, Walter Fenner

**Leonard, Charles L.**
See Heberden, Mary Violet

**Leonard, Cotton**
See Leonard, Jeffrey

**Leonard, David** 1740-1829
[FFF, PA]
*Chief-Justice of Bermuda*
* Massachusettensis

**Leonard, Dutch**
See Leonard, Emil John

**Leonard, Dutch**
See Leonard, Hubert Benjamin

**Leonard, Eddie**
See Toney, Lemuel Gordon

**Leonard, Edith Jewell** 1923-
[BEW]
*American talent representative and casting consultant*
* Leonard, Julie

**Leonard, Elmer Ellsworth** 1888-
[BE]
*American baseball player*
* Leonard, Tiny

**Leonard, Elmore** 1925- [CA]
*American author*
* Long, Emmett

**Leonard, Emil John** 1910-
[BE, DGS]
*American baseball player*
* Leonard, Dutch

**Leonard, Florence Peltier** [NAA]
*American writer*
* Peltier, Florence

**Leonard, Frederick** 1881-1954
[LC]
*British playwright*
* Lonsdale, Frederick

**Leonard, George H.** 20th c. [SFL]
*Author*
* Cooper, Hughes

**Leonard, Gus**
See Lerond, Gustav

**Leonard, H. C.** [PA]
*Author*
* H. C. L.

**Leonard, Harlan Quentin** 1905-
[WWJ]
*American jazz musician*
* Leonard, Mike

**Leonard, Helen Louise** 1861-1922
[BEW, EMT, F1]
*American actress and singer*
* Russell, Lillian

**Leonard, Hubert Benjamin**
1892-1952 [AS, BE, PB]
*American baseball player*
* Leonard, Dutch

**Leonard, Hugh**
See Byrne, John Keyes

**Leonard, Jack E.**
See Lebitsky, Leonard

**Leonard, Jeffrey** 1955- [SMG]
*American baseball player*
* Leonard, Cotton

**Leonard, Joe** 20th c.
*Auto racer*
* [The] Pelican
* [The] Penguin

**Leonard, John** 1901-1956 [SC]
*British-born actor, bandleader, singer*
* Little, Little Jack

**Leonard, Julie**
See Leonard, Edith Jewell

**Leonard, Mike**
See Leonard, Harlan Quentin

**Leonard, Nellie Mabel** 1875- ?
[NAA]
*American author*
* Stuart, Fay

**Leonard, Ray** 1956-
*American boxer*
* Leonard, Sugar Ray

**Leonard, Sheldon**
See Bershad, Sheldon Leonard

**Leonard, Slick**
See Leonard, Bob

**Leonard, Sugar Ray**
See Leonard, Ray

**Leonard, Susan** 1865-1944 [BEW]
*American entertainer*
* Westford, Susanne

**Leonard, Tiny**
See Leonard, Elmer Ellsworth

**Leonard, Walter Fenner** 1907-
[MK, PB]
*American baseball player*
* [The] Black Lou Gehrig
* Leonard, Buck

**Leonard-Boyne, Eva**
See Boyne, Eva

**Leonardi, Biki**
See Leonardi, Elvira

**Leonardi, Elvira** 20th c. [WFA]
*Italian fashion designer*
* Leonardi, Biki

**Leonardi, Leon**
See Leonardi, Leonid

**Leonardi, Leonid** 1901- [ASC]
*Russian-born American composer, conductor, pianist*
* Leonardi, Leon

**Leonardo da Pisa**
See Fibonacci, Leonardo

**Leonardo, Harry**
See Gottsacker, H. L.

**Leone, Sarah**
See Brown, Polly

**Leone, Scott**
See Bonnell, Kenneth

**Leone, Sergio** 1921- [FDG]
*Italian director*
* Robertson, Bob

**Leong, Gor Yun**
See Ellison, Virginia Howell

**Leonhardt, Anna** 20th c. [SC]
*Actress*
* Belle, Nancy

**Leonhart, [Dr.] Raphael W.**
See Wybraniec, Peter F[rank]

**Leoni, Gaspare** 1872-1926
[BX, RBE]
*Italian-born American boxer*
* Leon, Casper

**Leoni, Leone**
See Osborne, John D.

**Leoni, Leone** 1509-1590 [WBD]
*Italian medalist, goldsmith, sculptor*
* [Il] Cavaliere Aretino

**Leonid**
See Bosworth, Willan George

**Leonidas**
See Da Silva, Leonidas

**Leonidas** 5th c. BC [FFF]
*King of Sparta*
* [The] Defender of Thermopylae

**[The] Leonidas of Hungary**
See Nicholas

**[The] Leonidas of Modern Greece**
See Bozzaris, Marco

**[The] Leonidas of the Day**
See Peel, [Sir] Robert

**Leonide [or Leonid]**
See Berman, Leonide [or Leonid]

**Leontes**
See Bindley, James

**Leont'ev, A.**
See Leont'ev, Lev Abramovich

**Leont'ev, Lev Abramovich**
1901-1974 [B10]
*Russian economist*
* Leont'ev, A.

**Leontius of Byzantium** 485?- 543?
[WBD]
*Byzantine monk*
* Byzantinus
* [The] First of the Scholastics
* Scholasticus

**Leopold** [RH]
*Prince*
* Peu-a-Peu

**Leopold, Babe**
See Leopold, Nathan F.

**Leopold, Carolyn Clugston** 1923-
[CA]
*American author*
* Michaels, Carolyn Leopold

**Leopold, Emmanuel-Flavia**
1896-1962 [CW]
*West Indian poet and author*
* Lavigne, Mark

**Leopold, Isaiah Edwin** 1886-1966
[F2, FC, IPA]
*American entertainer*
* Wynn, Ed

**Leopold, Nathan F.** 1904-1971
[BLB, CA, CAP]
*American murderer and author*
* Ballard, Morton D.
* Johnson, George
* Lanne, William F.
* Lawrence, Richard A.
* Leopold, Babe

**Leopold, Winnie** 1896- [THR]
*British actress and singer*
* Collins, Winnie

**Leopold I** 1640-1705 [HN, SN]
*Emperor of Germany*
* [The] Great
* [The] Little Man in Red Stockings

**Leopold I** 1676-1747
[DEP, DNNF, SN]
*Prince of Anhalt-Dessau*
* [Der] Alte Dessauer
* [The] Old Dessauer

**Leopold I** 1790-1865
[DEP, DNNS, FFF]
*King of Belgium*
* [The] Nestor of Europe

**Leopold II**
See Louis Philippe Marie Victor

**Leopold II** 15th c. [SN]
*Duke of Austria*
* [The] Big
* [The] Courtly

**Leopold III** 1096-1136 [WBD]
*Margrave of Austria*
* [The] Pious

**Leopold VI** 1176-1230 [WBD]
*Duke of Austria*
* [Der] Glorreiche [The Glorious]

**Lepcio, Ted**
See Lepcio, Thaddeus Stanley

**Lepcio, Thaddeus Stanley** 1930-
[BE]
*American baseball player*
* Lepcio, Ted

**Lepel, H.**
*See* Gurster, Eugen

**[The] Leper**
*See* Amalrich

**[The] Leper**
*See* Baldwin IV

**Lepin, Ella-Marta**
*See* Egorova, Evgeniia Nikolaevna

**Lepine, Alfred** 1901-1955
[CEI, FHE]
*Canadian-born hockey player*
* Lepine, Pit

**Lepine, Ernest** [PA]
*Author*
* Manuel
* Quatrelles

**LePine, Louis Joseph** 1876-1949
[BE]
*Canadian-born baseball player*
* LePine, Pete

**LePine, Pete**
*See* LePine, Louis Joseph

**Lepine, Pit**
*See* Lepine, Alfred

**Lepley, Jean Elizabeth** 1934- [CA]
*British-born author and educator*
* Darcy, Jean

**Lepofsky, Manfred** 1905-1971
[AW, CA, EMD]
*American author and editor*
* Lee, Manfred B[ennington]
* Queen, Ellery [joint pseudonym
  with Daniel Nathan]
* Queen, Ellery, Jr. [joint
  pseudonym with Daniel Nathan]
* Ross, Barnaby [joint pseudonym
  with Daniel Nathan]

**Leppert, Alice Jeanne** 1912?-
[CED, FC, OCF]
*American actress and singer*
* Faye, Alice

**Leppert, Don Eugene** 1930- [BE]
*American baseball player*
* Leppert, Tiger

**Leppert, Tiger**
*See* Leppert, Don Eugene

**Leppoc, Derfla**
*See* De Marini y Coppel, Alfredo
Jose

**Leprohon, Pierre** 1903- [CA]
*French film critic and historian*
* Valbonne, Jean

**Lerchbaum, Dora** 20th c. [NAA]
*Polish-born writer*
* Love, D.

**Lerchen, Bertram Roe** 1889-1962
[BE]
*American baseball player*
* Lerchen, Dutch

**Lerchen, Dutch**
*See* Lerchen, Bertram Roe

**Lerian, Peck**
*See* Lerian, Walt[er Irvin]

**Lerian, Walt[er Irvin]** 1903-1929
[BE]
*American baseball player*
* Lerian, Peck

**Leriche, Jeanne** 1869-1934 [SC]
*French actress*
* Cheirel, Jeanne

**Leris, Claire Josephe** 1723-1803
[SN, WBD]
*French actress*
* Clairon, Claire Josephe Hippolyte
  de la Tude
* [The] Queen of Carthage

**L'Ermite, Daniel** 1584-1613 [PA]
*Author*
* Eremita

**Lermoliev, Ivan**
*See* Morelli, Giovanni

**Lernier, Luke**
*See* Leighton, F. S.

**Lerond, Gustav** 1856-1939 [SC]
*French-born actor*
* Leonard, Gus

**LeRos, Christian**
*See* Sorel, W. J.

**Leroux, Etienne**
*See* Le Roux, S. P. Daniel

**Leroy**
*See* Barnwell, Annie M.

**Leroy**
*See* Chatman, John Len

**Leroy from Eloy**
*See* Malone, Art Lee

**LeRoy, Hal**
*See* Schotte, John LeRoy

**LeRoy, Ken**
*See* Klopfenstein, Kenneth
Vladimir

**Leroy, Louis** [PA]
*Author*
* Regius

**Leroy's Buddy**
*See* Gaither, Bill

**Lerrovitch**
*See* Hersey, Harold

**Lerski, George Jan** 1917- [CA]
*Polish-born American historian and
author*
* Jur, Jerzy

**Lerteth, Oban**
*See* Fanthorpe, R[obert] Lionel

**Lesbia**
*See* Clodia

**[The] Lesbian Citizen**
*See* Alcaeus

**Lescaille, Catherine** 1649-1711
[DNNF]
*Dutch poet*
* [The] Dutch Sappho

**Lesdiguieres, Duc de**
*See* De Bonne, Francois

**Leser, Tina**
*See* Smith, Tina Shillard

**LeShan, Lawrence L[ee]** 1920-
[CA]
*American author*
* Grendon, Edward

**Lesher, Phyllis** 1912- [IAW]
*American author*
* Livingston-Matthews, Asenath

**Lesizwe, Ilizwi**
*See* Lee, Franz John Tennyson

**Lesky, John** 1888-1955 [BX, RBE]
*American boxer*
* Buff, Johnny

**Lesley, Carole**
*See* Rippingale, Maureen

**Lesley, J. P.**
*See* Lesley, Peter

**Lesley, Peter** 1819-1903 [WBD]
*American geologist*
* Lesley, J. P.

**Lesley, W. W.**
*See* Mason, William Lasley

**Leslie, A. L.**
*See* Lazarus, Arnold Leslie

**Leslie, Alfred** 1874-1925 [THR]
*British actor*
* Lester, Alfred

**Leslie, Amy**
*See* West, Lillie

**Leslie, Arthur**
*See* Grieve, Christopher Murray

**Leslie, Blake**
*See* Duckworth, Leslie Blakey

**Leslie, Captain**
*See* Bradley, J. J. G.

**Leslie, Cecilie** 1914- [CA]
*British author and critic*
* MacAdam, Eve

**Leslie, Doris**
*See* Fergusson Hannay, [Lady]

**Leslie, Emma**
*See* Dixon, Mrs.

**Leslie, Frank**
*See* Carter, Henry

**Leslie, Frank**
*See* Collier, Frank

**Leslie, Gene**
*See* Halverson, Leslie Eugene

**Leslie, Henrietta**
*See* Schuetze, Gladys Henrietta
[Raphael]

**Leslie, Joan**
*See* Brodell, Joan

**Leslie, John**
*See* Howitt, John Leslie Despard

**Leslie, John Randolph** 1885-
[WWL]
*British author*
* Leslie, Shane

**Leslie, Josephine Aimee Campbell**
1898-1979 [AW, CA]
*British author*
* Dick, R. A.

**Leslie, Lawrence**
*See* Rathborne, St. George

**Leslie, Lew**
*See* Lessinsky, Lewis

**Leslie, Lilian** [joint pseudonym with
Violet Lilian Perkins]
*See* Hood, Archer Leslie

**Leslie, Lilian** [joint pseudonym with
Arthur Leslie Hood]
*See* Perkins, Violet Lilian

**Leslie, Madeline**
*See* Baker, Mrs. H. N. Woods

**Leslie, Mary Isabel** 1899- ?
[DIL, SFL, WGT]
*Irish author and poet*
* Lane, Temple

**Leslie, O. H.**
*See* Slesar, Henry

**Leslie, Peter** 1922- [ESF, WGT]
*British author, journalist, actor*
* MacNee, Patrick

**Leslie, Robert**
*See* Roberts, Sonia Leslie

**Leslie, Rochelle**
*See* Diamond, Graham

**Leslie, Sambo**
*See* Leslie, Samuel Andrew

**Leslie, Samuel Andrew** 1905- [BE]
*American baseball player*
* Leslie, Sambo

**Leslie, San**
*See* Crook, Bette [Jean]

**Leslie, Shane**
*See* Leslie, John Randolph

**Leslie, Sylvia**
*See* Ward, Sylvia

**Leslie, Tom**
*See* Veale, Thomas

**Leslie, Val**
*See* Knights, Leslie Douglas

**Leslie, Walter**
*See* Levinsky, Walter

**Leslie, Ward S.**
*See* Ward, Elizabeth Honor
[Shedden]

**Leslie-Stuart, May**
*See* Stuart, May

**Lesman, Boleslaw** 1878-1937
[CD, TCL]
*Polish poet*
* Lesmian, Boleslaw

**Lesmian, Boleslaw**
*See* Lesman, Boleslaw

**Lesnevich, Gus** 1915-1964 [WBC]
*American boxer*
* [The] Russian Lion

**Lesperance, David** 20th c. [WGT]
*Author*
* Davidson, Gene A.

**Lespes, Napoleon** 1811- ? [PA]
*Author*
* Trimm, Timothy

**[The] Lesser**
*See* James

**Lesser, Columbus**
*See* Cowen, Laurence

**Lesser, Derwin**
*See* Hornig, Charles D.

**Lesser, Milton** 1928-
[CA, WD, WGT]
*American author*
* Chase, Adam [joint pseudonym
  with Paul W. Fairman]
* Frazer, Andrew
* Granger, D. J.
* Marlowe, Stephen
* Ridgway, Jason

**Lesser, Milton** (Continued)
* Tenneshaw, S. M. [house pseudonym, Ziff-Davis]
* Thames, C[hristopher] H.

**Lesser, Roger Harold** 1928- [CA]
*British-born author and clergyman*
* Damor, Hakji

**Lessing, Bruno**
*See* Block, Rudolph

**Lessing, Gotthold Ephraim**
1729-1781 [DEP, DNNF, FFF]
*German playwright and critic*
* [The] Aesop of Germany
* [The] Father of German Literature
* [The] Frederick the Great of Thought

**Lessinsky, Lewis** 1886-1963
[BEW, EMT]
*American producer and director*
* Leslie, Lew

**Lester, Alfred**
*See* Leslie, Alfred

**Lester, Andrew**
*See* Greenhough, Terence [Terry]

**Lester, Anthony**
*See* Boyce, Christopher John

**Lester, Bruce**
*See* Lister, Bruce

**Lester, Charles Edward** 1815- ?
[PA]
*Author*
* Berkeley

**Lester, Frank**
*See* Usher, Frank Hugh

**Lester, Gene**
*See* Mercer, Jean

**Lester, Irvin**
*See* Pratt, [Murray] Fletcher

**Lester, James**
*See* Blake, Leslie James

**Lester, Jane**
*See* Walker, Emily Kathleen

**Lester, Katherine** 1911- [FC]
*American actress*
* De Mille, Katherine

**Lester, Ketty**
*See* Frierson, Revoyda

**Lester, Louise**
*See* Nathal, Mrs.

**Lester, Mark**
*See* Russell, Martin

**Lester-Rands, A.**
*See* Judd, Frederick Charles

**Lestocq, William**
*See* Wooldridge, Lestocq Boileau

**L'Estoilo, Pierre**
*See* Housset, Arsene

**L'Estrange, Anna**
*See* Ellerbeck, Rosemary

**L'Estrange, Charles James**
1880?-1947 [LC, SFL]
*Author*
* Strang, Herbert [joint pseudonym with George Herbert Ely]

**L'Estrange, Dick**
*See* Von Strensch, Gunther

**L'Estrange, [Sir] Roger** 1616-1704
[HN, RH, SN]
*British journalist*
* Old Noll's Fiddler
* Oliver's Fiddler

**Lesueur, Daniel**
*See* Lapauze, Jeanne

**Lesueur, Nicolas** 1545-1594 [PA]
*Author*
* Sudorius

**Lesuk, Bill** 1946- [SMG]
*Canadian-born hockey player*
* Lesuk, Tractor

**Lesuk, Tractor**
*See* Lesuk, Bill

**Lesure, Thomas B[arbour]** 1923-
[CA]
*American author*
* Barbour, Thomas L.

**Leszlei, Marta**
*See* Dosa, Marta Leszlei

**Let-'em-Go Joe**
*See* Durant, Joseph

**Lethaby, John W.** 20th c. [WGT]
*Author*
* J. W. L.

**Lethbridge, Rex**
*See* Meyers, Roy [Lethbridge]

**Lethington, Secretary**
*See* Maitland, William

**Letine**
*See* Gorin, George

**Letob, O. H.**
*See* Botelho, Francis Martin

**Letoriere, Georges**
*See* Peyronney, Vicomtesse de

**Letory, John Bruno** 1918- [IBW]
*American clergyman and musician*
* Sayles, Bartholomew

**Letromache, Maeng**
*See* Lee, Franz John Tennyson

**Letrusco**
*See* Martini, Virgilio

**Lettieri, Al**
*See* Lettieri, Alfredo

**Lettieri, Alfredo** 1928-1975 [SC]
*American actor and screenwriter*
* Lettieri, Al

**Letz, George Montgomery** 1916-
[FC, ITA, SW]
*American actor*
* Montgomery, George

**Leucadio Doblado, Don**
*See* White, Joseph Blanco

**Leumas, William S.**
*See* Scantlan, Samuel William

**LeVake, Dorothy Jean** 1925-
[BEW]
*American singer and actress*
* Darling, Jean

**Levance, Cal**
*See* Waite, Charles

**Levane, Andrew** 1920- [BB, MEB]
*American basketball player*
* Levane, Fuzzy

**Levane, Fuzzy**
*See* Levane, Andrew

**Levary, Tibor**
*See* Tiberiu, Farkas

**Levater, Louis**
*See* Spach, M. Louis Adolph

**Levee Joe**
*See* Weldon, Will

**Levee, Pauline Marion Goddard**
1911-
*American actress*
* Goddard, Paulette

**Leven, Benny**
*See* Levin, Benjamin

**Levene, Ben** 1938- [ART]
*British painter*
* B. L.

**Levene, Phoebus A. T.**
*See* Levin, Fishel

**Levene, Sam**
*See* Levine, Samuel

**Leventhal, Albert Rice** 1907-1976
[CA]
*American publisher, editor, author*
* Rice, Albert

**Leventhal, Ronald** 1927- [ASC]
*American musician and author*
* Lee, Ronny

**Leventon, Vladimir Ivan** 1904-1951
[BDF, OCF, WEF]
*Russian-born American producer*
* Lewton, Val

**Lever, Charles James** 1809-1872
[DEP, PA, SN]
*Irish author*
* Gosebett, Paul
* [The] Irish Smollett
* Lorrequer, Harry
* O'Dowd, Cornelius
* [The] Prince of Neck-or-Nothing Novelists

**Lever, J. K.**
*See* Lever, John Kenneth

**Lever, Jake**
*See* Lever, John Kenneth

**Lever, John Kenneth** 1949- [DC]
*British cricketer*
* Lever, J. K.
* Lever, Jake

**Leverenz, Tiny**
*See* Leverenz, Walt[er Fred]

**Leverenz, Walt[er Fred]** 1888-1973
[BE]
*American baseball player*
* Leverenz, Tiny

**Leverett, Dixie**
*See* Leverett, Gorham Vance

**Leverett, Gorham Vance**
1894-1957 [BE]
*American baseball player*
* Leverett, Dixie

**Leverette, Hod**
*See* Leverette, Horace William

**Leverette, Horace William**
1889-1958 [BE]
*American baseball player*
* Leverette, Hod

**Leverson, Ada** 1865-1936 [LC]
*British author*
* Elaine
* [The] Sphinx

**Leveson, Henry Astbury**
1828-1875 [DEL]
*British author*
* H. A. L., The Old Shekarry
* [The] Old Shekarry

**Leveson-Gower, [Sir] Henry Dudley Gresham** 1873-1954 [EC]
*British cricketer*
* Leveson-Gower, Shrimp

**Leveson-Gower, Shrimp**
*See* Leveson-Gower, [Sir] Henry Dudley Gresham

**Levesque, Leo A.** 1905- [NAA]
*American poet*
* Dion-Levesque, Rosaire

**Levesque, Rene** 1922-
*Canadian politician*
* Rene the Red

**Levey, Ethel**
*See* Fowler, Ethelia

**Levi**
*See* Dowling, Levi H.

**Levi, Aristotle**
*See* Schoeb, Erika

**Levi ben Gershon** [or Gerson]
1288?-1344? [WBD]
*French mathematician and philosopher*
* Gersonides

**Levi, Eliphas**
*See* Constant, Alphonse Louis

**Levi, Isaac** [FFF]
*Musician*
* Levy, Jules

**Levi, Peter** 1931- [DLE]
*British poet*
* Tigar, Chad

**Levi, Renato** 1926- [B10]
*Italian boat-builder*
* Levi, Sonny

**Levi, Sonny**
*See* Levi, Renato

**[The] Leviathan**
*See* Walpole, [Sir] Robert [First Earl of Orford]

**[The] Leviathan of Book-Collectors**
*See* Rawlinson, Thomas

**[The] Leviathan of Literature**
*See* Johnson, Samuel

**Levick, Mrs. Gustavus** [FFF]
*Entertainer*
* Bartling, Ada

**Levie, Isaac** 1867?-1945 [BEW]
*American theatrical performer and producer*
* Watson, Billy

**Levielle** [or Leuvielle?], **Gabriel**
1883-1925 [CU, FI, FC]
*French actor and director*
* Linder, Max
* Lonesome Luke

**Levien, Ilse** 1852-1908 [WBD]
*German author*
* Frapan-Akunian, Ilse

**Levien, Sonya**
See Hovey, Sonya Levien

**Levin, Benjamin** 1903- [BMH]
*British comedian and singer*
* Bonn, Issy
* Leven, Benny

**Levin, Edwina**
See Macdonald, Edwina Le Vin

**Levin, Fishel** 1869-1940 [JL]
*Russian-born chemist*
* Levene, Phoebus A. T.

**Levin, Kim** 20th c. [CA]
*American artist and writer*
* Pateman, Kim

**Levin, Marcia Obrasky** 1918-
[CA, SAT]
*American author*
* Martin, Jeremy [joint pseudonym
  with Martin P. Levin]
* Martin, Marcia

**Levin, Martin P.** 20th c. [CA, SAT]
*American author*
* Martin, Jeremy [joint pseudonym
  with Marcia Obrasky Levin]

**Levin, Richard** 20th c. [WGT]
*Author*
* Mand, Cyril [joint pseudonym
  with George R. Hahn]

**Levine, Ben** 20th c. [EJS]
*American boxer*
* [The] Grand Old Man

**Levine, Betty K[rasne]** 1933- [CA]
*American author*
* Krasne, Betty

**Levine, Henry** 1907- [PMJ, WWJ]
*American jazz musician*
* Levine, Hot Lips

**Levine, Hot Lips**
See Levine, Henry

**Levine, Isaac Don** 1892- [NAA]
*Russian-born author*
* Monitor

**Levine, Lawrence** 20th c. [MS]
*American musician*
* Lee, Larry

**Levine, Mara** 1914-1965 [SC]
*American actress*
* Alexander, Mara

**Levine, Philip** 1928- [CA]
*American poet*
* Poe, Edgar

**Levine, Pretty**
See Levine, Sam

**Levine, Red**
See Levine, Sam

**Levine, Sam** 20th c. [BLB, PHM]
*American underworld figure*
* Levine, Pretty
* Levine, Red

**Levine, Samuel** 1905- [BEW, EMT]
*American actor*
* Levene, Sam

**Levine, William** 1881- ? [WW]
*Author*
* Levinrew, Will

**Levinger, Lowell** 1946- [RO2]
*American musician*
* Banana

**Levinrew, Will**
See Levine, William

**Levinsky, Alexander H.** 1910?-
[CEI, EJS, FHE]
*American hockey player*
* Levinsky, Kingfish
* Levinsky, Mein Boy

**Levinsky, Battling**
See Lebrowitz, Barney

**Levinsky, Kingfish**
See Levinsky, Alexander H.

**Levinsky, Mein Boy**
See Levinsky, Alexander H.

**Levinsky, Walter** 1929- [ASC]
*American musician*
* Leslie, Walter

**Levinson, Bob**
See Wells, Robert

**Levinson, Irene**
See Zahava, Irene

**Levinson, Jerry** 1909- [PMJ]
*American composer*
* Livingston, Jerry

**Levinson, Norman** 1900-1972
[IPA, WFA]
*American fashion designer*
* [The] Dean of American Fashion
  Designers
* Norell, Norman

**Levis, Oscal**
See Levis, Oscar

**Levis, Oscar** 20th c. [OBW]
*American baseball player*
* Levis, Oscal

**Levise, William S., Jr. [Billy]** 1947-
[RO2]
*American singer*
* Lee, Billy
* Ryder, Mitch

**Levison, J.** [PA]
*Author*
* Hannibal, Julius Caesar

**Levister, Wendell W.** 1926- [IBW]
*American-born transport pilot and
flight instructor*
* [The] Ebon Eagle

**Levitch, Gary** 1946- [RO2]
*American musician*
* Lewis, Gary

**Levitch, Joseph** 1926-
[BDF, FC, HT]
*American actor, producer, director*
* Lewis, Jerry

**Levitin, George** 1916- [CA]
*Russian-born American author*
* Levitine, George

**Levitine, George**
See Levitin, George

**Levitt, Bunny**
See Levitt, Harold

**Levitt, Harold** 1911?- [BB]
*American basketball free-throw
expert*
* Levitt, Bunny

**Levitt, I. M.**
See Levitt, Israel Monroe

**Levitt, Israel Monroe** 1908- [WYA]
*American author*
* Levitt, I. M.

**Levitzka, Sarah** 1858?-1953
[BEW]
*Russian-born actress*
* Adler, Sarah

**Levkowitz, Isidore** 1881- ?
[BEW, PMJ]
*German-born actor and vaudevillian*
* Howard, Eugene

**Levkowitz, Wilhelm** 1886-1949
[BEW, EMT, PMJ]
*German-born vaudevillian*
* Howard, Willie

**Levon, Fred**
See Ayvazian, L. Fred

**Levsen, Dutch**
See Levsen, Emil Henry

**Levsen, Emil Henry** 1898-1972
[BE, PB]
*American baseball player*
* Levsen, Dutch

**Levshin, Peter** 1737-1812 [WBD]
*Russian prelate*
* Platon

**Levy, Adele** [FFF]
*Entertainer*
* Belgarde, Adele

**Levy, Arthur** 1878-1946 [JL]
*German philosopher*
* Liebert, Arthur

**Levy, Brigid Antonia Brophy** 1929-
[WGT]
*British author*
* Brophy, Brigid

**Levy, Burton** 1912-
[BEW, EMT, TR]
*American composer*
* Lane, Burton

**Levy, Butch**
See Levy, Leonard

**Levy, Charles** 1913- [CA]
*American author*
* Lee, Charles

**Levy, Ed[ward Clarence]**
See Whitner, Edward Clarence

**Levy, Estelle**
*Actress*
* Davies, Gwen

**Levy, Frederick** 1878?-1938
[F1, F2, FC]
*American actor*
* Tearle, Conway

**Levy, George Morton** 20th c.
[BBH]
*American harness racing pioneer*
* [The] Father of Modern Harness
  Racing

**Levy, Henry** 1813-1900 [JL]
*British composer*
* Russell, Henry

**Levy, Herbert I.** 1900?- [FC, FD]
*American director*
* Leeds, Herbert I.

**Levy, Herta Hess**
See Kahn, Herta Hess

**Levy, Irish**
See Levy, Milton Lambert

**Levy, Jacques Fromental Elie**
1799-1862 [WBD]
*French composer*
* Halevy

**Levy, Jules**
See Levi, Isaac

**Levy, Julien** 1906?-1981
*American art dealer*
* [The] Modernist Maestro

**Levy, Julius** 1831-1914 [WBD]
*German poet and author*
* Rodenberg, Julius

**Levy, Leonard** 20th c. [EJS]
*American football player and
wrestler*
* Levy, Butch

**Levy, Lorelei**
See Schwalberg, Carol[yn
Ernestine Stein]

**Levy, Louis Henry** 1883-1960
[EJS]
*American football historian*
* Baker, L. H.

**Levy, Milton** 1894-1948 [SC]
*American actor and bandleader*
* Britton, Milt

**Levy, Milton Lambert** ?-1958
[EJS]
*American football player*
* Levy, Irish

**Levy, Newman** 1888- [WWL]
*American author*
* Flaccus

**Levy, Paul** 1889-1932 [FC]
*American director*
* Bern, Paul

**Levy, Phil**
See Fox, Phil

**Levy, Roland Alexis Manuel**
1891-1966 [BBD, JL]
*French composer and author*
* Roland-Manuel, Alexis

**Levy, Samuel** 1890-1968 [EMT]
*American choreographer and dancer*
* Lee, Sammy

**Levy, Stephen** 1939- [FC]
*Canadian actor*
* Young, Stephen

**Lew**
See Clayton, Cyril James

**Lewald, Fanny**
See Stahr, Mme. Adolf W. T.

**Lewandowski, Herbert** 1896-
[WGT]
*Author*
* Van Dovski, Lee

**Lewes, George Henry** 1817-1878
[DEL, PA]
*British author, critic, historian*
* Churchill, Frank
* Lawrence, Slingsby
* Vivian

**Lewes, Lettie**
See Cleveland, Philip Jerome

**Lewes, William James**
See Fine, David

**Lewesdon, John**
See Daniell, Albert Scott

**Lewin, Arthur** [FFF]
*Entertainer*
* Terriss, William

**Lewin, C. L.**
*See* Brister, Richard

**Lewin, Dore** 1879-1932 [THR]
*Polish-born actor*
* Mannering, Dore Lewin

**Lewin, Ellaline** 1871-1971 [EMT]
*British actress and singer*
* Terriss, Ellaline

**Lewin, Kurt Z.** 1890-1947 [JL]
*German-born psychologist*
* [The] Father of Field Theory

**Lewin, Leonard C[ase]** 1916- [CA]
*American writer and editor*
* Case, L. L.

**Lewing, Anthony Charles** 1933-
[AW]
*British author*
* Bannerman, Mark

**Lewins, C. A.** 20th c. [MBF]
*British author*
* Rivers, Tex

**Lewis, Abby**
*See* Lewis, Camelia Albon

**Lewis, Albert Ehrlich** 1908- [BEW]
*American educator, critic, director*
* Lewis, Allan

**Lewis, Alfred Henry** 1858-1914
[EMD]
*American editor and author*
* Quin, Dan

**Lewis, Allan**
*See* Lewis, Albert Ehrlich

**Lewis, Alma** [FFF]
*Entertainer*
* Ormsby, Clara

**Lewis, Alonzo** 1794-1861 [PA]
*Author*
* [The] Lynn Bard

**Lewis, Alvin** 1943- [IBW]
*American boxer*
* Lewis, Blue

**Lewis, Angelo J.** 20th c. [BS, MBF]
*British author*
* Hoffmann, [Professor] Louis

**Lewis, Art** 1911-1962 [FB]
*American football coach*
* Lewis, Pappy

**Lewis, Ben**
*See* Smolar, Boris

**Lewis, Big Ed**
*See* Lewis, Edward

**Lewis, Big Lewie**
*See* Lewis, David R.

**Lewis, Blue**
*See* Lewis, Alvin

**Lewis, Bob**
*See* Lubbers, Robert

**Lewis, Bubbles**
*See* Lewis, R. S.

**Lewis, Buddy**
*See* Lewis, [William] Morgan

**Lewis, Buddy**
*See* Lewis, John Kelly

**Lewis, Buddy**
*See* Lewis, William Henry [Bill]

**Lewis, C. S.**
*See* Lewis, Clive Staples

**Lewis, Camelia Albon** 1910-
[BEW]
*American actress*
* Lewis, Abby

**Lewis, Caroline** [joint pseudonym
with (James) Stafford Ransome and
M. H. Temple]
*See* Begbie, [Edward] Harold

**Lewis, Caroline** [joint pseudonym
with (Edward) Harold Begbie and
M. H. Temple]
*See* Ramsome, [James] Stafford

**Lewis, Caroline** [joint pseudonym
with James S. Ransome and
(Edward) Harold Begbie]
*See* Temple, M. H.

**Lewis, Carson**
*See* Milton, John R.

**Lewis, Catherine**
*See* Robertson, Mrs. Donald

**Lewis, Charles**
*See* Dixon, Roger

**Lewis, Charles**
*See* Rowe, John Gabriel

**Lewis, Charles Bertrand** 1842-1924
*American journalist*
* [The] Free Press Man
* Quad, M.

**Lewis, Clarence** 20th c. [OBW]
*American baseball player*
* Lewis, Foots

**Lewis, Clifford** 1912- [AW]
*British author*
* Berrisford, Judith M. [joint
pseudonym with Judith Mary
(Berrisford) Lewis]

**Lewis, Clive Staples** 1898-1963
[LC, SAT, WGT]
*British author*
* Clerk, N. W.
* Hamilton, Clive
* Lewis, C. S.
* Whilk, Nat

**Lewis, Connie**
*See* Wilson, Constance

**Lewis, Country**
*See* Lewis, Gaston F.

**Lewis, Curigwen**
*See* Jones-Lewis, Curigwen

**Lewis, Cyclone Louis**
*See* Lewis, Vach

**Lewis, D. B.**
*See* Bixby, Jerome Lewis

**Lewis, D. B. Wyndham**
*See* Lewis, Dominic Bevan
Wyndham

**Lewis, D. D.**
*See* Lewis, Dwight Douglas

**Lewis, Daddy**
*See* Lewis, James H.

**Lewis, David** 1942- [CA]
*British-born author and journalist*
* Hodgson, David

**Lewis, David R.** 1953- [SMG]
*Canadian-born hockey player*
* Lewis, Big Lewie

**Lewis, Dominic Bevan Wyndham**
1894-1969 [DLE, LC, TC]
*British author and columnist*
* Beachcomber [newspaper column
pseudonym, 1919-1924]
* Lewis, D. B. Wyndham
* Shy, Timothy [joint pseudonym
with Ronald William Fordham
Searle]

**Lewis, Don** 1934- [IBW]
*American jazz musician and
political activist*
* Lewis, Sports

**Lewis, Duffy**
*See* Lewis, George Edward

**Lewis, Dwight Douglas** 1945-
[SMG]
*American football player*
* Lewis, D. D.

**Lewis, E. M.** 20th c. [CA]
*British educator, playwright, author*
* Melwood, Mary

**Lewis, Ed**
*See* Friedrich, Robert

**Lewis, Edward** 1909- [EJ, NP]
*American jazz musician*
* Big D
* Lewis, Big Ed
* Lewis, Rags

**Lewis, Edward Morgan** 1872-1936
[BE]
*Welsh-born American baseball
player*
* Lewis, Parson

**Lewis, Elliott**
*See* Remley, Frank

**Lewis, Eric**
*See* Tuffley, Fred Eric Lewis

**Lewis, Ernest** 20th c. [NBB]
*American musician*
* Country Slim

**Lewis, Estelle Anna Blanche
Robinson** 1824-1880 [PA]
*Author*
* Stella

**Lewis, Fielding**
*See* Byars, William Vincent

**Lewis, Foots**
*See* Lewis, Clarence

**Lewis, Francine**
*See* Weinstock, Helen

**Lewis, Fred**
*See* Till, Fred

**Lewis, Fred** 1944- [B10, BB]
*American basketball player*
* Lewis, Fritz

**Lewis, Fred** 20th c. [SA]
*American handball player*
* Lewis, Steady Freddie

**Lewis, Fritz**
*See* Lewis, Fred

**Lewis, Furry**
*See* Lewis, Walter

**Lewis, Gary**
*See* Levitch, Gary

**Lewis, Gaston F.** 1904- [IBW]
*American track and field coach*
* Lewis, Country

**Lewis, Gentleman**
*See* Lewis, William Thomas

**Lewis, George**
*See* Zenon [or Zeno], George Louis
Francis

**Lewis, George Edward** 1888- [BE]
*American baseball player*
* Lewis, Duffy

**Lewis, Harry**
*See* Besterman, Henry

**Lewis, Henry**
*See* Gehrig, [Henry] Lou[is]

**Lewis, Ian**
*See* Bensman, Joseph

**Lewis, Ida** 1841-1911 [DEP, FFF]
*American lighthouse keeper*
* [The] Grace Darling of America

**Lewis, Ida** 1869-1950 [BEW]
*Canadian-born actress*
* Arthur, Julia

**Lewis, J. R.**
*See* Lewis, Roy

**Lewis, Jack** 20th c. [MBF]
*British author and editor*
* Hood, Stephen
* Jackson, Lewis
* Lewis, Phylis

**Lewis, James H.** ?-1928 [SC]
*American actor*
* Lewis, Daddy

**Lewis, Janet**
*See* Winters, Janet Lewis

**Lewis, Jeffreys**
*See* Mainhall, Mrs. Henry

**Lewis, Jerry**
*See* Levitch, Joseph

**Lewis, Jerry Lee** 1935- [CME]
*American singer and musician*
* [The] Killer

**Lewis, John Delaware** [PA]
*Author*
* Smith, John

**Lewis, John Kelly** 1916- [BE]
*American baseball player*
* Lewis, Buddy

**Lewis, John Noel Claude** 1912-
[IAW]
*Welsh-born author*
* Venner, J. G.

**Lewis, Johnny**
*See* Hill, Lester

**Lewis, Joseph** [OBW]
*American baseball player*
* Lewis, Sleepy

**Lewis, Judith Mary [Berrisford]**
1912- [AW, IAW, WD]
*British author*
* Berrisford, Judith M. [joint
pseudonym with Clifford Lewis]
* Farr, Fiona
* Hope, Amanda

**Lewis, Julius Warren** 1833-1920
[PA, WW]
*Author*
* Barrington, F. Clinton

**Lewis, Julius Warren** (Continued)
* Constellano, Illion
* Lewis, Leon

**Lewis, Kate**
See Cox, Ida

**Lewis, Kid**
See Mendeloff, Gershon

**Lewis, Lange**
See Brandt, Jane Lewis

**Lewis, Lefty**
See Lewis, Wilmarth

**Lewis, Leo** [CFH]
*American-born football player*
* [The] Lincoln Locomotive

**Lewis, Leo Rich** 1865- ? [NAA]
*American educator and author*
* Rich, C. B.

**Lewis, Leon**
See Lewis, Julius Warren

**Lewis, Leonard** 20th c. [WFA]
*British hairstylist*
* Leonard

**Lewis, Lesley** 1909- [WD]
*British author*
* Lawrence, Lesley

**Lewis, Lucia Z.**
See Anderson, Lucia [Lewis]

**Lewis, Lux**
See Lewis, Meade Anderson

**Lewis, Mabel** 1872-1957 [THR]
*British actress*
* Terry-Lewis, Mabel

**Lewis, Margaret Cameron** 1867- ?
[ALY]
*American author*
* Cameron, Margaret

**Lewis, Mary**
See Kidd, Mary

**Lewis, Mary Christianna [Milne]**
1907- [CC, EMD, WW]
*British author*
* Brand, Christianna
* Roland, Mary
* Thompson, China

**Lewis, Mary Christianna [Milne]**
1907- [CA, TCC]
*British author*
* Ashe, Mary Ann
* Jones, Annabel

**Lewis, Mary Edmonia** 1845-1890
[IBW]
*American sculptor*
* Lewis, Wildfire

**Lewis, Mary F. W.**
See Bond, Mary Fanning Wickham

**Lewis, Matthew Gregory**
1775-1818 [DEP, HN, RH]
*British poet, playwright, author*
* Lewis, Monk

**Lewis, May**
See Goldstone, Aline Lewis

**Lewis, Meade Anderson** 1905-1964
[HDM, WWJ]
*American jazz musician*
* [The] Duke of Luxembourg
* Lewis, Lux

**Lewis, Mel**
See Sokoloff, Melvin

**Lewis, Mildred D.** 1912- [CA]
*American author*
* DeWitt, James

**Lewis, Monk**
See Lewis, Matthew Gregory

**Lewis, [William] Morgan**
1906-1968 [EMT]
*American composer*
* Lewis, Buddy

**Lewis, Nina?**
See Buck, Marilyn Jean

**Lewis, Pappy**
See Lewis, Art

**Lewis, Parson**
See Lewis, Edward Morgan

**Lewis, Paul**
See Gerson, Noel Bertram

**Lewis, Pete**
See Crown, Peter J.

**Lewis, Phylis**
See Lewis, Jack

**Lewis, R. S.** 20th c. [OBW]
*American baseball player*
* Lewis, Bubbles

**Lewis, Rags**
See Lewis, Edward

**Lewis, Robert** 1900-1965 [NOJ]
*American jazz musician*
* Son Fewclothes

**Lewis, Roger**
See Zarchy, Harry

**Lewis, Roy** 1933- [AW]
*British barrister and author*
* Lewis, J. R.
* Springfield, David

**Lewis, Sabby**
See Lewis, William Sebastian

**Lewis, Shari**
See Hurwitz, Shari

**Lewis, Sherman** 1942- [FB]
*American football player*
* Lewis, Tank

**Lewis, [Harry] Sinclair** 1885-1951
[ANT]
*American author and playwright*
* Graham, Tom

**Lewis, Sleepy**
See Lewis, Joseph

**Lewis, Smiley**
See Lemons, Overton Amos

**Lewis, Smiling**
See Lemons, Overton Amos

**Lewis, Sports**
See Lewis, Don

**Lewis, Steady Freddie**
See Lewis, Fred

**Lewis, Stephen** 1946?- [B10]
*American author*
* Sills, Jennifer

**Lewis, Strangler**
See Friedrich, Robert

**Lewis, Tank**
See Lewis, Sherman

**Lewis, Ted**
See Friedman, Theodore Leopold

**Lewis, Ted**
See Mendeloff, Gershon

**Lewis, Thomas H.** 20th c. [WWL]
*British editor and poet*
* Riot, Pat

**Lewis, Tommy**
See Watts, Lou[is Thomas]

**Lewis, Vach** 20th c. [BLB]
*American underworld figure*
* Lewis, Cyclone Louis

**Lewis, Vance**
See Vanzi, Luigi

**Lewis, Voltaire**
See Ritchie, Edwin

**Lewis, W. W.** [PA]
*Author*
* Binnacle

**Lewis, Waller** 1711-1781 [FFF]
*British author and physician*
* Cam

**Lewis, Walter** 1893-1981 [BWW]
*American singer*
* Lewis, Furry

**Lewis, Whitey**
See Siedenschner, Jacob

**Lewis, Wildfire**
See Lewis, Mary Edmonia

**Lewis, William Henry [Bill]** 1904-
[BE]
*American baseball player*
* Lewis, Buddy

**Lewis, William Sebastian** 1914-
[WWJ]
*American jazz musician*
* Lewis, Sabby

**Lewis, William Thomas** 1748-1811
[DEP, RH, WBD]
*British comedian*
* Lewis, Gentleman
* [The] Mercutio of Actors

**Lewis, William Waller** 1860-1915
[BEW]
*Spanish-born actor and producer*
* Waller, Lewis

**Lewis, Wilmarth** 1896-
*American editor of Walpole letters*
* Lewis, Lefty

**Lewiton, Mina**
See Simon, Mina Lewiton

**Lewittes, Mordecai Henry**
See Lewittes, Morton H[enry]

**Lewittes, Morton H[enry]** 1911-
[CA]
*American educator and author*
* Lewittes, Mordecai Henry

**Lewton, Val**
See Leventon, Vladimir Ivan

**Lewyn, Joey Marion**
*Actor*
* Mack, Marion

**Lexau, Joan M.** 20th c. [CA, SAT]
*American author*
* Nodset, Joan L.

**Lexy, Edward**
See Little, Edward Gerald

**Ley, Arthur Gordon** 1921-1968
[ESF, SFL, WGT]
*British author*
* Luther, Ray
* Sellings, Arthur

**Ley, Brea R.**
See McCalment, Maebelle
[Brearley]

**Ley, Willy** 1906-1969 [CA, SAT]
*German-born American author*
* Willey, Robert

**Leybourne, George**
See Saunders, Joe

**Leyel, Carl F.**
See Leijel, Carl F.

**Leyhart, Edward**
See Edwards, Elwyn Hartley

**Leynard, Martin**
See Berger, Ivan [Bennett]

**Leypoldt, Frederick** 1837?-1884
[FFF]
*German-born American publisher
and bibliographer*
* Pylodet, L.

**Leys, Simon**
See Ryckmans, Pierre

**Leyva, Fred F.** ?-1921 [SC]
*Actor*
* Lyons, Fred

**Leyva, Ricardo**
See Valdes, Nelson P.

**Lezama, Jose**
See Lima, Jose Lezama

**L'Hermite, Francois** 1601-1655
[WBD]
*French poet, playwright, author*
* L'Hermite, Tristan

**L'Hermite, Tristan**
See L'Hermite, Francois

**L'homme-Eclair [The Top Man]**
See Morenz, Howarth William

**L'Hospital [or L'Hopital], Michel de**
1507-1573 [SN]
*French jurist and statesman*
* [A] Second Cato the Censor

**Li Chin-yang** 1917- [WOA]
*Chinese-American author and
journalist*
* Lee, C. Y.

**Li Erh** 5th c. BC [WBD]
*Chinese philosopher*
* Lao-tzu [or Lao-tse]

**Li Hung-chang** 1823-1901
[DEP, DHA, DNNS]
*Chinese statesman*
* [The] Bismarck of Asia

**Li Lorenzo, Maurizio** 1933?-1979
*Italian actor and faith healer*
* Arena, Maurizio

**Li, Shu-T'ien** 1900- [IAW]
*Chinese-born engineer and writer*
* Lee, John
* Lee, Keng-Yen

**Li Yuan** 565- 635 [WBD]
*Chinese emperor*
* Kao Tsu

**[The] Liar**
See Aswad, al-

[The] Liar
See Moseilma

Libb, Richard 1890-1935 [SC]
Canadian-born actor
* Travers, Richard C.

Libbey, Pauline 1885-1938 [BEW]
American actress
* Frederick, Pauline

Liberace
See Liberace, Wladziu Valentino

[The] Liberace of London
See Atwell, Winifred

Liberace, Wladziu Valentino 1919-
[BMH, FC, ITA]
American pianist
* Liberace
* [The] Rhinestone Rubinstein

[The] Liberal Conscience of
Washington
See Barth, Alan

[The] Liberator
See Bolivar, Simon

[The] Liberator
See O'Connell, Daniel

[The] Liberator of Chile
See O'Higgins, Bernardo

[The] Liberator of Genoa
See Doria, Andrea

[The] Liberator of Italy
See Garibaldi, Giuseppe

[The] Liberator of Missouri
See Pillow, Gideon Johnson

[The] Liberator of the New World
See Franklin, Benjamin

Liberi, Pietro 1605-1687 [WBD]
Venetian painter
* [Il] Libertino

Liberito, Joe 20th c. [PHM]
American underworld figure
* [The] Baker

[El] Libertador
See Bolivar, Simon

[Il] Libertino
See Liberi, Pietro

Libke, Al[bert Walter] 1918- [BE]
American baseball player
* Libke, Big Al

Libke, Big Al
See Libke, Al[bert Walter]

Libose, Jean
See Ambroise, Lys

[The] Librarian of the Republic of
Letters
See Fabricius, John Albert

[The] Libyan Sibyl
See Van Wagener, Isabelle

Licavoli, Horseface
See Licavoli, Peter, Sr.

Licavoli, Jack
See Licavoli, James

Licavoli, James 20th c.
American underworld figure
* Licavoli, Jack

Licavoli, Peter, Sr. 20th c.
American underworld figure
* Licavoli, Horseface

Licavoli, Thomas 20th c. [MM]
American underworld figure
* Licavoli, Yonnie

Licavoli, Yonnie
See Licavoli, Thomas

[El] Licenciado Tome de Burguillos
See Vega Carpio, Lope Felix de

Lichenstein, Irving Herbert 1923-
[BEW]
American actor and fencing master
* Colbin, Rod

Lichine, David
See Lichtenstein, David

Licht, Hans
See Brandt, Paul

Lichtenberg, Elisabeth Jacoba
1913- [CA]
Dutch-born British author
* Van Someren, Liesje

Lichtenstein, David 1909?-1972
[JL, THR]
Russian-born dancer and
choreographer
* Lichine, David

Lichtenstein, George Maurice
1905- [WEC]
American cartoonist
* Lichty

Lichtenstein, Mortimer Haig 1918-
[BEW]
American actor
* Marshall, Mort

Lichtheim, George 1912-1973 [CA]
German-born historian and author
* Arnold, G. L.

Lichtman, Joseph 1931-
[BEW, EMT, TR]
American director and
choreographer
* Layton, Joe

Lichtveld, [Dr.] L. A. M. 1906-
[CW]
Surinamese author, poet, playwright
* Helman, Albert

Lichty
See Lichtenstein, George Maurice

Lickfold, Charles 1846-1909
[BEW]
British-born actor
* Warner, Charles

Lickfold, Henry Bryon 1876-1958
[BEW]
British-born actor
* Warner, Henry Bryon

Lickshingle, Grandfather
See Criswell, Robert W.

Liddell, C. H. [joint pseudonym with
Catherine Lucile Moore]
See Kuttner, Henry

Liddell, C. H. [joint pseudonym with
Henry Kuttner]
See Moore, Catherine Lucile

Liddell Hart, B. H.
See Liddell Hart, [Sir] Basil Henry

Liddell Hart, [Sir] Basil Henry
1895-1970 [LC]
British journalist, lecturer, military
advisor
* Liddell Hart, B. H.

Liddington, Liddie
See Liddington, Robert Allen

Liddington, Robert Allen 1948-
[SMG]
Canadian-born hockey player
* Liddington, Liddie

Liddy, Eleanor Jane 1870-1948
[BEW, BMH, THR]
Scottish-born actress, singer, dancer
* [The] Essence of Eccentricity
* [La] Petite Nellie
* Wallace, Nellie

Liddy, James [Daniel Reeves] 1934-
[CA, DLE]
Irish author and poet
* Lynch, Brian
* O'Connor, Liam
* Reeves, Daniel

Lidin, Vladimir
See Gomberg, Vladimir
Germanovich

Lieb, Dick
See Lieb, Ziskind

Lieb, Michael 1844-1900
[FFF, WBD]
Hungarian painter
* Munkacszy, Mihaly von

Lieb, Ziskind 1930- [ASC]
American musician
* Lieb, Dick

Liebeler, Jean [Mayer] 20th c.
[WW]
Author
* Mather, Virginia

Lieber, Charles Edwin 1909-1961
[BE]
American baseball player
* Lieber, Dutch

Lieber, Dutch
See Lieber, Charles Edwin

Lieber, Francis 1800-1872
[FFF, PA]
German-born historian and author
* Americus

Lieber [or Liebler], Thomas
1524-1583 [DHA, WBD]
German-Swiss theologian, physician,
philosopher
* Erastus, Thomas

Lieberman, M. I. 20th c. [CSH]
Canadian football player
* Lieberman, Moe

Lieberman, Moe
See Lieberman, M. I.

Lieberman, Mortimer 1905?-1963
[BEW]
American columnist
* Mortimer, Lee

Liebermann, David 1887-1971
[FC]
American actor
* Mann, Hank

Liebert, Arthur
See Levy, Arthur

Liebhardt, Glenn Ignatius 1910-
[BE]
American baseball player
* Liebhardt, Sandy

Liebhardt, Sandy
See Liebhardt, Glenn Ignatius

Liebling, A. J.
See Liebling, Abbott Joseph

Liebling, Abbott Joseph 1904-1963
[LC, TC1]
American journalist
* Liebling, A. J.

Liebmann, Yisrol Paul Mann 1915-
[BEW]
Canadian-born actor, director,
educator
* Mann, Paul

Liebowitz, Sidney 1935-
[BEW, EMT]
American singer
* Lawrence, Steve

Liebstein, Jacov 1898- [JL]
Lithuanian-born American political
activist
* Lovestone, Jay

Lieknis, Edvarts 1883-1940 [EWL]
Latvian poet
* Virza, Edvarts

Lien, Chi
See Wong, Elizabeth

Lieven, Albert
See Lieven-Lieven, Albert Fritz

Lieven, Dariya Khristoforovna
1784-1857 [WBD]
Latvian-born society leader
* [The] Sibyl of Europe

Lieven-Lieven, Albert Fritz 1906-
[THR]
German-born actor
* Lieven, Albert

Life, John
See Chadwick, Charles

Liggett, Genevieve Gauntier 1885-
[CU, NAA]
American author and actress
* Gauntier, Gene
* [The] Kalem Girl

Liggins, Ethel 1886- [BBD]
British pianist
* Leginska, Ethel

Liggins, Joe 1915- [PMJ]
American singer and bandleader
* [The] Honeydripper

Light Bulb Johnson
See Johnson, Lyndon Baines

Light, Daisy Mae 1883-1965 [SC]
American actress
* Harte, Betty

Light Horse Harry
See Lee, Henry

Light Horse Harry Cooper
See Cooper, Harry E.

Light Horse Harry Wilson
See Wilson, Harry E.

Light, Maud 1881-1934 [BEW]
American actress
* Illington, Margaret

[The] Light of the Age
See Maimonides [or Moses ben Maimon]

[The] Light of the Town
See Oates, Titus

[The] Light of the West
See Maimonides [or Moses ben Maimon]

[The] Light of the World
See Jesus Christ

[The] Light of the World
See Sigismund

Light, Walter Herrod 1888-
[MBF, WWL]
British author and editor
* Herrod, Walter
* Willson, Wingrove

Lightfoot, Alexander 1924-1971
[BWW]
American singer
* Lightfoot, George
* Lightfoot, Papa
* Little Papa Walter
* Papa George

Lightfoot, George
See Lightfoot, Alexander

Lightfoot, Hannah 18th c.
[DEP, DHA, DNNS]
Wife of King George III of England
* [The] Fair Quakeress

Lightfoot, Papa
See Lightfoot, Alexander

Lightner, A. M.
See Hopf, Alice L[ightner]

Lightner, Winnie
See Hanson, Winifred

Lightnin'
See Mitchell, Doris

Lightnin' Joe Collins
See Collins, Joseph Lawton

Lightnin' Jr.
See Dupree, William Thomas

Lightnin' Jr.
See Williams, L. C.

Lightnin' Slim
See Hicks, Otis V.

Lightning
See Hamilcar

[The] Lightning
See Stephen II

Lightning Destroyer
See Foreman, George

Lightning Hutch Hutchinson
See Hutchinson, Charles

[The] Lightning Story-Writer
See Crawford, Francis Marion

Lightstone, Pauline 1882- [BBD]
Canadian opera singer
* Donalda, Pauline

Ligne, Charles Joseph 1735-1814
[DNNF, FFF, SN]
Austrian army officer
* [The] Prince of Coxcombs

Ligon, Jim 20th c. [IBW]
American basketball player
* [The] Great Goose

Ligonier
See Burleigh, William Henry

Liguest, Pierre Laclede
1724?-1778 [WBD]
French-born fur trader and pioneer in America
* Laclede, Pierre

Liguquka, Iphiva Elilala
See Mazibuko, Mandla Thomas

[The] Ligurian Sage
See Persius Flaccus, Aulus

Lijn, Liliane
See Segall, Liliane

Like, Jim [GW]
American rodeo performer
* Like, Powder Horn

Like, Powder Horn
See Like, Jim

Lil
See Ormsby, Waterman L., Jr.

Li'l Abner
See Erickson, Paul Walford

Lil Abner
See Hagan, Cliff

Li'l Jackie Paterson
See Paterson, Jackie

Li'l Lou Kaplan
See Kaplan, Louis

Li'l Papa Moliere
See Moliere, Frank

Lil Son Jackson
See Jackson, Melvin

Lil Ty Barkley
See Barkley, Tyrone

Lilburne, John 1613-1657
[DNNS, FFF, RH]
British republican
* Freeborn John

Liletts [or Liletta], Marta Maria
1897- [F1, F2, FC]
German actress
* Daghofer, Lillitts
* Dagover, Lil

Liliencron, Friedrich [Axel Adolf]
1844-1909 [EWL]
German poet and author
* Von L., Detlev

Lilienthal, David E. 20th c.
American author
* Ely, David

Lilina, Maria Petrovna
See Perevozchikova, Maria Petrovna

Liljenfors, Bennie Mads Carl
1938- [IAW]
Swedish author
* Matiason, K. G.
* Wilding, Sten

Lillebakken, J. P. 1879-1967
[EWL]
Norwegian author
* Falkberget, Johan [Petter]

Lilley, Alan William 1959- [DC]
British cricketer
* Lilley, Peanut

Lilley, Arthur Frederick Augustus
1867-1929 [EC]
British cricketer
* Lilley, Dick

Lilley, Dick
See Lilley, Arthur Frederick Augustus

Lilley, Peanut
See Lilley, Alan William

Lilley, Peter 20th c. [CC, WW]
Author
* Buckingham, Bruce [joint pseudonym with Anthony Stansfeld]
* Chandos, Dane [joint pseudonym with N. Stansbury-Millett, later with A. Stansfeld]

Lillie, Beatrice
See Munston, Constance Sylvia

Lillie, Grasshopper
See Lillie, James J. [Jim]

Lillie, James J. [Jim] 1862-1890
[BE]
American baseball player
* Lillie, Grasshopper

Lillies, Arthur 1858-1932 [THR]
British theatrical manager
* Chudleigh, Arthur

Lillo
See Galante, Carmine

[A] Lillo Among Painters
See Hogarth, William

Lilly, Isabella Purvis 1907- [IAW]
New Zealand author
* Allan, Ann
* Cousin Ann

Lilly, John 1553?-1600? [SN]
British author
* [The] Euphuist

Lilly, Lambert
See Goodrich, Samuel G.

Lilly, Leon 1884-1960 [THR]
British actor and playwright
* Gordon, Leon

Lilly, Patrick J. 1949-
American police officer
* LaRocca, Pasquale
* LaRocca, Patty

Lilly, Robert 20th c.
American football player
* Lilly, Tiger

Lilly, Tiger
See Lilly, Robert

Lilly, William 1602-1681
[DEP, DNNS, FFF]
British astrologer
* [The] English Merlin
* [The] Last Astrologer
* [The] Merlin of England
* Merlinus Anglicus
* Sidrophel

Lily [code name used during World War II]
See Carre, Mathilde [Belard]

[The] Lily of the Mohawks
See Tekakwitha, Kateri

Lima, Jose Lezama 1911?-1976
[CA]
Cuban poet, author, editor
* Lezama, Jose

Limbach, Cornelius 1889-1965
[SC]
American actor
* Edwards, Neely

Limeno [From Lima]
See Garate y Hernandez, Jose

Limeno [From Lima]
See Garate Echenique, Enrique

Limentani, Giacoma
See Limentani Cantatore, Giacometta

Limentani Cantatore, Giacometta
1927- [IAW]
Italian translator
* Limentani, Giacoma

Liminana, Eva 1899-1953 [SC]
Mexican actress, producer, screenwriter
* Duchess Olga

Limmer, Luke, Esq.
See Leighton, Frederick

Limnelius, George
See Robinson, Lewis George

Limner, Luke
See Leighton, John

Lin, Adet J[usu] 1923- [CA]
Chinese-born author
* Tan Yun

Lin, Anor 1926- [CA]
Chinese editor, author, translator
* Lin, Tai-yi
* Lin, Wu-shuang

Lin Cho-Liang
Musician
* Lin, Jimmy

Lin, Frank
See Atherton, Gertrude [Franklin Horn]

Lin, Jimmy
See Lin Cho-Liang

Lin, Richard
See Lin Show Yu

Lin Show Yu 1933- [CAR]
British artist
* Lin, Richard

Lin, Tai-yi
See Lin, Anor

Lin, Wu-shuang
See Lin, Anor

Lincoln, Abbey
See Woolridge, Anna Marie

Lincoln, Abe
See Pearson, Charles M.

Lincoln, Abraham 1809-1865
[DEP, FAP, SN]
American president
* [The] Ancient
* [The] Buffoon
* Caesar
* Father Abraham
* [The] Flatboat Man
* [The] Grand Wrestler
* [The] Great Emancipator
* Honest Abe
* [The] Illinois Baboon

**Lincoln, Abraham** (Continued)
* [The] Jester
* [The] Long 'Un
* [The] Man of the People
* [The] Martyr President
* Old Abe
* [The] Rail Splitter
* [The] Sage of Springfield
* [The] Sectional President
* [The] Tycoon
* [The] Tyrant
* Uncle Abe

**Lincoln, Charlie**
See Hicks, Charlie

**Lincoln, E. K.**
See Lincoln, Edward Kline

**Lincoln, E. R.**
See Van Horn, Dale R.

**Lincoln, Edward Kline** ?-1958
[SC]
American actor
* Lincoln, E. K.

**Lincoln, Elmo**
See Linkenhelter, Otto Elmo

**Lincoln, Geoffrey**
See Mortimer, John [Clifford]

**Lincoln, George**
See Freda, Riccardo

**Lincoln, Howard**
See Harbaugh, Thomas Chalmers

**Lincoln, Isaac**
See Trebitsch, Isaac

**Lincoln, Jane Elizabeth** [Larcombe]
1829- ? [FFF]
American author
* Campbell, Kate

**[The] Lincoln Locomotive**
See Lewis, Leo

**[A] Lincolnshire Grazier**
See Horne, Thomas Hartwell

**Lind, Abraham** 1933- [OP]
American opera singer
* Lind-Oquendo, Abraham

**Lind, Jack**
See Lind, Jackson Hugh

**Lind, Jackson Hugh** 1946- [BE]
American baseball player
* Lind, Jack

**Lind, Jakov**
See Landwirth, Heinz

**Lind, Jenny**
See Lind, Johanna Maria

**Lind, Johanna Maria** 1820-1887
[DNNF, FFF, WBD]
Swedish singer
* Lind, Jenny
* [The] Swedish Nightingale

**Lind, Joseph Conrad** 1915- [BEW]
American actor
* Hayes, Peter Lind

**Lind, Letty**
See Rudge, Letty

**Lind, Ragnar Godfrey** 1909-
[BEW, FC]
American actor
* Lynn, Jeffrey

**Lind, Ruby**
See Lindsay, Ruby

**Lind-Oquendo, Abraham**
See Lind, Abraham

**Lindars, Barnabas**
See Lindars, Frederick Chevallier

**Lindars, Frederick Chevallier**
1923- [WD]
British clergyman and author
* Lindars, Barnabas

**Lindbeck, Em**
See Lindbeck, Emerit Desmond

**Lindbeck, Emerit Desmond** 1935-
[BE]
American baseball player
* Lindbeck, Em

**Lindberg, Armas Emanuel** 1884-
[BBD]
Finnish musicologist and composer
* Launis, Armas Emanuel

**Lindberg, Karl Sivert** 1933- [IAW]
Swedish author and poet
* Veits, Ulf

**Lindbergh, Charles Augustus**
1902-1974
American aviator
* Lindy
* [The] Lone Eagle
* Lucky Lindy

**[The] Lindbergh of the Sea**
See D'Aboville, Gerard

**Lindbergh, Richard Franklin**
See Speck, Richard Franklin

**Lindegger, Albert** 1904- [GA]
Swiss graphic artist
* Lindi

**Lindemann, Frederick Alexander**
1886-1957
British physicist
* [The] Prof

**Linden, Erik Hugo Emanuel** 1918-
[IAW]
Swedish author and poet
* Lowo, Hans
* Ristare, Bo

**Linden, Hal**
See Lipshitz, Harold

**Linden, Oliver**
See Abrahams, Doris Caroline

**Linden, Robert**
See Jacobson, Robert Navra

**Linden, Sara**
See Bartlett, Marie [Swan]

**Linder, Max**
See Levielle [or Leuvielle?],
Gabriel

**Linderman, Bill** 1920-1965 [GW]
American rodeo performer
* [The] King

**Linderman, Bud**
See Linderman, Elmer

**Linderman, Elmer** 20th c. [GW]
American rodeo performer
* Linderman, Bud

**Linders, Carl**
See Geibel, Adam

**Lindfors, Viveca**
See Torstensdotter, Elsa Viveca

**Lindholm, Anna Chandler** 1870- ?
[WW]
Author
* Fay, Dorothy

**Lindi**
See Lindegger, Albert

**Lindley, Erica**
See Quigley, Aileen

**Lindley, Louis Bert, Jr.** 1919-
[FC, ITA, SW]
American actor and rodeo performer
* Pickens, Slim

**Lindner, D. Berry**
See DuBreuil, Elizabeth Lorinda

**Lindo, Mark Prager** 1819-1879
[WBD]
Dutch author
* [De] Oude Heer Smits [Old Mr.
Smits]

**Lindon-Travers, Florence** 1913-
[FC]
British actress
* Travers, Linden

**Lindquist, Carl Emil** 1919- [BE]
American baseball player
* Lindquist, Lindy

**Lindquist, Lindy**
See Lindquist, Carl Emil

**Linds, Mark Prager** [PA]
Author
* Smitts, Mr.

**Lindsay, Barbara** 20th c. [CA]
Author
* James, Josephine [joint
pseudonym with Emma Gelders
Sterne]

**Lindsay, Christian H.** 1878-1941
[BE]
American baseball player
* Lindsay, Pinky

**Lindsay, D'Auvergne Sharon**
1904-1963
American actress and songwriter
* Lynn, Sharon E.

**Lindsay [or Lyndsay], [Sir] David**
1490-1555 [WBD]
Scottish poet
* Lindsay of the Mount

**Lindsay, Frog**
See Lindsay, Robert

**Lindsay, Harold Arthur** 1900-
[CA]
Australian author
* Bogaduck
* Carrick, A. B.
* Ex-R.S.M.

**Lindsay, Harry**
See Hudson, H. Lindsay

**Lindsay, Jack** 1900- [CA, WD]
Australian historian, author, editor
* Meadows, Peter
* Preston, Richard

**Lindsay, John**
See Muriel, John Saint Clair

**Lindsay, Josephine**
See Story, Rosamond Mary

**Lindsay, Kathleen** 1903-
[AW, WW]
British author
* Cameron, Margaret
* Richmond, Mary

**Lindsay, Lord** 1812- ? [PA]
Author
* Crawford, A. W.

**Lindsay, Margaret**
See Kies, Margaret

**Lindsay, [John] Maurice** 1918-
[CA]
Scottish poet, editor, author
* Brock, Gavin

**Lindsay of the Mount**
See Lindsay [or Lyndsay], [Sir]
David

**Lindsay, Perry**
See Dern, Peggy Gaddis

**Lindsay, Pinky**
See Lindsay, Christian H.

**Lindsay, Robert** 20th c. [OBW]
American baseball player
* Lindsay, Frog

**Lindsay, Robert Blake Theodore**
[Ted] 1925- [CEI, FHE, HK]
Canadian-born hockey player and
executive
* Lindsay, Scarface
* Lindsay, Terrible Ted

**Lindsay, Robert James** 1832-1901
[WBD]
British army officer
* Loyd-Lindsay, Robert James
* Wantage, Baron

**Lindsay, Ruby** 1887-1919 [DBA]
British painter and illustrator
* Lind, Ruby

**Lindsay, Sadi** ?-1969 [SC]
French-born actress and writer
* Leduc, Claudine

**Lindsay, Scarface**
See Lindsay, Robert Blake
Theodore [Ted]

**Lindsay, Terrible Ted**
See Lindsay, Robert Blake
Theodore [Ted]

**Lindsay, Vera**
See Poliakoff, Vera

**Lindsay-Thomson, Beatrix** 1900-
[THR]
British actress
* Thomson, Beatrix

**Lindsey, Joseph** 1899- ? [NOJ]
American jazz musician
* Lindsey, Little Joe
* Lindsey, Seefus

**Lindsey, Little Joe**
See Lindsey, Joseph

**Lindsey, Seefus**
See Lindsey, Joseph

**Lindsley, Mary F[lora]** 20th c.
[CA]
American educator and author
* Jaffee, Mary L.

**Lindstroem, Kirsten**
See Fischer, Marie Louise

**Lindstrom, Alf**
See Lundholm, Anja

**Lindstrom, Frederick Charles**
1905-1981 [BE, DGS]
*American baseball player*
* Lindstrom, Lindy

**Lindstrom, Lindy**
*See* Lindstrom, Frederick Charles

**Lindstrom, Willy** 1951- [SMG]
*Swedish-born hockey player*
* Willy the Wisp

**Lindy**
*See* Lindbergh, Charles Augustus

**Linebarger, Paul M[yron] A[nthony]**
1913-1966 [CA, ESF, SF]
*American author*
* Bearden, Anthony
* Forest, Felix C.
* Smith, Carmichael
* Smith, Cordwainer

**Linebarger, Paul Myron Wentworth**
1871- ? [NAA]
*American author*
* Myron, Paul

**Linecar, Arthur** 20th c. [WWL]
*British author*
* Grim, Anthony

**Linedecker, Clifford L.** 1931- [CA]
*American author*
* Clifton, Lewis

**Lineham, Richard** 20th c. [BBH]
*Boxer*
* [The] Lion

**Linesman**
*See* Grant, Maurice Harold

**Linfield, Mary Barrow** 1891-
[NAA]
*American author*
* Highland, Lawrence

**Linfield, Sam**
*See* Clifton, Sam

**Lingard, Dickey**
*See* Dunning, Harriet Sarah

**Lingard, Mrs. William** [FFF]
*Entertainer*
* Dunning, Alice

**Lingard, Nellie**
*See* Burbeck, Mrs. F. M.

**Lingeman, Richard R[oberts]** 1931-
[CA]
*American author*
* Chignon, Niles
* Hirsch, William Randolph [joint
    pseudonym with Marvin Kitman
    and Victor S. Navasky]

**Lingenfelter, Charles David**
1887-1934 [SC]
*American actor*
* Percival, Walter C.

**[The] Lingerer**
*See* Fabius Maximus Verrucosus,
Quintus

**Lingley, Big Bill**
*See* Lingley, William

**Lingley, William** ?-1915 [BLB]
*American murderer and gangster*
* Lingley, Big Bill

**Linhart, Anton Hansjorg** 1942-
[SMG]
*Austrian-born football player*
* Linhart, Toni

**Linhart, Toni**
*See* Linhart, Anton Hansjorg

**Linington, Elizabeth** 1921-
[AW, CA, CC]
*American author*
* Blaisdell, Anne
* Egan, Lesley
* O'Neill, Egan
* Shannon, Dell

**Linke, Babe**
*See* Linke, Ed[ward Karl]

**Linke, Ed[ward Karl]** 1911- [BN]
*American baseball player*
* Linke, Babe

**Linke, Fred[erick L.]** 20th c. [BE]
*American baseball player*
* Linke, Laddie

**Linke, Laddie**
*See* Linke, Fred[erick L.]

**Linke Poot**
*See* Doeblin, Alfred

**Linkenhelter, Otto Elmo**
1889-1952 [BEW, F1, FC]
*American actor*
* Lincoln, Elmo

**Linkensale**
*See* Ingersoll, L. D.

**Linkinwater, Tim**
*See* Waldo, James Curtis

**Linklater, J. Lane**
*See* Watkins, Alex

**Linley, Elizabeth Ann** 1754-1792
[DNNF, RH, SN]
*British singer*
* [The] Maid of Bath

**Linley, Julian**
*See* Pearson, Alec George

**Linley, Mark**
*See* Samways, George Richmond

**Linn, Bambi**
*See* Linnemier, Bambina Aennchen

**Linn, Bud**
*See* Linn, Grafton E.

**Linn, Grafton E.** 1909-1968 [SC]
*American actor and singer*
* Linn, Bud

**[The] Linnaeus of Hogarth**
*See* Ireland, John

**Linnankoski, Johannes**
*See* Peltonen, Vihtori

**Linnemier, Bambina Aennchen**
1926- [BEW]
*American actress and dancer*
* Linn, Bambi

**Lino**
*See* Martinez, Lino

**Linseman, Ken** 1958-
*Canadian-born hockey player*
* [The] Rat

**Linskill, Doris Joy** 1908- [IAW]
*British author and playwright*
* Trevor, Joy

**Linsley, Ladd. E.**
*See* Sellers, Connie Leslie, Jr.

**Linton, A. H.**
*See* Hopkins, Alphonso A.

**Linton, Barbara Leslie** 1945- [CA]
*American author*
* Austin, Barbara Leslie

**Linton, Bob**
*See* Linton, Claud C.

**Linton, Claud C.** 1902- [BE]
*American baseball player*
* Linton, Bob

**Linton, Mabel** 1905- [F2, ITA]
*American actress*
* Morley, Karen

**Linton, Phyllis Margaret** 1929-
[SWI]
*British swimmer*
* Linton, Pip

**Linton, Pip**
*See* Linton, Phyllis Margaret

**Linton, William James** 1812- ?
[PA]
*Author*
* Spartacus

**Linus** ?- 76 [HN]
*Pope*
* [The] Great Light [Llever Mawr]

**Linval, Paule Cassius de**
1890-1970 [CW]
*West Indian author*
* Marx, Jean

**Linwood, Lottie**
*See* Cooke, Helen M.

**Linwood, Lucy-Anne**
*See* Ellwood, Gracia-Fay

**Linz, Philip Francis** 1939- [BE]
*American baseball player*
* Linz, Supersub

**Linz, Supersub**
*See* Linz, Philip Francis

**[The] Lion**
*See* Damelowicz

**[The] Lion**
*See* Henry

**[The] Lion**
*See* Lineham, Richard

**[The] Lion**
*See* Louis VIII

**[The] Lion**
*See* Nomelleni, Leo

**[The] Lion**
*See* Otto I [or Otho]

**[The] Lion**
*See* Smith, William Henry Joseph
Berthol Bonaparte Bertholoff

**[The] Lion**
*See* Thompson, William

**[The] Lion**
*See* William

**[The] Lion Hearted**
*See* Richard I

**[The] Lion Hunter**
*See* Cumming, Roualeyn George
Gordon

**[The] Lion Killer**
*See* Gerard, Jules

**[The] Lion King of Assyria**
*See* Arioch al Asser

**[The] Lion of Defence**
*See* Model, Walther

**[The] Lion of God**
*See* Ali

**[The] Lion of God and His Prophet**
*See* Hamza

**[The] Lion of Janina**
*See* Ali

**[The] Lion of Judah**
*See* Makonnen, Ras Tafari

**[The] Lion of Justice**
*See* Henry I

**[The] Lion of Munster**
*See* Galen, Graf Clemens von

**[The] Lion of Paris**
*See* Paderewski, Ignace Jan

**[The] Lion of Swaziland**
*See* Sobhuza II

**[The] Lion of Sweden**
*See* Baner [Banier or Banner],
Johan

**[The] Lion of the Caribbean**
*See* Bustamante, [Sir] William
Alexander

**[The] Lion of the Fold of Judah**
*See* MacHale, John

**[The] Lion of the Lyceum**
*See* Price, Joseph Charles

**[The] Lion of the North**
*See* Gustavus Adolphus

**[The] Lion of the Punjab**
*See* Ranjit [or Runjeet], Singh

**[Le] Lion Rouge**
*See* Ney, Michel [Duc
d'Elchingen]

**[The] Lion Tamer**
*See* Goulding, Edmund

**Lionel, Robert**
*See* Fanthorpe, R[obert] Lionel

**[La] Lionne**
*See* Paulet, Mlle.

**Liotta, Leonardo** 1932-
[BX, RBE, WBC]
*American boxer*
* [The] Boston Bomber
* Demarco, Tony

**[The] Lip**
*See* Durocher, Leo Ernest

**[The] Lip**
*See* Schmidt, Helmut

**Lipchitz, Chaim Jacob** 1891-1973
[CAR]
*French sculptor*
* Lipchitz, Jacques

**Lipchitz, Jacques**
*See* Lipchitz, Chaim Jacob

**Lipkind, William** 1904-1974
[SAT, TCC]
*American author*
* Will

**Lipon, John Joseph** 1922- [BE, PB]
*American baseball player and
manager*
* Lipon, Skids

**Lipon, Skids**
See   Lipon, John Joseph

**Lipp, Helen Louise** 1917-
[BEW, TR]
*American singer and actress*
* Bliss, Helena

**Lipp, Joseph Julius**
See   Lipski, Joseph Julius

**Lippard, George** 1822-1854   [PA]
*Author*
* Darppil

**Lipper, Bette** 1922?-1954   [BEW]
*Actress*
* Grayson, Bette

**Lippert, Clarissa Start** 1917-   [CA]
*American author*
* Davidson, Clarissa Start
* Start, Clarissa

**Lippi, [Fra] Filippo** 1406?-1469
[WBD]
*Florentine painter*
* Filippo del Carmine

**Lippi, Lorenzo** 1606-1664   [WBD]
*Florentine poet and painter*
* Zipoli, Perlone

**Lippincott, Sara**
See   Richards, Sara Lippincott

**Lippincott, Sara Jane [Clarke]**
1825?-1904   [DEL, DNNF, FFF]
*American journalist*
* Greenwood, Grace

**[Il] Lippo [The Blear-Eyed]**
See   Brandolini, Aurelius

**Lipschitz, [Rabbi] Chaim U.** 1912-
[AW]
*Israeli-born author and clergyman*
* Yerushalmi, Chaim

**Lipscomb, Big Daddy**
See   Lipscomb, [Eu]gene

**Lipscomb, Dickey** 1941-   [ECM]
*American singer and songwriter*
* Lee, Dickey

**Lipscomb, [Commander] F. W.**
See   Lipscomb, Frank Woodgate

**Lipscomb, Frank Woodgate** 1903-
[CA]
*British naval officer and author*
* Lipscomb, [Commander] F. W.

**Lipscomb, [Eu]gene** 1931-1963
[AS, FB]
*American football player*
* Lipscomb, Big Daddy

**Lipscomb, Gerard** 1911-   [BE]
*American baseball player*
* Lipscomb, Nig

**Lipscomb, Nig**
See   Lipscomb, Gerard

**Lipsett, Marianne** 20th c.   [THR]
*British actress*
* Caldwell, Marianne

**Lipshitz, Harold** 1931-
[BEW, EMT, TR]
*American actor and singer*
* Linden, Hal

**Lipsitz, Dean** 1919-   [CA]
*American author*
* Lipton, Dean

**Lipsius, Marie** 1837-1927
[BBD, WBD]
*German author*
* [La] Mara

**Lipski, Joseph Julius** 1889-1958
[EJS]
*American football official*
* Lipp, Joseph Julius

**Lipson, Fredda** 1926-   [JL, RO1]
*American singer*
* Gibbons, Fredda
* Gibbs, Georgia
* Gibson, Fredda [or Freddie]
* Her Nibs

**Lipson, Gertrude** 20th c.   [DLE]
*British author*
* Charles, Gerda

**Lipton, Dean**
See   Lipsitz, Dean

**Lipton, Robert** 20th c.   [SFL]
*Author*
* Sterling, Barry

**Lipton, Thomas**
*British merchant and yachtsman*
* Tea, Sir

**Liranzo, Pedro Rafael** 1953-
[SMG]
*Dominican-born baseball player*
* Liranzo, Raf

**Liranzo, Raf**
See   Liranzo, Pedro Rafael

**Lisboa, Antonio Francisco**
1730-1814   [IBW]
*Brazilian architect and sculptor*
* [The] Little Cripple

**Lisbona, Edward** 1915-   [ASC]
*British-born American composer and pianist*
* Miller, Eddie
* Miller, Piano

**Lisciotti, Larry** 20th c.
*American billiard player*
* Lisciotti, Oil Can

**Lisciotti, Oil Can**
See   Lisciotti, Larry

**Liscombe, Carl**
See   Liscombe, Harry Carlyle

**Liscombe, Harry Carlyle** 1915-
[CEI, FHE, HK]
*Canadian-born hockey player*
* Liscombe, Carl

**Lisenbee, Hod**
See   Lisenbee, Horace Milton

**Lisenbee, Horace Milton** 1898-
[BE]
*American baseball player*
* Lisenbee, Hod

**Lisi, Virna**
See   Pieralisi, Virna

**Lisle, Lester**
See   Walker, Emmeline Lisle

**Lisle, Mary**
See   Cornish, [Doris] Mary

**Lisle, Seward D.**
See   Ellis, Edward S[ylvester]

**[The] Lisping**
See   Eric XI

**Liss, Peggy K[orn]** 1927-   [CA]
*American historian and author*
* Korn, Peggy

**Lissandrino**
See   Magnasco, Alessandro

**Lissenden, George B.** 1879- ?
[WWL]
*British author*
* Whitstable, George

**Lissitzky, El.**
See   Lissitzky, Lazar Markovich

**Lissitzky, Lazar Markovich**
1890-1941   [CAR]
*Russian artist*
* Lissitzky, El.

**List, Ilka Katherine** 1935-
[CA, SAT]
*American artist and author*
* Maidoff, Ilka List

**[The] Listener**
See   Chamberlain, Nathan Henry

**Lister, Bruce** 1912-   [FC]
*South African actor*
* Lester, Bruce

**Lister, Eve**
See   Watson, Eve

**Lister, Lance**
See   Watson, Solomon Lancelot
Inglis

**Lister, Morris Elmer** 1881-1948
[BE]
*American baseball player*
* Lister, Pete

**Lister, Pete**
See   Lister, Morris Elmer

**Liston, B. E.**
See   Livingston, Berkeley

**Liston, Big Lis**
See   Liston, Emil S.

**Liston, Charles** 1932?-1970?
[AS, B10, BX]
*American boxer*
* [The] Bear
* Liston, Sonny

**Liston, Emil S.** 1890-1949   [BBH]
*American basketball coach*
* Liston, Big Lis
* Liston, Liz

**Liston, Harry** 1843-1929   [BMH]
*British comedian*
* [The] Stage-Struck Hero

**Liston, Jack**
See   Maloney, Ralph Liston

**Liston, Liz**
See   Liston, Emil S.

**Liston, Sonny**
See   Liston, Charles

**Liston, Victor** ?-1913   [BMH]
*British comic singer*
* [The] Robson of the Halls

**Lite, Jams**
See   Schneck, Stephen

**[A] Literary Antiquary**
See   Fairholt, F. W.

**[The] Literary Anvil**
See   Johnson, Samuel

**[The] Literary Baker**
See   Jeacock, Caleb

**[The] Literary Bull-Dog**
See   Warburton, William

**[The] Literary Castor**
See   Johnson, Samuel

**[The] Literary Colossus**
See   Johnson, Samuel

**[The] Literary Leather-Dresser**
See   Dowse, Thomas

**[A] Literary Machiavel**
See   Addison, Joseph

**[A] Literary Proteus**
See   Hill, [Sir] John

**[A] Literary Sinbad**
See   Hall, Basil

**[A] Literary Sycophant**
See   Hurd, Richard

**Lithotomus**
See   Ammonius

**Litri**
See   Baez y Quintero, Miguel

**Litri**
See   Baez Espuny, Miguel

**Littell, Country**
See   Littell, Mark Alan

**Littell, Mark Alan** 1953-   [SMG]
*American baseball player*
* Littell, Country

**[The] Little**
See   Dionysius Exiguus

**[The] Little**
See   John of Salisbury

**[The] Little**
See   Procop

**Little, A. Edward**
See   Klein, Aaron E.

**Little Abbie Brunies**
See   Brunies, Albert

**Little Al Gunter**
See   Gunter, Al

**Little Albie Booth**
See   Booth, Albert James, Jr.

**Little Alec Bannerman**
See   Bannerman, Alexander
Chambers

**Little All Right**
See   Ritchey, Claude Cassius

**Little Andrew Odom**
See   Odom, Andrew

**Little Angie Tuminaro**
See   Tuminaro, Angelo

**Little Ann Bunn**
See   Bunn, Ann

**Little Anthony**
See   Gourdine, Anthony

**Little Apples**
See   Reggione, Michael

**Little Artha Johnson**
See   Johnson, John Arthur [Jack]

**Little Augie Carfano**
See   Carfano, Anthony

**Little Augie Orgen**
See Orgen, Jacob

**Little Augie Pisano**
See Carfano, Anthony

**[The] Little Beagle**
See Cecil, William [First Baron Burleigh]

**Little Bear Zardis**
See Zardis, Chester

**Little Beaver Rowe**
See Rowe, Frank

**Little Ben**
See Harrison, Benjamin

**Little Benny Harris**
See Harris, Benjamin

**Little, Big Devil**
See Little, John

**Little Big Man**
See Minacore, Calogero

**Little, Big Tiny**
See Little, Dudley

**Little Bill Johnston**
See Johnston, William M.

**Little, Billy**
See Rhodes, Billy

**Little Billy Smith**
See Smith, Billy

**Little Bird**
See Heath, James Edward [Jimmy]

**[The] Little Blue-Cloak**
See Champion, Edme

**Little Bo**
See Robinson, Fannie Clay

**[The] Little Boswell of His Day**
See Aubrey, John

**Little Box o' Tricks**
See Palmer, Thomas

**Little Boy Blue**
See Booth, Albert James, Jr.

**Little Boy Blue**
See Ford, Aleck

**Little Boy Fuller**
See Trice, Rich[ard]

**Little Bozo**
See Pizzo, John F.

**[The] Little Bronze Statue from Florida**
See Desjardins, Pete[r]

**Little Brother Griffin**
See Griffin, Roosevelt

**Little Brother Montgomery**
See Montgomery, Eurreal Wilford

**[The] Little Bugler**
See Roger, George Munroe

**Little, Byrd**
See Lomax, E. Victoria

**Little Caesar**
See Burnett, Carl

**Little Caesar**
See DiVarco, Joseph Vincent

**Little Caesar**
See Saperstein, Abraham M. [Abe]

**[The] Little Captain**
See George II

**Little Carl Carlton**
See Carlton, Carl

**Little, Chicken**
See Little, Larry

**Little Chink Martin**
See Abraham, Martin, Jr.

**Little Chis Chism**
See Chism, Elijah

**Little Chocolate**
See Dixon, George

**Little Chrissie Evert**
See Evert, Chris[tine Marie]

**[The] Little Colonel**
See Reese, Harold Henry

**Little Comedy**
See Horneck, Catharine [Kate]

**Little, Constance** 20th c. [CC]
*Author*
* Little, Conyth [joint pseudonym with Gwenyth Little]

**Little, Conyth** [joint pseudonym with Gwenyth Little]
See Little, Constance

**Little, Conyth** [joint pseudonym with Constance Little]
See Little, Gwenyth

**[The] Little Corporal**
See Bonaparte, Napoleon

**[The] Little Cowboy**
See Gobel, George Leslie

**[The] Little Cripple**
See Lisboa, Antonio Francisco

**Little Daddy**
See Braddix, Ben

**[The] Little Dauphin**
See De Bourgogne, Louis

**Little David**
See Felton, John

**Little David Alexander**
See Alexander, David

**[The] Little Deacon**
See John of Salisbury

**Little Do Doherty**
See Doherty, Hugh Lawrence

**[The] Little Doctor**
See Meanwell, Walter E.

**[The] Little Dragon**
See Lee Yuen Kam

**Little Dud Vincent**
See Vincent, Clarence

**Little, Dudley** 1930- [ASC, DAM]
*American musician*
* Little, Big Tiny
* Little, Tiny

**[The] Little Duke**
See Scott, James

**[The] Little Dutchman**
See Zuppke, Robert C.

**[The] Little Dynamo**
See Faulkner, Walt

**Little Eagle** 1913-
*American-Indian actor*
* Cody, Iron Eyes

**Little Eddie Boyd**
See Boyd, Edward Riley

**Little Eddie Burns**
See Burns, Eddie

**Little Eddie Kirkland**
See Kirkland, Eddie

**Little Eddie Spann**
See Spann, Charles Edward, III

**Little, Edward Gerald** 1897- [FC]
*British actor*
* Lexy, Edward

**Little Elsie**
See Bierbower [or Bierbauer], Elsie

**Little Esther**
See Jones, Esther Mae

**Little Eva**
See Boyd, Eva Narcissus

**Little Eva Lange**
See Lange, William Alexander

**Little Eva Wilhelm**
See Wilhelm, Irvin Key

**Little Farvel Kovolick**
See Kovolick, Philip

**[The] Little Flower**
See La Guardia, Fiorello Henry

**Little Flower of Jesus**
See Martin, Therese

**[The] Little Flying Devil**
See Kestner, Paul

**Little, Frances**
See Macaulay, Fannie Caldwell

**[The] Little General**
See Theobald, Ron[ald M.]

**Little, George A.** 1883- [NAA]
*Canadian clergyman and editor*
* Graham, Homer

**Little George Buford**
See Buford, George

**Little George Smith**
See Smith, George

**Little Georgie Gobel**
See Gobel, George Leslie

**[The] Little Giant**
See Douglas, Stephen Arnold

**[The] Little Giant**
See Green, David

**[The] Little Giant**
See Howard, Frank J.

**[The] Little Giant**
See Hurt, Edward Paisley [Eddie]

**[The] Little Giant**
See Joliat, Aurel Emile

**Little Giant**
See Margo, Peter

**Little Giant**
See Morgan, Joseph Leonard [Joe]

**[The] Little Giant of the Blues**
See Blackmore, Amos

**[The] Little Globetrotter**
See Earle, William Moffat

**Little Gloria Vanderbilt**
See Vanderbilt, Gloria

**Little, Gordon W.** 1860-1942 [SC]
*American actor and circus performer*
* Pawnee Bill

**Little, Gwenyth** 20th c. [CC]
*Author*
* Little, Conyth [joint pseudonym with Constance Little]

**[The] Little Hebrew**
See Attell, Abraham Washington

**Little Henry**
See Gray, Henry

**Little Hercules**
See Wilding, Anthony F.

**Little Hillock**
See Confucius [or K'ung Fu-tzu]

**Little Hudson**
See Shower, Hudson

**Little Hymie Weiss**
See Wajcieckowski, Earl

**[The] Little Indian**
See Moore, Wilbur

**Little, Jack**
See Little, William Arthur

**Little Jack Little**
See Leonard, John

**Little Jack McGill**
See McGill, John Edward

**Little Jackie Sharkey**
See Cervati, Giovanni

**Little Jazz Eldridge**
See Eldridge, [David] Roy

**Little, Jim**
See Brown, Sidney

**Little Jim Folsom**
See Folsom, Jim

**Little Jim Rushing**
See Rushing, James Andrew [Jimmy]

**Little Jimmie Turrell**
See Turrell, James Archie [Jim]

**Little Jimmy Dempsey**
See Dempsey, James Clifford

**Little Jimmy Dickens**
See Dickens, Jimmy

**Little Jimmy Sizemore**
See Sizemore, Jimmy

**Little, Joan** 1954- [IBW]
*American prison rape victim*
* Nadir, Hadiyah Joan

**Little Joe**
See Cook, Joe

**Little Joe**
See Hill, Lester

**Little Joe Blue**
See Valery, Joseph, Jr.

**Little Joe Bonanno**
See Bonanno, Joseph, Jr.

**Little Joe Calabriese**
See Calabriese, Joseph

**Little Joe Gehrig**
See Gehrig, [Henry] Lou[is]

**Little Joe Lindsey**
See Lindsey, Joseph

**Little Joe Montoya**
See Montoya, Joseph M.

**Little Joe Presko**
See Presko, Joseph Edward

**Little Joe Yeager**
See Yeager, Joseph F.

**Little Joey**
See Hall, Joseph

**Little John**
See Nailor, John

**Little, John** 1947- [SMG]
*American football player*
* Little, Big Devil

**Little John Badanjek**
See Badanjek, John

**Little John Hartman**
See Hartman, John

**Little Johnny Jones**
See Jones, John

**Little Johnny Taylor**
See Young, Johnny

**Little Jr.**
See Johnson, Luther, Jr.

**Little Junior Parker**
See Parker, Herman

**Little Junior Wells**
See Blackmore, Amos

**Little Junior Williams**
See Williams, Emery H.

**Little Katie Crippen**
See Crippen, Catherine [Katie]

**Little, Kenneth**
See Scotland, James

**[The] Little Lady of the Stars**
See Proctor, Mary

**Little, Larry** 1945- [SMG]
*American football player*
* Little, Chicken

**Little Laura Dukes**
See Dukes, Laura

**Little Lauro Salas**
See Salas, Lauro

**Little, Lawrence** 1893- [FB]
*American football coach*
* Little, Lou

**Little Linda Ludgrove**
See Ludgrove, Linda

**Little, Little Jack**
See Leonard, John

**Little Looie Aparicio**
See Aparicio, Luis Ernesto

**Little, Lou**
See Little, Lawrence

**Little Lou Goldstein**
See Goldstein, Lou

**Little Loving Henry**
See Byrd, Henry Roeland

**Little Luther**
See Johnson, Lucius Brinson

**Little Mac**
See McClellan, George Brinton

**Little Mac Macullar**
See Macullar, James F.

**Little Maceo**
See Merriweather, Rozier

**[A] Little Machiavelli**
See Galiani, Ferdinand

**Little Mack McCarthy**
See McCarthy, Thomas Francis
Michael [Tommy]

**Little Mack Simmons**
See Simmons, Mack

**Little Mackey Sanders**
See Sanders, Charlie

**[The] Little Magician**
See Van Buren, Martin

**[The] Little Magnet**
See Deagon, Lyda

**Little, Malcolm** 1925-1965
[CBS, IBW, NAD]
*American Black Muslim leader*
* Detroit Red
* El Shabazz, El-Hajj Malik
* Malcolm X

**Little Man**
See Johnson, James

**[The] Little Man**
See Minacore, Calogero

**[The] Little Man in Red Stockings**
See Leopold I

**Little Man Wagner**
See Wagner, Danny, Jr.

**[The] Little Marlborough**
See Schwerin, Kurt Christoph von.

**[The] Little Master**
See Beham, Hans Sebald

**Little Mike McKendrick**
See McKendrick, Gilbert Michael

**Little Milton**
See Campbell, Milton James

**Little Milton Anderson**
See Anderson, Milton

**Little Miss Dynamite**
See Tarpley, Brenda Mae

**Little Miss Poker Face**
See Wills, Helen Newington

**Little Miss Sharecropper**
See Baker, LaVern

**Little Mr. Everywhere**
See Huggins, Miller James

**Little Mo Connolly**
See Connolly, Maureen

**Little Mo Modzelewski**
See Modzelewski, Richard [Dick]

**[The] Little Mother of Colored Drama**
See Bush, Anita

**Little Mouse Metidieri**
See Metidieri, Carlos

**Little, Mrs. J. Z.** [FFF]
*Entertainer*
* Campbell, Lizzie

**[The] Little Napoleon**
See Beauregard, Pierre Gustave
Toutant

**Little Napoleon**
See Chadd, Archie

**Little Napoleon**
See Kaplan, Louis

**[The] Little Napoleon**
See McClellan, George Brinton

**[The] Little Napoleon**
See McGraw, John Joseph

**[The] Little Napoleon of the West
Coast Bar**
See Delmas, Delphin

**Little Nemo**
See Hill, Bennett

**Little Nemo Stephens**
See Stephens, James Walter

**Little New York**
See Campagna, Louis

**[The] Little Nightingale**
See Pope, Alexander

**Little Otis**
See Rush, Otis

**[The] Little Pale Star from Georgia**
See Stephens, Alexander Hamilton

**Little Papa Joe**
See Williams, Joseph Leon [Joe]

**Little Papa Walter**
See Lightfoot, Alexander

**Little Patsy Doyle**
See Doyle, Patrick

**Little, Paul H.**
See Litwinsky, Paul

**Little, Paula**
See Litwinsky, Paul

**Little Peetie Wheatstraw**
See Hogg, Andrew

**Little Peggy March**
See March, Peggy

**Little Phil**
See Sheridan, Philip Henry

**Little Phil Geier**
See Geier, Louis Phillip

**Little Pod Ellingsen**
See Ellingsen, H. Bruce

**[The] Little Poet**
See Oldys, Alexander

**Little Poison**
See Runyan, Paul Scott

**Little Poison**
See Waner, Lloyd James

**[The] Little Potato**
See Pascual, Camilo Alberto

**[The] Little Preacher**
See De Marets, Samuel

**[The] Little Prince of Soul**
See Jackson, Michael Joseph

**[The] Little Professor**
See DiMaggio, Dominic Paul

**[The] Little Professor of the Piney
Woods**
See Jones, Laurence Clifton

**[The] Little Queen**
See Isabella of Valois

**Little Ray**
See Agee, Ray[mond Clinton]

**Little Red Cagney**
See Cagney, James Francis
[Jimmy]

**[The] Little Red Fox**
See Alexander II

**Little Red Lopez**
See Lopez, Danny

**Little Richard**
See Penniman, Richard

**Little, Ruby A. Black** 1896- [NAA]
*American journalist*
* Black, Ruby Aurora

**Little Sam**
See Broonzy, William Lee Conley

**Little Sax Crowder**
See Crowder, Robert Henry [Bob]

**Little Sister**
See Scruggs, Irene

**Little Smokey Smothers**
See Smothers, Abraham

**Little Son**
See Broonzy, William Lee Conley

**Little Son Joe**
See Lawlars, Ernest

**Little Son Willis**
See Willis, Aaron

**Little Son Willis**
See Willis, Malcolm

**Little Sonny Brown**
See Brown, Samuel

**[The] Little Spaniard**
See Ribera, Jose

**[The] Little Sparrow**
See Gassion, Edith Giovanna

**[The] Little Steam Engine**
See Galvin, James Francis

**Little Stevie Wonder**
See Cauthen, Steve

**Little Stevie Wonder**
See Morris, Steveland

**Little Stevie Wright**
See Wright, Steve

**Little Sure Shot**
See Moses, Annie

**Little Susy**
See Prentiss, Mrs.

**Little Sylvia**
See Vanderpool, Sylvia

**Little T Bone**
See Gaines, Roy

**Little T Bone**
See Rankin, R. S.

**Little T Teagarden**
See Teagarden, Charlie

**Little Temple**
See Jenkins, Gus

**Little, Thomas**
See Moore, Thomas

**Little Tich**
See Hanif Mohammad

**Little Tich**
See Relph, Harry

**Little Tiger Thompson**
See Thompson, Esau

**Little, Tiny**
See Little, Dudley

**Little, Tobe**
See Slaughter, Marion T.

**Little Tom Jefferson**
See Jefferson, Thomas

**Little Tom Maguire**
See Maguire, Tom

**[The] Little Tramp**
See Chaplin, Charles Spencer

**Little Tubby Raskin**
See Raskin, Julius

**Little Van**
See Van Buren, Martin

**[The] Little Van Dyck**
See Dyck [or Dijk], Philip van

**[The] Little Vermin**
See Laud, William

**Little Victoria**
See Lawrence, Vesta

**Little Victoria**
See Monks, Victoria

**Little Walter**
See Jacobs, Marion Walter

**Little Walter J**
See Jacobs, Marion Walter

**Little Walter J.**
See Westbrook, Walter J.

**Little Walter Jr.**
See Smith, George

**[The] Little Whig**
See Anne

**Little, William Arthur** 1891-1961
[BE]
*American baseball player*
* Little, Jack

**Little Willie**
See Friedrich Wilhelm

**Little Willie Foster**
See Foster, Willie [or Willy]

**Little Willie John**
See Woods, William J.

**Little Willie Johnson**
See Johnson, William Edward John

**Little Willie Littlefield**
See Littlefield, Willie

**Little Wolf**
See Shines, John Ned [Johnny]

**Littleboy, Sheila M.**
See Ary, Sheila M[ary Littleboy]

**Littlefield, Little Willie**
See Littlefield, Willie

**Littlefield, Willie** 1931- [BWW]
*American singer*
* Littlefield, Little Willie

**Littlejohn**
See Mackenzie, R. Shelton

**Littlejohn**
See Tomlins, Frederick Guest

**Littlejohn, Hugh**
See Lockhart, John Hugh

**Littlejohn, John**
See Funchess, John

**Littler, [Eu]gene [Alex]** 1930- [GF]
*American golfer*
* Gene the Machine

**Littleton, Classy Cleo**
See Littleton, Cleophus

**Littleton, Cleophus** 1932- [BB]
*American basketball player*
* Littleton, Classy Cleo

**Littleton, Mark**
See Kennedy, John Pendleton

**Littlewit, Humphrey**
See Lovecraft, Howard Phillips

**Littlewood, Alan** 1936- [IAW]
*British writer*
* Ceres

**Littlewood, S. R.**
See Littlewood, Samuel Robinson

**Littlewood, Samuel Robinson**
1875-1963 [LC]
*British author and drama critic*
* Littlewood, S. R.

**Littricebey, Clara Alma Allen** 20th
c. [BWW]
*American entertainer*
* Littricebey, Granny

**Littricebey, Granny**
See Littricebey, Clara Alma Allen

**Litvak, Anatole**
See Lutwak, Michael Anatol

**Litvinne, Felia**
See Schuetz, Francoise-Jeanne

**Litvinov, Ivy** 1890?-1977 [CA]
*British-born author*
* Low, Ivy

**Litvinov, Maxim M.**
See Wallach, Meir

**Litwack, Harry** 1907- [BB]
*Austrian-born American basketball player*
* [The] Chief

**Litwinsky, Paul** 1915- [CA, SFL]
*American author*
* Little, Paul H.
* Little, Paula
* Paul, Hugo

**Litwos**
See Sienkiewicz, Henryk [Adam Aleksander Pius]

**Liu An** 2nd c. BC [WBD]
*Chinese ruler and scholar*
* Huai-nan Tzu

**Liu, James T[zu] C[hien]**
See Liu, Tzu-chien

**Liu, Tzu-chien** 1919- [CA]
*Chinese-born educator and author*
* Liu, James T[zu] C[hien]

**Liu, Wu-chi** 1907- [CA, WD]
*Chinese-born American historian, critic, author*
* Hsia Hsiao

**Liutprand [or Liudprand]** 922?-972? [WBD]
*Italian prelate and historian*
* Liutprand of Cremona

**Liutprand of Cremona**
See Liutprand [or Liudprand]

**Livandais, Augustus M. D.** [PA]
*Author*
* Knutt, A. P.

**Live Oak George**
See Law, George

**Lively, Bud**
See Lively, Everett Adrian

**Lively, Everett Adrian** 1925- [BE]
*American baseball player*
* Lively, Bud
* Lively, Red

**Lively, Henry Everett** 1885-1967
[BE]
*American baseball player*
* Lively, Jack

**Lively, Jack**
See Lively, Henry Everett

**Lively, Red**
See Lively, Everett Adrian

**Lively, Walter**
See Elliott, Bruce [Walter Gardner Lively Stacy]

**Livermore, Jean**
See Sanville, Jean

**[The] Livermore Larruper**
See Baer, Max[imilian Adelbert]

**[The] Liverpool Landseer**
See Huggins, William

**Livers, Virgil Chester, Jr.** 1952-
[SMG]
*American football player*
* Mighty Mouse

**Liverton, Joan** 1913- [AW, CAP]
*British author*
* Medhurst, Joan

**[The] Livery Muse**
See Dodsley, Robert

**Livi, Ivo [or Yvo]** 1921-
[BDF, ITA, WEF]
*French actor and singer*
* Montand, Yves

**[The] Living Archive**
See Traglia, Luigi

**[The] Living Cyclopaedia**
See Longinus, Dionysius Cassius

**[A] Living Dictionary**
See Leibnitz [or Leibniz], Gottfried Wilhelm von

**[The] Living Legend**
See Morganfield, McKinley

**[A] Living Library**
See Toussain, Jacques

**[The] Living Sophism**
See Robespierre, Maximilien

**Livingston, Berkeley** 1908-
[ESF, SFP, WGT]
*American writer*
* Barclay, Lester
* Blade, Alexander [house pseudonym, Ziff-Davis]
* Hickey, H. B.
* Liston, B. E.
* Steele, Morris J. [house pseudonym, Ziff-Davis]

**Livingston, Don Leslie** 1892-
[NAA]
*American author*
* Gable, Rufe

**Livingston, Fud**
See Livingston, Joseph Anthony

**Livingston, Goo Goo**
See Livingston, L. D.

**Livingston, Herb** 1916- [WGT]
*American author*
* Blade, Alexander [house pseudonym, Ziff-Davis]
* Hickey, H. B.

**Livingston, Jerry**
See Levinson, Jerry

**Livingston, John Henry** 1746-1825
[FFF]
*American clergyman*
* [The] Father of the Dutch Reformed Church in America

**Livingston, Joseph Anthony**
1906-1957 [ASC, EJ, PMJ]
*American jazz musician*
* Livingston, Fud

**Livingston, Kenneth**
See Stewart, Kenneth Livingston

**Livingston, L. D.** 20th c. [OBW]
*American baseball player*
* Livingston, Goo Goo

**Livingston, Libby**
See Livingston, Warren

**Livingston, Mary**
See Marks, Sadie

**Livingston, Mickey**
See Livingston, Thompson Orville

**Livingston, Mollie Parnis** 1905-
[IPA]
*American fashion designer*
* Parnis, Mollie

**Livingston, Paddy**
See Livingston, Patrick Joseph

**Livingston, Patrick Joseph** 1880- ?
[BE]
*American baseball player*
* Livingston, Paddy

**Livingston, Peter Van Rensselaer**
See Townsend, James B[arclay] J[ermain]

**Livingston, Thompson Orville**
1914- [ALR, BE]
*American baseball player*
* Livingston, Mickey

**Livingston, Warren**
*American football player*
* Livingston, Libby

**Livingston, William** 1723-1790
[FFF]
*American politician*
* [The] Don Quixote of New Jersey

**Livingston, William** (Continued)
* [The] Itinerant Dey of New Jersey
* [The] Whipping Post

**Livingston-Matthews, Asenath**
See   Lesher, Phyllis

**Livingstone, Harrison Edward** 1937-   [CA, WD]
*American author and poet*
* Fairfield, John

**Livingstone, Margaret**
See   Flynn, Mary Margaret

**[The] Livy of France**
See   Mariana, Juan de [or John]

**[The] Livy of Portugal**
See   Barros, Joao de

**[The] Livy of Spain**
See   Ginez de Sepulveda, Juan

**[The] Livy of Spain**
See   Mariana, Juan de [or John]

**Lizana, Curly**
See   Lizana, Florin J.

**Lizana, Florin J.** 1895-1967   [NOJ]
*American jazz musician*
* Lizana, Curly

**[The] Lizard King**
See   Morrison, Jim

**Lizzani, Carlo** 1922-   [FDG]
*Italian director*
* Beaver, Lee

**Llavarito**
See   Leal y Casado, Eduardo

**Llenas, Chilote**
See   Llenas, Winston Enriquillo

**Llenas, Winston Enriquillo** 1943- [BE]
*Dominican-born baseball player*
* Llenas, Chilote

**Llerena, Mario** 1913-   [CA]
*Cuban-born American author*
* Niemoller, Ara

**Llero, Auguste**
See   Rolle, Christian

**Llewellyn**
See   Saunders, Robert

**Llewellyn, Clement Manly** 1895- [BE]
*American baseball player*
* Llewellyn, Lew

**Llewellyn, D[avid] W[illiam] Alun** 1903-   [CA]
*British author*
* Taffy

**Llewellyn, Fewlass**
See   Jones, Fewlass

**Llewellyn, Frederick** 1924-   [FC]
*British actor*
* Bartholemew, Freddie

**Llewellyn, Lew**
See   Llewellyn, Clement Manly

**Llewellyn, M. J.**
See   Llewellyn, Michael John

**Llewellyn, Michael John** 1953- [DC]
*Welsh cricketer*
* Llewellyn, M. J.

**Llewellyn, Richard**
See   Llewellyn Lloyd, Richard Dafydd Vyvyan

**Llewellyn Lloyd, Richard Dafydd Vyvyan** 1906?-   [CA, LC, SAT]
*Welsh-born author, playwright, journalist*
* Llewellyn, Richard

**Llewelyn ab Iorwerth**   ?-1240 [WBD]
*Prince of Wales*
* [The] Great

**Llewelyn, T. Harcourt**
See   Hamilton, Charles Harold St. John

**Lloyd, Alice**
See   Wood, Alice

**Lloyd, Alison** 1905-1935   [F2]
*Actress*
* Todd, Thelma

**Lloyd, Arthur** 1840-1904   [BMH]
*Scottish-born entertainer*
* [The] Last of the Lion Comiques

**Lloyd, Barry John** 1953-   [DC]
*Welsh cricketer*
* Lloyd, Lloydy

**Lloyd, Bumble**
See   Lloyd, David

**Lloyd, Charles**
See   Birkin, Charles [Lloyd]

**Lloyd, Clive Hubert** 1944-   [DC]
*Guyanese-born cricketer*
* Big C

**Lloyd, David** 1947-   [DC]
*British cricketer*
* Lloyd, Bumble

**Lloyd, Dennis** 1915-   [CA]
*British barrister and author*
* Lloyd of Hampstead, Baron

**Lloyd, Duke**
See   Lloyd, Harold Clayton, Jr.

**Lloyd, Grace**
See   Hyman, Grace Lloyd

**Lloyd, Harold Clayton, Jr.** 1931-1971   [SC]
*American actor and singer*
* Lloyd, Duke

**Lloyd, Herbert**
See   Fearn, John Russell

**Lloyd, Hugh**
See   Fitzhugh, Percy Keese

**Lloyd, Ian**
See   Buonconciglio, Ian

**Lloyd, Jane**
See   Roberts, John S[torm]

**Lloyd, Jasper**
See   Lloyd, Timothy Andrew

**Lloyd, Jerome [Jerry]**
See   Hurwitz, Jerome

**Lloyd, Joe** 20th c.   [EG]
*British golfer*
* [The] General

**Lloyd, John Henry** 1884-1965 [AS, BAB, MK]
*American baseball player*
* [The] Black Wagner
* [El] Cuchara [The Shovel]

**Lloyd, John Henry** (Continued)
* Lloyd, Pops

**Lloyd, Joseph H.** 20th c.   [WWL]
*Irish author, editor, poet*
* Laoide, Seosamh

**Lloyd, Kathleen**
See   Gackle, Kathleen

**Lloyd, Lloydy**
See   Lloyd, Barry John

**Lloyd, Marie**
See   Wood, Matilda Alice Victoria

**Lloyd, Marie, Jr.**
See   Courtney, Marie

**Lloyd, Mary** 1890-1973 [F2, FC, THR]
*British actress*
* Merrall, Mary
* Merrall, Queenie

**Lloyd of Hampstead, Baron**
See   Lloyd, Dennis

**Lloyd, Pops**
See   Lloyd, John Henry

**Lloyd, Richard**
See   Brotherton, Alice Williams

**Lloyd, Ronald**
See   Friedland, Ronald Lloyd

**Lloyd, Rosie**
See   Wood, Rosie

**Lloyd, Samuel Jones** 1796-1883 [FFF]
*British economist*
* Mercator

**Lloyd, Stephanie**
See   Golding, Morton J[ay]

**Lloyd, Stephen**
See   Bond, Stephen

**Lloyd, Teflon**
See   Lloyd, Timothy Andrew

**Lloyd, Timothy Andrew** 1956- [DC]
*British cricketer*
* Lloyd, Jasper
* Lloyd, Teflon

**Lloyd George, David** 1863-1945 [NN]
*British prime minister*
* [The] Welsh Wizard

**Lloyd-Thomas, Catherine** 1917- [CA]
*British playwright and director*
* Muschamp, Thomas

**Lo**
See   Second element of name for further listings

**Lo**
See   Piccolo, Fillippo

**Loader, William Reginald** 1916- [AW, CA]
*British author*
* Nash, Daniel

**Loan, Mike**
See   Loan, William Joseph

**Loan, William Joseph** 1895-1966 [BE]
*American baseball player*
* Loan, Mike

**Lobaugh, Elma K.** 1907-   [WW]
*Author*
* Lowe, Kenneth

**Lobb, Stephen** 17th c.   [SN]
*Jesuit leader*
* [The] Hypocrite

**Lobert, Hans**
See   Lobert, John Bernard

**Lobert, Honus**
See   Lobert, John Bernard

**Lobert, John Bernard** 1881-1968 [AS, BE, PB]
*American baseball player*
* Lobert, Hans
* Lobert, Honus

**Lobingier, Elizabeth Miller** 1889- [NAA]
*American educator and author*
* Miller, Elizabeth Erwin

**Lobo**
See   Lavoie, Kent

**Lobo, George Edmund** 1894- [WWL]
*British author and editor*
* Sherry, Oliver

**Lobsang Rampa, Tuesday**
See   Hoskin, Cyril Henry

**[La] Loca**
See   Juana [Joanna or Jane]

**Locas, Jacques** 1954-   [SMG]
*Canadian-born hockey player*
* [The] Jet Man

**Loch, Joice NanKivell** 1893-   [CA]
*Australian-born relief worker and author*
* NanKivell, Joice M.

**Lochard, Doc**
See   Lochard, Metz Tullus Paul

**Lochard, Metz Tullus Paul** 20th c. [IBW]
*Haitian-born journalist*
* Lochard, Doc

**Locher, Charles** 1913-1979   [FC]
*American actor*
* Hall, Jon

**Locher, Donald** 1902-   [FC]
*American actor*
* Terry, Don

**Locher, Jacob** 1470-1528   [PA]
*Author*
* Philomessus

**Lochlons, Colin**
See   Jackson, C[aary] Paul

**Lock, Arnold Charles Cooper** 20th c.   [WW]
*Author*
* Cooper, Charles

**Lock, Thomas**
See   Land, George Thomas Lock

**Lockard, Francis Marion [Frank]** 1855- ?   [NAA]
*American author*
* F. M.

**Lockard, Leonard**
See   Thomas, Theodore L. [Ted]

**Lockart, Lucia A[licia] Fox** 1930-
[CA]
*Peruvian-born author and educator*
* Ugaro De Fox, Lucia

**Locke, Arthur D'Arcy** 1917-
[BWG, EG, GF]
*South African golfer*
* Locke, Bobby

**Locke, Bobby**
*See* Locke, Arthur D'Arcy

**Locke, Bobby**
*See* Locke, Lawrence Donald

**Locke, Charles F.** 20th c. [WGT]
*Author*
* McLociard, George

**Locke, Clinton W.** [house pseudonym] [Stratemeyer Syndicate]
*See* Stratemeyer, Edward L.

**Locke, David Ross** 1833-1888
[DEL, DNNF, FFF]
*American author*
* Nasby, [Rev.] Petroleum Vesuvius

**Locke, George [Walter]** 1936-
[ESF, SFP]
*British author*
* Walters, Gordon

**Locke, Gipper**
*See* Locke, Roland A.

**Locke, John** ?-1889 [FFF]
*Irish poet and journalist*
* Southern Gael

**Locke, Lawrence Donald** 1934-
[BE]
*American baseball player*
* Locke, Bobby

**Locke, Lucie**
*See* Price, Lucie Locke

**Locke, Martin**
*See* Duncan, W[illiam] Murdoch

**Locke, Peter**
*See* McCutchan, J[ohn] Wilson

**Locke, R. E.**
*See* Raffelock, David

**Locke, Robert Donald** 20th c.
[WGT]
*Author*
* Arcot, Roger

**Locke, Roland A.** 1903?-1952 [AS]
*American track and field athlete*
* Locke, Gipper

**Locke, Una**
*See* Bailey, Mrs. V. L.

**Locke, W. J.**
*See* Locke, William John

**Locke, William John** 1863-1930
[LC]
*British author*
* Locke, W. J.

**Locke-Elliott, Sumner**
*See* Elliott, Sumner Locke

**Locker, Arthur**
*See* Forbes, J. H.

**Locker, Frederick** 1821-1895
[WBD]
*British poet*
* Locker-Lampson, Frederick

**Locker-Lampson, Frederick**
*See* Locker, Frederick

**Lockett, Buck**
*See* Lockett, Lester

**Lockett, Lester** 1912- [MK]
*American baseball player*
* Lockett, Buck

**Lockhart, Carl Ford** 1943-
[FB, SMG]
*American football player*
* Lockhart, Spider

**Lockhart, Frank** ?-1928
*Auto racer*
* [The] Boy Wonder

**Lockhart, Holes**
*See* Lockhart, Howard

**Lockhart, Howard** 20th c. [CEI]
*Hockey player*
* Lockhart, Holes

**Lockhart, John Gibson** 1794-1854
[DEL, FFF, RH]
*Scottish author and critic*
* [The] Aristarch of British Criticism
* Morris, Peter
* Peter
* Wastle, William

**Lockhart, John Hugh** 19th c.
[FFF, PA]
*Grandson of Scottish author, Sir Walter Scott*
* Littlejohn, Hugh

**Lockhart, Spider**
*See* Lockhart, Carl Ford

**Lockhart, T. C.**
*See* Stammel, Heinz-Josef

**Locklear, Chief**
*See* Locklear, Gene

**Locklear, Gene** 1949- [SMG]
*American baseball player*
* Locklear, Chief

**Lockman, Carroll Walter** 1926-
[BE, PB]
*American baseball player*
* Lockman, Whitey

**Lockman, Whitey**
*See* Lockman, Carroll Walter

**Lockridge, Frances Louise [Davis]**
20th c. [CC, WW]
*Author*
* Richards, Francis [joint pseudonym with Richard (Orson) Lockridge]

**Lockridge, Hildegarde [Dolson]**
1908-1981 [CA]
*American author*
* Dolson, Hildegarde

**Lockridge, Norman**
*See* Roth, Samuel

**Lockridge, Richard [Orson]** 1898-
[CC, WW]
*Author*
* Richards, Francis [joint pseudonym with Frances Louise (Davis) Lockridge]

**Lockroy, Joseph Philippe**
*See* Simon, Joseph Philippe

**[The] Locksmith King**
*See* Louis XVI

**Lockwood, Claude Edward** 1946-
[BE, SMG, WWB]
*American baseball player*
* Lockwood, Skip

**Lockwood, Gary**
*See* Yusolfsky, John Gary

**Lockwood, Margaret**
*See* Day, Margaret

**Lockwood, Mary**
*See* Spelman, Mary

**Lockwood, Skip**
*See* Lockwood, Claude Edward

**Lockyer, Roger Walter** 1927-
[CA, WD]
*British author and historian*
* Francis, Philip

**Loco, Joe**
*See* Esteves, Jose, Jr.

**Lode, Rex**
*See* Goldstein, William Isaac

**Loden, James [Jimmie]** 1929-
[CME, CWG]
*American country-western performer*
* James, Sonny
* [The] Southern Gentleman

**Loder, John**
*See* Lowe, John

**Loder, Vernon**
*See* Vahey, John George Haslette

**Lodge, Mrs. Benjamin** [FFF]
*Entertainer*
* Maddigan, Gertie

**Lodge, Thomas** 1555-1625
[DEP, DNNS, RH]
*British author, playwright, poet*
* [The] Young Juvenal

**Lodigiani, Dario Joseph** 1916-
[BE]
*American baseball player*
* Lodigiani, Lodi

**Lodigiani, Lodi**
*See* Lodigiani, Dario Joseph

**Loeb, Albert Lorch** 1890- [EJS]
*American football player*
* [Der] Yiddisher Vild-Kat

**Loeb, Richard A.** 1907-1936 [BLB]
*American murderer and kidnapper*
* Johnson, George
* Mason, Louis

**Loehr, Dolores** 1926-1971
[BEW, FC]
*American actress*
* Lynn, Diana

**Loening, Sarah Larkin** 1896- [CA]
*American author and poet*
* Larkin, Sarah

**Loennquist, Carl Adolph** 20th c.
[ALY]
*Swedish-born clergyman and author*
* Teofilus

**Loeper, John J[oseph]** 1929-
[CA, SAT]
*American educator and author*
* Lowe, Jay, Jr.

**Loewe Kalbe**
*See* Loewe, Wilhelm

**Loewe, Wilhelm** 1814-1886 [WBD]
*German politician*
* Loewe Kalbe

**Loewenbrugger, Nikolaus**
1417-1487 [WBD]
*Swiss hermit*
* Bruder Klaus
* Nicholas of Flue

**Loewenstein, Laszlo** 1904-1964
[BDF, FC]
*Hungarian-born actor*
* Lorre, Peter

**Loewenthal, Leonard Joseph Alfonso**
1903- [CA]
*British physician and author*
* Lowe, Alfonso

**Loff, Jeanette**
*See* Lov, Janette

**Lofft, Capel** 1751-1824 [SN]
*British author*
* [The] Maecenas of Shoemakers

**Lofland, John** [PA]
*Author*
* [The] Milford Bard

**Loftin, J. C.** [FFF, PA]
*Author*
* Ace Clubs

**Loftin, Louis Santop** 1890-1945
[MK]
*American baseball player*
* Loftin, Top
* Santop, Louis

**Loftin, Top**
*See* Loftin, Louis Santop

**Lofton, Clarence** 1896-1956?
[BWW, EJ, WWJ]
*American jazz musician*
* Clemens, Albert?
* Lofton, Cripple Clarence

**Lofton, Cripple Clarence**
*See* Lofton, Clarence

**Lofton, Lawrence** 1930- [DAM]
*American musician*
* Lofton, Tricky

**Lofton, Tricky**
*See* Lofton, Lawrence

**Lofts, Norah [Robinson]** 1904-
[CA, CC, WGT]
*British author*
* Astley, Juliet
* Curtis, Peter

**Loftus, Cissie**
*See* Loftus, Marie Cecilia

**Loftus, Marie** 1857-1940 [THR]
*Scottish-born comedienne*
* [The] Hibernian Hebe

**Loftus, Marie Cecilia** 1876-1943
[BEW]
*Scottish-born actress*
* Loftus, Cissie

**Loftus, Mrs. W. F.** [FFF]
*Entertainer*
* Adair, Marie

**Lofty**
*See* Isaacs, Marcel Godfrey

**Log Cabin Harrison**
*See* Harrison, William Henry

**[The] Log Cabin President**
*See* Harrison, William Henry

**Logan**
See Ward, Townsend

**Logan, Agnes**
See Adams, Agnes

**Logan, Celia** [PA]
*Author*
* C. L.

**Logan, Don**
See Crawford, William [Elbert]

**Logan, Ella**
See Armour-Allan, Ella

**Logan, Ford**
See Newton, Dwight Bennett

**Logan, Harvey** ?-1903 [BLB]
*American criminal*
* Curry, Kid

**Logan, Jake** [house pseudonym,
Playboy Press]
See Krepps, Robert W[ilson]

**Logan, Jake** [house pseudonym,
Playboy Press]
See Rifkin, Shepard

**Logan, James [or John]**
See Tah-gah-jute

**Logan, John Alexander** 1826-1886
[DNNS, SN]
*American army officer and
statesman*
* Jack of Spades

**Logan, John, Jr. [Johnny]** 1927-
[PB]
*American baseball player*
* Logan, Yachta

**Logan, Lefty**
See Logan, Robert Dean

**Logan, Lillian Mee** 1909- [IAW]
*American-born educator and author*
* Nagol [joint pseudonym with
Virgil Glen Logan]

**Logan, M. C.** [PA]
*Author*
* Vincent, Ellerton

**Logan, Mark**
See Nicole, Christopher Robin

**Logan, Olive** 1841- ? [FFF, PA]
*American writer*
* Belle, Clara
* Chroniquense

**Logan, Robert Dean** 1910- [BE]
*American baseball player*
* Logan, Lefty

**Logan, Thomas A.** [PA]
*Author*
* Gloan

**Logan, Virgil Glen** 1904- [IAW]
*American-born educator and author*
* Nagol [joint pseudonym with
Lillian Mee Logan]

**Logan, William**
See Harris, Larry M[ark]

**Logan, Yachta**
See Logan, John, Jr. [Johnny]

**Logau, Friedrich von** 1604-1655
[WBD]
*German poet and author*
* Golaw, Salomon von

**Loghem, Martinus Gesinus Lambert
van** 1849-1934 [WBD]
*Dutch poet and author*
* Fiore della Neve

**Logroller**
See Le Gallienne, Richard

**Logroscino [or Lo Groscino], Nicola**
1700?-1763? [WBD]
*Italian composer*
* [Il] Dio dell'Opera Buffa

**Logue, Christopher** 1926-
[CA, WD]
*British author, poet, playwright*
* Vicarion, [Count] Palmiro

**Lohier, Michel** 1891-1973 [CW]
*West Indian author*
* Oubo, Irac

**Lohman, George F.** 1864-1928
[BE]
*American baseball player*
* Lohman, Pete

**Lohman, Pete**
See Lohman, George F.

**Lohrke, Jack Wayne** 1924- [BE]
*American baseball player*
* Lohrke, Lucky

**Lohrke, Lucky**
See Lohrke, Jack Wayne

**Lohrman, Paul** [house pseudonym,
Ziff-Davis]
See Fairman, Paul W.

**Lohrman, Paul** [house pseudonym,
Ziff-Davis]
See Shaver, Richard S[harpe]

**Loinger, Silvia Mary** 1917- [IAW]
*Austrian author*
* Simalo

**Loison, Louis Henri** 1770?-1816
[SN]
*French army officer*
* [The] Bloody One-Handed
* Maneta

**Lokayat, Suri**
See Chaudhari, Raghuveer

**Loknayak [The Peoples Hero]**
See Narayan, Jayaprakash

**Lolewski-Cassini, Oleg** 1913- [IPA]
*French fashion designer*
* Cassini, Oleg

**Lolita**
See Ditta, Lolita

**Lollard, Walter** ?-1322 [SN]
*Leader of religious cult*
* [The] Morning Star of the
Reformation in Germany

**Lolli, Countess** 1850-1922 [FFF]
*Italian opera singer*
* Scalchi, Sofia

**[The] Lollipop Governor**
See Milliken, William Grawn

**Lollobrigida, Guido** 20th c. [WF]
*Italian actor*
* Burton, Lee

**L'Olonnois, Francois**
See Nau, Jacques Jean David

**Lolordo, Pasquale** ?-1929 [PHM]
*American underworld figure*
* Lolordo, Patsy

**Lolordo, Patsy**
See Lolordo, Pasquale

**Lom, Herbert**
See Kuchacevich Ze
Schluderpacheru, Herbert Charles
Angelo

**Lom, Josephine**
See Lomnicka, [Azdis] Josephine

**Lomas, Doris** 1900-1975 [SC]
*British actress*
* Pender, Doris

**Lomas, Steve**
See Brennan, Joseph L[omas]

**Lomax, Bliss**
See Drago, Harry Sinclair

**Lomax, E. Victoria** [PA]
*Author*
* Little, Byrd

**Lomax, W. J.** 20th c. [MBF]
*British author*
* Fulke, Commissioner
* Maxwell, Herbert

**Lombard, Carole**
See Peters, Jane Alice

**Lombard, Nap** [joint pseudonym
with Neil Stewart]
See Johnson, Pamela Hansford

**Lombard, Nap** [joint pseudonym
with Pamela Hansford Johnson]
See Stewart, Neil

**Lombard, Peter**
See Benham, William

**Lombard, Peter [or Pietro]**
1100-1164 [DNNF, DNNS, HN]
*Italian theologian*
* Magister Sententiarum
* [The] Master of Sentences

**Lombardi, Alfonso**
See Cittadella, Alfonso

**Lombardi, Beezer**
See Lombardi, Ernesto Natali

**Lombardi, Bocci**
See Lombardi, Ernesto Natali

**Lombardi, Claudio** 1922- [EJ]
*American jazz musician*
* Lombardi, Clyde

**Lombardi, Clyde**
See Lombardi, Claudio

**Lombardi, Cynthia**
See Lombardi, Georgina M.
[Richmond]

**Lombardi, Ernesto Natali** 1908-
[BE, BN, PB]
*American baseball player*
* Lombardi, Beezer
* Lombardi, Bocci
* Lombardi, Ernie
* Lombardi, Lom
* Lombardi, Schnozz

**Lombardi, Ernie**
See Lombardi, Ernesto Natali

**Lombardi, Georgina M. [Richmond]**
20th c. [NAA, WW]
*American author*
* Lombardi, Cynthia

**Lombardi, Lella** 1943- [SA]
*Italian auto racer*
* [The] Tigress of Turin

**Lombardi, Lom**
See Lombardi, Ernesto Natali

**Lombardi, Schnozz**
See Lombardi, Ernesto Natali

**Lombardo, Antonio** ?-1928 [PHM]
*Italian-born American underworld
figure*
* Lombardo, Tony

**Lombardo, Gaetano Alberto**
1902-1977 [BEW]
*Canadian bandleader*
* Lombardo, Guy

**Lombardo, Guy**
See Lombardo, Gaetano Alberto

**Lombardo, Lombo**
See Lombardo, Thomas A.

**Lombardo, Thomas A.** 1922-1950
[AS, FB]
*American football player*
* Lombardo, Lombo

**Lombardo, Tony**
See Lombardo, Antonio

**Lombino, Salvatore A.** 1926-
[CA, EMD, WGT]
*American author*
* Cannon, Curt
* Collins, Hunt
* Hunter, Evan
* Marsten, Richard
* McBain, Ed
* Rice, Craig [joint pseudonym
with Georgiana Ann Randolph]

**Lome, Mike**
See Pinkwater, Daniel Manus

**Lomenie de Brienne, Etienne Charles**
1727-1794 [HN]
*French prelate and statesman*
* [Le] Cardinal de l'Ignominie

**Lomnicka, [Azdis] Josephine** 20th
c. [WD]
*Polish-born artist and writer*
* Lom, Josephine

**Lomov, A.**
See Lomov-Oppokov, Georgii
Ippolitovich

**Lomov-Oppokov, Georgii Ippolitovich**
1888-1938 [B10]
*Russian Communist leader*
* Lomov, A.

**Lomski, Leo** 1903?-1975 [B10]
*American boxer*
* [The] Aberdeen Assassin

**Lon, Alice** ?-1981
*American singer*
* [The] Champagne Lady

**Lonardo, Big Joe**
See Lonardo, Joseph

**Lonardo, Joseph** 20th c. [MM]
*American underworld figure*
* Lonardo, Big Joe
* Lonardo, Peppino

**Lonardo, Peppino**
See Lonardo, Joseph

**Lonati** 17th c. [HN]
*Italian musician*
* [Il] Gobbo [The Hunchback]

**Lonborg, Arthur** 1899- [BB]
*American basketball coach*
* Lonborg, Dutch

**Lonborg, Dutch**
See Lonborg, Arthur

**Lonborg, Gentleman Jim**
See Lonborg, James Reynold

**Lonborg, James Reynold** 1943-
[SMG]
*American baseball player*
* Lonborg, Gentleman Jim
* Lonborg, Lonnie

**Lonborg, Lonnie**
See Lonborg, James Reynold

**Lonchar, John Anthony** 1952-
[SMG]
*American baseball player*
* Lonchar, Lonch

**Lonchar, Lonch**
See Lonchar, John Anthony

**Lonchit [or Loncit], Vilma?**
See Baulsy, Banky Vilma

**[A] London Antiquary**
See Hotten, John Camden

**London, Art**
See Lund, Arthur

**[The] London Bach**
See Bach, Johann Christian

**London, George**
See Burnstein, George

**[The] London Hermit**
See Parke, F.

**[The] London Idol**
See Powles, Matilda Alice

**London, Jane**
See Geis, Darlene [Stern]

**London, John**
See Kuehne, John

**London, Julie**
See Peck, Julie

**London, Lisa**
See Martin, Gloria Ann

**[The] London Physician**
See Guy, William Augustus

**[A] London Physician**
See Howard, James

**[The] London Star**
See De Melvin, Henri

**London, Stewart**
See Wilson, Roger C.

**London, Tom**
See Clapham, Leonard

**[The] Londoner**
See Barron, Oswald

**London's Lancashire Comedian**
See Stansfield, Thomas

**Londos, Jim** 20th c. [CSH]
*Boxer*
* [The] Golden Greek

**Lone Cat Fuller**
See Fuller, Jesse

**[The] Lone Cowboy**
See Aliff, Hamilton C.

**[The] Lone Eagle**
See Lindbergh, Charles Augustus

**Lone Pine, Hal**
See Breau, Harold

**Lone Star Dietz**
See Dietz, William

**[The] Lone Star Ranger**
See Slaughter, Marion T.

**[The] Lone Star Ranger**
See White, John I[rwin]

**[The] Lone Wolf**
See Woods, Oscar

**[The] Lone Wolf of Uruguayan Letters**
See Onetti, Juan Carlos

**[The] Lone Wolf Politician**
See Mitchell, Clarence M., III

**[The] Lonely Cowboy**
See Fletcher, Tex

**Lonergan, Peg Leg**
See Lonergan, Richard

**Lonergan, Richard** 20th c. [BLB]
*American gangster*
* Lonergan, Peg Leg

**[The] Lonesome Cowboy**
See White, John I[rwin]

**Lonesome Dave**
See Peverett, David

**Lonesome George**
See Gobel, George Leslie

**Lonesome George Weiss**
See Weiss, George Martin

**Lonesome Luke**
See Levielle [or Leuvielle?], Gabriel

**[The] Lonesome Road Racer**
See Wiltshire, George

**[The] Lonesome Singer of the Air**
See Marvin, Johnny

**Lonesome Sundown**
See Green, Cornelius

**Loney, Glenn [Meredith]** 1928-
[CA]
*American educator and author*
* Meredith, Jeff

**[Le] Long**
See Philip V [or Philippe]

**Long, Amelia Reynolds** 1904-
[WGT, WW]
*Author*
* Coxe, Kathleen Buddington [joint pseudonym with Edna McHugh]
* Laing, Patrick
* Reynolds, Adrian
* Reynolds, Peter
* Weir, Mordred

**Long, Andy Iona** 1902- [ASC]
*Hawaiian composer*
* Iona, Andy

**Long, Ann Marie**
See Jensen, Pauline Marie [Long]

**Long, Arnold** 1940- [DC]
*British cricketer*
* Long, Buzby
* Long, Oblong

**Long Bob Ewing**
See Ewing, George Lemuel

**Long Bob Meusel**
See Meusel, Robert William [Bob]

**Long, Buzby**
See Long, Arnold

**Long, Don** 1910?- [WWJ]
*American jazz musician*
* Long, Slats

**Long, Emmett**
See Leonard, Elmore

**Long, Frank Belknap** 1903-
[SFL, WGT]
*American author*
* Long, Lyda Belknap
* Northern, Leslie [house pseudonym]

**Long, Fred T.** 20th c. [IBW]
*American football coach*
* Long, Pop

**Long, Frederick** 1940-1969 [RO2]
*American singer*
* Long, Shorty

**Long, Gabrielle Margaret Vere [Campbell]** 1886-1952
[LAO, TC, WGT]
*British author and playwright*
* Bowen, Marjorie
* Campbell, Margaret
* Costanza, Senora
* Paye, Robert
* Preedy, George
* Shearing, Joseph
* Vere, Margaret
* Winch, John

**Long, Germany**
See Long, Herman C.

**Long, Gerry**
See Larkins, William Frederick

**Long, Glynn Lea** 1895-1945 [NOJ]
*American jazz musician*
* Long, Red

**Long Gone Miles**
See Miles, Luke

**Long Hair**
See Custer, George Armstrong

**[The] Long Haired Samian**
See Pythagoras

**Long Harry**
See Wilkinson, Henry, Jr.

**Long, Helen Beecher [house pseudonym] [Stratemeyer Syndicate]**
See Stratemeyer, Edward L.

**Long Herm Besse**
See Besse, Herman

**Long, Herman C.** 1866-1909
[AS, BE]
*American baseball player*
* Long, Germany

**Long, Huey**
See Long, Sumner

**Long, Huey Pierce** 1893-1935
*American politician*
* [The] Kingfish

**Long, Huey Pierce, Jr.** 1918-
*American politician*
* Billiu, Russell

**[The] Long Island Farmer Poet**
See Cutter, Bloodgood H.

**Long, James Sebastian** 1954-
[IBW]
*American jockey*
* [The] Black Shoemaker

**Long Jim Barnes**
See Barnes, James M.

**Long Jim Holdsworth**
See Holdsworth, James [Jim]

**Long Jim Whitney**
See Whitney, James E.

**Long John**
See Wentworth, John

**Long, John** 1956-
*American basketball player*
* B. B.
* Long, Lightning

**Long John Andre**
See Andre, John Edward

**Long John Baldry**
See Baldry, John

**Long, John Frederick Lawrence** 1917- [CA, IAW]
*British air force officer and author*
* Longo, Juan
* Longsword, John

**Long John Henderson**
See Henderson, John Duncan

**Long John Reilly**
See Reilly, John Good

**Long John Woodruff**
See Woodruff, John

**Long, Juanita** 1901-1968 [EMT]
*American actress and singer*
* Hall, Juanita

**Long, Lep**
See Long, Lester

**Long, Lester** 1888-1958 [BE]
*American baseball player*
* Long, Lep

**Long Levi Meyerle**
See Meyerle, Levi Samuel

**Long, Lightning**
See Long, John

**Long, Lily Augusta** ?-1927 [WW]
*Author*
* Doubleday, Roman

**Long, Lucile**
See Brandt, Lucile [Long Strayer]

**Long, Lyda Belknap**
See Long, Frank Belknap

**Long, Naomi Cornelia**
See Madgett, Naomi Long

**Long Neck Woman**
See Cheatham, K[aryn] Follis

**Long, Nelson** 1876-1929 [BE]
*Canadian-born baseball player*
* Long, Red

**Long, Oblong**
See Long, Arnold

**Long Peter**
See Aartsen, Peter

**Long, Peter**
See Hecht, Ben

**Long, Pop**
See Long, Fred T.

**Long, Red**
See Long, Glynn Lea

**Long, Red**
See Long, Nelson

**Long, Richard A[lexander]** 1927-
[CA]
*American educator and author*
* Alexander, Ric

**Long, Russell** 20th c.
*American politician*
* Long, Sugar Ray

**Long Sam Thompson**
See Thompson, Samuel Tommy

**[The] Long Scribe**
See Dowling, Vincent

**Long, Shorty**
See Long, Frederick

**Long Sir Thomas**
See Robinson, [Sir] Thomas

**Long, Slats**
See Long, Don

**Long, Sugar Ray**
See Long, Russell

**Long, Sumner** 20th c.
*American shipping broker and sailboat racer*
* Long, Huey

**Long Tom**
See Jefferson, Thomas

**Long Tom Hughes**
See Hughes, Thomas J.

**Long Tom Parsons**
See Parsons, Thomas Anthony [Tom]

**Long Tom Winsett**
See Winsett, John Thomas

**[The] Long 'Un**
See Lincoln, Abraham

**Long, Wesley**
See Smith, George O[liver]

**Long, William Stuart**
See Stuart, Vivian [Finlay]

**Long-Holloway, A.**
See Holloway, Arthur Thomas

**Longabaugh, Harry** ?-1909? [B10]
*American outlaw*
* [The] Sundance Kid

**Longalius**
See De Longueil, Christophe

**Longbaugh, Harry**
See Goldman, William W.

**Longbeard**
See FitzOsbert, William

**Longbeard, Frederick**
See Longyear, Barry Brookes

**Longden, Johnny** 1910- [CSH]
*Canadian jockey*
* [The] Pumper

**Longdon, George**
See Rayer, Francis G.

**Longfellow, Henry Wadsworth**
1807-1882 [FFF, PA, SN]
*American poet*
* Coffin, Joshua
* Drift-Wood

**Longfellow, Henry Wadsworth**
(Continued)
* Hammergafferstein, Hans
* [The] Poet of the Commonplace

**[The] Longfellow of the South**
See Hayne, Paul Hamilton

**Longhair, Dr.**
See Byrd, Henry Roeland

**Longhair, Professor**
See Byrd, Henry Roeland

**Longhi, Pietro**
See Falca, Pietro

**Longhurst, Percy William** 1874- ?
[MBF]
*British author*
* Agent 55
* Hockley, Lewis
* Kingston, Brian
* Spence, Hubert

**Longimanus [The Long-Handed]**
See Artaxerxes I

**Longinus**
See Dlugosz, Jean

**Longinus, Dionysius Cassius** 213-
273 [FFF, RH, SN]
*Roman philosopher*
* [The] Living Cyclopaedia
* [The] Walking Library
* [The] Walking Museum

**Longleigh, Peter J., Jr.**
See Korges, James

**Longley, Clint** 1952- [SMG]
*American football player*
* [The] Mad Bomber

**Longley, Red**
See Longley, Wyman

**Longley, Wyman** 20th c. [OBW]
*American baseball player*
* Longley, Red

**Longo, Germano** 20th c. [WF]
*Italian actor*
* Laramy, Grant

**Longo, Juan**
See Long, John Frederick Lawrence

**Longomontanus**
See Severin, Christian

**Longrigg, Jane Chichester** 1929-
[CA]
*British author*
* Chichester, Jane

**Longrigg, Roger [Erskine]** 1929-
[AW, CA, WD]
*Scottish-born author*
* Drummond, Ivor
* Erskine, Rosalind

**Longshanks**
See Edward I

**Longstreet, A. B.** 1790-1870 [PA]
*American author*
* [A] Native Georgian
* Short, Bob

**Longstreet, James** 1821-1904
[FFF]
*American army officer*
* Old Pete

**Longstreet, [Henry] Stephen [Weiner]**
1907- [CA, TC1, WW]
*American author and playwright*
* Burton, Thomas
* Haggard, Paul
* Ormsbee, David
* Weiner, Henri

**Longsword**
See Henry II

**Longsword**
See William

**Longsword**
See William I

**Longsword, John**
See Long, John Frederick Lawrence

**Longway, A. Huge**
See Lang, Andrew

**Longworth, Alice Roosevelt**
1884?-1980
*Daughter of American president, Theodore Roosevelt*
* Princess Alice

**Longworth, Nicholas** 1782-1863
[WBD]
*American horticulturist*
* [The] Father of American Grape Culture

**Longyear, Barry Brookes** 1942-
[CA]
*American author*
* Ango, Fan D.
* Longbeard, Frederick
* Rant, Tol E.
* Ringdahl, Mark
* Vinest, Shaw

**Lonnen, Beatrice Helen** 1886-
[THR]
*British actress*
* Lonnen, Jessie

**Lonnen, Ellen Farren** 1887- [THR]
*British actress*
* Lonnen, Nellie

**Lonnen, Jessie**
See Lonnen, Beatrice Helen

**Lonnen, Nellie**
See Lonnen, Ellen Farren

**Lonnon, Alice**
See Perkins, Alice

**Lonsberry, Roscoe** 1947- [SMG]
*Canadian-born hockey player*
* Lonsberry, Ross

**Lonsberry, Ross**
See Lonsberry, Roscoe

**Lonsdale, Frederick**
See Leonard, Frederick

**Lonsdale, Gordon Arnold**
See Molody, Konon Trofimovich

**Lonsdale, Mrs.** [FFF]
*Entertainer*
* Eyre, Sophie

**Lonzo**
See George, Lloyd

**Lonzo**
See Hooten, David

**Lonzo**
See Sullivan, John Y.

**Looker, Antonina [Hansell]** 1898-
[CA]
*American author and poet*
* Hansell, Antonina
* Jones, Orlando
* Macdonald, Nina Hansell

**Lookout**
See Noble, John [Appelbe]

**Loomis, Alfred Fullerton**
1890-1968 [B10]
*American author*
* Spun Yarn

**Loomis, Amy**
See Brooks, Amy

**Loomis, Noel M[iller]** 1905-1969
[CA]
*American author*
* Allison, Sam
* Miller, Benj.
* Miller, Frank
* Water, Silas

**Loomis, Rae**
See Steger, Shelby

**Loonie, Janice Hays**
See Hays, Janice Nicholson

**[The] Loose Girt Boy**
See Caesar, [Gaius] Julius

**Loose, H.**
See Lourie, Dick

**Loose, Katharine Riegel** 1877- ?
[NAA]
*American author*
* Schock, George

**Lopana**
See De La Llana, Pedro

**Lopat, Ed**
See Lopatnyski, Edmund Walter

**Lopat, Steady Eddie**
See Lopatnyski, Edmund Walter

**Lopatnyski, Edmund Walter** 1918-
[BE, SR]
*American baseball player*
* [The] Junk Man
* Lopat, Ed
* Lopat, Steady Eddie

**Lopes, Tony**
See Lopez, Tony

**Lopez, Al**
See Lopez, Alfonso Raymond

**Lopez, Alfonso Raymond** 1908-
[BAB, BE]
*American baseball player and manager*
* Lopez, Al
* [The] Senor

**Lopez, Antonio** 20th c. [GS]
*Spanish bullfighter*
* [El] Ronquillo [The Raucous One]

**Lopez, Art**
See Lopez, Arturo

**Lopez, Arturo** 1937- [BE]
*Puerto Rican-born baseball player*
* Lopez, Art

**Lopez, Aurelio Alejandro** 1948-
[BE, SMG]
*Mexican-born baseball player*
* [El] Lanzallama
* Rios, Aurelio

**Lopez, Aurelio Alejandro**
(Continued)
* Smoke, Senor

**Lopez, Carlos**
See   Lopez y Valles, Carlos Chaflan

**Lopez, Danny**
American boxer
* Lopez, Little Red

**Lopez, Emerito, Jr.** 1945-   [SMG]
American baseball player
* Lopez, Junior

**Lopez, Encarnacion** 1905-1945
[BEW]
Argentinian-born dancer
* Argentinita

**Lopez, Enrique** 20th c.   [SFL]
Author
* Lopez, Hank

**Lopez, Felix** 20th c.   [GS]
Spanish bullfighter
* [El] Regio [The Gorgeous One]

**Lopez, Hank**
See   Lopez, Enrique

**Lopez, Joseph** 1890-1959
[BEW, EMT, PMJ]
American entertainer
* Cook, Joe

**Lopez, Junior**
See   Lopez, Emerito, Jr.

**Lopez, Little Red**
See   Lopez, Danny

**Lopez, Magda**
See   Lopez de Victoria y Fernandez,
Magdalena

**Lopez, Perfecto Macabata** 1924-
[EJ]
American jazz musician
* Lopez, Perry

**Lopez, Perry**
See   Lopez, Perfecto Macabata

**Lopez, Richard** 20th c.   [RO2]
American musician
* Lopez, Scar

**Lopez, Scar**
See   Lopez, Richard

**Lopez, Tony** 20th c.   [RBE]
American boxer
* Lopes, Tony

**Lopez, Trini**
See   Lopez, Trinidad, III

**Lopez, Trinidad, III** 1937-   [IPA]
American singer
* Lopez, Trini

**Lopez de Victoria y Fernandez,
Magdalena** 1900-   [CW]
Puerto Rican poet
* Lopez, Magda

**Lopez Llergo, Josefina Pellicer**
1940-1964   [SC]
Mexican actress
* Pellicer, Pina

**Lopez Ostoloza, Beatriz** 20th c.
[WFA]
Mexican writer
* Trixie

**Lopez Parejo, Francisco**
1899-1932   [GS]
Spanish bullfighter
* Parejito [Little Smooth One]

**Lopez Pinillos, Jose** 1875-1922
[HDM]
Spanish author and playwright
* Parmeno

**Lopez-Portillo y Rojas, Jose** 1850-
?   [ALY]
Mexican author
* Ben Issa, Isuf

**Lopez y Portal, Gabriel** 1855-1902
[GS]
Spanish bullfighter
* Mateito [Little Matthew]

**Lopez y Valles, Carlos Chaflan**
1887-1942   [SC]
Mexican actor
* Lopez, Carlos

**Lopokoff, Lydia** 1892-   [THR]
Russian-born dancer and actress
* Lopokova, Lydia

**Lopokova, Lydia**
See   Lopokoff, Lydia

**Lopresti, Lucia Longhi** 1895-   [B10]
Italian author and critic
* Banti, Anna

**Lora Trejo, Francisco** 1907-   [GS]
Mexican bullfighter
* Pericas

**Lorac, E. C. R.**
See   Rivett, Edith Caroline

**Lorac, H. R. C.?**
See   Crossen, Ken[dell Foster]

**Loraine, Philip**
See   Estridge, Robin

**Loran, Martin** [joint pseudonym with
Ron Smith]
See   Baxter, John

**Loran, Martin** [joint pseudonym with
John Baxter]
See   Smith, Ron[ald] L[oran]

**Lorand, Colette**
See   Grauaug, Colette

**Lorber, Max J.** 20th c.   [EJS]
American football player
* Lorber, Mugs

**Lorber, Mugs**
See   Lorber, Max J.

**Lord, Barbara**
See   Gratz, Barbara Jeannette

**Lord Barrymore's Tiger**
See   Lee, Alexander

**Lord, Bris**
See   Lord, Bristol Robotham

**Lord, Bristol Robotham** 1883-1964
[BE]
American baseball player
* Lord, Bris

**Lord Byron**
See   Nelson, Byron

**Lord, Carl**
See   Lord, Carleton

**Lord, Carleton** 1900-1947   [BE]
American baseball player
* Lord, Carl

**Lord, Douglas** 1904-   [WD]
British author, poet, translator
* Ireland, Doreen

**Lord, Elaezar** 1788-1871   [PA]
Author
* E. L.

**Lord Fanny**
See   Hervey, John [Baron Hervey
of Ickworth]

**Lord, Garland** [joint pseudonym with
Mindret Lord]
See   Garland, [Mary] Isabel

**Lord, Garland** [joint pseudonym with
(Mary) Isabel Garland]
See   Lord, Mindret

**Lord George**
See   Sanger, George

**Lord God the Pope**
See   Borghese, Camillo

**Lord, Grace V.**   [DNNF]
Author
* Champlin, Virginia

**Lord, Halkett**   [FFF]
Author
* Klett, Harold

**[The] Lord High Executioner**
See   Anastasia, Albert

**Lord, Jack**
See   Ryan, John Joseph

**Lord, Jeffrey** [house pseudonym]
See   Engel, Lyle Kenyon

**Lord, Jeffrey** [house pseudonym]
See   Green, Roland [James]

**Lord, Jeremy**
See   Redman, Ben Ray

**Lord John**
See   Sanger, John

**Lord, Justin**
See   Cook, Justin Lord

**Lord, Lonnie**
See   Haydock, Ron

**Lord Mayor of the Theatric Sky**
See   Hunt, [James Henry] Leigh

**Lord, Mindret**   [WW]
Author
* Lord, Garland [joint pseudonym
with (Mary) Isabel Garland]

**Lord, Nancy**
See   Titus, Eve

**[The] Lord of Crazy Castle**
See   Hall, John

**[The] Lord of his Age**
See   Suleiman II [or Soliman]

**[The] Lord of Leasowes**
See   Shenstone, William

**[The] Lord of the British
Pandemonium**
See   Shakespeare, William

**Lord of the Isles**
See   Donald

**Lord Oxford's Miss**
See   Davenport, Elizabeth

**Lord, Phillips Haynes** 1902-1975
[SC]
American actor, producer, writer
* Parker, Seth

**Lord, Shirley**
See   Anderson, Shirley Lord

**Lord Ted**
See   Dexter, Roy Evatt

**Lord Timothy**
See   Dexter, Timothy

**Lord, Vivian**
See   Wallace, Pat

**Lorde, Audre** 1934-   [CA]
American educator and author
* Domini, Rey

**Lorel, Phil**
See   De Pietro, Albert

**Loren, Sophia**
See   Scicolone, Sofia Villani

**Lorenz, Ellen Jane** 1907-   [ASC]
American composer
* James, Allen

**Lorenz, Sarah E.**
See   Winston, Sarah

**Lorenzen, Adolph Andreas**
1893-1963   [BE]
American baseball player
* Lorenzen, Lefty

**Lorenzen, Lefty**
See   Lorenzen, Adolph Andreas

**Lorenzetti, Ambrogio**
1300?-1348?   [WBD]
Italian painter
* Di Lorenzo, Ambrogio

**Lorenzetti, Pietro** 1280?-1348?
[WBD]
Italian painter
* Laurati, Pietro

**Lorenzini, Carlo** 1826-1890   [WBD]
Italian author
* Collodi, Carlo

**[The] Lorenzo de Medici of Hungary**
See   Matthias Corvinus

**Lorenzo, El Magnifico [Lorenzo the
Magnificent]**
See   Garza Arrambide, Lorenzo

**Lorenzo, Francisco** 1940?-
American business executive
* Lorenzo, Pancho

**Lorenzo, Pancho**
See   Lorenzo, Francisco

**Lorenzon, Livio** 1926-1971   [SC]
Italian actor
* Lawrence, Charlie

**Loreto, Giorgio** 1941-   [OP]
Italian opera singer
* Lormi, Giorgio

**Lorimer, Adam**
See   Watson, William Lorimer

**Lorimer, Mary**
See   Dunning, M. O. B.

**Lorimer, Maxwell George** 1908-
[TR]
British actor and dancer
* Wall, Max

**Lorimer, Scat**
See   Fuentes, Martha Ayers

**Lorin, Kenneth** 1909-  [AM]
*American vocal arranger and composer*
* Darby, Ken

**Loring, Andrew**
See  Lathrop, Lorin Andrews

**Loring, Emilie [Baker]**  ?-1951
[ANT, WW]
*American author*
* Story, Josephine

**Loring, Eugene**
See  Kerpestein, Leroy

**Loring, J. M.**
See  Crozetti, Ruth G. Warner
[Lora]

**Loring, Laurie**
See  Pratt, L. Maria

**Loring Pasha**
See  Loring, William Wing

**Loring, Peter**
See  Shellabarger, Samuel

**Loring, William Wing** 1818-1886
[FFF]
*American army officer*
* Loring Pasha
* Old Blizzard

**Loriot**
See  Buelow, Bernhard-Viktor von

**Loris**
See  Hofmannsthal, Hugo
Hofmann, Edler Von

**Loris, Heinrich** 1488-1563  [WBD]
*Swiss scholar*
* Glareanus, Henricus

**Lorm, Hieronymus**
See  Landesmann, Heinrich

**Lormi, Giorgio**
See  Loreto, Giorgio

**Lorne, Charles**
See  Brand, [Charles] Neville

**Lorne, Constance**
See  MacLaurin, Constance

**Lorne, Marion**
See  MacDougall, Marion Lorne

**Lorne, Tommy**
See  Corcoran, Hugh Gallagher

**Lorner**
See  Stoddart, Jane T.

**Lornquest, Olaf**
See  Rips, Ervine M[ilton]

**Lorrain, Camille**
See  Babou, Hippolyte

**Lorrain [or Lorraine], Claude**
See  Gellee [or Gelee], Claude

**Lorrain, Jean**
See  Duval, Paul

**Lorraine, Alden**
See  Ackerman, Forrest J[ames]

**Lorraine, Anne**
See  Chisholm, Lilian Mary

**Lorraine, Francois de** 1519-1563
[HN, WBD]
*French soldier and politician*
* [Le] Balafre [The Scarred]
* [The] Butcher of Vassy
* Guise, 2nd Duc de

**Lorraine, Francois de** (Continued)
* [The] Preserver of His Country

**Lorraine, Harry**
See  Herd, Henry

**Lorraine, Henry I [or Henri] de**
1550-1589?  [FFF, HN, SN]
*French soldier*
* [Le] Balafre [The Scarred]
* [The] Gashed
* Guise, 3rd Duc de
* [The] King of Paris
* [The] People's King

**Lorraine, Henry II [or Henri] de**
1614-1664  [DEP, FFF, RH]
*French soldier*
* Guise, Duc de
* [The] Hero of Fable

**Lorraine, Irma**
See  Berenyi, Maria

**Lorraine, Lilith**
See  Wright, Mary M.

**Lorraine, Lillian**
See  De Jacques, Ealallean [or
Eulallean?]

**Lorraine, Paul** [house pseudonym,
Curtis Warren]
See  Bird, William Henry Fleming

**Lorraine, Paul** [house pseudonym,
Curtis Warren]
See  Fearn, John Russell

**Lorraine, Paul** [joint pseudonym
with Arthur O. Roberts] [house
pseudonym, Curtis Warren]
See  Glasby, John [Stephen]

**Lorraine, Paul** [joint pseudonym
with John (Stephen) Glasby] [house
pseudonym, Curtis Warren]
See  Roberts, Arthur O.

**Lorraine, Sid**
See  Johnson, Sidney Richard

**Lorre, Peter**
See  Loewenstein, Laszlo

**Lorrequer, Harry**
See  Lever, Charles James

**Lorrimer, Laura**
See  Shelton, Julia Finley

**Lorring, Joan**
See  Ellis, Dellie Madeline [or
Magdalen?]

**Lorrnel, Marlise** ?-1978  [FIR]
*Actress*
* Rey, Anita

**Los, George**
See  Amabile, George

**Losada, Manuel** 1825-1873  [FFF]
*Mexican bandit*
* [The] Tiger of Alica

**Loscalzo, Joseph Robert**
1910-1955  [AS, BX, RBE]
*American boxer*
* Wolgast, Midget

**Losch, Ottilie Ethel** 1902-1975
[BEW, EMT, TR]
*Austrian-born dancer, actress,
choreographer*
* Losch, Tilly

**Losch, Tilly**
See  Losch, Ottilie Ethel

**Loscutoff, James** 1930-  [BB]
*American basketball player*
* Loscutoff, Jungle Jim

**Loscutoff, Jungle Jim**
See  Loscutoff, James

**[The] Losing Pitcher**
See  Mulcahy, Hugh Noyes

**Lot, Arthur**
See  Bunner, Henry Cuyler

**Lot, Parson**
See  Kingsley, Charles

**Lotarev, Igor Vasilyevich**
1887-1942  [CD]
*Russian poet*
* Severyanin, Igor

**Lothair II** 1070?-1137
[DNNS, WBD]
*King of Germany and Holy Roman
emperor*
* [The] Saxon

**Lothar, Ernst**
See  Mueller, Ernst

**Lothar, Louis**
See  Dupin, Paul

**Lothian, Jane** 1863?-1938  [BEW]
*American actress*
* Kennard, Jane

**Lothrop, Amy**
See  Warner, Anna Bartlett

**Lothrop, Harriet Mulford Stone**
1844-1924  [SAT]
*American author*
* Sidney, Margaret

**Loti, Pierre**
See  Viaud, Louis Marie Julien

**Lotich, Peter** 1528-1560  [PA]
*Author*
* Secundus

**Lotinga, Ernest** 1876-1951  [F2]
*British actor, screenwriter, producer*
* Roy, Dan

**Lott, Monroe**
See  Howard, Edwin

**Lotta, Charlotte**
See  Crabtree, Carlotta

**Lotte** [code name used during World
War II]
See  Bonnesen, Edith

**Lottich, Kenneth V[erne]** 1904-
[AW, CA]
*American educator and author*
* Conrad, Kenneth

**Lottman, Eileen** 1927-  [CA]
*American author and screenwriter*
* Willis, Maud

**Lotz, Joseph Peter [Joe]** 1891-1971
[BE]
*American baseball player*
* Lotz, Smokey

**Lotz, Smokey**
See  Lotz, Joseph Peter [Joe]

**Lou**
See  Leatham, Louis Salisbury

**Loubat**
See  Bohan, Francois-Phillippe

**Louden, Baldy**
See  Louden, William

**Louden, William** 1885-1935  [BE]
*American baseball player*
* Louden, Baldy

**Loudermilk, Charlie** 1927-  [ECM]
*American country-western performer*
* Louvin, Charlie

**Loudermilk, Ira** 1924-1965  [ECM]
*American country-western performer*
* Louvin, Ira

**Loudermilk, John D.** 1934-  [PAC]
*American composer*
* Dee, Johnny

**Louie the Lump**
See  Pioggi, Louis

**Louis [or Ludwig]** 1042- ?
[DNNF, DNNS, SN]
*Margrave of Thuringia*
* Ludwig der Springer
* [The] Springer

**Louis** 14th c.  [WBD]
*King of Hungary and Poland*
* [The] Great

**Louis** 1661-1711
[DNNS, HN, RH]
*Son of King Louis XIV of France*
* [Le] Grand Dauphin
* [The] Great Dauphin
* Monseigneur

**Louis** 1729-1765  [HN]
*Son of King Louis XV of France*
* [The] French Germanicus

**Louis de France** 1682-1712
[DNNS]
*Grandson of King Louis XIV of
France*
* Bourgogne, Duc de
* [The] Second Dauphin

**Louis de Male**
See  Louis II

**Louis, Jean**
See  Berthault, Jean Louis

**Louis, Joe**
See  Barrow, Joseph Louis

**Louis, Joe Hill**
See  Hill, Lester

**Louis, [Father] M.**
See  Merton, Thomas [James]

**Louis, Marilyn** 1922?-
[BDF, FC, IPA]
*American actress*
* Fleming, Rhonda

**Louis, Morris**
See  Bernstein, Morris Louis

**Louis Napoleon**
See  Bonaparte, Charles Louis
Napoleon

**Louis of Nassau** 1538-1574
[DNNS, HN, RH]
*Founder of the Dutch Republic*
* [The] Bayard of the Netherlands

**Louis Philippe** 1773-1850
[DEP, HN, SN]
*King of France*
* [The] Citizen King
* Corby, M.
* [The] King of the Barricades
* Latour, M. Chabaud
* Lebrun, M.
* Mueller, Herr
* [The] Napoleon of Peace

**Louis Philippe** (Continued)
* [La] Poire
* [Le] Roi Bourgeois
* [Le] Roi Citoyen
* [Le] Roi des Barricades
* Smith, King
* Smith, William

**Louis Philippe Marie Victor**
1835-1909   [WBD]
*King of Belgium*
* Leopold II

**Louis, Pierre-Felix** 1870-1925
[CD, EWL, LC]
*French poet and author*
* Louys, Pierre

**Louis, Ray Baldwin** 1949-   [CA]
*American author, filmmaker,
playwright*
* Saltboy, Razor

**Louis, Tommy**
*See*   Watts, Lou[is Thomas]

**Louis William I** 1655-1707   [SN]
*German soldier and military
engineer*
* [Der] Tuerken Louis

**Louis X**
*See*   Walcott, Louis Gene

**Louis I** 778- 840
[DNNS, FFF, SN]
*King of France and Holy Roman
emperor*
* [Le] Debonnaire
* [The] Meek
* [Le] Pieux
* [The] Pious

**Louis I** 1326-1382
[DNNS, SN, WBD]
*King of Hungary*
* [The] Great

**Louis II [or Ludwig]** 804?- 876
[DNNS, HN, WBD]
*King of Germany*
* [The] German

**Louis II [or Ludwig]** 822?- 874?
[HN]
*King of Lorraine and Holy Roman
emperor*
* [The] Young

**Louis II** 846-879   [FFF, RH, SN]
*King of France*
* [Le] Begue
* [The] Stammerer

**Louis II** 1228-1294   [WBD]
*Duke of Bavaria*
* [The] Strict

**Louis II** 1330-1384?   [HN]
*Count of Flanders*
* Louis de Male

**Louis II [or Ludwig]** 1845-1886
*King of Bavaria*
* [The] Dream King

**Louis III [or Ludwig]** 880- 923?
[HN, SN]
*Emperor of Germany*
* [The] Blind

**Louis III [or Ludwig]** 893- 911
[DNNS, HN, WBD]
*King of Germany*
* [The] Child
* [The] Infant

**Louis IV** 921- 954
[HN, SN, WBD]
*King of France*
* D'Outremer
* [The] Foreigner
* Transmarine

**Louis IV** 1287?-1347   [DNNS]
*King of Germany and Holy Roman
emperor*
* [The] Bavarian

**Louis IX** 1215?-1270
[DHA, HN, SN]
*King of France*
* St. Louis
* [The] Solomon of France

**Louis IX** 15th c.   [SN]
*Duke of Bavaria*
* [The] Rich

**Louis V** 966- 987   [HN, SN, WBD]
*King of France*
* [Le] Faineant
* [The] Indolent
* [The] Sluggard

**Louis VI** 1081-1137
[DNNS, FFF, SN]
*King of France*
* [The] Fat
* [Le] Gros
* [The] Wide Awake

**Louis VII** 1121?-1180
[DNNS, SN, WBD]
*King of France*
* [The] Foolish
* [Le] Jeune
* [Le] Pieux [The Pious]
* [The] Young

**Louis VIII** 1187-1226
[DNNS, FFF, SN]
*King of France*
* Coeur de Lion [Lion-Hearted]
* [The] Lion

**Louis X** 1289-1316
[RH, SN, WBD]
*King of France*
* [Le] Hutin
* [The] Quarreler

**Louis XI** 1423-1483
[DNNS, FFF, HN]
*King of France*
* Christianissimus Rex
* [The] French Tiberius
* Most Christian King
* [The] Universal Spider

**Louis XII** 1462-1515
[DNNS, FFF, HN]
*King of France*
* [The] Father of Letters
* [The] Father of the People
* [The] Just
* [Le] Pere du Peuple

**Louis XIII** 1601-1643
[DNNS, HN, SN]
*King of France*
* [The] Just

**Louis XIV** 1638-1715
[DNNS, FFF, SN]
*King of France*
* Baboon, Lewis
* [The] Destroyer of Heresy
* Dieu-Donne [God-Given]
* [Le] Grand Monarque
* [The] Great
* [The] New Constantine
* Old Bonafide
* [Le] Roi Soleil

**Louis XIV** (Continued)
* [The] Sun God
* [The] Sun King
* That Wolf of France

**Louis XV** 1710-1774
[DEP, FF, SN]
*King of France*
* [Le] Bien Aime
* [The] Well Beloved

**Louis XVI** 1754-1793
[DEP, HN, SN]
*King of France*
* [The] Baker
* [The] Crowned Sancho
* [Le] Desire
* [The] Locksmith King
* [The] Martyr King
* [The] Restorer of French Liberty
* Veto, Monsieur

**Louis XVIII** 1755-1824
[HN, RH, SN]
*King of France*
* [Le] Desire
* [The] Father of His Country
* [The] Father of the People
* Jehu
* [The] King of England's Viceroy
* [The] King of Slops
* [Le] Roi Panade

**Louisa**
*See*   Wallace, Lewis

**Louisa Henrietta** 1627-1667   [SN]
*Queen of Prussia*
* Armida

**Louise, Anita**
*See*   Fremault, Anita Louise

**Louise, Edouard** 1941-   [EJ7]
*French jazz musician*
* Louiss, Eddy

**Louise Ellen**
*See*   Moulton, Ellen Louise
Chandler

**Louise, Tina**
*See*   Blacker, Tina

**Louiseboulanger**
*See*   Boulanger, Louise

**Louisiana Earl Nelson**
*See*   Nelson, Earl

**[The] Louisiana Lady**
*See*   Nickerson, Camille Lucie

**[The] Louisiana Lark**
*See*   Jones, Ernest Mahlon

**Louisiana Lightning**
*See*   Guidry, Ron[ald Ames]

**Louisiana Red**
*See*   Minter, Iverson

**Louiss, Eddy**
*See*   Louise, Edouard

**[The] Louisville Legend**
*See*   Griffith, Darrell

**[The] Louisville Lip**
*See*   Clay, Cassius Marcellus, Jr.

**Lounds, Stanley Samuel** 1906-
[ART]
*British artist*
* S. L.

**Lounger**
*See*   Curtis, George William

**[The] Lounger**
*See*   Gilder, Joseph B.

**Lounger at the Clubs**
*See*   Yates, Edmund Hodgson

**Lounger in the Lobby**
*See*   Merrill, Royal W.

**Lourant, Arthur** 20th c.   [IBW]
*American actor*
* Lourant, Chico

**Lourant, Chico**
*See*   Lourant, Arthur

**Lourens-Koop, Adriana Luberta
Klazina** 1920-   [IAW]
*Dutch author*
* Toussaint, Jackie

**Lourie, Dick** 1937-   [CA]
*American poet and educator*
* Loose, H.
* Wonder, Alvin

**Lourie, Helen**
*See*   Storr, Catherine [Cole]

**[The] Louse**
*See*   Cohen, Mickey

**Louvier, Pierre**
*See*   Lucas, Gerald

**Louvigny, Andre**
*See*   Ruellan, Andre

**Louvin, Charlie**
*See*   Loudermilk, Charlie

**Louvin, Ira**
*See*   Loudermilk, Ira

**Louvish, Misha** 1909-   [CA]
*Rumanian-born editor and
translator*
* Bar-Natan, Moshe

**Louwen, Jan** 1924-   [IAW]
*Dutch author*
* Viking, Ted

**Louys, Pierre**
*See*   Louis, Pierre-Felix

**Lov, Janette** 1906-1942
*American actress*
* Loff, Jeanette

**Love, Bessie**
*See*   Horton, Juanita

**Love, Billy** 20th c.
[BWW, NBB, RO1]
*American musician*
* Love, Red

**Love, Bob** 1942-   [BB]
*American basketball player*
* Love, Butterbean

**Love, Butterbean**
*See*   Love, Bob

**Love, Christopher** 1618-1651   [SN]
*British theologian*
* Venn's Principal Fireman at
Windsor

**Love, D.**
*See*   Lerchbaum, Dora

**Love, Elmer Haughton** 1893-1942
[BE]
*American baseball player*
* Love, Slim

**[The] Love Goddess**
*See*   Cansino, Margarita Carmen

**Love, Janet**
See Ferrier, Janet Mackay

**Love, Larry**
See Khaury, Herbert

**Love, Mabel**
See Watson, Mabel

**Love, Red**
See Love, Billy

**Love, Slim**
See Love, Elmer Haughton

**LoVecchio, Frank Paul** 1913-
[FC, IPA, PMJ]
*American singer*
* Laine, Frankie

**Lovechild, Mrs.**
See Fenn, Eleanor

**Lovecraft, H. P.**
See Lovecraft, Howard Phillips

**Lovecraft, Howard Phillips**
1890-1937 [SF, WGT]
*American author*
* Appleton, Laurence
* Bickerstaffe, Isaac, Jr.
* Dunne, John T.
* Houdini?
* Jones, John J.
* Littlewit, Humphrey
* Lovecraft, H. P.
* Maynwaring, Archibald
* Paget-Lowe, H[enry]
* Phillips, Ward
* Raleigh, Richard
* Rowley, Ames Dor[r]ance
* Senectissimus, Theobaldus, Esq.
* Softly, Edward
* Swift, Augustus T.
* Theobald
* Theobald, Lewis, Jr.
* Theobaldus
* Willie, Albert Frederic
* Zoilus

**Lovecraft, Linda**
See Parry, Michel Patrick

**Loveday, John** [FFF]
*Writer*
* Academicus
* Scrutator

**Lovehill, C. B.**
See Nutt, Charles

**Lovejoy, Cornelia** [PA]
*Author*
* Everett, Paul

**Lovejoy, Elijah Parish** 1802-1837
[WBD]
*American abolitionist*
* [The] Martyr Abolitionist

**Lovelace, Linda**
See Traynor, Linda

**[The] Lovelace of His Time**
See Du Plessis, Armand Jean

**Loveland, Joy**
See Wasmansdoff, Joyce

**Lovell, Arthur**
See Lovell-Williams, David Arthur

**Lovell, Ingraham**
See Bacon, Josephine Dodge
[Daskam]

**Lovell, Marc**
See McShane, Mark

**Lovell, Mark**
See Tollemache, David

**Lovell, Mark** 1934- [CA]
*British author*
* Rowlands, Peter

**Lovell, Mrs.** 19th c. [PA]
*Author*
* Halm

**Lovell, Raymond**
See Lovell-Robinson, Raymond

**Lovell-Robinson, Raymond**
1900-1953 [THR]
*Canadian-born actor*
* Lovell, Raymond

**Lovell-Williams, David Arthur** 1864-
? [WWL]
*British author*
* Lovell, Arthur

**[The] Lovely Bessie**
See Raleigh, Elizabeth

**[The] Lovely Georgius**
See Washington, George

**Lovely, Louise**
See Welch, Louise

**Lovely, Maureen Patey** 1906-
[ART]
*British painter, engraver, designer*
* Proudman, M. Eyre

**[A] Lover of Literature**
See Greene, Thomas

**Lover of the Fine Arts**
See Brooks, Maria Gowen

**Loveridge, Marguerite**
See Marsh, Margaret

**Lovesey, Peter** 1936- [CA]
*British author*
* Lear, Peter

**Lovestone, Jay**
See Liebstein, Jacov

**Lovett, Blue**
See Lovett, Winifred

**Lovett, Eddie** 1916- [IBW]
*American farmer*
* [The] Piney Woods Thoreau

**Lovett, Mem**
See Lovett, Merritt Marwood

**Lovett, Merritt Marwood** 1912-
[BE]
*American baseball player*
* Lovett, Mem

**Lovett, W. L.** ?-1923 [BLB]
*American gangster*
* Lovett, Wild Bill

**Lovett, Wild Bill**
See Lovett, W. L.

**Lovett, Winifred** 1943- [RO2]
*American singer*
* Lovett, Blue

**Lovey Joe Powell**
See Powell, Joe

**Lovin' Putty Annixter**
See Annixter, Julius

**Lovin, Roger Robert** 1941-
[CA, IAW]
*American writer*
* Brighton, Wesley, Jr.
* Driver, C. C.

**Lovin, Roger Robert** (Continued)
* Zweit, Adam

**Lovingood, Alvin** 1892- [NAA]
*American writer*
* Kole, A. K.

**Lovingood, Sut**
See Harris, George W.

**Lovley, Jim**
See Lovley, Leonard

**Lovley, Leonard** 1900- [BB]
*American basketball player*
* Lovley, Jim

**Low, Dorothy Mackie**
See Low, Lois Dorothea

**Low, Gardner**
See Rodda, Charles

**Low, Ivy**
See Litvinov, Ivy

**Low, Lois Dorothea** 1916-
[AW, CA, WD]
*Scottish-born author*
* Low, Dorothy Mackie
* Paxton, Lois

**Low, Rachael**
See Whear, [Dr.] Rachael

**Lowdermilk, Grover Cleveland**
1885-1968 [BE]
*American baseball player*
* Lowdermilk, Slim

**Lowdermilk, Slim**
See Lowdermilk, Grover Cleveland

**Lowe, Alfonso**
See Loewenthal, Leonard Joseph
Alfonso

**Lowe, Anne** 1899-1966 [IBW]
*American fashion designer*
* [The] Dean of Black American
Designers

**Lowe, Bennett** [PA]
*Author*
* Justitia

**Lowe, Charles K.**
See Swicegood, Thomas L. P.

**Lowe, Claud D.** 20th c. [MBF]
*British scriptwriter*
* Clifford, Martin [house
pseudonym]
* Griffiths, Maurice
* Hardy, Phillip

**Lowe, Corke**
See Pepper, Choral

**Lowe, Florence** 1902-1975 [SC]
*American stunt performer*
* Barnes, Florence
* Barnes, Pancho

**Lowe, Helen Porter** 1876- ?
[WWL]
*British author*
* Lowe-Porter, H. T.

**Lowe, Jay, Jr.**
See Loeper, John J[oseph]

**Lowe, John** 1898- [F2, FC]
*British actor*
* Loder, John

**Lowe, Kenneth**
See Lobaugh, Elma K.

**Lowe, Kevin** 1959- [SMG]
*Canadian-born hockey player*
* Lowe, Viscious

**Lowe, Link**
See Lowe, Robert Lincoln

**Lowe, Norman E.** 1928- [CEI]
*Canadian-born hockey player*
* Lowe, Odie

**Lowe, Odie**
See Lowe, Norman E.

**Lowe, Robert Lincoln** 1868-1951
[BE]
*American baseball player*
* Lowe, Link

**Lowe, Viscious**
See Lowe, Kevin

**Lowe, William Herman** 1897-
[NAA]
*American writer*
* Suds

**Lowe-Porter, H. T.**
See Lowe, Helen Porter

**Lowell, Alan**
See Thomas, William B. [Bill]

**Lowell, Amy** 1874-1925 [CAA]
*American poet*
* [A] Dreamer
* [A] Poker of Fun

**Lowell, Helen**
See Robb, Helen

**Lowell, J. R.** [joint pseudonym with
Robert Lowell]
See Lowell, Jan

**Lowell, J. R.** [joint pseudonym with
Jan Lowell]
See Lowell, Robert

**Lowell, James Russell** 1819-1891
[DEL, DNNF, PA]
*American author, poet, diplomat*
* Biglow, Hosea
* Wilbur, Homer
* [A] Wonderful Quiz

**Lowell, Jan** 20th c. [SFL]
*Author*
* Lowell, J. R. [joint pseudonym
with Robert Lowell]

**Lowell, Joan** 1900-1967 [SC]
*Actress and author*
* Trask, Helen

**Lowell, John**
See Russell, John L.

**Lowell, John** 1769-1840 [FFF, PA]
*American attorney and author*
* [The] Boston Rebel
* [A] Bostonian
* [A] Citizen of Massachusetts
* [A] Citizen of New England
* [The] Columella of New England
* [A] Friend to Peace
* [A] Layman
* [A] Massachusetts Lawyer
* [A] New England Farmer
* No bel-esprit
* [An] Old Farmer
* [A] Roxbury Farmer
* [A] Yankee Farmer

**Lowell, Robert** 20th c. [SFL]
*Author*
* Lowell, J. R. [joint pseudonym
with Jan Lowell]

**Lowell, Tex**
See Turner, George E[ugene]

**Lowenkopf, Shelly A[lan]** 1931-
[CA]
*American editor and author*
* Chambers, Howard V.

**Lowenstein, Kenneth** 1919-   [ITA]
*American television executive*
* Lowenstein, Larry

**Lowenstein, Larry**
See Lowenstein, Kenneth

**Lowenthal, Marjorie Fiske** 20th c.
[CA]
*American author*
* Fiske, Marjorie

**Lower, Richard** 1631-1691   [PA]
*Author*
* Cladpole, Tim

**Lowery, Nick** 1956-
*German-born football player*
* Nick the Kick

**Lowery, Robert**
See Hanks, Robert Lowery

**Lowing, Anne**
See Geach, Christine

**Lown, Omar Joseph** 1924-
[BE, BTB, SMG]
*American baseball player*
* Lown, Turk

**Lown, Turk**
See Lown, Omar Joseph

**Lowndes, Doc**
See Lowndes, Robert Augustine
Ward

**Lowndes, R. W.**
See Lowndes, Robert Augustine
Ward

**Lowndes, Robert Augustine Ward**
1916-   [ESF, SF, WGT]
*American author and editor*
* Cooke, Arthur [joint pseudonym
with E. Balter, C. Kornbluth, J.
Michel, D. Wollheim]
* Gottesman, S. D. [joint
pseudonym with Cyril M.
Kornbluth and Frederik Pohl]
* Grey, Carol
* Kent, Mallory
* Lavond, Paul Dennis [joint
pseudonym with J. H. Dockweiler,
C. Kornbluth, F. Pohl]
* Lowndes, Doc
* Lowndes, R. W.
* MacDougal, John [joint
pseudonym with James
(Benjamin) Blish]
* Morley, Wilfred Owen
* Morrison, Richard
* Morrison, Robert
* Sherman, Michael
* Sherman, Peter Michael
* Woods, Lawrence [joint
pseudonym with Donald A(llen)
Wollheim]
* Wright, Robert [joint pseudonym
with Forrest J. Ackerman]

**Lowndes, Susan**
See Lowndes Marques, Susan

**Lowndes Marques, Susan** 20th c.
[AW]
*British-born author*
* Lowndes, Susan

**Lowo, Hans**
See Linden, Erik Hugo Emanuel

**Lowrey, Harry Lee** 1918-
[BE, PB, SMG]
*American baseball player and coach*
* Lowrey, Peanuts

**Lowrey, Peanuts**
See Lowrey, Harry Lee

**Lowry, Henry Dawson** 1869- ?
[WWL]
*Author*
* [The] Impertinent

**Lowry, Joan [Catlow]** 1911-
[CA, WD]
*British author*
* Catlow, Joanna
* Lea, Joan

**Lowry, Mose**
See Lowry, Sam[uel Joseph]

**Lowry, Nan**
See MacLeod, Ruth

**Lowry, Robert [James Collas]**
1919-   [CA]
*American author*
* Caldwell, James

**Lowry, Sam[uel Joseph]** 1920-   [BE]
*American baseball player*
* Lowry, Mose

**Lowther, [Sir] James** 1736-1802
[SN]
*British politician*
* Farthing Jamie

**Loxley, Raymond**
See Murray, C. Geoffrey

**Loxley, Violet**
See Humphreys, Violet

**Loxmith, John**
See Brunner, John [Kilian
Houston]

**Loy, Barbara**
See Gentilini, Maria Teresa

**Loy, Mino** 20th c.   [WF]
*Italian director*
* Donan, J. Lee

**Loy, Myrna**
See Williams, Myrna

**Loyacano, Arnold** 1889-1962
[NOJ]
*American jazz musician*
* Loyacano, Deacon

**Loyacano, Bud**
See Loyacano, John

**Loyacano, Deacon**
See Loyacano, Arnold

**Loyacano, Hook**
See Loyacano, Joe

**Loyacano, Joe** 1893-1967   [NOJ]
*American jazz musician*
* Loyacano, Hook

**Loyacano, John** 1879-1960   [NOJ]
*American jazz musician*
* Loyacano, Bud

**[La] Loyale Epee [The Loyal Sword]**
See MacMahon, Marie Edme
Patrice Maurice de

**Loyd, E. P.**   [PA]
*Author*
* [A] Clergyman's Daughter

**Loyd, Ed**
See Kirkeby, Wallace Theodore

**Loyd-Lindsay, Robert James**
See Lindsay, Robert James

**Loys, Captain**
See Labe, Louise

**Loyson, Charles Jean Marie**
1827-1912   [DNNS, WBD]
*French clergyman*
* Hyacinthe, Pere

**Lozovskii, Aleksandr**
See Dridzo, Solomon Abramovich

**Lozzi, Edmondo** 20th c.   [WF]
*Italian film editor*
* Zimmerwal, Edmond

**Lu ch'iao**
See Wu, Nelson I[kon]

**Lu Hsun**
See Chou Shu-jen

**Lu, K'uan-yu**
See Luk, Charles

**Lu Liang Huan** 1936-   [EG]
*Golfer*
* Lu, Mr.

**Lu, Mr.**
See Lu Liang Huan

**Luaces, Joaquin Lorenzo**
1826-1867   [CW]
*Cuban poet, playwright, author*
* Fornaris y Joaquin, lorenzo
Luaces

**Luahne, Iolani** 1915?-1978   [FIR]
*Hawaiian actress and dancer*
* Auntie Io

**Luandrew, Albert** 1907-   [BWW]
*American singer*
* Delta Joe
* Doctor Clayton's Buddy
* Sunnyland Slim

**Luard, Nicholas Lambert** 1937-
[CA, WWS]
*British author*
* [The] King of Satire
* McVean, James

**Luba**
See Marks, Rudenko

**Lubbers, Robert** 1922-   [WECO]
*American cartoonist*
* Lewis, Bob

**Luber, Jet**
See Meulenbelt-Luber, Henrietta
C. A.

**Lubin, Howard** 20th c.   [RO2]
*British musician*
* Lubin, Lem

**Lubin, Lem**
See Lubin, Howard

**Lubin, Maurice Alcibiade** 1917-
[CW]
*Haitian author and critic*
* Malu

**Luboshits, Lea** 1887-   [BBD]
*Russian musician*
* Luboshutz, Lea

**Luboshutz, Lea**
See Luboshits, Lea

**Lubotsky, Charlotte Rae** 1926-
[BEW, TR]
*American actress and singer*
* Rae, Charlotte

**Luby, Hal**
See Luby, Hugh Max

**Luby, Hugh Max** 1913-   [BE]
*American baseball player*
* Luby, Hal

**Luby, John Perkins** 1868-1899
[BE]
*American baseball player*
* Luby, Pat

**Luby, Kate**   [PA]
*Author*
* O'Dowd, Darby

**Luby, Pat**
See Luby, John Perkins

**Luc [Luke]**
See Frederick II

**Luc Gabrielle, [Sister]**
See Deckers, Jeannine

**Luca, Cleve**
See Luca, Cleveland O.

**Luca, Cleveland O.** 1827-1872
[IBW]
*American musician*
* Luca, Cleve

**Luca da Cortona**
See Signorelli, Luca d'Egidio di
Ventura de

**Lucan, Arthur**
See Towle, Arthur

**Lucanese, Dominic** 1898?-
*American singer*
* Lucas, Nick

**Lucania, Salvatore** 1897-1962
[B10]
*American underworld figure*
* [The] King of the Pimps
* Lane, Charles
* Luciano, Charles
* Luciano, Lucky
* Ross, Charles
* Three Twelve

**Lucas, Barbara**
See Wall, Barbara

**Lucas, Buster**
See Lucas, John Charles [Johnny]

**Lucas, Charles** 1713-1771   [HN]
*Irish politician*
* [The] Incorruptible Lucas

**Lucas, Charles Fred** 1902-
[BE, PB]
*American baseball player*
* Lucas, Red
* [The] Nashville Narcissus

**Lucas, Christopher Norman** 1912-
[ASC]
*British-born songwriter and
recording executive*
* Davis, Norman

**Lucas, E. V.**
See Lucas, Edward Verrall

**Lucas, Edward Verrall** 1868-1938
[LC, WWL]
*British author*
* E. V. L.
* Lucas, E. V.

**Lucas, Emily Beatrix Coursolles**
See   Jones, Emily Beatrix
Coursolles

**Lucas, Eugene** 1901-1972   [SC]
*American actor, singer, songwriter*
* Austin, Gene
* [The] Whispering Tenor

**Lucas, F. L.**
See   Lucas, Frank Laurence

**Lucas, Francois** 1812- ?   [PA]
*Author*
* Brugensis

**Lucas, Frank Laurence** 1894-1967
[LC]
*British author, scholar, critic*
* Lucas, F. L.

**Lucas, Gerald** 1935-   [IAW]
*Swiss author*
* Louvier, Pierre
* Melvier, Laurent

**Lucas, Hans**
See   Godard, Jean-Luc

**Lucas, Jane**
See   Spivey, Victoria Regina
[Vicky]

**Lucas, John Charles [Johnny]**
1903-1970   [BE]
*American baseball player*
* Lucas, Buster

**Lucas, Jonathan**
See   Giarraputo, Lucas Thomas
Aco

**Lucas, Laddie**
See   Lucas, Percy Belgrave

**Lucas, Lazy Bill**
See   Lucas, William [Bill]

**Lucas, Luke**
See   Lucas, Ray Wesley

**Lucas, Nick**
See   Lucanese, Dominic

**Lucas, Percy Belgrave** 1915-
[EG, OCS]
*British politician and golfer*
* Lucas, Laddie

**Lucas, Ray Wesley** 1908-1969
[BE]
*American baseball player*
* Lucas, Luke

**Lucas, Red**
See   Lucas, Charles Fred

**Lucas, Richard** 1648-1715   [HN]
*British clergyman*
* [The] Blind Prebendary of
  Westminster

**Lucas, Robert**
See   Ehrenzweig, Robert

**Lucas van Leyden**
See   Hugensz, Lucas

**Lucas, Victoria**
See   Plath, Sylvia

**Lucas, William [Bill]** 1918-   [BWW]
*American singer*
* Lucas, Lazy Bill

**Lucca, Pauline**
See   Von Walhofen, Baroness

**Lucchese, Thomas Gaetano**
1903-1967   [BLB, PHM]
*American underworld figure*
* Brown, Three Finger

**Lucci, Mike** 20th c.
*American football player*
* Lucci, Owl

**Lucci, Owl**
See   Lucci, Mike

**Lucciola, John** 1926-   [ASC]
*American musician*
* Luce, Johnnie

**Luce, Johnnie**
See   Lucciola, John

**Luce, Polly**
See   Marion, Pauline

**Lucero, Roberto**
See   Meredith, Robert C[hidester]

**Lucey, James D[ennis]** 1923-
[CA, WD]
*American author*
* James, Matthew

**Lucey, Joseph Earl [Joe]** 1897-
[BE]
*American baseball player*
* Lucey, Scootch

**Lucey, Scootch**
See   Lucey, Joseph Earl [Joe]

**Lucia**
See   Hunting, M. E.

**Lucian** ?- 290   [HN]
*Saint*
* [The] Apostle of Beauvais

**Lucian** 120- 180   [DEP, FFF]
*Greek author*
* [The] Cerberus of the Muses
* [The] Philosopher of Samosata
* [The] Samosatian Philosopher

**Lucian** 240?- 312   [WBD]
*Syrian-born theologian*
* Lucian of Antioch
* [The] Martyr

**Lucian of Antioch**
See   Lucian

**[The] Lucian of France**
See   Rabelais, Francois

**Luciani, Albino** 1912-1978
*Pope*
* Gianpaolo
* John Paul I

**Luciani, Sebastiano** 1485?-1547
[WBD]
*Italian painter*
* Sebastiano del Piombo

**Luciano, Charles**
See   Lucania, Salvatore

**Luciano, Lucky**
See   Lucania, Salvatore

**Lucid, Pate** 1912-1981   [FC, ITA]
*American actor*
* Hayden, Lucky
* Hayden, Russell
* [The] Rootin', Tootin', Ridin'
  Romeo of the Screen

**Lucie-Smith, [John] Edward**
[McKenzie] 1933-   [WD]
*British poet, translator, writer*
* Kershaw, Peter

**Lucien, Jon**
See   Harrigan, Jon Lucien

**Lucier, Mrs. Frederick**   [FFF]
*Entertainer*
* Archmere, Halie

**Lucifer**
See   Ball, John

**Lucile**
See   Sutherland, Lucy Christina

**Lucilius, Caius** 2nd c. BC
[DEP, DNNS, FFF]
*Roman poet*
* [The] Father of Roman Satire

**Lucinda B.**
See   Bowser, L.

**Lucio**
See   Phillips, Gordon

**Luciolli, Mario** 1910-   [IAW]
*Italian-born author*
* Donosti, Mario

**Lucis Amator**
See   Burton, Doris

**Lucius II**
See   Caccianemici, Gerardo

**Lucius III**
See   Allucingoli, Ubaldo

**Luck, Lucky**
See   Luck, Robert

**Luck, Robert** ?-1977   [FIR]
*Actor*
* Luck, Lucky

**Luckless, John** [joint pseudonym
with Clifford Irving]
See   Burkholz, Herbert

**Luckless, John** [joint pseudonym
with Herbert Burkholz]
See   Irving, Clifford Michael

**Lucky Eddie Rosenbaum**
See   Rosenbaum, Edward

**Lucky Lindy**
See   Lindbergh, Charles Augustus

**Lucrece**
See   Daniels, Coralin

**Lucretius Carus, Titus** 1st c. BC
[SN]
*Roman poet*
* [The] Sculptor Poet

**Lucullus**
See   Bennis, Wessel Johannes

**Lucullus**
See   Bernard, Samuel

**Lucy** [code name used during World
War II]
See   Roesseler, Rudolf

**Lucy, [Sir] Henry William**
1845-1924   [FFF, WWL]
*British author*
* Member of the Chiltern
  Hundreds
* My Baritone
* Toby, M. P.

**Lucy, Thomas Elmore** 1874- ?
[NAA]
*American author*
* Elmore, Carol

**Luddeckens, Werner Louis Georg**
1889?-1945   [SC]
*German actor*
* Alexander, Georg

**Luder, Doctor**
See   Luther, Martin

**Luders, Catherine** 1828?- ?
[FFF, PA]
*American poet*
* Hermann, Emily

**Ludgrove, Linda** 1947-   [SWI]
*British swimmer*
* Ludgrove, Little Linda

**Ludgrove, Little Linda**
See   Ludgrove, Linda

**Ludlow, Dwight** 1889-   [CU]
*American actor*
* Washburn, Bryant

**Ludlow, Geoffrey**
See   Meynell, Laurence [Walter]

**Ludlow, George**
See   Kay, Ernest

**Ludlum, Mabel Cleland**
See   Widdemer, Mabel Cleland

**Ludlum, Robert** 1927-   [CA, WD]
*American author*
* Ryder, Jonathan

**Ludolph, Wee Willie**
See   Ludolph, William Francis
[Willie]

**Ludolph, William Francis [Willie]**
1900-1952   [BE]
*American baseball player*
* Ludolph, Wee Willie

**Ludovici, Anthony M[ario]** 1882- ?
[CAP]
*British author and illustrator*
* Cobbett
* Paterson, Huntley
* Valentine, David

**Ludovisi, Alessandro** 1554-1623
[WBD]
*Pope*
* Gregory XV

**Ludvigsen, Karl [Eric]** 1934-   [CA]
*American writer*
* Miles, Elliot
* Nielssen, Eric

**Ludwell, Bernice**
See   Stokes, Manning Lee

**Ludwig der Springer**
See   Louis [or Ludwig]

**Ludwig, Emil**
See   Cohn, Emil

**Ludwig, Eric**
See   Grunwald, Stefan

**Ludwig, Frederic**
See   Grunwald, Stefan

**Ludwig, Myles Eric** 1942-   [CA]
*American author*
* Williams, J. X.

**Lueders, Charles Henry**   [FFF]
*American writer*
* Karlsten, Henry

**Lueth, Julia** 1864?-1950 [BEW]
*Danish-born actress and playwright*
* Anderson, Julia

**Luff, Stanley George Anthony**
1921- [CA]
*British author*
* Farnash, Hugh

**Lufft, Hans** 1495-1584 [WBD]
*German printer*
* [The] Bible Printer

**Luganski, Kosak**
See Dahl, Vladimir Ivanovitch

**Lugard, Flora Louisa Shaw**
1852-1929 [SAT]
*Irish-born journalist and author*
* Shaw, Flora Louisa

**[El] Lugareno**
See Betancourt Cisneros, Gaspar

**Lugosi, Bela**
See Blasko, Bela Lugosi

**Lugow**
See Gow, Lucienne

**Luhar, Tribhuvandas Purushottandas**
20th c. [IAW]
*Indian author and poet*
* Sundaram

**Luhrsen, Wild Bill**
See Luhrsen, William Ferdinand
[Bill]

**Luhrsen, William Ferdinand [Bill]**
1884-1973 [BE]
*American baseball player*
* Luhrsen, Wild Bill

**Luigi**
See Facciuto, Eugene Louis

**Luimardel**
See Martinez-Delgado, Luis

**Luisetti, Angelo Enrico** 1916-
[B10, BB, OCS]
*American basketball player*
* Luisetti, Hank

**Luisetti, Hank**
See Luisetti, Angelo Enrico

**Luisinus**
See Luvigini, Francesco

**Luiz, Washington**
See Pereira de Souza, Washington
Luiz

**Luk, Charles** 1898- [AW, CA]
*Chinese editor and translator*
* Lu, K'uan-yu

**Lukacs, Pal** 1891?-1971
[FC, WEF]
*Hungarian-born actor*
* Lukas, Paul

**Lukas, Charlotte Koplinka** 1954-
[CA]
*American author and poet*
* Koplinka, Charlotte

**Lukas, Paul**
See Lukacs, Pal

**Luke**
See Clarke, Gordon Luke

**Luke** 1st c. [DEP, DNNF, FF]
*Saint*
* [The] Beloved Physician

**Luke the Drifter**
See Williams, Hiram King

**Lukeman, Alex** 20th c. [SFL]
*Author*
* Dain, Alex

**Lukens, Adam**
See De Reyna, Diane Detzer

**Lukens, Alan R., III** 20th c. [BBH]
*American sailboat racer*
* Lukens, Doc

**Lukens, Doc**
See Lukens, Alan R., III

**Lukens, Henry Clay** 1838- ?
[FFF, PA]
*American author*
* Erratic Enrique
* Snekul, Heinrich Yale

**Lukon, Edward Paul [Eddie]** 1920-
[BE]
*American baseball player*
* Lukon, Mongoose

**Lukon, Mongoose**
See Lukon, Edward Paul [Eddie]

**Lully, Jean Baptiste** 1632-1687
[SN]
*French composer*
* [Le] Coeur Bas [The Base Heart]
* [Un] Coquin Tenebreux [A Dark
Knave]

**Lully, Raymond** 1234?-1315
[FFF, HN]
*Spanish philosopher*
* [The] Enlightened Doctor
* [The] Illuminated Doctor
* Illuminatus, Doctor
* [The] Most Enlightened Doctor

**Lulu**
See Bonaparte, Napoleon Eugene
Louis Jean Joseph

**Lulu**
See Lawrie, Marie McDonald
McLaughlin

**Lulu Belle**
See Wiseman, Myrtle Eleanor
Cooper

**Lum, Peter**
See Crowe, [Lady] Bettina [Lum]

**Lumb, Emmeline** 20th c. [WWL]
*British author*
* Brittain, Noel

**Lumb, Lummy**
See Lumb, Richard Graham

**Lumb, Richard Graham** 1950-
[DC]
*British cricketer*
* Lumb, Lummy

**[The] Lumber King**
See Weyerhaeuser, Frederick

**Lumberjack**
See Lambert, T. H.

**Lumenti, Commuter**
See Lumenti, Ralph Anthony

**Lumenti, Ralph Anthony** 1936-
[BE]
*American baseball player*
* Lumenti, Commuter

**Luminus**
See Melling, Leonard

**Lumley, Apple Cheeks**
See Lumley, Harry

**Lumley, B.** 19th c. [PA]
*Author*
* Hermes

**Lumley, Dave** 1954- [SMG]
*Canadian-born hockey player*
* Lumley, Lummer

**Lumley, Harry** 1926-
[CEI, FHE, HK]
*Canadian-born hockey player*
* Lumley, Apple Cheeks

**Lumley, Harry G.** 1880-1938 [BN]
*American baseball player*
* Lumley, Yock

**Lumley, Lummer**
See Lumley, Dave

**Lumley, Yock**
See Lumley, Harry G.

**Lun**
See Rich, John

**Luna, Donyale**
See Freeman, Peggy Anne Donyale
Aragonea Pegeon

**Luna, Guillermo Romero** 1930-
[BE]
*Mexican-born baseball player*
* Luna, Memo

**Luna, Kris [house pseudonym, Curtis
Warren]**
See Bird, William Henry Fleming

**Luna, Kris [house pseudonym, Curtis
Warren]**
See O'Brien, David

**Luna, Memo**
See Luna, Guillermo Romero

**Lunaeus, Peter** 1586-1638 [PA]
*Author*
* Van der Kun

**Lunar, Dennis**
See Mungo, Raymond

**[A] Lunar Wray**
See Savage, M. J.

**Lunchbasket, Roger**
See Reeve-Jones, Alan Edmond

**Lund, A. Morten** 1926- [CA]
*American author*
* Borch, Ted

**Lund, Arthur** 1915- [MY]
*American singer*
* London, Art

**Lund, Francis L.** 1913- [FB]
*American football player*
* Lund, Pug

**Lund, Penny**
See Lund, Pentti Alexander

**Lund, Pentti Alexander** 1925-
[CEI]
*Finnish-born hockey player*
* Lund, Penny

**Lund, Philip R[eginald]** 1938- [CA]
*New Zealand-born author*
* Confucius

**Lund, Pug**
See Lund, Francis L.

**Lund, Troels Frederik** 1840-1921
[WBD]
*Danish historian*
* Troels-Lund

**Lundberg, Eleanor Jewett** 1892-
[NAA]
*American journalist*
* Jewett, Eleanor

**Lundberg, Kai**
See Potthoff, Margot Maria

**Lunden, Joan**
See Blunden, Joan

**Lundgren, Paul Arthur** 1925-
[IAW]
*American writer*
* McCutcheon, James

**Lundholm, Anja** 20th c. [IAW]
*German-born author*
* Lindstrom, Alf

**Lundy, Richard** 1898-1965 [MK]
*American baseball player*
* King Richard

**Lunn, Arnold [Henry Moore]**
1888-1974 [CA, CAT]
*British author*
* Croft, Sutton
* Rubicon

**Lunn, Hugh Kingsmill** 1889-1949
[LC, TC, TC1]
*British author and critic*
* Kingsmill, Hugh

**Lunn, Robert** 1912-1966 [ECM]
*American country-western performer*
* [The] Talking Blues Boy
* [The] Talking Blues Man

**Lunt, Arthur Milton** 1881-1971
[F1, FC, SC]
*British actor*
* Rosmer, Milton

**Lunt, George** 1807- ? [FFF]
*American attorney and author*
* Brooke, Wesley

**Lunt, Irene**
See Bradbury, Irene

**Lunt, Lois**
See Metz, Lois Lunt

**Luola**
See Niller, Mary Ager

**Lupescu, Elena** 1896?-1977
*Wife of King Carol of Rumania*
* [The] Jewish Pompadour
* Lupescu, Magda

**Lupescu, Magda**
See Lupescu, Elena

**Lupien, Tony**
See Lupien, Ulysses John

**Lupien, Ulysses John** 1917- [BE]
*American baseball player*
* Lupien, Tony

**Lupino, Henry George** 1892-1959
[F2, FC, SC]
*British actor*
* Lane, Lupino
* Lane, Nipper

**Lupino, Wallace** 1898-1961 [SC]
*Scottish-born actor*
* Lane, Wallace

**Lupo, Joseph**
See Saietta, Ignazio

**Lupo the Wolf**
*See* Saietta, Ignazio

**Lupoff, Richard Allen** [Dick] 1935-
[CA, ESF, SFP]
*American author*
* Hamlet, Ova
* O'Donnell, Dick [joint pseudonym with Don(ald) (Arthur) Thompson]
* Steele, Addison, II

**Lupton, Marie** 1875-1930    [THR]
*British actress*
* Studholme, Marie

**Lupton, Netta** 1893?-1953    [BEW]
*British-born actress*
* Westcott, Netta

**Lupulus**
*See* Woelflein, Heinrich

**Luque, Adolfo** 1890-1957
[BE, DGS]
*Cuban-born baseball player*
* Luque, Dolf
* [The] Pride of Havana

**Luque, Dolf**
*See* Luque, Adolfo

**Lurgan, Lester**
*See* Knowles, Mabel Winifred

**Lurye, Mikhail** 1882-1932    [JL]
*Russian economist and politician*
* Larin, Yuri

**[The] Lusian Scipio**
*See* Nunio

**Luska, Sidney**
*See* Harland, Henry

**Lussier, Yvonne**
*Actress*
* D'Orsay, Fifi

**Lussu, Joyce** [Salvadori] 1912-
[CA]
*Italian writer and translator*
* Salvadori, Joyce

**Luster, Shirley** 1925-    [PMJ]
*American singer*
* Christy, June

**Lustiger, Aaron** 1927?-
*French clergyman*
* Lustiger, Jean-Marie

**Lustiger, Jean-Marie**
*See* Lustiger, Aaron

**Lutchman, Martinus Haridat**
1926-    [CW]
*Surinamese poet*
* Shrinivasi, Asjantenu

**Lutenberg, Charles William**
1864-1938    [BE]
*American baseball player*
* Lutenberg, Luke

**Lutenberg, Luke**
*See* Lutenberg, Charles William

**Luther, Frank**
*See* Crow, Francis Luther [Frank]

**Luther, Irene** 1891?-    [F1, F2, FC]
*American actress*
* Rich, Irene

**Luther, Martin** 1483-1546
[DEP, HN, SN]
*German religious reformer*
* [The] German Paul
* [The] Great Iconoclast

**Luther, Martin** (Continued)
* Luder, Doctor
* [The] Michael Angelo of the Reformation
* [The] Monk of Eisleben
* [The] Monk of Wittenberg
* [The] Nightingale of Wittenberg
* [The] Solitary Monk
* [The] Third Elias
* [The] Wittenberg Monk

**[The] Luther of England**
*See* Cranmer, Thomas

**Luther, Ray**
*See* Ley, Arthur Gordon

**Lutoslawski, Wincenty** 1863- ?
[WWL]
*British philosopher and author*
* Ezami, Henri

**Lutschitsch-Dalmatoff, B.** 1862- ?
[THR]
*Russian actor*
* Dalmatoff, B.

**Luttringer, Al**
*See* Luttringer, Alfonse

**Luttringer, Alfonse** 1879-1953
[SC]
*American actor*
* Luttringer, Al

**Luttwak, Edward Nicolae** 1942-
[IAW]
*Rumanian-born author*
* Ignotus, Miles

**Lutwak, Michael Anatol** 1902-
[FD, WEF]
*Russian-born director*
* Litvak, Anatole

**Lutyens, Mary** 1908-    [CA, WD]
*British author and editor*
* Wyndham, Esther

**Lutz, E. O.**
*See* Lutz, Edward Oscar

**Lutz, Edward Oscar** 1919-    [BEW]
*American accountant, educator, executive*
* Lutz, E. O.

**Lutz, Louis William** 1898-    [BE]
*American baseball player*
* Lutz, Red

**Lutz, Michael** 1949-    [RO2]
*American musician*
* Lutz, Sam

**Lutz, Red**
*See* Lutz, Louis William

**Lutz, Sam**
*See* Lutz, Michael

**Lutzke, Rube**
*See* Lutzke, Walter John

**Lutzke, Walter John** 1897-1938
[BE]
*American baseball player*
* Lutzke, Rube

**Luvigini, Francesco** 1523-1568
[PA]
*Author*
* Luisinus

**Lux**
*See* Jones, Lucy M.

**Lux, Adam**
*See* Pic, Ulysse

**Lux Dux**
*See* Howard, Anna H. C.

**Lux Mundi**
*See* Wessel, Johann [or John]

**Luxemburg, Rosa** 1870-1919
[WBD]
*German Socialist leader*
* Red Rosa

**Luxton, Leonora Kathrine** 1895-
[CA]
*American astrologer and author*
* Howard, Nona

**Luz y Caballero, Jose Cipriano de la**
1800-1862    [CW]
*Cuban author*
* Filolezes

**Luzinski, Gregory Michael** 1950-
[SMG]
*American baseball player*
* [The] Bull
* Luzinski, Hoss

**Luzinski, Hoss**
*See* Luzinski, Gregory Michael

**Lyall, David**
*See* Reeves, Helen Buckingham [Mathers]

**Lyall, David**
*See* Swan, Annie S[hepherd]

**Lyall, Edna**
*See* Bayly, Ada Ellen

**Lyall, Katharine Elizabeth** 1928-
[CA]
*British journalist and author*
* Whitehorn, Katharine

**Lycidas**
*See* Milton, John

**[The] Lycurgus of the Lower House**
*See* Russell, [Lord] John Earl

**Lycurgus, Solon**
*See* Clemens, Samuel Langhorne

**Lydgate, John** 1375-1460
[HN, RH, SN]
*British poet*
* [The] Monk of Bury

**[The] Lydgate of His Day**
*See* Jean [or Jehan] de Meung

**[The] Lydian Poet**
*See* Alcman

**Lydon, John** 20th c.
*British musician*
* Rotten, Johnny

**Lyel, Viola**
*See* Watson, Violet

**Lygo, Mary**
*See* Goodall, Irene

**Lying Dick Talbot**
*See* Talbot, Richard

**[The] Lying Scot**
*See* Burnet, Gilbert

**Lykiard, Alexis** [Constantine]
1940-    [CA]
*Greek-born poet and author*
* Piano, Celeste

**Lyle, Albert Walter** 1944-
[BE, PB, WWB]
*American baseball player*
* Lyle, Sparky

**Lyle, Cecil** 1892?-1955    [BEW]
*Magician*
* [The] Great Lyle

**Lyle, Gwladys M.** [Morgan] 1888-
[NAA]
*American author and poet*
* Morgan, Gwladys M.

**Lyle, Lyston**
*See* Gibson, Edward

**Lyle, Sparky**
*See* Lyle, Albert Walter

**Lyly, John** 1554?-1606    [SN]
*British author*
* [The] Ape of Envie

**Lyman, Abe**
*See* Simon, Abraham

**Lyman, Albert Robison** 1880-1973
[CAP]
*American author*
* [The] Old Settler

**Lyman, G. H.**    [PA]
*Author*
* De Leon, Stuart

**Lyman, Helen Hoyt** 20th c.    [NAA]
*American author and poet*
* Hoyt, Helen

**Lyman, Link**
*See* Lyman, William Roy

**Lyman, William Roy** 1898-1972
[BBH, FB, SMG]
*American football player*
* Lyman, Link

**Lymington, John**
*See* Chance, John Newton

**Lynam, Joan** 20th c.    [IAW]
*Irish author*
* Lynam, Shevawn

**Lynam, Shevawn**
*See* Lynam, Joan

**Lynch, Brian**
*See* Liddy, James [Daniel Reeves]

**Lynch, Brid**
*See* Ni Loinsigh, Brid

**Lynch, Dummy**
*See* Lynch, Matthew Daniel

**Lynch, Eric**
*See* Bingley, David Ernest

**Lynch, Frances**
*See* Compton, David Guy

**Lynch, Gentleman Jack**
*See* Lynch, John

**Lynch, Grey**
*See* Dorworth, Alice Grey

**Lynch, Harriet Louise** 20th c.
[NAA]
*American author*
* St. Felix, Marie

**Lynch, Hester** 1740-1821    [PA]
*Author*
* Matilda, Anna

**Lynch, James**
*See* Andreyev, Leonid [Nikolaevich]

**Lynch, John** 1918?-
*Irish politician*
* Lynch, Gentleman Jack

**Lynch, John Gilbert Bohun** 20th c.
[MBF]
*British author*
* Bloomer, Jack

**Lynch, Lawrence L.**
*See* Van Deventer, Emma
Murdock

**Lynch, Marilyn** 1938- [CA]
*American author*
* Ward, Melanie

**Lynch, Matthew Daniel** 1927- [BE]
*American baseball player*
* Lynch, Dummy

**Lynch, Mrs. Samuel** [FFF]
*Entertainer*
* Meserole, Fannie

**Lynd, Robert** 1879-1949 [LC]
*Irish-born author*
* Y. Y.

**Lynd, Rosa**
*See* Secor, Rosa

**Lyndon**
*See* Bright, Matilda A.

**Lyndon, Barre?**
*See* Edgar, Alfred

**Lynds, Dennis** 1924-
[AW, SFL, WGT]
*American author*
* Arden, William
* Collins, Michael
* Crowe, John
* Grant, Maxwell [house
   pseudonym]

**Lyne, Joseph Leycester** 1837- ?
[RH]
*Monk*
* Ignatius, [Father]

**Lyngstad, Sverre** 1922- [IAW]
*Norwegian-born author*
* Larr, Sven

**Lynk, Warder**
*See* Bowman, Gerald

**Lynley, Carol**
*See* Jones, Carol

**Lynn**
*See* Brown, Velma Darbo

**Lynn, Barbara**
*See* Ozone, Barbara Lynn

**[The] Lynn Bard**
*See* Lewis, Alonzo

**Lynn, Benjamin** 18th c. [FFF]
*American pioneer*
* [The] Daniel Boone of Southern
   Kentucky
* [The] Hunter Preacher

**Lynn, Cheryl**
*See* Smith, Cherry George

**Lynn, Cora**
*See* Cunati, Caroline

**Lynn, Diana**
*See* Loehr, Dolores

**Lynn, Eddie**
*See* Meminger, Edward Lynn

**Lynn, Elwyn Augustus** 1917- [AW]
*Australian author and editor*
* Augustus

**Lynn, Escott**
*See* Lawrence, Christopher George
Holman

**Lynn, Frank**
*See* Leisy, James Franklin

**Lynn, Gerrie**
*See* Robeck, Geraldine Cecilia

**Lynn, Irene**
*See* Rowland, D[onald] S[ydney]

**Lynn, Jane Thursten** 1915- [ASC]
*American composer*
* Willadsen, Gene

**Lynn, Janet**
*See* Salomon, Janet Lynn
[Nowicki]

**Lynn, Japhet Monroe** 1913- [BE]
*American baseball player*
* Lynn, Red

**Lynn, Jeffrey**
*See* Lind, Ragnar Godfrey

**Lynn, Mara**
*See* Mosier, Marilyn

**Lynn, Margaret**
*See* Battye, Gladys

**Lynn, Mary**
*See* Brokamp, Marilyn

**Lynn, Max**
*See* Anderson, G. J. B.

**Lynn, Patricia**
*See* Watts, Mabel Pizzey

**Lynn, Red**
*See* Lynn, Japhet Monroe

**Lynn, Sharon E.**
*See* Lindsay, D'Auvergne Sharon

**Lynn, Vera** 1916- [NN]
*British singer*
* [The] Forces' Sweetheart

**Lynne, Becky**
*See* Zawadsky, Patience

**Lynne, Carole**
*See* Haymen, Helen Violet Carolyn

**Lynne, Glenys** 20th c. [RO2]
*South African singer*
* Jill

**Lynne, James Broom** 1920- [WD]
*British author and playwright*
* Quartermain, James

**Lynott, Jessica** 1930- [NAD]
*Yoga instructor*
* Savitri Priya, [Swami]

**Lynton, Ann**
*See* Rayner, Claire

**Lynton, Harriet Ronken** 1920-
[CA]
*American author*
* Ronken, Harriet

**LYNX**
*See* Angermayer, Fred Antoine

**Lynx**
*See* Fairfield, Cecily Isabel

**Lyon, Elinor**
*See* Wright, Elinor Bruce

**Lyon, Francis D.** 20th c. [ITA]
*American director*
* Lyon, Pete

**Lyon, Isaac S.** 19th c. [FFF]
*American writer*
* Old Cartman

**Lyon, Jessica**
*See* De Leeuw, Cateau Wilhelmina

**Lyon, John** 1951- [DC]
*British cricketer*
* Lyon, Lenny

**Lyon, Katherine**
*See* Mix, Katherine Lyon

**Lyon, Lenny**
*See* Lyon, John

**Lyon, Lyman R.**
*See* De Camp, L[yon] Sprague

**Lyon, Marjorie**
*See* Meredyth-Starmer, Marjorie

**Lyon, Pete**
*See* Lyon, Francis D.

**Lyons, Alexander M.** 1863-1945
[SC]
*British-born actor*
* Crimmins, Dan[iel]

**Lyons, Clifford Williams**
1902-1974 [SC]
*American actor, director, stunt
performer*
* Lyons, Tex

**Lyons, Delphine C.**
*See* Smith, Evelyn E.

**Lyons, Ed[ward Hoyte]** 1923- [BE]
*American baseball player*
* Lyons, Mouse

**Lyons, Francis Lunakiaki**
1909-1960 [SC]
*American actor, musician, singer*
* Lyons, Freckles

**Lyons, Freckles**
*See* Lyons, Francis Lunakiaki

**Lyons, Fred**
*See* Leyva, Fred F.

**Lyons, George Tony** 1891- [BE]
*American baseball player*
* Lyons, Smooth

**Lyons, J. B.** 1922- [CA]
*Irish physician and author*
* Fitzwilliam, Michael

**Lyons, John Maguire** 1926- [IAW]
*Scottish-born author and cartoonist*
* O'Liathain, Sesu

**Lyons, Lady, of Strathmore** [PA]
*Author*
* L.

**Lyons, Luella B.** 1897- [NAA]
*American writer*
* La Plante, Sandra
* Rider, Jane

**Lyons, Marc**
*American football player*
* Lyons, Mountain

**Lyons, Marcus**
*See* Blish, James [Benjamin]

**Lyons, Mountain**
*See* Lyons, Marc

**Lyons, Mouse**
*See* Lyons, Ed[ward Hoyte]

**Lyons, Smooth**
*See* Lyons, George Tony

**Lyons, Tex**
*See* Lyons, Clifford Williams

**Lyons, Thomas A.** 1869-1920 [BE]
*American baseball player*
* Lyons, Toby

**Lyons, Toby**
*See* Lyons, Thomas A.

**Lyra, Nicholas de** 1270-1340 [HN]
*French monk and author*
* Utilis, Doctor

**[The] Lyric Muse**
*See* Corinna

**Lys, Christian**
*See* Brebner, Percy James

**Lyte, Richard**
*See* Whelpton, [George] Eric

**Lytell, Jimmy**
*See* Sarrapede, James

**Lytle, Dad**
*See* Lytle, Edward Benson

**Lytle, Donald** 1941- [CME]
*American country-western performer*
* [The] Ohio Kid
* Paycheck, Johnny
* Young, Donnie

**Lytle, Edward Benson** 1862-1950
[BE]
*American baseball player*
* Lytle, Dad
* Lytle, Pop

**Lytle, Pop**
*See* Lytle, Edward Benson

**Lyttelton, Thomas [Second Baron
Lyttelton]** 1744-1779 [WBD]
*British politician*
* [The] Wicked Lord Lyttelton

**Lyttle, Jean**
*See* Garrett, Eileen J[eanette]

**Lyttle, Richard B[ard]** 1927- [CA]
*American author*
* Lang, Rex

**Lyttleton, Edith J.** 1873-1945
[WBD]
*New Zealand author*
* Lancaster, G. B.

**Lytton, Doris**
*See* Partington, Doris

**Lytton, Edward**
*See* Morris, Charles Smith

**Lytton, Jane**
*See* Clarke, Percy A.

# M

**M.**
*See* Gillison, Margaret

**M.**
*See* MacPherson, George Gordon

**M.**
*See* Moody, Michael David

**M**
*See* Stone, Susan Berch

**M**
*See* Warner, Cornell

**M. A.**
*See* Andrews, Marcia

**M. A.**
*See* Blagdon, Francis William

**M. A. C.**
*See* MacFayden, Dugald

**M. A. D.**
*See* Denison, Mary Andrews

**M. A. T.**
*See* Tincker, Mary Agnes

**M. B.**
*See* Balfour, Maria

**M. B.**
*See* Drew, Mona

**M. B.**
*See* Faust, Frederick [Schiller]

**M. B.**
*See* Lamb, Mary

**M. C.**
*See* Cooper, Mary

**M. D.**
*See* Black, F. R.

**M. D.**
*See* Davis, Marcus

**M. D. C.**
*See* Brooks, Erastus

**M. della R. W.**
*See* Whitehead, Margaret della Rovere

**M. E. B.**
*See* Gillie, Mary E.

**M. E. L.**
*See* Lee, Mary Elizabeth

**M. E. M.**
*See* Powell, H. W.

**M. E. M. J.**
*See* Jones, Margaret Elizabeth Mary

**M. E. W. S.**
*See* Sherwood, Mary Elizabeth Wilson

**M. F.**
*See* Fisher, Myrta

**M. F. A.**
*See* Atkinson, Marshall Foster

**M. F. D.**
*See* Douglas, Marguerite France

**M. G.**
*See* Giergielewicz, Mieczyslaw

**M. G.**
*See* Gillison, Margaret

**M. H.**
*See* Hadfield, Miles

**M. H.**
*See* Hullah, Mrs.

**M. H. B.**
*See* Burnham, Mary Hewins

**M. H. S.**
*See* Seymour, Mary H.

**M. H. S.**
*See* Spielmann, Marion Harry Alexander

**M. H. T.**
*See* Fiske, Mrs. Stephen

**M. K.**
*See* Kreeger, Marianne

**M. L. R.**
*See* Smith, May Riley

**M. M.**
*See* Baker [or Mortenson?], Norma Jean

**M. M.**
*See* Meredith, Mark

**M. M. C.**
*See* Coatman, Maureen Margaret

**M. M. D.**
*See* Dodge, Mary Mapes

**M. M. M.**
*See* Tooke, W.

**M. N. M.**
*See* Bleecker, Mary Noel

**M. P.**
*See* Patrick, Marion

**M. P.**
*See* Potter, Mary

**M. P. H.**
*See* Heaslip, Mark Patrick

**M. R. B.**
*See* Bethel, Marion Ross

**M. S.**
*See* Safford, Mary J.

**M. S.**
*See* Smedley, Menella Bute

**M. T. F.**
*See* Porter, Katherine Anne

**M. W.**
*See* Woodthorpe, Patricia Mariella

**M. W. H.**
*See* Hazeltine, Mayo H.

**M. W. T.**
*See* Tileston, Mary W.

**Ma-ka-tae-mish-kia-kiak**
1767-1838 [WBD]
*American Indian chieftain*
* Black Hawk

**Maartens, Maarten**
*See* Schwartz, Jozua Marius Willem Van Der Poorten

**Maas, Duane Frederick** 1931- [BE]
*American baseball player*
* Maas, Duke

**Maas, Duke**
*See* Maas, Duane Frederick

**Mabel**
*See* Hazen, M. P.

**Mabley, Edward [Howe]** 1906-
[CA]
*American playwright*
* Ware, John

**Mabley, Jackie**
*See* Aiken, Loretta Mary

**Mabley, Moms**
*See* Aiken, Loretta Mary

**Mabon, Willie** 1925- [BWW]
*American singer*
* Big Willie

**Mabrouk, Djelloul** 1934- [CA]
*Algerian-born American author*
* Marbrook, Del
* Marbrook, Djelloul

**Mabuse [or Malbodius]**
*See* Gossaert [Gossart], Jan

**Mac**
*See* MacManus, Seumas

**Mac**
*See* McConnell, Wallace Robert

**Mac**
*See* McGeachy, C. E. A.

**Mac A'Ghobhainn, Iain**
*See* Smith, Iain Crichton

**Mac A'Ghobhainn, Seamus**
*See* Smith, Iain Crichton

**Mac A'Ghreidhir, Gillechriosd**
*See* Grieve, Christopher Murray

**Mac An Bhaird, Seaghan**
*See* Ward, John C.

**Mac Gilla Cuddy**
*See* Archdekin, Richard

**Mac Giolla Eain, Eoin**
*See* MacErlean, John C.

**Mac, Mr.**
*See* McDonnell, James Smith

**Mac, Mr.**
*See* McLaughlin, Walter T.

**Mac the Knife**
*See* Macmillan, Harold

**MacAdam, [Reginald] Al[an]** 1952?-
*Canadian-born hockey player*
* MacAdam, Spud

**MacAdam, Eve**
*See* Leslie, Cecilie

**Macadam, Ian**
*See* Adamson, Iaian Beaton

**Macadam, John Loudon**
1756-1836 [DEP, DNNS, SN]
*Scottish engineer*
* [The] King of Roads

**MacAdam, Spud**
*See* MacAdam, [Reginald] Al[an]

**MacAedhagan, Eamon**
*See* Egan, Edward Welstead

**Macallan, Daniel** [PA]
*Author*
* Scrutator

**MacAlpin, Rory**
*See* MacKinnon, Charles Roy

**MacAlpine**
*See* Kenneth I

**MacAlpine, Margaret H[esketh Murray]** 1907-   [CAP]
*Scottish-born author*
* Carmichael, Ann

**Macalpine, Simon** 1917-   [TR]
*Scottish actor*
* Lack, Simon

**Macandro**
See   Rubio, Antonio

**MacApp, C. C.**
See   Capps, Carroll M.

**MacArno, Mat**
See   Cook, Theodore P.

**Macarone**
See   Arnold, George

**MacArthur, Burke**
See   Burks, Arthur J.

**MacArthur, D[avid] Wilson** 1903-
[CA, WD, WWL]
*Scottish-born author and journalist*
* Sinclair, Gavin
* Wilson, David

**MacArthur, Douglas** 1880-1964
*American military leader*
* Dugout Doug

**Macartney, Charles George**
1886-1958   [EC]
*Australian cricketer*
* [The] Governor General

**Macaulay**
See   Frothingham, Washington

**Macaulay, Aula**   [FFF]
*Writer*
* Academicus

**Macaulay, Fannie Caldwell**
1863-1941   [ALY, WBD]
*American author*
* Little, Frances

**Macaulay, Thomas Babington [First Baron Macaulay]** 1800-1859
[DEL, DEP, RH]
*British statesman and author*
* Benengeli, Cid Hamet
* [A] Book in Breeches
* Merton, Tristram

**Macauley, Easy Ed**
See   Macauley, Edward C.

**Macauley, Edward C.** 1928-   [BB]
*American basketball player*
* Macauley, Easy Ed

**Macauley, Robie [Mayhew]** 1919-
[CN]
*American author*
* Dumbarton, A.

**Macaw**
See   Hannays, Kitty

**Macbeath, Innis [Stewart]** 1928-
[IAW]
*Irish-born author*
* Maloney, Tighe
* Stewart, Rattray
* Tissant-Bernac, Mathieu

**Macbeth, Lydia** 1888-   [THR]
*British actress*
* Bilbrooke, Lydia

**MacBeth the Great**
See   MacDonald, Patrick

**MacBride, Melchoir**
See   Quinton, John P[urcell]

**Maccabaeus**
See   Judas Asmonaeus

**Maccabee, Dan**
See   Segal, Samuel

**Maccall, Isobel**
See   Boyd, Elizabeth Orr

**MacCall, Libby**
See   Machol, Libby

**Maccall, William** 1812- ?   [FFF]
*British author*
* Atticus

**MacCarthy, [Sir] Desmond**
1878-1952   [LC, TC1]
*British author, editor, critic*
* Affable Hawk

**MacCathmhaoil, Seaghan**
See   Campbell, John Patrick

**MacCathmhaoil, Seosamh**
See   Campbell, Joseph

**MacClure, Victor** 1887-   [CC, WW]
*Scottish author*
* Craig, Peter

**MacColl, Malcolm** 1838- ?
[PA, WWL]
*British author*
* Expertus
* Scrutator

**MacCraig, Hugh**
See   Ward, Craig

**MacDaniel, Charles**
See   Garrison, Charles M.

**MacDermot, Robert**
See   Barbour, Robert MacDermot

**MacDermot, Thomas H.**
1870-1933   [CW]
*Jamaican-born poet, journalist, author*
* Redcam, Tom

**Macdermott, G. H.**
See   Farrell, Gilbert Hastings

**MacDiarmid, Hugh**
See   Grieve, Christopher Murray

**MacDonald, Aeneas**
See   Thomson, George Malcolm

**MacDonald, Andrew** 1755?-1788?
[FFF, PA]
*Scottish poet*
* Bramble, Matthew

**MacDonald, Angus**
See   MacDonald Douglas, Ronald Angus

**MacDonald, Anson**
See   Heinlein, Robert A[nson]

**MacDonald, B. J.**
See   MacDonald, Blair

**Macdonald, Blackie**
See   Emrich, Duncan [Black Macdonald]

**MacDonald, Blair** 1953-   [SMG]
*Canadian-born hockey player*
* MacDonald, B. J.

**Macdonald, Edwina Le Vin** 1886-
[WWL]
*American author*
* Levin, Edwina

**MacDonald, Eric**
See   Allan, F. Carney

**MacDonald, Flora** 20th c.
*Canadian politician*
* [The] Red Tory

**Macdonald, George**   [PA]
*Author*
* Dalmocand

**MacDonald, Golden**
See   Brown, Margaret Wise

**Macdonald, J. Hay**   [PA]
*Author*
* Jambon, Jean

**Macdonald, [Sir] James**   [SN]
*Seventh Baronet of Sleat*
* [The] Scottish Marcellus

**Macdonald, John**
See   Millar, Kenneth

**Macdonald, John** 1779-1849
[WBD]
*Scottish clergyman*
* [The] Apostle of the North

**Macdonald, [Sir] John Alexander**
1815-1891   [DNNS]
*Canadian prime minister*
* Old To-morrow

**MacDonald, John D[ann]** 1916-
[EMD]
*American author*
* Farrell, John Wade [house pseudonym]
* Henry, Robert [house pseudonym]
* Lane, John [house pseudonym]
* O'Hara, Scott [house pseudonym]
* Reed, Peter [house pseudonym]
* Rieser, Henry [house pseudonym]

**Macdonald, John Ross**
See   Millar, Kenneth

**MacDonald, Katherine** 1894-1956
[CU]
*American actress*
* [The] American Beauty

**Macdonald, Malcolm John Ross**
1932-   [CA, WD]
*British author, playwright, editor*
* Ross-Macdonald, Malcolm J[ohn]

**MacDonald, Marcia**
See   Hill, Grace [Livingston]

**Macdonald, Mrs. Edmond**   [FFF]
*Entertainer*
* Howard, Cordelia

**Macdonald, Mrs. W. H.**   [FFF]
*Entertainer*
* Stone, Marie

**MacDonald, Murray**
See   Honeyman, Walter MacDonald

**Macdonald, Nina Hansell**
See   Looker, Antonina [Hansell]

**Macdonald of Glengarry** 17th c.
[DNNF]
*Scottish chieftain*
* Glengarry

**MacDonald, Patrick** 20th c.   [IBW]
*American bandleader*
* MacBeth the Great

**MacDonald, Philip** 1896?-
[CA, EMD, LC]
*British author*
* Fleming, Oliver [joint pseudonym with Ronald MacDonald]
* Lawless, Anthony
* Porlock, Martin
* Stuart, W. J.
* Stuart, Warren

**MacDonald, Ronald** 20th c.
*Scottish playwright and author*
* Fleming, Oliver [joint pseudonym with Philip MacDonald]

**Macdonald, Ross**
See   Millar, Kenneth

**MacDonald, S. W.**
See   MacDonald, Stuart Wyllie

**MacDonald, Stuart Wyllie** 1948-
[ART]
*Scottish painter*
* MacDonald, S. W.

**Macdonald, Wilson** 1880- ?   [FFF]
*Canadian poet*
* Spiral Groove

**Macdonald, Zillah K[atherine]**
1885-   [CAP, SAT]
*Canadian-born author*
* Zillah

**MacDonald Douglas, Ronald Angus**
1906-   [IAW]
*Scottish author and playwright*
* MacDonald, Angus

**Macdonell, Alastair Ruadh**
1725?-1761   [WBD]
*Scottish soldier*
* Pickle the Spy

**Macdonell, Archibald Gordon**
1895-1941   [CC, TC, WW]
*Scottish author*
* Cameron, John
* Gordon, Neil

**Macdonnaill, Brian**
See   McDonald, Bernard

**Macdonnell, James Edmond** 1917-
[CA]
*Australian author*
* MacNell, James

**MacDonnell, James Francis Carlin**
1881-1945   [CAT]
*American poet*
* Carlin, Francis

**MacDouall, Robertson**
See   Mair, George Brown

**MacDougal, John** [joint pseudonym with Robert Augustine Ward Lowndes]
See   Blish, James [Benjamin]

**MacDougal, John** [joint pseudonym with James (Benjamin) Blish]
See   Lowndes, Robert Augustine Ward

**MacDougall, Fiona**
See   MacLeod, Robert F.

**MacDougall, Leslie Grahame**
See   Grahame-Thomson, Leslie

**Macdougall, Margaret** ?-1943
[SFL]
*Author*
* Armour, Margaret

**MacDougall, Marion Lorne**
1886?-1968 [BEW, FC]
*American actress*
* Lorne, Marion

**MacDuff, Andrew**
*See* Fyfe, Horace Brown

**Mace, Harry L.** 19th c. [BE]
*American baseball player*
* Mace, Jimmy

**Mace, Jimmy**
*See* Mace, Harry L.

**[The] Macedonian**
*See* Basil I [or Basilius]

**[The] Macedonian**
*See* Polyaenus, Julius

**Macedonia's Madman**
*See* Alexander III

**Macedonicus**
*See* Aemilius Paulus, Lucius

**Macedonicus**
*See* Metellus, Quintus Caecilius

**MacElroy, Andrew Jackson** 20th c.
[NAA]
*American publisher and writer*
* MacGregor, Jack

**MacEnri, Seaghan**
*See* Henry, John Patrick

**Maceo, Antonio** 1848-1896 [IBW]
*American-born leader of the Cuban revolution, 1849*
* [The] Bronze Titan

**MacErlean, John C.** 20th c.
[WWL]
*Irish editor*
* Mac Giolla Eain, Eoin

**Macero, Attilio Joseph** 1925- [EJ]
*American jazz musician and composer*
* Macero, Teo

**Macero, Teo**
*See* Macero, Attilio Joseph

**MacFadden, Gertrude** 1900-1967
[SC]
*American actress*
* MacFadden, Mickey

**MacFadden, Mickey**
*See* MacFadden, Gertrude

**MacFall, Haldane** 1860- ? [WWL]
*British author*
* Hal, Dane

**Macfarlane, Ian** 1888-1969 [THR]
*Australian-born actor*
* Fleming, Ian

**Macfarlane, John** 20th c. [WWL]
*Canadian author and poet*
* Arbory, John

**MacFarlane, Kenneth**
*See* Walker, Kenneth MacFarlane

**Macfarlane, Robert** ?-1883 [FFF]
*Scottish-born journalist and author*
* Rutherglen

**MacFarlane, Stephen**
*See* Cross, John Keir

**MacFayden, Daniel Knowles**
1905-1972 [BE, PB]
*American baseball player*
* MacFayden, Deacon Danny

**MacFayden, Deacon Danny**
*See* MacFayden, Daniel Knowles

**MacFayden, Dugald** 1867- ?
[LAO]
*British clergyman, author, poet*
* M. A. C.

**MacFee, Maxwell**
*See* Rennie, James Alan

**MacFhionnlaoich, Peadar**
*See* MacGinley, Peter T.

**MacGeachy, Charles E. A.** [PA]
*Author*
* [The] Danburian

**MacGibbon, Jean** 1913- [TCC]
*British author*
* Howard, Jean

**MacGill, Moyna**
*See* McIldowie, Chattie

**MacGillivray, James Pittendrigh**
1856- ? [LAO]
*Scottish sculptor and writer*
* Maitland, Peter
* P. M.

**MacGinley, Peter T.** 20th c.
[WWL]
*Irish author and playwright*
* MacFhionnlaoich, Peadar

**MacGlashan, Helen** ?-1969 [SC]
*American actress and screenwriter*
* Meredyth, Bess

**MacGregor, Alasdair Alpin [Douglas]**
1899-1970 [CA, CAP]
*Scottish journalist and poet*
* Featherstonehaugh, Francis

**MacGregor, Chummy**
*See* MacGregor, John Chalmers

**MacGregor, D. R.**
*See* MacGregor, David Roy

**MacGregor, David Roy** 1925-
[ART]
*British artist*
* MacGregor, D. R.

**MacGregor, Irvine T.** 1915- [ASC]
*Scottish-born musician*
* MacGregor, Scotty

**Macgregor, J.** 1797-1857 [PA]
*Author*
* South, Simeon

**MacGregor, Jack**
*See* MacElroy, Andrew Jackson

**MacGregor, James [Murdoch]**
1925- [AW, CA, WGT]
*Scottish author*
* Francis, Gregory [joint
  pseudonym with Frank Parnell]
* McIntosh, J. T.

**Macgregor, John** 1825-1892
[WBD]
*British author and canoe designer*
* Rob Roy

**MacGregor, John** 1848- ? [LAO]
*Scottish author*
* Ralph

**MacGregor, John Chalmers** 1903-
[ASC, EJ]
*American musician*
* MacGregor, Chummy

**Macgregor, Malcolm**
*See* Mason, William

**MacGregor, Mary**
*See* Jameson, Malcolm

**MacGregor, Sandy**
*See* White, John

**MacGregor, Scotty**
*See* MacGregor, Irvine T.

**MacGregory**
*See* Gregory, Malcolm

**MacGrian, Michael**
*See* West, Anthony C.

**MacGuire, Philip**
*See* Burton, Harry McGuire

**Machado, Paulo Sergio Mastrotti**
1947- [IAW]
*Brazilian author*
* Rocket, Captain

**Machado y Ruiz, Antonio**
1875-1939 [TLC]
*Spanish poet and playwright*
* Cabellera

**MacHale, John** [SN]
*Archbishop of Tuam*
* [The] Lion of the Fold of Judah

**Machan, Tibor R[ichard]** 1939-
[CA]
*Hungarian-born author and educator*
* Polony, Raymond

**Machaquito [Little Strong One]**
*See* Gonzalez y Madrid, Rafael

**MacHaye, Eric**
*See* Roche, Arthur Somers

**Machemer, David Ritchie** 1951-
[SMG]
*American baseball player*
* Machemer, Mac

**Machemer, Mac**
*See* Machemer, David Ritchie

**Machen, Arthur**
*See* Jones, Arthur Llewellyn

**[Der] Macher [The Doer]**
*See* Schmidt, Helmut

**Macher, Daniel J.** [FFF]
*Entertainer*
* Shelby, Daniel

**Macheside, Candia**
*See* Mario, Giuseppe

**Machiavelli**
*See* McCready, Warren T[homas]

**[A] Machiavelli**
*See* Necker, Jacques [or James]

**Machiavelli, Niccolo [or Nicholas]**
1469-1527 [HN, SN]
*Italian statesman and political philosopher*
* [The] Prince of Politicians
* [Il] Segretario

**[The] Machiavellian Belshazzar**
*See* Van Buren, Martin

**Machine Gun Butera**
*See* Butera, Lou

**Machine Gun Jack**
*See* De Mora, James Vincenzo

**Machine Gun Kelly**
*See* Kelly, George R.

**Machine, Mr.**
*See* Burton, Mike

**Machito**
*See* Grillo, Frank

**Machlin, Milton Robert** 1924-
[AW]
*American author*
* Jason, Wm.
* Roberts, McLean

**Machlis, Joseph** 1906- [AW]
*Latvian-born author*
* Selcamm, George

**Machol, Libby** 1916- [CA]
*American writer*
* MacCall, Libby

**MacHugh, Edward** 20th c.
*Singer*
* Your Gospel Singer

**Machuisdean, Hamish** 1883-
[WWL]
*Scottish author*
* Gates, Michael

**Maciarz, Joseph John** 1915- [BE]
*American baseball player*
* Mack, Joseph John [Joe]

**Macias, Raton**
*See* Macias, Raul

**Macias, Raul** 1934- [BX]
*Mexican boxer*
* Macias, Raton

**Macie, James Lewis [or Louis]**
1765-1829 [WBD]
*British chemist and mineralogist*
* Smithson, James

**Maciel, Judi[th Anne]** 1942- [CA]
*American educator and author*
* Stewart, Judith Anne

**MacInnes, Helen** 1907- [SAT]
*Scottish-born American author*
* Highet, Helen

**Macinnes, Tom** 1867- ? [WWL]
*Canadian author*
* Roy, Julien

**Macintosh, Edith Joan [Burbridge]**
1919- [WW]
*Author*
* Cockin, Joan

**MacIntosh, Peter** 1944- [IBW]
*Jamaican-born singer and musician*
* Tosh, Peter

**Macintyre, Duncan** [SN]
*Gaelic poet*
* [The] Fair Haired

**Macioci, Nicholas** 1935- [RO1]
*American musician*
* Massi, Nick

**Macip, Vicente Juan** 1500?-1579
[WBD]
*Spanish painter*
* De Juanes [or Joanes], Juan
* [The] Spanish Raphael

**MacIre, Esor B.**
*See* Ambrose, Eric [Samuel]

**Maciste**
*See* Pagano, Bartolomeo

**Maciulevicius-Maciulis, Jonas**
1862-1932 [EWL]
*Lithuanian author*
* Maironis

**MacIver, Muriel** 1888-1950   [BEW]
*Canadian-born actress*
* Starr, Muriel

**Mack**
See   McCullough, Joseph B.

**Mack**
See   Menchan, W. McKinley

**Mack, Andrew**
See   McAloon, William Andrew

**Mack, Billy**
See   McBride, William

**Mack, Brearley**
See   McCalment, Maebelle
[Brearley]

**Mack, Buck**
See   Mack, James

**Mack, Cecil**
See   McPherson, Richard C.

**Mack, Charles**
See   McGaughey, Charles

**Mack, Charles**
See   Sellers, Charles E.

**Mack, Claire** 1921?-1978   [FIR]
*Comedienne*
* Mack, Cookie

**Mack, Connie**
See   McGillicuddy, Cornelius
Alexander

**Mack, Cookie**
See   Mack, Claire

**Mack, Dennis Joseph [Denny]**
See   McCrohan, Dennis Joseph

**Mack, Earle Thaddeus**
See   McGillicuddy, Earle Thaddeus

**Mack, Edwin** 1946-   [RBE]
*Dutch boxer*
* Mack, Fighting

**Mack, Ernest**
See   Stone, Ernest

**Mack, Evalina**
See   McNamara, Lena Randolph
[Brooke]

**Mack, Fighting**
See   Mack, Edwin

**Mack, Frank George** 1900-   [BE]
*American baseball player*
* Mack, Stubby

**Mack, Hughie**
See   McGowan, Hugh

**Mack, James** ?-1959   [SC]
*American actor*
* Mack, Buck

**Mack, Jerry**
See   Johnson, Jerry Mack

**Mack, Joseph**
See   McNamara, Joseph

**Mack, Joseph John [Joe]**
See   Maciarz, Joseph John

**Mack, Kirby**
See   McEvoy, Harry K[irby]

**Mack, Lonnie**
See   McIntosh, Lonnie

**Mack, Maebelle**
See   McCalment, Maebelle
[Brearley]

**Mack, Marion**
See   Lewyn, Joey Marion

**Mack, Marjorie**
See   Dixon, Marjorie [Mack]

**Mack, Mrs. Will H.**   [FFF]
*Entertainer*
* Woodson, Kittie

**Mack, Nila**
See   MacLoughlin, Nila

**Mack, Noreen**
See   O'Flynn, Honoria

**Mack, Ray**
See   Mlckovsky, Raymond James

**Mack, Reddy**
See   McNamara, Joseph

**Mack, Stubby**
See   Mack, Frank George

**Mack the Knife**
See   Jones, Mack

**Mack the Knife**
See   Mouskos, Mikhail

**Mack, Warner**
See   McPherson, Warner

**Mack, Willard**
See   McLaughlin, Charles W.

**Mackail, J. W.**
See   Mackail, John William

**Mackail, John William** 1859-1945
[LC]
*Scottish educator and author*
* Mackail, J. W.

**Mackarness, Mrs. M. A.**   [PA]
*Author*
* Planche, Miss

**MacKay, Baldy**
See   MacKay, Calum

**MacKay, Calum** 1927-   [CEI]
*Canadian-born hockey player*
* MacKay, Baldy

**Mackay, Charles** 1812- ?   [PA]
*Author*
* Wagstaffe, Launcelot, Jr.

**MacKay, Duncan McMillan**
1894?-1943?   [CEI, FHE, HK]
*Canadian-born hockey player*
* MacKay, Mickey
* [The] Wee Scot

**Mackay, Elsie** ?-1928   [BF]
*Scottish-born actress*
* Wyndham, Poppy

**Mackay, James [Alexander]** 1936-
[CA, WD]
*Scottish writer and translator*
* Angus, Ian
* Finlay, William
* Garden, Bruce
* Whittington, Peter

**Mackay, Lewis Hugh** 1897-
[SFL, WGT]
*Author*
* Matheson, Hugh

**Mackay, Mary** 1855-1924
[B10, LC, TC]
*British author and musician*
* Corelli, Marie

**MacKay, Mickey**
See   MacKay, Duncan McMillan

**Mackay, Miss**   [PA]
*Author*
* Dods, Jeanie

**Mackay, Mrs. John A.**   [FFF]
*Entertainer*
* Bennett, Lavinia

**Mackay, Rita Eleanore** 1928-
[BEW]
*American actress*
* Gam, Rita

**Mackaye, Alberigh** 1849-1881
[FFF]
*British author*
* Ali Baba

**MacKeever, Maggie**
See   Clark, Gail

**MacKellar, Billie**
See   MacKellar, Lillian

**MacKellar, Lillian** 20th c.   [BBH]
*New Zealand-born swimmer and
coach*
* MacKellar, Billie

**MacKellar, Thomas** 1812- ?   [PA]
*Author*
* Tam

**Mackelworth, R. W.**
See   Mackelworth, Ronald Walter

**Mackelworth, Ronald Walter**
1930-   [SF]
*British author*
* Mackelworth, R. W.

**Mackendrick, Alexander** 1912-
[FC]
*American-born director*
* Mackendrick, Sandy

**Mackendrick, Sandy**
See   Mackendrick, Alexander

**MacKendrick, William Gordon** 1864-
?   [NAA]
*Canadian author*
* [The] Roadbuilder

**MacKenna, Kenneth**
See   Mielziner, Leo, Jr.

**Mackenzie, Alexander Slidell**
See   Slidell, Alexander

**Mackenzie, Bloody**
See   Mackenzie, [Sir] George

**Mackenzie, Compton**
See   Compton, [Sir] Edward
Montagu

**Mackenzie, Edward** 1854-1918
[BEW]
*British-born actor and producer*
* Compton, Edward

**Mackenzie, Francis Sidney**
1885-1964   [BEW]
*British actor*
* Compton, Francis

**Mackenzie, G. A.**   [FFF]
*Canadian writer*
* Dale, Ellis

**Mackenzie, [Sir] George**
1636-1691   [SN, WBD]
*Scottish attorney and author*
* Mackenzie, Bloody
* [The] Noble Wit of Scotland

**Mackenzie, H. H.** ?-1916   [BEW]
*Producer and actor*
* Morrell, H. H.

**Mackenzie, H. Millicent** 1863- ?
[WWL]
*British educator and author*
* H. M. K.

**Mackenzie, Henry** 1745-1831
[DNNS, DEL, PA]
*Scottish author*
* [The] Addison of the North
* H. M. K.
* [The] Man of Feeling

**MacKenzie, Joan** 1925-   [AW, CA]
*Canadian author and poet*
* Bedard, Michelle
* Finnigan, Joan

**Mackenzie, K. R. H.**   [PA]
*Author*
* Cryptonymus

**Mackenzie, Kenneth** 1913-1955
[TCL]
*Australian author and poet*
* Mackenzie, Seaforth

**Mackenzie, R. Shelton** 1809-1881
[PA]
*Author*
* Littlejohn
* Sholto

**MacKenzie, Rhoda Elizabeth**
1939?-   [CW]
*Jamaican poet*
* Auntie Lizzie

**MacKenzie, Robert**   [SMG]
*American football coach*
* MacKenzie, Sarge

**MacKenzie, Sarge**
See   MacKenzie, Robert

**Mackenzie, Seaforth**
See   Mackenzie, Kenneth

**Mackenzie, [Dr.] Willard**
See   Stratemeyer, Edward L.

**Mackey, Biz**
See   Mackey, Raleigh

**Mackey, Charles** 1812- ?   [PA]
*Author*
* Grimbosh, Herman

**Mackey, Ernan**
See   McInerny, Ralph

**Mackey, Guy** ?-1971   [BBH]
*American collegiate athletic director*
* Mackey, Red

**Mackey, Mrs. F. A.**   [FFF]
*Entertainer*
* Sylvester, Louise

**Mackey, Raleigh** 1897-   [MK]
*American baseball player*
* Mackey, Biz

**Mackey, Red**
See   Mackey, Guy

**Mackie, Albert D[avid]** 1904-
[AW, CAP, WD]
*Scottish poet and playwright*
* MacNib

**Mackie, Bert**
See Mackie, Robert James

**Mackie, Frank** 1904-1969 [NOJ]
*American jazz musician*
* Mackie, Red

**Mackie, George** 1920- [ART]
*Scottish graphic artist*
* G. M.

**Mackie, Maron**
See McNeely, Jeannette

**Mackie, Pauline Bradford**
See Hopkins, Pauline Mackie

**Mackie, Red**
See Mackie, Frank

**Mackie, Robert James** 1893-1967
[SC]
*American actor*
* Mackie, Bert

**Mackie, S. G.**
See Mackie, Sheila Gertrude

**Mackie, Sheila Gertrude** 1928-
[ART]
*British artist*
* Mackie, S. G.

**Mackin, Anita**
See Donson, Cyril

**Mackinlay, Leila Antoinette Sterling**
1910- [CAP, WD]
*British author*
* Grey, Brenda

**Mackinlock, Duncan**
See Watts, Peter Christopher

**MacKinnon, Charles Roy** 1924-
[AW, CA, IAW]
*Scottish-born author*
* Conte, Charles
* Donald, Vivian
* MacAlpin, Rory
* Montrose, Graham
* Rose, Hilary
* Stuart, Charles
* Torr, Iain

**Mackintosh, Craig M.** 20th c.
[ESF]
*Author*
* Craig, Brian [joint pseudonym
  with Brian M(ichael) Stableford]

**Mackintosh, Elizabeth** 1896-1952
[BEW, CC, EMD]
*Scottish-born playwright and author*
* Daviot, Gordon
* Tey, Josephine

**Mackintosh, [Sir] James**
1765-1832 [SN]
*Scottish philosopher and historian*
* [The] Apostate

**Mackintosh, Kevin Scott** 1957-
[DC]
*British cricketer*
* Mackintosh, Mac
* Mackintosh, Toffo

**Mackintosh, Mac**
See Mackintosh, Kevin Scott

**Mackintosh, Toffo**
See Mackintosh, Kevin Scott

**Mackle, Jeff**
See McLeod, John F[reeland]

**Macklem, Friday**
See Macklem, Roy

**Macklem, Roy** 20th c. [SMG]
*American football team staff
member*
* Macklem, Friday

**Macklin, Charles**
See MacLaughlin, Charles

**MacKnight, Ninon** 1908-
[IBY, ICB]
*Australian-born illustrator*
* Ninon

**Macksey, [Major] K. J.**
See Macksey, Kenneth J.

**Macksey, Kenneth J.** 1923- [CA]
*British author and editor*
* Macksey, [Major] K. J.

**Mackworth**
See Rhondda, [Viscountess]
Margaret Haig

**Mackworth, Cecily** 1911- [CAT]
*Welsh-born author and columnist*
* Rhiannon

**MacLachlan, Kenneth D.**
1902-1972 [SC]
*Canadian-born actor and stunt
performer*
* Duncan, Keene

**Maclagan, Bridget**
See Borden, Mary

**Maclagan, Dorothea F.** 1895-
[ART]
*British painter*
* D. F. M.

**MacLaine, Shirley**
See Beaty, Shirley Maclean

**MacLane, Armand Ralph**
See McLane, Armand Ralph

**MacLaren, Gordon**
See Patten, William George

**Maclaren, Ian**
See Watson, John

**MacLaren, James**
See Grieve, Christopher Murray

**MacLaughlin, Charles** 1690-1797
[RH]
*British actor*
* Macklin, Charles

**MacLaurin, Constance** 1914-1969
[SC]
*Scottish-born actress*
* Lorne, Constance

**MacLean, Alistair [Stuart]** 1922-
[CA, WD, WWS]
*Scottish author*
* Stuart, Ian

**MacLean, Art**
See Shirreffs, Gordon D[onald]

**Maclean, Arthur**
See Tubb, Edwin Charles

**MacLean, Arthur George** 20th c.
[MBF]
*British author*
* Kirby, Arthur

**Maclean, Christina**
See Casement, Christina

**MacLean, Katherine** 1925-
[CA, ESF]
*American author*
* Dye, Charles

**MacLean, Katherine** (Continued)
* Morris, G. A.

**MacLean, R. D.**
See MacLean, Rezin Donald

**MacLean, Rezin Donald**
1859-1948 [SC]
*American actor and director*
* MacLean, R. D.

**Maclehose, Agnes** 1759-1841
[DEL, RH, SN]
*Corresponded with Scottish poet,
Robert Burns*
* Clarinda

**MacLennan, Harry** 1870-1950
[BMH, IPA]
*Scottish singer*
* [The] Laird of the Halls
* Lauder, Harry

**MacLeod, Charlotte [Matilda
Hughes]** 1922- [CA]
*Canadian-born author*
* Hughes, Matilda

**MacLeod, Ellen Jane** 1916-
[AW, SAT, WD]
*Scottish-born author and playwright*
* Anderson, Ella

**Macleod, Fiona**
See Sharp, William

**Macleod, Jean Sutherland** 1908-
[AW, CA]
*Scottish author*
* Airlie, Catherine

**Macleod, Joseph [Todd Gordon]**
1903- [CA, WD]
*British author, poet, playwright*
* Drinan, Adam

**MacLeod, Robert**
See Knox, William [Bill]

**MacLeod, Robert F.** 1917- [CA]
*American publisher and illustrator*
* MacDougall, Fiona

**MacLeod, Ruth** 1903- [CA]
*American author*
* Lowry, Nan

**MacLiammoir, Micheal**
See Willmore, Alfred

**Maclise, Daniel** 1811?-1870
[FFF, PA, WBD]
*Irish painter*
* Croquis, Alfred

**Macliver, Colin** 1792-1863 [WBD]
*British army officer*
* Campbell, [Sir] Colin

**MacLoughlin, Nila** 1891?-1953
[BEW]
*American actress, writer, producer*
* Mack, Nila

**Maclure, William** 1763-1840
[FFF]
*American geologist*
* [The] Father of American
  Geology

**MacMahon, Marie Edme Patrice
Maurice de** 1808-1893
[DEP, DHA]
*French president*
* [La] Loyale Epee [The Loyal
  Sword]

**MacMahon, Paul** 1924- [FC]
*American dancer*
* Gilbert, Paul

**MacMahon, Robert Carrier** 1924-
*American-born restaurateur*
* Carrier, Robert

**Macmann, Elaine**
See Willoughby, Elaine Macmann

**MacManus, James**
See MacManus, Seumas

**MacManus, Seumas** 1869-1960
[CA]
*Irish author, playwright, poet*
* Mac
* MacManus, James

**MacMillan, Annabelle**
See Quick, Annabelle

**Macmillan, Douglas** 1884- [WWL]
*British author*
* Cary, D. M.

**Macmillan, Georgina Fitzgerald** 20th
c. [WWL]
*British author*
* Fitzgerald, Ena

**Macmillan, Harold** 1894- [NN]
*British prime minister*
* Mac the Knife
* Supermac

**MacMillan, Mac**
See MacMillan, William Stewart

**MacMillan, William Stewart**
1943- [SMG]
*Canadian-born hockey player*
* MacMillan, Mac
* MacMillan, Yaky

**MacMillan, Yaky**
See MacMillan, William Stewart

**MacMullan, Charles Walden
Kirkpatrick** 1889-1973 [LAO, LC]
*Irish-born playwright*
* Munro, C[harles] K[irkpatrick]

**Macmurchada, Diarmaid**
See MacMurrough, Dermot

**MacMurray, John** 1745-1793
[WBD]
*British publisher*
* Murray, John

**MacMurrough, Dermot**
1110?-1171 [HN, WBD]
*King of Leinster*
* [The] Foreigners' Friend
* Macmurchada, Diarmaid

**MacNab, Barney**
See MacNab, L. B.

**MacNab, L. B.** 1902-1968 [BBH]
*American ski patrol founder*
* MacNab, Barney

**MacNamara, Brinsley**
See Weldon, John

**MacNamara, Gerald**
See Morrow, Harry C.

**MacNeal, F. A.**
See MacNeal, Frank Ashby

**MacNeal, Frank Ashby** 1867-1918
[SC]
*American actor*
* MacNeal, F. A.

**MacNee, Patrick**
See Leslie, Peter

**MacNeice, [Frederick] Louis**
1907-1963 [CA, LC, TC]
*Irish poet*
* Malone, Louis

**MacNeil, Al**
See MacNeil, Allister Wences

**MacNeil, Allister Wences** 1935-
[FHE, HK]
*Canadian-born hockey player and coach*
* MacNeil, Al

**MacNeil, Duncan**
See McCutchan, Philip [Donald]

**MacNeil, Neil**
See Ballard, [Willis] Todhunter

**MacNeill, Dand**
See Fraser, George MacDonald

**Macneill, Janet**
See McNeely, Jeannette

**MacNell, James**
See Macdonnell, James Edmond

**MacNib**
See Mackie, Albert D[avid]

**Macnie, John** 1836-1909
[ESF, SFL, WGT]
*American author*
* Thiusen, Ismar

**Macnish, Robert** 1802-1837
[FFF, PA]
*Scottish author and physician*
* Modern Pythagorean

**Macomber, Daria**
See Robinson, Patricia Colbert

**Macomber, George** 1927- [BBH]
*American skier*
* [The] Cat

**Macon, David Harrison** 1870-1952
[CME, ECM, DAM]
*American country-western performer*
* [The] Dixie Dew Drop
* [The] Grand Old Man
* King of the Banjo Players
* King of the Hillbillies
* Macon, Uncle Dave

**Macon, John Wesley** 1923-1973
[BWW]
*American singer*
* Shortstuff, Mr.

**Macon, Uncle Dave**
See Macon, David Harrison

**MacOrlan, Pierre**
See Dumarchais, Pierre MacOrlan

**Macouba, Auguste**
See Armeth, Auguste

**MacPatterson, F.**
See Ernsting, Walter

**MacPeek, Walter G.** 1902-1973
[CAP, NAA, SAT]
*American author and editor*
* Jumpp, Hugo

**MacPhail, James A.** 20th c. [WW]
*Author*
* Crockett, James [joint pseudonym with Cornelia Warriner]

**MacPhail, Larry**
See MacPhail, Leland Stanford

**MacPhail, Leland Stanford** 1890-
[PB]
*American baseball executive*
* MacPhail, Larry

**MacPhee, Waddy**
See MacPhee, Walter Scott

**MacPhee, Walter Scott** 1899- [BE]
*American baseball player*
* MacPhee, Waddy

**MacPherson, Bruce Ian** 1954-
[SMG]
*American baseball player*
* MacPherson, Mac

**MacPherson, Bud**
See MacPherson, James Albert

**MacPherson, George Gordon**
1910- [ART]
*British sculptor and painter*
* M.

**Macpherson, Ian**
See Macpherson, John Cook

**Macpherson, James** 1738-1796
[PA]
*Author*
* Ossian

**MacPherson, James Albert** 1927-
[CEI]
*Canadian-born hockey player*
* MacPherson, Bud

**Macpherson, Jessie Ingram** 1893-
[AW]
*Scottish-born author*
* Kennie, Jessie

**Macpherson, John Cook** 20th c.
[SFL]
*Author*
* Macpherson, Ian

**MacPherson, Mac**
See MacPherson, Bruce Ian

**Macpherson, Quinton** 1871?-1940
[BEW]
*Actor*
* Hymack, Mr.

**MacPherson, Thomas George**
1915- [CA]
*British-born author*
* Parsons, Tom

**MacPiarais, Padraic**
See Pearse, Patrick Henry

**MacQueen, James William** 1900-
[WW]
*Author*
* Edwards, James G.
* McHugh, Jay

**Macrabin, Mark**
See Cunningham, Allan

**Macrae, Arthur**
See Schroepfer, Arthur

**MacRae, Donald G.** 1921- [CA]
*Scottish-born sociologist and author*
* Campbell, Clive

**Macrae, Hawk**
See Barker, Albert W.

**Macrae, Herbert**
See Fearn, C. Eaton

**MacRae, Travis**
See Feagles, Anita MacRae

**Macready, William Charles**
1793-1873 [SN]
*British actor*
* [The] King Arthur of the Stage

**Macrembolites**
See Eustathius [or Eumathius]

**Macri, Teresa [or Theresa]**
1797?-1876 [DNNS, SN]
*Friend of British poet, George Gordon Byron*
* [The] Maid of Athens

**Macrinus [or Salmon?], Jean**
1490-1557 [DEP, FFF, SN]
*French poet*
* [The] French Horace
* [The] Horace of France

**Macropedius, Georgius** ?-1558
[PA]
*Author*
* Langeveld

**MacSarin, Kenneth**
See Sarin, Max Kenneth

**Macswell**
See Russ, W. L.

**MacThomais, Ruaraidh**
See Thomson, Derick Smith

**MacTyre, Paul**
See Adam, Robert James

**Macullar, James F.** 1855-1924
[BE]
*American baseball player*
* Macullar, Little Mac

**Macullar, Little Mac**
See Macullar, James F.

**Macumber, Mari**
See Sandoz, Mari [Susette]

**Macurdy, John**
See McCurdy, John Edward

**MacVean, Phyllis** 1892- [WWL]
*British author*
* Hambledon, Phyllis

**MacVeigh, Sue**
See Nearing, Elizabeth [Custer]

**MacVicar, Martha** 1925-1971
[FC]
*American actress*
* Vickers, Martha

**MacWherter, Rod**
See McWherter, Rodney

**Macy, Dora**
See Oursler, Grace Perkins

**Mad Anthony Wayne**
See Wayne, Anthony

**Mad Bell**
See Lauchlan, Isabel

**[The] Mad Bomber**
See Fuqua, Richard

**[The] Mad Bomber**
See Longley, Clint

**[The] Mad Caliph**
See Hakim, al-

**[The] Mad Cavalier**
See Rupert

**[The] Mad Cornarus**
See Cornarus, John

**[The] Mad Diarist**
See Mew, Thomas Joseph, III
[Tommy]

**[The] Mad Dog**
See Tracy, Harry

**Mad Dog Carter**
See Carter, Fred

**Mad Dog Coll**
See Coll, Vincent

**Mad Dog Garner**
See Garner, Gary

**Mad Dog Manders**
See Manders, Dave

**Mad Dog Mandich**
See Mandich, Jim

**Mad Dog O'Billovich**
See O'Billovich, Jack

**Mad Dog Ross**
See Ross, Edgar

**Mad Dog Sanders**
See Sanders, Clarence

**Mad Dog White**
See White, Dwight

**[The] Mad Duck**
See Karras, Alex[ander G.]

**[The] Mad Hatter**
See Anastasia, Albert

**[The] Mad Hungarian**
See Hrabosky, Alan Thomas

**Mad Jack**
See Percival, John

**[The] Mad King of Lacedaemon**
See Cleomenes

**Mad Mab Barnet**
See Barnet, Charles Daly [Charlie]

**Mad Mad Joe Califano**
See Califano, Joseph Anthony, Jr.

**Mad Man**
See Rabelais, Francois

**Mad Marshall Goldberg**
See Goldberg, Marshall

**Mad Mike Calvert**
See Calvert, Michael

**[The] Mad Monk**
See Meyer, Russell Charles

**[The] Mad Monk**
See Rasputin, Grigori Efimovich

**[The] Mad Mullah**
See Bordino, Pietro

**[The] Mad Mullah**
See Mohammed ibn-Abdullah

**[The] Mad Parson**
See Swift, Jonathan

**[The] Mad Poet**
See Clarke [or Clark?], McDonald

**[The] Mad Poet**
See Lee, Nathaniel

**[The] Mad Priest of Kent**
See Ball, John

**[The] Mad Programmer**
See Antonowsky, Marvin

**[The] Mad Queen**
See Juana [Joanna or Jane]

**[The] Mad Russian**
See Gordon, Bert

**[The] Mad Russian**
See Novikoff, Lou[is Alexander]

**[The] Mad Russian**
See Vucerovich, William

**[The] Mad Socrates**
See Diogenes

**[The] Mad Stork**
See Hendricks, Ted

**Mada**
See Clark, Mary L.

**Madame Jenny**
See Sacerdote, Jenny

**Madame Queen**
See Randolph, Lillian

**Madame Simone**
See Benda, Simone

**Madame Spivy**
See Le Voe, Spivy

**Madau, Antonio** 1931- [OP]
*Italian opera producer, set designer, author*
* Madau Diaz, Antonello

**Madau Diaz, Antonello**
See Madau, Antonio

**Madcap Maxie Baer**
See Baer, Max[imilian Adelbert]

**[The] Madcap Princess of Monaco**
See Charlotte

**Madden, Bunny**
See Madden, Thomas J.

**Madden, Daniel Owen** 19th c. [PA]
*Author*
* North, Darby

**Madden, [Jerry] David** 1933- [CN]
*American author*
* Travis, Jack

**Madden, Dick**
See Sellers, Connie Leslie, Jr.

**Madden, [Sir] Frederick** 1801-1873
[PA]
*Author*
* F. M.

**Madden, Kid**
See Madden, Michael Joseph

**Madden, Lefty**
See Madden, Leonard Joseph
[Len]

**Madden, Leonard Joseph [Len]**
1890-1949 [BE]
*American baseball player*
* Madden, Lefty

**Madden, M. A.**
See Sadlier, Mary Anne

**Madden, Michael Joseph**
1866-1896 [BE]
*American baseball player*
* Madden, Kid

**Madden, Owen** 1892-1964
[BLB, MM]
*British-born American murderer and bootlegger*
* [The] Killer

**Madden, Owen** (Continued)
* Madden, Owney

**Madden, Owney**
See Madden, Owen

**Madden, T. E.** 20th c. [WWL]
*British author and journalist*
* Field Officer

**Madden, Thomas J.** 1884- [BE]
*American baseball player*
* Madden, Bunny

**Madden, Warren**
See Cameron, Kenneth Neill

**Maddern, Al**
See Ellison, Harlan [Jay]

**Maddern, Minnie**
See White, Mrs. Legrand

**Maddigan, Gertie**
See Lodge, Mrs. Benjamin

**Maddison, Angela Mary** 1923-
[AW, CA, SAT]
*British author and illustrator*
* Banner, Angela

**Maddock, Larry**
See Jardine, Jack Owen

**Maddock, Mrs. E. A.** 19th c. [PA]
*Author*
* E. A. M.

**Maddock, Stephen**
See Walsh, James Morgan

**Maddocks**
See Greenall, Jack

**Maddox, Buggy Whip**
See Maddox, Garry Lee

**Maddox, Carl**
See Tubb, Edwin Charles

**Maddox, Claude**
See Moore, J. E.

**Maddox, Garry Lee** 1949- [PB]
*American baseball player*
* Maddox, Buggy Whip

**Maddox, Lester**
See Hauss, Len

**Maddox, Max**
See Jeans, Herbert

**Maddox, May** 1877-1938 [SC]
*American actress*
* Wallace, May

**Maddox, Rose**
See Brogdon, Roseea Arbana

**Maddux, Rachel**
See Baker, Rachel Maddux

**Madeira, Antonio** 1905- [EWL]
*Portuguese poet, author, playwright*
* Branquinho Da Fonseca, Antonio Jose

**Madeleine** [code name used during World War II]
See Khan, Noor Inayat

**Madeleva, [Sister] M.**
See Wolff, Mary Evaline

**Mademoiselle**
See Orleans, Anne Marie Louise d'

**Mademoiselle Judith**
See Bernat, Julie

**Madetoja, Onerva** 1882- ? [WBD]
*Finnish author and poet*
* O'nerva, L.

**Madgett, Naomi Long** 1923- [CA]
*American author*
* Long, Naomi Cornelia
* Witherspoon, Naomi Long

**Madhavikutty**
See Das, Kamala

**Madhubuti, Haki R.**
See Lee, Don[ald] L[uther]

**Madiana**
See Ricord, J. B.

**Madigan, Anthony J.** 1868-1954
[BE]
*American baseball player*
* Madigan, Pony

**Madigan, Connie**
See Madigan, Cornelius Dennis

**Madigan, Cornelius Dennis** 1934-
[CEI]
*Canadian-born hockey player*
* Madigan, Connie

**Madigan, Edward P.** 1896?-1966
[AS, FB]
*American football coach*
* Madigan, Slip

**Madigan, Mrs. H. P.** [FFF]
*Entertainer*
* Yates, Mary E.

**Madigan, Pony**
See Madigan, Anthony J.

**Madigan, Slip**
See Madigan, Edward P.

**Madison, Frank**
See Hutchins, Francis Gilman

**Madison, Guy**
See Moseley, Robert

**Madison, Hank**
See Rowland, D[onald] S[ydney]

**Madison, James** 1751-1836 [FAP]
*American president*
* [The] Father of the Constitution
* [The] Sage of Montpelier

**Madison, James** 20th c. [NBB]
*American musician*
* Madison, Pee Wee

**Madison, Jane**
See Horne, Hugh Robert

**Madison, Joyce**
See Mintz, Joyce Lois

**Madison, Louis** 1899-1948
[EJ, WWJ]
*American jazz musician*
* Shots, Kid

**Madison, Marilyn**
See Picken, Mary Brooks

**Madison, Matilda**
See Denison, Mrs.

**Madison, Nat**
See Moscovitch, Nathaniel

**Madison, Noel**
See Moscovitch, Nathaniel

**Madison, Pee Wee**
See Madison, James

**Madison, Thomas A[lvin] [Tom]**
1926- [CA]
*American author*
* Campbell, Luke

**Madjeski, Ed[ward William]**
See Majewski, Edward William

**Madlee, Dorothy [Haynes]** 1917-
[CA]
*American author and journalist*
* Haynes, Anne
* Rogers, Wade

**Madlock, Bill, Jr.** 1951- [SMG]
*American baseball player*
* Madlock, Mad

**Madlock, Mad**
See Madlock, Bill, Jr.

**[The] Madman**
See Apollodorus

**[The] Madman**
See Sebastian

**[The] Madman of Donner Summitt**
See Buek, Richard

**[The] Madman of Halberstadt**
See Christian of Brunswick

**[The] Madman of the North**
See Charles XII

**Madonilla [or Madonella]**
See Astell, Mary

**[The] Madonna**
See Mary

**Madrid, Sal**
See Madrid, Salvador

**Madrid, Salvador** 1920- [BE]
*American baseball player*
* Madrid, Sal

**Madrilenito [Little Fellow from Madrid]**
See Diaz Cordero, Luis

**Madsen, Axel** 1930- [CA]
*Danish-born author and journalist*
* Brion, Guy

**Madsen, Carl** 20th c. [BBH, CSH]
*Canadian lacrosse player*
* Madsen, Gus

**Madsen, Gus**
See Madsen, Carl

**Madsen, Merdin Prince Gunnar**
1943- [RO2]
*Danish-born musician*
* Madsen, Mert

**Madsen, Mert**
See Madsen, Merdin Prince Gunnar

**Mae, Jimsey**
See Rawley, Charlotte

**[A] Maecenas**
See Blount, William [Fourth Baron Mountjoy]

**[A] Maecenas**
See Montagu, Charles [First Earl of Halifax]

**[The] Maecenas and Petronius of His Age**
See Stanhope, Philip

**[The] Maecenas of Book-Lovers**
See Grolier, Jean

[The] Maecenas of Danish Letters
See Rahbeck, Knud Lyne

[The] Maecenas of Embryo Players
See Hardham, John

[The] Maecenas of England
See Rogers, Samuel

[The] Maecenas of France
See Francis I or [Francois]

[The] Maecenas of His Day
See Mazarin, Jules

[The] Maecenas of His Time
See Visconti, Galeazzo II

[The] Maecenas of Shoemakers
See Lofft, Capel

Mael, Peter [joint pseudonym with
Charles Vincent]
See Causse, Charles

Mael, Peter [joint pseudonym with
Charles Causse]
See Vincent, Charles

[The] Maeonian Poet
See Homer

[The] Maeonian Swan
See Homer

Maeonides
See Homer

Maepen, Hugh
See Kuttner, Henry

Maepen, K. H.
See Kuttner, Henry

Maer, Stephen 1933- [ART]
British artist
* S. M.

Maera
See Garcia y Lopez, Manuel

Maerlant, Jakob 1235-1300
[DEP, DNNF, SN]
Belgian poet
* [The] Father of Dutch Poetry
* [The] Father of Flemish Poets

[El] Maestro [The Master]
See Dihogo, Martin

[Il] Maestro
See Fellini, Federico

[El] Maestro [The Teacher]
See Shoemaker, William [Willie]

[El] Maestro [The Master]
See Valdes, Angel

Maestro, Johnny
See Mastrangelo, Johnny

Maeterlinck, Georgette 1876-1941
[BEW]
French-born actress
* LeBlanc, Georgette

Maeterlinck, Maurice [Polydore
Marie Bernard] 1862-1949 [LC]
Belgian poet and playwright
* [The] Belgian Shakespeare

Maffei, Andrea [SN]
Italian author
* [The] Nestor of Modern Italian
Authors

Maga
See Blackwood, William

Magaddino, Stefano 1891- [BLB]
Italian-born American underworld
figure
* Magaddino, Steve

Magaddino, Steve
See Magaddino, Stefano

Magda F.
See Ferrer-Peralta, Magda

Magdalena
See Bay, Magdalena

Magdeleine
See Carbet, Marie-Magdalene

Magee, James 1929- [AW]
Irish author
* Taylor, John

Magee, Lee
See Hoernschemeyer, Leopold
Christopher

Magee, Leo Christopher
See Hoernschemeyer, Leopold
Christopher

Magee, Sherry
See Magee, Sherwood Robert

Magee, Sherwood Robert
1884-1929 [AS, BE]
American baseball player
* Magee, Sherry

Magee, William Kirkpatrick
1868-1961 [LC]
Irish author
* Eglinton, John

Maggio, Dante 20th c. [WF]
Italian actor
* May, Dan

Maghett, Sam[uel] 1937-1969
[BWW, DAM]
American singer
* Good Rocking Sam
* Magic Sam
* Magic Singing Sam

[The] Magic Lady
See Larsen, Geraldine

Magic, Mr.
See Monroe, Earl

Magic Sam
See Maghett, Sam[uel]

Magic Singing Sam
See Maghett, Sam[uel]

Magic Slim
See Holt, Morris

[The] Magician
See Abreu, Joseph Lawrence [Joe]

[The] Magician
See Briscoe, Marlin

[The] Magician
See Cawston, Mervyn

[The] Magician
See Peter Lee, Sidney

[The] Magician of the North
See Hamann, Johann Georg

[The] Magician of the North
See Scott, [Sir] Walter

Magill, Marcus [joint pseudonym
with Brian (Merrikin) Hill?]
See Giles, Joanna Elder

Magill, Marcus [joint pseudonym
with Joanna Elder Giles?]
See Hill, Brian [Merrikin]

Magill, Rory
See Faulkner, Dorothea M.

Maginn, William 1793-1842
[DEL, FFF, SN]
Irish author and journalist
* Bombardinio
* [The] Modern Rabelais
* Odoherty, [Sir] Morgan
* [The] Prince of Pedagogues

Magister Abstractionum
See De Mairone, Francois

Magister Contradictionis
See Grosseteste, Robert

Magister Contradictionum
See Wessel, Johann [or John]

Magister Islebius
See Sneider, Johannes

Magister, Joseph
See Goldberg, Louis T[heodore]

Magister, Juras
See Zagorski, Jerzy

Magister Scolarum
See Grosseteste, Robert

Magister Sententiarum
See Lombard, Peter [or Pietro]

Magito, Suria
See Saint Denis, Valia Maria
[Suria]

Magliabecchi, Antonio [or Anthony]
1633-1714 [RH, SN]
Florentine bibliophile
* [Il] Biblioteca Animata [The
Living Library]
* [The] Book Prodigy of His Age
* [Il] Divoratore de Libri [The
Devourer of Books]
* Helluo
* [The] Universal Index and Living
Cyclopaedia

Maglie, Salvatore Anthony 1917-
[BE, PB]
American baseball player
* [The] Barber
* Maglie, Sinister Sal
* [The] Renaissance Assassin

Maglie, Sinister Sal
See Maglie, Salvatore Anthony

Maglio, Paul
See DeLucia, Felice

Magliocco, Giuseppe ?-1963
[PHM]
Italian-born American underworld
figure
* Magliocco, Joseph

Magliocco, Joseph
See Magliocco, Giuseppe

Magloire, Auguste 1872-1948
[CW]
Haitian historian, journalist,
sociologist
* Fureteur, Jean Le

Magloire, Clement, fils 1912-1971
[CW]
Haitian poet and author
* Saint Aude, Magloire

Magloire, Francis L.
See Sejour-Magloire, Francis L.

Maglone, Barney
See Wilson, Robert A.

[El] Magnanimo
See Alfonso V [or Alphonso]

[The] Magnanimous
See Albert V [or Albrecht]

[The] Magnanimous
See Alfonso V [or Alphonso]

[The] Magnanimous
See John Frederick

[The] Magnanimous
See Khosru I [or Chosroes]

[The] Magnanimous
See Philip

[The] Magnanimous
See Philip II [or Philippe]

Magnasco, Alessandro 1667?-1749
[WBD]
Italian painter
* Lissandrino

Magner, Edmund Burke 1888-1956
[BE]
American baseball player
* Magner, Stubby

Magner, Stubby
See Magner, Edmund Burke

[The] Magnet
See Addy, Robert Edward [Bob]

[The] Magnetic Statesman
See Blaine, James Gillespie

Magnetica, Electra
See Fox, Hugh [Bernard, Jr.]

[The] Magnificent
See Alfonso III [or Alphonso]

[The] Magnificent
See Edmund I [or Eadmund]

[The] Magnificent
See George IV

[The] Magnificent
See Khosru I [or Chosroes]

[The] Magnificent
See Medici, Lorenzo de

[The] Magnificent
See Robert I

[The] Magnificent
See Suleiman II [or Soliman]

[The] Magnificent Heber
See Heber, Richard

[The] Magnificent Mongoose
See Wright, Archibald Lee

[The] Magnificent Vestvali
See Vestvali, Felicita

Magnin, Cyril 20th c.
American business executive
* San Francisco, Mr.

[EL] Magno
See Ferdinand I

Magnoeus
See Magnusson, Arne

Magnus
See Raviola, Antonio

**Magnus** [SN]
*Earl of Northumberland*
* Red Mane

**Magnus Eriksson**
*See* Magnus II

**Magnus, Gerald**
*See* Bowman, Gerald

**Magnus, John**
*See* Ellison, Harlan [Jay]

**Magnus, Jonas** 1583-1651 [PA]
*Author*
* Wexisnensis

**Magnus Ladulas [Barn Lock]**
*See* Magnus I

**Magnus, Philip**
*See* Magnus-Allcroft, [Sir] Philip [Montefiore]

**Magnus-Allcroft, [Sir] Philip [Montefiore]** 1906- [CAP]
*British author and editor*
* Magnus, Philip

**Magnus I** ?-1047 [DNNS, WBD]
*King of Norway and Denmark*
* [The] Good

**Magnus I** 1240-1290 [WBD]
*King of Sweden*
* Magnus Ladulas [Barn Lock]

**Magnus II** 1316-1374
[DNNS, WBD]
*King of Sweden*
* Magnus Eriksson
* Smek

**Magnus III** 1073-1103
[DNNS, WBD]
*King of Norway*
* Barefoot
* Barfod

**Magnus IV** 1115?-1139 [WBD]
*King of Norway*
* [The] Blind

**Magnus VI** 1238-1280
[DNNS, WBD]
*King of Norway*
* Lagaboeter [Reformer of the Laws]

**Magnusdottir, Magnea** 1930-
[IAW]
*Icelandic author*
* Kleifum, [Fra] Magnea

**Magnuson, Maggie**
*See* Magnuson, Warren G.

**Magnuson, Warren G.** 1905?-
*American politician*
* Magnuson, Maggie

**Magnusson, Arne** 1663-1730 [PA]
*Author*
* Magnoeus

**Magnusson, Guomundur**
1873-1918 [CD, EWL]
*Icelandic author and poet*
* Trausti, Jon

**[El] Mago [The Magician]**
*See* Gardes, Charles Romuald

**Magoogin**
*See* Jennings, John J.

**Magoon, Bob**
*See* Magoon, Eaton, Jr.

**Magoon, Carey** [joint pseudonym with Marian Austin (Waite) Magoon]
*See* Carey, Elisabeth

**Magoon, Carey** [joint pseudonym with Elisabeth Carey]
*See* Magoon, Marian Austin [Waite]

**Magoon, Eaton, Jr.** 1922- [ASC]
*American composer*
* Magoon, Bob

**Magoon, George Henry** 1875-1943
[BE]
*American baseball player*
* Magoon, Topsy

**Magoon, Marian Austin [Waite]**
1885- [WW]
*Author*
* Magoon, Carey [joint pseudonym with Elisabeth Carey]

**Magoon, Topsy**
*See* Magoon, George Henry

**Magor, W. L.**
*See* Magor, William Laurence

**Magor, William Laurence** 1913-
[ART]
*Welsh-born painter*
* Magor, W. L.

**Magpie**
*See* Webb, W. H.

**Magrath, E.** [PA]
*Author*
* E. M.

**Magraw, Beatrice Irene [May]**
1888- [AW]
*British author*
* Padeson, Mary

**Magraw, Lucy Cotton** 1891-1948
[SC]
*American actress*
* Cotton, Lucy

**Magriel, Paul** 1947?-
*Mathematician and backgammon player*
* [The] Human Computer
* X 22

**Magriska, Helene**
*See* Brockies, Enid Florence

**Magruder, Julia** 1854-1907 [FFF]
*American author*
* Kerr, Sherrill

**Magrum, Bud**
*See* Magrum, Francis

**Magrum, Francis** 1949- [SMG]
*American football player*
* Magrum, Bud

**Maguen, David**
*See* Markish, David

**Maguilevsky, Leonide** 1899- [FC]
*Russian producer and director*
* Moguy, Leonide

**Maguire, Anne**
*See* Munn, Meryl Lucile

**Maguire, Aunt**
*See* Berry, Frances Miriam

**Maguire, Francis** 1839- ?
[FFF, PA]
*Entertainer*
* Mayo, Frank

**Maguire, Little Tom**
*See* Maguire, Tom

**Maguire, Robert Augustine Joseph**
1898- [AW, CA]
*Irish-born author*
* Taaffe, Michael

**Maguire, Tom** 1869-1934 [SC]
*American actor*
* Maguire, Little Tom

**Magus aus dem Norden**
*See* Hamann, Johann Georg

**Magus of the North**
*See* Hamann, Johann Georg

**Mahaffey, Lee Roy** 1903-1969
[BE]
*American baseball player*
* Mahaffey, Popeye

**Mahaffey, Popeye**
*See* Mahaffey, Lee Roy

**Mahaffy-Wilson, Mary Ruth**
1902- [IAW]
*American columnist*
* Moms Musings

**Mahal, Taj**
*See* Fredricks, Henry Sainte Claire

**Mahan, Bull**
*See* Mahan, Larry

**Mahan, Edward W.** 1882- [FB]
*American football player*
* Mahan, Natick Eddie

**Mahan, Larry** 1943?- [B10, GW]
*American rodeo performer*
* Mahan, Bull

**Mahan, Natick Eddie**
*See* Mahan, Edward W.

**Mahan, Pat**
*See* Wheat, Patte

**Mahan, Patte Wheat**
*See* Wheat, Patte

**Maharg, S. A.**
*See* Graham, Angus A.

**[The] Mahatma**
*See* Rickey, [Wesley] Branch

**Mahavishnu**
*See* McLaughlin, John

**[The] Mahdi**
*See* Mohammed Ahmed

**Mahdi, Tarik Shakir**
*See* Audeh, Muhammad Daoud

**Maher, Beaver**
*See* Maher, Bruce D.

**Maher, Bruce D.** 1937- [FB]
*American football player*
* Maher, Beaver

**Maher, Ramona** 1934- [CA]
*American author*
* Mayer, Agatha

**Mahler-Kalkstein, Menaham** 1908-
[BBD]
*Israeli composer*
* Avidom, Menaham

**Mahmud** 971?-1030
[DNNS, WBD]
*Sultan of Ghazni*
* [The] Great
* [The] Idol Smasher

**Mahner-Mons, Hans** 20th c. [SFL]
*Author*
* Possendorf, Hans

**Mahon, Al[fred Gwin]** 1910- [BE]
*American baseball player*
* Mahon, Lefty

**Mahon, Charles James Patrick**
1800-1891 [DNNS, WBD]
*Irish politician and adventurer*
* [The] O'Gorman Mahon

**Mahon, Lefty**
*See* Mahon, Al[fred Gwin]

**Mahon, Natasha** 1917- [THR]
*Brazilian-born dancer and actress*
* Sokolova, Natasha

**Mahon, Tommy** 1880-1955
[BX, RBE]
*British boxer*
* Bowker, Joe

**Mahone, William** 1826-1895
[FFF, SN]
*American army officer*
* Hero of the Crater
* Skin and Bone

**Mahoney, Elizabeth** 1911- [AW]
*American author*
* Mara, Thalia

**Mahoney, Francis** 20th c. [SMG]
*American basketball player*
* Mahoney, Mo

**Mahoney, George W.** 1873-1940
[BE]
*American baseball player*
* Mahoney, Mike

**Mahoney, James Thomas** 1935-
[SMG]
*American baseball coach*
* Mahoney, Moe

**Mahoney, Jock**
*See* O'Mahoney, Jacques

**Mahoney, M. F.** [PA]
*Author*
* Stradling, Matthew

**Mahoney, Mike**
*See* Mahoney, George W.

**Mahoney, Mo**
*See* Mahoney, Francis

**Mahoney, Moe**
*See* Mahoney, James Thomas

**Mahony, Elizabeth Ann Katherine**
1857-1896 [BMH]
*Irish-born comedienne*
* Bellwood, Bessie

**Mahony, Elizabeth Winthrop**
1948- [CA, SAT]
*American editor and author*
* Winthrop, Elizabeth

**Mahony, Francis** 1804-1866
[DEL, PA]
*British journalist*
* Prout, Father
* Savonarola, Jeremy
* Yorke, Oliver, Esq.

**Mahony, Patrick** 1911- [CA]
*American author*
* O'Mahony, Patrick

**Mahovlich, Francis William [Frank]**
1938-   [HK, SMG]
*Canadian-born hockey player*
* [The] Big M

**Mahr, Curley**
See   Mahr, Herman Carl

**Mahr, Herman Carl** 1901-1964
[ASC, BEW]
*American composer and arranger*
* Mahr, Curley

**[The] Maid of Athens**
See   Macri, Teresa [or Theresa]

**[The] Maid of Bath**
See   Linley, Elizabeth Ann

**[The] Maid of Brittany**
See   Eleanor

**[The] Maid of Kent**
See   Bocher, Joan

**[The] Maid of Magic**
See   Thurston, Jane

**[The] Maid of Norway**
See   Margaret

**[The] Maid of Orleans**
See   Joan of Arc [or Jeanne d'Arc]

**[The] Maid of Saragossa [or Saragoza]**
See   Augustina

**Maida**
See   Crowe, Maida

**[The] Maiden**
See   Malcolm IV

**[The] Maiden King**
See   Malcolm IV

**[The] Maiden Queen**
See   Elizabeth I

**Maidoff, Ilka List**
See   List, Ilka Katherine

**Maier, Booby**
See   Maier, E.

**Maier, E.** 20th c.   [OET]
*Spanish tennis player*
* Maier, Booby

**Maigrot, Emile** 1889-1961   [WBD]
*French poet and author*
* Henriot, Emile

**Maik, Henri**
See   Hecht, Henri Joseph

**Mailho, Emil Pierre** 1909-   [BE]
*American baseball player*
* Mailho, Lefty

**Mailho, Lefty**
See   Mailho, Emil Pierre

**Maillart, Aime**
See   Maillart, Louis

**Maillart, Louis** 1817-1871   [WBD]
*French composer*
* Maillart, Aime

**Maillot, Antoine Francois**
1747-1814   [PA]
*Author*
* Eve

**Mails, Duster**
See   Mails, John Walter

**Mails, John Walter** 1895?-1974
[B10, BE, PB]
*American baseball player*
* [The] Great
* Mails, Duster

**Maimonides [or Moses ben Maimon]**
1135-1204   [DNNS, HN, RH]
*Spanish scholar, philosopher, author*
* [The] Great Eagle
* [The] Light of the Age
* [The] Light of the West
* Rambam

**Main, Alex**
See   Main, Miles Grant

**Main, Forrest Harry** 1922-   [BE]
*American baseball player*
* Main, Woody

**Main, Marjorie**
See   Krebs, Mary Tomlinson

**Main, Miles Grant** 1884-1965   [BE]
*American baseball player*
* Main, Alex

**Main, Woody**
See   Main, Forrest Harry

**Mainbocher**
See   Bocher, Main Rousseau

**Maine, Bruno**
See   Manninen, Bruno Jalmar

**Maine, C. E.**
See   McIlwain, David

**Maine, Charles Eric**
See   McIlwain, David

**Maine, David**
See   Avice, Claude

**Maine de Biran**
See   Gonthier de Biran, Marie
Francois Pierre

**Maine, Harry Carlton** 1899-
[NAA]
*American writer*
* Osofer, Phil

**Maine, Trevor**
See   Catherall, Arthur

**Mainhall, Mrs. Henry**   [FFF]
*Entertainer*
* Lewis, Jeffreys
* Virgil, Laura

**Mainprize, Don[ald Charles]** 1930-
[CA]
*American author*
* Rock, Richard

**Mainquene, Louise** 1885-   [THR]
*French actress*
* Sylvie, Louise

**Mains, Grasshopper**
See   Mains, Willard Eben

**Mains, Wee Willie**
See   Mains, Willard Eben

**Mains, Willard Eben** 1868-1923
[BN]
*American baseball player*
* Mains, Grasshopper
* Mains, Wee Willie

**Maintenon, Marquise de**
See   D'Aubigne, Francoise

**Mainwaring, Daniel** 1901?-1977
[CC, EMD, WW]
*American author and screenwriter*
* Homes, Geoffrey

**Maiorana, Victor E.** 1897-1964
[ASC]
*Italian-born musician*
* Lamont, Victor

**Mair, G. H.**
See   Mair, George Henry

**Mair, George Brown** 1914-
[AW, CA, WD]
*Scottish physician and author*
* Bok, Kooshti
* MacDouall, Robertson

**Mair, George Henry** 1887-1926
[LC]
*British author*
* Mair, G. H.

**Mair, Margaret**
See   Crompton, Margaret [Norah
Mair]

**Maironis**
See   Maciulevicius-Maciulis, Jonas

**Mais, S. P. B.**
See   Mais, Stuart Petre Brodie

**Mais, Stuart Petre Brodie** 1885-
[LC, TC]
*British author and radio broadcaster*
* Mais, S. P. B.

**Maisel, Flash**
See   Maisel, Frederick Charles

**Maisel, Frederick Charles**
1889-1967   [BE]
*American baseball player*
* Maisel, Flash
* Maisel, Fritz

**Maisel, Fritz**
See   Maisel, Frederick Charles

**Maisels, Maxine S.** 1939-   [CA]
*American author*
* Amishai-Maisels, Ziva

**Maisels, Misha** 20th c.   [CA]
*American author*
* Amishai, M. H.

**Maisky, Michael**
See   Maisky, Mischa

**Maisky, Mischa** 1948-   [IWM]
*Russian-born musician*
* Maisky, Michael

**Maison, Margaret M[ary Bowles]**
1920-   [CA]
*British author*
* Clare, Margaret

**[La] Maisonneuve**
See   Heroet, Antoine

**Maitland**
See   Bartlett, J.

**Maitland, E.**   [PA]
*Author*
* Ainslie, Herbert

**Maitland, Peter**
See   MacGillivray, James
Pittendrigh

**Maitland, Reginald T.** 20th c.
[EMD, SFP]
*Author*
* Scott, R. T. M.

**Maitland, Reginald T.** (Continued)
* Stockbridge, Grant [house
pseudonym]

**Maitland, Ruth**
See   Erskine, Ruth

**Maitland, T. G. Dowling** 20th c.
[MBF]
*British author*
* Chandos, Herbert
* Gale, H. Winter
* Monck, Tristam K.

**Maitland, Thomas**
See   Buchanan, Robert Williams

**Maitland, [Sir] Thomas**   [HN]
*Governor of the Ionian Islands*
* King Tom

**Maitland, William** 1528?-1573
[WBD]
*Scottish politician*
* Lethington, Secretary

**Maitre**
See   Des Essaut, M. Davrelle

**Maitre Adam**
See   Billaut, Adam

**Maizel, C. L.**
See   Maizel, Clarice Matthews

**Maizel, Clarice Matthews** 1919-
[CA]
*British author*
* Maizel, C. L.
* Maizel, Leah

**Maizel, Leah**
See   Maizel, Clarice Matthews

**Maj, M. A.**
See   Jacobson, Marcus A. I.

**Majeski, Heeney**
See   Majeski, Henry

**Majeski, Henry** 1916-   [BE]
*American baseball player*
* Majeski, Heeney

**Majeski, William [Bill]** 1927-   [CA]
*American author and playwright*
* Fredericks, Vic [house
pseudonym]

**Majewski, Edward William** 1909-
[BE]
*American baseball player*
* Madjeski, Ed[ward William]

**[The] Major**
See   Houk, Ralph George

**[The] Major**
See   Jackson, Robert R.

**[The] Major**
See   Poore, Benjamin Perley

**Major, Alan P[ercival]** 1929-   [CA]
*British author*
* John, Dane

**Major Bob**
See   Astles, Robert

**Major, Charles** 1856-1913   [WBD]
*American author*
* Caskoden, [Sir] Edwin

**Major, Dagney**
See   Major, J. D.

**Major, Geraldyn Hodges** 1894-
[CA]
*American author*
* Major, Gerri

**Major, Gerri**
*See* Major, Geraldyn Hodges

**Major, J. D.** 20th c.   [MBF]
*British author*
* Hayward, Dagney
* Major, Dagney

**Major, Jakab Gyula**
*See* Mayer, Jakab Gyula

**Major Mite**
*See* Howerton, Clarence

**Majorano, Gaetano** 1703-1783
[SN, WBD]
*Italian singer*
* Caffarelli
* [The] Insolent

**Majors, Lee**
*See* Yeary, Lee

**Majors, Simon**
*See* Fox, Gardner Francis

**Mak, Marii**
*See* Ferrari, Raquel

**Makanowitzky, Barbara**
*See* Norman, Barbara

**Makarios III**
*See* Mouskos, Mikhail

**Makary**
*See* Iranek-Osmecki, Kazimierz

**Makathini, Elijah**   [RBE]
*South African boxer*
* Makathini, Tap Tap

**Makathini, Tap Tap**
*See* Makathini, Elijah

**Makeles [The Butcher]**
*See* Leo I

**Makemson, Donald Emmet** 1915-
[CA]
*American historian and author*
* Worcester, Donald E[mmet]

**Makepeace, Joan**
*See* Joan

**[The] Maker of Champions**
*See* Cromwell, Dean

**Makgill, [Sir] George** 1868- ?
[WWL]
*British author*
* Grant, Francis
* Waite, Victor

**Maki, Chico**
*See* Maki, Ronald Patrick

**Maki, Ronald Patrick** 1939-
[CEI, FHE, HK]
*Canadian-born hockey player*
* Maki, Chico

**Makley, Charles** 20th c.   [BLB]
*American criminal*
* Makley, Fat Charley

**Makley, Fat Charley**
*See* Makley, Charles

**Makonnen, Ras Tafari** 1891-1975
[NN]
*Emperor of Ethiopia*
* Haile Selassie
* [The] Lion of Judah

**Makowicz, Adam**
*See* Matyszkowicz, Adam

**Makowsky, Harry Duquesne** 1923-
[EJS]
*French-born American baseball player*
* Markell, Duke
* Markell, Harry Duquesne

**Makumbi, Eseza** 20th c.   [IBW]
*Ugandan-born actress and educator*
* Makumbi, Esther

**Makumbi, Esther**
*See* Makumbi, Eseza

**Mal**
*See* Hancock, Malcolm

**Mala**
*See* Wise, Ray

**Mala, Yenomdrah**
*See* Byers, Charles Alma

**Malachi**
*See* Scott, [Sir] Walter

**Malacrida, Marchese** 1890-   [LAO]
*Italian-born author*
* Piermarini

**Malagrida**
*See* Petty, [Sir] William

**Malagrowther, Malachi**
*See* Scott, [Sir] Walter

**Malakoff**
*See* Johnson, Samuel

**Malakoff**
*See* Johnson, W. F.

**Malan, Adolph** 1910-   [BDW]
*South African fighter pilot*
* Malan, Sailor

**Malan, Cesar Jean Salomon**
1812-1894   [WBD]
*British scholar*
* Malan, Solomon Caesar

**Malan, Renato Marco** 1911-   [CA]
*Italian-born author*
* Mark Alan, Roy

**Malan, Sailor**
*See* Malan, Adolph

**Malan, Solomon Caesar**
*See* Malan, Cesar Jean Salomon

**Malaparte, Curzio**
*See* Suckert, Kurt Erich

**Malara**   [SN]
*Spanish poet*
* [The] Betisian Menander

**Malarcher, Cap**
*See* Malarcher, David Julius

**Malarcher, David Julius** 1894-
[MK]
*American baseball player*
* Malarcher, Cap
* Malarcher, Gentleman Dave

**Malarcher, Gentleman Dave**
*See* Malarcher, David Julius

**Malatesta, Guido** 20th c.   [FDG]
*Italian director*
* Read [or Reed?], James

**Malchus** 223- 304
[FFF, HN, WBD]
*Greek scholar*
* [The] Philosopher

**Malchus** (Continued)
* Porphyry

**Malcolm, Charles**
*See* Hincks, Cyril Malcolm

**Malcolm, Dan**
*See* Silverberg, Robert

**Malcolm, John**
*See* Uren, Malcolm John Leggoe

**Malcolm, Margaret**
*See* Kuether, Edith Lyman

**Malcolm X**
*See* Little, Malcolm

**Malcolm III** 1024-1093
[FFF, RH, SN]
*King of Scotland*
* Canmore
* Great Head

**Malcolm IV** 1141-1165
[DHA, FFF, SN]
*King of Scotland*
* [The] Maiden
* [The] Maiden King

**Malcolmson, Anne**
*See* Von Storch, Anne B.

**Malden, Henry** 19th c.   [PA]
*Author*
* Murray, Hamilton

**Malden, Karl**
*See* Sekulovich, Mladen

**Malden, R. H.**
*See* Malden, Richard Henry

**Malden, Richard Henry** 1879-1951
[HFF]
*British clergyman and author*
* Malden, R. H.

**Maldonado y Rodriguez, Edmundo**
1910-1964   [GS]
*Mexican bullfighter*
* Tato de Mexico [Lisper from Mexico]

**Malebranche, Nicolas** 1638-1715
[SN]
*French philosopher*
* [The] Plato of His Age

**Malefammi, Baron**
*See* Donati, Corso

**Malerich, Edward P.** 1940-
[CA, WD]
*American actor and author*
* Easton, Edward

**Malet, Lucas**
*See* Harrison, Mary St. Leger
[Kingsley]

**Malet, Oriel**
*See* Vaughan, Auriel Rosemary
Malet

**Malherbe, Francois de** 1555-1628
[SN]
*French poet*
* [The] Father of Modern French Poetry
* [The] Oracle of Good-Sense
* [The] Purist of Language

**Mali**
*See* Nair, V. Madhavan

**Maliades**
*See* Henry

**Malick, Terrence** 1943-   [CA]
*American screenwriter, producer, director*
* Whitney, David

**Malicky, Lillian Joyce** 1944-   [OP]
*American opera singer*
* Castle, Joyce

**[A] Malignant Plant**
*See* Philip IV [or Philippe]

**Malik, Abdul**
*See* De Coteau, Delano

**Malik, Michael Abdul**
*See* De Freitas, Michael

**Malik Shah** 11th c.   [WBD]
*Sultan of the Seljuk Turks*
* Jalal-al-Din [Majesty of Religion]

**Malin, Peter**
*See* Conner, [Patrick] Reardon

**Malinche**
*See* Marina, Dona Xaramillo

**Malinovsky, Alexander** 20th c.
[SFP]
*Author*
* Bogdanov, Alexander

**Malins, M. H.**
*See* Malins, Margery Helen

**Malins, Margery Helen** 20th c.
[ART]
*British painter and illustrator*
* Malins, M. H.

**Maliszewski, Miguel** 1948-   [AES]
*Argentinian-born soccer player*
* Maliszewski, Mike

**Maliszewski, Mike**
*See* Maliszewski, Miguel

**Malkoff, Buzz**
*See* Malkoff, Jay

**Malkoff, Jay** 20th c.   [SMG]
*American football team physician*
* Malkoff, Buzz

**[The] Mall of Italy**
*See* Hannibal

**Malla**
*See* Garcia y Diaz, Agustin

**Mallard, Bo**
*See* Mallard, Louis

**Mallard, Louis** 20th c.   [BBH]
*American basketball player and coach*
* Mallard, Bo

**Mallecho, Miching, Esq.**
*See* Shelley, Percy Bysshe

**Malleolus**
*See* Hammerlein, Felix

**Malleson, Lucy Beatrice**
1899-1973   [CA, CC, WW]
*British author*
* Egerton, Lucy
* Gilbert, Anthony
* Keith, J. Kilmeny
* Meredith, Anne

**Mallet, David**
*See* Malloch, David

**Malleus Arianorum**
*See* Hilary

**Malleus Hereticorum**
See   Ailly, Pierre d'

**Malleus Hereticorum**
See   Caster, Francois

**Malleus Hereticorum**
See   Heigerlin, Johannes

**Malleus Monachorum**
See   Cromwell, Thomas [Earl of Essex]

**Malleus Scotorum**
See   Edward I

**Malley, Ern** [joint pseudonym with Harold Stewart]
See   McAuley, James Phillip

**Malley, Ern** [joint pseudonym with James Phillip McAuley]
See   Stewart, Harold

**Malliard, Mlle.** 18th c.   [RH]
*French actress*
* [The] Goddess of Liberty

**Mallinson, Russell**
See   Stannard, Russell

**Mallison, William M.**   [FFF, PA]
*American writer*
* O'Pake

**Malloch, David** 1705-1765   [WBD]
*Scottish poet*
* Mallet, David

**Malloch, George Reston** 1875- ?
[WWL]
*British author, playwright, poet*
* Paulus, Jan

**Malloch, Peter**
See   Duncan, W[illiam] Murdoch

**Mallock, W. H.**
See   Mallock, William Hurrell

**Mallock, William Hurrell**
1849-1923   [LC]
*British author*
* Mallock, W. H.

**Mallon, Mary** ?-1938   [BL]
*American disease carrier*
* Typhoid Mary

**Mallonee, Ben**
See   Mallonee, Howard Bennett

**Mallonee, Howard Bennett** 1894-
[BE]
*American baseball player*
* Mallonee, Ben
* Mallonee, Lefty

**Mallonee, Lefty**
See   Mallonee, Howard Bennett

**Mallory, Boots**
See   Mallory, Patricia

**Mallory, James Baugh [Jim]** 1918-
[BE]
*American baseball player*
* Mallory, Sunny Jim

**Mallory, Mark**
See   Reynolds, Dallas McCord

**Mallory, Memphis Bill**
See   Mallory, William N.

**Mallory, Patricia** 1913?-1958
[BEW]
*American actress*
* Mallory, Boots

**Mallory, Sheldon** 1953-   [SMG]
*American baseball player*
* Mallory, Shell

**Mallory, Shell**
See   Mallory, Sheldon

**Mallory, Sunny Jim**
See   Mallory, James Baugh [Jim]

**Mallory, William N.** 1901-1945
[FB]
*American football player*
* Mallory, Memphis Bill

**Mallowan, A[gatha] C[hristie]**
See   Christie, Agatha [Mary Clarissa]

**Malloy, [Archibald] Alex[ander]**
1886-1961   [BE]
*American baseball player*
* Malloy, Lick

**Malloy, Durable Mike**
See   Malloy, Mike

**Malloy, John** 1888?-1940   [FC, SC]
*American actor*
* Wray, John

**Malloy, Lick**
See   Malloy, [Archibald] Alex[ander]

**Malloy, Mike** ?-1933   [CEC]
*American murder victim*
* Malloy, Durable Mike

**Malm, Margaretha**
See   Pettersson, H. Bertil N.

**Malmberg, Carl** 1904-   [CA, SAT]
*American author*
* Trent, Timothy

**Malmberg, Harry William** 1926-
[BE]
*American baseball player*
* Malmberg, Swede

**Malmberg, Swede**
See   Malmberg, Harry William

**Malmquist, Eve Theodor** 1915-
[IAW]
*Swedish educator and author*
* E. M.

**Malo, Gina**
See   Flynn, Janet

**Malone, Andrew E.**
See   Byrne, Laurence Patrick

**Malone, Art Lee** 20th c.
*American football player*
* Leroy from Eloy

**Malone, Carroll**
See   McBurney, M.

**Malone, Cement Head**
See   Malone, John F.

**Malone, Dorothy**
See   Maloney, Dorothy

**Malone, Elmer Taylor, Jr.** 1943-
[CA]
*American poet*
* Malone, Ted

**Malone, Ferguson G.** 1842-1905
[BE]
*American baseball player and manager*
* Malone, Fergy

**Malone, Fergy**
See   Malone, Ferguson G.

**Malone, John F.** 20th c.
*American FBI agent*
* Malone, Cement Head

**Malone, Lew[is Aloysius]**
1897-1973   [BE]
*American baseball player*
* Ryan, Lew

**Malone, Louis**
See   MacNeice, [Frederick] Louis

**Malone, Mervin Haskell** 1927-
[CWG]
*American country-western performer*
* Malone, Red

**Malone, Michael Francis** 1950-
[DC]
*Australian-born cricketer*
* Malone, Mick

**Malone, Mick**
See   Malone, Michael Francis

**Malone, Pat**
See   Malone, Perce Leigh

**Malone, Patricia**
See   Marsden-Clark, Patricia

**Malone, Perce Leigh** 1902-1943
[AS, BE, PB]
*American baseball player*
* Malone, Pat

**Malone, Percy Sylvester**
See   Caswell, Wilbur Larremore

**Malone, Pick**
See   Maloney, Andrew Pickens

**Malone, Red**
See   Malone, Mervin Haskell

**Malone, Ted**
See   Malone, Elmer Taylor, Jr.

**Malone, Ted**
See   Russell, Frank Alden

**Maloney, Andrew Pickens**
1893?-1962   [BEW]
*Theatrical performer*
* Malone, Pick

**Maloney, David Wilfred** 1956-
[SMG]
*Canadian-born hockey player*
* [The] Kid

**Maloney, Dorothy** 1925-
[BDF, FC, WEF]
*American actress*
* Malone, Dorothy

**Maloney, Francis [Joseph] T[erence]**
20th c.   [WGT]
*British author*
* Terry

**Maloney, Happy**
See   Maloney, Patrick

**Maloney, James Monte** 20th c.
[PMJ]
*American bandleader*
* Joy, Jimmy

**Maloney, Janette** 1905-   [THR]
*American-born actress and singer*
* Gilmore, Janette

**Maloney, Pat**
See   Markun, Patricia Maloney

**Maloney, Patrick** 20th c.   [BLB]
*American underworld figure*
* Maloney, Happy

**Maloney, Ralph Liston** 1927-1973
[CA]
*American author*
* Liston, Jack

**Maloney, Terry** 20th c.   [SFP]
*Author*
* Rubios, Jose

**Maloney, Tighe**
See   Macbeath, Innis [Stewart]

**Malossis, Auguste Paul Poulet**
[PA]
*Author*
* Rouillon, Paul

**Maloy, Biff**
See   Maloy, Paul Augustus

**Maloy, Paul Augustus** 1892-   [BE]
*American baseball player*
* Maloy, Biff

**Malpede, Karen**
See   Taylor, Karen Malpede

**Malpott, Virgule**
See   Ghnassia, Maurice [Jean-Henri]

**Malraux, [Georges-] Andre**
1901-1976   [CAP, EWL]
*French author*
* Berger, [Colonel] A.

**Malta, Alexander**
See   Lagger, Alexander

**Maltby, H. F.**
See   Maltby, Henry Francis

**Maltby, Henry Francis** 1880-1963
[LC]
*South African-born actor and playwright*
* Maltby, H. F.

**Malte-Brun [or Maltebrun], Conrad**
See   Bruun, Malte Conrad

**Malten, Therese**
See   Mueller, Therese

**Maltzan, Adolf Georg Otto von**
1877-1927   [WBD]
*German diplomat*
* Maltzan, Ago von

**Maltzan, Ago von**
See   Maltzan, Adolf Georg Otto von

**Maltzberger, Gordon Ralph**
1912-1974   [BE]
*American baseball player*
* Maltzberger, Maltzy

**Maltzberger, Maltzy**
See   Maltzberger, Gordon Ralph

**Malu**
See   Lubin, Maurice Alcibiade

**Malvern, Gladys** ?-1962   [CA]
*American author and actress*
* Corbin, Sabra Lee
* Von Klopp, Vahrah

**Malyon, Eily**
See   Lees-Craston, Eily Sophie

**Malzberg, Barry N[orman]** 1939-
[CA, SFL, SFP]
*American author*
* O'Donnell, K. M.

**Malzberg, Barry N[orman]**
(Continued)
* Schaefer, Robin

**Mama Can Can**
See Rainey, Gertrude Malissa Nix [Pridgett]

**Mama Cass**
See Cohen, Ellen Naomi

**Mama G.**
See Davis, Grania

**Mama Lu**
See Parks, Louise

**Mamalick, Gordon** 1931-	[IWM]
*Canadian musician*
* Mann, Gordie

**[The] Mama's Boy**
See Leiner, Benjamin

**[The] Mambo King**
See Prado, [Domase] Perez

**Mambrino**
See McKinney, H. D.

**Mamoun, al-** 786- 833	[SN]
*Seventh Caliph of Baghdad*
* [The] Augustus of Arabian Literature
* [The] Father of Arabic Literature

**[The] Man**
See Friedhofer, Hugo Wilhelm

**[The] Man**
See Morris, Steveland

**[The] Man**
See Musial, Stanislaus

**[The] Man about Town**
See Muldoon, William H.

**[The] Man from Missouri**
See Truman, Harry

**[The] Man from the North**
See Hobman, Joseph Burton

**Man in Claret**
See Gould, Edward Sherman

**[The] Man in the Brown Suit**
See Rupp, Adolph

**[The] Man in the Front-Row**
See Henderson, Henrietta

**[The] Man in the Green Suit**
See O'Doul, Francis Joseph [Frank]

**[The] Man in the Iron Mask?**
See Mattioli, Ercole Antonio

**[The] Man in the Velvet Suit**
See Williams, William Holt [Billy]

**[The] Man Milliner**
See Henry III [or Henri]

**Man Mountain Dean**
See Leavitt, Frank S.

**[The] Man Mountain of Professional Ball**
See Earp [or Earpe?], Francis

**Man o' War**
See Rice, Edgar Charles

**[The] Man of a Thousand Curves**
See Sain, John Franklin [Johnny]

**[The] Man of a Thousand Faces**
See Chaney, Alonso

**[The] Man of a Thousand Moves**
See Baylor, Elgin

**[The] Man of Bath**
See Allen, Ralph

**[The] Man of Blood**
See Charles I

**[The] Man of Blood**
See Simmons, Thomas

**[The] Man of Blood and Iron**
See Bismarck, Otto Eduard Leopold von

**[The] Man of Business**
See Decker, T.

**[The] Man of Business**
See Rathbone, William

**[The] Man of Chios**
See Homer

**[The] Man of December**
See Bonaparte, Charles Louis Napoleon

**[The] Man of Destiny**
See Bonaparte, Napoleon

**[The] Man of Destiny**
See Cleveland, [Stephen] Grover

**[The] Man of Feeling**
See Mackenzie, Henry

**[The] Man of Ghent**
See Guizot, M.

**[The] Man of God**
See Alexis [or Alexius]

**[The] Man of Great Heart**
See Hoover, Herbert Clark

**[The] Man of Independence**
See Truman, Harry

**[The] Man of One Thousand Voices**
See Chatton, Sydney

**[The] Man of Ross**
See Higginson, Stephen

**[The] Man of Ross**
See Kyrle, John

**[The] Man of Sedan**
See Bonaparte, Charles Louis Napoleon

**[The] Man of Sedition**
See Claude, Jean

**[The] Man of Silence**
See Bonaparte, Charles Louis Napoleon

**[The] Man of Sin**
See Cromwell, Oliver

**[The] Man of Steel**
See Zaleski, Anthony Florian

**[The] Man of the People**
See Fox, Charles James

**[The] Man of the People**
See Jefferson, Thomas

**[The] Man of the People**
See Lincoln, Abraham

**[The] Man of the Revolution**
See Adams, Samuel

**[The] Man of the Third Republic**
See Bonaparte, Charles Louis Napoleon

**[The] Man on Horseback**
See Boulanger, Georges Ernest Jean Marie

**[The] Man on Horseback**
See Roosevelt, Theodore [Teddy]

**[The] Man Salamander**
See Potter, Richard

**[The] Man to See**
See Rothstein, Arnold

**[The] Man Uptown**
See Rothstein, Arnold

**[The] Man Who Broke Purple**
See Friedman, William Frederic

**[The] Man Who Keeps his Eyes and Ears Open**
See Beecher, Henry Ward

**[The] Man Who Lit Up Broadway**
See Gaess, William C., Jr.

**[The] Man Who was a Private**
See Quincy, Samuel Miller

**[The] Man Who was Warned**
See Begbie, [Edward] Harold

**[The] Man with a Million Friends**
See Myrick, David Luke

**[The] Man with a Thousand Fingers**
See Hayes, Edgar Junius

**[The] Man with a Thousand Songs**
See Donovan, Tony

**[The] Man with a Thousand Voices**
See Graham, Frank

**[The] Man with a Thousand Voices**
See Masilongan, Christobal

**[The] Man with no Master but God**
See Delamarre, Victor

**[The] Man with the Funny Horn**
See Mosley, Lawrence Leo

**[The] Man with the Golden Arm**
See Davis, A. W.

**[The] Man with the Golden Gut**
See Silverman, Fred

**[The] Man with the Leather Breeches**
See Fox, George

**[The] Man with the Midas Touch**
See Rickard, George Lewis

**[The] Man with the Million Dollar Hands**
See Garcia, Frank

**[The] Man with the Sling**
See Randolph, John

**[The] Man without a Skin**
See Cumberland, Richard

**[A] Man without a Spleen**
See Chekhov, Anton [Pavlovich]

**Mana-Zucca**
See Zuckermann, Augusta

**Managing Clerk**
See Spero, Leopold

**[The] Manassa Mauler**
See Dempsey, William Harrison

**Manastersky, Timothy** 1929-	[CEI]
*Canadian-born hockey player*
* Manastersky, Tom

**Manastersky, Tom**
See Manastersky, Timothy

**Mance, Elizabeth Hope** 1883-
[WWL]
*British author*
* Hope, Elizabeth

**Mance, Julian Clifford, Jr.** 1928-
[DAM, EJ, PMJ]
*American jazz musician*
* Mance, Junior

**Mance, Junior**
See Mance, Julian Clifford, Jr.

**[El] Manchao [The Spotted One]**
See Parrondo, Tomas

**[El] Manchequito [The Little Fellow from La Mancha]**
See Martinez y Pingarron, Candido

**[A] Manchester Man**
See Lamb, J.

**[A] Manchester Manufacturer**
See Cobden, Richard

**[The] Manchester Poet**
See Swain, Charles

**[The] Manchester Prophet**
See Hall, Ellis

**Manchet, Eliane**
See Schaaf, Eliane

**Mancini, Boom Boom**
See Mancini, Lenny

**Mancini, Boom Boom**
See Mancini, Ray

**Mancini, Lenny** 20th c.
*American boxer*
* Mancini, Boom Boom

**Mancini, Ray** 1961?-
*American boxer*
* Mancini, Boom Boom

**Manco Capac** 1500?-1544	[WBD]
*Ruler of Peru*
* Manco Inca

**[El] Manco de Lapanto**
See Cervantes Saavedra, Miguel de

**Manco Inca**
See Manco Capac

**Mancuso, August Rodney** 1905-
[BE, PB]
*American baseball player*
* Mancuso, Blackie
* Mancuso, Gus

**Mancuso, Blackie**
See Mancuso, August Rodney

**Mancuso, Felix** 1913-	[CEI]
*Canadian-born hockey player*
* Mancuso, Gus

**Mancuso, Gus**
See Mancuso, August Rodney

**Mancuso, Gus**
See Mancuso, Felix

**Mancuso, Gus**
See Mancuso, Ronald Bernard

**Mancuso, Ronald Bernard** 1933-
[DAM, EJ]
*American jazz musician*
* Mancuso, Gus

**Mand, Cyril** [joint pseudonym with Richard Levin]
See   Hahn, George R.

**Mand, Cyril** [joint pseudonym with George R. Hahn]
See   Levin, Richard

**Mand [or Maend], Ewald [or Evald]** 1906-   [CA]
*Estonian-born clergyman and author*
* Kalmus, Ain

**Mandar, Michael Phillips** 1759-1823   [PA]
*Author*
* Theophile

**[The] Mandarin**
See   Navin, Frank

**Mandel, Georges**
See   Rothchild, Jeroboam

**Mandel, Joseph** 1880-1954 [BDF, FC, FD]
*Austrian-born director*
* May, Joe

**Mandel, Leon** 1928-   [CA]
*American author*
* Dalmas, John

**Mandelkorn, Eugenia Miller** 1916- [CA]
*American author*
* Miller, Eugenia

**Mandell, Sammy**
See   Mandella, Samuel R.

**Mandella, Samuel R.** 1904-1961? [BX, RBE, WBC]
*American boxer*
* Mandell, Sammy
* [The] Rockford Sheik

**Mander, Lionel** 1888-1946 [FI, FC, SC]
*British actor*
* Mander, Luther
* Mander, Miles
* Miles, Luther

**Mander, Luther**
See   Mander, Lionel

**Mander, Miles**
See   Mander, Lionel

**Manders, Automatic Jack**
See   Manders, John

**Manders, Dave** 20th c.
*American football player*
* Manders, Mad Dog

**Manders, Harry**
See   Farmer, Philip Jose

**Manders, John** 1910-   [FB]
*American football player*
* Manders, Automatic Jack

**Manders, Mad Dog**
See   Manders, Dave

**Mandeville, John**
See   Haines, E[dwin] Irvine

**Mandich, Jim** 1948-   [SMG]
*American football player*
* Mandich, Mad Dog

**Mandich, Mad Dog**
See   Mandich, Jim

**Mandot, Baker Boy**
See   Mandot, Joe

**Mandot, Joe** 1891-1956   [BX]
*American boxer*
* Mandot, Baker Boy

**Mandrake the Magician**
See   Mueller, Donald Frederick

**Mandrepelias, Loizos**
See   Hartocollis, Peter

**Manera, Jesus Franco** 20th c.   [WF]
*Director*
* Franco, Jess

**Manery, Randy** 1949-   [SMG]
*Canadian-born hockey player*
* Manery, Straw

**Manery, Straw**
See   Manery, Randy

**Maneta**
See   Loison, Louis Henri

**Manetta, Fess**
See   Manetta, Manuel

**Manetta, Manuel** 1889-1969 [WWJ]
*American jazz musician*
* Manetta, Fess

**Manetti, Lido** 1899-1928   [SC]
*Italian-born actor*
* Kent, Arnold

**Manfred, Frederick Feikema**
See   Feikema, Frederick

**Manfred, Robert**
See   Marx, Erica Elizabeth

**Mangano, Dago Lawrence**
See   Mangano, Lawrence

**Mangano, Lawrence** 20th c. [BLB, PHM]
*American underworld figure*
* Mangano, Dago Lawrence

**Mangasarian, Flora** 1880?-1968 [THR]
*Turkish-born actress and singer*
* Zabelle, Flora

**Mangeur [or Comeston]**
See   Pierre

**Mangione, Gap**
See   Mangione, Gaspare Charles

**Mangione, Gaspare Charles** 1938- [EJ7]
*American jazz musician*
* Mangione, Gap

**Mangrum, Dandy**
See   Mangrum, Jim

**Mangrum, Jim** 1948-   [RM, RO2]
*American singer*
* Mangrum, Dandy

**Mangual, Jose Manuel** 1952- [SMG, WWB]
*Puerto Rican-born baseball player*
* Mangual, Pepe

**Mangual, Pepe**
See   Mangual, Jose Manuel

**Mangum, Blackie**
See   Mangum, Leon Allen

**Mangum, Ernest G.** 20th c.   [SMG]
*American football player*
* Mangum, Pete

**Mangum, Leon Allen** 1898-1974 [BE]
*American baseball player*
* Mangum, Blackie

**Mangum, Pete**
See   Mangum, Ernest G.

**Manhattan**
See   Scoville, Joseph A.

**Manhoff, Bill**
See   Manhoff, Wilton

**Manhoff, Wilton** 1919-1974   [CA]
*American playwright*
* Manhoff, Bill

**Maniere, J. E.**
See   Giraudoux, Jean [Hippolyte]

**Manigault, G.** 19th c.   [PA]
*Author*
* Saint Cecilia

**Manik**
See   Memon, Munir Ahmed

**[The] Manikin**
See   Ellis, Welbore

**Manili**
See   Ruiz, Manuel

**Manion, Clyde Jennings** 1896-1967 [BE]
*American baseball player*
* Manion, Pete

**Manion, Pete**
See   Manion, Clyde Jennings

**Manion, Red**
See   Friedman, Max Motel

**Manivannan**
See   Naa Parthasarathy, Naarayana-Parthasarathy

**Mankad, Mulvantrai** 1917-   [EC]
*Indian cricketer*
* Mankad, Vinoo

**Mankad, Vinoo**
See   Mankad, Mulvantrai

**Mankiewicz, Herman** 1897-1953
*American screenwriter and journalist*
* Mankiewicz, Mank

**Mankiewicz, Mank**
See   Mankiewicz, Herman

**Mankittrick, Richard Kendall**   [PA]
*Author*
* R. K. M.

**Mankowska, Joyce Kells Batten** 1919-   [CAP]
*Scottish-born author*
* Batten, Joyce Mortimer

**Manley, Charles** 1830-1916   [SC]
*Irish-born actor*
* Manley, Daddy

**Manley, Daddy**
See   Manley, Charles

**Manley, Mary de la Riviere** 1663?-1724
*British playwright*
* Rivella

**Manley, Ruth Rodney King** 1907?-1973   [CA]
*American poet and author*
* King, Ruth Rodney

**Manly, Marline**
See   Rathborne, St. George

**Mann, Abel**
See   Creasey, John

**Mann, Anthony [or Anton]**
See   Bundsmann, Anton [or Emil]

**Mann, Avery**
See   Breetveld, Jim Patrick

**Mann, Ben Garth** 1915-   [BE]
*American baseball player*
* Mann, Red

**Mann, Bert**
See   Mann, Robert E.

**Mann, Charles**
See   Graham, Roger Phillips

**Mann, D. J.**
See   Freedman, James Dillet

**Mann, Deborah**
See   Bloom, Ursula [Harvey]

**Mann, Edward**
See   Fried, Emanuel

**Mann, Frank Hollister** 20th c. [BBH]
*American athletic trainer*
* Mann, Skipper

**Mann, Golo**
See   Mann, Gottfried

**Mann, Gordie**
See   Mamalick, Gordon

**Mann, Gottfried** 1909-   [CA]
*German historian and author*
* Mann, Golo

**Mann, H. Leigh**
See   Lehman, Helen Miller

**Mann, Hank**
See   Liebermann, David

**Mann, Henry J.** 1843-1878   [FFF]
*British actor*
* Montague, Harry

**Mann, Herbie**
See   Solomon, Herbert Jay

**Mann, Jack**
See   Vivian, Evelyn Charles H.

**Mann, Larnard** 20th c.   [BBH]
*American athletic trainer*
* Mann, Lon

**Mann, Lon**
See   Mann, Larnard

**Mann, Manfred**
See   Leibowitz, Michael

**Mann, Milton**
See   Graham, Roger Phillips

**Mann, Patricia**
See   Earnshaw, Patricia

**Mann, Patrick**
See   Waller, Leslie

**Mann, Paul**
See   Liebmann, Yisrol Paul Mann

**Mann, Peggy**
See   Germano, Margaret

**Mann, Red**
See   Mann, Ben Garth

**Mann, Rheta**
See   Zell, Mrs.

**Mann, Robert E.** 1902- [ASC]
*American composer and comedian*
\* Mann, Bert

**Mann, Skipper**
*See* Mann, Frank Hollister

**Mann, Theodore**
*See* Goldman, Theodore

**Mann, Thomas** 1875-1955 [TC]
*German author*
\* Thomas, Paul

**Mannan, Laila**
*See* Sanchez, Sonia Knight

**Manne, Macho**
*See* Omari, Cuthbert Kashingo

**Manne, Sheldon** 1920- [PMJ]
*American musician*
\* Manne, Shelly

**Manne, Shelly**
*See* Manne, Sheldon

**Mannering, Dore Lewin**
*See* Lewin, Dore

**Mannering, Julia**
*See* Bingham, Madeleine

**Mannering, Mary**
*See* Friend, Florence

**Mannering, Max**
*See* Holland, Josiah Gilbert

**Mannering, May**
*See* Nowell, H. P. H.

**Mannering, Moya**
*See* Doyle, Moya

**Manners, Alexandra**
*See* Rundle, Anne

**Manners, Charles**
*See* Mansergh, Southcote

**Manners, David**
*See* Acklom, Rauff De Ryther
Duan

**Manners, Dudley**
*See* Krupp, D. Dudley

**Manners, Julia**
*See* Greenaway, Gladys

**Manners, Lucille**
*See* McClinchy, Marie Emily

**Manners, Miss**
*See* Martin, Judith Sylvia

**Manners, Mrs.**
*See* Richards, Cornelia H.
[Bradley]

**Manners, Mrs. Horace**
*See* Swinburne, Algernon Charles

**Manners, Zeke**
*See* Mannes, Leo

**Mannes, Leo** 1911- [ASC]
*American composer and singer*
\* Manners, Zeke

**Mannes, Marya**
*See* Blow, Marya Mannes

**Manney, Henrietta** 1875-1942
[HCA]
*American actress*
\* Westley, Helen

**Manngian, Peter**
*See* Monger, [Ifor] David

**Mannheim, L. Andrew** 1925-
[IAW]
*Czech-born author*
\* Matheson, Andrew

**Manninen, Bruno Jalmar**
1896-1962 [BEW]
*Finnish-born designer*
\* Maine, Bruno

**Manning, Adelaide Frances Oke**
1891-1959 [CC, EMD, WW]
*British author*
\* Coles, Manning [joint pseudonym
with Cyril Henry Coles]
\* Gaite, Francis [joint pseudonym
with Cyril Henry Coles]

**Manning, Anne** 1807-1879 [PA]
*Author*
\* More, Margaret
\* Osborne, Edward
\* Powell, Mary

**Manning, Catharine**
*See* Frazier, Corinne Reid

**Manning, David**
*See* Faust, Frederick [Schiller]

**Manning, Ed**
*See* Manning, Ernest Devon
[Ernie]

**Manning, Ernest Devon [Ernie]**
1890- [BE]
*American baseball player*
\* Manning, Ed

**Manning, Frances Duncan** 20th c.
[NAA]
*American author and horticulturist*
\* Duncan, Frances

**Manning, Frederic** 1887-1935
[LC, TC]
*Australian-born author and poet*
\* Private 19022

**Manning, Henry E.** 1808- ? [PA]
*Author*
\* H. E. M.

**Manning, Hilda**
*See* Reach, James

**Manning, Irene**
*See* Harvuot, Inez

**Manning, Jack**
*See* Marks, Jack Wilson Manning

**Manning, Lee**
*See* Stokes, Manning Lee

**Manning, Leo**
*See* Hallbing, Kjell Kare

**Manning, Marie** 1875?-1945 [B10]
*American columnist*
\* Fairfax, Beatrice

**Manning, Mary Louise**
*See* Cameron, Lou

**Manning, Rosemary**
*See* Cole, Margaret Alice

**Manning, Rosemary Joy** 1911-
[AW, CA, IAW]
*British author*
\* Davys, Sarah
\* Voyle, Mary

**Manning, Rube**
*See* Manning, Walter S.

**Manning, Thomas** 1772-1840 [SN]
*British linguist and mathematician*
\* [The] Darling of the Nine

**Manning, Val**
*See* Miller, Val

**Manning, Walter S.** 1883-1930
[BE]
*American baseball player*
\* Manning, Rube

**Manning, William Henry**
1852-1929 [WW]
*Author*
\* Halliday, Ben
\* Inman, Robert Randolph?
\* Pierce, Jo
\* St. Vrain, [Major] E. L.
\* Waring, Marcus H.
\* Wilton, [Capt.] Mark

**Manningham, Basil**
*See* Homersham, Basil Henry

**Mannix, Mary Walsh** 1846-1938
[CAT]
*American poet*
\* Ashburton, Sarah Frances
\* Hunting, Sylvia
\* Willis, Hope

**Manno, Jeff**
*See* Manno, Nick

**Manno, Mousey**
*See* Manno, Tom

**Manno, Nick** 20th c. [PHM]
*American underworld figure*
\* Manno, Jeff

**Manno, Tom** 20th c. [PHM]
*American underworld figure*
\* Manno, Mousey

**Mannon, M. M.** [joint pseudonym
with Mary Ellen Mannon]
*See* Mannon, Martha

**Mannon, M. M.** [joint pseudonym
with Martha Mannon]
*See* Mannon, Mary Ellen

**Mannon, Martha** 1909- [WW]
*Author*
\* Mannon, M. M. [joint pseudonym
with Mary Ellen Mannon]

**Mannon, Mary Ellen** 1913- [WW]
*Author*
\* Mannon, M. M. [joint pseudonym
with Martha Mannon]

**Mannon, W.** 1891-1967 [BF]
*British actor and producer*
\* Ward, Warwick

**Mannon, Warwick**
*See* Hopkins, Kenneth

**Mannone, Joseph** 1900?-
[ASC, DAM, PMJ]
*American jazz musician*
\* Manone, Joseph
\* Manone, Wingy

**Mannstein, Fritz Erich von**
*See* Von Lewinski, Fritz Erich

**Mannyng, Robert** 1288-1338
[WBD]
*British author and poet*
\* De Brunne, Robert

**Manola, Marion**
*See* Mould, Mrs. Henry S.

**Manolete [Big Manuel]**
*See* Rodriguez Sanchez, Manuel

**Manolete [Big Manuel]**
*See* Rodriguez Sanchez, Manuel

**Manon, Marcia**
*See* Ankewich, Camille

**Manone, Joseph**
*See* Mannone, Joseph

**Manone, Wingy**
*See* Mannone, Joseph

**Manor, Jason**
*See* Hall, Oakley [Maxwell]

**Manos, Charley**
*See* Moustakas, Alkiviadis

**Manos de Piedra [Hands of Stone]**
*See* Duran, Roberto

**Manouche**
*See* Germain, Germaine

**Mansbridge, Pamela**
*See* Course, Pamela Mary

**Mansergh, Southcote** 1857-1935
[BBD]
*British opera singer and impresario*
\* Manners, Charles

**Mansfield, Arthur** 20th c. [BBH]
*American baseball coach*
\* Mansfield, Dynie

**Mansfield, Dynie**
*See* Mansfield, Arthur

**Mansfield, Edward Deering**
1801-1880? [FFF, PA]
*American journalist*
\* Veteran Observer

**Mansfield, Elizabeth**
*See* Schwartz, Paula

**Mansfield, Estrith**
*See* Harris, Edna Edith

**Mansfield, Jayne**
*See* Palmer, Vera Jane

**Mansfield, Joseph** 1889?-1971
[EMT, FD, PMJ]
*American actor and singer*
\* Santley, Joseph

**Mansfield, Joyce** 1920- [ICB]
*British illustrator*
\* Bee, Joyce

**Mansfield, Katherine**
*See* Beauchamp, Kathleen
Mansfield

**Mansfield, L. W.** [PA]
*Author*
\* Z. P.

**Mansfield, Lawrence**
*See* Forrest, William Mentzel

**Mansfield, Libby**
*See* Schwartz, Paula

**Mansfield, Martha**
*See* Ehrlich, Martha

**Mansfield, Mary Lou**
*See* Daly, Pauline

**Mansfield, Maynard** 1910- [PMJ]
*American jazz musician*
\* Mansfield, Saxie

**Mansfield, Norman**
*See* Gladden, E[dgar] Norman

**Mansfield, Portia**
*See* Swett, Portia

**Mansfield, Richard**
*See* Rudersdorff, Richard

**Mansfield, Saxie**
See   Mansfield, Maynard

**Mansfield, Walworth**
See   Walton, W. H.

**Mansfield, Willette** 1890-1960
[BEW]
*American actress and producer*
* Kershaw, Willette

**Manson, James B.**   [PA]
*Author*
* Warmley, Ernst

**Manson, Janet** 1922-1961   [SC]
*American actress*
* Kalionzes, Janet

**Manson, Margaret**
See   Aldiss, Margaret [Christie]

**Manson, [Sir] Patrick** 1844-1922
[WBD]
*British physician and parasitologist*
* [The] Father of Tropical
   Medicine

**Mansouri, Lotfi**
See   Mansouri, Lotfollah

**Mansouri, Lotfollah** 1929-   [OP]
*Iranian-born opera producer and
stage designer*
* Mansouri, Lotfi

**Mansur [or Hasan?], Abul Qasim**
940-1020   [DEP, HN, WBD]
*Persian poet*
* Firdusi [or Firdausi]
* [The] Homer of Khorasan
* [The] Homer of Persia
* [The] Oriental Homer

**Mant, Richard**
See   Hearne, George Richard Mant

**Mantell, Frank**
See   Mintell, Frank Otto

**Mantell, Robert Bruce** 1854-1928
[THR]
*Scottish-born actor and theatrical
manager*
* Hudson, Robert

**Mantilla, Felix Lamela** 1934-
*Puerto Rican-born baseball player*
* [The] Cat

**Mantinband, James H.** 20th c.
[WW]
*Author*
* Keystone, Oliver

**Mantle, Mickey Charles** 1931-
[ALR, BE]
*American baseball player*
* [The] Commerce Comet

**Mantle, Winifred Langford** 1911-
[AW, CA, WD]
*British author*
* Fellowes, Anne
* Lang, Frances
* Langford, Jane

**Manton, Jo**
See   Gittings, Jo [Grenville]
Manton

**Manton, Kate**
See   Knight, Mrs. S. G.

**Manton, Mr.**
See   Montrose, Duchess of

**Manton, Paul**
See   Walker, Peter Norman

**Manton, Peter**
See   Creasey, John

**Mantooth, Lawrence** 20th c.   [BBH]
*American wrestler*
* [The] Scissor King

**Mantovani**
See   Mantovani, Annunzio Paulo

**Mantovani, Annunzio Paulo**
1908-1980   [PMJ]
*British conductor*
* Mantovani

**[The] Mantuan**
See   Spagnolus, Baptista

**[The] Mantuan Bard**
See   Vergilius Maro, Publius

**[The] Mantuan Muse**
See   Vergilius Maro, Publius

**[The] Mantuan Swan**
See   Vergilius Maro, Publius

**Mantuano, Marco**
See   Benevides, Marco

**Manuel**
See   Lepine, Ernest

**Manuel, George** 1915-   [IAW]
*South African author*
* Gemel

**Manuel, Jose** 20th c.   [GS]
*Spanish bullfighter*
* Tinin

**Manuel, Nikolaus** 1484-1530
[WBD]
*Swiss painter and engraver*
* Deutsch, Nikolaus

**Manuel I Comnenus** 1120-1180
[FFF, HN, RH]
*Byzantine emperor*
* Captain
* [The] Great Captain

**Manuela**
See   De Rochechouart-Mortemart,
Marie Clementine

**Manugupta**
See   Shastri, Prithvinath

**Manush, Heinie**
See   Manush, Henry Emmett

**Manush, Henry Emmett**
1901-1971   [BE, CBS, DGS]
*American baseball player*
* Manush, Heinie

**Manville, George**
See   Fenn, George Manville

**Manville, W. H.**
See   Manville, William Henry

**Manville, William Henry** 1930-
[CA]
*American author*
* Manville, W. H.
* Williams, Henry

**Many, Seth E[dward]** 1939-   [CA]
*American author*
* NO, Dr.

**Many Treaties, Chief**
See   Hazlett, William

**Manyase, Lenchman Thozamile**
1915-   [IAW]
*South African author and poet*
* Joli-Ox

**Manzoni, Giacomo** 1908-   [CAR]
*Italian sculptor*
* Manzu, Giacomo

**Manzu, Giacomo**
See   Manzoni, Giacomo

**Mao?**
See   Addis, Hazel Iris Wilson

**Mao Tse-tung** 1893-1976
*Chinese Communist leader*
* [The] Great Helmsman

**Mao Tun [Contradiction]**
See   Shen Yen-ping

**Maore**
See   Inglis, J.

**Mapel, Lefty**
See   Mapel, Rolla Hamilton

**Mapel, Rolla Hamilton** 1890-1966
[BE]
*American baseball player*
* Mapel, Lefty

**Mapes, Cliff Franklin** 1922-   [BE]
*American baseball player*
* Mapes, Tiger

**Mapes, Mary A.**
See   Ellison, Virginia Howell

**Mapes, Tiger**
See   Mapes, Cliff Franklin

**Mapes, Victor** 1870- ?   [NAA]
*American playwright and author*
* Post, Maveric
* Sharp, Sidney

**Mapes, Walter** 1150-1196
[DEL, FFF, SN]
*Welsh poet*
* [The] Anacreon of the Twelfth
   Century
* [The] Jovial Toper

**Maphis, Joe**
See   Maphis, Otis W.

**Maphis, Otis W.** 1921-
[CWG, DAM]
*American country-western performer*
* [The] King of the Strings
* Maphis, Joe

**Maphis, Rose Lee** 1922-   [FCW]
*American country-western performer*
* Rose of the Mountains

**Maple, Eddie** 20th c.
*American jockey*
* [The] Anchor

**Maples, Evelyn Lucille [Palmer]**
1919-   [IAW]
*American author*
* Dalby, B. J.

**Maplesden, Ray**
See   Pearce, Raymond Maplesden

**Mapleton, S. E.**   [PA]
*Author*
* [A] Clergyman's Wife

**Mapother, Edith Rubel** 20th c.
[NAA]
*American educator, musician, poet*
* Rubel, Edith

**Mappelbeck, John**
See   Collins, James H.

**Mar, Helen**
See   Walker, Mrs. D. M. F.

**[La] Mara**
See   Lipsius, Marie

**Mara, Adele**
See   Delgado, Adelaida

**Mara, Barney**
See   Roth, Arthur J[oseph]

**Mara, Jeanette**
See   Cebulash, Mel

**Mara, Thalia**
See   Mahoney, Elizabeth

**Maraini, Yoi** 20th c.   [WWL]
*Author*
* Pawlowska, Yoi

**Marais**
See   Brown, Mary Rachel

**Marais, Jean**
See   Villain-Marais, Jean

**Marais, Miranda**
See   Baruch de la Pardo, Rosa Lily
Odette

**Marama**
See   Cilento, Phyllis Dorothy

**Marano, Doretta** 1928-1968
[BEW, EMT]
*American actress and singer*
* Morrow, Doretta

**Maranville, Rabbit**
See   Maranville, Walter James
Vincent

**Maranville, Walter James Vincent**
1891-1954   [AS, DGS, PB]
*American baseball player*
* Maranville, Rabbit

**Maras, Karl** [house pseudonym,
Comyns]
See   Bulmer, [Henry] Kenneth

**Maras, Karl** [house pseudonym]
See   Hawkins, Peter

**Marasmus, Seymour**
See   Rivoli, Mario

**Marat, Jean Paul** 1744-1793
[DNNF, FF, HN]
*French revolutionary leader*
* Ami du Peuple
* [The] Apostle of Massacre
* [The] Friend of the People
* [The] People's Friend
* [The] Republican Martyr

**Marathon**
See   McNish, James Thomas

**Marauder, Father**
See   De Vignerot du Plessis, Louis
Francois Armand

**Maravan, Lila**
See   Muschamp, Lila

**Maravich, Peter** 1948-   [BB]
*American basketball player*
* Maravich, Pistol Pete

**Maravich, Pistol Pete**
See   Maravich, Peter

**Maraviglia, Guiseppe Maria**
?-1684   [PA]
*Author*
* Mirabilia

**Marberry, Firpo**
See   Marberry, Fred

**Marberry, Fred** 1898-  [BE, PB]
*American baseball player*
* Marberry, Firpo

**Marble, Anna** 1881?-1946  [BEW]
*American author and press
representative*
* Pollock, Anna

**Marble, Harriet Clement**
1903-1975  [CA]
*American author*
* Jones, Harriet

**Marble, Major**
See  Cheever, Henry T.

**Marblestone, Eddie** 1907?-  [PMJ]
*American singer*
* Stone, Eddie

**Marbo, Camille**
See  Borel, Marguerite [Appell]

**Marbode, M.**  [PA]
*Author*
* Pellicarius

**Marbrook, Del**
See  Mabrouk, Djelloul

**Marbrook, Djelloul**
See  Mabrouk, Djelloul

**Marc, Elizabeth**
See  Mirza, Nusrat Ali

**Marca, Francois de**  [HN]
*Medieval scholar*
* Illustratus, Doctor

**Marcano, Jesus Manuel**
See  Trillo, Jesus Manuel

**Marcantonio**
See  Raimondi, Marcantonio

**Marceau, Felicien**
See  Carette, Louis Albert

**Marceau, Francois Severin**
See  Marceau-Desgraviers,
Francois Severin

**Marceau-Desgraviers, Francois
Severin** 1769-1796  [WBD]
*French army officer*
* Marceau, Francois Severin

**Marcel**
See  Allen, William Francis

**Marcel, Eugene** 1862-1941  [EWL]
*French author*
* Prevost, Marcel

**Marcel, Lucille**
See  Wasself, Lucille

**Marceline**
See  Orbes, Marceline

**Marcelino**
See  Agnew, Edith J[osephine]

**Marcella, Fatso Marco**
See  Marcella, Marco

**Marcella, Marco** 1909?-1962
[BEW]
*Theatrical performer*
* Marcella, Fatso Marco

**Marcelle, Ghost**
See  Marcelle, Oliver H.

**Marcelle, Oliver H.** 20th c.  [OBW]
*American baseball player*
* Marcelle, Ghost

**Marcelle-Maurette**
See  Maurette, Marcelle Marie
Josephine

**Marcellini, Siro** 1921-  [FDG]
*Italian director*
* Markson, Sean

**Marcellino, Jocko**
See  Marcellino, John

**Marcellino, John** 1950-  [RO2]
*American singer*
* Marcellino, Jocko

**Marcellinus, Animianus**
See  Nadel, Aaron

**Marcello**
See  D'Affry, Adele

**Marcello, Carlos**
See  Minacore, Calogero

**Marcellus, Marcus Claudius** 3rd c.
BC  [DEP, DNNF, DNNS]
*Roman general and statesman*
* [The] Sword of Rome

**[The] Marcellus of Spain**
See  John

**Marcellus, P. H.**
See  Cronmiller, George, Jr.

**Marcellus II**
See  Cervini, Marcello

**Marcet, Mary** 1769-1858  [PA]
*Author*
* Haldimand

**Marcetta, Mike**
See  Marcetta, Milan

**Marcetta, Milan** 1936-  [CEI]
*Canadian-born hockey player*
* Marcetta, Mike

**March, Anne**
See  Woolson, Constance Fenimore

**March, Ausias** 1397?-1460  [SN]
*Valencian poet*
* [The] Petrarch of Catalonia

**March, Charles W.** 1815-1864
[FFF, PA]
*American author*
* Pequot

**March, Fredric**
See  Bickel, Frederick McIntyre

**March, Hal**
See  Mendelson, Harold

**March Hare**
See  Walmsley, Leo

**March, Harold C.** 1908-
[CEI, FHE, HK]
*Canadian-born hockey player*
* March, Mush

**March, Hilary**
See  Adcock, Almey St. John

**March, Hilary**
See  Pulvertaft, Lalage Isobel

**March, Jermyn**
See  Webb, Dorothy Anna Maria

**[The] March King**
See  Sousa, John Philip

**March, Little Peggy**
See  March, Peggy

**March, Major**
See  Willcox, Orlando Bolivar

**March, Marjorie**
See  Leibich, Augusta

**March, Miles Standish** 1860-1932
[SC]
*American actor*
* Walsh, Frank

**March, Mush**
See  March, Harold C.

**March, Peggy** 1948-  [RO1]
*American singer*
* March, Little Peggy

**March, Stella**
See  Marshall, Marjorie Bell

**March, Walter**
See  Willcox, Orlando Bolivar

**March, William**
See  Campbell, William Edward
March

**Marchand, Marie Francoise**
1711-1803  [WBD]
*French actress*
* Dumesnil, Marie Francoise

**Marchant, Catherine**
See  Cookson, Catherine Ann
[McMullen]

**Marchant, Ella** 20th c.
[SFL, WGT]
*Author*
* Two Women of the West [joint
pseudonym with Alice Ilgenfritz
Jones]

**Marchant, R[omano Isabel]**
See  Colbron, Grace Isabel

**Marchant, R. A.**
See  Marchant, Rex Alan

**Marchant, Rex Alan** 1933-  [WYA]
*Author*
* Marchant, R. A.

**Marchaud, Alfred**
See  Kaufman, M.

**Marchbanks, Samuel**
See  Davies, Robertson

**Marchegiano, Rocco** 1923-1969
[AS, BX, RBE]
*American boxer*
* [The] Brockton Blockbuster
* Marciano, Rocky

**Marchelle, Ponce Kiah** 20th c.
*American columnist*
* Heloise

**Marchena de Leyba, Amelia
Francisco** 1850-1941  [CW]
*Dominican author*
* Francasi [or Francasci], Amelia

**Marchese, Paul** 20th c.  [BLB]
*American underworld figure*
* Di Cristina, Paul

**Marchi, Giacomo**
See  Bassani, Giorgio

**Marchioni, Mark** 20th c.  [SFP]
*Author*
* Marconette

**Marchmont, Frederick**
See  Torriano, Hugh Arthur

**Marciano, Rocky**
See  Marchegiano, Rocco

**Marcliffe, Theophilus**
See  Godwin, William

**Marco di Tiziano**
See  Vecelli, Marco

**Marco, Lou**
See  Gottfried, Theodore Mark

**Marco the Magi**
See  Pelaez, Cesareo

**Marco Gomez, Jaime** 1920-  [GS]
*Spanish bullfighter*
* [EL] Choni

**Marcol, Chester**
See  Marcol, Czelslaw C.

**Marcol, Czelslaw C.** 1949-  [FB]
*Polish-born American football
player*
* Marcol, Chester
* [The] Polish Messiah

**Marcombe, Edith Marion**
See  Shiffert, Edith [Marcombe]

**Marconette**
See  Marchioni, Mark

**Marcos, [Fray]**
See  Niza, Marcos de

**Marcos, Imelda** 1930-
*Wife of Philippine president
Ferdinand Marcos*
* [The] Iron Butterfly
* [The] Orchid

**Marcos, Jesus** 20th c.  [GS]
*Spanish bullfighter*
* Monedero [The Minter]

**Marcou-Ferrand, Juan Victor Sejour**
1817-1874  [IBW]
*American playwright and poet*
* Sejour, Victor

**Marcous, Louis** 1883-1941  [JL]
*French painter*
* Marcoussis, Louis

**Marcoussis, Louis**
See  Marcous, Louis

**Marcoux, Jean Emile Diogene**
1877-1962  [BBD]
*Italian-born opera singer*
* Marcoux, Vanni

**Marcoux, Vanni**
See  Marcoux, Jean Emile Diogene

**Marcoy, Paul**
See  De Saint Cricq, Lorenzo

**Marcum, Footsie**
See  Marcum, John Alfred

**Marcum, John Alfred** 1908-  [BE]
*American baseball player*
* Marcum, Footsie

**Marcus**
See  Davis, Matthew Livingston

**Marcus, Anne M[ulkeen]** 1927-
[CA]
*American author and educator*
* Mulkeen, Anne

**Marcus Aurelius**
See  Annius Verus, Marcus

**[The] Marcus Aurelius of the Base Empire**
See John II Comnenus

**Marcus, Carol** 20th c. [BEW]
*American actress*
* Grace, Carol

**Marcus, David** 1902-1948 [EJS]
*American boxer*
* Mars, Danny
* Mars, Mickey

**Marczali, Henrik**
See Morgenstern, Henrik

**Marczlewicz, Charles Anthony**
1919- [BE]
*American baseball player*
* Marshall, Charles Anthony [Charlie]

**[The] Mare**
See Ryan, Hermine Braunsteiner

**Marek**
See Zulawski, Marek

**Marek, Kurt W[illi]** 1915-1972
[AW, B10, CAP]
*German-born journalist, archaeologist, author*
* Ceram, C. W.

**Mareth, Glenville** [joint pseudonym with Jack Weinstock]
See Gomberg, William Gilbert

**Mareth, Glenville** [joint pseudonym with William Gilbert Gomberg]
See Weinstock, Jack

**Marevna**
See Vorobeva, Maria

**Margaret** 1283-1290
[DNNF, FFF, SN]
*Granddaughter of King Alexander III of Scotland*
* [The] Fair Maid of Norway
* [The] Maid of Norway

**Margaret** 1353-1412
[DEP, HN, SN]
*Queen of Denmark, Norway, and Sweden*
* [The] Northern Semiramis
* [The] Scandinavian Semiramis
* [The] Semiramis of the North

**Margaret [or Marguerite]**
1430-1482 [HN]
*Wife of King Henry VI of England*
* Anjou, Marguerite d'
* [The] She Wolf of France

**Margaret** 1489-1541 [SN]
*Wife of King James IV of Scotland*
* [The] Rose

**Margaret of Angouleme**
See Margaret [or Marquerite] of Navarre

**Margaret of Austria**
See Margaret of Parma

**Margaret of Carinthia** 1318-1369
[WBD]
*Daughter of Henry, Duke of Carinthia*
* Maultasch

**Margaret of Constantinople**
See Margaret of Flanders

**Margaret of Flanders** 1200?-1280
[WBD]
*Daughter of Emperor Baldwin I, Count of Flanders and Hainault*
* Margaret of Constantinople

**Margaret [or Marguerite] of France**
1523?-1574 [HN, RH, WBD]
*Daughter of King Francis I of France*
* Margaret of Savoy
* [La] Mere des Peuples
* [The] Mother of the People

**Margaret [or Marguerite] of Navarre**
1492-1549 [HN, WBD]
*Queen of Navarre*
* Margaret of Angouleme
* Margaret of Orleans
* Margaret of Valois
* Marguerite des Marguerites [Pearl of Pearls]
* [The] Tenth Muse

**Margaret of Orleans**
See Margaret [or Marquerite] of Navarre

**Margaret of Parma** 1522-1586
[WBD]
*Daughter of Emperor Charles V*
* Margaret of Austria

**Margaret of Savoy**
See Margaret [or Marguerite] of France

**Margaret of Valois**
See Margaret [or Marguerite] of Navarre

**Margaret Rose** 1930-
*British princess*
* P. M.

**Marge**
See Buell, Marjorie Henderson

**Margerison, John S.** 20th c. [MBF]
*British author*
* Grey, Gilbert
* Mellalieu, James S.

**Margerson, David**
See Davies, David Margerison

**Margery**
See Crandon, Mina [Stinson]

**Margetic, Magnetic**
See Margetic, Pato

**Margetic, Pato** 1961?-
*Argentinian soccer player*
* Margetic, Magnetic

**Margheriti, Antonio** 1916- [FDG]
*Italian director*
* Daisies, Anthony
* Dawson, Anthony

**Marginalia**
See Poe, Edgar Allan

**Margo**
See Boldao y Castilla, Maria Marguerita Guadalupe

**Margo, Peter** 20th c.
*American billiard player*
* Little Giant

**Margoliouth, George Edward**
1901- [THR]
*British theatrical press representative*
* Fearon, George Edward

**Margolis, Charles** 1874-1926 [SC]
*American actor*
* Margolis, Doc

**Margolis, Doc**
See Margolis, Charles

**Margrethe II** 1940-
*Queen of Denmark*
* Daisy
* Grathmer, Ingahild

**Marguerita**
See Bornstein, Marguerita

**Marguerite des Marguerites [Pearl of Pearls]**
See Margaret [or Marquerite] of Navarre

**Margulois, David** 1911-
[EMT, IPA]
*American producer*
* Merrick, David

**Marholm, Laura**
See Hansson, Laura

**Maria Christina** 1947-
*Dutch princess*
* Van Oranje, Christina

**Maria de Jesus**
See Fernandez Coronel, Maria

**Maria Del Rey, [Sister]**
See Danforth, Ethel M.

**Maria Di Gesu, [Sister]**
See Felicita, Maria

**Maria, Giuseppe**
See Racagni, Giovanni

**Maria, Jennie**
See Renard, Celine

**Maria Louisa** 1791-1847 [SN]
*Wife of Napoleon Bonaparte*
* [The] Deadly Austrian

**Maria Mour, Jean Hubert**
See Papailler, Hubert

**Maria Theresa** 1717-1780
[HN, SN]
*Queen of Austria*
* [The] Modern Hippolyta
* [The] Mother of Her Country

**Marian Anderson of the Blues**
See Hunter, Alberta

**Marian Dolores, [Sister]**
See Robinson, [Sister] Marian Dolores

**Marian, Sahle Sellassie Berhane**
1936-
*Ethiopian author*
* Sellassie, Sahle

**Mariana**
See Foster, Marian Curtis

**Mariana, Juan de [or John]**
1537-1624 [DNNS, RH, SN]
*Spanish historian*
* [The] Father of Spanish History
* [The] Livy of France
* [The] Livy of Spain

**Mariano, Luis**
See Gonzalez, Luis

**Mariano de Aguiar, Sinesio** 20th c.
[FIR]
*Brazilian actor*
* De Conde, Syn

**Marianus, Doctor**
See Duns Scotus, Johannes

**Maric, Boze**
See Maric, Bozidar

**Maric, Bozidar** 1942- [AES]
*Yugoslav soccer player*
* Maric, Boze

**Marichal, Juan Antonio Sanchez**
1937- [BE]
*Dominican-born baseball player*
* [The] Dominican Dandy
* Marichal, Manito

**Marichal, Manito**
See Marichal, Juan Antonio Sanchez

**Marichaud, Alphonse**
See Wilson, Florence Roma Muir

**Marie**
See Kindberg, Agnes Marie

**Marie**
See Skidmore, Harriet M.

**[Josephe Jeanne] Marie Antoinette**
1755-1793 [DEP, DHA, SN]
*Wife of King Louis XVI of France*
* [The] Austrian
* Autrichienne
* [The] Baker's Wife
* Deficit, Madame
* [The] Guardian Angel of France
* Veto, Madame
* [The] Widow Capet

**Marie Charlotte** 1724-1800
[DNNS]
*Countess of Boufflers-Rouveret*
* Idole du Temple [Idol of the Temple]

**Marie, Jeanne**
See Wilson, Marie B[eatrice]

**Marie St. Justin, [Mother]**
See Rene-Bazin, Marie

**Mariel**
See Moorien, M.

**Mariella, [Sister]**
See Gable, Mary

**Mariem, Sahala** 1844-1913 [IBW]
*Abyssinian emperor*
* Menelik II

**Marietta**
See Bradley, Harriet M.

**Marijac**
See Dumas, Jacques

**Marilue**
See Johnson, Marilue Carolyn

**[The] Marilyn Monroe of Burlesque**
See Evans, Dixie

**Marin, A. C.**
See De Marini y Coppel, Alfredo Jose

**Marin, Alfred**
See De Marini y Coppel, Alfredo Jose

**Marin, Jean**
See Morvan, Yves

**Marin, Richard** 1947- [RO2]
*American entertainer*
* Cheech

**Marina, Dona Xaramillo**
1505-1529 [PA]
*Author*
* Malinche

**Marinacci, Gloria**
*See* Cutsforth, Gloria

**[The] Marine**
*See* Blais, George

**Marine, Nick**
*See* Oursler, Will[iam Charles]

**Mariner, David**
*See* Smith, David MacLeod

**Mariner, Scott** [joint pseudonym
with Frederik Pohl]
*See* Kornbluth, Cyril M.

**Mariner, Scott** [joint pseudonym
with Cyril M. Kornbluth]
*See* Pohl, Frederik

**[El] Marinero [The Sailor]**
*See* Ortega y Ramirez, Antonio

**Maring, Helen**
*See* Samsel, Helen Maring

**Marini, Jean Baptiste** 1569-1625
[FFF]
*Italian poet*
* [The] Cavalier

**[El] Marino [The Mariner]**
*See* Palomares Del Pino, Francisco

**Marino, Big Bobby**
*See* Marino, Francis

**Marino, Dado**
*See* Marino, Salvador

**Marino, Enrico** 1889- [BBH]
*Italian-born American bowler*
* Marino, Hank

**Marino, Francis** ?-1976
*American labor union organizer*
* Marino, Big Bobby

**Marino, Hank**
*See* Marino, Enrico

**Marino, James** ?-1931 [BLB]
*American underworld figure*
* LaPore, James

**Marino, Rinaldo R.** 1916-1963
[ASC]
*American composer*
* Martin, Lennie

**Marino, Salvador** 1916- [BX, RBE]
*American boxer*
* Marino, Dado

**Marinoni, Rosa Zagnoni** 1890-
[NAA]
*Italian-born poet and author*
* Morrison, Ross Zane
* Rosca, the Jester

**Marinus**
*See* Martin, Jacques

**Marinus, R.**
*See* Jonah

**Mario**
*See* Baletti, Giuseppe

**Mario, Giuseppe** 1810- ? [PA]
*Author*
* Macheside, Candia

**Mario, Queena**
*See* Tillotson, Queena

**Marion, Dave**
*See* Graves, David Marion

**Marion, Edna**
*See* Hannam, Edna

**Marion, Elias** ?-1730 [PA]
*Author*
* Allut, Jean

**Marion, Francis** 1732?-1795
[SN, WBD]
*American army officer*
* [The] Swamp Fox

**Marion, Frieda** 1912- [CA]
*American author*
* Kent, Arden
* Von Castelhun, Friedl

**Marion, Henry**
*See* Alvarez Del Rey, Ramon
Felipe San Juan Mario Silvio Enrico

**Marion, Joan**
*See* Nicholls, Joan

**Marion, John Wyeth** 1914- [BE]
*American baseball player*
* Marion, Red

**Marion, Martin Whiteford** 1917-
[BE, BN, PB]
*American baseball player and
manager*
* Ely, Bones
* Marion, Slats
* [The] Octopus
* Shortstop, Mr.

**Marion, Pauline** ?-1973 [TR]
*Actress*
* Luce, Polly

**Marion, Red**
*See* Marion, John Wyeth

**Marion, Slats**
*See* Marion, Martin Whiteford

**Marion, Stella**
*See* Boyle, Mrs. Charles H.

**Mariotti, Luigi**
*See* Gallenga, Antonio Carlo
Napoleone

**Maris, Mona**
*See* Cap de Vielle, Maria

**Maris, Paul**
*See* Zelmanowitz, Gerald Martin

**Marisa**
*See* Nucera, Marisa Lonette

**Marisol**
*See* Marisol, Escobar

**Marisol, Escobar** 1930- [CAR]
*Venezuelan sculptor*
* Marisol

**Maritote, Frank** 20th c.
[BLB, PHM]
*American underworld figure*
* Diamond, Frank

**Maritz, Empie**
*See* Maritz, Magdalena Petronella

**Maritz, Magdalena Petronella**
1922- [IAW]
*South African author*
* Maritz, Empie

**Maritza, Sari**
*See* Detering-Nathan, Patricia

**Maritzburg, Pieter**
*See* Jackson, Thomas

**Mariucci, John** 1916- [FHE]
*American hockey player*
* Mariucci, Maroosh

**Mariucci, Maroosh**
*See* Mariucci, John

**Marius**
*See* Benedict, Steve

**Marius**
*See* Wells, William Charles

**Marius, Caius** 2nd c. BC
[FFF, HN, RH]
*Roman general*
* [The] Saviour of Rome
* [The] Third Founder of Rome

**Marius, Madame** [FFF]
*Entertainer*
* St. John, Florence

**Marius, Simon** 1564-1624 [PA]
*Author*
* Mayer

**Mark** ?- 74? [SN]
*Saint*
* [The] Stump Fingered

**Mark Alan, Roy**
*See* Malan, Renato Marco

**Mark, Edwina**
*See* Fadiman, Edwin, Jr.

**Mark, John**
*See* Tindall, Frederick Cryer

**Mark, Matthew**
*See* Babcock, Frederic

**Mark, Pauline [Dahlin]** 1913- [CA]
*American author*
* Mark, Polly

**Mark, Polly**
*See* Mark, Pauline [Dahlin]

**Mark, Ted**
*See* Gottfried, Theodore Mark

**[The] Mark Tapley of Kings**
*See* Charles VII

**[The] Mark Twain of Country Music**
*See* Hall, Tom T.

**[The] Mark Twain of France**
*See* Moinaux, Georges-Victor
Marcel

**Markandaya, Kamala**
*See* Taylor, Kamala [Purnaiya]

**Markell, Charles Frederick** 1855-
? [ALY]
*American author*
* Chaskell

**Markell, Duke**
*See* Makowsky, Harry Duquesne

**Markell, Harry Duquesne**
*See* Makowsky, Harry Duquesne

**Marker, Chris**
*See* Bouche-Villeneuve, Christian
Francois

**Marker, Clare**
*See* Witcombe, Rick Trader

**Markes, Albert Ernest** 1865-1901
[DBA]
*British painter*
* Albert

**Markewich, Maurice** 1936- [EJ]
*American jazz musician*
* Markewich, Reese

**Markewich, Reese**
*See* Markewich, Maurice

**Markham, David**
*See* Harrison, Peter Basil

**Markham, Dewey Alamo**
1904-1981 [IBW]
*American comedian*
* Markham, Pigmeat

**Markham, Gervasse** 1570-1655
[PA]
*Author*
* G. M.

**Markham, Howard**
*See* Hay, Mary Cecil

**Markham, Lucia Clark**
*See* Markham, Lula Clark

**Markham, Lula Clark** 1870- ?
[NAA]
*American poet*
* Markham, Lucia Clark

**Markham, Mrs.**
*See* Penrose, Elizabeth
[Cartwright]

**Markham, Pauline**
*See* Hall, Margaret

**Markham, Pigmeat**
*See* Markham, Dewey Alamo

**Markham, Robert**
*See* Amis, Kingsley [William]

**Markham, Russ**
*See* Hall, Steve

**Markins, W. S.**
*See* Jenkins, Marie M[agdalen]

**Markish, David** 1938- [CA]
*Russian-born author*
* Maguen, David

**Markland, [Cleneth Eu]gene** 1919-
[BE]
*American baseball player*
* Markland, Mousey

**Markland, Mousey**
*See* Markland, [Cleneth Eu]gene

**Markland, Russell** 1892- [WWL]
*British author and poet*
* Ingersley, R. M.

**Marko [or Markoski?], Vincent**
1903-1954 [SC]
*American actor*
* Tyler, Tom

**Markoosie**
*See* Patsauq, Markoosie

**Markova, Alicia**
*See* Marks, Lilian Alicia

**Markowitz, Ernest H.** 1919-
[BEW, EMT]
*American producer and playwright*
* Martin, Ernest H.

**Markowitz, Irvin** 1923- [EJ]
*American jazz musician*
* Markowitz, Marky

**Markowitz, Leila** 1936- [BEW]
*American actress and singer*
* Martin, Leila

**Markowitz, Marky**
See　Markowitz, Irvin

**Markowitz, Richard** 1926-　[ASC]
*American composer*
* Allen, Richard

**Markowitz, Sandra** 1937-
[SW, TR]
*American actress*
* Harris, Barbara

**Marks, Charlie** 1881-1971　[F2]
*Actor*
* Dale, Charlie

**Marks, Edith Bobroff** 1924-　[CA]
*American educator and author*
* Bobroff, Edith

**Marks, Elias J.** 1880-1960　[ASC]
*American composer and singer*
* Dawson, Eli

**Marks, Harry H.**　[FFF]
*American writer*
* Grinder

**Marks, J**
See　Highwater, Jamake

**Marks, Jack Wilson Manning**
1916-　[BEW]
*American actor, director, educator*
* Manning, Jack

**Marks, Lilian Alicia** 1910-　[CAP]
*British ballet dancer*
* Markova, Alicia

**Marks, Nora**
See　Atkinson, Eleanor
[Stackhouse]

**Marks, Peter**
See　Smith, Robert Kimmel

**Marks, Richard** 19th c.　[PA]
*Author*
* Aliquis

**Marks, Rudenko** 20th c.　[WFA]
*French-born fashion designer*
* Luba

**Marks, Sadie** 20th c.
*Actress*
* Livingston, Mary

**Marks, Sallie**
See　Showles, Mrs. William

**Marks, Stan[ley]** 1929-　[CA]
*Australian author*
* King, Martin

**Marks, Winston K[itchener]** 20th
c.　[WGT]
*Author*
* Winney, Ken

**Markson, Sean**
See　Marcellini, Siro

**Markun, Patricia Maloney** 1924-
[CA, SAT]
*American author*
* Forrest, Sybil
* Maloney, Pat
* Marroquin, Patricio
* O'Carroll, Ryan

**Marlay**
See　Chapman, D. W.

**Marlborough**
See　Oaksey, [Lord] John Geoffrey
Tristram

**Marlee, Paul**
See　Nijbroek, Paul Armand

**Marler, Walt A.**
See　Dawley, Thomas Robinson, Jr.

**Marley, Frank Elsworth** 1862- ?
[NAA]
*American author and editor*
* Historian

**Marlin, Henry**
See　Giggal, Kenneth

**Marlin, Morris Wayne** 1915-
[CWG, DAM]
*American country-western performer*
* Marlin, Sleepy

**Marlin, Roy**
See　Ashmore, Basil Norton

**Marlin, Sleepy**
See　Marlin, Morris Wayne

**Marling, Ilse**　[THR]
*German-born actress and singer*
* Marvenga, Ilse

**Marlinski, Cossack**
See　Bestuzhev [or Bestuschew],
Aleksandr Aleksandrovich

**Marlitt, E.**
See　John, Eugenie

**Marlow, Edwina**
See　Huff, Tom Elmer

**Marlow, Joyce**
See　Connor, Joyce Mary

**Marlow, Louis**
See　Wilkinson, Louis Umfreville

**Marlow, Lucy**
See　McAleer, Lucy Ann

**Marlowe, Amy Bell** [house
pseudonym] [Stratemeyer
Syndicate]
See　Stratemeyer, Edward L.

**Marlowe, Charles**
See　Jay, Harriet

**Marlowe, Christopher** 1564-1593
[SN]
*British playwright*
* [That] Atheist Tamburian
* [The] Father of English Dramatic
Poetry

**Marlowe, Dan J[ames]** 1914-
[EMD]
*American writer*
* Sandaval, Jaime

**Marlowe, Hugh**
See　Hipple, Hugh Herbert

**Marlowe, Hugh**
See　Patterson, Harry

**Marlowe, Jerry**
See　Mautner, Jerome

**Marlowe, Joan**
See　Mintz, Joan

**Marlowe, Julia**
See　Frost, Sarah Frances

**Marlowe, Kenneth** 1926-　[CA]
*American author and hair stylist*
* Mr. Kenneth
* Stuart, Leslie

**Marlowe, Louis J.**
See　Goetten, L. J.

**Marlowe, Stephen**
See　Lesser, Milton

**Marlowe, Webb**
See　McComas, J[esse] Francis

**Marly, Florence**
See　Smekalova, Hana

**Marmaduke, Sir**
See　Tilton, Theodore

**Marmarosa, Dodo**
See　Marmarosa, Michael

**Marmarosa, Michael** 1925-
[EJ, PMJ]
*American jazz musician*
* Marmarosa, Dodo

**Marmora, Dagoberto**
See　Bobadilla y Lunar, Emilio

**Marnell, Joseph** 20th c.
[SFL, WGT]
*Author*
* Koomoter, Zeno

**Marner, Robert**
See　Budrys, Algirdas Jonas

**Marnie, Hal**
See　Marnie, Harry Sylvester

**Marnie, Harry Sylvester** 1918-
[BE]
*American baseball player*
* Marnie, Hal

**Marno, Anne**
See　Italiano, Anna Maria Luisa

**Marolewski, Fred Daniel** 1928-
[BE]
*American baseball player*
* Marolewski, Fritz

**Marolewski, Fritz**
See　Marolewski, Fred Daniel

**Marontz, Louis Aston**
See　Simpson, Louis

**Marossi, Ruth**
See　Krefetz, Ruth

**Marot, Clement** 1484?-1544
[HN, SN]
*French poet*
* [The] Chaucer of France
* [The] French Chaucer
* [The] Poet of Princes
* [The] Valet Poet

**Marot, Jean**
See　Desmaretz, Jean

**Marotte, Jean Gilles** 1945-
[FHE, SMG]
*Canadian-born hockey player*
* Crunch, Captain

**Marprelate, Martin**
See　Penry, John

**Marquand, J. P.**
See　Marquand, John Phillips

**Marquand, John Phillips**
1893-1960　[LC, WW]
*American author*
* Marquand, J. P.
* Phillips, John

**Marquand, Josephine**
See　Gladstone, Josephine

**Marquard, Brick**
See　Marquard, Carl

**Marquard, Carl** ?-1978　[FIR]
*Cinematographer*
* Marquard, Brick

**Marquard, Leo[pold]** 1897-　[CA]
*South African author*
* Burger, John

**Marquard, Richard William**
1889-1980　[BAB, PB, SR]
*American baseball player*
* [The] Eleven Thousand Dollar
Beauty
* [The] Eleven Thousand Dollar
Lemon
* [The] Eleven Thousand Dollar
Wonder
* Marquard, Rube

**Marquard, Rube**
See　Marquard, Richard William

**Marquardt, Albert Ludwig**
1902-1968　[BE]
*American baseball player*
* Marquardt, Ollie

**Marquardt, Ollie**
See　Marquardt, Albert Ludwig

**Marques, Zaccaria**
See　Marques, Zacharias Cyrilo

**Marques, Zacharias Cyrilo** 1937-
[OP]
*Brazilian opera singer*
* Marques, Zaccaria

**Marquess, Clarence Emmett** 1925-
[CEI]
*Canadian-born hockey player*
* Marquess, Mark

**Marquess, Mark**
See　Marquess, Clarence Emmett

**Marquette, Bud**
See　Marquette, Clayton

**Marquette, Clayton** 20th c.　[BBH]
*American gymnastics coach*
* Marquette, Bud

**Marquez, Canena**
See　Marquez, Luis Angel

**Marquez, Francisco** 20th c.　[RBE]
*Mexican boxer*
* Marquez, Trompo

**Marquez, Gonzalo** 1946-　[PB]
*Venezuelan-born baseball player*
* Marquez, Hurricane

**Marquez, Hurricane**
See　Marquez, Gonzalo

**Marquez, Leonardo** 1818- ?
[DNNS, FFF]
*Mexican army officer*
* [The] Tiger of Tacayuba [or
Tacubaya?]

**Marquez, Luis Angel** 1925-　[BE]
*Puerto Rican-born baseball player*
* Marquez, Canena

**Marquez, Raymond** 20th c.　[PHM]
*American underworld figure*
* Marquez, Spanish Raymond

**Marquez, Spanish Raymond**
See　Marquez, Raymond

**Marquez, Trompo**
See　Marquez, Francisco

**Marquez Lopez, Francisca**
1888-1962   [BEW, CED]
*Spanish actress and singer*
* Meller, Raquel

**Marquez y Gispert, Matias Felipe**
1851-1887   [CW]
*Cuban author*
* Aclea, Damaso Gil

**Marquis au Courtnez**
See   Guillaume d'Orange

**[Le] Marquis de Brandenbourg**
See   Frederick II

**[The] Marquis Duke of Cadiz**
See   Ponce de Leon, Rodrigo

**Marquis, Jean-Robert** 20th c.   [WF]
*Film art director*
* Altan, Francesco Tullio

**Marquis, M.** 20th c.   [MBF]
*British author*
* Williams, Richard [house
   pseudonym]

**Marquis, Noonie**
See   Marquis, Roger Julian

**Marquis, Roger Julian** 1937-   [BE]
*American baseball player*
* Marquis, Noonie

**Marr, Charles W.** 1862-1912   [BE]
*American baseball player*
* Marr, Lefty

**Marr, Lefty**
See   Marr, Charles W.

**Marr, N. J.**
See   Marr-Johnson, Nancy

**Marr, William**
See   Dobie, William

**Marr-Johnson, Diana [Maugham]**
1908-   [CA]
*British author*
* Maugham, Diana

**Marr-Johnson, Nancy** 1921?-
[CW]
*British-born author and journalist*
* Marr, N. J.

**Marrack, J. F.** 20th c.   [CA]
*Author*
* Potiphar [joint pseudonym with
   (George) Anthony Hern]

**Marradi, Giovanni** 1852-1922
[WBD]
*Italian poet*
* Labronio, G.

**Marre, Albert**
See   Moshinski, Albert

**Marreco, Anne**
See   Wignall, Anne

**Marrero, Adriano** 20th c.   [RBE]
*Dominican boxer*
* Marrero, Nani

**Marrero, Connie**
See   Marrero, Conrado Eugenio
Ramos

**Marrero, Conrado Eugenio Ramos**
1917-   [BE]
*Cuban-born baseball player*
* Marrero, Connie

**Marrero, Nani**
See   Marrero, Adriano

**Marric, J. J.**
See   Creasey, John

**[A] Married Critic**
See   Janin, Jules Gabriel

**Marriner, Edythe** 1918-1975
[BDF, FC, WEF]
*American actress*
* Hayward, Susan

**Marriott, Alice**
See   Edgar, Mrs. R.

**Marriott, Buck**
See   Meagher, M.

**Marriott, James William**
1884-1953   [SFL]
*Author*
* Wray, Roger

**Marriott, Moore**
See   Moore-Marriott, George
Thomas

**Marrison, Leslie William** 1901-
[AW, CA, WD]
*Irish-born author*
* Dowley, D. M.

**Marron Eufrasio, Alejandro** 1916-
[GS]
*Mexican bullfighter*
* Farolito [Little Lighthouse]

**Marroquin, Patricio**
See   Markun, Patricia Maloney

**Marrou, Henri Irenee** 1904-   [IAW]
*French music critic*
* Davenson, Henri

**Marrow, Buck**
See   Marrow, Charles Kennon

**Marrow, Charles Kennon** 1909-
[BE]
*American baseball player*
* Marrow, Buck

**Marrs, Stella** 1932-   [EJ7]
*American singer*
* Soft Soul, Ms.

**Marryatt, Florence**
See   Ross-Church, Florence M.

**Marryatt, Frederick** 1792-1848
[PA]
*Author*
* Violet, M.

**Marryshow, Theophilus Albert**
1887-1958   [CW]
*Grenadan poet and legislator*
* Golden, Max T.

**Mars, Andre** 1515-1576   [PA]
*Author*
* Massius

**Mars, Danny**
See   Marcus, David

**Mars, E. C.**
See   Mazani, Eric C. F. Nhando

**Mars, Jean Price**
See   Price-Mars, Jean

**Mars, Marjorie**
See   Brown, Marjorie

**Mars, Mickey**
See   Marcus, David

**Mars, Mlle.**
See   Boutet, Anne Francoise
Hippolyte

**[The] Mars of China**
See   Quang-yoo

**[The] Mars of Portugal**
See   Albuquerque, Alfonso [or
Affonso] de

**Mars, W. T.**
See   Mars, Witold Tadeusz J.

**Mars, Witold Tadeusz J.** 1912-
[CA, SAT]
*Polish-born artist and illustrator*
* Mars, W. T.

**Marsala, Mario Salvatore**
1909-1975   [PMJ, WWJ]
*American jazz musician*
* Marsala, Marty

**Marsala, Marty**
See   Marsala, Mario Salvatore

**Marsano, Ramon**
See   Dinges, John [Charles]

**Marsden, Anthony**
See   Sutton, Eric Graham Sutton

**Marsden, Frederick**
See   Silver, W. A.

**Marsden, Gerrard** 1942-   [RO2]
*British musician*
* Gerry

**Marsden, James**
See   Creasey, John

**Marsden, John Howard**   [PA]
*Author*
* Philomon

**Marsden, Samuel** 1764-1838
[DNNF]
*Australian clergyman and
missionary*
* [The] Apostle of New Zealand

**Marsden-Clark, Patricia** 1899-
[THR]
*British actress and singer*
* Malone, Patricia

**Marse Henry**
See   Watterson, Henry

**Marse Joe McCarthy**
See   McCarthy, Joseph Vincent

**Marsee, Susanne**
See   Dowell, Susan Irene

**Marseilles' Good Bishop**
See   De Belsunce, Henri Francois
Xavier

**Marsh, A-Mo**
See   Marsh, Amos

**Marsh, Amos** 20th c.
*American football player*
* Marsh, A-Mo

**Marsh, Analyticus**
See   Morrison, Marsh

**Marsh, Andrew**
See   O'Donovan, John

**Marsh, Carol**
See   Simpson, Norma

**Marsh, Constance Crane** 19th c.
[FFF]
*American poet*
* Gabriel, Virginia

**Marsh, E.**   [PA]
*Author*
* Nellie

**Marsh, Edwin**
See   Schorb, Edwin Marsh

**Marsh, Garry**
See   Geraghty, Leslie March

**Marsh, Henry**
See   Saklatvala, Beram

**Marsh, J. E.**
See   Marshall, Evelyn

**Marsh, James** 1794-1842   [PA]
*Author*
* Philopolis

**Marsh, Jean**
See   Marshall, Evelyn

**Marsh, Joan**
See   Marsh, John

**Marsh, John** 1907-
[CAP, WD, WGT]
*British author and historian*
* Davis, Julia
* Elton, John
* Harley, John
* Hastings, Harrington
* Lawrence, Irene
* Marsh, Joan
* Richmond, Grace
* Sawley, Petra
* Ware, Monica
* Woodward, Lilian

**Marsh, Mae**
See   Marsh, Mary Warne

**Marsh, Margaret** 1892-1925   [SC]
*American actress*
* Loveridge, Marguerite

**Marsh, Margaret Munnerlyn
Mitchell** 1900-1949   [NAA]
*American author*
* Mitchell, Margaret

**Marsh, Marion**
See   Krauth, Violet

**Marsh, Mary Warne** 1895-1968
[BDF, F1, FC]
*American actress*
* Marsh, Mae

**Marsh, Muriel** 1898-   [THR]
*Irish-born actress*
* Alexander, Muriel

**Marsh, Patrick**
See   Hiscock, Leslie

**Marsh, Paul**
See   Hopkins, Kenneth

**Marsh, Rebecca**
See   Neubauer, William Arthur

**Marsh, Richard** 20th c.   [RO2]
*American singer*
* Saxon, Sky

**Marshal de Saxe**
See   Saxe, [Hermann] Maurice de

**Marshal, James**
See   Bounds, Sydney J[ames]

**[The] Marshal of the Army of God
and Holy Church**
See   FitzWalter, Robert

**Marshal, William** ?-1219   [SN]
*First Earl of Pembroke and Strigul*
* [The] Protector

**Marshall, Albert Leroy** 1943-
[SMG]
*Canadian-born hockey player*
* Marshall, Cat
* Marshall, Moose

**Marshall, Archibald**
See  Marshall, Arthur Hammond

**Marshall, Arthur C.** 20th c.   [MBF]
*British author and editor*
* Brooke, Arthur
* Crane, Berkeley
* Steele, Howard [house pseudonym]
* Yorke, Carras

**Marshall, Arthur Hammond**
1866-1934   [SFL]
*Author*
* Marshall, Archibald

**Marshall, B. R.**
See  Marshall, Brian Roberts

**Marshall, Bart**
See  Marshall, Herbert

**Marshall, Boisy**
See  Marshall, William

**Marshall, Brenda**
See  Ankerson, Ardis

**Marshall, Brian Roberts** 1935-
[ART]
*British artist*
* Marshall, B. R.

**Marshall, Buck**
See  Marshall, David

**Marshall, Buster**
See  Marshall, Vivian Burey

**Marshall, Cat**
See  Marshall, Albert Leroy

**Marshall, Catherine**
See  DuBreuil, Elizabeth Lorinda

**Marshall, Cecelia A. Suyat** 1928-
[IBW]
*Wife of American Supreme Court Justice, Thurgood Marshall*
* Marshall, Cissy

**Marshall, Charles** 1899?-1975
[SW]
*American actor*
* Marshall, Red

**Marshall, Charles** 19th c.   [PA]
*Author*
* Grey, Heraclitus
* Harkaway

**Marshall, Charles Anthony [Charlie]**
See  Marczlewicz, Charles Anthony

**Marshall, Charles C., III** 1945?-
*American student activist*
* Marshall, Chip

**Marshall, Charles Hunt** 20th c.
[WW]
*Author*
* Hunt, Peter [joint pseudonym with George Worthing Yates]

**Marshall, Chester Alan**
See  Chess, Stanley

**Marshall, Chip**
See  Marshall, Charles C., III

**Marshall, Christabel**  ?-1960   [LC]
*British author*
* St. John, Christopher Marie

**Marshall, Cissy**
See  Marshall, Cecelia A. Suyat

**Marshall, Clarence Westly** 1925-
[BE]
*American baseball player*
* Marshall, Cuddles

**Marshall, Cuddles**
See  Marshall, Clarence Westly

**Marshall, Cy**
See  Marshall, Roy DeVerne

**Marshall, David** 20th c.
[BBH, CSH]
*Canadian lacrosse player*
* Marshall, Buck

**Marshall, Denz**
See  Marshall, Malcolm Denzil

**Marshall, Doc**
See  Marshall, Edward Herbert

**Marshall, Doc**
See  Marshall, William Riddle

**Marshall, Douglas**
See  McClintock, Marshall

**Marshall, E. G.**
See  Marshall, Everett G.

**Marshall, E. P.**
See  Montgomery, Rutherford George

**Marshall, Edmund**
See  Hopkins, Kenneth

**Marshall, Edmund**   [FFF]
*Writer*
* Cantianus

**Marshall, Edward Herbert** 1906-
[BE]
*American baseball player*
* Marshall, Doc

**Marshall, Elizabeth Margaret**
1926-   [IAW]
*Scottish author*
* Sutherland, Elizabeth

**Marshall, Emily**
See  Hall, Bennie Caroline [Humble]

**Marshall, Evelyn** 1897-
[AW, CA, SAT]
*British author*
* Bourne, Lesley
* Marsh, J. E.
* Marsh, Jean

**Marshall, Everett G.** 1910-   [FC]
*American actor*
* Marshall, E. G.

**Marshall, Francis** 20th c.   [ART]
*British illustrator, painter, author*
* F. M.

**Marshall, Gary**
See  Snow, Charles Horace

**Marshall, George Catlett**
1880-1959   [CND]
*American military leader*
* Braid [code name used during World War II]
* Fourfold [code name used during World War II]
* Mell, Mr. [code name used during World War II]

**Marshall, H. P.** 20th c.   [MBF]
*British author*
* Stark, Jonathan

**Marshall, Henry**
See  Battcock, Marshall King

**Marshall, Herbert** 1890-
*British actor*
* Marshall, Bart

**Marshall, Iron Mike**
See  Marshall, Michael Grant

**Marshall, Jack**
See  Marshall, William

**Marshall, James Vance**
See  Payne, Donald Gordon

**Marshall, James Vance** 1887-1964
[CAP]
*Australian author*
* Doone, Jice

**Marshall, Jim** 20th c.   [IBW]
*American football player*
* Marshall, Wrong Way

**Marshall, Joanne**
See  La Cock, Joanne Letitia

**Marshall, Joanne**
See  Rundle, Anne

**Marshall, John**
See  Pepper, Frank S.

**Marshall, John** 1755-1835   [SN]
*American Supreme Court justice*
* [The] Expounder of the Constitution

**Marshall, Joseph** 1902-1948
[PMJ, WWJ]
*American jazz musician*
* Marshall, Kaiser

**Marshall, Kaiser**
See  Marshall, Joseph

**Marshall, Katherine Helen Maud**
?-1945   [LC]
*British author*
* Diver, Maud

**Marshall, Kim**
See  Marshall, Michael [Kimbrough]

**Marshall, Lloyd?**
See  Wilding, Philip

**Marshall, Lovat**
See  Duncan, W[illiam] Murdoch

**Marshall, Maco**
See  Marshall, Malcolm Denzil

**Marshall, Malcolm Denzil** 1958-
[DC]
*West Indian cricketer*
* Marshall, Denz
* Marshall, Maco

**Marshall, Margaret Lenore Wiley**
1908-   [CAP, WD]
*American author*
* Wiley, Margaret L.

**Marshall, Marguerite Mooers**
See  Dean, Marguerite Mooers Marshall

**Marshall, Marjorie Bell** 1916-
[AW]
*British author*
* March, Stella

**Marshall, Mel[vin]** 1911-   [CA]
*American author*
* Cory, Ray

**Marshall, Michael [Kimbrough]**
1948-   [CA]
*American author and educator*
* Marshall, Kim

**Marshall, Michael Grant** 1943-
[SMG]
*American baseball player*
* Marshall, Iron Mike

**Marshall, Moose**
See  Marshall, Albert Leroy

**Marshall, Mort**
See  Lichtenstein, Mortimer Haig

**Marshall, Mrs. Frank**   [FFF]
*Entertainer*
* Cavendish, Ada

**Marshall, Oliver P.**   [PA]
*Author*
* Revilo

**Marshall, Percy**
See  Young, Percy M[arshall]

**Marshall, Raymond**
See  Raymond, Rene

**Marshall, Red**
See  Marshall, Charles

**Marshall, Roy DeVerne** 1890-   [BE]
*American baseball player*
* Marshall, Cy
* Marshall, Rube

**Marshall, Rube**
See  Marshall, Roy DeVerne

**Marshall, S. L. A.**
See  Marshall, Samuel Lyman Atwood

**Marshall, Samuel Lyman Atwood**
1900-1977
*American general, historian, journalist*
* Marshall, S. L. A.
* Marshall, Slam

**Marshall, Slam**
See  Marshall, Samuel Lyman Atwood

**Marshall, Stephen** 1594?-1655
[DEP, DNNS, FFF]
*British clergyman*
* [The] Geneva Bull

**Marshall, T. W.** 19th c.   [PA]
*Author*
* Chausable, Archdeacon

**Marshall, Thoroughgood** 1908-
[IBW]
*American Supreme Court Justice*
* Civil Rights, Mr.
* Marshall, Thurgood

**Marshall, Thurgood**
See  Marshall, Thoroughgood

**Marshall, Tully**
See  Phillips, William

**Marshall, Vivian Burey**  ?-1955
[IBW]
*Wife of American Supreme Court Justice, Thurgood Marshall*
* Marshall, Buster

**Marshall, William**
See  Walpole, Horatio [Fourth Earl of Orford]

**Marshall, William** 1907-
[IBW, OBW]
*American baseball player and bowler*
* Marshall, Boisy
* Marshall, Jack

**Marshall, William Riddle**
1875-1959 [BE]
*American baseball player*
* Marshall, Doc

**Marshall, Willie**
See Marshall, Willmott Charles

**Marshall, Willmott Charles** 1931-
[CEI]
*Canadian-born hockey player*
* Marshall, Willie

**Marshall, Wrong Way**
See Marshall, Jim

**[The] Marshalltown Infant**
See Anson, Adrian Constantine

**Marshner, Connaught Coyne** 1951-
[CA]
*American writer*
* Sarsfield, C. P.

**Marsland, Bishop of**
See Duncan, Ronald [Frederick Henry]

**Marsland, Maj. Gen.**
See Duncan, Ronald [Frederick Henry]

**Marson, Aileen**
See Pitt-Marson, Aileen

**Marsten, Richard**
See Lombino, Salvatore A.

**Marston, Adelaide** [joint pseudonym with Lynn Stone]
See Richton, Addy

**Marston, Adelaide** [joint pseudonym with Addy Richton]
See Stone, Lynn

**Marston, Edward** 1825-1914
[WWL]
*British author and publisher*
* Amateur Angler

**Marston, Hyde**
See Carlton, Captain

**Marston, [Major] Jeffery Eardley**
1887- [LAO]
*Welsh-born author*
* Jeffery, Jeffery E.

**Marston, John** 1575-1634
[DEL, WBD]
*British playwright*
* Kinsayder, W.

**Marston, John Westland** 1819- ?
[PA]
*Author*
* Crispinus

**Marston, [Col.] Marvin R.** 20th c.
[BBH]
*American sled dog racer*
* Marston, Muktuk

**Marston, Max**
See Marston, Maxwell R.

**Marston, Maxwell R.** 1892- [EG]
*American golfer*
* Marston, Max

**Marston, Muktuk**
See Marston, [Col.] Marvin R.

**Marston, William Moulton**
1893-1947 [WECO]
*American author and cartoonist*
* Moulton, Charles

**Mart, Donovan**
See Martin, E. Le Breton

**[Le] Marteau des Heretiques**
See Ailly, Pierre d'

**Martel**
See Frothingham, Washington

**Martel, Charles**
See Charles [or Karl]

**Martel, Doc**
See Martel, Leon Alphonse

**Martel, Don Robert** 1939- [CWG]
*American country-western performer*
* Martel, Marty

**Martel, Leon Alphonse** 1883-1947
[BE]
*American baseball player*
* Martel, Doc
* Martel, Marty

**Martel, Marty**
See Martel, Don Robert

**Martel, Marty**
See Martel, Leon Alphonse

**Martel, Marty**
See Martel, Wilbert

**Martel, Wilbert** 1887-1958
[BBH, CSH]
*Canadian bowler*
* King of the Candlepins
* Martel, Marty

**Martel de Janville, Comtesse de**
See Riquetti de Mirabeau, Sibylle Gabrielle Marie Antoinette

**Martell, Charles**
See Delf, Thomas

**Martell, Claudia**
See Wolff, Victoria

**Martell, James**
See Bingley, David Ernest

**Martens, Adolphe-Adhemar-Louis-Michel**
1898-1962 [CA, TCL]
*Belgian playwright and author*
* De Ghelderode, Michel

**Martens, Fernand** 1904-1970 [FC]
*French actor*
* Gravet, Fernand

**Martens, Paul**
See Southwold, Stephen

**Martequilla, Angel** 1940- [BX]
*Cuban-born boxer*
* Napoles, Jose

**Martes, Jose Antonio** 1920- [CW]
*Curacaon poet and author*
* Lauffer, Pierre

**Martha, Henry**
See Finkelstein, Mark

**Martha Jean, the Queen**
See Steinberg, Martha Jean Jones

**Marti, Pepe**
See Marti Perez, Jose Julian

**Marti Perez, Jose Julian**
1853-1895 [CW]
*Cuban poet, playwright, author*
* Marti, Pepe

**Martin, [Frater]**
See Gillet, Stanislaus

**Martin** 316?- 397? [SN, WBD]
*Saint*
* [The] Apostle of Gaul
* Martin of Tours

**Martin, A. L.** 20th c. [MBF]
*British author*
* Reid, Desmond [house pseudonym]

**Martin, Abe**
See Hubbard, Frank McKinney

**Martin, Abe**
See Martin, Glen

**Martin, Albert**
See Mehan, Joseph Albert

**Martin, Albert**
See Nussbaum, Al[bert F.]

**Martin, Alexandre** 1815-1895
[WBD]
*French mechanic and politician*
* Albert the Workingman

**Martin, Alfred Manuel**
See Pesano, Alfred Manuel

**Martin, Alphonse Case** 1845-1933
[BE]
*American baseball player*
* Martin, Phoney

**Martin, Amos**
See Martin, Anthony

**Martin, Andre**
See Jacoby, Henry

**Martin, Anthony**
See Glynn, Anthony Arthur

**Martin, Anthony** 1949- [SMG]
*American football player*
* Martin, Amos

**Martin, April**
See Sherrill, Dorothy

**Martin, Babe**
See Martinovich, Boris Michael

**Martin, Barnes Robertson** 1923-
[BE]
*American baseball player*
* Martin, Barney

**Martin, Barney**
See Martin, Barnes Robertson

**Martin, Big Jim**
See Martin, James

**Martin, Bill**
See Joel, Billy

**Martin, Billy**
See Pesano, Alfred Manuel

**Martin, Blind George**
See Phelps, Arthur

**Martin, Bob** 1898- [BX, RBE]
*American boxer*
* Martin, Fighting Bob

**Martin, Bon Louis Henri** 1810- ?
[PA]
*Author*
* Felix
* Irner

**Martin, Butch**
See Martin, Oliver, Jr.

**Martin, Cannonball**
See Martino, Edward Vittorio

**Martin, Charles** 1917-1974 [B10]
*French fashion designer and composer*
* Esterel

**Martin, Chink**
See Abraham, Martin

**Martin, Chris-Pin**
See Martin Piaz, Ysabel Ponciana Chris-Pin

**Martin, Christopher**
See Hoyt, Edwin P[almer], Jr.

**Martin, Cort**
See Sherman, Jory [Tecumseh]

**Martin, Cye**
See Martin, Seymore

**Martin, Daisy**
See James, Daisy

**Martin, David** 1915- [TCC]
*Hungarian-born author and poet*
* Spinifex

**Martin, Dean**
See Crocetti, Dino

**Martin, Dickie**
See Martin, Harry B.

**Martin, Doc**
See Martin, Harold Winthrop

**Martin, Dorothea**
See Hewitt, Kathleen Douglas

**Martin, Dugie**
See Martin, Slater

**Martin, E. Le Breton** 1874-1944
[MBF]
*British author*
* Lee, Raymond
* Mart, Donovan
* Shaw, Martin

**Martin, Eddie**
See Martino, Edward Vittorio

**Martin, Egbert** 1859-1887 [CW]
*Guyanese poet*
* Leo

**Martin, Elizabeth** 1869-1941 [SC]
*American actress*
* Weldon, Lillian

**Martin, Elwood Goode** 1893- [BE]
*American baseball player*
* Martin, Speed

**Martin, Ernest H.**
See Markowitz, Ernest H.

**Martin, Eugene**
See De Vaux, Baron

**Martin, Eugene** [house pseudonym]
[Stratemeyer Syndicate]
See Stratemeyer, Edward L.

**Martin, Eugenie** 1879?-1959
[BEW]
*Russian-born actress*
* Geniat, Marcelle

**Martin, Fiddlin'**
See Martin, Frank

**Martin, Fiddlin' Joe**
See Martin, Joe

**Martin, Fighting Bob**
See Martin, Bob

**Martin, Francis**
See Reid, Charles [Stuart]

**Martin, Francois Xavier**
1764?-1846 [FFF]
*American jurist*
* [The] Father of the Jurisprudence
of Louisiana

**Martin, Frank** 20th c. [BWW]
*American musician*
* Martin, Fiddlin'

**Martin, Fredric**
See Christopher, Matt[hew F.]

**Martin, G. A.**
See Martin, Gloria Ann

**Martin, Ged**
See Martin, Gerald Warren

**Martin, George**
See Martin, Jorge

**Martin, George** 1889- [NAA]
*American editor and writer*
* Pepper, George

**Martin, George** 20th c. [GW]
*American rodeo performer*
* Martin, Tex

**Martin, George Alfred** 1911-
[BBH]
*American wrestling coach*
* [The] Father of High School
Wrestling

**Martin, Gerald Warren** 1945- [CA]
*British-born historian and author*
* Martin, Ged

**Martin, Glen** 20th c. [BBH]
*American baseball coach*
* Martin, Abe

**Martin, Gloria Ann** 1937- [IAW]
*American author and poet*
* London, Lisa
* Martin, G. A.
* Tramin, A. G.
* Tramin, Ed
* Tramin, Lisa

**Martin, Greg**
See Miller, George Louquet

**Martin, Harold Winthrop**
1887-1925 [BE]
*American baseball player*
* Martin, Doc

**Martin, Harry B.** 1874-1959 [GF]
*American golf writer*
* Martin, Dickie

**Martin, Harvey** 1950- [SMG]
*American football player*
* Martin, Too Mean

**Martin, [Sir] Henry** 17th c.
[FFF, PA]
*British author*
* Phoenix

**Martin, Herschel Ray** 1909- [BE]
*American baseball player*
* Martin, Hersh

**Martin, Hersh**
See Martin, Herschel Ray

**Martin, Honest Abe**
See Martin, Othol H.

**Martin, Hubert Jacques** 1943-
[B10, CEI, FHE]
*Canadian-born hockey player and
aviator*
* Martin, Pit

**Martin, Hugh Whitfield**
1874-1952 [BBD]
*American opera singer*
* Martin, Riccardo

**Martin, Humanity**
See Martin, Richard

**Martin, J. C.**
See Martin, Joseph Clifton

**Martin, J. F.** [FFF]
*American writer*
* Hydrant Chuck

**Martin, Jacques** ?-1562 [PA]
*Author*
* Marinus

**Martin, James** 1886- [IBW]
*American businessman*
* Martin, Big Jim

**Martin, James R.** 1919- [FB]
*American football player*
* Martin, Jungle Jim

**Martin, Janet**
See Garfinkel, Bernard

**Martin, Jay**
See Golding, Morton J[ay]

**Martin, Jean Baptiste** 1659-1735
[RH]
*French painter*
* [Des] Batailles [Of Battles]

**Martin, Jeremy** [joint pseudonym
with Martin P. Levin]
See Levin, Marcia Obrasky

**Martin, Jeremy** [joint pseudonym
with Marcia Obrasky Levin]
See Levin, Martin P.

**Martin, Joe** 1900-1975 [BWW]
*American singer*
* Martin, Fiddlin' Joe

**Martin, John**
See Shepard, Morgan Van
Roorbach

**Martin, John**
See Tatham, Laura

**Martin, John** 1791-1855 [PA]
*Author*
* J. M.

**Martin, John Leonard** 1904-1965
[AS, BE, PB]
*American baseball player*
* Martin, Pepper
* [The] Wild Horse of the Osage

**Martin, Jorge** 20th c. [WF]
*Actor*
* Martin, George

**Martin, Jose** 1843-1910 [GS]
*Spanish bullfighter*
* La Santera [The Sanctuary
Keeper]

**Martin, Jose L[uis]** 1921- [CA]
*Puerto Rican-born author and
educator*
* Yunkel, Ramar

**Martin, Joseph Clifton** 1936- [BE]
*American baseball player*
* Martin, J. C.

**Martin, Joseph Samuel** [Joe]
1876-1964 [BE]
*American baseball player*
* Martin, Silent Joe

**Martin, Joy** 1922- [CA]
*American author and educator*
* Crandall, Joy

**Martin, Judith Sylvia** 1938- [CA]
*American author and columnist*
* Manners, Miss

**Martin, Judy**
See Overstake, Eva Alaine

**Martin, June Hall**
See McCash, June Hall

**Martin, Jungle Jim**
See Martin, James R.

**Martin, Kevin**
See Pelton, Robert W[ayne]

**Martin, [Basil] Kingsley** 1897-1969
[CA]
*British editor and writer*
* Critic

**Martin, Lady Theodore** 19th c.
[FFF]
*British actress*
* Fawcitt, Helen

**Martin, Lance** 1918- [IAW]
*American author*
* Ancel, Martin

**Martin, Lawrence** 1895- [NAA]
*American educator and writer*
* Aylesworth, Allison
* Rutherford, Chas.

**Martin, Leila**
See Markowitz, Leila

**Martin, Lennie**
See Marino, Rinaldo R.

**Martin, Linda Lou**
See Martin, Wanda Frances
Arnold

**Martin, Little Chink**
See Abraham, Martin, Jr.

**Martin, Lloyd** 1916- [EJ, PMJ]
*American jazz musician*
* Martin, Skip

**Martin, Lucien**
See Gabel, Joseph

**[The] Martin Luther of Switzerland**
See Zwingli, Ulrich

**Martin, Lynn** 20th c.
*American politician*
* [The] Ax

**Martin, Malachi** 20th c. [CA]
*Irish-born American author*
* Serafian, Michael

**Martin, Marcia**
See Levin, Marcia Obrasky

**Martin, Maude**
See Bruno, Guido

**Martin, Morris** 20th c.
*American soil-conservation expert*
* Martin, Red

**Martin, Mrs. T. J.** [FFF]
*Entertainer*
* Fiske, Marion

**Martin, Nancy**
See Salmon, Annie Elizabeth
[Martin]

**Martin, Nancy** 20th c.
*American entertainer*
* [The] Pride of the West Virginia
Hills

**Martin, Nell Columbia Boyer**
1890- [WW]
*Author*
* Boyer, Columbia

**Martin, Netta** 20th c. [AW]
*Scottish journalist and broadcaster*
* Ashton, Lucy

**Martin, Octave**
See Maurras,
Charles-Marie-Photius

**Martin, Oliver**
See Davies, Ernest

**Martin, Oliver, Jr.** 1936- [IBW]
*American bicycle racer*
* Martin, Butch

**Martin, Othol H.** 1908- [FB]
*American football coach*
* Martin, Honest Abe

**Martin, Patricia Miles** 1899-
[CA, SAT, WD]
*American author and poet*
* Lane, Jerry
* Miles, Miska

**Martin, Paul**
See Deale, Kenneth Edwin Lee

**Martin, Paul**
See Rade, Paul Martin

**Martin, Paul R.**
See Martin-Dillon, Paul

**Martin, Pepper**
See Martin, John Leonard

**Martin, Pete**
See Halfpenny, Peter

**Martin, Pete**
See Martin, William Thornton

**Martin, Peter**
See Chaundler, Christine

**Martin, Peter**
See Leckie, Peter Martin

**Martin, Phoney**
See Martin, Alphonse Case

**Martin, Pit**
See Martin, Hubert Jacques

**Martin, R. Johnson**
See Mehta, Rustam Jehangir

**Martin, Ray** 20th c.
*American billiard player*
* Midnight Cowboy

**Martin, Red**
See Martin, Morris

**Martin of Tours**
See Martin

**Martin of Troppau** ?-1278 [WBD]
*Prelate and author*
* Martinus Polonus
* [The] Pole

**Martin, Reginald Alec** 1900-
[SFL, WGT]
*Author*
* Cameron, Brett

**Martin, Reginald Alec** (Continued)
* Dixon, Rex
* Eliott, E. C.
* Martin, Rex
* Martin, Robert
* Martin, Scott

**Martin, Rex**
*See* Martin, Reginald Alec

**Martin, Riccardo**
*See* Martin, Hugh Whitfield

**Martin, Richard**
*See* Creasey, John

**Martin, Richard** 1754- ? [HN]
*British politician*
* Martin, Humanity

**Martin, Richard A.**
*See* Rosenblatt, Richard Andrew

**Martin, Rick**
*See* Martin, Robert L.

**Martin, Robert**
*See* Martin, Reginald Alec

**Martin, Robert [Lee]** 1908- [CA]
*American author*
* Roberts, Lee

**Martin, Robert Bernard** 1918-
[CA, CC, WD]
*American author, critic, educator*
* Bernard, Robert

**Martin, Robert L.** 1919?- [B10]
*American gambler*
* Martin, Rick

**Martin, Robert W.**
*See* Pelton, Robert W[ayne]

**Martin, Ross**
*See* Rosenblatt, Martin

**Martin, Ruth** [house pseudonym]
*See* Rayner, Claire

**Martin, Sallie M. D.** [FFF]
*Writer*
* Sibyl

**Martin, Sam**
*See* Moskowitz, Sam

**Martin, Samuel** 18th c. [SN]
*British politician*
* [The] Duellist

**Martin, Sara**
*See* Dunn, Sara

**Martin, Scott**
*See* Martin, Reginald Alec

**Martin, Seymore** 1914-1972 [SC]
*American actor*
* Martin, Cye

**Martin, Shane**
*See* Johnston, George Henry

**Martin, Silent Joe**
*See* Martin, Joseph Samuel [Joe]

**Martin, Skip**
*See* Martin, Lloyd

**Martin, Slater** 1925- [BB]
*American basketball player*
* Martin, Dugie

**Martin, Smokey Joe**
*See* Martin, William Joseph [Joe]

**Martin, Speed**
*See* Martin, Elwood Goode

**Martin, Stella**
*See* Heyer, Georgette

**Martin, Tex**
*See* Martin, George

**Martin, [Sir] Theodore** 1816-1909
[WWL]
*Scottish-born British author*
* Gaultier, Bon [joint pseudonym
 with William Edmonstoune
 Aytoun]

**Martin, Therese** 1873-1897 [WBD]
*Saint*
* Little Flower of Jesus
* Therese de Lisieux

**Martin, Thomas Hector** 1913-
[ESF, SFL, WGT]
*British author*
* Saxon, Peter [house pseudonym]
* Thomas, Martin

**Martin, Tony**
*See* Morris, Alvin

**Martin, Too Mean**
*See* Martin, Harvey

**Martin, Vicky**
*See* Storey, Victoria Carolyn

**Martin, Violet Florence** 1865-1915
[LC, TC]
*Irish author*
* Ross, Martin
* Somerville and Ross [joint
 pseudonym with Edith Anna
 Oenone Somerville]

**Martin, W.** 20th c. [MBF]
*British author*
* Kingsley, Hamilton

**Martin, Wanda Frances Arnold**
1926- [CWG]
*American country-western performer*
* Martin, Linda Lou

**Martin, Webber**
*See* Silverberg, Robert

**Martin, Wendy**
*See* Martini, Teri

**Martin, William** [DEL, RH]
*Author*
* Parley, Peter

**Martin, William Joseph [Joe]**
1911-1960 [BE]
*American baseball player*
* Martin, Smokey Joe

**Martin, William Thornton**
1901?-1980
*American author and editor*
* Martin, Pete

**Martin Caro Cases, Francisco**
1915- [GS]
*Spanish bullfighter*
* Curro Caro [Dear Little Curro]

**Martin Caro Cases, Juan** 1910-
[GS]
*Spanish bullfighter*
* Chiquito de la Audiencia

**Martin-Dillon, Paul** 1886- [CAT]
*American author and journalist*
* Martin, Paul R.

**Martin IV**
*See* De Brie, Simon

**Martin Piaz, Ysabel Ponciana
Chris-Pin** 1893-1953 [F1, HCA]
*American actor*
* [El] Comico
* Martin, Chris-Pin

**Martin Ramos, Baldomero** 1940-
[GS]
*Spanish bullfighter*
* Terremoto de Malaga
 [Earthquake from Malaga]

**Martin Sanchez, Santiago** 1938-
[GS, OCS]
*Spanish bullfighter*
* [El] Viti

**Martin V**
*See* Colonna, Ottone [or Oddone]

**Martin y Solar, Vicente** 1754-1810
[WBD]
*Spanish composer*
* Martini, Vicente

**Martina, Joseph John [Joe]**
1889-1962 [BE]
*American baseball player*
* Martina, Oyster Joe

**Martina, Oyster Joe**
*See* Martina, Joseph John [Joe]

**Martindale, [Rev.] C. C.**
*See* Martindale, Cyril Charlie

**Martindale, Cyril Charlie**
1879-1963 [LC]
*British clergyman and author*
* Martindale, [Rev.] C. C.

**Martindale, Spencer**
*See* Wolff, William Deakin

**Martindale, Wink**
*See* Martindale, Winston Conrad

**Martindale, Winston Conrad** 1933-
*American television performer*
* Martindale, Wink

**Martineau, Harriet** 1802-1876
[DEL, PA]
*British author*
* Angelina
* H. M.
* [An] Invalid

**Martinelli, Viola** ?-1967 [SC]
*American actress*
* Holden, Viola

**Martines, Julia**
*See* O'Faolain, Julia

**Martinetti, Mme. Ignacio** [FFF]
*Entertainer*
* Murillo, Edith

**Martinetz, Vivian L.** 1927- [CA]
*American author*
* Broussard, Vivian L.

**Martinez, Buck**
*See* Martinez, John Albert

**Martinez, Felix Anthony** 1950-
[SMG, WWB]
*American baseball player*
* Martinez, Tippy

**Martinez, Gabriel Antonio** 1941-
[BE]
*Cuban-born baseball player*
* Martinez, Tony

**Martinez, Horacio** 20th c. [OBW]
*American baseball player*
* Martinez, Rabbit

**Martinez, Isidora**
*See* King, Mrs. John J.

**Martinez, John Albert** 1948-
[BE, SMG, WWB]
*American baseball player*
* Martinez, Buck

**Martinez, Julio** 1876-1930 [GS]
*Spanish bullfighter*
* Templaito [The Valiant One]

**Martinez, Limonar**
*See* Martinez, Rogelio Ulloa

**Martinez, Lino** 20th c. [WFA]
*Spanish fashion designer*
* Lino

**Martinez, Luis** 1930- [EJ7]
*American jazz musician*
* Martinez, Sabu

**Martinez, Marty**
*See* Martinez, Orlando Olivo

**Martinez, Orlando Olivo** 1941-
[BE]
*Cuban-born baseball player*
* Martinez, Marty

**Martinez, Rabbit**
*See* Martinez, Horacio

**Martinez, Rogelio Ulloa** 1918-
[BE]
*Cuban-born baseball player*
* Martinez, Limonar

**Martinez, Rudy** 1945- [RO2]
*American singer*
* Question Mark

**Martinez, Sabu**
*See* Martinez, Luis

**Martinez, Teddy**
*See* Martinez, Teodoro Noel

**Martinez, Teodoro Noel** 1947-
[BE]
*Dominican-born baseball player*
* Martinez, Teddy

**Martinez, Tippy**
*See* Martinez, Felix Anthony

**Martinez, Tony**
*See* Martinez, Gabriel Antonio

**Martinez Alvarez, Rafael**
1882-1959 [CW, NAA]
*Puerto Rican author and playwright*
* Alva, Martin

**Martinez Davila, Manuel**
1883-1934 [CW]
*Puerto Rican poet and author*
* Arce, Jose de

**Martinez de Hoz, Jose Alfredo**
*Argentinian landowner, industrialist,
government official*
* Dr. Joe

**Martinez de Jarava, Elio Antonio**
1444-1532 [WBD]
*Spanish author*
* Nebrija [or Lebrija], Elio Antonio
 de

**Martinez-Delgado, Luis** 1896-
[AW]
*Colombian author*
* Luimardel

**Martinez Gonzalez, Pedro** 1932-
[GS]
*Spanish bullfighter*
* Pedres [Big Pedro]

**Martinez Ruiz, Jose** 1873?-1967
[CD, CLC, EWL]
*Spanish author and playwright*
* Ahriman
* Azorin
* Candido

**Martinez y Pingarron, Candido**
1867-1925  [GS]
*Spanish bullfighter*
* [El] Manchequito [The Little
  Fellow from La Mancha]

**Martinez Zuviria, Gustavo Adolfo**
1883-1962  [EWL, TC, WBD]
*Argentinian author*
* Wast, Hugo

**Marting, Ruth Lenore** 1907-  [WW]
*Author*
* Bailey, Hilea

**Martingale, Hawser**
*See* Sleeper, John Sherburne

**Martini, George**
*See* Matrisciano, George

**Martini, Guido Joe** 1913-  [BE]
*American baseball player*
* Martini, Southern
* Martini, Wedo

**Martini il Tedesco**
*See* Schwarzendorf, Johann Paul
Agidius

**Martini, Jean Paul Egide**
*See* Schwarzendorf, Johann Paul
Agidius

**Martini, Southern**
*See* Martini, Guido Joe

**Martini, Teri** 1930-  [CA]
*American author*
* King, Alison
* Martin, Wendy
* Martini, Therese

**Martini, Therese**
*See* Martini, Teri

**Martini, Vicente**
*See* Martin y Solar, Vicente

**Martini, Virgilio** 1903-  [CA]
*Italian author*
* Letrusco

**Martini, Wedo**
*See* Martini, Guido Joe

**Martino, Al**
*See* Cini, Alfred

**Martino, Edward Vittorio** 1903-
[BX, RBE, SA]
*American boxer*
* Martin, Cannonball
* Martin, Eddie

**Martino, Pat**
*See* Azzara, Pat

**Martinot, Sadie**
*See* Stinson, Mrs. Frederick

**Martinovich, Boris Michael** 1920-
[BE]
*American baseball player*
* Martin, Babe

**Martins, Jay**
*See* Tener, Martin J.

**Martins de Miranda, David**
*Brazilian faith healer*
* [The] Envoy of the Messiah

**Martinson, Marty**
*See* Martinson, Michael Anthony

**Martinson, Michael Anthony**
1956-  [BR]
*American baseball player*
* Martinson, Marty

**Martinson, Moa**
*See* Svarts, Helga

**Martinus, [Efraim] Frank** 1936-
[CW, IAW]
*West Indian author*
* Arion, F. M.

**Martinus Polonus**
*See* Martin of Troppau

**Martinuzzi, George** 1482-1551
[HN, WBD]
*Hungarian statesman*
* Frater Georgius
* Utjesenovic, Juraj
* [The] Wolsey of Hungary

**Martius**
*See* Rose, Frederick W.

**Martlet**
*See* Davis, Richard Bingham

**Martlew, Mary**
*See* Greenhalgh, Mary

**Martoff, Nickoli** 1922-  [BEW]
*American producer and director*
* Mayo, Nick

**Marton, Francesca**
*See* Bellasis, Margaret Rosa

**Martorano, Joseph** 1927-1972
[SC]
*American actor*
* Corey, Joseph

**Martorell, John**  [SN]
*Spanish author*
* [The] Boccaccio of the Provencal
  Language

**Martov, Julius**
*See* Tsederbaum, Iulii O.

**Marttin, Paul** 1937-  [AW]
*German-born physician and writer*
* Plaut, Martin

**Martyn, Barry** 1941-  [EJ7]
*British-born jazz musician*
* Martyn, Kid

**Martyn, Edward** 1859-1923
[SFL, WGT]
*Irish author*
* Sirius

**Martyn, Henry**
*See* Perry, Martin Henry

**Martyn, Ivor**
*See* Smith, Bernard

**Martyn, Kid**
*See* Martyn, Barry

**Martyn, Myles**
*See* Elliott-Cannon, Arthur Elliott

**Martyn, Oliver**
*See* White, Herbert [Martyn]
Oliver

**Martyn, Phillip**
*See* Tubb, Edwin Charles

**Martyn, William** 1562-1617  [PA]
*Author*
* Old Chatty Cheerful

**Martyn, Wyndham** 1875- ?
[NAA, WW]
*British author*
* Grenvil, William

**Martyn-Green, William** 1899-1975
[BEW, TR]
*British actor and singer*
* Green, Martyn

**[The] Martyr**
*See* Edmund [or Eadmund]

**[The] Martyr**
*See* Edward [or Eadward]

**[The] Martyr**
*See* Justin

**[The] Martyr**
*See* Lucian

**[The] Martyr Abolitionist**
*See* Lovejoy, Elijah Parish

**[The] Martyr Earl**
*See* Stanley, James

**[The] Martyr King**
*See* Charles I

**[The] Martyr King**
*See* Henry VI

**[The] Martyr King**
*See* Louis XVI

**Martyr, Peter**
*See* Anghiera, Pietro Martire

**[The] Martyr President**
*See* Garfield, James Abram

**[The] Martyr President**
*See* Lincoln, Abraham

**[The] Martyr to Science**
*See* Berthollet, Claude Louis

**Marugg, Silvio A.** 1923-  [CW]
*Curacaon poet and author*
* Tip

**Maruna, Annikki**
*See* Aaltonen, [Ilta] Annikki
[Tyyne]

**Marut, Ret** 20th c.
*German actor and author*
* Croves, Hal?
* Torsvan, Traven?
* Traven, B.?

**Maruyama Okyo**
*See* Okyo

**Marvel, Carl Shipp** 1894-  [IAW]
*American chemist and writer*
* Speed

**Marvel, Ik**
*See* Mitchell, Donald Grant

**[The] Marvel of Hockey**
*See* Morenz, Howarth William

**Marvel, Scott**
*See* Findlay, J. Dawson

**Marvell, Andrew**
*See* Davies, Howell

**Marvell, Andrew**
*See* Middleton, Arthur

**Marvell, Andrew** 1620-1678
[DEL, HN, RH]
*British poet and satirist*
* [The] British Aristides
* [The] Incorruptible
* [The] Uncorruptible Commoner

**Marvell, Holt**
*See* Maschwitz, Eric

**[The] Marvellous Boy**
*See* Chatterton, Thomas

**Marvelous Mal Whitfield**
*See* Whitfield, Malvin Greston

**Marvelous Marv Galliher**
*See* Galliher, Marvin Gene

**Marvelous Marv Throneberry**
*See* Throneberry, Marvin Eugene

**Marvelous Marvin Hagler**
*See* Hagler, Marvin

**Marvelous Mel Parnell**
*See* Parnell, Melvin Lloyd

**Marvelous Mel Weldon**
*See* Weldon, Melvin

**Marvenga, Ilse**
*See* Marling, Ilse

**Marville, Pierre Nicolas**
1754-1815  [PA]
*Author*
* Andre

**Marvin, F. S.**
*See* Marvin, Francis Sydney

**Marvin, Francis Sydney** 1863-1943
[LC]
*British author*
* Marvin, F. S.

**Marvin, John T.** 1906-  [CA]
*American author and columnist*
* Richards, Charles

**Marvin, Johnny** 1898-1945  [ECM]
*American country-western performer*
* [The] Lonesome Singer of the Air

**Marvin, Ken**
*See* George, Lloyd

**Marvin the Magnificent**
*See* Barnes, Marvin

**Marvin, W. R.**
*See* Cameron, Lou

**Marwedi, Friedrich Carl** 20th c.
[EE]
*German intelligence agent*
* Dr. Pfalzgraf

**Marwick, Ernest Walker** 1915-
[IAW]
*Scottish author*
* E. W. M.

**Marx, Adolph Arthur** 1888-1964
[ASC, BDF, BEW]
*American comic actor*
* Marx, Harpo

**Marx, Albert A.** 1892-1960  [SC]
*American actor and clown*
* Almar the Clown

**Marx, Chico**
*See* Marx, Leonard

**Marx, Erica Elizabeth** 1909-1967
[CAP]
*British author*
* Manfred, Robert

**Marx, Groucho**
*See* Marx, Julius Henry

**Marx, Gummo**
*See* Marx, Milton

**Marx, Harpo**
See Marx, Adolph Arthur

**Marx, Herbert** 1901-1979
[BDF, BEW, EMT]
*American comic actor*
* Marx, Zeppo

**Marx, Jean**
See Linval, Paule Cassius de

**Marx, Jerry**
See Bernstein, Jerry Marx

**Marx, Julius Henry** 1890-1977
[BDF, BEW, EMT]
*American comic actor*
* Marx, Groucho

**Marx, Leonard** 1887-1961
[BDF, EMT, F2]
*American comic actor*
* Marx, Chico

**Marx, Milton** 1897-1977   [BEW]
*American comic actor*
* Marx, Gummo

**Marx, Zeppo**
See Marx, Herbert

**Mary**
See Jackson, Mary Hilliard

**Mary**   [HN, RH]
*Mother of Jesus*
* [The] Blessed Virgin
* [The] Madonna
* Our Lady of O
* [The] Queen of Heaven
* [The] Virgin Mary

**Mary Alfreda, [Sister]**
See Elsensohn, Edith M.

**Mary Aloysius, [Sister]**
See Becraft, Ann Marie

**Mary Aloysius, [Sister]**
See Schaldenbrand, Mary

**Mary Angelita, [Sister]**
See Stackhouse, Mary Agnes

**Mary Annette, [Sister]**
See Buttimer, Anne

**Mary Anthony, [Mother]**
See Weinig, Jean Maria

**Mary Aquina, [Sister]**
See Weinrich, Anna Katharina
Hildegard

**Mary Beatrice** 1658-1718
[DHA, FFF, WBD]
*Wife of King James II of England*
* Mary of Modena
* [The] Queen of Tears

**Mary Beth**
See Miller, Mary Beth

**Mary Catherine, [Sister]**
See Anderson, Kathleen Agness
Cicely

**Mary Consolata, [Sister]**
See Carroll, Alice Viola

**Mary Dominic, [Sister]**
See Gallagher, Mary Dominic

**Mary Dominic, [Sister]**
See Parker, Marion Dominica
Hope

**Mary Edward, [Sister]**
See Feehan, Agnes M.

**Mary Eleanor, [Sister]**
See Brosnahan, Katherine Mary

**Mary Estelle, [Sister]**
See Casalandra, Estelle

**Mary Francis, [Mother]**
See Aschmann,

**[The] Mary Garden of Ragtime**
See Abuza, Sophie

**Mary Gilbert, [Sister]**
See DeFrees, Madeline

**Mary Jane**
See Lampton, W. J.

**Mary Jean, [Sister]**
See Dorcy, Mary Jean

**Mary Justine, [Sister]**
See Sabourin, Anne Winifred

**Mary Lucille, [Sister]**
See Clark, Sylvia

**Mary Madeleva, [Sister]**
See Wolff, Mary Evaline

**Mary of Guise** 1515-1560   [WBD]
*Queen of Scotland*
* Mary of Lorraine

**Mary of Lorraine**
See Mary of Guise

**Mary of Modena**
See Mary Beatrice

**[The] Mary of the Gael**
See Bridget [or Brigette]

**Mary of the Incarnation**
See Guyard, Marie

**[The] Mary Pickford of France**
See Grandais, Susanne

**Mary, Queen of Scots** 1542-1587
[DEP, SN, WBD]
*Daughter of King James V of
Scotland*
* [The] Mermaid
* [La] Reine Blanche
* [The] Soft Medusa
* Stuart, Mary
* [The] White Queen

**Mary Salesia, [Sister]**
See Poggel, Mary

**Mary Scholastica, [Sister]**
See Jenkins, Marie M[agdalen]

**[The] Mary Stuart of Italy**
See Jane I

**Mary Theodore, [Sister]**
See Hegeman, Mary

**Mary I** 1516-1558
[DNNF, SN, WBD]
*Queen of England*
* Bloody Mary
* Tudor, Mary

**Maryanna, [Sister]**
See Childs, Maryanna

**Marynen, Joannes**
See Matthyssen, Joannes Michael

**Maryon, Edward**
See Maryon-D'Aulby, John
Edward

**Maryon-D'Aulby, John Edward**
1867-1954   [BBD]
*British composer*
* Maryon, Edward

**Masaccio**
See Guidi, Tommaso

**Masaniello**
See Aniello, Tommaso

**Mascall, Margery D.**
See Netherclift, Beryl Constance

**Mascara, Red**
See Mascari, Joseph Rocco

**Mascari, Joseph Rocco** 1922-
[ASC]
*American composer*
* Mascara, Red

**Maschler, Tom** 20th c.   [CA]
*Author*
* Caine, Mark [joint pseudonym
with Frederic (Michael) Raphael]

**Maschwitz, Eric** 1901-
[EMD, LAO, WW]
*British author*
* Marvell, Holt

**Masci, Girolamo** ?-1292   [CAL]
*Pope*
* Nicholas IV

**Masers d'Aubrespy**
See Latude, Jean Henry

**Masers de Latude**
See Latude, Jean Henry

**Masfar ben Bedreddin, Al-** 6th c.
[SN]
*Spanish orator*
* [The] Torch of Eloquence

**Masha**
See Stern, Marie

**Masilongan, Christobal** 1925-1974
[SC]
*Actor*
* De Vera, Cris
* [The] Man with a Thousand
Voices

**[The] Masked Marvel**
See Patton, Charley

**[The] Masked Singer of Country
Songs**
See Walker, William Marvin
[Billy]

**Mason, A. E. W.**
See Mason, Alfred Edward
Woodley

**Mason, Adelbert William**
1883-1962   [BE]
*American baseball player*
* Mason, Del

**Mason, Adrian**
See Lee, [Rev.] Albert

**Mason, Alfred Edward Woodley**
1865-1948   [LC, WWS]
*British author*
* Mason, A. E. W.

**Mason, Arthur Telford** 20th c.
[LC]
*Author*
* Artemas

**Mason, C. P.** 20th c.   [WGT]
*Author*
* Snooks, Epaminondas T.

**Mason, Carola**
See Zentner, Carola

**Mason, Caroline M.**   [PA]
*Author*
* Thekla

**Mason, Charles** 20th c.   [WW]
*Author*
* Mason, S. C.

**Mason, Chuck**
See Rowland, D[onald] S[ydney]

**Mason, Cryin**
See Mason, Norman

**Mason, Dan**
See Grassman, Dan

**Mason, Del**
See Mason, Adelbert William

**Mason, Douglas R[ankine]** 1918-
[AW, CA, SF]
*British author*
* Douglas, R. M.
* Rankine, John

**Mason, Edna Warren**
See Pfizenmayer, Edna Warren
Mason

**Mason, Ernst**
See Pohl, Frederik

**Mason, Eudo C[olecestra]**
1901-1969   [CAP]
*British educator and author*
* Maurer, Otto

**Mason, F. V. W.**
See Mason, F[rancis] Van Wyck

**Mason, F[rancis] Van Wyck**
1897?-1978   [ANT, CA, WGT]
*American author*
* Coffin, Geoffrey
* Mason, F. V. W.
* Mason, Frank W.
* Weaver, Ward

**Mason, Frank**
See De Masi, Francesco

**Mason, Frank W.**
See Mason, F[rancis] Van Wyck

**Mason, Frankie**
See McCan, Frank

**Mason, Fred** 1865-1895   [BMH]
*American-born entertainer*
* [The] Whistling Coster

**Mason, George C.** 1820- ?   [PA]
*Author*
* Champlin
* O'Lincoln, Robert

**Mason, Gregory** [joint pseudonym
with Doris Meek]
See Jones, Adrienne

**Mason, Gregory** [joint pseudonym
with Adrienne Jones]
See Meek, Doris

**Mason, Howard**
See Ramage, Jennifer

**Mason, Ida**
See Fisher, Eliza M. A.

**Mason, John** 1900-   [THR]
*American author and critic*
* Brown, John Mason

**Mason, John** 20th c.   [IBW]
*American comedian*
* Spider Bruce

**Mason, Louis**
See Loeb, Richard A.

**Mason, Madeline** 1913- [CA]
*American author and lecturer*
* Bartlett, David
* Mason, Tyler

**Mason, Michael Henry** 1900-
[AW]
*British author*
* Blake, Cameron

**Mason, Miriam Evangeline**
1900-1973 [IA]
*American author*
* Swain, Miriam

**Mason, Mrs. C. A. B.** [FFF]
*American poet*
* Caro

**Mason, Mrs. W. J.** [FFF]
*Entertainer*
* Temple, Victoria

**Mason, Norman** 20th c. [GW]
*American rodeo performer*
* Mason, Cryin

**Mason, Pamela**
See Kellino, Pamela

**Mason, Philip** 1906-
[AW, CA, WD]
*British author*
* Woodruff, Philip

**Mason, R. A. K.**
See Mason, Ronald Alison Kells

**Mason, Ronald Alison Kells** 1905-
[LC]
*New Zealand author*
* Mason, R. A. K.

**Mason, S. C.**
See Mason, Charles

**Mason, Shirley**
See Flugrath, Leona

**Mason, Smiling Billy**
See Mason, William C.

**Mason, Stuart**
See Millard, Christopher Sclater

**Mason, Tally**
See Derleth, August [William]

**Mason, Tyler**
See Mason, Madeline

**Mason, Val**
See Hackleman, Wauneta

**Mason, William** 1725?-1797
[DEL, SN]
*British poet*
* Macgregor, Malcolm
* Scroddles

**Mason, William C.** 1888-1941
[SC]
*American actor*
* Mason, Smiling Billy

**Mason, William Lasley** 1861- ?
[ALY]
*American author*
* Lesley, W. W.

**[The] Masque of Poets**
See Lathrop, G. P.

**Mass, William**
See Gibson, William

**Massa, Duke**
See Massa, Gordon Richard

**Massa, Gordon Richard** 1935- [BE]
*American baseball player*
* Massa, Duke
* Massa, Moose

**Massa, Moose**
See Massa, Gordon Richard

**Massachusettensis**
See Leonard, David

**Massachusetts**
See Derby, Elias Haskett

**[A] Massachusetts Lawyer**
See Lowell, John

**Massachusetts Yankee**
See Baggs, Lyman Hotchkiss

**Massalsky, Helen Koltzoff** [PA]
*Author*
* D'Istria, Dora

**Massarik, Friederike** 1882-1969
[JL, THR]
*Austrian-born actress and singer*
* Massary, Fritzi

**Massaro, Salvatore** 1902?-1933
[ASC, EJ, PMJ]
*American jazz musician*
* Lang, Eddie

**Massary, Fritzi**
See Massarik, Friederike

**Masse, Felix Marie** 1822-1884
[WBD]
*French composer*
* Masse, Victor

**Masse, Victor**
See Masse, Felix Marie

**Masselink, Ben** 1919- [CA]
*American author and television
scriptwriter*
* Toliver, George

**Massen, Mrs. L. F.** [FFF]
*Entertainer*
* Burroughs, Marie

**Massena, Andre** 1758-1817
[DNNS, HN, SN]
*French army officer*
* [The] Child of Fortune
* [L']Enfant Cheri de la Victorie
* [L']Enfant de la Fortune
* [The] Favored Child of Victory
* [The] Spoilt Child of Fortune

**Masseria, Giuseppe** ?-1931
[BLB, MM, PHM]
*Italian-born American underworld
figure*
* [The] Boss
* Masseria, Joseph

**Masseria, Joseph**
See Masseria, Giuseppe

**Massett, Stephen C.** [PA]
*American author and composer*
* Pipes, Jeemes, of Pipesville

**Massey, Big Bill**
See Massey, William Harry [Bill]

**Massey, E. C.** [FFF]
*Author*
* Whatshisname

**Massey, Erika** 1900- [CA]
*American author*
* Zastrow, Erika

**Massey, Guy**
See Slaughter, Marion T.

**Massey, Harry** [IBW]
*American football coach*
* King Leo

**Massey, Ilona**
See Hajmassy, Ilona

**Massey, Mike**
See Massey, William Herbert

**Massey, Red**
See Massey, Roy Hardee

**Massey, Roy Hardee** 1890-1954
[BE]
*American baseball player*
* Massey, Red

**Massey, Ruth**
See Tovell, Ruth Massey

**Massey, William Harry [Bill]**
1871-1940 [BE]
*American baseball player*
* Massey, Big Bill

**Massey, William Herbert**
1893-1971 [BE]
*American baseball player*
* Massey, Mike

**Massi, Gentile** 1370?-1427?
[WBD]
*Italian painter*
* Gentile da Fabriano

**Massi, Nick**
See Macioci, Nicholas

**Massicot, Butz**
See Massicot, Percy

**Massicot, Percy** 1910- [NOJ]
*American jazz musician*
* Massicot, Butz

**Massillon, Jean Baptiste**
1663-1742 [DEP, DNNS, SN]
*French prelate and orator*
* [The] Cicero of France
* [The] Peaceful Prelate

**Massine, Leonide**
See Myassin, Leonid Fedorovich

**Massinger, Philip** 1583-1640 [SN]
*British playwright*
* Apollo's Messenger

**Massingham, H. W.**
See Massingham, Henry William

**Massingham, Henry William**
1860-1924 [LC]
*British journalist*
* Massingham, H. W.

**Massis, Henri** 1886- [CAT]
*French author*
* Agathon

**Massius**
See Mars, Andre

**Masskoff, Maurice** 1871-1940
[BEW]
*Russian-born actor*
* Moscovitch, Maurice

**Masso, Justo** 1886-1971 [SC]
*Spanish actor*
* Oh Gran, Gilbert

**Masson, Barthelemy** 1485-1566
[PA]
*Author*
* Latonius

**Masson, Georgina**
See Johnson, Marion Georgina
[Wikeley]

**Masson, Mme. Clemence Harding**
[FFF]
*Author*
* Dixon

**Massopust, A. H.** 1895- [BBH]
*American volleyball player and
coach*
* Massopust, Dick

**Massopust, Dick**
See Massopust, A. H.

**Mastai-Ferretti, Giovanni Maria**
1792-1878 [DEP, DNNS, FFF]
*Pope*
* Pius IX
* [The] Prisoner of the Vatican

**Mastenbroek, Hendrika** 20th c.
[BBH, SWI]
*Dutch swimmer*
* Mastenbroek, Rie

**Mastenbroek, Rie**
See Mastenbroek, Hendrika

**[The] Master**
See Goethe, Johann Wolfgang von

**[The] Master**
See Hobbs, [Sir] John Berry

**Master Adam**
See Billaut, Adam

**[The] Master Among Masters**
See Read, Herbert

**Master Juba Lane**
See Lane, William Henry

**Master Melvin**
See Ott, Mel[vin Thomas]

**[The] Master of Air Defense**
See Kelly, James J.

**[The] Master of Ballyhoo**
See Rickard, George Lewis

**[The] Master of Contradiction**
See Wessel, Johann [or John]

**[The] Master of History**
See Comestor, Peter [or Petrus]

**[The] Master of Love**
See Ovidius Naso, Publius

**[The] Master of Sentences**
See Lombard, Peter [or Pietro]

**[The] Master of Stone-Cutting**
See Dolcebono, Giacomo

**[The] Master of Stories**
See Comestor, Peter [or Petrus]

**[The] Master of Suspense**
See Hitchcock, Alfred

**[The] Master of Those Who Knew**
See Aristotle

**[The] Master of Trinity**
See Wordsworth, Christopher

**Master Timothy**
See Reynolds, George W. M.

**Master X**
See Boland, Jesse Lee

**Masterman, C. F. G.**
See Masterman, Charles Frederick
Gurney

**Masterman, Charles Frederick Gurney** 1874-1927 [LC]
*British statesman and author*
* Masterman, C. F. G.

**Masterman, J. C.**
*See* Masterman, John Cecil

**Masterman, John Cecil** 1891-
[WWS]
*British author*
* Masterman, J. C.

**Masters, Anthony** 20th c. [CA]
*British author*
* Tate, Richard

**Masters, Bat**
*See* Buley, Bernard

**Masters, Edgar Lee** 1868?-1950
[CAA, TLC]
*American poet, author, playwright*
* Atherton, Lucius
* Chubb, Elmer
* Ford, Webster
* Prowler, Harley
* Puckett, Lute
* Wallace, Dexter

**Masters, Juan**
*See* Eames, Juanita

**Masters, Kelly R.** 1897-
[AW, CA, SAT]
*American author*
* Ball, Zachary

**Masters, Paul**
*See* Samways, George Richmond

**Masters, W. W.**
*See* Masters, William Walter

**Masters, William**
*See* Cousins, Margaret

**Masters, William Walter** 1894-
[AW]
*British author*
* Masters, W. W.

**Masterson, Bat**
*See* Masterson, Bernard E.

**Masterson, Bat**
*See* Masterson, William Barclay

**Masterson, Bernard E.** 1911-1963
[FB]
*American football player*
* Masterson, Bat

**Masterson, Lefty**
*See* Masterson, Paul Nickalis

**Masterson, Louis**
*See* Hallbing, Kjell Kare

**Masterson, Paul Nickalis** 1915-
[BE]
*American baseball player*
* Masterson, Lefty

**Masterson, Val**
*See* Wright, W. George

**Masterson, Whit** [joint pseudonym with Robert (Bob) Wade]
*See* Miller, Bill

**Masterson, Whit** [joint pseudonym with Bill Miller]
*See* Wade, Robert [Bob]

**Masterson, William Barclay** 1853-1921 [B10]
*American sheriff and sportswriter*
* Masterson, Bat

**Masterton, Bat**
*See* Masterton, William

**Masterton, William** 1938-1968
[CEI, FHE, HK]
*Canadian-born hockey player*
* Masterton, Bat

**Maston, T. B.**
*See* Maston, Thomas Bufford

**Maston, Thomas Bufford** 1897-
[WYA]
*American author*
* Maston, T. B.

**Mastrangelo, Johnny** 1939- [RO1]
*American singer*
* Maestro, Johnny
* Mastro, Johnny

**Mastro, Johnny**
*See* Mastrangelo, Johnny

**Masuccio di Salerno**
*See* Dei Guardati, Tommaso

**Masur, Harold Q.** 1909- [CA]
*American author*
* Fleming, Guy
* James, Edward

**Masurius**
*See* Desmasures, Louis

**Mata**
*See* Thompson, William R.

**Mata, Daya**
*See* Wright, Faye

**Mata Hari**
*See* Zelle, Margarete Gertrude

**Matalon, Isaac Moses** 1928-
[BEW]
*British actor, singer, dancer*
* Matalon, Zack

**Matalon, Zack**
*See* Matalon, Isaac Moses

**[The] Match King**
*See* Kreuger, Ivar

**Match, Pincus** 1904-1944 [EJS]
*American basketball player*
* Match, Pinky

**Match, Pinky**
*See* Match, Pincus

**Matcha, Jack** 1919- [CA]
*American author*
* Mitchel, Jackson
* Tanner, John

**[The] Matchless Orinda**
*See* Philips, Katherine

**Mate, Rudolph**
*See* Matheh, Rudolf

**Mateito [Little Matthew]**
*See* Lopez y Portal, Gabriel

**Matelot**
*See* Uren, Malcolm John Leggoe

**Mateo Salcedo, Miguel** 1939- [GS]
*Spanish bullfighter*
* Miguelin [Little Mike]

**Materfamilias**
*See* Bell, Mrs. C. M.

**Mateyko, G. M.** 20th c. [SFP]
*Author*
* Mayfield, M. I. [joint pseudonym with Henry I. Hirshfield]

**Mathalin**
*See* Taillasson, Gaillard

**Mathe, Albert**
*See* Camus, Albert

**Matheh, Rudolf** 1898-1964
[BDF, FD]
*Polish-born director*
* Mate, Rudolph

**Mather, Berkely**
*See* Davies, Jasper

**Mather, Margaret**
*See* Haberkom, Mrs. Emil

**Mather, Virginia**
*See* Liebeler, Jean [Mayer]

**Mathers, Edward Powys** 1892-
[WWL]
*British author*
* Torquemada

**Mathers, Helen**
*See* Reeves, Helen Buckingham [Mathers]

**Matheson, Andrew**
*See* Mannheim, L. Andrew

**Matheson, Hugh**
*See* Mackay, Lewis Hugh

**Matheson, Joan** 1924-
[SFL, WGT]
*American author*
* Transue, Jacob

**Matheson, Richard [Burton]** 1926-
[WGT]
*American author*
* Swanson, Logan

**Matheson, Rodney**
*See* Creasey, John

**Matheson, Sylvia A.**
*See* Schofield, Sylvia Anne

**Mathew, Theobald** 1790-1856
[DEP, FF, FFF]
*Irish clergyman*
* [The] Apostle of Temperance
* [The] Sinner's Friend

**Mathews, Albert** 1820-1903
[FFF, PA]
*Author*
* Siegvolk, Paul

**Mathews, Benjamin Kenny Ollard** 1889- [ART]
*British painter*
* B. M.

**Mathews, Charles** 1776-1835 [HN]
*British comedian*
* Prism, Brother

**Mathews, Evelyn Craw** 1906-
[CAP]
*Canadian author*
* Cleaver, Nancy

**Mathews, J. Brander** [PA]
*Author*
* Griffenhoof, Arthur

**Mathews, Mrs. Brander** [FFF]
*Entertainer*
* Harland, Ada

**Mathewson, Christopher** 1880-1925 [AS, DGS, PB]
*American baseball player*
* Big Six
* Mathewson, Christy

**Mathewson, Christy**
*See* Mathewson, Christopher

**Mathias, Carl Lynwood** 1936- [BE]
*American baseball player*
* Mathias, Stubby

**Mathias, Stubby**
*See* Mathias, Carl Lynwood

**Mathieson, Una Cooper**
*See* Gibson, Amanda Melvina Thorley

**Mathieu, J. P.** 1932?-1980
*Interior designer and painter*
* Mathieu, Pepe

**Mathieu, Noel** 1916- [EWL]
*French poet*
* Emmanuel, Pierre

**Mathieu, Pepe**
*See* Mathieu, J. P.

**Mathis, Big Bus**
*See* Mathis, Buster

**Mathis, Buster** 1944- [IBW]
*American boxer*
* Mathis, Big Bus

**Mathis, Dean**
*See* Mathis, Lewis

**Mathis, Lewis** 1939- [RO2]
*American singer*
* Mathis, Dean

**Mathur, Yaduvansh Bahadur** 1929-
[IAW]
*Indian author*
* Baby

**Mathura, Mustapha** 1939- [TR]
*West Indian author*
* Matura, Mustapha

**Matias**
*See* Henrioud, Charles

**Matiason, K. G.**
*See* Liljenfors, Bennie Mads Carl

**Matilda [or Maud]** 1080-1118
[HN]
*Wife of King Henry I of England*
* Godithe [or Godiva]
* [The] Good
* Good Queen Maud

**Matilda [or Maud]** 1102-1167
[DNNF, DNNS, HN]
*Daughter of King Henry I of England*
* Domina Anglorum
* [The] Lady of England

**Matilda, Anna**
*See* Cowley, Hannah

**Matilda, Anna**
*See* Lynch, Hester

**Matilda of Tuscany** 1046-1115
[WBD]
*Countess of Tuscany*
* [The] Great Countess

**Matilda, Rosa**
*See* Byrne, Charlotte Dacre

**Matison, Steven Martin** 20th c.
[WFA]
*Mexican fashion designer*
* Esteban

**Matlock, Alec**
*See* Cooper, Robert Andrew

**Matlock, Julian Clifton** 1907?-
[ASC, DA, MEJ]
*American jazz musician*
* Matlock, Matty

**Matlock, Matty**
*See* Matlock, Julian Clifton

**Matoaka** 1595?-1617 [SN, WBD]
*American Indian princess*
* Pocahontas
* Virginia's Tutelary Saint

**Matranga, Charles** 20th c. [BLB]
*American underworld figure*
* Matranga, Millionaire Charlie

**Matranga, Millionaire Charlie**
*See* Matranga, Charles

**Matray, Erno** 20th c.
*Hungarian-born director, writer, actor*
* Matray, Ernst

**Matray, Ernst**
*See* Matray, Erno

**Matrisciano, George** 20th c. [BLB]
*American underworld figure*
* Martini, George

**Matson, Randel** 1945- [TF]
*American track and field athlete*
* Matson, Randy

**Matson, Randy**
*See* Matson, Randel

**Matsuba, Moshe**
*See* Ben Yosef, Avraham Chaim

**Matsumoto, Hidehiko** 1926- [EJ]
*Japanese jazz musician and actor*
* Matsumoto, Sleepy

**Matsumoto, Sleepy**
*See* Matsumoto, Hidehiko

**Matsuno, Masako**
*See* Kobayashi, Masako Matsuno

**Matsuo Basho**
*See* Matsuo Munefusa

**Matsuo Munefusa** 1644-1694
[WBD]
*Japanese poet*
* Basho
* Matsuo Basho

**Matsys, Quentin** 1460-1529
[DNNF]
*Flemish painter*
* [The] Blacksmith of Antwerp

**Matt, Anton Josef** 20th c. [BBH]
*Austrian-born skier*
* Matt, Toni

**Matt, Toni**
*See* Matt, Anton Josef

**Mattaniah** 6th c. BC [WBD]
*King of Judah*
* Zedekiah

**Mattathias**
*See* Antigonus II

**Matte, Kid**
*See* Matte, Thomas R.

**Matte, Thomas R.** 1939- [FB]
*American football player*
* Matte, Kid

**Mattei, Bruno** 20th c. [WF]
*Film editor*
* Matthews, Jordan B.

**Matteo, P. B., Jr.**
*See* Ringgold, Gene

**Mattern, Al**
*See* Mattern, Alonzo Albert

**Mattern, Alonzo Albert** 1883-1958
[BE]
*American baseball player*
* Mattern, Al

**Matthau, Walter**
*See* Matuschanskayasky, Walter

**Matthew, Thomas**
*See* Rogers, John

**Matthew, Toby** 1546-1628 [SN]
*British prelate*
* [The] Preaching Bishop

**Matthew, Wentworth Arthur**
*See* Benyehuda, Yoseh Ben Moshea

**Matthews, A. E.**
*See* Matthews, Alfred Edward

**Matthews, Alfred Edward**
1869-1960 [BEW, SC]
*British actor*
* Matthews, A. E.
* Matthews, Matty

**Matthews, Anthony**
*See* Barker, Dudley

**Matthews, Banjo**
*See* Matthews, Edwin K.

**Matthews, Bebe**
*See* Matthews, Nathaniel

**Matthews, Bo**
*See* Matthews, William

**Matthews, Channing**
*See* Channing-Renton, Ernest Matthews

**Matthews, Chif**
*See* Matthews, Lewis

**Matthews, Clayton** 1918- [CA]
*American author*
* Brisco, Patty [joint pseudonym with Patricia (Brisco) Matthews]

**Matthews, Constance Mary** 1908-
[CA]
*New Zealand-born author*
* Carrington, Molly

**Matthews, Coots**
*See* Matthews, Edward

**Matthews, Dora** ?-1975 [SC]
*American actress*
* Merande, Doro

**Matthews, Edward** 1923-
*American oilwell troubleshooter*
* Matthews, Coots

**Matthews, Edwin K.** 1932- [EAR]
*American auto racer*
* Matthews, Banjo

**Matthews, George** 20th c. [NP]
*American jazz musician*
* Matthews, Truce

**Matthews, Ian**
*See* McDonald, Ian

**Matthews, Jacklyn Meek**
*See* Meek, Jacklyn O'Hanlon

**Matthews, John** 1859-1927 [SC]
*Welsh-born actor*
* Ray, Johnny

**Matthews, Jordan B.**
*See* Mattei, Bruno

**Matthews, Kevin**
*See* Fox, Gardner Francis

**Matthews, Lewis** 1885?- ? [NOJ]
*American jazz musician*
* Matthews, Chif

**Matthews, Matty**
*See* Matthews, Alfred Edward

**Matthews, Matty**
*See* Matthews, William R.

**Matthews, Nathaniel** 1890?-1961
[NOJ]
*American jazz musician*
* Matthews, Bebe

**Matthews, Pamela** 1930- [BF]
*British actress*
* Morris, Lana

**Matthews, Patricia [Brisco]** 1927-
[CA]
*American author*
* Brisco, Pat A.
* Brisco, Patty [joint pseudonym with Clayton Matthews]

**Matthews, Pauline** 1947- [RO2]
*British singer*
* Dee, Kiki

**Matthews, Rags**
*See* Matthews, Raymond

**Matthews, Raymond** 1905- [FB]
*American football player*
* Matthews, Rags

**Matthews, Stanley** 1915?- [SR]
*British soccer player*
* [The] Prince of Dribblers

**Matthews, Stanley G[oodwin]**
1924- [CA]
*Canadian-born author*
* Goodwin, Mark

**Matthews, Thomas Soady** 1864- ?
[LAO]
*British author*
* T. S. M.

**Matthews, Tom**
*See* Klewin, W[illiam] Thomas

**Matthews, Truce**
*See* Matthews, George

**Matthews, William** 1951- [SMG]
*American football player*
* Matthews, Bo

**Matthews, William R.** 1873-1948
[AS, BX, RBE]
*American boxer*
* Matthews, Matty

**Matthias Corvinus** 1442?-1490
[DNNS, SN, WBD]
*King of Hungary*
* [The] Cosmo de Medici of Hungary
* [The] Great
* [The] Lorenzo de Medici of Hungary
* Matyas Hollos

**Matthiessen, F. O.**
*See* Matthiessen, Francis Otto

**Matthiessen, Francis Otto**
1902-1950 [LC]
*American author and educator*
* Matthiessen, F. O.

**Matthyssen, Joannes Michael**
1902- [IAW]
*Belgian author*
* Marynen, Joannes

**Mattice, Butch**
*See* Mattice, Lionel

**Mattice, Lionel** 1941- [RO1]
*American musician*
* Mattice, Butch

**Mattick, Chick**
*See* Mattick, Walter Joseph
[Wally]

**Mattick, Walter Joseph [Wally]**
1887-1968 [BE]
*American baseball player*
* Mattick, Chick

**Mattioli, Ercole Antonio**
1640-1703 [WBD]
*Italian statesman and diplomat*
* [The] Man in the Iron Mask?

**Mattox, Cloy Mitchell** 1902- [BE]
*American baseball player*
* Mattox, Monk

**Mattox, Harold Henry** 1921-
[BEW]
*American dancer, singer, actor*
* Mattox, Matt

**Mattox, Hazel** ?-1973 [FIR]
*American actress and writer*
* Hancock, Hazel
* La Vinder, Gracille

**Mattox, Matt**
*See* Mattox, Harold Henry

**Mattox, Monk**
*See* Mattox, Cloy Mitchell

**Mattson, Eric**
*See* Mattson, Rudolph

**Mattson, Rudolph** 1908- [BEW]
*American producer and director*
* Mattson, Eric

**Matura, Mustapha**
*See* Mathura, Mustapha

**Maturin, Charles Robert**
1782-1824 [DEL, PA]
*Irish author and playwright*
* Murphy, Dennis Jasper

**Matus, Juan** 1891- [B10]
*Yaqui Indian*
* Don Juan

**Matuschanskayasky, Walter** 1920-
[BDF, IPA, SW]
*American actor*
* Matthau, Walter

**Matusow, Harvey Marshall** 1926-
[AW]
*American author, journalist, broadcaster*
* Muldoon, Omar

**Matuzak, Harry George** 1910-
[BE]
*American baseball player*
* Matuzak, Matty

**Matuzak, Matty**
*See* Matuzak, Harry George

**Matyas Hollos**
*See* Matthias Corvinus

**Matyszkowicz, Adam** 1940- [EJ7]
*Czech-born jazz musician*
* Makowicz, Adam

**Matz, Bertram Waldrom** 1865- ?
[WWL]
*British author*
* Sack, O.

**Matzo, Emma** 1922-  [FC, WEF]
*American actress*
* Scott, Lizabeth

**Mau-Mau Bett**
See   Baumfree, Betsy

**Mauch, Gene William** 1925-  [BE]
*American baseball player and manager*
* Mauch, Skip

**Mauch, Skip**
See   Mauch, Gene William

**Mauck, Alfred Maris** 1869-1921
[BE]
*American baseball player*
* Mauck, Hal

**Mauck, Hal**
See   Mauck, Alfred Maris

**Mauclair, Camille**
See   Faust, Camille

**Maud, Victoria** 20th c.  [SC]
*Actress*
* Ray, Thelma

**Maude, Lillian Nancy** 1880?-1970
[BF, SC]
*British actress and author*
* Price, Nancy

**Maudet, Christian** 1904-
[BDF, FC, OCF]
*French director*
* Christian Jaque

**Maugham, Diana**
See   Marr-Johnson, Diana
[Maugham]

**Maugham, Robert Cecil Romer**
1916-1981  [CA, LC, WD]
*British author*
* Griffin, David
* Maugham, Robin

**Maugham, Robin**
See   Maugham, Robert Cecil
Romer

**Maugham, W[illiam] Somerset**
1874-1965  [WWS]
*British author and playwright*
* Somerville

**Maughn, Donald** 20th c.  [RO2]
*Singer*
* Fardon, Don

**Maul, Albert Joseph** 1865-1958
[AS, BE]
*American baseball player*
* Maul, Smiling Al

**[The] Maul of Monks**
See   Cromwell, Thomas [Earl of
Essex]

**Maul, Smiling Al**
See   Maul, Albert Joseph

**Maulbetsch, John** 20th c.
*American football player*
* Maulbetsch, Maulie

**Maulbetsch, Maulie**
See   Maulbetsch, John

**Mauldin, Mark**
See   Mauldin, Marshall Reese

**Mauldin, Marshall Reese** 1914-
[BE]
*American baseball player*
* Mauldin, Mark

**Maule, Hamilton Bee** 1915-
[B10, CA]
*American sportswriter*
* Maule, Tex

**Maule, Tex**
See   Maule, Hamilton Bee

**Maule, Thomas** 1645-1724  [PA]
*Author*
* Theodorus Philalethes

**Maulnier, Thierry** 1909-  [IAW]
*French author and playwright*
* Talagrand, Jacques Louis

**Maultasch**
See   Margaret of Carinthia

**Maultsby, Emmaline** 1928-  [EJ]
*American singer*
* Moore, Debby

**Maupin, Helen Christine Bennett**
1881- ?  [NAA]
*American writer*
* Bennett, Helen Christine

**Maura, [Sister]**
See   Eichner, Maura

**Maura, [Sister]**
See   Power, Mary

**Maurault, Olivier** 1886-  [NAA]
*Canadian clergyman and author*
* Deligny, Louis

**Maurer, Maurice** 1914-  [ITA]
*American theatre executive*
* Maurer, Ziggy

**Maurer, Mrs. George W.**  [FFF]
*Entertainer*
* Quick, Ida

**Maurer, Otto**
See   Mason, Eudo C[olecestra]

**Maurer, Rose**
See   Somerville, Rose M[aurer]

**Maurer, Ziggy**
See   Maurer, Maurice

**Maurette, Marcelle Marie Josephine**
1903-  [BEW]
*French writer and playwright*
* Marcelle-Maurette

**Mauriac, Francois [Charles]**
1885-1970  [CAP]
*French author and journalist*
* Forez

**Maurice**
See   Mouvet, Maurice

**Maurice, David [John Kerr]** 1899-
[CAP]
*Australian author*
* Wunnakyawhtin U Ohn Ghine

**Maurice, Edmund**
See   Lenon, Edmund Fitz-Maurice

**Maurice, Mary** 1844-1918
[FI, SC]
*American actress*
* Maurice, Mother

**Maurice, Michael**
See   Skinner, Conrad Arthur

**Maurice, Mother**
See   Maurice, Mary

**Maurice, Roger**
See   Asselineau, Roger [Maurice]

**Mauricius [or Mauritius], Flavius
Tiberius** 539?- 602  [HN, WBD]
*Byzantine emperor*
* Avaricious Tyrant

**Mauriello, Ralph** 1934-  [BE]
*American baseball player*
* Mauriello, Tami

**Mauriello, Tami**
See   Mauriello, Ralph

**Maurina, Zenta**
See   Raudive-Maurina, Zenta

**[Il] Mauro**
See   Arcano, Giovanni

**Maurois, Andre**
See   Herzog, Emile [Salomon
Wilhelm]

**Maurras, Charles-Marie-Photius**
1868-1952  [EWL]
*French author*
* Garnier, Pierre
* Martin, Octave
* Rameau, Leon
* Xenophon XIII

**Maury, Chip**
See   Maury, Donald P.

**Maury, Donald P.** 1939?-  [B10]
*American photographer*
* Maury, Chip

**Maury, Matthew Fontaine**
1806-1873  [FFF]
*American oceanographer and author*
* Bluff, Harry

**Mauthe, J. L.** 1890-1967  [AS, FB]
*American football player*
* Mauthe, Pete

**Mauthe, Pete**
See   Mauthe, J. L.

**Mautner, Jerome** 1913-  [ASC]
*American musician*
* Marlowe, Jerry

**Mauzolli, Pietro Angelo**  [PA]
*Author*
* Palingenesius

**Maverick, Augustus**  [FFF, PA]
*Journalist*
* Peebles, Paul

**Mavin, John** [joint pseudonym with
(John) Edgell Rickword]
See   Garman, Douglas Mavin

**Mavin, John** [joint pseudonym with
Douglas Mavin Garman]
See   Rickword, [John] Edgell

**Mavity, Hubert**
See   Bond, Nelson S[lade]

**Mavor, Osborne Henry** 1888-1951
[LC, TCL, TLC]
*Scottish playwright*
* Bridie, James
* Henderson, Mary
* Kellock, Archibald P.

**Mavromichalis, Petros** 1775-1848
[PA, WBD]
*Greek patriot*
* Petro Bey

**Mawdsley, Norman**
See   Hargreaves-Mawdsley,
W[illiam] Norman

**Max**
See   Maxwell, W. H.

**Max, Lucy**
See   Bogue, Lucile Maxfield

**Max, Nicholas**
See   Asbell, Bernard

**Max, Raymond**
See   Hart, Cyril Charles

**Maxfield, Elizabeth**
See   Miller, Elizabeth Maxfield

**Maxfield, Prudence M.** 1921-
[AW]
*British author*
* Hill, Prudence

**Maxhim, Tristan**
See   Jones, [Max Him] Henri

**Maxim, Hudson**
See   Maxim, Isaac

**Maxim, Isaac** 1853-1927  [WBD]
*American engineer and inventor*
* Maxim, Hudson

**Maxim, Joey**
See   Berardinelli, Guiseppe Antonio

**Maximian** ?- 310  [WBD]
*Roman emperor*
* Herculius

**Maximilian Joseph** 1808-1888
[WBD]
*Bavarian duke, author, playwright*
* Phantasus

**Maximilian I** 1459-1519
[DNNF, FFF, HN]
*Emperor of Germany*
* [The] Last of the Knights
* [The] Penniless
* Pochi Danari
* [The] Taciturn
* Theuerdank [Dear Thanks]

**Maximilian I** 1573-1651
[DNNS, FFF, SN]
*Duke of Bavaria*
* [The] Great

**Maximilian II** 1527-1576
[DNNS, FF, SN]
*Archduke of Austria and Holy
Roman emperor*
* [The] Delight of Mankind
* [A] German Mithridates
* [The] Prince of Peace

**Maximinus, Gaius Julius Verus** 173-
238  [WBD]
*Roman emperor*
* Thrax [The Thracian]

**Maximinus, Galerius Valerius**
See   Daza

**Maximum John Sirica**
See   Sirica, John Joseph

**Maximum John Wood**
See   Wood, John H., Jr.

**Maximus** 580?- 662  [WBD]
*Saint*
* [The] Confessor

**Maxon, Anne**
See   Best, [Evangel] Allena
Champlin

**Maxton, Hugh**
See McCormack, William John

**Maxtone Graham, James Anstruther**
1924- [AW, CA]
*British writer*
* Anstruther, James

**Maxtone Graham, Joyce [Anstruther]**
1901- [TC]
*British author*
* Struther, Jan

**Maxvill, Charles Dallan** 1939- [BE]
*American baseball player*
* Maxvill, Dal

**Maxvill, Dal**
See Maxvill, Charles Dallan

**Maxwell, Allan**
See Bayfield, William John

**Maxwell, Anna Caroline**
1851-1929 [WBD]
*American nurse*
* [The] American Florence
Nightingale

**Maxwell, Bert** 20th c. [BMH]
*American entertainer*
* Bernard, Bert

**Maxwell, Billy**
See Maxwell, W. J.

**Maxwell, Cedric** 20th c.
*American basketball player*
* Maxwell, Cornbread

**Maxwell, Charles Richard** 1927-
[BE, SMG]
*American baseball player*
* Maxwell, Paw Paw
* Maxwell, Smokey

**Maxwell, Cornbread**
See Maxwell, Cedric

**Maxwell, Eddie**
See Cherkose, Eddie

**Maxwell, Edward**
See Herman, Alan

**Maxwell, Edward**
See Pollock, Courtnay

**Maxwell, Fred G.** 1890- [HK]
*Canadian-born hockey player and coach*
* Maxwell, Steamer

**Maxwell, Gerald**
See Braddon, Gerald

**Maxwell, Gordon**
See Shute, Walter

**Maxwell, Herbert**
See Lomax, W. J.

**Maxwell, Herbert M.**
See Wyman, Walter Forestus

**Maxwell, Jack**
See McKeag, Ernest L[ionel]

**Maxwell, Jiggs**
See Maxwell, Zearlee

**Maxwell, Joslyn**
See Ireland, M. J.

**Maxwell, Lois**
See Hooker, Lois

**Maxwell, Marilyn**
See Maxwell, Marvel

**Maxwell, Marina** 1934- [CW]
*Trinidadian singer, producer, poet*
* Omowale, Marina

**Maxwell, Marvel** 1921?-1972
[FC, PMJ]
*American singer and actress*
* Maxwell, Marilyn

**Maxwell, Mary Elizabeth [Braddon]**
1837-1915 [DEL, WGT]
*British author*
* Braddon, [Miss] Mary E.
* Lascelles, [Lady] Caroline
* White, Babington

**Maxwell, Mary Mortimer**
See Banks, Elizabeth

**Maxwell, Patricia Anne** 1942-
[CA, WD]
*American author*
* Blake, Jennifer
* Trehearne, Elizabeth [joint
pseudonym with Carol Albritton]

**Maxwell, Paul**
See Gian, Paolo

**Maxwell, Paw Paw**
See Maxwell, Charles Richard

**Maxwell, Richard** [FFF]
*Entertainer*
* Ogden, Richard D'Orsay

**Maxwell, Robert W.** 1884-1922
[FB]
*American football player and sportswriter*
* Maxwell, Tiny

**Maxwell, Ronald**
See Smith, Ronald Gregor

**Maxwell, Smokey**
See Maxwell, Charles Richard

**Maxwell, Steamer**
See Maxwell, Fred G.

**Maxwell Street Jimmy**
See Thomas, Charles

**Maxwell, Tiny**
See Maxwell, Robert W.

**Maxwell, Vicky**
See Worboys, Annette Isobel

**Maxwell, W. B.**
See Maxwell, William Babington

**Maxwell, W. H.** 1852- ? [PA]
*Author*
* Max

**Maxwell, W. J.** 1929- [EG]
*American golfer*
* Maxwell, Billy

**Maxwell, William Babington**
1866-1938 [LC]
*British author*
* Maxwell, W. B.

**Maxwell, Zearlee** 20th c. [OBW]
*American baseball player*
* Maxwell, Jiggs

**May, Ada**
See Weeks, Ada Mae

**May, Alice**
See Raymond, Mrs. Lewis

**May, Bernice**
See Cross, Zora Bernice May

**May, Bubba**
See May, Robert Earl, Jr.

**May, Buckshot**
See May, William Herbert

**May, Butler** 20th c. [BWW]
*American entertainer*
* May, Stringbeans

**May, Chopper**
See May, David LaFrance

**May, Dan**
See Maggio, Dante

**May, Dave**
See May, Davis Edwards

**May, David LaFrance** 1943-
[SMG]
*American baseball player*
* May, Chopper

**May, Davis Edwards** 1951- [SMG]
*American baseball player*
* May, Dave

**May, Edith**
See Drinker, Anna

**May, Edna**
See Pettie [or Petty], Edna May

**May, Elaine**
See Berlin, Elaine

**May, Frank Spuriell** 1895-1970
[AS, BE, PB]
*American baseball player*
* May, Jakie

**May, Hannah**
See Spivey, Addie

**May, Harley** 20th c. [GW]
*American rodeo performer*
* May, Ladder

**May, Henry John** 1903- [CA]
*Rhodesian-born barrister and author*
* Schlosberg, H[ershel] J[oshua]

**May, Herbert Richard Duffield** 1878-
? [WWL]
*British author*
* Hardy, Mark

**May, Ida**
See Pike, Mary H. Green

**May, J. C.**
See Dikty, Julian Chain May

**May, Jakie**
See May, Frank Spuriell

**May, Janine**
See Andonian, Jeanne [Beghian]

**May, Joe**
See Mandel, Joseph

**May, Joseph** 1916-1972 [IBW]
*American singer*
* Brother Joe
* Thunderbolt of the Middle West

**May, Julian [C.]**
See Dikty, Julian Chain May

**May, Julian** 1931- [SAT]
*American author*
* Feilen, John
* Grant, Matthew G.
* Thorne, Ian

**May, Ladder**
See May, Harley

**May, Margery Land**
See Foster, Margery Land May

**May, Mattie**
See Brown, Mrs. C. R.

**May, Merrill Glend** 1911- [BE]
*American baseball player*
* May, Pinky

**May, Paul**
See Ostermayr, Paul

**May, Pinky**
See May, Merrill Glend

**May, Red**
See May, Walter O.

**May, Robert Earl, Jr.** 1956- [IBW]
*American prison inmate*
* May, Bubba

**May, Robert Stephen** 1929-
[CA, WD]
*British author and journalist*
* May, Robin

**May, Robin**
See May, Robert Stephen

**May, Rudolph, Jr.** 1944- [SMG]
*American baseball player*
* [The] Dude

**May, Sophie**
See Clarke, Rebecca

**May, Sophie**
See Meyer, Sophie Frederika
Elizabeth

**May, Stewart**
See De Mejo, Carlo

**May, Stringbeans**
See May, Butler

**May, Thomas** 1595-1650
[FFF, SN]
*British poet and historian*
* [The] Historian of the Long
Parliament

**May, Val**
See May, Valentine

**May, Valentine** 1927- [TR]
*British director*
* May, Val

**May, Walter O.** 20th c. [SMG]
*American football player*
* May, Red

**May, William Herbert** 1899- [BE]
*American baseball player*
* May, Buckshot

**May, Winifred Arnold** 20th c.
[NAA]
*American author*
* Arnold, Winifred

**May, Winifred Jean** 1921- [IAW]
*South African author*
* Wynne, May

**Maya [or Moya?], Victoria** 1935?-
[FC, SW]
*Mexican actress*
* Cristal, Linda

**Mayakovsky, Vladimir Vladimirovich**
1893-1930 [MWD]
*Russian poet*
* [The] Iron Poet
* [The] Poet of the Revolution

**Mayall, John** 1933?- [BWW, PRS]
*British musician*
* [The] Father of British Blues
* [The] Grandfather of British Rock

**Mayberry, Big John**
*See* Mayberry, John Claiborn

**Mayberry, John Claiborn** 1950-
[SMG]
*American baseball player*
* Mayberry, Big John

**Maybray-King, Horace**
*See* King, Horace Maybray

**Maybrick, Michael** 1844-1913
[BBD, BEW, FFF]
*British singer and composer*
* Adams, Stephen

**Maye, Bernyce**
*See* Moore, Bernyce Atz

**Mayer**
*See* Marius, Simon

**Mayer, Agatha**
*See* Maher, Ramona

**Mayer, Arthur Loeb** 1887?-1981
*American film distributor, exhibitor, historian*
* [The] Merchant of Menace

**Mayer, Bernadette** 1945- [CA]
*American poet*
* Memory

**Mayer, Carl** 1894-1944 [FIR]
*Austrian-born screenwriter*
* [The] First Poet of the Screen

**Mayer, Charles E. E.** 1901-1971
[CSH]
*Canadian sportswriter, commentator, official*
* Trois Etoiles [Three Stars]
* Uncle Charles

**Mayer, Charles Leopold** 1881- ?
[CA]
*French scientist and author*
* Reyam

**Mayer, Christa Charlotte**
*See* Thurman, Christa C[harlotte]
Mayer

**Mayer, Ellen Moers**
*See* Moers, Ellen

**Mayer, Erskine**
*See* Erskine, James

**Mayer, Franz Xaver** [FFF]
*Author*
* Ackermann, Gottlieb

**Mayer, Hannelore** 1929- [IAW]
*Austrian author*
* Valencak, Hannelore

**Mayer, Henry** 1868-1954 [WEC]
*American cartoonist*
* Mayer, Hy

**Mayer, Hy**
*See* Mayer, Henry

**Mayer, Jakab Gyula** 1858-1925
[BBD]
*Hungarian pianist, conductor, composer*
* Major, Jakab Gyula

**Mayer, Jane Rothschild** 1903-
[ANT, AW, CA]
*American author*
* Jaynes, Clare [joint pseudonym with Clara Gatzert Spiegel]

**Mayer, Johann** 1486-1543
[SN, WBD]
*German theologian*
* Dreck [Dirt]
* Eck, Johann

**Mayer, Sam[uel Frankel]**
*See* Erskine, Samuel Frankel

**Mayer, Scissors**
*See* Erskine, James

**Mayer-Boerckel, Ferdy** 1920- [TR]
*British actor*
* Mayne, Ferdy

**Mayer-Thurman, Christa C.**
*See* Thurman, Christa C[harlotte]
Mayer

**Mayerl, Billy**
*See* Mayerl, Joseph W.

**Mayerl, Joseph W.** 1902-1959
[BEW]
*British-born composer and conductor*
* Mayerl, Billy

**Mayes, Adair Bushyhead**
1885-1962 [BE]
*American baseball player*
* Mayes, Paddy

**Mayes, Ethel**
*See* Moore, Monette

**Mayes, Paddy**
*See* Mayes, Adair Bushyhead

**Mayfair, Franklin**
*See* Mendelsohn, Felix, Jr.

**Mayfield, Ann Todd** 1932- [FC]
*American actress*
* Todd, Ann

**Mayfield, Catfish**
*See* Mayfield, Rufus

**Mayfield, Cleo**
*See* Empy, Cleo

**Mayfield, Frank**
*See* Starnes, Daniel

**Mayfield, Julia**
*See* Hastings, Phyllis Dora Hodge

**Mayfield, M. I.** [joint pseudonym with G. M. Mateyko]
*See* Hirshfield, Henry I.

**Mayfield, M. I.** [joint pseudonym with Henry I. Hirshfield]
*See* Mateyko, G. M.

**Mayfield, Millie**
*See* Homes, Mary Sophie Shaw

**Mayfield, Rufus** 20th c. [IBW]
*American community organizer*
* Mayfield, Catfish

**Mayflower, Minnie**
*See* Ladd, Catherine Stratton

**Mayhar, Ardath F[rances]** 1930-
[WD]
*American poet and author*
* Hurst, Ardath Frances

**Mayhew, Charles**
*See* Smith, Charles

**Mayhew, Elizabeth**
*See* Bear, Joan

**Mayhew, Katie**
*See* Widmer, Mrs. Harry

**Mayhew, Stella**
*See* Sadler, Izetta Estelle

**Maynard, Bill**
*See* Maynard, Christopher

**Maynard, Bob** 20th c. [GW]
*American rodeo performer*
* Maynard, Flash

**Maynard, Buster**
*See* Maynard, James Walter

**Maynard, Chick**
*See* Maynard, Leroy Evans

**Maynard, Christopher** 1958- [DC]
*British cricketer*
* Maynard, Bill
* Maynard, Fish

**Maynard, Claire**
*See* McCarthy, Marie

**Maynard, Colonel** [FFF]
*American writer*
* Kentucky Colonel

**Maynard, Donald** 1937- [FB]
*American football player*
* Maynard, Sunshine

**Maynard, Fish**
*See* Maynard, Christopher

**Maynard, Flash**
*See* Maynard, Bob

**Maynard, James Walter** 1913-
[BE]
*American baseball player*
* Maynard, Buster

**Maynard, Leroy Evans** 1896-1957
[BE]
*American baseball player*
* Maynard, Chick

**Maynard, Richard Wheeler** 20th c.
[BE]
*American baseball player*
* Wheeler, Richard [Dick]

**Maynard, Ruth**
*See* Coffin, Ruth Maynard

**Maynard, Sunshine**
*See* Maynard, Donald

**Maynard, Walter**
*See* Beale, Thomas Willert

**Mayne, Arthur**
*See* Batchelor, Richard A. C.

**Mayne, Clarice**
*See* Dulley, Clarice

**Mayne, Ernie**
*See* Barratt, Percy Ernest

**Mayne, Ethel Colburn** ?-1941
[LC]
*Irish author*
* Huntly, Frances E.

**Mayne, Ferdy**
*See* Mayer-Boerckel, Ferdy

**Mayne, H. H.**
*See* Wilson, Helen Helga

**Mayne, Rutherford**
*See* Waddell, Samuel J.

**Mayne, William** [James Carter]
1928- [CA, CLC, SAT]
*British author*
* Cobalt, Martin
* James, Dynely [joint pseudonym with R. D. Caesar]
* Molin, Charles

**Maynwaring, Archibald**
*See* Lovecraft, Howard Phillips

**Mayo, Cass**
*See* Stevens, Casandra Mayo

**Mayo, Edward Joseph**
*See* Mayoski, Edward Joseph

**Mayo, Frank**
*See* Maguire, Francis

**Mayo, Goat**
*See* Mayo, Paul

**Mayo, Harry A.**
*See* Sampson, Ray

**Mayo, Isabella Fyvie** ?-1914
[DEL, PA, WWL]
*Author*
* Garrett, Edward
* Garrett, Ruth

**Mayo, James**
*See* Coulter, Stephen

**Mayo, Johann** [FFF]
*German painter*
* [The] Bearded

**Mayo, Margaret**
*See* Clatten, Lilian

**Mayo, Mark**
*See* Lane, Yoti

**Mayo, Mary**
*See* Woodson, Mary Blake

**Mayo, Moose**
*See* Mayo, Paula

**Mayo, Mrs. William H.** [FFF]
*Entertainer*
* Sutherland, Josie

**Mayo, Nick**
*See* Martoff, Nickoli

**Mayo, Paul** 20th c. [GW]
*American rodeo performer*
* Mayo, Goat

**Mayo, Paula** 20th c.
*American basketball player*
* Mayo, Moose

**Mayo, Sam**
*See* Cowan, Samuel

**Mayo, Virginia**
*See* Jones, Virginia

**Mayoe, Franklin and Marian**
*See* Rosewater, Frank

**Mayor De Luxe**
*See* White, Kevin Hagan

**[The] Mayor of Gower Gulch**
*See* Dalroy, Harry

**[The] Mayor of Kneesville**
*See* Schleier, Gregory

**[The] Mayor of the Palace**
*See* Du Plessis, Armand Jean

**Mayoski, Edward Joseph** 1910-
[BE]
*American baseball player*
* Mayo, Edward Joseph

[The] Maypole
See Schulemberg, Erangard Melrose de [Duchess of Kendal]

Mayrant, Drayton
See Simons, Katherine Drayton Mayrant

Mayrseidl, Caroline 1902- [THR]
Austrian-born actress and singer
* Seidl, Lea

Mays, Carl William 1893-1971 [BE, DGS]
American baseball player
* Mays, Sub

Mays, Cedric Wesley 1907- [AW, CA]
British author
* Mays, Spike

Mays, Junie
See Mays, Junior Allen

Mays, Junior Allen 1914- [MY]
American musician
* Mays, Junie

Mays, Spike
See Mays, Cedric Wesley

Mays, Sub
See Mays, Carl William

Mays, William Howard, Jr. [Willie] 1931- [BE, PB]
American baseball player
* [The] Say-Hey Kid

Maysi, Kadra
See Simons, Katherine Drayton Mayrant

Mayson, Marina
See Rogers, Rosemary

Maytag, Bud
See Maytag, Lewis B.

Maytag, Lewis B. 1926-
American airline executive
* Maytag, Bud

Mayuto
See Correa, Mailto

Mazal Tov
See Czaczkes, Shmuel Yosef

Mazani, Eric C. F. Nhando 1948- [DLE]
Rhodesian poet
* Mars, E. C.

Mazarin, Jules 1602-1661 [SN]
French prelate and statesman
* [The] Maecenas of His Day

[The] Mazarin of Letters
See Alembert, Jean Le Rond d'

Maze, Henry 1956- [SMG]
Canadian-born hockey player
* Maze, Rocky

Maze, Rocky
See Maze, Henry

Mazeroski, Maz
See Mazeroski, William Stanley

Mazeroski, William Stanley 1936- [BE]
American baseball player
* Mazeroski, Maz

Mazibuko, Mandla Thomas 1946- [IAW]
South African poet
* Liguquka, Iphiva Elilala

Mazimoff, Alla 1879-1945 [CU]
Russian-born actress
* Nazimova, Alla

Mazquiaran y Torrontegui, Diego 1895-1940 [GS, OCS]
Spanish bullfighter
* Fortuna [Fortune]

Mazur, Edward Joseph 1929- [CEI, FHE]
Canadian-born hockey player
* Mazur, Spider

Mazur, Spider
See Mazur, Edward Joseph

Mazurki, Mike
See Mazurwski, Mikhail

Mazursky, Irwin 1930-
American screenwriter and director
* Mazursky, Paul

Mazursky, Paul
See Mazursky, Irwin

Mazurwski, Mikhail 1909- [FC]
American actor
* Mazurki, Mike

Mazza, Adriana 1928- [SAT]
Italian illustrator
* Saviozzi, Adriana

Mazzantinito [Little Mazzantino]
See Alarcon, Tomas

Mazzera, Melvin Leonard 1914- [BE]
American baseball player
* Mazzera, Mike

Mazzera, Mike
See Mazzera, Melvin Leonard

Mazzini, Giuseppe 1808?-1872 [HN]
Italian patriot
* [The] Stormy Petrel of European Politics

Mazzochi, Alessio Simmacho 1684-1771 [PA]
Author
* Mazzochole

Mazzochole
See Mazzochi, Alessio Simmacho

Mazzolari, Guiseppe Marione 1712-1786 [PA]
Author
* Parthenia

Mazzoletti, Collette Helene 1907-1968 [SC]
American actress
* Merton, Collette

Mazzoli [or Mazzuoli], Lodovico 1478?-1528 [WBD]
Italian painter
* [Il] Ferrarese
* Mazzolino

Mazzolino
See Mazzoli [or Mazzuoli], Lodovico

Mazzoni, Guido 1450-1518 [WBD]
Italian sculptor
* [Il] Modanino

Mazzuoli [or Mazzola], Girolamo Francesco Maria 1503-1540 [WBD]
Italian painter
* [Il] Parmigianino [or Parmigiano]

Mbali, Ona
See Omari, Cuthbert Kashingo

Mberi, Antar Sudan Katara
See Henderson, Thomas Louis

McAdams, George D. 1886-1937 [BE]
American baseball player
* McAdams, Jack

McAdams, Jack
See McAdams, George D.

McAdoo, Bob 1951- [SMG]
American basketball player
* McAdoo, Mac

McAdoo, Mac
See McAdoo, Bob

McAfee, B.
See Slaughter, Marion T.

McAfee, Carlos
See Slaughter, Marion T.

McAfee, George A. 1918- [BBH, FB]
American football player
* McAfee, Lefty
* McAfee, One Play

McAfee, Lefty
See McAfee, George A.

McAfee, Nella Marshall [PA]
Author
* San Souce

McAfee, One Play
See McAfee, George A.

McAleer, Lucy Ann 1932- [ITA]
American actress
* Marlow, Lucy

McAllister, Alister 1877-1943 [CC, EMD, WW]
Irish playwright and author
* Brock, Lynn
* Wharton, Anthony

McAllister, Amanda
See Hager, Jean

McAllister, Cassie
See McAllister, Lewis William

McAllister, Chip
See McAllister, Frank

McAllister, Frank 20th c. [OBW]
American baseball player
* McAllister, Chip

McAllister, Jack
See Coakley, Andrew James

McAllister, Lewis William 1874-1962 [BE, BN]
American baseball player
* McAllister, Cassie
* McAllister, Sport

McAllister, Mary H. 1947- [GF]
American golfer
* McAllister, Susie

McAllister, Sport
See McAllister, Lewis William

McAllister, Susie
See McAllister, Mary H.

McAloon, William Andrew 1864?-1931 [BEW]
American actor and singer
* Mack, Andrew

McAlpin, Grant
See McCulley, Johnston

McAlpine, Robert W. [FFF, PA]
American writer
* Ancient, Oliver
* Brittle, Gath
* Sonica
* Uncle Jake

McArdle, Brian 20th c. [MBF]
British author
* Reid, Desmond [house pseudonym]

McArthur, Dixie
See McArthur, Oland Alexander

McArthur, John
See Wise, Arthur

McArthur, Mac
See McArthur, Malcolm

McArthur, Malcolm 1862- ? [BE]
American baseball player
* McArthur, Mac

McArthur, Oland Alexander 1892- [BE]
American baseball player
* McArthur, Dixie

McAtee, Bub
See McAtee, Michael James

McAtee, Jerome 1920- [CEI]
Canadian-born hockey player
* McAtee, Jud

McAtee, Jud
See McAtee, Jerome

McAtee, Linus 20th c. [BBH]
American jockey
* McAtee, Pony

McAtee, Michael James 1845-1876 [BE]
American baseball player
* McAtee, Bub

McAtee, Pony
See McAtee, Linus

McAuley, Ike
See McAuley, James Earl

McAuley, James Earl 1893-1928 [BE]
American baseball player
* McAuley, Ike

McAuley, James Phillip 1917-1976 [CA]
Australian poet
* Malley, Ern [joint pseudonym with Harold Stewart]

McAuley, Kenneth Leslie 1921- [FHE]
Canadian-born hockey player
* McAuley, Tubby

McAuley, Tubby
See McAuley, Kenneth Leslie

McAuliffe, Muggs
See McAuliffe, Richard John [Dick]

**McAuliffe, Richard John [Dick]**
1939- [PB]
*American baseball player*
* McAuliffe, Muggs

**McAvoy, James Eugene** 1894-1973
[BE]
*American baseball player*
* McAvoy, Wickey

**McAvoy, Jock**
*See* Bamford, Joseph

**McAvoy, Wickey**
*See* McAvoy, James Eugene

**McBain, Ed**
*See* Lombino, Salvatore A.

**McBean, Alvin O'Neal** 1938-
[SMG]
*American baseball player*
* Double O
* [The] Gay Blade
* McBean, Jumping

**McBean, Jumping**
*See* McBean, Alvin O'Neal

**McBee, Lefty**
*See* McBee, Pryor Edward

**McBee, Pryor Edward** 1901-1965
[BE]
*American baseball player*
* McBee, Lefty

**McBride, Algernon Briggs**
1869-1956 [BE]
*American baseball player*
* McBride, Algie

**McBride, Algie**
*See* McBride, Algernon Briggs

**McBride, Arnold Ray** 1949-
[SMG, WWB]
*American baseball player*
* [The] Callaway Kid
* McBride, Bake

**McBride, Arthur** 1887-1972
[FB, MM, PHM]
*American football team owner*
* McBride, Mickey

**McBride, Bake**
*See* McBride, Arnold Ray

**McBride, Floyd** 1902- [BB]
*American basketball coach*
* McBride, Mickey

**McBride, Mickey**
*See* McBride, Arthur

**McBride, Mickey**
*See* McBride, Floyd

**McBride, Patricia**
*See* Bartz, Patricia McBride

**McBride, Peter** 1854- ? [LAO]
*German-born physician and author*
* E. C. M.

**McBride, William** 1889- [IBW]
*American comedian*
* Mack, Billy

**McBroom, Marden** 1914- [FC]
*American actor*
* Bruce, David

**McBroom, R. Curtis** 1910- [CAP]
*American author*
* Dring, Nathaniel

**McBurney, Alvin** 1911- [PMJ]
*American musician*
* Rey, Alvino

**McBurney, M.** [PA]
*Author*
* Malone, Carroll

**McCabe, Cameron**
*See* Borneman, Ernest Wilhelm Julius

**McCabe, James Arthur** 1881-1944
[BE]
*American baseball player*
* McCabe, Swat

**McCabe, Joseph** 1867-1955 [LC]
*British author and clergyman*
* Anthony, [Father]

**McCabe, Swat**
*See* McCabe, James Arthur

**McCaffree, Charles** 20th c. [BBH]
*American swimmer, coach, organization officer*
* McCaffree, Mac

**McCaffree, Mac**
*See* McCaffree, Charles

**McCaffrey, Charles P.** ?-1894
[BE]
*American baseball player*
* McCaffrey, Sparrow

**McCaffrey, John** 1938- [BB]
*American basketball player*
* McCaffrey, Pete

**McCaffrey, Pete**
*See* McCaffrey, John

**McCaffrey, Sparrow**
*See* McCaffrey, Charles P.

**McCahan, Robert C.** 1899-1958
[SC]
*American actor*
* Dease, Bobby

**McCaig, Edith** 20th c. [CA]
*American author*
* Engren, Edith [joint pseudonym with Robert Jesse McCaig]

**McCaig, Robert Jesse** 1907- [CA]
*American author*
* Engren, Edith [joint pseudonym with Edith McCaig]

**McCain, Boogie**
*See* McCain, Jerry

**McCain, Constance** 20th c. [ITA]
*American actress*
* Cain, Sugar

**McCain, Jerry** 1930- [BWW]
*American singer*
* McCain, Boogie

**McCall, Bam**
*See* McCall, Brian Allen

**McCall, Brian Allen** 1943- [BE]
*American baseball player*
* McCall, Bam

**McCall, C. W.**
*See* Fries, William [Bill]

**McCall, Creighton**
*See* Melcher, Gilbert W[ayne]

**McCall, Dutch**
*See* McCall, Robert Leonard

**McCall, John Corey**
*See* Morland, Nigel

**McCall, John William** 1925- [BE]
*American baseball player*
* McCall, Windy

**McCall, Lizzie**
*See* Lennon, Mrs. Nestor

**McCall, Robert Leonard** 1920-
[BE]
*American baseball player*
* McCall, Dutch

**McCall, Sidney**
*See* Fenollosa, Mary McNeil

**McCall, Vincent**
*See* Morland, Nigel

**McCall, Virginia Nielsen** 1909-
[CA, SAT]
*American author*
* Nielsen, Virginia

**McCall, Windy**
*See* McCall, John William

**McCallum, Colin Whitton**
1852-1945 [BEW, BMH, FC]
*British entertainer and songwriter*
* Coborn, Charlie
* [The] Comic of the Day
* [The] Father of the Profession

**McCalment, Maebelle [Brearley]**
20th c. [NAA]
*American writer*
* Ley, Brea R.
* Mack, Brearley
* Mack, Maebelle

**McCan, Frank** 1896- [BX, RBE]
*American boxer*
* Mason, Frankie

**McCann, Arthur**
*See* Campbell, John W[ood], Jr.

**McCann, Coolidge**
*See* Fawcett, F[rank] Dubrez

**McCann, Edson** [joint pseudonym with Frederik Pohl]
*See* Alvarez Del Rey, Ramon Felipe San Juan Mario Silvio Enrico

**McCann, Edson** [joint pseudonym with Ramon Felipe San Juan Mario Alvarez Del Rey]
*See* Pohl, Frederik

**McCann, Philip**
*See* Felstein, Ivor

**McCarren, Laurence Anthony**
1951- [SMG]
*American football player*
* McCarren, Rock

**McCarren, Rock**
*See* McCarren, Laurence Anthony

**McCarroll, James** 1814- ? [FFF]
*American author and editor*
* Finnegan, Terry

**McCarroll, Marion C[lyde]**
1893?-1977 [CA]
*American author and columnist*
* Fairfax, Beatrice

**McCarter, Jody** [joint pseudonym with Vermille McCarter]
*See* Demelikoff, Jodi

**McCarter, Jody** [joint pseudonym with Jodi Demelikoff]
*See* McCarter, Vermille

**McCarter, Vermille** 20th c. [SFP]
*Author*
* McCarter, Jody [joint pseudonym with Jodi Demelikoff]

**McCarter, Willie** 20th c.
*American basketball player*
* [The] Worm

**McCarthy, Babe**
*See* McCarthy, James

**McCarthy, Charles J.** 1903-1960
[ASC]
*American musician*
* McCarthy, Pat

**McCarthy, Charles L.** 1882-1962
[AS]
*American sportscaster*
* McCarthy, Clem

**McCarthy, Clean Gene**
*See* McCarthy, Eugene Joseph

**McCarthy, Clem**
*See* McCarthy, Charles L.

**McCarthy, Denis Florence** 1820- ?
[PA]
*Author*
* J. H.

**McCarthy, Eugene Joseph** 1916-
*American politician*
* McCarthy, Clean Gene

**McCarthy, Herbert** 20th c. [THR]
*British actor and playwright*
* Darnley, Herbert

**McCarthy, J. P.**
*See* McCarthy, Joseph Priestley

**McCarthy, J. T.**
*See* Torrio, John [Johnny]

**McCarthy, James** 1923-1975
[B10, BB]
*American basketball coach*
* McCarthy, Babe

**McCarthy, Joseph Priestley**
*American radio broadcaster*
* McCarthy, J. P.

**McCarthy, Joseph Raymond**
1908-1957
*American politician*
* Tail Gunner Joe

**McCarthy, Joseph Vincent**
1887-1978 [BE, DGS, PB]
*American baseball manager*
* McCarthy, Marse Joe

**McCarthy, Julia** 1897?-1974 [B10]
*American columnist*
* Randolph, Nancy

**McCarthy, Justine** 1926?-1959
[BDF, BEW, FC]
*British actress*
* Kendall, Kay

**McCarthy, Little Mack**
*See* McCarthy, Thomas Francis Michael [Tommy]

**McCarthy, Marie** 1912-1941 [SC]
*American actress*
* Maynard, Claire

**McCarthy, Marse Joe**
*See* McCarthy, Joseph Vincent

**McCarthy, Mrs. Daniel** [FFF]
*Entertainer*
* Coleman, Kitty

**McCarthy, Pat**
See   Cook, Patricia

**McCarthy, Pat**
See   McCarthy, Charles J.

**McCarthy, Shaun [Lloyd]** 1928-
[CA]
*British author and journalist*
* Callas, Theo
* Cory, Desmond

**McCarthy, Teresa**
See   Anderson, Teresa

**McCarthy, Thomas Francis Michael**
**[Tommy]** 1864-1922   [BAB]
*American baseball player*
* [The] Kid
* McCarthy, Little Mack

**McCartney, William H.**   [FFF, PA]
*American author*
* Muldoon, Major

**McCarty, Henry** 1859-1881
*American gunfighter*
* Antrim, Henry
* Antrim, Kid
* Antrim, William
* Billy the Kid
* Bonney, William

**McCarty, Norma**
See   Crandall, Norma

**McCarty, Wilson** 20th c.   [CA]
*Author*
* Chamberlain, Wilson [joint
   pseudonym with Norma
   Crandall]

**McCash, June Hall** 1938-   [CA]
*American author*
* Martin, June Hall

**McCauley, Elfrieda B[abnick]**
1915-   [CA]
*American editor*
* House, Anne W.

**McCauley, Mary** 1754?-1832
[WBD]
*American Revolutionary War
heroine*
* Pitcher, Molly

**McCaull, M. E.**
See   Bohlman, [Mary] Edna
McCaull

**McCay, Winsor** 1869-1934
[WECO]
*American cartoonist*
* Silas

**McChesney, Harry Vincent**
1880-1960   [BE]
*American baseball player*
* McChesney, Pud

**McChesney, Mary F.** 20th c.   [WW]
*Author*
* Rayter, Joe

**McChesney, Pud**
See   McChesney, Harry Vincent

**McClain, Boots**
See   McClain, Edward

**McClain, Edward** 20th c.   [OBW]
*American baseball player*
* McClain, Boots

**McClain, Houndog**
See   McClain, Ted

**McClain, Ted** 1947?-   [BB, SMG]
*American basketball player*
* [The] Hound
* McClain, Houndog

**McClannin, Mrs. R. F.**   [FFF]
*Entertainer*
* Skerrett, Emma

**McClary, Jane Stevenson** 1919-
[CA]
*American journalist and author*
* McIlvaine, Jane

**McClary, Thomas Calvert**
[ESF, WGT]
*American author*
* Peregoy, Calvin

**McClaskey, Harry** 20th c.   [PMJ]
*Canadian singer*
* Burr, Henry

**McClatchy, C. K.**
See   McClatchy, Charles Kenny

**McClatchy, Charles Kenny** 1858- ?
[NAA]
*American journalist*
* McClatchy, C. K.

**McClean, Kathleen**
See   Hale, Kathleen

**McCleary, Eleanor**
See   Picken, Mary Brooks

**McCleese, James** 1942-   [RO1]
*American singer*
* Soul, Jimmy

**McClellan, George Brinton**
1826-1885   [DEP, DNNS, SN]
*American army officer*
* Little Mac
* [The] Little Napoleon

**McClellan, William**
See   Strong, Charles Stanley

**McClelland, Richard Leeper** 1922-
[TR]
*Irish actor*
* Leech, Richard

**McClendon, Charles Y.** 1923-   [FB]
*American football coach*
* McClendon, Cholly Mac

**McClendon, Cholly Mac**
See   McClendon, Charles Y.

**McClendon, Ernestine**
See   Epps, Ernestine

**McClendon, Marie Millicent Dancy**
1900-   [NAA]
*American author*
* Dancy, M. M.

**McClendon, Rosalie Virginia Scott**
**[Rose]** 1884-1936   [IBW]
*American actress and poet*
* [The] Black Duse

**McClinchy, Marie Emily** 1912-
*American singer*
* Manners, Lucille

**McClintock, Harry Kirby**
1882-1957   [CME]
*American country-western performer*
* Haywire Mac

**McClintock, Marshall** 1906-1967
[CAP, SAT]
*American author*
* Duncan, Gregory
* Marshall, Douglas

**McClintock, Marshall** (Continued)
* McClintock, Mike
* Starret, William

**McClintock, Mike**
See   McClintock, Marshall

**McClintock, Minda Agnes** 1856- ?
[NAA]
*American physician and author*
* Agnes

**McClinton, O. B.**
See   McClinton, Obie Burnett

**McClinton, Obie Burnett** 1942-
[ECM]
*American country-western performer*
* McClinton, O. B.

**McCloskey, Honest John**
See   McCloskey, John

**McCloskey, John** 1862-1940   [BE]
*American baseball manager*
* McCloskey, Honest John

**McCloskey, John** 1898?-1947?
[NOJ]
*American jazz musician*
* Rogers, Emmett

**McCloskey, Paul N.** 1927-
*American politician*
* McCloskey, Pete

**McCloskey, Pete**
See   McCloskey, Paul N.

**McCloskey, [John] Robert** 1914-
[CA, SAT]
*American author and illustrator*
* Dangerfield, Balfour

**McCloud, David**
See   Coonradt, Paul Talbot

**McCloy, Helen [Worrell Clarkson]**
1904-   [CA]
*American author*
* Clarkson, Helen

**McClung, Bum**
See   McClung, Thomas Lee

**McClung, Thomas Lee**
1870-1914?   [AS, FB]
*American football player and U.S.
treasurer*
* McClung, Bum

**McClure, Adrienne Ruth**
1908?-1947   [BEW]
*American theatrical performer*
* Ames, Adrienne

**McClure, Greg**
See   Easton, Dale

**McClure, Harold Murray [Hal]**
1859-1919   [BE]
*American baseball player*
* McClure, Mac

**McClure, Mac**
See   McClure, Harold Murray
[Hal]

**McClure, Mac**
See   McClure, Robert Craig

**McClure, Robert Craig** 1953-
[SMG]
*American baseball player*
* McClure, Mac

**McCluskey, Harry Roberts**
1892-1962   [BE]
*American baseball player*
* McCluskey, Lefty

**McCluskey, Henry** 1827-1870
[PA]
*Author*
* Paddy

**McCluskey, Lefty**
See   McCluskey, Harry Roberts

**McCobb, Mary Selden**   [FFF, PA]
*Writer*
* Densel, Mary

**McColl, Alex[ander Boyd]** 1894-
[BE]
*American baseball player*
* McColl, Red

**McColl, Ewan**
See   Miller, Jimmy

**McColl, Red**
See   McColl, Alex[ander Boyd]

**McCollum, J. C.**   [PA]
*Author*
* Trumps

**McCollum, Robert Lee** 1909-1967
[BWW, NBB]
*American singer*
* McCoy, Robert Lee
* Nighthawk, Robert
* Pettie's Boy
* Ramblin' Bob

**McComas, I. V.** 20th c.   [WWL]
*British author*
* Somerville, H. B.

**McComas, J[esse] Francis**
1911-1978   [ESF, WGT]
*American author and editor*
* Marlowe, Webb

**McComb, Florence**
See   Melim, Mary M.

**McComb, Frederick Wilson Henry**
1927-   [IAW]
*Irish-born author*
* Habershon, Keith

**McComb, Katherine Woods** 1895-
[CA]
*American author*
* Woods, Constance

**McConn, Charles Maxwell** 1881- ?
[WWL]
*American educator and author*
* McConn, Max

**McConn, Max**
See   McConn, Charles Maxwell

**McConnell, Ambrose Moses**
1883-1942   [BE]
*American baseball player*
* McConnell, Amby

**McConnell, Amby**
See   McConnell, Ambrose Moses

**McConnell, Forrest W.**
1911?-1962   [BEW]
*American theatrical performer*
* McConnell, Peewee

**McConnell, James Douglas**
**Rutherford** 1915-   [CA, CC, EMD]
*Irish-born author*
* Rutherford, Douglas
* Temple, Paul [joint pseudonym
   with Francis Durbridge]

**McConnell, John Lithgow Chandos**
1918-   [CA]
*Scottish-born author*
* Chandos, John

McConnell, Peewee
See McConnell, Forrest W.

McConnell, Wallace Robert 1881-
? [WWL]
American geographer and author
* Mac

McConnell, Will
See Snodgrass, William DeWitt

McCook, Alexander McDowell
1831-1903 [SN]
American army officer
* McCook, Fighting

McCook, Fighting
See McCook, Alexander McDowell

McCord, Guy
See Reynolds, Dallas McCord

McCord, May Kennedy 1880-1943
[FFA]
American singer
* [The] Queen of the Hillbillies

McCord, Whip
See Norwood, Victor G[eorge]
C[harles]

McCord, William, Jr. 1944- [RO2]
American singer
* Vera, Billy

McCormac, Brian
See Swan, Cormac

McCormack, Billie
See Burke, Blanche E.

McCormack, Goose
See McCormack, John Ronald

McCormack, James 20th c. [MBF]
British author
* Patrick, Max

McCormack, John Ronald 1925-
[CEI]
Canadian-born hockey player
* McCormack, Goose

McCormack, John W. 1892?-1980
American politician
* [The] Fighting Irishman of South
  Boston

McCormack, Patty
See Russo, Patricia Ellen

McCormack, William John 1947-
[DIL]
Irish poet
* Maxton, Hugh

McCormick, Alyce 1904-1932
[SC]
American actress
* Auburn, Joy

McCormick, Barry
See McCormick, William J.

McCormick, Buck
See McCormick, Frank Andrew

McCormick, [George] Donald [King]
1911- [AW, CA, WD]
Welsh-born author and historian
* Deacon, Richard

McCormick, F. J.
See Judge, Peter

McCormick, Frank Andrew 1913-
[BE, PB]
American baseball player
* McCormick, Buck

McCormick, Harry Elwood
1881-1962 [BE]
American baseball player
* McCormick, Moose

McCormick, Hyannis Port
See McCormick, John

McCormick, Jerry
See McCormick, John

McCormick, John ?-1905 [BE]
American baseball player
* McCormick, Jerry

McCormick, John 20th c.
American football player
* McCormick, Hyannis Port

McCormick, Mary 1914- [CA]
American author
* McCormick, [Sister] Rose
  M[atthew]

McCormick, Merla Jean 1938-
[CA]
American author
* Sparks, Merla Jean

McCormick, Mike
See McCormick, Myron Winthrop

McCormick, Moose
See McCormick, Harry Elwood

McCormick, Mrs. Loudon [FFF]
Entertainer
* Miller, Maud

McCormick, Myron Winthrop
1917- [BE]
American baseball player
* McCormick, Mike

McCormick, [Sister] Rose M[atthew]
See McCormick, Mary

McCormick, Wilfred 1903- [CA]
American author
* Allison, Rand
* Dunlap, Lon

McCormick, William J. 1874-1956
[BE]
American baseball player
* McCormick, Barry

McCorquodale, Barbara
See Cartland, Barbara [Hamilton]

McCovey, Stretch
See McCovey, Willie Lee

McCovey, Wallopin Willie
See McCovey, Willie Lee

McCovey, Willie Lee 1938-
[BE, IBW, PB]
American baseball player
* McCovey, Stretch
* McCovey, Wallopin Willie

McCoy, Al
See Rudolph, Al[bert]

McCoy, Charles
See Selby, Norman

McCoy, Charles [Charlie]
1909-1950 [BWW]
American singer
* McCoy, Papa
* Mississippi Mudder
* Papa Charlie

McCoy, Chink
See McCoy, Frank

McCoy, Cyclone
See McCoy, Robert Jesse

McCoy, Elijah J. 1843-1929 [IBW]
American inventor
* [The] Real McCoy

McCoy, Flintstone
See McCoy, Leon

McCoy, Frank 1906- [MK]
American baseball player
* McCoy, Chink

McCoy, Iola Fuller 20th c.
[CA, SAT]
American author
* Fuller, Iola

McCoy, Joe 1905-1950 [BWW]
American singer
* Big Joe
* Georgia Pine Boy
* Hallelujah Joe
* Hamfoot Ham
* Kansas Joe
* Mississippi Mudder
* Mud Dauber Joe
* Wilber, Bill

McCoy, John 20th c. [WGT]
Author
* Commissioner, Lord

McCoy, Kathleen [Kathy] 1945-
[CA]
American author and actress
* McCoy, Kaylin

McCoy, Kaylin
See McCoy, Kathleen [Kathy]

McCoy, Kid
See McGee, Bill

McCoy, Kid
See Selby, Norman

McCoy, Leon 20th c. [GW]
American rodeo performer
* McCoy, Flintstone

McCoy, Malachy
See Caulfield, Malachy Francis

McCoy, Minnie
See Douglas, Lizzie

McCoy, Mrs. U. E. [FFF]
Entertainer
* Hodgson, Ethelyn

McCoy, Papa
See McCoy, Charles [Charlie]

McCoy, Robert Edward
See McCoy, Robert Jesse

McCoy, Robert Jesse 1910-
[BWW]
American singer
* McCoy, Cyclone
* McCoy, Robert Edward

McCoy, Robert Lee
See McCollum, Robert Lee

McCoy, Tim 1893- [CU]
American actor
* [The] White Eagle

McCoy, Van Allen 1941-1979
[IBW]
American dance creator, conductor,
singer
* [The] Disco Kid

McCoy, Viola 1900?-1956?
[BWW]
American singer
* Brown, Amanda
* Cliff, Daisy

McCoy, Viola (Continued)
* Johnson, Fannie
* Johnson, Gladys
* McCoy, Violet
* White, Clara
* Williams, Bessie
* Williams, Susan

McCoy, Violet
See McCoy, Viola

McCrabb, Buster
See McCrabb, Lester William

McCrabb, Lester William 1914-
[BE]
American baseball player
* McCrabb, Buster

McCracken, Elizabeth A. M. 20th
c. [WWL]
Irish journalist and author
* Priestley, L. A. M.

McCracken, James 1920?-
American opera singer
* McCracken, Moose

McCracken, John D. 1911-1958
[AS, BB]
American basketball player
* McCracken, Jumping Jack

McCracken, Jumping Jack
See McCracken, John D.

McCracken, Moose
See McCracken, James

McCrary, John Reagan 1910-
American entertainer and journalist
* McCrary, Tex

McCrary, Tex
See McCrary, John Reagan

McCravey, Leonard 20th c. [GW]
American rodeo performer
* McCravey, Sinner

McCravey, Sinner
See McCravey, Leonard

McCready, Jack
See Powell, Talmage

McCready, Warren T[homas]
1915- [CA]
American author
* Machiavelli

McCreary, Conn 1921- [BBH]
American jockey
* McCreary, Convertible Conn

McCreary, Convertible Conn
See McCreary, Conn

McCreary, Jay
See McCreary, Lawrence J.

McCreary, Lawrence J. 20th c.
[BBH]
American basketball player and
coach
* McCreary, Jay

McCree, Wade H. 1920?-
American solicitor general
* [The] Poet Laureate of the Sixth
  Circuit

McCreedie, Judge
See McCreedie, Walter Henry

McCreedie, Walter Henry
1876-1934 [BE]
American baseball player
* McCreedie, Judge

**McCreery, Bud**
See McCreery, Walker William

**McCreery, Thomas C.** [SN]
*American politician*
* [The] Silver Tongued Sluggard of the Senate

**McCreery, Walker William** 1921?-
[ASC, BEW]
*American composer*
* McCreery, Bud

**McCreigh [or MacCreigh], James**
See Pohl, Frederik

**McCrohan, Dennis Joseph**
1851-1888 [BE]
*American baseball player*
* Mack, Dennis Joseph [Denny]

**McCrory, Florence** 1917- [PMJ]
*American singer*
* Keene, Linda

**McCrum, Myra Daisy** [FFF, PA]
*Author*
* Howard, Daisy

**McCue, Lillian Bueno** 1902-
[CA, WD]
*American author and playwright*
* De La Torre, Lillian
* De La Torre-Bueno, Lillian

**McCulley, Johnston** 1883-1958
[EMD, NAA, MBF]
*American author*
* Brien, Raley
* Carter, Nicholas?
* Drayne, George
* McAlpin, Grant
* Morton, Monica
* Phelps, Frederic
* Pierson, Walter
* Raley, Rowena
* Stone, John Mack
* Strong, Harrington

**McCulloch, Derek** 1897- [MBF]
*British author*
* Uncle Mac

**McCulloch, Earl** 1936- [FB]
*American football player*
* McCulloch, Pearl

**McCulloch, Ernie** 1926- [BBH]
*Canadian skier*
* [The] Grand Slam Champion

**McCulloch, Hugh** [PA]
*Author*
* J. R. M.

**McCulloch, J. H.** 20th c. [MBF]
*British author*
* Rawlings, J. R.

**McCulloch, John Tyler**
See Burroughs, Edgar Rice

**McCulloch, Pearl**
See McCulloch, Earl

**McCullough, Big Bob**
See McCullough, Robert

**McCullough, Harold Taylor** 20th
c. [BBH]
*American basketball coach*
* McCullough, Mack

**McCullough, James H.**
See Clark, Neil McCullough

**McCullough, Joseph B.** [FFF, PA]
*American editor*
* Mack

**McCullough, Mack**
See McCullough, Harold Taylor

**McCullough, Phil**
See McCullough, Pinson Lamar

**McCullough, Pinson Lamar** 1917-
[BE]
*American baseball player*
* McCullough, Phil

**McCullough, Robert** 20th c. [PHM]
*American underworld figure*
* McCullough, Big Bob

**McCurdy, John Edward** 1929-
[OP]
*American opera singer*
* Macurdy, John

**McCurdy, Nancy**
See Parrish, [Emma] Kenyon

**McCurry, Clarence Earl** 20th c.
*American singer and songwriter*
* Ashley, Thomas Clarence

**McCutchan, J[ohn] Wilson** 1909-
[CA]
*American author and educator*
* Locke, Peter

**McCutchan, Philip [Donald]** 1920-
[CA, WD, WWS]
*British author*
* MacNeil, Duncan

**McCutcheon, George Barr**
1866-1928 [WGT]
*American author*
* Greaves, Richard

**McCutcheon, Hugh Davie-Martin**
1909- [IAW]
*Scottish author*
* Davie-Martin, Hugh

**McCutcheon, James**
See Lundgren, Paul Arthur

**McDaniel, David [Edward]** 1939-
[CA]
*American author*
* Johnstone, Ted

**McDaniel, Deacon**
See McDaniel, Sam[uel Rufus]

**McDaniel, Ed** 1938- [FB, SMG]
*American football player and wrestler*
* Chief Wahoo
* McDaniel, Wahoo

**McDaniel, Ellas**
See Bates, Otha Ellas

**McDaniel, Evelyn**
See Bryan, Evelyn McDaniel Frazier

**McDaniel, Hattie** 1895-1952
[BWW]
*American singer and actress*
* [The] Colored Sophie Tucker
* [The] Female Bert Williams
* Hi Hat Hattie

**McDaniel, James** 1915-1963
[CWG]
*American country-western performer*
* McDaniel, Sleepy

**McDaniel, Lindy**
See McDaniel, Lyndall Dale

**McDaniel, Lyndall Dale** 1935-
[BE]
*American baseball player*
* McDaniel, Lindy

**McDaniel, Sam[uel Rufus]**
1886-1962 [BWW, SC]
*American actor*
* McDaniel, Deacon

**McDaniel, Samuel Walton** [FFF]
*American writer*
* Parsonus Rusticus

**McDaniel, Sleepy**
See McDaniel, James

**McDaniel, Wahoo**
See McDaniel, Ed

**McDaniels, Booker T.** ?-1974?
[MK]
*American baseball player*
* McDaniels, Cannonball

**McDaniels, Cannonball**
See McDaniels, Booker T.

**McDaniels, Jim** 1948- [SMG]
*American basketball player*
* McDaniels, Mac

**McDaniels, Mac**
See McDaniels, Jim

**McDavid, Raven I[oor], Jr.** 1911-
[CA]
*American author*
* Darwin, M. B.
* Hatteras, Owen, III
* Pyles, Aitken

**McDermott, Aubrey [or Paul?]** 20th
c. [ESF, WGT]
*Author*
* McDermott, Dennis [joint pseudonym with Walter Dennis and P. Schuyler Miller]

**McDermott, Dennis** [joint pseudonym with P. Schuyler Miller and Aubrey McDermott]
See Dennis, Walter L.

**McDermott, Dennis** [joint pseudonym with Walter Dennis and P. Schuyler Miller]
See McDermott, Aubrey [or Paul?]

**McDermott, Dennis** [joint pseudonym with Aubrey McDermott and Walter Dennis]
See Miller, P[eter] Schuyler

**McDermott, Frank A.** 1889- [BE]
*American baseball player*
* McDermott, Red

**McDermott, Hugh F.** 1833- ? [PA]
*Author*
* Pax

**McDermott, Maurice Joseph**
1928- [BE]
*American baseball player*
* McDermott, Mickey

**McDermott, Michael** 20th c.
[BBH]
*American swimmer*
* McDermott, Turk

**McDermott, Mickey**
See McDermott, Maurice Joseph

**McDermott, Red**
See McDermott, Frank A.

**McDermott, Turk**
See McDermott, Michael

**McDole, Carol**
See Farley, Carol

**McDole, Ron** 20th c.
*American football player*
* [The] Dancing Bear
* McDole, Rubber Man

**McDole, Rubber Man**
See McDole, Ron

**McDonald, Ab**
See McDonald, Alvin Brian

**McDonald, Alvin Brian** 1936-
[CEI, FHE, HK]
*Canadian-born hockey player*
* McDonald, Ab

**McDonald, Babe**
See McDonald, Patrick J.

**McDonald, Bernard** 1923- [SFL]
*Author*
* Macdonnaill, Brian

**McDonald, Bucko**
See McDonald, Wilfred Kennedy

**McDonald, Cathy**
See Wallis, Geraldine McDonald

**McDonald, Charles E.**
See Crabtree, Charles C.

**McDonald, Daniel** 1847-1880 [BE]
*American baseball player*
* McDonald, Jack

**McDonald, Edward Richard** 1873-
? [SFL, WGT]
*Author*
* McDonald, Raymond [joint pseudonym with Raymond Alfred Leger]

**McDonald, Enos William**
1915-1968 [CWG, DAM]
*American country-western performer*
* McDonald, Skeets

**McDonald, Erwin L[awrence]**
1907- [CA]
*American clergyman and author*
* Hankins, Clabe

**McDonald, Garry** 1948?- [B10]
*Australian actor and television performer*
* Gunston, Norman

**McDonald, Gooseneck Bill**
See McDonald, William

**McDonald, Hot Rod**
See McDonald, James LeRoy

**McDonald, Ian** 20th c. [RO2]
*British singer*
* Matthews, Ian

**McDonald, Jack**
See McDonald, Daniel

**McDonald, James LeRoy** 1927-
[BE]
*American baseball player*
* McDonald, Hot Rod

**McDonald, James Preston** 1904-
[WWJ]
*American jazz musician*
* Jackson, Preston

**McDonald, Jamie**
See Heide, Florence Parry

McDonald, Joe 20th c. [B10]
*American singer*
* Country Joe

McDonald, Joseph E. 1819-1891
[FFF]
*American politician*
* Old Saddlebags

McDonald, Julie 1929- [CA]
*American author and playwright*
* Jensen, Julie

McDonald, Luther 20th c. [OBW]
*American baseball player*
* McDonald, Vet

McDonald, Mac
*See* McDonald, Webster

McDonald, Marie
*See* Frye, Marie

McDonald, Patrick J. 1878?-1954
[AS]
*Irish-born track and field athlete*
* McDonald, Babe

McDonald, Paula 1939?- [B10]
*American author*
* Herrigan, Jackie

McDonald, Raymond [joint
pseudonym with Edward Richard
McDonald]
*See* Leger, Raymond Alfred

McDonald, Raymond [joint
pseudonym with Raymond Alfred
Leger]
*See* McDonald, Edward Richard

McDonald, Richard C. 1935?-
[B10]
*American author*
* Herrigan, Jeff

McDonald, Skeets
*See* McDonald, Enos William

McDonald, Stump
*See* McDonald, Tommy

McDonald, Tex
*See* Crabtree, Charles C.

McDonald, Tommy 20th c.
*American football player*
* [The] Elf
* McDonald, Stump

McDonald, Vet
*See* McDonald, Luther

McDonald, Webster 1900-
[IBW, MK]
*American baseball player*
* [The] Giant Killer
* McDonald, Mac

McDonald, Wilfred Kennedy 1911-
[CEI, FHE, HK]
*Canadian-born hockey player*
* McDonald, Bucko

McDonald, William 1867-1950
[IBW]
*American banker*
* McDonald, Gooseneck Bill

[The] McDonald's of Con Men
*See* Weinberg, Melvin

McDonnell, Arthur 1883-1951
[BEW]
*Irish actor*
* Sinclair, Arthur

McDonnell, James Smith
1899?-1980
*American business executive*
* Mac, Mr.
* McDonnell, Old Mac

McDonnell, James William [Jim]
1922- [BE]
*American baseball player*
* McDonnell, Mack

McDonnell, John W. 1856- ? [FFF]
*American writer*
* Fitzgibbons, Patrick

McDonnell, Mack
*See* McDonnell, James William
[Jim]

McDonnell, Old Mac
*See* McDonnell, James Smith

McDonnell, Virginia B[leecker]
[Jinny] 1917- [CA]
*Author*
* Kirby, Jean [house pseudonym,
Whitman Publishing]

McDonough, Al
*See* McDonough, James Allison

McDonough, C. J. [PA]
*Author*
* Warwick, Charles

McDonough, James Allison 1950-
[CEI, HK, HR]
*Canadian-born hockey player*
* McDonough, Al

McDougal, James A. 1878-1910
[BE]
*American baseball player*
* McDougal, Sandy

McDougal, Lem
*See* McDougal, Lemuel

McDougal, Lemuel 20th c. [OBW]
*American baseball player*
* McDougal, Lem

McDougal, Sandy
*See* McDougal, James A.

McDougal, Stan
*See* Diamant, Lincoln

McDow, Gerald
*See* Scortia, Thomas N[icholas]

McDowall, Roddy
*See* McDowall, Roderick Andrew

McDowall, Roderick Andrew
1928- [BEW, TR]
*British actor*
* McDowall, Roddy

McDowell, Crosby
*See* Freeman, John Crosby

McDowell, Frederick 1904-1972
[DAM]
*American singer and composer*
* McDowell, Mississippi Fred

McDowell, Joseph 1756- ? [FFF]
*American revolutionary soldier*
* Quaker Meadows Joe

McDowell, Kate Sherwood
1849-1883 [FFF, WBD]
*American author*
* Bonner, Sherwood

McDowell, Malcolm
*See* Taylor, Malcolm

McDowell, Michael 1950- [CA]
*American author*
* Aldyne, Nathan [joint pseudonym
with Dennis Schuetz]

McDowell, Mississippi Fred
*See* McDowell, Frederick

McDowell, Mrs. E. A. [FFF]
*Entertainer*
* Reeves, Fannie

McDowell, Samuel Edward Thomas
1942- [BE, PB]
*American baseball player*
* McDowell, Sudden Sam

McDowell, Sudden Sam
*See* McDowell, Samuel Edward
Thomas

McDuff, Brother Jack
*See* McDuffy, Eugene

McDuffie, Terris 1911- [MK]
*American baseball player*
* Elmer the Great

McDuffy, Eugene 1926- [EJ7]
*American jazz musician*
* McDuff, Brother Jack

McEachern, Malcolm 1884?-1945
[BMH]
*Australian-born entertainer*
* Jetsam

McEdwards, William Blake 1922-
[FC]
*American writer, producer, director*
* Edwards, Blake

McElfresh, [Elizabeth] Adeline
1918- [CA, WW]
*American author*
* Cleveland, John
* Scott, Jane
* Wesley, Elizabeth

McElhanon, Kenneth Andrew
1939- [CA]
*American author*
* Saqorewec, E.

McElhenny, Hugh 1928- [B10, FB]
*American football player*
* McElhenny, King

McElhenny, King
*See* McElhenny, Hugh

McElhinney, Jane 1836-1874
[FFF, PA]
*American actress and author*
* Clare, Ada
* Noyes, Mrs. J. F.
* [The] Queen of Bohemia
* Stanfield, Agnes

McElmury, Jim 1949- [SMG]
*American hockey player*
* McElmury, Mac

McElmury, Mac
*See* McElmury, Jim

McElroy, Hercules
*See* McElroy, James Dennis

McElroy, James Dennis 1945-
[IBW]
*American strongman*
* McElroy, Hercules

McElroy, Jim 1953- [SMG]
*American basketball player*
* McElroy, Mac

McElroy, Lee
*See* Kelton, Elmer

McElroy, Mac
*See* McElroy, Jim

McElroy, William E. [PA]
*Author*
* Hubbell, Myron

McElveen, Humpy
*See* McElveen, Pryor Mynatt

McElveen, Pryor Mynatt
1880-1951 [BE]
*American baseball player*
* McElveen, Humpy

McElwee, Lee
*See* McElwee, Leland Stanford

McElwee, Leland Stanford
1894-1957 [BE]
*American baseball player*
* McElwee, Lee

McEnery, David 1914-
[ASC, CWG, DAM]
*American country-western performer*
* Red River Dave

McEnroe, John 1959?-
*American tennis player*
* McTantrum
* Superbrat

McEntee, Maurice Wurts ?-1883
[FFF]
*American author and journalist*
* Blue Jacket, Uncle

McEnvoy, C. N. 20th c. [MBF]
*British author*
* Strange, Kemble

McEver, Eugene T. 1908- [FB]
*American football player*
* McEver, Mack
* McEver, Wild Bull

McEver, Mack
*See* McEver, Eugene T.

McEver, Wild Bull
*See* McEver, Eugene T.

McEvoy, Arthur 1901-1957 [FC]
*British entertainer*
* Randle, Frank

McEvoy, Bernard 1842- ? [NAA]
*British-born journalist and author*
* Diogenes
* Redbarn, Thomas

McEvoy, Harry K[irby] 1910- [CA]
*American author*
* Mack, Kirby

McEvoy, J. P.
*See* McEvoy, Joseph Patrick

McEvoy, Joseph Patrick
1894-1958 [BEW]
*American librettist and playwright*
* McEvoy, J. P.

McEvoy, Mac
*See* McEvoy, Michael Stephen
Anthony

McEvoy, Marjorie Harte 20th c.
[AW, CA, WD]
*British author and journalist*
* Harte, Marjorie

McEvoy, Michael Stephen Anthony
1956- [DC]
*British cricketer*
* McEvoy, Mac

**McEwan, Cap**
See   McEwan, John J.

**McEwan, Geraldine**
See   McKeown, Geraldine

**McEwan, John J.** 1893-1970   [FB]
*American football player and coach*
* [The] Giant from Minnesota
* McEwan, Cap
* [The] Rover Center

**McEwan, Josephine** 1892-   [BF]
*American-born actress*
* Earle, Josephine

**McEwen, Tom** 20th c.
*American auto racer*
* [The] Mongoose

**McFadden, Elbows**
See   McFadden, George

**McFadden, Flash**
See   McFadden, Samuel

**McFadden, George** 20th c.   [RBE]
*Boxer*
* McFadden, Elbows

**McFadden, Gertrude V.** 20th c.
[WWL]
*British author*
* Milbrook, John

**McFadden, Samuel** 1952-   [RO2]
*American musician*
* McFadden, Flash

**McFadin, Bud**
See   McFadin, Lewis B.

**McFadin, Lewis B.** 1928-
[FB, SMG]
*American football player*
* McFadin, Bud

**McFall, Bim**
See   McFall, Donald Jefferson

**McFall, Donald Jefferson** 1951-
[HR]
*Canadian-born hockey player*
* McFall, Bim

**McFall, Frances Elizabeth [Clark]**
1862-1943   [LC, TC, TCI]
*Irish-born author*
* Grand, Sarah

**McFarland, Chappie**
See   McFarland, Charles Edward

**McFarland, Charles Edward** 1924-
[BE]
*American baseball player*
* McFarland, Chappie

**McFarland, Dorothy Tuck** 1938-
[CA]
*American author*
* Tuck, Dorothy

**McFarland, George Emmett** 1928-
[FC, WA]
*American actor*
* McFarland, Spanky

**McFarland, Herm**
See   McFarland, Hermus W.

**McFarland, Hermus W.**
1870-1935   [BE]
*American baseball player*
* McFarland, Herm

**McFarland, LaMont A.** 1871-1913
[BE]
*American baseball player*
* McFarland, Monte

**McFarland, Lester** 1902-
[CWG, DAM]
*American country-western performer*
* McFarland, Mac

**McFarland, Mac**
See   McFarland, Lester

**McFarland, Monte**
See   McFarland, LaMont A.

**McFarland, Packey**
See   McFarland, Patrick

**McFarland, Patrick** 1888-1938
[BX, RBE]
*American boxer*
* McFarland, Packey

**McFarland, Spanky**
See   McFarland, George Emmett

**McFarlane, Alexis** 1906-   [THR]
*Rhodesian-born actress*
* France, Alexis

**McFarlane, David** 1949-   [AW]
*British writer*
* Tyson, Teilo

**McFarlane, Elaine** 1942-   [RO2]
*American singer*
* McFarlane, Spanky

**McFarlane, Spanky**
See   McFarlane, Elaine

**McFerran, Douglass David** 1934-
[CA]
*American author*
* Farren, David

**McFlimsey, Flora**
See   Johnson, Evelyn Kimball

**McGaffigan, Martin A.** 1888-1940
[BE]
*American baseball player*
* McGaffigan, Patsy

**McGaffigan, Patsy**
See   McGaffigan, Martin A.

**McGann, Dan**
See   McGann, Dennis L.

**McGann, Dennis L.** 1872-1910
[AS, BE]
*American baseball player*
* McGann, Dan

**McGarr, Chippy**
See   McGarr, James B.

**McGarr, James B.** 1863-1904   [BE]
*American baseball player*
* McGarr, Chippy

**McGarr, James Vincent [Jim]**
1888-   [BE]
*American baseball player*
* McGarr, Reds

**McGarr, Reds**
See   McGarr, James Vincent [Jim]

**McGarrity, Mark** 1943-   [CA]
*American author*
* Gill, Bartholomew

**McGarry, William Rutledge** 1868?-
?   [WWS]
*American author*
* Smythe, James P.

**McGaughey, Charles** 1878-1956
[SC]
*American actor and producer*
* Mack, Charles

**McGaughy, Dudley Dean** 20th c.
[ESF, SFL, WGT]
*American author*
* Dean, Dudley
* Owen, Dean

**McGavin, Moyra**
See   Crichton, Eleanor Moyra
[McGavin]

**McGaw, Naomi Blanche Thoburn**
1920-   [CA]
*British author*
* Hervey, Jane

**McGeachy, C. E. A.**   [PA]
*Author*
* Mac

**McGeachy, Irving Harding** 1889-
[NAA]
*American columnist*
* Chatfield, Caroline

**McGee, Bill** 20th c.   [BBH]
*Boxer*
* McCoy, Kid

**McGee, Ernest Timothy** 1921-
*American Hanafi Muslim leader*
* Abdul Khaalis, Hamaas

**McGee, Fibber**
See   Jordan, James

**McGee, Fiddler Bill**
See   McGee, William Henry

**McGee, Francis D.** 1899-1934
[BE]
*American baseball player*
* McGee, Tubby

**McGee, Molly**
See   Jordan, Marian Driscoll

**McGee, Thomas D'Arcy**
1825-1868   [FFF]
*Canadian author and statesman*
* Backwoodsman

**McGee, Tubby**
See   McGee, Francis D.

**McGee, William Henry** 1909-   [BE]
*American baseball player*
* McGee, Fiddler Bill

**McGeehan, Conny**
See   McGeehan, Cornelius Bernard

**McGeehan, Cornelius Bernard**
1883-1907   [BE]
*American baseball player*
* McGeehan, Conny

**McGeoch, Andrew Jackson** 1900-
[AW]
*Scottish poet and playwright*
* Paul, Adrian

**McGhee, Brownie**
See   McGhee, Walter Brown

**McGhee, Donnie** 20th c.
*American football player*
* McGhee, Floater

**McGhee, Fibber**
See   McGhee, William Mac [Bill]

**McGhee, Floater**
See   McGhee, Donnie

**McGhee, Globetrotter**
See   McGhee, Granville H.

**McGhee, Granville H.** 1918-1961
[BWW, NBB]
*American singer*
* McGhee, Globetrotter
* McGhee, Stick[s]

**McGhee, Howard** 1918-   [IBW]
*American jazz musician*
* McGhee, Maggie

**McGhee, Maggie**
See   McGhee, Howard

**McGhee, Norman L., Jr.** 1928-
[IBW]
*American astrologer*
* Ke-Kumbha, Kanya

**McGhee, Stick[s]**
See   McGhee, Granville H.

**McGhee, Walter Brown** 1915-
[BWW, DAM, FCW]
*American musician*
* Brother George
* Collins, Big Tom
* Fuller, Blind Boy, 2
* Johnson, Henry
* McGhee, Brownie
* Spider Sam
* Tennessee Gabriel
* Williams, Blind Boy

**McGhee, William Mac [Bill]** 1908-
[BE]
*American baseball player*
* McGhee, Fibber

**McGill, Big Jack**
See   McGill, John George

**McGill, Bill** 1939-   [BB]
*American basketball player*
* [The] Hill

**McGill, Ian**
See   Allegro, John Marco

**McGill, John Edward** 1923-   [FHE]
*Canadian-born hockey player*
* McGill, Little Jack

**McGill, John George** 1921-
[CEI, FHE]
*Canadian-born hockey player*
* McGill, Big Jack

**McGill, Kid**
See   McGill, William Vaness

**McGill, Little Jack**
See   McGill, John Edward

**McGill, Marci**
See   Balterman, Marcia Ridlon

**McGill, Parson**
See   McGill, William John [Bill]

**McGill, William John [Bill]**
1880-1959   [BE]
*American baseball player*
* McGill, Parson

**McGill, William Vaness**
1873-1944   [BE]
*American baseball player*
* McGill, Kid

**McGillicuddy, Cornelius Alexander**
1862-1956   [BAB, BE, PB]
*American baseball manager*
* Mack, Connie
* McGillicuddy, Slats
* [The] Tall Tactician

**McGillicuddy, Earle Thaddeus**
1889-1967   [BE]
*American baseball player*
* Mack, Earle Thaddeus

**McGillicuddy, Mr.**
*See* Abisch, Roslyn Kroop [Roz]

**McGillicuddy, Slats**
*See* McGillicuddy, Cornelius Alexander

**McGilvery, Laurence** 1932-   [CA]
*American editor and publisher*
* Van Geil, Mercury E. C. L.

**McGilvray, Big Bill**
*See* McGilvray, William Alexander [Bill]

**McGilvray, William Alexander [Bill]**
1883-1952   [BE]
*American baseball player*
* McGilvray, Big Bill

**McGinn, Maureen Ann**
*See* Sautel, Maureen Ann

**McGinnis, Big Mac**
*See* McGinnis, George

**McGinnis, Duane** 1938-   [CA]
*American poet*
* Niatum, Duane

**McGinnis, George**   [SMG]
*American basketball player*
* McGinnis, Big Mac

**McGinnis, George W.** 1864-1934
[BE]
*American baseball player*
* McGinnis, Jumbo

**McGinnis, Jumbo**
*See* McGinnis, George W.

**McGinnis, K. K.**
*See* Page, Grover, Jr.

**McGinnity, Joseph Jerome**
1871-1929   [BE, DGS, PB]
*American baseball player*
* [The] Iron Man

**McGirr, Edmund**
*See* Giles, Kenneth

**McGirt, William Archibald** 1923-
[CA]
*American poet*
* Inman, Will

**McGiver, John**
*See* Morris, George

**McGivern, Maureen Daly** 20th c.
[CA]
*Irish-born author*
* Daly, Maureen

**McGivern, William P[eter]** 1924-
[EMD, ESF, WGT]
*American author and screenwriter*
* Blade, Alexander [house pseudonym, Ziff-Davis]
* Peters, Bill

**McGlinchy, Fabia Drake** 1904-
[FC]
*British actress*
* Drake, Fabia

**McGlinn, Dwight**
*See* Brannon, William T.

**McGloin, Joseph Thaddeus** 1917-
[CA, WW]
*American author and clergyman*
* O'Finn, Thaddeus

**McGlothen, Lynn Everratt** 1950-
[SMG]
*American baseball player*
* McGlothen, Mac

**McGlothen, Mac**
*See* McGlothen, Lynn Everratt

**McGlothin, Ezra Mac** 1920-   [BE]
*American baseball player*
* McGlothin, Pat

**McGlothin, Pat**
*See* McGlothin, Ezra Mac

**McGlothlin, James Milton [Jim]**
1943-   [BE, PB]
*American baseball player*
* McGlothlin, Red

**McGlothlin, Red**
*See* McGlothlin, James Milton [Jim]

**McGluphy**
*See* Harrison, Hank

**McGlynn, Christopher**
*See* Ginder, Richard

**McGlynn, Stoney**
*See* McGlynn, Ulysses Simpson Grant

**McGlynn, Ulysses Simpson Grant**
1872-1941   [BE]
*American baseball player*
* McGlynn, Stoney

**McGonegal, Alfred** 1900-1974
[FC, HCA]
*American actor*
* Jenkins, Allen

**McGoorty, Eddie**
*See* Van Dusart, Eddie

**McGoughy, Hugh Dilman** 20th c.
[FIR]
*American actor*
* Dilman, Hugh

**McGovern, Hugh** 20th c.
[BLB, PHM]
*American underworld figure*
* McGovern, Stubby

**McGovern, John Terrence**
1880-1918   [BX, RBE]
*American boxer*
* McGovern, Terrible Terry

**McGovern, Stubby**
*See* McGovern, Hugh

**McGovern, Terrible Terry**
*See* McGovern, John Terrence

**McGowan, Beauty**
*See* McGowan, Frank Bernard

**McGowan, Bridget**   [FFF]
*Entertainer*
* Vernon, Ida

**McGowan, Frank Bernard** 1901-
[BE]
*American baseball player*
* McGowan, Beauty

**McGowan, Hugh** 1884-1927   [SC]
*American actor*
* Mack, Hughie

**McGowan, Inez**
*See* Graham, Roger Phillips

**McGowan, Lieutenant Colonel** [code name used during World War II]
*See* Murphy, Robert

**McGowan, Mickey**
*See* McGowan, Tullis Earl

**McGowan, Tullis Earl** 1921-   [BE]
*American baseball player*
* McGowan, Mickey

**McGranary, Al**
*See* McGranary, Aloysius Cornelius

**McGranary, Aloysius Cornelius**
1902-1971   [SC]
*American actor*
* McGranary, Al

**McGraner, Howard** 1889-1952
[BE]
*American baseball player*
* McGraner, Muck

**McGraner, Muck**
*See* McGraner, Howard

**McGrath, Doyle**
*See* Schorb, Edwin Marsh

**McGrath, Fidgy**
*See* McGrath, Fulton

**McGrath, Fulton** 1908-1958
[WWJ]
*American jazz musician*
* McGrath, Fidgy

**McGrath, John James** 1919-   [EAR]
*American auto racer*
* McGrath, Smiling Jack

**McGrath, Mary**
*See* Murranka, Mary

**McGrath, Morgan**
*See* Rae, Hugh C[rauford]

**McGrath, Robert L[ee]** 1920-   [CA]
*American author*
* Lee, Bob
* Lee, Roberta

**McGrath, Smiling Jack**
*See* McGrath, John James

**McGraw, Donnie** 1953-   [SMG]
*American football player*
* McGraw, Quick Draw

**McGraw, Frank Edwin** 1944-
[B10, PB, SMG]
*American baseball player*
* McGraw, Tug

**McGraw, J. H.** 20th c.   [MBF]
*British author*
* Jackson, Howard

**McGraw, John Joseph** 1873-1934
[BE, DGS, PB]
*American baseball manager*
* [The] Little Napoleon
* McGraw, Muggsy

**McGraw, Muggsy**
*See* McGraw, John Joseph

**McGraw, Quick Draw**
*See* McGraw, Donnie

**McGraw, Tug**
*See* McGraw, Frank Edwin

**McGraw, William Corbin** 1916-
[CA, MJA, SAT]
*American author*
* Corbin, William

**McGreal, E. B.** 1905-   [ITA]
*American film executive*
* McGreal, Mike

**McGreal, Elizabeth**
*See* Yates, Elizabeth

**McGreal, Mike**
*See* McGreal, E. B.

**McGregor**
*See* Hurley, Doran

**McGregor, Charles** 1931-   [IBW]
*American actor*
* Fat Freddie

**McGregor, Donald Alexander**
1939-   [CEI]
*Canadian-born hockey player*
* McGregor, Sandy

**McGregor, Edward** 1873-1917
[BEW, CED]
*American entertainer*
* [The] Happy Tramp
* Wills, Nat M.

**McGregor, Parke**
*See* Cushnie, Parke

**McGregor, Sandy**
*See* McGregor, Donald Alexander

**McGrew, Alex** 1826- ?   [PA]
*Author*
* Brandywine

**McGrew, Fenn** [joint pseudonym with Julia McGrew]
*See* Fenn, Caroline K.

**McGrew, Fenn** [joint pseudonym with Caroline K. Fenn]
*See* McGrew, Julia

**McGrew, Julia** 20th c.   [WW]
*Author*
* McGrew, Fenn [joint pseudonym with Caroline K. Fenn]

**McGrew, Slim**
*See* McGrew, Walter Howard

**McGrew, Walter Howard**
1899-1967   [BE]
*American baseball player*
* McGrew, Slim

**McGuffy, Moaner**
*See* Reeve, Edward H. [Ted]

**McGuinn, James Joseph, III** 1942-
[RO2]
*American singer*
* McGuinn, Roger

**McGuinn, Roger**
*See* McGuinn, James Joseph, III

**McGuire, Biff**
*See* McGuire, William Joseph, Jr.

**McGuire, Deacon**
*See* McGuire, James Thomas

**McGuire, Edna**
*See* Boyd, Edna McGuire

**McGuire, Elmer**
*See* McGuire, Thomas Patrick [Tom]

**McGuire, Harp**
*See* McGuire, Henry Herbert

**McGuire, Henry Herbert**
1921-1966   [SC]
*American actor*
* McGuire, Harp

**McGuire, James Thomas**
1863-1936  [AS, BE]
*American baseball player and manager*
* McGuire, Deacon

**McGuire, M.**
See  McPherson, Malcolm

**McGuire, Marcy**
See  McGuire, Marilyn

**McGuire, Marilyn** 20th c.  [AM]
*American actress and singer*
* McGuire, Marcy

**McGuire, Mickey**
See  Yule, Joe, Jr.

**McGuire, Mrs. J. P.**  [PA]
*Author*
* Lady of Virginia

**McGuire, P.**
See  Penick, Clifton Hewitt

**McGuire, Richard** 1926-  [BB]
*American basketball player*
* McGuire, Tricky Dick

**McGuire, Thomas Patrick [Tom]**
1892-1959  [BE]
*American baseball player*
* McGuire, Elmer

**McGuire, Tricky Dick**
See  McGuire, Richard

**McGuire, William Joseph, Jr.**
1926?-  [BEW, TR]
*American actor and playwright*
* McGuire, Biff

**McGuirk, Harriet**
See  Nawrot, Harriet

**McGunnigle, Gunner**
See  McGunnigle, William Henry
[Bill]

**McGunnigle, William Henry [Bill]**
1855-1899  [BE]
*American baseball manager*
* McGunnigle, Gunner

**McGurk, Slater**
See  Roth, Arthur J[oseph]

**McGurn, Jack**
See  De Mora, James Vincenzo

**McGurn, Joseph** 1872?-1952
[BEW]
*American actor*
* Allen, Joseph

**McHale, Frank**  [PA]
*Author*
* Geraint

**McHale, John** 1791- ?  [PA]
*Author*
* Hierophilos

**McHargue, Georgess** 20th c.
[CA, SAT]
*American author*
* Chase, Alice
* Usher, Margo Scegge

**McHargue, James Eugene** 1907-
[EJ, PMJ, WWJ]
*American jazz musician*
* McHargue, Rosy

**McHargue, Rosy**
See  McHargue, James Eugene

**McHenry, Nellie**
See  Webster, Mrs. John

**McHouston, Ed**
See  Baker, McHouston

**McHugh, Edna** 20th c.  [WW]
*Author*
* Coxe, Kathleen Buddington [joint pseudonym with Amelia Reynolds Long]

**McHugh, Jay**
See  MacQueen, James William

**McHugh, Maxine Davis**
1899?-1978  [CA, IA]
*American journalist and author*
* Davis, Maxine

**McHugh, Ruth Nelson**
See  Nelson, Ruth

**McHugh, Stuart**
See  Rowland, D[onald] S[ydney]

**McIldowie, Chattie** 1895-1975
[SC, THR]
*Irish-born actress*
* MacGill, Moyna

**McIlraith, Dorothy Ann** 1937-
[OP]
*Canadian opera singer*
* Protero, Dodi

**McIlvaine, Charles** 1840-1909
[WGT]
*American author*
* Hodge, Toby

**McIlvaine, Jane**
See  McClary, Jane Stevenson

**McIlveen, Henry Cooke** 1880-1960
[BE]
*Irish-born baseball player*
* McIlveen, Irish

**McIlveen, Irish**
See  McIlveen, Henry Cooke

**McIlwain, David** 1921-
[ESF, SF, SFL]
*British author*
* Maine, C. E.
* Maine, Charles Eric
* Rayner, Richard
* Wade, Robert

**McIlwain, Smokey**
See  McIlwain, [William] Stover

**McIlwain, [William] Stover**
1939-1966  [BE]
*American baseball player*
* McIlwain, Smokey

**McIlwraith, Maureen Mollie Hunter**
1922-  [AW, CA, SAT]
*Scottish author and playwright*
* Hunter, Mollie

**McInerny, Ralph** 1929-  [CA]
*American philosopher and author*
* Austin, Harry
* Mackey, Ernan

**McInnis, John Phalen** 1890-1960
[AS, DGS, PB]
*American baseball player*
* McInnis, Stuffy

**McInnis, Stuffy**
See  McInnis, John Phalen

**McIntire, Harry**
See  McIntire, John Reed

**McIntire, John Reed** 1879-1949
[AS, BE]
*American baseball player*
* McIntire, Harry
* McIntire, Rocks

**McIntire, Rocks**
See  McIntire, John Reed

**McIntosh, Alec** 1907-1959  [B10]
*American artist*
* Blue Eagle, Acee

**McIntosh, Alexander** 1947-  [CA]
*American poet and editor*
* McIntosh, Sandy

**McIntosh, J. T.**
See  MacGregor, James [Murdoch]

**McIntosh, Kenneth** 20th c.  [WGT]
*Author*
* Casey, Kent

**McIntosh, Kinn Hamilton** 1930-
[AW, CA, EMD]
*British author*
* Aird, Catherine

**McIntosh, Lonnie** 1941-  [RO1]
*American musician*
* Mack, Lonnie

**McIntosh, Louis**
See  Johnson, Christopher

**McIntosh, Maria Jane** 1803-1878
[FFF, PA]
*American author*
* Aunt Kitty
* Cousin Kate

**McIntosh, Professor**
See  McIntosh, William
Carmichael

**McIntosh, Sandy**
See  McIntosh, Alexander

**McIntosh, William Carmichael** 20th
c.  [LAO]
*Scottish psychiatrist, zoologist, author*
* McIntosh, Professor

**McIntyre, Hugh D.**  [FFF, PA]
*Author*
* Aberdeen

**McIntyre, James Francis** 1886?-1979
*American religious leader*
* [The] Brick and Mortar Priest

**McIntyre, John** 1869- ?  [LAO]
*Scottish author and playwright*
* Brandane, John

**McIntyre, John T[homas]**
1871-1951  [CC, WW]
*Author*
* O'Neil, Kerry

**McIntyre, Marion**
See  Gray, Marion

**McIver, Jock**
See  Parrot, William

**McIver, Tennie Stewart** 1873- ?
[NAA]
*American writer*
* G. M., Mrs.

**McJames, Doc**
See  James, James McCutchen

**McJames, James McCutchen**
See  James, James McCutchen

**McKahan, Rufus Alan** 1892-1950
[F1, FC]
*American actor*
* Hale, Alan

**McKain, Archie Richard** 1911-
[BE]
*American baseball player*
* McKain, Happy

**McKain, Happy**
See  McKain, Archie Richard

**McKale, James Fritz** 20th c.  [BBH]
*American baseball coach and collegiate athletic director*
* McKale, Pop

**McKale, Pop**
See  McKale, James Fritz

**McKay, Eleanor Gough** 1915-1959
[BEW, EJ, WWJ]
*American singer*
* Day, Lady
* Holiday, Billie

**McKay, George W.**
See  Reuben, George

**McKay, Grif**
See  Kirkpatrick, M. Glen

**McKay, Jim**
See  McManus, James Kenneth

**McKay, Kevin**
See  Strong, Charles Stanley

**McKay, Scott**
See  Gose, Carl Chester

**McKeag, Ernest L[ionel]** 1896-
[CAP]
*British author*
* Braza, Jacque
* Griff [house pseudonym?]
* Grimshaw, Mark
* Haynes, Pat
* King, John
* Lacroix, Ramon
* Laroche, Rene
* Maxwell, Jack
* McKeay, Eileen
* Vane, Roland

**McKeay, Eileen**
See  McKeag, Ernest L[ionel]

**McKechnie, Deacon Bill**
See  McKechnie, William Boyd

**McKechnie, Florence** 1901-
[BEW, FC, IPA]
*American actress*
* Eldridge, Florence

**McKechnie, McKech**
See  McKechnie, Walter Thomas
John

**McKechnie, Walter Thomas John**
1947-  [SMG]
*Canadian-born hockey player*
* McKechnie, McKech

**McKechnie, William Boyd**
1887-1965  [BE, DGS, PB]
*American baseball player, coach, manager*
* McKechnie, Deacon Bill

**McKee, Eva Sue** 1926-
[ECM, FCW, RO1]
*American country-western performer*
* Thompson, Sue

**McKee, Lafayette Stocking**
1872-1959 [SC]
*American actor*
* McKee, Lafe

**McKee, Lafe**
See McKee, Lafayette Stocking

**McKee, Raymond Ellis** 1890- [BE]
*American baseball player*
* McKee, Red

**McKee, Red**
See McKee, Raymond Ellis

**McKeen, Lawrence D., Jr.**
1925-1933 [SC]
*American actor*
* McKeen, Snookums

**McKeen, Snookums**
See McKeen, Lawrence D., Jr.

**McKeever, Marcia**
See Laird, Jean E[louise]

**McKeever, Mrs. John T., Jr.** [FFF]
*Entertainer*
* Bishop, Frances

**McKeithan, Emmett James**
1906-1969 [BE]
*American baseball player*
* McKeithan, Tim

**McKeithan, Tim**
See McKeithan, Emmett James

**McKelway, St. Clair** 1905-1980
[CA]
*American author and editor*
* Hall, J. De P.

**McKendrick, Big Mike**
See McKendrick, Reuben Michael

**McKendrick, Gilbert Michael**
1903?-1961 [WWJ]
*American jazz musician*
* McKendrick, Little Mike

**McKendrick, Little Mike**
See McKendrick, Gilbert Michael

**McKendrick, Reuben Michael**
1901-1965 [WWJ]
*American jazz musician*
* McKendrick, Big Mike

**McKenna, A. Daniel**
See Finnerty, Adam Daniel

**McKenna, Evelyn**
See Joscelyn, Archie Lynn

**McKenna, James William** 1873- ?
[BE]
*American baseball player*
* McKenna, Kit

**McKenna, Kit**
See McKenna, James William

**McKenna, Margaret Mary** 1930-
[CA]
*American author*
* McKenna, [Sister] Mary
Lawrence

**McKenna, [Sister] Mary Lawrence**
See McKenna, Margaret Mary

**McKenna, Patricia**
See Goedicke, Patricia [McKenna]

**McKenna, R. M.**
See McKenna, Richard Milton

**McKenna, Richard Milton** 20th c.
[WGT]
*Author*
* McKenna, R. M.

**McKenney, R. Armstrong**
See Claiborne, Robert [Watson,
Jr.]

**McKenny, Howie**
See McKenny, Jim

**McKenny, Jim** 1946- [SMG]
*Canadian-born hockey player*
* McKenny, Howie

**McKenry, Frank Gordon**
1888-1956 [BE]
*American baseball player*
* McKenry, Limb

**McKenry, Limb**
See McKenry, Frank Gordon

**McKenzie, Altamont** 1951- [AES]
*Jamaican soccer player*
* McKenzie, Altie

**McKenzie, Altie**
See McKenzie, Altamont

**McKenzie, Christian**
See Duffell, Anne

**McKenzie, Grace E.** 1913- [NAA]
*British-born poet*
* Hastings, Elizabeth

**McKenzie, John Albert** 1937-
[FHE]
*Canadian-born hockey player*
* McKenzie, Pie

**McKenzie, Paige**
See Blood, Marje

**McKenzie, Pie**
See McKenzie, John Albert

**McKenzie, Ray?**
See Silverberg, Robert

**McKenzie, Red**
See McKenzie, William

**McKenzie, William** 1899?-1948
[DAM, EJ, PMJ]
*American singer*
* McKenzie, Red

**McKeown, Geraldine** 1932-
[BEW, TR]
*British actress*
* McEwan, Geraldine

**McKern, Leo**
See McKern, Reginald

**McKern, Reginald** 1920- [TR]
*Australian actor and director*
* McKern, Leo

**McKernan, John Leo** 1882-1963
[AS, BX]
*American boxing manager*
* Kearns, Doc
* Kearns, Jack

**McKernan, Pigpen**
See McKernan, Ron

**McKernan, Ron** 1946-1973 [RO2]
*American musician*
* McKernan, Pigpen

**McKerrow, R. B.**
See McKerrow, Ronald Brunlees

**McKerrow, Ronald Brunlees**
1872-1940 [LC]
*British author and editor*
* McKerrow, R. B.

**McKibbon, J. E.** 20th c. [MBF]
*British author*
* Ellis, John
* Probyn, Elise
* Probyn, John E.

**McKillop, Norman** 1892-1974
[CA]
*Scottish locomotive engineer and
author*
* Beg, Toran

**McKim, Ann** 1912-1979
[F2, FC, SW]
*American actress*
* Dvorak, Ann

**McKimmey, James** 1923- [CA]
*American author*
* Swift, Benjamin

**McKinley, Bill**
See Gillum, William McKinley
[Bill]

**McKinley, William** 1843-1901
[FAP]
*American president*
* [The] Idol of Ohio
* [The] Napoleon of Princeton
* Prosperity's Advance Agent
* [The] Stocking-Foot Orator
* Wobbly Willie

**McKinney, Bones**
See McKinney, Horace

**McKinney, Charles** 20th c. [SMG]
*American baseball player*
* McKinney, Rich

**McKinney, H. D.** [FFF]
*American writer*
* Mambrino

**McKinney, Horace** 1919-
[BB, SMG]
*American basketball player and
coach*
* McKinney, Bones

**McKinney, Kate Slaughter** 1859- ?
[NAA]
*American author and poet*
* Katydid

**McKinney, Mac**
See McKinney, William

**McKinney, Rich**
See McKinney, Charles

**McKinney, T. L.** ?-1859 [PA]
*Author*
* Aristides

**McKinney, William** 1895?- [MY]
*American musician and manager*
* McKinney, Mac

**McKinnies, Henry H.** 1925?-1969
[BDF, FC, WEF]
*American actor*
* Hunter, Jeffrey

**McKinnis, Gread** 1913- [MK]
*American baseball player*
* McKinnis, Lefty

**McKinnis, Lefty**
See McKinnis, Gread

**McKinnon, Neil** 1873?-1946
[BEW]
*Scottish-born comedian*
* Kenyon, Neil

**McKittrick, Anna Margaret**
1860-1939 [LC]
*Irish author*
* Ros, Amanda McKittrick

**McKnight, Harmen Packard** 1855-
? [WWL]
*American author*
* Browne, George N.

**McLachlan, Murray** 20th c. [SWI]
*South African swimmer*
* McLachlan, Tich

**McLachlan, Tich**
See McLachlan, Murray

**McLamore, Claire** 1927- [OP]
*American opera singer*
* Watson, Claire

**McLandress, Herschel**
See Galbraith, John Kenneth

**McLane, Armand Ralph** 1936-
[OP]
*American opera singer*
* MacLane, Armand Ralph

**McLaren, George W.** ?-1967
[AS, FB]
*American football player*
* McLaren, Tank

**McLaren, J. A.** 20th c. [MBF]
*British author*
* Adams, John

**McLaren, Tank**
See McLaren, George W.

**McLarnin, Baby Face**
See McLarnin, Jimmy

**McLarnin, Jimmy** 1905-
[BX, RBE]
*Irish-born boxer*
* McLarnin, Baby Face

**McLarry, Howard Bell** 1891-1971
[BE]
*American baseball player*
* McLarry, Polly

**McLarry, Polly**
See McLarry, Howard Bell

**McLarty, Margaret Elizabeth** 20th
c. [BEW]
*American actress and singer*
* Fulton, Eileen

**McLaughlin, Bill**
See Phillips, James W.

**McLaughlin, Bo**
See McLaughlin, Michael Duane

**McLaughlin, Charles W.**
1878-1934 [BEW]
*Canadian-born actor, playwright,
director*
* Mack, Willard

**McLaughlin, Emma Maude** 1901-
[CA]
*American author*
* Weir, Alice M.

**McLaughlin, James Anson**
1888-1934 [BE]
*American baseball player*
* McLaughlin, Kid

**McLaughlin, John** 1942-   [NAD]
*British musician*
* Mahavishnu

**McLaughlin, Jud**
*See* McLaughlin, Justin Theodore

**McLaughlin, Justin Theodore**
1912-1964   [BE]
*American baseball player*
* McLaughlin, Jud

**McLaughlin, Katherine Elizabeth**
1921-1975   [ITA, SC]
*American actress*
* Ryan, Sheila

**McLaughlin, Kid**
*See* McLaughlin, James Anson

**McLaughlin, Mercia** 1901-   [THR]
*South African-born actress*
* Gregori, Mercia

**McLaughlin, Michael Duane** 1953-
[SMG]
*American baseball player*
* McLaughlin, Bo

**McLaughlin, Walter T.** 20th c.
[BBH]
*American collegiate athletic director*
* Mac, Mr.

**McLaughry, DeOrmond**
1893-1974   [B10, FB]
*American football coach*
* McLaughry, Tuss

**McLaughry, Tuss**
*See* McLaughry, DeOrmond

**McLaverty, Edmund** 1882-1951
[FC]
*British actor*
* Breon, Edmund

**McLean, Barney**
*See* McLean, Robert L.

**McLean, Caroline Crawford** 20th
c.   [NAA]
*American author and educator*
* Crawford, Caroline

**McLean, Eric W.** 1900-
[MBF, WWL]
*British author*
* Rayle, Geoffrey
* Townsend, Eric W.

**McLean, J. Sloan** [joint pseudonym
with Josephine M. Wunsch]
*See* Gillette, Virginia M[ary]

**McLean, J. Sloan** [joint pseudonym
with Virginia M(ary) Gillette]
*See* Wunsch, Josephine M.

**McLean, John Bannerman**
1881-1921   [BE, BN]
*American baseball player*
* McLean, Larry
* McLean, Slashaway
* McLean, Slasher

**McLean, John David Ruari** 1917-
[IAW]
*Scottish author*
* Hardie, David

**McLean, Kathryn** [Anderson]
1909-1966   [CAP, SAT]
*American author*
* Forbes, Kathryn

**McLean, Larry**
*See* McLean, John Bannerman

**McLean, Raymond** 1915-1964
[AS, SMG]
*American football player and coach*
* McLean, Scooter

**McLean, Robert L.** 1917-   [BBH]
*American skier*
* McLean, Barney

**McLean, Scooter**
*See* McLean, Raymond

**McLean, Slashaway**
*See* McLean, John Bannerman

**McLean, Slasher**
*See* McLean, John Bannerman

**McLean, Virginia Katherine** 1916-
[MY]
*American singer*
* Verrill, Virginia

**McLeish, Garen**
*See* Stine, Whitney Ward

**McLeland, Nubbin**
*See* McLeland, Wayne Gaffney

**McLeland, Wayne Gaffney** 1924-
[BE]
*American baseball player*
* McLeland, Nubbin

**McLellan, C. M. S.**
*See* Morton, Hugh

**McLendon, Benson Rayfield, Jr.**
1945-   [BWG, GF]
*American golfer*
* McLendon, Mac

**McLendon, Mac**
*See* McLendon, Benson Rayfield,
Jr.

**McLennan, J.**   [FFF]
*Author*
* Pungent, Pierce

**McLeod, Alexander D'Avila**
1896-1973   [SC]
*American actor, circus and rodeo
performer*
* McLeod, Tex

**McLeod, Allan S.** 1949-   [SMG]
*Canadian-born hockey player*
* McLeod, Moose

**McLeod, Barbara**
*See* Fielding, Barbara

**McLeod, John F[reeland]** 1917-
[CA]
*American journalist*
* Freeland, Jay
* Mackle, Jeff

**McLeod, Margaret Vail**
*See* Holloway, Teresa [Bragunier]

**McLeod, Moose**
*See* McLeod, Allan S.

**McLeod, Mrs. G. A.** 19th c.   [FFF]
*Writer*
* Neale, Flora

**McLeod, Mrs. J. F.**   [FFF]
*Entertainer*
* Wilkes, Ada

**McLeod, Ross**
*See* Feldman, Herbert [H. S.]

**McLeod, Tex**
*See* McLeod, Alexander D'Avila

**McLiam, John**
*See* Williams, John Joseph

**McLish, Bus** [or Buster]
*See* McLish, Calvin Coolidge
Julius Caesar Tuskahoma

**McLish, Calvin Coolidge Julius
Caesar Tuskahoma** 1925-   [BE, PB]
*American baseball player*
* McLish, Bus [or Buster]

**McLlelan, George H. H.** 1907?-
[CW]
*Guyanese folklorist and journalist*
* Puncuss, Pugagee

**McLlhargey, Jack** 1952-   [SMG]
*Canadian-born hockey player*
* McLlhargey, Wolfman

**McLlhargey, Wolfman**
*See* McLlhargey, Jack

**McLociard, George**
*See* Locke, Charles F.

**McLoughlin, Maurice E.**
1890-1957   [AS, OET]
*American tennis player*
* [The] California Comet

**McLowery, Frank**
*See* Keevill, Henry J[ohn]

**McLure, R.** 20th c.   [MBF]
*British author*
* Knowles, Thomas E.

**McMacken, Bill** 20th c.   [GW]
*American rodeo performer*
* [The] Count

**McMahon, Andrew** 1926-   [BWW]
*American singer*
* McMahon, Blueblood

**McMahon, Blueblood**
*See* McMahon, Andrew

**McMahon, Doc**
*See* McMahon, Henry John

**McMahon, Henry John** 1886-1929
[BE]
*American baseball player*
* McMahon, Doc

**McMahon, J. A.** 20th c.   [CSH]
*Canadian lacrosse player*
* McMahon, Wandy

**McMahon, James, Jr.** 1912-1974
[BBH]
*American bowler*
* McMahon, Junie

**McMahon, John Joseph** 1867-1954
[AS, BE, DGS]
*American baseball player*
* McMahon, Sadie

**McMahon, Junie**
*See* McMahon, James, Jr.

**McMahon, Pat**
*See* Hoch, Edward D.

**McMahon, Robert**
*See* Weverka, Robert

**McMahon, Sadie**
*See* McMahon, John Joseph

**McMahon, Wandy**
*See* McMahon, J. A.

**McMakin, John Weaver**
1878-1956   [BE]
*American baseball player*
* McMakin, Spartanburg John

**McMakin, Spartanburg John**
*See* McMakin, John Weaver

**McManus, Declan Patrick** 1955?-
*British musician*
* Costello, Elvis

**McManus, George** 20th c.   [BLB]
*American gambler*
* McManus, Hump

**McManus, Hump**
*See* McManus, George

**McManus, James Kenneth** 1921-
[CA]
*American sports commentator and
author*
* McKay, Jim

**McManus, Joab Logan** 1887-1955
[BE]
*American baseball player*
* McManus, Joe

**McManus, Joe**
*See* McManus, Joab Logan

**McMath, Virginia Katherine** 1911-
[BDF, BEW, EMT]
*American actress, singer, dancer*
* Rogers, Ginger

**McMeekan, Wayne James** 1914-
[BEW, EMT, TR]
*American actor*
* Wayne, David

**McMeekin, Clark** [joint pseudonym
with Isabel (McLennan) McMeekin]
*See* Clark, Dorothy [Park]

**McMeekin, Clark** [joint pseudonym
with Dorothy (Park) Clark]
*See* McMeekin, Isabel
[McLennan]

**McMeekin, Isabel** [McLennan]
1895-   [ANT, CA, SAT]
*American author*
* McMeekin, Clark [joint
pseudonym with Dorothy (Park)
Clark]

**McMichen, Clayton** 1900-   [B10]
*American musician*
* McMichen, Pappy

**McMichen, Pappy**
*See* McMichen, Clayton

**McMickle, Mick**
*See* McMickle, R. D.

**McMickle, R. D.** 1907-   [MY]
*American jazz musician*
* McMickle, Mick

**McMillan, Bub**
*See* McMillan, Norman Alexis

**McMillan, George A.** 20th c.   [BE]
*American baseball player*
* McMillan, Reddy

**McMillan, James** 1925-
[AW, WD]
*Scottish-born author*
* Coriolanus

**McMillan, Lida**
*See* Snow, Lida

**McMillan, Norman Alexis**
1895-1969 [BE]
*American baseball player*
* McMillan, Bub

**McMillan, Rebel**
*See* McMillan, Thomas Law
[Tommy]

**McMillan, Reddy**
*See* McMillan, George A.

**McMillan, Thomas Law [Tommy]**
1888-1966 [BE]
*American baseball player*
* McMillan, Rebel

**McMillian, Butterball**
*See* McMillian, Jim

**McMillian, Jim** 20th c.
*American basketball player*
* McMillian, Butterball

**McMillin, Alvin N.** 1895-1952
[AS, FB, SMG]
*American football player and coach*
* McMillin, Bo

**McMillin, Bo**
*See* McMillin, Alvin N.

**McMinn, Ursula** 1906-1973
[F2, FC]
*British actress*
* Jeans, Ursula

**McMorrow, Fred** 1925- [CA]
*American writer*
* Redfield, Clark

**McMullen, Catherine**
*See* Cookson, Catherine Ann
[McMullen]

**McMullen, John F.** 1849-1881
[BE]
*American baseball player*
* McMullen, Lefty

**McMullen, Joseph Carl** 1882-
[NAA]
*American playwright*
* Carlton, Joseph

**McMullen, Kenneth Lee** 1942-
[SMG]
*American baseball player*
* McMullen, Pound Cake

**McMullen, Lefty**
*See* McMullen, John F.

**McMullen, Pound Cake**
*See* McMullen, Kenneth Lee

**McMullin, Ruth R[oney]** 1942-
[CA]
*American author and editor*
* Roney, Ruth Anne

**McMurray, Nancy A[rmistead]**
1936- [CA]
*American author and illustrator*
* Yowa

**McMurrogh-Kavanagh, Douglas
Gerrard** 1888-1950 [SC]
*Irish-born actor and director*
* Gerrard, Douglas

**McMurry, Lolita** 1908- [F2]
*Actress*
* Grey, Lita

**McNab, Frances**
*See* Fraser, Agnes Maude

**McNabb, Carl Mac** 1917- [BE]
*American baseball player*
* McNabb, Skinny

**McNabb, Skinny**
*See* McNabb, Carl Mac

**McNair, Boob**
*See* McNair, Donald Eric

**McNair, Donald Eric** 1909-1949
[BE]
*American baseball player*
* McNair, Boob

**McNally, Blood**
*See* McNally, John V.

**McNally, Curtis**
*See* Birchall, Ian H[arry]

**McNally, Horace** 1913-
[FC, ITA, SW]
*American actor*
* McNally, Stephen

**McNally, John V.** 1904-
[FB, SMG]
*American football player*
* Blood, Johnny
* McNally, Blood
* [The] Vagabond Halfback

**McNally, Stephen**
*See* McNally, Horace

**McNally, Walter** [FFF]
*Entertainer*
* Wilson, George

**McNamara, Barbara Willard**
1913- [AW]
*Australian author*
* O'Conner, Elizabeth

**McNamara, Big Mac**
*See* McNamara, Gerry

**McNamara, Dinny**
*See* McNamara, John Raymond

**McNamara, Gerry** 20th c. [SMG]
*Hockey scout*
* McNamara, Big Mac

**McNamara, John Raymond**
1905-1963 [BE]
*American baseball player*
* McNamara, Dinny

**McNamara, Joseph** 1866-1916
[BE]
*Irish-born baseball player*
* Mack, Joseph
* Mack, Reddy

**McNamara, Lena Randolph [Brooke]**
1891- [CAP, WW]
*American author and illustrator*
* Mack, Evalina

**McNamara, [Sister] Marie Aquinas**
*See* Schaub, Marilyn McNamara

**McNaught, Rosamond Livingstone**
20th c. [NAA]
*American writer and poet*
* Hancock, Frances

**McNaughton, Gus**
*See* Le Clerq, Augustus Howard

**McNaughton, John H.** [FFF]
*American poet*
* Babble Brook

**McNaughton, Violet** 1873?-1953
[BEW]
*Canadian-born actress*
* Adair, Jean

**McNeal, Harry**
*See* McNeal, John Harley

**McNeal, John Harley** 1878-1945
[BE]
*American baseball player*
* McNeal, Harry

**McNeely, Big Jay**
*See* McNeely, Cecil

**McNeely, Cecil** 1928- [EJ]
*American musician*
* McNeely, Big Jay

**McNeely, Jeannette** 1918- [CA]
*American author*
* Mackie, Maron
* Macneill, Janet

**McNeil, Brownie**
*See* McNeil, Norman L.

**McNeil, Clifton A.** 1940- [FB]
*American football player*
* McNeil, Spider
* McNeil, Sticks

**McNeil, Minnie**
*See* Dayton, Mrs. Peter

**McNeil, Norman L.** 1915- [FFA]
*American singer*
* McNeil, Brownie

**McNeil, Spider**
*See* McNeil, Clifton A.

**McNeil, Sticks**
*See* McNeil, Clifton A.

**McNeile, Herman Cyril** 1888-1937
[EMD, LC, TC]
*British author*
* Sapper

**McNeill, Janet**
*See* Alexander, Janet

**McNeillie, John** 20th c. [B10]
*British author*
* Niall, Ian

**McNeilly, Mildred Masterson**
1910- [ANT]
*American author*
* Dewey, James
* Kelly, Glenn

**McNeilly, Wilfred Glassford** 1921-
[CA, ESF, SFL]
*Scottish-born author*
* Baker, W[illiam] Howard
* Ballinger, W. A.
* Glassford, Wilfred
* Gregg, Martin
* Hunter, Joe
* Lecale, Errol
* Reid, Desmond
* Saxon, Peter [house pseudonym]

**McNish, George** 1660-1722 [FFF]
*American clergyman*
* [The] Father of Presbyterianism
   in New York

**McNish, James Thomas** 1898-
[IAW]
*South African author*
* Marathon

**McNulty, Dorothy** 1908-
[FC, ITA]
*American actress*
* Singleton, Penny

**McNulty, Eugene Dennis** 1917-
[PMJ, SW]
*American singer*
* Day, Dennis

**McNutt, Charles**
*See* Nutt, Charles

**McPadden, Gunner**
*See* McPadden, William

**McPadden, William** 20th c. [BLB]
*American underworld figure*
* McPadden, Gunner

**McPartland, Kid**
*See* Lawrence, William

**McPeake, Big Red**
*See* McPeake, William Curtis

**McPeake, William Curtis** 1927-
[CWG, DAM]
*American country-western performer*
* McPeake, Big Red

**McPhail, Larry**
*See* McPhail, Leland Stanford

**McPhail, Leland Stanford**
1890-1975 [B10]
*American baseball official*
* McPhail, Larry

**McPhee, Bid [or Biddy]**
*See* McPhee, John Alexander

**McPhee, John Alexander**
1859-1943 [AS, BE, DGS]
*American baseball player*
* McPhee, Bid [or Biddy]

**McPherrin, Jones**
*See* Day, Thomas Franklin

**McPherson, Aimee Semple**
1890-1944
*Canadian-born evangelist*
* Aimee, [Sister]
* [The] World's Most
   Pulchritudinous Evangelist

**McPherson, [Captain] Angus**
*See* Colinski, A. J.

**McPherson, Hugh** 1921- [CA]
*Canadian author*
* McPherson, Hugo [Archibald]

**McPherson, Hugo [Archibald]**
*See* McPherson, Hugh

**McPherson, Malcolm** 1850- ? [PA]
*Author*
* McGuire, M.

**McPherson, Richard C.** 1883-1944
[ASC, PMJ]
*American composer*
* Mack, Cecil

**McPherson, Warner** 1936- [CWG]
*American country-western performer*
* Mack, Warner

**McQuade, Ann Aikman** 1928-
[CA]
*American author*
* Aikman, Ann

**McQuail, Thursty**
*See* Bruce, Wallace

**McQueen, Butterfly**
*See* McQueen, Thelma

**McQueen, Mildred Hark** 1908-
[CAP, SAT]
*American author and playwright*
* Hark, Mildred

**McQueen, Thelma** 1911-    [FC]
*American actress*
* McQueen, Butterfly

**McQuery, Mox**
*See* McQuery, William Thomas

**McQuery, William Thomas**
1861-1900    [BE]
*American baseball player*
* McQuery, Mox

**McQuillan, Handsome Hugh**
*See* McQuillan, Hugh A.

**McQuillan, Hugh A.** 1897-1947
[BE, BN]
*American baseball player*
* [The] Astoria Eagle
* McQuillan, Handsome Hugh

**McQuillen, Glen Richard** 1915-
[BE]
*American baseball player*
* McQuillen, Red

**McQuillen, Red**
*See* McQuillen, Glen Richard

**McQuoid, Rose Lee** 20th c.    [SC]
*American actress*
* Lee, Rose

**M'Cracken, Mike**
*See* Landsborough, G. H.

**McRae, Cassius**
*See* McRae, Graham

**McRae, Ellen**
*See* Gillooly, Edna Rae

**McRae, Graham** 1940-    [EAR]
*New Zealand auto racer*
* McRae, Cassius

**McRae, Lindsay**
*See* Sowerby, Arthur Lindsay
McRae

**McRae, Roy**
*See* Buley, Bernard

**M'cready, Max**
*See* M'cready, Samuel Maxwell

**M'cready, Samuel Maxwell** 1918-
[EG]
*British golfer*
* M'cready, Max

**McRuer, Helen** ?-1945    [SC]
*American actress and playwright*
* Mitchell, Helen

**McShane, Mark** 1929?-    [CA, WD]
*Australian-born author*
* Lovell, Marc

**McShann, Hootie**
*See* McShann, Jay

**McShann, Jay** 1909-
[DAM, EJ, PMJ]
*American jazz musician*
* McShann, Hootie

**McSorley, John Bernard**
1858-1936    [BE]
*American baseball player*
* McSorley, Trick

**McSorley, Trick**
*See* McSorley, John Bernard

**McSpaden, Harold** 1908-
[BWG, GF]
*American golfer*
* McSpaden, Jug

**McSpaden, Jug**
*See* McSpaden, Harold

**McSweeney, Virginia** 1898-1968
[F1, F2, FC]
*American actress*
* Valli, Virginia

**McTantrum**
*See* McEnroe, John

**McTell, Blind Willie**
*See* McTell, Willie Samuel

**McTell, Willie Samuel** 1901-1959
[BWW]
*American singer*
* Barrelhouse Sammy
* Blind Doogie
* Blind Sammy
* Georgia Bill
* Glaze, Red Hot Willie
* Hot Shot Willie
* McTell, Blind Willie
* Pig 'n' Whistle Red
* Red Hot Willie

**McTurk, Michael** 1858?- ?    [CW]
*Guyanese folklorist*
* Quow

**McVea, Samuel** 1885-1921
[BX, IBW]
*American boxer*
* [The] Black Globetrotter
* McVey, Sam

**McVean, James**
*See* Luard, Nicholas Lambert

**McVeigh, Charles** 1898-
[CEI, HK]
*Canadian-born hockey player*
* McVeigh, Rabbit

**McVeigh, Rabbit**
*See* McVeigh, Charles

**McVey, Lucille** 1868-1925    [FC]
*American actress*
* Drew, Mrs. Sidney

**McVey, Sam**
*See* McVea, Samuel

**McVicker, Brock**    [PA]
*Author*
* Edgerton, Wild

**McVicker, Mrs. Horace**    [FFF]
*Entertainer*
* Weaver, Effie

**McVicor, John** 20th c.    [CEI]
*Hockey player*
* McVicor, Slim

**McVicor, Slim**
*See* McVicor, John

**McWeeny, Buzz**
*See* McWeeny, Douglas Lawrence

**McWeeny, Douglas Lawrence**
1896-1953    [BE]
*American baseball player*
* McWeeny, Buzz

**McWherter, Rodney** 1936-    [OP]
*American opera singer*
* MacWherter, Rod

**McWhirter, Glenna S.** 1929-    [CA]
*American columnist*
* McWhirter, Nickie

**McWhirter, Nickie**
*See* McWhirter, Glenna S.

**McWilliams, Calm Daddy**
*See* McWilliams, Stanley W.

**McWilliams, Stanley W.** 1939-
[IBW]
*American Air Patrol pilot*
* McWilliams, Calm Daddy

**McWorter, Gerald** 20th c.
*American educator*
* Alkalamit, Abdul

**Mea**
*See* Angerer, Mea

**Meabey, Leonard**
*See* Gander, Leonard Marsland

**Meachum, Dad**
*See* Meachum, James H.

**Meachum, James H.** 1893?-1963
[BEW]
*American theatrical performer*
* Meachum, Dad

**Mead, Jude** 1919-    [CA]
*American clergyman, educator,
author*
* Jude, [Father]

**Mead, Matt**
*See* Richards, Ross

**Mead, Russell**
*See* Koehler, Margaret [Hudson]

**Mead, Sidney Moko** 1927-    [AW]
*New Zealand author*
* Moko

**Meade, Claire**
*See* Fields, Marguerite

**Meade, Ellen**
*See* Roddick, Ellen

**Meade, George Gordon** 1815-1872
[DNNS, FFF, SN]
*American army officer*
* Four Eyed George

**Meade, Julia**
*See* Kunze, Julia

**Meade, L[illie] T[homas]**
*See* Smith, Elizabeth Thomasina
[Meade]

**Meade, Mary**
*See* Church, Ruth Ellen [Lovrien]

**Meade, Richard**
*See* Haas, Ben[jamin] L[eopold]

**Meader, Vaughn** 1936?-
*American entertainer*
* Sunday, Johnny

**Meadley, George Wilson**    [PA]
*Author*
* G. W. M.

**Meador, James H.** 1912-    [FC, SW]
*American actor*
* Craig, James

**Meadowcroft, Enid LaMonte**
*See* Wright, Enid Meadowcroft
[LaMonte]

**Meadowcroft, Ernest [William]**
1914-    [WD]
*British author and poet*
* William, Arnold

**Meadowes, Pauline**
*See* Megroz, Phyllis

**Meadows, Country**
*See* Meadows, Edward

**Meadows, Edward** 1932-    [FB]
*American football player*
* Meadows, Country

**Meadows, Henry Lee** 1894-1963
[BE, DGS, PB]
*American baseball player*
* Meadows, Specs

**Meadows, Jayne**
*See* Cotter, Jane

**Meadows, Lindon**
*See* Greatrex, Charles

**Meadows, Peter**
*See* Lindsay, Jack

**Meadows, Specs**
*See* Meadows, Henry Lee

**Meagher, M.** 20th c.    [MBF]
*British author*
* Marriott, Buck

**Meagher of the Sword**
*See* Meagher, Thomas Francis

**Meagher, Thomas Francis**
1823-1867    [HN]
*Irish-born American politician and
army officer*
* Meagher of the Sword

**Meaker, M. J.**
*See* Meaker, Marijane

**Meaker, Marijane** 1927-
[CLC, FBJ, SAT]
*American author*
* Aldrich, Ann
* Kerr, M. E.
* Meaker, M. J.
* Packer, Vin

**[The] Meal Ticket**
*See* Hubbell, Carl Owen

**Mean Joe Greene**
*See* Greene, Charles Edward

**Means, Mary** 20th c.    [WW]
*Author*
* Scott, Denis [joint pseudonym
  with Theodore Saunders]

**Meanwell, Walter E.** 1884-1953
[AS, BB]
*British-born American basketball
coach*
* [The] Little Doctor

**Meany, Big George**
*See* Meany, [William] George

**Meany, [William] George** 1894-1980
*American labor leader*
* Meany, Big George

**Meara, Charles Edward [Charlie]**
1891-    [BE]
*American baseball player*
* Meara, Goggy

**Meara, Goggy**
*See* Meara, Charles Edward
[Charlie]

**Mearns, David Chambers** 1899-
[CA]
*American author*
* Fraddle, Farragut

**Measday, George**
*See* Soderberg, Percy Measday

**Mease, John** 1746-1826    [FFF]
*American soldier*
* [The] Last of the Cocked Hats

**Meason, Gilbert Laing** 19th c.   [PA]
*Author*
* G. L. M.

**Measor, Adele**
*See*   Buckstone, Mrs. J. C.

**Measor, C. P.**   [PA]
*Author*
* Scrutator

**Meat Loaf**
*See*   Aday, Marvin Lee

**Mebane, John [Harrison]** 1909-
[CA]
*American author*
* DeVilbiss, Philip
* Heartman, Harold

**Mec, Dinah** 1920-   [BF]
*British actress*
* Sheridan, Dinah

**[Il] Meccherino**
*See*   Di Pace, Domenico

**Mecham, William** 1853-1902
[WEC]
*British cartoonist*
* Merry, Tom

**[The] Mechanical Man**
*See*   Gehringer, Charles Leonard

**[The] Mechanical Man**
*See*   Nelson, Byron

**Meco**
*See*   Monardo, Meco

**Mecom, Big John**
*See*   Mecom, John W., Sr.

**Mecom, John W., Sr.** 1911?-1981
*American industrialist*
* Mecom, Big John

**Medard, Yves**
*See*   Labuchin, Rassoul

**Medaris, John B.** 1902-
*American army officer and priest*
* Bruce, [Father]

**Medary, Samuel** 1801-1864   [FFF]
*American editor*
* [The] Old Wheel Horse of
   Democracy

**Medbury, Jessie Royse** 1904-1972
[BEW, FC]
*American actress*
* Landis, Jessie Royce

**[The] Meddler**
*See*   Roosevelt, Theodore [Teddy]

**Mede, Joseph**
*See*   Garland, David John

**Medeiros, Pep**
*See*   Medeiros, Ray Antone

**Medeiros, Ray Antone** 1926-   [BE]
*American baseball player*
* Medeiros, Pep

**Medford, Kay**
*See*   Regan, Kathleen Patricia

**Medhurst, Joan**
*See*   Liverton, Joan

**Mediana, Patricia** 1923-   [BEW]
*British actress*
* Medina, Patricia

**Medical Mother**
*See*   Cilento, Phyllis Dorothy

**Medich, Doc**
*See*   Medich, George Francis

**Medich, George Francis** 1948-
[SMG]
*American baseball player*
* Medich, Doc

**Medici, Alessandro Ottaviano de**
1535-1605   [WBD]
*Pope*
* Leo XI

**Medici, Anna Maria Ludovica de**
1667-1743   [WBD]
*Daughter of Cosimo III, Grand
Duke of Tuscany*
* [The] Last of the Medici

**Medici, Cosmo [or Cosimo] de**
1389-1464   [DHA, HN, WBD]
*Florentine ruler*
* Cosimo the Elder
* [The] Father of His Country
* [The] Invincible

**Medici, Cosmo [or Cosimo] de**
1519-1574   [DNNS, FFF, SN]
*Grand Duke of Tuscany*
* [The] Great

**Medici, Francesco de** 1541-1587
[SN]
*Son of Cosmo, Grand Duke of
Tuscany*
* [The] Second Brutus

**Medici, Giovanni Angelo**
1499-1565   [WBD]
*Pope*
* Pius IV

**Medici, Giovanni de** 1475-1521
[RH, WBD]
*Pope*
* Divine Majesty
* Husband of the Church
* [The] Key of all the Universe
* Leo X
* Prince of the Apostles

**Medici, Giovanni de** 1498-1526
[HN, SN, WBD]
*Italian general*
* [The] Devil
* Giovanni delle Bande Nere [John
   of the Black Bands]
* [Il] Gran Diavolo

**Medici, Giulio de** 1478-1534
[WBD]
*Pope*
* Clement VII

**Medici, Lorenzino de**
*See*   Medici, Lorenzo de

**Medici, Lorenzo de** 1395-1440
[WBD]
*Florentine banker*
* [The] Elder

**Medici, Lorenzo de** 1448-1492
[DNNF, HN, RH]
*Florentine ruler*
* [The] Father of Letters
* [The] Magnificent
* [The] Patron of the Fine Arts
* [The] Restorer of Learning

**Medici, Lorenzo de** 1463-1507
[WBD]
*Florentine politician*
* [The] Younger

**Medici, Lorenzo de** 1514-1548
[WBD]
*Murdered Alessandro de Medici,
First Duke of Florence*
* Medici, Lorenzino de

**[The] Medici of the Middle West**
*See*   Miller, J. Irwin

**Medici, Piero de** 1414-1469   [WBD]
*Ruler of Florence*
* [The] Gouty

**Medicine Bill Mountjoy**
*See*   Mountjoy, William R. [Billy]

**Medicus II**
*See*   Philipp, Elliot Elias

**Medina, Hector** 20th c.   [RBE]
*Mexican boxer*
* Casanova, Young

**Medina, Patricia**
*See*   Mediana, Patricia

**Meding, Oskar** 1829-1903   [PA]
*Author*
* Samarow, Gregor

**Medley?**
*See*   Etherege, [Sir] George

**Medley, Anne**
*See*   Borchard, Ruth [Berendsohn]

**Medlicott, Margaret P[aget]** 1913-
[CA]
*British author*
* Paget, Margaret

**Mednick, Stanley Robert** 1930-
[BEW]
*American playwright*
* Roberts, Meade

**Medolla [or Meldolla], Andrea**
1522?-1582   [WBD]
*Italian painter*
* Schiavone, Andrea

**Medveczky**
*See*   Hatar, Gyozo Victor John

**Medvedev, Mikhail**
*See*   Bernstein, Meyer Y.

**Medwick, Ducky**
*See*   Medwick, Joseph Michael

**Medwick, Joseph Michael**
1911-1975   [BE, PB, SR]
*American baseball player*
* [The] Hungarian Rhapsody
* Medwick, Ducky
* Medwick, Muscles

**Medwick, Muscles**
*See*   Medwick, Joseph Michael

**Mee, Arthur** 1875- ?   [WWL]
*British author*
* Idris

**Mee, Judge**
*See*   Mee, Thomas William
[Tommy]

**Mee, Mary**
*See*   Dean, Mary

**Mee, Thomas William [Tommy]**
1890-   [BE]
*American baseball player*
* Mee, Judge

**Meech, Edward Raymond** ?-1952
[SC]
*American actor and circus performer*
* Meech, Montana

**Meech, Montana**
*See*   Meech, Edward Raymond

**Meegan, Pete[r J.]** 1863-1905   [BE]
*American baseball player*
* Meegan, Steady Pete

**Meegan, Steady Pete**
*See*   Meegan, Pete[r J.]

**Meehan, Chick**
*See*   Meehan, John Francis

**Meehan, Francis** 1898-1968   [BB]
*American basketball player*
* Meehan, Stretch

**Meehan, Francis Joseph** 1881- ?
[CAT]
*American author and critic*
* Scarlet, Will
* Zachary Leo, [Brother]

**Meehan, John Francis** 1893-1972
[B10, FB]
*American football coach*
* Meehan, Chick

**Meehan, Stretch**
*See*   Meehan, Francis

**Meehan, Willie**
*See*   Walcott, Eugene

**[The] Meek**
*See*   Frederick II

**[The] Meek**
*See*   Louis I

**Meek, Dad**
*See*   Meek, Frank J.

**Meek, Doris** 20th c.   [WW]
*Author*
* Gregory, Mason [joint
   pseudonym with Adrienne Jones]
* Mason, Gregory [joint
   pseudonym with Adrienne Jones]

**Meek, Frank J.** ?-1922   [BE]
*American baseball player*
* Meek, Dad

**Meek, Freddie**
*See*   Meek, Fredericka

**Meek, Fredericka** 1971-   [IBW]
*American child prodigy*
* Meek, Freddie

**Meek, Jacklyn O'Hanlon** 1933-
[CA, WYA]
*American author*
* Matthews, Jacklyn Meek
* O'Hanlon, Jacklyn

**Meek, Lois Hayden**
*See*   Stolz, Lois Meek

**Meek, [Major] S. P.**
*See*   Meek, Sterner St. Paul

**Meek, [Captain] S. P.**
*See*   Meek, Sterner St. Paul

**Meek, Sterner St. Paul** 1894-
[NAA, SF]
*American author*
* Meek, [Captain] S. P.
* Meek, [Major] S. P.
* St. Paul, Sterner

**Meeker, Mildred**
*See*   Bruno, Guido

**Meeker, Ralph**
*See*   Rathgeber, Ralph

**Meeker, W. Johns** 20th c. [WGT]
*Author*
* Johns, Willy

**Meeks, Linda A.**
See Brower, Linda A.

**Meeropol, Abel** 20th c. [ASC]
*American composer and educator*
* Allan, Lewis

**Meeropol, Michael**
See Rosenberg, Michael

**Meeropol, Robert**
See Rosenberg, Robert

**Meers, Babe**
See Meers, Russ[ell Harlan]

**Meers, Russ[ell Harlan]** 1918- [BE]
*American baseball player*
* Meers, Babe

**Mees, Steve**
See Flexner, Stuart Berg

**Meeus, Marcel** 1934- [IAW]
*Belgian writer*
* Cremer, Samuel

**Megard, Andree**
See Chamonal, Marie

**Megerdichian, Vahan Leon** 1923-
[EJ]
*American jazz musician*
* Merian, Leon

**Megerle, Hans Ulrich** 1644-1709
[WBD]
*Austrian clergyman and satirist*
* Abraham a Sancta [or Santa]
  Clara

**Megged [or Meged], Aharon [or Aron]**
1920- [CA]
*Israeli journalist*
* A. M.

**Meghor, Camillo**
See Van Peteghem, Camille

**Mego, Al**
See Roberts, Arthur O.

**Megroz, Phyllis** 20th c. [WWL]
*British author*
* Meadowes, Pauline

**Megson, Neil Andrew** 1950- [CAR]
*British artist*
* P-Orridge, Genesis

**Mehan, Joseph Albert** 1929- [CA]
*American author*
* Martin, Albert

**Mehboob**
See Mehboobkhan, Ramjankhan

**Mehboobkhan, Ramjankhan** 1907-
[FC]
*Indian director*
* Mehboob

**Mehemet [or Mohammed] Ali**
1769?-1848? [DNNS, HN, RH]
*Viceroy of Egypt*
* [The] Napoleon of the East
* [The] Peter the Great of Egypt

**Mehemet Ali Pasha**
See Detroit, Karl

**Meher, [Baba]**
See Irani, Merwan S.

**Mehle, Aileen** 20th c. [B10]
*American columnist*
* Knickerbocker, Suzy
* Suzy

**Mehlhorn, Wild Bill**
See Mehlhorn, William

**Mehlhorn, William** 1894?-
[EG, GF]
*American golfer*
* Mehlhorn, Wild Bill

**Mehmed Namik** 1840-1888 [WBD]
*Turkish poet, author, patriot*
* Kemal Bey

**Mehmet Suleiman** ?-1572? [WBD]
*Turkish poet*
* Fuzuli

**Mehta, Rustam Jehangir** 1912-
[AW, CA]
*Indian author*
* Hartman, Roger
* Martin, R. Johnson
* Plutonius

**Mei Sheng** 2nd c. BC [WBD]
*Chinese poet*
* [The] Father of Modern Chinese
  Poetry

**Meibes, Joseph** 1927- [BEW, FC]
*German-born actor*
* Ericson, John

**Meidinger-Geise, Inge**
See Meidinger-Geise, Ingeborg
Lucie

**Meidinger-Geise, Ingeborg Lucie**
1923- [IAW]
*German author*
* Meidinger-Geise, Inge

**Meier, Arthur Ernst** 1879- ? [BE]
*American baseball player*
* Meier, Dutch

**Meier, Dutch**
See Meier, Arthur Ernst

**Meighan, Thaddeus W.** [PA]
*Author*
* Asmodeus

**Meigs, Cornelia Lynde** 1884-1973
[CA, SAT]
*American author*
* Aldon, Adair

**Meikle, Arthur Francis** 1871-1945
[BE]
*American baseball player*
* Nichols, Arthur Francis

**Meikle, Buster**
See Meikle, David

**Meikle, Clive**
See Brooks, Jeremy

**Meikle, David** 20th c. [RO2]
*British musician*
* Meikle, Buster

**Meiklejohn, J. M. D.**
See Meiklejohn, John Miller Dow

**Meiklejohn, John Miller Dow**
1836-1902 [LC]
*Scottish educator and author*
* Meiklejohn, J. M. D.

**Mein Boy Levinsky**
See Levinsky, Alexander H.

**Meine, Heinie**
See Meine, Henry William

**Meine, Henry William** 1896-1968
[AS, BE]
*American baseball player*
* [The] Count of Luxemburg
* Meine, Heinie

**Meineke, Don** 1930- [BB]
*American basketball player*
* Meineke, Monk

**Meineke, Monk**
See Meineke, Don

**Meir, Golda**
See Meyerson, Golda [Mabovitz]

**Meiring, Desmond**
See Rice, Desmond Charles

**Meissner, Hans-Otto** 1909- [CA]
*German author*
* Roos, Hans

**[Der] Meister**
See Goethe, Johann Wolfgang von

**[Der] Meister**
See Wieland, Christoph Martin

**Meister, Dutch**
See Meister, Karl Daniel

**Meister Karl**
See Leland, Charles Godfrey

**Meister, Karl Daniel** 1891-1967
[BE]
*American baseball player*
* Meister, Dutch

**Meister Leu**
See Jud, Leo

**Meistermann, Georg** 1911- [ART]
*German painter and stained-glass
window designer*
* G. M.

**Meistier, Gilbert** 1900- [NOJ]
*American jazz musician*
* Blind Gilbert

**Meistrell, Harland W.** 1900-1962
[BBH]
*American lacrosse coach*
* Meistrell, Tots

**Meistrell, Tots**
See Meistrell, Harland W.

**Meixel, Merten Merrill** 1887- [BE]
*American baseball player*
* Meixel, Moxie

**Meixel, Moxie**
See Meixel, Merten Merrill

**Mejias y Jimenez, Antonio**
1922-1975 [GS, OCS]
*Venezuelan-born bullfighter*
* Bienvenida [Welcome]

**Mejias y Jimenez, Manuel**
1912-1938 [GS]
*Spanish bullfighter*
* Bienvenida [Welcome]

**Mejias y Rapela, Manuel**
1884-1964 [GS]
*Spanish bullfighter*
* Bienvenida [Welcome]

**Mejorcito [Best Little One]**
See Ortega, Santiago

**Mekum, Friedrich** 1491-1546
[WBD]
*German theologian*
* Myconius [or Mykonius],
  Friedrich

**Melamed, Samuel Max** 1885-
[NAA]
*Russian-born editor and author*
* Krieger, Maxime
* Krieger, William

**[The] Melancholy**
See Cowley, Abraham

**[The] Melancholy Jacques**
See Rousseau, Jean-Jacques

**Melanchthon, Philip**
See Schwarzert, Philipp

**Melanie**
See Safka, Melanie

**Melanie, [Sister]**
See Willingham, Saundra

**Melaro, Constance L[oraine]** 1929-
[CA]
*American educator and author*
* Bruce, Monica

**Melaro, H. J. M.** 1928- [ASC]
*American composer and producer*
* Melaro, Speed

**Melaro, Speed**
See Melaro, H. J. M.

**Melati Van Java**
See Sloot, Marie

**Melba, Nellie**
See Mitchell, Helen Porter

**Melbourne, Ivor**
See Ransome, L. E.

**Melcher, Bertha Corbett** 1872- ?
[NAA]
*American writer and poet*
* Mother of the Sun-Bonnet Babies

**Melcher, Gilbert W[ayne]** 1910-
[NAA]
*American writer*
* Aachen, C. V.
* Burt, Gill
* G. W. M.
* McCall, Creighton

**Melchiorre, Eugene** 1927- [BB]
*American basketball player*
* Melchiorre, Squeaky

**Melchiorre, Squeaky**
See Melchiorre, Eugene

**Meldrum, Helen Myers**
See Scott, Helen Myers

**Meldrum, James**
See Broxholme, John Franklin

**Mele, Albert Ernest** 1915- [BE]
*American baseball player*
* Mele, Dutch

**Mele, Dutch**
See Mele, Albert Ernest

**Mele, Sabath Anthony** 1922-
[BE, PB, SMG]
*American baseball manager*
* Mele, Sam

**Mele, Sam**
See Mele, Sabath Anthony

**Melekh, Igor Yakovlevich** 20th c.
[EE]
*Russian intelligence agent*
* Stephens, Peter

**Melendez Melendez, Gabriel** 1930-
[GS]
*Mexican bullfighter*
* Coca Cola

**Melendez Valdes, Juan** 1754-1817
[DNNF, DNNS, FFF]
*Spanish poet*
* Restaurador del Parnaso
* [The] Restorer of Parnassus

**Melesh, Alex**
See Melesher, Alexander

**Melesher, Alexander** 1890-1949
[SC]
*Russian-born actor*
* Melesh, Alex

**Melesigenes**
See Homer

**Melesville**
See Duveyrier, Anne Honore
Joseph

**Melford**
See Reeve, John

**Melhorn, Nathan R.** 1871- ?
[NAA]
*American clergyman, editor, author*
* Etan, Raymond

**Meli, Giovanni** 1740-1815
[DNNS, FFF, SN]
*Sicilian poet*
* [The] Anacreon of Sicily
* [The] Sicilian Anacreon
* [The] Sicilian Theocritus

**Melillo, Oscar Donald** 1899-1963
[AS, BE]
*American baseball player*
* Melillo, Ski
* Melillo, Spinach

**Melillo, Ski**
See Melillo, Oscar Donald

**Melillo, Spinach**
See Melillo, Oscar Donald

**Melim, Mary M.** 19th c. [PA]
*Author*
* McComb, Florence

**Melin, A. K.** 20th c.
*American frisbee manufacturer*
* Melin, Spud

**Melin, Spud**
See Melin, A. K.

**Melis, Jose**
See Melis Guiu, Jose

**Melis Guiu, Jose** 1920- [ASC]
*Cuban-born American musician*
* Melis, Jose

**Melissa**
See Brereton, Jane Hughes

**Mell**
See Lazarus, Mel

**Mell, Mr.** [code name used during
World War II]
See Marshall, George Catlett

**Mellalieu, James S.**
See Margerison, John S.

**Melland, Frank Hulme** [WWL]
*British author*
* Africanus

**Melland, Sylvia** 20th c. [ART]
*British painter and etcher*
* S. M.

**Melle**
See Oldeboerrigter, Melle
Johannes

**Mellen, Grenville** 1799-1841 [PA]
*Author*
* Reverie, Reginauld

**Mellen, Ida M[ay]** 1877- ? [CA]
*American author*
* De Mar, Esmeralda
* Otis, George

**Mellenbruch, Giles Edward** 1911-
[ASC]
*American musician*
* Giles, Johnny

**Meller, Raquel**
See Marquez Lopez, Francisca

**Mellett, John Calvin** 1888- [IA]
*American author and journalist*
* Brooks, Jonathan

**[The] Mellifluous Doctor**
See Bernard of Clairvaux

**Mellilo, James** 1880?-1946 [AS]
*American bowler*
* Smith, James

**Mellin, Jeanne** 1929- [CA]
*American horsewoman, artist,
illustrator*
* Herrick, Jean Mellin

**Melling, Leonard** 1913- [AW]
*British author*
* Luminus

**Mellinger, Max**
See Mellinger, Maxon

**Mellinger, Maxon** 1906-1968 [SC]
*American actor*
* Mellinger, Max

**Mellody, Honey**
See Mellody, William [Billy]

**Mellody, William [Billy]**
1884-1919 [AS, BX, RBE]
*American boxer*
* Mellody, Honey

**Mellon, Bunny**
See Mellon, Rachel

**Mellon, Rachel** 20th c.
*Wife of American financier Paul
Mellon*
* Mellon, Bunny

**Mellos, Ilias** 1904- [EWL]
*Greek author*
* Venezis, Ilias

**Melmoth, Courtney**
See Pratt, Samuel Jackson

**Melmoth, Sebastian**
See Wilde, Oscar Fingal
O'Flahertie Wills

**Melmoth, William** 1710-1799
[DEL, FFF, PA]
*British author*
* Fitzosborne, [Sir] Thomas

**Meloan, Molly**
See Meloan, Paul

**Meloan, Paul** 1888-1950 [BE]
*American baseball player*
* Meloan, Molly

**Melon, Miss**
See St. Albans, Duchess of

**Meloney, Franken** [joint pseudonym
with William Brown Meloney]
See Franken, Rose

**Meloney, Franken** [joint pseudonym
with Rose Franken]
See Meloney, William Brown

**Meloney, William Brown** 1903-
[AW]
*American author, producer, director*
* Grant, Margaret [joint
pseudonym with Rose Franken]
* Meloney, Franken [joint
pseudonym with Rose Franken]

**Melrose, Julia**
See Lemon, Mrs. Henry W.

**Melton, Barry** 1949- [RO2]
*American musician*
* [The] Fish

**Melton, Clifford George** 1912-
[BE]
*American baseball player*
* Melton, Mountain Music

**Melton, Mountain Music**
See Melton, Clifford George

**Melton, Mrs. William** [FFF]
*Entertainer*
* Mitchell, Dolly

**Melton, Reuben Franklin**
1917-1971 [BE]
*American baseball player*
* Melton, Rube

**Melton, Rube**
See Melton, Reuben Franklin

**Melton, William Edwin** 1945-
[SMG]
*American baseball player*
* Belt'n Melt'n

**Meltzer, Bernard** 1917?-
*American radio broadcaster*
* Uncle Bernie

**Meltzer, Gregor** 1501-1531 [WBD]
*German jurist*
* Haloander, Gregor

**Melvier, Laurent**
See Lucas, Gerald

**Melville, Ada**
See Hazleton, Mrs. J. H.

**Melville, Alan**
See Caverhill, William Melville

**Melville, Andrew**
See Emm, Andrew

**Melville, Anne**
See Potter, Margaret [Newman]

**Melville, Emily**
See Jones, Emily

**Melville, Jean**
See Cummins, Mary Warmington

**Melville, Jean-Pierre**
See Grumbach, Jean-Pierre

**Melville, Jennie**
See Butler, Gwendoline [Williams]

**Melville, Kathleen** 1904- [F2]
*Actress*
* O'Regan, Katherine

**Melville, Lewis** [joint pseudonym
with Reginald Hargreaves]
See Benjamin, Lewis Saul

**Melville, Lewis** [joint pseudonym
with Lewis Saul Benjamin]
See Hargreaves, Reginald
[Charles]

**Melville, Maud**
See Anderson, Mrs. Oscar

**Melville, Pearl**
See Baldwin, Mrs. Walter S.

**Melville, Virginia**
See Murray, Mrs. J. J.

**Melville, Winifred**
See Wright, Winifred

**Melvin, G. S.** 1886-1946 [BMH]
*Scottish-born comedian*
* Donovan, Hugh

**Melwood, Mary**
See Lewis, E. M.

**Member for Paris**
See Murray, Eustace Clare
Grenville

**Member for Treorky**
See Bowen-Rowlands, Ernest
Bowen Brown

**[A] Member of CSMV**
See Lawson, Ruth Penelope

**Member of the Burton Hunt**
See Braddon, [Sir] Henry Yule

**Member of the Chiltern Hundreds**
See Lucy, [Sir] Henry William

**Meminger, Dean** 1948- [BB]
*American basketball player*
* [The] Dream

**Meminger, Edward Lynn**
1905-1975 [SC]
*American actor and producer*
* Lynn, Eddie

**Memnon**
See Ramses V [or Rameses]

**Memon, Fahmida** 1948- [IAW]
*Pakistani writer and poet*
* Yakub, Tasnim

**Memon, Munir Ahmed** 1943-
[IAW]
*Pakistani author*
* Manik

**[The] Memorable**
See Eric II

**Memory**
See Mayer, Bernadette

**[The] Memory Man**
See Bottle, J. M.

**Memphis Bill Mallory**
See Mallory, William N.

**Memphis Bill Terry**
See Terry, William Harold

**Memphis Blues Boy**
See Nix, Willie

**[The] Memphis Heat**
See Parrish, Larry

**Memphis Jim**
See Dorsey, Thomas A[ndrew]

**Memphis Ma Rainey**
See Glover, Lilian

**Memphis Minnie**
See Douglas, Lizzie

**Memphis Mose**
See Dorsey, Thomas A[ndrew]

**Memphis Pal Moore**
See Moore, Thomas Wilson

**Memphis Slim**
See Chatman, John Len

**Memphis Slim**
See Davenport, Charles [Edward]

**Memphis Willie B**
See Borum, William [Willie]

**Mena, Juan de** 1411-1456
[DEP, DNNS, SN]
*Spanish poet*
* [The] Spanish Ennius

**Mena, Maria Cristina**
See Chambers, Maria Cristina

**[The] Menace**
See Conner, Dennis

**[The] Menace**
See Tueart, Dennis

**Menander**
See Morgan, Charles [Langbridge]

**Menander** 4th c. BC [DNNS, RH]
*Athenian poet*
* Creator of the New Comedy
* [The] Prince of New Comedy

**Menander** 2nd c. BC [WBD]
*Greek king of India*
* Milinda

**Menantes**
See Hunold, Christian Friedrich

**Menaptus, Wilhelm** [PA]
*Author*
* Insulaneus

**Menasco, John**
See Sellers, Connie Leslie, Jr.

**Menasco, Norman**
See Guin, Wyman [Woods]

**Menchan, W. McKinley** 1898-
[IAW]
*American educator and writer*
* Judge
* Mack

**Mencher, Murray** 1898-
[ASC, PMJ]
*American composer*
* Murry, Ted

**Mencke [or Mencken], Johann
Burkhard** 1674-1732 [WBD]
*German author and historian*
* Von der Linde, Philander

**Mencken, H. L.**
See Mencken, Henry Louis

**Mencken, Henry Louis** 1880-1956
[CAA, LC]
*American author and editor*
* Hatteras, Owen [joint pseudonym
with George Jean Nathan]
* Mencken, H. L.
* [The] Sage of Baltimore

**Mendel**
See Smith, James Samuel

**Mendel, David** 1789-1850 [WBD]
*German historian and theologian*
* Neander, Johann August
Wilhelm

**Mendel, Jo** [house pseudonym,
Albert Whitman & Co.]
See Bond, Gladys Baker

**Mendel, Jo** [house pseudonym,
Albert Whitman & Co.]
See Gilbertson, Mildred [Geiger]

**Mendele Mocher Sforim [Mendele
the Bookseller]**
See Abromowitz, Sholem Yakob

**Mendeloff, Gershon** 1894-1970
[BX, EJS, RBE]
*British boxer*
* [The] Aldgate Sphinx
* Lewis, Kid
* Lewis, Ted

**Mendelsohn, Felix, Jr.** 1906- [CA]
*American author*
* Mayfair, Franklin

**Mendelsohn, Oscar [Adolf]** 1896-
[CA]
*Australian author and composer*
* Milsen, Oscar

**Mendelson, Harold** 1920-1970
[BEW]
*American actor*
* March, Hal

**Mendelssohn, [Jakob Ludwig] Felix**
1809-1847 [SN, WBD]
*German composer*
* Mendelssohn-Bartholdy, Felix
* [The] Mozart of the Nineteenth
Century

**Mendelssohn, Moses** 1729-1785
[HN, SN, WBD]
*German philosopher*
* [The] German Socrates
* [The] Jewish Socrates
* [The] Plato of Germany
* [The] Socrates of the Jews

**Mendelssohn-Bartholdy, Felix**
See Mendelssohn, [Jakob Ludwig]
Felix

**Mendenhall, John Rufus** 1948-
[SMG]
*American football player*
* Mendenhall, Mendy

**Mendenhall, Mendy**
See Mendenhall, John Rufus

**Mendes, Black Cat**
See Mendes, Joe

**Mendes, Catulle** 1841-1909 [CD]
*French poet, author, playwright*
* Valerius, C.

**Mendes, Joe** [GW]
*American rodeo performer*
* Mendes, Black Cat

**Mendez, Cachin**
See Mendez, Oscar

**Mendez, Joe**
See Mendez, Jose

**Mendez, Jose** 20th c. [OBW]
*American baseball player*
* Mendez, Joe

**Mendez, Oscar** 1945- [RBE]
*Argentinian boxer*
* Mendez, Cachin

**Mendez Pinto, Ferdinand**
1509?-1583 [DNNF, FFF, SN]
*Portuguese traveller*
* [The] Prince of Liars

**Mendicant, Arch?**
See Aldiss, Brian W[ilson]

**Mendis, Gehan Dixon** 1955- [DC]
*Sri Lankan cricketer*
* Mendis, Jack
* Mendis, Mendo
* Mendis, Sergio

**Mendis, Jack**
See Mendis, Gehan Dixon

**Mendis, Judith** [PA]
*Author*
* Chailness

**Mendis, Mendo**
See Mendis, Gehan Dixon

**Mendis, Sergio**
See Mendis, Gehan Dixon

**Mendl, Gladys**
See Schuetze, Gladys Henrietta
[Raphael]

**Mendonca, Susan** 1950- [CA]
*British-born author*
* Sinclair, Rose

**Mendoza, Mario** 1950- [BE]
*Mexican-born baseball player*
* Aizpuru, Mario

**Mendoza Romero, Maria Luisa**
1934- [IAW]
*Mexican author*
* Catay
* China

**Mendrock, William**
See Nicote, Piere

**Menedemos** 4th c. BC [RH, SN]
*Greek philosopher*
* [The] Eretrian Bull

**Menefee, Jocko**
See Menefee, John

**Menefee, John** 1868-1953 [BE]
*American baseball player*
* Menefee, Jocko

**Meneghel, Antonietta** 1893- [BBD]
*Italian opera singer*
* Monte, Toti Dal

**Menelik II**
See Mariem, Sahala

**Menen, Aubrey**
See Menon, Salvator Aubrey
Clarence

**Meneses, Enrique** 1929- [CA]
*Spanish journalist*
* Carvajal, Ricardo
* Crain, Jeff

**Mengele, [Dr.] Josef** 20th c.
*German physician during Nazi
regime*
* [The] Angel of Death

**[Il] Menghino del Violoncello**
See Gabrielli, Domenico

**Mengs, Anton Rafael** 1728-1779
[SN]
*German painter*
* [The] Prince of Bohemian Artists

**Menken, Adah Isaacs** 1835?-1868
[FFF]
*American actress*
* [The] Queen of the Plaza

**Mennin, Peter**
See Mennini, Peter

**Mennini, Peter** 1923- [BBD, IPA]
*American composer*
* Mennin, Peter

**Menon, Salvator Aubrey Clarence**
1912- [EWL]
*British author*
* Menen, Aubrey

**Menor, Gypsy Marpessa Dawn**
1935- [IBW]
*American singer and actress*
* Dawn, Marpessa

**Menosky, Leaping Mike**
See Menosky, Michael William

**Menosky, Michael William** 1894-
[BE]
*American baseball player*
* Menosky, Leaping Mike

**Menot, Michael** 15th c. [SN]
*French clergyman*
* [The] Golden Tongued

**Menter, Sophie**
See Popper, Frau

**Mentor**
See Jones, Frank H.

**Mentor**
See Quincy, Josiah

**Mentzer**
See Fischart, Johann

**Menzel, Johanna**
See Meskill, Johanna Menzel

**Menzel, Roderich** 1907-
[CA, IAW]
*Czech-born author*
* Morawa, Michael
* Parma, Clemens

**Meoli, Randolph Bart, Jr.** 1951-
[SMG]
*American baseball player*
* Meoli, Rudy

**Meoli, Rudy**
See Meoli, Randolph Bart, Jr.

**Merak, A. J.**
See Glasby, John [Stephen]

**Merande, Doro**
See Matthews, Dora

**Merante, Mrs. Louis** [FFF]
*Entertainer*
* Richard, Zina

**Merauges**
See Chanorrier, Antoine

**Mercado, Jose Ramon** 1863-1911
[CW]
*Puerto Rican poet and journalist*
* Momo

**Mercantelli, Eugene Rudolph**
1906- [BE]
*American baseball player*
* Rye, Eugene Rudolph
* Rye, Half-Pint

**Mercator**
See Brewer, William A.

**Mercator**
See Lloyd, Samuel Jones

**Mercator, John**
See Kaufmann, Walter

**Mercator, Nicolaus**
See Kaufmann, Nicolaus

**Merce, Antonia** 1891?-1936
[BEW]
*Argentinian-born dancer*
* Argentina

**Mercein, Eleanor**
See Kelly, Eleanor Mercein

**Mercer, Cecil William** 1885-1960
[CC, EMD, LC]
*British author*
* Yates, Dornford

**Mercer, Frances**
See Hills, Frances Elizabeth

**Mercer, George Barclay**
1874-1903 [AS, BE]
*American baseball player*
* Mercer, Win

**Mercer, Jean** 1941- [CA]
*American author*
* Lester, Gene

**Mercer, Jessie** 20th c. [CA]
*American author*
* Shannon, Terry

**Mercer, Joan Bodger** 1923- [CA]
*American-born author*
* Bodger, Joan

**Mercer, John Louis** 1869-1941
[BE]
*American baseball player*
* Johnson, John Louis
* Johnson, Youngy

**Mercer, Mike**
*American football player*
* Mercer, Moco

**Mercer, Moco**
See Mercer, Mike

**Mercer, Win**
See Mercer, George Barclay

**Merchant, Andy**
See Merchant, James Anderson

**Merchant, James Anderson** 1950-
[SMG]
*American baseball player*
* Merchant, Andy

**Merchant, Matthew**
See Wood, W. S.

**[The] Merchant of Menace**
See Mayer, Arthur Loeb

**Merchant, Paul**
See Ellison, Harlan [Jay]

**Merchant, Vivien**
See Thomson, Ada

**Merchantius**
See Le Marchant, Jacques

**Mercier, Bartholomew** 1734-1799
[SN]
*French bibliographer*
* [The] Ulysses of Bibliographers

**Mercurial Miles Davis**
See Davis, Miles Dewey, Jr.

**Mercurio, Skang**
See Mercurio, Walter

**Mercurio, Walter** 1896-1972
[BBH]
*Italian-born American bowler*
* Mercurio, Skang

**Mercurius** ?- 535 [DNNS]
*Pope*
* John II

**Mercurius Rusticus**
See Dibdin, Thomas Frognall

**Mercury**
See Allen, Cecil J[ohn]

**Mercury**
See Baird, George D.

**Mercury**
See Bruce, L. C.

**Mercury, Fred**
See Bulsara, Frederick

**Mercutio**
See Winter, William

**[The] Mercutio of Actors**
See Lewis, William Thomas

**[The] Mere Dandini**
See George IV

**Mere des Pauvres [Mother of the Poor]**
See Epremesnil, Francoise Augustine d'

**[La] Mere des Peuples**
See Margaret [or Marguerite] of France

**Meredith, Anne**
See Malleson, Lucy Beatrice

**Meredith, Arnold**
See Hopkins, Kenneth

**Meredith, Billy** 20th c. [NN]
*British soccer player*
* [The] Welsh Wizard

**Meredith, Buford** 20th c. [OBW]
*American baseball player*
* Meredith, Geetchie

**Meredith, Burgess**
See Burgess, George

**Meredith, Dandy Don**
See Meredith, Joe Don

**Meredith, David William**
See Miers, Earl Schenck

**Meredith, Geetchie**
See Meredith, Buford

**Meredith, Hal**
See Blyth, Harry

**Meredith, James E.** 1892-1957
[AS, TF]
*American track and field athlete*
* Meredith, Ted

**Meredith, Jeff**
See Loney, Glenn [Meredith]

**Meredith, Joe Don** 1938- [FB]
*American football player and sportscaster*
* Meredith, Dandy Don

**Meredith, Lee**
See Sauls, Judi Lee

**Meredith, Louisa** 1812- ? [PA]
*Author*
* Twomby, Louisa

**Meredith, Lucille**
See Couch, Lizzie

**Meredith, Mark** 20th c. [WWL]
*British writer*
* M. M.

**Meredith, Mary G.**
See Webb, Mary

**Meredith, Nicolete**
See Stack, Nicolete Meredith

**Meredith, Owen**
See Bulwer-Lytton, Edward Robert

**Meredith, Peter**
See Worthington-Stuart, Brian Arthur

**Meredith, Robert C[hidester]** 1921-
[CA]
*American educator and author*
* Lucero, Roberto

**Meredith, Scott**
See Feldman, Scott

**Meredith, Ted**
See Meredith, James E.

**Meredyth, Bess**
See MacGlashan, Helen

**Meredyth-Starmer, Marjorie**
1914- [IAW]
*British author*
* Lyon, Marjorie

**Merena, John Joseph** 1909- [BE]
*American baseball player*
* Merena, Spike

**Merena, Spike**
See Merena, John Joseph

**Meretricious**
See Watkinson, Frank

**Merewether, Art[hur Francis]**
1902- [BE]
*American baseball player*
* Merewether, Merry

**Merewether, Merry**
See Merewether, Art[hur Francis]

**Merezhkovskaya, Zinaida
Nikolaevna** 1869-1945 [WBD]
*Russian poet, author, critic*
* Hippius

**Merian, Leon**
See Megerdichian, Vahan Leon

**Merillat, Louis A., Jr.** ?-1948 [FB]
*American football player*
* [The] Forward Pass King

**Merin, Peter**
See Bihalji-Merin, Oto

**Merisi [or Merisio], Michelangelo**
1565?-1609 [WBD]
*Italian painter*
* Caravaggio, Michelangelo da

**Meriton, Peter**
See Hunter, [Alfred] John

**Meritt, Lucy Shoe** 1906- [CA]
*American archaeologist and author*
* Shoe, Lucy T.

**Meriwether, Del**
See Meriwether, Wilhelm Delano

**Meriwether, Wilhelm Delano**
1943- [IBW]
*American physician*
* Meriwether, Del

**Merkle, Bonehead**
See Merkle, Fred[erick Charles]

**Merkle, Fred[erick Charles]**
1888-1956 [SR]
*American baseball player*
* Merkle, Bonehead
* Merkle, George

**Merkle, George**
See Merkle, Fred[erick Charles]

**Merland, Oliver** 20th c. [MBF]
*British author*
* Collins, Colin
* Grant, Douglas
* Pound, Singleton

**Merlin**
See Tennyson, Alfred [First Baron Tennyson]

**Merlin**
See Wilder, Alexander

**Merlin, Antoine Christophe**
1762-1833 [WBD]
*French politician*
* Merlin de Thionville

**Merlin, David**
See Moreau, David Merlin

**Merlin de Douai**
See Merlin, Philippe Antoine

**Merlin de Thionville**
See Merlin, Antoine Christophe

**Merlin, Jean Raymond** 1510-1578
[PA]
*Author*
* Mouray

**Merlin, Joanna**
See Ratner, Joann

**[The] Merlin of England**
See Lilly, William

**[The] Merlin of Scotland**
See Learmont, Thomas

**Merlin, Philippe Antoine**
1754-1838 [WBD]
*French jurist and politician*
* Merlin de Douai

**Merlini, [The] Great**
See Rawson, Clayton

**Merlino, Merlin Mesmer**
See Carpenter, Donald G.

**Merlinus Anglicus**
See Lilly, William

**Merlotti, Claudio** 1533-1604
[WBD]
*Italian musician and composer*
* Da Correggio, Claudio
* Merulo, Claudio

**Merlyn, Arthur**
See Blish, James [Benjamin]

**[The] Mermaid**
See Mary, Queen of Scots

**Merman, Ethel**
See Zimmerman, Ethel Agnes

**Mero, Caldius Biberius**
See Domitius Ahenobarbus, Lucius

**Meronek, Smiley**
See Meronek, William

**Meronek, William** 1917- [CEI]
*Canadian-born hockey player*
* Meronek, Smiley

**Merrall, Mary**
See Lloyd, Mary

**Merrall, Queenie**
See Lloyd, Mary

**Merrick, David**
See Margulois, David

**Merrick, Hugh**
See Meyer, Harold Albert

**Merrick, Jim**
See Fearn, C. Eaton

**Merrick, John** ?-1890
*British victim of neurological disorder*
* [The] Elephant Man

**Merrick, Leonard**
See Miller, Leonard

**Merrick, M. M.**
See Cecily, [Mother]

**Merrick, Mark**
See Rathborne, St. George

**Merrick, Williston**
See Ford, Williston Merrick

**Merridew, Arthur**
See Gaskoin, Charles Jacinth Bellairs

**Merril, Judith**
See Grossman, Josephine Judith

**Merrill, Al**
See Merrill, C. Allison

**Merrill, Antoinette June** 1912-
[CA]
*American author*
* Merrill, Toni

**Merrill, Bob**
See Lavan, Henry

**Merrill, C. Allison** 1924- [BBH]
*American skiing coach*
* Merrill, Al

**Merrill, Dina**
See Hutton, Nedinia

**Merrill, H. R.** [PA]
*Author*
* Old Scout

**Merrill, Helen**
See Milcetic, Helen

**Merrill, Jan** 1956-
*American track and field athlete*
* [The] Mummy

**Merrill, Linda**
See Rosenthal, Linda

**Merrill, Linda** 1951?-
*American ballerina*
* Ashley, Merrill

**Merrill, P. J.**
See Roth, Holly

**Merrill, Robert**
See Miller, Morris

**Merrill, Royal W.** [FFF]
*American writer*
* Lounger in the Lobby

**Merrill, Toni**
See Merrill, Antoinette June

**Merriman, Alex**
See Silverberg, Robert

**Merriman, Beth**
See Taylor, Demetria

**Merriman, Citation**
See Merriman, Lloyd Archer

**Merriman, Henry Seton**
See Scott, Hugh Stowell

**Merriman, Lloyd Archer** 1924-
[BE]
*American baseball player*
* Merriman, Citation

**Merriman, Maurice**
See Hook, Samuel Clarke

**Merriman, Pat**
See Atkey, Philip

**Merrit, Katarin Markov**
See Ackerman, Forrest J[ames]

**Merritt, Aime**
See Ackerman, Forrest J[ames]

**Merritt, E. B.**
See Waddington, Miriam

**Merritt, [John] Howard** 1894-1955
[BE]
*American baseball player*
* Merritt, Lefty

**Merritt, Lefty**
See Merritt, [John] Howard

**Merritt, Si**
See Hoyer, Mildred N.

**Merriweather, Bob**
See Merriweather, Rozier

**Merriweather, Maceo**
See Merriweather, Major

**Merriweather, Magnus**
See Talbot, Charles R.

**Merriweather, Major** 1905-1953
[BWW, EJ]
*American singer*
* Big Maceo
* Merriweather, Maceo

**Merriweather, Rozier** 20th c.
[BWW]
*American musician*
* Little Maceo
* Merriweather, Bob

**Merry Andrew**
See Borde, Andrew

**Merry Andrew**
See Freeman, John Henry Gordon

**Merry, Doctor**
See Wyndham, J.

**Merry Droll**
See Killigrew, Thomas

**Merry, Felix**
See Duyckinck, Evert Augustus

**[The] Merry Magician**
See Christman, Paul C.

**Merry, Malcolm James** 20th c.
[MBF]
*British author*
* Errym, Malcolm J.
* Rymer, James Malcolm

**[The] Merry Monarch**
See Bodie, Sam

**[The] Merry Monarch**
See Charles II

**[The] Merry Mortician**
See Hoyt, Waite Charles

**Merry, Robert**
See Stearns, J. N.

**Merry, Robert** 1755-1798
[DEP, FFF, RH]
*British poet and playwright*
* Della Crusca
* O. P. Q.

**Merry, Tom**
See Mecham, William

**Merryfellow, Malthus**
See Clark, Charles

**Merson, Billy**
See Thompson, William Henry

**Merson, H. A.**
See Watson, Harold

**Mertes, Bernard James** 1923-
[SMG]
*American football player and coach*
* Mertes, Bus

**Mertes, Bus**
See Mertes, Bernard James

**Mertes, Samuel Blair** 1872-1945
[BE]
*American baseball player*
* Mertes, Sandow

**Mertes, Sandow**
See Mertes, Samuel Blair

**Merton, Collette**
See Mazzoletti, Collette Helene

**Merton, Giles**
See Curran, Mona [Elisa]

**Merton, John**
See La Varre, John Merton

**Merton, Thomas [James]**
1915-1968 [B10, CA, LC]
*French-born clergyman, author, poet*
* Louis, [Father] M.

**Merton, Tristram**
See Macaulay, Thomas Babington
[First Baron Macaulay]

**Mertz, Barbara [Gross]** 1927-
[AW, CA, WD]
*American author and historian*
* Michaels, Barbara
* Peters, Elizabeth

**Mertz, George**
See Mushrush, Obadiah

**Merulo, Claudio**
See Merlotti, Claudio

**Merville, Pierre Francois**
1783-1853 [PA]
*Author*
* Camus

**Mervyn, William**
See Pickwoad, William

**Merwin, [W.] Sam[uel], Jr.** 1910-
[ESF, SFP, WGT]
*American author*
* Curson, Stanley
* Lee, Matt

**Merwin, [W.] Sam[uel], Jr.**
(Continued)
* Saturn, Sergeant [house pseudonym]
* Sprague, Carter

**Merwin, W. S.**
See Merwin, William Stanley

**Merwin, William Stanley** 1927-
[WYA]
*American author*
* Merwin, W. S.

**Mesa**
See Selimovic, Mehmed

**Mesa, Johnny**
See Meza, Johnny

**Mesaros, Stjepan** 1903?-
*Croatian-born political activist*
* Nelson, Steve

**[La] Meschinerie**
See Enoch, Pierre

**Meserole, Fannie**
See Lynch, Mrs. Samuel

**Meservey, Robert Preston** 1918-
[BEW, EMT, IPA]
*American actor and singer*
* Preston, Robert

**[El] Mesias [The Messiah]**
See Benete, Antonio

**Mesirow, Milton** 1899-1972
[DAM, PMJ, WWJ]
*American jazz musician*
* Mezzrow, Mezz
* Mezzrow, Milton

**Meske, Eunice Boardman** 1926-
[CA]
*American author and educator*
* Boardman, Eunice

**Meskill, Johanna Menzel** 1930-
[CA]
*German-born historian and author*
* Menzel, Johanna

**Meskin, Morton** 1916- [WECO]
*American cartoonist*
* Morton, Mort, Jr.

**Meslin, Michael Neure** ?-1677
[PA]
*Author*
* Laurent

**Mesmer, Friedrich Anton**
1734-1815 [HN, SN]
*Austrian physician*
* [The] Father of Mesmerism

**Mesritz, Andre** 1909- [FC]
*British actor*
* Morell, Andre

**Messager, Charles** 1882-1971
[CA, CD]
*French poet, author, playwright*
* Vildrac, Charles

**[The] Messalina of Germany**
See Barbara of Cilley

**[The] Messalina of the North**
See Catherine II

**Messell, Hank**
See Everts, Henry

**Messenger, Andrew Warren** 1898-
[BE]
*American baseball player*
* Messenger, Bud

**Messenger, Bob**
See Messina, Roberto

**Messenger, Bobby**
See Messenger, Charles Walter

**Messenger, Bud**
See Messenger, Andrew Warren

**Messenger, Charles Walter**
1884-1951 [BE]
*American baseball player*
* Messenger, Bobby

**Messenger, Lilian T. R.** [FFF]
*American writer*
* Clifton, Zena

**Messenger of Allah**
See Poole, Elijah

**[The] Messenger of Wandsbeck**
See Claudius, Matthias

**Messent, Charles** 1857- ? [WWL]
*British author*
* Baring, Max

**Messer, August** 1867-1937 [WBD]
*German philosopher and author*
* Friedwalt, A.

**Messer, Mona Naomi Anne**
[Hocking] 20th c. [WW]
*Author*
* Hocking, Anne

**Messer, Samuel G.** 1911-
[FC, HT, ITA]
*American actor*
* Middleton, Robert

**Messersmith, Andy**
See Messersmith, John Alexander

**Messersmith, Bluto**
See Messersmith, John Alexander

**Messersmith, Channel**
See Messersmith, John Alexander

**Messersmith, John Alexander**
1945- [BE, PB, SMG]
*American baseball player*
* Messersmith, Andy
* Messersmith, Bluto
* Messersmith, Channel

**[The] Messiah**
See Crowley, Edward Alexander

**Messick, Dale**
See Messick, Dalia

**Messick, Dalia** 1906-
*American cartoonist*
* Messick, Dale

**Messier, Mark** 1961- [SMG]
*Canadian-born hockey player*
* Messier, Mess

**Messier, Mess**
See Messier, Mark

**Messina, Roberto** 20th c. [WF]
*Italian actor*
* Messenger, Bob

**Messina, Santo** 1927- [ITA]
*American entertainment executive*
* Sina, Sandy

**[La] Messine**
See Adam, Juliette

**Messinger, Buddy**
See Messinger, Melvin Joe

**Messinger, Melvin Joe** 1909-1965
[SC]
*American actor*
* Messinger, Buddy

**Messino, Wee Willie**
See Messino, William

**Messino, William** 1917- [BLB]
*American underworld figure*
* Messino, Wee Willie

**Messmann, John** 20th c. [SFL]
*Author*
* Nicole, Claudette

**Mestayer, Mrs. W. A.** [FFF]
*Entertainer*
* Vaughn, Theresa

**Mestayer, William**
See Hoppe, William

**Meta**
See Tomkiewicz, Mina

**Metacomet** ?-1676 [WBD]
*American Indian chieftain*
* Philip

**Metador**
See Alden, William L.

**Metastasio**
See Trapassi, Pietro Antonio
Domenico Bonaventura

**Metcalf, George**
See Johnson, George Metcalf

**Metcalf, Suzanne**
See Baum, L[yman] Frank

**Metcalfe, Francis**
See Egerton, J. K.

**Metcalfe, Thomas** 1780-1855
[FFF]
*American politician*
* Old Stone Hammer

**Metcalfe, [Captain] W. C.**
See Lawrence, Christopher George
Holman

**Metellus, Quintus Caecilius** 2nd c.
BC [WBD]
*Roman general and politician*
* Numidicus

**Metellus, Quintus Caecilius** 2nd c.
BC [WBD]
*Roman general and politician*
* Macedonicus

**Metellus, Quintus Caecilius** 1st c.
BC [SN, WBD]
*Roman general*
* Creticus

**Metellus, Quintus Caecilius** 1st c.
BC [WBD]
*Roman general and politician*
* Pius

**Metesky, George**
See Hoffman, Abbie

**Meteyard, Eliza** 1824?-1879
[DEL, DNNF, FFF]
*British author*
* Silverpen

**Metha, Frank Joseph** 1913- [BE]
*American baseball player*
* Metha, Scat

**Metha, Scat**
See Metha, Frank Joseph

**Metheny, Arthur Beauregard**
1915- [BE]
*American baseball player*
* Metheny, Bud

**Metheny, Bud**
See Metheny, Arthur Beauregard

**Methodicus, Doctor**
See Bassol, John

**Methodius** 826- 885 [DNNS]
*Saint*
* [The] Apostle of the Slavs

**Methold, Kenneth Walter** 1931-
[AW, CA]
*British author*
* Cade, Alexander

**Methuen, [Sir] Algernon Methuen
Marshall**
See Stedman, Algernon Methuen
Marshall

**Methuen, John**
See Bell, John Keble

**Methven, Ralph**
See Thomson, Ralph Methven

**Metidieri, Carlos** 1942- [AES]
*Brazilian soccer player*
* Metidieri, Little Mouse
* Metidieri, Topolino

**Metidieri, Little Mouse**
See Metidieri, Carlos

**Metidieri, Topolino**
See Metidieri, Carlos

**Metius, Adriaan** 1571-1635 [WBD]
*Dutch mathematician*
* Adriaanszoon, Adriaan

**Metkovich, Catfish**
See Metkovich, George Michael

**Metkovich, Catso**
See Metkovich, George Michael

**Metkovich, George Michael** 1921-
[BE, BN]
*American baseball player*
* Metkovich, Catfish
* Metkovich, Catso

**Metlova, Maria** 20th c.
[SFL, WGT]
*Author*
* Hathaway, Louise

**Metro, Charles [Charlie]**
See Moreskonich, Charles

**Metropolitan Opera, Mr.**
See Robinson, Francis [Arthur]

**Metsanurk, Mait**
See Hubel, Eduard

**Metternich, Clemens Wenzel Lothar**
1773-1859 [SN]
*Austrian statesman*
* [The] Autocrat of Austria

**Metz, Alice** [FFF]
*Entertainer*
* Harrison, Alice

**Metz, Lois Lunt** 1906- [CAP]
*American author and educator*
* Lunt, Lois

**Metz, Louis** [FFF]
*Entertainer*
* Harrison, Louis

**Metzetti, Sylvester Ricardo** 1896-
[F1, F2, FC]
*American actor*
* Talmadge, Richard

**Metzger, Butch**
See Metzger, Clarence Edward

**Metzger, Clarence Edward** 1952-
[SMG, WWB]
*American baseball player*
* Metzger, Butch

**Metzger, Ros**
See Metzger, Roswell William

**Metzger, Roswell William** 1906-
[ASC]
*American musician*
* Metzger, Ros

**Meulenbelt-Luber, Henrietta C. A.**
1889- [LAO]
*Dutch author*
* Luber, Jet

**Meunier, Francois**
See Miller, Francis Trevelyn

**Meurisse, Lucien** 1890-1972 [SC]
*Actor*
* Mussiere, Luciene

**Meusel, Emil Frederick** 1893-1963
[AS, DGS, PB]
*American baseball player*
* Meusel, Irish

**Meusel, Irish**
See Meusel, Emil Frederick

**Meusel, Languid Bob**
See Meusel, Robert William [Bob]

**Meusel, Long Bob**
See Meusel, Robert William [Bob]

**Meusel, Robert William [Bob]**
1896- [BE]
*American baseball player*
* Meusel, Languid Bob
* Meusel, Long Bob

**Meux, [Sir] Hedworth**
See Lambton, Hedworth

**Mew, Thomas Joseph, III [Tommy]**
1942- [CAR]
*American artist*
* [The] Mad Diarist

**Mewburn, Martin**
See Hitchin, Martin Mewburn

**[The] Mexican Nightingale**
See Peralta, Angela

**[The] Mexican Spitfire**
See Velez De Villalobos,
Guadelupe

**[The] Mexican Washington**
See Juarez, Benito Pablo

**[The] Mexican Wildcat**
See Ybarra, Jose

**Meyer, Adolph**
See Goldschmidt, M. A.

**Meyer, Benny**
See Meyer, Bernhard

**Meyer, Bernhard** 1888-1974 [BE]
*American baseball player*
* Meyer, Benny
* Meyer, Earache

**Meyer, Berta** 1878-1952 [BBD]
*German opera singer*
* Morena, Berta

**Meyer, Bonnie**
*See* Thorne, Mrs. J. H.

**Meyer, Charles R[obert]** 1926-
[CA]
*American writer, photographer,*
*public relations consultant*
* Jay, Donald

**Meyer, Conrad Ferdinand**
1825-1898 [WBD]
*Swiss poet and author*
* Meyer-Ziegler, Conrad Ferdinand

**Meyer, David** 1930-1980
[HT, SW]
*American actor*
* Janssen, David

**Meyer, Dorothy Quick** 1900-
[WGT]
*American author*
* Quick, Dorothy

**Meyer, Dutch**
*See* Meyer, Lambert Daniel

**Meyer, Dutch**
*See* Meyer, Leo Robert

**Meyer, Earache**
*See* Meyer, Bernhard

**Meyer, Edward** 20th c.
*American army officer*
* Meyer, Shy

**Meyer, Gustav** 1868-1932
[HFF, SFP]
*Austrian-born author*
* Meyrink, Gustave

**Meyer, H. K. Houston**
*See* Meyer, Heinrich

**Meyer, Hans**
*See* Meyer, John F.

**Meyer, Harold Albert** 1898-
[CA, WD]
*British author, photographer,*
*translator*
* Merrick, Hugh

**Meyer, Heinrich** 1904- [CA]
*German-born author*
* Barlow, Robert O.
* Meyer, H. K. Houston

**Meyer, Hy**
*See* Meyer, Hyman

**Meyer, Hyman** 1875-1945 [SC]
*American actor*
* Meyer, Hy

**Meyer, Jean Shepherd** 1929- [SAT]
*American author and illustrator*
* Berwick, Jean

**Meyer, Jerome Sydney** 1895-1975
[CA, SAT]
*American editor and writer*
* Jennings, S. M.

**Meyer, Johann Georg** 1813-1886
[WBD]
*German painter*
* Meyer von Bremen

**Meyer, John F.** 20th c. [BBH]
*American sailboat racer*
* Meyer, Hans

**Meyer, John M.** 1897- [NAA]
*German-born naturalist, author,*
*editor*
* Morley, Mathew

**Meyer, June**
*See* Jordan, June

**Meyer, Lambert Daniel** 1915- [BE]
*American baseball player*
* Meyer, Dutch

**Meyer, Leo Robert** 1898-
[B10, FB]
*American football coach*
* Meyer, Dutch
* Old Iron Pants
* [The] Saturday Fox

**Meyer, Mathilde** 1851-1933
[BEW]
*German-born theatrical performer*
* Cottrelly, Mathilde

**Meyer, Russell Charles** 1923- [BE]
*American baseball player*
* [The] Mad Monk

**Meyer, Shy**
*See* Meyer, Edward

**Meyer, Sophie Frederika Elizabeth**
[FFF]
*Author*
* May, Sophie

**Meyer the Bug**
*See* Suchowljansky, Maier

**Meyer von Bremen**
*See* Meyer, Johann Georg

**Meyer-Ziegler, Conrad Ferdinand**
*See* Meyer, Conrad Ferdinand

**Meyerbeer, Giacomo**
*See* Beer, Jakob Liebmann

**Meyerle, Levi Samuel** 1849-1921
[BE]
*American baseball player*
* Meyerle, Long Levi

**Meyerle, Long Levi**
*See* Meyerle, Levi Samuel

**Meyers, Chief**
*See* Meyers, John Tortes

**Meyers, John Tortes** 1880-1971
[BE, PB]
*American baseball player*
* Meyers, Chief

**Meyers, Louie**
*See* Myers, Louis

**Meyers, Roy [Lethbridge]**
1910-1974 [CAP]
*British physician and author*
* Lethbridge, Rex

**Meyers, Sidney** 1906-1969 [B10]
*American director*
* Stebbins, Robert

**Meyerson, Golda [Mabovitz]**
1898-1978 [B10, CA, IPA]
*Israeli prime minister*
* Meir, Golda

**Meyerson, Tuvia**
*See* Shulvass, Moses A.

**Meyerstein, E. H. W.**
*See* Meyerstein, Edward Harry
William

**Meyerstein, Edward Harry William**
1889-1952 [MBL, WWL]
*British author*
* E. H. W. M.
* Meyerstein, E. H. W.

**Meynell, Clyde**
*See* Van Straubenzee, Clyde

**Meynell, Laurence [Walter]** 1899-
[CC, WW]
*British author and editor*
* Baxter, Valerie
* Eton, Robert
* Ludlow, Geoffrey
* Tring, A. Stephen

**Meynell, Wilfrid** 1852-1948 [FFF]
*British author and journalist*
* Oldcastle, John

**Meyrick, [Canon]**
*See* Meyrick, Frederick James

**Meyrick, Frederick James** 1871- ?
[LAO]
*British clergyman and author*
* Meyrick, [Canon]

**Meyrink, Gustave**
*See* Meyer, Gustav

**Meysenburg, Janet B.** 1884-1955
[FC, HCA]
*American actress*
* Beecher, Janet

**Meza, Johnny** 20th c. [RBE]
*American boxer*
* Mesa, Johnny

**Mezzofanti, Giuseppe** 1774-1849
[DHA, FFF, SN]
*Italian linguist and prelate*
* [The] Briareus of Languages
* [A] Monster of Languages
* [La] Pentecote Vivante
* [The] Walking Polyglot

**Mezzrow, Mezz**
*See* Mesirow, Milton

**Mezzrow, Milton**
*See* Mesirow, Milton

**M'Govan, James**
*See* Honeyman, William C.

**Mia**
*See* Parsons-Irwin, Maureen

**Miali, Roberto** 20th c. [WF]
*Italian actor*
* Wilson, Jerry

**Miall, Robert**
*See* Burke, John [Frederick]

**Micantoni, Adriano** 20th c. [WF]
*Italian actor*
* Anthony, Mike

**Micelotta, Mickey**
*See* Micelotta, Robert Peter [Bob]

**Micelotta, Robert Peter [Bob]**
1928- [BE]
*American baseball player*
* Micelotta, Mickey

**Michael**
*See* Wheeler, Joseph Trank

**Michael Angelo de Kermesses**
*See* Laar [or Laer], Pieter van

**[The] Michael Angelo of America**
*See* Cabrera, Miguel

**[The] Michael Angelo of Battle
Scenes**
*See* Cerquozzi, Michael Angelo

**[The] Michael Angelo of France**
*See* Cousin, Jean

**[The] Michael Angelo of France**
*See* Puget, Pierre

**[The] Michael Angelo of Modern
Literature**
*See* Hugo, Victor Marie

**[The] Michael Angelo of Music**
*See* Gluck, Christoph Willibald

**[The] Michael Angelo of Opera**
*See* Wagner, [Wilhelm] Richard

**[The] Michael Angelo of Sculptors**
*See* Puget, Pierre

**[The] Michael Angelo of Sculptors**
*See* Slodtz, Rene Michael

**[The] Michael Angelo of Spain**
*See* Cano, Alonso [or Alonzo]

**[The] Michael Angelo of the Lyre**
*See* Palestrina, Giovanni

**[The] Michael Angelo of the Middle
Ages**
*See* Arnolfo di Cambio

**[The] Michael Angelo of the
Reformation**
*See* Luther, Martin

**Michael, Big Mike**
*See* Michael, J. E.

**Michael, Gene Richard** 1938- [BE]
*American baseball player*
* Michael, Stick

**Michael, J. E.** 20th c.
*American football player*
* Michael, Big Mike

**Michael, James**
*See* Scagnetti, Jack

**Michael, Jerry Dean** 1938?- [B10]
*American automobile executive and*
*transvestite*
* Carmichael, Geraldine Elizabeth

**Michael, John**
*See* Sempill, Ernest

**Michael, Judith** [joint pseudonym
with Michael Fain]
*See* Barnard, Judith

**Michael, Judith** [joint pseudonym
with Judith Barnard]
*See* Fain, Michael

**Michael, Manfred**
*See* Winterfeld, Henry

**Michael of Walachia** ?-1601
[WBD]
*Prince of Walachia*
* [The] Bold

**Michael, Paul**
*See* Sempill, Ernest

**Michael, Ralph**
*See* Shotter, Ralph Champion

**Michael, Stick**
*See* Michael, Gene Richard

**Michael X**
*See* De Freitas, Michael

**Michael II** ?- 829
[DNNS, FFF, WBD]
*Byzantine emperor*
* [The] Amorian
* [Le] Begue
* [The] Stammerer

**Michael III** 9th c. [WBD]
*Byzantine emperor*
* [The] Drunkard

**Michael IV** 11th c. [DNNS, WBD]
*Byzantine emperor*
* [The] Paphlagonian

**Michael V Calaphrates** 11th c.
[DNNS]
*Byzantine emperor*
* [The] Calker

**Michael VI Stratioticus** 11th c.
[DNNS]
*Byzantine emperor*
* [The] Warrior

**Michaeles, M. M.**
*See* Golding, Morton J[ay]

**Michaelis, Karin**
*See* Stangeland, Katharina Marie
[Bech-Brondum] Michaelis

**Michaels, Barbara**
*See* Mertz, Barbara [Gross]

**Michaels, Carolyn Leopold**
*See* Leopold, Carolyn Clugston

**Michaels, Casimir Eugene**
*See* Kwietniewski, Casimir Eugene

**Michaels, Cass**
*See* Kwietniewski, Casimir Eugene

**Michaels, Dale**
*See* Rifkin, Shepard

**Michaels, Joe**
*See* Saltzman, Joseph [Joe]

**Michaels, Kristin**
*See* Williams, Jeanne

**Michaels, Lynn**
*See* Strongin, Lynn

**Michaels, Peter**
*See* Jackson, Carol

**Michaels, Ruth Gruber**
*See* Gruber, Ruth

**Michaels, Steve**
*See* Avallone, Michael [Angelo],
Jr.

**Michaelson, John August**
1893-1968 [BE]
*Finnish-born baseball player*
* Michaelson, Mike

**Michaelson, Mike**
*See* Michaelson, John August

**Michalska, Marianna** 1899?-1959
[F1, F2, FC]
*Polish-born American entertainer*
* Gray, Gilda

**Michalske, August** 1903-
[FB, SMG]
*American football player*
* Michalske, Iron Mike
* Michalske, Mike

**Michalske, Iron Mike**
*See* Michalske, August

**Michalske, Mike**
*See* Michalske, August

**Michaud, Georges** 1888-1970 [SC]
*French actor*
* Milton, Georges

**Michaux, Elder**
*See* Michaux, Solomon Lightfoot

**Michaux, Solomon Lightfoot**
*Evangelist*
* Michaux, Elder

**Miche, Giuseppe**
*See* Bochenski, Joseph M.

**Michel**
*See* Churchill, Peter

**[Le] Michel Ange des Bamboches**
*See* Laar [or Laer], Pieter van

**[Le] Michel Ange Francais**
*See* Cousin, Jean

**[Le] Michel Ange Francais**
*See* Puget, Pierre

**Michel, Claude** 1738-1814 [WBD]
*French sculptor*
* Clodion

**Michel, Ferdinaid** 19th c. [PA]
*Author*
* Real, Antony

**Michel, John B.** 1917- [ESF, WGT]
*American author*
* Conway, Bowen
* Cooke, Arthur [joint pseudonym
  with C. Kornbluth, R. Lowndes,
  E. Balter, D. Wollheim]
* Raymond, Hugh
* Tara, John
* Woods, Lawrence [joint
  pseudonym with Donald A(llen)
  Wollheim]

**Michel, Maria Johanna** 1932- [OP]
*Dutch-born opera singer*
* Bazuky, Maya

**Michelangeli**
*See* Michelangeli, Arturo Benedetti

**Michelangeli, Arturo Benedetti**
1920- [MS]
*Italian musician*
* Michelangeli

**Michelangelo [or Michael Angelo]**
*See* Buonarroti, Michelangelo [or
Michael Angelo]

**Micheli, Ornella** 20th c. [WF]
*Italian film editor*
* Christie, Donna

**Michels, Nicholas Aloysius** 20th c.
[SFL, WGT]
*Author*
* Mikalowitch, Nicolai

**Michieli [or Micheli], Dominico**
?-1130 [HN]
*Doge of Venice*
* [The] Terror of the Greeks

**[The] Michigan Assassin**
*See* Kiecal, Stanislaus

**[The] Michigan Wildcat**
*See* Wolgust, Adolphus

**Michnick, Irwin S.** 1928- [EJ]
*American jazz musician*
* Leigh, Mitch

**Michon, Pierre** 1610-1685 [PA]
*Author*
* Bocadelot, Abbe

**Mick**
*See* Wilson, Michael

**Mick the Quick**
*See* Rivers, John Milton

**Mickel, Owen Harlan** [B10]
*American horseman*
* Montana, Montie

**Mickens, Robert** 20th c. [RO2]
*American musician*
* Mickens, Spike

**Mickens, Spike**
*See* Mickens, Robert

**Mickey Mouse Haefner**
*See* Haefner, Milton Arnold

**Mickiewicz, Adam** 1798-1855
[DEP, DNNF, SN]
*Polish poet*
* [The] Polish Byron

**Mickle, Elmon** 1919-1977
[BWW, NBB]
*American singer*
* Driftin' Slim
* Harmonica Harry
* Model T Slim
* Smith, Drifting

**Micklewhite, Maurice** 1933-
[BDF, FC, IPA]
*British actor*
* Caine, Michael

**Micky the Magician**
*See* Hades, Micky

**[The] Microphone of God**
*See* Sheen, Fulton J.

**Micyllus**
*See* Moltzer, Jacob

**Middle Wallop**
*See* Sprake, Leslie

**Middlebrook, David**
*See* Rosenus, Alan [Harvey]

**Middlecoff, Cary** 1921- [GF]
*American golfer*
* Middlecoff, Doc

**Middlecoff, Doc**
*See* Middlecoff, Cary

**Middlesex**
*See* Robinson, William Stevens

**Middleton, Arthur**
*See* O'Brien, Edward Joseph
Harrington

**Middleton, Arthur** 1743-1788 [PA]
*Author*
* Marvell, Andrew

**Middleton, Doc**
*See* Riley, James

**Middleton, Edgar Charles** 1894-
[WWL]
*British author and journalist*
* [An] Air Pilot

**Middleton, Ellis** 20th c. [WWL]
*British author*
* Lees, John Morton

**Middleton, George** 1880- ? [BEW]
*American playwright*
* Saisson, Pierre [joint pseudonym
  with St. George Guy Reginald
  Bolton]

**Middleton, Guy**
*See* Middleton-Powell, Guy

**Middleton, Harry** [WD]
*Author*
* Kiefer, Middleton [joint
  pseudonym with Warren David
  Kiefer]

**Middleton, James Blaine [Jim]**
1889-1974 [BE]
*American baseball player*
* Middleton, Rifle Jim

**Middleton, John** 1578- ?
[DNNF, FFF, HN]
*British giant*
* [The] Child of Hale

**Middleton, Josephine**
*See* Alcock, Josephine

**Middleton, Julia** 20th c. [IBW]
*American culture center organizer*
* Aunt Bee

**Middleton, Peggy Yvonne** 1922-
[BDF, FC, WEF]
*Canadian actress*
* De Carlo, Yvonne

**Middleton, Richard** ?-1304
[DNNF, DNNS, HN]
*British theologian*
* Fundatus et Copiosus, Doctor
* [The] Profound Doctor
* Profundus, Doctor
* [The] Solid Doctor
* Solidus, Doctor

**Middleton, Rifle Jim**
*See* Middleton, James Blaine [Jim]

**Middleton, Robert**
*See* Messer, Samuel G.

**Middleton-Murry, Colin** 1926-
[CA, SF, WD]
*British author*
* Cowper, Richard
* Murry, Colin

**Middleton-Powell, Guy** 1907-
[THR]
*British actor*
* Middleton, Guy

**Midgely, R. L.**
*See* Pulsifer, D.

**Midgett, Elwin W.** 1911- [CAP]
*American author*
* Midgett, Wink

**Midgett, Wink**
*See* Midgett, Elwin W.

**Midkiff, Ezra Millington**
1882-1957 [BE]
*American baseball player*
* Midkiff, Salt Rock

**Midkiff, Salt Rock**
*See* Midkiff, Ezra Millington

**Midler, Bette** 1945-
*American singer and actress*
* [The] Divine Miss M

**Midnight, Captain**
*See* Tibbs, Casey

**Midnight Cowboy**
*See* Martin, Ray

**[The] Midnight Express**
*See* Tolan, Eddie

**[The] Midnight Idol**
*See* Newton, Wayne

[The] Midwife of Men's Thoughts
See Socrates

Mieczislaw, Jan 1850-1925 [WBD]
Polish opera singer
* Reszke, Jean de

Mieczyslawa
See Radzyminska, Jozefa

Mieg, Peter 1906- [ART]
Swiss painter
* P. M.

Miel [or Meel], Jan 1599-1663
[WBD]
Flemish painter and engraver
* Della Vite, Giovanni

Mielants, Florent Constant Albert
1917- [MWD]
Belgian poet and playwright
* Hensen, Herwig

Mielziner, Leo, Jr. 1899-1962
[BEW]
American actor, director, editor
* MacKenna, Kenneth

Mier Jimenez, Ramon 1925- [GS]
Mexican bullfighter
* Nino de la Rose [Boy of the Rose]

Mierkowicz, Butch
See Mierkowicz, Edward Frank

Mierkowicz, Edward Frank 1924-
[BE]
American baseball player
* Mierkowicz, Butch

Miers, Earl Schenck 1910-1972
[CA, SAT, WW]
American author and editor
* Meredith, David William

Miesel, Sandra [CA]
American author
* Black, Roberta [joint pseudonym
with Robert (Stratton) Coulson]

Miggins, Irish
See Miggins, Lawrence Edward
[Larry]

Miggins, Lawrence Edward [Larry]
1925- [BE]
American baseball player
* Miggins, Irish

Miggy, Mrs.
See Krentel, Mildred White

Mighels, Ella Sterling Cummins
1853- ? [NAA]
American author
* Esmeralda, Aurora

[The] Mighty Atom
See Booth, Albert James, Jr.

[The] Mighty Atom
See Bradford, David

[The] Mighty Atom
See Grant, Bryan

[The] Mighty Atom
See Greenstein, Joseph L.

[The] Mighty Atom
See Joliat, Aurel Emile

[The] Mighty Atom
See Wilde, James [Jimmy]

Mighty Flea Conners
See Conners, Gene

Mighty Joe Young
See Young, Joseph

[The] Mighty Leviathan
See Hobbes, Thomas

Mighty Little Mo
See Connolly, Maureen

Mighty Maggie Thatcher
See Thatcher, Margaret Hilda
[Roberts]

[The] Mighty Manager
See Huggins, Miller James

[The] Mighty Midget of Corsicana
See Wilson, Robert E. [Bobby]

[The] Mighty Mite
See Booth, Albert James, Jr.

[The] Mighty Mite
See Huggins, Miller James

Mighty Mouse
See Livers, Virgil Chester, Jr.

Mighty Mouse
See Tanner, Elaine

[The] Mighty Sparrow
See Slinger, Francisco

Migliaccio, Edward 1881-1946
[SC]
Italian-born actor
* Farfariello

Mignard, Pierre 1610-1695 [SN]
French painter
* [The] Roman

[Le] Mignon
See Henry III [or Henri]

Mignonette
See Moore, Emily H.

Miguelin [Little Mike]
See Mateo Salcedo, Miguel

Mihalek, Jim 20th c. [GW]
American rodeo performer
* Mihalek, Weasel

Mihalek, Weasel
See Mihalek, Jim

Mihilakis, Ulysses George 20th c.
[WGT]
Author
* Hassen, Silaki Ali

Mik
See Mikkelsen, Henning Dahl

Mik, Al
See Plastino, Al

Mikado Milt Scott
See Scott, Milt[on Parker]

Mikalowitch, Nicolai
See Michels, Nicholas Aloysius

Mikan, Baron
See Barba, Harry

Mike
See Donnet, [Baron] Michael
Gabriel Libert Marie

Mike
See Hughes, Patrick C.

Mike
See Muir, Mary

Mike the Pike
See Heitler, Michael

Mike-Mayer, Istvan 1947- [SMG]
Hungarian-born football player
* Mike-Mayer, Steve

Mike-Mayer, Steve
See Mike-Mayer, Istvan

Mikes, George
See Mikes, Gyorgy

Mikes, Gyorgy 1912- [SFL]
Author
* Mikes, George

Miketta, Bob
See Morris, Robert

Mikhailov, Peter
See Peter I [Petr Alekseevich]

Mikhoels, Salomon
See Vovsky, Salomon Mikhailovich

Mikkelsen, Henning Dahl 20th c.
[WECO]
Danish cartoonist
* Mik

Mikkelson, Mick
See Mikkelson, Peter J.

Mikkelson, Peter J. 1939- [SMG]
American baseball player
* Mikkelson, Mick

Miklos, Hank
See Miklos, John Joseph

Miklos, John Joseph 1910- [BE]
American baseball player
* Miklos, Hank

Mikol, Jim
See Mikol, John Stanley

Mikol, John Stanley 1938- [CEI]
Canadian-born hockey player
* Mikol, Jim

[The] Milan Bach
See Bach, Johann Christian

Milan, Deerfoot
See Milan, Jesse Clyde

Milan, Jesse Clyde 1887-1953
[AS, DGS, PB]
American baseball player
* Milan, Deerfoot
* Milan, Zeb

Milan, Zeb
See Milan, Jesse Clyde

[The] Milanese
See Bach, Johann Christian

Milani, Chef
See Milani, Joseph L.

Milani, Joseph L. 1892-1965 [SC]
American actor and cooking-show
host
* Milani, Chef

Milbrook, John
See McFadden, Gertrude V.

Milburn, William Henry 1823- ?
[DNNF, FF, SN]
American clergyman
* [The] Blind Preacher

Milcetic, Helen 1929- [EJ]
American singer
* Merrill, Helen

[The] Mild
See Frederick II

Mildred, [Sister] M.
See Hill, Margaret Shirley

Mile a Minute Murphy
See Murphy, Charles W.

Milecete, Helen
See Jones, Susan Carleton

Miles
See Southwold, Stephen

Miles, Allan
See Dellinger, Allan Miles

Miles, Buddy
See Miles, George

Miles, Butch
See Thornton, Charles J.

Miles, Charles J.
See Thornton, Charles J.

Miles, Dee
See Miles, Wilson Daniel

Miles, Dorien K[lein] 1915- [CA]
American author
* Miles, Sylva [joint pseudonym
with Sylva Mularchyk]

Miles, Elliot
See Ludvigsen, Karl [Eric]

Miles, Frederic James 1869- ?
[LAO]
British writer and editor
* Rangefinder

Miles, Garry
See Cason, James

Miles, George 1948- [IBW]
American musician
* Miles, Buddy

Miles, Gertrude Elizabeth 1860- ?
[NAA]
American author
* Arnold, Faith Stewart

Miles, John
See Bickham, Jack M[iles]

Miles, John 20th c. [OBW]
American baseball player
* Miles, Mule

Miles, Josephine [Josie] 1900?-
[BWW]
American singer
* Flowers, Evangelist Mary
* Harris, Pearl
* Jones, Augusta

Miles, Keith
See Tralins, S[andor] Robert
[Bob]

Miles, Lily Pearl ?-1957 [SC]
American actress
* Shelby, Charlotte

Miles, Lizzie
See Landreaux, Elizabeth Mary

Miles, Long Gone
See Miles, Luke

Miles, Lotta
See Court, Florence

Miles, Luke 1925- [DAM]
American singer
* Miles, Long Gone

Miles, Luther
See Mander, Lionel

Miles, Miska
See Martin, Patricia Miles

Miles, Mule
See Miles, John

Miles, Otis 1949- [RO2]
American singer
* Williams, Otis

Miles, Peter
See Perreau, Gerald

Miles, Pliny 1818-1865 [FFF, PA]
American journalist
* Communipaw

Miles, Susan 1887- [WWL]
British author
* Roberts, Ursula

Miles, Sylva [joint pseudonym with
Sylva Mularchyk]
See Miles, Dorien K[lein]

Miles, Sylva [joint pseudonym with
Dorien K(lein) Miles]
See Mularchyk, Sylva

Miles, Vera
See Ralston, Vera

Miles, Wilson Daniel 1909- [BE]
American baseball player
* Miles, Dee

Miley, Bubber
See Miley, James Wesley

Miley, James Wesley 1903-1932
[DAM, EJ, PMJ]
American jazz musician
* Miley, Bubber

[The] Milford Bard
See Lofland, John

Milford, Jake
See Milford, John

Milford, John 20th c. [SMG]
American hockey manager
* Milford, Jake

Milforde, Marie
See Fisher, Mary

Milhailovitch, Boris 1891-1963
[FC]
Russian-born producer
* Morros, Boris

Milic, Jan ?-1374 [WBD]
Moravian-born prelate
* Milic of Kremsier

Milic of Kremsier
See Milic, Jan

Milinda
See Menander

Militant
See Sandburg, Carl [August]

[The] Military Ventriloquist
See Whitaker, Thomas

Militello, Pietro
See Natali, Alfred Maxim

Miljus, John Kenneth 1895- [BE]
American baseball player
* [The] Big Serb

[The] Milk Snatcher
See Thatcher, Margaret Hilda
[Roberts]

Milkman Jim Turner
See Turner, James Riley

Milkomane, George Alexis
Milkomanovich 1903-
[CC, LC, WW]
Russian-born British physician and
author
* Bankoff, George Alexis
* Borodin, George
* Braddon, George
* Conway, Peter
* Sava, George

Milkowski, Zygmunt 1824-1915
[WBD]
Polish author
* Jez, Teodor Tomasz

Milks, Herbert 1902- [CEI]
Canadian-born hockey player
* Milks, Hib

Milks, Hib
See Milks, Herbert

[The] Milkwoman of Bristol
See Yearsley, Ann

Milky the Clown
See Fox, Karrell

Mill
See Butler, William M.

[The] Mill Boy of the Slashes
See Clay, Henry

Mill, C. R.
See Crnjanski, Milos

Mill, Garrett
See Miller, Margaret

Mill, Ian St. John
See Mills, Terry Kenneth

Millaird, M. Albert [PA]
Author
* Grimm, Baron

Millan Diaz, Antonio 1947-1976
[GS]
Spanish bullfighter
* Carnicerito de Ubeda [Little
Butcher from Ubeda]

Milland, Jack
See Truscott-Jones, Reginald

Milland, Ray
See Truscott-Jones, Reginald

Milland, Spike
See Truscott-Jones, Reginald

Millar, James Primrose Malcolm
1893- [IAW]
Scottish-born author
* White, G. A.

Millar, Kenneth 1915-
[CA, CC, EMD]
American author
* Macdonald, John
* Macdonald, John Ross
* Macdonald, Ross

Millar, Mary
See Wetton, Mary

Millar, Minna Henrietta Joy 1914-
[AW]
British-born author
* Collier, Joy

Millard, Alice
See Bullivant, Cecil Henry

Millard, Christopher Sclater 1872-
? [LC, WWL]
British author
* Mason, Stuart

Millard, E. E. 19th c. [PA]
Author
* E. M. E.

Millard, Edward R. ?-1963 [BEW]
Theatrical performer
* Millard, Rocky

Millard, Harry W.
See Williams, Harry Millard

Millard, Joseph 20th c. [SFP]
Author
* Westwood, N. J.

Millard, Rocky
See Millard, Edward R.

Millard, Ursula
See Coulter, Ursula

Millarde, June Elizabeth
1899-1936 [BEW]
American actress
* Caprice, June

Millaud, M. Albert [PA]
Author
* Himery, Paul

Millay, Edna St. Vincent
1892-1950 [LC]
American author
* Boyd, Nancy

Millbank, F. T.
See Holmes, Geoffrey Andrew

Millbank, Mrs. George [FFF]
Entertainer
* Paine, Lizzie

Millburn, Cynthia
See Brooks, Anne Tedlock

Miller, Abraham Joseph, Jr. 20th
c. [RO2]
American musician
* Miller, Onion

Miller, Al 20th c.
Auto racer
* Clean, Mr.

Miller, Albert 1913- [FFA]
Canadian singer
* [The] Canadian Burl Ives
* Mills, Alan

Miller, Alex
See Ford, Aleck

Miller, Alexander R. G.
1875?-1940 [BEW]
Theatrical performer
* Karson, Kit

Miller, Alice Moore 1916-1960
[SC]
American actress
* Moore, Alice

Miller, Allen L., III 1948- [GF]
American golfer
* [The] Other Miller

Miller, Ann
See Collier, Lucille Ann

Miller, B. [PA]
Author
* B. M.

Miller, Benj.
See Loomis, Noel M[iller]

Miller, Benny
See Kaplan, Louis

Miller, Big
See Miller, Clarence H.

Miller, Bill 1920-1961
[CC, EMD, WW]
American author
* Masterson, Whit [joint
pseudonym with Robert (Bob)
Wade]
* Miller, Wade [joint pseudonym
with Robert (Bob) Wade]
* Wilmer, Dale [joint pseudonym
with Robert (Bob) Wade]

Miller, Bill 20th c. [BLB]
American criminal
* [The] Killer

Miller, Bing
See Miller, Edmund John

Miller, Bing
See Miller, John E.

Miller, Bob 1895-1955 [CWG]
American singer and songwriter
* Burnett, Bob
* Ferguson, Bob
* Kackley, Bob
* Palmer, Bill

Miller, Buck
See Miller, Clarence

Miller, Buck
See Miller, Eddie

Miller, Bullet
See Miller, Frank Lee

Miller, Buzz
See Miller, Vernal Philip

Miller, Calliope
See Miller, George Frederick

Miller, Calvin E. 1914- [CWG]
American country-western performer
* Miller, Curley

Miller, Carl Grover 1893- [NAA]
American educator and author
* Ballard, Cyrus

Miller, Carmen 1944- [BF]
British actress
* Miller, Mandy

Miller, Charles 20th c. [SMG]
American football player
* Miller, Ookie

Miller, Charles Bradley 1868-1945
[BE]
American baseball player
* Miller, Dusty

Miller, Charles C. 1831- ? [ALY]
American author
* Benson, P., Sr.

Miller, Charles Henry 1842-1922
[WBD]
American etcher, painter, author
* De Muldor, Carl

Miller, Christine
See Van Walree, Mrs. E. C. W.

Miller, Cincinnatus Heine
1848-1913 [BEW, LC, PA]
American poet and playwright
* Miller, Joaquin

Miller, Clarence 1923- [BBH]
American softball player
* Miller, Buck

**Miller, Clarence H.** 1923-    [EJ]
*American jazz musician*
* Miller, Big

**Miller, Cotton**
See   Miller, Hugh Stanley [Hughie]

**Miller, Curley**
See   Miller, Calvin E.

**Miller, Curly**
See   Miller, George

**Miller, Cyclone**
See   Miller, Joseph H.

**Miller, Dais**
See   Miller, Lloyd Tevis

**Miller, Davy** 20th c.    [BLB]
*American boxer and referee*
* Miller, Yiddles

**Miller, Dempsey** 20th c.    [OBW]
*American baseball player*
* Miller, Dimp

**Miller, Dimp**
See   Miller, Dempsey

**Miller, Doc**
See   Miller, Roy Oscar

**Miller, Doggie**
See   Miller, George Frederick

**Miller, Doris R.**
See   Mosesson, Gloria R[ubin]

**Miller, Dots**
See   Miller, John Barney

**Miller, Dusty**
See   Miller, Charles Bradley

**Miller, Dusty**
See   Miller, Geoffrey

**Miller, E. F.**
See   Pohle, Robert W[arren], Jr.

**Miller, E. G.**
See   Miller, Edward George

**Miller, Eddie**
See   Lisbona, Edward

**Miller, Eddie** 20th c.    [OBW]
*American baseball player*
* Miller, Buck

**Miller, Edgar E.**    [FB]
*American football player*
* Miller, Rip

**Miller, Edmund John** 1894-1966
[AS, DGS, PB]
*American baseball player*
* Miller, Bing

**Miller, Edward George** 1883-1948
[SC]
*American actor*
* Miller, E. G.

**Miller, Edward Robert** 1916-    [BE]
*American baseball player*
* Miller, Eppie

**Miller, Elizabeth Beecher**    [NAA]
*American journalist*
* Beecher, Elizabeth [Betty]

**Miller, Elizabeth Erwin**
See   Lobingier, Elizabeth Miller

**Miller, Elizabeth Maxfield** 1910-
[CA]
*American author, educator,
translator*
* Maxfield, Elizabeth

**Miller, Eppie**
See   Miller, Edward Robert

**Miller, Ernest** 1894?-1971
[DAM, EJ, PMJ]
*American jazz musician*
* Miller, Punch
* Punch, Kid

**Miller, Eschal** 1918-    [FC]
*American actress*
* Grey, Nan

**Miller, Eugene** 20th c.    [BBH]
*American football player*
* Miller, Shorty

**Miller, Eugenia**
See   Mandelkorn, Eugenia Miller

**Miller, Evelyn**
See   Berger, Evelyn Miller

**Miller, F. F.** 1834- ?    [PA]
*Author*
* Ardboe

**Miller, Fish Bait**
See   Miller, William Mosley

**Miller, Flash**
See   Miller, Leroy

**Miller, Florence Fenwick** 1854- ?
[LAO]
*British author and editor*
* Filomena

**Miller, Foghorn**
See   Miller, George Frederick

**Miller, Francis Trevelyn** 1877- ?
[ALY]
*American author*
* Meunier, Francois

**Miller, Frank**
See   Loomis, Noel M[iller]

**Miller, Frank Lee** 1886-1974    [BE]
*American baseball player*
* Miller, Bullet

**Miller Fred[erick Holman]**
1886-1953    [BE]
*American baseball player*
* Miller, Speedy

**Miller, Frederick [Walter Gascoyne]**
1904-    [CA]
*New Zealand journalist*
* [The] Gascon

**Miller, G. R.**
See   Judd, Frederick Charles

**Miller, Gameboy**
See   Miller, Samuel

**Miller, Gary Neil** 1934?-
[BEW, FC, HT]
*American actor and singer*
* Dunn, Michael

**Miller, Gene**
See   Miller, Truman

**Miller, Geoffrey** 1952-    [DC]
*British cricketer*
* Miller, Dusty
* Miller, Mills

**Miller, George**
See   Moran, George

**Miller, George** 1909-    [IBW]
*American dancer*
* Miller, Curly

**Miller, George Frederick**
1864-1909    [AS, BE]
*American baseball player*
* Miller, Calliope
* Miller, Doggie
* Miller, Foghorn

**Miller, George Louquet** 1934-    [CA]
*American clergyman and author*
* Martin, Greg

**Miller, H. V.**
See   Miller, Harry Vye

**Miller, Hack**
See   Miller, James Eldridge

**Miller, Hack**
See   Miller, Lawrence

**Miller, Harriet** 1831-1918    [WBD]
*American ornithologist and author*
* Miller, Olive Thorne

**Miller, Harry Vye** 1907-    [ART]
*New Zealand painter*
* Miller, H. V.

**Miller, Helen Hill** 1899-    [CA]
*American author*
* Hill, Helen

**Miller, Hooks**
See   Miller, William Paul [Bill]

**Miller, Hope Ridings**
See   Ridings, Hope Dupre

**Miller, Hub**
See   Miller, Pleas

**Miller, Hugh** 1802-1856    [DEP]
*Scottish geologist and author*
* [The] Stonemason of Cromarty

**Miller, Hugh Stanley [Hughie]**
1887-1945    [BE]
*American baseball player*
* Miller, Cotton

**Miller, Isabel**
See   Routsong, Alma

**Miller, J. Irwin** 1909?-
*American industrialist*
* [The] Medici of the Middle West

**Miller, Jack** 1895-1941    [SC]
*American actor*
* Miller, Shorty

**Miller, James [Jim]** ?-1937    [BE]
*American baseball player*
* Miller, Rabbit

**Miller, James Edward** 1913-
*American jazz musician*
* Miller, Sing

**Miller, James Eldridge** 1911-1966
[BE]
*American baseball player*
* Miller, Hack

**Miller, Jason**
See   Miller, John

**Miller, Jim**
See   Moss, Eugene

**Miller, Jimmy** 20th c.    [HDM]
*British actor, singer, director*
* McColl, Ewan

**Miller, Joan Maxine** 1922-
[BEW, TR]
*American actress and singer*
* Copeland, Joan

**Miller, Joaquin**
See   Miller, Cincinnatus Heine

**Miller, Joe**
See   Mottley, John

**Miller, Joe, II**
See   Ballantyne, James

**Miller, Joe, Jr.**
See   Westcott, Thompson

**Miller, John**
See   Samachson, Joseph

**Miller, John** 1939?-    [IPA]
*American playwright*
* Miller, Jason

**Miller, John Anthony** 1915-    [BE]
*American baseball player*
* Miller, Ox

**Miller, John Barney** 1886-1923
[AS, BE]
*American baseball player*
* Miller, Dots

**Miller, John E.** 1903-1964    [AS]
*American football player*
* Miller, Bing

**Miller, Joseph [Joe]** 1684-1738
[DEL, FFF, RH]
*British comic actor*
* [The] Father of Jests

**Miller, Joseph** 20th c.    [ASC]
*American musician*
* Miller, Taps

**Miller, Joseph H.** 1859-1916    [BE]
*American baseball player*
* Miller, Cyclone

**Miller, Kathlyn** 1896-1933    [THR]
*Scottish-born actress and singer*
* Hilliard, Kathlyn

**Miller, Ken[neth Albert]** 1915-    [BE]
*American baseball player*
* Miller, Whitey

**Miller, Lanora** 1932-    [CA]
*American editor and author*
* Welzenbach, Lanora F.

**Miller, Laura Owen**
See   Bamberger, Laura Owen
Miller

**Miller, Lawrence**
See   Alais, Ernest W.

**Miller, Lawrence** 1894-1971
[BE, PB]
*American baseball player*
* Miller, Hack

**Miller, Lefty**
See   Miller, Ralph Henry

**Miller, Leo Alphonso** 1897-    [BE]
*American baseball player*
* Miller, Red

**Miller, Leonard** 1864-1939
[LC, TC]
*British author*
* Merrick, Leonard

**Miller, Leroy** 20th c.    [OBW]
*American baseball player*
* Miller, Flash

**Miller, Lloyd Tevis** 1875- ?    [IBW]
*American physician*
* Miller, Dais

**Miller, Louis** 1898-1962    [SC]
*Actor*
* Mills, Guy

**Miller, Lowell Otto** 1889-1962
[BE]
*American baseball player*
* Miller, Moonie

**Miller, Lydia F. F.** 1805- ?
[DEL, FFF]
*Author*
* Myrtle, Harriet

**Miller, Mandy**
See   Miller, Carmen

**Miller, Marc**
See   Baker, Marceil Genee
[Kolstad]

**Miller, Margaret** 20th c.    [SFL]
*Author*
* Mill, Garrett

**Miller, Margaret J.**
See   Dale, Margaret J[essy] Miller

**Miller, Marilyn**
See   Reynolds, Mary Ellen

**Miller, Marsha**
See   Baker, Marceil Genee
[Kolstad]

**Miller, Martha**
See   Ivan, Martha Miller Pfaff

**Miller, Martin**
See   Muller, Rudolph

**Miller, Marvin**
See   Mueller, Marvin

**Miller, Mary**
See   Northcott, [William] Cecil

**Miller, Mary Beth** 1942-
[CA, SAT]
*American author and actress*
* Mary Beth

**Miller, Mary Britton** 1883-1975
[ANT, CA, LC]
*American author and poet*
* Bolton, Isabel

**Miller, Mary Ester** 1876- ?    [CAN]
*Canadian author*
* Keith, Marion

**Miller, Maud**
See   McCormick, Mrs. Loudon

**Miller, Max**
See   Sargent, Thomas Henry

**Miller, May**
See   Hues, Mrs. Frank

**Miller, Merrill**
See   Miller, Morris

**Miller, Mills**
See   Miller, Geoffrey

**Miller, Moonie**
See   Miller, Lowell Otto

**Miller, Morris** 1890-1957    [SC]
*American actor*
* De Costa, Morris

**Miller, Morris** 1919-    [CA, OP]
*American opera singer*
* Merrill, Robert
* Miller, Merrill

**Miller, Mrs. Henry**    [FFF]
*Entertainer*
* Heron, Bijou

**Miller, Mrs. John A.**    [PA]
*Author*
* Latimer, Faith

**Miller, Nicole Puleo** 1944-    [CA]
*American author*
* Puleo, Nicole

**Miller, Norman** 20th c.    [IBW]
*American actor*
* Miller, Porto Rico

**Miller, Olive Thorne**
See   Miller, Harriet

**Miller, Onion**
See   Miller, Abraham Joseph, Jr.

**Miller, Ookie**
See   Miller, Charles

**Miller, Otis Louis** 1901-1959
*American baseball player*
* Miller, Otto

**Miller, Otto**
See   Miller, Otis Louis

**Miller, Ox**
See   Miller, John Anthony

**Miller, P[eter] Schuyler** 1912-1974
[ESF, WGT]
*American author and critic*
* McDermott, Dennis [joint
   pseudonym with Aubrey
   McDermott and Walter Dennis]
* Nihil

**Miller, Perry** 1944-    [RO2]
*American musician*
* Young, Jesse Colin

**Miller, Piano**
See   Lisbona, Edward

**Miller, Pleas** 20th c.    [OBW]
*American baseball player*
* Miller, Hub

**Miller, Porto Rico**
See   Miller, Norman

**Miller, Punch**
See   Miller, Ernest

**Miller, R. S.** 1936-    [CA]
*American author*
* Huston, Fran

**Miller, Rabbit**
See   Miller, James [Jim]

**Miller, Ralph Henry** 1899-1967
[BE]
*American baseball player*
* Miller, Lefty

**Miller, Red**
See   Miller, Leo Alphonso

**Miller, Red**
See   Miller, Robert

**Miller, Rice**
See   Ford, Aleck

**Miller, Richard**
See   Pietschmann, Richard John,
III

**Miller, Rip**
See   Miller, Edgar E.

**Miller, Robert** 1927-    [SMG]
*American football coach*
* Miller, Red

**Miller, Roland Arthur** 1918-    [BE]
*American baseball player*
* Miller, Ronnie

**Miller, Ronnie**
See   Miller, Roland Arthur

**Miller, Roscoe Clyde** 1876-1913
[BE]
*American baseball player*
* Miller, Roxy
* Miller, Rubberlegs

**Miller, Roxy**
See   Miller, Roscoe Clyde

**Miller, Roy Oscar** 1883-1938    [BE]
*American baseball player*
* Miller, Doc

**Miller, Rubberlegs**
See   Miller, Roscoe Clyde

**Miller, Rudel Charles** 1900-    [BE]
*American baseball player*
* Miller, Rudy

**Miller, Rudy**
See   Miller, Rudel Charles

**Miller, Ruth**
See   Jacobs, Ruth Harriet

**Miller, Samuel** 20th c.
[MM, PHM]
*American underworld figure*
* Miller, Gameboy

**Miller, Seymour** 1908-    [ASC]
*American musician*
* Miller, Sy

**Miller, Shorty**
See   Miller, Eugene

**Miller, Shorty**
See   Miller, Jack

**Miller, Sing**
See   Miller, James Edward

**Miller, Speedy**
See   Miller Fred[erick Holman]

**Miller, Susan** 1946-    [FC]
*American actress*
* Saint James, Susan

**Miller, Sy**
See   Miller, Seymour

**Miller, Taps**
See   Miller, Joseph

**Miller, Thomas** 1807?-1874
[DEL, DNNS, SN]
*British author and poet*
* [The] Basket Maker

**Miller, Tobias Ham**    [PA]
*Author*
* Uncle Toby

**Miller, Truman** 1924?-1963    [BEW]
*Stage manager and actor*
* Miller, Gene

**Miller, Val** 1942-    [IAW]
*British author*
* Manning, Val

**Miller, Velna Lou** 1935-    [BEW]
*American actress and singer*
* Miller, Wynne

**Miller, Vernal Philip** 1928-    [BEW]
*American dancer, choreographer,
actor*
* Miller, Buzz

**Miller, Wade** [joint pseudonym with
Robert (Bob) Wade]
See   Miller, Bill

**Miller, Wade** [joint pseudonym with
Bill Miller]
See   Wade, Robert [Bob]

**Miller, Ward Taylor** 1884-1958
[BE]
*American baseball player*
* Miller, Windy

**Miller, Warne**
See   Rathborne, St. George

**Miller, Warren** 1921-1966    [B10]
*American author*
* Vail, Amanda

**Miller, Whitey**
See   Miller, Ken[neth Albert]

**Miller, Wild Bill**
See   Miller, William Francis [Bill]

**Miller, William** 1781?-1849
[FFF, HN]
*American religious leader*
* [The] American Prophet
* [The] Poet of Low Hampton

**Miller, William** 1928-
[FC, SW, WEF]
*Irish-born American actor*
* Boyd, Stephen

**Miller, William Francis [Bill]**
1910-    [BE]
*American baseball player*
* Miller, Wild Bill

**Miller, William Mosley**    [B10]
*Former Congressional doorkeeper*
* Miller, Fish Bait

**Miller, William Paul [Bill]** 1926-
[BE]
*American baseball player*
* Miller, Hooks

**Miller, Willie**
See   Ford, Aleck

**Miller, Windy**
See   Miller, Ward Taylor

**Miller, Wright W[atts]** 1903-
[AW, CA]
*British author and editor*
* North, Mark

**Miller, Wynne**
See   Miller, Velna Lou

**Miller, Yiddles**
See   Miller, Davy

**Milles, [Vilhelm] Carl [Emil]**
See   Anderson, Vilhelm Carl Emil

**Millet [or Mile], Jean Francois**
1642?-1679    [SN, WBD]
*Flemish painter*
* Francisque
* [A] Jupiter in Sabots

**Millet, Kadish** 1923-    [ASC]
*American composer*
* Millet, Kay

**Millet, Kay**
See   Millet, Kadish

**Millett, Nigel Stansbury** 1904-
[LAO]
*British author*
* Oke, Richard

**Milligan, Frances J. G.**
See   Watkins, Frances Jane
Grierson

**Milligan, Jocko**
See Milligan, John

**Milligan, John** 1861-1923
[AS, BE]
*American baseball player*
* Milligan, Jocko

**Milligan, Mary** 1882-1966 [SC]
*Irish actress*
* Milligan, Min

**Milligan, Min**
See Milligan, Mary

**Milligan, Spike**
See Milligan, Terence Alan

**Milligan, Terence Alan** 1918-
[AW, CA, TR]
*British actor, director, author*
* Milligan, Spike

**Millikan, Robert** 20th c.
*American physicist*
* Millikan, Tinker

**Millikan, Tinker**
See Millikan, Robert

**Milliken, Bobo**
See Milliken, Robert Fogle [Bob]

**Milliken, Robert Fogle [Bob]** 1926-
[BE]
*American baseball player*
* Milliken, Bobo

**Milliken, William Grawn** 1922-
*American politician*
* Boy Scout Bill
* [The] Lollipop Governor
* Milquetoast, Governor

**Millinder, Lucius** 1900-1966
[DAM, PMJ, WWJ]
*American bandleader*
* Millinder, Lucky

**Millinder, Lucky**
See Millinder, Lucius

**Millington, Philip** [FFF]
*Author*
* Cento

**[The] Million Dollar Mermaid**
See Kellerman, Annette

**Millionaire Charlie Matranga**
See Matranga, Charles

**[The] Millionaire Gorilla**
See Capone, Al[phonse]

**[El] Millonario [The Millionaire]**
See Segura, Vicente

**Millor**
See Fernandes, Millor

**Mills, Abbott Paige** 1889- [BE]
*American baseball player*
* Mills, Jack

**Mills, Alan**
See Miller, Albert

**Mills, Algernon Victor** 1905-
[WW]
*Author*
* Latimer, Rupert

**Mills, Dorothy**
See Howard, Dorothy Gray

**Mills, Enos Abijah** 1870-1922
[WBD]
*American author*
* [The] Father of the Rocky
  Mountain National Park

**Mills, Ferocious Fred**
See Mills, Freddie

**Mills, Florence Winfrey**
1895-1927 [IBW]
*American singer, actress, dancer*
* Baby Florence

**Mills, Frank**
See Ransom, Frank

**Mills, Freddie** 1919-1965 [WBC]
*British boxer*
* Mills, Ferocious Fred

**Mills, Frederick Allen** 1869-1948
[ASC, BEW, DAM]
*American composer*
* Mills, Kerry

**Mills, Guy**
See Miller, Louis

**Mills, Howard Robertson** 1910-
[BE]
*American baseball player*
* Mills, Lefty

**Mills, Hugh [Travers]** 20th c. [CC]
*Author*
* Travers, Hugh

**Mills, Jack**
See Mills, Abbott Paige

**Mills, Janet Melanie Ailsa** 1894-
[CA]
*British author*
* Challoner, H. K.

**Mills, Kerry**
See Mills, Frederick Allen

**Mills, Lefty**
See Mills, Howard Robertson

**Mills, Martin**
See Boyd, Martin

**Mills, Osmington**
See Brooks, Vivian Collin

**Mills, P'lla**
See Mills, Priscilla

**Mills, Priscilla** 1918-1964 [IBW]
*American painter and sculptor*
* Mills, P'lla

**Mills, Samuel John** 1783-1818
[FFF]
*American clergyman*
* [The] Father of Foreign Mission
  Work

**Mills, Terry Kenneth** 1949- [IAW]
*British author*
* Mill, Ian St. John

**Mills, Wee Willie**
See Mills, William Grant [Willie]

**Mills, William Grant [Willie]**
1877-1914 [BE]
*American baseball player*
* Mills, Wee Willie

**Mills, Yaroslava Surmach** 1925-
[ICB]
*American illustrator*
* Yaroslava

**Millsap, Marjorie** 1911- [F2]
*Actress*
* Lee, Dorothy

**Millsaps, Daniel W., III** 1919-
[IAW]
*American author*
* Nuki
* Web, Dan

**Millspaugh, Charles Frederick** 1854-
? [ALY]
*American botanist and author*
* Pesthe

**Millstein, Rose Silverman**
1903?-1975 [CA]
*Russian-born American author,
journalist, playwright*
* Silverman, Rose

**Miln, H. Crichton** ?-1957 [MBF]
*British author*
* Crichton, Jack
* Harper, Gillis

**Milnar, Albert Joseph** 1913- [BE]
*American baseball player*
* Milnar, Happy

**Milnar, Happy**
See Milnar, Albert Joseph

**Milne, A. A.**
See Milne, Alan Alexander

**Milne, Alan Alexander** 1882-1956
[LC, TC, WWL]
*British author and playwright*
* A. A. M.
* Milne, A. A.

**Milne, John Erskine** 1931- [ART]
*British sculptor*
* J. E. M.

**Milne, Pete**
See Milne, William James

**Milne, William James** 1925- [BE]
*American baseball player*
* Milne, Pete

**Milner, D. E.**
See Milner, Donald Ewart

**Milner, Donald Ewart** 1898- [ART]
*British artist*
* Milner, D. E.

**Milner, Florence Cushman** 20th c.
[NAA]
*American author and editor*
* Cushman, Evelyn

**Milner, George**
See Hardinge, George Edward
Charles

**Milner, Hammer**
See Milner, John David

**Milner, J.** 1744-1797 [PA]
*Author*
* J. M.

**Milner, John** 1752-1826 [WBD]
*British prelate*
* [The] English Athanasius

**Milner, John David** 1949- [BE]
*American baseball player*
* Milner, Hammer

**Milner, Marion [Blackett]** 1900-
[AW, CA, WD]
*British psychoanalyst and author*
* Field, Joanna

**Milner, Michael**
See Cooper, Saul

**Milnes, Richard Monckton [First
Baron Houghton]** 1809-1885 [DEL]
*British author and poet*
* [A] Layman

**Milnes, Thomas Wray** 1894-
[WWL]
*British author, poet, playwright*
* Jig-Saw

**[La] Milo**
See Montague, Pansy

**Milo** 6th c. BC [HN]
*Greek athlete*
* [The] Italian Samson

**Milo, George**
See Vescia, George Milo

**Miloradowitch, Michael**
1770-1820 [DNNF, FFF, RH]
*Russian army officer*
* [The] Murat of Russia
* [The] Russian Murat

**Milos, Milos**
See Milosevic, Milos

**Milosevic, Milos** 1941-1966 [SC]
*Yugoslav-born actor*
* Milos, Milos

**Milosevich, Michael [Mike]**
1915-1966 [BE]
*American baseball player*
* Milosevich, Mollie

**Milosevich, Mollie**
See Milosevich, Michael [Mike]

**Milosz, Czeslaw** 1911- [CA]
*Polish poet and author*
* Syruc, J.

**Milquetoast, Governor**
See Milliken, William Grawn

**Milsen, Oscar**
See Mendelsohn, Oscar [Adolf]

**Milsom, Charles Henry** 1926-
[WD]
*British author and journalist*
* Weston, William

**Milstead, Cowboy**
See Milstead, George Earl

**Milstead, George Earl** 1903- [BE]
*American baseball player*
* Milstead, Cowboy

**Miltenberg**
See Lafontaine, August Heinrich
Julius

**Miltiades** 6th c. BC [FFF, SN]
*Athenian general*
* [The] Tyrant of the Chersonese

**Milto** 5th c. BC [WBD]
*Greek beauty*
* Aspasia

**Milton, Byron** 1931-1973 [IBW]
*American racer*
* Milton, Doc

**Milton, Doc**
See Milton, Byron

**Milton, Ernest** 1905-    [NOJ]
*American jazz musician*
* Milton, Kid

**Milton, Georges**
See   Michaud, Georges

**Milton, Gladys Alexandra** 20th c.
[WW]
*Author*
* Carlyle, Anthony

**Milton, Hamilton Pirie Matt** 1938-
[SWI]
*British swimmer*
* Milton, Tony

**Milton, Jack**
See   Kimbro, John M.

**Milton, John** 1608-1674
[FFF, HN, PA]
*British poet*
* [The] Blind Tiresias of Modern
   Times
* [The] British Homer
* [The] Homer of Britain
* [The] Lady of Christ College
* Lycidas
* [The] Pedagogue
* [The] Prince of Poets
* [The] Trader in Faction

**Milton, John R.** 1924-    [IAW]
*American author*
* Garrard, Christopher
* Lewis, Carson

**Milton, Kid**
See   Milton, Ernest

**Milton, Mark**
See   Pelton, Robert W[ayne]

**Milton, Mark**
See   Shepherd, S. Rossiter

**[The] Milton of Germany**
See   Klopstock, Friedrich Gottlieb

**[The] Milton of Painting**
See   Fuseli, Johann Kaspar

**Milton, Oliver**
See   Hewitt, Cecil Rolph

**Milton, Robert**
See   Davidor, Robert

**Milton, Saul** 20th c.    [SFL]
*Author*
* Flinders, Karl

**Milton, Tommy** 20th c.
*Auto racer*
* [The] Great Milton

**Milton, Tony**
See   Milton, Hamilton Pirie Matt

**Milverton, Charles A.**
See   Penzler, Otto

**Milwaukee Phil Alderisio**
See   Alderisio, Felix Anthony

**Mimenza Castillo, Ricardo** 1888-
[NAA]
*Mexican poet, writer, publisher*
* Blas, Ruy

**Mimi**
See   Dancourt, Marie Anne Carton

**Mimnermus** 7th c. BC    [DNNS]
*Greek poet*
* [The] Smyrnean Poet

**Minacore, Calogero** 1910-
*American underworld figure*
* Little Big Man
* [The] Little Man
* Marcello, Carlos

**Minahan, Cotton**
See   Minahan, Edmund Joseph

**Minahan, Edmund Joseph**
1882-1958    [BE]
*American baseball player*
* Minahan, Cotton

**Minarcin, Buster**
See   Minarcin, Rudy Anthony

**Minarcin, Rudy Anthony** 1930-
[BE]
*American baseball player*
* Minarcin, Buster

**Minasi, Dom**
See   Minasi, Dominic

**Minasi, Dominic** 1943-    [EJ7]
*American jazz musician*
* Minasi, Dom

**Mince, Johnny**
See   Muenzenberger, John Henry

**Mincher, Don[ald Ray]** 1938-    [PB]
*American baseball player*
* Mincher, Mule

**Mincher, Mule**
See   Mincher, Don[ald Ray]

**Mincho** 1352-1431    [WBD]
*Japanese painter*
* Cho Densu

**Mincieli, Rose Laura** 1912-    [CA]
*American author, educator,
librarian*
* Ross, Laura

**Mincius, John** 11th c.    [WBD]
*Pope*
* Benedict X

**Mind, Gottfried [or Godefroi]**
1768-1814    [DNNS, FFF, RH]
*Swiss painter*
* [The] Bernese Friedli
* [The] Raphael of Cats

**[The] Mind of the School**
See   Aristotle

**Mindt, Heinz R.** 1940-    [IAW]
*German author*
* Paturi, Felix R.

**Mineo, Art**
See   Mineo, Attilio

**Mineo, Attilio** 1918-    [ASC]
*American musician*
* Mineo, Art

**Miner, Budd**
See   Miner, William

**Miner, California Billy**
See   Miner, William

**Miner, Charles** 1800-1865    [PA]
*Author*
* Harwood, John
* Poor Robert the Scribe

**Miner, Lefty**
See   Miner, Ray[mond Theadore]

**Miner, Matthew**
See   Wallmann, Jeffrey M[iner]

**Miner, Old Bill**
See   Miner, William

**Miner, Ray[mond Theadore]**
1897-1963    [BE]
*American baseball player*
* Miner, Lefty

**Miner, Virginia Scott** 1901-    [IA]
*American author*
* Hoosier Hank
* Hoosier Hannah
* Kay, Phoebe
* Kiplinger, David
* Thatcher, Amelia
* Wilcox, Hannah Simms

**Miner, William** 1847-1913    [BLB]
*American stage and train robber*
* Anderson, George
* Anderson, Sam
* Edwards, G. W.
* Miner, Budd
* Miner, California Billy
* Miner, Old Bill
* Morgan, William

**Minerva**
See   Montagu, Mary Wortley

**Minerve, Geezil**
See   Minerve, Harold

**Minerve, Harold** 1922-    [EJ7]
*American jazz musician*
* Minerve, Geezil

**Mines, John Flavel** 1835-1891
[FFF]
*American author*
* Oldboy, Felix

**Mines, Samuel** 1909-    [WD]
*American author and editor*
* Field, Peter

**Mingle, Belle** 1858-1900    [BEW]
*American actress*
* Archer, Belle

**Mingston, R. Gresham**
See   Stamp, Roger

**Mingus, Charles [Charlie]**
1923?-1979
*American jazz musician*
* Jazz's Angry Man

**Minh, Big**
See   Minh, Duong Van

**Minh, Duong Van** 1916-
*South Vietnamese military leader*
* Minh, Big

**Mini Tank Hughes**
See   Hughes, Leroy

**[The] Miniature King of Swing**
See   Short, Bobby

**Minier, Nelson** [joint pseudonym
with Adrien (Pearl) Stoutenburg]
See   Baker, Laura Nelson

**Minier, Nelson** [joint pseudonym
with Laura Nelson Baker]
See   Stoutenburg, Adrien [Pearl]

**Miniggio, Riccardo** 20th c.    [WF]
*Italian actor*
* Ric

**Minimus, Lord**
See   Hudson, Jeffrey

**[La] Ministerie**
See   Babinot, Albert

**Minkovitz, Moshe** 1936-    [CA]
*Israeli anthropologist and author*
* Shokeid, Moshe

**Minnaar-Vos, Anna**
See   Vos, Anna Beyera

**[The] Minneapolis Tomboy**
See   Berg, Patricia J. [Patty]

**Minner, Lefty**
See   Minner, Paul Edison

**Minner, Paul Edison** 1923-    [BE]
*American baseball player*
* Minner, Lefty

**Minnesota Fats**
See   Wanderone, Rudolf, Jr.

**Minogue, Dennis** 20th c.
*American singer, songwriter,
baseball player*
* Cashman, Terry

**Minor, Dan** 20th c.    [NP]
*American jazz musician*
* Big D

**Minor, Fred** 1913-    [NOJ]
*American jazz musician*
* Minor, H. E.

**Minor, H. E.**
See   Minor, Fred

**Minoso, Minnie**
See   Minoso, Saturnino Orestes
Arrieta Armas

**Minoso, Saturnino Orestes Arrieta
Armas** 1922-    [BE, IBW]
*Cuban-born baseball player*
* [The] Cuban Comet
* Minoso, Minnie

**Minot, Laurence** 1300?-1352    [HN]
*British poet*
* [The] English Tyrtaeos

**Minski, Nikolai Maksimovich**
See   Vilenkin, Nikolai Maksimovich

**Minsky, Betty Jane [Toebe]** 1932-
[CA]
*American author*
* Toby, Liz

**Minson, Roland** 20th c.    [MEB]
*American basketball player*
* [The] Cat

**[The] Minstrel of the Border**
See   Scott, [Sir] Walter

**Mintell, Frank Otto** 1886-1951
[BX, RBE]
*German-born boxer*
* Mantell, Frank

**Minter, Davide C.** 1892-    [WWL]
*British author and editor*
* Caroline

**Minter, Iverson** 1936-    [BWW, EJ7]
*American singer*
* Bey, Iverson
* Cryin' Red
* Fuller, Playboy
* Fuller, Richard Lee
* Fuller, Rocky
* Guitar Red
* James, Elmore, Jr.
* Louisiana Red
* Minter, Red
* Rockin' Red
* Walkin' Slim

**Minter, Mary Miles**
See Shelby, Juliet

**Minter, Red**
See Minter, Iverson

**Minto-Cowen, Frances**
See Munthe, Frances

**Mintwood**
See Wager, Mary A. E.

**Mintz, David** 1927-  [FC, TR]
*American actor*
* Knight, David

**Mintz, Joan** 1920-  [BEW]
*American publisher and writer*
* Marlowe, Joan

**Mintz, Joyce Lois** 1933-  [CA]
*American author and editor*
* Madison, Joyce

**Minus**
See Engh, Bjorg Larsen

**[A] Minute Philosopher**
See Kingsley, Charles

**Minuto [Minute]**
See Vargas y Gonzalez, Enrique

**Minzesheimer, Blanche** 1891-1963
[BEW]
*American theatrical performer*
* Blanche, Belle

**Miomandre, Francis de**
See Durand, Francois

**Mione, Peter** 20th c.  [BLB]
*American underworld figure*
* Muggins, Petey

**Mira**
See Brunet, Jean Joseph

**Mirabeau, Barrel**
See Riquetti, [Andre] Boniface
[Louis]

**Mirabeau, Comte de**
See Riquetti, Honore Gabriel
Victor

**Mirabeau, Marquis de**
See Riquetti, Victor

**[The] Mirabeau of the Gironde**
See Vergniaud, Pierre Victurnien

**[The] Mirabeau of the Markets**
See Danton, Georges Jacques

**[The] Mirabeau of the Mob**
See Danton, Georges Jacques

**[The] Mirabeau of the Sans Culottes**
See Danton, Georges Jacques

**Mirabeau Tonneau**
See Riquetti, [Andre] Boniface
[Louis]

**Mirabeau, Tub**
See Riquetti, Honore Gabriel
Victor

**Mirabeau, Vicomte de**
See Riquetti, [Andre] Boniface
[Louis]

**Mirabella, Gesualdo** 1915-  [OP]
*Italian producer, singer, actor*
* Vassallo, Aldo Mirabella

**Mirabilia**
See Maraviglia, Guiseppe Maria

**Mirabilis, Doctor**
See Bacon, Roger

**[The] Miracle Man**
See Brown, Jerald Ray

**[The] Miracle Man**
See Stallings, George Tweedy

**[The] Miracle Man of the Rockies**
See Albeck, Stan

**[The] Miracle of Nature**
See Christina

**[The] Miracle of Our Age**
See Sidney, [Sir] Philip

**[The] Miracle of the Age**
See Bacon, Roger

**[The] Miraculous Child**
See D'Artois, Henri Charles
Ferdinand Marie

**Miraglia, Emilio** 20th c.  [WF]
*Italian director*
* Brady, Hal

**Miramant, Yves**
See Romanette, Irmine

**Mirambo** ?-1885  [FFF]
*East African chieftain*
* [The] Napoleon of Africa

**Mirana, Paul** 20th c.  [SG]
*Boxer*
* Moran, Pal

**Miranda, Carmen**
See Da Cunha, Maria Do Carmo

**Miranda, Guillermo Perez** 1926-
[BE]
*Cuban-born baseball player*
* Miranda, Willie

**Miranda, Isa**
See Sampietro, Ines Isabella

**Miranda, Javier**
See Bioy-Casares, Adolfo

**Miranda, Maria**
See Krenz-Senior, Ethel Rosabelle

**Miranda, Willie**
See Miranda, Guillermo Perez

**Miranda da Silva Filho, Sebastio**
1952-  [AES]
*Brazilian soccer player*
* Mirandinha

**Mirande, Yves**
See Le Querrec, A. Charles

**Mirandinha**
See Miranda da Silva Filho,
Sebastio

**[The] Mirandola of His Age**
See Digby, [Sir] Kenelm

**Mircea** ?-1418  [WBD]
*Prince of Walachia*
* [The] Great

**Mirecourt, Eugene de**
See Jacquot, Charles Jean Baptiste

**Mirglip, Knarf**
See Pilgrim, Frank

**Miriam**
See Heath, Maggie E.

**Miriam**
See Przesmycki, Zenon

**Miriam of the Holy Spirit, [Sister]**
See Powers, Jessica

**Miroeus**
See Lemire, Aubert

**Miron**
See Hazeltine, Miron J.

**Miroslava**
See Stern, Miroslava

**[The] Mirror of all Martial Men**
See Montacute [or Montagu],
Thomas de

**[The] Mirror of Courtesy**
See Sidney, [Sir] Philip

**[The] Mirror of Justice**
See Victoria

**Mirus, Ludmilla** 1905-  [IAW]
*Austrian-born author*
* Egger, Ellen
* Mirus-Kauba, Ludmilla

**Mirus-Kauba, Ludmilla**
See Mirus, Ludmilla

**Mirza Muhammad Ali** 1676-1756
[WBD]
*Nawab of Bengal*
* Ali Vardi Khan
* Allahvardi Khan

**Mirza, Nusrat Ali** 1882- ?  [WWL]
*Welsh author*
* Marc, Elizabeth

**Mischievous Andy**
See Jackson, Andrew

**Miserocchi, Anna** 20th c.  [WF]
*Italian actress*
* Wart, Helen

**Mises, Dr.**
See Fechner, Gustav Theodor

**Mishima, Yukio**
See Hiraoka, Kimitake

**Mishra, Vidhata** 1934-  [IAW]
*Indian author*
* Shrividhata

**Miske, Billy**
See Miskel, William

**Miskel, William** 20th c.  [SG]
*Boxer*
* Miske, Billy

**Miss Bess**
See Farmer, Bess

**Miss Frances**
See Horwich, Frances R[appaport]

**Miss Juliet**
See Delf, Juliet

**Miss Lillian**
See Carter, Lillian [Gordy]

**Miss Lou**
See Bennett, Louise Simone

**Miss Mit**
See Talmadge, Mattie

**Miss Nancy**
See Oldfield, Anna

**Miss Vicky**
See Khaury, Mrs. Herbert
Buckingham

**Miss X**
See Goodrich-Freer, Adela M.

**Miss Z**
See Cusseaux, Zulema

**Mississippi Big Joe**
See Williams, Joe

**Mississippi Fred McDowell**
See McDowell, Frederick

**Mississippi Joe Callicott**
See Callicott, Joe

**Mississippi John Jackson**
See Jackson, John H.

**Mississippi Matilda**
See Witherspoon, Matilda

**[The] Mississippi Mockingbird**
See Harris, Wynonie

**[The] Mississippi Mudcat**
See Bush, Guy Terrell

**Mississippi Mudder**
See McCoy, Charles [Charlie]

**Mississippi Mudder**
See McCoy, Joe

**Missoni, Ottavio**
*Italian fashion designer*
* Missoni, Tai

**Missoni, Tai**
See Missoni, Ottavio

**Mr. A.**
See Rothstein, Arnold

**Mr. B**
See Balanchivadze, Gyorgi
Melitonovitch

**Mr. B**
See Eckstein, William Clarence

**Mr. Bo**
See Collins, Louis Bo

**Mr. Buddy**
See Durham, Edward Lee

**Mr. C**
See Chambers, Wallace

**Mr. Cliff**
See Roberts, Clifford

**Mr. Eli**
See Robinson, Eli

**Mr. Joe**
See Wright, Joseph, Sr.

**Mr. Joe**
See Zerilli, Joseph

**Mr. Kenneth**
See Marlowe, Kenneth

**Mr. P.**
See Prysock, Arthur

**Mr. Rick**
See Randall, Richard

**Mr. T.**
See Tero, Lawrence

**Mr. X**
See Barber, Miller

**Mr. X**
See Hoch, Edward D.

**Mr. X**
See Rescigno, Xavier Frederick

**Mistinguett**
See Bourgeois, Jeanne Marie

**[The] Mistletoe Politician**
See   Van Buren, Martin

**Mistral, Gabriela**
See   Godoy Alcayaga, Lucila

**Mistral, George**
See   Mistral, Jorge

**Mistral, Jorge** 1923-1972   [SC]
*Actor*
* Mistral, George

**Mitcham, Gilroy**
See   Newton, William Simpson

**Mitchel, Jackson**
See   Matcha, Jack

**Mitchel, Ormsby McKnight**
1810-1862   [DNNF, DNNS, SN]
*American army officer and astronomer*
* Old Stars

**Mitchell, Adam**
See   Pyle, Hilary

**Mitchell, Adrian** 1932-   [CA, IAW]
*British author, poet, playwright*
* Hewitt, Ben
* Jones, Volcano
* Mudgeon, Apeman
* Treacle, Uncle

**Mitchell, Arthur Adam** 1934-
[IBW]
*American choreographer*
* Poet in Motion

**Mitchell, Billy** 1917?-1978   [FIR]
*Entertainer*
* Postime, Mr.

**Mitchell, Blue**
See   Mitchell, Richard Allen

**Mitchell, Bunny**
See   Mitchell, Martha

**Mitchell, Cameron**
See   Mitzell, Cameron M.

**Mitchell, Carolyn**
See   Thomason, Barbara Ann

**Mitchell, Charles** 20th c.
*American banker*
* Mitchell, Sunshine Charlie

**Mitchell, Charles J.**
See   O'Dea, Patrick J.

**Mitchell, Charlotte Grimes** 1872- ?
[NAA]
*American author*
* Twain, Minerva Mark

**Mitchell, Clarence M., III** 1940-
[IBW]
*American politician*
* [The] Lone Wolf Politician

**Mitchell, Clarence M., Jr.** 1911-
[IBW]
*American attorney, congressional lobbyist, former boxer*
* [The] 101st Senator
* [The] Shamrock Kid

**Mitchell, Clyde** [house pseudonym, Ziff-Davis]
See   Ellison, Harlan [Jay]

**Mitchell, Clyde** [joint pseudonym with Robert Silverberg] [house pseudonym, Ziff-Davis]
See   Garrett, [Gordon] Randall [Philip David]

**Mitchell, Clyde** [joint pseudonym with Randall Garrett] [house pseudonym, Ziff-Davis]
See   Silverberg, Robert

**Mitchell, Dolly**
See   Melton, Mrs. William

**Mitchell, Donald Grant** 1822- ?
[DEL, FFF, PA]
*American author*
* Caius
* Marvel, Ik
* [An] Opera Goer
* Timon, John

**Mitchell, Doris** 20th c.   [NBB]
*American musician*
* Lightnin'

**Mitchell, Elizabeth Harcourt**   [PA]
*Author*
* E. H. R.

**Mitchell, Ewan**
See   Janner, Greville Ewan

**Mitchell, Frederick Francis**
See   Yapp, Frederick Francis

**Mitchell, G.**   [PA]
*Author*
* One from the Plow

**Mitchell, Gene**
See   Hoadley, H. O[rlo]

**Mitchell, George** 1899-   [MY]
*American jazz musician*
* Mitchell, Mitch

**Mitchell, Ginger**
See   Mitchell, Rhea

**Mitchell, Gladys [Maude Winifred]**
1901-   [CA, CC, EMD]
*British author*
* Hockaby, Stephen
* Torrie, Malcolm

**Mitchell, Gordon B.** 1932-
[DAM, EJ]
*American jazz musician*
* Mitchell, Whitey

**Mitchell, Guy**
See   Cernick, Al

**Mitchell, Helen**
See   McRuer, Helen

**Mitchell, Helen Porter** 1861-1931
[BBD, IPA, LC]
*Australian opera singer*
* Melba, Nellie

**Mitchell, Isabel Mary** 1893-   [AW]
*Australian author*
* Plain, Josephine

**Mitchell, Jack**
See   Sellers, Connie Leslie, Jr.

**Mitchell, James** 1926-   [AW, CA]
*British author*
* Munro, James

**Mitchell, James Leslie** 1901-1935
[LC, TC, TC1]
*Scottish author, archaeologist, historian*
* Gibbon, Lewis Grassic

**Mitchell, John**
See   Lamy, Douglas N.

**Mitchell, John** 1794-1870   [PA]
*Author*
* Chester, John

**Mitchell, John** 1946-   [RO2]
*British musician*
* Mitchell, Mitch

**Mitchell, John Hanlon** 1897-
[NAA]
*Canadian author*
* Hanlon, John

**Mitchell, John Kearsley** 1798-1858
[FFF]
*American physician and poet*
* [A] Yankee

**Mitchell, Joni**
See   Anderson, Roberta Joan

**Mitchell, K. L.**
See   Lamb, Elizabeth Searle

**Mitchell, Keith Moore** 1927-
[DAM, EJ, PMJ]
*American jazz musician*
* Mitchell, Red

**Mitchell, Kerry**
See   Wilkes-Hunter, Richard

**Mitchell, Langdon [Elwin]** 1862- ?
[NAA]
*American playwright*
* Varley, John Philip

**Mitchell, Lottie Pearl** ?-1974
[IBW]
*American civil rights leader*
* AKA, Miss
* Lady Pearl
* NAACP, Miss

**Mitchell, Maggie**
See   Paddock, Mrs.

**Mitchell, Margaret**
See   Marsh, Margaret Munnerlyn Mitchell

**Mitchell, Martha** 1941-
*Administrative aide to American president Jimmy Carter*
* Mitchell, Bunny

**[The] Mitchell Meteor**
See   Morenz, Howarth William

**Mitchell, Mitch**
See   Mitchell, George

**Mitchell, Mitch**
See   Mitchell, John

**Mitchell, Myron** 1899-   [BX, RBE]
*American boxer*
* Mitchell, Pinkey

**Mitchell, Oliver** 1876-1945   [BEW]
*American producer, director, author*
* Morosco, Oliver

**Mitchell, P. J.**
See   Mitchell, Parren James

**Mitchell, Paige**
See   Ginnes, Judith S.

**Mitchell, Parren James** 1938-
[IBW]
*American politician*
* Mitchell, P. J.

**Mitchell, Pinkey**
See   Mitchell, Myron

**Mitchell, Priscilla** 1941-   [FCW]
*American singer*
* Sadina

**Mitchell, R. C.**   [FFF, PA]
*British writer*
* Creighton, Rob

**Mitchell, R. C.** (Continued)
* Vigilant

**Mitchell, R. J.**
See   Mitchell, Robert James

**Mitchell, Red**
See   Mitchell, Keith Moore

**Mitchell, Red**
See   Mitchell, William Dickie

**Mitchell, Rhea** 1905-1957   [SC]
*American actress*
* Mitchell, Ginger

**Mitchell, Richard Allen** 1930-1979
[DAM, EJ]
*American jazz musician*
* Mitchell, Blue

**Mitchell, Robert** 19th c.   [PA]
*Author*
* Bomeair, D. H.

**Mitchell, Robert James** 1930-
[ART]
*British sculptor*
* Mitchell, R. J.

**Mitchell, Roscoe** 20th c.   [IBW]
*American actor and comedian*
* Mitchell, Scoey

**Mitchell, Ruth**
See   Kornfeld, Ruth

**Mitchell, S. Valentine**
See   Gammell, Susanna Valentine Mitchell

**Mitchell, Scoey**
See   Mitchell, Roscoe

**Mitchell, Scott**
See   Godfrey, Lionel Robert Holcombe

**Mitchell, Stanley**
See   Albertini, Adalberto

**Mitchell, Sunshine Charlie**
See   Mitchell, Charles

**Mitchell, Ugo** 1883-   [BX]
*Italian-born boxer*
* Kelly, Hugo

**Mitchell, Whitey**
See   Mitchell, Gordon B.

**Mitchell, William** 18th c.
[DNNF, RH, SN]
*Scottish tin-plate worker and author*
* [The] Great Tinclarian Doctor

**Mitchell, William [Bill]** 1853-1928
[B10, BLB]
*American murderer*
* Russell, Baldy

**Mitchell, William** 1916-1977
[BDF, FC, WEF]
*British actor*
* Finch, Peter
* Finchy

**Mitchell, William Dickie** 1930-
[CEI]
*Canadian-born hockey player*
* Mitchell, Red

**Mitchell, Young**
See   Herget, John L.

**Mitchell, Yvonne**
See   Joseph, Yvonne

Mitchell-Cotts, [Sir] William
Campbell 1903?-1964 [BEW]
*Actor*
* Cotts, Campbell

Mitchelson, Marvin 1929?-
*American attorney*
* [The] Paladin of Paramours

[The] Mite Manager
*See* Huggins, Miller James

Mitelberg, Louis 1919- [WEC]
*French cartoonist*
* Tim

Mitford, John [FFF]
*Author*
* Burton, Alfred

Mitford, Nancy 1904-1973 [CA]
*British author*
* Rodd, Nancy Freeman-Mitford

Mithridates I 2nd c. BC [WBD]
*King of Parthia*
* Arsaces VI

Mithridates II 2nd c. BC [WBD]
*King of Parthia*
* [The] Great

Mithridates VI Eupator 1st c. BC
[WBD]
*King of Parthia*
* [The] Great

[El] Mito [The Myth]
*See* Rodriguez, Carlos

Mitra, Sarada Prasanna
1865-1915 [NAD]
*Spiritual teacher*
* Trigunatita, [Swami]

[The] Mitre Courtier
*See* Lamb, Charles

[The] Mitred Ass
*See* Potier, Augustin

Mitred Dulness
*See* Parker, Samuel

Mitru, Alexandru 1914- [IAW]
*Rumanian author*
* Piraianu, Alexandru

Mitry, Jean
*See* Goetgheluck Le Rouge
Taillard Des Acres De Presfontaines,
Jean Rene

Mitscher, Marc Andrew 1887-
[BDW]
*American naval officer*
* Mitscher, Mich

Mitscher, Mich
*See* Mitscher, Marc Andrew

Mitskevich, A. P. 20th c. [SFP]
*Author*
* Dneprov, Anatoly

Mitsuyori, Kimura 1559-1635
[WBD]
*Japanese painter*
* Sanraku, Kano

Mittarilli, Nicolo Gracome
1707-1777 [PA]
*Author*
* Benedetto, Giovanni

Mittelholzer, Edgar 1909-1965
[CW]
*Guyanese-born author, playwright,
poet*
* Woodsley, H. Austin

Mitterling, Ralph 1890-1956 [BE]
*American baseball player*
* Mitterling, Sarge

Mitterling, Sarge
*See* Mitterling, Ralph

Mitterrand, Francois Maurice Adrien
Marie 1916-
*French president*
* Morland

Mitton, G. E.
*See* Scott, Geraldine Edith

Mitzell, Cameron M. 1918-
[BEW, ITA]
*American actor*
* Mitchell, Cameron

Mitzou
*See* Izquierdo, Mitzou

Mix, Katherine Lyon [CA]
*American author*
* Lyon, Katherine

Mix-Up, Professor
*See* Fox, Karrell

Mixter, Elisabeth W.
*See* Morss, Elizabeth W.

Miyazaki, Toshio 20th c. [EE]
*Japanese intelligence agent*
* Tanni

Mize, John Robert 1913-
[BE, BN, PB]
*American baseball player*
* [The] Big Cat
* Mize, Skippy

Mize, Skippy
*See* Mize, John Robert

Mizell, Vinegar Bend
*See* Mizell, Wilmer David

Mizell, Wilmer David 1930-
[BE, PB]
*American baseball player*
* Mizell, Vinegar Bend

Mizerak, Miz
*See* Mizerak, Steve

Mizerak, Steve 20th c.
*American billiard player*
* Mizerak, Miz

Mizner, Elizabeth Howard 1907-
[CA]
*American author*
* Howard, Elizabeth

Mlad-Miltijad
*See* Djuricic, Uladen St.

Mlckovsky, Raymond James
1916-1969 [BE]
*American baseball player*
* Mack, Ray

Mmcoatman
*See* Coatman, Maureen Margaret

Mnemon
*See* Artaxerxes II

Mo, Billy
*See* Joachim, Peter Mico

Moanin' Matty Bell
*See* Bell, Madison

[The] Mobile Magician
*See* Cousy, Robert J. [Bob]

Mobutu, Joseph Desire 1930-
[B10, IBW]
*President of Zaire*
* [Le] Guide
* Mobutu, Sese Seko

Mobutu, Sese Seko
*See* Mobutu, Joseph Desire

Mocatta, Dorothy Allen 1900-
[WWL]
*British author*
* Mocatta, Frances

Mocatta, Frances
*See* Mocatta, Dorothy Allen

Mocky, Jean-Pierre
*See* Mokiejeswki, Jean

Moco [joint pseudonym with Jorgen
Morgenson]
*See* Cornelius, Cosper

Moco [joint pseudonym with Cosper
Cornelius]
*See* Morgenson, Jorgen

Modak, Manorama Ramkrishna
*See* Grove, Marguerite

[Il] Modanino
*See* Mazzoni, Guido

Model T Slim
*See* Mickle, Elmon

Model, Walther 1891-1945 [BDW]
*German army officer*
* [The] Lion of Defence

Modell, Merriam 1908- [WW]
*Author*
* Piper, Evelyn

Modena, Maria
*See* Kreis, Erna

Modenos, John Philip
*See* Modinos, Ioannis Philip

Moderator?
*See* Francis, [Sir] Philip

[The] Modern Admirable Crichton
*See* Burton, Richard

[The] Modern Antigone
*See* Bourbon, Marie Therese
Charlotte de

[The] Modern Aristophanes
*See* Foote, Samuel

[The] Modern Burns
*See* Grieve, Christopher Murray

[The] Modern Charlemagne
*See* Bonaparte, Napoleon

[The] Modern Congreve
*See* Sheridan, Richard Brinsley

[The] Modern Croesus
*See* Morrison, James

[The] Modern Galen
*See* Fernel, Jean

[The] Modern Gracchus
*See* Riquetti, Honore Gabriel
Victor

[The] Modern Greek
*See* Mudie, Robert

[The] Modern Hippolyta
*See* Maria Theresa

[The] Modern Hogarth
*See* Cruikshank, George

[The] Modern Jugurtha
*See* Abd-el-Kader

[The] Modern K. O. King
*See* Chaney, George

[The] Modern Messalina
*See* Catherine II

[The] Modern Miracle Worker
*See* Bodie, Sam

[The] Modern Newton
*See* Laplace, Pierre Simon de

[The] Modern Nimrod
*See* Bonaparte, Napoleon

[The] Modern Pilate
*See* Philip IV [or Philippe]

[The] Modern Pliny
*See* Gesner, Konrad von

[The] Modern Plutarch
*See* La Mothe Le Vayer, Francois
de

Modern Pythagorean
*See* Macnish, Robert

[The] Modern Quintus Curtius
*See* Aubert, Rene

[The] Modern Rabelais
*See* Maginn, William

[The] Modern Roscius
*See* Betty, William Henry West

[The] Modern Sage
*See* K'ang Yu-wei

[The] Modern Sesostris
*See* Bonaparte, Napoleon

[The] Modern Wagner
*See* Humperdink, Engelbert

[The] Modernist Maestro
*See* Levy, Julien

Moderwell, Hiram K. 1888-
[WWL]
*American author*
* Motherwell, Hiram

Modesto
*See* Ruiz, Henry

Modestus
*See* Draper, [Sir] William

Modini, Robert 1919- [FC]
*American actor*
* Stack, Robert

Modinos, Ioannis Philip 1930-
[OP]
*American opera singer*
* Modenos, John Philip

Modjeska [or Modrzejewska], Helena
*See* Opido, Helena

Modjeski, Ralph
*See* Modrzejewski, Ralph

Modoc
*See* Doyle, Jefferson E. P.

Modrzejewski, Ralph 1861-1940
[WBD]
*Polish-born engineer*
* Modjeski, Ralph

Modzelewski, Big Mo
*See* Modzelewski, Ed

**Modzelewski, Ed** 20th c. [BBH]
*American football player*
* Modzelewski, Big Mo

**Modzelewski, Little Mo**
See Modzelewski, Richard [Dick]

**Modzelewski, Mo**
See Modzelewski, Richard [Dick]

**Modzelewski, Richard [Dick]**
1931- [FB, SMG]
*American football player and coach*
* Modzelewski, Little Mo
* Modzelewski, Mo

**Modzelewski, Stan** 20th c. [MEB]
*American basketball player*
* Modzelewski, Stutz

**Modzelewski, Stutz**
See Modzelewski, Stan

**Moe, Angelo**
See Moe, Chris

**Moe, Chris** 1949- [RO2]
*American musician*
* Moe, Angelo

**Moebius**
See Giraud, Jean

**Moeckl, Christiane** 1947- [OP]
*German opera singer*
* Zinkler, Christiane

**Moeller, Joseph Douglas** 1943-
[SMG]
*American baseball player*
* Moeller, Skeeter

**Moeller, Lucky**
See Moeller, W. E.

**Moeller, Ron[ald Ralph]** 1938-
[BE]
*American baseball player*
* [The] Kid

**Moeller, Skeeter**
See Moeller, Joseph Douglas

**Moeller, Sweat**
See Moeller, Thomas

**Moeller, Thomas** 20th c. [RO2]
*British musician*
* Moeller, Sweat

**Moeller, W. E.** 1912- [FCW]
*American music executive*
* Moeller, Lucky

**Moendved [or Menved]**
See Eric VI [or VIII]

**Moer, Paul**
See Moerschbacher, Paul E.

**Moers, Ellen** 1928-1979 [CA]
*American educator, critic, author*
* Mayer, Ellen Moers

**Moerschbacher, Paul E.** 1916- [EJ]
*American jazz musician*
* Moer, Paul

**Moeser, Justus** 1720-1794 [SN]
*German author, historian, jurist*
* [The] Franklin of Germany

**Moffa, Paolo** 20th c. [WF]
*Italian director*
* Byrd, John

**Moffat, Margaret**
See Bury, Margaret

**Moffatt, James**
See Hughes, Robert J.

**Moffett, Anthony J.** 1945?- [CBS]
*American politician*
* Moffett, Toby

**Moffett, Toby**
See Moffett, Anthony J.

**Moffitt, De Loyce** 1906- [ASC]
*American composer, conductor,
arranger*
* Moffitt, Deke

**Moffitt, Deke**
See Moffitt, De Loyce

**Mofussillite**
See Lang, Thomas

**Moggridge, Helen** 20th c. [ART]
*British artist*
* H. M. M.

**Mogridge, George** 1802-1854
[DEL, DNNF, FFF]
*British author*
* Holding, Ephraim
* Jaunt, Jeremy
* Old Humphrey
* Parley, Peter

**Mogridge, Stephen** 1915- [AW]
*British author and journalist*
* Stevens, Jill

**Moguy, Leonide**
See Maguilevsky, Leonide

**Mohammed [or Mahomet]** 570-
632 [DEP, FF, FFF]
*Religious teacher and founder of
Mohammedanism*
* [The] Apostle of the Sword
* [The] Camel Driver of Mecca
* [The] Father of Believers
* [The] Prophet
* Thaumaturgus

**Mohammed** 1029-1072 [WBD]
*Sultan of the Seljuk Turks*
* Alp Arslan [Courageous Lion]

**Mohammed** 20th c.
*Saudi Arabian prince*
* Abu Sharein [Father of the
Double Evil]

**Mohammed Ahmed** 1843?-1885
[DNNS, WBD]
*Moslem agitator*
* [The] False Prophet
* [The] Mahdi

**Mohammed, Elijah**
See Bogan, Gulam

**Mohammed ibn-Abdullah** ?-1920
[WBD]
*Somali religious leader*
* [The] Mad Mullah

**Mohammed ibn-Ibrahim**
1119-1229? [WBD]
*Persian poet*
* Attar [Druggist]
* Farid ud-din Attar

**Mohammed Nadir Khan**
1880-1933 [WBD]
*King of Afghanistan*
* Nadir Shah

**Mohammed of Ghor**
See Muizz-ad-din

**Mohammed II [or Mahomet]**
1430-1481 [DEP, FFF]
*Sultan of Turkey*
* [The] Conqueror
* [The] Father of Good Works

**Mohammed II [or Mahomet]**
(Continued)
* [The] Great

**Mohammed X** 1445?-1500?
[WBD]
*King of Granada*
* [The] Brave

**Mohammed XI**
See Abu Abdallah [or Abdullah]

**Mohan, P. Nath**
See Shastri, Prithvinath

**Mohan, Rajneesh Chandra** 1932?-
*Indian spiritual teacher*
* Bhagwan Shree Rajneesh [Good
Sir Rajneesh]

**Moharaj, Soncu** 1931- [IAW]
*Indian author*
* Jyotirmoy, Ghosh Dastider

**Mohawk**
See Rowe, Nicholas

**Mohican**
See Fisher, Joseph E.

**Mohieddin, Khaled** 20th c.
*Egyptian politician*
* [The] Red Major

**Mohler, Ernest Follette** 1874-1961
[BE]
*American baseball player*
* Mohler, Kid

**Mohler, Kid**
See Mohler, Ernest Follette

**Mohlmann, [Father] Michael**
1920?- [CW]
*Curacaon author and poet*
* Van Nuland, Wim

**Mohns, Diesel**
See Mohns, Douglas Allen

**Mohns, Douglas Allen** 1933- [FHE]
*Canadian-born hockey player*
* Mohns, Diesel

**Mohr, Clare Eloise** 1901-1959
[SC]
*American actress*
* Del Mar, Claire

**Mohr, Frederick**
See Leidhof, Charles

**Mohr, Gordon** 1916- [CA]
*American army officer and writer*
* Mohr, Jack

**Mohr, Jack**
See Mohr, Gordon

**Moiloa, James Jantjies** 1916-
[IAW]
*South African author and poet*
* Ntate, J. J.

**Moina**
See Dinnies, Anna Peyre

**Moina**
See Ryan, Abram Joseph

**Moinaux, Georges-Victor Marcel**
1860-1929 [CD, EWL, WBD]
*French author, playwright, poet*
* Courteline, Georges
* [The] Mark Twain of France

**Moir, David Macbeth** 1798-1851
[DEL, RH]
*British author and poet*
* Delta

**Moir, David Macbeth** (Continued)
* Wauch, Mansie

**Moise, Isaac** 1796-1880 [WBD]
*French attorney and politician*
* Cremieux, Adolphe

**Mojica, Jose** 1896-1974 [CA]
*Mexican-born Peruvian monk,
author, actor*
* Jose De Guadaloupe, [Brother]

**Mojo**
See Buford, George

**Mokanna, al-**
See Hakim ben Allah

**Mokanna the Veiled**
See Hakim ben Allah

**Mokiejeswki, Jean** 1929-
[FC, WEF]
*French director and actor*
* Mocky, Jean-Pierre

**Moko**
See Mead, Sidney Moko

**Mola di Roma**
See Mola, Pierfrancesco

**Mola, Pierfrancesco** 1612-1666
[WBD]
*Italian painter*
* Mola di Roma

**[The] Mole**
See Ray, James Earl

**Mole, Fenton LeRoy** 1925- [BE]
*American baseball player*
* Mole, Muscles

**Mole, Irving Milfred** 1898-1961
[DAM, EJ, PMJ]
*American jazz musician*
* Mole, Miff

**Mole, Mathieu** 1584-1656 [DNNS]
*French jurist and politician*
* [The] Pym of France

**Mole, Miff**
See Mole, Irving Milfred

**Mole, Muscles**
See Mole, Fenton LeRoy

**Mole, William**
See Younger, William Anthony

**Moleri**
See Demoliere, M. Hippolyte Jules

**Molesworth, Keith F.** 1906-1966
[AS]
*American football player*
* Molesworth, Rabbit

**Molesworth, Mary Louisa Stewart**
1839-1921 [LC]
*Dutch-born author*
* Graham, Ennis

**Molesworth, Rabbit**
See Molesworth, Keith F.

**Moliere**
See Poquelin, Jean Baptiste

**Moliere, Ernest** 1902?- [NOJ]
*American jazz musician*
* Moliere, Kid

**Moliere, Frank** 1914- [NOJ]
*American jazz musician*
* Moliere, Li'l Papa

**Moliere, Kid**
See Moliere, Ernest

**Moliere, Li'l Papa**
See Moliere, Frank

**[The] Moliere of Italy**
See Goldoni, Carlo

**[The] Moliere of Music**
See Gretry, Andre Ernest Modeste

**[The] Moliere of Spain**
See Moratin, Leandro Fernandez

**Molin, Charles**
See Mayne, William [James Carter]

**Molina, Manuel** ?-1927 [GS]
*Spanish bullfighter*
* Algabeno-Chico [Little One from Algaba]

**Molina y Martinez, Rafael** 1880-1910 [GS]
*Spanish bullfighter*
* Lagartijo [Lizard]
* Lagartijo Chico [Little Lizard]

**Molina y Sanchez, Rafael** 1841-1900 [GS]
*Spanish bullfighter*
* Lagartijo [Lizard]

**Molinar, Demostines** 1933- [IBW]
*Panamanian-born scuba diver*
* Jones, Davy
* Molinar, Mo

**Molinar, Mo**
See Molinar, Demostines

**Molineaux, the Morocco Prince**
See Wharton, Jim

**Molinos, Miguel de** 1640-1697? [SN]
*Spanish clergyman*
* [The] Quietist

**Mollegen, Anne Rush**
See Smith, Anne Mollegen

**Mollwitz, Frederick August** 1890-1967 [BE]
*German-born baseball player*
* Mollwitz, Fritz
* Mollwitz, Zip

**Mollwitz, Fritz**
See Mollwitz, Frederick August

**Mollwitz, Zip**
See Mollwitz, Frederick August

**Molnar, Ferenc**
See Neumann, Ferenc

**Molody, Konon Trofimovich** 20th c. [EE]
*Intelligence agent for Russia*
* Lonsdale, Gordon Arnold

**Molon**
See Apollonius

**Molotov, Vyacheslav Mikhailovich**
See Skryabin, Vyacheslav Mikhailovich

**Moltke, Hellmuth Karl Bernhard von** 1800-1891 [DNNS, FFF, SN]
*Prussian army officer*
* Hellmuth the Taciturn
* [Der] Schweigsame
* [The] Silent One

**Moltzer, Jacob** 1503-1558 [PA]
*Author*
* Micyllus

**Molyneaux, John William Henry** [PA]
*Author*
* J. W. H. M.

**Molyneux**
See Molyneux, Edward

**Molyneux, Edward** 1891-1974 [WFA]
*British fashion designer*
* Molyneux

**Mombrizio, Bonino** 1424-1484 [PA]
*Author*
* Momritius

**Momi, Winifred Lei** 1899- [AM]
*American singer and actress*
* Shaw, Winnie

**Momo**
See Mercado, Jose Ramon

**[El] Momo**
See Soto, Gabriel

**Momritius**
See Mombrizio, Bonino

**Moms Musings**
See Mahaffy-Wilson, Mary Ruth

**Mon**
See Pountney, Monica Brailey

**Mon Soldat [My Soldier]**
See Henry IV [or Henri]

**Mona, Alli** 20th c. [IBW]
*American magician*
* Prince Alli

**Mona Lisa**
See Gherardini, Lisa di Anton Maria

**Monaco, James** 1885-1945 [AM]
*American composer*
* Ragtime Jimmy

**Monaco, Richard** 1940- [CA]
*American author, poet, editor*
* Robhs, Dwight

**Monadnock**
See Nicholas, Dr.

**Monaghan, James** 1891- [IAW]
*American author*
* Monaghan, Jay

**Monaghan, Jay**
See Monaghan, James

**Monaghan, John Joseph** 1920- [BX, RBE]
*Irish boxer*
* Monaghan, Rinty

**Monaghan, Rinty**
See Monaghan, John Joseph

**[El] Monaguillo [The Altar Boy]**
See Torres Jimenez, Andres

**Monahan, Bubs**
See Monahan, Harold

**Monahan, Edward Francis** 1928- [BE]
*American baseball player*
* Monahan, Rinty

**Monahan, Harold** 20th c. [SR]
*Bobsled racer*
* Monahan, Bubs

**Monahan, Hart**
See Monahan, Hartland Patrick

**Monahan, Hartland Patrick** 1951- [HR]
*Canadian-born hockey player*
* Monahan, Hart

**Monahan, Rinty**
See Monahan, Edward Francis

**Monar, Motilall Rooplalln** 1944?- [CW]
*Guyanese poet and editor*
* Greene, Eustace

**[The] Monarch**
See Giscard d'Estaing, Valery

**Monarch of Christendom**
See Borghese, Camillo

**Monarch of Letters**
See Selden, John

**[The] Monarch of Mont Blanc**
See Smith, Albert Richard

**[The] Monarch of the Musical Kingdom**
See Handel, Georg Friedrich

**Monardo, Meco** 1939- [RO2]
*American entertainer*
* Meco

**Monbouquette, Monbo**
See Monbouquette, William Charles

**Monbouquette, William Charles** 1936- [SMG]
*American baseball player*
* Monbouquette, Monbo

**Moncamp, Arthur**
See Pilgrim, Thomas

**Monceau, Lucie** 1871?-1948 [BEW]
*French actress*
* Moreno, Marguerite

**Moncho y Gilabert, Antonio** 20th c. [SFP]
*Author*
* Gautisolo, Miguel

**Monck, Tristam K.**
See Maitland, T. G. Dowling

**Moncorge, Jean-Alexis** 1904- [BDF, OCF, WEF]
*French actor*
* Gabin, Jean

**Moncrief, Robert** 20th c. [RO1]
*American singer*
* Edwards, Bobby

**Moncrieff, Ernest**
See Chi, Richard Hu See-Yee

**Moncrieff, [Sir] Henry** 1750-1827 [PA]
*Author*
* Welwood

**Moncrieff, [Sir] James Wellwood** 1776-1851 [RH]
*Scottish attorney and jurist*
* [The] Whole Duty of Man

**Moncrieff, Robert Hope** 20th c. [MBF]
*British author*
* Hope, Ascott R.

**Moncure, Jane Belk** 20th c. [SAT]
*American educator and author*
* Wannamaker, Bruce

**Monda, Richard** 20th c. [RO2]
*American singer and songwriter*
* Daddy Dewdrop

**Mondale, Fritz**
See Mondale, Walter Frederick

**Mondale, Joan**
*Wife of American vice president Walter Mondale*
* Joan of Art

**Mondale, Walter Frederick** 1928-
*American vice president*
* Mondale, Fritz

**Monday Boanerges**
See Cook, Flavius Josephus

**Monday, Michael**
See Ginder, Richard

**Monday, Paul**
See Gadd, Paul

**Monday, Rick**
See Monday, Robert James, Jr.

**Monday, Robert James, Jr.** 1945- [PB, SMG, WWB]
*American baseball player*
* Monday, Rick

**Mondelle, Wendayne**
See Ackerman, Wendayne

**Mondello, Nuncio** 1910?- [EJ, PMJ, WWJ]
*American jazz musician*
* Mondello, Toots

**Mondello, Toots**
See Mondello, Nuncio

**Mondeno [The Clean One]**
See Garcia Jimenez, Juan

**Mondey, David [Charles]** 1917- [CA]
*British air force officer and author*
* Charles, David

**Mondose, Alex**
See Onsmonde, Alexandre

**Mondschein, Irving** 1925- [EJS]
*American track and field athlete*
* Mondschein, Moon

**Mondschein, Moon**
See Mondschein, Irving

**Mondy, Pierre**
See Cuq, Pierre

**Monedero [The Minter]**
See Marcos, Jesus

**Monett, Lireve**
See Worrell, Everil

**Money Bags Qualters**
See Qualters, Thomas Francis [Tom]

**Money, Brooks**
See Money, Donald Wayne

**Money, Donald Wayne** 1947- [BE]
*American baseball player*
* Money, Brooks

**Money-Coutts, Francis** 1851- ? [WWL]
*British author*
* Coutts, Francis

**Mong, Yuk** 1908-1933 [SC]
*Actor*
* Fook, Monte

**Monge, Isidro Pedroza** 1951-
[SMG]
*Mexican-born baseball player*
* Monge, Sid

**Monge, Sid**
See Monge, Isidro Pedroza

**Monger, [Ifor] David** 1908-
[AW, CA]
*Welsh physician and playwright*
* Manngian, Peter
* Richards, Peter

**[The] Mongolian Bonaparte**
See Timur [or Timour]

**[The] Mongoose**
See McEwen, Tom

**Monheimer, A.** [PA]
*Author*
* Hackle, B.

**Monica, Maestro**
See Monica, Manuel [or Antonio?]

**Monica, Manuel [or Antonio?]**
1731?- ? [CW]
*Dominican poet and singer*
* Monica, Maestro
* Monica, Meso

**Monica, Meso**
See Monica, Manuel [or Antonio?]

**Monig, Christopher**
See Crossen, Ken[dell Foster]

**Monique**
See Benoit, Alice P.

**Monitor**
See Levine, Isaac Don

**Monjo, F. N.**
See Monjo, Ferdinand Nicolas, III

**Monjo, Ferdinand Nicolas, III**
1924- [TCC]
*American author*
* Monjo, F. N.

**[The] Monk**
See Alfonso IV [or Alphonso]

**[The] Monk**
See Casimir I

**[The] Monk**
See Ramiro II

**Monk [or Monkey]**
See Ruth, George Herman

**Monk, Alan**
See Kendall, Willmoore

**Monk, Galdo**
See Riseley, Jerry B[urr, Jr.]

**Monk, George [Duke of Albemarle]**
1608-1670 [DEP, DNNS, SN]
*British army officer*
* Honest George
* Old George
* [The] Thinking Silent General

**[The] Monk of Bury**
See Lydgate, John

**[The] Monk of Eisleben**
See Luther, Martin

**[The] Monk of the Golden Islands**
See Cybo of Genoa

**[The] Monk of Westminster**
See Richard of Cirencester

**[The] Monk of Wittenberg**
See Luther, Martin

**Monk, Thelonious Sphere**
1920-1982 [IBW]
*American jazz musician*
* [The] High Priest of Bebop

**[The] Monkey King**
See Trefflich, Henry

**Monkland, George**
See Whittet, George Sorley

**Monkman, Phyllis**
See Harrison, Phyllis

**Monks, Victoria** 1884-1927 [BMH]
*British singer*
* John Bull's Girl
* Little Victoria

**Monkshood, G. F.**
See Clarke, William James

**Monmouth**
See Henry V

**Monmouth, Duke of**
See Scott, James

**Monmouth, Elizabeth H.** [PA]
*Author*
* Homespun, Sophia

**Monnet, Jean** 1888-1979
*French political economist*
* [The] Father of Europe
* [The] Father of the European
   Community

**Monnow, Peter**
See Croudace, Glynn

**Monomachus [Who Fights in Single
Combat]**
See Constantine IX

**Monomachus**
See Vladimir II

**Mononen, Larry**
See Mononen, Lauri Ilmari

**Mononen, Lauri Ilmari** 1950-
[SMG]
*Finnish-born hockey player*
* Mononen, Larry

**Monongo**
See Clytus, John

**Monophthalmos [The One-Eyed]**
See Antigonus I

**Monro, Alexander** 1697-1767 [PA]
*Author*
* Primus

**Monro, Gavin**
See Monro-Higgs, Gertrude

**Monro-Higgs, Gertrude** 1905-
[AW, WD]
*British author*
* Monro, Gavin

**Monroe, Alex**
*American football player*
* Monroe, Mole

**Monroe, Donald** 1888-
[SFL, WGT]
*American author*
* Keith, Donald [joint pseudonym
   with Keith Monroe]

**Monroe, Earl** 1944- [BB, SR]
*American basketball player*
* Magic, Mr.

**Monroe, Earl** (Continued)
* [The] Pearl

**Monroe, Ed[ward Oliver]**
1893-1969 [BE]
*American baseball player*
* Monroe, Peck

**Monroe, Forest**
See Wiechmann, Ferdinand
Gerhard

**Monroe, George H.** [FFF]
*American journalist*
* Templeton

**Monroe, James** 1758-1831 [FAP]
*American president*
* [The] Era of Good Feeling
   President
* [The] Last of the Cocked Hats

**Monroe, John Alexander**
1874-1942 [RBE]
*Canadian boxer*
* Munroe, Jack

**Monroe, Keith** 1917-
[CA, SFL, WGT]
*American author*
* Cochran, Rice E.
* Colombo, Dale
* Keith, Donald [joint pseudonym
   with Donald Monroe]

**Monroe, Lyle**
See Heinlein, Robert A[nson]

**Monroe, Marilyn**
See Baker [or Mortenson?],
Norma Jean

**Monroe, Mole**
See Monroe, Alex

**Monroe, Peck**
See Monroe, Ed[ward Oliver]

**Monroe, Vince**
See Vincent, Monroe

**Monroe, William [Bill]** 1911-
[CWG, FCW]
*American country-western performer*
* [The] Father of Bluegrass Music

**Monrose, Louis**
See Barizan, Louis Martial

**Monseigneur**
See Louis

**Monsell, Margaret E[mma Irwin]**
1917- [WGT]
*American author*
* Irwin, Margaret E.

**Monserrat, Mrs. George** [FFF]
*Entertainer*
* Ottolengui, Helen

**Monsieur**
See Orleans, Philippe II d'

**Monsieur Charles**
See Chop, Max

**[Le] Monsieur de l'Orchestre**
See Mortier, Arnold

**Monsieur le Coadjuteur**
See Gondi, Jean Francois Paul de

**Monsieur le Duc**
See Bourbon, Henri Jules de

**Monsieur le Duc**
See Bourbon, Louis Henri de

**Monsieur le Prince**
See Bourbon, Louis II de [Prince
de Conde]

**Monsieur X**
See Howard, Joseph

**Monsieur X**
See Moutis, Patrice Des

**[The] Monster**
See Howard, Frank Oliver

**[The] Monster**
See Radatz, Richard Raymond
[Dick]

**[The] Monster**
See Williams, Renwick

**[The] Monster Man**
See Eddy, Everett

**[The] Monster Man**
See Mundus, [Captain] Frank

**[A] Monster of Languages**
See Mezzofanti, Giuseppe

**[The] Monster of Nature**
See Vega Carpio, Lope Felix de

**[El] Monstruo [The Monster]**
See Rodriguez Sanchez, Manuel

**Montacute [or Montagu], Thomas de**
1388-1428 [HN, RH]
*Fourth Earl of Salisbury*
* [The] Mirror of all Martial Men

**Montagna, Luigi** 1887-1950
[CU, FC, SC]
*Italian-American actor*
* [The] Bull
* Montana, Bull

**Montagu, Charles [First Earl of
Halifax]** 1661-1715 [SN]
*British statesman and patron of the
arts*
* [A] Maecenas

**Montagu, John [Fourth Earl of
Sandwich]** 1718-1792
[DNNF, DNNS, RH]
*British diplomat*
* Twitcher, Jemmy

**Montagu, Mary Wortley**
1689-1762 [DEL, FFF, SN]
*British author and poet*
* Artemisia
* [The] Female Maecenas
* Minerva

**Montagu, Robert**
See Hampden, John

**Montague, Alphonsus Joseph-Mary
Augustus** 1880-1948 [BEW]
*British-born historian and editor*
* Summers, Rey

**Montague, Basil** 1770-1851 [PA]
*Author*
* [The] Water Drinker

**Montague, Bruce Alexander** 1939-
[IAW]
*British author and playwright*
* Alexander, Bruce
* Bruce, Martin
* O'Toole, Kate
* Savage, Oscar

**Montague, C. E.**
See Montague, Charles Edward

**Montague, Charles Edward**
1867-1928    [LC, TC]
*Irish journalist, author, critic*
* Montague, C. E.

**Montague, E. L.**
*See*  Hervey, E. L.

**Montague, Eleonora Louisa** 1811-
?    [PA]
*Author*
* [The] Landgrave
* Russell, Margaret

**Montague, Harold**
*See*  Smith, Harold

**Montague, Harry**
*See*  Mann, Henry J.

**Montague, John**
*See*  Moore, LaVerne M.

**Montague, Pansy** 20th c.    [THR]
*Australian-born entertainer*
* [La] Milo

**[The] Montaigne of Geneva**
*See*  Bonnivard, Francois de

**Montalban, Ricardo**
*See*  Montalban Merino, Ricardo

**Montalban Merino, Ricardo** 1920-
[BEW]
*Mexican-born actor*
* Montalban, Ricardo

**Montalte, Louis de**
*See*  Pascal, Blaise

**Montana**
*See*  Williams, Reginald Gordon

**Montana, Bull**
*See*  Montagna, Luigi

**Montana, Montie**
*See*  Mickel, Owen Harlan

**Montana, Patsy**
*See*  Blevins, Rubye

**Montana Red Tate**
*See*  Tate, Don

**Montana Slim**
*See*  Carter, Wilf

**Montana, Small**
*See*  Gan, Benjamin

**[The] Montana Wonder**
*See*  Kiecal, Stanislaus

**Montanari, Sergio** 20th c.    [WF]
*Italian film editor*
* Hillman, Sergius

**Montand, Yves**
*See*  Livi, Ivo [or Yvo]

**Montanez, Guillermo Naranjo**
1948-    [BE, SMG, WWB]
*Puerto Rican-born baseball player*
* Montanez, Willie

**Montanez, Willie**
*See*  Montanez, Guillermo Naranjo

**Montani, Virgil** 1880?-1956
[BEW]
*Actor and dancer*
* Clifford, Jack

**Montano Arriola, Gustavo** 1917-
[WECO]
*American cartoonist*
* Arriola, Gus

**Montanus**
*See*  Van der Berghe, Robert

**Montayne, Harold B.** 20th c.    [SFP]
*Author*
* Eaton, George L.

**Montbars** 1645- ?
[DNNF, DNNS, FFF]
*French buccaneer*
* [The] Exterminator

**Montclair, Dennis**
*See*  Sladen, Norman St. Barbe

**[The] Montclair Mailman**
*See*  Cestone, Michael

**Monte, Toti Dal**
*See*  Meneghel, Antonietta

**Montefusco, John Joseph, Jr.**
1950-    [SMG]
*American baseball player*
* [The] Count

**Monteith, Owen**
*See*  Hook, Samuel Clarke

**Montejo, Manny**
*See*  Montejo, Manuel

**Montejo, Manuel** 1936-    [BE]
*Cuban-born baseball player*
* Montejo, Manny
* Montejo, Pete

**Montejo, Pete**
*See*  Montejo, Manuel

**Montella, Sonny**
*See*  Montella, William

**Montella, William** 20th c.
*American underworld figure*
* Montella, Sonny

**Montemayor, Felipe Angel** 1930-
[BE]
*Mexican-born baseball player*
* Montemayor, Monty

**Montemayor, Monty**
*See*  Montemayor, Felipe Angel

**Monterey, Carlotta**
*See*  Taasinge, Hazel Neilson

**Montero, Roberto Bianchi** 1907-
[FDG]
*Italian director*
* White, M. Robert

**Monterose, Frank Anthony, Jr.**
1927-    [EJ]
*American jazz musician*
* Monterose, J. R.

**Monterose, J. R.**
*See*  Monterose, Frank Anthony, Jr.

**Montes, Emeterio**
*See*  Corretjer, Juan Antonio

**Montes, Fabian**
*See*  De Elzaburu, Manuel

**Montez, Lola**
*See*  Gilbert, Marie Dolores Eliza
Rosanna

**Montez, Maria**
*See*  Gracia Vidal de Santo Silas,
Maria Africa Antonia

**Montford, Simon de** 1150?-1218
[HN]
*French military leader*
* [The] French Maccabaeus

**Montfort, Auguste** 1913-    [CA]
*French author*
* Le Breton, Auguste

**Montfort, Simon de [Earl of
Leicester]** 1200?-1265    [HN, WBD]
*British statesman and soldier*
* Simon the Righteous

**Montgaillard, Comte de**
*See*  Roques, Maurice Jacques

**Montgelas, Maximilian Joseph von**
*See*  De Garnerin, Maximilian
Joseph

**Montgomerie, Alexander**
1588-1661    [WBD]
*Sixth Earl of Eglinton*
* Greysteel

**Montgomery, Bernard Law**
1887-1976    [CA]
*British military leader*
* Montgomery of Alamein
* Monty

**Montgomery, Bob** 1919-    [IBW]
*American boxer*
* Montgomery, Bobcat

**Montgomery, Bobcat**
*See*  Montgomery, Bob

**Montgomery, Buddy**
*See*  Montgomery, Charles F.

**Montgomery, Charles F.** 1930-
[DAM, EJ]
*American jazz musician*
* Montgomery, Buddy

**Montgomery, Charlotte Baker**
1910-    [IAW]
*American author*
* Baker, Charlotte

**Montgomery, Constance**
*See*  Cappel, Constance

**Montgomery, Eurreal Wilford**
1906?-    [EJ, WWJ]
*American jazz musician*
* Montgomery, Little Brother

**Montgomery, Florence** 20th c.    [F2]
*Actress*
* Arliss, Florence

**Montgomery, G. V.** 20th c.    [IPA]
*American politician*
* Montgomery, Sonny

**Montgomery, George**
*See*  Letz, George Montgomery

**Montgomery, Gerald**
*See*  Moultrie, John

**Montgomery, Girard**
*See*  Moultrie, George

**Montgomery, Henry, Jr.**
1904-1981    [BEW, F2, FC]
*American actor, producer, director*
* Montgomery, Robert

**Montgomery, James** 1771-1854
[DNNS, PA, SN]
*Scottish poet*
* Alcaeus
* [The] Bard of Sheffield
* [A] Poet

**Montgomery, John Leslie**
1925-1968    [DAM]
*American jazz musician*
* Montgomery, Wes

**Montgomery, L. M.**
*See*  Montgomery, Lucy Maude

**Montgomery, Leslie Alexander**
1873-1961    [LC]
*Irish author*
* Doyle, Lynn

**Montgomery, Little Brother**
*See*  Montgomery, Eurreal Wilford

**Montgomery, Lucy Maude**
1874-1942    [LC]
*Canadian author*
* Montgomery, L. M.

**Montgomery, Mamie Elizabeth**
1891-    [IAW]
*American author*
* Wakefield, Elizabeth

**Montgomery, Max**
*See*  Davenport, Guy [Mattison],
Jr.

**Montgomery, Monk**
*See*  Montgomery, William Howard

**Montgomery, Monty**
*See*  Montgomery, Robert Edward

**Montgomery of Alamein**
*See*  Montgomery, Bernard Law

**Montgomery, Peggy** 1918-    [F2]
*Actress*
* Baby Peggy

**Montgomery, Raymond A., Jr.**
1936-    [CA]
*American author*
* Mountain, Robert

**Montgomery, Richard** 1736-1775
[HN]
*British army officer*
* [The] Wolf of America

**Montgomery, Richmond Ames** 20th
c.    [NAA]
*American clergyman and author*
* Kilbourn, Timothy

**Montgomery, Robert**
*See*  Montgomery, Henry, Jr.

**Montgomery, Robert Bruce**
1921-1978    [CC, EMD, SF]
*British author and composer*
* Crispin, Edmund

**Montgomery, Robert Douglass**
1908-1966    [SC]
*American actor*
* Douglas, Kent

**Montgomery, Robert Edward**
1944-    [SMG]
*American baseball player*
* Montgomery, Monty

**Montgomery, Roselle Mercier** 20th
c.    [NAA]
*American poet and writer*
* Allen, Glen

**Montgomery, Rutherford George**
1894-    [NAA, TCC]
*American author*
* Avery, A. A.
* Avery, Al
* Elder, Art
* Marshall, E. P.
* Proctor, Everitt

**Montgomery, Sonny**
*See*  Montgomery, G. V.

**Montgomery, Thomasina**
1946-1970   [IBW, RO2]
*American singer*
* Terrell, Tammi

**Montgomery, Wes**
*See*  Montgomery, John Leslie

**Montgomery, William Howard**
1921-   [DAM, EJ]
*American jazz musician*
* Montgomery, Monk

**Monti, Luigi** 19th c.   [PA]
*Author*
* Sampleton, Samuel

**Montifaud, Marc de**
*See*  Quivogne de Montifaud, Marie
Amelie

**Montigny, L.**
*See*  Lemoine, Adolph

**Montini, Giovanni Battista Enrico
Antonio Maria** 1897-1978   [CBS]
*Pope*
* Paul VI
* [The] Pilgrim Pope

**Montluc, Seigneur de**
*See*  De Lasseran-Massencome,
Blaise

**Montmorency, Anne de** 1493-1567
[DNNF, FFF, HN]
*Constable of France*
* [The] Conqueror
* [The] Fabius of France
* [The] French Fabius

**Montmorency-Bouteville, Francois
Henri de [Duc de Luxembourg]**
1628-1695   [DNNS, SN]
*French marshal*
* [Le] Tapissier de Notre-Dame
* [The] Upholsterer of Notre Dame

**Montoliu, Tete**
*See*  Montoliu, Vincente

**Montoliu, Vincente** 1933-   [EJ7]
*Spanish jazz musician*
* Montoliu, Tete

**Montoya, Joseph M.** 1915-1978
*American politician*
* [The] Barefoot Boy from Pena
Blanca
* Montoya, Little Joe

**Montoya, Little Joe**
*See*  Montoya, Joseph M.

**Montreal, Young**
*See*  Billingkoff, Morris

**Montreal's Liberace**
*See*  Richer, Donald [Donny]

**Montrose, David** 1904-
[BX, EJS, RBE]
*Russian-born boxer*
* Brown, Newsboy

**Montrose, Duchess of** 19th c.
[FFF]
*Racehorse owner*
* Manton, Mr.

**Montrose, First Marquis of**
*See*  Graham, James

**Montrose, Graham**
*See*  MacKinnon, Charles Roy

**Montrose, James St. David**
*See*  Appleman, John Alan

**Montrose, Kate**
*See*  Faust, Mrs. A. J.

**Montrose, Muriel**
*See*  Andrews, Muriel

**Montrose, Second Marquis of**
*See*  Graham, James

**Montross, David**
*See*  Backus, Jean L[ouise]

**Monty**
*See*  Montgomery, Bernard Law

**Monvel**
*See*  Boutet, Jacques Marie

**Monzant, Ramon Segundo** 1933-
[BE]
*Venezuelan-born baseball player*
* Monzant, Ray

**Monzant, Ray**
*See*  Monzant, Ramon Segundo

**Moodie, Edwin**
*See*  Williams, Edwin Alfred

**Moodnick, Ronald** 1924-
[EMT, FC, TR]
*British actor*
* Moody, Ron

**Moody, Big Train**
*See*  Moody, John Clifford

**Moody, Clyde** 1915-   [CWG]
*American country-western performer*
* [The] Hillbilly Waltz King
* [The] Woodchopper

**Moody, Granville** 1812-1887   [FFF]
*American clergyman and army
officer*
* [The] Fighting Parson

**Moody, John Clifford** 1917-   [IBW]
*American football player*
* Moody, Big Train

**Moody, Juice**
*See*  Moody, Keith

**Moody, Keith** 1953-   [SMG]
*American football player*
* Moody, Juice

**Moody, Michael David** 1946-
[ART]
*British artist*
* M.

**Moody, Orville** 1933-   [GF]
*American golfer*
* Moody, Sarge

**Moody, Ron**
*See*  Moodnick, Ronald

**Moody, Sarge**
*See*  Moody, Orville

**Moolic, George Henry** 1867-1915
[BE]
*American baseball player*
* Moolic, Prunes

**Moolic, Prunes**
*See*  Moolic, George Henry

**Moolson, Melusa**
*See*  Solomon, Samuel

**Moon, George P.** 20th c.   [MBF]
*British author*
* Pembury, Montague

**Moon, Jack**
*See*  Elliott, John B.

**Moon, Lefty**
*See*  Moon, Leo

**Moon, Leo** 1899-1970   [BE]
*American baseball player*
* Moon, Lefty

**[The] Moon Maniac**
*See*  Fish, Hamilton

**Moonbeam, Governor**
*See*  Brown, Edmund Gerald,
Jr.[Jerry]

**Moonblood, Q.**
*See*  Stallone, Sylvester [Enzio]

**Moondog**
*See*  Hardin, Louis Thomas

**Mooney, Bernard** 1897-   [BBH]
*American wrestling coach*
* Mooney, Spike

**Mooney, Canice [Albert James]**
1911-1963   [CA]
*Irish clergyman, librarian, author*
* O Maonaigh, Cainneach

**Mooney, Harry**
*See*  Goodchild, Harry

**Mooney, Paul** 20th c.   [IBW]
*American author*
* [The] Black Tornado

**Mooney, Sam**
*See*  Giancana, Salvatore

**Mooney, Spike**
*See*  Mooney, Bernard

**Mooney, Thomas** 1806-1888   [FFF]
*Irish journalist*
* Trans-Atlantic

**Moonlight Ace Fussell**
*See*  Fussell, Fred[erick Morris]

**Moonshine Kate Carson**
*See*  Carson, Rosa Lee

**Moor, D. S.**
*See*  Orlov, Dimitry Stakhiyevich

**[The] Moor of Venice**
*See*  Haywood, Spencer

**Moorcock, Michael John**
1939-1978   [CA, ESF, WGT]
*British author*
* Barclay, Bill
* Barrington, Michael [joint
pseudonym with Barrington
J(ohn) Bayley]
* Bradbury, E[dward] P.
* Colvin, James
* Reid, Desmond [house
pseudonym]

**Moore, Adelaide**
*See*  Valentine, Mrs.

**Moore, Alexander Herman** 1899-
[BWW]
*American singer*
* Moore, Whistling Alex
* Papa Chittlins

**Moore, Alice**
*See*  Miller, Alice Moore

**Moore, Alton** 1908-   [WWJ]
*American jazz musician*
* Moore, Slim

**Moore, Alvin Earl** 1953-   [BR]
*American baseball player*
* Moore, Junior

**Moore, Anacreon**
*See*  Moore, Thomas

**Moore, Andrew**
*See*  Binder, Frederick Moore

**Moore, Andrew C., Jr.** 1902-1971
[FB]
*American football coach*
* Moore, Scrappy

**Moore, Ann** 19th c.   [FF]
*Claimed to have fasted for 20
months*
* [The] Fasting Woman of Tutbury

**Moore, Anon**
*See*  Galloway, James M.

**Moore, Archie**
*See*  Wright, Archibald Lee

**Moore, Arnold Dwight** 1913?-
[BWW, IBW]
*American singer*
* Blues, Mr.
* Moore, Eldermo
* Moore, Gatemouth

**Moore, Arthur** 20th c.   [SFL]
*Author*
* Moore, Harris [joint pseudonym
with Alf(red) Harris]
* Oriel, Antrim

**Moore, Austin**
*See*  Muir, [Charles] Augustus

**Moore, Bartholomew Figures**
1801-1878   [FFF]
*American attorney*
* [The] Father of the North
Carolina Bar

**Moore, Bernyce Atz** 1910?-1962
[BEW]
*American theatrical performer*
* Maye, Bernyce

**Moore, Beryl**
*See*  Smith Woods, Dorothy Beryl

**Moore, Big Chief**
*See*  Moore, Russell

**Moore, Big Sol**
*See*  Moore, Wayne

**Moore, Blue Goose**
*See*  Moore, Eugene, Sr.

**Moore, Brew**
*See*  Moore, Milton Aubrey, Jr.

**Moore, Bud**
*See*  Moore, Edgar Augustine

**Moore, Bud**
*See*  Moore, Walter

**Moore, Buster**
*See*  Moore, Robert

**Moore, C. L.**
*See*  Moore, Catherine Lucile

**Moore, Catherine Lucile** 1911-
[HFF, SFL, WGT]
*American author*
* Hammond, Keith [joint
pseudonym with Henry Kuttner]
* Hastings, Hudson [joint
pseudonym with Henry Kuttner]
* Liddell, C. H. [joint pseudonym
with Henry Kuttner]
* Moore, C. L.
* O'Donnell, Lawrence [joint
pseudonym with Henry Kuttner]

**Moore, Catherine Lucile** (Continued)
* Padgett, Lewis [joint pseudonym with Henry Kuttner]

**Moore, Charles**
See Moore, Reginald Charles Arthur

**Moore, Chief**
See Moore, Euel Walton

**Moore, Clara [Jessup]** [FFF]
*American author*
* Moreton, Clara

**Moore, Clayton**
See Brandner, Gary

**Moore, Clayton**
See Granbeck, Marilyn

**Moore, Colleen**
See Morrison, Kathleen

**Moore, Cory**
See Sturgeon, Wina

**Moore, Crossfire**
See Moore, Earl Alonzo

**Moore, Cy**
See Moore, William Austin

**Moore, Cy**
See Moore, William Wilcy

**Moore, Debby**
See Maultsby, Emmaline

**Moore, Dennie**
See Moore, Florence

**Moore, Dick[ie]**
See Moore, John Richard, Jr.

**Moore, Dinty**
See Moore, James

**Moore, Dinty**
See Moore, William H., III

**Moore, Dobie**
See Moore, Walter

**Moore, E. W.**
See Kelly, George R.

**Moore, Earl Alonzo** 1878-1961 [BE]
*American baseball player*
* Moore, Crossfire

**Moore, Edgar Augustine** 1918- [CWG]
*American country-western performer*
* Moore, Bud

**Moore, Edward**
See Muir, Edwin

**Moore, Edward** 1835-1916 [WBD]
*British scholar*
* [The] Oxford Dante

**Moore, Eldermo**
See Moore, Arnold Dwight

**Moore, Elizabeth**
See Atkins, Meg Elizabeth

**Moore, Elsie**
See O'Loughlin, Louise T.

**Moore, Emily H.** [FFF, PA]
*Author*
* Mignonette

**Moore, Erica Maria** 20th c. [SFL]
*Author*
* Akira

**Moore, Euel Walton** 1908- [BE]
*American baseball player*
* Moore, Chief

**Moore, Eugene, Jr.** 1909- [BE]
*American baseball player*
* Moore, Rowdy

**Moore, Eugene, Sr.** 1885-1938 [BE]
*American baseball player*
* Moore, Blue Goose

**Moore, F. L.** [PA]
*Author*
* F. L. M.

**Moore, Farmer**
See Moore, Raymond Leroy

**Moore, Fenworth** [house pseudonym] [Stratemeyer Syndicate]
See Stratemeyer, Edward L.

**Moore, Florence** 1907- [BEW]
*American actress*
* Moore, Dennie

**Moore, G. E.**
See Moore, George Edward

**Moore, Garry**
See Morfit, Thomas Garrison

**Moore, Gatemouth**
See Moore, Arnold Dwight

**Moore, George Edward** 1873-1958 [LC]
*British author and philosopher*
* Moore, G. E.

**Moore, Hannah** 1744-1833 [PA]
*Author*
* Z.

**Moore, Harris** [joint pseudonym with Arthur Moore]
See Harris, Alf[red]

**Moore, Harris** [joint pseudonym with Alf(red) Harris]
See Moore, Arthur

**Moore, Harry** 20th c. [OBW]
*American baseball player*
* Moore, Mike

**Moore, Harry R.** 1888-1958? [IBW, SC]
*American entertainer and boxer*
* Bosco
* Moore, Kingfish
* Moore, Tim
* Noble, Kid
* Young Klondyke

**Moore, Ivy Lee** 1953- [SMG]
*American football player*
* Moore, Moe

**Moore, J. E.** ?-1958 [BLB]
*American underworld figure*
* Maddox, Claude
* Moore, Screwy

**Moore, J. S.** 19th c. [FFF, PA]
*American writer*
* Parsee Merchant

**Moore, James** 1869?-1952 [B10]
*American restaurateur*
* Moore, Dinty

**Moore, James** 1924-1970 [BWW, NBB]
*American singer*
* Harmonica Slim
* Harpo, Slim

**Moore, James** 1928- [CA]
*British author, editor, translator*
* Balfour, John

**Moore, James** 20th c. [OBW]
*American baseball player*
* Moore, Red

**Moore, Jane L.** [PA]
*Author*
* Ione

**Moore, Jo-Jo**
See Moore, Joe Gregg

**Moore, Joe Gregg** 1908- [BE]
*American baseball player*
* [The] Gause Ghost
* Moore, Jo-Jo

**Moore, John** 1644-1714 [SN]
*British prelate and book collector*
* [The] Father of Black Letter Collectors

**Moore, John C.** [FFF]
*American writer*
* Snooks, Peter

**Moore, John Richard, Jr.** 1925- [CA]
*American actor and author*
* Moore, Dick[ie]

**Moore, John Travers** 1908- [CA]
*American author and poet*
* Tripp, John

**Moore, Joseph Solomon** 19th c. [PA]
*American author*
* Adersey Curiosibhoy

**Moore, Julia A.** 1847-1920 [PA, WBD]
*American poet*
* [The] Sweet Singer of Michigan

**Moore, Junior**
See Moore, Alvin Earl

**Moore, Kenneth**
See La Due, Hubert

**Moore, Kieron**
See O'Hanrahan, Kieron

**Moore, Kingfish**
See Moore, Harry R.

**Moore, Lander**
See Fensch, Thomas

**Moore, LaVerne M.** 1906-1972 [EG, GF]
*American golfer*
* Montague, John
* [The] Mysterious Montague
* [The] Rake and Shovel Golfer

**Moore, Leonard** 20th c.
*American football player*
* Moore, Spats

**Moore, Lloyd Albert** 1912- [BE]
*American baseball player*
* Moore, Whitey

**Moore, Maggie**
See Williamson, Mrs. J. C.

**Moore, Melba**
See Moorman, Beatrice

**Moore, Memphis Pal**
See Moore, Thomas Wilson

**Moore, Michael**
See Harris, Herbert

**Moore, Mike**
See Moore, Harry

**Moore, Milton Aubrey, Jr.** 1924-1973 [DAM, EJ, EJ7]
*American jazz musician*
* Moore, Brew

**Moore, Moe**
See Moore, Ivy Lee

**Moore, Monette** 1902-1962 [BWW]
*American singer*
* [The] Girl of Smiles
* Mayes, Ethel
* Potter, Nettie
* Smith, Susie
* White, Grace

**Moore, Mrs. Bloomfield H.** [PA]
*Author*
* Ward, Mrs. H. O.

**Moore, Muriel Sarah** 20th c. [LAO]
*British author*
* Glynn, Bill

**Moore, Nell**
See Morfit, Eleanor Borum [Little]

**Moore, Nicholas**
See Nicolaeff, Ariadne

**Moore, Nicholas** 1918- [CA]
*British author and poet*
* Kelly, Guy

**Moore, Numa Smith** 1928- [EJ]
*American jazz musician*
* Moore, Pee Wee

**Moore, Oliver**
See Perry, Oliver Curtis

**Moore, Pee Wee**
See Moore, Numa Smith

**Moore, Pete**
See Moore, Warren

**Moore, Raymond Leroy** 1926- [BE]
*American baseball player*
* Moore, Farmer

**Moore, Red**
See Moore, James

**Moore, Reg**
See Moore, Reginald Charles Arthur

**Moore, Regina**
See Dunne, Mary Collins

**Moore, Reginald Charles Arthur** 1930- [WD]
*British author, journalist, poet*
* Moore, Charles
* Moore, Reg

**Moore, Richard E. M.** 1938- [ART]
*British medical artist*
* R. E. M. M.
* R. M.

**Moore, Robert**
See Williams, Robert Moore

**Moore, Robert** 1898?-1966 [NOJ]
*American jazz musician*
* Moore, Buster

**Moore, Robert E. [Bobby]** 1949- [FB, SMG]
*American football player*
* Rashad, Ahmad

**Moore, Robert L[owell], Jr.** 1925-
[B10, CA]
*American author*
* Moore, Robin

**Moore, Robin**
See  Moore, Robert L[owell], Jr.

**Moore, Roger**
See  O'More, Rory

**Moore, Rosalie**
See  Brown, Rosalie [Gertrude]
Moore

**Moore, Rowdy**
See  Moore, Eugene, Jr.

**Moore, Russell** 1912?-
[DAM, EJ, WWJ]
*American jazz musician*
* Moore, Big Chief

**Moore, Scrappy**
See  Moore, Andrew C., Jr.

**Moore, Scrappy**
See  Moore, William Allen

**Moore, Screwy**
See  Moore, J. E.

**Moore, Slim**
See  Moore, Alton

**Moore, Spats**
See  Moore, Leonard

**Moore, Square**
See  Moore, Squire

**Moore, Squire** 20th c.  [OBW]
*American baseball player*
* Moore, Square

**Moore, Terry**
See  Koford, Helen

**Moore, Thomas**
See  Girolami, Enzo

**Moore, Thomas** 1779-1852
[DEL, FFF, PA]
*Irish poet*
* [The] Bard of Erin
* Brown, Thomas, the Younger
* Cribb, Tom
* [The] Fudge Family
* [An] Irish Man
* [The] Lansdowne Laureate
* Little, Thomas
* Moore, Anacreon
* Moore, Trumpet
* One of the Fancy
* Rock, Captain

**Moore, Thomas Wilson** 1894-1953
[BX, RBE]
*American boxer*
* Moore, Memphis Pal

**Moore, Tim**
See  Moore, Harry R.

**Moore, Tomiwitta** 1930-  [IBW]
*American actress*
* Moore, Tommie

**Moore, Tommie**
See  Moore, Tomiwitta

**Moore, Tony** 20th c.  [MBF]
*British author*
* Morris, Tony

**Moore, Trumpet**
See  Moore, Thomas

**Moore, Wallace**
See  Conway, Gerard F.

**Moore, Walter** ?-1932  [MK]
*American baseball player*
* Moore, Dobie

**Moore, Walter** 1926-  [EAR]
*American auto racer*
* Moore, Bud

**Moore, Warren** 1939-  [IBW, RO1]
*American singer, musician,
songwriter*
* Moore, Pete

**Moore, Wayne** 1945-  [SMG]
*American football player*
* Moore, Big Sol

**Moore, Whistling Alex**
See  Moore, Alexander Herman

**Moore, Whitey**
See  Moore, Lloyd Albert

**Moore, Wilbur** 1916-1965  [AS]
*American football player*
* [The] Little Indian

**Moore, Wild Willie**
See  Moore, Willie

**Moore, William Allen** 1892-1964
[BE]
*American baseball player*
* Moore, Scrappy

**Moore, William Austin** 1905-  [BE]
*American baseball player*
* Moore, Cy

**Moore, William H., III** 1900-
[BBH]
*American lacrosse coach*
* Moore, Dinty

**Moore, William Wilcy** 1897-1963
[BE, PB]
*American baseball player*
* Moore, Cy

**Moore, Willie**
See  Moretti, William

**Moore, Willie** 20th c.  [BWW]
*American musician*
* Moore, Wild Willie

**Moore, Willie C.** 1913-1971
[BWW]
*American singer*
* Boll Weenie Bill
* Boll Weevil Bill

**Moore, Winston Lee** 1919-1966
[CWG]
*American country-western performer*
* Willet, Slim

**Moore-Marriott, George Thomas**
1885-1949  [F2, FC]
*British actor*
* Marriott, Moore

**Mooreau, M.**  [PA]
*Author*
* Beaubien

**Moorer, Boom Boom**
See  Moorer, Elkcanna

**Moorer, Elkcanna** 20th c.  [RBE]
*American boxer*
* Moorer, Boom Boom

**Moorhouse, Herbert Joseph** 1882-
[NAA, WW]
*Canadian author*
* Moorhouse, Hopkins

**Moorhouse, Hilda Vansittart** 20th
c.  [CAP]
*British author*
* Vansittart, Jane

**Moorhouse, Hopkins**
See  Moorhouse, Herbert Joseph

**Moorien, M.**  [PA]
*Author*
* Mariel

**Moorman, Beatrice** 1945-
[IPA, SSS]
*American singer and actress*
* Moore, Melba

**Moorshead, Henry**
See  Pine, Leslie Gilbert

**[The] Moose**
See  Boros, Julius Nicholas

**Moose John**
See  Walker, John Mayon [Johnny]

**Moppert, Gabrielle** 1880- ?  [FC]
*French actress*
* Dorziat, Gabrielle

**Mora, Chato [Pug-Nose Mora]**
See  Mora y Garcia, Jose Antonio

**Mora, Josie** 1948-  [IAW]
*American author*
* Nada, Alivia

**Mora, Vera**
See  Sesan, Karolina Vera

**Mora, Victor** 20th c.  [WECO]
*Spanish cartoonist*
* Alcazar, Victor

**Mora y Garcia, Jose Antonio** 1926-
[GS]
*Spanish bullfighter*
* Mora, Chato [Pug-Nose Mora]

**[A] Moral Byron**
See  Proctor, Bryan Waller

**[The] Moral Censor of China**
See  Confucius [or K'ung Fu-tzu]

**[The] Moral Gower**
See  Gower, John

**[The] Moral Surface**
See  Peel, [Sir] Robert

**Morales, Esy**
See  Morales, Ishmael

**Morales, Ishmael** 1917-1950  [SC]
*Puerto Rican-born actor and
bandleader*
* Morales, Esy

**Morales, Jerry**
See  Morales, Julio Ruben

**Morales, Jorge** 20th c.  [RBE]
*American boxer*
* Dynamita, Kid

**Morales, Julio Ruben** 1949-
[BE, SMG, WWB]
*Puerto Rican-born baseball player*
* Morales, Jerry

**Morales, Luis de** 1509?-1586
[FFF, RH, WBD]
*Spanish painter*
* [The] Divine

**Morales y Mula, Jose** 1883-1939
[GS]
*Spanish bullfighter*
* Ostioncito [Little Oyster]

**Moralisto**
See  Dill, J. M.

**Moran**  [RH, SN]
*King of Ireland*
* [The] Just

**Moran, Albert Thomas** 1912-  [BE]
*American baseball player*
* Moran, Hiker

**Moran, Bugs**
See  Moran, Carl William, II

**Moran, Bugs**
See  Moran, George

**Moran, Butterfingers**
See  Moran, Thomas B.

**Moran, Carl William, II** 1950-
[SMG]
*American baseball player*
* Moran, Bugs

**Moran, Carlo**  [PA]
*Author*
* Bloodgood, Harry

**Moran, Charles B.** 1879-1949
[AS, FB]
*American baseball player and
umpire, football coach*
* Uncle Charlie

**Moran, Charles McMoran Wilson**
See  Wilson, Charles McMoran

**Moran, D.**  [PA]
*Author*
* Murray, Dominick

**Moran, Deedle**
See  Moran, Roy Ellis

**Moran, George**
See  Searcy, George

**Moran, George** 1893-1957  [BLB]
*American underworld figure*
* Miller, George
* Moran, Bugs

**Moran, Gertrude Augusta** 1923-
[B10]
*American tennis player*
* Moran, Gussie

**Moran, Gussie**
See  Moran, Gertrude Augusta

**Moran, Hiker**
See  Moran, Albert Thomas

**Moran, James Edward** 1900-
[BX, RBE]
*American boxer*
* Goodrich, Jimmy

**Moran, Judy**
See  Sellers, Connie Leslie, Jr.

**Moran, Lois**
See  Dowling, Lois Darlington

**Moran, Mae**
See  Beaman, Lottie Kimbrough

**Moran, Mike**
See  Ard, William [Thomas]

**Moran, Owen** 1884-1949
[BX, RBE]
*British boxer*
* [The] Fearless

**Moran, Paddy**
See  Moran, Patrick Joseph

**Moran, Pal**
See  Mirana, Paul

**Moran, Pat**
*See* Mudgett, Helen

**Moran, Patrick Joseph** 1887-1966
[HK]
*Canadian-born hockey player*
* Moran, Paddy

**Moran, Pauline Theresa**
1885-1952    [BEW, F1, F2]
*American actress*
* Moran, Polly

**Moran, Polly**
*See* Moran, Pauline Theresa

**Moran, Roy Ellis** 1884-1966    [BE]
*American baseball player*
* Moran, Deedle

**Moran, Thomas B.** 1892-1971
[BLB]
*American pickpocket*
* Moran, Butterfingers

**Morando, Paolo** 1486-1522  [WBD]
*Veronese painter*
* [Il] Cavazzola [or Cavazzuola]

**Morar**
*See* Fraser, [Sir] William A.

**Morasawa, Chiyo** 20th c.    [EE]
*Japanese intelligence agent*
* Osawa, Lola

**Moratin, Leandro Fernandez**
1760-1828    [DNNF, FFF, SN]
*Spanish playwright and poet*
* [The] Moliere of Spain
* [The] Spanish Moliere

**Moravia, Charles**
*See* Darlouze, Rene

**Morawa, Michael**
*See* Menzel, Roderich

**Moray, Dugald**
*See* Cumming-Skinner, Dugald
Matheson

**Moray, John S.**
*See* Cazauran, Augustus R.

**Morck, Paal** 1876-1931    [EWL]
*Norwegian-American author*
* Rolvaag, Ole Edvaart

**Mordaunt, Charles [Third Earl of
Peterborough]** 1658-1735    [FFF]
*British army and naval officer,
diplomat*
* Smith, Matthew

**Mordaunt, Eleanor [or Elinor]**
*See* Mordaunt, Evelyn May
[Clowes]

**Mordaunt, Evelyn May [Clowes]**
1877?-1942    [TC, TCI, WW]
*British author*
* Mordaunt, Eleanor [or Elinor]
* Riposte, A.

**Mordaunt, Mrs. F. S.**    [FFF]
*Entertainer*
* Fleming, Marion

**Mordechai, Ben**
*See* Gerber, Israel J[oshua]

**Mordichai**
*See* Nathan, Isaac

**Mordvinoff, Nicolas** 1911-1973
[CA]
*Russian-born American author,
artist, illustrator*
* Nicolas

**[The] More**
*See* Sforza, Lodovico [or Ludovico]

**More, Alexandre** 1616-1670    [PA]
*Author*
* Morus

**More, Anthony**
*See* Clinton, Edwin M.

**More, Atherton**
*See* Child, Herbert

**More, Caroline [joint pseudonym
with Margaret Pitcairn Strachan]**
*See* Cone, Molly [Lamken]

**More, Caroline [joint pseudonym
with Molly (Lamken) Cone]**
*See* Strachan, Margaret Pitcairn

**More, Euston**
*See* Bloomer, Arnold Euston More

**More, Henry** 1614-1687    [SN]
*British clergyman and philosopher*
* [The] Chrysostom of Christ's
College
* [An] Intellectual Epicure

**More, Margaret**
*See* Manning, Anne

**More, Phantom**
*See* Smith, James Moore

**More the Great**
*See* Fitzgerald, Gerald

**Moreas, Jean**
*See* Papadiamantopoulos, Iannis

**Moreau, David Merlin** 1927-
[AW, WD]
*British business executive and
author*
* Merlin, David

**Morecambe, Eric**
*See* Bartholomew, [John] Eric

**Morehead, Albert H[odges]**
1909-1966    [CAP]
*American author and editor*
* Hodges, Turner

**Morehead, David Michael** 1943-
[BE]
*American baseball player*
* Morehead, Moe

**Morehead, Moe**
*See* Morehead, David Michael

**Morehead, Moe**
*See* Morehead, Seth Marvin

**Morehead, Seth Marvin** 1934-  [BE]
*American baseball player*
* Morehead, Moe

**Moreira, Ruben** 20th c.  [WECO]
*Cartoonist*
* Rubimor

**Morel**
*See* Deschamps, Eustache

**Morel, Dighton**
*See* Warner, Kenneth [Lewis]

**Morel, Francois Xavier** 20th c.
[FDG]
*Belgian director*
* Rental, J. W.

**Moreland, Margaret Elizabeth**
*See* Cooksley, Margaret Elizabeth

**Morell, Andre**
*See* Mesritz, Andre

**Morell, [Sir] Charles**
*See* Ridley, James

**Morelle, Maureen**
*See* Fullam, Maureen Nina

**Morellet, Andre** 1727-1819    [SN]
*French satirist*
* Bite 'em

**Morelli, Carlo**
*See* Zanelli, Carlos

**Morelli, Giovanni** 1816-1891
[WBD]
*Italian art critic*
* Lermoliev, Ivan

**Morelli, Mme.**    [FFF]
*Entertainer*
* Cornalba, Mlle.

**Morello, Pete**
*See* Morello, Piddu

**Morello, Piddu** ?-1930
[MM, PHM]
*American underworld figure*
* [The] Clutching Hand
* Morello, Pete

**Morely, Ralph**
*See* Hinton, Henry L.

**Moren, Hicks**
*See* Moren, Lewis Howard

**Moren, Lewis Howard** 1883-1966
[BE]
*American baseball player*
* Moren, Hicks

**Moren, Sally M[oore]** 1947-  [CA]
*American author*
* Morgan, Jane

**Morena, Berta**
*See* Meyer, Berta

**Morency, Buster**
*See* Morency, Robert

**Morency, Robert** 1932-1937    [SC]
*Actor*
* Morency, Buster

**Morency, Suzanne Giroux** 1772- ?
[PA]
*Author*
* Quillet, Dame

**Morenito de Algeciras [Little Dark
One from Algeciras]**
*See* Olive Rodas, Diego

**Morenito de Seville, Gino**
*See* Gilmore, Eugene, Airman

**Moreno, Antonio** 1879-1942    [GS]
*Spanish bullfighter*
* Moreno de Alcala [Moreno from
Alcala]

**Moreno, Bento**
*See* Teixeira De Queiroz, Francisco

**Moreno, Francisco** 20th c.    [FIR]
*Actor*
* Moreno, Paco

**Moreno, Marguerite**
*See* Monceau, Lucie

**Moreno, Mario** 1911-
[FC, IPA, OCF]
*Mexican entertainer*
* Cantinflas

**Moreno, Martin**
*See* Swartz, Harry [Felix]

**Moreno, Paco**
*See* Moreno, Francisco

**Moreno, Pajarito**
*See* Moreno, Ricardo

**Moreno, Ricardo** 20th c.    [WBC]
*Mexican boxer*
* Moreno, Pajarito

**Moreno, Rita**
*See* Alverio, Rosita Dolores

**Moreno, Sky Ball**
*See* Moreno, Thomas

**Moreno, Thomas** 1895-1938    [SC]
*American actor and stunt performer*
* Moreno, Sky Ball

**Moreno, Tomas** 20th c.    [GS]
*Spanish bullfighter*
* [El] Tempranillo [The Little
Early One]

**Moreno, Virginia [Reyes]** 1925-
[DLE]
*Filipino poet and playwright*
* Pile

**Moreno, Wenceslas** 1899-    [BMH]
*Spanish ventriloquist*
* Senor Wences

**Moreno, Yen Ye'**
*See* Moreno Quintero, Omar
Renan

**Moreno de Alcala [Moreno from
Alcala]**
*See* Moreno, Antonio

**Moreno del Moral, Jose** 1884-1941
[GS]
*Spanish bullfighter*
* Lagartijillo-Chico [Tiny Lizard]

**Moreno Quintero, Omar Renan**
1953-    [BR]
*Panamanian-born baseball player*
* Moreno, Yen Ye'

**Moreno y Fernandez, Antonio**
1866-1929    [GS]
*Spanish bullfighter*
* Lagartijillo [Little Lizard]

**Morentz, Ethel Irene** 1925-
[CA, IAW]
*American author, poet, educator*
* Fischer, Jakob
* Morentz, Pat

**Morentz, Pat**
*See* Morentz, Ethel Irene

**Morenz, Howarth William**
1902-1937    [CEI, FHE, SR]
*Canadian-born hockey player*
* [The] Babe Ruth of Hockey
* [The] Canadian Catapult
* L'homme-Eclair [The Top Man]
* [The] Marvel of Hockey
* [The] Mitchell Meteor
* Morenz, Howie
* Morenz, Le Grand
* [The] Stratford Streak

**Morenz, Howie**
*See* Morenz, Howarth William

**Morenz, Le Grand**
*See* Morenz, Howarth William

**Moresby, Louis**
*See* Beck, Eliza Louisa Moresby

**Moreskonich, Charles** 1919-    [BE]
*American baseball player*
* Metro, Charles [Charlie]

**Moret, Gallo**
*See*   Moret, Rogelio Torres

**Moret, Neil**
*See*   Daniels, Charles N.

**Moret, Rogelio Torres** 1949-
[BE, SMG]
*Puerto Rican-born baseball player*
* Moret, Gallo
* Moret, Roger

**Moret, Roger**
*See*   Moret, Rogelio Torres

**Moreton, Andrew**
*See*   Foe, Daniel

**Moreton, Clara**
*See*   Moore, Clara [Jessup]

**Moreton, Douglas Arthur** 1928-
[IAW, WD]
*British author*
* Douglas, Arthur
* Douglas, Joyce

**Moreton, John**
*See*   Cohen, Morton N[orton]

**Moretti, Eleanor**
*See*   Rogers, Eleanor

**Moretti, William**  ?-1951
[BLB, PHM]
*American underworld figure*
* Moore, Willie

**[Il] Moretto da Brescia**
*See*   Bonvicino, Alessandro [or
Alexander]

**Morey, Charles**
*See*   Fletcher, Helen Jill

**Morfit, Eleanor Borum [Little]**
1917?-1974    [B10]
*American interior decorator*
* Moore, Nell

**Morfit, Thomas Garrison** 1915-
[IPA, ITA]
*American entertainer*
* Moore, Garry

**Morford, Henry** 1823-1881    [PA]
*Author*
* [The] Governor

**Morgan, Allen D.** 20th c.    [SFP]
*Author*
* Smith, Hogan

**Morgan, Bassett**
*See*   Morgan, Grace Jones

**Morgan, Bruce**
*See*   Hueston, Billy

**Morgan, Charles [Langbridge]**
1894-1958    [LC]
*British author*
* Menander

**Morgan, Chester Collins [Chet]**
1910-    [BE]
*American baseball player*
* Morgan, Chick

**Morgan, Chick**
*See*   Morgan, Chester Collins
[Chet]

**Morgan, Claire**
*See*   Highsmith, [Mary] Patricia

**Morgan, Claudia**
*See*   Wupperman, Claudeigh Louise

**Morgan, Cy**
*See*   Morgan, Harry Richard

**Morgan, De Wolfe**
*See*   Williamson, Thames Ross

**Morgan, Dennis**
*See*   Morner, Stanley

**Morgan, Edwin Willis [Eddie]**
1914-    [BE]
*American baseball player*
* Morgan, Pepper

**Morgan, Emanuel**
*See*   Bynner, Witter

**Morgan, Frank**
*See*   Wupperman, Francis Philip

**Morgan, Fred Troy** 1926-    [CA]
*American author*
* Bleeker, Mordecia

**Morgan, G. J.**
*See*   Rowland, D[onald] S[ydney]

**Morgan, Gene**
*See*   Schwartzkopf, Eugene

**Morgan, Grace Jones** 1885-
[WWL]
*American author*
* Morgan, Bassett

**Morgan, Gwladys M.**
*See*   Lyle, Gwladys M. [Morgan]

**Morgan, Gwyneth**
*See*   Beal, Gwyneth Morgan

**Morgan, Harold Lansford** 1934-
[DAM]
*American jazz musician*
* Morgan, Lanny

**Morgan, Harry**
*See*   Bratsburg, Harry

**Morgan, Harry Richard**
1878-1962    [AS, BE]
*American baseball player*
* Morgan, Cy

**Morgan, Henry**
*See*   Von Ost, Henry Lerner

**Morgan, Hilda Campbell** 20th c.
[LAO]
*Welsh-born author*
* Vaughan, Hilda

**Morgan, Howard** 1936-    [EJ7]
*American jazz musician*
* Morgan, Sonny

**Morgan, Irene**
*See*   Morse, Irl

**Morgan, James Edward** 1883-    [BE]
*American baseball player*
* Morgan, Red

**Morgan, Jane**
*See*   Moren, Sally M[oore]

**Morgan, Jaye P.**
*See*   Morgan, Mary

**Morgan, Jinx**
*See*   Morgan, Judith A[dams]

**Morgan, Joan** 1905-    [BF]
*British actress, author, playwright*
* North, Iris
* Wood, Joan Wentworth

**Morgan, Joseph Leonard [Joe]**
1943-    [IBW]
*American baseball player*
* Little Giant

**Morgan, Judith A[dams]** 1939-
[CA, IAW]
*American author*
* Adams, Judith
* Kragen, Jinx
* Morgan, Jinx

**Morgan, Justina**
*See*   Freeman, Jean Todd

**Morgan, Lady Sidney** 1783-1859
[PA]
*Author*
* Owenson

**Morgan, Lanny**
*See*   Morgan, Harold Lansford

**Morgan, Lee**
*See*   Hallbing, Kjell Kare

**Morgan, Lewis Henry** 1818-1881
[FFF]
*American anthropologist*
* [The] Father of American
  Anthropology

**Morgan, Maggie**
*See*   Cone, Mrs.

**Morgan, Margo**
*See*   Rockwood, Margaret

**Morgan, Marjorie**
*See*   Chibnall, Marjorie
[McCallum]

**Morgan, Mary** 1932-    [RO1]
*American singer*
* Morgan, Jaye P.

**Morgan, McKayla**
*See*   Basile, Gloria Vitanza

**Morgan, Memo**
*See*   Avallone, Michael [Angelo],
Jr.

**Morgan, Michael** [joint pseudonym
with Dean M. Dorn]
*See*   Carle, C. E.

**Morgan, Michael** [joint pseudonym
with C. E. Carle]
*See*   Dorn, Dean M.

**Morgan, Michael**
*See*   Morgenstern, Dan M[ichael]

**Morgan, Michaela**
*See*   Basile, Gloria Vitanza

**Morgan, Michele**
*See*   Roussel, Simone

**Morgan, Murray Cromwell** 1916-
[ANT, WW]
*American author*
* Murray, Cromwell

**Morgan Mwynvawr** 10th c.    [SN]
*Welsh prince and warrior*
* [The] Courteous

**Morgan, Nicholas**
*See*   Morgan, Thomas Bruce

**Morgan, Pepper**
*See*   Morgan, Edwin Willis [Eddie]

**Morgan, Phillip**
*See*   Phillips, Morgan

**Morgan, Piero**
*See*   Piccioni, Piero

**Morgan, Plowboy**
*See*   Morgan, Tom Stephen

**Morgan, Ralph**
*See*   Wupperman, Raphael Kuhner

**Morgan, Red**
*See*   Morgan, James Edward

**Morgan, Robert**
*See*   Turner, Robert [Harry]

**Morgan, Scott**
*See*   Kuttner, Henry

**Morgan, Sharon A[ntonia]** 1951-
[CA]
*American author*
* Fufuka, Karama

**Morgan, Shirley**
*See*   Kiepper, Shirley Morgan

**Morgan, Sonny**
*See*   Morgan, Howard

**Morgan, Sydney** 1783?-1859    [SN]
*Irish author and poet*
* [The] Irish De Stael

**Morgan, Ted**
*See*   De Gramont, Sanche

**Morgan, Thomas Bruce** 1926-1972
[CA]
*American author*
* David, Nicholas
* Morgan, Nicholas

**Morgan, Thomas Christopher**
1914-    [AW, WW]
*British author*
* Muir, John

**Morgan, Tod**
*See*   Pilkington, Bert

**Morgan, Tom**
*See*   Morganelli, Tom

**Morgan, Tom Stephen** 1930-
[ALR, BE]
*American baseball player*
* Morgan, Plowboy

**Morgan, Wesley**
*See*   Bennett, Isadora

**Morgan, Wild Bill**
*See*   Morgan, William

**Morgan, William**
*See*   Miner, William

**Morgan, William** 20th c.    [OBW]
*American baseball player*
* Morgan, Wild Bill

**Morgan, William Sacheus** 20th c.
[ALY]
*Welsh-born author*
* Webley, Pelagian

**Morgan-Grenville, Gerard
[Wyndham]** 1931-    [CA]
*British author*
* Ross, George

**Morgan-Jones, David Sylvanus**
1900-    [ART]
*British painter*
* Voel, David

**Morganelli, Tom** 1909-    [MY]
*American jazz musician*
* Morgan, Tom

**Morganfield, McKinley** 1915-
[BWW, EJ]
*American singer*
* Boss Man
* [The] Living Legend
* Waters, Muddy

**Morganstern, Carl** 1859- ? [THR]
*American-born entertainer*
* Hertz, Carl
* [The] King of Cards

**Morganweck, Frank** 1875-1941
[BB, BBH]
*American basketball promoter,
financier, manager*
* [The] Connie Mack of Pro
Basketball
* Morganweck, Morgie
* Morganweck, Pop

**Morganweck, Morgie**
See Morganweck, Frank

**Morganweck, Pop**
See Morganweck, Frank

**Morgenson, Jorgen** 20th c.
[WECO]
*Danish cartoonist*
* Moco [joint pseudonym with
Cosper Cornelius]

**Morgenstern, Albert** 1926- [BEW]
*American actor*
* Sterne, Morgan

**Morgenstern, Dan M[ichael]** 1929-
[IAW]
*German-born author*
* Morgan, Michael

**Morgenstern, Henrik** 1856-1940
[WBD]
*Hungarian historian*
* Marczali, Henrik

**Morgenthau, Hans J.** 1904- [JL]
*German-born political scientist and
author*
* [The] Father of Power Politics

**Morgenthau, Henry J.** 1891-
[BDW]
*American government official*
* Henry the Morgue

**Morhardt, Meredith Goodwin**
1937- [BE]
*American baseball player*
* Morhardt, Moe

**Morhardt, Moe**
See Morhardt, Meredith Goodwin

**Mori, Ogai**
See Mori, Rintaro

**Mori, Rintaro** 1862-1922 [B10]
*Japanese author, playwright, critic*
* Mori, Ogai

**Morial, Dutch**
See Morial, Ernest Nathan

**Morial, Ernest Nathan** 1929-
[IBW]
*American politician*
* Morial, Dutch

**Moriale, [Fra]**
See D'Albano, Montreal

**Moriarty, Denis Ignatius**
See Daunt, William Joseph O'Neill

**Moriarty, Ellen** [FFF]
*Writer*
* Ellice, Lucy

**Moriarty, Ellen** (Continued)
* Evangeline

**Moriarty, John Singleton**
See Moriarty, W[illia]m Daniel

**Moriarty, Joseph** 1911?-1979
*American underworld figure*
* Moriarty, Newsboy

**Moriarty, Newsboy**
See Moriarty, Joseph

**Moriarty, Patrick Eugene**
1804-1875 [FFF]
*American clergyman and writer*
* Ermite
* Hierophilos

**Moriarty, Tom** 1878- ? [THR]
*Irish-born comedian*
* Stuart, Tom

**Moriarty, W[illia]m Daniel** 1877- ?
[NAA]
*American economist and author*
* Darragh, Darrach
* Moriarty, John Singleton

**Morich, Stanton**
See Griffith-Jones, George
Chetwynd

**Morien, Sydney**
See Archibald, Edith Jessie

**Morier, James Justinian**
1780-1849 [DEL, PA]
*British author and diplomat*
* Hajji Baba of Ispahan
* Persic, Peregrine

**Morimura, Tadasi**
See Yoshikawa, Takeo

**Morin, Claire**
See Dore, Claire [Morin]

**Morin, Etienne** 1899-1966 [MWD]
*French playwright*
* Passeur, Steve

**Morin, Leo-Pol** 1892- [NAA]
*Canadian writer and composer*
* Callihou, James

**Morine, Hoder**
See Conroy, John Wesley [Jack]

**Moriner, Ida** 1876-1937 [THR]
*American actress*
* Conquest, Ida

**Morison, Eileen** 1915- [FC]
*American actress*
* Morison, Patricia

**Morison, Frank**
See Ross, Albert Henry

**Morison, Patricia**
See Morison, Eileen

**Moritz** 1572-1632 [WBD]
*Landgrave of Hesse-Cassel*
* [Der] Gelehrte [The Scholar]

**Morkovin, Bela V.**
See Morkovin, Boris V[ladimir]

**Morkovin, Boris V[ladimir]**
1882-1968 [CAP]
*Russian-born author*
* Morkovin, Bela V.

**Morland**
See Mitterrand, Francois Maurice
Adrien Marie

**Morland, Bart**
See Burrage, Edwin Harcourt

**Morland, Dick**
See Hill, Reginald [Charles]

**Morland, George** 1763-1804
[DEP, DNNS, RH]
*British painter*
* [The] English Teniers

**Morland, Nigel** 1905-
[CA, EMD, IAW]
*British author and editor*
* Dane, Mary
* De Sola, John
* Donavan, John
* Forrest, Norman
* Garnett, Roger
* Kimberley, Hugh
* McCall, John Corey
* McCall, Vincent
* Shepherd, Neal

**Morland, Peter Henry**
See Faust, Frederick [Schiller]

**Morlay, Gaby**
See Fumoleau, Blanche

**Morley, Brian**
See Bradley, Marion Zimmer

**Morley, Charles** 1855-1916 [BEW]
*British-born actor*
* Cartwright, Charles

**Morley, Countess of** 19th c. [PA]
*Author*
* Spruggins, Richard Sucklethum

**Morley, John** 1942- [ART]
*British painter*
* J. M.

**Morley, Karen**
See Linton, Mabel

**Morley, Leroy** 1906- [BB]
*American basketball coach*
* Morley, Stix

**Morley, Mathew**
See Meyer, John M.

**Morley, Mrs.**
See Anne

**Morley, Stix**
See Morley, Leroy

**Morley, Susan**
See Cross, John Keir

**Morley, Wilfred Owen**
See Lowndes, Robert Augustine
Ward

**Mormonenko, Grigori** 1903-
[FC, WEF]
*Russian director*
* Alexandrov, Grigori

**Morna**
See Ladd, Catherine Stratton

**Mornay, Philippe de [Seigneur du
Plessis-Marly]** 1549-1623
[DNNF, RH, WBD]
*Supporter of the French Protestants*
* Duplessis Mornay
* [The] Huguenot Pope
* [Le] Pape des Huguenots
* [The] Pope of the Huguenots

**Morner, Stanley** 1910?-
[FC, ITA, PMJ]
*American actor*
* Morgan, Dennis

**[The] Morning Star of Reformation**
See Waldo, Pierre

**[The] Morning Star of Song**
See Chaucer, Geoffrey

**[The] Morning Star of Stepney**
See Burroughs, Jeremiah

**[The] Morning Star of the
Reformation**
See Wycliffe [or Wyclif], John

**[The] Morning Star of the
Reformation in Germany**
See Lollard, Walter

**Mornington, Edor**
See Roberts, Cecil Edric
Mornington

**[El] Morocho del Abasto [The
Brown-Haired Man from the Market]**
See Gardes, Charles Romuald

**Morogh, Dominick** [FFF]
*Entertainer*
* Murray, Dominick

**Morojo**
See Douglas, Myrtle R.

**Moroni-Celsi, Guido** 1885-1962
[WECO]
*Italian cartoonist*
* Sterny, F.

**Morosco, Oliver**
See Mitchell, Oliver

**Morotius**
See Morozzo, Carlo Giuseppe

**Morozzo, Carlo Giuseppe**
1645-1729 [PA]
*Author*
* Morotius

**Morpurgo, Nelly**
See Morpurgo, Pieternella

**Morpurgo, Pieternella** 1940- [OP]
*Dutch opera singer*
* Morpurgo, Nelly

**Morra, Egidio** 1906- [ASC]
*Italian-born musician*
* Morra, Gene

**Morra, Gene**
See Morra, Egidio

**Morrah, Dermot [Michael
Macgregor]** 1896-1974 [CAP]
*British journalist and author*
* Yorkist

**Morrall, Earl** 1934- [SMG]
*American football player*
* Morrall, Old Bones

**Morrall, Old Bones**
See Morrall, Earl

**Morrell, H. H.**
See Mackenzie, H. H.

**Morrell, John**
See Olsen, Thomas Carl Morrell

**Morrell, Wallace**
See Garrish, Harold J.

**Morren, Theophil**
See Hofmannsthal, Hugo
Hofmann, Edler Von

**Morrill, Honest John**
See Morrill, John Francis

**Morrill, John Francis** 1855-1932
[BE]
*American baseball player and manager*
* Morrill, Honest John

**Morrill, Richard**
*See* Schreck, Everett M.

**Morris**
*See* Bevere, Maurice

**Morris, Alan B.** 1910- [BBH]
*Canadian football player and coach*
* Morris, Teddy

**Morris, Alvin** 1912?- [FC, PMJ]
*American singer and actor*
* Martin, Tony

**Morris, Anthony Paschal** 1849- ?
[WW]
*Author*
* Newton, Nat?

**Morris, Barboura** 1932-1975 [SC]
*American actress*
* O'Neil, Barbour

**Morris, Bert De Wayne** 1914-1959
[FC]
*American actor*
* Morris, Wayne

**Morris, Bugs**
*See* Bennett, Joseph Harley

**Morris, C. A.**
*See* Morris, Charles Alfred

**Morris, Cannonball**
*See* Morris, Edward

**Morris, Captain**
*See* Morris, Charles

**Morris, Carl B.** 1887-1951 [SG]
*American boxer*
* [The] Sapulpa Giant

**Morris, Carrie Finnell** 1893?-1963
[BEW]
*American theatrical performer*
* Finnell, Carrie

**Morris, Charles** 1740?-1838?
[DEL]
*British songwriter*
* Morris, Captain

**Morris, Charles** 1784-1856 [WBD]
*American naval officer*
* [The] Statesman of the American Navy

**Morris, Charles** 1919- [IBW]
*American community organizer*
* Charles 37X
* Kenyatta, Charles

**Morris, Charles Alfred** 1898-
[ART]
*British painter*
* Morris, C. A.

**Morris, Charles Smith** 1833-1922
[WW]
*Author*
* Allen, Hugh
* Ballard, J. D.
* Blake, Redmond?
* Dare, Roland
* Frazier, S. M.
* Inman, Robert Randolph?
* Kaine, George S.
* Lytton, Edward
* Murry, William
* Pastnor, Paul
* Pierce, Jo

**Morris, Charles Smith** (Continued)
* Preston, Paul
* Southard, J. H.
* Tripp, C. E.
* Vincent, E. L.

**Morris, Clara**
*See* Morrison, Clara

**Morris, Corbet**
*See* Thompson, Louis McClanahan

**Morris, Edward** 1859-1937
[AS, BE]
*American baseball player*
* Morris, Cannonball

**Morris, Elizabeth Woodbridge** 1870-
? [NAA]
*American author*
* Woodbridge, Elizabeth

**Morris, Elwin Gordon** 1921- [CEI]
*Canadian-born hockey player*
* Morris, Moe

**Morris, Eph**
*See* Morris, Evan

**Morris, Eugene** 1947-
[FB, IPA, SMG]
*American football player*
* Morris, Mercury

**Morris, Evan** 20th c. [CSH]
*American rowboat racer*
* Morris, Eph

**Morris, G. A.**
*See* MacLean, Katherine

**Morris, George** 1913-1975 [SC]
*American actor*
* McGiver, John

**Morris, Gwendolen Sutherland**
[SFL]
*Author*
* Sutherland, Morris

**Morris, Harold** 20th c. [OBW]
*American baseball player*
* Morris, Yellowhorse

**Morris, Harry**
*See* Birkenhead, Harry

**Morris, Harry** 1918- [IBW]
*Liberian-born industrialist and politician*
* [The] Rubber King

**Morris, Hugh**
*See* Herman, Lewis

**Morris, James Humphrey** 1926-
[CA]
*British author*
* Morris, Jan

**Morris, Jan**
*See* Morris, James Humphrey

**Morris, Jane**
*See* Ardmore, Jane Kesner

**Morris, John** [joint pseudonym with
John Hearne]
*See* Cargill, Morris

**Morris, John** [joint pseudonym with
Morris Cargill]
*See* Hearne, John

**Morris, Johnnie**
*See* Erickson, John Morris

**Morris, Joseph Christopher
Columbus** 1903- [EJ, WWJ]
*American jazz musician*
* Columbus, Chris

**Morris, Joseph Harley**
*See* Bennett, Joseph Harley

**Morris, Julian**
*See* West, Morris L[anglo]

**Morris, Kate** ?-1918 [THR]
*British actress*
* Serjeantson, Kate

**Morris, Katherine**
*See* Pike, Mrs. F. A. M.

**Morris, Kenneth** 1879-1937 [SFL]
*Author*
* Morus, Cenydd

**Morris, Lana**
*See* Matthews, Pamela

**Morris, Leo** 1939- [EJ7]
*American jazz musician*
* Muhammad, Idris

**Morris, [Sir] Lewis** 1833- ? [WWL]
*Author*
* New Writer

**Morris, Mercury**
*See* Morris, Eugene

**Morris, Michael** 1942- [CAR]
*Canadian painter*
* Dot, Marcel
* General Idea, Miss
* Idea, Marcel

**Morris, Moe**
*See* Morris, Elwin Gordon

**Morris, Mrs. Austin W.** [FFF]
*Entertainer*
* Toucey, Kate

**Morris, Myron**
*See* Stearns, Myron Morris

**Morris, Nobuko**
*See* Albery, Nobuko

**Morris, Old Tom**
*See* Morris, Thomas, Sr.

**Morris, Olive** 1884- [THR]
*British actress*
* Terry, Olive

**Morris, Patrick**
*See* Bouchard De Montmerency,
William Geoffrey

**Morris, Patsy** 1930?-
*American opponent of capital punishment*
* [The] Queen of Death Row

**Morris, Peter**
*See* Lockhart, John Gibson

**Morris, Robert** 1818- ? [FFF]
*Author*
* [The] Poet Laureate of
Freemasonry

**Morris, Robert** 1911- [ASC]
*American composer*
* Miketta, Bob

**Morris, Ruby Turner** 1908- [CA]
*American economist and author*
* Norris, Ruby Turner

**Morris, Ruth**
*See* Webb, Ruth Enid Borlase
Morris

**Morris, Samuel** 1700-1770? [FFF]
*American clergyman*
* [The] Father of Presbyterianism
in Virginia

**Morris, Samuel V.** [FFF]
*Writer*
* Hoosier

**Morris, Sara**
*See* Burke, John [Frederick]

**Morris, Stephen**
*See* Nussbaum, Morris

**Morris, Steveland** 1950-
[IBW, IPA, SSS]
*American singer and composer*
* [The] Man
* Wonder, Little Stevie
* Wonder, Stevie

**Morris, Teddy**
*See* Morris, Alan B.

**Morris, Thomas, Jr.** 1850-1875
[BWG, EG, GF]
*Scottish golfer*
* Morris, Young Tom

**Morris, Thomas, Sr.** 1821-1908
[BWG, EG, GF]
*Scottish golfer*
* Morris, Old Tom

**Morris, Tony**
*See* Moore, Tony

**Morris, Wayne**
*See* Morris, Bert De Wayne

**Morris, William**
*See* Fluhrer, John L.

**Morris, Yellowhorse**
*See* Morris, Harold

**Morris, Young Tom**
*See* Morris, Thomas, Jr.

**Morris-Goodall, Vanne** 1909- [CA]
*British author*
* Goodall, Vanne Morris

**Morrison, Arthur** 1863- ? [WWL]
*British author*
* Hewitt, Martin

**Morrison, C. T.**
*See* Morrison, Charles Theodore

**Morrison, Charles Theodore** 1936-
[LBA]
*American author*
* Morrison, C. T.

**Morrison, Clara** 1846-1925
[BEW, FFF]
*Canadian-born actress and writer*
* Morris, Clara

**Morrison, Crutchy**
*See* Morrison, John

**Morrison, Curley**
*See* Morrison, Fred

**Morrison, Dwight** 20th c. [SMG]
*American basketball player*
* Morrison, Red

**Morrison, Eula Atwood** 1911-
[CA, WD]
*American author*
* Atwood, Drucy
* Delmonico, Andrea

**Morrison, Fred** [SMG]
*American football player*
* Morrison, Curley

**Morrison, Fred** 1923-    [IBW]
*American underwater demolition expert*
* Morrison, Tiz

**Morrison, George** 1891-1973    [SC]
*American actor*
* Morrison, Pete

**Morrison, Gert W.** [house pseudonym] [Stratemeyer Syndicate]
*See* Stratemeyer, Edward L.

**Morrison, Heady** 19th c.    [PA]
*Author*
* Juvinell, Uncle

**Morrison, Irving**
*See* Morse, Irl

**Morrison, James** 19th c.    [SN]
*British financier*
* [The] Modern Croesus

**Morrison, Jeanette Helen** 1927-
[BDF, FC, IPA]
*American actress*
* Leigh, Janet

**Morrison, Jim** 1943-1971    [PRS]
*American singer*
* [The] Lizard King

**Morrison, John** 17th c.    [PA]
*Author*
* Struys, John

**Morrison, John** 20th c.    [CEI]
*Hockey player*
* Morrison, Crutchy

**Morrison, John A.** 1919-    [EJ]
*American jazz musician*
* Morrison, Peck

**Morrison, John Dewey** 1895-1966
[BE, BTB]
*American baseball player*
* Morrison, Jughandle Johnny

**Morrison, Jughandle Johnny**
*See* Morrison, John Dewey

**Morrison, Kathleen** 1900-    [F1, F2]
*American actress*
* Moore, Colleen

**Morrison, Margaret Mackie**
?-1973    [CA]
*Scottish-born author*
* Cost, March
* Morrison, Peggy

**Morrison, Marion Michael**
1907-1979    [BDF, F2, FC]
*American actor*
* [The] Duke
* Wayne, John

**Morrison, Marsh** 1902-    [CA]
*American chiropractor and author*
* Marsh, Analyticus

**Morrison, Mary**
*See* Washburne, Mary B.

**Morrison, Michael A.** 1934-    [ITA]
*American producer and film executive*
* Wayne, Michael A.

**Morrison, Mrs. Lewis**    [FFF]
*Entertainer*
* Wood, Rose

**Morrison, Paul Fix** 1902-    [FC]
*American actor*
* Fix, Paul

**Morrison, Peck**
*See* Morrison, John A.

**Morrison, Peggy**
*See* Morrison, Margaret Mackie

**Morrison, Pete**
*See* Morrison, George

**Morrison, Red**
*See* Morrison, Dwight

**Morrison, Richard**
*See* Lowndes, Robert Augustine Ward

**Morrison, Richard James**
1795-1874    [DNNF, RH, WBD]
*British astrologer*
* Zadkiel

**Morrison, Robert**
*See* Lowndes, Robert Augustine Ward

**Morrison, Roberta**
*See* Webb, Jean Francis

**Morrison, Ross Zane**
*See* Marinoni, Rosa Zagnoni

**Morrison, Thomas James** 20th c.
[AW]
*Scottish author*
* Muir, Alan

**Morrison, Tiz**
*See* Morrison, Fred

**Morrison, Toni**
*See* Wofford, Chloe Anthony

**Morrison, Velma Ford** 1909-    [CA]
*American publisher and author*
* Ford, Hildegarde

**Morrison, Victor**
*See* Glut, Donald F[rank]

**Morrison, William**
*See* Samachson, Joseph

**Morrison, William** 1888-1960    [SC]
*Irish-born actor*
* Rainey, Norman

**Morriss, J. H.**
*See* Ghnassia, Maurice [Jean-Henri]

**Morrissey, Deacon**
*See* Morrissey, Frank Frederick

**Morrissey, Frank Frederick** 20th c.
[BE]
*American baseball player*
* Morrissey, Deacon

**Morrissey, Jo-Jo**
*See* Morrissey, Joseph Anselm

**Morrissey, John Albert** [Jack]
1877-1936    [BE]
*American baseball player*
* Morrissey, King

**Morrissey, Joseph Anselm**
1904-1950    [BE]
*American baseball player*
* Morrissey, Jo-Jo

**Morrissey, Joseph Laurence** 1905-
[ESF, SFL, WGT]
*American author*
* Richards, Henry
* Saxon, Richard

**Morrissey, King**
*See* Morrissey, John Albert [Jack]

**Morros, Boris**
*See* Milhailovitch, Boris

**Morrough, E. R.** 20th c.    [SFL]
*Author*
* Abu Nadaar

**Morrow, Betty**
*See* Bacon, Elizabeth

**Morrow, Buddy**
*See* Zudekoff, Muni

**Morrow, Charlotte**
*See* Kirwan, Molly [Morrow]

**Morrow, Doretta**
*See* Marano, Doretta

**Morrow, Harry C.** 1866-1938
[DIL]
*Irish playwright and actor*
* MacNamara, Gerald

**Morrow, W. C.**
*See* Morrow, William Chambers

**Morrow, William Chambers**
1853-1923    [HFF]
*American author*
* Morrow, W. C.

**Morse, Anne Christensen** 1915-
[CA]
*American author*
* Head, Ann

**Morse, Bud**
*See* Morse, Newell Obediah

**Morse, Carol**
*See* Yeakley, Marjory Hall

**Morse, Dolly**
*See* Morse, Theodora

**Morse, H[enry] Clifton, IV** 1924-
[CA]
*American author*
* Clifton Fourth

**Morse, Hap**
*See* Morse, Peter R.

**Morse, Irl** 1894-    [NAA]
*American editor, poet, critic*
* Baldwin, Douglas
* Morgan, Irene
* Morrison, Irving

**Morse, Jedediah** 1761-1826
[FFF, WBD]
*American clergyman and author*
* [The] Father of American Geography

**Morse, Katharine Duncan** 1888-
[WGT]
*American author*
* Doane, Jerry

**Morse, Martha Wilson** 1900-
[AW]
*American author*
* Wilson, Martha

**Morse, Newell Obediah** 1904-    [BE]
*American baseball player*
* Morse, Bud

**Morse, Peter R.** 20th c.    [BE]
*American baseball player*
* Morse, Hap

**Morse, Richard**
*See* Eastman, Fred

**Morse, Samuel Finley Breese**
1791-1872    [FFF]
*American inventor*
* [The] Father of the Telegraph

**Morse, Theodora** 1890-1953
[ASC, DAM]
*American lyricist*
* Esrom, D. A.
* Morse, Dolly
* Terriss, Dorothy

**Morse, Withrow** 1880- ?    [NAA]
*American chemist and writer*
* Rankin, John

**Morsell, Mrs. Herndon**    [FFF]
*Entertainer*
* Burton, Lizzie

**Morss, Elizabeth W.** 1918-    [CA]
*American artist*
* Mixter, Elisabeth W.

**Mort, Vivian**
*See* Cromie, Alice Hamilton

**Mortensen, Lee**
*See* Mortensen, Leland

**Mortensen, Leland** 20th c.    [BBH]
*American horseshoe pitcher*
* Mortensen, Lee

**Mortensson, Ivar** 1857-1934
[WBD]
*Norwegian author, journalist, theologian*
* Mortensson-Egnund, Ivar

**Mortensson-Egnund, Ivar**
*See* Mortensson, Ivar

**[The] Mortician**
*See* Gotshalk, Len

**Mortier, Arnold**    [PA]
*Author*
* [Le] Monsieur de l'Orchestre

**Mortier, Marie Antoinette** 1882- ?
[WBD]
*French author*
* Aurel

**Mortimer**
*See* Cade, John [Jack]

**Mortimer**
*See* Murphey, J. M.

**Mortimer, Chapman**
*See* Chapman-Mortimer, William Charles

**Mortimer, Charles**
*See* Chapman-Mortimer, William Charles

**Mortimer, Gilbert**
*See* Gibbs, Montgomery

**Mortimer, Grace**
*See* Stuart, M. B.

**Mortimer, Henry**
*See* Rennie, John O. D.

**Mortimer, January**
*See* Gallichan, Walter M.

**Mortimer, John** [Clifford] 1923-
[B10, WD]
*British playwright and author*
* Lincoln, Geoffrey

**Mortimer, John Hamilton**
1741-1779    [DEP, DNNS, RH]
*British painter*
* [The] English Salvator Rosa

**Mortimer, Lee**
See   Lieberman, Mortimer

**Mortimer, Lottie**
See   Paff, Mrs. Charles

**Mortimer, Mrs. N. E.**   [PA]
*Author*
* Rayland, Rose

**Mortimer, Penelope [Ruth]** 1918-
[CA, WD]
*British author and columnist*
* Dimont, Penelope
* Temple, Ann

**Mortimer, Peter**
See   Roberts, Dorothy James

**Morton, A. Q.** 1919-   [AW]
*Scottish clergyman and author*
* Kew, Andrew

**Morton, Air Mail**
See   Morton, William H.

**Morton, Anthony**
See   Creasey, John

**Morton, Benny**
See   Morton, Henry Sterling

**Morton, Bubba**
See   Morton, Wycliffe Nathaniel

**Morton, Burley**
See   Morton, George

**Morton, Carl Wendle** 1944-   [SMG]
*American baseball player*
* Morton, Mo

**Morton, Charles**
See   Mudge, Carl

**Morton, Charles** 1819- ?   [DNNS]
*Music hall manager*
* [The] Father of the Halls

**Morton, Craig** 1943-
*American football player*
* Morton, Curly

**Morton, Curly**
See   Morton, Craig

**Morton, Eleanor**
See   Stern, Elizabeth Gertrude
[Levin]

**Morton, Flutes**
See   Morton, Norvel E.

**Morton, George** 20th c.   [RO2]
*American record producer*
* Morton, Shadow

**Morton, George** 20th c.   [IBW]
*American horse trainer*
* Morton, Burley

**Morton, Guy, Jr.** 1930-   [BE]
*American baseball player*
* Morton, Moose

**Morton, Guy Mainwaring**
1896-1968   [LAO, LC, WW]
*British author and playwright*
* Forrest, Mark
* Traill, Peter

**Morton, H. V.**
See   Morton, Henry Canova Vollam

**Morton, Helen Marie** 1936-   [CAR]
*American artist*
* Morton, Ree

**Morton, Henry Canova Vollam**
1892-   [LC, TC]
*British author*
* Morton, H. V.

**Morton, Henry Sterling** 1907-
[DAM, EJ, NP]
*American jazz musician*
* Bones, Mr.
* Morton, Benny

**Morton, Hugh** 1865-1916   [BEW]
*American-born playwright, librettist,
lyricist*
* McLellan, C. M. S.

**Morton, J. B.**
See   Morton, John [Cameron
Andrieu] Bingham [Michael]

**Morton, Jelly Roll**
See   La Menthe, Ferdinand Joseph

**Morton, John** 1724?-1777   [FFF]
*American financier*
* [The] Rebel Banker

**Morton, John [Cameron Andrieu]
Bingham [Michael]** 1893-1979
[B10, CA, LC]
*British author and columnist*
* Beachcomber [newspaper column
    pseudonym, 1924- ]
* Morton, J. B.

**Morton, Joseph**
See   Richman, Al

**Morton, Maxine**
See   West, Katherine

**Morton, Mo**
See   Morton, Carl Wendle

**Morton, Moose**
See   Morton, Guy, Jr.

**Morton, Mort, Jr.**
See   Meskin, Morton

**Morton, Nails**
See   Morton, Samuel J.

**Morton, Norvel E.** 1900?-1962
[WWJ]
*American jazz musician*
* Morton, Flutes

**Morton, Oliver [Hazard] Perry
[Throck]** 1823-1877   [FF, SN]
*American politician*
* [The] Devil on Two Sticks

**Morton, Patience**
See   Govan, [Mary] Christine
Noble

**Morton, Patricia**
See   Golding, Morton J[ay]

**Morton, Ree**
See   Morton, Helen Marie

**Morton, Samuel J.** ?-1923   [BLB]
*American underworld figure*
* Morton, Nails

**Morton, Sarah Wentworth**
1752?-1806?   [FFF, WBD]
*American poet*
* [The] American Mrs. Montague
* Philenia [or Phililenia?]

**Morton, Shadow**
See   Morton, George

**Morton, Sparrow**
See   Morton, William H.

**Morton, Thomas** ?-1646?   [SN]
*British author*
* [A] Troubler of Israel

**Morton, William**
See   Ferguson, William Blair
Morton

**Morton, William Ferdinand Joseph**
See   La Menthe, Ferdinand Joseph

**Morton, William H.** 19th c.   [BE]
*American baseball player*
* Morton, Sparrow

**Morton, William H.** 1909-   [FB]
*American football player*
* Morton, Air Mail

**Morton, Wycliffe Nathaniel** 1931-
[BE]
*American baseball player*
* Morton, Bubba

**Mortson, Gus**
See   Mortson, James Angus Gerald

**Mortson, James Angus Gerald**
1925-   [CEI, FHE]
*Canadian-born hockey player*
* Mortson, Gus

**Morum, William** 20th c.   [AW]
*British author and playwright*
* Smith, Surrey [joint pseudonym
    with William Dinner]

**Morus**
See   More, Alexandre

**Morus, Cenydd**
See   Morris, Kenneth

**Morvan, Yves** 1909-   [IAW]
*French journalist and author*
* Marin, Jean

**Moryn, Moose**
See   Moryn, Walter Joseph

**Moryn, Walter Joseph** 1926-   [BE]
*American baseball player*
* Moryn, Moose

**Mosa**
See   Gribaldi, Matteo

**Mosbacher, Bus**
See   Mosbacher, Emil

**Mosbacher, Emil** 20th c.
*American sailboat racer*
* Mosbacher, Bus

**Moscherosch [or Mosenrosh], Johann
Michael** 1601-1669   [WBD]
*German author*
* [The] Dreamer
* Von Sittewald, Philander

**Moscovitch, Maurice**
See   Masskoff, Maurice

**Moscovitch, Nathaniel** 1905?-   [FC]
*American actor*
* Madison, Nat
* Madison, Noel

**Moscowitz, Jennie**
See   Silverstein, Jennie

**Mose**
See   Depond, Moise

**Moseilma** 7th c.   [RH]
*Claimed to be a prophet*
* [The] Liar

**Moseka, Aminata**
See   Woolridge, Anna Marie

**Mosel, George Ault, Jr.** 1922-
[BEW]
*American playwright*
* Mosel, Tad

**Mosel, Tad**
See   Mosel, George Ault, Jr.

**Moseley, Hallam Reynold** 1948-
[DC]
*West Indian cricketer*
* [The] Black Flash
* Moseley, Mojo
* Moses the Lawgiver

**Moseley, Mojo**
See   Moseley, Hallam Reynold

**Moseley, Robert** 1922-
[FC, IPA, ITA]
*American actor*
* Madison, Guy

**Moselly, Emile** 1870-1918   [WBD]
*French author*
* Chenin, Emile

**Moser, Hans**
See   Juliet, Jean

**Moses, Anna Mary Robertson**
1860?-1961
*American artist*
* Moses, Grandma

**Moses, Annie** 1860-1926   [AS, NN]
*American sharpshooter*
* Little Sure Shot
* Mozee, Annie
* Oakley, Annie

**Moses, Bob**
See   Parris, Bob

**Moses, Grandma**
See   Moses, Anna Mary Robertson

**Moses, Hilda Theresa** 20th c.
[BEW]
*American actress*
* Simms, Hilda

**Moses, Louis**   [FFF]
*American actor and playwright*
* Aldrich, Louis

**[The] Moses of Athens**
See   Aristocles

**[The] Moses of Mesopotamia**
See   Jacobus

**Moses, Peepsight**
See   Moses, Wallace [Wally]

**Moses, Ruben**
See   Wurmbrand, Richard

**Moses the Lawgiver**
See   Moseley, Hallam Reynold

**Moses the Son of Jehoshar**
See   Ebel, Henry

**Moses to Her People**
See   Tubman, Harriet Araminta
Ross Davis

**Moses, Wallace [Wally]** 1910-
[BN]
*American baseball player*
* Moses, Peepsight

**Mosesson, Gloria R[ubin]** 20th c.
[CA]
*American editor*
* French, Kathryn

**Mosesson, Gloria R[ubin]**
(Continued)
* Miller, Doris R.

**Moshe, David**
*See* Winkelman, Donald M.

**Mosher, Frederick C.** 1913- [IAW]
*American author*
* Fritz

**Mosher, L. E.** [FFF]
*American writer*
* Wagoner, Hank

**Mosher, T. B.**
*See* Mosher, Thomas Bird

**Mosher, [Christopher] Terry** 1942-
[CA]
*Canadian author and cartoonist*
* Aislin

**Mosher, Thomas Bird** 1852-1923
[LC]
*Publisher*
* Mosher, T. B.

**Moshinski, Albert** 1925- [EMT]
*American director*
* Marre, Albert

**Mosier, Marilyn** 1929- [BEW]
*American actress, dancer,
comedienne*
* Lynn, Mara

**Mosina, Czecho**
*See* Mosina, Tarcisio

**Mosina, Tarcisio** 1951- [AES]
*Yugoslav soccer player*
* Mosina, Czecho

**Moskiman, Doc**
*See* Moskiman, William Bankhead

**Moskiman, William Bankhead**
1879-1953 [BE]
*American baseball player*
* Moskiman, Doc

**Moskowitz, Harry** 1904- [EJS]
*American basketball coach*
* Moskowitz, Jammy

**Moskowitz, Jammy**
*See* Moskowitz, Harry

**Moskowitz, Sam** 1920- [CA, CC]
*American author and editor*
* Martin, Sam

**Moskvitin, Jurij**
*See* Hansen, Jurij

**Mosley, Baptiste** 1893-1965 [NOJ]
*American jazz musician*
* Mosley, Bat

**Mosley, Bat**
*See* Mosley, Baptiste

**Mosley, Lawrence Leo** 1909-
[EJ, PMJ, WWJ]
*American jazz musician*
* [The] Man with the Funny Horn
* Mosley, Snub

**Mosley, [Sir] Oswald [Ernald]**
1896-1980 [CAP]
*British legislator and author*
* European

**Mosley, Snub**
*See* Mosley, Lawrence Leo

**Moss, Buddy**
*See* Moss, Eugene

**Moss, Crazy Horse**
*See* Moss, Robert

**Moss, Eugene** 1906- [BWW]
*American singer*
* Miller, Jim
* Moss, Buddy

**Moss, John** 20th c.
*American poker player*
* Moss, Texas Johnny

**Moss, Nancy**
*See* Moss, Robert [Alfred]

**Moss, Robert [Alfred]** 1903- [CAP]
*British author*
* Moss, Nancy
* Moss, Roberta

**Moss, Robert** 20th c. [SMG]
*American football player*
* Moss, Crazy Horse

**Moss, Roberta**
*See* Moss, Robert [Alfred]

**Moss, Rose** 1937- [CA]
*South African-born educator and
author*
* Johannes, R.

**Moss, Texas Johnny**
*See* Moss, John

**Mossbank** [code name used during
World War II]
*See* Laval, Pierre

**Mosser, Ann J.** 1912-
*American author*
* Allwood, Edith
* Brown, M. E.
* Hall, B. K.
* Ressom, J. Ann

**Mossi, Donald Louis** 1929- [BE]
*American baseball player*
* [The] Sphinx

**Mossman, Dow** 1943- [CA]
*American author*
* O'Quill, Scarlett

**Mossop, Irene**
*See* Swatridge, Irene Maude
[Mossop]

**[The] Most Beautiful Girl on Radio**
*See* Eden, Ann

**[The] Most Christian Doctor**
*See* Charlier, Jean

**[The] Most Christian Doctor**
*See* De Cusa, Nicholas

**[The] Most Christian King**
*See* Charles I

**Most Christian King**
*See* Louis XI

**Most Christian King**
*See* Pepin III

**[The] Most Enlightened Doctor**
*See* Lully, Raymond

**Most Erudite of the Romans**
*See* Varro, Marcus Terentius

**Most Faithful Majesty**
*See* John V

**[The] Most Learned Fool in
Christendom**
*See* James I

**Most Learned of the Romans**
*See* Varro, Marcus Terentius

**[The] Most Methodical Doctor**
*See* Bassol, John

**[The] Most Profound Doctor**
*See* Aegidius [or Giles] of Colonna

**[The] Most Remarkable Man on
Earth**
*See* Bodie, Sam

**[The] Most Resolute Doctor**
*See* Durand de St. Pourcain,
Guillaume

**Mostel, Samuel Joel** 1915-1977
[BEW, EMT, IPA]
*American actor*
* Mostel, Zero

**Mostel, Zero**
*See* Mostel, Samuel Joel

**Mostil, Bananas**
*See* Mostil, John Anthony

**Mostil, John Anthony** 1896-1970
[DGS, PB]
*American baseball player*
* Mostil, Bananas

**Mostyn-Owen, Gaia**
*See* Servadio, Gaia [Cecilia
Gemmalina]

**Mota, Manny**
*See* Mota, Manuel Rafael

**Mota, Manuel Rafael** 1938-
[BE, PB, SMG]
*Dominican-born baseball player*
* Mota, Manny
* Mota, Mickey
* Mota, Pee Wee

**Mota, Mickey**
*See* Mota, Manuel Rafael

**Mota, Pee Wee**
*See* Mota, Manuel Rafael

**Motassem, Al-** [HN]
*Caliph*
* [The] Eight

**Motaung, Boy-Boy**
*See* Motaung, Kaiser

**Motaung, Kaiser** 1944- [AES]
*South African soccer player*
* Motaung, Boy-Boy

**Moten, Benny**
*See* Moten, Clarence Lemont

**Moten, Clarence Lemont** 1916-
[EJ]
*American jazz musician*
* Moten, Benny

**Moth**
*See* Fleming, [Robert] Peter

**Mothell, Carroll Ray** 1897- [MK]
*American baseball player*
* Mothell, Dink

**Mothell, Dink**
*See* Mothell, Carroll Ray

**[A] Mother**
*See* Bird, Sarah

**[The] Mother**
*See* Richard, Mira

**Mother Ann**
*See* Lee, Ann

**Mother Goose**
*See* Bowen, Ruth J. Baskerville

**Mother Goose**
*See* Fleet, Thomas

**Mother Goose**
*See* Foster, Elizabeth

**Mother Goose**
*See* Perrault, Charles

**Mother Hubbard**
*See* Spenser, Edmund

**Mother Julia**
*See* Billiart, Marie R. J.

**Mother Maybelle**
*See* Carter, Maybelle

**Mother MD**
*See* Cilento, Phyllis Dorothy

**[The] Mother of Believers**
*See* Ayesha [or Ayeshah]

**[The] Mother of Gospel Music**
*See* Smith, Willie Mae Ford

**[The] Mother of Her Country**
*See* Maria Theresa

**[The] Mother of Mod**
*See* Quant, Mary

**[The] Mother of Tennis**
*See* Outerbridge, Mary Ewing

**[The] Mother of the Blues**
*See* Rainey, Gertrude Malissa Nix
[Pridgett]

**[The] Mother of the Camps**
*See* Victoria [or Victorina]

**[The] Mother of the Civil Rights
Movement**
*See* Parks, Rose

**[The] Mother of the Gracchi**
*See* Cornelia

**[The] Mother of the Irish Drama**
*See* Gregory, [Lady] Isabella
Augusta Persse

**[The] Mother of the Mountains**
*See* Hance, Margaret

**[The] Mother of the Movies**
*See* Cogan, Fanny Hay

**[The] Mother of the People**
*See* Margaret [or Marguerite] of
France

**[The] Mother of the Salvation Army**
*See* Booth, Catherine Mumford

**Mother of the Sun-Bonnet Babies**
*See* Melcher, Bertha Corbett

**[The] Mother of the World**
*See* Bojaxhiu, Agnes Gonxha

**Motherwell, Hiram**
*See* Moderwell, Hiram K.

**Motley, Arthur Harrison** 1900-
[B10]
*American publisher*
* Motley, Red

**Motley, Marion** 1921- [IBW]
*American football player*
* Motley, Tank

**Motley, Mary**
*See* De Reneville, Mary Margaret
Motley Sheridan

**Motley, Mrs.** [PA]
*Author*
* Derrick, Frances

**Motley, Red**
See Motley, Arthur Harrison

**Motley, Tank**
See Motley, Marion

**Motolinicafoutli**
See Davila Garibi, Jose Ignacio

**[The] Motor City Cobra**
See Hearns, Thomas

**[The] Motor City Madman**
See Nugent, Ted

**Motor Mouth**
See Young, Andrew Jackson, Jr.

**[The] Motorized Cowboy**
See Bryan, Jimmy

**Mott, Alfred Julius** [PA]
*Author*
* Barrowcliffe, A. J.

**Mott, Bitsy**
See Mott, Elisha Matthew

**Mott, Edward Spencer** 1844-1910
[WW]
*Author*
* Gubbins, Nathaniel
* Spencer, Edward

**Mott, Elisha Matthew** 1918- [BE]
*American baseball player*
* Mott, Bitsy

**Mott, Michael** 1930- [DLE]
*British poet and author*
* Alston, Charles

**Mott, Vincent Valmon** 1916- [CA]
*American economist and author*
* St. Andre, Lucien

**Motte, Peter**
See Harrison, Richard [Motte]

**Mottley, John** 1692-1750 [PA]
*Author*
* Miller, Joe

**Mottola, Tony** 1918- [PMJ]
*American musician*
* Big, Mr.

**Motton, Curt**
See Motton, Curtell Howard

**Motton, Curtell Howard** 1940-
[BE]
*American baseball player*
* Motton, Curt

**Mottram, R. H.**
See Mottram, Ralph Hale

**Mottram, Ralph Hale** 1883-1971
[LC, TC]
*British author*
* Mottram, R. H.

**Motz, Josephine** 1891-1964 [SC]
*American actress*
* Taylor, Josephine

**Mouhadjou [or Mahdjou], [Said]
Moustapha**
See Denard, Robert [Bob]

**Mouillot, Gertrude**
See Davison, Gertrude

**Mould, Mrs. Henry S.** [FFF]
*Entertainer*
* Manola, Marion

**Moule, H.** 19th c. [PA]
*Author*
* [A] Country Parson

**Moule, Winifred Ruby** 1920- [TR]
*British actress and singer*
* Lee, Vanessa

**Moules, Peter** 20th c. [RO2]
*British singer*
* [The] Count

**Moulie, Charles** 1890- [WBD]
*French author*
* Sandre, Thierry

**Mouligneau, Michel** 1935- [IAW]
*Belgian author*
* De Guy Latteur

**Moulin, Louis du** 1603?-1680?
[FFF]
*Historian and author*
* Philalethes, Irenaeus

**Moulton, Albert Theodore** 1886-
[BE]
*American baseball player*
* Moulton, Ollie

**Moulton, Carl**
See Tubb, Edwin Charles

**Moulton, Charles**
See Marston, William Moulton

**Moulton, Ellen Louise Chandler**
1835-1908 [FFF, PA]
*American poet*
* Ellen Louise
* L. C. M.
* Louise Ellen

**Moulton, Mabel**
See Noyes, Mrs. A. C.

**Moulton, Ollie**
See Moulton, Albert Theodore

**Moultrie, George** 19th c. [PA]
*Author*
* Montgomery, Girard

**Moultrie, John** 1804?- ? [FFF]
*British poet*
* Montgomery, Gerald

**Mounet, Jean Sully** 1841-1916
[BEW]
*French-born actor*
* Mounet-Sully, Jean

**Mounet-Sully, Jean**
See Mounet, Jean Sully

**Mount Cashel, Earl of** 1791?-1883
[FFF]
*Irish aristocrat*
* [The] Father of the House of
Lords

**Mount, Elisabeth**
See Dougherty, Betty

**Mount Washington**
See Washington, Russell

**[The] Mountain Brutus**
See Tell, William

**[The] Mountain Evangelist**
See Jones, Sam[uel Porter]

**Mountain Fern**
See Williamson, LaVerne

**[The] Mountain Man**
See Walton, Bill

**Mountain Man Roberts**
See Roberts, Dale

**Mountain Music Melton**
See Melton, Clifford George

**Mountain, Robert**
See Montgomery, Raymond A., Jr.

**[The] Mountain Tiger of Nepaul**
See Ranjit [or Runjeet], Singh

**Mountbatten, Richard**
See Wallmann, Jeffrey M[iner]

**Mountcastle, Fanny**
See Thorp, Mrs. Charles R.

**[A] Mountebank in Criticism**
See Warburton, William

**Mountfield, David**
See Grant, Neil

**[The] Mountie of American
Corporate Chiefs**
See Bradshaw, Thornton

**Mountjoy, Desmond**
See Chapman-Huston, D. M.

**Mountjoy, Earl** 16th c. [FFF]
*British aristocrat*
* [The] Kitchen Maid in Ireland

**Mountjoy, Medicine Bill**
See Mountjoy, William R. [Billy]

**Mountjoy, William R. [Billy]**
1857-1894 [BE]
*American baseball player*
* Mountjoy, Medicine Bill

**Moura, Joaq** 20th c.
*Brazilian eccentric*
* [The] Kisser

**Mouravieff, Nicholas** 1793-1866
[FFF]
*Russian army officer and governor
of Lithuania*
* [The] Hangman of Lithuania

**Mouray**
See Merlin, Jean Raymond

**Mourdaunt, Mrs. Frank** [FFF]
*Entertainer*
* Wallace, Laura

**Mourer, Marie-Louise-Jeanne**
1922-1967 [BDF, OCF, WEF]
*French actress*
* Arley, Catherine
* Arley, Maryse
* Carol, Martine
* Mourer, Maryse

**Mourer, Maryse**
See Mourer, Marie-Louise-Jeanne

**Mouron, Adolphe Jean Marie**
1901-1968 [B10]
*French illustrator*
* Cassandre, A. M.

**Mouskos, Mikhail** 1913-1977
*Archbishop and president of Cyprus*
* [The] Dark Priest
* Mack the Knife
* Makarios III

**Moussard, Jacqueline** 1924- [CA]
*French author*
* Cervon, Jacqueline

**Moustakas, Alkiviadis** 1923- [CA]
*American journalist*
* Manos, Charley

**Mouth**
See Duyn, Willem

**[The] Mouth of the South**
See Turner, Robert Edward, III

**Mouthpiece**
See Porter, Maurice Malcolm

**Moutis, Patrice Des** 1919?-1975
[B10]
*French gambler*
* Monsieur X

**Mouvet, Maurice** 1886?-1927
[BEW]
*Dancer*
* Maurice

**Move Up Joe**
See Gerhardt, John Joseph

**Movshovitz, Israel** 1870-1939
[WBD]
*Russian-born scholar*
* Davidson, Israel

**Mowat, Robert Case** 1913- [IAW]
*British author*
* Mowat, Robin

**Mowat, Robin**
See Mowat, Robert Case

**Mowbray, Henry**
See Sweeney, Harry E.

**Mowbray, John**
See Hadath, John Edward Gunby

**Mowbray, John**
See Vahey, John George Haslette

**Mowbray, W. J.** 20th c. [MBF]
*British author*
* Gascoigne, Eric

**Mower, Mrs. Fred** [FFF]
*Entertainer*
* Page, Lutie

**Mowrey, Harry Harlan** 1884-1947
[BE]
*American baseball player*
* Mowrey, Mike

**Mowrey, Mike**
See Mowrey, Harry Harlan

**Mowshay, Ben**
See Summerfield, Woolfe

**Moya, Natalie**
See Mullaly, Natalie

**Moya, Pedro** 20th c. [GS]
*Spanish bullfighter*
* [El] Nino de la Capea [The Boy
of the Bull-Capings]

**Moyano, Sebastian** 1495?-1550?
[WBD]
*Spanish conquistador*
* Belalcazar [or Benalcazar],
Sebastian de

**Moyne**
See Toussaint-Desessarts, Nicholas

**Moyne, Bryan Walter Guinness**
1905- [IAW]
*British author and poet*
* Guinness, Bryan

**Moyridge, George** [FFF]
*Author*
* Uncle Adam

**Mozart, Franz Xaver Wolfgang**
1791-1844 [WBD]
*Austrian composer, musician,
conductor*
* Mozart, Wolfgang Amadeus

**Mozart, George**
*See* Gillings, David

**Mozart, Johannes Chrysostom
Wolfgangus Theophilus** 1756-1791
[HN, SN, WBD]
*Austrian composer*
* [The] Father of Modern Music
* Mozart, Wolfgang Amadeus
* [The] Raphael of Music
* [The] Raphael of Opera

**Mozart, Maria Anna** 1751-1829
[WBD]
*Austrian musician*
* Mozart, Nannerl

**Mozart, Nannerl**
*See* Mozart, Maria Anna

**[The] Mozart of the Nineteenth
Century**
*See* Mendelssohn, [Jakob Ludwig]
Felix

**Mozart, Wolfgang Amadeus**
*See* Mozart, Franz Xaver
Wolfgang

**Mozart, Wolfgang Amadeus**
*See* Mozart, Johannes Chrysostom
Wolfgangus Theophilus

**Mozee, Annie**
*See* Moses, Annie

**[El] Mozo**
*See* Herrera, Francisco de

**Mozzi, Marco Antonio** 1678-1736
[PA]
*Author*
* Mutius

**Mphahlele, Ezekiel** 1919- [CA]
*South African author*
* Eseki, Bruno

**M'Pherson, Samuel** [SN]
*Scottish commander*
* [A] Second Xenophon

**Mraz, George** 1944- [EJ7]
*Czech-born jazz musician*
* Mraz, Jiri

**Mraz, Jiri**
*See* Mraz, George

**Mrs. T**
*See* Thatcher, Margaret Hilda
[Roberts]

**Mrs. Thomas's Favourite Husband**
*See* Thomas, Alf

**M'Taggart, J. M.**
*See* M'Taggart, John M'Taggart
Ellis

**M'Taggart, John M'Taggart Ellis**
1866-1925 [LC]
*British lecturer and author*
* M'Taggart, J. M.

**Mu Minin, Ameru al-**
*See* Brown, Eugene

**Mu, Yang**
*See* Wang, Ching Hsien

**Muazzim, Prince**
*See* Bahadur Shah I

**Mubarak, Hosni** 1928?-
*Egyptian president*
* [The] Court Jester
* Empty Face
* Sadat's Sadat

**Mucius, Caius** [DNNF]
*Roman patrician*
* Scaevola

**Mud Dauber Joe**
*See* McCoy, Joe

**Mudd, Alice F.** [PA]
*Author*
* Peach Bloom

**Mudd, Richard** 20th c.
*American basketball player*
* Mudd, Suds

**Mudd, Suds**
*See* Mudd, Richard

**Mude, O.**
*See* Gorey, Edward [St. John]

**Mudge, Carl** 20th c.
*American actor*
* Morton, Charles

**Mudgeon, Apeman**
*See* Mitchell, Adrian

**Mudgett, Helen** 1934- [EJ]
*American jazz musician*
* Moran, Pat

**Mudgett, Herman W.**
*See* White, William A[nthony]
P[arker]

**Mudie, Leonard**
*See* Cheetham, Leonard M.

**Mudie, Robert** 1777-1842 [PA]
*Author*
* [The] Modern Greek

**[El] Mudo [The Mute]**
*See* Fernandez Navarrete, Juan

**Muehfeldt, Freddie** 20th c. [BLB]
*American gangster*
* [The] Kid

**Muehlbach, Luise [or Louise]**
*See* Mundt, Clara M.

**Muelier**
*See* Higgins, Charles Eli

**Mueller, Adam Heinrich**
1779-1829 [WBD]
*German political economist*
* Mueller von Nitersdorf

**Mueller, Clarence Franklin**
1899-1975 [B10, BE]
*American baseball player*
* Mueller, Heinie

**Mueller, Donald Frederick** 1927-
[BE]
*American baseball player*
* Mandrake the Magician

**Mueller, Dorothy** 1901- [CA]
*British-born author*
* Bowick, Dorothy Mueller

**Mueller, Emmett Jerome** 1912-
[BE]
*American baseball player*
* Mueller, Heinie

**Mueller, Ernst** 1890- [JL]
*Austrian author*
* Lothar, Ernst

**Mueller, Ernst** 20th c. [SFL]
*Author*
* West, Julian

**Mueller, Frederick** 1867-1925
[BMH]
*German-born gymnast and
strongman*
* Sandow, Eugen[e]
* [The] Strongest Man in the
World

**Mueller, Friedrich** 1749-1825
[WBD]
*German poet, painter, engraver*
* Mueller, Maler

**Mueller, Gerald F[rancis]** 1927-
[CA]
*American author*
* Roberto, [Brother]

**Mueller, Gerhardt**
*See* Bickers, Richard Leslie
Townshend

**Mueller, Gestapo**
*See* Mueller, Heinrich

**Mueller, Gussie**
*See* Mueller, Gustave

**Mueller, Gustave** 1890-1965 [NOJ]
*American jazz musician*
* Mueller, Gussie

**Mueller, Hawk**
*See* Mueller, William Lawrence
[Bill]

**Mueller, Heinie**
*See* Mueller, Clarence Franklin

**Mueller, Heinie**
*See* Mueller, Emmett Jerome

**Mueller, Heinrich** 1896- [BDW]
*German Nazi leader*
* Mueller, Gestapo

**Mueller, Hermann** 1876-1931
[WBD]
*German politician*
* Mueller-Franken

**Mueller, Herr**
*See* Louis Philippe

**Mueller, Iron Man**
*See* Mueller, Ray Coleman

**Mueller, Johann** 1436-1476
[PA, WBD]
*German mathematician and
astronomer*
* Regiomontanus

**Mueller, Johann von** 1752-1809
[SN]
*Swiss historian*
* [The] Thucydides of Germany

**Mueller, Maler**
*See* Mueller, Friedrich

**Mueller, Marvin** 1913- [FC]
*American actor, radio and television
announcer*
* Miller, Marvin
* Warren, Charlie

**Mueller, Merrill**
*Newscaster*
* Mueller, Red

**Mueller, Ray Coleman** 1912- [BE]
*American baseball player*
* Mueller, Iron Man

**Mueller, Red**
*See* Mueller, Merrill

**Mueller, Therese** 1855-1930
[WBD]
*German opera singer*
* Malten, Therese

**Mueller von Koenigswinter**
*See* Mueller, Wolfgang

**Mueller von Nitersdorf**
*See* Mueller, Adam Heinrich

**Mueller, William Lawrence [Bill]**
1920- [BE]
*American baseball player*
* Mueller, Hawk

**Mueller, Wolfgang** 1816-1873
[WBD]
*German poet and author*
* Mueller von Koenigswinter

**Mueller-Franken**
*See* Mueller, Hermann

**Mueller-Guttenbrunn, Adam**
1852-1923 [WBD]
*Austrian author, playwright, theatre
director*
* Ignotus

**Mueller-Harlin, Wolfgang Johannes**
1940- [IAW]
*German author*
* Thomas, Manuel

**Mueller-Tannewitz, Anna** 1899-
[IAW]
*German author*
* Juergen, Anna

**[The] Muenchausen of the West**
*See* Crockett, David [Davy]

**Muenster, Sebastian** 1489-1552
[DNNS, HN, RH]
*German theologian, geographer,
mathematician*
* [The] German Strabo
* [The] Strabo of Germany

**Muensterberg, Maximilian**
*See* Nentwich, Max

**Muenzenberger, John Henry** 1912-
[EJ, PMJ, WWJ]
*American jazz musician*
* Mince, Johnny

**Muffett, Billy Arnold** 1930- [BE]
*American baseball player*
* Muffett, Muff

**Muffett, Muff**
*See* Muffett, Billy Arnold

**Muggable Mary**
*See* Glatzle, Mary

**Muggeridge, Edward James**
1830-1904 [WBD, WEF]
*British photographer*
* Muybridge, Eadweard

**Muggeson, Margaret Elizabeth**
1942- [AW, IAW, WD]
*British author*
* Dickinson, Margaret
* Jackson, Everatt

**Muggins, Petey**
*See* Mione, Peter

[El] Muhajir
See   Jackman, Marvin X.

Muhammad Ghori
See   Muizz-ad-din

Muhammad, Idris
See   Morris, Leo

Muhammad, Matthew Saad
See   Franklin, Matthew

Muhammed, Elijah
See   Poole, Elijah

Muich, Ignatius Andrew 1903-
[BE]
American baseball player
* Muich, Joe

Muich, Joe
See   Muich, Ignatius Andrew

Muir, Alan
See   Morrison, Thomas James

Muir, [Charles] Augustus 1892-
[CA, CC, WD]
Scottish-born author
* Moore, Austin

Muir, Barbara K[enrick Gowing]
1908-   [CA]
British author
* Kaye, Barbara

Muir, Dexter
See   Gribble, Leonard R[eginald]

Muir, Edwin 1887-1959   [TLC]
Scottish poet and author
* Moore, Edward

Muir, Jane
See   Petrone, Jane Muir

Muir, Jean
See   Fullerton, J. M.

Muir, John
See   Morgan, Thomas Christopher

Muir, John   [PA]
Author
* J. M.

Muir, Kenneth [Arthur] 1907-   [CA]
British educator and author
* Finney, Mark

Muir, Marie Agnes 1904-
[AW, CA]
British author
* Blake, Monica
* Clynder, Monica
* Scott, Jean

Muir, Mary 20th c.   [WWL]
British writer
* Mike

Muir, Wardrop Openshaw
1878-1927   [MBF]
British author
* Lang, Stewart

Muirhead, Thorburn
See   Thorburn-Muirhead, James

Muizz-ad-din ?-1206   [WBD]
Sultan of Ghazni
* Mohammed of Ghor
* Muhammad Ghori

Mul
See   Muldoon, William H.

Mularchyk, Sylva 20th c.   [CA]
American author
* Miles, Sylva [joint pseudonym
  with Dorien K(lein) Miles]

Mulargia, Edoardo 20th c.   [WF]
Italian director
* Muller, Edward G.

Mulcahy, A. E. 1913-
American singer
* Dover, Fostoria
* [The] Queen of the Torchers

Mulcahy, Hugh Noyes 1913-   [BE]
American baseball player
* [The] Losing Pitcher

Mulcahy, Lucille Burnett 20th c.
[CA, SAT]
American author
* Hale, Helen

Muldaur, Maria
See   D'Amato, Maria Grazia Rosa
Domenica

Mulder, Connie
See   Mulder, Cornelius

Mulder, Cornelius 1925?-
South African politician
* Mulder, Connie

Mulder, Herman
See   Mulder, Johannes Hermanus

Mulder, Johannes Hermanus 1894-
[IWM]
Dutch composer and educator
* Mulder, Herman

Muldoon, Dennis
See   Goodwin, George B.

Muldoon, Major
See   McCartney, William H.

Muldoon, Omar
See   Matusow, Harvey Marshall

Muldoon, Piggy
See   Muldoon, Robert David

Muldoon, Robert David 20th c.
New Zealand prime minister
* Muldoon, Piggy

Muldoon, William H.   [PA]
Author
* [The] Man about Town
* Mul

Muldowney, Cha Cha
See   Muldowney, Shirley

Muldowney, Shirley 1940?-
American auto racer
* Muldowney, Cha Cha

Muldrow, Baby Face
See   Muldrow, Gail

Muldrow, Gail 20th c.   [RO2]
American singer
* Muldrow, Baby Face

Mulesko, Angelo
See   Oglesby, Joseph

Mulet, Paul
See   Rivers, Louis

Mulford, Ralph 20th c.
Auto racer
* [The] Parson

Mulier, Pieter 1637-1701   [WBD]
Dutch painter
* Cavaliere Tempesta

Mulkeen, Anne
See   Marcus, Anne M[ulkeen]

Mulkor, Pioter
See   Hlojzy, Nagel

Mullaly, Charles J. 1877-1949
[CAT]
American author and editor
* Goodwin, Francis
* Winslow, Paul

Mullaly, Mrs. W. S.   [FFF]
Entertainer
* Weber, Lisa

Mullaly, Natalie 1900-   [THR]
Irish-born actress
* Moya, Natalie

Mullane, Anthony John 1859-1944
[BE, DGS]
Irish-born American baseball player
* [The] Apollo of the Box
* Mullane, Count Tony

Mullane, Count Tony
See   Mullane, Anthony John

Mullany, Azarius   [PA]
Author
* B. A. M.

Mulla's Bard
See   Spenser, Edmund

Mulle, Maude
See   Bell, Mrs. A. M.

Mulleavy, Greg[ory Thomas] 1905-
[BE]
American baseball player
* Mulleavy, Moe

Mulleavy, Moe
See   Mulleavy, Greg[ory Thomas]

Mullen, Bud
See   Mullen, Francis

Mullen, C. J. J.
See   Mullen, Cyril J.

Mullen, Cyril J. 1908-   [CA]
American author
* Mullen, C. J. J.

Mullen, Ford Parker 1917-   [BE]
American baseball player
* Mullen, Moon

Mullen, Francis 20th c.
American government official
* Mullen, Bud

Mullen, M.   [PA]
Author
* North, Oliver

Mullen, Moon
See   Mullen, Ford Parker

Mullen, Moon
See   Mullen, Thomas Patrick

Mullen, Stanley [B.] 1911-1973
[WGT]
American author
* Beecher, Lee
* Beecher, Stanley
* Drummond, John Peter

Mullen, Thomas Patrick 1951-
[SMG]
American football player
* Mullen, Moon

Mullenger, Donna 1921-
[BDF, FC, WEF]
American actress
* Adams, Donna
* Reed, Donna

Mullens, Edward 1916-   [EJ, WWJ]
American jazz musician
* Mullens, Moon

Mullens, Moon
See   Mullens, Edward

Muller, Billex
See   Ellis, Edward S[ylvester]

Muller, Brick
See   Muller, Harold

Muller, Charles G[eorge] 1897-
[CA, IAW]
American author
* Geoffrey, Charles
* Gilliland, Charles

Muller, Charles Louis 1815-1892
[WBD]
French painter
* Muller de Paris

Muller de Paris
See   Muller, Charles Louis

Muller, Edward G.
See   Mulargia, Edoardo

Muller, Harold 1901-1962
[AS, FB]
American football player
* Muller, Brick

Muller, John E. [house pseudonym]
See   Fanthorpe, R[obert] Lionel

Muller, John E. [house pseudonym]
See   Glynn, Anthony Arthur

Muller, Paul
See   King, Albert

Muller, Paul 1898-   [IWM]
Swiss composer
* Muller-Zurich, Paul

Muller, Rudolph 1899-   [FC]
Czech-born actor
* Miller, Martin

Muller-Zurich, Paul
See   Muller, Paul

Mullican, Aubrey Wilson
1909-1967   [CWG, DAM]
American country-western performer
* [The] King of the Hillbilly Piano
  Players
* Mullican, Moon

Mullican, Dorothy 1906-1981
American actress
* Lane, Lola

Mullican, Moon
See   Mullican, Aubrey Wilson

Mullican, Priscilla 1917-   [PMJ]
American actress
* Lane, Priscilla

Mullican, Rosemary 1916-   [PMJ]
American actress
* Lane, Rosemary

Mulligan, Big Joe
See   Mulligan, Joseph Ignatius
[Joe]

**Mulligan, Gerald Joseph [Gerry]**
1927- [EJ7]
*American jazz musician*
* Mulligan, Jeru

**Mulligan, Hugh A.** 1925- [IAW]
*American-born author*
* H. A. M.

**Mulligan, James** 1874?-1962
[BEW]
*American theatrical performer*
* Valdare, Sunny Jim

**Mulligan, Jeru**
See Mulligan, Gerald Joseph
[Gerry]

**Mulligan, Joseph Ignatius [Joe]**
1913- [BE]
*American baseball player*
* Mulligan, Big Joe

**Mulligan, Paddy**
See Mulligan, Patrick

**Mulligan, Patrick** 1945- [AES]
*Irish soccer player*
* Mulligan, Paddy

**Mullin, George Joseph** 1880-1944
[BE]
*American baseball player*
* Mullin, Wabash George

**Mullin, Wabash George**
See Mullin, George Joseph

**Mullins, Ann**
See Dally, Ann Gwendolen Mullins

**Mullins, Jeff** 1942- [BB]
*American basketball player*
* Mullins, Pork Chop

**Mullins, Pork Chop**
See Mullins, Jeff

**Mullins, Rossana E.** ?-1878 [PA]
*Author*
* R. E. L.
* R. E. M.

**Mullion, Mordecai**
See Wilson, John

**Mullner**
See Collin, Jacques Albin Simon

**Mulock, Miss**
See Craik, Mrs. George Lillie

**Multatuli**
See Dekker, Eduard Douwes

**[The] Multi-Media Person**
See Brown, Mary Richardson

**Mulvey, Ruth Watt**
See Harmer, Ruth Mulvey

**Mumbles**
See Horton, Walter

**Mumford, Angelina S.** 1830- ?
[FFF, PA]
*American poet*
* Picciola

**Mumford, Ethel Watts**
See Grant, Ethel Watts Mumford

**Mummius, Lucius** 2nd c. BC
[WBD]
*Roman general and politician*
* Achaicus

**[The] Mummy**
See Merrill, Jan

**Mummy Daddy**
See Khan, Javed Miandad

**Mun**
See Leaf, [Wilbur] Munro

**Muna el Hussein [Desire of Hussein]**
See Gardiner, Toni

**Munby, A. N. L.**
See Munby, Alan Noel Latimer

**Munby, Alan Noel Latimer**
1913-1974 [HFF, SFL]
*British author*
* Munby, A. N. L.

**Munce, Ruth Hill** 1898-
[CAP, SAT]
*American author*
* Hill, Ruth Livingston

**Munch, Andreas** 1811-1884 [SN]
*Norwegian poet and playwright*
* Norway's First Skald

**Munchausen, Baron**
See Gernsback, Hugo

**[The] Muncie Mortar**
See Bonham, Ron

**Mundanschaffter, Juan Carlos**
1916- [FC]
*Argentinian actor*
* Thompson, Carlos

**Munday, John William** 20th c.
[SFP]
*Author*
* Seeley, Charles S.

**Mundt, Clara M.** 1814-1873
[DNNF, FFF, WBD]
*German author*
* Muehlbach, Luise [or Louise]

**Mundus, [Captain] Frank** 1926?-
*American shark fisherman*
* [The] Monster Man

**Mundus, Jakob**
See Vetsch, Jakob

**Mundy, Bingo**
See Mundy, Ronald

**Mundy, Max**
See Schofield, Sylvia Anne

**Mundy, Ronald** 20th c. [RO1]
*American singer*
* Mundy, Bingo

**Mundy, Talbot**
See Gribbon, William Lancaster

**Mundy, W. P.**
See Mundy, William Percy

**Mundy, William Percy** 1936-
[ART]
*British painter*
* Mundy, W. P.

**Munger, Al**
See Unger, Maurice Albert

**Munger, George David** 1918- [BE]
*American baseball player*
* Munger, Red

**Munger, Gordon C.** 1891-1947
[SC]
*American actor*
* Daly, Pat

**Munger, Hortense Roberta**
See Roberts, Hortense Roberta

**Munger, Red**
See Munger, George David

**Mungo, Raymond** 1946- [CA]
*American author*
* Lunar, Dennis

**Munguia, Miguel** 20th c. [GS]
*Spanish bullfighter*
* [El] Inspirado [The Inspired One]

**Muni, Narad**
See Anand, Mulk Raj

**Muni, Paul**
See Weisenfreund, Muni

**Muniz, Manny**
See Muniz Rodriquez, Manuel

**Muniz Rodriquez, Manuel** 1947-
[SMG]
*Puerto Rican-born baseball player*
* Muniz, Manny

**Munk, Kaj**
See Petersen, Kaj Harald
Leininger

**Munkacsi, Martin** 1895?-1963
[WFA]
*Rumanian-born photographer*
* [The] High Priest of Fashion in
Motion

**Munkaczsy, Mihaly von**
See Lieb, Michael

**Munkittrick, Howard** 1865-1928
[BBD, BEW, EMT]
*American composer*
* Talbot, Howard

**Munn, Biggie**
See Munn, Clarence Lester

**Munn, Clarence Lester** 1908-1975
[B10]
*American football coach*
* Munn, Biggie

**Munn, Hart**
See Hardy, C. Colburn

**Munn, Marguerite** 1870- ? [WWL]
*British author*
* Bryant, M.

**Munn, Meryl Lucile** 1916- [CA]
*American author*
* Maguire, Anne
* Nearing, Penny

**Munnings, Hilda** ?-1974 [TR]
*Dancer*
* Sokolova, Lydia

**Munns, Big Ed**
See Munns, Les[lie Ernest]

**Munns, Les[lie Ernest]** 1908- [BE]
*American baseball player*
* Munns, Big Ed
* Munns, Nemo

**Munns, Nemo**
See Munns, Les[lie Ernest]

**Munoz, Felipe** 1951- [SWI]
*Mexican swimmer*
* Tibio [Luke-Warm]

**Munoz, Joe**
See Munoz, Jose

**Munoz, Jose** 20th c. [OBW]
*American baseball player*
* Munoz, Joe

**Munoz, Juan Antonio** 1922- [FDG]
*Spanish director*
* Bardem, Juan Antonio

**Munoz Marin, Luis** 1898?-1980
*Puerto Rican governor*
* God's Pamphleteer

**Munoz y Gonzalez, Fermin**
1879-1942 [GS]
*Spanish bullfighter*
* Corchaito [Little Cork]

**Munoz y Marin, Bernardo**
1895-1969 [GS]
*Spanish bullfighter*
* Carnicerito [Little Butcher]

**Munro, C[harles] K[irkpatrick]**
See MacMullan, Charles Walden
Kirkpatrick

**Munro, David**
See Devine, David McDonald

**Munro, Duncan H.**
See Russell, Eric Frank

**Munro, H. H.**
See Munro, Hector Hugh

**Munro, Hector Hugh** 1870-1916
[HFF, LC, TC]
*British author*
* Munro, H. H.
* Saki

**Munro, [Macfarlane] Hugh** 20th c.
[CA, IAW]
*Scottish author*
* Farlane, Jason
* Jason
* Wyvis, Ben

**Munro, James**
See Cave, Roderick [George James
Munro]

**Munro, James**
See Mitchell, James

**Munro, Kathryn**
See Tupper, Kathryn Munro

**Munro, Mary**
See Howe, Doris Kathleen

**Munro, Neil** 1864-1930 [WW]
*Author*
* Foulis, Hugh

**Munro, Robert**
See Hale-Monro, John Robert

**Munro [or Monro], Robert** ?-1633
[WBD]
*Scottish army officer*
* [The] Black Baron

**Munro, Ronald Eadie**
See Glen, Duncan Munro

**Munro-Noble, Maisie** 1883-1945
[BEW, EMT]
*British actress and singer*
* Gay, Maisie

**Munroe, Elizabeth L[ee]** 1900-
[CA]
*American poet*
* Grenelle, Lisa

**Munroe, Jack**
See Monroe, John Alexander

**Munroe, R.**
See Cheyne, [Sir] Joseph Lister
Watson

**Munsel, Patrice**
*See* Munsil, Patrice Beverly

**Munsey, Cecil [Richard, Jr.]** 1935-
[CA]
*American educator and author*
* Richardson, C.

**Munshi**
*See* Soomro, Mohammad Ibrahim

**Munshi, Shehnaaz**
*See* Skagen, Kiki

**Munsil, Patrice Beverly** 1925-
[MS]
*American opera singer*
* Munsel, Patrice

**Munson, Clarence Hanford** 1883-
[BE]
*American baseball player*
* Munson, Red

**Munson, Joseph Martin Napoleon
[Joe]**
*See* Carlson, Joseph Martin
Napoleon

**Munson, Ona**
*See* Wolcott, Ona

**Munson, Red**
*See* Munson, Clarence Hanford

**Munson, Squatty**
*See* Munson, Thurman Lee

**Munson, Thurman Lee** 1947-1979
[PB]
*American baseball player*
* Munson, Squatty

**Munster**
*See* O'Sullivan, Farrar

**Munster, Minnie**
*See* Burleigh, Harriet E.

**Munston, Constance Sylvia** 1898-
[FC]
*British actress*
* Lillie, Beatrice

**Munthe, Frances** 1915?-
[AW, CA, WD]
*British author*
* Cowen, Frances
* Hyde, Eleanor
* Minto-Cowen, Frances

**Muntz, [Isabelle] Hope** 1907-
[IAW]
*Canadian-born author*
* Langland, William

**Muntz, James**
*See* Crowcroft, Peter

**Mur**
*See* Murschetz, Luis Marian

**Mura, Corrine**
*See* Wall, Corinna

**Murad Efendi**
*See* Werner, Franz von

**Muraguri, Nicholas** 1934-    [IAW]
*Kenyan author*
* Ruheni, Mwangi

**Muraire, Jules** 1883-1946
[FC, WEF]
*French actor*
* Raimu

**Murat, Joachim** 1767?-1815
[DNNS, HN, SN]
*King of Naples*
* [Le] Beau Sabreur
* [The] Dandy King
* Franconi, King
* [The] Good Swordsman
* [The] Handsome Swordsman
* [Un] Roi de Theatre

**[The] Murat of Russia**
*See* Miloradowitch, Michael

**[The] Murat of the Magyar Army**
*See* Kinisi, Paul

**Murcer, Bobby Ray** 1946-    [PB]
*American baseball player*
* Murcer, Okie

**Murcer, Okie**
*See* Murcer, Bobby Ray

**Murch, Simeon T.** 1880-1939    [BE]
*American baseball player*
* Murch, Simmy

**Murch, Simmy**
*See* Murch, Simeon T.

**Murchison, Thomas Malcolm**
1896-1962    [BE]
*American baseball player*
* Murchison, Tim

**Murchison, Tim**
*See* Murchison, Thomas Malcolm

**Murcia [From Murcia]**
*See* Jimenez y Najar, Bartolome

**Murdoch, Doc**
*See* Murdoch, Donald Walter

**Murdoch, Donald Walter** 1956-
[SMG]
*Canadian-born hockey player*
* Murdoch, Doc
* Murdoch, Murder

**Murdoch, Frank**
*See* Hitchcock, Francis

**Murdoch, Mud**
*See* Murdoch, Robert John

**Murdoch, Murder**
*See* Murdoch, Donald Walter

**Murdoch, Robert John** 1946-
[SMG]
*Canadian-born hockey player*
* Murdoch, Mud

**Murdock, Ann**
*See* Coleman, Irene

**Murdock, Laurette P.** 1900-    [CA]
*American author*
* Eustis, Laurette

**Murdock, William**
*See* Humberger, William

**Muredach, Myles**
*See* Kelley, Francis Clement

**Murff, John Robert** 1921-    [BE]
*American baseball player*
* Murff, Red

**Murff, Red**
*See* Murff, John Robert

**Murfree, Mary Noailles**
1850-1922    [SFL, WGT]
*American author*
* Craddock, Charles Egbert
* Denbry, R. Emmet?

**Muriel, John Saint Clair** 1909-
[WW]
*British author*
* Dewes, Simon
* Lindsay, John

**Murielle, Constance**
*See* Bennett, Mrs. Clement

**Murillo, Edith**
*See* Martinetti, Mme. Ignacio

**Murio-Celli, Mme.**
*See* D'Elpeux, Ravin

**Muris, Johannes de** 14th c.    [WBD]
*British musical theorist, astronomer,
mathematician*
* Normanus

**Muris, Johannes [or Julianus] de** 14th
c.    [WBD]
*French musical theorist*
* De Francia

**Murman, George**
*See* Heirens, William

**Murnau, F[riedrich] W[ilhelm]**
*See* Plumpe, Friedrich Wilhelm

**Murph the Surf**
*See* Murphy, Jack Ronald

**Murphey, Anna** 1797-1860    [PA]
*Author*
* [An] Ennuyee

**Murphey, Big Tim**
*See* Murphey, Timothy

**Murphey, J. M.**    [PA]
*Author*
* Mortimer

**Murphey, Timothy** ?-1928
[BLB, MM, PHM]
*American politician*
* Murphey, Big Tim

**Murphy, Audie** 1924-    [BDW]
*American army officer*
* Murphy, Baby

**Murphy, Baby**
*See* Murphy, Audie

**Murphy, Beatrice M.** 1908-    [CA]
*American editor and author*
* Campbell, Beatrice Murphy

**Murphy, Billy**
*See* Murphy, Thomas W.

**Murphy, Billy J.** 1921-    [FB]
*American football coach*
* Murphy, Spook

**Murphy, Brian** 1949?-
*American behavior therapist*
* Sunshine, Leo

**Murphy, Buck**
*See* Whitcomb, Ian

**Murphy, Buzz**
*See* Murphy, Robert R.

**Murphy, Calvin** 1948-    [IBW]
*American basketball player*
* [The] Tiny Giant

**Murphy, Charles** 1907-    [BB]
*American basketball player*
* Murphy, Stretch

**Murphy, Charles W.** 1871-1950
[BBH]
*American bicycle racer*
* Murphy, Mile a Minute

**Murphy, Cicero** 1936-    [IBW]
*American billiard player*
* [The] Brooklyn Kid

**Murphy, Con**
*See* Murphy, Cornelius B.

**Murphy, Connie**
*See* Murphy, Cornelius David

**Murphy, Cornelius B.** 1863-1914
[BE]
*American baseball player*
* Murphy, Con
* Murphy, Razzle Dazzle

**Murphy, Cornelius David**
1870-1945    [BE]
*American baseball player*
* Murphy, Connie

**Murphy, Dennis Jasper**
*See* Maturin, Charles Robert

**Murphy, Dummy**
*See* Murphy, Herbert C.

**Murphy, E[mmett] Jefferson** 1926-
[CA, SAT]
*American author*
* Murphy, Pat

**Murphy, Emily F.** 20th c.    [NAA]
*Canadian author*
* Canuck, Janey

**Murphy, Fireman**
*See* Murphy, John Joseph

**Murphy, Fordham Johnny**
*See* Murphy, John Joseph

**Murphy, Frank J.** 20th c.    [BE]
*American baseball player*
* Murphy, Tony

**Murphy, Gentle Willie**
*See* Murphy, William N. [Willie]

**Murphy, Grandma**
*See* Murphy, John Joseph

**Murphy, Guffer**
*See* Murphy, John T.

**Murphy, Harlem Tommy**
*See* Murphy, Tommy

**Murphy, Hazel**
*See* Thurston, Hazel [Patricia]

**Murphy, Herbert C.** 1890-    [BE]
*American baseball player*
* Murphy, Dummy

**Murphy, Honest Eddie**
*See* Murphy, John Edward

**Murphy, Ike**
*See* Burns, Isaac Murphy

**Murphy, Irish Bob**
*See* Conarty, Edward Lee

**Murphy, Isaac**
*See* Burns, Isaac Murphy

**Murphy, Jack Ronald** 1937-    [B10]
*American thief*
* Murph the Surf

**Murphy, James [Jimmy]** ?-1924
*Auto racer*
* [The] Smiling Irishman

**Murphy, John**
*See* Grady, Ronan Calistus, Jr.

**Murphy, John Daly**
*See* Conlon, John Daly

**Murphy, John Edward** 1891-1969
[BE]
*American baseball player*
* Murphy, Honest Eddie

**Murphy, John Joseph** 1908-1970
[BE, PB]
*American baseball player*
* Murphy, Fireman
* Murphy, Fordham Johnny
* Murphy, Grandma

**Murphy, John P.** 1879-1914    [BE]
*American baseball player*
* Murphy, Soldier Boy

**Murphy, John T.** 1900?-1964
[BEW]
*Theatrical performer*
* Murphy, Guffer

**Murphy, Kid**
See   Frascella, Peter

**Murphy, Leo Joseph** 1889-1960
[BE]
*American baseball player*
* Murphy, Red

**Murphy, Lyle** 1908-
[ASC, DAM, EJ]
*American jazz musician*
* Murphy, Spud

**Murphy, Melvin E.** 1915-
[DAM, EJ, PMJ]
*American jazz musician*
* Murphy, Turk

**Murphy, Mike**
See   Hribar, Erneytsck

**Murphy, Mile a Minute**
See   Murphy, Charles W.

**Murphy, Pat**
See   Murphy, E[mmett] Jefferson

**Murphy, Razzle Dazzle**
See   Murphy, Cornelius B.

**Murphy, Red**
See   Murphy, Leo Joseph

**Murphy, Robert [Bob]**
See   Dunnell, Duke Foster

**Murphy, Robert** 20th c.    [CND]
*American diplomat*
* McGowan, Lieutenant Colonel
  [code name used during World
  War II]

**Murphy, Robert R.** 1895-1938
[BE]
*American baseball player*
* Murphy, Buzz

**Murphy, Rose** 20th c.    [PMJ]
*American singer*
* [The] Chee Chee Girl

**Murphy, Soldier Boy**
See   Murphy, John P.

**Murphy, Spook**
See   Murphy, Billy J.

**Murphy, Spud**
See   Murphy, Lyle

**Murphy, Stretch**
See   Murphy, Charles

**Murphy, Thomas W.** 1863-1939
[BX, RBE, WBC]
*New Zealand boxer*
* Murphy, Billy
* Murphy, Torpedo Billy

**Murphy, Tommy** 1885-1958    [RBE]
*American boxer*
* Murphy, Harlem Tommy

**Murphy, Tony**
See   Murphy, Frank J.

**Murphy, Torpedo Billy**
See   Murphy, Thomas W.

**Murphy, Turk**
See   Murphy, Melvin E.

**Murphy, William Henry**
1869-1906    [BE]
*American baseball player*
* Murphy, Yale

**Murphy, William N. [Willie]** 20th
c.    [BE]
*American baseball player*
* Murphy, Gentle Willie

**Murphy, Yale**
See   Murphy, William Henry

**Murranka, Mary** 1944-    [WD]
*British author*
* McGrath, Mary

**Murray**
See   Saunders, Robert

**Murray, A. C.** 20th c.    [MBF]
*British author*
* Feveril, Hubert
* Gray, Andrew

**Murray, Adrian**
See   Curran, Mona [Elisa]

**Murray, Adrian** 20th c.    [MBF]
*British author*
* Gordon, Richard

**Murray, Alfalfa Bill**
See   Murray, William H.

**Murray, Aline**
See   Kilmer, Aline

**Murray, Alma**
See   Pinero, Mrs. A. W.

**Murray, Ambrose Joseph** 1913-
[BE]
*American baseball player*
* Murray, Amby

**Murray, Amby**
See   Murray, Ambrose Joseph

**Murray, Andrew Nicholas**
1880-1929    [MBF]
*British author*
* Arnold, Malcolm
* Deane, Vesey
* Islay, Nicholas

**Murray, Anne** 1947-    [RO2]
*Canadian singer*
* [The] Singing Sweetheart of
  Canada

**Murray, Arthur**
See   Teichman, Arthur

**Murray, Athol** 1892-    [CSH]
*Canadian clergyman and college
founder*
* Murray, Pere

**Murray, Bearcat**
See   Murray, Jim

**Murray, Beatrice**
See   Posner, Richard

**Murray, Big Jim**
See   Murray, James Francis [Jim]

**Murray, Braham**
See   Goldstein, Braham

**Murray, Brian**
See   Bell, Brian

**Murray, Bud**
See   Murray, Julian

**Murray, C. Geoffrey** 20th c.    [MBF]
*British author*
* Gray, Geoffrey
* Kingsford, Guy
* Loxley, Raymond

**Murray, Charles T.**    [PA]
*Author*
* Wright, Samuel

**Murray, Cromwell**
See   Morgan, Murray Cromwell

**Murray, D. L.**
See   Murray, David Leslie

**Murray, David** 1955-    [IBW]
*American jazz musician*
* Murray, Sunny

**Murray, David Leslie** 1888-1962
[LC]
*British author*
* Murray, D. L.

**Murray, David Stark** 1900-    [IAW]
*British pathologist and author*
* Brown, Irwin

**Murray, Deacon**
See   Murray, Raymond Lee

**Murray, Dominick**
See   Moran, D.

**Murray, Dominick**
See   Morogh, Dominick

**Murray, Donald**
See   Bloom, Murray

**Murray, Donald**
See   Vivarelli, Piero

**Murray, E. C. Greenville**  ?-1882
[PA]
*Author*
* [The] Roving Englishman

**Murray, Edgar Joyce** 1878- ?
[MBF]
*British author*
* Drew, Sidney
* Rover, Max

**Murray, Edna**
See   Rowland, D[onald] S[ydney]

**Murray, Edna**    [BLB]
*American criminal*
* [The] Kissing Bandit

**Murray, Eustace Clare Grenville**
1828?-1881    [FFF, PA]
*British journalist and author*
* Hope, Mark
* Member for Paris
* Scampington, Duke of
* Trois Etoiles

**Murray, Frances**
See   Booth, Rosemary Frances

**Murray, George King** 1898-1955
[BE]
*American baseball player*
* Murray, Smiler

**Murray, Gilbert**
See   Wycherley, Richard Newman

**Murray, Hamilton**
See   Malden, Henry

**Murray, Irene**
See   Witherspoon, Irene Murray

**Murray, J. Harold**
See   Roulon, Harry

**Murray, Jack** 20th c.    [CEI]
*Hockey player*
* Murray, Muzz

**Murray, James Arthur** 1927-
[DAM]
*American jazz musician*
* Murray, Sunny

**Murray, James Francis [Jim]** 1898-
[BE]
*American baseball player*
* Murray, Big Jim

**Murray, Jeanne** 1923-
[BEW, IPA, TR]
*American actress*
* Stapleton, Jean

**Murray, Jeremiah J.** 1865-1922
[BE]
*American baseball player*
* Murray, Miah

**Murray, Jill**
See   Walker, Emily Kathleen

**Murray, Jim**
See   Murray, Philip Jesse, Jr.

**Murray, Jim** 20th c.    [SMG]
*Hockey team trainer*
* Murray, Bearcat

**Murray, Joan** 1904-    [AW]
*British author*
* Wildeblood, Joan

**Murray, John**
See   MacMurray, John

**Murray, John**
See   Pfeferstein, John

**Murray, John** 1741-1815
[FFF, WBD]
*British-born clergyman*
* [The] Father of Universalism in
  America

**Murray, John** 1778-1843
[DNNF, FFF, SN]
*British publisher*
* [The] Anak of Publishers
* [The] Emperor of the West

**Murray, John F[rancis]** 1923-1977
[CA, CAP]
*American author and playwright*
* Backgammon, Daisy
* Carryaway, Nick
* Combs, Robert

**Murray, John Joseph** 1884-1958
[AS, BE]
*American baseball player*
* Murray, Red

**Murray, Johnny**
See   Sloves, Herman

**Murray, Julian** 1888-1952    [SC]
*American actor and director*
* Murray, Bud

**Murray, K. F.**
See   Carlisle, Fred

**Murray, Ken**
See   Court, Don

**Murray, Ken**
*See* Turner, Robert [Harry]

**Murray, Leo** 20th c.    [GW]
*American rodeo performer*
* Murray, Pickhandle

**Murray, Leslie** 20th c.    [SFL]
*Author*
* Leo, Bessie

**Murray, Lindley** 1745-1826    [WBD]
*Scottish-American grammarian*
* [The] Father of English
   Grammar

**Murray, Louise Spigler** 1875-1956
[F1, F2]
*Actress*
* Carver, Louise

**Murray, Mae**
*See* Koenig, Marie Adrienne

**Murray, Miah**
*See* Murray, Jeremiah J.

**Murray, Mrs. J. J.**    [FFF]
*Entertainer*
* Melville, Virginia

**Murray, Mrs. John**    [FFF]
*Entertainer*
* Hawthorne, Grace

**Murray, Muzz**
*See* Murray, Jack

**Murray, Nicholas** 1803-1861
[DEL, FFF, PA]
*American clergyman and author*
* Kirwan

**Murray, Pere**
*See* Murray, Athol

**Murray, Peter**
*See* James, Peter

**Murray, Philip Jesse, Jr.** 1925-
[FFA]
*American singer*
* Murray, Jim

**Murray, Pickhandle**
*See* Murray, Leo

**Murray, Raymond Lee** 1917-    [BE]
*American baseball player*
* Murray, Deacon

**Murray, Red**
*See* Murray, John Joseph

**Murray, Robert**
*See* Graydon, Robert Murray

**Murray, Robert**
*See* Twyman, Harold William

**Murray, Rosalind**
*See* Toynbee, Rosalind

**Murray, Ruth Hilary** 1933-    [CA]
*Irish-born educator and author*
* Finnegan, Ruth H.

**Murray, Sinclair**
*See* Sullivan, Edward Alan

**Murray, Smiler**
*See* Murray, George King

**Murray, Sunny**
*See* Murray, David

**Murray, Sunny**
*See* Murray, James Arthur

**Murray, T. C.**
*See* Murray, Thomas C.

**Murray the K**
*See* Kaufman, Murray

**Murray, Thomas C.** 1873-1959
[LC]
*Irish playwright*
* Murray, T. C.

**Murray, William**
*See* Graydon, William Murray

**Murray, William [First Earl of
Mansfield]** 1705-1793    [WBD]
*British jurist*
* [The] Father of Modern Toryism

**Murray, William H.** 20th c.    [BLB]
*American politician*
* Murray, Alfalfa Bill

**Murrell, Elsie Kathleen Seth-Smith**
1883-    [CAP]
*British author*
* Seth-Smith, Elsie K.

**Murrell, Phil** 1933-    [BB]
*American basketball player*
* Murrell, Red

**Murrell, Red**
*See* Murrell, Phil

**Murrells, Joseph** 1904-    [IAW]
*British author and songwriter*
* Temple, Edith

**Murrow, Edward Roscoe**
*See* Murrow, Egbert Roscoe

**Murrow, Egbert Roscoe** 1908-1965
[WBD]
*American television journalist*
* Murrow, Edward Roscoe

**Murry, Colin**
*See* Middleton-Murry, Colin

**Murry, Ted**
*See* Mencher, Murray

**Murry, William**
*See* Morris, Charles Smith

**Murschetz, Luis Marian** 1936-
[IAW]
*Austrian-born author and cartoonist*
* Mur

**Musaeus** 5th c.    [WBD]
*Greek poet*
* Grammaticus

**Musaeus, Johann Karl August**
1735-1787    [FFF]
*German author*
* Schellenburg

**Musafir**
*See* Tagore, Amitendranath

**Muschamp, Lila** 1896?-1950
[BEW]
*Actress*
* Maravan, Lila

**Muschamp, Thomas**
*See* Lloyd-Thomas, Catherine

**Muscles, Mr.**
*See* Jackson, Reginald [Reggie]

**[The] Muscovy General**
*See* Dalyell [or Dalzell], Thomas

**[La] Muse de la Patrie [The Country's
Muse]**
*See* Gay, Delphine

**Muse, Lewis Anderson** 1908-
[BWW]
*American singer*
* Muse, Rabbit

**[La] Muse Limonadiere**
*See* Bourette, Charlotte

**[The] Muse of Cumberland**
*See* Blamire, Susanna

**[The] Muse of Greece**
*See* Xenophon

**[The] Muse of Tragedy**
*See* Siddons, Sarah

**Muse, Patricia [Alice]** 1923-    [CA]
*American author*
* Walters, Nell

**Muse, Rabbit**
*See* Muse, Lewis Anderson

**Musgrave-Wood, John** 1915-
[WEC]
*British cartoonist*
* Emmwood

**Musgrove, Nancye** 1893-    [THR]
*British actress*
* Stewart, Nancye

**Mushafir, Kartikeya Skylark**
*See* Tikekar, Shripad Ramchandra

**Mushrush, Obadiah** 1875-1938
*American underworld figure*
* Mertz, George

**Musial, Stan[ley Frank]**
*See* Musial, Stanislaus

**Musial, Stanislaus** 1920-
[BAB, SR]
*American baseball player*
* [The] Man
* Musial, Stan[ley Frank]
* Stan the Man

**Music, Dr.**
*See* Riley, Doug[las Brian]

**Musica, Philip** 1877-1938    [BLB]
*Italian-born American swindler*
* Costa, Frank
* Coster, F[rank] Donald

**[The] Musical Small-Coal Man**
*See* Britton, Thomas

**Musidora**
*See* Roques, Jeanne

**Musikara**
*See* Parikh, Rasiklal Chhotalal

**Musketoeren**
*See* Wirtanen, Atos Kasimir

**Muskrat Bill Shipke**
*See* Shipke, William M. [Bill]

**Muslih-ud-Din [or Moslehedin]**
1184?-1291    [DNNS, SN, WBD]
*Persian poet*
* [The] Nightingale of a Thousand
   Songs
* [The] Oriental Catullus
* [The] Oriental Homer
* Saadi [or Sadi]

**Musolino, Vincenzo** 20th c.    [WF]
*Italian director*
* Davis, Glen Vincent

**Muspratt, Rosalie Helen**
1906-1976    [HFF, SFL, WGT]
*British author*
* John, Jasper

**Mussa, Hawaja**
*See* Smilansky, Moshe

**Musselman, Johnson J.** 1890-1958
[SC]
*American actor and magician*
* Aska the Magician

**Musset, [Louis Charles] Alfred de**
1810-1857    [DNNS, HN, RH]
*French poet*
* [The] French Byron

**Mussey, Virginia T. H.**
*See* Ellison, Virginia Howell

**Mussi, Mary** 1907-    [AW, CA]
*British author*
* Edgar, Josephine
* Howard, Mary

**Mussiere, Luciene**
*See* Meurisse, Lucien

**Musso, George F.** 20th c.    [FB]
*American football player*
* Musso, Moose

**Musso, John, Jr.** 1950-    [SMG]
*American football player*
* [The] Italian Stallion

**Musso, Moose**
*See* Musso, George F.

**Mussolini, Benito** 1883-1945
[CBS, NN]
*Italian dictator*
* [The] Bullfrog of the Pontine
   Marshes
* [Il] Duce

**Mussot**
*See* Arnould, Jean-Francois

**Mussulli, Boots**
*See* Mussulli, Henry W.

**Mussulli, Henry W.** 1917-1967
[EJ, PMJ]
*American jazz musician*
* Mussulli, Boots

**Mustache George Huber**
*See* Huber, George

**Mustache Mike Contino**
*See* Contino, Michael

**Mustafa ibn-Abdallah** 1600?-1658
[WBD]
*Turkish historian and bibliographer*
* Hajji Khalfah [Assessor Who Has
   Made the Pilgrimage]
* Katib Chelebi [Noble Secretary]

**Mustafa [or Mustapha], Kemal**
1881-1938    [CBS, WBD]
*Turkish military leader and
statesman*
* Kemal Ataturek
* Kemal Pasha

**Mustafavi, Ruhollah** 1900?-
*Iranian head of state*
* Hindi
* [The] Imam
* Khomeini, [Ayatollah] Ruhollah

**Mustapha** 1755-1808    [HN]
*Sultan of Turkey*
* Bairaktar [Standard Bearer]

**Musto, Barry** 1930-    [AW, WD]
*British author*
* Simon, Robert

**Musus**
*See* Daniel, Samuel

**Muter, Mela**
See   Mutermilch, Mela

**Mutermilch, Mela** 1873-1967   [JL]
*Polish-born artist*
* Muter, Mela

**Mutesa, Edward, II** 1924-1969
*President of Uganda*
* King Freddie

**Muth, Conrad** 1471?-1526   [WBD]
*German scholar*
* Mutian
* Mutianus Rufus, Conradus

**Muti, Ornella**
See   Rivelli, Francesca

**Mutian**
See   Muth, Conrad

**Mutianus Rufus, Conradus**
See   Muth, Conrad

**Mutius**
See   Mozzi, Marco Antonio

**Mutrie, James J. [Jim]** 1851-1938
[BE]
*American baseball manager*
* Mutrie, Truthful Jim

**Mutrie, Truthful Jim**
See   Mutrie, James J. [Jim]

**[The] Mutton Eating King**
See   Charles II

**Mutwa, Baba**
See   Mutwa, Gado Vusa Mazulu

**Mutwa, Gado Vusa Mazulu** 1922-
[IBW]
*South African witch doctor,
sculptor, painter*
* Mutwa, Baba

**Mutz**
See   Kuenstler, Morton

**Muybridge, Eadweard**
See   Muggeridge, Edward James

**Muziano, Girolamo** 1528?-1592
[WBD]
*Italian painter*
* Bressano [or Brescianino],
   Girolamo

**Muzio [or Mutio]**
See   Nuzio, Girolamo

**Muzio, Claudia**
See   Muzzio, Claudina

**Muzorewa, Abel Tendekayi** 1925-
*Prime Minister of Zimbabwe
Rhodesia*
* Muzorewa, Muzzy

**Muzorewa, Muzzy**
See   Muzorewa, Abel Tendekayi

**Muzquiz, Carlos** 1906-1960   [SC]
*Mexican actor*
* Muzquiz, Compadre

**Muzquiz, Compadre**
See   Muzquiz, Carlos

**Muzzio, Claudina** 1889-1936
[BBD]
*Italian opera singer*
* Muzio, Claudia

**Muzzio, Girolamo** 1496-1576   [PA]
*Author*
* Nuzio

**Muzzy, L. R.**   [PA]
*Author*
* Aunt Prudence

**Mwamba, Pal**
See   Roberts, John S[torm]

**Mwandishi [Composer]**
See   Hancock, Herbert Jeffrey
[Herbie]

**Mwanga**
See   Stark, Claude Alan

**My Baritone**
See   Lucy, [Sir] Henry William

**My Book, Doctor**
See   Abernethy, John

**My Brother's Brother**
See   Chekhov, Anton [Pavlovich]

**My Fancy**
See   Baker, Mae Rose

**My Pen**
See   Dunn, Caleb

**My Philosophical Poet**
See   Alexander, [Sir] William
[First Earl of Stirling]

**Myassin, Leonid Fedorovich**
1895-1979   [CA]
*Russian-born dancer and
choreographer*
* Massine, Leonide

**Myatt, Foghorn**
See   Myatt, George Edward

**Myatt, George Edward** 1914-   [BE]
*American baseball player*
* Myatt, Foghorn
* Myatt, Mercury
* Myatt, Stud

**Myatt, Mercury**
See   Myatt, George Edward

**Myatt, Nellie** 20th c.   [AW]
*British author*
* Kirkham, Nellie

**Myatt, Stud**
See   Myatt, George Edward

**Myconius [or Mykonius], Friedrich**
See   Mekum, Friedrich

**Myconius [or Mykonius], Oswald**
See   Geishuesler, Oswald

**Mycroft**
See   Holmes, Geoffrey Andrew

**Myddleton, Robert**
See   Hebblethwaite, Peter

**Myer, Buddy**
See   Myer, Charles Solomon

**Myer, Charles Solomon** 1904-1974
[B10, DGS, PB]
*American baseball player*
* Myer, Buddy

**Myers, Albert** 1863-1927   [BE]
*American baseball player*
* Myers, Cod

**Myers, Allen O.**   [FFF]
*American writer*
* Pickaway

**Myers, Bumps**
See   Myers, Hubert Maxwell

**Myers, C. F.**
See   Fairbanks, Carol

**Myers, Carl** 20th c.   [GW]
*American rodeo performer*
* Myers, Curly

**Myers, Carol Fairbanks**
See   Fairbanks, Carol

**Myers, Cod**
See   Myers, Albert

**Myers, Curly**
See   Myers, Carl

**Myers, F. W. H.**
See   Myers, Frederic William
Henry

**Myers, Frederic William Henry**
1843-1901   [LC]
*British author and poet*
* Myers, F. W. H.

**Myers, Hap**
See   Myers, Harold Robert

**Myers, Hap**
See   Myers, Ralph Edward

**Myers, Harold Robert** 1947-   [CEI]
*Canadian-born hockey player*
* Myers, Hap

**Myers, Harriet Kathryn**
See   Whittington, Harry

**Myers, Henry Harrison** 1889-1965
[AS, BE, PB]
*American baseball player*
* Myers, Hy

**Myers, Howard L.** 20th c.   [SFP]
*Author*
* Foray, Verge

**Myers, Hubert Maxwell**
1912-1968   [EJ, WWJ]
*American jazz musician*
* Myers, Bumps

**Myers, Hy**
See   Myers, Henry Harrison

**Myers, James E.** 20th c.   [ASC]
*American composer*
* DeKnight, Jimmy

**Myers, L. H.**
See   Myers, Leopold Hamilton

**Myers, Leopold Hamilton**
1881-1944   [LC]
*British author*
* Myers, L. H.

**Myers, Linwood Lincoln** 1914-
[BE]
*American baseball player*
* Myers, Lynn

**Myers, Louis** 1929-   [BWW]
*American singer*
* Meyers, Louie

**Myers, Lynn**
See   Myers, Linwood Lincoln

**Myers, Mary Cathcart** 1906-   [AW]
*British author*
* Cathcart, Mary

**Myers, Michael** 20th c.   [IPA]
*American politician*
* Myers, Ozzie

**Myers, Ozzie**
See   Myers, Michael

**Myers, P. Hamilton** 1812- ?   [PA]
*Author*
* [The] First of the Knickerbockers

**Myers, Pop**
See   Myers, Theodore E.

**Myers, Ralph Edward** 1888-   [BE]
*American baseball player*
* Myers, Hap

**Myers, Ramona** 1909?-   [PMJ]
*American singer*
* Davies, Ramona
* Ramona

**Myers, Richard**
See   Myers, Richardson

**Myers, Richardson** 1901-   [BEW]
*American composer and producer*
* Myers, Richard

**Myers, Serious**
See   Myers, Wilson Ernest

**Myers, Stanley** 1918-   [JL]
*American playwright and critic*
* Richards, Stanley

**Myers, Theodore E.** 1874-1954
[AS]
*American auto racing promoter and
official*
* Myers, Pop

**Myers, Wilson Ernest** 1906-
[WWJ]
*American jazz musician*
* Myers, Serious

**Mykolaitis, Vincas** 1893-   [EWL]
*Lithuanian poet, author, playwright*
* Putinas

**Myles, Symon**
See   Follett, Kenneth Martin

**Mylin, Edward Everett** 1895-1975
[B10, FB]
*American football player and coach*
* Mylin, Hook [or Hooks]

**Mylin, Hook [or Hooks]**
See   Mylin, Edward Everett

**Myra**
See   Fairbanks, Mrs. A. W.

**Myra**
See   Newburgh, Countess of

**Myrander**
See   Stevenson, James Alexander

**Myrddin, Fardd**
See   Jones, John Daniel

**Myre, Louis Philippe** 1948-   [FHE]
*Canadian-born hockey player*
* Myre, Phil

**Myre, Phil**
See   Myre, Louis Philippe

**Myrick, David Luke** 1916-1971
[CME, ECM, FCW]
*American country-western performer*
* [The] Man with a Million Friends
* Tyler, T. Texas

**Myrivilis, Stratis**
See   Stamatopoulos, Stratis

**Myron, Paul**
See   Linebarger, Paul Myron
Wentworth

**Myrtil, Odette**
See   Quignard, Odette

**Myrtle, Harriet**
See   Gillies, Mary

**Myrtle, Harriet**
*See* Miller, Lydia F. F.

**Myrtle, May**
*See* Holden, Maria

**Myrtle, Minnie**
*See* Bryan, Sarah M. L.

**Myrtle, Minnie**
*See* Dyer, Minnie Theresa

**Myrtle, Minnie**
*See* Johnson, Anna C.

**Myrtle, Mollie**
*See* Bacon, Julia

**Myslivecek [or Mysliweczek], Josef**
1737-1781    [WBD]
*Czech composer*
* [Il] Boemo
* Venatorini

**Mysterious Bachelor**
*See* Clark, Dana Board

**Mysterious Billy Smith**
*See* Smith, Amos

**[The] Mysterious Montague**
*See* Moore, LaVerne M.

**[The] Mysterious Rhinestone Cowboy**
*See* Coe, David Allan

**Mystery**
*See* Westmoreland, Maria
Elizabeth [Jourdan]

**Mystifizinsky, Deutobold
Symbolizetti Allegoriowitsch**
*See* Vischer, Friedrich Theodor von

**Mzee [Grand Old Man]**
*See* Ngengi, Kamau wa

# N

**N. A.**
See Ansell, Norah

**N. K.**
See Kay, Nora

**N. of Arkansas**
See Noland, C. M. F.

**N. T.**
See Truebner, Nicolas

**N. T. G.**
See Granlund, Nils Thor

**[A] N. Y. Detective**
See Doughty, Francis W.

**N. Y. Times Man**
See Alden, William L.

**Na Gopaleen [or Na gCopaleen], Myles**
See O'Nuallain, Brian

**Naa Parthasarathy, Naarayana-Parthasarathy** 1932- [IAW]
*Indian author and poet*
* Alagan, Koodal
* Dheeran
* Manivannan
* Pon Mudi

**NAACP, Miss**
See Mitchell, Lottie Pearl

**Naber, Charles R.**
See Hall, Frank Richards

**Nabokov, Vladimir Vladimirovich** 1899-1977 [ANT, CA, CD]
*Russian-born American author, poet, playwright*
* [The] Black Swan of Lac Leman
* Siren, V[ladimir]

**Nabonidus** 6th c. BC [WBD]
*King of Babylonia*
* [The] Antiquarian King

**Nacchiante, Giacome** [PA]
*Author*
* Naclautus

**Nachez, Tivadar**
See Naschitz, Theodor

**Nacht, Max** 1881-1973 [B10]
*American author and journalist*
* Nomad, Max

**Nacional [National]**
See Anllo y Orrio, Ricardo

**Nacional II [National, the Second]**
See Anllo y Orrio, Juan

**Naclautus**
See Nacchiante, Giacome

**Nada, Alivia**
See Mora, Josie

**Nada Yolanda**
See Sharpe, Pauline

**Nadar**
See Tournachon, [Gaspard] Felix

**Nadel, Aaron** 20th c. [SFP]
*Author*
* Marcellinus, Animianus

**Nadel, Warren** 1930- [ASC]
*American composer*
* Starr, Randy

**Nader, Owen**
See Ackerman, Forrest J[ames]

**Nader, Seena**
See Ackerman, Forrest J[ames]

**Nader, William, S. X. Q.**
See Douglas, William

**Nadir, A. A.?**
See Romanoff, Alexander Nicholayevitch

**Nadir, Hadiyah Joan**
See Little, Joan

**Nadir, Moishe**
See Reiss, Isaac

**Nadir Shah**
See Mohammed Nadir Khan

**Nadir Shah** 1688-1747 [FFF, WBD]
*King of Persia*
* Tahmasp Kuli Khan [Slave of Tahmasp]
* [The] Wallace of Persia

**Nadja**
See Wanger, Beatrice

**Nadler, Susan**
See Gantry, Susan Nadler

**Naftali, Ch.**
See Brandwein, Chaim N[aftali]

**Nagai, Kafu**
See Nagai, Sokichi

**Nagai, Sokichi** 1879-1959 [WOA]
*Japanese author and critic*
* Nagai, Kafu

**Nagel, Anne**
See Dolan, Ann

**Nagel, Endre** 1909- [CAR]
*Swedish painter*
* Nemes, Endre

**Nagele, Anton** 1876- ? [LAO]
*German author*
* Clavell, Stauffer

**Nageleisen, Louis Marcellus** 1887-1965 [BE]
*American baseball player*
* Nagelsen, Lou[is Marcellus]

**Nagelsen, Lou[is Marcellus]**
See Nageleisen, Louis Marcellus

**Nagelson, Russell Charles** 1944- [BE]
*American baseball player*
* Nagelson, Rusty

**Nagelson, Rusty**
See Nagelson, Russell Charles

**Nagle, Arthur**
See Sullivan, Edmund

**Nagle, J. E.** [PA]
*Author*
* Cousin Nourma

**Nagle, Judge**
See Nagle, Walter Harold

**Nagle, Kel**
See Nagle, Kelvin David George

**Nagle, Kelvin David George** 1920- [EG, GF]
*Australian golfer*
* Nagle, Kel

**Nagle, Lucky**
See Nagle, Walter Harold

**Nagle, Walter Harold** 1880-1971 [BE]
*American baseball player*
* Nagle, Judge
* Nagle, Lucky

**Nagle-Healy, James Anthony** 1916- [IAW]
*Irish author, actor, producer*
* Hay, Nigel
* Healy, James N.

**Nagler, A. M.**
See Nagler, Alois M.

**Nagler, Alois M.** 1907- [BEW]
*Austrian-born educator, theatrical historian, drama critic*
* Nagler, A. M.

**Nagol** [joint pseudonym with Virgil Glen Logan]
See Logan, Lillian Mee

**Nagol** [joint pseudonym with Lillian Mee Logan]
See Logan, Virgil Glen

**Nagurski, Bronislaw** 1908- [FB, OCS]
*Canadian-born American football player*
* Nagurski, Bronko

**Nagurski, Bronko**
See Nagurski, Bronislaw

**Naidorf, Mendel** 1914- [EJS]
*Argentinian chess master*
* Najdorf, Miguel

**Naidu, [Rama] Murti** 20th c. [BL]
*Indian strong man*
* [The] Indian Hercules

**Naidu, Sarojini [Chattopadhyay]** 1879-1949 [LC]
*Indian political leader and poet*
* [The] Nightingale of India

**Naigeon, Jacques Andre** 1738-1810 [HN, SN]
*French author*
* [The] Inquisitor of Atheists

**Nailor, John** 12th c. [HN]
*British outlaw*
* Little John

**Naipaul, V. S.**
See Naipaul, Vidiadhar Surajprasad

**Naipaul, Vidiadhar Surajprasad** 1932- [LC]
*British author*
* Naipaul, V. S.

**Nair, Krishnapillai Krishnan** 1918- [IAW]
*Indian author*
* Chaitanya, Krishna

**Nair, V. Madhavan** 1915- [IAW]
*Indian author*
* Mali

**Naish, Carrol Patrick** 1901- [BEW]
*American actor*
* Naish, J. Carrol

**Naish, J. Carrol**
See Naish, Carrol Patrick

**Naismith, Helen** 1929-    [CA]
*American writer*
* Eppie

**Naismith, Horace**
See   Helmer, William J[oseph]

**Naismith, Laurence**
See   Johnson, Laurence Bernard

**Najam**
See   Shastri, Prithvinath

**Najdorf, Miguel**
See   Naidorf, Mendel

**Nakae, Noriko** 1940-    [CA]
*Japanese artist and illustrator*
* Ueno, Noriko

**Naksok**
See   Sung-Tai, Kim

**Nakulan**
See   Doraiswajy, Trivandrum
Krishna Iyer

**Naldi, Nita**
See   Dooley, Anita Donna

**Naleway, Chick**
See   Naleway, Frank

**Naleway, Frank** 1901-1949    [BE]
*American baseball player*
* Naleway, Chick

**Nall, Hiram Abiff** 1950-    [CA]
*American author and editor*
* Wadinasi, Sedeka

**Nallaperumal, Ravanasamudram
Subbiah** 1931-    [IAW]
*Indian author*
* Charan, Sakthi

**Nalle**
See   Valtiala, Kaarle-Juhani Bertel

**Nam Suk**
See   Ahn, Soo-gil

**Namary, Genevieve** ?-1956    [SC]
*Canadian-born actress*
* Blinn, Genevieve

**Namath, Broadway Joe**
See   Namath, Joseph W.

**Namath, Joseph W.** 1943-    [FB]
*American football player*
* Gerber, Mr.
* Namath, Broadway Joe

**Namby-Pamby**
See   Philips, Ambrose

**[A] Nameless Nobleman**
See   Austin, Jane Goodwin

**Namier, Julia** 1893-    [CA]
*Russian-born author*
* De Beausobre, Julia Mikhailovna

**Namier, [Sir] Lewis**
See   Bernstein-Namierowski, Lewis

**Namovicz, Gene Inyart** 1927-    [CA]
*American author and librarian*
* Inyart, Gene

**Nana Sahib**
See   Dandhu Panth

**Nanak** 1469-1538    [WBD]
*Indian religious leader*
* Guru [Teacher]

**Nance, Bo**
See   Nance, James S.

**Nance, Doc**
See   Cooper, William G.

**Nance, Floor Show**
See   Nance, Willis

**Nance, James S.** 1942-    [FB]
*American football player*
* Nance, Bo

**Nance, Kid**
See   Cooper, William G.

**Nance, Ray**
See   Nance, Willis

**Nance, William G.**
See   Cooper, William G.

**Nance, Willis** 1913-1976
[DAM, IBW, PMJ]
*American jazz musician*
* Nance, Floor Show
* Nance, Ray

**Nanchoff, Crazy Horse**
See   Nanchoff, George

**Nanchoff, George** 1954-
*American soccer player*
* Nanchoff, Crazy Horse

**Nanda Kumar**
See   Nuncomar

**Nandakumar, Prema** 1939-    [CA]
*Indian author*
* Aswin

**Nankin, Eileen** 20th c.    [OP]
*American opera singer*
* Shelle, Eileen

**NanKivell, Joice M.**
See   Loch, Joice NanKivell

**Nanni, Giovanni**
See   Annius of Viterbo

**Nano, Hervis**
See   Leach, Harvey

**Nanton, Joseph [Joe]** 1904-1946?
[DAM, EJ, PMJ]
*American jazz musician*
* Nanton, Tricky Sam

**Nanton, Tricky Sam**
See   Nanton, Joseph [Joe]

**Naoroji, Dadabhai** 1825-1917
[DEP]
*Indian political reformer*
* [The] Father of Indian
Nationalism
* [The] Grand Old Man of India

**Nap**
See   Bonaparte, Napoleon

**Napier, Alan**
See   Napier-Clavering, Alan

**Napier, Buddy**
See   Napier, Skelton LeRoy

**Napier, Diana**
See   Ellis, Molly

**Napier, Eudie**
See   Napier, Euthumn

**Napier, Euthumn** 1915-    [MK]
*American baseball player*
* Napier, Eudie

**Napier, Geoffrey**
See   Glemser, Bernard

**Napier, Geraldine**
See   Glemser, Bernard

**Napier, Macveigh** 1776-1847    [SN]
*Scottish editor*
* [The] Bacon Fly

**Napier, Marita**
See   Jacobs, Marita

**Napier, Mark**
See   Laffin, John [Alfred Charles]

**Napier, Mary**
See   Wright, [Mary] Patricia

**Napier, Priscilla** 1908-    [CA]
*British author*
* Hunt, Penelope
* Stewart, Eve

**Napier, Skelton LeRoy** 1889-1968
[BE]
*American baseball player*
* Napier, Buddy

**Napier, William**
See   Seymour, William Napier

**Napier-Clavering, Alan** 1903-    [FC]
*British-born actor*
* Napier, Alan

**Napjus, Alice James** 1913-    [CA]
*American author*
* Napjus, James

**Napjus, James**
See   Napjus, Alice James

**Naples, Al**
See   Naples, Aloysius Francis

**Naples, Aloysius Francis** 1927-
[BE]
*American baseball player*
* Naples, Al

**Napoleon, Art**
See   Sudhalter, Richard M[errill]

**Napoleon, George** 1914-1964
[WWJ]
*American jazz musician*
* Napoleon, Teddy

**Napoleon le Petit**
See   Bonaparte, Charles Louis
Napoleon

**[The] Napoleon of Africa**
See   Mirambo

**[The] Napoleon of Essayists**
See   Greeley, Horace

**[The] Napoleon of Finance**
See   Ouyrard, Gabriel Julien

**[The] Napoleon of Finance**
See   Ward, Ferdinand

**[The] Napoleon of Liverpool Finance**
See   Ranger, Morris

**[The] Napoleon of Mexico**
See   Iturbide, Agusto

**[The] Napoleon of Oratory**
See   Gladstone, William Ewart

**[The] Napoleon of Peace**
See   Louis Philippe

**[The] Napoleon of Princeton**
See   McKinley, William

**[The] Napoleon of the Drama**
See   Bunn, Alfred

**[The] Napoleon of the Drama**
See   Elliston, Robert William

**[The] Napoleon of the Drama**
See   Frohman, Charles

**[The] Napoleon of the East**
See   Mehemet [or Mohammed] Ali

**[The] Napoleon of the Indian Race**
See   Hinmaton-Yalaktit

**[The] Napoleon of the Stump**
See   Polk, James Knox

**[The] Napoleon of the Turf**
See   Bentinck, [Lord] George

**Napoleon, Phil**
See   Napoli, Filippo

**Napoleon, Prince**
See   Bonaparte, Napoleon Joseph
Charles Paul

**Napoleon, Teddy**
See   Napoleon, George

**Napoleon the Little**
See   Bonaparte, Charles Louis
Napoleon

**Napoleon I**
See   Bonaparte, Francois Charles
Joseph [Duc de Reichstadt]

**Napoleon I**
See   Bonaparte, Napoleon

**Napoleon III**
See   Bonaparte, Charles Louis
Napoleon

**Napoleon XIV**
See   Samuels, Jerry

**Napoles, Jose**
See   Martequilla, Angel

**Napoles Fajardo, Juan Cristobal**
1829-1862    [CW]
*Cuban poet and playwright*
* [El] Cucalambe

**Napoli, Filippo** 1901-    [WWJ]
*American jazz musician*
* Napoleon, Phil

**Napoli, Vincent** 20th c.    [SFP]
*Author*
* Vincent

**Narain, Jai Prakash**
See   Narayan, Jayaprakash

**Naranjo, Cholly**
See   Naranjo, Lazaro Ramon
Gonzalo

**Naranjo, Lazaro Ramon Gonzalo**
1934-    [BE]
*Cuban-born baseball player*
* Naranjo, Cholly

**Narayan, Jayaprakash** 1902-1979
[CA]
*Indian political leader and author*
* J. P.
* Loknayak [The Peoples Hero]
* Narain, Jai Prakash

**Narayan, R. K.**
See   Narayan, Rasipuram
Krishnaswami

**Narayan, Rasipuram Krishnaswami**
1907?-    [WYA]
*Indian author*
* Narayan, R. K.

**Narcejac, Thomas**
See Ayraud, Pierre

**Narcissa**
See Oldfield, Anna

**Narcisse, Louis H.** 1921-  [IBW]
*American clergyman*
* King Louis

**[The] Narcissus of France**
See Lamartine, Alphonse Marie
Louis de Prat de

**Narell, Irena** 1923-  [CA]
*Polish-born American author*
* Penzik, Irena

**Nares, Edward** 1762-1848  [PA]
*Author*
* Cecil, William
* It Matters Not Who

**Nares, Owen**
See Ramsay, Owen Nares

**Narino, Henry** 1889-1965  [THR]
*French-born actor and singer*
* De Bray, Henry

**Narleski, Cap**
See Narleski, William Edward
[Bill]

**Narleski, William Edward [Bill]**
1899-1964  [BE]
*American baseball player*
* Narleski, Cap

**Narsanmor**
See Sanchez Morales, Narciso

**Narssius**
See Van Naerssen, Jan

**Narum, Buster**
See Narum, Leslie Ferdinand

**Narum, Leslie Ferdinand** 1940-
[BE, SMG]
*American baseball player*
* Narum, Buster

**Narvestad, Joerund** 1894-  [NAA]
*Norwegian-born author and
educator*
* Jorgenson, Theodore

**Nasby, [Rev.] Petroleum Vesuvius**
See Locke, David Ross

**Naschitz, Theodor** 1859-1930  [JL]
*Hungarian musician*
* Nachez, Tivadar

**Nascimento, Francisco Manoel do**
1734-1819  [WBD]
*Portuguese poet*
* Elysio, Filinto

**Nash, B. A.**
See Banash, Joseph

**Nash, Beau**
See Nash, Richard

**Nash, Chandler**
See Hunt, Katherine Chandler

**Nash, Charles** 1942-  [BB]
*American basketball player*
* Nash, Cotton

**Nash, Cotton**
See Nash, Charles

**Nash, Daniel**
See Loader, William Reginald

**Nash, Frank** 20th c.  [BLB]
*American bank robber*
* Nash, Jelly

**Nash, James Edwin** 1945-  [PB]
*American baseball player*
* Nash, Jumbo

**Nash, Jelly**
See Nash, Frank

**Nash, John** 1830-1901  [BMH]
*British comedian*
* [The] Laughing Blacksmith
* Nash, Jolly John

**Nash, Jolly John**
See Nash, John

**Nash, Jumbo**
See Nash, James Edwin

**Nash, Lemoine** 1898-1969  [BWW]
*American singer*
* [The] Banjo Boy
* Nash, Lemon

**Nash, Lemon**
See Nash, Lemoine

**Nash, Linell**
See Smith, Linell Nash

**Nash, Mary**
See Ryan, Mary

**Nash, N. Richard**
See Nusbaum, Nathaniel Richard

**Nash, Newlyn** [joint pseudonym with
Muriel Howe]
See Howe, Doris Kathleen

**Nash, Newlyn** [joint pseudonym with
Doris Kathleen Howe]
See Howe, Muriel

**Nash, Richard** 1674-1762
[FF, HN, SN]
*British fashion leader*
* [Le] Grand Nash
* [The] King of Bath
* Nash, Beau

**Nash, Simon**
See Chapman, Raymond

**Nash [or Nashe?], Thomas**
1567-1601  [PA, SN, WBD]
*British author and playwright*
* [The] Ape of Greene
* Our English Rabelais
* Pasquil
* Pennilesso, Pierre
* Young Juvenal

**Nash, Willard G.**  [PA]
*Author*
* Dusty

**[The] Nashville Narcissus**
See Lucas, Charles Fred

**Nasier, Alcofribas**
See Rabelais, Francois

**Nasmyth, Alexander** 1758-1840
[WBD]
*Scottish painter*
* [The] Father of Scottish
Landscape Art

**Nasmyth, Patrick [or Peter?]**
1787-1831  [DEP, FFF, SN]
*Scottish painter*
* [The] English Hobbema
* [The] Hobbema of Scotland
* [The] Scotch Hobbema

**Nason, Arthur Huntington** 1877- ?
[NAA]
*American author and editor*
* Van Dyke, Anthony

**Nason, Leonard Hastings** 1895-
[WW]
*Author*
* Steamer

**[The] Nassau Nugget**
See Kazmaier, Richard W., Jr.

**Nasser's Poodle**
See Sadat, Anwar

**Nast, Elsa Ruth**
See Watson, Jane Werner

**Nastase, Ilie** 1949-  [SA]
*Rumanian tennis player*
* Nastase, Nasty

**Nastase, Nasty**
See Nastase, Ilie

**Nasworthy, Frank**
*American skateboard designer*
* Cadillac, Captain

**Nat King Cole**
See Coles, Nathaniel Adams

**Natale, Anthony** 20th c.  [BBH]
*American horseshoe pitcher*
* Natale, Ginger

**Natale, Ginger**
See Natale, Anthony

**Natali, Alfred Maxim** 1915-  [CA]
*Italian-born American author*
* Militello, Pietro

**Natchez**
See Broonzy, William Lee Conley

**Nate the Great**
See Thurmond, Nate

**Nathal, Mrs.**  [FFF]
*Entertainer*
* Lester, Louise

**Nathan, Daniel** 1905-
[CA, CC, EMD]
*American author*
* Dannay, Frederic
* Queen, Ellery [joint pseudonym
with Manfred Lepofsky]
* Queen, Ellery, Jr. [joint
pseudonym with Manfred
Lepofsky]
* Ross, Barnaby [joint pseudonym
with Manfred Lepofsky]

**Nathan, G. J.**
See Nathan, George Jean

**Nathan, George Jean** 1882-1958
[CAA, LC]
*American author and critic*
* Hatteras, Owen [joint pseudonym
with Henry Louis Mencken]
* Nathan, G. J.

**Nathan, Isaac** ?-1492  [PA]
*Author*
* Mordichai

**Nathan, Max** 1916-1968  [SC]
*American actor*
* Newmark, Stewart

**Nathan, Vivian**
See Firko, Vivia

**[The] Natick Cobbler**
See Colbath, Jeremiah Jones

**Natick Eddie Casey**
See Casey, Edward L.

**Natick Eddie Mahan**
See Mahan, Edward W.

**[A] Native Georgian**
See Longstreet, A. B.

**[A] Native of the South**
See Cooper, Myles

**Natonek, Hans** 1892-  [LAO]
*Czech-born editor and author*
* Nek

**Natsume, Kinnosuke** 1867-1916
[EWL, TLC]
*Japanese author*
* Gudabutsu
* Natsume, Soseki

**Natsume, Soseki**
See Natsume, Kinnosuke

**Natti, Mary Lee** 1919-  [CA, SFL]
*American author*
* Kingman, Lee

**Nature's Glory**
See Elizabeth I

**Nau, Jacques Jean David**
1634-1671  [FFF]
*French buccaneer*
* L'Olonnois, Francois
* [The] Scourge of the Spaniards

**Nau, John Antoine**
See Torquet, Andre

**[The] Naugatuck Nugget**
See O'Shea, Frank Joseph

**Naughton, Mortimer J.**
1889?-1958  [BEW]
*American actor*
* Norton, Jack

**Naughton, Owen** 20th c.  [WWL]
*Irish author and editor*
* O Neachtain, Eoghan

**Nauni, Remigo** 1521-1581  [PA]
*Author*
* Remi de Florence

**Nauticus**
See Clowes, [Sir] William Laird

**Nauticus**
See Seaman, [Sir] Owen

**Nauticus**
See Waltari, Mika [Toimi]

**Nava, Franz**
See Rimbault, Edward Francis

**Nava, Sandy**
See Nava, Vincent P.

**Nava, Vincent P.** 1850-1906  [BE]
*American baseball player*
* Nava, Sandy

**Navarchus** [joint pseudonym with
James Woods]
See Vaux, Patrick

**Navarchus** [joint pseudonym with
Patrick Vaux]
See Woods, James

**[The] Navarrais**
See Charles II

**Navarre, Andre**
See Wright, Alexander

**Navarro, Fats**
See Navarro, Theodore

**Navarro, Joaquin** 1873-1936 [GS]
*Spanish bullfighter*
* Quinito

**Navarro, Julio Ventura** 1936-
[BE, SMG]
*Puerto Rican-born baseball player*
* Navarro, Whiplash

**Navarro, Osvaldo** 1893-1954
[WEC]
*Brazilian cartoonist*
* Osvaldo

**Navarro, Ruben** 20th c. [AES]
*Argentinian soccer player*
* [The] Hatchet

**Navarro, Theodore** 1923-1950
[DAM, EJ, PMJ]
*American jazz musician*
* Navarro, Fats

**Navarro, Whiplash**
See Navarro, Julio Ventura

**Navarrus**
See Azpeleneta, Martimius ab

**Navasky, Victor S.** 1932- [CA]
*American author and editor*
* Hirsch, William Randolph [joint
pseudonym with Marvin Kitman
and R. Lingeman]

**[The] Navigator**
See Henry [or Don Henrique]

**Navin, Frank**
*American baseball team owner*
* [The] Mandarin

**Navratilova, Martina** 1957?-
*Czech-born tennis player*
* [The] Iron Maiden

**Nawaz, Malik Sarfraz** 1948- [DC]
*Pakistani-born cricketer*
* Nawaz, Saf

**Nawaz, Saf**
See Nawaz, Malik Sarfraz

**Nawe, Izabella**
See Binek, Izabella

**Nawrot, Harriet** 1903-1975 [SC]
*American actress and roller skater*
* McGuirk, Harriet

**Nayar, S.**
See Doraiswajy, Trivandrum
Krishna Iyer

**Naylor, Eliot**
See Frankau, Pamela

**Naylor, Jerry** 1939- [ECM]
*American country-western performer*
* Garrard, Jackie

**Naylor, John** 1920- [CA]
*British astrologer and author*
* Orion

**Naylor, Roleine Cecil** 1892-1966
[BE]
*American baseball player*
* Naylor, Rollie

**Naylor, Rollie**
See Naylor, Roleine Cecil

**Nayudu, Cottari Kanakayia**
1895-1967 [EC]
*Indian cricketer*
* [The] Indian Bradman

**Nazareth, Peter** 1940- [CA]
*Ugandan-born author*
* Wako, Mdogo

**Nazarian, Nikki**
See Nichols, Cecilia Fawn

**[The] Nazarite**
See Parr, Samuel

**Nazimova, Alla**
See Mazimoff, Alla

**Nazzaro**
See Nazzaro, Erminio

**Nazzaro, Erminio** 1912- [BMH]
*Italian-born impressionist*
* Nazzaro

**NCA, Mr.**
See Callaghan, Dennis

**Ndugu**
See Chancler, Leon

**Neafie**
See Purple, Edwin R.

**Neagle, Anna**
See Robertson, Marjorie

**Neagu, Paul** 1938- [CAR]
*British sculptor*
* Belmood, Husny
* Honeysuckle, Philip
* Larsocchi, Eduard
* Paidola, Anton

**Neal, Adeline Phyllis** 1894- [WW]
*Author*
* Grey, A. F.

**Neal, Gavin**
See Tubb, Edwin Charles

**Neal, Harry**
See Bixby, Jerome Lewis

**Neal, Hilary**
See Norton, Olive Marion
[Claydon]

**Neal, James** [FFF]
*British author*
* Nemesis

**Neal, James T[homas]** 1936- [CA]
*American geologist and author*
* James, Thomas N.

**Neal, Jennie** [FFF]
*Entertainer*
* Garrison, Maude

**Neal, John** 1793-1876
[DEL, DNNF, PA]
*American author*
* Adams, Will
* Allen, Paul
* O'Cataract, Jehu
* O'Cataract, John

**Neal, Offa**
See Neal, Theophilus Fountain

**Neal, [Sir] Paul** [PA]
*Author*
* Sidrophel

**Neal, Theophilus Fountain**
1876-1950 [BE]
*American baseball player*
* Neal, Offa

**Neale, Alfred Earle** 1891-1973
[B10, BE, FB]
*American football player and coach*
* Neale, Greasy

**Neale, Alice Clay** 1828-1863 [PA]
*Author*
* Alice

**Neale, C. Goodliffe** 20th c. [BS]
*British magazine publisher*
* Goodliffe the Magician

**Neale, Erskine** 1805- ? [PA]
*Author*
* [A] Coroner's Clerk
* [A] Country Curate
* [A] Gaol Chaplain

**Neale, Flora**
See McLeod, Mrs. G. A.

**Neale, Greasy**
See Neale, Alfred Earle

**Neale, J. E.**
See Neale, [Sir] John Ernest

**Neale, [Sir] John Ernest** 1890- [LC]
*British author and educator*
* Neale, J. E.

**Neale, Nettie**
See Heath, Maggie E.

**Neander, Johann August Wilhelm**
See Mendel, David

**[The] Neapolitan**
See Tischbein, Johann Heinrich
Wilhelm

**Nearing, Elizabeth [Custer]** 1898?-
[ANT, CC]
*American author*
* MacVeigh, Sue

**Nearing, John Scott** 1912-1976
[SAT]
*American author*
* Scott, John

**Nearing, Penny**
See Munn, Meryl Lucile

**Neave, A. H.**
See Headley-Neave, Alice

**[Der] Nebelmeister**
See Rosemeyer, Bernd

**[The] Nebraska Wildcat**
See Hudkins, Ace

**Nebrija [or Lebrija], Elio Antonio de**
See Martinez de Jarava, Elio
Antonio

**Neckam [or Necham], Alexander**
1157-1217 [WBD]
*British scholar*
* Nequam

**Necker, Jacques [or James]**
1732-1804 [HN, SN]
*French statesman and financier*
* [A] Machiavelli
* [The] Virtuous Genevese

**Necker, Olivier** 1440?-1484 [WBD]
*Adviser to King Louis XI of France*
* Olivier le Dain [or le Daim]
* Olivier le Diable

**Nederveen Hendriks, Wietske** 20th
c. [IAW]
*Dutch author and poet*
* Wytske

**Nedlo the Gypsy Violinist**
See Olden, Charles

**Nee, Brett de Bary** 1943- [CA]
*American author*
* De Bary, Brett

**Needham, David** 1951- [RBE]
*British boxer*
* [The] Artful Dodger

**Needham, Deerfoot**
See Needham, Thomas J.

**Needham, Marchamont** 1620-1678
[SN]
*British author*
* [The] Cobbett of His Day

**Needham, Marchmont**
See Quincy, Josiah

**Needham, Thomas J.** 1879-1926
[BE]
*Irish-born American baseball player*
* Needham, Deerfoot

**Neef, Elton T.**
See Fanthorpe, R[obert] Lionel

**Neek, Hugh**
See Olden, Charles

**Neels, Marc** 1922- [WECO]
*Flemish cartoonist*
* Sleen, Marc

**Neely, Bob** 1953- [SMG]
*Canadian-born hockey player*
* Neely, Waldo

**Neely, Waldo**
See Neely, Bob

**[The] Neem**
See Nemo, Henry

**Neeper, Carolyn** 1937- [CA]
*American author*
* Neeper, Cary

**Neeper, Cary**
See Neeper, Carolyn

**Neera**
See Zuccari, Anna Radius

**Neerskov, Hans Kristian** 1932-
[CA]
*Danish author and clergyman*
* Kristian, Hans

**Neethling, J. S.**
See Neethling, Jacobus Stephanus

**Neethling, Jacobus Stephanus** 20th
c. [IAW]
*South African author*
* Neethling, J. S.
* Neethling, Kobus

**Neethling, Kobus**
See Neethling, Jacobus Stephanus

**Neeves, Thyrza** 1884- [THR]
*British actress*
* Norman, Thyrza

**Nef, Evelyn Stefansson** 1913- [CA]
*American geographer and author*
* Stefansson, Evelyn

**Nefe, Gaspard** 1514-1580 [PA]
*Author*
* Noevius

**Neff, Felix** 1798-1829
[DNNF, FFF, HN]
*Swiss missionary*
* [The] Apostle of the Alps

**Neff, Hildegarde**
See Knef, Hildegard

**Negri, Pola**
See Chalupec, Apolonia

[El] Negro
See Nino, Pedro Alonso

Negron Munoz, Mercedes
1895-1973 [CW]
*Cuban poet*
* Lair, Clara

Nehemiah, Renaldo
*American track and field athlete*
* Nehemiah, Skeets

Nehemiah, Skeets
See Nehemiah, Renaldo

Neidhart Fuchs [Neidhart the Fox]
See Neidhart von Reuenthal

Neidhart von Reuenthal 13th c.
[WBD]
*Bavarian knight and poet*
* Neidhart Fuchs [Neidhart the Fox]

Neighbors, Cecil F. 1880-1964
[BE]
*American baseball player*
* Neighbors, Cy

Neighbors, Cy
See Neighbors, Cecil F.

Neil, [Judge] Henry 1863- ? [NAA]
*American author*
* Everett, Marshall

Neil, Ross
See Harwood, Isabella

Neilhams, Terence 1940- [FC]
*British actor and singer*
* Faith, Adam

Neill, A. S.
See Neill, Alexander Sutherland

Neill, Alexander Sutherland
1883-1973 [LC]
*British educator and author*
* Neill, A. S.

Neill, Beau
See Neill, Thomas Hewson

Neill, Beverly Louise 1929-
[FC, IPA, ITA]
*American actress*
* Blake, Amanda

Neill, Roy William
See De Gostrie, Roland

Neill, Thomas Hewson 1826-1885
[FFF]
*American soldier*
* Neill, Beau

Neilson, Cora
See Carver, Mrs. J. H.

Neilson, Francis
See Butters, Francis

Neilson, James Anthony 1940-
[CEI, FHE, HK]
*Canadian-born hockey player*
* [The] Chief

Neilson, Lilian Adelaide
See Brown, Elizabeth Ann

Neilson, Marguerite
See Tompkins, Julia [Marguerite
Hunter Manchee]

Neilson, Perlita
See Sowden, Margaret

Neilson, Vernon
See Clarke, Percy A.

Neilson-Terry, Dennis
See Terry, Dennis

Neilson-Terry, Hazel 1918-1974
[SC, THR]
*British actress*
* Terry, Hazel

Neilson-Terry, Phyllis
See Terry, Phyllis

Neish, Duncan
See Allan, F. Carney

Neiswanger, Marion 1879- ?
[THR]
*American playwright*
* Fairfax, Marion

Nek
See Natonek, Hans

Nekola, Bots
See Nekola, Francis Joseph

Nekola, Francis Joseph 1907- [BE]
*American baseball player*
* Nekola, Bots

Nellie
See Marsh, E.

Nelms, Henning [WW]
*Author*
* Talbot, Hake

Nelson, Abbott Willie
See Nelson, Willie

Nelson, Albert 1923- [BWW]
*American singer*
* King, Albert

Nelson, Albert Francis
See Horazdovsky, Albert W.

Nelson, Andrew [Andy] 20th c.
[BE]
*American baseball player*
* Nelson, Peaches

Nelson, Babe
See Nelson, Robert Sidney [Bob]

Nelson, Baby Face
See Gillis, Lester

Nelson, Barry
See Nielson, Robert

Nelson, Barry
See Thomas, Reginald George

Nelson, Battling
See Nielson, Oscar M.

Nelson, Benjamin Earl 1938-
[PRS, RO1]
*American singer and songwriter*
* King, Ben E.

Nelson, Big Eye
See Nelson, Louis Delisle

Nelson, Big George
See Gillis, Lester

Nelson, Bob 1944- [BWW]
*American singer*
* Nelson, Chicago Bob

Nelson, Byron 1912- [BWG, EG]
*American golfer*
* Lord Byron
* [The] Mechanical Man

Nelson, Charles A. 19th c. [FFF]
*American journalist*
* Chelsea

Nelson, Chicago Bob
See Nelson, Bob

Nelson, Country Willie
See Nelson, Willie

Nelson, Dave
See Nelson, Davidson C.

Nelson, Davidson C. 1905-1946
[WWJ]
*American jazz musician*
* Nelson, Dave

Nelson, Dixie Kay 1933-
[ITA, SW]
*American actress*
* Nelson, Lori

Nelson, Doc
See Nelson, George

Nelson, Earl 20th c. [BWW]
*American musician*
* Nelson, Louisiana Earl

Nelson, Earle Leonard 1897-1928
[BLB]
*American murderer*
* Wilson, Roger

Nelson, Eddie 1894-1940 [SC]
*American actor*
* Nelson, Sunkist

Nelson, [George] Emmett
1905-1967 [BE]
*American baseball player*
* Nelson, Ramrod

Nelson, Emmett 20th c. [BWW]
*American musician*
* Rush, Bobby

Nelson, Eric Hilliard 1940-
[DAM, IPA, ITA]
*American singer and actor*
* Nelson, Ricky

Nelson, Ethel Florence 1913?-
[AW, CA]
*Canadian-born author*
* Nelson, Nina

Nelson, Evelyn 1918?- [PMJ]
*American singer*
* Baker, Bonnie
* Baker, Wee Bonnie

Nelson, Frankie
See Valerio, Michael

Nelson, Gene
See Berg, Leander

Nelson, George
See Gillis, Lester

Nelson, George 20th c. [BBH]
*American collegiate athletic trainer*
* Nelson, Doc

Nelson, Gertrude
See Bobin, John William [Jack]

Nelson, Glenn Richard 1924- [BE]
*American baseball player*
* Nelson, Rocky

Nelson, Harold 1880-1965 [SC]
*American actor and singer*
* Reed, Gus

Nelson, Harriet Hilliard
See Snyder, Peggy Lou

Nelson, Harrison 1925?- [BWW]
*American singer*
* Harris, Peppermint

Nelson, Horace 1916?- [MY]
*American jazz musician*
* Nelson, Steady

Nelson, Horatio 1758-1805
[DNNS, FFF, HN]
*British naval officer*
* [The] Duke of Thunder
* [The] Hero of a Hundred Fights
* [The] Hero of the Nile

Nelson, Ira 1913?-1978 [FIR]
*American country-western performer*
* Nelson, Pop

Nelson, Iromeio 1902-1974 [BWW]
*American singer*
* Nelson, Romeo

Nelson, Jack
See Nelson, Jackson W.

Nelson, Jack Alton 1927-1978
[SMG]
*American football coach*
* Nelson, Jocko

Nelson, Jackson W. 1849-1910
[AS, BE]
*American baseball player*
* Nelson, Jack

Nelson, Jane
See Wright, M. Jane

Nelson, Jimmie
See Gillis, Lester

Nelson, Jimmy
See Irvin, Monford Merrill

Nelson, Jocko
See Nelson, Jack Alton

Nelson, [Hugh] Lawrence 1907-
[WW]
*Author*
* Trent, Peter

Nelson, Line Drive
See Nelson, Lynn Bernard

Nelson, Lori
See Nelson, Dixie Kay

Nelson, Louis Delisle 1885-1949
[DAM, EJ, WWJ]
*American jazz musician*
* DeLisle, Louis
* Nelson, Big Eye

Nelson, Louisiana Earl
See Nelson, Earl

Nelson, Lyle 20th c.
*American biathlete*
* Nelson, Vile Lyle

Nelson, Lynn Bernard 1905-1955
[BE]
*American baseball player*
* Nelson, Line Drive

Nelson, Marguerite
See Floren, Lee

Nelson, Michael Harrington 1921-
[CA]
*British author, television
scriptwriter, interviewer*
* Stratton, Henry

Nelson, Nina
See Nelson, Ethel Florence

Nelson, Oswald George 1907-1975
[CA, DAM, IPA]
*American actor, producer, director*
* Nelson, Ozzie

**Nelson, Ozzie**
*See* Nelson, Oswald George

**Nelson, Papoose**
*See* Nelson, Walter

**Nelson, Peaches**
*See* Nelson, Andrew [Andy]

**Nelson, Peter**
*See* Solow, Martin

**Nelson, Pop**
*See* Nelson, Ira

**Nelson, R. F.**
*See* Nelson, Radell Faraday

**Nelson, Radell Faraday** 1931-
[CA, ESF]
*American author*
* Elson, R. N.
* Nelson, R. F.
* Nelson, Ray

**Nelson, Ramrod**
*See* Nelson, [George] Emmett

**Nelson, Ray[mond Nelson]**
*See* Kellogg, Raymond N.

**Nelson, Ray**
*See* Nelson, Radell Faraday

**Nelson, Red**
*See* Horazdovsky, Albert W.

**Nelson, Ricky**
*See* Nelson, Eric Hilliard

**Nelson, Robert Sidney [Bob]** 1936-
[BE]
*American baseball player*
* Nelson, Babe
* Nelson, Tex

**Nelson, Rocky**
*See* Nelson, Glenn Richard

**Nelson, Roger Eugene** 1944-
[BE, PB, SMG]
*American baseball player*
* Nelson, Spider

**Nelson, Romeo**
*See* Nelson, Iromeio

**Nelson, Roy**
*See* Nelson-Smith, Alan Roy Vere

**Nelson, Ruth** 1914-  [CA]
*American educator and author*
* McHugh, Ruth Nelson

**Nelson, Sandy**
*See* Egnatzik, Joseph

**Nelson, Spider**
*See* Nelson, Roger Eugene

**Nelson, Steady**
*See* Nelson, Horace

**Nelson, Steve**
*See* Bobin, John William [Jack]

**Nelson, Steve**
*See* Mesaros, Stjepan

**Nelson, Sunkist**
*See* Nelson, Eddie

**Nelson, T.** 20th c.  [MBF]
*British author*
* Brown, Duncan

**Nelson, Tex**
*See* Nelson, Robert Sidney [Bob]

**Nelson, Victor**
*See* Bobin, John William [Jack]

**Nelson, Vile Lyle**
*See* Nelson, Lyle

**Nelson, Virginia**
*See* Tallent, Virginia

**Nelson, Walter** 20th c.  [RO2]
*American musician*
* Nelson, Papoose

**Nelson, Willie** 1933-  [FCW]
*American singer and songwriter*
* Nelson, Abbott Willie
* Nelson, Country Willie

**Nelson-Smith, Alan Roy Vere**
1905-  [WWL]
*British author*
* Nelson, Roy

**Nemes, Endre**
*See* Nagel, Endre

**Nemesis?**
*See* Francis, [Sir] Philip

**Nemesis**
*See* Neal, James

**Nemesis**
*See* Watre, Antony

**Nemeth, Janos** 20th c.  [BBH]
*Hungarian-born water polo player*
* Nemeth, Jim

**Nemeth, Jim**
*See* Nemeth, Janos

**Nemo**
*See* Browne, Hablot Knight

**Nemo**
*See* Coffin, Roland F.

**Nemo, Henry** 1914-  [PMJ]
*American composer*
* [The] Neem

**Nemo, Omen**
*See* Rehm, Warren S.

**Nenadovic, Matija** 1777-1854
[WBD]
*Serbian clergyman and patriot*
* Prota Matija

**Nennius** 8th c.  [DEP]
*Welsh historian*
* [The] British Hector

**Nentwich, Max** 1868- ?  [LAO]
*German author and playwright*
* Muensterberg, Maximilian

**Neos Philopator [New Philopator]**
*See* Ptolemy VII

**Neptune**
*See* Taylor, Benjamin Ogle

**Neptune, Father**
*See* Cavill, Dick

**Neptunus**
*See* Bruce, Benjamin

**Nepveu, Andre** 1881-1959  [WBD]
*French author*
* Durtain, Luc

**Nepveu [or Neveu], Pierre** ?-1542?
[WBD]
*French architect*
* Trinqueau

**Nequam**
*See* Neckam [or Necham],
Alexander

**Neri Tanfucio**
*See* Fucini, Renato

**Nericault, Philippe** 1680-1754
[WBD]
*French playwright*
* Destouches, Philippe

**Nero**
*See* Bonaparte, Charles Louis
Napoleon

**Nero [Claudius Caesar Drusus
Germanicus]**
*See* Domitius Ahenobarbus, Lucius

**[A] Nero**
*See* Leclerc du Tremblay, Francois

**[The] Nero of Germany**
*See* Wenceslaus [or Wenceslas]

**[The] Nero of Persia**
*See* Sefi [or Sophi]

**[The] Nero of the North**
*See* Christian II

**Nero, Paul**
*See* Polnarioff, Kurt

**Nero, Peter**
*See* Nierow, Bernard

**Nero Caesar, Tiberius Claudius** ?-
37?  [DEP, FFF, SN]
*Roman emperor*
* [The] Imperial Machiavelli
* [The] Prince of Hypocrites
* Tiberius

**Nerone, Giuseppe** ?-1925?
[BLB, PHM]
*American underworld figure*
* [The] Cavalier
* Nerone, Joseph
* Pavia, Joe
* Spano, Tony

**Nerone, Joseph**
*See* Nerone, Giuseppe

**Nerses** 310?- 374  [WBD]
*Patriarch of Armenia*
* [The] Great

**Nerses** 1098-1173  [WBD]
*Patriarch of Armenia*
* [The] Gracious

**Neruda, Pablo**
*See* Reyes Basualto, [Ricardo
Eliezer] Neftali

**Nerval, Gerard de**
*See* Labrunie, Gerard

**Nervo, Jimmy**
*See* Holloway, James

**[The] Nervous Greek**
*See* Skizas, Lou[is Peter]

**Nervy Nick Nichols**
*See* Nichols, Charles Augustus

**Nerys**
*See* Prys Williams, Nerys Mair
Sioned

**Nesbit, Edith** 1858-1924
[FFF, LC, TC]
*British author and poet*
* Bland, Fabian [joint pseudonym
with Hubert Bland]
* Carisbrooke

**Nesbit, Troy**
*See* Folsom, Franklin [Brewster]

**Nesbitt, Miriam Anne**
*See* Skancke, Miriam Anne

**Neshamith, Sara**
*See* Dushnitzky-Shner, Sara

**Nesmith, Robert I.** 1891-  [CA]
*American author*
* Clarke, [Captain] Jafah

**Nesmy, Jean**
*See* Surchamp, Henry

**Ness, Richard Derby**  [PA]
*Author*
* W. D.

**Nestle, John Francis** 1912-
[CA, IAW]
*British author*
* Falcon

**Nestor**
*See* Steele, [Sir] Richard

**Nestor** 1056?-1114?
[DNNS, HN, RH]
*Russian historian and monk*
* [The] Father of Russian History

**[The] Nestor Girl**
*See* Rhodes, Billie

**[The] Nestor of America**
*See* Franklin, Benjamin

**[The] Nestor of Canadian Politicians**
*See* Baldwin, Robert

**[The] Nestor of English Authors**
*See* Rogers, Samuel

**[The] Nestor of English Scholarship**
*See* Kennedy, Benjamin Hall

**[The] Nestor of Europe**
*See* Leopold I

**[The] Nestor of German Philosophy**
*See* Platner, Ernst

**[The] Nestor of German Poesy**
*See* Tiedge, Christoph August

**[The] Nestor of German Sculptors**
*See* Dannecker, John Heinrich

**[The] Nestor of Modern Italian
Authors**
*See* Maffei, Andrea

**[The] Nestor of the Chemical
Revolution**
*See* Black, James

**[The] Nestor of the Confederacy**
*See* Stephens, Alexander Hamilton

**[The] Nestor of the German Book
Trade**
*See* Frommann, Friedrich
Johannes

**[The] Nestor of the House of
Commons**
*See* Ellice, Edward

**Netamuxwe**
*See* Bock, William Sauts

**Netherclift, Beryl Constance** 1911-
[IAW]
*British author*
* Mascall, Margery D.

**Neto, Edvaldo** 20th c.  [AES]
*Brazilian soccer player*
* Vava

**Nettell, Richard [Geoffrey]** 1907-
[CAP, WD]
*British author*
* Kenneggy, Richard

**Netterville, Luke**
*See* O'Grady, Standish James

**Nettl, John Peter** 1926-1968  [CAP]
*German-born author*
* Norwood, Paul

**Nettles, Bonnie Lu**
*American religious cult leader*
* Peep

**Neubauer, William Arthur** 1916-
[CA]
*American author*
* Arthur, William
* Bennett, Christine
* Bligh, Norman
* Carter, Ralph
* Garrison, Joan
* Hathaway, Jan
* Marsh, Rebecca
* Newcomb, Norma
* Semple, Gordon

**Neuberger, Sigmund** 1872-1911
[BMH]
*German-born magician and
illusionist*
* [The] Great Lafayette

**Neuer, John S.** 1880- ?   [BE]
*American baseball player*
* Neuer, Tacks

**Neuer, Tacks**
*See* Neuer, John S.

**Neuffer, Irene LaBorde** 1919-   [CA]
*American author*
* LaBorde, Rene

**Neumaier, Horst R.** 1939-   [OP]
*German opera singer*
* Laubenthal Horst R.

**Neuman, Butch**
*See* Neuman, Paul William

**Neuman, Paul William**  ?-1964
[BBH]
*American basketball player and
coach*
* Neuman, Butch

**Neumann, Ferenc** 1878-1952
[JL, MWD]
*Hungarian playwright and director*
* Molnar, Ferenc

**Neumann, Vera** 1910-   [WFA]
*American designer*
* Vera

**Neustadtl, Hermine**
*See* Stich, Hermine Neustadtl

**Neuwert**
*See* Nowaczynski, Adolf

**Nevada, Emma**
*See* Wixom, Emma

**Nevada Jack Rose**
*See* Rose, Jack

**Nevanlinna, Sinikka Sisko** 1917-
[IAW]
*Finnish author and poet*
* Kallio, Sinikka
* Kallio-Visapaa, Sinikka

**Nevaro**
*See* Willkomm, Otto

**Nevers, C. O.**
*See* Converse, Charles Crozat

**Nevetz**
*See* Cox, Stephen Bernard

**Neville, Anne**
*See* Farleigh, Elsie

**Neville, Arthur**   [RM]
*Musician*
* Neville, Red

**Neville, B[arbara] Alison [Boodson]**
1925-   [CA, CC, WW]
*British author*
* Candy, Edward

**Neville, C. J.**
*See* Franklin, Cynthia

**Neville, Cecily [or Cicely]** 15th c.
[DNNS, FFF]
*Wife of Richard, Duke of York*
* [The] White Rose of Raby

**Neville, Derek** 1911-   [IAW]
*British author and poet*
* Salt, Jonathan

**Neville, [Thomas] Henry**
*See* Gartside, Thomas Henry

**Neville, Kris [Ottman]** 1925-
[ESF, WGT]
*American author*
* Starke, Henderson

**Neville, Lee**
*See* Richards, Lela Horn

**Neville, Margaret**
*See* Smith, Margaret

**Neville, Margot** [joint pseudonym
with Neville (Goyder) Joske]
*See* Goyder, Margot

**Neville, Margot** [joint pseudonym
with Margot Goyder]
*See* Joske, Neville [Goyder]

**Neville, Mary**
*See* Foster, Mary A.

**Neville, Mary**
*See* Woodrich, Mary Neville

**Neville, Red**
*See* Neville, Arthur

**Neville, Richard** 1428-1471
[DEP, DHA, HN]
*Earl of Warwick*
* [The] Kingmaker
* [The] Last of the Barons

**Neville, Robert**   [HN]
* [The] Peacock of the North

**Nevin, Evelyn C.**
*See* Ferguson, Evelyn

**Nevins, Francis, Jr.** 20th c.
*American author and attorney*
* Nevins, Mike

**Nevins, Mike**
*See* Nevins, Francis, Jr.

**Nevinson, H. W.**
*See* Nevinson, Henry Woodd

**Nevinson, Henry Woodd**
1856-1941   [LC]
*British author*
* Nevinson, H. W.

**[The] New Alexandre Dumas**
*See* Feval, Paul Henri

**[The] New Aristarchus**
*See* Sallo, Denis de

**[The] New Constantine**
*See* Louis XIV

**[The] New Dress-Improver**
*See* Wilde, Oscar Fingal
O'Flahertie Wills

**[The] New Empress of the Blues**
*See* Brown, Olive

**[A] New England Farmer**
*See* Lowell, John

**[A] New England Housekeeper**
*See* Howard, Caroline K.

**[A] New England Man**
*See* Paulding, James Kirke

**[The] New Heresiarch**
*See* Toland, Junius Janus

**[The] New Luther**
*See* Du Plessis, Armand Jean

**[The] New Moses**
*See* Anastasius

**[The] New Samson**
*See* Delamarre, Victor

**New Writer**
*See* Morris, [Sir] Lewis

**[The] Newark Adonis**
*See* Weinert, Charley

**Newbern, Frances** 1913?-   [PMJ]
*American singer*
* Langford, Frances

**Newberry, Oliver** 1789-1860   [FFF]
*American shipbuilder*
* [The] Admiral of the Lakes
* [The] Steamboat King

**Newbold, Anna Heckscher** 1898-
[NAA]
*American author and poet*
* Baden, Katia

**Newbold, Stokes**
*See* Adams, Richard N[ewbold]

**Newborn, Venezuela** 20th c.   [IBW]
*American editor*
* Newborn, Vinnie

**Newborn, Vinnie**
*See* Newborn, Venezuela

**Newbound, Bernard Slade** 1930-
[CA]
*Canadian-born playwright*
* Slade, Bernard

**Newburgh, Countess of**   [SN]
* Myra

**Newbury, Herbert**
*See* Herbert, S. A. F.

**Newby, George Eric** 1919-   [DLE]
*British author*
* Parker, James

**Newby, P. H.**
*See* Newby, Percy Howard

**Newby, Percy Howard** 1918-   [LC]
*British author*
* Newby, P. H.

**Newchurch, Harold Everett** 1937-
[IBW]
*American journalist*
* Newchurch, Tack Towne

**Newchurch, Tack Towne**
*See* Newchurch, Harold Everett

**Newcomb, Ada**
*See* Hamlin, Mrs. Paul

**Newcomb, Duane G[raham]** 1929-
[CA]
*American author*
* Firestone, Tom

**Newcomb, Ellsworth**
*See* Kenny, Ellsworth Newcomb

**Newcomb, Kerry** 1946-   [CA]
*American author*
* Carrol, Shana [joint pseudonym
   with Frank Schaefer]
* Gentry, Peter [joint pseudonym
   with Frank Schaefer]
* Savage, Christina [joint
   pseudonym with Frank Schaefer]

**Newcomb, Norma**
*See* Neubauer, William Arthur

**Newcomb, Theresa**
*See* Jackson, Mrs. T. J.

**Newcombe, Donald** 1926-   [BE, PB]
*American baseball player*
* Newcombe, Newk

**Newcombe, Louis**
*See* Stobbs, John Louis Newcombe

**Newcombe, Newk**
*See* Newcombe, Donald

**Newcome, Colin**
*See* Young, Fred W.

**Newell, Charles M.**   [PA]
*Author*
* Barnacle, [Captain] B.

**Newell, Crosby**
*See* Bonsall, Crosby Barbara
[Newell]

**Newell, Hope Hockenberry**
1896-1965   [CA]
*American author*
* Hockenberry, Hope

**Newell, Ma**
*See* Newell, Marshall

**Newell, Marshall** 1871-1897
[AS, FB]
*American football player*
* Newell, Ma

**Newell, Mrs. Atkins**   [FFF]
* Palma, [Signora] Sara

**Newell, Pinky**
*See* Newell, William E.

**Newell, Robert Henry** 1836-1901
[DEL, DNNF, FFF]
*American author and journalist*
* Kerr, Orpheus C.

**Newell, Rosemary** 1922-   [CA]
*American author*
* Gibson, Rosemary

**Newell, Roy**
*See* Raymond, Harold Newell

**Newell, S.** 1824- ?   [PA]
*Author*
* North, W. Savage

**Newell, William E.** 1920-   [BBH]
*American collegiate athletic trainer*
* Newell, Pinky

**Newhall, C. S.** [PA]
*Author*
* Carl

**Newhouser, Harold [Hal]** 1921-
[ARL, BE]
*American baseball player*
* Prince Hal

**Newkirk, Foster**
*See* Tucker, John F[rancis]

**Newland, Mary**
*See* Oldland, Lilian

**Newlight, [Rev] Aristarchus**
*See* Fitzgerald, William

**Newlight, Aristarchus**
*See* Whately, Richard

**Newlin, Margaret Rudd** 1925-
[CA, WD]
*American poet and critic*
* Rudd, Margaret

**Newlin, Maurice Milton [Maury]**
1914- [BE]
*American baseball player*
* Newlin, Mickey

**Newlin, Mickey**
*See* Newlin, Maurice Milton
[Maury]

**Newlon, Clarke** 20th c.
[B10, CA, SAT]
*American author*
* Clarke, Michael

**Newman, A.**
*See* Pim, Herbert Moore

**Newman, Adrien Ann** 1941- [CA]
*American author*
* Arpel, Adrien

**Newman, Allan Scott** 1950?-1978
*American entertainer*
* Scott, William

**Newman, Bernard [Charles]**
1897-1968 [CC, LC, WW]
*British author*
* Betteridge, Don

**Newman, Brains**
*See* Newman, David

**Newman, Dangerous Dan**
*See* Newman, Kenneth Daniel

**Newman, David** 1933-
[DAM, EJ, IBW]
*American jazz musician*
* Newman, Brains
* Newman, Fathead

**Newman, Ernest**
*See* Roberts, William

**Newman, Fathead**
*See* Newman, David

**Newman, Frank**
*See* Abrams, Sam[uel]

**Newman, John** 20th c. [CA, WGT]
*British author*
* Johns, Kenneth [joint pseudonym
with (Henry) Kenneth Bulmer]

**Newman, John Henry** 1801-1890
[HN, PA]
*British theologian*
* Catholicus
* J. H. N.
* [The] Recluse of Edgbaston

**Newman, Kenneth Daniel** 1952-
[SMG]
*Canadian-born hockey player*
* Newman, Dangerous Dan

**Newman, Kenneth E.** 20th c.
[MBF]
*British author and editor*
* Clifford, Martin [house
pseudonym]
* Conquest, Owen [house
pseudonym]
* Richards, Frank [house
pseudonym]

**Newman, M. W.** [PA]
*Author*
* [The] Exile of Erin

**Newman, Margaret**
*See* Potter, Margaret [Newman]

**Newman, Meta [Pennock]** 1891-
[NAA]
*American author and editor*
* Pennock, Meta

**Newman, Mona Alice Jean** 1910-
[WD]
*British author*
* Fitzgerald, Barbara
* Stewart, Jean

**Newmar, Julie**
*See* Newmeyer, Julia Charlene

**Newmar, Rima**
*See* Wagman, Naomi

**Newmark, Stewart**
*See* Nathan, Max

**[The] Newmarket Oracle**
*See* Ogden

**Newmeyer, Julia Charlene** 1930?-
[BEW, FC, SW]
*American actress, singer, dancer*
* Newmar, Julie

**Newquist, Roy** 1925- [SFL]
*Author*
* Sterland, Carl

**Newsom, Bobo**
*See* Newsom, Norman Louis

**Newsom, Buck**
*See* Newsom, Norman Louis

**Newsom, Norman Louis**
1907-1962 [AS, BN, PB]
*American baseball player*
* Newsom, Bobo
* Newsom, Buck
* Ol' Showboat

**Newsome, Arden J[eanne]** 1932-
[CA]
*American author and columnist*
* Sebastian, Jeanne

**Newsome, Dick**
*See* Newsome, Heber Hampton

**Newsome, Heber Hampton**
1909-1965 [BE]
*American baseball player*
* Newsome, Dick

**Newsome, Lamar Ashby** 1910-
[BE]
*American baseball player*
* Newsome, Skeeter

**Newsome, Skeeter**
*See* Newsome, Lamar Ashby

**Newsons, Albert** 1891- [WWL]
*British author*
* Bands, Paul

**Newton, A. E.**
*See* Newton, Alfred Edward

**Newton, Alfred Edward** 1863-1940
[LC]
*American book collector and author*
* Newton, A. E.

**Newton, Charles E.**
*See* Perine, C. E.

**Newton, Clark**
*See* Harmon, Jim

**Newton, David C.**
*See* Chance, John Newton

**Newton, Doc**
*See* Newton, Eustace James

**Newton, Dwight Bennett** 1916-
[CA]
*American author*
* Bennett, Dwight
* Hardin, Clement
* Logan, Ford
* Temple, Dan

**Newton, Eustace James** 1877-1931
[BE]
*American baseball player*
* Newton, Doc

**Newton, Fig**
*See* Newton, Lloyd

**Newton, Fig**
*See* Newton, Robert Lee

**Newton, Francis**
*See* Hobsbawm, Eric J[ohn Ernest]

**Newton, Henry Chance** 1854-1931
[BEW, THR]
*British-born critic and playwright*
* Carados
* Gawain

**Newton, I. M.**
*See* Newton, Irene Margaret

**Newton, Irene Margaret** 1915-
[ART]
*British artist*
* Newton, I. M.

**Newton, [Sir] Isaac** 1642-1727
[DEP, DNNS, HN]
*British mathematician and
philosopher*
* [The] Priest of Nature

**Newton, Jean**
*See* Stich, Hermine Neustadtl

**Newton, Lloyd** 1943- [IBW]
*American air force officer*
* Newton, Fig

**Newton, Macdonald**
*See* Newton, William Simpson

**Newton, Nat?**
*See* Morris, Anthony Paschal

**[The] Newton of Harmony**
*See* Rameau, Jean Philippe

**Newton, Robert Lee** 1949- [SMG]
*American football player*
* Newton, Fig

**Newton, Stu**
*See* Whitcomb, Ian

**Newton, Wayne** 1942?-
*American singer*
* [The] Midnight Idol

**Newton, William Simpson** 1923-
[CA]
*British author*
* Mitcham, Gilroy
* Newton, Macdonald

**Ney, Marie**
*See* Fix, Marie

**Ney, Michel [Duc d'Elchingen]**
1769-1815 [DEP, DHA, FF]
*French army officer*
* [The] Bravest of the Brave
* [Le] Lion Rouge
* [Le] Plus Brave des Braves

**Ney, Patrick**
*See* Bolitho, [Henry] Hector

**Ney, Wolfgang**
*See* Harranth, Wolf

**Ngagoyeanes, Nicholas** 1939- [CA]
*Greek-born journalist*
* Gage, Nicholas

**Ngengi, Kamau wa** 1891?-1978
*Kenyan president*
* Kamau, Johnstone
* Kenyatta, Jomo
* Mzee [Grand Old Man]

**Ngugi, James T[hiong'o]** 1938-
[CA, CLC]
*Kenyan-born author and playwright*
* Thiong'o, Ngugi wa

**Nguyen-Anh** ?-1820 [WBD]
*King of Annam, Indo-China*
* Gialong

**Ni Fhaircheallaigh, Una**
*See* O'Farrelly, Agnes

**Ni Loinsigh, Brid** 1913-1968 [SC]
*Irish actress*
* Lynch, Brid

**Niall** ?- 405 [HN]
*King of Ireland*
* [The] Great
* [The] Hero of the Nine Hostages

**Niall, Ian**
*See* McNeillie, John

**Niarhos, Constantine Gregory**
1920- [BE]
*American baseball player*
* Niarhos, Gus

**Niarhos, Gus**
*See* Niarhos, Constantine Gregory

**Niatum, Duane**
*See* McGinnis, Duane

**Niazi, A. A. K.** 20th c.
*Pakistani army officer*
* Niazi, Tiger

**Niazi, Immie**
*See* Niazi, Imran Ahmad Khan

**Niazi, Imran Ahmad Khan** 1952-
[DC]
*Pakistani cricketer*
* Niazi, Immie

**Niazi, Tiger**
*See* Niazi, A. A. K.

**[The] Nibbler**
*See* Hibbler, Albert George

**Niblo, Fred**
See Nobile, Frederico

**Nibor, Kay**
See Tucker, Robin

**Niboyet, Pauline Fortunio** [PA]
*Author*
* Fortunio, P. N.

**Nibrah**
See Hardin, L. S.

**Nic Leodhas, Sorche**
See Alger, Leclaire [Gowans]

**Nicander**
See Williams, Morris

**Nicander, Edwin**
See Rau, Nicander Edwin

**Nicator**
See Demetrius II

**Nicator**
See Seleucus I

**Niccolo**
See Isouard, Nicolas

**Nicetas**
See Ignatius

**Nichevo**
See Dawes, Angela Kathleen

**Nicholas** 4th c. [DNNF, RH]
*Saint*
* Kriss Kringle [or Christ Kinkle]
* Santa Claus

**Nicholas** 16th c. [HN]
*Count of Zriny*
* [The] Leonidas of Hungary

**Nicholas, Big Nick**
See Nicholas, George Walker

**Nicholas, Dr.** [PA]
*Author*
* Monadnock

**Nicholas, Don**
See De Collibus, Nicholas

**Nicholas, George Walker** 1922-
[EJ]
*American jazz musician*
* Nicholas, Big Nick

**Nicholas, Joseph [Joe]** 1883-1957
[EJ]
*American jazz musician*
* Nicholas, Wooden Joe

**Nicholas of Flue**
See Loewenbrugger, Nikolaus

**Nicholas, Philip Norborne**
1773-1849 [FFF]
*American writer*
* Agricola

**Nicholas, William** [joint pseudonym
with Nicholas Palen (Nick)
Thimmesch]
See Johnson, William O.

**Nicholas, William** [joint pseudonym
with William O. Johnson]
See Thimmesch, Nicholas Palen
[Nick]

**Nicholas, Wooden Joe**
See Nicholas, Joseph [Joe]

**Nicholas I** 800?- 867
[DNNS, FFF, SN]
*Pope*
* [The] Great

**Nicholas I [Nikolai Pavlovich]**
1796-1855 [DEP, DHA, HN]
*Czar of Russia*
* [The] Iron Emperor

**Nicholas II**
See Gerard of Burgundy

**Nicholas III**
See Orsini, Giovanni Gaetano

**Nicholas IV**
See Masci, Girolamo

**Nicholas V**
See Parentucelli [or da Sarzana],
Tommaso

**Nicholas V**
See Rainalducci, Pietro

**Nicholls, Anthony**
See Parsons, Anthony

**Nicholls, Joan** 1908-1945 [THR]
*British actress*
* Marion, Joan

**Nicholls, Muriel** 1920?-1975?
[BWW]
*American singer*
* Booze, Beatrice
* Booze, Wee Bea
* [The] Queen Bea of Blues Singers
* [The] See See Rider Blues Girl

**Nichols, Adelaide**
See Baker, Adelaide Nichols

**Nichols, Alvin** 1947- [BWW]
*American singer*
* Jones, B. B.
* Nichols, Youngblood

**Nichols, Arthur Francis**
See Meikle, Arthur Francis

**Nichols, Barbara**
See Nickeraeur, Barbara

**Nichols, Cecilia Fawn** 1906- [CAP]
*American author and playwright*
* Nazarian, Nikki

**Nichols, Charles Augustus**
1869-1953 [AS, BAB, PB]
*American baseball player*
* Nichols, Kid
* Nichols, Nervy Nick

**Nichols, Dale [William]** 1904-
[CAP]
*American-born artist, designer,
illustrator*
* De Polman, Willem

**Nichols, Dave**
See Frost, Helen

**Nichols, Dolan Levon** 1930- [BE]
*American baseball player*
* Nichols, Nick

**Nichols, Ernest Loring** 1905-1965
[ASC, BBD, DAM]
*American jazz musician*
* Nichols, Red

**Nichols, Fan**
See Hanna, Frances [Nichols]

**Nichols, Frederick C.** 19th c. [BE]
*American baseball player*
* Nichols, Tricky

**Nichols, George Herbert Fosdike**
1883- [LAO]
*British author and journalist*
* Quex

**Nichols, Jimmy**
See Nicholson, James David

**Nichols, John** [SN]
*British editor*
* [The] Prosper Marchand of
English Literature

**Nichols, Kid**
See Nichols, Charles Augustus

**Nichols, Mary Sergeant Gove** 1810-
? [FFF]
*American author*
* Orme, Mary

**Nichols, Mike**
See Peschkowsky, Michael Igor

**Nichols, Nervy Nick**
See Nichols, Charles Augustus

**Nichols, Nicholas**
See Lathe, Herbert William

**Nichols, Nick**
See Nichols, Dolan Levon

**Nichols, Paul**
See Dallis, Nicholas Peter

**Nichols, Peter**
See Youd, Christopher Samuel

**Nichols, Rebecca S. Reed**
1819-1903 [FFF]
*American author and poet*
* Cleaveland, Kate
* Ellen

**Nichols, Red**
See Nichols, Ernest Loring

**Nichols, Richard William** 1930-
[ART]
*American-born painter*
* R. W. N.

**Nichols, Scott**
See Scortia, Thomas N[icholas]

**Nichols, Thomas** [PA]
*Author*
* Asmodeus

**Nichols, Tricky**
See Nichols, Frederick C.

**Nichols, Youngblood**
See Nichols, Alvin

**Nicholson, Christina**
See Nicole, Christopher Robin

**Nicholson, Dorothy**
See Smith, Gladys Mary

**Nicholson, Eliza Jane Poitevent**
1849-1896 [FFF, PA]
*American writer*
* Eliza
* Rivers, Pearl

**Nicholson, Francis** 1753-1844
[WBD]
*British painter*
* [The] Father of Water Color
Painting

**Nicholson, J. D.**
See Nicholson, James David

**Nicholson, James David** 1917-
[BWW]
*American singer*
* Nichols, Jimmy
* Nicholson, J. D.

**Nicholson, James William Augustus**
1821-1887 [FFF]
*American naval officer*
* War Horse

**Nicholson, Jane**
See Steen, Marguerite

**Nicholson, John**
See Parcell, Norman H[owe]

**Nicholson, John** [SN]
*British poet*
* [The] Airedale Poet

**Nicholson, Louise** [FFF]
*Entertainer*
* Nikita, Mlle.

**Nicholson, Mal**
See Nicholson, Mallagy

**Nicholson, Mallagy** 1909- [IBW]
*Canadian-born business executive*
* Nicholson, Mal

**Nicholson, Margaret**
See Shelley, Percy Bysshe

**Nicholson, Margaret Beda [Larminie]**
1924- [AW, CA, WD]
*British author*
* Yorke, Margaret

**Nicholson, Mrs. Paul** [FFF]
*Entertainer*
* Thornton, Adelaide

**Nicholson, Nick**
See Nicholson, Robert

**Nicholson, Parson**
See Nicholson, Thomas C.

**Nicholson, Robert** 20th c. [ITA]
*American producer*
* Nicholson, Nick

**Nicholson, Swish**
See Nicholson, William Beck

**Nicholson, Thomas C.** 1862-1917
[BE]
*American baseball player*
* Nicholson, Parson

**Nicholson, William** ?-1849 [DEL]
*British poet*
* [The] Galloway Poet

**Nicholson, William** 1816-1865
[WBD]
*Australian statesman*
* [The] Father of the Australian
Ballot

**Nicholson, William Beck** 1914-
[DGS]
*American baseball player*
* Nicholson, Swish

**Nicholson, [Sir] William Newzam
Prior** 1872-1949 [DBA]
*British painter*
* Beggarstaff, W.

**Nichopoulos, George C.** 1928?-
*American physician who treated
Elvis Presley*
* Nick, Dr.

**Nick**
See Whitley, Jonas E.

**Nick, Dr.**
See Nichopoulos, George C.

**Nick the Kick**
See Lowery, Nick

**Nick the Quick**
See Werkman, Nick

**Nickalls, Gully**
See Nickalls, Guy Oliver

**Nickalls, Guy Oliver** 1899- [B10]
*British rower*
* Nickalls, Gully

**Nickeraeur, Barbara** 1932-1976
[HCA]
*American actress*
* Nichols, Barbara

**Nickerson, Camille Lucie** 1888-
[FFA, IBW]
*American singer*
* [The] Louisiana Lady

**Nickerson, Hammie**
See Davis, Hammie

**Nicklaus, Jack William** 1940- [EG]
*American golfer*
* [The] Golden Bear

**Nicklin, Philip Holbrook**
1786-1842 [FFF]
*American author*
* Prolix, Peregrine

**Nicklin, Samuel Strang** 1876-1932
[BE]
*American baseball player*
* [The] Dixie Thrush
* Strang, Samuel Nicklin

**Nickson, Hilda** 1912- [IAW]
*British author*
* Pressley, Hilda
* Preston, Hilary

**Nico**
See Jungman, Nico

**Nicol, Abioseh**
See Nicol, Davidson [Sylvester
Hector Willoughby]

**Nicol, Ann**
See Turnbull, Ann [Christine]

**Nicol, Davidson [Sylvester Hector
Willoughby]** 1924- [CA, WD]
*Sierra Leonean author*
* Nicol, Abioseh

**Nicol, Eric [Patrick]** 1919-
[AW, CA]
*Canadian author and playwright*
* Jabez

**Nicolaeff, Ariadne** 1915- [WD]
*British playwright and translator*
* Moore, Nicholas

**Nicolai, Christopher Friedrich**
1733-1811 [SN]
*German author*
* Erz-Philister

**Nicolaie, Louis Francois**
1811-1879 [WBD]
*French playwright*
* Clairville, Louis Francois

**Nicolas**
See Mordvinoff, Nicolas

**Nicolas, F. R. E.**
See Freeling, Nicolas

**Nicolas, Jean** 1740-1823 [DNNS]
*French politician*
* [The] Tartuffe of the Revolution

**Nicolas, [Sir] Nicholas Harris**
1799-1848 [FFF]
*British author and historian*
* Clionas

**Nicolas, P.** ?-1649 [PA]
*Author*
* Peltrel

**Nicole, Christopher Robin** 1930-
[AW, CA, IAW]
*British author*
* Cade, Robin
* Grange, Peter
* Logan, Mark
* Nicholson, Christina
* York, Andrew

**Nicole, Claudette**
See Messmann, John

**Nicoll, [Henry] Maurice [Dunlop]**
1884-1953 [ESF, SFL, WGT]
*British author*
* Swayne, Martin

**Nicoll, [Sir] William Robertson**
1851-1923 [WBD]
*Scottish clergyman and editor*
* Clear, Claudius

**Nicolson, John Urban** 1885- [WW]
*Author*
* [The] King of the Black Isles

**Nicolson, Victoria Mary**
See Sackville-West, Victoria Mary

**Nicomedes II** 2nd c. BC
[FFF, SN, WBD]
*King of Bithynia*
* Epiphanes
* [The] Illustrious

**Nicosia, Francesco M[ichael]**
1933- [CA]
*Italian-born American author and
educator*
* Nicosia, Franco M.

**Nicosia, Franco M.**
See Nicosia, Francesco M[ichael]

**Nicoson, Angus** 20th c. [BBH]
*American basketball player and
coach*
* Nicoson, Nick

**Nicoson, Nick**
See Nicoson, Angus

**Nicote, Piere** 1625-1695 [PA]
*Author*
* Mendrock, William

**Niebergall, Charles Arthur [Charlie]**
1899- [BE]
*American baseball player*
* Niebergall, Nig

**Niebergall, Nig**
See Niebergall, Charles Arthur
[Charlie]

**Niekro, Knucksie**
See Niekro, Philip Henry

**Niekro, Philip Henry** 1939- [SMG]
*American baseball player*
* Niekro, Knucksie

**Nielsen, Alice**
See Ivarius, Alice

**Nielsen, Asta** 1882-1972 [SC]
*Danish actress and producer*
* [Die] Asta

**Nielsen, Bent Rosenkilde** 1904-
[ART]
*Danish author, journalist, art critic*
* Don Benito

**Nielsen, Helen Berniece** 1918-
[CA, CC, EMD]
*American author and scriptwriter*
* Giles, Kris

**Nielsen, Jean Sarver** 1922- [CA]
*American author*
* Sarver, Hannah

**Nielsen, Virginia**
See McCall, Virginia Nielsen

**Nielson, Ingrid**
See Bancroft, Iris [Nelson]

**Nielson, Oscar M.** 1882-1954
[AS, BX, RBE]
*Danish-born boxer*
* [The] Durable Dane
* Nelson, Battling

**Nielson, Robert** 1925-
[BEW, SW, TR]
*American actor*
* Nelson, Barry

**Nielssen, Eric**
See Ludvigsen, Karl [Eric]

**Nieman, Butch**
See Nieman, Elmer LeRoy

**Nieman, Elmer LeRoy** 1918- [BE]
*American baseball player*
* Nieman, Butch

**Niembsch von Strehlenau, Nikolaus**
1802-1850 [WBD]
*Hungarian-born poet*
* Lenau, Nikolaus

**Niemes, Jack**
See Niemes, Jacob Leland

**Niemes, Jacob Leland** 1919-1966
[BE]
*American baseball player*
* Niemes, Jack

**Niemeyer, Mrs.** [FFF]
*Entertainer*
* Chalfaut, May

**Niemi, Finn**
See Niemi, Laurie

**Niemi, Laurie** 1925-1968 [AS]
*American football player*
* Niemi, Finn

**Nieminen, Anna-Maija** 1928-
[IAW]
*Finnish author*
* Raittila, Anne-Maija

**Niemoller, Ara**
See Llerena, Mario

**Nienaber, Christoffel Johannes
Michael** 1918- [IAW]
*South African author*
* Nienaber, Stoffel

**Nienaber, Petrus Johannes** 1910-
[IAW]
*South African author*
* De Villiers, Ryno B.
* Rousseau, J. J.
* Van Niekerk, I. R.

**Nienaber, Stoffel**
See Nienaber, Christoffel Johannes
Michael

**Nienstedt, Stanley Grover** 1926-
[BEW]
*American actor and singer*
* Grover, Stanley

**Nierow, Bernard** 1934- [EPM]
*American musician*
* Nero, Peter

**Niese, Charlotte** 1854- ? [WBD]
*German author*
* Buerger, Lucian

**Nieto, Jose** 20th c. [FIR]
*Actor*
* Nieto, Pepe

**Nieto, Manuel** 1869-1942 [GS]
*Spanish bullfighter*
* Gorete [Little Cap]

**Nieto, Pepe**
See Nieto, Jose

**Nieuwenhuysen, Van**
See Vaez, Jean N. Gustave

**Nievens, Big Daddy**
See Nievens, Roosevelt

**Nievens, Roosevelt** 20th c.
*American football coach*
* Nievens, Big Daddy

**Nifo, Augustine** 1473-1538 [PA]
*Author*
* Niphas

**Nigel** 12th c. [WBD]
*British monk and author*
* Wireker, Nigel

**Niger**
See Fox, Charles James

**Niger, Emilius**
See Roumer, Emile

**Nigh, Bonnie Lenora** 1926- [ITA]
*American actress*
* Nigh, Jane

**Nigh, Jane**
See Nigh, Bonnie Lenora

**Nighbor, Dutch**
See Nighbor, Frank

**Nighbor, Frank** 1893-1966 [FHE]
*Canadian-born hockey player*
* Nighbor, Dutch

**Night Train Lane**
See Lane, Dick

**Night Train Lane**
See Lane, Richard

**Nighthawk, Robert**
See McCollum, Robert Lee

**Nightingale, Florence** 1820-1910
[FFF, NN]
*British nurse, hospital reformer,
philanthropist*
* Filomena, Saint
* [The] Lady with the Lamp

**[The] Nightingale of a Thousand
Songs**
See Muslih-ud-Din [or
Moslehedin]

**[The] Nightingale of India**
See Naidu, Sarojini
[Chattopadhyay]

**[The] Nightingale of the Twrch**
See Edwards, John

[The] Nightingale of Twickenham
See  Pope, Alexander

[The] Nightingale of Wittenberg
See  Luther, Martin

[The] Nightingale of Wittenberg
See  Sachs, Hans

[The] Nightmare of Europe
See  Bonaparte, Napoleon

Nightrate, Emil
See  Spielmann, Peter James

Nigro, Laura 1947-  [RO2]
American singer
* Nyro, Laura

Nihil
See  Miller, P[eter] Schuyler

Niininen, Margit
See  Toernudd, Margit

Nijbroek, Paul Armand 1938-
[CW]
Surinamese poet
* Marlee, Paul

Nijsni, K. M.
See  Cox-George, Noah Arthur
William

Nik
See  Lee, Francis Nigel

Nikita, Mlle.
See  Nicholson, Louise

Nil Admirari, Esq.
See  Shelton, Frederick William

Niland, Big John
See  Niland, John H.

Niland, Gorgo
See  Niland, John H.

Niland, Honest Tom
See  Niland, Thomas James [Tom]

Niland, John H. 1944-  [FB]
American football player
* Niland, Big John
* Niland, Gorgo

Niland, Thomas James [Tom]
1870-1950  [BE]
American baseball player
* Niland, Honest Tom

Nile, Dorothea
See  Avallone, Michael [Angelo],
Jr.

Nilense, Baron
See  Collin, Jacques Albin Simon

Niles, Johnny
See  Nilsson, Harry Edward, III

Nill, George Charles 1881-1962
[BE]
American baseball player
* Nill, Rabbit

Nill, Rabbit
See  Nill, George Charles

Nilla
See  Allin, Abby

Niller, Mary Ager  [FFF]
Author and poet
* Luola

Nillo
See  Curtiss, A. A.

Nilson, Alice 1924-  [EJ7]
Swedish singer
* Babs, Alice

Nilson, Amabel Rhoda 1908-  [AW]
New Zealand-born home economist
and author
* Nilson, Bee

Nilson, Bee
See  Nilson, Amabel Rhoda

Nilsson
See  Nilsson, Harry Edward, III

Nilsson, Birgit
See  Svensson, Marta Birgit

Nilsson, Harry Edward, III 1941-
[LRR, RO2]
American singer
* Niles, Johnny
* Nilsson

Nilsson, Usha Saksena 1930-
[B10, CA]
Indian-born author
* Priyamvada, Usha

Nimrod
See  Apperley, Charles James

Nimrod
See  Reynolds, John Hamilton

Nina
See  Campbell-Quine, Nina

Ninety Six
See  Voiselle, William Symmes

Ninian  ?- 432?  [FFF]
Saint
* [The] Apostle of the Picts

[El] Nino de la Capea [The Boy of the
Bull-Capings]
See  Moya, Pedro

Nino de la Estrella [Child of the Star]
See  Zafon, Silvino

Nino de La Palma [Boy from La
Palma]
See  Ordonez y Aguilera, Cayetano

Nino de la Rose [Boy of the Rose]
See  Mier Jimenez, Ramon

Nino, Pedro Alonso 1468-1505?
[WBD]
Spanish navigator
* [El] Negro

[El] Nino Sabio [The Wise Child]
See  Camino Sanchez, Francisco

Ninon
See  MacKnight, Ninon

Ninon de Lenclos
See  L'Enclos, Anne

Niphas
See  Nifo, Augustine

Nips, Nick
See  Bennett, John Michael

Nirt, Red
See  Trinder, Tommy

Nishi, Noriko 1943-
Japanese-born fashion designer
* Noriko

Nishri, Zvi
See  Orlvov, Zvi

Nisidas
See  Urena de Mendoza, Nicolas

Niska, Maralin Fae
See  Dice, Maralin Fae

Nisot, Mavis Elizabeth [Hocking]
1893-  [WW]
Author
* Penmare, William

Nissen, Greta
See  Rutz-Nissen, Grethe

Nistico, Sal
See  Nistico, Salvatore

Nistico, Salvatore 1940-  [EJ7]
American jazz musician
* Nistico, Sal

Nitch',o|as, Nick
See  Nitcholas, Otho James

Nitcholas, Otho James 1908-  [BE]
American baseball player
* Nitcholas, Nick

Nitgenockle
See  Galt, William Hamilton

[The] Nitrate King
See  North, John Thomas

Nitro Nellie Goins
See  Goins, Nellie Louise

Nitti, Frank  ?-1944?  [BLB, PHM]
American underworld figure
* [The] Enforcer

Niva, Rosa
See  Noel, Victoire

Nivedita, [Sister]
See  Noble, Margaret Elizabeth

Niven, Frank 20th c.  [BBH]
American horseshoe pitching
promoter
* Niven, Hands

Niven, Hands
See  Niven, Frank

Niven, Marian
See  Alston, Mary Niven

Nix, Willie 1922-  [BWW]
American singer
* Memphis Blues Boy

Nixon, Clint
See  Hecht, Clinton James

Nixon, Elmo
See  Nixon, Elmore

Nixon, Elmore 1933-1975?  [BWW]
American singer
* Nixon, Elmo

Nixon, Hammie
See  Davis, Hammie

Nixon, K.
See  Nixon, Kathleen Irene
[Blundell]

Nixon, Kathleen Irene [Blundell] 20th
c.  [CA]
British author and artist
* Nixon, K.

Nixon, Marni
American singer
* [The] Ghostess with the Mostest

Nixon, Richard Milhous 1913-
[FAP, NN]
American president
* Gloomy Gus
* Richard the Chicken-Hearted
* Tricky Dick [or Dickie]

Nixon, Wm. Penn
See  Tourgee, Albion W[inegar]

Nixson, Maisie Mayer 1890-
[WWL]
British author
* Lennox, Edward

Niza, Marcos de  ?-1558  [WBD]
French-born missionary and
explorer
* Marcos, [Fray]

Nizzi, Guido 1900-  [SFL]
Italian-born author
* Nizzi, Skipper

Nizzi, Skipper
See  Nizzi, Guido

Nkrumah, Kwame 1909-1972
[IBW]
Prime minister of Ghana
* Osagyefo [Redeemer]

No bel-esprit
See  Lowell, John

NO, Dr.
See  Many, Seth E[dward]

No, Dr.
See  Treurnicht, Andries

No Flint Grey
See  Grey, Charles [First Earl
Grey]

No Kid Glover
See  Glover, Frederick Austin
[Freddie]

No Name
See  Burleigh, Cecil

No Neck Williams
See  Williams, Walter Allen

No Splash Browning
See  Browning, David

Noack, Armond A. 1930-  [ECM]
American country-western performer
* Noack, Eddie
* Wood, Tommy

Noack, Eddie
See  Noack, Armond A.

Noah, Mordecai Manuel
1785-1851  [FFF]
American journalist and politician
* Howard

Noailles, Duchesse de 18th c.
[DNNS, FFF, RH]
French courtier
* Etiquette, Madame

Nobel, Phil
See  Fanthorpe, R[obert] Lionel

Nobile, Frederico 1874-1948
[BDF, FC]
American director
* Niblo, Fred

Nobilis Mathematicus
See  Dee, John

Nobis, Booger Red
See  Nobis, Thomas H., Jr.

Nobis, Thomas H., Jr. 1943-
American football player
* Nobis, Booger Red

[The] Noble
See  Alfonso VIII [or Alphonso]

[The] Noble
See   Charles III

[The] Noble
See   Frederick William

[El] Noble
See   Sancho IV

[The] Noble
See   Suleiman I [or Soliman]

[The] Noble Buzzard
See   Burnet, Dr.

Noble, Charles
See   Pawley, Martin Edward

Noble, Clarke Randolph 20th c.
[BBH]
American baseball coach and
collegiate athletic director
* Noble, Dudy

Noble, Dudy
See   Noble, Clarke Randolph

Noble, James
See   Holloway, Ernest A.

Noble, James 1907-   [MY]
American jazz musician
* Noble, Jiggs

Noble, Jiggs
See   Noble, James

Noble, John
See   Griffin, Frank

Noble, John [Appelbe] 1914-   [CA]
British-born mariner and author
* Jan
* Lookout

Noble, Kid
See   Moore, Harry R.

Noble, Kitty
See   Killingsworth, Katherine

Noble, Margaret Elizabeth
1867-1911   [B10]
Irish disciple of Swami Vivekananda
* Nivedita, [Sister]

Noble, Rafael Miguel 1922-
[BE, OBW]
Cuban-born baseball player
* Noble, Ray

Noble, Ray
See   Noble, Rafael Miguel

Noble, Samuel 1859- ?   [WWL]
Scottish author and poet
* Nomie

[The] Noble Soul
See   Khosru I [or Chosroes]

[The] Noble Wit of Scotland
See   Mackenzie, [Sir] George

[A] Nobleman's Son
See   Barrett, T. W.

Nobles, Milton
See   Tamey, Milton

[The] Noblest Roman of the National
Baseball Field
See   Comiskey, Charles Albert

Noceni, Erle
See   Sellers, Connie Leslie, Jr.

Nocentelli, Breeze
See   Nocentelli, Leo

Nocentelli, Leo 20th c.   [RM]
Musician
* Nocentelli, Breeze

Nocona Slim Burnett
See   Burnett, John

Nodset, Joan L.
See   Lexau, Joan M.

Noe, Amedee de 1819-1879
[FFF, RH, WBD]
French caricaturist
* Cham

[The] Noel Coward of Russia
See   Kataev, Valentin Petrovich

Noel, Ella Marguerite 1943-   [OP]
American opera singer
* Noel, Rita

Noel, Hilda Bloxton, Jr.
See   Schroetter, Hilda Noel

Noel, John
See   Bird, Dennis Leslie

Noel, L.
See   Barker, Leonard Noel

Noel, Lucien 20th c.
French actor
* Noel Noel

Noel Noel
See   Noel, Lucien

Noel, Rita
See   Noel, Ella Marguerite

Noel, Victoire 1815-1903   [BBD]
French opera singer
* Niva, Rosa
* Stoltz, [Mademoiselle] Heloise
* Stoltz, Rosine
* Ternaux, Mademoiselle

Noel-Baker, Philip John
See   Baker, Philip John

Noel-Cooper, George W.
See   Cooper, George William Noel

Noel Hume, Ivor 1927-   [IAW]
British-born archaeologist and
author
* Akerman, Richard

Noelita Marie, [Sister]
See   Blakely, Delois

Noevius
See   Nefe, Gaspard

Nogaret de la Valette, Jean Louis de
1554-1642   [SN]
French courtier and politician
* Epernon, Duc d'
* [Le] Valet du Cardinal

Noguera, Magdalena
See   Conde Abellan, Carmen

Nogues i Cases, Xavier 1873-1941
[WEC]
Spanish cartoonist and illustrator
* Babel

Nohain, Franc
See   Le Grand, Franc

Noir, Jean
See   Cassou, Jean

Nojiri, Kiyohiko 1897-1973   [CA]
Japanese author and historian
* Osaragi, Jiro

Nokes, George Augustus 1867- ?
[WWL]
British author
* Sekon, George Augustus

Nokes, James 17th c.   [DNNS]
British actor
* Nokes, Nurse

Nokes, Nurse
See   Nokes, James

Nolamo, Stanley
See   Cohen, Stanley Irving

[The] Nolan
See   Bruno, Giordano

Nolan, Brian
See   O'Nuallain, Brian

Nolan, Chuck
See   Edson, John Thomas

Nolan, [Violet] Cynthia 1914-
[WD]
Australian author
* Reed, Cynthia

Nolan, Dixie
See   Scruggs, Irene

Nolan, Edward Sylvester
1857-1913   [BE]
American baseball player
* [The] Only Nolan

Nolan, F.   [PA]
Author
* Search, Sarah

Nolan, George Brent 1904-   [FC]
Irish-born actor
* Brent, George

Nolan, Jeannette Covert
1897-1974   [CA, SAT]
American author and critic
* Tucker, Caroline

Nolan, Mary
See   Robertson, Mary Imogene

Nolan, Mrs. James   [FFF]
Entertainer
* Ryan, Kate

Nolan, S. E.   [PA]
Author
* Gerrard, Kenner

Nolan, William F[rancis] 1928-
[CA, WGT]
American author
* Anmar, Frank
* Cahill, Mike?
* Edwards, F. E.
* Phillips, Michael

Noland, C. M. F.   [PA]
Author
* N. of Arkansas

Noland, John T. 1896-1931
[BLB, CEC, MM]
American underworld figure
* [The] Clay Pigeon of the
   Underworld
* Diamond, John Thomas [Jack]
* Diamond, Legs
* Hart, John
* Higgins, John

Nolarci, Vigilio
See   Carnoli, Luigi

Nolde, Emil
See   Hansen, Emil

Noll, Bink
See   Noll, Lou Barker

Noll, John Francis 1875- ?   [NAA]
American clergyman and author
* J. F. N.

Noll, Lou Barker 1927-   [CA]
American poet and editor
* Noll, Bink

Noll, Martin David 1912-   [CA]
American author and poet
* Buxbaum, Martin

Nomad
See   Custer, George Armstrong

Nomad, Max
See   Nacht, Max

Nomdet, Nylla
See   Tedmon, Allyn Henry

Nomelleni, Leo 1924-
Italian-born American football
player
* [The] Lion

Nomentanus
See   Crescentius, Johannes [or
John]

Nomie
See   Noble, Samuel

Nomistake
See   Partee, W. B.

Nompar de Caumont, Antonin
1633-1723   [RH]
French soldier
* [The] Dancing Chancellor
* Lauzun, Duc de

[The] Non Such
See   Hutchinson, Ann

Noname [house pseudonym]
See   Enton, Harry

Noname
See   Senarens, Luis Philip

Nonnenkamp, Leo William 1911-
[BE]
American baseball player
* Nonnenkamp, Red

Nonnenkamp, Red
See   Nonnenkamp, Leo William

Nonni
See   Sveinsson, Jon

Nonnius
See   Nunez, Ludwig

[The] Nonpareil
See   Kelly, John

Noon, Brian 1919-   [CA]
British artist, graphologist, poet
* Kurdsen, Stephen

Noon, Ed
See   Avallone, Michael [Angelo],
Jr.

Noon Ghunna
See   Khan, Javed Miandad

Noon, T. R.
See   Norton, Olive Marion
[Claydon]

Noon, Thomas 1921-1968   [FC]
American actor
* Noonan, Tommy

Noonan, Robert 1868-1911 [LC]
British author
* Tressell, Robert

Noonan, Suzanne Dobson 1911-
American actress
* O'Day, Molly

Noonan, Tommy
See Noon, Thomas

Noonan, Virginia Louise
1910?-1968 [F2, FC]
American actress
* O'Neil, Sally

Noone, Edwina
See Avallone, Michael [Angelo],
Jr.

Noone, Peter Blair Denis Bernard
1947- [EPM, PRS, RO2]
British singer
* Herman

Noordung, Hermann
See Potocnik, Captain

Nora [or Norma]
See Aiken, Elizabeth

Norbert, [Father]
See Parisot, Pierre

Norbert, W.
See Wiener, Norbert

Norbury, Earl of 19th c.
[DNNF, FFF, SN]
Irish jurist
* [The] Hanging Judge

Norcross, Elizabeth
See Gladstone, Arthur M.

Norcross, John
See Conroy, John Wesley [Jack]

[Le] Nord
See Colbert, Jean Baptiste de

Nord, Amiral [code name used
during World War II]
See Abrial, [Vice Admiral]

Nord, Pierre
See Brouillard, Andre Leon

Nordau, Max Simon
See Suedfeld, Max Simon

Norden, Charles
See Durrell, Lawrence [George]

Norden, Christine
See Thornton, Mary

Nordenhjelm [DEP]
* [The] Father of Swedish
Eloquence

Nordhausen, Richard 1868?- ?
[WBD]
German author
* Caliban

Nordhof, Daniel Georg 1639-1691
[PA]
Author
* Polyhistor

Nordhoff, Charles [FFF]
American writer
* Holmes, Charles

Nordica, Lillian
See Norton, Lillian

Nordicus
See Snyder, Louis L.

Nordström, Andrew Arthur 1931-
[BE]
American baseball player
* Carey, Andy

Norell, Norman
See Levinson, Norman

Norena, Eide
See Hansen, Kaja Andrea Karoline
Eide

[The] Norfolk Boy
See Porson, Richard

[The] Norfolk Gamester
See Walpole, [Sir] Robert [First
Earl of Orford]

Norfolk, Kid
See Ward, William [Willie]

Noriac, Jules
See Cayron, C. A. J.

Noricus
See Tockler, Conrad

Noriko
See Nishi, Noriko

Norma Jean
See Beasler, Norma Jean

[The] Norma Shearer of Sweden
See Gustafsson, Greta Lovisa

[The] Norman
See William I

Norman, Ames
See Ames, Norma

Norman, Barbara 1927- [CA, WD]
American author and translator
* Makanowitzky, Barbara

Norman, Bill
See Norman, Henry Willis Patrick

Norman, Coniel 20th c. [SMG]
American basketball player
* Norman, Popcorn

Norman, Don[ald] 20th c. [RO2]
American musician and songwriter
* Storball, Don

Norman, Fredie Hubert 1942-
[SMG]
American baseball player
* Norman, Top Cat

Norman, Geraldine [Lucia] 1940-
[CA]
British author
* Keen, Geraldine

Norman, Harold Christopher Francis
1879- ? [WWL]
British author
* Hill, Warren

Norman, Henry Willis Patrick
1910-1962 [BE]
American baseball player and
manager
* Norman, Bill

Norman, J. H.
See Norman, John Henry

Norman, James
See Schmidt, James Norman

Norman, Joe
See Heard, J[oseph] Norman

Norman, John
See Lange, John Frederick, Jr.

Norman, John Henry 1896- [ART]
British painter
* Norman, J. H.

Norman, Josephine
See Arrich, Josephine

Norman, Kerry
See Le Pelley, Guernsey

Norman, Louis
See Whittemore, Don

Norman, Norman V.
See Norman-Burt, Norman V.

Norman, Philip
See Philips, George Norman

Norman, Popcorn
See Norman, Coniel

Norman, Richard
See Briefer, Richard [Dick]

Norman, Robert
See Gardner, Maurice

Norman, Shin
See Norman, William

Norman, Steve
See Pashko, Stanley

Norman, Thyrza
See Neeves, Thyrza

Norman, Top Cat
See Norman, Fredie Hubert

Norman, Victor
See Ransome, L. E.

Norman, W. S.
See Wilson, N[orman] Scarlyn

Norman, William 1935-1976
[IBW]
American entertainer
* Fat Alburt

Norman, William 20th c. [OBW]
American baseball player
* Norman, Shin

Norman-Burt, Norman V.
1864-1943 [THR]
British actor and theatrical manager
* Norman, Norman V.

Normand, Cisco
See Normand, Emile R.

Normand, Emile R. 1936- [EJ7]
Canadian jazz musician
* Normand, Cisco

Normand, Mabel
See Fortescue, Mabel

Normannus
See Tonnies, Ferdinand Julius

Normanus
See Muris, Johannes de

Normyx
See Douglas, George Norman

Norna
See Brooks, Mary Elizabeth
[Aiken]

Norris, Alexander M.
See Nosseck, Max

Norris, Benjamin Franklin, Jr.
1870-1902 [LC, TC]
American author
* Norris, Frank

Norris, Clarence 1913- [IBW]
Defendant in celebrated
"Scottsboro" trial
* Norris, Willie

Norris, Dead Eye
See Norris, William James

Norris, Edgar Poe
See Kinnaird, Clark

Norris, Frank
See Norris, Benjamin Franklin, Jr.

Norris, George William 1861-1944
[WBD]
American politician
* [The] Father of the Twentieth
Amendment

Norris, Harris
See Swindell, Minnie Harris

Norris, Henry 1665-1730? [SN]
British actor
* Heigh-Ho
* Jubilee Dicky

Norris, [Sir] John ?-1746
[DNNF, FFF, SN]
British naval officer
* Foul Weather Jack

Norris, John 1657-1711
[DNNS, HN, RH]
British philosopher and clergyman
* [The] English Plato

Norris, Kid
See Norris, Walter Oster

Norris, Ruby Turner
See Morris, Ruby Turner

Norris, Walter Oster 1904-1958
[BBH]
American lacrosse player and coach
* [The] Kid
* Norris, Kid

Norris, William
See Block, William Norris

Norris, William James 1951-
[BWW]
American singer
* Norris, Dead Eye

Norris, Willie
See Norris, Clarence

North, Andrew
See Norton, Alice Mary

North, Barclay
See Hudson, William Cadwalader

North, Bob
See Young, Harold

North, Charles W.
See Bauer, Erwin A.

North, Christopher
See Wilson, John

North, Colin
See Bingley, David Ernest

North, Colonel
See Bullivant, Cecil Henry

[The] North Country Angler
See Doubleday, Thomas

North, Darby
See Madden, Daniel Owen

North, Eric
See Cronin, Bernard [Charles]

**North, [Captain] George**
See Stevenson, Robert Louis Balfour

**North, Gil**
See Horne, Geoffrey

**North, Grace May**
See North-Monfort, Grace May

**North, Hattie**
See Johnson, Edith North

**North, Howard**
See Dudley-Smith, Trevor

**North, Iris**
See Morgan, Joan

**North, Jack**
See Pentelow, John Nix

**North, John Thomas** 1844-1896
[DNNS, FFF]
*British industrialist*
* [The] Nitrate King

**North, Laurence**
See Symon, James David

**North, Lionel**
See Northcroft, George J. H.

**North, Marilla**
See Wilson, Marilla

**North, Mark**
See Miller, Wright W[atts]

**North, Oliver**
See Mullen, M.

**North, Paul** 1889?-1968 [THR]
*British artist and designer*
* Shelving, Paul

**North, Pearson**
See Pearson, T. E.

**North, Robert**
See Withers, Carl A.

**North, Sara**
See Hager, Jean

**North, Sheree**
See Bethel, Dawn

**North, W. Savage**
See Newell, S.

**North, William** 1869- ? [WW]
*Author*
* Rodd, Ralph
* Vanner, John

**[The] North Wind**
See Colbert, Jean Baptiste de

**North-Monfort, Grace May** 20th c.
[NAA]
*American author*
* North, Grace May
* Norton, Carol

**[The] Northamptonshire Peasant Poet**
See Clare, John

**[The] Northamptonshire Poet**
See Clare, John

**[The] Northamptonshire Poet**
See Plummer, John

**Northcote**
See Boulting, Sydney

**Northcott, Baldy**
See Northcott, Laurence

**Northcott, [William] Cecil** 1902-
[CA]
*British clergyman and author*
* Miller, Mary
* Temple, Arthur

**Northcott, Laurence** 1907- [CEI]
*Canadian-born hockey player*
* Northcott, Baldy

**Northcroft, Dorothea M.** 20th c.
[WWL]
*British author*
* Ford, D. M.

**Northcroft, E. Florence** ?-1914
[WWL]
*British author*
* Cheerful, [Mrs.] Mary

**Northcroft, George J. H.** [WWL]
*British author*
* North, Lionel

**Northe, Margaret Scott Copeland**
20th c. [NAA]
*American musician, poet, editor*
* Copeland, Margaret Scott

**Northen, Hub**
See Northen, Hubbard Elwin

**Northen, Hubbard Elwin**
1885-1947 [BE]
*American baseball player*
* Northen, Hub

**[The] Northern Harlot**
See Elizabeth Petrovna

**Northern, Leslie** [house pseudonym]
See Long, Frank Belknap

**[A] Northern Man**
See Ingersoll, Charles Jared

**[The] Northern Phidias**
See Thorvaldsen, Bertel [or Albert]

**[The] Northern Semiramis**
See Catherine II

**[The] Northern Semiramis**
See Margaret

**[The] Northern Telemaque**
See Alexander I [Aleksandr Pavlovich]

**[The] Northern Victor**
See Gustavus Adolphus

**Northerner**
See Hughes, William Jesse

**Northey, Ronald James** 1920-1971
[BE]
*American baseball player*
* [The] Round Man

**Northgrave, Anne**
See Tibble, Anne

**Northmore, Elizabeth Florence**
1906-1974 [CAP]
*British author*
* Stucley, Elizabeth

**Northrop, George Howard**
1888-1945 [BN]
*American baseball player*
* Northrop, Jake
* Northrop, Jerky Jake

**Northrop, Jake**
See Northrop, George Howard

**Northrop, Jerky Jake**
See Northrop, George Howard

**Northrup, [Capt.] B. A.**
See Hubbard, Lafayette Ronald

**Northrup, Doc**
See Northrup, M. A.

**Northrup, Edwin Fitch** 1866-1940
[ESF, SFL, WGT]
*American author*
* Pseudoman, Akkad

**Northrup, M. A.** 20th c. [BBH]
*American wrestler*
* Northrup, Doc

**Northshield, Robert** 20th c. [ET]
*Producer and television scriptwriter*
* Northshield, Shad

**Northshield, Shad**
See Northshield, Robert

**[The] Northumberland Piper**
See Allen, James

**[The] Northumbrian Gentleman**
See Tegner, Henry [Stuart]

**Norton, Alice Mary** 1912-
[CA, MJA, WYA]
*American author*
* North, Andrew
* Norton, Andre
* Norton, Andrew
* Weston, Allen [joint pseudonym with Grace Weston Hogarth]

**Norton, Alice Whitson** 1897-
[NAA]
*American writer*
* Barry, Alice Montgomery
* Slater, Elizabeth Anne

**Norton, Andre**
See Norton, Alice Mary

**Norton, Andrew**
See Norton, Alice Mary

**Norton, Barry**
See De Biraben, Alfredo

**Norton, Bess**
See Norton, Olive Marion [Claydon]

**Norton, Browning**
See Norton, Frank R. B.

**Norton, Carol**
See North-Monfort, Grace May

**Norton, Caroline Elizabeth Sarah**
1808-1877 [FFF, PA]
*British author*
* Aunt Carry
* Hi Ski Hi
* Sheridan, C. E.

**Norton, Chico**
See Norton, Forrest

**Norton, Daniel** 20th c. [RO1]
*American singer*
* Norton, Sonny

**Norton, Edith Eliza Ames** 1864- ?
[NAA]
*American writer*
* Dunn, Eliza

**Norton, Fletcher [First Baron Grantley]** 1716-1789 [SN]
*British jurist*
* Bull Face Double-Fee, Sir

**Norton, Forrest** 20th c. [SMG]
*American football team staff member*
* Norton, Chico

**Norton, Frank R. B.** 1909- [WYA]
*Author*
* Norton, Browning

**Norton, J.** 1606-1663 [PA]
*Author*
* [A] Layman

**Norton, J. J.** 1849- ? [BE]
*American baseball player and manager*
* Carey, Thomas John [Tom]

**Norton, Jack**
See Naughton, Mortimer J.

**Norton, Lillian** 1857-1914
[BBD, BEW, FFF]
*American opera singer*
* Nordica, Lillian

**Norton, Olive Marion [Claydon]**
1913- [AW, CA]
*British author*
* Neal, Hilary
* Noon, T. R.
* Norton, Bess
* Norway, Kate

**Norton, Sonny**
See Norton, Daniel

**Norton, Sybil**
See Cournos, Helen Kestner Satterthwaite

**Norton, Thomas** 1532-1584 [FFF]
*British barrister and poet*
* Archcarnifex

**Norton, Victor**
See Dalton, Gilbert

**Norval**
See Noyes, E. H.

**Norville, Kenneth** 1908-
[EJ, PMJ, WWJ]
*American jazz musician*
* Norvo, Red

**Norvo, Red**
See Norville, Kenneth

**Norvus, Nervous**
See Drake, Jimmy

**Norway, Kate**
See Norton, Olive Marion [Claydon]

**Norway, Nevil Shute** 1899-1960
[LC, TC, TCL]
*British author*
* Shute, Nevil

**Norway's First Skald**
See Munch, Andreas

**[The] Norwegian Doll**
See Henie, Sonja

**[The] Norwich Weaver Boy**
See Fox, William Johnson

**Norwood, Abraham** 19th c. [PA]
*Author*
* Abraham

**Norwood, Ellie**
See Brett, Anthony

**Norwood, John**
See Stark, [Delbert] Raymond

**Norwood, One Leg**
See Norwood, Sam

**Norwood, Paul**
See Nettl, John Peter

**Norwood, Peg Leg**
See  Norwood, Sam

**Norwood, Pig**
See  Norwood, Sam

**Norwood, R. D.**
See  Norwood, Sam

**Norwood, Sam** 1900?-1967?
[BWW]
*American singer*
* Norwood, One Leg
* Norwood, Peg Leg
* Norwood, Pig
* Norwood, R. D.

**Norwood, Victor G[eorge] C[harles]**
1920-  [CA, WD]
*British author, playwright, poet*
* Banton, Coy
* Baxter, Shane V.
* Bowie, Jim
* Brand, Clay
* Cody, Walt
* Colter, Shayne
* Corteen, Wes
* Dangerfield, Clint
* Dark, Johnny
* Destry, Vince
* Fargo, Doone
* Fisher, Wade
* Gearing-Thomas, G.
* Hampton, Mark
* Janson, Hank [house pseudonym?]
* Karta, Nat
* McCord, Whip
* Rand, Brett
* Regan, Brad
* Russell, Shane
* Shane, Mark
* Shane, Rhondo
* Strange, Dillon
* Tressidy, Jim
* Tyrone, Paul
* Willard, Portman

**Norwood, Wheelbarrow**
See  Norwood, Willie

**Norwood, Willie** 1947-  [SMG]
*American basketball player*
* Norwood, Wheelbarrow

**Nosey**
See  Wellesley, Arthur

**Nosille, Nalrah**
See  Ellison, Harlan [Jay]

**Nosseck, Max** 1902-1972  [SC]
*Polish-born actor, director, producer*
* Norris, Alexander M.

**Nostalgia**
See  Bentley, James William Benedict

**Nostradamus, Merlin**
See  Cobbe, Frances Power

**[The] Nostradamus of Portugal**
See  Bandarra, Goncalo Annes

**Nostro, Nick** 20th c.  [WF]
*Italian director*
* Howard, Nick

**Nosworthy, A. L.**
See  Nosworthy, Ann Louise

**Nosworthy, Ann Louise** 1929-
[ART]
*Scottish-born artist*
* Nosworthy, A. L.

**Notabilis, Doctor**
See  Peter de l'Isle

**Notger [or Notker]** 830?-912
[RH, SN, WBD]
*Swiss monk*
* Balbulus
* [Le] Begue
* [The] Stammerer

**Nothing Venture**
See  Finney, Humphrey S.

**Nothus [Bastard]**
See  Ochus

**Notker** 952?-1022  [WBD]
*Swiss-German scholar*
* Labeo [The Thick-Lipped]

**Notlep, Robert**
See  Pelton, Robert W[ayne]

**Noto, Lore**
See  Noto, Lorenzo

**Noto, Lorenzo** 1923-  [BEW]
*American actor and producer*
* Noto, Lore

**Nott, Barry**
See  Hurren, Bernard John

**[The] Nottingham Captain**
See  Brandreth, Jeremiah

**Nottingham, Don** 1949-  [SMG]
*American football player*
* [The] Human Bowling Ball

**[The] Nottingham Poet**
See  Bailey, Philip James

**Noureddin-Mahmud** 1116-1174
[FFF, HN, RH]
*Sultan of Syria and Egypt*
* [The] Scourge of Christians

**Nourse, Alan E[dward]** 1928-  [CA]
*American author, columnist, medical expert*
* Dr. X
* Edwards, Al

**Nous-Terre, Jean**
See  Gratiant, Gilbert

**Nous-Tous, Jean**
See  Gratiant, Gilbert

**Nouveau, Arthur**
See  Whitcomb, Ian

**Novachovitch, Lippe Benzion**
1856-1932  [WBD]
*Lithuanian-born author, poet, playwright*
* Ben-Nez
* Benedict, Leopold
* Winchevsky, Morris

**Novack, George [Edward]** 1905-
[CA]
*American author and lecturer*
* Warde, William F.

**Novaes, Guiomar** 1895-1979
*Brazilian pianist*
* [The] Paderewska of the Pampas

**Novag, Novi** 20th c.  [RM]
*Musician*
* Novi

**Novak, Joseph**
See  Kosinski, Jerzy [Nikodem]

**Novak, Kim**
See  Novak, Marilyn

**Novak, Marilyn** 1933-
[BDF, FC, HT]
*American actress*
* Novak, Kim

**Novakovsky, Alexander** 1915-
[CA]
*Russian-born economist and author*
* Nove, Alec

**Novalis**
See  Hardenberg, Friedrich von

**Novanglus**
See  Adams, John

**Novarro, Ramon**
See  Samaniegos, Ramon Gil

**Nove, Alec**
See  Novakovsky, Alexander

**Novel, Edward**
See  De Maune, Edward

**Novella, Rita** 1920-  [FC]
*Mexican actress, singer, dancer*
* Drake, Dona
* Rio, Rita

**Novelli, Enrico** 1876-1943  [WEC]
*Italian cartoonist, author, illustrator*
* Yambo

**Novelli, Mario** 20th c.  [WF]
*Italian actor*
* Freeman, Anthony

**Novello, Armando** 1888-1938
[BMH, SC]
*Swiss-born actor and circus performer*
* Toto the Clown

**Novello, Clara A.** 1818- ?  [PA]
*Author*
* Gigliucci, Countess

**Novello, Ivor**
See  Davies, David Ivor

**Novello, Mary** 1809- ?  [PA]
*Author*
* Baun, Kit, Mariner

**[Le] Noven de mon Oncle**
See  Collin, Jacques Albin Simon

**Novi**
See  Novag, Novi

**Novikoff, Lou[is Alexander]**
1915-1970  [BE, PB]
*American baseball player*
* [The] Mad Russian

**Novikov, Olga** 1840-1925  [WBD]
*Russian journalist*
* O. K.

**Novomirsky**
See  Gordin, Morris

**Novotney, Ralph Joseph** 1924-
[BE]
*American baseball player*
* Novotney, Rube

**Novotney, Rube**
See  Novotney, Ralph Joseph

**Nowaczynski, Adolf** 1876-1944
[CD]
*Polish playwright and pamphleteer*
* Neuwert
* Przyjaciel

**Nowak, Mariette** 1941-  [CA]
*American author*
* Ronsman, M. M.

**Nowatzke, Thomas M. [Tom]** 1942-
*American football player*
* [The] Struggler

**Nowedonah** 1903?-1975  [B10]
*American Indian lecturer*
* Hunter, Lois

**Nowel, Samuel**  [SN]
*American clergyman*
* [The] Fighting Chaplain

**Nowell, Elizabeth Cameron** 20th c.
[SAT]
*American author*
* Cameron, Elizabeth
* Clemons, Elizabeth

**Nowell, H. P. H.**  [PA]
*Author*
* Mannering, May

**Nowlan, George** 20th c.  [ECM]
*American country-western performer*
* Davis, Danny
* Yankee Irishman

**Nowlan, Phil[ip Francis]**
1888-1940  [WGT]
*American author*
* Phillips, Frank

**Noyce, Elisha** 19th c.  [PA]
*Author*
* Uncle John

**Noyes, Arthur**
*American chemist*
* Noyes, Stinker

**Noyes, Charles Henry**  [PA]
*Author*
* Quiet, Charles

**Noyes, E. H.**  [PA]
*Author*
* Norval

**Noyes, James O.** 1829- ?  [FFF]
*American author*
* Our Own Correspondent

**Noyes, MacLeod**
See  Palton, Francis T.

**Noyes, Mrs. A. C.**  [FFF]
*Entertainer*
* Moulton, Mabel

**Noyes, Mrs. J. F.**
See  McElhinney, Jane

**Noyes, Stinker**
See  Noyes, Arthur

**Noyes, W. H.**  [FFF]
*American editor*
* Saxon

**Noyes, Winfield Charles** 1889-
[BE]
*American baseball player*
* Noyes, Wynn

**Noyes, Wynn**
See  Noyes, Winfield Charles

**Noyes-Kane, Dorothy** 1906-  [CAP]
*American author and columnist*
* Sproul, Dorothy Noyes

**Noziere, Fernand**
See  Weyl, Fernand

**Ntate, J. J.**
See  Moiloa, James Jantjies

**Ntsoelengoe, Ace**
See  Ntsoelengoe, Patrick

**Ntsoelengoe, Patrick** 1956-    [AES]
*South African soccer player*
* Ntsoelengoe, Ace

**Nuad**    [HN]
*Irish chieftain*
* Silver Hand

**Nubin, Rosetta** 1915?-1973
[EJ, PMJ]
*American singer*
* Tharpe, [Sister] Rosetta

**Nucera, Marisa Lonette** 1959-
[CA]
*American poet*
* Marisa

**Nuetzel, Charles [Alexander]** 1934-
[ESF, SFL, WGT]
*American author*
* Augustus, Albert, Jr.
* English, Charles
* Rivere, Alec

**Nuevo Ciclon de Mexico [New Cyclone of Mexico]**
*See*  Arruza, Manolo

**Nugent, Basil** 1894-1968    [THR]
*British actor*
* Sydney, Basil

**Nugent, John Peer** 1930-    [CA]
*American author and journalist*
* Exall, Barry

**Nugent, Nancy** 1938-    [CA]
*American writer and photographer*
* Hawke, Nancy

**Nugent, Ted** 1948?-
*American singer*
* [The] Motor City Madman

**Nu'i [The Great]**
*See*  Kamehameha I

**Nuitter**
*See*  Truinet, Charles Louis Etienne

**Nuki**
*See*  Millsaps, Daniel W., III

**Numano, Allen Stanislaus Motoyuki** 1908-    [IAW]
*Japanese-born author and translator*
* Corenanda, A. L. A.

**Number 48**
*See*  Booth, Albert James, Jr.

**Number 1**
*See*  Douglas, Leon

**Number 30**
*See*  Gehlen, Reinhard

**Number 12, Mrs.**
*See*  Starbuck, Alicia Jo

**Number 24**
*See*  Sonsteby, Gunnar

**Numidicus**
*See*  Metellus, Quintus Caecilius

**Numkena, Anthony** 20th c.
*American actor*
* Holliman, Earl

**[The] Nun of Duelmen**
*See*  Emmerich [or Emmerick], Anna Katharina

**[The] Nun of Kent**
*See*  Barton, Elizabeth

**Nuncomar** ?-1775    [WBD]
*Indian government official*
* Nanda Kumar

**Nunes de Caceres, Jose** 1772-1846
[CW]
*Dominican author and poet*
* [El] Fabulista Principiante

**Nunez, Alcide** 1884-1934    [WWJ]
*American jazz musician*
* Nunez, Yellow

**Nunez, Francisco** 20th c.    [GS]
*Spanish bullfighter*
* Curillo

**Nunez, Ludwig** 1555- ?    [PA]
*Author*
* Nonnius

**Nunez, William Loring** 19th c.
[FFF]
*Author*
* Spencer, Major

**Nunez, Yellow**
*See*  Nunez, Alcide

**Nunez de Arce, Gaspar** 1834-1903
[DNNS]
*Spanish poet*
* [The] Spanish Tennyson

**Nunez de Guzman, Fernan [or Fernando]** 1470?-1553
[DNNS, SN, WBD]
*Spanish scholar*
* [El] Comendador Griego
* [The] Greek Commentator
* [El] Pinciano

**Nunio**    [SN]
* [The] Lusian Scipio

**Nunley, Maggie Rennert**
*See*  Rennert, Maggie

**Nunn, William Curtis** 1908-
[CA, WD]
*American historian, poet, author*
* Curtis, Will
* Twist, Ananias

**Nunn May, Allan** 20th c.    [EE]
*British physicist and intelligence agent for Russia*
* Alek [code name]

**Nunnemacher, Mrs. Jacob**    [FFF]
*Entertainer*
* Webster, Lizzie

**Nuppenau, Tonny Landy** 1937-
[OP]
*Danish opera singer*
* Landy, Tonny

**Nur el Hussein [Light of Hussein]**
*See*  Halaby, Elizabeth

**Nur, Queen**
*See*  Halaby, Elizabeth

**Nura**
*See*  Ulreich, Nura Woodson

**Nuraini**
*See*  Sim, Katharine [Thomasset]

**Nurmi, Paavo** 1897-1973
[NN, SR, TF]
*Finnish track and field athlete*
* [The] Flying Finn
* [The] Phantom Finn

**Nurse, Malcolm** 1903-1959    [IBW]
*West Indian-born diplomat*
* Padmore, George A.

**[The] Nurse of Antiquity**
*See*  Camden, William

**[The] Nursing Mother of Philosophy**
*See*  Boufflers, Mme. de

**Nusbaum, Nathaniel Richard**
1913-    [BEW, TR]
*American playwright, author, producer*
* Nash, N. Richard

**Nusic, Branislav** 1864-1938    [CD]
*Serbian playwright and author*
* Akiba, Ben

**Nussbaum, Al[bert F.]** 1934?-    [CA]
*American bank robber and author*
* Avellano, Alberto
* Frederick, Lee
* Hiller, Doris
* Martin, Albert
* Oreshnik, A. F.

**Nussbaum, Morris** 1897-1964    [SC]
*American actor and director*
* Ankrum, Morris
* Morris, Stephen

**Nutbrown, Maurice** 20th c.    [MBF]
*British author*
* Denbigh, Maurice

**Nutt, Charles** 1929-1967
[CA, HFF, SF]
*American author*
* Beaumont, Charles
* Beaumont, E. J.
* Grantland, Keith
* Lovehill, C. B.
* McNutt, Charles
* Phillips, Michael
* Tenneshaw, S. M. [house pseudonym]

**Nutt, Lily Clive** 1888-    [AW]
*British author*
* Arden, Clive

**Nuttall, Jeff** 1933-    [CA]
*British author and poet*
* Church, Peter
* Homoras

**Nuttall-Smith, Margaret Emily Noel**
1919-    [ART, FBJ]
*British illustrator*
* Fortnum, Peggy
* P. F.

**Nutter, Dizzy**
*See*  Nutter, Everett Clarence

**Nutter, Edna May Cox-Oliver**
1883?-1942    [BEW, F2, OCF]
*American actress*
* Oliver, Edna May

**Nutter, Everett Clarence**
1892-1958    [BE]
*American baseball player*
* Nutter, Dizzy

**Nutting, Mary O.** 19th c.    [PA]
*Author*
* Barrett, Mary

**Nuverbis**
*See*  Spotswood, Dillon Jordan

**Nuvolari, Tazio**
*Auto racer*
* [The] Flying Mantuan

**Nuyen, France**
*See*  Vannga, France

**Nuzio**
*See*  Muzzio, Girolamo

**Nuzio, Girolamo** 1496-1576
[WBD]
*Italian author and diplomat*
* Muzio [or Mutio]

**Nxeleafrika, Mnguni**
*See*  Jaffe, Hosea

**Nyberg, Julia Christina** 1785- ?
[PA]
*Author*
* Sveeadstroem

**Nydahl, Mally**
*See*  Nydahl, Malvin J.

**Nydahl, Malvin J.** 1906-    [FB]
*American football player*
* Nydahl, Mally

**Nye, Bill**
*See*  Nye, Edgar Wilson

**Nye, Edgar Wilson** 1850-1896
[FFF, WBD]
*American author*
* Nye, Bill

**Nye, Harold G.**
*See*  Harding, Lee

**Nye, Miriam [Maurine Hawthorn] Baker** 1918-    [CA]
*American author and columnist*
* Baker, Miriam Hawthorn

**Nye, Nelson C[oral]** 1907-    [CA]
*American author*
* Colt, Clem
* Denver, Drake C.
* Rockingham, Montague

**Nyerere, Julius Kambarage** 1922-
*Tanzanian president*
* [The] Father of African Socialism

**Nyers, Amelia Kathryn** 1907-    [IA]
*American writer*
* Raw, Kathryn

**Nyman, Nyls Wallace** 1954-    [BE]
*American baseball player*
* Nyman, Rex

**Nyman, Rex**
*See*  Nyman, Nyls Wallace

**Nyren, Dorothy**
*See*  Curley, Dorothy Nyren

**Nyro, Laura**
*See*  Nigro, Laura

**Nystrom, Knuckles**
*See*  Nystrom, Thore Robert

**Nystrom, Thore Robert** 1952-
[SMG]
*Swedish-born hockey player*
* Nystrom, Knuckles

**Nyvall, David** 1863- ?    [NAA]
*Swedish-born educator, author, poet*
* A. N.

# O

**O.**
See   James, Lionel

**O. A.**
See   Andersson, Oskar Emil

**O and W [Oldest and Wisest]**
See   Reagan, Ronald Wilson

**O. B.**
See   Brown, Ollie Lee

**O. B.**
See   Obradovich, James Robert

**O Breanndain, Cathaoir**
See   Brennan, Charles

**O Ceallaigh, Sean**
See   O'Kelly, John J.

**O Ceallaigh, Tomas**
See   O'Kelly, Thomas

**O Ceithearnaigh, Seamus**
See   Carney, James [Patrick]

**O Conaire, Padraic**
See   Conroy, Patrick

**O Concheanainn, Tomas**
See   Concannon, Thomas

**O Danachair, Caoimhin**
See   Danaher, Kevin

**O Donnchadha, Tadhg**
See   O'Donoghue, Tadhg

**O Dubh, Cathal**
See   Duff, Charles [St. Lawrence]

**O Dubhghaill, Seamus**
See   Doyle, James J.

**O Duinnin, Padraig**
See   Dinneen, Patrick Stephen

**O Farachain, Roibeard**
See   Farren, Robert

**O Flannghaile, Tomas**
See   Flannery, Thomas

**O. H. I. O.**
See   Frankenstein, George L.

**O hAimhirgin, Osborn**
See   Bergin, Osborn J.

**O hAodha, Tomas**
See   Hayes, Thomas

**O. Jr.**
See   Omsby, Waterman L., Jr.

**O. K.**
See   King, Oliver

**O. K.**
See   Kireeff, O.

**O. K.**
See   Novikov, Olga

**O Laoghaire, Peadar**
See   O'Leary, Peter

**O Maille, Micheal**
See   O'Malley, Michael

**O Maonaigh, Cainneach**
See   Mooney, Canice [Albert James]

**O Neachtain, Eoghan**
See   Naughton, Owen

**O. P. F.**
See   Buchanan, James

**O. P. Q.**
See   Merry, Robert

**O. S.**
See   Seaman, [Sir] Owen

**O Seaghdha, Padraig**
See   O'Shea, Patrick

**O Seaghdha, Padraig**
See   O'Shea, Patrick J.

**O Siochain, P[adraig] A[ugustine**
See   Sheehan, Patrick Augustine

**[The] Oak**
See   Connor, Roger

**Oak Cliff T-Bone**
See   Walker, Aaron Thibeaux

**Oak, Purushottam Nagesh** 1917-
[IAW]
*Indian author*
* Amarnath
* Hansraj Bhatia
* Peno
* Uttam

**Oaker, Jane**
See   Peper, Minnie Dorothy

**Oakes, A. H.**
See   Bunner, Henry Cuyler

**Oakes, Elizabeth**   [PA]
*Author*
* Halfenstein, Ernest

**Oakes, Ennis Talmadge** 1886-1948
[BE]
*American baseball player*
* Oakes, Rebel

**Oakes, James** 1807-1878
[FFF, PA]
*Author*
* Acorn

**Oakes, Rebel**
See   Oakes, Ennis Talmadge

**Oakes, Vanya**
See   Oakes, Virginia Armstrong

**Oakes, Virginia Armstrong** 1909-
[B10]
*American author*
* Oakes, Vanya

**Oakie, Jack**
See   Offield, Lewis Delaney

**Oakland, Vivian**
See   Anderson, Vivian

**Oakland, Will**
See   Hinrichs, Herman

**Oakley, Annie**
See   Moses, Annie

**Oakley, Daisy**
See   Harding, Mrs. Roger

**Oakley, Eric Gilbert** 1916-   [CA]
*British author and publisher*
* Capon, Peter
* Grapho
* Gregson, Paul

**Oakley, Frederick**   [PA]
*Author*
* Short, Joshua

**Oakley, Mrs. J. R.**   [FFF]
*Entertainer*
* Vaughn, Cora

**[The] Oakmont Orator**
See   Dykes, James Joseph [Jimmy]

**Oaksey, [Lord] John Geoffrey Tristram** 1929-   [IAW]
*British author*
* Audax
* Marlborough

**Oakum, John**
See   Phillips, Walter P.

**Oana, Henry Kauhane** 1908-   [BE]
*American baseball player*
* Oana, Prince

**Oana, Prince**
See   Oana, Henry Kauhane

**Oastler, Richard** 1789-1861
[DEP, DNNS, HN]
*British social reformer*
* [The] Factory King

**Oates, Alice**
See   Titus, Tracy

**Oates, C. T.**
See   Oates, Christine Tate

**Oates, Christine Tate** 1913-   [ART]
*British painter*
* Oates, C. T.

**Oates, Felix**
See   Catlin, George L.

**Oates, Joyce Carol** 1938-   [CN]
*American author, playwright, poet*
* Fernandes/Oates

**Oates, Titus**
See   Bell, Martin

**Oates, Titus** 1649-1705   [SN]
*British imposter*
* [The] Knight of the Post
* [The] Light of the Town
* [An] Orthodox Beast
* [The] Scorn of the Court
* Telltroth, Titus
* Thou Shred of a Loom

**Obadele, Imari Abubakaru, I**
See   Henry, Richard

**Obadia, Hakki**
See   Obadia, Heskel H.

**Obadia, Heskel H.** 1924-   [IWM]
*Iraqi-born musician*
* Obadia, Hakki

**O'Bannion, Charles Dion**
1892-1924   [BLB]
*American underworld figure*
* O'Bannion, Deanie

**O'Bannion, Deanie**
See   O'Bannion, Charles Dion

**Obata, Yojiro**
See   Uetake, Yojiro

**Obed, Elisha** 1952-   [IBW]
*Bahamian boxer*
* [The] Bahamian Fighting Machine

**Obee, Lois** 1909-1976   [FC, TR]
*British actress*
* Dresdel, Sonia

**O'Beirne, Brian**
See   Donn-Byrne, Brian Oswald

[The] Obelisk
See Thurman, Allen Granbery

Oberhansli, Trudi
See Schlapbach-Oberhansli, Trudi

Oberholtzer, Peter
See Brannon, William T.

Oberlander, Andrew J. 1905-1968
[AS, FB]
American football player
* Oberlander, Swede

Oberlander, Doc
See Oberlander, Hartman Louis

Oberlander, Hartman Louis
1864-1922 [BE]
American baseball player
* Oberlander, Doc

Oberlander, Swede
See Oberlander, Andrew J.

Oberlin, Flossie
See Oberlin, Frank Rufus

Oberlin, Frank Rufus 1876-1952
[BE]
American baseball player
* Oberlin, Flossie

Oberndorff, [Count] Charles 1876-
? [LAO]
German-born author
* Von Oberndorff, Carl

Oberon, Merle
See Thompson, Estelle Merle
O'Brien

O'Berta, Dingbat
See Oberta, John

Oberta, John [BLB]
American gangster
* O'Berta, Dingbat

Obertraut, Johann Michael 17th c.
[SN]
Danish army officer
* [Der] Deutsche Michael

O'Billovich, Jack 20th c.
American football player
* O'Billovich, Mad Dog

O'Billovich, Mad Dog
See O'Billovich, Jack

O'Blather, Count
See O'Nuallain, Brian

Oboe, Peter
See Jacobs, Walter Darnell

Obolenski, [Prince] Dimitri Romanoff
See Gerguson, Harry

Obotunde, Ijimere
See Beier, Ulli

Obradovic, Dimitrije 1742?-1811
[WBD]
Serbian author
* Dositheus

Obradovich, Buffy
See Obradovich, James Robert

Obradovich, James Robert 1953-
[SMG]
American football player
* O. B.
* Obradovich, Buffy

O'Brady, Frederic Michel Maurice
See Abel, Frederic Michel Maurice

O'Brian, Frank
See Garfield, Brian [Francis]
Wynne

O'Brian, Hugh
See Krampe, Hugh Charles

O'Brien, Angela Maxine 1937-
[FC, IPA, SW]
American actress
* O'Brien, Margaret

O'Brien, Buck
See O'Brien, Thomas Joseph

O'Brien, C. G.
See O'Brien, Charlotte Grace

O'Brien, Charlotte Grace ?-1909
[WWL]
Irish author
* O'Brien, C. G.

O'Brien, Chewing Gum
See O'Brien, John J.

O'Brien, Clifford Edward 20th c.
[SFL, WGT]
Author
* O'Brien, Larry Clinton

O'Brien, Conor Cruise 1917-
[B10, CA]
Irish author and diplomat
* Cruise O'Brien, Conor
* O'Donnell, Donat

O'Brien, Cyril C[ornelius] 1906-
[CA]
Canadian author, educator,
composer
* Wilson, Crane

O'Brien, Darby
See O'Brien, John F.

O'Brien, Dave
See Fronabarger, David Poole

O'Brien, David
See Herd, David

O'Brien, David 20th c. [SFL]
Author
* Cameron, Berl [house
    pseudonym, Curtis Warren]
* Le Page, Rand [house
    pseudonym, Curtis Warren]
* Luna, Kris [house pseudonym,
    Curtis Warren]
* Shaw, Brian [house pseudonym,
    Curtis Warren]

O'Brien, David Wright ?-1944
[ESF, WGT]
American author
* Blade, Alexander [house
    pseudonym, Ziff-Davis]
* Cabot, John York
* Dennis, Bruce
* Farnsworth, Duncan
* Garson, Clee [house pseudonym,
    Ziff-Davis]
* Vardon, Richard

O'Brien, Dean D. [joint pseudonym
with Otto O(scar) Binder]
See Binder, Earl Andrew

O'Brien, Dean D. [joint pseudonym
with Earl Andrew Binder]
See Binder, Otto O[scar]

O'Brien, Dee
See Bradley, Marion Zimmer

O'Brien, Donough [Baron of Ibrickan]
?-1624 [WBD]
Irish politician
* [The] Great Earl

O'Brien, E. G.
See Clarke, Arthur C[harles]

O'Brien, Edward Joseph Harrington
1890- [WWL]
American author
* Middleton, Arthur

O'Brien, Edward Stephenson
See Butt, Isaac

O'Brien, Ellard John 1930- [CEI]
Canadian-born hockey player
* O'Brien, Obie

O'Brien, Flann
See O'Nuallain, Brian

O'Brien, Frank Aloysius 1894-
[BE]
American baseball player
* O'Brien, Mickey

O'Brien, Gladys ?-1920 [SC]
American actress
* Field, Gladys

O'Brien, Hod
See O'Brien, Walter Howard

O'Brien, Howard Vincent
1888-1947 [WW]
Author
* Perrin, Clyde

O'Brien, Jack
See Hagen, Joseph F.

O'Brien, Jane 1918- [FC]
American actress
* Bryan, Jane

O'Brien, Joey
See Aiuppa, Joseph John [Joe]

O'Brien, John 1836-1887
[FFF, WBD]
American comedian
* Raymond, John T.

O'Brien, John F. 1867-1892 [BE]
American baseball player
* O'Brien, Darby

O'Brien, John J. 1870-1913 [BE]
Canadian-born baseball player
* O'Brien, Chewing Gum

O'Brien, John K.
See Byrne, John K.

O'Brien, Larry Clinton
See O'Brien, Clifford Edward

O'Brien, Margaret
See O'Brien, Angela Maxine

O'Brien, Marian P[lowman] 1915-
[CA]
American author
* Bryan, Mavis

O'Brien, Mary 20th c. [LRR]
British-born singer
* Springfield, Dusty

O'Brien, Mickey
See O'Brien, Frank Aloysius

O'Brien, Obie
See O'Brien, Ellard John

O'Brien, Obie
See O'Brien, Thomas Edward

O'Brien, Pat
See O'Brien, William Joseph, Jr.

O'Brien, Patria Gene 1916-1970
[FC]
American actress
* Ellis, Patricia

O'Brien, Peter 1842-1914 [DEP]
Irish jurist
* Peter the Packer

O'Brien, Philadelphia Jack
See Hagen, Joseph F.

O'Brien, Queenie
See Thompson, Estelle Merle
O'Brien

O'Brien, Robert C.
See Conly, Robert Leslie

O'Brien, Shots
See Brennan, Charles

O'Brien, Thomas Edward 1918-
[BE]
American baseball player
* O'Brien, Obie

O'Brien, Thomas Joseph
1882-1959 [BE]
American baseball player
* O'Brien, Buck

O'Brien, Tom
See Aiuppa, Joseph John [Joe]

O'Brien, Walter Howard 1936-
[EJ]
American jazz musician
* O'Brien, Hod

O'Brien, William Joseph, Jr. 1899-
[F2, IPA]
American actor
* O'Brien, Pat

O'Bryan, Leonel [Campbell]
?-1938 [B10]
American newspaper publisher
* Pry, Polly

O'Bryen, W. J.
See Wheeler-O'Bryen, Wilfrid
James

O'Brynt, Jon
See Barnum, W[illiam] Paul

[The] Obscure Philosopher
See Heraclitos [or Heraclitus]

Observer
See Bruce, Benjamin

Observer
See Taylor, Benjamin Ogle

Obukhova, Lidiia Alekseevna 20th
c. [SFL]
Author
* Obukhova, Lydia

Obukhova, Lydia
See Obukhova, Lidiia Alekseevna

O'Byrne, Dermot
See Bax, [Sir] Arnold [Edward
Trevor]

O'Callaghan, Brigid 1870-1955
[BEW, PMJ]
American entertainer
* Friganza, Trixie

**Ocampo, Victoria** 1891?-1979
[CA]
*Argentinian author, editor,*
*translator*
* [The] Queen of Letters

**O'Carolan, Turloch** 1670-1738
[DNNS, SN]
*Irish poet and musician*
* [The] Irish Anacreon
* [The] Last True Bard of Ireland
* [The] Orpheus of the Green Isle

**O'Carroll, Marie-Madeleine**
**Bernadette** 1906-
[BEW, FC, WEF]
*British actress*
* Carroll, Madeleine

**O'Carroll, Ryan**
See Markun, Patricia Maloney

**O'Casey, Sean**
See Casey, John

**O'Cataract, Jehu**
See Neal, John

**O'Cataract, John**
See Neal, John

**O'Cathasaigh, Donal**
See Casey, Daniel J[oseph]

**O'Cathasaigh, Shaun**
See Casey, John

**Occam [or Ockham], William of**
1276?-1347 [DNNS, FFF, HN]
*British philosopher*
* Invincibilis, Doctor
* [The] Invincible Doctor
* [The] Singular Doctor
* Singularis, Doctor
* Venerabilis, Doctor
* Venerabilis Inceptor
* [The] Venerable Initiator

**Occasional**
See Bruce, Sanders D.

**Occasional**
See Forney, John W.

**Occidente, Maria dell'**
See Brooks, Maria Gowen

**Ocean, Julian**
See De Mesne, Eugene [Frederick]

**[The] Ocean Shepherd**
See Raleigh, [Sir] Walter

**Oceans, Lucky**
See Gosfield, Reuben

**Ochus** 5th c. BC [WBD]
*King of Persia*
* Darius II
* Nothus [Bastard]

**Ochus** 4th c. BC [WBD]
*King of Persia*
* Artaxerxes III

**Ock, Harold David** 1912- [BE]
*American baseball player*
* Ock, Whitey

**Ock, Whitey**
See Ock, Harold David

**Ockey, Footie**
See Okypch, Walter Andrew

**Ockey, Walter Andrew**
See Okypch, Walter Andrew

**Ockleman, Constance Frances Marie**
1919-1973 [BDF, FC, WEF]
*American actress*
* Keane, Constance
* Lake, Veronica

**Ockside, Knight Russ**
See Underhill, Edward Fitch

**O'Clery, Michael**
See O'Clery, Tadhg

**O'Clery, Tadhg** 1575-1643 [WBD]
*Irish clergyman and scholar*
* O'Clery, Michael

**O'Connell, Charles J.** 20th c.
[BBH]
*American handball organization*
*officer*
* [The] Father of One Wall
   Handball

**O'Connell, Daniel** 1775-1847
[DEP, HN, RH]
*Irish political agitator*
* [The] Big Beggarman
* [The] Great O
* [The] Irish Agitator
* [The] Liberator
* [The] Uncrowned Monarch

**O'Connell, Dermie**
See O'Connell, Dermott

**O'Connell, Dermott** [SMG]
*American basketball player*
* O'Connell, Dermie

**O'Connell, Peg**
See Ahern, Margaret McCrohan

**O'Connell, R. F.**
See Van De Gohm, Richard

**O'Connell's Head Pacificator**
See Steel, Tom

**O'Conner, Barrett Willoughby** 20th
c. [NAA]
*American author*
* Willoughby, Barrett

**O'Conner, Elizabeth**
See McNamara, Barbara Willard

**O'Conner, Roger** [PA]
*Author*
* Rock, Captain

**O'Connor, Alma Mabel** 1927-
[FC, ITA]
*American actress*
* Gillis, Ann

**O'Connor, Bucky**
See O'Connor, Frank

**O'Connor, Buddy**
See O'Connor, Herbert William

**O'Connor, Cathal** ?-1010 [HN]
*King of Connaught*
* O'Connor of the Bloody Hand

**O'Connor, Claxton J.** 1907- [BBH]
*American lacrosse player and coach*
* O'Connor, Okie

**O'Connor, Frank**
See O'Donovan, Michael

**O'Connor, Frank** 1913-1958 [BB]
*American basketball coach*
* O'Connor, Bucky

**O'Connor, Herbert William** 1916-
[CEI, FHE, HK]
*Canadian-born hockey player*
* O'Connor, Buddy

**O'Connor, James F. [Jim]**
1893?-1963 [BEW]
*American journalist*
* Knight, Gene

**O'Connor, James Matthew**
1865-1950 [BE]
*American baseball player*
* Connor, James Matthew [Jim]

**O'Connor, John Joseph** 1867-1937
[BE]
*American baseball player*
* O'Connor, Peach Pie

**O'Connor, Liam**
See Liddy, James [Daniel Reeves]

**O'Connor, [Sister] Mary Catharine**
20th c. [CAP]
*American author and educator*
* Farrell, Catharine

**O'Connor of the Bloody Hand**
See O'Connor, Cathal

**O'Connor, Okie**
See O'Connor, Claxton J.

**O'Connor, Paddy**
See O'Connor, Patrick Francis

**O'Connor, Patrick**
See Wibberley, Leonard [Patrick
O'Connor]

**O'Connor, Patrick Francis**
1879-1950 [BE]
*American baseball player*
* O'Connor, Paddy

**O'Connor, Patrick Joseph** 1924-
[AW, WD]
*Irish poet and editor*
* Fiacc, Padraic

**O'Connor, Peach Pie**
See O'Connor, John Joseph

**O'Connor, Philip**
See Bancroft, Marie Constant

**O'Connor, Richard** 1915-1975
[B10, CA]
*American author, actor, journalist*
* Archer, Frank
* Burke, John
* Wayland, Patrick

**O'Connor, Sandra Day** 1930?-
*American Supreme Court justice*
* [The] Bitch Queen

**O'Connor, Stacy**
See Rollins, William

**O'Connor, T. P.**
See O'Connor, Thomas Power

**O'Connor, Terrible Tommy**
See O'Connor, Thomas

**O'Connor, Thomas** 1886- ? [BLB]
*Irish-born American murderer and*
*robber*
* O'Connor, Terrible Tommy

**O'Connor, Thomas Power**
1848-1929 [CBS, LC, WBD]
*Irish journalist and politician*
* [The] Father of the House of
   Commons
* O'Connor, T. P.
* Tay Pay

**O'Connor, Vincent Clarence Scott**
20th c. [WWL]
*British author*
* Odysseus

**O'Connor, William** 1891?-1964
[BEW]
*Theatrical performer*
* Conlin, Ray, Sr.

**Oconomowoc**
See Henshall, James A.

**Octavia**
See Ives, Mary Alice

**Octavianus, Gaius Julius Caesar**
See Octavius, Gaius

**Octavio, Francesco** 1447-1490
[PA]
*Author*
* Cliophile

**Octavius** 937?- 964 [CAL]
*Pope*
* John XII

**Octavius** 12th c. [WBD]
*Antipope*
* Victor IV

**Octavius, Gaius** ?- 14
[HN, RH, SN]
*Roman emperor*
* Augustus
* [The] Father of His Country
* Octavianus, Gaius Julius Caesar

**October, John**
See Portway, Christopher [John]

**October, Mr.**
See Jackson, Reginald [Reggie]

**[An] Octogenarian**
See Roche, James

**Octopus**
See Drachman, Julian M[oses]

**[The] Octopus**
See Marion, Martin Whiteford

**O'Cuilleanain, Eilis Dillon** 1920-
[TBJ]
*Irish author*
* Dillon, Eilis

**O'Daly, Cormac**
See Forbes, Dick

**O'Daniel, Iron Mike**
See O'Daniel, John Wilson

**O'Daniel, Janet** 20th c. [WD]
*American author*
* Janet, Lillian [joint pseudonym
   with Lillian Ressler]

**O'Daniel, John Wilson** 1894-1975
[B10]
*American military leader*
* O'Daniel, Iron Mike

**O'Daniel, Pappy**
See O'Daniel, Wilbert Lee

**O'Daniel, Wilbert Lee** 1890-1969
[CWG, DAM]
*American country-western performer*
*and politician*
* O'Daniel, Pappy

**O'Dare, Kerry**
See Starr, Richard Harry

**O'Day, Anita**
See Colton, Anita

**O'Day, Dawn**
See Paris, Dawn Evelyeen

**O'Day, Molly**
See Noonan, Suzanne Dobson

**O'Day, Molly**
See Williamson, LaVerne

**O'Day, Mrs. William** [FFF]
*Entertainer*
* Wells, Sadie

**O'Day, Peggy**
See Reis, Peggy

**[The] Odcombian Legstretcher**
See Coryat, Thomas

**Oddo, Sandra [Schmidt]** 1937-
[CA]
*American writer*
* Schmidt, Sandra

**Odds and Ends**
See Quevedo, Walter C.

**O'Dea, Anne Caldwell** 1867-1936
[PMJ]
*American lyricist and librettist*
* Caldwell, Anne

**O'Dea, Lefty**
See O'Dea, Paul

**O'Dea, Patrick J.** 1872-1962 [FB]
*Australian-born American football player*
* Mitchell, Charles J.

**O'Dea, Paul** 1920- [BE]
*American baseball player*
* O'Dea, Lefty

**Odell, Carol** [CAP]
*Author*
* Odell, Gill [joint pseudonym with Traviss Gill]

**O'Dell, Digger**
See Brown, John H.

**O'Dell, Digger**
See O'Dell, William Oliver [Billy]

**O'Dell, Digger**
See Smith, Herbert O'Dell

**Odell, Gill** [joint pseudonym with Carol Odell]
See Gill, Traviss

**Odell, Gill** [joint pseudonym with Traviss Gill]
See Odell, Carol

**O'Dell, Kenny**
See Gist, Kenneth, Jr.

**O'Dell, Mac** 1916- [CWG]
*American country-western performer*
* [The] Old Country Boy

**Odell, Shorty**
See Schwartz, Solomon

**O'Dell, William Oliver [Billy]** 1933-
[BE, BTB]
*American baseball player*
* O'Dell, Digger

**Odem, J.**
See Rubin, Jacob A.

**Oden, James Burke [Jimmy]**
1903-1977 [BWW]
*American singer*
* Big Bloke
* Oden, Old Man
* Poor Boy
* St. Louis Jimmy

**Oden, Old Man**
See Oden, James Burke [Jimmy]

**Odenwald, Lefty**
See Odenwald, Theodore Joseph [Ted]

**Odenwald, Theodore Joseph [Ted]**
1902-1965 [BE]
*American baseball player*
* Odenwald, Lefty

**Odescalchi, Benedetto** 1611-1689
[WBD]
*Pope*
* Innocent XI

**Odetta**
See Holmes, Odetta

**Odette**
See Fortin, Marie Des Neiges

**Odette, Mary**
See Goimbault, Odette

**O'Dhu, Fergus**
See Trotter, [Canon] John Crawford

**Odin**
See Burvik, Mabel Odin

**Odington, Walter**
See Walter of Evesham

**O'do [or U'do]** 1042?-1099 [WBD]
*Pope*
* Urban II

**Ododonus**
See Wolton, Edward

**O'Doherty, Eileen**
See Walker, Anna

**Odoherty, [Sir] Morgan**
See Maginn, William

**O'Doire, Annraoi**
See Beechhold, Henry F[rank]

**Odom, Andrew** 1936- [BWW]
*American singer*
* B. B. Jr.
* Big Voice
* Blues Boy
* Odom, King
* Odom, Little Andrew
* Odom, Voice

**Odom, Blue Moon**
See Odom, Johnny Lee

**Odom, David Everett [Dave]** 1918-
[BE]
*American baseball player*
* Odom, Porky

**Odom, Heinie**
See Odom, Herman Boyd

**Odom, Herbert** 1933- [IBW]
*American boxer*
* Doc O

**Odom, Herman Boyd** 1900- [BE]
*American baseball player*
* Odom, Heinie

**Odom, Johnny Lee** 1945-
[PB, SMG, WWB]
*American baseball player*
* Odom, Blue Moon

**Odom, King**
See Odom, Andrew

**Odom, Leprechaun**
See Odom, Steve Talmage

**Odom, Little Andrew**
See Odom, Andrew

**Odom, Porky**
See Odom, David Everett [Dave]

**Odom, Steve Talmage** 1952-
[SMG]
*American football player*
* Odom, Leprechaun

**Odom, Voice**
See Odom, Andrew

**Odon, Gerard** [HN]
*Medieval scholar*
* Scolasticus, Doctor

**O'Donald, Donald**
See Cooksley, S[idney] Bert

**O'Donnell, Cathy**
See Steely, Ann

**O'Donnell, Dick** [joint pseudonym with Don(ald) (Arthur) Thompson]
See Lupoff, Richard Allen [Dick]

**O'Donnell, Dick** [joint pseudonym with Richard Allen (Dick) Lupoff]
See Thompson, Don[ald Arthur]

**O'Donnell, Donat**
See O'Brien, Conor Cruise

**O'Donnell, Edward** ?-1923 [BLB]
*American gangster*
* O'Donnell, Spike

**O'Donnell, Emmett** 1906-1971
[WA]
*American military leader*
* O'Donnell, Rosy

**O'Donnell [or O'Donell?], Hugh**
1571?-1602 [HN]
*Irish chieftain*
* Red Hugh

**O'Donnell, John Thomas, Jr.**
1899-1940 [SC]
*American actor*
* Ward, Hap, Jr.

**O'Donnell, John Thomas, Sr.**
1868?-1944 [BEW, SC]
*American actor and producer*
* Ward, Hap

**O'Donnell, K. M.**
See Malzberg, Barry N[orman]

**O'Donnell, Klondike**
See O'Donnell, William

**O'Donnell, Lawrence** [joint pseudonym with Catherine Lucile Moore]
See Kuttner, Henry

**O'Donnell, Lawrence** [joint pseudonym with Henry Kuttner]
See Moore, Catherine Lucile

**O'Donnell, Peter** 20th c. [MBF]
*British author*
* Barnes, John

**O'Donnell, Rosy**
See O'Donnell, Emmett

**O'Donnell, Spike**
See O'Donnell, Edward

**O'Donnell, William** 20th c.
[BLB, PHM]
*American underworld figure*
* O'Donnell, Klondike

**O'Donnevan, Finn**
See Sheckley, Robert

**O'Donoghue, Tadhg** 20th c.
[WWL]
*Irish poet and editor*
* O Donnchadha, Tadhg

**O'Donovan, Gerald**
See O'Donovan, Jeremiah

**O'Donovan, Jeremiah** 1871-1942
[DIL]
*Irish author*
* O'Donovan, Gerald

**O'Donovan, John** 1921- [CA]
*Irish author, playwright, broadcaster*
* Marsh, Andrew

**O'Donovan, Michael** 1903-1966
[CBS, LC, TC1]
*Irish author*
* O'Connor, Frank

**O'Donovan, Mrs.**
See Rossa, Mrs. O'Donovan

**O'Doul, Francis Joseph [Frank]**
1897-1969 [AS, DGS, PB]
*American baseball player*
* [The] Man in the Green Suit
* O'Doul, Lefty

**O'Doul, Lefty**
See O'Doul, Francis Joseph [Frank]

**O'Dowd, Cornelius**
See Lever, Charles James

**O'Dowd, Darby**
See Luby, Kate

**O'Dowd, Mike** 1895-1957
[BX, RBE]
*American boxer*
* [The] St. Paul Cyclone

**O'Dreams, John**
See Wallace, Henry

**Odwell, Fred[erick William]**
1872-1948 [BE]
*American baseball player*
* Odwell, Fritz

**Odwell, Fritz**
See Odwell, Fred[erick William]

**Odysseus**
See O'Connor, Vincent Clarence Scott

**Oecolampadius, Johannes**
See Heussgen [or Huessgen], Johannes

**Oedipus**
See Bassianus

**Oehlenschlaeger, Adam Gottlob**
1779-1850 [SN, WBD]
*Danish poet and playwright*
* [The] King of the Scandinavian Singers
* [The] Poet King of Scandinavia

**Oehmke, Thomas Harold** 1947-
[CA]
*American author*
* Plain, Warren

**Oelrichs, Blanche** 1890-1950
[BEW]
*American actress, author, poet*
* Strange, Michael

**Oertel, Charles Frank [Chuck]**
1931- [BE]
*American baseball player*
* Oertel, Ducky
* Oertel, Snuffy

**Oertel, Ducky**
See Oertel, Charles Frank [Chuck]

**Oertel, Philipp Friedrich Wilhelm**
1798-1867 [WBD]
*German author*
* Von Horn, W. O.

**Oertel, Snuffy**
See Oertel, Charles Frank [Chuck]

**Oesteren, Friedrich Werner Van**
1874- ? [LAO]
*German author and poet*
* Oestern, Fr. W. V.

**Oestern, Fr. W. V.**
See Oesteren, Friedrich Werner Van

**Oestman, Nan Inger** 1923- [IAW]
*Swedish author*
* Inger, Nan

**Oettinger, Louella** 1880?-1972
[F2, FC, OCF]
*American columnist*
* Parsons, Louella O.

**O'Faolain, Julia** 20th c. [CA, CN]
*Irish author and translator*
* Martines, Julia

**O'Faolain, Sean**
See Whelan, John

**O'Farrell, M. J.** 1832- ? [PA]
*Author*
* Irish Priest

**O'Farrell, Talbot**
See Parrot, William

**O'Farrell, William** 1904- [CC]
*Author*
* Grew, William

**O'Farrelly, Agnes** 20th c. [WWL]
*Irish author*
* Ni Fhaircheallaigh, Una

**O'Farrill, Arturo** 1921-
[ASC, DAM, EJ]
*Cuban-born composer*
* O'Farrill, Chico

**O'Farrill, Chico**
See O'Farrill, Arturo

**O'Feeney, Francis** 1883-1953
*American actor, screenwriter, director, producer*
* Ford, Francis [Frank]

**O'Feeney, Sean** 1895-1973
*American director, producer, screenwriter*
* Ford, John
* Ford, Pappy

**Ofek, Uriel**
See Popik, Uriel

**Ofer, Harold** ?-1978 [FIR]
*Actor*
* Renard, Roy

**Offard, Cecil** [PA]
*Author*
* Thornton, Harold

**Offerman, George, Sr.** 1880-1938
[SC]
*American actor*
* [The] Original Singing Nut

**Offerre, M.**
See Shamir, Moshe

**Office, Rollie**
See Office, Rowland Johnnie

**Office, Row**
See Office, Rowland Johnnie

**Office, Rowland Johnnie** 1952-
[BE, SMG]
*American baseball player*
* Office, Rollie
* Office, Row

**[An] Officer**
See Gleig, George Robert

**Offield, Lewis Delaney** 1903-1978
[CED, F2, FC]
*American actor*
* Oakie, Jack

**Offord, Lenore Glen** 1905- [CA]
*American author*
* Durrant, Theo [joint pseudonym]

**Offutt, A. J.**
See Offutt, Andrew Jefferson

**Offutt, Andrew Jefferson** 1934-
[CA, ESF, SFL]
*American author*
* Cleve, John
* Douglas, Jeff [joint pseudonym with Douglas Bruce Berry]
* Offutt, A. J.
* Williams, J. X. [house pseudonym, Greenleaf Classics]

**O'Fihely, Maurice** ?-1513 [PA]
*Author*
* De Portu

**O'Finn, Thaddeus**
See McGloin, Joseph Thaddeus

**O'Flaherty, Barney** 1823-1876
[FFF, PA]
*Entertainer*
* Williams, Barney

**O'Flaherty, John Benedict** 1918-
[CEI]
*Canadian-born hockey player*
* O'Flaherty, Peanuts

**O'Flaherty, Peanuts**
See O'Flaherty, John Benedict

**O'Flinn, Peter**
See Fanthorpe, R[obert] Lionel

**O'Flynn, Honoria** 1909- [ASC]
*Irish composer*
* Mack, Noreen

**O'Flynn, Jimmy**
See Graydon, Robert Murray

**O'Flynn, Peter**
See Fanthorpe, R[obert] Lionel

**O'Francis, Mary** [PA]
*Author*
* Blount, Margaret

**Og, Liam**
See O'Neill, William

**O'Galop [At the Gallop]**
See Rossillon, Marius

**Ogan, George F.** 1912- [CA, SAT]
*American author*
* Castle, Lee [joint pseudonym with Margaret E. (Nettles) Ogan]
* Keefer, Catherine [joint pseudonym with Margaret E. (Nettles) Ogan]
* Ogan, M. G. [joint pseudonym with Margaret E. (Nettles) Ogan]
* Stowe, Rosetta [joint pseudonym with Margaret E. (Nettles) Ogan]

**Ogan, M. G.** [joint pseudonym with Margaret E. (Nettles) Ogan]
See Ogan, George F.

**Ogan, M. G.** [joint pseudonym with George F. Ogan]
See Ogan, Margaret E. [Nettles]

**Ogan, Margaret E. [Nettles]**
1923-1979 [CA, SAT]
*American author*
* Castle, Lee [joint pseudonym with George F. Ogan]
* Keefer, Catherine [joint pseudonym with George F. Ogan]
* Ogan, M. G. [joint pseudonym with George F. Ogan]
* Stowe, Rosetta [joint pseudonym with George F. Ogan]

**Ogarkov, Nikolai** 1918?-
*Russian military leader*
* [The] Father of the Modern Soviet Army

**O'Gatty, Jimmy**
See Agati, James

**O'Gatty, Packey**
See Agati, Pasquale

**Ogawa, Pelorhanke Ai**
See Anthony, Florence

**Ogden** 18th c. [HN]
*Gambler*
* [The] Newmarket Oracle

**Ogden, Anna Cora** 1819-1870 [PA]
*Author*
* Berkeley, Helen
* Isabel

**Ogden, Bud**
See Ogden, Carlos

**Ogden, C. K.**
See Ogden, Charles Kay

**Ogden, Carlos** 1946- [BB]
*American basketball player*
* Ogden, Bud

**Ogden, Charles Kay** 1889-1957
[LC]
*British author, editor, inventor of Basic English*
* Ogden, C. K.

**Ogden, Curly**
See Ogden, Warren Harvey

**Ogden, R. L.** [PA]
*Author*
* Podgers

**Ogden, Richard D'Orsay**
See Maxwell, Richard

**Ogden, Warren Harvey** 1901-1964
[BE]
*American baseball player*
* Ogden, Curly

**Ogilvie, Clare M.**
See Clifford, Clare

**Ogilvy, Arthur James** 20th c. [SFL]
*Author*
* A. J. O.

**Ogilvy, Gavin**
See Barrie, [Sir] James Matthew

**Ogle, Anne** [PA]
*Author*
* Owen, Ashelford

**Oglesby, Joseph** 1931- [CA]
*American author*
* Kain, Malcolm
* Mulesko, Angelo
* Vale, Lewis
* Woodson, Jeff

**Oglesby, Richard James**
1824-1899 [FFF]
*American politician*
* Uncle Dick

**Ognall, Leopold Horace** 1908-
[AW, CA, CC]
*Canadian-born author*
* Carmichael, Harry
* Howard, Hartley

**Ognev [or Ognyov?], N[ikolai]**
See Rosanov [or Rozanov?], Mikhail Grigorievich

**[The] O'Gorman Mahon**
See Mahon, Charles James Patrick

**O'Gorman, Samuel F.**
See Cusack, Michael J[oseph]

**O'Gotham, Bob**
See Greely, Robert H.

**O'Grady, Elizabeth Anne** 20th c.
[AW, CA]
*Australian photojournalist and author*
* Scollan, E. A.

**O'Grady, Felix**
See Hadath, John Edward Gunby

**O'Grady, Rohan**
See Skinner, June Margaret O'Grady

**O'Grady, Sean** 1959?-
*American boxer*
* [The] Bubblegum Bomber
* [The] Green Machine

**O'Grady, Standish James**
1846-1928 [SFL, WGT]
*Irish author*
* Clive, Arthur
* Netterville, Luke

**O'Grady, Tony**
See Clemens, Brian Horace

**Ogrodowski, Ambrose Francis**
1912-1956 [BE]
*American baseball player*
* Ogrodowski, Brusie

**Ogrodowski, Brusie**
See Ogrodowski, Ambrose Francis

**Ogunseye, Obalumi**
See Garrett, Irving

**Ogus, Joyce** 1932- [TR]
*British actress and dancer*
* Blair, Joyce

**Ogus, Lionel** 1931- [TR]
*Canadian actor, dancer, choreographer*
* Blair, Lionel

**O'Gwynn, James** 20th c.   [ECM]
*American country-western performer*
* [The] Smiling Irishman

**Oh Gran, Gilbert**
See  Masso, Justo

**Oh Red Washington**
See  Washington, George

**Oh Yeah Rogers**
See  Aiverum, Timothy Louis

**O'Hair, Iva N. Smith** 20th c.
[NAA]
*American poet*
* O'Hair, Nolanne

**O'Hair, Nolanne**
See  O'Hair, Iva N. Smith

**Ohanian, Krekor** 1925-  [FC, IPA]
*American actor*
* Connors, Michael

**O'Hanlon, George**
See  Rice, George

**O'Hanlon, George Samuel**
1874-1946  [SC]
*American actor*
* [The] King of Burlesque
* Rice, Sam

**O'Hanlon, Jacklyn**
See  Meek, Jacklyn O'Hanlon

**O'Hanlon, John** 19th c.  [PA]
*Author*
* Lageniensis

**O'Hannegan, Larry**
See  Harris, Lee O.

**O'Hanrahan, Kieron** 1925-  [FC]
*Irish actor*
* Moore, Kieron

**O'Hara, Barnes**
See  Banim, Michael, Jr.

**O'Hara, Dale**
See  Gillese, John Patrick

**O'Hara, David**
See  Snell, Roy Judson

**O'Hara, James Francis** 1875-1954
[BE]
*American baseball player*
* O'Hara, Kid

**O'Hara, John [Henry]** 1905-1970
[CA]
*American author*
* Delaney, Franey

**O'Hara, Joy**
See  Farquar, Agnes Stephens

**O'Hara, Kareen**
See  Careddu, Stefania

**O'Hara, Kenneth**
See  Walton, Bryce

**O'Hara, Kevin**
See  Cumberland, Marten

**O'Hara, Kid**
See  O'Hara, James Francis

**O'Hara, Mary**
See  Alsop, Mary O'Hara

**O'Hara, Maureen**
See  Fitzsimmons [or Fitzsimons?],
Maureen

**O'Hara, Scott** [house pseudonym]
See  MacDonald, John D[ann]

**Ohara, Yutaka** 1908-  [IAW]
*Japanese author*
* Houn

**O'Harris, Pixie**
See  Pratt, Rhona Olive

**O'Harro, Mike** 20th c.
*American nightclub owner*
* [The] Singles King of
  Washington

**O'Hearn, Donald Edwin** 1928-
[FHE]
*Canadian-born hockey player*
* O'Hearn, Nipper

**O'Hearn, Nipper**
See  O'Hearn, Donald Edwin

**O'Henry, Henry**
See  Dominguez Aragones,
Edmundo

**O'Herlihy, Eileen** 1922-  [BEW]
*Scottish-born actress*
* Herlie, Eileen

**O'Higgins, [Don] Ambrosio**
See  Higgins, Ambrose

**O'Higgins, Bernardo** 1778-1842
[WBD]
*Chilean soldier and statesman*
* [The] Liberator of Chile

**O'Higgins, Hyacinth Hazel**
1922?-1970  [EMT, FC]
*British actress and singer*
* Hazell, Hy

**[The] Ohio Gong**
See  Allen, William

**[The] Ohio Kid**
See  Lytle, Donald

**Ohira, Masayoshi** 1910-1980
*Japanese prime minister*
* [The] Bull
* Otochan [Daddy]

**Ohiyesa**
See  Eastman, Charles A[lexander]

**Ohl, Hans**
See  Kusenberg, Kurt

**Ohm, Peter** 1923-  [FC]
*British actor*
* Vaughan, Peter

**Ohnet, Georges**
See  Henot, Georges

**Ohon**
See  Barba, Harry

**Ohsawa, Georges**
See  Sakurazawa, Yukikazu

**Ohser, Erich** 1903-1944  [WECO]
*German cartoonist*
* Plauen, E. O.

**Oil Can Eddie**
See  Sadlowski, Edward

**Oil Can Lisciotti**
See  Lisciotti, Larry

**Ojeda, Chucho**
See  Ojeda, Jesus

**Ojeda, Jesus** 1892-1943  [SC]
*Mexican actor*
* Ojeda, Chucho

**Oka**
See  Kuzmowycz, Olha

**Okada, Hideki**
See  Glassco, John [Stinson]

**Oke, Richard**
See  Millett, Nigel Stansbury

**O'Keefe, Dennis**
See  Flanagan, Edward Vanes, Jr.

**O'Keefe, Joseph** 20th c.  [BLB]
*American underworld figure*
* O'Keefe, Specs

**O'Keefe, Lester** 1896-  [ASC]
*American composer and advertising
executive*
* Form, Tom

**O'Keefe, Specs**
See  O'Keefe, Joseph

**O'Kelly, Don**
See  Kelly, Donald Patrick

**O'Kelly, John J.** 20th c.  [WWL]
*Irish author*
* O Ceallaigh, Sean

**O'Kelly, Thomas** 20th c.  [WWL]
*Irish poet and author*
* O Ceallaigh, Tomas

**O'Key**
See  Radwanski, Pierre A[rthur]

**Oklahoma Bob Albright**
See  Albright, Bob

**Oklahoma Jack Clark**
See  Clark, Jim

**Oklahoma Peddler**
See  Gilles, Albert S[imeon], Sr.

**Oklahoma's Singing Cowboy**
See  Autry, [Orvon] Gene

**Okrie, Frank Anthony** 1896-1959
[BE]
*American baseball player*
* Okrie, Lefty

**Okrie, Lefty**
See  Okrie, Frank Anthony

**Okyo** 1733-1795  [WBD]
*Japanese painter*
* Maruyama Okyo

**Okypch, Walter Andrew** 1920-
[BE]
*American baseball player*
* Ockey, Footie
* Ockey, Walter Andrew

**Ol' Blue Eyes**
See  Sinatra, Francis Albert
[Frank]

**Ol' Cement Hands**
See  Caster, Richard

**Ol' Ironsides**
See  Tobin, James Anthony [Jim]

**Ol' Man River**
See  Wright, Archibald Lee

**Ol' Showboat**
See  Newsom, Norman Louis

**Olaf** 11th c.  [DNNS]
*King of Sweden*
* [The] Lap King

**Olaf** 13th c.  [HN]
*Poet*
* [The] White Poet

**Olaf Haraldsson**
See  Olaf II [or Olaus]

**Olaf Haraldsson**
See  Olaf III [or Olaus]

**Olaf Kyrre [The Quiet]**
See  Olaf III [or Olaus]

**Olaf Magnusson**
See  Olaf IV

**Olaf, Pierre**
See  Trivier, Pierre-Olaf

**Olaf Sitricson** ?- 981  [WBD]
*Danish king of Northumbria and
Dublin*
* [The] Red

**Olaf Tryggvesson**
See  Olaf I

**Olaf I** ?-1095  [WBD]
*King of Denmark*
* Hunger

**Olaf I** 969-1000  [WBD]
*King of Norway*
* Olaf Tryggvesson

**Olaf II [or Olaus]** 992-1030
[HN, WBD]
*King of Norway*
* [The] Fat
* Olaf Haraldsson
* [The] Saint
* Saint Olaf
* Skotkoenung [The Tax-King]

**Olaf III [or Olaus]** ?-1093
[FFF, RH, WBD]
*King of Norway*
* Olaf Haraldsson
* Olaf Kyrre [The Quiet]
* [The] Pacific

**Olaf IV** 1100?-1115  [WBD]
*King of Norway*
* Olaf Magnusson

**Olai, Georgius** 1598-1672
[HN, WBD]
*Swedish poet*
* [The] Father of Modern Swedish
  Poetry
* Stiernhielm [or Stjernhjelm],
  Georg

**Olander, Joan Lucille** 1933-
[FC, ITA, SW]
*American actress*
* Van Doren, Mamie

**O'Lanus, Corry**
See  Stanton, John

**O'Laoghaire, Liam**
See  O'Leary, Liam

**Olausson, Rune Erland** 1933-
[IAW]
*Swedish author*
* Alm, Monica

**Olbracht, Ivan**
See  Zeman, Kamil

**Olcott, Chancellor John**
1858?-1932  [BEW, WBD]
*American-born actor, singer,
songwriter*
* Olcott, Chauncey

**Olcott, Chauncey**
See  Olcott, Chancellor John

**Olcott, Sidney**
See  Alcott, John S.

**Olczewska, Maria**
See  Berchtenbreiter, Marie

[The] Old
See Gorm

[The] Old
See Haakon IV Haakonsson

Old Abe
See Lincoln, Abraham

Old Aches and Pains
See Appling, Lucius Benjamin

Old Actor
See Shelly, Mortimer M.

[The] Old Admiral
See Columbus, Christopher

Old Andy
See Johnson, Andrew

[An] Old Angler and Bibliopole
See Thomas, Boosey

[The] Old Arbitrator
See Klimm, William Joseph

[The] Old Ascraean
See Hesiod

Old Bachelor
See Curtis, George William

Old Bachelor
See Wirt, William

Old Bags
See Scott, John

Old Bags
See Vansittart, Nicholas

Old Beeswax
See Semmes, Raphael

Old Bill Miner
See Miner, William

Old Billy Gray
See Gray, William

Old Bird
See Clarke, Cecil

Old Blinky Howe
See Howe, Gordon [Gordie]

Old Blizzard
See Loring, William Wing

Old Blood and Guts
See Patton, George Smith, Jr.

Old Bonafide
See Louis XIV

Old Bones Brown
See Brown, Joe

Old Bones Morrall
See Morrall, Earl

Old Borax
See Dvorak, Antonin

Old Bory
See Beauregard, Pierre Gustave Toutant

Old Boy
See Blanchard, E. E.

Old Boy
See Hughes, Thomas

Old Brains
See Halleck, Henry Wager

Old Brown of Osawatomie
See Brown, John

Old Buck
See Buchanan, James

[The] Old Buddha
See Tzu Hsi [or Tze-hsi]

Old Buena Vista
See Taylor, Zachary

Old Bullion
See Benton, Thomas Hart

OLd Burchell
See Burritt, Elihu

Old Bushman
See Wheelwright, W.

Old Cabinet
See Gilder, Richard Watson

Old Cartman
See Lyon, Isaac S.

Old Celt
See Bottrell, W.

Old Chalk
See Chadwick, Henry

Old Chapultepec
See Scott, Winfield

Old Chatty Cheerful
See Martyn, William

Old Chickamauga
See Steedman, James B.

Old Chief
See Clay, Henry

Old, Chilly
See Old, Christopher Middleton

Old Chocolate
See Williams, Feab. S.

Old, Christopher Middleton 1948-
[DC]
British cricketer
* Old, Chilly

Old Chrysanthemum
See Bernal, John Desmond

Old Colonel Draper
See Draper, T. Waln-Morgan

Old Colony
See Zabriskie, F. N.

Old Coonskin Davis
See Davis, Curt[is Benton]

Old Corporal
See Coan, Leander S.

[The] Old Country Boy
See O'Dell, Mac

Old Creepy Karpis
See Karpowicz, Alvin

Old Dad
See Crosby, Harry Lillis

Old Daph
See Davenant, [Sir] William

Old Denmark
See Febiger, Christian

[The] Old Dessauer
See Leopold I

[The] Old Dog
See Bartlett, Frederick Orin

[The] Old Dog
See Cunnington, Charles Leslie

Old Dog Ritter
See Ritter, Louis Elmer

Old Douro
See Wellesley, Arthur

Old Dreadnought
See Boscawen, Edward

Old Eagle Eye
See Beckley, Jacob Peter [Jake]

Old Ebony
See Blackwood, William

Old Eight to Seven
See Hayes, Rutherford Birchard

[An] Old Farmer
See Lowell, John

Old Father Ephraim
See Poget [or Pagit?], Ephraim

Old Folks Arntzen
See Arntzen, Orie Edgar

Old Folks Kinder
See Kinder, Ellis Raymond

Old Folks Pillette
See Pillette, Herman

[The] Old Fox
See Griffith, Clark Calvin

[The] Old Fox
See Soult, Nicolas Jean de Dieu

[The] Old Fox
See Washington, George

[The] Old Fox of the Balkans
See Pasic, Nikola

Old Fritz
See Frederick II

Old George
See Monk, George [Duke of Albemarle]

Old Glorious
See William III

Old Glory
See Burdett, [Sir] Francis

Old Goldy
See Goldwater, Barry [Morris]

Old Granddad Kinder
See Kinder, Ellis Raymond

Old Granny
See Harrison, William Henry

Old Gravel Voice
See Harmon, Ernest Nason

Old Gravity
See Thurlow, Edward [First Baron Thurlow]

[The] Old Gray Fox
See Case, Everett

Old Grimes
See Greene, Albert Gorton

Old Groaner
See Crosby, Harry Lillis

[The] Old Groaner
See Reeve, Edward H. [Ted]

Old Grog
See Vernon, Edward

Old Grover
See Cleveland, [Stephen] Grover

Old Harlo
See Abbott, Charles Edwards

Old Harry
See Henry VIII

Old Harve Bailey
See Bailey, Harvey

[The] Old Hero
See Jackson, Andrew

Old Hewson the Cobbler
See Hewson, John

Old Hickory
See Jackson, Andrew

[The] Old Home Remedy
See Barger, Eros Bolivar

Old Horace
See Walpole, Horatio [First Baron Walpole of Wolterton]

Old Hoss Ardner
See Ardner, Joseph A. [Joe]

Old Hoss Radbourn
See Radbourn, Charles Gardner

Old Hoss Stephenson
See Stephenson, Jackson Riggs

Old Hoss Twineham
See Twineham, Arthur W.

Old Humphrey
See Mogridge, George

Old Hurrygraph
See Robinson, James A.

Old Hutch
See Hutchinson, Benjamin Peters

Old Indestructible Hein
See Hein, Mel

Old Iron Head
See Johnson, Roy

Old Iron Pants
See Cronkite, Walter

Old Iron Pants
See Meyer, Leo Robert

Old Jack
See Jackson, Thomas Jonathan

Old Jacob
See Tonson, Jacob

[That] Old Jew of Eton
See Rous [or Rowse], Francis

Old Jock
See Wilson, John

Old Joe Clark
See Clark, Manuel D., Jr.

Old, John M.
See Bava, Mario

Old Kinderhook
See Van Buren, Martin

[The] Old Lamplighter
See Blake, Hector

Old Leatherface
See Chennault, Claire Lee

[The] Old Lefthander
See Sanders, Joe

Old Lev Saltonstall
See Saltonstall, Leverett

**[The] Old Lion**
See Roosevelt, Theodore [Teddy]

**Old Mac McDonnell**
See McDonnell, James Smith

**[An] Old Maid**
See Phillips, Miss

**[The] Old Man**
See Broz, Josip

**[The] Old Man**
See Fangio, Juan Manuel

**[The] Old Man**
See Fry, Bob

**[The] Old Man**
See Grace, William Gilbert

**[An] Old Man**
See Head, [Sir] Francis Bond

**[The] Old Man**
See Travis, Walter J.

**Old Man Eloquent**
See Adams, John Quincy

**[The] Old Man Eloquent**
See Coleridge, Samuel Taylor

**[The] Old Man Eloquent**
See Gladstone, William Ewart

**[The] Old Man Eloquent**
See Isocrates

**[The] Old Man Eloquent**
See Socrates

**[That] Old Man Eloquent**
See Wilson, John

**Old Man Oden**
See Oden, James Burke [Jimmy]

**[The] Old Man of the Mountain**
See Hassan-ben-Sabah

**[The] Old Man of the Mountain**
See Roberts, Floyd

**Old Man of the Mountain**
See Rogers, Nathaniel P.

**[The] Old Man of the Mountain**
See Timmis, Brian

**Old Man River**
See Boros, Julius Nicholas

**[The] Old Man River**
See Skelton, Jimmy

**[The] Old Master**
See Gaines, Joseph

**[The] Old Master**
See Oldfield, Berna Eli

**Old Mathematics**
See Humphreys, Andrew Atkinson

**Old Merry**
See Hodder, Edwin

**[An] Old Modern**
See Pegge, Samuel

**Old Morality**
See Smith, William Henry

**[The] Old Mortality in His Line**
See Upcott, William

**[The] Old Mortality of Pictures**
See Vertue, George

**Old Mose Grove**
See Grove, Robert Moses

**Old Mother Hancock**
See Hancock, John

**Old Nick**
See Forgues, Paul Emile Durand

**Old 98**
See Harmon, Thomas D.

**Old Noll**
See Cromwell, Oliver

**Old Noll's Fiddler**
See L'Estrange, [Sir] Roger

**Old Pam**
See Temple, Henry John

**Old Pard**
See Ballou, Noble Winfield

**Old Patch**
See Price, Charles

**Old Pete**
See Longstreet, James

**Old Pete Alexander**
See Alexander, Grover Cleveland

**Old Peveril**
See Scott, [Sir] Walter

**Old Poison Stewart**
See Stewart, Nelson

**Old Possum**
See Eliot, Thomas Stearns

**[The] Old Pretender**
See Stuart, James Francis Edward

**Old Private**
See Gerrish, T.

**[The] Old Professor**
See Stengel, Charles Dillon

**[The] Old Public Functionary**
See Buchanan, James

**Old Put**
See Putnam, Israel

**Old Q**
See Douglas, William

**Old Reliable**
See Henrich, Thomas David

**Old Reliable**
See Start, Joseph

**Old Reliable**
See Thomas, George Henry

**Old Robin**
See Devereux, Robert [Third Earl of Essex]

**[The] Old Roman**
See Comiskey, Charles Albert

**[The] Old Roman**
See Thurman, Allen Granbery

**Old Rosey**
See Rosecrans, William Starke

**Old Rough and Ready**
See Taylor, Zachary

**Old Rowley**
See Charles II

**Old Saddlebags**
See McDonald, Joseph E.

**Old Sailor**
See Barker, Matthew Henry

**Old Sailor**
See Coffin, Roland F.

**Old Sarah**
See Churchill, Sarah Jennings

**Old Sarge Street**
See Street, Charles Evard

**Old Sarum**
See Salisbury, Marchioness of

**[The] Old Satyr**
See De Marguetel de Saint-Denis, Charles

**Old Scout**
See Merrill, H. R.

**[The] Old Settler**
See Lyman, Albert Robison

**Old 77**
See Grange, Harold E.

**[The] Old Shah**
See Pahlavi, Reza

**[The] Old Shekarry**
See Leveson, Henry Astbury

**[The] Old Shoe**
See Wilson, Thornton Arnold

**Old Shoes Shoemaker**
See Shoemaker, William

**Old Si**
See Small, Samuel White

**Old Sink and Swim**
See Adams, John

**Old Sleuth**
See Halsey, Harlan Page

**[An] Old Soldier**
See Butler, [Sir] William Francis

**Old Soupbone Hubbell**
See Hubbell, Carl Owen

**Old South**
See Austin, Benjamin

**Old Stager**
See Field, Munsell B.

**Old Stars**
See Mitchel, Ormsby McKnight

**Old Stay Maker**
See Thomson, Alexander

**Old Steady**
See Steedman, James B.

**Old Stone**
See Stone, Henry

**Old Stone Hammer**
See Metcalfe, Thomas

**Old Stonewall Collins**
See Collins, George M.

**Old Straws**
See Field, Joseph M.

**Old Stubblebeard Grimes**
See Grimes, Burleigh Arland

**Old Subtlety**
See Fiennes, William [First Viscount Saye and Sele]

**Old Tecumseh**
See Sherman, William Tecumseh

**Old Thad**
See Stevens, Thaddeus

**Old Three Stars**
See Grant, Hiram Ulysses

**Old Times**
See Davis, James D.

**Old Tip**
See Harrison, William Henry

**Old Tippecanoe**
See Harrison, William Henry

**Old To-morrow**
See Macdonald, [Sir] John Alexander

**Old Tom Morris**
See Morris, Thomas, Sr.

**Old Tomato Face**
See Hartnett, Charles Leo

**Old Tommy**
See Devin, Thomas C.

**Old True Blue**
See Richardson, Abram [or Arthur?] Harding

**Old 'Un**
See Durivage, Francis Alexander

**Old United States**
See Grant, Hiram Ulysses

**Old Usufruct**
See Tilden, Samuel Jones

**Old Veto**
See Cleveland, [Stephen] Grover

**Old Veto**
See Johnson, Andrew

**Old Vicar**
See Warter, John Wood

**Old War-Horse**
See Devin, Thomas C.

**[The] Old Wheel Horse of Democracy**
See Medary, Samuel

**Old Wigs**
See Dunstan, [Sir] Jeffrey

**[The] Old Wizard**
See Carver, George Washington

**[The] Old Woman in the Red Cap**
See Pabor, Charles Henry

**Old Wrinkle-Boots**
See Willis, Browne

**[The] Old Yorkshire Turfman**
See Herbert, Henry William

**Old Zach**
See Buchanan, James

**Old Zach**
See Taylor, Zachary

**Oldacre, Cedric, of Saxe Normanby**
See Warter, John Wood

**Oldboy, Felix**
See Mines, John Flavel

**Oldbug, Jonathan**
See Withington, Leonard

**Oldcastle, Humphrey**
See St. John, Henry

**Oldcastle, John**
See Meynell, Wilfrid

Oldcastle, [Sir] John 1360?-1417
[FFF, HN, SN]
*Leader of religious sect in England*
* [The] Father of Political
   Dissenters
* [The] Good Lord Cobham

Oldeboerrigter, Melle Johannes
1908-1976   [CAR]
*Dutch painter*
* Melle

Olden, Charles 1909?-   [BMH, FC]
*British entertainer*
* Nedlo the Gypsy Violinist
* Neek, Hugh
* Ray, Ted

Olden, Georg 1921-   [IBW]
*American graphic artist*
* [The] Dean of TV Art Directors

Oldest Inspector
*See* Bently, J.

Oldfeld, Peter [joint pseudonym with
P. Jacobsson]
*See* Bartlett, Vernon

Oldfeld, Peter, [joint pseudonym
with Vernon Bartlett]
*See* Jacobsson, P.

Oldfield, Anna 1683-1730   [RH]
*British actress*
* Miss Nancy
* Narcissa

Oldfield, Barney
*See* Oldfield, Berna Eli

Oldfield, Berna Eli 1878-1946
[AS, FC]
*American auto racer*
* [The] Old Master
* Oldfield, Barney

Oldfield, Claude Houghton
1889-1961   [LAO, LC, TC]
*British author*
* Houghton, Claude

Oldham, Derek
*See* Oldham, John Stephens

Oldham, Esso
*See* Oldham, Stephen

Oldham, Hugh R.
*See* Whitford, Joan

Oldham, John 1653-1683
[DEL, FFF, PA]
*British poet*
* Astrophel
* [The] English Juvenal
* Grubendol
* [The] Juvenal of England

Oldham, John Cyrus 1893-1961
[BE, BN]
*American baseball player*
* Oldham, Red
* Oldham, Rube

Oldham, John Stephens 1893-1968
[SC]
*British actor and opera singer*
* Oldham, Derek

Oldham of Greystones, Dr.
*See* Henry, Caleb Sprague

Oldham, Red
*See* Oldham, John Cyrus

Oldham, Rube
*See* Oldham, John Cyrus

Oldham, Stephen 1948-   [DC]
*British cricketer*
* Oldham, Esso

Oldland, Lilian 1905-   [F2]
*Actress*
* Newland, Mary

Oldmeadow, E. J.
*See* Oldmeadow, Ernest James

Oldmeadow, Ernest James
1867-1949   [LC]
*British author*
* Oldmeadow, E. J.

Oldring, Reuben Henry 1884-1961
[BE]
*American baseball player*
* Oldring, Rube

Oldring, Rube
*See* Oldring, Reuben Henry

Oldschool, Oliver
*See* Dennie, Joseph

Oldschool, Oliver
*See* Sargent, Nathan

Oldstyle, Jonathan
*See* Irving, Washington

Oldys, Alexander   [SN]
*British poet*
* [The] English Scarron
* [The] Little Poet

Oldys, Francis
*See* Chalmers, George

Oldys, William 1696-1761   [PA]
*Author*
* Hayward, Thomas

Ole Bootnose Abel
*See* Abel, Sid[ney Gerald]

Ole-Luk-Oie [Olaf Shut-Eye]
*See* Swinton, [Sir] Ernest Dunlop

Olearius
*See* Von Oleuschtaeger, Johann
Daniel

O'Leary, Big Jim
*See* O'Leary, Jim

O'Leary, Chester F.
*See* Kuehnelt-Leddihn, Erik
[Ritter Von]

O'Leary, Daniel 1856-1922   [BE]
*American baseball player*
* O'Leary, Hustling Dan

O'Leary, Hustling Dan
*See* O'Leary, Daniel

O'Leary, Jim 20th c.   [BLB]
*American underworld figure*
* O'Leary, Big Jim

O'Leary, John
*See* Panzram, Carl

O'Leary, Liam 1910-   [WD]
*Irish author*
* O'Laoghaire, Liam

O'Leary, Pat
*See* Guerisse, Albert

O'Leary, Peter 20th c.   [WWL]
*Irish author*
* O Laoghaire, Peadar

Oleastro, Hieronimo ?-1563   [PA]
*Author*
* De Azambuya

Olemy, P. T.
*See* Baker, George

Olenius, Elsa Victoria 1896-   [IAW]
*Swedish author*
* Bergius, Elsa Britt

Oleson, John 1899-   [FC]
*Canadian-born actor*
* Qualen, John

Olga
*See* Erteszek, Olga

Olga
*See* Phillips, Olga Somech

Olguin Rangel, Eduardo 1918-
[GS]
*Mexican bullfighter*
* [El] Fantasma [The Ghost]

O'Liathain, Sesu
*See* Lyons, John Maguire

[The] Oliday King
*See* Butlin, [Sir] Billy

O'Lincoln, Robert
*See* Mason, George C.

Oliphant, Carolina [Baroness Nairne]
1766-1845   [DNNS, SN]
*Scottish poet*
* [The] Flower of Strathearn

Oliphant, Elmer Q. 1892?-
[BB, FB]
*American basketball and football
player*
* Oliphant, Ollie

Oliphant, Ollie
*See* Oliphant, Elmer Q.

Oliphant, William 1906-   [PMJ]
*American bandleader*
* Osborne, Will

Olitski, Jules
*See* Demikovosky, Jevel

Oliva, Antonio Pedro 1940-
[BE, WWB]
*Cuban-born baseball player*
* Oliva, Tony

Oliva, Tony
*See* Oliva, Antonio Pedro

Olivares, Conde de
*See* De Guzman, Gaspar [Duque
de Sanlucar]

Olive, Martin 1958-   [DC]
*British cricketer*
* Olive, Palm

Olive, May
*See* Wheeler, Mrs. S. T.

Olive, Palm
*See* Olive, Martin

Olive-Branch, [Rev] Simon
*See* Roberts, William

Olive Rodas, Diego 1872-1950
[GS]
*Spanish bullfighter*
* Morenito de Algeciras [Little
   Dark One from Algeciras]

Oliven, Fritz 1874- ?   [LAO]
*German author*
* Rideamus

Oliver
*See* Gibbs, Oliver

Oliver
*See* Swofford, William Oliver

Oliver, Al[bert, Jr.] 1946-   [BE, PB]
*American baseball player*
* Scoop, Mr.

Oliver, Amy Roberta [Ruck] 1878-
?   [AW, CA, LAO]
*British author*
* Ruck, Berta

Oliver, C. W.
*See* Oliver, Charles William

Oliver, Chad
*See* Oliver, Symes Chadwick

Oliver, Charles William 1911-
[ART]
*American-born painter*
* Oliver, C. W.

Oliver, Clarence
*See* LaGrone, Oliver

Oliver, Dean 20th c.   [GW]
*American rodeo performer*
* Oliver, Wope

Oliver, Dick
*See* Barrett, Tracey Souter

Oliver, Dora Dana 1881- ?   [NAA]
*American writer*
* Shipman, Elydia Foss

Oliver, Dude
*See* Oliver, Philip Robert

Oliver, Edith
*See* Goldsmith, Edith

Oliver, Edna May
*See* Nutter, Edna May Cox-Oliver

Oliver, Edward S. 1916?-1961
[AS, EG, GF]
*American golfer*
* Oliver, Porky

Oliver, Eugene   [FFF]
*Entertainer*
* Revillo, Eugene

Oliver, Gail
*See* Scott, Marian [Gallagher]

Oliver, Gay
*See* Owen, Garnet

Oliver, George
*See* Onions, [George] Oliver

Oliver, Gertrude Kent 20th c.
[MBF]
*British author*
* Carr, Kent

Oliver, Harold 1898-   [FHE]
*Canadian-born hockey player*
* Oliver, Harry

Oliver, Harry
*See* Oliver, Harold

Oliver, Henry Kemble
*See* Oliver, Thomas Henry

Oliver, Hugh ?-1569   [PA]
*Author*
* Witweyke

Oliver, Jane
*See* Rees, Helen Christina Easson
[Evans]

Oliver, John Rathbone 1872-1943
[TC1]
*Author*
* Roland, John

**Oliver, Joseph** 1885-1938
[BBD, DAM, IBW]
*American jazz musician*
* Oliver, King
* Papa Joe

**Oliver, Kine**
*See* Alexander, Alger

**Oliver, King**
*See* Oliver, Joseph

**Oliver, Mark**
*See* Tyler-Whittle, Michael Sidney

**Oliver, Melvin James** 1910-
[DAM, EJ, IBW]
*American jazz musician*
* [The] Charming Vocalist
* Oliver, Sy

**Oliver, Mert**
*See* Oliver, Merton A.

**Oliver, Merton A.** 1917-    [EJ]
*American jazz musician*
* Oliver, Mert

**Oliver, Nathaniel** 1940-    [BE, SMG]
*American baseball player*
* Oliver, Pee Wee

**Oliver, Olly**
*See* Oliver, Philip Robert

**Oliver, Owen**
*See* Flynn, [Sir] J. Albert

**Oliver, Pee Wee**
*See* Oliver, Nathaniel

**Oliver, Pen**
*See* Thompson, [Sir] Henry

**Oliver, Peter**
*See* Oliver, William Pynchon

**Oliver, Philip Robert** 1956-    [DC]
*British cricketer*
* Oliver, Dude
* Oliver, Olly

**Oliver, Porky**
*See* Oliver, Edward S.

**Oliver, Rebel**
*See* Oliver, Thomas Noble [Tom]

**Oliver, Rochelle**
*See* Olshever, Rochelle

**Oliver, Stephen**
*See* Chatto, William Andrew

**Oliver, Susan**
*See* Gercke, Charlotte

**Oliver, Sy**
*See* Oliver, Melvin James

**Oliver, Symes Chadwick** 1928-
[SF]
*American anthropologist and author*
* Oliver, Chad

**Oliver, Thelma** 20th c.    [IBW]
*Yoga disciple*
* Kaur, Krishna

**Oliver, Thomas Henry** 1800-1885
[WBD]
*American educator, composer,
industrialist*
* Oliver, Henry Kemble

**Oliver, Thomas Noble [Tom]** 1903-
[BE]
*American baseball player*
* Oliver, Rebel

**Oliver, Tim**
*See* Wilkins, [Robert] Tim[othy]

**Oliver, Vic**
*See* Samek, Viktor Oliver

**Oliver, William Pynchon**
1821-1855    [PA]
*Author*
* Oliver, Peter

**Oliver, Wope**
*See* Oliver, Dean

**Oliveras, Frank**
*See* Pesce, Franco

**Oliveria, Flash**
*See* Oliveria, Miranda

**Oliveria, Miranda** 20th c.    [AES]
*Soccer player*
* Oliveria, Flash

**Olivero, Magda**
*See* Olivero, Maria Maddalena

**Olivero, Maria Maddalena** 1916-
[OP]
*Italian opera singer*
* Olivero, Magda

**Oliver's Fiddler**
*See* L'Estrange, [Sir] Roger

**Olivia**
*See* Briggs, Emily Edson

**Olivier, Jacques**
*See* Guyonnet, Jacques

**Olivier le Dain [or le Daim]**
*See* Necker, Olivier

**Olivier le Diable**
*See* Necker, Olivier

**Olivo, Chi Chi**
*See* Olivo, Federico Emilio

**Olivo, Federico Emilio** 1928-    [BE]
*Dominican-born baseball player*
* Olivo, Chi Chi

**Ollapod**
*See* Clark, Willis Gaylord

**Ollie Papa**
*See* Thomas, Charles

**Olliver, Tom**
*See* Graydon, William Murray

**Olmedo y Vazquez, Antonio**
1874-1901    [GS]
*Spanish bullfighter*
* Valentin

**Olmo, Chico**
*See* Olmo, Luis Francisco
Rodriguez

**Olmo, Jibaro**
*See* Olmo, Luis Francisco
Rodriguez

**Olmo, Luis Francisco Rodriguez**
1919-    [BE, BN]
*Puerto Rican-born baseball player*
* Olmo, Chico
* Olmo, Jibaro

**Olmsted, Charlotte**
*See* Kursh, Charlotte Olmsted

**Olney, Ross Robert** 1929-    [IAW]
*American author*
* Wilson, Pat

**Olofsson, Nils Phillip** 1906?-1974
[B10]
*American wrestler*
* [The] Swedish Angel

**O'London, John**
*See* Whitten, Wilfred

**O'Loughlin, Louise T.**    [FFF]
*Entertainer*
* Moore, Elsie

**Olsen, Albert William** 1921-    [BE]
*American baseball player*
* Olsen, Ole

**Olsen, Alfred Johannes, Jr.**
1884-1956    [SF]
*American writer*
* Olsen, Bob

**Olsen, Arthur** 1894-    [BE]
*American baseball player*
* Olsen, Ole

**Olsen, Bob**
*See* Olsen, Alfred Johannes, Jr.

**Olsen, Bud**
*See* Olsen, Enoch

**Olsen, Cruster Aud** 1889-1938
[SC]
*American actor*
* Cruster, Aud

**Olsen, D. B.**
*See* Hitchens, Dolores [Birk]

**Olsen, Enoch** 20th c.    [SMG]
*American basketball player*
* Olsen, Bud

**Olsen, Harold G.** 1895-1953    [AS]
*American basketball player and
coach*
* Olsen, Ole

**Olsen, Ib Spang** 1921-    [CA, SAT]
*Danish-born author and illustrator*
* Detine, Padre [joint pseudonym
with Erik E. Frederiksen]

**Olsen, John Edward [Jack]** 1925-
[CA]
*American author*
* Rhoades, Jonathan

**Olsen, John Siguard** 1892-1963
[BEW, EMT, IPA]
*American entertainer*
* Olsen, Ole

**Olsen, Ole**
*See* Olsen, Albert William

**Olsen, Ole**
*See* Olsen, Arthur

**Olsen, Ole**
*See* Olsen, Harold G.

**Olsen, Ole**
*See* Olsen, John Siguard

**Olsen, Theodore Victor** 1932-
[CA, WD]
*American author*
* Stark, Joshua
* Storm, Christopher
* Willoughby, Cass

**Olsen, Thomas Carl Morrell** 1912-
[IAW]
*Scottish-born author*
* Morrell, John

**Olsen, Tracy** 1940-    [ITA]
*American actress*
* Carter, Tracy

**Olsheski, Gail** 1952-    [CA]
*Canadian author*
* Henley, Gail

**Olshever, Rochelle** 1937-    [BEW]
*American actress*
* Oliver, Rochelle

**Olson, Ann Margret** 1941-
[BDF, FC, HT]
*Swedish-born American actress*
* Ann Margret

**Olson, Bobo**
*See* Olson, Carl

**Olson, Carl** 1928-    [B10, RBE, WA]
*American boxer*
* Olson, Bobo

**Olson, Eugene E.** 1936-    [CA]
*American author*
* Steiger, Brad

**Olson, Helene Dean** 20th c.    [IAW]
*American writer*
* Betty

**Olson, Henry Russell** 1913-    [ASC]
*American musician*
* Russell, Henry

**Olson, Ivan Massie** 1885-1965
[AS, BE]
*American baseball player*
* Olson, Ivy

**Olson, Ivy**
*See* Olson, Ivan Massie

**Olson, Karl Arthur** 1930-    [BE]
*American baseball player*
* Olson, Ole

**Olson, Marv[in Clement]** 1907-
[BE]
*American baseball player*
* Olson, Sparky

**Olson, Ole**
*See* Olson, Karl Arthur

**Olson, Robert G.** 1913-    [ASC]
*American composer and educator*
* Roberts, Jon
* Rollins, Glenn

**Olson, Sparky**
*See* Olson, Marv[in Clement]

**Olson, Willis S.** 1930-    [BBH]
*American skier*
* Billy the Kid

**Olsson, Anna** 1866- ?    [NAA]
*Swedish-born author*
* Aina

**Olt, Arisztid**
*See* Blasko, Bela Lugosi

**Olugebefola, Ademola?**
*See* Thomas, Harold Alexander

**Olvera, Ernesto Hill**
*See* Olvera Gonzalez, Hermengildo

**Olvera Gonzalez, Hermengildo**
1937-1967    [SC]
*Mexican actor and musician*
* Olvera, Ernesto Hill

**Olvero Lara, Francisco** 1883-    [GS]
*Mexican bullfighter*
* Berrinches [Bad-Tempered]

**Olympia, Mr.**
*See* Zane, Frank

**Oma, Lee**
*See* Czjewski, Frank

**O'Mahoney, Jacques** 1919-
[FC, ITA, SW]
*American actor*
* Mahoney, Jock

**O'Mahoney, Rich**
*See* Crozetti, Ruth G. Warner
[Lora]

**O'Mahoney, Thaddeus** [PA]
*Author*
* A. M.

**O'Mahony, C. K.** 1884- [WWL]
*British author*
* Ellis, Julian
* Kingston, Charles

**O'Mahony, Patrick**
*See* Mahony, Patrick

**O'Malley, Ellen**
*See* Jones, Ellen

**O'Malley, Frank** 1916-
[SFL, WGT]
*Author*
* O'Rourke, Frank

**O'Malley, J. Patrick**
*See* O'Malley, Patrick H., Jr.

**O'Malley, Kevin**
*See* Hossent, Harry

**O'Malley, Mary Dolling** [Sanders]
1889?-1974 [CA, LC, TC]
*British author*
* Bridge, Ann

**O'Malley, Michael** 20th c. [WWL]
*Irish author and editor*
* O Maille, Micheal

**O'Malley, Patrick H., Jr.**
1891-1966 [F1]
*Actor*
* O'Malley, J. Patrick

**Oman, Carola** [Mary Anima]
1897-1978 [CA]
*British author*
* Lenanton, Carola Mary Anima
Oman

**O'Mant, Hedley Percival Angelo**
1899-1955 [MBF]
*British author*
* Clifford, Martin [house
pseudonym]
* Conquest, Owen [house
pseudonym]
* Hawke, [Captain] Robert
* Owen, Hedley
* Richards, Frank [house
pseudonym]
* Scott, Hamilton
* Scott, Hedley

**Omar Khayyam** 11th c.
[DEP, DNNF]
*Persian poet*
* [The] Astronomer Poet
* [The] Great Tentmaker
* [The] King of Wisdom
* [The] Persian Horace

**Omar, the Magnificent**
*See* Kotkin, David

**Omar I** 581- 644
[DNNF, FFF, SN]
*Caliph of the Mussulman empire*
* [The] Commander of the Faithful
* [The] Emperor of Believers

**O'Mara, Pat**
*See* O'Mara, Timothy Joseph

**O'Mara, Timothy Joseph** 1901-
[NAA]
*British-born author*
* O'Mara, Pat

**Omari, Cuthbert Kashingo** 1936-
[IAW]
*Tanzanian sociologist and author*
* Manne, Macho
* Mbali, Ona

**Omchery**
*See* Pillai, Narayana Narayana

**O'Meara, Dermand** ?-1620 [PA]
*Author*
* Dermitius

**O'Meara, Kathleen** [PA]
*Author*
* Ramsay, Grace

**Omedy, Eugene**
*See* Roper, Neil Campbell
Ommanney

**Omega**
*See* Bradbury, Ray [Douglas]

**Omer** [or Omar] **Pasha**
*See* Lattas, Michael

**Omiccioli, Palmina** 1925-
[FC, WEF]
*Italian actress*
* Rossi-Drago, Eleonora

**Omichund**
*See* Amir Chand

**Ommanney, F. D.**
*See* Ommanney, Francis Downes

**Ommanney, Francis Downes** 1903-
[LC]
*British zoologist and author*
* Ommanney, F. D.

**[The] Omniscious Doctor**
*See* Agrippa, [Cornelius] Heinrich

**Omnium, Jacob**
*See* Higgins, Matthew James

**Omohundro, John** 1943- [SMG]
*American football trainer*
* Johnny O

**O'Moore, Barry**
*See* Yost, Herbert A.

**O'More, Peggy**
*See* Blocklinger, Peggy O'More

**O'More, Rory** 17th c. [WBD]
*Irish chieftain*
* Moore, Roger

**Omowale, Marina**
*See* Maxwell, Marina

**Ompteda, [Baron] Georg von**
1863-1931 [WBD]
*German author, poet, playwright*
* Egestorff, Georg

**Omsby, Waterman L., Jr.** 1834- ?
[PA]
*Author*
* O. Jr.

**On the Go**
*See* Steimer, Francis Alfred

**On The Spot Spooner**
*See* Spooner, Ed

**Onadipe, Kola**
*See* Onadipe, Nathaniel Kolawole

**Onadipe, Nathaniel Kolawole**
1922- [CA, TCC]
*Nigerian author*
* Kolon, Nita
* Onadipe, Kola

**O'Nair, Mairi**
*See* Evans, Constance May

**Onassis, Jacqueline Lee** [Bouvier]
[Kennedy] 1929-
*Widow of Greek tycoon A. Onassis
and American president J. Kennedy*
* Jackie O

**[The] Once and Future Prime
Minister**
*See* Soares, Mario

**Ondra, Anny**
*See* Ondrakova, Anny

**Ondrakova, Anny** 1903- [FC, OCF]
*Polish-born actress*
* Ondra, Anny

**One Arm Daily**
*See* Daily, Hugh Ignatius

**[The] One Armed Devil**
*See* Kearny, Philip

**One Armed John**
*See* Wrencher, John Thomas

**One Armed Phil**
*See* Kearny, Philip

**One Eye Babe**
*See* Philip, Joseph

**One Eye Dotson**
*See* Dotson, Clarence

**[The] One Eyed**
*See* Hermippus

**[The] One Eyed**
*See* Zisca, John

**One from the Plow**
*See* Mitchell, G.

**One Grand Schmidt**
*See* Schmidt, Ernest J.

**[The] 101st Senator**
*See* Mitchell, Clarence M., Jr.

**One Leg Norwood**
*See* Norwood, Sam

**[The] One Man Trio**
*See* Bonner, Weldon H. Philip

**One of No Party**
*See* Grant, James

**One of the Barclays**
*See* Otis, Mrs. Harrison Gray

**One of the Fancy**
*See* Moore, Thomas

**One of the Fancy**
*See* Taylor, F.

**One Play McAfee**
*See* McAfee, George A.

**One Round Tilden**
*See* Tilden, William Tatem, II

**One Who has Whistled at the Plow**
*See* Somerville, Alexander

**One Who is But an Attorney**
*See* Butt, George

**One Who is Really an Englishman**
*See* Smith, C. W.

**O'Neal, Blackie**
*See* O'Neal, Charles

**O'Neal, Charles** 1904?-
*American author*
* O'Neal, Blackie

**O'Neal, Ernie** [RBE]
*American boxer*
* O'Neal, Pope

**O'Neal, Oran Herbert** 1899- [BE]
*American baseball player*
* O'Neal, Skinny

**O'Neal, Pope**
*See* O'Neal, Ernie

**O'Neal, Skinny**
*See* O'Neal, Oran Herbert

**O'Neal, Zelma**
*See* Schroeder, Zelma

**O'Neddy, Philothie**
*See* Donday, Auguste Marie

**O'Neil, Barbour**
*See* Morris, Barboura

**O'Neil, Buck**
*See* O'Neil, John Jordan

**O'Neil, Dennis** 1939- [WECO]
*American cartoonist and editor*
* O'Shaugnessey, Sergius

**O'Neil, Eric**
*See* Barnum, W[illiam] Paul

**O'Neil, John Jordan** 1911- [MK]
*American baseball player*
* O'Neil, Buck

**O'Neil, Kerry**
*See* McIntyre, John T[homas]

**O'Neil, Nance**
*See* Lamson, Gertrude

**O'Neil, Nancy**
*See* Smith, Nancy

**O'Neil, Sally**
*See* Noonan, Virginia Louise

**O'Neil, Simon**
*See* Simonelli, Giovanni

**O'Neill, Archie**
*See* Henaghan, Jim

**O'Neill, Buck**
*See* O'Neill, Frank J.

**O'Neill, C. M.**
*See* Wilkes-Hunter, Richard

**O'Neill, Cabby**
*See* O'Neill, Leo C.

**O'Neill, Con** 1484?-1559? [WBD]
*First Earl of Tyrone*
* Bacach [The Lame]

**O'Neill, Daniel** [PA]
*Author*
* D. O. N.

**O'Neill, Dodie**
*See* O'Neill, Dolores

**O'Neill, Dolores** 1917- [PMJ]
*American singer*
* O'Neill, Dodie

**O'Neill, Egan**
*See* Linington, Elizabeth

**O'Neill, [Robert] Emmett** 1918-
[BE]
*American baseball player*
* O'Neill, Pinky

**O'Neill, Father**
See Dellacroce, Aniello

**O'Neill, Francis J.** 20th c.    [ALR]
*American baseball team owner*
* O'Neill, Steve

**O'Neill, Frank J.** 1875-1958
[AS, FB]
*American football player and coach*
* O'Neill, Buck

**O'Neill, Hattie**
See Russell, Mrs. R. F.

**O'Neill, James Beaton** 1913-   [CEI]
*Canadian-born hockey player*
* O'Neill, Peggy

**O'Neill, James Edward** 1858-1915
[AS, DGS, PB]
*Canadian-born baseball player*
* O'Neill, Tip

**O'Neill, James Keith** 1920-    [BF]
*British actor*
* Edwards, Jimmy

**O'Neill, Leo C.** 20th c.    [BBH]
*American basketball coach*
* O'Neill, Cabby

**O'Neill, Marie**
See Allgood, Marie

**O'Neill, [Sister] Mary Agatha**
1886-  [CAT]
*Canadian-born author*
* Gaule, Beatrice

**O'Neill, Michael Joyce** 1877-1959
[BE]
*Irish-born baseball player*
* Joyce, Mike

**O'Neill, Mickey**
See Dion, Clarence J. H.

**O'Neill, Moira**
See Skrine, Agnes

**O'Neill, Peaches**
See O'Neill, Philip Bernard

**O'Neill, Peggy**
See O'Neill, James Beaton

**O'Neill, Philip Bernard** 1879-1955
[BE]
*American baseball player*
* O'Neill, Peaches

**O'Neill, Pinky**
See O'Neill, [Robert] Emmett

**O'Neill, Rose Cecil** 1874- ?    [TC]
*American illustrator, poet, author*
* Latham, O'Neill

**O'Neill, Scott**
See Scott, Peg O'Neill

**O'Neill, Shane**
See O'Neill, William

**O'Neill, Steve**
See O'Neill, Francis J.

**O'Neill, Thomas** 1923-    [CEI]
*Canadian-born hockey player*
* O'Neill, Windy

**O'Neill, Thomas Philip** 1912-   [B10]
*American politician*
* O'Neill, Tip

**O'Neill, Tip**
See O'Neill, James Edward

**O'Neill, Tip**
See O'Neill, Thomas Philip

**O'Neill, William** 1927-    [CA]
*British-born educator and author*
* Og, Liam
* O'Neill, Shane
* O'Remus, Seamus

**O'Neill, Windy**
See O'Neill, Thomas

**O'nerva, L.**
See Madetoja, Onerva

**Onesimus**
See Courtier, P. L.

**Onetti, Juan Carlos** 1909-    [CLC]
*Uruguayan author*
* [The] Lone Wolf of Uruguayan
  Letters

**Onfroy de Breville, Jacques**
1858-1931   [WEC]
*French cartoonist and illustrator*
* Job

**Onghill**
See Creswell, John

**Onion Head**
See Pericles

**Onions, C. T.**
See Onions, Charles Talbut

**Onions, Charles Talbut** 1873-1965
[LC]
*British editor*
* Onions, C. T.

**Onions, [George] Oliver** 1873-1961
[CC, LC, TC]
*British author*
* Oliver, George

**Onis, Curly**
See Onis, Manuel Dominguez

**Onis, Manuel Dominguez** 1908-
[BE]
*American baseball player*
* Onis, Curly
* Onis, Ralph

**Onis, Ralph**
See Onis, Manuel Dominguez

**Onkel Adam**
See Wetterbergh, Carl Anton

**Onkel Danny**
See Turell, Dan

**Onkel Franz**
See Frisch, Frank Francis

**Onkel Tom**
See Hevesi, Ludwig

**Onkelos** 1st c.    [WBD]
*Author*
* [The] Proselyte

**Onlooker**
See Grange, Cyril

**Onlooker**
See Parsons, Edward

**[The] Only**
See Richter, Jean Paul Friedrich

**[The] Only Aretino**
See Accolti, Bernardo

**[The] Only Nolan**
See Nolan, Edward Sylvester

**O'Nolan, Brian**
See O'Nuallain, Brian

**Onorato, Glauco** 20th c.    [WF]
*Italian actor*
* Stark, Richard

**Onoto Watanna**
See Babcock, Winnifred Eaton

**Onsmonde, Alexandre** 1894-1972
[SC]
*Belgian actor and singer*
* Mondose, Alex

**O'Nuallain, Brian** 1911-1966
[AW, CAP, DIL]
*Irish author*
* Barnabas, Brother
* Doe, John James
* Knowall, George
* Na Gopaleen [or Na gCopaleen],
  Myles
* Nolan, Brian
* O'Blather, Count
* O'Brien, Flann
* O'Nolan, Brian

**Onwhyn, Thomas**    [PA]
*Author*
* Palette, Peter

**Onyx**
See Ward, Elizabeth Stuart
[Phelps]

**Oom Paul**
See Kruger, Stephanus Johannes

**Oom Paul Derringer**
See Derringer, Paul

**Oom Paul Krueger**
See Krueger, Arthur William

**[The] Oomph Girl**
See Sheridan, Clara Lou

**Oosterman, Gordon** 1927-    [CA]
*American educator and author*
* Eastman, G. Don

**O'Pake**
See Mallison, William M.

**O'Pake, Mr.**
See Beckner, S. W. E.

**Opatoshu, David**
See Opatovsky, David

**Opatoshu, Joseph**
See Opatovsky, Joseph

**Opatovsky, David** 1918-    [TR]
*American actor*
* Opatoshu, David

**Opatovsky, Joseph** 1886-1954
[EWL]
*Polish-born author*
* Opatoshu, Joseph

**Opdycke, John Baker** 1878- ?
[ALY]
*American author*
* Opdyke, Oliver

**Opdyke, Oliver**
See Opdycke, John Baker

**Opdyke, [Doctor] Underhill**
See Tyler, Royal

**Openshaw, G. H.** 20th c.    [MBF]
*British author*
* Gale, John

**Openshaw, G. H.** (Continued)
* Shaw, Dick
* Shaw, Justin
* Sterne, Duncan

**[An] Opera Goer**
See Mitchell, Donald Grant

**Ophuls, Marcel**
See Oppenheimer, Marcel

**Ophuls, Max**
See Oppenheimer, Max

**Opido, Helena** 1844-1909    [BEW]
*Polish-born actress*
* Modjeska [or Modrzejewska],
  Helena

**Opie, John** 1761-1807
[DEP, FFF, SN]
*British painter*
* [The] Cornish Wonder

**Opimius**
See Fitzhugh, William Henry

**Opitz, Martin** 1597-1639
[RH, SN, WBD]
*German author and poet*
* [The] Beau Brummel of
  Language
* [The] Dryden of Germany
* [The] Father of Modern German
  Poetry
* Opitz von Boberfeld
* [The] Restorer of German Poetry

**Opitz von Boberfeld**
See Opitz, Martin

**Opp, Francis**
See Oppenheimer, Francis J.

**Oppenheim, E[dward] Phillips**
1866-1946    [CC, EMD, WW]
*British author*
* Partridge, Anthony

**Oppenheim, Jill** 1940-
[FC, HT, SW]
*American actress*
* St. John, Jill

**Oppenheim, Joel Lester** 1930-
[DLE]
*American poet*
* Aquarius

**Oppenheimer, Erika**
See Fromm, Erika

**Oppenheimer, Francis J.** 1881- ?
[NAA]
*American author*
* Opp, Francis

**Oppenheimer, J[ulius] Robert**
1904-1967
*American physicist*
* [The] Father of the A-Bomb

**Oppenheimer, Marcel** 1927-    [OCF]
*German-born director*
* Ophuls, Marcel

**Oppenheimer, Max** 1902-1957
[BDF, FC, FD]
*German director*
* Ophuls, Max

**Opper, Adolf** 1825-1903    [JL]
*Bohemian-born journalist*
* De Blowitz, Henri

**OPS**
See Rabago, Andres

Optic, Oliver [joint pseudonym with Edward L. Stratemeyer]
See Adams, William Taylor

Optic, Oliver [joint pseudonym with William Taylor Adams]
See Stratemeyer, Edward L.

Optimus, Doctor
See De Bulhoes, Fernando

O'Quill, Maurice
See Denslow, Martin Van Buren

O'Quill, Scarlett
See Mossman, Dow

O'Quinn, Vithaldas H.
See Santesson, Hans Stefan

Oracle
See Pearce, Ethel Katherine

[The] Oracle of Delft
See Grotius, Hugo

[The] Oracle of Denmark
See Bernstorff, Johann Hartwig Ernst von

[The] Oracle of France
See Bernard of Clairvaux

[The] Oracle of Good-Sense
See Malherbe, Francois de

[The] Oracle of Law
See Coke, [Sir] Edward

[The] Oracle of the Church
See Bernard of Clairvaux

[L']Oracolo delle Battaglie
See Falcone, Aniello

Orage, A. R.
See Orage, Alfred Richard

Orage, Alfred Richard 1873-1934 [LC]
British editor, lecturer, author
* Orage, A. R.

Oram, John
See Thomas, Jack

Oran
See Otis, F. N.

O'Randa, Jack
See Stone, Ena Margaret

Orange, Clyde
See Orange, Walter

Orange Juice
See Simpson, Orenthal James

Orange, Walter 1947- [RO2]
American musician
* Orange, Clyde

Oraquill
See Bornemann, Mary

[The] Orator
See O'Rourke, James Henry

Orator Jim O'Rourke
See O'Rourke, James Henry

[The] Orator of Free-Dirt
See Julian, George W.

[The] Orator of Nature
See Henry, Patrick

[The] Orator of the Human Race
See Du Val-de-Grace, Jean [or Johann] Baptiste

Orb, Clay
See Conrow, Herbert

Orbes, Marceline 1873-1927 [BEW]
Spanish-born clown
* Marceline

Orbis, Victor
See Powell-Smith, Vincent [Walter Francis]

Orbison, Keck [joint pseudonym with Olive Orbison]
See Keck, Maud

Orbison, Keck [joint pseudonym with Maud Keck]
See Orbison, Olive

Orbison, Olive 20th c. [WW]
Author
* Orbison, Keck [joint pseudonym with Maud Keck]

Orcagna
See Di Cione, Andrea

Orchard, Eliza
See Connor, Mrs. E. A.

[The] Orchid
See Marcos, Imelda

[The] Orchid Man
See Carpentier, Georges

[The] Orchid of the Screen
See Griffith, Corinne

Orczy, Baroness
See Barstow, Emma Magdalena Rosalina Marie Josepha Barbara

Ord, Robert
See Ostlere, Edith

Ordenana, Antonio Rodriguez 1920- [BE]
Cuban-born baseball player
* Ordenana, Tony

Ordenana, Tony
See Ordenana, Antonio Rodriguez

Ordinatissimus, Doctor
See Bassol, John

Ordonez, Valeriano 1924- [IAW]
Spanish author and poet
* Is-Orval

Ordonez y Aguilera, Cayetano 1904-1961 [GS]
Spanish bullfighter
* Nino de La Palma [Boy from La Palma]

Ordunez, E. A. 20th c. [GW]
Rodeo performer
* Ordunez, Yaqui

Ordunez, Yaqui
See Ordunez, E. A.

Ordway, Roger
See Pauker, John

Oreco
See Rodrigues Martins, Waldemar

O'Regan, Katherine
See Melville, Kathleen

O'Reilly, Jack 20th c.
American sportscaster
* O'Reilly, Legs

O'Reilly, Legs
See O'Reilly, Jack

O'Reilly, [Private] Miles
See Halpine, Charles Graham

O'Reilly, Montagu
See Andrews, Wayne

O'Reilly, Navan
See Franks, Tom

O'Reilly, Tiger
See O'Reilly, William Joseph

O'Reilly, William Joseph 1905- [OCS]
Australian cricketer
* O'Reilly, Tiger

O'Rell, Max
See Blouet, Paul

O'Remus, Seamus
See O'Neill, William

Orenburgsky, Sergey Ivanovich
See Gusev, Sergey Ivanovich

Oreshnik, A. F.
See Nussbaum, Al[bert F.]

[An] Orestes of Exile
See Stael, Anne Louise Germaine de

Orfebre Tapatio
See Ortiz Puga, Jose

Orga, Ates
See D'Arcy-Orga, Ates

Orga, Irfan 1909- [AW]
Turkish-born author
* Riza, Ali

Organ, John 1925- [CA]
British author and illustrator
* Ashley, Graham
* Farrell, Desmond

[The] Organizer of Victory
See Carnot, Lazare-Nicolas-Marquerite

Orgel, Doris 1929- [CA, SAT]
Austrian-born author
* Adelberg, Doris

Orgen, Jacob ?-1927 [BLB, PHM]
American underworld figure
* Orgen, Little Augie

Orgen, Little Augie
See Orgen, Jacob

Orgeni, Aglaja
See St. Jorgen, Goerger

Orgill, Douglas 1922- [CA]
British author
* Gilman, J. D. [joint pseudonym with Jack Fishman]

O'Riain, Liam P.
See Ryan, William Patrick

Oriana
See Anne of Denmark

Oriana
See Elizabeth I

Oricellarius
See Ruccellai, Benardo

Oriel, Antrim
See Moore, Arthur

Orient
See Kidder, Frederic

[The] Oriental Catullus
See Muslih-ud-Din [or Moslehedin]

[The] Oriental Homer
See Mansur [or Hasan?], Abul Qasim

[The] Oriental Homer
See Muslih-ud-Din [or Moslehedin]

Origen 185- 253 [DNNS, FFF, HN]
Greek theologian
* Adamantius
* [The] Father of Biblical Criticism

[The] Original Authentic Folk Singer
See Kincaid, Bradley

[The] Original Dinah
See Waters, Ethel

[The] Original Gay 90's Gal
See Thomas, Lillian

[The] Original Genius
See Cook, Will Marion

[The] Original Radio Girl
See De Leath, Vaughn

[The] Original Singing Cowboy
See Sprague, Carl T.

[The] Original Singing Nut
See Offerman, George, Sr.

[The] Original Tramp Cyclist
See Clark, P. L.

O'Riley, Warren
See Richardson, Gladwell

Orinda
See Philips, Katherine

Orinifo, Mrs. [FFF]
Entertainer
* Tournier, Millie

Orion
See Hammerton, [Sir] John Alexander

Orion
See Naylor, John

Orion
See Tullock, W. W.

O'Riordan, Conal O'Connell 1874-1948 [BEW, LC, TC]
Irish-born playwright, author, actor
* Connell, F. Norreys

Orkan, Wladyslaw
See Szmaciarz-Smreczynski, Franciszek

Orlando
See Hall, James

Orlando, Emanuels 1927- [CW]
Surinamese poet
* Cyrano

Orleans, Anne Marie Louise d' 1627-1693 [FFF, RH, SN]
Duchess of Montpensier
* [La] Grande Mademoiselle
* Mademoiselle

Orleans, Henri Eugene Philippe Louis d' 1822- ? [HN]
Son of King Louis Philippe of France
* [L']Homme du Lit de Fer

Orleans, Louis Philippe Albert d'
1838-1894    [FFF]
*Pretender to crown of France and author*
* Langel
* Paris, Comte de

Orleans, Louis Philippe Joseph d'
1747-1793    [DHA, DNNF, HN]
*French political leader*
* Egalite, Monsieur
* Egalite, Philippe
* Gamelle

Orleans, Philippe II d' 1674-1723
[DEP, FFF]
*Brother of King Louis XIV of France*
* Monsieur

Orlev, Uri
*See* Orlowski, Jerzy Henryk

Orley, John 1899-    [IPA]
*American poet and critic*
* Tate, Allen

Orliac, Mme. J. M. S.    [PA]
*Author*
* Daurignac, J. M. S.

Orlier, Blaise
*See* Sylvestre, [Joseph Jean] Guy

Orlik, Ivan A. 1898-1953    [SC]
*Russian-born actor and dancer*
* Orlik, Vanya

Orlik, Vanya
*See* Orlik, Ivan A.

Orloff, Max
*See* Crowcroft, Peter

Orlov, Dimitry Stakhiyevich
1883-1946    [WEC]
*Russian cartoonist*
* Moor, D. S.

Orlowski, Jerzy Henryk 1931-
[CA]
*Polish-born author*
* Orlev, Uri

Orlvov, Zvi 1878- ?    [EJS]
*Russian-born Israeli educator*
* Nishri, Zvi

Orman, Felix
*See* Abraham, Gus

Ormandy, Eugene
*See* Blau, Eugene

Orme, Denise
*See* Smither, Jessie

Orme, Eve 1894-    [AW]
*Irish-born author*
* Day, Irene

Orme, K. 20th c.    [MBF]
*British author*
* Clifford, Martin [house pseudonym]

Orme, Mary
*See* Nichols, Mary Sergeant Gove

Orme, Michael
*See* Greeven, Alice Augusta

Orme, Rowan
*See* Rowan-Hamilton, Sydney Orme

Ormiston, Margaret
*See* Curle, M. O.

Ormiston, Roberta
*See* Fletcher, Adele [Whitely]

Ormond, Frederic
*See* Dey, Frederic Van Rensselaer

Ormond, Pierce 1467?-1539    [HN]
*Lord lieutenant of Ireland*
* Red Peter

Ormonde, Duke of
*See* Butler, James

Ormsbee, David
*See* Longstreet, [Henry] Stephen [Weiner]

Ormsby, Clara
*See* Lewis, Alma

Ormsby, Waterman L., Jr. 1834- ?
[FFF, PA]
*American writer*
* Lil

[An] Ornament of Italy
*See* Bentivoglio, Guido

Ornest, Ota
*See* Ornstein, Ota

Ornig, Graef
*See* Ackerman, Forrest J[ames]

Ornis
*See* Winchester, Clarence

Ornstein, But
*See* Ornstein, George

Ornstein, George 1917?-1978
[FIR]
*Film executive*
* Ornstein, But

Ornstein, Honora 1883?-1975
[B10]
*American pioneer*
* Diamond Tooth Lil

Ornstein, J. L.
*See* Ornstein, Jacob Leonard

Ornstein, Jacob Leonard 1915-
[CA]
*American linguist and author*
* Ornstein, J. L.
* Ornstein-Galicia, J[acob] L[eonard]

Ornstein, Ota 1912-    [JL]
*Czech director*
* Ornest, Ota

Ornstein, Richard W. 1880-1963
[FC, WEF]
*German director*
* Oswald, Richard

Ornstein-Galicia, J[acob] L[eonard]
*See* Ornstein, Jacob Leonard

Orosmades
*See* Gray, Thomas

O'Rourke, Blackie
*See* O'Rourke, Francis James

O'Rourke, Charles C. 1917-    [FB]
*Canadian-born football player*
* O'Rourke, Chuckin' Charley

O'Rourke, Charlie
*See* O'Rourke, James Patrick

O'Rourke, Chuckin' Charley
*See* O'Rourke, Charles C.

O'Rourke, Edmund 19th c.
[DEL, RH]
*Irish playwright*
* Falconer, Edmund

O'Rourke, Francis James 1891-
[BE]
*Canadian-born baseball player*
* O'Rourke, Blackie

O'Rourke, Frank
*See* O'Malley, Frank

O'Rourke, James Henry
1852-1919    [BAB, BBH, PB]
*American baseball player*
* [The] Orator
* O'Rourke, Orator Jim
* Uncle Jeems

O'Rourke, James Patrick 1937-
[BE]
*American baseball player*
* O'Rourke, Charlie

O'Rourke, James Stephen
1889-1955    [BE]
*American baseball player*
* O'Rourke, Queenie

O'Rourke, Joseph Leo, Sr.
1881-1956    [BE]
*American baseball player*
* O'Rourke, Patsy

O'Rourke, Orator Jim
*See* O'Rourke, James Henry

O'Rourke, Patsy
*See* O'Rourke, Joseph Leo, Sr.

O'Rourke, Queenie
*See* O'Rourke, James Stephen

O'Rourke, Ruth Carol 1914-
[BEW, FC]
*American actress*
* Hussey, Ruth

O'Rourke, Timothy Patrick
1864-1938    [BE]
*American baseball player*
* O'Rourke, Voiceless Tim

O'Rourke, Voiceless Tim
*See* O'Rourke, Timothy Patrick

Orovida
*See* Pissarro, Orovida Camille

Orowitz, Eugene Maurice 1936?-
[FC, SW]
*American actor*
* Landon, Michael

Orphan Annie
*See* D'Aquino, Iva Ikuko [Toguri]

[The] Orphan of the Temple
*See* Bourbon, Marie Therese Charlotte de

[The] Orpheus of Arabia
*See* Farabi, Abu Nasr Mohammed al-

[The] Orpheus of Highwaymen
*See* Gay, John

[The] Orpheus of Scotland
*See* James I

[The] Orpheus of the Eighteenth Century
*See* Handel, Georg Friedrich

[The] Orpheus of the Green Isle
*See* O'Carolan, Turloch

Orr, Isaac 1793-1844    [FFF, PA]
*American clergyman and writer*
* Hambden
* Timoleon

Orr, James Lawrence 1822-1873
[SN]
*American politician and diplomat*
* [That] Prince of Demagogues

Orr, Mary
*See* Denham, Mary Orr

Orrell, Forrest Gordon 1917-    [BE]
*American baseball player*
* Orrell, Joe

Orrell, Joe
*See* Orrell, Forrest Gordon

Orrente, Pedro 1570?-1644    [WBD]
*Spanish painter*
* [The] Spanish Bassano

Orrico, Carmen 1935-    [FC, SW]
*American actor*
* Saxon, John

Orrmont, Arthur 1922-    [CA]
*American author*
* Hunter, Anson

Orsatti, Ernesto Ralph 1903-1968
[BE]
*American baseball player*
* Orsatti, Ernie

Orsatti, Ernie
*See* Orsatti, Ernesto Ralph

Orsay, Alfred Guillaume Gabriel d'
1801-1852    [DEP]
*French artist and fashion leader*
* [The] Last of the Dandies

Orsin, Floro
*See* Townsend, Alice

Orsini, Giovanni Gaetano
1216?-1280    [SN, WBD]
*Pope*
* [The] Accomplished
* [Il] Compirito
* Nicholas III

Orsini, Giulio
*See* Gnoli, Domenico

Orsini, Pietro Francesco
1649-1730    [HN]
*Pope*
* Benedict XIII
* [The] Pacificator of Europe

Orsino, Horse
*See* Orsino, John Joseph

Orsino, John Joseph 1938-    [BE]
*American baseball player*
* Orsino, Horse

Orszagh, Pavol 1849-1921    [CD]
*Slovak poet*
* Hviezdoslav

Ort, Ana
*See* Andrews, Arthur [Douglas, Jr.]

Ort, Ivan
*See* Dodge, Ossian E.

Orta, Pedro 20th c.    [SMG]
*Cuban-born baseball player*
* [The] Babe Ruth of Cuba

Ortea, Francisco Carlos 1845-1899
[CW]
*Dominican author*
* Franck, Dr.

**Ortea, Virginia Elena** 1866-1903
[CW]
*Dominican-born author and playwright*
* Kennedy, Elena

**Ortega, Filomeno Coronado** 1939-
[BE]
*American baseball player*
* Ortega, Kemo
* Ortega, Phil

**Ortega, Gaspar**
*See* Benitez, Gaspar

**Ortega, Kemo**
*See* Ortega, Filomeno Coronado

**Ortega, Phil**
*See* Ortega, Filomeno Coronado

**Ortega, Santiago** 1917- [GS]
*Spanish bullfighter*
* Mejorcito [Best Little One]

**Ortega y Ramirez, Antonio**
1857-1910 [GS]
*Spanish bullfighter*
* [El] Marinero [The Sailor]

**Orth, Albert Lewis** 1872-1948 [BE]
*American baseball player*
* [The] Curveless Wonder

**Orth, Bennington**
*See* Hoar, Roger Sherman

**Orth, Johann**
*See* John Nepomuk Salvator

**Orth, Richard** 1931- [CA, WD]
*American author*
* Anderson, Clifford [joint pseudonym with Robert Anderson and Clifford Irving]
* Carver, John
* Cummings, Richard
* Gardner, Richard [or Dic]

**[An] Orthodox Beast**
*See* Oates, Titus

**Ortin, Chato**
*See* Ortin, Leopoldo

**Ortin, Leopoldo** 1893-1953 [SC]
*Mexican actor*
* Ortin, Chato

**Ortiz, Angel** 20th c. [RBE]
*American boxer*
* Ortiz, Ruby

**Ortiz, Baby**
*See* Ortiz, Olivrio Nunez

**Ortiz, Elisabeth Lambert** 1928-
[CA]
*British author*
* Lambert, Elisabeth

**Ortiz, J. M.** 20th c. [GS]
*Spanish bullfighter*
* Gallito de Zafra [Little Rooster from Zafra]

**Ortiz, Olivrio Nunez** 1919- [BE]
*Cuban-born baseball player*
* Ortiz, Baby

**Ortiz, Ruby**
*See* Ortiz, Angel

**Ortiz De Montellano**
*See* Ortiz De Montellano, Bernardo

**Ortiz De Montellano, Bernardo**
1899- [NAA]
*Mexican author*
* Ortiz De Montellano

**Ortiz Puga, Jose** 1902- [GS]
*Mexican bullfighter*
* Orfebre Tapatio

**Ortman, E[lmore] Jan** 1884- [CAP]
*American educator and author*
* Ortman, Elmer John

**Ortman, Elmer John**
*See* Ortman, E[lmore] Jan

**Ortmanns, Pauline Ronacher** 1912-
[WEF]
*Austrian actress*
* Romance, Viviane

**Orton, Arthur** 1834-1898 [WBD]
*British imposter*
* Castro, Thomas

**Orton, James** 1826- ? [PA]
*Author*
* Alaster

**Orton, Joe**
*See* Orton, John Kingsley

**Orton, John Kingsley** 1933-1967
[LC]
*British playwright*
* Orton, Joe

**Orton, Thora Margaret** 20th c.
[AW]
*British author*
* Colson

**Ortuno Duplaix, Emilio** 1933- [GS]
*Spanish bullfighter*
* Jumillano

**Ortyx**
*See* Eaton, David H.

**Orwell, George**
*See* Blair, Eric Arthur

**Ory, Edward** 1886-1973
[ASC, DAM, EJ]
*American jazz musician*
* Ory, Kid

**Ory, Kid**
*See* Ory, Edward

**Oryah, Yehudith**
*See* Schochet, J. Immanuel

**Osadchey, Edward P.** 20th c.
[PHM]
*American underworld figure*
* Spitz, Eddie

**Osagyefo [Redeemer]**
*See* Nkrumah, Kwame

**Osaragi, Jiro**
*See* Nojiri, Kiyohiko

**Osawa, Lola**
*See* Morasawa, Chiyo

**Osborn, Barbara M.**
*See* Henkel, Barbara Osborn

**Osborn, Fred**
*See* Osborn, Wilfred P.

**Osborn, Laughton** 1809-1878
*Author*
* Alethitheras

**Osborn, Wilfred P.** 1883-1954
[BE]
*American baseball player*
* Osborn, Fred

**Osborne, Adrienne**
*See* Eisbein, Adrienne

**Osborne, Alma** 20th c. [SC]
*Actress*
* Delmar, Ethel

**Osborne, Bobo**
*See* Osborne, Lawrence Sidney

**Osborne, Bud**
*See* Osborne, Lennie

**Osborne, Charles Humfrey Caulfeild**
1891- [CA]
*British educator and author*
* Humfrey, C.

**Osborne, D. H.**
*See* Osborne, Denis Henry

**Osborne, David**
*See* Silverberg, Robert

**Osborne, Denis Henry** 1919- [ART]
*British painter*
* Osborne, D. H.

**Osborne, Dorothy [Gladys] Yeo**
1917- [AW, CA, WD]
*British author*
* Arthur, Gladys

**Osborne, Edward**
*See* Manning, Anne

**Osborne, Ernest Preston**
1893-1969 [BE]
*American baseball player*
* Osborne, Tiny

**Osborne, George**
*See* Silverberg, Robert

**Osborne, James Henry** 1949-
[SMG]
*American football player*
* Osborne, Jaws

**Osborne, Jaws**
*See* Osborne, James Henry

**Osborne, Jefferson**
*See* Schroeder, J. W.

**Osborne, Jimmie** 1923-1957 [CM]
*American country-western performer*
* [The] Kentucky Folk Singer

**Osborne, John D.** [FFF]
*American journalist*
* Gamma
* Leoni, Leone

**Osborne, Lawrence Sidney** 1935-
[BE]
*American baseball player*
* Osborne, Bobo

**Osborne, Lennie** 1881?-1964
[BEW, F1, F2]
*American actor*
* Osborne, Bud
* Osborne, Miles

**Osborne, Mark**
*See* Bayfield, William John

**Osborne, Mark**
*See* Bobin, John William [Jack]

**Osborne, Michael** 20th c. [RO2]
*British musician*
* Osborne, Oz

**Osborne, Miles**
*See* Osborne, Lennie

**Osborne, Ossie**
*See* Osborne, Wayne Harold

**Osborne, Oz**
*See* Osborne, Michael

**Osborne, Sydney Godolphin**
1808-1889 [DEL, PA, RH]
*British author and clergyman*
* S. G. O.

**Osborne, Tiny**
*See* Osborne, Ernest Preston

**Osborne, Wayne Harold** 1912-
[BE]
*American baseball player*
* Osborne, Ossie

**Osborne, Will**
*See* Oliphant, William

**Osbourne, John** 1948- [RO2]
*British singer*
* Osbourne, Ozzie

**Osbourne, Ozzie**
*See* Osbourne, John

**Oscar**
*See* Sullivan, Rollin

**Oscar, Henry**
*See* Wale, Henry

**Oscar of the Waldorf**
*See* Tschirky, Oscar

**Oscard, Fernanda** 1921- [BEW]
*American talent representative*
* Oscard, Fifi

**Oscard, Fifi**
*See* Oscard, Fernanda

**Osceola**
*See* Blixen, Karen [Christentze Dinesen]

**Oscotean**
*See* Kent, [William] Charles [Mark]

**Osenburg, Richard** 20th c. [SFP]
*Author*
* Lauler, Michael

**Osgood, Frances Sargent Locke**
1811-1850 [FFF]
*American poet*
* Florence

**Osgood, Irene**
*See* Harvey, Irene

**Osgood, Kate Putman** [PA]
*Author*
* Putman, Kate

**Osgood, Win**
*See* Osgood, Winchester D.

**Osgood, Winchester D.** 1870- ?
[FB]
*American football player*
* Osgood, Win

**O'Shaugnessey, Sergius**
*See* O'Neil, Dennis

**O'Shea, Blackjack**
*See* Rellaford, Jack

**O'Shea, Frank Joseph** 1920- [BE]
*American baseball player*
* [The] Naugatuck Nugget
* Shea, Spec

O'Shea, Jack
See  Rellaford, Jack

O'Shea, Kittie
See  Scanlan, Kate

O'Shea, Patrick 20th c.    [WWL]
Irish author
* O Seaghdha, Padraig

O'Shea, Patrick J. 20th c.    [WWL]
Irish author and playwright
* O Seaghdha, Padraig

O'Shea, Sean
See  Tralins, S[andor] Robert
[Bob]

O'Shea, Tessie 1914-    [BMH]
Welsh-born comedienne
* Two Ton Tessie

Osiander, Andreas
See  Hosemann, Andreas

Oski
See  Conti, Oscar

Osman Nuri Pasha 1837?-1900
[WBD]
Turkish army officer
* Ghazi, al- [The Conqueror]

Osman Pasha
See  Ripperda, Jan Willem

Osman, T. Embly    [PA]
Author
* Ayers, Alfred

Osman I [or Othman] 1259-1326
[RH, SN, WBD]
Founder of the Turkish empire
* [The] Conqueror
* Ghazi, al-

Osmond, Andrew Philip Kingsford
1938-    [CA, WWS]
British author
* Reid, Philip [joint pseudonym
  with Richard Ingrams]

Osmun, Thomas Embly 1834-1902
[FFF]
American author and critic
* Ayres, Alfred

Osnovyanenko
See  Kvitka, Grigori Petrovich

Osofer, Phil
See  Maine, Harry Carlton

Osorgin, Mikhail Andreyevich
See  Ilyin, Mikhail Andreyevich

Ossenbrink, Luther W. 1915-
[CWG, ECM]
American country-western performer
* [The] Arkansas Woodchopper
* Arkie

Ossian
See  Macpherson, James

Ossian 3rd c.    [FFF, RH, SN]
Gaelic bard and warrior
* [The] Celtic Homer
* [The] Gaelic Homer
* [The] Homer of the Celts
* [The] Poet of the Vague

Ossian-Nilsson, Karl Gustav 1875-
?    [WBD]
Swedish poet and author
* Ossiannilsson, Karl Gustav

Ossiannilsson, Karl Gustav
See  Ossian-Nilsson, Karl Gustav

Ossit
See  Deslandes, [Baroness] M.

Ossman, Sylvester Louis 20th c.
[PMJ]
Musician
* Ossman, Vess

Ossman, Vess
See  Ossman, Sylvester Louis

Ossoli
See  Fuller, Margaret Sarah

Ossorio, Carlos 20th c.    [GS]
Venezuelan bullfighter
* Rayito [Little Beam]

[The] Ostade of Literary History
See  Wood, Anthony

Osteen, Champ
See  Osteen, James Champlin

Osteen, Claude Wilson 1939-
[PB, SMG]
American baseball player
* Osteen, Gomer

Osteen, Gomer
See  Osteen, Claude Wilson

Osteen, James Champlin
1877-1962    [BE]
American baseball player
* Osteen, Champ

Osten, M.    [PA]
Author
* Eyler, Emile

Osterberg, Jim 20th c.    [DAM]
American musician
* Stooge, Iggy

Ostergaard, Geoffrey Nielsen
1926-    [CA]
British political scientist and author
* Gerard, Gaston

Ostergard, Red
See  Ostergard, Robert Lund

Ostergard, Robert Lund 1898-    [BE]
American baseball player
* Ostergard, Red

Osterman, Edward Monk  ?-1920
[BLB]
American underworld figure
* Eastman, Edward Monk

Osterman, Jack
See  Rosenthal, Jack

Osterman, Paula Marie 1908-
[F2, FC]
American actress
* Torres, Raquel

Ostermayr, Paul 1909-    [FDG]
German director
* May, Paul

Ostermueller, Frederick Raymond
1907-1957    [AS, BE]
American baseball player
* Ostermueller, Fritz

Ostermueller, Fritz
See  Ostermueller, Frederick
Raymond

Ostertag, Barna
See  Ostertag, Bernard

Ostertag, Bernard 1902-    [BEW]
American artists representative and
actor
* Ostertag, Barna

Osterwald, Bibi
See  Osterwald, Margaret Virginia

Osterwald, Margaret Virginia 20th
c.    [BEW]
American actress
* Osterwald, Bibi

Ostioncito [Little Oyster]
See  Morales y Mula, Jose

Ostlere, Edith 20th c.    [THR]
Playwright and actress
* Ord, Robert

Ostlere, Gordon 1921-    [DLE]
British author
* Gordon, Richard

Ostlund, Island
See  Ostlund, Petur David

Ostlund, Petur David 1943-    [EJ7]
American-born jazz musician
* Ostlund, Island

Ostrander, Isabel [Egenton]
1883?-1924    [CC, WW]
Author
* Chipperfield, Robert Orr
* Fox, David
* Grant, Douglas

Ostrander, Mrs. Clarence    [FFF]
Entertainer
* Wentworth, Mae

Ostransky, Big Leroy
See  Ostransky, Leroy

Ostransky, Leroy 1918-
American composer and educator
* Ostransky, Big Leroy

Ostrowski, Joseph Paul 1916-    [BE]
American baseball player
* Ostrowski, Professor

Ostrowski, Professor
See  Ostrowski, Joseph Paul

Ostrowsky
See  Holmquist, Anders

Ostrus, Merrill 1919-    [ASC]
American composer
* Staton, Merrill

O'Suilleabhain, Sean 1903-    [CA]
Irish archivist and author
* O'Sullivan, Sean

O'Sullivan, Dennis Patrick Terence
Joseph 1906-1971
[EJ, PMJ, WWJ]
American jazz musician
* Sullivan, Joe

O'Sullivan, Eugene 1892-1971    [FC]
British entertainer
* Gerrard, Gene

O'Sullivan, Farrar    [PA]
Author
* Munster

O'Sullivan, Gilbert
See  O'Sullivan, Raymond Edward

O'Sullivan, Paul 1917-    [BEW]
American producer, theatre
manager, press representative
* Vroom, Paul

O'Sullivan, Raymond Edward
1946-    [RO2]
Irish-born singer
* O'Sullivan, Gilbert

O'Sullivan, Sean
See  O'Suilleabhain, Sean

O'Sullivan, Seumas
See  Starkey, James Sullivan

Osusky, Stefan 1889-1973    [CA]
Czech diplomat and author
* Argus

Osvaldo
See  Navarro, Osvaldo

Oswald, Lee Harvey 1939-1963
[BLB]
American who assassinated
President John F. Kennedy
* Lee, O. H.

Oswald, Maude
See  Hawley, Mrs. D. R.

Oswald, Richard
See  Ornstein, Richard W.

Oswalda, Ossi
See  Staglich, Oswalda

Otero, Reggie
See  Otero, Regino Joseph Gomez

Otero, Regino Joseph Gomez 1915-
[BE]
Cuban-born baseball player
* Otero, Reggie

[The] Other Eye of Florence
See  Cavalcanti, Guido

[The] Other Miller
See  Miller, Allen L., III

[The] Other One
See  Bonaparte, Napoleon

Othere
See  Windsor-Garnett, John
Raynham

Otis, Belle
See  Woods, C. H.

Otis, Bill
See  Otis, Paul Franklin

Otis, Cannonball
See  Otis, Harry George

Otis, F. N.    [FFF]
American writer
* Oran

Otis, George
See  Mellen, Ida M[ay]

Otis, Harry George 1886-    [BE]
American baseball player
* Otis, Cannonball

Otis, James
See  Kaler, James Otis

Otis, Johnny, Jr. 1953-    [EJ7]
American jazz musician
* Otis, Shuggie

Otis, Mrs. Harrison Gray 19th c.
[PA]
Author
* One of the Barclays

Otis, Paul Franklin 1889-    [BE]
American baseball player
* Otis, Bill

Otis, Shuggie
See  Otis, Johnny, Jr.

**Otley, Barbara Kathleen** 1918-
[ART]
*British painter*
* Fiennes-Foster

**Otochan [Daddy]**
*See* Ohira, Masayoshi

**O'Toole, [Father]**
*See* Synnott, Ed. Fitzgerald

**O'Toole, Kate**
*See* Montague, Bruce Alexander

**O'Toole, Laurence** ?-1180    [HN]
*Archbishop of Dublin*
* [The] Father of His Country

**O'Toole, Rex**
*See* Tralins, S[andor] Robert
[Bob]

**Otrepieff, Gregory** ?-1606?    [HN]
*Russian monk*
* [The] Pretender
* [The] Warbeck of the North

**Otsuka, George**
*See* Otsuka, Keiji

**Otsuka, Keiji** 1938-    [EJ7]
*Japanese jazz musician*
* Otsuka, George

**Ott, Maggie Glenn**
*See* Ott, Virginia

**Ott, Mel[vin Thomas]** 1909-1958
[BE, BTB]
*American baseball player and
manager*
* Master Melvin

**Ott, Peter**
*See* Von Hildebrand, Dietrich

**Ott, Virginia** 1917-    [CA]
*American author*
* Ott, Maggie Glenn

**Ottaviano, Thomas** 1936-    [BEW]
*American producer and director*
* Cimber, Matt

**Ottenheimer, Florette Regina**
1924-    [BEW]
*American actress*
* Hayes, Maggie

**Ottesen, Thea Tauber** 1913-    [CA]
*Hungarian-born educator and
author*
* Bank-Jensen, Thea

**Otto**    [SN]
*Earl of Ascania and Ballenstedt*
* [The] Rich

**Otto**    [SN]
*Margrave of Meissen*
* [The] Rich

**Otto [or Otho]**    [SN]
*Duke of Austria*
* [The] Jovial

**Otto** 1204-1252    [WBD]
*Margrave of Brandenburg*
* [The] Child

**Otto, August J.** 1943-    [FB]
*American football player*
* Otto, Gus

**Otto, Gus**
*See* Otto, August J.

**Otto of Bamberg** 1060?-1139
[WBD]
*Saint*
* [The] Father of the Monks

**Otto, Young**
*See* Susskind, Arthur

**Otto I [or Otho]** 912- 973
[DNNS, FFF, SN]
*King of Germany and Holy Roman
emperor*
* [The] Great
* [The] Lion

**Otto II** ?-1253    [WBD]
*Duke of Bavaria*
* [The] Illustrious

**Otto II [or Otho]** 955- 983
[FFF, HN, SN]
*Holy Roman emperor*
* [The] Bloody
* [The] Pale Death of the Saracens
* [The] Red
* Rufus

**Otto III [or Otho]** 980-1002
[DEP, DNNS, SN]
*Holy Roman emperor*
* [The] Wonder of the World

**Otto IV [or Otho]** 1175?-1218
[FFF, RH, SN]
*Holy Roman emperor*
* [The] Proud

**Ottoboni, Pietro** 1610-1691    [CAL]
*Pope*
* Alexander VIII

**Ottokar II** 1230?-1278    [WBD]
*King of Bohemia*
* [The] Great

**Ottolengui, Helen**
*See* Monserrat, Mrs. George

**O'Tyne, Nicholas**
*See* Foster, Leroy A.

**Oubo, Irac**
*See* Lohier, Michel

**[De] Oude Heer Smits [Old Mr.
Smits]**
*See* Lindo, Mark Prager

**Oudeis**
*See* Darby, Christopher Lovett

**Oudenarde, Dominie Nicholas
Aegidius**
*See* Paulding, James Kirke

**Oudin, Mrs. Eugene**    [FFF]
* Parker, Louise

**Oudraadt, Jean** 1540-1606    [PA]
*Author*
* Gerobulus

**Ouellette, Adeland** 1911-    [CEI]
*Canadian-born hockey player*
* Ouellette, Eddie

**Ouellette, Eddie**
*See* Ouellette, Adeland

**Ouida**
*See* Rame, Marie Louise

**Ounskowsky, Mischa** 1905-1967
[F2, FC]
*Russian-born actor*
* Auer, Mischa

**Our American Cruikshank**
*See* Johnston, David Claypole

**Our Champion for Homer**
*See* Boileau-Despreaux, Nicolas

**Our Chet**
*See* Arthur, Chester Alan

**Our Domestic Raphael**
*See* Stothard, Thomas

**Our English Corot**
*See* Peppercorn, Arthur Douglas

**Our English Homer**
*See* Warner, William

**Our English Marcellus**
*See* Henry

**Our English Rabelais**
*See* Nash [or Nashe?], Thomas

**Our Fritz**
*See* Frederick William

**Our Gracie**
*See* Stansfield, Grace

**Our Hebrew Friend**
*See* Rose, Julian

**Our Lady of Mercy**
*See* Tallien, Jeanne Marie Ignace
Theresa

**Our Lady of O**
*See* Mary

**Our Marie**
*See* Wood, Matilda Alice Victoria

**Our Mary**
*See* Anderson, Mary Antoinette

**Our Mary**
*See* Ewen, Mary Cecilia

**Our Member for Paris**
*See* Labouchere, Henry

**Our Mock Ovid**
*See* Coypeau, Charles [Sieur
d'Assouci]

**Our only General**
*See* Wolseley, Garnet Joseph [First
Viscount Wolseley]

**Our Own Correspondent**
*See* Noyes, James O.

**Our Own Evarts**
*See* Evarts, William Maxwell

**Our Scottish Bodoni**
*See* Ballantyne, John

**Our Second Ciceronian**
*See* Southwell, Robert

**Our Talatamtana**
*See* Harvey, Gabriel

**Our Tender**
*See* Hamlen, Georgia

**Our Will**
*See* Shakespeare, William

**Ouroussow, Eugenie** 1908-1975
[CA]
*Russian-born American educator,
administrator, author*
* Lehovich, Eugenie Ouroussow

**Oursler, [Charles] Fulton**
1893-1952    [CC, EMD, TC1]
*American playwright, journalist,
author*
* Abbot, Anthony
* Armstrong, April
* Frikell, Samri

**Oursler, Grace Perkins** 1900-
[NAA]
*American author*
* Macy, Dora
* Perkins, Grace

**Oursler, Will[iam Charles]** 1913-
[CA]
*American author*
* Gallager, Gale
* Marine, Nick

**Oury, Gerard**
*See* Tannenbaum, Max-Gerard
Houry

**Ouseley, Gideon Jasper Richard**
1835-1906    [WGT]
*Author*
* Theosopho

**Ousley, Curtis** 1935-1971
[EJ7, RM, RO1]
*American musician*
* Curtis, King

**Outen, Chick**
*See* Outen, William Austin

**Outen, William Austin** 1905-1961
[BE]
*American baseball player*
* Outen, Chick

**Outerbridge, Mary Ewing** 20th c.
[SA]
*American tennis player*
* [The] Mother of Tennis

**Outi**
*See* Honkanen, Hilja Loviisa
Valkeapaa

**Outis, U. Donough**
*See* White, Richard Grant

**Outland, John H.** 1871-1947    [FB]
*American football player*
* [The] Father of Kansas Relays

**[The] Outlaw**
*See* Edward

**[The] Outlaw**
*See* Jennings, Waylon

**Outrageous, Captain**
*See* Turner, Robert Edward, III

**Outram, [Sir] James** 1803?-1861
[DEP, DNNS, HN]
*British army officer*
* [The] Bayard of India
* [The] Bayard of the East
* [The] Bayard of the Indian Army

**Outside, Mr.**
*See* Caroline, James Calvin

**Outside, Mr.**
*See* Davis, Glenn W.

**Ouvard, Jacques**
*See* Guichardan, Roger
Jean-Baptiste

**[L']Ouvreuse du Cirque**
*See* Gauthier-Villars, Henri

**Ouyrard, Gabriel Julien** 1770-1846
[SN]
*French banker and merchant*
* [The] Napoleon of Finance

**Ovary, Geza**
*See* Paskandi, Geza

**Oved, Mosheh**
*See* Good, Morris Edward

**Oveissi, Gholam Ali** 20th c.
*Iranian military leader*
* [The] Butcher of Teheran

**Overacker, Le Roy** 1931- [FC]
*American actor*
* Baby Le Roy

**Overall, Jeff**
*See* Overall, Orval

**Overall, Orval** 1881-1947 [BN]
*American baseball player*
* Overall, Jeff

**Overholser, Wayne D.** 1906-
[AW, CA]
*American author*
* Daniels, John S.
* Leighton, Lee
* Roberts, Wayne
* Stevens, Dan J.
* Wayne, Joseph

**Overmire, Frank** 1919-
[BE, BTB, SMG]
*American baseball player and coach*
* Overmire, Stub [or Stubby]

**Overmire, Stub [or Stubby]**
*See* Overmire, Frank

**Overstake, Eva Alaine** 1918-1952
[CWG]
*American country-western performer*
* Martin, Judy

**Overstreet, Bonaro Wilkinson**
1902- [NAA]
*American poet*
* Wilkinson, Bonara

**Overstreet, Tommy** 1937- [ECM]
*American country-western performer*
* Dean, Tommy

**Overtheway, Mrs.**
*See* Ewing, Juliana Horatia

**Overton, Max**
*See* Wilcox, Don

**Overy, Claire May**
*See* Bass, Clara May

**Ovesen, Ellis**
*See* Smith, Shirley M[ae]

**Ovid**
*See* Ovidius Naso, Publius

**[The] Ovid of France**
*See* Bellay, Joachim du

**[The] Ovid of the English Nation**
*See* Drayton, Michael

**Ovidius Naso, Publius** ?- 17?
[DEP, WBD]
*Roman poet*
* [The] Master of Love
* Ovid

**Owain, Owain** 1929- [IAW]
*Welsh author*
* Herco
* Humphreys, John

**Owanda**
*See* Robinson, Edgar Williams

**Owen, Arnold Malcolm** 1916?-
[B10, BE, PB]
*American baseball player*
* Owen, Mickey

**Owen, Ashelford**
*See* Ogle, Anne

**Owen, Bill**
*See* Rowbotham, William

**Owen, Caroline Dale**
*See* Snedeker, Caroline Dale

**Owen, Clifford**
*See* Hamilton, Charles Harold St.
John

**Owen, [Harry] Collinson**
1882-1956 [WGT, WW]
*Author*
* Addison, Hugh
* Collinson, Owen?

**Owen, D. E.** 20th c. [MBF]
*British author*
* English, Don

**Owen, Dean**
*See* McGaughy, Dudley Dean

**Owen, Edmund**
*See* Teller, Neville

**Owen, Frank** 1893-1968
[ESF, HFF, WGT]
*American author*
* Abner, Gerald
* Braithwaite, Raymond
* Hung Long Tom
* Kent, Richard
* Williams, Roswell

**Owen, Frank** 1907?-1979 [CA]
*British author and broadcaster*
* Cato [joint pseudonym with Peter
 D(unsmore) Howard and Michael
 Foote]

**Owen, Frank Malcolm** 1879-1942
[BE]
*American baseball player*
* Owen, Yip

**Owen, Freck**
*See* Owen, Marv[in James]

**Owen, Garnet** 20th c. [IAW]
*American author*
* Oliver, Gay

**Owen, Hedley**
*See* O'Mant, Hedley Percival
Angelo

**Owen, Hugh**
*See* Faust, Frederick [Schiller]

**Owen, J. A.**
*See* Visger, Jean A. Owen

**Owen, Jack** 1929- [AW]
*British author*
* Dykes, Jack

**Owen, John Pickard**
*See* Butler, Samuel

**Owen, Joseph B.** [PA]
*Author*
* Alter

**Owen, Marsha**
*See* Busby, Mabel Janice

**Owen, Marv[in James]** 1906- [BN]
*American baseball player*
* Owen, Freck

**Owen, Mickey**
*See* Owen, Arnold Malcolm

**Owen, Norman**
*See* Walters, J.

**Owen, Richard**
*See* Roberts, Edna

**Owen, Robert N. [Bob]**
*See* Geis, Richard E[rwin]

**Owen, Roderic**
*See* Fenwick-Owen, Roderic
Franklin Rawnsley

**Owen, Seena**
*See* Auen, Signe

**Owen, Steve** 20th c.
*American football coach*
* Owen, Stout Steve

**Owen, Stout Steve**
*See* Owen, Steve

**Owen, Tom**
*See* Watts, Peter Christopher

**Owen, Tom, the Bee Hunter**
*See* Thorpe, Thomas Bangs

**Owen, Vincent**
*See* Cook, Fred Gordon

**Owen, William**
*See* Pughe, William Owen

**Owen, William Charles** 1854- ?
[WWL]
*British author*
* Senex

**Owen, Yip**
*See* Owen, Frank Malcolm

**Owens, A.**
*See* Hersey, Harold

**Owens, Alvis Edgar, Jr.** 1929-
[CME, CWG, DAM]
*American country-western performer*
* Owens, Buck

**Owens, Artie** 1953- [SMG]
*American football player*
* Owens, Flea

**Owens, Bear**
*See* Owens, James Philip

**Owens, Black Widow**
*See* Owens, Milton

**Owens, Brig** 20th c.
*American football player*
* Owens, Twiggy

**Owens, Buck**
*See* Owens, Alvis Edgar, Jr.

**Owens, Charles M.**
*See* Brown, Charles M.

**Owens, Charles Wayne** 1954?-
[B10, SMG]
*American football player*
* Owens, Tinker

**Owens, Cotton**
*See* Owens, Everett

**Owens, Doye H.** 1892-1962 [ASC]
*American musician*
* Owens, Tex

**Owens, Eddie**
*See* Abram, Eddie

**Owens, Everett** 1924- [EAR]
*American auto racer*
* Owens, Cotton

**Owens, Flea**
*See* Owens, Artie

**Owens, Furman Lee** 1910- [BE]
*American baseball player*
* Owens, Jack

**Owens, Jack**
*See* Owens, Furman Lee

**Owens, James Cleveland**
1913-1980 [BBH, CA, TF]
*American track and field athlete*
* [The] Ebony Antelope
* Owens, Jesse

**Owens, James Philip** 1934- [BE]
*American baseball player*
* Owens, Bear

**Owens, Jesse**
*See* Owens, James Cleveland

**Owens, Milton** 1954- [RBE]
*American boxer*
* Owens, Black Widow

**Owens, Paul** 1924- [SMG]
*American baseball team personnel
director*
* [The] Pope

**Owens, R. C.**
*See* Owens, Raleigh C.

**Owens, Raleigh C.** 1933- [FB]
*American football player*
* Owens, R. C.

**Owens, Raymond** ?-1942 [MK]
*American baseball player*
* Owens, Smoky

**Owens, Red**
*See* Owens, Thomas Llewellyn

**Owens, Richard**
*See* Chentres, Federico

**Owens, Robert** 1941- [IBW]
*American clergyman*
* Owens, [Father] Vladimir

**Owens, Rochelle**
*See* Bass, Rochelle

**Owens, Ruby** 1908-1963 [CM]
*American country-western performer*
* Radio's Original Texas Cowgirl
* Texas Ruby

**Owens, Smoky**
*See* Owens, Raymond

**Owens, Steve E.** 1947- [FB]
*American football player*
* Ki He Gha [Leader]

**Owens, Tex**
*See* Owens, Doye H.

**Owens, Thelma** 1905- [CA]
*American author*
* Grafton, Ann

**Owens, Thomas Llewellyn**
1874-1952 [BE]
*American baseball player*
* Owens, Red

**Owens, Tinker**
*See* Owens, Charles Wayne

**Owens, Twiggy**
*See* Owens, Brig

**Owens, [Father] Vladimir**
*See* Owens, Robert

**Owenson**
*See* Morgan, Lady Sidney

**[The] Owl**
*See* Banghart, Basil

**[The] Owl**
*See* Hooton, Burt Carlton

[The] Owl
See   Polizzi, Alfred

Owl, Sebastian
See   Thompson, Hunter S[tockton]

Owlglass, Dr.
See   Blaich, Hans Erich

[The] Ox
See   Zampieri, Domenico

Oxberry, William 1784-1824
[DNNS, FFF, SN]
British poet, printer, publisher,
publican, player
* [The] Five P's

Oxenbury, Helen
See   Burningham, Helen Oxenbury

Oxenbury, Thomas Bernard 1904-
[ART]
British artist
* T. B. O.

Oxenford, John 1812-1877   [PA]
Author
* [An] English Play-Goer

Oxenham, Elsie
See   Dunkerley, Elsie Jeanette

Oxenham, John
See   Dunkerley, William Arthur

Oxenstierna, Axel Gustafsson
1583-1654   [SN]
Swedish statesman
* [The] Eagle of the North

[The] Oxford Dante
See   Moore, Edward

Oxley, Kate
See   Whitehead, Kate

Oxley, William 1939-   [CA]
British poet
* Hardy, Jason

Oxoniae Poeta Laureatus
See   Skelton, John

Oy-vik
See   Holmvik, Oyvind

Oyler, Andrew Paul [Andy] 1880- ?
[BE]
American baseball player
* Oyler, Pepper

Oyler, Pepper
See   Oyler, Andrew Paul [Andy]

Oyra, Jan
See   Wojcieszko, Jan

Oyster Joe Martina
See   Martina, Joseph John [Joe]

Ozaki, Milton K. 20th c.
[CC, WW]
American author
* Saber, Robert O.

[The] Ozark Bear
See   Tesreau, Charles Monroe

Ozark, Daniel Leonard 1923-
[BE, PB]
American baseball coach and
manager
* Ozark Ike

Ozark Ike
See   Kiner, Ralph McPherran

Ozark Ike
See   Ozark, Daniel Leonard

Ozark Ike
See   Zernial, Gus Edward

Ozbekhan, Anne Binkley Rand 20th
c.   [TBJ]
American author
* Rand, Anne

Ozdemir 16th c.   [HN]
* [The] Iron Ogli
* [The] Turkish Samson

Ozdenak, Yasin Erol 1948-   [AES]
Turkish soccer player
* Yasin, Erol

Ozgun, Faruk
See   Agca, Mehmet Ali

Ozmer, Doc
See   Ozmer, Horace Robert

Ozmer, Horace Robert 1901-   [BE]
American baseball player
* Ozmer, Doc

Ozone, Barbara Lynn 1942-   [RO1]
American singer and songwriter
* Lynn, Barbara

Ozy
See   Rosset, Benjamin Charles

# P

**P. A.**
*See* Ainslie, Peter

**P. B. St. J.**
*See* St. John, Percy Boyle

**P. F.**
*See* Nuttall-Smith, Margaret
Emily Noel

**P. G.**
*See* Gardner, Peter

**P. G.**
*See* Giggle, Philip

**P. G.**
*See* Gyllenhammar, Pehr

**P. H.**
*See* Hempton, Paul Andrew Keates

**P. H.**
*See* Hogarth, Arthur Paul

**P. J.**
*See* Johnson, Pamela P.

**P. J. G.**
*See* Garrard, Peter John

**P. L. K. [Plucky Little King]**
*See* Hussein

**P. M.**
*See* MacGillivray, James
Pittendrigh

**P. M.**
*See* Margaret Rose

**P. M.**
*See* Mieg, Peter

**P. P., A Parish Clerk**
*See* Arbuthnot, John

**P. P. C. R.**
*See* Watts, Thomas

**P. P., Clerk of this Parish**
*See* Aburthnot, John

**P. P. J.**
*See* Pickard Jenkins, Percy

**P. R.**
*See* Page Roberts, James

**P. T.**
*See* Thursby, Peter

**P. V. B.**
*See* Bradshaw, Percival Vanner

**P. W.**
*See* Strasser, Bernard Paul

**P. W. W.**
*See* Wilson, Philip Whitwell

**P-Orridge, Genesis**
*See* Megson, Neil Andrew

**[The] Pa**
*See* Stevens, Siaka

**Pa, Choon**
*See* Kwak, Chong Won

**Paaltjens, Piet**
*See* Haverschmidt, Francois

**Pab**
*See* Blooman, Percy A.

**Pablo, Augustus**
*See* Swaby, Horace

**Pabon Pabon, Rosemberg** 20th c.
*Colombian guerrilla leader*
* Uno, Comandante

**Pabor, Charles Henry** 1846-1913
[BE]
*American baseball player and
manager*
* [The] Old Woman in the Red
Cap

**Pabst, G. W.**
*See* Pabst, George Wilhelm

**Pabst, George Wilhelm** 1885-1967
[FC]
*German director*
* Pabst, G. W.

**Pace, Peter**
*See* Burnett, David [Benjamin
Foley]

**Pacelli, Eugenio Maria Giovanni**
1876-1958   [CBS, WBD]
*Pope*
* [The] Fighting Pope
* Pius XII
* [The] Pope of Peace

**Pachal, Clay**
*See* Pachal, Clayton

**Pachal, Clayton** 1956-   [HR]
*Canadian-born hockey player*
* Pachal, Clay

**Pacheco, Assis**
*See* De Assis Pacheco, Armando

**Pacheco, Luis**
*See* Fatio, Louis

**Pachin Marin**
*See* Gonzalez Marin, Francisco

**Pachter, Henry M[aximilian]**
*See* Paechter, Henry M[aximilian]

**[The] Pacific**
*See* Amadeus VIII

**[The] Pacific**
*See* Frederick III

**[The] Pacific**
*See* Olaf III [or Olaus]

**[The] Pacific**
*See* Pedro II

**[Le] Pacificateur de la Vendee**
*See* Hoche, [Louis] Lazarus

**[The] Pacificator of Europe**
*See* Orsini, Pietro Francesco

**Pacificator of the Occident**
*See* Gonzalez, Manuel

**Pacificus**
*See* Giddings, Joshua Reed

**Pacificus**
*See* Hamilton, Alexander

**Pacioli [or Paccioli], Luca**
1450?-1520?   [WBD]
*Italian mathematician*
* Di Borgo, Luca

**Paciorek, Thomas Marian** 1946-
[SMG]
*American baseball player*
* Paciorek, Wimpy

**Paciorek, Wimpy**
*See* Paciorek, Thomas Marian

**Pacis, Vicente Albano** 1900-
[NAA]
*Filipino editor*
* Pradas, Virginia

**Packard, Gilian E.** 1938-   [ART]
*British artist*
* G. E. P.

**Packer, Alfred** 1847-1907   [BLB]
*American murderer and robber*
* Schwartze, John

**Packer, Joy [Petersen]** 1905-   [CA]
*South African author*
* Packer, Lady

**Packer, Lady**
*See* Packer, Joy [Petersen]

**Packer, Vin**
*See* Meaker, Marijane

**Paco De Oro [Paco the Golden One]**
*See* Diez, Francisco

**Paco Frascuelo**
*See* Sanchez, Francisco

**Paco d'Arcos, J.**
*See* Correa da Silva, Joaquim
Belford

**Pacorro**
*See* Diaz y Perez, Francisco

**Padden, Brains**
*See* Padden, Richard J. [Dick]

**Padden, Gunner**
*See* Padden, William

**Padden, Richard J. [Dick]**
1870-1922   [BN]
*American baseball player*
* Padden, Brains

**Padden, William** 20th c.   [BLB]
*American underworld figure*
* Padden, Gunner

**Paddie Kak**
*See* Kirtland, Ethel Schwartz

**Paddock, Charles W.** 1900-1943
[BBH]
*American track and field athlete*
* [The] World's Fastest Human

**Paddock, Mrs.**   [FFF]
*Entertainer*
* Mitchell, Maggie

**Paddu, Antonio** 1944-   [BX]
*Italian boxer*
* Paddu, Tonino

**Paddu, Tonino**
*See* Paddu, Antonio

**Paddy**
*See* McCluskey, Henry

**Paddywhiski**
*See* Fox, Will H.

**Padecopeo, Gabriel**
*See* Vega Carpio, Lope Felix de

**Paden, Clifton** 1874-1956   [SC]
*American actor, playwright,
screenwriter*
* Emerson, John

**[The] Paderewska of the Pampas**
*See* Novaes, Guiomar

**Paderewski, Ignace Jan** 1860-1941
[MS]
*Polish pianist*
* [The] Lion of Paris

**Padeson, Mary**
*See* Magraw, Beatrice Irene [May]

**Padget, Calvin Jackson**
*See* Ferroni, Giorgio

**Padgett, Don Wilson** 1911-    [BE]
*American baseball player*
* Padgett, Red

**Padgett, Ernest Kitchen [Ernie]**
1899-1957    [BE, PB]
*American baseball player*
* Padgett, Red

**Padgett, Lewis** [joint pseudonym
with Catherine Lucile Moore]
*See* Kuttner, Henry

**Padgett, Lewis** [joint pseudonym
with Henry Kuttner]
*See* Moore, Catherine Lucile

**Padgett, Red**
*See* Padgett, Don Wilson

**Padgett, Red**
*See* Padgett, Ernest Kitchen
[Ernie]

**Padgett, Ron** 1942-    [CA]
*American poet*
* Dangerfield, Harlan
* Veitch, Tom

**Padilla [Small Oven]**
*See* Garcia De La Flor, Angel

**Padilla, Eduardo**
*See* Figueroa, Eduardo

**Padilla, Jose Gualberto** 1829-1886
[CW]
*Puerto Rican poet*
* [El] Caribe

**Padilla de Sanz, Trina** 1880?- ?
[CW]
*Puerto Rican poet*
* [La] Hija del Caribe

**[The] Padishah of the Padishah**
*See* Canning, [Sir] Stratford [First
Viscount Stratford de Redcliffe]

**Padjan, Jack** 1888-1960    [SC]
*Actor*
* Duane, Jack

**Padmore, George A.**
*See* Nurse, Malcolm

**[Il] Padovanino**
*See* Varotari, Alessandro

**[The] Padre of Hollywood**
*See* Dodd, Neal

**[El] Padrino**
*See* Alvero Cruz, Jose Medrano

**Padula, Vicente** 1900-1967    [SC]
*Argentinian-born actor*
* Padula, Vincent

**Padula, Vincent**
*See* Padula, Vicente

**Padva, Vladimir**
*Musician*
* Padwa, Vee

**Padwa, Vee**
*See* Padva, Vladimir

**Paechter, Henry M[aximilian]**
1907-    [CA]
*German-born historian and author*
* Pachter, Henry M[aximilian]
* Rabasseire, Henry

**Paetel, Erich** 1875- ?    [LAO]
*German editor and author*
* Her, Erich

**Paff, Mrs. Charles**    [FFF]
*Entertainer*
* Mortimer, Lottie

**Pafko, Andrew** 1921-    [BE, BN]
*American baseball player*
* [The] Brow
* Pafko, Handy Andy
* Pafko, Pruschka

**Pafko, Handy Andy**
*See* Pafko, Andrew

**Pafko, Pruschka**
*See* Pafko, Andrew

**Pagan, Jose**
*See* Rivera, Jose

**Pagan, Kristian**
*See* Sebelien, John Robert Francis

**Pagan y Ferrer, Gloria Maria**
1920-    [CA]
*Puerto Rican poet*
* Palma, Marigloria

**Paganelli [or Pignatelli], Bernardo**
?-1153    [WBD]
*Pope*
* Eugenius III

**Paganini, Nicolo** 1782-1840    [SN]
*Italian musician*
* [The] Devil

**Pagano, Bartolomeo** 1878-1947
[WEF]
*Italian actor*
* Maciste

**Page, Alan** 1946-    [IBW]
*American football player*
* Page, War Whoop

**Page, Anita**
*See* Pomares, Anita

**Page, Arthur W.**
*See* Wellington, Arthur

**Page, Big 'Un**
*See* Page, Walter

**Page, Catherine** 20th c.    [AW]
*Irish-born author*
* Armstrong, Cathleen

**Page, Don**
*See* Paige, Jose

**Page, Eileen**
*See* Heal, Edith

**Page, Eleanor**
*See* Coerr, Eleanor [Beatrice]

**Page, Elizabeth Lawson** 20th c.
[IBW]
*American educator*
* Page, Hot Lips

**Page, Evelyn** 1902-
[CA, WD, WW]
*American author*
* Scarlett, Roger [joint pseudonym
with Dorothy Blair]

**Page, Fireman**
*See* Page, Joseph Francis [Joe]

**Page, [Sir] Francis** 1718-1741
[HN, RH]
*British jurist*
* [The] Hanging Judge

**Page, G. S.**
*See* Galbraith, Georgie Starbuck

**Page, Gale**
*See* Rutter, Sally

**Page, Gerald W[ilburn]** 1939-
[CA, HFF, WGT]
*American author and editor*
* Grindle, Carleton
* Jones, Harold
* Lee, Eric
* Pembrooke, Kenneth
* Tifton, Leo

**Page, Grover, Jr.** 1918-    [CA]
*American author and librarian*
* McGinnis, K. K.

**Page, H. A.**
*See* Yapp, Alexander

**Page, Harlan O.** 1887-1965
[AS, BB]
*American basketball player*
* Page, Pat

**Page, Horse**
*See* Page, Walter

**Page, Hot Lips**
*See* Page, Elizabeth Lawson

**Page, Hot Lips**
*See* Page, Oran Thaddeus

**Page, Jake**
*See* Page, James K[eena], Jr.

**Page, James K[eena], Jr.** 1936-
[CA]
*American author and editor*
* Page, Jake

**Page, John Arthur** 1910-    [FC, ITA]
*American actor*
* Paige, Robert [Bob]

**Page, John Percy** 1877-1973
[CSH]
*Canadian basketball coach*
* Page, Papa

**Page, Joseph Francis [Joe]** 1917-
[BE, PB]
*American baseball player*
* [The] Gay Reliever
* Page, Fireman

**Page, Kenneth Calvin**
*See* Hogben, Lancelot Thomas

**Page, La Wanda** 1920-    [IBW]
*American entertainer*
* [The] Bronze Goddess of Fire

**Page, LeRoy Robert** 1906-    [BAB]
*American baseball player*
* Paige, LeRoy Robert
* Paige, Satchel

**Page, Lips**
*See* Page, Oran Thaddeus

**Page, Lorna**
*See* Rowland, D[onald] S[ydney]

**Page, Lucille**
*See* Berdell, Lucille

**Page, Lutie**
*See* Mower, Mrs. Fred

**Page, Marco**
*See* Kurnitz, Harry

**Page, Mary**
*See* Heal, Edith

**Page, Norvell W.** 1904-1961
[EMD, ESF, WGT]
*American author*
* Craig, Randolph
* Stockbridge, Grant

**[The] Page of State to the Muses**
*See* Spenser, Edmund

**[A] Page on Father Page**
*See* Fitzgerald, Gerald M.

**Page, Oran Thaddeus** 1908-1954
[BWW, DAM, EJ]
*American jazz musician*
* Page, Hot Lips
* Page, Lips
* Papa Snow White

**Page, Papa**
*See* Page, John Percy

**Page, Pat**
*See* Page, Harlan O.

**Page, Patricia Kathleen** 1916-
[CA, WD]
*British-born poet and artist*
* Cape, Judith
* Irwin, P. K.

**Page, Patti**
*See* Fowler, Clara Ann

**Page, Paul**
*See* Hicks, Campbell U.

**Page, Richard**    [PA]
*Author*
* Hardcastle, Daniel

**Page, Stanton**
*See* Fuller, Henry Blake

**Page, Thomas** [joint pseudonym with
Daniel T. Streib]
*See* Jones, Robert Page

**Page, Thomas** [joint pseudonym with
Robert Page Jones]
*See* Streib, Daniel T.

**Page, Tilsa**
*See* Stubbs, Tilsa

**Page, Vicki**
*See* Avey, Ruby

**Page, Walter** 20th c.    [NP]
*American jazz musician*
* Page, Big 'Un
* Page, Horse

**Page, Walter Hines** 1855-1918
[WBD]
*American journalist*
* Worth, Nicholas

**Page, War Whoop**
*See* Page, Alan

**Page Roberts, James** 1925-    [ART]
*British painter and sculptor*
* P. R.

**Pagery, Francois**
*See* Klein, Gerard

**Pages, Pedro** 1916-    [CA]
*Spanish-born educator and author*
* Alba, Victor

**Paget, Debra**
*See* Griffin, Debralee

**Paget, Francis Edward** 1806- ?
[FFF, PA]
*British clergyman and author*
* Churne, William
* F. E. P.

**Paget, George Charles Henry Victor**
1922- [CA]
*British author*
* Anglesey, Marquess of

**Paget, John**
*See* Aiken, John [Kempton]

**Paget, Margaret**
*See* Medlicott, Margaret P[aget]

**Paget, Violet** 1856-1935
[HDM, LC, TC]
*British author*
* Lee, Vernon

**Paget-Lowe, H[enry]**
*See* Lovecraft, Howard Phillips

**Pagett, Nicola**
*See* Scott, Nicola

**Pagliaroni, James Vincent** 1937-
[BE]
*American baseball player*
* Pagliaroni, Pag

**Pagliaroni, Pag**
*See* Pagliaroni, James Vincent

**Pahlavi, Reza** 20th c.
*Iranian ruler*
* [The] Old Shah

**Pahlow, Mannfried Otto Siegfried**
1926- [IAW]
*German chemist and writer*
* Hagen, Martin S.

**Pahz, [Anne] Cheryl Suzanne**
*See* Goldfeder, [Anne] Cheryl
Suzanne

**Pahz, James Alon**
*See* Goldfeder, [Kenneth] James

**Paicovich, Yigal** 1918- [CA]
*Israeli politician and author*
* Allon, Yigal

**Paidagogos, Petros**
*See* Brickman, William W.

**Paidola, Anton**
*See* Neagu, Paul

**Paiement, Wilf**
*See* Paiement, Wilfred

**Paiement, Wilfred** 1955-
[FHE, SMG]
*Canadian-born hockey player*
* Paiement, Wilf

**Paige, Elbridge Gerry** 1816-1859
[PA]
*American author*
* Dow Jr.

**Paige, Evelyn**
*See* Gold, Evelyn Paige

**Paige, George L.** 1885- [BE]
*American baseball player*
* Paige, Pat

**Paige, Janis**
*See* Jaden, Donna Mae

**Paige, Jose** 1900?-1967
[F2, FC, SC]
*American actor*
* Alvarado, Don
* Page, Don

**Paige, Leo**
*See* Cochrane, William E.

**Paige, LeRoy Robert**
*See* Page, LeRoy Robert

**Paige, Mabel**
*See* Roberts, Mabel

**Paige, Norman**
*See* Seltzer, Norman Murray

**Paige, Pat**
*See* Paige, George L.

**Paige, Patsy**
*See* Brilhante, Patricia

**Paige, Robert [Bob]**
*See* Page, John Arthur

**Paige, Satchel**
*See* Page, LeRoy Robert

**Paikert, Imre** 1917- [OP]
*Hungarian opera singer*
* Palos, Imre

**Paillere, Madeleine Dominique**
1916- [CW]
*Haitian poet, author, art critic*
* Fraeniel

**Paine, A. G. Amye** 1864- ? [NAA]
*British-born writer*
* A. G. A. P.
* Clarke, Gertrude

**Paine, Allie**
*See* Paine, Alva

**Paine, Alva** 1919- [BB]
*American basketball player*
* Paine, Allie

**Paine, Flip**
*See* Paine, Phillips Steere

**Paine, Guthrie?**
*See* Tremaine, F[rederick] Orlin

**Paine, Hammond**
*See* Hook, H. Clarke

**Paine, J. Lincoln**
*See* Kramish, Arnold

**Paine, Lauran [Bosworth]** 1916-
[ESF, SFL, SFP]
*British author*
* Carrel, Mark
* Howard, Troy

**Paine, Leslie Harold William**
1921- [IAW]
*British author*
* Paine, Nicky

**Paine, Lizzie**
*See* Millbank, Mrs. George

**Paine, Nicky**
*See* Paine, Leslie Harold William

**Paine, Phillips Steere** 1930- [BE]
*American baseball player*
* Paine, Flip

**Paine, Thomas** 1737-1809 [PA]
*Author*
* Duchatelet

**Painter, Mary C.** 1841- ? [PA]
*Author*
* Dawdle, Dolly

**[The] Painter of Coolness**
*See* Hobbema, Minderhout

**[The] Painter of Jansenism**
*See* Champagne, Philippe de

**[The] Painter of Nature**
*See* Belleau, Remi

**[The] Painter of Pageants**
*See* Cagliari [or Caliari?], Paolo

**[The] Painter of the Graces**
*See* Appiani, Andrea

**[The] Painter of the Graces**
*See* Boucher, Francois

**[The] Painter of the National Parks**
*See* Widforss, Gunnar Mauritz

**[The] Painter of the Soil**
*See* Wood, Grant

**Painter Pug**
*See* Hogarth, William

**[The] Painting Moralist**
*See* Hogarth, William

**[The] Painting Nun**
*See* Kent, Corita

**Painton, Ivan Emory** 1909- [IAW]
*American poet and painter*
* Zarello, Florian

**Pair, Ronald R.** 20th c.
*American inventor and entrepreneur*
* R. P.

**Pairault, Pierre** 1922- [CA]
*French author*
* Wul, Stefan

**Paisley, Tom**
*See* Passailaigue, Thomas E.

**Pak, Chan-Ki**
*See* Park, Chan-Ki

**Pakenham, Francis Aungier** 1905-
[NN]
*British diplomat*
* Porn, Lord

**Pakington, [Sir] John** ?-1560
[SN, WBD]
*British barrister and courtier*
* Her Temperance
* Pakington, Lusty

**Pakington, [Sir] John Somerset**
*See* Russell, John Somerset

**Pakington, Lusty**
*See* Pakington, [Sir] John

**Pal, Rudrendra Kumar** 1902-
[IAW]
*Indian physician and writer*
* Parulkumar

**Palacio, Lino** 1910?- [WECO]
*Argentinian cartoonist*
* Flax

**[The] Paladin of Paramours**
*See* Mitchelson, Marvin

**Palance, Jack**
*See* Palanuik, Walter

**Palander af Vega**
*See* Palander, Louis

**Palander, Louis** 1842-1902 [WBD]
*Swedish naval officer and Arctic
explorer*
* Palander af Vega

**Palanuik, Walter** 1920?-
[FC, SW, WEF]
*American actor*
* Palance, Jack

**Palazzeschi, Aldo**
*See* Giurlani, Aldo

**Paldi, Zelda** 1873-1935 [BEW]
*American actress and playwright*
* Sears, Zelda

**[The] Pale Death of the Saracens**
*See* Otto II [or Otho]

**Palermo, Alex**
*See* Palermo, Alfonse Lawrence

**Palermo, Alfonse Lawrence** 1929-
[BEW]
*American director, choreographer,
actor*
* Palermo, Alex

**Palermo, Blinky**
*See* Palermo, Frank

**Palermo, Bucky**
*See* Palermo, Charles

**Palermo, Charles** 1932?-
*American underworld figure*
* Allen, Charlie
* Buck, Charlie
* Palermo, Bucky

**Palermo, Frank** 20th c.
*American boxing promoter,
convicted of extortion*
* Palermo, Blinky

**Palestrant, Simon S.** 1907-
[AW, CAP]
*American author*
* Edwards, Stephen
* Stevens, S. P.
* Strand, Paul E.

**Palestrina, Giovanni** 1525?-1594
[DEP, HN, SN]
*Italian composer*
* [The] Father of Music
* [The] Michael Angelo of the Lyre
* [The] Prince of Music

**Palethorpe-Todd, Richard** 1919-
[BF]
*Irish-born actor*
* Todd, Richard

**Palette, Billy**
*See* Robinson, William

**Palette, Peter**
*See* Onwhyn, Thomas

**Paley, Babe**
*See* Paley, Barbara Cushing

**Paley, Barbara Cushing** 1915?-1978
*American socialite*
* Paley, Babe

**Palfrey, Sarah G.** 19th c. [PA]
*Author*
* Foxton, E.

**Palgrave, Francis Turner**
1824-1897 [DEL]
*British author and editor*
* Thurston, Henry T.

**Palica, Ervin Martin**
*See* Pavliecivich, Ervin Martin

**Palickar, Stephen J.** 1896- [NAA]
*American author and journalist*
* Carr, Stephen J.
* Stephens, S. J.

**Palingenesius**
*See* Mauzolli, Pietro Angelo

**Palinurus**
*See* Connolly, Cyril [Vernon]

**Palisier, John** 1885?- ? [NOJ]
*American jazz musician*
* Palisier, Pujol

**Palisier, Pujol**
See Palisier, John

**Pall, Ellen Jane** 1952- [CA]
*American author*
* Hill, Fiona

**Pall, Etienne**
See Platel, Felix

**Palladino, Joseph Anthony** 1910-
[BEW, TR]
*American actor*
* Faye, Joey

**Pallant, Norman C.** 20th c. [SFP]
*Author*
* Crouch, Charles Alban

**Pallante, Aladdin Abdullah Achmed Anthony** 1913-1970 [SC]
*American actor and comic singer*
* Aladdin

**[The] Pallas of Sweden**
See Key, Ellen Karoline Sofia

**Palli, Pitsa**
See Hartocollis, Peter

**Palm, Clarence** 20th c. [OBW]
*American baseball player*
* Palm, Spoony

**Palm, Gene**
See Palmisano, Luigi

**Palm, Mike**
See Palm, Richard Paul

**Palm, Richard Paul** 1925- [BE]
*American baseball player*
* Palm, Mike

**Palm, Spoony**
See Palm, Clarence

**Palma Giovane**
See Palma, Jacopo

**Palma, Jacopo** 1480?-1528 [WBD]
*Venetian painter*
* Palma Vecchio
* [Il] Vecchio [The Elder]

**Palma, Jacopo** 1544-1628 [WBD]
*Venetian painter*
* [Il] Giovane [The Younger]
* Palma Giovane

**Palma, Marigloria**
See Pagan y Ferrer, Gloria Maria

**Palma, [Signora] Sara**
See Newell, Mrs. Atkins

**Palma Vecchio**
See Palma, Jacopo

**Palma y Romay, Ramon de**
1812-1860 [CW]
*Cuban poet, playwright, author*
* [El] Bachiller Alfonso de Maldonado

**Palmara, Mimmo** 20th c. [WF]
*Italian actor*
* Palmer, Dick

**Palmeno [Man from Palma Del Rio]**
See Garcia, Julio

**Palmeno [Man from Palma Del Rio]**
See Garcia, Manuel

**Palmer**
See Powers, Francis Gary

**Palmer, B. C.**
See Schmidt, Laura M[arie]

**Palmer, Baldy**
See Palmer, Edwin Henry [Eddie]

**Palmer, Bernard** 1914- [CA]
*American author*
* Runyan, John

**Palmer, Betsy**
See Hrunek, Patricia Betsy

**Palmer, Bill**
See Miller, Bob

**Palmer, Cleveland**
See Bradley, William Aspenwall

**Palmer, Dick**
See Palmara, Mimmo

**Palmer, Ding**
See Palmer, Winthrop H.

**Palmer, Edwin Henry [Eddie]**
1893- [BE]
*American baseball player*
* Palmer, Baldy

**Palmer, Elsie Pavitt** 1922- [CA]
*American author*
* Palmer, Peter

**Palmer, Fred** 1851-1927 [BEW]
*British-born actor*
* Grove, Fred

**Palmer, Gregg**
See Lee, Palmer

**Palmer, Gretta**
See Clark, Gretta Palmer

**Palmer, Hackle**
See Key, R. Blake

**Palmer, Halleck**
See Watson, Evelyn Mabel

**Palmer, Henrietta Eliza Vaughan**
1856-1911 [LC]
*British author*
* Winter, John Strange

**Palmer, James Shedden** 1810-1867
[FFF]
*American naval officer*
* Palmer, Pie Crust

**Palmer, John Leslie** 1885-1944
[CC, EMD, LC]
*British author*
* Beeding, Francis [joint pseudonym with Hilary Aidan St. George Saunders]
* Haddon, Christopher
* Pilgrim, David [joint pseudonym with Hilary Aidan St. George Saunders]

**Palmer, Laura**
See Schmidt, Laura M[arie]

**Palmer, Lilli**
See Peiser, Maria Lilli

**Palmer, Lucienne** 20th c.
[BEW, TR]
*British playwright and translator*
* Hill, Lucienne

**Palmer, Lynde**
See Peebles, Mary

**Palmer, M.** [PA]
*Author*
* Varick

**Palmer, Madelyn** 1910- [IAW]
*Australian-born author*
* Peters, Geoffrey

**Palmer, Minnie**
See Rogers, Mrs. John R.

**Palmer, P. K.** ?-1973? [SFL]
*Author*
* Parnell, Keith

**Palmer, Pamela Lynn** 1951- [CA]
*American poet*
* Leigh, Palmer

**Palmer, Patricia** 1895-1964 [SC]
*American actress*
* Gibson, Margaret

**Palmer, Pedlar**
See Palmer, Thomas

**Palmer, Peter**
See Palmer, Elsie Pavitt

**Palmer, Pie Crust**
See Palmer, James Shedden

**Palmer, Pot-Pie**
See Sanford, Edward

**Palmer, Raymond A[rthur]**
1910-1977 [ESF, SF, WGT]
*American editor and writer*
* Gade, Henry [house pseudonym]
* Irwin, G. H.
* Patton, Frank
* Pelkie, Joe Walter
* Quitman, Wallace
* Steber, A. R.
* Steele, Morris J. [house pseudonym, Ziff-Davis]
* Webster, Robert N.
* Winters, Rae?

**Palmer, Stuart [Hunter]** 1905-1968
[CC, WW]
*American author*
* Stewart [or Stuart], Jay

**Palmer, Thomas** 1876-1949
[BX, RBE]
*British boxer*
* Little Box o' Tricks
* Palmer, Pedlar

**Palmer, Tobias**
See Weathers, Winston

**Palmer, Vera Jane** 1932?-1967
[BDF, FC, IPA]
*American actress*
* Mansfield, Jayne

**Palmer, William Claud Michel**
1891?-1970 [F2, FC]
*British actor*
* Allister, Claud

**Palmer, William Henry** 1830-1878
[PA]
*Author*
* Heller, Robert

**Palmer, William Thomas** 1877- ?
[WWL]
*British author*
* Kent, Christopher
* W. T. P.

**Palmer, Winthrop H.** 1906-1970
[BBH]
*American hockey player*
* Palmer, Ding

**Palmerston, Viscount**
See Temple, Henry John

**Palmezeaux**
See Cubieres, Michael

**Palmier, Remo**
See Palmieri, Remo

**Palmieri, Remo** 1923- [EJ]
*American jazz musician*
* Palmier, Remo

**Palmisano, Luigi** 20th c.
[SFL, SFP]
*Author*
* Palm, Gene

**Palmyra's Queen**
See Stanhope, Hester Lucy

**Palomares Del Pino, Francisco** 20th
c. [GS]
*Spanish bullfighter*
* [El] Marino [The Mariner]

**Palomo Linares [Palomo from Linares]**
See Palomo Martinez, Sebastian

**Palomo Martinez, Sebastian** 1947-
[GS]
*Spanish bullfighter*
* Palomo Linares [Palomo from Linares]

**Palos, Imre**
See Paikert, Imre

**Palsgrave, Goodman**
See Frederick V

**Palsgrave, Goody**
See Elizabeth

**Palsson, Hermann** 1921- [IAW]
*Icelandic-born author*
* Cadwr

**Paltenghi, Madeleine**
See Anderson, Madeleine Paltenghi

**Paltock, Robert** 18th c. [PA]
*Author*
* R. P.
* Wilkins, Peter

**Palton, Francis T.** [PA]
*Author*
* Noyes, MacLeod

**[A] Paltry Dunghill**
See Hill, [Sir] John

**Pam**
See Temple, Henry John

**Pambelecito**
See Cervantes, Jose

**Pamela**
See FitzGerald, Lady

**Pamfili, Giovanni Battista**
1574-1655 [WBD]
*Pope*
* Innocent X

**Pamjean, Louis**
See Bedford-Jones, Henry [James O'Brien]

**Pamphili**
See Eusebius of Caesarea

**Pan**
See Beresford, Leslie

**Pan, Peter**
See Bartier, Pierre

**Panaetius**
See De Ferrare, Baptiste

**Panama Al Brown**
See Brown, Alphonse Theo

**Panard, Charles-Francois**
1694-1765 [DEP, FFF, SN]
*French poet and playwright*
* [The] Father of Modern French Song
* [The] La Fontaine of the Vaudeville

**[The] Panard of the 19th Century**
See Gouffe, Armand

**[The] Panavision Kid**
See Bowering, George

**Panbourne, Oliver**
See Rockey, Howard

**Pancho**
See Cook, Enoch

**Pancoast, Ace**
See Pancoast, Asa

**Pancoast, Asa** 1905- [ASC]
*American musician*
* Pancoast, Ace

**Panconcelli-Calzia, Giulio** 1878- ?
[LAO]
*Italian-born educator and author*
* G. P. C.

**Paner, George Washington**
1871-1950 [BE]
*American baseball player*
* Paynter, George Washington

**Panfili, Mirella** 20th c. [WF]
*Italian actress*
* Sullivan, Mary

**Pangborn, Edgar** 1909-1976
[SFL, WGT]
*American author*
* Harrison, Bruce

**Pangloss**
See Hendie, Paul

**Panica, John** 1893- [BX, RBE]
*American boxer*
* Wilson, Johnny

**Panikkar, K[avalam] Madhava**
1895-1963 [CAP]
*Indian author*
* Chanakya
* Putra, Kerala

**Panneton, Philippe** 1895-1960
[WBD]
*Canadian author*
* Ringuet

**Panomita**
See Beccadelli, Antonio

**Panonius, Janus**
See Cisinge, Johann

**Panova, Vera [Federovna]**
1905-1973 [CA]
*Russian author, playwright, journalist*
* Veltman, Vera

**Panowski, Eileen [Janet] Thompson**
1920- [CA, WD]
*American author*
* Thompson, Eileen

**Pansey**
See Reid, Esther

**Panshin, Alexei** 1940- [ESF]
*American author*
* Adams, Louis J. A. [joint pseudonym with Joe Louis Hensley]

**Pansy**
See Alden, Isabella Macdonald

**Pansy**
See Donisthorpe, Ida Margaret Loder

**Pantaleon, Jacques** ?-1264 [WBD]
*Pope*
* Urban IV

**Pantarch**
See Andrews, Stephen Pearl

**Panting, Arnold Clement** ?-1917
[MBF]
*British author and editor*
* Arnold, Clement

**Panting, James Harwood** 20th c.
[MBF, WWL]
*British author*
* Heathcote, Claud

**Pantolabus, Ponce**
See Huntingdon, John

**Panzarella, Anthony John** 1915-
[BEW]
*American producer and director*
* Parella, Anthony

**Panzer, Paul Wolfgang**
See Panzerbeiter, Paul

**Panzerbeiter, Paul** 1872-1958
*German-born actor*
* Panzer, Paul Wolfgang

**Panzram, Carl** 1891-1930 [BLB]
*American murderer*
* Allen, Jack
* Baldwin, Jeff
* Copper John, II
* Davis, Jeff
* O'Leary, John
* Rhoades, Jefferson

**Paolella, Alfred** 1905-
[PMJ, WWJ]
*American composer and bandleader*
* James, Freddy
* Powell, Teddy

**Paoli, Betty**
See Glueck, Barbara Elisabeth

**Paoli, Corsica**
See Paoli, Pasquale de

**Paoli, Pasquale de** 1726-1807
[DNNF, FFF, SN]
*Corsican patriot*
* Paoli, Corsica

**Paolinelli, Rinaldo Angelo** 1895-
[BE]
*American baseball player*
* Pinelli, Babe
* Pinelli, Ralph Arthur

**Paolo, [Fra]**
See Sarpi, Pietro

**Paolotti, John**
See Wilson, Guthrie Edward

**Paolotto, [Fra]**
See Ghislandi, [Fra] Vittore

**Pap**
See Paprocki, Thomas

**Papa Bear Banks**
See Banks, Earl

**Papa Bear Halas**
See Halas, George S.

**Papa Charlie**
See Davis, Charlie

**Papa Charlie**
See McCoy, Charles [Charlie]

**Papa Charlie Jackson**
See Jackson, Charlie

**Papa Chittlins**
See Moore, Alexander Herman

**Papa Doc**
See Duvalier, Francois

**Papa George**
See Lightfoot, Alexander

**Papa Henry Brown**
See Brown, Henry

**Papa Jac**
See Assunto, Jacob

**Papa Jack**
See Laine, George Vitelle

**Papa Joe**
See Oliver, Joseph

**Papa John**
See Joseph, John

**Papa John**
See Phillips, John

**Papa John Creach**
See Creach, John

**Papa Johnny Torrio**
See Torrio, John [Johnny]

**Papa la Violette**
See Bonaparte, Napoleon

**Papa Mutt Carey**
See Carey, Thomas

**Papa Snow White**
See Page, Oran Thaddeus

**Papa Tono**
See Alix, Juan Antonio

**Papadiamantopoulos, Iannis**
1856-1910 [CD, EWL, HDM]
*Greek-born poet, playwright, author*
* Moreas, Jean

**Papadimitriou, Theodoros** 1931-
[CAR]
*Greek sculptor*
* Theodoros

**Papailler, Hubert** 1916- [CW]
*Haitian poet and author*
* Maria Mour, Jean Hubert

**Papaleo, Anthony** 1928-
[BEW, FC, IPA]
*American actor*
* Franciosa, Anthony [Tony]

**Papaleo, William** 1922- [BX, RBE]
*American boxer*
* Pep, Willie
* Will o' the Wisp

**Paparella, Attilio** 1874-1944
[BBD]
*Italian conductor and composer*
* Parelli, Attilio

**Papareschi, Gregorio** ?-1143
[WBD]
*Pope*
* Innocent II

**Pape, D. L.**
See Pape, Donna [Lugg]

**[Le] Pape des Huguenots**
See Mornay, Philippe de [Seigneur du Plessis-Marly]

**Pape, Donna [Lugg]** 1930- [CA]
*American author*
* Pape, D. L.

**[El] Papelero [The Paper Seller]**
See Alvarado Luvianos, Victor

**[The] Paper King**
See Law, John

**Paper Saving Pope**
See Pope, Alexander

**Paperito**
See Jiminez, Marcos

**[The] Paperknife**
See Tullock, W. W.

**[The] Paphlagonian**
See Michael IV

**Papillon**
See Charriere, Henri

**Papineau, Louis Joseph** 1786-1871
[HN]
*French-Canadian politician*
* [The] Canadian O'Connell

**Papini, Giovanni** 1881-1956 [CAT]
*Italian author*
* Falco, Gian

**Papirius, Lucius** 4th c. BC [WBD]
*Roman general and politician*
* Cursor

**Papirofsky, Joseph** 1921-
[BEW, EMT, IPA]
*American director and producer*
* Papp, Joseph

**Papish, Frank Richard** 1917-1965
[BE]
*American baseball player*
* Papish, Pap

**Papish, Pap**
See Papish, Frank Richard

**Papke, William Herman [Billy]**
1886-1936 [BX, RBE]
*American boxer*
* [The] Illinois Thunderbolt
* [The] Thunderbolt

**Papoulkas, Sotirios** 1943- [OP]
*Greek opera singer*
* Papulkas, Soto

**Papp, Joseph**
See Papirofsky, Joseph

**Pappas, Angelos** 1883- [SFL]
*Author*
* Pappazisis, Evangelos

**Pappas, George Stephen** 1930-
[WD]
*Australian author and educator*
* Justificus

**Pappas, Gimpy**
See Pappas, Milt[on Steven]

**Pappas, Milt[on Steven]** 1939-   [PB]
*American baseball player*
* [The] Golden Greek
* Pappas, Gimpy

**Pappazisis, Evangelos**
*See* Pappas, Angelos

**Paprika**
*See* Holmvik, Oyvind

**Paprocki, Thomas** 1901-1973
[WEC]
*American cartoonist*
* Pap

**Papulkas, Soto**
*See* Papoulkas, Sotirios

**Papus**
*See* Encausse, Gerard

**Paquirri**
*See* Rivera Perez, Francisco

**Parabellum**
*See* Grautoff, Ferdinand
[Heinrich]

**Paracelsus, Philippus Aureolus**
*See* Von Hohenheim, Theophrastus
Bombastus

**Paradise, Mary**
*See* Eden, Dorothy Enid

**Paragraph, Peter**
*See* Faulkner, George

**[The] Parakeet**
*See* Fuentes, Rigoberto

**Parallax**
*See* Robotham, Samuel Birley

**[The] Paramount Wildcat**
*See* Rainey, Gertrude Malissa Nix
[Pridgett]

**Parans, Cato**
*See* Heber, Richard

**Parasara**
*See* De Silva, David

**Parbury, Kathleen Ophir Theodora**
1901-   [ART]
*British sculptor*
* K. O. T. P.

**Parcell, Norman H[owe]** 20th c.
[SFL, WGT]
*British author*
* Fairleigh, Christopher
* Nicholson, John
* Percival, Norman

**Pardee, C. W.** 1885-1975
[FIR, SC]
*American actor, rodeo performer,
trainer*
* Pardee, Doc

**Pardee, Doc**
*See* Pardee, C. W.

**Pardee, Gabby**
*See* Pardee, John P. [Jack]

**Pardee, John P. [Jack]** 1936-
*American football player*
* Pardee, Gabby

**Pardon, George Frederick**
1824-1884   [DEL, FFF, PA]
*British author and critic*
* Crawley, [Captain] Rawdon
* G. F. P.

**Pare, Ambroise** 1517-1590
[DEP, DNNS, HN]
*French surgeon*
* [The] Father of French Surgery

**Pareja, Juan de** 1606?-1670
[WBD]
*Spanish painter*
* [El] Esclavo [The Slave]

**Parejito [Little Smooth One]**
*See* Lopez Parejo, Francisco

**Parella, Anthony**
*See* Panzarella, Anthony John

**Parelli, Attilio**
*See* Paparella, Attilio

**[The] Parent of Canal Navigation**
*See* Egerton, Francis

**[The] Parent of English Verse**
*See* Waller, Edmund

**Parentucelli [or da Sarzana],
Tommaso** 1397?-1455   [WBD]
*Pope*
* Nicholas V

**Pares, Marion Stapylton** 1914-
[AW, CA]
*British author*
* Campbell, Judith

**Paret, Benny**
*See* Paret, Bernardo

**Paret, Bernardo** 1937-1962
[RBE, WBC]
*Cuban-born boxer*
* Paret, Benny
* Paret, Kid

**Paret, Kid**
*See* Paret, Bernardo

**Paretti, Tony** 20th c.   [BLB]
*American underworld figure*
* [The] Shoemaker

**Parfouru, Paul Desire** 1843-1917
[BEW]
*French producer and actor*
* Porel, Paul

**Pargeter, Edith Mary** 1913-
[AW, CA, CC]
*British author*
* Peters, Ellis

**Parham, Charles Valdez** 1913-
[DAM, EJ, WWJ]
*American jazz musician*
* Parham, Truck

**Parham, Hartzell Strathdene**
1900-1943   [EJ, PMJ, WWJ]
*American jazz musician*
* Parham, Tiny

**Parham, Robert Randall** 1943-
[CA]
*American poet and writer*
* Roberts, Rand

**Parham, Tiny**
*See* Parham, Hartzell Strathdene

**Parham, Truck**
*See* Parham, Charles Valdez

**Pariani, Bill**
*See* Pariani, Cino

**Pariani, Cino** 20th c.   [BBH]
*Soccer player*
* Pariani, Bill

**Paricciuoli, Walter** 1917-   [BBH]
*American soccer player*
* Peters, Wally

**Parikh, Rasiklal Chhotalal** 1897-
[IAW]
*Indian author*
* Musikara

**Parilli, Babe**
*See* Parilli, Vito

**Parilli, Vito** 1930-   [FB, SMG]
*American football player*
* Parilli, Babe

**Parin, A. P. L.**
*See* Faxon, Henry W.

**Pario, James** 20th c.   [SG]
*Boxer*
* Bazzano, Tommy

**Paris, Comte de**
*See* Orleans, Louis Philippe Albert
d'

**Paris, Dawn Evelyeen** 1918-
[F2, FC]
*American actress*
* O'Day, Dawn
* Shirley, Anne

**Paris, Diacre**
*See* Paris, Francois de

**Paris, Francois de** 1690-1727
[WBD]
*French theologian*
* Paris, Diacre

**Paris, John**
*See* Ashton-Gwatkin, Frank
Trelawny Arthur

**Paris, John Aryton** 1785-1856
[PA]
*Author*
* [A] Physician

**Paris, Manuel**
*See* Conesa, Manuel R.

**Parise, J. P.**
*See* Parise, Jean Paul

**Parise, Jean Paul** 1941-
[CEI, SMG]
*Canadian-born hockey player*
* Parise, J. P.
* Parise, Jeep

**Parise, Jeep**
*See* Parise, Jean Paul

**Parish, Townsend**
*See* Pietschmann, Richard John,
III

**Parisian Bob Caruthers**
*See* Caruthers, Robert Lee

**Parisot, Pierre** 1697-1769
[FFF, SN]
*French missionary*
* Norbert, [Father]

**Parisse, Louis Peter** 1911-1956
[BE]
*American baseball player*
* Parisse, Tony

**Parisse, Tony**
*See* Parisse, Louis Peter

**[The] Park Avenue Hillbilly**
*See* Shay, Dorothy

**Park, Chan-Ki** 1928-   [IAW]
*Korean author*
* Pak, Chan-Ki

**Park, Chung Hee** 1917-1979
*South Korean president*
* [The] Patriarch? [code name]
* Takagi, Masao

**Park, Fanny** 1852- ?   [WWL]
*British author*
* Heslop, F.

**Park, James Allen**   [PA]
*Author*
* [A] Layman

**Park, Jordan** [joint pseudonym with
Frederik Pohl]
*See* Kornbluth, Cyril M.

**Park, Jordan** [joint pseudonym with
Cyril M. Kornbluth]
*See* Pohl, Frederik

**Park, Maeva**
*See* Dobner, Maeva Park

**Park, Tongsun** 20th c.
*South Korean businessman*
* [The] Asian Great Gatsby

**Parke, F.**   [PA]
*British author*
* [The] London Hermit

**Parke, Harry**
*See* Einstein, Harry

**Parker, Ace**
*See* Parker, Clarence McKay

**Parker, Adele**
*See* Von Ohl, Adele

**Parker, Admiral**
*See* Parker, Richard

**Parker, Anthony**
*See* Tull, Anthony

**Parker, Beatrice**
*See* Huff, Tom Elmer

**Parker, Bently**
*See* Benjamin, Park

**Parker, Bert**
*See* Ellison, Harlan [Jay]

**Parker, Big Jim**
*See* Parker, Jim

**Parker, Big Train**
*See* Parker, Thomas [Tom]

**Parker, Bird**
*See* Parker, Charles Christopher,
Jr. [Charlie]

**Parker, Bonnie** 1911-1934   [BLB]
*American murderer and robber*
* Suicide Sal

**Parker, Buddy**
*See* Parker, Raymond

**Parker, Caroline**
*See* Fenton, Mrs. Charles

**Parker, Cecelia** 1932?-
[FC, ITA, SW]
*American actress*
* Parker, Suzy

**Parker, Cecil**
*See* Schwabe, Cecil

**Parker, Charles Christopher, Jr.**
**[Charlie]** 1920-1955
[BBD, EJ, PMJ]
*American jazz musician*
* Parker, Bird
* Parker, Yardbird

**Parker, Clarence McKay** 1913-
[FB]
*American football player*
* Parker, Ace

**Parker, Clarence Perkins**
1893-1967   [BE]
*American baseball player*
* Parker, Pat

**Parker, Cobra**
*See* Parker, David Gene [Dave]

**Parker, David Gene [Dave]** 1951-
[IBW]
*American baseball player*
* Parker, Cobra

**Parker, Dixie**
*See* Parker, Douglas Wooley

**Parker, Doc**
*See* Parker, Harley Park

**Parker, Dom Anselm** 1880- ?
[WWL]
*British clergyman and writer*
* Stanislaus, Edward

**Parker, [Sister] Dominic**
*See* Parker, Marion Dominica
Hope

**Parker, Dorothy**
*See* Rothschild, Dorothy

**Parker, Douglas Wooley** 1895-
[BE]
*American baseball player*
* Parker, Dixie

**Parker, Elizabeth [Chandler]**   [FFF]
*Author*
* Chandler, Bessie

**Parker, Eric** 1870- ?   [LAO]
*British author and journalist*
* Cheviot

**Parker, Fitzgerald Sale** 1863- ?
[NAA]
*American clergyman, author, editor*
* Teche, L. A.

**Parker, Francis James** 1913-   [PB]
*American baseball player*
* Francis, Charles
* Parker, Salty

**Parker, Frank**
*See* Ciccio, Frank

**Parker, Harley Park** 1874-1941
[BE]
*American baseball player*
* Parker, Doc

**Parker, Helen F.**   [PA]
*Author*
* H. F. P.

**Parker, Henry Taylor** 1867-1934
[BEW]
*American critic*
* H. T. P.

**Parker, Herman** 1932-1971
[BWW, DAM]
*American singer*
* Parker, Junior
* Parker, Little Junior

**Parker, Hershel** 1935-   [CA]
*American educator and author*
* Willis, Samuel

**Parker, Isaac** 20th c.   [BLB]
*American jurist*
* [The] Hanging Judge

**Parker, James**
*See* Newby, George Eric

**Parker, Jean**
*See* Green, Mae

**Parker, Jean**
*See* Sharat Chandra, G[ubbi]
S[hankara Chetty]

**Parker, Jim** 1934-   [IBW]
*American football player*
* Parker, Big Jim

**Parker, John** 1875- ?   [WWL]
*British author*
* J. P.

**Parker, John William, Jr.** 1918-
[EJ, PMJ, WWJ]
*American jazz musician*
* Parker, Knocky

**Parker, Junior**
*See* Parker, Herman

**Parker, Knocky**
*See* Parker, John William, Jr.

**Parker, Lefty**
*See* Parker, Paul

**Parker, Lew**
*See* Jacobs, Austin Lewis

**Parker, Linda** 20th c.   [ECM]
*American country-western performer*
* [The] Sunbonnet Girl

**Parker, Little Junior**
*See* Parker, Herman

**Parker, Louise**
*See* Oudin, Mrs. Eugene

**Parker, M. E. Frances**
*See* Bellerby, [Mary Eireen]
Frances

**Parker, Marion Dominica Hope**
1914-   [WD]
*British poet, author, critic,
translator*
* Hope, Marion
* Mary Dominic, [Sister]
* Parker, [Sister] Dominic

**Parker, Maurice Wesley** 1939-
[SMG]
*American baseball player*
* Parker, Tiger

**Parker, Mrs. Benton**   [FFF]
*Entertainer*
* Buchanan, Virginia

**Parker, Mrs. Harry D.**   [FFF]
*Entertainer*
* Blair, Lottie

**Parker, Mrs. Richard E.**   [FFF]
*Entertainer*
* Dillon, Fannie

**Parker, Murray** 1896-1965   [SC]
*American actor*
* Uncle Murray

**Parker, Nathaniel** 1922-   [IBW]
*American actor*
* [El] Shadow Negro

**Parker, Pat**
*See* Parker, Clarence Perkins

**Parker, Paul**
*See* Blunt, Paul

**Parker, Paul** 20th c.   [BLB]
*American bank robber*
* Parker, Lefty

**Parker, Paul William Giles** 1956-
[DC]
*Rhodesian-born cricketer*
* Parker, Polly
* Parker, Porky

**Parker, Pinky**
*See* Ciccio, Frank

**Parker, Polly**
*See* Parker, Paul William Giles

**Parker, Porky**
*See* Parker, Paul William Giles

**Parker, Raymond** 1913-
[FB, SMG]
*American football coach*
* Parker, Buddy

**Parker, Richard** ?-1797   [HN]
*British seaman*
* Parker, Admiral

**Parker, Robert**
*See* Boyd, Waldo T.

**Parker, Robert** 20th c.   [SMG]
*American basketball player*
* Parker, Sonny
* Sonny P.

**Parker, Robert LeRoy** 1867-1937
[BLB]
*American bank and train robber*
* Cassidy, Butch
* Cassidy, George

**Parker, Rosa Abbott**   [FFF, PA]
*Author*
* Abbott, Rosa

**Parker, Salty**
*See* Parker, Francis James

**Parker, Samuel** 1640-1688   [SN]
*British author*
* Mitred Dulness

**Parker, Seth**
*See* Lord, Phillips Haynes

**Parker, Sonny**
*See* Parker, Robert

**Parker, Suzy**
*See* Parker, Cecelia

**Parker, Theodore** 1810-1860   [FFF]
*American clergyman and author*
* Blodgett, Levi

**Parker, Thomas [Tom]** 20th c.
[OBW]
*American baseball player*
* Parker, Big Train

**Parker, Tiger**
*See* Parker, Maurice Wesley

**Parker, [Captain] Tom**
*See* Van Kuijk, Andreas Cornelis

**Parker, Tomcat**
*See* Parker, Willie

**Parker, Willard**
*See* Van Eps, Worster

**Parker, Willie** 20th c.   [NBB]
*American singer*
* Parker, Tomcat

**Parker, Yardbird**
*See* Parker, Charles Christopher,
Jr. [Charlie]

**Parkes, Frank Kobina** 1932-   [AW]
*Ghanaian author*
* Dompo, Kwesi

**Parkes, James William** 1896-
[IAW]
*British clergyman and author*
* Hadham, John

**Parkes, Lucas**
*See* Harris, John [Wyndham
Parkes Lucas] Beynon

**Parkes, Terence** 1927-   [AW]
*British cartoonist*
* Larry

**Parkes, Wyndham**
*See* Harris, John [Wyndham
Parkes Lucas] Beynon

**Parkinson, Cornelia M.** 1925-   [CA]
*American author*
* Taylor, Day [joint pseudonym
with Sharon Salvato]

**Parkinson, Elizabeth** 1882-1922
[DAM]
*American singer*
* Parkinson, Parkina

**Parkinson, H. B.**
*See* Parkinson, Henry Broughton

**Parkinson, Henry Broughton**
1884-1970   [BF]
*British director*
* Parkinson, H. B.

**Parkinson, Parkina**
*See* Parkinson, Elizabeth

**Parkinson-Fortescue, Chichester
Samuel**
*See* Fortescue, Chichester Samuel

**Parks**
*See* Price, Charles

**Parks, Larry**
*See* Klausman, Samuel

**Parks, Louise** 20th c.   [IBW]
*American dance troupe leader*
* Mama Lu

**Parks, Rose**
*American civil rights activist*
* [The] Mother of the Civil Rights
Movement

**Parks, Slicker**
*See* Parks, Vernon Henry

**Parks, Vernon Henry** 1895-   [BE]
*American baseball player*
* Parks, Slicker

**Parkyakarkus**
*See* Einstein, Harry

**Parkyn, Walter A.** 1862- ?   [WWL]
*British author*
* Homo

**Parley, Peter**
*See* Goodrich, Samuel Griswold

**Parley, Peter**
*See* Kettell, Samuel

**Parley, Peter**
See  Martin, William

**Parley, Peter**
See  Mogridge, George

**Parlin, John**
See  Graves, Charles Parlin

**Parlo, Dita**
See  Kornstadt, Grethe Gerda

**Parly, Ticho**
See  Christiansen, Ticho Parly
Frederik

**Parma, Clemens**
See  Menzel, Roderich

**Parmelee, LeRoy Earl** 1907-    [BE]
*American baseball player*
* Parmelee, Tarzan

**Parmelee, Tarzan**
See  Parmelee, LeRoy Earl

**Parmeno**
See  Lopez Pinillos, Jose

**Parmer, J. N.**
See  Parmer, Jess Norman

**Parmer, Jess Norman** 1925-
[WYA]
*American author*
* Parmer, J. N.

**[Il] Parmigianino [or Parmigiano]**
See  Mazzuoli [or Mazzola],
Girolamo Francesco Maria

**Parnell, Charles Stewart**
1846-1891    [DEP, DHA, DNNS]
*Irish statesman*
* [The] Uncrowned King of Ireland

**Parnell, Dusty**
See  Parnell, Melvin Lloyd

**Parnell, Francis**
See  Pragnell, Festus

**Parnell, Frank**    [WGT]
*Author*
* Francis, Gregory [joint
  pseudonym with James
  (Murdoch) MacGregor]
* Richardson, Francis [joint
  pseudonym with L. E. Bartle]

**Parnell, Frederick Russell**
1889-1973    [BMH]
*British ventriloquist*
* Carr, Russ

**Parnell, Keith**
See  Palmer, P. K.

**Parnell, Marvelous Mel**
See  Parnell, Melvin Lloyd

**Parnell, Melvin Lloyd** 1922-    [BE]
*American baseball player*
* Parnell, Dusty
* Parnell, Marvelous Mel

**Parnell, Red**
See  Parnell, Roy

**Parnell, Roy** 20th c.    [OBW]
*American baseball player*
* Parnell, Red

**Parnell, Thomas Frederick**
1862-1957    [BMH]
*British ventriloquist*
* [The] Father of the Profession
* Russell, Fred

**Parnell, Val**
See  Parnell, Valentine Charles

**Parnell, Valentine Charles** 1894-
[THR]
*British theatrical manager*
* Parnell, Val

**Parnham, James Arthur** 1894-1963
[BE]
*American baseball player*
* Parnham, Rube

**Parnham, Rube**
See  Parnham, James Arthur

**Parnis, Mollie**
See  Livingston, Mollie Parnis

**Paroisse-Pougin, Francois-Auguste
Arthur** 1834-1921    [BBD]
*French author and music critic*
* Pougin, Arthur

**Parolini, Gianfranco** 20th c.    [FDG]
*Italian director*
* Kramer, Frank

**Parr, Harriet** 1837- ?    [DEL, FFF]
*British author*
* Lee, Holme

**Parr, [Dr.] John Anthony**
See  Anthony, [Dr.] E.

**Parr, Julian F.** 20th c.    [SFP]
*Author*
* Ragatzy, Anton

**Parr, Lucy** 1924-    [CA, SAT]
*American writer*
* Carroll, Laura

**Parr, Old**
See  Parr, Thomas

**Parr, Olive Katharine** 1874-1955
[B10]
*British author*
* Chase, Beatrice

**Parr, Robert**
See  Gardner, Erle Stanley

**Parr, Samuel** 1747-1825
[DEL, DEP, DNNF]
*British scholar*
* [The] Birmingham Doctor
* Johnson, Brummagem
* [The] Nazarite
* Phileleutherus Norfolciensis
* Philopatris Varvicensis
* [The] Whig Johnson

**Parr, Thomas** 1483?-1635
[DEP, DNNS, RH]
*British centenarian*
* Parr, Old

**Parra, Luis** 20th c.    [GS]
*Spanish bullfighter*
* [El] Jerezano [The Man from
  Jerez]

**Parra Duenas, Augustin** 1924-
[GS]
*Spanish bullfighter*
* Parrita [Little Parra]

**Parran**
See  Garlow, Clarence Joseph

**Parrao [Spreading]**
See  Hernandez y Castro, Joaquin

**Parrhasius** 5th c. BC
[DEP, DNNS, FFF]
*Greek painter*
* [The] King of Painters

**Parrhasius** (Continued)
* [The] Prince of Painters

**[The] Parricide**
See  Henry V [or Heinrich]

**[The] Parricide**
See  John [or Johannes] of Swabia

**Parris, Bob** 1944-    [NAD]
*American civil rights organizer*
* Moses, Bob

**Parrish, Eugene**
See  Harding, Donald Edward

**Parrish, Judy**
See  Donohue, Dorothy Howell

**Parrish, [Emma] Kenyon** 1849- ?
[NAA]
*American writer*
* Gamelyn
* McCurdy, Nancy

**Parrish, Larry** 1943-
*American attorney*
* Clean, Mr.
* [The] Memphis Heat

**Parrish, Mary**
See  Cousins, Margaret

**Parrish, Mary Frances**
See  Fisher, Mary Frances Kennedy

**Parrita [Little Parra]**
See  Parra Duenas, Augustin

**Parrondo, Tomas** 1857-1900    [GS]
*Spanish bullfighter*
* [El] Manchao [The Spotted One]

**Parrot, William** 1878-1952    [BMH]
*British comedian and singer*
* McIver, Jock
* O'Farrell, Talbot

**Parrott, Charles**
See  Chase, Charles [Charley]

**Parrott, George** 20th c.    [BLB]
*American bandit*
* Curry, Big Nose
* Curry, Flat Nose
* Curry, George L.

**Parrott, James [Jimmy]**
See  Chase, James [Jimmy]

**Parrott, Jiggs**
See  Parrott, Walter E.

**Parrott, Michael Everett Arch**
1954-    [SMG]
*American baseball player*
* [The] Birdman

**Parrott, Paul?**
See  Chase, Charles [Charley]

**Parrott, Tacky Tom**
See  Parrott, Thomas William
[Tom]

**Parrott, Thomas William [Tom]**
1868-1932    [BE]
*American baseball player*
* Parrott, Tacky Tom

**Parrott, Walter E.** 1871-1898    [BE]
*American baseball player*
* Parrott, Jiggs

**Parry, David Harold** 1868-1950
[MBF]
*British author*
* Blake, [Captain] Wilton
* Pike, Morton

**Parry, Hugh J[ones]** 1916-
[CA, WD, WW]
*American author*
* Cross, James

**Parry, John**
See  Whelpton, [George] Eric

**Parry, John Humphreys** 1787-1825
[PA]
*Author*
* Griffenhoof, Anthony

**Parry, Michel Patrick** 1947-
[HFF, WGT]
*British author*
* Cassaba, Carlos
* Fury, Nick
* Lee, Steve
* Lovecraft, Linda
* Pendragon, Eric

**Parsee Merchant**
See  Moore, J. S.

**Parsifal**
See  Curl, James Stevens

**[The] Parson**
See  Mulford, Ralph

**Parson Frank**
See  Jacox, Francis

**Parson, Jiggs**
See  Parson, William Edwin

**[The] Parson of the Islands**
See  Thomas, Joshua

**Parson, William Edwin** 1885-1967
[BE]
*American baseball player*
* Parson, Jiggs

**Parsons, Anthony** 1893-1963
[MBF]
*British author*
* Nicholls, Anthony

**Parsons, B.** 20th c.    [MBF]
*British author*
* Hunt, Maurice
* Young, Warwick

**Parsons, Baby**
See  Parsons, Harriet

**Parsons, Buzz**
See  Parsons, Les

**Parsons, C. L.** 20th c.    [BBH]
*American sports editor and
basketball organization officer*
* Parsons, Poss

**Parsons, David** 1915-    [THR]
*British actor*
* Tree, David

**Parsons, Dixie**
See  Parsons, Edward Dixon

**Parsons, Edward** 1900-    [IAW]
*British-born author*
* Onlooker

**Parsons, Edward Dixon** 1916-    [BE]
*American baseball player*
* Parsons, Dixie

**Parsons, Elizabeth** 1749-1807
[WBD]
*British imposter*
* [The] Cock Lane Ghost

**[The] Parson's Emperor**
See  Charles IV [or Karl]

**Parsons, Gram**
*See* Connor, Cecil

**Parsons, Harriet** 20th c. [FI]
*Actress*
* Parsons, Baby

**Parsons, Les** 1950- [AES]
*Canadian soccer player*
* Parsons, Buzz

**Parsons, Long Tom**
*See* Parsons, Thomas Anthony
[Tom]

**Parsons, Louella O.**
*See* Oettinger, Louella

**Parsons, Patrick** 1912- [FC]
*British actor*
* Holt, Patrick

**Parsons, Poss**
*See* Parsons, C. L.

**Parsons [or Persons?], Robert**
1546-1610 [FFF, PA, SN]
*British missionary and author*
* Crowbuck, Robert
* Doleman, Robert
* Howlett, John
* Philopater, Andreas
* [A] Proteus

**Parsons, Smiling Bill**
*See* Parsons, William [Billy]

**Parsons, Thomas Anthony [Tom]**
1939- [BE]
*American baseball player*
* Parsons, Long Tom

**Parsons, Tom**
*See* MacPherson, Thomas George

**Parsons, William [Billy]** 1878-1919
[FI, SC]
*American actor and producer*
* Parsons, Smiling Bill

**Parsons-Irwin, Maureen** 1935-
[ART]
*British artist*
* Mia

**Parsonus Rusticus**
*See* McDaniel, Samuel Walton

**Partch, Virgil Franklin, II** 1916-
[WEC]
*American cartoonist*
* VIP

**Partee, W. B.** [PA]
*Author*
* Nomistake

**Partenheimer, Harold Philip**
1891-1971 [BE]
*American baseball player*
* Partenheimer, Steve

**Partenheimer, Party**
*See* Partenheimer, Stanwood
Wendell

**Partenheimer, Stan**
*See* Partenheimer, Stanwood
Wendell

**Partenheimer, Stanwood Wendell**
1922- [BE]
*American baseball player*
* Partenheimer, Party
* Partenheimer, Stan

**Partenheimer, Steve**
*See* Partenheimer, Harold Philip

**Parthenia**
*See* Mazzolari, Guiseppe Marione

**Parthian**
*See* Grimshaw, Roland William
Wrigley

**Partington, Doris** 1893-1953
[BEW]
*British-born actress*
* Lytton, Doris

**Partington, F. H.**
*See* Yoxall, Harry W[aldo]

**Partington, Mrs.**
*See* Avery, Samuel P.

**Partington, Mrs.**
*See* Shillaber, Benjamin Penhallow

**[The] Partisan of Independence**
*See* Adams, John

**Parton, Sara Payson Willis**
1811-1872 [DEL, WBD]
*American author*
* Fern, Fanny

**Partridge, Anthony**
*See* Oppenheim, E[dward] Phillips

**Partridge, [Sir] Bernard** 1861-1945
[BEW, LC, WEC]
*British actor, cartoonist, painter*
* Gould, Bernard

**Partridge, Edward Bellamy**
1877-1960 [SFL, WGT]
*Author*
* Bailey, Thomas

**Partridge, Eric Honeywood**
1894-1979 [IAW]
*British literary critic and
lexicographer*
* Denison, Corrie
* Vigilans
* [The] Word King

**Partridge, Fez**
*See* Partridge, Martin David

**Partridge, Martin David** 1954-
[DC]
*British cricketer*
* Partridge, Fez

**Parulkumar**
*See* Pal, Rudrendra Kumar

**Parulski, George R[ichard], Jr.**
1954- [CA]
*American author*
* Brian, Alan B.
* Taylor, George

**Parva Laus [Little Laud]**
*See* Laud, William

**Parviz**
*See* Ghylichkhani, Parviz

**Parviz**
*See* Khosru II [or Chosroes]

**Pary, C. C.**
*See* Gilmore, Christopher Cook

**Pascal, Andre**
*See* De Rothschild, [Baron] Henri

**Pascal, Blaise** 1623-1662 [RH]
*French philosopher*
* Montalte, Louis de
* Thaumaturgus

**Pascal, Gabor** 1894-1954 [BEW]
*Hungarian-born director*
* Pascal, Gabriel

**Pascal, Gabriel**
*See* Pascal, Gabor

**[The] Pascal of Germany**
*See* Hardenberg, Friedrich von

**Pascarel**
*See* Warner, B. Ellison

**Paschal, Nancy**
*See* Trotter, Grace V[iolet]

**Paschal II**
*See* Ranieri

**Paschal III**
*See* Guido of Crema

**Pascin, Jules**
*See* Pincas, Julius

**Pascoe, Amy Bennet** 20th c. [EG]
*British golfer*
* Pascoe, Polly

**Pascoe, Polly**
*See* Pascoe, Amy Bennet

**Pascual**
*See* Garcia Sanchez, Jesus

**Pascual, Camilo Alberto** 1934-
[BE]
*Cuban-born baseball player*
* [The] Little Potato

**Pascual y Olmos, Jose** 1870-1943
[GS]
*Spanish bullfighter*
* [El] Valenciano [The Valencian]

**Pasdeloup, Jean-Marie**
*See* Durben, Wolfgang Johannes
Maria

**Pasha, Khalil Sheriff** [PA]
*Author*
* Fridolin, Major

**Pashko, Stanley** 1913- [CA]
*American author*
* Norman, Steve
* Robbins, Tony

**Pasic, Nikola** 1845?-1926 [WBD]
*Serbian and Yugoslav statesman*
* [The] Old Fox of the Balkans

**[La] Pasionaria**
*See* Ibarruri, Dolores

**Pasiphilus**
*See* Busche, Hermann von dem

**Paskandi, Geza** 1933- [IAW]
*Rumanian-born poet, playwright,
translator*
* Ovary, Geza

**Paskert, Dode**
*See* Paskert, George Henry

**Paskert, George Henry** 1881-1959
[AS, BE, PB]
*American baseball player*
* Paskert, Dode

**Pasko, W. W.** [FFF]
*American writer*
* Seneca

**Pasquale, Geraldine Ann** 1947-
[RO1]
*American singer*
* Stevens, Dodie

**Pasquier, Bach**
*See* Pasquier, Charles Joseph

**Pasquier, Charles Joseph**
1881?-1953 [BEW, SC]
*French actor*
* Bach, Fernand
* Pasquier, Bach

**Pasquil**
*See* Nash [or Nashe?], Thomas

**Pasquin, Anthony [Tony]**
*See* Williams, John

**Pass, Joe**
*See* Passalaqua, Joseph Anthony

**Passailaigue, Thomas E.** 1932-
[CA, SAT]
*American writer, singer, composer*
* Bethancourt, T. Ernesto
* Paisley, Tom

**Passalaqua, Joseph Anthony** 1929-
[EJ7]
*American jazz musician*
* Pass, Joe

**[Un] Passant**
*See* D'Hervilly, Ernest

**Passante, Dom**
*See* Fearn, John Russell

**Passarelli, Eduardo** 1900- [WEF]
*Italian director*
* De Filippo, Eduardo

**[Il] Passatore**
*See* Bellino

**Passeau, Claude William** 1909-
[BN]
*American baseball player*
* Passeau, Deacon

**Passeau, Deacon**
*See* Passeau, Claude William

**Passel, Anne W[onders]** 1918- [CA]
*American poet and writer*
* Wonders, Anne

**Passeur, Steve**
*See* Morin, Etienne

**Passingham, Kenneth** 20th c. [SFP]
*Author*
* Slack

**[The] Passion Orator**
*See* Andrews, John Urkhardt

**Passmore, Aileen Esther**
*See* Griffiths, Aileen Esther

**Passy, Colonel**
*See* De Wavrin, Andre

**Pasternak, Mike** 1936- [JL]
*British disc jockey*
* Rosko, Emperor

**Pastnor, Paul**
*See* Morris, Charles Smith

**Paston, George**
*See* Symonds, Emily Morse

**Paston, [Sir] William** 1378-1444
[WBD]
*British jurist*
* [The] Good Judge

**[A] Pastor**
*See* Dibdin, Thomas Frognall

**Pastor, Antonio [Tony]** 1837-1908
*American actor and theatre manager*
* [The] Father of Vaudeville

**Pastor, Tony**
*See* Halsey, Harlan Page

**Pastor, Tony**
See Pestritto, Antonio

**Pastor X**
See Johnson, Merle Allison

**Pastor y Duran, Vicente**
1879-1966 [GS]
*Spanish bullfighter*
* [El] Chico de la Blusa [The Boy of the Blouse]

**Pastora Gomez, Eden** 20th c.
*Nicaraguan guerrilla leader*
* Zero, Commander

**Pastoret [Shepherd]**
See Ferrer y Rodriguez, Francisco

**Pastorini, Signor**
See Walmesley, Charles

**[A] Pastor's Wife**
See Hubbell, Martha Stone

**Pastrano, Wilfred Raleigh** 1935-
[BX, RBE]
*American boxer*
* Pastrano, Willie

**Pastrano, Willie**
See Pastrano, Wilfred Raleigh

**Pastrone, Giovanni** 1883-1959
[OCF]
*Italian director and producer*
* Fosco, Piero

**Pastry, Mr.**
See Hearne, Richard

**Paszkiewicz, Mieczyslaw** 1925-
[IAW]
*Polish-born author and poet*
* Wizbor, Jakub Horczak

**[The] Pat Boone of Country Music**
See Anderson, Bill

**Patanne, Maria**
See LaPietra, Mary

**Patatero [Potato Seller]**
See Cosio Tesero, Alberto

**Patch, Jim** 20th c. [GW]
*American rodeo performer*
* Patch, Scrapiron

**Patch, Scrapiron**
See Patch, Jim

**Patch, Wally**
See Vinicombe, Walter

**Patchett, M. E.**
See Patchett, Mary Osborne Elwyn

**Patchett, Mary Osborne Elwyn**
1897- [SFL, TCC]
*Australian author*
* Bruce, David
* Patchett, M. E.

**Patchin, Patch**
See Patchin, Steven Earl

**Patchin, Steven Earl** 1950- [BR]
*American baseball player*
* Patchin, Patch

**Patek, Freddie Joe** 1944- [BE, PB]
*American baseball player*
* [The] Flea
* Patek, Midge
* Patek, Moochie

**Patek, Midge**
See Patek, Freddie Joe

**Patek, Moochie**
See Patek, Freddie Joe

**Patel, Dip**
See Patel, Dipak Narshi

**Patel, Dipak Narshi** 1958- [DC]
*Kenyan-born cricketer*
* Patel, Dip
* Patel, Dipstick

**Patel, Dipstick**
See Patel, Dipak Narshi

**Patelin**
See Leclerc du Tremblay, Francois

**Pateman, Kim**
See Levin, Kim

**Patenaude, Edgar Arnold** 1949-
[HR, SMG]
*Canadian-born hockey player*
* Patenaude, Rusty

**Patenaude, Rusty**
See Patenaude, Edgar Arnold

**Pater, Elias**
See Friedman, Jacob Horace

**Pater Patrum**
See Gregory of Nyssa

**Pater, [Philip] Roger**
See Hudleston, Gilbert Roger

**Paterson, A. B.**
See Paterson, Andrew Barton

**Paterson, Andrew Barton**
1864-1941 [LC, WWL]
*Australian songwriter and author*
* [The] Banjo
* Paterson, A. B.
* Paterson, Banjo

**Paterson, Anne**
See Einselen, Anne F.

**Paterson, Banjo**
See Paterson, Andrew Barton

**Paterson, Huntley**
See Ludovici, Anthony M[ario]

**Paterson, Jackie** 1920-1966
[WBC]
*Scottish boxer*
* Paterson, Li'l Jackie
* [The] Swattin' Scot

**Paterson, Li'l Jackie**
See Paterson, Jackie

**Paterson, Paul** 19th c. [PA]
*Author*
* Playfair, Hugo

**Paterson, Samuel** 1728-1802 [PA]
*Author*
* Coryot Junior

**Paterson, William Romaine** 1870-
? [LAO]
*Scottish-born author*
* Swift, Benjamin

**[The] Pathfinder**
See Fremont, John Charles

**[The] Patient**
See Albert IV

**Patin, Guy** 1601?-1672 [SN]
*French physician*
* [The] Rabelaisian Doctor

**Patmore, Coventry K. Dighton** 1823-
? [PA]
*Author*
* [The] Unknown Eros

**Paton, Emilie** [PA]
*Author*
* Rozier, Jacques

**Paton, [Sir] Noel** [PA]
*Author*
* Strivelyne, Elsie

**Paton Walsh, Gillian Honoinne Mary**
1937?- [AW, SAT, TCC]
*British author*
* Paton Walsh, Jill

**Paton Walsh, Jill**
See Paton Walsh, Gillian Honoinne
Mary

**[The] Patriarch?** [code name]
See Park, Chung Hee

**[The] Patriarch of Dorchester**
See White, John

**[The] Patriarch of Ferney**
See Arouet, Francois Marie

**[The] Patriarch of Harmony**
See Porpora, Nicholas

**[The] Patriarch of New England**
See Cotton, John

**[The] Patriarch of Shifters**
See Greene, Robert

**Patrice, Ann**
See Galbraith, Georgie Starbuck

**[The] Patrician of Rome**
See Pepin III

**Patricius**
See Adler, Philip

**Patrick**
See Byrne, John [Patrick]

**Patrick, [Father]**
See Cummins, John Thomas
Benedict

**Patrick** 389?- 461?
[DNNF, DNNS, FFF]
*Saint*
* [The] Apostle of Ireland

**Patrick, [Brother] Benilde**
See Feeney, Gerard Martin

**Patrick, Diana**
See Wilson, Desemea

**Patrick, Frederick Murray** 1916-
[CEI, FHE]
*Canadian-born hockey player*
* Patrick, Muzz

**Patrick, Gail**
See Fitzpatrick, Margaret

**Patrick, Gilbert** 20th c. [BBH]
*Jockey*
* Gilpatrick

**[The] Patrick Henry of New England**
See Phillips, Wendell

**Patrick, John**
See Avallone, Michael [Angelo],
Jr.

**Patrick, John**
See Christ, Ronald John

**Patrick, John**
See Goggan, John Patrick

**Patrick, Johnstone G[illespie]**
1918- [CA]
*Scottish-born clergyman and author*
* Forward, Luke
* Star Man's Padre

**Patrick, Keats**
See Karig, Walter

**Patrick, Leal**
See Stone, Patti

**Patrick, Lester** 1883-1960 [FHE]
*Canadian-born hockey player*
* Hockey, Mr.
* [The] Silver Fox

**Patrick, Lilian**
See Keogh, Lilian Gilmore

**Patrick, Lilian** 1889?-1962 [BEW]
*Theatrical performer*
* Diamond, Lillian

**Patrick, Marion** 1940- [ART]
*British painter*
* M. P.

**Patrick, Max**
See McCormack, James

**Patrick, Muzz**
See Patrick, Frederick Murray

**Patrick, Nigel**
See Wemyss, Nigel

**Patrick, Q.** [joint pseudonym with
Richard Wilson Webb]
See Aswell, Mary Louise

**Patrick, Q.** [joint pseudonym with
Richard Wilson Webb]
See Kelly, Martha Mott [Patsy]

**Patrick, Q.** [joint pseudonym with
Mary L. Aswell, Martha Kelly, and
Hugh Wheeler]
See Webb, Richard Wilson

**Patrick, Q.** [joint pseudonym with
Richard Wilson Webb]
See Wheeler, Hugh Callingham

**Patrick, Ted** 1930-
*American "deprogrammer" of
religious cultists*
* Black Lightning
* Black Satan

**Patridge, S. W.** [PA]
*Author*
* S. W. P.

**[A] Patriot**
See Guy, L.

**[The] Patriot**
See Russell, William

**[The] Patriot King**
See George III

**[The] Patriot King**
See St. John, Henry

**[The] Patriot of Humanity**
See Grattan, Henry

**[The] Patriot Printer of 1776**
See Bradford, William

**Patris, Louis**
See Patsouras, Louis

**[The] Patron**
See Starr, George

**[The] Patron of the Fine Arts**
See Medici, Lorenzo de

**[The] Patron Saint of Queens**
*See* Elizabeth

**[The] Patron Saint of Smiths and Artists**
*See* Eloi [or Eligius]

**[The] Patron Saint of Wuerzburg**
*See* Kilian

**Patry, M.** 20th c. [WBD]
*British author*
* Williams, Patry [joint pseudonym with D. Williams]

**Patsauq, Markoosie** 1942- [CA]
*Canadian author*
* Markoosie

**Patsouras, Louis** 1931- [CA]
*American historian and author*
* Patris, Louis

**Patt, Babe**
*See* Patt, Maurice

**Patt, Frank** 1928- [BWW]
*American singer*
* Honeyboy

**Patt, Maurice** 20th c. [EJS]
*American football player*
* Patt, Babe

**Patte, Harold** 20th c.
*American politician*
* Patte, Porque

**Patte, Porque**
*See* Patte, Harold

**Pattee, David E.** 20th c. [SFP]
*Author*
* Davis, Pat

**Patten, Case L.** 1876-1935 [BE]
*American baseball player*
* Patten, Casey

**Patten, Casey**
*See* Patten, Case L.

**Patten, Clinton A.** 20th c. [WGT]
*Author*
* Rock, James

**Patten, Gilbert**
*See* Patten, William George

**Patten, Lewis B[yford]** 1915- [CA]
*American author*
* Ford, Lewis B.

**Patten, William George** 1866-1945
[TC, WGT, WW]
*American author*
* Bell, Emerson
* Bellwood, Herbert
* Dangerfield, Harry
* MacLaren, Gordon
* Patten, Gilbert
* St. Dare, Julian
* Standish, Burt L.
* Wilder, William West

**Patterson, Arthur E.** 20th c. [SMG]
*American baseball executive*
* Patterson, Red

**Patterson, Arthur W.** 1888-
[WWL]
*British author*
* Davidson, Wilder Bristol

**Patterson, Charlotte [Buist]** 1942-
[CA]
*American author*
* Buist, Charlotte

**Patterson, Claude, Jr.** 1925-1972
[BBH]
*American bowler*
* Patterson, Pat

**Patterson, Daryl Alan** 1943-
[SMG]
*American baseball player*
* Patterson, Pat

**Patterson, Eleanor Medill**
1884-1948 [WBD]
*American journalist and author*
* Gizycka, Eleanor M.

**Patterson, Elmer Calvin** 1888-1975
[SC]
*American actor*
* Patterson, Hank

**Patterson, Hal** 20th c. [CFH]
*Canadian football player*
* Prince Hal

**Patterson, Hank**
*See* Patterson, Elmer Calvin

**Patterson, Harry** 1929-
[AW, CA, WD]
*British author*
* Fallon, Martin
* Graham, James
* Higgins, Jack
* Marlowe, Hugh

**Patterson, Jane**
*See* Britton, Mattie Lula Cooper

**Patterson, Jimmy Dale** 1935-
[CWG, DAM]
*American singer and songwriter*
* Patterson, Pat

**Patterson, John** 1856-1936 [BMH]
*Scottish-born animal trainer*
* Duncan, Professor

**Patterson, John W.** 20th c. [OBW]
*American baseball player*
* Patterson, Pat

**Patterson, Lila**
*See* Rainey, Gertrude Malissa Nix
[Pridgett]

**Patterson, Margaret**
*See* Grant, Maude Margaret

**Patterson, Olive**
*See* Rowland, D[onald] S[ydney]

**Patterson, Ottilie**
*See* Barber, Anna-Ottilie Patterson

**Patterson, Pat**
*See* Patterson, Claude, Jr.

**Patterson, Pat**
*See* Patterson, Daryl Alan

**Patterson, Pat**
*See* Patterson, Jimmy Dale

**Patterson, Pat**
*See* Patterson, John W.

**Patterson, Pat**
*See* Patterson, William Jennings
Bryan

**Patterson, Peter** 1932- [B10, WD]
*British playwright*
* Terson, Peter

**Patterson, Red**
*See* Patterson, Arthur E.

**Patterson, Roy Lewis** 1876-1953
[BE]
*American baseball player*
* [The] Boy Wonder

**Patterson, Sarah** 20th c. [IBW]
*American boxing manager*
* Patterson, Tiny

**Patterson, Sheila** 20th c. [IBW]
*American basketball player*
* Patterson, Too Tall

**Patterson, Tiny**
*See* Patterson, Sarah

**Patterson, Too Tall**
*See* Patterson, Sheila

**Patterson, Troy**
*See* Corvino, Ettore

**Patterson, Vance** 20th c. [BWW]
*American musician*
* Piano Red

**Patterson, William Jennings Bryan**
1901- [BE]
*American baseball player*
* Patterson, Pat

**Patti, Adela Juana Maria**
1843-1919 [PA]
*Spanish-born opera singer*
* Patti, Adelina

**Patti, Adelina**
*See* Patti, Adela Juana Maria

**Patti, Carlotta**
*See* De Muenck, Carlotta Patti

**Pattieson, Peter**
*See* Scott, [Sir] Walter

**Pattin, Duck**
*See* Pattin, Martin William

**Pattin, Martin William** 1943-
[SMG]
*American baseball player*
* Pattin, Duck

**Pattinson, Nancy Evelyn** 20th c.
[AW]
*British author*
* Asquith, Nan

**Pattison, Dorothy Wyndlow**
1832-1878 [PA, WBD]
*British philanthropist*
* Sister Dora

**Patton, Big John**
*See* Patton, John

**Patton, Charles H.** 1901?-1962
[BEW]
*Actor*
* Sheldon, Jerry

**Patton, Charley** 1887-1934 [BWW]
*American singer*
* [The] Masked Marvel
* Peters, Charley

**Patton, Frank**
*See* Palmer, Raymond A[rthur]

**Patton, Frank** [house pseudonym]
*See* Shaver, Richard S[harpe]

**Patton, Fred** 1911- [IAW]
*American producer and scriptwriter*
* Guinn, Pat

**Patton, George Smith, Jr.**
1885-1945 [CND]
*American military leader*
* Old Blood and Guts

**Patton, John** 1936- [DAM]
*American musician*
* Patton, Big John

**Patton, John** 20th c. [PHM]
*American underworld figure*
* [The] Boy Mayor

**Patton, Marion**
*See* Waldron, Marion Patton

**Paturi, Felix R.**
*See* Mindt, Heinz R.

**Patyn, William** 1395?-1486
[WBD]
*British prelate*
* Waynflete [or Wainfleet],
William of

**Paufichet, Jules** 1883?-1951
[FC, OCF, WEF]
*French actor*
* Berry, Jules

**Pauker, John** 1920- [CA]
*Hungarian-born author and poet*
* Griffiths, Robert L., III
* Ordway, Roger
* Rowley, Thomas
* Somes, Jethro

**Paul, [Father]**
*See* Dhorme, Edouard

**Paul** [code name used during World
War II]
*See* Dourlein, Pieter

**Paul**
*See* Hildebrand, Ray

**Paul** [code name used during World
War II]
*See* Kiffer, Raoul

**Paul, [Father]**
*See* Sarpi, Pietro

**Paul**
*See* Saul of Tarsus

**Paul**
*See* Scott, [Sir] Walter

**Paul, Adrian**
*See* McGeoch, Andrew Jackson

**Paul, Arthur Stuart** 1943- [CEI]
*Canadian-born hockey player*
* Paul, Butch

**Paul, Auren**
*See* Uris, Auren

**Paul, Betty**
*See* Percheron, Betty

**Paul, Billy**
*See* Williams, Paul

**Paul, Bonnie Ann** 1941- [BEW]
*American actress, singer, dancer*
* Scott, Bonnie

**Paul, Butch**
*See* Paul, Arthur Stuart

**Paul, Cedar**
*See* Davenport, Gertrude Mary

**Paul, Daniel**
*See* Kessel, Lipmann

**Paul, Elliot Harold** 1891-1958
[CC, WW]
*Author and journalist*
* Rutledge, Brett

**Paul, Emily**
*See* Eicher, [Ethel] Elizabeth

**Paul, Ernest**
See Focke, Ernest Paul Walter

**Paul, F. W.**
See Fairman, Paul W.

**Paul, Genay**
See Webster, Ester Luise

**Paul, Hugo**
See Litwinsky, Paul

**Paul, James**
See Kocsis, James C.

**Paul James Francis, [Father]**
See Wattson, Lewis Thomas

**Paul, Jean**
See Richter, Jean Paul Friedrich

**Paul, John**
See Webb, Charles Henry

**Paul, John** 1747-1792 [WBD]
*American naval officer*
* Jones, John Paul

**Paul, Judith Edison** 1939- [CA]
*American author*
* Edison, Judith

**Paul, Les**
See Polfus, Lester

**Paul, Lyn**
See Belcher, Lynda Susan

**Paul, M. B.**
See Paul, Morrison Bloomfield

**Paul, Marco**
See Abbot, Jacob

**Paul, Morrison Bloomfield** 20th c.
[ITA]
*Canadian-born director and cameraman*
* Paul, M. B.

**Paul of the Cross**
See Danei, Paolo Francesco

**Paul of Thebes** 3rd c. [WBD]
*Saint*
* [The] Hermit

**Paul of Venice**
See Sarpi, Pietro

**Paul, Robert**
See Abelson, Robert

**Paul, Robert**
See Roberts, John G[aither]

**Paul, Sheri**
See Resnick, Sylvia [Safran]

**Paul, Stefanie [or Taffy?]** 1942-
[HT]
*American actress*
* Powers, Stefanie

**Paul, William**
See Eicher, [Ethel] Elizabeth

**Paul II**
See Barbo, Pietro

**Paul III**
See Farnese, Alessandro

**Paul IV**
See Caraffa, Giovanni Pietro

**Paul V**
See Borghese, Camillo

**Paul VI**
See Montini, Giovanni Battista
Enrico Antonio Maria

**Paula**
See Jackson, Jill

**Paulding, Frederick**
See Dodge, Frederick

**Paulding, James Kirke** 1778-1860
[DEL, FFF, PA]
*American author and poet*
* Bull-us, Hector
* [A] Doubtful Gentleman
* Langstaff, Launcelot [joint
  pseudonym with Washington
  Irving and William Irving]
* [A] New England Man
* Oudenarde, Dominie Nicholas
  Aegidius
* Tickler, Timothy

**Paulet, John** 1598-1675 [WBD]
*Fifth Marquis of Winchester*
* [The] Great Loyalist

**Paulet, Mlle.** 17th c. [HN]
*Friend of King Henry IV of France*
* [La] Lionne

**Paulin, Doc**
See Paulin, Ernest

**Paulin, Ernest** 1902?- [NOJ]
*American jazz musician*
* Paulin, Doc

**Paull, Harry Major** 1854- ? [MBF]
*British author*
* Blake, Paul

**Paulo the Magic Clown**
See Klingler, Paul

**Paulsen, Gil**
See Paulsen, Guilford Paul Hans

**Paulsen, Guilford Paul Hans** 1902-
[BE]
*American baseball player*
* Paulsen, Gil

**Paulson, Jack**
See Jackson, C[aary] Paul

**Paultz, Billy** 20th c.
*American basketball player*
* [The] Whopper

**Paulus Aeginela** 7th c. [SN]
*Greek physician*
* [The] Father of Obstetric Surgery

**Paulus, Jan**
See Malloch, George Reston

**Paulus Servita**
See Sarpi, Pietro

**Paulus Venetus**
See Sarpi, Pietro

**Pauly, Rosa**
See Pollak, Rose

**Paumier, Alfred**
See Hodgson, Alfred

**Pauper et Ignotus**
See Thatcher, John Wells

**[The] Pausanias of Britain**
See Camden, William

**Pavageau, Alcide** 1888-1969
[EJ, WWJ]
*American jazz musician*
* Pavageau, Slow Drag

**Pavageau, Slow Drag**
See Pavageau, Alcide

**Pavan, Marisa**
See Pierangeli, Marisa

**Pavarotti, Luciano** 1935- [MS]
*Italian-born opera singer*
* King of the High C's

**Pavelich, Blackie**
See Pavelich, Martin Nicholas
[Marty]

**Pavelich, Martin Nicholas [Marty]**
1927- [FHE]
*Canadian-born hockey player*
* Pavelich, Blackie

**Paveskovich, John Michael** 1919-
[BE]
*American baseball player and
manager*
* Pesky, Johnny
* Pesky, Needlenose

**Pavia, Joe**
See Nerone, Giuseppe

**Pavia y Alburquerque, Manuel**
1828?-1895 [DHA]
*Spanish army officer*
* [The] Dictator of a Day

**Pavius**
See Pouw, Pietro

**Pavlenko, Petr Andreevich**
1899-1951 [SFL]
*Author*
* Pavlenko, Piotr

**Pavlenko, Piotr**
See Pavlenko, Petr Andreevich

**Pavletich, Donald Stephen** 1938-
[SMG]
*American baseball player*
* Pavletich, Pav

**Pavletich, Pav**
See Pavletich, Donald Stephen

**Pavliecivich, Ervin Martin** 1928-
[BE]
*American baseball player*
* Palica, Ervin Martin

**Pavlik, Evelyn Marie** 1954- [CA]
*American author*
* Sheridan, Adora [joint
  pseudonym with Jane Fay Hong]

**Pavsic, Vladimir** 1913- [EWL]
*Slovene poet and playwright*
* Bor, Matej

**Pawelek, Porky**
See Pawelek, Theodore John [Ted]

**Pawelek, Theodore John [Ted]**
1919-1964 [BE]
*American baseball player*
* Pawelek, Porky

**Pawle, Gerald** 1913- [CA]
*British columnist*
* Atticus

**Pawley, Eric**
See Pawley, Frederick Arden

**Pawley, Frederick Arden** 1907-
[BEW]
*American educator and architect*
* Pawley, Eric

**Pawley, Martin Edward** 1938-
[WD]
*British author*
* Noble, Charles
* Spade, Rupert

**Pawlikowska, Marja [Kossak]**
1899-1945 [CD]
*Polish poet and playwright*
* Jasnorzewska, Marja
* [The] Polish Sappho
* [The] Queen of Polish Lyricists

**Pawlowska, Yoi**
See Maraini, Yoi

**Pawnee Bill**
See Little, Gordon W.

**Pax**
See Cholmondeley, Mary

**Pax**
See McDermott, Hugh F.

**Paxinou, Katina**
See Konstantopoulou, Katina

**Paxton, Gary** 20th c. [RO1]
*American singer*
* Flip

**Paxton, Jack**
See Lawton, Sherman P[axton]

**Paxton, [Dr.] John**
See Lawton, Sherman P[axton]

**Paxton, John** 1923- [IAW]
*British author and editor*
* Cherrill, Jack

**Paxton, Lois**
See Low, Lois Dorothea

**Paxton, Sydney**
See Hood, Sydney Paxton

**Paycheck, Johnny**
See Lytle, Donald

**Paye, Robert**
See Long, Gabrielle Margaret Vere
[Campbell]

**Payelle, Raymond-Gerard**
1898-1971 [CA]
*French author, critic, playwright*
* Heriat, Philippe

**Payes, Rachel C[osgrove]** 1922-
[CA]
*American author*
* Arch, E. L.
* Cosgrove, Rachel

**Payn, James** [PA]
*Author*
* Found Dead

**Payne, Alan**
See Jakes, John W[illiam]

**Payne, Alban S.** 1822- ? [FFF, PA]
*Author*
* Spicer, Nicholas

**Payne, Alma Smith**
See Ralston, Alma

**Payne, Andrew H.** 20th c. [OBW]
*American baseball player*
* Payne, Jap

**Payne, B. J.**
See Payne, Betty

**Payne, Betty** 1950- [IBW]
*American air force officer*
* Payne, B. J.

**Payne, Buckner H.**   [PA]
*Author*
* Ariel

**Payne, Cecil McKenzie** 1922-
[EJ7]
*American jazz musician*
* Payne, Zodiac

**Payne, Coal Oil**
See   Payne, Henry B.

**Payne, Crutchley**
See   Evans, Frank Howel

**Payne, Doc**
See   Payne, William

**Payne, Donald Gordon** 1924-
[CA, WD]
*British author*
* Cameron, Ian
* Gordon, Donald
* Marshall, James Vance

**Payne, Hazel Belle [Saulisberry]**
1892-   [WW]
*Author*
* Gay, Greer

**Payne, Henry B.** 1810-1896   [FFF]
*American politician*
* Payne, Coal Oil

**Payne, Jap**
See   Payne, Andrew H.

**Payne, John** 1940-   [SW]
*Australian actor*
* Thompson, Jack

**Payne, Percival** 1926-1979
[DAM, EJ, IBW]
*American jazz musician*
* Payne, Sonny

**Payne, [Pierre Stephen] Robert**
1911-   [CA]
*British-born author*
* Cargoe, Richard
* Devon, John Anthony
* Horne, Howard
* Tikhonov, Valentin
* Young, Robert

**Payne, Roger** 1739-1797   [SN]
*British bookbinder*
* [The] Coryphaeus of Bookbinders

**Payne, Sonny**
See   Payne, Percival

**Payne, William**   [OBW]
*American baseball player*
* Payne, Doc

**Payne, Zodiac**
See   Payne, Cecil McKenzie

**Paynter, George Washington**
See   Paner, George Washington

**[Le] Paysan du Danube**
See   Legendre, Louis

**Payson, George**   [PA]
*Author*
* Romaine, Robert Dexter

**Payton, Sweetness**
See   Payton, Walter Jerry

**Payton, Walter Jerry** 1954-   [SMG]
*American football player*
* Payton, Sweetness
* Payton, Wonderful Walter

**Payton, Wonderful Walter**
See   Payton, Walter Jerry

**Paz, A.**
See   Goldfeder, [Kenneth] James

**Paz, Zan**
See   Goldfeder, [Anne] Cheryl
Suzanne

**Paz-Soldan y Unanue, Pedro**   [PA]
*Author*
* De Arona, Juan

**Pazzetti, Pat**
See   Pazzetti, Vincent J.

**Pazzetti, Vincent J.** 1890-1972
[FB]
*American football player*
* Pazzetti, Pat

**Pea Ridge Day**
See   Day, Clyde Henry

**Pea Soup Dumont**
See   Dumont, George Henry

**Peabody, Chub**
See   Peabody, Endicott

**Peabody, Eddy** 1912-1970   [SC]
*American actor and musician*
* King of the Banjo

**Peabody, Endicott** 1920-   [FB]
*American football player*
* [The] Baby Faced Assassin
* Peabody, Chub

**Peace Bertha Von Suttner**
See   Von Suttner, Bertha

**Peace, Frank**
See   Cook, William Everett

**[The] Peaceful**
See   Casimir I

**[The] Peaceful**
See   Edgar [or Eadgar]

**[The] Peaceful**
See   Kang-wang

**[The] Peaceful Prelate**
See   Massillon, Jean Baptiste

**Peaceful Valley Denzer**
See   Denzer, Roger

**[The] Peacemaker**
See   Edward VII

**[The] Peacemaker**
See   Isabel [or Elizabeth]

**Peach Bloom**
See   Mudd, Alice F.

**Peach Pie O'Connor**
See   O'Connor, John Joseph

**Peache**
See   Hernandez, Jose P. H.

**Peaches**
See   Barker [or Hurd?], Francine

**Peaches**
See   Greene, Linda

**Peacock, Marie** 1893-   [THR]
*British actress and singer*
* Blanche, Marie

**[The] Peacock of the North**
See   Neville, Robert

**Peacock, Thomas Love** 1785-1866
[DEL, PA]
*British author and poet*
* Peppercorn, Peter

**Peaker, E. J.**
See   Peaker, Edra Jeanne

**Peaker, Edra Jeanne** 20th c.   [ITA]
*American actress, singer, dancer*
* Peaker, E. J.

**Peale, Patrick**
See   Seckendorf, Gustav Anton von

**[The] Peanut Bard**
See   Canning, Josiah D., of Gill

**[The] Peanut Farmer**
See   Carter, James Earl, Jr.
[Jimmy]

**Peanut, Mr.**
See   Carver, George Washington

**[The] Pear**
See   Harvey, William King

**Pearce**   [HN]
*Prize-fighter*
* [The] Game Chicken

**Pearce, A. H.**
See   Quibell, Agatha Hunt

**Pearce, A[nn] Philippa**
See   Christie, Ann Philippa Pearce

**Pearce, Brian Leonard** 1915-
[AW, IAW]
*British author*
* Farnborough
* Hussey, Leonard
* Redman, Joseph

**Pearce, Charles Louis St. John** 20th
c.   [MBF]
*British author*
* Fairbanks, Nat

**Pearce, Ducky**
See   Pearce, William C.

**Pearce, Ethel Katherine** 1856- ?
[WWL]
*British journalist*
* Discipulus
* Oracle

**Pearce, Gracie**
See   Pearce, Grayson S.

**Pearce, Grayson S.** ?-1894   [BE]
*American baseball player*
* Pearce, Gracie

**Pearce, Guy**
See   Pilley, Charles

**Pearce, Pard**
See   Pearce, W.

**Pearce, Raymond Maplesden**
1894-   [AW]
*British physician and author*
* Maplesden, Ray

**Pearce, W.** 20th c.   [SMG]
*American football player*
* Pearce, Pard

**Pearce, William C.** 1885-1933
[BE]
*American baseball player*
* Pearce, Ducky

**Peard, F. M.**   [PA]
*Author*
* F. M. P.

**Pearl**
See   Joplin, Janis

**[The] Pearl**
See   Monroe, Earl

**Pearl, Eric**
See   Elman, Richard

**Pearl, Esther Elizabeth**
See   Ritz, David

**Pearl, Eula**
See   Ferrand, Eula Pearl

**Pearl, Irene**
See   Guyonvarch, Irene Cecilia

**Pearl, Jack**
See   Pearl, Jacques Bain

**Pearl, Jacques Bain** 1923-
[SFL, WYA]
*American author*
* Pearl, Jack

**Pearl, Lee**
See   Pearl, Leo J.

**Pearl, Leo J.** 1907-   [ASC]
*American composer*
* Pearl, Lee

**Pearl, Minnie**
See   Cannon, Sarah Ophelia Colley

**[The] Pearl of Brittany**
See   Eleanor

**[The] Pearl of Ireland**
See   Bridget [or Brigette]

**[The] Pearl of Normandy**
See   Emma

**[The] Pearl of the East**
See   Zenobia

**[The] Pearl of Zealand**
See   Coomans, Joanna

**Pearlman, Irving Ralph** 1898-
[EJS]
*American football player*
* Pearlman, Red

**Pearlman, Red**
See   Pearlman, Irving Ralph

**Pearlson, Marion S.** 1922-1956
[SC]
*American actress*
* Richman, Marian

**Pearlstein, Howard J.** 1942-   [CA]
*American poet and author*
* Rush, Joshua

**Pearse, Patrick Henry** 20th c.
[WWL]
*Irish author and editor*
* MacPiarais, Padraic

**Pearson, Alec George** 20th c.
[MBF]
*British author*
* Linley, Julian
* Scott, [Captain] Russell

**Pearson, Andrew Russel**
1897-1969   [IPA]
*American journalist*
* Pearson, Drew

**Pearson, Charles M.** 1920-1944
[FB]
*American football player*
* Lincoln, Abe
* Pearson, Senator
* Pearson, Stubby

**Pearson, Columbus Calvin, Jr.**
1932-   [DAM, EJ]
*American jazz musician*
* Pearson, Duke

**Pearson, Dave**
See Barraclough, David Pearson

**Pearson, David P. [Dave]**
See Pierson, David P.

**Pearson, Drew**
See Pearson, Andrew Russel

**Pearson, Duke**
See Pearson, Columbus Calvin, Jr.

**Pearson, Emily C.** [PA]
*Author*
* Ervie

**Pearson, Francis Gates** 1855-1942
[BEW]
*British actor*
* Gerald, Frank

**Pearson, Hoot**
See Pearson, Montgomery
Marcellus

**Pearson, Lester Bowles, Jr.** 1897-
*Canadian prime minister*
* Pearson, Mike

**Pearson, Lon**
See Pearson, Milo Lorentz

**Pearson, Martin** [joint pseudonym
with Donald A(llen) Wollheim]
See Kornbluth, Cyril M.

**Pearson, Martin** [joint pseudonym
with Cyril M. Kornbluth]
See Wollheim, Donald A[llen]

**Pearson, Mike**
See Pearson, Lester Bowles, Jr.

**Pearson, Milo Lorentz** 1939- [CA]
*American author and educator*
* Pearson, Lon

**Pearson, Monte**
See Pearson, Montgomery
Marcellus

**Pearson, Montgomery Marcellus**
1909- [BE, BN]
*American baseball player*
* Pearson, Hoot
* Pearson, Monte

**Pearson, Preston** 1945- [SMG]
*American football player*
* [The] Cinderella Man

**Pearson, Senator**
See Pearson, Charles M.

**Pearson, Shepperd**
See Hadath, John Edward Gunby

**Pearson, Stubby**
See Pearson, Charles M.

**Pearson, T. E.** 20th c. [MBF]
*British author*
* North, Pearson

**Peart, Biscuits**
See Peart, Clarence

**Peart, Clarence** 20th c. [CSH]
*Canadian lacrosse promoter*
* Peart, Biscuits

**Peary, Marie Ahnighito**
See Kuhne, Marie [Ahnighito
Peary]

**[The] Peasant**
See Traina, Giuseppe

**[The] Peasant Bard**
See Burns, Robert

**[The] Peasant Bard**
See Cummings, Josiah D.

**[The] Peasant Bard**
See Hill, George

**[The] Peasant Boy Philosopher**
See Ferguson, James

**[The] Peasant of Cotignola**
See Attendolo, Giacomuzo d'

**[The] Peasant of the Danube**
See Legendre, Louis

**[The] Peasant Painter of Sweden**
See Hoerberg, Peter

**[The] Peasant Philosopher**
See Deubler, Konrad

**[The] Peasant Poet of
Northamptonshire**
See Clare, John

**[The] Peasant Poet of Suffolk**
See Bloomfield, Robert

**[The] Peasant Poetess**
See Hamilton, Janet

**[The] Peasant Pope**
See Sarto, Giuseppe Melchiorre

**[The] Peasants' King**
See Casimir III

**Pease, Alfa**
See Crouse, Mrs. Charles E.

**Pease, [Lt.] John**
See Hoar, Roger Sherman

**Pease, Lillie**
See Chrissie, Mrs. Edward

**Peay, Benjamin Franklin** 1931-
[RO1]
*American singer*
* Benton, Brook

**Pebbly Jack Glasscock**
See Glasscock, John Wesley

**Peccadille**
See Bandovin, E.

**Peccadille**
See Doubled, Victor

**Pecci, Gioacchino Vincenzo**
1810-1903 [CBS, WBD]
*Pope*
* Leo XIII

**Pechey, Archibald Thomas**
1876-1961 [LAO, WW]
*British author and playwright*
* Cross, Mark
* Valentine

**Peck, Abe**
See Peckolick, Abe

**Peck, Dutch**
See Peck, Hubert

**Peck, Eileen**
See Cline, Eileen Peck

**Peck, Ellen [or Catherine?]** [PA]
*Author*
* Pine, Cuyler

**Peck, George W.** 1817-1859 [PA]
*Author*
* Bigly, Cantell A.

**Peck, Hubert** 1898- [BB]
*American basketball player*
* Peck, Dutch

**Peck, Julie** 1926- [FC, IPA, ITA]
*American actress and singer*
* London, Julie

**Peck, Leonard**
See Hardy, C. Colburn

**Peck, Lillie** ?-1878 [PA]
*Author*
* Elliot, Ruth

**Peck, Wallace**
See Walter, Charles T.

**Peck, Winifred Frances [Knox]** 20th
c. [WW]
*Author*
* Knox, Winifred Frances

**Peckham, Richard**
See Holden, Raymond [Peckham]

**Peckolick, Abe** 1945- [CA]
*American writer*
* Peck, Abe

**Pecora, Santo**
See Pecoraro, Santo J.

**Pecoraro, Santo J.** 1902-
[EJ, PMJ, WWJ]
*American jazz musician*
* Pecora, Santo

**Pecsok, Mary Bodell** 1919- [CA]
*American author*
* Bodell, Mary

**[The] Pedagogue**
See Milton, John

**Peddell, Maud Clement** 20th c.
[NAA]
*American playwright*
* Clement, Kay

**Pedder, James** 1755-1859 [PA]
*Author*
* Frank

**Peden, Rachel Mason** 1901- [IA]
*American columnist*
* R. F. D., Mrs.

**Peden, Torchy**
See Peden, William John

**Peden, William John** 1906-
[BBH, CSH]
*Canadian bicycle racer*
* Peden, Torchy

**Pederneiras, Raul Paranhos**
1874-1953 [WEC]
*Brazilian cartoonist, author,
educator*
* Raul

**Pedersen, Knut** 1859-1952
[LC, TCL]
*Norwegian author and playwright*
* Hamsun, Knut

**Pedersen, Sven** 1917- [CA]
*Danish author*
* Hassel, Sven

**Pedersoli, Carlo** 20th c. [WF]
*Italian actor*
* Spencer, Bud

**Pederson, Carl** 1895-1958
[BEW, CED, EMT]
*Danish actor, dancer, singer*
* Brisson, Carl

**Pederson, Lily** ?-1919 [SC]
*American actress*
* Gray, Beata
* Gray, Betty

**Pederson, Pullman G.** 1920- [EJ]
*American jazz musician*
* Pederson, Tommy

**Pederson, Tommy**
See Pederson, Pullman G.

**Pedler, Christopher Magnus Howard**
1927- [ESF, SFL]
*British author and scientist*
* Pedler, Kit

**Pedler, Kit**
See Pedler, Christopher Magnus
Howard

**Pedres [Big Pedro]**
See Martinez Gonzalez, Pedro

**Pedrick, Jean** 1922- [CA]
*American poet and author*
* Kefferstan, Jean

**Pedrick, Robert, Jr.** 20th c. [RO2]
*American singer*
* John, Robert

**Pedro** 1334-1369
[DNNS, RH, SN]
*King of Castile and Leon*
* [The] Cruel

**Pedro I** 1320-1367
[DNNS, FFF, WBD]
*King of Portugal*
* [The] Just
* [The] Justiciary
* [The] Severe

**Pedro II** 1648-1706 [WBD]
*King of Portugal*
* [The] Pacific

**Pedro III [or Peter]** 1239-1285
[DNNS, SN, WBD]
*King of Aragon*
* [The] Great

**Pedro IV [or Peter]** 1319-1387
[FFF, SN, WBD]
*King of Aragon*
* [The] Ceremonious

**Pedroes, Charles P.** 20th c. [BE]
*American baseball player*
* Pedroes, Chick

**Pedroes, Chick**
See Pedroes, Charles P.

**Pedrosa, Amilde** 1920- [WEC]
*Brazilian cartoonist*
* Appe

**Pedrucho [Big Pedro]**
See Basauri Paguaga, Pedro

**Pedrucho [Big Pedro]**
See Garcia, Francisco

**Peebles, Hap**
See Peebles, Harry

**Peebles, Harry** 1913- [CM]
*American concert promoter*
* Peebles, Hap

**Peebles, Mary** 1839- ? [FFF]
*American author*
* Palmer, Lynde

**Peebles, McKinley** 1897- [BWW]
*American singer*
* Sweet Papa Stovepipe

**Peebles, Paul**
See Maverick, Augustus

**Peebles, William** 1767-1823 [PA]
*Author*
* [A] Clergyman of the Church of
 Scotland

**Peek, Coyle, Jr.** 1950- [IBW]
*American auto racer*
* Black Helmet

**Peekskill Pete Cregan**
*See* Cregan, Pete[r James]

**Peel, Frederick** 1888- [WW]
*Author*
* Slingsby, Rufus [joint pseudonym
 with Charles Siddle]

**Peel, Hazel Mary [Wallis]** 1930-
[AW, CA]
*British author*
* Hayman
* Peel, Wallis

**Peel, [Captain] Jonathan**
1799-1854 [PA]
*Author*
* Dinks

**Peel, Norman Lemon**
*See* Hirsch, Paul

**Peel, Orange**
*See* Peel, [Sir] Robert

**Peel, Parsley**
*See* Peel, [Sir] Robert

**Peel, [Sir] Robert** 1788-1850
[FFF, RH, SN]
*British statesman*
* [The] Leonidas of the Day
* [The] Moral Surface
* Peel, Orange
* Peel, Parsley
* [The] Run Away Spartan

**Peel, Wallis**
*See* Peel, Hazel Mary [Wallis]

**Peele, Biscuits**
*See* Peele, Clarence

**Peele, Clarence** 20th c.
[BBH, CSH]
*Canadian lacrosse player*
* Peele, Biscuits

**Peele, George** 1556-1596 [SN]
*British playwright and poet*
* [The] Atlas of Poetrie

**Peep**
*See* Nettles, Bonnie Lu

**Peeping Tom**
*See* Kettell, Samuel

**Peerce, Jan**
*See* Perelmuth, Jacob Pincus

**Peerless Annabelle**
*See* Buchan, Annabelle Whitford

**Peerless Hal Chase**
*See* Chase, Harold Harris [Hal]

**[The] Peerless Leader**
*See* Chance, Frank Leroy

**Peers, Donald** 1909?-1973 [FIR]
*British singer*
* [The] Cavalier of Song

**Peers, Frank** 1874- ? [THR]
*British lyricist, composer,
entertainer*
* Leo, Frank

**Peerson, Eliza O.** [PA]
*Author*
* Aliqua

**Peery, George A.** 1906- [BE]
*American baseball player*
* Peery, Red

**Peery, Red**
*See* Peery, George A.

**Peeslake, Gaffer**
*See* Durrell, Lawrence [George]

**Peete, Charles [Charlie]** 1931-1956
[BE, IBW]
*American baseball player*
* Peete, Mule

**Peete, Mule**
*See* Peete, Charles [Charlie]

**Peetie Wheatstraw's Brother**
*See* Gordon, Jimmy

**Peetie Wheatstraw's Buddy**
*See* Ray, Harmon

**Peg Leg Elliot**
*See* Elliot, Frank

**Peg Leg Howell**
*See* Howell, Joshua Barnes

**Peg Leg Lonergan**
*See* Lonergan, Richard

**Peg Leg Norwood**
*See* Norwood, Sam

**Peg Leg Sam**
*See* Jackson, Arthur

**Peg Pete**
*See* Jackson, Arthur

**Pegasus**
*See* Benson, Nathaniel Anketell

**Pegge, Samuel** 1704-1796 [SN]
*British antiquary*
* [An] Old Modern

**Peguy, Charles Pierre** 1873-1914
[EWL]
*French poet, journalist, philosopher*
* Baudouin, Charles Pierre
* Deloire, Pierre

**Peichl, Gustav** 1928- [WEC]
*Austrian cartoonist and architect*
* Ironimus

**Peil, Charles Edward** 1908?-1962
[BEW]
*Actor*
* Jones, Johnny

**Peiresc, Nicolas Claude Fabi de**
1580-1637 [SN]
*French scholar*
* [The] Attorney General of the
 Republic of Letters

**Peiser, Maria Lilli** 1914-
[BDF, TR, WEF]
*German-born actress*
* Palmer, Lilli

**Peitz, Heinie**
*See* Peitz, Henry Clement

**Peitz, Henry Clement** 1870-1943
[AS, BE]
*American baseball player*
* Peitz, Heinie

**Peladan, Joseph** 1858-1918 [WBD]
*French author*
* Peladan, Josephin

**Peladan, Josephin**
*See* Peladan, Joseph

**Peladeau, Pierre** 1925?-
*Canadian publisher*
* Pile o Dough

**Pelaez, Cesareo** 1932?-
*Cuban-born magician*
* Marco the Magi

**Pelagius II** ?- 590 [DHA]
*Pope*
* Infallible

**Pelau**
*See* Auguste, Arsene

**Pele**
*See* Arantes Do Nascimento,
Edson

**Peletier, Andrew Arthur**
1884-1921 [BX, RBE]
*Canadian-born boxer*
* Pelkey, Arthur

**Pelham, Alfred Montgomery** 1900-
[IBW]
*American accountant and college
administrator*
* Fix It, Mr.

**Pelham, John** 1838-1863 [SN]
*American army officer*
* [The] Gallant

**Pelham, M.**
*See* Phillips, [Sir] Richard

**Pelican**
*See* Kurschner, Conrad

**[The] Pelican**
*See* Leonard, Joe

**Pelikan, Lillian Alize Elianore**
1891-1931 [BEW]
*German-born aerial performer*
* Leitzel, Lillian

**Pelissier, H. G.**
*See* Pelissier, Harry Gabriel

**Pelissier, Harry Gabriel** 1874-1913
[BMH]
*British entertainer*
* Pelissier, H. G.

**Pelissier De Bujac, Jacques Etienne**
1904-1972 [FC]
*American actor*
* Cabot, Bruce

**Pelkey, Arthur**
*See* Peletier, Andrew Arthur

**Pelkie, Joe Walter**
*See* Palmer, Raymond A[rthur]

**Pelkonen, Elina**
*See* Honkanen, Hilja Loviisa
Valkeapaa

**Pell, Franklyn**
*See* Pelligrin, Frank E.

**Pell, John W.**
*See* Fish, Hamilton

**Pellan, Alfred**
*See* Pelland, Alfred

**Pelland, Alfred** 1906- [CAR]
*Canadian painter*
* Pellan, Alfred

**Pellegrin**
*See* La Motte-Fouque, Friedrich
Heinrich Karl de

**Pellegrini, Carlo** ?-1889
[FFF, HN, RH]
*British caricaturist*
* Ape

**Pellerano Castro, Arturo Bautista**
1865-1916 [CW]
*West Indian poet, author, playwright*
* Byron

**Pelletier, Marcel** 20th c. [SMG]
*French-born hockey player and
coach*
* [The] Gypsy Goalie

**Pelletier, Marie-Therese**
1886?-1934 [BEW]
*French-born actress*
* Pierat, Marie-Therese

**Pellicanus, Konrad**
*See* Kuerschner, Konrad

**Pellicarius**
*See* Marbode, M.

**Pellicer, Pina**
*See* Lopez Llergo, Josefina Pellicer

**Pelligrin, Frank E.** 20th c. [WW]
*Author*
* Pell, Franklyn

**Pellisson-Fontanier, Paul**
1624-1693 [HN, SN]
*French author*
* Convertisseur
* [The] King's Convertisseur

**Pelot, Pierre** 1945- [ESF]
*French author*
* Suragne, Pierre

**Pelovitz, Morton Herbert** 1925-
[EJ]
*American jazz musician*
* Herbert, Mort

**Peltier, Florence**
*See* Leonard, Florence Peltier

**Pelto, Bert**
*See* Pelto, Pertti J[uho]

**Pelto, Pertti J[uho]** 1927- [CA]
*American author and anthropologist*
* Pelto, Bert

**Pelton, Beverly Jo** 1939- [CA]
*American author*
* Jensen, Jo

**Pelton, Robert W[ayne]** 1937- [CA]
*American author*
* Arthur, Tiffany
* Martin, Kevin
* Martin, Robert W.
* Milton, Mark
* Notlep, Robert
* Sonero, Devi

**Peltonen, Vihtori** 1869-1913
[WBD]
*Finnish playwright and poet*
* Linnankoski, Johannes

**Peltrel**
*See* Nicolas, P.

**Pelty, Barney** 1880-1939 [EJS]
*American baseball player*
* [The] Yiddish Curver

**Pember-Devereux, Margaret R[ose
Roy McAdam]** 1877- ? [WGT]
*Author*
* Devereux, Roy

**Pemberton, Col.** 19th c.   [PA]
*Author*
* Leo

**Pemberton, Edgar**   [PA]
*Author*
* Burton, P. M.

**Pemberton, Israel** 1715-1779
[FFF]
*American Quaker leader*
* [The] King of the Quakers
* Wampum, King

**Pemberton, Renfrew**
*See* Busby, F. M.

**Pembroke, George**
*See* Prud'homme, George

**Pembroke, Thomas**
*See* Hopkinson, Henry Thomas
[Tom]

**Pembrooke, Kenneth**
*See* Page, Gerald W[ilburn]

**Pembury, Bill**
*See* Groom, Arthur William

**Pembury, Grosvenor**
*See* Haydon, N. G.

**Pembury, Montague**
*See* Moon, George P.

**Pemjean, Lucian**
*See* Bedford-Jones, Henry [James
O'Brien]

**[The] Pen of the Revolution**
*See* Jefferson, Thomas

**Pen, Steel**
*See* Penn, Colonel

**Pena Rego, Jesus** 20th c.   [WECO]
*Spanish cartoonist*
* Suso

**Pencil**
*See* Sowden, [Sir] William John

**Pendarves, G. G.**
*See* Trenery, Gladys Gordon

**Pendennis, Arthur, Esquire**
*See* Thackeray, William
Makepeace

**Pendenys, Arthur**
*See* Humphreys, Arthur L.

**Pender, Doris**
*See* Lomas, Doris

**Pender, Lex**
*See* Pendower, Jacques

**Pendergrass, Theodore [Teddy]**
1951-   [IBW]
*American singer, musician,
composer*
* Svengali
* Teddy Bear

**Penders, Marilyn**
*See* Pendower, Jacques

**Pendle, Nicholas**
*See* Birtill, George Arthur

**Pendleton, Conrad Padraic**
*See* Kidd, Walter Evans

**Pendleton, Don[ald Eugene]** 1927-
[CA]
*American author*
* Britain, Dan
* Gregory, Stephan

**Pendleton, George Hunt**
1825-1889   [FFF, SN]
*American politician*
* Gentleman George

**Pendower, Jacques** 1899-1976
[AW, CA, MBF]
*British author*
* Carstairs, Kathleen
* Curtis, Tom
* Dower, Penn
* Jacobs, T[homas] C[urtis]
  H[icks]
* Pender, Lex
* Penders, Marilyn
* Penn, Anne
* Stagg, James

**Pendragon**
*See* Sampson, Henry

**Pendragon, Eric**
*See* Parry, Michel Patrick

**Pendray, G[eorge] Edwards** 1901-
[NAA, WGT]
*American author, journalist, editor*
* Edwards, Gawain

**Penfield, Cornelia**
*See* Lathrop, Cornelia Sterrett
[Penfield]

**Penguin** [code name]
*See* Ahern, Thomas

**[The] Penguin**
*See* Cey, Ronald Charles

**[The] Penguin**
*See* Leonard, Joe

**Penhafirme, Count of**
*See* Sartorius, [Sir] G. R.

**Penholder**
*See* Eggleston, Edward

**Peniakoff, Vladimir** 1897-   [BDW]
*Belgian-born British army officer*
* Popski

**Penick, Clifton Hewitt** 1885-
[NAA]
*American journalist*
* McGuire, P.

**Penick, Mary Frances** 1931-
[CME, CWG]
*American country-western performer*
* Davis, Skeeter

**Penklub**
*See* Lange, Carl Gustav Albert

**Penlake, Richard**
*See* Salmon, Percy R.

**Penman**
*See* Hallock, Charles

**Penmare, William**
*See* Nisot, Mavis Elizabeth
[Hocking]

**Penn, Anne**
*See* Pendower, Jacques

**Penn, Arthur**
*See* Bunner, Henry Cuyler

**Penn, Christopher**
*See* Lawlor, Pat[rick Anthony]

**Penn, Colonel**   [FFF]
*British army officer*
* Pen, Steel

**Penn, Mr.**
*See* Colwell, Stephen

**Penn, Ruth Bonn**
*See* Rosenberg, Ethel [Clifford]

**Penn, William**
*See* Evarts, Jeremiah

**Penn, William** 1644-1718   [SN]
*British Quaker leader and founder
of Pennsylvania*
* That Jesuit

**Penn-Gaskell, Patricia** 1916-
[THR]
*British actress*
* Hilliard, Patricia

**Pennage, E. M.**
*See* Finkel, George [Irvine]

**Pennanen, Lea Airi-Sirkka** 1929-
[IAW]
*Finnish author*
* Pikkumolliainen, Leena

**Penner, Bumps**
*See* Pinter, Josef

**Penner, Joe**
*See* Pinter, Josef

**Pennes, Jean** 1894-   [WEC]
*French cartoonist*
* Sennep, J.

**Penney, Annette Culler** 1916-   [CA]
*American author*
* Culler, Annette Lorena

**Penni, Giovanni Francesco**
1488?-1528?   [SN]
*Italian painter*
* [Il] Fattore [The Steward]

**Pennibb**
*See* Sibley, Inez K.

**Pennick, Jack**
*See* Pennick, Ronald

**Pennick, Ronald** 1895?-1964
[BEW]
*American actor*
* Pennick, Jack

**Pennie, Frank** 20th c.
*American football player*
* Pennie, Ox

**Pennie, Ox**
*See* Pennie, Frank

**[The] Penniless**
*See* Maximilian I

**[The] Penniless**
*See* Walter

**Pennilesso, Pierre**
*See* Nash [or Nashe?], Thomas

**Penniman, Major**
*See* Dennison, Charles W.

**Penniman, Richard** 1935-
[EJ, SSS]
*American singer*
* Little Richard

**Pennington, Ann** 1895?-   [AM]
*American actress and dancer*
* [The] Shimmy Queen

**Pennington, George Louis** 1896-
[BE]
*American baseball player*
* Pennington, Kewpie

**Pennington, Kewpie**
*See* Pennington, George Louis

**Pennington, Penny**
*See* Galbraith, Georgie Starbuck

**Pennington, Stuart**
*See* Galbraith, Georgie Starbuck

**Pennington-Richards, C. M.** 1911-
[BF]
*British director*
* Richards, Pennington

**Pennochio, Tommy** 20th c.   [CEC]
*American underworld figure*
* [The] Bull

**Pennock, Herb[ert Jefferis]**
1894-1948   [ALR, BAB, BE]
*American baseball player*
* [The] Knight of Kennett Square
* [The] Squire of Kennett Square

**Pennock, Meta**
*See* Newman, Meta [Pennock]

**Pennot, [Rev.] Peter**
*See* Round, William Marshall Fitts

**[The] Pennsylvania Farmer**
*See* Dickinson, John

**Penny, Johnny** 20th c.   [RBE]
*American boxer*
* Pinney, Johnny

**Penny, Richard**
*See* Lasser, David

**Penny, William** 19th c.   [PA]
*Author*
* Denarius

**[The] Pennyless**
*See* Frederic IV

**Peno**
*See* Oak, Purushottam Nagesh

**Penrose, Elizabeth [Cartwright]**
1790-1837   [DEL, FFF, RH]
*British author*
* Markham, Mrs.

**Penrose, Llewellyn**
*See* Eagles, John

**Penrose, Margaret** [house
pseudonym] [Stratemeyer
Syndicate]
*See* Stratemeyer, Edward L.

**Penry, John** 1559-1593   [PA]
*British author*
* Marprelate, Martin
* Priest, Martin

**[The] Pensioned Dauber**
*See* Hogarth, William

**Pentecost, Hugh**
*See* Philips, Judson Pentecost

**Pentecost, Martin**
*See* Hearn, John

**[La] Pentecote Vivante**
*See* Mezzofanti, Giuseppe

**Pentelow, John Nix** 1872-1931
[MBF]
*British author and editor*
* Clifford, Martin [house
  pseudonym]
* Huntingdon, Harry
* North, Jack
* Randolph, Richard
* Richards, Frank [house
  pseudonym]
* Ryle, Randolph
* West, John

**Pentland, Mary**
See Tilton, Mrs. E. L.

**Pentreath, Doll** 1686-1777 [RH]
* [The] Last who Spoke Cornish

**Pentz, Jacob** [PA]
Author
* Gopher

**Penzik, Irena**
See Narell, Irena

**Penzler, Otto** 1942- [CA]
German-born author
* Adler, Irene
* Ferrier, Lucy
* Gregory, Stephen
* Milverton, Charles A.

**People, Granville Church** 20th c.
[WW]
Author
* Church, Granville

**[The] People's Artist**
See Douglas, Emory

**[The] People's Captain**
See Garibaldi, Giuseppe

**[The] People's Cherce**
See Walker, Frederick E.

**[The] People's Friend**
See Gordon, William

**[The] People's Friend**
See Marat, Jean Paul

**[The] People's Friend**
See Robespierre, Maximilien

**Peoples, James E. [Jimmy]**
1863-1920 [BN]
American baseball player
* Peoples, Kid

**Peoples, Kid**
See Peoples, James E. [Jimmy]

**[The] People's King**
See Lorraine, Henry I [or Henri]
de

**[The] People's President**
See Cleveland, [Stephen] Grover

**[The] People's President**
See Jackson, Andrew

**[The] People's William**
See Gladstone, William Ewart

**Peoples, Woodrow** 1943- [FB]
American football player
* Peoples, Woody

**Peoples, Woody**
See Peoples, Woodrow

**Pep, Willie**
See Papaleo, William

**Pepe Hillo [Little Joe]**
See Leal y Casado, Cayetano

**Peper, Minnie Dorothy** 1880- ?
[THR]
American actress
* Oaker, Jane

**Pepete [Big Joe]**
See Gallego Mateo, Jose

**Pepin** ?- 640? [WBD]
Frankish ruler
* [The] Elder
* Pepin of Landern

**Pepin of Herstal**
See Pepin II

**Pepin of Landern**
See Pepin

**Pepin II** ?- 714 [WBD]
Frankish ruler
* Pepin of Herstal

**Pepin III** 714?- 768
[DNNS, HN, SN]
King of the Franks
* [Le] Bref
* Most Christian King
* [The] Patrician of Rome
* [The] Short

**Pepino**
See Carre, Freddy

**Pepito the Spanish Clown**
See Perez, Pepito

**Pepitone, Joseph Anthony** 1940-
[BE]
American baseball player
* Pepitone, Pepi

**Pepitone, Pepi**
See Pepitone, Joseph Anthony

**Peploe, Denis Frederic Neil** 1914-
[ART]
Scottish painter
* Denis P.

**Peploski, Joseph Aloysius** 1891-
[BE]
American baseball player
* Peploski, Pepper

**Peploski, Pepper**
See Peploski, Joseph Aloysius

**Pepper, Bill**
See Pepper, Curtis G.

**Pepper, Choral** 1918- [CA]
American writer
* Lowe, Corke
* Rollins, Royce

**Pepper, Curtis G.** 1920- [CA]
American author
* Pepper, Bill

**Pepper, Frank S.** 20th c. [MBF]
British author
* Marshall, John
* Wilton, Hal

**Pepper, Gary** 1949-
British jazz musician
* Pepper, Woody

**Pepper, George**
See Martin, George

**Pepper, Hugh McLaurin** 1931-
[BE]
American baseball player
* Pepper, Laurin

**Pepper, Joan**
See Wetherell-Pepper, Joan
Alexander

**Pepper, Laurin**
See Pepper, Hugh McLaurin

**Pepper, Woody**
See Pepper, Gary

**Pepperbox, Peter**
See Fessenden, Thomas Green

**Peppercorn, Arthur Douglas**
1847-1924 [DBA]
British painter
* Our English Corot

**Peppercorn, H., M.D.**
See Barham, Richard Harris

**Peppercorn, Peter**
See Peacock, Thomas Love

**Peppergrass, Paul**
See Boyce, J.

**Peppermint Cane**
See Harris, Wynonie

**Pepperpod, Pip**
See Stoddard, Charles Warren

**Peppler, Alice Stolper**
See Stolper, Alice

**Pepys in Essex**
See Tompkins, Herbert
Winckworth

**[The] Pepys of His Age**
See De Bourdeille, Pierre

**Pepys, Samuel** 1633-1703
[DEP, DNNS, SN]
British author and politician
* [The] Father of Black Letter Lore
* [The] Prince of Gossips
* [The] Weather Glass of His Time

**Pequot**
See March, Charles W.

**Per Aera**
See Boothby, Frederick Lewis
Maitland

**Per Mare**
See Boothby, Frederick Lewis
Maitland

**Peralta, Angela** 1843?-1883 [FFF]
Mexican singer
* [The] Mexican Nightingale

**Peralta, Goyo**
See Peralta, Gregorio

**Peralta, Gregorio** 1935- [BX]
Argentinian boxer
* Peralta, Goyo

**Peralta Seleron, Francisco**
1900-1930 [GS]
Spanish bullfighter
* Facultades [Abilities]

**Perceval, Maxwell**
See Perceval-Maxwell, Michael

**Perceval-Maxwell, Michael** [WD]
Historian and author
* Perceval, Maxwell

**Perch, Philemon**
See Johnston, Richard Malcolm

**Percheron, Betty** 1921- [THR]
British actress
* Paul, Betty

**Percival**
See Raphael, John N.

**Percival, Fanny**
See Percy, Mrs. F. A.

**Percival, Hayward**
See Hayward, Percy Roy

**Percival, John** 1779-1862
[FFF, WBD]
American naval officer
* Mad Jack

**Percival, John** (Continued)
* Roaring Jack

**Percival, Norman**
See Parcell, Norman H[owe]

**Percival, Walter C.**
See Lingenfelter, Charles David

**Percy, Charles Henry**
See Smith, Dorothy Gladys

**Percy, Edward**
See Smith, Edward Percy

**Percy, Florence**
See Allen, Elizabeth Akers

**Percy, George**
See Groves-Raines, George Percy

**Percy, Henry** 1364-1403
[DHA, DNNS, SN]
British army officer
* Hotspur

**Percy, Henry** 1564-1632 [WBD]
Ninth Earl of Northumberland
* [The] Wizard Earl

**Percy, [Sir] Hugh**
See Smithson, Hugh

**Percy, Marvin** 1925- [ECM]
American singer and songwriter
* Rainwater, Marvin

**Percy, Mrs. F. A.** [PA]
Author
* Percival, Fanny

**Percy, Reuben**
See Byerley, Thomas

**Percy, Sholto**
See Robertson, Joseph Clinton

**Percy, Thomas** 1729-1811 [SN]
British author and poet
* [The] Father of Poetical Taste

**Perdiguero Perez, Fernando** 1929-
[IAW]
Spanish author
* Pin, Oscar

**Perdita**
See Robinson, Mary Darby

**Perdomo y Heredia, Josefa Antonia**
1834-1896 [CW]
Dominican poet
* Laura

**Perdoni, Renso** 1941- [FB]
Italian-born American football
player
* Perdoni, Rock

**Perdoni, Rock**
See Perdoni, Renso

**Perdue, Hubbard E.** 1882-1968
[BE]
American baseball player
* [The] Gallatin Squash

**[Le] Pere aux Rondeaux**
See Davaux, Jean Baptiste

**Pere de la Patrie**
See Suger

**[Le] Pere de la Patrie**
See Vincent de Paul

**[Le] Pere de la Pensee**
See Catinat, Nicholas

**Pere de l'Eloquence**
See Jean [or Jehan] de Meung

[Le] Pere de l'Histoire de France
See Duchesne, Andre

[Le] Pere des Lettres
See Francis I or [Francois]

[Le] Pere du Peuple
See Louis XII

[Le] Pere Duchesne
See Hebert, Jacques Rene

[Le] Pere Enfantin
See Enfantin, Barthelemy Prosper

Pere la Pudeur
See Berenger, Rene

Peregoy, Calvin
See McClary, Thomas Calvert

[La] Peregrina
See Avellaneda y Arteaga,
Gertrudis Gomez de

Peregrine, [Brother]
See Blewitt, Octavius

Peregrine
See Deutscher, Isaac

Peregrinus
See Vincent of Lerins

Pereira, Harold Bertram 1890-
[CA]
British author
* Askari, Hussaini Muhammad
* Yeates, Mabel

Pereira, Jacob Rodrigue
1715-1780 [WBD]
Spanish educator
* Pereire, Jacob Rodrigue

Pereira, Nunez Alvarez 1360-1431
[FFF, RH, SN]
Portuguese army officer and
diplomat
* [The] Cid of Portugal
* [The] Portuguese Cid

Pereira, W. D.
See Pereira, Wilfred Dennis

Pereira, Wilfred Dennis 1921-
[SFL]
British author
* Pereira, W. D.

Pereira de Souza, Washington Luiz
1869-1957 [WBD]
Brazilian statesman
* Luiz, Washington

Pereire, Jacob Rodrigue
See Pereira, Jacob Rodrigue

Perelman, S. J.
See Perelman, Sidney Joseph

Perelman, Sidney Joseph
1904-1979 [BEW, IPA, LC]
American playwright and author
* Perelman, S. J.
* [El] Sid

Perelmuth, Jacob Pincus 1904-
[BBD]
American opera singer
* Peerce, Jan

Perera, Padma
See Hejmadi, Padma

Pereria Saromenho, Auguste
?-1878 [PA]
Author
* Abdallah

Peres, Shimon
See Persky, Shimon

Peresitch, [Colonel] 20th c. [CND]
Yugoslav military leader
* Hope, Mr. [code name used
during World War II]

Pereszlenyi, Martin 1918- [BEW]
Hungarian writer
* Esslin, Martin

Peretti, Felice 1521-1590
[HN, WBD]
Pope
* [The] Second Founder of Rome
* Sixtus V

Peretto
See Pomponazzi, Pietro

Peretz, Yitskhok Leybush
1852-1915 [MWD]
Polish author and poet
* [The] Colossus of Yiddish
Literature
* [The] Father of Yiddish
Literature

Perevozchikova, Maria Petrovna
1866-1954 [BEW]
Actress
* Lilina, Maria Petrovna

Perey, Lucien
See Herpin, Clara Adele Luce

Perez, Atanasio Rigal 1942-
[PB, SMG, WWB]
Cuban-born baseball player
* Perez, Doggie
* Perez, Tony

Perez, Cap
See Perez Rodriguez, Carlos
Andres

Perez, Doggie
See Perez, Atanasio Rigal

Perez, Jose Maria 20th c.
Spanish cartoonist
* Peridis

Perez, Juan
See Wellman, Manly Wade

Perez, Martin Roman 1947-
[SMG]
American baseball player
* Perez, Taco

Perez, Pepito 1896-1975 [FIR, SC]
Spanish-born actor
* Pepito the Spanish Clown

Perez, Taco
See Perez, Martin Roman

Perez, Tony
See Perez, Atanasio Rigal

Perez, Victor 1911-1942
[BX, RBE, WBC]
Tunisian boxer
* Perez, Young
* [The] Tunis Terror

Perez, Young
See Perez, Victor

Perez de Guzman, Alphonso [or
Alonso] 1258?-1320?
[DNNF, FFF, WBD]
Spanish army officer
* [El] Bueno
* [The] Spanish Brutus

Perez de Leon, Hermina
1894-1953 [SC]
Mexican actress
* Derba, Mimi

Perez Rodriguez, Carlos Andres
1922?-
Venezuelan president
* Perez, Cap

Perez y Hoyos, Angel 1898- [GS]
Spanish bullfighter
* Angelillo de Triana [Little Angel
of Triana]

[The] Perfect
See John II

Perforatus
See Borde, Andrew

[The] Perfume Burglar
See Wajcieckowski, Earl

Pergarth, Peter
See Goddard, Norman Molyneux

Pericas
See Lora Trejo, Francisco

Pericles 5th c. BC [DEP, SN]
Athenian statesman
* [The] G. O. M. of Athens
* Onion Head
* Schinocephalus

Pericoli, Niccolo 1485-1550
[WBD]
Italian sculptor and architect
* [Il] Tribolo

Peridis
See Perez, Jose Maria

Perier, Auguste Casimir
1811-1878 [WBD]
French politician
* Casimir Perier, Auguste

Perier, Francois
See Pilu, Francois

Periere, Inez
See Huntington, Mrs. Wright

Peril, Milton R.
See Jones, Francis

[Le] Perin
See Daly, Augustin

Perine, C. E. [PA]
Author
* Newton, Charles E.

Periquin
See Espinosa de los Monteros,
Armando

Periwinkle, Paul
See St. John, Percy Boyle

Perk, Abner
See Twombly, A. Stevenson

Perkerson, Medora [Field] 20th c.
[WW]
Author
* Field, Medora

Perkins, Abigail
See Kaler, James Otis

Perkins, Alice 1872- ? [THR]
American actress
* Lonnon, Alice

Perkins, Buck
See Perkins, Clayton

Perkins, Charles Sullivan [Charlie]
1905- [BE]
American baseball player
* Perkins, Lefty

Perkins, Clayton 20th c. [FCW]
American musician
* Perkins, Buck

Perkins, Cy
See Perkins, Ralph Foster

Perkins, Don[ald A.] 20th c.
American football player
* Perkins, Perk

Perkins, Eli
See Landon, Melville De Lancey

Perkins, Faith
See Bramer, Jennie [Perkins]

Perkins, Frederick Beecher [PA]
Author
* Budlong, Pharaoh

Perkins, Grace
See Oursler, Grace Perkins

Perkins, Joe Willie 1913- [BWW]
American singer
* Perkins, Pinetop

Perkins, Justin 1805-1869 [WBD]
American missionary
* [The] Apostle of Persia

Perkins, Kenneth 1890- [WWL]
American author
* Phillips, King

Perkins, Lefty
See Perkins, Charles Sullivan
[Charlie]

Perkins, Newton Stephens 1925-
[CA]
American sportswriter
* Perkins, Steve

Perkins, O. C. 20th c.
American singer
* Perkins, Perk

Perkins, Perk
See Perkins, Don[ald A.]

Perkins, Perk
See Perkins, O. C.

Perkins, Pinetop
See Perkins, Joe Willie

Perkins, Ralph Foster 1896-1963
[BE, PB]
American baseball player
* Perkins, Cy

Perkins, Sam 20th c.
American basketball player
* [The] Plastic Man

Perkins, Steve
See Perkins, Newton Stephens

Perkins, Violet Lilian 20th c.
[SFL, WGT]
Author
* Leslie, Lilian [joint pseudonym
with Arthur Leslie Hood]

Perkins, Virginia Chase 1902-
[CAP, WD]
American author
* Chase, Virginia Lowell

Perle, George
See Perlman, George

**Perley**
See Poore, Benjamin Perley

**Perley, Mrs. Frank** [FFF]
*Entertainer*
* Glenn, Ida

**Perlinger, Jeff** 1953- [SMG]
*American football player*
* Perlinger, Pearl

**Perlinger, Pearl**
See Perlinger, Jeff

**Perlman, George** 1915- [CA]
*American composer and author*
* Perle, George

**Perlman, Jess** 1891- [CA]
*American poet*
* Gray, Philip

**Perls, Frederick S[alomon]**
1893?-1970 [CA]
*German-born author and
psychotherapist*
* Perls, Fritz

**Perls, Fritz**
See Perls, Frederick S[alomon]

**Pernoll, Henry Hubbard**
1888-1944 [BE]
*American baseball player*
* Pernoll, Hub

**Pernoll, Hub**
See Pernoll, Henry Hubbard

**Peron, Eva** 1919?-1952
*Wife of Argentinian president Juan
Peron*
* Peron, Evita

**Peron, Evita**
See Peron, Eva

**Peronne**
See Thompson, Ellen Perronet

**Peropadre, Miguel** 20th c. [GS]
*Spanish bullfighter*
* Cincovillas [Five Villas]

**Perowne, Barry**
See Atkey, Philip

**[The] Perpetual Candidate**
See Cleveland, [Stephen] Grover

**Perpetual Motion**
See Jackson, Henry

**Perrault, Charles** 1628-1703
[PA, SN]
*French author*
* Immortal Pindar's Foe
* Mother Goose

**Perrault, Jumping Joe**
See Perrault, Paul Joseph

**Perrault, Paul Joseph** 20th c.
[BBH]
*American skier*
* Perrault, Jumping Joe

**Perreau, Gerald** 1938- [FC]
*American actor*
* Miles, Peter

**Perreau, Ghislaine** 1941-
[FC, ITA, SW]
*American actress*
* Perreau, Gigi

**Perreau, Gigi**
See Perreau, Ghislaine

**Perreault, Miche**
See Perreault, Robert

**Perreault, Robert** 1931- [CEI]
*Canadian-born hockey player*
* Perreault, Miche

**Perrers [or Pierce?], Alice** ?-1400
[DNNF, FFF, RH]
*Mistress of King Edward III of
England*
* [The] Lady of the Sun

**Perri, Leslie**
See Wilson, Doris Marie Claire
Baumgardt Pohl

**Perrier, Anna** 19th c. [PA]
*Author*
* [An] Irish Woman

**Perrier, Rose-Marie**
See Casias, Rose-Marie Perrier

**Perrin, Claude Victor [Duc de
Bellune]** 1766-1841 [WBD]
*French army officer*
* Victor [or Victor-Perrin], Claude

**Perrin, Clyde**
See O'Brien, Howard Vincent

**Perrin, Jack**
See Rayart, Jack Perrin

**Perrin, Lefty**
See Perrin, William Joseph [Bill]

**Perrin, William Joseph [Bill]**
1911-1974 [BE]
*American baseball player*
* Perrin, Lefty

**Perrine, John Grover** 1885-1948
[BE]
*American baseball player*
* Perrine, Nig

**Perrine, Nig**
See Perrine, John Grover

**Perrinot, Jeanne** 1906- [THR]
*French actress and singer*
* Aubert, Jeanne

**Perritt, Pol**
See Perritt, William Dayton

**Perritt, William Dayton**
1892-1947 [AS, BE]
*American baseball player*
* Perritt, Pol

**Perrone, Sam**
See Perrone, Santo

**Perrone, Santo** ?-1966 [PHM]
*American underworld figure*
* Perrone, Sam

**Perrot, Gervase**
See Jones, Arthur Llewellyn

**Perry, A. T.** 1887- [WGT]
*Ukrainian-born British author*
* Ack-Lak, General

**Perry, Albert** 20th c. [GW]
*American rodeo performer*
* Perry, Coyote

**Perry, Annette**
See Perry, Antoinette

**Perry, Antoinette** 1888-1946 [SC]
*American actress and director*
* Perry, Annette

**Perry, Aulcie** 20th c. [IBW]
*American-born basketball player*
* Ben Avraham, Elisha

**Perry, Bob**
See Perry, Melvin Gray

**Perry, Brighton**
See Sherwood, Robert Emmet

**Perry, Clair Willard** 1887- [NAA]
*American author*
* Perry, Clay

**Perry, Clay**
See Perry, Clair Willard

**Perry, Clifford Albyn** 1891-1937
[EMT]
*British-born actor, producer,
director*
* Cliff, Laddie

**Perry, Coyote**
See Perry, Albert

**Perry, Dick** 1922- [SFL]
*Author*
* Winfield, Dick

**Perry, Elaine**
See Frueauff, Elaine Storrs

**Perry, Ernest Thomas** 1908- [ART]
*Irish-born painter*
* E. P.

**Perry, Fletcher** 1927-
[B10, FB, IBW]
*American football player*
* Joe the Jet
* Perry, Joe
* Perry, Jolting Joe

**Perry, Harry Dennies**
See Ingraham, Prentiss

**Perry, Irene**
See Brady, Irene

**Perry, Irma**
See Le Gallienne, Irma Hinton

**Perry, James Curtis**
See Perry, Oliver Curtis

**Perry, Joe**
See Perry, Fletcher

**Perry, Jolting Joe**
See Perry, Fletcher

**Perry, Junebug**
See Perry, Vernon, Jr.

**Perry, Lincoln Theodore** 892?-
[B10, F2, FC]
*American entertainer*
* Stepin Fetchit

**Perry, Margaret**
See Frueauff, Margaret Hall

**Perry, Martin Henry** 1903- [AW]
*British author*
* Martyn, Henry

**Perry, Melvin Gray** 1934- [BE]
*American baseball player*
* Perry, Bob

**Perry, Montanye** 20th c. [NAA]
*American author*
* Lambert, Marion

**Perry, Neil James** 1958- [DC]
*British cricketer*
* Perry, Ziggy

**Perry, Oliver Curtis** 1864-1930
[BLB]
*American train robber*
* Moore, Oliver
* Perry, James Curtis

**Perry, Ritchie [John Allen]** 1942-
[CA]
*British author*
* Allen, John

**Perry, Ruth** 1892-
*Author*
* Campion, Rose [joint pseudonym
with Arthur LeRoy Kaser and
Jean Lee Latham]

**Perry, Socks**
See Perry, William Henry [Hank]

**Perry, Vernon, Jr.** 1953- [SMG]
*American football player*
* Perry, Junebug

**Perry, Vic[tor]** 1920-1974 [SC]
*British-born actor*
* [The] World's Greatest
Pickpocket

**Perry, William** [FFF]
*British boxer*
* [The] Tipton Slasher

**Perry, [Captain] William B.**
See Brown, William Perry

**Perry, William Henry [Hank]**
1886-1956 [BE]
*American baseball player*
* Perry, Socks

**Perry, Ziggy**
See Perry, Neil James

**Perryman, Art**
See Perryman, Stephen Peter

**Perryman, Emmett Key** 1888-1966
[BE]
*American baseball player*
* Perryman, Parson

**Perryman, Parson**
See Perryman, Emmett Key

**Perryman, Rufus G.** 1892-1973
[BWW, EJ]
*American jazz musician*
* Detroit Red
* Speckled Red

**Perryman, Stephen Peter** 1955-
[DC]
*British cricketer*
* Perryman, Art

**Perryman, William Lee [Willie]**
1911- [BWW]
*American singer*
* Boogie 'n' Blues, Mr.
* Feelgood, Doctor
* Piano Red

**Pershing, Black Jack**
See Pershing, John Joseph

**Pershing, John Joseph** 1860-1948
[CND]
*American military leader*
* Pershing, Black Jack

**Pershing, Marie**
See Schultz, Pearle Henriksen

**[The] Persian Alexander**
See Sandjar

**[The] Persian Anacreon**
See Hafiz, Mohammed

[The] Persian Horace
See Omar Khayyam

[The] Persian King
See Cyrus

Persiani, Andre Paul Stephane
1927- [EJ]
French jazz musician
* Persiany, Andre Paul Stephane

Persiany, Andre Paul Stephane
See Persiani, Andre Paul Stephane

Persic, Peregrine
See Morier, James Justinian

Persico, Carmine 20th c. [PHM]
American underworld figure
* [The] Snake

Persico, Salvatore Giuseppe 1893-
[BE]
American baseball player
* Smith, Joe
* Smith, Salvatore Giuseppe

Persis
See Haime, Agnes Irvine
Constance [Adams]

Persius Flaccus, Aulus 34- 62
[FFF, RH, SN]
Roman satirist
* [The] Ligurian Sage

Perske, Betty Joan 1924-
[BDF, BEW, EMT]
American actress
* Bacall, Lauren

Persky, Mordecai 1931- [CA]
American editor
* Persky, Mort

Persky, Mort
See Persky, Mordecai

Persky, Shimon 1923- [CA]
Israeli politician and author
* Peres, Shimon

[A] Person about Town
See Webb, Cornelius

Person, Muscles
See Person, Norman

Person, Norman 20th c. [GW]
American rodeo performer
* Person, Muscles

Personne
See Wilkins, E. G. P.

[The] Perspicuous Doctor
See Burleigh, [or Burley?], Walter

Perspicuus, Doctor
See Bonet, Nicholas

Persson, Harry Arnold 1920- [EJ]
Swedish jazz musician
* Arnold, Harry

Pertinax
See Geraud, [Charles Joseph]
Andre

Pertinax
See Gerault, Charles

Pertinax
See Haws, Duncan

Pertinax, Publius Helvius 126-
193 [DEP, FFF]
Roman emperor
* [The] Tennis Ball of Fortune

Pertinez, Zoilo 20th c. [GS]
Spanish bullfighter
* Terremoto [Big Earthquake]

Pertzel, Mrs. [FFF]
Entertainer
* Prescott, Marie

Perugini, Signor
See Chatterton, John

[Il] Perugino
See Bartoli, Pietro Santi

[Il] Perugino
See Vannucci, Pietro

Perus, Francoise 1936- [IAW]
French-born author
* Cueva, Francoise
* Perus-Cueva, Francoise

Perus-Cueva, Francoise
See Perus, Francoise

Pesano, Alfred Manuel 1928-
[BE, IPA, SMG]
American baseball player and
manager
* Martin, Alfred Manuel
* Martin, Billy

[Il] Pesarese
See Cantarini [or da Pesaro],
Simone

Pesce, Franco 20th c. [WF]
Italian actor
* Oliveras, Frank

Peschkowsky, Michael Igor 1931-
[BEW, FC, FD]
German-born American entertainer
and director
* Nichols, Mike

[Il] Pesellino
See Di Stefano, Francesco

Peshkov [or Pyeshkoff], Alexei
Maximovich 1868-1936
[OCF, TC, TCL]
Russian author and playwright
* Chlamyda, Jehudiil
* Gorky, Maxim

Peskay, Edward 1899?-1978 [FIR]
Film industry pioneer
* Peskay, Pop

Peskay, Pop
See Peskay, Edward

Pesky, Johnny
See Paveskovich, John Michael

Pesky, Needlenose
See Paveskovich, John Michael

Pessen, Beth 1943- [CA]
American author
* Shub, Beth

Pessl, Gabriela Elsa 1906- [BBD]
Austrian-born musician
* Pessl, Yella

Pessl, Yella
See Pessl, Gabriela Elsa

Pessoa, Fernando [Antonio Nogueira]
1888-1935 [WOA]
Portuguese poet
* Caeiro, Alberto
* De Campos, Alvaro
* Reis, Ricardo

Pestalozzi
See Peters, Bernard

Pesthe
See Millspaugh, Charles Frederick

Pestritto, Antonio 1907-1969
[EJ, PMJ, WWJ]
American jazz musician
* Pastor, Tony

Petaja, Emil [Theodore] 1915-
[ESF]
American author
* Pine, Theodore [joint pseudonym
with Henry L. Hasse]

Pete the Hermit
See Howard, Peter

Peter
See Lockhart, John Gibson

Peter
See Simon

Peter [HN]
Bishop of Argos
* Thaumaturgus

Peter ?-1012 [CAL]
Pope
* Bucca Porci [Pig's Snout]
* Sergius IV

Peter [or Pietro] 406- 450
[FFF, HN]
Saint
* Chrysologus
* Golden Speech
* [The] Golden Tongued

Peter 19th c. [DNNS, RH]
Calabrian robber chief
* [The] Emperor of the Mountains

Peter Claver 1580-1654 [WBD]
Saint
* [The] Apostle of the Negroes

Peter de l'Isle [HN]
Medieval scholar
* Notabilis, Doctor

Peter Lee, Sidney 20th c.
British forger
* [The] Magician

Peter of Amiens 1050?-1115?
[SN, WBD]
French monk
* [The] Hermit

Peter [or Pierre] of Cluny
1092?-1156 [FFF, HN, WBD]
French-born monk
* Peter of Montboissier
* Venerabilis, Doctor
* [The] Venerable Doctor

Peter of Montboissier
See Peter [or Pierre] of Cluny

Peter of Tarentaise [Pietro di
Tarantasia] 1245-1277 [CAL, HN]
Pope
* Famosissimus, Doctor
* Innocent V

[The] Peter Pan of Politics
See Brown, Edmund Gerald,
Jr.[Jerry]

Peter, R. C.
See Peter, Robert Charles

Peter, Robert Charles 1888- [ART]
British painter and engraver
* Peter, R. C.

Peter the Great
See Pund, Henry R.

[The] Peter the Great of Egypt
See Mehemet [or Mohammed] Ali

Peter the Packer
See O'Brien, Peter

Peter I [Petr Alekseevich]
1672-1725 [DNNS, SN, WBD]
Czar of Russia
* [The] Great
* Mikhailov, Peter

Peterkiewicz, Jerzy
See Pietrkiewicz, Jerzy

Peterkin, Alexander 19th c. [PA]
Author
* Anti Harmonicus
* Civis

Peterkin, Daisy 1884-1952 [BEW]
American theatrical performer
* Dazie, Mademoiselle

Peterman, Roberta 1930-
[IPA, OP]
American opera singer
* Peters, Roberta

Peters, Alexander
See Hollander, Zander

Peters, Arthur Anderson
1913-1979 [CA]
American author
* Peters, Fritz

Peters, Barney
See Bauer, Erwin A.

Peters, Bernadette
See Lazzara, Bernadette

Peters, Bernard 1827- ? [FFF, PA]
American editor
* Pestalozzi

Peters, Bill
See McGivern, William P[eter]

Peters, Brock
See Fisher, Brock

Peters, Bryan
See George, Peter [Bryan]

Peters, Caroline
See Betz, Eva Kelly

Peters, Charley
See Patton, Charley

Peters, Curtis Arnoux, Jr.
1904?-1968 [CA, LC]
American cartoonist
* Arno, Peter

Peters, Donald L. 1925- [CA]
American educator and author
* Peters, Leslie

Peters, Elizabeth
See Mertz, Barbara [Gross]

Peters, Elizabeth 1926- [SW]
American actress
* Peters, Jean

Peters, Ellis
See Pargeter, Edith Mary

Peters, Fred
See Tuite, Frederick P.

Peters, Fritz
See Peters, Arthur Anderson

Peters, Gary Charles 1937- [PB]
American baseball player
* Peters, Pete

**Peters, Geoffrey**
See Palmer, Madelyn

**Peters, Geoffrey**
See Trippe, Peter

**Peters [or Peter?], Hugh**
1599-1660 [DNNS, HN]
*British clergyman*
* Cromwell's Mad Chaplain
* [The] Pulpit Buffoon

**Peters, Jane Alice** 1908-1942
[BDF, F1, FC]
*American actress*
* Lombard, Carole

**Peters, Jean**
See Peters, Elizabeth

**Peters, John William** 1893-1932
[BE]
*American baseball player*
* Peters, Shotgun

**Peters, L. T.** [joint pseudonym with
Jo-Ann Klainer]
See Klainer, Albert S.

**Peters, L. T.** [joint pseudonym with
Albert S. Klainer]
See Klainer, Jo-Ann

**Peters, Lane**
See Lapidus, Elaine

**Peters, Lawrence**
See Davies, Leslie Purnell

**Peters, Leslie**
See Peters, Donald L.

**Peters, Linda**
See Catherall, Arthur

**Peters, Ludovic**
See Brent, Peter [Ludwig]

**Peters, Marcia**
See Gouled, Vivian G[loria]

**Peters, Maureen** 1935-
[AW, CA, WD]
*Welsh-born author*
* Black, Veronica
* Darby, Catherine
* Rothman, Judith
* Whitby, Sharon

**Peters, Oscar C.** 1886- [BE]
*American baseball player*
* Peters, Rube

**Peters, Pete**
See Peters, Gary Charles

**Peters, Roberta**
See Peterman, Roberta

**Peters, Rube**
See Peters, Oscar C.

**Peters, Russell Dixon** 1914- [BE]
*American baseball player*
* Peters, Rusty

**Peters, Rusty**
See Peters, Russell Dixon

**Peters, S. H.**
See Porter, William Sydney

**Peters, S. T.**
See Brannon, William T.

**Peters, Shotgun**
See Peters, John William

**Peters, Steven**
See Geiser, Robert L[ee]

**Peters, Susan**
See Carnahan, Suzanne

**Peters, W. A.** [PA]
*Author*
* Bronson, Doctor

**Peters, Wally**
See Paricciuoli, Walter

**Petersen, Gwenn Boardman** 1924-
[CA]
*British-born author*
* Boardman, Gwenn R.

**Petersen, Kaj Harald Leininger**
1898-1944 [BEW]
*Danish playwright and clergyman*
* Munk, Kaj

**Petersen, Robert Storm** 1882-1949
[WEC]
*Danish cartoonist, painter, actor,
author*
* Storm P.

**Petersham, Miska**
See Petersham, Petrezselyem
Mikaly

**Petersham, Petrezselyem Mikaly**
1888-1960 [CA]
*Hungarian-born American author
and illustrator*
* Petersham, Miska

**Petersilea, Carlyle** 1844-1903
[SFL, WGT]
*Author*
* Von Himmel, Ernst

**Peterson, Anna**
See Rundquist, Anna Olivia

**Peterson, Beatrice** 1916- [FC]
*American actress*
* Brooke, Hillary

**Peterson, Buddy**
See Peterson, Carl Francis

**Peterson, Cap**
See Peterson, Charles Andrew

**Peterson, Carl Francis** 1925- [BE]
*American baseball player*
* Peterson, Buddy

**Peterson, Charles Andrew** 1942-
[BE]
*American baseball player*
* Peterson, Cap

**Peterson, Corinna** 1923- [AW]
*British author*
* Cochrane, Corinna

**Peterson, Firecracker**
See Peterson, Herman

**Peterson, Fred Ingels** 1942-
[BE, PB]
*American baseball player*
* Peterson, Fritz

**Peterson, Fritz**
See Peterson, Fred Ingels

**Peterson, Harding** 1930- [SMG]
*American baseball player and
manager*
* Peterson, Pete

**Peterson, Herman** ?-1975 [BBH]
*American trapshooter*
* Peterson, Firecracker

**Peterson, James**
See Zeiger, Henry A[nthony]

**Peterson, Jim**
See Crawford, William [Elbert]

**Peterson, John Victor** 20th c.
[WGT]
*Author*
* Valding, Victor [joint pseudonym
with Allan Ingvald Benson]

**Peterson, Judge Kenneth** 1966-
[IBW]
*American musician*
* Peterson, Lucky

**Peterson, Lenka**
See Isacson, Betty Ann

**Peterson, Lucky**
See Peterson, Judge Kenneth

**Peterson, Margaret**
See Fischer, Margaret Ann
Peterson

**Peterson, Marvin** 1948- [IBW]
*American jazz musician*
* Hannibal

**Peterson, Maud Howard**
See Hoopes, Mary Howard

**Peterson, Pete**
See Peterson, Harding

**Peterson, Pete**
See Peterson, Wilbur

**Peterson, Ralph Howard**
1915?-1976 [B10]
*American journalist and television
newscaster*
* Howard, Ralph

**Peterson, Robert E[ugene]** 1928-
[CA]
*American author*
* Saya, Peter

**Peterson, Roger Tory** 1908?-
*American author and illustrator of
bird guides*
* King Penguin

**Peterson, Wilbur** 1915-1960 [SC]
*American actor*
* Peterson, Pete

**Petie, Haris**
See Petty, Roberta

**Petiot, Henry Jules** 1901-1965
[CAT, EWL]
*French author*
* Daniel Rops

**Petit, Adrien** 1500- ? [PA]
*Author*
* Coelicus

**[Le] Petit Albert**
See Albert [Count of Bollstadt]

**Petit, Anne-Marie** 1938- [FC]
*French actress*
* Petit, Pascale

**[Le] Petit Bernard**
See Bernard, Solomon

**Petit, Buddy**
See Crawford, Joseph

**[Le] Petit Caporal**
See Bonaparte, Napoleon

**[The] Petit Chef**
See Sukulov, Victor

**[Le] Petit Fils de Voltaire**
See About, Edmond Francois
Valentin

**[Le] Petit Homme Rouge**
See Vizetelly, Ernest Alfred

**[Le] Petit Manteau Bleu**
See Champion, Edme

**Petit, Pascale**
See Petit, Anne-Marie

**[Le] Petit Roi de Bourges**
See Charles VII

**[La] Petite Nellie**
See Liddy, Eleanor Jane

**Petkov, Khristo Botyov** 1847-1876
[WBD]
*Bulgarian patriot and poet*
* Botyov, Khristo

**Peto**
See White, Stanley

**Peto, James**
See White, Stanley

**Petofi, Sandor**
See Petrovics, Sandor

**Petosky, Fred Lee** 1911- [BE]
*American baseball player*
* Petosky, Ted

**Petosky, Ted**
See Petosky, Fred Lee

**Petracco, Francesco** 1304-1374
[FFF, WBD]
*Italian poet*
* Petrarch
* [The] Prince of the Sonnet

**Petrarch**
See Petracco, Francesco

**[The] Petrarch of Catalonia**
See March, Ausias

**[The] Petrarch of England**
See Sidney, [Sir] Philip

**[The] Petrarch of France**
See Ronsard, Pierre de

**[The] Petrarch of Spain**
See Garcilaso de la Vega

**Petri, Elio**
See Petri, Eraclio

**Petri, Eraclio** 1929- [FDG]
*Italian director*
* Petri, Elio

**Petri, Gerlacus**
See Gerlac, Peterson

**Petri, Sjurd Peeters** 1527-1597
[PA]
*Author*
* Suffridus

**Petrie, Mildred McClary** 1912-
[CA]
*Canadian-born author*
* Tymeson, Mildred McClary

**Petrie, Rhona**
See Buchanan, Marie

**Petrilli, Dominick** ?-1953 [PHM]
*American underworld figure*
* [The] Gap

**Petro Bey**
See Mavromichalis, Petros

**Petrocelli, Americo Peter** 1943-
[BE, SMG]
*American baseball player*
* Petrocelli, Rico

**Petrocelli, Orlando R[alph]** 1930-
[CA]
*American publisher and author*
* Dyer, Brian [joint pseudonym
  with Brian Rothery]

**Petrocelli, Rico**
See Petrocelli, Americo Peter

**Petrolle, Billy** 1905- [BX, RBE]
*American boxer*
* [The] Fargo Express

**Petrone, Jane Muir** 1929- [CA]
*American author*
* Muir, Jane

**[El] Petronio de los Toreros [The
Petronio of the Bullfighters]**
See Gaona y Jimenez, Rodolfo

**Petronius**
See Larsen, Erik

**Petronius, Caius [or Gaius]** 1st c.
[FFF, RH, SN]
*Roman courtier*
* Arbiter Elegantiae [or
  Elegantiarum]
* [A] Roman Beau Brummel

**[The] Petronius of France**
See Jolyot de Crebillon, Claude
Prosper

**Petroselli, Luigi** 1932?-
*Italian politician*
* Bananas, Joe

**Petrosky, James** 1927- [BE]
*American baseball player*
* Clark, James [Jim]

**Petrov, Eugene [or Yevgeni]**
See Katayev, Yevgeni Petrovich

**Petrova, Olga**
See Harding, Muriel

**Petrovics, Sandor** 1823-1849
[WBD]
*Hungarian poet*
* Petofi, Sandor

**Petrovitsch [or Petrovic], George**
1766?-1817 [HN, WBD]
*Serbian peasant leader*
* Black George
* Czerny Djordje
* Karageorge [or Karadjordje]

**Petrovskaya, Kyra**
See Wayne, Kyra Petrovskaya

**Petrovsky, N.**
See Poltoratzky, N[ikolai]
P[etrovich]

**Petry, Daniel Joseph** 1958- [SMG]
*American baseball player*
* Petry, Peaches

**Petry, Peaches**
See Petry, Daniel Joseph

**Petschler, Erik** 20th c.
*Swedish director*
* [The] Swedish Mack Sennett

**Pettersson, H. Bertil N.** 1932-
[IAW]
*Swedish author*
* Malm, Margaretha

**Pettes, George W.** 19th c. [PA]
*Author*
* G. W. P.

**[The] Petticoat Pet**
See Van Buren, Martin

**Pettie [or Petty], Edna May**
1875?-1948 [BEW, CED, EMT]
*American actress and singer*
* May, Edna

**Pettie's Boy**
See McCollum, Robert Lee

**Pettigrew, Leola B.** 1893- [BWW]
*American singer*
* Grant, Coot
* Grant, Leola B.
* Hunter, Patsy

**Pettinger, Cowboy**
See Pettinger, Eric

**Pettinger, Eric** 20th c. [CEI]
*Canadian-born hockey player*
* Pettinger, Cowboy

**Pettingill, Amos**
See Harris, William Bliss

**Pettit, Lefty**
See Pettit, [George William] Paul

**Pettit, Lefty**
See Pettit, Leon Arthur

**Pettit, Leon Arthur** 1902- [BE]
*American baseball player*
* Pettit, Lefty

**Pettit, [George William] Paul**
1931- [BE]
*American baseball player*
* Pettit, Lefty

**Pettitt, Mrs.** [FFF]
*Entertainer*
* Buckingham, Fanny Louise

**Pettus, William T.** ?-1924 [MK]
*American baseball player*
* Pettus, Zack

**Pettus, Zack**
See Pettus, William T.

**Petty, Jesse Lee** 1894-1971 [BE]
*American baseball player*
* [The] Silver Fox

**Petty, King**
See Petty, Richard

**Petty, Richard** 1938?-
*American auto racer*
* [The] King
* Petty, King

**Petty, Roberta** 1915- [CA]
*American artist and illustrator*
* Petie, Haris

**Petty, [Sir] William** 1623-1687
[DNNS, SN]
*British statistician and political
economist*
* [The] Universal Genius

**Petty, [Sir] William** 1737-1805
[FFF, RH, SN]
*British statesman*
* Lansdowne, Marquis of
* Malagrida

**Petzholdt, J.** [PA]
*Author*
* Philalethes

**Peu-a-Peu**
See Leopold

**Peverett, David** 20th c. [RM, RO2]
*British musician*
* Lonesome Dave

**[The] Peveril of the Peak**
See Scott, [Sir] Walter

**Pevsner, Naum Neemia** 1890-
[CAP]
*Russian-born sculptor and author*
* Gabo, Naum

**Peyo**
See Culliford, Pierre

**Peyronney, Vicomtesse de** 1841- ?
[FFF]
*French author*
* Etincelle
* Letoriere, Georges
* Trilby

**Peyton, Benny**
See Peyton, Benton E.

**Peyton, Benton E.** 1890?-1965
[WWJ]
*American jazz musician*
* Peyton, Benny

**Peyton, Green**
See Wertenbaker, G. Peyton

**Peyton, K. M.**
See Peyton, Kathleen Wendy
[Herald]

**Peyton, Kathleen Wendy [Herald]**
1929- [AW, CA, WD]
*British author*
* Herald, Kathleen
* Peyton, K. M.

**Peyzaret, Richard** 20th c. [WEC]
*French cartoonist*
* F'Murr

**Pezet, [Dr.] F.**
See Zauner, Franz Paul

**Pezold, Larry**
See Pezold, Lorenz Johannes

**Pezold, Lorenz Johannes**
1893-1957 [BE]
*American baseball player*
* Pezold, Larry

**Pezza, Michele** 1771?-1806
[WBD]
*Italian gangleader*
* Angelo, [Fra]
* Diavolo, [Fra]

**Pezzolo, Francesco Stefano**
1887-1961 [BE, PB]
*American baseball player*
* Bodie, Frank Stephan
* Bodie, Ping

**Pezzullo, John** 1911- [BE]
*American baseball player*
* Pezzullo, Pretzels

**Pezzullo, Pretzels**
See Pezzullo, John

**Pfaal, Hans**
See Poe, Edgar Allan

**[Der] Pfaffen Kaiser**
See Charles IV [or Karl]

**Pfalzgraf, Florence Leighton** 1902-
[WW]
*Author*
* Leighton, Florence

**Pfeferstein, John** 1906- [BEW]
*American playwright, lyricist,
composer*
* Murray, John

**Pfeffer, Big Jeff**
See Pfeffer, Francis Xavier

**Pfeffer, Dandelion**
See Pfeffer, Nathaniel Frederick

**Pfeffer, Edward Joseph** 1888-1972
[BE]
*American baseball player*
* Pfeffer, Jeff

**Pfeffer, Francis Xavier** 1882-1954
[BE]
*American baseball player*
* Pfeffer, Big Jeff

**Pfeffer, Jeff**
See Pfeffer, Edward Joseph

**Pfeffer, Nathaniel Frederick**
1860-1932 [BE]
*American baseball player*
* Pfeffer, Dandelion

**Pfeifer, Allan Cameron** 1896-
[BEW]
*American press representative*
* Dalzell, Allan C.

**Pfeiffer, C. Boyd** 1937- [IAW]
*American author*
* Fletcher, Scott

**Pfeiffer, Ida** 1797-1858 [PA]
*Author*
* Ryer

**Pfeiffer, Jane Cahill** 1933?-
*American television executive*
* Attila the Nun
* [The] Ayatullah
* Clean, Mrs.
* St. Jane

**Pfeiffer, Marcella**
See Syracuse, Marcella Pfeiffer

**Pfeiffer, Tillie**
See Fuber, Mrs. Edward

**Pfeil, Donald J.** 20th c.
[ESF, WGT]
*American author*
* Arrow, William [house
  pseudonym, Ballantine Books]

**Pfeister, Jack**
See Pfiestenberger, John Theodore
Joseph [Jack]

**Pfiestenberger, John Theodore
Joseph [Jack]** 1878-1953 [AS, BE]
*American baseball player*
* Jack the Giant Killer
* Pfeister, Jack

**Pfizenmayer, Edna Warren Mason**
1885- [NAA]
*American writer*
* Mason, Edna Warren

**Pfoutz, Shirley Eclov** 1922- [CA]
*American author*
* Eclov, Shirley

**Pfund, Lee**
See Pfund, LeRoy Herbert

**Pfund, LeRoy Herbert** 1919- [BE]
*American baseball player*
* Pfund, Lee

**Pfyl, Meinhard Charles** 1884-1945
[BE]
*American baseball player*
* Pfyl, Monte

**Pfyl, Monte**
*See* Pfyl, Meinhard Charles

**Phaedra**
*See* Inghirami, Tommaso

**Phaintin' Phil Scott**
*See* Suffling, Philip

**Phal, Louis** 1897-1925 [BX]
*Senegalese-born boxer*
* Siki, Battling
* [The] Singular Senegalese

**Phalaris?**
*See* Francis, [Sir] Philip

**Phalaris Junior**
*See* Boyle, Charles [Fourth Earl of Orrery]

**Phantastes**
*See* Hazlitt, William

**Phantasus**
*See* Maximilian Joseph

**[The] Phantom**
*See* Javier, [Manuel] Julian Liranzo

**[The] Phantom Finn**
*See* Nurmi, Paavo

**[The] Phantom Major**
*See* Stirling, David

**Pharboeus**
*See* Verwey, Hans

**Pharoah, Jaarone**
*See* Jenkins, Gus

**Pharr, Robert D[eane]** 1916- [CA]
*American author*
* Washington, C.

**Phazma**
*See* Field, Matthew C.

**Pheasant, [Dr.] Lundy**
*See* Cooper, Robert Andrew

**Phelan, Arthur Thomas** 1887-1964
[BE]
*American baseball player*
* Phelan, Dugan

**Phelan, Dick**
*See* Phelan, James D.

**Phelan, Dugan**
*See* Phelan, Arthur Thomas

**Phelan, James D.** 1854-1931 [BE]
*American baseball player*
* Phelan, Dick

**Phelan, Jeremiah**
*See* King, Charles Daly

**Phelon, Mira M.** 20th c. [SFL]
*Author*
* [The] Phelons [joint pseudonym with William P. Phelon]

**Phelon, William P.** 20th c. [SFL]
*Author*
* [The] Phelons [joint pseudonym with Mira M. Phelon]

**[The] Phelons** [joint pseudonym with William P. Phelon]
*See* Phelon, Mira M.

**[The] Phelons** [joint pseudonym with Mira M. Phelon]
*See* Phelon, William P.

**Phelps, Arthur** 1890?-1933?
[BWW]
*American singer*
* Blind Arthur
* Blind Blake
* Gorgeous Weed
* James, Billy
* Martin, Blind George

**Phelps, Babe**
*See* Phelps, Ernest Gordon

**Phelps, Blimp**
*See* Phelps, Ernest Gordon

**Phelps, Cornelius Carman**
1840-1885 [BE]
*American baseball player*
* Phelps, Neal

**Phelps, Digger**
*See* Phelps, Richard

**Phelps, Elizabeth Stuart**
*See* Ward, Elizabeth Stuart [Phelps]

**Phelps, Ernest Gordon** 1908-
[BE, DGS, PB]
*American baseball player*
* Phelps, Babe
* Phelps, Blimp

**Phelps, Frederic**
*See* McCulley, Johnston

**Phelps, George H[amilton]** 1854- ?
[WGT]
*Author*
* Tangent, Patrick Quinn

**Phelps, L. L.** [PA]
*Author*
* Alpha

**Phelps, Neal**
*See* Phelps, Cornelius Carman

**Phelps, Richard** 20th c. [B10]
*American basketball coach*
* Phelps, Digger

**Phelps, W. D.** [PA]
*Author*
* Webfoot

**Philadelphia Jack O'Brien**
*See* Hagen, Joseph F.

**[A] Philadelphian**
*See* Williams, W.

**Philadelphos [Brother-Lover]**
*See* Ptolemy II

**Philadelphus**
*See* Attalus II

**Philagathus** ?-1013? [WBD]
*Antipope*
* John XVI

**Philalethes**
*See* Amherst, Nicholas

**Philalethes**
*See* Fellows, Robert

**Philalethes**
*See* Horton, [Sir] R. J. W.

**Philalethes**
*See* John [or Johann] Nepomuk Maria Joseph

**Philalethes**
*See* Petzholdt, J.

**Philalethes, Irenaeus**
*See* Moulin, Louis du

**[The] Philanthropist**
*See* Howard, John

**Philanthropos**
*See* Ladd, William

**Philaret**
*See* Drozdov, Vasili Mikhailovich

**Philaret**
*See* Romanov, Fedor Nikitich

**Philaretes**
*See* Cooper, John Gilbert

**Philaretus**
*See* Toplady, Augustus Montagu

**Philargos, Petros** 1339-1410
[HN, WBD]
*Pope*
* Alexander V
* Refulgidus, Doctor

**Philbin, Silent Steve**
*See* Philbin, Stephen H.

**Philbin, Stephen H.** 1888-1973
[FB]
*American football player*
* Philbin, Silent Steve

**Philby, Harold** 1912-
*British intelligence agent for Russia*
* Philby, Kim

**Philby, Kim**
*See* Philby, Harold

**Phileleutherus Lipsiensis**
*See* Bentley, Richard

**Phileleutherus Norfolciensis**
*See* Parr, Samuel

**Philenia [or Phililenia?]**
*See* Morton, Sarah Wentworth

**Philes, George P.** 1828- ? [PA]
*Author*
* Silentiarius, Paulus

**Philibert I** 1464-1482 [WBD]
*Duke of Savoy*
* [The] Hunter

**[An] Philibin**
*See* Pollock, John H[ackett]

**Philidor**
*See* Danican, Francois Andre

**Philip**
*See* Metacomet

**Philip** ?- 34 [WBD]
*Son of Herod, King of Judea*
* Herod Philip

**Philip [Marcus Julius Philippus]** ?-
249 [WBD]
*Roman emperor*
* [The] Arabian

**Philip** 1st c. [DNNS]
*Early Christian deacon*
* [The] Evangelist

**Philip [or Philippe]** 1342-1404
[DNNS, SN, WBD]
*First Duke of Burgundy*
* [The] Bold
* [Le] Hardi

**Philip [or Philippe]** 1396-1467
[DNNS, SN, WBD]
*Third Duke of Burgundy*
* [Le] Bon
* [The] Good
* [The] Great Duke of the West

**Philip** 1504-1567 [DNNS]
*Landgrave of Hesse*
* [The] Magnanimous

**Philip, Gerard** 1922-1959
[BDF, WEF]
*French actor*
* Philipe, Gerard

**Philip, James** 1858-1911 [B10]
*American rancher and conservationist*
* Philip, Scotty

**Philip, Joseph** 1879-1960 [NOJ]
*American jazz musician*
* One Eye Babe

**Philip, Lotte Brand**
*See* Foerster, Lotte B[rand]

**Philip, Scotty**
*See* Philip, James

**Philip I [or Philippe]** 1052-1108
[FFF, HN, SN]
*King of France*
* [The] Amorous

**Philip I** 1478-1506
[DNNS, SN, WBD]
*King of Spain*
* [The] Handsome

**Philip II [or Philippe]** 1165-1223
[FFF, HN, SN]
*King of France*
* Augustus
* [The] Gift of God
* [The] Magnanimous

**Philip II** 1527-1598 [HN]
*King of Spain*
* [The] Demon of the South

**Philip III [or Philippe]** 1245-1285
[DNNS, HN, SN]
*King of France*
* [The] Bold
* [The] False Coiner
* [Le] Hardi

**Philip IV [or Philippe]** 1268-1314
[DNNS, SN, WBD]
*King of France*
* [Le] Bel
* [The] Fair
* [A] Malignant Plant
* [The] Modern Pilate

**Philip V [or Philippe]** 1294?-1322
[DNNS, HN, WBD]
*King of France*
* [Le] Long
* [The] Tall

**Philip V** 1683-1746
[DNNF, DNNS, SN]
*King of Spain*
* Baboon, Philip

**Philip VI [or Philippe]** 1293-1350
[HN, SN]
*King of France*
* [Le] Bien Fortune
* [The] Fortunate

**Philipe, Gerard**
*See* Philip, Gerard

**Philipp, Adolph** 1864-1936 [BEW]
*German-born playwright, composer, actor*
* Briquet, Jean

**Philipp, Elliot Elias** 1915-
[CA, WD]
*British physician and author*
* Embey, Philip
* Havil, Anthony
* Medicus II
* Tempest, Victor

**Philippe, Claudius Charles**
1911?-1978
*British-born caterer*
* Philippe of the Waldorf

**Philippe of the Waldorf**
*See* Philippe, Claudius Charles

**Philippi [or Philippson?]**
1506-1556 [DNNS, SN, WBD]
*German historian*
* [The] Prophet of the Syrians
* [The] Protestant Livy
* Sleidan [or Sleidanus], John

**Philippi, Mark**
*See* Bender, Arnold

**Philippicus**
*See* Bardanes

**Philips, Ambrose** 1671?-1749
[SN, WBD]
*British poet and playwright*
* Namby-Pamby

**Philips, George Norman** 1888?-
[MBF]
*British author*
* Fremlin, Victor
* Norman, Philip
* Skene, Anthony [Juan]

**Philips, Judson Pentecost** 1903-
[CC, EMD, WW]
*American author*
* Pentecost, Hugh

**Philips, Katherine** 1631-1664
[DEL, SN, WBD]
*British poet*
* [The] Incomparable Orinda
* [The] Matchless Orinda
* Orinda

**Philips, Thomas**
*See* Davies, Leslie Purnell

**Philiscos** 3rd c. BC [HN, SN]
*Alexandrian poet*
* Homer the Younger

**Philisides**
*See* Sidney, [Sir] Philip

**Philkins, Ike**
*See* Bowen, William Abraham

**Phillifent, John Thomas** 1916-1976
[IAW, SF, SFL]
*British author*
* Colson, Dorothea
* Johnson, Alan
* Rackham, John

**Phillimon, Harriet Eleanor** [PA]
*Author*
* H. E. P.

**Phillip, Nobbie**
*See* Phillip, Norbert

**Phillip, Norbert** 1948- [DC]
*West Indian cricketer*
* Phillip, Nobbie
* Phillip, Zidi

**Phillip, Zidi**
*See* Phillip, Norbert

**Philippe, Charles Louis**
1872?-1952 [AS, DGS, PB]
*American baseball player*
* Phillippe, Deacon

**Phillippe, Deacon**
*See* Phillippe, Charles Louis

**Phillips, Alan**
*See* Stauderman, Albert P[hilip]

**Phillips, Alan Meyrick Kerr** 1916-
[CA]
*British author*
* Phillips, Mickey

**Phillips, Albert Abernathy**
1904-1964 [BE]
*American baseball player*
* Phillips, Buz

**Phillips, Alexander Forbes**
1866-1917 [WWL]
*British author and playwright*
* Forbes, Athol

**Phillips, Anne G[arvey]** 1929- [CA]
*American educator and author*
* Dye, Anne G.

**Phillips, Ardith Lowell** 20th c.
[BBH]
*American basketball coach*
* Phillips, Pete

**Phillips, Aubrey Clyde** 20th c.
[SMG]
*American football player and coach*
* Phillips, Red

**Phillips, Barty**
*See* Phillips, Elizabeth Margaret Ann

**Phillips, Batt**
*See* Phillips, W. J.

**Phillips, Bill**
*See* Phillips, Merlyn J.

**Phillips, Bubba**
*See* Phillips, John Melvin

**Phillips, Bum**
*See* Phillips, Oail

**Phillips, Buz**
*See* Phillips, Albert Abernathy

**Phillips, Clarence Lemuel** 1908-
[BE]
*American baseball player*
* Phillips, Red

**Phillips, Dad**
*See* Phillips, Festus

**Phillips, Damon Roswell** 1919-
[BE]
*American baseball player*
* Phillips, Dee

**Phillips, David Atlee** 1922- [CA]
*American intelligence officer, editor, author*
* Spelvin, George

**Phillips, Dee**
*See* Phillips, Damon Roswell

**Phillips, Dennis John Andrew**
1924- [AW, CA, CC]
*British author*
* Chambers, Peter
* Chester, Peter

**Phillips, Elizabeth Margaret Ann**
1933- [IAW]
*British author*
* Phillips, Barty

**Phillips, Esther**
*See* Jones, Esther Mae

**Phillips, Festus** 1872-1955 [SC]
*American actor and makeup artist*
* Phillips, Dad

**Phillips, Flip**
*See* Filipelli, Joseph Edward

**Phillips, Frank**
*See* Nowlan, Phil[ip Francis]

**Phillips, Fuzz**
*See* Phillips, Leo

**Phillips, George Searle** 1817- ?
[DEL, DNNF, FFF]
*American author and journalist*
* Searle, January

**Phillips, George Spencer** [PA]
*Author*
* Dix, J. R.

**Phillips, Gerald William** 1884-
[WW]
*Author*
* Huntingdon, John

**Phillips, Gordon** 1890- [LAO]
*British journalist*
* Lucio

**Phillips, H. C.**
*See* Honey, Philip

**Phillips, Harold Ross** 1919-1972
[PB]
*American baseball coach and manager*
* Phillips, Lefty

**Phillips, Horace** 1853- ? [BE]
*American baseball manager*
* Phillips, Hustling Horace

**Phillips, Horace** 20th c. [MBF]
*British author and editor*
* Duke, Derek
* Hope, Walter
* Stanton, Marjorie

**Phillips, Howard S.** 1894- [NAA]
*British-born editor and writer*
* Rivas, Guillermo

**Phillips, Hugh** 1886- [WWL]
*British author*
* Hughes, Philip

**Phillips, Hustling Horace**
*See* Phillips, Horace

**Phillips, Irna** ?-1974 [ET]
*Scriptwriter*
* [The] Queen of the Soaps

**Phillips, Irv[ing W.]** 1908- [SAT]
*American cartoonist, illustrator, author*
* Sabuso

**Phillips, Ivan Keith** 1943- [OP]
*American scenic and lighting designer*
* Phillips, Van

**Phillips, J. B.**
*See* Phillips, John Bertram

**Phillips, [Doctor] J. P.**
*See* Durand, J. P.

**Phillips, Jack**
*See* Sandburg, Carl [August]

**Phillips, Jack Dorn** 1921- [BE]
*American baseball player*
* Phillips, Stretch

**Phillips, James [Jim]** 1936-
[FB, SMG]
*American football player and coach*
* Phillips, Red

**Phillips, James W.** 1922- [CA]
*American author*
* Eblis, J. Philip
* McLaughlin, Bill

**Phillips, Jerome C.**
*See* Cleveland, Philip Jerome

**Phillips, John**
*See* Marquand, John Phillips

**Phillips, John** 1941- [DAM]
*American singer*
* Papa John

**Phillips, John Bertram** 1906- [LC]
*British author and prelate*
* Phillips, J. B.

**Phillips, John Henry, Sr.**
1877-1948 [NOJ]
*American jazz musician*
* Fischer, Johnny

**Phillips, John Melvin** 1930-
[BE, SMG]
*American baseball player*
* Phillips, Bubba

**Phillips, Kate**
*See* Goldney, Kate

**Phillips, Kathleen** 20th c.
[CA, SAT]
*Author*
* Cole, Annette [joint pseudonym with Barbara A(nnette) Steiner]
* D'Andrea, Kate [joint pseudonym with Barbara A(nnette) Steiner]

**Phillips, King**
*See* Perkins, Kenneth

**Phillips, Lefty**
*See* Phillips, Harold Ross

**Phillips, Leo** 1916?-1977 [FIR]
*American jazz musician*
* Phillips, Fuzz

**Phillips, Leon**
*See* Gerson, Noel Bertram

**Phillips, Lin** 1947- [RO2]
*American musician*
* Phillips, Spike

**Phillips, Mac**
*See* Phillips, Maurice J[ack]

**Phillips, Mark** [joint pseudonym with Laurence M(ark) Janifer]
*See* Garrett, [Gordon] Randall [Philip David]

**Phillips, Mark** [joint pseudonym with Randall Garrett]
*See* Harris, Larry M[ark]

**Phillips, Maurice J[ack]** 1914-
[CA]
*American author*
* Phillips, Mac

**Phillips, Merlyn J.** 20th c. [CEI]
*Canadian-born hockey player*
* Phillips, Bill

**Phillips, Michael**
See Nolan, William F[rancis]

**Phillips, Michael**
See Nutt, Charles

**Phillips, Michael Joseph** 1937-
[WD]
*American poet, critic, writer*
* Fairplay, Roger
* Swift, Farguar

**Phillips, Michelle**
See Gilliam, Holly

**Phillips, Mickey**
See Phillips, Alan Meyrick Kerr

**Phillips, Miss** 19th c. [PA]
*Author*
* [An] Old Maid

**Phillips, Morgan** [PA]
*Author*
* Morgan, Phillip

**Phillips, Mrs. Henry** [FFF]
*Entertainer*
* Castleton, Kate

**Phillips, Nibs**
See Phillips, Thomas Neil

**Phillips, O. A.**
See Phillips, Oail

**Phillips, Oail** 1923?- [B10, SMG]
*American football coach and manager*
* Phillips, Bum
* Phillips, O. A.

**Phillips, Olga Somech** 1901- [AW]
*British author*
* Olga

**Phillips, Osborne**
See Barcynski, Leon Roger

**Phillips, Pauline Esther [Friedman]**
1918- [CA]
*American columnist*
* Dear Abby
* Phillips, Popo
* Van Buren, Abigail

**Phillips, Pete**
See Phillips, Ardith Lowell

**Phillips, Peter** [house pseudonym]
See Browne, Howard

**Phillips, Phil**
See Baptiste, John Phillip

**Phillips, Philip** 1834-1895 [WBD]
*American singer and music publisher*
* [The] Singing Pilgrim

**Phillips, Pop**
See Phillips, R. H.

**Phillips, Popo**
See Phillips, Pauline Esther [Friedman]

**Phillips, R. H.** 20th c. [CSH]
*Canadian lacrosse promoter*
* Phillips, Pop

**Phillips, Red**
See Phillips, Aubrey Clyde

**Phillips, Red**
See Phillips, Clarence Lemuel

**Phillips, Red**
See Phillips, James [Jim]

**Phillips, Richard**
See Dick, Philip K[indred]

**Phillips, [Sir] Richard** 1767-1840
[DEL, FFF]
*British journalist*
* Adair, James
* Barrow, [Rev.] S.
* Blair, [Rev.] David
* Bossut, M. L'Abbe
* Clarke, [Rev.] C. C.
* Goldsmith, [Rev.] J.
* Pelham, M.

**Phillips, Rog**
See Graham, Roger Phillips

**Phillips, Silver Bill**
See Phillips, William Corcoran

**Phillips, Spike**
See Phillips, Lin

**Phillips, Steve**
See Whittington, Harry

**Phillips, Stretch**
See Phillips, Jack Dorn

**Phillips, Tay**
See Phillips, William Taylor

**Phillips, Thomas Neil** 1880-1923
[BBH]
*Canadian-born hockey player*
* Phillips, Nibs

**Phillips, Tom**
See Drotning, Phillip T[homas]

**Phillips, Van**
See Phillips, Ivan Keith

**Phillips, Vel**
See Phillips, Velvalea R.

**Phillips, Velvalea R.** 1924- [IBW]
*American politician*
* Phillips, Vel

**Phillips, W.**
See Dodge, Wendell Phillips

**Phillips, W. J.** 20th c. [CEI]
*Canadian-born hockey player*
* Phillips, Batt

**Phillips, Walter P.** [PA]
*Author*
* Oakum, John

**Phillips, Ward**
See Lovecraft, Howard Phillips

**Phillips, Watts** [PA]
*Author*
* Balfour, Fairfax

**Phillips, Wendell** 1811-1884 [SN]
*American abolitionist*
* [The] Patrick Henry of New England

**Phillips, Whoa Bill**
See Phillips, William Corcoran

**Phillips, William** 1864-1943
[HCA, SC]
*American actor*
* Marshall, Tully

**Phillips, William Corcoran**
1868-1941 [BE]
*American baseball player*
* Phillips, Silver Bill
* Phillips, Whoa Bill

**Phillips, William Taylor** 1933-
[BE]
*American baseball player*
* Phillips, Tay

**Phillips-Birt, Douglas** 1920-1977
[CA]
*British author*
* Argus
* Hextall, David
* Hogarth, Douglas

**Phillipson, Christopher Paul** 1952-
[DC]
*British cricketer*
* Phillipson, Phillipo

**Phillipson, Phillipo**
See Phillipson, Christopher Paul

**Phillpotts, [Mary] Adelaide [Eden]**
1896- [LC, WD]
*British author, poet, playwright*
* Ross, Mary Adelaide Eden

**Phillpotts, Eden** 1862-1960
[CC, EMD, LC]
*British author, poet, playwright*
* Hext, Harrington

**Philly Joe Jones**
See Jones, Joseph Rudolph

**Philmore, R.**
See Howard, Herbert Edmund

**Philo**
See Frend, William Hugh Clifford

**Philo Judaeus** 1st c.
[DEP, DNNF, DNNS]
*Hellenistic philosopher*
* [The] Jewish Plato

**Philochristus**
See Abbott, Edwin Abbott

**Philologer, A. B.**
See Sterne, Laurence

**Philologos [A Lover of Words]**
See Bailey, Nathan

**Philomela**
See Rowe, Elizabeth

**Philomessus**
See Locher, Jacob

**Philometor**
See Antiochus VIII

**Philometor**
See Attalus III

**Philometor**
See Demetrius III

**Philometor [Mother-Lover]**
See Ptolemy VI

**Philomneste, Junior**
See Brunet, Gustave

**Philomon**
See Marsden, John Howard

**Philomythes**
See Gonzalez, Gonzalo

**Philopacificus**
See Worcester, N.

**Philopater, Andreas**
See Parsons [or Persons?], Robert

**Philopator**
See Antiochus IX

**Philopator [Father-Lover]**
See Ptolemy IV

**Philopator**
See Seleucus IV

**Philopator Neos Dionysos**
See Ptolemy XII [or X]

**Philopator Philometor Caesar**
See Ptolemy XV [XIV or XVI]

**Philopatris Varvicensis**
See Parr, Samuel

**Philopoemen** 3rd c. BC
[DEP, DNNS, SN]
*Greek army officer*
* [The] Last of the Greeks

**Philopolis**
See Marsh, James

**Philopoliteius**
See Skene, [Sir] John

**[Le] Philosophe Inconnu**
See Saint Martin, Louis Claude de

**[The] Philosopher**
See Alfonso X [or Alphonso]

**[The] Philosopher**
See Alfred [or Alured]

**[The] Philosopher**
See Annius Verus, Marcus

**Philosopher**
See Contarini, Marc Antoine

**[The] Philosopher**
See De Serment, Louise Anastasie

**[The] Philosopher**
See Justin

**[The] Philosopher**
See Leo VI

**[The] Philosopher**
See Malchus

**[The] Philosopher of Chelsea**
See Carlyle, Thomas

**[The] Philosopher of China**
See Confucius [or K'ung Fu-tzu]

**[The] Philosopher of Democracy**
See Jefferson, Thomas

**[The] Philosopher of Disenchantment**
See Schopenhauer, Arthur

**[The] Philosopher of Ferney**
See Arouet, Francois Marie

**[The] Philosopher of Malmesbury**
See Hobbes, Thomas

**[The] Philosopher of Persia**
See Avicenna [or Abou-ibn-Sina]

**[The] Philosopher of Samosata**
See Lucian

**[The] Philosopher of Sans Souci**
See Frederick II

**[The] Philosopher of Sunshine and Rain**
See Griffith, Lawrence Rector

**[The] Philosopher of the Arabs**
See Kindi, al- [Abu Yusef al-Kindi]

**[The] Philosopher of the Christians**
See Aristocles

**[The] Philosopher of the Unknown**
See Saint Martin, Louis Claude de

[The] Philosopher of Wimbledon
See   Horne, John

[The] Philosopher Prince
See   Frederick II

[The] Philosopher with the Golden Thigh
See   Pythagoras

[The] Philosophic Bard
See   Euripides

[The] Philosophical
See   Strode, Ralph

Philosophus Anglorum
See   Athelard of Bath

Philosophus Teutonicus
See   Boehme, Jacob

Philp, Kenward 19th c.   [FFF]
American writer
* Flaneur

Philpot, J. H.
See   Philpot, Joseph Henry

Philpot, Joseph Henry 1850-1939
[SFL, WGT, WWL]
British author
* Lafargue, Philip
* Philpot, J. H.

Philpott, Margaret 1903-   [F2]
American actress
* Bellamy, Madge

Philps, Arthur Carlton 1880-1942
[BMH, THR]
British entertainer
* Carlton
* [The] Great Carlton
* [The] Human Hairpin

Phineas
See   Hanifin, J.

Phipps, Beatrix
See   Kemp, Mrs. Maurice F.

Phipps, [Sir] Constantine
1656-1723   [SN]
Chancellor of Ireland
* [The] Impudent

Phipps, Joyce Irene 1910-1979
[EMT, FC]
British actress
* Grenfell, Joyce

Phipps, Margaret
See   Tatham, Laura

Phipson, Joan
See   Fitzhardinge, Joan Margaret

Phiseldeck
See   Schmidt, Christoph

Phiz
See   Browne, Hablot Knight

Phiz, Francis
See   Smedley, Francis Edward
[Frank]

Phlogobombos, Terentius
See   Judah, Samuel Benjamin
Helbert

Phocian
See   Hamilton, Alexander

Phoebus
See   Gaston III

Phoenix
See   Martin, [Sir] Henry

Phoenix Donald Weaver
See   Weaver, William [Bill]

Phoenix, John, Gentleman
See   Derby, George Horatio

[The] Phoenix of His Age
See   Kindi, al- [Abu Yusef
al-Kindi]

[The] Phoenix of Literature
See   Grotius, Hugo

[The] Phoenix of Spain
See   Vega Carpio, Lope Felix de

[The] Phoenix of Wit
See   Rabelais, Francois

Photius Junior
See   Sherlock, William

Phra
See   Arnold, Edwin Lester

[The] Phrasemaker
See   Wilson, [Thomas] Woodrow

Phrynicus 2nd c.   [WBD]
Greek grammarian
* Arabius

Phusin, Kate
See   Ruskin, John

Physcon [Big-Belly]
See   Ptolemy VIII [or VII]

[A] Physician
See   Dickson, Samuel Henry

[A] Physician
See   Paris, John Aryton

Physick, Edward Harold
1878-1972   [SFL, WGT]
British author
* Visiak, E. H.

Physick, Philip Syng 1768-1837
[FFF, WBD]
American surgeon
* [The] Father of American
Surgery

Physics
See   Crawford, Samuel W.

Piaf, Edith
See   Gassion, Edith Giovanna

[A] Pianist
See   Gottschalk, Louis M.

Piano, Celeste
See   Lykiard, Alexis [Constantine]

Piano Legs Gore
See   Gore, George F.

Piano Legs Hickman
See   Hickman, Charles Taylor

[The] Piano Playing Baron
See   Samek, Viktor Oliver

Piano Red
See   Harrison, Vernon

Piano Red
See   Patterson, Vance

Piano Red
See   Perryman, William Lee
[Willie]

Piano Sam Vinson
See   Vinson, Sam

Piano Slim
See   Burton, Willard

Piatigorsky, Gregor 1903-1976
[MS]
Russian musician
* [The] Russian Casals

Piatt, Iron Man
See   Piatt, Wiley Harold

Piatt, Louise Kirby 1812-1864
[FFF]
American author
* Smith, Bell

Piatt, Wiley Harold 1874-1946
[BE]
American baseball player
* Piatt, Iron Man

Piatti, Girolomo 1547-1591   [PA]
Author
* Platus

Piazza, Ben
See   Piazza, Benito Daniel

Piazza, Benito Daniel 1934-
[BEW]
American actor and writer
* Piazza, Ben

Pic
See   Higgins, Charles S.

Pic, Ulysse   [PA]
Author
* Lux, Adam

Pica, Peter
See   Aldiss, Brian W[ilson]

Picard, Dorothy Young 1906-   [CA]
American author
* Croman, Dorothy Young

Picariello, Fredrick Anthony 1940-
[RO1]
American singer
* Cannon, Boom Boom
* Cannon, Freddy

Picaroon
See   Ballantyne, John

Picart, Stephen [or Etienne]
1631-1721   [FFF, RH, SN]
French engraver
* [The] Roman

[The] Picasso of Flowers
See   Teshigahara, Sofu

Picasso, Pablo [Ruiz]
See   Ruiz, Pablo Diego Jose
Francisco de Paula Juan
Nepomuceno Cipriano

Piccadilly
See   Gerard, Pierre S.

[The] Piccadilly Patriot
See   Burdett, [Sir] Francis

Piccinino, Jacopo 20th c.   [SN]
Italian army officer
* [The] Thunderbolt of War

Picciola
See   Mumford, Angelina S.

Piccioni, Piero 20th c.   [WF]
Italian composer
* Morgan, Piero

Piccolo, Fillippo ?-1769   [PA]
Author
* Lo

Piccolo, L. Brian 1943-1970   [FB]
American football player
* Piccolo, Pic

Piccolo Pete Elko
See   Elko, Peter

Piccolo, Pic
See   Piccolo, L. Brian

Pichegru, Charles 1761-1804   [SN]
French army officer
* [The] Savior of His Country

Pichon, Fats
See   Pichon, Walter

Pichon, Thomas ?-1781   [PA]
Author
* Tyrrell, Thomas Signis

Pichon, Walter 1906-1967   [WWJ]
American jazz musician
* Pichon, Fats

Picinich, Val
See   Picinich, Valentine John

Picinich, Valentine John
1896-1942   [BE]
American baseball player
* Picinich, Val

Pick, Mr.
See   Scoville, Joseph A.

Pickard, Dad
See   Pickard, Obey

Pickard, Obey ?-1958   [DAM]
American musician
* Pickard, Dad

Pickard Jenkins, Percy 20th c.
[ART]
Welsh designer and painter
* P. P. J.

Pickaway
See   Myers, Allen O.

Pickel, Konrad 1459-1508   [WBD]
German poet
* Celtis [or Celtes], Conradus

Picken, Mary Brooks 1886-   [NAA]
American author
* Joan, Mary
* Madison, Marilyn
* McCleary, Eleanor
* Wells, Jane Warren

Pickens, Buster
See   Pickens, Edwin Goodwin

Pickens, Edwin Goodwin
1916-1964   [BWW]
American singer
* Pickens, Buster

Pickens, Slim
See   Burns, Eddie

Pickens, Slim
See   Lindley, Louis Bert, Jr.

Pickering, Dick
See   Pickering, Urbane Henry

Pickering, Ellen   [PA]
Author
* Daniel, Mrs. Mackenzie

Pickering, Oliver Dan 1870-1952
[BE]
American baseball player
* Pickering, Ollie

Pickering, Ollie
See   Pickering, Oliver Dan

Pickering, Percival
See   Stirling, Anna Maria Diana
Wilhelmina [Pickering]

**Pickering, Stephen** 1947-    [CA]
*American author*
* Ben Avraham, Chofetz Chaim

**Pickering, Urbane Henry**
1899-1970    [BE]
*American baseball player*
* Pickering, Dick

**Pickering, William** 1796-1854
[SN]
*British publisher*
* Discipulus Aldi

**Picket**
*See*   Tomlinson, B. W.

**Pickett, Bobby** 1940-    [RO1]
*American singer and songwriter*
* Pickett, Boris

**Pickett, Boris**
*See*   Pickett, Bobby

**Pickett, Wilson** 1941-    [IBW]
*American singer and songwriter*
* [The] Wicked

**Pickford, Jack**
*See*   Smith, Jack

**Pickford, Lottie**
*See*   Smith, Lottie

**Pickford, Mary**
*See*   Smith, Gladys Mary

**Pickle, Peregrine**
*See*   Upton, George Putnam

**Pickle the Spy**
*See*   Macdonell, Alastair Ruadh

**Pickles, Frank K.** 1893-    [WWL]
*Scottish writer*
* Quiz

**Pickles, M[abel] Elizabeth** 1902-
[CAP, WD]
*British author*
* Burgoyne, Elizabeth

**Pickup, Clarence William** 1897-
[BE]
*American baseball player*
* Pickup, Ty

**Pickup, Ty**
*See*   Pickup, Clarence William

**Pickwoad, William** 1912-1976
[TR]
*British actor*
* Mervyn, William

**Pickworth, H. O.** 1920-    [EG]
*Australian golfer*
* Pickworth, Ossie

**Pickworth, Ossie**
*See*   Pickworth, H. O.

**Pico, John Baptist** 1688-1740
[HN]
*Italian educator*
* [The] Dante of Philosophy

**Picone, Babe**
*See*   Picone, Mario Peter

**Picone, Mario Peter** 1926-    [BE]
*American baseball player*
* Picone, Babe

**Picou, Alphonse**
*See*   Ghnassia, Maurice
[Jean-Henri]

**Picou, Alphonse Floristan**
1879-1961    [IBW]
*American jazz musician*
* Picou, Peak

**Picou, Peak**
*See*   Picou, Alphonse Floristan

**Picquet, Francois** 1708-1781    [FFF]
*Missionary*
* [The] Great Jesuit of the West

**Picton, Bernard**
*See*   Knight, Bernard

**Picton, Nina** 20th c.    [WGT]
*Author*
* Dearborn, Laura

**Picton, Thomas** 1822- ?    [FFF, PA]
*American journalist*
* [An] Ex Editor
* Gothamite
* Juvenile
* Preston, Paul
* [Le] Viola

**Picus, John Quinn** 1884-1946
[AS, BE]
*American baseball player*
* Quinn, John Picus [Jack]

**Pidgeon, William Edwin** 1909-
[WEC]
*Australian painter, illustrator,
cartoonist*
* Wep

**Pie Crust Palmer**
*See*   Palmer, James Shedden

**[The] Pie Lady**
*See*   Reveron, Saundra

**Piechota, Al**
*See*   Piechota, Aloysius Edward

**Piechota, Aloysius Edward** 1914-
[BE]
*American baseball player*
* Piechota, Al

**Pied Piper**
*See*   Williams, Dorian

**[The] Pied Piper of Harlem**
*See*   Edinboro, Arlington

**[The] Pied Piper of Love**
*See*   White, Barry

**Pieh, Cy**
*See*   Pieh, Edwin John

**Pieh, Edwin John** 1886-1945    [BE]
*American baseball player*
* Pieh, Cy

**Pieralisi, Virna** 1937-    [FC]
*Italian actress*
* Lisi, Virna

**Pierangeli, Anna Maria** 1932-1971
[FC, IPA]
*Italian actress*
* Angeli, Pier

**Pierangeli, Marisa** 1932-
[FC, ITA, SW]
*Italian actress*
* Pavan, Marisa

**Pierat, Marie-Therese**
*See*   Pelletier, Marie-Therese

**Pierce, Billie**
*See*   Goodson, Wilhelmina Madison

**Pierce, Carl Webster** 1898-    [NAA]
*American playwright and actor*
* Applebud, Adam

**Pierce, Dede**
*See*   Pierce, Joseph De Lacrois

**Pierce, Edith Gray** 1893-    [CA]
*American author*
* Gray, Marian

**Pierce, Emma**
*See*   Schulz, Mrs. Warren

**Pierce, Franklin** 1804-1869
[FAP, SN]
*American president*
* Handsome Frank
* Purse
* Young Hickory

**Pierce, Jo**
*See*   Manning, William Henry

**Pierce, Jo**
*See*   Morris, Charles Smith

**Pierce, John Leonard, Jr.** 1921-
[CA]
*German-born author*
* Bramlett, John

**Pierce, John Robinson** 1910-
[CA, ESF]
*American author*
* Coupling, J. J.
* Roberts, John

**Pierce, Joseph De Lacrois**
1904-1973    [DAM, EJ7, IBW]
*American jazz musician*
* Pierce, Dede

**Pierce, Katherine**
*See*   St. John, Wylly Folk

**Pierce, Lefty**
*See*   Pierce, Ray[mond Lester]

**Pierce, Marvin** 20th c.    [RO2]
*American musician*
* Pierce, Merve

**Pierce, Merve**
*See*   Pierce, Marvin

**Pierce, Ray[mond Lester]**
1897-1963    [BE]
*American baseball player*
* Pierce, Lefty

**Pierce, Ronald** 1938-    [SW]
*American actor*
* Ely, Ron

**Pierce, Thomas** 1786-1850    [PA]
*Author*
* Horace in Cincinnati
* Idestone

**Piercy, Mrs.**    [FFF]
*Entertainer*
* Dargon, Augusta

**Piercy, Wild Bill**
*See*   Piercy, William Benton

**Piercy, William Benton** 1896-1951
[BE]
*American baseball player*
* Piercy, Wild Bill

**Pieretti, Chick**
*See*   Pieretti, Marino Paul

**Pieretti, Marino Paul** 1920-    [BE]
*Italian-born baseball player*
* Pieretti, Chick

**Pierian Dick**
*See*   Harvey, Richard

**Pierleoni, Pietro** 12th c.    [WBD]
*Antipope*
* Anacletus II

**Piermarini**
*See*   Malacrida, Marchese

**Piero di Cosimo** 1462-1521    [WBD]
*Florentine painter*
* Piero di Lorenzo

**Piero di Lorenzo**
*See*   Piero di Cosimo

**Pierotti, Piero** 1912-    [FDG]
*Italian director*
* Stanley, Peter E.

**Pierozzi, Antonio** 1389-1459
[WBD]
*Saint*
* Antoninus
* De Forciglioni, Antonio

**Pierre, [Abbe]**
*See*   Groues, Henri Antoine

**Pierre** ?-1180    [HN]
*Medieval scholar*
* Mangeur [or Comeston]

**[The] Pierre Cardin of Korea**
*See*   Kim, Andre

**Pierre, Paul**
*See*   Calle, Paul

**Pierre Benoit, Louis Marie** 1936-
[CW]
*Haitian poet and author*
* Fardin, Dieudonne

**Pierrepoint, Albert**
*See*   Andrews, Allen

**Pierro, Wild Bill**
*See*   Pierro, William Leonard [Bill]

**Pierro, William Leonard [Bill]**
1926-    [BE]
*American baseball player*
* Pierro, Wild Bill

**Pierrot**
*See*   Arnold, George

**Piers, Ashdown** [joint pseudonym
with John James Pitcairn]
*See*   Freeman, Richard

**Piers, Ashdown** [joint pseudonym
with Richard Freeman]
*See*   Pitcairn, John James

**Pierson, David P.** 1855-1922    [BE]
*American baseball player*
* Pearson, David P. [Dave]

**Pierson, Dick**
*See*   Pierson, Edmund Dana

**Pierson, Edmund Dana** ?-1922
[BE]
*American baseball player*
* Pierson, Dick

**Pierson, John H[erman] G[roesbeck]**
1906-    [CA]
*American author and economist*
* Hand, John

**Pierson, Walter**
*See*   McCulley, Johnston

**Pierson, Wild Bill**
*See*   Pierson, William Morris [Bill]

**Pierson, William Morris [Bill]**
1899-1959   [BE]
*American baseball player*
* Pierson, Wild Bill

**Pieseio**
*See* Beardslee, L. A.

**Piestre, Fernand Anne** 1845-1924
[WBD]
*French painter*
* Cormon

**Piet, Anthony Francis**
*See* Pietruszka, Anthony Francis

**Pieters, Eddie** 1936?-   [CW]
*Curacaon author and playwright*
* Heyliger

**Pieterszoon, Jan**
*See* Sweelinck [or Swelinck], Jan
Pieters

**Pieterszoon, Nicolaes**
1593?-1674?   [WBD]
*Dutch anatomist*
* Tulp, Claes Pieterszoon

**Pietrkiewicz, Jerzy** 1916-
[ESF, SFL]
*Polish author*
* Peterkiewicz, Jerzy

**Pietro Aquila** 1350-1420   [HN]
*Medieval scholar*
* Scotus Minor
* Sufficens, Doctor

**Pietrosante, Nicholas V. [Nick]** 1937-
*American football player*
* [The] Plunger

**Pietruszka, Anthony Francis** 1906-
[BE]
*American baseball player*
* Piet, Anthony Francis

**Pietschmann, Richard John, III**
1940-   [CA]
*American author and columnist*
* Miller, Richard
* Parish, Townsend

**[Le] Pieux**
*See* Louis I

**[Le] Pieux [The Pious]**
*See* Louis VII

**[Le] Pieux**
*See* Robert II

**Piez, Charles William** 1892-1930
[BE]
*American baseball player*
* Piez, Sandy

**Piez, Sandy**
*See* Piez, Charles William

**Piff, Charles** 1930-   [TR]
*British actor*
* Kay, Charles

**Pig 'n' Whistle Red**
*See* McTell, Willie Samuel

**Pigalle, Jean Baptiste** 1714-1785
[DEP, DNNS, SN]
*French sculptor*
* [The] French Phidias

**Pigault de l'Epiney** 1753-1835
[WBD]
*French author*
* Pigault-Lebrun

**Pigault-Lebrun**
*See* Pigault de l'Epiney

**Piggott, C. M.**
*See* Guido, [Cecily] Margaret

**Pigmeat Pete**
*See* Wilson, Wesley

**Pignatari, Baby**
*See* Pignatari, Francisco

**Pignatari, Francisco** 1917?-1977
*Brazilian industrialist*
* Pignatari, Baby

**Pignatelli, Antonio** 1615-1700
[WBD]
*Pope*
* Innocent XII

**Pigott, Anthony Charles Shackleton**
1958-   [DC]
*British cricketer*
* Pigott, Lester

**Pigott, E. F. S.**   [FFF]
*British writer*
* Chat-Huant

**Pigott, Lester**
*See* Pigott, Anthony Charles
Shackleton

**Pigott, Mimi** 1905?-1966   [THR]
*British actress, singer, dancer*
* Crawford, Mimi

**Pigott, William** 1870-1943   [LC]
*British author*
* Wales, Hubert

**Pigozzi, Luciano** 20th c.   [WF]
*Italian actor*
* Collins, Alan

**Pigtail Billy Riley**
*See* Riley, William James [Billy]

**Pihos, Big Dog**
*See* Pihos, Peter L.

**Pihos, Peter L.** 1923-   [FB]
*American football player*
* Pihos, Big Dog

**Pike, Charles R.**
*See* Harknett, Terry

**Pike, Lip**
*See* Pike, Lipman Emanuel

**Pike, Lipman Emanuel** 1845-1893
[AS, BE]
*American baseball player*
* Pike, Lip

**Pike, Mary Caroline**   [FFF, PA]
*Author*
* Hyde, Sidney

**Pike, Mary H. Green** 1827- ?
[FFF]
*American author*
* Langdon, Mary
* May, Ida
* Story, Sydney A., Jr.

**Pike, Morton**
*See* Parry, David Harold

**Pike, Mrs.**   [FFF]
*Entertainer*
* Sackett, Millie

**Pike, Mrs. F. A. M.**   [PA]
*Author*
* Morris, Katherine

**Pike, Noah W.** 1838- ?   [PA]
*Author*
* Gordox

**Pike, Robert L.**
*See* Fish, Robert L.

**Pike, William Ernest** 20th c.
[MBF]
*British author and editor*
* Conquest, Owen [house
pseudonym]
* James, Ernest
* Richards, Frank [house
pseudonym]

**Pikestaff**
*See* Baker, Thomas

**Pikkumolliainen, Leena**
*See* Pennanen, Lea Airi-Sirkka

**Pilbeam, Margery** 1919-   [BF]
*British actress*
* Pilbeam, Nova

**Pilbeam, Nova**
*See* Pilbeam, Margery

**Pilcher, Rosamunde** 1924-
[AW, CA, WD]
*British author and playwright*
* Fraser, Jane

**Pile**
*See* Moreno, Virginia [Reyes]

**Pile, D. W.** 20th c.   [MBF]
*British author*
* Webber, Stawford

**Pile o Dough**
*See* Peladeau, Pierre

**[The] Pilgrim**
*See* Daniel

**Pilgrim, Anne**
*See* Allan, Mabel Esther

**Pilgrim, David** [joint pseudonym
with Hilary Aidan St. George
Saunders]
*See* Palmer, John Leslie

**Pilgrim, David** [joint pseudonym
with John Leslie Palmer]
*See* Saunders, Hilary Aidan St.
George

**Pilgrim, Derral**
*See* Zachary, Hugh

**Pilgrim, Frank** 1926-   [CW]
*Guyanese journalist, playwright,
broadcaster*
* Mirglip, Knarf

**Pilgrim, Paul**
*See* Strodach, Paul Zeller

**Pilgrim, Peter**
*See* Bird, Robert Montgomery

**[The] Pilgrim Pope**
*See* Montini, Giovanni Battista
Enrico Antonio Maria

**Pilgrim, Thomas** 19th c.   [PA]
*Author*
* Moncamp, Arthur

**Pilgrim, William Lepper**
1859-1918   [THR]
*British actor*
* Abingdon, W. L.

**Pilio, Gerone**
*See* Whitfield, John Humphreys

**Pilk, Henry**
*See* Campbell, Ken

**Pilkington, Bert** 1902-1953
[BX, RBE]
*American boxer*
* Morgan, Tod

**Pilkington, Betty** 20th c.   [CA]
*American journalist*
* Alsterlund, Betty

**Pilkington, Cynthia**
*See* Horne, Cynthia Miriam

**Pillai, Narayana Narayana** 1924-
[IAW]
*Indian author and playwright*
* Omchery

**[The] Pillar of Doctors**
*See* William of Champeaux

**Pilleteri, Tony** 1917-   [BX, RBE]
*American boxer*
* [The] Garfield Gunner
* Larkin, Tippy

**Pillette, Dee**
*See* Pillette, Duane Xavier

**Pillette, Duane Xavier** 1922-   [BE]
*American baseball player*
* Pillette, Dee

**Pillette, Herman** 1895-1960
*American baseball player*
* Pillette, Old Folks

**Pillette, Old Folks**
*See* Pillette, Herman

**Pilley, Charles** 1885-   [LAO]
*British barrister and journalist*
* Pearce, Guy

**Pillion, Cecil Randolph** 1894-1962
[BE]
*American baseball player*
* Pillion, Squiz

**Pillion, Squiz**
*See* Pillion, Cecil Randolph

**Pillow, Gideon Johnson** 1806-1878
[SN]
*American army officer*
* [The] Liberator of Missouri

**Pilney, Andrew James** 1913-   [BE]
*American baseball player*
* Pilney, Anoy

**Pilney, Anoy**
*See* Pilney, Andrew James

**Pilnyak, Boris**
*See* Vogau, Boris Andreyevich

**Pilon, Germain** 1515?-1590
[FFF, RH, SN]
*French sculptor*
* [The] Father of French Sculpture

**Pilot, James**   [FB]
*American football player*
* Pilot, Preacher

**Pilot, Preacher**
*See* Pilot, James

**[The] Pilot who Weathered the Storm**
*See* Pitt, William

**Pilotin, Michael** 20th c.   [SFP]
*Author*
* Spriel, Stephen

**Pilou**
*See* Bardot, Louis

**Pilu, Francois** 1919-    [FC]
*French actor*
* Perier, Francois

**Pim, Herbert Moore** 1883-    [WWL]
*British author*
* Newman, A.

**Pimpernel**
See   Beaver, W. H.

**Pin, Oscar**
See   Perdiguero Perez, Fernando

**Pin-Tin**
See   Craveri, Sebastiano

**Pincas, Julius** 1885-1930    [WEC]
*American artist*
* Pascin, Jules

**Pincay, Laffit** 20th c.
*Jockey*
* [The] Pirate

**[El] Pinciano**
See   Nunez de Guzman, Fernan [or Fernando]

**Pinckert, Jeane** 1918-    [IPA]
*American clairvoyant*
* Dixon, Jeane

**Pincus, Jacob** 1838-1918    [EJS]
*American horse trainer and jockey*
* Jacob the Silent

**Pindar** 5th c. BC
[DNNS, FFF, HN]
*Greek poet*
* [The] Dircaean Swan
* [The] Prince of Lyric Poets
* [The] Theban Bard
* [The] Theban Eagle
* [The] Theban Lyre

**[The] Pindar, Horace, and Virgil of England**
See   Cowley, Abraham

**[The] Pindar of England**
See   Cowley, Abraham

**[The] Pindar of England**
See   Gray, Thomas

**[The] Pindar of England**
See   Villiers, George

**[The] Pindar of France**
See   Dorat, Jean

**[The] Pindar of France**
See   Lebrun, Ponce Denis Ecouchard

**[The] Pindar of France**
See   Ronsard, Pierre de

**[The] Pindar of Italy**
See   Chiabrera, Gabriello

**Pindar, Paul**
See   Akerman, John Yonge

**Pindar, Peter?**
See   Lawler, C. F.

**Pindar, Peter**
See   Wolcot, John

**Pindemonte, Ippolito** 1753-1828
[SN]
*Italian poet*
* [The] Italian Gray

**Pinder, Callie**
See   Pinder, Cyril

**Pinder, Cyril** 1946-    [IBW]
*American football player*
* Pinder, Callie

**Pinder, J. M.**
See   Pinder, John Michael

**Pinder, John Michael** 1948-    [ART]
*British artist*
* Pinder, J. M.

**Pine, Arthur** 1917-    [ASC]
*American public relations executive*
* Richards, Jay

**Pine, Cuyler**
See   Peck, Ellen [or Catherine?]

**Pine, Leslie Gilbert** 1907-    [CA]
*British author*
* Moorshead, Henry

**Pine, Theodore** [joint pseudonym with Emil (Theodore) Petaja]
See   Hasse, Henry L.

**Pine, Theodore** [joint pseudonym with Henry L. Hasse]
See   Petaja, Emil [Theodore]

**Pine, William**
See   Harknett, Terry

**Pineapple, Johnny**
See   Kaonohi, David

**Pineau, Gabriel du** 1573-1644
[DEP, FFF, SN]
*French jurist*
* [The] Cato of Anjou
* [The] Father of the People

**Pinelli, Babe**
See   Paolinelli, Rinaldo Angelo

**Pinelli, Ralph Arthur**
See   Paolinelli, Rinaldo Angelo

**Pinelo**
See   De Leon, Antonio

**Pinero, A. W.**
See   Pinero, [Sir] Arthur Wing

**Pinero, [Sir] Arthur Wing** 1855-1934    [LC]
*British playwright*
* Pinero, A. W.

**Pinero, Mrs. A. W.**    [FFF]
*Entertainer*
* Murray, Alma

**Pinetop**
See   Sparks, Aaron

**Pineux-Duval, Eugene Emmanuel** 1808-1885    [WBD]
*French painter*
* Amaury-Duval, Eugene Emmanuel

**Pinewood Tom**
See   White, Josh[ua Daniel]

**[The] Piney Woods Thoreau**
See   Lovett, Eddie

**Ping Pong**
See   Thompson, William Henry

**[The] Ping Pong Diplomat**
See   Braithwaite, George

**Pinheiro, Paulo Henrique Barbara** 1933-    [IAW]
*Brazilian author*
* Barbara, Paulo Henrique

**Piniella, Louis Victor** 1943-    [PB]
*American baseball player*
* Piniella, Piney

**Piniella, Piney**
See   Piniella, Louis Victor

**[The] Pink Powder Puff**
See   Guglielmi Di Valentina D'Antonguolla, Rodolpho Alfonso Raffaelo P.

**Pinkerton, John** 1758-1826    [DEL]
*Scottish author and historian*
* Heron, Robert

**Pinkerton, W. Anson**
See   Steele, Henry

**Pinkney, Miles**
See   Carre, Thomas

**Pinkston, Clarence** 1900-1965
[BBH]
*American swimming coach*
* Pinkston, Pinky

**Pinkston, Pinky**
See   Pinkston, Clarence

**Pinkwater, Daniel Manus** 1941-
[IAW]
*American author and illustrator*
* Duck, Captain
* Lome, Mike
* Tress, Arthur

**Pinner, Joma**
See   Werner, Herma

**Pinney, Johnny**
See   Penny, Johnny

**Pino, E.**
See   Wittermans, Elizabeth [Pino]

**Pintard, Lewis** 1732-1818    [FFF]
*American merchant*
* [The] Father of Historical Societies

**Pinter, Harold** 1930-    [CA]
*British playwright and actor*
* Baron, David

**Pinter, Josef** 1904-1941
[BEW, FC]
*Hungarian-born American comedian*
* Penner, Bumps
* Penner, Joe

**Pinto, Cecilia** 20th c.    [WEC]
*Brazilian cartoonist*
* Cica

**Pinto, Jacqueline** 1927-    [WD]
*British author*
* Blairman, Jacqueline

**Pinto, Peter**
See   Bernstein, Eric [Lennard]

**Pinto, Ziraldo Alves** 1932-    [WEC]
*Brazilian cartoonist*
* Ziraldo

**Pinturicchio, Bernardo**
See   Betti [or Di Biagio?], Bernardino

**Pinza, Ezio**
See   Pinza, Fortunato

**Pinza, Fortunato** 1892?-1957
[BBD, FC]
*Italian-born American opera singer*
* Pinza, Ezio

**Pioche de la Vergne, Marie Madeleine** 1634-1693    [SN]
*French author*
* [The] Fog
* La Fayette, Comtesse de

**Pioggi, Louis** 20th c.    [BLB]
*American underworld figure*
* Louie the Lump

**Pioneer**
See   Yates, Raymond Francis

**Piot, Lazarus**
See   Silvayn, Alexander

**[The] Pious**
See   Albert [or Albrecht]

**[The] Pious**
See   Albert IV

**[The] Pious**
See   Annius Verus, Marcus

**[The] Pious**
See   Canute II

**[The] Pious**
See   Edward VI

**[The] Pious**
See   Eric IX

**[The] Pious**
See   Ernest I [or Ernst]

**[The] Pious**
See   Frederick III

**[The] Pious**
See   Henry

**[The] Pious**
See   Leopold III

**[The] Pious**
See   Louis I

**[The] Pious**
See   Robert II

**[The] Pious**
See   Skippon, Philip

**[The] Pious**
See   William I

**Pious Jeems**
See   Gordon, James

**[Il] Piovano**
See   Arlotto Mainardi

**Piper, David Towry** 1918-    [AW]
*British author*
* Towry, Peter

**Piper, Evelyn**
See   Modell, Merriam

**Piper, Louis B.** 20th c.    [IBW]
*American fashion designer*
* Piper, Scotty

**Piper, Peter**
See   Langbehn, Theo

**Piper, Roger**
See   Fisher, John [Oswald Hamilton]

**Piper, Scott** 1954-    [SMG]
*American football player*
* Clutch, Mr.

**Piper, Scotty**
See   Piper, Louis B.

**Pipes, Jeemes, of Pipesville**
See   Massett, Stephen C.

**Pipgras, George** 1899- [BN]
*American baseball player*
* [The] American Peasant
* [The] Danish Viking

**Pipkin, Lefty**
*See* Pipkin, Robert

**Pipkin, Robert** 20th c. [OBW]
*American baseball player*
* Pipkin, Lefty

**Pipo**
*See* Sofman, Gustave

**Pippen, Cotton**
*See* Pippen, Henry Harold

**Pippen, Henry Harold** 1910- [BE]
*American baseball player*
* Pippen, Cotton

**Pipper, Pippia**
*See* Whaling, Thornton

**Pippi de Gianuzzi, Giulio**
1492?-1546 [FFF, RH, WBD]
*Italian painter*
* [The] Roman
* Romano, Giulio

**Pipps, Mr.**
*See* Leigh, Percival

**Piquet, Francois** 1708-1781
[DEP, DNNS]
*Clergyman*
* [The] Apostle of the Iroquois

**Piquetort, Jean**
*See* Routhier, [Sir] Adolphe Basile

**Piraianu, Alexandru**
*See* Mitru, Alexandru

**[The] Pirate**
*See* Pincay, Laffit

**[The] Pirate of the Gulf**
*See* Lafitte, Jean

**[The] Pirate Patriot**
*See* Koxinga

**[El] Pireo**
*See* Cano Ruiz, Manuel

**Pires, Joe**
*See* Stout, Robert Joe

**Pirie, Alexander K.** 1942- [EG]
*Scottish golfer*
* Pirie, Sandy

**Pirie, Sandy**
*See* Pirie, Alexander K.

**Pirie-Gordon, C. H. C.**
*See* Pirie-Gordon, Charles Harry
Clinton

**Pirie-Gordon, Charles Harry Clinton**
1883-1969 [SFL, WGT]
*British author*
* Pirie-Gordon, C. H. C.
* Prospero and Caliban [joint
pseudonym with Frederick
William Serafino Austin Rolfe]

**[Il] Pisanello**
*See* Pisano, Antonio

**Pisani, Carmen**
*See* Frapolli, Madame

**Pisano, Andrea** 1270?-1348 [WBD]
*Italian sculptor*
* Da Pontedera, Andrea

**Pisano, Antonio** 1397?-1455?
[WBD]
*Veronese painter*
* [Il] Pisanello
* Pisano, Vittore

**Pisano, Leonardo**
*See* Fibonacci, Leonardo

**Pisano, Little Augie**
*See* Carfano, Anthony

**Pisano, Vittore**
*See* Pisano, Antonio

**Piscator**
*See* Lathy, Thomas P.

**Piscator**
*See* Walton, Izaak

**Piscator, Paganus**
*See* Fisher, Payne

**Piscinarius**
*See* Wier, Johannes

**[The] Pisistratos of Rome**
*See* Caesar, [Gaius] Julius

**Pismire, Osbert**
*See* Hivnor, Robert

**Pissarro, Orovida Camille**
1893-1968 [DBA]
*British painter and etcher*
* Orovida

**[The] Pistol**
*See* Rulewski, Jan

**Pistol Pete Albright**
*See* Albright, Thomas

**Pistol Pete Maravich**
*See* Maravich, Peter

**Pistol Pete Reiser**
*See* Reiser, Harold Patrick

**Pistorius, Pieter** 1920- [IAW]
*South African author*
* Hendriks, P. G.

**Pitcairn, Frank**
*See* Cockburn, [Francis] Claud

**Pitcairn, John James** 1860-1936
[CC, EMD, WGT]
*British physician and author*
* Ashdown, Clifford [joint
pseudonym with Richard
Freeman]
* Piers, Ashdown [joint pseudonym
with Richard Freeman]

**Pitcher, Evelyn G[oodenough]**
1915- [CA]
*American author and educator*
* Goodenough, Evelyn

**Pitcher, Gladys** 1890- [CAP]
*American editor*
* Adams, Betsy
* Wentworth, Barbara
* Weston, Ann

**Pitcher, Molly**
*See* McCauley, Mary

**Pitcher, William John Charles**
1859?-1925 [BEW]
*Designer and artist*
* Wilhelm, C.

**Pitchford, Richard Valentine**
1895-1973 [B10]
*Welsh-born American magician*
* Cardini

**Pitchin' Paul Christman**
*See* Christman, Paul C.

**[The] Pitching Poet**
*See* Kenna, Ed[ward Benninghaus]

**Pithawalla, Maneck B.** 1886-
[WWL]
*Indian poet*
* Ruby

**Pitkin, Sylvia Sherman** 1895-
[NAA]
*American playwright*
* Sherman, Sylvia

**Pitko, Alex[ander]** 1914- [BE]
*American baseball player*
* Pitko, Spunk

**Pitko, Spunk**
*See* Pitko, Alex[ander]

**Pitlock, Lee Patrick Thomas** 1947-
[SMG]
*American baseball player*
* Pitlock, Skip

**Pitlock, Skip**
*See* Pitlock, Lee Patrick Thomas

**Pitman, Margaret J.** [PA]
*Author*
* Deane, Margery

**[Il] Pitocchetto [The Beggar]**
*See* Ceruti, Giacomo

**Pitre, Cannonball**
*See* Pitre, Didier

**Pitre, Didier** 1884-1934
[FHE, HK]
*Canadian-born hockey player*
* Pitre, Cannonball
* Pitre, Pit

**Pitre, Pit**
*See* Pitre, Didier

**Pitt, Archie**
*See* Selinger, Archie

**Pitt, Diamond**
*See* Pitt, Thomas

**Pitt, Jeremy**
*See* Wynne-Tyson, [Timothy] Jon
[Lyden]

**Pitt Lips Epps**
*See* Epps, Eugene

**Pitt, Mrs. H. M.** [FFF]
*Entertainer*
* Addison, Fannie

**Pitt, Thomas** 1653-1726 [WBD]
*British merchant and governor of
Madras*
* Pitt, Diamond

**Pitt, Valerie**
*See* Hall, Valerie

**Pitt, William [Earl of Chatham]**
1708-1778 [DEP, DNNS, WBD]
*British statesman*
* [The] British Cicero
* [The] Distressed Statesman
* [The] Elder Pitt
* [The] Great Commoner
* [The] Terrible Cornet of Horse

**Pitt, William** 1759-1806
[FFF, HN, WBD]
*British prime minister*
* [The] Heaven-Sent Minister
* [The] Pilot who Weathered the
Storm

**Pitt, William** (Continued)
* [The] Younger Pitt

**Pitt-Marson, Aileen** 1912- [THR]
*British actress*
* Marson, Aileen

**Pitt-Rivers, Augustus Henry**
*See* Lane Fox, Augustus Henry

**Pittard, Helene** 1874-1953
[ESF, SFL, WGT]
*French author*
* Roger, Noelle

**Pittenger, Clarke Alonzo** 1899-
[BE]
*American baseball player*
* Pittenger, Pinky

**Pittenger, Pinky**
*See* Pittenger, Clarke Alonzo

**Pittinger, Charles Reno** 1871-1909
[AS, BE]
*American baseball player*
* Pittinger, Togie

**Pittinger, Togie**
*See* Pittinger, Charles Reno

**Pittman, Jack** [IBW]
*American religious leader*
* John the Prophet

**Pitts, [Rev.] Alfred**
*See* Watson, Johnny

**Pitts, Donny**
*See* Hathaway, Donny

**Pitts, Eliza Susan** 1898-1963
[BEW]
*American actress*
* Pitts, Zasu

**Pitts, Frank** 1943- [FB]
*American football player*
* Pitts, Riddler

**Pitts, Riddler**
*See* Pitts, Frank

**Pitts, Zasu**
*See* Pitts, Eliza Susan

**Pittsburg Phil**
*See* Smith, George

**[The] Pittsburgh Kid**
*See* Conn, Billy

**Pittsburgh Phil Strauss**
*See* Strauss, Harry

**[The] Pittsburgh Stealer**
*See* Taveras, Franklin Fabian

**[The] Pittsburgh Windmill**
*See* Greb, Edward Henry

**Pitusin**
*See* Hurtado, Alfredo

**Pius**
*See* Metellus, Quintus Caecilius

**Pius II**
*See* De Piccolomini, Enea Silvio

**Pius III**
*See* Todeschini-Piccolomini,
Francesco

**Pius IV**
*See* Medici, Giovanni Angelo

**Pius IX**
*See* Mastai-Ferretti, Giovanni
Maria

Pius V
See Ghislieri, Michele

Pius VI
See Braschi, Giovanni Angelo

Pius VII
See Chiaramonti, Luigi Barnaba

Pius VIII
See Castiglioni, Francesco Saverio

Pius X
See Sarto, Giuseppe Melchiorre

Pius XI
See Ratti, Ambrogio Damiano
Achille

Pius XII
See Pacelli, Eugenio Maria
Giovanni

Pixerecourt, Rene Charles Guilbert
de 1773-1844 [DNNS, SN]
French playwright
* [The] Corneille of the Boulevards
* [The] Shakespeare of the
Boulevards

Pixley, Frank M. [FFF]
American writer
* Podrida, Olla

Pizarro, Francisco 1475?-1541
[DNNS, FFF, RH]
Spanish explorer
* [The] Conqueror
* Conquistador

Pizzarelli, Bucky
See Pizzarelli, John

Pizzarelli, John 1926- [EJ7]
American jazz musician
* Pizzarelli, Bucky

Pizzarno, Madame [FFF]
Entertainer
* Giuri, Adele

Pizzat, Frank J[oseph] 1924- [CA]
American psychologist and author
* Venafro, Mark

Pizzo, John F. 1907-1952 [SC]
American actor and circus performer
* Little Bozo

Pizzo, Vito 1929- [EJ]
American jazz musician
* Price, Vito

Place, Benjamin
See Thring, Edward

Place, Marian T[empleton] 1910-
[CA, SAT]
American author
* White, Dale
* Whitinger, R. D.

Placere, Morris N.
See Gupta, Sushil Kumar

Placide, Alice
See Emmett, Mrs. Charles E.

Placido
See Valdes, Gabriel de la
Concepcion

Pladner, Emile 1906- [BX, RBE]
French boxer
* Pladner, Spider

Pladner, Spider
See Pladner, Emile

Plaidy, Jean
See Hibbert, Eleanor Alice
[Burford]

[The] Plain and Perspicuous Doctor
See Burleigh, [or Burley?], Walter

[The] Plain Dealer
See Wycherly, William

Plain, Josephine
See Mitchell, Isabel Mary

Plain, Warren
See Oehmke, Thomas Harold

Planche, Miss
See Mackarness, Mrs. M. A.

Planchet, Roger Anthony 1923-
[CWG]
Canadian country-western performer
* Rogers, Smiling Slim

Plancus, Janus
See Bianchi, Giovanni

Plane, Anne
See Seymour, Marjorie F.

[The] Planet Prince
See Haggard, J. Harvey

Plank, Edward Stewart 1875-1926
[BE, BTB]
American baseball player
* Plank, Gettysburg Eddie

Plank, Gettysburg Eddie
See Plank, Edward Stewart

Plantagenet
See Geoffrey IV

Plantagenet, Edith 12th c.
[DNNF, DNNS, SN]
Wife of David, Prince Royal of
Scotland
* [The] Fair Maid of Anjou

Plantagenet, Edmund 1241?-1296
[DNNS, HN, WBD]
First Earl of Lancaster
* Crouchback

Plante, [Joseph] Jacques 1929-
[CEI, FHE, HK]
Canadian-born hockey player
* Jake the Snake
* Plante, Omer

Plante, Omer
See Plante, [Joseph] Jacques

Plantin, Christopher 1520?-1589
[SN]
Flemish typographer and printer
* [The] Cellini of Printing

Planus et Perspicuus, Doctor
See Burleigh, [or Burley?], Walter

Plaskitt, Dorothy 1874?-1950
[THR]
British actress
* Hammond, Dorothy

[The] Plastic Man
See Perkins, Sam

Plastino, Al 20th c. [WECO]
Cartoonist
* Mik, Al

Platak, Joseph 1909?-1954 [AS]
American handball player
* [The] Blond Panther

Platel, Felix ?-1888 [PA]
French writer
* Ignotus
* Pall, Etienne

Platerito [Little Silversmith]
See Taravilla y Amoros, Gregorio

Plath, Sylvia 1932-1963
[B10, CAP, LC]
American author and poet
* Lucas, Victoria

Platner, Ernst 1744-1818
[HN, SN]
German physician and philosopher
* [The] German Nestor of
Philosophy
* [The] Nestor of German
Philosophy

Plato
See Aristocles

Plato
See Coventry, Henry

Plato
See De Quincey, Thomas

[The] Plato of Germany
See Jacobi, Friedrich Heinrich

[The] Plato of Germany
See Mendelssohn, Moses

[The] Plato of His Age
See Malebranche, Nicolas

[The] Plato of the Christian World
See Herder, Johann Gottfried von

[The] Plato of the Eighteenth Century
See Arouet, Francois Marie

[The] Plato of the Puritans
See Howe, John

Platon
See Levshin, Peter

[The] Platonic Puritan
See Howe, John

[The] Platonist
See Taylor, Thomas

Platonov, Andrei
See Klimentov, Andrei Platonovich

Platt, Charles 1945- [ESF]
British author and editor
* St. James, Blakely [house
pseudonym, Playboy Press]

Platt, Edward
See Greenberg, Edward

Platt, J. G.
See Platt, John Gerald

Platt, John Gerald 1892- [ART]
British painter, engraver, etcher
* Platt, J. G.

Platt, Kin 1911- [SFL]
Author
* York, Wesley Simon

Platt, Mizell George 1920- [BE]
American baseball player
* Platt, Whitey

Platt, Whitey
See Platt, Mizell George

Platts, Beryl 1918- [CA]
British author and editor
* Seaton, Beryl

Platus
See Piatti, Girolomo

Plauen, E. O.
See Ohser, Erich

Plaut, Martin
See Marttin, Paul

Plautus
See Wilder, Alexander

Plawin, Paul 1938- [CA]
American author
* Godly, J. P.
* Steele, Dirk

Playboy Dick Cavill
See Cavill, Dick

[The] Player
See Bach, Hans

Player, Eddie [MBF]
British author
* Reid, Desmond [house
pseudonym]

Playfair, Hugo
See Paterson, Paul

Pleasant, Cousin Joe
See Joseph, Pleasant

Pleasant Joe
See Joseph, Pleasant

Pleasant, Tommy Lee
See Smith, Pleasant

Pleasant Willy
See Shakespeare, William

Pleasants, Jack 1874-1923 [BMH]
British comedian
* [The] Bashful Limit

Pleasants, Mammy
See Pleasants, Mary Ellen Smith

Pleasants, Mary Ellen Smith
?-1904 [IBW]
American abolitionist
* Pleasants, Mammy

Pleasure, King
See Beeks, Clarence

[The] Plebeian Child of the Revolution
See Bonaparte, Napoleon

[The] Plebeian Count
See Riquetti, Honore Gabriel
Victor

Plemiannikov, Roger Vadim 1928-
[BDF, FC, FDG]
French director
* Vadim, Roger

Plendello, Leo
See Saint, Andrew [John]

Plenipo, Rummer
See Prior, Matt[hew]

Pleon, Alec 1911- [BMH]
British comedian
* Funny Face

Pletikosic, Ante 1939- [AES]
Yugoslav soccer player
* Pletikosic, Tony

Pletikosic, Tony
See Pletikosic, Ante

Plews, Arthur Gordon Lane 1867-
? [THR]
British actor
* Poulton, A. G.

**Pleydell, George**
See Bancroft, George Pleydell

**Pleydell, Susan**
See Senior, Isabel J[anet] C[ouper] Syme

**Plick et Plock**
See Simenon, Georges [Joseph Christian]

**Plieksans, Janis** 1865-1929 [EWL]
*Latvian poet, playwright, translator*
* Rainis, Janis

**Plimsoll, Samuel** 1824-1898 [DEP, WBD]
*British politician, author, shipping reformer*
* [The] Sailor's Friend

**Pliny [Gaius Plinius Secundus]** 23-79 [WBD]
*Roman scholar*
* [The] Elder

**Pliny [Gaius Plinius Caecilius Secundus]** 62-113 [WBD]
*Roman politician*
* [The] Younger

**[The] Pliny of the East**
See Ibn-Muhammed, Zakarija

**Pliny the Youngest**
See Wilson, Stanley Kidder

**Plon-Plon**
See Bonaparte, Napoleon Joseph Charles Paul

**Plotinus** 205?- 270 [RH]
*Roman philosopher*
* Thaumaturgus

**[The] Plotter**
See Ferguson, Robert

**Ploug, Parmo Carl**
See Rytter, Poul

**Ploughman, John**
See Spurgeon, Charles Haddon

**Ploughman, Nina**
See Sutcliffe, Pavella Dolores

**[The] Ploughman of Madrid**
See Isidore [or Isidro]

**Ploughpenny**
See Eric IV [or VI]

**Ploughshare, Peter**
See Beach, S. B.

**Plover**
See Wise, John S.

**Plowman, Giles**
See Sutcliffe, Joseph Robert

**Pluckrose, Henry [Arthur]** 1931- [CA, SAT]
*British educator and editor*
* Cobbett, Richard

**Pluff, Barbara Littlefield** 1926- [CA]
*American author*
* Clayton, Barbara

**Plum, J.**
See Wodehouse, Pelham Grenville

**Plum, Jennifer**
See Kurland, Michael

**Plumb, Beatrice**
See Hunzicker, Beatrice Plumb

**Plumb, Hay**
See Hay-Plumb, Edward

**Plumb, J. H.**
See Plumb, John Harold

**Plumb, John Harold** 1911- [LC]
*British historian and author*
* Plumb, J. H.

**Plumb, Plumber**
See Plumb, Ron

**Plumb, Ron** 1950- [SMG]
*Canadian-born hockey player*
* Plumb, Plumber

**[The] Plumber**
See DeCavalcante, Simone Rizzo

**[The] Plumed Knight**
See Blaine, James Gillespie

**Plumer, William** 1759-1850 [FFF, PA]
*Author*
* Cincinnatus

**Plumley, Ernest Frederick** 1909- [AW, WD]
*British playwright and actor*
* Clevedon, John

**Plumm, Norman D.**
See Hornback, Bert G[erald]

**Plummer, Ben**
See Bingley, David Ernest

**Plummer, Clare [Emsley]** 1912- [AW, CA, WD]
*British author*
* Emsley, Clare

**Plummer, John** 1831- ? [PA]
*Author*
* [The] Northamptonshire Poet

**Plummer, Thomas Arthur** 20th c. [WW]
*Author*
* Sarne, Michael

**Plummy**
See Dellbridge, John

**Plumpe, Friedrich Wilhelm** 1889-1931 [BDF, FC, FD]
*German director*
* Murnau, F[riedrich] W[ilhelm]

**[The] Plunger**
See Pietrosante, Nicholas V. [Nick]

**Plunkett, Henry** [RH]
*Writer*
* Fusbos

**Plunkett, J. M.**
See Plunkett, Joseph Mary

**Plunkett, James**
See Kelly, James Plunkett

**Plunkett, Joseph Mary** 1887-1916 [LC]
*Irish editor, poet, nationalist*
* Plunkett, J. M.

**[Le] Plus Brave des Braves**
See Ney, Michel [Duc d'Elchingen]

**Plutarch** 46?- 120? [DNNS, FFF, SN]
*Greek historian*
* [The] Cheronean Sage

**[The] Plutarch of France**
See La Mothe Le Vayer, Francois de

**Plutonius**
See Mehta, Rustam Jehangir

**Plymley, Peter**
See Smith, Sydney

**[The] Plymouth Sound**
See White, James

**Po Joe Williams**
See Williams, Joe

**Poage, Scott T[abor]** 1931- [CA]
*American engineer and author*
* Scott, P. T.

**Pocahontas**
See Matoaka

**Poccetti, Bernardino**
See Barbatelli, Bernardino [or Bernardo]

**Poche**
See Deschamps, M. Pierre

**Pochi Danari**
See Maximilian I

**Pochonet, Dave**
See Pochonet, Gerard

**Pochonet, Gerard** 1924- [EJ]
*French jazz musician*
* Pochonet, Dave

**[The] Pocket Rocket**
See Richard, [Joseph] Henri

**[The] Pocket Sims Reeves**
See Powles, Matilda Alice

**Pocock, Carmichael Charles** 1920?-1979
*British-born oil company executive*
* Pocock, Mike

**Pocock, Cyrene Sue** 1896?-1964 [BEW]
*American opera singer*
* Van Gordon, Cyrena

**Pocock, Mike**
See Pocock, Carmichael Charles

**Pocock, Nicholas Edward Julian** 1951- [DC]
*Venezuelan-born cricketer*
* Pocock, Pokers

**Pocock, Patrick Ian** 1946- [DC]
*Welsh-born cricketer*
* Pocock, Percy

**Pocock, Percy**
See Pocock, Patrick Ian

**Pocock, Pokers**
See Pocock, Nicholas Edward Julian

**Pocoroba, Biff**
See Pocoroba, Bill

**Pocoroba, Bill** 1953- [SMG]
*American baseball player*
* Pocoroba, Biff
* Pocoroba, Poco

**Pocoroba, Poco**
See Pocoroba, Bill

**Podbielan, Bud**
See Podbielan, Clarence Anthony

**Podbielan, Clarence Anthony** 1924- [BE]
*American baseball player*
* Podbielan, Bud

**Podgajny, John Sigmund [Johnny]** 1920- [BE, PB]
*American baseball player*
* Podgajny, Specs

**Podgajny, Specs**
See Podgajny, John Sigmund [Johnny]

**Podgers**
See Ogden, R. L.

**Podmarsh, Rollo**
See Salter, Donald P. M.

**Podoliak, Boris**
See Kostiuk, Hryhory

**Podrida, Olla**
See Pixley, Frank M.

**Poe, Edgar**
See Levine, Philip

**Poe, Edgar Allan** 1809-1849 [PA, SN]
*American author and poet*
* [The] American Richard Savage
* [A] Bostonian
* Marginalia
* Pfaal, Hans
* Quarles

**Poel, William**
See Pole, William

**[A] Poet**
See Montgomery, James

**[The] Poet at the Breakfast Table**
See Holmes, Oliver Wendell

**[The] Poet Bishop**
See Taylor, Jeremy

**[The] Poet Genius of His People**
See Dunbar, Paul Laurence

**Poet in Motion**
See Mitchell, Arthur Adam

**[The] Poet King of Scandinavia**
See Oehlenschlaeger, Adam Gottlob

**[The] Poet Laureate of Democracy**
See Riley, James Whitcomb

**[The] Poet Laureate of Freemasonry**
See Morris, Robert

**[The] Poet Laureate of Georgia**
See Stanton, Frank Lebby

**[The] Poet Laureate of Harlem**
See Hughes, [James] Langston

**[The] Poet Laureate of Modern Jazz**
See Hendricks, John Carl

**[The] Poet Laureate of Oxford**
See Skelton, John

**[The] Poet Laureate of the Bees**
See Evans, John

**[The] Poet Laureate of the Little Smokies**
See Hickman, Herman M., Jr.

**[The] Poet Laureate of the Revolution**
See Esenin, Sergei Aleksandrovich

**[The] Poet Laureate of the Sixth Circuit**
See McCree, Wade H.

[The] Poet 'o the Plains
See  Eberhardt, John J.

[The] Poet of Childhood
See  Eberhardt, John J.

[The] Poet of France
See  Ronsard, Pierre de

[The] Poet of Greta Hall
See  Southey, Robert

[The] Poet of Haslemere
See  Tennyson, Alfred [First Baron Tennyson]

[The] Poet of Hygiene
See  Dumas, Jean Baptiste Andre

[The] Poet of Kings
See  Ronsard, Pierre de

[The] Poet of Kirkintilloch
See  Watson, Walker

[The] Poet of Kissing
See  Sidney, [Sir] Philip

[The] Poet of Languedoc
See  Boe, Jacques

[The] Poet of Liberty
See  Schiller, Johann Christoph Friedrich von

[The] Poet of Low Hampton
See  Miller, William

[The] Poet of Methodism
See  Wesley, Charles

[The] Poet of Poets
See  Shelley, Percy Bysshe

[The] Poet of Princes
See  Marot, Clement

[The] Poet of St. Honore
See  Beranger, Pierre Jean de

[The] Poet of the American Revolution
See  Freneau, Philip Morin

[The] Poet of the Chase
See  Somerville, William

Poet of the Chicago Slums
See  Algren, Nelson

[The] Poet of the Commonplace
See  Longfellow, Henry Wadsworth

[The] Poet of the Confederacy
See  Ryan, Abram Joseph

[The] Poet of the Excursion
See  Wordsworth, William

[The] Poet of the Future
See  Ronsard, Pierre de

[The] Poet of the Inquisition
See  Calderon de la Barca, Pedro

[The] Poet of the Organ
See  Crawford, Jesse

[The] Poet of the Piano
See  Cavallaro, Carmen

[The] Poet of the Poor
See  Crabbe, George

[The] Poet of the Revolution
See  Mayakovsky, Vladimir Vladimirovich

Poet of the Slaves
See  Alves, Antonio De Castro

[The] Poet of the Sword
See  Skobeleff, Michael Dimitrievitch

[The] Poet of the Vague
See  Ossian

[The] Poet of Wicomisco
See  Dennis, Amanda E.

[The] Poet Pug
See  Pope, Alexander

[The] Poet Scout
See  Crawford, J. W.

[The] Poet Sire of Italy
See  Alighieri, Durante

[The] Poet Squab
See  Dryden, John

[Le] Poete des Rois
See  Ronsard, Pierre de

[The] Poetical Father of Waller
See  Fairfax, Edward

[The] Poetical Milkmaid
See  Yearsley, Ann

[A] Poetical Rochefoucault
See  Davenant, [Sir] William

[A] Poetical Spagnoletto
See  Grahame, James

[The] Poet's Poet
See  Spenser, Edmund

Poff, Alonzo M. 1870-1952  [SC]
American actor
* Poff, Lon

Poff, Lon
See  Poff, Alonzo M.

Poffenberger, Boots
See  Poffenberger, Cletus Elwood

Poffenberger, Cletus Elwood 1915-
[PB]
American baseball player
* Poffenberger, Boots

Poget [or Pagit?], Ephraim 17th c.
[SN]
Clergyman and author
* Old Father Ephraim

Poggel, Mary 1851-1907  [IA]
American author
* Ave
* Mary Salesia, [Sister]

Poggenburg, Edward Francis
1901?-1963  [BEW]
American theatrical performer
* Gardner, Ed

Poggi, Emil J. 1928-  [CA]
American educator and author
* Poggi, Jack

Poggi, Jack
See  Poggi, Emil J.

Pogo
See  Gray, Patricia [Clark]

Pogodin, Nikolai Fyodorovich
See  Stukalov, Nikolai Fyodorovich

Pogonatus
See  Constantine IV

Pohl, Frederik 1919-
[ESF, SF, WGT]
American author and editor
* Andrews, Elton V.
* Fleur, Paul

Pohl, Frederik (Continued)
* Gottesman, S. D. [joint pseudonym with Cyril M. Kornbluth and Robert Lowndes]
* Gregor, Lee [joint pseudonym with Milton A. Rothman]
* Howard, Warren F.
* Judd, Cyril [joint pseudonym with Cyril M. Kornbluth]
* Lavond, Paul Dennis [joint pseudonym with J. Dockweiler, C. Kornbluth, R. Lowndes]
* Mariner, Scott [joint pseudonym with Cyril M. Kornbluth]
* Mason, Ernst
* McCann, Edson [joint pseudonym with Ramon Felipe San Juan Mario Alvarez Del Rey]
* McCreigh [or MacCreigh], James
* Park, Jordan [joint pseudonym with Cyril M. Kornbluth]
* Satterfield, Charles [joint pseudonym with Ramon Felipe San Juan Alvarez Del Rey]
* Wylie, Dirk [joint pseudonym with Joseph Harold Dockweiler and Cyril M. Kornbluth]

Pohle, Robert W[arren], Jr. 1949-
[CA]
American author
* Farnsworth, James
* Lee, Devon
* Miller, E. F.

Pohler, Joseph C. 1892-  [F2]
Actor
* Pollar, Gene

Pohlman, Max Edward 1911-  [IA]
American physician, playwright, author
* Benjamin, Claude
* Edwards, Max
* George, Marion E.

Poignart, J.  [PA]
Author
* [L']Homme Qui-Let

Poile, Bud
See  Poile, Norman Robert

Poile, Norman Robert 1924-
[CEI, FHE, HK]
Canadian-born hockey player
* Poile, Bud

Poindexter, Albert 1902?-
[CWG, PMJ]
American country-western performer
* Dexter, Al

Poindexter, [Chester] Jennings
1910-  [BE]
American baseball player
* Poindexter, Jinx

Poindexter, Jinx
See  Poindexter, [Chester] Jennings

Poindexter, Norwood 1926-
[DAM, EJ]
American jazz musician
* Poindexter, Pony

Poindexter, Pony
See  Poindexter, Norwood

Poinsot, Austin Edward  [PA]
Author
* D'Heylli, Georges

Pointed Arrow
See  Jackson, Andrew

Pointer, Aaron Elton 1942-  [BE]
American baseball player
* Pointer, Hawk

Pointer, Bonnie
See  Pointer, Patricia

Pointer, Hawk
See  Pointer, Aaron Elton

Pointer, Patricia 1950-  [EJ7]
American jazz musician
* Pointer, Bonnie

Pointkowski, Thomas Max 1926-
[OP]
American opera singer
* Tipton, Thomas

Pointon, Robert
See  Rooke, Daphne [Marie]

[La] Poire
See  Louis Philippe

Poire, Emmanuel 1859-1909
[WEC]
French cartoonist
* D'Ache, Caran

Poirie, Jean-Aurele Pierre
1795-1855  [CW]
West Indian poet
* Saint Aurele, Poirie de

Poirier, Louis 1910-  [EWL, TC1]
French author, playwright, poet
* Gracq, Julien

Poison, David
See  Kotey, David

Poison Ivy Andrews
See  Andrews, Ivy Paul

Poison Joe Brennan
See  Brennan, Joseph R.

[A] Poker of Fun
See  Lowell, Amy

Pol Pot
See  Saloth Sar

POLA
See  Watson, Pauline

Polachanin, Nicholas Joseph 1917-
[BE]
American baseball player
* Polly, Nicholas Joseph [Nick]

Polaire, Mademoiselle
See  Bouchard, Emilie Marie

Poland, Dorothy Elizabeth Hayward
1937-  [AW, WD]
Welsh author
* Farely, Alison
* Hammond, Jane

Polatschek-Williams, Jolan
See  Williams, Jolan

Polcher, Egon
See  Anschel, Eugene

Polder, Markus
See  Kruess, James

Poldowski
See  Wieniawska, Irene Regine

[The] Pole
See  Martin of Troppau

Pole, Michael de la 1330?-1389
[DNNF, DNNS, HN]
First Earl of Suffolk
* [The] Beloved Merchant

**Pole, William** 1852-1934
[BEW, LC, WBD]
*British actor, director, producer*
* Poel, William

**Poles, E.** 20th c. [OBW]
*American baseball player*
* Poles, Possum

**Poles, Possum**
*See* Poles, E.

**Poles, Spot**
*See* Poles, Spotswood

**Poles, Spotswood** 1887-1962 [MK]
*American baseball player*
* Poles, Spot

**Polfus, Lester** 1916- [ECM, EJ]
*American jazz musician*
* Hot Rod Red
* Paul, Les
* Rhubarb Red

**Polhem, Christopher** 1661-1751
[WBD]
*Swedish engineer and inventor*
* [The] Father of Swedish
  Mechanics

**Poli, Maurice** 20th c. [WF]
*Italian actor*
* Greenwood, Monty

**Poli, Umberto** 1883-1957
[B10, EWL, TCL]
*Italian poet*
* Saba, Umberto

**Poliakoff, Vera** 1911- [THR]
*Russian-born actress*
* Lindsay, Vera

**Poliarchus**
*See* Cotterell, [Sir] Charles

**Policeman Paul**
*See* Blyth, Harry

**Polidor**
*See* Guillaume, Ferdinando

**Poliorcetes**
*See* Demetrius I

**Polis, Gregory Linn** 1950- [SMG]
*Canadian-born hockey player*
* Polis, Indiana
* Polis, Pole-Eye

**Polis, Indiana**
*See* Polis, Gregory Linn

**Polis, Pole-Eye**
*See* Polis, Gregory Linn

**[The] Polish Bayard**
*See* Poniatowski, Joseph

**[The] Polish Byron**
*See* Mickiewicz, Adam

**[The] Polish Cato**
*See* Reyten, Thaddeus

**[The] Polish Franklin**
*See* Czacki, Thaddeus

**[The] Polish Messiah**
*See* Marcol, Czeslaw C.

**[The] Polish Moliere**
*See* Fredro, Alexander

**[The] Polish Pindar**
*See* Szymonowicz, Szymon

**[The] Polish Prince**
*See* Stemkowski, Peter David

**[The] Polish Rifle**
*See* Jaworski, Ron

**[The] Polish Sappho**
*See* Pawlikowska, Marja [Kossak]

**[The] Polish Voltaire**
*See* Krasicki, Ignatius

**[The] Polite Lunatic**
*See* Sullivan, James E.

**Politella, Dario** 1921- [CA, WD]
*American author*
* Granite, Tony
* Stewart, David

**Polith, M.** 19th c. [PA]
*Author*
* [A] Russian

**Politian**
*See* Ambrogini, Angelo

**[The] Political Grimalkin**
*See* Van Buren, Martin

**[The] Political Minstrel**
*See* Glazer, Joe

**[The] Politician**
*See* Castiglia, Francesco

**Politicus**
*See* Kulski, Wladyslaw W[szebor]

**Politzer, Heinrich** 1910-1978 [CA]
*Austrian-born author*
* Politzer, Heinz

**Politzer, Heinz**
*See* Politzer, Heinrich

**Poliuto**
*See* Wilkie, F. B.

**Poliziano, Angelo**
*See* Ambrogini, Angelo

**Polizzi, Alfred** 1900-
[BLB, MM, PHM]
*Italian-born American underworld
figure*
* [The] Owl
* Polizzi, Big Al

**Polizzi, Big Al**
*See* Polizzi, Alfred

**Polk, Bob**
*See* Polk, James

**Polk, James** 1915- [BB]
*American basketball coach*
* Polk, Bob

**Polk, James Knox** 1795-1849
[FAP]
*American president*
* [The] First Dark Horse
* [The] Napoleon of the Stump

**Polk, Josiah F.** 19th c. [PA]
*Author*
* Kroates

**Polka Dot Slim**
*See* Vincent, Monroe

**[The] Polka King**
*See* Budry, Chester

**Polkinghorne, Margaret** 1939-
[OP]
*British opera singer*
* Kingsley, Margaret

**Pollack, Michael John, Jr.** 1939-
[BEW, FC]
*American actor*
* Pollard, Michael J.

**Pollaiuolo, Simone** 1454?-1508?
[WBD]
*Florentine architect*
* [Il] Cronaca [The Chronicler]

**Pollak, Felix** 1909- [CA]
*Austrian-born poet*
* Anselm, Felix

**Pollak, Rose** 1894- [JL]
*Hungarian-born opera singer*
* Pauly, Rosa

**Polland, Madeleine A[ngela]** 1918-
[TCC]
*Irish-born author*
* Adrian, Frances

**Pollar, Gene**
*See* Pohler, Joseph C.

**Pollard, A. F.**
*See* Pollard, Albert Frederick

**Pollard, A. W.**
*See* Pollard, Alfred William

**Pollard, Albert Frederick**
1869-1948 [LC]
*British historian and author*
* Pollard, A. F.

**Pollard, Alfred William** 1859-1944
[LC]
*British author and editor*
* Pollard, A. W.

**Pollard, Dock**
*See* Pollard, Samuel

**Pollard, Frederick Douglass, Sr.**
1894- [FB, IBW]
*American football player*
* Pollard, Fritz

**Pollard, Frederick, Jr.** 20th c.
[IBW]
*American football player, track and
field athlete*
* Pollard, Fritz

**Pollard, Fritz**
*See* Pollard, Frederick Douglass,
Sr.

**Pollard, Fritz**
*See* Pollard, Frederick, Jr.

**Pollard, Jim** 1922- [BB]
*American basketball player*
* [The] Kangaroo Kid

**Pollard, John X.** [house pseudonym]
*See* Browne, Howard

**Pollard, Michael J.**
*See* Pollack, Michael John, Jr.

**Pollard, Samuel** 1938- [IBW]
*American clergyman*
* Pollard, Dock

**Pollard, Snub**
*See* Fraser, Harold

**Polli, Crip**
*See* Polli, Lou[is Americo]

**Polli, Lou[is Americo]** 1901- [BE]
*American baseball player*
* Polli, Crip

**Pollini, Mme.**
*See* Poole, Clara

**Pollock, Anna**
*See* Marble, Anna

**Pollock, Courtnay** 1877- ? [WWL]
*British author*
* Maxwell, Edward

**Pollock, Guy**
*See* Hamilton, Robert Douglas

**Pollock, John H[ackett]** 1887-
[WGT]
*Author*
* [An] Philibin

**Pollock, Martin**
*See* Gardner, Maurice

**Pollock, Mary**
*See* Blyton, Enid [Mary]

**Polly, Nicholas Joseph [Nick]**
*See* Polachanin, Nicholas Joseph

**Polnarioff, Kurt** 1917-1958 [PMJ]
*German-born American musician*
* Nero, Paul

**Polo, Articum**
*See* Higinbotham, John D.

**Polock Joe Saltis**
*See* Saltis, Joseph

**Polonsky, Abraham** 20th c. [WW]
*Author*
* Hogarth, Emmett [joint
  pseudonym with Mitchell A.
  Wilson]

**Polony, Raymond**
*See* Machan, Tibor R[ichard]

**Polsby, Nelson W[oolf]** 1934- [CA]
*American political scientist and
author*
* Clun, Arthur

**Poltoratzky, N[ikolai] P[etrovich]**
1921- [CA]
*Turkish-born American educator
and author*
* Petrovsky, N.

**Poltroon, Milford**
*See* Bascom, David

**Poluski, Byno** 1908- [F2, FC]
*British actress*
* Ward, Polly

**Polva, Anni**
*See* Polviander, Anni Kyllikki

**Polviander, Anni Kyllikki** 1915-
[IAW]
*Finnish author*
* Heino, Kyllikki
* Polva, Anni

**Polyaenus, Julius** 2nd c. [SN]
*Greek scholar*
* [The] Macedonian

**Polycarp** 72?- 156? [HN]
*Saint*
* Doctor of Asia
* Doctor of the Holy Church of
  Smyrna

**Polygnotus** 5th c. BC
[FFF, RH, SN]
*Greek painter*
* [The] Father of Ecclesiastical
  History
* [The] Father of Historic Painting

**Polyhistor**
*See* Nordhof, Daniel Georg

**Polyhistor**
*See* Thordsen, Theodori

[The] Polyphemus of Literature
See Johnson, Samuel

Polyphile
See La Fontaine, Jean de

Polypus
See Barrett, Eaton Stannard

Pomares, Anita 1910-
American actress
* Page, Anita

Pombal, Marques de
See Carvalho e Mello, Sebastiao Jose de

Pomeran, David Sheldon 1931-
[BEW]
American producer, director, playwright
* Sheldon, David

Pomeranus
See Bugenhagen, Johann

Pomeranz, Joseph 1895-1955
[BEW]
Russian-born director
* Pomeroy, Jay

Pomeroy, Brick
See Pomeroy, Mark M.

Pomeroy, Eugene
See Donnelly, Thomas F.

Pomeroy, Florence Mary
See Powley, Florence Mary Pomeroy

Pomeroy, Hub[bard]
See Claassen, Harold

Pomeroy, Iola
See Howard, Mrs. L.

Pomeroy, Jay
See Pomeranz, Joseph

Pomeroy, Mark M. 1840- ?
[FFF, PA]
American journalist
* Pomeroy, Brick

Pomeroy, Pete
See Roth, Arthur J[oseph]

Pomfret, Baron
See Dame, Lawrence

Pomfret, Joan
See Townsend, Joan

Pomfret, Peter
See Graves, Richard

Pommer, Dr.
See Bugenhagen, Johann

Pomona?
See Francis, [Sir] Philip

Pompeius Magnus, Sextus 1st c.
BC [WBD]
Roman soldier
* [The] Younger

Pompeo, John Anthony 1934- [EJ]
American jazz musician
* Rae, Johnny

Pompey [or Pompeius], Cneius 1st c.
BC [DNNS, HN]
Roman general
* [The] Great
* Sampsiceranus, Alabarches, the Jerusalemite

Pompez, Alex
See Pompez, Allesandro

Pompez, Allesandro 20th c. [OBW]
American baseball player
* Pompez, Alex

Pomponazzi, Pietro 1462-1525
[SN]
Italian philosopher
* Peretto

Pomponio, Leto
See Vilelleschi, Marchese Francesco

Pomponius, Lucius 1st c. BC
[WBD]
Latin author
* Bononiensis [Of Bononia]

Pomus, Doc
See Pomus, Jerome

Pomus, Jerome 1925- [PRS]
American songwriter
* Pomus, Doc

Pon Mudi
See Naa Parthasarathy, Naarayana-Parthasarathy

Ponce de Leon, Rodrigo 1443-1492
[HN]
Spanish general
* [The] Marquis Duke of Cadiz

Pond, Arlie
See Pond, Erasmus Arlington

Pond, Ducky
See Pond, Raymond

Pond, Erasmus Arlington
1872-1930 [BE]
American baseball player
* Pond, Arlie

Pond, Frederick Eugene 1856- ?
[FFF, PA]
Writer
* Red Wing
* Wildwood, Will

Pond, George E. [FFF, PA]
Author
* Quilibet, Philip

Pond, Myron [PA]
Author
* [The] Commodore

Pond, Paul 1942?- [RO2, TR]
British actor and singer
* Jones, Paul

Pond, Raymond 1903-
American football coach
* Pond, Ducky

Pond, S. T. R. 20th c. [MBF]
British author
* Reay, Trevace

Pond, Wilf Pocklington 20th c.
[NAA]
British-born editor
* Cottingham, Henry
* Cousans, S. W.
* Slight, John

Poniatowski, Joseph 1763-1814
[DNNF, FFF, HN]
Polish general
* [The] Bayard of Poland
* [The] Polish Bayard

Poningoe
See Dunn, Caleb

Pons, Alice Josephine 1904- [BBD]
French-born opera singer
* Pons, Lily

Pons, Lily
See Pons, Alice Josephine

Ponselle, Carmela
See Ponzillo, Carmela

Ponselle, Rosa Melba
See Ponzillo, Rosa Melba

Ponsford, Ponny
See Ponsford, William Harold

Ponsford, William Harold 1900-
[EC]
Australian cricketer
* Ponsford, Ponny

Ponsin, Mlle.
See Prevost, Madame Henri

Ponsonby, Doris Almon 1907-
[CA, WD]
British author
* Rybot, Doris
* Tempest, Sarah

Ponsonby, [Sir] Henry Frederick
1825-1894? [RH]
British statesman and author
* Sebastian

Ponsonby, Spencer Cecil Brabazon
[FFF]
Author
* Row, Bolton

Pont
See Laidler, Gavin Graham

Pont, Keith Rupert 1953- [DC]
British cricketer
* Pont, Monty
* Pont, Plod

Pont, Monty
See Pont, Keith Rupert

Pont, Plod
See Pont, Keith Rupert

Pontanus
See Dupont, Dennis

Ponte, Jacopo [or Giacomo] da
1510-1592 [WBD]
Venetian painter
* Bassano, Jacopo [or Giacomo] da

Pontecorvo, Gilberto 1919-
[BDF, FDG]
Italian director
* Pontecorvo, Gillo

Pontecorvo, Gillo
See Pontecorvo, Gilberto

Pontiac
See Knight, Oliver

Ponticus
See Aquila

[The] Pontiff of Calvinists
See Du Plessis, Armand Jean

Pontius, Brute
See Pontius, Miller

Pontius, Miller 20th c.
American football player
* Pontius, Brute

Pontormo, Jacopo da
See Carrucci, Jacopo

Ponzi, Charles 1878-1949 [BLB]
Italian-born American swindler
* [The] Great Ponzi

Ponzillo, Carmela 1892- [BBD]
American opera singer
* Ponselle, Carmela

Ponzillo, Rosa Melba 1897-1981
[WBD]
American opera singer
* [The] Caruso in Petticoats
* Ponselle, Rosa Melba

Pool, Harlin Welty 1908-1963
[BE]
American baseball player
* Pool, Samson

Pool, Maria L. [FFF]
American writer
* Earnshaw, Catharine

Pool, Samson
See Pool, Harlin Welty

Poole, Buster
See Poole, James E.

Poole, Clara [FFF]
Entertainer
* Pollini, Mme.

Poole, Easy
See Poole, James Ralph [Jim]

Poole, Elijah 1897-1975
[HDM, IBW, IPA]
American Black Muslim leader
* Karriam, Elijah
* Messenger of Allah
* Muhammed, Elijah

Poole, Frederick King 1934- [CA]
American writer and consultant
* Harris, Andrew

Poole, James E. 1915- [FB]
American football player
* Poole, Buster

Poole, James Ralph [Jim] 1895-
[BE]
American baseball player
* Poole, Easy

Poole, Joseph [RH]
British clergyman
* Fiddler Joss

Poole, Michael
See Poole, Reginald Heber

Poole, Reginald Heber 1885-
[MBF, WW]
British author
* Heber, Austin
* Heber, Reginald
* Poole, Michael
* Thomas, Anthony
* Valentine, Henry

Poole, Seth
See Riemer, George

Poole, Virginia Sherman 1919-
[BEW, FC, SW]
American actress
* Gilmore, Virginia

Poole, Vivian
See Jaffe, Gabriel Vivian

Pooler, James Anthony 1954-
[SMG]
American football player
* Pooler, Pooh

**Pooler, Pooh**
See Pooler, James Anthony

**Poolla, Tirupati Raju**
See Raju, Poolla Tirupati

**Poor Bernard**
See Bernard, Claude

**Poor Bob**
See Woodfork, Robert

**Poor Boy**
See Oden, James Burke [Jimmy]

**Poor Charlie**
See West, Charles [Charlie]

**Poor Con**
See Jackson, William

**[The] Poor Devil**
See Freron, Elie-Catherine

**[The] Poor Fish Peddler**
See Vanzetti, Bartolomeo

**Poor Jim**
See Rachell, James

**Poor Little Rich Girl**
See Hutton, Barbara

**[The] Poor Man's Friend**
See Symcott, Margaret

**[The] Poor Man's Priest**
See Dolling, Richard Radclyffe

**[The] Poor Priest**
See Bernard, Claude

**Poor Richard**
See Franklin, Benjamin

**Poor Robert the Scribe**
See Miner, Charles

**Poor Robin**
See Herrick, Robert

**Poor Robin**
See Winstanley, William

**Poore, Benjamin Perley** 1820-1887
[FFF, PA, WBD]
*American journalist*
* [The] Major
* Perley
* Raconteur

**Poot, Huibert Cornelisz[oon]**
1689-1733 [WBD]
*Dutch poet*
* [The] Dutch Hesiod

**Pooter**
See Hamilton, Alex

**Pooton, James** 1834- ? [PA]
*Author*
* Unit, Matthew

**Poots-Booby, Edna**
See Larsen, Carl

**Pop Boy Smith**
See Smith, Clarence Ossie

**[The] Pope**
See Barr, Alfred Hamilton, Jr.

**[The] Pope**
See Owens, Paul

**Pope, Alexander** 1688-1744
[DNNS, FFF, SN]
*British poet*
* [An] Apothecary
* [The] Bard of Twickenham
* [The] Best Poet of England

**Pope, Alexander** (Continued)
* Distich, Dick
* [The] English Horace
* [The] Little Nightingale
* [The] Nightingale of Twickenham
* [The] Poet Pug
* Pope, Paper Saving
* [The] Portentous Cub
* Scriblerus, Martinus
* [That] True Deacon of the Craft
* [The] Twickenham Bard

**Pope, F. W.** 20th c. [MBF]
*British author*
* Hulbert, Lloyd

**Pope, Henry** [PA]
*Author*
* Gavilan, Peak

**[The] Pope in Worsted Stockings**
See Crabbe, George

**Pope Joan**
See John VIII

**Pope, John** 1822-1892 [FFF, SN]
*American army officer*
* Saddle-Bag John

**[The] Pope of Africa**
See Carr, Burgess

**[The] Pope of Geneva**
See Chauvin [or Caulvin?], Jean

**[The] Pope of Peace**
See Pacelli, Eugenio Maria Giovanni

**[The] Pope of Philosophy**
See Aristotle

**[The] Pope of the Huguenots**
See Du Plessis, Armand Jean

**[The] Pope of the Huguenots**
See Mornay, Philippe de [Seigneur du Plessis-Marly]

**[The] Pope of the Reformation**
See Chauvin [or Caulvin?], Jean

**Pope, Paper Saving**
See Pope, Alexander

**Pope, Pat** 1918- [THR]
*British actress and singer*
* Taylor, Pat

**Pope-Hennessy, J. W.**
See Pope-Hennessy, John Wyndham

**Pope-Hennessy, John Wyndham**
1913- [LC]
*British author*
* Pope-Hennessy, J. W.

**Popel, Stefan**
See Bandera, Stefan

**[The] Pope's Kaiser**
See Charles IV [or Karl]

**Popescu, Christine** 1930-
[CA, SAT]
*British author*
* Keir, Christine
* Pullein-Thompson, Christine

**Popiel, Paul**
See Popiel, Poul Peter

**Popiel, Poul Peter** 1943- [HR]
*Danish-born hockey player*
* Popiel, Paul

**Popik, Uriel** 1926- [CA]
*Israeli author, editor, translator*
* Ofek, Uriel

**[The] Popinjay**
See Henry II [or Henri]

**[The] Popish Duke**
See James II

**Poplicola?**
See Francis, [Sir] Philip

**Popov, Alexander Serafimovich** 1863-
? [CD]
*Russian author*
* Serafimovich, Alexander

**Popov, Dusko** 1912?-1981
*Yugoslav-born British intelligence agent*
* Tricycle

**Popovic, Nenad D[ushan]** 1909-
[CAP]
*Yugoslavian-born educator and author*
* Spectator

**Popovich, Paul** 1940- [SMG]
*American baseball player*
* Popovich, Pop

**Popovich, Pavel** 20th c. [CND]
*Russian cosmonaut*
* Golden Eagle

**Popovich, Pop**
See Popovich, Paul

**Popowski, Edward Joseph [Eddie]**
1913- [BE]
*American baseball manager*
* Popowski, Pop

**Popowski, Pop**
See Popowski, Edward Joseph [Eddie]

**Poppa [or Poppy] Hop**
See Wilson, Harding

**Popper, Frau** [FFF]
*Entertainer*
* Menter, Sophie

**Popplewell, Nigel Francis Mark**
1957- [DC]
*British cricketer*
* Popplewell, Poppers
* Popplewell, Pops

**Popplewell, Poppers**
See Popplewell, Nigel Francis Mark

**Popplewell, Pops**
See Popplewell, Nigel Francis Mark

**Poppo** ?-1048 [CAL]
*Pope*
* Damasus II

**Pops, Mr.**
See Fiedler, Arthur

**Popski**
See Peniakoff, Vladimir

**Poquelin, Jean Baptiste** 1622-1673
[HN, SN, WBD]
*French playwright*
* [The] Anatomist of Humanity
* [The] Aristophanes of His Age
* [Le] Contemplateur
* [The] Father of French Comedy
* [The] French Aristophanes
* Gelaste

**Poquelin, Jean Baptiste** (Continued)
* [L']Hypochondre
* Moliere

**Poquette, Pierre**
See Poquette, Thomas Arthur

**Poquette, Thomas Arthur** 1951-
[SMG]
*American baseball player*
* Poquette, Pierre

**Por, Odon** 1883- [WWL]
*Author and journalist*
* [Un] Gildista

**Porat, Yosef**
See Foerder, Heinz

**Porcari, Constance Kwolek** 1933-
[CA]
*American author*
* Kwolek, Constance

**Porcher, Mary F. Wickham**
See Bond, Mary Fanning Wickham

**Porcupine, Peter**
See Cobbett, William

**Pordenone, Giovanni Antonio da**
See De Sacchi, Giovanni Antonio

**Porel, Paul**
See Parfouru, Paul Desire

**Porges, Arthur** 1915-
[ESF, HFF, WGT]
*American author*
* Arthur, Peter
* Rogers, Pat

**Pork Chop Hoffman**
See Hoffman, John Edward

**Pork Chop Lee**
See Green, Lee

**Pork Chop Mullins**
See Mullins, Jeff

**Pork Chop Smith**
See Smith, Jerome

**Porlock, Martin**
See MacDonald, Philip

**Porn, Lord**
See Pakenham, Francis Aungier

**Porphyrogenitus [Born in the Purple]**
See Constantine VII

**Porphyry**
See Malchus

**Porpora, Nicholas** 1685?-1767?
[HN]
*Italian composer*
* [The] Patriarch of Harmony

**Porrata Doria de Rincon, Providencia**
1910-1968 [CW]
*Puerto Rican poet*
* Rubens, Alma

**Porrata Dorio de Aponte, Carmen**
1911- [CW]
*Puerto Rican poet*
* Demar, Carmen

**Porsche, Ferdinand** 1909- [CA]
*German industrialist and author*
* Porsche, Ferry

**Porsche, Ferry**
See Porsche, Ferdinand

**[The] Porson of Old English and French Literature**
See Douce, Francis

**Porson, Richard** 1759-1808
[DNNS, FFF, SN]
*British scholar and critic*
* Cantabrigiensis
* [That] Coryphaeus of Learning
* Devil Dick
* [The] Norfolk Boy

**Port, Wymar**
*See* Judy, Will[iam Lewis]

**Portal, Ellis**
*See* Powe, Bruce

**Portal, V. E.** 1893-    [WWL]
*British author*
* Bannisdale, V. E.

**Porte-Crayon**
*See* Strother, David Hunter

**[The] Portentous Cub**
*See* Pope, Alexander

**[The] Porter**
*See* DeLucia, Felice

**Porter, Alan**
*See* Clark, Ruth C[ampbell]

**Porter, Alice**
*See* Edwards, Margaret Marie

**Porter, Allen** 1895?-1944    [WWJ]
*American jazz musician*
* Porter, Yank

**Porter, Alvin**
*See* Rowland, D[onald] S[ydney]

**Porter, Curtis** 1929-    [EJ]
*American jazz musician*
* Hadi, Shafi

**Porter, David John** 1948-    [IAW]
*British playwright*
* Gladwyn, Edward

**Porter, Dorothy Louise Burnett**
1905-    [IBW]
*American author and librarian*
* [The] Dean of Black Research
  Bibliographers

**Porter, Eleanor [Hodgman]**
1868-1920    [TC]
*American author*
* Stewart, Eleanor

**Porter, Elise** 20th c.    [THR]
*American actress*
* Bartlett, Elise

**Porter, Freak Man**
*See* Porter, George

**Porter, Frederick** 1871- ?    [MBF]
*Scottish author and playwright*
* Watson, Frederick

**Porter, Geezer**
*See* Porter, Howard

**Porter, Gene Stratton**
*See* Stratton, Geneva Grace

**Porter, George** 20th c.    [RM]
*Musician*
* Porter, Freak Man

**Porter, H. V.**
*See* Porter, Henry V.

**Porter, Harold Everett** 1887-1936
[NAA, TC, WW]
*American author*
* Hall, Holworthy

**Porter, Henry V.** 1891-
*American basketball executive*
* Porter, H. V.

**Porter, Howard** 1948-
*American basketball player*
* Porter, Geezer

**Porter, J. W.** 1933-    [BE]
*American baseball player*
* Porter, Jay

**Porter, Jack Nusan**
*See* Puchtik, Yakov Nusan

**Porter, Jake**
*See* Porter, Vernon

**Porter, Jay**
*See* Porter, J. W.

**Porter, Katherine Anne** 1890-    [CN]
*American author*
* M. T. F.

**Porter, Kathryn**
*See* Swinford, Betty [June Wells]

**Porter, Linn Boyd** 1851-1916
[WGT]
*American author*
* Ross, Albert

**Porter, Madeline** 20th c.
*American author*
* Habersham, Elizabeth [joint
  pseudonym with Shannon
  Harper]
* James, Anna [joint pseudonym
  with Shannon Harper]

**Porter, Mark**
*See* Leckie, Robert [Hugh]

**Porter, Maurice Malcolm** 1909-
[AW]
*British dentist and writer*
* Mouthpiece

**Porter, Mrs. Robert P.**    [FFF]
*American writer*
* Detective's Daughter

**Porter, Richard Twilley** 1901-1974
[BE]
*American baseball player*
* Porter, Twitchy
* Porter, Wiggles

**Porter, Sheena**
*See* Lane, Sheena Porter

**Porter, T. B.** 20th c.    [GW]
*American rodeo performer*
* Porter, Teaberry

**Porter, Teaberry**
*See* Porter, T. B.

**Porter, Twitchy**
*See* Porter, Richard Twilley

**Porter, Vernon** 1910?-    [WWJ]
*American jazz musician*
* Porter, Jake

**Porter, Wiggles**
*See* Porter, Richard Twilley

**Porter, William Sydney** 1862-1910
[EMD, EWL, WYA]
*American author*
* Henry, O.
* Henry, Oliver
* Peters, S. H.

**Porter, William Trotter** 1809-1858
[FFF, PA]
*American journalist*
* York's Tall Son

**Porter, Yank**
*See* Porter, Allen

**Porterfield, Bob**
*See* Porterfield, Erwin Coolidge

**Porterfield, Erwin Coolidge** 1923-
[BE]
*American baseball player*
* Porterfield, Bob

**Portia**
*See* Adams, Abigail Smith

**Portman, Arthur Fitzhardinge**
1861-1940    [OCS]
*British horse racing authority and
editor*
* Audax

**Porto, Al[fred]** 1926-    [BE]
*American baseball player*
* Porto, Lefty

**Porto, Lefty**
*See* Porto, Al[fred]

**Porto, Louis**
*See* Rousseau, Camille

**Portobello, Petronella**
*See* Anderson, [Lady] Flavia

**[The] Portuguese Apollo**
*See* Camoens, Luis de

**[The] Portuguese Cid**
*See* Pereira, Nunez Alvarez

**[The] Portuguese Fernandel**
*See* Felipe, Alfredo

**[The] Portuguese Horace**
*See* Ferreira, Antonio

**[The] Portuguese Joan of Arc**
*See* Almeida, Brites de

**[The] Portuguese Livy**
*See* Barros, Joao de

**[The] Portuguese Maecenas of Arts
and Sciences**
*See* Emanuel I [Manuel or
Manoel]

**[The] Portuguese Mars**
*See* Albuquerque, Alfonso [or
Affonso] de

**[The] Portuguese Nostradamus**
*See* Bandarra, Goncalo Annes

**[The] Portuguese Nun**
*See* Alcaforada, Mariana

**[The] Portuguese Pindar**
*See* Diniz da Cruz e Silva, Antonio

**[The] Portuguese Plautus**
*See* Vicente, Gil

**[The] Portuguese Theocritus**
*See* Sa de Miranda, Francisco da

**[The] Portuguese Titian**
*See* Sanchez Coello, Alonzo

**Portway, Christopher [John]** 1923-
[CA]
*British author*
* October, John

**Posada, Leo**
*See* Posada, Leopoldo Jesus

**Posada, Leopoldo Jesus** 1936-    [BE]
*Cuban-born baseball player*
* Posada, Leo
* Posada, Popy

**Posada, Popy**
*See* Posada, Leopoldo Jesus

**Posateri, Mike** 1900?-1977    [FIR]
*Film set dresser and boxer*
* Dundee, Mike

**Posedel, Barnacle Bill**
*See* Posedel, William John

**Posedel, Chief**
*See* Posedel, William John

**Posedel, Porthole**
*See* Posedel, William John

**Posedel, Sailor Bill**
*See* Posedel, William John

**Posedel, William John** 1906-    [PB]
*American baseball player*
* Posedel, Barnacle Bill
* Posedel, Chief
* Posedel, Porthole
* Posedel, Sailor Bill

**Poser, Bob**
*See* Poser, John Falk

**Poser, John Falk** 1910-    [BE]
*American baseball player*
* Poser, Bob

**Posey, C. W.**
*See* Posey, Cumberland Willis, Sr.

**Posey, Cum**
*See* Posey, Cumberland Willis

**Posey, Cumberland Willis**
1890?-1946    [AS, MK]
*American baseball player*
* Posey, Cum

**Posey, Cumberland Willis, Sr.** 1858-
?    [IBW]
*American businessman*
* Posey, C. W.

**Posner, Jacob D.** 1883-    [WW]
*Author*
* Dean, Gregory

**Posner, Richard** 1944-    [CA, WD]
*American author*
* Craig, Jonathan
* Foster, Iris
* Murray, Beatrice
* Todd, Paul
* Wine, Dick

**Possendorf, Hans**
*See* Mahner-Mons, Hans

**Possumtrot, Eli**
*See* Ferguson, Robert B.

**Post, A. H.**
*See* Badger, Joseph E.

**Post, F. A.**
*See* Post-Nikov, Feodor A.

**Post, Henry** 1948-    [CA]
*American author*
* Spot, Ryhen

**Post, J. B.**
*See* Post, Jerry Benjamin

**Post, Jerry Benjamin** 1937-    [SFL]
*American author*
* Post, J. B.

**Post, Maveric**
*See* Mapes, Victor

**Post, Mortimer**
*See* Blair, Walter

**Post, Sarah L.** [FFF, PA]
*American writer*
* Graham, Rosa

**Post-Nikov, Feodor A.** 1872- ?
[NAA]
*Russian-born editor and author*
* Post, F. A.

**Posta, Adrienne**
See Poster, Adrienne

**Poste, Denver**
See Cox, Charles Roy

**Postelnich, Joana**
See Banu, Eugenia

**Poster, Adrienne** 1948-   [FC]
*British actress*
* Posta, Adrienne

**Postime, Mr.**
See Mitchell, Billy

**Postl, Karl Anton** 1793-1864
[WBD]
*Moravian-born author*
* Sealsfield, Charles

**Postma, Magdalena Jacomina**
1908-   [CA]
*South African author*
* Postma, Minnie

**Postma, Minnie**
See Postma, Magdalena Jacomina

**[The] Postman Poet**
See Capern, Edward

**Poston, Doc**
See Poston, Joseph E.

**Poston, Joseph E.** 1895?-1942
[WWJ]
*American jazz musician*
* Poston, Doc

**Pot, Philippe** 1428-1494
[FF, FFF, HN]
*French prime minister*
* Cicero's Mouth

**Pothecary, Raymond** 20th c.
[MBF]
*British author*
* Ford, Quinton

**Potier, Augustin** 17th c.   [SN]
*Bishop of Beauvais*
* [The] Mitred Ass

**Potiphar**
See Curtis, George William

**Potiphar** [joint pseudonym with J. F.
Marrack]
See Hern, [George] Anthony

**Potiphar** [joint pseudonym with
(George) Anthony Hern]
See Marrack, J. F.

**Potocnik, Captain** 20th c.   [SFP]
*Author*
* Noordung, Hermann

**Potoco [Large Pot]**
See Villegas, Jose

**Potokinova, Bohd. J.**
See Botto, Jan

**Pott, Lefty**
See Pott, Nelson Adolph

**Pott, Leon Vince Philip** 1896-1913
[BMH]
*British comedian*
* Fragson, Harry

**Pott, Nellie**
See Pott, Nelson Adolph

**Pott, Nelson Adolph** 1899-1963
[BE]
*American baseball player*
* Pott, Lefty
* Pott, Nellie

**[The] Pottawatomie Giant**
See Willard, Jess

**Potter, A. K.**   [PA]
*Author*
* Six

**Potter, Barnabas [or Barnaby?]**
1578-1642   [SN]
*British prelate*
* [The] Puritanical Bishop

**Potter, Faith**
See Toperoff, Sam

**Potter, George William, Jr.** 1930-
[AW, CA, CC]
*American author*
* Withers, E. L.

**Potter, H. C.**
See Potter, Henry C.

**Potter, Henry C.** 1904-   [BEW]
*American director and producer*
* Potter, H. C.

**Potter, Henry Glasford** 19th c.
[SAT]
*British author*
* Democritus

**Potter, Hilda** 1888-   [THR]
*British actress*
* Bruce-Potter, Hilda

**Potter, Margaret [Newman]** 1926-
[AW, CA, SAT]
*British author*
* Betteridge, Anne
* Melville, Anne
* Newman, Margaret

**Potter, Mary** 1900-   [ART]
*British painter*
* M. P.

**Potter, Nettie**
See Moore, Monette

**Potter, Phillip A.** 20th c.   [IBW]
*American clergyman*
* [The] Black Pope

**Potter, Richard** 1783-1835   [IBW]
*American magician*
* [The] Black Houdini
* [The] Man Salamander
* Professor of Legerdemain

**Potter, Robert** 20th c.   [ESF, SFL]
*Australian author and clergyman*
* Easterley, Robert and
  Wilbraham, John

**Potter, Robert H. [Bob]** 1902-   [BE]
*American baseball player*
* Potter, Squire

**Potter, Squire**
See Potter, Robert H. [Bob]

**Potthoff, Margot Maria** 20th c.
[IAW]
*German author*
* Lundberg, Kai

**Pottios, Mike**
See Pottios, Myron J.

**Pottios, Myron J.** 1939-   [FB]
*American football player*
* Pottios, Mike

**Pottle, F. A.**
See Pottle, Frederick Albert

**Pottle, Frederick Albert** 1897-
[LC]
*American educator and author*
* Pottle, F. A.

**Pottle, Gilbert Emery Bensley**
1875?-1945   [BEW, F2, FC]
*American actor and playwright*
* Emery, Gilbert

**Pottle, Juliet Wilbor Tompkins** 1871-
?   [NAA]
*American author*
* Tompkins, Juliet Wilbor

**Potts, Arthur** 20th c.   [WECO]
*British cartoonist*
* Spot

**Potts, Thomas Richard** 1915-1944
[SC]
*American actor*
* Fiske, Richard

**Potvin, Damase** 1879- ?   [NAA]
*Canadian journalist and author*
* Sainte Foy

**Potvin, Jean Rene** 1949-   [SMG]
*Canadian-born hockey player*
* Potvin, Potsy

**Potvin, Potsy**
See Potvin, Jean Rene

**Pou, Genevieve [Long]** 1919-
[CC, WW]
*Author*
* Holden, Genevieve

**Pouch, Captain**
See Reynolds, John

**Pougatcheff, Emilian** 1726-1775
[HN]
*Russian rebel leader*
* [The] Pretender

**[The] Poughkeepsie Seer**
See Davis, Andrew Jackson

**Pougin, Arthur**
See Paroisse-Pougin,
Francois-Auguste Arthur

**Pougny, Jean**
See Puni, Ivan Albert

**Poulton, A. G.**
See Plews, Arthur Gordon Lane

**Poulton, Harry** 20th c.   [BBH]
*Boxer*
* Poulton, Kid

**Poulton, Kid**
See Poulton, Harry

**Poulton, Ronald William**
1889-1915   [OCS]
*British rugby player*
* Poulton Palmer, Ronald William

**Poulton Palmer, Ronald William**
See Poulton, Ronald William

**Pouly**
See Boudin y Martin, Pierre

**Pound Cake McMullen**
See McMullen, Kenneth Lee

**Pound, Ezra [Loomis]** 1885-1972
[CA, CAA]
*American poet and critic*
* Atheling, William
* E. P.
* Venison, Alfred

**Pound, Reginald** 20th c.   [WWL]
*British writer*
* Renthwaite, Robert

**Pound, Singleton**
See Merland, Oliver

**Pountney, Monica Brailey** 20th c.
[ART]
*British painter*
* Mon

**Poupard, Henri-Pierre** 1901-
[BBD, HDM]
*French composer*
* Sauguet, Henri

**Pournelle, Jerry [Eugene]** 1933-
[CA, ESF, SFP]
*American author*
* Curtis, Wade

**Poussin, Gaspar**
See Dughet, Gaspar

**Poussin, Nicolas** 1594-1665
[HN, SN]
*French painter*
* [The] Intellectual Artist

**[The] Poussin of England**
See Cooper, Richard

**[The] Poussin of France**
See Dughet, Gaspar

**Pouw, Pietro** 1564-1611   [PA]
*Author*
* Pavius

**Poveda y Armenteros, Francisco**
1796-1879   [CW]
*Cuban poet and playwright*
* [El] Trovador Cubano

**Powder Face Eckert**
See Eckert, Tom

**Powder Horn Like**
See Like, Jim

**Powe, Bruce** 1925-   [CA]
*Canadian author*
* Portal, Ellis

**Powel**
See Price, Charles

**Powell, Adam Clayton, III** 1946-
[IBW]
*American radio and television
journalist*
* Powell, Skipper

**Powell, Albert** 1900-   [BF]
*British actor*
* Powell, Sandy

**Powell, Altivia Edwards** 1924-
[IBW]
*American singer and columnist*
* [The] Left Bank Mother
  Confessor
* Powell, Buttercup

**Powell, Big Red**
See Powell, Edward D.

**Powell, Boche**
*See* Powell, Edward D.

**Powell, Boog**
*See* Powell, John Wesley

**Powell, Brian** 1934-    [CA]
*Canadian educator and author*
* Brian

**Powell, Bud**
*See* Powell, Earl

**Powell, Buttercup**
*See* Powell, Altivia Edwards

**Powell, Clive** 20th c.    [LRR]
*British jazz musician*
* Fame, Georgie

**Powell, Earl** 1924-1966
[DAM, EJ, PMJ]
*American jazz musician*
* Powell, Bud

**Powell, Edward D.** 1912-    [MK]
*American baseball player*
* Powell, Big Red
* Powell, Boche

**Powell, Eric Frederick William**
1899-    [WD]
*British author*
* Rusholm, Peter

**Powell, Everard Stephen, Sr.** 1907-
[DAM, NP, PMJ]
*American jazz musician*
* Karweem, Musheed
* Powell, Rudy
* Powell, Tooty

**Powell, Frank**
*See* Ingraham, Prentiss

**Powell, Geoffrey Stewart** 1914-
[CA]
*British army officer and author*
* Angus, Tom

**Powell, Glennon** 1947-    [SMG]
*American football team staff
member*
* Powell, Silky

**Powell, Gordon** 1922-    [EJ, PMJ]
*American jazz musician*
* Powell, Specs

**Powell, H. W.**    [PA]
*Author*
* M. E. M.

**Powell, Jane**
*See* Burce, Suzanne

**Powell, Jimmy** 20th c.    [NP]
*American jazz musician*
* Powell, Neat

**Powell, Jody**
*See* Powell, Joseph Lester, Jr.

**Powell, Joe** 1952-    [IBW]
*American dancer*
* Powell, Lovey Joe

**Powell, John Wesley** 1941-
[IPA, PB, SMG]
*American baseball player*
* Powell, Boog

**Powell, Joseph Lester, Jr.** 1944?-
[B10]
*Administrative aide to American
president Jimmy Carter*
* Powell, Jody

**Powell, Lee**
*See* Lee, Alfred E.

**Powell, Lovey Joe**
*See* Powell, Joe

**Powell, Mary**
*See* Manning, Anne

**Powell, Melvin** 20th c.    [OBW]
*American baseball player*
* Powell, Put

**Powell, Mousie**
*See* Powell, Walter

**Powell, Neat**
*See* Powell, Jimmy

**Powell, Neil**
*See* Innes, Brian

**Powell, Ollie** 1890?-1928    [WWJ]
*American jazz musician*
* Powers, Ollie

**Powell, Peewee**
*See* Powell, William Ernest

**Powell, Peter** 1928-
*American clergyman*
* Powell, Stone Forehead

**Powell, Philip Wayne** 1913-    [CA]
*American historian and author*
* Wayne, Philip

**Powell, Piggie**
*See* Powell, William Ernest

**Powell, Pigmeat**
*See* Powell, William Ernest

**Powell, Put**
*See* Powell, Melvin

**Powell, Rabbit**
*See* Powell, Raymond Reath

**Powell, Raymond Reath**
1888-1962    [BE]
*American baseball player*
* Powell, Rabbit

**Powell, Richard [Pitts]** 1908-    [CA]
*American author*
* Kirk, Jeremy

**Powell, Richard Stillman**
*See* Barbour, Ralph Henry

**Powell, Ruben** 20th c.    [BBH]
*American archer*
* Flight Archer, Mr.

**Powell, Rudy**
*See* Powell, Everard Stephen, Sr.

**Powell, Sandy**
*See* Powell, Albert

**Powell, Silky**
*See* Powell, Glennon

**Powell, Skipper**
*See* Powell, Adam Clayton, III

**Powell, Sonny**
*See* Bester, Alfred

**Powell, Specs**
*See* Powell, Gordon

**Powell, Stone Forehead**
*See* Powell, Peter

**Powell, Talmage** 1920-    [CA, WW]
*American author*
* McCready, Jack
* Talmage, Anne

**Powell, Teddy**
*See* Paolella, Alfred

**Powell, Tiny**
*See* Powell, Vance

**Powell, Tooty**
*See* Powell, Everard Stephen, Sr.

**Powell, Vance** 1928?-    [BWW]
*American singer*
* Powell, Tiny

**Powell, Walter** 20th c.    [BEW]
*American orchestra leader*
* Powell, Mousie

**Powell, Wee Willie**
*See* Powell, William Ernest

**Powell, William** ?-1803    [HN]
*British eccentric*
* [The] Highgate Prophet

**Powell, William Ernest** 1903-
[MK]
*American baseball player*
* Powell, Peewee
* Powell, Piggie
* Powell, Pigmeat
* Powell, Wee Willie

**Powell-Smith, Vincent [Walter
Francis]** 1939-    [AW, CA, WD]
*British author, reviewer, critic*
* Elphinstone, Francis
* Justiciar
* Orbis, Victor
* Santa Maria

**Power, Arthur**
*See* Dudden, Arthur P[ower]

**Power, Cecil**
*See* Allen, [Charles] Grant
[Blairfindie]

**Power, Marguerite A.** 19th c.    [PA]
*Author*
* Honoria

**Power, Mary** 1881-1957    [CAT]
*Canadian-born author*
* Maura, [Sister]

**Power, Nelson**
*See* Judd, Alfred

**Power, Norman S[andiford]** 1916-
[CA]
*British clergyman and author*
* Kratos

**Power, Paul**
*See* Vestergard, Luther

**Power, Rex**
*See* Langley, Roger

**Power, Richard** 1928-1970    [CAP]
*Irish author*
* De Paor, Risteard

**Power, Samuel Browning**    [PA]
*Author*
* S. B. P.

**Power, Susan C. Dunning** 19th c.
[FFF]
*American author*
* Dare, Shirley

**Power-Ross, Robert W.**
*See* Ross, Robert W.

**Power-Waters, Brian** 1922-    [CA]
*British-born American airline pilot
and author*
* Captain X

**Powers, Anne**
*See* Schwartz, Anne Powers

**Powers, Barbara Hudson**
*See* Dudley, Barbara Hudson

**Powers, C. F., Jr.** 1923-    [ITA]
*American film executive*
* Powers, Mike

**Powers, Chester** 20th c.    [LRR]
*American singer*
* Valenti, Dino

**Powers, Dick**
*See* Sellers, Connie Leslie, Jr.

**Powers, Ellis Foree** 1906-    [BE]
*American baseball player*
* Powers, Mike

**Powers, Francis Gary** 1929-    [EE]
*American intelligence agent*
* Palmer

**Powers, George**
*See* Infield, Glenn [Berton]

**Powers, Grandmother**
*See* Powers, Philip J.

**Powers, Ike**
*See* Powers, John Lloyd

**Powers, J. F.**
*See* Powers, James Farl

**Powers, J. L.**
*See* Glasby, John [Stephen]

**Powers, James Farl** 1917-    [WYA]
*American author*
* Powers, J. F.

**Powers, Jessica** 20th c.    [CAT]
*American poet*
* Miriam of the Holy Spirit,
[Sister]

**Powers, Jet**
*See* Smith, James Marcus

**Powers, John A.** 1923?-1980
*American air force officer*
* Powers, Shorty
* [The] Voice of Mission Control
* [The] Voice of the Astronauts

**Powers, John J[ames]** 1945-    [CA]
*American author*
* Powers, John R.

**Powers, John Lloyd** 1906-1968
[BE]
*American baseball player*
* Powers, Ike

**Powers, John R.**
*See* Powers, John J[ames]

**Powers, Johnny**
*See* De Pow, Johnny

**Powers, Julia**
*See* Cox, Ida

**Powers, Julius**
*See* Cox, Ida

**Powers, M. L.**
*See* Tubb, Edwin Charles

**Powers, Mala**
*See* Powers, Mary Ellen

**Powers, Margaret**
*See* Heal, Edith

**Powers, Mary Ellen** 1931-
[FC, ITA, SW]
*American actress*
* Powers, Mala

**Powers, Mike**
See Powers, C. F., Jr.

**Powers, Mike**
See Powers, Ellis Foree

**Powers, Mrs. William** [FFF]
*Entertainer*
* Booth, Rachel

**Powers, Ollie**
See Powell, Ollie

**Powers, Philip J.** 1853-1914 [BE]
*American baseball player*
* Powers, Grandmother

**Powers, Richard**
See Duryea, George

**Powers, Richard M.** 1921- [IBY]
*American author, illustrator, painter*
* Gorman, Terry

**Powers, S. Rugeley** [PA]
*Author*
* S. R. P.

**Powers, Shorty**
See Powers, John A.

**Powers, Stefanie**
See Paul, Stefanie [or Taffy?]

**Powerscourt, Sheila**
See Wingfield, Sheila [Viscountess Powerscourt]

**Powhatan**
See Wa-hun-sen-a-cawh [or Wahunsonacook]

**Powis, Carl Edgar** 1928- [BE]
*American baseball player*
* Powis, Jug

**Powis, Jug**
See Powis, Carl Edgar

**Powles, Harry** ?-1888 [BMH]
*British comic singer*
* Ball, Harry
* [The] Tramp Musician

**Powles, Matilda Alice** 1864-1952
[BMH, THR]
*British theatrical performer*
* [The] Great Little Tilley
* [The] London Idol
* [The] Pocket Sims Reeves
* Tilley, Vesta

**Powley, Faith Hinckley** 1891-
[NAA]
*American author*
* Jayne, Faith

**Powley, Florence Mary Pomeroy**
1892- [CAP]
*British poet*
* Pomeroy, Florence Mary

**Powley, Jean [Makins]** 20th c.
[WW]
*Author*
* Cardwell, Ann

**Powys, J. C.**
See Powys, John Cowper

**Powys, John Cowper** 1872-1963
[LC]
*British author*
* Powys, J. C.

**Powys, Stephen**
See De Lanty, Virginia

**Powys, T. F.**
See Powys, Theodore Francis

**Powys, Theodore Francis**
1875-1953 [LC, TC]
*British author*
* Powys, T. F.

**Poy**
See Fearon, Percy Arthur

**Poynder, John** 1779-1849 [PA]
*Author*
* [A] Layman

**Poynter, James William** 1885-
[WWL]
*British author*
* Indicator

**Poznanski, Alfred** 1883?-1934
[BEW]
*Polish-born playwright*
* Savoir, Alfred

**Pozo, Chano**
See Pozo y Gonzales, Luciano

**Pozo, Chino**
See Pozo, Francisco

**Pozo, Francisco** 1915- [EJ]
*Cuban-born jazz musician*
* Pozo, Chino

**Pozo y Gonzales, Luciano**
1915-1948 [EJ]
*Cuban-born jazz musician*
* Pozo, Chano

**Prabhupada, Bhaktivedanta** 1896-
[CA]
*Indian spiritual teacher and author*
* Bhaktivedanta, A. C.
* Bhaktivedanta Swami, A. C.

**Prada, Benny Kid**
See Prada, Bernardo

**Prada, Bernardo** 1950- [RBE]
*Colombian boxer*
* Prada, Benny Kid

**Pradas, Virginia**
See Pacis, Vicente Albano

**Praderito [Little Meadow]**
See Diaz Del Busto, Severiano

**Prado, [Domase] Perez** 1922-
[EPM, IBW]
*Cuban-born bandleader, arranger, composer*
* [The] Mambo King
* [El] Rey del Mambo [The King of Mambo]

**Praeceptor Germaniae**
See Schwarzert, Philipp

**Praeceptor Humilis**
See West, Luther Shirley

**Praed, Winthrop Mackworth**
1802-1839 [DEL, FFF]
*British poet*
* Courtenay, Peregrine
* Joyeuse, Vyvian

**Praestantissimus Mathematicus**
See Dee, John

**Praetorius, Michael**
See Schultheiss [or Schulz], Michael

**Pragnell, Festus** 1905- [ESF]
*British author*
* Parnell, Francis

**Prairie Bird**
See Willenan, M. W.

**Prairie Dog Finley**
See Finley, Larry

**[The] Prairie Star**
See Bedra, Julie Marlene

**Prajadhipok** 1893-1941 [WBD]
*King of Siam*
* Rama VII

**Prance, June E[lizabeth]** 1929-
[CA]
*British-born author and illustrator*
* Shaw, Elizabeth

**Prateolus**
See Duprean, Gabriel

**Prather, Richard S[cott]** 1921-
[CA, CC, WW]
*American author*
* Knight, David
* Ring, Douglas

**Pratt, Agnes Rothery** 20th c.
[NAA]
*American author*
* Edwards, Agnes
* Rothery, Agnes Edwards

**Pratt, Al[bert G.]** 1847-1937 [BE]
*American baseball manager*
* Uncle Al

**Pratt, Babe**
See Pratt, Walter

**Pratt, Cornelia Atwood**
See Comer, Cornelia Atwood

**Pratt, D. E. H.**
See Pratt, Derrick Edward Henry

**Pratt, Daniel** 1809-1887
[DNNF, DNNS, FFF]
*American eccentric*
* [The] Great American Traveller

**Pratt, Del**
See Pratt, Derrill Burnham

**Pratt, Dennis** 1897-1971
[EMT, FC, PMJ]
*British-born actor and singer*
* King, Dennis

**Pratt, Derrick Edward Henry**
1895- [ART]
*British painter*
* Pratt, D. E. H.

**Pratt, Derrill Burnham** 1888- [BE]
*American baseball player*
* Pratt, Del

**Pratt, E. J.**
See Pratt, Edwin John

**Pratt, Edwin John** 1883-1964 [LC]
*Canadian educator and poet*
* Pratt, E. J.

**Pratt, Eleanor Blake [Atkinson]**
1899- [NAA, WW]
*American author*
* Atkinson, Eleanor Blake
* Blake, E. A.
* Blake, Eleanor

**Pratt, F. Alcott** 19th c. [FFF]
*American author*
* Demijohn

**Pratt, [Murray] Fletcher**
1897-1956 [ESF, SF, WGT]
*American author*
* Fletcher, George U.
* Lester, Irvin
* Ruby, B. F.

**Pratt, Francis Bruce [Frank]** 1897-
[BE]
*American baseball player*
* Pratt, Truckhorse

**Pratt, Inga Stephens** 20th c. [SFP]
*Author*
* Stephens, I. M.

**Pratt, J. Loring** [PA]
*Author*
* L. I.

**Pratt, John** 1931- [AW, CA]
*British naval officer and author*
* Winton, John

**Pratt, L. Maria** [PA]
*Author*
* Loring, Laurie

**Pratt, Larry**
See Pratt, Lester John

**Pratt, Leonard E.** 20th c. [MBF]
*British author and editor*
* Smith, Fenton

**Pratt, Lester John** 1887-1969 [BE]
*American baseball player*
* Pratt, Larry

**Pratt, Rhona Olive** 1903- [IAW]
*Welsh-born author*
* O'Harris, Pixie

**Pratt, Samuel Jackson** 1749-1814
[DEL, PA]
*British author and poet*
* Melmoth, Courtney

**Pratt, Theodore** 1901-
[ANT, CC, TC1]
*American author*
* Brace, Timothy

**Pratt, Truckhorse**
See Pratt, Francis Bruce [Frank]

**Pratt, Walter** 1916-
[CEI, FHE, HK]
*Canadian-born hockey player*
* Pratt, Babe

**Pratt, William Henry** 1887-1969
[BDF, BEW, F1]
*British actor*
* Karloff, Boris

**Pratza, Nicholas** 1904?-1973 [F2]
*Rumanian-born actor*
* Stuart, Nick

**Pravda, Frantisek**
See Hlinka, Vojtech

**[The] Praying Millionaire**
See Johnson, Wallace

**[The] Praying Puncher**
See Cream, Arnold Raymond

**Praz, Mario** 1896- [CA]
*Italian author, editor, translator*
* Alcibiade
* Di Guisa, Giano

**[The] Preacher**
See Grande, Juan

**[The] Preacher President**
See Garfield, James Abram

**[The] Preaching Bishop**
See Matthew, Toby

**Prebble, John Edward Curtis** 1915-
[CA]
*British author*
* Curtis, John

**Prebble, Marjorie Mary Curtis**
1912-   [CA]
*British author*
* Compton, Ann
* Conway, Denise
* Curtis, Marjorie

**Preece, T. Evan**   [HN, RH]
*Prophet of South Wales*
* Shipton, Mother

**Preedy, George**
*See* Long, Gabrielle Margaret Vere
[Campbell]

**Preibisch, Mel[vin Adolphus]** 1914-
[BE]
*American baseball player*
* Preibisch, Primo

**Preibisch, Primo**
*See* Preibisch, Mel[vin Adolphus]

**[Le] Premier Grenadier de France**
*See* La Tour [or Latour]
d'Auvergne, Theophile Malo Corret
de

**[Le] Premier Grenadier de la
Republique**
*See* La Tour [or Latour]
d'Auvergne, Theophile Malo Corret
de

**Premont, [Brother] Jeremy**
*See* Willett, [Brother] Franciscus

**Prenaier, Paul**
*See* Sperry, Reginald

**Prendergast** 12th c.   [HN]
*Protector of MacGallapatrick of
Ossory*
* [The] Faithful Norman

**Prendergast, Paul**
*See* Jerrold, Douglas William

**Prentice, Cecil** 1903-1971   [BMH]
*British entertainer*
* Granada, Cecil

**Prentice, Charles W.** 1898-   [THR]
*Scottish-born composer*
* Prentice, Jock

**Prentice, Fry**
*See* Prentice, Jo Ann

**Prentice, Jo Ann** 1933-   [GF]
*American golfer*
* Prentice, Fry

**Prentice, Jock**
*See* Prentice, Charles W.

**Prentiss, George Pepper**
*See* Wilson, George Pepper

**Prentiss, Kitten**
*See* Wilson, George Pepper

**Prentiss, Mrs.** 19th c.   [PA]
*Author*
* Little Susy

**Prentiss, Paula**
*See* Ragusa, Paula

**Presberg, Miriam Goldstein** 1919-
[CA, WD]
*American author*
* Gilbert, Miriam

**Presbyter**
*See* Turner, Samuel Hurlburt

**Presbyter, Ignotus**
*See* Van Allen, William Harman

**[The] Presbyterian Paul-Pry**
*See* Edwards, Thomas

**[The] Presbyterian Ulysses**
*See* Campbell, Archibald

**Prescot, Julian**
*See* Budd, John

**Prescott, Bobby**
*See* Prescott, George Bertrand

**Prescott, Caleb**
*See* Bingley, David Ernest

**Prescott, George Bertrand** 1931-
[BE]
*Panamanian-born baseball player*
* Prescott, Bobby

**Prescott, H. F. M.**
*See* Prescott, Hilda Frances
Margaret

**Prescott, Hilda Frances Margaret**
1896-1972   [LC]
*British author*
* Prescott, H. F. M.

**Prescott, Marie**
*See* Pertzel, Mrs.

**[The] Preserver**
*See* Ptolemy I

**[The] Preserver of His Country**
*See* Lorraine, Francois de

**President**
*See* Sanden, Thomas

**President Bob**
*See* Spencer, Robert [Second Earl
of Sunderland]

**President De Facto**
*See* Hayes, Rutherford Birchard

**[Le] President Je Dis Ca**
*See* Charton, Louis

**[The] President Maker**
*See* Clay, Henry

**Presko, Joseph Edward** 1928-   [BE]
*American baseball player*
* Presko, Little Joe

**Presko, Little Joe**
*See* Presko, Joseph Edward

**Presland, John**
*See* Bendit, Gladys Williams

**Presle, Micheline**
*See* Chassagne, Micheline

**Presley, Elvis Aaron** 1935-1977
[FCW, NN, RO1]
*American singer*
* Burrows, [Colonel] Jon [FBI code
name]
* Elvis the Pelvis
* [The] Father of Rock 'n Roll
* [The] Hillbilly Cat
* [The] King
* [The] King of Rock 'n Roll
* Swivel Hips

**Press, Red**
*See* Press, Seymour

**Press, Seymour** 1924-   [EJ]
*American jazz musician*
* Press, Red

**Presser, Charles** 20th c.   [SG]
*Boxer*
* Burke, Sailor

**Presser, [Gerrit] Jacob** 1899-1970
[CAP]
*Dutch historian and author*
* Drukker, J.
* Van Dam, J.
* Van Wageningen, J.

**Pressler, Franz** 1927-   [EJ]
*Austrian jazz musician*
* Fatty George

**Pressley, Hilda**
*See* Nickson, Hilda

**Pressnell, Forest Charles** 1906-
[BE]
*American baseball player*
* Pressnell, Tot

**Pressnell, Tot**
*See* Pressnell, Forest Charles

**Pressoir, Carlo**
*See* Pressoir, Charles Fernand

**Pressoir, Charles Fernand**
1910-1973   [CW]
*French-born poet and author*
* Pressoir, Carlo

**Prest, T.**   [PA]
*Author*
* Angelina

**Prestel, Jim** 20th c.
*American football player*
* Prestel, Primo

**Prestel, Primo**
*See* Prestel, Jim

**Prester John**
*See* Togrul Wang Khan

**Presti, Tony**
*See* Vander Linden, Anthony

**Prestigiocomo, Pasquale** 20th c.
[BLB]
*American underworld figure*
* Presto, Pasquale

**Prestnia, Frank** 20th c.   [RO2]
*American musician*
* Prestnia, Rocco

**Prestnia, Rocco**
*See* Prestnia, Frank

**Presto**
*See* Swift, Jonathan

**Presto, Pasquale**
*See* Prestigiocomo, Pasquale

**Preston, Arthur**
*See* Hankins, Arthur Preston

**Preston, Edward**
*See* Guess, Edward Preston

**Preston, Frank** 1860?-1939   [BEW]
*American producer and press
representative*
* Weadon, Percy

**Preston, Hilary**
*See* Nickson, Hilda

**Preston, Hugh**
*See* Wilson, Derek Alan

**Preston, James** 1913-   [CAP]
*Australian author*
* James, Ronald

**Preston, Mrs. M. J.**   [PA]
*Author*
* Junkin, Margaret

**Preston, Newt**
*See* Preston, Ray

**Preston, Paul**
*See* Cooper, Alfred Benjamin

**Preston, Paul**
*See* Morris, Charles Smith

**Preston, Paul**
*See* Picton, Thomas

**Preston, Ray** 1954-   [SMG]
*American football player*
* Preston, Newt

**Preston, Richard**
*See* Lindsay, Jack

**Preston, Robert**
*See* Meservey, Robert Preston

**Preston, Roger**   [PA]
*Author*
* Widdrington, Roger

**Preston, Terry**
*See* Husky, Ferlin

**Preston, Thomas Austin** 1929?-
[B10]
*American gambler*
* Amarillo Slim

**Preston, Walford**
*See* Townley, Houghton

**Preston-Muddock, Joyce Emmerson**
1843-1934   [EMD, WW]
*British journalist and author*
* Donovan, Dick

**Prestopnik, Irving Henry**
1912-1949   [NOJ, PMJ, WWJ]
*American jazz musician*
* Fazola, Faz
* Fazola, Irving Henry

**[Il] Prete Genovese**
*See* Strozzi [or Strozza], Bernardo

**[The] Pretender**
*See* Cleveland, [Stephen] Grover

**[The] Pretender**
*See* Otrepieff, Gregory

**[The] Pretender**
*See* Pougatcheff, Emilian

**Preti, Mattia** 1613-1699   [WBD]
*Italian painter*
* [Il] Calabrese
* [Il] Cavaliere Calabrese

**Pretorius, Hertha**
*See* Kouts, Hertha Pretorius

**Pretty Boy**
*See* Covay, Don

**Pretty Boy Floyd**
*See* Floyd, Charles Arthur

**Pretty, Violet** 1931?-   [FC, SW]
*British actress*
* Heywood, Anne

**Pretzel, Karl**
*See* Harris, Charles H.

**Preuss, Phyllis** 1939-
[BWG, EG, GF]
*American golfer*
* Preuss, Tish

**Preuss, Tish**
*See* Preuss, Phyllis

**Previn, Andre**
*See* Previn, George

**Previn, George** 1929- [JL]
*American conductor*
* Previn, Andre

**Prevost, Alain** 1930?-1971 [CA]
*French journalist and author*
* D'Hugues, Varnac

**Prevost, Francis**
*See* Prevost Battersby, H. F.

**Prevost, Madame Henri** [FFF]
*Entertainer*
* Ponsin, Mlle.

**Prevost, Marcel**
*See* Marcel, Eugene

**Prevost, Marie**
*See* Dunn, Marie Bickford

**Prevost Battersby, H. F.** 20th c.
[WWL]
*British author*
* Prevost, Francis

**Prez Kenneth**
*See* Kidd, Kenneth

**Prezihov, Voranc**
*See* Kuhar, Lovro

**Priam**
*See* Collins, C. J.

**Price, Benton**
*See* Wilson, Roger C.

**Price, Beverley Joan** 1931-
[AW, WD]
*New Zealand editor and author*
* Randell, Beverley

**Price, Charles** 18th c. [HN]
*Banknote forger*
* Bond
* Brank
* Old Patch
* Parks
* Powel
* Schutz
* Wigmore
* Wilmott

**Price, Clarence** 1889-1968 [BB]
*American basketball coach*
* Price, Nibs

**Price, Dennis**
*See* Rose-Price, Dennistoun John
Franklyn

**Price, Edgar Hoffman** 1898-
[HFF, WGT]
*American author*
* Daly, Hamlin

**Price, Emerson Field** 1902- [NAA]
*American writer*
* Hanley, Hugh

**Price, Ernest Cutler** 1891-1942
[BX, RBE]
*American boxer*
* Dillon, Jack
* Jack the Giant Killer

**Price, Evadne**
*See* Smith, Helen Zenna

**Price, Frank J.** 1860- ? [ALY]
*American author and editor*
* Conway, Faulkner

**Price, George [Henry]** 1910- ?
[CAP]
*Welsh-born clergyman, educator,
author*
* Price, Rhys

**Price, Jennifer**
*See* Hoover, Helen [Drusilla
Blackburn]

**Price, Jimmie**
*See* White, John I[rwin]

**Price, Joseph Charles** 1854-1893?
[IBW]
*American clergyman and college
administrator*
* [The] Lion of the Lyceum

**Price, Joseph Preston [Joe]**
1897-1961 [BE]
*American baseball player*
* Price, Lumber

**Price, Kate**
*See* Duffy, Kate

**Price, Kenny** 1931- [ECM]
*American country-western performer*
* [The] Round Mound of Sound

**Price, Leontyne**
*See* Price, Mary Violet Leontine

**Price, Lucie Locke** 1904-
[CA, SAT, WD]
*American artist and poet*
* Locke, Lucie

**Price, Lumber**
*See* Price, Joseph Preston [Joe]

**Price, Mary Violet Leontine** 1927-
[IPA]
*American opera singer*
* Price, Leontyne

**Price, Mrs. E. H.** [FFF]
*Entertainer*
* Davenport, Fanny

**Price, Nancy**
*See* Maude, Lillian Nancy

**Price, Nibs**
*See* Price, Clarence

**[The] Price of Roman Poets**
*See* Vergilius Maro, Publius

**Price, Olive** 1903- [CA, SAT]
*American author and playwright*
* Cherryholmes, Anne
* West, Barbara

**Price, Pat** 1955- [SMG]
*Canadian-born hockey player*
* Price, Pricey

**Price, Pricey**
*See* Price, Pat

**Price, Ray Noble** 1926- [CWG]
*American country-western performer*
* [The] Cherokee Cowboy

**Price, Rhys**
*See* Price, George [Henry]

**Price, Robert** 1900- [CA]
*American educator, author, poet*
* Drew, Morgan

**Price, Virginia Williams** 20th c.
[NAA]
*American writer*
* Pride, Ginia

**Price, Vito**
*See* Pizzo, Vito

**Price, Walter**
*See* Wilson, Roger C.

**Price, Walter Travis** 1917-
[BWW, NBB]
*American singer*
* Big Walter
* [The] Thunderbird from Coast to
Coast

**Price, William Raleigh** 1875- ?
[NAA]
*American educator and author*
* Bonner, Raleigh

**Price-Mars, Jean** 1876-1969 [CW]
*Haitian author*
* Mars, Jean Price

**Priceman, James**
*See* Kirkland, Winifred
Margaretta

**Prichard, Hesketh Vernon Hesketh**
1876-1922 [WW]
*British author*
* Heron, H.

**Prichard, K.**
*See* Prichard, Kate O'Brien
Hesketh

**Prichard, Kate O'Brien Hesketh** 20th
c. [EMD, WW]
*Author*
* Heron, E.
* Prichard, K.

**Prichard, Katharine Susannah**
*See* Throssell, Katharine Susannah
Prichard

**Priddy, Al**
*See* Brown, Frederick Kenyon

**Pride, Charley** 1938- [FCW, RO2]
*American country-western performer*
* Pride, Country Charley

**Pride, Country Charley**
*See* Pride, Charley

**Pride, Ginia**
*See* Price, Virginia Williams

**[The] Pride of Havana**
*See* Luque, Adolfo

**[The] Pride of Pontypridd**
*See* Thomas, Frederick Hall

**[The] Pride of the Ghetto**
*See* Bernstein, Joe

**[The] Pride of the Phillipines**
*See* Coleman, James L.

**[The] Pride of the West Virginia Hills**
*See* Martin, Nancy

**[The] Pride of the Yankees**
*See* Gehrig, [Henry] Lou[is]

**Pride, Thomas** ?-1658 [SN]
*British parliamentary officer*
* Pride, Yeasty
* [The] Purging Colonel

**Pride, Yeasty**
*See* Pride, Thomas

**Pridgeon, Alan Paul** 1954- [DC]
*British cricketer*
* Pridgeon, Pridge

**Pridgeon, Pridge**
*See* Pridgeon, Alan Paul

**Pridvorov, Yefim** 1883- [CD]
*Russian poet*
* Bedny, Demyan

**[The] Priest**
*See* Konrad

**[The] Priest**
*See* Lamprecht

**Priest Hater**
*See* Eric II

**Priest, John**
*See* Kotschnig, John Walter

**Priest, Martin**
*See* Penry, John

**[The] Priest of Nature**
*See* Newton, [Sir] Isaac

**[A] Priest of the English Church**
*See* Smith, Clement Ogle

**Priestley, Clive Ryland** 1892-
[WW]
*Author*
* Ryland, Clive

**Priestley, J. B.**
*See* Priestley, John Boynton

**Priestley, John Boynton** 1894-
[BEW, CA, IPA]
*British playwright and author*
* Goldsmith, Peter
* Priestley, J. B.

**Priestley, Joseph** 1733-1804 [SN]
*British clergyman and chemist*
* Priestley, Proteus

**Priestley, L. A. M.**
*See* McCracken, Elizabeth A. M.

**Priestley, Leslie Avoca** 1908-
[IWM]
*British musician*
* Carew, Leslie

**Priestley, Proteus**
*See* Priestley, Joseph

**Priestley, Robert**
*See* Wiggins, David

**Prieto Barrera, Diego** 1856-1918
[GS]
*Spanish bullfighter*
* Cuatro Dedos [Four Fingers]

**Prieur de la Cote-d'Or**
*See* Prieur-Duvernois, Claude
Antoine

**[Le] Prieur de Vendome**
*See* Vendome, Philippe de

**Prieur-Duvernois, Claude Antoine**
1763-1827 [WBD]
*French scholar and politician*
* Prieur de la Cote-d'Or

**Priggins, Peter**
*See* Hewlett, J.

**Prignani, Bartolommeo** 1318-1389
[WBD]
*Pope*
* Urban VI

**Priley, Margaret Hubbard** 1909-
[CA]
*American author*
* Hubbard, Margaret Ann

**Prim, Pop**
*See* Prim, Raymond Lee

**Prim, Raymond Lee** 1906- [BE]
*American baseball player*
* Prim, Pop

**Prime, C. T.**
See   Prime, Cecil Thomas

**Prime, Cecil Thomas** 1909-   [WYA]
*Author*
* Prime, C. T.

**Prime, Edward Dorr Griffith**
1814-1891   [FFF, PA]
*American clergyman and writer*
* Eusebius

**Prime, Lord**
See   Reynolds, Walter Doty

**[The] Prime Minister**
See   Castiglia, Francesco

**[The] Prime Minister of Mirth**
See   Wade, George Edward

**Prime, Samuel Irenaeus** 1812-1885
[FFF, PA, WBD]
*American clergyman and writer*
* Irenaeus

**Prime, William Cowper** 1825- ?
[PA]
*Author*
* W.

**Primm, [Brother] Orrin**
See   Willett, [Brother] Franciscus

**[The] Primrose Sphynx**
See   Disraeli, Benjamin

**Primus**
See   Monro, Alexander

**Primus Baronetorum Angliae**
See   Bacon, [Sir] Nicholas

**[The] Prince**
See   Judah I [or Jehudah]

**Prince**
See   Salmon, Leon N.

**Prince, Adelaide**
See   Rubenstein, Adelaide

**Prince Alli**
See   Mona, Alli

**Prince, Arthur** 1881-1948   [BMH]
*British ventriloquist*
* [The] Court Magician and
    Ventriloquist

**[Le] Prince de la Critique**
See   Janin, Jules Gabriel

**Prince, Dorris** 1899-1927   [SC]
*American actress*
* Dare, Dorris

**Prince, Edward Ernest** 1858- ?
[NAA]
*British-born writer*
* Bessarion

**Prince, F. T.**
See   Prince, Frank Templeton

**Prince, Frank Templeton** 1912-
[MBL]
*British poet*
* Prince, F. T.

**Prince Hal**
See   Chase, Harold Harris [Hal]

**Prince Hal**
See   Newhouser, Harold [Hal]

**Prince Hal**
See   Patterson, Hal

**Prince Hal**
See   Schumacher, Harold Henry

**[The] Prince Imperial**
See   Bonaparte, Napoleon Eugene
Louis Jean Joseph

**Prince, J. H.**
See   Prince, Jack Harvey

**Prince, Jack Harvey** 1908-
[CA, SAT]
*British-born author and illustrator*
* Aquillo, Don
* Clinton, Jon
* Prince, J. H.
* Wardell, Dean

**Prince John**
See   Van Buren, John

**Prince, John Critchley** 19th c.   [SN]
*British poet*
* [The] Bard of Hyde

**Prince Kuroki**
See   Brezinski, Max Frederick

**Prince Leonard**
See   Casley, Leonard

**[The] Prince of Accompanists**
See   Harty, [Sir] Hamilton

**[The] Prince of Alchemy**
See   Rudolf II [or Rudolph]

**[The] Prince of Ancient Comedy**
See   Aristophanes

**[The] Prince of Artists**
See   Duerer, Albrecht [or Albert]

**[The] Prince of Beaux**
See   Brummel, George Bryan

**[The] Prince of Bibliomaniacal
Writers**
See   Dibdin, Thomas Frognall

**[The] Prince of Bohemian Artists**
See   Mengs, Anton Rafael

**[The] Prince of Castilian Poets**
See   Garcilaso de la Vega

**[The] Prince of Centres**
See   Wagstaff, Harold

**[The] Prince of Cookery**
See   Snowden, John

**[The] Prince of Coxcombs**
See   Ligne, Charles Joseph

**[The] Prince of Critics**
See   Aristarchus

**[The] Prince of Dandies**
See   Brummel, George Bryan

**[The] Prince of Darkness**
See   Firbank, Louis

**[That] Prince of Demagogues**
See   Orr, James Lawrence

**[The] Prince of Destruction**
See   Timur [or Timour]

**[The] Prince of Diplomatists**
See   Talleyrand-Perigord, Charles
Maurice de

**[The] Prince of Dribblers**
See   Matthews, Stanley

**[The] Prince of Fools**
See   Angoulevant

**[The] Prince of Gossips**
See   Pepys, Samuel

**[The] Prince of Grammarians**
See   Appollonius of Alexandria

**[The] Prince of Hebrew Grammarians**
See   Chajug, Jehuda

**[The] Prince of Historians**
See   Herrera, Antonio de

**[The] Prince of Hypocrites**
See   Nero Caesar, Tiberius
Claudius

**[The] Prince of Liars**
See   Mendez Pinto, Ferdinand

**[The] Prince of Light**
See   Jesus Christ

**[The] Prince of Literature**
See   Han Yu

**[The] Prince of Lyric Poets**
See   Duperier, Charles

**[The] Prince of Lyric Poets**
See   Pindar

**[The] Prince of Music**
See   Palestrina, Giovanni

**[The] Prince of Neck-or-Nothing
Novelists**
See   Lever, Charles James

**[The] Prince of New Comedy**
See   Menander

**[The] Prince of Novelists**
See   Fielding, Henry

**[The] Prince of Orators**
See   Demosthenes

**[The] Prince of Painters**
See   Apelles

**[The] Prince of Painters**
See   Parrhasius

**[The] Prince of Paragraphists**
See   Greeley, Horace

**[The] Prince of Peace**
See   King, Michael Luther, Jr.

**[The] Prince of Peace**
See   Maximilian II

**[The] Prince of Pedagogues**
See   Maginn, William

**[The] Prince of Philosophers**
See   Aristocles

**[The] Prince of Physicians**
See   Avicenna [or Abou-ibn-Sina]

**[The] Prince of Poets**
See   Goethe, Johann Wolfgang von

**[The] Prince of Poets**
See   Milton, John

**[The] Prince of Poets**
See   Spenser, Edmund

**[The] Prince of Poets**
See   Vergilius Maro, Publius

**[The] Prince of Politicians**
See   Machiavelli, Niccolo [or
Nicholas]

**[The] Prince of Priests**
See   Henry V

**[The] Prince of Princes**
See   Jesus Christ

**[The] Prince of Quarrellers**
See   Caron, Pierre Augustin

**[The] Prince of Red-Nosed
Comedians**
See   Simmons, James

**[The] Prince of Satirists**
See   Sachs, Hans

**[The] Prince of Science**
See   Tehuhe

**[The] Prince of Scoffers**
See   Arouet, Francois Marie

**[The] Prince of Showmen**
See   Barnum, Phineas Taylor

**[The] Prince of Silesian Poets**
See   Greif [Griphius or Gryphius],
Andreas

**[The] Prince of Spanish Poetry**
See   Garcilaso de la Vega

**[The] Prince of Story-Tellers**
See   Boccaccio, Giovanni

**Prince of the Apostles**
See   Medici, Giovanni de

**[The] Prince of the Apostles**
See   Simon

**[The] Prince of the New Pharisees**
See   Gaetano [or Caetani],
Benedetto

**[The] Prince of the Ode**
See   Ronsard, Pierre de

**[The] Prince of the Peace**
See   Godoy, Manuel de

**[The] Prince of the Sonnet**
See   Bellay, Joachim du

**[The] Prince of the Sonnet**
See   Petracco, Francesco

**[The] Prince of the Youth**
See   Gonzalvo di Cordova,
Hernandez

**[The] Prince of Wails**
See   Ray, John Alvin [Johnny]

**[The] Prince of Wicket-Keepers**
See   Blackham, John McCarthy

**[The] Prince of Wits**
See   Stanhope, Philip

**Princeps Theologorum**
See   Aegidius [or Giles] of Colonna

**Princess Alice**
See   Longworth, Alice Roosevelt

**[The] Princess of Ahlden**
See   Sophia Dorothea

**[The] Princess of Black Poetry**
See   Giovanni, Yolande Cornelia,
Jr.

**[The] Princess of the Blues**
See   Brown, Olive

**Princess of the Press**
See   Barnett, Ida Baker Wells

**Princeton Charlie Reilly**
See   Reilly, Charles Thomas

**Principe de la Paz**
See   Godoy, Manuel de

**Principe del Toreo [Prince of
Bullfighting]**
See   Leal Kuri, Alfredo

**Pring-Mill, Robert D[uguid] F[orrest]**
1924- [CA]
*British educator and author*
* Duguid, Robert

**Pringle, Aileen**
See Bisbee, Aileen

**Pringle, John** 1895?-1936
[BDF, BEW, F1]
*American actor*
* Gilbert, John

**Pringle, Laurence P.** 1935-
[CA, SAT]
*American author, editor, photographer*
* Edmund, Sean

**Pringle-Pattison, Andrew**
See Seth, Andrew

**Prins, Co**
See Prins, Jacob

**Prins, Jacob** 1938- [AES]
*Dutch soccer player*
* Prins, Co

**Printemps, Yvonne**
See Wigniolle, Yvonne

**Prior, Harry**
See Knightley, D. G.

**Prior, James**
See Kirk, James Prior

**Prior, Lulu**
See De Nyse, Mrs. Edward

**Prior, Matt[hew]** 1664-1721 [SN]
*British poet and diplomat*
* Plenipo, Rummer
* [The] State Proteus

**Prior, Samuel**
See Galt, John

**Prism, Brother**
See Mathews, Charles

**[The] Prisoner of Chillon**
See Bonnivard, Francois de

**[The] Prisoner of Ham**
See Bonaparte, Charles Louis
Napoleon

**[The] Prisoner of Spandau**
See Hess, Rudolf

**[The] Prisoner of the Vatican**
See Mastai-Ferretti, Giovanni
Maria

**Pritchard, Buddy**
See Pritchard, Harold William

**Pritchard, Harold William** 1936-
[BE]
*American baseball player*
* Pritchard, Buddy

**Pritchard, John Laurence** 1885-
[WW]
*Author*
* Laurence, John

**Pritchard, John Wallace** 1912-
[CA, ESF, SFL]
*American author and psychologist*
* Wallace, Ian

**Pritchard, Norman** 1877-1929
[THR]
*British actor*
* Trevor, Norman

**Pritchard, William Thomas** 1909-
[ESF, SFL, WGT]
*British author*
* Dexter, William

**Pritchett, V. S.**
See Pritchett, Victor Sawdon

**Pritchett, Victor Sawdon** 1900-
[IPA, LC]
*British author and critic*
* Pritchett, V. S.

**Pritkin, Ron** 1920- [ASC]
*American entertainer*
* Terry, Ron

**Private 19022**
See Manning, Frederic

**Privateer**
See Foster, Charles J.

**Privett, Booger Red**
See Privett, Sam

**Privett, Sam** 1858-1926 [GW]
*American rodeo performer*
* Privett, Booger Red

**Priyamvada, Usha**
See Nilsson, Usha Saksena

**Pro Football, Mr.**
See Halas, George S.

**Probst, Colonel**
See Probst, Otto

**Probst, Nicholas David** 1935-
[BEW]
*American actor*
* Pryor, Nicholas

**Probst, Otto** 1889- [GF]
*American collector of golf memorabilia*
* Probst, Colonel

**Proby, P. J.**
See Smith, James Marcus

**Probyn, Elise**
See McKibbon, J. E.

**Probyn, John E.**
See McKibbon, J. E.

**Proceviat, Pro**
See Proceviat, Richard Peter

**Proceviat, Richard Peter** 1946-
[SMG]
*Canadian-born hockey player*
* Proceviat, Pro

**Proclus** 410- 485 [RH]
*Greek philosopher*
* Thaumaturgus

**Procop** ?-1434 [WBD]
*Hussite leader*
* [The] Little

**Procop [or Procopius], Andrew**
1380?-1434 [DNNS, WBD]
*Hussite leader*
* [The] Great

**Procope-Couteau, Michael**
1684-1753 [PA]
*Author*
* Colteli

**Procopio, Mariellen**
See Grutz, Mariellen Procopio

**[The] Procopius of France**
See Siri, Victor

**Procter, Adelaide Anne** 1825-1864
[WBD]
*British poet*
* Berwick, Mary

**Procter, Michael John** 1946- [DC]
*South African-born cricketer*
* Procter, Prock

**Procter, Prock**
See Procter, Michael John

**Proctor, Bryan Waller** 1787-1874
[FFF, PA, SN]
*British poet*
* Cornwall, Barry
* Jessamine, James
* [A] Moral Byron

**Proctor, Cub**
See Proctor, James

**Proctor, Everitt**
See Montgomery, Rutherford
George

**Proctor, Ezekiel** 1831-1907 [B10]
*American Indian leader*
* Proctor, Zeke

**Proctor, James** 20th c. [OBW]
*American baseball player*
* Proctor, Cub

**Proctor, Mary** 20th c. [LAO]
*Irish-born author*
* [The] Little Lady of the Stars

**Proctor, Miller**
See Huggins, Miller James

**Proctor, Noah Richard** 1900-1967
[BE]
*American baseball player*
* Proctor, Red

**Proctor, Paul**
See Samways, George Richmond

**Proctor, Red**
See Proctor, Noah Richard

**Proctor, Richard A.** [FFF]
*Author*
* Five of Clubs

**Proctor, Zeke**
See Proctor, Ezekiel

**Procureur de la Lanterne**
See Desmoulins, [Lucie Simplice]
Camille [Benoit]

**Prodgers, George** 1892-
[CEI, FHE]
*Canadian-born hockey player*
* Prodgers, Goldie

**Prodgers, Goldie**
See Prodgers, George

**[The] Prodigal**
See Albert VI

**[The] Prodigy of France**
See Bude, Guillaume

**[The] Prodigy of Learning**
See Hahnemann, [Christian
Friedrich] Samuel

**[The] Prof**
See Blood, Ernest A.

**[The] Prof**
See Lindemann, Frederick
Alexander

**[The] Professor**
See Cavill, Fred

**[The] Professor**
See Scott, Benny

**Professor**
See Sityana, Alfred Mama Sikhefu

**[The] Professor**
See Smith, Oliver Prince

**[The] Professor**
See Verner, David

**[The] Professor**
See Whaling, Thornton

**[The] Professor**
See Wilson, [Thomas] Woodrow

**[The] Professor**
See Woodcock, Leonard

**[The] Professor at the Breakfast
Table**
See Holmes, Oliver Wendell

**Professor of Legerdemain**
See Potter, Richard

**Professor X**
See Boorstin, Daniel Joseph

**Professor X**
See Faulk, Odie B.

**Proffitt, Josephine Moore** 1914-
[ASC]
*American composer and author*
* Dee, Sylvia

**Profitabilis, Doctor**
See Bonet, Nicholas

**[The] Profound Doctor**
See Bradwardine, Thomas

**[The] Profound Doctor**
See Middleton, Richard

**Profundissimus, Doctor**
See Aegidius [or Giles] of Colonna

**Profundus, Doctor**
See Bradwardine, Thomas

**Profundus, Doctor**
See Jacobus de Ascoli

**Profundus, Doctor**
See Middleton, Richard

**Prog**
See Scott, Thomas J.

**Prognostes**
See Fosco, Placide

**[The] Projector**
See Law, John

**Prole, Lozania** [joint pseudonym
with Charles Eade]
See Bloom, Ursula [Harvey]

**Prole, Lozania** [joint pseudonym
with Ursula (Harvey) Bloom]
See Eade, Charles

**Prolix, Peregrine**
See Nicklin, Philip Holbrook

**Prometheus**
See Steimer, Francis Alfred

**Pronzini, Bill** 1943- [CA]
*American author*
* Foxx, Jack
* Saxon, Alex

**Proper, Adolph** 1886?-1950 [BEW]
*Austrian-born clown*
* Robins, Adolph

[The] Prophet
See Brothers, Richard

[The] Prophet
See Joachim

[The] Prophet
See Lalawethika

[The] Prophet
See Mohammed [or Mahomet]

[The] Prophet of the Northwest
See Riel, Louis David

[The] Prophet of the Syrians
See Ephraem

[The] Prophet of the Syrians
See Philippi [or Philippson?]

[The] Prophetess
See Ayesha [or Ayeshah]

[The] Prophetess of Exeter
See Southcott, Joanna

[A] Prose Ariosto
See Bandello, Matteo [or Matthew]

[The] Prose Burns of Ireland
See Carleton, William

[The] Prose Homer of Human Nature
See Fielding, Henry

[The] Proselyte
See Onkelos

[The] Prosk
See Proski, Joe

Proski, Joe 1939- [SMG]
American basketball trainer
* [The] Prosk

Prosner, G. W. [PA]
Author
* Z.

Prosper, John [joint pseudonym with John C(hipman) Farrar]
See Buranelli, Prosper

Prosper, John [joint pseudonym with Prosper Buranelli]
See Farrar, John C[hipman]

Prosper, Lincoln
See Cannon, Helen

[The] Prosper Marchand of English Literature
See Nichols, John

Prosper of Aquitaine 5th c. [WBD]
Author
* Prosper Tiro

Prosper Tiro
See Prosper of Aquitaine

Prosperi, Francesco 20th c. [WF]
Director
* Shannon, Frank

Prosperity's Advance Agent
See McKinley, William

Prospero
See Douce, Francis

Prospero
See West, Tristram Frederick

Prospero and Caliban [joint pseudonym with Frederick William Serafino Austin Rolfe]
See Pirie-Gordon, Charles Harry Clinton

Prospero and Caliban [joint pseudonym with Charles Harry Clinton Pirie-Gordon]
See Rolfe, Frederick William [Serafino Austin Lewis Mary]

Prota Matija
See Nenadovic, Matija

[The] Protector
See Cromwell, Oliver

[The] Protector
See Marshal, William

[The] Protector
See Richard III

[The] Protector
See Seymour, Edward

[The] Protector of Peru
See San Martin, Jose de

Protector of the Indians
See Las Casas, Bartolome de

Protero, Dodi
See McIlraith, Dorothy Ann

[The] Protestant Duke
See Scott, James

[The] Protestant Hero
See Frederick II

[The] Protestant Joiner
See Colledge

[The] Protestant Livy
See Philippi [or Philippson?]

[The] Protestant Martyr
See Godfrey, [Sir] Edmund bury

[The] Protestant Pope
See Ganganelli, Giovanni Vincenzo Antonio

Proteus
See Carvalho, S. S.

[A] Proteus
See Parsons [or Persons?], Robert

Protheroe, Cyril 20th c. [SFL]
Author
* Le Page, Rand [house pseudonym, Curtis Warren]

Protheroe, Ernest 20th c. [MBF]
British author
* Henley, P. A.

Prothro, Doc
See Prothro, James Thompson

Prothro, James Thompson 1893-1971 [BE, PB]
American baseball player
* Prothro, Doc

[The] Proto Rebel
See Douglas, William

Protovates Angliae
See Whittington [or Whitynton?], Robert

[The] Proud
See Albert I [or Albrecht]

[The] Proud
See Henry X

[The] Proud
See Otto IV [or Otho]

[The] Proud
See Tarquin II [or Tarquinius]

[The] Proud African
See Hall, Ian

[The] Proud Duke
See Seymour, Charles

Proudfit, David L. [FFF, PA]
American author
* Arkwright, Peleg

Proudfit, Fairfax 1887- [BEW]
American educator, costume designer, writer
* Walkup, Fairfax Proudfit

Proudfoot, Walter
See Vahey, John George Haslette

Proudman, M. Eyre
See Lovely, Maureen Patey

Prough, Bill
See Prough, H. Clinton

Prough, H. Clinton 1888- [BE]
American baseball player
* Prough, Bill

Prout, Father
See Mahony, Francis

Prout, Geoffrey 1894- ? [MBF]
British author
* Spencer, Roland [joint pseudonym with Francis Alister Warwick]
* Valentine, Henry

Prouting, Frederick James [FFF]
British writer and editor
* Brown, Vandyke
* Verite sans Peur

Provence, Marcel
See Jouhandeau, Marcel Henri

Provenzano, Anthony 1917-
American underworld figure
* Provenzano, Tony Pro

Provenzano, Tony Pro
See Provenzano, Anthony

Prowler, Harley
See Masters, Edgar Lee

Prowse, R. O.
See Prowse, Richard Orton

Prowse, Richard Orton 1862-1949 [LC]
British author
* Prowse, R. O.

Prude, Agnes George 1905- [CA]
American choreographer, director, dancer, author
* De Mille, Agnes

Prudence Penny
See Young, Norma

Prudentius, Aurelius Clemens 348-410? [DEP, SN]
Spanish poet
* [The] Virgil and Horace of the Christians

Prudhomme, Augie
See Prudhomme, John Olgus

Prudhomme, Don 20th c.
American auto racer
* [The] Snake

Prud'homme, George 1901-1972 [FIR, SC]
American actor and opera singer
* Pembroke, George

Prudhomme, John Olgus 1902- [BE]
American baseball player
* Prudhomme, Augie

Prudhomme, Rene Francois Armand 1839-1907 [CD]
French poet
* Sully-Prudhomme

Prudhon, Pierre-Paul
See Prudon, Pierre

Prudon, Pierre 1758-1823 [WBD]
French painter
* Prudhon, Pierre-Paul

Pruess, Earl Henry 1895- [BE]
American baseball player
* Pruess, Gibby

Pruess, Gibby
See Pruess, Earl Henry

Pruett, Gene 20th c. [GW]
American rodeo performer
* Pruett, Stiffy

Pruett, Hub
See Pruett, Hubert Shelby

Pruett, Hubert Shelby 1900- [BE, PB]
American baseball player
* Pruett, Hub
* Pruett, Shucks

Pruett, Shucks
See Pruett, Hubert Shelby

Pruett, Stiffy
See Pruett, Gene

Pruiett, Charles LeRoy 1883-1953 [BE]
American baseball player
* Pruiett, Tex

Pruiett, Tex
See Pruiett, Charles LeRoy

Pruitt, Alan
See Rose, Alvin Emanuel

Pruning Knife
See Allen, Henry Francis

Prus, Boleslaw
See Glowacki, Aleksander

Prusias I 3rd c. BC [WBD]
King of Bithynia
* [The] Lame

Prusias II 2nd c. BC [WBD]
King of Bithynia
* [The] Horseman

[The] Prussian Boot
See Bismarck, Otto Eduard Leopold von

[The] Prussian Pindar
See Willamow, Johann Gottlieb

Prussing, M. Jean
See Burden, Jean

Prutkov, Kozma
See Snodgrass, William DeWitt

Pry, Polly
See O'Bryan, Leonel [Campbell]

Pryde, Anthony
See Weekes, Agnes Russell

**Pryde, James Ferrier** 1866-1941
[DBA]
*British painter, lithographer, poster
designer*
* Beggarstaff, J.

**Pryde, Peggy**
*See* Woodley, Letitia Matilda

**Prynne, Marginal**
*See* Prynne, William

**[The] Prynne of His Day**
*See* Stubbs, Philip

**Prynne, Voluminous**
*See* Prynne, William

**Prynne, William** 1600-1669
[RH, SN]
*British pamphleteer*
* [The] Cato of the Age
* Prynne, Marginal
* Prynne, Voluminous
* S. L.

**Pryor, Bubba**
*See* Pryor, James Edward

**Pryor, Jacqueline**
*See* Williamson, Connie

**Pryor, James Edward** 1921-
[BWW]
*American singer*
* Pryor, Bubba
* Pryor, Snooky

**Pryor, Martha**
*See* Waters, Ethel

**Pryor, Nicholas**
*See* Probst, Nicholas David

**Pryor, Paul**
*See* Taggard, E. T.

**Pryor, Snooky**
*See* Pryor, James Edward

**Prys Williams, Nerys Mair Sioned**
1913- [DBA]
*British painter and potter*
* Nerys

**Pryse, Hugh**
*See* Pryse, John Hwfa

**Pryse, John Hwfa** 1910-1955
[BEW]
*British-born actor*
* Pryse, Hugh

**Prysock, Arthur** 1925- [IBW]
*American singer*
* Mr. P.

**Przesmycki, Zenon** 1861-1944
[WBD]
*Polish editor and poet*
* Miriam

**Przybyszewski, Stanislaw**
1868-1927 [MWD]
*Polish editor, author, playwright*
* [The] Founder of Polish
Modernism

**Przyjaciel**
*See* Nowaczynski, Adolf

**Psenka, R. Jaromir** 1875- ? [NAA]
*German-born author*
* Dore, Gabriel

**Pseudo Demetrius**
*See* Demetrius I

**Pseudoman, Akkad**
*See* Northrup, Edwin Fitch

**Psifidis, Billy**
*See* Psifidis, Vasillis

**Psifidis, Vasillis** 1944- [AES]
*Greek soccer player*
* Psifidis, Billy

**Psigoloog**
*See* Visser, Willem Johannes
Conradie

**Psycho Ann**
*See* Barrows, [Ruth] Marjorie

**Pteleon**
*See* Grieve, Christopher Murray

**Ptolemy** 3rd c. BC [RH, WBD]
*King of Macedonia*
* Keraunos [or Ceraunus]
* [The] Thunderbolt

**Ptolemy I** 4th c. BC
[FFF, HN, SN]
*King of Egypt*
* [The] Preserver
* Soter

**Ptolemy II** 3rd c. BC [HN]
*King of Egypt*
* Philadelphos [Brother-Lover]

**Ptolemy III** 3rd c. BC [HN, WBD]
*King of Egypt*
* Euergetes [Benefactor]

**Ptolemy IV** 3rd c. BC [HN, WBD]
*King of Egypt*
* Philopator [Father-Lover]

**Ptolemy IX [or VIII]** 1st c. BC
[HN, WBD]
*King of Egypt*
* Lathyros
* Soter II

**Ptolemy V** 2nd c. BC
[FFF, HN, SN]
*King of Egypt*
* Epiphanes
* [The] Illustrious

**Ptolemy VI** 2nd c. BC [WBD]
*King of Egypt*
* Philometor [Mother-Lover]

**Ptolemy VII** 2nd c. BC [WBD]
*King of Egypt*
* Neos Philopator [New
Philopator]

**Ptolemy VIII [or VII]** 2nd c. BC
[HN, WBD]
*King of Egypt*
* Euergetes II
* Physcon [Big-Belly]

**Ptolemy X [IX or XI]** 1st c. BC
[WBD]
*King of Egypt*
* Alexander I

**Ptolemy XI [X or XII]** 1st c. BC
[WBD]
*King of Egypt*
* Alexander II

**Ptolemy XII [or X]** 1st c. BC
[HN, WBD]
*King of Egypt*
* Auletes [Flute Player]
* Philopator Neos Dionysos

**Ptolemy XV [XIV or XVI]** 1st c.
BC [WBD]
*Son of Cleopatra, Queen of Egypt*
* Cesarion
* Philopator Philometor Caesar

**P'u-yi, Henry**
*See* Hsuan T'ung

**Public Utility, Mr.**
*See* Sporn, Philip

**Publicola**
*See* Adams, John Quincy

**Publicola**
*See* Fox, William Johnson

**Publicola**
*See* Smith, Sydney

**Publicola**
*See* Williams, D. E.

**Publicola**
*See* Williams, John

**Publicus**
*See* Fraleck, Edison Baldwin

**Publius**
*See* Hamilton, Alexander

**Puccinelli, Count**
*See* Puccinelli, George Lawrence

**Puccinelli, George Lawrence**
1906-1956 [BE]
*American baseball player*
* Puccinelli, Count

**[La] Pucelle**
*See* Joan of Arc [or Jeanne d'Arc]

**Puchtik, Yakov Nusan** 1944- [CA]
*Russian-born American sociologist
and author*
* Porter, Jack Nusan

**Puchungo**
*See* Henriquez, Rafael Americo

**Puck**
*See* Ryan, William

**[The] Puck of Commentators**
*See* Steevens, George

**Puckett, Gary** 1942- [RO2]
*American singer*
* Puckett, General

**Puckett, General**
*See* Puckett, Gary

**Puckett, Lute**
*See* Masters, Edgar Lee

**Puechner, Ray** 1935- [CA, WD]
*American author*
* Haddo, Oliver
* Tiger, Jack
* Victor, Charles B.

**Puente, Ernest, Jr.** 1925- [EJ]
*American jazz musician*
* Puente, Tito

**Puente, Tito**
*See* Puente, Ernest, Jr.

**Puetz, Ruth-Margret**
*See* Doerkes, Ruth-Margret

**Pufendorf, Samuel von** 1632-1694
[WBD]
*German jurist and historian*
* Severinus de Monzambano

**Puga, Ricardo** [GS]
*Spanish bullfighter*
* [El] Cateto [The Yokel]

**Puget, Pierre** 1623-1694
[DNNF, DNNS, FFF]
*French sculptor, painter, architect*
* [The] Michael Angelo of France

**Puget, Pierre** (Continued)
* [The] Michael Angelo of
Sculptors
* [Le] Michel Ange Francais

**Pugh, Buzz**
*See* Pugh, Jethro, Jr.

**Pugh, Eliza Lofton [Phillips]** 1841-
? [FFF, PA]
*American writer*
* Arria

**Pugh, Gordon Scott** 1909-1969
[BBH]
*American lacrosse player and coach*
* Pugh, Willie

**Pugh, Jethro, Jr.** 1944- [SMG]
*American football player*
* Pugh, Buzz

**Pugh, Joe Bennie** 1926-1960
[BWW]
*American singer*
* Forrest City Joe

**Pugh, Roger** 20th c. [MBF]
*British author*
* Rogers, Ben

**Pugh, Willie**
*See* Pugh, Gordon Scott

**Pugh, Wynette** 1942- [CME]
*American country-western performer*
* Wynette, Tammy

**Pughe, William Owen** 1759-1835
[WBD]
*Welsh antiquarian and
lexicographer*
* Owen, William

**Puig y de la Puente, Francisco**
1839-1917 [CW]
*Cuban author*
* Rosas, Julio

**Pujol, Pierre Leon** 1867- ? [THR]
*French playwright*
* Flers, P. L.

**Pulaski, Isme Beringer** ?-1948
[BEW]
*American journalist, editor, critic*
* Pulaski, Jack

**Pulaski, Jack**
*See* Pulaski, Isme Beringer

**Pulcher**
*See* Claudius, Appius

**Pulcher**
*See* Claudius, Publius

**Pulcher**
*See* Clodius [or Claudius], Publius

**Puleo, Nicole**
*See* Miller, Nicole Puleo

**Pulitzer, Margaret Leech**
*See* Leech, Margaret

**Pullein-Thompson, Christine**
*See* Popescu, Christine

**Pullein-Thompson, Denis** 1919-
[LC]
*British playwright*
* Cannan, Denis

**Pullein-Thompson, Diana**
*See* Farr, Diana Pullein-Thompson

**Pullen, George Frederick** [AW]
*British translator*
* Culpeper, Martin

**Pulling, Albert Van Siclen** 1891-
[CA]
*American author*
* Pulling, Pierre

**Pulling, Christopher Robert Druce**
1893- [CAP]
*British author*
* Druce, Christopher

**Pulling, Pierre**
*See* Pulling, Albert Van Siclen

**Pulos, William Leroy** 1920- [IAW]
*American psychologist and author*
* Anderson, Alfred

**[The] Pulpit Buffoon**
*See* Peters [or Peter?], Hugh

**[A] Pulpit Physician**
*See* Sacheverell, Henry

**Pulsford, Norman George** 1902-
[WW]
*Author*
* Trevor, A. C.

**Pulsifer, D.** 19th c. [PA]
*Author*
* Midgely, R. L.

**Pulteney**
*See* Amherst, Nicholas

**Pulteney, William [Earl of Bath]**
1684-1764 [SN]
*British politician*
* [That] Weather Cock

**Pulteney's Toad-Eater**
*See* Vane, Henry

**Pultz, Adele** 1874-1930 [THR]
*American actress and singer*
* Ritchie, Adele

**Pulvertaft, Lalage Isobel** 1925-
[AW, WD]
*British author*
* March, Hilary

**[The] Pumper**
*See* Longden, Johnny

**Punch**
*See* Vassy, Gaston

**Punch, Kid**
*See* Miller, Ernest

**Puncuss, Pugagee**
*See* McLlelan, George H. H.

**Pund, Henry R.** 1907- [FB]
*American football player*
* Peter the Great
* Pund, Peter

**Pund, Peter**
*See* Pund, Henry R.

**Punever, Peter**
*See* Greenleaf, Lawrence N.

**Pungent, Pierce**
*See* McLennan, J.

**Puni, Ivan Albert** 1892-1956
[CAR]
*French painter*
* Pougny, Jean

**Punnett, Ivar** [CC, WW]
*Author*
* Simons, Roger [joint pseudonym
with Margaret Punnett]

**Punnett, Margaret** [CC]
*Author*
* Simons, Roger [joint pseudonym
with Ivar Punnett]

**[El] Puno**
*See* Gonzalez, Jaime

**Punteret [Sharpshooter]**
*See* Cecilio y Villanueva, Juan

**Pupper, Johann** 1400?-1475
[WBD]
*German monk and theologian*
* Johannes von Goch

**Puracal, John T[homas]** 1931-
[CA]
*Australian economist and author*
* Purcal, John T[homas]

**Purcal, John T[homas]**
*See* Puracal, John T[homas]

**Purcell, Blondie**
*See* Purcell, William Aloysius

**Purcell, Estelle**
*See* Fielders, Mrs. Frank M.

**Purcell, J. S.** 20th c. [MBF]
*British author*
* Stapleton, Maurice

**Purcell, James A.** 1906-1966
[BBH]
*American auto racing manager and
promoter*
* Purcell, Pat

**Purcell, Pat**
*See* Purcell, James A.

**Purcell, Victor William Williams
Saunders** 1896-1965 [CA, LC]
*British author*
* Buttle, Myra

**Purcell, William Aloysius** [BE]
*American baseball player and
manager*
* Purcell, Blondie

**Purdell, Reginald**
*See* Grasdorf, Reginald

**Purdie, Bernard** 1939- [EJ7, LRR]
*American jazz musician*
* Purdie, Pretty

**Purdie, Pretty**
*See* Purdie, Bernard

**Purdom, C. B.**
*See* Purdom, Charles Benjamin

**Purdom, Charles Benjamin**
1883-1965 [BEW, LC]
*British author and critic*
* Purdom, C. B.

**Purdy, Everett Virgil** 1904-1951
[BE]
*American baseball player*
* Purdy, Pid

**Purdy, Pid**
*See* Purdy, Everett Virgil

**[The] Pure**
*See* Baffo

**[The] Purging Colonel**
*See* Pride, Thomas

**[El] Puri**
*See* Castellano Martinez, Agustin

**[The] Purist of Language**
*See* Malherbe, Francois de

**[The] Puritan Captain**
*See* Standish, Miles

**[A] Puritan Pepys**
*See* Sewall, Samuel

**[The] Puritan Plato**
*See* Howe, John

**[The] Puritanical Bishop**
*See* Potter, Barnabas [or
Barnaby?]

**Purley, John**
*See* Thomas, Reginald George

**Purnell, Idella** 1901- [CA]
*Mexican-born author*
* Stone, Idella Purnell
* Stone, Ikey

**Purnell, Jesse Rhoades** 1879-1966
[BE]
*American baseball player*
* Purnell, Scrappy

**Purnell, Keg**
*See* Purnell, William

**Purnell, Scrappy**
*See* Purnell, Jesse Rhoades

**Purnell, Thomas** 19th c. [PA]
*Author*
* Q.

**Purnell, William** 1915-1965
[DAM, EJ, WWJ]
*American jazz musician*
* Purnell, Keg

**Purple, Edwin R.** 1831-1879 [PA]
*Author*
* Neafie

**[The] Purple Streak**
*See* Boynton, Ben L.

**Purpur, Clifford** 1916- [CEI]
*American-born hockey player*
* Purpur, Fido

**Purpur, Fido**
*See* Purpur, Clifford

**Pursch, Friedrich Traugott**
1774-1820 [WBD]
*German-born botanist and
horticulturist*
* Pursh, Frederick

**Purse**
*See* Pierce, Franklin

**Pursh, Frederick**
*See* Pursch, Friedrich Traugott

**Purtell, William Patrick [Billy]**
1886-1962 [BN]
*American baseball player*
* [The] Child Athlete

**Purtill, Maurice** 1916-
[PMJ, WWJ]
*American jazz musician*
* Purtill, Moe

**Purtill, Moe**
*See* Purtill, Maurice

**Purwitsky, Marcus** ?-1963 [EJS]
*Russian-born South African horse
trainer*
* Purwitsky, Paddy

**Purwitsky, Paddy**
*See* Purwitsky, Marcus

**Push 'em Up Tony**
*See* Lazzeri, Anthony Michael
[Tony]

**Pushcart Tony Cermack**
*See* Cermack, Anton

**Pushful Joe**
*See* Chamberlain, Joseph

**Pushkin, Alexander Sergeivitch**
1799-1837 [DNNF, FFF, IBW]
*Russian poet*
* Belkine, Ivan
* [The] Father of Russian
Literature
* [The] Russian Byron

**Putinas**
*See* Mykolaitis, Vincas

**Putman, Kate**
*See* Osgood, Kate Putman

**Putnam, Eleanor**
*See* Bates, Harriet L. Vose

**Putnam, George H[aven]**
1844-1930 [WGT]
*British-born American author*
* G. H. P.

**Putnam, Isra**
*See* La Spina, Greye Bragg

**Putnam, Israel** 1718-1790
[DNNF, FFF, SN]
*American army officer*
* Old Put

**Putnam, John**
*See* Beckwith, Burnham Putnam

**Putnam, Kenneth**
*See* Klass, Philip

**Putnam, Mary Lowell** 1810- ?
[PA]
*Author*
* Colvil, Edward

**Putnam, Mrs. S. W.** [FFF]
*Entertainer*
* Amond, Nellie

**Putnam, S. W.** [FFF]
*Entertainer*
* Sedgwick, Billy

**Putnam, Sarah A.** 19th c. [FFF]
*Author*
* Brock, Sallie A.

**Putney, Gail J.**
*See* Fullerton, Gail Putney

**Putney, Henry M.** 19th c.
[FFF, PA]
*American writer*
* Snoggins

**Putra, Kerala**
*See* Panikkar, K[avalam] Madhava

**Puzzle "Nom"**
*See* Tingley, Richard Hoadley

**Pyatt, Frederick Nelson** 1953-
[SMG]
*Canadian-born hockey player*
* Pyatt, Nelly

**Pyatt, Nelly**
*See* Pyatt, Frederick Nelson

**Pycroft, Nita** 1902- [THR]
*British actress and singer*
* Croft, Nita

**Pyle, Cash and Carry**
See   Pyle, Charles C.

**Pyle, Charles C.** 1881-1939
[AS, FB]
*American football promoter*
* Pyle, Cash and Carry

**Pyle, Firpo**
See   Pyle, Harlan Albert

**Pyle, Harlan Albert** 1905-    [BE]
*American baseball player*
* Pyle, Firpo

**Pyle, Harry Thomas** 1861-1908
[BE]
*American baseball player*
* Pyle, Shadow

**Pyle, Herbert Ewald** 1910-    [BE]
*American baseball player*
* Pyle, Lefty

**Pyle, Hilary** 1936-    [CA]
*Irish art critic and author*
* Cullen, Peta
* Mitchell, Adam

**Pyle, Lefty**
See   Pyle, Herbert Ewald

**Pyle, Shadow**
See   Pyle, Harry Thomas

**Pyles, Aitken**
See   McDavid, Raven I[oor], Jr.

**Pylkowski, Henry** 1911-1957
[AS, BX, RBE]
*American boxer*
* Risko, Babe
* Risko, Eddie

**Pylodet, L.**
See   Leypoldt, Frederick

**Pym, Beatrice Angela Carrington**
20th c.    [THR]
*British actress*
* Cromwell, Cecil

**Pym, John** 1584-1643
[FFF, HN, SN]
*British politician*
* [The] English Aristides
* Pym, King

**Pym, King**
See   Pym, John

**[The] Pym of France**
See   Mole, Mathieu

**Pym, T.**
See   Creed, Clara

**Pynchon, Adeline Lobdell Atwater**
20th c.    [NAA]
*American writer*
* Atwater, Caroline Lobdell

**Pyne, John** 17th c.    [SN]
*Regicide*
* [The] King of the West

**Pyne, William Henry** 1770-1843
[PA]
*Author*
* Hardcastle, Ephraim

**Pyricus**    [SN]
*Painter*
* [The] Ryparographer

**Pythagoras** 6th c.
[DEP, DNNS, RH]
*Greek philosopher and
mathematician*
* Crotona's Sage

**Pythagoras** (Continued)
* [The] Long Haired Samian
* [The] Philosopher with the
  Golden Thigh
* [The] Sage of Crotona
* [The] Sage of Samos
* [The] Samian Sage

**Python**
See   Dennis, John

# Q

**Q**
*See* Buckner, Quinn

**Q**
*See* Jones, Quincy Delight, Jr.

**Q.**
*See* Purnell, Thomas

**Q.**
*See* Quiller-Couch, [Sir] Arthur Thomas

**Q.**
*See* Rosenberg, Charles G.

**Q.**
*See* Yates, Edmund Hodgson

**Q. B.**
*See* Buckner, Quinn

**Q. Q.**
*See* Taylor, Jane

**[A] Quack in Commentatorship**
*See* Warburton, William

**Quackenbush, Bill**
*See* Quackenbush, Hubert George

**Quackenbush, Hubert George**
1922- [CEI, FHE]
*Canadian-born hockey player*
* Quackenbush, Bill

**Quad, Doctor**
*See* Blackall, Christopher Rubey

**Quad, M.**
*See* Lewis, Charles Bertrand

**Quaker Meadows Joe**
*See* McDowell, Joseph

**[The] Quaker Poet**
*See* Barton, Bernard

**[The] Quaker Poet**
*See* Whittier, John Greenleaf

**[The] Quaker Soldier**
*See* Biddle, Clement

**Qualen, John**
*See* Oleson, John

**Quallon**
*See* Bradbury, Stephen Henry

**Qualters, Marguerite** 1895-1974
[SC]
*American actress*
* Qualters, Tot

**Qualters, Money Bags**
*See* Qualters, Thomas Francis [Tom]

**Qualters, Thomas Francis [Tom]**
1935- [BE]
*American baseball player*
* Qualters, Money Bags

**Qualters, Tot**
*See* Qualters, Marguerite

**Quang-yoo** ?- 265 [HN]
*Chinese general*
* [The] Mars of China

**Quant, Mary** 1934- [WFA]
*British fashion designer*
* [The] Mother of Mod

**Quarles**
*See* Poe, Edgar Allan

**[The] Quarreler**
*See* Louis X

**[The] Quarrelsome**
*See* Henry II

**Quartararo, Gladys** 20th c.
*Actress*
* Quartaro, Nena

**Quartaro, Nena**
*See* Quartararo, Gladys

**Quarterback** [code name used during World War II]
*See* Stilwell, Joseph W.

**Quarterback, Mr.**
*See* Starr, Bryan Bartlett

**Quartermain, James**
*See* Lynne, James Broom

**Quatrelles**
*See* Lepine, Ernest

**Quayle, Mary Jane Ward** 1905-
[NAA]
*American author*
* Ward, Mary Jane

**Quedens, Eunice** 1912-
[BEW, EMT, FC]
*American actress*
* Arden, Eve

**[The] Queen**
*See* Spivey, Victoria Regina [Vicky]

**[The] Queen**
*See* Steinberg, Martha Jean Jones

**Queen Anne's Great Captain**
*See* Churchill, John [First Duke of Marlborough]

**[The] Queen Bea of Blues Singers**
*See* Nicholls, Muriel

**Queen Bess**
*See* Elizabeth I

**Queen, Billy Eddleman** 1928- [BE]
*American baseball player*
* Queen, Doc

**Queen Dick**
*See* Cromwell, Richard

**Queen, Doc**
*See* Queen, Billy Eddleman

**Queen Elleezee**
*See* Landreaux, Elizabeth Mary

**Queen, Ellery** [joint pseudonym with Daniel Nathan]
*See* Lepofsky, Manfred

**Queen, Ellery** [joint pseudonym with Manfred Lepofsky]
*See* Nathan, Daniel

**Queen, Ellery, Jr.**
*See* Holding, James [Clark Carlisle, Jr.]

**Queen, Ellery, Jr.** [joint pseudonym with Daniel Nathan]
*See* Lepofsky, Manfred

**Queen, Ellery, Jr.** [joint pseudonym with Manfred Lepofsky]
*See* Nathan, Daniel

**Queen Henry**
*See* Henrietta Maria

**Queen, Mrs. Frederick E.** [FFF]
*Entertainer*
* Lascelles, Emma

**[The] Queen of Beauty**
*See* Somerset, Duchess of

**[The] Queen of Blues**
*See* Brown, Ada

**[The] Queen of Bohemia**
*See* McElhinney, Jane

**[The] Queen of Carthage**
*See* Leris, Claire Josephe

**[The] Queen of Civil Rights**
*See* Hurley, Ruby

**[The] Queen of Coins**
*See* Ford, Mary

**[The] Queen of Country Music**
*See* Deason, Muriel Ellen

**[The] Queen of Crime**
*See* Christie, Agatha [Mary Clarissa]

**[The] Queen of Death Row**
*See* Morris, Patsy

**[The] Queen of Disco**
*See* Gaines, Donna

**[The] Queen of Hearts**
*See* Elizabeth

**Queen of Hearts**
*See* Keplinger, Mrs. E. M. Patterson

**[The] Queen of Heaven**
*See* Mary

**[The] Queen of Heaven**
*See* Voo-chee

**[The] Queen of Horror**
*See* Radcliffe, Anne

**[The] Queen of Letters**
*See* Ocampo, Victoria

**[The] Queen of Limbo**
*See* Croney, Roz

**Queen of Palmyra**
*See* Stanhope, Hester Lucy

**[The] Queen of Polish Lyricists**
*See* Pawlikowska, Marja [Kossak]

**[The] Queen of Protest**
*See* Baez, Joan

**[The] Queen of Queens**
*See* Cleopatra

**[The] Queen of Rock 'n Rouge**
*See* Furnier, Vincent Damon

**[The] Queen of Shepherds**
*See* Elizabeth I

**[The] Queen of Song**
*See* Catalani, Angelica

**[The] Queen of Soul**
*See* Franklin, Aretha

**[The] Queen of Soul**
*See* Hightower, Donna

**[The] Queen of Staccato**
*See* Selika, Marie

**[The] Queen of Tears**
*See* Mary Beatrice

**[The] Queen of Tennis**
*See* Washington, Ora

**Queen of the Alligator Wrestlers**
*See* Edstrom, Katherine

**[The] Queen of the American Stage**
*See* Duff, Mary Ann

[The] Queen of the Autoharp
See   Carter, Maybelle

[The] Queen of the Blues
See   Dunn, Sara

[The] Queen of the Blues
See   Edwards, Susie

[The] Queen of the Blues
See   Jones, Ruth [Lee]

[The] Queen of the Blues
See   Smith, Mamie

[The] Queen of the Blues
See   Spivey, Victoria Regina
[Vicky]

[The] Queen of the Blues
See   Thomas, Blanche

[The] Queen of the Blues
See   Waters, Ethel

Queen of the Crystal Tank
See   Webb, Ada

Queen of the Desert
See   Stanhope, Hester Lucy

[The] Queen of the Discotheques
See   Gaynor, Gloria

[The] Queen of the East
See   Zenobia

[The] Queen of the Folksingers
See   Baez, Joan

[The] Queen of the Hillbillies
See   McCord, May Kennedy

[The] Queen of the Ice
See   Blanchard, Theresa Weld

[The] Queen of the Ice
See   Henie, Sonja

[The] Queen of the Memphis Sound
See   Thomas, Carla

[The] Queen of the Moaners
See   Gibbons, Irene

[The] Queen of the Moaners
See   Smith, Clara

[The] Queen of the Night Clubs
See   Alix, Liza Mae

[The] Queen of the Northern Seas
See   Elizabeth I

[The] Queen of the Plaza
See   Menken, Adah Isaacs

Queen of the Radio
See   Guillot, Olga

[The] Queen of the Soaps
See   Phillips, Irna

Queen of the South
See   Broil, Arlette B.

[The] Queen of the Torchers
See   Mulcahy, A. E.

[The] Queen of the Yodelers
See   Bedra, Julie Marlene

[The] Queen of Thriller Writers
See   Christie, Agatha [Mary
Clarissa]

[The] Queen of Virgins
See   Elizabeth I

Queen Rachel
See   Canevaro, Barbara

Queen Sarah
See   Churchill, Sarah Jennings

[The] Queen Square Hermit
See   Bentham, Jeremy

Queen Willa
See   Dickson, Willa

[The] Queen's Earl of Desmond
See   Fitzgerald, James

[The] Queen's Favorite Physician
See   Arbuthnot, John

[The] Queen's Poisoner
See   Rene, Master

Queerfellow, Quintin
See   Clark, Charles

Queerquill
See   Waggamon, Mary T.

Quencher, Mark
See   Conolly, Charles M.

Quennell, C. H.
See   Quennell, Charles Henry
Bourne

Quennell, Charles Henry Bourne
1872-1935   [LC]
Architect and author
*  Quennell, C. H.

Quentin, Patrick [joint pseudonym
with Hugh Callingham Wheeler]
See   Webb, Richard Wilson

Quentin, Patrick [joint pseudonym
with Richard Wilson Webb]
See   Wheeler, Hugh Callingham

Querard, Joseph-Maria 1797-1865
[PA]
Author
*  D'Erquar, Mar. Jozon

Querculus
See   Chesnan, Nicolas

Quercus
See   Kingsley, O. A.

[El] Queretaro [The Man from
Queretaro]
See   Sanroman, Ernesto

Query
See   Brady, James T.

Query, Peter, Esq.
See   Tupper, Martin Farquhar

Quesnay de Beaurepaire, Jules
1837-1923   [WBD]
French jurist and author
*  De Glouvet, Jules

Questal, Mae 20th c.   [CED]
American entertainer
*  [The] Betty Boop Girl

Question Mark
See   Martinez, Rudy

Quevedo
See   Wright, R. W.

Quevedo, Walter C.   [FFF, PA]
American writer
*  Odds and Ends

Quex
See   Nichols, George Herbert
Fosdike

Queyroul, Henri 1857-1921   [BEW]
French-born playwright
*  Keroul, Henri

Quibell, Agatha Hunt 1921-
[AW, WD]
Canadian-born author
*  Pearce, A. H.

Quichot, Dona
See   Tomkiewicz, Mina

Quick, Annabelle 1922-   [CA]
American translator
*  MacMillan, Annabelle

Quick, Dorothy
See   Meyer, Dorothy Quick

Quick Draw McGraw
See   McGraw, Donnie

Quick Hands Torres
See   Torres, Jose Luis

Quick, Ida
See   Maurer, Mrs. George W.

Quick, John 1748-1831   [RH]
British comedian
*  [The] Retired Diocletian of
Islington

Quick, Lyman 1907-   [EG, GF]
American golfer
*  Quick, Smiley

Quick, Philip
See   Strage, Mark

Quick, Smiley
See   Quick, Lyman

Quick, Tom
See   Wooldridge, George B.

Quicksell, Howard 1901-1953
[WWJ]
American jazz musician
*  Quicksell, Howdy

Quicksell, Howdy
See   Quicksell, Howard

Quid
See   Fitzgerald, Robert Allan

[Un] Quidam
See   Turla, Leopoldo

Quidam
See   Weintraub, Wiktor

Quiellens, Maurice 20th c.   [RBE]
American boxer
*  Quiellens, Tiger

Quiellens, Tiger
See   Quiellens, Maurice

Quien Sabe?
See   Bates, Harry Arthur

Quiet, Charles
See   Noyes, Charles Henry

[The] Quiet Corruptor
See   Remus, George

Quiet Joe Knight
See   Knight, Jonas William

[A] Quiet Man
See   Thayer, Alexander Wheelock

Quiet Observer
See   Wilson, Erasmus

[The] Quiet Tiger
See   Charles, Ezzard

[The] Quietist
See   Molinos, Miguel de

Quievreux, Jean-Francois 1926-
[EJ7]
French jazz musician
*  Gilson, Jef

Quigley, Aileen 1930-   [IAW]
British author
*  Fabian, Ruth
*  Lindley, Erica

Quigley, Eileen Elliott
See   Vivers, Eileen Elliott

Quigley, Ernest C. 1880-1968
Canadian-born basketball official
*  Quigley, Quig

Quigley, Jane 1939-   [TR]
American actress
*  Alexander, Jane

Quigley, Joan 20th c.   [CA]
American astrologer and author
*  Star, Angel

Quigley, Margery 1886-
American author
*  Clark, Margery [joint pseudonym
with Mary E. Clark]

Quigley, Quig
See   Quigley, Ernest C.

Quigley, Thomas James 1860-1913
[BEW]
American theatrical performer
*  Seabrooke, Thomas Q.

Quignard, Odette 1898-   [BEW]
French actress
*  Myrtil, Odette

Quilibet, Philip
See   Pond, George E.

Quilici, Frank Ralph 1939-   [BE]
American baseball player
*  Quilici, Guido

Quilici, Guido
See   Quilici, Frank Ralph

Quill
See   Grange, Cyril

Quill, Barnaby
See   Brandner, Gary

[The] Quill Man
See   Johnson, William B.

Quill, Timothy
See   Warren, Arthur

Quiller, Andrew
See   Bulmer, [Henry] Kenneth

Quiller-Couch, [Sir] Arthur Thomas
1863-1944   [CC, LC, TC]
British author
*  Q.

Quillet, Dame
See   Morency, Suzanne Giroux

Quilter, Eddie
See   Woodman, Thomas

Quilty, Silver
See   Quilty, Sylvester Patrick

Quilty, Sylvester Patrick 1891-
[BBH, CSH]
Canadian football player
*  Quilty, Silver

Quin, Dan
See   Lewis, Alfred Henry

**Quin, James** 1693-1766
[DNNS, RH]
*Irish actor*
\* [The] Whitfield of the Stage

**Quin, Mike**
*See* Ryan, Paul William

**Quince, Peter**
*See* Day, George Harold

**Quince, Peter**
*See* Story, Isaac

**Quince, Peter Lum**
*See* Ritchie, [Harry] Ward

**Quincunx, [Ms.] Ramona J.**
*See* Borgmann, Dmitri A[lfred]

**Quincy, Edmund** 1808-1877
[FFF, PA]
*American writer*
\* Byles
\* D. Y.

**Quincy, Josiah** 1744-1775
[FFF, PA]
*American author and patriot*
\* Hyperion
\* [An] Independent
\* Mentor
\* Needham, Marchmont
\* Sexby, Edward

**Quincy, Samuel Miller** 1833- ?
[PA]
*Author*
\* [The] Man Who was a Private

**Quinichette, Paul** 1921-  [PMJ]
*American jazz musician*
\* Quinichette, Vice Pres

**Quinichette, Vice Pres**
*See* Quinichette, Paul

**Quinito**
*See* Navarro, Joaquin

**Quinlan, Finners**
*See* Quinlan, Thomas Aloysius

**Quinlan, Red**
*See* Quinlan, Sterling C.

**Quinlan, Runty**
*See* Quinlan, Walter

**Quinlan, Sterling C.** 1916-  [CA]
*American author*
\* Quinlan, Red

**Quinlan, Thomas Aloysius**
1887-1966  [BE]
*American baseball player*
\* Quinlan, Finners

**Quinlan, Walter** 20th c.  [BLB]
*American gangster*
\* Quinlan, Runty

**Quinn, Edwin McIntosh**
1906-1952?  [WWJ]
*American jazz musician*
\* Quinn, Snoozer

**Quinn, Elisabeth** 1881-1962  [SAT]
*American author and editor*
\* Adams, Dale
\* Quinn, Vernon
\* Vequin, Capini

**Quinn, Ethel**
*See* Russell, Lindsay Patricia

**Quinn, Jimmy** 20th c.  [BLB]
*American underworld figure*
\* Hot Stove Jimmy

**Quinn, John Edward Pick**
1884-1956  [BE]
*American baseball player*
\* Quinn, Pit

**Quinn, John Picus [Jack]**
*See* Picus, John Quinn

**Quinn, Kitty**
*See* Wilkinson, Mrs. R. O.

**Quinn, Maire Roden**  ?-1947
[BEW]
*Irish-born actress*
\* Quinn, Mary

**Quinn, Mary**
*See* Quinn, Maire Roden

**Quinn, Paddy**
*See* Quinn, Patrick

**Quinn, Pat** 20th c.
*Hockey player and coach*
\* Crunch, Captain

**Quinn, Patrick** 19th c.  [BE]
*American baseball player*
\* Quinn, Paddy

**Quinn, Pit**
*See* Quinn, John Edward Pick

**Quinn, Simon**
*See* Smith, William Martin

**Quinn, Snoozer**
*See* Quinn, Edwin McIntosh

**Quinn, Vernon**
*See* Quinn, Elisabeth

**Quinn, Wellington Hunt**
1918-1954  [BE]
*American baseball player*
\* Quinn, Wimpy

**Quinn, Wimpy**
*See* Quinn, Wellington Hunt

**Quino**
*See* Lavado, Joaquin

**Quinones, Francisco Mariano**
1830-1903  [CW]
*Puerto Rican author*
\* Kadosh, A.

**Quint, Jeanne**
*See* Benoliel, Jeanne Quint

**Quintana, Luis Joaquin** 1951-  [BE]
*Puerto Rican-born baseball player*
\* Santos, Luis Joaquin

**Quintana, Manuel Jose** 1772-1857
[DEP, HN, SN]
*Spanish poet and orator*
\* [The] Spanish Tyrtaeus
\* [The] Tyrtaeus of Spain

**Quintanilla, Chinito**
*See* Quintanilla, Roberto

**Quintanilla, Luis** 1900-  [NAA]
*French-born author and poet*
\* Taniya, Kyn

**Quintanilla, Maria Aline Griffith y
Dexter, Condesa De**
*See* Griffith, Maria Aline

**Quintanilla, Roberto** 20th c.  [RBE]
*Mexican boxer*
\* Quintanilla, Chinito

**Quintin, Rex**
*See* Hardinge, Charles Wrexe

**Quinton, John P[urcell]** 1879- ?
[WGT]
*British author*
\* MacBride, Melchoir

**Quinton, Paul**
*See* Wright, W. George

**Quintus Icilius**
*See* Guichard [or Guischard], Karl
Gottlieb

**Quinzano**
*See* Conti, Giovanni-Francesca

**Quiroule, Pierre [Rolling Stone]**
*See* Sayer, Walter William

**Quisenberry, Dan**
*American baseball player*
\* [The] Quiz

**Quitman, Wallace**
*See* Palmer, Raymond A[rthur]

**Quittenton, Bertram** 20th c.  [MBF]
*British author*
\* Quiz, Roland, Jr.

**Quittenton, Richard Martin Howard**
1833-1914  [MBF]
*British author*
\* Quiz, Roland

**Quivas, Manuel**
*See* Quivers, Emanual

**Quiver**
*See* Dyson, Timothy J.

**Quivers, Emanual** 19th c.  [IBW]
*American pioneer*
\* Quivas, Manuel

**Quivey, Grace** 1873-1927  [BEW]
*American singer*
\* Van Studdiford, Grace

**Quivogne de Montifaud, Marie
Amelie** 1850- ?
*French author*
\* [The] Boccaccio of the
   Nineteenth Century
\* Montifaud, Marc de

**[The] Quixote of the North**
*See* Charles XII

**Quiz**
*See* Caswall, Edward

**Quiz**
*See* Dickens, Charles

**Quiz**
*See* Pickles, Frank K.

**[The] Quiz**
*See* Quisenberry, Dan

**Quiz, Roland**
*See* Quittenton, Richard Martin
Howard

**Quiz, Roland, Jr.**
*See* Quittenton, Bertram

**Quod, John**
*See* Irving, John Treat

**Quodlibets**
*See* Hayman, Robert

**Quoirez, Francoise** 1935-
[CA, FC, LC]
*French author and playwright*
\* Sagan, Francoise

**Quondam**
*See* Stevens, Charles McClellan

**Quousque**
*See* Atkins, Frederick Anthony

**Quow**
*See* McTurk, Michael

# R

* Indicates Assumed Name

**R**
*See* Rees, [Morgan] Goronwy

**R.**
*See* Rosselet, Andre

**R. B.**
*See* Barrett, Roderic

**R. B.**
*See* Beaver, Robert Atwood

**R. B.**
*See* Beverly, Robert

**R. B.**
*See* Bradford, Robert

**R. B. G.**
*See* Ganly, Rosaleen Brigid

**R. C. H.**
*See* Hoare, [Sir] Richard Colt

**R. E. L.**
*See* Mullins, Rossana E.

**R. E. M.**
*See* Mullins, Rossana E.

**R. E. M. M.**
*See* Moore, Richard E. M.

**R. E. M. W.**
*See* Whitaker, Rogers Ernest Malcolm

**R. F.**
*See* Fendt, Rene

**R. F. D., Mrs.**
*See* Peden, Rachel Mason

**R. F. K.**
*See* Kennedy, Robert Francis [Bobby]

**R. G. W.**
*See* White, Richard Grant

**R. H.**
*See* Hawker, Robert

**R. H.**
*See* Hobson, Robert

**R. H. L.**
*See* Humphrey, L. J.

**R. J.**
*See* Jeffries, Richard

**R. K.**
*See* Kent, Rockwell

**R. K. M.**
*See* Mankittrick, Richard Kendall

**R. L. S.**
*See* Stevenson, Robert Louis Balfour

**R. M.**
*See* Moore, Richard E. M.

**R. M. B.**
*See* Broadfield, Robina Margaret

**R. M. C. E.**
*See* Eagar, Richard Michael Cardwell

**R. P.**
*See* Pair, Ronald R.

**R. P.**
*See* Paltock, Robert

**R. P. H. G.**
*See* Howgrave-Graham, Robert P.

**R. R.**
*See* Reynolds, Ruth Evelyn Millicent

**R. W.**
*See* Whitaker, Rogers Ernest Malcolm

**R. W. G.**
*See* Gammon, Robert William

**R. W. N.**
*See* Nichols, Richard William

**Raabe, Wilhelm** 1831-1910 [WBD]
*German poet and author*
* Corvinus, Jakob

**Rab**
*See* Abba Arika

**Rab Roy Gaston**
*See* Gaston, Robert

**Rabagliati, Alberto**
*See* Rabagliati-Vinata, Alberto

**Rabagliati-Vinata, Alberto**
1906-1974 [SC]
*Italian actor and singer*
* Rabagliati, Alberto

**Rabago, Andres** 1947- [WEC]
*Spanish cartoonist*
* OPS

**Rabajos, Andy** 20th c. [PMJ]
*American singer*
* Russell, Andy

**Rabasseire, Henry**
*See* Paechter, Henry M[aximilian]

**Rabb, Theodore**
*See* Rabinowicz, Theodore

**Rabbi**
*See* Judah I [or Jehudah]

**[The] Rabbi of Swat**
*See* Solomon, Moses H.

**Rabbie**
*See* Towers, Maxwell

**[The] Rabbit**
*See* Huggins, Miller James

**Rabbit's Foot Williams**
*See* Coleman, Burl C.

**Rabbitt, Eddie**
*See* Thomas, Edward

**Rabdau, Marianne**
*See* Bakker-Rabdau, Marianne K[atherine]

**Rabe, Florence** 1888-1954
[BEW, FC]
*American actress*
* Bates, Florence

**Rabe, Folke**
*See* Reinhold, Alvar Harald

**Rabelais, Francois** 1494?-1553
[FFF, RH, SN]
*French satirist*
* [The] Father of Ridicule
* [The] Lucian of France
* Mad Man
* Nasier, Alcofribas
* [The] Phoenix of Wit
* [The] Ryparographer of Wits
* [The] Socrates of the French Renaissance

**[The] Rabelais of England**
*See* Sterne, Laurence

**[The] Rabelais of England**
*See* Swift, Jonathan

**[The] Rabelais of Geneva**
*See* Bonnivard, Francois de

**[The] Rabelais of Germany**
*See* Fischart, Johann

**[The] Rabelais of Good Society**
*See* Swift, Jonathan

**[The] Rabelaisian Doctor**
*See* Patin, Guy

**Rabi, I. I.**
*See* Rabi, Isidor Isaac

**Rabi, Isidor Isaac** 1898- [IPA]
*Austrian physicist*
* Rabi, I. I.

**Rabia, Aliyah** 1932- [EJ, IBW]
*American singer*
* Staton, Dakota
* Trucking Kid

**Rabin, Fishy**
*See* Rabinowitz, Philip

**Rabin, Philip**
*See* Rabinowitz, Philip

**Rabinowicz, Theodore** 1937- [JL]
*Czech-born historian and author*
* Rabb, Theodore

**Rabinowitsch, Lydia**
*See* Kempner, Lydia Rabinowitsch

**Rabinowitz, Jerome** 1918-
[BEW, EMT, IPA]
*American choreographer, dancer, director*
* Robbins, Jerome

**Rabinowitz, Philip** 20th c. [EJS]
*American basketball player*
* Rabin, Fishy
* Rabin, Philip

**Rabinowitz, Solomon J.** 1859-1916
[LC, TC, TLC]
*Russian-born author and playwright*
* Aleichem, Shalom
* [The] Jewish Mark Twain

**Rabinowitz, William Edward** 1915-
[BEW]
*American stage manager and director*
* Ross, Bill

**Raboy, Emanuel** 1914-1967
[WECO]
*American cartoonist*
* Raboy, Mac

**Raboy, Mac**
*See* Raboy, Emanuel

**Racagni, Giovanni** 1741-1822 [PA]
*Author*
* Maria, Giuseppe

**Racan, Marquis de**
*See* De Bueil, Honorat

**Rachel**
*See* Ferguson, Rachel

**Rachel, Mlle.**
*See* Felix, Elisa

**Rachell, James** 1910-
[BWW, NBB]
*American singer*
* Poor Jim
* Rachell, Yank

**Rachell, Yank**
See Rachell, James

**Rachilde**
See Vallette, Marguerite

**Rachman, Stanley Jack** 1934- [CA]
*South African-born psychologist and author*
* Durac, Jack

**Racina, Thom** 1946- [CA]
*American author and playwright*
* Anicar, Tom

**Racine, Jean Baptiste** 1639-1699
[DEP, DNNS, SN]
*French poet*
* Acante
* [L']Historien Trop Paye
* [L']Hypocrite Rimeur
* [The] Virgil of the French Drama

**[The] Racine of Italy**
See Trapassi, Pietro Antonio Domenico Bonaventura

**[The] Racine of Music**
See Sacchini, Antonio Maria Gaspare

**Racine's Monkey**
See Campistron, Jean Galbert de

**Racing, Mr.**
See Speers, James [Jim]

**Racke, Henry** 1883-1940 [SC]
*American actor*
* Gordon, C. Henry

**Rackham, John**
See Phillifent, John Thomas

**Raconteur**
See Poore, Benjamin Perley

**Racot, Adolph** [PA]
*Author*
* Dancourt

**Radatz, Richard Raymond [Dick]**
1937- [BE, PB]
*American baseball player*
* [The] Monster

**Radbourn, Charles Gardner**
1853?-1897 [AS, BBH, PB]
*American baseball player*
* Radbourn, Old Hoss
* Radbourn, Rad

**Radbourn, Dordy**
See Radbourn, George B.

**Radbourn, George B.** 1856-1904
[BE]
*American baseball player*
* Radbourn, Dordy

**Radbourn, Old Hoss**
See Radbourn, Charles Gardner

**Radbourn, Rad**
See Radbourn, Charles Gardner

**Radcliff, Raymond Allen**
1902?-1962 [AS, DGS, PB]
*American baseball player*
* Radcliff, Rip

**Radcliff, Rip**
See Radcliff, Raymond Allen

**Radcliffe, Anne** 1764-1823 [SN]
*British author*
* [The] Queen of Horror
* [The] Shakespeare of Romance Writers

**Radcliffe, Double Duty**
See Radcliffe, Theodore [Ted]

**Radcliffe, [Henry] Garnett** 1899-
[WW]
*Author*
* Travers, Stephen

**Radcliffe, Henry**
See Sims, Henry R.

**Radcliffe, Jack**
See Smith, Charles

**Radcliffe, Janette**
See Roberts, Janet Louise

**Radcliffe, Theodore [Ted]** 1904-
[B10, MK]
*American baseball player*
* Radcliffe, Double Duty

**Radcliffe, Virginia**
See Hurst, Virginia Radcliffe

**Rade, Paul Martin** 1857-1940
[WBD]
*German theologian*
* Martin, Paul

**Radebaugh, Roy** 1910-1960
[BEW, FC]
*American actor*
* Cromwell, Richard

**Radek, Karl Bernardovich**
See Sobelsohn, Karl

**Rademacher, Erich** 20th c. [BBH]
*German swimmer and water polo player*
* Rademacher, Ete

**Rademacher, Ete**
See Rademacher, Erich

**Rader, David M.** 1948- [PB]
*American baseball player*
* Rader, Rooster

**Rader, Douglas Lee** 1944-
[BE, PB]
*American baseball player*
* Rader, Rojo
* Rader, Rooster
* [The] Red Rooster

**Rader, Drew Leon** 1901- [BE]
*American baseball player*
* Rader, Lefty

**Rader, Lefty**
See Rader, Drew Leon

**Rader, Rojo**
See Rader, Douglas Lee

**Rader, Rooster**
See Rader, David M.

**Rader, Rooster**
See Rader, Douglas Lee

**Radetzky Von Radetz, [Countess] Berta Leonarz De Harding** 1902-
[AW]
*German-born author*
* Harding, Bertita

**Radford, Ruby L[orraine]**
1891-1971 [CA, SAT, WW]
*American author*
* Bailey, Matilda
* Ford, Marcia

**Radha**
See Smith, Mary

**Radical**
See Jones, Leslie Grove

**Radilovic, Julio** 1928- [WECO]
*Yugoslav cartoonist*
* Jules

**Radimsky, Ladislaw** 1898-1970
[CA]
*Czech diplomat, editor, author*
* Den, Petr

**Radio's Dream Girl**
See Joy, Alice

**Radio's Original Texas Cowgirl**
See Owens, Ruby

**Radla, Astrik** 954?-1044?
[DNNF, DNNS, FFF]
*Saint*
* Anastasius
* [The] Apostle of Hungary
* [The] Apostle of the Hungarians
* Astericus

**Radley, Clive Thornton** 1944- [DC]
*British cricketer*
* Radley, Grizzly

**Radley, Grizzly**
See Radley, Clive Thornton

**Radley, Harry John** 1910- [CEI]
*Canadian-born hockey player*
* Radley, Yip

**Radley, Yip**
See Radley, Harry John

**Radmilovic, Paul**
See Radmilovic, Paulo

**Radmilovic, Paulo** 1886-1968
[BBH, SWI]
*British swimmer*
* Radmilovic, Paul
* Radmilovic, Raddy

**Radmilovic, Raddy**
See Radmilovic, Paulo

**Rado, Agi**
See Rado, Agnes

**Rado, Agnes** 1931- [IWM]
*Hungarian-born musician*
* Rado, Agi

**Rado, Alexander**
See Radolfi, Alexander

**Radocchia, Emilio Joseph** 1932-
[ASC, EJ]
*American jazz musician*
* Richards, Emil

**Radolfi, Alexander** 20th c.
[EE, WWW]
*Russian intelligence agent*
* Kulichev, Ignati
* Rado, Alexander

**Radwanski, Pierre A[rthur]** 1903-
[CAP, WD]
*Canadian author and poet*
* Al-Van-Gar
* Chochlik
* O'Key
* Radwanski-Szinagel, [Dr.] Pierre A.

**Radwanski-Szinagel, [Dr.] Pierre A.**
See Radwanski, Pierre A[rthur]

**Radway, Ann**
See Geis, Richard E[rwin]

**Radyr, Tomos**
See Stevenson, James Patrick

**Radziwill, Catherine** 1858-1941
[WBD]
*Russian author*
* Vassili, [Count] Paul

**Radziwill, Nicholas** 1515-1565
[WBD]
*Prince of Nieswiez*
* [The] Black

**Radzyminska, Jozefa** 1921- [IAW]
*Polish author and poet*
* Mieczyslawa

**Rae, Charlotte**
See Lubotsky, Charlotte Rae

**Rae, Hugh C[rauford]** 1935-
[AW, CA, IAW]
*Scottish author and playwright*
* Crawford, Robert
* Houston, R. B.
* McGrath, Morgan
* Stern, Stuart
* Stirling, Jessica

**Rae, Jack**
See Sampley, Alton

**Rae, Johnny**
See Pompeo, John Anthony

**Rae, Milford Andersen** 1946- [CA]
*American author*
* Rae, Rusty

**Rae, Nan**
See Clark, Nan

**Rae, Rusty**
See Rae, Milford Andersen

**Rae, Scott**
See Hammill, Cicely Mary

**Raeburn, David**
See Herring, Paul

**Raeburn, [Sir] Henry** 1756-1823
[WBD]
*Scottish painter*
* [The] Scottish Reynolds

**Raeder, Cap**
See Raeder, Robert

**Raeder, Robert** 1953- [HR]
*American hockey player*
* Raeder, Cap

**Raemsdonck**
See De Ghesquiere, Joseph Jean

**Raether, Bud**
See Raether, Harold Herman [Hal]

**Raether, Harold Herman [Hal]**
1932- [BE]
*American baseball player*
* Raether, Bud

**Raevsky, Iosif Moiseevich**
See Gradus, Iosif Moiseevich

**Rafael, Beulah K.** 1893?-1964
[BEW]
*American theatrical performer*
* Kennedy, Beulah

**Rafael de Paula [Rafael from Paula]**
See Soto Moreno, Rafael

**Rafael, Juan Vicente**
See Rivera Viera, [Padre] Juan

**Raffaelino del Garbo**
See Capponi, Raffaello

**Raffaelli, Giuliano** 20th c.  [WF]
*Italian actor*
* Rafferty, Julian

**Raffaellino**
*See* Colle, Raffaello dal

**Raffalovich, George** 1880- ?
[WWL]
*British author*
* Sands, Bedwin

**Raffelock, David** 1897-  [CAP]
*American author*
* Locke, R. E.

**Rafferty, Chips**
*See* Goffage, John

**Rafferty, Julian**
*See* Raffaelli, Giuliano

**Raffety, Gordon Edward** 1907-
[NAA]
*American author and poet*
* Gray, John

**Raffles Bill**
*See* Aglassinger, Andreas

**Rafinesque, Constantine Samuel**
1783-1840  [WBD]
*Turkish-born naturalist*
* Rafinesque-Schmaltz,
  Constantine Samuel

**Rafinesque-Schmaltz, Constantine
Samuel**
*See* Rafinesque, Constantine
Samuel

**Raft, George**
*See* Ranft, George

**Rag, Captain**
*See* Smith, Edmund Neale

**[The] Rag Man**
*See* Burrows, Hermann

**Ragatzy, Anton**
*See* Parr, Julian F.

**[Il] Ragazzo**
*See* Broschi, Carlo

**Ragg, Thomas Murray** 1897-
[WW]
*Author*
* Thomas, Murray

**Ragged, Hyder**
*See* Biron, [Sir] Henry Chartres

**Ragged Staff**
*See* Coley, Rex

**[The] Ragin' Cajun**
*See* Guidry, Ron[ald Ames]

**Raglan, Baron**
*See* Raglan, FitzRoy

**Raglan, Baron**
*See* Somerset, Fitzroy James
Henry

**Raglan, Clarence Eldon** 1927-
[CEI]
*Canadian-born hockey player*
* Raglan, Rags

**Raglan, FitzRoy** 1885-1964  [CA]
*British author*
* Raglan, Baron
* Somerset, FitzRoy Richard

**Raglan, James**
*See* Cornwall-Walker, Thomas
James Raglan

**Raglan, Rags**
*See* Raglan, Clarence Eldon

**Ragland, John Morgan** 1906-1946
[BEW, WA]
*American theatrical performer*
* Ragland, Rags

**Ragland, Rags**
*See* Ragland, John Morgan

**Raglin, Alvin Redrick** 1917-1955
[EJ, WWJ]
*American jazz musician*
* Raglin, Junior

**Raglin, Junior**
*See* Raglin, Alvin Redrick

**Ragonese, Don** 1920-  [ASC]
*American composer, singer,
musician*
* Rodney, Don

**Ragsdale, Bob** 20th c.  [GW]
*American rodeo performer*
* Ragsdale, Rags

**Ragsdale, Lulah**
*See* Ragsdale, Tallulah

**Ragsdale, Rags**
*See* Ragsdale, Bob

**Ragsdale, Ray** 1939-  [ECM]
*American singer and songwriter*
* Stevens, Ray

**Ragsdale, Tallulah** 20th c.  [NAA]
*American author*
* Ragsdale, Lulah

**[The] Ragtime Girl**
*See* Barlow, Maud

**Ragtime Jimmy**
*See* Monaco, James

**Ragtime Jimmy Durante**
*See* Durante, James Francis
[Jimmy]

**Ragtime Joe Howard**
*See* Howard, Joseph

**[The] Ragtime Kid**
*See* Campbell, S. Brunson

**[The] Ragtime King**
*See* Greene, Gene

**Ragtime Texas Thomas**
*See* Thomas, Henry

**Ragusa, Paula** 1939-
[BDF, FC, HT]
*American actress*
* Prentiss, Paula

**Rahbeck, Knud Lyne** 1760-1830
[SN]
*Danish poet, author, critic*
* [The] Maecenas of Danish
  Letters

**Rahman, Abdul**
*See* Wayman, Tony Russell

**Rahner, Raymond M.** 20th c.  [CA]
*American actor, television
performer, author*
* Rayner, Ray

**Rahsaan Roland Kirk**
*See* Kirk, Ronald T.

**Rahsepar**
*See* Yar-Shater [or Yarshater],
Ehsan O[llah]

**Rahv, Philip**
*See* Greenberg, Ivan

**[The] Raider**
*See* Kilpatrick, [Hugh] Judson

**[The] Rail Splitter**
*See* Lincoln, Abraham

**Railroad Bill**
*See* Dorsey, Thomas A[ndrew]

**[The] Railway King**
*See* Gould, Jason

**[The] Railway King**
*See* Hudson, George

**[The] Railway King**
*See* Vanderbilt, William Henry

**Raimann, Ferdinand** 1790-1836
[WBD]
*Austrian actor and playwright*
* Raimund, Ferdinand

**Raimar, Freimund**
*See* Rueckert, Friedrich

**Raimbourg, Andre** 1917-1970
[FC, OCF, WEF]
*French actor and singer*
* Bourvil

**Raimon, Louis Albert Alexandre**
1922-
*French hairstylist*
* Alexandre

**Raimond**
*See* Hurlburt, William Henry

**Raimond, C. E.**
*See* Robins, Elizabeth

**Raimondi, Marcantonio**
1475?-1534?  [WBD]
*Italian engraver*
* Marcantonio

**Raimu**
*See* Muraire, Jules

**Raimund, Ferdinand**
*See* Raimann, Ferdinand

**Raimund, Golo**
*See* Dannenberg, George

**Rainalducci, Pietro** 14th c.  [WBD]
*Antipope*
* Nicholas V

**Rainbow [Secret Service code name]**
*See* Reagan, Nancy Davis

**Raine, Jack**
*See* Raine, Thomas Foster

**Raine, Nancy Greene** 1943-  [BBH]
*Canadian skier*
* Tiger of the Slopes

**Raine, Thomas Foster** 1897-
[BEW]
*British actor*
* Raine, Jack

**Rainer, Jerome**
*See* Goode, Gerald

**Rainer, Julia**
*See* Goode, Ruth

**Raines, Ella**
*See* Raubes, Ella Wallace

**Raines, Tim** 1961?-
*American baseball player*
* [The] Rock

**Rainey, Bill G.** 1926-  [CA]
*American author*
* Rainey, Buck

**Rainey, Buck**
*See* Rainey, Bill G.

**Rainey, Gertrude Malissa Nix
[Pridgett]** 1886-1939
[BWW, DAM, EJ]
*American singer*
* [The] Black Nightingale
* [The] Golden Necklace of the
  Blues
* Mama Can Can
* [The] Mother of the Blues
* [The] Paramount Wildcat
* Patterson, Lila
* Rainey, Ma
* Rainey, Madame
* Smith, Anne
* [The] Songbird of the South

**Rainey, Ma**
*See* Rainey, Gertrude Malissa Nix
[Pridgett]

**Rainey, Madame**
*See* Rainey, Gertrude Malissa Nix
[Pridgett]

**Rainey, Memphis Ma**
*See* Glover, Lilian

**Rainey, Norman**
*See* Morrison, William

**Rainey, Pa**
*See* Rainey, William

**Rainey, W. B.**
*See* Blassingame, Wyatt Rainey

**Rainey, William** 20th c.
[DAM, EJ, PMJ]
*American entertainer*
* Rainey, Pa

**Rainger, Ralph**
*See* Reichenthal, Ralph

**Rainham, Thomas**
*See* Barren, Charles

**Rainis, Janis**
*See* Plieksans, Janis

**Raintree, Lee**
*See* Sellers, Connie Leslie, Jr.

**Rainwater, Marvin**
*See* Percy, Marvin

**Rainy Day Smith**
*See* Smith, John Thomas

**Raisa, Rosa**
*See* Burchstein, Rosa Raisa

**Raittila, Anne-Maija**
*See* Nieminen, Anna-Maija

**Raj**
*See* Kalra, Rajinder Mohan

**Rajagopalacharia, Chakravarti**
1879-1972  [WBD]
*Indian politician*
* C. R.
* [The] Tamil Mahatma

**[The] Rajah**
*See* Hornsby, Rogers

**[The] Rajah**
*See* Roy, Rammohun

**Rajah, Raboid**
*See* Boyd, Ray

**Rajneesh, Acharya** 1931-    [CA]
*Indian mystic and author*
* Rajneesh, Bhagwan Shree

**Rajneesh, Bhagwan Shree**
See   Rajneesh, Acharya

**Rajonsky, Milton M.** 1924-    [IEJ]
*American jazz musician*
* Rogers, Shorty

**Raju**
See   Ahmed, Raju

**Raju, Poolla Tirupati** 1904-    [CA]
*Indian educator and author*
* Poolla, Tirupati Raju

**[The] Rake and Shovel Golfer**
See   Moore, LaVerne M.

**Raker, Hugh**
See   Endfield, Cyril Raker

**Raknes, Ola** 1887-1975    [CAP]
*Norwegian author*
* Arnold, Carl

**Rakosi, Carl** 1903-    [CA]
*German-born poet*
* Rawley, Callman

**Rakow, Edward Charles** 1936-
[BE]
*American baseball player*
* Rakow, Rock

**Rakow, Rock**
See   Rakow, Edward Charles

**Raleigh, Alan**
See   Brown, Elijah

**Raleigh, Bones**
See   Raleigh, James Donald

**Raleigh, Cecil**
See   Rowlands, Cecil

**Raleigh, Elizabeth** ?-1603    [SN]
*Wife of British courtier, Sir Walter
Raleigh*
* [The] Lovely Bessie

**Raleigh, James Donald** 1926-
[CEI, FHE]
*Canadian-born hockey player*
* Raleigh, Bones

**Raleigh, Richard**
See   Lovecraft, Howard Phillips

**Raleigh, [Sir] Walter** 1552?-1618
[DEP, DNNS]
*British courtier, explorer, statesman*
* [The] Knight of the Cloak
* [The] Ocean Shepherd
* [The] Shepherd of the Ocean

**Raleigh, Walter S.** 18th c.    [PA]
*Author*
* W. S. R.

**Raley, Rowena**
See   McCulley, Johnston

**Ralp, Howard**
See   Bretherton, Ralph Harold

**Ralph**
See   MacGregor, John

**Ralph, Jessie**
See   Chambers, Jessie Ralph

**Ralph, Julian E.** 1853-1903    [FFF]
*American journalist*
* German Barber

**Ralph 124E41**
See   Ackerman, Forrest J[ames]

**Ralph 124TL41**
See   Ackerman, Forrest J[ames]

**Ralston, Alma** 20th c.    [CA]
*American author*
* Payne, Alma Smith

**Ralston, Doc**
See   Ralston, Samuel Beryl

**Ralston, Gilbert A[lexander]** 1912-
[CA]
*American author*
* Alexander, Gil

**Ralston, Jan**
See   Dunlop, Agnes M. R.

**Ralston, Samuel Beryl** 1885-    [BE]
*American baseball player*
* Ralston, Doc

**Ralston, Vera** 1929?-
[BDF, FC, HT]
*American actress*
* Miles, Vera

**Ram Dass, [Baba] [Servant of God]**
See   Alpert, Richard

**Ram, Immanuel**
See   Velikovsky, Immanuel

**Ram John Holder**
See   Holder, John Wesley

**Rama**
See   Gupta, Ram Chandra

**Rama Rau, Santha**
See   Bowers, Santha Rama Rau

**Rama I**
See   Chao P'ya Chakri

**Rama VI**
See   Chao Fa Maha Vajiravudh

**Rama VII**
See   Prajadhipok

**Ramadhin, K. T.** 1930-    [EC]
*West Indian cricketer*
* Ramadhin, Sonny

**Ramadhin, Sonny**
See   Ramadhin, K. T.

**Ramage, Alan** 1957-    [DC]
*British cricketer*
* Ramage, Rod

**Ramage, Jennifer** 20th c.    [WW]
*Author*
* Mason, Howard

**Ramage, Rod**
See   Ramage, Alan

**Ramal, Walter**
See   De La Mare, Walter [John]

**Ramanan**
See   Venkateswaran, Taruvai
Anantaramaseshan

**Ramanujan, Molly** 1932-    [CA]
*Indian-born author*
* Daniels, Shouri
* Ramanujan, Shouri

**Ramanujan, Shouri**
See   Ramanujan, Molly

**Rambach, Miriam** 1888-    [JL]
*Polish-born ballet teacher*
* Rambert, [Dame] Marie

**Rambam**
See   Maimonides [or Moses ben
Maimon]

**Rambaud, Yveling**
See   Gilbert, Frederic

**Rambaut, A. Beatrice** 20th c.
[WWL]
*Irish author*
* Romney, A. B.

**Rambeau, Eddie**
See   Flurie, Edward Cletus

**Rambeau, Marjorie** 1889-1970
[FIR]
*American actress*
* [The] Bernhardt of the Klondike

**Rambert, Elmer Donald** 1917-    [BE]
*American baseball player*
* Rambert, Pep

**Rambert, [Dame] Marie**
See   Rambach, Miriam

**Rambert, Pep**
See   Rambert, Elmer Donald

**[The] Rambler**
See   Barton, George

**[The] Rambler**
See   Deutzman, Lawrence
F[rederick]

**Rambler**
See   Fullerton, George H.

**Rambler**
See   Holden, Luther L.

**Rambler**
See   Thatcher, John Wells

**Ramblin' Bob**
See   McCollum, Robert Lee

**Ramblin' Jack Elliott**
See   Adnopoz, Elliott Charles

**Rambling King Floyd**
See   Floyd, Frank

**Rambo, Pete**
See   Rambo, Warren Dawson

**Rambo, Warren Dawson** 1906-
[BE]
*American baseball player*
* Rambo, Pete

**Ramboldini [or de Ramboldoni],
Vittorino** 1378-1446    [WBD]
*Italian educator*
* Vittorino da Feltre

**Rambova, Natacha**
See   Shaunessy, Winifred

**Rame, David**
See   Divine, Arthur Durham

**Rame, Marie Louise** 1839-1908
[SAT]
*British author*
* De La Ramee, [Marie] Louise
* Ouida

**Rameau, Jean**
See   Labaigt, Laurent

**Rameau, Jean Philippe**
1683-1764?    [FFF, HN, SN]
*French musician and composer*
* [The] Newton of Harmony

**Rameau, Leon**
See   Maurras,
Charles-Marie-Photius

**[La] Ramee**
See   Ramus, Pierre

**Ramenghi, Bartolommeo**
1484-1542    [WBD]
*Italian painter*
* [Il] Bagnacavallo

**Ramey, Ben N.** 1921-1977    [ESF]
*American writer*
* Hollis, H. H.

**Ramirez, Alice Louise** 20th c.
[SFL]
*Author*
* Tiny Alice

**Ramirez, Jose** 1898-    [GS]
*Mexican bullfighter*
* Gaonita [Little Gaona]

**Ramirez, Orlando** 1950-    [BE]
*Colombian-born baseball player*
* Leal, Orlando

**Ramirez, Ram**
See   Ramirez, Roger J.

**Ramirez, Roger J.** 1913-
[ASC, WWJ]
*Puerto Rican-born jazz musician*
* Ramirez, Ram

**Ramirez Alonso, Alfonso** 1916-
[GS]
*Mexican bullfighter*
* [El] Calesero [The Buggy Driver]

**Ramirez-Sanchez, Ilyich** 1947?-
*Venezuelan-born terrorist*
* Carlos
* [The] Jackal

**Ramiro II** ?-1147    [WBD]
*King of Spain*
* [The] Monk

**Ramistella, John** 1942-
[PRS, RO2]
*American singer and songwriter*
* Rivers, Johnny

**Ramler, Charles William**
1725-1798    [SN]
*German poet*
* [The] German Horace

**Rammelsberg, Kate**    [FFF]
*Entertainer*
* Rolla, Mlle.

**Ramon**
See   Gomez de la Serna, Ramon

**Ramon, Boris**
See   Hawkins, Peter

**Ramon, Laon** 1917-    [F2]
*Actor*
* Janney, Leon

**Ramona**
See   Myers, Ramona

**Ramone, Dee Dee**
See   Colvin, Douglas

**Ramone, Joey**
See   Hyman, Jeffrey

**Ramone, Johnny**
See   Cummings, Johnny

**Ramone, Marky**
See   Bell, Mark

**Ramone, Tommy**
See   Erdelyi, Tommy

**Ramos, Armando** 1948-    [BX, RBE]
*American boxer*
* Ramos, Mando

**Ramos, Chucho**
See Ramos, Jesus Manuel Garcia

**Ramos, Jesus Manuel Garcia**
1918- [BE]
*Venezuelan-born baseball player*
* Ramos, Chucho

**Ramos, Mando**
See Ramos, Armando

**Ramos, Pedro Guerra** 1935- [BE]
*Cuban-born baseball player*
* Ramos, Pete

**Ramos, Pete**
See Ramos, Pedro Guerra

**Ramos, Sugar**
See Ramos Zaqueira, Urtiminio

**Ramos Lopez, Leopoldo** 1913-
[GS]
*Mexican bullfighter*
* Ahijado del Matadero
  [God-Child of the
  Slaughter-House]

**Ramos Zaqueira, Urtiminio** 1941-
[BX, RBE]
*Cuban boxer*
* Ramos, Sugar

**Ramp, James** 1898- [NAA]
*British-born author*
* Ames, Woodforde

**Rampo, Edogawa**
See Hirai, Taro

**Ramsay, Alexander** 1754-1824
[FFF]
*British-born anatomist*
* [The] Caliban of Science

**Ramsay, Allan** 1686-1758
[DEL, FFF, SN]
*Scottish poet*
* [The] Scottish Theocritus

**Ramsay, Andrew Michael**
1686-1743 [FFF, RH, WBD]
*Scottish author*
* [The] Cavalier

**Ramsay, Fay**
See Eastwood, Helen

**Ramsay, Fox**
See Ramsay, Maule

**Ramsay, Grace**
See O'Meara, Kathleen

**Ramsay, Joan**
See Wilson, Louise Bruguiere
Church

**Ramsay, Maule** 20th c. [BBH]
*Scottish-born sled dog racer*
* Ramsay, Fox

**Ramsay, Owen Nares** 1888-1943
[F1, F2, FC]
*British actor*
* Nares, Owen

**Ramsbottom, Mrs.**
See Hook, Theodore Edward

**Ramsdell, James Willard**
1918-1969 [BE]
*American baseball player*
* Willie the Knuck

**Ramsden, E. H.**
See Ramsden, Hartley

**Ramsden, F. E.** [FFF]
*American writer*
* Kalula

**Ramsden, Hartley** 20th c. [AW]
*British author*
* Ramsden, E. H.

**Ramsden, Lewis**
See Dowding, A. L.

**Ramses III [or Rameses]**
[DEP, WBD]
*King of Egypt*
* [The] Egyptian Solomon
* Rhampsinitus

**Ramses V [or Rameses]** [HN]
*King of Egypt*
* Memnon

**Ramsey, George?**
See Dorsey, Thomas A[ndrew]

**Ramsey, Joseph McCray** 1890-
[NAA]
*American editor*
* J. M. R.

**Ramsey, Square Jaw**
See Ramsey, William Thrace [Bill]

**Ramsey, Thomas A.** 1864-1906
[AS, BE, PB]
*American baseball player*
* Ramsey, Toad

**Ramsey, Toad**
See Ramsey, Thomas A.

**Ramsey, William Thrace [Bill]**
1921- [BE]
*American baseball player*
* Ramsey, Square Jaw

**Ramskill, Valerie Patricia
Roskams** [AW, CAP, WD]
*British author*
* Brooke, Carol

**Ramsome, [James] Stafford**
1860-1931 [SFL]
*Author*
* Lewis, Caroline [joint pseudonym
  with (Edward) Harold Begbie and
  M. H. Temple]

**Ramus, Pierre** 1515-1572 [PA]
*Author*
* [La] Ramee

**Rana, J.**
See Bhatia, Jamunadevi

**Rance, Janet Mary** 1928- [IAW]
*British writer*
* Graham, Janet

**[El] Ranchero [The Rancher]**
See Aguilar Gonzalez, Jorge

**Rand, Anne**
See Ozbekhan, Anne Binkley Rand

**Rand, Bill**
See Engler, William George

**Rand, Brett**
See Norwood, Victor G[eorge]
C[harles]

**Rand, Ellen**
See Fleming, Nellie

**[The] Rand Goal Mine**
See Geffin, Aaron

**Rand, J. H.**
See Holland, James R.

**Rand, James S.**
See Attenborough, Bernard George

**Rand, John**
See Reach, James

**Rand, Lionel**
See Van Clouser, Lionel

**Randall, Addison Owen** 1907-1945
[SC]
*American actor*
* Randall, Jack

**Randall, Anne Frances**
See Robinson, Mary Darby

**Randall, Arkle**
See Randall, Derek William

**Randall, Bo**
See Randall, W. D.

**Randall, Clay**
See Adams, Clifton

**Randall, Derek William** 1951-
[DC]
*British cricketer*
* Randall, Arkle

**Randall, Jack**
See Randall, Addison Owen

**Randall, Janet** [joint pseudonym with
Robert W(illiam) Young]
See Young, Jan[et Randall]

**Randall, Janet** [joint pseudonym with
Jan(et Randall) Young]
See Young, Robert W[illiam]
[Bob]

**Randall, Joseph** 1931-1970 [SC]
*American stunt performer*
* Starr, Randy

**Randall, Mary**
See Colver, Alice Mary [Ross]

**Randall, Rae**
See Salvason, Sigrum

**Randall, Richard** 20th c. [IBW]
*American dog breeder, hair stylist,
fashion designer*
* Mr. Rick

**Randall, Robert** [joint pseudonym
with Robert Silverberg]
See Garrett, [Gordon] Randall
[Philip David]

**Randall, Robert** [joint pseudonym
with Randall Garrett]
See Silverberg, Robert

**Randall, Robert Lee** 1948- [SMG]
*American baseball player*
* B. R.

**Randall, Rona**
See Shambrook, Rona

**Randall, Steven**
See Andrews, Clarence A[delbert]

**Randall, W. D.** 1909?- [B10]
*American knife maker*
* Randall, Bo

**Randall, William**
See Gwinn, William R.

**Randel, Adelaide**
See Atwood, Mrs.

**Randell, Benny** 20th c. [BBH]
*Boxer*
* Randell, Red

**Randell, Beverley**
See Price, Beverley Joan

**Randell, Red**
See Randell, Benny

**Randi, Don**
See Schwartz, Don

**Randi, James** 20th c.
*Magician*
* [The] Amazing Randi

**Randle, Frank**
See McEvoy, Arthur

**Randle, Sonny**
See Randle, Ulmo

**Randle, Ulmo** 1936- [FB]
*American football player*
* Randle, Sonny

**Randles, Anthony V[ictor], Jr.**
1942- [CA]
*American journalist*
* Randles, Slim

**Randles, Slim**
See Randles, Anthony V[ictor], Jr.

**Randolph, Arthur C.**
See Greene, Alvin Carl

**Randolph, Asa Philip** 1889-1979
[IBW]
*American labor leader*
* [The] Grand Old Man of Black
  Liberation

**Randolph, Big Jim**
See Randolph, James Lyle

**Randolph, Boots**
See Randolph, Homer Louis, III

**Randolph, Dorothy**
See Cohen, Dorothy

**Randolph, Ellen**
See Ross, William Edward Daniel

**Randolph, Georgiana Ann**
1908-1957 [CC, EMD, WGT]
*American author and screenwriter*
* Rice, Craig [joint pseudonym
  with Salvatore A. Lombino]
* Sanders, Daphne
* Venning, Michael

**Randolph, Gordon**
See Von Block, Sylvia

**Randolph, Homer Louis, III** 20th c.
[CME]
*American musician*
* Randolph, Boots

**Randolph, Irving** 1909-
[DAM, EJ, PMJ]
*American jazz musician*
* Randolph, Mouse

**Randolph, [Lieutenant] J. H.**
See Ellis, Edward S[ylvester]

**Randolph, James Lyle** 1930-1970
[IBW]
*American disc jockey*
* Randolph, Big Jim

**Randolph, Jerry**
See Brannon, William T.

**Randolph, John**
See Cohen, Emanuel Hirsch

**Randolph, John** 1773-1833 [FFF]
*American statesman*
* Jack the Giant-Killer

**Randolph, John** (Continued)
\* [The] Man with the Sling

**Randolph, Josie Lee**
See Beers, Mrs. J. Newton

**Randolph, Lillian** 20th c.   [IBW]
American actress and conductor
\* Madame Queen

**Randolph, Marion**
See Rodell, Marie F[reid]

**Randolph, Mouse**
See Randolph, Irving

**Randolph, Nancy**
See McCarthy, Julia

**Randolph, Nancy**
See Robb, Inez [Callaway]

**Randolph, Paschal Beverly** 1825- ?
[FFF]
Author
\* Lee, Griffin

**Randolph, Randy**
See Randolph, Zilner T.

**Randolph, Richard**
See Pentelow, John Nix

**Randolph, Thomas, Jr. [Tom]**
1943-   [IBW]
American track and field athlete
\* Speed, Mr.

**Randolph, Zilner T.** 1899-   [MY]
American jazz musician
\* Randolph, Randy

**Random, Alan**
See Kay, Ernest

**Random, Alex**
See Rowland, D[onald] S[ydney]

**Rands, William Brightly** ?-1882
[DEL, PA]
British writer
\* Browne, Matthew
\* Fieldmouse, Timon
\* Holbeach, Henry

**Randy Andy**
See Andrew

**Raney, Butch**
See Raney, Gordon

**Raney, Frank Robert Donald**
See Raniszewski, Frank Robert
Donald

**Raney, Gordon** ?-1953   [BBH]
American basketball player and
coach
\* Raney, Butch

**Raney, Ribs**
See Raniszewski, Frank Robert
Donald

**Raney, Sue**
See Claussen, Raelene

**Ranft, George** 1895-
[BDF, F2, FC]
American actor
\* Raft, George

**Rangefinder**
See Miles, Frederic James

**Rangely, Olivia**
See Zachary, Hugh

**[The] Ranger**
See Flack, Captain

**Ranger Bill**
See William, Joseph

**Ranger, Ken**
See Creasey, John

**Ranger, Morris**   [SN]
British speculator
\* [The] Napoleon of Liverpool
Finance

**Ranieri** 1050?-1118   [WBD]
Pope
\* Paschal II

**Raniszewski, Frank Robert Donald**
1923-   [BE]
American baseball player
\* Raney, Frank Robert Donald
\* Raney, Ribs

**Ranjee**
See Shahani, Ranjee

**Ranji**
See Ranjitsinhji, Kumar Shri

**Ranjit [or Runjeet], Singh**
1780-1839   [HN, WBD]
Maharaja
\* [The] Lion of the Punjab
\* [The] Mountain Tiger of Nepaul

**Ranjitsinhji, Kumar Shri**
1872-1933   [NN]
Cricketer and Maharajah of
Nawanagar
\* Ranji

**Rank, Otto**
See Rosenfeld, Otto

**Rankin, Arthur**
See Davenport, Arthur Rankin

**Rankin, Arthur McKee** 1841-1914
[THR]
Canadian-born actor and theatrical
manager
\* Henley, George

**Rankin, Fannie W.**   [PA]
Author
\* F. W. R.

**Rankin, Hugh Doak** 20th c.   [WGT]
American author
\* Doak

**Rankin, John**
See Morse, Withrow

**Rankin, Mrs. McKee**   [FFF]
Entertainer
\* Blanchard, Kittie

**Rankin, R. S.** 1933-   [BWW]
American singer
\* Little T Bone
\* Walker, T Bone, Jr.

**Rankin, Ruth [DeLone] I[rvine]**
1924-   [CA]
American author
\* DeLone, Ruth

**Rankin, Stella** 1915-   [ART]
British painter
\* S. R.

**Rankine, John**
See Mason, Douglas R[ankine]

**Rann, John** ?-1774
[DNNF, DNNS, RH]
British highwayman
\* Sixteen-String Jack

**Ranney, Agnes V.** 1916-
[B10, CA, SAT]
American author
\* Reeves, Ruth Ellen

**Ransenthaler, Peter** 1929-   [SW]
German actor
\* Carsten, Peter

**Ransford, Oliver Neil** 1914-   [AW]
British-born physician and author
\* Wylcotes, John

**Ransom, Frank** 1870-1921   [BEW]
American actor
\* Mills, Frank

**Ransom, Jay Ellis** 1914-   [CA]
American author
\* Adams, Henry T.

**Ransom, Olive**
See Stephens, Kate

**Ransome, Charles A.**
See Rowe, John Gabriel

**Ransome, L. E.** 20th c.   [MBF]
British author
\* Clifford, Martin [house
pseudonym]
\* Hayes, Ivor
\* Melbourne, Ivor
\* Norman, Victor
\* Richards, Frank [house
pseudonym]
\* Stirling, Tom

**Ransome, Mrs. J. W.**   [FFF]
Entertainer
\* Bordeaux, Ella

**Ransome, Stephen**
See Davis, Frederick Clyde

**Ransome-Davies, Basil**
See Colley, Iain

**Rant, Tol E.**
See Longyear, Barry Brookes

**Rantipole**
See Bonaparte, Charles Louis
Napoleon

**Ranyard, Ellen Henrietta White**
1810-1879   [DEL, FFF]
British author
\* L. N. R.

**Ranzini, Addis Durning** 1909-
[NAA]
American author and columnist
\* Ames, Elinor

**Raoul** [code name used during World
War II]
See Churchill, Peter

**Raoul, Anthony**
See Wilmot, Anthony

**Raoul, M.** ?-1274   [PA]
Author
\* De Ferriers

**Rapagnetto-D'Annunzio, Gabriele**
[original family surname?]
See D'Annunzio, Gabriele

**Rapaport, Jerome L.** 1928-   [CA]
American historian and author
\* Clark, Jerome L.

**Raper, Jack**
See Raper, Julius Rowan

**Raper, Julius Rowan** 1938-   [CA]
American author
\* Raper, Jack

**Raphael**
See Santi [or Sanzio?], Raffaello

**Raphael, Chaim** 1908-
[CA, CC, WW]
British author
\* Davey, Jocelyn
\* Raphael, Rab

**Raphael, Elaine**
See Bolognese, Elaine Raphael
[Chionchio]

**Raphael, Frederic [Michael]** 1931-
[CA]
American-born author
\* Caine, Mark [joint pseudonym
with Tom Maschler]

**Raphael, Jay**
See Josephs, Ray

**Raphael, John N.** 1868-1917
[BEW]
Playwright, critic, journalist
\* Percival

**Raphael, [Father] M.**
See Goldgraber, Kenneth

**[The] Raphael of Cats**
See Mind, Gottfried [or Godefroi]

**[The] Raphael of Domestic Art**
See Wilkie, [Sir] David

**[The] Raphael of England**
See Reynolds, [Sir] Joshua

**[The] Raphael of France**
See Le Sueur [or Lesueur],
Eustache

**[The] Raphael of Holland**
See Van Hemskerck, Martin

**[The] Raphael of Music**
See Mozart, Johannes Chrysostom
Wolfgangus Theophilus

**[The] Raphael of Opera**
See Mozart, Johannes Chrysostom
Wolfgangus Theophilus

**[The] Raphael of the Parc-aux-Cerfs**
See Boucher, Francois

**Raphael, Rab**
See Raphael, Chaim

**Raphaela, Cornelius [Nechi]**
1914?-   [CW]
Curacaon author and poet
\* Hernandez, Victor P.

**Raphaelle**
See Guertin, Raphaelle-Berthe

**Rapid Robert Feller**
See Feller, Robert William
Andrew

**Rapid, Young**
See Brown, T. Allston

**[The] Rapier of the North**
See Chapdelaine, Ovila

**Rapp, Butler** 1898?-1931   [NOJ]
American jazz musician
\* Rapp, Guye

**Rapp, Goldie**
See Rapp, Joseph Aloysius

**Rapp, Guye**
See Rapp, Butler

**Rapp, Joseph Aloysius** 1892-   [BE]
American baseball player
\* Rapp, Goldie

**Rapp, Louis** 1909-1970 [PMJ]
*American singer*
* Wood, Barry

**Rappaport, Solomon** 1863-1920
[BEW]
*Playwright*
* Ansky, S. A.

**Rapuzzi, G. L.** 20th c. [SFP]
*Author*
* Gray, Woody
* Renna, G.

**Raq**
*See* Evens, Glyn Kinnaird

**Raquenue, Izmael**
*See* Zequiera y Arango, Manuel de

**Rare Ben Jonson**
*See* Jonson, Ben[jamin]

**Rarey, John Solomon** 1827?-1866
[FFF]
*American horse-tamer and author*
* Scrutator

**Rariden, Bedford Bill**
*See* Rariden, William Angel

**Rariden, William Angel** 1888-1942
[BE]
*American baseball player*
* Rariden, Bedford Bill

**Rasch, C. M.**
*See* Rasch, Catherine Margaret

**Rasch, Catherine Margaret** 1891-
[ART]
*British painter*
* Rasch, C. M.

**Raschi, Victor John Angelo** 1919-
[BE]
*American baseball player*
* [The] Springfield Rifle

**Rascoe, Jesse Ed**
*See* Bartholomew, Ed[ward
Ellsworth]

**Rasey, Ruth M.**
*See* Simpson, Ruth Mary Rasey

**Rash, Dora Eileen Agnew [Wallace]**
1897- [AW, CA]
*British author*
* Wallace, Doreen

**Rashad, Ahmad**
*See* Moore, Robert E. [Bobby]

**Rasheed, [Rev.] Hakeem**
*See* Jones, Clifford

**Rashid al-Din** 1250?-1318 [WBD]
*Arabic historian*
* Tabib, al- [The Physician]

**Raskin, Big Tubby**
*See* Raskin, Morris

**Raskin, Julius** 1906- [EJS]
*American basketball player*
* Raskin, Little Tubby

**Raskin, Little Tubby**
*See* Raskin, Julius

**Raskin, Morris** 20th c. [EJS]
*American basketball coach*
* Raskin, Big Tubby

**Raskind, Richard** 1935-
*American ophthalmologist and
tennis pro who underwent sex-
change surgery*
* Richards, Renee

**Rasley, John M.** 1913- [ASC]
*American composer*
* Johnston, Randolph

**Rasmussen, Deerfoot**
*See* Rasmussen, Wayne

**Rasmussen, Eric Ralph**
*See* Rasmussen, Harold Ralph

**Rasmussen, Harold Ralph** 1952-
[SMG]
*American baseball player*
* [The] Great Dane
* Rasmussen, Eric Ralph

**Rasmussen, Juliana**
*See* Galcai, Lalauga Malana Au
Faoa Taupou O. Tuffle Tuimanua

**Rasmussen, Wayne** 20th c.
*American football player*
* Rasmussen, Deerfoot

**Rasofsky, Barnet David** 1909-1967
[AS, BX, EJS]
*American boxer*
* Ross, Barney

**Rasputin, Grigori Efimovich**
1871?-1916 [BL]
*Russian mystic*
* [The] Holy Satyr
* [The] Mad Monk

**Rasputin, Maria**
*See* Bern, Maria Rasputin Soloviev

**Rassoul, Mohammed**
*See* Bogan, Gulam

**Rastelli, Oreste** 1900- [BMH]
*Italian-born acrobat*
* Voltige a la Richard

**Rastelli, Philip** 20th c.
*American underworld figure*
* Rastelli, Rusty

**Rastelli, Rusty**
*See* Rastelli, Philip

**Rasulala, Thalmus**
*See* Crowder, Jack

**[The] Rat**
*See* Linseman, Ken

**[The] Rat**
*See* Ratcliffe, [Sir] Richard

**Rata-Langa**
*See* Galantara, Gabriele

**Ratatoskr**
*See* Blaich, Hans Erich

**Ratazzi, Mme.** 1830- ? [PA]
*Author*
* D'Albans, Vicompte
* Stack, Baron

**Ratcliffe, Patricia** 1940- [IAW]
*British author*
* King, Teri

**Ratcliffe, Ratters**
*See* Ratcliffe, Robert Malcolm

**Ratcliffe, [Sir] Richard** [SN]
* [The] Rat

**Ratcliffe, Robert Malcolm** 1951-
[DC]
*British cricketer*
* Ratcliffe, Ratters

**Ratcliffe, Samuel Kirkham** 1868- ?
[WWL]
*American journalist*
* Kirkman, Francis

**Ratcliffe, Wilton Calvert** 1903-
[BEW]
*American actor*
* Graff, Wilton

**Rath, E. J.** [joint pseudonym with
Edith Rathbone (Jacobs) Brainerd]
*See* Brainerd, Chauncey Corey

**Rath, E. J.** [joint pseudonym with
Chauncey Corey Brainerd]
*See* Brainerd, Edith Rathbone
[Jacobs]

**Rathbone, William** 19th c. [PA]
*Author*
* [The] Man of Business

**Rathborne, St. George** 1854-1938
[NAA, WW]
*American author*
* Adams, Harrison
* Burton, Andy
* Carter, Herbert
* Clifton, Oliver Lee
* Dale, Dash
* Duncan, Duke
* Edwards, Ward
* Forbes, Aleck
* Howard, Jack
* Langley, John Prentice
* Lawson, W. B.
* Leslie, Lawrence
* Manly, Marline
* Merrick, Mark
* Miller, Warne
* Robertson, Alex
* St. George, Harry
* Sharpe, Jack
* Stewart, Gordon

**Rather, Bo**
*See* Rather, David Elmer

**Rather, David Elmer** 1950- [SMG]
*American football player*
* Rather, Bo

**Rathgeber, Ralph** 1920-
[BDF, BEW, FC]
*American actor*
* Meeker, Ralph

**Rathjen, Carl H[enry]** 1909-
[IAW, SAT]
*American author*
* Russell, Charlotte
* Russell, Clinton

**Ratigan, Eleanor Eldridge** 1916-
[CA]
*American author*
* Wharton, Virginia

**Ratisbonne, Louis Fortune Gustave**
1827-1900 [WBD]
*French author*
* Trim

**Ratner, Joann** 1931- [BEW]
*American actress*
* Merlin, Joanna

**Rato [Rat]**
*See* Fittipaldi, Emerson

**Ratsch, Fred E.** 1891-1933 [SC]
*American actor*
* Rooney, Pat

**Rattenberry, William A.**
1857-1933 [SC]
*American actor*
* White, Bill

**Ratti, Ambrogio Damiano Achille**
1857-1939 [CBS]
*Pope*
* Pius XI

**Rattlebrain**
*See* Halse, G.

**[The] Rattler**
*See* Riley, Ken

**Rattler, Morgan**
*See* Banks, Percival Weldon

**Rattray, Henrietta Barbara** 20th c.
[WWL]
*British author*
* Jehan, Noor

**Rattray, Simon**
*See* Dudley-Smith, Trevor

**Rau, Bayone**
*See* Rau, Douglas James

**Rau, Douglas James** 1948- [SMG]
*American baseball player*
* Rau, Bayone

**Rau, Nicander Edwin** 1877?-1951
[BEW]
*American entertainer*
* Nicander, Edwin

**Raubenheimer, George Harding**
1923- [AW, WD]
*South African author and
screenwriter*
* Harding, George

**Raubes, Ella Wallace** 1921- [FC]
*American actress*
* Raines, Ella

**Rauch, Billy**
*See* Rauch, Russell

**Rauch, Russell** 1910- [PMJ]
*American musician*
* Rauch, Billy

**Raudive-Maurina, Zenta** 1897-
[IAW]
*Latvian-born author*
* Maurina, Zenta

**Raudman, Robert Joyce [Bob]**
1942- [BE]
*American baseball player*
* Raudman, Shorty

**Raudman, Shorty**
*See* Raudman, Robert Joyce [Bob]

**Raul**
*See* Pederneiras, Raul Paranhos

**Rault, Walter**
*See* Gorham, Maurice Anthony
Coneys

**Rausse**
*See* Franke, H. F.

**Rautakallio, Pekka Olavi** 1953-
[SMG]
*Finnish-born hockey player*
* Rautakallio, Rocky

**Rautakallio, Rocky**
*See* Rautakallio, Pekka Olavi

**Rautzhan, Clarence George** 1952-
[SMG]
*American baseball player*
* Rautzhan, Lance

**Rautzhan, Lance**
See Rautzhan, Clarence George

**Ravales, Robin** 1935- [CW]
*Surinamese poet and playwright*
* Dobru, R.

**Ravazza, Carl** 1912?-1968 [PMJ]
*American singer and bandleader*
* Ravell, Carl

**[The] Rave**
See Stallworth, Dave

**Ravell, Carl**
See Ravazza, Carl

**[The] Raven**
See Frey, A. R.

**[The] Raven Knight**
See Hunyadi, Janos [or Huniades, John]

**Ravenel, Charles, Jr.** 1938?-
*American banker and politician*
* Ravenel, Pug

**Ravenel, John**
See Upshur, Donald M.

**Ravenel, Pug**
See Ravenel, Charles, Jr.

**Ravenglass, Hal**
See Wood, Samuel Andrew

**Ravenhall, Mrs.**
See Keiser, Robert

**Ravenscroft, Howard H.**
1902-1969 [SC]
*American actor*
* Barcroft, Roy

**Ravenswood**
See Beebee, Charles Washington

**Ravesteyn, Josse** 1506-1571 [PA]
*Author*
* Tiletanus

**Raviola, Antonio** 20th c. [WECO]
*Italian cartoonist*
* Magnus

**Ravlengherio, Francois** 1539-1597
[PA]
*Author*
* Ruphelenguis

**Raw, Kathryn**
See Nyers, Amelia Kathryn

**Raw Meat Bill**
See Rodgers, Wilbur Kincaid

**Rawford, W. C.**
See Crawford, William [Elbert]

**Rawhide [Secret Service code name]**
See Reagan, Ronald Wilson

**Rawley, Callman**
See Rakosi, Carl

**Rawley, Charlotte** 1894-1908 [SC]
*American actress*
* Mae, Jimsey

**Rawlings, Harry**
See Downing, George

**Rawlings, J. R.**
See McCulloch, J. H.

**Rawlings, John W.** 1892-1972 [PB]
*American baseball player*
* Rawlings, Red

**Rawlings, Marjorie Kinnan**
See Baskin, Marjorie Kinnan Rawlings

**Rawlings, Red**
See Rawlings, John W.

**Rawlins, E[ustace]**
See Barton, [Dr.] Eustace Robert

**Rawlins, Judith [Judy]**
See Riedel, Judith Ellen

**Rawlins, Lester**
See Rosenberg, Lester

**Rawlinson, A. R.**
See Rawlinson, Arthur Richard

**Rawlinson, Arthur Richard** 1894-
[THR]
*British playwright*
* Rawlinson, A. R.

**Rawlinson, Thomas** 1681-1725
[DEP, DNNS, SN]
*British book collector*
* Folio, Tom
* [The] Leviathan of Book-Collectors

**Rawls, Katherine** 1918- [BBH]
*American swimmer and diver*
* Rawls, Peggy

**Rawls, Peggy**
See Rawls, Katherine

**Rawson, Clayton** 1906-1971
[AW, CA, CC]
*American magician and author*
* Merlini, [The] Great
* Towne, Stuart

**Ray**
See Howard-Jones, Ray

**Ray, Aldo**
See DaRe, Aldo

**Ray, Allene**
See Burch, Allene

**Ray, Ambrose**
See Ray, Tom

**Ray, Andrew**
See Aureli, Andrea

**Ray, Baby**
See Ray, Buford

**Ray, Big Black**
See Ray, Danny

**Ray, Buddy**
See Ray, Robert J.

**Ray, Buford** 1916- [FB, SMG]
*American football player*
* Ray, Baby

**Ray, Cadillac**
See Ray, Eddie

**Ray, Chesty Joie**
See Ray, Joie

**Ray, Danny** 1934- [DAM]
*American musician*
* Ray, Big Black

**Ray, De Witt Grinnell** [PA]
*Author*
* Gray, Widett

**Ray, Eddie** 20th c.
*American football player*
* Ray, Cadillac

**Ray, Farmer**
See Ray, Robert Henry

**Ray, Gabrielle**
See Cook, Gabrielle

**Ray, Harmon** 1914- [BWW]
*American singer*
* Peetie Wheatstraw's Buddy
* Ray, Herman

**Ray, Herman**
See Ray, Harmon

**Ray, Hugh L.** 1884-1956 [AS, FB]
*American football official*
* Ray, Shorty

**Ray, Irene**
See Beebe, Rachel Irene

**Ray, Irv[ing Burton]** 1864-1947
[BE]
*American baseball player*
* Ray, Stubby

**Ray, Isom**
See Agee, Ray[mond Clinton]

**Ray, James Earl** 1928- [BLB]
*American assassin of civil-rights activist Martin Luther King, Jr.*
* Galt, Eric S.
* [The] Mole
* Sneyd, Ramon George
* Willard, John

**Ray, James Francis** 1944- [BE, PB]
*American baseball player*
* Ray, Sting

**Ray, Jaybird**
See Ray, Otto

**Ray, Jean**
See De Kremer, Jean Raymond

**Ray, Jimmy**
See Genovese, James

**Ray, John**
See Wray, John

**Ray, John Alvin [Johnny]** 1927-
[NN]
*American singer*
* [The] Prince of Wails

**Ray, John Lamar** 1944- [IBW]
*American attorney and politician*
* Ray, St. Peter

**Ray, Johnny**
See Matthews, John

**Ray, Joie** 1884- [BBH]
*American track and field athlete*
* Ray, Chesty Joie

**Ray, Larry**
See Hayes, Larry Ray

**Ray, Nicholas**
See Kienzle, Raymond Nicholas

**Ray, Otto** ?-1976 [MK]
*American baseball player*
* Ray, Jaybird

**Ray, R. J.**
See Brophy, Robert

**Ray, Rene**
See Creese, Irene

**Ray, Robert Henry** 1886-1963
[BE]
*American baseball player*
* Ray, Farmer

**Ray, Robert J.** 1919- [ASC]
*American composer*
* Ray, Buddy

**Ray, Russell**
See Strait, Raymond

**Ray, St. Peter**
See Ray, John Lamar

**Ray, Shorty**
See Ray, Hugh L.

**Ray, Sting**
See Ray, James Francis

**Ray, Stubby**
See Ray, Irv[ing Burton]

**Ray, Ted**
See Olden, Charles

**Ray, Terry** 1915- [FC, ITA, SW]
*American actress*
* Drew, Ellen

**Ray, Thelma**
See Maud, Victoria

**Ray, Tom** 20th c. [RO2]
*American musician*
* Ray, Ambrose

**Ray, Violet**
See Irvine, Edward James

**Ray, Wesley**
See Gaulden, Ray

**Ray, William Porter** [PA]
*Author*
* Tewksbury

**Rayall, Mrs. A.** ?-1854 [PA]
*Author*
* [A] Traveler

**Rayart, Jack Perrin** 1896-1968
[F1, F2]
*Actor*
* Perrin, Jack

**Raybaud, Maxime** [PA]
*Author*
* D'Alaux, Gustave

**Raycraft, Stan**
See Shaver, Richard S[harpe]

**Raye, Carol**
See Corkrey, Kathleen

**Raye, Don**
See Wilhoite, Donald MacRae, Jr.

**Raye, Martha**
See Reed, Margaret Theresa Yvonne

**Rayer, Francis G.** 20th c. [SFP]
*Author*
* Longdon, George

**Rayford, Big John**
See Rayford, John

**Rayford, John** 1943- [RO2]
*American musician*
* Rayford, Big John

**Rayito [Little Flash]**
See Del Pozo y Jimenez, Manuel

**Rayito [Little Beam]**
See Ossorio, Carlos

**Rayl, Jim** 1941-   [BB]
*American basketball player*
* [The] Splendid Splinter

**Rayland, Rose**
*See*   Mortimer, Mrs. N. E.

**Rayle, Geoffrey**
*See*   McLean, Eric W.

**Raymond, Arthur Lawrence**
1882-1912   [BE, PB]
*American baseball player*
* Raymond, Bugs

**Raymond, Augusta**
*See*   Kidder, Mrs. Edward E.

**Raymond, Bob**
*See*   Infascelli, Roberto

**Raymond, Bugs**
*See*   Raymond, Arthur Lawrence

**Raymond, Charles** [joint pseudonym
with Raymond Koch]
*See*   Koch, Charlotte

**Raymond, Charles** [joint pseudonym
with Charlotte Koch]
*See*   Koch, Raymond

**Raymond de Jesus, [Mother]**
*See*   Dion, [Sister] Anita

**Raymond de Saint-Gilles**
*See*   Raymond IV

**Raymond, E. V.**
*See*   Gallun, Raymond Z[inke]

**Raymond, Frenchy**
*See*   Raymond, Joseph Claude
Marc

**Raymond, G. Alison**
*See*   Lanier, Alison Raymond

**Raymond, Gene**
*See*   Guion, Raymond

**Raymond, Harold Newell**
1884-1957   [ASC]
*American composer*
* Newell, Roy

**Raymond, Harold R.** 1925-   [FB]
*American football coach*
* Raymond, Tubby

**Raymond, Harry H.**
*See*   Truman, Harry H.

**Raymond, Henry Augustus**
*See*   Scott, Sarah

**Raymond, Henry S.**   [PA]
*Author*
* Bowline, Billy

**Raymond, Hugh**
*See*   Michel, John B.

**Raymond, Ida**
*See*   Tardy, May. T.

**Raymond, Jack**
*See*   Caines, John

**Raymond, Jack**
*See*   Feder, George

**Raymond, John T.**
*See*   O'Brien, John

**Raymond, Joseph Claude Marc**
1937-   [BE, PB]
*Canadian-born baseball player*
* Raymond, Frenchy

**Raymond, Lee**
*See*   Hill, Mary Raymond

**Raymond, Louise**
*See*   Daniels, Mrs.

**Raymond, [Father] M.**
*See*   Flanagan, Joseph David
Stanislaus

**Raymond, Mary**
*See*   Keegan, Mary Heathcott

**Raymond, Mrs. Lewis**   [FFF]
*Entertainer*
* May, Alice

**Raymond, Paula**
*See*   Wright, Paula Ramona

**Raymond, Rene** 1906-
[CC, EMD, WW]
*British author*
* Chase, James Hadley
* Docherty, James L.
* Grant, Ambrose
* Marshall, Raymond

**Raymond, Robert**
*See*   Alter, Robert Edmond

**Raymond, Rossiter Worthington**
1840- ?   [PA]
*Author*
* Grey, Robertson

**Raymond, Tubby**
*See*   Raymond, Harold R.

**Raymond, Walter** 1852- ?   [WWL]
*British author*
* Cobbleigh, Tom

**Raymond, William Lee** 1877- ?
[NAA]
*American author*
* X

**Raymond IV** ?-1105   [WBD]
*Count of Toulouse*
* Raymond de Saint-Gilles

**Raynal, Louis**
*See*   Hoffman, Josef

**Rayne, Alan**
*See*   Tobin, James Edward

**Rayner, Augustus Alfred** 1894-
[WW]
*Author*
* Hall, Whyte

**Rayner, Chuck**
*See*   Rayner, Claude Earl

**Rayner, Claire** 1931-
[AW, CA, WD]
*British author and columnist*
* Brandon, Sheila
* Chetwynd, Berry
* Lynton, Ann
* Martin, Ruth [house pseudonym]
* Saxe, Isobel

**Rayner, Claude Earl** 1920-
[CEI, FHE, HK]
*Canadian-born hockey player*
* Bonnie Prince Charlie
* Rayner, Chuck

**Rayner, Guy**
*See*   Clarke, S. Dacre

**Rayner, Ray**
*See*   Rahner, Raymond M.

**Rayner, Richard**
*See*   McIlwain, David

**Raynes, Frederica Rozelle Ridgway**
1925-   [IAW]
*British author*
* Castweazle, Eleanor

**Rayo**
*See*   Schmied, Rudolf

**Rayson, Paul**
*See*   Jennings, Leslie Nelson

**Rayter, Joe**
*See*   McChesney, Mary F.

**Razaf, Andy**
*See*   Razafinkeriefo,
Andreamenentania Paul

**Razafinkeriefo, Andreamenentania
Paul** 1895-1973   [ASC, EJ, IBW]
*American lyricist*
* Crooning Andy
* Razaf, Andy

**[El] Razi**
*See*   Ben-Fares, Almed

**Razonador, Amable**
*See*   Henriquez y Alfau, Enrique

**[The] Razor**
*See*   Tojo, Eiki

**[Il] Re**
*See*   Arantes Do Nascimento,
Edson

**[Il] Re dei Cantatori**
*See*   Bernacchi, Antonio

**Re Galantuomo**
*See*   Victor Emmanuel II

**Re Lavrador [Farmer or Laborer
King]**
*See*   Diniz

**Rea, John Huntingdon** 1909-1968
[FC]
*American actor*
* Ridgeley, John

**Reach, James** 20th c.   [WW]
*Author*
* Abbott, Bruce
* Bremer, Ward
* Manning, Hilda
* Rand, John
* Ressieb, George
* Sutton, Thomas
* West, Tom
* Williams, Pete
* Williams, Richard

**Read, Buck**
*See*   Read, Herbert

**Read, E. A.**
*See*   Read, Edwin Alfred

**Read, Edwin Alfred** 1918-   [ART]
*British stonemason and painter*
* Read, E. A.

**Read, Herbert** 1883-1970   [BB]
*British-born American basketball
player*
* [The] Master Among Masters
* Read, Buck
* [The] Silver Fox

**Read [or Reed?], James**
*See*   Malatesta, Guido

**Read, Jan**
*See*   Read, John Hinton

**Read, John Hinton** 1917-
[AW, WD]
*Australian-born author and
playwright*
* Read, Jan

**Read, Melvin Dean** 1922-   [CEI]
*Canadian-born hockey player*
* Read, Pee Wee

**Read, Miss**
*See*   Saint, Dora Jessie [Shafe]

**Read, O.** 1886-   [WWL]
*British journalist*
* Reed, Hal

**Read, Pee Wee**
*See*   Read, Melvin Dean

**Read-Tucker, L.**
*See*   Tucker, Loraine Read

**Reade, Hamish**
*See*   Gray, Simon

**Reade, Lang**
*See*   Carter, David C[harles]

**Reade, Regina**
*See*   Richardson, Randell

**Reade, William Winwood**
1838-1875   [FFF]
*British author*
* Abati, Francesco

**Reader, Paul**
*See*   Arce Robledo, Carlos De

**[A] Reader Therein**
*See*   Cristadoro, Andrew

**[The] Reading Rifle**
*See*   Furillo, Carl Anthony

**Ready Money Spencer**
*See*   Spencer, Elihu

**Reagan, Arthur** 1882- ?   [BE]
*American baseball player*
* Reagan, Rip

**Reagan, Bobby**
*See*   Ruehle, George Robert

**Reagan, Dutch**
*See*   Reagan, Ronald Wilson

**Reagan, Moon**
*See*   Reagan, Neil

**Reagan, Nancy Davis** 20th c.
*Wife of American president, Ronald
Reagan*
* Rainbow [Secret Service code
name]

**Reagan, Neil** 1909?-
*Brother of American president,
Ronald Reagan*
* Reagan, Moon

**Reagan, Patricia** 1953?-
*American actress and daughter of
President Ronald Reagan*
* Davis, Patti

**Reagan, Rip**
*See*   Reagan, Arthur

**Reagan, Ronald Wilson** 1911-
[ET, FAP]
*American president and former actor*
* [The] Great Communicator
* O and W [Oldest and Wisest]
* Rawhide [Secret Service code
name]
* Reagan, Dutch
* Ronald the Right

Reagan, Thomas [James] B[utler]
1916-   [AW, CA]
*American author*
* Thomas, Jim

Real, Antony
*See*   Michel, Ferdinaid

[The] Real McCoy
*See*   McCoy, Elijah J.

Reaney, James Crerar 1926-   [AW]
*Canadian author*
* Spoonhill

Reardon, Beans
*See*   Reardon, John Edward

Reardon, John Edward
*American baseball official*
* Reardon, Beans

Reason, Rex
*See*   Roberts, Bart

Reaves, John
*See*   Reaves, T. Johnson

Reaves, T. Johnson 1950-   [FB]
*American football player*
* Reaves, John

Reavis, James Addison   ?-1908
[BLB]
*American swindler and forger*
* De Arizonac, Baron
* De Los Colorados, Caballero
* [The] Red Baron of Arizona

Reavis, T. M.   [FFF]
*Advocated shifting U. S. capital to
St. Louis, Mo.*
* [The] Capital Mover

Reay, Trevace
*See*   Pond, S. T. R.

[The] Rebbetzin [Rabbi's Wife]
*See*   Jungreis, Esther

[A] Rebel
*See*   Eggleston, George Cary

[The] Rebel Banker
*See*   Morton, John

[The] Rebel Poet
*See*   Islam, Kazi Nazrul

Rebennack, Malcolm John 1940-
[NAD]
*Singer*
* Dr. John, the Night Tripper

Reberger, Crane
*See*   Reberger, Frank Beall

Reberger, Frank Beall 1944-   [BE]
*American baseball player*
* Reberger, Crane

Rebholz, Russ 20th c.   [CFH]
*American-born football player*
* [The] Wisconsin Wrath

Reboul, Jean 1796-1864
[FFF, PA, WBD]
*French poet*
* [The] Baker Poet
* [Le] Boulanger de Nimes

Rebozo, Bebe
*See*   Rebozo, Charles Gregory

Rebozo, Charles Gregory 1912-
[B10]
*American real estate executive*
* Rebozo, Bebe

Recamier, Jeanne Francoise Julie
Adelaide 1777-1849   [SN]
*French society beauty*
* [A] Second Helen

Recapper
*See*   Abbott, Thomas C.

[Le] Rechin
*See*   Fulk IV

Reckoner
*See*   Strachan, John

[The] Recluse of Edgbaston
*See*   Newman, John Henry

Recour, Charles
*See*   Bott, Henry

Rectez, Ian
*See*   Weisinger, Mort[imer]

Rector, Connie
*See*   Rector, Cornelius

Rector, Cornelius 20th c.   [OBW]
*American baseball player*
* Rector, Connie

Rector, Red
*See*   Rector, William Eugene

Rector, William Eugene 1929-
[CWG, DAM]
*American country-western performer*
* Rector, Red

[The] Red
*See*   Amadeus VII

[The] Red
*See*   Conrad

[The] Red
*See*   Fulk I

[The] Red
*See*   Olaf Sitricson

[The] Red
*See*   Otto II [or Otho]

[The] Red Baron
*See*   Berenson, Gordon Arthur

[The] Red Baron
*See*   Berenson, Harold

[The] Red Baron
*See*   Von Richthofen, Manfred
Freiherr

[The] Red Baron of Arizona
*See*   Reavis, James Addison

Red Beard
*See*   Frederick I [or Friedrich]

Red Beard
*See*   Horush [Arouj, Horuc or
Koruk]

Red Beard
*See*   Khizr

[The] Red Bishop
*See*   Camara, Helder Pessoa

Red Butterfly
*See*   Lauritsen, John [Phillip]

[The] Red Comyn
*See*   Comyn, [Sir] John

Red Cross
*See*   Grant, Charles

[The] Red Cross Knight
*See*   George

[The] Red Dean
*See*   Johnson, Hewlett

[The] Red Devil
*See*   Jenatzy, Camille

Red Devil
*See*   Wilborn, Nelson

Red Dog Dougherty
*See*   Dougherty, Edward

Red Eagle
*See*   Weatherford, William

[The] Red Earl
*See*   Burke [or Burgo?], Richard

Red Eye Hay
*See*   Hay, James Alexander

Red Eye Jessie
*See*   Bell, Jessie

[The] Red Feather Girl
*See*   Bryant, Anita

[The] Red Fox
*See*   Casimir I

[The] Red Fox
*See*   Edgar [or Eadgar]

[The] Red Fox
*See*   Jefferson, Thomas

[The] Red Fox of Kinderhook
*See*   Van Buren, Martin

[The] Red Headed Music Maker
*See*   Hall, Wendell

[The] Red Headed Rooster of the
Rockies
*See*   Belford, Senator

[The] Red Headed Tomboy
*See*   Berg, Patricia J. [Patty]

Red Hot Willie
*See*   McTell, Willie Samuel

Red Hot Willie Glaze
*See*   McTell, Willie Samuel

Red Hott Bergen
*See*   Bergen, Stuart

Red Hugh
*See*   O'Donnell [or O'Donell?],
Hugh

Red Jacket
*See*   Sagoyewatha

[The] Red King
*See*   William II

[The] Red Light Bandit
*See*   Chessman, Caryl

[The] Red Major
*See*   Mohieddin, Khaled

Red Mane
*See*   Magnus

Red Mike Edson
*See*   Edson, Merritt Austin

Red Nelson
*See*   Wilborn, Nelson

Red Peter
*See*   Ormond, Pierce

[The] Red Prince
*See*   Frederick Charles

[The] Red Prince
*See*   Salameh, Ali Hassan

Red River Dave
*See*   McEnery, David

[The] Red Rooster
*See*   Rader, Douglas Lee

Red Rosa
*See*   Luxemburg, Rosa

Red Rudi Dutschke
*See*   Dutschke, Rudi

[The] Red Sultan
*See*   Abdul-Hamid II

Red Ted Heslin
*See*   Heslin, Ted

Red Ted Knight
*See*   Knight, Ted

Red Top Johnston
*See*   Johnston, Wilfred Ivy

[The] Red Tory
*See*   MacDonald, Flora

Red Wing
*See*   Pond, Frederick Eugene

Red Wing, Princess
*See*   St. Cyr, Lillian

ReDaK
*See*   Kimchi, David

Redax
*See*   Vingedal, Sven Erik Axel

Redaxela
*See*   Cropper, Mrs.

Redbarn, Thomas
*See*   McEvoy, Bernard

Redcam, Tom
*See*   MacDermot, Thomas H.

Redd, Elvira 1930-   [EJ7]
*American jazz musician*
* Redd, Vi

Redd, Vi
*See*   Redd, Elvira

Reddaway, W[illiam] Brian 1913-
[CA]
*British economist and author*
* Academic Investor

Redder, George
*See*   Drummond, Jack

Reddick
*See*   Kidder, Joseph

Reddin, Kenneth Shiels 1895-1967
[DIL]
*Irish author and playwright*
* Sarr, Kenneth

Redding, Cannon Ball
*See*   Redding, Richard

Redding, Otis 1941-1967   [PRS]
*American singer and songwriter*
* [The] King of Soul Singers

Redding, Richard 1891-1938?
[MK]
*American baseball player*
* Redding, Cannon Ball

[The] Redeemed Captive
*See*   Williams, John

Reden, Karl
*See*   Converse, Charles Crozat

Redfern, Buck
*See*   Redfern, George Howard

**Redfern, George Howard**
1902-1964 [BE]
*American baseball player*
* Redfern, Buck

**Redfern, Peter Irvine** 1954- [SMG]
*American baseball player*
* Redfern, Red

**Redfern, Red**
*See* Redfern, Peter Irvine

**Redfern, Ruth** 1908- [F2]
*Actress*
* Hiatt, Ruth

**Redfield, Clark**
*See* McMorrow, Fred

**Redfield, Jennifer**
*See* Hoskins, Robert

**Redfield, Malissa**
*See* Elliott, Malissa Childs

**Redfield, Martin**
*See* Brown, Alice

**[The] Redhead**
*See* Reuther, Walter Philip

**Redlich, Marcellus Donald**
*See* Von Redlich, Marcellus
Donald A. R.

**Redman, Ben Ray** 1896-1961
[AW, CC, WBD]
*American author and journalist*
* Lord, Jeremy

**Redman, Joseph**
*See* Pearce, Brian Leonard

**Redmayne, Barbara**
*See* Howe, Muriel

**Redmayne, Mary Priestley** 1902-
[WWL]
*British author*
* Rodney, M.

**Redmon, Jim** 1947- [SMG]
*American baseball player*
* Redmon, Rat

**Redmon, Rat**
*See* Redmon, Jim

**Redmond, John McKittrick [Jack]**
1910-1968 [BE]
*American baseball player*
* Redmond, Red

**Redmond, Juanita**
*See* Hipps, Juanita Redmond

**Redmond, Red**
*See* Redmond, John McKittrick
[Jack]

**Redo**
*See* Hill, Anthony

**Redpath, James** 1833-1891
[FFF, PA]
*Scottish-born journalist*
* Berwick

**Redstone, Sylvia**
*See* Honnor, Sylvia Crofts

**Redus, Frog**
*See* Redus, Wilson R.

**Redus, Wilson R.** 1905- [MK]
*American baseball player*
* Redus, Frog

**Redway, Ralph**
*See* Hamilton, Charles Harold St.
John

**Redway, Ridley**
*See* Hamilton, Charles Harold St.
John

**Redwine, Skip**
*See* Redwine, Wilbur

**Redwine, Wilbur** 1926- [ASC]
*American musician*
* Redwine, Skip

**Redwood, John**
*See* Search, Preston Willis

**Redwood, Ralph**
*See* Holden, J. G. P.

**Redwood, Rosaline**
*See* Staples, Marjory Charlotte

**Reece, Alphonso Son** 1931-
[DAM, EJ]
*Jamaican-born jazz musician*
* Reece, Dizzy

**Reece, Alys [Tracy]** 1912-
[AW, WD]
*British author*
* Wingfield, Susan

**Reece, Dizzy**
*See* Reece, Alphonso Son

**Reece, Reggie** 20th c. [BBH]
*Boxer*
* Reece, Roughie

**Reece, Roughie**
*See* Reece, Reggie

**Reed, A. C.**
*See* Reed, Aaron Corthen

**Reed, Aaron Corthen** 20th c.
[BWW]
*American musician and singer*
* Reed, A. C.

**Reed, Alan**
*See* Bergman, Teddy

**Reed, Alexander Wyclif** 1908-
[CA]
*New Zealand author*
* Harlequin

**Reed, Allan**
*See* Eisfeld, Rainer

**Reed, Blair** 20th c. [WW]
*Author*
* Ring, Adam

**Reed, Bob** 20th c.
*American football player*
* [The] Ski Cat

**Reed, C. H.** [PA]
*Author*
* Hazelton, Mabel

**Reed, Cynthia**
*See* Nolan, [Violet] Cynthia

**Reed, David V.**
*See* Vern, David

**Reed, Diz**
*See* Reed, Howard Dean

**Reed, Donald** 1939- [IBW]
*American army officer*
* [The] Black Tiger

**Reed, Donna**
*See* Mullenger, Donna

**Reed, Edward Charles** 1891-
[WWL]
*British author*
* Brangwyn, Charles

**Reed, Eliot** [joint pseudonym with
Charles Rodda]
*See* Ambler, Eric

**Reed, Eliot** [joint pseudonym with
Eric Ambler]
*See* Rodda, Charles

**Reed, Elizabeth Stewart** 1914-
[CA]
*American author*
* Stewart, Elizabeth Grey

**Reed, Emeline** [PA]
*Author*
* Roseau, Emie

**Reed, Emmett X.**
*See* King, Florence

**Reed, Frank**
*See* Ciorciolini, Marcello

**Reed, Gus**
*See* Nelson, Harold

**Reed, Hal**
*See* Read, O.

**Reed, Howard Dean** 1936- [BE]
*American baseball player*
* Reed, Diz

**Reed, Isabella** 1893?-
[BEW, F2, FC]
*British actress*
* Elsom, Isobel

**Reed, Ishmael** 1938- [CN]
*American author and poet*
* Coleman, Emmett

**Reed, Jerry**
*See* Hubbard, Jerry Reed

**Reed, Kit**
*See* Reed, Lillian Craig

**Reed, Lillian Craig** 1932- [CA]
*American journalist and author*
* Reed, Kit

**Reed, Lou**
*See* Firbank, Louis

**Reed, Lucy**
*See* DeRidder, Lucille

**Reed, Margaret Theresa Yvonne**
1916- [BEW, EMT, IPA]
*American actress, singer,
comedienne*
* Raye, Martha

**Reed, Mary J.** 1830- ? [FFF]
*American poet*
* Roseau, Marie

**Reed, Mrs. Samuel** [FFF]
*Entertainer*
* Boeckel, Mary

**Reed, Nathaniel** 1862?-1950 [B10]
*American reformed outlaw*
* Texas Jack

**Reed, Nora**
*See* Hall, Vera

**Reed, Peter** [house pseudonym]
*See* MacDonald, John D[ann]

**Reed, Van** [house pseudonym, Curtis
Warren]
*See* Hughes, Den[n]is [Talbot]

**Reed, Veronica**
*See* Sherman, Theresa

**Reed-Smith, Ida** 1868- ? [NAA]
*American author*
* Warrington, Dan

**Reeder, Cat**
*See* Reeder, Tom

**Reeder, Icicle**
*See* Reeder, James Edward

**Reeder, James Edward** 1865- ?
[BE]
*American baseball player*
* Reeder, Icicle

**Reeder, Nicholas [Nick]**
*See* Herchenroeder, Nicholas

**Reeder, Page, Sr.** 1921?-1977
[FIR]
*Radio producer and announcer*
* Reeder, Scoop

**Reeder, [Colonel] Red**
*See* Reeder, Russell P., Jr.

**Reeder, Russell P., Jr.** 1902-
[CA, SAT]
*American army officer and author*
* Reeder, [Colonel] Red

**Reeder, Scoop**
*See* Reeder, Page, Sr.

**Reeder, Tom** 1934- [CM]
*American radio broadcaster*
* Reeder, Cat

**Reeds, F. Anton** 20th c. [WGT]
*Author*
* Riker, Anthony

**Reeman, Douglas [Edward]** 1924-
[AW, WD]
*British author*
* Kent, Alexander

**Reems, Harry**
*See* Streicher, Herbert

**Reens, Mary**
*See* Singleton, Betty

**Rees, Dai**
*See* Rees, David James

**Rees, David**
*See* Wignall, Trevor

**Rees, David James** 1913- [EG, GF]
*Scottish golfer*
* Rees, Dai

**Rees, Dilwyn**
*See* Daniel, Glyn [Edmund]

**Rees, [Morgan] Goronwy** 1909-
[CA]
*Welsh-born author, columnist,
translator*
* R

**Rees, Helen Christina Easson [Evans]**
1903-1970 [CA]
*British author*
* Oliver, Jane

**Rees, Ioan Bowen** 1929- [CA]
*Welsh author*
* Rhys, Ioan

**Rees, Joan** 1927- [AW, WD]
*British author*
* Avery, June
* Bedford, Ann
* Strong, Susan

**Rees, Meriel**
*See* Lambot, Isobel Mary

**Rees, Stella**
See Allen, Mrs. William W.

**Reese, Della**
See Early, Deloreese Patricia

**Reese, Don** 1951-    [SMG]
*American football player*
* [The] Undertaker

**Reese, Donk**
See Reese, James Harrison

**Reese, Harold Henry** 1919-
[BE, DGS, IPA]
*American baseball player*
* [The] Little Colonel
* Reese, Pee Wee

**Reese, Harvey**
See Roeder, Adolph

**Reese, Heloise [Bowles]** 1919-1977
[CA]
*American columnist*
* Heloise

**Reese, James Harrison** 1905-
[SMG]
*American baseball coach*
* Reese, Donk

**Reese, James Hymie**
See Solomon, James Hymie

**Reese, John [Henry]** 20th c.    [CA]
*American author*
* Carpenter, John Jo

**Reese, Pee Wee**
See Reese, Harold Henry

**Reeve, Ada**
See Isaacs, Adelaide Mary

**Reeve, Edward H. [Ted]** 1902-
[CSH]
*Canadian journalist*
* Fagan, Nutsy
* McGuffy, Moaner
* [The] Old Groaner
* Snippersnapper, Alice
* [The] Squire of Squawg Hollow

**Reeve, Goodie** 1898?-1978    [FIR]
*Australian radio performer*
* [The] First Lady of Sydney Radio

**Reeve, Joel**
See Cox, William R[obert]

**Reeve, John** ?-1540    [PA]
*Author*
* Melford

**Reeve, Joseph** 1937-    [CA]
*American author and journalist*
* Albright, Joseph [Medill Patterson]

**Reeve-Jones, Alan Edmond** 1914-
[AW, IAW]
*Norwegian-born author, scriptwriter, lyricist*
* Allen, Edmund
* Lunchbasket, Roger

**Reeves, Clarence** 20th c.    [SG]
*Boxer*
* [The] Alabama Kid

**Reeves, Daniel**
See Liddy, James [Daniel Reeves]

**Reeves, Daniel E.** 1944-    [FB]
*American football player*
* Reeves, Deacon Dan

**Reeves, Deacon Dan**
See Reeves, Daniel E.

**Reeves, Del**
See Reeves, [Franklin] Delano

**Reeves, [Franklin] Delano** 1933-
[CWG, DAM, ECM]
*American country-western performer*
* [The] Dean Martin of Country Music
* Reeves, Del

**Reeves, Fannie**
See McDowell, Mrs. E. A.

**Reeves, Gentleman Jim**
See Reeves, James Travis [Jim]

**Reeves, George**
See Besselo, George

**Reeves, Goebel** 1899-1959    [ECM]
*American country-western performer*
* [The] Texas Drifter

**Reeves, Gunner**
See Reeves, Robert Edwin

**Reeves, Helen Buckingham [Mathers]**
1853-1920    [WGT, WW]
*British author*
* Lyall, David
* Mathers, Helen

**Reeves, James**
See Reeves, John Morris

**Reeves, James Travis [Jim]**
1923-1964    [BEW, ECM]
*American singer and actor*
* Bimbo Boy
* Reeves, Gentleman Jim

**Reeves, John Morris** 1909-
[SFL, TCL]
*British poet, author, critic*
* Reeves, James

**Reeves, Joyce**
See Gard, Joyce

**Reeves, Justin** 20th c.    [WGT]
*Author*
* Septama, Aladra

**Reeves, Marian Calhoun Legare** 19th
c.    [FFF, PA]
*American author*
* Fadette

**Reeves, Red**
See Reeves, Reuben

**Reeves, Reuben** 1905-    [WWJ]
*American jazz musician*
* Reeves, Red
* Reeves, River

**Reeves, River**
See Reeves, Reuben

**Reeves, Robert Edwin** 1904-    [BE]
*American baseball player*
* Reeves, Gunner

**Reeves, Ruth Ellen**
See Ranney, Agnes V.

**[The] Referee**
See Gordon, Archibald F.

**[The] Reform Governor**
See Cleveland, [Stephen] Grover

**[The] Reform Pope**
See Chauvin [or Caulvin?], Jean

**[The] Reformed Michael Angelo**
See Tibaldi, Pellegrino

**[The] Reformed Minstrel**
See Sutherland, Robert

**[The] Reformer of a Kingdom**
See Knox, John

**[The] Reformer of Astronomy**
See Copernicus, Nicolaus

**Refugitta**
See Harrison, Constance Cary

**Refulgidus, Doctor**
See Philargos, Petros

**Regaldo, Hector** 20th c.    [RO2]
*Venezuelan musician*
* Regaldo, Rudy

**Regaldo, Rudy**
See Regaldo, Hector

**Regan, Brad**
See Norwood, Victor G[eorge] C[harles]

**Regan, Donald Thomas** 1918-
*American government official*
* [The] Barracuda

**Regan, Kathleen Patricia**
1920-1980    [BEW, TR]
*American actress*
* Medford, Kay

**Regan, Phil[lip Raymond]** 1937-
[BE, PB]
*American baseball player*
* [The] Vulture

**Regard, Paul**
See Sheehan, Perley Poore

**Regas, Panagiotis** 1882-1974    [SC]
*Greek-born actor*
* Regas, Pedro

**Regas, Pedro**
See Regas, Panagiotis

**Regaterin [The Little Bargainer]**
See Boto y Recatero, Antonio

**Regazzoni, Clay**
See Regazzoni, Gianclaudio Giuseppe

**Regazzoni, Gianclaudio Giuseppe**
1939-    [EAR]
*Swiss auto racer*
* Regazzoni, Clay

**[The] Regenerator of Cookery**
See Careme, Marie Antoine

**Regenmeister**
See Caracciola, Rudi

**Regester, Seeley**
See Victor, Metta Victoria Fuller

**Reggione, Michael** ?-1932    [BLB]
*American underworld figure*
* Little Apples

**Regillo**
See De Sacchi, Giovanni Antonio

**Reginald, R[obert]**
See Burgess, Michael Roy

**Reginaldus**
See Regnauld, Valire

**Regine**
See Zylberberg, Regina

**[El] Regio [The Gorgeous One]**
See Lopez, Felix

**Regio, Jose**
See Dos Reis Pereira, Jose Maria

**Regiomontanus**
See Mueller, Johann

**Regis**
See Grise, Jeanne

**Regius**
See Leroy, Louis

**Regnauld, Valire** 1543-1623    [PA]
*Author*
* Reginaldus

**Regnault, Jeanne Julia** 1854-1941
[WBD]
*French actress*
* Bartet, Jeanne Julia

**Regnier, Jeanne-Marie**
See Khan, Noor Inayat

**Regnier, Mathurin** 1573-1613
[DNNS, FFF, SN]
*French poet*
* [The] Father of French Satire

**Regnier, Michel** 1931-    [WECO]
*Belgian cartoonist and editor*
* Albert, Louis
* Greg

**Rego, Anthony [Tony]**
See DeRego, Anthony

**Rehan, Ada**
See Crehan, Ada

**Rehm, Warren S.** 20th c.    [WGT]
*Author*
* Nemo, Omen

**Rei, Kosumi**
See Shibano, Takumi

**Reibel, Dutch**
See Reibel, Earl

**Reibel, Earl** 1930-    [CEI]
*Canadian-born hockey player*
* Reibel, Dutch

**Reiber, Frank Bernard** 1909-    [BE]
*American baseball player*
* Reiber, Tubby

**Reiber, Tubby**
See Reiber, Frank Bernard

**Reich, Edwin** 1926-    [BEW]
*American producer*
* Rich, Eddie

**Reichardt, Frederic C.** 1943-    [PB]
*American baseball player*
* Reichardt, Rick

**Reichardt, Rick**
See Reichardt, Frederic C.

**Reichenbach, Berke**
See Reichenbach, Harold

**Reichenbach, Harold** 20th c.
[SMG]
*American baseball player*
* Reichenbach, Berke

**Reichenthal, Laura** 1901-
[CN, LC, WD]
*American author and poet*
* Gottschalk, Laura Riding
* Jackson, Laura [Riding]
* Rich, Barbara [joint pseudonym with Robert Von Ranke Graves]
* Riding, Laura

**Reichenthal, Ralph** 1901-1942
[AM]
*American composer*
* Rainger, Ralph

**Reichert, Herbert W[illiam]** 1917-
[CA]
*American educator, author, translator*
* Schad, Wilhelm

**Reichman, Arthur** 1886-1944
[THR]
*American playwright*
* Richman, Arthur

**Reichman, Harry** 1895-1972
[BEW, EMT, PMJ]
*American singer and actor*
* Richman, Harry

**Reichner, Bix**
See Reichner, S. Bickley

**Reichner, S. Bickley** 20th c. [ASC]
*American composer*
* Reichner, Bix

**Reichow, Corncob**
See Reichow, Jerry

**Reichow, Hayseed**
See Reichow, Jerry

**Reichow, Jerry**
*American football player*
* Reichow, Corncob
* Reichow, Hayseed

**Reid, Breezy**
See Reid, Floyd

**Reid, Charles [Stuart]** 1900- [CA]
*British author and journalist*
* Davidson, John
* Martin, Francis
* Staurt, Charles

**Reid, Charlotte T.** 20th c. [ET]
*American politician and singer*
* King, Annette

**Reid, Christian**
See Fisher, Frances C.

**Reid, Desmond** [house pseudonym]
See Bounds, S. J.

**Reid, Desmond** [house pseudonym]
See Browne, Noel

**Reid, Desmond** [house pseudonym]
See Burke, John [Frederick]

**Reid, Desmond** [house pseudonym]
See Chance, John Newton

**Reid, Desmond** [house pseudonym]
See Dolphin, Reginald Charles
[Rex]

**Reid, Desmond** [house pseudonym]
See Douse, Anthony

**Reid, Desmond** [house pseudonym]
See Francis, Stephen D.

**Reid, Desmond** [house pseudonym]
See Garstin, A.

**Reid, Desmond** [house pseudonym]
See Hanson, V. J.

**Reid, Desmond** [house pseudonym]
See Lambe, F.

**Reid, Desmond** [house pseudonym]
See Martin, A. L.

**Reid, Desmond** [house pseudonym]
See McArdle, Brian

**Reid, Desmond**
See McNeilly, Wilfred Glassford

**Reid, Desmond** [house pseudonym]
See Moorcock, Michael John

**Reid, Desmond** [house pseudonym]
See Player, Eddie

**Reid, Desmond** [house pseudonym]
See Richards, Ross

**Reid, Desmond** [house pseudonym]
See Roberts, Lee

**Reid, Desmond** [house pseudonym]
See Robertson, Colin

**Reid, Desmond** [house pseudonym]
See Sowman, Gordon

**Reid, Desmond** [house pseudonym]
See Stagg, James

**Reid, Desmond** [house pseudonym]
See Story, Rosamond Mary

**Reid, Desmond** [house pseudonym]
See Teed, George Heber Hamilton

**Reid, Edgeworth Blair** 1920-
[BEW]
*American actor*
* Reid, Elliott

**Reid, Eleanor**
See Smith, Constance Isabel

**Reid, Elliott**
See Reid, Edgeworth Blair

**Reid, Esther** 19th c. [PA]
*Author*
* Pansey

**Reid, Floyd** 20th c. [SMG]
*American football player*
* Reid, Breezy

**Reid, Frances P[ugh]** 1910- [CA]
*American author*
* Allison, Marian

**Reid, Hal**
See Reid, James Hallock

**Reid, Hartlaw**
See Hardie, Robert

**Reid, Helen Grace** 20th c. [NAA]
*American author*
* Carlisle, Helen Grace

**Reid, Ike**
See Cauldwell, Ike Reid

**Reid, James Hallock** 1860?-1920
[BEW]
*Playwright*
* Reid, Hal

**Reid, James Macarthur** 1900-1970
[CAP]
*Scottish author*
* Walkinshaw, Colin

**Reid, John Cowie** 1916- [AW, CA]
*New Zealand educator and author*
* Caliban

**Reid, Max**
See Reid, Maxwell

**Reid, Maxwell** 1903-1969 [SC]
*American actor and musician*
* Reid, Max

**Reid, Patricia Kimberly** 1921?-
[BEW, FC, IPA]
*American actress*
* Stanley, Kim

**Reid, Philip** [joint pseudonym with Andrew Philip Kingsford Osmond]
See Ingrams, Richard

**Reid, Philip** [joint pseudonym with Richard Ingrams]
See Osmond, Andrew Philip Kingsford

**Reid, Sandy**
See Reid, William A.

**Reid, Sarah Addington** 1891-
[NAA]
*American author*
* Addington, Sarah

**Reid, T. W.** [PA]
*Author*
* [The] Extinguished Exile

**Reid, V. S.**
See Reid, Victor Stafford

**Reid, Victor Stafford** 1913- [LC]
*Jamaican author*
* Reid, V. S.

**Reid, Wallace Q.**
See Goodchild, George

**Reid, Whitelaw** 1837- ? [PA]
*Author*
* Agate

**Reid, William A.** 1857- ? [BE]
*Canadian-born baseball player*
* Reid, Sandy

**Reifsnyder, Reef**
See Reifsnyder, Robert H.

**Reifsnyder, Robert H.** 1937- [FB]
*American football player*
* Reifsnyder, Reef

**Reigle, Edmond** 1924- [CEI]
*Canadian-born hockey player*
* Reigle, Rags

**Reigle, Rags**
See Reigle, Edmond

**Reignolds, Kate**
See Winslow, Mrs. Irving

**Reile, Louis Anthony** 1925- [IAW]
*American author*
* Curran, John

**Reiling, Netty** 1900- [TC]
*German author*
* Seghers, Anna

**Reilley, Alexander Aloysius**
1884-1968 [BE]
*American baseball player*
* Reilley, Duke
* Reilley, Midget

**Reilley, Duke**
See Reilley, Alexander Aloysius

**Reilley, Midget**
See Reilley, Alexander Aloysius

**Reilly, Charles** 1868-1938 [BE]
*American baseball player*
* Reilly, Josh

**Reilly, Charles Thomas** 1855-1937
[BE]
*American baseball player*
* Reilly, Princeton Charlie

**Reilly, Edwin J.** [PA]
*Author*
* Clio

**Reilly, Helen [Abby Kieran]**
1881?-1962 [CC, WW]
*Author*
* Abbey, Kieran

**Reilly, John Good** 1858-1937
[BE, PB]
*American baseball player*
* Reilly, Long John

**Reilly, Josh**
See Reilly, Charles

**Reilly, Long John**
See Reilly, John Good

**Reilly, Mrs. James** [FFF]
*Entertainer*
* Templeton, May

**Reilly, Princeton Charlie**
See Reilly, Charles Thomas

**Reilly, Sidney**
See Rosenblum, Sigmund G.

**Reilly, William K.**
See Creasey, John

**Reimann, Dutch**
See Reimann, Harry

**Reimann, Harry** 20th c. [BBH]
*American basketball player*
* Reimann, Dutch
* Reimann, Wally

**Reimann, Wally**
See Reimann, Harry

**Rein, Bo**
See Rein, Robert

**Rein, Orestes Pearle**
See Rhyne, Orestes Pearle

**Rein, Richard**
See Smith, Richard Rein

**Rein, Robert** 1946?-
*American football coach*
* Rein, Bo

**Reina, Gaetano** ?-1930 [BLB]
*American underworld figure*
* Reina, Tom

**Reina, Tom**
See Reina, Gaetano

**Reindeer Bill Killefer**
See Killefer, William Levier, Jr.

**[La] Reine Blanche**
See Mary, Queen of Scots

**Reiner, Max**
See Caldwell, [Janet] Taylor

**Reiners, Dennis** 20th c. [GW]
*American rodeo performer*
* Reiners, Ringtail

**Reiners, Ringtail**
See Reiners, Dennis

**Reinfeld, Fred** 1910-1964
[CAP, SAT]
*American author*
* Young, Edward

**Reinhardt, Django**
See Reinhardt, Jean Baptiste

**Reinhardt, Jean Baptiste**
1910-1953 [EJ, PMJ]
*Belgian-born jazz musician*
* Reinhardt, Django

**Reinhardt, Max**
See Goldmann, Max

**Reinhardt, S. Louis, Sr.** 1899-
[EJS]
*American football player*
* Reinhardt, Spider

**Reinhardt, Spider**
*See* Reinhardt, S. Louis, Sr.

**Reinhold, Alvar Harald** 1935-
[IWM]
*Swedish musician*
* Rabe, Folke

**Reinhold, C.**
*See* Koestlin, Christian Reinhold

**Reinicker, Walter [Wally]**
*See* Smith, Walter

**Reiniger, Robert Meredith** 1902-
[BEW, EMT]
*American composer, lyricist,
librettist*
* Willson, Meredith

**Reinikka, Oliver Mathias** 1901-
[CEI]
*Canadian-born hockey player*
* Reinikka, Rocco

**Reinikka, Rocco**
*See* Reinikka, Oliver Mathias

**Reinmar der Alte**
*See* Reinmar von Hagenau

**Reinmar von Hagenau** ?-1210?
[WBD]
*Minnesinger and knight*
* Reinmar der Alte

**Reinsmith, Richard**
*See* Smith, Richard Rein

**Reis, Harrie Crane** 1890-1939 [BE]
*American baseball player*
* Reis, Jack

**Reis, Jack**
*See* Reis, Harrie Crane

**Reis, Peggy** 1900-1964 [SC]
*American actress and stunt
performer*
* O'Day, Peggy

**Reis, Ricardo**
*See* Pessoa, Fernando [Antonio
Nogueira]

**Reiser, Harold Patrick**
1919?-1981 [B10, BE, PB]
*American baseball player*
* Reiser, Pete
* Reiser, Pistol Pete

**Reiser, Pete**
*See* Reiser, Harold Patrick

**Reiser, Pistol Pete**
*See* Reiser, Harold Patrick

**Reisigl, Bugs**
*See* Reisigl, Jacob

**Reisigl, Jacob** 1887-1957 [BE]
*American baseball player*
* Reisigl, Bugs

**Reisling, Doc**
*See* Reisling, Frank Carl

**Reisling, Frank Carl** 1874-1955
[BE]
*American baseball player*
* Reisling, Doc

**Reiss, Barbara Eve** 1941- [CA]
*American poet*
* Eve, Barbara

**Reiss, Isaac** 1885-1943 [BEW]
*Austrian-born playwright*
* Nadir, Moishe

**Reit, Seymour** 20th c. [SAT]
*American author, cartoonist, editor*
* Reit, Sy

**Reit, Sy**
*See* Reit, Seymour

**Reitci, Jack** 20th c. [CA]
*Author*
* Ritchie, Jack

**Reitci, Rita Krohne** 1930- [CA]
*American author*
* Ritchie, Rita

**Reiter, Virginia**
*See* Reiterer, Virginia

**Reiterer, Virginia** 20th c. [THR]
*Italian actress*
* Reiter, Virginia

**Reitz, Heinie**
*See* Reitz, Henry P.

**Reitz, Henry P.** 1867-1914 [BE]
*American baseball player*
* Reitz, Heinie

**Reitz, Kenneth John** 1951- [SMG]
*American baseball player*
* [The] Zamboni Machine

**Reizenstein, Elmer L.** 1892-1967
[EWL, LC, TC]
*American playwright and author*
* Rice, Elmer

**Rejane, Gabrielle**
*See* Reju, Gabrielle Charlotte

**Reju, Gabrielle Charlotte**
1857-1920 [BEW, LC, THR]
*French actress*
* Rejane, Gabrielle

**Relampaguito [Little Lightning Flash]**
*See* Gomez y Canete, Julio

**Reles, Abe** ?-1940
[BLB, MM, PHM]
*American underworld figure and
police informant*
* Twist, Kid

**Relgis, Eugene**
*See* Siegler, Eugene

**[A] Religious of CSMV**
*See* Lawson, Ruth Penelope

**[The] Religious Revolutionary**
*See* Ikhnaton [or Akhenaten]

**Rellaford, Jack** 1906-1967 [SC]
*American actor*
* O'Shea, Blackjack
* O'Shea, Jack

**Rellihan, Gernie Floss Hunter**
1888- [IAW]
*American poet*
* Hunter, Gernie

**Relonde, Maurice**
*See* Jagendorf, M.

**Relph, Harry** 1868-1928
[BEW, BMH, NN]
*British comedian*
* [The] Great Little Mackney
* Little Tich

**Rem Doxfud**
*See* Hill, Anthony

**Remacle, Stephane**
*See* Javeau, Claude A.

**Remar, Frits** 1932- [IAW]
*Danish author*
* Dahl, John

**Remark, Erich Paul** 1898-1970
[EWL, TCL]
*German author*
* Remarque, Erich Maria

**Remarque, Erich Maria**
*See* Remark, Erich Paul

**Remback, William**
*See* Valigursky, Ed

**Rembrandt**
*See* Van Rijn [or Ryn], Rembrandt
Harmensz [or Harmenszoon]

**[The] Rembrandt of the Comic Strip**
*See* Caniff, Milton

**[The] Rembrandt of the Prairies**
*See* Zuppke, Robert C.

**Remenham, John**
*See* Vlasto, John Alexander

**Rementer, Butch**
*See* Rementer, Willis J.

**Rementer, Willis J.** 20th c. [BE]
*American baseball player*
* Rementer, Butch

**Remenyi, Ede**
*See* Hoffmann, Ede

**Remer, Helen** 1877-1939 [THR]
*American actress*
* Ware, Helen

**Remerond**
*See* De Saulieu, Thierry

**Remi [or Remigius]** 439?- 535?
[HN, RH, WBD]
*Saint*
* [The] Apostle of the Franks
* [The] Great Apostle of the
French
* [The] Second St. Paul

**Remi de Florence**
*See* Nauni, Remigo

**Remi [or Remy], Georges** 1907-
[CA, SAT]
*Belgian author and illustrator*
* Herge

**Remi, Philippe de** 1250?-1296
[SN]
*French jurist*
* Beaumanoir, Sire de
* [The] French Justinian

**Remick, Ann** 1935- [IPA]
*American actress*
* Remick, Lee

**Remick, Lee**
*See* Remick, Ann

**Remington, Ella-Carrie** 1914- [CA]
*American author*
* Alden, Carella

**Remington, Mark**
*See* Bingley, David Ernest

**Remley, Frank** 1902-1967 [SC]
*American actor and musician*
* Lewis, Elliott

**Remnant, Ernest** 1910-1973
[BMH]
*British comedian*
* Wheeler, Jimmy

**Rempe, Jim**
*American billiard player*
* King James

**Rempt, Jan Dirk** 1907- [AW]
*Dutch-born author*
* De Jong Van Hage, T. P. Merkrid

**Remus, George** 1873- ? [MM]
*German-born American underworld
figure*
* [The] Gentle Grafter
* King of the Bootleggers
* [The] Quiet Corruptor

**Remy, Dominique** 1886?- [NOJ]
*American jazz musician*
* Remy, T-Boy

**Remy, Pierre-Jean** 1937- [IAW]
*French author*
* Angremy, Jean-Pierre

**Remy, T-Boy**
*See* Remy, Dominique

**Rena**
*See* Crossley, Mrs. M. L. R.

**Rena, Henry**
*See* Rene, Henry

**Rena, Kid**
*See* Rene, Henry

**Renad, Frederick**
*See* Cooper, Frederick

**[The] Renaissance Assassin**
*See* Maglie, Salvatore Anthony

**Renaldo, Duncan**
*See* Duncan, Renault Renaldo

**Renard, Celine** [PA]
*Author*
* Maria, Jennie

**Renard, Jules** 1864-1910 [EWL]
*French author*
* Drauer

**Renard, Rachelle**
*See* Secor, Mrs. George J.

**Renard, Roy**
*See* Ofer, Harold

**Renaud**
*See* Crosneau, Maurice Arnold

**Renaud, Mme. Rene** [FFF]
*Entertainer*
* Hill, Rosa

**Renault**
*See* Laurent, Emmanuel

**Renault, Mary**
*See* Challans, Mary

**Renavent, George**
*See* De Cheux, Georges

**Renay, Diane**
*See* Kushner, Renee Diane

**Rencelaw, Brian**
*See* Russell, Ray

**Render, Bill**
*See* Fletcher, Tex

**Rene, Googie**
See   Rene, Leon

**Rene, Hans Evert**
See   Renerius, Hans-Evert

**Rene, Henry** 1900-1949
[DAM, EJ, WWJ]
*American jazz musician*
* Rena, Henry
* Rena, Kid

**Rene, Jules**
See   De Cassamajor, Marquis

**Rene, Leon** 20th c.   [RO1]
*American musician*
* Rene, Googie

**Rene, Master** 16th c.   [HN]
*Poisoned Jeanne d'Albret, mother of
King Henri IV*
* [The] Queen's Poisoner

**Rene, Natalia** 1908?-1977   [CA]
*Russian dance historian, critic,
author*
* Roslavleva, Natalia

**Rene the Red**
See   Levesque, Rene

**Rene-Bazin, Marie** 1883-   [CAT]
*French author*
* Marie St. Justin, [Mother]

**Rene I** 1408?-1480
[DNNS, SN, WBD]
*Titular King of Naples*
* [Le] Bon Roi Rene
* [The] Good
* [The] Good King Rene
* [The] Last of the Troubadours

**Renerius, Hans-Evert** 1941-   [IAW]
*Swedish author*
* Rene, Hans Evert

**Renfroe, Chico**
See   Renfroe, Othello Nelson

**Renfroe, Gangster**
See   Renfroe, Othello Nelson

**Renfroe, Martha Kay** 1938-   [CA]
*American author*
* Wren, M. K.

**Renfroe, Othello Nelson** 1923-
[IBW, MK]
*American baseball player*
* Renfroe, Chico
* Renfroe, Gangster

**Renggli, Josef**
*Swiss chef*
* Renggli, Seppi

**Renggli, Seppi**
See   Renggli, Josef

**Renick, Cab**
See   Renick, Jesse

**Renick, Jesse** 1917-   [BB]
*American basketball player*
* Renick, Cab

**Renier, Elizabeth**
See   Baker, Betty D[oreen Flook]

**Renier, G. J.**
See   Renier, Gustaaf Johannes

**Renier, Gustaaf Johannes**
1892-1962   [LC]
*Dutch-born historian and author*
* Renier, G. J.

**Reniff, Harold Eugene** 1938-   [BE]
*American baseball player*
* Reniff, Porky

**Reniff, Porky**
See   Reniff, Harold Eugene

**Renin, Paul**
See   Goyne, Richard

**Renn, Casey**
See   Crim, Keith R[enn]

**Renn, Ludwig**
See   Vieth Von Golssenau, Arnold
Friedrich

**Renn, Thomas E[dward]** 1939-
[CA]
*American author*
* Strike, Jeremy

**Renna, Big Bill**
See   Renna, William Beneditto

**Renna, G.**
See   Rapuzzi, G. L.

**Renna, William Beneditto** 1924-
[BE]
*American baseball player*
* Renna, Big Bill

**Rennell, Thomas** 1753-1840
[DEP, DNNS, HN]
*British clergyman*
* [The] Demosthenes of the Pulpit

**Renner, A. M.**
See   Gatterman, Eugen Ludwig

**Renner, Karl** 1870-1950   [WBD]
*Austrian statesman and author*
* Springer, Rudolf
* Synopticus

**Rennert, Dutch**
See   Rennert, Laurence Henry, Jr.

**Rennert, Laurence Henry, Jr.**
1934-   [NLG]
*American baseball official*
* Rennert, Dutch

**Rennert, Maggie** 1922-   [CA]
*American author*
* Nunley, Maggie Rennert

**Rennie, Christopher**
See   Ambrose, Eric [Samuel]

**Rennie, Eric Alexander** 1909-
[BEW]
*British actor and director*
* Rennie, Michael

**Rennie, James Alan** 1899-1969
[CAP]
*Scottish author*
* Cleland, Morton
* Denver, Boone
* MacFee, Maxwell

**Rennie, John O. D.** 1875-1952   [SC]
*Actor*
* Mortimer, Henry

**Rennie, Michael**
See   Rennie, Eric Alexander

**Renny**
See   Barber, Raymond

**Reno, Clint**
See   Ballard, [Willis] Todhunter

**Rensa, Pug**
See   Rensa, Tony George

**Rensa, Tony George** 1901-   [BE]
*American baseball player*
* Rensa, Pug

**Renshaw, William Charles**
1861-1904   [OCS]
*British tennis player*
* [The] Father of Modern Lawn
Tennis

**Rensie, Willis**
See   Eisner, Will[iam Erwin]

**Rental, J. W.**
See   Morel, Francois Xavier

**Renthwaite, Robert**
See   Pound, Reginald

**Rentner, Ernest** 20th c.   [SMG]
*American football player*
* Rentner, Pug

**Rentner, Pug**
See   Rentner, Ernest

**Renton, Cam**
See   Armstrong, Richard

**Renton, Julia**
See   Cole, Margaret Alice

**Renzelman, Marilyn**
See   Ferguson, Marilyn

**Renzi, Emma**
See   Scheepers, Emmerentia

**Repo, Seppo** 1947-   [SMG]
*Finnish-born hockey player*
* [The] Fox

**Repp, Ed[ward] Earl** 1900-
[SFL, WGT]
*American author*
* Buckner, Brad
* Cody, John
* Field, Peter

**Reppeteau, Carey Harrison**
1890-1957   [SC]
*American actor*
* Harrison, Carey

**[The] Republican Martyr**
See   Marat, Jean Paul

**[The] Republican Queen**
See   Sophie Charlotte

**Repulski, Eldon John** 1927-   [BE]
*American baseball player*
* Repulski, Rip

**Repulski, Rip**
See   Repulski, Eldon John

**Rerre**
See   Gonzalez Buzon, Manuel

**Resch, Chico**
See   Resch, Glenn Allan

**Resch, Glenn Allan** 1948-
[B10, SMG]
*Canadian-born hockey player*
* Resch, Chico

**Rescigno, Xavier Frederick** 1913-
[BE]
*American baseball player*
* Mr. X

**Resetar, Dorothy L.** 1899?-1979
*American actress*
* Bergere, Dorothy

**[A] Resident of San Domingo**
See   Fabens, J. W.

**Reskind, John**
See   Wallmann, Jeffrey M[iner]

**Resnick, Lee**
See   Resnick, Leon

**Resnick, Leon** 1923-   [ASC]
*American musician*
* Resnick, Lee

**Resnick, Sylvia [Safran]** 1927-
[CA]
*American author and columnist*
* Paul, Sheri

**[The] Resolute**
See   Florio, John

**[The] Resolute Doctor**
See   Baconthorp [Bacon or
Bacondorp], John

**Resolutissimus, Doctor**
See   Durand de St. Pourcain,
Guillaume

**Ressel, Franco** 20th c.   [WF]
*Italian actor*
* Ressel, Frank

**Ressel, Frank**
See   Ressel, Franco

**Ressich, John [Sellar Matheson]**
1877- ?   [WW]
*Author*
* Baxter, Gregory [joint pseudonym
with Eric De Banzie]

**Ressieb, George**
See   Reach, James

**Ressler, Alice** 1918-   [CA]
*American author*
* Wayne, Alice

**Ressler, Lillian** 20th c.   [WD]
*Author*
* Janet, Lillian [joint pseudonym
with Janet O'Daniel]

**Ressom, J. Ann**
See   Mosser, Ann J.

**Resta, Dario**  ?-1924
*British-born auto racer*
* [The] Conquering Invader
* [The] Foreign Invader

**Restalrig**
See   Symons, J. B.

**Restani, Big Bird**
See   Restani, Kevin

**Restani, Kevin** 1951-   [SMG]
*American basketball player*
* Restani, Big Bird

**Restaurador del Parnaso**
See   Melendez Valdes, Juan

**Restelli, Dingo**
See   Restelli, Dino Paul

**Restelli, Dino Paul** 1924-   [BE]
*American baseball player*
* Restelli, Dingo

**Restif de La Bretonne**
See   Restif, Nicolas Edme

**Restif, Nicolas Edme** 1734-1806
[DNNS, WBD]
*French author*
* [The] French Defoe
* Restif de La Bretonne
* [The] Rousseau of the Gutter
* [The] Voltaire of Chambermaids

**Restitutor Orbis**
See Aurelian [Claudius Lucius Valerius Domitius Aurelianus]

**Restless, Jimmy**
See Hull, James

**Reston, James** 1910-
*American journalist*
* Reston, Scotty

**Reston, Scotty**
See Reston, James

**[The] Restorer of Cities**
See Sancho I

**[The] Restorer of French Liberty**
See Louis XVI

**[The] Restorer of German Poetry**
See Opitz, Martin

**[The] Restorer of Learning**
See Medici, Lorenzo de

**[The] Restorer of Letters**
See Heigius, Alexander

**[The] Restorer of Parnassus**
See Melendez Valdes, Juan

**[The] Restorer of Poland**
See Casimir I

**[The] Restorer of Science in Germany**
See Sturm, Johann Christoph

**[The] Restorer of the Protestantism of France**
See Court, Antoine

**[The] Restorer of the Roman Empire**
See Aurelian [Claudius Lucius Valerius Domitius Aurelianus]

**Reszke, Jean de**
See Mieczislaw, Jan

**Rethberg, Elisabeth**
See Sattler, Lisbeth

**[The] Retired Diocletian of Islington**
See Quick, John

**[A] Retired Guardian**
See Bradley, William

**Retla, Robert**
See Alter, Robert Edmond

**Retlaw, S. P.**
See Steinhaeuser, Walter Philip

**Retner, Beth A.**
See Brown, Beth

**Retnuh X**
See Hunter, William F.

**Retnyw, Werdna**
See Winter, Andrew

**Rettig, Adolph John** 1894- [BE]
*American baseball player*
* Rettig, Otto

**Rettig, Otto**
See Rettig, Adolph John

**Retz, Cardinal de**
See Gondi, Jean Francois Paul de

**Retz, Catiline**
See Gondi, Jean Francois Paul de

**Retzlaff, Palmer** 1931- [FB]
*American football player*
* Retzlaff, Pete

**Retzlaff, Pete**
See Retzlaff, Palmer

**Reuben, George** 1880-1945 [SC]
*Russian-born actor*
* McKay, George W.

**Reulbach, Big Ed**
See Reulbach, Edward Marvin

**Reulbach, Edward Marvin**
1882-1961 [BE, PB]
*American baseball player*
* Lawson, Edward
* Reulbach, Big Ed

**Reurslag, Guurtje Johanna Hendrika**
1886- [LAO]
*Dutch educator and author*
* Riemens-Reurslag, J.

**Reuter, Paul Julius von**
See Josaphat, Israel Beer

**Reuther, Walter Philip** 1907-1970
*American labor leader*
* [The] Redhead

**Rev. B**
See Eisner, Betty Grover

**Reval, Jacques**
See Laver, James

**Revel, Harry**
See Floyd, Gilbert

**[Le] Revele**
See Artaud, Antonin

**Revelle, Arthur Hamilton**
See Engstroem, Arthur Hamilton

**Revere, M. P.**
See Williamson, Alice Muriel [Livingston]

**Revere, Paul**
See Abarbanell, Jacob

**[The] Reverend**
See Brezina, Greg

**Reverend Billy**
See Robinson, William

**Reverend Ike**
See Eikerenkoetter, Frederick J.

**Reverend Levi**
See Dryden, John

**Reverie, Reginauld**
See Mellen, Grenville

**Revermort, J. A.**
See Cramb, John Adam

**Reveron, Saundra** 1942- [IBW]
*American caterer*
* [The] Pie Lady

**Reverse, Sir**
See Buller, [Sir] Redvers Henry

**Revertito [Little Reverte]**
See Garcia Reverte, Manuel

**Revier, Dorothy**
See Velegra, Doris

**Revile, E. B.**
See Byrne, Oliver

**Revillo, Eugene**
See Oliver, Eugene

**Revilo**
See Marshall, Oliver P.

**[El] Revolucionario del Toreo [The Revolutionary Bullfighter]**
See Belmonte y Garcia, Juan

**Revons, E. C.**
See Converse, Charles Crozat

**Revorg, Trebla**
See Grover, Albert

**Revson, Champagne Peter**
See Revson, Peter Jeffrey

**Revson, Peter Jeffrey** 1939-1974
[EAR]
*American auto racer*
* Revson, Champagne Peter

**Rexford, John**
See Bailey, Prentiss

**Rey, Alvino**
See McBurney, Alvin

**Rey, Anita**
See Lorrnel, Marlise

**[El] Rey del Mambo [The King of Mambo]**
See Prado, [Domase] Perez

**[El] Rey del Temple**
See Solorzano Davalos, Jesus

**Rey, Fernando**
See Arambillet, Fernando

**Rey, Frederico**
See Koning, Fred Wittop

**Rey, Hans Augusto** 1898-1977
[CA, SAT]
*German-born illustrator and author*
* Uncle Gus

**Rey, Louis-Etienne-Ernest**
1823-1909 [BBD]
*French composer*
* Reyer, Louis-Etienne-Ernest

**Rey, Pepe**
See Cornyn, John Hubert

**Rey, Roberto**
See Colas Iglesias, Roberto

**Rey, Russell** [house pseudonym, Curtis Warren]
See Hughes, Den[n]is [Talbot]

**Rey Tigre [King Tiger]**
See Tijerina, Reies

**Rey-Stolle, Alejandro** 1910- [IAW]
*Spanish author*
* Xavier, Adro

**Reyam**
See Mayer, Charles Leopold

**Reybaud, Marie Roch Louis** 1799-? [PA]
*Author*
* Dwrocher, Leon

**Reyburn, Wallace [Macdonald]**
1913- [IAW]
*New Zealand-born author*
* Scott, William

**Reyer, Louis-Etienne-Ernest**
See Rey, Louis-Etienne-Ernest

**Reyes, Dr.** [code name]
See Rogers, William Pierce

**Reyes, Eva**
See Ardura, Adaljina

**Reyes, Fernando De Los** 1930-
[GS]
*Mexican bullfighter*
* Callao [Pebble]

**Reyes, Miguel Angel**
See Dilone, Miguel Angel

**Reyes, Nap**
See Reyes, Napoleon Aguilera

**Reyes, Napoleon Aguilera** 1919-
[BE]
*Cuban-born baseball player*
* Reyes, Nap

**Reyes Basualto, [Ricardo Eliezer] Neftali** 1904-1973
[CLC, EWL, TCL]
*Chilean poet*
* [The] Latin Walt Whitman
* Neruda, Pablo

**Reyhaud, [Madam] C.**
See Arnaud, Henrietta

**Reymond, Louis**
See Daudet, Ernest

**Reymont, Ladislas**
See Reymont, Wladyslaw Stanislaw

**Reymont, Wladyslaw Stanislaw**
1867-1925 [TLC]
*Author*
* Reymont, Ladislas

**Reyna, Ruth** 1904- [IAW]
*American author*
* Abbott, Evelyn
* Abbott, Orrina
* Ana, Ray

**Reynard**
See Fox, Myron

**Reynard**
See Foxcroft, Frank

**Reynold, Thomas, Physition**
See Rhodion [or Roeslin], Eucharius

**Reynolds, Adrian**
See Long, Amelia Reynolds

**Reynolds, Allie Pierce** 1915-
[BE, DGS, PB]
*American baseball player*
* Reynolds, Chief
* Superchief

**Reynolds, Bart**
See Emblen, Donald Lewis

**Reynolds, Charles** 1879?-1942
[BMH, THR]
*British comedian*
* Austin, Charles

**Reynolds, Chief**
See Reynolds, Allie Pierce

**Reynolds, Craig**
See Enfield, Harold Hugh

**Reynolds, Dallas McCord** 1917-
[CA, ESF, WGT]
*American author*
* Collins, Clark
* Mallory, Mark
* McCord, Guy
* Reynolds, Mack
* Ross, Dallas

**Reynolds, Daniel Vance [Danny]**
1919- [BE]
*American baseball player*
* Reynolds, Squirrel

**Reynolds, Debbie**
See Reynolds, Mary Frances

**Reynolds, Dickson**
*See* Reynolds, Helen Mary
Greenwood Campbell

**Reynolds, George W. M.** 19th c.
[PA]
*Author*
* Bos
* Master Timothy

**Reynolds, Hacksaw**
*See* Reynolds, Jack

**Reynolds, Helen Mary Greenwood
Campbell** 1884- [CA, NAA]
*Canadian author and illustrator*
* Dickson, Helen
* Reynolds, Dickson

**Reynolds, Horse**
*See* Reynolds, Robert Odell

**Reynolds, Jack** 20th c.
*American football player*
* Reynolds, Hacksaw

**Reynolds, John**
*See* Whitlock, Ralph

**Reynolds, John** ?-1607 [HN]
*Leader of a religious sect in Britain*
* Pouch, Captain

**Reynolds, John Hamilton**
1794-1842 [FFF]
*British poet*
* Herbert, Edward
* Nimrod

**Reynolds, Joseph** [FFF]
*American railroad owner*
* Diamond Joe

**Reynolds, [Sir] Joshua** 1723-1792
[DNNS, SN]
*British painter*
* [The] Raphael of England

**Reynolds, L. Major**
*See* Leipiar, Louise

**Reynolds, Liggett**
*See* Simon, Robert Alfred

**Reynolds, Mack**
*See* Reynolds, Dallas McCord

**Reynolds, Madge**
*See* Whitlock, Ralph

**Reynolds, Marjorie**
*See* Goodspeed, Marjorie

**Reynolds, Mary Ellen** 1898-1936
[BEW, EMT, PMJ]
*American actress, dancer, singer*
* Miller, Marilyn

**Reynolds, Mary Frances** 1932-
[BDF, EMT, FC]
*American actress, singer, dancer*
* Reynolds, Debbie

**Reynolds, Mrs. James** [FFF]
*Entertainer*
* Rivers, Olive

**Reynolds, Myra Rolfe** 20th c.
[NAA]
*American writer*
* Alden, Betty [house pseudonym?]

**Reynolds, Peter**
*See* Horrocks, Peter

**Reynolds, Peter**
*See* Long, Amelia Reynolds

**Reynolds, Robert Odell** 20th c.
[BBH]
*American football player*
* Reynolds, Horse

**Reynolds, Ron**
*See* Bradbury, Ray [Douglas]

**Reynolds, Ruth Evelyn Millicent**
1915- [ART]
*British painter and sculptor*
* R. R.

**Reynolds, Squirrel**
*See* Reynolds, Daniel Vance
[Danny]

**Reynolds, Vivian**
*See* Snyder, Mrs.

**Reynolds, Walter Doty** 1860- ?
[SFL, WGT]
*Author*
* Prime, Lord

**Reynolds-Stephens, [Sir] William**
*See* Stephens, William

**Reys, Maria Everdina** 1924- [EJ]
*Dutch singer*
* Reys, Rita

**Reys, Rita**
*See* Reys, Maria Everdina

**Reyten, Thaddeus** 18th c. [HN]
*Resisted the partition of Poland*
* [The] Polish Cato

**Rhaeticus [or Rheticus]**
*See* Von Lauchen, Georg Joachim

**Rhampsinitus**
*See* Ramses III [or Rameses]

**Rhapsody, Miss**
*See* Wells, Viola Gertrude

**Rhawn, Robert John [Bobby]** 1919-
[BE]
*American baseball player*
* Rhawn, Rocky

**Rhawn, Rocky**
*See* Rhawn, Robert John [Bobby]

**Rhea, Don** 20th c. [CM]
*American radio broadcaster*
* Uncle Don

**Rhea, Nicholas**
*See* Walker, Peter Norman

**Rheal**
*See* Cesena, Sebastian Gayet

**Rheam, Cy**
*See* Rheam, Kenneth Johnston

**Rheam, Kenneth Johnston**
1893-1947 [BE]
*American baseball player*
* Rheam, Cy

**Rhem, Charles Flint** 1903-
[BE, BN, PB]
*American baseball player*
* Rhem, Shad
* Rhem, Zorie

**Rhem, Shad**
*See* Rhem, Charles Flint

**Rhem, Zorie**
*See* Rhem, Charles Flint

**Rhene Baton**
*See* Baton, Rene

**Rhiannon**
*See* Mackworth, Cecily

**Rhine, Alice Hyneman** [PA]
*Author*
* A. H. R.
* Alice

**Rhines, Bunker**
*See* Rhines, William P. [Billy]

**Rhines, William P. [Billy]**
1869-1922 [PB]
*American baseball player*
* Rhines, Bunker

**[The] Rhinestone Rubinstein**
*See* Liberace, Wladziu Valentino

**Rhinewine, Abraham** 1887- [NAA]
*Polish-born journalist and author*
* Ero

**Rhiney, Bambi**
*See* Rhiney, Delores Francine

**Rhiney, Delores Francine** 20th c.
[IBW]
*American fashion model*
* Rhiney, Bambi

**Rhinotmetus [With the Nose Cut Off]**
*See* Justinian II

**Rho, Stella**
*See* Vitelleschi, Stella

**Rhoades, Dusty**
*See* Rhoades, Robert Barton

**Rhoades, Geoffrey H.** 1898- [ART]
*British painter*
* G. H. R.

**Rhoades, Jefferson**
*See* Panzram, Carl

**Rhoades, Jonathan**
*See* Olsen, John Edward [Jack]

**Rhoades, Judith G[rubman]** 1935-
[CA]
*American author*
* Dilling, Judith

**Rhoades, Robert Barton**
1879-1967 [BE, PB]
*American baseball player*
* Rhoades, Dusty

**Rhodan, Forry**
*See* Ackerman, Forrest J[ames]

**Rhode, Austen**
*See* Francis, Basil [Hoskins]

**Rhode, John**
*See* Street, Cecil John Charles

**Rhode, Winslow**
*See* Roe, F[rederic] Gordon

**Rhodes, Alfred** ?-1948 [SC]
*American actor*
* Rhodes, Dusty

**Rhodes, Billie** 1894- [CU]
*American actress*
* [The] Nestor Girl

**Rhodes, Billy** 1895-1967 [SC]
*American actor*
* Little, Billy

**Rhodes, Donald Wayne** 1954-
[SMG]
*American football player*
* Rhodes, Skid

**Rhodes, Dusty**
*See* Rhodes, Alfred

**Rhodes, Dusty**
*See* Rhodes, James Lamar

**Rhodes, Dusty**
*See* Rhodes, John Gordon

**Rhodes, Dusty**
*See* Rhodes, William Clarence
[Bill]

**Rhodes, Erik**
*See* Sharpe, Ernest Rhoades

**Rhodes, Ethmer Cletus** 1913-1966
[CWG]
*American country-western performer*
* Rhodes, Slim

**Rhodes, Fella**
*See* Rhodes, William

**Rhodes, Izora** 20th c. [IBW]
*American singer*
* Two Tons of Fun

**Rhodes, James Lamar** 1927-
[B10, BE, PB]
*American baseball player*
* Rhodes, Dusty

**Rhodes, John Gordon** 1907-1960
[BE]
*American baseball player*
* Rhodes, Dusty

**Rhodes, Laura**
*See* Robinson, Lisa

**Rhodes, Oakmead**
*See* Burke, Thomas

**Rhodes, Orville J.** 1930-
[ECM, RM]
*American musician*
* Rhodes, Red

**Rhodes, Red**
*See* Rhodes, Orville J.

**Rhodes, Ruth** 1896-1975 [SC]
*American actress*
* Lee, Ruth

**Rhodes, Skid**
*See* Rhodes, Donald Wayne

**Rhodes, Slim**
*See* Rhodes, Ethmer Cletus

**Rhodes, W. H.** 20th c. [SFP]
*Author*
* Caxton

**Rhodes, William** 20th c.
*American football player*
* Rhodes, Fella

**Rhodes, William Clarence [Bill]** 19th
c. [BE]
*American baseball player*
* Rhodes, Dusty

**Rhodes, Zandra Lindsey** 1940-
[WFA]
*British fashion and textile designer*
* [The] Girl with Green Hair

**[The] Rhodian Master**
*See* Ennius, Quintus

**Rhodiginenus, Lingi Richiere**
1450-1525 [PA]
*Author*
* Cielius

**Rhodion [or Roeslin], Eucharius**
1540-1598 [FFF]
*British author*
* Reynold, Thomas, Physition

**Rhodopis**
*See* Doricha

**Rhody**
*See* Burnside, Ambrose Everett

**Rhody, Louis**
*See* Rothkopf, Louis

**Rhondda, [Viscountess] Margaret Haig** 1884- [WWL]
*British author*
* Mackworth

**Rhone, Earnest** 1953- [SMG]
*American football player*
* Rhone, Ironman

**Rhone, Ironman**
*See* Rhone, Earnest

**[The] Rhone of Christian Eloquence**
*See* Bossuet, Jacques Benigne

**[The] Rhone of Christian Eloquence**
*See* Hilary

**[The] Rhone of Latin Eloquence**
*See* Hilary

**Rhoscomyl, Owen**
*See* Vaughan, Owen

**Rhubarb, Colonel**
*See* Worthington, Robert Lee [Bob]

**Rhubarb Red**
*See* Polfus, Lester

**Rhuddlau, John**
*See* Blanden, Charles Granger

**Rhue, Morton**
*See* Strassar, Todd

**Rhydderch, Ieuan**
*See* Jones, Evan David

**[The] Rhyming Barber**
*See* Di Giovanni, Domenico

**Rhyndacenus**
*See* Lascaris, Andreas Johannes [or Janus]

**Rhyne, Orestes Pearle** 1885- [NAA]
*American author and educator*
* Rein, Orestes Pearle

**Rhys, Horton** [PA]
*Author*
* Imported Sparrow

**Rhys, Ioan**
*See* Rees, Ioan Bowen

**Rhys, Megan**
*See* Williams, Jeanne

**Rhys-Jones, Dilys** 1946- [TR]
*British actress*
* Watling, Dilys

**[The] Rhythm and Blues King**
*See* Frost, Frank Otis

**Rhythm, Miss**
*See* Brown, Ruth

**Rhythm, Mr.**
*See* Williams, Andre

**Ribeiro, Antonio**
*See* Guarghias, Aloysius George

**Ribera, Jose** 1588-1652 [SN, WBD]
*Spanish painter*
* [The] Little Spaniard
* Spagnoletto

**Ric**
*See* Miniggio, Riccardo

**Ricardel, Molly**
*See* Boehnel, Molly

**Ricardo, Don**
*See* Ridgely, Richard

**Ricasoli, Bettino [Baron of Brolio]** 1809-1880 [SN]
*Italian statesman*
* [The] Baron

**Ricault, Charles Joseph de** 1823-1899 [WBD]
*French historian and author*
* Hericault, Charles d'

**Ricca, Mops**
*See* DeLucia, Felice

**Ricca, Paul**
*See* DeLucia, Felice

**Riccardo, John** 1924-
*American automobile executive*
* [The] Flamethrower

**Ricci, Marie Nielli** 1883-1970 [WFA]
*Italian-born fashion designer*
* Ricci, Nina

**Ricci, Nina**
*See* Ricci, Marie Nielli

**Ricciarelli, Daniele** 1509-1566 [SN, WBD]
*Italian painter*
* [Il] Braccatone
* [The] Breeches Maker
* Volterra, Daniele da

**Riccio, Andrea**
*See* Briosco, Andrea

**Riccio, Domenico** 1494-1567 [WBD]
*Italian painter*
* [Il] Brusasorci

**Riccoboni, Adrienne** 1930- [FC]
*British actress*
* Corri, Adrienne

**Riccoboni, Lelio**
*See* Riccoboni, Lodovico

**Riccoboni, Lodovico** 1675?-1753 [WBD]
*Italian-born actor and playwright*
* Riccoboni, Lelio

**Riccoboni, Luigi** 1674-1753 [PA]
*Author*
* Lelio

**Riccobono, Joseph S.** 1893?-1975 [B10]
*American underworld figure*
* Bono, Joe

**Rice, Albert**
*See* Leventhal, Albert Rice

**Rice, Allison** [joint pseudonym with Jane Rice]
*See* Allison, Ruth

**Rice, Allison** [joint pseudonym with Ruth Allison]
*See* Rice, Jane

**Rice, Brian K.** 1932- [IAW]
*British author*
* Vigilans

**Rice, Clive Edward Butler** 1949- [DC]
*South African-born cricketer*
* Rice, Ricie

**Rice, Craig** [joint pseudonym with Georgiana Ann Randolph]
*See* Lombino, Salvatore A.

**Rice, Craig** [joint pseudonym with Salvatore A. Lombino]
*See* Randolph, Georgiana Ann

**Rice, Del**
*See* Rice, Delbert W.

**Rice, Delbert W.** 1922- [BE]
*American baseball player*
* Rice, Del

**Rice, Desmond Charles** 1924- [CA]
*British author*
* Meiring, Desmond

**Rice, Dicey**
*See* Rice, John Michael

**Rice, Dorothy Mary** 1913- [CA]
*Irish-born author*
* Borne, Dorothy
* Vicary, Dorothy

**Rice, Edgar Charles** 1892-1974 [BAB, DGS, PB]
*American baseball player*
* Man o' War
* Rice, Sam

**Rice, Elinor**
*See* Hays, Elinor Rice

**Rice, Elmer**
*See* Reizenstein, Elmer L.

**Rice, George** 1917- [FC]
*American actor*
* O'Hanlon, George

**Rice, Granny**
*See* Rice, H. Grantland

**Rice, H. Grantland** 1880-1954 [FB]
*American sportswriter*
* Rice, Granny

**Rice, Harold** 20th c. [BS]
*American educator and owner of silk magic business*
* [The] Silk King

**Rice, Harold Housten** 1924- [BE]
*American baseball player*
* Rice, Hoot

**Rice, Hoot**
*See* Rice, Harold Housten

**Rice, Howard** 1897-1954 [SC]
*American actor*
* Carney, Don
* Uncle Don

**Rice, Isaac L.** 1850- ? [PA]
*Author*
* Ecir

**Rice, James** 19th c. [SAT]
*British author*
* Legrand, Martin

**Rice, Jane** 20th c. [WGT]
*Author*
* Austin, Mary
* Rice, Allison [joint pseudonym with Ruth Allison]

**Rice, Jim Crow**
*See* Rice, Thomas Dartmouth

**Rice, Joan Odette** 1919- [AW]
*British writer and broadcaster*
* Hallam, Jay

**Rice, John Michael** 1949- [DC]
*British cricketer*
* Rice, Dicey

**[The] Rice Paddy Ranger**
*See* Curless, Richard [Dick]

**Rice, Ricie**
*See* Rice, Clive Edward Butler

**Rice, Rosella** [FFF]
*Writer*
* Brooks, Chatty

**Rice, Sam**
*See* O'Hanlon, George Samuel

**Rice, Sam**
*See* Rice, Edgar Charles

**Rice, Thomas Dartmouth** 1808-1860 [DNNF, SN, WBD]
*American songwriter and minstrel-show pioneer*
* [The] Father of American Minstrelsy
* Rice, Jim Crow

**[The] Rich**
*See* Canute II

**Rich**
*See* Fairfield, Richard Ivan

**[The] Rich**
*See* Fugger, Jakob, II

**[The] Rich**
*See* George

**[The] Rich**
*See* Louis IX

**[The] Rich**
*See* Otto

**[The] Rich**
*See* Otto

**Rich, Barbara** [joint pseudonym with Laura Reichenthal]
*See* Graves, Susan B[ernard]

**Rich, Barbara** [joint pseudonym with Robert Von Ranke Graves]
*See* Reichenthal, Laura

**Rich, Bernard** 1917- [IEJ, PMJ, WWJ]
*American jazz musician*
* Baby Traps
* Rich, Buddy
* Traps the Drum Wonder

**Rich, Buddy**
*See* Rich, Bernard

**Rich, C. B.**
*See* Lewis, Leo Rich

**Rich, D. Coleman**
*See* Richardson, Darrell C.

**Rich, Eddie**
*See* Reich, Edwin

**Rich, Edith J. R.** 1878-1956 [BEW]
*American editor and author*
* Isaacs, Edith J. R.

**Rich, Henry K.**
*See* Goddard, Norman Molyneux

**Rich, Irene**
*See* Luther, Irene

**Rich, John** 1692-1761
[DNNF, DNNS, SN]
*British actor*
* [The] Father of Harlequins
* Lun

**Rich, Robert**
*See* Trumbo, Dalton

**Rich, Woodrow Earl** 1917- [BE]
*American baseball player*
* Rich, Woody

**Rich, Woody**
*See* Rich, Woodrow Earl

**Richard, A.** 1809- ? [PA]
*Author*
* Du Cental

**Richard, Bee-Bee**
*See* Richard, Lee Edward

**Richard, Bill**
*See* Van Horn, Dale R.

**Richard, Cliff**
*See* Webb, Harold

**Richard D.**
*See* Dent, Richard

**Richard, George**
*See* Stubbs, Harry C[lement]

**Richard, [Joseph] Henri** 1936-
[FHE]
*Canadian hockey player*
* [The] Pocket Rocket

**Richard, J. R.**
*See* Richard, James Rodney

**Richard, Jacques** 1952- [SMG]
*Canadian-born hockey player*
* Costeau

**Richard, James Robert**
*See* Bowen, Robert Sydney

**Richard, James Rodney** 1950-
[BE, NLG]
*American baseball player*
* Richard, J. R.

**Richard, Jean-Marius** 1905- [FC]
*French screenwriter and director*
* Carlo-Rim

**Richard, Kent?**
*See* Crossen, Ken[dell Foster]

**Richard, Lee**
*See* Le Pelley, Guernsey

**Richard, Lee David** 1926- [BEW]
*American actor*
* Richardson, Lee

**Richard, Lee Edward** 1948- [SMG]
*American baseball player*
* Richard, Bee-Bee

**Richard, [Joseph Henri] Maurice**
1921- [CEI, FHE, SR]
*Canadian hockey player*
* [The] Babe Ruth of Hockey
* Richard, Rocket
* [The] Rocket

**Richard, Mira** 1878?-1973 [B10]
*French religious leader*
* [The] Mother

**Richard of Cirencester** 14th c.
[DNNF, FFF, HN]
*British historian*
* [The] Monk of Westminster

**Richard, Rocket**
*See* Richard, [Joseph Henri] Maurice

**Richard the Chicken-Hearted**
*See* Nixon, Richard Milhous

**Richard, Zina**
*See* Merante, Mrs. Louis

**Richard I** ?- 996 [DNNS, WBD]
*Duke of Normandy*
* [The] Fearless

**Richard I** 1157-1199
[DHA, HN, SN]
*King of England*
* Coeur de Lion
* [The] Dickon of the Broom
* [The] Lion Hearted

**Richard II** ?-1026?
[DNNS, FFF, SN]
*Duke of Normandy*
* [The] Good

**Richard II** 1367?-1400 [HN, SN]
*King of England*
* Bordeaux
* [The] Coxcomb
* [Le] Jeune Damoisel Richart
* [The] Skinless Prince of Wales

**Richard III** 1452-1485
[FFF, SN, WBD]
*King of England*
* [The] Boar
* Crouchback
* [The] Hogge
* [The] Protector

**Richards, Al**
*See* Shubin, Seymour

**Richards, Alfred [Luther]** 1939-
[CA]
*American psychologist and author*
* Richards, Fred

**Richards, Allen**
*See* Rosenthal, Richard A.

**Richards, Ann**
*See* Kenton, Margaret Ann Borden

**Richards, Beah**
*See* Richardson, Beulah

**Richards, Charles**
*See* Marvin, John T.

**Richards, Charles** 1912-
[DAM, EJ, WWJ]
*American jazz musician*
* Richards, Red

**Richards, Clay**
*See* Crossen, Ken[dell Foster]

**Richards, Clifton James** 1958-
[DC]
*British cricketer*
* Richards, Jack

**Richards, Cornelia H. [Bradley]**
1822- ? [FFF]
*American author*
* Manners, Mrs.

**Richards, Curley Top**
*See* Richards, Ruby

**Richards, David**
*See* Bickers, Richard Leslie
Townshend

**Richards, Dick** 20th c. [SFL]
*Author*
* Wells, Barry

**Richards, Duane**
*See* Hurley, Vic

**Richards, Emil**
*See* Radocchia, Emilio Joseph

**Richards, Ezek**
*See* Savage, John

**Richards, Frances** 1903- [ART]
*British artist*
* F. R.

**Richards, Francis** [joint pseudonym
with Richard (Orson) Lockridge]
*See* Lockridge, Frances Louise
[Davis]

**Richards, Francis** [joint pseudonym
with Frances Louise (Davis)
Lockridge]
*See* Lockridge, Richard [Orson]

**Richards, Frank** [house pseudonym]
*See* Austin, Stanley E.

**Richards, Frank** [house pseudonym]
*See* Barnard, Richard Innes

**Richards, Frank** [house pseudonym]
*See* Barrie, S.

**Richards, Frank** [house pseudonym]
*See* Brooks, Edwy Searles

**Richards, Frank** [house pseudonym]
*See* Catchpole, William Leslie

**Richards, Frank** [house pseudonym]
*See* Cook, Fred Gordon

**Richards, Frank** [house pseudonym]
*See* Davis, A. W.

**Richards, Frank** [house pseudonym]
*See* Down, C. Maurice

**Richards, Frank** [house pseudonym]
*See* Duffy, Michael Francis

**Richards, Frank** [house pseudonym]
*See* Gibbons, William

**Richards, Frank**
*See* Hamilton, Charles Harold St.
John

**Richards, Frank** [house pseudonym]
*See* Herman, Julius

**Richards, Frank** [house pseudonym]
*See* Hinton, Herbert Allan

**Richards, Frank** [house pseudonym]
*See* Hook, H. Clarke

**Richards, Frank** [house pseudonym]
*See* Hope, William Edward
Stanton

**Richards, Frank** [house pseudonym]
*See* Kemp, Alec M.

**Richards, Frank** [house pseudonym]
*See* Kirkham, Reginald S.

**Richards, Frank** [house pseudonym]
*See* Newman, Kenneth E.

**Richards, Frank** [house pseudonym]
*See* O'Mant, Hedley Percival
Angelo

**Richards, Frank** [house pseudonym]
*See* Pentelow, John Nix

**Richards, Frank** [house pseudonym]
*See* Pike, William Ernest

**Richards, Frank** [house pseudonym]
*See* Ransome, L. E.

**Richards, Frank** [house pseudonym]
*See* Samways, George Richmond

**Richards, Frank** [house pseudonym]
*See* Shepherd, S. Rossiter

**Richards, Frank** [house pseudonym]
*See* Twyman, Harold William

**Richards, Frank** [house pseudonym]
*See* Wood-Smith, Noel

**Richards, Fred**
*See* Richards, Alfred [Luther]

**Richards, Fred Charles** 1927- [BE]
*American baseball player*
* Richards, Fuzzy

**Richards, Fuzzy**
*See* Richards, Fred Charles

**Richards, Henry**
*See* Morrissey, Joseph Laurence

**Richards, Henry**
*See* Stoddard, Richard Henry

**Richards, Hilda**
*See* Hamilton, Charles Harold St.
John

**Richards, Hilda**
*See* Wheway, John W.

**Richards, I. A.**
*See* Richards, Ivor Armstrong

**Richards, Ivor Armstrong**
1893-1979 [LC, TC]
*British critic*
* [The] Guru of Cambridge
* Richards, I. A.

**Richards, J. R.**
*See* Richards, James Rodney

**Richards, Jack**
*See* Richards, Clifton James

**Richards, James Rodney** 1950-
[IBW]
*American baseball player*
* Richards, J. R.

**Richards, Jason**
*See* Bock, Fred

**Richards, Jay**
*See* Pine, Arthur

**Richards, Jeff**
*See* Taylor, Richard Mansfield

**Richards, Johnny**
*See* Cascales, John

**Richards, Kenny**
*See* Broderick, Richard
L[awrence]

**Richards, Lela Horn** 1870- ?
[NAA]
*American author*
* Neville, Lee

**Richards, Leslie**
*See* Green, Richard

**Richards, Lillian**
*See* Richardson, Mrs. Leander

**Richards, Mrs. George** [FFF]
*Entertainer*
* Goodwin, Maude

**Richards, Parke**
*See* Fewell, Laura R.

**Richards, Paul**
*See* Buddee, Paul Edgar

**Richards, Pennington**
See Pennington-Richards, C. M.

**Richards, Peter**
See Monger, [Ifor] David

**Richards, Phyllis**
See Auty, Phyllis

**Richards, Red**
See Richards, Charles

**Richards, Renee**
See Raskind, Richard

**Richards, Robert [Bob]** 1926- [TF]
*American track and field athlete*
* [The] Vaulting Vicar

**Richards, Ronald Charles William**
1923- [AW, CA, WD]
*British author and playwright*
* Saddler, K. Allen

**Richards, Ross** 20th c. [MBF]
*British author*
* Mead, Matt
* Reid, Desmond [house pseudonym]

**Richards, Ruby** 20th c. [IBW]
*American entertainer*
* Richards, Curley Top

**Richards, Sara Lippincott** 1875- ?
[NAA]
*American author*
* Lippincott, Sara
* Stein, J. J.

**Richards, Stanley**
See Myers, Stanley

**Richards, Stephen**
See Stevens, Mark

**Richards, Thomas**
See Bergman, Richard Thomas

**Richards, William Upton** [PA]
*Author*
* W. U. R.

**Richardson, Abram [or Arthur?]**
**Harding** 1855-1931 [BE, DGS, PB]
*American baseball player*
* Old True Blue
* Richardson, Hardy

**Richardson, Anne**
See Roiphe, Anne Richardson

**Richardson, Anthony** 1899- [AW]
*British author*
* Currie, Thomas Stewart

**Richardson, Antonio** 1928- [BF]
*British director*
* Richardson, Tony

**Richardson, Arleta**
See Wright, Arleta

**Richardson, Beth**
See Gutcheon, Beth R[ichardson]

**Richardson, Beulah** 20th c. [IBW]
*American actress, author, director*
* Richards, Beah

**Richardson, Bill**
See Richardson, Hubert Leon

**Richardson, C.**
See Munsey, Cecil [Richard, Jr.]

**Richardson, C. C.**
See Richardson, Clarence Clifford

**Richardson, Claibe**
See Richardson, Claiborne F.

**Richardson, Claiborne F.** 1929-
[ASC]
*American composer*
* Richardson, Claibe

**Richardson, Clarence Clifford**
1918- [BWW]
*American singer*
* Richardson, C. C.
* Richardson, Peg

**Richardson, Darrell C.** 20th c.
[SFP]
*Author*
* Rich, D. Coleman

**Richardson, Emory Aaron** ?-1965
[IA]
*American poet*
* Big Rich

**Richardson, Flavia**
See Thomson, Christine Campbell

**Richardson, Francis** [joint pseudonym with Frank Parnell]
See Bartle, L. E.

**Richardson, Francis** [joint pseudonym with L. E. Bartle]
See Parnell, Frank

**Richardson, Gabriel** 18th c. [SN]
*Friend of Scottish poet, Robert Burns*
* Brewer Gabriel

**Richardson, Garnet** 1933- [CSH]
*Canadian curler*
* Richardson, Sam

**Richardson, Gladwell** 20th c.
[MBF]
*British author*
* Blacksnake, George
* Clarkson, Orman
* Grant, Maxwell [house pseudonym]
* Haines, John
* Jones, Calico
* Kent, Pete
* Kildare, Maurice
* O'Riley, Warren
* Warner, Frank
* Winslowe, John

**Richardson, Grace Lee**
See Dickson, Naida

**Richardson, H. B.** 20th c. [SMG]
*American baseball manager*
* Richardson, Spec

**Richardson, Hardy**
See Richardson, Abram [or Arthur?] Harding

**Richardson, Harold Edward** 1929-
[IAW]
*American author*
* Cumberland, Cass

**Richardson, Henry Handel**
See Robertson, Ethel Florence [Lindesay Richardson]

**Richardson, Henry V-M** 1923-
[CA]
*American author*
* Richardson, Vokes

**Richardson, Hubert Leon** 20th c.
*American politician*
* Richardson, Bill

**Richardson, Isabella** 1782-1878
[PA]
*Author*
* Shiels, Tibbie

**Richardson, Israel Bush** 1815-1862
[FFF]
*American army officer*
* Fighting Dick

**Richardson, J. P.**
See Richardson, Jape

**Richardson, James** 1760-1850 [PA]
*Author*
* Stevin, Adam

**Richardson, Jape** 1935-1959 [RO1]
*American singer and songwriter*
* [The] Big Bopper
* Richardson, J. P.

**Richardson, Julian** 1916- [IBW]
*American printer and bookstore owner*
* Richardson, Rich

**Richardson, Leander** [FFF]
*American writer*
* Town Listener

**Richardson, Lee**
See Richard, Lee David

**Richardson, Midge Turk** 1930-
[CA]
*American author*
* Turk, Midge

**Richardson, Mrs. Leander** [FFF]
*Entertainer*
* Andrews, Carrie
* Gilman, Ada
* Richards, Lillian

**[The] Richardson of Athens**
See Thespis

**Richardson, Peg**
See Richardson, Clarence Clifford

**Richardson, Randell** 1921- [ASC]
*American singer*
* Reade, Regina
* Rogers, Rosalind

**Richardson, Rich**
See Richardson, Julian

**Richardson, Robert S[hirley]** 1902-
[CA, SAT]
*American author*
* Latham, Philip

**Richardson, Sam**
See Richardson, Garnet

**Richardson, Samuel** 1689-1761
[DEP, DNNS, RH]
*British author*
* [The] English Marivaux
* [The] Founder of the English Domestic Novel
* [The] Shakespeare of Prose Fiction

**Richardson, Sandy**
See Richardson, Thomas F.

**Richardson, Spec**
See Richardson, H. B.

**Richardson, Thomas F.** 1907?-1980
*American robber*
* Richardson, Sandy

**Richardson, Tony**
See Richardson, Antonio

**Richardson, Vokes**
See Richardson, Henry V-M

**Richardson, William** 18th c.
[DNNS]
*Writer*
* [The] Father of War Correspondents

**Richelieu**
See Robinson, William Erigena

**Richelieu, Cardinal de**
See Du Plessis, Armand Jean

**Richelieu, Duc de**
See De Vignerot du Plessis, Louis Francois Armand

**Richenbacher, Edward** 1890-1973
*American aviator and businessman*
* Ace of Aces
* Rickenbacker, Edward Vernon [Eddie]

**Richer, Donald [Donny]** 20th c.
[WFA]
*Canadian fashion designer*
* Montreal's Liberace

**Richey, David** 1939- [CA]
*American author*
* Davey, John
* Johnson, Richard

**Richey, Robert Keith** 1898- [BEW]
*American actor, playwright, director*
* Keith, Robert

**Richfield, Mai**
See Ryan, Mrs. Thomas

**Richman, Abraham Samuel** 1921-
[EJ, PMJ]
*American jazz musician*
* Richman, Boomie

**Richman, Ace**
See Richman, Milton Harry

**Richman, Al** 1913- [CA]
*British-born author*
* Morton, Joseph
* Richmond, Al

**Richman, Arthur**
See Reichman, Arthur

**Richman, Boomie**
See Richman, Abraham Samuel

**Richman, Harry**
See Reichman, Harry

**Richman, Marian**
See Pearlson, Marion S.

**Richman, Mark**
See Richman, Marvin Jack

**Richman, Marvin Jack** 1927-
[BEW]
*American actor*
* Richman, Mark

**Richman, Milton Harry** 1916-
[CWG]
*American country-western performer*
* Richman, Ace

**Richmond**
See Sheppard, Jacob R.

**Richmond, Al**
See Richman, Al

**Richmond, Bill** 1763-1829 [IBW]
*American-born boxer*
* [The] Black Terror

**Richmond, Bud**
See Richmond Ray[mond S.]

**Richmond, Charles D.** 1935- [EJ]
*American jazz musician*
* Richmond, Dannie

**Richmond, Dannie**
*See* Richmond, Charles D.

**Richmond, George**
*See* Brister, Richard

**Richmond, George**
*See* Samways, George Richmond

**Richmond, Grace**
*See* Marsh, John

**Richmond, H. B.**
*See* Bungay, E. Newton

**Richmond, Harry**
*See* Boyle, Henry

**Richmond, Hattie L.**
*See* Canfield, Mrs. Eugene

**Richmond, John Peter**
*See* Carradine, Richmond Reed

**Richmond, Kane**
*See* Bowditch, Frederick W.

**Richmond, Mary**
*See* Lindsay, Kathleen

**Richmond Ray[mond S.]** 1896-
[BE]
*American baseball player*
* Richmond, Bud

**Richmond, Rod**
*See* Glut, Donald F[rank]

**Richmond, William**
*See* Fell, William Richmond

**Richstein, Larry** 20th c. [RM]
*Musician*
* Tabin, Rube

**Richter, Emil Henry** 1888-1934
[BE]
*German-born baseball player*
* Richter, Reggie

**Richter, Ernst H.** 1901-1959
[WGT]
*German author*
* Brown, William
* Terridge, Ernest

**Richter, Eugen** 1838-1906 [SFL]
*Author*
* Richter, Eugene

**Richter, Eugene**
*See* Richter, Eugen

**Richter, J. H.**
*See* Richter-Altschaffer, John
Hans

**Richter, Jean Paul Friedrich**
1763-1825 [DEP, RH, SN]
*German author*
* [Der] Einzige
* [The] Only
* Paul, Jean
* [The] Unique

**Richter, Reggie**
*See* Richter, Emil Henry

**Richter, Vernon**
*See* Hutchcroft, Vera

**Richter-Altschaffer, John Hans**
1901- [WD]
*American economist and author*
* Richter, J. H.

**Richton, Addy**
*Radio scriptwriter*
* Marston, Adelaide [joint
pseudonym with Lynn Stone]

**Ricimer** ?- 472 [HN]
*Roman general*
* [The] Roman King-Maker

**Rickard, Cole**
*See* Barrett, Geoffrey John

**Rickard, George Lewis**
1870?-1929 [AS, BX, OCS]
*American boxing promoter*
* [The] Man with the Midas Touch
* [The] Master of Ballyhoo
* Rickard, Tex

**Rickard, Tex**
*See* Rickard, George Lewis

**Rickenbacker, Edward Vernon**
**[Eddie]**
*See* Richenbacher, Edward

**Ricker, Elswyth Thane** 20th c.
[THR]
*Playwright and author*
* Thane, Elswyth

**Rickert, Corinne Holt**
*See* Sawyer, Corinne Holt

**Rickert, Diamond Joe**
*See* Rickert, Joseph Francis [Joe]

**Rickert, Joseph Francis [Joe]**
1876-1943 [BE]
*American baseball player*
* Rickert, Diamond Joe

**Rickert, Marvin August** 1921- [BE]
*American baseball player*
* Rickert, Twitch

**Rickert, Shirley Jean** 20th c. [FIR]
*American entertainer*
* Gilda

**Rickert, Twitch**
*See* Rickert, Marvin August

**Rickerts, Helen** 1923- [FC]
*American actress*
* Carter, Helena

**Rickey, [Wesley] Branch**
1881-1965 [BE, PB]
*American baseball player, manager,
executive*
* [The] Mahatma

**Rickover, Hyman** 1900- [JL]
*American military leader*
* [The] Father of the Atomic
Submarine

**Ricks, James** 20th c. [MEB]
*American basketball player*
* Ricks, Pappy

**Ricks, Jonathan**
*See* Flanagan, Edward Vanes, Jr.

**Ricks, Pappy**
*See* Ricks, James

**Rickword, [John] Edgell** 1898-
[CA]
*British author, editor, translator*
* Mavin, John [joint pseudonym
with Douglas Mavin Garman]

**Rico, Alfredo Cruz** 1944- [BE]
*American baseball player*
* Rico, Fred

**Rico, Fred**
*See* Rico, Alfredo Cruz

**Ricord, J. B.** [FFF]
*Author*
* Madiana

**Ricord, Philippe** 1800-1889 [FFF]
*American-born physician*
* [The] Great American Doctor

**Ricordi, Giulio** 1840-1912 [WBD]
*Italian composer*
* Burgmein

**Rictus, Jehan**
*See* De Saint Amand, Gabriel
Randon

**Ridarelli, Robert Lewis** 1942-
[EPM, RO1]
*American singer*
* Rydell, Bobby

**Riddell, Charlotte Eliza Lawson**
**[Cowan]** 1832-1906
[HFF, WGT, WW]
*Irish author*
* Hawthorne, Rainey
* Trafford, F. G.

**Riddell, John**
*See* Ford, Corey

**Riddell, William Renwick** 1852- ?
[WWL]
*Canadian author*
* Williams, Rendall

**Riddick, Crow**
*See* Riddick, Walter H.

**Riddick, Margaret** 20th c. [THR]
*British actress*
* Bennett, Faith

**Riddick, Walter H.** 20th c. [IBW]
*American housing development
planner*
* Riddick, Crow

**Riddle, Charles** 20th c. [SMG]
*American baseball scout*
* Riddle, Chase

**Riddle, Chase**
*See* Riddle, Charles

**Riddle, Hugh Joseph** 1912-
[ART, DBA]
*British painter*
* Riddle, Huseph

**Riddle, Huseph**
*See* Riddle, Hugh Joseph

**Riddle, Jit**
*See* Riddle, Marshall Lewis

**Riddle, John Ludy** 1905- [BE]
*American baseball player*
* Riddle, Mutt

**Riddle, Marshall Lewis** 1918-
[MK]
*American baseball player*
* Riddle, Jit

**Riddle, Mutt**
*See* Riddle, John Ludy

**Riddle, Richard**
*See* Ainley, Richard

**Riddolls, Brenda Harks** 20th c.
[AW]
*British author*
* English, Brenda H.

**Rideamus**
*See* Oliven, Fritz

**Rideaux, Charles De Balzac** 1900-
[WW]
*Author*
* Chancellor, John

**Rider, Jane**
*See* Lyons, Luella B.

**Ridgeley, John**
*See* Rea, John Huntingdon

**Ridgely, Richard** 1910- [ASC]
*American musician*
* Ricardo, Don

**Ridges, R.**
*See* Smith, Bridges W.

**Ridgeway, Philip**
*See* Bower, Philip

**Ridgley, Bebe**
*See* Ridgley, William

**Ridgley, William** 1882-1961 [NOJ]
*American jazz musician*
* Ridgley, Bebe

**Ridgway, Jason**
*See* Lesser, Milton

**Riding, Laura**
*See* Reichenthal, Laura

**Ridings, Hope Dupre** 1906- [NAA]
*American writer*
* Miller, Hope Ridings
* Vincent, Ann

**Ridl, Buzz**
*See* Ridl, Charles

**Ridl, Charles** 1920- [BB]
*American basketball coach*
* Ridl, Buzz

**Ridley, James** 1736-1765
[DEL, RH]
*British author*
* Morell, [Sir] Charles
* Van Scelter, Helter

**Ridley, M. R.**
*See* Ridley, Maurice Roy

**Ridley, Maurice Roy** 1890-1969
[LC]
*British author and educator*
* Ridley, M. R.

**Ridley, Nat, Jr.** [house pseudonym]
[Stratemeyer Syndicate]
*See* Stratemeyer, Edward L.

**Ridlon, Marcia**
*See* Balterman, Marcia Ridlon

**Ridste, Frances Lillian Mary**
1919-1948 [BEW, FC]
*American actress*
* Landis, Carole

**Rie, May**
*See* Crean, Mary Walsingham

**Riebe, Hank**
*See* Riebe, Harvey Donald

**Riebe, Harvey Donald** 1921- [BE]
*American baseball player*
* Riebe, Hank

**Riedel, Judith Ellen** 1936-1974
[SC]
*American actress*
* Rawlins, Judith [Judy]

**Riedman, Sarah R[egal]** 1902-
[SAT]
*Rumanian-born American author*
* Gustafson, Sarah R.

**Riefe, Alan** 1925-    [CA]
*American author*
* Riefe, Barbara

**Riefe, Barbara**
*See* Riefe, Alan

**Riefenstahl, Helene Bertha Amalie**
1902-    [FDG]
*German director*
* Riefenstahl, Leni

**Riefenstahl, Leni**
*See* Riefenstahl, Helene Bertha
Amalie

**Riegel, Robert Henry** 1914-
[EG, GF]
*American golfer*
* Riegel, Skee

**Riegel, Skee**
*See* Riegel, Robert Henry

**Riegels, Roy** 20th c.    [SR]
*American football player*
* Riegels, Wrong Way

**Riegels, Wrong Way**
*See* Riegels, Roy

**Rieger, August** 20th c.    [WF]
*German director*
* Aurive, Jean Charles

**Riel, Louis David** 1844-1885    [FFF]
*Canadian insurgent*
* [The] Prophet of the Northwest

**Riemens-Reurslag, J.**
*See* Reurslag, Guurtje Johanna
Hendrika

**Riemer, George** 1920-1973    [CAP]
*American author*
* Poole, Seth
* Schirmerhorn, Clint

**Rienzi, Cola di**
*See* Gabrini, Niccolo

**Riepenhausen, Christian**
1789-1860    [WBD]
*German painter, designer, etcher*
* Riepenhausen, Johannes

**Riepenhausen, Franz**
*See* Riepenhausen, Friedrich

**Riepenhausen, Friedrich**
1786-1831    [WBD]
*German painter, designer, etcher*
* Riepenhausen, Franz

**Riepenhausen, Johannes**
*See* Riepenhausen, Christian

**Ries, Lulu** 20th c.    [BEW]
*American singer and actress*
* Bates, Lulu

**Riese, Felicia** 1918-    [FC]
*British actress*
* Roc, Patricia

**Rieser, Henry** [house pseudonym]
*See* MacDonald, John D[ann]

**Riffe, Ernest**
*See* Bergman, [Ernst] Ingmar

**Rifkin, Shepard** 1918-    [CA, WD]
*American author*
* Logan, Jake [house pseudonym,
Playboy Press]

**Rifkin, Shepard** (Continued)
* Michaels, Dale

**Rifkin, Stanley Mark** 1946?-
*American computer expert, accused
of fraud*
* Hansen, Mike

**Rifle**
*See* Butler, George H.

**[The] Rifle**
*See* Etcheverry, Sam

**[The] Rifle**
*See* Strickland, Roger

**Rifle Jim Middleton**
*See* Middleton, James Blaine [Jim]

**Rift, Valerie**
*See* Bartlett, Marie [Swan]

**Rigau y Ros, Hyacinthe Francois
Honorat Mathias Pierre Martyr
Andre** 1659-1743
[DEP, DNNS, WBD]
*French painter*
* [The] French Van Dyck
* Rigaud, Hyacinthe
* [The] Van Dyck of France

**Rigaud, Hyacinthe**
*See* Rigau y Ros, Hyacinthe
Francois Honorat Mathias Pierre
Martyr Andre

**Rigby, Arthur**
*See* Turner, William

**Rigby, Edward**
*See* Coke, Edward

**Rigdum Funnidos**
*See* Ballantyne, John

**Rigg, Henry Kilburn** 1911-1980
[CA]
*American editor and author*
* Kilburn, Henry

**Riggs, Betty**
*See* Riggs, Mary Elizabeth

**Riggs, Dorothy**
*See* Riggs, Mary Elizabeth

**Riggs, Lee Aubrey**
*Auctioneer*
* Riggs, Speed

**Riggs, Mary Elizabeth** 1899-1975
[F1, FC, SC]
*American actress*
* Brent, Evelyn
* Riggs, Betty
* Riggs, Dorothy

**Riggs, Speed**
*See* Riggs, Lee Aubrey

**Righi, Massimo** 20th c.    [WF]
*Italian actor*
* Dean, Max

**Right Cross**
*See* Armstrong, Paul

**Rignall, Lionel** 1850?-1919    [BEW]
*British-born actor and producer*
* Rignold, Lionel

**Rigney, Emory Elmo** 1897-    [BE]
*American baseball player*
* Rigney, Topper

**Rigney, Specs**
*See* Rigney, William Joseph

**Rigney, Topper**
*See* Rigney, Emory Elmo

**Rigney, William Joseph** 1919-    [BE]
*American baseball manager*
* [The] Cricket
* Rigney, Specs

**Rignold, Lionel**
*See* Rignall, Lionel

**Rignold, Marie**
*See* D'Altra, Marie

**Rigolo**
*See* Thieblin, Napoleon [or
Nicolas?] Leon

**Rigoni, Orlando [Joseph]** 1897?-
[CA, WD]
*American author*
* Ames, Leslie
* Bell, Carolyn
* Wesley, James

**Rigsby, Howard** 1909-    [CA, WW]
*American author*
* Howard, Mark
* Howard, Vechel

**Riis**
*See* Bohr, Russell LeRoi

**Rijsbergen, Wilhelmus** 1952-
[AES]
*Dutch soccer player*
* Rijsbergen, Wim

**Rijsbergen, Wim**
*See* Rijsbergen, Wilhelmus

**Riker, Anthony**
*See* Reeds, F. Anton

**Rikhoff, James C.** 1931-    [CA]
*American author*
* Cornwall, Jim
* Fargo, Joe
* Kincaid, Alan

**Rikki**
*See* Ducornet, Erica

**Riley, Doug[las Brian]** 1945-    [EJ7]
*Canadian jazz musician*
* Music, Dr.

**Riley, Frank**
*See* Ryhlick, Frank

**Riley, Jack** 1895-1933    [SC]
*American actor*
* Riley, Slim

**Riley, James** 1851?-1913    [B10]
*American outlaw*
* Middleton, Doc

**Riley, James Whitcomb** 1849-1916
[FFF, SAT, WBD]
*American author and poet*
* [The] Hoosier Poet
* Johnson, Benjamin F., of Boone
* [The] Poet Laureate of
Democracy

**Riley, Ken** 1947-    [SMG]
*American football player*
* [The] Rattler

**Riley, Pigtail Billy**
*See* Riley, William James [Billy]

**Riley, Slim**
*See* Riley, Jack

**Riley, Tex**
*See* Creasey, John

**Riley, William James [Billy]**
1857-1887    [BE]
*American baseball player*
* Riley, Pigtail Billy

**Rill, Eli**
*See* Schectman, Elias Maxwell

**Rimbault, Edward Francis** 1816-
[PA]
*Author*
* Nava, Franz

**Rimel, Duane [Weldon]** 1915-    [CA]
*American author*
* Biggs, Peter
* Leggett, Eric
* Lemir, Andre
* Weldon, Rex

**Rimmer, W. J.**
*See* Rowland, D[onald] S[ydney]

**Rinaldini, Angiolo**
*See* Battisti, Eugenio

**Ring, Adam**
*See* Reed, Blair

**Ring, Douglas**
*See* Prather, Richard S[cott]

**[The] Ring Gorilla**
*See* Bloom, Phil

**Ringbolt**
*See* Codman, John

**Ringdahl, Mark**
*See* Longyear, Barry Brookes

**Ringelnatz, Joachim**
*See* Boetticher, Hans

**Ringer, Ada**    [FFF]
*Entertainer*
* Knowles, Marie

**Ringgold, Gene** 1918-    [CA]
*American author*
* Lawrence, Kenneth G.
* Matteo, P. B., Jr.

**Ringi, Kjell Arne Soerensen** 1939-
[CA, SAT]
*Swedish author and illustrator*
* S-Ringi, Kjell

**Ringlets**
*See* Custer, George Armstrong

**Ringletub, Jeremiah**
*See* Styles, John

**Ringling, A. T.**
*See* Rungeling, Alf

**Ringling, Alfred J.**
*See* Rungeling, Alfred J.

**Ringling, Charles**
*See* Rungeling, Charles

**Ringling, John**
*See* Rungeling, John

**Ringmann, Christoph** 1940-    [MS]
*German musician*
* Eschenbach, Christoph

**Ringo, Johnny**
*See* Keevill, Henry J[ohn]

**Ringold, Clay**
*See* Hogan, [Robert] Ray

**Ringoold, Fred**
*See* Cerchio, Fernando

**Ringuet**
*See* Panneton, Philippe

**Rink, Doris** 1910-1925 [SC]
*American actress*
* Wynn, Doris

**Rinker, Mildred** 1907-1951
[BEW, CED]
*American singer*
* Bailey, Mildred

**Rinnan, Henry Oliver** 20th c. [EE]
*Norwegian traitor*
* Wist, Olav

**Rinzler, Carol Eisen** 1941- [CA]
*American author*
* Eisen, Carol G.

**Rio, Frank** 20th c. [BLB, PHM]
*American underworld figure*
* Cline, Frank
* Gline, Frank
* Kline, Frank
* Rio, Slippery

**Rio, Rita**
*See* Novella, Rita

**Rio, Slippery**
*See* Rio, Frank

**Riopelle, Howard Joseph** 1922-
[CEI]
*Canadian-born hockey player*
* Riopelle, Rip

**Riopelle, Rip**
*See* Riopelle, Howard Joseph

**Riordan, Bags**
*See* Riordan, Mike

**Riordan, Dan**
*See* Cook, William Everett

**Riordan, Irene** 1903-1973 [FC]
*American comedienne*
* Ryan, Irene

**Riordan, Mike** 1945- [SMG]
*American basketball player*
* Riordan, Bags

**Rios, Aurelio**
*See* Lopez, Aurelio Alejandro

**Rios, Tere**
*See* Versace, Marie Teresa Rios

**Riot, Pat**
*See* Lewis, Thomas H.

**Riperton, Minnie** 1948-1980 [RO2]
*American singer*
* Davis, Andrea

**Ripley, Allen Stevens** 1952- [SMG]
*American baseball player*
* Ripley, Rip

**Ripley, Elmer** 1891- [BB]
*American basketball player and coach*
* Ripley, Rip

**Ripley, Julia C.**
*See* Dorr, Mrs. J. C.

**Ripley, Rip**
*See* Ripley, Allen Stevens

**Ripley, Rip**
*See* Ripley, Elmer

**Ripman, Penelope** ?-1973 [TR]
*Actress, director, stage manager*
* Jenner, Caryl

**Ripman, Walter**
*See* Rippmann, Walter

**Ripon, John Scott**
*See* Byerley, John Scott

**Riposte, A.**
*See* Mordaunt, Evelyn May
[Clowes]

**Rippay, Benjamin Wesley** 1850- ?
[DGS, BE]
*American baseball player*
* Jones, Charles Wesley

**Rippelmeyer, Raymond** 1933-
[SMG]
*American baseball coach*
* Rippelmeyer, Rip

**Rippelmeyer, Rip**
*See* Rippelmeyer, Raymond

**Ripperda, Jan Willem** 1680-1737
[WBD]
*Dutch-born adventurer*
* Osman Pasha

**Ripperger, Henrietta**
*See* Hawley, Henrietta Ripperger

**Rippingale, Maureen** 1935-1974
[SC]
*British actress and dancer*
* Lesley, Carole

**Rippmann, Walter** 1869-1947
[WBD]
*British educator*
* Ripman, Walter

**Rips, Ervine M[ilton]** 1921- [CA]
*American author*
* Farnum, K. T.
* Lornquest, Olaf

**Riq**
*See* Atwater, Richard Tupper

**Riquetti, [Andre] Boniface [Louis]**
1754-1792 [DNNF, DNNS, FFF]
*French soldier and politician*
* Mirabeau, Barrel
* Mirabeau Tonneau
* Mirabeau, Vicomte de

**Riquetti, Honore Gabriel Victor**
1749-1791 [DHA, HN, SN]
*French orator and revolutionary leader*
* [The] Demosthenes of France
* [The] Hurricane .
* Mirabeau, Comte de
* Mirabeau, Tub
* [The] Modern Gracchus
* [The] Plebeian Count
* [The] Shakespeare of Eloquence
* [The] Tub

**Riquetti, Victor** 1715-1789
[DEP, DHA, SN]
*French soldier and economist*
* [L']Ami des Hommes
* [The] Friend of Man
* Mirabeau, Marquis de

**Riquetti de Mirabeau, Sibylle
Gabrielle Marie Antoinette**
1850-1932 [FFF, WBD]
*French author*
* Gyp
* Martel de Janville, Comtesse de

**Risberg, Charles August**
1894-1975 [B10, BE, PB]
*American baseball player*
* Risberg, Swede

**Risberg, Swede**
*See* Risberg, Charles August

**Riscoe, Arthur**
*See* Boorman, Arthur

**Risdon, Elizabeth**
*See* Evans, Elizabeth

**Riseley, Jerry B[urr, Jr.]** 1920-
[CA]
*American columnist and author*
* Monk, Galdo

**Rishton, William**
*See* Wright, W. George

**Rising, Perry Sumner** 20th c. [BE]
*American baseball player*
* Rising, Pop

**Rising, Pop**
*See* Rising, Perry Sumner

**Riskit, Jack**
*See* Evans, John

**Risko, Babe**
*See* Pylkowski, Henry

**Risko, Eddie**
*See* Pylkowski, Henry

**Risko, Johnny** 1902-1953 [BX]
*American boxer*
* [The] Cleveland Rubber Man
* [The] Spoiler

**Risner, James Robinson** 1924?-
*American air force pilot*
* Risner, Robbie

**Risner, Robbie**
*See* Risner, James Robinson

**Ristare, Bo**
*See* Linden, Erik Hugo Emanuel

**Ristaud**
*See* Cottin, Sophie

**Ristori, Adelaide**
*See* Capranica del Grillo,
Marchioness

**Rita**
*See* Humphreys Booth, Eliza
Margaret J. [Gollan]

**Ritchard, Cyril**
*See* Trimnell-Ritchard, Cyril

**Ritcher, Rene** 1910- [TR]
*British actress*
* Collier, Patience

**Ritchey, Claude Cassius**
1873-1951 [BE]
*American baseball player*
* Little All Right

**Ritchie, Adele**
*See* Pultz, Adele

**Ritchie, Alvin** 1890- [BBH, CFH]
*Canadian football team builder*
* [The] Silver Fox

**Ritchie, Balfour** 20th c. [MBF]
*British author*
* Baldwin, Basil

**Ritchie, Barbara** 20th c.
*Author*
* Arden, Barbie [joint pseudonym
with Adrien (Pearl) Stoutenburg]

**Ritchie, Bill**
*See* Edgar, Frank Terrell Rhoades

**Ritchie, David** 1926-1952 [BX]
*Australian boxer*
* Sands, Dave

**Ritchie, Douglas** 1905- [BDW]
*British radio broadcaster*
* Britton, Colonel

**Ritchie, Edwin** 1931- [CA, WD]
*American columnist and author*
* Lewis, Voltaire

**Ritchie, Jack**
*See* Reitci, Jack

**Ritchie, John Simon** 1957?-1979
*British musician*
* Vicious, Sid

**Ritchie, [Sir] Lewis**
*See* Da Costa Ricci, Lewis
Anselmo

**Ritchie, [Mary] Lily Munsell** 1867-
? [NAA]
*American author*
* Briarly, Mary

**Ritchie, Nellie Claire**
*See* Stephens, Mrs. Thomas C.

**Ritchie, Rita**
*See* Reitci, Rita Krohne

**Ritchie, Ruth** 1900- [CA]
*American author*
* Juline, Ruth Bishop

**Ritchie, Thomas** 1778-1854 [SN]
*American journalist*
* [The] Father of Democracy in
Virginia

**Ritchie, [Harry] Ward** 1905- [CA]
*American author and poet*
* Quince, Peter Lum

**Ritchie, Willie**
*See* Steffen, Gerhardt A.

**Ritchie-Calder, Peter Ritchie**
*See* Calder, Peter Ritchie

**Ritson, Claire** 1907- [DBA]
*British painter*
* Claire

**Ritson, Joseph** 1752-1803
[DEL, SN]
*British antiquary and critic*
* [The] Learned Cabbage-Eater
* Sycorax
* [The] Word Catcher

**Ritsos, Giannes**
*See* Ritsos, Yannis

**Ritsos, Yannis** 1909- [CA]
*Greek poet*
* Ritsos, Giannes

**Rittenhouse, David** 1732-1792?
[HN]
*American astronomer*
* [The] American Newton

**Ritter, Bud**
*See* Ritter, Julius

**Ritter, Felix**
*See* Kruess, James

**Ritter, Hank**
*See* Ritter, William Herbert

**Ritter, Julius** 20th c. [BBH]
*American basketball player and coach*
* Ritter, Bud

**Ritter, Louis Elmer** 1875-1952
[BE]
*American baseball player*
* Ritter, Old Dog

**Ritter, Maurice Woodward**
1906?-1974   [DAM, FC, PMJ]
*American country-western performer*
* Ritter, Tex

**Ritter, Old Dog**
*See*  Ritter, Louis Elmer

**Ritter, Tex**
*See*  Ritter, Maurice Woodward

**Ritter, William Herbert** 1893-1964
[BE]
*American baseball player*
* Ritter, Hank

**Rittman, Gertrud** 20th c.   [BEW]
*German-born composer and arranger*
* Rittman, Trude

**Rittman, Trude**
*See*  Rittman, Gertrud

**Ritvala, M.**
*See*  Waltari, Mika [Toimi]

**Ritz, Al**
*See*  Joachim, Al

**Ritz, David** 1943-   [CA]
*American author*
* Pearl, Esther Elizabeth

**Ritz, Sally**
*See*  Henderson, Rosa [Rose]

**Rius**
*See*  Del Rio, Eduardo

**Rivail, Leon Hippolyte Denisart**
[PA]
*Author*
* Kardec, Allan

**Rivas, Guillermo**
*See*  Phillips, Howard S.

**Rivaz, Alice**
*See*  Golay, Alice

**Rive, Jean Joseph** 1730-1791   [SN]
*French bibliographer*
* [An] Ajax Flagellifer
* [The] Bull Dog of la Valliere
* [The] French Ritson

**Rivella**
*See*  Manley, Mary de la Riviere

**Rivelli, Francesca** 1956?-
*Italian actress*
* [The] Italian Sex Bomb
* Muti, Ornella

**Rivels, Charles** 20th c.   [BMH]
*British acrobatic clown*
* [The] Chaplin of the Trapeze

**[The] River of Paradise**
*See*  Bernard of Clairvaux

**Rivera, Bombo**
*See*  Rivera Torres, Jesus, Jr.

**Rivera, Chita**
*See*  Figueroa Del Rivero, Dolores
Conchita

**Rivera, Jim**
*See*  Rivera, Manuel Joseph

**Rivera, Jose** 20th c.   [RBE]
*American boxer*
* Pagan, Jose

**Rivera, Jungle Jim**
*See*  Rivera, Manuel Joseph

**Rivera, Manuel Joseph** 1922-
[BE, PB]
*American baseball player*
* Rivera, Jim
* Rivera, Jungle Jim

**Rivera, Scarlet**
*See*  Shea, Donna

**Rivera Perez, Francisco** 1948-
[GS]
*Spanish bullfighter*
* Paquirri

**Rivera Torres, Jesus, Jr.** 1952-
[SMG]
*Puerto Rican-born baseball player*
* Rivera, Bombo

**Rivera Viera, [Padre] Juan**
1885-1953   [CW]
*Puerto Rican poet*
* Rafael, Juan Vicente

**Rivere, Alec**
*See*  Nuetzel, Charles [Alexander]

**Rivers, Georgia**
*See*  Clark, Marjorie

**Rivers, Guy**
*See*  Simms, William Gilmore

**Rivers, Joe**
*See*  Ybarra, Jose

**Rivers, John Milton** 1948-   [WWB]
*American baseball player*
* Mick the Quick
* Rivers, Mickey

**Rivers, Johnny**
*See*  Ramistella, John

**Rivers, Larry**
*See*  Grossberg, Irving

**Rivers, Laurence**
*See*  Stebbins, Rowland

**Rivers, Lord**   [RH]
*Gambler*
* [The] Wellington of Gamblers

**Rivers, Louis** 1922-   [IBW]
*American author*
* Mulet, Paul

**Rivers, Mickey**
*See*  Rivers, John Milton

**Rivers, Olive**
*See*  Reynolds, Mrs. James

**Rivers, Pearl**
*See*  Nicholson, Eliza Jane
Poitevent

**Rivers, Tex**
*See*  Lewins, C. A.

**Riverside, John**
*See*  Heinlein, Robert A[nson]

**Riverside Visitor**
*See*  Wright, Thomas

**Riverton, Stein**
*See*  Elvestad, Sven

**Rives, Amelie**
*See*  Troubetzkoy, Princess

**Rives, Leigh**
*See*  Seward, William W[ard], Jr.

**Rivett, Edith Caroline** 1894-1958
[CC, EMD, LC]
*British author*
* Carnac, Carol
* Lorac, E. C. R.

**Riviere, Arthur Bernard** 1899-1965
[BE]
*American baseball player*
* Riviere, Tink

**Riviere, Curly**
*See*  Riviere, Fred

**Riviere, Fred** 1875-1935   [SC]
*American actor*
* Riviere, Curly

**Riviere, Tink**
*See*  Riviere, Arthur Bernard

**Rivington, Charles**   [PA]
*Author*
* Scrutator

**Rivington, William**   [PA]
*Author*
* [A] Layman

**Rivinus, August Quirinus**
*See*  Bachmann, August Quirinus

**Rivoli, Mario** 1943-   [SAT]
*American illustrator*
* Koutoukas, H. M.
* Marasmus, Seymour

**Rix, Donna**
*See*  Rowland, D[onald] S[ydney]

**Rixey, Epp**
*See*  Rixey, Eppa P.

**Rixey, Eppa Jeptha**
*See*  Rixey, Eppa P.

**Rixey, Eppa P.** 1891-1963
[BE, DGS, PB]
*American baseball player*
* Rixey, Epp
* Rixey, Eppa Jeptha
* Rixey, Jeptha

**Rixey, Jeptha**
*See*  Rixey, Eppa P.

**Rixon, Annie**
*See*  Studdert, Annie Louisa

**Riza, Ali**
*See*  Orga, Irfan

**Rizzi, Tony**
*See*  Rizzi, Trefoni

**Rizzi, Trefoni** 1923-   [DAM, EJ]
*American jazz musician*
* Rizzi, Tony

**Rizzo, Anthony** 1937-   [ASC]
*American musician*
* Rizzo, Bob

**Rizzo, Bob**
*See*  Rizzo, Anthony

**Rizzo, Frank Lazarro** 1921-
*American politician*
* [The] Cisco Kid

**Rizzoti, Antonio**
*See*  Dragna, Jack

**Rizzotti, Madame**   [FFF]
*Entertainer*
* Giuri, Marie

**Rizzuto, Flea**
*See*  Rizzuto, Phil[lip Francis]

**Rizzuto, Phil[lip Francis]** 1918-
[BE, BN, PB]
*American baseball player*
* Rizzuto, Flea
* Rizzuto, Scooter

**Rizzuto, Scooter**
*See*  Rizzuto, Phil[lip Francis]

**Ro Tae-yong**
*See*  Rutt, Richard

**Roach, John**
*See*  Roche, John

**Roach, Jonathan**
*See*  Endfield, Cyril Raker

**Roach, Max**
*See*  Roach, Maxwell

**Roach, Maxwell** 1925-   [EJ7]
*American jazz musician*
* Roach, Max

**Roach, Portia**
*See*  Takakjian, Portia

**Roach, Robert W. A.** 1933-   [WGT]
*British author*
* Jorgensson, A. K.

**Roach, Roxy**
*See*  Roach, Wilbur C.

**Roach, Skel**
*See*  Weichbrodt, Rudolph C.

**Roach, Wilbur C.** 1884-1947   [BE]
*American baseball player*
* Roach, Roxy

**Road Runner**
*See*  Garr, Ralph Allen

**Road Runner Ferguson**
*See*  Ferguson, Rufus

**[The] Roadbuilder**
*See*  MacKendrick, William
Gordon

**Roadrunner**
*See*  Cournoyer, Yvan Serge

**Roane, Peter**
*See*  Campbell, C[larence] Samuel

**Roaring Bill Hassamaer**
*See*  Hassamaer, William Louis
[Bill]

**Roaring Bob of the Garden**
*See*  Bensley, Robert

**Roaring Jack**
*See*  Percival, John

**Roark, Garland** 1904-   [CA]
*American author*
* Garland, George

**Rob Roy**
*See*  Campbell [or Macgregor?],
Robert

**Rob Roy**
*See*  Macgregor, John

**Robard, Jackson**
*See*  Wallmann, Jeffrey M[iner]

**Robards, Sherman M[arshall]**
1939-   [CA]
*American journalist and author*
* Robards, Terry

**Robards, Terry**
*See*  Robards, Sherman M[arshall]

**Robarge, John F.** 1922-   [CWG]
*American country-western performer*
* Roe, Tex

**Robb, Helen** 1866-1937   [BEW]
*American actress*
* Lowell, Helen

**Robb, Inez [Callaway]** 1901?-1979
[CA]
*American author and columnist*
* Randolph, Nancy

**Robb, John**
See   Robson, Norman

**Robb, John S.**   [FFF]
*Writer*
* Solitaire

**[The] Robber**
See   Edward IV

**Robbins, Alfred Farthing**   [FFF]
*British author*
* Dunheved

**Robbins, Austin** 1944-   [BB]
*American basketball player*
* Robbins, Red

**Robbins, C. A**
See   Robbins, Clarence Aaron

**Robbins, Clarence Aaron**
1888-1949   [WGT, WW]
*American author*
* Robbins, C. A
* Robbins, Tod

**Robbins, Harold**
See   Kane, Francis

**Robbins, Henry**
See   Slavitt, David Rytman

**Robbins, Jerome**
See   Rabinowitz, Jerome

**Robbins, June** 20th c.   [CA]
*American poet*
* Julie
* Julie of Colorado Springs

**Robbins, Marty**
See   Robinson, Martin D.

**Robbins, Raleigh**
See   Hamilton, Charles Harold St.
John

**Robbins, Red**
See   Robbins, Austin

**Robbins, Rollin**
See   Sherwood, Roland H.

**Robbins, Ruth**
See   Schein, Ruth Robbins

**Robbins, Tod**
See   Robbins, Clarence Aaron

**Robbins, Tony**
See   Pashko, Stanley

**Robby the Robber**
See   Robinson, Brooks [Calbert,
Jr.]

**Robeck, Geraldine Cecilia** 1928-
[CWG]
*American country-western performer*
* Lynn, Gerrie

**Robello, Thomas Vardasco [Tommy]**
1913-   [BE]
*American baseball player*
* Robello, Tony

**Robello, Tony**
See   Robello, Thomas Vardasco
[Tommy]

**Roberds, Fred A.** 1941-   [ASC]
*American composer, singer, actor*
* Roberds, Smokey

**Roberds, Smokey**
See   Roberds, Fred A.

**Roberge, Joseph Albert Armand**
1917-   [BE]
*American baseball player*
* Roberge, Skippy

**Roberge, Skippy**
See   Roberge, Joseph Albert
Armand

**Roberson, Marie**
See   Hamm, Marie Roberson

**Roberson, Orlando** 1910?-   [WWJ]
*American jazz musician*
* Robeson, Orlando

**Roberson, Rocky**
See   Roberson, Rudolph

**Roberson, Rudolph** 20th c.   [IBW]
*American athlete*
* Roberson, Rocky

**Robert** ?- 866   [WBD]
*Count of Anjou*
* [The] Strong

**Robert, Felix**
See   Cazenave, [or Cacenabe],
Pierre

**Robert Fleury**
See   Fleury, Joseph Nicolas Robert

**Robert, Friedrich**
See   Ehlers, Friedrich Robert

**Robert of Anjou** 1275-1343
[DNNS, HN]
*King of Naples*
* [The] Solomon of His Age
* [The] Wise

**Robert of Geneva** 1342?-1394
[WBD]
*Antipope*
* Clement VII

**Robert the Devil**
See   Damiens, Robert Francois

**Robert the Red**
See   Campbell [or Macgregor?],
Robert

**Robert the Rhymer**
See   Williams, Alan Moray

**Robert I**   [SN]
*First Duke of Calabria*
* [The] Cunning
* Guiscard
* [The] Terror of the Faithless

**Robert I** ?-1035
[DNNF, DNNS, RH]
*Duke of Normandy*
* [The] Devil
* [Le] Diable
* [The] Magnificent

**Robert I** 1274-1329   [HN, WBD]
*King of Scotland*
* [The] Bruce
* Hob [or Hobbe], King
* [The] Joshua of Scotland
* [The] Summer King

**Robert II**   [SN]
*Count of Sicily*
* [The] Terror of the Faithless

**Robert II** 971?-1031
[DNNS, FFF, RH]
*King of France*
* [Le] Pieux

**Robert II** (Continued)
* [The] Pious

**Robert II** 1054?-1134
[DNNF, WBD]
*Duke of Normandy*
* Curt-Hose [Short-Shanks]

**Robert II** 1316-1390   [DNNS]
*King of Scotland*
* [The] Steward

**Robert III**
See   Stewart, John

**Roberta of Venice**
See   Di Camerino, Giuliana

**Robertaille, Anthony F.** 1879-1947
[BE]
*American baseball player*
* Robertaille, Chick

**Robertaille, Chick**
See   Robertaille, Anthony F.

**Robertjeot**
See   Sanderson, John

**Roberto, [Brother]**
See   Mueller, Gerald F[rancis]

**Roberts, Anthony**
See   Watney, John B[asil]

**Roberts, Archie**
See   Roberts, Arthur J.

**Roberts, Arthur Guy** 1903-   [WWL]
*British author*
* Clifford, Guy

**Roberts, Arthur J.** 20th c.   [FB]
*American football player*
* Roberts, Archie

**Roberts, Arthur O.** 1923-
[CA, SFL]
*American author*
* Cameron, Berl [joint pseudonym
with John (Stephen) Glasby]
[house pseudonym, Curtis
Warren]
* Le Page, Rand [joint pseudonym
with John (Stephen) Glasby]
[house pseudonym, Curtis
Warren]
* Lorraine, Paul [joint pseudonym
with John (Stephen) Glasby]
[house pseudonym, Curtis
Warren]
* Mego, Al

**Roberts, Bart** 1928-   [FC]
*American actor*
* Reason, Rex

**Roberts, [Carl Eric] Bechhofer**
1894-1949   [LC, WW, WWL]
*British author*
* Bechhofer, C. E.
* Ephesian

**Roberts, Ben**
See   Eisenberg, Ben

**Roberts, Big Jim**
See   Roberts, James Newson [Jim]

**Roberts, Block Buster**
See   Roberts, Lenerte

**Roberts, Bo**
See   Roberts, S. H.

**Roberts, C. D. G.**
See   Roberts, [Sir] Charles George
Douglas

**Roberts, Captain**
See   Hobart, Augustus C.

**Roberts, Catherine Alice**   [PA]
*Author*
* C. A. R.

**Roberts, Cecil Edric Mornington**
1892-   [TC, WWL]
*British author and playwright*
* Beresford, Russell
* Mornington, Edor
* Seer

**Roberts, Charles Emory** 1918-
[BE]
*American baseball player*
* Roberts, Red

**Roberts, [Sir] Charles George
Douglas** 1860-1943   [LC]
*Canadian author and poet*
* Roberts, C. D. G.

**Roberts, Charles Luckeyeth**
1887?-1968   [ASC, DAM, WWJ]
*American jazz musician*
* Roberts, Luckey

**Roberts, Clarence Ashley**
1888-1963   [BE]
*American baseball player*
* Roberts, Skipper

**Roberts, Clifford** 1893?-1977
*American golfer*
* Mr. Cliff

**Roberts, Cyril D.** 1939-   [IBW]
*American insurance agent*
* Roberts, Sonny

**Roberts, Dale** 1942-   [BE]
*American baseball player*
* Roberts, Mountain Man

**Roberts, Dan**
See   Ross, William Edward Daniel

**Roberts, David**
See   Cox, John Roberts [Jack]

**Roberts, Dell**
See   Fendell, Bob

**Roberts, Dorothy James** 1903-
[CAP]
*American author*
* Mortimer, Peter

**Roberts, Edith**
See   Roberts, Elizabeth [Kneipple]

**Roberts, Edna** 1912-   [IAW]
*British writer*
* Finlay, Michael
* Hilton, Josephine
* Owen, Richard

**Roberts, Edward** 1904-   [BF]
*British director and screenwriter*
* Dryhurst, Edward

**Roberts, Edwin F.**   [PA]
*Author*
* Happy John

**Roberts, Elizabeth [Kneipple]** 20th
c.   [CA]
*Author*
* Roberts, Edith

**Roberts, Eric** 1914-   [AW, CA]
*British author and playwright*
* Robin

**Roberts, Fireball**
See   Roberts, [Edward] Glenn, [Jr.]

**Roberts, Floyd** 20th c.
*Auto racer*
* [The] Old Man of the Mountain

**Roberts, Frederick Sleigh**
1832-1914  [NN]
*British military leader*
* Bobs
* Bobs Bahadur

**Roberts, George**
*See* Walters, Robert

**Roberts, George Edward Theodore**
1877-1953  [WW]
*Author*
* Goodridge Roberts, Theodore

**Roberts, Glen**
*See* Freeman, Leonard

**Roberts, [Edward] Glenn, [Jr.]**
1927?-1964  [AS, EAR, OCS]
*American auto racer*
* Roberts, Fireball

**Roberts, Grant**
*See* Wallmann, Jeffrey M[iner]

**Roberts, Helen**
*See* Hunter, Alberta

**Roberts, Holt**
*See* Draper, Ben

**Roberts, Hortense Roberta** 20th c.
[CA]
*American author*
* Munger, Hortense Roberta

**Roberts, Irene M.** 1925?-
[AW, CA, WD]
*British author*
* Carr, Roberta
* Harle, Elizabeth
* Roberts, Ivor
* Rowland, Iris
* Shaw, Irene

**Roberts, Ivor**
*See* Roberts, Irene M.

**Roberts, J. P.**  [PA]
*Author*
* Happy, John

**Roberts, James Hall**
*See* Duncan, Robert Lipscomb

**Roberts, James M.** 1900-1945  [FB]
*American football player*
* Roberts, Red

**Roberts, James Newson [Jim]**
1895-  [BE]
*American baseball player*
* Roberts, Big Jim

**Roberts, James William** 1918-
[CWG]
*American singer*
* Carson, James

**Roberts, Jane** 1929-  [CA]
*American author*
* Butts, Jane Roberts

**Roberts, Janet Louise** 1925-  [CA]
*American author*
* Bronte, Louisa
* Danton, Rebecca
* Radcliffe, Janette

**Roberts, Jim**
*See* Bates, Barbara S[nedeker]

**Roberts, Jim**
*See* Caudle, James Robert

**Roberts, Jimmy**
*See* Edmeades, Robert Thomas

**Roberts, Joan**
*See* Seagrist, Josephine

**Roberts, Joe**
*See* Saltzman, Joseph [Joe]

**Roberts, John**
*See* Bingley, David Ernest

**Roberts, John**
*See* Pierce, John Robinson

**Roberts, John**
*See* Swinerton, Thomas

**Roberts, John** 18th c.  [PA]
*Author*
* Anti Scriblerus Histronicus

**Roberts, John G[aither]** 1913-  [CA]
*American author*
* Paul, Robert

**Roberts, John Peter** 1925-  [IAW]
*Welsh-born author*
* Welsh, Robert

**Roberts, John S[torm]** 1936-  [CA]
*British author*
* Anthony, John
* Lloyd, Jane
* Mwamba, Pal
* Storm, Anthony

**Roberts, Johnny**
*See* Robilotto, John

**Roberts, Jon**
*See* Olson, Robert G.

**Roberts, Julian**
*See* Bardens, Dennis [Conrad]

**Roberts, Keith [John Kingston]**
1935-  [CA, WGT]
*British author*
* Bevan, Alistair
* Kingston, John
* Stringer, David

**Roberts, Ken**
*See* Lake, Kenneth R[obert]

**Roberts, Kenneth**
*See* Dent, Lester

**Roberts, Kenneth [Lewis]** 1885-
[CAA]
*American author*
* Kilgallen, Milton

**Roberts, Lee**
*See* Martin, Robert [Lee]

**Roberts, Lee** 20th c.  [MBF]
*British author*
* Reid, Desmond [house
  pseudonym]

**Roberts, Lenerte** 20th c.  [IBW]
*American realtor*
* Roberts, Block Buster

**Roberts, Lionel**
*See* Fanthorpe, R[obert] Lionel

**Roberts, Lisa**
*See* Turner, Robert [Harry]

**Roberts, Luckey**
*See* Roberts, Charles Luckeyeth

**Roberts, Mabel** 1880?-1954  [BEW]
*American actress*
* Paige, Mabel

**Roberts, MacLennan**
*See* Terrall, Robert

**Roberts, Maggie**  [PA]
*Author*
* Strebor, Eiggam

**Roberts, Mark** 20th c.  [CA]
*Author*
* Derrick, Lionel [joint pseudonym
  with Chet Cunningham]

**Roberts, Martin**
*See* Wells, [Frank Charles] Robert

**Roberts, Marty**
*See* Schopp, Martin Robert

**Roberts, McLean**
*See* Machlin, Milton Robert

**Roberts, Meade**
*See* Mednick, Stanley Robert

**Roberts, Moe**
*See* Roberts, Morris

**Roberts, Morris** 1907-  [CEI]
*American hockey player*
* Roberts, Moe

**Roberts, Mountain Man**
*See* Roberts, Dale

**Roberts, Murray**
*See* Graydon, Robert Murray

**Roberts, Nancy**
*See* Finley, Annette

**Roberts, Ralph**
*See* Barent, Ralph

**Roberts, Rand**
*See* Parham, Robert Randall

**Roberts, Red**
*See* Roberts, Charles Emory

**Roberts, Red**
*See* Roberts, James M.

**Roberts, Rinalda**
*See* Cudlipp, Edythe

**Roberts, Robert Evan** 1926-  [BE]
*American baseball player*
* Roberts, Robin

**Roberts, Robin**
*See* Roberts, Robert Evan

**Roberts, Rose**
*See* Calvert, Mrs. Louis

**Roberts, S. C.**
*See* Roberts, [Sir] Sydney Castle

**Roberts, S. H.** 20th c.
*American business executive*
* Roberts, Bo

**Roberts, Sally**
*See* Dunn, Sara

**Roberts, Sally**
*See* Jones, Sally Roberts

**Roberts, Skipper**
*See* Roberts, Clarence Ashley

**Roberts, Snitcher**
*See* Johnson, James

**Roberts, Sonia Leslie** 1934-  [IAW]
*British author*
* Leslie, Robert
* Trevor, Charlotte

**Roberts, Sonny**
*See* Roberts, Cyril D.

**Roberts, [Sir] Sydney Castle**
1887-1966  [LC]
*British educator and author*
* Roberts, S. C.

**Roberts, Terence**
*See* Sanderson, Ivan T[erence]

**Roberts, Thom[as Sacra]** 1940-
[CA]
*American author*
* Lawrence, Thomas

**Roberts, Tom**
*See* Thomas, R[obert] Murray

**Roberts, Tommy** 20th c.  [WFA]
*British fashion designer*
* Freedom, Mr.

**Roberts, Ursula**
*See* Miles, Susan

**Roberts, Virginia**
*See* Dean, Nell Marr

**Roberts, Walt** 20th c.  [IBW]
*American football player*
* [The] Flea

**Roberts, Wayne**
*See* Overholser, Wayne D.

**Roberts, Will** 20th c.  [BLB]
*American train robber*
* Dixon

**Roberts, Will** 20th c.  [ART]
*Welsh painter*
* Will R.

**Roberts, William** 1767-1849  [PA]
*Author*
* Olive-Branch, [Rev] Simon

**Roberts, William** 1868-1959
[LC, TC]
*British author and music critic*
* Newman, Ernest

**Roberts, William Hedley** 1864- ?
[THR]
*British weightlifter*
* Atlas

**Roberts-Jones, Phillipe John A. G.**
1924-  [IAW]
*Belgian author*
* Jones, Phillipe

**Robertshaw, [James] Denis** 1911-
[AW, CA]
*British author*
* Gaunt, Michael

**Robertson, A. J.**
*See* Robertson, Alfred

**Robertson, Agnes**
*See* Boucicault, Agnes Kelly
Robertson

**Robertson, Alex**
*See* Rathbone, St. George

**Robertson, Alexander Campbell**
1887-  [B10]
*American musician*
* Robertson, Eck

**Robertson, Alfred** 1891-1948  [BB]
*American basketball coach*
* Robertson, A. J.

**Robertson, Alice Alberthe** 1871- ?
[SFL, WGT]
*American author*
* David, K.
* St. Luz, Berthe

**Robertson, Amy**
See   Cooper, Robert Andrew

**Robertson, Bob**
See   Leone, Sergio

**Robertson, Butch**
See   Robertson, Isaiah

**Robertson, C. Alvin** 1891-1943
[WWJ]
*American jazz musician*
* Robertson, Zue

**Robertson, Colin** 1906-   [MBF]
*British author and playwright*
* Reid, Desmond [house
  pseudonym]

**Robertson, Constance [Pierrepont
Noyes]** 1897-   [ANT, CA, WD]
*American author*
* Scott, Dana

**Robertson, Creole Pete**
See   Robertson, Peter

**Robertson, Doc**
See   Robertson, Elbert K.

**Robertson, E. Arnot**
See   Robertson, Eileen Arbuthnot

**Robertson, Eck**
See   Robertson, Alexander
Campbell

**Robertson, Eileen Arbuthnot**
1903-1961   [LC, TC]
*British author*
* Robertson, E. Arnot

**Robertson, Eileen Arnot**
See   Turner, Eileen Arbuthnot
Robertson

**Robertson, Elbert K.** 20th c.   [IBW]
*American inventor*
* Robertson, Doc

**Robertson, Ellis** [joint pseudonym
with Robert Silverberg]
See   Ellison, Harlan [Jay]

**Robertson, Ellis** [joint pseudonym
with Harlan (Jay) Ellison]
See   Silverberg, Robert

**Robertson, Elspeth**
See   Ellison, Joan Audrey
[Anderson]

**Robertson, Ethel Florence [Lindesay
Richardson]** 1870-1946
[EWL, TC, TCL]
*Australian author*
* Richardson, Henry Handel

**Robertson, Forbes**
See   Forbes-Robertson, [Sir]
Johnston

**Robertson, Frank C[hester]** 1890-
[CA, NAA]
*American author*
* Crane, Robert
* Field, Frank Chester
* Hill, King

**Robertson, Helen**
See   Edmiston, Helen Jean Mary

**Robertson, Henry** 1890?-   [NOJ]
*American jazz musician*
* Robertson, Sleepy

**Robertson, Ian**
See   Forbes-Robertson, Ian

**Robertson, Isaiah** 1949-   [IBW]
*American football player*
* Robertson, Butch

**Robertson, J. G.**
See   Robertson, John George

**Robertson, J. M.**
See   Robertson, John Mackinnon

**Robertson, Jaime** 1944-   [RO2]
*Canadian-born musician*
* Robertson, Robbie

**Robertson, James** 1859-1936   [SC]
*American actor*
* Robertson, Scotty

**Robertson, James B.** 1909?-1966
[ASC, CWG]
*American country-western performer*
* Robertson, Texas Jim

**Robertson, James Logie** 1846- ?
[WWL]
*Scottish author and poet*
* Haliburton, Hugh

**Robertson, John George** 1867-1933
[LC]
*British author and educator*
* Robertson, J. G.

**Robertson, John Henry** 1889-1965
[BE]
*American baseball player*
* Robinson, John Henry
* Robinson, Rube

**Robertson, John Henry** 1909-1965
[LC]
*British author and journalist*
* Connell, John

**Robertson, John Mackinnon**
1856-1933   [LC]
*Scottish-born journalist and author*
* Robertson, J. M.

**Robertson, John Wylie** 1889-1966
[FC]
*British actor*
* Watson, Wylie

**Robertson, Joseph Clinton**
1788-1852   [FFF]
*British editor*
* Percy, Sholto

**Robertson, Keith [Carlton]** 1914-
[CA, SAT, WW]
*American author*
* Keith, Carlton

**Robertson, Lawson** 1883-1951
[TF]
*Scottish-born track and field athlete
and coach*
* Robertson, Robbie

**Robertson, Margaret** 1849-1935
[BEW]
*British actress*
* Kendal, [Dame] Madge

**Robertson, Margery Ellen** 1906-
[WD]
*British author*
* Thorp, Ellen
* Thorp, Morwenna

**Robertson, Marion Gordon** 1930?-
[B10]
*American television performer and
executive*
* Robertson, Pat

**Robertson, Marjorie** 1904-
[BDF, BEW, FC]
*British actress*
* Neagle, Anna

**Robertson, Mary Imogene**
1905?-1948   [BEW, F2, FIR]
*American actress*
* [The] Hard Luck Girl
* Nolan, Mary
* Wilson, Bubbles
* Wilson, Imogene

**Robertson, Mrs. Donald**   [FFF]
*Entertainer*
* Lewis, Catherine

**Robertson, Oscar** 1938-   [BB]
*American basketball player*
* [The] Big O

**Robertson, Pat**
See   Robertson, Marion Gordon

**Robertson, Peter** 1907-   [IBW]
*American baseball player*
* Robertson, Creole Pete

**Robertson, R. R.**
See   Robertson, Richard Ross

**Robertsson, Richard Ross** 1914-
[ART]
*Scottish sculptor*
* Robertson, R. R.

**Robertson, Robbie**
See   Robertson, Jaime

**Robertson, Robbie**
See   Robertson, Lawson

**Robertson, S. M.**
See   Robertson, Sheila Macleod

**Robertson, Scotty**
See   Robertson, James

**Robertson, Seonaid Mairi** 1912-
[ART]
*Scottish-born artist*
* S. M. R.

**Robertson, Sheila Macleod** 1927-
[ART]
*British painter and sculptor*
* Robertson, S. M.

**Robertson, Sherrard Alexander**
1919-1970   [BE]
*Canadian-born baseball player*
* Robertson, Sherry

**Robertson, Sherry**
See   Robertson, Sherrard
Alexander

**Robertson, Sleepy**
See   Robertson, Henry

**Robertson, Texas Jim**
See   Robertson, James B.

**Robertson, Zue**
See   Robertson, C. Alvin

**Robertson-Glasgow, R. C.**
See   Robertson-Glasgow, Raymond
Charles

**Robertson-Glasgow, Raymond
Charles** 1901-1965   [LC]
*British author and cricket
correspondent*
* Robertson-Glasgow, R. C.

**Robertsson, Sigurdur** 1909-   [IAW]
*Icelandic author and playwright*
* Alfur Utangaros

**Robeson, Eslanda Cardoza Goode**
1896-1965   [IBW]
*American pathologist, chemist,
author*
* Robeson, Essie

**Robeson, Essie**
See   Robeson, Eslanda Cardoza
Goode

**Robeson, Kenneth** [house
pseudonym, Street & Smith]
See   Bogart, William G.

**Robeson, Kenneth** [house
pseudonym, Street & Smith]
See   Daniels, Norman [A.]

**Robeson, Kenneth** [house
pseudonym, Street & Smith]
See   Dent, Lester

**Robeson, Kenneth** [house
pseudonym, Street & Smith]
See   Donovan, Laurence

**Robeson, Kenneth** [house
pseudonym, Street & Smith]
See   Ernst, Paul Frederick

**Robeson, Kenneth** [house
pseudonym, Street & Smith]
See   Goulart, Ron[ald Joseph]

**Robeson, Kenneth** [house
pseudonym, Street & Smith]
See   Hathaway, Alan

**Robeson, Kenneth** [house
pseudonym, Street & Smith]
See   Johnson, W. Ryerson

**Robeson, Kenneth** [house
pseudonym, Street & Smith]
See   Tepperman, Emile

**Robeson, Orlando**
See   Roberson, Orlando

**Robeson, Reed**
See   Robeson, Reeve

**Robeson, Reeve** 20th c.   [IBW]
*American businessman*
* Robeson, Reed

**Robespierre, Maximilien**
1759?-1794   [HN, RH, SN]
*French revolutionary leader*
* [The] Cromwell of France
* [The] Incorruptible
* [The] King of Terror
* [The] Living Sophism
* [The] People's Friend
* Robespierre, Seagreen
* [The] Seagreen Incorruptible

**Robespierre, Seagreen**
See   Robespierre, Maximilien

**Robey, [Sir] George**
See   Wade, George Edward

**Robhs, Dwight**
See   Monaco, Richard

**Robic, Ivo**
See   Robish, Eevo

**Robidoux, Florent** 1960-
*Canadian-born hockey player*
* Robidoux, Robey

**Robidoux, Robey**
See   Robidoux, Florent

**Robilotto, John** ?-1958
[BLB, PHM]
*American underworld figure*
* Roberts, Johnny

**Robin**
*See* Denard, Robert [Bob]

**Robin**
*See* Roberts, Eric

**[The] Robin Hood of the Cookson Hills**
*See* Floyd, Charles Arthur

**[The] Robin Hood of the Lowlands**
*See* Campbell [or Macgregor?], Robert

**Robin of Redesdale**
*See* Hilyard, Robert

**Robinet, Lee**
*See* Browne, F. G.

**Robinett, Stephen [Allen]** 1941-
[CA, WGT]
*American author*
* Hallus, Tak

**Robins, Adolph**
*See* Proper, Adolph

**Robins, Denise [Naomi]** 1897-
[CA, WD]
*British author and playwright*
* French, Ashley
* Gray, Harriet
* Kane, Julia
* Wright, Francesca

**Robins, Dorothy B.**
*See* Robins-Mowry, Dorothy B[ernice]

**Robins, Edward H.**
*See* Haas, Edward

**Robins, Elizabeth** 1862-1952
[LC, TC, WW]
*American actress and author*
* Raimond, C. E.

**Robins, Fenton**
*See* Gammon, D. J.

**Robins, Seelin**
*See* Ellis, Edward S[ylvester]

**Robins-Mowry, Dorothy B[ernice]** 1921- [CA]
*American author*
* Robins, Dorothy B.

**Robinson, Alfred** 1936?-
*American political organizer*
* Robinson, Skip

**Robinson, Annie Douglas** 1842- ?
[FFF]
*American poet*
* Douglas, Marian

**Robinson, Arthur** 1888-1935?
[FDG]
*American-born director*
* Robison, Arthur

**Robinson, Banjo**
*See* Robinson, Ikey L.

**Robinson, Bat**
*See* Robinson, James

**Robinson, Beezer**
*See* Robinson, Bob

**Robinson, Bernard Whitfield** 1918-1972 [IBW]
*American physician, naval officer, hospital administrator*
* Robinson, Robby

**Robinson, Big Ike**
*See* Robinson, Isaiah

**Robinson, Big Jim**
*See* Robinson, Nathan

**Robinson, Bill**
*See* Robinson, Luther

**Robinson, Bill** 20th c. [OBW]
*American baseball player*
* Robinson, Bojangles

**Robinson, Billy**
*See* Robinson, Wilbert

**Robinson, Black Rusie**
*See* Robinson, James

**Robinson, Blondie**
*See* Robinson, Graydon

**Robinson, Bob** 20th c. [GW]
*American rodeo performer*
* Robinson, Beezer

**Robinson, Bojangles**
*See* Robinson, Bill

**Robinson, Brooks [Calbert, Jr.]** 1937- [SMG]
*American baseball player*
* Impossible, Mr.
* Robby the Robber
* Robinson, Hoover
* [The] Vacuum Cleaner

**Robinson, Budd**
*See* Robinson, David

**Robinson, Chaille Howard [Payne]** 20th c. [CA]
*American author*
* Kirby, Jean [house pseudonym, Whitman Publishing]
* Robinson, Kathleen

**Robinson, Cleophus** 1932- [IBW]
*American clergyman and songwriter*
* [The] King of Gospel Music

**Robinson, Clyde** ?-1915 [BE]
*American baseball player*
* Robinson, Rabbit

**Robinson, Cornelius** 1902- [IBW]
*American tour guide*
* Robinson, Robby

**Robinson, Cynthia** 1946- [SSS]
*Musician*
* Robinson, Ecco

**Robinson, David** 1915- [CA]
*American author, playwright, screenwriter*
* Robinson, Budd

**Robinson, Derek** 1932- [WD]
*British author*
* Robson, Dirk

**Robinson, Doctor**
*See* Hannegan, Dennis

**Robinson, Dora** 20th c. [THR]
*British theatrical business manager*
* Fellowes-Robinson, Dora

**Robinson, Ecco**
*See* Robinson, Cynthia

**Robinson, Ed** 1882?- [NOJ]
*American jazz musician*
* Robinson, Rabbit

**Robinson, Eddie** 1919- [IBW]
*American football player and coach*
* Football, Mr.

**Robinson, Edgar Williams** 1794-1863 [PA]
*Author*
* Owanda

**Robinson, Edward G.**
*See* Goldenberg, Emanuel

**Robinson, Edward N.** 1873-1945
[FB]
*American football coach*
* Robinson, Robbie
* [The] Walter Camp of Brown Football

**Robinson, Edwin Meade** 1878- ?
[NAA]
*American author and poet*
* Robinson, Ted

**Robinson, Eli** 20th c. [NP]
*American jazz musician*
* Mr. Eli

**Robinson, Ezekial R.** 20th c. [IBW]
*American magician*
* Ezekiel the Great

**Robinson, Fannie Clay** 20th c. [IBW]
*Wife and business manager of American entertainer, Bill "Bojangles" Robinson*
* Little Bo

**Robinson, Fat**
*See* Robinson, Freddy

**Robinson, Frances**
*See* Ladd, Marion Frances

**Robinson, Francis [Arthur]** 1910-1980 [CA]
*American opera executive and author*
* Metropolitan Opera, Mr.

**Robinson, Frank Isaac** 1938-
[IBW]
*American musician*
* Robinson, Sugar Chile

**Robinson, Frank M[alcolm]** 1926-
[CA]
*American author*
* Benji, Thomas
* Courtney, Robert
* Walsh, James

**Robinson, Freddy** 20th c. [RBE]
*American boxer*
* Robinson, Fat

**Robinson, Frederick John [Viscount Goderich and Earl of Ripon]** 1782-1859 [DNNF, DNNS, SN]
*British statesman*
* Goderich, Goosey
* Robinson, Prosperity

**Robinson, Geoffrey** 1921- [TR]
*British actor*
* Chater, Geoffrey

**Robinson, George** 20th c. [OBW]
*American baseball player*
* Robinson, Sis

**Robinson, George Geoffrey** 1874-1944 [LC]
*British editor*
* Dawson, Geoffrey

**Robinson, Good Rockin'**
*See* Robinson, Louis Charles

**Robinson, Graydon** 1928-
[BBH, CSH]
*Canadian bowler*
* Robinson, Blondie

**Robinson, Herbert Spencer** 20th c.
[CA]
*American author*
* Hespro, Herbert

**Robinson, Herk**
*See* Robinson, Spencer T.

**Robinson, Hoover**
*See* Robinson, Brooks [Calbert, Jr.]

**Robinson, Ignatius Loyola**
*See* Knapp, Samuel Lorenzo

**Robinson, Ikey L.** 1904- [WWJ]
*American jazz musician*
* Robinson, Banjo

**Robinson, Isaiah** 1892-1962 [NOJ]
*American jazz musician*
* Robinson, Big Ike

**Robinson, Jack**
*See* Robinson, Robert

**Robinson, James** 1903-1957
[BWW]
*American singer*
* Bat the Humming-Bird
* Robinson, Bat

**Robinson, James** 20th c. [OBW]
*American baseball player*
* Robinson, Black Rusie

**Robinson, James A.** 19th c. [PA]
*Author*
* Old Hurrygraph

**Robinson, James D., III** 1935-
*American business executive*
* Jimmy Three Sticks

**Robinson, Jan M.** 1933-
[B10, SAT]
*American author*
* Flood, Flash

**Robinson, Jill** 1936- [CA]
*American author*
* Schary, Jill
* Zimmer, Jill Schary

**Robinson, Jim**
*See* Robinson, Nathan

**Robinson, Jimmy Lee** 1931-
[BWW]
*American singer*
* Aliomar, Latif
* Lee, Jimmy
* Lee, Lonesome

**Robinson, Joan [Mary] G[ale Thomas]** 1910- [CA, SAT]
*British author and illustrator*
* Thomas, Joan Gale

**Robinson, John C.** 1907- [IBW]
*Ethiopian air force officer*
* [The] Brown Condor

**Robinson, John Henry**
*See* Robertson, John Henry

**Robinson, Josie**
*See* Hayward, Mrs. Louis

**Robinson, Kathleen**
*See* Robinson, Chaille Howard [Payne]

**Robinson, L. C.**
*See* Robinson, Louis Charles

**Robinson, Leonard [Len]** 1951-
[SMG]
*American basketball player*
* Robinson, Truck

**Robinson, Lewis George** 1886-
[CC, WW]
*Author*
* Braha, George
* Limnelius, George

**Robinson, Lisa** 1936-    [CA]
*American author*
* Rhodes, Laura

**Robinson, Louis Charles**
1915-1976    [BWW]
*American singer*
* Robinson, Good Rockin'
* Robinson, L. C.

**Robinson, Luther** 1878-1949
[EMT, IPA, PMJ]
*American actor and dancer*
* Bojangles
* Robinson, Bill

**Robinson, Mack**
See Robinson, Matthew

**Robinson, Madeleine**
See Svoboda, Madeleine

**Robinson, [Sister] Marian Dolores**
1916-    [CA]
*American psychologist and author*
* Marian Dolores, [Sister]

**Robinson, Martin D.** 1925-
[ECM, RO1]
*American singer*
* Robbins, Marty
* Teardrop, Mr.

**Robinson, Mary** 19th c.
[DNNS, FFF, RH]
*Wife of John Hatfield, who was
executed for forgery*
* [The] Beauty of Buttermere

**Robinson, Mary Darby** 1758-1800
[DHA, FFF, SN]
*British actress, author, poet*
* [The] English Sappho
* [The] Fair Perdita
* Perdita
* Randall, Anne Frances

**Robinson, Matthew** 20th c.    [IBW]
*American track and field athlete*
* Robinson, Mack

**Robinson, Mike** 20th c.    [IBW]
*American basketball player*
* Tiny Darkhorse

**Robinson, Mogul**
See Robinson, Remus G.

**Robinson, Mrs. Forrest**    [FFF]
*Entertainer*
* Blair, Eugenia

**Robinson, Mrs. George**    [FFF]
*Entertainer*
* Baldwin, Florence

**Robinson, Nathan** 1892-1976
[IBW, PMJ, WWJ]
*American jazz musician*
* Robinson, Big Jim
* Robinson, Jim

**Robinson, Nugent**    [FFF]
*American writer*
* Clover, Sam
* Rugby, Nym

**Robinson, Patricia Colbert** 1923-
[CA]
*American author and playwright*
* Duval, Margaret
* Macomber, Daria

**Robinson, Patrick**    [SN]
* Diminutive Peter

**Robinson, Paul** 1944-    [SMG]
*American football player*
* [The] Cactus Comet
* Robinson, Robby

**Robinson, Prosperity**
See Robinson, Frederick John
[Viscount Goderich and Earl of
Ripon]

**Robinson, Rabbit**
See Robinson, Clyde

**Robinson, Rabbit**
See Robinson, Ed

**Robinson, Ray**
See Smith, Walker

**Robinson, Ray Charles** 1930?-
[BBD, BWW, LRR]
*American musician*
* Charles, Ray
* [The] Genius
* [The] Senior Diplomat of Soul

**Robinson, Remus G.** 20th c.    [IBW]
*American physician and school
administrator*
* Robinson, Mogul

**Robinson, Richard Blundell** 1905-
[WW]
*Author*
* Leaderman, George

**Robinson, Robbie**
See Robinson, Edward N.

**Robinson, Robbo**
See Robinson, Robert Timothy

**Robinson, Robby**
See Robinson, Bernard Whitfield

**Robinson, Robby**
See Robinson, Cornelius

**Robinson, Robby**
See Robinson, Paul

**Robinson, Robert** 1927-    [BB]
*American basketball player*
* Robinson, Jack

**Robinson, Robert Murray** 1949-
[SMG]
*American baseball player*
* Robinson, Smokey

**Robinson, Robert Timothy** 1958-
[DC]
*British cricketer*
* Robinson, Robbo

**Robinson, Roland Edward** 1912-
[IAW]
*Irish-born author and poet*
* [The] Bastard from the Bush

**Robinson, Rube**
See Robertson, John Henry

**Robinson, Sis**
See Robinson, George

**Robinson, Skindown**
See Robinson, Walter

**Robinson, Skip**
See Robinson, Alfred

**Robinson, Smith** 1909-    [IBW]
*American editor*
* Robinson, Smitty

**Robinson, Smitty**
See Robinson, Smith

**Robinson, Smokey**
See Robinson, Robert Murray

**Robinson, Smokey**
See Robinson, William

**Robinson, Solon** 1803-1880
[FFF, PA]
*American author*
* Blythe, White, Jr.
* [A] Layman

**Robinson, Spencer T.** 1941-    [SMG]
*American baseball executive*
* Robinson, Herk

**Robinson, Spider** 1948-    [CA]
*American author*
* Wyatt, B. D.

**Robinson, Sugar Chile**
See Robinson, Frank Isaac

**Robinson, Sugar Ray**
See Smith, Walker

**Robinson, Sylvia Vanderpool** 1936-
[RO2]
*American singer and songwriter*
* Sylvia

**Robinson, T. H.**
See Robinson, Theodore Henry

**Robinson, Ted**
See Robinson, Edwin Meade

**Robinson, Theodore Henry**
1881-1964    [LC]
*British educator and author*
* Robinson, T. H.

**Robinson, Therese Albertine Louise
von Iakob** 1797-1870
[DEL, DNNF, RH]
*German-born philologist and author*
* Talvi

**Robinson, [Sir] Thomas**    [SN]
* Long Sir Thomas

**Robinson, Truck**
See Robinson, Leonard [Len]

**Robinson, Walter** 20th c.    [OBW]
*American baseball player*
* Robinson, Skindown

**Robinson, Wilbert** 1863?-1934
[BAB, DGS, PB]
*American baseball player and
manager*
* Fish, Billy
* Robinson, Billy
* Uncle Robbie [or Robby]

**Robinson, William** ?-1963    [BEW]
*British theatrical performer*
* Palette, Billy

**Robinson, William** 18th c.    [SN]
*British clergyman*
* Reverend Billy

**Robinson, William** 1940-
[PRS, RO2]
*American singer and songwriter*
* Robinson, Smokey

**Robinson, William Ellsworth**
1861-1918    [BMH]
*American-born magician*
* Ben Ali, Achmed

**Robinson, William Ellsworth**
(Continued)
* Foo, Chung Ling
* Khan, Abdul
* Sahib, Nana
* Soo, Chung Ling
* Soo, Hop Ling

**Robinson, William Erigena**
1814-1892    [PA]
*American author and journalist*
* Richelieu

**Robinson, William H.** 1859-1894
[BE]
*American baseball player*
* Robinson, Yank

**Robinson, William Stevens**
1818-1876    [FFF, PA]
*American author and journalist*
* Gilbert
* Kremlin
* Middlesex
* Warrington

**Robinson, Yank**
See Robinson, William H.

**Robion, Jean**
See Lanier, [Dr.] Clement

**Robish, Eevo** 1931-    [RO1]
*Yugoslav singer*
* Robic, Ivo

**Robison, Arthur**
See Robinson, Arthur

**Robison, Carson J.** 1890-1957
[CWG]
*American country-western performer*
* [The] Granddaddy of the
Hillbillies

**Robison, David Victor** 1911?-1978
[FIR]
*Screenwriter*
* David, Paul

**Robison, Mary** 1865-1942
[BEW, F1, OCF]
*Australian-born actress*
* Robson, May

**Robison, Ruth** 20th c.    [BEW]
*American actress and producer*
* Bailey, Ruth

**Robison, Willard** 1894-1968
*American bandleader and singer*
* [The] Evangelist of Rhythm

**Robjohn, William James**
1843-1920    [BBD]
*British-born musician*
* Florio, Caryl

**Robles Soler, Antonio** 1897-
[SFL, WGT]
*Spanish author*
* Antoniorrobles

**Robley, Rob**
See Robley, Wendell

**Robley, Wendell** 1916-    [CA]
*American author*
* Robley, Rob

**Robotham, Samuel Birley**    [FFF]
*Astronomer and writer*
* Parallax

**Robson, Dirk**
See Robinson, Derek

**Robson, Frederick**
See Brownbill, Thomas Robson

**Robson, H. M.**
See Robson, Hugh Mather

**Robson, Hugh Mather** 1929-
[ART]
*British artist*
* Robson, H. M.

**Robson, May**
See Robison, Mary

**Robson, Norman** 20th c.    [SFL]
*Author*
* Robb, John

**[The] Robson of the Halls**
See Liston, Victor

**Robson, Stuart**
See Stuart, Henry Robson

**Robusti, Jacopo** 1518-1594
[DNNS, SN, WBD]
*Italian painter*
* [Il] Furioso
* [The] Thunderbolt of Painting
* Tintoretto

**Robyn, Wee Willie**
See Robyn, William

**Robyn, William**
*Singer*
* Robyn, Wee Willie

**Roc, Patricia**
See Riese, Felicia

**Rocco, Gaetano** 1914-1952    [SC]
*American actor*
* Tano, Guy

**Roch, Dalby**
See Webb, Ethel

**Rocha, Ephraim** 1923-    [BB]
*American basketball player*
* Rocha, Red

**Rocha, Red**
See Rocha, Ephraim

**Rochard, Henri**
See Charlier, Roger H[enri]

**Rochdale, Thomas**
See Hinde, Alfred

**[The] Rochdale Thunderbolt**
See Bamford, Joseph

**Roche, A. K.** [joint pseudonym with
Boche Kaplan]
See Abisch, Roslyn Kroop [Roz]

**Roche, A. K.** [joint pseudonym with
Roslyn Kroop Abisch]
See Kaplan, Boche

**Roche, Arthur Somers** 1883-1935
[WW]
*Author*
* MacHaye, Eric

**Roche, Eric**
See Rochester, George Ernest

**Roche, Hester**
See Rochester, George Ernest

**Roche, James** 1770-1853
[DEL, PA]
*British author*
* J. R.
* [An] Octogenarian

**Roche, John**
See Le Roi, David [De Roche]

**Roche, John** 1813-1887
[FFF, WBD]
*Irish-born American shipbuilder*
* [The] Father of American
Shipbuilding
* [The] Father of Iron Shipbuilding
in America
* Roach, John

**Roche, John Joseph [Jack]** 1890-
[BE]
*American baseball player*
* Roche, Red

**Roche, Red**
See Roche, John Joseph [Jack]

**Rochefort, Bennett Harold**
See Gilbert, Bennett Harold
Rochefort

**Rochefort, Julian** 20th c.    [MBF]
*British author*
* Stevens, Christopher

**Rochelle**
See Flacon, Joseph Henry

**Rochester**
See Anderson, Edmund Lincoln
[Eddie]

**Rochester, Earl of**
See Wilmot, John

**Rochester, George Ernest** 1905?-
[MBF, SFL]
*British author*
* Beresford, John
* Chatham, Frank
* Frazer, Allison
* Furze, Barton
* Gaunt, Jeffrey
* Hale, Martin
* Kent, Elizabeth
* Roche, Eric
* Roche, Hester
* Smith, Hamilton
* West, Mary

**Rochester, Mark**
See Kent, [William] Charles
[Mark]

**Rochette, Raoul**
See Rochetto, Raoul Desire

**Rochetto, Raoul Desire** 1790-1854
[PA]
*Author*
* Rochette, Raoul

**Rochfort, Alfred**
See Calhoun, Alfred R.

**Rochon, Francois Jean** 1953-
[SMG]
*Canadian-born hockey player*
* Rochon, Frank

**Rochon, Frank**
See Rochon, Francois Jean

**[The] Rock**
See Averill, [Howard] Earl

**[The] Rock**
See Raines, Tim

**[The] Rock**
See Zeidel, Lawrence [Larry]

**Rock, Blossom**
See Blake, Marie

**Rock, C. V.**
See Rocken, Kurt Walter

**Rock, Captain**
See Moore, Thomas

**Rock, Captain**
See O'Conner, Roger

**Rock, Charles**
See Rock De Fabeck, Arthur
Charles

**Rock, David John** 1957-    [DC]
*British cricketer*
* Rock, Jungle
* Rock, Rocky

**Rock, James**
See Patten, Clinton A.

**Rock, Jungle**
See Rock, David John

**Rock, Lester Henry**
See Schwarzrock, Lester Henry

**[The] Rock of Chickamauga**
See Thomas, George Henry

**Rock, Pebbles**
See Rock, Walter

**Rock, Richard**
See Mainprize, Don[ald Charles]

**Rock, Rocky**
See Rock, David John

**Rock, Walter** 20th c.
*American football player*
* Rock, Pebbles
* Rock, Zeke

**Rock, Zeke**
See Rock, Walter

**Rock De Fabeck, Arthur Charles**
1866-1919    [BEW]
*Indian-born actor*
* Rock, Charles

**Rockafeller, Harry J.** 20th c.
[BBH]
*American collegiate athletic director*
* Rockafeller, Rocky

**Rockafeller, Rocky**
See Rockafeller, Harry J.

**Rockafeller, David** 1916?-
*American banking executive*
* D. R.

**Rockefeller, Happy**
See Rockefeller, Margaretta Large
[Fitler Murphy]

**Rockefeller, Jay**
See Rockefeller, John D., IV

**Rockefeller, John D., IV** 1937?-
*American politician*
* Rockefeller, Jay

**Rockefeller, John Davison, III**
1906-1978
*American industrialist and
philanthropist*
* J. D. R. 3

**Rockefeller, Margaretta Large [Fitler
Murphy]** 1926-    [B10]
*Wife of American vice president,
Nelson Rockefeller*
* Rockefeller, Happy

**Rockefeller, Nelson Aldrich**
1908-1979    [B10]
*American vice president*
* Rockefeller, Rocky

**Rockefeller, Rocky**
See Rockefeller, Nelson Aldrich

**Rocken, Kurt Walter** 1906-    [WGT]
*German author*
* Rock, C. V.
* Walter, Henry

**[The] Rocket**
See Larose, Claude

**[The] Rocket**
See Richard, [Joseph Henri]
Maurice

**Rocket, Captain**
See Machado, Paulo Sergio
Mastrotti

**Rockey, Howard** 1886-1934    [WW]
*Author*
* Bryce, Ronald
* Panbourne, Oliver

**Rockfeller, Roger**
See Deodato, Ruggero

**[The] Rockford Sheik**
See Mandella, Samuel R.

**Rockin' Red**
See Minter, Iverson

**Rockin' Reggie Vincent**
See Vincent, Reggie

**Rockin' Sydney**
See Semien, Sidney

**Rockingham, Montague**
See Nye, Nelson C[oral]

**Rocklin, Ross Louis** 1913-    [CA]
*American author*
* Cente, H. F.
* Rocklynne, Ross
* Smith, Carlton

**Rocklynne, Ross**
See Rocklin, Ross Louis

**Rockwell, Kiffin Ayres**
See Hayes, Kiffin Ayres

**Rockwell, Matt**
See Rowland, D[onald] S[ydney]

**Rockwood, Harry**
See Young, Ernest A.

**Rockwood, Margaret** 1897-1962
[SC]
*American actress and singer*
* Morgan, Margo

**Rockwood, Roy** [house pseudonym]
[Stratemeyer Syndicate]
See Stratemeyer, Edward L.

**Roda Roda, Alexander Friedrich
Ladislaus**
See Rosenfeld, Alexander
Friedrich Ladislaus

**Rodberg, Lillian** 1936-    [CA]
*American author and columnist*
* Boehme, Lillian R.

**Rodd, Kylie Tennant** 1912-    [CA]
*Australian author*
* Tennant, Kylie

**Rodd, Nancy Freeman-Mitford**
See Mitford, Nancy

**Rodd, Ralph**
See North, William

Rodda, Charles 1891-
[AW, CA, WW]
*Australian-born author*
* Holt, Gavin
* Low, Gardner
* Reed, Eliot [joint pseudonym with Eric Ambler]

Rodda, Peter [Gordon] 1937- [CA]
*South African-born playwright and poet*
* Tudhope, Richard

Roddick, Ellen 1936- [CA]
*American author and columnist*
* Meade, Ellen

Roddy the Rover
See De Blacam, Hugh [Aodh]

Rode, [Jacques] Pierre [Joseph] 1774-1830 [SN]
*French musician*
* [The] Correggio of the Violin

Rodell, Marie F[reid] 1912-1975 [CA, CC, WW]
*American author, literary agent, editor*
* Randolph, Marion

Rodenberg, Julius
See Levy, Julius

Roderick ?- 711
[DEP, DNNS, SN]
*King of the Visigoths*
* [The] Last of the Goths

Rodes, Alfred 1905- [BMH]
*Argentinian-born entertainer*
* [L']enfant Paganini

Rodgers, Andy
See Rodgers, Kenneth Andre Ian

Rodgers, Bill
See Rodgers, Wilbur Kincaid

Rodgers, Buck
See Rodgers, Francis G.

Rodgers, Buck
See Rodgers, Robert L. [Bob]

Rodgers, Francis G. 20th c.
*American business executive*
* Rodgers, Buck

Rodgers, Frank
See Infield, Glenn [Berton]

Rodgers, Franklin C. 1931- [FB]
*American football coach*
* Rodgers, Pepper

Rodgers, Ira E. 1895-1963 [AS, FB]
*American football player*
* Rodgers, Rat

Rodgers, James Charles [Jimmie] 1897-1933 [CWG]
*American country-western performer*
* America's Blue Yodeler
* [The] Father of Commercial Hillbilly Music
* [The] Father of Country Music
* [The] Singing Brakeman

Rodgers, Joann Ellison 1941- [CA]
*American journalist*
* Scott, Eve

Rodgers, [Sir] John [Charles] 1906- [IAW]
*British politician and author*
* Scrambled Ego

Rodgers, Kenneth Andre Ian 1934- [BE]
*American baseball player*
* Rodgers, Andy

Rodgers, Pepper
See Rodgers, Franklin C.

Rodgers, Rat
See Rodgers, Ira E.

Rodgers, Robert L. [Bob] 1938- [PB]
*American baseball player*
* Rodgers, Buck

Rodgers, W. R.
See Rodgers, William Robert

Rodgers, Wilbur Kincaid 1887- [BE]
*American baseball player*
* Raw Meat Bill
* Rodgers, Bill

Rodgers, William Robert 1909-1969 [LC]
*Irish poet*
* Rodgers, W. R.

Rodinson, Maxime 1915- [CA]
*French author*
* Ronsin, Jean

Rodman, Ella
See Church, Eliza Rodman

Rodman, Emerson
See Ellis, Edward S[ylvester]

Rodman, Eric
See Silverberg, Robert

Rodman, Howard 20th c. [WF]
*American screenwriter*
* Simoun, Henri

Rodman, Maia
See Wojciechowska, Maia [Teresa]

Rodney, Bob
See Rodrigo, Robert

Rodney, Don
See Ragonese, Don

Rodney, M.
See Redmayne, Mary Priestley

Rodney, Red
See Chudnick, Robert

Rodrigo, Robert 1928- [CA]
*British sportswriter and author*
* Rodney, Bob

Rodrigues, Vilmar Silva 1931- [WEC]
*Brazilian cartoonist*
* Vilmar

Rodrigues Ferreira, Alexander 1756-1815 [FFF]
*Brazilian traveller*
* [The] Brazilian Humboldt

Rodrigues Martins, Waldemar 1937- [AES]
*Brazilian soccer player*
* Oreco

Rodriguez, Angel
See Schmid, Charles Howard, Jr.

Rodriguez, Antonio Hector 1920- [BE]
*Cuban-born baseball player*
* Rodriguez, Hec

Rodriguez, Aurelio Ituarte 1947- [BE]
*Mexican-born baseball player*
* Rodriguez, Leo

Rodriguez, Bobby
See Rodriguez, Roberto Munoz

Rodriguez, Braulio 20th c. [WECO]
*Spanish cartoonist*
* Bayo

Rodriguez, Brito
See Rodriguez, Sebastian

Rodriguez, Carlos [GS]
*Venezuelan bullfighter*
* [El] Mito [The Myth]

Rodriguez, Chi Chi
See Rodriguez, Juan

Rodriguez, Eliseo C. 1946- [SMG]
*Puerto Rican-born baseball player*
* Rodriguez, Ellie

Rodriguez, Ellie
See Rodriguez, Eliseo C.

Rodriguez, Fernando Pedro 1928- [BE]
*Cuban-born baseball player*
* Rodriguez, Freddy

Rodriguez, Freddy
See Rodriguez, Fernando Pedro

Rodriguez, Guillermo 1914-1951 [GS]
*Peruvian bullfighter*
* [El] Sargento [The Sergeant]

Rodriguez, Hec
See Rodriguez, Antonio Hector

Rodriguez, Jesus Rafael
See Hernaiz, Jesus Rafael

Rodriguez, Johnny
See Rodriguez, Juan Raul Davis

Rodriguez, Juan 1935- [B10, BWG, GF]
*Puerto Rican golfer*
* Rodriguez, Chi Chi

Rodriguez, Juan Raul Davis 1952- [ECM]
*American country-western performer*
* Rodriguez, Johnny

Rodriguez, Leo
See Rodriguez, Aurelio Ituarte

Rodriguez, Nicholas Goodwin 1904?- [WWJ]
*Cuban-born jazz musician*
* Rodriguez, Rod

Rodriguez, Roberto Munoz 1943- [BE]
*Venezuelan-born baseball player*
* Rodriguez, Bobby

Rodriguez, Rod
See Rodriguez, Nicholas Goodwin

Rodriguez, Sebastian 1642- ? [IBW]
*American musician*
* Rodriguez, Brito

Rodriguez, Tito 1923-1973 [SC]
*Actor, singer, bandleader*
* [The] Frank Sinatra of Latin Music

Rodriguez Alvarez, Alejandro 1903-1965 [CA, EWL]
*Spanish poet, playwright, screenwriter*
* Casona, Alejandro

Rodriguez Sanchez, Guadalupe 1899- [GS]
*Mexican bullfighter*
* Guero Guadalupe [Blonde Guadalupe]

Rodriguez Sanchez, Jose 1870-1922 [GS]
*Spanish bullfighter*
* Bebe Chico [Little Baby]

Rodriguez Sanchez, Manuel 1883-1923 [GS, SA]
*Spanish bullfighter*
* Manolete [Big Manuel]

Rodriguez Sanchez, Manuel 1917-1947 [GS, OCS]
*Spanish bullfighter*
* [The] Caliph of Cordoba
* Manolete [Big Manuel]
* [El] Monstruo [The Monster]

Rodriguez Ucares, Fray Jose 1725?- ? [CW]
*Cuban poet and playwright*
* [El] Capacho
* Capacho, Padre
* Ucres [or Ucares], Rodriguez

Rodriguez Valades, Jesus 1908- [GS]
*Mexican bullfighter*
* Simonillo [Little Simon]

Rodriguez y Ortega, Joaquin 1903- [GS, OCS]
*Spanish bullfighter*
* Cagancho

Rodt, Rudolf
See Eichrodt, Ludwig

Rodwell, James 19th c. [PA]
*Author*
* Uncle James

Rodziewiczowna, Marja 1863-1944 [CD]
*Polish author*
* Zmogas

Roe [Frederick] Clay 1901- [BE]
*American baseball player*
* Roe, Shad

Roe, Elwin Charles 1915- [BE, PB]
*American baseball player*
* Roe, Preacher

Roe, F[rederick] Gordon 1894- [CA, LAO, WD]
*British author*
* Criticus
* F. G. R.
* Rhode, Winslow
* Uncle Gordon

Roe, Harry Mason [house pseudonym] [Stratemeyer Syndicate]
See Stratemeyer, Edward L.

Roe, Ivan 1917- [AW, WD]
*British author*
* Savage, Richard

Roe, Leonard
See Douglas, John

Roe, M. S.
See Thomson, Daisy Hicks

**Roe, Mary A.** 19th c.   [PA]
*Author*
* Cornwall, C. M.

**Roe, Preacher**
*See* Roe, Elwin Charles

**Roe, Richard**
*See* Cowper, Francis Henry

**Roe, Shad**
*See* Roe [Frederick] Clay

**Roe, Tex**
*See* Robarge, John F.

**Roe, William J[ames]** 1843-1915
[SFL, WGT]
*American author*
* Cervus, G. I.
* Genone, Hudor

**Roebuck, John Arthur** 1801-1879
[DNNS]
*British politician*
* Tear 'em

**Roebuck, Peter Michael** 1956-
[DC]
*British cricketer*
* Roebuck, Professor
* Roebuck, Roger

**Roebuck, Professor**
*See* Roebuck, Peter Michael

**Roebuck, Roger**
*See* Roebuck, Peter Michael

**Roeder, Adolph** 1857- ?   [ALY]
*American author and clergyman*
* Reese, Harvey

**Roeder, Pat**
*See* Ellison, Harlan [Jay]

**Roehrich, William** 1912-   [TR]
*American actor and author*
* Roerick, William

**Roelas [Ruelas], Juan de las**
1560?-1625   [WBD]
*Spanish painter*
* [El] Clerigo

**Roemer, Buddy**
*See* Roemer, Charles, III

**Roemer, Charles, III** 1944?-
*American businessman*
* Roemer, Buddy

**Roemers, Anna**   [SN]
* [A] Dutch Sappho

**Roerick, William**
*See* Roehrich, William

**Roesseler, Rudolf** 1897-1958
[EE, WWW]
*German publisher and intelligence
agent for Russia*
* Lucy [code name used during
World War II]

**Roest, Rust**
*See* Elkan, Sophie

**Roeterdink, Hubert**
*See* Roeterdink, Hubertus
Johannus Albertus

**Roeterdink, Hubertus Johannus
Albertus** 1948-   [IWM]
*Dutch musician*
* Roeterdink, Hubert

**Roetter, Charles Frederick** 1919-
[CA]
*German-born columnist and author*
* Satiricus

**Rogan, Bullet Joe**
*See* Rogan, Wilbur

**Rogan, Wilbur** 1893?-1967
[AS, MK]
*American baseball player*
* Rogan, Bullet Joe

**Roger**
*See* Toutain, Jose

**Roger Ferdinand**
*See* Ferdinand, Roger

**Roger, George Munroe**   [PA]
*Author*
* [The] Little Bugler

**Roger, Mae Durham** 20th c.   [CA]
*American author and librarian*
* Durham, Mae

**Roger, Noelle**
*See* Pittard, Helene

**Roger of Bruges**
*See* Van der Weyde, Roger

**Roger, Pierre** 1291-1352   [WBD]
*Pope*
* Clement VI

**Roger the Dodger**
*See* Ward, Roger

**Roger I** 1031-1101   [SN]
*Count of Sicily and Calabria*
* [The] Great Count
* [The] Terror of the Faithless

**Rogers, Ben**
*See* Pugh, Roger

**Rogers, Buck**
*See* Rogers, Everett

**Rogers, Buck**
*See* Rogers, Lee Otis

**Rogers, Buck**
*See* Rogers, Orlin Woodrow

**Rogers, Buddy**
*See* Rogers, Charles

**Rogers, Charles** 1904-
[F2, FC, IPA]
*American actor*
* Rogers, Buddy

**Rogers, Clara Kathleen** 1844- ?
[NAA]
*British-born singer, composer,
author*
* Doria, Clara

**Rogers, D. J.**
*See* Rogers, Dewayne Julius

**Rogers, Dewayne Julius** 20th c.
[IBW]
*American singer*
* Rogers, D. J.

**Rogers, Don**
*See* Degler, Claude

**Rogers, Don**
*See* Schieldge, Ernest

**Rogers, Doug**
*See* Bradbury, Ray [Douglas]

**Rogers, Duke?**
*See* Williams, Egbert Austin

**Rogers, Eleanor**   [FFF]
*Entertainer*
* Moretti, Eleanor

**Rogers, Emmett**
*See* McCloskey, John

**Rogers, Emmett**
*See* Sweet, Emmett Martine

**Rogers, Everett** 1891-1952   [NOJ]
*American jazz musician*
* Rogers, Buck

**Rogers, Floyd**
*See* Spence, William John Duncan

**Rogers, Genevieve**
*See* Aiken, Mrs. Frank E.

**Rogers, Ginger**
*See* McMath, Virginia Katherine

**Rogers, Gus**
*See* Solomon, Gus

**Rogers, Henry** 1806-1877   [PA]
*Author*
* Greyson, R. E. H.
* Vindex

**Rogers, James [Jimmy]**
*See* Lane, James A.

**Rogers, John**
*See* Rogers, Thomas Percy

**Rogers, John**
*See* Snow Cloud

**Rogers, John** 1500-1555
[FFF, WBD]
*British martyr*
* [The] Deritend Martyr
* Matthew, Thomas

**Rogers, Keith**
*See* Harris, Marion Rose [Young]

**Rogers, Lee**
*See* Wilson, Roger C.

**Rogers, Lee Otis** 1913-   [BE]
*American baseball player*
* Rogers, Buck
* Rogers, Lefty

**Rogers, Lefty**
*See* Rogers, Lee Otis

**Rogers, Lefty**
*See* Rogers, Orlin Woodrow

**Rogers, Levi** 1887-1963   [B10]
*Canadian rower and coxswain*
* Rogers, Shotty

**Rogers, Lorain**   [FFF]
*Entertainer*
* Thompson, Charlotte

**Rogers, Loula K.**   [FFF]
*Author*
* Leola

**Rogers, Max**
*See* Solomon, Max

**Rogers, Melva**
*See* Graham, Roger Phillips

**Rogers, Mick**
*See* Glut, Donald F[rank]

**Rogers, Milt**
*See* Adelstein, Milton

**Rogers, Mrs. Charles S.**   [FFF]
*Entertainer*
* Vickers, Mattie

**Rogers, Mrs. John R.**   [FFF]
*Entertainer*
* Palmer, Minnie

**Rogers, Nat**
*See* Rogers, William Richard

**Rogers, Nathaniel P.** 1794-1846
[FFF]
*American journalist*
* Old Man of the Mountain

**Rogers, Oh Yeah**
*See* Aiverum, Timothy Louis

**Rogers, Orlin Woodrow** 1912-   [BE]
*American baseball player*
* Rogers, Buck
* Rogers, Lefty

**Rogers, Packy**
*See* Hazinski, Stanley Frank

**Rogers, Pat**
*See* Porges, Arthur

**Rogers, Paul [Patrick]** 1900-   [CA]
*American author and editor*
* Hardwick, Homer

**Rogers, Phillips**
*See* Idell, Albert E.

**Rogers, Robert**
*See* Hamilton, Charles Harold St.
John

**Rogers, Rosalind**
*See* Richardson, Randell

**Rogers, Rosemary** 1932-
[CA, WD]
*American author*
* Mayson, Marina

**Rogers, Roy**
*See* Slye, Leonard

**Rogers, Ruth** 1890-   [WW]
*Author*
* Alexander, Ruth

**Rogers, Samuel** 1763-1855
[DEP, FFF, SN]
*British poet*
* [The] Banker Poet
* [The] Bard of Memory
* [The] Last English Maecenas
* [The] Maecenas of England
* [The] Nestor of English Authors

**Rogers, Samuel Shepard** 1943-
[CA, TR]
*American playwright*
* Shadow, Slim
* Shepard, Sam

**Rogers, Sarah** 1819- ?   [PA]
*Author*
* [A] Lady of New York

**Rogers, Shorty**
*See* Rajonsky, Milton M.

**Rogers, Shotgun**
*See* Rogers, Thomas Andrew

**Rogers, Shotty**
*See* Rogers, Levi

**Rogers, Smiling Slim**
*See* Planchet, Roger Anthony

**Rogers, Stanley Frank**
*See* Hazinski, Stanley Frank

**Rogers, Steve**
*See* Clarke, Percy A.

**Rogers, Thomas Andrew**
1895-1936   [BE]
*American baseball player*
* Rogers, Shotgun

**Rogers, Thomas Percy** 1897-
[IAW]
*British author*
* Rogers, John

**Rogers, Timmie**
See   Aiverum, Timothy Louis

**Rogers, Tom**
See   Edgar, Alfred

**Rogers, W. G.**
See   Rogers, William Garland

**Rogers, Wade**
See   Madlee, Dorothy [Haynes]

**Rogers, Warren**
See   Brucker, Roger W[arren]

**Rogers, Will[iam Penn Adair]**
1879-1935   [BMH]
*American actor and comedian*
* [The] Cherokee Kid
* [The] World's Number One
  Wisecracker

**Rogers, William Garland**
1896-1978   [WYA]
*American author*
* Rogers, W. G.

**Rogers, William Pierce** 1913-
*American secretary of state*
* Reyes, Dr. [code name]

**Rogers, William Richard** 1893-
[MK]
*American baseball player*
* Rogers, Nat

**Rognan, Roy**  ?-1943   [SC]
*Actor and dancer*
* Rognoni

**Rognoni**
See   Rognan, Roy

**Rogow, Lee** 20th c.   [SFP]
*Author*
* Ellis, Craig [house pseudonym]

**Rogoz, Viorica-Georgina** 1927-
[IAW]
*Rumanian author*
* Huber

**[A] Rogue of a Scot**
See   Erskine, John

**Roguery, Doctor**
See   Smith, Thomas

**Rohatyn, Felix** 1929?-
*American investment banker*
* Felix the Fixer
* Fixit, Mr.

**Rohe, Vera-Ellen Westmeyr**
1926-1981   [FC, PMJ, SW]
*American actress and dancer*
* Vera Ellen

**Rohen, Edward** 1931-   [CA, WD]
*British poet and author*
* Connors, Bruton

**Rohl, Wolf Detlef**
See   Eisfeld, Rainer

**Rohlfs, Anna Katharine [Green]**
1846-1935   [NAA, WW]
*American author*
* Green, Anna Katharine

**Rohmer, Elizabeth Sax**
See   Ward, Rose Elizabeth Knox

**Rohmer, Eric**
See   Scherer, Jean Marie Maurice

**Rohmer, Sax**
See   Ward, Arthur Henry

**Rohrbach, Peter Thomas** 1926-
[WD]
*American author*
* Cody, James R.

**[Le] Roi**
See   Whitaker, Thomas

**[Le] Roi Bourgeois**
See   Louis Philippe

**[Le] Roi Citoyen**
See   Louis Philippe

**[Un] Roi de Theatre**
See   Murat, Joachim

**[Le] Roi des Barricades**
See   Louis Philippe

**[Le] Roi des Braves**
See   Henry IV [or Henri]

**[Le] Roi des Feuilletons**
See   Janin, Jules Gabriel

**[Le] Roi des Halles**
See   Vendome, Francois de

**[Le] Roi des Predicateurs**
See   Bourdaloue, Louis

**[Le] Roi des Reptiles**
See   De la Ville, Bernard Germain
Etienne

**[Le] Roi des Versailles**
See   Thiers, Louis Adolphe

**[Le] Roi du Roi**
See   Du Plessis, Armand Jean

**[Le] Roi Panade**
See   Louis XVIII

**[Le] Roi Soleil**
See   Louis XIV

**Roig, Anton Ambrose** 1928-   [BE]
*American baseball player*
* Roig, Tony

**Roig, Tony**
See   Roig, Anton Ambrose

**Roiphe, Anne Richardson** 1935-
[CA]
*American author*
* Richardson, Anne

**Rojan**
See   Rojankovsky, Feodor
Stepanovich

**Rojankovsky, Feodor Stepanovich**
1891-1970   [CA]
*Russian-born author and illustrator*
* Rojan

**Rojas, Alejandro M.** 1938-   [PB]
*Cuban-born baseball player*
* Rojas, Minnie

**Rojas, Cookie**
See   Rojas, Octavio Rivas

**Rojas, Jose**   [GS]
*Spanish bullfighter*
* El Melenas [The Long-Haired
  One]

**Rojas, Minnie**
See   Rojas, Alejandro M.

**Rojas, Octavio Rivas** 1939-
[PB, SMG, WWB]
*Cuban-born baseball player*
* Rojas, Cookie

**Rojatt, Rick** 1947-
*Canadian stunt artist*
* [The] Human Fly

**Roker, Granville William** 1932-
[EJ7]
*American jazz musician*
* Roker, Mickey

**Roker, Mickey**
See   Roker, Granville William

**Roland**
See   Zacherle, John

**Roland, Gilbert**
See   Damaso De Alonso, Luis
Antonio

**Roland, John**
See   Oliver, John Rathbone

**Roland, Marion**
See   Ross, Marion

**Roland, Mary**
See   Lewis, Mary Christianna
[Milne]

**Roland, Nicholas**
See   Walmsley, Arnold Robert

**[The] Roland of the Army**
See   Le Blond, Louis Vincent
Joseph [Comte de St. Hilaire]

**Roland, Ruth** 1893-1937   [CU]
*American actress*
* [The] Serial Queen

**Roland de La Platiere, Jean Marie**
1734-1793   [SN]
*French revolutionary leader*
* [The] Just

**Roland de La Platiere, Jeanne Manon**
1754-1793   [DEP, DNNS, FF]
*French social leader*
* [The] Circe of the Revolution

**Roland-Manuel, Alexis**
See   Levy, Roland Alexis Manuel

**Rolant, Rene**
See   Fanthorpe, R[obert] Lionel

**Roldan, Enrique**
See   Garcia, Andres

**Rolf, Frederick**
See   Friedrichs, Frederick

**Rolfe, Father**
See   Rolfe, Frederick William
[Serafino Austin Lewis Mary]

**Rolfe, Frederick William [Serafino
Austin Lewis Mary]** 1860-1913
[LC, SFL, TC]
*British author*
* Corvo, Baron
* Prospero and Caliban [joint
  pseudonym with Charles Harry
  Clinton Pirie-Gordon]
* Rolfe, Father

**Rolfe, James** 20th c.   [BLB]
*American politician*
* Rolfe, Sunny Jim

**Rolfe, Red**
See   Rolfe, Robert Abial

**Rolfe, Robert Abial** 1908-1969
[AS, BE, PB]
*American baseball player*
* Rolfe, Red

**Rolfe, Sunny Jim**
See   Rolfe, James

**Rolla, Mlle.**
See   Rammelsberg, Kate

**Rolle, Christian** 1929-   [CW]
*West Indian poet*
* Llero, Auguste

**Rolle, Richard** 1290?-1349
[SN, WBD]
*British poet*
* [The] Hermit of Hampole

**Rolle, Tony** 1960-   [IBW]
*American musician*
* [The] Twentieth Century Mozart

**Rollin, Charles** 1661-1741   [SN]
*French educator*
* [The] Bee of France
* Thucydides

**Rollin, Frank A.**
See   Whipper, Frances E. Rollin

**Rolling-Pin, Commodore**
See   Carter, John Hanson

**Rollings, Red**
See   Rollings, William Russell

**Rollings, William Russell**
1904-1964   [BE]
*American baseball player*
* Rollings, Red

**Rollington, Ralph**
See   Allingham, John W.

**Rollins, Al**
See   Rollins, Elwin Ira

**Rollins, Ellen H.** 19th c.   [PA]
*Author*
* Arr, E. H.

**Rollins, Elwin Ira** 1926-
[CEI, FHE, SMG]
*Canadian-born hockey player*
* Rollins, Al

**Rollins, Glenn**
See   Olson, Robert G.

**Rollins, Jack**
See   Rollins, Walter E.

**Rollins, Kathleen** 20th c.
[EMD, WW]
*Author*
* Debrett, Hal [joint pseudonym
  with Davis Dresser]

**Rollins, Red**
See   Rollins, Richard John

**Rollins, Richard John** 1938-   [BE]
*American baseball player*
* Rollins, Red

**Rollins, Royce**
See   Pepper, Choral

**Rollins, Sonny**
See   Rollins, Theodore Walter

**Rollins, Theodore Walter** 1929?-
[DAM, EJ, PMJ]
*American jazz musician*
* Rollins, Sonny

**Rollins, Walter E.** 1907-1973
[DAM]
*American lyricist*
* Rollins, Jack

**Rollins, William** 1897- [WW]
*Author*
* O'Connor, Stacy

**Rollo [Rolf or Hrolf]** 860?- 931?
[WBD]
*Norse chieftain*
* [The] Ganger [or Walker]

**Rolls, Anthony**
*See* Vulliamy, C[olwyn] E[dward]

**Rolls, M. M.** [PA]
*Author*
* His Mother

**[The] Rolls Royce of Country Singers**
*See* Jones, George

**Rolo**
*See* Greenhalgh, Fred

**Rolph, C. H.**
*See* Hewitt, Cecil Rolph

**Rolt, L. T. C.**
*See* Rolt, Lionel Thomas Caswell

**Rolt, Lionel Thomas Caswell**
1910-1974 [HFF]
*British author*
* Rolt, L. T. C.

**Rolvaag, Ole Edvaart**
*See* Morck, Paal

**Rolyat, Dan**
*See* Taylor, Herbert

**Roma, Clarice**
*See* Hann, Roma

**Romack, D. M.**
*See* Hammack, Robert Dean
Michael

**[Le] Romain**
*See* Dumont, Jean

**Romain, Roy**
*See* Romain, Royston

**Romain, Royston** 1918- [SWI]
*British swimmer*
* Romain, Roy

**Romaine, David**
*See* Bohme, David M.

**Romaine, Lawrence B.** 1900-
[CAP]
*American author*
* [The] Weathercock

**Romaine, Linton**
*See* Lee, [Rev.] Albert

**Romaine, Robert Dexter**
*See* Payson, George

**Romains, Jules**
*See* Farigoule, Louis

**[The] Roman**
*See* Dumont, Jean

**[The] Roman**
*See* Mignard, Pierre

**[The] Roman**
*See* Picart, Stephen [or Etienne]

**[The] Roman**
*See* Pippi de Gianuzzi, Giulio

**[The] Roman**
*See* Van Roomen, Adrian

**[The] Roman Achilles**
*See* Dentatus, Sicinius

**[A] Roman Beau Brummel**
*See* Petronius, Caius [or Gaius]

**[The] Roman Chaucer**
*See* Ennius, Quintus

**Roman, Daniel [David]**
*See* Romanow, Daniel David

**Roman, Eric**
*See* Herzog, Eric

**[The] Roman Hercules**
*See* Commodus, Lucius Aelius

**[The] Roman Hippocrates**
*See* Celsus, Aulus Cornelius

**Roman, Johan Helmich** 1694-1758
[WBD]
*Swedish musician and composer*
* [The] Father of Swedish Music

**[The] Roman King-Maker**
*See* Ricimer

**[The] Roman Roland**
*See* Dentatus, Sicinius

**[The] Roman Socrates**
*See* Laelius, Gaius

**Roman, William**
*See* Wills, Garry

**Romance, Viviane**
*See* Ortmanns, Pauline Ronacher

**Romanette, Irmine** 1895?- [CW]
*West Indian poet and author*
* Miramant, Yves

**Romani, Girolamo** 1485-1566
[WBD]
*Italian painter*
* [Il] Romanino

**[Il] Romanino**
*See* Romani, Girolamo

**Romanis, George Zackery**
*See* Roumanis, George Zackery

**Romanne-James, C.**
*See* Romanne-James, Helena
Constance

**Romanne-James, Helena
Constance** [LAO]
*British author, editor, journalist*
* Romanne-James, C.

**Romano, Deane Louis** 1927- [CA]
*American author*
* Cairo, Jon

**Romano, Don**
*See* Turner, Robert [Harry]

**Romano, Emanuel**
*See* Glicenstein, Emanuel

**Romano, Giulio**
*See* Pippi de Gianuzzi, Giulio

**Romano, Honey**
*See* Romano, John Anthony

**Romano, John Anthony** 1934- [BE]
*American baseball player*
* Romano, Honey

**Romano, Paolo**
*See* Alatri, Paolo

**Romanoff, Alexander Nicholayevitch**
1881-1945 [EMD, TC, WGT]
*Russian-born British author*
* Abdullah, Achmed
* Nadir, A. A.?

**Romanoff, Mike**
*See* Gerguson, Harry

**Romanones, Countess of**
*See* Griffith, Maria Aline

**Romanov, Fedor Nikitich**
1553?-1633 [WBD]
*Patriarch of Moscow*
* Philaret

**Romanow, Daniel David** 1921-
[CA]
*American author*
* Roman, Daniel [David]

**[The] Romantic Fiddler**
*See* Trini, Anthony

**Romanus**
*See* Lenihan, F. J.

**Romanus IV** ?-1071 [FFF, SN]
*Byzantine emperor*
* Diogenes

**Romayne, Leicester**
*See* Guimaraens, Manoel Pedro

**Romberger, Allen Isaiah** 1927-
[BE]
*American baseball player*
* Romberger, Dutch

**Romberger, Dutch**
*See* Romberger, Allen Isaiah

**Rome, Alger** [joint pseudonym with
Algirdas Jonas Budrys]
*See* Bixby, Jerome Lewis

**Rome, Alger** [joint pseudonym with
Jerome Lewis Bixby]
*See* Budrys, Algirdas Jonas

**Rome, Anthony**
*See* Albert, Marvin H.

**Rome, Fred**
*See* Toplis, Fred

**Rome, Stewart**
*See* Ryott, Septimus William

**Romeo**
*See* Fellowes, G. W.

**Romeral**
*See* Fernandez, Armando

**Romero, Curro**
*See* Romero Lopez, Francisco

**Romero, Gary**
*See* Catsos, Nicholas A.

**Romero Lopez, Francisco** 1935-
[GS]
*Spanish bullfighter*
* Romero, Curro

**Rommel, Erwin** 1891-1944
[CBS, CND]
*German military leader*
* [The] Desert Fox

**Romnes, Doc**
*See* Romnes, Elwin N.

**Romnes, Elwin N.** 1909-
[CEI, FHE, HK]
*American hockey player*
* Romnes, Doc

**Romney, A. B.**
*See* Rambaut, A. Beatrice

**Romney, Dick**
*See* Romney, Ernest L.

**Romney, Edana**
*See* Rubenstein, Edana

**Romney, Elwood** 1911-1970 [BB]
*American basketball player*
* Romney, Woody

**Romney, Ernest L.** 1895-1969
[BB, FB]
*American football and basketball
coach*
* Romney, Dick

**Romney, Steve**
*See* Bingley, David Ernest

**Romney, Woody**
*See* Romney, Elwood

**Romo, Huevo**
*See* Romo, Vicente Navarro

**Romo, Vicente Navarro** 1943-
[BE, SMG]
*Mexican-born baseball player*
* Romo, Huevo

**Romoff, Woodrow Wilson** 1918-
[BEW]
*American actor*
* Romoff, Woody

**Romoff, Woody**
*See* Romoff, Woodrow Wilson

**Romondt, Marcus**
*See* Brandt, Johanna

**Romualdez, Benjamin** 20th c.
*Filipino newspaper owner and
provincial governor*
* Romualdez, Kokoy

**Romualdez, Kokoy**
*See* Romualdez, Benjamin

**[The] Romulus of Brandenburg**
*See* Henry I [or Heinrich]

**Ronald, David William** 1937- [CA]
*Scottish-born writer*
* Williams, D.

**Ronald, E. B.**
*See* Barker, Ronald Ernest

**Ronald, [Sir] Landon**
*See* Russell, Landon R.

**Ronald the Right**
*See* Reagan, Ronald Wilson

**Ronalds, Danby**
*See* Frankau, Ronald

**Ronalds, Mary Teresa** 1946-
[IAW]
*British author*
* Sheridan, Teresa

**Ronan, Erskine** 20th c. [FHE]
*Canadian hockey player*
* Ronan, Skene

**Ronan, Georgia**
*See* Crampton, Georgia Ronan

**Ronan, Skene**
*See* Ronan, Erskine

**Roncalli, Angelo Giuseppe**
1881-1963 [CBS]
*Pope*
* John XXIII

**[Le] Rondie**
See Gaillard, Angier

**Ronet, E.** ?-1972 [FIR]
*French actress*
* De Breteuil, Gilberte

**Roney, Ruth Anne**
See McMullin, Ruth R[oney]

**Ronge [or Ronger], Florimond**
1825-1892 [WBD]
*French composer*
* Herve

**Ronken, Harriet**
See Lynton, Harriet Ronken

**Ronn, Yuval** 20th c. [SFL]
*Author*
* Ionel

**Ronns, Edward**
See Aarons, Edward S[idney]

**[El] Ronquillo [The Raucous One]**
See Lopez, Antonio

**Ronsard, Pierre de** 1524-1585
[DNNS, RH, SN]
*French poet*
* [L']Apollon de la Source des
  Muses [The Apollo of the
  Fountain of Muses]
* [The] French Chaucer
* [The] French Poet
* [The] Horace of France
* [The] King of Poets
* [The] Petrarch of France
* [The] Pindar of France
* [The] Poet of France
* [The] Poet of Kings
* [The] Poet of the Future
* [Le] Poete des Rois
* [The] Prince of the Ode

**Ronsin, Jean**
See Rodinson, Maxime

**Ronsman, M. M.**
See Nowak, Mariette

**Rood, Jack**
See Van Horn, Dale R.

**Rooke, Daphne [Marie]** 1914-
[CA, SAT]
*South African-born author*
* Pointon, Robert

**Rooke, Valentine**
See Brooke, Valentine

**Rooks, George Brinton McClellan**
See Ruckser, George Brinton
McClellan

**Rooney, Alderman**
See Townley, Daniel O'Connell

**Rooney, Arthur J.** 1901- [BBH]
*American football team owner and
administrator*
* [The] Grand Old Man

**Rooney, Mickey**
See Yule, Joe, Jr.

**Rooney, Pat**
See Ratsch, Fred E.

**Roope, Cyril**
See Roope, Graham Richard
James

**Roope, Graham Richard James**
1946- [DC]
*British cricketer*
* Roope, Cyril

**Roos, Audrey [Kelley]** 1912- [WW]
*Author*
* Kelley, Audrey
* Roos, Kelley [joint pseudonym
  with William Roos]

**Roos, Hans**
See Meissner, Hans-Otto

**Roos, Kelley [joint pseudonym with
William Roos]**
See Roos, Audrey [Kelley]

**Roos, Kelley [joint pseudonym with
Audrey (Kelley) Roos]**
See Roos, William

**Roos, William** 1911- [WW]
*Author*
* Roos, Kelley [joint pseudonym
  with Audrey (Kelley) Roos]

**Roosevelt, Buddy**
See Sanderson, Kent

**Roosevelt, [Anna] Eleanor** 1884-1962
*American lecturer, writer, and wife
of President Franklin Roosevelt*
* [The] Assistant President

**Roosevelt, Franklin Delano**
1882-1945 [CND, FAP]
*American president*
* Admiral Q [code name used
  during World War II]
* [The] Boss
* F. D. R.
* [The] Houdini in the White
  House
* King Franklin
* [The] Sphinx
* [The] Squire of Hyde Park
* That Man in the White House

**Roosevelt, Haroun al-**
See Roosevelt, Theodore [Teddy]

**Roosevelt, Robert Barnwell**
1829-1906 [FFF, PA]
*American author and politician*
* Barnwell
* Zell, Ira

**Roosevelt, Theodore [Teddy]**
1858-1919 [DNNS, FAP]
*American president*
* [The] Bull Moose
* [The] Driving Force
* [The] Dynamo of Power
* Four Eyes
* [The] Great White Chief
* [The] Happy Warrior
* [The] Hero of San Juan Hill
* [The] Man on Horseback
* [The] Meddler
* [The] Old Lion
* Roosevelt, Haroun al-
* [The] Rough Rider
* [The] Sage of Princeton
* T. R.
* Telescope Teddy
* [The] Trust Buster
* [The] Typical American

**Root, Charles Henry** 1899-1970
[BE, DGS, PB]
*American baseball player*
* Root, Chinski

**Root, Chinski**
See Root, Charles Henry

**Root, Jack**
See Ruthaly, Janos

**Roote, Mike**
See Fleischer, Leonore

**[The] Rootin', Tootin', Ridin' Romeo
of the Screen**
See Lucid, Pate

**[The] Rope**
See Boyd, Robert Richard

**[The] Rope Dancer**
See De Grantmesnil, Yvo

**Roper, Laura Wood** 1911-
[CA, WD]
*American author*
* Wood, Laura N[ewbold]

**Roper, Loring**
See Colvin, Fred Herbert

**Roper, Neil Campbell Ommanney**
1941- [IAW]
*Scottish-born poet and translator*
* Omedy, Eugene

**Roper, Ronnalie J.** 1936- [CA]
*American author*
* Howard, Ronnalie Roper

**Roper, Susan Bonthron** 1948- [CA]
*American author*
* Brand, Susan

**Roper, William L[eon]** 1897- [CA]
*American author*
* Fry, David
* Sparkman, William

**Ropes, Arthur Reed** 1859-1933
[EMT]
*British lyricist and librettist*
* Ross, Adrian

**Ropshin, V.**
See Savinkov, Boris Viktorovich

**Roquero Dominguez, Juan**
1825-1885 [CW]
*Cuban playwright*
* Arrugado

**Roques, Jeanne** 1889-1957 [SC]
*French actress and director*
* Musidora

**Roques, Maurice Jacques**
1761-1841 [WBD]
*French intelligence agent*
* Montgaillard, Comte de

**Rorvik, David M[ichael]** 1946-
[CA]
*American author*
* Davidson, Michael

**Ros, Amanda McKittrick**
See McKittrick, Anna Margaret

**Rosa**
See Bonheur, Rosalie

**Rosa**
See Jeffrey, Rosa Vertner

**Rosa, Carl August Nicholas**
See Rose, Carl August Nicholas

**Rosa di Tivoli**
See Ross, Philipp Peter

**Rosa, Patti**
See Buckingham, Jessie

**Rosa, Salvator** 1615-1673
[HN, WBD]
*Italian painter and poet*
* Salvatoriello
* [The] Shakespeare of Painting

**Rosanov [or Rozanov?], Mikhail
Grigorievich** 1888-1938 [CD, LAO]
*Russian author*
* Ognev [or Ognyov?], N[ikolai]

**Rosar, Buddy**
See Rosar, Warren Vincent

**Rosar, Warren Vincent** 1914-
[BE, PB]
*American baseball player*
* Rosar, Buddy

**Rosario, Angel Ramon** 1945- [BE]
*Puerto Rican-born baseball player*
* Rosario, Jimmy

**Rosario, Jimmy**
See Rosario, Angel Ramon

**Rosas, Julio**
See Puig y de la Puente, Francisco

**Rosavella**
See Tucker, Blanch

**Rosay, Francoise**
See Bandy De Naleche, Francoise

**Rosca, the Jester**
See Marinoni, Rosa Zagnoni

**Roscelin de Compiegne**
See Roscellinus [or Rucelinus]

**Roscellinus [or Rucelinus]** 12th c.
[WBD]
*Philosopher*
* Roscelin de Compiegne

**Roscius Britannicus**
See Betterton, Thomas

**Roscius Britannicus**
See Garrick, David

**Roscius Britannicus**
See Tarlton, Richard

**[The] Roscius of England**
See Betterton, Thomas

**[The] Roscius of England**
See Garrick, David

**[The] Roscius of France**
See Boyron, Michel [or Michael]

**Roscius, Quintus** 1st c. BC [SN]
*Roman actor*
* [The] Jewel

**Roscoe, Charles**
See Rowland, D[onald] S[ydney]

**Roscoe, Deane**
See Yates, Frederic B.

**Roscoe, John** 1921- [WW]
*Author*
* Roscoe, Mike [joint pseudonym
  with Michael Ruso]

**Roscoe, Mike [joint pseudonym with
Michael Ruso]**
See Roscoe, John

**Roscoe, Mike [joint pseudonym with
John Roscoe]**
See Ruso, Michael

**[The] Roscommon Giant**
See Coffey, Jim

**[The] Rose**
See Margaret

**[The] Rose**
See Rozema, David Scott [Dave]

Rose, Alex
See Royz, Olesh

Rose, Alvin Emanuel 20th c.    [WW]
Author
* Pruitt, Alan

Rose, Arthur 1890-1968    [THR]
British actor
* Rose, Clarkson

Rose, Billy
See Rosenberg, William Samuel

Rose, Camille Davied 1893-    [CAP]
American writer and editor
* Davied, Camille

Rose, Carl August Nicholas
1843-1889    [WBD]
German operatic impresario
* Rosa, Carl August Nicholas

Rose, Charles E. 1860- ?    [WWL]
British author
* Eddy, Charles

Rose, Clarkson
See Rose, Arthur

Rose, Della
See Bullion, Laura

Rose, [Lady] Dorothy Violet
Frederica 1910-    [AW]
British-born author and journalist
* Carrington, Dorothy

Rose, Florella
See Carlson, Vada F.

Rose, Francis [Frank]
See Fearn, John Russell

Rose, Fred
See Rosenberg, Fred

Rose, Fred 1897-1954    [ECM]
American songwriter and music
publisher
* Dawson, Bart
* Jenkins, Floyd

Rose, Frederick W. 1849- ?
[WWL]
British author
* Martius

Rose, George 1830-1883
[DEL, FFF, RH]
British author
* Sketchley, Arthur

Rose, Hilary
See MacKinnon, Charles Roy

Rose, Ian 1920-    [WD]
Canadian physician and author
* Rose, Robert

Rose, Irving
See Browne, Ernest D.

Rose, J. H.
See Rose, John Holland

Rose, Jack 20th c.    [BLB]
American underworld figure
* Billiard Ball Jack

Rose, Jack 20th c.    [GW]
American rodeo performer
* Rose, Nevada Jack

Rose, Jennifer
See Weber, Nancy

Rose, John Holland 1855-1942
[LC]
British author and educator
* Rose, J. H.

Rose, Julian 1879-1935    [BMH]
American comedian
* Our Hebrew Friend

Rose, Kathleen Mary 1892?-1975
[FIR]
Entertainer
* Delores

Rose, Laurence F.
See Fearn, John Russell

Rose, Marie
See Brady, Alice

Rose, Morris
See Stacher, Joseph

Rose, Nevada Jack
See Rose, Jack

[La] Rose Noire de Paris [The Black
Rose of Paris]
See Landreaux, Elizabeth Mary

Rose of the Mountains
See Maphis, Rose Lee

[The] Rose of York
See Elizabeth

Rose, Pamela
See Koevoets, Pamela

Rose, Pete[r Edward] 1941-
[B10, BE, PB]
American baseball player
* Hustle, Charlie

Rose, Philip
See Rosenberg, Philip

Rose, Phyllis
See Hoge, Phyllis

Rose, Robert
See Rose, Ian

Rose, Wendy 1948-    [CA, SAT]
American author and illustrator
* Edwards, Bronwen Elizabeth
* Khanshendel, Chiron

Rose-Price, Dennistoun John
Franklyn 1915-1973
[BEW, FC, OCF]
British actor
* Price, Dennis

Roseau, Emie
See Reed, Emeline

Roseau, Marie
See Reed, Mary J.

Rosebery, Lilian
See Routledge, Lilian

Roseboro, Gabby
See Roseboro, John H.

Roseboro, John H. 1933-    [PB]
American baseball player
* Roseboro, Gabby

Rosebrough, Eli E. 19th c.    [BE]
American baseball player
* Rosebrough, Zeke

Rosebrough, Zeke
See Rosebrough, Eli E.

Rosecrans, William Starke
1819-1898    [DNNS, SN]
American army officer
* Old Rosey

Rosecrans, William Starke
(Continued)
* Rosey

Rosedale, Ivan
See Ditmas, Francis Ivan Leslie

Rosegger, P. K.
See Rosegger, Petri Kettenfeier

Rosegger, Peter
See Rosegger, Petri Kettenfeier

Rosegger, Petri Kettenfeier
1843-1918    [WBD]
Austrian poet and author
* Rosegger, P. K.
* Rosegger, Peter

Roselle, Agnes 1870-1948    [BEW]
Canadian-born actress
* Knott, Roselle

Roselle, Amy
See Dacre, Mrs. Arthur

Roseller, David
See Timms, Edward Vivian

Roselli, John
See Sacco, Fillippo

Roseman, Chief
See Roseman, James J.

Roseman, James J. 1856- ?
[BE, EJS]
American baseball player and
manager
* Roseman, Chief

Rosemeyer, Bernd 1909-1938
[EAR]
German auto racer
* [Der] Nebelmeister

Rosen, Albert Leonard 1925-
[BE, EJS, PB]
American baseball player
* Rosen, Flip

Rosen, Doc
See Stacher, Joseph

Rosen, Flip
See Rosen, Albert Leonard

Rosen, Frenchy
See Rosen, William

Rosen, Goodwin George 1912?-
[BE, EJS]
Canadian-born baseball player
* Rosen, Goody

Rosen, Goody
See Rosen, Goodwin George

Rosen, Harry
See Siegel, Benjamin

Rosen, [Captain] James 1894?-
Actor
* [The] King of the Midgets

Rosen, Joseph
See Stacher, Joseph

Rosen, Martin Meyer
See Rosen, Moishe

Rosen, Michael 1946-    [AW]
British author
* [The] Landgrave of Hesse

Rosen, Moishe 1932-    [CA]
American clergyman and author
* Rosen, Martin Meyer

Rosen, Nig
See Stromberg, Harry

Rosen, Stanley 20th c.    [EJS]
American football player
* Rosen, Tex

Rosen, Tex
See Rosen, Stanley

Rosen, William 1882-1961    [EJS]
American horse trainer
* Rosen, Frenchy

Rosenbach, A. S.
See Rosenbach, Abraham Simon
Wolf

Rosenbach, Abraham Simon Wolf
1876-1952    [LC]
American rare book dealer and
author
* Rosenbach, A. S.

Rosenbaum, Borge 1909-    [BBD]
Danish-born pianist
* Borge, Victor

Rosenbaum, Edward 20th c.    [PHM]
American underworld figure
* Rosenbaum, Lucky Eddie

Rosenbaum, Hercel 1902-1937
[JL]
Polish author
* Drzewiecki, Henryk

Rosenbaum, Lucky Eddie
See Rosenbaum, Edward

Rosenberg, Aaron 20th c.
American football player
* Rosenberg, Rosy

Rosenberg, Alexander 20th c.    [EJS]
American basketball player
* Rosenberg, Petey

Rosenberg, Charles G. 19th c.    [PA]
Author
* Q.

Rosenberg, Charley Phil
See Green, Charles

Rosenberg, Elinor Blaisdell 1904-
[WGT]
American author
* Blaisdell, Anne
* Blaisdell, Elinor

Rosenberg, Ethel [Clifford]
[CA, SAT]
American author
* Clifford, Eth
* Penn, Ruth Bonn

Rosenberg, Fred 20th c.    [EE]
Polish-born intelligence agent for
Russia
* Rose, Fred

Rosenberg, George 1864-1936
[ASC]
German-born composer
* Rosey, George

Rosenberg, Gill
See Koestler, Gisela Maria

Rosenberg, Harry 1903-    [FC]
American singer
* [The] Street Singer
* Tracy, Arthur

Rosenberg, Ina 1937-    [FC]
American actress
* Balin, Ina

**Rosenberg, Jerold** 1926-1955
[BEW, EMT]
*American composer and lyricist*
* Ross, Jerry

**Rosenberg, John Paul [Jack]** 1935-
[NAD]
*American educator and developer of
"est" therapy*
* Erhard, Werner

**Rosenberg, Lefty Louis**
*See* Rosenberg, Louis

**Rosenberg, Leon Nikolaevich**
1867-1924 [WBD]
*Russian painter*
* Bakst, Leon Nikolaevich

**Rosenberg, Lester** 1924-    [TR]
*American actor*
* Rawlins, Lester

**Rosenberg, Louis** 20th c.    [BLB]
*American underworld figure*
* Rosenberg, Lefty Louis

**Rosenberg, Michael** 1943?-    [B10]
*American author*
* Meeropol, Michael

**Rosenberg, Nancy Sherman** 1931-
[CA, SAT]
*American author*
* Sherman, Nancy

**Rosenberg, Petey**
*See* Rosenberg, Alexander

**Rosenberg, Philip** 1921-
[BEW, TR]
*American producer*
* Rose, Philip

**Rosenberg, Robert** 1947?-    [B10]
*American author*
* Meeropol, Robert

**Rosenberg, Rosy**
*See* Rosenberg, Aaron

**Rosenberg, William Samuel**
1899-1966    [BEW, EMT]
*American producer and lyricist*
* Rose, Billy

**Rosenblatt, Fred** 1914-    [CA]
*American author*
* Dreyfus, Fred

**Rosenblatt, Martin** 1920-    [FC]
*Polish-American actor*
* Martin, Ross

**Rosenblatt, Richard Andrew** 1925-
[BEW]
*American stage manager, actor,
director*
* Grayson, Richard
* Martin, Richard A.

**Rosenbloom, Maxie** 1904-1956
[BX, EJS, RBE]
*American boxer*
* Rosenbloom, Slapsie Maxie

**Rosenbloom, Slapsie Maxie**
*See* Rosenbloom, Maxie

**Rosenblum, Lawrence** 1908-
[CAP, WW]
*American author*
* Knight, Adam
* Lariar, Lawrence
* Lawrence, Michael
* Stark, Michael

**Rosenblum, Sigmund G.** 1874- ?
[JL]
*Russian-born intelligence agent*
* Reilly, Sidney

**Rosenbusch, Harry**
*See* Rosenbusch, Karl Heinrich
Ferdinand

**Rosenbusch, Karl Heinrich Ferdinand**
1836-1914    [WBD]
*German geologist*
* Rosenbusch, Harry

**Rosenfeld, Alexander Friedrich
Ladislaus** 1872-1945 [WBD]
*Slavonian-born author and
journalist*
* Roda Roda, Alexander Friedrich
    Ladislaus

**Rosenfeld, Bobbie**
*See* Rosenfeld, Fanny

**Rosenfeld, Fanny** 1903-1969
[B10, EJS]
*Canadian track and field athlete*
* Rosenfeld, Bobbie

**Rosenfeld, Friedrich** 1902-    [IAW]
*Austrian-born author*
* Feld

**Rosenfeld, Henry** 1918?-
*American writer*
* Henry, Gig

**Rosenfeld, Lev Borisovich**
1883-1936    [JL, WBD]
*Russian Communist leader*
* Kamenev, Lev Borisovich

**Rosenfeld, Louis Zara** 1910-
[NAA]
*American author*
* Zara, Louis

**Rosenfeld, Lulla** 1914-    [CA]
*American actress and author*
* Adler, Lulla

**Rosenfeld, Monroe H.** 1861-1918
[DAM]
*American composer*
* Belasco, F.

**Rosenfeld, Otto** 1884-1939    [JL]
*Austrian-born psychologist*
* Rank, Otto

**Rosenfelder, Charles H.** 1947-    [FB]
*American football player*
* Rosenfelder, Rosey

**Rosenfelder, Rosey**
*See* Rosenfelder, Charles H.

**Rosehgren, Frank Duane** 1926-
[BEW]
*American playwright*
* Duane, Frank

**Rosenheimer, Arthur** 1916-    [CA]
*American author*
* Knight, Arthur

**Rosenkrantz, Linda** 1934-    [CA]
*American author and columnist*
* Damiano, Laila

**Rosenman, Samuel** 20th c.
*American jurist and advisor to
President Franklin Roosevelt*
* Sammy the Rose

**Rosenmeyer, Alan Otto** 1921-    [CA]
*German-born American psychologist
and author*
* Ross, Alan O[tto]

**Rosenstock, Sami** 1896-1963
[EWL, TCL]
*Rumanian-born French poet and
author*
* Tzara, Tristan

**Rosenthal, Andrew** 20th c.    [CA]
*Author*
* Warren, Andrew [joint
    pseudonym with Warren
    (Stanley) Tute]

**Rosenthal, Beansie**
*See* Rosenthal, Herman

**Rosenthal, Carolyn** 20th c.    [BEW]
*American lyricist*
* Leigh, Carolyn

**Rosenthal, Elinor Marilyn** 1932-
[OP]
*American opera singer*
* Ross, Elinor

**Rosenthal, Eugenie** 1912-    [BEW]
*American lighting and scenic
designer*
* Rosenthal, Jean

**Rosenthal, Herman** ?-1912    [BLB]
*American gambler*
* Rosenthal, Beansie

**Rosenthal, Jack** 1902?-1939
[BEW]
*American comedian*
* Osterman, Jack

**Rosenthal, Jean**
*See* Rosenthal, Eugenie

**Rosenthal, Linda** 20th c.
*American ballerina*
* Merrill, Linda

**Rosenthal, Lyova Haskell** 1929-
[BEW, FC, IPA]
*American actress*
* Grant, Lee

**Rosenthal, M. L.**
*See* Rosenthal, Macha Louis

**Rosenthal, Macha Louis** 1917-
[WYA]
*American author*
* Rosenthal, M. L.

**Rosenthal, Richard A.** 1925-
[CA, WW]
*American author*
* Richards, Allen

**Rosenus, Alan [Harvey]** 1940-    [CA]
*American author*
* Middlebrook, David

**Rosenzweig, Harry** 20th c.
*American politician*
* [The] Diamond Man

**Roser, Bunny**
*See* Roser, John Joseph

**Roser, Emerson Corey** 1918-    [BE]
*American baseball player*
* Roser, Steve

**Roser, John Joseph** 1901-    [BE]
*American baseball player*
* Roser, Bunny

**Roser, Steve**
*See* Roser, Emerson Corey

**Rosevear, John** 1936-    [CA]
*American author*
* Circus, Jim

**Rosewater, Frank** 1856- ?
[SFL, WGT]
*American author*
* Mayoe, Franklin and Marian

**Rosey**
*See* Rosecrans, William Starke

**Rosey, George**
*See* Rosenberg, George

**Roshanara**
*See* Craddock, Olive

**Rosi, Paolo** 1928-    [BX]
*Italian-born boxer*
* Rosi, Paulo

**Rosi, Paulo**
*See* Rosi, Paolo

**Rosicrucian**
*See* Frothingham, Washington

**Rosing, Bodil**
*See* Hammerich, Bodil

**Rosio, Giovanni Vittorio**
1577-1647    [PA]
*Author*
* Erythroeus, James Ficias

**Rosius**
*See* Koes, Friedrick

**Roskam, Karel Lodewijk** 1931-
[IAW]
*Dutch author*
* Dutchman, Kalamu

**Rosko, Emperor**
*See* Pasternak, Mike

**Roskolenko, Harry** 1907-1980
[CA]
*American author*
* Ross, Colin

**Roslavleva, Natalia**
*See* Rene, Natalia

**Roslyn, Guy**
*See* Hatton, Joshua

**Rosmer, Ernst**
*See* Bernstein, Elsa

**Rosmer, Milton**
*See* Lunt, Arthur Milton

**Rosmini-Serbati, Antonio**
1797-1855    [DEP]
*Italian philosopher*
* [The] Italian Froebel

**Rosner, Johnny** 1895-1974
[EJS, RBE]
*American boxer*
* Rosner, Young

**Rosner, Young**
*See* Rosner, Johnny

**Rosny, J. H.** [joint pseudonym with
Seraphin Justin Francois Boex]
*See* Boex, Joseph-Henri Honore

**Rosny, J. H.** [joint pseudonym with
Joseph-Henri Honore Boex]
*See* Boex, Seraphin Justin Francois

**Rosny aine, J. H.**
*See* Boex, Joseph-Henri Honore

**Rosny jeune, J. H.**
*See* Boex, Seraphin Justin Francois

**Rospigliosi, Giulio** 1600-1669
[WBD]
*Pope*
* Clement IX

**Ross, Adrian**
See Ropes, Arthur Reed

**Ross, Alan O[tto]**
See Rosenmeyer, Alan Otto

**Ross, Albert**
See Porter, Linn Boyd

**Ross, Albert Henry** 1891-
[SFL, WGT]
*Author*
* Morison, Frank

**Ross, Allan**
See Warwick, Alan Ross

**Ross, Angus**
See Giggal, Kenneth

**Ross, Annie**
See Short, Annabelle

**Ross, Barnaby** [joint pseudonym with
Daniel Nathan]
See Lepofsky, Manfred

**Ross, Barnaby** [joint pseudonym with
Manfred Lepofsky]
See Nathan, Daniel

**Ross, Barney**
See Rasofsky, Barnet David

**Ross, Betty** 1880-1947 [SC]
*American actress*
* Clarke, Betty Ross

**Ross, Beverly Morgan** 1914-
[CWG, DAM]
*American country-western performer*
* Ross, Buddy

**Ross, Bill**
See Rabinowitz, William Edward

**Ross, Bitter Herb**
See Ross, Herbert George

**Ross, Buck**
See Ross, Lee Ravon

**Ross, Buddy**
See Ross, Beverly Morgan

**Ross, Buster**
See Ross, Chester Franklin

**Ross, Catherine**
See Beaty, Betty

**Ross, Charles**
See Lucania, Salvatore

**Ross, Charles Henry** 1836- ?
[FFF, PA]
*British author*
* Sloper, Ally

**Ross, Charles Isaiah** 1925-
[BWW, NBB]
*American singer*
* [The] Flying Eagle
* Ross, Doc [or Doctor]

**Ross, Charles J.**
See Kelly, Charles J.

**Ross, Chester Franklin** 1903- [BE]
*American baseball player*
* Ross, Buster

**Ross, Chuck** 20th c.
*American author*
* Demos, Erik

**Ross, Churchill**
See Weigle, Ross

**Ross, Clarissa**
See Ross, William Edward Daniel

**Ross, Colin**
See Roskolenko, Harry

**Ross, Curly**
See Ross, Ernest Bertram [Ernie]

**Ross, Dallas**
See Reynolds, Dallas McCord

**Ross, Dana**
See Ross, William Edward Daniel

**Ross, Doc [or Doctor]**
See Ross, Charles Isaiah

**Ross, Edgar** 1949- [RBE]
*American boxer*
* Ross, Mad Dog

**Ross, Elinor**
See Rosenthal, Elinor Marilyn

**Ross, Elizabeth**
See Kuebler-Ross, Elizabeth

**Ross, Ellen** [PA]
*Author*
* Brook, Nelsie

**Ross, Ernest Bertram [Ernie]**
1880-1950 [BE]
*Canadian baseball player*
* Ross, Curly

**Ross, Eulalie Steinmetz** 1910- [CA]
*American author and librarian*
* Steinmetz, Eulalie

**Ross, Eva Florence**
See Stevens, Mrs. Victor

**Ross, Frank [Xavier], Jr.** 1914-
[CA]
*American author*
* Frank, R., Jr.

**Ross, George**
See Morgan-Grenville, Gerard
[Wyndham]

**Ross, George**
See Ross, Isaac

**Ross, Harold Wallace** 1892-1951
[LC]
*American editor*
* Ross, Roughhouse

**Ross, Helaine**
See Daniels, Dorothy

**Ross, Helena**
See Young, Patricia Helena

**Ross, Herbert**
See Tait, Herbert

**Ross, Herbert George** 1931-
*American basketball player*
* Ross, Bitter Herb

**Ross, Howard**
See Rossini, Renato

**Ross, Ian**
See Rossmann, John F[rancis]

**Ross, Isaac** 1907- [WD]
*British playwright*
* Ross, George

**Ross, Ivan T.**
See Rossner, Robert

**Ross, James** [joint pseudonym with
Tony Halliwell]
See Darrington, Hugh

**Ross, James** [joint pseudonym with
Hugh Darrington]
See Halliwell, Tony

**Ross, Jean**
See Hewson, Irene Dale

**Ross, Jerry**
See Rosenberg, Jerold

**Ross, John**
See Coowescoowe [or
Kooweskoowe]

**Ross, Jonathan**
See Rossiter, John

**Ross, Joseph**
See Wrzos, Joseph Henry

**Ross, Katherine**
See Walter, Dorothy Blake

**Ross, Keith** 1899-1960 [F2, FC]
*American actor*
* Keith, Ian

**Ross, Lancelot Patrick** 1906-
[PMJ]
*American singer*
* Ross, Lanny

**Ross, Lanny**
See Ross, Lancelot Patrick

**Ross, Laura**
See Mincieli, Rose Laura

**Ross, Laurence**
See Hyland, Ann

**Ross, Leah**
See Webb, Mary Haydn

**Ross, Lee Ravon** 1915- [BE]
*American baseball player*
* Ross, Buck

**Ross, Leonard [Q.]**
See Rosten, Leo C[alvin]

**Ross, Lucas Tunia** 20th c. [RO2]
*American musician*
* Ross, Tawl

**Ross, Mad Dog**
See Ross, Edgar

**Ross, Marilyn**
See Ross, William Edward Daniel

**Ross, Marilyn Heimberg** 1939-
[CA]
*American author*
* Heimberg, Marilyn Markham

**Ross, Marion** 1898-1966 [SC]
*American actress*
* Roland, Marion

**Ross, Martin**
See Martin, Violet Florence

**Ross, Mary Adelaide Eden**
See Phillpotts, [Mary] Adelaide
[Eden]

**Ross, Mother**
See Davies, Mrs. Christian

**Ross, Mrs. W. S.** [FFF]
*Entertainer*
* Wood, Lillian

**Ross, Nancy**
See DeRoin, Nancy

**Ross, Oriel**
See Swinstead, Muriel

**Ross, Patricia**
See Wood, Patricia E. W.

**Ross, Paul**
See Crawford, William [Elbert]

**Ross, Philipp Peter** 1657-1705
[WBD]
*German painter*
* Rosa di Tivoli

**Ross, Robert W.** 1922- [CA]
*American author and clergyman*
* Power-Ross, Robert W.

**Ross, Roughhouse**
See Ross, Harold Wallace

**Ross, Shirley**
See Gaunt, Bernice

**Ross, Sutherland**
See Callard, Thomas Henry

**Ross, T. J.**
See Ross, Theodore John

**Ross, Tawl**
See Ross, Lucas Tunia

**Ross, Theodore John** 1924- [SFL]
*American author*
* Ross, T. J.

**Ross, Virginia**
See Conolly, Mrs. Edward J.

**Ross, W. E. D.**
See Ross, William Edward Daniel

**Ross, Ward**
See Fearn, John Russell

**Ross, William**
See Gonzalez, Gonzalo

**Ross, William Edward Daniel**
1912- [CA, SFL]
*Canadian author*
* Ames, Leslie
* Dana, Rose
* Dorset, Ruth
* Gilmer, Ann
* Randolph, Ellen
* Roberts, Dan
* Ross, Clarissa
* Ross, Dana
* Ross, Marilyn
* Ross, W. E. D.
* Rossiter, Jane
* Steel, Tex
* Williams, Rose

**Ross, William Stewart** 20th c.
[WWL]
*British author*
* Saladin

**Ross, Z. H.**
See Ross, Zola Helen

**Ross, Zola Helen** 1912- [CA, WW]
*American author*
* Arre, Helen
* Iles, Bert
* Ross, Z. H.

**Ross-Church, Florence M.** 19th c.
[FFF]
*Author*
* Marryatt, Florence

**Ross-Craig, Stella** 1906- [ART]
*British artist*
* S. R. C.

**Ross-Macdonald, Malcolm J[ohn]**
See Macdonald, Malcolm John
Ross

**Ross Williamson, Hugh** 1901-
[CA]
*British playwright*
* Rossiter, Ian

**Rossa, Mrs. O'Donovan**   [PA]
*Author*
* O'Donovan, Mrs.

**Rosse, Ian**
*See* Straker, John Foster

**Rosse, Susanna**
*See* Connolly, Vivian

**Rossel, Roger**
*See* Vandeputte, Roger

**Rosselet, Andre** 1915-   [ART]
*Swiss artist*
* R.

**Rossen, Punch**
*See* Rossen, Ronnie

**Rossen, Ronnie** 20th c.   [GW]
*American rodeo performer*
* Rossen, Punch

**Rosser, Lee** 20th c.   [GW]
*American rodeo performer*
* Rosser, Rounder

**Rosser, Rounder**
*See* Rosser, Lee

**Rosset, Barnet Lee, Jr.** 1922-
[BEW]
*American editor*
* Rosset, Barney

**Rosset, Barney**
*See* Rosset, Barnet Lee, Jr.

**Rosset, Benjamin Charles** 1910-
[CA]
*Russian-born author*
* Ozy

**Rossetti, Christina Georgina**
1830-1894   [FFF, WBD]
*British poet*
* Alleyne [or Allyn?], Ellen

**Rossetti, Gino**
*See* Rossetti, Louis A.

**Rossetti, Louis A.** 1930?-   [B10]
*American architect*
* Rossetti, Gino

**Rossetti, Minerva**
*See* Rowland, D[onald] S[ydney]

**Rossi, Aga**
*See* Agarossi, Elena

**Rossi, Francis** 20th c.   [RO2]
*British musician*
* Rossi, Mike

**Rossi, Francois**
*See* Abiatt, Roland

**Rossi, Girolamo** 1539-1607   [PA]
*Author*
* Rubens

**Rossi, Mike**
*See* Rossi, Francis

**Rossi, Salomone** 1565?-1628?
[WBD]
*Italian-born composer*
* [L']Ebreo

**Rossi, Sanna Morrison Barlow**
1917-   [CA]
*American author*
* Barlow, Sanna Morrison

**Rossi, Tommy**
*See* Cuiringione, Tommy

**Rossi-Drago, Eleonora**
*See* Omiccioli, Palmina

**Rossignol, Felix Ludger** 1839-1903
[BBD]
*French composer*
* De Joncieres, Victorin

**Rossignol, Jean Antoine** 1759-1802
[HN]
*French army officer*
* [The] Devil of Vendee

**Rossillon, Marius** 1880?-1946
[WEC]
*French cartoonist*
* O'Galop [At the Gallop]

**Rossini, Gioachino Antonio**
1792-1868   [DNNS, SN]
*Italian composer*
* [The] Swan of Pesaro

**Rossini, Renato** 20th c.   [WF]
*Italian actor*
* Ross, Howard

**Rossiter, Anna M. S.**   [PA]
*Author*
* Cushman, Lilla N.

**Rossiter, Anthony** 1926-   [ART]
*British painter*
* A. R.

**Rossiter, Ian**
*See* Ross Williamson, Hugh

**Rossiter, Jane**
*See* Ross, William Edward Daniel

**Rossiter, John** 1916-   [CA]
*British author*
* Ross, Jonathan

**Rossiter, Oscar**
*See* Skeels, Vernon H.

**Rossiter, Will**
*See* Williams, W. R.

**Rossler, Ernestine** 1861-1936   [SC]
*Czech-born actress and opera singer*
* Schumann-Heink, Ernestine

**Rossman, Evelyn**
*See* Rothchild, Sylvia

**Rossmann, John F[rancis]** 1942-
[CA]
*American author*
* Ross, Ian

**Rossner, Robert** 1932-   [CA]
*American author and educator*
* Ross, Ivan T.

**[Il] Rosso Fiorentino**
*See* De Rossi, Giovanni Battista

**Rosso, Gustavo** 1881-1950   [WEC]
*Italian cartoonist and illustrator*
* Gustavino [Little Gustave]

**Rostand, Louise Rose Etiennette**
1871-1953   [WBD]
*French poet*
* Gerard, Rosemonde

**Rostand, Robert**
*See* Hopkins, Robert

**Rosten, Leo C[alvin]** 1908-
[AW, CA, LC]
*American author and playwright*
* Ross, Leonard [Q.]

**Rostrevor, George**
*See* Hamilton, George Rostrevor

**Rostron, P. R.**
*See* Hulbert, Joan Margery

**Rostron, Primrose**
*See* Hulbert, Joan Margery

**Rostropovich, Mstislav** 1927?-
*Russian musician*
* Rostropovich, Slava

**Rostropovich, Slava**
*See* Rostropovich, Mstislav

**Rotarius**
*See* Kerekes, Tibor

**Rotation Slim**
*See* Hairston, George

**Rotella, Domenico** 1918-   [CAR]
*Italian artist*
* Rotella, Mimmo

**Rotella, Mimmo**
*See* Rotella, Domenico

**Roth, Alexander**
*See* Dunner, Joseph

**Roth, Arthur J[oseph]** 1925-   [CA]
*American author*
* Mara, Barney
* McGurk, Slater
* Pomeroy, Pete

**Roth, Bobby**
*See* Roth, Herman

**Roth, Braggo**
*See* Roth, Robert Frank

**Roth, Christian** 1945-   [IAW]
*Swiss author and columnist*
* Brdlbrmpft

**Roth, Herman** 20th c.   [OBW]
*American baseball player*
* Roth, Bobby

**Roth, Holly** 1916-1964
[CA, CC, EMD]
*American author*
* Ballard, K. G.
* Merrill, P. J.

**Roth, Karen**
*See* Sellers, Connie Leslie, Jr.

**Roth, Lillian**
*See* Rutstein, Lillian

**Roth, Robert**
*See* Sellers, Connie Leslie, Jr.

**Roth, Robert Frank** 1892-1936
[BE]
*American baseball player*
* Roth, Braggo

**Roth, Samuel** 1894-1974   [CA]
*Austrian-born American poet, editor, publisher*
* Lockridge, Norman

**Rothafel, Roxy**
*See* Rothapfel, Samuel L.

**Rothafel, S. L.**
*See* Rothapfel, Samuel L.

**Rothapfel, Samuel L.** 1882-1936
[WA, WEF]
*American theatre manager*
* Rothafel, Roxy
* Rothafel, S. L.

**Rothchild, Jeroboam** 1885-1944
[JL]
*French government official*
* Mandel, Georges

**Rothchild, Sylvia** 1923-   [CA]
*American author*
* Rossman, Evelyn

**Rothenstein, Albert Daniel**
1883-1953   [THR]
*British artist and designer*
* Rutherston, Albert Daniel

**Rotherham, Thomas** 1423-1500
[WBD]
*British prelate*
* Scott, Thomas

**Rothermel, Bobby**
*See* Rothermel, Edward Hill

**Rothermel, Edward Hill** 1870- ?
[BE]
*American baseball player*
* Rothermel, Bobby

**Rothery, Agnes Edwards**
*See* Pratt, Agnes Rothery

**Rothery, Brian** 1934-   [WD]
*Irish author*
* Dyer, Brian [joint pseudonym
with Orlando R(alph) Petrocelli]

**Rothko, Mark**
*See* Rothkowitz [or Rothkovich],
Marcus

**Rothkopf, Louis** 20th c.   [PHM]
*American underworld figure*
* Rhody, Louis
* Zarumba, Louis

**Rothkowitz [or Rothkovich], Marcus**
1903-1970
*Russian-born American artist*
* Rothko, Mark

**Rothmaler, Karl von**
*See* Einem, Karl von

**Rothman, Arnold** 1925-   [ITA]
*American actor and writer*
* Arnold, Danny

**Rothman, Judith**
*See* Peters, Maureen

**Rothman, Milton A.** 1919-   [WGT]
*American author*
* Gregor, Lee [joint pseudonym
with Frederik Pohl]

**Rothmuller, Aron Marko** 1908-
[CA]
*Yugoslav-born American opera singer and educator*
* Kinor, Jehuda

**Rothmund, Wilhelmino** 1917-
[BEW]
*American actress*
* Worth, Billie

**Rothschild, Dorothy** 1893-1967
[IPA]
*American author*
* Parker, Dorothy

**Rothschild, J. Monroe** 1891-1963
[SC]
*American actor*
* Childs, Monroe

**Rothstein, Arnold** 1882-1928
[BLB, MM]
*American underworld figure*
* A. R.
* [The] Big Bankroll
* Big, Mr.
* [The] Brain
* [The] Man to See
* [The] Man Uptown

**Rothstein, Arnold** (Continued)
* Mr. A.

**Rothweiler, Paul R[oger]** 1931-
[CA]
*American author*
* Ruyerson, James Paul

**Rothwell, Henry Talbot** 1921-
[AW]
*British author*
* Talbot, Henry

**Rothwell, William H.** 1880-1927
[BX, RBE]
*American boxer*
* Corbett, Young

**Rotrou, Jean de** 1609-1650
[HN, SN]
*French playwright*
* [The] Father of the French
  Drama
* [The] Founder of the French
  Theatre

**Rotsler, William** 1926-
[ESF, WGT]
*American author and artist*
* Arrow, William [house
  pseudonym, Ballantine Books]
* Hall, John Ryder

**Rotten, Johnny**
See Lydon, John

**Roudebush, Earl David** 1891- ?
[BBH]
*American basketball coach*
* Roudebush, Roudie

**Roudebush, Roudie**
See Roudebush, Earl David

**Rouel, Joseph Jules** [PA]
*Author*
* J. J. R.

**Rouget de Lisle, Claude Joseph**
1760-1836 [HN]
*French army officer and composer*
* [The] Tyrtaeus of France

**Rough and Ready**
See Taylor, Zachary

**Rough Hewer**
See Yates, Robert

**Rough House Haynes**
See Haynes, Leroy H.

**[The] Rough Rider**
See Roosevelt, Theodore [Teddy]

**Roughsey, Dick** 1921?-
[ICB]
*Australian illustrator*
* Goobalathaldin [tribal name]

**Rouher, Eugene** 1813-1884 [FFF]
*French prime minister*
* Vice Emperor

**Rouillon, Paul**
See Malossis, Auguste Paul Poulet

**Roulon, Harry** 1891-1940 [SC]
*American actor*
* Murray, J. Harold

**Roulston, Rolly**
See Roulston, William Orville

**Roulston, William Orville** 1911-
[CEI]
*Canadian-born hockey player*
* Roulston, Rolly

**Roumanis, George Zackery** 1929-
[EJ]
*American jazz musician*
* Romanis, George Zackery

**Roumer, Emile** 1903- [CW]
*Haitian poet*
* Niger, Emilius

**Roumi**
See Aiwas, Dzati

**[The] Round Man**
See Northey, Ronald James

**[The] Round Mound of Sound**
See Price, Kenny

**[The] Round Mound of Sound**
See Sawell, Larry

**Round, William Marshall Fitts**
1845-1906 [PA]
*American author and journalist*
* Pennot, [Rev.] Peter

**Rounesville, Robert** 1914-1974
[SC]
*American actor and opera singer*
* Field, Robert

**Rourke, James**
See Trimble, Louis P[reston]

**Rourke, Louise Musgrave** 20th c.
[WWL]
*British author*
* Dickerson-Watkins, L.

**Rous [or Rowse], Francis**
1579-1659 [SN]
*British politician*
* Another Proteus
* [That] Old Jew of Eton

**Rous, Helen**
See Shaw, Helen

**Rouse, Raymond** 1936- [AES]
*Welsh soccer player*
* Rouse, Vic

**Rouse, Rebel**
See Rouse, Stephen John

**Rouse, Stephen John** 1949- [DC]
*Welsh-born cricketer*
* Rouse, Rebel

**Rouse, Vic**
See Rouse, Raymond

**Rousseau, Camille** 1921- [CW]
*West Indian poet*
* Porto, Louis

**Rousseau, Henri** 1844-1910 [WBD]
*French painter*
* [Le] Douanier

**Rousseau, J. J.**
See Nienaber, Petrus Johannes

**Rousseau, Jean-Jacques**
1712-1778 [DNNF, DNNS, SN]
*Swiss-French philosopher*
* [The] Citizen of Geneva
* [The] Father of Sentiment
* J. J.
* [The] Melancholy Jacques

**Rousseau, Odette** 1901-1974
[FIR, SC]
*French actress and singer*
* Florelle [or Florette?]

**[The] Rousseau of China**
See K'ang Yu-wei

**[The] Rousseau of the Gutter**
See Restif, Nicolas Edme

**Rousseau, Victor**
See Emanuel, Victor Rousseau

**Roussel, Simone** 1920-
[BDF, FC, ITA]
*French actress*
* Morgan, Michele

**Roussimoff, Andre** 20th c.
*French wrestler*
* Andre the Giant

**Roustabout**
See Hoffmann, Phil

**Routhier, [Sir] Adolphe Basile** 1839-
? [ALY]
*Canadian author*
* Piquetort, Jean

**Routledge, Lilian** 20th c. [THR]
*British actress*
* Rosebery, Lilian

**Routsong, Alma** 1924- [CA]
*American author*
* Miller, Isabel

**Rouverol, Jean**
See Butler, Jean Rouverol

**Roux, Paul Pierre** 1861-1940
[EWL]
*French poet and playwright*
* Saint Pol-Roux

**Rouzier, Maximilien Louis Severin**
1846-1927 [CW]
*Haitian journalist and author*
* Saint Mexant
* Semexant

**[The] Rover Center**
See McEwan, John J.

**Rover, Max**
See Murray, Edgar Joyce

**Rovin, Alex**
See Russo, Albert

**Rovin, Ben**
See Clevenger, Ernest Allen, Jr.

**[The] Roving Englishman**
See Murray, E. C. Greenville

**Rovira**
See Acha Sanz, Raul

**Row, Bolton**
See Ponsonby, Spencer Cecil
Brabazon

**Row, Saville**
See Clark, Saville

**Rowan, David [Dave]**
See Drohan, David

**Rowan, Deirdre**
See Williams, Jeanne

**Rowan-Hamilton, Sydney Orme**
1877- ? [LAO]
*British author and playwright*
* Orme, Rowan

**Rowans, Virginia**
See Tanner, Edward Everett, III

**Rowbotham, Sheila** 1943- [CA]
*British author and political activist*
* Turner, Sheila

**Rowbotham, William** 1914?-
[BF, FC]
*British comic actor*
* Owen, Bill

**Rowdy Bill Coughlin**
See Coughlin, Bill

**Rowdy Richard Bartell**
See Bartell, Richard William

**Rowe, Alice E.**
See Rowe, John Gabriel

**Rowe, Bolton**
See Stephenson, Benjamin Charles

**Rowe, Elizabeth** 1674-1737
[DEL, PA]
*British author*
* Philomela

**Rowe, Frank** 20th c. [GW]
*American rodeo performer*
* Rowe, Little Beaver

**Rowe, Harland Stimson** 1896-1969
[BE]
*American baseball player*
* Rowe, Hypie

**Rowe, Homie**
See Rowe, Norman

**Rowe, Hypie**
See Rowe, Harland Stimson

**Rowe, John Gabriel** 1873- ? [MBF]
*British author*
* Austin, Mortimer
* Bright, James
* Dunstan, Gregory
* Ferris, Arthur
* Gabriel, John
* Lewis, Charles
* Ransome, Charles A.
* Rowe, Alice E.
* Walters, T. B.

**Rowe, Little Beaver**
See Rowe, Frank

**Rowe, Lynwood Thomas**
1910?-1961 [AS, BE, PB]
*American baseball player*
* Rowe, Schoolboy

**Rowe, Margaret [Kevin]** 1920-
[CA]
*Australian-born author*
* Teresa Margaret, [Sister]

**Rowe, Nicholas** [FFF, PA]
*American writer*
* Mohawk

**Rowe, Norman** 20th c. [GW]
*American rodeo performer*
* Rowe, Homie

**Rowe, Saville**
See Scott, Clement William

**Rowe, Schoolboy**
See Rowe, Lynwood Thomas

**Rowe, Stephen**
See Stares, John Edward Spencer

**Rowe, Vivian C[laud]** 1902-1978
[CA]
*British author*
* Hooton, Charles

**Rowe, W.** 20th c. [MBF]
*British author*
* Bingham, [Major] Arthur

**Rowell, Bama**
See Rowell, Carvel William

**Rowell, Carvel William** 1916-   [BE]
*American baseball player*
* Rowell, Bama

**Rowing U.S.A., Mr.**
See   Goes, Clifford T.

**Rowland, Clarence Henry**
1879-1969   [AS, BTB, PB]
*American baseball executive*
* Rowland, Pants
* Svengali

**Rowland, D.** 1778-1859   [PA]
*Author*
* [A] Layman

**Rowland, D[onald] S[ydney]** 1928-
[CA]
*British author*
* Adams, Annette
* Bassett, Jack
* Baxter, Hazel
* Benton, Karla
* Berry, Helen
* Brant, Lewis
* Bray, Alison
* Brayce, William
* Brockley, Fenton
* Bronson, Oliver
* Buchanan, Chuck
* Caley, Rod
* Carlton, Roger
* Cleve, Janita
* Court, Sharon
* Craig, Vera
* Craille, Wesley
* Dryden, John
* Fenton, Freda
* Field, Charles
* Garner, Graham
* Kroll, Burt
* Langley, Helen
* Lansing, Henry
* Lant, Harvey
* Lynn, Irene
* Madison, Hank
* Mason, Chuck
* McHugh, Stuart
* Morgan, G. J.
* Murray, Edna
* Page, Lorna
* Patterson, Olive
* Porter, Alvin
* Random, Alex
* Rimmer, W. J.
* Rix, Donna
* Rockwell, Matt
* Roscoe, Charles
* Rossetti, Minerva
* Scott, Norford
* Scott, Valerie
* Segundo, Bart
* Shaul, Frank
* Spurr, Clinton
* Starr, Roland
* Stevens, J. D.
* Suffling, Mark
* Talbot, Kay
* Travers, Will
* Vine, Sarah
* Vinson, Elaine
* Walters, Rick
* Webb, Neil

**Rowland, E. G.**
See   Girolami, Enzo

**Rowland, Grey**
See   Rowland-Brown, Lilian

**Rowland, Iris**
See   Roberts, Irene M.

**Rowland, Pants**
See   Rowland, Clarence Henry

**Rowland, Roland** 1918?-
*British industrialist*
* Rowland, Tiny

**Rowland, Tiny**
See   Rowland, Roland

**Rowland, W.**
See   Winter, Holmes Edwin
Cornelius

**Rowland-Brown, Lilian** 1863- ?
[LAO]
*British author*
* Rowland, Grey

**Rowlands, Cadwallader**
See   Hotten, John Camden

**Rowlands, Cecil** 1856-1914   [BEW]
*Playwright*
* Raleigh, Cecil

**Rowlands, Effie Adelaide**
See   Albanesi, [Madame] Effie
Maria [Henderson]

**Rowlands, John** 1841-1904
[FFF, IPA]
*Welsh explorer*
* [The] Cortez of Africa
* Stanley, Henry Morton

**Rowlands, Peter**
See   Lovell, Mark

**Rowles, Mary Elizabeth** 20th c.
[BEW]
*American actress*
* Rowles, Polly

**Rowles, Polly**
See   Rowles, Mary Elizabeth

**Rowley, Ames Dor[r]ance**
See   Lovecraft, Howard Phillips

**Rowley, Charles, Jr.**   [PA]
*Author*
* Gilderoy, Roland

**Rowley, Herbert** 1883?-1964
[BEW]
*Theatrical performer*
* Bond, Bert

**Rowley, Richard**
See   Williams, Richard Valentine

**Rowley, Thomas**
See   Chatterton, Thomas

**Rowley, Thomas**
See   Pauker, John

**Rowse, A. L.**
See   Rowse, Alfred Leslie

**Rowse, Alfred Leslie** 1903-   [LC]
*British author and historian*
* Rowse, A. L.

**Roxalana**
See   Davenport, Elizabeth

**[A] Roxbury Farmer**
See   Lowell, John

**Roy**
See   Willis, Nathaniel Parker

**Roy, Brandon**
See   Barclay, Florence Louisa
Charlesworth

**Roy, Dan**
See   Lotinga, Ernest

**Roy, Ewell Paul** 1929-   [CA]
*American agricultural economist
and author*
* Bonnette, Victor
* Lemoine, Ernest

**Roy, Gordon**
See   Wallace, Helen

**Roy, Jack**
See   Cohen, Jacob

**Roy, Julien**
See   Macinnes, Tom

**Roy, Jumbo**
See   Roy, Norm[an Brooks]

**Roy, Lee**
See   Antonini, Leo

**Roy, Liam**
See   Scarry, Patricia [Murphy]
[Patsy]

**Roy, Luxymon**
See   Homan, Samuel H.

**Roy, Norm[an Brooks]** 1928-   [BE]
*American baseball player*
* Roy, Jumbo

**Roy, Percy Gordon**
See   Wolfgang, Otto

**Roy, Ralph**
See   Badger, Joseph E.

**Roy, Ramala Pratap**
See   Bhosale, Yeshwantrao P.

**Roy, Rammohun** 1780-1833   [PA]
*Author*
* [The] Rajah

**Royaards, Wilhelm** 1867?-1929
[BEW]
*Actor and director*
* Royaards, William

**Royaards, William**
See   Royaards, Wilhelm

**[The] Royal Butcher**
See   Henry VIII

**Royal, D.**
See   DuBreuil, Elizabeth Lorinda

**[A] Royal Field Leech**
See   Symonds, Francis Addington

**[The] Royal Martyr**
See   Charles I

**[The] Royal Midas**
See   Dennis, John

**Royal 'Prentice in the Art of Poesy**
See   James I

**Royal, Ralph**
See   Abarbanell, Jacob

**Royal, Ted**
See   Dewar, Ted Royal

**[The] Royal Violinist**
See   Southgate, Elsie

**[The] Royalist Butcher**
See   De Lasseran-Massencome,
Blaise

**Royce, Forrest** 1911-1965   [SC]
*American stunt performer*
* Royce, Frosty

**Royce, Frosty**
See   Royce, Forrest

**Royce, Julian**
See   Gardner, Julian

**Royce, Kenneth**
See   Gandley, Kenneth Royce

**Royde, Frank**
See   Howroyd, Frank

**Royer**
See   Hastings, Louis Royer

**Royer, Harry** 1889-1951   [SC]
*American actor*
* Royer, Missouri

**Royer, Missouri**
See   Royer, Harry

**Royer, Robb** 20th c.   [RO2]
*American musician and songwriter*
* Wilson, Robb

**Royster, Jeron Kennis** 1952-
[SMG]
*American baseball player*
* Bird, J.
* Royster, Jerry

**Royster, Jerry**
See   Royster, Jeron Kennis

**Royston, Roy**
See   Crowden, Roy

**Royz, Olesh** 1898-1976   [JL]
*Polish-born American political
figure*
* Rose, Alex

**Roze, Raymond**
See   Roze-Perkins, J. H. Raymond

**Roze-Perkins, J. H. Raymond**
1875-1920   [BBD]
*British composer*
* Roze, Raymond

**Rozelle, Alvin Ray** 1926-   [FB, IPA]
*American football commissioner*
* [The] Boy Commissioner
* Rozelle, Pete

**Rozelle, Pete**
See   Rozelle, Alvin Ray

**Rozelle, Richard** 20th c.   [RBE]
*American boxer*
* [The] Fly

**Rozema, David Scott [Dave]** 1956-
[SMG]
*American baseball player*
* [The] Rose

**Rozier, Jacques**
See   Paton, Emilie

**Ruano, Argimiro** 1924-   [CA]
*Spanish-born author*
* Ruano, Nazario

**Ruano, Nazario**
See   Ruano, Argimiro

**Rubashov, Schneor Zalman**
1889-1974   [CA]
*Israeli president, poet, historian*
* Shazar, [Schneor] Zalman

**[The] Rubber Duck**
See   Fries, William [Bill]

**[The] Rubber King**
See   Morris, Harry

**[The] Rubber Lion**
See   Blomberg, Werner von

**Rubber Man McDole**
See   McDole, Ron

**Rubel, Edith**
See Mapother, Edith Rubel

**Ruben, Lynsey** 1951-
British composer and singer
* De Paul, Lynsey

**Ruben, William S.** 20th c.
[SFL, WGT]
Author
* Shannon, Fred

**Rubens**
See Rossi, Girolamo

**Rubens, Alma**
See Porrata Doria de Rincon,
Providencia

**Rubens, Alma**
See Smith, Alma

**[The] Rubens of France**
See Delacroix, Ferdinand Victor
Eugene

**Rubens, Peter Paul** 1577-1640
[HN, RH]
Flemish painter
* [Le] Gentilhomme de la Peinture
* [The] Gentleman Painter

**Rubenstein, Adelaide** 1857?-1941
[BEW]
British actress
* Prince, Adelaide

**Rubenstein, Edana** 1919-  [FC]
South African-born actress
* Romney, Edana

**Rubenstein, Jacob** 1911-1967  [JL]
American nightclub owner who
killed Lee Harvey Oswald
* Ruby, Jack

**Ruberto, John Edward** 1946-
[SMG]
American baseball coach
* Ruberto, Sonny

**Ruberto, Sonny**
See Ruberto, John Edward

**Rubicon**
See Lunn, Arnold [Henry Moore]

**Rubimor**
See Moreira, Ruben

**Rubin, Charles J.** 1950-  [CA]
American author
* Buzzle, Buck

**Rubin, Cynthia Elyce** 1944-  [CA]
American author
* Alplaus, N. Y. [joint pseudonym
with Jerome Rubin]

**Rubin, Gail** 1942-  [CA]
American author
* Bereny, Gail Rubin

**Rubin, Harold**
See Kane, Francis

**Rubin, Jacob A.** 1910-1972  [CA]
Austrian-born American editor,
journalist, author
* Odem, J.

**Rubin, Jerome** 20th c.   [CA]
American author
* Alplaus, N. Y. [joint pseudonym
with Cynthia Elyce Rubin]

**Rubin, Michael Stewart** 1929-
[BEW, EMT, TR]
American playwright and librettist
* Stewart, Michael

**Rubini, Diane** 1890-1969   [SC]
American actress
* De Aubry, Diane

**Rubino, Matthew** 20th c.
American underworld figure
* Rubino, Mike

**Rubino, Mike**
See Rubino, Matthew

**Rubinstein, Chip**
See Rubinstein, Matthew N.

**Rubinstein, Harry** 1895-1974
[BEW, EMT]
American composer and librettist
* Ruby, Harry

**Rubinstein, Matthew N.** 1921-
[WFA]
American clothing manufacturer
* Rubinstein, Chip

**Rubinstein, S[amuel] Leonard**
1922-  [CA]
American author
* Weber, Rubin [joint pseudonym
with Robert G. Weaver]

**Rubio, Antonio** 20th c.   [GS]
Spanish bullfighter
* Macandro

**Rubio de Valencia [Redhead of
Valencia]**
See Villa y Mari, Francisco

**Rubio, Julio**
See Buyana, Mohamed

**Rubios, Jose**
See Maloney, Terry

**Ruby**
See Pithawalla, Maneck B.

**Ruby, B. F.**
See Pratt, [Murray] Fletcher

**Ruby, Harry**
See Rubinstein, Harry

**Ruby, Jack**
See Rubenstein, Jacob

**Ruby, Martin** 1922-  [CFH]
American-born football player
* Ruby, Rube

**Ruby Robert Fitzsimmons**
See Fitzsimmons, Robert [Bob]

**Ruby, Rube**
See Ruby, Martin

**Ruby, Texas**
See Fox, Ruby Owens

**Ruby, Thelma**
See Wigoder, Thelma

**Ruccellai, Benardo** 1449-1514
[PA]
Author
* Oricellarius

**Ruchrath [or Ruchrad], Johannes**
?-1481?  [WBD]
German religious reformer
* John of Wesel

**Ruck, Berta**
See Oliver, Amy Roberta [Ruck]

**Rucker, Annabelle** 1904-1967   [SC]
American actress
* Williams, Annabelle

**Rucker, George Napoleon**
1884-1970   [BE, PB]
American baseball player
* Rucker, Nap

**Rucker, Henry** 1921-   [IBW]
American psychic
* [The] Ghost Breaker

**Rucker, John Joel** 1917-   [BE]
American baseball player
* [The] Crabapple Comet

**Rucker, Nap**
See Rucker, George Napoleon

**Ruckser, George Brinton McClellan**
1863-1935   [BE]
American baseball player
* Rooks, George Brinton McClellan

**Ruckstull, F[red] Wellington** 1853-
?  [NAA]
French-born writer and editor
* Arbeiter, Petronius

**Rudd, Margaret**
See Newlin, Margaret Rudd

**Rude, Ike** 1894-  [GW]
American rodeo performer
* Rude, Jitney

**Rude, Jitney**
See Rude, Ike

**Rudensky, Morris**
See Friedman, Max Motel

**Rudensky, Red**
See Friedman, Max Motel

**Ruderman, Rudy**
See Ruderman, Seymour George

**Ruderman, Seymour George** 1926-
[ASC]
American composer
* Ruderman, Rudy

**Rudersdorff, Richard**   [FFF]
Entertainer
* Mansfield, Richard

**Rudge, Letty** 1862-1923   [THR]
British actress and dancer
* Lind, Letty

**Rudhyar, Dane**
See Chenneviere, Daniel

**Rudie, Evelyn**
See Bernauer, Evelyn Rudie

**Rudloff, Leo**
See Von Rudloff, Alfred Felix

**Rudnick, George** ?-1940
[BLB, PHM]
American underworld figure
* Rudnick, Whitey

**Rudnick, Whitey**
See Rudnick, George

**Rudolf II [or Rudolph]** 1552-1612
[DHA, FFF, SN]
Emperor of Germany
* [The] German Trimegistus
* [The] Hermes Trismegistus of
Germany
* [The] Prince of Alchemy

**Rudolph, Al[bert]** 1894-1966
[AS, BX, EJS]
American boxer
* McCoy, Al

**Rudolph, Baldy**
See Rudolph, Richard

**Rudolph, Dutch**
See Rudolph, John Herman

**Rudolph, John Herman** 1882-1967
[BE]
American baseball player
* Rudolph, Dutch

**Rudolph, Marvin** 1938-1979   [BB]
American basketball official
* Hollywood, Mr.
* Rudolph, Mendy

**Rudolph, Mendy**
See Rudolph, Marvin

**Rudolph, Richard** 1887-1949
[BE, PB]
American baseball player
* Rudolph, Baldy

**Rudolph, Skeeter**
See Rudolph, Wilma Glodean
Ward

**Rudolph, Wilma Glodean Ward**
1940-  [BBH, IBW, SR]
American track and field athlete
* [The] Black Gazelle
* [The] Black Pearl
* [La] Gazelle
* Rudolph, Skeeter
* Rudolph, Wondrous Wilma
* [The] World's Fastest Woman

**Rudolph, Wondrous Wilma**
See Rudolph, Wilma Glodean
Ward

**Rudomin, Esther**
See Hautzig, Esther Rudomin

**Rudstrom, Calvin** 1895-   [CA]
American author
* Rutstrum, Calvin

**Rueckert, Friedrich** 1788-1866
[WBD]
German poet
* Raimar, Freimund

**Ruedi, Norma Paul**
See Ainsworth, Norma

**Ruehle, George Robert** 1932-
[CWG]
American country-western performer
* Reagan, Bobby

**Ruel, Herold Dominic** 1896-1963
[AS, BE, PB]
American baseball player
* Ruel, Muddy

**Ruel, Muddy**
See Ruel, Herold Dominic

**Rueleus, Mme. C.** ?-1878   [PA]
Author
* Graviere, Caroline

**Ruell, Patrick**
See Hill, Reginald [Charles]

**Ruellan, Andre** 1922-   [ESF]
French author
* Dupont, Kurt
* Louvigny, Andre
* Steiner, Kurt
* Vigan, Luc
* Wargar, Kurt

**Ruether, Dutch**
See Ruether, Walter Henry

**Ruether, Walter Henry** 1893-1970
[AS, BE, PB]
American baseball player
* Ruether, Dutch

**Ruf, Frank** 1909-  [HCA]
*American actor*
* Faylen, Frank

**Ruffin, David** 20th c.  [IBW]
*American singer, dancer, bandleader*
* King David

**Ruffin, Penelope** 20th c.  [IBW]
*American tour guide*
* Ruffin, Penny

**Ruffin, Penny**
See Ruffin, Penelope

**Ruffing, Charles Herbert** 1904-
[BE, DGS, PB]
*American baseball player*
* Ruffing, Red

**Ruffing, Red**
See Ruffing, Charles Herbert

**[The] Ruffle**
See Tegner, Henry [Stuart]

**Ruffner, Budge**
See Ruffner, Lester Ward

**Ruffner, Lester Ward** 1918-  [CA]
*American author*
* Ruffner, Budge

**Ruffo, Titta**
See Titta, Ruffo Cafiero

**Rufus [The Red]**
See Clare, Gilbert de

**Rufus**
See Otto II [or Otho]

**Rufus**
See William II

**Rugby, Nym**
See Robinson, Nugent

**[The] Rugged Lion [Al Haidara]**
See Ali

**Ruhamah**
See Scudamore, Lily

**Ruhamah**
See Skidmore, Harriet M.

**Ruheni, Mwangi**
See Muraguri, Nicholas

**Ruhland, Stanley** 20th c.  [BEW]
*American actor*
* Gaige, Truman

**Ruhlmann, Eugene Augustus**
1861-1918  [BEW, BMH, CED]
*American entertainer*
* [The] Dandy Coloured Coon
* Stratton, Eugene

**Ruhnke, Claude**
See Ruhnke, Kent

**Ruhnke, Kent** 1952-  [SMG]
*Canadian-born hockey player*
* Ruhnke, Claude

**Ruiz, Chico**
See Ruiz, Hiraldo Sablon

**Ruiz, Henry** 20th c.
*Nicaraguan guerrilla leader*
* Modesto

**Ruiz, Hiraldo Sablon** 1938-1972
[BE, PB]
*Cuban-born baseball player*
* Ruiz, Chico

**Ruiz, Jose** 20th c.  [GS]
*Spanish bullfighter*
* [El] Calatraveno [The Man from Calatrava]

**Ruiz, Juan** 1283?-1351?  [WBD]
*Spanish poet*
* [The] Archpriest of Hita

**Ruiz, Manuel** 20th c.  [GS]
*Spanish bullfighter*
* Manili

**Ruiz, Pablo Diego Jose Francisco de Paula Juan Nepomuceno Cipriano**
1881-1973  [CA]
*Spanish-born painter and sculptor*
* Picasso, Pablo [Ruiz]

**Ruiz, Poppa**
See Ruiz, Silvino

**Ruiz, Silvino** 20th c.  [OBW]
*American baseball player*
* Ruiz, Poppa

**Ruiz Camino, Carlos** 1920-1966
[GS]
*Mexican bullfighter*
* Arruza, Carlos
* [El] Ciclon Mexicano [The Mexican Cyclone]

**Ruiz De La Torre, Victor** 1940-
[GS]
*Spanish bullfighter*
* [El] Satelite [The Satellite]

**Ruiz y Vargas, Juan** 1855-1910
[GS]
*Spanish bullfighter*
* Lagartija [The Rogue]

**Rukeyser, Bud**
See Rukeyser, M. S., Jr.

**Rukeyser, M. S., Jr.** 20th c.  [ET]
*Television executive*
* Rukeyser, Bud

**Rule, William Harris** 19th c.  [PA]
*Author*
* W. H. R

**Ruler, Alexander John** 1936-
[IAW]
*British author*
* Alexander, John

**[The] Ruler of the Ausonian Lyre**
See Ambrogini, Angelo

**Rulewski, Jan** 20th c.
*Polish labor leader*
* [The] Pistol

**Rulfs, Helen** 1907?-  [FC]
*American actress*
* Vinson, Helen

**Rullianus**
See Fabius Maximus, Quintus

**Ruman, Sig**
See Rumann, Siegfried

**Rumann, Siegfried** 1884?-1967
[F2, FC]
*German actor*
* Ruman, Sig

**Rumbold-Gibbs, Henry St. John Clair**
1909-1975  [AW, CA, CC]
*British author*
* Gibbs, Henry
* Harvester, Simon
* Saxon, John

**Rumford, Count**
See Thompson, Benjamin

**Rumsey, Bert**
See Rumsey, Burtis Harold

**Rumsey, Burtis Harold** 1892-1968
[SC]
*American actor*
* Rumsey, Bert

**Rumsey, Julian Sidney** 1823-1886
[FFF]
*American merchant*
* [The] Father of Grain Inspection

**Rumsey, Murray**
See Rumshinsky, Murray

**Rumsfeld, Donald** 1932-
*American politician*
* Rumsfeld, Rummy

**Rumsfeld, Rummy**
See Rumsfeld, Donald

**Rumshinsky, Murray** 1907-  [ASC]
*American composer and conductor*
* Rumsey, Murray

**[The] Run Away Spartan**
See Peel, [Sir] Robert

**Runciman, A., pinx**
See Cummings, Albert Arratoon Runciman

**Runciman, James Cochran Stevenson**
1903-  [LC]
*British author and educator*
* Runciman, [Sir] Steven

**Runciman, John**
See Aldiss, Brian W[ilson]

**Runciman, [Sir] Steven**
See Runciman, James Cochran Stevenson

**Rundell, Mrs.** 19th c.  [RH]
*Author*
* [A] Lady

**Rundle, Anne** 20th c.
[AW, CA, WD]
*British author*
* Lamont, Marianne
* Manners, Alexandra
* Marshall, Joanne
* Sanders, Jeanne

**Rundquist, Anna Olivia** 1871-1951
[MS]
*Swedish-born opera singer*
* Fremstad, Olive
* Peterson, Anna

**Runeskold-Baner, Johan Gustaf**
1861- ?  [NAA]
*Swedish-born author*
* Sagabard, Raven

**Rungeling, Alf** 1862?-1919  [BEW]
*American circus proprietor*
* Ringling, A. T.

**Rungeling, Alfred J.** 1853?-1916
[BEW]
*American circus proprietor*
* Ringling, Alfred J.

**Rungeling, Charles** 1864-1926
[BEW]
*American circus proprietor*
* Ringling, Charles

**Rungeling, John** 1866?-1936
[BEW]
*American circus performer and proprietor*
* Ringling, John

**Runkle, Janice** 1953?-1981
*American veterinarian*
* Clark, M.

**Runkle, Lucia Gilbert**  [PA]
*Author*
* Calhoun, Mrs.

**Runnels, James Edward** 1928-
[BE, PB]
*American baseball player*
* Runnels, Pete

**Runnels, Mrs. Frederick**  [FFF]
*Entertainer*
* Somerville, Amelia

**Runnels, Pete**
See Runnels, James Edward

**Runnymede**
See Disraeli, Benjamin

**Runyan, John**
See Palmer, Bernard

**Runyan, Paul Scott** 1908-
[BWG, GF]
*American golfer*
* Little Poison

**Runyon, Charles W.** 1928-  [CA]
*American author*
* West, Mark

**Rupert [Rupertus or Ruprecht]** 650?-
?  [WBD]
*Saint*
* [The] Apostle of the Bavarians

**Rupert** 1352-1410  [SN]
*King of Germany*
* [The] Straitened

**Rupert** 1619-1682
[DNNF, RH, SN]
*Duke of Bavaria and British royalist general*
* [The] Mad Cavalier

**[The] Rupert of Debate**
See Stanley, Edward George Geoffrey Smith

**Rupert, Raphael Rudolph** 1910-
[CAP]
*Hungarian-born writer*
* Tatray, Istvan

**Ruphelenguis**
See Ravlengherio, Francois

**Rupolo, Ernest** ?-1964
[BLB, PHM]
*American underworld figure*
* [The] Hawk

**Rupp, Adolph** 1901-  [BB]
*American basketball coach*
* [The] Baron
* [The] Man in the Brown Suit

**Ruppert, Charles** 1914-
[FC, ITA, SW]
*American actor*
* Drake, Charles

**Ruppert, Chester**
See Graham, Roger Phillips

**[Un] Rural**
See De Cavagnac, G.

**Rural**
See Dunlap, M. L.

**[The] Rural Postman of Bideford**
See Capern, Edward

**Ruric, Peter** 20th c. [EMD]
*Author*
* Cain, Paul

**Rush, Andy**
See Rush, Jess Howard

**Rush, Bobby**
See Nelson, Emmett

**Rush, Jess Howard** 1889- [BE]
*American baseball player*
* Rush, Andy

**Rush, Joshua**
See Pearlstein, Howard J.

**Rush, Otis** 1934- [BWW]
*American singer*
* Little Otis

**Rushing, James Andrew [Jimmy]**
1902-1972 [BWW, NP]
*American singer*
* Five By Five, Mr.
* Honey Bunny Boo
* Rushing, Little Jim

**Rushing, Little Jim**
See Rushing, James Andrew
[Jimmy]

**Rusholm, Peter**
See Powell, Eric Frederick William

**Rushton, Charles**
See Shortt, Charles Rushton

**Rusie, Amos Wilson** 1871-1942
[AS, BE, PB]
*American baseball player*
* [The] Hoosier Thunderbolt

**Rusin, Jack**
See Russin, Jack

**Rusinol y Prats, Santiago**
1861-1931 [BEW]
*Spanish-born playwright and artist*
* Rusinyol, Santiago

**Rusinyol, Santiago**
See Rusinol y Prats, Santiago

**Ruskin, John** 1819-1900
[DEL, PA]
*British author and art critic*
* [A] Graduate of Oxford
* Phusin, Kate

**Ruslander, Mark** 1933?-
*American comedian*
* Russell, Mark

**Ruso, Michael** 20th c. [WW]
*Author*
* Roscoe, Mike [joint pseudonym
with John Roscoe]

**Russ, Lavinia** 1904- [CA]
*American author and editor*
* Faxon, Lavinia

**Russ, Paula**
See Ignatiev, Pauline

**Russ, W. L.** [FFF]
*American writer*
* Macswell

**Russell**
See Connell, Russell H.

**Russell, Albert**
See Bixby, Jerome Lewis

**Russell, Amanda**
See Feldman, Ellen [Bette]

**Russell, Andy**
See Rabajos, Andy

**Russell, Ann**
See Dosch, Audrey Ann

**Russell, Anna**
See Russell-Brown, Anna Claudia

**Russell, Arthur**
See Goode, Arthur Russell

**Russell, Baldy**
See Mitchell, William [Bill]

**Russell, Big Jim**
See Russell, James Wyman

**Russell, Billy**
See Brown, Adam George

**Russell, Bob**
See Russell, Sidney Keith

**Russell, Bull Run**
See Russell, [Sir] William Howard

**Russell, Byron**
See Russell, Patrick Joseph

**Russell, C.** 20th c. [MBF]
*British author*
* Clifford, Martin [house
pseudonym]
* Wood, Geoffrey

**Russell, Campy**
See Russell, Michael

**Russell, Charles Ellsworth**
1906-1969 [ASC, DAM, EJ]
*American jazz musician*
* Russell, Pee Wee

**Russell, Charlotte**
See Rathjen, Carl H[enry]

**Russell, Clarence Dixon** 1890-1962
[BE]
*American baseball player*
* Russell, Lefty

**Russell, Clinton**
See Rathjen, Carl H[enry]

**Russell, Curly**
See Russell, Dillon

**Russell, Dillon** 1920- [EJ, PMJ]
*American jazz musician*
* Russell, Curly

**Russell, E. J. C.**
See Russell, Edwin John Cumming

**Russell, Edwin John Cumming**
1939- [ART]
*British sculptor*
* Russell, E. J. C.

**Russell, Elizabeth Mary**
1866-1941 [WBD]
*Australian-born author*
* Elizabeth

**Russell, Eric Frank** 1905-1978
[ESF]
*British author*
* Craig, Webster
* Munro, Duncan H.

**Russell, Erle?**
See Wilding, Philip

**Russell, Ernestine** 1921- [AM]
*American actress*
* Russell, Jane

**Russell, Ewell Albert** 1889-
[BE, PB]
*American baseball player*
* Russell, Reb

**Russell, Frank** 20th c. [OBW]
*American baseball player*
* Russell, Junior

**Russell, Frank Alden** 20th c.
*American poet, philosopher, radio
personality*
* Malone, Ted

**Russell, Fred**
See Parnell, Thomas Frederick

**Russell, G. W. E.**
See Russell, George William
Erskine

**Russell, George William**
1867-1935 [EWL, TC, TLC]
*Irish author, poet, playwright*
* A. E.
* Y. O.

**Russell, George William Erskine**
1853-1919 [LC]
*British author and politician*
* Russell, G. W. E.

**Russell, Glen David** 1915-1973
[BE]
*American baseball player*
* Russell, Rip

**Russell, Hattie**
See Labadie, Mrs. Francis

**Russell, Henry**
See Levy, Henry

**Russell, Henry**
See Olson, Henry Russell

**Russell, Honey**
See Russell, John D.

**Russell, Isaac Ed** 1913- [EJ]
*American jazz musician*
* Russell, Snookum

**Russell, J.**
See Bixby, Jerome Lewis

**Russell, James**
See Craythorne, James

**Russell, James**
See Harknett, Terry

**Russell, James Wyman** 1912-
[CWG]
*American country-western performer*
* Russell, Big Jim

**Russell, Jane**
See Russell, Ernestine

**Russell, John**
See Fearn, John Russell

**Russell, John** 1885-1956 [WW]
*Author*
* Thrice, Luke

**Russell, John D.** 1903-1973
[B10, BB, SMG]
*American basketball player and
coach*
* Russell, Honey

**Russell, [Lord] John Earl**
1792-1878 [DEL, DNNF, SN]
*British statesman and author*
* Finality John
* [A] Gentleman who has Left his
Lodgings
* [The] Lycurgus of the Lower
House

**Russell, John Henry** 1893-1972
[MK]
*American baseball player*
* Russell, Pistol

**Russell, John J.** 1886- [RBE]
*American boxer*
* Russell, Unk

**Russell, John L.** ?-1937 [SC]
*American actor and director*
* Lowell, John

**Russell, John Somerset** 1799-1880
[WBD]
*British politician*
* Pakington, [Sir] John Somerset

**Russell, Junior**
See Russell, Frank

**Russell, Kathleen Barbara** 1940-
[ART]
*Scottish-born painter*
* K.

**Russell, Landon R.** 1873-1938
[BBD]
*British conductor*
* Ronald, [Sir] Landon

**Russell, Lefty**
See Russell, Clarence Dixon

**Russell, Leon**
See Wilson, Hank

**Russell, Lillian**
See Leonard, Helen Louise

**Russell, Lindsay Patricia** 20th c.
[WWL]
*Author and poet*
* Quinn, Ethel

**Russell, Lloyd Opal** 1913-1968
[BE]
*American baseball player*
* Russell, Tex

**Russell, Mabel**
See Scott, Mabel

**Russell, Margaret**
See Montague, Eleonora Louisa

**Russell, Mark**
See Ruslander, Mark

**Russell, Martin** 1934- [CA]
*British author*
* Lester, Mark

**Russell, Michael** 1952-
[NBA, SMG]
*American basketball player*
* Russell, Campy

**Russell, Mrs. R. F.** [FFF]
*Entertainer*
* O'Neill, Hattie

**Russell, Nipsey** 20th c. [IBW]
*American comedian*
* Harlem's Son of Fun

**Russell, Norma Hull Lewis** 1902-
[CA]
*British author*
* Hodgson, Norma

**Russell, Patrick**
See Sammis, John

**Russell, Patrick Joseph**
1884?-1963 [BEW]
*Irish-born actor*
* Russell, Byron

**Russell, Pee Wee**
See Russell, Charles Ellsworth

**Russell, Pistol**
See Russell, John Henry

**Russell, Ray** 20th c. [SFP]
*Author*
* Rencelaw, Brian
* Thorne, Roger

**Russell, Raymond**
See Balfour, William Raymond
John Evelyn

**Russell, Reb**
See Russell, Ewell Albert

**Russell, Rex**
See Langdon, John [Franklin
Coasten]

**Russell, Rip**
See Russell, Glen David

**Russell, Ropes**
See Russell, William Ellis [Bill]

**Russell, Rufus Rufty** 1940?- [B10]
*American cinematographer*
* Russell, Rusty

**Russell, Rusty**
See Russell, Rufus Rufty

**Russell, S. K.**
See Russell, Sidney Keith

**Russell, Sarah**
See Laski, Marghanita

**Russell, Sarah**
See Wright, Mabel Osgood

**Russell, Shane**
See Norwood, Victor G[eorge]
C[harles]

**Russell, Sidney Keith** 1914-
[ASC, PMJ]
*American lyricist*
* Russell, Bob
* Russell, S. K.

**Russell, Snookum**
See Russell, Isaac Ed

**Russell, Tex**
See Russell, Lloyd Opal

**Russell, Thomas**
See Laslett, Peter

**Russell, Unk**
See Russell, John J.

**Russell, William** 1639-1683 [WBD]
*British politician*
* [The] Patriot

**Russell, William** 19th c. [WW]
*British author*
* Inspector F.
* Waters
* Waters, Thomas?

**Russell, William Clark** 1844-1911
[WWL]
*British author*
* [A] Seafarer

**Russell, William Ellis [Bill]** 1948-
[PB, SMG]
*American baseball player*
* Russell, Ropes
* Russell, Young Blood
* Super Rook

**Russell, William Felton [Bill]** 1934-
[IBW]
*American basketball player, coach,
manager*
* Basketball, Mr.

**Russell, [Sir] William Howard**
1820-1907 [SN]
*British journalist*
* Russell, Bull Run

**Russell, Winifred Brent** 20th c.
[NAA]
*American author*
* Stait, Virginia

**Russell, Young Blood**
See Russell, William Ellis [Bill]

**Russell-Brown, Anna Claudia**
1911- [BEW]
*British actress, singer, lyricist*
* Russell, Anna

**Russi, Luciano** 1914- [IAW]
*Italian author*
* Ellerre

**[A] Russian**
See Polith, M.

**[The] Russian Byron**
See Pushkin, Alexander
Sergeivitch

**[The] Russian Casals**
See Piatigorsky, Gregor

**[The] Russian Lion**
See Hackenschmidt, George

**[The] Russian Lion**
See Lesnevich, Gus

**[The] Russian Livy**
See Karamzin, Nicholas
Michaelovitch

**[The] Russian Messalina**
See Catherine II

**[The] Russian Murat**
See Miloradowitch, Michael

**[The] Russian Palestrina**
See Bortniansky, Dmitri

**[The] Russian Voltaire**
See Somorokof [or Sumorokow],
Alexander Petrovitch

**Russin, Babe**
See Russin, Irving

**Russin, Irving** 1911-
[ASC, EJ, PMJ]
*American jazz musician*
* Russin, Babe

**Russin, Jack** 20th c.
*American jazz musician*
* Rusin, Jack

**Russo, Albert** 1943- [IAW]
*Belgian author and poet*
* Rovin, Alex

**Russo, Andy**
See Russo, Anthony C.

**Russo, Anthony C.** 1903-1958 [EJ]
*American jazz musician*
* Russo, Andy

**Russo, Lefty**
See Russo, Marius Ugo

**Russo, Marius Ugo** 1914- [BE]
*American baseball player*
* Russo, Lefty

**Russo, Patricia Ellen** 1945- [BEW]
*American actress*
* McCormack, Patty

**Russo, Santo** 1929- [EJ]
*American jazz musician*
* Russo, Sonny

**Russo, Sonny**
See Russo, Santo

**[The] Russophobist**
See Urquhart, David

**Russworm**
See Gluchen, Freidrich Wilhelm

**[The] Rustic Bard**
See Dinsmoor, Robert

**Rusticus**
See Jenkins, MacGregor

**Rustyface**
See Cunnington, Charles Leslie

**Rutgers, Lispenard**
See Smith, Henry Erskine

**Rutgers, Rudy**
See Torborg, Jeffrey Allen

**Rutgers van der Loeff, An[na]
Basenau** 1910- [SAT]
*Dutch author and translator*
* Bas, Rutger

**Ruth, Babe**
See Ruth, George Herman

**Ruth, George Herman** 1895-1948
[AS, OCS, SR]
*American baseball player*
* [The] Babe
* [The] Bambino
* Monk [or Monkey]
* Ruth, Babe
* Ruth, Jidge
* [The] Sultan of Swat

**Ruth, Jidge**
See Ruth, George Herman

**Ruthaly, Janos** 1876-1963
[AS, BX, RBE]
*Austrian-born boxer*
* Root, Jack

**Ruther, Bull**
See Ruther, Wyatt

**Ruther, Wyatt** 1923- [EJ]
*American jazz musician*
* Ruther, Bull

**Rutherford, Alvord** 20th c. [AES]
*American soccer player*
* Rutherford, Skip

**Rutherford, Austin** 20th c. [GW]
*American rodeo performer*
* Rutherford, Buck

**Rutherford, Buck**
See Rutherford, Austin

**Rutherford, Chas.**
See Martin, Lawrence

**Rutherford, Doc**
See Rutherford, John William
[Johnny]

**Rutherford, Douglas**
See McConnell, James Douglas
Rutherford

**Rutherford, Edward James** 1927-
[IAW]
*British author*
* Rutherford, Ward

**Rutherford, Elman** 1912?- [WWJ]
*American jazz musician*
* Rutherford, Rudy

**Rutherford, John**
See Baker, Evelyn Greenleaf

**Rutherford, John William [Johnny]**
1925- [BE]
*Canadian-born baseball player*
* Rutherford, Doc

**Rutherford, Joseph Franklin**
1869-1941 [WBD]
*American religious leader*
* Rutherford, Judge

**Rutherford, Judge**
See Rutherford, Joseph Franklin

**Rutherford, Laurette** 1914-1968
[SC]
*American actress*
* Arlen, Judith

**Rutherford, Mark**
See White, William Hale

**Rutherford, Rudy**
See Rutherford, Elman

**Rutherford, Skip**
See Rutherford, Alvord

**Rutherford, Ward**
See Rutherford, Edward James

**Rutherglen**
See Macfarlane, Robert

**Rutherston, Albert Daniel**
See Rothenstein, Albert Daniel

**Ruthin, Margaret**
See Catherall, Arthur

**Ruthven, Lord** [HN]
*Scottish aristocrat*
* Greysteil

**Ruthven, Richard David** 1951-
[SMG]
*American baseball player*
* Ruthven, Rufus

**Ruthven, Rufus**
See Ruthven, Richard David

**Rutland, Arthur**
See Adcock, [Arthur] St. John

**Rutland, Dodge**
See Singleton, Betty

**Rutledge, Brett**
See Paul, Elliot Harold

**Rutledge, [Dom] Denys**
See Rutledge, Edward William

**Rutledge, Edward William** 1906-
[CA, WD]
*British clergyman and author*
* Rutledge, [Dom] Denys

**Rutledge, Maryse**
See Gibson, Marice Louise

**Rutledge, Nancy** 20th c. [WW]
*Author*
* Bryson, Leigh

**Rutstein, Lillian** 1910-1980　[FC]
*American actress*
* Roth, Lillian

**Rutstrum, Calvin**
*See* Rudstrom, Calvin

**Rutt, M. E.**
*See* Shah, Amina

**Rutt, Richard** 1925-　[CA]
*British-born clergyman and author*
* Ro Tae-yong

**Rutter, Grace** 1878?-1950　[BEW]
*American actress*
* Elliston, Grace

**Rutter, Sally** 1913?-　[FC, ITA]
*American actress*
* Page, Gale

**Ruttkay, Arnold** 1923-　[IAW]
*Hungarian-born author*
* So, Bernat

**Rutty, Herbert Waring** 1857-1932
[THR]
*British actor*
* Waring, Herbert

**Rutz-Nissen, Grethe** 1906?-
[F2, FC]
*Norwegian actress*
* Nissen, Greta

**Ruyerson, James Paul**
*See* Rothweiler, Paul R[oger]

**Ruysbroek, Jean de** 1293-1381
[DNNF, FFF, HN]
*Flemish mystic*
* [The] Divine Doctor
* Divinus, Doctor
* [The] Ecstatic Doctor
* Ecstaticus, Doctor

**Ruyslinck, Ward**
*See* De Belser, Reimond Karel
Maria

**Ruze**
*See* Coiffier, Antoine

**Ruzicka, Lavoslav** 1887-　[WBD]
*Yugoslav-born chemist*
* Ruzicka, Leopold

**Ruzicka, Leopold**
*See* Ruzicka, Lavoslav

**Ruzkova, Jana** 1943-　[OP]
*Czech opera singer*
* Jonasova, Jana

**[Il] Ruzzante**
*See* Beolco, Angelo

**Ryall, G. F. T.**
*See* Ryall, George Francis Trafford

**Ryall, George Francis Trafford**
1887?-1979　[CA]
*American columnist*
* Audax Minor
* Ryall, G. F. T.

**Ryall, William Bolitho** 1890-1920
[LC, TC]
*British author and journalist*
* Bolitho, William

**Ryan, Abram Joseph** 1838-1886
[FFF, WBD]
*American clergyman and poet*
* Moina
* [The] Poet of the Confederacy
* [The] Tom Moore of the
Confederacy

**Ryan, Blondy**
*See* Ryan, John Collins

**Ryan, Buddy**
*See* Ryan, James

**Ryan, Bunny**
*See* Ryan, Elizabeth

**Ryan, Chew Tobacco**
*See* Ryan, Frank

**Ryan, Chico**
*See* Ryan, Dave

**Ryan, Connie**
*See* Ryan, Cornelius Joseph

**Ryan, Cornelius Joseph** 1920-
[BE, SMG]
*American baseball player, coach,
manager*
* Ryan, Connie

**Ryan, Cyclone**
*See* Ryan, Daniel R.

**Ryan, Daniel R.** 1866-1917　[BE]
*Irish-born baseball player*
* Ryan, Cyclone

**Ryan, Dave** 1948-　[RO2]
*American singer*
* Ryan, Chico

**Ryan, Elizabeth** 20th c.　[OET]
*Tennis player*
* Ryan, Bunny

**Ryan, Ernest** 1897-　[CAT]
*American author*
* Ernest, [Brother]

**Ryan, Frank** 20th c.　[PHM]
*American underworld figure*
* Ryan, Chew Tobacco

**Ryan, Frederick** 1876-1913　[DIL]
*Irish journalist and editor*
* Finian
* Irial

**Ryan, Gerald**　[FFF]
*Entertainer*
* Eyre, Gerald

**Ryan, Gulfport**
*See* Ryan, John Francis [Jack]

**Ryan, Hermine Braunsteiner** 1920?-
*Austrian concentration camp guard
during the Nazi era*
* [The] Mare
* [The] Stomping Mare

**Ryan, Irene**
*See* Riordan, Irene

**Ryan, James** 1934-　[SMG]
*American football coach*
* Ryan, Buddy

**Ryan, John** 20th c.　[GW]
*American rodeo performer*
* Ryan, Paddy

**Ryan, John Collins** 1906-1959　[BE]
*American baseball player*
* Ryan, Blondy

**Ryan, John Fergus** 1931-　[CA]
*American author and playwright*
* Thames, Jack

**Ryan, John Francis [Jack]**
1884-1949　[BE]
*American baseball player*
* Ryan, Gulfport

**Ryan, John Joseph** 1922?-
[FC, SW]
*American actor*
* Lord, Jack

**Ryan, Joseph B.** 1902-　[BBH]
*Canadian football team manager*
* Ryan, Rufus

**Ryan, Kate**
*See* Nolan, Mrs. James

**Ryan, Lew**
*See* Malone, Lew[is Aloysius]

**Ryan, Little**
*See* Ryan, Melvin

**Ryan, Mary** 1885-1976　[HCA]
*American actress*
* Nash, Mary

**Ryan, Melvin** 1914-　[MY]
*American singer*
* Ryan, Little

**Ryan, Merven J.** 20th c.　[OBW]
*American baseball player*
* Ryan, Red

**Ryan, Mrs. Thomas**　[FFF]
*Entertainer*
* Conway, Mai
* Richfield, Mai

**Ryan, [Lynn] Nolan** 1947-　[BE, PB]
*American baseball player*
* [The] Express

**Ryan, Paddy**
*See* Ryan, John

**Ryan, Paul William** 1906-1947
[WW]
*Author*
* Finnegan, Robert
* Quin, Mike

**Ryan, Red**
*See* Ryan, Merven J.

**Ryan, Rosy**
*See* Ryan, Wilfred Patrick Dolan

**Ryan, Rufus**
*See* Ryan, Joseph B.

**Ryan, Sgt.**
*See* Coryell, John Russell

**Ryan, Sheila**
*See* McLaughlin, Katherine
Elizabeth

**Ryan, Tim**
*See* Dent, Lester

**Ryan, Tommy**
*See* Eboli, Thomas

**Ryan, Tommy**
*See* Youngs, Joseph, Jr.

**Ryan, Wilfred Patrick Dolan**
1898-　[BE]
*American baseball player*
* Ryan, Rosy

**Ryan, William** ?-1848　[HN]
*Irish murderer*
* Puck

**Ryan, William Patrick** 20th c.
[WWL]
*Irish author*
* O'Riain, Liam P.

**Ryba, Dominic Joseph** 1903-1970
[BE, PB]
*American baseball player*
* Ryba, Mike

**Ryba, Mike**
*See* Ryba, Dominic Joseph

**Rybot, Doris**
*See* Ponsonby, Doris Almon

**Ryckmans, Pierre** 1935-　[CA]
*Belgian art historian and author*
* Leys, Simon

**Rycon**
*See* Savery, Constance Winifred

**Rydell, Bobby**
*See* Ridarelli, Robert Lewis

**Rydell, Forbes** [joint pseudonym with
Helen B. Rydell]
*See* Forbes, DeLoris [Florine]
Stanton

**Rydell, Forbes** [joint pseudonym with
DeLoris (Florine) Stanton Forbes]
*See* Rydell, Helen B.

**Rydell, Helen B.**　[EMD, WW]
*American author*
* Rydell, Forbes [joint pseudonym
with DeLoris (Florine) Stanton
Forbes]

**Rydell, Wendell**
*See* Rydell, Wendy

**Rydell, Wendy** 1927-1981
[CA, SAT, WD]
*American author*
* Rydell, Wendell

**Ryden, Ernest Edwin** 1886-　[NAA]
*American clergyman and editor*
* Augustson, Ernest

**Ryder, Alfred**
*See* Corn, Alfred Jacob

**Ryder, [Sir] Don**
*See* Ryder, [Sir] Sydney Thomas

**Ryder, Elliot**　[PA]
*Author*
* Ynetchi, Paul

**Ryder, [Prof.] G. W.**
*See* Grimm, Richard

**Ryder, Jonathan**
*See* Ludlum, Robert

**Ryder, Michael Lawson** 1927-
[WD]
*British writer*
* Lawson, Michael

**Ryder, Mitch**
*See* Levise, William S., Jr. [Billy]

**Ryder, Steven**
*See* Edgar, Alfred

**Ryder, [Sir] Sydney Thomas** 1916-
[B10]
*British publisher and editor*
* Ryder, [Sir] Don

**Rydz, Edward** 1886-1943　[BDW]
*Polish statesman and army officer*
* Smigly-Rydz, Edward

**Rye, Anthony**
*See* Youd, Christopher Samuel

**Rye, Eugene Rudolph**
*See* Mercantelli, Eugene Rudolph

**Rye, Half-Pint**
*See* Mercantelli, Eugene Rudolph

**Rye, Michael**
*See* Billsbury, Rye

**Ryer**
*See* Pfeiffer, Ida

**Ryer, Frederick R.** [PA]
*Author*
* Warwick

**Ryerson, Lowell**
*See* Van Atta, Winfred Lowell

**Ryhlick, Frank** 20th c. [SFP]
*Author*
* Riley, Frank

**Ryland, Clive**
*See* Priestley, Clive Ryland

**Ryland, Lee**
*See* Arlandson, Leone

**Ryle, Randolph**
*See* Pentelow, John Nix

**Rymer, James Malcolm**
*See* Merry, Malcolm James

**Rymer, Thomas** 1641-1713 [SN]
*British literary critic*
* Shakespeare's Critic

**Rymnikski**
*See* Suvorov [or Suwarof],
Aleksandr Vasilievich

**Rynas, Stephen A.** 20th c. [WGT]
*Author*
* Arr, Stephen

**Ryott, Septimus William**
1886?-1965 [F1, F2, FC]
*British actor*
* Rome, Stewart

**[The] Ryparographer**
*See* Pyricus

**[The] Ryparographer of Wits**
*See* Rabelais, Francois

**Ryse, Sherwood**
*See* Starey, Alfred B.

**Rytter, Poul** 1813-1894 [WBD]
*Danish poet and politician*
* Ploug, Parmo Carl

**Rywell, Martin** 1905-1971 [CAP]
*American author and editor*
* Hemingway, Taylor
* Sears, Deane

**Rzewuski, Stanislaw** 17th c.
[WBD]
*Polish soldier*
* [The] Grand Hetman of the
  Crown

# S

**S. A. M.**
*See* Vestal, Herman Beeson

**S. B. P.**
*See* Power, Samuel Browning

**S. C.**
*See* Crampton, Sean

**S. D. B.**
*See* Bruce, Sanders D.

**S. E. B.**
*See* Brydges, Samuel Egerton

**S. G.**
*See* Gordon, Susan

**S. G. O.**
*See* Osborne, Sydney Godolphin

**S. H.**
*See* Hall, Spencer T.

**S. K.**
*See* Kirby, K. Sarah N.

**S. L.**
*See* Lounds, Stanley Samuel

**S. L.**
*See* Prynne, William

**S. M.**
*See* Maer, Stephen

**S. M.**
*See* Melland, Sylvia

**S. M. C.**
*See* Anderson, Kathleen Agness Cicely

**S. M. R.**
*See* Robertson, Seonaid Mairi

**S. R.**
*See* Rankin, Stella

**S. R. C.**
*See* Ross-Craig, Stella

**S. R. P.**
*See* Powers, S. Rugeley

**S. S.**
*See* Clarkson, Anthony

**S. S. C.**
*See* Conant, Silliman S.

**S. S. D. D.**
*See* Farr, Florence

**S. S. E.**
*See* Sperry, [Sally] Baxter

**S. T. C.**
*See* Coleridge, Samuel Taylor

**S. W.**
*See* Ward, Sam[uel]

**S. W., Esq.**
*See* Scott, [Sir] Walter

**S. W. P.**
*See* Patridge, S. W.

**S-Ringi, Kjell**
*See* Ringi, Kjell Arne Soerensen

**Sa de Miranda, Francisco da**
1495?-1558 [DNNS]
*Portuguese poet*
* [The] Portuguese Theocritus

**Saadi [or Sadi]**
*See* Muslih-ud-Din [or Moslehedin]

**Saari, Uhro** 20th c. [BBH]
*American water polo coach*
* Saari, Whitey

**Saari, Whitey**
*See* Saari, Uhro

**Saba, Umberto**
*See* Poli, Umberto

**Sabbatini, Andrea** 1480?-1545
[WBD]
*Italian painter*
* Andrea da Salerno

**Saben, Gertrude Chetwynd Shallcross**
20th c. [WGT]
*Author*
* Saben, Gregory [joint pseudonym with Frederick Evelyn Burkitt]

**Saben, Gregory** [joint pseudonym with Gertrude Chetwynd Shallcross Saben]
*See* Burkitt, Frederick Evelyn

**Saben, Gregory** [joint pseudonym with Frederick Evelyn Burkitt]
*See* Saben, Gertrude Chetwynd Shallcross

**Saber, Robert O.**
*See* Ozaki, Milton K.

**Sabiad**
*See* White, Stanhope

**Sabich, Spider**
*See* Sabich, Vladimir

**Sabich, Vladimir** 1943?-1976 [B10]
*American skier*
* Sabich, Spider

**Sabin, A. K.**
*See* Sabin, Arthur Knowles

**Sabin, Arthur Knowles** 1879-1959
[LC]
*British poet*
* Sabin, A. K.

**Sabine, William Henry Waldo**
1903- [WWL]
*British author*
* [The] White Friar

**Sabini, John Anthony** 1921-
[AW, CA]
*American author*
* Anthony, John

**Sabino**
*See* Ballard, Edward

**Sabinus**
*See* Floridus, Francisco

**Sabinus Vespasianus, Titus Flavius**
40-81 [DNNS, RH, WBD]
*Roman emperor*
* [The] Darling of Mankind
* [The] Delight of Mankind
* Titus

**[El] Sabio [The Learned]**
*See* Alfonso X [or Alphonso]

**[El] Sabio**
*See* Ferdinand VI

**[El] Sabio [The Wise]**
*See* Sancho VI

**[Le] Sablonnier [The Sand-Dealer]**
*See* Frederick II

**Sabo, Alex[ander]**
*See* Szabo, Alexander

**Sabo, Giz**
*See* Szabo, Alexander

**Sabourin, Anne Winifred** 1910-
[CA]
*American author and nun*
* Mary Justine, [Sister]
* Sabourin, Justine

**Sabourin, Gary Bruce** 1943- [HK]
*Canadian-born hockey player*
* Sabourin, Gaye

**Sabourin, Gaye**
*See* Sabourin, Gary Bruce

**Sabourin, Justine**
*See* Sabourin, Anne Winifred

**Sabre, Dirk**
*See* Laffin, John [Alfred Charles]

**Sabre, Mark**
*See* Thomas, William B. [Bill]

**Sabu**
*See* Dastagir, Sabu

**Sabu, Frank**
*See* Konadu, Samuel Asare

**Sabuso**
*See* Phillips, Irv[ing W.]

**Sabut Jung [The Daring in War]**
*See* Clive, Robert [Baron Clive of Plassey]

**Saca Bona**
*See* Grimshaw, Ivan Gerould

**Sacastru, Martin**
*See* Bioy-Casares, Adolfo

**Saccas [Sack Bearer]**
*See* Ammonius

**Sacchini, Antonio Maria Gaspare**
1735?-1786 [DEP, FFF, RH]
*Italian composer*
* [The] Racine of Music

**Sacco, Fillippo** 1905- [BLB]
*Italian-born American underworld figure*
* Roselli, John

**Sacco, Lugee** 1943- [RO1]
*American singer and songwriter*
* Christie, Lou

**Sacco, Nicolo** 1891-1927
*Italian-born American political radical*
* [The] Good Shoemaker

**Sacerdote, Jenny** 20th c. [WFA]
*French fashion designer*
* Madame Jenny

**Sacharissa**
*See* Sidney, Dorothy

**Sacharuk, Lawrence William**
1952- [SMG]
*Canadian-born hockey player*
* Sacharuk, Satch

**Sacharuk, Satch**
*See* Sacharuk, Lawrence William

**Sachem, E. B.**
*See* Creel, Stephen Melville

**Sacheverell, Henry** 1674?-1724
[SN]
*British clergyman*
* [A] Pulpit Physician
* [The] Zealous Doctor

Sachs, Albert Louis 1935-  [CA]
*South African author*
* Sachs, Albie

Sachs, Albie
*See* Sachs, Albert Louis

Sachs, Edward Julius 1927-1964
[EAR]
*American auto racer*
* [The] Clown Prince of Auto
   Racing
* Sachs, Fast Eddie

Sachs, Fast Eddie
*See* Sachs, Edward Julius

Sachs, Georgia
*See* Adams, Georgia Sachs

Sachs, Hans 1494-1576
[HN, RH, SN]
*German poet*
* [The] Cobbler Poet
* [The] Laureate of the Gentle
   Craft
* [The] Nightingale of Wittenberg
* [The] Prince of Satirists

Sack, Ethel 1895?-1957  [BEW]
*American actress*
* Cody, Ethel

Sack, O.
*See* Matz, Bertram Waldrom

Sackerman, Henry
*See* Kahm, Harold S.

Sackett, Grenville A.  [FFF]
*American poet*
* Alfred

Sackett, Harry
*See* Dixon, Andrew

Sackett, Julia 1887-1975
[BEW, EMT, PMJ]
*American actress and singer*
* Sanderson, Julia

Sackett, Millie
*See* Pike, Mrs.

Sacks, Claire
*See* Sprague, Claire S[acks]

Sackville-West, V.
*See* Sackville-West, Victoria Mary

Sackville-West, Victoria Mary
1892-1962  [CA, LC, TC]
*British author and poet*
* Nicolson, Victoria Mary
* Sackville-West, V.

Sad Sam Gray
*See* Gray, Samuel David

Sad Sam Jones
*See* Jones, Samuel

Sad Sam Jones
*See* Jones, Samuel Pond

Sad Sam Zoldak
*See* Zoldak, Samuel Walter

Sadat, Anwar 1918-1981
*Egyptian president*
* [The] Hero of the Crossing
* Nasser's Poodle

Sadat's Sadat
*See* Mubarak, Hosni

Sadaukai, Owusu
*See* Fuller, Howard

Saddle-Bag John
*See* Pope, John

Saddler, A. C. 1935-   [EG]
*Golfer*
* Saddler, Sandy

Saddler, Dandy Sandy
*See* Saddler, Joseph

Saddler, Joseph 1926-
[BX, IBW, RBE]
*American boxer*
* Saddler, Dandy Sandy
* Saddler, Sandy

Saddler, K. Allen
*See* Richards, Ronald Charles
William

Saddler, Sandy
*See* Saddler, A. C.

Saddler, Sandy
*See* Saddler, Joseph

Sadeur, James
*See* De Foigny, Gabriel

Sadgrove, Sidney Henry 1920-
[AW, WD]
*British playwright*
* Torrance, Lee

Sadi, Fats
*See* Sadi, Lallemand

Sadi, Lallemand 1926-   [EJ]
*Belgian jazz musician*
* Sadi, Fats

Sadina
*See* Mitchell, Priscilla

Sadino, Elmano
*See* Bocage [or Boccage], Manuel
Maria Barbosa du

Sadleir, Michael
*See* Sadler, M. T. H.

Sadler, Clarice Laurence 20th c.
[WWL]
*British author*
* Laurence, Clarice

Sadler, Haskell Robert 1935-
[BWW]
*American singer*
* Cool Papa

Sadler, Izetta Estelle 1875?-1934
[BEW]
*American actress*
* Mayhew, Stella

Sadler, James Robert 1908-1967
[BMH]
*British entertainer*
* Desmonde, Jerry

Sadler, L. R.  [PA]
*Author*
* Larwood, Jacob

Sadler, M. T. H. 1888-  [WWL]
*British author*
* Sadleir, Michael

Sadlier, Mary Anne 1820- ?  [PA]
*Author*
* Madden, M. A.

Sadlowski, Edward 1939-
*American labor leader*
* Oil Can Eddie

Sadowski, Robert Frank [Bob]
1937-  [BE]
*American baseball player*
* Sadowski, Sid

Sadowski, Sid
*See* Sadowski, Robert Frank [Bob]

Sadyk Pasha
*See* Czajkowski, Michal

Saemund Sigfusson 1054?-1133
[RH, SN, WBD]
*Icelandic clergyman and poet*
* [The] Sage
* [The] Wise

Saetone [joint pseudonym]
*See* Camus, Albert

Saffah, al- [The Bloodshedder]
*See* Abbas, Abu-al-

Safford, Mary J.   [PA]
*Author*
* M. S.

Safian, Jill
*See* Jacobs, Jill

Safka, Melanie 1947-   [RO2]
*American singer*
* Melanie

Sagabard, Raven
*See* Runeskold-Baner, Johan
Gustaf

[The] Sagacious Terrier
*See* Bruce, James

Sagadahoc
*See* Kidder, Frederic

Sagan, Francoise
*See* Quoirez, Francoise

Sagan, Leontine
*See* Schlesinger, Leontine

[The] Sage
*See* Bernal, John Desmond

[Le] Sage
*See* Charles V

[Le] Sage
*See* John V [or Jean]

[Le] Sage
*See* Las Cases, Emmanuel
Augustin Dieudonne de

[The] Sage
*See* Saemund Sigfusson

Sage, Agnes Carolyn 20th c.   [ALY]
*American author*
* Sage, Agnes Carr

Sage, Agnes Carr
*See* Sage, Agnes Carolyn

[The] Sage and Serious Spenser
*See* Spenser, Edmund

Sage, Frances
*See* Satz, Frances

Sage, Juniper [joint pseudonym with
Edith (Thacher) Hurd]
*See* Brown, Margaret Wise

Sage, Juniper [joint pseudonym with
Margaret Wise Brown]
*See* Hurd, Edith [Thacher]

[The] Sage of Alexandria
*See* Euclid

[The] Sage of Auburn
*See* Seward, William Henry

[The] Sage of Baltimore
*See* Mencken, Henry Louis

[The] Sage of Chappaqua
*See* Greeley, Horace

[The] Sage of Chelsea
*See* Carlyle, Thomas

[The] Sage of Concord
*See* Emerson, Ralph Waldo

[The] Sage of Crotona
*See* Pythagoras

[The] Sage of Emporia
*See* White, William Allen

[The] Sage of Kinderhook
*See* Van Buren, Martin

[The] Sage of Lindenwald
*See* Van Buren, Martin

[The] Sage of Moberly
*See* Conroy, John Wesley [Jack]

[The] Sage of Monticello
*See* Jefferson, Thomas

[The] Sage of Montpelier
*See* Madison, James

[The] Sage of Mount Vernon
*See* Washington, George

[The] Sage of Princeton
*See* Cleveland, [Stephen] Grover

[The] Sage of Princeton
*See* Roosevelt, Theodore [Teddy]

[The] Sage of Samos
*See* Pythagoras

[The] Sage of Skinner Street
*See* Godwin, William

[The] Sage of Springfield
*See* Lincoln, Abraham

[The] Sage of Syracuse
*See* Archimedes

[The] Sage of the Hermitage
*See* Jackson, Andrew

[The] Sage of Wheatland
*See* Buchanan, James

Sager, Jane Olive 1914-   [MY]
*American jazz musician*
* Sager, Si

Sager, Pony
*See* Sager, Samuel B.

Sager, Samuel B. 1847- ?   [BE]
*American baseball player*
* Sager, Pony

Sager, Si
*See* Sager, Jane Olive

Sagglehorne, Sadie
*See* Chaillie, Jean Humphrey

[The] Saginaw Kid
*See* Lavigne, George

Sagittarius
*See* Katzin, Olga

Sagittarius
*See* Schutz, Heinrich

Sagoyewatha 1751?-1830
[FFF, WBD]
*American Indian chieftain*
* [The] Cowkiller
* Red Jacket

Sahafzadeh
*See* Efendi, Mohammed Esaad

Sahib, Nana
*See* Robinson, William Ellsworth

Sahm, Douglas Saldana 1942-
[RO2]
*American singer and musician*
* Sir Douglas

Saicho 767- 822 [WBD]
*Japanese religious leader*
* Dengyo Daishi

Sa'id, Ali Ahmad 1930- [B10]
*Lebanese poet*
* Adonis

Said, Bob
*See* Said, Boris

Said, Boris 1932- [EAR]
*American auto racer*
* Said, Bob

Saidy, Fareed Milhem 1907-
[BEW, EMT]
*American librettist*
* Saidy, Fred

Saidy, Fred
*See* Saidy, Fareed Milhem

Saietta, Ignazio 20th c.
[BLB, PHM]
*American underworld figure*
* Lupo, Joseph
* Lupo the Wolf

Sailil
*See* Tullock, W. W.

Sailor Bill Posedel
*See* Posedel, William John

Sailor Billy Vincent
*See* Vincent, William J.

Sailor Bob Shawkey
*See* Shawkey, Bob

Sailor Don Sauer
*See* Sauer, Don

[The] Sailor King
*See* William IV

Sailor, Leo 1895-1962
*American actor*
* Saylor, Sid

[The] Sailor's Friend
*See* Plimsoll, Samuel

Saimes, George 1941- [FB]
*American football player*
* Camus in Shoulder Pads
* [The] Existentialist Pass
 Defender

Sain, John Franklin [Johnny] 1917-
[BE, BTB]
*American baseball player*
* [The] Man of a Thousand Curves

Sainpolis, John
*See* St. Polis, John

[The] Saint
*See* Canute IV

[The] Saint
*See* Chin-tsou-jin

[The] Saint
*See* Edward VI

[The] Saint
*See* Eric IX

[The] Saint
*See* Ferdinand III

[The] Saint
*See* Henry II [or Heinrich]

[The] Saint
*See* Ladislas I

[The] Saint
*See* Olaf II [or Olaus]

St. Albans, Duchess of 1775-1837
[PA]
*Author*
* Melon, Miss

Saint Albin
*See* Balzac, Honore de

Saint Albin
*See* Collin, Jacques Albin Simon

Saint Amand
*See* Lacoste, Jean Amand

St. Andre, Lucien
*See* Mott, Vincent Valmon

Saint, Andrew [John] 1946- [CA]
*British writer*
* Plendello, Leo

St. Angel, Marjorie 1920-1969
[SC]
*American actress*
* Holliday, Marjorie

Saint Aubain, Andreas Nicolai de
1798-1865 [WBD]
*Danish author*
* Bernhard, Karl

Saint Aude, Magloire
*See* Magloire, Clement, fils

Saint Aurele, Poirie de
*See* Poirie, Jean-Aurele Pierre

St. Barbe
*See* Sladen, Douglas

Saint Benjamin
*See* White, Richard Grant

Saint Bernard Croly
*See* Croly, George

[The] Saint Beuve of English
Criticism
*See* Arnold, Matthew

St. Briavels, James
*See* Wood, James Playsted

St. Bruno, Albert Francis 1909-
[CAP]
*Australian-born author*
* Bruno, Frank

Saint Cecilia
*See* Manigault, G.

St. Clair, Byrd Hooper 1905- [CA]
*American author*
* Hooper, Byrd

St. Clair, Cecil
*See* Clark, Susie Champney

St. Clair, Elizabeth
*See* Cohen, Susan

St. Clair, Geek
*See* St. Clair, Robert B.

St. Clair, Katherine
*See* Huff, Tom Elmer

St. Clair, Leonard
*See* Cooper, Leonard

St. Clair, Mabel
*See* Hibbard, Carrie S.

St. Clair, Margaret 1911-
[ESF, SF, WGT]
*American author*
* Hazel, William?
* Hazzard, Wilton
* Seabright, Idris

St. Clair, Philip
*See* Howard, Munroe

St. Clair, Robert B. 1931- [FB]
*American football player*
* St. Clair, Geek

St. Clair, Victor
*See* Browne, George Waldo

St. Claire, Ebba
*See* St. Claire, Edward Joseph

St. Claire, Edward Joseph 1921-
[BE]
*American baseball player*
* St. Claire, Ebba

St. Cyr, Cyprian
*See* Bernstein, Eric [Lennard]

St. Cyr, Lillian 1873-1974
[F1, SC]
*American actress*
* Red Wing, Princess

St. Dare, Julian
*See* Patten, William George

Saint Denis, Michel Jacques
1897-1971 [AW, CAP]
*French-born producer, director,
author*
* Duchesne, Jacques

St. Denis, Ruth
*See* Dennis, Ruth

St. Denis, Teddie
*See* Denham, June Catherine
Church

Saint Denis, Valia Maria [Suria] 20th
c. [AW]
*Russian-born playwright*
* Magito, Suria

Saint, Dora Jessie [Shafe] 1913-
[AW, CA, WD]
*British author*
* Read, Miss

Saint Eden, Dennis
*See* Foster, Don[ald]

Saint Etienne
*See* De Villiers, Cosm

Saint Evremond, Seigneur de
*See* De Marguetel de Saint-Denis,
Charles

St. Felix, Marie
*See* Lynch, Harriet Louise

St. George, Harry
*See* Rathborne, St. George

St. George, Philip
*See* Avallone, Michael [Angelo],
Jr.

Saint Gildas the Wise
*See* Gildas [or Gildus]

St. Guillaume de Gellone
*See* Guillaume d'Orange

St. Helier, Ivy
*See* Aitchison, Ivy

St. Hereticus
*See* Brown, Robert McAfee

St. Hilaire, Marco de
*See* Hilaire, Emile Marc

Saint Hyacinthe, Cardonner
1684-1746 [PA]
*Author*
* De Themuseuil, Chevalier

St. Innocence, [Sister]
*See* Gerson, Vassily Vassilijevich

St. Jacques, Raymond
*See* Johnson, James Arthur

St. Jacques, Sterling 1951?-
*American fashion model and dancer*
* St. Jacques, Swirling Sterling

St. Jacques, Swirling Sterling
*See* St. Jacques, Sterling

St. James, Andrew
*See* Stern, James [Andrew]

St. James, Bernard
*See* Treister, Bernard W[illiam]

St. James, Blakely [house
pseudonym, Playboy Press]
*See* Platt, Charles

St. James, Fred
*See* Sullivan, John Florence

St. James of Compostela
*See* James

Saint James, Susan
*See* Miller, Susan

St. Jane
*See* Pfeiffer, Jane Cahill

Saint Jerome
*See* Edmunds, George Franklin

St. John, Al 1893-1963
[F1, FC, SC]
*American actor*
* Jones, Fuzzy Q.
* St. John, Fuzzy

St. John, Beth
*See* John, Elizabeth Beaman

St. John, Betta
*See* Streidler, Betty

St. John, Christopher Marie
*See* Marshall, Christabel

St. John, David
*See* Hunt, E[verette] Howard, Jr.

St. John, Dick
*See* Gosting, Richard

St. John, Eugenia
*See* Berry, Martha Eugenia

St. John, Florence
*See* Marius, Madame

St. John, Fuzzy
*See* St. John, Al

St. John, Henry
*See* Cooper, Charles Henry St.
John

St. John, Henry
*See* Creasey, John

**St. John, Henry** 1678-1751
[DEL, RH, SN]
*British statesman and writer*
* Bolingbroke, Proud
* Bolingbroke, Viscount
* High Mettled Harry
* Oldcastle, Humphrey
* [The] Patriot King

**St. John, J. Hector**
See Crevecoeur, Michel Guillaume
Jean de

**St. John, Jill**
See Oppenheim, Jill

**St. John, John**
See Sale, Richard [Bernard]

**St. John, Leonie** [joint pseudonym
with Nancy Harmon]
See Bayer, William

**St. John, Leonie** [joint pseudonym
with William Bayer]
See Harmon, Nancy

**St. John, Lily**
See Johnson, Lilian Clara

**St. John, Mabel**
See Cooper, Charles Henry St.
John

**Saint John, Marguerite**
See Wood, Mrs. G. M.

**St. John, Nellie**
See Van Auken, Mrs. Henry

**St. John, Oliver** 1598?-1673 [SN]
*British jurist*
* [The] Dark Lantern Man

**St. John, Percy Boyle** 1819- ? [PA]
*Author*
* P. B. St. J.
* Periwinkle, Paul

**St. John, Philip**
See Alvarez Del Rey, Ramon
Felipe San Juan Mario Silvio Enrico

**St. John, Sergius** 18th c. [PA]
*Author*
* Grandfather

**Saint John the Righteous**
See Anderson, John Bayard

**St. John, Wylly Folk** 1908-
[CA, SAT]
*American author*
* Fox, Eleanor
* Larson, Eve
* Pierce, Katherine
* Vincent, Mary Keith
* Williams, Michael

**St. Jorgen, Goerger** 1841-1926
[BBD]
*Hungarian-born opera singer*
* Orgeni, Aglaja

**St. Kames**
See Townsend, S. Nugent

**St. Laurence, A.**
See Felkin, Alfred Laurence

**St. Laurent, Ace**
See St. Laurent, Andre

**St. Laurent, Andre** 1953- [SMG]
*Canadian-born hockey player*
* St. Laurent, Ace

**Saint Laurent, Cecil**
See Laurent-Cely, Jacques

**Saint Laurent, Felix de**
See Ambroise, Fernand

**Saint Laurent, Yves** [Henri Donat
Mathieu] 1936-
*French fashion designer*
* Y. S. L.

**St. Leger, Elizabeth** 18th c.
[FFF, HN, RH]
*Daughter of Arthur, Lord Doneraile*
* [The] Female Freemason
* [The] Lady Freemason

**St. Lis** [or Liz]
See Senlis, Simon

**St. Louis**
See Louis IX

**[The] St. Louis born Flame of Paris**
See Baker, Josephine Carson

**St. Louis Jimmy**
See Oden, James Burke [Jimmy]

**St. Louis Mac**
See Simmons, Mack

**St. Luz, Berthe**
See Robertson, Alice Alberthe

**Saint Marc Girardin, Francois
Auguste**
See Girardin, Marc

**St. Mars, F.**
See Atkins, Frank, Jr.

**Saint Martin, Louis Claude de**
1743-1803 [DNNS, FFF, SN]
*French philosopher*
* [The] French Boehme
* [Le] Philosophe Inconnu
* [The] Philosopher of the
Unknown

**St. Maur, Harry** [FFF]
*American writer*
* Almaviva

**Saint Mexant**
See Rouzier, Maximilien Louis
Severin

**St. Myer, Ned**
See Stratemeyer, Edward L.

**[The] Saint of Selma**
See Jemison, David Victor

**[The] Saint of the Gutters**
See Bojaxhiu, Agnes Gonxha

**Saint Olaf**
See Olaf II [or Olaus]

**Saint Patrice**
See Harden-Hickey, James

**[The] St. Paul Cyclone**
See O'Dowd, Mike

**[The] St. Paul Phantom**
See Gibbons, Mike

**St. Paul, Sterner**
See Meek, Sterner St. Paul

**Saint Pierre, Abbe de**
See Castel, Charles Irenee

**Saint Pol-Roux**
See Roux, Paul Pierre

**St. Polis, John** 1873-1946 [SC]
*American actor*
* Sainpolis, John

**St. Raymond, Anne**
See Italiano, Anna Maria Luisa

**Saint Real, Abbe de**
See Vichard, Cesar

**St. Reynard, Geoff**
See Krepps, Robert W[ilson]

**Saint Robert**
See Viard, Felix

**Saint Saphorin**
See De Pesmes, Francois Louis

**Saint Subber, Arnold**
See Subber, Arnold

**St. Tamara**
See Kolba, Tamara

**St. Vivant, M.**
See Bixby, Jerome Lewis

**St. Vrain, [Major] E. L.**
See Manning, William Henry

**Saint-John, Perse**
See Leger, [Marie-Rene] Alexis
Saint-Leger

**Sainte Foy**
See Potvin, Damase

**Sainte Marie, Beverly** 1942?-
[IPA]
*Canadian-born singer*
* Sainte Marie, Buffy

**Sainte Marie, Buffy**
See Sainte Marie, Beverly

**Saintine**
See Boniface, Joseph Xavier

**Saisset-Schneider, Charlotte
Elisabeth Germaine** 1882-1942
[BDF, FC, FDG]
*French director*
* Dulac, Germaine

**Saisson, Pierre** [joint pseudonym
with George Middleton]
See Bolton, St. George Guy
Reginald

**Saisson, Pierre** [joint pseudonym
with St. George Guy Reginald
Bolton]
See Middleton, George

**Saitch, Bruiser**
See Saitch, Eyre

**Saitch, Eyre** 20th c. [MEB]
*American basketball player*
* Saitch, Bruiser

**Saito, Fred**
See Saito, Hiroyuki

**Saito, Hiroyuki** 1917- [CA]
*Japanese author and journalist*
* Saito, Fred

**Saito, Michiko**
See Fujiwara, Michiko

**Sakall, Cuddles**
See Szakall, Eugene Gero

**Sakall, S. Z.**
See Szakall, Eugene Gero

**Saki**
See Munro, Hector Hugh

**Saklatvala, Beram** 1911-1976
[CA, WD]
*British poet and author*
* Marsh, Henry

**Saks, Elmer Eliot**
See Fawcett, F[rank] Dubrez

**Saks, Gene**
See Saks, Jean Michael

**Saks, Jean Michael** 1921- [BEW]
*American actor and director*
* Saks, Gene

**Sakurazawa, Yukikazu** 1893-1966
[HDM, NAD]
*Cultist and founder of macrobiotics*
* Ohsawa, Georges

**Sakyamuni** [Sage of the Sakyas]
See Siddhartha

**Sal, Dizzy**
See Saldanha, Edward

**Sala, George Augustus** 1828-1895
[FFF, PA]
*British author*
* Cruiser, Benedict, M. M.
* G. A. S.

**Salaam, Kalamu Ya**
See Ferdinand, Val

**Salaam, Liaqat Ali**
See Clarke, Kenneth Spearman
[Kenny]

**Saladin**
See Ross, William Stewart

**Salahuddin, Daoud**
See Belfield, David

**Salamanca, D. F. Se**
See Ingram, John H.

**Salamanca, Lucy**
See Del Barco, Lucy Salamanca

**Salamatullah**
See Ullah, Salamat

**Salameh, Ali Hassan** 1943?-1979
*Palestinian terrorist*
* Abu Hassan
* [The] Red Prince

**Salas, Lauro** 1927- [WBC]
*Mexican boxer*
* Salas, Little Lauro

**Salas, Little Lauro**
See Salas, Lauro

**Salas, Paco**
See Lago Severino, Francisco

**Salathiel**
See Croly, George

**Salavina**
See Savane, Virgile

**Salazar, Lazaro** 1914-1957 [MK]
*American baseball player*
* [The] Blue Prince

**Salchichon** [The Sausage]
See Thomas

**Saldanha, Edward** 1934- [EJ]
*Burmese-born jazz musician*
* Sal, Dizzy

**Saldivar, Vicente**
See Saldivar Garcia, Vincente
Samuel

**Saldivar Garcia, Vincente Samuel**
1943- [BX, RBE]
*Mexican-born boxer*
* Saldivar, Vicente

**Sale, Aggie**
See Sale, Forest

**Sale, Charles** 1885-1936
[BEW, CED, F2]
*American comedian and author*
* Sale, Chic

**Sale, Chic**
*See* Sale, Charles

**Sale, Cornelius, Jr.** 1917?-
*American politician*
* Byrd, Robert Carlyle

**Sale, Forest** 1911-    [BB]
*American basketball player*
* Sale, Aggie

**Sale, Richard [Bernard]** 1911-    [CA]
*American author*
* St. John, John

**Saleeby, Caleb Williams** 1878- ?
[LAO]
*British physician and author*
* Crusader
* Lens

**Salerno, Anthony** 20th c.
*American gambler and loan shark*
* Salerno, Fat Tony

**Salerno, Fat Tony**
*See* Salerno, Anthony

**Sales, Soupy**
*See* Hines, Milton

**Saleski, Buffy**
*See* Saleski, Kathleen

**Saleski, Don** 1949-    [SMG]
*Canadian-born hockey player*
* [The] Bird

**Saleski, Kathleen** 1950-
*American author*
* Saleski, Buffy

**Saley, M. L.**    [FFF]
*American writer*
* Ditson, Dick

**[The] Salian**
*See* Conrad II

**[The] Salic**
*See* Conrad II

**Salim, Ahmad Khatab**
*See* Atkinson, A. K.

**Salinger, J. D.**
*See* Salinger, Jerome David

**Salinger, Jerome David** 1919-
[IPA, LC]
*American author*
* Salinger, J. D.

**Salisbury, Marchioness of**
1749?-1835    [HN]
*Grandmother of the prime minister*
* Old Sarum

**Salisbury, Marilla** 1908?-
*American track and field athlete*
* Sunbonnet Sue

**Salivarova, Zdena**
*See* Skvorecka, Zdena Salivarova

**Sallaska, Georgia Myrle** 1933-
[SFL]
*American author*
* Benedict, Myrle

**Sallaway, Myrtle May** 1893-
[NAA]
*American writer and poet*
* Cousin Gene
* Sallaway, Peggy Gene

**Sallaway, Peggy Gene**
*See* Sallaway, Myrtle May

**Sallee, Harry Franklin** 1885-1950
[AS, BE, PB]
*American baseball player*
* Sallee, Slim

**Sallee, Slim**
*See* Sallee, Harry Franklin

**Sallo, Denis de** 1626-1669    [SN]
*Founder of first literary journal*
* [The] New Aristarchus

**[The] Sallust of France**
*See* Vichard, Cesar

**Sally Bugs Briguglio**
*See* Briguglio, Salvatore

**Salma, Abu**
*See* Karmi, Abdul Karim

**Salmasius**
*See* Saumaise, Claude

**Salmon, Annie Elizabeth [Martin]**
1899-    [AW, CA, WD]
*British author*
* Ashley, Elizabeth
* Martin, Nancy

**Salmon, Chico**
*See* Salmon, Rutherford Eduardo

**Salmon, Geraldine Gordon** 1897-
[WW]
*Author*
* Sarasin, J. G.

**Salmon, Hamilton** 1893-1962    [BB]
*American basketball player*
* Salmon, June

**Salmon, June**
*See* Salmon, Hamilton

**Salmon, Leon N.** 1845- ?    [PA]
*Author*
* Ixion
* Prince

**Salmon, Louis J.** 1880-1965    [AS]
*American football player*
* Salmon, Red

**Salmon, Percy R.** 1872- ?    [WWL]
*British author*
* Penlake, Richard

**Salmon, Red**
*See* Salmon, Louis J.

**Salmon, Rutherford Eduardo** 1940-
[BE]
*Panamanian-born baseball player*
* Salmon, Chico

**Salola, Eeero** 1902-    [IAW]
*Finnish author*
* Diogenes
* Lauri
* Lauri, Pikku

**Salomon** 13th c.    [HN]
* [The] Jew of Tewkesbury

**Salomon, Janet Lynn [Nowicki]**
1953-    [CA]
*American figure skater and author*
* Lynn, Janet

**Salomons, Jean-Pierre** 1909-    [FC]
*French-born actor*
* Aumont, Jean-Pierre

**Saloth Sar** 1925?-
*Cambodian premier*
* Pol Pot

**Salpeter, Mechel** 1892-
[BEW, EMT]
*American producer*
* Gordon, Max

**Salsbury, Mrs. Nate**    [FFF]
*Entertainer*
* Samuels, Ray

**Salt, Henry** 1780-1827    [PA]
*Author*
* [A] Traveler

**Salt, Jonathan**
*See* Neville, Derek

**[The] Salt King**
*See* Corbett, John

**[The] Salt of Art**
*See* Buonarroti, Michelangelo [or
Michael Angelo]

**Salt Rock Midkiff**
*See* Midkiff, Ezra Millington

**Salt, Sarah**
*See* Hobson, Coralie [Von Werner]

**Saltboy, Razor**
*See* Louis, Ray Baldwin

**Salten, Felix**
*See* Salzmann, Felix

**Salter, Cedric**
*See* Knight, Francis Edgar [Frank]

**Salter, Donald P. M.** 1942-    [CA]
*British author*
* Podmarsh, Rollo

**Salter, Edith A.**    [FFF]
*Author*
* Howard, Assunta

**Salter, Mary D.**
*See* Ainsworth, Mary D[insmore]
Salter

**Salter, Sy** 1926-    [IBW]
*American boxer*
* Total Man

**Salter, T. F.** 19th c.    [PA]
*Author*
* T. F. S.

**Saltikoff, W.**    [PA]
*Author*
* Stchedrin, Nikolai

**Saltis, Joseph** 20th c.    [BLB, PHM]
*American gangster*
* Saltis, Polock Joe

**Saltis, Polock Joe**
*See* Saltis, Joseph

**Saltonstall, Leverett** 1893?-1979
*American politician*
* Saltonstall, Old Lev
* Saltonstall, Salty

**Saltonstall, Old Lev**
*See* Saltonstall, Leverett

**Saltonstall, Salty**
*See* Saltonstall, Leverett

**Salty Dog Sam**
*See* Collins, Samuel

**Saltykov, Mikhail Evgrafovich**
1826-1889    [WBD]
*Russian author*
* Shchedrin, N.

**Saltzgaver, Jack**
*See* Saltzgaver, Otto Hamlin

**Saltzgaver, Otto Hamlin** 1905-
[BE]
*American baseball player*
* Saltzgaver, Jack

**Saltzman, Joseph [Joe]** 1939-    [CA]
*American author, producer, editor*
* Laertes, Joseph
* Michaels, Joe
* Roberts, Joe

**Salustri, Carlo Alberto** 1873-1950
[EWL]
*Italian poet*
* Trilussa

**Salva, Pierre** 1900?-1980
*French gypsy leader*
* King of the Gypsies of Europe

**Salvadori, Joyce**
*See* Lussu, Joyce [Salvadori]

**Salvadori, Massimo**
*See* Salvadori-Paleotti, Massimo

**Salvadori, Max William**
*See* Salvadori-Paleotti, Massimo

**Salvadori-Paleotti, Massimo** 1908-
[CA]
*British-born educator and author*
* Salvadori, Massimo
* Salvadori, Max William

**Salvason, Sigrum** 1909-1934    [SC]
*American actress*
* Randall, Rae

**Salvato, Sharon** 20th c.    [CA]
*Author*
* Taylor, Day [joint pseudonym
with Cornelia M. Parkinson]

**[The] Salvator Rosa of the Sea**
*See* Scott, Michael

**Salvatoriello**
*See* Rosa, Salvator

**Salvi, Giovanni Battista** 1605-1685
[WBD]
*Italian painter*
* [Il] Sassoferrato

**Salvi, Paul**
*See* DeLucia, Felice

**Salviati, Cecco di**
*See* De Rossi, Francesco

**Salviati, Leonardo** 1540-1589
[WBD]
*Italian scholar*
* Infarinato

**Salvo, Gyp**
*See* Salvo, Manuel

**Salvo, Manuel** 1913-    [BE]
*American baseball player*
* Salvo, Gyp

**Salzedo, Carlos**
*See* Salzedo, Leon

**Salzedo, Leon** 1885-1961    [MS]
*French musician*
* Salzedo, Carlos

**Salzer, Beeb**
*See* Salzer, Clarence M., Jr.

**Salzer, Clarence M., Jr.** 1933-
[OP]
*American scenic and lighting
designer*
* Salzer, Beeb

**Salzmann, Felix** 1869-1945 [LC]
*Hungarian-born author*
* Salten, Felix

**Sam Bam Cunningham**
*See* Cunningham, Sam[uel Lewis, Jr.]

**Sam, Butch**
*See* Sam, Robert

**Sam, Robert** 20th c. [RO2]
*American musician*
* Sam, Butch

**Sam the Man**
*See* Taylor, Samuel L.

**Sam the Plumber**
*See* DeCavalcante, Simone Rizzo

**Sam the Sham**
*See* Samudio, Domingo

**Samachson, Joseph** 1906-
[CA, SAT, SF]
*American author*
* Miller, John
* Morrison, William
* Sterling, Brett [house pseudonym, Standard Magazines]

**Samaniegos, Ramon Gil** 1899-1968
[BDF, CED, F1]
*Mexican-born actor*
* Novarro, Ramon

**Samarakis, Antonis** 1919- [IAW]
*Greek author*
* Kyprianos, Iossif

**Samaroff, Olga**
*See* Hickenlooper, Lucie Mary Olga Agnes

**Samarow, Gregor**
*See* Meding, Oskar

**Sambrot, William [Anthony]** 1920-
[ESF, IAW]
*American writer*
* Ayes, Anthony
* Ayes, William

**Samek, Viktor Oliver** 1898-1964
[BEW, BMH]
*Austrian-born comedian and musician*
* Brown, Harry
* [The] Continental Wizard
* Oliver, Vic
* [The] Piano Playing Baron

**[The] Samian Poet**
*See* Simonides

**[The] Samian Sage**
*See* Pythagoras

**Samira [Beautiful Flower]**
*See* Stahl, Eva

**Sammis, John** 1942- [CA, SAT]
*American author*
* Russell, Patrick

**Sammon, Winona** 1909-1941
*American actress*
* Shannon, Peggy

**Sammons, Fur**
*See* Sammons, James

**Sammons, James** 20th c. [PHM]
*American underworld figure*
* Sammons, Fur

**Sammy the Publican**
*See* Adams, Samuel

**Sammy the Rose**
*See* Rosenman, Samuel

**Samo, Mrs.** [FFF]
*Entertainer*
* Seymour, Laura

**Samoiloff, Louise Cripps**
*See* Cripps, Louise Lilian

**[The] Samosatian Philosopher**
*See* Lucian

**Samperi, Anthony** 20th c. [SG]
*Boxer*
* [The] Gas House Tartar
* Young, Terry

**Sampietro, Ines Isabella** 1909-
[BDF, FC, ITA]
*Italian actress*
* Miranda, Isa

**Sampleton, Samuel**
*See* Monti, Luigi

**Sampley, Alton** 1899-1957 [SC]
*American actor*
* Rae, Jack

**Sampliner, Louis H.** 20th c. [WGT]
*Author*
* Blade, Alexander [house pseudonym, Ziff-Davis]

**Sampsiceranus, Alabarches, the Jerusalemite**
*See* Pompey [or Pompeius], Cneius

**Sampson, Edgar Melvin** 1907-
[WWJ]
*American jazz musician*
* [The] Lamb

**Sampson, Emma Speed** 1868- ?
[NAA]
*American author*
* Speed, Nell

**Sampson, Henry** 19th c. [PA]
*Author*
* Pendragon

**Sampson, Linda Joy** 1945- [RO1]
*American singer*
* Scott, Linda

**Sampson, Ray** 1898-1964 [SC]
*American actor*
* Mayo, Harry A.

**Sampson, Richard Henry**
1896-1973 [CC, EMD, LC]
*British author*
* Hull, Richard

**Sampson, Sammy**
*See* Broonzy, William Lee Conley

**Sampson, Virginia Reid** 1909-1955
[SC]
*American actress*
* Carver, Lynn

**Sams, Jessie Bennett** 20th c. [IBW]
*American author*
* Sams, Veanie

**Sams, Veanie**
*See* Sams, Jessie Bennett

**Samsel, Helen Maring** 1903-
[NAA]
*American poet*
* Maring, Helen

**Samson** [FFF]
*Biblical strongman*
* [The] Hercules of the Jews
* [The] Jewish Hercules

**Samson, George Alexander Gibb**
1858-1918 [BEW, WBD]
*British actor and stage manager*
* Alexander, [Sir] George

**[The] Samson of England**
*See* Topham, Thomas

**Samsonov, Samson**
*See* Edelstein, Samson Iosifovich

**Samudio, Domingo** 1940?-
[PRS, RM, RO1]
*American singer*
* Sam the Sham

**Samuel, Valerie** 1910- [THR]
*British actress*
* Tudor, Valerie

**Samuels Bacon**
*See* Samuels, Philip Francis

**Samuels, Calvin** 20th c. [RM]
*Musician*
* Samuels, Fuzzy

**Samuels, Fuzzy**
*See* Samuels, Calvin

**Samuels, Howie**
*See* Hoffman, Abbie

**Samuels, Ike**
*See* Samuels, Samuel Earl

**Samuels, Jerry** 20th c. [RO1]
*American singer and songwriter*
* Napoleon XIV

**Samuels, Joseph Jonas [Joe]** 1905-
[BE]
*American baseball player*
* Samuels, Skabotch

**Samuels, Miriam** 1925- [FC]
*British actress*
* Karlin, Miriam

**Samuels, Philip Francis** 1881- ?
[WGT]
*Author*
* Samuels Bacon

**Samuels, Ray**
*See* Salsbury, Mrs. Nate

**Samuels, Samuel Earl** 1876- ?
[EJS]
*American baseball player*
* Samuels, Ike

**Samuels, Skabotch**
*See* Samuels, Joseph Jonas [Joe]

**Samuels, Victor**
*See* Banis, Victor J[erome]

**Samuelson, Julian** 1878-1934
[BEW]
*British playwright, producer, director*
* Wylie, Julian

**Samuelson, Morris Laurence** 1880-
? [THR]
*British playwright and librettist*
* Wylie, Lauri

**Samways, George Richmond** 1895-
[MBF]
*British author*
* Clifford, Martin [house pseudonym]
* Conquest, Owen [house pseudonym]
* Linley, Mark
* Masters, Paul
* Proctor, Paul

**Samways, George Richmond**
(Continued)
* Richards, Frank [house pseudonym]
* Richmond, George

**Samwell, Gertrude Constance**
1860?-1946 [THR]
*British actress*
* Featherstonhaugh, Constance

**Samwell-Smith, Paul** 1943- [RO2]
*British musician*
* Samwell-Smith, Sam

**Samwell-Smith, Sam**
*See* Samwell-Smith, Paul

**San Francisco, Mr.**
*See* Magnin, Cyril

**San Martin, Jose de** 1778-1850
[FFF, WBD]
*South American patriot*
* [The] Protector of Peru

**San Souce**
*See* McAfee, Nella Marshall

**San Vicente y Navarro, Rufino**
1880-1963 [GS]
*Spanish bullfighter*
* Chiquito de Begona [Little Fellow from Begona]

**Sanborn, B. X.**
*See* Ballinger, William Sanborn
[Bill]

**Sanborn, Duane** 1914- [CA]
*American author*
* Bradley, Duane

**Sanchez, Antonio** 20th c. [RBE]
*American boxer*
* Sanchez, Tony

**Sanchez, Cocoa**
*See* Sanchez, Ezequiel

**Sanchez, Ezequiel** 20th c. [RBE]
*Puerto Rican boxer*
* Sanchez, Cocoa

**Sanchez, Francisco** 1845-1924
[GS]
*Spanish bullfighter*
* Paco Frascuelo

**Sanchez, Pablo** 20th c. [GS]
*Spanish bullfighter*
* Barajitas [The Little Card Player]

**Sanchez, Paul** 1935- [TR]
*American actor*
* Sand, Paul

**Sanchez, Pedro**
*See* Spalla, Ignazio

**Sanchez, Sonia Knight** 1934-
[IBW]
*American author, poet, playwright*
* Mannan, Laila

**Sanchez, Tony**
*See* Sanchez, Antonio

**Sanchez Coello, Alonzo** 1515-1590
[DEP, FFF, SN]
*Portuguese painter*
* [The] Portuguese Titian
* [The] Titian of Portugal

**Sanchez de Almodovar, Bachiller Toribo**
*See* Del Monte y Aponte, Domingo

**Sanchez De Leon, Leandro**
1859-1914 [GS]
*Spanish bullfighter*
* Cacheta [Lever]

**Sanchez Del Campo, Jose**
1848-1925 [GS]
*Spanish bullfighter*
* Cara Ancha [Wide-Face]

**Sanchez Morales, Narciso** 1915-
[IAW]
*Spanish author*
* Aletes
* Anteo
* Narsanmor

**Sanchez Munoz, Gil** 1380?-1446
[WBD]
*Antipope*
* Clement VIII

**Sanchez Olivares, Luis** 1927- [GS]
*Colombian bullfighter*
* Diamante Negro [Black
Diamond]

**Sanchez Rodriguez, Jose**
1895-1957 [GS]
*Spanish bullfighter*
* Hipolito

**Sancho I** 1154-1212 [HN, WBD]
*King of Portugal*
* [The] City Builder
* [The] Father of His Country
* [The] Restorer of Cities

**Sancho II** ?-1072 [DNNS, WBD]
*King of Castile*
* [El] Fuerte
* [The] Strong

**Sancho II** 1208-1248 [WBD]
*King of Portugal*
* Capelo

**Sancho III** 970-1035
[DNNS, WBD]
*King of Navarre*
* [The] Great

**Sancho IV** ?-1076 [WBD]
*King of Navarre*
* [El] Noble

**Sancho IV** 1258-1295 [WBD]
*King of Spain*
* [El] Bravo

**Sancho VI** ?-1194 [WBD]
*King of Navarre*
* [El] Sabio [The Wise]

**Sancho VII** ?-1234 [WBD]
*King of Navarre*
* [El] Fuerte [The Strong]

**Sancta Clara**
*See* Davenport, Christopher

**Sanctuary, Brenda** 1934- [WD]
*British author and columnist*
* Campbell, Bridget

**Sand, George**
*See* Dudevant, Amandine Lucille
Aurore Dupin

**Sand, Heinie**
*See* Sand, John Henry

**Sand, John Henry** 1897-1958 [BE]
*American baseball player*
* Sand, Heinie

**Sand, Maurice**
*See* Dudevant, Maurice

**Sand, Paul**
*See* Sanchez, Paul

**Sand, Warren B.?**
*See* Tremaine, F[rederick] Orlin

**Sanda, Dominique**
*See* Varaigne, Dominique

**Sandaval, Jaime**
*See* Marlowe, Dan J[ames]

**Sanday, Edgar**
*See* Faure, Edgar

**Sandblad-Haneson, Emelie Cecilia
Sofia** 1889- [IAW]
*Swedish author*
* Torpare, Tord

**Sandburg, Carl [August]**
1878-1967 [CA, SAT]
*American poet and author*
* Militant
* Phillips, Jack

**Sandburg, Helga**
*See* Crile, Helga Sandburg

**Sandby, Paul** 1725-1809 [WBD]
*British engraver and painter*
* [The] Father of Watercolor Art

**Sande, Earl** 20th c.
*Jockey*
* Sande, Handy

**Sande, Handy**
*See* Sande, Earl

**Sandel, Cora**
*See* Fabricius, Sara

**Sandell, Lynn**
*See* Wickdahl, Lillian

**Sanden, Thomas** 18th c. [PA]
*Author*
* [A] Layman
* President

**Sander, Peter**
*See* Szarvas, Peter

**Sanders, Albert**
*See* Davidson, David

**Sanders, Butch**
*See* Sanders, Roy Garvin

**Sanders, Byrne Hope**
*See* Sperry, Byrne Hope

**Sanders, Charlie** 1946- [IBW]
*American football player*
* Deep, Charlie
* Sanders, Little Mackey

**Sanders, Clarence** 1952- [SMG]
*American football player*
* Sanders, Mad Dog

**Sanders, Colonel**
*See* Sanders, Harland

**Sanders, Daffy**
*See* Sanders, Kenneth George

**Sanders, Daphne**
*See* Randolph, Georgiana Ann

**Sanders, Daryl** 20th c.
*American football player*
* Sanders, Skunk

**Sanders, Deac**
*See* Sanders, John Maurice

**Sanders, Dorothy Lucie** 1917-
[CA]
*Australian author*
* Walker, Lucy

**Sanders, Ed** 1939- [CA]
*American poet, editor, filmmaker*
* Black, Hobart

**Sanders, Edward S.** 1914?-1936
[BEW]
*American theatrical performer*
* Abbott, Edward S.

**Sanders, Farrell** 1940- [EJ7]
*American jazz musician*
* Sanders, Pharoah

**Sanders, Harland** 1890?-1980
*American business executive*
* Sanders, Colonel

**Sanders, Henry R.** 1905-1958
[AS, SMG]
*American football coach*
* Sanders, Red

**Sanders, Jeanne**
*See* Rundle, Anne

**Sanders, Joe** 1896-1965 [PMJ]
*American bandleader*
* [The] Old Lefthander

**Sanders, John** 20th c. [SFL]
*Author*
* Comer, Ralph

**Sanders, John Maurice** 1950-
[SMG]
*American football player*
* Sanders, Deac

**Sanders, Josephine** 1898- [EMT]
*American actress, dancer, singer*
* Delroy, Irene

**Sanders, Kenneth George** 1941-
[BE]
*American baseball player*
* Sanders, Daffy

**Sanders, Kent**
*See* Wilkes-Hunter, Richard

**Sanders, Leonard** 1929- [CA]
*American author and journalist*
* Thomas, Dan

**Sanders, Little Mackey**
*See* Sanders, Charlie

**Sanders, Mad Dog**
*See* Sanders, Clarence

**Sanders, Noah**
*See* Blount, Roy [Alton], Jr.

**Sanders, Pep**
*See* Sanders, Roy Garvin

**Sanders, Pharoah**
*See* Sanders, Farrell

**Sanders, Red**
*See* Sanders, Henry R.

**Sanders, Roy Garvin** 1892-1950
[BE]
*American baseball player*
* Sanders, Butch
* Sanders, Pep

**Sanders, Roy L.** 1894- [BE]
*American baseball player*
* Sanders, Simon

**Sanders, Satch**
*See* Sanders, Thomas E.

**Sanders, Simon**
*See* Sanders, Roy L.

**Sanders, Skunk**
*See* Sanders, Daryl

**Sanders, Thomas** 1904-1967 [FC]
*British actor*
* Conway, Tom

**Sanders, Thomas E.** 1938-
[B10, IBW]
*American basketball coach*
* Sanders, Satch

**Sanders, Winston P.**
*See* Anderson, Poul [William]

**Sanderson, Derek Michael** 1946-
[B10, HR]
*Canadian hockey player*
* Sanderson, Turk

**Sanderson, [Ronald] Douglas** 1922-
[WW]
*Author*
* Brett, Martin
* Douglas, Malcolm

**Sanderson, F. W.**
*See* Sanderson, Frederick William

**Sanderson, Frederick William**
1857-1922 [LC]
*British educator and author*
* Sanderson, F. W.

**Sanderson, H. P.** 20th c. [SFP]
*Author*
* Carr, Joan

**Sanderson, Ivan T[erence]**
1911-1973 [CA, SAT]
*Scottish-born author*
* Roberts, Terence

**Sanderson, John** 1783-1844 [PA]
*Author*
* Robertjeot

**Sanderson, Julia**
*See* Sackett, Julia

**Sanderson, Kent** 1898-1973
[F1, F2, SC]
*American actor*
* Roosevelt, Buddy

**Sanderson, Sabina W[arren]** 1931-
[CA]
*American editor*
* Fawcett, Marion

**Sanderson, Turk**
*See* Sanderson, Derek Michael

**Sandette**
*See* Walsh, Marie A.

**Sandford, Marjorie** 1910- [THR]
*British actress and singer*
* Dey, Marjorie

**Sandford, Nell Mary** 1936- [WD]
*British author*
* Dunn, Nell

**Sandford, Samuel** [SN]
*British actor*
* [The] Spagnolet of the Theatre

**Sandford, Stanley J.** 1894-1961
[SC]
*American actor*
* Sandford, Tiny

**Sandford, Tiny**
*See* Sandford, Stanley J.

**Sandison, Janet**
See Cameron, Elizabeth Jane

**Sandjar** 1117-1158
[DEP, FFF, SN]
*Seljuke sultan*
* [The] Alexander of Persia
* [The] Persian Alexander
* [The] Second Alexander

**Sandlin, Joann S[chepers] De Lora**
1935- [CA]
*American author and sociologist*
* De Lora, Joann S.

**Sandman, Peter M[ark]** 1945- [CA]
*American author*
* David, William

**Sandor, Alfred**
See Sandwina, Alfred Heymann

**Sandoval Alarcon, Mario** 20th c.
*Guatemalan politician*
* [The] Godfather

**Sandow, Eugen[e]**
See Mueller, Frederick

**Sandown, Margaret**
See Stone, Ena Margaret

**Sandoz, Mari [Susette]** 1901-1966
[B10, CA, SAT]
*American author*
* Macumber, Mari

**Sandre, Thierry**
See Moulie, Charles

**Sands, Bedwin**
See Raffalovich, George

**Sands, Dave**
See Ritchie, David

**Sands, Dave?** [house pseudonym?]
See Walton, Bryce

**Sands, Jimmy**
See Santucci, Jimmy

**Sands, John**
See Hutchinson, William

**Sands, Johnny**
See Harp, John

**Sands, Leo G[eorge]** 1912- [CA]
*American engineer and author*
* Craig, Lee
* Helmi, Jack

**Sands, Leonard**
See Sellers, Connie Leslie, Jr.

**Sands, Martin**
See Burke, John [Frederick]

**Sands, Piggy**
See Sands, Sam

**Sands, Robert Charles** 1799-1832
[FFF, PA]
*American author and journalist*
* Amphilogist
* Herbert, Francis, Esq.

**Sands, Sam** 20th c. [OBW]
*American baseball player*
* Sands, Piggy

**Sandwina, Alfred Heymann** 1918-
[BEW]
*Hungarian-born actor*
* Sandor, Alfred

**Sandy, Max**
See Saunders, Carl Maxon

**Sandy, Stephen**
See Sandys, Stephen

**Sandys, George Windle**
See Crawfurd, Oswald John
Frederick

**Sandys, K.** [PA]
*Author*
* Syndas, Kate

**Sandys, Oliver**
See Evans, Marguerite Florence
Helene Jervis

**Sandys, Stephen** 1935- [CA]
*American author and poet*
* Sandy, Stephen

**Sane, Jacques Noel** 1740-1832
[HN]
*French naval engineer*
* [Le] Vauban de la Marine

**Sanford, Edward** 1809- ? [PA]
*Author*
* Palmer, Pot-Pie

**Sanford, George F.** 1870-1938 [FB]
*American football player and coach*
* Sanford, Sandy

**Sanford, John Elroy** 1922-
[CA, IBW, IPA]
*American actor and comedian*
* Chicago Red
* Foxx, Redd
* Sanford, Smiley

**Sanford, Laura** [PA]
*Author*
* Fanchon

**Sanford, Sandy**
See Sanford, George F.

**Sanford, Smiley**
See Sanford, John Elroy

**Sang, Samantha**
See Gray, Cheryl

**Sangallo, Antonio Picconi da**
See Cordiani, Antonio

**Sangallo, Giuliano da**
See Giamberti, Giuliano

**Sangchilli, Baltazar**
See Belenguer Hevoas, Baltazar

**Sanger, Edward** 1882-1956
[F2, FC]
*British actor*
* Herbert, Holmes

**Sanger, George** 1825- 1911 [WBD]
*British circus owner*
* Lord George

**Sanger, Herbert**
See Hoffmann, Lothar

**Sanger, John** 1816-1889 [WBD]
*British circus owner*
* Lord John

**Sangerson, Margaret Love**
See Bedford-Jones, Henry [James
O'Brien]

**Sanglier des Ardennes**
See La Marck, Guillaume [or
William] de

**Sangodare, Asjantenu**
See Slory, Michael

**Sangster, Ann**
See Shennan, Victoria

**Sangster, Jimmy** 1927- [SFL]
*Welsh-born author*
* Sansom, John [joint pseudonym
with Alfred Edgar]

**Sanguillen, Manny**
See Sanguillen, Manuel DeJesus

**Sanguillen, Manuel DeJesus** 1944-
[BE, SMG]
*Panamanian-born baseball player*
* Sanguillen, Manny

**Sanicki, Butch**
See Sanicki, Ed[ward Robert]

**Sanicki, Ed[ward Robert]** 1924-
[BE]
*American baseball player*
* Sanicki, Butch

**Sanjay, Rajendra**
See Gupta, Rajendra Prasad

**Sannazaro, Jacopo [or Giacomo]**
1458-1530 [DEP, FFF, RH]
*Italian poet*
* Actius Sincerus
* [The] Christian Virgil

**Sannella, Andy**
See Sannella, Anthony

**Sannella, Anthony** 1900-1961?
[WWJ]
*American jazz musician*
* Sannella, Andy

**Sanraku, Kano**
See Mitsuyori, Kimura

**Sanroman, Ernesto** 20th c. [GS]
*Mexican bullfighter*
* [El] Queretaro [The Man from
Queretaro]

**Sans Gene, Madame**
See Lefebvre, Catherine Hubscher
[Duchess of Dantzig]

**Sans Malice**
See Akakia, Martin

**Sans Peur**
See John [or Jean]

**Sans Peur, Jean**
See Babou, Hippolyte

**Sansom, John** [joint pseudonym with
Jimmy Sangster]
See Edgar, Alfred

**Sansom, John** [joint pseudonym with
Alfred Edgar]
See Sangster, Jimmy

**Sansovino, Andrea**
See Contucci, Andrea

**Sansovino, Jacopo**
See Tatti, Jacopo

**Santa Claus**
See Nicholas

**Santa Maria**
See Powell-Smith, Vincent [Walter
Francis]

**Santamaria, Mongo**
See Santamaria, Ramon

**Santamaria, Nick** 1941- [RO1]
*American singer*
* Santo, Nick

**Santamaria, Ramon** 1922- [IBW]
*Cuban-born jazz musician*
* Santamaria, Mongo

**Santana, Blas Silverio** 1950-
[SMG]
*Dominican-born baseball player*
* Santana, Chi Chi

**Santana, Chi Chi**
See Santana, Blas Silverio

**Santee, Collier**
See Flexner, Stuart Berg

**Santell, Alfred** 1895- [WEF]
*American director*
* Sautell, Al

**Santerre, Antoine Joseph**
1752-1809 [SN]
*French politician and army officer*
* [The] Frothy General

**Santesson, H. S.**
See Santesson, Hans Stefan

**Santesson, Hans Stefan** ?-1975
[SF, SFP]
*American author and editor*
* O'Quinn, Vithaldas H.
* Santesson, H. S.

**Santi [or Sanzio?], Raffaello**
1483-1520 [FFF, RH, WBD]
*Italian painter*
* [The] Affable
* [The] Angel of the Sun
* [The] Divine
* Raphael
* [The] Sociable Spirit

**Santiago, Blackie**
See Santiago, Lester

**Santiago, Burnell** 1915-1944
[NOJ]
*American jazz musician*
* [The] King of Boogie Woogie

**Santiago, Captain**
See Irurzun, Hugo

**Santiago, Jose Guillermo** 1928-
[BE]
*Puerto Rican-born baseball player*
* Santiago, Pants

**Santiago, Lester** 1909-1965 [NOJ]
*American jazz musician*
* Santiago, Blackie

**Santiago, Pants**
See Santiago, Jose Guillermo

**Santiel, Powerpack**
See Santiel, Terral

**Santiel, Terral** 20th c. [RO2]
*American musician*
* Santiel, Powerpack

**Santley, Joseph**
See Mansfield, Joseph

**Santly, Banjo**
See Santly, Joseph H.

**Santly, Joseph H.** 1886-1962
[BEW]
*American theatrical performer and
songwriter*
* Santly, Banjo

**[El] Santo**
See Ferdinand III

**Santo, Nick**
See Santamaria, Nick

**Santoni, Espartaco B.** 20th c. [WF]
*Italian actor*
* Anthony, Robert

**Santop, Louis**
See Loftin, Louis Santop

**Santos, Alfred?**
See Tremaine, F[rederick] Orlin

**Santos, Domingo**
See Domingo, Pedro

**Santos, Enrique** 1859-1935 [GS]
*Spanish bullfighter*
* Tortero [Cake Maker]

**Santos, Helen** 1939- [AW]
*British author*
* Griffiths, Helen

**Santos, Luis Joaquin**
See Quintana, Luis Joaquin

**Santos Pue, Gaston** 1931- [GS]
*Mexican bullfighter*
* [El] Centauro Potosino [The
 Centaur from San Luis Potosi]

**[A] Sant'ring Bully**
See James II

**Santucci, Girolamo** 20th c.
[BLB, PHM]
*American underworld figure*
* Doyle, Bobby

**Santucci, Jimmy** 1922- [MY]
*American jazz musician*
* Sands, Jimmy

**Sanville, Jean** 1918- [CA]
*American psychotherapist and
author*
* Livermore, Jean

**Saperstein, Abraham M. [Abe]**
1901?-1966 [BB, EJS]
*American basketball coach and team
owner*
* [The] Barnum of Basketball
* Little Caesar

**Sapiens**
See Gildas [or Gildus]

**Sapiens**
See Laelius, Gaius

**Sapiens, Doctor**
See Wessel, Johann [or John]

**Sapon, Archie** 20th c. [SG]
*Boxer*
* Bell, Archie

**Sapper**
See McNeile, Herman Cyril

**Sappho** 7th c. BC
[FFF, HN, WBD]
*Greek poet*
* [The] Tenth Muse

**[The] Sappho of Brabant**
See Bijns [or Byns], Anna

**[The] Sappho of Toulouse**
See Isaure, Clemence

**Sapte, W.**
See Edwards, Robert Hamilton

**[The] Sapulpa Giant**
See Morris, Carl B.

**Saqorewec, E.**
See McElhanon, Kenneth Andrew

**Sara**
See Blake, Sally Mirliss

**Sarac, Roger**
See Caras, Roger A[ndrew]

**Saraceni, Eugene** 1902-
[GME, OCS]
*American golfer*
* Knickers, Mr.
* Sarazen, Gene

**Sarachek, Bernard** 20th c. [EJS]
*American basketball player*
* Sarachek, Red

**Sarachek, Red**
See Sarachek, Bernard

**[The] Sarah Bernhardt of the Cafe
Concert**
See Guilbert, Yvette

**Sarandon, Susan**
See Tomaling, Susan

**Sarasin, J. G.**
See Salmon, Geraldine Gordon

**Sarasqueta, Indalecio** 1860-1928
[OCS]
*Spanish pelota player*
* Chiquito D'Eibar [Little Fellow
 from Eibar]

**Saraswati, S. K.**
See Saraswati, Sarasi Kumar

**Saraswati, Sarasi Kumar** 1908-
[IAW]
*Indian author*
* Saraswati, S. K.

**Sarazen, Dolores**
See Hertzler, Edith DeVilliers

**Sarazen, Gene**
See Saraceni, Eugene

**Sarban**
See Wall, John William

**Sarbievius**
See Sarbiewski, Mathieu Cassimer

**Sarbiewski, Mathieu Cassimer**
1595-1640 [PA]
*Author*
* Sarbievius

**Sarbrow, Cepre**
See Barrows, P. S.

**Sarcey, Francisque** 1827-1899
[WBD]
*French journalist and critic*
* Binet, Satane

**[The] Sardanapalus of China**
See Cheo-tsin

**[The] Sardanapalus of Germany**
See Wenceslaus [or Wenceslas]

**Sardi, Ivan**
See Szepes, Ivan

**Sardina, Adolfo** 1933?- [B10]
*Cuban-born fashion designer*
* Adolfo

**Sardinias, Eligio** 1910- [BX, RBE]
*Cuban boxer*
* Chocolate, Kid
* [The] Cuban Bon Bon

**Sardon, F. J.** [PA]
*Author*
* Carle

**Sarfatti, Margherita** 1886-1961
[WBD]
*Italian author and critic*
* Cidie
* [El] Sereno

**Sargent, Aaron A.** 1827-1887
[FFF]
*American politician and diplomat*
* Sargent, Effigy

**Sargent, Brian [Lawrence]** 1927-
[CA]
*British music educator, author,
composer*
* Strange, N. Blair

**Sargent, Chic**
See Sargent, Epes Winthrop

**Sargent, Effigy**
See Sargent, Aaron A.

**Sargent, Ella S.** [PA]
*Author*
* Elliott, Elinor

**Sargent, Epes Winthrop**
1872?-1938 [BEW]
*Bahamian-born drama critic*
* Sargent, Chic

**Sargent, Gary** 1954- [SMG]
*American hockey player*
* Sargent, Sarge

**Sargent, Henry Jackson** 1809- ?
[FFF, PA]
*American poet*
* Anonym, Walter
* Legatee, Residuary

**Sargent, Horse Belly**
See Sargent, Joseph Alexander
[Joe]

**Sargent, Joseph**
See Sargente, Giuseppe Daniel

**Sargent, Joseph Alexander [Joe]**
1893-1950 [BE]
*American baseball player*
* Sargent, Horse Belly

**Sargent, Judith** 1751-1820 [PA]
*American author*
* Constantia

**Sargent, Lucius Manlius**
1786-1867 [FFF, PA]
*American poet and journalist*
* Sexton of the Old School
* Sigma

**Sargent, Mrs. H. J.** [FFF]
*Entertainer*
* Bailey, Hannah

**Sargent, Nathan** 1794-1875
[FFF, PA]
*American author*
* Oldschool, Oliver

**Sargent, Richard**
See Cox, Richard

**Sargent, Sarge**
See Sargent, Gary

**Sargent, Thomas Henry** 1895-1963
[BEW, FC]
*British entertainer*
* [The] Cheeky Chappie
* Miller, Max

**Sargente, Giuseppe Daniel** 1925-
[FIR]
*American director*
* Sargent, Joseph

**[El] Sargento [The Sergeant]**
See Rodriguez, Guillermo

**Sari**
See Fleur, Anne

**Sarin, Max Kenneth** 1912-1967
[SC]
*American actor*
* MacSarin, Kenneth

**Sarkar, P. R.** 1921- [NAD]
*Indian educator*
* Shrii Shrii Anandamurti

**Sarkia, Kaarlo Teodor**
See Sulin, Kaarlo Teodor

**Sarkis**
See Zabunyan, Serkis

**Sarle, Charles Spenser** 20th c.
[WWL]
*British author and journalist*
* Amory, Arthur R.

**Sarlo**
See King, Carroll E.

**Sarma, Challa Radhakrishna** 1929-
[IAW]
*Indian author*
* Krishna

**Sarment, Jean**
See Bellemere, Jean

**Sarmiento, Manny**
See Sarmiento Aponte, Manuel
Eduardo

**Sarmiento Aponte, Manuel Eduardo**
1956- [BR]
*Venezuelan-born baseball player*
* Sarmiento, Manny

**Sarne, Michael**
See Plummer, Thomas Arthur

**Sarnian**
See Falla, Frank W.

**Saroff, Morton** 1924- [ITA]
*American music executive*
* Jay, Morty

**Sarony, Leslie**
See Frye, Leslie

**Saroyan, William** 1908-1981
[CA, LC]
*American author*
* Goryan, Sirak

**Sarpi, Paolo**
See Sarpi, Pietro

**Sarpi, Pietro** 1552-1623
[FFF, SN, WBD]
*Italian prelate*
* Paolo, [Fra]
* Paul, [Father]
* Paul of Venice
* Paulus Servita
* Paulus Venetus
* Sarpi, Paolo

**Sarr, Kenneth**
See Reddin, Kenneth Shiels

**Sarrapede, James** 1904-1972
[PMJ, WWJ]
*American jazz musician*
* Lytell, Jimmy

**Sarrazin, Jacques Michel Andre**
1940- [ITA]
*Canadian-born actor*
* Sarrazin, Michael

**Sarrazin, Michael**
See Sarrazin, Jacques Michel
Andre

**Sarruf, Alexander** 1908-  [F2, FC]
*Egyptian actor*
* D'Arcy, Alex

**Sarsfield, C. P.**
*See* Marshner, Connaught Coyne

**Sartees, M. Edward**  [PA]
*Author*
* Jorrocks, John

**Sarti, Signor**
*See* Ashton, Knight

**Sarto, Andrea del**
*See* D'Agnolo di Francesco,
Andrea Domenico

**Sarto, Ben**
*See* Fawcett, F[rank] Dubrez

**Sarto, Giuseppe Melchiorre**
1835-1914  [CBS, DNNS, WBD]
*Pope*
* [The] Peasant Pope
* Pius X

**Sartorius**
*See* Snyders, Johann

**Sartorius, [Sir] G. R.** 1790- ?  [PA]
*Author*
* Penhafirme, Count of

**Sarver, Hannah**
*See* Nielsen, Jean Sarver

**Sarvis, Andrew** 20th c.  [OBW]
*American baseball player*
* Sarvis, Smoky

**Sarvis, Smoky**
*See* Sarvis, Andrew

**Saslavsky, Luis** 20th c.  [WF]
*Author*
* Fourcade, Simon

**Sass, Charles**  [FFF]
*American writer*
* Centaur

**Sass, George H.**  [FFF, PA]
*American writer*
* Gray, Barton

**Sass, Job**
*See* Foxcroft, George A.

**[Il] Sassoferrato**
*See* Salvi, Giovanni Battista

**Sassoon, Richa** 1858-1927  [JL]
*Indian-born publisher*
* Beer, Rachel

**Satane, Paul**
*See* Haill, Robert Godfrey

**Satanella**
*See* Burnham, Mary Hewins

**Satchell, Clarence** 20th c.  [RO2]
*American musician*
* Satchell, Satch

**Satchell, Satch**
*See* Satchell, Clarence

**Satchmo**
*See* Armstrong, [Daniel] Louis

**[El] Satelite [The Satellite]**
*See* Ruiz De La Torre, Victor

**Sathima**
*See* Benjamin, Bea

**Satiricus**
*See* Roetter, Charles Frederick

**Sato, Masahiko**
*See* Satoh, Masahiko

**Satoh, Masahiko** 1941-  [EJ7]
*Japanese-born jazz musician*
* Sato, Masahiko

**Satprem**
*See* Enginger, Bernard

**Satre, Magnus** 20th c.  [BBH]
*American skier*
* [The] Iron Man

**Satriano, Satch**
*See* Satriano, Thomas Victor

**Satriano, Thomas Victor** 1940-
[BE]
*American baseball player*
* Satriano, Satch

**Satterfield, Charles** [joint pseudonym
with Frederik Pohl]
*See* Alvarez Del Rey, Ramon
Felipe San Juan Mario Silvio Enrico

**Satterfield, Charles** [joint pseudonym
with Ramon Felipe San Juan
Alvarez Del Rey]
*See* Pohl, Frederik

**Satterly, Weston**
*See* Sunners, William

**Satterwhite, Collen Gray**
1920-1978  [ASC]
*American musician*
* Satterwhite, Tex

**Satterwhite, Tex**
*See* Satterwhite, Collen Gray

**Sattin, Lonnie**
*See* Staton, Alonzo Louis Lee

**Sattler, Lisbeth** 1894-1976  [BBD]
*German opera singer*
* Rethberg, Elisabeth

**[The] Saturday Fox**
*See* Meyer, Leo Robert

**Saturn, Sergeant** [house pseudonym]
*See* Friend, Oscar J[erome]

**Saturn, Sergeant** [house pseudonym]
*See* Merwin, [W.] Sam[uel], Jr.

**Saturn, Sergeant** [house pseudonym]
*See* Weisinger, Mort[imer]

**[The] Satyr**
*See* Charles II

**Satz, Frances** 1915-1963  [SC]
*American actress*
* Keating, Katherine
* Sage, Frances

**Saud, Sulaimon**
*See* Tyner, Alfred McCoy

**Sauer, Don** 20th c.  [RBE]
*Boxing promoter*
* Sauer, Sailor Don

**Sauer, Edward** 1920-  [BE]
*American baseball player*
* Sauer, Horn

**Sauer, Horn**
*See* Sauer, Edward

**Sauer, Joseph** 1901-  [FC]
*American actor*
* Sawyer, Joseph

**Sauer, Muriel Stafford** 20th c.
[CA]
*American graphologist and author*
* Stafford, Muriel

**Sauer, Sailor Don**
*See* Sauer, Don

**Sauget, J. S.** 1871- ?  [NAA]
*French-born naturalist and author*
* Leon, Frere

**Sauguet, Henri**
*See* Poupard, Henri-Pierre

**Saul, Beverly Jean** 1928-
[ITA, SW]
*American actress*
* Tyler, Beverly

**Saul of Tarsus** ?- 67?
[DEP, FF, WBD]
*Saint*
* [The] Apostle of the Gentiles
* Paul

**Saul, Oscar**
*See* Halpern, Oscar Saul

**Sauls, Judi Lee** 1947-  [SW]
*Actress*
* Meredith, Lee

**Sault, R. O.**
*See* Swan, Charles F.

**Saumaise, Claude** 1588-1658  [PA]
*Author*
* Salmasius

**Saunders, Allen** 1899-  [WECO]
*American cartoonist*
* Allen, Dale

**Saunders, Ann Loreille** 1930-  [WD]
*British author*
* Cox-Johnson, Ann

**Saunders, Caleb**
*See* Heinlein, Robert A[nson]

**Saunders, Carl Maxon** 1890-1974
[CA]
*American journalist*
* Sandy, Max

**Saunders, Carl McK.**
*See* Ketchum, Philip

**Saunders, David**
*See* Sontup, Dan[iel]

**Saunders, David**  [FFF]
*Author*
* [The] Shepherd of Salisbury
Plain

**Saunders, Edward** 1866-1910
[BMH]
*British comedian, singer, songwriter*
* Deane, Charles

**Saunders, Frederick** 1807- ?  [PA]
*Author*
* [An] Epicure

**Saunders, Hilary Aidan St. George**
1898-1951  [LC, TC, WW]
*British author*
* Beeding, Francis [joint
pseudonym with John Leslie
Palmer]
* Pilgrim, David [joint pseudonym
with John Leslie Palmer]

**Saunders, Ione**
*See* Cole, Margaret Alice

**Saunders, Jean** 1932-  [CA, WD]
*British author*
* Blake, Sally
* Innes, Jean
* Summers, Rowena

**Saunders, Joe** 1842-1884  [BMH]
*British entertainer*
* Leybourne, George

**Saunders, Killer**
*See* Saunders, Mark

**Saunders, Lawrence** [joint
pseudonym with Clarisy Musadore
(Ogden) Davis]
*See* Davis, Burton

**Saunders, Lawrence** [joint
pseudonym with Burton Davis]
*See* Davis, Clarisy Musadore
[Ogden]

**Saunders, Mark** 20th c.  [BBH]
*Boxer*
* Saunders, Killer

**Saunders, Red**
*See* Saunders, Theodore

**Saunders, Richard**
*See* Franklin, Benjamin

**Saunders, Robert** 1727-1783  [FFF]
*British author*
* Burlington
* Llewellyn
* Murray
* Spencer, Nat

**Saunders, Russell**
*See* Wiley, Carl A.

**Saunders, Russell Collier** 1906-
[BE]
*American baseball player*
* Saunders, Rusty

**Saunders, Rusty**
*See* Saunders, Russell Collier

**Saunders, Theodore** 1912-
[EJ, WWJ]
*American jazz musician*
* Saunders, Red

**Saunders, Theodore** 20th c.  [WW]
*Author*
* Scott, Denis [joint pseudonym
with Mary Means]

**Saunders, Wallace** 20th c.  [IBW]
*American songwriter*
* Saunders, Wash

**Saunders, Wash**
*See* Saunders, Wallace

**Saunders, Wes**
*See* Bounds, Sydney J[ames]

**Saura, Carlos**
*See* Altares Saura, Carlos

**Sauser-Hall, Frederic** 1887-1961
[EWL, LC, OCF]
*French-born poet and author*
* Cendrars, Blaise

**Saussure, Rene de** 20th c.  [WBD]
*Swiss-French philologist*
* Antido

**Sautel, Maureen Ann** 1951-  [CA]
*American author*
* McGinn, Maureen Ann

**Sautell, Al**
*See* Santell, Alfred

**Sautereau, Barry** 1932-    [TR]
*British actor*
* Kent, Barry

**Sauvage, Franck**
*See*  Horn, Maurice

**Sauvage, Sieur du**
*See*  Brissot, Roland

**Sauvageau, Juan** 1917-    [CA]
*Canadian-born author*
* Lavoix, Jean

**Sauval, Henri** 1620?-1669?    [SN]
*French historian*
* [The] Stowe of France

**Sava, George**
*See*  Milkomane, George Alexis
Milkomanovich

**Sava, Jimmy** 1895-1960    [BEW]
*American-born actor*
* Savo, Jimmy

**Savage, Blake**
*See*  Goodwin, Harold Leland [Hal]

**Savage, Catharine**
*See*  Brosman, Catharine Savage

**Savage, Christina** [joint pseudonym
with Frank Schaefer]
*See*  Newcomb, Kerry

**Savage, Christina** [joint pseudonym
with Kerry Newcomb]
*See*  Schaefer, Frank

**Savage, D. S.**
*See*  Savage, Derek Stanley

**Savage, David**
*See*  Hossent, Harry

**Savage, David Earle, Jr.** 1946-
[EAR]
*American auto racer*
* Savage, Swede

**Savage, Derek Stanley** 1917-
[MBL]
*British critic*
* Savage, D. S.

**Savage, Fred**
*See*  Savage, Richard LeQuesne

**Savage, Gordon** 1906-    [CEI]
*Canadian-born hockey player*
* Savage, Tony

**Savage, Houston**
*See*  DeBlasio, Gene

**Savage, Ian**
*See*  Giggal, Kenneth

**Savage, John**
*See*  Youngs, John

**Savage, John** 1828-1888    [FFF, PA]
*Irish-born journalist, poet,
playwright*
* Richards, Ezek
* Touchstone

**Savage, Leslie**
*See*  Duff, Douglas Valder

**Savage, M. J.** 19th c.    [PA]
*Author*
* [A] Lunar Wray

**Savage, Mary**
*See*  Dresser, Mary

**Savage, Mildred** [Spitz] 1919-    [CA]
*American author*
* Barrie, Jane

**Savage, Oscar**
*See*  Montague, Bruce Alexander

**Savage, Richard**
*See*  Roe, Ivan

**Savage, Richard** [Fourth Earl Rivers]
1660?-1712    [HN]
*British soldier*
* Tyburn Dick

**Savage, Richard LeQuesne** 1955-
[DC]
*British cricketer*
* Savage, Fred

**Savage, Swede**
*See*  Savage, David Earle, Jr.

**Savage Tom Thomas**
*See*  Thomas, Thomas W. [Tom]

**Savage, Tony**
*See*  Savage, Gordon

**Savalas, Aristotle** 1925-    [IPA, SW]
*American actor*
* Savalas, Telly

**Savalas, Telly**
*See*  Savalas, Aristotle

**Savane, Virgile** 1865-1920?    [CW]
*West Indian author and poet*
* Salavina

**Savarin**
*See*  Courtine, Robert

**Savelli, Cencio** 13th c.    [WBD]
*Pope*
* Honorius III

**Savelli, Giacomo** 1210?-1287
[WBD]
*Pope*
* Honorius IV

**Saverine, Rabbit**
*See*  Saverine, Robert Paul

**Saverine, Robert Paul** 1941-    [BE]
*American baseball player*
* Saverine, Rabbit

**Savery, Constance Winifred** 1897-
[IAW]
*British author*
* Cloberry, Elizabeth
* Rycon

**Savi, E. W.**
*See*  Savi, Ethel Winifred Bryning

**Savi, Ethel Winifred Bryning**
?-1954    [LC]
*British author*
* Savi, E. W.

**Savidge, Ralph Austin** 1879-1959
[BE]
*American baseball player*
* [The] Human Whipcord

**Savile**
*See*  Sothern, Henry

**Savile, [Sir] George** [Marquis of
Halifax] 1630?-1695    [SN]
*British statesman*
* [The] Trimmer

**Savile, [Sir] Henry** 1549-1622    [SN]
*British scholar*
* [The] Lay Bishop

**Savin, Una**
*See*  Hepworth, Mrs. George H.

**Savinkov, Boris Viktorovich**
1879-1925    [B10, CD]
*Russian terrorist and author*
* Ropshin, V.

**[The] Savior of His Country**
*See*  Pichegru, Charles

**[The] Savior of His Country**
*See*  Washington, George

**[The] Savior of Paris**
*See*  Gallieni, Joseph Simon

**[The] Savior of Protestantism**
*See*  Gustavus Adolphus

**Savior of the Texas League**
*See*  Hoskins, Dave

**[The] Saviour of Rome**
*See*  Marius, Caius

**[The] Saviour of Society**
*See*  Bonaparte, Charles Louis
Napoleon

**[The] Saviour of the Nation**
*See*  Cromwell, Oliver

**[The] Saviour of the Nations**
*See*  Wellesley, Arthur

**[The] Saviour of the People**
*See*  FitzOsbert, William

**Saviozzi, Adriana**
*See*  Mazza, Adriana

**Savitri Priya, [Swami]**
*See*  Lynott, Jessica

**Savo, Jimmy**
*See*  Sava, Jimmy

**Savoir, Alfred**
*See*  Poznanski, Alfred

**Savoldi, Joseph A.** 1909-1974    [FB]
*Italian-born football player*
* Savoldi, Jumpin' Joe

**Savoldi, Jumpin' Joe**
*See*  Savoldi, Joseph A.

**Savona, Leopoldo** 20th c.    [FDG]
*Italian director*
* Colman, L.

**Savonarola, Jeremy**
*See*  Mahony, Francis

**Savory, Kenneth** 1873?-1923
[BEW]
*British-born comedian*
* Douglas, Kenneth

**Savory, [Sir] Reginald Arthur**
1894-    [AW]
*British writer*
* Ledsam

**Savoy, Anne**
*See*  Brooks, Anne Sooy

**Savoy, Ashton** 20th c.    [NBB]
*American singer*
* Conroy, Ashton

**Savoy, Houston**
*See*  DeBlasio, Gene

**Savoy, Mark**
*See*  Turner, Robert [Harry]

**Savransky, Moe**
*See*  Savransky, Morris

**Savransky, Morris** 1929-    [BE]
*American baseball player*
* Savransky, Moe

**Saw, Buck**
*See*  Aby, Joe C.

**Sawamura, Kunitaro**
*See*  Kato, Tomoichi

**Sawatski, Carl Ernest** 1927-
[BE, PB]
*American baseball player and
manager*
* Sawatski, Swats

**Sawatski, Swats**
*See*  Sawatski, Carl Ernest

**Sawell, Larry**    [IBW]
*American disc jockey*
* [The] Round Mound of Sound
* [The] Sugar Pie Guy
* [The] Tokyo Giant

**Sawley, Petra**
*See*  Marsh, John

**Sawtelle, William Carter**
*See*  Graham, Roger Phillips

**Sawtille, Mrs. E. W.** 19th c.    [PA]
*Author*
* Towne, Tracy

**Sawtre, William** ?-1401    [HN]
*British heretic*
* [The] First English Martyr

**Sawyer**
*See*  Wirtanen, Atos Kasimir

**Sawyer, Buddy**
*See*  Estep, Harold

**Sawyer, Carl**
*See*  Schreuer, Carl

**Sawyer, Carl Everett** 1890-1957
[BE]
*American baseball player*
* Sawyer, Huck

**Sawyer, Corinne Holt** 20th c.    [CA]
*American author*
* Rickert, Corinne Holt

**Sawyer, Country**
*See*  Sawyer, John

**Sawyer, Eugene T.** 1846-1924
[EMD, WW]
*Author*
* Carter, Nicholas

**Sawyer, Frederick William** 1810- ?
[FFF]
*American legal writer*
* Canty Carl
* Carl

**Sawyer, Huck**
*See*  Sawyer, Carl Everett

**Sawyer, John**
*See*  Foley, [Cedric] John

**Sawyer, John** 1953-    [SMG]
*American football player*
* Sawyer, Country

**Sawyer, Joseph**
*See*  Sauer, Joseph

**Sawyer, Mark**
*See*  Greenhood, [Clarence] David

**Sawyer, Ray** 1937-    [RO2]
*American singer*
* [The] Hook
* Hook, Dr.

**Sawyers, Bo**
*See*  Sawyers, James

**Sawyers, James** 20th c.    [RO2]
*American musician*
* Sawyers, Bo

**Sax, Adolphe**
*See* Sax, Antoine Joseph

**Sax, Antoine Joseph** 1814-1894
[WBD]
*Belgian musical instrument maker*
* Sax, Adolphe

**Sax, Christian** 1714-1806    [PA]
*Author*
* Saxius

**Saxafragi**
*See* Thorne, Sheldon B.

**Saxe, Isobel**
*See* Rayner, Claire

**Saxe, [Hermann] Maurice de**
1696-1750   [SN, WBD]
*French marshal*
* [A] Homeric Ajax
* Marshal de Saxe
* [The] Turenne of Louis XV

**Saxe, Templer**
*See* Edeveain, Templer Edward

**Saxius**
*See* Sax, Christian

**[The] Saxon**
*See* Emma

**[The] Saxon**
*See* Henry I [or Heinrich]

**[The] Saxon**
*See* Lothair II

**Saxon**
*See* Noyes, W. H.

**Saxon, Alex**
*See* Pronzini, Bill

**Saxon, Bill**
*See* Wallmann, Jeffrey M[iner]

**Saxon, Carl**
*See* Day, A. Grove

**[The] Saxon Giant**
*See* Handel, Georg Friedrich

**Saxon, Gladys Relyea** 20th c.    [CA]
*American author*
* Borden, M.
* Seyton, Marion

**Saxon, John**
*See* Orrico, Carmen

**Saxon, John**
*See* Rumbold-Gibbs, Henry St.
John Clair

**Saxon, Lefty**
*See* Saxon, Thomas

**[The] Saxon Milton**
*See* Caedmon

**Saxon, Peter** [house pseudonym]
*See* Baker, William Arthur
Howard

**Saxon, Peter** [house pseudonym]
*See* Martin, Thomas Hector

**Saxon, Peter** [house pseudonym]
*See* McNeilly, Wilfred Glassford

**Saxon, Richard**
*See* Morrissey, Joseph Laurence

**Saxon, Sky**
*See* Marsh, Richard

**Saxon, Thomas** 20th c.    [OBW]
*American baseball player*
* Saxon, Lefty

**Saxon, Van**
*See* Granbeck, Marilyn

**Saxon, Van**
*See* Simpson, Evangeline M.

**Saxon, Vin**
*See* Haydock, Ron

**Saxton, Judith**
*See* Turner, Judy

**Say**
*See* Cheves, Langdon

**[The] Say-Hey Kid**
*See* Mays, William Howard, Jr.
[Willie]

**Saya, Peter**
*See* Peterson, Robert E[ugene]

**Sayao, Bidu**
*See* De Oliveira Sayao, Balduina

**Saye, Joe**
*See* Shulman, Joseph

**Sayel, Saed** 20th c.
*Military adviser to the Palestine
Liberation Organization*
* Abu Walid

**Sayer, Gerard** 1948-    [RO2]
*British singer*
* Sayer, Leo

**Sayer, H. W.**
*See* Sayer, Harold Wilfred

**Sayer, Harold Wilfred** 1913-
[ART]
*British painter and etcher*
* Sayer, H. W.

**Sayer, Leo**
*See* Sayer, Gerard

**Sayer, Nancy Margetts** 1913-
[WD]
*British author*
* Bradfield, Nancy

**Sayer, Wal**
*See* Sayer, Walter William

**Sayer, Walter William** 1892-
[MBF]
*British author*
* Quiroule, Pierre [Rolling Stone]
* Sayer, Wal

**Sayers, Ben**
*See* Sayers, Bernard

**Sayers, Bernard** 1857-1924    [EG]
*Scottish golfer*
* Sayers, Ben
* Sayers, Wee Ben

**Sayers, Dorothy L[eigh]** 1893-1957
[CC, WW]
*Author*
* Leigh, Johanna

**Sayers, Edgar**
*See* Edgar, Alfred

**Sayers, Gale E.** 1943-    [IBW]
*American football player*
* [The] Kansas Cyclone
* Sayers, Magic

**Sayers, James Denson** 20th c.
[MBF]
*British author*
* Bardwell, Denver

**Sayers, Magic**
*See* Sayers, Gale E.

**Sayers, Wee Ben**
*See* Sayers, Bernard

**Sayler, H. L.**
*See* Sayler, Harry Lincoln

**Sayler, Harry Lincoln** 1863- ?
[WGT]
*American author*
* Lamar, Ashton
* Sayler, H. L.
* Stuart, Gordon
* Whitney, Elliott [joint pseudonym
  with Henry Bedford-Jones]

**Sayles, Bartholomew**
*See* Letory, John Bruno

**Sayles, Edwin Booth** 1892-    [CAP]
*American author*
* Sayles, Ted

**Sayles, Hezekiah, Jr.** 1918-1974
[IBW]
*American boxing manager*
* Sayles, Kiah

**Sayles, Kiah**
*See* Sayles, Hezekiah, Jr.

**Sayles, Ted**
*See* Sayles, Edwin Booth

**Saylor, Lefty**
*See* Saylor, Phil[ip Andrew]

**Saylor, Phil[ip Andrew]** 1871-1937
[BE]
*American baseball player*
* Saylor, Lefty

**Saylor, Sid**
*See* Sailor, Leo

**Sayre, Gordon**
*See* Woolfolk, Josiah Pitts

**Sbarbaro, Anthony** 1897-1969
[ASC, EJ, WWJ]
*American jazz musician*
* Spargo, Tony

**Sbernia**
*See* Berni, Francesco

**Scaasi, Arnold**
*See* Isaacs, Arnold

**Scaccio, John**
*See* Talamo, W.

**Scaeva**
*See* Stubbes, John

**Scaevola**
*See* Mucius, Caius

**Scafone, Jack, Jr.** 1936-    [RO1]
*Canadian-born singer and songwriter*
* Scott, Jack

**Scaggs, Boz**
*See* Scaggs, William Royce

**Scaggs, William Royce** 1944-
[RO2]
*American musician*
* Scaggs, Boz

**Scagnetti, Jack** 1924-    [CA]
*American journalist*
* Michael, James

**Scala, Can Francesco della**
1291-1329   [WBD]
*Imperial vicar of Verona*
* Scala, Cane Grande della

**Scala, Cane Grande della**
*See* Scala, Can Francesco della

**Scala, Gia**
*See* Scoglio, Giovanna

**Scalchi, Sofia**
*See* Lolli, Countess

**Scale, Elizabeth Barry** 1889-    [CU]
*American actress*
* Barriscale, Bessie

**Scales, Prunella**
*See* Illingworth, Prunella

**Scalice, Frank** ?-1957    [PHM]
*American underworld figure*
* Cheech, Don

**Scaliger, Josephus Justus**
1540-1609   [HN, RH]
*Italian scholar*
* [The] Father of Chronology

**[The] Scaliger of the Age**
*See* Warburton, William

**Scalisi, Josefina** 1932-    [OP]
*Argentinian opera singer*
* Carini, Nina

**Scalpel, Aesculapius**
*See* Berdoe, Edward

**Scalzi, Frank Joseph** 1913-    [BE]
*American baseball player*
* Scalzi, Skeeter

**Scalzi, Skeeter**
*See* Scalzi, Frank Joseph

**Scampington, Duke of**
*See* Murray, Eustace Clare
Grenville

**Scanderbeg**
*See* Castriot [or Castriota?],
George

**Scanderbeg III**
*See* Ahmed Bey Zogu

**[The] Scandinavian Semiramis**
*See* Margaret

**Scanlan, Doc**
*See* Scanlan, William Dennis

**Scanlan, Dreamy**
*See* Scanlan, Frank Aloysius

**Scanlan, Frank Aloysius**
1890-1969   [BE]
*American baseball player*
* Scanlan, Dreamy

**Scanlan, Kate**    [FFF]
*Entertainer*
* O'Shea, Kittie

**Scanlan, William Dennis**
1881-1949   [AS, BE]
*American baseball player*
* Scanlan, Doc

**Scanlon, C. K. M.**
*See* Eliot, G. F.

**Scanlon, C. K. M.** [house
pseudonym]
*See* Gruber, Frank

**Scannabecchi, Lamberto** ?-1130
[WBD]
*Pope*
* Honorius II

**Scannabue, Aristarco**
*See* Baretti, Giuseppe
Marc'Antonio

**Scannell, Jan**
*See* Scannell, Johannes Petrus

**Scannell, Johannes Petrus** 1916-
[IAW]
*South African author*
* Scannell, Jan

**Scantlan, Samuel William** 1901-
[IAW]
*American clergyman and author*
* Leumas, William S.

**Scantlebury, Pat**
*See* Scantlebury, Patricio
Athelstan

**Scantlebury, Patricio Athelstan**
1925- [BE, OBW]
*Panamanian-born baseball player*
* Scantlebury, Pat

**Scarce, Guerrant McCurdy** 1949-
[SMG]
*American baseball player*
* Scarce, Mac

**Scarce, Mac**
*See* Scarce, Guerrant McCurdy

**Scarf, Maggi**
*See* Scarf, Maggie

**Scarf, Maggie** 1932- [CA, SAT]
*American author*
* Scarf, Maggi

**Scarface**
*See* Capone, Al[phonse]

**Scarff, William**
*See* Budrys, Algirdas Jonas

**Scargill, Andy** 20th c.
*British labor leader*
* King Arthur

**Scarlet, Rebecca**
*See* Burt, Katharine Newlin

**Scarlet, Will**
*See* Meehan, Francis Joseph

**Scarlett, Bill**
*See* Swartz, William

**Scarlett, [Sir] James [First Baron
Abinger]** 1769-1844 [SN]
*British jurist*
* Ex Officio Jemmy

**Scarlett, Roger** [joint pseudonym
with Evelyn Page]
*See* Blair, Dorothy

**Scarlett, Roger** [joint pseudonym
with Dorothy Blair]
*See* Page, Evelyn

**Scarpa, Salvatore** 1918- [ASC]
*American musician*
* Donson, Don

**Scarpelli**
*See* Scarpelli, Furio

**Scarpelli, Furio** 20th c. [WF]
*Screenwriter*
* Scarpelli

**Scarron, Paul** 1610-1660 [SN]
*French poet, author, playwright*
* [The] Father of French Burlesque
* [The] Invalid Laureate

**Scarrott, Michael**
*See* Fisher, Arthur Stanley
Theodore

**Scarry, Patricia [Murphy] [Patsy]**
1924- [CA, SAT]
*Canadian-born author*
* Roy, Liam

**Scat Man Crothers**
*See* Crothers, [Benjamin] Sherman
[Louis]

**Schaaf, Eliane** 1937- [OP]
*French opera singer*
* Manchet, Eliane

**Schaaf, Marilyn Brooke Goffstein**
1940- [FBJ, ICB]
*American author and illustrator*
* Goffstein, M. B.

**Schaber, Nicholas** 1858-1936 [SC]
*American actor*
* Woods, Nick

**Schabinger, Arthur A.** 1889-1972
*American basketball coach*
* Schabinger, Schabie

**Schabinger, Schabie**
*See* Schabinger, Arthur A.

**Schachner, Nat[han]** 1895-1955
[ESF, WGT]
*American author*
* Corbett, Chan
* Glamis, Walter

**Schacht, Al[exander]** 1892-
[BE, SR]
*American baseball player*
* [The] Clown Prince of Baseball

**Schacht, Henry** 1887?-1964
[BEW]
*Actor and educator*
* Sharp, Henry

**Schacht, Ray McKeown** 1929-
[CWG]
*American country-western performer*
* Stuart, Carl

**Schachterle, Nancy [Lange]** 1925-
[CA]
*Canadian-born author*
* Laing, Anne C.

**Schad, Wilhelm**
*See* Reichert, Herbert W[illiam]

**Schaefer, Frank** 1936- [CA]
*American author*
* Carrol, Shana [joint pseudonym
with Kerry Newcomb]
* Gentry, Peter [joint pseudonym
with Kerry Newcomb]
* Savage, Christina [joint
pseudonym with Kerry
Newcomb]

**Schaefer, Germany**
*See* Schaefer, Herman A.

**Schaefer, Herman A.** 1878-1919
[AS, BE, PB]
*American baseball player*
* Schaefer, Germany

**Schaefer, Hildegard** 1917- [IAW]
*German author*
* Gardener, Hilde

**Schaefer, Jacob, Sr.** 1855-1909
[AS]
*American billiards player*
* [The] Wizard

**Schaefer, Robin**
*See* Malzberg, Barry N[orman]

**Schaeffer, E. Carroll** 20th c. [BBH]
*American swimmer*
* Schaeffer, Midget

**Schaeffer, Harry Edward** 1924-
[BE]
*American baseball player*
* Schaeffer, Lefty

**Schaeffer, Lefty**
*See* Schaeffer, Harry Edward

**Schaeffer, Midget**
*See* Schaeffer, E. Carroll

**Schafer, Gertrude** 1880-1960 [SC]
*American actress*
* Bondhill, Gertrude

**Schafer, Gus**
*See* Stevens, Peter

**Schafer, Harry C.** 1846-1935 [BE]
*American baseball player*
* Schafer, Silk Stocking

**Schafer, Pinny**
*See* Schafer, William

**Schafer, Silk Stocking**
*See* Schafer, Harry C.

**Schafer, William** [RBE]
*Boxing agent*
* Schafer, Pinny

**Schaffenberger, Kurt** 1920-
[WECO]
*American cartoonist*
* Wahl, Lou

**Schakel, Pieter**
*See* Balluseck, Daniel J. Von

**Schakovskoy, [Princess] Zinaida**
1906- [CA]
*Russian-born author and poet*
* Croise, Jacques

**Schaldenbrand, Mary** 1922- [CA]
*American educator and author*
* Mary Aloysius, [Sister]

**Schalk, Cracker**
*See* Schalk, Raymond William

**Schalk, LeRoy John** 1908- [BE]
*American baseball player*
* Schalk, Roy

**Schalk, Raymond William**
1892-1970 [AS, DGS, PB]
*American baseball player*
* Schalk, Cracker

**Schalk, Roy**
*See* Schalk, LeRoy John

**Schaller, Biff**
*See* Schaller, Walter

**Schaller, Walter** 1889-1939 [BE]
*American baseball player*
* Schaller, Biff

**Schallick, August** 1858-1937 [BE]
*German-born baseball player*
* Shallix, August
* Shallix, Gus

**Schanfield, Lewis Maurice**
1867-1941 [BEW, EMT, PMJ]
*American actor, producer, director*
* Fields, Lew

**Schardt, Big Bill**
*See* Schardt, Wilburt

**Schardt, Wilburt** 1886-1964 [BE]
*American baseball player*
* Schardt, Big Bill

**Scharein, Art[hur Otto]** 1905-1969
[BE]
*American baseball player*
* Scharein, Scoop

**Scharein, George Albert** 1914-
[BE]
*American baseball player*
* Scharein, Tom

**Scharein, Scoop**
*See* Scharein, Art[hur Otto]

**Scharein, Tom**
*See* Scharein, George Albert

**Scharf, Boo-Boo**
*See* Scharf, Herman

**Scharf, Edward T.** 1859-1937 [BE]
*American baseball player*
* Scharf, Nick

**Scharf, Herman** 1901-1963 [SC]
*American actor and stunt performer*
* Scharf, Boo-Boo

**Scharf, Nick**
*See* Scharf, Edward T.

**Scharff, Lester** 1895-1962 [SC]
*American actor*
* Sharpe, Lester

**Scharlemann, Dorothy Hoyer**
1912- [CA]
*American author and playwright*
* Sharon, Donna Haye

**Schartenmeyer**
*See* Vischer, Friedrich Theodor von

**Schary, Dore**
*See* Schary, Isidore

**Schary, Isidore** 1905?-1980
*American screenwriter, playwright,
producer*
* [The] Boy Wonder of Hollywood
* Schary, Dore

**Schary, Jill**
*See* Robinson, Jill

**Schattner, Martine** 1911- [BEW]
*American publisher*
* Schattner, Meyer

**Schattner, Meyer**
*See* Schattner, Martine

**Schaub, Marilyn McNamara** 1928-
[CA]
*American translator*
* McNamara, [Sister] Marie
Aquinas

**Schauer, Alexander**
*See* Dimitrihoff, Dimitri Ivanovich

**Schauer, Rube**
*See* Dimitrihoff, Dimitri Ivanovich

**Schauffler, Margaret Widdemer** 20th
c. [WWL]
*American author*
* Widdemer, Margaret

**Schaumburg, Paul** 1884- [WBD]
*German author*
* Burg, Paul

**Schayes, Adolph** 1928-
*American basketball player*
* Schayes, Dolph

**Schayes, Dolph**
See Schayes, Adolph

**Schealtiel, Nochumm J.**
See Schochet, J. Immanuel

**Schechter, William** 1934- [CA]
*Austrian-born author*
* Williams, Chester

**Scheckter, Baby Bear**
See Scheckter, Jody

**Scheckter, Jody** 20th c. [EAR]
*Auto racer*
* Scheckter, Baby Bear

**Schectman, Elias Maxwell** 1926-
[BEW]
*American actor, director, playwright*
* Rill, Eli

**Schedel, Ferencz** 1805-1875
[WBD]
*Hungarian historian*
* Toldy, Ferencz

**Scheels, Rabode Hermann**
1622-1662 [PA]
*Author*
* Schelius

**Scheepers, Emmerentia** 20th c.
[OP]
*South African opera singer*
* Renzi, Emma

**Scheer, Heinie**
See Scheer, Henry William

**Scheer, Henry William** 1900- [EJS]
*American baseball player*
* Scheer, Heinie

**Scheer, K. H.**
See Scheer, Karl Herbert

**Scheer, Karl Herbert** 1928-
[SF, WGT]
*German author*
* Scheer, K. H.
* Turbojew, Alexej

**Scheer, Vincent Morris** 1905-
[B10, BX, EJS]
*American boxer*
* Callahan, Mushi [or Mushy]

**Scheeren, Dutch**
See Scheeren, Frederick

**Scheeren, Frederick** 1891- [BE]
*American baseball player*
* Scheeren, Dutch
* Scheeren, Fritz

**Scheeren, Fritz**
See Scheeren, Frederick

**Scheff, Friederike**
See Yager, Anna

**Scheff, Fritzi**
See Yager, Anna

**Scheffler, Johannes** 1624-1677
[WBD]
*German poet and mystic*
* Angelus Silesius

**Schein, Ruth Robbins** 1917- [TBJ]
*American author*
* Robbins, Ruth

**Scheinblum, Milton** 1927- [EJ]
*American jazz musician*
* Sheen, Mickey

**Scheinman, Walter Witcover** 1924-
[BEW]
*American actor, director, educator*
* Witcover, Walt

**Schelius**
See Scheels, Rabode Hermann

**Schell, Bunny**
See Schell, Rolfe F[inch]

**Schell, Rolfe F[inch]** 1916- [CA]
*American author*
* Schell, Bunny

**Schelle, Gerard Anthony** 1917-
[BE]
*American baseball player*
* Schelle, Jim

**Schelle, Jim**
See Schelle, Gerard Anthony

**Schellenburg**
See Musaeus, Johann Karl August

**Schemanske, Buck**
See Schemanske, Fred[erick
George]

**Schemanske, Fred[erick George]**
1903-1960 [BE]
*American baseball player*
* Schemanske, Buck

**Schembechler, Bo**
See Schembechler, Glenn Edward

**Schembechler, Glenn Edward**
1929- [B10, FB]
*American football coach*
* Schembechler, Bo

**[The] Schemer**
See Drucci, Vincent

**Schemm, Mildred Walker** 1905-
[CA]
*American author*
* Walker, Mildred

**Schenck, Anita A[llen]** 1909- [CA]
*American author*
* Allen, Anita

**Schenck, Leopold** [FFF]
*German editor*
* Schreier, Captain

**Schenck, William** 1893-1924 [BX]
*American boxer*
* Brennan, Bill

**Schenk, Frances Victoria** 1908-
[EMT]
*American actress and singer*
* Day, Frances

**Schepens, Martin** 1955- [DC]
*British cricketer*
* Schepens, Skep

**Schepens, Skep**
See Schepens, Martin

**Scheper, Nancy**
See Scheper-Hughes, Nancy

**Scheper-Hughes, Nancy** 1944-
[CA]
*American anthropologist and author*
* Scheper, Nancy

**Schere, Monroe** 1913- [CA]
*American author*
* Howard, Jessica
* Summerhill, J. K.
* Winter, Abigail

**Scherer, Edmond** 1815-1889 [FFF]
*French journalist*
* French Politician

**Scherer, Jean Marie Maurice**
1920- [BDF, FC, FDG]
*French director*
* Cordier, Gilbert
* Rohmer, Eric

**Scherer, Roy Harold, Jr.** 1925-
[BDF, FC, IPA]
*American actor*
* Fitzgerald, Roy
* Hudson, Rock

**Scherr, Marie** 20th c. [SFL, WGT]
*Author*
* Cher, Marie

**Schertzer [or Shertzer], Herman**
1909- [PMJ]
*American jazz musician*
* Schertzer, Hymie

**Schertzer, Hymie**
See Schertzer [or Shertzer],
Herman

**Schesler, Charles** 1900-1953 [BE]
*German-born baseball player*
* Schesler, Dutch

**Schesler, Dutch**
See Schesler, Charles

**Scheucher, Annemarie** 1935- [OP]
*Austrian costume designer and
architect*
* Skalicki, Amirei

**Scheuerman, Margaret** 20th c.
[BEW]
*American theatre executive*
* Sherman, Margaret

**Schiano, Anthony** 20th c. [B10]
*American detective*
* Solo, Tony

**Schiavone, Andrea**
See Medolla [or Meldolla], Andrea

**Schick, George Baldwin Powell**
1903- [IAW]
*American educator and author*
* Baldwin, George

**Schickel, Julia Whedon** 1936- [CA]
*American author*
* Whedon, Julia

**Schickele, Peter** 1935- [CA]
*American composer and author*
* Bach, P. D. Q.

**Schieldge, Ernest** 20th c. [BS]
*American magician*
* Rogers, Don

**Schieri, Friedrich Franz** 1922-
[IWM]
*German conductor and composer*
* Schieri, Fritz

**Schieri, Fritz**
See Schieri, Friedrich Franz

**Schiff, Else** 1878?-1961 [BEW]
*German actress and author*
* Basserman, Else

**Schiff, Sydney** 1869?-1944
[LC, TC]
*British author and translator*
* Hudson, Stephen

**Schiffmann, Meir** 1918- [CA]
*German-born American author*
* Ben Horin, Meir

**Schifrin, Boris** 1932- [EJ7]
*Argentinian-born jazz musician*
* Schifrin, Lalo

**Schifrin, Lalo**
See Schifrin, Boris

**Schildkraut, Joseph** 1896- [FIR]
*Austrian-born actor*
* Schildkraut, Pepi

**Schildkraut, Pepi**
See Schildkraut, Joseph

**Schillaci, Anthony**
See Schillaci, Peter Paul

**Schillaci, Peter Paul** 1929- [CA]
*American clergyman and author*
* Schillaci, Anthony

**Schiller, Craig** 1951- [CA]
*American author*
* Schiller, Mayer

**Schiller, Henry Carl** 19th c. [PA]
*Author*
* Grey, Anthony

**Schiller, Johann Christoph Friedrich
von** 1759-1805 [SN]
*German poet and playwright*
* [The] Poet of Liberty
* [The] Shakespeare of Germany

**Schiller, Mayer**
See Schiller, Craig

**Schiller, Rose Leiman**
See Goldemberg, Rose Leiman

**Schilling, August E.** 1908-1957
[SC]
*American actor*
* Schilling, Gus

**Schilling, Bertha** 1869-1935 [BBD]
*Swiss-born opera singer*
* Breval, Lucienne

**Schilling, George, Sr.** 1886-1964
[NOJ]
*American jazz musician*
* Schilling, Happy

**Schilling, Gus**
See Schilling, August E.

**Schilling, Happy**
See Schilling, George, Sr.

**Schillings, Elbert Isaiah** 1900-1954
[BE]
*American baseball player*
* Schillings, Red

**Schillings, Red**
See Schillings, Elbert Isaiah

**Schilperoort, Peter** 1919- [EJ]
*Dutch jazz musician*
* Bronx, Pat

**Schilsky, Austin** 1897- [FC]
*British actor*
* Trevor, Austin

**Schindell, Cy**
See Schindell, Seymore

**Schindell, Seymore** 1907-1948
[SC]
*American actor*
* Schindell, Cy

**Schiner, Herbert Arthur**
1918-1970 [SC]
*American actor*
* Shriner, Herb

**Schinocephalus**
*See* Pericles

**Schiott, Johannes** 1914- [BEW]
*American director*
* Fearnley, John

**Schipa, Raffaele Attilio Amadeo**
1889-1965 [MS]
*Italian opera singer*
* Schipa, Tito

**Schipa, Tito**
*See* Schipa, Raffaele Attilio
Amadeo

**Schire**
*See* Gardner, E. D.

**Schirick, Dutch**
*See* Schirick, Harry Ernest

**Schirick, Harry Ernest** 1890-1968
[BE]
*American baseball player*
* Schirick, Dutch

**Schirmer, Joe** 1916?-1975 [FIR]
*Musician*
* King of the Banjo

**Schirmerhorn, Clint**
*See* Riemer, George

**Schisgal, Oscar** 1901-
[CA, SAT, WW]
*Belgian-born author and
speechwriter*
* Cole, Jackson
* Hardy, Stuart

**Schittenhelm, Gisele Eve** 1906?-
[F2, FC, WEF]
*German actress*
* Helm, Brigette

**Schjelderup, Gerik** 20th c. [ART]
*Irish artist and actor*
* Gerik

**Schlachter, Susan**
*See* Thaler, Susan

**Schlapbach-Oberhansli, Trudi**
1944- [CA]
*Swiss author and illustrator*
* Oberhansli, Trudi

**Schlecker, Max** 1930- [IWM]
*Swiss publisher and editor*
* Schleo

**Schlee, Nicholaevna Sanina** 1904-
[WFA]
*Russian-born fashion designer*
* Valentina

**Schleger, Hans** 20th c. [GA]
*British graphic artist*
* Zero

**Schlei, Admiral**
*See* Schlei, George Henry

**Schlei, George Henry** 1878-1958
[BE]
*American baseball player*
* Schlei, Admiral

**Schleier, Gregory** 1918-1974 [SC]
*American actor*
* Dixon, Paul
* [The] Mayor of Kneesville

**Schlein, Miriam** 1926-
[CA, SAT, TCC]
*American author*
* Stanhope, Lavinia
* Weiss, Miriam

**Schlemihl, Peter**
*See* Thoma, Ludwig

**Schlemihl, Peter**
*See* Wood, George

**Schleo**
*See* Schlecker, Max

**Schlesinger, Bruno Walter**
1876-1962 [BBD, IPA]
*German conductor*
* Walter, Bruno

**Schlesinger, Leontine** 1889- [WEF]
*Austrian-born director*
* Sagan, Leontine

**Schlesinger, Rudy**
*See* Schlesinger, William Cordes

**Schlesinger, William Cordes** 1942-
[BE]
*American baseball player*
* Schlesinger, Rudy

**Schletz, Elke** 1940- [FC]
*German actress*
* Sommer, Elke

**Schliebner, Dutch**
*See* Schliebner, Frederick Paul

**Schliebner, Frederick Paul** 1894-
[BE]
*German-born baseball player*
* Schliebner, Dutch

**Schlink, [Mother] Basilea**
*See* Schlink, Klara

**Schlink, Klara** 1904- [CA]
*German author and religious leader*
* Basilea, [Mother]
* Schlink, [Mother] Basilea

**Schlitzer, Biff**
*See* Schlitzer, Victor Joseph

**Schlitzer, Victor Joseph** 1884-1948
[BE]
*American baseball player*
* Schlitzer, Biff

**Schloesser, Hendrik** 1943- [OP]
*Dutch opera singer*
* Van Ree, Jean

**Schlosberg, H[ershel] J[oshua]**
*See* May, Henry John

**Schloss, Arthur David** 1889-1966
[LC, TC]
*British translator*
* Waley, Arthur

**Schloss, William** 1914- [FC]
*American director*
* Castle, William

**Schmalz, Herbert Gustave**
1856-1935 [DBA]
*British painter*
* Angelico
* Carmichael, Herbert

**Schmees, George Edward** 1924-
[BE]
*American baseball player*
* Schmees, Rocky

**Schmees, Rocky**
*See* Schmees, George Edward

**Schmeisser, William C. [Bill]**
1880-1941 [BBH]
*American lacrosse coach*
* Father Bill

**Schmeling, Max[imilian Adolph Otto
Siegfried]** 1905- [BX, RBE]
*German-born boxer*
* [The] Black Uhlan

**Schmid, Charles Howard, Jr.** 1942-
[BLB]
*American murderer*
* Rodriguez, Angel

**Schmid, Eduard** 1890-1966
[CD, EWL]
*German author*
* Edschmid, Kasimir

**Schmide, John Bernhardt Vander
Kleine** 20th c. [BEW]
*American actor and stage manager*
* Barney, Jay

**Schmidt, Albert** 1902- [WECO]
*American cartoonist*
* Smith, Al

**Schmidt, Anton Franz** 1893-1955
[WBD]
*German playwright, author, critic*
* Dietzenschmidt

**Schmidt, Boss**
*See* Schmidt, Charles

**Schmidt, Butch**
*See* Schmidt, Charles John

**Schmidt, Charles** 1880-1932 [BE]
*American baseball player*
* Schmidt, Boss
* Schmidt, Dutch

**Schmidt, Charles John** 1887-1952
[BE]
*American baseball player*
* Schmidt, Butch

**Schmidt, Christoph** 1740-1801
[PA]
*Author*
* Phiseldeck

**Schmidt, Crazy**
*See* Schmidt, Frederick

**Schmidt, Dorothea**
*See* Wender, Dorothea

**Schmidt, Dutch**
*See* Schmidt, Charles

**Schmidt, Ernest J.** 1911-
*American basketball player*
* Schmidt, One Grand

**Schmidt, Frank Elmer** 1879-1952
[BE, PB]
*American baseball player*
* Smith, Frank Elmer
* Smith, Nig

**Schmidt, Frederick** 1866-1940
[BE]
*American baseball player*
* Schmidt, Crazy

**Schmidt, Helmut** 1918-
*West German chancellor*
* [The] Lip
* [Der] Macher [The Doer]
* Schmidt, Super
* Schmidt the Lip

**Schmidt, Herman** 20th c. [BE]
*American baseball player*
* Schmidt, Pete

**Schmidt, Ilse** ?-1963 [SC]
*German actress and dancer*
* Grace, Dinah

**Schmidt, James Norman** 1912-
[CA, WW]
*American author*
* Norman, James

**Schmidt, Kaspar** 1806-1856
[WBD]
*German philosopher*
* Stirner, Max

**Schmidt, Kate** 1954-
*American javelin thrower*
* Kate the Great

**Schmidt, Laura M[arie]** 1952-
[CA]
*American poet and editor*
* Palmer, B. C.
* Palmer, Laura

**Schmidt, One Grand**
*See* Schmidt, Ernest J.

**Schmidt, Otto Ernst** 1862-1926
[WBD]
*German author and playwright*
* Ernst, Otto

**Schmidt, Pete**
*See* Schmidt, Herman

**Schmidt, Sandra**
*See* Oddo, Sandra [Schmidt]

**Schmidt, Super**
*See* Schmidt, Helmut

**Schmidt the Lip**
*See* Schmidt, Helmut

**Schmidt, Wilhelm** 1876- ? [CD]
*German playwright, author, poet*
* Schmidtbonn, Wilhelm

**Schmidt, Willy** 1896- [WGT]
*German author*
* Gerhold, German

**Schmidtbonn, Wilhelm**
*See* Schmidt, Wilhelm

**Schmidtke, Rudi**
*See* Schmidtke, Ruediger

**Schmidtke, Ruediger** 1943- [BX]
*German boxer*
* Schmidtke, Rudi

**Schmied, Rudolf** 20th c. [B10]
*Austrian mystic*
* Rayo

**Schmit, Jean-Pierre** 1904- [IWM]
*Luxembourgian musicologist*
* Schmit, Jempy

**Schmit, Jempy**
*See* Schmit, Jean-Pierre

**Schmitt, Harrison Hagan** 1935-
[B10]
*American geologist and astronaut*
* Schmitt, Jack

**Schmitt, Jack**
See Schmitt, Harrison Hagan

**Schmitz, Bear Tracks**
See Schmitz, John Albert

**Schmitz, Ettore** 1861-1928
[CD, EWL, LC]
*Italian author*
* Svevo, Italo

**Schmitz, John Albert** 1920-
[BE, PB]
*American baseball player*
* Schmitz, Bear Tracks

**Schnabel, Johann Gottfried**
1690?-1750? [WBD]
*German author*
* Gisander

**Schnake**
See Hauser, Carl

**Schnaubelt, Franz Joseph** 1914-
[CA]
*American author*
* Joseph, Franz

**Schneck, Stephen** 1933- [CA]
*American entertainer and author*
* Bite, Ben
* Fite, Mack
* Kite, Larry
* Knight, James
* Lite, Jams
* Spit, Sam

**Schneeweiss, Amalie** 1839-1898
[WBD]
*Opera singer*
* Weiss, Amalie

**Schneider, Abram Leopoldovich**
1917- [BEW]
*Russian-born director*
* Schneider, Alan

**Schneider, Alan**
See Schneider, Abram
Leopoldovich

**Schneider, Betty Vance Humphreys**
1927- [AW, WD]
*American labor economist and
author*
* Humphreys, B. V.

**Schneider, Buzz**
See Schneider, William

**Schneider, Elmer Reuben** 1919-
[EJ]
*American jazz musician*
* Schneider, Moe

**Schneider, Emanuel Sebastian**
1853-1933 [BE]
*American baseball player*
* Snyder, Emanuel Sebastian
* Snyder, Redleg

**Schneider, Ethel** 1916-1964 [SC]
*American actress*
* Clark, Ethel

**Schneider, Guenther** 1890-1956
[BEW, F1, FC]
*American actor*
* Arnold, Edward

**Schneider, Hannes** 1890-1955
[BBH]
*Austrian-born skiing instructor*
* [The] Father of Modern Skiing

**Schneider, Isidor** 1896- [CAA]
*Polish-born poet, author, editor*
* I. S.

**Schneider, Laurie**
See Adams, Laurie

**Schneider, Leonard Alfred**
1925-1966 [CA, JL]
*American comedian, actor, author*
* Bruce, Lenny

**Schneider, Louis** 1805-1878
[WBD]
*German actor and author*
* Both, L. W.

**Schneider, Moe**
See Schneider, Elmer Reuben

**Schneider, Romy**
See Albach-Retty, Rosemarie

**Schneider, William** 1954- [HR]
*American hockey player*
* Schneider, Buzz

**Schneider-Green, Ann** 20th c. [OP]
*British opera singer*
* Green, Anna

**Schneidman, Biff**
See Schneidman, Herman

**Schneidman, Herman** 1913-
[EJS]
*American football player*
* Schneidman, Biff

**Schnellbacher, Claw**
See Schnellbacher, Otto O.

**Schnellbacher, Otto O.** 1923- [FB]
*American football player*
* Schnellbacher, Claw

**Schneyder, J. F.**
See Taylor, [Frank Herbert]
Griffin

**Schnitter, Johannes**
See Sneider, Johannes

**Schnittkind, Henry Thomas** 1888-
[NAA]
*Lithuanian-born author*
* Thomas, Henry

**Schnitzer, Eduard** 1840-1892
[WBD]
*German traveler and explorer*
* Emin Pasha, Mehmed

**[The] Schnoz**
See Durante, James Francis
[Jimmy]

**Schnozzle**
See Durante, James Francis
[Jimmy]

**Schnozzola**
See Durante, James Francis
[Jimmy]

**Schochen, Muriel Betty** 1920-
[BEW]
*American director, actress, educator*
* Sharon, Muriel

**Schochet, J. Immanuel** 1935-
[IAW]
*Swiss-born clergyman and author*
* Oryah, Yehudith
* Schealtiel, Nochumm J.

**Schock, George**
See Loose, Katharine Riegel

**Schockeor, Urbain Jacques**
1890-1928 [AS, BE]
*American baseball player*
* Shocker, Urban James

**Schoeb, Erika** 20th c. [SFL]
*Author*
* De Witt, Denise
* Levi, Aristotle
* Von Grau, Wernher

**Schoen, Martin**
See Schongauer, Martin

**Schoenberg, Alfred** 1868-1949
[BEW, EMT, F2]
*German-born entertainer*
* Shean, Al

**Schoendienst, Albert Fred** 1923-
[DGS, PB, SMG]
*American baseball player and
manager*
* Finn, Huckleberry
* Schoendienst, Red

**Schoendienst, Red**
See Schoendienst, Albert Fred

**Schoenduv, A. L.** 1858- ? [PA]
*Author*
* A. L. S.

**Schoene, Lotte**
See Bodenstein, Charlotte

**Schoenemann, Anna Elisabeth**
1758-1817 [WBD]
*Friend of German poet, Johann
Wolfgang von Goethe*
* Schoenemann, Lili

**Schoenemann, Lili**
See Schoenemann, Anna Elisabeth

**Schoenenberger, Gualtiero**
See Schoenenberger, Walter Louis
Frederic

**Schoenenberger, Walter Louis
Frederic** 1926- [IAW]
*Swiss art historian and author*
* Schoenenberger, Gualtiero

**Schoenfeld, William C.** 1893-
[ASC]
*American composer and arranger*
* Blake, Lowell
* Conrad, Hugh

**Schoenfield, Eugene** 1935- [NAD]
*American physician*
* Hippocrates, Dr.

**Schoening, Alwina** 1848-1925
[BBD]
*American opera singer*
* Valleria, Alwina

**Schoepflin, Harl Vincent**
1893-1968 [SF]
*American author*
* Vincent, Harl

**Schofield, Ducky**
See Schofield, John Richard

**Schofield, John Richard** 1935-
[BE]
*American baseball player*
* Schofield, Ducky

**Schofield, Paul**
See Tubb, Edwin Charles

**Schofield, Sylvia Anne** 1922-
[AW, CA, WD]
*British author*
* Matheson, Sylvia A.
* Mundy, Max

**Scholander, Fredrik Wilhelm** [FFF]
*Author*
* Acharius

**[The] Scholar Gypsy**
See Wade, George Alfred

**Scholarios, Georgios** 15th c.
[WBD]
*Greek scholar and prelate*
* Gennadius II

**[The] Scholastic**
See Epiphanius

**[The] Scholastic Divine**
See Anselm of Laon

**[The] Scholastic Doctor**
See Anselm of Laon

**Scholasticus**
See Evagrius

**Scholasticus**
See Leontius of Byzantium

**Scholasticus**
See Socrates

**Scholefield, Edmund O.**
See Butterworth, William
Edmund, III

**Scholefield, Lillia** ?-1954 [BEW]
*Playwright*
* Field, Lila

**Scholl, Jerry**
See Schutz, Joseph Willard

**Scholz, Winfried** 20th c. [SFP]
*Author*
* Sholes, W. W.

**Schomburg, Alex** 1905- [ESF]
*American illustrator*
* King of the Airbrush

**Schonestein, David** ?-1879 [PA]
*Author*
* Steune, Georges

**Schonfield, Hugh J[oseph]** 1901-
[CA, WD]
*British historian and author*
* Fielding, Hubert
* Hegesippus

**Schongauer, Martin** 1445?-1491
[WBD]
*German engraver and painter*
* Hipsch [or Huebsch] Martin
* Schoen, Martin

**School Master Camden**
See Camden, William

**Schoolboy Cleve**
See White, Cleve

**Schoolcraft, Henry R.** 1793-1864
[PA]
*Author*
* Colcroft, Henry Roeve

**[The] Schoolgirl Songstress**
See Kirkwood, Pat

**[The] Schoolmaster Comedian**
See Hay, Will

**Schoolmaster, John**
See Doudna, Edgar G.

**[The] Schoolmaster of Politics**
See Wilson, [Thomas] Woodrow

**[The] Schoolmaster of the Republic**
See Webster, Noah

**Schoonmaker, Ann** 1928- [CA]
*American author*
* Boyd, Ann S.

Schoonover, Gloria Jean 1928-
[FC, PMJ, SW]
*American singer and actress*
* Jean, Gloria

Schop, Le Baron
*See* Texier, Edward

Schopenhauer, Arthur 1788-1860
[SN]
*German philosopher*
* [The] Philosopher of
Disenchantment

Schopfer, Jean 1868-1931 [TC]
*Swiss-born author, playwright,
historian*
* Anet, Claude

Schopp, Martin Robert 1918-
[CWG]
*American country-western performer*
* Roberts, Marty

Schorb, Edwin Marsh 1940- [CA]
*American author and poet*
* Marsh, Edwin
* McGrath, Doyle

Schosberg, Paul A. 1938- [CA]
*American author*
* Allyn, Paul

Schotte, John LeRoy 1912?-
[EMT, PMJ]
*American dancer and actor*
* LeRoy, Hal

Schotte, Paulus
*See* Elbogen, Paul

Schrader, F. F. [FFF]
*Journalist*
* Keen, Royal

Schrage, Pops
*See* Schrage, Tom

Schrage, Tom 1947?-
*American basketball player*
* Schrage, Pops

Schragmueller, Elsbeth 20th c.
[EE]
*German intelligence agent*
* [The] Beautiful Blonde of
Antwerp
* [The] Blonde of Antwerp
* [The] Terrible Doctor Elsbeth
* Tiger Eyes

Schrall, Leo 20th c. [BBH]
*American baseball coach*
* Schrall, Scrapiron

Schrall, Scrapiron
*See* Schrall, Leo

Schreck, Everett M. 1897- [CAP]
*American actor and author*
* Morrill, Richard

Schreck, Max
*See* Abel, Alfred

Schreck, Ossee
*See* Schreckengost, Ossee Freeman

Schreckengost, Ossee Freeman
1875-1914 [BE]
*American baseball player*
* Schreck, Ossee

Schreiber, Barney
*See* Schreiber, David Henry

Schreiber, David Henry 1882- ?
[BE]
*American baseball player*
* Schreiber, Barney

Schreiber, Hermann O. L. 1920-
[CA, WD]
*Austrian historian and author*
* Bassermann, Lujo
* Buehnau, Ludwig

Schreiber, Le Anne 1945?-
*American sports editor*
* Schreiber, Swivel Hips

Schreiber, Paul Frederick 1902-
[BE]
*American baseball player*
* Schreiber, Von

Schreiber, Swivel Hips
*See* Schreiber, Le Anne

Schreiber, Von
*See* Schreiber, Paul Frederick

Schreier, Captain
*See* Schenck, Leopold

Schreiner, Olive [Emily Albertina]
1855-1920 [B10, LC]
*South African author*
* Iron, Ralph

Schreuer, Carl 1921- [BEW]
*American producer and stage
manager*
* Sawyer, Carl

Schrieber, Helmut 1903?-1963
[BEW]
*Magician*
* Kalanag

Schrift, Shirley 1922-
[BDF, BEW, FC]
*American actress*
* Winters, Shelley

Schriner, David 1911-
[CEI, FHE, HK]
*Canadian-born hockey player*
* Schriner, Sweeney

Schriner, Sweeney
*See* Schriner, David

Schriver, Pop
*See* Schriver, William F.

Schriver, William F. 1866-1932
[BE, PB]
*American baseball player*
* Schriver, Pop

Schroder, Helen 1904-1966
[CED, EMT, PMJ]
*American actress and singer*
* [The] Boop Boop A Doop Girl
* Kane, Helen

Schroeder, Frederick R. 1921-
[BBH, OET]
*American tennis player*
* Schroeder, Lucky
* Schroeder, Ted

Schroeder, J. W. 1871-1932 [SC]
*American actor*
* Osborne, Jefferson

Schroeder, John Henry 1784-1883
[FFF]
*German banker and financier*
* [The] German Peabody

Schroeder, Lucky
*See* Schroeder, Frederick R.

Schroeder, Richard C. 20th c. [CA]
*Columnist*
* Alfred, Richard [joint pseudonym
with Nathan Alfred Haverstock]

Schroeder, Ted
*See* Schroeder, Frederick R.

Schroeder, Zelma 1907- [EMT]
*American actress, singer, dancer*
* O'Neal, Zelma

Schroepfer, Arthur 1908-1962
[THR]
*British actor and playwright*
* Macrae, Arthur

Schroetter, Hilda Noel 1917- [CA]
*American editor and writer*
* Noel, Hilda Bloxton, Jr.

Schroll, Al[bert Bringhurst] 1933-
[BE]
*American baseball player*
* Schroll, Bull

Schroll, Bull
*See* Schroll, Al[bert Bringhurst]

Schryver, Corneilise 1482-1558
[PA]
*Author*
* Grapheus

Schryver, Pieter 1661-1743 [PA]
*Author*
* Scriverius

Schubart, Fannie Kilbourne 20th c.
[NAA]
*American author*
* Kilbourne, Fannie

Schubbert
*See* Strubberg, Friedrich Armand

Schubert, Emile H.
*See* Smith, Leonard B.

Schuble, Heinie
*See* Schuble, Henry George

Schuble, Henry George 1906- [BE]
*American baseball player*
* Schuble, Heinie

Schuchman, Joan 1934- [CA]
*American author*
* Brenner, Isabel
* Jones, Miriam
* Jones, Zelda

Schuck, F. H. P.
*See* Schuck, Frederick Hugh Paul

Schuck, Frederick Hugh Paul
1916- [SFL]
*American author*
* Schuck, F. H. P.

Schueler, Dorli-Maria 1940- [OP]
*German opera singer*
* Chryst, Dorothea

Schuerholz, Fred Peter 1889-1975
[BE]
*American baseball player*
* Sherry, Fred Peter

Schuette, Conrad Herman Louis
1843- ? [ALY]
*German-born clergyman and author*
* T. O. F.

Schuetz, Dennis 20th c. [CA]
*Author*
* Aldyne, Nathan [joint pseudonym
with Michael McDowell]

Schuetz, Francoise-Jeanne
1861-1936 [BBD]
*Russian opera singer*
* Litvinne, Felia

Schuetze, Gladys Henrietta [Raphael]
1881-1946 [TC]
*British author*
* Leslie, Henrietta
* Mendl, Gladys

Schulberg, B. P.
*See* Schulberg, Benjamin Percival

Schulberg, Benjamin Percival
1892-1957 [BEW]
*American producer*
* Schulberg, B. P.

Schulefand, Richard 1929?-
[FC, ITA, TR]
*American actor*
* Shawn, Dick
* Shawn, Richy

Schulemberg, Erangard Melrose de
[Duchess of Kendal] ?-1743
[DNNF, DNNS, FFF]
*Mistress of King George I of
England*
* [The] Maypole

Schulkers, Robert Franc
1890-1972 [B10]
*American author and critic*
* Hawkins, Sekatary

Schulman, L. M.
*See* Schulman, Lester Martin

Schulman, Lester Martin 1934-
[SFL]
*American author and editor*
* Schulman, L. M.

Schult, Arthur William 1928- [BE]
*American baseball player*
* Schult, Dutch

Schult, Dutch
*See* Schult, Arthur William

Schulte, Elaine L[ouise] 1934- [CA]
*American author*
* Young, Elaine L.

Schulte, Frank 1882-1949
[AS, BE, PB]
*American baseball player*
* Schulte, Wildfire

Schulte, Fred William 1904-
[BE, PB]
*American baseball player*
* Schulte, Fritz

Schulte, Fritz
*See* Schulte, Fred William

Schulte, Ham
*See* Schultehenrich, Herman
Joseph

Schulte, Herman Joseph
*See* Schultehenrich, Herman
Joseph

Schulte, Leonard William [Len]
*See* Schultehenrich, Leonard
William

Schulte, Wildfire
*See* Schulte, Frank

Schultehenrich, Herman Joseph
1912- [BE]
*American baseball player*
* Schulte, Ham
* Schulte, Herman Joseph

**Schultehenrich, Leonard William**
1916- [BE]
*American baseball player*
* Schulte, Leonard William [Len]

**Schultheiss [or Schulz], Michael**
1571-1621 [WBD]
*German composer and author*
* Praetorius, Michael

**Schultz, Barney**
See Schultz, George Warren

**Schultz, Bill**
See Schultz, Robert Duffy [Bob]

**Schultz, Buddy**
See Schultz, Charles Budd

**Schultz, Charles Budd** 1950-
[SMG]
*American baseball player*
* Schultz, Buddy

**Schultz, David [Dave]** 1949-
[FHE, SMG]
*Canadian-born hockey player*
* [The] Hammer

**Schultz, Dode**
See Schultz, Joseph Charles, Jr.

**Schultz, Dutch**
See Flegenheimer, Arthur

**Schultz, George Warren** 1926-
[BE, PB, SMG]
*American baseball player and coach*
* Schultz, Barney

**Schultz, Germany**
See Schultz, Joseph Charles, Sr.

**Schultz, Harry**
See Heinberg, Alexander

**Schultz, Hoe**
See Schultz, Joseph Charles, Jr.

**Schultz, Howard Henry** 1922- [BE]
*American baseball player*
* Schultz, Steeple
* Schultz, Stretch

**Schultz, James Willard** 1859-1947
[YAB]
*American author*
* Anderson, W. B.
* Apikuni [Far-Off White Robe]

**Schultz, Johann** 1595-1645 [PA]
*Author*
* Scultetus

**Schultz, Joseph Charles, Jr.** 1918-
[BE]
*American baseball player and
manager*
* Schultz, Dode
* Schultz, Hoe

**Schultz, Joseph Charles, Sr.**
1893-1941 [BE]
*American baseball player*
* Schultz, Germany

**Schultz, Pearle Henriksen** 1918-
[CA, SAT]
*American author*
* Pershing, Marie

**Schultz, Robert Duffy [Bob]** 1923-
[BE]
*American baseball player*
* Schultz, Bill

**Schultz, Steeple**
See Schultz, Howard Henry

**Schultz, Stretch**
See Schultz, Howard Henry

**Schultze, Carl Edward** 1866-1939
[WECO]
*American cartoonist*
* Bunny

**Schultze, Paul**
See Langer, Alfons

**Schulz, Adolph G.** 1883-1951
[AS, FB]
*American football player*
* Schulz, Germany

**Schulz, Albert C.** 1889-1931 [BE]
*American baseball player*
* Schulz, Lefty

**Schulz, Germany**
See Schulz, Adolph G.

**Schulz, Lefty**
See Schulz, Albert C.

**Schulz, Mrs. Warren** [FFF]
*Entertainer*
* Pierce, Emma

**Schulz Ewerth, Eckard** 1924-1961
[SC]
*Samoan-born actor and singer*
* Tuala, Mario

**Schulze, Alfred Otto Wolfgang**
1913-1951 [CAR]
*German painter*
* Wols

**Schumacher, Harold Henry** 1910-
[BE, PB]
*American baseball player*
* Prince Hal

**Schuman, Karen** 20th c.
*American editor*
* Blossom

**Schumann, Carl J.** 1884-1946 [BE]
*American baseball player*
* Schumann, Hack

**Schumann, Hack**
See Schumann, Carl J.

**Schumann, Maurice** 1911- [IAW]
*French author*
* Sidobre, Andre

**Schumann-Heink, Ernestine**
See Rossler, Ernestine

**Schura**
See Kollontay, Alexandra

**Schurgot, Helen** 20th c. [BEW]
*American actress and singer*
* Scott, Helena

**Schuster, Broadway**
See Schuster, William Charles

**Schuster, Sabu**
See Schuster, William Charles

**Schuster, William Charles** 1914-
[BE, BN]
*American baseball player*
* Schuster, Broadway
* Schuster, Sabu

**Schusterman, Ben** 1906- [BEW]
*American business executive*
* Sommers, Ben

**Schutte, Ethel** 1896- [THR]
*American actress and singer*
* Shutta, Ethel

**Schutz**
See Price, Charles

**Schutz, Emma**
See Harrison, Louise

**Schutz, Heinrich** 1585-1672 [FFF]
*German composer*
* [The] Father of German Music
* Sagittarius

**Schutz, Joseph Willard** 1912-
[ESF]
*American author and diplomat*
* Scholl, Jerry

**Schuyler, Keith C.** 1919- [IAW]
*American author*
* Bradley, Brian K.

**Schuyler, Sonny** 1913- [PMJ]
*American singer*
* Skylar, Sunny

**Schwab, Dutch**
See Schwab, Frank J.

**Schwab, Frank J.** 1895-1965
[AS, FB]
*American football player*
* Schwab, Dutch

**Schwabe, Cecil** 1897- [FC]
*British actor*
* Parker, Cecil

**Schwabe, Leo** ?-1889 [FFF]
*Philanthropist*
* [The] Soldiers' Friend

**Schwalberg, Carol[yn Ernestine
Stein]** 1930- [CA]
*American author*
* Bolling, Hal
* Jenkins, Phyllis
* La Fontaine, Blanche
* Levy, Lorelei
* Shorter, Carl
* Stein, Charles
* Ullman, Barbara

**Schwamb, Blackie**
See Schwamb, Ralph Richard

**Schwamb, Ralph Richard** 1926-
[BE]
*American baseball player*
* Schwamb, Blackie

**Schwamm, George S.** 1903-1966
[SC]
*American stunt performer*
* Schwamm, Tony

**Schwamm, Tony**
See Schwamm, George S.

**Schwandt, Wilbur** 1914- [ASC]
*American musician*
* Swan, Don

**Schwann, Duncan**
See Swann, Duncan

**Schwartz, Anne Powers** 1913-
[CA, SAT]
*American author*
* Powers, Anne

**Schwartz, Bernard** 1925-
[BDF, FC, HT]
*American actor*
* Curtis, Tony

**Schwartz, Betty** 1927- [CA]
*American author*
* Black, Betty

**Schwartz, Blab**
See Schwartz, William Charles
[Bill]

**Schwartz, Charles Henry**
1895-1925 [BLB]
*American murderer and swindler*
* Warren, Harold

**Schwartz, Don** 1937- [EJ7]
*American jazz musician*
* Randi, Don

**Schwartz, Frances** 20th c.
[CAP, WD]
*Author*
* Sylvin, Francis [joint pseudonym
with Sylvia S(ybil) Seaman]

**Schwartz, Jacob Lawrence** 1912-
[BEW]
*American composer, lyricist,
producer*
* Lawrence, Jack

**Schwartz, Jerome Lawrence** 1915-
[CA]
*American playwright, director,
producer*
* Lawrence, Jerome

**Schwartz, Jozua Marius Willem Van
Der Poorten** 1858-1915
[LC, TC, WW]
*Dutch author*
* Maartens, Maarten

**Schwartz, Marchmont** 1909-
[EJS, FB]
*American football player*
* Schwartz, Marchy

**Schwartz, Marchy**
See Schwartz, Marchmont

**Schwartz, Muriel A.**
See Eliot, Thomas Stearns

**Schwartz, Oscar** 1889-1967
[CED, EMT]
*American actor and singer*
* Shaw, Oscar

**Schwartz, Paula** 1925- [CA]
*American author and playwright*
* Mansfield, Elizabeth
* Mansfield, Libby

**Schwartz, Pop**
See Schwartz, William August

**Schwartz, Richard** 1928- [EJ]
*American jazz musician*
* Sutton, Dick

**Schwartz, Solomon** 1874?-1924
[SC]
*American actor*
* Odell, Shorty

**Schwartz, William August**
1864-1940 [BE]
*American baseball player*
* Schwartz, Pop

**Schwartz, William Charles [Bill]**
1884-1961 [BE]
*American baseball player*
* Schwartz, Blab

**Schwartzdorf, Jacob** 1909- [BEW]
*American musical director,
composer, conductor*
* Blackton, Jay

**Schwartze, John**
See Packer, Alfred

**Schwartzkopf, Eugene** 1892-1940
[SC]
*American actor and bandleader*
* Morgan, Gene

**Schwartzmann, Leo Isaakovich**
1868-1938 [CD]
*Russian philosopher and critic*
* Shestov, Leo

**Schwarz, Bertha** 1855-1947 [BBD]
*German opera singer*
* Bianchi, Bianca

**Schwarzenberg, Elisabeth**
See Czernohorsky, Elisabeth

**Schwarzendorf, Johann Paul Agidius**
1741-1816 [WBD]
*French composer*
* Martini il Tedesco
* Martini, Jean Paul Egide

**Schwarzeneggar, Arnold** 1947-
*Austrian bodybuilder*
* [The] Austrian Oak

**Schwarzert, Philipp** 1497-1560
[DEP, HN, WBD]
*German religious reformer*
* [The] German Proteus
* Melanchthon, Philip
* Praeceptor Germaniae
* [The] Teacher of Germany

**Schwarzkopf, Hans** 1910-
[BBD, OP]
*American opera director and linguist*
* White, John S.

**Schwarzrock, Lester Henry** 1912-
[BE]
*American baseball player*
* Rock, Lester Henry

**Schwegler, Paul** 1911- [FB]
*American football player*
* Schwegler, Schweg

**Schwegler, Schweg**
See Schwegler, Paul

**Schweickart, Russell L.** 1935-
*American astronaut*
* Schweickart, Rusty

**Schweickart, Rusty**
See Schweickart, Russell L.

**[Der] Schweigsame**
See Moltke, Hellmuth Karl
Bernhard von

**Schweitzer, Al[bert Casper]**
1882-1969 [BE]
*American baseball player*
* Schweitzer, Cheese

**Schweitzer, Byrd Baylor**
See Baylor, Byrd

**Schweitzer, Cheese**
See Schweitzer, Al[bert Casper]

**Schweizer, Marc** 1931- [IAW]
*French author*
* Generoso, Marc-Antoine
* Geneve, Pierre
* Larista, Pepe
* Laurac, Serge

**Schweizer, Richard Gene** 1930-
[BEW]
*American actor, singer, dancer*
* France, Richard

**Schwend, Friedrich** 1907?-
*German Nazi police official*
* Wendig, Dr.

**Schwerin, Kurt Christoph von.**
1684-1757 [DEP, DNNF, DNNS]
*Prussian army officer*
* [The] Little Marlborough

**Schwichtenberg, Wilbur** 1912-
[EJ, PMJ, WWJ]
*American jazz musician*
* Bradley, Will

**Schwitters, Cletus Lee** 20th c.
*Actor*
* Keith, Byron

**Sciacca, Anthony** 1921- [EJ, PMJ]
*American jazz musician*
* Scott, Tony

**[The] Scian Muse**
See Simonides

**Sciapiro, Michel** 1891-1962 [ASC]
*Russian-born musician*
* Fielding, Michael

**Scicolone, Sofia Villani** 1934-
[BDF, SW, WEF]
*Italian actress*
* Loren, Sophia

**Science Fiction, Mr.**
See Ackerman, Forrest J[ames]

**[The] Scientific Statesman**
See Burke, Edmund

**[The] Scintillating Sicilian**
See Trippi, Charles L. [Charlie]

**Scioppius, Gaspar** 1576-1649
[PA, SN]
*German scholar*
* [The] Grammatical Cynic
* Grammaticus, Caius

**Scio's Blind Old Bard**
See Homer

**Scipio**
See Watson, [John Hugh] Adam

**Scipio Aemilianus Africanus
Numantinus, Publius Cornelius** 2nd c.
BC [WBD]
*Roman general*
* [The] Younger

**Scipio Africanus, Publius Cornelius**
3rd c. BC [WBD]
*Roman general*
* [The] Elder

**Scipio, Lucius Cornelius** 3rd c. BC
[WBD]
*Roman politician*
* Barbatus

**Scipion**
See D'Arnal, Etienne

**[The] Scissor King**
See Mantooth, Lawrence

**Sclanders, Doorn**
See Fearn, John Russell

**Sclater, Ruth Leigh** 1895- [NAA]
*American author*
* Leigh, Ruth

**Scoffic, Lou[is]** 1913- [BE]
*American baseball player*
* Scoffic, Weaser

**Scoffic, Weaser**
See Scoffic, Lou[is]

**Scoggins, Jesse Leonard**
1891-1923 [BE]
*American baseball player*
* Scoggins, Jim
* Scoggins, Lefty

**Scoggins, Jim**
See Scoggins, Jesse Leonard

**Scoggins, Lefty**
See Scoggins, Jesse Leonard

**Scoglio, Giovanna** 1934-1972 [FC]
*Italian actress*
* Scala, Gia

**Scognamiglio, Vincenzio** 1922?-
[BEW, TR]
*Italian-born actor*
* Gardenia, Vincent

**Scolari, Paolo** ?-1191 [WBD]
*Pope*
* Clement III

**Scolasticus**
See John II

**Scolasticus, Doctor**
See Alfred [or Alured]

**Scolasticus, Doctor**
See Buridan, Jean

**Scolasticus, Doctor**
See Castro Novo, Hugh de

**Scolasticus, Doctor**
See Odon, Gerard

**Scollan, E. A.**
See O'Grady, Elizabeth Anne

**Scollin, James Arthur, Jr.** 1951-
*American disc jockey*
* Scols

**Scolnick, Sylvan** 20th c. [B10]
*American swindler and embezzler*
* Big Cherry

**Scols**
See Scollin, James Arthur, Jr.

**Scoop, Mr.**
See Oliver, Al[bert, Jr.]

**Scopulorum, Junipero**
See Aschwanden, Peter

**[The] Scorn of the Court**
See Oates, Titus

**Scortia, Thomas N[icholas]** 1926-
[CA]
*American author*
* Kurz, Artur R.
* McDow, Gerald
* Nichols, Scott

**Scortichini, Guido** 20th c. [WF]
*Italian actor*
* Burke, Samson

**[The] Scot**
See Thomson, Robert Brown
[Bobby]

**Scot, Alexander** 1525?-1584?
[DNNS, RH, SN]
*Scottish poet*
* [The] Anacreon of Ancient
  Scottish Poetry
* [The] Scottish Anacreon

**Scot, Chesman**
See Bulmer, [Henry] Kenneth

**[The] Scotch Hobbema**
See Nasmyth, Patrick [or Peter?]

**[The] Scotch Justinian**
See David I

**[The] Scotch Sappho**
See Cockburn, Catherine

**[The] Scotch Wop**
See Corrara, Joseph

**Scotchburn, Vernon** 1897-1957
[THR]
*British actor and playwright*
* Sylvaine, Vernon

**[The] Scotian Petrarch**
See Drummond, William

**Scotland, James** 1917- [CA]
*Scottish author and playwright*
* Emerson, Ronald
* Little, Kenneth

**Scotland, Jay**
See Jakes, John W[illiam]

**Scott, Adam** ?-1529
[DNNS, FFF, SN]
*Scottish marauder*
* [The] King of the Border
* [The] King of Thieves

**Scott, Alastair**
See Allen, Kenneth S[ydney]

**Scott, Andrew**
See Scotti, Andrea

**Scott, [Captain] Angus**
See Colinski, A. J.

**Scott, Anthony**
See Dresser, Davis

**Scott, Archer G.**
See Larbalestier, Philip George

**Scott, Arthur** 1890-1949
[DAM, PMJ, WWJ]
*American jazz musician*
* Scott, Bud

**Scott, Benny** 1945- [IBW]
*American auto racer*
* [The] Professor

**Scott, Billy** 1923- [BMH]
*British entertainer*
* Scott, Uke

**Scott, Bonnie**
See Paul, Bonnie Ann

**Scott, Bud**
See Scott, Arthur

**Scott, Bullet**
See Scott, Willie

**Scott, C. P.**
See Scott, Charles Prestwich

**Scott, Casey**
See Kubis, Pat

**Scott, Charles Prestwich**
1846-1932 [LC]
*British newspaper editor and owner*
* Scott, C. P.

**Scott, Charlie** 1947- [IBW]
*American athlete*
* Abdul-Aleem, Shaheed

**Scott, Christopher John** 1959-
[DC]
*British cricketer*
* Scott, Rock

**Scott, Churchill**
See Jackson, Joseph [Francis
Ambrose]

**Scott, Clement William** 1841-1904
[FFF, PA]
*British drama critic*
* Almaviva
* Rowe, Saville

**Scott, Clifford** 1913-    [IBW]
*American racehorse trainer*
* Scott, Scotty

**Scott, Clyde** 1924-    [FB]
*American football player*
* Scott, Smackover

**Scott, Cora Annett [Pipitone]**
1931-    [CA, SAT]
*American author*
* Annett, Cora

**Scott, Dan** [house pseudonym]
[Stratemeyer Syndicate]
*See* Barker, S[quire] Omar

**Scott, Dan** [house pseudonym]
[Stratemeyer Syndicate]
*See* Stratemeyer, Edward L.

**Scott, Dana**
*See* Robertson, Constance
[Pierrepont Noyes]

**Scott, Deacon**
*See* Scott, Lewis Everett

**Scott, Denis** [joint pseudonym with
Theodore Saunders]
*See* Means, Mary

**Scott, Denis** [joint pseudonym with
Mary Means]
*See* Saunders, Theodore

**Scott, Dixon**
*See* Scott, Walter

**Scott, Elise Aylen** 1904-    [NAA]
*Canadian writer*
* Aylen, Elise

**Scott, Ernest**
*See* Groves, William E.

**Scott, Ethel McCullough** 20th c.
[CA]
*Author*
* Clark, Garel [joint pseudonym
   with May Garelick]

**Scott, Eve**
*See* Rodgers, Joann Ellison

**Scott, Evelyn** 1893-    [WW]
*Author*
* Souza, Ernest

**Scott, Floyd John** 1898-1953    [BE]
*American baseball player*
* Scott, Pete

**Scott, Frances V.**
*See* Wing, Frances [Scott]

**Scott, G. Forrester** 20th c.    [WWL]
*Author*
* Halsham, John

**Scott, Genevia**
*See* Sylvester, Hannah

**Scott, George C., Jr.** 1944-
[PB, SMG]
*American baseball player*
* [The] Boomer

**Scott, Geraldine Edith** 20th c.
[LAO]
*British author*
* Mitton, G. E.

**Scott, Gordon**
*See* Werschkul, Gordon M.

**Scott, Hamilton**
*See* O'Mant, Hedley Percival
Angelo

**Scott, Hedley**
*See* O'Mant, Hedley Percival
Angelo

**Scott, Hedley**
*See* Young, Fred W.

**Scott, Helen Myers** 1876- ?
[WWL]
*Scottish author*
* Meldrum, Helen Myers

**Scott, Helena**
*See* Schurgot, Helen

**Scott, Hugh Stowell** 1862-1903
[LC]
*British author*
* Merriman, Henry Seton

**Scott, Ivan**
*See* Eppinoff, Ivan

**Scott, J. W. Robertson**
*See* Scott, John William Robertson

**Scott, Jack**
*See* Scafone, Jack, Jr.

**Scott, Jack S.**
*See* Escott, Jonathan

**Scott, James** 1649-1685
[DEP, DNNF, WBD]
*Claimant to British throne*
* Crofts, James
* Fitzroy, James
* [The] Little Duke
* Monmouth, Duke of
* [The] Protestant Duke

**Scott, James** 1888-1957    [BE, PB]
*American baseball player*
* Death Valley Jim

**Scott, Jane**
*See* McElfresh, [Elizabeth]
Adeline

**Scott, Jay** 1924-    [THR]
*British theatrical designer*
* Hutchinson Scott, Jay

**Scott, Jean**
*See* Muir, Marie Agnes

**Scott, Jeffrey**
*See* Usher, Shaun

**Scott, Jeremy**
*See* Dick, Kay

**Scott, Jody** 1923-    [WW]
*Author*
* Scott, Thurston [joint pseudonym
   with George Thurston Leite]

**Scott, John**
*See* Nearing, John Scott

**Scott, John**    [FFF]
*Horse trainer*
* [The] Wizard of the North

**Scott, John** 1751-1838
[DEP, FFF, SN]
*British jurist*
* Eldon, Earl of
* Old Bags
* [The] Stormy Petrel of Politics

**Scott, John** 1820-1907    [PA]
*American author and soldier*
* Barbarossa

**Scott, John William Robertson**
1866-1962    [LC]
*British author and editor*
* Scott, J. W. Robertson

**Scott, Latayne Colvett** 1952-    [CA]
*American author*
* Colvett, Latayne

**Scott, Lefty**
*See* Scott, Marshall

**Scott, Leslie**
*See* Abullah, Zakariya

**Scott, Lewis Everett** 1892-1960
[AS, BE, PB]
*American baseball player*
* Scott, Deacon

**Scott, Linda**
*See* Sampson, Linda Joy

**Scott, Lizabeth**
*See* Matzo, Emma

**Scott, Lloyd**
*See* Turner, George E[ugene]

**Scott, Mabel** 1872?-1908    [BEW]
*Actress*
* Russell, Mabel

**Scott, Malcolm** 1872-1929    [BMH]
*British comedian*
* [The] Woman who Knows

**Scott, Marco**
*See* Charlier, Roger H[enri]

**Scott, Marian [Gallagher]** 20th c.
[WW]
*Author*
* Oliver, Gail
* Wolffe, Katherine

**Scott, Marshall** 1915-1964    [BE]
*American baseball player*
* Scott, Lefty

**Scott, Martin**
*See* Gehman, Richard Boyd

**Scott, Mary**    [RH]
*Daughter of Sir William Scott of
Harden*
* [The] Flower of Yarrow

**Scott, Maxwell**
*See* Staniforth, [Dr.] John William

**Scott, Michael** 1789-1835    [SN]
*Scottish author*
* [The] Salvator Rosa of the Sea

**Scott, Mickey**
*See* Scott, Ralph Robert

**Scott, Mikado Milt**
*See* Scott, Milt[on Parker]

**Scott, Milt[on Parker]** 1866-1938
[BE]
*American baseball player*
* Scott, Mikado Milt

**Scott, Monica**
*See* Baber, Monica Mary

**Scott, Natalie Anderson**
*See* Sokoloff, Natalie B.

**Scott, Nicola** 1945-    [TR]
*British actress*
* Pagett, Nicola

**Scott, Norford**
*See* Rowland, D[onald] S[ydney]

**Scott, O. R.**
*See* Gottliebsen, Ralph Joseph

**[The] Scott of Ireland**
*See* Banim, John

**[The] Scott of the Sea**
*See* Cooper, James Fenimore

**Scott, P. T.**
*See* Poage, Scott T[abor]

**Scott, Peg O'Neill** 20th c.
[SFL, WGT]
*American author*
* O'Neill, Scott
* Werper, Barton [house
   pseudonym]

**Scott, Pete**
*See* Scott, Floyd John

**Scott, Peter Dale** 1929-    [CA]
*Canadian-born author*
* Greene, Adam
* Sproston, John

**Scott, Peter T.** 20th c.
[ESF, SFL, WGT]
*American author*
* Werper, Barton [house
   pseudonym]

**Scott, Phaintin' Phil**
*See* Suffling, Philip

**Scott, Phil**
*See* Suffling, Philip

**Scott, Phillippa** 1935-    [BEW]
*American actress*
* Scott, Pippa

**Scott, Pippa**
*See* Scott, Phillippa

**Scott, R. T. M.**
*See* Maitland, Reginald T.

**Scott, Ralph Robert** 1947-
[SMG, WWB]
*German-born baseball player*
* Scott, Mickey

**Scott, Randolph**
*See* Crane, Randolph

**Scott, Raymond**
*See* Warnow, Harry

**Scott, Robert** 20th c.    [WGT]
*British author*
* Blue Wolf

**Scott, Robin**
*See* Wilson, Robin S[cott]

**Scott, Rock**
*See* Scott, Christopher John

**Scott, Roland B.** 1911-    [IBW]
*American physician*
* [The] Father of Sickle Cell
   Anemia Research

**Scott, Roney**
*See* Gault, William Campbell

**Scott, [Captain] Russell**
*See* Pearson, Alec George

**Scott, [Major] S. S.**
*See* Harbaugh, Thomas Chalmers

**Scott, Sarah** ?-1795    [PA]
*Author*
* Raymond, Henry Augustus

**Scott, Scotty**
See Scott, Clifford

**Scott, Smackover**
See Scott, Clyde

**Scott, Stanley**
See Fagerstrom, Stan

**Scott, Steve**
See Crawford, William [Elbert]

**Scott, Stuart**
See Aitken, William Russell

**Scott, Thomas**
See Rotherham, Thomas

**Scott, Thomas J.** [PA]
*Author*
* Prog

**Scott, Thurston** [joint pseudonym with Jody Scott]
See Leite, George Thurston

**Scott, Thurston** [joint pseudonym with George Thurston Leite]
See Scott, Jody

**Scott, Titus**
See Ingram, Thomas Theodore Scott

**Scott, Tommy**
See Woodward, Thomas Jones

**Scott, Tony**
See Sciacca, Anthony

**Scott, Uke**
See Scott, Billy

**Scott, Valerie**
See Rowland, D[onald] S[ydney]

**Scott, Walter**
See Chestnutt, Edgar B.

**Scott, [Sir] Walter** 1771-1832
[DEL, RH, SN]
*Scottish author and poet*
* [The] Arioso of the North
* [A] Bard of Martial Lay
* [The] Border Minstrel
* Cleishbotham, Jedediah
* Clutterbuck, [Captain] Cuthbert
* Croftangry, Chrystal
* Dryasdust, [The] Rev. Dr.
* [The] Duke of Darnick
* Duns Scotus
* [The] Great Border Minstrel
* [The] Great Magician of the North
* [The] Great Unknown
* Grogg, Colonel
* [The] Homer of Modern Days
* [A] Layman
* [The] Magician of the North
* Malachi
* Malagrowther, Malachi
* [The] Minstrel of the Border
* Old Peveril
* Pattieson, Peter
* Paul
* [The] Peveril of the Peak
* S. W., Esq.
* Somnambulus
* Templeton, Laurence
* [The] Wizard of the North

**Scott, Walter** 1872-1954 [B10]
*American adventurer*
* Death Valley Scotty

**Scott, Walter** 1882-1915 [WWL]
*Author*
* Scott, Dixon

**Scott, Warwick**
See Dudley-Smith, Trevor

**Scott, Wendell, Sr.** 1922- [IBW]
*American auto racer*
* [The] Dean of Black Racing

**Scott, Will[iam Matthew]**
1894?-1964 [EMD]
*British author and artist*
* Watt, William

**Scott, William**
See Newman, Allan Scott

**Scott, William**
See Reyburn, Wallace [Macdonald]

**Scott, William R[alph]** 1918- [CA]
*American author and screenwriter*
* Hill, Weldon

**Scott, Willie** ?-1958 [IBW]
*American auto racer*
* Scott, Bullet

**Scott, Winfield** 1786-1866
[DNNS, SN]
*American army officer*
* Old Chapultepec

**Scott, Winifred Mary** 20th c.
[LAO]
*British author*
* Wynne, Pamela

**Scott-Fraser, Elizabeth**
See Fraser, Elizabeth Bertha [Liz]

**Scott-Heron, Gil** 1949- [IBW]
*American author, poet, musician*
* Spiderman

**Scott-James, R. A.**
See Scott-James, Rolfe Arnold

**Scott-James, Rolfe Arnold**
1878-1959 [LC]
*British author and editor*
* Scott-James, R. A.

**Scott-Moncrieff, C. K.**
See Scott-Moncrieff, Charles Kenneth Michael

**Scott-Moncrieff, Charles Kenneth Michael** 1889-1930 [LC]
*Scottish-born translator*
* Scott-Moncrieff, C. K.

**Scott-Taggart, Elizabeth Mary Josephine** 1927- [ART]
*British sculptor*
* Est

**Scott Thorn, Ronald**
See Wilkinson, Ronald

**Scotti, Andrea** 20th c. [WF]
*Italian actor*
* Scott, Andrew

**Scottie**
See Wilson, Robert

**[The] Scottish Anacreon**
See Scot, Alexander

**[The] Scottish Boanerges**
See Alexander, James

**[The] Scottish Boanerges**
See Haldane, Robert

**[The] Scottish Heliogabalus**
See James I

**[The] Scottish Hogarth**
See Allan, David

**[The] Scottish Homer**
See Wilkie, William

**[The] Scottish Hudibras**
See Colvil, Samuel

**[The] Scottish Marcellus**
See Macdonald, [Sir] James

**[The] Scottish Plato**
See Stewart, Dugald

**[The] Scottish Reynolds**
See Raeburn, [Sir] Henry

**[The] Scottish Sidney**
See Baillie, Robert

**[The] Scottish Solomon**
See James I

**[The] Scottish Teniers**
See Wilkie, [Sir] David

**[The] Scottish Theocritus**
See Ramsay, Allan

**[The] Scottish Vandyke**
See Jamesone, George

**[The] Scottish Walpole**
See Sharpe, Charles Kirkpatrick

**[The] Scotts Irishman**
See Bruce, William

**Scotty**
See Urquhart, C. H.

**Scotus, Johannes [or John]** 815?-875? [HN, RH, SN]
*Medieval philosopher and theologian*
* Erigena [The Irishman]
* [The] Last of the Platonists
* [The] Wise

**Scotus Minor**
See Pietro Aquila

**[The] Scourge**
See Tropea, Orassio [or Orazio]

**[The] Scourge of Christians**
See Noureddin-Mahmud

**[The] Scourge of Europe**
See Bonaparte, Napoleon

**[The] Scourge of Fanaticism**
See South, Robert

**[The] Scourge of God**
See Attila

**[The] Scourge of God**
See Charles VIII

**[The] Scourge of God**
See Genseric

**[The] Scourge of God**
See Timur [or Timour]

**[The] Scourge of Grammar**
See Jacob, Giles

**[The] Scourge of Homer**
See Zoilus [or Zoilos]

**[The] Scourge of Infidels**
See Khaled [or Khalid]

**[The] Scourge of Princes**
See Aretino, Pietro

**[The] Scourge of Scotland**
See Edward I

**[The] Scourge of the Propagators of the Faith**
See Drelincourt, Charles

**[The] Scourge of the Spaniards**
See Nau, Jacques Jean David

**[The] Scourge of Wales**
See Edward I

**Scovel, Juy**
See Fontana, Jean Pierre

**Scovel, Mrs.** [FFF]
*Entertainer*
* Fielding, May

**Scovell, Edward** [FFF]
* Scovello, Signor

**Scovello, Signor**
See Scovell, Edward

**Scoville, Joseph A.** 1815-1864
[DEL, FFF, PA]
*British author and journalist*
* Barrett, Walter, Clerk
* Manhattan
* Pick, Mr.

**Scram, Arthur N.**
See Guild, Leo

**Scrambled Ego**
See Rodgers, [Sir] John [Charles]

**Scramuzzo, Craig William** 1950-
[SMG]
*American baseball player*
* Scramuzzo, Moose

**Scramuzzo, Moose**
See Scramuzzo, Craig William

**Scrannel, Orpheus**
See Armstrong, Terence Ian Fytton

**Scrap Iron Beecher**
See Beecher, Ed[ward]

**Scrap Iron Courtney**
See Courtney, Clinton Dawson

**Scrap Iron Kenna**
See Kenna, Ed[ward Aloysious]

**Scrap Iron Stinson**
See Stinson, Gorrell R.

**Scrappy Bill Joyce**
See Joyce, William Michael

**Scratchley, Harry**
See Sherwood, John D.

**Scratt, Ivan**
See Scratuglia, Ivan

**Scratuglia, Ivan** 20th c. [WF]
*Italian actor*
* Scratt, Ivan

**Screamin' Jay Hawkins**
See Hawkins, Jalacy J.

**Scribble**
See Sowden, [Sir] William John

**[The] Scribe of the Revolution**
See Jefferson, Thomas

**Scribe, Simeon**
See Black, Adam

**Scriber, Peter**
See Davis, Charles Augustus

**Scriblerus, Martinus**
See Pope, Alexander

**Scrire. O. T. O. 4-7**
See Gardner, Gerald Brosseau

**Scrivener, Chuck**
See Scrivener, Wayne Allison

[The] Scrivener of Crosbiters
See Greene, Robert

Scrivener, Wayne Allison 1947-
[SMG, WWB]
American baseball player
* Scrivener, Chuck

Scriverius
See Schryver, Pieter

Scroddles
See Mason, William

Scroggie, Marcus Graham 1901-
[WD]
British engineer and writer
* Cathode Ray

Scrope, George Julius Poulett
See Thomson, George Julius
Poulett

Scruggs, Baby
See Scruggs, Leazar

Scruggs, Faye 20th c.   [RO1]
American singer
* Adams, Atomic
* Adams, Faye

Scruggs, Irene 1901-   [BWW]
American singer
* Brown, Chocolate
* Little Sister
* Nolan, Dixie

Scruggs, Leazar 1921-   [BWW]
American dancer
* Scruggs, Baby

Scrutator
See Ensor, [Sir] Robert Charles

Scrutator
See Harlock, K. W.

Scrutator
See Jerram, Charles

Scrutator
See Loveday, John

Scrutator
See Macallan, Daniel

Scrutator
See MacColl, Malcolm

Scrutator
See Measor, C. P.

Scrutator
See Rarey, John Solomon

Scrutator
See Rivington, Charles

Scrutton, Daphne 1922-   [FC]
British actress
* Anderson, Daphne

Scrymgeour Wedderburn, Janet
1941-   [ART]
British sculptor and stained-glass
window designer
* J. S. W.

Scudamore, Lily   [FFF]
American writer
* Ruhamah

Scudder, Kawliga
See Scudder, Pat

Scudder, Mildred Lee 1908-
[CA, TBJ]
American author
* Lee, Mildred

Scudder, Pat 20th c.   [GW]
American rodeo performer
* Scudder, Kawliga

Scuderi, Magdalen [or Madeleine] de
1607-1671   [DEP, DNNS, RH]
French poet
* [The] French Sappho
* [The] Tenth Muse

[The] Sculptor of American History
See Kelly, James Edward

[The] Sculptor Poet
See Lucretius Carus, Titus

Scultetus
See Schultz, Johann

Sczepkowski, Theodore Walter
1923-   [BE]
American baseball player
* Sepkowski, Theodore Walter
[Ted]

Sdt, E.
See Skarstedt, Ernest Teofil

[The] Se Baptist
See Smith [or Smyth?], John

Se De Kay
See Kirke, Charles D.

Sea
See Coffin, Roland F.

Sea Gull
See Chereshkova, Valentina
Vladimirovna

Sea Lion
See Bennett, Geoffrey [Martin]

Sea Lion Hall
See Clolo, Carlos

Sea Shell
See Clark, Jeremiah Simpson

Seab, Lenial
See Johnston, D. S. B.

Seabright, Idris
See St. Clair, Margaret

Seabright, John
See Tubb, Edwin Charles

Seabrooke, David
See Bedford-Jones, Henry [James
O'Brien]

Seabrooke, Edward   [FFF]
Entertainer
* Lee, Edward

Seabrooke, Thomas Q.
See Quigley, Thomas James

Seabury, Ynez 1909-1973
[FIR, SC]
American actress
* [The] Biograph Baby

Seacole, Mary ?-1881   [IBW]
Jamaican-born nurse
* [The] Yellow Doctress

Seadlund, John Henry 1910-1938
[BLB]
American murderer and kidnapper
* Anders, Peter

Seadoaghob, Nana 1936-   [WBC]
Thai boxer
* Kingpetch, Pone

[A] Seafarer
See Russell, William Clark

Seaforth
See Foster, George Cecil

Seaforth, A. Nelson
See Clarke, George Sydenham

Seagar, Joan
See Fearn, John Russell

Seager, Charles   [FFF]
* Academicus

Seagrave, Barbara Ann Garvey
See Jackson, Barbara Ann Garvey
Seagrave

[The] Seagreen Incorruptible
See Robespierre, Maximilien

Seagrist, Josephine 1922-   [BEW]
American actress and singer
* Roberts, Joan

Seagull
See Herzstein, Barbara

Seale, Johnny Ray 1938-   [BE]
American baseball player
* Durango Kid

Sealey, Leonard George William
1923-   [IAW]
British-born educator and author
* Britt, George

Seals, Danny 1950-   [RO2]
American singer
* England Dan

Seals, Frank Junior 1942-
[BWW, IBW]
American singer, songwriter,
musician
* Seals, Son

Seals, Jim 20th c.   [BWW]
American musician
* Seals, Son

Seals, Son
See Seals, Frank Junior

Seals, Son
See Seals, Jim

Sealsfield, Charles
See Postl, Karl Anton

Seaman, Augustus   [PA]
Author
* Brick, Titus

Seaman, Elizabeth [Cochrane]
1867-1922   [B10]
American journalist
* Bly, Nellie

Seaman, [Sir] Owen 1861- ?
[WWL]
British author
* Nauticus
* O. S.

Seaman, Sylvia S[ybil] 1910-
[CAP, WD]
American author
* Sylvin, Francis [joint pseudonym
with Frances Schwartz]

Seamark
See Small, Austin J.

Seames, C. O. 20th c.   [IBW]
American tennis player
* Seames, Mother

Seames, Mother
See Seames, C. O.

Search, Edward
See Hazlitt, William

Search, Edward
See Tucker, Abraham

Search, John
See Whately, Richard

Search Light
See Frank, Waldo David

Search, Preston Willis 1853- ?
[NAA]
American author and educator
* Redwood, John

Search, Sarah
See Nolan, F.

Search, Warner Christian
See Smith, Baron

[The] Searcher
See Fludd, Robert

Searcher, Leland
See Hebbard, William Wallace

Searchlight
See Eardley-Wilmot, [Sir] Sydney
Marow

Searcy, George ?-1949   [F2]
Actor
* Moran, George

Seare, Nicholas
See Whitaker, Rod

Searing, Laura C. Redden
1840-1923   [FFF]
American poet
* Glyndon, Howard

Searle, January
See Phillips, George Searle

Searle, Kathryn Adrienne 1942-
[CA, SAT]
British author and illustrator
* Kathryn

Searle, Louise
See Hunter, Mrs. Henry

Searle, Mrs. Cyril   [FFF]
Entertainer
* Eytinge, Rose

Searle, Ronald William Fordham
1920-   [DLE]
British artist, illustrator, author
* Shy, Timothy [joint pseudonym
with Dominic Bevan Wyndham
Lewis]

Sears, Deane
See Rywell, Martin

Sears, Isaac 1730-1786   [SN]
American merchant
* Sears, King

Sears, Ken[neth Eugene] 1917-
[BE]
American baseball player
* Sears, Ziggy

Sears, King
See Sears, Isaac

Sears, Mrs. Newton   [PA]
Author
* Kismet

Sears, Zelda
See Paldi, Zelda

Sears, Ziggy
See Sears, Ken[neth Eugene]

**Seastrom, Victor**
See Sjoestroem, Victor

**Seaton, Beryl**
See Platts, Beryl

**Seattle Bill James**
See James, William Lawrence

**Seattle Frank**
See DuBreuil, Elizabeth Lorinda

**Seaver, George Thomas [Tom]**
1944- [NLG]
*American baseball player*
* [The] Franchise
* Terrific, Tom

**Seaver, W. A.** [PA]
*Author*
* Editors Drawer

**Seawell, Molly Elliot** 1860-1916
[FFF]
*American author*
* Sydney

**Seaworthy, [Captain] Gregory**
See Gregory, James

**Sebastian**
See Ponsonby, [Sir] Henry
Frederick

**Sebastian** 1554-1578 [DNNS, SN]
*King of Portugal*
* [The] Madman

**Sebastian, Jeanne**
See Newsome, Arden J[eanne]

**Sebastian, John** 1944- [RO2]
*American singer*
* Benson, John

**Sebastian, Lee**
See Silverberg, Robert

**Sebastian, Margaret**
See Gladstone, Arthur M.

**Sebastiano del Piombo**
See Luciani, Sebastiano

**Sebelien, John Robert Francis** 1858-
? [LAO]
*Danish-born scientist and author*
* Pagan, Kristian

**Sebenthal, Roberta Elizabeth**
1917- [CA, WD]
*American author and poet*
* Kruger, Paul

**Sebley, Frances Rae** 1921- [WD]
*British author and critic*
* Jeffs, Rae

**Sebring, Jay**
See Kummer, Thomas Jay

**Sec**
See Blow, Marya Mannes

**Secchi, Luciano** 1939- [WEC]
*Italian cartoonist*
* Bunker, Max

**Sechrist, Doc**
See Sechrist, Theodore O'Hara

**Sechrist, Theodore O'Hara**
1876-1950 [BE]
*American baseball player*
* Sechrist, Doc

**Seckendorf, Gustav Anton von**
1775-1823 [FFF]
*German author and playwright*
* Peale, Patrick

**Seckener, Mrs. James A.** [FFF]
*Entertainer*
* Vogt, Marie

**[The] Second Achilles**
See Dentatus, Sicinius

**[The] Second Alexander**
See Sandjar

**[The] Second Aristotle**
See Achillini, Alessandro

**[A] Second Aristotle**
See Frederick II

**[The] Second Augustine**
See Aquinas, Thomas [Thomas of
Aquino]

**[The] Second Brutus**
See Medici, Francesco de

**[A] Second Cato the Censor**
See L'Hospital [or L'Hopital],
Michel de

**[The] Second Charlemagne**
See Charles V

**[The] Second Dauphin**
See Louis de France

**[The] Second Effulgence**
See Gotescalc

**[The] Second Founder of Rome**
See Peretti, Felice

**[A] Second Helen**
See Recamier, Jeanne Francoise
Julie Adelaide

**Second, Henry**
See Harrison, Henry Sydnor

**[The] Second Hogarth**
See Bunbury, Henry William

**[The] Second John**
See Adams, John Quincy

**[A] Second Mars**
See Della Rovere, Giuliano

**[The] Second Parent of the Reformed
Church**
See John [or Johann]

**[The] Second Romulus**
See Camillus, Marcus Furius

**[The] Second Romulus of
Brandenburg**
See Albert I [or Albrecht]

**[The] Second St. Augustine**
See Hughes de St. Victor

**[The] Second St. Paul**
See Remi [or Remigius]

**[The] Second Solomon**
See Henry VII

**[The] Second Solomon**
See James I

**Second Thoughts, Solomon**
See Kennedy, John Pendleton

**[The] Second Trajan**
See Claudius II [Marcus Aurelius
Claudius]

**[The] Second Washington**
See Clay, Henry

**[The] Second Washington**
See Juarez, Benito Pablo

**[A] Second Xenophon**
See M'Pherson, Samuel

**Secor, Helena**
See Tons, Helen

**Secor, Mrs. George J.** [FFF]
*Entertainer*
* Renard, Rachelle

**Secor, Rosa** 1884-1922 [THR]
*American actress*
* Lynd, Rosa

**Secrest, Meryle**
See Beveridge, Meryle Secrest

**[The] Secretary of Nature**
See Aristocles

**[The] Secretary of Nature**
See Aristotle

**[The] Secretary of Nature**
See Bacon, Francis [First Baron
Verulam]

**[The] Secretary of Nature**
See Socrates

**Secrist, Kelliher** [joint pseudonym
with W. G. Secrist]
See Kelliher, Dan T.

**Secrist, Kelliher** [joint pseudonym
with Dan T. Kelliher]
See Secrist, W. G.

**Secrist, W. G.** 20th c. [WW]
*Author*
* Secrist, Kelliher [joint pseudonym
with Dan T. Kelliher]

**Sectanus, Quintus**
See Sergardi, Ludovico

**[The] Sectional President**
See Lincoln, Abraham

**Secundus**
See Lotich, Peter

**Secundus, Asmodeus**
See Sotheran, Charles

**Secundus, Johannes**
See Everaerts, Jan Nicolai

**Secutor**
See Slater, John Herbert

**Sedges, John**
See Buck, Pearl S[ydenstricker]

**Sedgewick, Helen**
See Brady, Helen

**Sedgman, Frank** 20th c. [OET]
*Australian tennis player*
* [The] Gentleman

**Sedgwick, Anne Douglas**
See Selincourt, Anne De

**Sedgwick, Billy**
See Putnam, S. W.

**Sedgwick, Doomsday**
See Sedgwick, William

**Sedgwick, Duke**
See Sedgwick, Henry Kenneth

**Sedgwick, Henry Kenneth** 1899-
[BE]
*American baseball player*
* Sedgwick, Duke

**Sedgwick, Modwena**
See Glover, Modwena

**Sedgwick, Theodore, Jr.**
1780-1839 [FFF]
*American author and attorney*
* Veto

**Sedgwick, William** ?-1669? [SN]
*British clergyman*
* [The] Apostle of the Isle of Ely
* Sedgwick, Doomsday

**Sedolin, Sture**
See Hallstrom, Carl

**Sedran, Barney**
See Sedransky, Barney

**Sedransky, Barney** 1891-1969
[BB, EJS]
*American basketball player*
* Sedran, Barney

**Sedric, Con-Con**
See Sedric, Paul

**Sedric, [Eu]gene** 1907-1963
[EJ, PMJ, WWJ]
*American jazz musician*
* Sedric, Honey Bear

**Sedric, Honey Bear**
See Sedric, [Eu]gene

**Sedric, Paul** 20th c. [EJ, WWJ]
*American musician*
* Sedric, Con-Con

**Seduro, Vladimir** 1910- [CA]
*Russian-born author*
* Hlybinny, Vladimir

**Sedway, Moe**
See Sedwitz, Morris

**Sedwitz, Morris** 20th c. [BLB]
*American underworld figure*
* Sedway, Moe

**Sedych, Andrei**
See Zwibak, Jacques

**See, Chad**
See See, Charles Henry [Charlie]

**See, Charles Henry [Charlie]**
1896-1948 [BE]
*American baseball player*
* See, Chad

**[The] See See Rider Blues Girl**
See Nicholls, Muriel

**Seebord, G. R.**
See Soderberg, Percy Measday

**Seed, Cecile Eugenie** 1930- [WD]
*South African author*
* Seed, Jenny

**Seed, Jenny**
See Seed, Cecile Eugenie

**Seed, Sheila Turner** 1937?-1979
[CA]
*American editor, writer,
photographer*
* Turner, Sheila R.

**Seedo, Sonia**
See Fuchs, Sonia Husid

**Seeds, Robert Ira** 1907- [BE]
*American baseball player*
* Seeds, Suitcase Bob

**Seeds, Suitcase Bob**
See Seeds, Robert Ira

**Seeger, Pete[r R.]** 1919- [FCW]
*American singer and songwriter*
* Bowers, Pete

**Seelen, Arthur**
See Seelenfreund, Arthur

**Seelenfreund, Arthur** 1923-  [BEW]
*American actor and theatre bookseller*
* Seelen, Arthur

**Seeley, Charles S.**
See Munday, John William

**Seeley, John Robert** 1834- ?  [PA]
*Author*
* Ecce Homo

**Seeley, Robert B.** 19th c.  [PA]
*Author*
* [A] Layman

**Seelos, Annette**
See Wallis, Blanche

**Seer**
See Roberts, Cecil Edric Mornington

**Seers, Eugene** 1865- ?  [NAA]
*Canadian-born poet and author*
* Dantin, Louis

**Seestern**
See Grautoff, Ferdinand [Heinrich]

**Seferiades, Giorgos Stylianou** 1900-1971  [CA, EWL, TCL]
*Greek diplomat and poet*
* Seferis, George

**Seferis, George**
See Seferiades, Giorgos Stylianou

**Seff, Richard**
See Siff, Richard Philip

**Sefi [or Sophi]** ?-1642  [HN]
*Sultan of Persia*
* [The] Nero of Persia

**Sefrit, Sallie Mulholland** 1862-1941  [IA]
*American writer and poet*
* Waller, Virginia Harmon

**Segal, Marc** 1887-  [JL]
*Russian painter*
* Chagall, Marc

**Segal, Samuel** 20th c.  [EJS]
*American wrestler*
* Maccabee, Dan

**Segale, Rose** 1850-1941  [CAT]
*Italian-born American author*
* Blandina, [Sister]

**Segall, Don** 20th c.  [SFL]
*Author*
* August, Leo

**Segall, Liliane** 1939-  [CAR]
*American artist*
* Lijn, Liliane

**Seghers, Anna**
See Reiling, Netty

**Seghi, Phillip Dominic** 1918-  [SMG]
*Baseball manager*
* Seghi, Swapper

**Seghi, Swapper**
See Seghi, Phillip Dominic

**[Il] Segretario**
See Machiavelli, Niccolo [or Nicholas]

**Seguier, Pierre**  [RH]
*French prophet and clergyman*
* [The] Danton of the Cevennes

**Segundo, Bart**
See Rowland, D[onald] S[ydney]

**Segura, Francisco** 1921-  [B10]
*Ecuadorian tennis player*
* Segura, Pancho

**Segura, Pancho**
See Segura, Francisco

**Segura, Vicente** 1883-  [GS]
*Mexican bullfighter*
* [El] Millonario [The Millionaire]

**Segura y Campos, Antonio** 1880-1930  [GS]
*Spanish bullfighter*
* Segurita [Little Segura]

**Segurita [Little Segura]**
See Segura y Campos, Antonio

**Seibel, Werner** 1946-  [IAW]
*German author and poet*
* Lebies, Rene

**Seibold, Harry** 1896-1965  [BE]
*American baseball player*
* Seibold, Socks

**Seibold, Socks**
See Seibold, Harry

**Seid, Ruth** 1913-  [ANT, AW, CA]
*American author and playwright*
* Sinclair, Jo

**Seide, Diane** 1930-  [CA]
*American author*
* Seidner, Diane

**Seidl, Lea**
See Mayrseidl, Caroline

**Seidlitz, Julius**
See Jedteles, Itzig

**Seidman, J. S.**
See Seidman, Jacob Stewart

**Seidman, Jacob Stewart** 1901-  [BEW]
*American investor and accountant*
* Seidman, J. S.

**Seidner, Diane**
See Seide, Diane

**Seifert, Elizabeth**
See Gasparotti, Elizabeth Seifert

**Seiffert, Ernst** 1892-1948  [BBD, EMT]
*Austrian-born opera singer*
* Tauber, Richard

**Seignobosc, Francoise** 1897-1961  [CA, MJA]
*French author and illustrator*
* Francoise

**Seinfel, Ruth**
See Goode, Ruth

**Seitz, Carolyn Jane** 1928-  [BEW]
*American actress, singer, director*
* Seitz, Dran

**Seitz, Dran**
See Seitz, Carolyn Jane

**Seitz, Franz** 20th c.  [WF]
*German screenwriter*
* Laforet, Georg

**[The] Sejanus of England**
See Villiers, George

**Sejour, Victor**
See Marcou-Ferrand, Juan Victor Sejour

**Sejour-Magloire, Francis L.** 1940-  [CW]
*Haitian poet and author*
* Magloire, Francis L.

**Sekely, Steve**
See Szekely, Istvan

**Sekers, Miki**
See Sekers, Nicholas

**Sekers, Nicholas** ?-1972  [WFA]
*British fabric manufacturer*
* Sekers, Miki

**Sekon, George Augustus**
See Nokes, George Augustus

**Sekona, Fonomonu** 20th c.  [RBE]
*Tongan boxer*
* Sekona, Young

**Sekona, Young**
See Sekona, Fonomonu

**Seku, Yerba**
See Hooi, Richard

**Sekulovich, Mladen** 1914-  [BDF, HT, SW]
*American actor*
* Malden, Karl

**Selbach, Albert Karl** 1872-1956  [AS, BE, PB]
*American baseball player*
* Selbach, Kip

**Selbach, Kip**
See Selbach, Albert Karl

**Selbini, Lalla** ?-1942  [BMH]
*Entertainer*
* [The] Bathing Belle on the Bicycle

**Selby, Brit**
See Selby, Robert Briton

**Selby, Norman** 1873-1940  [AS, BX, RBE]
*American boxer*
* [The] Corkscrew Kid
* McCoy, Charles
* McCoy, Kid

**Selby, Percival M.**
See Short, Percival M.

**Selby, Robert Briton** 1945-  [CEI, FHE]
*Canadian-born hockey player*
* Selby, Brit

**Selcamm, George**
See Machlis, Joseph

**Selchow**
See Lafontaine, August Heinrich Julius

**Selden, Albert**
See Seldon, Albert Wiggin

**Selden, George**
See Thompson, George Selden

**Selden, John** 1584-1654  [SN]
*British jurist and statesman*
* [The] Learned Selden
* Monarch of Letters

**Seldes, Gilbert [Vivian]** 1893-1970  [CA, WW]
*American author*
* Bluphocks, Lucien

**Seldes, Gilbert [Vivian]** (Continued)
* Cauliflower, Sebastian
* Johns, Foster
* Shaw, Vivian

**Seldon, Albert Wiggin** 1922-  [BEW]
*American composer, producer, lyricist*
* Selden, Albert

**Seldon-Truss, Leslie**
See Truss, [Leslie] Seldon

**Seleucus I** 4th c. BC  [WBD]
*King of the Seleucidae*
* Nicator

**Seleucus II** 3rd c. BC  [WBD]
*King of the Seleucidae*
* Callinicus

**Seleucus III** 3rd c. BC  [WBD]
*King of the Seleucidae*
* Soter

**Seleucus IV** 2nd c. BC  [WBD]
*King of the Seleucidae*
* Philopator

**Seleucus VI** 2nd c. BC  [WBD]
*King of the Seleucidae*
* Epiphanes Nicator

**Selig, Allan H.** 20th c.  [SMG]
*American baseball executive*
* Selig, Bud

**Selig, Bud**
See Selig, Allan H.

**Seligman, Walter Herbert** 1902-  [OP]
*German conductor*
* Herbert, Walter

**Selika, Marie** 1852-1937  [IBW]
*American singer*
* [The] Queen of Staccato

**Selim II** 1524?-1574  [DNNS]
*Sultan of Turkey*
* [The] Sot

**Selimovic, Mehmed** 1910-  [IAW]
*Yugoslav author*
* Mesa

**Selincourt, Anne De** 1873- ?  [WWL]
*British author*
* Sedgwick, Anne Douglas

**Selinger, Archie** 1885-1940  [BEW]
*Actor and director*
* Pitt, Archie

**Selkirk, George Alexander** 1908-  [BE, BN, PB]
*American baseball player*
* Selkirk, Twink
* Selkirk, Twinkletoes

**Selkirk, J. B.**
See Brown, James

**Selkirk, Twink**
See Selkirk, George Alexander

**Selkirk, Twinkletoes**
See Selkirk, George Alexander

**Sell, Elwood Lester** 1897-1961  [BE]
*American baseball player*
* Sell, Epp

**Sell, Epp**
See Sell, Elwood Lester

**Sell, Hildegarde Loretta** 1906-
[IPA, PMJ]
*American singer*
* Hildegarde

**Sellar, Robert James Batchen**
1893- [WWL]
*British author*
* Chalfont, Peter

**Sellari, Girolamo de'** 1501-1556
[WBD]
*Italian painter*
* Carpi, Girolamo da

**Sellassie, Sahle**
*See* Marian, Sahle Sellassie
Berhane

**Sellers, Charles E.** 1887-1934
[BEW, F2]
*American entertainer*
* Mack, Charles

**Sellers, Con**
*See* Sellers, Connie Leslie, Jr.

**Sellers, Connie Leslie, Jr.** 1922-
[CA, SFL]
*American author*
* Adam, Don
* Adams, Rich
* Adonis, Michael
* Arana, Ric
* Bannion, Della
* Bates, Norman
* Bear, Joe
* Campbell, Fred
* Carre, Chuck
* Cellini, Cal
* Connaughton, Sam
* Conners, Selwyn
* Conniston, Sam
* Cotton, Jerri
* Crane, Robert
* Denning, Laurence
* DeVries, Con
* Dilli, Rick
* Downs, Bill
* Elliot, C. S.
* Gentry, Arthur
* Hall, Marcia
* Hawk, Jack
* Herman, Louis
* Higgins, Martyn
* Hurst, Brian
* Jacobs, Steven
* Lang, Jim
* Lark, Jody
* Linsley, Ladd. E.
* Madden, Dick
* Menasco, John
* Mitchell, Jack
* Moran, Judy
* Noceni, Erle
* Powers, Dick
* Raintree, Lee
* Roth, Karen
* Roth, Robert
* Sands, Leonard
* Sellers, Con
* Sellers, Mary
* Selwyn, Chuck
* Shannon, Leonard
* Simbeaux, L. L.
* Stanton, Chuck
* Steele, Charles
* Trent, Lawrence
* Trent, Leo
* Tully, Tom
* Ward, Tom

**Sellers, Isaiah** 1802?-1864 [WBD]
*American steamboat pilot and writer*
* Twain, Mark

**Sellers, Jingle Joints**
*See* Sellers, Ron

**Sellers, John** 1924- [BWW, EJ]
*American singer*
* Brother John
* Frank, Johnny

**Sellers, Mary**
*See* Sellers, Connie Leslie, Jr.

**Sellers, Naomi**
*See* Flack, Naomi John White

**Sellers, Oliver** 1881-1952 [BE]
*American baseball player*
* Sellers, Rube

**Sellers, Phil** 1953-
*American basketball player*
* [The] Thrill

**Sellers, Ron** 1947- [FB]
*American football player*
* Sellers, Jingle Joints
* Sellers, Weasel

**Sellers, Rube**
*See* Sellers, Oliver

**Sellers, Weasel**
*See* Sellers, Ron

**Sellings, Arthur**
*See* Ley, Arthur Gordon

**Selmair-Selwart, Antonio Franz
Thaeus** 1896- [BEW]
*German actor*
* Selwart, Tonio

**Selman, Elsie Emily** 1919- [IAW]
*British author*
* Taylor, Selman

**Selmark, George**
*See* Truss, [Leslie] Seldon

**Selten, Morton**
*See* Stubbs, Morton Richard

**Seltzer, Bromo**
*See* Seltzer, Leo A.

**Seltzer, Joe** 20th c. [F2]
*Actor*
* Smith, Joe

**Seltzer, Leo A.** 20th c. [BBH]
*American Roller Derby pioneer*
* Seltzer, Bromo

**Seltzer, Leon E[ugene]** 1918- [CA]
*American author*
* Leigh, Eugene

**Seltzer, Louis B[enson]** 1897-1980
[CA]
*American author, journalist, editor*
* Cleveland, Mr.

**Seltzer, Norman Murray** 1935-
[OP]
*American opera singer*
* Paige, Norman

**Selvaggio, John R.** 1937- [ASC]
*American musician*
* Carlo, Johnny

**Selwart, Tonio**
*See* Selmair-Selwart, Antonio
Franz Thaeus

**Selwyn, Chuck**
*See* Sellers, Connie Leslie, Jr.

**Selywn, John H.**
*See* Josephs, John

**Selz, Ralph Jerome Von Braun**
1909- [BLB]
*American murderer*
* [The] Laughing Killer

**Sem**
*See* Goursat, Georges

**Sembrich, Marcella**
*See* Kochanska, Praxede
Marcelline

**Semenko, Dave** 1957- [SMG]
*Canadian-born hockey player*
* Semenko, Semenk

**Semenko, Semenk**
*See* Semenko, Dave

**Semexant**
*See* Rouzier, Maximilien Louis
Severin

**Semien, Ivory Lee**
*See* Semien, Lee

**Semien, Lee** 1931- [BWW]
*American singer*
* King Ivory Lee
* Semien, Ivory Lee

**Semien, Sidney** 1938-
[BWW, NBB]
*American singer*
* Count Rockin' Sydney
* Rockin' Sydney

**Seminola**
*See* Cox-George, Noah Arthur
William

**[The] Semiramis of the North**
*See* Catherine II

**[The] Semiramis of the North**
*See* Margaret

**Semkiw, Virlyana**
*See* Shevchuk, Tetiana

**Semler, Johann Salomo** 1725-1791
[DNNS, WBD]
*German theologian*
* [The] Father of German
Rationalism

**Semmes, Raphael** 1809-1877
[DNNS, SN]
*American naval officer*
* Old Beeswax

**[Il] Semolei**
*See* Franco, Battista

**Semon, Ray**
*See* Beane, Mrs. George A., Jr.

**Sempell, Charlotte** 1909- [CA]
*German-born historian and author*
* Klenbort, Charlotte

**Sempill, Ernest** 20th c. [MBF]
*British author*
* Coles, Detective Inspector
* Gale, Alan
* Michael, John
* Michael, Paul
* Storm, Michael
* Storm, Rupert

**Semple, Dugald** 1884- [LAO]
*Scottish author and naturalist*
* Wheelhouse

**Semple, Gordon**
*See* Neubauer, William Arthur

**Semproch, Baby**
*See* Semproch, Roman Anthony

**Semproch, Ray**
*See* Semproch, Roman Anthony

**Semproch, Roman Anthony** 1931-
[BE]
*American baseball player*
* Semproch, Baby
* Semproch, Ray

**Semyonov, Iron Pants**
*See* Semyonov, Vladimir

**Semyonov, Vladimir** 20th c.
*Russian diplomat*
* Semyonov, Iron Pants

**Senarens, Lu**
*See* Senarens, Luis Philip

**Senarens, Luis Philip** 1865-1939
[ESF, SF, WGT]
*American author*
* Clyde, Kit?
* Doughty, Frank?
* Earle, W. J.?
* Garne, Gaston?
* Howard, Capt.?
* [The] Jules Verne of America
* Noname
* Senarens, Lu
* Sparling, Ned?

**Sencourt, Robert [Esmonde]**
*See* George, Robert Esmonde
Gordon

**Sendall, E.** [FFF, PA]
*Author*
* Caractacus

**Sendelbach, J. W.** [FFF]
*Entertainer*
* Shannon, Joseph W.

**Sendrey, Alfred**
*See* Szendrei, Aladar

**Seneca**
*See* Pasko, W. W.

**[The] Seneca of the East**
*See* Buzurg-Mihir

**Senectissimus, Theobaldus, Esq.**
*See* Lovecraft, Howard Phillips

**Senectus**
*See* Granger, Gideon

**Senerchia, Al** 1907- [MY]
*American jazz musician*
* Senner, Al

**Senerchia, Emanuel Robert** 1931-
[BE]
*American baseball player*
* Senerchia, Sonny

**Senerchia, Sonny**
*See* Senerchia, Emanuel Robert

**Senex**
*See* Anderson, James

**Senex**
*See* Owen, William Charles

**Senghor, Leopold Sedar** 1906-
[IBW]
*President of Senegal*
* [The] Father of the Constitution

**Seninho**
*See* Jardim, Arsenio

**[The] Senior Diplomat of Soul**
*See* Robinson, Ray Charles

**Senior, Isabel J[anet] C[ouper] Syme**
20th c. [CA]
*Scottish-born author*
* Pleydell, Susan

**Senior, William** 1790-1864
[FFF, PA]
*British author*
* Spinner, Red
* Uncle Hardy

**Senlis, Simon** ?-1109 [HN]
*Earl of Northampton and Huntingdon*
* St. Lis [or Liz]

**Sennachie**
See Whyte, Donald

**Sennep, J.**
See Pennes, Jean

**Senner, Al**
See Senerchia, Al

**Sennett, Mack**
See Sinnott, Michael

**Sennett, Ted**
See Sinitsky, Ted

**[The] Senor**
See Lopez, Alfonso Raymond

**Senor Wences**
See Moreno, Wenceslas

**Sensenderfer, Count**
See Sensenderfer, John Phillips Jenkins

**Sensenderfer, John Phillips Jenkins**
1847-1903 [BE]
*American baseball player*
* Sensenderfer, Count
* Sensenderfer, Sen-Sen

**Sensenderfer, Sen-Sen**
See Sensenderfer, John Phillips Jenkins

**Sentelle, Leopold Theodore**
1879-1923 [BE]
*American baseball player*
* Sentelle, Paul

**Sentelle, Paul**
See Sentelle, Leopold Theodore

**Sentencing Sam Leibowitz**
See Leibowitz, Samuel Simon

**Senter, Florence H.**
See Ellis, Florence Hawley

**[A] Sentimental Idler**
See Leach, Harry Harwood

**Sentinel**
See Bogart, William H.

**Sentry, John A.**
See Budrys, Algirdas Jonas

**Seoane, Manny**
See Seoane, Manuel Modesto

**Seoane, Manuel Modesto** 1955-
[SMG]
*American baseball player*
* Seoane, Manny

**Sepharial**
See Gorn-Old, Walter

**Sepia**
See Fryatt, Fanny

**Sepia**
See Holmvik, Oyvind

**[The] Sepia Mae West**
See Cox, Ida

**[The] Sepia Mae West**
See Fouche, Sam

**Sepkowski, Theodore Walter [Ted]**
See Sczepkowski, Theodore Walter

**Septama, Aladra**
See Reeves, Justin

**Sequoya [or Sequoyah]** 1770?-1843
[WBD]
*American Indian scholar*
* Guess, George

**Serafian, Michael**
See Martin, Malachi

**Serafimovich, Alexander**
See Popov, Alexander Serafimovich

**Serafin, Joseph Stanley** 1895-1947
[BE]
*American baseball player*
* Cobb, Joseph Stanley [Joe]

**Serafina Bacigalupi, Maria De La Concepcion Conchita** 1861?-1940
[BEW]
*Actress*
* Conchita

**Serafinowicz, Leszek** 1899- [CD]
*Polish poet and author*
* Lechon, Jan

**[The] Seraphic Doctor**
See Di Fidanza, Giovanni

**[The] Seraphic Saint**
See Bernardone, Giovanni Francesco

**Seraphicus, Doctor**
See Di Fidanza, Giovanni

**Serato, Massimo** 20th c. [WF]
*Italian actor*
* Barracuda, John

**Serebriakoff, Victor** 1912- [IAW]
*British author*
* Serry, Victor

**Serebroff, Munia** 1903- [BEW]
*Russian-born actor, singer, director*
* Seroff, Muni

**[El] Sereno**
See Sarfatti, Margherita

**Seretean, Bud**
See Seretean, M. B.

**Seretean, M. B.** [SMG]
*American basketball manager*
* Seretean, Bud

**Sergardi, Ludovico** 1660-1726
[PA]
*Author*
* Sectanus, Quintus

**Sergeant, Emily Frances Adeline**
1851-1904 [FFF]
*British author and poet*
* Adeline

**Serghi, Cella**
See Serghi Bogdan, Cella

**Serghi Bogdan, Cella** 1907- [IAW]
*Rumanian author*
* Serghi, Cella

**Sergi, Arturo**
See Kagan, Arthur

**Sergiev, Ioann** 1821-1908 [WBD]
*Russian clergyman*
* John of Kronstadt [or Cronstadt]

**Sergius II**
See Hogsmouth, Peter

**Sergius IV**
See Peter

**[The] Serial Queen**
See Roland, Ruth

**Seriel, Jerome**
See Vallee, Jacques

**Serjeant, Richard**
See Van Essen, William

**Serjeantson, Kate**
See Morris, Kate

**Serner, Martin G[unnar]**
1886-1947 [WGT]
*Swedish author*
* Heller, Frank

**Sernicoli, Davide**
See Trent, Ann

**Seroff, Muni**
See Serebroff, Munia

**Serov, Ivan A.** 1908- [EE]
*Russian secret police chief*
* [The] Butcher
* Ivan the Terrible

**[The] Serpent of Old Nile**
See Cleopatra

**Serpieres**
See Guillevic, Eugene

**Serra, Diana**
See Cary, Peggy-Jean Montgomery

**Serra, Junipero**
See Serra, Miguel Jose

**Serra, Miguel Jose** 1713-1784
[WBD]
*Spanish missionary in America*
* Serra, Junipero

**Serranito [Little Fellow from the Mountain]**
See Gonzalez y Delgado, Hilario

**Serrano, Carlos** 20th c. [GS]
*Mexican bullfighter*
* [El] Voluntario [The Ready One]

**Serranus**
See De Serres, Jean

**Serranus**
See Lambert, Francois

**Serrell, Bonnie**
See Serrell, William

**Serrell, William** 20th c. [OBW]
*American baseball player*
* Serrell, Bonnie

**Serrifile, F. O. O.**
See Holmes, William Kersley

**Serry, Victor**
See Serebriakoff, Victor

**Sert, Misia**
See Godebska, Marie Sophie Olga Zenaide

**Servadio, Gaia [Cecilia Gemmalina]**
1928- [WD]
*British author*
* Mostyn-Owen, Gaia

**[The] Servant of the Servants of God**
See Gregory I

**Service, R. W.**
See Service, Robert William

**Service, Robert William** 1876-1958
[LC]
*British-born poet*
* Service, R. W.

**Servius Tullius** 6th c. BC [HN]
*Legendary King of Rome*
* [The] Commons' King

**Servus Servorum Dei**
See Gregory I

**Serwischer, Kurt** 1913-1979
[CA, TR]
*Austrian actor*
* Kasznar, Kurt S.

**Sesan, Karolina Vera** 1908- [IWM]
*Russian-born opera singer and musicologist*
* Mora, Vera

**Sessi, Mathilde**
See Erlanger, Baroness

**Sessi, Walter Anthony** 1918- [BE]
*American baseball player*
* Sessi, Watsie

**Sessi, Watsie**
See Sessi, Walter Anthony

**Setaro, Peter D.** 1924- [ASC]
*American composer*
* Baxter, Larry

**Sete, Bola**
See De Andrada, Djalma

**Seth, Andrew** 1856-1931 [WBD]
*Scottish philosopher*
* Pringle-Pattison, Andrew

**Seth, Will**
See Bullock, William

**Seth-Smith, Elsie K.**
See Murrell, Elsie Kathleen Seth-Smith

**Seth-Smith, Leslie James** 1923-
[AW]
*British author*
* Brabazon, James

**Sethi, Denis**
See Sethi, Narendra Kumar

**Sethi, Narendra Kumar** 1935-
[IAW]
*Indian-born author*
* Sethi, Denis

**Sethunsa, Khotso** 1883- [IBW]
*South African medical practitioner*
* [The] Great One

**Seton, Anya**
See Chase, Anya Seton

**Seton, Ernest Thompson**
See Thompson, Ernest Evan Seton

**Seton, Graham**
See Hutchison, Graham Seton

**Seton-Watson, Robert William** 1879-
? [LAO]
*British author*
* Viator, Scotus

**Setoun, Gabriel**
See Hepburn, Thomas Nicoll

**Setterburg, Gabriel** 20th c. [SFP]
*Author*
* Crane, Eric

**Settle, Edith**
*See* Andrews, William Linton

**Settle, Elkanah** 1648-1724
[PA, SN]
*British playwright and poet*
* [The] City Laureate
* Doeg

**Settle, Joe**
*See* Settle, Josiah T.

**Settle, Josiah T.** 1850- ? [IBW]
*American attorney and government
official*
* Settle, Joe

**Settlemire, Lefty**
*See* Settlemire [Edgar] Merle

**Settlemire [Edgar] Merle** 1903-
[BE]
*American baseball player*
* Settlemire, Lefty

**Seume, Johann Gottfried**
1763-1810 [SN]
*German author and poet*
* [Der] Spaziergaenger nach
Syrakus

**Seuphor, Michel**
*See* Arp, Jean

**Seure, Cecile Emilie** 1874-1966
[SC]
*French actress*
* Sorel, Cecile

**Seuss, Dr.**
*See* Geisel, Theodor Seuss

**Seven Beauties**
*See* Frafuso, Pasqualino

**[The] Seven Days' King**
*See* Aniello, Tommaso

**[The] Seven Foot Cowboy**
*See* Harris, Homer William

**72 Cannon Chang**
*See* Chang Chung-Ch'ang

**Severance, Felix**
*See* Laumer, March

**[The] Severe**
*See* Pedro I

**Severin, Christian** 1562-1647
[WBD]
*Danish astronomer*
* Longomontanus

**Severinsen, Carl H.** 1927-
[ASC, B10, DAM]
*American jazz musician*
* Severinsen, Doc

**Severinsen, Doc**
*See* Severinsen, Carl H.

**Severinus de Monzambano**
*See* Pufendorf, Samuel von

**Severn, David**
*See* Unwin, David S[torr]

**Severne, Christian**
*See* Boulton, Anna

**Severson, Fred** 20th c. [BBH, CSH]
*Canadian lacrosse player*
* Severson, Whitey

**Severson, Jeff** 20th c.
*American football player*
* Severson, Peach

**Severson, Peach**
*See* Severson, Jeff

**Severson, Whitey**
*See* Severson, Fred

**Severud, Lloyd** 1918- [BBH]
*American skier and coach*
* Severud, Snoball

**Severud, Snoball**
*See* Severud, Lloyd

**Severyanin, Igor**
*See* Lotarev, Igor Vasilyevich

**Seville, David**
*See* Bagdasarian, Ross

**Sewall, Bud**
*See* Sewall, Grant

**Sewall, Grant** ?-1978 [FIR]
*Actor*
* Sewall, Bud

**Sewall, Samuel** 1652-1730 [SN]
*American jurist*
* [A] Puritan Pepys

**Seward, Alexander T. [Alec]**
1902-1972 [BWW]
*American singer*
* Blues Boy
* Blues King
* Georgia Slim
* Guitar Slim
* Seward, Slim

**Seward, Anna** 1747-1809 [DEL]
*British poet*
* [The] Swan of Lichfield

**Seward, Calgary Red**
*See* Seward, Roy

**Seward, Edward William**
*See* Sourhardt, Edward William

**Seward, Roy** 20th c. [GW]
*Rodeo performer*
* Seward, Calgary Red

**Seward, Slim**
*See* Seward, Alexander T. [Alec]

**Seward, William Henry** 1801-1872
[DEP, FFF]
*American statesman*
* [The] Sage of Auburn

**Seward, William W[ard], Jr.** 1913-
[CA]
*American author*
* Rives, Leigh

**Sewell, Elizabeth Missing** 1815- ?
[DEL]
*British author*
* [A] Lady

**Sewell, James Luther** 1901- [BE]
*American baseball manager*
* Sewell, Luke

**Sewell, Luke**
*See* Sewell, James Luther

**Sewell, Rip**
*See* Sewell, Truett Banks

**Sewell, Truett Banks** 1908-
[BE, PB]
*American baseball player*
* Sewell, Rip

**Sewgolum, Papwa**
*See* Sewgolum, Susunker

**Sewgolum, Susunker** 1929?-1978
[EG]
*South African golfer*
* Sewgolum, Papwa

**Sexby, Edward**
*See* Quincy, Josiah

**Sexten**
*See* Augustine, Richard

**Sexton of the Old School**
*See* Sargent, Lucius Manlius

**Sexton, Virginia Staudt** 1916-
[CA]
*American psychologist and author*
* Staudt, Virginia

**Sexy Rexy**
*See* Harrison, Reginald Carey

**Seybold, Ralph Orlando** 1870-1921
[AS, BE, PB]
*American baseball player*
* Seybold, Socks

**Seybold, Socks**
*See* Seybold, Ralph Orlando

**Seydel, Mildred [Wooley]** 20th c.
[CA]
*American publisher and author*
* Seydell, Mildred

**Seydell, Mildred**
*See* Seydel, Mildred [Wooley]

**Seyler, Athene**
*See* Hannen, Athene

**Seymour, A. J.**
*See* Seymour, Arthur James

**Seymour, Alan**
*See* Wright, Sydney Fowler

**Seymour, Alice** [FFF]
*Entertainer*
* Hensel, Octavia

**Seymour, Anne**
*See* Eckert, Anne Seymour

**Seymour, Arthur James** 1914-
[CW]
*Guyanese author, poet, critic*
* Seymour, A. J.

**Seymour, Caroline** [FFF]
*Writer*
* Spencer, Edward

**Seymour, Charles** 1662-1748
[DNNS, HN, SN]
*Sixth Duke of Somerset*
* [The] Proud Duke

**Seymour, Cy**
*See* Seymour, James Bentley

**Seymour, Dorothy Jane Z[ander]**
1928- [CA]
*American author*
* Johnson, Eleanor

**Seymour, Edward**
*See* Hiscocks, Richard

**Seymour, Edward** 1506?-1552
[HN, SN, WBD]
*First Duke of Somerset*
* [The] Good Duke
* [The] Protector

**Seymour, Edward** 1837-1877 [PA]
*Author*
* E. S.

**Seymour, Frederick H[enri]**
1850-1913 [WGT]
*Author*
* Gilhooley, Lord

**Seymour, George**
*See* Erby, John J.

**Seymour, Gordon**
*See* Waldstein, Charles

**Seymour, Henry**
*See* Hartmann, Helmut Henry

**Seymour, James Bentley**
1872-1919 [AS, BE, DGS]
*American baseball player*
* Seymour, Cy

**Seymour, Jane**
*See* Fitzpatrick, Marjorie Seymour

**Seymour, Jane**
*See* Frankenberg, Joyce Penelope
Wilhimena

**Seymour, Laura**
*See* Samo, Mrs.

**Seymour, Marjorie F.** 20th c.
[WWL]
*British author*
* Cynthia
* Plane, Anne

**Seymour, Mary H.** 1840-1881
[PA]
*Author*
* M. H. S.

**Seymour, Miranda**
*See* Sinclair, Miranda

**Seymour, Mrs. William** [FFF]
*Entertainer*
* Davenport, May

**Seymour, Stephen Andrew**
*See* Cohen, Seymour

**Seymour, Thomas** 1896- [FC]
*British director*
* Forde, Walter

**Seymour, William Napier** 1914-
[CA]
*British author*
* Napier, William

**Seyssel, Claude de** 1450-1520
[HN, RH]
*French historian*
* [The] Father of Modern French
Literature

**Seyton, Marion**
*See* Saxon, Gladys Relyea

**Sfondrati, Niccolo** 1535-1591
[CAL]
*Pope*
* Gregory XIV

**Sforza**
*See* Attendolo, Giacomuzo d'

**Sforza, James** 1369-1424
[FFF, SN]
*Italian army officer*
* [The] Great

**Sforza, Lodovico [or Ludovico]**
1451-1510? [HN, SN]
*Duke of Milan*
* [The] More

**Sgarlato, Nico** 1944-  [IAW]
*Italian author*
* Castellano, Franco

**Sgroi, Alfonso** 20th c.  [BLB]
*American underworld figure*
* [The] Butch

**Shackelford, Lynn** 1947-  [SMG]
*American sportscaster*
* Shackelford, Shack

**Shackelford, Shack**
*See* Shackelford, Lynn

**Shacket, Sheldon R[ubin]** 1941-
[CA]
*American author*
* Albran, Kehlog [joint pseudonym
  with Martin A. Cohen]

**Shackleton, C. C.**
*See* Aldiss, Brian W[ilson]

**Shackleton, Doris [Cavell]** 1918-
[CA]
*Canadian author*
* French, Doris

**Shackleton-Bailey, D[avid] R[oy]**
*See* Bailey, D[avid] R[oy]
Shackleton

**Shad, Bob** 20th c.  [NBB]
*American songwriter*
* Ellen, Robert

**Shade, Ellen**  [PA]
*Author*
* Ellwood, Ella

**Shade, R. D. B. M.** 1938-  [EG]
*Golfer*
* Shade, Ronnie

**Shade, Ronnie**
*See* Shade, R. D. B. M.

**Shade, Will** 1898-1966  [BWW, EJ]
*American jazz musician*
* Brimmer, Son

**Shadi, Dorothy Clotelle Clarke**
1908-  [CA, WD]
*American author, critic, translator*
* Clarke, Dorothy Clotelle

**[The] Shadow**
*See* Shed, Nevil

**Shadow, John**
*See* Byrom, John

**[El] Shadow Negro**
*See* Parker, Nathaniel

**Shadow, Slim**
*See* Rogers, Samuel Shepard

**[The] Shadower**
*See* Apollodorus

**Shadrin, Nicholas**
*See* Artamonov, Nikolai

**Shady Bill Leith**
*See* Leith, William [Bill]

**Shafer, Arthur Joseph** 1889-1962
[BE]
*American baseball player*
* Shafer, Tillie

**Shafer, Filomina**
*See* Shafer, Mina

**Shafer, Mina** 1872- ?  [NAA]
*American poet and writer*
* Shafer, Filomina

**Shafer, Phil** 20th c.
*Auto racer*
* [The] Texas Terror

**Shafer, Tillie**
*See* Shafer, Arthur Joseph

**Shaff, Monroe** 20th c.  [BEW]
*American producer and stage
manager*
* Shaff, Monty

**Shaff, Monty**
*See* Shaff, Monroe

**Shaffer, Anthony [Joshua]** 1926-
[CC, EMD, WD]
*British playwright and author*
* Anthony, Peter [joint pseudonym
  with Peter (Levin) Shaffer]

**Shaffer, George** 1852- ?  [BE]
*American baseball player*
* Shaffer, Orator

**Shaffer, Orator**
*See* Shaffer, George

**Shaffer, Peter [Levin]** 1926-
[CA, CC, EMD]
*British playwright and author*
* Anthony, Peter [joint pseudonym
  with Anthony (Joshua) Shaffer]

**Shaftesbury, Seventh Earl of**
*See* Cooper, Anthony Ashley

**Shaftsbury, Edmund**
*See* Edgerly, Webster

**Shah, Amina** 1918-  [CA]
*Scottish-born author*
* Rutt, M. E.

**Shah Jehan**
*See* Khorrum [or Khurram]

**Shahani, Ranjee** 1904-1968  [CA]
*Pakistani-born author*
* Ranjee

**Shahn, Bernarda Bryson**
*See* Bryson, Bernarda

**Shaiffer, Howard Charles**
1918-1967  [SC]
*American actor*
* Shaiffer, Tiny

**Shaiffer, Tiny**
*See* Shaiffer, Howard Charles

**Shake-Scene**
*See* Shakespeare, William

**Shaker**
*See* Adams, F. W.

**[The] Shakespeare of Divines**
*See* Taylor, Jeremy

**[The] Shakespeare of Eloquence**
*See* Riquetti, Honore Gabriel
Victor

**[The] Shakespeare of France**
*See* Corneille, Pierre

**[The] Shakespeare of Germany**
*See* Grossmann, Gustavus
Frederick William

**[The] Shakespeare of Germany**
*See* Kotzebue, August Friedrich
Ferdinand von

**[The] Shakespeare of Germany**
*See* Schiller, Johann Christoph
Friedrich von

**[The] Shakespeare of Harmony**
*See* Wagner, [Wilhelm] Richard

**[The] Shakespeare of India**
*See* Kalidasa

**[The] Shakespeare of Japan**
*See* Chikamatsu Monzaemon

**[The] Shakespeare of Painting**
*See* Rosa, Salvator

**[The] Shakespeare of Prose**
*See* Austen, Jane

**[The] Shakespeare of Prose Fiction**
*See* Richardson, Samuel

**[The] Shakespeare of Romance
Writers**
*See* Radcliffe, Anne

**[The] Shakespeare of Science Fiction**
*See* Wells, Herbert George

**[The] Shakespeare of Sweden**
*See* Strindberg, August

**[The] Shakespeare of the Boulevards**
*See* Pixerecourt, Rene Charles
Guilbert de

**Shakespeare, William** 1564-1616
[DEP, FFF, SN]
*British playwright and poet*
* Aetion
* [The] Bard of all Time
* [The] Bard of Avon
* [The] Homer of Dramatic Poets
* Johannes fac Totum [Jack of All
  Trades]
* [The] Lord of the British
  Pandemonium
* Our Will
* Pleasant Willy
* Shake-Scene
* [The] Swan of Avon
* [The] Sweet Swan of Avon
* [An] Upstart Crow
* [The] Young Apollo

**Shakespeare, William V.**
1912-1974  [FB]
*American football player*
* [The] Bard of Staten Island

**[A] Shakespeare Without Genius**
*See* Hardi, Alexandre

**Shakespeare's Critic**
*See* Rymer, Thomas

**[The] Shakesperian Scholar**
*See* White, Richard Grant

**Shakey Jake**
*See* Harris, James D. [Jimmie]

**Shakur, Assata**
*See* Chesimard, Joanne

**Shalhoub, Michel** 1932-
[BDF, FC, WEF]
*Egyptian-born actor*
* Sharif, Omar

**Shallix, August**
*See* Schallick, August

**Shallix, Gus**
*See* Schallick, August

**Shalmaneser II**  [WBD]
*King of Assyria*
* Shulmanuasharid

**Shalofsky, Henry** 1926-  [EJ]
*British jazz musician*
* Shaw, Hank

**Shalom, Shin** 1905-  [B10]
*Israeli poet and author*
* Shapira, Shalom Yosef

**Sham, Sir**
*See* Dawkins, Darryl

**Shambrick, Otto H.** 1864-1927
[BE]
*American baseball player*
* Shomberg, Otto H.

**Shambrook, Rona** 20th c.  [AW]
*British author and journalist*
* Randall, Rona

**Shamgar**
*See* Shamir, Moshe

**Shamir, Moshe** 1921-  [IAW]
*Israeli author*
* Keller, Asaph
* Offerre, M.
* Shamgar

**Shamlu, Ahmad** 1925-  [CLC]
*Iranian poet, critic, author*
* Bamdad, A.
* Sobh, A.

**Shamrock**
*See* Williams, R. D.

**[The] Shamrock Kid**
*See* Mitchell, Clarence M., Jr.

**Shan, Yeh**
*See* Wang, Ching Hsien

**Shand, Captain**
*See* Floyd, Gilbert

**Shandley, Sallie**
*See* Stivers, Mrs. J.

**Shandon, Captain**
*See* Cheltnam, C. Smith

**Shands, H. G.** 20th c.  [BBH]
*American basketball coach*
* Shands, Pete

**Shands, Pete**
*See* Shands, H. G.

**Shane, John**
*See* Durst, Paul

**Shane, Mark**
*See* Norwood, Victor G[eorge]
C[harles]

**Shane, Peggy**
*See* Boyd, [Margaret] Woodward
[Smith]

**Shane, Rhondo**
*See* Norwood, Victor G[eorge]
C[harles]

**Shane, Susannah**
*See* Ashbrook, Harriette [Cora]

**Shaner, Skinny**
*See* Shaner, Walter Dedaker
[Wally]

**Shaner, Walter Dedaker [Wally]**
1900-  [BE]
*American baseball player*
* Shaner, Skinny

**Shange, Ntozake**
*See* Williams, Paulette

**Shank, Bud**
*See* Shank, Clifford Everett, Jr.

**Shank, Clifford Everett, Jr.** 1926-
[ASC, EJ, PMJ]
*American jazz musician*
* Shank, Bud

**Shanklin, Ronnie Eugene** 1948-
[SMG]
*American football player*
* Shanklin, Shank

**Shanklin, Shank**
*See* Shanklin, Ronnie Eugene

**Shanks, Hank**
*See* Shanks, Howard Samuel

**Shanks, Howard Samuel**
1890-1941   [AS, BE, PB]
*American baseball player*
* Shanks, Hank

**Shanley, Doc**
*See* Shanley, Henry Roat

**Shanley, Henry Roat** 1889-1934
[BE]
*American baseball player*
* Shanley, Doc

**Shann, B. V.** 20th c.   [CAP]
*Author*
* Bevis, James [joint pseudonym
   with Marten Cumberland]

**Shann, Renee** 1907?-1979   [CA]
*British author*
* Gaye, Carol

**Shannon, A. Donnelly**
*See* Aitken, A. Donnelly

**Shannon, Carl**
*See* Hogue, Wilbur Owings

**Shannon, Del**
*See* Westover, Charles

**Shannon, Dell**
*See* Linington, Elizabeth

**Shannon, Elizabeth S.** 1914-1959
[SC]
*American actress*
* Sundmark, Betty

**Shannon, Ethel**
*See* Jackson, Ethel Shannon

**Shannon, Frank**
*See* Prosperi, Francesco

**Shannon, Frank**
*See* Shine, Dennis Francis Joseph

**Shannon, Frank E.** 20th c.   [BE]
*American baseball player*
* Shannon, Tod

**Shannon, Fred**
*See* Ruben, William S.

**Shannon, Joseph W.**
*See* Sendelbach, J. W.

**Shannon, Leonard**
*See* Sellers, Connie Leslie, Jr.

**Shannon, M.**
*See* Geddie, John

**Shannon, Maurice Joseph** 1895-
[BE]
*American baseball player*
* Shannon, Red

**Shannon, Moonman**
*See* Shannon, Thomas Michael
[Mike]

**Shannon, Peggy**
*See* Sammon, Winona

**Shannon, Red**
*See* Shannon, Maurice Joseph

**Shannon, Robert**
*See* Wieder, Robert S[hannon]

**Shannon, Spike**
*See* Shannon, William Porter

**Shannon, Terry**
*See* Mercer, Jessie

**Shannon, Thomas Michael [Mike]**
1939-   [BE, PB]
*American baseball player*
* Shannon, Moonman

**Shannon, Tod**
*See* Shannon, Frank E.

**Shannon, William Porter**
1878-1940   [BE]
*American baseball player*
* Shannon, Spike

**Shantry, Brian Keith** 1955-   [DC]
*British cricketer*
* Shantry, Shants

**Shantry, Shants**
*See* Shantry, Brian Keith

**Shantz, Billy**
*See* Shantz, Wilmer Ebert

**Shantz, Wilmer Ebert** 1927-   [BE]
*American baseball player*
* Shantz, Billy

**Shanwa**
*See* Haarer, Alec Ernest

**Shapira, Shalom Yosef**
*See* Shalom, Shin

**Shapiro, Dolph**
*See* Sharp, Dolph

**Shapiro, Gurrah**
*See* Shapiro, Jacob

**Shapiro, Jacob** 20th c.
[BLB, PHM]
*American underworld figure*
* Shapiro, Gurrah

**Shapiro, Max** 1911?-1981
*American editor, author, publisher*
* Stuart, Monroe

**Shapiro, Sammy** 1910-1975   [SC]
*American actor, bandleader,
musician*
* Spear, Sammy

**Shapiro, Samuel** 1927-   [CA]
*American historian and author*
* Falcon, Richard

**Shapoff, S. R.** 1918-   [B10, EJS]
*American horse trainer*
* Shapoff, Skippy

**Shapoff, Sherrill W.** 1921-1960
[EJS]
*American horse trainer*
* Shapoff, Skeeter

**Shapoff, Skeeter**
*See* Shapoff, Sherrill W.

**Shapoff, Skippy**
*See* Shapoff, S. R.

**Shappiro, Budd** 20th c.   [CAP]
*American author*
* Arthur, Budd

**Shappiro, Herbert [Arthur]**
1898?-1975   [B10, CAP]
*American author, playwright,
journalist*
* Arthur, Burt
* Arthur, Herbert
* Herbert, Arthur

**Shapur II [or Sapor]** 309- 379
[FFF, HN, WBD]
*Persian king*
* [The] Great
* [The] Shoulder Breaker
* Zoolactaf [or Dsulaktaf]

**Sharat Chandra, G[ubbi] S[hankara
Chetty]** 1938-   [CA]
*Indian-born poet*
* Parker, Jean

**Shard, Diana**
*See* Stearns, Peter N.

**Sharett, Moshe**
*See* Shertok, Moshe

**Sharif, Omar**
*See* Shalhoub, Michel

**Shark, Gill**
*See* Gillese, John Patrick

**[The] Shark of the Exchange**
*See* Fordyce, Alexander

**Sharkey, Jack**
*See* Cervati, Giovanni

**Sharkey, Jack**
*See* Cukoschay [or Zukauskas],
Joseph Paul

**Sharkey, John Michael** 1931-   [CA]
*American author and playwright*
* Abbot, Rick
* Johnson, Mike

**Sharkey, Little Jackie**
*See* Cervati, Giovanni

**Sharkey, Sailor**
*See* Sharkey, Tom

**Sharkey, Tom** 1873-1953   [SC]
*Irish-born boxer and actor*
* Sharkey, Sailor

**Sharlach, Marie** 1881-1938   [BEW]
*Russian-born theatrical performer*
* Dainton, Marie

**Sharman, Maisie**
*See* Bolton, Maisie Sharman

**Sharman, Miriam**
*See* Bolton, Maisie Sharman

**Sharon, Ariel** 1928?-
*Israeli army officer and government
official*
* [The] Bulldozer
* Sharon, Arik

**Sharon, Arik**
*See* Sharon, Ariel

**Sharon, Donna Haye**
*See* Scharlemann, Dorothy Hoyer

**Sharon, Muriel**
*See* Schochen, Muriel Betty

**Sharon, Rose**
*See* Grossman, Josephine Judith

**Sharookman, Bozo**
*See* Sharookman, Ed

**Sharookman, Ed** 20th c.
*American football player*
* Sharookman, Bozo

**Sharp, Blunt**
*See* Sharp, George

**Sharp, Conversation**
*See* Sharp, Richard

**Sharp, Dee Dee**
*See* LaRue, Dione

**Sharp, Dolph** 1914-   [CA]
*American writer*
* Shapiro, Dolph

**Sharp, George** 1950-   [DC]
*British cricketer*
* Sharp, Blunt
* Sharp, Sharpie

**Sharp, Henry**
*See* Schacht, Henry

**Sharp, [Sir] Henry** 1869- ?   [WWL]
*British author*
* Ainsworth, Oliver

**Sharp, James**
*See* Kinghorn, Alexander Manson

**Sharp, Kevin** 1959-   [DC]
*British cricketer*
* Action Man
* Sharp, Razor

**Sharp Knife**
*See* Jackson, Andrew

**Sharp, Luke**
*See* Barr, Robert

**Sharp, Margery**
*See* Castle, Margery Sharp

**[The] Sharp One**
*See* Bejart, Louis

**Sharp, Razor**
*See* Sharp, Kevin

**Sharp, Richard** 1760-1835   [DEL]
*British author and poet*
* Sharp, Conversation

**Sharp, Robert [George]** 20th c.
[SFL]
*Author*
* Deegan, Jon J. [house
   pseudonym, Hamilton]

**Sharp, Sharpie**
*See* Sharp, George

**Sharp, Sidney**
*See* Mapes, Victor

**Sharp, Thomas** 1693-1758   [FFF]
*British author*
* Coventry Antiquary

**Sharp, William** 1855-1905
[LC, WGT, WWL]
*Scottish-born poet and author*
* Brooks, W. H.
* Macleod, Fiona
* Tirebuck, W.

**Sharpe, Bayard Heston** 1881-1916
[BE]
*American baseball player*
* Sharpe, Bud

**Sharpe, Bud**
*See* Sharpe, Bayard Heston

**Sharpe, Charles Kirkpatrick**
1781-1849 [PA, SN]
*Scottish patron of the arts*
* [An] Amateur
* [The] Scottish Walpole

**Sharpe, D. Richard**
*See* Shaver, Richard S[harpe]

**Sharpe, Ernest Rhoades** 1906-
[BEW]
*American actor, singer, director*
* Rhodes, Erik

**Sharpe, Howard Lee** 20th c. [BBH]
*American basketball player and coach*
* Sharpe, Sharpie

**Sharpe, Jack**
*See* Rathborne, St. George

**Sharpe, Lester**
*See* Scharff, Lester

**Sharpe, Pauline** 1925- [NAD]
*Spiritual leader*
* Nada Yolanda

**Sharpe, Pepper**
*See* Sharpe, Robert

**Sharpe, Robert** 20th c. [OBW]
*American baseball player*
* Sharpe, Pepper

**Sharpe, Sharpie**
*See* Sharpe, Howard Lee

**Sharples, Robert** 1913- [IWM]
*British musician*
* Earley, Robert

**Sharrock, Linda**
*See* Chambers, Linda

**Sharrocks, Alfred Burgess** 1919-
[ART]
*British artist*
* A. B. S.

**Shashoua, Salim Samuel** 1930-
[IWM]
*Iraqi-born attorney and broadcasting editor*
* Shashoua, Shlomo

**Shashoua, Shlomo**
*See* Shashoua, Salim Samuel

**Shastri, Prithvinath** 1926- [IAW]
*Indian author and playwright*
* Manugupta
* Mohan, P. Nath
* Najam
* Vasistha, Mohan

**Shatt, Montague**
*See* Strong, Latham C.

**Shattuck, Ethel**
*See* Greenman, Ethel

**Shattuck, Meredith M.** 20th c.
[BBH]
*American roller skating organization officer*
* Shattuck, Red

**Shattuck, Red**
*See* Shattuck, Meredith M.

**Shattuck, Truly**
*See* Etrulia, Claire

**Shaughnessy, Clark D.** 1892-1970
[BBH]
*American football coach*
* [The] Father of the Modern T-Formation

**Shaughnessy, Francis Joseph [Frank]**
1883-1969 [AS, CFH]
*American baseball executive and football coach*
* Shaughnessy, Shag

**Shaughnessy, Shag**
*See* Shaughnessy, Francis Joseph [Frank]

**Shaul, Frank**
*See* Rowland, D[onald] S[ydney]

**Shaunessy, Winifred** 1897-1966
[SC]
*American actress, dancer, screenwriter*
* Hudnut, Winifred
* Rambova, Natacha

**Shaute, Joseph Benjamin**
1900-1970 [BE, PB]
*American baseball player*
* Shaute, Lefty

**Shaute, Lefty**
*See* Shaute, Joseph Benjamin

**Shavelson, Lydia** 1906- [THR]
*British actress*
* Sherwood, Lydia

**Shaver, Buster**
*See* Shaver, Floyd Herbert

**Shaver, C. L.**
*See* Shaver, Claude L.

**Shaver, Claude L.** 1905- [BEW]
*American educator*
* Shaver, C. L.

**Shaver, Floyd Herbert** 1905- [ASC]
*American entertainer and musician*
* Shaver, Buster

**Shaver, Gaius** 1910- [FB]
*American football player*
* Shaver, Gus

**Shaver, Gus**
*See* Shaver, Gaius

**Shaver, Richard S[harpe]**
1907-1975 [WGT]
*American author*
* Amherst, Wes
* Benson, Edwin
* Blade, Alexander [house pseudonym, Ziff-Davis]
* Dexter, Edwin?
* Dexter, Peter
* Dorot, Peter?
* Dorset, Richard
* Elclair, Mollie?
* English, Richard
* Irwin, G. H. [house pseudonym]
* Lohrman, Paul [house pseudonym, Ziff-Davis]
* Patton, Frank [house pseudonym]
* Raycraft, Stan
* Sharpe, D. Richard

**Shaw, Albert** 20th c. [NBB]
*American musician*
* Shaw, Honey Boy

**Shaw, Alfred** 1842-1907 [EC]
*British cricketer*
* [The] Emperor of Bowlers

**Shaw, Alfred** 1874-1958
*British-born baseball player*
* Shaw, Shoddy

**Shaw, Amelia M.** 1863?-1934
[BEW]
*Irish-born entertainer*
* Summerville, Amelia

**Shaw, Artie**
*See* Arshawsky, Arthur Jacob

**Shaw, Barton**
*See* Drummond, Patrick Hamilton

**Shaw, Brian** [house pseudonym, Curtis Warren]
*See* Fearn, John Russell

**Shaw, Brian** [house pseudonym, Curtis Warren]
*See* Griffiths, David Arthur

**Shaw, Brian** [house pseudonym, Curtis Warren]
*See* O'Brien, David

**Shaw, Brian** [house pseudonym, Curtis Warren]
*See* Tubb, Edwin Charles

**Shaw, Buck**
*See* Shaw, Lawrence T.

**Shaw, Bundles**
*See* Shaw, Everett

**Shaw, Bynum G[illette]** 1923- [WD]
*American author and screenwriter*
* Gillette, Bob

**Shaw, Charles** 1900- [WW]
*Author*
* Singer, Bant

**Shaw, David**
*See* Griffiths, David Arthur

**Shaw, Dawn**
*See* Shaw, Thelma

**Shaw, Dick**
*See* Openshaw, G. H.

**Shaw, Dupee**
*See* Shaw, Frederick Lander

**Shaw, Elijah W.** 1900- [WWJ]
*American jazz musician*
* Shaw, Lige

**Shaw, Elizabeth**
*See* Prance, June E[lizebeth]

**Shaw, Everett** 20th c. [GW]
*American rodeo performer*
* Shaw, Bundles

**Shaw, Flora Louisa**
*See* Lugard, Flora Louisa Shaw

**Shaw, Frank H.** 1878- ? [MBF]
*British author*
* Cleveland, Frank
* Guthrie, Archibald
* Hammerton, Grenville
* Hubert, Frank

**Shaw, Fred** 1867-1918 [BMH]
*British comic singer*
* Sheridan, Mark

**Shaw, Frederick Lander**
1859-1938 [AS, BE, PB]
*American baseball player*
* Shaw, Dupee

**Shaw, Fud**
*See* Shaw, Robert

**Shaw, George Bernard** 1856-1950
[LC, TC]
*Irish playwright, author, critic*
* Di Bassetto, Corno
* G. B. S.

**Shaw, Glen Byam**
*See* Shaw, Glencairn Alexander Byam

**Shaw, Glencairn Alexander Byam**
1904- [BEW]
*British actor and director*
* Shaw, Glen Byam

**Shaw, Grunting Jim**
*See* Shaw, James Aloysius

**Shaw, Hank**
*See* Shalofsky, Henry

**Shaw, Helen** 1863?-1934 [BEW]
*Irish-born actress*
* Rous, Helen

**Shaw, Henry Wheeler** 1818?-1885
[DEL, DNNF, FFF]
*American author*
* Billings, Josh
* Uncle Esek

**Shaw, Hollace**
*Singer*
* Vivien

**Shaw, Honey Boy**
*See* Shaw, Albert

**Shaw, Irene**
*See* Roberts, Irene M.

**Shaw, James Aloysius** 1893-1962
[BE]
*American baseball player*
* Shaw, Grunting Jim

**Shaw, Jane**
*See* Evans, Jean Bell Shaw

**Shaw, Joan**
*See* DeCosta, Joan

**Shaw, Joan** 1930- [EJ7]
*American jazz musician*
* Jones, Salena

**Shaw, Justin**
*See* Openshaw, G. H.

**Shaw, Lawrence T.** 1899- [FB]
*American football coach*
* Shaw, Buck
* [The] Silver Fox

**Shaw, Lawrence Taylor [Larry]**
1924- [SFL, SFP]
*American editor*
* Destiny, Archibald
* Thor, Terry

**Shaw, Lige**
*See* Shaw, Elijah W.

**Shaw, Marlena**
*See* Burgess, Marlena

**Shaw, Martin**
*See* Martin, E. Le Breton

**Shaw, Nate**
*See* Cobb, Ned

**Shaw, Oliver** 1776-1849 [FFF]
*American singer and songwriter*
* [The] Blind Singer

**Shaw, Oscar**
*See* Schwartz, Oscar

**Shaw, Robert** 1908- [BWW]
*American singer*
* Shaw, Fud

**Shaw, Sandie**
*See* Goodrich, Sandra

**Shaw, Sandra**
*See* Balfe, Veronica

**Shaw, Shoddy**
*See* Shaw, Alfred

**Shaw, Stanley Gordon** 1884-1938?
[MBF]
*British author*
* Dare, Captain
* Gordon, S. S.
* Gordon, Stanley
* Heritage, John
* Strange, Harry
* Wallace, Gordon

**Shaw, Susan**
*See* Sloots, Patsy

**Shaw, T. D. W.**
*See* Shaw, Thelma

**Shaw, Thelma** 1901-   [CA]
*American author and editor*
* Shaw, Dawn
* Shaw, T. D. W.

**Shaw, Thomas Edward**
*See* Lawrence, Thomas Edward

**Shaw, Victoria**
*See* Elphick, Jeanette

**Shaw, Vivian**
*See* Seldes, Gilbert [Vivian]

**Shaw, William Harlan** 1922-   [CA]
*American artist, author, educator*
* Harlan

**Shaw, Winnie**
*See* Momi, Winifred Lei

**Shawkey, Bob** 1890-
*American baseball player*
* Shawkey, Sailor Bob

**Shawkey, Sailor Bob**
*See* Shawkey, Bob

**Shawlee, Joan**
*See* Fulton, Joan

**Shawmut**
*See* Chamberlain, Nathan Henry

**Shawn, Dick**
*See* Schulefand, Richard

**Shawn, Edwin Meyers** 1891-1972
[CA]
*American dancer and choreographer*
* Shawn, Ted

**Shawn, Frank S.**
*See* Goulart, Ron[ald Joseph]

**Shawn, Richy**
*See* Schulefand, Richard

**Shawn, Semas**
*See* Gray, Whitley

**Shawn, Ted**
*See* Shawn, Edwin Meyers

**Shay, Arthur Joseph** 1898-1951
[BE]
*American baseball player*
* Shay, Marty

**Shay, Dorothy** 1923-1978   [ECM]
*American country-western performer*
* [The] Park Avenue Hillbilly

**Shay, Jerry**
*See* Dzedzeji, Jerry

**Shay, Marty**
*See* Shay, Arthur Joseph

**Shayback, Mr.**
*See* Barrows, Samuel June

**Shayback, Mrs.**
*See* Barrows, Catherine Isabel

**Shayne, Gordon**
*See* Winter, Bevis

**Shayne, Robert**
*See* Dawe, Robert Shaen

**Shazar, Rachel**
*See* Katznelson-Shazar, Rachel

**Shazar, [Schneor] Zalman**
*See* Rubashov, Schneor Zalman

**Shchedrin, N.**
*See* Saltykov, Mikhail Evgrafovich

**[The] She Majesty Generalissimo**
*See* Henrietta Maria

**[The] She Wolf of France**
*See* Isabella of France

**[The] She Wolf of France**
*See* Margaret [or Marguerite]

**Shea, Donna** 1950-
*American musician*
* Rivera, Scarlet

**Shea, Francis** 1912-   [CEI]
*American hockey player*
* Shea, Pat

**Shea, George Beverly** 1909-   [CWG]
*Canadian-born singer*
* America's Beloved Gospel Singer

**Shea, John Edward** 1874-1968
[BE]
*American baseball player*
* Shea, Nap

**Shea, John Gerald** 1906-   [CA]
*American author*
* Fitzgerald, Jack

**Shea, Nap**
*See* Shea, John Edward

**Shea, Pat**
*See* Shea, Francis

**Shea, Patrick Henry** 1898-   [BE]
*American baseball player*
* Shea, Red

**Shea, Red**
*See* Shea, Patrick Henry

**Shea, Robert [Joseph]** 1933-   [CA]
*American author*
* Eulenspiegel, Alexander
* Glass, Sandra

**Shea, Spec**
*See* O'Shea, Frank Joseph

**Shea, Timothy**
*See* Knipe, Alden Arthur

**Sheaffer, Louis**
*See* Slung, Louis Sheaffer

**Sheahan, D. B.** 1843- ?   [PA]
*Author*
* Bun
* Critique

**Sheahan, Henry Beston** 1888-   [TC]
*American author and naturalist*
* Beston, Henry

**Shean, Al**
*See* Schoenberg, Alfred

**Shearer, Moira**
*See* King, Moira

**Shearer, [Edith] Norma** 1904-
*Canadian-born actress*
* American Beauty Rose

**Shearing, Joseph**
*See* Long, Gabrielle Margaret Vere
[Campbell]

**Shears, Billie**
*See* Watson, O[scar] Michael

**Shears, George Penfield** 1890-
[BN]
*American baseball player*
* Shears, Scissors

**Shears, Scissors**
*See* Shears, George Penfield

**Sheats, Mary Boney** 1918-   [CA]
*American author and religious educator*
* Boney, Mary Lily

**Shebbeare, John** 1709-1788   [DEL]
*British author*
* Angeloni, Battista

**Sheckard, Jimmy**
*See* Sheckard, Samuel J. T.

**Sheckard, Samuel J. T.** 1878-1947
[AS]
*American baseball player*
* Sheckard, Jimmy

**Sheckley, Robert** 1928-
[ESF, WGT]
*American author*
* Barbee, Phillips
* Lange, Ned
* O'Donnevan, Finn

**Shed, Nevil** 20th c.
*American basketball player*
* [The] Shadow

**Sheehan, Biff**
*See* Sheehan, Timothy James

**Sheehan, Big Jim**
*See* Sheehan, James Thomas [Jim]

**Sheehan, James Thomas [Jim]**
1913-   [BE]
*American baseball player*
* Sheehan, Big Jim

**Sheehan, John** 1831- ?   [FFF, PA]
*Irish poet and author*
* Irish Whiskey Drinker
* [The] Knight of Innishowen

**Sheehan, John J.** 20th c.   [BBH]
*American boxer*
* Sheehan, Tan

**Sheehan, Patrick Augustine** 1905-
[CAP]
*Irish barrister and author*
* O Siochain, P[adraig] A[ugustine

**Sheehan, Perley Poore** 1875-1943
[WGT]
*American author*
* Regard, Paul

**Sheehan, Tan**
*See* Sheehan, John J.

**Sheehan, Timothy James**
1868-1923   [BE]
*American baseball player*
* Sheehan, Biff

**Sheehan, Valerie Harms** 1940-
[CA]
*American author*
* Harms, Valerie

**Sheehy-Skeffington, Francis**
*See* Skeffington, Francis

**Sheelah**
*See* Fletcher, A.

**Sheeler, Mark**
*See* Sheeler, Morris

**Sheeler, Morris** 1923-   [ITA]
*American actor*
* Sheeler, Mark

**Sheely, Bud**
*See* Sheely, Hollis Kimball

**Sheely, Earl Homer** 1893-1952
[BE, PB]
*American baseball player*
* Sheely, Whitey

**Sheely, Hollis Kimball** 1920-
[BE, PB]
*American baseball player*
* Sheely, Bud

**Sheely, Whitey**
*See* Sheely, Earl Homer

**Sheen, Chris**
*See* Shinfield, Christopher

**Sheen, Fulton J.** 1895-1979
*American clergyman*
* [The] Microphone of God

**Sheen, Martin**
*See* Estevez, Ramon

**Sheen, Mickey**
*See* Scheinblum, Milton

**[The] Sheepmaker**
*See* Smith, Joseph

**Sheeran, Big Irish**
*See* Sheeran, Frank

**Sheeran, Frank** 20th c.
*American labor union official*
* Sheeran, Big Irish

**Sheffield, Flora**
*See* Sheffield-Cassan, Flora

**Sheffield, John [Duke of Buckingham and Earl of Mulgrave]** 1648-1721
[SN]
*British politician and poet*
* All Pride, Lord

**Sheffield, Reginald**
*See* Sheffield-Cassan, Reginald

**Sheffield-Cassan, Flora** 1902-
[THR]
*British-born actress*
* Sheffield, Flora

**Sheffield-Cassan, Reginald**
1901-1957   [THR]
*British-born actor*
* Sheffield, Reginald

**[The] Sheik**
*See* Harroun, Ray

**Sheik, Kid**
*See* Colar, George

**[The] Sheik of Hollywood**
*See* Wonderlich, Jerry

**Sheinfeld, Leslie A.** 1926-   [CA]
*Canadian-born educator and author*
* Field, Leslie A.

**Sheinwold, Patricia**
*See* Fox-Sheinwold, Patricia

**Shekerjian, Regina Tor** 20th c.
[SAT]
*American author and illustrator*
* Tor, Regina

**Shekles, Gail** 1918-  [BEW, FC]
*American actor*
* Stevens, Craig

**Shelasky, George Irving** 1922-
[BEW, TR]
*American actor and singer*
* Irving, George S.

**Shelbourne, Cecily**
*See* Goodwin, Suzanne

**Shelby, Charlotte**
*See* Miles, Lily Pearl

**Shelby, Daniel**
*See* Macher, Daniel J.

**Shelby, James** 1927-  [BWW]
*American singer*
* Shelby, Son

**Shelby, Juliet** 1902-  [F2]
*American actress*
* Minter, Mary Miles

**Shelby, Son**
*See* Shelby, James

**Shelby, Susan**
*See* Kinnicutt, Susan Sibley

**Sheldon, Alice Bradley** 1915-
[ESF, SFL, WGT]
*American author and psychologist*
* Bradley, Alice
* Sheldon, Raccoona
* Tiptree, James, Jr.

**Sheldon, Ann** [house pseudonym]
[Stratemeyer Syndicate]
*See* Stratemeyer, Edward L.

**Sheldon, Bob Mitchell** 1950-
[SMG]
*American baseball player*
* Sheldon, Shellie

**Sheldon, C. M.**
*See* Sheldon, Charles Monroe

**Sheldon, Charles Monroe**
1857-1946  [LC]
*American author and clergyman*
* Sheldon, C. M.

**Sheldon, David**
*See* Pomeran, David Sheldon

**Sheldon, Eleanor Bernert** 1920-
[CA]
*American sociologist and author*
* Bernert, Eleanor H.

**Sheldon, George E.**
*See* Stahl, Le Roy

**Sheldon, Jerry**
*See* Patton, Charles H.

**Sheldon, John** [house pseudonym]
*See* Bloch, Robert [Albert]

**Sheldon, Lee**
*See* Lee, Wayne Cyril

**Sheldon, Muriel** 1926-  [CA]
*American author and illustrator*
* Batherman, Muriel

**Sheldon, Peter** 1922-  [CA]
*British author*
* Gaddes, Peter

**Sheldon, Raccoona**
*See* Sheldon, Alice Bradley

**Sheldon, Roy** [house pseudonym,
Hamilton]
*See* Brunner, John [Kilian
Houston]

**Sheldon, Roy** [house pseudonym,
Hamilton]
*See* Campbell, Herbert J.

**Sheldon, Roy** [house pseudonym,
Hamilton]
*See* Tubb, Edwin Charles

**Sheldon, Scott**
*See* Wallmann, Jeffrey M[iner]

**Sheldon, Shellie**
*See* Sheldon, Bob Mitchell

**Sheldon, Walt[er J.]** 1917-
[B10, CA]
*American author*
* James, Walter S.
* Walker, Shel
* Walters, Shelly

**Shell, Virginia Law** 1923-  [CA]
*American author*
* Law, Virginia W.

**Shellabarger, Samuel** 1888-1954
[ANT, CC, WW]
*American author*
* Esteven, John
* Loring, Peter

**Shelle, Eileen**
*See* Nankin, Eileen

**Shellenberger, Beechie**
*See* Shellenberger, Dave

**Shellenberger, Dave** 20th c.  [GW]
*American rodeo performer*
* Shellenberger, Beechie

**Shelley**
*See* Yeo-Thomas, Forest Frederick
Edward

**Shelley, Frances**
*See* Wees, Frances Shelley

**Shelley, Percy Bysshe** 1792-1822
[DEL, HN, SN]
*British poet*
* Ariel
* [The] Atheist
* Mallecho, Miching, Esq.
* Nicholson, Margaret
* [The] Poet of Poets

**Shelley, Peter**
*See* Dresser, Davis

**Shellogg, Alec**
*See* Shellogg, Frederick

**Shellogg, Frederick** 1916-1968
[AS]
*American football player*
* Shellogg, Alec

**Shelly, Carol Lee** 20th c.  [BS]
*American magician*
* Carroll, Shelley

**Shelly, Mortimer M.**  [PA]
*Author*
* Old Actor

**Shelton, Andrew Kemper**
1888-1954  [BE]
*American baseball player*
* Shelton, Skeeter

**Shelton, Frederick William** 1810- ?
[FFF]
*American author and clergyman*
* Nil Admirari, Esq.

**Shelton, Julia Finley**  [FFF]
*Writer*
* Lorrimer, Laura

**Shelton, Lola**
*See* Klaue, Lola Shelton

**Shelton, Miles**
*See* Wilcox, Don

**Shelton, Skeeter**
*See* Shelton, Andrew Kemper

**Shelton, Violet** 1892-1970  [THR]
*British actress*
* Campbell, Violet

**Shelving, Paul**
*See* North, Paul

**Shemo, Stan**
*See* Shemo, Stephen Michael

**Shemo, Stephen Michael** 1915-
[BE]
*American baseball player*
* Shemo, Stan

**Shen Yen-ping** 1896-  [EWL]
*Chinese author*
* Hsuan Chu
* Mao Tun [Contradiction]

**Shennan, Victoria** 1917-  [AW]
*British writer*
* Sangster, Ann

**Shenshin, Afanasi Afanasievich**
*See* Foeth, Afanasi Afanasievich

**Shenstone, William** 1714-1763
[SN]
*British poet*
* [The] Lord of Leasowes

**Shep**
*See* Sheppard, James

**Shepard, Benjamin Henry Jesse
Francis** 1848-1927  [TC]
*British-born American author and
musician*
* Grierson, Francis

**Shepard, Leslie Albert**
*See* Juhasz, Leslie Albert

**Shepard, Morgan Van Roorbach**
1865-1947  [NAA, SFL]
*American author and editor*
* Martin, John

**Shepard, Nathan**  [PA]
*Author*
* Key note

**Shepard, Sam**
*See* Rogers, Samuel Shepard

**Shephard, Bo**
*See* Shephard, Norman

**Shephard, Dorothea Alice**
*See* Farman, Ella

**Shephard, Norman** 1897-  [BB]
*American basketball coach*
* Shephard, Bo

**Shepheard-Walwyn, Hugh Wallwyn**
1874- ?  [WWL]
*British author*
* Venning, Normandy

**Shepherd, Ann**
*See* Kalish, Scheindel

**Shepherd, Berisford** 1917-  [WWJ]
*American jazz musician*
* Shepherd, Shep

**Shepherd, David Robert** 1940-
[DC]
*British cricketer*
* Shepherd, Shep

**Shepherd, Donald [Lee]** 1932-  [CA]
*American author, editor, literary
agent*
* Kevern, Barbara

**[The] Shepherd Earl of Cumberland**
*See* Clifford, Henry de

**Shepherd, Joan**
*See* Buchanan, Betty [Joan]

**Shepherd, John**
*See* Ballard, [Willis] Todhunter

**Shepherd, John Claridge**
*See* Campbell, John

**Shepherd, John Neil** 1943-  [DC]
*West Indian cricketer*
* Shepherd, Shep
* Shepherd, Walter

**[The] Shepherd Lord**
*See* Clifford, Henry de

**Shepherd, Neal**
*See* Morland, Nigel

**[The] Shepherd of Banbury**
*See* Campbell, John

**[The] Shepherd of Salisbury Plain**
*See* Saunders, David

**[The] Shepherd of the Ocean**
*See* Raleigh, [Sir] Walter

**Shepherd, S. Rossiter** 20th c.
[MBF]
*British author and editor*
* Milton, Mark
* Richards, Frank [house
pseudonym]

**Shepherd, Shep**
*See* Shepherd, Berisford

**Shepherd, Shep**
*See* Shepherd, David Robert

**Shepherd, Shep**
*See* Shepherd, John Neil

**Shepherd, Walter**
*See* Shepherd, John Neil

**Shepherd, William James** 1933-
[IAW]
*Australian author*
* James, Peregrine

**Shepherd, William James Affleck**
1867-1946  [WEC]
*British cartoonist*
* J. A. S.

**[The] Shepherdess of Dauphiny**
*See* Vincent, Isabeau

**Shepley, Michael**
*See* Shepley-Smith, Michael

**Shepley-Smith, Michael**
1907-1961  [FC]
*British actor*
* Shepley, Michael

**Sheppard, Charles** 20th c.   [GW]
*American rodeo performer*
* Sheppard, Snakehead

**Sheppard, Eli**
*See*   Young, Martha

**Sheppard, Elizabeth Sara**
1830-1862   [DNNF, FFF, PA]
*British author*
* Berger, Elizabeth
* Kinkel, Madame

**Sheppard, Gregory Wayne** 1949-
[SMG]
*Canadian-born hockey player*
* Sheppard, Shep

**Sheppard, Jacob R.**   [PA]
*Author*
* Richmond

**Sheppard, Jake O.** 20th c.   [CEI]
*Canadian-born hockey player*
* Sheppard, Johnny

**Sheppard, James** ?-1970   [RO1]
*American singer and songwriter*
* Shep

**Sheppard, Johnny**
*See*   Sheppard, Jake O.

**Sheppard, Lancelot C[apel]** 1906-
[CA]
*British author and translator*
* Capel, Roger

**Sheppard, Shep**
*See*   Sheppard, Gregory Wayne

**Sheppard, Snakehead**
*See*   Sheppard, Charles

**Sheppard, T. G.**
*See*   Browder, Bill

**Shepperd, John** 1907-   [FC]
*American actor*
* Strudwick, Shepperd

**Sherashevski, Boris**
*See*   Brown, John J.

**Sheraton, Neil**
*See*   Smith, Norman Edward Mace

**Sherdel, Wee Willie**
*See*   Sherdel, William Henry

**Sherdel, William Henry** 1896-1968
[AS, BE, PB]
*American baseball player*
* Sherdel, Wee Willie

**Sherer, Albert** 20th c.
*American diplomat*
* Sherer, Bud

**Sherer, Bud**
*See*   Sherer, Albert

**Sherid, Roy**
*See*   Sherid, Roydan Richard

**Sherid, Roydan Richard** 1908-
[BE]
*American baseball player*
* Sherid, Roy

**Sheridan**   [FFF]
* [The] Hero of Debt

**Sheridan, Adora** [joint pseudonym
with Evelyn Marie Pavlik]
*See*   Hong, Jane Fay

**Sheridan, Adora** [joint pseudonym
with Jane Fay Hong]
*See*   Pavlik, Evelyn Marie

**Sheridan, Ann**
*See*   Sheridan, Clara Lou

**Sheridan, C. E.**
*See*   Norton, Caroline Elizabeth
Sarah

**Sheridan, Clara Lou** 1915-1967
[BDF, CU, FC]
*American actress*
* Hellar, Gloria
* [The] Oomph Girl
* Sheridan, Ann

**Sheridan, Dinah**
*See*   Mec, Dinah

**Sheridan, [Eu]gene [Anthony]** 1896-
[BE]
*American baseball player*
* Sheridan, Red

**Sheridan, Helen Selina [Countess of
Dufferin]** 1807-1867   [RH, WBD]
*British poet*
* Gushington, Angelina
* Gushington, Impulsia

**Sheridan, Lee** [joint pseudonym with
Michael Sheridan]
*See*   Lee, Elsie

**Sheridan, Lee** [joint pseudonym with
Elsie Lee]
*See*   Sheridan, Michael

**Sheridan, Lionel Astor** 1927-   [CA]
*British barrister and author*
* Shoy, Lee Ang

**Sheridan, Mark**
*See*   Shaw, Fred

**Sheridan, Mary**
*See*   Graham, Daphne

**Sheridan, Michael** 20th c.   [CA]
*American author*
* Sheridan, Lee [joint pseudonym
with Elsie Lee]

**Sheridan, Mrs. W. H.**   [FFF]
*Entertainer*
* Davenport, Louise

**Sheridan, Neill Rawlins** 1921-   [BE]
*American baseball player*
* Sheridan, Wild Horse

**Sheridan, Philip Henry** 1831-1888
[DNNS, FFF, SN]
*American army officer*
* Jack of Clubs
* Little Phil

**Sheridan, Red**
*See*   Sheridan, [Eu]gene [Anthony]

**Sheridan, Richard Brinsley**
1751-1816   [RH, SN]
*Irish playwright*
* [The] Modern Congreve
* [A] Young Hercules

**Sheridan, Teresa**
*See*   Ronalds, Mary Teresa

**Sheridan, Thomas**
*See*   Gillings, Walter

**Sheridan, Wild Horse**
*See*   Sheridan, Neill Rawlins

**[The] Sheriff**
*See*   Constable, Jimmy Lee

**[The] Sheriff**
*See*   Young, Faron

**Sheriff, Paul**
*See*   Shouvalov, Paul

**Sheritier, M.** 1809- ?   [PA]
*Author*
* Thomas, Paul

**Sherling, Ed[ward Creech]**
1897-1965   [BE]
*American baseball player*
* Sherling, Shine

**Sherling, Shine**
*See*   Sherling, Ed[ward Creech]

**Sherlock, John Clinton** 1904-   [BE]
*American baseball player*
* Sherlock, Monk

**Sherlock, Monk**
*See*   Sherlock, John Clinton

**Sherlock, William** 1641-1707   [PA]
*Author*
* Photius Junior

**Sherman, Alex** 1923-   [FB]
*American football coach*
* Sherman, Allie

**Sherman, Allan**
*See*   Copelon, Allan

**Sherman, Allie**
*See*   Sherman, Alex

**Sherman, Babe**
*See*   Sherman, Daniel L.

**Sherman, Boogie-Woogie**
*See*   Sherman, Harry

**Sherman, Charles** 20th c.   [BLB]
*American underworld figure*
* Sherman, Chink

**Sherman, Charlotte A.**
*See*   Sherman, Jory [Tecumseh]

**Sherman, Chink**
*See*   Sherman, Charles

**Sherman, Daniel L.** 1892-   [BE]
*American baseball player*
* Sherman, Babe

**Sherman, Eleanor Rae** 1929-   [CA]
*American author and illustrator*
* Fleuridas, Ellie Rae

**Sherman, Elizabeth**
*See*   Friskey, Margaret Richards

**Sherman, Frank Dempster**
1860-1916   [SFL, WGT]
*American author*
* Two Wags [joint pseudonym with
John Kendrick Bangs]

**Sherman, Gail**
*See*   Dern, Peggy Gaddis

**Sherman, Harry** 1904?-1977   [FIR]
*Entertainer*
* Sherman, Boogie-Woogie

**Sherman, Joan**
*See*   Dern, Peggy Gaddis

**Sherman, John** 1823-1900   [FFF]
*American statesman*
* Honest John

**Sherman, Jory [Tecumseh]** 1932-
[CA]
*American author and columnist*
* Anvic, Frank
* Martin, Cort
* Sherman, Charlotte A.
* Tarrant, Wilma

**Sherman, Margaret**
*See*   Scheuerman, Margaret

**Sherman, Michael**
*See*   Lowndes, Robert Augustine
Ward

**Sherman, Nancy**
*See*   Rosenberg, Nancy Sherman

**Sherman, Peter Michael**
*See*   Lowndes, Robert Augustine
Ward

**Sherman, Sylvia**
*See*   Pitkin, Sylvia Sherman

**Sherman, Theresa** 1916-
[IBY, ICB]
*American illustrator*
* Reed, Veronica

**Sherman, William Tecumseh**
1820-1891   [DNNF, FFF, SN]
*American army officer*
* Old Tecumseh

**Sherock, Shorty**
*See*   Cherock, Clarence Francis

**Sherren, Wilkinson** 20th c.   [WWL]
*British author*
* Fay, Nicholas

**Sherriff, R. C.**
*See*   Sherriff, Robert Cedric

**Sherriff, Robert Cedric** 1896-
[LC, TC]
*British author and playwright*
* Sherriff, R. C.

**Sherrill, Dorothy** 1901-   [CA]
*American author and illustrator*
* Martin, April

**Sherrington, Alf**
*See*   Burrage, Alfred Sherrington

**Sherrod, Jane**
*See*   Singer, Jane Sherrod

**Sherry, Fred Peter**
*See*   Schuerholz, Fred Peter

**Sherry, Oliver**
*See*   Lobo, George Edmund

**Shertok, Moshe** 1894-1965   [WBD]
*Israeli prime minister*
* Sharett, Moshe

**Sherwin, Jeannette**
*See*   Gorlitz, Jeannette

**Sherwin, Sterling**
*See*   Hagen, John Milton

**Sherwood, Alice**
*See*   Haslam, Mrs. Charles A.

**[The] Sherwood Forester**
*See*   Hall, Spencer T.

**Sherwood, John D.** 1840- ?   [FFF]
*American author*
* Scratchley, Harry

**Sherwood, Josephine** 1884-1957
[FC]
*American actress*
* Hull, Josephine

**Sherwood, Lydia**
*See*   Shavelson, Lydia

**Sherwood, Mary Elizabeth Wilson**
[PA]
*Author*
* M. E. W. S.

**Sherwood, Mary Neal**   [FFF]
*Translator*
* Sterling, John

**Sherwood, Michael**
*See* Weathers, Philip Joseph

**Sherwood, Nelson**
*See* Bulmer, [Henry] Kenneth

**Sherwood, R. E.**
*See* Sherwood, Robert Emmet

**Sherwood, Robert Emmet**
1896-1955   [LC, TLC]
*American author and playwright*
* Perry, Brighton
* Sherwood, R. E.

**Sherwood, Roland H.** 1902-   [NAA]
*American-born writer*
* Robbins, Rollin

**Shestov, Leo**
*See* Schwartzmann, Leo Isaakovich

**Shevchuk, Tetiana** 1906-   [CAP]
*Canadian-born author*
* Bishop, Tania Kroitor
* Semkiw, Virlyana

**Shew, Bobby**
*See* Joratz, Robert

**Shewell, Mrs. L. R.**   [FFF]
*Entertainer*
* Skerrett, Rose

**Shewring, Walter** 1906-   [CAT]
*British author*
* Francis, Hayward

**Shibano, Takumi** 20th c.   [SFP]
*Author*
* Rei, Kosumi

**Shibukawa, Gyo**
*See* Yamasaki, Takeo

**Shiel, M. P.**
*See* Shiel, Matthew Phipps

**Shiel, Matthew Phipps** 1865-1947
[CC, EMD, LC]
*British author*
* Holmes, Gordon [joint
   pseudonym with Louis Tracy]
* Shiel, M. P.

**[The] Shield of Rome**
*See* Fabius Maximus Verrucosus,
Quintus

**Shields, Ben[jamin Cowan]** 1903-
[BE]
*American baseball player*
* Shields, Big Ben
* Shields, Lefty

**Shields, Big Ben**
*See* Shields, Ben[jamin Cowan]

**Shields, Charlie** 20th c.   [OBW]
*American baseball player*
* Shields, Lefty

**Shields, Cornelius** 1895?-1981
*American banker and yachtsman*
* [The] Gray Fox of Long Island
   Sound

**Shields, Ella**
*See* Buscher, Ella

**Shields, Francis LeRoy** 1891-1961
[BE]
*American baseball player*
* Shields, Pete

**Shields, G. O.** 1846- ?   [ALY, FFF]
*American author*
* Coquina

**Shields, Lefty**
*See* Shields, Ben[jamin Cowan]

**Shields, Lefty**
*See* Shields, Charlie

**Shields, Mrs. Bernard G.**   [FFF]
*Entertainer*
* Bernard, Bessie

**Shields, Pete**
*See* Shields, Francis LeRoy

**Shields, Sammy**
*See* Young, Sammy

**Shields, William Joseph** 1888-1961
[BDF, FC, IPA]
*Irish actor*
* Fitzgerald, Barry

**Shiels, Tibbie**
*See* Richardson, Isabella

**Shiffert, Edith [Marcombe]** 1916-
[CA]
*Canadian-born author and educator*
* Marcombe, Edith Marion

**Shifflett, Duck**
*See* Shifflett, Garland Jessie

**Shifflett, Garland Jessie** 1935-
[BE]
*American baseball player*
* Shifflett, Duck

**Shigeru, Tsuyuki**
*See* Kirkup, James

**Shih Chao-chi** 1877-1958   [WBD]
*Chinese diplomat*
* Sze Sao-ke, Alfred

**Shihab, Sahib**
*See* Gregory, Edmund

**Shillaber, Benjamin Penhallow**
1814-1890   [FFF]
*American author*
* Billaber, She P.
* Partington, Mrs.

**Shillaber, Ruth West** 1908-1955
[BEW]
*American actress*
* Weston, Ruth

**Shilling, Cal**
*See* Shilling, Carroll

**Shilling, Carroll** 1886?-1950
[BBH]
*American jockey*
* Shilling, Cal

**Shimi, Mac**
*See* Simpson, Archibald

**[The] Shimmy Queen**
*See* Pennington, Ann

**Shinault, Enoch Erskine**
1892-1930   [BE]
*American baseball player*
* Shinault, Ginger

**Shinault, Ginger**
*See* Shinault, Enoch Erskine

**Shine, Dennis Francis Joseph**
1908-   [SFL]
*Author*
* Shannon, Frank

**Shiner, Dick** 20th c.
*American football player*
* Shiner, Herbie

**Shiner, Herbie**
*See* Shiner, Dick

**Shines, John Ned [Johnny]** 1915-
[BWW]
*American singer*
* Little Wolf
* Shoe Shine Johnny

**Shinfield, Christopher** 1908-
[BMH]
*British female impersonator*
* Sheen, Chris

**Shingle, Solon**
*See* Dunn, Caleb

**Shinn, Earl** 1837-1886   [PA]
*Author*
* Strahan, Edward

**Shinso** 1460?-1530?   [WBD]
*Japanese painter*
* Soami

**Shinwell, Emmanuel** 1884-   [NN]
*British politician and labor leader*
* Sinbad the Tailor

**Ship Surgeon**
*See* Burton, Leonard Lamming

**Shipke, Muskrat Bill**
*See* Shipke, William M. [Bill]

**Shipke, William M. [Bill]**
1882-1940   [BE]
*American baseball player*
* Shipke, Muskrat Bill

**Shipley, David**
*See* Holden, David [Shipley]

**Shipley, Joseph Clark [Joe]** 1935-
[BE]
*American baseball player*
* Shipley, Moses

**Shipley, Joseph Twaddell** 1893-
[WD]
*American author*
* Goliard, Roy

**Shipley, Miriam Allen De Ford**
1888-1975   [WGT]
*American author*
* De Ford, Miriam Allen

**Shipley, Moses**
*See* Shipley, Joseph Clark [Joe]

**Shipman, Elydia Foss**
*See* Oliver, Dora Dana

**Shippen, William** ?-1742?
[HN, RH]
*British politician*
* [The] Incorruptible

**Shippen, Zoe**
*See* Varnum, Zoe Shippen

**Shipton, Anna** 19th c.   [PA]
*Author*
* A. S.

**Shipton, Mother**
*See* Preece, T. Evan

**Shirach, Baldur von** 1907-   [BDW]
*German Nazi leader*
* Falk, Richard

**Shiras, Wilmar H.** 1908-   [WGT]
*American author*
* Howes, Jane

**Shires, [Charles] Art[hur]**
1907-1967   [BE, PB]
*American baseball player*
* Art[hur] the Great
* Whattaman

**Shirey, Claire Lee** 1898-1962   [BE]
*American baseball player*
* Shirey, Duke

**Shirey, Duke**
*See* Shirey, Claire Lee

**Shirley**
*See* Skelton, John

**Shirley, Alvis Newman** 1918-   [BE]
*American baseball player*
* Shirley, Tex

**Shirley, Anne**
*See* Paris, Dawn Evelyeen

**Shirley, Ernest Raeford** 1901-1955
[BE]
*American baseball player*
* Shirley, Mule

**Shirley, Florence Henderson** 1883-
[NAA]
*American writer and editor*
* Leigh, Magda

**Shirley, James** 1596-1666
[DEP, DNNS, SN]
*British playwright*
* [The] Last Minstrel of the
   English Stage

**Shirley, Mule**
*See* Shirley, Ernest Raeford

**Shirley, R. O.**
*See* Shirley, Ralph Oakley

**Shirley, Ralph Oakley** 1918-   [ART]
*British potter and painter*
* Shirley, R. O.

**Shirley, Tex**
*See* Shirley, Alvis Newman

**Shiroyan, Haig Krikor** 1891-
[IAW]
*Armenian-born author and poet*
* Anoushavan

**Shirreffs, Gordon D[onald]** 1914-
[CA, SAT, WD]
*American author*
* Donalds, Gordon
* Flynn, Jackson
* Gordon, Stewart
* MacLean, Art

**Shiver, Chick**
*See* Shiver, Ivey Merwin

**Shiver, Ivey Merwin** 1906-   [BE]
*American baseball player*
* Shiver, Chick

**Shoals, Roger** 20th c.
*American football player*
* Shoals, Turtle

**Shoals, Turtle**
*See* Shoals, Roger

**Shocker, Urban James**
*See* Schockeor, Urbain Jacques

**[The] Shoe**
*See* Shoemaker, William [Willie]

**Shoe, Lucy T.**
*See* Meritt, Lucy Shoe

**Shoe Shine Johnny**
*See* Shines, John Ned [Johnny]

**Shoecraft, Robert K.** 1914-    [IBW]
*Micronesian chief justice*
* Shoecraft, Shoe

**Shoecraft, Shoe**
*See* Shoecraft, Robert K.

**Shoeffel, Mrs. John**    [FFF]
*Entertainer*
* Booth, Agnes

**Shoeless Joe Jackson**
*See* Jackson, Joseph Jefferson

**[The] Shoemaker**
*See* Paretti, Tony

**Shoemaker, Old Shoes**
*See* Shoemaker, William

**Shoemaker, William [Willie]** 1931-
*American jockey*
* [El] Maestro [The Teacher]
* [The] Shoe
* [The] Silent Shoe
* [El] Viejo [The Old One]
* [El] Zapatero [The Shoemaker]

**Shoemaker, William** 20th c.    [BLB]
*American detective*
* Shoemaker, Old Shoes

**Shoeneck, Jumbo**
*See* Shoeneck, Lewis N.

**Shoeneck, Lewis N.** 1862- ?    [BE]
*American baseball player*
* Shoeneck, Jumbo

**Shoenight, Aloise** 1914-    [CA]
*American poet*
* Tracy, Aloise

**Shoffner, Milburn James** 1905-
[BE]
*American baseball player*
* Shoffner, Milt

**Shoffner, Milt**
*See* Shoffner, Milburn James

**Shofner, Del**
*See* Shofner, Delbert M.

**Shofner, Delbert M.** 1934-    [FB]
*American football player*
* Shofner, Del

**Shofner, Frank Strickland** 1920-
[BE]
*American baseball player*
* Shofner, Strick

**Shofner, Grant Calvin** 1932-
[CWG]
*American country-western performer*
* Smith, Cal

**Shofner, Strick**
*See* Shofner, Frank Strickland

**Shokeid, Moshe**
*See* Minkovitz, Moshe

**Sholes, W. W.**
*See* Scholz, Winfried

**Sholl, Anna McClure** 20th c.    [WW]
*Author*
* Corson, Geoffrey

**Sholto**
*See* Mackenzie, R. Shelton

**Shomberg, Otto H.**
*See* Shambrick, Otto H.

**Shone, Patric**
*See* Hanley, James

**Shonin, Shodo** 8th c.    [HN]
*Japanese religious leader*
* [The] Buddhist St. Augustine

**Shooshan, Chip**
*See* Shooshan, Harry M., III

**Shooshan, Harry M., III**    [ET]
*American government counsel*
* Shooshan, Chip

**[The] Shootin' Fool**
*See* Drucci, Vincent

**Shor, Bernard** 1904-1977    [B10]
*American restaurateur*
* Shor, Toots

**Shor, Toots**
*See* Shor, Bernard

**Shore, Dinah**
*See* Shore, Frances Rose

**Shore, Edward William [Eddie]**
1902-    [SR]
*Canadian-born hockey player*
* [The] Babe Ruth of Hockey

**Shore, Frances Rose** 1917-
[FC, IPA, ITA]
*American entertainer*
* Shore, Dinah

**Shore, Hamby**
*See* Shore, Sam Hamilton

**Shore, Norman**
*See* Smith, Norman Edward Mace

**Shore, Philippa**
*See* Holbeche, Philippa [Jack]

**Shore, Sam Hamilton** 1886-1918
[FHE]
*Canadian-born hockey player*
* Shore, Hamby

**[The] Short**
*See* Pepin III

**Short, Annabelle** 1930-    [EJ]
*British-born American singer and*
*songwriter*
* Ross, Annie

**Short, Beth Campbell** 1908-    [NAA]
*American journalist*
* Campbell, Beth

**Short, Bob**
*See* Longstreet, A. B.

**Short, Bobby** 1924-
*American singer*
* [The] Miniature King of Swing

**Short, Charles Williams** 19th c.
[PA]
*Author*
* C. W. S.

**Short, Eleanor Talbot Kinkead** 20th
c.    [NAA]
*American author*
* Kinkead, Eleanor Talbot

**Short, J. D.** 1902-1962    [BWW]
*American singer*
* Short, Jaydee
* Short, Jelly Jaw

**Short, Jackson**
*See* Hochstein, Peter

**Short, Jaydee**
*See* Short, J. D.

**Short, Jelly Jaw**
*See* Short, J. D.

**Short, Joshua**
*See* Oakley, Frederick

**Short, Luke**
*See* Glidden, Frederick D[illey]

**Short, Mary Asenath**    [FFF, PA]
*American poet*
* True, Fanny

**Short, Percival M.** 1886-1955
[THR]
*British theatrical manager*
* Selby, Percival M.

**Short, Roger, Jr.**
*See* Eyen, Tom

**Shorten, Charles Henry** 1892-1965
[BE]
*American baseball player*
* Shorten, Chick

**Shorten, Chick**
*See* Shorten, Charles Henry

**Shorter, Aylward** 1932-    [CA]
*British anthropologist and author*
* Jensi, Muganwa Nsiku

**Shorter, Carl**
*See* Schwalberg, Carol[yn
Ernestine Stein]

**Shorthouse, Rebecca**
*See* Lea, Constance Nicholson

**Shortstop, Mr.**
*See* Marion, Martin Whiteford

**Shortstuff, Mr.**
*See* Macon, John Wesley

**Shortt, Charles Rushton** 1904-
[WW]
*Author*
* Rushton, Charles

**Shorty George**
*See* Johnson, James

**Shoshone Mike**
*See* Daggett, Mike

**[The] Shot**
*See* Foley, Jack

**Shots, Kid**
*See* Madison, Louis

**Shotter, Ralph Champion** 1907-
[FC, TR]
*British actor*
* Michael, Ralph

**Shotton, Barney**
*See* Shotton, Burton Edwin

**Shotton, Burton Edwin** 1884-1962
[BE, PB]
*American baseball player and*
*manager*
* Shotton, Barney

**[The] Shoulder Breaker**
*See* Shapur II [or Sapor]

**Shoun, Clyde Mitchell** 1912-1968
[AS, BE]
*American baseball player*
* Shoun, Hardrock

**Shoun, Hardrock**
*See* Shoun, Clyde Mitchell

**Shouvalov, Paul** 1903-1962    [FC]
*Russian-born film art director*
* Sheriff, Paul

**Shoveller, Shove**
*See* Shoveller, Stanley Howard

**Shoveller, Stanley Howard**
1882-1959    [OCS]
*British field hockey player*
* Shoveller, Shove

**Shovlin, Brode**
*See* Shovlin, John Joseph

**Shovlin, John Joseph** 1891-    [BE]
*American baseball player*
* Shovlin, Brode

**Shovlin, Joseph Kenneth**
1899?-1974    [FC, SC]
*American actor*
* Whalen, Michael

**Showalter, Max** 1917-
[FC, ITA, SW]
*American actor and composer*
* Adams, Casey

**Shower, Hudson** 1919-    [BWW]
*American singer*
* Little Hudson

**Showles, Mrs. William**    [FFF]
*Entertainer*
* Marks, Sallie

**Shoy, Lee Ang**
*See* Sheridan, Lionel Astor

**Shreve, Lev**
*See* Shreve, Leven Lawrence

**Shreve, Leven Lawrence** 1869-1942
[BE]
*American baseball player*
* Shreve, Lev

**Shreve, Tiffany**
*See* Everson, Carol

**Shrewsbury, Ralph**
*See* Jamieson, Leland Shattuck

**Shrii Shrii Anandamurti**
*See* Sarkar, P. R.

**[The] Shrimp**
*See* Shrimpton, Jean

**Shrimpton, Jean** 1943-
*British fashion model*
* [The] Shrimp

**Shriner, Herb**
*See* Schiner, Herbert Arthur

**Shrinivasi, Asjantenu**
*See* Lutchman, Martinus Haridat

**Shriver, Harry Graydon** 1896-    [BE]
*American baseball player*
* Shriver, Pop

**Shriver, Pop**
*See* Shriver, Harry Graydon

**Shrividhata**
*See* Mishra, Vidhata

**Shroyer, Frederick** 20th c.    [SFP]
*Author*
* Freyer, Erick

**Shtchirin, Jacob** 1890-    [BEW]
*Russian-born actor, director,*
*producer*
* Ben-Ami, Jacob

**Shu, Austin Chi-wei** 1915-    [CA]
*Chinese-born compiler and*
*translator*
* Chi-wei
* Yang-jen

**Shu, Eddie**
*See* Shulman, Edward

**Shub, Beth**
See Pessen, Beth

**Shuba, George Thomas** 1924- [BE]
*American baseball player*
* Shuba, Shotgun

**Shuba, Shotgun**
See Shuba, George Thomas

**Shubert, J. J.**
See Szemanski, Jacob

**Shubert, Lee**
See Szemanski, Levi

**Shubert, Sam S.**
See Szemanski, Samuel

**Shubin, Seymour** 1921- [IAW]
*American author*
* Richards, Al

**Shuff, Jean** 1929?- [BEW, FC, TR]
*British actress and singer*
* Carson, Jeannie

**Shufflebottom, Abel**
See Southey, Robert

**Shufflewick, Mrs.**
See Jamieson, Rex

**Shufflin' Phil Douglas**
See Douglas, Philips Brooks

**Shufflin' Sam**
See Brown, Robert

**Shugrue, Joe** 1894-1961
[BX, RBE]
*American boxer*
* [The] Jersey Bobcat
* Shugrue, Young Joe

**Shugrue, Young Joe**
See Shugrue, Joe

**Shulberg, Alan**
See Wilkes-Hunter, Richard

**Shull, Margaret Anne Wyse** 1940-
[CA]
*American author*
* Shull, Peg
* Windsor, Annie

**Shull, Peg**
See Shull, Margaret Anne Wyse

**Shulman, Edward** 1918- [EJ, PMJ]
*American jazz musician*
* Shu, Eddie

**Shulman, Joseph** 1923- [EJ]
*Scottish-born jazz musician*
* Saye, Joe

**Shulmanuasharid**
See Shalmaneser II

**Shultz, Gladys Denny** 1895- [CA]
*American author*
* Gardner, Anne

**Shultz, Toots**
See Shultz, Wallace Luther

**Shultz, Wallace Luther** 1888-1959
[BE]
*American baseball player*
* Shultz, Toots

**Shulvass, Moses A.** 1909- [IAW]
*Polish-born clergyman and author*
* Meyerson, Tuvia

**Shumsky, Zena Feldman** 1926-
[CA]
*British-born author*
* Collier, Jane

**Shumsky, Zena Feldman** (Continued)
* Collier, Zena

**Shumway, Lee**
See Shumway, Leonard C.

**Shumway, Leonard C.** 1884-1959
[SC]
*American actor*
* Shumway, Lee

**[The] Shunt**
See Hunt, James

**Shura, Kashina** 1937- [WFA]
*Korean-born fashion designer*
* Hardwick, Cathy

**Shura, Mary Francis**
See Craig, Mary Francis

**Shurman, Anna Maria von** 1607-1678
*German scholar*
* [The] Torch of Wisdom

**Shushtary, John** 1920- [CA]
*British editor*
* Canning, John

**Shuster, Bud**
See Shuster, E. G.

**Shuster, E. G.** 20th c. [IPA]
*American politician*
* Shuster, Bud

**Shute, Denny**
See Shute, Herman Densmore

**Shute, Herman Densmore**
1904-1974 [GF]
*American golfer*
* Shute, Denny

**Shute, Nevil**
See Norway, Nevil Shute

**Shute, Walter** 20th c. [MBF]
*British author*
* Edwards, Johnson
* Edwards, Walter
* Maxwell, Gordon
* Wentworth, Charles [house
pseudonym]

**Shutta, Ethel**
See Schutte, Ethel

**Shuttleworth, Kenneth** 1944- [DC]
*British cricketer*
* Shuttleworth, Shut

**Shuttleworth, Shut**
See Shuttleworth, Kenneth

**Shverubovich, Vasili Ivanovich**
1875-1948 [BEW]
*Actor*
* Kachalov, Vasili Ivanovich

**Shy Di**
See Diana

**Shy, Timothy** [joint pseudonym with
Ronald William Fordham Searle]
See Lewis, Dominic Bevan
Wyndham

**Shy, Timothy** [joint pseudonym with
Dominic Bevan Wyndham Lewis]
See Searle, Ronald William
Fordham

**Siano, Fiore** 20th c. [PHM]
*American underworld figure*
* Siano, Fury

**Siano, Fury**
See Siano, Fiore

**Siano, Joe**
See Valachi, Joseph Michael

**Sib**
See Ford, Aleck

**Sibbes, Richard** 1577-1635 [SN]
*British clergyman*
* Humble and Heavenly-Minded

**Sibelius, Jean**
See Sibelius, Johan Julius
Christian

**Sibelius, Johan Julius Christian**
1865-1957 [BEW, IPA]
*Finnish composer*
* Sibelius, Jean

**Sibert, Willa** 1873-1947 [EWL]
*American author, poet, critic*
* Cather, Willa

**Sibley, Ben** 1876- ? [THR]
*Irish-born entertainer*
* Albert, Ben

**Sibley, Henry H.** [PA]
*Author*
* Hal a Dacotah

**Sibley, Inez K.** 1908?- [CW]
*Jamaican author*
* Pennibb

**Sibley, Susan**
See Kinnicutt, Susan Sibley

**Sibyl**
See Martin, Sallie M. D.

**[The] Sibyl of Europe**
See Lieven, Dariya Khristoforovna

**[La] Sibylle du Faubourg
Saint-Germain**
See Lenormand, Marie Anne
Adelaide

**Siccone** ?-1003 [CAL]
*Pope*
* John XVII [or XVIII]

**[The] Sicilian Anacreon**
See Meli, Giovanni

**[The] Sicilian Ox**
See Aquinas, Thomas [Thomas of
Aquino]

**[The] Sicilian Theocritus**
See Meli, Giovanni

**Siciliano, Angelo** 1893-1972 [PE]
*Italian-born body builder*
* Atlas, Charles
* [The] World's Most Perfectly
Developed Man

**Siciliano, Mario** 20th c. [WF]
*Italian director*
* Sirko, Marlon

**[The] Sickly**
See Henry III

**Sickmann, Rocky**
See Sickmann, Rodney

**Sickmann, Rodney** 1958-
*American Marine who was held
hostage in Iran*
* Sickmann, Rocky

**Sicto, C.**
See Costi y Erro, Candido

**[El] Sid**
See Catlett, Sid L.

**[El] Sid**
See Perelman, Sidney Joseph

**Siddhartha** 6th c. BC [WBD]
*Indian philosopher and founder of
Buddhism*
* Gautama Buddha
* Sakyamuni [Sage of the Sakyas]

**Siddle, Charles** 1892- [WW]
*Author*
* Slingsby, Rufus [joint pseudonym
with Frederick Peel]

**[The] Siddons of America**
See Duff, Mary Ann

**Siddons, Sarah** 1755-1831 [HN]
*British actress*
* [The] Muse of Tragedy

**Sidebottom, Arnold [Arnie]** 1954-
[DC]
*British cricketer*
* Thanold, Woofer

**Siderocrates**
See Eisumenger, Samuel

**Sidetes**
See Antiochus VII

**[The] Sidewalk Poet**
See Crary, J. M.

**Sidis, William James** 1898- [NAA]
*American author*
* Folupa, Frank

**Sidnal, Emma**
See Freeman, Mrs. E. W.

**Sidney, Algernon**
See Granger, Gideon

**Sidney, Dorothy** 1617-1684 [WBD]
*Countess of Sunderland*
* Sacharissa

**Sidney, E. W.**
See Tucker, Nathaniel Beverley

**Sidney, Edward William**
See Tucker, Nathaniel Beverley

**Sidney, Frank**
See Warwick, Alan Ross

**Sidney, Frank**
See Warwick, Francis Alister

**Sidney, Frank**
See Warwick, Sidney

**Sidney, George**
See Bounds, S. J.

**Sidney, George**
See Greenfield, Sammy

**Sidney, Jonathan**
See Cooper, Emmanuel

**Sidney, Margaret**
See Lothrop, Harriet Mulford
Stone

**Sidney, Neilma**
See Gantner, Neilma

**Sidney, [Sir] Philip** 1554-1586
[FFF, HN, SN]
*British poet, statesman, soldier*
* Astrophel
* [The] British Bayard
* [The] Chevalier Bayard of Our
History
* [The] English Petrarch
* [The] Flower of Chivalry
* [The] Miracle of Our Age

**Sidney, [Sir] Philip** (Continued)
* [The] Mirror of Courtesy
* [The] Petrarch of England
* Philisides
* [The] Poet of Kissing
* [The] Warbler of Poetic Prose

**Sidney, Scott**
See   Siggins, Scott

**Sidney, Stuart?**
See   Avallone, Michael [Angelo], Jr.

**Sidney, Sylvia**
See   Kosow, Sophia

**Sidney-Fryer, Donald**
See   Fryer, Donald S[idney, Jr.]

**Sidobre, Andre**
See   Schumann, Maurice

**Sidrophel**
See   Lilly, William

**Sidrophel**
See   Neal, [Sir] Paul

**Sidrophel, Sir**
See   Walpole, [Sir] Robert [First Earl of Orford]

**Siebel, Frederick** 1913-   [ICB]
*Austrian-born industrial designer and illustrator*
* Siebel, Fritz

**Siebel, Fritz**
See   Siebel, Frederick

**Sieber, Sam Dixon** 1931-   [CA]
*American author*
* Kerr, Norman D.

**Siebert, Albert Charles** 1904-1939 [CEI, FHE, HK]
*Canadian-born hockey player*
* Siebert, Babe

**Siebert, Babe**
See   Siebert, Albert Charles

**Siebert, Eloise McElroy**
See   Hembling, Nina [Clark]

**Siebert, Sonny**
See   Siebert, Wilfred Charles

**Siebert, Wilfred Charles** 1937- [BE, PB, SMG]
*American baseball player*
* Siebert, Sonny

**Siedenschner, Jacob** 20th c.   [BLB]
*American underworld figure*
* Lewis, Whitey

**Sieg, W. M.**
See   Wulff, Sigismund

**Siege Gun Guilford**
See   Guilford, Jesse P.

**Siegel, Abe J.** 1914-1966 [BEW, SC]
*American actor*
* Stewart, David J.

**Siegel, Benjamin** 1906-1947
*American underworld figure*
* Rosen, Harry
* Siegel, Bugsy

**Siegel, Benjamin** 1914-   [WD]
*American author*
* Benn, Matthew

**Siegel, Bugsy**
See   Siegel, Benjamin

**Siegel, Doris** 20th c.   [CC, WW]
*Author*
* Wells, Susan

**Siegel, Jack**
See   Siegel, Jacob

**Siegel, Jacob** 1913-   [CA]
*American author*
* Siegel, Jack

**Siegel, Jerome** 20th c.   [SFP]
*Author*
* Kenton, Bernard J.

**Siegen, Ludwig von** 1609- ?   [WBD]
*German engraver*
* Von Sechten

**Siegler, Eugene** 1895-   [CA]
*Rumanian-born author*
* Relgis, Eugene

**Siegvolk, Paul**
See   Mathews, Albert

**Sielanski, Stanley** ?-1955   [SC]
*Polish-born actor*
* Stanislaw, Stanley

**Siemer, Cotton**
See   Siemer, Oscar Sylvester

**Siemer, Oscar Sylvester** 1901-1959 [BE]
*American baseball player*
* Siemer, Cotton

**Sienkiewicz, Henryk [Adam Aleksander Pius]** 1846-1916   [TLC]
*Polish author and journalist*
* Litwos

**Sierbois, R. Q.**
See   Boissier, Jeane B. Prudence

**Sierck, Detlef** 1900- [BDF, FC, FD]
*Danish-born director*
* Sirk, Douglas

**Siet, Gloria** 1930-   [OP]
*American opera singer*
* Lane, Gloria

**Sieveking, Lance**
See   Sieveking, Lancelot De Giberne

**Sieveking, Lancelot De Giberne** 1896-1972   [LC]
*British author and playwright*
* Sieveking, Lance

**Sievers, Roy Edward** 1926- [BE, DGS, PB]
*American baseball player*
* Sievers, Squirrel

**Sievers, Squirrel**
See   Sievers, Roy Edward

**Siew, William Leonard** 1888-1977 [CA]
*Lithuanian-born American journalist and author*
* Laurence, William Leonard

**Sifadda, Siful**
See   Wergeland, Henrik Arnold

**Siff, Richard Philip** 1927-   [BEW]
*American talent representative*
* Seff, Richard

**Sig**
See   Webber, George Harris

**Sigel, Franz** 1824-1902   [FFF, SN]
*German-born American army officer*
* Dutchy

**Sigel, Mike** 20th c.
*American billiard player*
* Hook, Captain

**Sigfusdottir, Greta**
See   Sigfusdottir, Lara Margret

**Sigfusdottir, Lara Margret** 1910- [IAW]
*Icelandic author*
* Sigfusdottir, Greta

**Siggins, Scott** 1872-1928   [SC]
*Actor and director*
* Sidney, Scott

**Sighele, Mariantonietta** 20th c. [OP]
*Italian opera singer*
* Sighele, Mietta

**Sighele, Mietta**
See   Sighele, Mariantonietta

**Sigismund**   [SN]
*Austrian monarch*
* [The] Simple

**Sigismund** 1368-1437 [DNNF, RH, SN]
*King of Germany*
* [The] Balaam of Modern History
* [The] Light of the World
* Super Grammaticam

**Sigismund I** 1467?-1548 [DNNS, FFF]
*King of Poland*
* [The] Great

**Sigismund II** 1520-1572 [FFF, RH, SN]
*King of Poland*
* Augustus

**Siglin, Paddy**
See   Siglin, Wesley Peter

**Siglin, Wesley Peter** 1891-1956 [BE]
*American baseball player*
* Siglin, Paddy

**Sigma**
See   Field, Julian Osgood

**Sigma**
See   Sargent, Lucius Manlius

**Signifyin' Mary Johnson**
See   Johnson, Mary

**Signorelli, Luca d'Egidio di Ventura de** 1441-1523   [WBD]
*Italian painter*
* Luca da Cortona

**Signoret, Simone**
See   Kaminker, Simone

**Sigourney, Lydia Howard** 1791-1865   [SN]
*American author*
* [The] Hemans of America

**Sigurd**
See   Hedenstierna, Alfred

**Sigurd Mund [Mouth]**
See   Sigurd II

**Sigurd I** 1089?-1130   [WBD]
*King of Norway*
* [The] Crusader

**Sigurd II** 1134-1155   [WBD]
*King of Norway*
* Sigurd Mund [Mouth]

**Siki, Battling**
See   Phal, Louis

**Silangan, Manuel**
See   Yabes, Leopoldo Y[abes]

**Silas**
See   McCay, Winsor

**Silbajoris, Frank**
See   Silbajoris, Rimvydas

**Silbajoris, Rimvydas** 1926-   [CA]
*Lithuanian-born educator and author*
* Silbajoris, Frank

**Silberberg, Leslie F[rances] Stone** 1905-   [WGT]
*American author*
* Stone, Leslie F.

**Silberman, Jerome** 1934-   [BEW]
*American actor*
* Wilder, Gene

**Silberschlag, Eisig** 1903-   [IAW]
*Austrian-born author*
* Strong, Eric

**Silberstein, Jay Jehiel** 1936-   [CA]
*Israeli-born author*
* Zif, Jay Jehiel

**Silbert, William M.** 1921-   [ITA]
*American entertainer*
* Bradley, Bill

**Silby, Charles** 1801-1863   [PA]
*Author*
* Tickletooth, Tabitha

**[The] Silent**
See   William I

**Silent Cal Benge**
See   Benge, Ray Adelphia

**Silent Cal Coolidge**
See   Coolidge, [John] Calvin

**Silent Frank Hinkey**
See   Hinkey, Frank A.

**Silent Gene Hairston**
See   Hairston, Gene

**Silent George Stone**
See   Stone, George Robert

**Silent George Twombly**
See   Twombly, George Frederick

**Silent Jake Volz**
See   Volz, Jacob Phillip [Jake]

**Silent Joe Martin**
See   Martin, Joseph Samuel [Joe]

**Silent John Gillespie**
See   Gillespie, John Patrick

**Silent John Hummel**
See   Hummel, John Edwin

**Silent John Titus**
See   Titus, John Franklin

**Silent John Whitehead**
See   Whitehead, John Henderson

**[The] Silent Laureate**
See   Bridges, Robert

**[The] Silent Man**
See   Gehringer, Charles Leonard

**[The] Silent Man**
See Grant, Hiram Ulysses

**Silent Mike Tiernan**
See Tiernan, Michael Joseph

**[The] Silent One**
See Moltke, Hellmuth Karl
Bernhard von

**[The] Silent Pole**
See Kowalewskie, Stanislaus

**[The] Silent Scot**
See Smith, Macdonald

**[The] Silent Shoe**
See Shoemaker, William [Willie]

**Silent Steve Philbin**
See Philbin, Stephen H.

**[The] Silent Swede**
See Stenmark, Ingemar

**Silent Tom Smith**
See Smith, Tom

**Silent Traveller**
See Chiang Yee

**Silent, William T.**
See Jackson, John William, Jr.

**Silentiarius, Paulus**
See Philes, George P.

**[The] Silentiary**
See Anastasius I

**[The] Silk King**
See Rice, Harold

**Silk Stocking Schafer**
See Schafer, Harry C.

**[The] Silken Lord**
See Fitzgerald, Thomas

**Silken Thomas**
See Fitzgerald, Thomas

**Sillah, Mododou Baikoro** 1935-
[IAW]
Gambian writer
* Baikoro

**Siller, Hilda**   [FFF]
American writer
* Hilda

**Siller, Van**
See Van Siller, Hilda

**Silliman, George Joseph L. W.**
[PA]
Author
* Hannibal

**Sills, Beverly**
See Silverman, Belle Miriam

**Sills, Jennifer**
See Lewis, Stephen

**Silly Billy**
See William Frederick

**Silly Billy**
See William IV

**[The] Silly Duke**
See Churchill, John [First Duke of
Marlborough]

**[The] Silly Kid**
See Floyd, Frank

**Silone, Ignazio**
See Tranquilli, Secondo

**Siltanen, Risto** 1958-   [SMG]
Finnish-born hockey player
* [The] Incredible Hulk

**Siluriensis, Leolinus**
See Jones, Arthur Llewellyn

**[The] Silurist**
See Vaughan, Henry

**Silva, Antonio Jose da** 1705-1739
[WBD]
Portuguese playwright
* [O] Judeu

**Silvani, Anita** 20th c.   [SFL, WGT]
Author
* A. F. S.

**Silvanus**
See Strasser, Bernard Paul

**Silvayn, Alexander** 16th c.   [FFF]
British author
* Piot, Lazarus

**Silve, Claude**
See Laforest-Divonne, Philomene
De

**Silver Bill Phillips**
See Phillips, William Corcoran

**[The] Silver Captain**
See Digby, [Sir] Henry

**Silver Donald Cameron**
See Cameron, Donald [Allan]

**[The] Silver Fox**
See Bierman, Bernard W. [Bernie]

**[The] Silver Fox**
See Jehan, Jean

**[The] Silver Fox**
See Kidd, E. Culver

**[The] Silver Fox**
See Patrick, Lester

**[The] Silver Fox**
See Petty, Jesse Lee

**[The] Silver Fox**
See Read, Herbert

**[The] Silver Fox**
See Ritchie, Alvin

**[The] Silver Fox**
See Shaw, Lawrence T.

**[The] Silver Fox**
See Snider, Edwin Donald

**[The] Silver Fox**
See Terry, William J.

**[The] Silver Fox of the Northland**
See Bierman, Bernard W. [Bernie]

**Silver, Fred**
See Silverberg, Frederick

**Silver Hand**
See Nuad

**Silver Kane**
See Ledesma, Gonzales

**Silver King of the Cowboys**
See Gray, Gene

**[The] Silver Masked Tenor**
See White, Joseph M.

**Silver, Monroe Burton** 1933-
[BEW]
American talent representative
* Silver, Monty

**Silver, Monty**
See Silver, Monroe Burton

**Silver, Nicholas**
See Faust, Frederick [Schiller]

**Silver, Ruth**
See Chew, Ruth

**[The] Silver Scot**
See Armour, Thomas Dickson
[Tommy]

**Silver Snaffle III**
See Cunningham, Margaret Isobel

**[The] Silver Tongue**
See Finch, Daniel [Second Earl of
Nottingham]

**[The] Silver Tongued**
See Barry, Spranger

**[The] Silver Tongued**
See Bates, William

**Silver Tongued**
See Booth, Barton

**[The] Silver Tongued**
See Hammond, Anthony

**[The] Silver Tongued**
See Smith, Henry

**[The] Silver Tongued**
See Sylvester, Joshua

**[The] Silver Tongued Orator of New
Hampshire**
See Gove, William Hazeltine

**[The] Silver Tongued Sluggard of the
Senate**
See McCreery, Thomas C.

**[The] Silver Trumpet of the House**
See Deering, [Sir] Edward

**Silver, W. A.**   [PA]
Author
* Marsden, Frederick

**Silver Whiskered Chapman**
See Chapman, George

**Silvera, Charles Anthony Ryan**
1924-   [BE]
American baseball player
* Silvera, Swede

**Silvera, Swede**
See Silvera, Charles Anthony Ryan

**Silverberg, Frederick** 1936-   [ASC]
American composer and pianist
* Silver, Fred

**Silverberg, Robert** 1936-
[CA, ESF, WGT]
American author
* Aghill, Gordon [joint pseudonym
with Randall Garrett]
* Arnette, Robert [house
pseudonym, Ziff-Davis]
* Bethlen, T. D.
* Blade, Alexander [joint
pseudonym with Randall Garrett]
[house pseudonym, Ziff-Davis]
* Burke, Ralph [joint pseudonym
with Randall Garrett]
* Chapman, Walker
* Clinton, Dirk
* Drummond, Walter
* Elliott, Don
* Greer, Richard [joint pseudonym
with Randall Garrett] [house
pseudonym, Ziff-Davis]

**Silverberg, Robert** (Continued)
* Jarvis, E. K. [house pseudonym,
Ziff-Davis]
* Jorgensen, Ivar [joint pseudonym
with Randall Garrett] [house
pseudonym, Ziff-Davis]
* Kastel, Warren [house
pseudonym, Ziff-Davis]
* Knox, Calvin M.
* Malcolm, Dan
* Martin, Webber
* McKenzie, Ray?
* Merriman, Alex
* Mitchell, Clyde [joint pseudonym
with Randall Garrett] [house
pseudonym, Ziff-Davis]
* Osborne, David
* Osborne, George
* Randall, Robert [joint pseudonym
with Randall Garrett]
* Robertson, Ellis [joint pseudonym
with Harlan (Jay) Ellison]
* Rodman, Eric
* Sebastian, Lee
* Spencer, Leonard G. [joint
pseudonym with Randall Garrett]
[house pseudonym, Ziff-Davis]
* Tenneshaw, S. M. [joint
pseudonym with Randall Garrett]
[house pseudonym, Ziff-Davis]
* Thornton, Hall
* Vance, Gerald [joint pseudonym
with Randall Garrett] [house
pseudonym, Ziff-Davis]
* Watson, Richard F.

**Silverblatt, Howard** 1909-
[BEW, EMT, FC]
American actor, director, producer
* Da Silva, Howard

**Silverlake, Arthur** 1905-
[FI, FC, ITA]
American actor
* Lake, Arthur

**Silverlake, Florence** 1905?-1980
American actress
* Lake, Florence

**Silverman, Belle Miriam** 1929-
[BBD, IPA, OP]
American opera singer
* Bubbles
* Sills, Beverly
* Silvery Bells

**Silverman, Fred** 1938?-
American television executive
* [The] Man with the Golden Gut

**Silverman, George** 20th c.   [EJS]
American basketball coach
* Silverman, Red

**Silverman, Harriet** ?-1975   [TR]
Columnist
* Silverman, Hattie

**Silverman, Hattie**
See Silverman, Harriet

**Silverman, Jesse Ormand** 1888-
[BE]
American baseball player
* Baker, Jesse Ormand

**Silverman, Red**
See Silverman, George

**Silverman, Rose**
See Millstein, Rose Silverman

**Silverpen**
See Meteyard, Eliza

**Silvers, Phil**
See Silversmith, Philip

**Silversmith, Philip** 1911?-
[BEW, IPA, SW]
*American actor*
* Silvers, Phil

**Silverstein, Alvin** 1933- [CA, SAT]
*American biologist, author,*
*columnist*
* Dr. A

**Silverstein, Benjamin Irving** 1919-
[BEW]
*American union executive*
* Irving, Ben

**Silverstein, Bullet Joe**
See Silverstein, Joseph L.

**Silverstein, Jennie** 1868?-1953
[BEW]
*Rumanian-born actress*
* Moscowitz, Jennie

**Silverstein, Joseph L.** 1898-1950
[EJS]
*American football player*
* Silverstein, Bullet Joe

**Silverstein, Ralph S.** 20th c. [EJS]
*American wrestler*
* Silverstein, Ruffy

**Silverstein, Ruffy**
See Silverstein, Ralph S.

**Silverstone, Alan** 1942?-
*American business executive*
* Uncle Al

**Silverstone, Jonas T.**
See Silverstone, Thomas

**Silverstone, Thomas** 1906- [BEW]
*American attorney and producer*
* Silverstone, Jonas T.

**Silvery Bells**
See Silverman, Belle Miriam

**Silvester, Frank**
See Bingley, David Ernest

**Silvestri, Hawk**
See Silvestri, Kenneth Joseph

**Silvestri, Kenneth Joseph** 1916-
[BE]
*American baseball player*
* Silvestri, Hawk

**Silveti, Juan** 1891-1956 [GS]
*Mexican bullfighter*
* [El] Tigre de Guanajuato [The
Tiger from Guanajuato]

**Silvette, Herbert** 1907- [AW]
*American author*
* Dogbolt, Barnaby

**Silvia, Charles** 20th c. [BBH]
*American swimmer and coach*
* Silvia, Red

**Silvia, Red**
See Silvia, Charles

**Silvius [or Sylvius], Aeneas**
See De Piccolomini, Enea Silvio

**Sim, Georges**
See Simenon, Georges [Joseph
Christian]

**Sim, Katharine [Thomasset]** 1913-
[CA, WW]
*British author*
* Nuraini

**Simalo**
See Loinger, Silvia Mary

**Siman, E. E., Jr.** 1921- [FCW]
*American music publisher, talent*
*scout, radio and recording executive*
* Siman, Si

**Siman, Si**
See Siman, E. E., Jr.

**Simbeaux, L. L.**
See Sellers, Connie Leslie, Jr.

**Simenon, Georges [Joseph Christian]**
1903- [CA, EMD, LC]
*Belgian author*
* Bobette
* Brulls, Christian
* D'Antibes, Germain
* Dersonnes, Jacques
* D'Isly, Georges
* Dorsan, Luc
* Dorsange, Jean
* Dossage, Jean
* Du Perry, Jean
* Georges, Georges Martin
* Gut, Gom
* Kim
* Plick et Plock
* Sim, Georges
* Vialis, Gaston
* Violis, G.

**Simeon, Omer** 1902- [MY]
*American jazz musician*
* Simeon, Simmie

**Simeon, Simmie**
See Simeon, Omer

**Simmonds, Michael Charles [Mike]**
1934- [AW]
*British author and journalist*
* Essex, Frank

**Simmons, Al**
See Szymanski, Aloysius Harry

**Simmons, Antennae Jimmy**
See Simmons, Jimmy

**Simmons, Blake**
See Wallmann, Jeffrey M[iner]

**Simmons, Bucketfoot Al**
See Szymanski, Aloysius Harry

**Simmons, Catherine**
See Duncan, Kathleen Mary

**Simmons, Cobra**
See Simmons, Gary

**Simmons, Daniel** 1891-1966 [SC]
*American actor*
* Yowlachie, Chief

**Simmons, David**
See Gold, Alan R[obert]

**Simmons, Dawn Langley**
See Hall, Gordon Langley

**Simmons, Flat Jack**
See Simmons, Jack

**Simmons, Gary** 1944- [SMG]
*Canadian-born hockey player*
* Simmons, Cobra

**Simmons, George Washington**
1885-1942 [BE]
*American baseball player*
* Simmons, Hack

**Simmons, Hack**
See Simmons, George Washington

**Simmons, Hi**
See Simmons, John

**Simmons, Huey** 1933- [EJ7]
*American jazz musician*
* Simmons, Sonny

**Simmons, Jack** 1941- [DC]
*British cricketer*
* Simmons, Flat Jack
* Simmons, Simmo

**Simmons, James** 1850-1923
[BMH, THR]
*British actor and comic singer*
* Fawn, James
* [The] Prince of Red-Nosed
Comedians

**Simmons, Jimmy** 20th c. [RM]
*Musician*
* Simmons, Antennae Jimmy

**Simmons, John** [BBH]
*American baseball coach*
* Simmons, Hi

**Simmons, Kim**
See Duncan, Kathleen Mary

**Simmons, Little Mack**
See Simmons, Mack

**Simmons, Lonnie**
See Simmons, Samuel

**Simmons, Mac**
See Simmons, Mack

**Simmons, Mack** 1934- [BWW]
*American singer*
* St. Louis Mac
* Simmons, Little Mack
* Simmons, Mac
* Sims, Mac

**Simmons, Malcolm Early** 1935-
[SMG]
*American baseball player*
* Simmons, Max

**Simmons, Max**
See Simmons, Malcolm Early

**Simmons, Pat[rick Clement]**
See Simoni, Patrick Clement

**Simmons, S. H.**
See Simmons, Sylvia

**Simmons, Samuel** 1915?- [WWJ]
*American jazz musician*
* Simmons, Lonnie

**Simmons, Simba**
See Simmons, Ted Lyle

**Simmons, Simmo**
See Simmons, Jack

**Simmons, Sonny**
See Simmons, Huey

**Simmons, Sylvia** 20th c. [CA]
*American advertising executive and*
*author*
* Simmons, S. H.

**Simmons, Ted Lyle** 1949- [SMG]
*American baseball player*
* Simmons, Simba

**Simmons, Thomas** ?-1808 [FFF]
*British murderer*
* [The] Man of Blood

**Simmons, William E.** 1850- ? [PA]
*Author*
* W. E. S.

**Simms, Ginny**
See Sims, Virginia

**Simms, Hilda**
See Moses, Hilda Theresa

**Simms, William Gilmore**
1806-1870 [FFF, PA]
*American author*
* Cooper, Frank
* Isabel
* Rivers, Guy

**Simms, Yvonne** 1928- [AW]
*British author and journalist*
* Simon

**Simon** [joint pseudonym with Roger
D'Este Burford]
See Blakeston, Oswell

**Simon** [joint pseudonym with Oswell
Blakeston]
See Burford, Roger D'Este

**Simon**
See Simms, Yvonne

**Simon** ?- 67? [DEP, DNNF]
*Saint*
* Cephas
* Peter
* [The] Prince of the Apostles

**Simon, Abraham** 1897-1957 [PMJ]
*American bandleader*
* Lyman, Abe

**Simon, Billy**
See Simon, Violet E.

**Simon, Charlie May**
See Fletcher, Charlie May Hogue

**Simon, Cully**
See Simon, John Cullen

**Simon, Doc**
See Simon, Neil

**Simon, Francois** 1895-1975
[BDF, F2, FC]
*Swiss-born actor*
* Simon, Michel

**Simon, Gus** 1881-1945 [SC]
*German-born actor, songwriter,*
*producer*
* Edwards, Gus

**Simon, Inge** 1921- [OP]
*German-born opera singer*
* Borkh, Inge

**Simon, Joe** 1947- [IBW]
*African singer and record producer*
* Chokin' Kind

**Simon, John**
See Simon, Jovan Ivan

**Simon, John Cullen** 1918- [CEI]
*Canadian-born hockey player*
* Simon, Cully

**Simon, Joseph Philippe** 1803-1891
[WBD]
*French comedian and playwright*
* Lockroy, Joseph Philippe

**Simon, Jovan Ivan** 1925- [BEW]
*Yugoslav-born theatre critic*
* Simon, John

**Simon, Jules**
See Suisse, J. F. S.

**Simon, Kenneth**
See Goldgraber, Kenneth

**Simon, Lionel** 1922- [CA]
*American author and publisher*
* Stuart, Lyle

**Simon, Mae** 20th c. [FIR]
*American actress*
* [The] Yiddish Sarah Bernhardt

**Simon, Michel**
*See* Simon, Francois

**Simon, Mina Lewiton** 1904-1970
[CAP, SAT]
*American author and educator*
* Lewiton, Mina

**Simon, Neil** 1927- [AN]
*American playwright*
* Simon, Doc

**Simon of Sudbury**
*See* Theobald [or Tybald], Simon

**Simon, Paul Frederick** 1941-
[RO2]
*American singer and songwriter*
* Landis, Jerry

**Simon, Pazuza**
*See* Simon, Stafford

**Simon, Richard** 1638-1712 [SN]
*French theologian*
* [The] Father of German Exegesis

**Simon, Robert**
*See* Musto, Barry

**Simon, Robert Alfred** 1897- [WW]
*Author*
* Reynolds, Liggett

**Simon, S. J.**
*See* Skidelsky, Simon Jasha

**Simon, Stafford** 1908?-1960
[WWJ]
*American jazz musician*
* Simon, Pazuza

**Simon, Sven**
*See* Springer, Axel, Jr.

**Simon the Righteous**
*See* Montfort, Simon de [Earl of Leicester]

**Simon, Violet E.** 20th c. [BBH]
*American bowler*
* Simon, Billy

**Simonds, William** 1822-1859
[FFF]
*American author*
* Aimwell, Walter

**Simone**
*See* Benda, Pauline

**Simone, Andre**
*See* Katz, Otto

**Simone, Nina**
*See* Waymon, Eunice Kathleen

**Simonelli, Giovanni** 20th c. [WF]
*Italian screenwriter*
* O'Neil, Simon

**Simonetta**
*See* Di Cesaro, Simonetta

**Simoni, Patrick Clement**
1908-1968 [BE]
*American baseball player*
* Simmons, Pat[rick Clement]

**Simonides** 7th c. BC [DEP, SN]
*Greek poet*
* [The] Samian Poet

**Simonides** 6th c. BC
[DNNS, RH, SN]
*Greek poet*
* [The] Cean Poet
* [The] Scian Muse

**Simonillo [Little Simon]**
*See* Rodriguez Valades, Jesus

**Simonim, Wilhelmina Josephine**
[PA]
*Author*
* Haller, Gustave

**Simons, Arthur D.** 1919?-1979
*American army officer*
* [The] Bull

**Simons, Butch**
*See* Simons, Melbern Ellis

**Simons, Claude, Jr.** 1914-1975
[B10, FB]
*American football player and coach*
* Simons, Monk

**Simons, Katherine Drayton Mayrant**
1892- [CA]
*American author and poet*
* Mayrant, Drayton
* Maysi, Kadra

**Simons, Melbern Ellis** 1900-1974
[BE]
*American baseball player*
* Simons, Butch

**Simons, Monk**
*See* Simons, Claude, Jr.

**Simons, Roger** [joint pseudonym with Margaret Punnett]
*See* Punnett, Ivar

**Simons, Roger** [joint pseudonym with Ivar Punnett]
*See* Punnett, Margaret

**Simonson, Mary Jane**
*See* Wheeler, Mary Jane

**Simoun, Henri**
*See* Rodman, Howard

**Simpkin**
*See* Webb, Arthur Patterson

**[The] Simple**
*See* Charles III

**[The] Simple**
*See* Frederick III

**[The] Simple**
*See* Sigismund

**[The] Simple Lombard**
*See* Di Castel, Guido

**Simpson, Adele**
*See* Smithline, Adele

**Simpson [or Sampson?], Agnes** 16th
c. [DNNF]
*Scottish woman executed for witchcraft*
* [The] Wise Wife of Keith

**Simpson, Archibald** [PA]
*Author*
* Shimi, Mac

**Simpson, Bertram Lennox** 1877- ?
[WWL]
*Author*
* Weale, B. L. Putnam

**Simpson, Bullet Joe**
*See* Simpson, Harold Joseph

**Simpson, Cass**
*See* Simpson, Cassino

**Simpson, Cassino** 1902- [MY]
*Italian-born jazz musician*
* Simpson, Cass

**Simpson, Clarence** 1915?- [B10]
*American basketball coach*
* Simpson, Snowy

**Simpson, Duke**
*See* Simpson, Thomas Leo

**Simpson, Edith Eva** 1902- [IAW]
*American poet*
* Felton, Eve

**Simpson, Edward** 19th c.
[DNNS, FFF, RH]
*Sold spurious flint arrowheads*
* Flint Jack

**Simpson, Evan** 1901-1953 [BEW]
*British-born actor, playwright, director*
* John, Evan

**Simpson, Evangeline M.** 19th c.
[FFF]
*Author*
* Saxon, Van

**Simpson, Harold Joseph** ?-1973
[BBH]
*Canadian-born hockey player*
* Simpson, Bullet Joe

**Simpson, Harry Leon** 1925- [BE]
*American baseball player*
* Simpson, Suitcase

**Simpson, Helen [de Guerry]**
*See* Browne, Helen de Guerry Simpson

**Simpson, Jane [Cross]** 1804- ?
[FFF]
*British poet*
* Gertrude

**Simpson, Jane** 1881-1935 [BEW]
*American actress*
* Wheatley, Jane

**Simpson, John Hampson** 20th c.
[WWL]
*British author*
* Hampson, John

**Simpson, Joseph** 20th c. [CME]
*American country-western performer*
* Simpson, Red

**Simpson, Louis** 1923- [CW]
*Jamaican-born poet*
* Marontz, Louis Aston

**Simpson, Mike**
*See* Simpson, Mitchell Louis

**Simpson, Mitchell Louis** 1916-
[MY]
*American jazz musician*
* Simpson, Mike

**Simpson, Myrtle L[illias]** 1931-
[CA]
*British author*
* Emslie, M. L.

**Simpson, N. F.**
*See* Simpson, Norman Frederick

**Simpson, Norma** 1926- [FC]
*British actress*
* Marsh, Carol

**Simpson, Norman Frederick** 1919-
[BEW]
*British playwright*
* Simpson, N. F.

**Simpson, O. J.**
*See* Simpson, Orenthal James

**Simpson, Orenthal James** 1947-
[FB, IPA, SMG]
*American football player*
* Juice
* Orange Juice
* Simpson, O. J.

**Simpson, Ralph** 1949-
*American basketball player*
* Simpson, Simp

**Simpson, Red**
*See* Simpson, Joseph

**Simpson, Ruth Mary Rasey** 1902-
[CA]
*American author and poet*
* Rasey, Ruth M.

**Simpson, Ryllis Barnes**
1899?-1978 [FIR]
*Dancer*
* Hasoutra

**Simpson, Shotgun**
*See* Simpson, Tom

**Simpson, Simp**
*See* Simpson, Ralph

**Simpson, Snowy**
*See* Simpson, Clarence

**Simpson, Stephen** 1789-1854 [PA]
*Author*
* Brutus

**Simpson, Suitcase**
*See* Simpson, Harry Leon

**Simpson, Thomas Leo** 1927- [BE]
*American baseball player*
* Simpson, Duke

**Simpson, Tom** 1952- [SMG]
*Canadian-born hockey player*
* Simpson, Shotgun

**Simpson, William** 20th c.
[ESF, SFL, WGT]
*American author*
* Blot, Thomas

**Sims, Clarence** 1891-1968 [BE]
*American baseball player*
* Sims, Pete

**Sims, D. N.**
*See* Sims, Denise Natalie

**Sims, Denise Natalie** 1940- [SFL]
*British author*
* Sims, D. N.

**Sims, Duane B.** 1941-
[BE, PB, SMG]
*American baseball player*
* Sims, Duke

**Sims, Duke**
*See* Sims, Duane B.

**Sims, George Robert** 1847-1922
[FFF, RH, WBD]
*British journalist and playwright*
* Dagonet

**Sims, Henry R.** 1893- [NAA]
*American editor and politician*
* Radcliffe, Henry

**Sims, John Haley [Jack]** 1925-
[DAM, EJ, PMJ]
*American jazz musician*
* Sims, Zoot

**Sims, Mac**
*See* Simmons, Mack

**Sims, Pete**
*See* Sims, Clarence

**Sims, Peter** 1938-   [EJ]
*American jazz musician*
* La Roca, Pete

**Sims, Virginia** 1916-   [FC]
*American singer*
* Simms, Ginny

**Sims, Zoot**
*See* Sims, John Haley [Jack]

**Sims-Errol, Leon** 1881-1951
[THR]
*Australian-born actor*
* Errol, Leon

**Simson, Eric Andrew** 1895-   [WW]
*Author*
* Kirk, Laurence

**Simson, Harold** 1878-1944   [THR]
*British composer*
* Fraser-Simson, Harold

**Simson, Lena Margaret**
1869?-1957   [NAA]
*British actress and author*
* Ashwell, Lena

**Sina, Sandy**
*See* Messina, Santo

**Sinatra, Francis Albert [Frank]**
1915?-   [NN]
*American singer and actor*
* [The] Chairman of the Board
* [The] Gov'nor
* Ol' Blue Eyes

**Sinbad**
*See* Dingle, Aylward Edward

**Sinbad the Tailor**
*See* Shinwell, Emmanuel

**Sinbaldi, Fosco**
*See* Kacew, Romain

**Sinbeth, Lesly**
*See* Bennis, Wessel Johannes

**Sinclair, Alasdair**
*See* Clyne, Douglas George Wilson

**Sinclair, Arthur**
*See* McDonnell, Arthur

**Sinclair, Bertha M[uzzy]**
1874-1940   [WGT]
*Author*
* Bower, B. M.

**Sinclair, Carrie Bell**   [FFF]
*American poet*
* Clara

**Sinclair, Clarence**
*See* Forshaw, Charles Frederick

**Sinclair, Duncan**
*See* Dunnett, Alastair MacTavish

**Sinclair, Edith**
*See* Favor, Mrs. Edward M.

**Sinclair, Emil**
*See* Hesse, Hermann

**Sinclair, Gavin**
*See* MacArthur, D[avid] Wilson

**Sinclair, Grace**
*See* Wallmann, Jeffrey M[iner]

**Sinclair, Heather**
*See* Johnston, William

**Sinclair, Ian**
*See* Foley, [Cedric] John

**Sinclair, James**
*See* Staples, Reginald Thomas

**Sinclair, Jo**
*See* Seid, Ruth

**Sinclair, Julian**
*See* Sinclair, Mary Amelia St. Clair

**Sinclair, Lottie**
*See* Kennedy, Mrs. Frank

**Sinclair, Mary**
*See* Cook, Mary

**Sinclair, Mary Amelia St. Clair**
1865?-1946   [TLC]
*British author and poet*
* Sinclair, Julian
* Sinclair, May

**Sinclair, May**
*See* Sinclair, Mary Amelia St. Clair

**Sinclair, Miranda** 1948-   [CA]
*British author*
* Seymour, Miranda

**Sinclair, Mrs. E. V.**   [FFF]
*Entertainer*
* Clifford, Maude

**Sinclair, Mrs. Harry**   [FFF]
*Entertainer*
* Vernon, Fanny

**Sinclair, Rose**
*See* Mendonca, Susan

**Sinclair, Upton [Beall]** 1878-1968
[CA, SAT]
*American author and politician*
* Fitch, Clarke
* Garrison, Frederick
* Stirling, Arthur

**Sinclair-Hill, Gerard Arthur**
1896-1945   [BEW]
*British director*
* Hill, Sinclair

**Sindall, B. R.**
*See* Sindall, Bernard Ralph

**Sindall, Bernard Ralph** 1925-
[ART]
*British sculptor*
* Sindall, B. R.

**Sinderby, Donald**
*See* Stephens, Donald Ryder

**Sine**
*See* Sinet, Maurice

**Sinet, Maurice** 1928-   [WEC]
*French cartoonist*
* Sine

**Sing-Sing**
*See* Singer, William Robert

**[Le] Singe de Racine**
*See* Campistron, Jean Galbert de

**Singer, Adam**
*See* Karp, David

**Singer, Al** 1907-1961   [EJS]
*American boxer*
* [The] Bronx Beauty

**Singer, Amanda**
*See* Brooks, Janice Young

**Singer, Bant**
*See* Shaw, Charles

**Singer, Bullet Bill**
*See* Singer, William Robert

**Singer, Burns**
*See* Singer, James Hyman

**Singer, Isaac Bashevis** 1904-
[CA, SAT]
*Polish-born American author*
* Bashevis, Isaac
* Warshofsky, Isaac

**Singer, James Hyman** 1928-1964
[B10]
*American poet and translator*
* Singer, Burns

**Singer, Jane Sherrod** 1917-
[CA, SAT]
*American author*
* Sherrod, Jane

**Singer, Kurt D[eutsch]**
*See* Deutsch, Kurt

**[The] Singer Throwing Machine**
*See* Singer, William Robert

**Singer, William Robert** 1944-
[BE, SMG]
*American baseball player*
* Billy No-No
* Sing-Sing
* Singer, Bullet Bill
* [The] Singer Throwing Machine

**Singh, Raj**
*See* Singh, Rajkumari

**Singh, Rajkumari** 1936?-   [CW]
*Guyanese poet and author*
* Singh, Raj

**Singin' Jack Smith**
*See* Smith, Jack

**Singin' Sam**
*See* Frankel, Harry

**[The] Singing Barber**
*See* Fairburn, Werly

**[The] Singing Brakeman**
*See* Rodgers, James Charles
[Jimmie]

**[The] Singing Christian**
*See* White, Josh[ua Daniel]

**[The] Singing Fisherman**
*See* Horton, Johnny

**[The] Singing Lady**
*See* Wicker, Ireene

**[The] Singing Nun**
*See* Deckers, Jeannine

**[The] Singing Pianist**
*See* Erby, John J.

**[The] Singing Pilgrim**
*See* Phillips, Philip

**[The] Singing Preacher**
*See* White, Booker T. Washington

**[The] Singing Ranger**
*See* Snow, Clarence Eugene

**Singing Sam Chatmon**
*See* Chatmon, Sam, Jr.

**Singing Sandie**
*See* Gordon, Alexander

**[The] Singing Sibyl**
*See* Victor, Metta Victoria Fuller

**[The] Singing Sweetheart of Canada**
*See* Murray, Anne

**[The] Singing Umpire**
*See* Byron, William

**Single Speech Hamilton**
*See* Hamilton, William Gerard

**[The] Singles King of Washington**
*See* O'Harro, Mike

**Singleton, Arthur James**
1898-1975   [DAM, EJ, PMJ]
*American jazz musician*
* Singleton, Zutty

**Singleton, Benjamin** 1809-1892
[IBW]
*American pioneer*
* Singleton, Pap

**Singleton, Bert Elmer** 1918-   [BE]
*American baseball player*
* Singleton, Smoky

**Singleton, Betty** 1910-   [CAP]
*British author*
* Reens, Mary
* Rutland, Dodge

**Singleton, Big**
*See* Singleton, Ron

**Singleton, John Edward** 1896-1937
[BE]
*American baseball player*
* Singleton, Sheriff

**Singleton, Mary, Spinster**
*See* Brooke, F.

**Singleton, Pap**
*See* Singleton, Benjamin

**Singleton, Penny**
*See* McNulty, Dorothy

**Singleton, Ron** 1952-   [SMG]
*American football player*
* Singleton, Big

**Singleton, Sheriff**
*See* Singleton, John Edward

**Singleton, Smoky**
*See* Singleton, Bert Elmer

**Singleton, Zutty**
*See* Singleton, Arthur James

**[The] Singular Doctor**
*See* Occam [or Ockham], William
of

**[The] Singular Senegalese**
*See* Phal, Louis

**Singularis, Doctor**
*See* Occam [or Ockham], William
of

**Siniavskii, Andrei Donatovich**
1925-   [B10]
*Russian author*
* Tertz, Abram

**Sini'letta, Vic**
*See* Smith, Victor A.

**Sinister Sal Maglie**
*See* Maglie, Salvatore Anthony

**Sinitsky, Ted** 1928-    [CA]
*American author*
* Sennett, Ted

**Sinjohn, John**
*See*  Galsworthy, John

**Sinjun**
*See*  John, Elizabeth Beaman

**Sinks, Rita Faye** 1944-    [CWG]
*American country-western performer*
* Faye, Rita

**Sinkwich, Fireball Frankie**
*See*  Sinkwich, Frank

**Sinkwich, Frank** 1920-    [FB]
*American football player*
* Sinkwich, Fireball Frankie

**Sinn, Mrs. William E.**    [FFF]
*Entertainer*
* Tanner, Cora

**Sinner Saved**
*See*  Huntington, William

**[The] Sinner's Friend**
*See*  Mathew, Theobald

**Sinno, Big Sal**
*See*  Sinno, Salvatore

**Sinno, Salvatore** 20th c.
*American underworld figure*
* Sinno, Big Sal

**Sinnott, Michael** 1880-1960
[BEW, F1, FC]
*Canadian-born director and
producer*
* [The] King of Comedy
* Sennett, Mack

**Sinoel**
*See*  Vies, Jen

**Sinuss, Z.**
*See*  Skujins, Zigmunds

**Siodmak, Curt**
*See*  Siodmak, Kurt

**Siodmak, Kurt** 1902-    [FD, FDG]
*German director*
* Siodmak, Curt

**Siodmak, Robert**
*See*  Siodmark, Robert

**Siodmark, Robert** 1900-1973    [SC]
*American-born actor, producer,
director*
* Siodmak, Robert

**Sipes, Leonard Raymond** 1930-
[CWG]
*American country-western performer*
* Collins, Tommy

**Sir, A.**
*See*  Sireborn, [Karl] Axel [Malte]

**Sir Bob**
*See*  Walpole, [Sir] Robert [First
Earl of Orford]

**Sir Charles**
*See*  Thompson, Charles Phillip

**Sir Douglas**
*See*  Sahm, Douglas Saldana

**Sir Len**
*See*  Slocombe, Philip Anthony

**Sir Richard**
*See*  Cooley, Duff C.

**Sir Timothy**
*See*  Keefe, Timothy John

**Sir Toby**
*See*  Sutton, Scott

**Sir Veto**
*See*  Johnson, Andrew

**Sir Walter**
*See*  Davis, Walter

**[The] Sir Walter Scott of Italy**
*See*  Ariosto, Lodovico

**Sireborn, [Karl] Axel [Malte]** 1915-
[IAW]
*Swedish author*
* Sir, A.

**Siren, V[ladimir]**
*See*  Nabokov, Vladimir
Vladimirovich

**Siri, Victor** 1615?-1685    [SN]
*Italian monk and historian*
* [The] Procopius of France

**Sirica, John Joseph** 1904-
*American jurist*
* Sirica, Maximum John

**Sirica, Maximum John**
*See*  Sirica, John Joseph

**Sirius**
*See*  Martyn, Edward

**Sirk, Douglas**
*See*  Sierck, Detlef

**Sirko, Marlon**
*See*  Siciliano, Mario

**Sirois, Jigger**
*See*  Sirois, Leon Duray

**Sirois, Leon Duray** 1935-    [EAR]
*American auto racer*
* Sirois, Jigger

**Sirone**
*See*  Jones, Norris

**Sirrom, Wes**
*See*  Weiss, Morris S[amuel]

**Sirveaux, Jules** 1882-1938    [OCF]
*French actor*
* Delphin

**Siseman, E. J.**
*See*  Siseman, Ernest James

**Siseman, Ernest James** 1920-
[ART]
*British painter*
* Siseman, E. J.

**Sisines**
*See*  Archelaus

**Sisler, George Harold** 1893-1973
[BE, DGS, PB]
*American baseball player*
* Sisler, Gorgeous George

**Sisler, Gorgeous George**
*See*  Sisler, George Harold

**Sissle, Noble** 20th c.    [BWW]
*American bandleader*
* Brown, Willie

**Sisson, C. J.**
*See*  Sisson, Charles Jasper

**Sisson, Charles Jasper** 1885-1966
[LC]
*British editor, author, educator*
* Sisson, C. J.

**Sisson, Jack** 18th c.    [IBW]
*American soldier*
* Sisson, Prince
* Watson, Guy

**Sisson, Prince**
*See*  Sisson, Jack

**Sister Dora**
*See*  Pattison, Dorothy Wyndlow

**[The] Sister of Shakespeare**
*See*  Baillie, Joanna

**Sisti, Sebastian Daniel** 1920-    [BE]
*American baseball player*
* Sisti, Sibby

**Sisti, Sibby**
*See*  Sisti, Sebastian Daniel

**Sistrunk, Otis** 1949-    [IBW]
*American football player*
* Sistrunk, Trunk

**Sistrunk, Trunk**
*See*  Sistrunk, Otis

**Sisyphus**
*See*  Barthelmes, [Albert] Wes[ley,
Jr.]

**Sitaramiah, Venkataramiah** 1899-
[IAW]
*Indian author, poet, playwright*
* Visee

**Sitko, Emil M.** 1923-1973    [FB]
*American football player*
* Sitko, Six Yards

**Sitko, Six Yards**
*See*  Sitko, Emil M.

**Sityana, Alfred Mama Sikhefu**
1907-    [IAW]
*South African author*
* Professor

**Sitzfleisch, Vladimir**
*See*  Spirer, Herbert F[rederick]

**Sivasankara Pillai, Thakazhi** 1912-
[IAW]
*Indian author*
* Thakazhi

**Sivertsen, Cort** 1622-1675    [WBD]
*Danish naval officer*
* Adelaer [or Adeler]

**Sivuca**
*See*  D'Oliviera, Severino

**Siward [Earl of Northumberland]**
?-1055    [WBD]
*Danish warrior*
* [The] Strong

**Six**
*See*  Potter, A. K.

**Six Yards Sitko**
*See*  Sitko, Emil M.

**Sixkiller, Alex** 1951-    [FB]
*American football player*
* Sixkiller, Sonny

**Sixkiller, Sonny**
*See*  Sixkiller, Alex

**Sixteen-String Jack**
*See*  Rann, John

**Sixtus IV**
*See*  Della Rovere, Francesco

**Sixtus V**
*See*  Peretti, Felice

**Sizemore, Chris[tine] Costner**
1927-    [CA]
*American author*
* Lancaster, Evelyn

**Sizemore, Jimmy** 1928-    [ECM]
*American country-western performer*
* Sizemore, Little Jimmy

**Sizemore, Little Jimmy**
*See*  Sizemore, Jimmy

**Sizemore, Pee Wee**
*See*  Sizemore, Ted Crawford

**Sizemore, Runt**
*See*  Sizemore, Ted Crawford

**Sizemore, Sizey**
*See*  Sizemore, Ted Crawford

**Sizemore, Ted Crawford** 1946-
[SMG]
*American baseball player*
* Sizemore, Pee Wee
* Sizemore, Runt
* Sizemore, Sizey

**Sjoberg, Lars-Erik** 1944-    [SMG]
*Swedish-born hockey player*
* Sjoberg, Shoe

**Sjoberg, Shoe**
*See*  Sjoberg, Lars-Erik

**Sjoeberg, Erik** 1794-1828
[DNNF, FFF, RH]
*Swedish poet*
* Vitalis

**Sjoeke, Eva** 1926-    [FC]
*Hungarian actress*
* Bartok, Eva

**Sjoestroem, Victor** 1879-1960
[BEW, FC, FD]
*Swedish actor and director*
* Seastrom, Victor

**Skaerbaek**
*See*  Fuechsel, Franz

**Skagen, Kiki** 1943-    [CA]
*American author*
* Munshi, Shehnaaz

**Skald**
*See*  Cray, Edward

**Skaldaspillir**
*See*  Eyvind Finnson

**Skalicki, Amirei**
*See*  Scheucher, Annemarie

**Skancke, Miriam Anne** 1879- ?
[THR]
*American actress*
* Nesbitt, Miriam Anne

**Skarbek, Krystyne** 1915?-1952
[B10]
*Polish underground leader during
World War II*
* Armand, Jacqueline
* Granville, Christine

**Skarstedt, Ernest Teofil** 1854- ?
[NAA]
*Swedish-born author*
* Sdt, E.

**[The] Skate**
*See*  Archibald, Nathaniel [Nate]

**Skawonius, Ses**
*See*  Skawonius, Sven Erik**

**Skawonius, Sven Erik** 20th c.
[ART]
*Swedish painter and theatre-set designer*
* Skawonius, Ses

**Skeat, W. W.**
See Skeat, Walter William

**Skeat, Walter William** 1834-1912
[LC]
*British philologist and author*
* Skeat, W. W.

**Skeels, Vernon H.** 1918- [ESF]
*American author and physician*
* Rossiter, Oscar

**Skeffington, Francis** 1878-1916
[DIL]
*Irish journalist*
* Sheehy-Skeffington, Francis

**Skeleton**
See Gicheru, Samuel Mwangi

**Skelley, Joseph Harold** 1891-
[THR]
*American actor*
* Skelly, Hal

**Skelly, Hal**
See Skelley, Joseph Harold

**Skelly, Madeleine** 1904- [BEW]
*American actress, producer, director*
* Skelly, Madge

**Skelly, Madge**
See Skelly, Madeleine

**Skelton, Herbert Sleath** 1870-1921
[BEW]
*Actor and producer*
* Sleath, Herbert

**Skelton, Jimmy** 1894?-1978 [FIR]
*Musician*
* [The] Old Man River

**Skelton, John** 1460?-1529
[DEL, PA, SN]
*British poet*
* [The] Inventive Skelton
* Oxoniae Poeta Laureatus
* [The] Poet Laureate of Oxford
* Shirley
* [The] Vicar of Hell

**Skelton, Red**
See Skelton, Richard Bernard

**Skelton, Richard Bernard** 1913-
[ASC, FC, IPA]
*American comedian and actor*
* Skelton, Red

**Skene, Anthony [Juan]**
See Philips, George Norman

**Skene, [Sir] John** 1540-1617 [FFF]
*Scottish advocate and writer*
* Philopoliteius

**Skerrett, Emma**
See McClannin, Mrs. R. F.

**Skerrett, Rose**
See Shewell, Mrs. L. R.

**Sketchley, Arthur**
See Rose, George

**Sketchley, Bud**
See Sketchley, Harry Clement

**Sketchley, Harry Clement** 1919-
[BE]
*Canadian-born baseball player*
* Sketchley, Bud

**[The] Ski Cat**
See Reed, Bob

**Ski, Mr.**
See Clair, John, Jr.

**Skiagraphos**
See Apollodorus

**Skibosh, Sky**
See Skibosh, Thomas A.

**Skibosh, Thomas A.** 20th c. [SMG]
*American baseball executive*
* Skibosh, Sky

**Skidelsky, Simon Jasha** 20th c.
[WW]
*Author*
* Simon, S. J.

**Skidmore, Harriet M.** [FFF, PA]
*American writer*
* Marie
* Ruhamah

**Skikne, Larushka Mischa**
1928-1973 [BDF, BEW, FC]
*Lithuanian-born actor*
* Harvey, Laurence

**Skillington, Nancy**
See Talbot, Nancy Wilfreda Hewitt

**Skillman, Ester Webster**
See Webster, Ester Luise

**Skin and Bone**
See Mahone, William

**Skingle, Kenneth Thomas** 1924-
[EJ]
*British jazz musician*
* Graham, Kenny

**[The] Skinless Prince of Wales**
See Richard II

**Skinner, Abby** 19th c. [FFF]
*American author*
* Aunt Abby

**Skinner, B. F.**
See Skinner, Burrhus Frederic

**Skinner, Burrhus Frederic** 1904-
[IPA]
*American psychologist*
* Skinner, B. F.

**Skinner, Camp**
See Skinner, Elisha Harrison

**Skinner, Charles M.** 1852- ? [PA]
*Author*
* Tramp

**Skinner, Conrad Arthur** 1889-
[WW]
*British author*
* Maurice, Michael

**Skinner, Dog**
See Skinner, Robert R.

**Skinner, Elisha Harrison**
1897-1944 [BE]
*American baseball player*
* Skinner, Camp

**Skinner, George** [PA]
*Author*
* Barnard, H. H.

**Skinner, I. G. M.** 1890- [DBA]
*British painter*
* Jacquier

**Skinner, J.** 1721- ? [PA]
*Author*
* [A] Layman

**Skinner, Jennifer** 1916-1962
[THR]
*British actress*
* Gray, Jennifer

**Skinner, June Margaret O'Grady**
1922- [AW, CA]
*Canadian author*
* O'Grady, Rohan

**Skinner, Robert R.** 1931- [PB]
*American baseball player and manager*
* Skinner, Dog

**Skinner, Salmon** 1818-1881 [PA]
*Author*
* Amigo

**Skip**
See Batton, Clyde

**Skipper, Betty**
See Barr, Betty

**Skippon, Philip** 17th c. [SN]
*British army officer*
* [The] Pious

**Skipworth, Alison**
See Groom, Alison

**Skirt, Buckley**
See Dress, Sue

**Skizas, Lou[is Peter]** 1932- [BE]
*American baseball player*
* [The] Nervous Greek

**Skladany, Joseph** 20th c. [BBH]
*American football player*
* Skladany, Muggsy

**Skladany, Muggsy**
See Skladany, Joseph

**Skobeleff, Michael Dimitrievitch**
1843-1882 [SN]
*Russian army officer*
* [The] Poet of the Sword

**Skoglund, Annika**
See Banfield, Britt Annika

**Skoog, Myer** 1926- [BB]
*American basketball player*
* Skoog, Whitey

**Skoog, Whitey**
See Skoog, Myer

**Skookum Chuck**
See Cumming, Robert Dalziel

**Skopec, Buckshot**
See Skopec, John S.

**Skopec, John S.** 1880-1912 [BE]
*American baseball player*
* Skopec, Buckshot

**Skorpios, Antares**
See Barlow, James William

**Skotkoenung [The Tax-King]**
See Olaf II [or Olaus]

**Skowron, Moose**
See Skowron, William Joseph, Jr.

**Skowron, William Joseph, Jr.**
1930- [BE, DGS, PB]
*American baseball player*
* Skowron, Moose

**Skrine, Agnes** 20th c. [WBD]
*Irish poet*
* O'Neill, Moira

**Skrine, Mary Nesta** 1905- [THR]
*Irish playwright and author*
* Farrell, M. J.

**Skrote, Z.**
See Skujins, Zigmunds

**Skryabin, Vyacheslav Mikhailovich**
1890- [CND, IPA]
*Russian diplomat*
* Dunker [code name used during World War II]
* Molotov, Vyacheslav Mikhailovich

**Skujins, Zigmunds** 1926- [IAW]
*Latvian author*
* Sinuss, Z.
* Skrote, Z.
* Zigis

**Skurdenis, Juliann V.**
See Skurdenis-Smircich, Juliann V[eronica]

**Skurdenis-Smircich, Juliann**
V[eronica] 1942- [CA]
*American author*
* Skurdenis, Juliann V.

**Skuse, Mrs.** [FFF]
*Entertainer*
* Whittingham, Mary

**Skvorecka, Zdena Salivarova** 1933-
[CA]
*Czech-born singer, actress, publisher*
* Salivarova, Zdena

**Sky Ball Moreno**
See Moreno, Thomas

**Skyland Scotty**
See Wiseman, Scott

**Skylar, Sunny**
See Schuyler, Sonny

**Slack**
See Passingham, Kenneth

**Slack, Slacky**
See Slack, Wilf[red Norris]

**Slack, Wilf[red Norris]** 1954- [DC]
*West Indian cricketer*
* Slack, Slacky

**Slade, Adam**
See Slade, Frank

**Slade, Bernard**
See Newbound, Bernard Slade

**Slade, Brownie**
See Slade, Eileen

**Slade, Eileen** 1920- [MY]
*American jazz musician*
* Slade, Brownie

**Slade, Frank** 1875- ? [DBA]
*British painter*
* Slade, Adam

**Slade, Gordon** 1904-1974 [BE]
*American baseball player*
* Slade, Oskie

**Slade, Gurney**
See Bartlett, Stephen

**Slade, Jack**
See Ballard, [Willis] Todhunter

**Slade, Oskie**
See  Slade, Gordon

**Sladek, John T[homas]** 1937-
[CA, ESF, WGT]
*American-born author*
* Demijohn, Thom [joint
　pseudonym with Thomas M.
　Disch]
* Knye, Cassandra [joint
　pseudonym with Thomas M.
　Disch]

**Sladen, Douglas** 20th c.　[WWL]
*British author*
* St. Barbe
* Wheelton, Brooke

**Sladen, Norman St. Barbe**  ?-1969
[CAP]
*British author and critic*
* Bullingham, Rodney
* Montclair, Dennis

**Slaettegard, Gunilla Lovisa**
See  Wallin, Gunilla Lovisa

**Slagle, James Franklin** 1873-1956
[BE, PB]
*American baseball player*
* [The] Human Mosquito
* Slagle, Rabbit
* Slagle, Shorty

**Slagle, Rabbit**
See  Slagle, James Franklin

**Slagle, Shorty**
See  Slagle, James Franklin

**Slaholt, Geswanouth** 1899-1981
[SW]
*Canadian-born actor*
* George, [Chief] Dan

**Slam, Sir**
See  Dawkins, Darryl

**[The] Slammer**
See  Snead, Sam[uel Jackson]

**Slammin Sam Snead**
See  Snead, Sam[uel Jackson]

**Slaney, George Wilson** 1884-
[AW, CAP, WW]
*British author*
* Woden, George
* Wouil, George

**Slapsie Maxie Rosenbloom**
See  Rosenbloom, Maxie

**Slate, John**
See  Fearn, John Russell

**Slater, Duke**
See  Slater, Frederick E.

**Slater, Elizabeth Anne**
See  Norton, Alice Whitson

**Slater, Ernest**  ?-1942
[SFL, WGT, WWL]
*British author*
* Gwynne, Paul

**Slater, Francis Carey** 1876-1958
[LC]
*South African author and poet*
* Van Avond, Jan

**Slater, Frederick E.** 1898-1966
[AS]
*American football player*
* Slater, Duke

**Slater, George** 1845- ?　[PA]
*Author*
* G. S.

**Slater, John Herbert** 20th c.
[WWL]
*British author*
* Secutor

**Slater, Nic**
See  Connolly, Charles M.

**Slater, Veronica**
See  Sullivan, Victoria

**Slatinaru, Maria**
See  Buzurin, Maria

**Slatoff, Stella B.**
See  Applebaum, Stella Balaban

**Slattery, James** 1948?-1974　[TR]
*Actor*
* Darling, Candy

**Slaughter, Barney**
See  Slaughter, Byron Atkins

**Slaughter, Byron Atkins**
1884-1961　[BE]
*American baseball player*
* Slaughter, Barney

**Slaughter, Country**
See  Slaughter, Enos Bradsher

**Slaughter, Elizabeth Blythe**
1893-1972　[F2, FC, SC]
*American actress*
* Blythe, Betty

**Slaughter, Enos Bradsher** 1916-
[B10, BE, PB]
*American baseball player*
* Slaughter, Country

**Slaughter, Frank G[ill]** 1908-
[CA, LC, WD]
*American author*
* Terry, C. V.

**Slaughter, Jean**
See  Doty, Jean Slaughter

**Slaughter, Marion T.** 1883-1948
[CME, CWG, PMJ]
*American country-western performer*
* Allen, Mack
* Ballard, Wolfe
* Calhoun, Jeff
* Carver, Al
* Dale, Vernon
* Dalhart, Vernon
* Evans, Frank
* Harris, Harry
* King, Fred
* Little, Tobe
* [The] Lone Star Ranger
* Massey, Guy
* McAfee, B.
* McAfee, Carlos
* Vernon, Bill
* Watson, Tom
* White, Bob

**Slaughter, N. Carter** 1885-1956
[BEW, FC]
*British actor and producer*
* Slaughter, Tod

**Slaughter, Tod**
See  Slaughter, N. Carter

**Slavic, Rosalind Welcher**
See  Welcher, Rosalind

**Slavitt, David Rytman** 1935-
[AW, CA, JL]
*American author, poet, translator*
* Robbins, Henry
* Sutton, Henry

**Slavutych, Yar**
See  Zhuchenko, Yar

**Slayback, Elbert** 1901-　[BE]
*American baseball player*
* Slayback, Scottie

**Slayback, Scottie**
See  Slayback, Elbert

**Slayback, Sly**
See  Slayback, William Grover

**Slayback, William Grover** 1948-
[SMG]
*American baseball player*
* Slayback, Sly

**[The] Slayer of the Bulgarians
[Bulgaroctonus]**
See  Basil II

**Slayton, Deke**
See  Slayton, Donald Kent

**Slayton, Donald Kent** 1924-
[B10, IPA]
*American astronaut*
* Slayton, Deke

**Slayton, Foster Herbert** 1902-　[BE]
*American baseball player*
* Slayton, Steve

**Slayton, Steve**
See  Slayton, Foster Herbert

**Sleath, Herbert**
See  Skelton, Herbert Sleath

**Sleen, Marc**
See  Neels, Marc

**Sleep, Michael William** 1955-
[SMG]
*Canadian-born hockey player*
* Sleep, Sleeper
* Sleep, Zee

**Sleep 'n Eat**
See  Best, Willie

**Sleep, Sleeper**
See  Sleep, Michael William

**Sleep, Zee**
See  Sleep, Michael William

**Sleeper, John Sherburne** 1794- ?
[PA]
*Author*
* Martingale, Hawser

**Sleepy Bill Burns**
See  Burns, William Thomas

**Sleepy Bill Johnson**
See  Johnson, William T.

**Sleepy Jim Crowley**
See  Crowley, James H.

**Sleepy John Estes**
See  Estes, John Adams

**Sleidan [or Sleidanus], John**
See  Philippi [or Philippson?]

**Slender, Robert**
See  Freneau, Philip Morin

**Slesar, Henry** 1927-
[CA, ESF, WW]
*American author*
* Harson, Sley [joint pseudonym
　with Harlan (Jay) Ellison]
* Leslie, O. H.
* Street, Jay

**Slick, Colonel**
See  Tittle, Yelberton Abraham

**Slick, Samuel**
See  Haliburton, Thomas Chandler

**Slidell, Alexander** 1803-1848
[PA, WBD]
*American naval officer*
* Mackenzie, Alexander Slidell
* [A] Young American

**Sliding Billy Hamilton**
See  Hamilton, William Robert

**Slifka, Lewis** 1920-　[ASC]
*American musician*
* Spence, Lew

**Slight, John**
See  Pond, Wilf Pocklington

**Slim**
See  Gicheru, Samuel Mwangi

**Slim Gray Gibson**
See  Gibson, Russell

**Slinger, Francisco** 1933?-　[CW]
*Trinidadian singer and poet*
* [The] Mighty Sparrow

**Slingin' Sammy Baugh**
See  Baugh, Samuel A.

**Slingsby, Jonathan Freke**
See  Waller, John Francis

**Slingsby, Philip**
See  Willis, Nathaniel Parker

**Slingsby, Rufus** [joint pseudonym
with Charles Siddle]
See  Peel, Frederick

**Slingsby, Rufus** [joint pseudonym
with Frederick Peel]
See  Siddle, Charles

**Slippers, Peggy**
See  Stevenson, Sara Yorke

**Sloan, Aloysius Martin** 1927-
[CEI, FHE, HK]
*Canadian-born hockey player*
* Sloan, Tod

**Sloan, [Adam] Bruce** 1914-　[BE]
*American baseball player*
* Sloan, Fatso

**Sloan, Fatso**
See  Sloan, [Adam] Bruce

**Sloan, George**　[FFF]
*Entertainer*
* Knight, George S.

**Sloan, J. Todhunter**
See  Sloan, James Forman

**Sloan, James Forman** 1874-1933
[AS, B10, BBH]
*American jockey*
* Sloan, J. Todhunter
* Sloan, Tod

**Sloan, Leni**
See  Sloan, Lenwood Ottis

**Sloan, Lenwood Ottis** 1948-   [IBW]
*American entertainer*
* Sloan, Leni

**Sloan, P. A.**
*See*  Sloan, Patrick Alan

**Sloan, Patrick Alan** 1908-   [WD]
*British economist and author*
* Sloan, P. A.

**Sloan, Stephen**
*See*  Solomon, Stephen

**Sloan, Tod**
*See*  Sloan, Aloysius Martin

**Sloan, Tod**
*See*  Sloan, James Forman

**Sloan, Tod**
*See*  Sloan, Yale Yeastman

**Sloan, Yale Yeastman** 1890-1956
[BE]
*American baseball player*
* Sloan, Tod

**Sloane, Olive** 1897?-1963   [THR]
*British actress*
* Baby Pearl

**Sloane, Sara**
*See*  Bloom, Ursula [Harvey]

**Sloat, Dwain Clifford** 1918-   [BE]
*American baseball player*
* Sloat, Lefty

**Sloat, Lefty**
*See*  Sloat, Dwain Clifford

**Sloathful Bill Lattimore**
*See*  Lattimore, William Hershel
[Bill]

**Slocombe, Philip Anthony** 1954-
[DC]
*British cricketer*
* Sir Len
* Slocombe, Slocs

**Slocombe, Slocs**
*See*  Slocombe, Philip Anthony

**Slocum, Hi**
*See*  Clemens, Samuel Langhorne

**Slodtz, Rene Michael** 1705-1764
[DEP, FFF, RH]
*French sculptor*
* [The] Michael Angelo of
  Sculptors

**Slokumb, Si**
*See*  Cheever, Henry P.

**Sloluck, J. Milton**
*See*  Bierce, Ambrose [Gwinett]

**Sloot, Marie** 1853- ?   [WWL]
*Dutch author*
* Melati Van Java

**Sloots, Patsy** 1929-   [FC]
*British actress*
* Shaw, Susan

**Slop, Doctor**
*See*  Stoddart, [Sir] John

**Sloper, Ally**
*See*  Ross, Charles Henry

**Sloper, Mace**
*See*  Leland, Charles Godfrey

**Slory, Michael** 1935-   [CW]
*Surinamese poet*
* Sangodare, Asjantenu

**Slosberg, Mike**
*See*  Slosberg, Myron

**Slosberg, Myron** 1934-   [CA]
*American author and advertising
executive*
* Slosberg, Mike

**Slotkin, Joseph**  ?-1929   [WGT]
*British author*
* Spie, Oliver?
* Tolz, Nick?

**Sloves, Herman** 1899-1957   [RBE]
*American boxer*
* [The] Bronx Bone-Crusher
* Murray, Johnny

**Slow Drag Pavageau**
*See*  Pavageau, Alcide

**Slow Joe Doyle**
*See*  Doyle, Judd Bruce

**Slow Kid Thompson**
*See*  Thompson, Ulysses

**Slow Trot**
*See*  Thomas, George Henry

**Slowitzky, Michael** 1893-1962
[ASC]
*American musician*
* Edwards, Michael

**Sluefoot Joe**
*See*  Gibson, Clifford

**[The] Sluggard**
*See*  Louis V

**Slumber, Baron**
*See*  Wodehouse, John

**Slung, Louis Sheaffer** 1912-   [CA]
*American author and journalist*
* Sheaffer, Louis

**Slusser, George Edgar** 1939-   [CA]
*American author*
* Anstey, Edgar

**Sly, Albert** 20th c.   [BLB]
*American train robber*
* Sly, Bertie

**Sly, Bertie**
*See*  Sly, Albert

**[The] Sly Fox**
*See*  Fox, Henry [First Baron
Holland]

**Slye, Leonard** 1912-
[CWG, FC, OCF]
*American actor and singer*
* [The] King of the Cowboys
* Rogers, Roy
* Weston, Dick

**Smadt, Jan** 1895-   [BE]
*American baseball player*
* Smith, John W.

**Small, Austin J.**  ?-1929
[ESF, SFL, WW]
*British author*
* Seamark

**[The] Small Beer Poet**
*See*  Fitzgerald, William Thomas

**Small, Blind Freddie**
*See*  Small, Freddie

**Small, Ernest**
*See*  Lent, Blair

**Small, Florence** 20th c.   [DBA]
*British painter*
* Hardy, Florence Deric

**Small, Freddie** 1898?-   [NOJ]
*American jazz musician*
* Small, Blind Freddie

**Small, George**   [FFF, PA]
*American author*
* Bricktop

**Small Light Throop**
*See*  Throop, Enos Thompson

**Small, Millie**
*See*  Smith, Millicent

**Small, Samuel White** 1851-1931
[FFF]
*American editor and clergyman*
* Old Si

**Small, William**
*See*  Eversley, David Edward
Charles

**Smallens, Alexander**
*See*  Smolensk, Alexander

**Smalley, George W.**   [PA]
*Author*
* G. W. S.

**Smalls, Cliff**
*See*  Smalls, Clifton Arnold

**Smalls, Clifton Arnold** 1918-   [EJ7]
*American jazz musician*
* Smalls, Cliff

**Smallwood, Jason**
*See*  Kisner, Jacob

**Smarrito**
*See*  Dati, Carlo Roberto

**Smart, Curly**
*See*  Smart, Wayne

**Smart, Wayne** 20th c.   [BBH]
*American harness racing trainer and
driver*
* Smart, Curly

**Smead, Mrs.**   [PA]
*Author*
* Fay

**Smeaton, Fred**
*See*  Cook, Fred Gordon

**Smeaton, Oliphant**
*See*  Smeaton, William Henry O.

**Smeaton, William Henry O.**
1856-1916   [WWL]
*Scottish author and journalist*
* Smeaton, Oliphant

**Smedley, Francis Edward [Frank]**
1818-1864   [DEL, FFF, RH]
*British author*
* Fairleigh, Frank
* Phiz, Francis

**Smedley, Menella Bute** 19th c.
[PA]
*Author*
* M. S.

**Smedsmo, Dale** 1951-   [SMG]
*American hockey player*
* Smedsmo, Smo

**Smedsmo, Smo**
*See*  Smedsmo, Dale

**Smeed, Frances**
*See*  Lasky, Jesse Louis, Jr.

**Smehoff, Aaron** 20th c.   [PHM]
*American underworld figure*
* Smiley, Allen

**Smejkal, Frank John** 1889-1950
[BE]
*American baseball player*
* Smykal, Frank John

**Smek**
*See*  Magnus II

**Smekalova, Hana** 1918-   [FC]
*Franco-Czech actress*
* Marly, Florence

**Smelfungus**
*See*  Alexander, Patrick Proctor

**Smelfungus**
*See*  Smollett, Tobias George

**Smidovich, Vikenti Vikentievich**
1867-1943   [WBD]
*Russian physician and author*
* Veresaev, Vikenti

**Smiff, O. P. Q. Philander**
*See*  Dowty, A. A.

**Smigly-Rydz, Edward**
*See*  Rydz, Edward

**Smik, Andrew J., Jr.** 1914-   [CWG]
*American country-western performer*
* Williams, Doc

**Smik, Jessie Wanda** 1919-   [CWG]
*American country-western performer*
* Williams, Chickie

**Smilansky, Moshe** 1874-1953
*Russian-born author*
* Mussa, Hawaja

**Smilansky, Yizhar**
*Israeli intelligence agent and author*
* Yizhar, S.

**Smiley, Allen**
*See*  Smehoff, Aaron

**Smiley, Arthur Lee, Jr.** 1925-1972
[DAM]
*American country-western performer*
* Smiley, Red

**Smiley, Charles Wesley** 1884-
[ALY]
*American author*
* Cascadananda, Anagaraca

**Smiley, Jim**
*See*  Spears, Raymond S[miley]

**Smiley, Red**
*See*  Smiley, Arthur Lee, Jr.

**Smiling Al Maul**
*See*  Maul, Albert Joseph

**Smiling Bill Donovan**
*See*  Donovan, William Edward

**Smiling Bill Parsons**
*See*  Parsons, William [Billy]

**Smiling Billy Mason**
*See*  Mason, William C.

**Smiling Bock Baker**
*See*  Baker, Charles

**[The] Smiling Cobra**
*See*  Aubrey, James T.

**Smiling Frank Farnum**
*See*  Smith, William

**[The] Smiling Irishman**
*See*  Murphy, James [Jimmy]

**[The] Smiling Irishman**
See O'Gwynn, James

**Smiling Jack McGrath**
See McGrath, John James

**Smiling Jimmy Sullivan**
See Sullivan, James A.

**Smiling Joe**
See Joseph, Pleasant

**Smiling Mickey Welch**
See Welch, Michael F.

**Smiling Slim Rogers**
See Planchet, Roger Anthony

**Smiling Stan Hack**
See Hack, Stanley Camfield

**Smith**
See Smith, Alice Maude

**Smith, A. De Herries** 1881- ?
[WWL]
*Canadian author*
* Finbar, Owen

**Smith, A. J. M.**
See Smith, Arthur James Marshall

**Smith, Ach**
See Smith, Anthony Charles

**Smith, Ada Beatrice Queen Victoria Louisa Virginia Du Conge** 1895-
[IBW]
*American entertainer*
* Smith, Brick Top

**Smith, Adam**
See Goodman, George J[erome] W[aldo]

**Smith, Adrian** 1936- [BB]
*American basketball player*
* Smith, Odie

**Smith, Al**
See Schmidt, Albert

**Smith, Al[fred Emanuel]** 1873-1944
*American politician*
* [The] Happy Warrior

**Smith, Al[phonse Eugene]** 1928-
[BE, PB]
*American baseball player*
* Smith, Fuzzy

**Smith, Al** 1945- [FHE]
*Canadian-born hockey player*
* Smith, Smitty

**Smith, Albert Richard** 1816-1860
[DNNS, PA, RH]
*British author and lecturer*
* Biddle, Jasper
* [The] Monarch of Mont Blanc

**Smith, Alexander**
See Adams, John

**Smith, Alexander Benjamin**
1871-1919 [BE, EJS]
*American baseball player*
* Smith, Broadway Aleck

**Smith, Alexis**
See Smith, Gladys

**Smith, Alf**
See Smith, Alfred E.

**Smith, Alfred Aloysius** 1861?-1931
[LC, TC, TC1]
*British author and adventurer*
* Horn, Alfred Aloysius
* Horn, Trader

**Smith, Alfred E.** 1873-1953 [FHE]
*Canadian-born hockey player*
* Smith, Alf

**Smith, Alice Maude** 1867- ?
[NAA]
*Canadian-born physician and playwright*
* Broome, Sutton
* Smith
* Smith, Scoville

**Smith, Allan E.** 20th c. [CND]
*Military leader*
* [The] Duke of Wonsan

**Smith, Alma** 1897-1931
[F1, F2, FC]
*American actress*
* Rubens, Alma

**Smith, Alvin K.** 1926- [BWW]
*American singer*
* King, Al

**Smith, Amos** 1871-1937
[BBH, BX, RBE]
*American boxer*
* Smith, Billy
* Smith, Mysterious Billy

**Smith, Andrew** 1836-1900 [WBD]
*British-born engineer and inventor*
* Hallidie, Andrew Smith

**Smith, Anne**
See Rainey, Gertrude Malissa Nix [Pridgett]

**Smith, Anne Mollegen** 1940- [CA]
*American editor and writer*
* Mollegen, Anne Rush

**Smith, Annie** [PA]
*Author*
* Herrin, Caller

**Smith, Anthony Charles** 1935-
[IAW]
*British author*
* Smith, Ach

**Smith, Arthur** 1921- [DAM]
*American bandleader and songwriter*
* Smith, Guitar Boogie

**Smith, Arthur** 20th c. [ECM, FCW]
*American country-western performer*
* Smith, Fiddlin' Arthur

**Smith, Arthur F.** [FFF]
*Entertainer*
* Arthur, Joseph

**Smith, Arthur James Marshall**
1902- [LC]
*Canadian-born author and educator*
* Smith, A. J. M.

**Smith, Arthur L.** 1942- [CA]
*American educator and author*
* Asante, Molefi K.

**Smith [or Schmet], Augustine**
See Gallitzin, Demetrius Augustine

**Smith, Babycakes**
See Smith, Jerry T.

**Smith, Baldy**
See Smith, William Farrar

**Smith, Barbara Herrnstein** 1932-
[CA, WD]
*American critic and editor*
* Herrnstein, Barbara

**Smith, Barbara Newman**
See Darrow, Alice Vicki

**Smith, Baron** 19th c. [PA]
*Author*
* Search, Warner Christian

**Smith, Beetle**
See Smith, Walter Bedell

**Smith, Bell**
See Piatt, Louise Kirby

**Smith, Bernard** 20th c. [MBF]
*British author and editor*
* Campbell, Harry
* Heath, Bernard
* Martyn, Ivor
* Smith, Jack
* Williams, Fred J.

**Smith, Bessie** 1894-1937 [BWW]
*American singer*
* [The] Empress of the Blues

**Smith, Billy**
See Smith, Amos

**Smith, Billy**
See Thomas, Will Madison

**Smith, Billy** 1903?-1963 [BEW]
*Theatrical performer*
* Smith, Little Billy

**Smith, Billy Ray** 1935- [FB]
*American football player*
* Smith, Black Rabbit

**Smith, Bingo**
See Smith, Bobby

**Smith, Black Rabbit**
See Smith, Billy Ray

**Smith, Blackjack**
See Smith, Harry E.

**Smith, Blue Smitty**
See Smith, Claude

**Smith, Boatswain**
See Smith, G. C.

**Smith, Bobby** 1946- [NBA, SMG]
*American basketball player*
* Smith, Bingo

**Smith, Bobus**
See Smith, Robert

**Smith, Boo**
See Smith, Bruce P.

**Smith, Brick Top**
See Smith, Ada Beatrice Queen Victoria Louisa Virginia Du Conge

**Smith, Bridges W.** [PA]
*Author*
* Ridges, R.

**Smith, Broadway Aleck**
See Smith, Alexander Benjamin

**Smith, Bruce P.** 1920-1967 [FB]
*American football player*
* Smith, Boo

**Smith, Bubba**
See Smith, Charles Aaron

**Smith, Bubba**
See Smith, George

**Smith, Bud**
See Smith, Wallace

**Smith, Buddy**
See Smith, Ivan

**Smith, Bull**
See Smith, Louis

**Smith, Bunty**
See Smith, Frances

**Smith, Buster**
See Smith, Henry

**Smith, C. Busby**
See Smith, John

**Smith, C. L.**
See Gascoigne, Mrs. C. L.

**Smith, C. Manby** 19th c. [PA]
*Author*
* Journeyman Printer

**Smith, C. Pritchard**
See Hoyt, Edwin P[almer], Jr.

**Smith, C. U.** 1901- [CA]
*American author and poet*
* Crowbate, Ophelia Mae

**Smith, C. W.** 19th c. [PA]
*Author*
* One Who is Really an Englishman

**Smith, Caesar**
See Dudley-Smith, Trevor

**Smith, Cal**
See Shofner, Grant Calvin

**Smith, Campbell Sherston** 1906-
[THR]
*British theatrical manager*
* Williams, Campbell

**Smith, Carl** 1908?- [WWJ]
*American jazz musician*
* Smith, Tatti

**Smith, Carlton**
See Rocklin, Ross Louis

**Smith, Carmichael**
See Linebarger, Paul M[yron] A[nthony]

**Smith, Carol Louise** 1935- [EJ7]
*American jazz musician*
* Kaye, Carol

**Smith, Caroline L.** [FFF, PA]
*American author*
* Aunt Carrie

**Smith, Catfish**
See Smith, Vernon

**Smith, Cecil [Howard, III]** 1917-
[CA]
*American columnist and playwright*
* Howard, Cecil

**Smith, Cedric** 20th c.
*American football player*
* Smith, Pat

**Smith, Charles** ?-1932? [MK]
*American baseball player*
* Smith, Chino

**Smith, Charles** 1900-1967 [SC]
*Scottish actor*
* Radcliffe, Jack

**Smith, Charles** 1908- [THR]
*British actor and singer*
* Mayhew, Charles

**Smith, Charles Aaron** 1945-
[FB, IPA, SMG]
*American football player*
* Smith, Bubba

**Smith, Charles Henry** 1826-1903
[FFF, PA, WBD]
*American author*
* Arp, Bill

**Smith, Charles J.** [FFF, PA]
*Writer*
* [The] Call Boy

**Smith, Charles Marvin** 1856-1927
[AS, BE]
*Canadian-born baseball player*
* Smith, Pop

**Smith, Charles Mitchell** 1855- ?
[NAA]
*American writer*
* Fowke, Gerard

**Smith, Charlotte** 1749-1806 [FFF]
*British author and poet*
* Deane, Kenner

**Smith, Cherry George** 1956- [IBW]
*American singer and songwriter*
* Lynn, Cheryl

**Smith, Chick**
See Smith, John William

**Smith, Chino**
See Smith, Charles

**Smith, Christopher Lyall** 1958-
[DC]
*South African cricketer*
* Smith, Kippy

**Smith, Christopher Martin**
See Forbes, Cabot L[owell]

**Smith, Cladys** 1908-
[DAM, EJ, PMJ]
*American jazz musician*
* Smith, Jabbo

**Smith, Clara** 1894?-1935 [BWW]
*American singer*
* Green, Violet
* [The] Queen of the Moaners
* Smith, Jolly Clara
* [The] World's Champion Moaner

**Smith, Clara Evelyn** 1886- [THR]
*British actress and singer*
* Evelyn, Clara

**Smith, Clarence** 1904-1929
[DAM, EJ, PMJ]
*American jazz musician*
* Smith, Pinetop

**Smith, Clarence Ossie** 1892-1924
[BE]
*American baseball player*
* Smith, Pop Boy

**Smith, Claude** 20th c. [BWW]
*American entertainer*
* Smith, Blue Smitty

**Smith, Claude M.** 20th c. [BBH]
*American collegiate athletic director*
* Smith, Tad

**Smith, Claudia Dell**
*Actress*
* Dell, Claudia

**Smith, Clay**
See Smith, Claydes

**Smith, Claydes** [RO2]
*American musician*
* Smith, Clay

**Smith, Clement Ogle** 19th c. [PA]
*Author*
* [A] Priest of the English Church

**Smith, Cleo**
See Smith, Cleopherus

**Smith, Cleo**
See Smith, Cleveland

**Smith, Cleopherus** 1953- [SMG]
*American baseball player*
* Smith, Cleo

**Smith, Cleveland** 20th c. [OBW]
*American baseball player*
* Smith, Cleo

**Smith, Clinton James** 1913-
[CEI, HK]
*Canadian-born hockey player*
* Smith, Snuffy

**Smith, Clipper**
See Smith, John

**Smith, Collie**
See Smith, O'Neill Gordon

**Smith, Columbia George**
See Smith, George Allen

**Smith, Constance**
See Smyth, Constance

**Smith, Constance [Connie]** 1941-
[FCW]
*American country-western performer*
* [The] Cinderella Girl of Country
  Music

**Smith, Constance Isabel** 1894-
[WW]
*Author*
* Reid, Eleanor

**Smith, Cordwainer**
See Linebarger, Paul M[yron]
A[nthony]

**Smith, Cotton Ed**
See Smith, Ellison DuRant

**Smith, Cura**
See Smith, Harold Raymond

**Smith, Cyril**
See Bruce-Smith, Cyril

**Smith, D. H.**
See Smith, David Henry

**Smith, David [Larmer]** 1899- [AW]
*Scottish author*
* Graham, Johnston

**Smith, David [Jeddie] [Dave]** 1942-
[CA]
*American author and poet*
* Cornwell, Smith

**Smith, David Henry** 1947- [ART]
*British artist*
* Smith, D. H.

**Smith, David MacLeod** 1920- [CA]
*Scottish author*
* Mariner, David

**Smith, David Mark** 1956- [DC]
*British cricketer*
* Smith, Smudger
* Smith, Smurf

**Smith, [Edgar] Dennis** 20th c.
[AW, WD]
*Author*
* Hathi

**Smith, Doc**
See Smith, Edward Elmer

**Smith, Dodie**
See Smith, Dorothy Gladys

**Smith, Don[ald A.]** 1946-
[BB, SMG]
*American basketball player*
* Abdul-Aziz, Zaid
* [The] Kangaroo

**Smith, Donald Robert** 1890-1973
[FC]
*American actor*
* Armstrong, Robert

**Smith, Donald Robin** 1942- [OP]
*Australian opera singer*
* Donald, Robin

**Smith, Doris** 20th c. [IBW]
*American fashion model*
* Smith, Toukie

**Smith, Dorothy**
*Actress*
* Dwan, Dorothy

**Smith, Dorothy [Stafford]** 1905-
[B10, CA, SAT]
*British author*
* Smith, Sarah Stafford

**Smith, Dorothy Gladys** 1896-
[CA, LC, WD]
*British author and playwright*
* Anthony, C. L.
* Percy, Charles Henry
* Smith, Dodie

**Smith, Dorothy June** 20th c. [ITA]
*American actress*
* Vincent, June

**Smith, Dorothy Loraine Blackburn**
[BEW]
*American actress*
* Blackburn, Dorothy

**Smith, Drifting**
See Mickle, Elmon

**Smith, Dutch**
See Smith, Harold

**Smith, E. E.**
See Smith, Edward Elmer

**Smith, Earl Sutton** 1897-
[BE, DGS, PB]
*American baseball player*
* Smith, Oil

**Smith, Edith Lillian**
See Webster, Edith Smith

**Smith, Edmund Neale** 1668-1710
[HN, SN]
*British poet*
* Rag, Captain
* Smith, Rag

**Smith, Edward Elmer** 1890-1965
[ESF, SF]
*American author*
* [The] Father of Space Opera
* Smith, Doc
* Smith, E. E.

**Smith, Edward Percy** 1891-1968
[BEW, LC]
*British playwright*
* Percy, Edward

**Smith, Eleanor** [FFF]
*Writer*
* Heatherbell

**Smith, Eleanor** 1875-1966 [SC]
*American actress*
* Lawson, Eleanor

**Smith, Elizabeth A.** 19th c. [PA]
*Author*
* Chester, Elizabeth S.
* [A] Clergyman's Daughter
* Honey Bee

**Smith, Elizabeth Bacheler** 20th c.
[BBH]
*American bicycling organization
founder*
* Smith, Isabel

**Smith, Elizabeth Thomasina [Meade]**
1854-1914 [CC, EMD, WW]
*British author*
* Meade, L[illie] T[homas]

**Smith, Ellison DuRant** 1864-1944
[WBD]
*American planter and politician*
* Smith, Cotton Ed

**Smith, Elmer Ellsworth** 1868-1945
[DGS, PB]
*American baseball player*
* Smith, Mike

**Smith, Elwood Hope** 1904- [BE]
*American baseball player*
* Smith, Mike

**Smith, Ernest Brammah**
1868?-1942 [EMD, LC, TC]
*British author*
* Bramah, Ernest

**Smith, Essex**
See Hope, [Frances] Essex
[Theodora]

**Smith, Evelyn E.** 1927- [SFL]
*Author*
* Lyons, Delphine C.

**Smith, F. R.** 1854- ? [WWL]
*British author*
* Ackworth, John

**Smith, Fannie N.** [PA]
*American author*
* Goldsmith, Christabel

**Smith, Farmer**
See Carten, Laura Paty

**Smith, Fenton**
See Pratt, Leonard E.

**Smith, Fiddlin' Arthur**
See Smith, Arthur

**Smith, Fireball**
See Smith, Theolic

**Smith, Florence Margaret**
1902-1971 [B10, CAP, LC]
*British author and poet*
* Smith, Stevie

**Smith, Floyd** 1917- [EJ]
*American jazz musician*
* Smith, Wonderful

**Smith, Ford**
See Friend, Oscar J[erome]

**Smith, Frances** 1912- [FC, SW]
*American actress and singer*
* Evans, Dale

**Smith, Frances** 1924- [EG]
*British golfer*
* Smith, Bunty

**Smith, Frances C[hristine]** 1904-
[CA, SAT]
*American author*
* Smith, Jean

**Smith, Frances Elizabeth** 1832?- ?
[FFF]
*American poet*
* Fales, Fanny

**Smith, Frances Scott [Fitzgerald]**
1921- [B10]
*Daughter of American author F.
Scott Fitzgerald*
* Smith, Scottie Fitzgerald

**Smith, Francis Shubael** 1819- ?
[PA]
*Author*
* Tenpin Boy

**Smith, Frank Elmer**
*See* Schmidt, Frank Elmer

**Smith, Frederick** 20th c. [CA]
*Musician*
* Sonic, Fred

**Smith, Frederick E[screet]** 1922-
[CA]
*British author*
* Farrell, David

**Smith, Frederick H.** 1889- [BE]
*American baseball player*
* Smith, Klondike

**Smith, Funny Papa**
*See* Smith, John T.

**Smith, Fuzzy**
*See* Smith, Al[phonse Eugene]

**Smith, G. C.** 1782-1863 [HN]
*Clergyman*
* Smith, Boatswain

**Smith, Gamaliel**
*See* Bentham, Jeremy

**Smith, Gentleman**
*See* Smith, William

**Smith, George** [FFF]
*"Plunger" on American racetrack*
* Pittsburg Phil

**Smith, George** 1924- [BWW, NBB]
*American singer*
* Allen, George
* Big Walter
* Harmonica King
* Hip Cat
* Little Walter Jr.
* Smith, Harmonica
* Smith, Little George

**Smith, George** 1945- [IBW]
*American football player*
* Smith, Bubba

**Smith, George Allen** 1892-1965
[BE]
*American baseball player*
* Smith, Columbia George

**Smith, George H[enry]** 1922-
[ESF, SFL, WGT]
*American author*
* Deer, M. J. [joint pseudonym with
    Mary J. Deer Smith]
* Hudson, Jan
* Jason, Jerry
* Smith, George Hudson
* Smith, Jan

**Smith, George Henry** 1871-1939
[BE]
*American baseball player*
* Smith, Heinie

**Smith, George Hudson**
*See* Smith, George H[enry]

**Smith, George J.** 1863-1927
[AS, BE]
*American baseball player*
* Smith, Germany

**Smith, George O[liver]** 1911-
[ESF, WGT]
*American author and engineer*
* Long, Wesley

**Smith, Gerald**
*See* Smith, Gerland Oliver

**Smith, Gerland Oliver** 1896-1974
[SC]
*British-born actor*
* Smith, Gerald

**Smith, Germany**
*See* Smith, George J.

**Smith, Gladys** 1921- [TR, WEF]
*Canadian-born actress*
* Smith, Alexis

**Smith, Gladys Mary** 1893-1979
[CU, FC, NN]
*Canadian-born actress*
* America's Sweetheart
* Nicholson, Dorothy
* Pickford, Mary
* [The] World's Sweetheart

**Smith, Goldwin** 1823-1910 [WWL]
*British-born historian and author*
* [The] Bystander

**Smith, Guitar Boogie**
*See* Smith, Arthur

**Smith, Gunboat**
*See* Smyth, Edward J.

**Smith, Guy**
*See* Erby, John J.

**Smith, H. W.**
*See* Goldschmidt, [Dr.] Hans

**Smith, Hal**
*See* Smith, James Harrell

**Smith, Hamilton**
*See* Rochester, George Ernest

**Smith, Hammond**
*See* Smith, John Robert

**Smith, Hap [or Happy]**
*See* Smith, Henry Joseph

**Smith, Harmonica**
*See* Smith, George

**Smith, Harold** 1874- ? [THR]
*British author and entertainer*
* Montague, Harold

**Smith, Harold** 1910- [WWJ]
*American jazz musician*
* Smith, Howard

**Smith, Harold** 20th c. [BBH]
*American diver*
* Smith, Dutch

**Smith, Harold J.**
*See* Fields, Ross Eugene

**Smith, Harold Raymond** 1931-
[BE]
*American baseball player*
* Smith, Cura

**Smith, Harry E.** 1918- [FB]
*American football player*
* Smith, Blackjack

**Smith, Heinie**
*See* Smith, George Henry

**Smith, Helen E.** [FFF, PA]
*American writer*
* Gale, Ethel

**Smith, Helen Zenna** 20th c.
[AW, WW]
*British playwright, author,
journalist*
* Price, Evadne

**Smith, Henry** 1550-1600
[FFF, RH]
*British clergyman*
* [The] Silver Tongued

**Smith, Henry** 1904-
[EJ, PMJ, WWJ]
*American jazz musician*
* Smith, Buster

**Smith, Henry Erskine** 20th c.
[NAA]
*American author and playwright*
* Rutgers, Lispenard

**Smith, Henry Joseph** 1883-1961
[BE]
*American baseball player*
* Smith, Hap [or Happy]

**Smith, Henry Welles** 1822-1881
[WBD]
*American attorney*
* Durant, Henry Fowle

**Smith, Herbert Huntington** 1851- ?
[ALY]
*American author*
* Huntington, H. S.

**Smith, Herbert O'Dell** 1915?-
*American stunt performer*
* O'Dell, Digger

**Smith, Hezekiah Leroy Gordon**
1909-1967 [ASC, DAM, EJ]
*American jazz musician*
* Smith, Stuff

**Smith, Hogan**
*See* Morgan, Allen D.

**Smith, Holland Metyeire**
1882-1967 [CND]
*American military leader*
* Smith, Howlin' Mad

**Smith, Honey Boy**
*See* Woodbridge, Hudson

**Smith, Hooley**
*See* Smith, Reginald Joseph

**Smith, Horace**
*See* Smith, Horatio

**Smith, Horatio** 1779-1849 [WBD]
*British poet*
* Chatfield, Paul, M.D.
* Smith, Horace

**Smith, Horton** 1908-1963 [GF]
*American golfer*
* [The] Joplin Ghost

**Smith, Howard**
*See* Smith, Harold

**Smith, Howard Van** 1910- [CA]
*American author*
* Sommers, David

**Smith, Howard Whitfield, Jr.**
1914- [BEW]
*American actor, stage manager,
director*
* Whitfield, Howard

**Smith, Howlin'**
*See* Smith, John T.

**Smith, Howlin' Mad**
*See* Smith, Holland Metyeire

**Smith, Huey** 1924- [RO1]
*American musician*
* Smith, Huey Piano

**Smith, Huey Piano**
*See* Smith, Huey

**Smith, Hugh Fangar**
*See* Fangareggi, Ugo

**Smith, Hurricane**
*See* Smith, Norman

**Smith, Iain Crichton** 1928-
[DLE, WOA]
*Scottish poet, author, playwright*
* Mac A'Ghobhainn, Iain
* Mac A'Ghobhainn, Seamus

**Smith, Ian** 1919-
*Rhodesian prime minister*
* Good Old Smitty
* Iron Man Ian

**Smith, Isabel**
*See* Smith, Elizabeth Bacheler

**Smith, Isadore Leighton Luce**
1901- [CA]
*American author*
* Leighton, Ann

**Smith, Ivan** 1919?-1981
*American country-western performer*
* Smith, Buddy

**Smith, J. D.** 20th c.
*American football player*
* [The] Wheatpicker

**Smith, J. T.**
*See* Smith, John T.

**Smith, Jabbo**
*See* Smith, Cladys

**Smith, Jack**
*See* Smith, Bernard

**Smith, Jack** 1896-1933
[BEW, F1, IPA]
*Canadian-born actor and producer*
* Pickford, Jack

**Smith, Jack** 1898-1950 [BEW, SC]
*American singer and actor*
* Smith, Whispering Jack
* [The] Whispering Baritone

**Smith, Jack** 20th c. [GW]
*American rodeo performer*
* Smith, Singin' Jack

**Smith, James**
*See* Mellilo, James

**Smith, James** 1887-1947 [BE]
*American baseball player*
* Bluejacket, James [Jim]

**Smith, James** 1935- [TR]
*British actor*
* Dale, Jim

**Smith, James** 20th c. [RM, RO2]
*American musician*
* Smith, Smitty

**Smith, James A.** 1876- ? [BE]
*American baseball player*
* Smith, Stub

**Smith, James Carlisle** 1890-1966
[AS, BE, PB]
*American baseball player*
* Smith, Red

**Smith, James Ellison** 1910-   [FC]
*American actor*
* Ellison, James

**Smith, James Harrell** 1923-   [CWG]
*American country-western performer*
* Smith, Hal

**Smith, James Marcus** 1938-   [RO2]
*American singer*
* Powers, Jet
* Proby, P. J.

**Smith, James Moore**   [SN]
* More, Phantom

**Smith, James Oscar [Jimmy]** 1926-
[IBW]
*American jazz musician*
* Jazz Organ, Mr.

**Smith, James Samuel** 1875- ?
[THR]
*British musician*
* Mendel

**Smith, Jan**
See   Smith, George H[enry]

**Smith, Jane**
See   Cox, Ida

**Smith, Jane Luella Dowd** 1847- ?
[NAA]
*American author*
* Lell, Jennie
* Ulla

**Smith, Jean**
See   Smith, Frances C[hristine]

**Smith, Jeff**
See   Jeffords, Jerome

**Smith, Jerome** 1895-   [NOJ]
*American jazz musician*
* Smith, Pork Chop

**Smith, Jerry Lee** 20th c.   [RO1]
*American musician and songwriter*
* Smith, Smoochee

**Smith, Jerry T.** 1943-   [FB]
*American football player*
* Smith, Babycakes
* Smith, Shane

**Smith, Jimmy Dee**
See   Smith, Pleasant

**Smith, Joe**
See   Persico, Salvatore Giuseppe

**Smith, Joe**
See   Seltzer, Joe

**Smith, John** [joint pseudonym with
Hoyt Hudson]
See   Herrick, Marvin Theodore

**Smith, John** [joint pseudonym with
Marvin Theodore Herrick]
See   Hudson, Hoyt

**Smith, John**
See   Lewis, John Delaware

**Smith, John**
See   Van Orden, Robert E.

**Smith [or Smyth?], John**
1570?-1612   [SN, WBD]
*British clergyman*
* [The] Father of English General
  Baptists

**Smith [or Smyth?], John** (Continued)
* [The] Se Baptist

**Smith, John** 1880?-1918   [NOJ]
*American jazz musician*
* Smith, Sugar Johnny

**Smith, John** 1924-   [AW, WD]
*British author, poet, playwright*
* Smith, C. Busby

**Smith, John** 20th c.   [BBH]
*American football player*
* Smith, Clipper

**Smith, John, Esq.**
See   Smith, Seba

**Smith, John Francis**
See   Gammon, John Francis

**Smith, John Joseph [Jack]**
See   Coffey, John Joseph

**Smith, John, Jr., of Arkansas**
See   Southworth, Sylvester S.

**Smith, John Robert** 1933-   [EJ7]
*American jazz musician*
* Hammond, Johnny
* Smith, Hammond

**Smith, John Stores**   [FFF]
*Author*
* Ackerlos, John

**Smith, John T.** 1890-   [BWW]
*American singer*
* Howlin' Wolf
* Smith, Funny Papa
* Smith, Howlin'
* Smith, J. T.

**Smith, John Thomas** 1766-1833
[FFF, RH, SN]
*British antiquary*
* Smith, Rainy Day

**Smith, John W.**
See   Smadt, Jan

**Smith, John William** 1892-1935
[BE]
*American baseball player*
* Smith, Chick

**Smith, Jolly Clara**
See   Smith, Clara

**Smith, Joseph**   [SN]
*British political organizer*
* [The] Sheepmaker

**Smith, Joseph**   [FFF]
*American naval officer*
* [The] Father of the Monitors

**Smith, Joseph Arthur** 1848-1906
[BEW]
*American playwright*
* Arthur, Joseph

**Smith, Joseph Edwards Adams**
[PA]
*Author*
* Greylock, Godfrey

**Smith, Kathryn Elizabeth [Kate]**
1908?-
*American singer*
* [The] Songbird of the South

**Smith, Kay Nolte** 1932-   [CA]
*American author and actress*
* Gillian, Kay

**Smith, Kenneth David** 1956-   [DC]
*British cricketer*
* Smith, Smithy

**Smith, Kester** 20th c.   [RM]
*Musician*
* Smith, Smitty

**Smith, King**
See   Louis Philippe

**Smith, King Edward, III** 1929-
[CWG]
*American country-western performer*
* Smith, Smitty

**Smith, Kippy**
See   Smith, Christopher Lyall

**Smith, Klondike**
See   Smith, Frederick H.

**Smith, L. D.**   [FFF]
*Author*
* Dog Whip

**Smith, L. H.** 1916-   [SFL, WGT]
*Author*
* Williams, Speedy

**Smith, Lafayette**
See   Higdon, Hal

**Smith, Larry** 20th c.   [RM]
*Musician*
* Smith, Legs Larry

**Smith, Laura Newton Rundless** 20th
c.   [IBW]
*American singer*
* Lee, Laura

**Smith, Lawrence E.** 1948-   [FB]
*American football player*
* Smith, Tody

**Smith, Lawrence Patrick** 1894-
[BE]
*American baseball player*
* Smith, Paddy

**Smith, Legs Larry**
See   Smith, Larry

**Smith, Lena [Kennedy]** 1914-   [CA]
*British author*
* Kennedy, Lena

**Smith, Leonard B.** 1915-   [ASC]
*American composer and conductor*
* Bingley, Richard
* Hemingway, Chas.
* Schubert, Emile H.

**Smith, LeRoi Tex** 1934-   [CA]
*American author*
* Ugama, LeRoi
* Welch, Charles Scott

**Smith, Lester** 1898-1952   [NOJ]
*American jazz musician*
* Smith, Monk

**Smith, Lew**
See   Floren, Lee

**Smith, Linell Nash** 1932-
[CA, SAT]
*American author and illustrator*
* Chenault, Nell
* Nash, Linell

**Smith, Little Billy**
See   Smith, Billy

**Smith, Little George**
See   Smith, George

**Smith, Lottie** 1895-1936
[BEW, F1, F2]
*Canadian-born actress*
* Pickford, Lottie

**Smith, Louis** 20th c.   [BE]
*American baseball player*
* Smith, Bull

**Smith, Lyle** 20th c.   [GW]
*American rodeo performer*
* Smith, Rom

**Smith, Mabel Louise** 1924-1972
[BWW, EJ]
*American singer*
* Big Maybelle
* Webster, Mamie

**Smith, Mac**
See   Smith, Macdonald

**Smith, Macdonald** 1880-1949   [GF]
*Scottish-born golfer*
* [The] Silent Scot
* Smith, Mac

**Smith, Mamie** 1883-1946   [BWW]
*American singer*
* [The] Queen of the Blues

**Smith, Mandy**
See   Landreaux, Elizabeth Mary

**Smith, Margaret**   [OP]
*British opera singer*
* Neville, Margaret

**Smith, Margaret** 1936?-   [EG, GF]
*American golfer*
* Smith, Wiffi

**Smith, Marguerite Alice Helene**
1875-1957   [BEW, CED]
*Belgian-born actress and opera
singer*
* Sylva, Marguerita

**Smith, Marion C.**   [PA]
*Author*
* Couthony, Marion

**Smith, Martin Cruz**
See   Smith, William Martin

**Smith, Marvin Harold** 1900-1961
[BE]
*American baseball player*
* Smith, Red

**Smith, Mary** 1918-   [AW, WD]
*British author*
* Drewery, Mary
* Radha

**Smith, Mary Ellen** 20th c.
[CA, SAT]
*American author*
* Smith, Mike

**Smith, Mary J. Deer** 20th c.
[WGT]
*American author*
* Deer, M. J. [joint pseudonym with
  George H(enry) Smith]

**Smith, Matthew**
See   Mordaunt, Charles [Third Earl
of Peterborough]

**Smith, Matthew Hale** 1810-1879
[FFF]
*American author and clergyman*
* Burleigh

**Smith, May Riley**   [PA]
*Author*
* M. L. R.

**Smith, Michael** 1939-   [CA]
*British psychologist and author*
* Apter, Michael J[ohn]

**Smith, Michael John** 1942-　[DC]
*British cricketer*
* Smith, Smudger

**Smith, Midget**
See　Smith, William Joseph

**Smith, Mike**
See　Smith, Elmer Ellsworth

**Smith, Mike**
See　Smith, Elwood Hope

**Smith, Mike**
See　Smith, Mary Ellen

**Smith, Millicent** 1946-　[RO2]
*Jamaican singer*
* Small, Millie

**Smith, Mr.**
See　Duleepsinhji, Kumar Shri

**Smith, Mona** 1909-　[FC]
*Australian-born actress*
* Barrie, Mona

**Smith, Monk**
See　Smith, Lester

**Smith, Mrs. Adolphe Jerrold**　[FFF]
*British writer*
* Corisande

**Smith, Mrs. Castle**　[PA]
*Author*
* Brenda

**Smith, Mrs. F. B.**　[PA]
*Author*
* Fanfan

**Smith, Mrs. John A.**　[PA]
*Author*
* Aunt Esther

**Smith, Mysterious Billy**
See　Smith, Amos

**Smith, Nancy** 1911-　[THR]
*Australian-born actress*
* O'Neil, Nancy

**Smith, Neil** 1949-　[DC]
*British cricketer*
* Smith, Sam
* Smith, Smudger

**Smith, Nig**
See　Schmidt, Frank Elmer

**Smith, Noland** 1943-　[FB]
*American football player*
* [The] Super Gnat

**Smith, Norma E[thel]** 20th c.
[NAA]
*Canadian author and poet*
* Bluenose

**Smith, Norman** 1923-　[RO2]
*British singer*
* Smith, Hurricane

**Smith, Norman Edward Mace**
1914-　[WD]
*British author*
* Sheraton, Neil
* Shore, Norman

**Smith, Norris** 1881-1969　[IBW]
*American-born actor and singer*
* [The] Boy Baritone

**Smith, O. C.**
See　Smith, Ocie Lee

**Smith, Ocie Lee** 1937-　[DAM]
*American singer*
* Smith, O. C.

**Smith, Odie**
See　Smith, Adrian

**Smith, Oil**
See　Smith, Earl Sutton

**Smith, Oliver Prince** 1894?-1978
*American military leader*
* [The] Professor

**Smith, O'Neill Gordon** 1933-1959
[EC]
*West Indian cricketer*
* Smith, Collie

**Smith, Ormond G.** 1860-1933
[WGT]
*American author*
* Carter, Nick [joint pseudonym
 with John Russell Coryell] [house
 pseudonym]

**Smith, Paddy**
See　Smith, Lawrence Patrick

**Smith, Pat**
See　Smith, Cedric

**Smith, Phenomenal**
See　Gammon, John Francis

**Smith, Pinetop**
See　Smith, Clarence

**Smith, Pinky**
See　Smith, Winthrop A.

**Smith, Pleasant** 1886-1969　[SC]
*American actor and wrestler*
* Pleasant, Tommy Lee
* Smith, Jimmy Dee

**Smith, Pop**
See　Smith, Charles Marvin

**Smith, Pop Boy**
See　Smith, Clarence Ossie

**Smith, Pops**
See　Smith, Russell T.

**Smith, Pork Chop**
See　Smith, Jerome

**Smith, Rabbi**
See　Smith, Thomas

**Smith, Rag**
See　Smith, Edmund Neale

**Smith, Rainy Day**
See　Smith, John Thomas

**Smith, Raymond Harley** 1945-
[IAW]
*American author*
* Del Norte, Scott

**Smith, Rebecca**
See　Lee, Rebecca Smith

**Smith, Red**
See　Smith, James Carlisle

**Smith, Red**
See　Smith, Marvin Harold

**Smith, Red**
See　Smith, Richard Paul

**Smith, Red**
See　Smith, Walter W[ellesley]

**Smith, Red**
See　Smith, Willard Jehu

**Smith, Reginald Joseph**
1903?-1963　[CEI, FHE, HK]
*Canadian-born hockey player*
* Smith, Hooley

**Smith, Richard Paul** 1904-　[BE]
*American baseball player*
* Smith, Red

**Smith, Richard Rein** 1930-　[CA]
*American author*
* Bond, Ray
* Castle, Damon
* Collins, Cindy
* Crossan, Darryl
* Davis, Cliff
* Davis, Jim
* Green, Robert
* Lane, Sherry
* Rein, Richard
* Reinsmith, Richard
* Stradley, Mark
* Taylor, Ann
* Taylor, Brad
* Tower, Diana
* Walters, Chad

**Smith, Riverboat**
See　Smith, Robert Walkup

**Smith, Robert**　[DNNF]
* Smith, Bobus

**Smith, Robert** 1914-　[AW]
*British author and journalist*
* Chattan, Robert

**Smith, Robert** 1938?-　[B10]
*American disk jockey*
* Wolfman Jack

**Smith, Robert A.** 1870?-1943
[BBH]
*American horse trainer*
* Smith, Whistling Bob

**Smith, Robert Charles** 1938-
[AW, CA]
*British author*
* Charles, Robert
* Leader, Charles

**Smith, Robert Dickie** 1928-　[IAW]
*American clergyman and author*
* Alexander, Justin

**Smith, Robert Edward** 1874- ?
[NAA]
*American author and clergyman*
* Brute, Q.

**Smith, Robert Gray** 1942-　[WEC]
*American cartoonist*
* Graysmith, Robert

**Smith, Robert Kimmel** 1930-
[CA, SAT]
*American author*
* Marks, Peter

**Smith, Robert Walkup** 1928-　[BE]
*American baseball player*
* Smith, Riverboat

**Smith, Robert Wilton** 1881-1957
[BMH]
*British comedian*
* Wilton, Robb

**Smith, Roger D.** 1936-　[FB]
*American football player*
* Smith, Zeke

**Smith, Rom**
See　Smith, Lyle

**Smith, Ron[ald] L[oran]** 1936-
[CA, WGT]
*American author*
* Loran, Martin [joint pseudonym
 with John Baxter]

**Smith, Ronald Gregor** 1913-1968
[CAP]
*Scottish author*
* Browne, Sam
* Maxwell, Ronald

**Smith, Ross** 1953-　[SMG]
*Canadian-born hockey player*
* Smith, Smitty

**Smith, Ross Alexander** 1907-1937
[BEW]
*American actor*
* Alexander, Ross

**Smith, Russell T.** 1890-1966
[WWJ]
*American jazz musician*
* Smith, Pops

**Smith, S. S.**
See　Williamson, Thames Ross

**Smith, Salvatore Giuseppe**
See　Persico, Salvatore Giuseppe

**Smith, Sam**
See　Smith, Neil

**Smith, Samuel** 1857- ?　[BE]
*American baseball player*
* Smith, Skyrocket

**Smith, Sarah** 1832-1911　[LC]
*British author*
* Stretton, Hesba

**Smith, Sarah Stafford**
See　Smith, Dorothy [Stafford]

**Smith, Scottie Fitzgerald**
See　Smith, Frances Scott
[Fitzgerald]

**Smith, Scoville**
See　Smith, Alice Maude

**Smith, Seba** 1792-1868
[FFF, PA, WBD]
*American author*
* Downing, [Major] Jack
* Smith, John, Esq.

**Smith, Shane**
See　Smith, Jerry T.

**Smith, Shelley**
See　Bodington, Nancy [Hermione]

**Smith, Sherrod Malone** 1891-1949
[AS, BE]
*American baseball player*
* Smith, Sherry

**Smith, Sherry**
See　Smith, Sherrod Malone

**Smith, Shirley M[ae]** 1923-　[CA]
*American author*
* Ovesen, Ellis

**Smith, Silent Tom**
See　Smith, Tom

**Smith, Singin' Jack**
See　Smith, Jack

**Smith, Skyrocket**
See　Smith, Samuel

**Smith, Smithy**
See　Smith, Kenneth David

Smith, Smitty
See   Smith, Al

Smith, Smitty
See   Smith, James

Smith, Smitty
See   Smith, Kester

Smith, Smitty
See   Smith, King Edward, III

Smith, Smitty
See   Smith, Ross

Smith, Smitty
See   Smith, William

Smith, Smitty
See   Smith, William John

Smith, Smoochee
See   Smith, Jerry Lee

Smith, Smudger
See   Smith, David Mark

Smith, Smudger
See   Smith, Michael John

Smith, Smudger
See   Smith, Neil

Smith, Smurf
See   Smith, David Mark

Smith, Snuffy
See   Smith, Clinton James

Smith, Soule 19th c.   [FFF]
American author
* Falcon

Smith, Stevie
See   Smith, Florence Margaret

Smith, Stub
See   Smith, James A.

Smith, Stuff
See   Smith, Hezekiah Leroy
Gordon

Smith, Sugar Johnny
See   Smith, John

Smith, Surrey [joint pseudonym with
William Morum]
See   Dinner, William

Smith, Surrey [joint pseudonym with
William Dinner]
See   Morum, William

Smith, Susie
See   Moore, Monette

Smith, Sydney 1771-1845
[DEL, PA]
British author and clergyman
* Plymley, Peter
* Publicola

Smith, T. D.
See   Dudley-Smith, Trevor

Smith, Tab
See   Smith, Talmadge

Smith, Tad
See   Smith, Claude M.

Smith, Talmadge 1909-1971
[EJ, PMJ, WWJ]
American jazz musician
* Smith, Tab

Smith, Tatti
See   Smith, Carl

Smith, Theolic 20th c.   [OBW]
American baseball player
* Smith, Fireball

Smith, Thomas   [SN]
Philologist
* Roguery, Doctor
* Smith, Rabbi
* Smith, Tograi

Smith, Thomas 1558?-1625   [WBD]
British merchant
* Smythe, [Sir] Thomas

Smith, Tina Shillard 1911-   [WFA]
American fashion designer
* Leser, Tina

Smith, Tody
See   Smith, Lawrence E.

Smith, Tograi
See   Smith, Thomas

Smith, Tom 1878?-1957   [AS]
American horse trainer
* Smith, Silent Tom

Smith, Tony 1927-   [IBW]
American musician
* Tony the Terror

Smith, Toukie
See   Smith, Doris

Smith, Trixie 1895-1943   [BWW]
American singer
* Ames, Tessie
* Lee, Bessie
* [The] Southern Nightingale

Smith, Verda T. 20th c.
American football player
* Smith, Vitamin T

Smith, Vernon 20th c.
American football player
* Smith, Catfish

Smith, Victor A. ?-1921   [SC]
American actor and circus performer
* Sini'letta, Vic

Smith, Vitamin T
See   Smith, Verda T.

Smith, W. B.   [PA]
Author
* Etheridge, Kelsic

Smith, W. J.
See   Smith, Walter James

Smith, Wade
See   Snow, Charles Horace

Smith, Walker 1920-
[BX, IBW, WBC]
American boxer
* [The] Harlem Hotshot
* [The] Harlem Hurricane
* Robinson, Ray
* Robinson, Sugar Ray

Smith, Wallace 1929-1973
[BX, RBE]
American boxer
* Smith, Bud

Smith, Walter   [BE]
American baseball player
* Reinicker, Walter [Wally]

Smith, Walter Bedell 1895-   [BDW]
American army officer
* [The] American Bulldog
* Smith, Beetle

Smith, Walter James 1917-   [SFL]
British author
* Smith, W. J.

Smith, Walter O.
See   Chattoram, Paul

Smith, Walter W[ellesley]
1905-1982   [B10, CA, IPA]
American sportswriter
* Smith, Red

Smith, Ward
See   Goldsmith, Howard

Smith, Webster
See   Coleman, Clayton W[ebster]

Smith, Whispering
See   Smith, Moses

Smith, Whispering Jack
See   Smith, Jack

Smith, Whistling Bob
See   Smith, Robert A.

Smith, Wib
See   Smith, Wilbur Floyd

Smith, Wiffi
See   Smith, Margaret

Smith, Wilbur Floyd 1886-1959
[BE]
American baseball player
* Smith, Wib

Smith, Willard Jehu 1892-   [BE]
American baseball player
* Smith, Red

Smith, Willard L[aurence] 1927-
[CA]
American author
* Laurence, Will

Smith, William
See   Louis Philippe

Smith, William 1730-1790
[DNNS, RH]
British actor
* Smith, Gentleman

Smith, William 1769-1839
[DNNS, FFF, SN]
British geologist
* [The] Father of English Geology

Smith, William 1796?-1887
[FFF, SN]
American politician
* Extra Billy

Smith, William 1883-1961   [F2]
Actor
* Farnum, Franklyn
* Farnum, Smiling Frank

Smith, William 20th c.   [RO2]
Canadian-born musician and
songwriter
* Smith, Smitty

Smith, William Augustus
1874-1944   [BMH]
British comedian
* Bard, Wilkie

Smith, William Dale 1929-   [CA]
American author
* Anthony, David

Smith, William Farrar 1824-1903
[FFF]
American army officer
* Smith, Baldy

Smith, William Henry 1825-1891
[DEP, DHA, DNNS]
British politician
* Old Morality

Smith, William Henry Joseph Berthol
Bonaparte Bertholoff 1897-1973
[ASC, DAM, EJ]
American jazz musician
* [The] Lion
* Willie the Lion

Smith, William John 1950-   [SMG]
Canadian-born hockey player
* Smith, Smitty

Smith, William Joseph 1899-
[BX, RBE]
American boxer
* Smith, Midget

Smith, William Joseph Thomas
1920-   [AW, IAW]
British author
* Ferrar, Gul

Smith, William Martin 1942-   [CA]
American author
* Quinn, Simon
* Smith, Martin Cruz

Smith, Willie 1939-   [BE]
American baseball player
* Smith, Wonderful Willie

Smith, Willie Mae Ford 1906-
[IBW]
American singer
* [The] Mother of Gospel Music

Smith, Winthrop A. 1907-   [BBH]
American lacrosse player and coach
* Smith, Pinky

Smith, Wonderful
See   Smith, Floyd

Smith, Wonderful Willie
See   Smith, Willie

Smith, Woodrow Wilson
See   Kuttner, Henry

Smith, Z. Z.
See   Westheimer, David

Smith, Zeke
See   Smith, Roger D.

Smith-Johannsen, Herman 1875- ?
[BBH]
Norwegian-born ski trail developer
* Smith-Johannsen, Jack Rabbit

Smith-Johannsen, Jack Rabbit
See   Smith-Johannsen, Herman

Smith-Masters, Margaret 1869- ?
[LAO]
British author
* Le Fevre, Felicite

Smith-Thomas, Eleanor Mary Tydfil
1910-   [THR]
Welsh-born actress and singer
* Fayre, Eleanor

Smith Woods, Dorothy Beryl
1904-   [AW]
British author
* Moore, Beryl

Smithells, Roger [William] 1905-
[CAP]
British author
* Cash, Sebastian

**Smither, Jessie** 1884-1960   [BEW]
*Actress*
* Orme, Denise

**Smithgall, Elizabeth**
See   Watts, Elizabeth [Bailey] Smithgall

**Smithline, Adele** 1903-   [IPA]
*American fashion designer*
* Simpson, Adele

**Smithson, Hugh** 1715-1786   [WBD]
*First Duke of Northumberland*
* Percy, [Sir] Hugh

**Smithson, James**
See   Macie, James Lewis [or Louis]

**Smithson, Noble** 1841- ?   [ALY]
*American author*
* Freeman, Frank

**Smithwick, Alfred Patrick**
1927?-1973   [BBH]
*Jockey*
* Smithwick, Paddy

**Smithwick, Paddy**
See   Smithwick, Alfred Patrick

**Smits, Teo**
See   Smits, Theodore R[ichard]

**Smits, Theodore R[ichard]** 1905-
[CA]
*American author*
* Smits, Teo

**Smitts, Mr.**
See   Linds, Mark Prager

**Smitz, Gaspar** ?-1689   [SN]
*Dutch painter*
* Smitz, Magdalen

**Smitz, Magdalen**
See   Smitz, Gaspar

**Smoke, Senor**
See   Lopez, Aurelio Alejandro

**Smokehouse Charley**
See   Dorsey, Thomas A[ndrew]

**Smokey Joe Finneran**
See   Finneran, Joseph Ignatius

**Smokey Joe Martin**
See   Martin, William Joseph [Joe]

**Smokey Joe Williams**
See   Williams, Joseph

**Smokey Joe Wood**
See   Wood, Joseph

**Smokin' Joe Frazier**
See   Frazier, Joseph [Joe]

**Smoky Babe**
See   Brown, Robert

**Smolar, Boris** 1897-   [IAW]
*Russian-born author and columnist*
* Lewis, Ben

**Smolens, Jay** 1927-   [BBD]
*American music critic and editor*
* Harrison, Jay

**Smolensk, Alexander** 1889-1972
[MS]
*Russian-born conductor*
* Smallens, Alexander

**Smoll, Clyde Hetrick** 1914-   [BE]
*American baseball player*
* Smoll, Lefty

**Smoll, Lefty**
See   Smoll, Clyde Hetrick

**[The] Smollett of the Stage**
See   Farquhar, George

**Smollett, Tobias George**
1721-1771   [DNNF, FFF, RH]
*British author*
* Smelfungus

**Smooth, Mr.**
See   Wallace, Jerry

**Smothers, Abraham** 20th c.
[BWW, NBB]
*American musician*
* Smothers, Little Smokey

**Smothers, Little Smokey**
See   Smothers, Abraham

**Smothers, Otis** 1929-   [BWW]
*American singer*
* Smothers, Smokey

**Smothers, Smokey**
See   Smothers, Otis

**Smowrey, Henry Neitz** 20th c.
[BE]
*American baseball player*
* Smoyer, Henry Neitz

**Smoyer, Henry Neitz**
See   Smowrey, Henry Neitz

**Smykal, Frank John**
See   Smejkal, Frank John

**Smyres, Clancy**
See   Smyres, Clarence Melvin

**Smyres, Clarence Melvin** 1922-
[BE]
*American baseball player*
* Smyres, Clancy

**[The] Smyrnean Poet**
See   Mimnermus

**Smyth, Constance** 20th c.   [ITA]
*Irish-born actress*
* Smith, Constance

**Smyth, Edward J.** 1887-1974
[BX, RBE]
*American boxer*
* Smith, Gunboat

**Smyth, Frank**   [FFF]
*American writer*
* Werter, Max

**Smyth, James Daniel** 1893-1958
[BE]
*American baseball player*
* Smyth, Red

**Smyth, Red**
See   Smyth, James Daniel

**Smythe, C. Stafford** 1921?-1971
[FHE]
*Canadian hockey executive*
* Smythe, Staff

**Smythe, Conn**
See   Smythe, Constantine Falkland Kerrys

**Smythe, Constantine Falkland Kerrys**
20th c.   [FHE]
*Canadian hockey executive*
* [The] David Harum of Hockey
* Smythe, Conn

**Smythe, James P.**
See   McGarry, William Rutledge

**Smythe, Staff**
See   Smythe, C. Stafford

**Smythe, [Sir] Thomas**
See   Smith, Thomas

**Snaith, J. C.**
See   Snaith, John Collis

**Snaith, John Collis** 1876-1936
[LC, TC]
*British author*
* [The] Gloomy Scribe
* Snaith, J. C.

**[The] Snake**
See   Persico, Carmine

**[The] Snake**
See   Prudhomme, Don

**Snap, Sylvanus**
See   Bergh, A. E.

**Snapper Jack Garrison**
See   Garrison, Edward

**[The] Snark**
See   Wood, Starr

**Snavely, Carl G.** 1894-   [FB]
*American football coach*
* King Carl

**Snead, Austine** ?-1888   [FFF]
*American journalist*
* Grundy, Miss

**Snead, J. C.**
See   Snead, Jesse Carlyle

**Snead, Jesse Carlyle** 1941-   [GF]
*American golfer*
* Snead, J. C.

**Snead, Sam[uel Jackson]** 1912-
[BBH, BWG]
*American golfer*
* [The] Slammer
* Snead, Slammin Sam
* [The] West Virginia Hillbilly

**Snead, Slammin Sam**
See   Snead, Sam[uel Jackson]

**Sneaky Pete**
See   Kleinow, Pete

**Sneddon, Robert W[illiam]** 20th c.
[NAA]
*Scottish-born author*
* Guillaume, Robert

**Snedeker, Caroline Dale**
1871-1956   [NAA, TCC]
*American author*
* Owen, Caroline Dale

**Sneed, Eddie** 20th c.   [OBW]
*American baseball player*
* Sneed, Lefty

**Sneed, Lefty**
See   Sneed, Eddie

**Sneider, Johannes** 1494?-1566
[WBD]
*German religious reformer*
* Agricola, Johannes
* Magister Islebius
* Schnitter, Johannes

**Snekul, Heinrich Yale**
See   Lukens, Henry Clay

**Snel, Billy**
See   Snell, William

**Snell, Doc**
See   Snell, Walter Henry [Wally]

**Snell, E. L.** 20th c.   [MBF]
*British author*
* Ellison, Ellis
* Ellsen, Ellis

**Snell, Hannah** 1723-1792
[DEP, RH]
*British soldier*
* [The] Female Marine
* Grey, James

**Snell, Roy Judson** 1878- ?   [NAA]
*American author*
* O'Hara, David

**Snell van Royen**
See   Snellius, Willebrord

**Snell, Walter Henry [Wally]** 1889-
[BE]
*American baseball player*
* Snell, Doc

**Snell, William** 1938-   [ASC]
*American composer, author, illustrator*
* Snel, Billy

**Snelling, Oswald Frederick** 1916-
[CA]
*British author*
* Frederick, Oswald

**Snelling, William Joseph**
1804-1848   [FFF, PA]
*American journalist*
* Bell, Solomon

**Snellings, Rolland** 20th c.   [IBW]
*American author*
* Toure, Askia Muhammed

**Snellius, Willebrord** 1591-1626
[WBD]
*Dutch mathematician*
* Snell van Royen

**Sneve, Virginia Driving Hawk**
1933-   [CA, SAT]
*American author*
* Driving Hawk, Virginia

**Sneyd, Ramon George**
See   Ray, James Earl

**Snider, Christopher** ?-1770   [HN]
*Killed by British soldiers*
* [The] First Martyr of Liberty

**Snider, Duke**
See   Snider, Edwin Donald

**Snider, Edwin Donald** 1926-
[BE, IPA, PB]
*American baseball player*
* [The] Duke
* [The] Silver Fox
* Snider, Duke

**Sniff, Mr.**
See   Abisch, Roslyn Kroop [Roz]

**Sniper**
See   Forty, Cecil Heber

**Snipes, Rock**
See   Snipes, Wyatt Eure

**Snipes, Roxy**
See   Snipes, Wyatt Eure

**Snipes, Wyatt Eure** 1896-1941
[BE]
*American baseball player*
* Snipes, Rock
* Snipes, Roxy

**Snippersnapper, Alice**
See   Reeve, Edward H. [Ted]

**Snod, E.**
See Dodd, E. A.

**Snodgrass, Fred Carlisle**
1887-1974 [BE]
*American baseball player*
* Snodgrass, Snow

**Snodgrass, Snow**
See Snodgrass, Fred Carlisle

**Snodgrass, W. D.**
See Snodgrass, William DeWitt

**Snodgrass, William DeWitt** 1926-
[DLE, WD]
*American poet, critic, translator*
* Gardons, S. S.
* McConnell, Will
* Prutkov, Kozma
* Snodgrass, W. D.

**Snoggins**
See Putney, Henry M.

**Snooks, Epaminondas T.**
See Mason, C. P.

**Snooks, Peter**
See Moore, John C.

**Snouckaert, William** 1510-1560
[PA]
*Author*
* Tenocarus

**Snover, Bosco**
See Snover, Colonel Lester

**Snover, Colonel Lester** 1895- [BE]
*American baseball player*
* Snover, Bosco

**Snow, C. P.**
See Snow, Charles Percy

**Snow, Charles Horace** 1877- ?
[WW]
*Author*
* Averill, H. C.
* Ballew, Charles
* Hardy, Russ
* Lee, Ranger
* Marshall, Gary
* Smith, Wade
* Wardle, Dan
* Wills, Chester

**Snow, Charles Percy** 1905-1980
[LC]
*British author*
* Snow, C. P.

**Snow, Clarence Eugene** 1914-
[CME, ECM, DAM]
*Canadian-born American country-
western performer*
* [The] Singing Ranger
* Snow, Hank
* [The] Yodeling Ranger

**Snow Cloud** 20th c. [B10]
*American Indian chieftain*
* Rogers, John

**Snow, Donald Clifford** 1917-
[CA, SAT, WYA]
*American author*
* Fall, Thomas

**Snow, Gilbert Wilson** 1915?-1953
[BEW]
*Actor*
* Gill, Paul

**Snow, Hank**
See Snow, Clarence Eugene

**Snow, Helen Foster** 1907-
[CA, WD]
*American author and poet*
* Wales, Nym

**Snow, Jane**
See Brandenburg, Margaret
Johnston

**[The] Snow King**
See Frederick V

**[The] Snow King**
See Gustavus Adolphus

**Snow, Lida** 1869?-1940 [BEW]
*American actress*
* McMillan, Lida

**Snow, Lyndon**
See Ansle, Dorothy Phoebe

**Snow, Phoebe**
See Laub, Phoebe

**[The] Snow Queen**
See Christina

**[The] Snow Queen**
See Elizabeth

**Snow, Sandy**
See Snow, William Alexander

**Snow, Terry**
See Woolsey, Maryhale

**Snow, Valaida** 20th c. [THR]
*American actress and singer*
* Valaida

**Snow White** [code name used during
World War II]
See Soong, Mei-ling [or Mayling]

**Snow, William Alexander** 1946-
[CEI]
*Canadian-born hockey player*
* Snow, Sandy

**Snowden, Elmer Chester**
1900-1973 [EJ, EJ7, IBW]
*American jazz musician*
* Snowden, Pops

**Snowden, Fred** 1937- [IBW]
*American basketball coach*
* [The] Fox

**Snowden, James** 1860- ? [LAO]
*British author and journalist*
* Snowden, Keighley

**Snowden, John** 20th c. [IBW]
*American editor and cooking school
operator*
* [The] Prince of Cookery

**Snowden, Keighley**
See Snowden, James

**Snowden, Pops**
See Snowden, Elmer Chester

**[The] Snowshoe Expressman**
See Johnson, Albert A.

**[The] Snowshoe Itinerant**
See Dyer, John Lewis

**Snyder, Charles N.** 1854-1924
[AS, BE]
*American baseball player*
* Snyder, Pop

**Snyder, Clifford Gilpin** 1917-
[ECM, FCW]
*American country-western performer*
* Stone, Cliffie

**Snyder, Cooney**
See Snyder, Frank C.

**Snyder, E. V.**
See Snyder, Eugene Vincent

**Snyder, Eloise C[olleen]**
See Bartos, Eloise C[olleen]

**Snyder, Emanuel Sebastian**
See Schneider, Emanuel Sebastian

**Snyder, Eugene Vincent** 1943-
[SFL]
*American author*
* Snyder, E. V.

**Snyder, Fairmont**
See Beebe, Ethel Fairmont

**Snyder, Frank C.** ?-1917 [BE]
*Canadian baseball player*
* Snyder, Cooney

**Snyder, Frank Elton** 1893-1962
[BE, PB]
*American baseball player*
* Snyder, Pancho

**Snyder, Gene**
See Snyder, M. G.

**Snyder, James**
See Synodinos, Dimitrios

**Snyder, John** 20th c.
*American lobbyist*
* Snyder, Magnum

**Snyder, Louis L.** 1907- [CA]
*American author and historian*
* Nordicus

**Snyder, M. G.** 20th c. [IPA]
*American politician*
* Snyder, Gene

**Snyder, Magnum**
See Snyder, John

**Snyder, Mrs.** [FFF]
*Entertainer*
* Reynolds, Vivian

**Snyder, Pancho**
See Snyder, Frank Elton

**Snyder, Peggy Lou** 1912?-
[IPA, PMJ, SW]
*American actress and singer*
* Nelson, Harriet Hilliard

**Snyder, Pop**
See Snyder, Charles N.

**Snyder, Redleg**
See Schneider, Emanuel Sebastian

**Snyders, Johann** ?-1568 [PA]
*Author*
* Sartorius

**So, Bernat**
See Ruttkay, Arnold

**Soa, Imamu Etheridge Knight**
See Knight, Etheridge

**Soami**
See Shinso

**Soapy Sam**
See Wilberforce, Samuel

**Soares, Chubby Cheeks**
See Soares, Mario

**Soares, Mario** 20th c.
*Portuguese premier*
* [The] Once and Future Prime
Minister

**Soares, Mario** (Continued)
* Soares, Chubby Cheeks

**Soares Correia, Artur Manuel**
1950- [AES]
*Portuguese soccer player*
* Artur

**Sobchuk, Dennis** 1954-
*Hockey player*
* [The] Greyhound

**Sobchuk, Gene** 1951- [SMG]
*Canadian-born hockey player*
* Sobchuk, Geno

**Sobchuk, Geno**
See Sobchuk, Gene

**Sobelsohn, Karl** 1885- ? [JL]
*Russian politician*
* Radek, Karl Bernardovich

**Sobh, A.**
See Shamlu, Ahmad

**Sobhuza II** 1899?-
*King of Swaziland*
* [The] Bull
* [The] Father of His Country
* [The] Great Crocodile
* [The] Great Mountain
* [The] Inexplicable
* [The] Lion of Swaziland
* Son of the She Elephant

**Sobotta, Kurt** 1907- [IAW]
*German author*
* Kurt, K. S.
* Straub, Otto

**Soccer, Mr.**
See Gonsalves, Bill

**Socci, Gianni**
See Socci, Giovanni

**Socci, Giovanni** 1939- [OP]
*Italian opera singer*
* Socci, Gianni

**[The] Sociable Spirit**
See Santi [or Sanzio?], Raffaello

**Society Kid Hogan**
See De Lorenzo, Salvatore

**Socius Ejectus**
See Baker, Thomas

**Sock, A.**
See Sulzberger, Arthur Ochs

**Sockalexis, Chief**
See Sockalexis, Louis Francis

**Sockalexis, Louis Francis**
1873-1913 [BE, PB]
*American baseball player*
* Sockalexis, Chief

**Socrates** 5th c. BC
[DEP, DNNS, FFF]
*Greek philosopher*
* [The] Bearded Master
* [The] Midwife of Men's Thoughts
* [The] Old Man Eloquent
* [The] Secretary of Nature
* [The] Wisest Man of Greece

**Socrates** 5th c. [WBD]
*Greek historian*
* Scholasticus

**[The] Socrates of His Age**
See Gabrielli, Trifone

**[The] Socrates of the French
Renaissance**
See Rabelais, Francois

[The] Socrates of the Jews
See Mendelssohn, Moses

[The] Socrates of the Musulmans
See Abou Hanifa

Soderberg, Percy Measday
1901-1969 [CAP]
British author
* Archer, S. E.
* Measday, George
* Seebord, G. R.
* Underhill, Peter

Soderland, M.
See Gandy, Mabel

[Il] Sodoma
See Bazzi, Giovanni Antonio de

Soederhjelm, Kai 1918- [IAW]
Finnish-born author
* Bergman, Jonas

Soerensen
See Vellejus, Andre Severin

Soeur Louise de la Misericorde
See Baume Le Blanc, Francoise
Louise de la

Soeur Sourire [Sister Smile]
See Deckers, Jeannine

Sofia
See Zeiger, Sophia

Sofman, Gustave 1902-1970 [SC]
French actor and circus performer
* Pipo

[The] Soft Medusa
See Mary, Queen of Scots

Soft Soul, Ms.
See Marrs, Stella

Softly, Edward
See Lovecraft, Howard Phillips

Sohl, Gerald Allan [Jerry] 1913-
[CA, ESF]
American author
* Butler, Nathan
* Sullivan, Sean Mei

Sohlke, Augustus 1865-1924
[BEW]
Director
* Sohlke, Gus

Sohlke, Gus
See Sohlke, Augustus

Sohr [or Sore], Martin 1486-1556
[WBD]
German musician and composer
* Agricola, Martin

[Il] Soiaro
See Gatti, Bernardino

Sojin
See Kamiyama, Sojin

Sokoloff, Melvin 1929- [EJ, PMJ]
American jazz musician
* Lewis, Mel

Sokoloff, Natalie B. 1906- [CAP]
Russian-born American author
* Scott, Natalie Anderson

Sokolov, Alexander V[sevolodovich]
1943- [CA]
Canadian-born author and educator
* Sokolov, Sasha

Sokolov, Sasha
See Sokolov, Alexander
V[sevolodovich]

Sokolova, Lydia
See Munnings, Hilda

Sokolova, Natasha
See Mahon, Natasha

Sola
See Anderson, Olive San Louie

Solaita, Tolia 1947- [SMG, WWB]
Samoan-born baseball player
* Solaita, Tony

Solaita, Tony
See Solaita, Tolia

Solari, Andrea 1470-1527
[FFF, RH, SN]
Italian painter
* [Del] Gobbo
* [The] Humpback

Solari [or Solario], Christoforo 15th
c. [WBD]
Italian sculptor and architect
* [Il] Gobbo [The Hunchback]

Solario, Antonio 1382-1455?
[FFF, HN, SN]
Italian painter
* [The] Gypsy
* [Il] Zingaro

Solario, Isadore 20th c. [EJS]
American basketball coach
* Solario, Spin

Solario, Spin
See Solario, Isadore

Solbelli, Olga 1898-1976 [FIR]
Italian actress
* Sunbeauty, Olga

Solberg, David 1943-
American actor
* Soul, David

Solbert, Romaine G. 1925- [CA]
American author and illustrator
* Solbert, Ronni

Solbert, Ronni
See Solbert, Romaine G.

[El] Soldado [The Soldier]
See Castro Sandoval, Luis

Soldano, Anthony 1927- [ASC]
American musician
* Dano, Tony

[Il] Soldatino [The Little Soldier]
See Barazzutti, Corrado

Soldier Boy Curry
See Curry, George James

Soldier Boy Murphy
See Murphy, John P.

[The] Soldier of the Andes
See Espinosa, Juan

[The] Soldiers' Friend
See Frederick Augustus

[The] Soldiers' Friend
See Schwabe, Leo

[The] Solemn Doctor
See Goethals, Henry

[The] Solemn Old Judge
See Hay, George Dewey

Solemnis, Doctor
See Goethals, Henry

Soler, Domingo
See Diaz Pavia, Domingo

Soler y Gisbert, Manuel 1913-1944
[GS]
Spanish bullfighter
* Vaquerito [Little Cowboy]

Soletanus, Matthoeus
See Tafuri, Malteo

Solicitor
See Hodgkinson, Conway
Loveridge

[The] Solid Doctor
See Middleton, Richard

Solidity, Madame
See D'Aubigne, Francoise

Solidus, Doctor
See Middleton, Richard

Soliman the Magnificent
See Jennens, Charles

Solitaire
See Robb, John S.

[El] Solitario
See Estebanez Calderon, Serafin

[The] Solitary Monk
See Luther, Martin

Sollima, Sergio 1921- [FDG]
Italian director
* Sterling, Simon

Solo, Jay
See Ellison, Harlan [Jay]

Solo, Tony
See Schiano, Anthony

Sologub, Fyodor
See Teternikov, Fyodor Kuzmich

Solomon
See Cutner, Solomon

Solomon, Abba 1915- [CA]
Israeli diplomat and author
* Eban, Abba
* Eban, Aubrey

Solomon, Charles 20th c.
[BLB, MM, PHM]
American underworld figure
* Solomon, King

Solomon, Eddie, Jr. 1951- [SMG]
American baseball player
* [The] King

Solomon, Gus 1869-1908
[BEW, CED]
American actor
* Rogers, Gus

Solomon, Hans
See Solomon, Johann

Solomon, Herbert Jay 1930- [EJ]
American jazz musician
* Mann, Herbie

Solomon, Hickory
See Solomon, Moses H.

Solomon, James B. 1921-1966 [SC]
American actor
* James, Ben

Solomon, James Hymie 1904-
[EJS]
American baseball player
* Reese, James Hymie

Solomon, Janis Little 1938- [CA]
American writer
* Gellinek, Janis Little

Solomon, Johann 1933- [EJ]
Austrian jazz musician
* Solomon, Hans

Solomon, King
See Solomon, Charles

Solomon, Max 1873-1932
[BEW, CED]
American actor
* Rogers, Max

Solomon, Moe
See Solomon, Moses H.

Solomon, Moses H. 1900-1966
[BE, EJS]
American baseball player
* [The] Rabbi of Swat
* Solomon, Hickory
* Solomon, Moe

Solomon, Mrs. Fred [FFF]
Entertainer
* Sutton, Mamie

[The] Solomon of China
See Lee chee-men

[The] Solomon of England
See Henry VII

[The] Solomon of England
See James I

[The] Solomon of France
See Charles V

[The] Solomon of France
See Louis IX

[The] Solomon of Great Britain
See George III

[The] Solomon of His Age
See Robert of Anjou

Solomon, Samuel 1904- [CA, WD]
British poet and translator
* Britindian
* Moolson, Melusa

Solomon, Stephen 1936- [CA]
American political scientist and
author
* Sloan, Stephen

Solomons, Ikey, Jun.
See Thackeray, William
Makepeace

[The] Solon of French Prose
See Balzac, Jean Louis Guez de

[The] Solon of Parnassus
See Boileau-Despreaux, Nicolas

Solorzano Davalos, Jesus 1907-
[GS]
Mexican bullfighter
* [El] Rey del Temple

Solow, Martin 1920- [CA]
American author
* Nelson, Peter

Solters, Julius Joseph
See Soltesz, Julius Joseph

Solters, Moose
See Soltesz, Julius Joseph

**Soltesz, Julius Joseph** 1908-
[BE, PB]
*American baseball player*
* Solters, Julius Joseph
* Solters, Moose

**Solwoska, Mara**
*See* French, Marilyn

**Soma, Ito**
*See* Doihara, Kenji

**Soman, Shirley** 1922-   [CA]
*American author*
* Camper, Shirley

**Some French Angel**
*See* De Salluste [or Salustius?],
Guillaume

**Somerby, Frederick**   [PA]
*Author*
* Cymon

**Somers, Bart**
*See* Fox, Gardner Francis

**Somers, Carole**
*See* Cosgrove, Judy

**Somers, Jonathan Swift, III**
*See* Farmer, Philip Jose

**Somers, Paul**
*See* Winterton, Paul

**Somers, Rosalie**
*See* Stephens, Harriet Marion

**Somers, Suzanne**
*See* Daniels, Dorothy

**Somerset, Duchess of**   [HN]
* [The] Queen of Beauty

**Somerset, Fitzroy James Henry**
1788-1855   [HN]
*British army officer*
* [The] Invisible Commander
* Raglan, Baron

**Somerset, FitzRoy Richard**
*See* Raglan, FitzRoy

**Somerset, Frances Thynne [Countess
of Hertford]** 1699-1754   [FFF]
*British author*
* Eusebia

**Somerset, Patrick**
*See* Holme-Sumner, Patrick

**Somervell, D. C.**
*See* Somervell, David Churchill

**Somervell, David Churchill**
1885-1965   [LC]
*British historian and author*
* Somervell, D. C.

**Somerville**
*See* Maugham, W[illiam]
Somerset

**Somerville, Alexander** 1811- ?   [PA]
*Author*
* One Who has Whistled at the
Plow

**Somerville, Amelia**
*See* Runnels, Mrs. Frederick

**Somerville and Ross** [joint
pseudonym with Edith Anna Oenone
Somerville]
*See* Martin, Violet Florence

**Somerville and Ross** [joint
pseudonym with Violet Florence
Martin]
*See* Somerville, Edith Anna
Oenone

**Somerville, Charles Ross** 1903-
[B10, GF]
*Canadian golfer*
* Somerville, Sandy

**Somerville, Edith Anna Oenone**
1858?-1949   [LC, TC]
*Irish author*
* Somerville and Ross [joint
pseudonym with Violet Florence
Martin]

**Somerville, H. B.**
*See* McComas, I. V.

**Somerville, Rose M[aurer]** 1908-
[CA]
*American sociologist and author*
* Maurer, Rose

**Somerville, Sandy**
*See* Somerville, Charles Ross

**Somerville, William** 1675-1742
[SN]
*British poet*
* [The] Poet of the Chase

**Somes, Jethro**
*See* Pauker, John

**[The] Sominex Kid**
*See* Hayakawa, Samuel Ichiye

**Sommer, Elke**
*See* Schletz, Elke

**Sommer, Hans**
*See* Zincke, Hans

**Sommer, Richard Jerome** 1934-
[IAW]
*American-born author and poet*
* Henningsson, Rik

**Sommers, Ben**
*See* Schusterman, Ben

**Sommers, David**
*See* Smith, Howard Van

**Sommers, Joseph Andrews**
1866-1908   [BE]
*American baseball player*
* Sommers, Pete

**Sommers, Kid**
*See* Sommers, William

**Sommers, Pete**
*See* Sommers, Joseph Andrews

**Sommers, William** ?-1895   [BE]
*Canadian baseball player*
* Sommers, Kid

**Sommerville, Andrew Henry [Andy]**
*See* Summersgill, Henry Travers

**Sommerville, Frankfort**
*See* Story, A. M. Sommerville

**Somnambulus**
*See* Scott, [Sir] Walter

**Somorokof [or Sumorokow],
Alexander Petrovitch** 1727?-1777
[DEP, DNNS, RH]
*Russian poet*
* [The] Russian Voltaire

**Somoza Debayle, Anastasio**
1925-1980
*Nicaraguan president*
* [The] Last Marine
* Somoza Debayle, Tachito [or
Tacho]

**Somoza Debayle, Tachito [or Tacho]**
*See* Somoza Debayle, Anastasio

**Somoza Garcia, Anastasio**
1896-1956
*Nicaraguan president*
* Somoza Garcia, Tacho

**Somoza Garcia, Tacho**
*See* Somoza Garcia, Anastasio

**Somoza Portocarrero, Anastasio**
1951?-1980
*Son of Nicaraguan president,
Anastasio Somoza*
* Somoza Portocarrero, Tachito

**Somoza Portocarrero, Tachito**
*See* Somoza Portocarrero,
Anastasio

**Son Fewclothes**
*See* Lewis, Robert

**Son Joe**
*See* Lawlars, Ernest

**[The] Son of His Grandfather**
*See* Harrison, Benjamin

**Son of Sam**
*See* Berkowitz, David R.

**[The] Son of the Devil**
*See* Ezzelino IV

**[The] Son of the Last Man**
*See* Charles II

**[A] Son of the Marshes**
*See* Visger, Jean A. Owen

**Son of the She Elephant**
*See* Sobhuza II

**Son of the Soil**
*See* Fletcher, Joseph Smith

**[A] Son of Thunder**
*See* Irving, Edward

**[The] Son of Toil**
*See* Brown, Adam George

**Son White Washington**
*See* Washington, Edward

**Soncinus**
*See* Barbus, Paolo

**Sondergaard, Edith Holm** 1900-
[BEW, FC, TR]
*American actress*
* Sondergaard, Gale

**Sondergaard, Gale**
*See* Sondergaard, Edith Holm

**Sonero, Devi**
*See* Pelton, Robert W[ayne]

**[The] Songbird of the South**
*See* Rainey, Gertrude Malissa Nix
[Pridgett]

**[The] Songbird of the South**
*See* Smith, Kathryn Elizabeth
[Kate]

**Songin, Butch**
*See* Songin, Ed[ward]

**Songin, Ed[ward]** 1923?-1976
[B10, SMG]
*American football player*
* Songin, Butch

**Sonia**
*See* Hamburger, Ursula-Maria

**Sonic, Fred**
*See* Smith, Frederick

**Sonica**
*See* McAlpine, Robert W.

**Sonnenberg, Dynamite Gus**
*See* Sonnenberg, Gustave

**Sonnenberg, Gustave** 1898-1944
[FB]
*American football player*
* Sonnenberg, Dynamite Gus

**Sonneveld, William**
*See* Sonneveld, Wim

**Sonneveld, Wim** 1918-1974   [SC]
*Dutch actor*
* Sonneveld, William

**Sonntag, Erik Nicholas** 1925-
[ART]
*German-born sculptor and painter*
* E. S.

**Sonntag, Uschi**
*See* Wiegand, Ursula

**Sonny Boy Williamson**
*See* Ford, Aleck

**Sonny Boy Williamson**
*See* Williamson, John Lee

**Sonny Ford Thomas**
*See* Thomas, James

**Sonny P.**
*See* Parker, Robert

**Sonny Red Kyner**
*See* Kyner, Junior Sylvester

**Sonny T**
*See* Terrell, Saunders

**Sono, Ephraim** 1955-   [SMG]
*South African soccer player*
* Sono, Jomo

**Sono, Jomo**
*See* Sono, Ephraim

**Sonsteby, Gunnar** 1918-   [BDW]
*Norwegian intelligence agent*
* Broch
* Fjeld, Erling
* Kjaken
* Number 24

**Sontup, Dan[iel]** 1922-   [CA]
*American author*
* Clarke, John
* Saunders, David

**[Le] Sony'r Ra**
*See* Blount, Herman

**Soo, Chung Ling**
*See* Robinson, William Ellsworth

**Soo, Hop Ling**
*See* Robinson, William Ellsworth

**Soomro, Mohammad Ibrahim**
1934-   [IAW]
*Pakistani author*
* Munshi

**Soong, Mei-ling [or Mayling]**
1899- [CND]
*Wife of Taiwanese president Chiang Kai-shek*
* Chiang Kai-shek, Madame
* Snow White [code name used during World War II]

**Soper, Oro M.** 1910?- [WWJ]
*American jazz musician*
* Soper, Tut

**Soper, Tut**
*See* Soper, Oro M.

**Sophia Dorothea** 1666-1726 [WBD]
*Wife of King George I of England*
* [The] Princess of Ahlden

**Sophie**
*See* Gimbel, Sophie

**Sophie Charlotte** 1668-1705
[DEP, DNNS, FFF]
*Queen of Prussia*
* [The] Republican Queen

**Sophocardus**
*See* Wishart [or Wiseheart?], George

**Sophocles** 5th c. BC
[DNNS, FFF, RH]
*Greek playwright*
* [The] Attic Bee
* [The] Attic Homer
* [The] Bee of Attica

**Sophonisba** 3rd c. BC [HN]
*Queen of Numidia*
* [The] Catharine de Medici of Africa

**Sorabji, Kaikhosru**
*See* Sorabji, Leon Dudley

**Sorabji, Leon Dudley** 1892- [BBD]
*British composer*
* Sorabji, Kaikhosru

**[El] Sordillo de Pereda**
*See* Arco, Alonso del

**Soreil, [Joseph] Arsene** 1893-
[IAW]
*Belgian author*
* Delaisne, Jean

**Sorel, Agnes** 1409?-1450
[DNNS, HN, SN]
*Mistress of King Charles VII of France*
* [La] Dame de Beaute

**Sorel, Byron**
*See* Yatron, Michael

**Sorel, Cecile**
*See* Seure, Cecile Emilie

**Sorel, Jean**
*See* De Rochbrune, Jean

**Sorel, Julia**
*See* Drexler, Rosalyn

**Sorel, W. J.** 19th c. [SAT]
*British author*
* LeRos, Christian

**Sorensen, Harald** 1905- [BBH]
*Norwegian-born skier, ski instructor, official, coach*
* Sorensen, Pop

**Sorensen, Pop**
*See* Sorensen, Harald

**Sorenson, Doc**
*See* Sorenson, J. C.

**Sorenson, Flemming** 20th c. [WFA]
*Danish-born fashion designer*
* Flemming

**Sorenson, J. C.** 20th c. [GW]
*American rodeo performer*
* Sorenson, Doc

**Sorey, Revie Cee, Jr.** 1953- [SMG]
*American football player*
* Hollywood, Rock

**Sorge, Anthony**
*See* Valachi, Joseph Michael

**Sorl, Ernest James** [FFF]
*Entertainer*
* Sutton, Ernest

**Sorokin, Pitirim A[lexandrovitch]**
1889-1968 [CA]
*Russian-born American sociologist and author*
* Tchaadaieff

**Sorrells, Buckshot**
*See* Sorrells, Marvin H.

**Sorrells, Chick**
*See* Sorrells, Raymond Edwin

**Sorrells, Marvin H.** 20th c. [GW]
*American rodeo performer*
* Sorrells, Buckshot

**Sorrells, Raymond Edwin** 1896-
[BE]
*American baseball player*
* Sorrells, Chick
* Sorrells, Red

**Sorrells, Red**
*See* Sorrells, Raymond Edwin

**[La] Sorrentina**
*See* Frasca, Mary

**Sortor, June Elizabeth** 1939-
[CA, SAT]
*American author*
* Sortor, Toni

**Sortor, Toni**
*See* Sortor, June Elizabeth

**Sorya, Francoise** 1932-
[BDF, FC, WEF]
*French actress*
* Aimee, Anouk
* Anouk

**Soseki, Natsume**
*See* Kinnosuke, Natsume

**Soskin, V. H.**
*See* Ellison, Virginia Howell

**Sosthenes**
*See* Coad, Frederick Roy

**[The] Sot**
*See* Selim II

**Soter [The Preserver]**
*See* Antiochus I

**Soter**
*See* Attalus I

**Soter [Preserver]**
*See* Demetrius I

**Soter**
*See* Ptolemy I

**Soter**
*See* Seleucus III

**Soter II**
*See* Ptolemy IX [or VIII]

**Sotheran, Charles** 1847- ? [PA]
*Author*
* C. S.
* Colmolyn
* Secundus, Asmodeus
* Southernwood

**Sothern, Ann**
*See* Lake, Harriette

**Sothern, Edward Askew**
*See* Stewart, Douglas

**Sothern, Ella**
*See* Willard, Mrs. Charles

**Sothern, George Evelyn Augustus**
1870- ? [THR]
*British actor*
* Sothern, Sam

**Sothern, Henry** 1819- ? [PA]
*Author*
* Savile

**Sothern, Hugh** 1882?-1947
[BEW, SC]
*American actor*
* Sutherland, Roy

**Sothern, Janet Evelyn** 20th c.
[THR]
*British actress*
* Evelyn, Janet

**Sothern, Mrs. Lytton** [FFF]
*Entertainer*
* Hewitt, Agnes

**Sothern, Sam**
*See* Sothern, George Evelyn Augustus

**Sothoron, Allen Sutton** 1893-1939
[BN]
*American baseball player*
* Sothoron, Fidge

**Sothoron, Fidge**
*See* Sothoron, Allen Sutton

**Soto, Gabriel** [GS]
*Mexican bullfighter*
* [El] Momo

**Soto, Roberto** 1888-1960 [SC]
*Mexican actor*
* El Panzon [The Belly]

**Soto Moreno, Rafael** 1940- [GS]
*Spanish bullfighter*
* Rafael de Paula [Rafael from Paula]

**Soubirous, Bernadette** 1844-1879
[WBD]
*Saint*
* Bernadette of Lourdes

**Souchak, Burly Mike**
*See* Souchak, Mike

**Souchak, Mike** 20th c.
*American football player*
* Souchak, Burly Mike

**Souchock, Bud**
*See* Souchock, Stephen

**Souchock, Stephen** 1919- [BE]
*American baseball player*
* Souchock, Bud

**Souchon, Doc**
*See* Souchon, Edmond, II

**Souchon, Edmond, II** 1897-1968
[EJ, EJ7]
*American jazz musician*
* Souchon, Doc

**Soudley, Henry**
*See* Wood, James Playsted

**Soul Brother Number 1**
*See* Brown, James

**Soul, David**
*See* Solberg, David

**Soul, Jimmy**
*See* McCleese, James

**Soul, Lady**
*See* Franklin, Aretha

**[The] Soul Man**
*See* Bland, Robert Calvin [Bobby]

**[The] Soul of the Black Liberation Army**
*See* Chesimard, Joanne

**Soulas, Josias de [Sieur de Primefosse]** 1608?-1672 [WBD]
*French actor*
* Floridor

**Souli, Charles George**
*See* Bedford-Jones, Henry [James O'Brien]

**Soulouque**
*See* Bonaparte, Charles Louis Napoleon

**Soult, Nicolas Jean de Dieu**
1769-1851 [DEP, DHA, FFF]
*Marshal of France*
* [The] Old Fox
* Vieux Renard

**Sour Mash Daniels**
*See* Daniels, [Harold] Jack

**Sourhardt, Edward William**
1867-1947 [AS, BE]
*American baseball player*
* Seward, Edward William

**Sousa, John Philip** 1854-1932
[WBD]
*American bandleader and composer*
* [The] March King

**Sousa, [Frei] Luiz de**
*See* Sousa Countinho, Manoel de

**Sousa Countinho, Manoel de**
1555-1632 [WBD]
*Portuguese monk and author*
* Sousa, [Frei] Luiz de

**Souster, Raymond** 1921-
[CA, WD]
*Canadian poet and author*
* Holmes, John
* Holmes, Raymond

**Soutar, Gwendoline Amy** 1904-
[AW]
*British author*
* Deane, Sonia

**South, Clark**
*See* Swain, Dwight V[reeland]

**South, Eddie** 1904-1962 [IBW]
*American jazz musician*
* Dark Angel of the Violin

**South, Elma**
*See* Cheesborough, Essie B.

**South, Grace**
*See* Clark, Gail

South, Robert 1634-1716 [SN]
*British clergyman*
* [The] Scourge of Fanaticism

South, Simeon
See Macgregor, J.

South, Theophilus
See Chitty, Edward

Southard, Helen Fairbairn 1906-
[CA]
*American psychologist and author*
* Fairbairn, Helen

Southard, J. H.
See Morris, Charles Smith

Southcote, George
See Ashton, [Sir] George Grey

Southcott, Joanna 1750-1814
[HN, SN]
*British religious leader*
* [The] Prophetess of Exeter
* [The] Spiritual Mother

Southerland, Katherine Virden 20th
c. [WWL]
*American author*
* Virden, Katherine

Southerland, Myrtella
See Harkness, Edith Myrtella

Southern Gael
See Locke, John

[The] Southern Gentleman
See Loden, James [Jimmie]

Southern, Jack
See Southworth, John Van Duyn

[A] Southern Matron
See Howard, Caroline K.

[The] Southern Nightingale
See Smith, Trixie

[The] Southern Scott
See Ariosto, Lodovico

Southern, Terry 1924?- [CA, WD]
*American author and screenwriter*
* Kenton, Maxwell [joint
pseudonym with Mason
Hoffenberg]

[A] Southerner
See Dake, Seymour R.

Southernwood
See Sotheran, Charles

Southey, Robert 1774-1843
[DEL, DEP, FFF]
*British author and poet*
* Bion
* Espriella, Manuel Alvarez
* [The] Poet of Greta Hall
* Shufflebottom, Abel

Southgate, Elsie 1890-1946 [BMH]
*British musician*
* [The] Royal Violinist

Southouse-Cheney, Reginald Evelyn
Peter 1896-1951 [LC]
*Irish author*
* Cheney, Peter

Southwell, Robert 1561-1595 [SN]
*British poet*
* Our Second Ciceronian

Southwold, Stephen 1887-1964
[LC, SFL, TC]
*British author*
* Bell, Neil

Southwold, Stephen (Continued)
* Lambert, S. H.
* Martens, Paul
* Miles

Southworth, Billy 20th c. [GSH]
*American baseball player*
* Billy the Kid

Southworth, Emma Dorothy Eliza
[Nevitte] 1818?-1899 [FFF]
*American author*
* E. D. E. N.

Southworth, John Van Duyn 1904-
[NAA]
*American author and educator*
* Southern, Jack

Southworth, Louis
See Grealey, Thomas Louis

Southworth, Sylvester S. [PA]
*Author*
* Smith, John, Jr., of Arkansas

Soutter, Fred
See Lake, Kenneth R[obert]

Souza, Carlos Estevao de 1921-
[WEC]
*Brazilian cartoonist*
* Estevao, Carlos

Souza, Ernest
See Scott, Evelyn

Souzay, Gerard
See Tisserand, Gerard Marcel

Sovine, Red
See Sovine, Woodrow Wilson

Sovine, Woodrow Wilson 1918-
[CME, CWG, DAM]
*American country-western performer*
* Sovine, Red

Sowande, Fela 1905- [IBW]
*Nigerian composer*
* [The] High Priest of Music

Sowden, Margaret 1933- [TR]
*British actress*
* Neilson, Perlita

Sowden, [Sir] William John 1858-
? [LAO]
*Australian author*
* Pencil
* Scribble

Sowder, Martin 1874-1931 [GW]
*American rodeo performer*
* Sowder, Thad

Sowder, Thad
See Sowder, Martin

Sowells, Petey
See Sowells, Rich

Sowells, Rich 20th c. [SMG]
*American football player*
* Sowells, Petey

Sowerby, Arthur Lindsay McRae
1899- [CAP]
*British author and editor*
* McRae, Lindsay

Sowerby, Githa
See Kendall, Katherine Githa

Sowman, Gordon 20th c. [MBF]
*British author*
* Reid, Desmond [house
pseudonym]

[The] Soybean Chemist
See Julian, Percy Lavon

Soyinka, Akinwande Oluwole
1934- [CLC, IBW, WOA]
*Nigerian playwright, director, poet,
author*
* Soyinka, Wole

Soyinka, Wole
See Soyinka, Akinwande Oluwole

Sozzo
See Albina, Giuseppe

Spaatz, Carl 1891-1974 [WWW]
*American air force officer*
* Spaatz, Tooey

Spaatz, Tooey
See Spaatz, Carl

Spacek, Mary Elizabeth 1950?-
[B10]
*American actress*
* Spacek, Sissy

Spacek, Sissy
See Spacek, Mary Elizabeth

Spach, M. Louis Adolph [PA]
*Author*
* Levater, Louis

Spade, Mark
See Balchin, Nigel [Marlin]

Spade, Rupert
See Pawley, Martin Edward

Spaeth, Helen Elizabeth 1924-
[OP]
*American opera singer*
* Vanni, Helen Elizabeth

[Lo] Spagna
See Di Pietro, Giovanni

[The] Spagnolet of the Theatre
See Sandford, Samuel

Spagnoletto
See Ribera, Jose

Spagnolus, Baptista 1443-1516
[RH]
*Italian poet*
* [The] Mantuan

[Lo] Spagnuolo
See Crespi, Giuseppe Maria

[Lo] Spagnuolo dei Pesci
See Herrera, Francisco de

Spahr, Juerg 1925- [WEC]
*Swiss cartoonist*
* Juesp

Spain, John
See Adams, Cleve F[ranklin]

Spalatin, Georg
See Burckhardt, Georg

Spalding, Charles Harry
1893-1950 [BE]
*American baseball player*
* Spalding, Dick

Spalding, Dick
See Spalding, Charles Harry

Spalding, Henry D. 1915- [CA]
*American author*
* Sping, Dan

Spalding, Keith
See Spalt, Karl Heinz G.

Spalding, Lucile
See Spalding, Ruth

Spalding, Ruth 20th c. [AW]
*British author and playwright*
* Jay, Marion
* Spalding, Lucile

Spalla, Ignazio 20th c. [WF]
*Italian actor*
* Sanchez, Pedro

Spalla, Joseph Salvatore 1923-
[ITA]
*American executive and producer*
* Spalla, Rick

Spalla, Rick
See Spalla, Joseph Salvatore

Spalt, Karl Heinz G. 1913- [WD]
*British author*
* Spalding, Keith

Span, Norman 20th c. [ASC]
*West Indian composer and singer*
* King Radio

Spang
See Spangler, Frank M.

Spang Gipe
See Huston, Henry Augustus

Spangenberg, Judith [Dunn] 1942-
[CA, SAT]
*American author*
* Dunn, Judy

Spangler, Frank M. 1881-1946
[WEC]
*American cartoonist*
* Spang

[The] Spaniard
See Healy, Patrick Francis

Spanier, Francis Joseph 1906-1967
[DAM, WWJ]
*American jazz musician*
* Spanier, Muggsy

Spanier, Muggsy
See Spanier, Francis Joseph

[The] Spanish Addison
See Feyjoo [or Feijoo] y
Montenegro, Frey Benito

[The] Spanish Bassano
See Orrente, Pedro

[The] Spanish Bayard
See Garcia de Paredes, Diego

[The] Spanish Brutus
See Perez de Guzman, Alphonso
[or Alonso]

[The] Spanish Byron
See Espronceda, Jose de

[The] Spanish Cellini
See Arfe y Villafane, Juan de

[The] Spanish Cicero
See Arguelles, Agustin

[The] Spanish Ennius
See Mena, Juan de

[The] Spanish Horace
See Argensola, Bartolome
Leonardo de

[The] Spanish Horace
See Argensola, Lupercio Leonardo
de

Spanish Jack
See Gonzales, Bli

**Spanish, Johnny**
See Weyler, Joseph

**[The] Spanish Moliere**
See Moratin, Leandro Fernandez

**[The] Spanish Petrarch**
See Garcilaso de la Vega

**[The] Spanish Phoenix**
See Vega Carpio, Lope Felix de

**[The] Spanish Raphael**
See Macip, Vicente Juan

**Spanish Raymond Marquez**
See Marquez, Raymond

**[The] Spanish Shakespeare**
See Calderon de la Barca, Pedro

**[The] Spanish Tennyson**
See Nunez de Arce, Gaspar

**[The] Spanish Tyrtaeus**
See Quintana, Manuel Jose

**[The] Spanish Victor Hugo**
See Zorilla, Jose

**Spann, Charles Edward, III** 1948-
[IBW]
*American swimmer*
* Spann, Little Eddie

**Spann, Little Eddie**
See Spann, Charles Edward, III

**Spanner, Valerie**
See Grayland, Valerie Merle
[Spanner]

**Spano, James**
See Aiuppa, Joseph John [Joe]

**Spano, Tony**
See Nerone, Giuseppe

**Spanpinato, Salvatore Willard**
1942- [RO2]
*American singer*
* Valentino, Sal

**Sparando, Ace**
See Sparando, Tony

**Sparando, Tony** 1906- [BBH]
*American bowler*
* Sparando, Ace

**Spargo, Tony**
See Sbarbaro, Anthony

**Spark Plug Adams**
See Adams, Earl John

**Sparkia, Roy [Bernard]** 1924- [CA]
*American author*
* Caine, Mitchell

**Sparkle, Sophie**
See Hicks, Jennie E.

**Sparkman, Edward A.** 1883-1957
[BEW, FC]
*Canadian-born actor*
* Sparks, Ned

**Sparkman, William**
See Roper, William L[eon]

**Sparks, Aaron** 20th c. [BWW]
*American musician*
* Pinetop

**Sparks, Don** 20th c. [SMG]
*American basketball team trainer*
* Sparks, Sparky

**Sparks, Jesse Wadlington** 1867- ?
[NAA]
*American attorney and writer*
* Jump, A.

**Sparks, Merla Jean**
See McCormick, Merla Jean

**Sparks, Ned**
See Sparkman, Edward A.

**Sparks, Sparky**
See Sparks, Don

**Sparks, Timothy**
See Dickens, Charles

**Sparling, Ned?**
See Senarens, Luis Philip

**Sparre, Nicolas** ?-1761 [PA]
*Author*
* Hiersingius

**Sparrow, Kid**
See Gassion, Edith Giovanna

**Sparrow, Rory** 20th c.
*American basketball player*
* [The] Buzzer Beater

**Sparrowgrass, Mr.**
See Cozzens, Frederick Swartwout

**Spartacus**
See Linton, William James

**Spartacus, Deutero**
See Fanthorpe, R[obert] Lionel

**Spartanburg John McMakin**
See McMakin, John Weaver

**Spaulding, Douglas**
See Bradbury, Ray [Douglas]

**Spaulding, Elbridge Gerry**
1809-1897 [FFF, WBD]
*American politician and banker*
* [The] Father of Greenbacks

**Spaulding, William** 1809- ? [PA]
*Author*
* W. S.

**Spavento**
See Hendie, Paul

**[Der] Spaziergaenger nach Syrakus**
See Seume, Johann Gottfried

**Speake, Robert Charles [Bob]**
1930- [BE]
*American baseball player*
* Speake, Spook

**Speake, Spook**
See Speake, Robert Charles [Bob]

**Speaker, Spoke**
See Speaker, Tristram E.

**Speaker, Tris**
See Speaker, Tristram E.

**Speaker, Tristram E.** 1888-1958
[AS, DGS, PB]
*American baseball player and
manager*
* [The] Gray Eagle
* Speaker, Spoke
* Speaker, Tris

**Spear, Benjamin**
See Henisch, Heinz K.

**Spear, Sammy**
See Shapiro, Sammy

**Spearman, Clyde** 20th c. [OBW]
*American baseball player*
* Spearman, Splo

**Spearman, Henry** 20th c. [OBW]
*American baseball player*
* Spearman, Splo

**Spearman, Splo**
See Spearman, Clyde

**Spearman, Splo**
See Spearman, Henry

**Spears, Clarence W.** 1894-1964
[AS, FB]
*American football player and coach*
* Spears, Cupid
* Spears, Doc
* Spears, Fat

**Spears, Cupid**
See Spears, Clarence W.

**Spears, Doc**
See Spears, Clarence W.

**Spears, Fat**
See Spears, Clarence W.

**Spears, Raymond S[miley]** 1876- ?
[NAA]
*American author*
* Smiley, Jim

**Special Duty Agent Three-Three**
See Granville, Clive

**Special K**
See Kelser, Greg

**Speck, Richard Benjamin**
See Speck, Richard Franklin

**Speck, Richard Franklin** 1941-
[BLB]
*American murderer*
* Brian, B.
* Lindbergh, Richard Franklin
* Speck, Richard Benjamin

**Speckled Red**
See Perryman, Rufus G.

**Spectator**
See Bellew, Henry Walter

**Spectator**
See Popovic, Nenad D[ushan]

**Spectator**
See Walkley, Arthur Bingham

**Spector, Isadore** 20th c. [EJS]
*American football player*
* Spector, Spook

**Spector, Spook**
See Spector, Isadore

**Speece, By**
See Speece, Byron Franklin

**Speece, Byron Franklin** 1897- [BE]
*American baseball player*
* Speece, By

**Speed**
See Marvel, Carl Shipp

**Speed Ball Cannon**
See Cannon, Richard

**Speed Demon**
See Agati, Pasquale

**[The] Speed Merchant**
See Laviolette, Jean Baptiste

**Speed Merchant of the Pulps**
See Burks, Arthur J.

**Speed, Mr.**
See Randolph, Thomas, Jr. [Tom]

**Speed, Nell**
See Sampson, Emma Speed

**Speer, G. T.**
See Speer, George Thomas

**Speer, George Nathan** 1886-1946
[BE]
*American baseball player*
* Speer, Kid

**Speer, George Thomas** 1891-1966
[DAM]
*American singer*
* Speer, G. T.

**Speer, Jack** 20th c. [SFP]
*Author*
* Bristol, John A.

**Speer, Kid**
See Speer, George Nathan

**Speer, Lena Brock** ?-1967 [DAM]
*American singer*
* Speer, Mom

**Speer, Mom**
See Speer, Lena Brock

**Speers, James [Jim]** 1882-1955
[CSH]
*Canadian racehorse breeder*
* Racing, Mr.

**Speicher, Helen Ross [Smith]** 1915-
[CA, SAT]
*American author*
* Abbott, Alice [joint pseudonym
  with Kathryn Kilby Borland]
* Land, Jane and Ross [joint
  pseudonym with Kathryn Kilby
  Borland]

**Spektor, [Dr.] Adam**
See Glut, Donald F[rank]

**Spellman, Leora** 1891-1945 [SC]
*American actress*
* Spellmeyer, Leora

**Spellmeyer, Leora**
See Spellman, Leora

**Spelman, Mary** 1934- [CA]
*American author*
* Lockwood, Mary
* Towne, Mary

**Spelvin, George**
See Phillips, David Atlee

**Spelvin, Georgina**
See Graham, Chele

**Spence, Alexander** 20th c. [LRR]
*Musician*
* Spence, Skip

**Spence, Duncan**
See Spence, William John Duncan

**Spence, Harrison L.** 1856-1908
[BE]
*American baseball manager*
* Spence, Harry

**Spence, Harry**
See Spence, Harrison L.

**Spence, Hubert**
See Longhurst, Percy William

**Spence, J. A. D.**
See Eliot, Thomas Stearns

**Spence, James Mudie**   [PA]
*Author*
* Leevitt, Don T. B.

**Spence, Joseph** 1698-1768   [DEL]
*British author*
* Beaumont, [Sir] Harry

**Spence, Lew**
*See* Slifka, Lewis

**Spence, Skip**
*See* Spence, Alexander

**Spence, William John Duncan**
1923-   [WD]
*British author*
* Bowden, Jim
* Ford, Kirk
* Rogers, Floyd
* Spence, Duncan

**Spencer**
*See* Herz, Jerome Spencer [Jerry]

**Spencer, Anne**
*See* Bannister, Annie Bethel Scales

**Spencer, Big Dee**
*See* Spencer, Daryl Dean

**Spencer, Brian** 1949-   [SMG]
*Canadian-born hockey player*
* Spencer, Spinner

**Spencer, Bud**
*See* Pedersoli, Carlo

**Spencer, Captain**
*See* Tuite, Hugh

**Spencer, Cornelia**
*See* Yaukey, Grace S[ydenstricker]

**Spencer, Daryl Dean** 1929-   [BE]
*American baseball player*
* Spencer, Big Dee

**Spencer, Diana**
*See* Diana

**Spencer, Edward**
*See* Mott, Edward Spencer

**Spencer, Edward**
*See* Seymour, Caroline

**Spencer, Edward**
*See* Stares, John Edward Spencer

**Spencer, Edward Russell**
1884-1945   [BE]
*American baseball player*
* Spencer, Tubby

**Spencer, Elihu** 1721-1784   [FFF]
*American clergyman*
* Spencer, Ready Money

**Spencer, Fred**
*See* Bretherton, Fred Spencer

**Spencer, Geoffrey**
*See* Wilson, Alexander [Douglas Chesney]

**Spencer, George** 1799-1864
[PA, RH]
*Clergyman and author*
* Ignatius, [Father]

**Spencer, Georgiana** 18th c.
*Duchess of Devonshire*
* [The] Duchess of Dimples

**Spencer, Henry** ?-1406
[FFF, RH, SN]
*Bishop of Norwich*
* [The] Fighting Prelate

**Spencer, Irvin James** 1937-   [CEI]
*Canadian-born hockey player*
* Spencer, Spinner

**Spencer, John**
*See* Vickers, Roy

**Spencer, John** 1949-   [DC]
*British cricketer*
* Spencer, Spud

**Spencer, John Charles [Lord Althorp]**
1782-1845   [DNNS]
*British politician*
* Honest John [or Jack]

**Spencer, Leonard G.** [joint
pseudonym with Robert Silverberg]
[house pseudonym, Ziff-Davis]
*See* Garrett, [Gordon] Randall
[Philip David]

**Spencer, Leonard G.** [joint
pseudonym with Randall Garrett]
[house pseudonym, Ziff-Davis]
*See* Silverberg, Robert

**Spencer, Lillian**
*See* Clayburgh, Mrs. Edward

**Spencer, Major**
*See* Nunez, William Loring

**Spencer, Mr.**   [PA]
*Author*
* Allyn, Enylla

**Spencer, Nat**
*See* Saunders, Robert

**Spencer, Norman D.**
*See* Factor, John

**Spencer, Oneill**
*See* Spencer, William

**Spencer, P. M.**
*See* Spencer, Pamela Mary

**Spencer, Pamela Mary** 1924-
[ART]
*British artist*
* Spencer, P. M.

**Spencer, Parke**
*See* Wright, Sewell Peaslee

**Spencer, Ready Money**
*See* Spencer, Elihu

**Spencer, Robert [Second Earl of
Sunderland]** 1640-1702   [SN]
*British politician*
* President Bob

**Spencer, Roland** [joint pseudonym
with Francis Alister Warwick]
*See* Prout, Geoffrey

**Spencer, Roland** [joint pseudonym
with Geoffrey Prout]
*See* Warwick, Francis Alister

**Spencer, Spinner**
*See* Spencer, Brian

**Spencer, Spinner**
*See* Spencer, Irvin James

**Spencer, Spud**
*See* Spencer, John

**Spencer, Tubby**
*See* Spencer, Edward Russell

**Spencer, Warren**
*See* Lengel, William Charles

**Spencer, William** 1909-1944
[WWJ]
*American jazz musician*
* Spencer, Oneill

**Spender, J. A.**
*See* Spender, John Alfred

**Spender, John Alfred** 1862-1942
[LC]
*British author*
* Spender, J. A.

**Spendlove, G. H.**
*See* Spendlove, Gerald Hugh

**Spendlove, Gerald Hugh** 1929-
[ART]
*British artist*
* Spendlove, G. H.

**Spenser, Edmund** 1552-1599
[FFF, RH, SN]
*British poet*
* [The] Bard of Mulla's Silver
    Stream
* [The] Child of Fancy
* [The] Child of the Ausonian
    Muse
* Clout, Colin
* [The] Father of the Poets
* Mother Hubbard
* Mulla's Bard
* [The] Page of State to the Muses
* [The] Poet's Poet
* [The] Prince of Poets
* [The] Sage and Serious Spenser

**Spenser, James**
*See* Guest, Francis Narold

**Spenser, [Sir] John** 16th c.   [SN]
*British politician*
* Spenser, Rich

**[The] Spenser of English
Prose-Writers**
*See* Taylor, Jeremy

**Spenser, Rich**
*See* Spenser, [Sir] John

**Speranza**
*See* Wilde, Jane Francesca Elgee

**Speranza, Norma Jean** 1935-
[RO1]
*American singer*
* Corey, Jill

**Speraw, Birdie**
*See* Speraw, Paul Bachman

**Speraw, Paul Bachman** 1893-1962
[BE]
*American baseball player*
* Speraw, Birdie
* Speraw, Polly

**Speraw, Polly**
*See* Speraw, Paul Bachman

**Spero, Leopold** 1887-   [WWL]
*British author*
* Hope, Cecil
* Managing Clerk

**Sperry, [Sally] Baxter** 1914-   [CA]
*German-born American author*
* S. S. E.

**Sperry, Byrne Hope** 1902-   [CA]
*South African-born author and
journalist*
* Sanders, Byrne Hope

**Sperry, J. E.**
*See* Eisenstat, Jane Sperry

**Sperry, Raymond, Jr.** [house
pseudonym] [Stratemeyer
Syndicate]
*See* Stratemeyer, Edward L.

**Sperry, Reginald**   [FFF]
*Prestidigitator*
* Prenaier, Paul

**Spewack, Samuel** 1899-   [WW]
*Author*
* Abbott, A. A.

**Speyrer, Charles W.** 1949-   [FB]
*American football player*
* Speyrer, Cotton

**Speyrer, Cotton**
*See* Speyrer, Charles W.

**[The] Sphinx**
*See* Baeza, Braulio

**[The] Sphinx**
*See* Gustafsson, Greta Lovisa

**[The] Sphinx**
*See* Leverson, Ada

**[The] Sphinx**
*See* Mossi, Donald Louis

**[The] Sphinx**
*See* Roosevelt, Franklin Delano

**Spicer, Anne Higginson** 1871- ?
[NAA]
*American author and poet*
* Anchusa

**Spicer, Bart** 1918-   [CC, WW]
*Author*
* Barbette, Jay

**Spicer, Nicholas**
*See* Payne, Alban S.

**Spicer, Seth**
*See* Gould, Benjamin F.

**Spickler, Charles A[braham]** 1880-
?   [WGT]
*American author*
* Brogan the Scribe

**Spider Bruce**
*See* Mason, John

**Spider Sam**
*See* McGhee, Walter Brown

**[The] Spiderman**
*See* Allen, Jimmy

**Spiderman**
*See* Scott-Heron, Gil

**Spie, Oliver?**
*See* Slotkin, Joseph

**Spiegel, Clara Gatzert** 1904-
[ANT]
*American author*
* Jaynes, Clare [joint pseudonym
    with Jane Rothschild Mayer]

**Spiel, Hilde**
*See* De Mendelssohn, Hilde Maria

**Spielberg, Hanns von**
*See* Zobeltitz, Hanns von

**Spielman, Fred**
*See* Spielman, Fritz

**Spielman, Fritz** 20th c.   [ASC]
*Austrian-born composer*
* Spielman, Fred

**Spielmann, M. H.**
See Spielmann, Marion Harry
Alexander

**Spielmann, Marion Harry Alexander**
1858-1948 [LAO, LC]
*British author and critic*
* M. H. S.
* Spielmann, M. H.

**Spielmann, Peter James** 1952-
[CA]
*American author*
* Nightrate, Emil

**Spike, Ethan**
See Whittier, Matthew F.

**Spiker, Ray**
See Faust, Ray

**Spikes**
See Botts, Randolph

**Spikes, Charley** 20th c. [IBW]
*American baseball player*
* [The] Bogalusa Bomber

**Spilhaus, Phyllis Margaret** 20th c.
[IAW]
*South African author*
* Whiting Spilhaus, M.

**Spillane, Frank Morrison** 1918-
[CA, CC, EMD]
*American author*
* Spillane, Mickey

**Spillane, Mickey**
See Spillane, Frank Morrison

**Spillius, Elizabeth Jane [Bott]**
1924- [AW]
*Canadian-born anthropologist and
author*
* Bott, Elizabeth

**Spillman, Barbara** 1927- [FFA]
*American singer*
* Dane, Barbara

**Spilotro, Anthony** 20th c.
*American underworld figure*
* Tony the Ant

**Spinella, Barney** 1893- [BBH]
*Italian-born American bowler*
* Spinella, Jumping Jack

**Spinella, Jumping Jack**
See Spinella, Barney

**Spinello Aretino**
See Spinello, Luca

**Spinello, Luca** 1330?-1410 [WBD]
*Florentine painter*
* Spinello Aretino

**Sping, Dan**
See Spalding, Henry D.

**Spinifex**
See Martin, David

**Spinks, Leon** 1954?-
*American boxer*
* Spinks, Mess-Over

**Spinks, Mess-Over**
See Spinks, Leon

**Spinner, Alice**
See Fraser, Augusta Zelia

**Spinner, Red**
See Senior, William

**Spinossimus**
See White, William, Jr.

**Spinther**
See Lentulus, Publius Cornelius

**[The] Spiral Ascensionist**
See Ethardo

**Spiral Groove**
See Macdonald, Wilson

**Spirer, Herbert F[rederick]** 1925-
[CA]
*American author and educator*
* Sitzfleisch, Vladimir

**Spires, Arthur** 1912- [BWW, NBB]
*American singer*
* Spires, Big Boy

**Spires, Benjamin** 1931- [BWW]
*American musician*
* Spires, Bud

**Spires, Big Boy**
See Spires, Arthur

**Spires, Bud**
See Spires, Benjamin

**[The] Spirit**
See Davis, Mickey

**[The] Spirit of Hampden**
See Fellowes, Robert

**[The] Spirit of Nashville**
See Collins, Lucretia

**[Lo] Spirito [The Ghost]**
See Valente, Umberto

**[The] Spiritual Mother**
See Southcott, Joanna

**Spiro, Edward** 1908- [CA]
*Austrian-born author*
* Cookridge, E. H.

**Spirt, Diana L[ouise]** 1925- [CA]
*American librarian and author*
* Lembo, Diana L.

**Spit, Sam**
See Schneck, Stephen

**Spitlera, Joseph P., Jr.** 1938?-
[NOJ]
*American jazz musician*
* Spitlera, Pee Wee

**Spitlera, Pee Wee**
See Spitlera, Joseph P., Jr.

**Spitteler, Carl** 1845-1924 [WBD]
*Swiss author*
* Tandem, Felix

**Spittin' Bill Doak**
See Doak, William Leopold

**Spitz, Eddie**
See Osadchey, Edward P.

**Spivey, Addie** 1910-1943 [BWW]
*American singer*
* May, Hannah
* Sweet Peas[e]

**Spivey, Elton Island** 1900-1971
[BWW]
*American singer*
* Spivey, Za Zu
* [The] Za Zu Girl

**Spivey, Victoria Regina [Vicky]**
1906-1976 [BWW]
*American singer*
* Lucas, Jane
* [The] Queen
* [The] Queen of the Blues

**Spivey, Za Zu**
See Spivey, Elton Island

**Splane, Elza K.**
See Temary, Elza

**[The] Splendid Splinter**
See Rayl, Jim

**[The] Splendid Splinter**
See Williams, Theodore Samuel
[Ted]

**Spo-Dee-O-Dee**
See Theard, Sam

**Spofforth, Frederick Robert**
1853-1926 [EC, OCS, WBD]
*Australian cricketer*
* [The] Demon Bowler

**Spognardi, Andrea Ettore** 1908-
[BE]
*American baseball player*
* Spognardi, Andy

**Spognardi, Andy**
See Spognardi, Andrea Ettore

**[The] Spoiler**
See Risko, Johnny

**[The] Spoilt Child of Fortune**
See Massena, Andre

**Sponagle, Barry** 20th c. [RBE]
*Canadian boxer*
* Sponagle, Kid

**Sponagle, Kid**
See Sponagle, Barry

**Spondanus**
See De Sponde, Jean

**Sponge, Mr.**
See Herbert, Henry William

**[The] Spoon**
See Witherspoon, James [Jimmy]

**Spooner, Ed** 20th c. [CSH]
*Bicycle racing pioneer*
* Spooner, On The Spot

**Spooner, John D.** 1937- [CA]
*American author*
* Brutus

**Spooner, On The Spot**
See Spooner, Ed

**Spoonhill**
See Reaney, James Crerar

**Spoopendyke**
See Huntly, Stanley

**Sporn, Philip** 1897?-1978
*Austrian-born American
industrialist*
* Public Utility, Mr.

**[The] Sportsman Ventriloquist**
See Clark, Johnson

**Sporus**
See Hervey, John [Baron Hervey
of Ickworth]

**Spot**
See Potts, Arthur

**Spot, Ryhen**
See Post, Henry

**Spotswood, Alexander** 1676-1740
[SN]
*British colonial governor*
* [The] Tubal Cain of America

**Spotswood, Dillon Jordan** 20th c.
[WGT]
*Author*
* Nuverbis

**Spotswood, John**
See Stanard, John Dandridge
Spotswood

**Spoturno, Francesco Giuseppe**
1874-1934 [WBD]
*Corsican-born French industrialist
and newspaper owner*
* Coty, Francois

**Sprackling, Sprack**
See Sprackling, William E.

**Sprackling, William E.** 1890- [FB]
*American football player*
* Sprackling, Sprack

**Sprague, Bud**
See Sprague, Mortimer E.

**Sprague, Carl T.** 1895- [ECM]
*American country-western performer*
* [The] Original Singing Cowboy

**Sprague, Carter**
See Merwin, [W.] Sam[uel], Jr.

**Sprague, Charles** 1791-1876 [PA]
*Author*
* [The] Banker Poet

**Sprague, Claire S[acks]** 1926- [CA]
*American educator and author*
* Sacks, Claire

**Sprague, Frank Julian** 1857-1934
[WBD]
*American engineer and inventor*
* [The] Father of Electric Traction

**Sprague, Mortimer E.** 1904- [FB]
*American football player*
* Sprague, Bud

**Sprague, Thomas A.**
See Fish, Hamilton

**Sprague, W. D.**
See Von Block, Sylvia

**Sprake, Leslie** 20th c. [WWL]
*British author*
* Middle Wallop

**Spratt, Henry Lee** 1888- [BE]
*American baseball player*
* Spratt, Jack

**Spratt, Jack**
See Cobb, Jack

**Spratt, Jack**
See Spratt, Henry Lee

**Sprecher, Karl**
See Bloch, David

**Sprecher, Muggsy**
See Sprecher, Robert J. [Bob]

**Sprecher, Robert J. [Bob]** 1921-
[EJ]
*American jazz musician*
* Sprecher, Muggsy

**Sprecher, William Gunther** 1924-
[ASC]
*German-born musician*
* Gunther, William

**Spreckels, Anthony** 1950?-1977
[FIR]
*Producer*
* Spreckels, Bunker

**Spreckels, Bunker**
See Spreckels, Anthony

**Spreckels, Claus** 1828-1908 [WBD]
*German-born sugar manufacturer*
\* [The] Sugar King

**Spreull, John** [SN]
*Religious dissenter*
\* Bass John

**Spriel, Stephen**
See Pilotin, Michael

**Sprigel, Olivier**
See Avice, Claude

**Sprigg, C[hristopher] St. John**
1907-1937 [EMD, LC, TC]
*British author and poet*
\* Caudwell, Christopher

**Spring, Clifford** 20th c.
[BBH, CSH]
*Canadian lacrosse player*
\* Spring, Doughy

**Spring, Doughy**
See Spring, Clifford

**Spring, Gerald M[ax]** 1897- [CA]
*German-born American educator
and author*
\* Bodwell, Richard

**Spring, Gordon** 20th c.
[BBH, CSH]
*Canadian lacrosse promoter*
\* Spring, Grumpy

**Spring, Grumpy**
See Spring, Gordon

**Springall, Charles** 1925- [FC]
*British entertainer*
\* Drake, Charlie

**[The] Springer**
See Louis [or Ludwig]

**Springer, Axel, Jr.** 1942?-1980
*German photojournalist*
\* Simon, Sven

**Springer, Barbara** 1871-1937 [SC]
*Hungarian-born actress*
\* DeBozoky, Barbara

**Springer, Marilyn Harris** 1931-
[CA]
*American author*
\* Harris, Marilyn

**Springer, Rudolf**
See Renner, Karl

**Springfield**
See Kelly, Maurice Anthony

**Springfield, David**
See Lewis, Roy

**Springfield, Dusty**
See O'Brien, Mary

**[The] Springfield Rifle**
See Raschi, Victor John Angelo

**Springmeyer, Charles E., Jr.** 1912-
[BEW]
*American actor, stage manager,
director*
\* Durand, Charles

**Sprinz, Joseph Conrad [Joe]** 1902-
[BE]
*American baseball player*
\* Sprinz, Mule

**Sprinz, Mule**
See Sprinz, Joseph Conrad [Joe]

**Sproston, John**
See Scott, Peter Dale

**Sproul, Dorothy Noyes**
See Noyes-Kane, Dorothy

**Sproule, Zibra**
See Trask, George F.

**Sproull, Lefty**
See Sproull, Ralph

**Sproull, Ralph** 1893- [BB]
*American basketball player*
\* Sproull, Lefty

**Sprouts**
See Whiteing, E.

**Spruggins, Richard Sucklethum**
See Morley, Countess of

**Spun Yarn**
See Loomis, Alfred Fullerton

**Spurgeon, Charles Haddon**
1834-1892 [DEL]
*British author and clergyman*
\* Ploughman, John

**Spurin-Calleia, Joseph** 1897-1975
[BEW, FC, HCA]
*Maltese-born actor*
\* Calleia, Joseph

**Spurr, Clinton**
See Rowland, D[onald] S[ydney]

**Spy**
See Ward, [Sir] Leslie

**Spy in Washington**
See Davis, Matthew Livingston

**Spykman, E. C.**
See Spykman, Elizabeth Choate

**Spykman, Elizabeth Choate**
1896-1943 [TCC]
*American author*
\* Spykman, E. C.

**[The] Squab Poet**
See Dryden, John

**[A] Square**
See Abbott, Edwin Abbott

**Square Jaw Ramsey**
See Ramsey, William Thrace [Bill]

**Squatter Sovereignty**
See Calhoun, John Caldwell

**[The] Squealer**
See Bioff, Willie

**[La] Squelette des Graces**
See Guimard, [Marie] Madeleine

**Squibob**
See Derby, George Horatio

**Squier, Emma Lindsay**
See Bransby, Emma Lindsay
Squier

**Squier, Ephraim George** 1821- ?
[DEL, PA]
*British author*
\* Bard, Samuel A.

**Squier, Lucita**
See Williams, Lucita Squier

**[The] Squint-Eyed**
See Barbieri, Giovanni [or Gian]
Francesco

**Squintum, Doctor**
See Irving, Edward

**Squintum, Doctor**
See Whitefield, George

**[The] Squire**
See Adams, Derek John

**[The] Squire**
See Clark, Johnson

**Squire**
See Coleman, John Winston, Jr.

**[The] Squire**
See Howe, Lyman

**Squire, J. C.**
See Squire, John Collings

**Squire, John Collings** 1884-1958
[LC, NAA]
*British author and journalist*
\* Eagle, Solomon
\* Squire, J. C.

**[The] Squire of Hyde Park**
See Roosevelt, Franklin Delano

**[The] Squire of Kennett Square**
See Pennock, Herb[ert Jefferis]

**[The] Squire of Squawg Hollow**
See Reeve, Edward H. [Ted]

**Squire, Ronald**
See Squirl, Ronald

**Squires, Eric**
See Ball, Sylvia Patricia

**Squires, Frederick** 20th c. [CAA]
*American author*
\* Thumtack, Tom

**Squires, Patricia**
See Ball, Sylvia Patricia

**Squires, Phil**
See Barker, S[quire] Omar

**Squires, Theodore** 1907-1942 [BS]
*American magician*
\* Anneman the Enigma
\* Annemann, Theodore
\* [The] Father of Modern Mental
Magic

**Squirl, Ronald** 1886-1958 [FC]
*British actor*
\* Squire, Ronald

**Squirrell, L. R.**
See Squirrell, Leonard Russell

**Squirrell, Leonard Russell** 1893-
[ART]
*British painter and etcher*
\* Squirrell, L. R.

**Sreenivasapuram, Sesha Charlu**
1921- [IAW]
*Indian author and poet*
\* Subhasree

**Sri Aurobindo**
See Ghose, Aurobindo

**Sri-Rajputra**
See Bera, Sudhir

**Sse-ma-Thsian** 1st c. [HN]
*Chinese historian*
\* [The] Herodotus of China

**Stabile, Jack** 20th c. [BLB]
*American underworld figure*
\* Stabile, Stick 'em Up

**Stabile, Stick 'em Up**
See Stabile, Jack

**Stabile, Theresa Maria** 1919-
[ASC, PMJ]
*American singer and composer*
\* Dawn, Dolly

**Stableford, Brian M[ichael]** 1948-
[ESF]
*British author and critic*
\* Craig, Brian [joint pseudonym
with Craig M. Mackintosh]

**Stabler, J. L.** [PA]
*Author*
\* Woodville, Jennie

**Stabler, Ken** 20th c.
*American football player*
\* Stabler, Snake

**Stabler, Snake**
See Stabler, Ken

**Stacek, Albert John** 1900- [BE]
*American baseball player*
\* Stokes, Al[bert John]

**Stacher, Doc**
See Stacher, Joseph

**Stacher, Joseph** 1902- [BLB, MM]
*Polish-born American underworld
figure*
\* Goldman, Harry
\* Harris, Doc
\* Harris, J. P.
\* Kent, George
\* Rose, Morris
\* Rosen, Doc
\* Rosen, Joseph
\* Stacher, Doc
\* Stein, Joe J.
\* Weiner, Doc

**Stachys, Dimitris**
See Constantelos, Demetrios J.

**Stack, Baron**
See Ratazzi, Mme.

**Stack, Frank H[untington]** 1937-
[CA]
*American artist*
\* Sturgeon, Foolbert

**Stack, Nicolete Meredith** 1896-
[CA]
*American author*
\* Hill, Elleen
\* Kenny, Kathryn [house
pseudonym]
\* Meredith, Nicolete

**Stack, Robert**
See Modini, Robert

**Stackhouse, Lefty**
See Stackhouse, Wilburn Artist

**Stackhouse, Mary Agnes**
1878-1934 [CAT]
*American author and poet*
\* Mary Angelita, [Sister]

**Stackhouse, Ruby** 20th c. [IBW]
*American singer*
\* Andrews, Ruby

**Stackhouse, Wilburn Artist**
1911-1973 [GF]
*American golfer*
\* Stackhouse, Lefty

**Stacy, Brian**
See Browder, Bill

**Stacy, Bruce**
See Elliott, Bruce [Walter Gardner Lively Stacy]

**Stacy, Terry**
See Lea, Terrea

**Stacy, Walter**
See Elliott, Bruce [Walter Gardner Lively Stacy]

**Stadelman, S. L.**
See Stadelman, Sara Lee

**Stadelman, Sara Lee** 1917- [CA]
American playwright and poet
* Harris, Sara Lee
* Stadelman, S. L.

**Stael, Anne Louise Germaine de**
1766-1817 [SN]
French author
* Corinne
* [An] Orestes of Exile

**Stafford, Caroline**
See Watjen, Carolyn L. T.

**Stafford, General**
See Stafford, James Joseph

**Stafford, Hanley**
See Austin, John

**Stafford, Harrison** 20th c. [BBH]
American football player
* Stafford, Harry

**Stafford, Harry**
See Stafford, Harrison

**Stafford, Heinie**
See Stafford, Henry Alexander

**Stafford, Henry Alexander** 1891-
[BE]
American baseball player
* Stafford, Heinie

**Stafford, James Joseph** 1868-1923
[BE]
American baseball player
* Stafford, General

**Stafford, Jo** 1920-
American singer
* Edwards, Darlene

**Stafford, Muriel**
See Sauer, Muriel Stafford

**Stafford, Peter**
See Tabori, Pal

**Stafford-Northcote, Iris** 1909-
[THR]
Irish-born actress and singer
* Ashley, Iris

**Staffordshire Knot**
See Wrottesley, Arthur John Francis

**[The] Stage-Struck Hero**
See Liston, Harry

**Stagg, Amos Alonzo** 1862-1965
[BB, BBH]
American football and basketball coach
* [The] Grand Old Man of Football
* [The] Grand Old Man of the Midway

**Stagg, J. R.** 20th c. [MBF]
British author
* Barnet, John
* Harte, Oliver

**Stagg, James**
See Pendower, Jacques

**Stagg, James** 20th c. [MBF]
British author and journalist
* Johns, Gilbert
* Reid, Desmond [house pseudonym]

**Stagge, Jonathan** [joint pseudonym with Hugh Callingham Wheeler]
See Webb, Richard Wilson

**Stagge, Jonathan** [joint pseudonym with Richard Wilson Webb]
See Wheeler, Hugh Callingham

**[The] Stagirite**
See Aristotle

**Staglich, Oswalda** 1899-1948 [SC]
German actress
* [The] German Mary Pickford
* Oswalda, Ossi

**Stahan, Butch**
See Stahan, Frank Ralph

**Stahan, Frank Ralph** 1915- [CEI]
Canadian-born hockey player
* Stahan, Butch

**Stahl, Charles Sylvester** 1873-1907
[AS, DGS, PB]
American baseball player
* Stahl, Chick

**Stahl, Chick**
See Stahl, Charles Sylvester

**Stahl, Eva** 1949-
Swedish nurse who served in Palestinian refugee camp, 1974-76
* Samira [Beautiful Flower]

**Stahl, Fred Alan** 1944- [CA]
American computer scientist and writer
* Feur, D. Cy

**Stahl, Garland** 1879-1922
[AS, BE, PB]
American baseball player and manager
* Stahl, Jake

**Stahl, Heinrich**
See Temme, Jodocus Donatus Hubertus

**Stahl, Jake**
See Stahl, Garland

**Stahl, Jesse** 20th c. [IBW]
American rodeo performer
* Stahl, Peerless

**Stahl, Karl**
See Goedeke, Karl

**Stahl, Le Roy** 1908- [CAP]
American author
* Sheldon, George E.
* Wood, Kirk

**Stahl, P. J.**
See Hetzel, Pierre Jules

**Stahl, Peerless**
See Stahl, Jesse

**Stahl, Pierre Jules**
See Hetzel, Pierre Jules

**Stahl-Nachbaur, Ernest**
See Guggenheimer, Ernest

**Stahr, Arthur**
See Voight, Valeska

**Stahr, Mme. Adolf W. T.** [PA]
Author
* Lewald, Fanny

**Staiger, Elizabeth Anne** 1928-
[BEW]
American actress and singer
* Staiger, Libi

**Staiger, Libi**
See Staiger, Elizabeth Anne

**Stainback, George Tucker** 1910-
[BE, PB]
American baseball player
* Stainback, Tuck

**Stainback, Macklin** 1911- [CA]
American attorney and author
* Fleming, Macklin

**Stainback, Tuck**
See Stainback, George Tucker

**Stainer, Leslie Howard** 1893-1943
[BDF, BEW, WEF]
British actor, director, playwright
* Howard, Leslie

**Staines, Trevor**
See Brunner, John [Kilian Houston]

**Stainforth, Frank** [PA]
Author
* Forsith, Nat

**Stainless Stephen**
See Baynes, Arthur Clifford

**Stairs, Gordon**
See Austin, Mary [Hunter]

**Stait, Virginia**
See Russell, Winifred Brent

**Stakman, Elvin C.** 1886?-1979
American plant pathologist
* Stakman, Stak

**Stakman, Stak**
See Stakman, Elvin C.

**Stalcup, Sparky**
See Stalcup, Wilbur

**Stalcup, Wilbur** 1910-1972 [BB]
American basketball coach
* Stalcup, Sparky

**Staley, Gale**
See Staley, George Gaylord

**Staley, George Gaylord** 1899- [BE]
American baseball player
* Staley, Gale

**Staley, Harry**
See Staley, Henry E.

**Staley, Henry E.** 1866-1910 [AS]
American baseball player
* Staley, Harry

**Stalin, Joseph**
See Dzhugashvili, Iosif Vissarionovich

**Stallard, Evan T.** 1937- [PB]
American baseball player
* Stallard, Tracy

**Stallard, Tracy**
See Stallard, Evan T.

**Stallcup, Red**
See Stallcup, Thomas Virgil

**Stallcup, Thomas Virgil** 1922- [BE]
American baseball player
* Stallcup, Red

**Staller, George Walborn** 1916-
[BE]
American baseball player
* Staller, Stopper

**Staller, Stopper**
See Staller, George Walborn

**Stallings, Big Chief**
See Stallings, George Tweedy

**Stallings, George Tweedy**
1867-1929 [BE, BTB]
American baseball player and manager
* [The] Miracle Man
* Stallings, Big Chief

**Stallone, Sylvester [Enzio]** 1946-
[CA]
American actor, director, screenwriter
* Moonblood, Q.

**Stallworth, Bud**
See Stallworth, Isaac

**Stallworth, Dave** 1941- [BB]
American basketball player
* [The] Rave

**Stallworth, Isaac** 1950- [BB]
American basketball player
* Stallworth, Bud

**Stamatopoulos, Stratis** 1892-
[EWL]
Greek author
* Myrivilis, Stratis

**Stammel, Heinz-Josef** 1926- [IAW]
German author
* Hagen, Christopher
* Lockhart, T. C.

**[The] Stammerer**
See Louis II

**[The] Stammerer**
See Michael II

**[The] Stammerer**
See Notger [or Notker]

**Stamp, Roger** 1913- [AW]
Scottish author
* Mingston, R. Gresham

**Stampede**
See Kelly, Jonathan F.

**Stamper, Alex**
See Kent, Arthur [William Charles]

**Stamper, Pete**
See Stamper, Wallace Logan

**Stamper, Wallace Logan** 1930-
[CWG, DAM]
American country-western performer
* Stamper, Pete

**Stamps, Hulan** 20th c. [OBW]
American baseball player
* Stamps, Lefty

**Stamps, Lefty**
See Stamps, Hulan

**Stan the Man**
See Musial, Stanislaus

**Stan the Man**
See Turner, Spurgeon, Jr.

**Stanard, John Dandridge Spotswood**
1905- [WWL]
American author and poet
* Spotswood, John

**Standaert**
See Bloemen, Pieter van

**Standing, Dorothy** 1909-    [F2, FC]
*British actress*
* Hammond, Kay

**Standing, John**
See Leon, John

**Standish, Burt L.**
See Patten, William George

**Standish, J. O.**
See Horler, Sydney

**Standish, John**    [SN]
*Opposed translation of Bible into English*
* Inkpot, Doctor

**Standish, Miles** 1584?-1656    [SN]
*American colonist*
* [The] Puritan Captain

**Standish, Richard**
See Goyne, Richard

**Standish, Robert**
See Gerahty, Digby George

**Stanek, Al** 1943-    [BE]
*American baseball player*
* Stanek, Lefty

**Stanek, Lefty**
See Stanek, Al

**Stanelli**
See De Groot, Edward Stanley

**Stanes, Muriel**
See Stevens, Muriel Phyllis

**Stanfield, Agnes**
See McElhinney, Jane

**Stanford, Jack** 1900-    [BMH]
*British comic dancer*
* [The] Dancing Fool

**Stanford, John Keith** 1892-    [CA]
*British author*
* Issachar

**Stanford, R. A. S.** 1892-1971    [SC]
*Actor*
* Grahame, Bert

**Stanford, Sally**
See Busby, Mabel Janice

**Stang, Judit** 1921-    [CA]
*Hungarian-born author and artist*
* Varga, Judy

**Stangeland, Katharina Marie [Bech-Brondum] Michaelis** 1872-1950    [EWL, TC]
*Danish author*
* Michaelis, Karin

**Stanhope, Ada**
See Bothner, Mrs. A.

**Stanhope, Adeline**
See Wheatcroft, Mrs. Nelson

**Stanhope, Douglas**
See Duff, Douglas Valder

**Stanhope, Eric**
See Hamilton, Charles Harold St. John

**Stanhope, Hester Lucy** 1770-1839 [HN]
*British eccentric*
* Palmyra's Queen
* Queen of Palmyra
* Queen of the Desert

**Stanhope, Lavinia**
See Schlein, Miriam

**Stanhope, Philip** 1755-1815    [SN]
*British statesman and author*
* Chesterfield, Earl of
* [The] Maecenas and Petronius of His Age
* [The] Prince of Wits

**Stanhope, Philip Dormer** 1694-1773    [DEP, SN, WBD]
*British statesman and author*
* Broadbottom, Geffery
* Chesterfield, Fourth Earl of
* [The] La Rochefoucauld of England
* [A] Tea Table Scoundrel

**Stanhouse, Don[ald Joseph]** 1951-
*American baseball player*
* Stanhouse, Full Pack

**Stanhouse, Full Pack**
See Stanhouse, Don[ald Joseph]

**Stanier, Maida Euphemia Kerr** 1909-    [CA]
*Scottish-born author, poet, playwright*
* Culex

**Staniforth, [Dr.] John William** 1863-1927    [MBF]
*British author*
* Scott, Maxwell

**Stanis, Ber Nadette**
See Stanislaus, Bernadette

**Stanislaus, Bernadette** 1953- [IBW]
*American actress, fashion model, dancer*
* Stanis, Ber Nadette

**Stanislaus, Edward**
See Parker, Dom Anselm

**Stanislavsky, Konstantin Sergeivitch**
See Alexeyev, Konstantin Sergeivitch

**Stanislaw, Stanley**
See Sielanski, Stanley

**Stankiewicz, Michal**
See Bystrzycki, Przemyslaw

**Stankiewicz, Mike**
See Stankiewicz, Myron

**Stankiewicz, Myron** 1935-    [CEI]
*Canadian-born hockey player*
* Stankiewicz, Mike

**Stanky, Edward Raymond** 1916- [BE, PB]
*American baseball player and manager*
* [The] Brat
* Stanky, Muggsy

**Stanky, Muggsy**
See Stanky, Edward Raymond

**Stanlaws, Penrhyn**
See Adamson, Penrhyn Stanley

**Stanley, Alixe Russell**
See Grant, Maude Margaret

**Stanley, Alma Stuart**
See De Garmo, Mrs. Charles

**Stanley, Barney**
See Stanley, Russell

**Stanley, Bennett**
See Hough, Stanley Bennett

**Stanley, Buck**
See Stanley, John Leonard

**Stanley, Chuck**
See Strong, Charles Stanley

**Stanley, Dave**
See Dachs, David

**Stanley, Dean** 1815-1881    [PA]
*Author*
* Anglicanus

**Stanley, Digger**
See Stanley, George

**Stanley, Edward George Geoffrey Smith** 1799-1869 [DEL, DNNF, FFF]
*British statesman and author*
* Derby, 14th Earl of
* [The] Hotspur of Debate
* [The] Rupert of Debate

**Stanley, Edward H. Smith** 1806- ? [PA]
*Author*
* E. H. S.

**Stanley, Fay Grissom [Shulman]** 1925-    [CA]
*American author*
* Fay, Stanley

**Stanley, Francis**
See Crocchiola, Francis Stanley

**Stanley, George** 1883-    [BX]
*British boxer*
* Stanley, Digger

**Stanley, Henry Morton**
See Rowlands, John

**Stanley, James** 1607-1651    [WBD]
*Seventh Earl of Derby*
* [The] Martyr Earl

**Stanley, John Leonard** 1889-1940 [BE]
*American baseball player*
* Stanley, Buck

**Stanley, John Wesley** 1903-    [MK]
*American baseball player*
* Stanley, Neck

**Stanley, Kim**
See Reid, Patricia Kimberly

**Stanley, Marge**
See Weinbaum, Stanley G[rauman]

**Stanley, Mickey**
See Stanley, Mitchell Jack

**Stanley, Milton O.** 1940-    [CM]
*American radio program director*
* Bailey, Bill

**Stanley, Mitchell Jack** 1942- [PB, SMG, WWB]
*American baseball player*
* Stanley, Mickey

**Stanley, Neck**
See Stanley, John Wesley

**Stanley, Nick**
See Stanley, Ralph

**Stanley, Nora Kathleen Begbie Strange** 1885?-    [AW, CAP]
*British author*
* Strange, Nora K.

**Stanley, Olin**
See Honeywell, E. L.

**Stanley, Peter E.**
See Pierotti, Piero

**Stanley, Phil**
See Ind, Allison

**Stanley, Phyllis**
See Knapman, Phyllis

**Stanley, Ralph** 1914-1972    [SC]
*American actor*
* Stanley, Nick

**Stanley, Reginald Fitz-Roy**
See Cowton, Robert

**Stanley, Robert**
See Hamilton, Charles Harold St. John

**Stanley, Russell** 1893-1971 [FHE, HK]
*Canadian-born hockey player*
* Stanley, Barney

**Stanley, Warwick**
See Hilton, John Buxton

**Stannard, Lane**
See Taurasi, James V., Sr.

**Stannard, Russell** 20th c.    [MBF]
*British author*
* Mallinson, Russell

**Stannus, Austin**
See Greaves, Clotilda

**Stannus, Edris** 1898-    [THR]
*Irish-born dancer*
* De Valois, [Dame] Ninette

**Stannus, [James] Gordon [Dawson]** 1902-    [CA]
*British author*
* Anthony, Gordon
* Jason

**Stansberger, Richard** 1950-    [CA]
*American poet and playwright*
* Grant, Venzo

**Stansbury, Alec**
See Higgs, Alec Stansbury

**Stansbury-Millett, Nigel** ?-1946
*Author*
* Chandos, Dane [joint pseudonym with Peter Lilley]

**Stansfeld, Anthony** 20th c. [CC, WW]
*Author*
* Buckingham, Bruce [joint pseudonym with Peter Lilley]
* Chandos, Dane [joint pseudonym with Peter Lilley]

**Stansfield, Grace** 1898-1979 [CED, FC]
*British singer and comedienne*
* Fields, Gracie
* Our Gracie

**Stansfield, Thomas** 1908-    [BMH]
*British comedian*
* Fields, Tommy
* London's Lancashire Comedian

**Stanstead, John**
See Groom, Arthur William

**Stanton, Baby Bull**
See Stanton, Leroy Bobby

**Stanton, Borden?**
See Wilding, Philip

**Stanton, Buck**
See Stanton, George Washington

**Stanton, C.** [PA]
*Author*
* C. S.

**Stanton, Chuck**
See Sellers, Connie Leslie, Jr.

**Stanton, Coralie**
See Hosken, Alice Cecil Seymour

**Stanton, Frank Lebby** 1857-1927
[WBD]
*American journalist and poet*
* [The] Poet Laureate of Georgia

**Stanton, George Washington** 1906-
[BE]
*American baseball player*
* Stanton, Buck

**Stanton, John**
See Wallis, George C.

**Stanton, John** 1826-1871 [PA]
*Author*
* O'Lanus, Corry

**Stanton, Lee**
See Stanton, Leroy Bobby

**Stanton, Leroy Bobby** 1946-
[BE, PB]
*American baseball player*
* Stanton, Baby Bull
* Stanton, Lee

**Stanton, Marjorie**
See Phillips, Horace

**Stanton, Paul**
See Beaty, [Arthur] David

**Stanton, Vance**
See Avallone, Michael [Angelo], Jr.

**Stanton, William**
See Hope, William Edward Stanton

**Stanwood, Brooks** [joint pseudonym with Susan Stanwood Kaminsky]
See Kaminsky, Howard

**Stanwood, Brooks** [joint pseudonym with Howard Kaminsky]
See Kaminsky, Susan Stanwood

**Stanwyck, Barbara**
See Stevens, Ruby

**Staples, Boo**
See Staples, Cleotha

**Staples, Bunnie**
See Staples, Yvonne

**Staples, Cleotha** 1934- [IBW]
*American singer*
* Staples, Boo
* Staples, Roberta

**Staples, Marjory Charlotte** 20th c.
[AW]
*New Zealand author*
* Redwood, Rosaline

**Staples, Pop**
See Staples, Roebuck

**Staples, Reginald Thomas** 1911-
[CA]
*British author*
* Bridges, Howard
* Sinclair, James
* Stevens, Robert Tyler

**Staples, Roberta**
See Staples, Cleotha

**Staples, Roebuck** [IBW, RO2, SSS]
*American singer*
* Staples, Pop

**Staples, Yvonne** 1938- [IBW]
*American singer*
* Staples, Bunnie

**Stapleton, D.** [joint pseudonym with Douglas Stapleton]
See Stapleton, Dorothy

**Stapleton, D.** [joint pseudonym with Dorothy Stapleton]
See Stapleton, Douglas

**Stapleton, Dorothy** 20th c. [WW]
*Author*
* Stapleton, D. [joint pseudonym with Douglas Stapleton]

**Stapleton, Douglas** 20th c. [WW]
*Author*
* Stapleton, D. [joint pseudonym with Dorothy Stapleton]

**Stapleton, Jean**
See Murray, Jeanne

**Stapleton, Maurice**
See Purcell, J. S.

**Stapleton, Pat[rick James]** 1940-
[FHE]
*Canadian-born hockey player*
* Stapleton, Whitey

**Stapleton, Vivian S.** 1921?-
[BEW, EMT, ITA]
*American actress and singer*
* Blaine, Vivian

**Stapleton, Whitey**
See Stapleton, Pat[rick James]

**Stapleton, Zoe Margaret** 20th c.
[THR]
*South African-born actress and dancer*
* Gail, Zoe

**Stapley, Richard**
See Wyler, Richard

**Stapulensis**
See Lefevre d'Etaples, Jacques

**[The] Star and Luminary of Law and Latern of Equity**
See Bartoli [or Bartolus]

**Star, Angel**
See Quigley, Joan

**Star Man's Padre**
See Patrick, Johnstone G[illespie]

**[The] Star of the North**
See Gustavus Adolphus

**Starbird, Kaye** 1916- [CA, SAT]
*American author*
* Jennison, C. S.

**Starbuck, Alicia Jo** 1951-
*American figure skater*
* Number 12, Mrs.
* Starbuck, Jo Jo

**Starbuck, Jo Jo**
See Starbuck, Alicia Jo

**Starch Johnny**
See Crowne, John

**Stares, John Edward Spencer**
1947- [IAW]
*British author*
* Rowe, Stephen
* Spencer, Edward

**Starey, Alfred B.** [FFF]
*Writer*
* Ryse, Sherwood

**Stargell, Papa**
See Stargell, Wilver Dornell

**Stargell, Pops**
See Stargell, Wilver Dornell

**Stargell, Willie**
See Stargell, Wilver Dornell

**Stargell, Wilver Dornell** 1941-
[BE, IPA, SMG]
*American baseball player*
* Stargell, Papa
* Stargell, Pops
* Stargell, Willie

**Stark, Albert M.** 1897- [EJS]
*American basketball coach*
* Stark, Dolly

**Stark, Claude Alan** 1935- [CA]
*French-born American author*
* Mwanga

**Stark, Dolly**
See Stark, Albert M.

**Stark, Dolly**
See Stark, Monroe Randolph

**Stark, Fortney H.**
*American politician*
* Stark, Pete

**Stark, James**
See Goldston, Robert Conroy

**Stark, John**
See Godwin, John

**Stark, Jonathan**
See Marshall, H. P.

**Stark, Joshua**
See Olsen, Theodore Victor

**Stark, Michael**
See Rosenblum, Lawrence

**Stark, Monroe Randolph**
1885-1924 [BE]
*American baseball player*
* Stark, Dolly

**Stark, Pesach** 1905- [JL]
*Polish author*
* Stryjkowski, Juljan

**Stark, Pete**
See Stark, Fortney H.

**Stark, Phil**
See Stork, Philipp

**Stark, [Delbert] Raymond** 1919-
[CA, WW]
*American author and poet*
* Norwood, John

**Stark, Richard**
See Onorato, Glauco

**Stark, Richard**
See Westlake, Donald E[dwin]

**Starke, Henderson**
See Neville, Kris [Ottman]

**Starkey, Digley Pilot** [PA]
*Author*
* Advena
* Theoria

**Starkey, Geoffrey** 15th c. [SN]
*British author and clergyman*
* [The] Grammarian

**Starkey, James Sullivan** 1879-1958
[EWL, LC, TC]
*Irish poet*
* O'Sullivan, Seumas

**Starkey, Richard** 1940-
[BBD, IPA, OCF]
*British musician*
* Starr, Ringo

**Starks, Kathryn** 1922- [EJ, IPA]
*American singer*
* Starr, Kay

**Starks, Lefty**
See Starks, Otis

**Starks, Otis** 20th c. [OBW]
*American baseball player*
* Starks, Lefty

**Starling, Thomas**
See Hayton, Richard Neil

**Starnagel, George Henry**
See Steurnagel, George Henry

**Starnes, Daniel** [PA]
*Author*
* Mayfield, Frank

**Starowieyski, Franciszek** 1930-
[GA]
*Polish graphic artist*
* Byk, Jan

**Starr, Bart**
See Starr, Bryan Bartlett

**Starr, Bryan Bartlett** 1934-
[B10, FB, SMG]
*American football player and coach*
* Quarterback, Mr.
* Starr, Bart

**Starr, Cecile** 1921- [CA]
*American filmmaker and editor*
* Boyajian, Cecile

**Starr, Chick**
See Starr, William

**Starr, Edwin**
See Hatcher, Charles

**Starr, George** 20th c. [EE]
*Intelligence agent*
* [The] Patron

**Starr, Henry**
See Bingley, David Ernest

**Starr, Iron Man**
See Starr, Raymond Francis

**Starr, John**
See Aycock, Roger Dee

**Starr, John A.**
See Gillese, John Patrick

**Starr, Judy**
See Gelfman, Judith S[chlein]

**Starr, Kay**
See Starks, Kathryn

**Starr, Laura B.** [FFF]
*American journalist*
* Fanchon

**Starr, Mark**
See Klein, Gerard

**Starr, Mrs. George O.** [FFF]
* Zarzel

**Starr, Muriel**
See MacIver, Muriel

**Starr, Randy**
See Nadel, Warren

**Starr, Randy**
See Randall, Joseph

**Starr, Raymond Francis**
1906-1963 [BE]
*American baseball player*
* Starr, Iron Man

**Starr, Richard Harry** 1878- ?
[MBF, WW, WWL]
*British author*
* Essex, Captain
* Essex, Richard
* Godwin, Frank
* O'Dare, Kerry

**Starr, Ringo**
See Starkey, Richard

**Starr, Roland**
See Rowland, D[onald] S[ydney]

**Starr, Tramp**
See Wilson, William Carl

**Starr, William** 1911- [EJS]
*American baseball player*
* Starr, Chick

**Starret, William**
See McClintock, Marshall

**Start, Clarissa**
See Lippert, Clarissa Start

**Start, Joseph** 1842?-1927 [BE, PB]
*American baseball player*
* Old Reliable
* Start, Rocks

**Start, Rocks**
See Start, Joseph

**Stasek, Antal**
See Zeman, Antonin

**Stasheff, Edward**
See Korostasheffsky, Adolphe
Borisovitch

**Stashynsky, Bogdan** 1931- [EE]
*Russian intelligence agent*
* Draeger, Siegfried

**Stasz, Clarice** 20th c. [CA]
*American sociologist and author*
* Stoll, Clarice Stasz

**[The] State Apothecary**
See Beresford, John Claudius

**[The] State Proteus**
See Prior, Matt[hew]

**[The] Staten Island Scot**
See Thomson, Robert Brown
[Bobby]

**[The] Statesman Bishop**
See Williams, John

**[The] Statesman of the American
Navy**
See Morris, Charles

**Statham, George**
See Statham, John Brian

**Statham, John Brian** 1930- [EC]
*British cricketer*
* Statham, George

**Staton, Alonzo Louis Lee** [BEW]
*American actor and singer*
* Sattin, Lonnie

**Staton, Dakota**
See Rabia, Aliyah

**Staton, Joseph [Joe]** 1948- [BE]
*American baseball player*
* Staton, Slim

**Staton, Merrill**
See Ostrus, Merrill

**Staton, Slim**
See Staton, Joseph [Joe]

**Statten, Vargo**
See Fearn, John Russell

**Statz, Arnold John** 1897-
[BE, BTB]
*American baseball player*
* Statz, Jigger

**Statz, Jigger**
See Statz, Arnold John

**Staub, Daniel Joseph** 1944-
[PB, SMG, WWB]
*American baseball player*
* [Le] Grand Orange
* Staub, Rusty

**Staub, Rusty**
See Staub, Daniel Joseph

**Stauderman, Albert P[hilip]** 1910-
[CA]
*American author*
* Phillips, Alan

**Staudt, Virginia**
See Sexton, Virginia Staudt

**Stauffer, Don**
See Berkebile, Fred D[onovan]

**Staunton, Schuyler**
See Baum, L[yman] Frank

**Staurt, Charles**
See Reid, Charles [Stuart]

**Stautner, Ernie** 20th c.
*American football player*
* [The] Horse

**Stavropoulos**
See Stavropoulos, George Peter

**Stavropoulos, George Peter** 20th c.
[WFA]
*Greek-born fashion designer*
* Stavropoulos

**Stavros, Niko**
See King, Florence

**[The] Stay Maker**
See Thomson, Alexander

**Stchedrin, Nikolai**
See Saltikoff, W.

**Stead, Thistle Yolette** 1902-
[AW, WD]
*Australian biologist and author*
* Harris, Thistle Y.

**Stead, W. T.**
See Stead, William Thomas

**Stead, William Thomas** 1849-1912
[LC]
*British journalist*
* Stead, W. T.

**Steady Eddie Lopat**
See Lopatnyski, Edmund Walter

**Steady Freddie Lewis**
See Lewis, Fred

**Steady Pete Meegan**
See Meegan, Pete[r J.]

**Steady Roll Johnson**
See Johnson, James

**Steady Steve Vickers**
See Vickers, Stephen James

**Steagall, Red**
See Steagall, Russell

**Steagall, Russell** [CME]
*American country-western performer*
* Steagall, Red

**Stealingworth, Slim**
See Wesselmann, Tom

**[The] Steamboat King**
See Newberry, Oliver

**Steamer**
See Nason, Leonard Hastings

**Stearns, Albert**
See Stearns, Edgar Franklin

**Stearns, Edgar Franklin** 1879- ?
[ESF, SFL, WGT]
*American author*
* Franklin, Edgar
* Stearns, Albert

**Stearns, J. N.** [FFF]
*American author*
* Merry, Robert

**Stearns, Myron Morris** 1884-
[NAA]
*American author and editor*
* Amid, John
* Morris, Myron

**Stearns, Norman Thomas** 1901-
[MK]
*American baseball player*
* Stearns, Turkey

**Stearns, Peter N.** 1936- [IAW]
*British-born author*
* Shard, Diana

**Stearns, Turkey**
See Stearns, Norman Thomas

**Stebbins, G. S.** [PA]
*Author*
* Izax, Ickabod

**Stebbins, Mrs. S. B.** [FFF]
*American poet*
* Bridges, Sallie

**Stebbins, Robert**
See Meyers, Sidney

**Stebbins, Rowland** 1882-1948
[BEW]
*American producer*
* Rivers, Laurence

**Stebel, Sidney Leo** 1924- [CA]
*American author*
* Bergson, Leo

**Stebelski, Julian**
See Stoberski, Zygmunt Julian

**Steber, A. R.** [house pseudonym,
Ziff-Davis]
See Graham, Roger Phillips

**Steber, A. R.**
See Palmer, Raymond A[rthur]

**Stecchetti, Lorenzo**
See Guerrini, Olindo

**Steckling, Adri** 20th c. [WFA]
*American fashion designer*
* Adri

**Steding, Peggy** 20th c. [SA]
*American racquetball player*
* Super Duper Tex

**Stedman**
See Dodge, Elizabeth C.

**Stedman, Algernon Methuen
Marshall** 1856-1924 [WBD]
*British publisher*
* Methuen, [Sir] Algernon
Methuen Marshall

**Stedman, Charles Ellery**
1831-1905 [B10]
*American physician and
lithographer*
* Chinks

**Stedman, Edmund Clarence**
1833-1908 [DEP, DNNS, FF]
*American poet*
* [The] Banker Poet

**Steed, Mabel A.** 1894- [WW]
*Author*
* Hughes, M. Alison

**Steedman, James B.** 1818-1883
[DNNS, SN]
*American army officer*
* Old Chickamauga
* Old Steady

**Steegmuller, Francis** 1906-
[CA, CC, TC1]
*American author*
* Keith, David
* Steel, Byron

**Steel Arm Davis**
See Davis, Walter

**Steel Arm Johnny**
See Taylor, John

**Steel Arm Tyler**
See Tyler, William

**Steel, Byron**
See Steegmuller, Francis

**Steel, Howard**
See Hayter, Cecil Goodenough

**Steel, Kurt**
See Steel, Rudolph Hornaday

**[The] Steel Magnolia**
See Carter, Rosalynn Smith

**Steel, Rudolph Hornaday** 1904-
[WW]
*Author*
* Kagey, Rudolf
* Steel, Kurt

**Steel, Tex**
See Ross, William Edward Daniel

**Steel, Tom** [HN]
* O'Connell's Head Pacificator

**Steel, Vernon**
See Antonietti, Vernon

**Steele, Addison, II**
See Lupoff, Richard Allen [Dick]

**Steele, Big Bill**
See Steele, William Mitchell

**Steele, Bob**
See Bradbury, Robert

**Steele, Charles**
See Sellers, Connie Leslie, Jr.

**Steele, Chester K.**
See Stratemeyer, Edward L.

**Steele, Curtis**
See Tepperman, Emile

**Steele, Dale**
See Glut, Donald F[rank]

**Steele, Daniel**
See Chadwick, Charles

**Steele, David Stanley** 1941- [DC]
*British cricketer*
* Steele, Stainless

**Steele, Dirk**
See Plawin, Paul

**Steele, Edward** 1915- [MK]
*American baseball player*
* Steele, Stainless

**Steele, Erskine**
See Henderson, Archibald

**Steele, Francesca Maria** 1848- ?
[LAO]
*British author*
* Dale, Darley

**Steele, Fred I[rving]** 1938- [CA]
*American author*
* Steele, Fritz

**Steele, Fritz**
See Steele, Fred I[rving]

**Steele, Henry** 1931- [CA]
*American economist and author*
* Pinkerton, W. Anson

**Steele, Howard** [house pseudonym]
See Brooks, Leonard Harold

**Steele, Howard** [house pseudonym]
See Edgar, Alfred

**Steele, Howard** [house pseudonym]
See Marshall, Arthur C.

**Steele, Howard** [house pseudonym]
See Symonds, Francis Addington

**Steele, John** [FFF]
*American industrialist*
* Coal Oil Johnny

**Steele, John Frederick** 1946- [DC]
*British cricketer*
* Steele, Steeley

**Steele, Larry** 1916- [IBW]
*American entertainer*
* [The] Black Flo Ziegfeld

**Steele, Mary Q[uintard Govan]**
1922- [CA, SAT, TBJ]
*American author*
* Gage, Wilson

**Steele, Morris J.** [house pseudonym, Ziff-Davis]
See Livingston, Berkeley

**Steele, Morris J.** [house pseudonym, Ziff-Davis]
See Palmer, Raymond A[rthur]

**Steele, [Sir] Richard** 1672-1729
[DEL, FFF, SN]
*British author and playwright*
* Bickerstaff, Isaac
* Edgar, [Sir] John
* [The] First of the British
  Periodical Essayists
* Ironside, Nestor
* Jay
* Nestor
* [A] Twopenny Author

**Steele, Stainless**
See Steele, David Stanley

**Steele, Stainless**
See Steele, Edward

**Steele, Steeley**
See Steele, John Frederick

**Steele, Tommy**
See Hicks, Thomas

**Steele, William [Bill]**
See Gettinger, William A.

**Steele, William Mitchell**
1885-1949 [BE]
*American baseball player*
* Steele, Big Bill

**Steelman, Farmer**
See Steelman, Morris James

**Steelman, Morris James**
1875-1944 [BE]
*American baseball player*
* Steelman, Farmer

**Steely, Ann** 1923-1970 [FC]
*American actress*
* O'Donnell, Cathy

**Steen, Frank**
See Felstein, Ivor

**Steen, Malcolm Harold** 1928- [CA]
*American actor and author*
* Steen, Mike

**Steen, Marguerite** 1894-1975 [CA]
*British author and playwright*
* Dryden, Lennox
* Nicholson, Jane

**Steen, Mike**
See Steen, Malcolm Harold

**Steenberg, Rise** 1913- [MS]
*American opera singer*
* Stevens, Rise

**Steenie**
See Villiers, George

**Steer, Charlotte**
See Hunter, Maud L[ily]

**Steers, Les**
See Steers, Lester

**Steers, Lester** 1917- [TF]
*American track and field athlete*
* Steers, Les

**Steevens, G. W.**
See Steevens, George Warrington

**Steevens, George** 1736-1800
[PA, SN]
*British Shakespearian commentator*
* Amner
* [The] Puck of Commentators

**Steevens, George Warrington**
1869-1900 [LC]
*British journalist*
* Steevens, G. W.

**Stefani [or di Stefano], Ambrogio**
15th c. [WBD]
*Italian painter*
* Borgognone, Ambrogio

**Stefansson, Evelyn**
See Nef, Evelyn Stefansson

**Stefansson, Magnus** 1884-1942
[EWL]
*Icelandic poet*
* Arnarson, Oern

**Steffan, Alice Kennedy** 1907- [CA]
*American author*
* Steffan, Jack

**Steffan, Jack**
See Steffan, Alice Kennedy

**Steffanson, Con** [house pseudonym]
See Cassiday, Bruce [Bingham]

**Steffanson, Con** [house pseudonym]
See Goulart, Ron[ald Joseph]

**Steffen, Anthony**
See De Teffe, Antonio

**Steffen, Gerhardt A.** 1891-
[BX, RBE]
*American boxer*
* Ritchie, Willie

**Steffens, Arthur** 1873- ? [MBF]
*British author*
* Cooper, Freemont
* Dee, Dare
* Glyn, Harrison
* Hale, Clement
* Hardy, Arthur S.
* Leigh, [Capt.] Arthur
* Walters, W. G.
* Wentworth, Charles [house
  pseudonym]

**Stegeman, H. J.**
See Stegeman, Herman J.

**Stegeman, Herman J.** 1891-1939
[FB]
*American football coach*
* Stegeman, H. J.

**Steger, Shelby** 1906- [CA]
*American author*
* Loomis, Rae

**Steiger, Brad**
See Olson, Eugene E.

**Steimer, Francis Alfred** 1854- ?
[FFF, PA]
*Author*
* On the Go
* Prometheus

**Stein, Aaron Marc** 1906-
[CA, CC, EMD]
*American author*
* Bagby, George
* Stone, Hampton

**Stein, Bird** 1868-1944 [JL]
*American educator*
* Gans, Bird

**Stein, Charles**
See Schwalberg, Carol[yn
Ernestine Stein]

**Stein, Frank N.**
See Briefer, Richard [Dick]

**Stein, George** 1903-1967
[F1, F2, FC]
*Polish-born actor*
* Stone, George E.

**Stein, Henry Eugene** 1945-
[ESF, WGT]
*American author*
* Stine, Hank
* Whyte, Sibley

**Stein, J. H.** 20th c. [MBF]
*British author*
* Dixon, Don

**Stein, J. J.**
See Richards, Sara Lippincott

**Stein, Jacob** 20th c. [MM]
*American underworld figure*
* Drew, John

**Stein, Jan**
See Hegeler, Sten

**Stein, Joe J.**
See Stacher, Joseph

**Stein, Johann Saville**
See Stone, John Saville

**Stein, Johnny**
See Hountha, John Philip

**Stein, Jules W. Arndt** 20th c. [MM]
*American underworld figure*
* Arnstein, Nicky

**Stein, Julius Kerwin** 1905-
[BEW, EMT, ITA]
*British-born composer and producer*
* Styne, Jule

**Stein, Justin Marion** 1911- [BE]
*American baseball player*
* Stein, Ott

**Stein, Lloyd** 20th c. [BBH]
*American athletic trainer*
* Stein, Snapper

**Stein, Ott**
See Stein, Justin Marion

**Stein, Randy**
See Stein, William Randolph

**Stein, Robert Jack** 1930-1980
[AM, EMT]
*American actor, dancer, singer*
* Van, Bobby

**Stein, Snapper**
See Stein, Lloyd

**Stein, William Randolph** 1953-
[BR]
*American baseball player*
* Stein, Randy

**Steinbeck, John [Ernst]** 1902-1968
[CA]
*American author*
* Glasscock, Amnesia

**Steinberg, Aaron Zacharovich**
1891-1975 [CA]
*Russian-born British author and educator*
* Avrelin, M.

**Steinberg, Amy**
See Douglas, Mrs. John

**Steinberg, Edna** 1905-1965 [SC]
*Canadian-born actress*
* Gregory, Edna

**Steinberg, Elsy** 1929- [FC]
*American actress*
* Stewart, Elaine

**Steinberg, Hans Wilhelm**
1899-1978 [MS]
*German conductor*
* Steinberg, William

**Steinberg, Martha Jean Jones** 20th
c. [IBW]
*American radio performer and
community organizer*
* Martha Jean, the Queen
* [The] Queen

**Steinberg, Paul** 1880- ? [EJS]
*American football player*
* Steinberg, Twister

**Steinberg, Twister**
See Steinberg, Paul

**Steinberg, William**
See Steinberg, Hans Wilhelm

**Steinbrunner, Chris**
See Steinbrunner, Peter Christian

**Steinbrunner, Peter Christian**
1933- [CA, SFL]
*American author*
* Christian, Peter
* Steinbrunner, Chris

**Steiner, Abraham Albert** 1921-
[CA]
*Czech-born American author*
* Avni, Abraham Albert

**Steiner, Barbara A[nnette]** 1934-
[CA, SAT]
*American author*
* Cole, Annette [joint pseudonym with Kathleen Phillips]
* D'Andrea, Kate [joint pseudonym with Kathleen Phillips]
* Daniel, Anne

**Steiner, Gerolf** 1908- [CA]
*German educator and author*
* Andereich, Justus
* Stuempke, Harald
* Wiederump, Trotzhard

**Steiner, James Harry** 1917- [BE]
*American baseball player*
* Steiner, Red

**Steiner, Kurt**
See Ruellan, Andre

**Steiner, Red**
See Steiner, James Harry

**Steinfeldt, Battleaxe**
See Steinfeldt, Harry M.

**Steinfeldt, Harry M.** 1876-1914
[BN]
*American baseball player*
* Steinfeldt, Battleaxe

**Steinhaeuser, Walter Philip** 1878-
? [NAA]
*American author and educator*
* Retlaw, S. P.

**Steinhauer, H. A.** [PA]
*Author*
* Cozinski, Mary

**Steinhausen, H.**
See Gurster, Eugen

**Steinmetz, Charles Proteus**
See Steinmetz, Karl August Rudolf

**Steinmetz, Christian** 1882-1963
[BB]
*American basketball player*
* [The] Father of Wisconsin Basketball

**Steinmetz, Eulalie**
See Ross, Eulalie Steinmetz

**Steinmetz, Karl August Rudolf**
1865-1923 [WBD]
*American engineer*
* Steinmetz, Charles Proteus

**Steinschneider, Hermann**
1869-1933 [NAD]
*German psychic and astrologer*
* Hanussen, Eric

**Steinway, Henry Engelhard**
See Steinweg, Heinrich Engelhard

**Steinweg, Heinrich Engelhard**
1797-1871 [WBD]
*German-born piano manufacturer*
* Steinway, Henry Engelhard

**Steinwendner, Kurt** 1920- [CAR]
*Austrian artist*
* Stenvert, Curt

**Stell, Mrs. Martin** [FFF]
*Entertainer*
* Wheeler, Fanny

**Stella**
See Bowen-Graves, Mrs.

**Stella**
See Devereux, Penelope

**Stella**
See Hanania, Stella

**Stella**
See Johnson, Esther

**Stella**
See Lewis, Estelle Anna Blanche Robinson

**Stella, Luciano** 20th c. [WF]
*Italian actor*
* Kendall, Tony

**Stelzle, Jacob Charles** 1867-1919
[AS, BE]
*American baseball player*
* Stenzel, Jacob Charles

**Stembler, May**
See Iasigi, Mrs. A. D.

**Stemkowski, Peter David** 1943-
[SMG]
*Canadian-born hockey player*
* [The] Polish Prince
* Stemkowski, Stemmer

**Stemkowski, Stemmer**
See Stemkowski, Peter David

**Stemp, Isay**
See Stempnitzky, Isay

**Stempasius**
See Baron, Pierre

**Stempnitzky, Isay** 1922- [CA]
*Russian-born American business executive and author*
* Stemp, Isay

**Sten, Anna**
See Sujakevitch, Anjuschka Stenski

**Stender, Jan** [BBH]
*Dutch swimming coach*
* [The] Hangman of Hilversum

**Stendhal**
See Beyle, Marie Henri

**Stengel, Casey**
See Stengel, Charles Dillon

**Stengel, Charles Dillon**
1889?-1975 [BAB, BE, OCS]
*American baseball player and manager*
* [The] Old Professor
* Stengel, Casey
* Stengel, Dutch

**Stengel, Dutch**
See Stengel, Charles Dillon

**Stenmark, Ingemar** 20th c.
*Swedish skier*
* [The] Silent Swede

**Stennett, Renaldo Antonio** 1951-
[BE, SMG]
*Panamanian-born baseball player*
* Stennett, Rennie

**Stennett, Rennie**
See Stennett, Renaldo Antonio

**Steno**
See Vanzina, Stefano

**Stensch, Gunther Siegmund** 1924-
[CA]
*German-born American biologist and author*
* Stent, Gunther S[iegmund]

**Stensland, Inger** 1934?-1970
[BEW, FC]
*Swedish-born actress*
* Stevens, Inger

**Stent, Gunther S[iegmund]**
See Stensch, Gunther Siegmund

**Stentor, Ivy**
See Keller, H. A.

**Stenus**
See Huxley, Herbert H[enry]

**Stenvall, Alexis** 1834-1872 [WBD]
*Finnish playwright and author*
* Kivi, Alexis

**Stenvert, Curt**
See Steinwendner, Kurt

**Stenzel, Jacob Charles**
See Stelzle, Jacob Charles

**Step, Edward** 1855- ? [WWL]
*British author*
* Weston, James

**[The] Stepfather of His Country**
See Washington, George

**Stephan, Agnes**
See Kreuter-Trankel, Margot

**Stephanowitch, Dantri**
See De Riallo, J. Girard

**Stephen**
See Cox, Stephen Bernard

**Stephen, Alexander R.** 1954- [EG]
*Scottish golfer*
* Stephen, Sandy

**Stephen, Buzz**
See Stephen, Louis Roberts

**Stephen Dushan**
See Stephen Nemanya IX

**Stephen, [Sir] George** 1794- ? [PA]
*Author*
* [An] Attorney

**Stephen, [Sir] James Fitzjames**
1829-1894 [DEL, PA]
*British jurist and author*
* [A] Barrister

**Stephen, James Kenneth**
1859-1892 [WBD]
*British poet*
* J. K. S.

**Stephen, Joyce Alice** 20th c. [AW]
*New Zealand-born author*
* Thomas, J. Bissell

**Stephen, [Sir] Leslie** 1832-1904
[B10]
*British author and philosopher*
* [A] Don

**Stephen, Louis Roberts** 1944- [BE]
*American baseball player*
* Stephen, Buzz

**Stephen, Mary**
See Grimes, Katharine A.

**Stephen Nemanya IX** 1308?-1355
[WBD]
*King of Serbia*
* Stephen Dushan

**Stephen of Moldavia** 1433?-1504
[WBD]
*Prince of Moldavia*
* [The] Great

**Stephen, Sandy**
See Stephen, Alexander R.

**Stephen I** 979?-1038 [HN, WBD]
*King of Hungary*
* [The] Apostle of Hungary

**Stephen II** 1100-1131
[DNNS, FFF, HN]
*King of Hungary*
* [The] Lightning
* Thunder and Lightning
* [The] Thunderer

**Stephen IX [or X]**
See Frederick

**Stephens, Alexander Hamilton**
1812-1883 [SN]
*American politician*
* [The] Little Pale Star from Georgia
* [The] Nestor of the Confederacy

**Stephens, Arthur**
See Agnew, Stephen Hamilton

**Stephens, Buster**
See Stephens, Vernon Decatur

**Stephens, Charles**
See Goldin, Stephen

**Stephens, Clara** 1870-1907 [BEW]
*American actress*
* Bloodgood, Clara

**Stephens, Clifford** 1953- [RBE]
*American boxer*
* Stephens, Randy

**Stephens, Donald Ryder** 1898-
[MBF, SFL]
*British author*
* Sinderby, Donald

**Stephens, Edna** 1883- [THR]
*American actress*
* Goodrich, Edna

**Stephens, Frances**
See Bentley, Margaret

**Stephens, Francis H.**
See Driscoll, Annette Sophia

**Stephens, George** 1800-1851 [PA]
*Author*
* Caveat Emptor

**Stephens, George** 1922- [SMG]
*American football team staff member*
* Stephens, Tex

**Stephens, Harold** 20th c. [SMG]
*American football player*
* Stephens, Hayseed

**Stephens, Harriet Marion**
1823-1858 [FFF, PA]
*Author*
* H. M. S.

**Stephens, Harriet Marion**
(Continued)
* Somers, Rosalie
* Ward, Marion

**Stephens, Hayseed**
*See* Stephens, Harold

**Stephens, I. M.**
*See* Pratt, Inga Stephens

**Stephens, James Walter** 1883-1965
[BE]
*American baseball player*
* Stephens, Little Nemo

**Stephens, Jeanne**
*See* Hager, Jean

**Stephens, Junior**
*See* Stephens, Vernon Decatur

**Stephens, Kate** 1853- ?    [ALY]
*American author*
* Ransom, Olive

**Stephens, Kenneth**
*See* Agnew, Stephen Hamilton

**Stephens, Lawrence Sterne** 20th c.
[ESF, WGT]
*American illustrator*
* Lawrence
* Lawrence, Stephen

**Stephens, Little Nemo**
*See* Stephens, James Walter

**Stephens, Mike** 1885?-1927?
[NOJ]
*American jazz musician*
* [The] Father of Dixieland Drums
* Stephens, Ragbaby

**Stephens, Mrs. Thomas C.**    [FFF]
*Entertainer*
* Ritchie, Nellie Claire

**Stephens, Mrs. W. T.**    [FFF]
*Entertainer*
* Gray, Minnie Oscar

**Stephens, Peter**
*See* Melekh, Igor Yakovlevich

**Stephens, R. L.**
*See* Hoch, Edward D.

**Stephens, Ragbaby**
*See* Stephens, Mike

**Stephens, Randy**
*See* Stephens, Clifford

**Stephens, Reed**
*See* Donaldson, Stephen R.

**Stephens, Richard Waring** 1912?-
[BEW, TR]
*British actor*
* Waring, Richard

**Stephens, Rosemary** 1924-    [CA]
*American author*
* Carswell, Leslie

**Stephens, S. J.**
*See* Palickar, Stephen J.

**Stephens, Tex**
*See* Stephens, George

**Stephens, Vernon Decatur**
1920-1968    [AS, BE, PB]
*American baseball player*
* Stephens, Buster
* Stephens, Junior

**Stephens, W. C.** 20th c.    [BBH]
*Horse trainer*
* Stevens, Woody

**Stephens, William** 1862-1943
[WBD]
*British sculptor*
* Reynolds-Stephens, [Sir] William

**Stephenson, Andrew M.** 1946-
[ESF]
*British author and illustrator*
* Ames

**Stephenson, Benjamin Charles** 19th
c.    [FFF]
*Playwright*
* Rowe, Bolton

**Stephenson, Calvin** 20th c.    [RO2]
*American singer*
* Stephenson, Dhaakk

**Stephenson, Dhaakk**
*See* Stephenson, Calvin

**Stephenson, Dummy**
*See* Stephenson, Reuben Crandol

**Stephenson, George James** ?-1888
[FFF]
*British author and journalist*
* Albion

**Stephenson, Henry**
*See* Garroway, Henry Stephenson

**Stephenson, Jackson Riggs** 1898-
[BE, BN, PB]
*American baseball player*
* Stephenson, Old Hoss
* Stephenson, Warhorse

**Stephenson, Old Hoss**
*See* Stephenson, Jackson Riggs

**Stephenson, Reuben Crandol**
1869-1924    [BE]
*American baseball player*
* Stephenson, Dummy

**Stephenson, Tarzan**
*See* Stephenson, Walter McQueen

**Stephenson, Valentine**
*See* Hamlen, Georgia

**Stephenson, Walter McQueen**
1911-    [BE]
*American baseball player*
* Stephenson, Tarzan

**Stephenson, Warhorse**
*See* Stephenson, Jackson Riggs

**Stephenson, [Sir] William Samuel**
1896-    [B10]
*British intelligence official*
* Intrepid [code name]

**Stephson, Arthur Lee** 1926-    [NBB]
*American musician*
* Kansas City Red

**Stepin Fetchit**
*See* Perry, Lincoln Theodore

**Stepka, Milan**
*See* Benes, Jan

**Stepniak**
*See* Dragomanoff, Michael

**Stepnyak, Sergei Mikhailovich**
*See* Kravchinski, Sergei
Mikhailovich

**Steptoe, Lydia**
*See* Barnes, Djuna

**Sterland, Carl**
*See* Newquist, Roy

**Sterling, Anthony**
*See* Caesar, [Eu]gene [Lee]

**Sterling, Barry**
*See* Lipton, Robert

**Sterling, Brett** [house pseudonym]
*See* Bradbury, Ray [Douglas]

**Sterling, Brett** [house pseudonym,
Standard Magazines]
*See* Hamilton, Edmond [Moore]

**Sterling, Brett** [house pseudonym,
Standard Magazines]
*See* Samachson, Joseph

**Sterling, Edward** 1773-1847
[DEL, SN]
*British journalist*
* [The] Thunderer of the Times
* Vetus

**Sterling, Ford**
*See* Stitch, George Ford

**Sterling, Helen**
*See* Hoke, Helen L.

**Sterling, Jan [or Jane]**
*See* Adriance, Jane Sterling

**Sterling, Jean**
*See* Taylor, Mary Virginia

**Sterling, John**
*See* Sherwood, Mary Neal

**Sterling, John** 1806-1844    [FFF]
*British author and poet*
* Archeus

**Sterling, Richard**
*See* Leggatt, Albert G.

**Sterling, Robert**
*See* Hart, William Sterling

**Sterling, [Maria] Sandra**
*See* Floren, Lee

**Sterling, Simon**
*See* Sollima, Sergio

**Sterling, Stewart**
*See* Winchell, Prentice

**Sterling X**
*See* Stuckey, Sterling

**Sterling-Jones, M.**
*See* Jones, Mary R.

**[The] Stern**
*See* Frederick

**[The] Stern**
*See* Harold III

**Stern, Alfred** 1899-    [CA]
*Austrian-born American philosopher
and author*
* Alstern, Fred

**Stern, Baroness**    [FFF]
*French actress*
* Croizette, Sophie

**Stern, Bill** 20th c.    [FB]
*Sportscaster*
* Lateral Pass

**Stern, Daniel**
*See* De Flavigny, Marie Catherine
Sophie

**Stern, David** 1909-    [ANT, WW]
*American author*
* Stirling, Peter

**Stern, Elizabeth**
*See* Uhr, Elizabeth

**Stern, Elizabeth Gertrude [Levin]**
1890-1954    [B10]
*American author*
* Morton, Eleanor

**Stern, G. B.**
*See* Stern, Gladys Bertha
[Bronwyn]

**Stern, Georges** 1882-1928    [EJS]
*French jockey*
* [The] King of the Derbies
* [The] King of the Jockeys

**Stern, Gladys Bertha [Bronwyn]**
1890-    [LC, TC]
*British author*
* Stern, G. B.

**Stern, James [Andrew]** 1904-
[WD, WW]
*British author and translator*
* St. James, Andrew

**Stern, Jay B.** 1929-    [CA]
*American educator and author*
* Kohavi, Y.

**Stern, Marie** 1909-    [CA]
*American artist, author, illustrator*
* Masha

**Stern, Maximilian Enric** 1926-
[OP]
*Israeli opera singer*
* Ben-Schachar, Mordecai Enric

**Stern, Miroslava** 1930-1955    [SC]
*Czech-born actress*
* Miroslava

**Stern, Paul Frederick**
*See* Ernst, Paul Frederick

**Stern, Philip Van Doren** 1900-
[CA, NAA, TC1]
*American author*
* Storme, Peter

**Stern, Stuart**
*See* Rae, Hugh C[rauford]

**Sternaman, Dutch**
*See* Sternaman, Edward D.

**Sternaman, Edward D.** 1873- ?
[FB]
*American football player*
* Sternaman, Dutch

**Sternberg, Alexander von**
*See* Ungern-Sternberg, Alexander
von

**Sternberg, Jonas** 1894-1969
[CA, WEF]
*Austrian-born director*
* Von Sternberg, Josef

**Sterne, Duncan**
*See* Openshaw, G. H.

**Sterne, Emma Gelders** 1894-1971
[CA, SAT]
*American author*
* Broun, Emily
* James, Josephine [joint
pseudonym with Barbara
Lindsay]

**Sterne, Karl**
*See* Daudet, Julie Rosalie Celeste

**Sterne, Laurence** 1713-1768
[DEP, DNNF, FFF]
*British author*
* [The] English Rabelais
* [The] English Seneca
* Philologer, A. B.
* [The] Rabelais of England
* Yorick, Mr.

**Sterne, Morgan**
*See* Morgenstern, Albert

**Sterne, Stuart**
*See* Bloede, Gertrude

**Sterny, F.**
*See* Moroni-Celsi, Guido

**Sterrett, Charles Hurlbut**
1889-1965    [BE]
*American baseball player*
* Sterrett, Dutch

**Sterrett, Dutch**
*See* Sterrett, Charles Hurlbut

**Stesichorus** 6th c. BC    [FFF, SN]
*Greek poet*
* [The] Father of Choral Epode

**Stet**
*See* Welby, Thomas Earle

**Stetson, Mrs. John**    [FFF]
* Stokes, Katie

**Stettinius, Edward Reilley, Jr.**
1900-1949    [CND]
*American secretary of state*
* Collodion [code name used during
    World War II]

**Steune, Georges**
*See* Schonestein, David

**Steurnagel, George Henry**
1873-1946    [BE]
*American baseball player*
* Starnagel, George Henry

**Stevens, Alfred Peck** 1839-1888
[BMH, WBD]
*British entertainer*
* [The] Great Vance
* Vance, Alfred Glenville

**Stevens, Big Ed**
*See* Stevens, Edward Lee

**Stevens, Casandra Mayo** ?-1966
[ASC]
*American composer and dancer*
* Mayo, Cass

**Stevens, Cat**
*See* Georgiou, Stephen Demetre

**Stevens, Cat**
*See* Stevens, Charles A.

**Stevens, Charles A.**    [PA]
*Author*
* Stevens, Cat

**Stevens, Charles McClellan** 1861-
?    [SFL]
*Author*
* Quondam

**Stevens, Christopher**
*See* Rochefort, Julian

**Stevens, Christopher**
*See* Tabori, Pal

**Stevens, Clifford**
*See* Weisse, Clifford Stevens

**Stevens, Clysle** 1927-    [CA]
*American poet*
* Wade, John Stevens

**Stevens, Con**
*See* Stevens, Constantine Augustus
Lucy

**Stevens, Connie**
*See* Ingolia, Concetta Ann

**Stevens, Constance** 1918-    [BF]
*British actress*
* Gray, Sally

**Stevens, Constantine Augustus Lucy**
1900-    [OCS]
*Greyhound racing pioneer*
* Stevens, Con

**Stevens, Craig**
*See* Shekles, Gail

**Stevens, Dan J.**
*See* Overholser, Wayne D.

**Stevens, Dodie**
*See* Pasquale, Geraldine Ann

**Stevens, E. S.**
*See* Drower, Ethel Stefana May

**Stevens, Edward**
*See* Cosgrove, Stephen E[dward]

**Stevens, Edward Lee** 1925-    [BE]
*American baseball player*
* Stevens, Big Ed

**Stevens, Fae Hewston**
*See* Stevens, Frances Isted

**Stevens, Frances Isted** 1907-
[AW, CAP]
*Australian author*
* Stevens, Fae Hewston

**Stevens, Frances Moyer [Ross]**
1895-    [WW]
*Author*
* Hale, Christopher

**Stevens, Francis**
*See* Bennett, Gertrude Barrows

**Stevens, Franklin** 1933-    [CA, SAT]
*American author*
* Franklin, Steve

**Stevens, George** 19th c.    [PA]
*Author*
* Collins
* Whipple, Wade

**Stevens, Harry**
*See* Stevens, James Arthur [Jim]

**Stevens, Inger**
*See* Stensland, Inger

**Stevens, J. D.**
*See* Rowland, D[onald] S[ydney]

**Stevens, Jake**
*See* Stevens, Paul Eugene

**Stevens, James Arthur [Jim]**
1889-1966    [BE]
*American baseball player*
* Stevens, Harry

**Stevens, Jill**
*See* Mogridge, Stephen

**Stevens, Jimmy** 20th c.
*New Hebridean leader*
* Stevens, Moly

**Stevens, Joe** 20th c.    [WWJ]
*American jazz musician*
* Stevens, Ragababy

**Stevens, John**
*See* Tubb, Edwin Charles

**Stevens, John** 1919-    [FC, SW]
*American actor*
* Brodie, Steve

**Stevens, John** 20th c.    [SFL]
*Author*
* Hatfield, Frank

**Stevens, K. T.**
*See* Wood, Gloria

**Stevens, Lee** 1931-    [BMH]
*British female impersonator*
* Avid, Alan
* [The] Bird with the Feathers

**Stevens, Lynn**
*See* Feeney, Franklin

**Stevens, Mal**
*See* Stevens, Marvin Allen

**Stevens, Margaret Dean**
*See* Aldrich, Bess Streeter

**Stevens, Mark** 1916?-    [FC]
*American actor*
* Richards, Stephen

**Stevens, Marvin Allen** 1900?-
[B10, FB]
*American football player and coach*
* Stevens, Mal

**Stevens, Moly**
*See* Stevens, Jimmy

**Stevens, Mrs. Victor**    [FFF]
*Entertainer*
* Ross, Eva Florence

**Stevens, Muriel Phyllis** 1914-
[ART]
*British painter and illustrator*
* Stanes, Muriel

**Stevens, Onslow**
*See* Stevenson, Onslow Ford

**Stevens, Pam**
*See* Gelberg, George

**Stevens, Paul**
*See* Gattoni, Paul Steven

**Stevens, Paul Eugene** 1900-    [MK]
*American baseball player*
* Stevens, Jake

**Stevens, Peter** [joint pseudonym with
Darlene (Stern) Geis]
*See* Geis, Bernard

**Stevens, Peter** [joint pseudonym with
Bernard Geis]
*See* Geis, Darlene [Stern]

**Stevens, Peter** 20th c.    [BLB]
*American underworld figure*
* Schafer, Gus

**Stevens, Ragababy**
*See* Stevens, Joe

**Stevens, Ray**
*See* Ragsdale, Ray

**Stevens, Rise**
*See* Steenberg, Rise

**Stevens, Robert Tyler**
*See* Staples, Reginald Thomas

**Stevens, Ruby** 1907-
[BDF, BEW, F2]
*American actress*
* Stanwyck, Barbara

**Stevens, S. P.**
*See* Palestrant, Simon S.

**Stevens, Sarah**
*See* Heenan, Mrs. John C.

**Stevens, Siaka** 1906?-
*President of Sierra Leone*
* [The] Pa

**Stevens, Stella**
*See* Eggleston, Estelle

**Stevens, Thaddeus** 1773?-1868
[DNNS, FFF, SN]
*American politician*
* [The] Great Commoner
* Old Thad

**Stevens, Walter** 1877-1939    [BLB]
*American underworld figure*
* [The] Dean of Chicago Gunmen

**Stevens, William**    [FFF]
*Author*
* Ain

**Stevens, William [Carey]** 1881- ?
[NAA]
*American writer*
* Twelve o'Clock

**Stevens, William Christopher**
*See* Allen, Stephen Valentine
[Steve]

**Stevens, Woody**
*See* Stephens, W. C.

**Stevens, Yvette Marie** 1954-    [IBW]
*American singer*
* Khan, Chaka

**Stevenson**
*See* Gaskell, Elizabeth Cleghorn

**Stevenson, Anne**
*See* Elvin, Anne Katharine
Stevenson

**Stevenson, D. E.**
*See* Stevenson, Dorothy Emily

**Stevenson, Dorothy Emily**
1892-1973    [SFL]
*Scottish-born author*
* Stevenson, D. E.

**Stevenson, Florence** 20th c.    [CA]
*American author and playwright*
* Curzon, Lucia
* Faire, Zabrina

**Stevenson, Graham Barry** 1955-
[DC]
*British cricketer*
* Stevenson, Moonbeam

**Stevenson, J. P.**
*See* Stevenson, James Patrick

**Stevenson, James Alexander**
1881-1937    [DBA]
*British sculptor*
* Myrander

**Stevenson, James Patrick** 1910-
[CA, WD]
*Welsh-born clergyman and author*
* Haldane-Stevenson, James
    Patrick
* Radyr, Tomos
* Stevenson, J. P.

**Stevenson, John** 1853- ?
[SFL, WGT]
*American author*
* Jackson, Stephen

**Stevenson, John Hall**
See Hall, John

**Stevenson, John P.**
See Grierson, Edward

**Stevenson, Keith** 1950- [DC]
British cricketer
* Stevenson, Stevo

**Stevenson, Moonbeam**
See Stevenson, Graham Barry

**Stevenson, Mrs. Charles** [FFF]
Entertainer
* Claxton, Kate

**Stevenson, Onslow Ford** 1902?-
[BEW, FC]
American actor and director
* Stevens, Onslow

**Stevenson, Robert Louis Balfour**
1850-1894 [DEP, FFF, WBD]
Scottish author and poet
* North, [Captain] George
* R. L. S.
* Tusitala [Teller of Tales]
* [The] Virgil of Prose

**Stevenson, Sara Yorke** 1847- ?
[ALY]
French-born author
* Slippers, Peggy

**Stevenson, Steve**
See Stevenson, Tommy

**Stevenson, Steve**
See Stevenson, Vincent M.

**Stevenson, Stevo**
See Stevenson, Keith

**Stevenson, Tommy** 1914?-1944
[WWJ]
American jazz musician
* Stevenson, Steve

**Stevenson, Vincent M.** 1884-1962
[AS, FB]
American football player
* Stevenson, Steve

**Stevenson, William** 1925- [CA]
British author
* Chen Hwei

**Stevenson, William Adell** 1948-
[IBW]
American playwright and television
scriptwriter
* Adell, Ilunga

**Stevin, Adam**
See Richardson, James

**[The] Steward**
See Robert II

**Steward, Alexander** 1343?-1405?
[HN, WBD]
Earl of Buchan and Lord of
Badenoch
* [The] Wolf of Badenoch

**Steward, Sable** 1876- ? [THR]
British comedienne
* Fern, Sable

**Stewart, A. C.**
See Stewart, Agnes Charlotte

**Stewart, Ace**
See Stewart, Asa

**Stewart, Agnes Charlotte** 20th c.
[TCC]
British author
* Stewart, A. C.

**Stewart, Albert** 1904-
Canadian-born hockey player
* Stewart, Babe

**Stewart, Albert** 20th c. [GW]
American rodeo performer
* Stewart, Whitey

**Stewart, Alfred Walter** 1880-1947
[CC, EMD, WW]
British author
* Connington, J[ohn] J[ervis]

**Stewart, Anita**
See Converse, Anita Marie
[Stewart]

**Stewart, Anita**
See Stewart, Anna May

**Stewart, Anna May** 1895-1961
[F1, F2, FC]
American actress
* Stewart, Anita

**Stewart, Asa** 1869-1912 [BE]
American baseball player
* Stewart, Ace

**Stewart, Babe**
See Stewart, Albert

**Stewart, Babs**
See Stewart, Rosalind

**Stewart, Black Jack**
See Stewart, John Sherratt

**Stewart, Bob** 1950- [SMG]
Canadian-born hockey player
* Stewart, Stewie

**Stewart, Bud**
See Stewart, Edward Perry

**Stewart, Bunky**
See Stewart, Veston Goff

**Stewart, Catherine**
See Zeigle, Kate M.

**Stewart, Charles**
See Zurhorst, Charles [Stewart,
Jr.]

**Stewart, Charles** [CEI, SMG]
Hockey player
* Stewart, Doc

**Stewart, Charles Eugene**
1883-1934 [BE]
American baseball player
* Stewart, Tuffy

**Stewart, Clinton** [FFF]
American writer
* Walsingham

**Stewart, David**
See Politella, Dario

**Stewart, David J.**
See Siegel, Abe J.

**Stewart, Doc**
See Stewart, Charles

**Stewart, Donald** 1950- [IBW]
American circus performer
* Stewart, Keywash

**Stewart, Douglas** 1830-1880 [PA]
Author
* Sothern, Edward Askew

**Stewart, Dugald** 1753-1828 [HN]
Scottish philosopher
* [The] Scottish Plato

**Stewart, Edward Perry** 1916- [BE]
American baseball player
* Stewart, Bud

**Stewart, Elaine**
See Steinberg, Elsy

**Stewart, Eleanor**
See Porter, Eleanor [Hodgman]

**Stewart, Elizabeth Grey**
See Reed, Elizabeth Stewart

**Stewart, Eve**
See Napier, Priscilla

**Stewart, Evelyn**
See Galli, Ida

**Stewart, Frances**
See Wilmot, James Reginald

**Stewart, Fred** 1946- [RO2]
American musician
* Stone, Fred

**Stewart, Gabby**
See Stewart, Glen Weldon

**Stewart, Gene**
See Hallowell, Russell F.

**Stewart, Geraldine**
See Barry, Mrs. Shiel

**Stewart, Glen Weldon** 1912- [BE]
American baseball player
* Stewart, Gabby

**Stewart, Gordon**
See Rathborne, St. George

**Stewart, Harold** 20th c. [CA]
Australian poet
* Malley, Ern [joint pseudonym
with James Phillip McAuley]

**Stewart, Harris B[ates], Jr.** 1922-
[CA]
American oceanographer and author
* Benthic, Arch E.

**Stewart, Hod**
See Stewart, Horace

**Stewart, Horace** ?-1907
Canadian-born hockey player
* Stewart, Hod

**Stewart, Isabella**
See Chesne-Dauphine, Isabella

**Stewart, J. C.**
See Crossey, J. S.

**Stewart, J. I. M.**
See Stewart, John Innes
Mackintosh

**Stewart, Jackie** 1939- [EAR]
Scottish auto racer
* [The] Flying Scot

**Stewart [or Stuart], James** ?-1592
[SN, WBD]
Second Earl of Moray
* [The] Bonny Earl

**Stewart [or Stuart], James**
1531?-1570 [DNNF, FFF, HN]
First Earl of Moray
* [The] Good Regent

**Stewart, James L.** 1913-
[BDF, FC, WEF]
British actor
* Granger, Stewart

**Stewart [or Stuart], Jay**
See Palmer, Stuart [Hunter]

**Stewart, Jean**
See Newman, Mona Alice Jean

**Stewart, John** 1340?-1406 [WBD]
King of Scotland
* Robert III

**Stewart, John** 1749-1822
[DNNF, RH, SN]
British traveller
* Stewart, Walking

**Stewart, John [William]** 1920-
[CA]
American author
* Cole, Jack

**Stewart, John Allan** 1838- ?
[FFF, PA]
American writer
* Taswert

**Stewart, John Franklin** 1894- [BE]
American baseball player
* Stewart, Stuffy

**Stewart, John Innes Mackintosh**
1906- [CC, EMD, LC]
Scottish-born author
* Innes, Michael
* Stewart, J. I. M.

**Stewart, John Sherratt** 1917-
[FHE, HK]
Canadian-born hockey player
* Stewart, Black Jack

**Stewart, Judith Anne**
See Maciel, Judi[th Anne]

**Stewart, Kaye**
See Howe, Doris Kathleen

**Stewart, Kenneth Livingston** 1894-
[CC, WW]
Author
* Livingston, Kenneth

**Stewart, Kerry**
See Stewart, Linda

**Stewart, Keywash**
See Stewart, Donald

**Stewart, Lefty**
See Stewart, Walter Cleveland

**Stewart, Leroy** 1914-
[DAM, EJ, PMJ]
American jazz musician
* Stewart, Slam

**Stewart, Linda** 20th c. [CA]
American author
* Stewart, Kerry
* Stewart, Sam

**Stewart, Logan**
See Wilding, Philip

**Stewart, Mack**
See Stewart, William Macklin

**Stewart, Margaret**
See Wilson, Margaret Campell

**Stewart, Margaret** 1897-
[BF, THR]
British actress
* Stuart, Madge

**Stewart, Marie Kathryn**
1882-1956 [BEW, F2, FC]
American actress
* Doro, Marie

**Stewart, Martha**
See Haworth, Martha

**Stewart, Michael**
*See* Rubin, Michael Stewart

**Stewart, Nancye**
*See* Musgrove, Nancye

**Stewart, Neb**
*See* Stewart, Walter Nesbitt

**Stewart, Neil** 20th c. [WW]
*Author*
* Lombard, Nap [joint pseudonym with Pamela Hansford Johnson]

**Stewart, Nels**
*See* Stewart, Nelson

**Stewart, Nelson** 1902-1957
[FHE, HK]
*Canadian-born hockey player*
* Stewart, Nels
* Stewart, Old Poison

**Stewart, Old Poison**
*See* Stewart, Nelson

**Stewart, Paul A.** 1885- [IBW]
*American scout program organizer*
* Stewart, Pop

**Stewart, Paula**
*See* Zurndorfer, Dorothy Paula

**Stewart, Pop**
*See* Stewart, Paul A.

**Stewart, Ralph Donald** 1948-
[SMG]
*Canadian-born hockey player*
* Stewart, Stewie

**Stewart, Rattray**
*See* Macbeath, Innis [Stewart]

**Stewart, Rex**
*See* Stewart, William

**Stewart, Robert [Viscount Castlereagh]** 1769-1822
[DNNS, FFF, SN]
*British statesman*
* [The] Derrydown Triangle

**Stewart, Rosalind** 1922- [MY]
*American singer*
* Stewart, Babs

**Stewart, Rose** 1945- [RO2]
*American musician*
* Stone, Rose

**Stewart, Sam**
*See* Stewart, Linda

**Stewart, Sandy**
*See* Galitz, Sandra Ester

**Stewart, Slam**
*See* Stewart, Leroy

**Stewart, Stephen** 1869- ? [THR]
*British actor*
* Ewart, Stephen T.

**Stewart, Stewie**
*See* Stewart, Bob

**Stewart, Stewie**
*See* Stewart, Ralph Donald

**Stewart, Stuffy**
*See* Stewart, John Franklin

**Stewart, Sylvester** 1944- [RO2]
*American musician*
* Stone, Sly

**Stewart, Tuffy**
*See* Stewart, Charles Eugene

**Stewart, Veston Goff** 1931- [BE]
*American baseball player*
* Stewart, Bunky

**Stewart, Walking**
*See* Stewart, John

**Stewart, Walter Cleveland** 1900-
[BE, PB]
*American baseball player*
* Stewart, Lefty

**Stewart, Walter Nesbitt** 1918-
[BE]
*American baseball player*
* Stewart, Neb

**Stewart, Wendall**
*See* Eklund, Gordon

**Stewart, Whitey**
*See* Stewart, Albert

**Stewart, Will**
*See* Williamson, John Stewart
[Jack]

**Stewart, William** 1907-1967 [IBW]
*American jazz musician*
* Stewart, Rex

**Stewart, William Macklin** 1913-
[BE]
*American baseball player*
* Stewart, Mack

**Stewart-Cockerton, Josephine**
1895- [WWL]
*British author*
* Herne, Thomas

**Stibbes, Agnes Jean** [FFF]
*Writer*
* Fairfax, Ruth

**Stich, Hermine Neustadtl** 1897-
[NAA]
*American journalist*
* Neustadtl, Hermine
* Newton, Jean

**[The] Stick**
*See* Kovolick, Philip

**Stick 'em Up Stabile**
*See* Stabile, Jack

**Stickles, Montford** 1938- [FB]
*American football player*
* Stickles, Monty

**Stickles, Monty**
*See* Stickles, Montford

**Stickney, Sarah**
*See* Ellis, Mrs.

**Stiehm, Ewald O.** 1885-1923 [FB]
*American football coach*
* Stiehm, Jumbo

**Stiehm, Jumbo**
*See* Stiehm, Ewald O.

**Stiernhielm [or Stjernhjelm], Georg**
*See* Olai, Georgius

**Stierwell, Jay**
*See* Swicegood, Thomas L. P.

**Stiff, Dorothy Aileen** 1921- [AW]
*British writer*
* Kendal, June

**Stiger, Jim** 20th c.
*American football player*
* Stiger, Smiley

**Stiger, Smiley**
*See* Stiger, Jim

**Stilicho, Flavius** 359?- 408 [RH]
*Roman general and statesman*
* [The] Last of the Romans

**Still Bill Hill**
*See* Hill, William C.

**Still, William Grant** 1895-1978
[IBW]
*American composer and musician*
* [The] Dean of Afro-American Composers

**Stille, Karl**
*See* Demme, Hermann Christoph Gottfried

**Stiller, Mauritz**
*See* Stiller, Mosche [or Mowscha]

**Stiller, Mosche [or Mowscha]**
1883-1928 [FD]
*Finnish director*
* [The] Iron Duke
* Stiller, Mauritz

**Stilling, Heinrich [or John Henry]**
*See* Jung, Heinrich

**Stillman, Lou**
*See* Ingber, Lou

**[The] Stilt**
*See* Chamberlain, Wilt[on]

**Stilwell, Joseph W.** 1883-1946
[CND, WA]
*American military leader*
* Inwall [code name used during World War II]
* Quarterback [code name used during World War II]
* Stilwell, Vinegar Joe

**Stilwell, Silas Moore** 1800-1881
[FFF]
*American politician*
* Caucus, King

**Stilwell, Vinegar Joe**
*See* Stilwell, Joseph W.

**Stimmel, Archibald May [Archie]**
1873-1958 [BE]
*American baseball player*
* Stimmel, Lumbago

**Stimmel, Lumbago**
*See* Stimmel, Archibald May
[Archie]

**Stimson, Frederic Jesup** 1855-1943
[NAA]
*American diplomat and author*
* J. S. of Dale

**Stinchcomb, Gaylord R.** 1896-1973
[B10, FB]
*American football player*
* Stinchcomb, Pete

**Stinchcomb, Pete**
*See* Stinchcomb, Gaylord R.

**Stine, G[eorge] Harry** 1928-
[CA, SAT]
*American author*
* Correy, Lee

**Stine, Hank**
*See* Stein, Henry Eugene

**Stine, Whitney Ward** 1930- [CA]
*American author*
* McLeish, Garen
* Ward, Jonathon

**Stinson, Gorrell R.** 1945- [SMG]
*American baseball player*
* Stinson, Scrap Iron

**Stinson, Mrs. Frederick** [FFF]
*Entertainer*
* Martinot, Sadie

**Stinson, Scrap Iron**
*See* Stinson, Gorrell R.

**Stipetic, Werner H.** 1942- [CA]
*German screenwriter, producer, director*
* Herzog, Werner

**Stires, Garrett** 1849-1933 [BE]
*American baseball player*
* Stires, Gat

**Stires, Gat**
*See* Stires, Garrett

**Stirling, A. M. W.**
*See* Stirling, Anna Maria Diana Wilhelmina [Pickering]

**Stirling, Anna Maria Diana Wilhelmina [Pickering]** 1865-1965
[CAP, LC]
*British author*
* Pickering, Percival
* Stirling, A. M. W.

**Stirling, Arthur**
*See* Sinclair, Upton [Beall]

**Stirling, Bummer**
*See* Stirling, Hugh

**Stirling, David** 1915-
[BDW, WWW]
*British military leader*
* [The] Phantom Major

**Stirling, Gordon** [SMG]
*American sportswriter and basketball team president*
* Stirling, Scotty

**Stirling, Hugh** 1910- [CFH]
*Canadian football player*
* Stirling, Bummer

**Stirling, James** 1692-1770 [WBD]
*Scottish mathematician*
* [The] Venetian

**Stirling, Jessica**
*See* Rae, Hugh C[rauford]

**Stirling, Peter**
*See* Stern, David

**Stirling, Peter Lee** 20th c. [RO2]
*British singer*
* Boone, Daniel

**Stirling, Scotty**
*See* Stirling, Gordon

**Stirling, Tom**
*See* Ransome, L. E.

**Stirner, Max**
*See* Schmidt, Kaspar

**Stirnweiss, George Henry**
1918?-1958 [AS, BE, PB]
*American baseball player*
* Stirnweiss, Snuffy

**Stirnweiss, Snuffy**
*See* Stirnweiss, George Henry

**Stirrup**
*See* Brent, Henry J.

**Stitch, George Ford** 1884?-1939
[BEW, F1, F2]
*American actor*
* Sterling, Ford

**Stitch, Wilhelmina**
*See* Collie, Ruth

**Stith, Edith Mae** 1907-
[BEW, IBW]
*American singer, dancer, actress*
* Barnes, Mae
* Brownskin Mama

**Stitt, Edward** 1924-
[DAM, EJ, PMJ]
*American jazz musician*
* Stitt, Sonny

**Stitt, J. M.** 1930- [AW]
*Scottish author*
* Brunswick, James

**Stitt, Sonny**
*See* Stitt, Edward

**Stivens, Dal**
*See* Stivens, Dallas George

**Stivens, Dallas George** 1911- [SFL]
*Author*
* Stivens, Dal

**Stivers, Jeremiah** [FFF]
*Entertainer*
* Watson, Will

**Stivers, Mark** 20th c. [SFL]
*Author*
* Disrobeson, Kin I.

**Stivers, Mrs. J.** [FFF]
*Entertainer*
* Shandley, Sallie

**Stivetts, Happy Jack**
*See* Stivetts, John Elmer

**Stivetts, John Elmer** 1868-1930
[BE]
*American baseball player*
* Stivetts, Happy Jack

**Sto**
*See* Tofano, Sergio

**Stobbs, John Louis Newcombe**
1921- [IAW]
*British author*
* Newcombe, Louis

**Stoberski, Zygmunt Julian** 1916-
[IAW]
*Polish author*
* Boroniecki, Miroslaw
* Stebelski, Julian

**Stockard, Susan** 1944- [SW]
*American actress*
* Channing, Stockard

**Stockbridge, Frank Parker** 1870- ?
[NAA]
*American author and journalist*
* Johnson, Caleb

**Stockbridge, Grant** [house
pseudonym]
*See* Gruber, Frank

**Stockbridge, Grant** [house
pseudonym]
*See* Maitland, Reginald T.

**Stockbridge, Grant**
*See* Page, Norvell W.

**Stockbridge, Grant** [house
pseudonym]
*See* Tepperman, Emile

**Stockdale, Carl**
*See* Stockdale, Carlton

**Stockdale, Carlton** 1874-1953 [SC]
*American actor*
* Stockdale, Carl

**Stockdale, Percival** 1736-1811
[FFF]
*British author*
* Agricola

**Stocken, Frank** 1867-1937 [THR]
*British actor*
* Lacy, Frank

**Stocker, Helen** 1887- [WWL]
*British poet*
* Cash, Helen

**[The] Stocking-Foot Orator**
*See* McKinley, William

**Stockton, F. R.**
*See* Stockton, Francis Richard

**Stockton, Francis Richard**
1834-1902 [LC]
*American author*
* Stockton, F. R.

**Stockton, Mrs. Frank R.** [FFF]
*Writer*
* Dunn, Deborah

**Stockwell, George A.** [PA]
*Author*
* Archer

**Stockwell, Mrs. L. R.** [FFF]
*Entertainer*
* Brandon, Ethel

**Stoddard, Betsy**
*See* Zimmerman, Elizabeth S.

**Stoddard, Charles** [house
pseudonym]
*See* Kuttner, Henry

**Stoddard, Charles** [house
pseudonym]
*See* Strong, Charles Stanley

**Stoddard, Charles Augustus** 1833-
? [ALY]
*American author*
* Augustus

**Stoddard, Charles Warren**
1843-1909 [WBD]
*American author and poet*
* Pepperpod, Pip

**Stoddard, [Major] Henry B.**
*See* Ingraham, Prentiss

**Stoddard, Richard Henry**
1825-1903 [FFF]
*American poet and critic*
* Richards, Henry

**Stoddard, Sandol**
*See* Warburg, Sandol Stoddard

**Stoddart, Jane T.** 20th c. [WWL]
*British author*
* Lorner

**Stoddart, [Sir] John** 1773-1856
[DEL, PA]
*British journalist*
* J. S.
* Slop, Doctor

**Stoeffler, Johann** 1425-1531 [PA]
*Author*
* Stofflerinus

**Stoepel, Helene** 1862?-1937
[BEW]
*American actress*
* Heron, Bijou

**Stoepfel, Mrs. Robert** [FFF]
*Entertainer*
* Heron, Matilda

**Stofflerinus**
*See* Stoeffler, Johann

**Stoil, Michael Jon** 1950- [CA]
*German-born educator and author*
* Augustine, Erich

**Stojanov, Stojan**
*See* Gancev, Stojan

**Stokely, Wilma Dykeman** 1920-
[CA]
*American author*
* Dykeman, Wilma

**Stoker, Abraham** 1847-1912
[CC, EMD, LC]
*British author*
* Stoker, Bram

**Stoker, Alan** 1930- [CA, WD]
*British author*
* Evans, Alan

**Stoker, Bram**
*See* Stoker, Abraham

**Stoker, H. G.**
*See* Stoker, Hew Gordon Dacre

**Stoker, Hew Gordon Dacre**
1885-1966 [SC]
*Irish-born actor and playwright*
* Gordon, Hew
* Stoker, H. G.

**Stoker, Willard**
*See* Stoker, William Richard

**Stoker, William Richard** 1905-
[TR]
*British director*
* Stoker, Willard

**Stokes, Al[bert John]**
*See* Stacek, Albert John

**Stokes, Big Mo**
*See* Stokes, Maurice

**Stokes, Cedric**
*See* Beardmore, George

**Stokes, Ella**
*See* Doris, Mrs. John B.

**Stokes, Francis William** 1883-
[WW]
*Author*
* Everton, Francis

**Stokes, Katie**
*See* Stetson, Mrs. John

**Stokes, Manning Lee** 20th c.
[WGT, WW]
*Author*
* Ludwell, Bernice
* Manning, Lee

**Stokes, Maurice** 1933-1970
[BB, IBW]
*American basketball player*
* Stokes, Big Mo
* Stokes, Mo

**Stokes, Mo**
*See* Stokes, Maurice

**Stokes, Pee Wee**
*See* Stokes, Tony

**Stokes, Robert [Bob]**
*See* Wilkening, Howard [Everett]

**Stokes, Simpson**
*See* Fawcett, F[rank] Dubrez

**Stokes, Tony** 20th c. [RBE]
*American boxer*
* Stokes, Pee Wee

**Stoll, Clarice Stasz**
*See* Stasz, Clarice

**Stoll, Dennis G[ray]** 1912- [CA]
*British author*
* Craig, Denys

**Stoll, [Sir] Oswald**
*See* Gray, Oswald

**Stolper, Alice** 1934- [IAW]
*American author*
* Peppler, Alice Stolper

**Stolterfoth, Georg**
*See* Bonus, Arthur

**Stoltz, Adley** 1946- [ITA]
*American actress*
* Dupont, Adley

**Stoltz, [Mademoiselle] Heloise**
*See* Noel, Victoire

**Stoltz, Rosine**
*See* Noel, Victoire

**Stolz, Lois Meek** 1891- [CAP]
*American psychologist and author*
* Meek, Lois Hayden

**[The] Stomping Mare**
*See* Ryan, Hermine Braunsteiner

**Stone, Alan** [house pseudonym]
[Stratemeyer Syndicate]
*See* Stratemeyer, Edward L.

**Stone, Alan** [house pseudonym]
[Stratemeyer Syndicate]
*See* Svenson, Andrew E.

**Stone, Arthur**
*See* Gladstone, Arthur

**Stone, Barbara Haskins**
1924?-1979 [CA]
*British editor*
* Haskins, Barbara

**Stone, Butch**
*See* Stone, Henry

**Stone, Carol**
*See* Stone, Fredeline Montgomery

**Stone, Cliffie**
*See* Snyder, Clifford Gilpin

**Stone, Eddie**
*See* Marblestone, Eddie

**Stone, Elna** 20th c. [CA]
*American author*
* Daniel, Elna Worrell

**Stone, Ena Margaret** 1911- [IAW]
*South African-born author*
* O'Randa, Jack
* Sandown, Margaret

**Stone, Ernest** 20th c. [BMH]
*British comedian*
* Mack, Ernest

**Stone, Eugenia** 1879-1971
[CA, SAT]
*American author*
* Stone, Gene

Stone, Ezra
See Feinstone, Ezra Chaim

Stone Forehead Powell
See Powell, Peter

Stone, Fred
See Stewart, Fred

Stone, Fredeline Montgomery
1915- [BEW]
American actress and director
* Stone, Carol

Stone, Gene
See Stone, Eugenia

Stone, George E.
See Stein, George

Stone, George H. 1946- [PB]
American baseball player
* Stone, Stoney

Stone, George Robert 1876-1945
[EJS]
American baseball player
* Stone, Silent George

Stone, Grace Zaring 1896?-
[ANT, CAP, CC]
American author
* Vance, Ethel

Stone, Hampton
See Stein, Aaron Marc

Stone, Henry ?-1653
[FFF, RH, SN]
British painter and sculptor
* Old Stone

Stone, Henry 1913- [PMJ]
American musician
* Stone, Butch

Stone, Hoyt E[dward] 1935- [CA]
American author and clergyman
* Vernon, Eddie

Stone, I. F.
See Stone, Isidor Feinstein

Stone, Idella Purnell
See Purnell, Idella

Stone, Ikey
See Purnell, Idella

Stone, Irving
See Tennenbaum, Irving

Stone, Isidor Feinstein 1907- [IPA]
American journalist and author
* Stone, I. F.

Stone, John Christopher 1923-
[ART]
British artist
* J. C. S.

Stone, John Mack
See McCulley, Johnston

Stone, John Saville [FFF, PA]
Author
* Stein, Johann Saville

Stone, John Vernon 1918- [BE]
American baseball player
* Stone, Rocky

Stone, Jonathan Thomas
1905-1955 [AS, BE, PB]
American baseball player
* Stone, Rocky

Stone, Leslie F.
See Silberberg, Leslie F[rances]
Stone

Stone, Lyle 1931- [IBW]
American athlete
* Stone, Toni

Stone, Lynn
Radio scriptwriter
* Marston, Adelaide [joint
pseudonym with Addy Richton]

Stone, Marie
See Macdonald, Mrs. W. H.

Stone, Oliver
See Bowdoin, William Goodrich

Stone, Patti 1926- [CA]
American author
* Patrick, Leal

Stone, Peter 20th c. [WF]
American screenwriter
* Werty, Quentin

Stone, Raymond [house pseudonym]
[Stratemeyer Syndicate]
See Stratemeyer, Edward L.

Stone, Richard
See Delaney, Jack J[ames]

Stone, Richard A. [house
pseudonym] [Stratemeyer
Syndicate]
See Stratemeyer, Edward L.

Stone, Rocky
See Stone, John Vernon

Stone, Rocky
See Stone, Jonathan Thomas

Stone, Rose
See Stewart, Rose

Stone, Silent George
See Stone, George Robert

Stone, Simon
See Barrington, Howard

Stone, Sly
See Stewart, Sylvester

Stone, Stoney
See Stone, George H.

Stone, Stoney
See Stone, Wayne

Stone, Susan Berch 1944- [CA]
American author
* M
* Whitefield, Ann

Stone, Thomas H.
See Harknett, Terry

Stone, Tiger [or Tige]
See Stone, William Arthur

Stone, Toni
See Stone, Lyle

Stone, Wayne 20th c. [RO2]
Canadian-born musician
* Stone, Stoney

Stone, William Arthur 1901-1960
[BE]
American baseball player
* Stone, Tiger [or Tige]

Stone, William Joel 1848-1918
[WBD]
American politician
* Gum-Shoe Bill

Stonebraker, Homer 20th c. [BBH]
American basketball player
* Stonebraker, Stoney

Stonebraker, Stoney
See Stonebraker, Homer

Stoneham, Charles Thurley 1895-
[WW]
Author
* Thurley, Norgove

Stonehenge
See Walsh, John Henry

Stoneman, Ernest V. 1893-1968
[CWG, DAM]
American country-western performer
* Stoneman, Pop

Stoneman, Pop
See Stoneman, Ernest V.

Stoneman, Stoney
See Stoneman, William A.

Stoneman, William A. 1944- [PB]
American baseball player
* Stoneman, Stoney

[The] Stonemason of Cromarty
See Miller, Hugh

Stoner, Lil
See Stoner, Ulysses Simpson Grant

Stoner, Michael S. 1911- [ASC]
American composer
* Stoner, Mickey

Stoner, Mickey
See Stoner, Michael S.

Stoner, Mother
See Stoner, Winifred Sackville

Stoner, Ulysses Simpson Grant
1899-1966 [BE]
American baseball player
* Stoner, Lil

Stoner, Winifred Sackville [NAA]
Author and songwriter
* Stoner, Mother

[The] Stonewall of the West
See Cleburne, Patrick Ronayne

Stong, Clair L. 1902?-1975
[B10, CA]
American engineer, columnist, writer
* Stong, Red

Stong, Red
See Stong, Clair L.

Stonor, Oliver 1903- [CAP]
British author, journalist, critic
* Bishop, E. Morchard
* Bishop, Morchard

Stooge, Iggy
See Osterberg, Jim

Stookey, Noel 1937- [RO1]
American singer
* Stookey, Paul

Stookey, Paul
See Stookey, Noel

Stooping Jack Gorman
See Gorman, John F. [Jack]

Stoopnagle, [Colonel] Lemuel Q.
See Taylor, F. Chase

Stopelman, Francis
See Stoppelman, Frans

Stopes, Marie Carmichael 20th c.
[LAO]
Scottish author and scientist
* Carmichael, Marie

Stoppard, Tom
See Straussler, Thomas

Stoppelman, Francis
See Stoppelman, Frans

Stoppelman, Frans 1921- [CAP]
Dutch author
* Stopelman, Francis
* Stoppelman, Francis

Stoppelmoor, Cheryl 1951?-
American actress
* Ladd, Cheryl

[The] Stopper
See Calhoun, David

Storball, Don
See Norman, Don[ald]

Storey, Edward Francis 1901- [EG]
Golfer
* Storey, Eustace

Storey, Eustace
See Storey, Edward Francis

Storey, Red
See Storey, Roy Alvin

Storey, Roy Alvin 1918-
[CFH, HK]
Canadian-born football and hockey
official
* Storey, Red

Storey, Victoria Carolyn 1945-
[CA]
British author
* Martin, Vicky

[The] Stork
See Hendricks, Ted

Stork, Philipp 1929- [OP]
Canadian opera singer
* Stark, Phil

Storm
See Townsend, Storm Diana

Storm, Anthony
See Roberts, John S[torm]

Storm, Brian [house pseudonym,
Curtis Warren]
See Holloway, Brian

Storm, Christopher
See Olsen, Theodore Victor

Storm, Duncan
See Floyd, Gilbert

Storm, Eric
See Tubb, Edwin Charles

Storm, Gale
See Cottle, Josephine

Storm, Hyemeyohsts 1935- [CA]
American author
* Golden Silver

[The] Storm in Norman
See Van Lier, Norm[an, III]

Storm, Ivan
See Thomas, Reginald George

Storm, Jannick
See Jorgensen, J. S.

[The] Storm King
See Espy, James Pollard

Storm, Lesley
See Clark, Mabel Margaret
[Cowie]

**Storm, Mallory**
See Fairman, Paul W.

**Storm, Michael**
See Sempill, Ernest

**Storm P.**
See Petersen, Robert Storm

**Storm, Robert**
See Trell, Max

**Storm, Rupert**
See Sempill, Ernest

**Storm, Russell**
See Williams, Robert Moore

**Storm, Virginia**
See Swatridge, Irene Maude
[Mossop]

**Storme, Peter**
See Stern, Philip Van Doren

**[The] Stormy Petrel of European
Politics**
See Mazzini, Giuseppe

**[The] Stormy Petrel of Politics**
See Brougham, Henry Peter

**[The] Stormy Petrel of Politics**
See Scott, John

**Storr, Catherine [Cole]** 1913-
[CA, SAT]
*British author*
* Adler, Irene
* Lourie, Helen

**Storti, Lin**
See Storti, Lindo Ivan

**Storti, Lindo Ivan** 1906- [BE]
*American baseball player*
* Storti, Lin

**Story, A. M. Sommerville** 20th c.
[WGT, WWL]
*Author*
* Sommerville, Frankfort

**Story, Adeline E.** [FFF]
*American writer*
* Dixon, Helena

**Story, E. M.**
See Cassidy, James

**Story, Isaac** 1774-1803?
[FFF, PA, WBD]
*American poet*
* Quince, Peter

**Story, Josephine**
See Loring, Emilie [Baker]

**[The] Story Lady**
See Faulkner, Georgene

**Story, Richard**
See Gold, Horace Leonard

**Story, Rosamond Mary** 20th c.
[MBF]
*British author*
* Jeskins, Richard
* Lee, Charles H.
* Lindsay, Josephine
* Reid, Desmond [house
pseudonym]
* Tracy, Catherine
* Woods, Ross

**Story, Sydney A., Jr.**
See Pike, Mary H. Green

**[The] Stot**
See Stuart, James

**Stothard, Thomas** 1755-1834 [SN]
*British illustrator and painter*
* [The] English Raphael
* Our Domestic Raphael

**Stott, Mr.** 19th c. [RH]
*Journalist*
* Hafiz

**Stoughton, Blaine** 20th c.
*Hockey player*
* Stoughton, Stash

**Stoughton, Stash**
See Stoughton, Blaine

**Stout, Allyn McClelland**
1904-1974 [BE]
*American baseball player*
* Stout, Fish Hook

**Stout, Fish Hook**
See Stout, Allyn McClelland

**Stout Harry**
See Henry VIII

**Stout, Robert Joe** 1936- [CA]
*American author*
* Pires, Joe

**Stout Steve Owen**
See Owen, Steve

**Stoutenburg, Adrien [Pearl]** 1916-
[CA, SAT, TBJ]
*American author*
* Arden, Barbie [joint pseudonym
with Barbara Ritchie]
* Kendall, Lace
* Minier, Nelson [joint pseudonym
with Laura Nelson Baker]

**Stovall, Babe**
See Stovall, Jewell

**Stovall, Firebrand**
See Stovall, George Thomas

**Stovall, George Thomas** 1878-1951
[BE, PB]
*American baseball player and
manager*
* Stovall, Firebrand

**Stovall, Jesse Cranmer** 1876-1955
[BE]
*American baseball player*
* Stovall, Scout

**Stovall, Jewell** 1907-1974 [BWW]
*American singer*
* Stovall, Babe

**Stovall, Scout**
See Stovall, Jesse Cranmer

**Stovenour, June** 1926- [FC, PMJ]
*American actress*
* Haver, June

**Stovey, Harry Duffield**
See Stowe, Harry Duffield

**Stovold, Andrew Willis** 1953- [DC]
*British cricketer*
* Stovold, Squeak
* Stovold, Stov
* Stovold, Stovers

**Stovold, Bubble**
See Stovold, Martin Willis

**Stovold, Martin Willis** 1955- [DC]
*British cricketer*
* Stovold, Bubble

**Stovold, Squeak**
See Stovold, Andrew Willis

**Stovold, Stov**
See Stovold, Andrew Willis

**Stovold, Stovers**
See Stovold, Andrew Willis

**Stow, John** 1525-1605
[DEP, FFF, SN]
*British historian*
* [The] Herodotus of Old London
* Trudger and Trencher

**Stowasser, Friedrich** 1928- [B10]
*Austrian artist*
* Hundertwasser, Fritz

**Stowe, Harriet Beecher** 1811-1896
[DEL]
*American author*
* Crowfield, Christopher

**Stowe, Harry Duffield** 1856-1937
[BE, DGS]
*American baseball player*
* Stovey, Harry Duffield

**[The] Stowe of France**
See Sauval, Henri

**Stowe, Rosetta** [joint pseudonym
with Margaret E. (Nettles) Ogan]
See Ogan, George F.

**Stowe, Rosetta** [joint pseudonym
with George F. Ogan]
See Ogan, Margaret E. [Nettles]

**Stowell, Augustus**
See Legge, Alfred Owen

**Stowell, Baron** 1745-1836 [PA]
*Author*
* Civis

**[The] Strabo of Britain**
See Camden, William

**[The] Strabo of Germany**
See Muenster, Sebastian

**Strabolgi, Bartolomeo**
See Tucci, Niccolo

**Strachan, John** 1778-1867 [PA]
*Author*
* Reckoner

**Strachan, Margaret Pitcairn** 1908-
[CA, WD]
*American author*
* More, Caroline [joint pseudonym
with Molly (Lamken) Cone]

**Straci, Joseph** 20th c. [PHM]
*American underworld figure*
* Stretch, Joe

**Strader, Norman** 1902?-1956 [AS]
*American football player*
* Strader, Red

**Strader, Red**
See Strader, Norman

**Stradley, Mark**
See Smith, Richard Rein

**Stradling, Matthew**
See Mahoney, M. F.

**Straesser, Joep**
See Straesser, Joseph Willem
Frederik

**Straesser, Joseph Willem Frederik**
1934- [IWM]
*Dutch composer*
* Straesser, Joep

**Strafford**
See Johnson, Harriet Laight C.

**Strage, Mark** 1927- [CA]
*Manchurian-born American author*
* Hazlitt, Joseph
* Quick, Philip

**Strahan, Edward**
See Shinn, Earl

**Strahler, Michael Wayne** 1947-
[SMG]
*American baseball player*
* Strahler, Spider
* [The] Thin Man

**Strahler, Spider**
See Strahler, Michael Wayne

**Strahorn, Robert E.** [PA]
*Author*
* Aleter, Esq.

**Straight, Douglas** [PA]
*Author*
* Daryl, Sydney

**Straight Tongue**
See Whipple, Henry Benjamin

**Strain, R. W. M.**
See Strain, Robert William Magill

**Strain, Robert William Magill**
1907- [ART]
*Irish-born painter*
* Strain, R. W. M.

**Straine, Doc**
See Straine, James

**Straine, James** 20th c. [BWW]
*American entertainer*
* Straine, Doc

**Strait, Raymond** 1924- [CA]
*American author*
* Ray, Russell

**[The] Straitened**
See Rupert

**Straiton, Edward Cornock** 1917-
[CA]
*Scottish veterinarian and author*
* Vet, T. V.

**Straker, John Foster** 1904- [CA]
*British author*
* Rosse, Ian

**Strand, Les**
See Strandt, Leslie Roy

**Strand, Mark**
See Strand, Marthinius A.

**Strand, Marthinius A.** 1887-1965
[BBH]
*Norwegian-born skiing organization
founder and officer*
* Strand, Mark

**Strand, Paul E.**
See Palestrant, Simon S.

**Strandberg, Carl Vilhelm August**
1818-1877 [WBD]
*Swedish poet and journalist*
* Talis Qualis

**Strandt, Leslie Roy** 1924- [EJ]
*American jazz musician*
* Strand, Les

**Strang, Herbert** [joint pseudonym
with Charles James L'Estrange]
See Ely, George Herbert

**Strang, Herbert** [joint pseudonym with George Herbert Ely]
*See* L'Estrange, Charles James

**Strang, Samuel Nicklin**
*See* Nicklin, Samuel Strang

**Strange, Alan Cochrane** 1909- [BE]
*American baseball player*
* Strange, Inky

**Strange, Dillon**
*See* Norwood, Victor G[eorge] C[harles]

**Strange, Harry**
*See* Shaw, Stanley Gordon

**Strange, Inky**
*See* Strange, Alan Cochrane

**Strange, John Stephen**
*See* Tillet, Dorothy [Stockbridge]

**Strange, Joseph**
*See* Crawfurd, Oswald John Frederick

**Strange, Kemble**
*See* McEnvoy, C. N.

**Strange, Michael**
*See* Oelrichs, Blanche

**Strange, N. Blair**
*See* Sargent, Brian [Lawrence]

**Strange, Nora K.**
*See* Stanley, Nora Kathleen Begbie Strange

**Strangeglove, Dr.**
*See* Stuart, Richard Lee

**[The] Stranger**
*See* Walton, Bill

**Stranger, Joyce**
*See* Wilson, Joyce M[uriel Judson]

**Stranger, Ralph**
*See* Judson, Ralph

**Stranks, Charles James** 1901- [AW]
*British author*
* Hillyer, Richard

**Strapontin**
*See* Burain, Paul

**Strasberg, Lee** 1901-1982 [JL]
*Austrian-born actor and director*
* [The] Father of Method Acting

**Strassar, Todd** 20th c.
*American author*
* Rhue, Morton

**Strasser, Bernard Paul** 1895- [CAP]
*German-born author and clergyman*
* P. W.
* Silvanus

**Strataki, Anastasia** 1938- [BBD]
*Canadian opera singer*
* Stratas, Teresa

**Stratas, Teresa**
*See* Strataki, Anastasia

**Stratemeyer, Edward L.** 1862-1930 [CAP, EMD, SAT]
*American author*
* Abbott, [Manager] Henry
* Adams, Harrison
* Appleton, Victor [house pseudonym] [Stratemeyer Syndicate]

**Stratemeyer, Edward L.** (Continued)
* Appleton, Victor, II [house pseudonym] [Stratemeyer Syndicate]
* Barnum, Richard [house pseudonym] [Stratemeyer Syndicate]
* Bartlett, Philip A. [house pseudonym] [Stratemeyer Syndicate]
* Barton, May Hollis [house pseudonym] [Stratemeyer Syndicate]
* Beach, Charles Amory [house pseudonym] [Stratemeyer Syndicate]
* Bonehill, [Captain] Ralph
* Bowie, Jim
* Calkins, Franklin
* Carson, [Captain] James [house pseudonym] [Stratemeyer Syndicate]
* Chadwick, Lester [house pseudonym] [Stratemeyer Syndicate]
* Chapman, Allen [house pseudonym] [Stratemeyer Syndicate]
* Charles, Louis
* Cooper, James A.
* Cooper, John R. [house pseudonym] [Stratemeyer Syndicate]
* Daly, Jim
* Davenport, Spencer
* Dawson, Elmer A. [house pseudonym] [Stratemeyer Syndicate]
* Dixon, Franklin W. [house pseudonym] [Stratemeyer Syndicate]
* Duncan, Julia K. [house pseudonym] [Stratemeyer Syndicate]
* Edison, Theodore?
* Edwards, Julie
* Emerson, Alice B. [house pseudonym] [Stratemeyer Syndicate]
* Ferris, James Cody [house pseudonym] [Stratemeyer Syndicate]
* Forbes, Graham B. [house pseudonym] [Stratemeyer Syndicate]
* Ford, Albert Lee
* Frank?
* Gordon, Frederick [house pseudonym] [Stratemeyer Syndicate]
* Hamilton, Robert W.
* Hardy, Alice Dale [house pseudonym] [Stratemeyer Syndicate]
* Harkaway, Hal
* Hawley, Mabel C. [house pseudonym] [Stratemeyer Syndicate]
* Henderley, Brooks [house pseudonym] [Stratemeyer Syndicate]
* Hicks, Harvey
* Hill, Grace Brooks [house pseudonym] [Stratemeyer Syndicate]
* Hope, Laura Lee [house pseudonym] [Stratemeyer Syndicate]
* Hunt, Francis [house pseudonym] [Stratemeyer Syndicate]
* Jack?
* Judd, Frances K. [house pseudonym] [Stratemeyer Syndicate]

**Stratemeyer, Edward L.** (Continued)
* Keene, Carolyn [house pseudonym] [Stratemeyer Syndicate]
* Lawson, W. B.?
* Locke, Clinton W. [house pseudonym] [Stratemeyer Syndicate]
* Long, Helen Beecher [house pseudonym] [Stratemeyer Syndicate]
* Mackenzie, [Dr.] Willard
* Marlowe, Amy Bell [house pseudonym] [Stratemeyer Syndicate]
* Martin, Eugene [house pseudonym] [Stratemeyer Syndicate]
* Moore, Fenworth [house pseudonym] [Stratemeyer Syndicate]
* Morrison, Gert W. [house pseudonym] [Stratemeyer Syndicate]
* Optic, Oliver [joint pseudonym with William Taylor Adams]
* Penrose, Margaret [house pseudonym] [Stratemeyer Syndicate]
* Ridley, Nat, Jr. [house pseudonym] [Stratemeyer Syndicate]
* Rockwood, Roy [house pseudonym] [Stratemeyer Syndicate]
* Roe, Harry Mason [house pseudonym] [Stratemeyer Syndicate]
* St. Myer, Ned
* Scott, Dan [house pseudonym] [Stratemeyer Syndicate]
* Sheldon, Ann [house pseudonym] [Stratemeyer Syndicate]
* Sperry, Raymond, Jr. [house pseudonym] [Stratemeyer Syndicate]
* Steele, Chester K.
* Stone, Alan [house pseudonym] [Stratemeyer Syndicate]
* Stone, Raymond [house pseudonym] [Stratemeyer Syndicate]
* Stone, Richard A. [house pseudonym] [Stratemeyer Syndicate]
* Strayer, E. Ward
* Thorndyke, Helen Louise [house pseudonym] [Stratemeyer Syndicate]
* Warner, Frank A. [house pseudonym] [Stratemeyer Syndicate]
* Webster, Frank V. [house pseudonym] [Stratemeyer Syndicate]
* West, Jerry [house pseudonym] [Stratemeyer Syndicate]
* Wheeler, Janet D. [house pseudonym] [Stratemeyer Syndicate]
* White, Ramy Allison [house pseudonym] [Stratemeyer Syndicate]
* Winfield, Allen?
* Winfield, Arthur M.
* Winfield, Edna
* Woods, Nat
* Young, Clarence [house pseudonym] [Stratemeyer Syndicate]

**Stratford, Philip**
*See* Bulmer, [Henry] Kenneth

**[The] Stratford Streak**
*See* Morenz, Howarth William

**Stratten, John**
*See* Alldridge, John Stratten

**Stratton, Charles Sherwood** 1838-1883 [DNNS, FFF, WBD]
*American dwarf*
* Thumb, Tom

**Stratton, Chris**
*See* Hubbard, Richard

**Stratton, Eugene**
*See* Ruhlmann, Eugene Augustus

**Stratton, Gander**
*See* Stratton, Monty Franklin Pierce

**Stratton, Geneva Grace** 1868-1924 [LC]
*American author*
* Porter, Gene Stratton

**Stratton, Henry**
*See* Nelson, Michael Harrington

**Stratton, Monty Franklin Pierce** 1912- [BE]
*American baseball player*
* Stratton, Gander

**Stratton, Richard A.** 1932-
*American naval officer and Vietnam POW*
* [The] Beak

**Stratton, Thomas** [joint pseudonym with Eugene DeWeese]
*See* Coulson, Robert [Stratton]

**Stratton, Thomas** [joint pseudonym with Robert (Stratton) Coulson]
*See* DeWeese, Eugene

**Straub, Otto**
*See* Sobotta, Kurt

**Straus**
*See* Fields, J. M.

**Straus, Oscar**
*See* Strauss, Oscar

**Strauss, Dutch**
*See* Strauss, Joseph

**Strauss, Frances** 1904- [CAP]
*American author*
* Wiley, Bell

**Strauss, Harry** ?-1941 [BLB, PHM]
*American underworld figure*
* Strauss, Pittsburgh Phil

**Strauss, Joseph** 1844-1906 [EJS]
*Hungarian-born American baseball player*
* Strauss, Dutch

**Strauss, Jr.**
*See* Field, Kate

**Strauss, [Mary] Lucille Jackson** 1908- [CAP]
*American librarian and author*
* Jackson, Lucille

**Strauss, Oscar** 1870-1954 [JL]
*Austrian-born composer*
* Straus, Oscar

**Strauss, Pittsburgh Phil**
*See* Strauss, Harry

**Strauss, Yawcob**
*See* Adams, Charles Follen

**Straussler, Thomas** 1937-
[CA, MWD, WOA]
*British playwright*
* Stoppard, Tom

**Strawberry Bill Bernhard**
*See* Bernhard, William Henry

**Straws**
*See* Field, Joseph M.

**Straws, Jr.**
*See* Field, Mary Katherine Keemle
[Kate]

**Strayer, E. Ward**
*See* Stratemeyer, Edward L.

**Strayhorn, Swee'Pea**
*See* Strayhorn, William [Billy]

**Strayhorn, William [Billy]**
1915-1967    [EJ, EJ7, IBW]
*American jazz musician*
* Strayhorn, Swee'Pea

**Streaker, John A.** 1859- ?    [BE]
*American baseball player*
* Stricker, Cub
* Stricker, John A.

**Strebor, Eiggam**
*See* Roberts, Maggie

**Streefkerf, Hendrick**
*See* Verkuyl, Gerrit

**Streep, Mary Louise** 1950?-
*American actress*
* Streep, Meryl

**Streep, Meryl**
*See* Streep, Mary Louise

**Street, A. G.**
*See* Street, Arthur George

**Street, Arthur George** 1892-1966
[CAP, LC]
*British author*
* Brian, James
* Street, A. G.

**Street, Bobbie Lee** 1944-
[PAC, RO2]
*American singer and songwriter*
* Gentry, Bobbie

**Street, C. J. C.**
*See* Street, Cecil John Charles

**Street, Cecil John Charles**
1884-1964    [CC, EMD, WGT]
*British author*
* Burton, Miles
* F. O. O.
* Rhode, John
* Street, C. J. C.

**Street, Charles Evard** 1882-1951
[AS, BE, PB]
*American baseball player and
manager*
* Street, Gabby
* Street, Old Sarge

**Street, G. S.**
*See* Street, George Slythe

**Street, Gabby**
*See* Street, Charles Evard

**Street, George Slythe** 1867-1936
[LC]
*British author*
* Street, G. S.

**Street, Jay**
*See* Slesar, Henry

**Street, Jonathan**
*See* Tiner, John Hudson

**Street, Lee**
*See* Hampton, Kathleen

**Street, Old Sarge**
*See* Street, Charles Evard

**Street, Robert**
*See* Thomas, Gordon

**[The] Street Rustler**
*See* Woods, Oscar

**[The] Street Singer**
*See* Rosenberg, Harry

**Streeter, Lefty**
*See* Streeter, Samuel

**Streeter, Samuel** 1900-    [MK]
*American baseball player*
* Streeter, Lefty

**Streib, Daniel T.** 20th c.    [SFP]
*Author*
* Page, Thomas [joint pseudonym
  with Robert Page Jones]

**Streicher, Herbert** 20th c.
*American actor*
* Reems, Harry

**Streidler, Betty** 1930-    [FC]
*American actress*
* St. John, Betta

**Streisand, Barbara** 1942-    [AM]
*American singer and actress*
* Streisand, Barbra

**Streisand, Barbra**
*See* Streisand, Barbara

**Strephon**
*See* Bradbury, Edward

**Stretch, Joe**
*See* Straci, Joseph

**Stretton, Charles**
*See* Dyer, Charles [Raymond]

**Stretton, Hesba**
*See* Smith, Sarah

**Stretton, Renshaw**
*See* Dyer, Charles [Raymond]

**Streuvels, Stijn**
*See* Lateur, Frank

**Stribling, T. S.**
*See* Stribling, Thomas Sigismund

**Stribling, Thomas Sigismund**
1881-1965    [LC, TC]
*American author*
* Stribling, T. S.

**Stribling, William Lawrence**
1904-1933    [BX, RBE]
*American boxer*
* [The] Georgia Peach
* [The] King of the Canebrakes
* Stribling, Young

**Stribling, Young**
*See* Stribling, William Lawrence

**Stricker, Cub**
*See* Streaker, John A.

**Stricker, John A.**
*See* Streaker, John A.

**Strickland, Bo**
*See* Strickland, George Bevan

**Strickland, Enfield** 1870?-1964
[BEW]
*Theatrical performer*
* Strickland, Rube

**Strickland, George Bevan** 1926-
[BE]
*American baseball player*
* Strickland, Bo

**Strickland, Howard** 1952-    [SMG]
*American football player*
* Strickland, Strick

**Strickland, Roger** 1940-    [BB]
*American basketball player*
* [The] Rifle

**Strickland, Rube**
*See* Strickland, Enfield

**Strickland, Strick**
*See* Strickland, Howard

**Stricklin, Al**
*See* Stricklin, Alton Meeks

**Stricklin, Alton Meeks** 1908-    [B10]
*American musician*
* Stricklin, Al

**[The] Strict**
*See* Louis II

**Stride, Madeline** 1909-    [THR]
*British actress*
* Gibson, Madeline

**Strike, Jeremy**
*See* Renn, Thomas E[dward]

**Striker, Jake**
*See* Striker, Wilbur Scott

**Striker, Wilbur Scott** 1933-    [BE]
*American baseball player*
* Striker, Jake

**Strincevich, Jumbo**
*See* Strincevich, Nicholas
Mihailovich

**Strincevich, Nicholas Mihailovich**
1915-    [BE]
*American baseball player*
* Strincevich, Jumbo

**Strindberg, August** 1849-1912
[WBD]
*Swedish playwright and author*
* [The] Shakespeare of Sweden

**Stringbean**
*See* Akeman, David

**Stringer, David**
*See* Roberts, Keith [John
Kingston]

**Stripp, Jersey Joe**
*See* Stripp, Joseph Valentine

**Stripp, Joseph Valentine** 1903-
[BE, PB]
*American baseball player*
* Stripp, Jersey Joe

**Stritzl, Siegfried** 1944-    [AES]
*Yugoslav-born American soccer
player*
* Stritzl, Siggy

**Stritzl, Siggy**
*See* Stritzl, Siegfried

**Strivelyne, Elsie**
*See* Paton, [Sir] Noel

**Strix**
*See* Fleming, [Robert] Peter

**Strix**
*See* Howes, George W.

**Strodach, Paul Zeller** 1876- ?
[NAA]
*American clergyman and author*
* Pilgrim, Paul

**Strode, Ralph** 14th c.    [DEL, SN]
*British scholar and poet*
* [The] Philosophical

**Strode, Woodrow Wilson** 1915-
[IBW]
*American athlete and actor*
* Strode, Woody

**Strode, Woody**
*See* Strode, Woodrow Wilson

**Strollo, Anthony C.** 1899-1962
[BLB, PHM]
*American underworld figure*
* Bender, Tony

**Stromberg, Harry**    [BLB, MM]
*American underworld figure*
* Rosen, Nig

**Stromberg, Honey**
*See* Stromberg, John

**Stromberg, John** 1853-1902
[BEW, DAM]
*American composer*
* Stromberg, Honey

**Stromme, Floyd Marvin** 1916-    [BE]
*American baseball player*
* Stromme, Rock

**Stromme, Rock**
*See* Stromme, Floyd Marvin

**[The] Strong**
*See* Augustus II

**[The] Strong**
*See* Robert

**[The] Strong**
*See* Sancho II

**[The] Strong**
*See* Siward [Earl of
Northumberland]

**[The] Strong Arm**
*See* Danton, Georges Jacques

**Strong Bow**
*See* Campbell, John Beautiste

**Strong, Charles**
*See* Epstein, Samuel

**Strong, Charles Stanley** 1906-1962
[CAT, NAA, SFL]
*American author and editor*
* Bartlett, Nancy
* Keats, Myron
* McClellan, William
* McKay, Kevin
* Stanley, Chuck
* Stoddard, Charles [house
  pseudonym]
* Sturdy, Carl

**Strong, Eric**
*See* Silberschlag, Eisig

**Strong, Harrington**
*See* McCulley, Johnston

**Strong, James**
*See* Hervey, Hedley

**Strong, L. A. G.**
*See* Strong, Leonard Alfred George

**Strong, Latham C.** [PA]
*Author*
* Shatt, Montague

**Strong, Leonard Alfred George**
1896-1958 [LC]
*British author*
* Strong, L. A. G.

**[The] Strong Man**
See Topham, Thomas

**Strong, Pat**
See Hough, Richard [Alexander]

**Strong, Solange**
See Hertz, Solange [Strong]

**Strong, Spencer**
See Ackerman, Forrest J[ames]

**Strong, Susan**
See Rees, Joan

**Strongblood, Casper**
See Webster, David Endicott

**Strongbow**
See Clare, Gilbert de

**Strongbow**
See Clare, Richard de

**[The] Strongest Man in the World**
See Cyr, Louis

**[The] Strongest Man in the World**
See Mueller, Frederick

**[The] Strongest Man Who Ever Lived**
See Cyr, Louis

**Strongheart, [Chief] Nipo**
See Tahchenum, Neeahpouw

**Strongin, Lynn** 1939- [CA]
*American author and poet*
* Michaels, Lynn

**Strongi'th'arm, Charles**
See Armstrong, Charles Wicksteed

**Stroock, Geraldine** 1925-1977
[BEW, FC, IPA]
*American actress*
* Brooks, Geraldine

**Strother, David Hunter** 1817-1888
[DEL, DNNF, FFF]
*American author and illustrator*
* Porte-Crayon

**Strother, Pat Wallace**
See Wallace, Pat

**Strothotte, Maurice Arnold**
1865-1937 [BBD]
*American musician*
* Arnold, Maurice

**Stroud, Albert**
See Budrys, Algirdas Jonas

**Stroud, Edwin Marvin** 1939- [BE]
*American baseball player*
* [The] Creeper

**Stroud, Ralph Vivian** 1885- [BE]
*American baseball player*
* Stroud, Sailor

**Stroud, Robert Franklin**
1887-1963 [BLB]
*American murderer*
* [The] Birdman of Alcatraz

**Stroud, Sailor**
See Stroud, Ralph Vivian

**Stroughter, Le Roy** 1969- [IBW]
*American trapeze performer*
* Stroughter, Pee Wee

**Stroughter, Pee Wee**
See Stroughter, Le Roy

**Strout, Richard L[ee]** 1898- [CA]
*American journalist*
* T. R. B.

**Strover, Dorothea** 1900- [CA, WD]
*British author and illustrator*
* Tinne, Dorothea
* Tinne, E. D.

**Strozzi [or Strozza], Bernardo**
1581-1644 [WBD]
*Italian painter and engraver*
* [Il] Capuccino
* [Il] Prete Genovese

**Strozzi, Filippo** 1426-1491 [WBD]
*Florentine banker*
* [The] Elder

**Strozzi, Giambattista** 1488-1538
[WBD]
*Led attack against Medici family of
Florence*
* Filippo II

**Strubberg, Friedrich Armand**
1806-1889 [WBD]
*German-born author*
* Armand
* Schubbert

**Struble, Virginia**
See Burlingame, Virginia [Struble]

**Struck, Dutch**
See Struck, Raymond F.

**Struck, Raymond F.** 20th c. [BBH]
*American basketball player and
coach*
* Struck, Dutch

**Strudwick, Shepperd**
See Shepperd, John

**Struebe, Hermann** 1879- ?
[CD, LAO]
*German playwright, author, poet*
* Burte, Hermann

**Strug, Andrzej**
See Galecki, Tadeusz

**[The] Struggler**
See Nowatzke, Thomas M. [Tom]

**Strunck, Nicolas Adam** 1640-1700
[SN]
*German composer*
* Archdiavolo

**Strung, Norman** 1941- [CA]
*American author*
* Barkee, Asouff
* Yaeger, Bart

**Strunk, Jud**
See Strunk, Justin Roderick, Jr.

**Strunk, Justin Roderick, Jr.** 1936-
[B10, RO2]
*American singer and songwriter*
* Strunk, Jud

**Struss, Clarence Herbert** 1909-
*American baseball player*
* Struss, Steamboat

**Struss, Steamboat**
See Struss, Clarence Herbert

**Struther, Jan**
See Maxtone Graham, Joyce
[Anstruther]

**Strutt, Lord**
See Charles II

**Struys, John**
See Morrison, John

**Strydonck, Victor van** 1876-1953
[BDW]
*Belgian army officer*
* Strydonck de Burkel, Victor van

**Strydonck de Burkel, Victor van**
See Strydonck, Victor van

**Stryjkowski, Juljan**
See Stark, Pesach

**Stryker, Dutch**
See Stryker, Sterling Alpa

**Stryker, Sterling Alpa** 1895-1964
[BE]
*American baseball player*
* Stryker, Dutch

**Stuart, Alex**
See Stuart, Vivian [Finlay]

**Stuart, Alex R.**
See Stuart, Richard Gordon

**Stuart, Anthony**
See Hale, Julian A[nthony]
S[tuart]

**Stuart, Athenian**
See Stuart, James

**Stuart, Brian**
See Worthington-Stuart, Brian
Arthur

**Stuart, Carl**
See Schacht, Ray McKeown

**Stuart, Charles**
See MacKinnon, Charles Roy

**Stuart, Charles Edward Louis Philip
Casimir** 1720-1788
[DEP, DNNS, SN]
*British prince*
* [The] Bonnie Chevalier
* Bonnie Prince Charlie
* Charles Edward
* [The] Highland Laddie
* [The] King Over the Water
* [The] Young Adventurer
* [The] Young Chevalier
* [The] Young Pretender

**Stuart, Charlotte** 1863- ? [THR]
*British actress*
* Granville, Charlotte

**Stuart, Chauncey**
See Stuart, William Alexander
[Bill]

**Stuart, Clay**
See Whittington, Harry

**Stuart, Cosmo**
See Gordon-Lennox, Cosmo
Charles

**Stuart, D[orothy] M[argaret]**
See Browne, Dorothy Margaret
Stuart

**Stuart, David**
See Hoyt, Edwin P[almer], Jr.

**Stuart, Don A.**
See Campbell, John W[ood], Jr.

**Stuart, Donald** 20th c. [MBF]
*British author and playwright*
* Stuart, Ronald
* Verner, Gerald

**Stuart, Fay**
See Leonard, Nellie Mabel

**Stuart [or Stewart], Frances Teresa**
1647-1702 [WBD]
*Mistress of King Charles II of
England*
* [La] Belle Stuart

**Stuart, Frederick**
See Tomlin, Eric Walter Frederick

**Stuart, Giacomo Rossi** 20th c.
[WF]
*Italian actor*
* Stuart, Jack

**Stuart, Gilbert** 1746?-1786 [SN]
*Scottish author and journalist*
* Zoilus

**Stuart, Gilbert Charles** 1755-1828
[SN]
*American painter*
* [The] American Stuart

**Stuart, Gloria**
See Finch, Gloria Stuart

**Stuart, Gordon**
See Bedford-Jones, Henry [James
O'Brien]

**Stuart, Gordon**
See Sayler, Harry Lincoln

**Stuart, Henry Benedict Maria
Clemens** 1725-1807
[DEP, DHA, SN]
*King of England*
* Henry IX
* [The] Last of the Stuarts
* York, Cardinal

**Stuart, Henry Robson** 1836-1903
[BEW]
*American actor and producer*
* Robson, Stuart

**Stuart, Hod**
See Stuart, Horace Hodgson

**Stuart, Hod**
See Stuart, William

**Stuart, Horace Hodgson**
1880-1907 [HK]
*Canadian-born hockey player*
* Stuart, Hod

**Stuart, Ian**
See MacLean, Alistair [Stuart]

**Stuart, Ina** 1907- [F2]
*Actress*
* La Roy, Rita

**Stuart, Jack**
See Stuart, Giacomo Rossi

**Stuart, James** 1713-1788 [DNNF]
*British painter and architect*
* Stuart, Athenian

**Stuart, James** 1776-1849 [FFF]
*Scottish traveller*
* [The] Stot

**Stuart, James Ewell Brown**
1833-1864 [WBD]
*American army officer*
* Stuart, Jeb

**Stuart, James Francis Edward**
1688-1766 [DEP, SN, WBD]
*Son of King James II*
* [The] Chevalier de St. George
* James Edward
* James III
* [The] King Over the Water
* [The] Old Pretender
* [The] Warming Pan Child
* [The] Warming Pan Hero

**Stuart, Jane** 1942- [CA]
*American author and translator*
* Juergensmeyer, Jane Stuart

**Stuart, Jay Allison**
See Tait, Dorothy

**Stuart, Jean**
See Leisenring, Margaret

**Stuart. Jeanne**
See Sweet, Jeanne

**Stuart, Jeb**
See Stuart, James Ewell Brown

**Stuart, Jeff** 1952- [RO2]
*American musician*
* Stuart, Wally

**Stuart, John**
See Croall, John Alfred Louden

**Stuart, John [Third Earl of Bute]**
1713-1792 [HN, SN]
*British prime minister*
* Boot Jack
* [The] Wire Master

**Stuart, John Davis [Johnny]**
1901-1970 [BE]
*American baseball player*
* Stuart, Stud

**Stuart, Kenneth**
See Wesander, Bjoern Kenneth

**Stuart, Leslie**
See Barrett, Thomas Augustine

**Stuart, Leslie**
See Marlowe, Kenneth

**Stuart, Logan?**
See Wilding, Philip

**Stuart, Lyle**
See Simon, Lionel

**Stuart, M. B.** [PA]
*Author*
* Mortimer, Grace

**Stuart, Madge**
See Stewart, Margaret

**Stuart, Mary**
See Mary, Queen of Scots

**Stuart, Maude**
See Grubbs, Maude

**Stuart, May** 20th c. [THR]
*British actress*
* Leslie-Stuart, May

**Stuart, Michael**
See Thomas, Reginald George

**Stuart, Monroe**
See Shapiro, Max

**Stuart, Morna** 1905- [AW]
*British author*
* Campbell, C. J.

**Stuart, Mrs. Everard** [FFF]
*Entertainer*
* Branscombe, Maud

**Stuart, Nick**
See Pratza, Nicholas

**Stuart, Otho**
See Andreae, Otto Stuart

**Stuart, Red**
See Stuart, William

**Stuart, Richard Gordon** 1947-
[ESF]
*Scottish author*
* Gordon, Stuart
* Stuart, Alex R.

**Stuart, Richard Lee** 1932-
[BE, DGS, PB]
*American baseball player*
* [The] Iron Glove
* Strangeglove, Dr.
* Stuart, Stonefingers

**Stuart, Ronald**
See Stuart, Donald

**Stuart, Sheila**
See Baker, Mary Gladys Steel

**Stuart, Sidney**
See Avallone, Michael [Angelo],
Jr.

**Stuart, Stonefingers**
See Stuart, Richard Lee

**Stuart, Stud**
See Stuart, John Davis [Johnny]

**Stuart, Tom**
See Moriarty, Tom

**Stuart, V. A.**
See Stuart, Vivian [Finlay]

**Stuart, Vivian [Finlay]** 1914-
[CA, WD]
*British author*
* Allen, Barbara
* Finlay, Fiona
* Long, William Stuart
* Stuart, Alex
* Stuart, V. A.

**Stuart, W. J.**
See MacDonald, Philip

**Stuart, Wally**
See Stuart, Jeff

**Stuart, Warren**
See MacDonald, Philip

**Stuart, William** 20th c.
[CBH, CEI, CSH]
*Canadian-born hockey player*
* Stuart, Hod
* Stuart, Red

**Stuart, William Alexander [Bill]** 20th
c. [BE]
*American baseball player*
* Stuart, Chauncey

**Stuart-Baker, Iris** 1901- [THR]
*British actress*
* Baker, Iris

**Stubbes, John** 1541-1600
[DEL, PA]
*British author*
* Scaeva

**Stubbing, Newton Haydn** 1921-
[CAR]
*British painter*
* Stubbing, Tony

**Stubbing, Tony**
See Stubbing, Newton Haydn

**Stubbings, Hilda Uren**
See U'Ren-Stubbings, Hilda

**Stubborn Old Grover**
See Cleveland, [Stephen] Grover

**Stubbs, Harry C[lement]** 1922-
[CA, ESF, SF]
*American author*
* Clement, Hal
* Richard, George

**Stubbs, Morton Richard**
1860-1939 [BEW, FC]
*British actor*
* Selten, Morton

**Stubbs, Philip** 15th c. [SN]
*Puritan pamphleteer*
* [The] Prynne of His Day

**Stubbs, Tilsa** 1926- [THR]
*British actress*
* Page, Tilsa

**Stubby, Captain**
See Fouts, Tom C.

**Stuber, Abe**
See Stuber, Emmett R.

**Stuber, Emmett R.** 1904- [FB]
*American football coach*
* Stuber, Abe

**Stuber, Stanley I[rving]** 1903-
[CAP]
*American author*
* Erasmus, M. Nott

**Stuckey, Sterling** 1932- [IBW]
*American author and historian*
* Sterling X

**Stucley, Elizabeth**
See Northmore, Elizabeth Florence

**Stucley, Lusty**
See Stucley, [Sir] Thomas

**Stucley, [Sir] Thomas** 1525?-1578
[SN]
*British adventurer*
* Stucley, Lusty

**Studdert, Annie Louisa** 1885-
[AW]
*Author*
* Rixon, Annie

**Studebaker, Don** 20th c. [SFP]
*Author*
* Decles, Jon

**[A] Student of Law**
See Hunt, Frederick Knight

**[A] Student of Occultism**
See Hartmann, Franz

**Studer, Steven Paul** 1953- [SMG]
*American football player*
* Studer, Stu

**Studer, Stu**
See Studer, Steven Paul

**Studholme, Marie**
See Lupton, Marie

**Studley, Seymour L.** 19th c. [BE]
*American baseball player*
* Studley, Warhorse

**Studley, Warhorse**
See Studley, Seymour L.

**Studstill, Monkey**
See Studstill, Pat[rick L.]

**Studstill, Pat[rick L.]** 1938-
*American football player*
* Studstill, Monkey

**Stuempke, Harald**
See Steiner, Gerolf

**[The] Stuffed Prophet**
See Cleveland, [Stephen] Grover

**Stuffel, Paul Harrington** 1927-
[BE]
*American baseball player*
* Stuffel, Stu

**Stuffel, Stu**
See Stuffel, Paul Harrington

**Stukalov, Nikolai Fyodorovich**
1900-1962 [MWD]
*Russian playwright*
* Pogodin, Nikolai Fyodorovich

**Stukeley, William** 1687-1765
[WBD]
*British antiquary and author*
* [The] Arch Druid

**Stukus, Annis** 20th c. [CFH]
*Canadian football player and coach*
* Stukus, Stuke

**Stukus, Stuke**
See Stukus, Annis

**[The] Stump Fingered**
See Mark

**[The] Stupid Boy**
See Aquinas, Thomas [Thomas of
Aquino]

**Sturdivant, Snake**
See Sturdivant, Thomas Virgil

**Sturdivant, Thomas Virgil** 1930-
[BE, PB]
*American baseball player*
* Sturdivant, Snake

**Sturdy, Carl**
See Strong, Charles Stanley

**Sture-Vasa, Mary**
See Alsop, Mary O'Hara

**Sturgeon, Foolbert**
See Stack, Frank H[untington]

**Sturgeon, Theodore Hamilton**
See Waldo, Edward Hamilton

**Sturgeon, Wina** 20th c. [CA]
*American author*
* Moore, Cory

**Sturges, Preston**
See Biden, Edmond P.

**Sturgill, Virgil Leon** 1897- [NAA]
*American writer and poet*
* Edgewood, Henry

**Sturgis, Colin** [joint pseudonym with
Mel(vin) Sturgis]
See Cole, Les[ter]

**Sturgis, Colin** [joint pseudonym with
Les(ter) Cole]
See Sturgis, Mel[vin]

**Sturgis, H. O.**
*See* Sturgis, Howard Overing

**Sturgis, Howard Overing**
1855-1920 [LC]
*British author*
* Sturgis, H. O.

**Sturgis, Mel[vin]** 20th c. [WGT]
*Author*
* Sturgis, Colin [joint pseudonym with Les(ter) Cole]

**Sturm, Johann Christoph**
1507-1589 [DEP, FFF, SN]
*German scholar*
* [The] Cicero of Germany
* [The] German Cicero
* [The] Restorer of Science in Germany

**Sturrock, Jeremy**
*See* Healey, Benjamin James

**Sturt, George** 1863-1927
[B10, LC, TCL]
*British author*
* Bourne, George

**Sturton, Hugh**
*See* Johnston, Hugh Anthony Stephen

**Sturtzel, Howard A[llison]** 1894-
[CA, SAT]
*American author*
* Annixter, Paul

**Sturtzel, Jane Levington** 1903-
[CA, SAT]
*American author*
* Annixter, Jane
* Comfort, Jane Levington

**Sturzwage, Leopold** 1879-1968
[CAR]
*French painter*
* Survage, Leopold

**Stutz, George** 1893-1930 [BE]
*American baseball player*
* Stutz, Kid

**Stutz, Kid**
*See* Stutz, George

**Stuyvesant, Alice** [joint pseudonym with Charles Norris Williamson]
*See* Williamson, Alice Muriel [Livingston]

**Stuyvesant, Alice** [joint pseudonym with Alice Muriel (Livingston) Williamson]
*See* Williamson, Charles Norris

**Stuyvesant, Peter**
*See* Stuyvesant, Petrus

**Stuyvesant, Petrus** 1592-1672
[WBD]
*Dutch administrator in America*
* Stuyvesant, Peter

**Stydahar, Joseph L.** 1912- [FB]
*American football player*
* Stydahar, Jumbo Joe

**Stydahar, Jumbo Joe**
*See* Stydahar, Joseph L.

**Styles, Frank Showell** 1908-
[CA, CC, SAT]
*British author*
* Carr, Glyn
* Howell, S.

**Styles, John** 1770-1860 [FFF]
*British clergyman*
* Ringletub, Jeremiah

**Styles, Lena**
*See* Styles, William Graves

**Styles, William Graves** 1897-1956
[BE]
*American baseball player*
* Styles, Lena

**Stylites, Simeon**
*See* Caldwell, William A.

**Stylla, Joanne**
*See* Branden, Victoria [Fremlin]

**Stymie**
*See* Beard, Matthew

**Styne, Jule**
*See* Stein, Julius Kerwin

**Stynes, Cornelius William**
1868-1944 [BE]
*American baseball player*
* Stynes, Neil

**Stynes, Neil**
*See* Stynes, Cornelius William

**Su Kuo-feng** 20th c.
*Chinese prime minister*
* Hua Kuo-feng

**Su Man-shu** 1884-1918 [EWL]
*Chinese poet and author*
* Su Yuan-ying

**Su Shih** 1036-1101 [WBD]
*Chinese poet and statesman*
* Su Tung-po

**Su Tung-po**
*See* Su Shih

**Su Yuan-ying**
*See* Su Man-shu

**Suardi, Bartolommeo** 1460?-1536?
[WBD]
*Italian painter and architect*
* [Il] Bramantino

**Suarez, Carlos** 1913- [GS]
*Mexican bullfighter*
* Tototoro [All Bull]

**Suarez, Francisco [or Francois]**
1548-1617 [DNNS, FFF]
*Spanish theologian and philosopher*
* [The] Last of the Schoolmen

**Suarez Lynch, B.** [joint pseudonym with Jorge Luis Borges]
*See* Bioy-Casares, Adolfo

**Suarez Lynch, B.** [joint pseudonym with Adolfo Bioy-Casares]
*See* Borges, Jorge Luis

**Subber, Arnold** 1918- [BEW]
*American producer*
* Saint Subber, Arnold

**Subhadra-Nandan**
*See* Das, Prafulla Chandra

**Subhasree**
*See* Sreenivasapuram, Sesha Charlu

**Sublett, Bubbles**
*See* Sublett, John William

**Sublett, John William** 1902- [IBW]
*American entertainer*
* Sublett, Bubbles

**[The] Sublime Child**
*See* Hugo, Victor Marie

**Sublimis et Illuminatus, Doctor**
*See* Tauler, Johann

**Subond, Valerie**
*See* Grayland, Valerie Merle [Spanner]

**Subotai [or Sabutai]** 1172?-1245
[WBD]
*Mongol general*
* Bagatur [The Valiant]

**Subtilis, Doctor**
*See* Duns Scotus, Johannes

**Subtilissimus, Doctor**
*See* Duns Scotus, Johannes

**[The] Subtle Doctor**
*See* Duns Scotus, Johannes

**Suchowljansky, Maier** 1902- [BLB]
*Russian-born American underworld figure*
* Lansky, Meyer
* Meyer the Bug

**Suck All Cream**
*See* Clarke, Samuel

**Suckert, Kurt Erich** 1898-1957
[CD, EWL]
*Italian author, poet, playwright*
* Malaparte, Curzio

**Suckling, John** 1926- [TR]
*British lighting designer and theatre consultant*
* Wyckham, John

**Suckling, Robert** 1933- [TR]
*British actor and director*
* Chetwyn, Robert

**Sudakis, Suds [or Sudsy]**
*See* Sudakis, William Paul, Jr.

**Sudakis, William Paul, Jr.** 1946-
[BE, SMG]
*American baseball player*
* Sudakis, Suds [or Sudsy]

**Sudbury, Richard**
*See* Gibson, Charles Hammond

**Suddaby, [William] Donald**
1900-1964 [ESF, LC, TCC]
*British author*
* Griff, Alan

**Sudden Death Hill**
*See* Hill, John Melvin

**Sudden Sam McDowell**
*See* McDowell, Samuel Edward Thomas

**Suddith, Arnold Eugene** 20th c.
[BBH]
*American basketball player*
* Suddith, Sally

**Suddith, Sally**
*See* Suddith, Arnold Eugene

**Suddoth, J. Guy**
*See* Erby, John J.

**Suder, Pecky**
*See* Suder, Pete[r]

**Suder, Pete[r]** 1916- [BE, PB]
*American baseball player*
* Suder, Pecky

**Sudhalter, Richard M[errill]** 1938-
[CA]
*American author and music critic*
* Napoleon, Art

**Sudhoff, John William** 1874-1917
[BE]
*American baseball player*
* Sudhoff, Wee Willie

**Sudhoff, Wee Willie**
*See* Sudhoff, John William

**Sudkamp, [Sister] Augustine**
*See* Sudkamp, Cora May

**Sudkamp, Cora May** 1914- [IWM]
*American music educator*
* Sudkamp, [Sister] Augustine

**Sudlow, Bessie**
*See* Gunn, Mrs. Michael

**Sudlow, Elizabeth Williams** 1878-
? [NAA]
*Canadian-born journalist and author*
* Waldus, Edythe

**Sudorius**
*See* Lesueur, Nicolas

**Suds**
*See* Lowe, William Herman

**Sue, Eugene**
*See* Sue, Marie Joseph

**Sue, Marie Joseph** 1804-1857
[WBD]
*French author*
* Sue, Eugene

**Suedfeld, Max Simon** 1849-1923
[WBD]
*German physician and author*
* Nordau, Max Simon

**Suedfeld, Peter**
*See* Field, Peter

**Suess, Hans** 476?-1522 [WBD]
*German painter*
* Kulmbach, Hans von

**Sufana, Eugene** 1928- [EJ]
*American jazz musician*
* Allen, Gene

**Sufficens, Doctor**
*See* Pietro Aquila

**Suffling, Mark**
*See* Rowland, D[onald] S[ydney]

**Suffling, Philip** 1902- [RBE, SG]
*British boxer*
* Scott, Phaintin' Phil
* Scott, Phil

**Suffolk Coast**
*See* Cooper, Ernest Read

**Suffridus**
*See* Petri, Sjurd Peeters

**Suga**
*See* Yusuke, Suga

**Sugar Bear Blanks**
*See* Blanks, Larvell

**Sugar Bear Clemons**
*See* Clemons, Craig Lynn

**Sugar Bear Crowder**
*See* Crowder, Randy

**Sugar Bear Hamilton**
*See* Hamilton, Raymond Lee

**Sugar Bear Young**
See Young, Willie Lull

**Sugar, Bert Randolph** 1937- [CA]
*American author*
* Brooks, John
* Davis, Suzanne

**Sugar Boy Dougherty**
See Dougherty, Thomas James
[Tom]

**Sugar Boy Williams**
See Williams, Joseph Leon [Joe]

**Sugar Chile Robinson**
See Robinson, Frank Isaac

**Sugar Jim Henry**
See Henry, Samuel James

**Sugar Johnny Smith**
See Smith, John

**[The] Sugar King**
See Spreckels, Claus

**Sugar, Leo T.** 1929- [FB]
*American football player*
* Sugar, Shug

**Sugar Lip**
See Hafiz, Mohammed

**[The] Sugar Pie Guy**
See Sawell, Larry

**Sugar Ray Long**
See Long, Russell

**Sugar Ray Robinson**
See Smith, Walker

**Sugar, Shug**
See Sugar, Leo T.

**Sugarhouse Pete DiGiovanni**
See DiGiovanni, Peter

**Suger** 1081?-1151 [WBD]
*French statesman*
* [The] Father of His Country
* Pere de la Patrie

**Suggs, Chick**
See Suggs, Edward Murray

**Suggs, Edward Murray** 1901- [BX]
*American boxer*
* Suggs, Chick

**Suggs, Simon**
See Hooper, Johnson J.

**Sugimoto, Tsunetaro** 1879-1924
[SC]
*Japanese-born actor*
* Tomamoto, Thomas

**Suhr, August Richard** 1906- [BE]
*American baseball player*
* Suhr, Gus

**Suhr, Gus**
See Suhr, August Richard

**Suicide Sal**
See Parker, Bonnie

**Suisse, J. F. S.** [PA]
*Author*
* Simon, Jules

**Suitcase Bob Seeds**
See Seeds, Robert Ira

**Suiter, Arlendo D.** 1919- [ASC]
*American composer*
* Suiter, Don

**Suiter, Don**
See Suiter, Arlendo D.

**Suitger** ?-1047 [CAL]
*Pope*
* Clement II

**Sujakevitch, Anjuschka Stenski**
1908?- [F2, FC]
*Russian-born actress*
* Sten, Anna

**Sukeforth, Clyde LeRoy** 1901-
[BE]
*American baseball player*
* Sukeforth, Sukey

**Sukeforth, Sukey**
See Sukeforth, Clyde LeRoy

**Sukulov, Victor** 20th c. [EE]
*Latvian-born intelligence agent*
* Kent, Edward
* [The] Petit Chef

**Sularz, Bronislaw** 1942- [AES]
*Polish soccer player*
* Sularz, Jerry

**Sularz, Jerry**
See Sularz, Bronislaw

**Suleiman I [or Soliman]** ?-1410?
[FFF, RH]
*Sultan of Turkey*
* [The] Noble

**Suleiman II [or Soliman]**
1493?-1566 [FFF, RH, WBD]
*Sultan of Turkey*
* Canuni
* [The] Conqueror
* [The] Law Giver
* [The] Lord of his Age
* [The] Magnificent

**Sulin, Kaarlo Teodor** 1902-1945
[EWL]
*Finnish poet*
* Sarkia, Kaarlo Teodor

**Sulky**
See Arcularius, Henry W.

**Sulla, Lucius Cornelius** 2nd c. BC
[WBD]
*Roman general and politician*
* Felix

**Sullivan, Barry**
See Barry, Patrick

**Sullivan, Big Mike**
See Sullivan, Michael Joseph

**Sullivan, Bonar** 1924-1958 [FC]
*American actor*
* Colleano, Bonar, Jr.

**Sullivan, Brian**
See Sullivan, Harry Joseph

**Sullivan, Carl Mancel** 1918- [BE]
*American baseball player*
* Sullivan, Jack

**Sullivan, Chub**
See Sullivan, John Frank

**Sullivan, Cynthia Jan** 1937- [GF]
*American golfer*
* Sullivan, Silky

**Sullivan, Dan** 20th c. [BMH]
*British strongman*
* [The] Wonder of the Age

**Sullivan, Daniel** 1855-1910 [BEW]
*American actor and playwright*
* Sully, Daniel

**Sullivan, Daniel C.** 1857-1893 [BE]
*American baseball player*
* Sullivan, Link

**Sullivan, Des**
See Sullivan, Thomas Desmond

**Sullivan, Eddie**
See Collins, Edward Trowbridge,
Sr. [Eddie]

**Sullivan, Edgar James** 1890?-1957
[BEW]
*British theatrical performer*
* Colleano, Bonar, Sr.

**Sullivan, Edmund** 20th c. [WWL]
*British author*
* Nagle, Arthur

**Sullivan, Edward Alan** 1868-1947
[CAN, WW]
*Canadian author*
* Murray, Sinclair

**Sullivan, Elizabeth** 1902-
[F2, FC, OCF]
*British-born American actress*
* Lanchester, Elsa

**Sullivan, Eric Harrison**
See Hickey, Madelyn Eastlund

**Sullivan, Frank**
See Dillinger, John Herbert

**Sullivan, Frank** 1910-1975
[SC, SW]
*American actor*
* Sully, Frank

**Sullivan, Frank Taylor** 1929- [CEI]
*Canadian-born hockey player*
* Sullivan, Sully

**Sullivan, George James** 1929-
[CEI, FHE, HK]
*Canadian-born hockey player*
* Sullivan, Red

**Sullivan, Harry Joseph** 1919-1969
[SC]
*American-born actor and opera singer*
* Sullivan, Brian

**Sullivan, Jack**
See Sullivan, Carl Mancel

**Sullivan, Jack** 1878-1947
[BX, RBE]
*American boxer*
* Sullivan, Twin

**Sullivan, James A.** 20th c. [PHM]
*American sheriff*
* Sullivan, Smiling Jimmy

**Sullivan, James E.** 1864?-1931
[BEW]
*Comedian*
* [The] Polite Lunatic

**Sullivan, Joe**
See O'Sullivan, Dennis Patrick
Terence Joseph

**Sullivan, John Florence** 1894-1956
[EMT, FC, SC]
*American entertainer*
* Allen, Fred
* Huckle, Paul
* James, Freddie
* St. James, Fred

**Sullivan, John Frank** 1856-1881
[BE]
*American baseball player*
* Sullivan, Chub

**Sullivan, John L[awrence]**
1858-1918 [AS, BX, RBE]
*American boxer*
* [The] Boston Strong Boy

**Sullivan, John Peter** 1941- [SMG]
*American baseball player*
* Sullivan, Sully

**Sullivan, John Y.** 1917-1967
[CWG, DAM]
*American country-western performer*
* Lonzo

**Sullivan, Kid**
See Tricamo, Stephen J.

**Sullivan, Lefty**
See Sullivan, Paul Thomas

**Sullivan, Link**
See Sullivan, Daniel C.

**Sullivan, Mary**
See Panfili, Mirella

**Sullivan, Maxine**
See Williams, Marietta

**Sullivan, Michael Joseph**
1866-1906 [BE]
*American baseball player*
* Sullivan, Big Mike

**Sullivan, Mike** 1878-1937
[AS, BX, RBE]
*American boxer*
* Sullivan, Twin

**Sullivan, Paul Thomas** 1916- [BE]
*American baseball player*
* Sullivan, Lefty

**Sullivan, Peter** 1951- [SMG]
*Canadian-born hockey player*
* Sullivan, Silky

**Sullivan, Red**
See Sullivan, George James

**Sullivan, Robert Baldwin** 19th c.
[FFF]
*Canadian writer*
* Cinna

**Sullivan, Rollin** 1919-
[CWG, DAM]
*American country-western performer*
* Oscar

**Sullivan, Sean Mei**
See Sohl, Gerald Allan [Jerry]

**Sullivan, Sheila** 1927- [CA]
*British author and editor*
* Bathurst, Sheila

**Sullivan, Silky**
See Sullivan, Cynthia Jan

**Sullivan, Silky**
See Sullivan, Peter

**Sullivan, Sleeper**
See Sullivan, Thomas Jefferson

**Sullivan, Smiling Jimmy**
See Sullivan, James A.

**Sullivan, Steve**
See Tricamo, Stephen J.

**Sullivan, Sully**
See Sullivan, Frank Taylor

**Sullivan, Sully**
See Sullivan, John Peter

**Sullivan, Thomas Desmond** 1913-
[GF]
*American sportswriter*
* Sullivan, Des

**Sullivan, Thomas Jefferson** ?-1899
[BE]
*American baseball player*
* Sullivan, Sleeper

**Sullivan, Twin**
*See* Sullivan, Jack

**Sullivan, Twin**
*See* Sullivan, Mike

**Sullivan, Vernon**
*See* Vian, Boris

**Sullivan, Victoria** 1943- [CA]
*American poet and playwright*
* Slater, Veronica

**Sullivan, Yankee**
*See* Ambrose, James

**Sully, Daniel**
*See* Sullivan, Daniel

**Sully, Frank**
*See* Sullivan, Frank

**Sully-Prudhomme**
*See* Prudhomme, Rene Francois
Armand

**Sultan El Osman, Chareh**
*See* Bullock-Webster, Llewelyn

**[The] Sultan of Magic**
*See* Wishner, Sam

**[The] Sultan of Swat**
*See* Ruth, George Herman

**Sulzberger, Arthur Hays** 1891-1968
*American newspaper publisher*
* Aitchess, A.

**Sulzberger, Arthur Ochs** 1926?-
*American newspaper publisher*
* Sock, A.
* Sulzberger, Punch

**Sulzberger, C. L.**
*See* Sulzberger, Cyrus Leo, III

**Sulzberger, Cyrus Leo, III** 1912-
[WYA]
*American author*
* Sulzberger, C. L.

**Sulzberger, Punch**
*See* Sulzberger, Arthur Ochs

**Sumac, Yma**
*See* Chavarri, Emperatriz

**Summer, Donna**
*See* Gaines, Donna

**[The] Summer King**
*See* Amadeus

**[The] Summer King**
*See* Robert I

**Summerall, George** 20th c. [FB]
*American football player*
* Summerall, Pat

**Summerall, Pat**
*See* Summerall, George

**Summerfield, Charles**
*See* Arrington, Alfred W.

**Summerfield, Charles**
*See* Foster, Theodore

**Summerfield, Woolfe** 1897-
[WWL]
*British author and barrister*
* Mowshay, Ben

**Summerforest, Ivy B.**
*See* Kirkup, James

**Summerhayes, Prudence**
*See* Alan Turner, Violet Prudence

**Summerhill, J. K.**
*See* Schere, Monroe

**Summerly, Felix**
*See* Cole, [Sir] Henry

**Summerly, Mrs. Felix**
*See* Cole, Marian Fairman

**Summers, A. Leonard** 20th c.
[WWL]
*British author and journalist*
* Cue

**Summers, Champ**
*See* Summers, John J.

**Summers, Colin**
*See* Agnew, Stephen Hamilton

**Summers, Colleen** 1928-
[ECM, RO1]
*American singer*
* Ford, Mary

**Summers, Gordon**
*See* Hornby, John [Wilkinson]

**Summers, Hollis [Spurgeon, Jr.]**
1916- [CA, CN, WD]
*American author and poet*
* Hollis, Jim [joint pseudonym with
Louis P(reston) Trimble]

**Summers, John A.**
*See* Lawson, Horace Lowe

**Summers, John J.** 1948- [BR]
*American baseball player*
* Summers, Champ

**Summers, Kickapoo**
*See* Summers, Oron Edgar

**Summers, Oron Edgar** 1884-1953
[BE]
*American baseball player*
* Summers, Kickapoo

**Summers, Rey**
*See* Montague, Alphonsus
Joseph-Mary Augustus

**Summers, Rowena**
*See* Saunders, Jean

**Summersales, Rowland** 1912-
[AW]
*British author*
* Gaines, Robert

**Summersgill, Henry Travers**
1876-1931 [BE]
*American baseball player*
* Sommerville, Andrew Henry
[Andy]

**Summerskill, Edith** 1902?-1980?
*British politician*
* Dr. Edith

**Summerville, Amelia**
*See* Shaw, Amelia M.

**Summerville, George J.** 1892-1946
[BEW, F1, FC]
*American actor*
* Summerville, Slim

**Summerville, Slim**
*See* Summerville, George J.

**Summey, James C.** 1914-1976
[CWG, ECM]
*American country-western performer*
* Cousin Jody

**[The] Summoned**
*See* Ferdinand IV

**Sumner, David [W. K.]** 1937- [CA]
*American author*
* Kaiser, Bill

**Sumner, Eldon**
*See* Bruno, James Edward

**Sumner, J. D.**
*See* Sumner, John David

**Sumner, John David** 1924- [DAM]
*American singer and songwriter*
* Sumner, J. D.

**Sumter, Thomas** 1734-1832 [SN]
*American army officer*
* [The] Carolina Game-Cock

**[The] Sun God**
*See* Louis XIV

**[The] Sun King**
*See* Louis XIV

**Sun Ra**
*See* Blount, Herman

**Sun Wen**
*See* Sun Yat-sen

**Sun Yat-sen** 1866-1925 [WBD]
*Chinese statesman*
* Chung Shan
* [The] Father of the Revolution
* Sun Wen

**Sunbeauty, Olga**
*See* Solbelli, Olga

**[The] Sunbonnet Girl**
*See* Parker, Linda

**Sunbonnet Sue**
*See* Salisbury, Marilla

**[The] Sundance Kid**
*See* Csonka, Lawrence R. [Larry]

**[The] Sundance Kid**
*See* Longabaugh, Harry

**Sundaram**
*See* Luhar, Tribhuvandas
Purushottandas

**Sunday, Art[hur]**
*See* Wacher, August

**[The] Sunday Gentleman**
*See* Foe, Daniel

**Sunday, Johnny**
*See* Meader, Vaughn

**Sunday, Parson**
*See* Sunday, William Ashley
[Billy]

**Sunday, William Ashley [Billy]**
1862-1935 [BE, PB]
*American evangelist and baseball
player*
* [The] Evangelist
* Sunday, Parson

**Sundmark, Betty**
*See* Shannon, Elizabeth S.

**Sundra, Smokey**
*See* Sundra, Stephen Richard

**Sundra, Stephen Richard**
1910-1952 [BE]
*American baseball player*
* Sundra, Smokey

**Sunesson, Lambert** 1918- [IAW]
*Swedish author*
* Frykberg, August

**Sung Chiao**
*See* Chou, Eric

**Sung, P. M.**
*See* Chun, Jinsie K[yung] S[hien]

**Sung-Tai, Kim** 1907- [IWM]
*Korean composer, educator,
conductor*
* Naksok

**Sungei, Anak**
*See* Brooke, Gilbert Edward

**Sunkel, Lefty**
*See* Sunkel, Thomas Jacob

**Sunkel, Thomas Jacob** 1912- [BE]
*American baseball player*
* Sunkel, Lefty

**Sunna**
*See* Larusdottir, Elinborg

**Sunners, William** 1903- [CAP]
*American author*
* Keith, Lee
* Satterly, Weston

**Sunni-Ali, Fulani**
*See* Boston, Cynthia Priscilla

**Sunny Jack Sutthoff**
*See* Sutthoff, John Gerhard

**Sunny Jim**
*See* Watson, Johnny

**Sunny Jim Bottomley**
*See* Bottomley, James Leroy

**Sunny Jim Callaghan**
*See* Callaghan, Leonard James

**Sunny Jim Coffroth**
*See* Coffroth, James W. [Jimmy]

**Sunny Jim Cosmano**
*See* Cosmano, Vincenzo

**Sunny Jim Dygert**
*See* Dygert, James Henry

**Sunny Jim Fitzsimmons**
*See* Fitzsimmons, James

**Sunny Jim Hackett**
*See* Hackett, James Joseph [Jim]

**Sunny Jim Mallory**
*See* Mallory, James Baugh [Jim]

**Sunny Jim Rolfe**
*See* Rolfe, James

**Sunny Jim Valdare**
*See* Mulligan, James

**Sunnyland Slim**
*See* Luandrew, Albert

**Sunset Jimmy Burke**
*See* Burke, James Timothy

**Sunshine**
*See* Abbott, Wenonah Stevens

**Sunshine, Baby**
*See* Flood, Pauline

**Sunshine Charlie Mitchell**
*See* Mitchell, Charles

**Sunshine, Leo**
See Murphy, Brian

**Sunshine, Marion**
See Ijames, Mary Tunstall

**Sunshine, Mr.**
See Banks, Ernest [Ernie]

**Suomalainen, Kari Yrjana** 1920-
[WEC]
*Finnish cartoonist*
* Kari

**Super Duper Tex**
See Steding, Peggy

**[The] Super Gnat**
See Smith, Noland

**Super Grammaticam**
See Sigismund

**Super Joe**
See Charboneau, Joe

**Super Kraut**
See Kissinger, Henry Alfred

**Super Mex**
See Trevino, Lee

**Super Rook**
See Russell, William Ellis [Bill]

**Super Sub**
See Kennedy, John Edward

**Super Tex**
See Foyt, Anthony Joseph, Jr.

**[The] Superb**
See Hancock, Winfield Scott

**Superbow**
See Clements, Vassar

**Superbrat**
See McEnroe, John

**Superbus**
See Tarquin II [or Tarquinius]

**Superchief**
See Reynolds, Allie Pierce

**[The] Superior Person**
See Horsman, Edward

**Superjew**
See Epstein, Michael Peter

**Supermac**
See Macmillan, Harold

**Superman**
See Bollerman, Howard

**Superman**
See Hartung, Clinton Clarence

**Supporter of the Papal Omnipotence**
See Borghese, Camillo

**Supraner, Robyn** 1930- [CA, SAT]
*American author*
* Blake, Olive
* Frost, Erica
* Warren, Elizabeth

**Sur, Atul Krishna** 1904- [IAW]
*Indian author*
* Chandravati
* Yama

**Sura**
See Lentulus, Publius Cornelius

**Suragne, Pierre**
See Pelot, Pierre

**Suraiya, Jagdish Chatrabhuj** 1946-
[IAW]
*Indian author*
* Suraiya, Jug

**Suraiya, Jug**
See Suraiya, Jagdish Chatrabhuj

**Surchamp, Henry** 1876- ? [CAT]
*French author*
* Nesmy, Jean

**Sure Shot Dunlap**
See Dunlap, Frederick C.

**Surfaceman**
See Anderson, Alexander

**[The] Surgeon General of Baseball**
See Hyland, [Dr.] Robert F.

**Surkont, Matthew Constantine**
1922- [BE]
*American baseball player*
* Surkont, Max

**Surkont, Max**
See Surkont, Matthew Constantine

**Surmelian, Leon [Zaven]** 1907-
[CAP]
*Turkish-born author and educator*
* Vandour, Cyril

**Surrebutter, John, Esq.**
See Anstey, John

**Surrey, Richard**
See Brooker, Bertram

**Surtees, Fanny** 19th c. [PA]
*Author*
* Cherith

**Survage, Leopold**
See Sturzwage, Leopold

**[The] Surveyor President**
See Washington, George

**Susa, Charlotte**
See Wagmuller, Charlotte

**Susan**
See Graham, [Maude Fitzgerald]
Susan

**Susce, George Cyril Methodius**
1908- [BE]
*American baseball player*
* Susce, Good Kid

**Susce, Good Kid**
See Susce, George Cyril Methodius

**Suso**
See Pena Rego, Jesus

**Suso [or Seuse], Heinrich**
See Berg, Heinrich

**Sussex, Gordon**
See Volk, Gordon

**Susskind, Arthur** 1886- [BX, EJS]
*American boxer*
* Otto, Young

**Sussman, Cornelia Silver** 1914-
[CA]
*American author*
* Jessey, Cornelia

**Sutcliffe, Butch**
See Sutcliffe, Charles Inigo

**Sutcliffe, Charles Inigo** 1915- [BE]
*American baseball player*
* Sutcliffe, Butch

**Sutcliffe, Edward Elmer**
1863-1893 [BE]
*American baseball player*
* Sutcliffe, Sy

**Sutcliffe, Joseph Robert** 1911-
[IAW]
*British writer*
* Plowman, Giles

**Sutcliffe, Pavella Dolores** 20th c.
[IAW]
*British writer*
* Ploughman, Nina

**Sutcliffe, Peter** 1946?-
*British murderer*
* [The] Yorkshire Ripper

**Sutcliffe, Sy**
See Sutcliffe, Edward Elmer

**Sutherland, Conrad James** 1901- ?
[BBH]
*American lacrosse player and
official*
* Sutherland, Suds

**Sutherland, Dizzy**
See Sutherland, Howard Alvin

**Sutherland, Elizabeth**
See Marshall, Elizabeth Margaret

**Sutherland, Evelyn Greenleaf**
See Baker, Evelyn Greenleaf

**Sutherland, Gary Lynn** 1944-
[SMG]
*American baseball player*
* Sutherland, Suds

**Sutherland, Harvey Scott** 1894-
[BE]
*American baseball player*
* Sutherland, Suds

**Sutherland, Howard Alvin** 1923-
[BE]
*American baseball player*
* Sutherland, Dizzy

**Sutherland, James T.** 1870-1955
[BBH]
*Canadian hockey pioneer*
* [The] Father of Hockey

**Sutherland, Jock**
See Sutherland, John Bain

**Sutherland, John Bain** 1889-1948
[AS, B10, FB]
*Scottish-born American football
coach*
* [The] Dour Scot
* Sutherland, Jock

**Sutherland, Josie**
See Mayo, Mrs. William H.

**Sutherland, Lucy Christina**
1864?-1935 [WFA]
*British fashion designer*
* Lucile

**Sutherland, Morris**
See Morris, Gwendolen Sutherland

**Sutherland, Robert** ?-1888 [FFF]
*Entertainer and evangelist*
* Hart, [Senator] Bob
* [The] Reformed Minstrel

**Sutherland, Roy**
See Sothern, Hugh

**Sutherland, Suds**
See Sutherland, Conrad James

**Sutherland, Suds**
See Sutherland, Gary Lynn

**Sutherland, Suds**
See Sutherland, Harvey Scott

**Sutherland, William**
See Cooper, John Murray

**Suthinee**
See Ambhanwong, Suthilak

**Sutor, Harry G.** 20th c. [BE]
*American baseball player*
* Sutor, Rube

**Sutor, Rube**
See Sutor, Harry G.

**Sutthoff, John Gerhard** 1873-1942
[BE]
*American baseball player*
* Sutthoff, Sunny Jack

**Sutthoff, Sunny Jack**
See Sutthoff, John Gerhard

**Suttles, Bubbles**
See Suttles, George

**Suttles, George** 1901-1968 [MK]
*American baseball player*
* Suttles, Bubbles
* Suttles, Mule

**Suttles, Mule**
See Suttles, George

**Suttles, Shirley [Smith]** 1922- [CA]
*American author*
* Conger, Lesley

**Sutton, Clarence R.** 1931- [IBW]
*American bobsled racer*
* Sutton, Clay

**Sutton, Clay**
See Sutton, Clarence R.

**Sutton, Cochise**
See Sutton, Lloyd

**Sutton, Dick**
See Schwartz, Richard

**Sutton, Donald Howard** 1945-
[SMG]
*American baseball player*
* Sutton, Elmer
* Sutton, Sut

**Sutton, Eliza Warren** 1865-1935
[SC]
*American actress*
* Warren, Eliza

**Sutton, Elmer**
See Sutton, Donald Howard

**Sutton, Eric Graham Sutton** 1892-
[WGT]
*British author*
* Marsden, Anthony

**Sutton, Ernest**
See Sorl, Ernest James

**Sutton, Eugenia Geneva** 1917-
[SFL]
*American author*
* Sutton, Jean

**Sutton, Henry**
See Slavitt, David Rytman

**Sutton, I. M.**
See Coad, Frederick Roy

**Sutton, Jean**
See Sutton, Eugenia Geneva

**Sutton, Jeff**
See Sutton, Jefferson Howard

**Sutton, Jefferson Howard** 1913-
[CA]
*American author*
* Sutton, Jeff

**Sutton, John**
See Tullett, Denis

**Sutton, Lloyd** 20th c. [BBH]
*Boxer*
* Sutton, Cochise

**Sutton, Mamie**
See Solomon, Mrs. Fred

**Sutton, Margaret [Beebe]**
See Beebe, Rachel Irene

**Sutton, Maurice Lewis** 1927- [CA]
*American author*
* Sutton, Stack

**Sutton, Penny**
See Wood, Christopher [Hovelle]

**Sutton, Pepe**
See Sutton, Pierre Monte

**Sutton, Pierre Monte** 1947- [IBW]
*American broadcasting company
executive and publisher*
* Sutton, Pepe

**Sutton, Scott** [PA]
*Author*
* Sir Toby

**Sutton, Stack**
See Sutton, Maurice Lewis

**Sutton, Sut**
See Sutton, Donald Howard

**Sutton, Thomas**
See Reach, James

**Sutton, William** 1877-1955 [SC]
*American actor and magician*
* [The] Great Fontonelle

**Sutton, William Francis [Willie]**
1901-1980 [BLB, CEC]
*American bank robber*
* [The] Actor
* [The] Babe Ruth of Bank
Robbers
* Willie the Actor

**Sutton-Vane, V. H.**
See Sutton-Vane, Vane Hunt

**Sutton-Vane, Vane Hunt**
1888-1963 [BEW, LC]
*Playwright and actor*
* Sutton-Vane, V. H.
* Vane, Sutton

**Suvorov [or Suwarof], Aleksandr
Vasilievich** 1729-1800 [HN, WBD]
*Russian army officer*
* [The] Invincible
* Italiski
* Rymnikski

**Suzuki, Guts**
See Suzuki, Ishimatsu

**Suzuki, Ishimatsu** 1948- [RBE]
*Japanese boxer*
* Suzuki, Guts

**Suzuki, Shuji** 1927- [WEC]
*Japanese cartoonist and illustrator*
* Cho, Shinta

**Suzuki, Zenko** 1911?-
*Japanese prime minister*
* Fish, Mr.

**Suzy**
See Mehle, Aileen

**Svare, Harland** 20th c.
*Norwegian-American football coach*
* [The] Swede

**Svarts, Helga** 1890- [CD]
*Swedish author and poet*
* Martinson, Moa

**Svedberg, Emanuel** 1688-1772
[HN, WBD]
*Swedish scientist, philosopher,
author*
* [The] Apostle of the New
Jerusalem
* Swedenborg, Emanuel

**Sveeadstroem**
See Nyberg, Julia Christina

**Sveinsson, Aslakur**
See Indridason, Indridi

**Sveinsson, Jon** 1857-1944 [CAT]
*Icelandic-born author*
* Nonni

**Svengali**
See Pendergrass, Theodore
[Teddy]

**Svengali**
See Rowland, Clarence Henry

**Svennberg, Olof Teodor** 1852- ?
[THR]
*Swedish actor*
* Svennberg, Tore

**Svennberg, Tore**
See Svennberg, Olof Teodor

**Svenson, Andrew E.** 1910-1975
[CA, SAT]
*American author*
* Dixon, Franklin W. [house
pseudonym] [Stratemeyer
Syndicate]
* Stone, Alan [house pseudonym]
[Stratemeyer Syndicate]
* West, Jerry [house pseudonym]
[Stratemeyer Syndicate]

**Svensson, Marta Birgit** 1918- [OP]
*Swedish opera singer*
* Nilsson, Birgit

**Svensson, Sven**
See Bolay, Karl H.

**Sverkers, Stig**
See Foghammar, Stig Sverker

**Sverre [or Swerro]** 1152?-1202
[WBD]
*King of Norway*
* Sverre Sigurdsson

**Sverre Sigurdsson**
See Sverre [or Swerro]

**Svevo, Italo**
See Schmitz, Ettore

**Svoboda, Madeleine** 1916- [FC]
*French actress*
* Robinson, Madeleine

**Swaby, Horace** 20th c.
*Jamaican musician*
* Pablo, Augustus

**Swacina, Harry Joseph** 1881-1944
[BE]
*American baseball player*
* Swacina, Swats

**Swacina, Swats**
See Swacina, Harry Joseph

**Swadling, Ann Pauline** 1936- [OP]
*British opera singer*
* Howard, Ann

**Swaim, Cy**
See Swaim, John Hillary

**Swaim, John Hillary** 1874-1918
[BE]
*American baseball player*
* Swaim, Cy

**Swain, Charles** 1803-1874 [DEL]
*British poet*
* [The] Manchester Poet

**Swain, Dwight V[reeland]** 1915-
[CA]
*American author*
* South, Clark

**Swain, E. G.**
See Swain, Edmund Gill

**Swain, Edmund Gill** 1861-1938
[HFF]
*British author*
* Swain, E. G.

**Swain, Garry**
See Swain, Garth Frederick Arthur

**Swain, Garth Frederick Arthur**
1947- [HR]
*Canadian-born hockey player*
* Swain, Garry

**Swain, Mark**
See Clemens, Samuel Langhorne

**Swain, Miriam**
See Mason, Miriam Evangeline

**Swallow, Norman** 1921-
[AW, CA, WD]
*British author*
* Leather, George

**Swamp Baby Wilson**
See Wilson, Charles Woodrow
[Charlie]

**[The] Swamp Fox**
See Marion, Francis

**[The] Swamp Fox**
See Vinson, Carl

**Swamp Rat Garlits**
See Garlits, Donald Glenn

**Swan, Annie S[hepherd]** 1860-1943
[LC]
*Scottish author*
* Lyall, David

**Swan, Charles F.** [PA]
*Author*
* Sault, R. O.

**Swan, Cormac** 1916- [AW]
*British physician and writer*
* McCormac, Brian
* Tynan, Philip

**Swan, Don**
See Schwandt, Wilbur

**Swan, Marie**
See Bartlett, Marie [Swan]

**[The] Swan of Avon**
See Shakespeare, William

**[The] Swan of Cambray**
See Fenelon, Francois de Salignac
de la Mothe

**[The] Swan of Lichfield**
See Seward, Anna

**[The] Swan of Mantua**
See Vergilius Maro, Publius

**[The] Swan of Padua**
See Algarotti, Francesco

**[The] Swan of Pesaro**
See Rossini, Gioachino Antonio

**[The] Swan of the Meander**
See Homer

**[The] Swan of the Thames**
See Taylor, John

**Swander, Edward O.** 1880-1944
[BE]
*American baseball player*
* Swander, Pinky

**Swander, Pinky**
See Swander, Edward O.

**Swann, Donald [Ibrahim]** 1923-
[CA]
*British songwriter and entertainer*
* Tablet, Hilda

**Swann, Ducky**
See Swann, Henry

**Swann, Duncan** 1878- ? [WWL]
*British author*
* Schwann, Duncan

**Swann, Henry** 1892- [BE]
*American baseball player*
* Swann, Ducky

**Swann, Peggy**
See Geis, Richard E[rwin]

**Swanson, Arthur Leonard** 1936-
[BE]
*American baseball player*
* Swanson, Red

**Swanson, Gloria**
See Swenson, Josephine May

**Swanson, Logan**
See Matheson, Richard [Burton]

**Swanson, Red**
See Swanson, Arthur Leonard

**Swanstrom, Nils**
See Brannon, William T.

**Swanwick, Anna** 19th c. [PA]
*Author*
* A. S.

**Swanwick, Catherine** 19th c. [PA]
*Author*
* L.

**Swarbrook, Frederick William**
1950- [DC]
*British cricketer*
* Swarbrook, Swarby

**Swarbrook, Swarby**
See Swarbrook, Frederick William

**Swarsbrick, Robert** 1740-1824
[HN]
* [The] Hermit of Lathom

**Swartz, Bud**
See Swartz, Sherwin Merle

**Swartz, Dan** 1934-   [BB]
*American basketball player*
* Swartz, Dogpatch

**Swartz, Dazzy**
*See* Swartz, Monroe

**Swartz, Dogpatch**
*See* Swartz, Dan

**Swartz, Harry [Felix]** 1911-   [CA]
*American author*
* Moreno, Martin
* Valcoe, H. Felix

**Swartz, Monroe** 1897-   [BE]
*American baseball player*
* Swartz, Dazzy
* Swartz, Monty

**Swartz, Monty**
*See* Swartz, Monroe

**Swartz, Sherwin Merle** 1929-   [EJS]
*American baseball player*
* Swartz, Bud

**Swartz, William** ?-1978   [FIR]
*Actor*
* Scarlett, Bill

**Swasey, Charles James** 1847-1908
[BE]
*American baseball player*
* Sweasy, Charles James

**Swatridge, Charles** 20th c.
[CA, WW]
*British author*
* Charles, Theresa [joint
  pseudonym with Irene Maude
  (Mossop) Swatridge]

**Swatridge, Irene Maude [Mossop]**
[CA, WD, WW]
*British author*
* Chandos, Fay
* Charles, Theresa [joint
  pseudonym with Charles
  Swatridge]
* Mossop, Irene
* Storm, Virginia
* Tempest, Jan

**[The] Swattin' Scot**
*See* Paterson, Jackie

**Swayne, Geoffrey**
*See* Campion, Sidney Ronald

**Swayne, Martin**
*See* Nicoll, [Henry] Maurice
[Dunlop]

**Swayzee, Edwin** 1903-1935   [WWJ]
*American jazz musician*
* Swayzee, King

**Swayzee, King**
*See* Swayzee, Edwin

**Sweasy, Charles James**
*See* Swasey, Charles James

**[The] Sweater Girl**
*See* Turner, Julia Jean Mildred
Frances

**Sweatt, George** 1905-   [IBW]
*American baseball player*
* Sweatt, Never

**Sweatt, Never**
*See* Sweatt, George

**[The] Swede**
*See* Svare, Harland

**Swedenborg, Emanuel**
*See* Svedberg, Emanuel

**[The] Swedish Amazon**
*See* Christina

**[The] Swedish Angel**
*See* Olofsson, Nils Phillip

**[The] Swedish Dickens**
*See* Bergman, Hjalmar [Fredrik
Elgerus]

**[The] Swedish Douglas Fairbanks**
*See* Jahr, Adolf

**[The] Swedish Express**
*See* Hedberg, Anders

**[The] Swedish Maccabaeus**
*See* Gustavus Adolphus

**[The] Swedish Mack Sennett**
*See* Petschler, Erik

**[The] Swedish Nightingale**
*See* Lind, Johanna Maria

**Sweelinck [or Swelinck], Jan Pieters**
1562-1621   [WBD]
*Dutch musician and composer*
* Pieterszoon, Jan

**Sweeney, Barry**
*See* Hand, Geoffrey Joseph Philip
Macaulay

**Sweeney, Charles** 1922-   [CA]
*British author*
* Sweeney, R. C. H.

**Sweeney, Claire Cynthia** 1928-
[BEW]
*American literary representative*
* Degener, Claire S.

**Sweeney, Harry E.** 1882-1960   [SC]
*Australian-born actor*
* Mowbray, Henry

**Sweeney, John J.** 1860- ?   [BE]
*American baseball player*
* Sweeney, Rooney

**Sweeney, R. C. H.**
*See* Sweeney, Charles

**Sweeney, Rooney**
*See* Sweeney, John J.

**Sweet, Adolphus Jean** 1920-   [BEW]
*American actor and director*
* Sweet, Dolph

**Sweet, Blanche**
*See* Wayne, Daphne

**Sweet Charlie Brown**
*See* Brown, Charlie

**Sweet Daddy Grace**
*See* Grace, Charles Manuel

**Sweet, Dolph**
*See* Sweet, Adolphus Jean

**Sweet Emma**
*See* Barrett, Emma

**Sweet Emma the Bell Gal**
*See* Barrett, Emma

**Sweet, Emmett Martine** 1915-
[BEW]
*American actor, producer, director*
* Rogers, Emmett

**Sweet Eyes**
*See* Chamanan, Kriangsak

**Sweet, Jeanne** 1908-   [THR]
*British actress*
* Stuart. Jeanne

**[The] Sweet Little Fellow**
*See* Van Buren, Martin

**Sweet Lou Johnson**
*See* Johnson, Louis Brown

**Sweet Lou Whitaker**
*See* Whitaker, Louis Rodman

**Sweet Lovin Galloway**
*See* Galloway, Charles

**[The] Sweet Lyrist of Peter House**
*See* Gray, Thomas

**Sweet Mama Stringbean**
*See* Waters, Ethel

**Sweet Papa Stovepipe**
*See* Peebles, McKinley

**Sweet Pea Jefferson**
*See* Jefferson, Roy

**Sweet Peas[e]**
*See* Spivey, Addie

**[The] Sweet Singer of Michigan**
*See* Moore, Julia A.

**[The] Sweet Singer of the Temple**
*See* Herbert, George

**[The] Sweet Swan of Avon**
*See* Shakespeare, William

**Sweet Vinny Bourne**
*See* Bourne, Vincent

**Sweet William**
*See* Draper, William Henry

**Sweetland, Lester Leo** 1901-1974
[BE]
*American baseball player*
* Sweetland, Sugar

**Sweetland, Sugar**
*See* Sweetland, Lester Leo

**Sweetman, Grace** 1865?-1962
[BEW]
*American actress*
* Filkins, Grace

**Sweetman, M. E.** 1858?-1930
[THR]
*Irish playwright*
* Francis, M. E.

**Sweetser, Mary [Chisholm]** 1894-
[CA]
*American author*
* Sweetser, Ted

**Sweetser, Ted**
*See* Sweetser, Mary [Chisholm]

**[The] Sweetwater Swatter**
*See* Jenks, Verlin

**Swemmer, B. Northling** 1897-
[WWL]
*South African author*
* Africa, Ben

**Swenson, Josephine May** 1899?-
[BEW, FC, IPA]
*American actress*
* Swanson, Gloria

**Swenson, Peggy**
*See* Geis, Richard E[rwin]

**Swentor, Augie**
*See* Swentor, August William

**Swentor, August William** 1899-
[BE]
*American baseball player*
* Swentor, Augie

**Swetenham, Violet Hilda**   [WD]
*British author*
* Drummond, V. H.

**Swett, Charles A.** 1868- ?   [BE]
*American baseball player*
* Swett, Pop

**Swett, Pop**
*See* Swett, Charles A.

**Swett, Portia** 1887-   [BEW]
*American educator*
* Mansfield, Portia

**Sweven, Godfrey**
*See* Brown, John Macmillan

**Sweyn I [or Sueno]** ?-1014
[HN, WBD]
*King of Denmark*
* Forkbeard

**Sweyn II** ?-1075   [WBD]
*King of Denmark*
* Estrithson

**Swicegood, Thomas L. P.** 1930-
[CA]
*American author*
* Lowe, Charles K.
* Stierwell, Jay

**Swift, Alexandra** 1886-1936
[BEW]
*British-born actress*
* Carlisle, Alexandra

**Swift, Anthony**
*See* Farjeon, J[oseph] Jefferson

**Swift, Augustus T.**
*See* Lovecraft, Howard Phillips

**Swift, Benjamin**
*See* McKimmey, James

**Swift, Benjamin**
*See* Paterson, William Romaine

**Swift, David**
*See* Kaufmann, John

**Swift, Farguar**
*See* Phillips, Michael Joseph

**Swift, Jonathan** 1667-1745
[FFF, HN, PA]
*British author*
* Bickerstaff, Isaac, Esq.
* Cadenus
* [The] Copper Farthing Dean
* [The] Dean of St. Patrick's
* Drapier, M. B.
* [The] English Rabelais
* Gulliver, Lemuel
* [The] Mad Parson
* Presto
* [The] Rabelais of England
* [The] Rabelais of Good Society

**Swift, Julian**
*See* Applin, Arthur

**Swift, Merlin**
*See* Leeming, Joseph

**Swift, Tom**
*See* Kneafcy, Thomas

**Swigart, Oad**
*See* Swigart, Oadis Vaughn

**Swigart, Oadis Vaughn** 1915-   [BE]
*American baseball player*
* Swigart, Oad

**[The] Swimming Machine**
*See* Wenden, Michael

[The] Swimming Nun
See   Taylor, Stella

Swinburne, Algernon Charles
1837-1909   [FFF, PA]
British poet
* Manners, Mrs. Horace

Swinburne, Nora
See   Johnson, Elinore

Swindell, Minnie Harris 1889-   [IA]
American author
* Norris, Harris

Swinerton, Thomas ?-1554   [PA]
Author
* Roberts, John

Swinford, Betty [June Wells] 1927-
[CA]
American author
* Haynes, Linda
* Porter, Kathryn
* Swinford, Bob
* Wells, June

Swinford, Bob
See   Swinford, Betty [June Wells]

Swing Brother
See   Burns, Eddie

Swing, Mr.
See   Bondu, David [Dave]

Swing, Mrs.
See   Bondu, Mayme

Swinstead, Muriel 1907-   [THR]
British actress
* Ross, Oriel

Swinton, E. D.
See   Swinton, [Sir] Ernest Dunlop

Swinton, [Sir] Ernest Dunlop
1868-1951   [LC, WGT]
British author
* Backsight-Forethought
* Ole-Luk-Oie [Olaf Shut-Eye]
* Swinton, E. D.

Swirling Sterling St. Jacques
See   St. Jacques, Sterling

Swisher, Steven Eugene 1951-
[SMG]
American baseball player
* Swisher, Swish

Swisher, Swish
See   Swisher, Steven Eugene

[The] Swiss Walter Scott
See   Zoschokke

Swisshelm, Jane Grey   [FFF]
American writer
* Deans, Jennie

Swithin ?- 862   [DEP]
Saint
* [The] Weeping Saint

Switzer, Alfalfa
See   Switzer, Carl

Switzer, Benjamin 1880-1933   [SC]
Canadian-born actor and director
* Bertram, William

Switzer, Carl 1926-1959   [SC]
American actor
* Switzer, Alfalfa

Swivel Hips
See   Presley, Elvis Aaron

Swivel Hips Schreiber
See   Schreiber, Le Anne

Swivett, R. G. O.
See   Trippett, Frank

Swix, Mr.
See   Wictorin, John

Swoboda, Rocky
See   Swoboda, Ron[ald Alan]

Swoboda, Ron[ald Alan] 1944-
[BE, PB]
American baseball player
* Swoboda, Rocky

Swofford, William Oliver 1945-
[PRS, RO2]
American singer and songwriter
* Oliver

[The] Sword of Allah
See   Khaled [or Khalid]

[The] Sword of God
See   Khaled [or Khalid]

[The] Sword of Mars
See   Attila

[The] Sword of Rome
See   Marcellus, Marcus Claudius

[The] Sword of the Revolution
See   Washington, George

Swoyer, Anna Myrtle 1921?-
[BEW, EMT, IPA]
American actress
* Walker, Nancy

Swoyer, Dewey Stewart 20th c.
[BEW]
American entertainer
* Borto, Dewey

Sycorax
See   Ritson, Joseph

Sydell, Rose
See   Emmett, Mrs. Charles E.

Sydenham, Thomas 1624-1689
[HN, SN, WBD]
British physician
* [The] British Hippocrates
* [The] English Hippocrates
* [The] Father of Modern Practice
   in Medicine

Sydney
See   Seawell, Molly Elliot

Sydney, Basil
See   Nugent, Basil

Sydney, Carol
See   Fraser, Shelagh

Sydney, Charles 1872?-1922
[BEW]
British-born actor
* Ainsworth, Sydney

Sydney, Cynthia
See   Tralins, S[andor] Robert
[Bob]

Sydney, Frank
See   Warwick, Alan Ross

Sydney, Frank
See   Warwick, Francis Alister

Sydney, Frank
See   Warwick, Sidney

Sydney, Jon
See   Brady, John Walter

[The] Sydney Smith of the Gallic
Church
See   Apollinaris Sidonius, Gaius
Sollius

Sygrianus
See   De Bologne, Michele

Sykes, Arthur Alkin 1861- ?   [LAO]
British author
* Zigzag
* ZYX

Sykes, Bobbi 1945-   [IBW]
Australian political organizer
* Australia's Angela Davis

Sykes, Christopher [Hugh] 1907-
[CA]
British author
* Waughburton, Richard [joint
   pseudonym with Robert Byron]

Sykes, Doc
See   Sykes, Melvin

Sykes, George 1822-1880   [FFF]
American army officer
* Sykesey

Sykes, Melvin 20th c.   [OBW]
American baseball player
* Sykes, Doc

Sykes, Roosevelt 1906-   [BWW]
American singer
* Bey, Roosevelt Sykes
* [The] Blues Man
* Bragg, Dobby
* [The] Honeydripper
* Johnson, Easy Papa
* Kelly, Willie

Sykesey
See   Sykes, George

Sylva, Carmen
See   Elizabeth, [Queen]

Sylva, Ilena
See   Thimblethorpe, Ilena

Sylva, Marguerita
See   Smith, Marguerite Alice
Helene

Sylvaine, Vernon
See   Scotchburn, Vernon

[The] Sylvan Scribe
See   Forbes, Seloftus D.

Sylvan, Urbanus
See   Beeching, Henry Charles

Sylvander
See   Burns, Robert

Sylvane, Andre
See   Gerard, Paul Emile

Sylvester, Arthur
See   Tubbs, Arthur Lewis

Sylvester, Hannah 1900?-1973
[BWW]
American singer
* Harlem's Mae West
* Scott, Genevia

Sylvester, James Joseph
See   Joseph, James

Sylvester, John
See   Hawton, Hector

Sylvester, Joshua
See   Hotten, John Camden

Sylvester, Joshua 1563-1618
[DEL, DNNF, RH]
British poet and translator
* [The] Silver Tongued

Sylvester, Louise
See   Mackey, Mrs. F. A.

Sylvester, Philip
See   Worner, Philip Arthur
Incledon

Sylvester II
See   Gerbert

Sylvester III
See   John

Sylvestre, [Joseph Jean] Guy 1918-
[CA]
Canadian librarian and author
* Bruneau, Jean
* Orlier, Blaise

Sylvestri, Armaud   [PA]
Author
* Grimaud

Sylvestris
See   Bernard de Chartres

Sylvia
See   Douglas, Syble G.

Sylvia
See   Henderson, Sylvia

Sylvia
See   Robinson, Sylvia Vanderpool

Sylvia T
See   Treadgold, Sylvia

Sylvie
See   Sylvie, Therese

Sylvie, Louise
See   Mainquene, Louise

Sylvie, Therese 1883-1970   [OCF]
French actress
* Sylvie

Sylvin, Francis [joint pseudonym
with Sylvia S(ybil) Seaman]
See   Schwartz, Frances

Sylvin, Francis [joint pseudonym
with Frances Schwartz]
See   Seaman, Sylvia S[ybil]

Sylviolus
See   Forestier, Antoine,

Sylvius, C.
See   Coscia, Silvio

Sylvius, Franciscus
See   De la Boe, Franz

Symcott, Margaret 1642?-1691?
[HN, RH, WBD]
British actress and mistress of King
Charles II
* Gwyn [or Gwynne], Eleanor
* Gwyn [or Gwynne], Nell
* [The] Poor Man's Friend

Syme, Robert 1795- ?   [FFF]
Scottish author
* Tickler, Timothy

Symington, Charlotte   [PA]
Author
* Symington, Maggie

Symington, David 1904-
[AW, CAP]
British author
* Halliday, James

**Symington, Maggie**
See Symington, Charlotte

**Symmonds, John**
See Gonzales, Bli

**Symon, James David** 1867- ?
[WWL]
*British author*
* North, Laurence

**Symonds, Emily Morse** ?-1936
[BEW, LC]
*British author and playwright*
* Paston, George

**Symonds, Francis Addington** 1893-
[MBF, WWL]
*British author and editor*
* Danesford, Earle
* [A] Royal Field Leech
* Steele, Howard [house
   pseudonym]

**Symonds, Margaret** 1902-    [THR]
*British actress*
* Davey, Nuna

**Symons, A. J. A.**
See Symons, Alphonse James
Albert

**Symons, Albert James Alroy**
See Symons, Alphonse James
Albert

**Symons, Alphonse James Albert**
1900-1941    [LC]
*British author*
* Symons, A. J. A.
* Symons, Albert James Alroy

**Symons, [Dorothy] Geraldine** 1909-
[CA, LC]
*British author*
* Groves, Georgina

**Symons, J. B.** 20th c.    [WWL]
*Scottish editor and poet*
* Restalrig

**Symons, Thomas William**
1849-1920    [WBD]
*American engineer*
* [The] Father of the Barge Canal

**Symphony Sid**
See Torin, Sidney

**Syncellus**
See George

**Syndas, Kate**
See Sandys, K.

**Synge, Don**
See Edelstein, Hyman

**Synge, J. M.**
See Synge, John Millington

**Synge, John Millington** 1871-1909
[LC]
*Irish author*
* Synge, J. M.

**Synnott, Ed. Fitzgerald** 1873- ?
[WWL]
*British author*
* O'Toole, [Father]

**Synodinos, Dimitrios** 1919-    [B10]
*American columnist and former
gambler*
* Jimmy the Greek
* Snyder, James

**Synopticus**
See Renner, Karl

**Syntax**
See Ash, Edward Cecil

**Syntax, Dr.**
See Combe [or Coombe], William

**Syntax, Doctor**
See Gordon, Archibald F.

**Syntax, Dr.**
See Vizetelly, Francis Horace
[Frank]

**Syntax, John**
See Dennett, Herbert Victor

**Syracuse, Marcella Pfeiffer** 1930-
[CA]
*American author*
* Pfeiffer, Marcella

**[The] Syren of Antiquity**
See Xenophon

**Syrokomla, Wladyslaw**
See Kondratowicz, Ludwik
Wladyslaw

**Syruc, J.**
See Milosz, Czeslaw

**Szabo, Alexander** 1910-    [BE]
*American baseball player*
* Sabo, Alex[ander]
* Sabo, Giz

**Szabo, Istvan** 1863-1924    [WBD]
*Hungarian politician*
* Szabo-Nagyatad

**Szabo-Nagyatad**
See Szabo, Istvan

**Szacsvay-Feher, Tibor** 1907-
[IAW]
*Hungarian author*
* Feher, Tibor

**Szadall, Szdke**
See Szakall, Eugene Gero

**Szajkowski, Zosa**
See Frydman, Szajko

**Szakall, Eugene Gero** 1884-1955
[BEW, FC, SC]
*Hungarian-born actor*
* Sakall, Cuddles
* Sakall, S. Z.
* Szadall, Szdke

**Szaniawski, Jerzy** 1886-1966
[MWD]
*Polish playwright and author*
* [The] Dean of Polish Dramatists

**Szarvas, Peter** 1933-    [IWM]
*Hungarian-born musician*
* Sander, Peter

**Szatmary**
See Szigligetti, Joseph

**Sze Sao-ke, Alfred**
See Shih Chao-chi

**Szekely, Istvan** 1889?-1979
[FC, FD]
*Hungarian-born director*
* Sekely, Steve

**Szelenyi, Laszlo** 1935-    [IWM]
*Hungarian-born musician*
* Farago

**Szemanski, Jacob** 1878-1963
[EMT]
*Lithuanian-born producer*
* Shubert, J. J.

**Szemanski, Levi** 1873-1953    [EMT]
*Lithuanian-born producer*
* Shubert, Lee

**Szemanski, Samuel** 1876-1905
[EMT]
*Lithuanian-born producer*
* Shubert, Sam S.

**Szendrei, Aladar** 1884-    [BBD]
*Hungarian-born conductor and
composer*
* Sendrey, Alfred

**Szepes, Ivan** 1930-    [OP]
*Italian opera singer*
* Sardi, Ivan

**Szigeti, Joseph** 1892-1972    [MS]
*Hungarian musician*
* Szigeti, Joska

**Szigeti, Joska**
See Szigeti, Joseph

**Szigligetti, Joseph** 1814- ?    [PA]
*Author*
* Szatmary

**Szmaciarz-Smreczynski, Franciszek**
1876-1930    [CD]
*Polish poet and author*
* Orkan, Wladyslaw

**Szymanski, Aloysius Harry**
1902?-1956    [AS, BE, DGS]
*American baseball player*
* [The] Duke of Milwaukee
* Simmons, Al
* Simmons, Bucketfoot Al

**Szymanski, Ignatius S.**    [PA]
*Author*
* Harring, Harro

**Szymonowicz, Szymon** 1558-1629
[WBD]
*Polish poet*
* [The] Polish Pindar

**Szymonowska, Marie** 1790- ?    [PA]
*Author*
* Woloweki

# T

**T**
See  Tatlow, Tissington

**T**
See  Thorp, Joseph Peter

**T.**
See  Tupper, Martin Farquhar

**T.**
See  Tyler, Terry

**T. B.**
See  Bates, Thomas

**T. B.**
See  Brightwell, Thomas

**T. B. D.**
See  James, William Milbourne

**T. B. O.**
See  Oxenbury, Thomas Bernard

**T. C. B.**
See  Bridges, Thomas Charles

**T. F.**
See  Ashby, George

**T. F.**
See  Faulkner, Robert Trevor

**T. F. S.**
See  Salter, T. F.

**T. H.**
See  Hamilton, [Capt.] Thomas

**T. J.**
See  John, Thomas Edward

**T. J., Esq.**
See  Croker, John Wilson

**T. L.**
See  Laws, Tony

**T. N. T.**
See  Thomas, Cornelius Dickinson

**T. O. F.**
See  Schuette, Conrad Herman
Louis

**T. R.**
See  Roosevelt, Theodore [Teddy]

**T. R. B.**
See  Strout, Richard L[ee]

**T. S.**
See  Travers-Smith, Dorothea

**T. S. H.**
See  Henderson, Thulia Susannah

**T. S. M.**
See  Matthews, Thomas Soady

**T. T.**
See  Tilton, Theodore

**T. W.**
See  Weed, Thurlow

**Taabes, Kamil Amin**
See  Cohen, Elie

**Taafe, Alice Frances** 1896?-
[F1, F2, FC]
*American actress*
* Terry, Alice

**Taaffe, Michael**
See  Maguire, Robert Augustine
Joseph

**Taasinge, Hazel Neilson**
1888-1970  [SC]
*American actress*
* Monterey, Carlotta

**Tabaksblat, Alexander** 1921-  [OP]
*Israeli conductor and composer*
* Tarski, Alexander

**Tabard, Peter**
See  Blake, Leslie James

**Tabarin**
See  Duval, Georges

**[The] Tabasco Kid**
See  Elberfeld, Norman Arthur

**Taber, Edward Timothy** 1900-
[BE]
*American baseball player*
* Taber, Lefty

**Taber, Lefty**
See  Taber, Edward Timothy

**Tabib, al- [The Physician]**
See  Rashid al-Din

**Tabiensis**
See  Caynazzo, Jean

**Tabin, Rube**
See  Richstein, Larry

**Tablet, Hilda**
See  Swann, Donald [Ibrahim]

**Tabor, James Reubin** 1916-1953
[BE, PB]
*American baseball player*
* Tabor, Rawhide
* Tabor, Rube

**Tabor, Paul**
See  Tabori, Pal

**Tabor, Rawhide**
See  Tabor, James Reubin

**Tabor, Rube**
See  Tabor, James Reubin

**Tabori, Pal** 1908-1974
[AW, CA, WD]
*Hungarian-born British author,
journalist, scriptwriter*
* Stafford, Peter
* Stevens, Christopher
* Tabor, Paul

**[The] Taciturn**
See  Maximilian I

**Tacitus**
See  Haines, Charles Glidden

**[The] Tacitus of Sicily**
See  Falcandus, Hugo

**Tack Towne Newchurch**
See  Newchurch, Harold Everett

**Tacky Tom Parrott**
See  Parrott, Thomas William
[Tom]

**Tad**
See  Dorgan, Thomas Aloysius

**[Der] Tadler [The Fault-Finder]**
See  Gottsched, Johann Christoph

**Tadrack, Moss**
See  Caryl, Warren

**Tae-tsong I**
See  Lee chee-men

**Taffrail**
See  Dorling, Henry Taprell

**Taffy**
See  Llewellyn, D[avid] W[illiam]
Alun

**Taft, Jim** 1907?-  [MY]
*American jazz musician*
* Taft, Slim

**Taft, Slim**
See  Taft, Jim

**Tafuri, Malteo** 1492-1585  [PA]
*Author*
* Soletanus, Matthoeus

**Tag, Rag, and Bobtail, Messrs.**
See  Disraeli, Isaac

**Taggard, E. T.** 1839- ?  [PA]
*Author*
* Pryor, Paul

**Taggart, Robert John** 1890-  [BE]
*American baseball player*
* Kelly, James Robert [Jim]

**Tagge, Jerry L.** 1950-  [FB]
*American football player*
* Tagge, Tags

**Tagge, Tags**
See  Tagge, Jerry L.

**Tagger, Theodor** 1891-1958
[MGL]
*Austrian playwright*
* Bruckner, Ferdinand

**Tagliapetra, Madame**  [HN]
* Carreno, Teresa

**Tagliere, Signor**
See  Tyler, George

**Taglioni, Maria** 1804- ?  [PA]
*Author*
* De Voisons, [Countess] Gilbert

**Tagore, Amitendranath** 1922-  [CA]
*Indian-born educator and author*
* Musafir

**Tagore, Rabindranath**
See  Thakura, Ravindranatha

**Tah-gah-jute** 1725?-1780  [WBD]
*American Indian chieftain*
* Logan, James [or John]

**Tahchenum, Neehahpouw**
1891-1966  [SC]
*American actor*
* Strongheart, [Chief] Nipo

**Tahlaquah, David**
See  LeMond, Alan

**Tahmasp Kuli Khan [Slave of
Tahmasp]**
See  Nadir Shah

**Taieb, Heliane** 1929-  [ESF]
*French writer*
* Verlanger, Julia

**Tail Gunner Joe**
See  McCarthy, Joseph Raymond

**Taillandier, Rene Gaspard Ernest**
1817-1879  [WBD]
*French journalist and scholar*
* Taillandier, Saint Rene

**Taillandier, Saint Rene**
See  Taillandier, Rene Gaspard
Ernest

**Taillasson, Gaillard** 1580-1647
[PA]
*Author*
* Mathalin

**Taine, John**
See   Bell, Eric Temple

**Taira, Koji**
See   Kiyomura, Koji

**Tait, Archibald Campbell** 1811- ?
[PA]
*Author*
* [The] Bishop of London

**Tait, Dorothy** 1902?-1972   [CA]
*American author and journalist*
* Fairbairn, Ann
* Stuart, Jay Allison

**Tait, Euphemia Margaret** 20th c.
[WW]
*Author*
* Ironside, John

**Tait, George B.** 20th c.
[SFL, WGT]
*Author*
* Barclay, Alan

**Tait, Herbert** 1865-1934   [BEW]
*Indian-born actor*
* Ross, Herbert

**Taitt, Doug[las John]** 1902-   [BE]
*American baseball player*
* Taitt, Poco

**Taitt, Poco**
See   Taitt, Doug[las John]

**Taj Mahal**
See   Henry, Fredericks

**Tajiri, Larry S.**
See   Tajiri, Taneyoshi

**Tajiri, Taneyoshi** 1914-   [BEW]
*American drama editor and critic*
* Tajiri, Larry S.

**Takada, Kenzo** 1940-   [WFA]
*Japanese-born fashion designer*
* [The] Idea Man of French
   Ready-to-Wear

**Takagi, Masao**
See   Park, Chung Hee

**Takahashi, Korekiyo**
See   Kawamura, Korekiyo

**Takakjian, Portia** 1930-   [SAT]
*American illustrator*
* Johnston, Portia
* Roach, Portia
* Wiesner, Portia

**Takis**
See   Vassilakis, Panayotis

**Tal, Joseph**
See   Gruenthal, Joseph

**Tal-Coat, Pierre**
See   Jacob, Pierre

**Talagrand, Jacques Louis**
See   Maulnier, Thierry

**Talal bin Abdul Azziz al-Saud** 1930?-
*Saudi prince*
* [The] Humanitarian Prince

**Talamo, W.** 20th c.   [BLB]
*American underworld figure*
* Scaccio, John

**Talbert, Coo Coo**
See   Talbert, Elmer

**Talbert, Diron** 20th c.
*American football player*
* Crunch, Captain

**Talbert, Elmer** 1900-1950   [NOJ]
*American jazz musician*
* Talbert, Coo Coo

**Talbot, Bubby**
See   Talbot, Fred Lealand

**Talbot, Carl**
See   Hipkins, Charles Hammond

**Talbot, Carol Terry** 1913-   [CA]
*American author*
* Terry, Carol

**Talbot, Charles** 1660-1718   [SN]
*Duke of Shrewsbury*
* [The] King of Hearts

**Talbot, Charles R.** 19th c.   [PA]
*Author*
* Brownjohn, John
* Merriweather, Magnus

**Talbot, Edmund Bernard**
See   Fitzalan-Howard, Edmund
Bernard

**Talbot, Elizabeth** 1518-1608
[HN, WBD]
*Countess of Shrewsbury*
* Bess of Hardwick

**Talbot, Fred Lealand** 1941-   [BE]
*American baseball player*
* Talbot, Bubby

**Talbot, Hake**
See   Nelms, Henning

**Talbot, Henry**
See   Rothwell, Henry Talbot

**Talbot, Howard**
See   Munkittrick, Howard

**Talbot, Hugh**
See   Alington, Argentine Francis

**Talbot, John** 1373-1453
[DEP, DNNS, RH]
*First Earl of Shrewsbury*
* [The] Achilles of England
* [The] English Achilles
* [The] Terror of France

**Talbot, John William** 1869- ?
[NAA]
*American author and poet*
* Anonymous

**Talbot, Joseph Bovelle** 1896-1973
[SC]
*American actor and stunt performer*
* Talbot, Slim

**Talbot, Kay**
See   Rowland, D[onald] S[ydney]

**Talbot, Lawrence**
See   Bryant, Edward [Winslow, Jr.]

**Talbot, Lying Dick**
See   Talbot, Richard

**Talbot, Lyle**
See   Henderson, Lisle

**Talbot, Mary Lee Keister** 20th c.
[NAA]
*American writer*
* Dyer, Sabine

**Talbot, Nancy Wilfreda Hewitt**
1925-   [ART]
*British painter and stage designer*
* Skillington, Nancy

**Talbot, Richard** 1630-1691
[DNNF, DNNS, HN]
*Duke of Tyrconnel and Lord-
Lieutenant of Ireland*
* Talbot, Lying Dick

**Talbot, Slim**
See   Talbot, Joseph Bovelle

**Talbot Kelly, C. E.**
See   Talbot Kelly, Chloe Elizabeth

**Talbot Kelly, Chloe Elizabeth**
1927-   [ART]
*British illustrator*
* Talbot Kelly, C. E.

**Talcott, John** 1630-1688   [FFF]
*Commanded troops in 1676 Indian
War*
* [The] Indian Fighter

**Talcott, LeRoy Everett** 1921-   [BE]
*American baseball player*
* Talcott, Roy

**Talcott, Roy**
See   Talcott, LeRoy Everett

**Talender**
See   Bohse, August

**Talent, Leo** 1906-   [ASC]
*American musician*
* Winters, Jack

**[The] Talent of the Academy**
See   Aristotle

**Taliaferro, George** 1927-   [FB]
*American football player*
* Taliaferro, Scoop

**Taliaferro, Mike**
See   Taliaferro, Myron E.

**Taliaferro, Myron E.** 1941-   [FB]
*American football player*
* Taliaferro, Mike

**Taliaferro, Scoop**
See   Taliaferro, George

**Talis Qualis**
See   Strandberg, Carl Vilhelm
August

**[The] Talkative**
See   William II [Friedrich Wilhelm
Viktor Albert]

**[The] Talkies Only Rival**
See   Bodie, Sam

**[The] Talking Blues Boy**
See   Lunn, Robert

**[The] Talking Blues Man**
See   Lunn, Robert

**[The] Tall**
See   Albert [or Albrecht]

**[The] Tall**
See   Philip V [or Philippe]

**Tall Paul Hankins**
See   Hankins, Paul

**Tall, Stephen**
See   Crook, Compton N.

**[The] Tall Tactician**
See   McGillicuddy, Cornelius
Alexander

**[The] Tall Texan**
See   Gray, Claude

**[The] Tall Texan**
See   Kilpatrick, Ben

**Tall, Tom**
See   Guthrie, Tommie Lee

**Tallent, Virginia** 1911-1968   [SC]
*American actress*
* Nelson, Virginia

**Talleyrand-Perigord, Charles
Maurice de** 1754-1838
[DNNS, RH]
*French statesman*
* [The] Prince of Diplomatists

**Tallien, Jeanne Marie Ignace Theresa**
1774?-1831?   [HN]
*French lady of fashion and politician*
* Our Lady of Mercy

**Tallis [or Tallys], Thomas**
1510?-1585   [DEP, DNNS]
*British composer and musician*
* [The] Father of English
   Cathedral Music

**Talma, Francois Joseph** 1763-1826
[DNNS, HN]
*French actor*
* [The] French Roscius

**Talma, Mercedes**
See   Ford, Mary

**[The] Talma of the Boulevards**
See   Lemaitre, Antoine Louis
Prosper

**Talmadge, Mattie** 1881?-1981
*Mother of American politician,
Herman Talmadge*
* Miss Mit

**Talmadge, Richard**
See   Metzetti, Sylvester Ricardo

**Talmage, Anne**
See   Powell, Talmage

**Talmon, Thrace**
See   Hale, Edith

**Talton, Marion Lee** 1939-   [BE]
*American baseball player*
* Talton, Tim

**Talton, Tim**
See   Talton, Marion Lee

**Talvi**
See   Robinson, Therese Albertine
Louise von Iakob

**Tam**
See   MacKellar, Thomas

**Tam of the Cowgate**
See   Hamilton, [Sir] Thomas

**Tamai, Katsunori** 1903-1960
[WBD]
*Japanese soldier and author*
* Hino, Ashihei

**Tamara**
See   Drasin, Tamara Swann

**[La] Tamara**
See   Karsavin, Tamara

**Tamarin, Shirley Astor Glubok**
1933-   [TBJ]
*Author*
* Glubok, Shirley

**Tambs, Lewis Arthur**
See   Jones, Lewis Arthur

**Tamer, James** 1913-
*American underworld figure*
* Tamer, Occo

**Tamer, Occo**
See Tamer, James

**Tamerlan a Lunettes**
See Thiers, Louis Adolphe

**Tamerlane [or Tamburlaine]**
See Timur [or Timour]

**Tames, Richard Lawrence** 1946-
[WD]
*British economist, historian, author*
* Lawrence, James

**Tamey, Milton** 1847-1924 [BEW]
*American actor*
* Nobles, Milton

**[The] Tamil Mahatma**
See Rajagopalacharia, Chakravarti

**Tamiris, Helen**
See Becker, Helen

**Tamminen, Juhani** 1950- [SMG]
*Finnish-born hockey player*
* Tamminen, Tommy

**Tamminen, Tommy**
See Tamminen, Juhani

**Tammsaare, A. H.**
See Hansen, Anton

**Tammuz, Benjamin**
See Kammerstein, Benjamin

**Tamo**
See Bodhidharma

**Tamor, Caspipini**
See Duchi, Jacob

**Tampa Red**
See Woodbridge, Hudson

**Tamulis, Vitautis Casimirus**
1911-1974 [BE]
*American baseball player*
* Tamulis, Vito

**Tamulis, Vito**
See Tamulis, Vitautis Casimirus

**Tan Ku**
See Bailey, George W.

**Tan Yun**
See Lin, Adet J[usu]

**Tanaquil, Paul**
See Le Clercq, Jacques George
Clemenceau

**Tandem, Felix**
See Spitteler, Carl

**Tandler, [Dr.] Leo**
See Trebitsch, Isaac

**Tandon, Horace B. A. Moquin**
[PA]
*Author*
* Fredol

**Tangent, Patrick Quinn**
See Phelps, George H[amilton]

**Tangle Eye**
See Horton, Walter

**Tanguay, Eva** 1878-1947 [SC]
*Canadian-born actress*
* [The] I Don't Care Girl

**Tania**
See Bunke, Haydee Tamara

**Tania**
See Hearst, Patricia Campbell
[Patty]

**Tania B.**
See Blixen, Karen [Christentze
Dinesen]

**Taniya, Kyn**
See Quintanilla, Luis

**Tankersley, Lawrence William**
1901- [BE]
*American baseball player*
* Tankersley, Leo

**Tankersley, Leo**
See Tankersley, Lawrence William

**Tannenbaum, Albert** 20th c. [BLB]
*American underworld figure*
* Tannenbaum, Allie

**Tannenbaum, Allie**
See Tannenbaum, Albert

**Tannenbaum, Max-Gerard Houry**
1919- [FC, FDG]
*French actor and director*
* Oury, Gerard

**Tanner, Cora**
See Sinn, Mrs. William E.

**Tanner, Edward Everett, III**
1921-1976 [B10, CA]
*American author*
* Dennis, Patrick
* Rowans, Virginia

**Tanner, Elaine** 1951-
[BBH, CSH, SWI]
*Canadian swimmer*
* Mighty Mouse

**Tanner, Gid**
See Tanner, James Gideon

**Tanner, James Gideon** 1885-1960
[CWG, DAM, PMJ]
*American country-western performer*
* Tanner, Gid

**Tanner, James T.** 20th c. [THR]
*British librettist*
* Leader, James

**Tanner, John**
See Matcha, Jack

**Tanner, John** 1930-1963 [SC]
*American actor*
* Eager, Johnney

**Tanner, Lightnin'**
See Tanner, Paul

**Tanner, Lina** 1923- [IWM]
*British musician*
* Vincent, Lina

**Tanner, Paul** 1917- [MY]
*American jazz musician*
* Tanner, Lightnin'

**[The] Tanner President**
See Grant, Hiram Ulysses

**Tanner-Rutherford, C.**
See Winchester, Clarence

**Tanni**
See Miyazaki, Toshio

**Tano, Guy**
See Rocco, Gaetano

**Tanswell, Albert Henry Silas Russell**
1908- [BEW]
*British-born actor and director*
* Tanswell, Bertram

**Tanswell, Bertram**
See Tanswell, Albert Henry Silas
Russell

**Tante, Dilly**
See Kunitz, Stanley [Jasspon]

**Tantrist**
See Wesander, Bjoern Kenneth

**Tao-tse** 6th c. BC [FFF, HN, SN]
*Chinese philosopher*
* [The] Epicurus of China

**Tap City Harris**
See Harris, Arthur

**Tapio, Pat Decker**
See Kines, Pat Decker

**[Le] Tapissier de Notre-Dame**
See Montmorency-Bouteville,
Francois Henri de [Duc de
Luxembourg]

**Tappe, El**
See Tappe, Elvin Walter

**Tappe, Elvin Walter** 1927- [BE]
*American baseball player and
manager*
* Tappe, El

**Tapping, Sydney** 1873-1941
[F1, F2, FC]
*British actress*
* Fairbrother, Sydney

**Tar, Gyula** 1928- [OP]
*Hungarian opera singer*
* Tarnay, Gyula

**Tara, John**
See Michel, John B.

**Taral, Fred** 1867-1925 [BBH]
*Jockey*
* [The] Dutch Demon

**Tarasc, Gilbert**
See Best, Tharratt Gilbert

**Tarassoff [or Tarassov], Lev** 1911-
[B10, CA, EWL]
*French author*
* Troyat, Henri

**Taravilla y Amoros, Gregorio**
1882-1943 [GS]
*Spanish bullfighter*
* Platerito [Little Silversmith]

**Tarbert, Arlie**
See Tarbert, Wilber Arlington

**Tarbert, Wilber Arlington**
1904-1946 [BE]
*American baseball player*
* Tarbert, Arlie

**Tarde, Gabriel**
See De Tarde, Gabriel

**Tardieu, Andre Pierre Gabriel
Amedee** 1876-1945 [WBD]
*French politician*
* Villiers, George

**Tardieu, Antoine Francois**
1757-1822 [WBD]
*French engraver*
* [De L']Estrapade

**Tardieu, Charles Jean** 1765-1830
[WBD]
*French painter*
* Tardieu Cochin

**Tardieu Cochin**
See Tardieu, Charles Jean

**Tardieu, J. R.** [PA]
*Author*
* Granella, Victor

**Tardiveau, Rene Marie Auguste**
1867-1926 [CD, TC]
*French author*
* Boylesve, Rene

**Tardy, May. T.** [PA]
*Author*
* Raymond, Ida

**Targ, William**
See Torgownik, William

**Tarheel Slim**
See Bunn, Alden

**Tarkenton, Cindy**
See Tarkenton, Fran[cis]

**Tarkenton, Fran[cis]** 1940-
*American football player*
* Tarkenton, Cindy

**Tarkington, [Newton] Booth**
1869-1946 [CAA]
*American author*
* Van Loot, Cornelius Obenchain

**[Il] Tarlo**
See Cecchi, Emilio

**Tarlton, Richard** ?-1588 [DEP]
*British comedian*
* [The] English Roscius
* Roscius Britannicus

**Tarnacre, Robert**
See Cartmell, Robert

**Tarnawsky, Patricia W[arren]**
1936- [CA]
*American editor, author, poet*
* Kilina, Patricia

**Tarnay, Gyula**
See Tar, Gyula

**Tarne, Rosina**
See Fearn, John Russell

**Tarnower, Lydia** 20th c. [BEW]
*American editor*
* Joel, Lydia

**Tarpley, Brenda Mae** 1944-
[CME, ECM, RO1]
*American singer*
* Lee, Brenda
* Little Miss Dynamite

**Tarquin II [or Tarquinius]** 6th c.
BC [FFF, RH, SN]
*Legendary King of Rome*
* [The] Proud
* Superbus

**Tarrant, Wilma**
See Sherman, Jory [Tecumseh]

**Tarrok, Peer**
See Zwerenz, Gerhard

**Tarsis, Valerii Iakovievich** 1900-
[B10, WOA]
*Russian author*
* Veleriy, Ivan

**Tarski, Alexander**
See Tabaksblat, Alexander

**Tarski, Alfred** 1902- [JL]
*Polish-born philosopher*
* [The] Father of Logical
Semantics

**Tartaglia, Niccolo**
See Fontana, Nicola

**Tarto, Joe**
See Tortoriello, Joseph

**Tartuffe, Kaiser**
See William I [Wilhelm Friedrich Ludwig]

**[The] Tartuffe of the Revolution**
See Nicolas, Jean

**Tasco, Rai**
See Tasco, Ridgeway

**Tasco, Ridgeway** 1917- [ITA]
*American actor and announcer*
* Tasco, Rai

**Tashrak**
See Zevin, Israel Joseph

**Tashunca-Uitco** 1849?-1877
[WBD]
*American Indian chieftain*
* Crazy Horse

**[The] Tasmanian Devil**
See Lee, Ron

**Tassinari, Berte Danyell**
1870-1917 [SC]
*Italian-born actor*
* Dansey, Herbert

**Tasso, Torquato** 1544-1595 [SN]
*Italian poet*
* [The] Father of Tuscan Poetry

**Tassy, Tamas** 1920- [IWM]
*Hungarian-born composer,
conductor, arranger*
* Legrady, Thomas Theodore
* Thomas, Ted

**Taswert**
See Stewart, John Allan

**Tate, Allen**
See Orley, John

**Tate, B. H.**
See Boyer, Bruce Hatton

**Tate, Baby**
See Tate, Charles Henry

**Tate, Bennie**
See Tate, Henry Bennett

**Tate, Buddy**
See Tate, George Holmes

**Tate, Charles Henry** 1916-1972
[BWW]
*American singer*
* Tate, Baby

**Tate, Dimples**
See Tate, Edward Christopher

**Tate, Don** 20th c. [GW]
*American rodeo performer*
* Tate, Montana Red

**Tate, Edward**
See Dransfield, Michael [John]
Pender

**Tate, Edward Christopher**
1861-1932 [BE]
*American baseball player*
* Tate, Dimples
* Tate, Pop

**Tate, Ellalice**
See Hibbert, Eleanor Alice
[Burford]

**Tate, George Holmes** 1914?-
[EJ, NP, PMJ]
*American jazz musician*
* Tate, Buddy
* Tate, Moon

**Tate, Hal**
See Teitelman, Alex

**Tate, Harry, Jr.**
See Hutchison, Ronald

**Tate, Henry [or Harry]**
See Hutchison, Ronald Macdonald

**Tate, Henry Bennett** 1901-1973
[BE]
*American baseball player*
* Tate, Bennie

**Tate, Lee Willie** 1932- [BE]
*American baseball player*
* Tate, Skeeter

**Tate, Margaret** 1888?-
[BBD, EMT]
*British actress and singer*
* Teyte, Maggie

**Tate, Mary Anne**
See Hale, Arlene

**Tate, Montana Red**
See Tate, Don

**Tate, Moon**
See Tate, George Holmes

**Tate, Pop**
See Tate, Edward Christopher

**Tate, Richard**
See Masters, Anthony

**Tate, Robin**
See Fanthorpe, R[obert] Lionel

**Tate, Roosevelt** 20th c. [OBW]
*American baseball player*
* Tate, Speed

**Tate, Skeeter**
See Tate, Lee Willie

**Tate, Speed**
See Tate, Roosevelt

**Tate, Velma** 1913- [CA]
*American author*
* Davenport, Francine
* Taylor, Valerie
* Young, Nacella

**Tatham, Campbell**
See Elting, Mary

**Tatham, Laura** 1919- [AW]
*British author and journalist*
* Martin, John
* Phipps, Margaret

**Tati, Jacques**
See Tatischeff, Jacques

**Tatischeff, Jacques** 1908-
[BDF, FC, IPA]
*French director, writer, actor*
* Tati, Jacques

**Tatlow, Tissington** 1876- ? [LAO]
*Irish-born clergyman, editor, writer*
* T

**Tato de Mexico [Lisper from Mexico]**
See Maldonado y Rodriguez,
Edmundo

**Tatray, Istvan**
See Rupert, Raphael Rudolph

**Tattersall, Muriel Joyce** 1931-
[AW, CAP, WD]
*British author*
* Waud, Elizabeth

**Tatti, Jacopo** 1486-1570 [WBD]
*Italian sculptor and architect*
* Sansovino, Jacopo

**[The] Tattooed Man**
See Blaine, James Gillespie

**Tatu, Elizabeth A.** 1866-1944 [SC]
*American actress*
* Allyn, Lilly

**Tatum, Earl** 20th c. [NBA]
*American basketball player*
* [The] Black Jerry West

**Tatum, Goose**
See Tatum, Reece

**Tatum, Reece** 1919?-1967
[AS, BB]
*American basketball player*
* [The] Clown Prince of Basketball
* Tatum, Goose

**Taubenhaus, Eugene** 1909- [BEW]
*American actor, songwriter, business
representative*
* Doyle, Gene

**Taubensee, Fred Joseph** 1906-1955
[BE]
*American baseball player*
* Tauby, Fred Joseph

**Tauber, Richard**
See Seiffert, Ernst

**Tauby, Fred Joseph**
See Taubensee, Fred Joseph

**Tauler, Johann** 1300-1361
[DEP, HN, SN]
*German mystic*
* [The] Illuminated Doctor
* Illuminatus, Doctor
* Sublimis et Illuminatus, Doctor

**Taunton, Eric**
See Jones, Kenneth Westcott

**Taurasi, James V., Sr.** 20th c.
[SFP]
*Author*
* Stannard, Lane
* Vincent, J. Harry

**Taurus**
See Honey, Philip

**Tausen, Hans** 1494-1561
[DNNS, HN, RH]
*Danish religious reformer*
* [The] Danish Luther

**Taussig, J. J.** 20th c. [EJS]
*American boxing manager and
trainer*
* Taussig, Moose

**Taussig, Moose**
See Taussig, J. J.

**Tavares, Antone** 1950- [RO2]
*American singer*
* Tavares, Chubby

**Tavares, Arthur** 1949- [RO2]
*American singer*
* Tavares, Pooch

**Tavares, Butch**
See Tavares, Feliciano

**Tavares, Chubby**
See Tavares, Antone

**Tavares, Feliciano** 1953- [RO2]
*American singer*
* Tavares, Butch

**Tavares, Perry Lee** 1954- [RO2]
*American singer*
* Tavares, Tiny

**Tavares, Pooch**
See Tavares, Arthur

**Tavares, Tiny**
See Tavares, Perry Lee

**Tavener, John Adam [Jackie]**
1897-1969 [BN]
*American baseball player*
* Tavener, Rabbit

**Tavener, Rabbit**
See Tavener, John Adam [Jackie]

**Taveral, John**
See Howard, Robert Ervin

**Taveras, Alex**
See Taveras Betances, Alejandro
A.

**Taveras, Frank**
See Taveras, Franklin Fabian

**Taveras, Franklin Fabian** 1950-
[SMG]
*Dominican-born baseball player*
* [The] Pittsburgh Stealer
* Taveras, Frank

**Taveras Betances, Alejandro A.**
1955- [BR]
*Dominican-born baseball player*
* Taveras, Alex

**Tavernier, Mrs. Albert** [FFF]
*Entertainer*
* Van Cortlandt, Ida

**Tavis, Alec**
See Dunnett, Alastair MacTavish

**Taviss, Irene**
See Thomson, Irene Taviss

**Tavo, Gus** [joint pseudonym with
Martha Miller Pfaff Ivan]
See Ivan, Gustave E.

**Tavo, Gus** [joint pseudonym with
Gustave E. Ivan]
See Ivan, Martha Miller Pfaff

**Tawney, R. H.**
See Tawney, Richard Henry

**Tawney, Richard Henry** 1880-1962
[LC]
*British historian and author*
* Tawney, R. H.

**[The] Tawny**
See Bonvicino, Alessandro [or
Alexander]

**Tay Pay**
See O'Connor, Thomas Power

**Taylor, A. J. P.**
See Taylor, Alan John Percivale

**Taylor, Aaron** [BWW]
*American singer*
* Taylor, Buddy

**Taylor, Alan John Percivale** 1906-
[LC]
*British historian and author*
* Taylor, A. J. P.

**Taylor, Alec** 1862-1943    [OCS]
*British horse trainer*
* [The] Wizard of Manton

**Taylor, [Capt.] Alfred B.**
*See*   Ingraham, Prentiss

**Taylor, Ann**
*See*   Smith, Richard Rein

**Taylor, Antonio Sanchez** 1935-
[BE, SMG]
*Cuban-born baseball player*
* Taylor, Tony

**Taylor, Arthur** 1903-    [BWW]
*American singer*
* Taylor, Montana

**Taylor, Barbara G.** 1942-    [CA]
*American editor and writer*
* Desmarais, Barbara G.

**Taylor, Bayard** 1825-1878    [PA]
*Author*
* Echo Club

**Taylor, Benjamin Franklin**
1819-1887    [FFF]
*American author*
* [The] Goldsmith of America

**Taylor, Benjamin Ogle**    [PA]
*Author*
* Neptune
* Observer
* Viator

**Taylor, Bert Leston** 1866-1921
[TC]
*American columnist*
* B. L. T.

**Taylor, Bill**
*See*   Taylor, Joseph Cephus

**Taylor, Blues**
*See*   Taylor, Johnny

**Taylor, Bollicky**
*See*   Taylor, William Henry

**Taylor, Bones**
*See*   Taylor, Hugh

**Taylor, Brad**
*See*   Smith, Richard Rein

**Taylor, Brenda Forbes** 1909-
[BEW]
*British actress*
* Forbes, Brenda

**Taylor, Brewery Jack**
*See*   Taylor, John B.

**Taylor, Bruce**
*See*   Yin, Leslie Charles Bowyer

**Taylor, Bud**
*See*   Taylor, Charles B.

**Taylor, Buddy**
*See*   Taylor, Aaron

**Taylor, C. I.**
*See*   Taylor, Charles I.

**Taylor, Candy Jim**
*See*   Taylor, James

**Taylor, Cash**
*See*   Taylor, Joseph Cephus

**Taylor, Charles B.** 1903-1962
[AS, BX, RBE]
*American boxer*
* [The] Blond Terror of Terre
  Haute
* Taylor, Bud

**Taylor, Charles B.** (Continued)
* [The] Terre Haute Terror

**Taylor, Charles H. [Chuck]**
1901-1969    [AS]
*American basketball player and
editor*
* [The] Ambassador of Basketball

**Taylor, Charles I.** 1872-1922    [MK]
*American baseball player*
* Taylor, C. I.

**Taylor, Chat**
*See*   Taylor, Robert William

**Taylor, Chink**
*See*   Taylor, Leo Thomas

**Taylor, Chip**
*See*   Voigt, James Wesley

**Taylor, Constance Lindsay** 1907-
[WW]
*Author*
* Cullingford, Guy

**Taylor, Cora Walton** 1935-    [BWW]
*American singer*
* Taylor, Koko

**Taylor, Cyclone**
*See*   Taylor, Fred

**Taylor, D. M.** 1915-    [CM]
*American radio broadcaster*
* Taylor, Sammy

**Taylor, Day** [joint pseudonym with
Sharon Salvato]
*See*   Parkinson, Cornelia M.

**Taylor, Day** [joint pseudonym with
Cornelia M. Parkinson]
*See*   Salvato, Sharon

**Taylor, Demetria** 1903-1977    [CA]
*American author, educator, editor*
* Merriman, Beth

**Taylor, Dummy**
*See*   Taylor, Luther Haden

**Taylor, E. D.**    [PA]
*Author*
* Jenkins, S. Joshua

**Taylor, Eddie** 1923-    [BWW]
*American singer*
* Taylor, Playboy

**Taylor, Elizabeth Tebbetts** 20th c.
*Author*
* Tebbets-Taylor, Elizabeth

**Taylor, Estelle**
*See*   Boylan, Estelle

**Taylor, Eva**
*See*   Gibbons, Irene

**Taylor, F.**    [PA]
*Author*
* One of the Fancy

**Taylor, F. Chase** 1897-1950    [SC]
*American actor*
* Stoopnagle, [Colonel] Lemuel Q.

**Taylor, Fatty**
*See*   Taylor, Roland

**Taylor, Fred** 1883?-
[CEI, FHE, HK]
*Canadian-born hockey player*
* Taylor, Cyclone

**Taylor, Frederick Winslow**
1856-1915    [DEP]
*American engineer and efficiency
expert*
* [The] Father of Business
  Efficiency

**Taylor, Gay Stuart**   ?-1970    [B10]
*British diarist*
* Hurnscot, Loran

**Taylor, George**
*See*   Parulski, George R[ichard], Jr.

**Taylor, [Frank Herbert] Griffin**
1917-    [CA]
*British-born author*
* Schneyder, J. F.

**Taylor, H. Baldwin**
*See*   Waugh, Hillary Baldwin

**Taylor, Handsome Harry**
*See*   Taylor, Harry Warren

**Taylor, Harry**
*See*   Granick, Harry

**Taylor, Harry Warren** 1907-1969
[BE]
*American baseball player*
* Taylor, Handsome Harry

**Taylor, Hartford Connecticut**
1905-1963    [CWG]
*American country-western performer*
* Taylor, Harty

**Taylor, Harty**
*See*   Taylor, Hartford Connecticut

**Taylor, Hawk**
*See*   Taylor, Robert Dale

**Taylor, Herbert** 1872-1927    [BEW]
*British actor*
* Rolyat, Dan

**Taylor, Hound Dog**
*See*   Taylor, Theodore

**Taylor, Howard Langdon**
1920-1974    [B10]
*American author*
* Taylor, Tim

**Taylor, Hugh** 20th c.    [SMG]
*American football coach*
* Taylor, Bones

**Taylor, J. G.** 20th c.    [BBH]
*American sportswriter*
* Taylor, Stink

**Taylor, J. H.**
*See*   Taylor, John Henry

**Taylor, J. R.** 20th c.    [SMG]
*American football player*
* Taylor, Tarz

**Taylor, J. S.**
*See*   Taylor, James Spencer

**Taylor, Jack** 20th c.    [CC]
*Author*
* Gray, Jonathan

**Taylor, James** 1884-1948
[IBW, MK]
*American baseball player*
* Taylor, Candy Jim

**Taylor, James Spencer** 1921-
[ART]
*British painter*
* J. S. T.
* J. T.
* Taylor, J. S.

**Taylor, James Wren** 1898-1974
[B10, BE, PB]
*American baseball player and
manager*
* Taylor, Zack

**Taylor, Jane** 1783-1824    [PA]
*Author*
* Q. Q.

**Taylor, Jelly**
*See*   Taylor, Olan

**Taylor, Jeremy** 1613-1667
[PA, RH, SN]
*British author and prelate*
* [The] Beauty of Holiness
* [The] English Chrysostom
* [A] Layman
* [The] Poet Bishop
* [The] Shakespeare of Divines
* [The] Spenser of English
  Prose-Writers

**Taylor, Jerome**
*See*   Krejci, Jerome

**Taylor, Jesse**
*See*   Amidon, Bill [Vincent]

**Taylor, Joe**
*See*   Taylor, William Michael

**Taylor, Joe Carl** 1921-    [CWG]
*American country-western performer*
* [The] Cowboy Auctioneer

**Taylor, John**
*See*   Magee, James

**Taylor, John**    [SN]
*Oculist*
* Taylor, Liar

**Taylor, John** 1580-1654
[DEP, DNNF, FFF]
*British poet*
* [The] Swan of the Thames
* [The] Water Poet

**Taylor, John [Alfred]** 1931-    [CA]
*American poet and author*
* Coppe, Abiezer
* Dupin, August Dupont
* Ward, Charles Dexter

**Taylor, John** 20th c.    [OBW]
*American baseball player*
* Steel Arm Johnny

**Taylor, John B.** 1873-1900
[BE, PB]
*American baseball player*
* Taylor, Brewery Jack

**Taylor, John Henry** 1871-1963
[GF]
*British golfer*
* Taylor, J. H.

**Taylor, John M[axwell]** 1930-    [CA]
*American diplomat and author*
* Allen, Richard C.

**Taylor, Johnny** 20th c.    [BWW]
*American singer*
* Taylor, Blues

**Taylor, Johnny Lamar**
*See*   Young, Johnny

**Taylor, Joseph Cephus** 1926-    [BE]
*American baseball player*
* Taylor, Bill
* Taylor, Cash

**Taylor, Josephine**
*See*   Motz, Josephine

**Taylor, Joyce Barbara** 1921-
[ART]
*British artist*
* J. B. T.

**Taylor, Kamala [Purnaiya]** 1924-
[B10]
*Indian author*
* Markandaya, Kamala

**Taylor, Karen Malpede** 1945-    [CA]
*American author and editor*
* Malpede, Karen

**Taylor, Kent**
See   Weiss, Louis

**Taylor, Koko**
See   Taylor, Cora Walton

**Taylor, Laurette**
See   Cooney, Laurette

**Taylor, Leo Thomas** 1901-    [BE]
*American baseball player*
* Taylor, Chink

**Taylor, Les**
See   Taylor, Lionel

**Taylor, Liar**
See   Taylor, John

**Taylor, Lionel** 1916-    [ASC]
*American musician*
* Taylor, Les

**Taylor, Little Johnny**
See   Young, Johnny

**Taylor, Luther Haden** 1875?-1958
[AS, BE, PB]
*American baseball player*
* Taylor, Dummy

**Taylor, Major**
See   Taylor, Marshall W.

**Taylor, Malcolm** 1943-    [SW]
*British actor*
* McDowell, Malcolm

**Taylor, Margaret**
See   Burroughs, Margaret Taylor

**Taylor, Margaret**
See   Kenyon, [Margaret] Doris

**Taylor, Margaret Stewart** 20th c.
[CA]
*British author*
* Collier, Margaret

**Taylor, Marshall W.** 1878-1932
[BBH]
*American bicycle racer*
* Taylor, Major

**Taylor, Mary Ann** 1912-    [CA]
*American author*
* Bowe, Kate

**Taylor, Mary Virginia** 1912-
[ASC]
*American songwriter*
* Sterling, Jean
* Wood, Sue

**Taylor, Michael Angelo** 18th c.
[DNNS, HN, RH]
*Barrister*
* [The] Chicken

**Taylor, Michael Norman Somerset**
1942-    [DC]
*British cricketer*
* Taylor, Tay

**Taylor, Montana**
See   Taylor, Arthur

**Taylor, Moose**
See   Taylor, William Michael

**Taylor, Mrs. Tom**    [PA]
*Author*
* Barker, Laura

**Taylor, N. J.** 1946-    [BBH, CFH]
*Canadian football team president*
* Taylor, Piffles

**Taylor, Newton**
See   Taylor, William Henry

**Taylor, Norman**
See   Wood-Smith, Noel

**Taylor, Olan** 20th c.    [OBW]
*American baseball player*
* Taylor, Jelly

**Taylor, Pat**
See   Pope, Pat

**Taylor, Pete**
See   Taylor, Vernon Charles

**Taylor, Phoebe [Atwood]**
1909-1976    [CA, CC, EMD]
*American author*
* Tilton, Alice

**Taylor, Piffles**
See   Taylor, N. J.

**Taylor, Playboy**
See   Taylor, Eddie

**Taylor, Ralph** 1905-1951    [THR]
*British actor*
* Forbes, Ralph

**Taylor, Red**
See   Taylor, Walter

**Taylor, Richard** 1919-    [CA]
*American educator and author*
* Cronus, Diodorus

**Taylor, Richard Mansfield** 20th c.
[ITA, SW]
*American actor*
* Richards, Jeff

**Taylor, Robert**
See   Brough, Spangler Arlington

**Taylor, Robert** 1923-    [ECM]
*American country-western performer*
* Taylor, Tut

**Taylor, Robert** 1930-    [SW]
*Australian-born actor*
* Taylor, Rod

**Taylor, Robert Dale** 1939-    [BE]
*American baseball player*
* Taylor, Hawk

**Taylor, Robert William** 1941-    [DC]
*British cricketer*
* Taylor, Chat

**Taylor, Rod**
See   Taylor, Robert

**Taylor, Roland** 1946-    [NBA, SMG]
*American basketball player*
* Taylor, Fatty

**Taylor, Roosevelt** 1937-    [FB]
*American football player*
* Taylor, Rosey

**Taylor, Rosey**
See   Taylor, Roosevelt

**Taylor, Sam**
See   Alex, Gus

**Taylor, Sam**
See   Goodyear, Stephen Frederick

**Taylor, Sammy**
See   Taylor, D. M.

**Taylor, Samuel L.** 1916-    [EJ]
*American jazz musician*
* Sam the Man

**Taylor, Selman**
See   Selman, Elsie Emily

**Taylor, Seymour** 1912-    [ASC]
*American musician*
* Taylor, Sy

**Taylor, Slats**
See   Taylor, Virgil

**Taylor, Stella** 1932?-
*Former nun and expert swimmer*
* [The] Swimming Nun

**Taylor, Stink**
See   Taylor, J. G.

**Taylor, Sy**
See   Taylor, Seymour

**Taylor, Tarz**
See   Taylor, J. R.

**Taylor, Tay**
See   Taylor, Michael Norman
Somerset

**Taylor, Theodore**
See   Hotten, John Camden

**Taylor, Theodore** 1916?-1975
[B10]
*American musician*
* Taylor, Hound Dog

**Taylor, Theodore** 1921-    [CA]
*American author and screenwriter*
* Lang, T. T.

**Taylor, Thomas** 1758-1835
[SN, WBD]
*British scholar*
* [The] Platonist

**Taylor, Tim**
See   Taylor, Howard Langdon

**Taylor, Tony**
See   Taylor, Antonio Sanchez

**Taylor, Tut**
See   Taylor, Robert

**Taylor, Valerie**
See   Tate, Velma

**Taylor, Vernon Charles** 1927-    [BE]
*American baseball player*
* Taylor, Pete

**Taylor, Virgil** ?-1978    [FIR]
*Actor*
* Taylor, Slats

**Taylor, W. T.** 20th c.    [MBF]
*British author*
* Bredon, John
* Gregory, Dave
* Whitehouse, Arch

**Taylor, Walter** 20th c.    [IBW]
*American track and field athlete*
* Taylor, Red

**Taylor, Walter G.**
See   Geibel, Adam

**Taylor, William Desmond**
See   Deane-Turner, William
Cunningham

**Taylor, William Henry** 1855-1900
[BE]
*American baseball player*
* Taylor, Bollicky

**Taylor, William Henry** 1911-
[DBA]
*British painter, etcher, engraver*
* Taylor, Newton

**Taylor, William Michael** 1929-
[BE]
*American baseball player*
* Taylor, Joe
* Taylor, Moose

**Taylor, Zachary** 1784-1850
[DNNS, DNNF, SN]
*American president and army officer*
* Old Buena Vista
* Old Rough and Ready
* Old Zach
* Rough and Ready

**Taylor, Zack**
See   Taylor, James Wren

**Tchaadaieff**
See   Sorokin, Pitirim
A[lexandrovitch]

**Tchicaya, Gerald Felix** 1931-
[WOA]
*Congolese poet*
* U Tam'si

**Tea, Sir**
See   Lipton, Thomas

**[A] Tea Table Scoundrel**
See   Stanhope, Philip Dormer

**Teach, Edward** ?-1718
[CEC, WBD]
*British pirate*
* Blackbeard

**[The] Teacher of Germany**
See   Schwarzert, Philipp

**[The] Teacher of the Catholic Church**
See   Dionysius

**[The] Teacher President**
See   Garfield, James Abram

**Teachout, Arthur John** 1904-    [BE]
*American baseball player*
* Teachout, Bud

**Teachout, Bud**
See   Teachout, Arthur John

**Teachwell, Mrs.**
See   Fenn, Eleanor

**Teagarden, Big T**
See   Teagarden, Weldon Leo

**Teagarden, Charlie** 1913-    [PMJ]
*American jazz musician*
* Teagarden, Little T

**Teagarden, Clois Lee** 1915-    [EJ]
*American jazz musician*
* Teagarden, Cub

**Teagarden, Cub**
See   Teagarden, Clois Lee

**Teagarden, Jack**
See   Teagarden, Weldon Leo

**Teagarden, Little T**
See   Teagarden, Charlie

**Teagarden, Norma Louise**
See   Friedlander, Norma

**Teagarden, Weldon Leo** 1905-1964
[DAM, PMJ, WWJ]
*American jazz musician*
* Teagarden, Big T
* Teagarden, Jack

**Teague, George Herbert** 20th c.
[WWL]
*British author*
* Galway, Herbert

**Teague, John Jessop** 1856-1929
[WW]
*Author*
* Gerard, Morice

**Teague, Olin** 1911?-1981
*American politician and army officer*
* Teague, Tiger

**Teague, Tiger**
*See* Teague, Olin

**Teal, Allen Leslie** 1933-
[CEI, SMG]
*Canadian-born hockey player*
* Teal, Skip

**Teal, G. Donn** 1932- [WD]
*American author*
* Forsythe, Ronald

**Teal, Skeeter**
*See* Teal, Victor

**Teal, Skip**
*See* Teal, Allen Leslie

**Teal, Victor** 1949- [HR]
*Canadian-born hockey player*
* Teal, Skeeter

**Tear 'em**
*See* Roebuck, John Arthur

**Teardrop, Mr.**
*See* Robinson, Martin D.

**Tearle, Conway**
*See* Levy, Frederick

**Tearle, Minnie** [FFF]
*Entertainer*
* Conway, Minnie

**Teasdale, Joseph** 1936?-
*American politician*
* Teasdale, Walkin' Joe

**Teasdale, Sara Filsinger**
*See* Filsinger, Sara Teasdale

**Teasdale, Walkin' Joe**
*See* Teasdale, Joseph

**Tebar Perez, Gregorio** 1946- [GS]
*Spanish bullfighter*
* [El] Inclusero [The Foundling]

**Tebbets-Taylor, Elizabeth**
*See* Taylor, Elizabeth Tebbetts

**Tebbetts, Birdie**
*See* Tebbetts, George Robert

**Tebbetts, George Robert** 1909?-
[BE, IPA, PB]
*American baseball player and manager*
* Tebbetts, Birdie

**Tebeau, Charles Albert** 20th c.
[BE]
*American baseball player*
* Tebeau, Pussy

**Tebeau, George E.** 1862-1923 [BE]
*American baseball player*
* Tebeau, White Wings

**Tebeau, Oliver Wendell** 1864-1918
[AS, BE, PB]
*American baseball player and manager*
* Tebeau, Patsy

**Tebeau, Patsy**
*See* Tebeau, Oliver Wendell

**Tebeau, Pussy**
*See* Tebeau, Charles Albert

**Tebeau, White Wings**
*See* Tebeau, George E.

**Teche, L. A.**
*See* Parker, Fitzgerald Sale

**Tecosky, Morton** 1914-
[BEW, FC, TR]
*American director, producer, actor*
* Da Costa, Morton

**Teddy Bear**
*See* Pendergrass, Theodore
[Teddy]

**Teddy Boy Atkinson**
*See* Atkinson, Ted

**[Il] Tedesco**
*See* Elsheimer, Adam

**Tedmon, Allyn Henry** 1884- [NAA]
*American writer*
* Allen, Ted
* Nomdet, Nylla

**Tee-Van, Helen Damrosch** 1893-
[SAT]
*American artist, illustrator, writer*
* Damrosch, Helen Therese

**Teed, Cyrus Reed** 1839-1908
[SFL, WGT]
*American author*
* Chester, Lord
* Cyrus
* Koresh

**Teed, George Heber Hamilton**
1878-1939 [MBF]
*Canadian-born author*
* Brittany, Louis
* Hamilton, George
* Hamilton, Murray [joint pseudonym with Robert Murray Graydon]
* Reid, Desmond [house pseudonym]

**Tefft, Lyman Beecher** 1833- ?
[ALY]
*American author*
* Vindex

**Tegner, Henry [Stuart]** 1901- [CA]
*British author*
* [The] Northumbrian Gentleman
* [The] Ruffle

**Tehuhe** ?-1200 [HN, RH, SN]
*Chinese philosopher*
* [The] Aristotle of China
* [The] Prince of Science

**[The] Teian Muse [or Poet]**
*See* Anacreon

**Teichman, Arthur** 1895- [JL]
*American dancing instructor*
* Murray, Arthur

**Teichner, Hans H.** 1908-1957
[BBH]
*American ski instructor and promoter of skiing programs*
* Teichner, Peppi

**Teichner, Peppi**
*See* Teichner, Hans H.

**Teilhet, Darwin L[e Ora]**
1904-1964 [ANT, ESF]
*American author*
* Fisher, Cyrus T.

**Teitelman, Alex** 1912- [ASC]
*American entertainer and composer*
* Tate, Hal

**Teixeira De Pascoais, Joaquim**
*See* Teixeira De Vasconcelos, Joaquim Pereira

**Teixeira De Queiroz, Francisco**
1848-1919 [CD]
*Portuguese author*
* Moreno, Bento

**Teixeira De Vasconcelos, Joaquim
Pereira** 1877?-1952 [CD, EWL]
*Portuguese poet and author*
* Teixeira De Pascoais, Joaquim

**Tejada, Raquel** 1940?-
[FC, HT, IPA]
*American actress*
* Welch, Raquel

**Tekakwitha, Kateri** 1656-1680
[WBD]
*Saint*
* [The] Lily of the Mohawks

**Tekulve, Kent**
*See* Tekulve, Kenton Charles

**Tekulve, Kenton Charles** 1947-
[SMG]
*American baseball player*
* Tekulve, Kent

**Tela, Josephus**
*See* Webb, Joseph

**Telenga, Suzette** 1915- [CA]
*German-born author*
* Yorke, Susan

**Telescope Teddy**
*See* Roosevelt, Theodore [Teddy]

**Television, Mr.**
*See* Berlinger, Milton

**Telfer, Dariel** 1905- [CAP]
*American author*
* Forrest, Caleb

**Telford, Thomas** [FFF]
*Scottish poet*
* Eskdale Tam

**Tell, Muni**
*See* Griffin, Alice McClure

**Tell, William** 1282-1350 [HN, RH]
*Legendary Swiss hero*
* [The] Mountain Brutus

**Tellefsen, Carl** 1854-1908 [BBH]
*Norwegian-born skiing organization officer*
* [The] Father of American Organized Skiing

**Tellegen, Lou**
*See* Van Dammeler, Isador Louis Bernard

**Teller, Edward** 1908-
*Hungarian-born American physicist*
* [The] Father of the Hydrogen Bomb

**Teller, Neville** 1931- [IAW]
*British author*
* Owen, Edmund

**Tellez, Gabriel** 1570?-1648
[DNNF, RH, WBD]
*Spanish playwright*
* De Molina, Tirso

**Tellier, Jacques**
*See* Foy, Louis Andre

**Telltale, George**
*See* Holmes, Isaac Edward

**Telltroth, Titus**
*See* Oates, Titus

**Telmann, Konrad**
*See* Zitelmann, Konrad

**Telva, Marion**
*See* Toucke, Marion

**Temary, Elza** 1905-1968 [SC]
*American actress*
* Splane, Elza K.

**[Le] Temeraire**
*See* Charles

**Temme, Jodocus Donatus Hubertus**
1798-1881 [WBD]
*German jurist, criminologist, author*
* Stahl, Heinrich

**Temny**
*See* Basil II [or Vasili]

**Temothie**
*See* Escoffer, Tremim M.

**[The] Tempest**
*See* Junot, Andoche

**Tempest, Evelyn**
*See* Cuming, Edward William Dirom

**Tempest, J. Fletcher**
*See* Fletcher, John Arthur

**Tempest, Jan**
*See* Swatridge, Irene Maude [Mossop]

**Tempest, [Dame] Marie**
*See* Etherington, Mary Susan

**Tempest, Sarah**
*See* Ponsonby, Doris Almon

**Tempest, Theresa**
*See* Kent, Louise Andrews

**Tempest, Victor**
*See* Philipp, Elliot Elias

**[La] Tempete**
*See* Junot, Andoche

**Templaito [The Valiant One]**
*See* Martinez, Julio

**Templar**
*See* Kent, [William] Charles [Mark]

**Templar, John**
*See* Garbutt, John L.

**Templar, Maurice**
*See* Groom, Arthur William

**Temple, Ann**
*See* Mortimer, Penelope [Ruth]

**Temple, Arthur**
*See* Northcott, [William] Cecil

**Temple Bar**
*See* Fox-Davies, Arthur Charles

**Temple, Dan**
*See* Newton, Dwight Bennett

**Temple, Edith**
See   Murrells, Joseph

**Temple, Geechie**
See   Temple, Johnny

**Temple, Henry John** 1784-1865
[DEP, DNNS, HN]
*British statesman*
* Evergreen Pam
* Old Pam
* Palmerston, Viscount
* Pam

**Temple, James**
See   Bell, Eric Temple

**Temple, Johnny** 1906-1968   [BWW]
*American singer*
* Temple, Geechie

**Temple, Lafayette Parker** 1911-
[FFA]
*American singer*
* Temple, Pick

**Temple, Launcelot**
See   Armstrong, John

**Temple, M. H.** 20th c.   [SFL]
*Author*
* Lewis, Caroline [joint pseudonym
   with James S. Ransome and
   (Edward) Harold Begbie]

**Temple, Mattie**
See   Clark, Mrs. Henry

**Temple, Mrs. Edward P.**   [FFF]
*Entertainer*
* Winner, Polly

**Temple, Neville**
See   Fane, Julian Charles Henry

**Temple, Paul** [joint pseudonym with
James Douglas Rutherford
McConnell]
See   Durbridge, Francis

**Temple, Paul** [joint pseudonym with
Francis Durbridge]
See   McConnell, James Douglas
Rutherford

**Temple, Pick**
See   Temple, Lafayette Parker

**Temple, Ralph**
See   Alexander, Robert William

**Temple, Robin**
See   Wood, Samuel Andrew

**Temple, Victoria**
See   Mason, Mrs. W. J.

**Temple-Ellis, N. A.**
See   Holdaway, Neville Aldridge

**Templeton**
See   Monroe, George H.

**Templeton, Dink**
See   Templeton, Robert L.

**Templeton, Faith**
See   Barber, Harriet Booner

**Templeton, Fay**
See   West, Mrs. William

**Templeton, Garry Lewis** 1956-
[SMG]
*American baseball player*
* Templeton, Jump Steady

**Templeton, Herminie**
See   Kavanagh, Herminie
Templeton

**Templeton, Jesse**
See   Goodchild, George

**Templeton, Jump Steady**
See   Templeton, Garry Lewis

**Templeton, Laurence**
See   Scott, [Sir] Walter

**Templeton, May**
See   Reilly, Mrs. James

**Templeton, Mrs. John**   [FFF]
*Entertainer*
* Vane, Alice

**Templeton, Robert L.** 1897?-1962
[AS, TF]
*American track and field coach*
* Templeton, Dink

**Templeton, Ruth**
See   Bullivant, Margaret D.

**Templeton, Timothy**
See   Adams, Charles Baker

**Templeton, Tristram**
See   Davin, Nicholas Francis Flood

**Templeton, W. P.**
See   Templeton, William Pettigrew

**Templeton, William Pettigrew**
1915-   [BEW]
*Scottish playwright*
* Templeton, W. P.

**[The] Temporizing Statesman**
See   Whitelocke, Bulstrode

**[El] Tempranillo [The Little Early
One]**
See   Moreno, Tomas

**Temujin [or Temuchin]** 1162-1227
[WBD]
*Mongol chieftain*
* Genghis Khan

**Ten Cent Jimmy**
See   Buchanan, James

**Ten Eyck, Edward H.** 1879-1956
[AS]
*American rower*
* Ten Eyck, Ned

**Ten Eyck, Ned**
See   Ten Eyck, Edward H.

**10 4**
See   Correll, Victor Crosby

**[The] Ten Thousand Dollar Beauty**
See   Kelly, Michael Joseph

**Tenace, Fury G.** 1946-   [PB]
*American baseball player*
* Tenace, Gene

**Tenace, Gene**
See   Tenace, Fury G.

**Tenax**
See   Lean, Garth Dickinson

**Tenbrook, Harry**
See   Hansen, Henry Olaf

**Tench, Charles Victor** 1895-
[NAA]
*British-born writer*
* C. V. T.
* Truscott, Charles

**Tendron, Marcel** 1884- ?   [WBD]
*French author*
* Elder, Marc

**Tenella**
See   Clarke, Mary Bayard
Devereux

**Tenenbaum, Joseph** 1887-   [NAA]
*Polish-born physician and author*
* Bendow, Josef

**Tener, Martin J.** 1935-   [ASC]
*American composer, author,
educator*
* Martins, Jay

**Teneyck, Edward**   [PA]
*Author*
* Ed

**Teng Hsiao-ping [Little Peace]**
See   Kan Tse-kao

**Tengberg, Violet** 1920-   [ART]
*Swedish artist*
* V. T.

**Teniers, David** 1582-1649   [WBD]
*Flemish painter*
* [The] Elder

**Teniers, David** 1610-1690   [WBD]
*Flemish painter*
* [The] Younger

**[The] Teniers of Comedy**
See   Dancourt, Florent Carton

**Tenn, William**
See   Klass, Philip

**Tennant, Catherine**
See   Crozier, Kathleen Muriel
[Eyles]

**Tennant, Emma** 1937-   [ESF]
*British author and editor*
* Aydy, Catherine

**Tennant, Kylie**
See   Rodd, Kylie Tennant

**Tennant, Nora Jackson** 1915-   [CA]
*British educator and author*
* Jackson, Nora

**Tennenbaum, Irving** 1903-
[IPA, LC, TC]
*American author*
* Stone, Irving

**Tennent, [Sir] James Emerson** 1804-
?   [PA]
*Author*
* Emerson

**Tenneshaw, S. M.** [joint pseudonym
with Robert Silverberg] [house
pseudonym, Ziff-Davis]
See   Garrett, [Gordon] Randall
[Philip David]

**Tenneshaw, S. M.** [house pseudonym,
Ziff-Davis]
See   Geier, Chester S.

**Tenneshaw, S. M.** [house pseudonym,
Ziff-Davis]
See   Hamilton, Edmond [Moore]

**Tenneshaw, S. M.** [house pseudonym,
Ziff-Davis]
See   Lesser, Milton

**Tenneshaw, S. M.** [house
pseudonym]
See   Nutt, Charles

**Tenneshaw, S. M.** [joint pseudonym
with Randall Garrett] [house
pseudonym, Ziff-Davis]
See   Silverberg, Robert

**Tenness, George**
See   Delk, Robert Carlton

**Tennesse Ernie Ford**
See   Ford, Ernest Jennings

**Tennessee Gabriel**
See   McGhee, Walter Brown

**[The] Tennessee Plowboy**
See   Arnold, Richard Edward
[Eddy]

**[The] Tennessee Tailor**
See   Johnson, Andrew

**[The] Tennessee Terror**
See   Hickman, Herman M., Jr.

**Tennille**
See   Tennille, Toni

**Tennille, Toni**
*American singer*
* Tennille

**[The] Tennis Ball of Fortune**
See   Pertinax, Publius Helvius

**Tennis, Mr.**
See   Jones, Perry

**Tennov, Dorothy**
See   Tennow, Dorothy

**Tennow, Dorothy** 1928-   [CA]
*American psychologist and author*
* Hoffman, D. T.
* Tennov, Dorothy

**Tennyson, Alfred [First Baron
Tennyson]** 1809-1892
[DEL, DEP, FFF]
*British poet*
* Alcibiades
* [The] Bard of Arthurian
   Romance
* [The] English Virgil
* Merlin
* [The] Poet of Haslemere

**Tennyson, Harold Alfred** 1918-
[MY]
*American jazz musician*
* Tennyson, Tenny

**Tennyson, Joe** ?-1926   [BMH]
*British comedian*
* Devine

**Tennyson, Tenny**
See   Tennyson, Harold Alfred

**Tenocarus**
See   Snouckaert, William

**Tenpin Boy**
See   Smith, Francis Shubael

**[The] Tenpin Tattler**
See   Weinstein, Sam

**Tenskwatawa**
See   Lalawethika

**Tent, Ned**
See   Dennett, Herbert Victor

**[The] Tenth Muse**
See   Bradstreet, Anne

**[The] Tenth Muse**
See   Christina

**[The] Tenth Muse**
See   De Gournay, Marie Lejars

**[The] Tenth Muse**
See   De La Cruz, Juana Ines

[The] Tenth Muse
See Deshoulieres, Antoinette du Ligier de la Garde

[The] Tenth Muse
See Gay, Delphine

[The] Tenth Muse
See Margaret [or Marguerite] of Navarre

[The] Tenth Muse
See Sappho

[The] Tenth Muse
See Scuderi, Magdalen [or Madeleine] de

Teodomofilo
See Cardenas y Rodriguez, Nicolas

Teodorescu, Ion N. 1880-1967
[EWL, TCL]
Rumanian poet and author
* Arghezi, Tudor

Teofilus
See Loennquist, Carl Adolph

Tepper, M. B.
See Tepper, Matthew Bruce

Tepper, Matthew Bruce 1953-
[SFL]
American composer and writer
* Tepper, M. B.

Tepperman, Emile 20th c.
[SFL, SFP]
Author
* Robeson, Kenneth [house pseudonym, Street & Smith]
* Steele, Curtis
* Stockbridge, Grant [house pseudonym]

Ter Balkt, Herman Hendrik 1938-
[IAW]
Dutch author
* Aos, Foel
* De Balker, Habakuk, II

Terada, Torahiko 1878- ? [LAO]
Japanese physicist and writer
* Yosimura, Huyukiko

Teramond, Edmond Gautier de 1869-1957 [SFL]
Author
* Teramond, Guy de

Teramond, Guy de
See Teramond, Edmond Gautier de

Terek, A.
See Fors, Olga Dmitrievna

[The] Terence of England
See Cumberland, Richard

Teresa, [Mother]
See Bojaxhiu, Agnes Gonxha

Teresa, Big Vinnie
See Teresa, Vincent

Teresa Margaret, [Sister]
See Rowe, Margaret [Kevin]

Teresa, Vincent 20th c.
American underworld figure
* Teresa, Big Vinnie

Terhune, Mary Virginia [Hawes] 1835?-1922 [DNNF, FFF, WBD]
American author
* Harland, Marion

Terhune, Virginia Belle
See Van De Water, Virginia Belle Terhune

Terlecki, Robert Joseph 1945-
[SMG]
American baseball player
* Terlecki, Terk

Terlecki, Terk
See Terlecki, Robert Joseph

Terme, Hilary
See Hay, Jacob

Termen, Leon 1896- [BBD]
Russian inventor
* Theremin, Leon

Ternaux, Mademoiselle
See Noel, Victoire

Terni, Fausta Cialente 1900- [CA]
Italian author
* Cialente, Fausta

Tero, Lawrence
American actor and bodyguard
* Mr. T.

Terpander 7th c. BC
[DEP, DNNS, FFF]
Greek musician and poet
* [The] Father of Greek Music

Terrail, Pierre du 1476-1524
[DNNF, DNNS, SN]
French hero
* Bayard, Seigneur de
* [Le] Chevalier Sans Peur et Sans Reproche
* [The] Flower of Chivalry
* [The] Good Knight Without Fear and Without Reproach

Terrall, Robert 1914- [CA]
American author
* Gonzales, John
* Halliday, Brett
* Kyle, Robert
* Roberts, MacLennan

Terranova, Ciro 1891-1938
[BLB, PHM]
Italian-born American underworld figure
* [The] Artichoke King

Terranova, Dino
See Vacirca, Corrado

[The] Terre Haute Terror
See Taylor, Charles B.

Terrell, St. John
See Eccles, George Clinton

Terrell, Saunders 1911- [BWW]
American singer
* Sonny T
* Terry, Sanders
* Terry, Sonny

Terrell, Tammi
See Montgomery, Thomasina

Terremoto [Big Earthquake]
See Pertinez, Zoilo

Terremoto de Malaga [Earthquake from Malaga]
See Martin Ramos, Baldomero

[The] Terrible
See Ivan IV Vasilievich

[The] Terrible
See Touhy, Roger

[The] Terrible Cornet of Horse
See Pitt, William [Earl of Chatham]

[The] Terrible Doctor Elsbeth
See Schragmueller, Elsbeth

Terrible Ted Lindsay
See Lindsay, Robert Blake Theodore [Ted]

Terrible Ted Turner
See Turner, Robert Edward, III

Terrible Ted Williams
See Williams, Theodore Samuel [Ted]

Terrible Teddy Tetzlaff
See Tetzlaff, Teddy

Terrible Terry McGovern
See McGovern, John Terrence

Terrible Tommy Bolt
See Bolt, Tommy

Terrible Tommy O'Connor
See O'Connor, Thomas

Terrible Tommy Touhy
See Touhy, Tommy

Terridge, Ernest
See Richter, Ernst H.

Terrific, Tom
See Seaver, George Thomas [Tom]

Terris, Norma
See Allison, Norma

Terris, Sid 1904- [EJS]
American boxer
* [The] Ghost of the Ghetto

Terriss, Dorothy
See Morse, Theodora

Terriss, Ellaline
See Lewin, Ellaline

Terriss, William
See Lewin, Arthur

[The] Terror
See Cline, Donald Biff

[The] Terror
See Johnson, Daniel

[The] Terror of France
See Talbot, John

[The] Terror of the Faithless
See Robert I

[The] Terror of the Faithless
See Robert II

[The] Terror of the Faithless
See Roger I

[The] Terror of the Greeks
See Michieli [or Micheli], Dominico

[The] Terror of the Infield
See Dakoske, Edwin P.

[The] Terror of the World
See Attila

Terry
See Duncan, Terence Edward

Terry
See Maloney, Francis [Joseph] T[erence]

Terry, Adonis
See Terry, William J.

Terry, Al
See Theriot, Allison Joseph

Terry, Alice
See Taafe, Alice Frances

Terry, Buddy
See Terry, Eldin

Terry, C. V.
See Slaughter, Frank G[ill]

Terry, Carol
See Talbot, Carol Terry

Terry, Clarence Agee 20th c.
[IBW]
American football player
* Terry, Terrible

Terry, Dan
See Kostraba, Daniel

Terry, Dennis 1895-1932 [THR]
British actor, theatrical manager, producer
* Neilson-Terry, Dennis

Terry, Doc
See Adail, Terry

Terry, Don
See Locher, Donald

Terry, Edward Gordon 1872-1966
[LC]
British producer, director, stage designer
* Craig, Gordon

Terry, Eldin 1941- [IBW]
American jazz musician
* Terry, Buddy

Terry, Hazel
See Neilson-Terry, Hazel

Terry, Henry Machu
See Imbert-Terry, [Sir] Henry Machu

Terry, Memphis Bill
See Terry, William Harold

Terry, Noel
See Wood-Smith, Noel

Terry, Olive
See Morris, Olive

Terry, Phyllis 1892- [THR]
British actress
* Neilson-Terry, Phyllis

Terry, Ron
See Pritkin, Ron

Terry, Rose
See Cooke, Rose Terry

Terry, Sanders
See Terrell, Saunders

Terry, Saralee
See Kaye, Marvin [Nathan]

Terry, Sheila
See Clark, Kay

Terry, Sonny
See Terrell, Saunders

Terry, Terrible
See Terry, Clarence Agee

Terry the Blue-Eyed Irish Boy
See Casey, James

Terry Thomas
See Hoar-Stevens, Thomas Terry

**Terry, William**
See Harknett, Terry

**Terry, William Harold** 1898-    [BE]
*American baseball player and manager*
* Terry, Memphis Bill

**Terry, William J.** 1864-1915
[AS, NLG, PB]
*American baseball player*
* [The] Silver Fox
* Terry, Adonis

**Terry, Zeb**
See Terry, Zebulon Alexander

**Terry, Zebulon Alexander** 1891-
[BE]
*American baseball player*
* Terry, Zeb

**Terry-Lewis, Mabel**
See Lewis, Mabel

**Terson, Peter**
See Patterson, Peter

**Terstegge, Mabel Alice** 1905-    [CA]
*American author and educator*
* Georgiana, [Sister]

**Tertz, Abram**
See Siniavskii, Andrei Donatovich

**Terwagne, Anne Joseph** 1762-1817
[DNNS, WBD]
*Heroine of the French Revolution*
* [The] Amazon of Liberty
* [The] Amazon of the Revolution
* [La] Belle Liegeoise
* [The] Fury of the Gironde
* Theroigne de Mericourt

**Terwilliger, Twig**
See Terwilliger, Willard Wayne

**Terwilliger, Willard Wayne** 1925-
[BE]
*American baseball player*
* Terwilliger, Twig

**Terzian, Kathryn**
See Cramer, Kathryn

**Tesch, Al[bert John]** 1891-1947
[BE]
*American baseball player*
* Tesch, Tiny

**Tesch, Tiny**
See Tesch, Al[bert John]

**Teshigahara, Sofu** 1901?-
*Japanese flower arranger*
* [The] Picasso of Flowers

**Teshome, Alem** 1952?-    [IBW]
*Ethiopian actress and producer*
* Teshome, Ali

**Teshome, Ali**
See Teshome, Alem

**Tesone, William N.** 1927-    [ASC]
*American composer and singer*
* Duke, Billy

**Tesreau, Charles Monroe**
1889-1946    [AS, BN, PB]
*American baseball player*
* [The] Ozark Bear
* Tesreau, Jeff

**Tesreau, Jeff**
See Tesreau, Charles Monroe

**Tessier, Ernest Maurice**
1885-1973    [CC, LC]
*French author*
* Dekobra, Maurice

**Tessimond, A. S. J.**
See Tessimond, Arthur Seymour John

**Tessimond, Arthur Seymour John**
?-1962    [LC]
*British poet*
* Tessimond, A. S. J.

**Testerman, Don** 1952-    [SMG]
*American football player*
* Testerman, Hi Test

**Testerman, Hi Test**
See Testerman, Don

**Testis**
See Blondel, Maurice

**Testis?**
See Francis, [Sir] Philip

**Teswod**
See Dowsett, Joseph Morewood

**Tete Bottee**
See Comines [or Commines], Philippe de

**Teternikov, Fyodor Kuzmich**
1863-1927    [CD, EWL]
*Russian poet and author*
* Sologub, Fyodor

**Tetley, Mrs. William**    [FFF]
*Entertainer*
* Cushman, Josephine

**Tetsu**
See Yamauchi, Tetsu

**Tettelbach, Richard Morley [Dick]**
1929-    [BE]
*American baseball player*
* Tettelbach, Tut

**Tettelbach, Tut**
See Tettelbach, Richard Morley [Dick]

**Tettemer, John Moynihan**
1876-1949    [B10]
*American monk*
* Ildefonso, [Father]

**Tetzel, John [or Johann]**
1465?-1519    [PA, SN]
*German monk*
* [A] Holy Autolycus
* Texelius

**Tetzlaff, Teddy** 20th c.
*Auto racer*
* Tetzlaff, Terrible Teddy

**Tetzlaff, Terrible Teddy**
See Tetzlaff, Teddy

**Tetzner, Martha Helene** 1872- ?
[LAO]
*German author*
* Von Einsiedel, R.

**Tetzner, Ruth** 1917-    [IAW]
*German author*
* Hallard, Ruth

**Teufelsdroeckh, Herr**
See Carlyle, Thomas

**Teutha**
See Jerdau, William

**[The] Teutonic Theosopher**
See Boehme, Jacob

**Tewksbury**
See Ray, William Porter

**Tex, Joe**
See Arrington, Joseph, Jr.

**Texas Dolly Brunson**
See Brunson, Doyle

**[The] Texas Drifter**
See Reeves, Goebel

**Texas Guitar Slim**
See Winter, Johnny

**Texas Jack**
See Reed, Nathaniel

**Texas Jack Kraus**
See Kraus, John William

**Texas Jim Robertson**
See Robertson, James B.

**Texas Johnny Moss**
See Moss, John

**[The] Texas Kid**
See Knuckles, Grafton

**[The] Texas Nightingale**
See Barnes, Fae

**[The] Texas Nightingale**
See Wallace, Beulah Thomas

**Texas Ranger**
See Wallace, John

**[The] Texas Rattlesnake**
See Barrow, Clyde

**Texas Ruby**
See Owens, Ruby

**Texas Slim**
See Hooker, John Lee

**[The] Texas Terror**
See Shafer, Phil

**Texas Tessie**
See Douglas, Lizzie

**Texas Tommy**
See Dorsey, Thomas A[ndrew]

**[The] Texas Tornado**
See DeBakey, Michael

**[The] Texas Tornado**
See Foyt, Anthony Joseph, Jr.

**[The] Texas Wonder**
See Hoffman, Frank J.

**Texelius**
See Tetzel, John [or Johann]

**Texier, Edward**    [PA]
*Author*
* Kel-Kun
* Schop, Le Baron

**Textor, George Bernhardt**
1888-1954    [BE]
*American baseball player*
* Textor, Tex

**Textor, Tex**
See Textor, George Bernhardt

**Textu**
See Duprey de la Ruffiniere, Pierre

**Tey, Josephine**
See Mackintosh, Elizabeth

**Teyte, Maggie**
See Tate, Margaret

**Thacker, Moe**
See Thacker, Morris Benton

**Thacker, Morris Benton** 1934-
[BE]
*American baseball player*
* Thacker, Moe

**Thackeray, William Makepeace**
1811-1863    [DEL, SAT, WBD]
*British author*
* Brown, Mr.
* Clarence, Fitzroy
* [The] Fat Contributor
* Fitzboodle, George
* Jeames
* Pendennis, Arthur, Esquire
* Solomons, Ikey, Jun.
* Titmarsh, M. A.
* Titmarsh, Michael Angelo
* Wagstaff, Theophile
* Yellowplush, Charles James

**Thakazhi**
See Sivasankara Pillai, Thakazhi

**Thakura, Ravindranatha**
1861-1941    [EWL]
*Indian poet, playwright, author*
* Tagore, Rabindranath

**Thalberg, Sigismund** 1812-1871
[FFF]
*Swiss-born musician and composer*
* [The] Attila of the Piano

**Thalberg, T. B.**
See Corbett, Thalberg

**Thaler, M. N.**
See Kerner, Fred

**Thaler, Susan** 1939-    [CA]
*American author*
* Schlachter, Susan

**Thames, C[hristopher] H.**
See Lesser, Milton

**Thames, Jack**
See Ryan, John Fergus

**Thane, Elswyth**
See Ricker, Elswyth Thane

**Thane, Francois**
See Hennesy, James Albert

**Thanelian**
See Coffin, N. W.

**Thanet, Neil**
See Fanthorpe, R[obert] Lionel

**Thanet, Octave**
See French, Alice

**[The] Thanhouser Kid**
See Eline, Marie

**[The] Thanhouser Kidlet**
See Badgley, Helen

**Thanie, C. G.**    [FFF]
*American writer*
* Clyde, Kate

**Thanold, Woofer**
See Sidebottom, Arnold [Arnie]

**Tharaud, Lucien Rostaing, Jr.**
1953-    [CA]
*American poet*
* Tharaud, Ross

**Tharaud, Ross**
See Tharaud, Lucien Rostaing, Jr.

**Tharp, Corky**
See Tharp, Tom

**Tharp, Tom** 20th c. [SMG]
*American football player*
* Tharp, Corky

**Tharpe, [Sister] Rosetta**
See Nubin, Rosetta

**That Fox**
See Antipas

**That Jesuit**
See Penn, William

**That Limping Old Bard**
See Denham, [Sir] John

**That Man in the White House**
See Roosevelt, Franklin Delano

**That Wolf of France**
See Louis XIV

**Thatcher, Amelia**
See Miner, Virginia Scott

**Thatcher, Eva**
See Thatcher, Evelyn

**Thatcher, Evelyn** 1862-1942 [SC]
*American actress*
* [The] Irish Lady
* Thatcher, Eva

**Thatcher, John Wells** 1856- ?
[LAO]
*British barrister and author*
* Pauper et Ignotus
* Rambler

**Thatcher, Margaret Hilda [Roberts]**
1925- [NN, SC]
*British prime minister*
* Attila the Hen
* [The] Cold War Witch
* [The] Grocer's Daughter
* [The] Iron Lady of British
Politics
* [The] Iron Maiden
* [The] Milk Snatcher
* Mrs. T
* Thatcher, Mighty Maggie
* TINA [There is No Alternative]

**Thatcher, Mighty Maggie**
See Thatcher, Margaret Hilda
[Roberts]

**Thaumaturgus**
See Alexander Leopold

**Thaumaturgus**
See Apollonius of Tyana

**Thaumaturgus**
See Bernardone, Giovanni
Francesco

**Thaumaturgus**
See Gassner, Johann Joseph

**Thaumaturgus**
See Gregory of Neocaesarea

**Thaumaturgus**
See Isidore of Alexandria

**Thaumaturgus**
See Jamblichus

**Thaumaturgus**
See Mohammed [or Mahomet]

**Thaumaturgus**
See Pascal, Blaise

**Thaumaturgus**
See Peter

**Thaumaturgus**
See Plotinus

**Thaumaturgus**
See Proclus

**Thaumaturgus**
See Vespasian, Titus Flavius
Sabinus

**Thaumaturgus**
See Vincent de Paul

**[The] Thaumaturgus of His Age**
See De Bulhoes, Fernando

**[The] Thaumaturgus of the West**
See Bernard of Clairvaux

**Thaw, Evelyn Nesbit** 1885-1967
[SC]
*American actress*
* [The] Girl in the Red Velvet
Swing

**Thayendanegea** 1742-1807 [WBD]
*American Indian chieftain*
* Brant, Joseph

**Thayer, Alexander Wheelock**
1817-1897 [FFF]
*American author and diplomat*
* Diarist
* [A] Quiet Man

**Thayer, Charles** [SMG]
*Hockey team trainer*
* Thayer, Skip

**Thayer, Emma R[edington] Lee**
1874-1973 [CAP, EMD, NAA]
*American author and artist*
* Thayer, Lee

**Thayer, Frederick C[lifton], Jr.**
1924- [CA]
*American author*
* Walker, Jack

**Thayer, Geraldine**
See Daniels, Dorothy

**Thayer, Jane**
See Woolley, Catherine

**Thayer, Lee**
See Thayer, Emma R[edington]
Lee

**Thayer, Peter**
See Ames, Rose Wyler

**Thayer, Skip**
See Thayer, Charles

**Thayer, Sylvanus** 1785-1872
[WBD]
*American army officer and educator*
* [The] Father of the Military
Academy

**Thayer, Tiffany Ellsworth** 1902-
[TC, WW]
*American author*
* Doe, John
* Ellsworth, Elmer, Jr.

**Thayer, William Roscoe**
1859-1923 [FFF]
*American author*
* Hermes, Paul

**Thearcher**
See Hodgson, William Archer

**Theard, Harry L., Jr.** 1939- [OP]
*American opera singer*
* Theyard, Harry

**Theard, Sam** 20th c. [IBW]
*American songwriter, dancer,
comedian*
* Spo-Dee-O-Dee

**Theates**
See Weintraub, Wiktor

**[The] Theban Bard**
See Pindar

**[The] Theban Eagle**
See Pindar

**[The] Theban Lyre**
See Pindar

**Thede, Marion Draughon** 1903-
[CAP]
*American archivist and author*
* Unger, Marion

**Thee, Marek** 1918- [CA]
*Polish-born author*
* Gdanski, Marek

**Theimer, Joseph Michael**
1923-1955 [EJ]
*American jazz musician*
* Timer, Joe

**Theiner, George** 1927- [CA]
*Czech-born author*
* George, Jonathan [joint
pseudonym with John (Frederick)
Burke]

**Thekla**
See Mason, Caroline M.

**Thelwall, Citizen**
See Thelwall, John

**Thelwall, John** 1764-1834 [SN]
*British author and political reformer*
* Thelwall, Citizen

**Themaninthemoon**
See Eagles, John

**[The] Themistocles of Modern Greece**
See Kanaris, Constantine

**Thenon, Georges** ?-1941 [BEW]
*Author*
* Thenon, Rip

**Thenon, Rip**
See Thenon, Georges

**Theobald**
See Lovecraft, Howard Phillips

**Theobald, Alfred Herbert**
See Tubby, Alfred Herbert

**Theobald, Lewis, Jr.**
See Lovecraft, Howard Phillips

**Theobald, Ron[ald M.]** 1943- [PB]
*American baseball player*
* [The] Little General

**Theobald [or Tybald], Simon**
?-1381 [WBD]
*British prelate*
* Simon of Sudbury

**Theobaldus**
See Lovecraft, Howard Phillips

**Theodamus**
See Glass, Theodore

**Theodore**
See Kasa [or Kassa]

**Theodoric** 454- 526
[DNNS, FFF, WBD]
*King of the Ostrogoths*
* Dietrich von Bern [Theodoric of
Verona]
* [The] Great

**Theodoros**
See Papadimitriou, Theodoros

**Theodorus**
See Aristides [or Aristeides],
Publius Aelius

**Theodorus Philalethes**
See Maule, Thomas

**Theodosius I** 346- 395
[DNNS, FFF, SN]
*Roman emperor*
* [The] Great

**Theodosius II** 401- 450 [DNNS]
*Byzantine emperor*
* [The] Calligrapher

**[The] Theologian**
See Gregory of Nazianzus

**[The] Theologian**
See Isidore of Seville

**Theologicus, Doctor**
See Clemenges, Matthieu Nicholas
de

**Theologus**
See Gregory of Nazianzus

**Theophanes** 758?- 818 [WBD]
*Saint*
* [The] Confessor

**Theophile**
See Mandar, Michael Phillips

**Theophilus Secundus**
See Wilberforce, Robert Isaac

**Theophorus**
See Ignatius

**Theophrastos**
See Tyrtamos

**[The] Theophrastus of France**
See La Bruyere, Jean de

**Theophylactus** ?-1024 [CAL]
*Pope*
* Benedict VIII

**Theophylactus** 11th c. [CAL]
*Pope*
* Benedict IX

**Theoria**
See Starkey, Digley Pilot

**Theos [The Divine]**
See Antiochus II

**Theos**
See Antiochus VI

**Theosopho**
See Ouseley, Gideon Jasper
Richard

**Theotine**
See Bayle, Marc Antoine

**Theotokopoulos, Domenikos**
1548?-1614? [WBD]
*Greek-born Spanish painter*
* [El] Greco

**Theremin, Leon**
See Termen, Leon

**Therese de Lisieux**
See Martin, Therese

**Theriot, Allison Joseph** 1922-
[CWG]
*American country-western performer*
* Terry, Al

**Theroigne de Mericourt**
See Terwagne, Anne Joseph

**Thesenga, Arnold Joseph** 1914-
[BE]
*American baseball player*
* Thesenga, Jug

**Thesenga, Jug**
*See* Thesenga, Arnold Joseph

**Thespis** 6th c. BC [FFF, RH, SN]
*Greek poet*
* [The] Father of Greek Tragedy
* [The] Father of the Greek Drama
* [The] Richardson of Athens

**Theta**
*See* Thorne, William

**Theuerdank [Dear Thanks]**
*See* Maximilian I

**Thevenin, Denis**
*See* Duhamel, Georges

**Theyard, Harry**
*See* Theard, Harry L., Jr.

**T'Hezan, Arlette C.** 1934- [OP]
*French opera singer*
* T'Hezan, Helia

**T'Hezan, Helia**
*See* T'Hezan, Arlette C.

**Thiard, Pontus de** 1521-1605
[DNNS, FFF, SN]
*French poet*
* [The] Anacreon of France
* [The] French Anacreon

**Thibault, Jacques-Anatole-Francois**
1844-1924 [EWL, IPA, LC]
*French author, poet, critic*
* France, Anatole

**Thibaut IV** 1210?-1253 [HN, SN]
*Count of Champagne and King of
Navarre*
* [The] Father of French Poetry

**Thibeaux, Acklin** 1941- [IBW]
*American sociologist*
* Thibeaux, T-Bone

**Thibeaux, T-Bone**
*See* Thibeaux, Acklin

**Thieblin, Napoleon [or Nicolas?]**
Leon ?-1888 [FFF, PA, RH]
*British journalist and author*
* Azamat Batuk
* Rigolo

**[The] Thief**
*See* Capuzzi, Nick

**Thiele, Wilhelm** 1890- [FD]
*Austrian director*
* Thiele, William

**Thiele, William**
*See* Thiele, Wilhelm

**Thielemans, Jean** 1922- [EJ, PMJ]
*Belgian-born jazz musician*
* Thielemans, Toots

**Thielemans, Toots**
*See* Thielemans, Jean

**Thielhelm, Emil** 1950- [RO2]
*American musician*
* Thielhelm, Peppy

**Thielhelm, Peppy**
*See* Thielhelm, Emil

**Thielman, Jack**
*See* Thielman, John Peter

**Thielman, John Peter** 1879-1928
[BE]
*American baseball player*
* Thielman, Jack

**[Der] Thier Wolff**
*See* Wolff, Wilhelm

**Thiers, Louis Adolphe** 1797-1877
[HN]
*French historian*
* Attila le Petit
* Boum, General
* Cameleon
* [Le] Roi des Versailles
* Tamerlan a Lunettes

**Thiery, Herman** 1912- [EWL]
*Belgian poet, author, critic*
* Daisne, Johan

**Thies, Jake**
*See* Thies, Vernon Arthur

**Thies, Vernon Arthur** 1926- [BE]
*American baseball player*
* Thies, Jake

**Thimblethorpe, Ilena** 1916- [THR]
*British actress*
* Sylva, Ilena

**Thimblethorpe, June Sylvia** 1926-
[AW]
*British author*
* Thorpe, Sylvia

**Thimmesch, Nicholas Palen [Nick]**
1927- [CA, IAW]
*American author*
* Nicholas, William [joint
pseudonym with William O.
Johnson]

**[The] Thin Man**
*See* Strahler, Michael Wayne

**Thin Man Watts**
*See* Watts, Noble

**[The] Thing**
*See* Thomas, Lafayette Jerl

**[The] Thinking Silent General**
*See* Monk, George [Duke of
Albemarle]

**Thiong'o, Ngugi wa**
*See* Ngugi, James T[hiong'o]

**[The] Third Elias**
*See* Luther, Martin

**[The] Third Founder of Rome**
*See* Marius, Caius

**Third Round Diegel**
*See* Diegel, Leo

**Thirlmere, Rowland**
*See* Walker, John

**Thirlwell, George** 1902- [BEW]
*British actor*
* Turner, George

**[The] Thirteen Inch Shell**
*See* Bezdek, Hugo F.

**[The] Thirteenth Apostle**
*See* John

**31 Knot Burke**
*See* Burke, Arleigh

**This Mud Born Bubble**
*See* Harvey, Gabriel

**This Phoenix Among Kings**
*See* Frederick II

**This Ropemaker**
*See* Harvey, Gabriel

**Thistle, Donald**
*See* Brown, H. Clark

**Thistle, Mel[ville William]** 1914-
[CA]
*Canadian author*
* Bohr, Theophilus

**Thistle, Timothy**
*See* Ellsworth, O.

**Thiusen, Ismar**
*See* Macnie, John

**Thoene, Peter**
*See* Bihalji-Merin, Oto

**Thoeny, John** 1880-1948 [BE]
*American baseball player*
* Thoney, Bullet Jack
* Thoney, John

**Thole, Carolus Adrianus Maria**
1914- [ESF]
*Dutch-born illustrator*
* Thole, Karel

**Thole, Karel**
*See* Thole, Carolus Adrianus
Maria

**Thom, Robert**
*See* Flatow, Robert

**Thom, William** 1799-1850
[DNNS, RH]
*Scottish poet*
* [The] Weaver Poet of Inverurie

**Thoma, Frank** 1896- [BBH]
*American bowler*
* Thoma, Sykes

**Thoma, Ludwig** 1867-1921 [WBD]
*German journalist and author*
* Schlemihl, Peter

**Thoma, Sykes**
*See* Thoma, Frank

**Thomas** 19th c. [DHA]
*Duke of Genoa*
* Salchichon [The Sausage]

**Thomas, Alf** 20th c. [BMH]
*British comedian*
* Mrs. Thomas's Favourite
Husband

**Thomas, Alfred** 1870- ? [LAO]
*Welsh clergyman and author*
* Gwalia, Alfred

**Thomas, Alonzo** 20th c. [SMG]
*American football player*
* Thomas, Skip

**Thomas, Alphonse** 1899- [BE, PB]
*American baseball player*
* Thomas, Tommy

**Thomas, Amos Leon, Jr.** 1937-
[EJ7]
*American jazz musician*
* Thomas, Leone

**Thomas, Andrea**
*See* Hill, Margaret [Ohler]

**Thomas, Annie**
*See* Cudlip, Annie Thomas

**Thomas, Anthony**
*See* Poole, Reginald Heber

**Thomas, Augustus** 1857-1934
[MWD]
*American playwright*
* [The] Dean of American
Playwrights

**Thomas, B. J.**
*See* Thomas, Billy Joe

**Thomas, Baby Face**
*See* Thomas, Jesse

**Thomas, Billy Joe** 1942-
[PRS, RO2]
*American singer*
* Thomas, B. J.

**Thomas, Blanche** 1922-1977
[BWW]
*American singer*
* [The] Queen of the Blues

**Thomas, Boosey** [PA]
*Author*
* [An] Old Angler and Bibliopole

**Thomas, Bud**
*See* Thomas, John Tillman

**Thomas, Bud**
*See* Thomas, Luther Baxter

**Thomas, Cairo**
*See* Thomas, James

**Thomas, Carl H.**
*See* Doerffler, Alfred

**Thomas, Carla** 1942-
[BWW, IBW, SSS]
*American singer*
* [The] Queen of the Memphis
Sound

**Thomas, Carolyn**
*See* Duncan, Actea

**Thomas, Charles** 1900?- [NOJ]
*American jazz musician*
* Ollie Papa

**Thomas, Charles** 1918- [BB]
*American basketball player*
* Thomas, Red

**Thomas, Charles** 1925- [BWW]
*American singer*
* Davis, James [Jimmy]
* Maxwell Street Jimmy

**Thomas, Chester David** 1888-1953
[BE]
*American baseball player*
* Thomas, Pinch

**Thomas, Clarence Franklin**
1903-1952 [BE]
*American baseball player*
* Thomas, Lefty

**Thomas, Claude Alfred** 1890-1946
[BE]
*American baseball player*
* Thomas, Lefty

**Thomas, Cornelius Dickinson**
1920-1972 [CAP]
*American author*
* T. N. T.
* Thomas, Neal

**Thomas, Cotton**
*See* Jaxon, Frankie

**Thomas, Curtis** 20th c. [WW]
*Author*
* Kinney, Thomas

**Thomas, Dan**
*See* Sanders, Leonard

**Thomas, Daniel B.**
*See* Bluestein, Daniel Thomas

**Thomas, Danny**
*See* Jacobs, Amos

**Thomas, David** 1904-   [MK]
*American baseball player*
\* Thomas, Showboat

**Thomas, David John** 1959-   [DC]
*British cricketer*
\* Thomas, Teddy

**Thomas, Dennis** 20th c.   [RO2]
*American musician*
\* Dee Tee

**Thomas, Doris**
*See* Vancel, Doris

**Thomas, [Philip] Edward**
1878-1917   [LC]
*British author*
\* Eastaway, Edward

**Thomas, Edward** 1941-   [ECM]
*American country-western performer*
\* Rabbitt, Eddie

**Thomas, Elizabeth** 1675-1730
[SN]
*British author and poet*
\* Corinna

**Thomas, Elton**
*See* Ulman, Douglas Elton

**Thomas, Ernest Lewis** 1904-   [DLE]
*Welsh author*
\* Vaughn, Richard

**Thomas, Eugene** 1894-   [WW]
*Author*
\* Grey, Donald

**Thomas, Fannie Crawford** 1923-
[IBW]
*American singer and musician*
\* Thomas, Frantic Fay

**Thomas, Fathead**
*See* Thomas, George

**Thomas, Fay Wesley** 1904-   [BE]
*American baseball player*
\* Thomas, Scow

**Thomas, Foots**
*See* Thomas, Walter Purl

**Thomas, Forrest** 1881- ?   [BE]
*American baseball player*
\* Thomas, Frosty

**Thomas, Frantic Fay**
*See* Thomas, Fannie Crawford

**Thomas, Frederick Hall** 1886-1927
[BX, RBE, WBC]
*Welsh-born boxer*
\* [The] Pride of Pontypridd
\* Welsh, Freddy
\* [The] Welsh Wizard

**Thomas, Frosty**
*See* Thomas, Forrest

**Thomas, G. K.**
*See* Davies, Leslie Purnell

**Thomas, Gary** 20th c.   [RBE]
*American boxer*
\* Thomas, Tiger

**Thomas, Gary Philip** 1958-   [DC]
*British cricketer*
\* Thomas, Tight Lines

**Thomas, George** ?-1930   [WWJ]
*American jazz musician*
\* Thomas, Fathead

**Thomas, George Henry** 1816-1870
[DNNS, FFF, SN]
*American army officer*
\* Old Reliable
\* [The] Rock of Chickamauga
\* Slow Trot
\* Thomas, Pap
\* Washington, George

**Thomas, Gordon** 1933-   [CA]
*British author and editor*
\* Gordon, Tom
\* Street, Robert

**Thomas, H. C.**
*See* Keating, Lawrence A.

**Thomas, Harlan C.**
*See* Hale, William Harlan

**Thomas, Harold Alexander** 1941-
[IBW]
*American artist*
\* Olugebefola, Ademola?

**Thomas, Henry**
*See* Johnson, Leslie

**Thomas, Henry**
*See* Schnittkind, Henry Thomas

**Thomas, Henry**
*See* Townsend, Henry

**Thomas, Henry** 1874- ?   [BWW]
*American singer*
\* Thomas, Ragtime Texas

**Thomas, Isaiah** 1750-1831   [SN]
*American printer*
\* [The] Didot of America

**Thomas, Ivor**
*See* Bulmer-Thomas, Ivor

**Thomas, J. Bissell**
*See* Stephen, Joyce Alice

**Thomas, J. F.**
*See* Fleming, Thomas J[ames]

**Thomas, Jack** 20th c.   [SFL]
*Author*
\* Oram, John

**Thomas, James** 1926-   [BWW]
*American singer*
\* Thomas, Cairo
\* Thomas, Son
\* Thomas, Sonny Ford

**Thomas, James Leroy** 1936-   [BE]
*American baseball player*
\* Thomas, Lee

**Thomas, Jeannette Grise** 1935-
[CA]
*American author*
\* Grise, Jeannette

**Thomas, Jesse** 20th c.   [BWW]
*American musician*
\* Thomas, Baby Face

**Thomas, Jim**
*See* Reagan, Thomas [James]
B[utler]

**Thomas, Joan Gale**
*See* Robinson, Joan [Mary] G[ale
Thomas]

**Thomas, Joe**
*See* Daly, Joseph

**Thomas, Joe** 1902-   [NOJ]
*American jazz musician*
\* Brother Cornbread

**Thomas, John Peter** 1928-   [CA]
*American author*
\* Thomas, Piri

**Thomas, John Tillman** 1929-   [BE]
*American baseball player*
\* Thomas, Bud

**Thomas, Josephine**
*See* Henderson, Rosa [Rose]

**Thomas, Joshua**   [FFF]
*American clergyman*
\* [The] Parson of the Islands

**Thomas, K.**
*See* Fearn, John Russell

**Thomas, K. H.**
*See* Kirk, Thomas Hobson

**Thomas, Keith Marshall** 1924-
[BE]
*American baseball player*
\* Thomas, Kite

**Thomas, Kid**
*See* Valentine, Thomas

**Thomas, Kid**
*See* Watts, Lou[is Thomas]

**Thomas, Kite**
*See* Thomas, Keith Marshall

**Thomas, Lafayette Jerl** 1928-1977
[BWW]
*American singer*
\* [The] Thing

**Thomas, Lawrence Buckley**   [PA]
*Author*
\* L. B. T.

**Thomas, Lee**
*See* Floren, Lee

**Thomas, Lee**
*See* Thomas, James Leroy

**Thomas, Lefty**
*See* Thomas, Clarence Franklin

**Thomas, Lefty**
*See* Thomas, Claude Alfred

**Thomas, Leo Raymond** 1924-   [BE]
*American baseball player*
\* Thomas, Tommy

**Thomas, Leone**
*See* Thomas, Amos Leon, Jr.

**Thomas, Lillian** 1885-1969
[BWW, IBW]
*American singer*
\* Baker, Fannie
\* Brown, Lillian [or Lillyn]
\* Elbrown
\* Fernandez, Mildred
\* [The] Indian Princess
\* [The] Jazzbo Syncopator
\* Jones, Maude
\* [The] Kate Smith of Harlem
\* [The] Original Gay 90's Gal
\* [The] Youngest Interlocutor in
the World

**Thomas, Lowell Jackson**
1892-1981   [BBH]
*American radio broadcaster, author,
skier*
\* Thomas, Tommy

**Thomas, Luther Baxter** 1910-   [BE]
*American baseball player*
\* Thomas, Bud

**Thomas, M.**   [PA]
*Author*
\* Aptomas

**Thomas, M. L.**
*See* Jeier, Thomas

**Thomas, Manuel**
*See* Mueller-Harlin, Wolfgang
Johannes

**Thomas, Marlo**
*See* Jacobs, Margaret

**Thomas, Martin**
*See* Martin, Thomas Hector

**Thomas, Mary Alice** 20th c.
[WWL]
*Welsh author*
\* Eustace, Alice

**Thomas, Maurice** 1876-1961
[BDF, BEW, FC]
*French-born director*
\* Tourneur, Maurice

**Thomas, Mervyn**
*See* Curran, Mona [Elisa]

**Thomas, Michael Wolf** 1945-
[IAW]
*German film editor*
\* Wolf, Dieter

**Thomas, Murray**
*See* Ragg, Thomas Murray

**Thomas, Neal**
*See* Thomas, Cornelius Dickinson

**Thomas of Erceldoune**
*See* Learmont, Thomas

**Thomas of Woodstock** 1355-1397
[SN]
*Duke of Gloucester*
\* Cignus de Corde Benignus

**Thomas, Olive**
*See* Duffy, Olive

**Thomas, Pap**
*See* Thomas, George Henry

**Thomas, Paul**
*See* Mann, Thomas

**Thomas, Paul**
*See* Sheritier, M.

**Thomas, Pinch**
*See* Thomas, Chester David

**Thomas, Piri**
*See* Thomas, John Peter

**Thomas, R[obert] Murray** 1921-
[CA]
*American educator and author*
\* Roberts, Tom

**Thomas, R. S.**
*See* Thomas, Ronald Stuart

**Thomas, Ragtime Texas**
*See* Thomas, Henry

**Thomas, Ralph** 1840- ?
[DEL, FFF]
*British bibliographer*
\* Hamst, Olphar

**Thomas, Ramblin'**
*See* Thomas, Willard

**Thomas, Red**
See   Thomas, Charles

**Thomas, Red**
See   Thomas, Robert William

**Thomas, Reginald George** 1899- ?
[MBF]
*British author*
* Nelson, Barry
* Purley, John
* Storm, Ivan
* Stuart, Michael
* Wilson, Reg.

**Thomas, Robert William**
1898-1962   [BE]
*American baseball player*
* Thomas, Red

**Thomas, Ronald Stuart** 1913-      [LC]
*Welsh clergyman and poet*
* Thomas, R. S.

**Thomas, Ronald Wills** 1910-      [WW]
*Author*
* Bogar, Jeff
* Cadell, James
* Wills, Ronald

**Thomas, Ross** 1926-
[AW, CA, EMD]
*American author*
* Bleeck, Oliver

**Thomas, Savage Tom**
See   Thomas, Thomas W. [Tom]

**Thomas, Scow**
See   Thomas, Fay Wesley

**Thomas, Sherilyn** 1948-   [CA]
*American author*
* Thomas, Sherry

**Thomas, Sherry**
See   Thomas, Sherilyn

**Thomas, Showboat**
See   Thomas, David

**Thomas, Showboy**
See   Thomas, Worthia

**Thomas, Skip**
See   Thomas, Alonzo

**Thomas, Son**
See   Thomas, James

**Thomas, Sonny Ford**
See   Thomas, James

**Thomas, Stanley** 1933-   [CA]
*British-born author*
* Wyandotte, Steve

**Thomas, Ted**
See   Tassy, Tamas

**Thomas, Teddy**
See   Thomas, David John

**Thomas the Bastard**
See   Fauconberg [or Falconberg],
Thomas

**Thomas the Rhymer**
See   Learmont, Thomas

**Thomas, Theodore L. [Ted]** 1920-
[CA]
*American author*
* Lockard, Leonard

**Thomas, Thomas W. [Tom]**
1873-1942   [BE]
*American baseball player*
* Thomas, Savage Tom

**Thomas, Tiger**
See   Thomas, Gary

**Thomas, Tight Lines**
See   Thomas, Gary Philip

**Thomas, Tommy**
See   Thomas, Alphonse

**Thomas, Tommy**
See   Thomas, Leo Raymond

**Thomas, Tommy**
See   Thomas, Lowell Jackson

**Thomas, Virginia Castleton**
See   Castleton, Virginia

**Thomas, Walter Purl** 1907-
[EJ, PMJ, WWJ]
*American jazz musician*
* Thomas, Foots

**Thomas, Will Madison** 1905-
[IBW]
*American author*
* Smith, Billy

**Thomas, Willard** 20th c.   [BWW]
*American musician*
* Thomas, Ramblin'

**Thomas, William B. [Bill]** 1934-
[IAW]
*American author*
* Lowell, Alan
* Sabre, Mark
* Williams, Tom

**Thomas, William M.** 1878-1947
[BX, RBE]
*British boxer*
* Broad, Kid

**Thomas, Worthia** 1907-   [NOJ]
*American jazz musician*
* Thomas, Showboy

**Thomasius, Christian** 1655-1728
[SN]
*German philosopher and jurist*
* [The] Apostle of Enlightenment

**Thomason, Alkali Ike**
See   Thomason, Ike

**Thomason, Barbara Ann**
1937-1966   [SC]
*American actress*
* Mitchell, Carolyn

**Thomason, Ike**   [GW]
*American rodeo performer*
* Thomason, Alkali Ike

**Thomasson, H. L.** 1903-      [B10]
*American dairy scientist*
* Thomasson, Red

**Thomasson, Red**
See   Thomasson, H. L.

**Thompson, Alexander Mattock** 1861-
?   [LAO]
*German-born playwright and
journalist*
* Dangle

**Thompson, Alfred** 1926-   [EAR]
*American auto racer*
* Thompson, Speedy

**Thompson, Alvin Clarence**
1892-1974   [GF]
*American gambler and golfer*
* Thompson, Titanic

**Thompson, Anthony A.** 20th c.
[ESF, SFL, WGT]
*Author*
* Alban, Anthony

**Thompson, Arthur Leonard Bell**
1917-1975   [B10, CA]
*British author*
* Clifford, Francis

**Thompson, Aundra** 1953-   [SMG]
*American football player*
* Thompson, Boomer

**Thompson, Bendigo**
See   Thompson, William

**Thompson, Benjamin** 1753-1814
[PA]
*Author*
* Rumford, Count

**Thompson, Beryl Antonia**
1918-1970   [WEC]
*British cartoonist*
* Anton [joint pseudonym with
Harold Thompson]

**Thompson, Big Bill**
See   Thompson, William Hale

**Thompson, Big Jim**
See   Thompson, James R.

**Thompson, Big Sam**
See   Thompson, Samuel L.

**Thompson, Boomer**
See   Thompson, Aundra

**Thompson, Brute Force**
See   Thompson, George

**Thompson, Carlos**
See   Mundanschaffter, Juan Carlos

**Thompson, Cat**
See   Thompson, John A.

**Thompson, Cecil** 1905-
[CEI, FHE, HK]
*Canadian-born hockey player*
* Thompson, Tiny

**Thompson, Cecil Lewis** 1904-1946
[AS, BX, RBE]
*American boxer*
* Thompson, Young Jack

**Thompson, Charles** 20th c.   [SMG]
*American baseball team scout*
* Thompson, Tim

**Thompson, Charles John Samuel**
1862-1943   [SFL]
*Author*
* Thompson, Creswick J.

**Thompson, Charles Phillip** 1918-
[EJ, WWJ]
*American jazz musician*
* Sir Charles

**Thompson, Charlotte**
See   Rogers, Lorain

**Thompson, China**
See   Lewis, Mary Christianna
[Milne]

**Thompson, Corner Memory**
See   Thompson, John

**Thompson, Creswick J.**
See   Thompson, Charles John
Samuel

**Thompson, Cyclone**
See   Thompson, John

**Thompson, David** 1955-   [IBW]
*American basketball player*
* Thompson, Hotshot

**Thompson, Denman** 1833-1911
[BEW]
*American actor, playwright,
producer*
* Whitcomb, Joshua

**Thompson, Derby Dick**
See   Thompson, Herbert John

**Thompson, Derroll Lewis** 1925-
[FCW]
*American country-western performer*
* Adams, Derroll

**Thompson, Don[ald Arthur]** 1935-
[CA]
*American author and editor*
* O'Donnell, Dick [joint pseudonym
with Richard Allen (Dick)
Lupoff]

**Thompson, Edith** 20th c.   [WWL]
*British author*
* Tod, Evelyn

**Thompson, Eileen**
See   Panowski, Eileen [Janet]
Thompson

**Thompson, Eli** 1924-
[DAM, EJ, PMJ]
*American jazz musician*
* Thompson, Lucky

**Thompson, Ellen Perronet** 20th c.
[WWL]
*British author*
* Peronne

**Thompson, Ernest Evan Seton**
1860-1946   [LC, TC]
*American author*
* Seton, Ernest Thompson

**Thompson, Esau** 1949-   [IBW]
*American disc jockey*
* Thompson, Little Tiger

**Thompson, Estelle Merle O'Brien**
1911-1979   [BDF, IPA, WEF]
*British actress*
* Oberon, Merle
* O'Brien, Queenie

**Thompson, Eugene Earl** 1917-   [BE]
*American baseball player*
* Thompson, Junior

**Thompson, F. J.** 19th c.   [SN]
*British army officer*
* Thompson, Skikari

**Thompson, Frank**
*American politician*
* Thompson, Thompy

**Thompson, Frank** 20th c.   [OBW]
*American baseball player*
* Thompson, Groundhog

**Thompson, George**   [PA]
*Author*
* Civis
* Greenhorn

**Thompson, George** 20th c.   [MEB]
*American basketball player*
* Thompson, Brute Force

**Thompson, George Selden** 1929-
[B10, CA, SAT]
*American author*
* Selden, George

**Thompson, Grace E.** 20th c.
[WWL]
*British author*
* Hope, Camilla

**Thompson, Groundhog**
See  Thompson, Frank

**Thompson, Harlan Howard** 1894-
[CAP, SAT]
*American author*
* Holt, Stephen

**Thompson, Harold** 20th c.   [WEC]
*British cartoonist*
* Anton [joint pseudonym with
    Beryl Antonia Thompson]
* Botterill, H.

**Thompson, [Sir] Henry** 19th c.
[FFF]
*British author*
* Oliver, Pen

**Thompson, Herbert John** 1881- ?
[BBH]
*American horse trainer*
* Thompson, Derby Dick

**Thompson, Herman Lee** 1923-
[CWG]
*American country-western performer*
* Thompson, Tommy

**Thompson, Hippolita** ?-1933   [SC]
*American actress*
* Thompson, Polly

**Thompson, Hotshot**
See  Thompson, David

**Thompson, Hugh** 1943-   [BWG]
*American golfer*
* Thompson, Rocky

**Thompson, Hunter S[tockton]**
1939-   [CA, IAW]
*American author*
* Duke, Raoul
* Owl, Sebastian

**Thompson, J. J.**
See  Thompson, Jesse Jackson

**Thompson, Jack**
See  Payne, John

**Thompson, James Alfred** 1893-
[BE]
*American baseball player*
* Thompson, Shag

**Thompson, James H.**
See  Freeman, Graydon La Verne

**Thompson, James R.** 1937-
*American politician*
* Thompson, Big Jim

**Thompson, Jane Maude Evelyn De
Gourey Ireland** 1869- ?   [WWL]
*British author*
* Ireland, Maude

**Thompson, Jay**
See  Thompson, Jennings Lewis, Jr.

**Thompson, Jean M.** 20th c.   [NAA]
*American author*
* [The] Jack Frost Lady

**Thompson, Jennings Lewis, Jr.**
1927-   [ASC, BEW]
*American composer, playwright,
lyricist*
* Thompson, Jay

**Thompson, Jesse Jackson** 1919-
[IAW]
*American author*
* Thompson, J. J.

**Thompson, Jimmy** 1848-1931
[ECM]
*American country-western performer*
* Thompson, Uncle Jimmy

**Thompson, Jocko**
See  Thompson, John Samuel

**Thompson, John**   [SN]
*British auctioneer*
* Thompson, Corner Memory
* Thompson, Memory

**Thompson, John** 1767-1789   [PA]
*Author*
* Casca
* Gracchus

**Thompson, John** 1876-1951
[AS, RBE]
*American boxer*
* Thompson, Cyclone

**Thompson, John A.** 1906-   [BB]
*American basketball player*
* Thompson, Cat

**Thompson, John Dall** 1918-1971
[SC]
*American actor*
* Dall, John

**Thompson, John Dudley**
1898-1963   [BE]
*American baseball player*
* Thompson, Lee
* Thompson, Lefty

**Thompson, John H.** 1890-   [NAA]
*American author and editor*
* Headen, John
* Johns, Thompson

**Thompson, John P.** ?-1895   [BE]
*American baseball player*
* Thompson, Tug

**Thompson, John Samuel** 1920-
[BE]
*American baseball player*
* Thompson, Jocko

**Thompson, Joseph Parrish**
1819-1879   [FFF, PA]
*American clergyman and author*
* Berliner
* Egypt

**Thompson, Junior**
See  Thompson, Eugene Earl

**Thompson, Lafayette Fresco**
1902-1968   [BE, PB]
*American baseball player*
* Thompson, Tommy

**Thompson, Lee**
See  Thompson, John Dudley

**Thompson, Lefty**
See  Thompson, John Dudley

**Thompson, Little Tiger**
See  Thompson, Esau

**Thompson, Long Sam**
See  Thompson, Samuel Tommy

**Thompson, Louis McClanahan**
1881-1951   [SC]
*American actor*
* Morris, Corbet

**Thompson, Lucky**
See  Thompson, Eli

**Thompson, Lydia**
See  Henderson, Mrs. Alexander

**Thompson, Madeline**
See  Greig, Maysie

**Thompson, Marian Lee** 1928-
[EAR]
*American auto racer*
* Thompson, Mickey

**Thompson, Memory**
See  Thompson, John

**Thompson, Mickey**
See  Thompson, Marian Lee

**Thompson, Moose**
See  Thompson, Wilbur

**Thompson, Mrs. E. S. L.**   [PA]
*Author*
* Broderick, Mark

**Thompson, Mrs. William**   [FFF]
*American writer*
* Clara Belle

**Thompson, Percy Henry**
1875?-1953   [BEW, BMH]
*Theatrical performer*
* Honri, Percy

**Thompson, Peter**   [PA]
*Author*
* Dodger

**Thompson, Phillips**   [PA]
*Author*
* Briggs, Jimuel

**Thompson, Phyllis Hoge**
See  Hoge, Phyllis

**Thompson, Polly**
See  Thompson, Hippolita

**Thompson, Richard Wigginton**
1809-1900   [FFF]
*American politician*
* [The] Ancient Mariner of the
    Wabash

**Thompson, Rocky**
See  Thompson, Hugh

**Thompson, Rupert Luckhart**
1910-1971   [BE]
*American baseball player*
* Thompson, Tommy

**Thompson, Samuel L.** 1860-1922
[BE, DGS, PB]
*American baseball player*
* Thompson, Big Sam

**Thompson, Samuel Tommy** 1908-
[MK]
*American baseball player*
* Thompson, Long Sam

**Thompson, Shag**
See  Thompson, James Alfred

**Thompson, Skikari**
See  Thompson, F. J.

**Thompson, Slow Kid**
See  Thompson, Ulysses

**Thompson, Speedy**
See  Thompson, Alfred

**Thompson, Stephen**
See  Dell, Draycot Montagu

**Thompson, Sue**
See  McKee, Eva Sue

**Thompson, Sylvester** 1937-   [BWW]
*American singer*
* Johnson, Syl

**Thompson, Thompy**
See  Thompson, Frank

**Thompson, Tim**
See  Thompson, Charles

**Thompson, Tiny**
See  Thompson, Cecil

**Thompson, Titanic**
See  Thompson, Alvin Clarence

**Thompson, Tommy**
See  Thompson, Herman Lee

**Thompson, Tommy**
See  Thompson, Lafayette Fresco

**Thompson, Tommy**
See  Thompson, Rupert Luckhart

**Thompson, Tug**
See  Thompson, John P.

**Thompson, Ulysses** 20th c.   [BMH]
*American entertainer*
* Thompson, Slow Kid

**Thompson, Uncle Jimmy**
See  Thompson, Jimmy

**Thompson, Wilbur** 1921-   [TF]
*American track and field athlete*
* Thompson, Moose

**Thompson, William** 20th c.   [SG]
*Boxer*
* [The] Lion
* Thompson, Bendigo

**Thompson, William C. L.**
See  Edwards, William B[ennett]

**Thompson, William Hale**
1869?-1944   [BLB, PHM]
*American politician with underworld
ties*
* Thompson, Big Bill

**Thompson, William Henry**
1881-1947   [BEW, F1, THR]
*British actor*
* Merson, Billy
* Ping Pong

**Thompson, William R.**   [PA]
*Author*
* Mata

**Thompson, William Theodore**   [PA]
*Author*
* Jones, Major

**Thompson, Young Jack**
See  Thompson, Cecil Lewis

**Thomson, A. A.**
See  Thomson, Arthur Alexander

**Thomson, Ada** 1929-   [FC, TR]
*British actress*
* Merchant, Vivien

**Thomson, Alexander**   [SN]
* Old Stay Maker
* [The] Stay Maker

**Thomson, Arthur Alexander**
1894-1968   [LC]
*British author*
* Thomson, A. A.

**Thomson, Audrey**
See  Gwynn, Audrey Jean

**Thomson, Beatrix**
See  Lindsay-Thomson, Beatrix

**Thomson, Charles** 1729-1824 [SN]
*Irish-born American politician*
* Truth Teller

**Thomson, Christine Campbell**
1897- [HFF, MBF, SFP]
*British author*
* Alexander, Dair
* Campbell, Molly
* Hartley, Christine
* Richardson, Flavia

**Thomson, Daisy Hicks** 1918-
[AW, WD]
*Scottish author*
* Roe, M. S.
* Thomson, Jonathan H.

**Thomson, Derick Smith** 1921-
[CA, WD]
*Scottish poet and literary critic*
* MacThomais, Ruaraidh

**Thomson, Edward**
*See* Tubb, Edwin Charles

**Thomson, Floyd Harvey** 1949-
[SMG]
*Canadian-born hockey player*
* Thomson, White Pine

**Thomson, George Julius Poulett**
1797-1876 [WBD]
*British geologist*
* Scrope, George Julius Poulett

**Thomson, George Malcolm** 1899-
[CA]
*Scottish-born journalist and author*
* MacDonald, Aeneas

**Thomson, Irene Taviss** 1941- [CA]
*American sociologist and author*
* Taviss, Irene

**Thomson, J. A. K.**
*See* Thomson, James Alexander
Kerr

**Thomson, James** 1834-1882
[WBD]
*Scottish poet*
* B. V.
* Bysshe Vanolis

**Thomson, James Alexander Kerr**
1879-1959 [LC]
*Scottish-born scholar and author*
* Thomson, J. A. K.

**Thomson, James C[utting]** 1909-
[CA]
*American musicologist and author*
* Chase, Adam

**Thomson, Joan**
*See* Charnock, Joan Paget

**Thomson, John** 1778-1840 [DEP]
*Scottish painter*
* [The] Father of Scotch
  Landscape Painting

**Thomson, John Cockburn** 19th c.
[DNNF]
*British author*
* Wharton, Philip

**Thomson, Jonathan H.**
*See* Thomson, Daisy Hicks

**Thomson, Katherine Byerley**
1810-1862 [DEL, DNNF, FFF]
*British author*
* Grace, Eliza
* Wharton, Grace

**Thomson, Louis**
*See* Thomson, Louisa Emily

**Thomson, Louisa Emily** 1883-
[DBA]
*British painter, etcher, lithographer*
* Thomson, Louis

**Thomson, Meldrim** 1912?-
*American politician*
* Half-Mast Mel

**Thomson, Mortimer** 1832?-1875
[WBD]
*American author*
* Doesticks, Q. K. Philander

**Thomson, Neil**
*See* Johnson, Henry T.

**Thomson, Ralph Methven** 1875- ?
[NAA]
*American poet and writer*
* Methven, Ralph

**Thomson, Richard** 1795- ? [PA]
*Author*
* [An] Antiquary

**Thomson, Robert Brown [Bobby]**
1923- [BE, PB]
*Scottish-born baseball player*
* [The] Flying Scot
* [The] Scot
* [The] Staten Island Scot

**Thomson, White Pine**
*See* Thomson, Floyd Harvey

**Thoney, Bullet Jack**
*See* Thoeny, John

**Thoney, John**
*See* Thoeny, John

**Thor, Johannes**
*See* Lang, Isaac

**Thor, Terry**
*See* Shaw, Lawrence Taylor
[Larry]

**Thor, Tristan**
*See* Lang, Isaac

**Thorburn, Grant** 1773?-1863 [FFF]
*Scottish-born author*
* Todd, Laurie

**Thorburn, John**
*See* Goldsmith, John Herman
Thorburn

**Thorburn-Muirhead, James** 1899-
[IAW]
*Scottish-born author*
* Muirhead, Thorburn

**Thordsen, Theodori** [PA]
*Author*
* Polyhistor

**Thore, T. J. E.** [PA]
*Author*
* Baerger, W.

**Thormahlen, Hank**
*See* Thormahlen, Herbert Ehler

**Thormahlen, Herbert Ehler**
1896-1955 [BE]
*American baseball player*
* Thormahlen, Hank
* Thormahlen, Lefty

**Thormahlen, Lefty**
*See* Thormahlen, Herbert Ehler

**Thormodsgard, Paul Gayton** 1953-
[SMG]
*American baseball player*
* Thormodsgard, Thor

**Thormodsgard, Thor**
*See* Thormodsgard, Paul Gayton

**Thorn, John** 1947- [CA]
*German-born American author*
* Jones, Sanford W.

**Thornberry, William A.**
*See* Thornley, William A.

**Thornborough, Bishop** ?-1641
[SN]
*British clergyman*
* Denarius Philosophorum

**Thornborough, Laura**
*See* Thornburgh, Laura

**Thornburg, Elizabeth June** 1921-
[BEW, OCF, SW]
*American singer and actress*
* [The] Blonde Bombshell
* Hutton, Betty

**Thornburg, Marion** 1919?-
[FC, MY, PMJ]
*American singer and actress*
* Hutton, Butch
* Hutton, Marion

**Thornburgh, Laura** 20th c. [NAA]
*American author, film editor,
director*
* Thornborough, Laura

**Thornbury, William A.**
*See* Thornley, William A.

**Thorndyke, Helen Louise** [house
pseudonym] [Stratemeyer
Syndicate]
*See* Stratemeyer, Edward L.

**Thorndyke, Louise**
*See* Boucicault, Agnes Kelly
Robertson

**Thorne, Alice**
*See* Craythorne, Mrs. James

**Thorne, Bradley D.**
*See* Glut, Donald F[rank]

**Thorne, Brinck**
*See* Thorne, Samuel B.

**Thorne, Grace**
*See* Coulter, Mrs. Frazer

**Thorne, Guy**
*See* Gull, Cyril Arthur Edward
Ranger

**Thorne, Hart**
*See* Carhart, Arthur Hawthorne

**Thorne, Ian**
*See* May, Julian

**Thorne, Kate**
*See* Gray, Louisa M.

**Thorne, Mrs. J. H.** [FFF]
*Entertainer*
* Meyer, Bonnie

**Thorne, P.**
*See* Wells, Mary P.

**Thorne, Ramsay**
*See* Cameron, Lou

**Thorne, Roger**
*See* Russell, Ray

**Thorne, Samuel B.** ?-1930 [FB]
*American football player*
* Thorne, Brinck

**Thorne, Sheldon B.** [PA]
*Author*
* Saxafragi

**Thorne, Sterling**
*See* Fuller, Dorothy Mason

**Thorne, Whyte**
*See* Whiteing, Richard

**Thorne, William** 1558-1629 [FFF]
*British scholar*
* Theta

**Thornhill, Claude E.** 1893-1956
[AS, FB]
*American football player and coach*
* Thornhill, Tiny

**Thornhill, Tiny**
*See* Thornhill, Claude E.

**Thornley, William A.** 20th c.
[DBA]
*British painter*
* Thornberry, William A.
* Thornbury, William A.

**Thornton, Adelaide**
*See* Nicholson, Mrs. Paul

**Thornton, Andre** 1949- [BR]
*American baseball player*
* Thornton, Andy

**Thornton, Andy**
*See* Thornton, Andre

**Thornton, Argonne Dense** 1921-
[EJ]
*American jazz musician*
* Hakim, Sadik

**Thornton, Big Mama**
*See* Thornton, Willie Mae

**Thornton, Bill** 20th c. [SMG]
*American football coach*
* Thornton, Thunder

**Thornton, Buns**
*See* Thornton, Charles Inglis

**Thornton, Charles Inglis**
1850-1929 [EC]
*British cricketer*
* Thornton, Buns

**Thornton, Charles J.** 1944- [EJ7]
*American jazz musician*
* Miles, Butch
* Miles, Charles J.

**Thornton, Cyril**
*See* Hamilton, [Capt.] Thomas

**Thornton, Edward**
*See* Brooks, Edwy Searles

**Thornton, Frank**
*See* Ball, Frank

**Thornton, Hall**
*See* Silverberg, Robert

**Thornton, Harold**
*See* Offard, Cecil

**Thornton, Maimee**
*See* Jeffrey-Smith, May Thornton

**Thornton, Mary** 1924- [BF]
*British actress and singer*
* Norden, Christine

**Thornton, Thunder**
*See* Thornton, Bill

**Thornton, W. B.**
*See* Burgess, Thornton Waldo

**Thornton, Willie Mae** 1926-
[BWW, NBB, PRS]
*American singer*
* Thornton, Big Mama

**Thorogood, Albert** 1928?- [B10]
*British nonworker*
* Thorogood, Idle Albert

**Thorogood, Idle Albert**
*See* Thorogood, Albert

**[The] Thorough Doctor**
*See* Varro, William

**Thorp, Edward** 20th c.
*Mathematician and gambler*
* [The] Father of Card Counting

**Thorp, Ellen**
*See* Robertson, Margery Ellen

**Thorp, Joseph Peter** 1873- ?
[LAO, LC]
*British journalist and critic*
* T

**Thorp, Morwenna**
*See* Robertson, Margery Ellen

**Thorp, Mrs. Charles R.** [FFF]
*Entertainer*
* Mountcastle, Fanny

**Thorpe, Dobbin**
*See* Disch, Thomas M.

**Thorpe, E. G.**
*See* Thorpe, George

**Thorpe, George** 1916- [IAW]
*British author*
* Thorpe, E. G.

**Thorpe, Henry** 1841- ? [PA]
*Author*
* Walton

**Thorpe, Kampa**
*See* Bellamy, Mrs. E. W.

**Thorpe, Richard**
*See* Thorpe, Rollo Smolt

**Thorpe, Rollo Smolt** 1896-
[FC, FD, WEF]
*American director*
* Thorpe, Richard

**Thorpe, Sylvia**
*See* Thimblethorpe, June Sylvia

**Thorpe, Thomas Bangs** 1815-1878
[PA]
*American journalist*
* Owen, Tom, the Bee Hunter

**Thorpe, Trebor**
*See* Fanthorpe, R[obert] Lionel

**Thorpe, Trevor**
*See* Fanthorpe, R[obert] Lionel

**Thorson, Delos Russell** 1906-
[WW]
*Author*
* Christian, Kit [joint pseudonym
with Sara Winfree Thorson]

**Thorson, Sara Winfree** 1906-
[WW]
*Author*
* Christian, Kit [joint pseudonym
with Delos Russell Thorson]

**Thorstein, Eric**
*See* Grossman, Josephine Judith

**Thorvaldsen, Bertel [or Albert]**
1770?-1844 [HN]
*Danish sculptor*
* [The] Northern Phidias

**Thorwald, Juergen**
*See* Bongartz, Heinz

**Thou Shred of a Loom**
*See* Oates, Titus

**[The] Thoughtful Father**
*See* Catinat, Nicholas

**Thoyson, David** 1864-1951 [SC]
*Scottish-born actor*
* Torrence, David

**Thoyson, Ernest** 1878-1933 [SC]
*Scottish-born actor and singer*
* Torrence, Ernest

**[The] Thracian**
*See* Leo I

**[The] Thracian Dog**
*See* Zoilus [or Zoilos]

**Thrasher, Buck**
*See* Thrasher, Frank Edward

**Thrasher, Frank Edward**
1889-1938 [BE]
*American baseball player*
* Thrasher, Buck

**Thrax [The Thracian]**
*See* Maximinus, Gaius Julius
Verus

**[The] 3 Dog**
*See* Davis, William Henry [Willie]

**Three Finger Brown**
*See* Brown, Mordecai Peter
Centennial

**Three Finger Brown**
*See* Lucchese, Thomas Gaetano

**Three Fingered Jack**
*See* Hamilton, John

**Three Fingered Jack**
*See* White, William Jack

**Three Star Hennessey**
*See* Hennessey, George

**Three to Nothing Jack**
*See* Dalton, John P. [Jack]

**Three Twelve**
*See* Lucania, Salvatore

**Thrice, Luke**
*See* Russell, John

**[The] Thrill**
*See* Sellers, Phil

**Thring, Edward** 19th c. [PA]
*Author*
* Place, Benjamin

**Throneberry, Marvelous Marv**
*See* Throneberry, Marvin Eugene

**Throneberry, Marvin Eugene** 1933-
[BE, PB]
*American baseball player*
* Throneberry, Marvelous Marv

**Throop, Enos Thompson**
1784-1874 [SN]
*American politician*
* Throop, Small Light

**Throop, Small Light**
*See* Throop, Enos Thompson

**Thropp, Florence**
*See* Bulkley, Mrs. Edward A.

**Throssell, Katharine Susannah
Prichard** 1884- [LAO]
*Australian author*
* Prichard, Katharine Susannah

**Thrower, Hammer**
*See* Thrower, James

**Thrower, James** 20th c.
*American football player*
* Thrower, Hammer

**Thucydides**
*See* Rollin, Charles

**[The] Thucydides of Germany**
*See* Mueller, Johann von

**Thuitleru, Francois Jean**
1653-1688 [PA]
*Author*
* Juvenon

**Thumb, Thomas, Esq.**
*See* Church, Benjamin

**Thumb, Tom**
*See* Alden, Darius Adner

**Thumb, Tom**
*See* Bonaparte, Charles Louis
Napoleon

**Thumb, Tom**
*See* Stratton, Charles Sherwood

**[The] Thumper**
*See* Harris, Carrol Wayne

**[The] Thumper**
*See* Williams, Theodore Samuel
[Ted]

**Thumtack, Tom**
*See* Squires, Frederick

**Thuna, Lee**
*See* Thuna, Leonora

**Thuna, Leonora** 1929- [CA]
*American playwright*
* Thuna, Lee

**Thunder and Lightning**
*See* Stephen II

**[The] Thunderbird from Coast to
Coast**
*See* Price, Walter Travis

**[The] Thunderbolt**
*See* Bajazet I [Bayazid or Bajasid]

**[The] Thunderbolt**
*See* Handel, Georg Friedrich

**[The] Thunderbolt**
*See* Papke, William Herman
[Billy]

**[The] Thunderbolt**
*See* Ptolemy

**[The] Thunderbolt of France**
*See* De Gontaut, Charles

**[The] Thunderbolt of Italy**
*See* Foix, Gaston de [Duc de
Nemours]

**[The] Thunderbolt of Painting**
*See* Robusti, Jacopo

**Thunderbolt of the Middle West**
*See* May, Joseph

**[The] Thunderbolt of War**
*See* Piccinino, Jacopo

**Thundercloud, Chief**
*See* Daniels, Victor

**Thundercloud, Chief**
*See* Williams, Scott T.

**Thundercloud, Katherine**
*See* Witt, Shirley Hill

**[The] Thunderer**
*See* Gorovitz, Vladimir

**[The] Thunderer**
*See* Homer

**[The] Thunderer**
*See* Stephen II

**[The] Thunderer of the Times**
*See* Sterling, Edward

**Thundertentronckh, Arminius Von**
*See* Arnold, Matthew

**Thundy, Zacharias Pontian**
*See* Thundyil, Zacharias Pontian

**Thundyil, Zacharias Pontian** 1936-
[CA]
*Indian-born author and clergyman*
* Thundy, Zacharias Pontian

**Thurgood, Albert** 1875?-1935
[OCS]
*Australian soccer player*
* Albert the Great

**Thurley, Norgove**
*See* Stoneham, Charles Thurley

**Thurlow, Edward [First Baron
Thurlow]** 1731?-1806 [HN, SN]
*British jurist and politician*
* Old Gravity
* [The] Tiger

**Thurman, Allen Granbery**
1813-1895 [FFF]
*American politician*
* [The] Gladstone of America
* [The] Obelisk
* [The] Old Roman

**Thurman, Christa C[harlotte] Mayer**
1934- [CA]
*German-born author and museum
curator*
* Mayer, Christa Charlotte
* Mayer-Thurman, Christa C.

**Thurmond, Nate** 1941- [BB]
*American basketball player*
* Nate the Great

**Thursby, Peter** 1930- [ART]
*British sculptor*
* P. T.

**[The] Thurso Baker**
*See* Dick, Robert

**Thurston, Frederick C.** 1933- [FB]
*American football player*
* Thurston, Fuzzy

**Thurston, Fuzzy**
*See* Thurston, Frederick C.

**Thurston, Harry**
*See* Cowan, Marcus

**Thurston, Hazel [Patricia]** 1906-
[CA]
*Irish-born author*
* Murphy, Hazel

**Thurston, Henry T.**
*See* Palgrave, Francis Turner

**Thurston, Hollis John** 1899-1973
[BE, PB]
*American baseball player*
* Thurston, Sloppy

**Thurston, Howard**
*See* Gibson, Walter B[rown]

**Thurston, Jane** 20th c. [BS]
*American magician*
* [The] Maid of Magic

**Thurston, Laura M. Hawley**
1812-1842 [FFF]
*American poet and journalist*
* Viola

**Thurston, Sloppy**
*See* Thurston, Hollis John

**Thynne, Thomas** ?-1682
[HN, RH]
*British aristocrat*
* Tom of Ten Thousand

**Thynne [or Boteville?], William**
?-1546 [SN]
*British scholar*
* Aulicus

**Thyselius, Thorborg Elin**
**Tryggvesdotter** 1906- [IAW]
*Swedish author and poet*
* Castenius, Sigrid

**Thyson, A. C.**
*See* Aitchison, George

**Tiant, Lefty**
*See* Tiant, Luis E.

**Tiant, Luis E.** 1906-1976 [MK]
*American baseball player*
* Tiant, Lefty

**Tibaldi, Pellegrino** [SN, WBD]
*Italian artist*
* Da Bologna, Pellegrino
* [The] Reformed Michael Angelo

**Tibber, Robert**
*See* Friedman, Eve Rosemary

**Tibber, Rosemary**
*See* Friedman, Eve Rosemary

**Tibbetts, John C[arter]** 1946- [CA]
*American author*
* Ketch, Jack

**Tibbetts, William**
*See* Brannon, William T.

**Tibble, Anne** 1912- [CA]
*British author*
* Northgrave, Anne

**Tibbs, Casey** 20th c. [GW]
*American rodeo performer*
* Midnight, Captain

**Tibbs, Lillian Evans** 1890-1967
[IBW]
*American opera singer*
* Evanti, [Madame] Lillian

**Tiberiu, Farkas** 1914- [IWM]
*Rumanian-born musician*
* Levary, Tibor

**Tiberius**
*See* Nero Caesar, Tiberius
Claudius

**Tibet**
*See* Gascard, Gilbert

**Tibio [Luke-Warm]**
*See* Munoz, Felipe

**[The] Tibullus of France**
*See* Desforges, Evariste Desire
[Chevalier de Parny]

**Tich**
*See* Amey, Ian

**Tichborne, Cheviot**
*See* Ainsworth, W. H.

**Tichenor, J. C.**
*See* Kelly, George R.

**Ticker, Reuben** 1913-1975 [BBD]
*American opera singer*
* Tucker, Richard

**Tickler, Timothy**
*See* Paulding, James Kirke

**Tickler, Timothy**
*See* Syme, Robert

**Tickletooth, Tabitha**
*See* Silby, Charles

**Tiddy Doll**
*See* Grenville, Richard Temple
[First Earl Temple]

**Tiedge, Christoph August**
1752-1841 [HN]
*German poet*
* [The] Nestor of German Poesy

**Tielsch, Ilse** 1929- [IAW]
*Austrian author*
* Tielsch-Felzmann, Ilse

**Tielsch-Felzmann, Ilse**
*See* Tielsch, Ilse

**T'ien-wang [Heavenly Prince]**
*See* Hung Hsiu-ch'uan

**Tieri, Frank** 1904?-1981
*American underworld figure*
* Tieri, Funzi

**Tieri, Funzi**
*See* Tieri, Frank

**Tiernan, Michael Joseph**
1867-1918 [BE, DGS, PB]
*American baseball player*
* Tiernan, Silent Mike

**Tiernan, Silent Mike**
*See* Tiernan, Michael Joseph

**Tierney, Cotton**
*See* Tierney, James Arthur

**Tierney, Gerald** 1924-
[FC, ITA, SW]
*American actor*
* Brady, Scott

**Tierney, James Arthur** 1894-1953
[BE]
*American baseball player*
* Tierney, Cotton

**Tierney, John Lawrence** 1892-1972
[CAP]
*Australian author*
* James, Brian

**Tietje, Leslie William** 1911- [BE]
*American baseball player*
* Tietje, Toots

**Tietje, Toots**
*See* Tietje, Leslie William

**Tifew, H. C.**
*See* Fitch, William Edward

**Tiffin, Pamela**
*See* Wonso, Pamela

**Tifton, Leo**
*See* Page, Gerald W[ilburn]

**Tigar, Chad**
*See* Levi, Peter

**[The] Tiger**
*See* Clemenceau, Georges

**[The] Tiger**
*See* Thurlow, Edward [First Baron
Thurlow]

**Tiger, Derry**
*See* Ellison, Harlan [Jay]

**Tiger, Dick**
*See* Ihetu, Richard

**Tiger Eyes**
*See* Schragmueller, Elsbeth

**Tiger, Jack**
*See* Puechner, Ray

**Tiger Jack Fox**
*See* Fox, John Linwood

**Tiger, John**
*See* Wager, Walter Herman

**Tiger Lily**
*See* Blake, Lillie Devereux

**[The] Tiger of Alica**
*See* Losada, Manuel

**[The] Tiger of Central America**
*See* Guardiola, Santos

**[The] Tiger of Honduras**
*See* Guardiola, Santos

**[The] Tiger of Malaya**
*See* Yamashita, Tomoyuki

**[The] Tiger of Tacayuba [or
Tacubaya?]**
*See* Marquez, Leonardo

**[The] Tiger of the Philippines**
*See* Yamashita, Tomoyuki

**Tiger of the Slopes**
*See* Raine, Nancy Greene

**Tiger Tom**
*See* Woodward, Thomas Jones

**Tight Lines Thomas**
*See* Thomas, Gary Philip

**Tigranes** 1st c. BC [WBD]
*King of Armenia*
* [The] Great

**[El] Tigre de Guanajuato [The Tiger
from Guanajuato]**
*See* Silveti, Juan

**[The] Tigress of Turin**
*See* Lombardi, Lella

**Tigrina**
*See* Eide, Edith

**Tihoti**
*See* Calderon, George

**Tijerina, Reies** 20th c.
*Mexican-American political
organizer*
* Rey Tigre [King Tiger]

**Tikekar, Shripad Ramchandra**
1901- [AW]
*Indian author*
* Mushafir, Kartikeya Skylark

**Tikhon**
*See* Belyavin, Vasili Ivanovich

**Tikhonov, Valentin**
*See* Payne, [Pierre Stephen]
Robert

**Tiktiner**
*See* Viterbo, Dina Tiktiner

**Til, Sonny**
*See* Tilghman, Earlington

**Tilbury, Quenna**
*See* Walker, Emily Kathleen

**Tilden, Big Bill**
*See* Tilden, William Tatem, II

**Tilden, One Round**
*See* Tilden, William Tatem, II

**Tilden, Samuel Jones** 1814-1886
[FFF, SN]
*American politician*
* [The] Graystone Sage
* Old Usufruct

**Tilden, William Tatem, II**
1893-1953 [AS, OET, SR]
*American tennis player*
* King of the Nets
* Tilden, Big Bill
* Tilden, One Round

**Tildsley, Peter** 1898-1962
[BEW, FC]
*British actor, author, theatre
manager*
* Haddon, Peter

**Tilelli, Carmine Orlando** 1930-
[BX, RBE]
*American boxer*
* Giardello, Joey

**Tilesius, G.**
*See* Gistl, Johannes N. Franz
Xavier

**Tileston, Mary W.** 19th c. [PA]
*Author*
* M. W. T.

**Tiletanus**
*See* Ravesteyn, Josse

**Tilghman, Earlington** 20th c.
[RO1]
*American singer*
* Til, Sonny

**Tilken, Felix** 1860?-1921
[BEW, EMT, PMJ]
*Belgian-born composer*
* Caryll, Ivan

**Till, Bobo**
*See* Till, Emmett Louis

**Till, Emmett Louis** 1941-1955
[IBW]
*American lynching victim*
* Till, Bobo

**Till, Fred** 1860-1927 [BEW]
*British actor*
* Lewis, Fred

**Tillet, Dorothy [Stockbridge]** 1896-
[CC, WW]
*Author*
* Strange, John Stephen

**Tilley, Vesta**
*See* Powles, Matilda Alice

**Tilling, Mabel** 1880?-1957 [BEW]
*British-born actress and playwright*
* Constanduros, Mabel

**Tillinghast, A. W.**
*See* Tillinghast, Albert Warren

**Tillinghast, Albert Warren**
1875-1942    [GF]
*American golf course architect and golf writer*
* Tillinghast, A. W.

**Tillinghast, Joseph Leonard** 19th c.
[FFF]
*American jurist and author*
* Carroll
* Dion

**Tillinghast, Oliver Louis** 20th c.
[BBH]
*American roller skating planner, builder, flooring expert*
* Tillinghast, Tilli

**Tillinghast, Tilli**
*See* Tillinghast, Oliver Louis

**Tillis, James** 1957?-
*American boxer*
* Tillis, Quick

**Tillis, Quick**
*See* Tillis, James

**Tillman, Bad Dude**
*See* Tillman, Rusty

**Tillman, Benjamin Ryan** 1847-1918
*American politician*
* Tillman, Pitchfork

**Tillman, Nathaniel Patrick, Sr.**
1898-1965    [IBW]
*American educator*
* Tillman, Tic

**Tillman, Pitchfork**
*See* Tillman, Benjamin Ryan

**Tillman, Rusty** 20th c.
*American football player*
* Tillman, Bad Dude

**Tillman, Tic**
*See* Tillman, Nathaniel Patrick, Sr.

**Tilloch, Alexander** 1759-1825
[FFF]
*Scottish author and journalist*
* Biblicus

**Tillotson, Joe W.** 20th c.    [WGT]
*Author*
* Fuqua, Robert

**Tillotson, Queena** 1896-1951
[BBD]
*American opera singer and author*
* Mario, Queena

**Tillray, Les**
*See* Gardner, Erle Stanley

**Tilly**
*See* Kannan, Lakshmi

**Tillyard, E. M. W.**
*See* Tillyard, Eustace Mandeville Wetenhall

**Tillyard, Eustace Mandeville Wetenhall** 1889-1962    [LC]
*British author*
* Tillyard, E. M. W.

**Tilt, Julia** 19th c.    [PA]
*Author*
* Hamilton, May

**Tiltman, Hugh Hessell** 1897-
[MBF]
*British author*
* Davenport, Tex
* Hessell, Henry

**Tiltman, Ronald Frank** 1901-
[CAP]
*British author and journalist*
* Fraser, Ronald

**Tilton, Alice**
*See* Taylor, Phoebe [Atwood]

**Tilton, Mrs. E. L.**    [FFF]
*Entertainer*
* Pentland, Mary

**Tilton, Stephen W.**    [PA]
*Author*
* Uncle Willis

**Tilton, Theodore** 1835- ?    [PA]
*Author*
* Marmaduke, Sir
* T. T.

**Tim**
*See* Mitelberg, Louis

**Timbs, John** 1801-1875    [PA]
*Author*
* Welby, Horace

**Time Honored Lancaster**
*See* John of Gaunt

**Time, Mark**
*See* Irwin, H. C.

**Timer, Joe**
*See* Theimer, Joseph Michael

**[The] Times Bee-Master**
*See* Cumming, John

**Timm, Cap**
*See* Timm, L. C.

**Timm, L. C.** 20th c.    [BBH]
*American baseball coach*
* Timm, Cap

**Timmis, Brian** 20th c.    [CFH]
*Football player*
* [The] Old Man of the Mountain

**Timms, Edward Vivian** 1895-
[WWL]
*Australian author*
* Dane, Zel
* Roseller, David

**Timoleon**
*See* Orr, Isaac

**Timon**
*See* De Cormenin, Viscount

**Timon, John**
*See* Mitchell, Donald Grant

**Timony, Arthur N.**
*See* Vahey, John George Haslette

**Timur [or Timour]** 1336-1405
[DEP, HN, RH]
*Tartar conqueror*
* [The] Destroying Prince
* [The] Firebrand of the Universe
* Ghengis Khan
* [The] Mongolian Bonaparte
* [The] Prince of Destruction
* [The] Scourge of God
* Tamerlane [or Tamburlaine]
* Timur Lenk [Timur the Lame]

**Timur Lenk [Timur the Lame]**
*See* Timur [or Timour]

**TINA [There is No Alternative]**
*See* Thatcher, Margaret Hilda [Roberts]

**Tincker, Mary Agnes**    [PA]
*Author*
* M. A. T.

**Tincrowdor, Leo Queequeg**
*See* Farmer, Philip Jose

**Tindale, Mrs. Acton** 19th c.    [PA]
*Author*
* Butler, Diana

**Tindall, Frederick Cryer** 1900-
[IAW]
*British author*
* Mark, John

**Tindall, William York** 1903-    [CA]
*American educator and author*
* Yorick, A. P.

**Tineman [or Tyneman]**
*See* Douglas, Archibald

**Tiner, John Hudson** 1944-    [CA]
*American author*
* Street, Jonathan

**Tinglehoff, H. Michael** 1940-    [FB]
*American football player*
* Tinglehoff, Mick

**Tinglehoff, Mick**
*See* Tinglehoff, H. Michael

**Tingley, Richard Hoadley** 1856- ?
[NAA]
*American author*
* Lee, Ting
* Puzzle "Nom"

**[The] Tiniest Star in Films**
*See* Flood, Pauline

**Tinin**
*See* Manuel, Jose

**Tinker, C. B.**
*See* Tinker, Chauncey Brewster

**Tinker, Chauncey Brewster**
1876-1963    [LC]
*American author and educator*
* Tinker, C. B.

**Tinker, Gerald** 1951-    [SMG]
*American football player*
* Tinker, Tink

**Tinker, Tink**
*See* Tinker, Gerald

**[The] Tinley Park Express**
*See* Bettenhausen, Melvin E.

**Tinne, Dorothea**
*See* Strover, Dorothea

**Tinne, E. D.**
*See* Strover, Dorothea

**Tinning, Bud**
*See* Tinning, Lyle Forrest

**Tinning, Lyle Forrest** 1906-1961
[BE]
*American baseball player*
* Tinning, Bud

**[El] Tino [The Tank]**
*See* Blau Gisbert, Vicente

**Tinquette, Miss**
*See* Bourgeois, Jeanne Marie

**Tinsley, Gaynell C.** 1915-    [FB]
*American football player*
* Tinsley, Gus

**Tinsley, Gus**
*See* Tinsley, Gaynell C.

**Tinsley, Theodore** 20th c.    [SFP]
*Author*
* Grant, Maxwell [house pseudonym]

**Tinto, Dick**
*See* Goodrich, Frank Boott

**[La] Tintoretta**
*See* Tintoretto, Marietta

**Tintoretto**
*See* Robusti, Jacopo

**Tintoretto, Domenico** 1565-1637
[WBD]
*Italian painter*
* [The] Younger

**Tintoretto, Marietta** 1560-1590
[WBD]
*Italian painter*
* [La] Tintoretta

**[The] Tintoretto of England**
*See* Dobson, William

**[The] Tintoretto of Switzerland**
*See* Huber, Johann [or John] Rudolphe

**Tiny**
*See* Kelly, James

**Tiny Alice**
*See* Ramirez, Alice Louise

**Tiny Darkhorse**
*See* Robinson, Mike

**[The] Tiny Giant**
*See* Murphy, Calvin

**Tiny Tim**
*See* Khaury, Herbert

**Tio, Luis** 1863?-1927    [NOJ]
*Mexican-born jazz musician*
* Tio, Papa

**Tio, Papa**
*See* Tio, Luis

**[El] Tio Porsupuesto**
*See* Bolivar, Simon

**Tioga George Burns**
*See* Burns, George Henry

**Tip**
*See* Marugg, Silvio A.

**Tipoo Tib [or Tip]**
*See* Hamidi bin Muhammad

**Tippecanoe**
*See* Harrison, William Henry

**Tipple, Big Dan**
*See* Tipple, Dan[iel Slaughter]

**Tipple, Dan[iel Slaughter]**
1890-1960    [BE]
*American baseball player*
* Tipple, Big Dan
* Tipple, Rusty

**Tipple, Rusty**
*See* Tipple, Dan[iel Slaughter]

**Tippou-Saib** 1749-1799    [PA]
*Author*
* Behadour

**Tippy Toes Karras**
*See* Karras, Alex[ander G.]

**Tiptoft, John** 1427?-1470
[DNNS, HN, RH]
*Earl of Worcester*
* [The] Butcher of England

**Tipton, Dukie**
See Tipton, Eric Gordon

**Tipton, Eric Gordon** 1915-
[BE, FB]
*American football and baseball player*
* [The] Blue Devil
* Eric the Red
* Tipton, Dukie

**[The] Tipton Slasher**
See Angone, Frank

**[The] Tipton Slasher**
See Perry, William

**Tipton, Thomas**
See Pointkowski, Thomas Max

**Tiptree, James, Jr.**
See Sheldon, Alice Bradley

**Tirabeque**
See Lafuente [or La Fuente], Modesto

**Tirado, Victor Manuel**
See Tirado Lopez, Victor

**Tirado Lopez, Victor** 1940-
*Mexican-born guerrilla leader in Nicaragua*
* Tirado, Victor Manuel

**Tirebuck, W.**
See Sharp, William

**Tiridates III** 238?- 314 [WBD]
*King of Aremenia*
* [The] Great

**Tiroff, James [Jim]** ?-1975 [SC]
*Actor*
* Harper, James

**Tironi, Carla** 1926- [IAW]
*Italian author and photographer*
* Cerati, Carla

**Tirzah, Mademoiselle**
See Clewe, Belle Ragnar Parsons

**Tisanthrope, Ter**
See Gillespie, William Houyman

**Tischbein, Johann Heinrich Wilhelm** 1751-1829 [WBD]
*German painter*
* Goethe-Tischbein
* [The] Neapolitan

**Tisdom, James** 20th c. [NBB]
*American singer*
* Tisdom, Smokestack

**Tisdom, Smokestack**
See Tisdom, James

**Tisi [or Tisio], Benvenuto** 1481?-1559 [WBD]
*Italian painter*
* Garofalo, Benvenuto da

**Tisner**
See Artis Gener, Aveli

**Tissant-Bernac, Mathieu**
See Macbeath, Innis [Stewart]

**Tisserand, Gerard Marcel** 1920-
[BBD, OP]
*French opera singer*
* Souzay, Gerard

**Tisserand, Jacques**
See Barnes, Jim Weaver

**Titan, Earl**
See Fearn, John Russell

**Titania**
See Blixen, Karen [Christentze Dinesen]

**Titcomb, Cannonball**
See Titcomb, Ledell

**Titcomb, Ledell** 1865-1950 [BE]
*American baseball player*
* Titcomb, Cannonball

**Titcomb, Timothy**
See Holland, Josiah Gilbert

**Tite Amedie Ardoin**
See Ardoin, Amedie

**Tite, Prince**
See George II

**Titi, Prince**
See Frederick Louis

**Titian**
See Vecelli [or Vecellio], Tiziano

**[The] Titian of France**
See Blanchard, Jacques

**[The] Titian of Portugal**
See Sanchez Coello, Alonzo

**Titmarsh, M. A.**
See Thackeray, William Makepeace

**Titmarsh, Michael Angelo**
See Thackeray, William Makepeace

**Tito, Josip Broz**
See Broz, Josip

**[The] Tito of the Arab World**
See Assad, Hafez

**Titta, Ruffo Cafiero** 1877-1953 [MS]
*Italian opera singer*
* Ruffo, Titta

**Titterington, Mrs. S. B.** [PA]
*Author*
* Graham, Grace

**Titterton, W. R.**
See Titterton, William Richard

**Titterton, William Richard** 1876-1963 [LC]
*British author*
* Titterton, W. R.

**Titterwell, Timothy**
See Kettell, Samuel

**Tittle, Y. A.**
See Tittle, Yelberton Abraham

**Tittle, Yelberton Abraham** 1926-
[FB, IPA]
*American football player*
* Bald Eagle
* Slick, Colonel
* Tittle, Y. A.

**Titus**
See Sabinus Vespasianus, Titus Flavius

**Titus Aurelius Fulvus Boionius Arrius** 86- 161 [WBD]
*Roman emperor*
* Antoninus Pius

**Titus, Eve** 1922- [CA, TBJ]
*American author*
* Lord, Nancy

**Titus, John Franklin** 1876-1943
[BE, PB]
*American baseball player*
* Titus, Silent John

**[The] Titus of Germany**
See Joseph II

**Titus, Silent John**
See Titus, John Franklin

**Titus, Tracy** [FFF]
*Entertainer*
* Oates, Alice

**Tityrus**
See Chaucer, Geoffrey

**Tivag**
See Gavit, Daniel E.

**Tivoli**
See Bleakley, Horace William

**[Il] Tizianello**
See Vecelli, Tiziano

**Tjader, Cal**
See Tjader, Callen Radcliffe, Jr.

**Tjader, Callen Radcliffe, Jr.** 1925-
[EJ, PMJ]
*American jazz musician*
* Tjader, Cal

**Tkaczuk, Edward Terrance** 1920-
[BE]
*American baseball player*
* Kazak, Edward Terrance

**Toal, Mike** 1959- [SMG]
*Canadian-born hockey player*
* Toal, Toaler

**Toal, Toaler**
See Toal, Mike

**[The] Toastmaster General of the United States**
See Jessel, George

**Tobacco Bill Crosby**
See Crosby, William R.

**Tobacco Chewin' Johnny**
See Lanning, John Young

**Tobey, David** 1898- [EJS]
*American basketball player and coach*
* [The] Coach of Coaches
* Tobey, Pep

**Tobey, Pep**
See Tobey, David

**Tobias, Katherine**
See Gottfried, Theodore Mark

**Tobias, Lenore** 1912- [BEW]
*American theatre party agent*
* Tobin, Lenore

**Tobik, David Vance** 1953- [SMG]
*American baseball player*
* Tobik, Tobe

**Tobik, Tobe**
See Tobik, David Vance

**Tobin, Abba Dabba**
See Tobin, James Anthony [Jim]

**Tobin, James Anthony [Jim]** 1912-1969 [BE, BN, PB]
*American baseball player*
* Ol' Ironsides
* Tobin, Abba Dabba

**Tobin, James Edward** 1905-1968
[CAP]
*American poet, editor, educator*
* Rayne, Alan

**Tobin, John H.** [PA]
*Author*
* John of York

**Tobin, John Martin [Johnny]** 1906-
[BE]
*American baseball player*
* Tobin, Tip

**Tobin, Lenore**
See Tobias, Lenore

**Tobin, Marion Brooks** 1916- [BE]
*American baseball player*
* Tobin, Pat

**Tobin, Pat**
See Tobin, Marion Brooks

**Tobin, Tip**
See Tobin, John Martin [Johnny]

**Tobler, Oscar** 1897-1961
[EJS, RBE]
*American boxer*
* Jackson, Willie

**Toby, Liz**
See Minsky, Betty Jane [Toebe]

**Toby, M. P.**
See Lucy, [Sir] Henry William

**Toby, Simeon**
See Trask, George F.

**Toche, Raoul** [PA]
*Author*
* Tovel, Raoul
* Triet, Robert
* Trinsome

**Tockler, Conrad** 1495-1530 [PA]
*Author*
* Noricus

**Tod, Evelyn**
See Thompson, Edith

**Tod, Osma Gallinger** 1898- [CAP]
*American author*
* Couch, Osma Palmer
* Gallinger, Osma Couch

**Todd, A. L.**
See Todd, Alden

**Todd, Alden** 1918- [IAW]
*American author*
* Todd, A. L.

**Todd, Ann**
See Mayfield, Ann Todd

**Todd, Anne Ophelia**
See Dowden, Anne Ophelia [Todd]

**Todd, Arthur** 1914- [CED]
*Canadian singer*
* [The] Canadian Crosby
* Todd, Dick

**Todd, Barbara Euphan** ?-1976
[TCC]
*British author*
* Bower, Barbara
* Euphan

**Todd, Charles** 1872-1955 [THR]
*British actor and theatrical manager*
* Windermere, Charles

**Todd, Dick**
See Todd, Arthur

**Todd, Eric**
*See* DuBreuil, Elizabeth Lorinda

**Todd, H. E.**
*See* Todd, Herbert Eatton

**Todd, Herbert Eatton** 1908-    [TCC]
*British author*
* Todd, H. E.

**Todd, John M[urray]** 1918-    [CA]
*British author*
* Fox, John

**Todd, Laurie**
*See* Thorburn, Grant

**Todd, Margaret** 1859-1918    [LC]
*Scottish author*
* Travers, Graham

**Todd, Michael**
*See* Goldbogen [or Goldenborgen],
Avrom

**Todd, Nick**
*See* Boone, Nick

**Todd, Paul**
*See* Posner, Richard

**Todd, Paul Adrian** 1953-    [DC]
*British cricketer*
* Todd, Tubs

**Todd, Richard**
*See* Palethorpe-Todd, Richard

**Todd, Ruthven** 1914-    [CC, WD]
*American author and poet*
* Campbell, R. T.

**Todd, Sarah Manning**
*See* Freeman, Jean Todd

**Todd, Silas** 18th c.    [FFF]
*Assistant of British evangelist, John
Wesley*
* [The] Good Samaritan of London

**Todd, Thelma**
*See* Lloyd, Alison

**Todd, Tubs**
*See* Todd, Paul Adrian

**Todeschini-Piccolomini, Francesco**
1439-1503    [CAL]
*Pope*
* Pius III

**[The] Toe**
*See* Groza, Louis

**Toenes, Hal**
*See* Toenes, William Harrel

**Toenes, William Harrel** 1917-    [BE]
*American baseball player*
* Toenes, Hal

**Toernudd, Margit** 1905-    [IAW]
*Finnish author*
* Niininen, Margit

**Tofano, Sergio** 1886-1973    [WEC]
*Italian cartoonist, filmmaker, actor*
* Sto

**Tofte, Arthur** 1902-    [IAW]
*American author*
* Andersson, Nic
* Babcock, Florence
* Boles, Nick

**Tofujin**
*See* Kabashima, Katsuichi

**Togo, Hashimura**
*See* Irwin, Wallace Admah

**Togrul Wang Khan** 12th c.    [HN]
*Mongol chieftain*
* Prester John

**Tojo, Eiki** 1885-1948    [WBD]
*Japanese prime minister and army
officer*
* Tojo, Hideki
* [The] Razor

**Tojo, Hideki**
*See* Tojo, Eiki

**Tokarski, E. F.**
*See* Freund, Edward

**Tokle, Torger** 20th c.    [BBH]
*Norwegian-born skier*
* [The] Babe Ruth of Skiing

**Tokohama, Charlie**
*See* Grant, Charles

**[The] Tokyo Giant**
*See* Sawell, Larry

**Tokyo Rose?**
*See* D'Aquino, Iva Ikuko [Toguri]

**Tolan, Eddie** 1908-1967    [BBH]
*American track and field athlete*
* [The] Midnight Express

**Tolan, Michael**
*See* Tuchow, Michael

**Toland, John**
*See* Toland, Junius Janus

**Toland, Junius Janus** 1670-1722
[SN, WBD]
*Irish author*
* [The] New Heresiarch
* Toland, John

**Tolar, Cannonball**
*See* Tolar, Charles G.

**Tolar, Charles G.** 1937-    [FB]
*American football player*
* Tolar, Cannonball

**Tolby, Arthur**
*See* Infield, Glenn [Berton]

**Tolchard, Roger William** 1946-
[DC]
*British cricketer*
* Tolchard, Tolly

**Tolchard, Tolly**
*See* Tolchard, Roger William

**Tolderlund, Hother**    [PA]
*Author*
* Lau, Viggo

**Toldy, Ferencz**
*See* Schedel, Ferencz

**Toler, John [Earl of Norbury]**
?-1831    [HN]
*Irish jurist*
* [The] Hanging Judge

**Toliver, George**
*See* Masselink, Ben

**Tolkien, J. R. R.**
*See* Tolkien, John Ronald Reuel

**Tolkien, John Ronald Reuel**
1892-1973    [LC]
*British author*
* J. R. R. T.
* Tolkien, J. R. R.

**Tollemache, David** 20th c.    [WWL]
*British author*
* Lovell, Mark

**Toller, Kate Caffrey**
*See* Caffrey, Kate

**Tolliver, Steve** 20th c.    [ESF]
*Author*
* Davies, Fredric [joint pseudonym
with Ron(ald C.) Ellik]

**Tolmage, Gerald**
*See* Gardner, Maurice

**Tolnai, Karoly**
*See* De Tolnay, Charles Erich

**Tolnai, Vagujhelyi Karoly**
*See* De Tolnay, Charles Erich

**Tolson, Chester Julius** 1901-    [BE]
*American baseball player*
* Tolson, Chick
* Tolson, Slug

**Tolson, Chick**
*See* Tolson, Chester Julius

**Tolson, Dean** 1951-    [SMG]
*American basketball player*
* [The] Twig

**Tolson, Dover**
*See* Tolson, Marion

**Tolson, Marion** 1927-    [IBW]
*American racehorse trainer*
* Tolson, Dover

**Tolson, Slug**
*See* Tolson, Chester Julius

**Tolstoy, Leo**
*See* Tolstoy, Lev Lvovich

**Tolstoy, Leo**
*See* Tolstoy, Lev Nikolayevich

**Tolstoy, Lev Lvovich** 1869-1945
*Russian author*
* Tolstoy, Leo

**Tolstoy, Lev Nikolayevich**
1828-1910    [LC]
*Russian author*
* Tolstoy, Leo

**Tolz, Nick?**
*See* Slotkin, Joseph

**Tom**
*See* Garfunkel, Art

**[The] Tom Moore of France**
*See* Amfrye, Guillaume

**[The] Tom Moore of the Confederacy**
*See* Ryan, Abram Joseph

**Tom of Ten Thousand**
*See* Thynne, Thomas

**Tomacelli, Pietro** ?-1404    [WBD]
*Pope*
* Boniface IX

**Tomalin, Ruth** 20th c.    [WD]
*British author and poet*
* Leaver, Ruth

**Tomaling, Susan** 1946-    [SW]
*American actress*
* Sarandon, Susan

**Tomamoto, Thomas**
*See* Sugimoto, Tsunetaro

**Tomanek, Bones**
*See* Tomanek, Richard Carl

**Tomanek, Richard Carl** 1931-    [BE]
*American baseball player*
* Tomanek, Bones

**Tomaras, William [Bill]** 20th c.
[BBH]
*American wrestler and coach*
* [The] Father of High School
Wrestling

**Tomasic, Niccolo** 1802-1874
[WBD]
*Italian author*
* Tommaseo, Niccolo

**Tomato Face Cullop**
*See* Cullop, Henry

**Tombo, Monsieur**
*See* Armstrong, John

**Tombs, Harry**
*See* Walley, David Gordon

**Tomfool**
*See* Farjeon, Eleanor

**Tomkiewicz, Mina** 1917-1975
[CAP]
*Polish-born journalist and author*
* Meta
* Quichot, Dona

**Tomkinson, Constance**
*See* Weeks, Constance Tomkinson

**Tomlin, Eric Walter Frederick**
1913-    [AW]
*British author*
* Stuart, Frederick

**Tomlin, Felicity** 1910-    [TR]
*British playwright*
* Douglas, Felicity

**Tomlin, Lily**
*See* Tomlin, Mary Jean

**Tomlin, Mary Jean** 1939-
*American comedienne and actress*
* Tomlin, Lily

**Tomlin, Pinky**
*See* Tomlin, Truman

**Tomlin, Truman** 1908-    [PMJ]
*American composer, singer,
bandleader*
* Tomlin, Pinky

**Tomline, F.**
*See* Gilbert, [Sir] William
Schwenck

**Tomlins, Frederick Guest**
1804-1867    [FFF]
*British journalist*
* Littlejohn

**Tomlins, Keith Patrick** 1957-    [DC]
*British cricketer*
* Tomlins, Tommo

**Tomlins, Tommo**
*See* Tomlins, Keith Patrick

**Tomlinson, B. W.**    [FFF]
*Writer*
* Picket

**Tomlinson, Frederick Charles** 1867?-
?    [CW]
*Jamaican author*
* Charles, Frederick

**Tomlinson, H. M.**
*See* Tomlinson, Henry Major

**Tomlinson, Henry Major**
1873-1958   [LC, TC]
*British author*
* Tomlinson, H. M.

**Tomlinson, Ike**
*See*   Tomlinson, J. A.

**Tomlinson, J. A.** 20th c.   [BBH]
*American baseball coach*
* Tomlinson, Ike

**Tomlison, Henry** 1865- ?   [WWL]
*British poet*
* George, Henry Stephen

**Tommaseo, Niccolo**
*See*   Tomasic, Niccolo

**Tommy the Cork**
*See*   Corcoran, Thomas G.

**Tompion, Thomas** 1639-1713
[SN, WBD]
*British clockmaker*
* [The] Father of Clock-Making
* [The] Father of English
   Watchmaking

**Tompkins, Harry** 20th c.   [GW]
*American rodeo performer*
* Tompkins, Uppy

**Tompkins, Herbert Winckworth**
1867- ?   [LAO]
*British author and journalist*
* Pepys in Essex

**Tompkins, Julia [Marguerite Hunter
Manchee]** 1909-   [CA, WD]
*British author*
* Neilson, Marguerite

**Tompkins, Juliet Wilbor**
*See*   Pottle, Juliet Wilbor Tompkins

**Tompkins, Ron[ald Everett]** 1944-
[BE]
*American baseball player*
* Tompkins, Stretch

**Tompkins, Stretch**
*See*   Tompkins, Ron[ald Everett]

**Tompkins, Uppy**
*See*   Tompkins, Harry

**Tompkins, Yewell** 1909-
[BEW, IPA, ITA]
*American actor*
* Ewell, Tom

**Toms, Tubby**
*See*   Toms, William L.

**Toms, William L.** 20th c.   [BLB]
*American journalist*
* Toms, Tubby

**Tomson, Graham R.**
*See*   Watson, Rosamund [Ball]
Marriott

**Tomson, Tommy**
*See*   Tomson, W. R.

**Tomson, W. R.** 20th c.
*American advertising salesman*
* Tomson, Tommy

**Ton Duc Thang** 1889?-1980
*Vietnamese president*
* Uncle Ton

**Ton Ven**
*See*   Bordewijk, Ferdinand

**Tonans, Jupiter**
*See*   Erskine, Thomas

**Tonashi**
*See*   Harrington, Mark Raymond

**Tonawanda, Jackie** 1948-   [IBW]
*American boxer*
* [The] Female Ali

**Toney, Lemuel Gordon** 1875-1941
[ASC, BEW, CED]
*American entertainer and songwriter*
* Leonard, Eddie

**Tongue, Cornelius**   [PA]
*Author*
* Cecil

**Tonkin, Doc**
*See*   Tonkin, Harry Glenville

**Tonkin, Harry Glenville** 1881-1959
[BE]
*American baseball player*
* Tonkin, Doc

**[Le] Tonkinois**
*See*   Ferry, Jules Francois Camille

**Tonks, John** 1927-   [ART]
*British sculptor*
* J. T.

**Tonna, Charlotte Elizabeth**
1792-1846   [DEL, FFF]
*British author*
* Charlotte-Elizabeth

**Tonneman, Charles Richard**
1881-1951   [BE]
*American baseball player*
* Tonneman, Tony

**Tonneman, Tony**
*See*   Tonneman, Charles Richard

**Tonnies, Ferdinand Julius** 1855- ?
[LAO]
*German educator and author*
* Normannus

**Tons, Helen**   [FFF]
*Entertainer*
* Secor, Helena

**Tonson, Jacob**
*See*   Bennett, [Enoch] Arnold

**Tonson, Jacob** 1656?-1736   [SN]
*British publisher*
* Old Jacob

**Tonti, Henri de** 17th c.   [SN]
*Explorer of the Mississippi Valley*
* [The] Iron Hand

**Tony C.**
*See*   Conigliaro, Anthony Richard

**Tony Ducks Corallo**
*See*   Corallo, Antonio

**Tony Pro Provenzano**
*See*   Provenzano, Anthony

**Tony the Ant**
*See*   Spilotro, Anthony

**Tony the Gentleman**
*See*   Genna, Antonio

**Tony the Terror**
*See*   Smith, Tony

**Too Mean Martin**
*See*   Martin, Harvey

**Too Strong Boyd**
*See*   Boyd, Gregory Earl

**Too Tall Jones**
*See*   Jones, Ed

**Too Tall Patterson**
*See*   Patterson, Sheila

**Too Tight Henry**
*See*   Castle, Henry Lee

**Too Tight Henry**
*See*   Townsend, Henry

**Took, Belladonna**
*See*   Chapman, Vera

**Tooke, Horne**
*See*   Horne, John

**Tooke, W.** 1774-1820   [PA]
*Author*
* M. M. M.

**Tooker, Richard** 1902-   [WGT]
*American author*
* Lemke, Henry E.

**Toole, Rex**
*See*   Tralins, S[andor] Robert
[Bob]

**Tooley, John** 20th c.   [IBW]
*American playwright, producer,
actor*
* Ashby, John

**Toom Tabard [Empty Jacket]**
*See*   Baliol [or Balliol], John

**Toomay, Pat** 20th c.
*American football player*
* Toomay, Ropes

**Toomay, Ropes**
*See*   Toomay, Pat

**Toonder, Martin**
*See*   Groom, Arthur William

**Toorop, Annie Caroline** 1891-1955
[CAR]
*Dutch painter*
* Toorop, Charley

**Toorop, Charley**
*See*   Toorop, Annie Caroline

**Tootell, Hugh** ?-1745   [PA]
*British author*
* Dodd, Charles

**Toothpick Sam Jones**
*See*   Jones, Samuel

**Top Cat Jackson**
*See*   Jackson, Cubby

**Top Cat Norman**
*See*   Norman, Fredie Hubert

**Toperoff, Sam** 1933-   [CA]
*American author and poet*
* Potter, Faith

**Topham, Anthony** 20th c.   [RO2]
*British musician*
* Topham, Top

**Topham, Thomas** 1710-1753?
[DNNS, FFF, RH]
*British strongman*
* [The] British Samson
* [The] English Milo
* [The] Samson of England
* [The] Strong Man

**Topham, Top**
*See*   Topham, Anthony

**Topi**
*See*   Vikstedt, Toivo Alarik

**Toplady, Augustus Montagu**
1740-1778   [FFF]
*British clergyman*
* Philaretus

**Toplis, Fred** 1874- ?   [THR]
*British comedian*
* Rome, Fred

**Topol**
*See*   Topol, Chaim

**Topol, Chaim** 1935-   [FC, SW]
*Israeli actor*
* Topol

**Topolski, Feliks** 1907-   [ART]
*Polish-born painter and draftsman*
* F. T.

**Toporcer, George** 1899-   [BE, PB]
*American baseball player*
* Toporcer, Specs

**Toporcer, Specs**
*See*   Toporcer, George

**Topperwein, Elizabeth** ?-1945
[AS]
*American trapshooter*
* Topperwein, Plinky

**Topperwein, Plinky**
*See*   Topperwein, Elizabeth

**Toppin, Rupe**
*See*   Toppin, Ruperto

**Toppin, Ruperto** 1941-   [BE]
*Panamanian-born baseball player*
* Toppin, Rupe

**Tor, Regina**
*See*   Shekerjian, Regina Tor

**Torakis, Louis** 1928-   [BEW]
*American costume designer*
* Travis, Michael

**Torberg, Friedrich**
*See*   Kantor-Berg, Friedrich

**Torbett, Harvey Douglas Louis**
1921-   [CA]
*British author*
* Dee, Henry
* Isis

**Torbett, John Walter** 1871- ?
[NAA]
*American physician, poet, writer*
* Uncle Peter

**Torborg, Jeffrey Allen** 1941-
[SMG]
*American baseball player*
* Rutgers, Rudy

**[The] Torch of Eloquence**
*See*   Masfar ben Bedreddin, Al-

**[The] Torch of Pengwern**
*See*   Gwenwyn

**[The] Torch of Wisdom**
*See*   Shurman, Anna Maria von

**Torday, Ursula** 20th c.
[CC, WD, WW]
*British author*
* Allardyce, Paula
* Blackstock, Charity
* Blackstock, Lee

**Tordenskiol [Thunder Shield]**
*See*   Wessel, Peder

**Torello, James** 1931-
*American underworld figure*
* Torello, Turk

**Torello, Turk**
See Torello, James

**Torerito [Little Bullfighter]**
See Bejarano y Carrasco, Rafael

**Torga, Miguel**
See Coelho Da Rocha, Adolfo

**Torgeson, [Clifford] Earl** 1924-
[BE, PB]
*American baseball player*
* [The] Earl of Snohomish
* Torgeson, Torgie

**Torgeson, Lavern** 1929- [SMG]
*American football coach*
* Torgeson, Torgy

**Torgeson, Torgie**
See Torgeson, [Clifford] Earl

**Torgeson, Torgy**
See Torgeson, Lavern

**Torgosi, Karlon**
See Ackerman, Forrest J[ames]

**Torgosi, Vespertina**
See Ackerman, Forrest J[ames]

**Torgownik, William** 1907- [CA]
*American publisher, author, poet*
* Targ, William
* Yu, Charles

**Torigi, Richard**
See Tortorigi, Santo V.

**Torin, Sidney** 1909- [B10]
*American disk jockey*
* Symphony Sid

**Torkelson, Chester LeRoy**
1894-1964 [BE]
*American baseball player*
* Torkelson, Red

**Torkelson, Red**
See Torkelson, Chester LeRoy

**Torley, Luke**
See Blish, James [Benjamin]

**Torme, Mel[vin Howard]** 1925-
*American singer and songwriter*
* Butterscotch, Mr.
* [The] Kid with the Gauze in His
  Jaws
* [The] Velvet Fog
* [The] Velvet Frog
* Wyatt, Wesley Butler

**Torn, Elmore Rual, Jr.** 1931-
[BEW, FC, TR]
*American actor and director*
* Torn, Rip

**Torn, Rip**
See Torn, Elmore Rual, Jr.

**Tornado Jake Weimer**
See Weimer, Jacob

**Toro, Fermin** 1807-1865 [FFF]
*Venezuelan statesman and editor*
* Kastos, Emiro

**Torok, Lou** 1927- [CA]
*American author*
* [The] Convict Writer

**Torpare, Tord**
See Sandblad-Haneson, Emelie
Cecilia Sofia

**Torphy, Red**
See Torphy, Walter Anthony

**Torphy, Walter Anthony** 1891-
[BE]
*American baseball player*
* Torphy, Red

**Torquemada**
See Mathers, Edward Powys

**Torquemada, Juan de [or John]**
1388-1468 [HN]
*Spanish monk and prelate*
* Defender of the Faith

**Torquet, Andre** 1873-1918 [WBD]
*French poet and author*
* Nau, John Antoine

**Torquito [Little Torco]**
See Vigiola Del Torco, Serafin

**Torr, Iain**
See MacKinnon, Charles Roy

**Torr, Joan Rosita** 1893?-1967
[LAO, LC]
*British author*
* Forbes, Rosita

**Torrance, Baby Jack**
See Torrance, Jack

**Torrance, Jack** 1912-1970 [TF]
*American track and field athlete*
* [The] Baby Elephant
* Torrance, Baby Jack

**Torrance, Lee**
See Sadgrove, Sidney Henry

**[The] Torre of Poetry**
See Gray, Thomas

**Torre Lopez, Fernando** 1927-
[IAW]
*Mexican-born author*
* Grimaldo, Benjamin

**Torrence, David**
See Thoyson, David

**Torrence, Ernest**
See Thoyson, Ernest

**Torres, Alacran** 20th c. [BX, RBE]
*Mexican boxer*
* Torres, Efren

**Torres, Don Gilberto Nunez** 1915-
[BE]
*Cuban-born baseball player*
* Torres, Gil

**Torres, Efren**
See Torres, Alacran

**Torres, Gil**
See Torres, Don Gilberto Nunez

**Torres, Jose Luis** 1936- [WBC]
*Puerto Rican-born boxer*
* Torres, Quick Hands

**Torres, Quick Hands**
See Torres, Jose Luis

**Torres, Raquel**
See Osterman, Paula Marie

**Torres, Rosendo, Jr.** 1948- [SMG]
*Puerto Rican-born baseball player*
* Torres, Rusty

**Torres, Rusty**
See Torres, Rosendo, Jr.

**Torres, Tereska [Szwarc]** 20th c.
[CA, WD]
*French author*
* Achard, George

**Torres Jimenez, Andres** 1945- [GS]
*Spanish bullfighter*
* [El] Monaguillo [The Altar Boy]

**Torres y Feria, Manuel de**
1833-1892 [CW]
*Cuban playwright*
* De La Flor, Serafin

**Torres y Reina, Emilio** 1874-1947
[GS]
*Spanish bullfighter*
* Bombita [Little Bomb]

**Torres y Reina, Manuel** 1884-1936
[GS]
*Spanish bullfighter*
* Bombita III [Little Bomb the
  Third]

**Torres y Reina, Ricardo** 1879-1936
[GS, OCS]
*Spanish bullfighter*
* Bombita [Little Bomb]

**Torrey, Amos** [PA]
*Author*
* B. T.

**Torrey, Marjorie**
See Chanslor, Marjorie Torrey
[Hood]

**Torrey, Therese Von Hohoff**
1898?-1974 [CA]
*American author and editor*
* Hohoff, Tay

**Torrey, Ware** 1905- [WW]
*Author*
* Crosby, Lee

**Torriano, Hugh Arthur** 1860- ?
[WWL]
*British author*
* Marchmont, Frederick

**Torrie, Malcolm**
See Mitchell, Gladys [Maude
Winifred]

**Torrio, John [Johnny]** 1882-1957
[BLB, MM]
*Italian-born American underworld
figure*
* [The] Father of Modern
  American Gangsterdom
* [The] Fox
* J. T.
* Langley, Frank
* McCarthy, J. T.
* Torrio, Papa Johnny

**Torrio, Papa Johnny**
See Torrio, John [Johnny]

**Torro, Pel**
See Fanthorpe, R[obert] Lionel

**Torsi, Tristan**
See Lang, Isaac

**Torstensdotter, Elsa Viveca** 1920-
[BDF, WEF]
*Swedish-born actress*
* Lindfors, Viveca

**Torsvan, Traven?**
See Marut, Ret

**Tortero [Cake Maker]**
See Santos, Enrique

**Tortoriello, Joseph** 1902-
[EJ, PMJ, WWJ]
*American jazz musician*
* Tarto, Joe

**Tortorigi, Santo V.** 1917- [OP]
*American opera singer*
* Torigi, Richard

**[The] Tory Terrier**
See Churchill, John [First Duke of
Marlborough]

**Tosh, Peter**
See MacIntosh, Peter

**Toson, Shimazaki**
See Haruki, Shimazaki

**Tosswill, Leonard R. Major** 1880-
? [WWL]
*British author*
* Kyrle

**Tot, Endre**
See Toth, Endre

**Totah, Knobby**
See Totah, Nabil Marshall

**Totah, Nabil Marshall** 1930- [EJ]
*Jordanian-born jazz musician*
* Totah, Knobby

**Total Man**
See Salter, Sy

**Toth, Andreas** 1910?-
[BDF, FD, WEF]
*Hungarian-born director*
* De Toth, Andre

**Toth, Endre** 1937- [CAR]
*Hungarian artist*
* Tot, Endre

**Totham, Mary**
See Breinburg, Petronella

**Totila**
See Baduila

**Toto**
See De Curtis-Gagliardi, Antonio
Furst

**Toto the Clown**
See Novello, Armando

**Tototoro [All Bull]**
See Suarez, Carlos

**Totten, Charles Adiel Lewis** 1851-
? [FFF]
*American inventor and author*
* Alcott, Ten

**Totten, W. Fred** 1905- [IAW]
*American educator and author*
* Worthington Ball, John

**Totts, Kid**
See Blaise, Ed

**Toucey, Kate**
See Morris, Mrs. Austin W.

**Touchatout**
See Bienvenu, Leon

**Touchdown Tony Adams**
See Adams, Anthony L.

**Touchdown Tony Baker**
See Baker, Tony

**[The] Touchdown Twin**
See Bates, Mickey

**[The] Touchdown Twin**
See Caroline, James Calvin

**Touch'em, Timothy**
See Beck, Thomas

**Touchstone**
See Boote, Henry Ernest

**Touchstone**
See Burton, Claude Edward
Cole-Hamilton

**Touchstone**
See Durcie, John

**Touchstone**
See Savage, John

**Touchwood**
See Garner, Katherine Minta

**Toucke, Marion** 1898?-1962
[BEW]
*American opera singer*
* Telva, Marion

**Tough Tony Anastasio**
See Anastasio, Anthony

**Tough Tony Capezio**
See Capezio, Anthony

**Tough Tony Foyt**
See Foyt, Anthony Joseph, Jr.

**Touhy, Roger** 1898-1959
[BLB, PHM]
*American underworld figure*
* [The] Terrible

**Touhy, Terrible Tommy**
See Touhy, Tommy

**Touhy, Tommy** 20th c. [BLB]
*American underworld figure*
* Touhy, Terrible Tommy

**Toulman, C.**
See Crosland, Mrs. C.

**Toulouse Lautrec**
See Curcio, Renato

**Toumanova, Tamara**
See Khacidovitch, Tamara

**Tourbillon, Ratsy**
See Tourbillon, Robert Arthur

**Tourbillon, Robert Arthur** 1885- ?
[BLB]
*American swindler and robber*
* Collins, Dapper Don
* Hussey, Harry
* Tourbillon, Ratsy

**Toure, Askia Muhammed**
See Snellings, Rolland

**Toure, Kwame**
See Carmichael, Stokeley

**Tourel, Jennie**
See Davidson, Jennie

**Tourgee, Albion W[inegar]**
1838-1905 [SFL, WBD, WGT]
*American author and politician*
* Churton, Henry
* Henry, Edgar
* Nixon, Wm. Penn

**Tournachon, [Gaspard] Felix**
1820-1910 [B10, WEC]
*French artist and balloonist*
* Nadar

**Tournebu, Adrien** 1512-1565
[WBD]
*French scholar*
* Turnebe, Adrien

**Tournefort, Joseph Pittou de**
1656-1708 [DEP, HN]
*French botanist*
* [The] Father of Botany

**Tourneur, Maurice**
See Thomas, Maurice

**Tournier, Luc**
See Engels, Christiaan J. H.

**Tournier, Millie**
See Orinifo, Mrs.

**Tournimparte, Alessandra**
See Ginzburg, Natalia

**Toussain, Jacques** ?-1547 [SN]
*French scholar*
* [A] Living Library

**Toussaint, Gertrude**
See Clark, Mrs. W. H.

**Toussaint, Jackie**
See Lourens-Koop, Adriana
Luberta Klazina

**Toussaint-Desessarts, Nicholas**
1744-1810 [PA]
*Author*
* Moyne

**Tousseul, Jean**
See Degee, Olivier

**Tout, Hazel Dawn** 1891?- [BEW]
*American actress*
* Dawn, Hazel

**Toutain, Jose** 20th c. [WECO]
*Spanish cartoonist*
* Roger

**Tovar, Cesar Leonardo** 1940- [BE]
*Venezuelan-born baseball player*
* Tovar, Pepito

**Tovar, Pepito**
See Tovar, Cesar Leonardo

**Tovel, Raoul**
See Toche, Raoul

**Tovell, Ruth Massey** 1889- ?
[CAN]
*Canadian author*
* Massey, Ruth

**Tovey, R. L.**
See Tovey, Robert Lawton

**Tovey, Robert Lawton** 1924-
[ART]
*British painter*
* Tovey, R. L.

**Tower, Allen**
See Coggeshall, John Allen

**Tower, Diana**
See Smith, Richard Rein

**Tower, Don**
See Bower, Donald E[dward]

**[The] Tower Earl**
See Fitzgerald, James

**Tower, Joseph L.**
See La Torre, Giuseppe

**Tower, Stella Mary [Hodgson]**
1891- [WW]
*Author*
* Wolseley, Faith

**Towers, Ivar** [house pseudonym]
See Wilson, Richard

**Towers, Maxwell** 1909- [CA]
*Scottish-born author and poet*
* Rabbie

**Towers, Tricia**
See Ivison, Elizabeth

**Towle, Arthur** 1887-1954 [FC]
*British comedian and actor*
* Lucan, Arthur

**Towler, Daniel L.** 1928- [FB]
*American football player*
* Towler, Deacon Dan

**Towler, Deacon Dan**
See Towler, Daniel L.

**Town Crier**
See Byrne, Charles A.

**[The] Town Crier**
See Woollcott, Alexander

**Town Listener**
See Richardson, Leander

**Towne, Ada** 1868?-1931 [BEW]
*American actress*
* Fenton, Mabel

**Towne, Artie**
See Johnson, Henry

**Towne, Babe**
See Towne, Jay King

**Towne, Jay King** 1880-1938 [BE]
*American baseball player*
* Towne, Babe

**Towne, Mary**
See Spelman, Mary

**Towne, Stuart**
See Rawson, Clayton

**Towne, Tracy**
See Sawtille, Mrs. E. W.

**Townley, Carol**
See Townley-Parker, Caroline
Townley

**Townley, Daniel O'Connell**
1824-1873 [FFF]
*American author*
* Rooney, Alderman

**Townley, Houghton** 20th c. [MBF]
*British author*
* Preston, Walford

**Townley, Michael Vernon** 20th c.
*American suspected of involvement
in Chilean assassination plot*
* Williams

**Townley-Parker, Caroline Townley**
1891- [WWL]
*British author*
* Townley, Carol

**Towns, Forrest** 1914- [BBH]
*American track and field athlete*
* Towns, Speck

**Towns, Speck**
See Towns, Forrest

**Townsend, Alice** [PA]
*Author*
* Orsin, Floro

**Townsend, Eric W.**
See McLean, Eric W.

**Townsend, George Alfred**
1841-1914 [FFF, PA]
*American author and journalist*
* Bouquet, Johnny

**Townsend, George Alfred**
(Continued)
* Gath
* Laertes

**Townsend, George Henry**
1835-1869 [PA]
*British author*
* [An] English Critic
* Green, John

**Townsend, Happy**
See Townsend, John

**Townsend, Henry** 1909- [BWW]
*American singer*
* Thomas, Henry
* Too Tight Henry

**Townsend, Ira Dance** 1894-1965
[BE]
*American baseball player*
* Townsend, Pat

**Townsend, James B[arclay] J[ermain]**
1910- [CA]
*American author*
* Livingston, Peter Van Rensselaer

**Townsend, Joan** 1913- [IAW]
*British author*
* Pomfret, Joan

**Townsend, John** 1879-1963 [BE]
*American baseball player*
* Townsend, Happy

**Townsend, John** 1916- [BB]
*American basketball player*
* [The] Houdini of the Hardwood

**Townsend, Lefty**
See Townsend, Leo Alphonse

**Townsend, Leo Alphonse** 1891-
[BE]
*American baseball player*
* Townsend, Lefty

**Townsend, Mark**
See Wallmann, Jeffrey M[iner]

**Townsend, Mary Ashely [Van
Voorhis]** 1836?-1901 [FFF, PA]
*American poet*
* Xariffa

**Townsend, Pat**
See Townsend, Ira Dance

**Townsend, S. Nugent** [PA]
*Author*
* St. Kames

**Townsend, Storm Diana** 1937-
[ART]
*British-born sculptor*
* Storm

**Townsend, Virginia Frances**
1836-1920 [FFF]
*American author*
* Cousin Virginia

**Townshend, Charles** 1725-1767
[DNNS, WBD]
*British politician*
* [The] Weathercock

**Townshend, Richard**
See Bickers, Richard Leslie
Townshend

**Towry, Peter**
See Piper, David Towry

**Toxophilus**
See Faddis, William L.

[The] Toy Bull Dog
See Courtney, Clinton Dawson

[The] Toy Bulldog
See Walker, Edward Patrick

[The] Toy Cannon
See Wynn, James Sherman [Jim]

[The] Toy Tiger
See Howatt, Garry Robert Charles

Toyen
See Cerminova, Marie

Toynbee, Lawrence 1922- [ART]
British painter
* L. L. T.

Toynbee, Rosalind 1890- [WWL]
British author
* Murray, Rosalind

Tozer, Basil 20th c. [WWL]
British author
* Villain, Regardant

Tozzo, Rocco 1895-1954
[AS, BX, RBE]
American boxer
* Kansas, Rocky

Trabert, Marion 1930- [BBH]
American tennis player
* Trabert, Tony

Trabert, Tony
See Trabert, Marion

Trace, Al[bert J.] [ASC]
American composer, conductor,
singer
* Hart, Bob
* Watts, Clem

Tracewski, Richard Joseph 1935-
[SMG]
American baseball player and coach
* Tracewski, Tracy
* Tracewski, Trixie

Tracewski, Tracy
See Tracewski, Richard Joseph

Tracewski, Trixie
See Tracewski, Richard Joseph

Tracey, Thomas F.
See Flynn, Thomas W.

Trachsel, Myrtle Jamison 20th c.
[NAA]
American writer
* Jamison, Jane

[The] Tractor King
See House, Eddie James, Jr.

Tracts, Hartley Wintney
See Gifford, F. O.

Tracy, Aloise
See Shoenight, Aloise

Tracy, Arthur
See Rosenberg, Harry

Tracy, Benjamin Franklin
1830-1915 [WBD]
American Secretary of the Navy
* [The] Father of the American
Navy

Tracy, Catherine
See Story, Rosamond Mary

Tracy, Don[ald Fiske] 1905- ? [CA]
American author
* Fuller, Roger

Tracy, Harry 20th c. [BLB]
American criminal
* [The] Mad Dog

Tracy, Hetty
See Williams, Mrs. Jesse

Tracy, Leland
See Tralins, S[andor] Robert
[Bob]

Tracy, Louis 1863-1928
[CC, EMD, WW]
British author and journalist
* Holmes, Gordon [joint
pseudonym with Matthew Phipps
Shiel]

Tracy, Lucy Bradshaw 20th c.
[NAA]
American writer
* Alden, Betty [house pseudonym?]

Tracy, Mrs. [FFF]
Entertainer
* Ethel, Agnes

Tracy, Powers
See Ward, Don[ald G.]

Tracy, Roger Sherman 1841-1926
[ESF, SFL]
American author
* Hodge, T. Shirby

[The] Trader in Faction
See Milton, John

Trader Vic
See Bergeron, Victor

Trafford, F. G.
See Riddell, Charlotte Eliza
Lawson [Cowan]

Trafton, Adelina [FFF]
American author
* American Girl Abroad

Trafton, Edwin H. [PA]
Author
* Count, Noah

Trafton, George 1896-1971 [BBH]
American football player
* [The] Brute

Tragett, Margaret Rivers 1885-
[WWL]
British author
* Larminie, Margaret Rivers

Traglia, Luigi 1895?-1977
Italian cardinal
* [The] Living Archive

Tragus
See Bock, Hieronymus

Traherne, Michael
See Watkins-Pitchford, Denys
James

Trahey, Jane 1923- [CA]
American author
* Erlanger, Baba

Traill, Peter
See Morton, Guy Mainwaring

Traill, Robert 1642-1716
[FFF, SN]
Scottish clergyman
* [The] Venomous Preacher

Trailrider
See Hyland, Ann

Train, Arthur 1875- ? [WWL]
American author
* Lency, C.

Traina, Giuseppe 20th c. [BLB]
American underworld figure
* [The] Peasant

Trainor, Richard
See Tralins, S[andor] Robert
[Bob]

Trainor, Thomas Weston 1922-
[CEI]
Canadian-born hockey player
* Trainor, Wes

Trainor, Wes
See Trainor, Thomas Weston

[A] Traitor to Freedom
See Webster, Daniel

Tralins, Robert S.
See Tralins, S[andor] Robert
[Bob]

Tralins, S[andor] Robert [Bob]
1926- [CA, WD]
American author
* Bixby, Ray Z.
* King, Norman A.
* Miles, Keith
* O'Shea, Sean
* O'Toole, Rex
* Sydney, Cynthia
* Toole, Rex
* Tracy, Leland
* Trainor, Richard
* Tralins, Robert S.
* Traube, Ruy
* Verdon, Dorothy

Tramback, Red
See Tramback, Stephen Joseph

Tramback, Stephen Joseph 1915-
[BE]
American baseball player
* Tramback, Red

Tramin, A. G.
See Martin, Gloria Ann

Tramin, Ed
See Martin, Gloria Ann

Tramin, Lisa
See Martin, Gloria Ann

[The] Tramp
See Anderson, Arthur Henry

Tramp
See Skinner, Charles M.

[The] Tramp Musician
See Powles, Harry

Tran-nam-Trung
See Tran-van-Tra

Tran-van-Tra 1913- [B10]
Vietnamese military leader
* Tran-nam-Trung

Trankel, Margot
See Kreuter-Trankel, Margot

Tranquilli, Secondo 1900-
[CAP, EWL, IPA]
Italian author and playwright
* Silone, Ignazio

Trans-Atlantic
See Mooney, Thomas

Translator General
See Holland, Philemon

Transmarine
See Louis IV

Transue, Jacob
See Matheson, Joan

Trant, Martin
See White, Trentwell Mason

Tranter, Nigel [Godwin] 1909-
[CA, WWS]
Scottish author
* Tredgold, Nye

Trantina, Barbara 20th c. [BBH]
American swimmer
* Trantina, Bede

Trantina, Bede
See Trantina, Barbara

Trapassi, Pietro Antonio Domenico
Bonaventura 1698-1782
[FFF, RH, WBD]
Italian poet and playwright
* Metastasio
* [The] Racine of Italy

Trapp, George 1949-
American basketball player
* Trapp, Heat

Trapp, Heat
See Trapp, George

Trappier, Arthur Benjamin 1910-
[EJ, WWJ]
American jazz musician
* Trappier, Traps

Trappier, Traps
See Trappier, Arthur Benjamin

Traprock, Walter E.
See Chappell, George S.

Traps the Drum Wonder
See Rich, Bernard

Trask, George F. 1797-1875
[FFF, PA]
Clergyman and author
* Sproule, Zibra
* Toby, Simeon

Trask, Helen
See Lowell, Joan

Trask, Kate 1844-1909
[FFF, WBD]
American author
* Augusta, Clara
* Trask, Katrina

Trask, Katrina
See Trask, Kate

Trask, Merrill
See Colton, Mel

Traube, Ruy
See Tralins, S[andor] Robert
[Bob]

Traudl
See Flaxman, Traudl

Traugott, Elizabeth Closs 1939-
[CA]
American linguist and author
* Closs, Elizabeth

Trausti, Jon
See Magnusson, Guomundur

Travascio, Nicholas Anthony
1925-1964 [EJ, PMJ]
American jazz musician
* Travis, Nick

**[A] Traveler**
See Bavin, John

**[A] Traveler**
See Rayall, Mrs. A.

**[A] Traveler**
See Salt, Henry

**[A] Traveling Bachelor**
See Cooper, James Fenimore

**[A] Traveling Showman**
See Dilks, John M.

**[The] Traveling Texan**
See Walker, William Marvin
[Billy]

**Traveller**
See Dowsett, Joseph Morewood

**[The] Travelling Netminder**
See Conacher, Lionel Pretoria

**Traven, B.?**
See Marut, Ret

**Traven, Beatrice**
See Goldemberg, Rose Leiman

**Traver, Robert**
See Voelker, John Donaldson

**Travers, Allan**
See Travers, Aloysius Joseph

**Travers, Aloysius Joseph**
1892-1968 [BE]
*American baseball player*
* Travers, Allan

**Travers, Graham**
See Todd, Margaret

**Travers, Henry**
See Heagerty, Travers John

**Travers, Hugh**
See Mills, Hugh [Travers]

**Travers, Kenneth**
See Hutchin, Kenneth Charles

**Travers, Linden**
See Lindon-Travers, Florence

**Travers, P. L.**
See Travers, Pamela Lyndon

**Travers, Pamela Lyndon** 1904?-
[LC, TC]
*British author and poet*
* Travers, P. L.

**Travers, Phebe** [PA]
*Author*
* Aunt Florida

**Travers, Richard C.**
See Libb, Richard

**Travers, Stephen**
See Radcliffe, [Henry] Garnett

**Travers, Will**
See Rowland, D[onald] S[ydney]

**Travers-Smith, Dorothea** 20th c.
[ART]
*British painter*
* T. S.

**Traverse, Madlaine**
See Businsky, Madlaine

**Travis, Gerry**
See Trimble, Louis P[reston]

**Travis, Jack**
See Madden, [Jerry] David

**Travis, June**
See Grabiner, June Dorothea

**Travis, Lawrence**
See Deutzman, Lawrence
F[rederick]

**Travis, Michael**
See Torakis, Louis

**Travis, Nick**
See Travascio, Nicholas Anthony

**Travis, Richard**
See Justice, William

**Travis, Walter J.** 1862-1927
[BWG, EG, GF]
*Australian-born golfer*
* [The] Old Man

**Traylor, Bill** 20th c. [IBW]
*American painter*
* Uncle Bill

**Traynor, Alex**
See Lagerwall, Edna

**Traynor, Earl Richard** ?-1944
[SC]
*American actor*
* Hogan, Earl
* Hogan, Hap

**Traynor, Harold Joseph** 1899-1972
[BE, DGS, PB]
*American baseball player and manager*
* Traynor, Pie

**Traynor, Linda** 20th c.
*American actress*
* Lovelace, Linda

**Traynor, Pie**
See Traynor, Harold Joseph

**Treacher, Arthur**
See Veary, Arthur T.

**Treacle, Uncle**
See Mitchell, Adrian

**Treadgold, Sylvia** 1918- [ART]
*British artist*
* Sylvia T

**Treadway, Red**
See Treadway, Thadford Leon

**Treadway, Thadford Leon** 1920-
[BE]
*American baseball player*
* Treadway, Red

**Treat, Ida**
See Bergeret, Ida Treat

**Treat, Lawrence**
See Goldstone, Lawrence Arthur

**Trebitsch, Isaac** 1872?-1943 [EE]
*Hungarian-born intelligence agent*
* Chao kung, Abbot
* Lincoln, Isaac
* Tandler, [Dr.] Leo
* Trebitsch-Lincoln, Isaac

**Trebitsch-Lincoln, Isaac**
See Trebitsch, Isaac

**Trebor**
See Davis, Robert S.

**Trebor, Eidrah**
See Hardie, Robert

**Trechmann, Emma** 1909- [THR]
*British actress*
* Treckman, Emma

**Trecker, Janice Law** 1941- [CA]
*American author*
* Law, Janice

**Treckman, Emma**
See Trechmann, Emma

**Tredez, Alain** 1926- [CA, TBJ]
*French cartoonist, author, illustrator*
* Trez, Alain

**Tredez, Denise Laugier** 1930-
[CA, TBJ]
*French author*
* Trez, Denise

**Tredgold, Nye**
See Tranter, Nigel [Godwin]

**Tree, David**
See Parsons, David

**Tree, Gregory**
See Bardin, John Franklin

**Tree, [Sir] Herbert Draper Beerbohm**
See Beerbohm, Herbert

**Trefflich, Henry** 1908?-1978
*American animal importer*
* [The] Monkey King

**Trefor, Eirlys**
See Williams, Eirlys O[lwen]

**Trefossa**
See De Ziel, Henri Frans

**Trefouret, Jeanne Alfredine**
1859-1941 [BEW, WBD]
*French actress*
* Hading, Jane

**Tregellis, John**
See Gowing, Sidney Floyd

**Trehearne, Elizabeth** [joint
pseudonym with Patricia Anne
Maxwell]
See Albritton, Carol

**Trehearne, Elizabeth** [joint
pseudonym with Carol Albritton]
See Maxwell, Patricia Anne

**Treibich, S. J.**
See Treibich, Stephen John

**Treibich, Stephen John** 1936-1972
[SFL]
*Author*
* Treibich, S. J.

**Treister, Bernard W[illiam]** 1932-
[CA]
*American author*
* St. James, Bernard

**Trelawney, Hubert**
See Tuite, Hugh

**Trelawny, Edward** ?-1630 [HN]
* [The] Honest Lawyer

**Treleaven, R. B.**
See Treleaven, Richard Barrie

**Treleaven, Richard Barrie** 1920-
[ART]
*British artist*
* Treleaven, R. B.

**Trell, Max** 20th c. [WECO]
*American cartoonist*
* Storm, Robert

**Trelos, Tony**
See Crechales, Anthony George

**Tremaine, D. Lerium**
See Bradbury, Ray [Douglas]

**Tremaine, F[rederick] Orlin**
1899-1956 [ESF, SFP, WGT]
*American author and editor*
* Beale, Anne?
* Frederick, Orlin
* Lane, Arthur
* Paine, Guthrie?
* Sand, Warren B.?
* Santos, Alfred?
* Van Lorne, Warner

**Tremaine, Herbert**
See Deuchar, Maude

**Tremaine, Nelson** 20th c. [WGT]
*Author*
* Van Lorne, Warner

**Tremayne, Hartley**
See Armour, R. Coutts

**Tremayne, Jonathan**
See Forrest-Webb, Robert

**Tremayne, Peter**
See Ellis, Peter Berresford

**Tremblay, J. C.**
See Tremblay, Jean Claude

**Tremblay, Jean Claude** 1939-
[CEI, FHE, HK]
*Canadian-born hockey player*
* Tremblay, J. C.

**Trembly, Edward J.** 1860- ? [BE]
*American baseball player*
* Trumbull, Ed[ward J.]

**Tremel, Mumbles**
See Tremel, William Leonard
[Bill]

**Tremel, William Leonard [Bill]**
1929- [BE]
*American baseball player*
* Tremel, Mumbles

**Tremendous, Sir**
See Dennis, John

**Tremlett, Hurricane**
See Tremlett, Timothy Maurice

**Tremlett, Timothy Maurice** 1956-
[DC]
*British cricketer*
* Tremlett, Hurricane
* Tremlett, Tremers

**Tremlett, Tremers**
See Tremlett, Timothy Maurice

**Tremoille, [Vicomte] de Thouars
[Prince de Talmont]** 1460-1525
[WBD]
*French army officer*
* Chevalier sans Reproche

**Trenchard, Asa**
See Watterson, Henry

**Trenchard, John** 1662?-1723 [FFF]
*British author and journalist*
* Cato
* Diogenes

**Trenchard, Sarah**
See Chanfrau, Mrs. H. T.

**Trenery, Gladys Gordon**
1885?-1938 [HFF, WGT]
*British author*
* Pendarves, G. G.

**Trent, Al[phonso E.]** 1905-   [EJ]
*American jazz musician*
* Trent, Fonnie

**Trent, Ann** 20th c.   [AW, IAW]
*British author*
* Blythe, Joyce
* Carlton, Ann
* Crosse, Elaine
* Desana, Dorothy
* Sernicoli, Davide

**Trent, Clive?**
See  Emanuel, Victor Rousseau

**Trent, Fonnie**
See  Trent, Al[phonso E.]

**Trent, Gregory**
See  Williamson, Thames Ross

**Trent, John**
See  Brown, LaVerne

**Trent, Lawrence**
See  Sellers, Connie Leslie, Jr.

**Trent, Leo**
See  Sellers, Connie Leslie, Jr.

**Trent, Olaf**
See  Fanthorpe, R[obert] Lionel

**Trent, Paul** 1872- ?   [WWL]
*British author*
* Kaye, Wilmot

**Trent, Peter**
See  Nelson, [Hugh] Lawrence

**Trent, Roy**
See  Coe, Charles Francis

**Trent, Timothy**
See  Malmberg, Carl

**Trentworth, Fisher**
See  Ackerman, Forrest J[ames]

**Trepagnier, Ernest** 1885?-1968
[NOJ]
*American jazz musician*
* Trepagnier, Ninesse

**Trepagnier, Ninesse**
See  Trepagnier, Ernest

**Trepper, Leopold** 1904-1982
[EE, JL, WWW]
*Polish-born intelligence agent*
* [The] Big Chef
* Domb, Leiba
* [The] Grand Chef

**Tresilian, Liz**
See  Green, Elisabeth Sara

**Tress, Arthur**
See  Pinkwater, Daniel Manus

**Tressell, Robert**
See  Noonan, Robert

**Tressidy, Jim**
See  Norwood, Victor G[eorge]
C[harles]

**Tressilian, Charles**
See  Atcheson, Richard

**Trester, A. L.**
See  Trester, Arthur L.

**Trester, Arthur L.** 1878-1944
*American basketball executive*
* Trester, A. L.

**Treurnicht, Andries** 20th c.
*South African politician*
* No, Dr.

**Trevarthen, Hal P.**
See  Heydon, Joseph Kentigern

**Trevelyan, G. M.**
See  Trevelyan, George Macaulay

**Trevelyan, George Macaulay**
1876-1962   [LC]
*British historian and author*
* Trevelyan, G. M.

**Trevelyan, Hilda**
See  Tucker, Hilda

**Trevelyan, Katharine** 1908-   [CAP]
*British author*
* Goetsch-Trevelyan, Katharine

**Trevelyan, Robert**
See  Forrest-Webb, Robert

**Trevena, John**
See  Henham, Ernest George

**Treves, Kathleen**
See  Walker, Emily Kathleen

**Trevethick, Richard** 1771-1833
[DNNS]
*British engineer*
* [The] Father of the Locomotive

**Trevi, Christina**
See  Benitez Trevino, Christina

**Trevino, Bobby**
See  Trevino, Carlos Castro

**Trevino, Carlos Castro** 1945-   [BE]
*Mexican-born baseball player*
* Trevino, Bobby

**Trevino, Lee** 1939-   [SA]
*American golfer*
* Super Mex

**Trevision, Torquay**
See  Bedford-Jones, Henry [James
O'Brien]

**Trevor, A. C.**
See  Pulsford, Norman George

**Trevor, Ann**
See  Trilnick, Annie

**Trevor, Austin**
See  Schilsky, Austin

**Trevor, Charlotte**
See  Roberts, Sonia Leslie

**Trevor, Claire**
See  Wemlinger, Claire

**Trevor, Edward**
See  Bulwer-Lytton, Edward
Robert

**Trevor, Edward**
See  Fane, Julian Charles Henry

**Trevor, Elleston**
See  Dudley-Smith, Trevor

**Trevor, Glen**
See  Hilton, James

**Trevor, Joy**
See  Linskill, Doris Joy

**Trevor, Norman**
See  Pritchard, Norman

**Trevor, Ralph**
See  Wilmot, James Reginald

**Trevor, Van**
See  Boulanger, Robert F.

**Trevor, William**
See  Cox, William Trevor

**Trevor-Roper, H. R.**
See  Trevor-Roper, Hugh Redwald

**Trevor-Roper, Hugh Redwald**
1914-   [LC]
*British historian and writer*
* Trevor-Roper, H. R.

**Trew, Dighton**
See  Jones, J. G.

**Trez, Alain**
See  Tredez, Alain

**Trez, Denise**
See  Tredez, Denise Laugier

**[The] Tri-State Terror**
See  Underhill, Wilbur

**Triangle**
See  Bellew, Frank P. W.

**[Il] Tribolo**
See  Pericoli, Niccolo

**Triboniam**
See  Fraleck, Edison Baldwin

**Tribune**
See  Armstrong, Douglas Albert

**Tribune of Liberty, Peace, and
Justice**
See  Gabrini, Niccolo

**[The] Tribune of the People**
See  Babeuf, Francois Noel

**[The] Tribune of the People**
See  Bright, John

**[El] Tribuno Popular**
See  Deschamps, Eugenio

**Tricamo, Stephen J.** 1897-
[BX, RBE]
*American boxer*
* Sullivan, Kid
* Sullivan, Steve

**Trice, Borough**
See  Allen, Arthur Bruce

**Trice, Marguerite Gwynne** 1918-
[FC, ITA]
*American actress*
* Gwynne, Anne

**Trice, Rich[ard]** 1917-   [BWW]
*American singer*
* Fuller, Little Boy

**Trice, Welly**
See  Trice, William Augusta
[Willie]

**Trice, William Augusta [Willie]**
1910-1976   [BWW]
*American singer*
* Trice, Welly

**Tricky Dick [or Dickie]**
See  Nixon, Richard Milhous

**Tricky Dick McGuire**
See  McGuire, Richard

**Tricky Sam Nanton**
See  Nanton, Joseph [Joe]

**Tricotrin**
See  Henderson, N. J.

**Tricycle**
See  Popov, Dusko

**Triebel, George W.** 1855-1886
[BE]
*American baseball player*
* Creamer, George W.

**Triem, Paul Ellsworth** 1882-   [WW]
*Author*
* Ellsworth, Paul

**Triet, Robert**
See  Toche, Raoul

**Trietsch, Hezzie**
See  Trietsch, Paul

**Trietsch, Paul**
*Musician*
* Trietsch, Hezzie

**Trifonov, Georgy** 1926-   [B10]
*Russian author and poet*
* Dyomin, Mikhail

**Trigg, Harry Davis** 1927-   [CA]
*American author and television
scriptwriter*
* Clark, Parlin

**Trigger Mike Coppola**
See  Coppola, Michael

**Trigunatita, [Swami]**
See  Mitra, Sarada Prasanna

**Trihey, Harry**
See  Trihey, Henry Judah

**Trihey, Henry Judah** 1877-1942
[HK]
*Canadian hockey player*
* Trihey, Harry

**Trilby**
See  Peyronney, Vicomtesse de

**Trillo, Indio**
See  Trillo, Jesus Manuel

**Trillo, Jesus Manuel** 1950-
[BE, SMG]
*Venezuelan-born baseball player*
* Marcano, Jesus Manuel
* Trillo, Indio
* Trillo, Manny

**Trillo, Manny**
See  Trillo, Jesus Manuel

**Trilnick, Annie** ?-1970   [THR]
*British actress*
* Trevor, Ann

**Trilussa**
See  Salustri, Carlo Alberto

**Trim**
See  Ratisbonne, Louis Fortune
Gustave

**Trim, Corporal**
See  Bolger, Philip C[unningham]

**Trim, Geoffrey Edward** 1956-   [DC]
*British cricketer*
* Trim, Trimy

**Trim, Trimy**
See  Trim, Geoffrey Edward

**Trimble, Jacquelyn W[hitney]**
1927-   [CA]
*American author*
* Whitney, J. L. H.

**Trimble, Louis P[reston]** 1917-
[CA, NAA, WW]
*American author*
* Brock, Stuart
* Hollis, Jim [joint pseudonym with
Hollis (Spurgeon) Summers]

**Trimble, Louis P[reston]** (Continued)
* Rourke, James
* Travis, Gerry

**Trimiar, Lady**
See Trimiar [or Trimar?], Marion

**Trimiar [or Trimar?], Marion**
1953- [IBW]
*American boxer*
* Trimiar, Lady
* Trimiar, Tyger

**Trimiar, Tyger**
See Trimiar [or Trimar?], Marion

**Trimm, Thomas** 1884-
*German author, playwright, journalist*
* Welk, Ehm

**Trimm, Timothy**
See Lespes, Napoleon

**[The] Trimmer**
See Savile, [Sir] George [Marquis of Halifax]

**Trimmer, Eric James** 1923-
[AW, CA, WD]
*British physician and author*
* Jameson, Eric
* Lawson, [Dr.] Philip

**Trimnell-Ritchard, Cyril**
1897-1977 [BEW]
*Australian-born actor and director*
* Ritchard, Cyril

**Trinculo**
See Wheeler, Andrew Carpenter

**Trinder, Tommy** 1909- [BMH]
*British comedian*
* Nirt, Red

**Tring, A. Stephen**
See Meynell, Laurence [Walter]

**Trini, Anthony**
*Musician and singer*
* [The] Romantic Fiddler

**Trinidad, Corky**
See Trinidad, Francisco D., Jr.

**Trinidad, Francisco D., Jr.** 1939-
[CA]
*Filipino-born cartoonist*
* Trinidad, Corky

**[A] Trinity Man**
See Wright, Thomas

**Trinkle, Sybil** 1907-1947 [SC]
*American actress*
* Borden, Olive

**Trinqueau**
See Nepveu [or Neveu], Pierre

**Trinsome**
See Toche, Raoul

**Triolet, Elsa**
See Blick, Elsa

**Tripe**
See Hamilton, Mrs.

**Triple Threat Trippi**
See Trippi, Charles L. [Charlie]

**Triplet, William Samuel** 1899-
[SFL, WGT]
*Author*
* Bull, [Sergeant] Terry

**Triplett, Ernie** 20th c.
*Auto racer*
* [The] Blond Terror

**Tripp, C. E.**
See Morris, Charles Smith

**Tripp, John**
See Moore, John Travers

**Tripp, June Howard** 1901- [EMT]
*British actress, dancer, singer*
* June

**Tripp, Karen** 1923- [AW, CA]
*German-born author and poet*
* Gershon, Karen

**Tripp, Miles [Barton]** 1923- [CA]
*British author*
* Brett, John Michael
* Brett, Michael

**Tripp, Tom**
See Jones, Giles

**Tripp, Walter John** 1874- ?
[WWL]
*Author*
* Carroder, C. H.

**Trippe, Peter** [CC]
*Author*
* Peters, Geoffrey

**Trippenmeker, Heinrich**
1502-1560? [WBD]
*German painter, engraver, goldsmith*
* Aldegrever, Heinrich

**Trippett, Frank** 1926- [CA]
*American author and editor*
* Swivett, R. G. O.

**Trippetts, Mrs. Henry** [FFF]
*Entertainer*
* Belden, Clara

**Trippi, Charles L. [Charlie]** 1922-
[FB]
*American football player*
* [The] Scintillating Sicilian
* Trippi, Triple Threat

**Trippi, Triple Threat**
See Trippi, Charles L. [Charlie]

**Trips, Captain**
See Garcia, Jerry

**Trismegistus [Thrice Greatest]**
See Hermes

**Trissino, Giulio** 16th c. [SN]
*Son of Italian author, Giovanni Giorgio Trissino*
* Agrilupo

**Trissotin**
See Cotin, Charles

**Tritheim, Johannes**
See Heidendberg, Johannes

**Triton, A. N.**
See Barclay, Oliver R[ainsford]

**Trivier, Pierre-Olaf** 1928-
[BEW, TR]
*French actor*
* Olaf, Pierre

**Trixie**
See Lopez Ostoloza, Beatriz

**Trocchi, Alexander** 1925- [CA]
*Scottish author*
* Lengel, Frances

**Troels-Lund**
See Lund, Troels Frederik

**Trog**
See Fawkes, Walter Ernest

**Trois Etoiles [Three Stars]**
See Mayer, Charles E. E.

**Trois Etoiles**
See Murray, Eustace Clare Grenville

**[The] Trojan**
See Evers, John Joseph

**Trojanowicz, John M[ichael]** 1936-
[CA]
*American educator and author*
* Troyanovich, John M[ichael]

**Troll, Gustav**
See Brestowski, Carl August

**Trolley Line Butler**
See Butler, John Stephen [Johnny]

**Trollope, Mrs. Thomas Adolphus**
1810- ? [PA]
*Author*
* Garrow

**Troloppe, Francis**
See Feval, Paul Henri

**Tromlitz, A. von**
See Witzleben, Karl August Friedrich von

**Tronche, Philippe** 1929- [ESF]
*French author and journalist*
* Curval, Philippe

**Troncoso de la Concha, Manuel de
Jesus** 1878-1955 [CW]
*Dominican author*
* Buscon, Juan

**Trone, Roland** 20th c. [RO1]
*American singer*
* Don

**Tropea, Orassio [or Orazio]**
?-1926? [BLB, PHM]
*American underworld figure*
* [The] Scourge

**Tropica**
See Wolcott, Mary Adella

**Trosky, Harold Arthur, Jr. [Hal]**
See Troyavesky, Harold Arthur, Jr.

**Trosky, Harold Arthur, Sr.**
See Troyavesky, Harold Arthur, Sr.

**Trosky, Hoot**
See Troyavesky, Harold Arthur, Jr.

**Trossi, Carlo Felice** ?-1949 [EAR]
*Italian auto racer*
* Trossi, Didi

**Trossi, Didi**
See Trossi, Carlo Felice

**Trotere, Henry**
See Trotter, Henry

**Trotsky, Leon**
See Bronstein, Lev Davidovich

**Trotter, Dale** 20th c. [GW]
*American rodeo performer*
* Trotter, Trapper

**Trotter, Grace V[iolet]** 1900-
[CA, SAT]
*American author*
* Paschal, Nancy

**Trotter, Henry** 1855-1912 [BBD]
*British composer*
* Trotere, Henry

**Trotter, [Canon] John Crawford**
1848- ? [LAO]
*Irish clergyman and writer*
* O'Dhu, Fergus

**Trotter, Sallie**
See Crawford, Sallie Wallace Brown

**Trotter, Trapper**
See Trotter, Dale

**Trottier, Bryan** 1956- [SMG]
*Canadian-born hockey player*
* Trottier, Trots

**Trottier, Trots**
See Trottier, Bryan

**Trotzendorf, Valentin**
See Friedland, Valentin

**[The] Troubador of the Violin**
See Lande, Jules

**[The] Troubadour**
See Woods, Oscar

**Troubetzkoy, Princess** 1864?-1945
[BEW]
*American author and playwright*
* Rives, Amelie

**[A] Troubler of Israel**
See Morton, Thomas

**Troubles, Kid**
See Bargordes, Benjamin

**Trout, Dink**
See Trout, Francis

**Trout, Dizzy**
See Trout, Paul Howard

**Trout, Francis** 1898-1950 [SC]
*American actor and musician*
* Trout, Dink

**Trout, Kilgore**
See Farmer, Philip Jose

**Trout, Paul Howard** 1915-1972
[BE, PB, SMG]
*American baseball player*
* Trout, Dizzy

**Trout, Rainbow**
See Trout, Steve[n Russell]

**Trout, Steve[n Russell]** 1957-
*American baseball player*
* Trout, Rainbow

**[El] Trovador Cubano**
See Poveda y Armenteros, Francisco

**Trovatore**
See Williams, William Francis

**Trowbridge, John Townsend**
1827-1916 [DEL, DNNF, FFF]
*American author*
* Creyton, Paul

**Troy, Bun**
See Troy, Robert

**Troy, Dasher**
See Troy, John Joseph

**Troy, Forrest** 1933?- [B10]
*American journalist*
* Troy, Frosty

**Troy, Frosty**
See Troy, Forrest

**Troy, John Joseph** 1856-1938 [BE]
*American baseball player*
* Troy, Dasher

**Troy, Robert** 1888-1918 [BE]
*German-born baseball player*
* Troy, Bun

**Troy, Simon**
See Warriner, Thurman

**Troyanovich, John M[ichael]**
See Trojanowicz, John M[ichael]

**Troyat, Henri**
See Tarassoff [or Tarassov], Lev

**Troyavesky, Harold Arthur, Jr.**
1936- [BE]
*American baseball player*
* Trosky, Harold Arthur, Jr. [Hal]
* Trosky, Hoot

**Troyavesky, Harold Arthur, Sr.**
1912- [BE]
*American baseball player*
* Trosky, Harold Arthur, Sr.

**Troyer, Byron L[eRoy]** 1909- [CA]
*American author*
* Hamilton, Dave

**Truby, Bird Eye**
See Truby, Harry Garvin

**Truby, Harry Garvin** 1870-1953
[BE]
*American baseball player*
* Truby, Bird Eye

**Trucking Kid**
See Rabia, Aliyah

**Trucks, Butch**
See Trucks, Claude Hudson

**Trucks, Claude Hudson** 20th c.
[RO2]
*American musician*
* Trucks, Butch

**Trucks, Fire [or Fireball]**
See Trucks, Virgil Oliver

**Trucks, Virgil Oliver** 1919-
[BE, PB]
*American baseball player*
* Trucks, Fire [or Fireball]

**Trudeau, Garretson Beekman**
1948- [CA]
*American cartoonist and author*
* Trudeau, Garry B.

**Trudeau, Garry B.**
See Trudeau, Garretson Beekman

**Trudger and Trencher**
See Stow, John

**Trudix, Marty**
See Truman, Ruth

**[That] True Deacon of the Craft**
See Pope, Alexander

**True, Fanny**
See Short, Mary Asenath

**True Gun Hart**
See Hart, William Woodrow [Bill]

**True, Kate**
See Woods, Kate Tannant

**True Thomas**
See Learmont, Thomas

**Truebner, Nicolas** 1817- ? [PA]
*Author*
* N. T.

**Truempy, Balz**
See Truempy, Johann Balthasar

**Truempy, Johann Balthasar** 1946-
[IWM]
*Swiss composer*
* Truempy, Balz

**Truinet, Charles Louis Etienne**
1828-1899 [WBD]
*French playwright*
* Nuitter

**Trujillo, Boom Boom**
See Trujillo, Lorenzo

**Trujillo, Chel**
See Trujillo, Lorenzo L.

**Trujillo, Lorenzo** 20th c. [RBE]
*American boxer*
* Trujillo, Boom Boom

**Trujillo, Lorenzo L.** 1906?-1962
[BEW]
*Actor*
* Trujillo, Chel

**Truman, Harry** 1884-1972
[CND, FAP]
*American president*
* Give 'Em Hell Harry
* H. S. T.
* Haberdasher Harry
* High Tax Harry
* Kilting [code name used during
  World War II]
* [The] Man from Missouri
* [The] Man of Independence

**Truman, Harry H.** 1866-1925 [BE]
*American baseball player*
* Raymond, Harry H.

**Truman, Marcus George** 1890-
[WW]
*Author*
* Beckett, Mark

**Truman, Ruth** 1931- [CA]
*American author*
* Trudix, Marty

**Trumbauer, Frankie** 1900?-1956
[EJ, PMJ]
*American jazz musician*
* Trumbauer, Tram [or Trum]

**Trumbauer, Tram [or Trum]**
See Trumbauer, Frankie

**Trumble, Alfred** [FFF]
*American writer*
* Babbler

**Trumbo, Dalton** 1905-1976
[CA, WD]
*American screenwriter and author*
* Jackson, Sam
* Rich, Robert

**Trumbull, Ed[ward J.]**
See Trembly, Edward J.

**Trumbull, Jonathan** 1710-1785
[WBD]
*American statesman*
* Brother Jonathan

**Trumper, Hubert Bagster** 1902-
[CAP]
*British author*
* Bagster, Hubert

**Trumps**
See Dick, William Brisbane

**Trumps**
See McCollum, J. C.

**Trundlett, Helen B.**
See Eliot, Thomas Stearns

**Trungpa, Chogyam**
See Gyamtso, Choskyi

**Truscott, Charles**
See Tench, Charles Victor

**Truscott-Jones, Reginald** 1905?-
[BDF, F2, WEF]
*Welsh-born actor and director*
* Milland, Jack
* Milland, Ray
* Milland, Spike

**Trusler, Margaret**
See Fisher, Margaret Trusler

**Truss, [Leslie] Seldon** 1892-
[CA, CC]
*British author*
* Seldon-Truss, Leslie
* Selmark, George

**[The] Trust Buster**
See Roosevelt, Theodore [Teddy]

**Trusta**
See Ward, Elizabeth Stuart
[Phelps]

**Trusty Anthony**
See Aston, Anthony

**Truth, Sojourner**
See Van Wagener, Isabelle

**Truth Teller**
See Thomson, Charles

**Truthful Jim Mutrie**
See Mutrie, James J. [Jim]

**Tsai T'ien [Glorious Succession]**
See Kuang Hsu [or Kwang Hsu]

**Ts'ao Yu**
See Wan Chia-Pao

**Tsatsos, Ioanna** 1909- [CA]
*Greek author and poet*
* Tsatsos, Jeanne

**Tsatsos, Jeanne**
See Tsatsos, Ioanna

**Tschegerleb**
See Hafiz, Mohammed

**Tschernek, Viktor** 1913- [IAW]
*German author*
* Bergauer, Johannes

**Tschiffely, A. F.**
See Tschiffely, Aime Felix

**Tschiffely, Aime Felix** 1895-1954
[LC]
*Swiss-born author*
* Tschiffely, A. F.

**Tschirky, Oscar** 1866-1950 [WBD]
*Swiss-born hotel headwaiter*
* Oscar of the Waldorf

**Tschudi, Aegidius [or Gilg von]**
1505-1572 [DNNS, WBD]
*Swiss historian and theologian*
* [The] Father of Swiss History

**Tsederbaum, Iulii O.** 1873- ? [JL]
*Russian journalist and political
theorist*
* Martov, Julius

**Tseng Chi-tse** 1839-1890
[FFF, WBD]
*Chinese diplomat*
* [The] Celestial Talleyrand
* Tseng, Marshall

**Tseng, Marshall**
See Tseng Chi-tse

**Tseng Yu-ho**
See Ecke, Betty Tseng Yu-ho

**Tsubouchi, Shoyo**
See Tsubouchi, Yuzo

**Tsubouchi, Yuzo** 1859-1935
[MWD]
*Japanese director and playwright*
* Tsubouchi, Shoyo

**Tsukahara, Nobuo** 1926- [EJ7]
*Japanese jazz musician*
* Hara, Nobuo

**Tsukinabe, Isao**
See Vermeule, Cornelius Clarkson,
III

**Tsushima, Shuji** 1909-1948
[B10, TCL]
*Japanese author*
* Dazai, Osamu

**Tua Fault, Frank**
See Bullock-Webster, Llewelyn

**Tua, Teresina**
See Felicita, Maria

**Tuala, Mario**
See Schulz Ewerth, Eckard

**Tuan**
See Campbell, John Beautiste

**Tuann, Lucy H[siu-mei] C[hen]**
1938- [CA]
*Taiwanese-born author*
* Chen Jo-hsi

**[The] Tub**
See Riquetti, Honore Gabriel
Victor

**[The] Tubal Cain of America**
See Spotswood, Alexander

**Tubalcain**
See Watson, Mary

**Tubb, E. C.**
See Tubb, Edwin Charles

**Tubb, Edwin Charles** 1919-
[CA, ESF, SF]
*British author*
* Adams, Chuck
* Armstrong, Anthony
* Bain, Ted
* Beecham, Alice
* Blake, Anthony
* Carey, Julian
* Carpenter, Morley
* Cary, Jud
* Clarkson, J. F.
* Dale, Norman
* Farrow, James S.
* Fenner, James R.
* Godfrey, R. H.
* Graham, Charles S.
* Gray, Charles
* Gridban, Volsted [house
  pseudonym, Scion Publications]
* Guthrie, Alan
* Holt, George
* Hunt, Gill [house pseudonym,
  Curtis Warren]
* Innes, Alan
* Jackson, E. F.

**Tubb, Edwin Charles** (Continued)
* Kent, Gordon
* Kern, Gregory [house pseudonym]
* Lamont, Duncan
* Lang, King [house pseudonym, Curtis Warren]
* Lantry, Mike
* Lawrence, P.
* Lawson, Chet
* Maclean, Arthur
* Maddox, Carl
* Martyn, Phillip
* Moulton, Carl
* Neal, Gavin
* Powers, M. L.
* Schofield, Paul
* Seabright, John
* Shaw, Brian [house pseudonym, Curtis Warren]
* Sheldon, Roy [house pseudonym, Hamilton]
* Stevens, John
* Storm, Eric
* Thomson, Edward
* Tubb, E. C.
* Wainwright, Ken
* Weight, Frank
* West, Douglas
* Wilding, Eric
* Winnard, Frank

**Tubb, Ernest Dale** 1914-
[ECM, FCW]
*American country-western performer*
* [The] Gold Chain Troubador

**Tubbs, Arthur Lewis** 1867- ?
[ALY]
*American playwright*
* Sylvester, Arthur

**Tubbs, Jerry** 20th c.
*American football player*
* Tubbs, Tubby

**Tubbs, Tubby**
*See* Tubbs, Jerry

**Tubby, Alfred Herbert** 1862- ?
[LAO]
*British physician and author*
* Theobald, Alfred Herbert

**Tubman, Harriet Araminta Ross Davis** 1821-1913 [IBW]
*American abolitionist*
* Moses to Her People

**Tucci, Niccolo** 1908- [CA]
*Swiss-born American author and playwright*
* Strabolgi, Bartolomeo

**Tuchow, Michael** 20th c. [BEW]
*American actor*
* Tolan, Michael

**Tuck, Dorothy**
*See* McFarland, Dorothy Tuck

**Tucker, Abraham** 1705-1774
[DEL, DNNF, FFF]
*British author*
* Comment, Cuthbert
* Search, Edward

**Tucker, Agnes Kent Carruth** 1910-
[AW]
*American author*
* Carruth, Agnes K.

**Tucker, Ann**
*See* Giudici, Ann Couper

**Tucker, Blanch** [PA]
*Author*
* Rosavella

**Tucker, Bob**
*See* Tucker, [Arthur] Wilson

**Tucker, Caroline**
*See* Nolan, Jeannette Covert

**Tucker, Charlotte Maria**
1821?-1893 [DNNF, RH, WBD]
*British author*
* A. L. O. E. [A Lady of England]

**Tucker, Foghorn**
*See* Tucker, Thomas J.

**Tucker, Gabe**
*See* Tucker, Gaylord Bob

**Tucker, Gaylord Bob** 1915-
[CWG, DAM]
*American country-western performer*
* Tucker, Gabe

**Tucker, Georgina P.** 1911- [CA]
*American author*
* Tucker, Gina

**Tucker, Gina**
*See* Tucker, Georgina P.

**Tucker, Herbert** 1855- ? [WWL]
*South African author*
* H. T.

**Tucker, Hilda** 1880-1959 [BEW]
*Actress*
* Trevelyan, Hilda

**Tucker, Hubert Coutts** ?-1921
[DBA]
*British painter*
* Coutts, Hubert

**Tucker, [Allan] James** 1929-
[AW, CA, WD]
*Welsh author and journalist*
* Craig, David

**Tucker, John F[rancis]** 1871- ?
[ALY]
*American author*
* Newkirk, Foster

**Tucker, Josiah [or Joseph?]**
1711-1799 [HN]
*British author, clergyman, economist*
* Garlic, Parson

**Tucker, LaCosta** 20th c. [ECM]
*American country-western performer*
* LaCosta

**Tucker, Lael**
*See* Wertenbaker, Lael Tucker

**Tucker, Link**
*See* Bingley, David Ernest

**Tucker, Loraine Read** 1910- [ART]
*British industrial designer*
* Read-Tucker, L.

**Tucker, Lorenzo** 1907- [IBW]
*American actor*
* [The] Black Valentino

**Tucker, Mary**
*See* Clayton, Mrs. Albert

**Tucker, Nathaniel Beverley**
1784-1851 [FFF, PA]
*American author*
* Sidney, E. W.
* Sidney, Edward William

**Tucker, Richard**
*See* Ticker, Reuben

**Tucker, Robin** 1950- [CA]
*American author and editor*
* Nibor, Kay

**Tucker, Samuel** [IBW]
*American magician*
* [The] Great Sante

**Tucker, Sophie**
*See* Abuza, Sophie

**Tucker, Tee**
*See* Higgenbotham, Robert

**Tucker, Thomas J.** 1863-1935 [PB]
*American baseball player*
* Tucker, Foghorn

**Tucker, Thurman Lowell** 1917-
[BE, PB]
*American baseball player*
* Joe E.

**Tucker, Tommy**
*See* Higgenbotham, Robert

**Tucker, William George**
1905-1964 [BWW, NBB]
*American singer*
* Barbee, John Henry

**Tucker, [Arthur] Wilson** 1914-
[CA, SFL, WGT]
*American author*
* Hoy Ping Pong
* Tucker, Bob
* Vaid, Sanford

**Tucker-Fettner, Ann**
*See* Giudici, Ann Couper

**Tuckwell, Margaret** 20th c. [IAW]
*British author*
* Bacon, Margaret

**Tudhope, Richard**
*See* Rodda, Peter [Gordon]

**Tudor, Mary**
*See* Mary I

**Tudor, Rowan**
*See* Koster, Cornelius

**Tudor, Tasha**
*See* Burgess, Starling

**Tudor, Valerie**
*See* Samuel, Valerie

**Tudoran, Radu**
*See* Bogza, Nicolae

**Tueart, Dennis** 1949- [AES]
*British soccer player*
* [The] Menace

**[Der] Tuerken Louis**
*See* Louis William I

**Tuffley, Fred Eric Lewis**
1855-1935 [BEW]
*British-born actor*
* Lewis, Eric

**Tufts, Bowen Charleston**
1911-1970 [FC]
*American actor*
* Tufts, Sonny

**Tufts, Sonny**
*See* Tufts, Bowen Charleston

**Tufty, Barbara Jean** 1923- [IAW]
*American author*
* Jeans, Barbara

**Tuite, Frederick P.** 1885?-1963
[BEW]
*Actor*
* Peters, Fred

**Tuite, Hugh** 20th c. [MBF]
*British author*
* Spencer, Captain
* Trelawney, Hubert

**Tukesbury, Joe**
*See* Wright, Joseph X.

**Tulane, Anne**
*See* Italiano, Anna Maria Luisa

**Tulasne, Louis Rene** 1815-1885
[WBD]
*French botanist*
* [The] Founder of Modern Mycology

**Tull, Anthony** 1912- [THR]
*British author and director*
* Parker, Anthony

**Tullett, Denis** 1928- [WD]
*British poet*
* Sutton, John

**Tulloch, [Sir] A. M.** [HN]
*British writer*
* Dalgetty, Dugald

**Tullock, W. W.** ?-1920 [WWL]
*Author*
* [The] Booktaster
* Bridge, Bonar
* Goosequill, Gregory
* Hill, Arthur
* Orion
* [The] Paperknife
* Sailil

**Tully**
*See* Cicero, Marcus Tullius

**Tully, J. M.**
*See* Tully, Joyce Mary

**Tully, Joyce Mary** 20th c. [ART]
*British painter*
* Tully, J. M.

**Tully, Tom**
*See* Sellers, Connie Leslie, Jr.

**Tulp, Claes Pieterszoon**
*See* Pieterszoon, Nicolaes

**Tulsa Red**
*See* Fulson, Lowell

**Tumarin, Boris**
*See* Tumarinson, Boris

**Tumarinson, Boris** 1910-
[BEW, TR]
*Latvian-born actor, director, educator*
* Tumarin, Boris

**Tumble-Down Dick**
*See* Cromwell, Richard

**[The] Tumbleweed Kid**
*See* Curless, Richard [Dick]

**Tuminaro, Angelo** 20th c. [PHM]
*American underworld figure*
* Tuminaro, Little Angie

**Tuminaro, Little Angie**
*See* Tuminaro, Angelo

**[The] Tunis Terror**
*See* Perez, Victor

**Tunnell, Emlen** 1925-1975    [IBW]
*American football player and coach*
* [The] Gremlin

**Tunnell, George N.** 1903-1975
[PMJ, WWJ]
*American singer*
* Bon Bon

**Tunnell, Mavis** 1916-    [THR]
*British actress*
* Clair, Mavis

**Tunnell, Peggy Joye** 20th c.    [CWG]
*American country-western performer*
* Allen, Barbara

**Tunney, Gene**
*See* Tunney, James Joseph

**Tunney, James Joseph** 1897?-1978
[B10, BX, RBE]
*American boxer*
* [The] Fighting Marine
* Tunney, Gene

**Tunnicliffe, Colin John** 1951-    [DC]
*British cricketer*
* Tunnicliffe, Tunners

**Tunnicliffe, Howard Trevor** 1950-
[DC]
*British cricketer*
* Tunnicliffe, Pally

**Tunnicliffe, Pally**
*See* Tunnicliffe, Howard Trevor

**Tunnicliffe, Tunners**
*See* Tunnicliffe, Colin John

**Tunstall, Shana Barrett**
*See* Tunstall, Velma [Barrett]

**Tunstall, Velma [Barrett]** 1914-
[CA, WD]
*American poet*
* Tunstall, Shana Barrett

**Tupac Amaru**
*See* Condorcanqui, Jose Gabriel

**Tupper, Kathryn Munro** 20th c.
[NAA]
*Canadian poet*
* Munro, Kathryn

**Tupper, Martin Farquhar**
1810-1889    [DEL, PA]
*British poet*
* Query, Peter, Esq.
* T.

**Tupper, Mary**
*See* Jones, Mary Tupper

**Tur-Malka**
*See* Greenberg, Uri Zvi

**Turbojew, Alexej**
*See* Scheer, Karl Herbert

**Turchin, Edward Lawrence [Eddie]**
1917-    [BE]
*American baseball player*
* Turchin, Smiley

**Turchin, Smiley**
*See* Turchin, Edward Lawrence
[Eddie]

**Turell, Dan** 20th c.    [IAW]
*Danish poet*
* Onkel Danny

**[The] Turenne of Louis XV**
*See* Saxe, [Hermann] Maurice de

**Turgeon, Eugene Joseph** 1897-
[BE]
*American baseball player*
* Turgeon, Pete

**Turgeon, Jean** 1952-    [WEC]
*Canadian cartoonist*
* Gite

**Turgeon, [Madame] Leonida F.**
1883-    [NAA]
*Canadian author*
* Des Ormes, Renee

**Turgeon, Pete**
*See* Turgeon, Eugene Joseph

**Turicchia, Signor**
*See* Alunni, Corrado

**Turk, Chief**
*See* Turk, Lucas Newton

**Turk Gregory**
*See* Hildebrand

**Turk, Lucas Newton** 1898-    [BE]
*American baseball player*
* Turk, Chief

**Turk, Midge**
*See* Richardson, Midge Turk

**Turkel, Pauline**
*See* Kesselman, Judi R[osenthal]

**Turkey Mike Donlin**
*See* Donlin, Michael Joseph

**Turkiewicz, Jim** 1955-    [SMG]
*Canadian-born hockey player*
* Turkiewicz, Turk

**Turkiewicz, Turk**
*See* Turkiewicz, Jim

**[The] Turkish Samson**
*See* Ozdemir

**Turla, Leopoldo** 1818-1877    [CW]
*Cuban playwright and poet*
* [Un] Quidam

**Turleigh, Veronica**
*See* Turley, Veronica

**Turley, Bullet Bob**
*See* Turley, Robert Lee

**Turley, Robert Lee** 1930-    [BE, PB]
*American baseball player*
* Turley, Bullet Bob

**Turley, Veronica** 1903-    [THR]
*Irish-born actress*
* Turleigh, Veronica

**Turmair [or Thurmayr], Johannes**
1477-1534    [WBD]
*Bavarian historian*
* Aventinus, Johannes

**Turn Coat Meres**
*See* Booth, Henry

**Turn 'Em Loose Bruce**
*See* Wright, Bruce McMarion

**Turnbull, Alex** 20th c.    [BBH]
*Canadian lacrosse player*
* Turnbull, Dad

**Turnbull, Ann [Christine]** 1943-
[CA]
*British author*
* Nicol, Ann

**Turnbull, Dad**
*See* Turnbull, Alex

**Turnbull, Dora Amy Elles Dillon**
1878-1961    [CC, EMD, LC]
*British author*
* Delta
* Wentworth, Patricia

**Turnbull, John Iglehart**  ?-1944
[BBH]
*American lacrosse player*
* [The] Babe Ruth of Lacrosse

**Turnbull, Robert James** 1775-1833
[WBD]
*American author and attorney*
* Brutus

**Turnebe, Adrien**
*See* Tournebu, Adrien

**Turner, Annie Mae Bullock** 1939-
[DAM, SSS]
*American singer*
* Turner, Tina

**Turner, B. K.**
*See* Turner, Babe Kyro Lemon

**Turner, Babe Kyro Lemon**
1907-1972    [BWW]
*American singer*
* Black Ace
* Turner, B. K.
* Turner, Buck

**Turner, Bake**
*See* Turner, Robert

**Turner, Big Joe**
*See* Turner, Joseph [Vernon]

**Turner, Birdy**
*See* Turner, David Roy

**Turner, Blind Squire**
*See* Darby, Theodore [Teddy]

**Turner, Buck**
*See* Turner, Babe Kyro Lemon

**Turner, Bulldog**
*See* Turner, Clyde

**Turner, Cactus Jack**
*See* Turner, Jack

**Turner, Carrie**
*See* His, Mrs. Albert

**Turner, Claramae**
*See* Haas, Claramae

**Turner, Clay**
*See* Ballard, [Willis] Todhunter

**Turner, Clyde** 1919-
[B10, SMG, WA]
*American football player and coach*
* Turner, Bulldog

**Turner, Cotton**
*See* Turner, Terrence Lamont

**Turner, Curtis Morton** 1924-1970
[B10, BBH]
*American auto racer*
* Turner, Pops

**Turner, Daddy**
*See* Turner, Otis

**Turner, David Roy** 1949-    [DC]
*British cricketer*
* Turner, Birdy

**Turner, Dwight D.** 20th c.    [RO2]
*American singer*
* Turner, Spyder

**Turner, E. C.** 20th c.    [OBW]
*American baseball player*
* Turner, Pop

**Turner, Ed** 20th c.    [RBE]
*American boxer*
* Turner, Savage

**Turner, Eileen Arbuthnot Robertson**
1903-    [WGT]
*British author*
* Robertson, Eileen Arnot

**Turner, Florence** 1885-1946    [SC]
*American actress*
* [The] Vitagraph Girl

**Turner, George**
*See* Thirlwell, George

**Turner, George A.** 1870- ?    [BE]
*American baseball player*
* Turner, Tuck

**Turner, George E[ugene]** 1925-
[CA]
*American author and illustrator*
* Lowell, Tex
* Scott, Lloyd

**Turner, Happy**
*See* Turner, John C.

**Turner, Harley** 20th c.    [SMG]
*American football player*
* Turner, Rocky

**Turner, Jack** 20th c.
*Auto racer*
* Turner, Cactus Jack

**Turner, James Riley** 1904-
[BE, PB]
*American baseball player and coach*
* Turner, Milkman Jim

**Turner, Jerry**
*See* Turner, John Webber

**Turner, Joan** 1922-    [BMH]
*Irish-born actress, singer,
comedienne*
* [The] Girl with a Thousand
  Voices
* [The] Whacky Warbler

**Turner, John** 20th c.    [RM]
*Musician*
* Turner, Red

**Turner, John C.** 1896-1949    [ASC]
*American musician*
* Turner, Happy

**Turner, John M.**    [PA]
*Author*
* Head, Archibald

**Turner, John Victor** 1900-1945
[CC, MBF, WW]
*British author*
* Brady, Nicholas
* Hume, David

**Turner, John Webber** 1954-    [SMG]
*American baseball player*
* Turner, Jerry

**Turner, Joseph [Vernon]** 1911-
[BWW, EJ, RO1]
*American singer*
* Big Vernon
* [The] Boss of the Blues
* Turner, Big Joe
* [The] World's Greatest Blues
  Shouter

**Turner, Josie**
*See* Crawford, Phyllis

**Turner, Judy** 1936- [WD]
*British author*
* Saxton, Judith

**Turner, Julia Jean Mildred Frances**
1920- [BDF, SW, WEF]
*American actress*
* [The] Sweater Girl
* Turner, Lana

**Turner, Lana**
*See* Turner, Julia Jean Mildred
Frances

**Turner, Len**
*See* Floren, Lee

**Turner, Leopold McClintock** 20th
c. [THR]
*British journalist and theatre critic*
* Godfrey-Turner, L.

**Turner, Lily** 20th c. [BMH]
*British singer*
* Bush, Rose

**Turner, Lloyd** 1884- [BBH]
*Canadian-born hockey player*
* Hockey, Mr.

**Turner, Mary**
*See* Lambot, Isobel Mary

**Turner, Milkman Jim**
*See* Turner, James Riley

**Turner, Orpha** [PA]
*Author*
* Hammond, Orpha

**Turner, Otis** 1862-1918 [SC]
*American actor and director*
* Turner, Daddy

**Turner, Peter Paul**
*See* Jeffery, Grant

**Turner, Philip [William]** 1925-
[FBJ, IAW, TCC]
*British author and playwright*
* Chance, Stephen

**Turner, Plum**
*See* Turner, Richard

**Turner, Pop**
*See* Turner, E. C.

**Turner, Pops**
*See* Turner, Curtis Morton

**Turner, Red**
*See* Turner, John

**Turner, Richard** [SN]
*Miser*
* Turner, Plum

**Turner, Robert [Harry]** 1915- [CA]
*American author*
* Calhoun, Eric
* Klein, K. K.
* Lawson, Steve
* Lee, Parker
* Morgan, Robert
* Murray, Ken
* Roberts, Lisa
* Romano, Don
* Savoy, Mark

**Turner, Robert** 20th c. [SMG]
*American football player*
* Turner, Bake

**Turner, Robert Edward, III** 1939?-
*American business executive and
yacht racer*
* [The] Capsize Kid
* [The] Mouth of the South

**Turner, Robert Edward, III**
(Continued)
* Outrageous, Captain
* Turner, Ted
* Turner, Terrible Ted

**Turner, Rocky**
*See* Turner, Harley

**Turner, Samuel Hurlburt**
1790-1861 [PA]
*Author*
* Presbyter

**Turner, Sandbag**
*See* Turner, Sheadrick B.

**Turner, Savage**
*See* Turner, Ed

**Turner, Sheadrick B.** 1854- ?
[IBW]
*American politician*
* Turner, Sandbag

**Turner, Sheila**
*See* Rowbotham, Sheila

**Turner, Sheila R.**
*See* Seed, Sheila Turner

**Turner, Spurgeon, Jr.** 1924- [IBW]
*American disc jockey*
* Stan the Man

**Turner, Spyder**
*See* Turner, Dwight D.

**Turner, Ted**
*See* Turner, Robert Edward, III

**Turner, Terrence Lamont**
1881-1960 [BE]
*American baseball player*
* Turner, Cotton

**Turner, Terrible Ted**
*See* Turner, Robert Edward, III

**Turner, Thomas Lovatt** 1890-1962
[BE]
*American baseball player*
* Turner, Tink

**Turner, Tina**
*See* Turner, Annie Mae Bullock

**Turner, Tink**
*See* Turner, Thomas Lovatt

**Turner, Tuck**
*See* Turner, George A.

**Turner, W. J.**
*See* Turner, Walter James Redfern

**Turner, Walter James Redfern**
1889-1946 [LC, TC]
*British author, poet, music critic*
* Turner, W. J.

**Turner, William** 1520?-1568
[DEP]
*British clergyman, physician,
botanist*
* [The] Father of English Botany

**Turner, William** 1870-1944 [BEW]
*British comedian and playwright*
* Rigby, Arthur

**Turnesa, William P.** 1914- [BBH]
*American golfer*
* [The] Wedge

**Turngren, Annette** 1902-1980
[CA, WW]
*American author*
* Hopkins, A. T.

**[The] Turnip-Hoer**
*See* George I

**Turofsky, Riki**
*See* Turofsky, Rita Nan

**Turofsky, Rita Nan** 1944- [OP]
*Canadian opera singer*
* Turofsky, Riki

**Turpin, Ben**
*See* Turpin, Bernard

**Turpin, Bernard** 1869-1940
[FIR, SC]
*American actor*
* Turpin, Ben

**Turpin, Richard [Dick]** 1706?-1739
[HN]
*British robber*
* [The] Flying Highwayman

**Turpinszky, Bela** 1933- [OP]
*Hungarian opera singer*
* Adolbert, Bela

**Turquito**
*See* Betruz, Miguel

**Turrell, Big Jim**
*See* Turrell, James Archie [Jim]

**Turrell, James Archie [Jim]** 1943-
[CAR]
*American artist*
* [The] Arch
* Turrell, Big Jim
* Turrell, Little Jimmie

**Turrell, Little Jimmie**
*See* Turrell, James Archie [Jim]

**Turton, Thomas** 19th c. [PA]
*Author*
* Cantabrigiensis, Crito

**Turton-Jones, Edith Constance
[Bradshaw]** 1904-1968 [CAP]
*British author*
* Gillespie, Susan

**Turville, Henry**
*See* Bullivant, Cecil Henry

**[The] Tuscan Poet**
*See* Ariosto, Lodovico

**Tusitala [Teller of Tales]**
*See* Stevenson, Robert Louis
Balfour

**[The] Tuskegee Cowboy**
*See* Dawkins, Whit M.

**Tusser, Thomas** 1515?-1580
[RH, SN]
*British poet*
* [The] British Varro
* [The] Husbandman

**Tustin, Elizabeth**
*See* White, Celia

**Tut, King**
*See* Tut, Richard

**Tut, Richard** 20th c. [OBW]
*American baseball player*
* Tut, King

**Tute, G. W.**
*See* Tute, George William

**Tute, George William** 1933- [ART]
*British artist*
* Tute, G. W.

**Tute, Warren [Stanley]** 1914- [CA]
*British author and playwright*
* Warren, Andrew [joint
pseudonym with Andrew
Rosenthal]

**Tutt, William Thayer** 1902- [BBH]
*American hockey organization
officer*
* [The] Father of the NCAA
Hockey Tournament

**Tuttiett, Mary Gleed** ?-1923
[WWL]
*British author and poet*
* Gray, Maxwell

**Tuttle, E. C.** [FFF]
*Writer*
* Vernon, Judge

**Tuttle, Henry** 20th c. [SG]
*Boxer*
* King Tut

**Tuvim, Judith** 1921?-1965
[BDF, BEW, EMT]
*American actress and singer*
* Holliday, Judy

**Tuyuchi**
*See* Leito, Arturo

**TV Slim**
*See* Wills, Oscar

**Twain, Mark**
*See* Clemens, Samuel Langhorne

**Twain, Mark**
*See* Sellers, Isaiah

**Twain, Minerva Mark**
*See* Mitchell, Charlotte Grimes

**Tweed, J. H.**
*See* Knight, Vick R[alph], Jr.

**Tweedale, J.**
*See* Bickle, Judith Brundrett

**[The] 12 Million Dollar Man**
*See* Amouzegar, Jamshid

**Twelve o'Clock**
*See* Stevens, William [Carey]

**Twelvetrees, Helen**
*See* Jurgen, Helen Marie

**[The] Twentieth Century Gabriel**
*See* Hawkins, Erskine Ramsey

**[The] Twentieth Century Minstrel**
*See* Dyer-Bennet, Richard

**[The] Twentieth Century Mozart**
*See* Rolle, Tony

**20/1631**
*See* Upward, Allen

**[The] Twickenham Bard**
*See* Pope, Alexander

**[The] Twig**
*See* Tolson, Dean

**Twiggs, James** 1933- [SFL]
*Author*
* Jameson, Twiggs

**Twiggy**
*See* Hornby, Lesley

**Twilight Ed Killian**
*See* Killian, Edwin Henry

**Twinberrow, William Henry** 1877-
? [THR]
*British actor*
* Wolston, Henry

**Twineham, Arthur W.** 1866- ? [BE]
*American baseball player*
* Twineham, Old Hoss

**Twineham, Old Hoss**
*See* Twineham, Arthur W.

**Twiney, Harrie**
*See* Twiney, Harriette M. E.

**Twiney, Harriette M. E.**
1867-1953 [CW]
*Jamaican poet*
* Twiney, Harrie

**Twining, Doc**
*See* Twining, Howard Earle

**Twining, Howard Earle** 1894- [BE]
*American baseball player*
* Twining, Doc
* Twining, Twink

**Twining, Thomas** 1734-1804 [SN]
*British clergyman*
* [The] Country Clergyman of the
Eighteenth Century

**Twining, Twink**
*See* Twining, Howard Earle

**Twinkle Toes**
*See* LeFlore, Ron[ald]

**Twist, Ananias**
*See* Nunn, William Curtis

**Twist, Kid**
*See* Reles, Abe

**Twist, Kid**
*See* Zwerbach, Max

**[The] Twisting Vocalist**
*See* Woodward, Thomas Jones

**Twistleton-Wykeham-Fiennes, [Sir]
Ranulph** 1944- [WD]
*British author*
* Fiennes, Ranulph

**Twistleton-Wykeham-Fiennes,
Richard Nathaniel** 1909- [WD]
*British author and editor*
* Fiennes, Richard

**Twitchell, A. R.**
*See* Brandon, Michael

**Twitchell, Archie**
*See* Brandon, Michael

**Twitchell, Twitch**
*See* Twitchell, Wayne Lee

**Twitchell, Wayne Lee** 1948-
[SMG]
*American baseball player*
* Twitchell, Twitch

**Twitcher, Harry**
*See* Brougham, Henry Peter

**Twitcher, Jemmy**
*See* Montagu, John [Fourth Earl of
Sandwich]

**Twitty, Conway**
*See* Jenkins, Harold

**Two Gun Alterie**
*See* Alterie, Leland Verain

**Two Gun Cohen**
*See* Cohen, Morris A.

**Two Gun Collins**
*See* Collins, Harry Warren

**Two Gun Crowley**
*See* Crowley, Francis

**Two Gun Guardino**
*See* Guardino, Johnny

**Two Gun Pete**
*See* Washington, Sylvester

**Two, Mr.**
*See* Henry, Josiah F.

**Two Ton Baker**
*See* Baker, Richard E.

**Two Ton Tessie**
*See* O'Shea, Tessie

**Two Ton Tony Galento**
*See* Galento, Tony

**Two Tons of Fun**
*See* Rhodes, Izora

**Two Tons of Fun**
*See* Wash, Martha

**Two Wags** [joint pseudonym with
Frank Dempster Sherman]
*See* Bangs, John Kendrick

**Two Wags** [joint pseudonym with
John Kendrick Bangs]
*See* Sherman, Frank Dempster

**Two Women of the West** [joint
pseudonym with Ella Marchant]
*See* Jones, Alice Ilgenfritz

**Two Women of the West** [joint
pseudonym with Alice Ilgenfritz
Jones]
*See* Marchant, Ella

**Twogood, Forrest** 1907-1972 [BB]
*American basketball player and
coach*
* Twogood, Twogie

**Twogood, Twogie**
*See* Twogood, Forrest

**Twombly, A. Stevenson** [PA]
*Author*
* Perk, Abner

**Twombly, Babe**
*See* Twombly, Clarence Edward

**Twombly, Clarence Edward**
1896-1974 [BE]
*American baseball player*
* Twombly, Babe

**Twombly, Cy**
*See* Twombly, Edwin Parker

**Twombly, Deacon**
*See* Twombly, Henry B.

**Twombly, Edwin Parker**
1897?-1974 [B10]
*American baseball player and coach*
* Twombly, Cy

**Twombly, George Frederick** 1892-
[BE]
*American baseball player*
* Twombly, Silent George

**Twombly, Henry B.** 1862-1955
[FB]
*American football player*
* Twombly, Deacon

**Twombly, Silent George**
*See* Twombly, George Frederick

**Twomby, Louisa**
*See* Meredith, Louisa

**[A] Twopenny Author**
*See* Steele, [Sir] Richard

**Twyman, Harold William** 1898-
[MBF]
*British author*
* Cartwright, A.
* Forge, John
* Murray, Robert
* Richards, Frank [house
pseudonym]

**Tyard, Pontus de** 1521-1605 [DEP]
*French poet*
* [The] Anacreon of the French

**Tyburn Dick**
*See* Savage, Richard [Fourth Earl
Rivers]

**[A] Tycho Brahe**
*See* Dyer, George

**[The] Tycoon**
*See* Lincoln, Abraham

**Tydeus**
*See* Walpole, Horatio [Fourth Earl
of Orford]

**Tyler, A. E.**
*See* Armstrong, [Annette]
Elizabeth

**Tyler, Alvin** 20th c. [RM]
*Musician*
* Tyler, Red

**Tyler, Audrey Patterson** 20th c.
[IBW]
*American track and field athlete and
coach*
* Tyler, Mickey

**Tyler, Beverly**
*See* Saul, Beverly Jean

**Tyler, Bubba**
*See* Tyler, Lamar

**Tyler, George** [FFF]
* Tagliere, Signor

**Tyler, George Albert** 1889-1953
[AS, BE, PB]
*American baseball player*
* Tyler, Lefty

**Tyler, Harold McAfee** 1896-
[IBW]
*American attorney*
* Tyler, Tippy

**Tyler, John** 1790-1862 [FAP]
*American president*
* [The] Accidental President
* His Accidency
* Young Hickory

**Tyler, John Anthony [Johnnie]**
1906- [BE]
*American baseball player*
* Tyler, Ty Ty

**Tyler, Lamar** 20th c. [SMG]
*American football team trainer*
* Tyler, Bubba

**Tyler, Lefty**
*See* Tyler, George Albert

**Tyler, Mickey**
*See* Tyler, Audrey Patterson

**Tyler, Odette**
*See* Kirkland, Odette

**Tyler, R.** [PA]
*American author*
* [A] Virginian

**Tyler, Red**
*See* Tyler, Alvin

**Tyler, Royal** 1756-1826 [PA]
*Author*
* Opdyke, [Doctor] Underhill

**Tyler, Steel Arm**
*See* Tyler, William

**Tyler, T. Texas**
*See* Myrick, David Luke

**Tyler, Terry** 1956-
*American basketball player*
* T.
* Tyler, Thunder

**Tyler, Theodore**
*See* Ziegler, Edward William

**Tyler, Thunder**
*See* Tyler, Terry

**Tyler, Tippy**
*See* Tyler, Harold McAfee

**Tyler, Tom**
*See* Marko [or Markoski?],
Vincent

**Tyler, Ty Ty**
*See* Tyler, John Anthony [Johnnie]

**Tyler, William** 20th c. [OBW]
*American baseball player*
* Tyler, Steel Arm

**Tyler-Whittle, Michael Sidney**
1927- [CA]
*British author*
* Oliver, Mark
* Whittle, Tyler

**Tymeson, Mildred McClary**
*See* Petrie, Mildred McClary

**Tynan, Katharine**
*See* Hinkson, Katherine Tynan

**Tynan, Philip**
*See* Swan, Cormac

**Tyner, Alfred McCoy** 1938- [EJ7]
*American jazz musician*
* Saud, Sulaimon

**Tyng, Florence** [FFF]
*Writer*
* Florence

**Typhoid Mary**
*See* Mallon, Mary

**[The] Typical American**
*See* Roosevelt, Theodore [Teddy]

**Tyran de Blanc**
*See* Grimm, Friedrich Melchior
von

**[The] Tyrant**
*See* Lincoln, Abraham

**[The] Tyrant Basilides**
*See* Ivan IV Vasilievich

**[The] Tyrant of the Chersonese**
*See* Miltiades

**[The] Tyrant of the New England**
*See* Andros, [Sir] Edmund

**Tyrconnel, Duchess of** 17th c. [RH]
*Wife of Richard Talbot, Lord-
Lieutenant of Ireland*
* [The] White Widow

**Tyrone, Paul**
See Norwood, Victor G[eorge] C[harles]

**Tyrrell, Mary E.** 1883-1944 [BEW]
*American actress*
* Grey, Jane

**Tyrrell, Thomas Signis**
See Pichon, Thomas

**Tyrtaeus** 7th c. BC [RH, SN]
*Greek poet*
* [The] Hobbler
* [The] Lame

**[The] Tyrtaeus of France**
See Rouget de Lisle, Claude Joseph

**[The] Tyrtaeus of Germany**
See Koerner, Karl Theodor [or Carl Theodore]

**[The] Tyrtaeus of Spain**
See Quintana, Manuel Jose

**[The] Tyrtaeus of the British Navy**
See Dibdin, Charles

**Tyrtamos** 4th c. BC
[FFF, RH, SN]
*Greek philosopher and scientist*
* [The] Divine Speaker
* Theophrastos

**Tyrwhitt, Gerald Hugh** 1883-1950
[WBD]
*British composer and painter*
* Tyrwhitt-Wilson, Gerald Hugh

**Tyrwhitt-Wilson, Gerald Hugh**
See Tyrwhitt, Gerald Hugh

**Tyselling, Babe**
See Tyselling, Richard

**Tyselling, Richard** 1910- [BB]
*American basketball player and coach*
* Tyselling, Babe

**Tyshler, Alexandr Grigorievich** 1898- [CAR]
*Russian painter*
* Dzhin-Dzhikh-Shivil

**Tyson, A.**
See Hersey, Harold

**Tyson, Albert Thomas** 1892-1953
[BE]
*American baseball player*
* Tyson, Ty

**Tyson, Cecil Washington** 1914-
[BE]
*American baseball player*
* Tyson, Turkey

**Tyson, Coco**
See Tyson, James

**Tyson, James** 20th c. [RO1]
*American singer*
* Tyson, Coco

**Tyson, Teilo**
See McFarlane, David

**Tyson, Turkey**
See Tyson, Cecil Washington

**Tyson, Ty**
See Tyson, Albert Thomas

**Tytla, Bill**
See Tytla, Vladimir

**Tytla, Vladimir** 1904-1968 [WEC]
*American animator*
* Tytla, Bill

**Tytler, Anne Fraser** [PA]
*Author*
* A. F. T.

**Tytler, Balloon**
See Tytler, James

**Tytler, James** 1747-1805
[FFF, SN, WBD]
*Scottish-born scholar*
* Tytler, Balloon

**Tytler, Sarah**
See Keddie, Henrietta

**Tyus, Ansa**
See Tyus, Margaret

**Tyus, Margaret** 1947- [IBW]
*American educator*
* Tyus, Ansa

**Tzara, Tristan**
See Codrescu, Andrei

**Tzara, Tristan**
See Rosenstock, Sami

**Tzimeas, John** ?-1978 [FIR]
*Actor*
* Zimeas, John

**Tzu Hsi [or Tze-hsi]** 1835-1908
[WBD]
*Chinese empress dowager*
* [The] Old Buddha
* Yehonala

# U

**U. E.**
See Edgcumbe, Ursula

**U Tam'si**
See Tchicaya, Gerald Felix

**Uale, Frank** 1885-1927
[BLB, PHM]
*American underworld figure*
* Yale, Frankie

**Ubertini, Francesco** 1494?-1557
[WBD]
*Italian painter*
* [Il] Bachiacca

**Ubique**
See Gillmore, Parker

**Ubique**
See Guggisberg, [Sir] F. G.

**Uccello, Paolo**
See Di Dono, Paolo

**Uchida, Bomber**
See Uchida, Shoji

**Uchida, Shoji** 20th c. [RBE]
*Japanese boxer*
* Uchida, Bomber

**Ucres [or Ucares], Rodriguez**
See Rodriguez Ucares, Fray Jose

**Udall, Jan Beaney** 1938-
[CA, SAT]
*American artist and author*
* Beaney, Jan

**Udall, Lyn**
See Keating, John Henry

**Ueberroth, Harry** 1909-1953
[BEW]
*American actor*
* Curtis, Alan

**Ueno, Noriko**
See Nakae, Noriko

**Uetake, Yojiro** 20th c. [BBH]
*Japanese wrestler and coach*
* Obata, Yojiro

**Ugama, LeRoi**
See Smith, LeRoi Tex

**Ugaro De Fox, Lucia**
See Lockart, Lucia A[licia] Fox

**Ugolino [Count of Segni]**
1147?-1241 [WBD]
*Pope*
* Gregory IX

**Ugolino da Pisa**
See Gherardesca, Ugolino della
[Conte di Donoratico]

**Uhalt, Bernard Bartholomew** 1910-
[BE]
*American baseball player*
* Uhalt, Frenchy

**Uhalt, Frenchy**
See Uhalt, Bernard Bartholomew

**Uhl, Friedrich Ludwig** 1928- [OP]
*Austrian opera singer*
* Uhl, Fritz

**Uhl, Fritz**
See Uhl, Friedrich Ludwig

**[The] Uhlan King**
See Alfonso XII

**Uhland, Johann Ludwig** 1787-1862
[SN]
*German poet*
* [The] Genre Poet of Germany

**Uhle, George Ernest** 1898-
[BE, PB]
*American baseball player*
* [The] Bull

**Uhle, Lefty**
See Uhle, Robert Ellwood [Bob]

**Uhle, Robert Ellwood [Bob]** 1913-
[BE]
*American baseball player*
* Uhle, Lefty

**Uhr, Elizabeth** 1929- [CA]
*American author*
* Stern, Elizabeth

**Ukelele Ike**
See Edwards, Cliff

**Ukelele, Johnny**
See Kaaihue, Johnny

**Ukelele Kid**
See Burse, Charlie

**Ukrainka, Lesya**
See Kvitka, Laryssa Petrovna

**Ulacia, Gabino** 1919- [IBW]
*Cuban military leader*
* Ulacia, Le Grande

**Ulacia, Le Grande**
See Ulacia, Gabino

**Ulatowski, Clement Lambert**
1886-1967 [BE]
*American baseball player*
* Clemens, Clem

**Ulatowski, Clement Lambert**
(Continued)
* Clemens, Clement Lambert

**Ulbach, Louis** 1822- ? [PA]
*Author*
* Ferragus

**Ulfilas [or Uphilas]** 311?- 381?
[HN, SN]
*Bishop of the Goths*
* [The] Apostle of the Goths

**Ulisney, Michael Edward [Mike]**
1917- [BE]
*American baseball player*
* Ulisney, Slugs

**Ulisney, Slugs**
See Ulisney, Michael Edward
[Mike]

**Ulla**
See Smith, Jane Luella Dowd

**Ullah, Salamat** 1913- [CA]
*Indian educator and author*
* Salamatullah

**Ullithorne, Aida** 20th c. [THR]
*British actress*
* Jenoure, Aida

**Ullman, Barbara**
See Schwalberg, Carol[yn
Ernestine Stein]

**Ullrich, Carlos Santiago Castello**
1922- [BE]
*Cuban-born baseball player*
* Ullrich, Sandy

**Ullrich, Sandy**
See Ullrich, Carlos Santiago
Castello

**Ulman, Douglas Elton** 1883-1939
[BEW, WEF]
*American actor*
* Fairbanks, Douglas, Sr.
* Thomas, Elton

**Ulreich, Nura Woodson** 1899-1950
[IBY, ICB]
*American author and illustrator*
* Nura

**Ulric, Lenore**
See Ulrich, Lenore

**Ulrich, Charles, Jr.**
See Galt, William Hamilton

**Ulrich, Dutch**
See Ulrich, Frank W.

**Ulrich, Frank W.** 1899-1929 [BE]
*American baseball player*
* Ulrich, Dutch

**Ulrich, Lenore** 1892-1970
[BEW, FC]
*American actress*
* Ulric, Lenore

**Ultimus Anglorum**
See Bedell, William

**Ultimus Romanorum**
See Congreve, William

**Ultimus Romanorum [Last of the
Romans]**
See Hollis, Thomas

**Ultimus Romanorum**
See Johnson, Samuel

**Ultimus Romanorum**
See Walpole, Horatio [Fourth Earl
of Orford]

**Ultimus Scholasticorum, Doctor**
See Biel [or Byll], Gabriel

**Ulvaeus, Agnetha Faltskog** 1950-
[RO2]
*Swedish singer*
* Ulvaeus, Anna

**Ulvaeus, Anna**
See Ulvaeus, Agnetha Faltskog

**Ulyanov, Vladimir Ilich** 1870-1924
[IPA, OCF]
*Russian Communist leader*
* Lenin, Nicolai

**[The] Ulysses**
See Albert III [or Albrecht]

**Ulysses**
See George III

**Ulysses, Mohammed**
See Gernsback, Hugo

**[The] Ulysses of Bibliographers**
See Mercier, Bartholomew

**[The] Ulysses of the Highlands**
See Cameron, [Sir] Evan

**Umbach, Arnold J.** 20th c. [BBH]
*American wrestling coach*
* Umbach, Swede

**Umbach, Swede**
See Umbach, Arnold J.

**Umbehr, Otto** 1902- [B10]
*Austrian photojournalist*
* Umbo

**Umbellus, T.**
See  Eaton, David H.

**Umbo**
See  Umbehr, Otto

**[An] Umbrian Gozzoli**
See  Betti [or Di Biagio?],
Bernardino

**Un**
See     Second element of name

**Una**
See  Ford, Mary Anne McMullen

**Unada**
See  Gliewe, Unada [Grace]

**Uncle Abe**
See  Lincoln, Abraham

**Uncle Adam**
See  Moyridge, George

**Uncle Al**
See  Pratt, Al[bert G.]

**Uncle Al**
See  Silverstone, Alan

**Uncle Bernie**
See  Meltzer, Bernard

**Uncle Bill**
See  Alvord, William C.

**Uncle Bill**
See  Traylor, Bill

**Uncle Billy**
See  Courtright, William

**Uncle Charles**
See  Johnston, Charles Haven Ladd

**Uncle Charles**
See  Mayer, Charles E. E.

**Uncle Charlie**
See  Moran, Charles B.

**Uncle Cola**
See  Gentile, Nicola

**Uncle Constantchin**
See  Anson, Adrian Constantine

**Uncle Cyp**
See  Brasfield, L. L.

**Uncle Dan**
See  Anderson, Frank

**Uncle Dave Macon**
See  Macon, David Harrison

**Uncle Dick**
See  Oglesby, Richard James

**Uncle Don**
See  Rhea, Don

**Uncle Don**
See  Rice, Howard

**Uncle Ed**
See  Kempf, Edward J.

**Uncle Esek**
See  Shaw, Henry Wheeler

**Uncle Ezra**
See  Barrett, Patrick J.

**Uncle Gordon**
See  Roe, F[rederic] Gordon

**Uncle Gus**
See  Rey, Hans Augusto

**Uncle Hardy**
See  Senior, William

**Uncle Henry Warren**
See  Warren, Henry

**Uncle Herbert**
See  Arthur, Timothy Shay

**Uncle Ho**
See  Ho Chi Mihn

**Uncle Jack**
See  Dey, John William

**Uncle Jack**
See  Joel, Jack Bernato

**Uncle Jake**
See  King, Oswin Kerryn

**Uncle Jake**
See  McAlpine, Robert W.

**Uncle James**
See  Rodwell, James

**Uncle Jeems**
See  O'Rourke, James Henry

**Uncle Jerry**
See  Emerson, Anne

**Uncle Jimmy Thompson**
See  Thompson, Jimmy

**Uncle Joe**
See  Barnes, Joe

**Uncle Joe**
See  Cannon, Joseph Gurney

**Uncle Joe**
See  Dzhugashvili, Iosif
Vissarionovich

**Uncle John**
See  Chapman, Edwin O.

**Uncle John**
See  Noyce, Elisha

**Uncle Johnny Williams**
See  Williams, Johnny

**Uncle Jumbo**
See  Cleveland, [Stephen] Grover

**Uncle Kwesi**
See  Lamptey, Jonathan Kwesi

**Uncle Mac**
See  McCulloch, Derek

**Uncle Miltie**
See  Berlinger, Milton

**Uncle Monty**
See  Hamilton-Wilkes, Edwin
Montague

**Uncle Mose**
See  Goldblatt, Mose

**Uncle Murray**
See  Parker, Murray

**Uncle Paul**
See  Barham, Samuel, Jr.

**Uncle Paul**
See  Kruger, Paul [or Paulus]

**Uncle Peter**
See  Torbett, John Walter

**Uncle Philip**
See  Hawks, Francis Lister

**Uncle Ray**
See  Coffman, Ramon Peyton

**Uncle Remus**
See  Harris, Joel Chandler

**Uncle Robbie [or Robby]**
See  Robinson, Wilbert

**Uncle Robert**
See  Lee, Robert Edward

**Uncle Sam**
See  Wilson, Samuel

**Uncle Sam Grant**
See  Grant, Hiram Ulysses

**Uncle Sam Ward**
See  Ward, Sam[uel]

**Uncle Skipper?**
See  Jordan, Charles [Charley]

**Uncle Toby**
See  Miller, Tobias Ham

**Uncle Tom**
See  Bannon, Thomas Edward
[Tom]

**Uncle Ton**
See  Ton Duc Thang

**Uncle Will**
See  Wells, William

**Uncle Will, V. M.**
See  Crafts, W. F.

**Uncle Willis**
See  Tilton, Stephen W.

**Uncle Yoolus**
See  Blegen, Julius P.

**Uncles, Ewart Charles** 1919-
[ART]
*British artist*
* E. U.

**Uncommercial Traveler**
See  Dickens, Charles

**Unconditional Surrender Grant**
See  Grant, Hiram Ulysses

**[The] Uncorruptible Commoner**
See  Marvell, Andrew

**[The] Uncrowned King**
See  Gordon, Charles George

**[The] Uncrowned King of Ireland**
See  Parnell, Charles Stewart

**[The] Uncrowned Monarch**
See  O'Connell, Daniel

**[The] Uncrowned Queen of the Blues**
See  Cox, Ida

**Undercliffe, Errol**
See  Campbell, John Ramsey

**Underhill, Charles**
See  Hill, Reginald [Charles]

**Underhill, Edward** 16th c.
[HN, SN]
*Protestant supporter*
* [The] Hot Gospeller

**Underhill, Edward Bean**     [FFF]
*American writer*
* Fant, Eli

**Underhill, Edward Fitch** 1830-1898
*American author*
* Ockside, Knight Russ

**Underhill, Peter**
See  Soderberg, Percy Measday

**Underhill, Viola**
See  Wells, Viola Gertrude

**Underhill, Wilbur** 1897-1934
[BLB]
*American bank robber*
* [The] Tri-State Terror

**[The] Undersigned**
See  Arnold, George

**[The] Undertaker**
See  Reese, Don

**[The] Undertaker**
See  Woodcock, Leonard

**Underwood, Deadly**
See  Underwood, Derek Leslie

**Underwood, Derek Leslie** 1945-
[DC]
*British cricketer*
* Underwood, Deadly

**Underwood, Grace** 1911-     [THR]
*British actress*
* Barry, Christine

**Underwood, Keith Alfred** 1934-
[ART]
*British artist*
* K. A. U.

**Underwood, Lewis Graham**
See  Wagner, C[harles] Peter

**Underwood, Mavis Eileen** 1916-
[AW]
*British author*
* Kilpatrick, Sarah

**Underwood, Michael**
See  Evelyn, [John] Michael

**Underwood, Miles**
See  Glassco, John [Stinson]

**[The] Unfair Preacher**
See  Barrow, Isaac

**[The] Unfortunate**
See  Joseph II

**Unger, Marion**
See  Thede, Marion Draughon

**Unger, Maurice Albert** 1917-     [CA]
*American educator and author*
* Munger, Al

**Ungerer, Jean Thomas** 1931-
[CA, SAT, TBJ]
*French-born author and illustrator*
* Ungerer, Tomi

**Ungerer, Tomi**
See  Ungerer, Jean Thomas

**Ungern-Sternberg, Alexander von**
1806-1868    [WBD]
*Esthonian-born author*
* Sternberg, Alexander von

**[The] Ungodly**
See  Aetius of Antioch

**Uniacke, Evelyn Catherine** 1884-
[WWL]
*British author*
* Clark, Catherine

**Unicus [Alone]**
See  Joergensen, Johannes

**Union Man Holke**
See  Holke, Walter Henry

**Union Safeguard Grant**
See  Grant, Hiram Ulysses

[The] Unique
See Richter, Jean Paul Friedrich

Unit, Matthew
See Pooton, James

Unitas, Johnny 20th c.
*American football player*
* Johnny U

United States Grant
See Grant, Hiram Ulysses

United We Stand Grant
See Grant, Hiram Ulysses

[The] Universal Aristarchus
See Hoskins, John

[The] Universal Doctor
See Alain de Lille [or Alan de l'Isle]

[The] Universal Doctor
See Aquinas, Thomas [Thomas of Aquino]

[The] Universal Genius
See Petty, [Sir] William

[The] Universal Index and Living Cyclopaedia
See Magliabecchi, Antonio [or Anthony]

[The] Universal Philosopher
See Harriot, Thomas

[The] Universal Provider
See Whiteley, William

[The] Universal Spider
See Louis XI

Universalis, Doctor
See Alain de Lille [or Alan de l'Isle]

Universalis, Doctor
See Albert [Count of Bollstadt]

Universalis, Doctor
See Aquinas, Thomas [Thomas of Aquino]

Unk
See White, Cecil

[The] Unknown Eros
See Patmore, Coventry K. Dighton

Uno, Comandante
See Pabon Pabon, Rosemberg

Unofficial Observer
See Carter, John Franklin

Unpa
See Won-Sik, Lim

Unprecedented Strategist Grant
See Grant, Hiram Ulysses

Unquestionably Skilled Grant
See Grant, Hiram Ulysses

[The] Unready
See Ethelred II

Unseld, Westley 1947- [IBW]
*American basketball player*
* [The] Jolly Green Giant

Unser Choe Hauser
See Hauser, Joseph John

Unser, Del
See Unser, Delbert Bernard

Unser, Delbert Bernard 1944- [SMG]
*American baseball player*
* Unser, Del

Unser Fritz
See Frederick William

[The] Untaught Poetess
See Leapor, Mary

Unthank, Luisa-Teresa 1924- [AW, CA]
*British-born writer*
* Unthank, Tessa Brown

Unthank, Tessa Brown
See Unthank, Luisa-Teresa

Untouchable, Mr.
See Barnes, Leroy

Unwin, David S[torr] 1918- [AW, CA, WD]
*British author*
* Severn, David

Upchurch, Boyd Bradfield 1919- [CA, SF, WD]
*American author*
* Boyd, John

Upchurch, Jefferson Woodrow 1911-1971 [BE]
*American baseball player*
* Upchurch, Woody

Upchurch, Woody
See Upchurch, Jefferson Woodrow

Upcott, William 1779-1845 [SN]
*British bibliographer*
* [The] Old Mortality in His Line

Updyke, James
See Burnett, William Riley

[The] Upholsterer of Notre Dame
See Montmorency-Bouteville, Francois Henri de [Duc de Luxembourg]

Upp, George Henry 1883-1937 [BE]
*American baseball player*
* Upp, Jerry

Upp, Jerry
See Upp, George Henry

Upper, Joseph
See Harris, Joseph Upper

[The] Upright
See Frederick IV

Upright, Dixie
See Upright, Roy T.

Upright, Roy T. 1926- [BE]
*American baseball player*
* Upright, Dixie

Upright Telltruth, Esq.
See Lamb, Charles

Upshur, Donald M. 1912-1950 [SC]
*American actor and producer*
* Ravenel, John

Upshur, Mary J. S. [FFF, PA]
*Author*
* Fielding, Fanny

[The] Upside Down Comedian
See Lawrence, Joe

Upson, Norma 1919- [CA]
*American author*
* Kimball, Nancy

[An] Upstart Crow
See Shakespeare, William

Upton, George Putnam 1834-1919 [WBD]
*American journalist and music critic*
* Pickle, Peregrine

Upton, Margaret 1894?-1957 [BEW]
*American theatrical performer*
* Joyce, Peggy Hopkins

Upton, Muscles
See Upton, Thomas Herbert [Tom]

Upton, Thomas Herbert [Tom] 1926- [BE]
*American baseball player*
* Upton, Muscles

Upward, Allen 20th c. [WWL]
*British author*
* 20/1631

Upward, Edward Falaise 1903- [AW]
*British author*
* Chalmers, Allen

[El] Uqsor
See Borgmann, Dmitri A[lfred]

Urban, Louis John 1898- [BE]
*American baseball player*
* Urban, Luke

Urban, Luke
See Urban, Louis John

Urban, Sylvanus, Gent.
See Cave, Edward

Urban II
See O'do [or U'do]

Urban III
See Crivelli, Uberto

Urban IV
See Pantaleon, Jacques

Urban V
See De Grimoard, Guillaume

Urban VI
See Prignani, Bartolommeo

Urban VII
See Castagna, Giovanni Battista

Urban VIII
See Barberini, Maffeo

Urbanczyk, Andrew Andrzej 1936- [IAW]
*Russian-born author*
* A. U.

Urch, Elizabeth 1921- [WD]
*British author*
* Brogan, Elise

[The] Urchin
See Laud, William

Urell, William Francis 20th c. [WW]
*Author*
* Francis, William

U'Ren, Hilda
See U'Ren-Stubbings, Hilda

Uren, Hilda
See U'Ren-Stubbings, Hilda

Uren, Malcolm John Leggoe 1900- [AW]
*Australian author*
* Malcolm, John
* Matelot

U'Ren-Stubbings, Hilda 1914- [CA]
*British-born writer and bibliographer*
* Stubbings, Hilda Uren
* U'Ren, Hilda
* Uren, Hilda

Urena de Henriquez, Salome 1850-1897 [CW]
*Dominican poet*
* Herminia

Urena de Mendoza, Nicolas 1822-1875 [CW]
*Dominican poet and folklorist*
* Castulo
* Nisidas

Urfe, Honore d' 1567-1625 [HN, RH]
*French author*
* [The] Father of Pastoral Romance

Urich, Doc
See Urich, Richard

Urich, Richard 1929- [SMG]
*American football coach*
* Urich, Doc

Urick, Ed 20th c. [PMJ]
*American singer and actor*
* Ames, Ed

Urick, Gene 20th c. [PMJ]
*American singer*
* Ames, Gene

Urick, Joe 20th c. [PMJ]
*American singer*
* Ames, Joe

Urick, Vic 20th c. [PMJ]
*American singer*
* Ames, Vic

Uriel
See Da Veiga Fontoura, Uriel

Uriel, Henry
See Faust, Frederick [Schiller]

Uris, Auren 1913- [CA]
*American author*
* Paul, Auren

Urista, Alberto H. 1947- [CA]
*Mexican-born author*
* Alurista

Urmuz
See Codrescu, Andrei

Urn, Althea
See Ford, Consuelo Urisarri

Urner, Mabel Herbert
See Harper, Mabel Herbert

Urner, Nathan D. [PA]
*Author*
* Brentford, Burke

Urquhart, C. H. 1855- ? [FFF]
*American writer*
* Scotty

Urquhart, David 1805-1877 [SN]
*British diplomat*
* [The] Russophobist

**Urquhart, Paul**
*See* Black, Ladbroke Lionel Day

**Ursa Major**
*See* Johnson, Samuel

**Ursinus, Zacharias**
*See* Beer [or Baer], Zacharias

**Ursula, Sanna**
*See* Honkanen, Hilja Loviisa
Valkeapaa

**Urtisius**
*See* Wursteisen, Christian

**Urwin, Ranald Keith** 1942- [OP]
*British opera singer*
* Erwen, Keith

**Urziceanu, Aura** 1946- [EJ7]
*Rumanian-born jazz musician*
* Aura
* Lee, Aura

**Uscatescu, George** 1919- [IAW]
*Rumanian-born author*
* Aluta, Juan De

**Useless, Ipecac, M.D.**
*See* Houston, Eugene A.

**Usher, Frank Hugh** 1909-
[CA, WW]
*British author*
* Franklin, Charles
* Lester, Frank

**Usher, Margo Scegge**
*See* McHargue, Georgess

**Usher, Shaun** 1937- [CA]
*British author*
* Scott, Jeffrey

**Ushewokunze, Herbert** 20th c.
*Zimbabwe Rhodesian government
official*
* Herbie the Herbalist

**Usikota**
*See* Brinitzer, Carl

**Uspenskii, Petr Dem'yanovich**
1878-1947 [LC]
*Russian-born author*
* Uspensky, P. D.

**Uspensky, P. D.**
*See* Uspenskii, Petr Dem'yanovich

**Ussat, Dutch**
*See* Ussat, William August

**Ussat, William August** 1904-1959
[BE]
*American baseball player*
* Ussat, Dutch

**Usselmann, James** 1876-1938
[WBD]
*American actor*
* Carew, James

**Ustinov, Nicolai** 1925- [MS]
*Swedish opera singer*
* Gedda, Nicolai

**Uston, Kenneth** 1934?-
*American blackjack player*
* [The] King of the Card Counters

**[The] Usurper**
*See* Wang Mang

**Uticensis**
*See* Cato, Marcus Porcius

**Utilis, Doctor**
*See* Lyra, Nicholas de

**Utjesenovic, Juraj**
*See* Martinuzzi, George

**Utley, Fred Burton** 1863- ? [NAA]
*Canadian writer*
* Gordon, Ralph

**Utley, Ralph**
*See* Cairns, Huntington

**Utrerito [Little Fellow from Utrera]**
*See* Garcia, Antonio

**Uttam**
*See* Oak, Purushottam Nagesh

**Uttley, Alice Jane [Taylor]**
1884-1976 [CA, SAT]
*British author*
* Uttley, Alison

**Uttley, Alison**
*See* Uttley, Alice Jane [Taylor]

**Uzcudun, Paolino** 1899- [BX]
*Spanish boxer*
* [The] Basque Woodchopper

**Uzes, Duchesse d'**
*See* De Rochechouart-Mortemart,
Marie Clementine

# V

**V.**
*See* Clive, Mrs. Archer

**V. B.**
*See* Brooks, Vincent

**V. B. K.**
*See* Van Breda Kolff, Bill

**V. B. K.**
*See* Van Breda Kolff, Jan

**V. C. C. W.**
*See* Williams, Vivian Claud
Craddock

**V. F.**
*See* Foot, Victorine Anne

**V. N. G.**
*See* Garrod, Violet Nellie

**V. T.**
*See* Tengberg, Violet

**Vaccarelli, Horn**
*See* Vaccarelli, Joe J.

**Vaccarelli, Joe J.** 20th c. [RBE]
*Boxing agent*
* Vaccarelli, Horn

**Vaccarelli, Paolo Antonini** 20th c.
[BLB, PHM]
*Italian-born American underworld
figure*
* Kelly, Paul

**Vaccaro, Ernest B.** 1905?-1979
[CA]
*American journalist*
* Vaccaro, Tony

**Vaccaro, Tony**
*See* Vaccaro, Ernest B.

**Vacchi, Augustus Victor** 1842- ?
[LAO]
*French-born author*
* La Bolina, Jack

**Vace, Geoffrey**
*See* Cave, Hugh B[arnett]

**Vache, Ernest Lewis** 1895-1953
[BE]
*American baseball player*
* Vache, Tex

**Vache, Tex**
*See* Vache, Ernest Lewis

**Vachon, Rogatien Rosaire** 1945-
[FHE, HK, SMG]
*Canadian-born hockey player*
* Vachon, Rogie

**Vachon, Rogie**
*See* Vachon, Rogatien Rosaire

**Vacirca, Corrado** 1904-1969 [SC]
*Italian-born actor*
* Terranova, Dino

**[The] Vacuum Cleaner**
*See* Robinson, Brooks [Calbert,
Jr.]

**Vaczek, Louis Charles** 1913-
[CA, WW]
*Hungarian-born author*
* Hardin, Peter

**Vadianus, Joachim**
*See* Von Watt, Joachim

**Vadim, Roger**
*See* Plemiannikov, Roger Vadim

**Vadnais, Carol Marcel** 1945-
[SMG]
*Canadian-born hockey player*
* Vadnais, Vad

**Vadnais, Vad**
*See* Vadnais, Carol Marcel

**Vaeth, Martin**
*See* Kummer, Frederic Arnold

**Vaez, Jean N. Gustave** 1812- ?
[PA]
*Author*
* Nieuwenhuysen, Van

**Vaga, Perino del**
*See* Buonaccorsi, Pietro

**[The] Vagabond**
*See* Badeau, Adam

**Vagabond**
*See* Blake, George

**[The] Vagabond Halfback**
*See* McNally, John V.

**[The] Vagabond Lover**
*See* Vallee, Hubert P[rior]

**Vagramian, Aram** 1921- [ASC]
*American musician*
* Vega, Al

**Vagrant**
*See* Duffus, Louis George

**Vague, Vera**
*See* Allen, Barbara Jo

**Vahey, John George Haslette** 1881-
? [WW, WWL]
*British author*
* Clandon, Henrietta
* Haslette, John

**Vahey, John George Haslette**
(Continued)
* Lang, Anthony
* Loder, Vernon
* Mowbray, John
* Proudfoot, Walter
* Timony, Arthur N.

**Vahrer, M.** [PA]
*Author*
* Frederick

**Vaid, Sanford**
*See* Tucker, [Arthur] Wilson

**Vaidon, Lawdom**
*See* Woolman, David S.

**Vail, Amanda**
*See* Miller, Warren

**Vail, Dad**
*See* Vail, Harry Emerson

**Vail, Doc**
*See* Vail, Robert Garfield [Bob]

**Vail, Eric** 1953- [SMG]
*Canadian-born hockey player*
* Vail, Train

**Vail, Floyd** 19th c. [FFF]
*American writer*
* Flambeau
* Valentine, Floyd

**Vail, Harry Emerson** 1859-1928
[BBH]
*American rowing coach*
* Vail, Dad

**Vail, John Cooper** [PA]
*Author*
* Allspice, Zekel

**Vail, Kay Boyle** 1903- [WGT]
*Author*
* Boyle, Kay

**Vail, Melville** 1906- [CEI]
*Canadian-born hockey player*
* Vail, Sparky

**Vail, Robert Garfield [Bob]**
1881-1953 [BE]
*American baseball player*
* Vail, Doc

**Vail, Sparky**
*See* Vail, Melville

**Vail, Train**
*See* Vail, Eric

**Vaka, Demetra**
*See* Brown, Demetra Kenneth

**Vala, Katri Wadenstroem**
*See* Heikel, Karin Alice

**Valachi, Joseph Michael**
1904-1971 [BLB]
*American underworld figure*
* Cago, Joe
* Cargo, Joe
* Kato, Joe
* Siano, Joe
* Sorge, Anthony

**Valaida**
*See* Snow, Valaida

**Valasco, David** 1859-1931
[JL, TLC]
*American producer and playwright*
* Belasco, David
* [The] Bishop of Broadway

**Valbert, G.**
*See* Cherbuliez, Victor

**Valbonne, Jean**
*See* Leprohon, Pierre

**Valcoe, H. Felix**
*See* Swartz, Harry [Felix]

**Valda, [Mme.] Giulia**
*See* Cameron, Julia

**Valdare, Sunny Jim**
*See* Mulligan, James

**Valdarfer, Christopher**
*See* Haslewood, Joseph

**Valdeau, Vintie**
*See* Wheeler, Mrs. James

**Valdemoro**
*See* Fernandez Perez, Angel

**Valdes, Angel** 1838- ? [GS]
*Peruvian bullfighter*
* [El] Maestro [The Master]

**Valdes, Gabriel de la Concepcion**
1809-1844 [IBW, WBD]
*Cuban poet*
* Placido

**Valdes, Latigo**
*See* Valdes, Rene Gutierrez

**Valdes, Nelson P.** 1945- [CA]
*Cuban-born American educator and
author*
* Leyva, Ricardo

**Valdes, Rene Gutierrez** 1929- [BE]
*Cuban-born baseball player*
* Valdes, Latigo

**Valdes, Rodrigo**
See  Valdez, Rodrigo

**Valdes Machuca, Ignacio**
1792-1851  [CW]
*Cuban poet, playwright, journalist*
* Desval

**Valdespino, Hilario Borroto** 1939-
[BE]
*Cuban-born baseball player*
* Valdespino, Sandy

**Valdespino, Sandy**
See  Valdespino, Hilario Borroto

**Valdez, Carlos** 1926-  [EJ]
*Cuban-born jazz musician*
* Valdez, Potato

**Valdez, Potato**
See  Valdez, Carlos

**Valdez, Rodrigo** 1946-  [RBE]
*Colombian boxer*
* Valdes, Rodrigo

**Valdez, Strico** 20th c.  [OBW]
*American baseball player*
* Valdez, Swat

**Valdez, Swat**
See  Valdez, Strico

**Valding, Victor** [joint pseudonym
with John Victor Peterson]
See  Benson, Allan Ingvald

**Valding, Victor** [joint pseudonym
with Allan Ingvald Benson]
See  Peterson, John Victor

**Valdivia y Sisay, Aniceto**
1859-1927  [CW]
*Cuban playwright and poet*
* Kostia, Conde

**Vale, [Henry] Edmund [Theodoric]**
1888-1969  [CAP]
*Welsh author*
* Bledlow, John

**Vale, Jerry**
See  Vitaliano, Genaro Louis

**Vale, Keith**
See  Clegg, W. Paul

**Vale, Lewis**
See  Oglesby, Joseph

**Vale, Marguerite** 20th c.  [BEW]
*Playwright*
* Vale, Martin

**Vale, Martin**
See  Vale, Marguerite

**Valencak, Hannelore**
See  Mayer, Hannelore

**Valencia**
See  Cuevas Roger, Victoriano

**Valencia, Cookie**
See  Valencia, Jose

**Valencia, Flaco [Skinny Valencia]**
See  Valencia Orozco, Ignacio

**Valencia, Jose** 20th c.  [RBE]
*American boxer*
* Valencia, Cookie

**Valencia Orozco, Ignacio** 1907-
[GS]
*Mexican bullfighter*
* Valencia, Flaco [Skinny
Valencia]

**[El] Valenciano [The Valencian]**
See  Pascual y Olmos, Jose

**Valens, Ritchie**
See  Valenzuela, Richard

**Valente, Umberto**  [MM]
*American underworld figure*
* [Lo] Spirito [The Ghost]

**Valenti, Dino**
See  Powers, Chester

**Valentin**
See  Olmedo y Vazquez, Antonio

**Valentin, Karl**
See  Fey, Valentin Ludwig

**Valentina**
See  Schlee, Nicholaevna Sanina

**Valentine**
See  Pechey, Archibald Thomas

**Valentine, Alec**
See  Isaacs, Alan

**Valentine, Benjamin Bennaton**
1843-1926  [FFF]
*British-born journalist and
playwright*
* Fitznoodle, Francis
* Iredale, John

**Valentine, Bubba**
See  Valentine, Ellis Clarence

**Valentine, Corky**
See  Valentine, Harold Lewis

**Valentine, David**
See  Ludovici, Anthony M[ario]

**Valentine, Douglas**
See  Williams, [George] Valentine

**Valentine, Ellis Clarence** 1954-
[SMG]
*American baseball player*
* Valentine, Bubba

**Valentine, Floyd**
See  Vail, Floyd

**Valentine, Fred Lee** 1935-  [BE]
*American baseball player*
* Valentine, Squeaky

**Valentine, Harold Lewis** 1929-
[BE]
*American baseball player*
* Valentine, Corky

**Valentine, Helen** 1909-  [CAP]
*American educator and author*
* Valentine, [Sister] Mary Hester

**Valentine, Henry**
See  Poole, Reginald Heber

**Valentine, Henry**
See  Prout, Geoffrey

**Valentine, James C[heyne]** 1935-
[CA]
*American author*
* Valentine, Tom

**Valentine, Jo**
See  Armstrong, Charlotte

**Valentine, Joseph**
See  Valentino, Guiseppe

**Valentine, [Sister] Mary Hester**
See  Valentine, Helen

**Valentine, Mrs.**  [FFF, PA]
*Entertainer*
* Aunt Louisa

**Valentine, Mrs.** (Continued)
* Moore, Adelaide

**Valentine, Paul**
See  Daixel, William Wolf

**Valentine, Raymond** 1908-  [WWJ]
*American jazz musician*
* Valentine, Syd

**Valentine, Roger**
See  Duke, Donald Norman

**Valentine, Squeaky**
See  Valentine, Fred Lee

**Valentine, Syd**
See  Valentine, Raymond

**Valentine, Thomas** 1896-
*American jazz musician*
* Thomas, Kid

**Valentine, Tom**
See  Valentine, James C[heyne]

**Valentino**
See  Garavani, Valentino

**Valentino, Guiseppe** 1903-1948
[FC]
*Italian-American cinematographer*
* Valentine, Joseph

**Valentino, Mark**
See  Busillo, Anthony

**Valentino, Rudolph**
See  Guglielmi Di Valentina
D'Antonguolla, Rodolpho Alfonso
Raffaelo P.

**Valentino, Sal**
See  Spanpinato, Salvatore Willard

**Valentova, Ivona**
See  Gedzikova, Ivona

**Valenzuela, Benjamin Beltran**
[Benny] 1933-  [BE]
*Mexican-born baseball player*
* Valenzuela, Papelero

**Valenzuela, Papelero**
See  Valenzuela, Benjamin Beltran
[Benny]

**Valenzuela, Richard** 1940?-1959
[LRR]
*American musician*
* Valens, Ritchie

**Valeriano, Napoleon D[iestro]**
1917?-1975  [CA]
*Filipino-born American army officer
and author*
* Valeriano Serrano, Napoleon
Diestro

**Valeriano Serrano, Napoleon Diestro**
See  Valeriano, Napoleon D[iestro]

**Valerie**
See  Fould, Wilhelmine Josephine
Simonin

**Valerie, Louis**
See  Barko, Louis

**Valerio, Juan Francisco**
1829?-1878  [CW]
*Cuban author and playwright*
* Valor y Fe, Narciso

**Valerio, Michael** 20th c.  [SG]
*Boxer*
* Nelson, Frankie

**Valerius?**
See  Francis, [Sir] Philip

**Valerius, C.**
See  Mendes, Catulle

**Valery, Joseph, Jr.** 1934-  [BWW]
*American singer*
* Blue, Joe
* Blue, Little Joe

**Valestin, Edward Joseph** 1908-
[BE]
*American baseball player*
* Fallenstin, Ed[ward Joseph]
* Fallenstin, Jack

**[Le] Valet des Princes**
See  Froissart, Jean

**[Le] Valet du Cardinal**
See  Nogaret de la Valette, Jean
Louis de

**[The] Valet Poet**
See  Marot, Clement

**[The] Valiant**
See  Alfonso VI [or Alphonso]

**[The] Valiant**
See  John IV [or Jean]

**[The] Valiant Lion**
See  Alep Arslan

**Valigursky, Ed** 20th c.  [SFP]
*Author*
* Remback, William

**Valiquette, Big Jack**
See  Valiquette, Jack

**Valiquette, Jack** 1956-  [SMG]
*Canadian hockey player*
* Valiquette, Big Jack

**Valle-Inclan, Ramon Del**
See  Valle y Pena, Ramon Del

**Valle y Pena, Ramon Del**
1866-1936  [TCL]
*Spanish author, playwright, poet*
* Valle-Inclan, Ramon Del

**Vallee, Hubert P[rior]** 1901-
[AM, BEW, CA]
*American actor and singer*
* [The] Vagabond Lover
* Vallee, Rudy

**Vallee, Jacques** 1939-  [ESF]
*French author*
* Seriel, Jerome

**Vallee, Rudy**
See  Vallee, Hubert P[rior]

**Valleita, Leo**
See  Anselmi, Teodero

**Vallejo Gonzalez, Carmen** 1939-
[OP]
*Italian opera singer*
* Gonzalez, Carmen Pagliaro

**Valleria, Alwina**
See  Schoening, Alwina

**Vallette, Marguerite** 1860?-1953
[WBD]
*French author and critic*
* Rachilde

**Valli**
See  Van De Bovencamp, Valli

**Valli, Alida**
See  Altenburger, Alida Maria

**Valli, Frankie**
See  Castelluccio, Frank

**Valli, Valli**
See  Knust, Valli

**Valli, Virginia**
See  McSweeney, Virginia

**Valliquietto, Margaret Rose** 1911-
[EMT]
*American actress, singer, dancer*
* Knight, June

**Valmain, Frederic** 1931-  [AW]
*French playwright and author*
* Baulat, Paul
* Carter, James

**Valnay, Raoul**
See  Herve, Aime Marie Edouard

**Valor y Fe, Narciso**
See  Valerio, Juan Francisco

**Valter, M.**  [PA]
*Author*
* Domino

**Valtiala, Kaarle-Juhani Bertel**
1938-  [IAW]
*Finnish author*
* Nalle

**Valvrojenski, Bernard** 1865-1959
[JL]
*Lithuanian-born art historian and author*
* B. B.
* Berenson, Bernard

**Vambery, Armin**
See  Bamberger, Hermann

**Vamvoras, Clyde** 20th c.  [GW]
*American rodeo performer*
* Vamvoras, Vinegar Roan

**Vamvoras, Vinegar Roan**
See  Vamvoras, Clyde

**Van**
See  Second element of name for further listings

**Van**
See  Bartlett, David W.

**Van Aeken [or Van Aken], Hieronymus** 1450?-1516  [WBD]
*Dutch painter*
* Bosch, Hieronymus

**Van Allan, Richard**
See  Jones, Alan Philip

**Van Allen, William Harman** 1870-
?  [WWL]
*American author and clergyman*
* Presbyter, Ignotus

**Van Alstyne, Clayton Emery**
1900-1960  [BE]
*American baseball player*
* Van Alstyne Spike

**Van Alstyne Spike**
See  Van Alstyne, Clayton Emery

**Van Anrooy, Francine** 1924-  [CA]
*Dutch author*
* Van Anrooy, Frans

**Van Anrooy, Frans**
See  Van Anrooy, Francine

**Van Arden, J. Howard** 1856- ?
[PA]
*Author*
* Braddon, Paul

**Van Arnam, Dave** 20th c.  [SFP]
*Author*
* Archer, Ron [joint pseudonym with Theodore Edwin (Ted) White]

**Van Arsdale, Wirt**
See  Davis, Martha [Wirt]

**Van Atta, Russell** 1906-  [BE]
*American baseball player*
* Van Atta, Sheriff

**Van Atta, Sheriff**
See  Van Atta, Russell

**Van Atta, Winfred Lowell** 1910-
[CA, WW]
*American author*
* Ryerson, Lowell

**Van Auken, Mrs. Henry**  [FFF]
*Entertainer*
* St. John, Nellie

**Van Avond, Jan**
See  Slater, Francis Carey

**Van Bairle, Gaspard** 1584-1648
[PA]
*Author*
* Barloeus

**Van Bedacht, Rudy** 1932-  [CW]
*Surinamese poet, critic, journalist*
* Verlooghen, Corly

**Van Beever, Robert F.** 20th c.
[SFL]
*Author*
* Gordon, Fritz [joint pseudonym with Fred(erick) G(ordon) Jarvis, Jr.]

**Van Berg, Marion Harold**  ?-1971
[BBH]
*American horse trainer*
* Van, Mr.

**Van Beverloo, Cornelis Guillaume**
1922-  [CAR]
*Dutch painter*
* Corneille

**Van, Billy**
See  Coppola, Vito

**Van, Billy B.**
See  Vandegrift, Billy B.

**Van, Bobby**
See  Stein, Robert Jack

**Van Boxmeer, Boxy**
See  Van Boxmeer, John Martin

**Van Boxmeer, John Martin** 1952-
[SMG]
*Canadian-born hockey player*
* Van Boxmeer, Boxy

**Van Breda Kolff, Bill** 1922-
[BB, SMG]
*American basketball player and coach*
* V. B. K.
* Van Breda Kolff, Butch

**Van Breda Kolff, Butch**
See  Van Breda Kolff, Bill

**Van Breda Kolff, Jan** 1951-  [SMG]
*American basketball player*
* V. B. K.

**Van Briggle, Margaret F[rances] Jessup** 1917-  [CA]
*American author*
* Jessup, Frances

**Van Brocklin, Norm[an]** 1926-  [FB]
*American football player*
* [The] Dutchman

**Van Brugge, Jan**
See  Joris, David

**Van Buren, Abigail**
See  Phillips, Pauline Esther [Friedman]

**Van Buren, Deacon**
See  Van Buren, Edward Eugene

**Van Buren, Edward Eugene**
1870-1957  [BE]
*American baseball player*
* Van Buren, Deacon

**Van Buren, John** 1810-1866
[DNNS, SN]
*American attorney*
* [The] Jove of Jolly Fellows
* [The] Jupiter Tonans of His Party
* Prince John

**Van Buren, Martin** 1782-1862
[DEP, FAP, FFF]
*American president*
* [The] American Talleyrand
* [The] Enchanter
* [The] Follower in the Footsteps
* [The] Fox
* [The] Kinderhook Fox
* King Martin the First
* [The] Little Magician
* Little Van
* [The] Machiavellian Belshazzar
* [The] Mistletoe Politician
* Old Kinderhook
* [The] Petticoat Pet
* [The] Political Grimalkin
* [The] Red Fox of Kinderhook
* [The] Sage of Kinderhook
* [The] Sage of Lindenwald
* [The] Sweet Little Fellow
* [The] Weazel
* Whiskey Van
* [The] Wizard of Kinderhook
* [The] Wizard of the Albany Regency
* Young Hickory

**Van Buren, Steve** 20th c.
*American football player*
* Van Buren, Wham Bam

**Van Buren, Wham Bam**
See  Van Buren, Steve

**Van Calster, A. M.** 20th c.  [FDG]
*Belgian director*
* Calster, Og

**Van Campen, Karl**
See  Campbell, John W[ood], Jr.

**Van Clouser, Lionel** 1909-1942
[SC]
*American actor, songwriter, bandleader*
* Rand, Lionel

**Van Coevering, Jack**
See  Van Coevering, Jan Adrian

**Van Coevering, Jan Adrian** 1900-
[CAP]
*Dutch-born author*
* Van Coevering, Jack

**Van Cortlandt, Ida**
See  Tavernier, Mrs. Albert

**Van Dall, Harold?**
See  Budrys, Algirdas Jonas

**Van Dam, J.**
See  Presser, [Gerrit] Jacob

**Van Dam, Jose**
See  Van Damme, Joseph

**Van Damme, Joseph** 1940-  [OP]
*Belgian opera singer*
* Van Dam, Jose

**Van Dammeler, Isador Louis Bernard**
1881-1934  [BEW, F2]
*Dutch-born actor*
* Tellegen, Lou

**Van De Bovencamp, Valli** 20th c.
[IBY]
*Rumanian-born illustrator and designer*
* Valli

**Van De Gohm, Richard** 1919-
[IAW]
*British-born author*
* Gohm, D. C.
* Gohm, Douglas
* O'Connell, R. F.

**Van De Water, Virginia Belle Terhune** 20th c.  [NAA]
*American author*
* Terhune, Virginia Belle

**Van Dekker, Albert** 1904-1968
*American actor*
* Dekker, Albert

**Van Den Bogaerde, Derek Niven**
1920?-  [BDF, IPA, WEF]
*British actor*
* Bogarde, Dirk

**Van den Bogaert, Martin**  ?-1694
[WBD]
*Dutch sculptor*
* Desjardins, Martin

**Van Den Heuvel, Cornelisz A.**
1931-  [CA]
*American poet*
* corneliszavandenheuvel

**Van der Berghe, Robert**  ?-1580
[PA]
*Author*
* Montanus

**Van der Faes, Pieter** 1618-1680
[WBD]
*Dutch painter*
* Lely, [Sir] Peter

**Van Der Hurk, Peter** 1911-  [NAD]
*Dutch clairvoyant*
* Hurkos, Peter

**Van der Kun**
See  Lunaeus, Peter

**Van Der Meer, Anton**
See  Van Der Meer, Antonius Wiebe

**Van Der Meer, Antonius Wiebe**
1908-  [IWM]
*Dutch musician*
* Van Der Meer, Anton

**Van der Meer van Delft, Jan**
See  Vermeer, Jan

**Van Der Meersch, Maxence**
See  Cardijn, Josef

**Van der Mersch, Jean Andre**
1734-1792  [DNNF]
*Belgian patriot*
* [The] Brave Fleming

**Van Der Merwe, Derik**
*See* Van Der Merwe, Frederik
Johannes

**Van Der Merwe, Frederik Johannes**
1924- [IWM]
*South African musician*
* Van Der Merwe, Derik

**Van der Weyde, Roger** ?-1529
[FFF, SN]
*Flemish painter*
* Roger of Bruges

**Van Der Zee, Barbara Blanche**
1932- [IAW]
*British author*
* Griggs, Barbara

**Van Deventer, Emma Murdock** 20th
c. [EMD, WW]
*American author*
* Lynch, Lawrence L.

**Van Devere, Trish**
*See* Dressel, Patricia

**Van Dewall, Johannes**
*See* Kuehne, August

**Van Dine, S. S.**
*See* Wright, Willard Huntington

**Van Doesburg, Theo**
*See* Kupper, Christiaan Emil
Marie

**Van Dongen, Cornelis Theodorus
Marie** 1877-1968 [CAR]
*French painter*
* Van Dongen, Kees

**Van Dongen, Kees**
*See* Van Dongen, Cornelis
Theodorus Marie

**Van Doornik, Piet**
*See* Fransen, Piet Frans

**Van Doren, Dirck**
*See* Dey, Frederic Van Rensselaer

**Van Doren, Mamie**
*See* Olander, Joan Lucille

**Van Dorne, R.**
*See* Wallmann, Jeffrey M[iner]

**Van Dovski, Lee**
*See* Lewandowski, Herbert

**Van Dungen, Fritz** 1905- [FC]
*Dutch-born actor*
* Dorn, Philip

**Van Dusart, Eddie** 1889-1929
[BX, RBE]
*American boxer*
* McGoorty, Eddie

**[The] Van Dyck of France**
*See* Rigau y Ros, Hyacinthe
Francois Honorat Mathias Pierre
Martyr Andre

**Van Dyke, Anthony**
*See* Nason, Arthur Huntington

**Van Dyke, J.**
*See* Edwards, Frederick Anthony

**Van Dyke, W. S.**
*See* Van Dyke, Woodbridge
Strong, II

**Van Dyke, Woodbridge Strong, II**
1887-1943 [SC]
*American actor and director*
* Van Dyke, W. S.

**Van Dyne, Edith**
*See* Baum, L[yman] Frank

**Van Eijk, Kees** 20th c. [WF]
*Dutch actor*
* Guilty, Joseph

**Van Eps, Worster** 1912-
[FC, ITA, SW]
*American actor*
* Parker, Willard

**Van Erpe, Thomas** 1584-1624
[WBD]
*Dutch linguist*
* Erpenius

**Van Essen, William** 1910-
[AW, WD]
*British physician and author*
* Serjeant, Richard

**Van Eyck, Jan [or John]** 1385-1440
[DEP, FFF, RH]
*Flemish painter*
* [The] Father of Modern Oil
  Painting
* John of Bruges

**Van Geil, Mercury E. C. L.**
*See* McGilvery, Laurence

**Van Goeree, Irina**
*See* Huygh-De Keuster,
Maria-Frieda

**Van Gordon, Cyrena**
*See* Pocock, Cyrene Sue

**Van Grasshoff, Carl Louis**
1865-1919 [NAD]
*Religious leader*
* Heindel, Max

**Van Haltren, George E.** 1866-1945
[PB]
*American baseball player*
* Van Haltren, Rip

**Van Haltren, Rip**
*See* Van Haltren, George E.

**Van Haren, Wouter**
*See* Kolff, Roelof Coenraad

**Van Hassen, Amy**
*See* High-Smith, Domini

**Van Heller, Marcus**
*See* Zachary, Hugh

**Van Hemskerck, Martin**
1498-1574 [DEP, HN, RH]
*Dutch painter*
* [The] Raphael of Holland

**Van Herp, Jacques** 1923- [ESF]
*Belgian critic, editor, author*
* Jansen, Michel

**Van Heusen, James [Jimmy]**
*See* Babcock, Edward Chester

**Van Hoddis, Jakob**
*See* Davidsohn, Hans

**Van Horn, Dale R.** 1895- [NAA]
*American author*
* Covington, Chester
* Dale, V. R.
* Dalton, Howard
* Engell, Dee
* Lincoln, E. R.
* Richard, Bill
* Rood, Jack
* Vance, Gale
* Virginia, Daisy

**Van Horn, Douglas** 1944- [SMG]
*American football player*
* Van Horn, Reggie

**Van Horn, Reggie**
*See* Van Horn, Douglas

**Van Horne, Harry Randall** 1924-
[ASC]
*American composer and conductor*
* Van Horne, Randy

**Van Horne, Randy**
*See* Van Horne, Harry Randall

**Van Hulsteyn, Marda** ?-1970
[THR]
*South African-born actress*
* Vanne, Marda

**Van Iterson, S. R.**
*See* Van Iterson, Siny Rose Van
Der Breggen

**Van Iterson, Siny Rose Van Der
Breggen** 20th c. [FBJ]
*Dutch author*
* Van Iterson, S. R.

**Van Ith, Lily**
*See* Friedli, Emilie Ida

**Van Kampen, Oscar** 1928?- [CW]
*Surinamese author*
* Banana, Azijn

**Van Kriedt, David**
*See* Kriedt, David N.

**Van Kuijik, Andreas Cornelis** 1909?-
*Dutch-born business manager of
Elvis Presley*
* Parker, [Captain] Tom

**Van Laerhoven, Robert Victor Flora**
1953- [IAW]
*Belgian author*
* Ashmind, Kim

**Van Lake, Turk**
*See* Hovsepian, Vanig

**Van Lawick-Goodall, Jane** 1934-
[CA]
*British ethologist and author*
* Goodall, Jane

**Van Lhin, Erik**
*See* Alvarez Del Rey, Ramon
Felipe San Juan Mario Silvio Enrico

**Van Lier, Norm[an, III]** 1947-
[IBW]
*American basketball player*
* [The] Storm in Norman

**Van Lierde, John** 1907- [CAP]
*Belgian-born author*
* Van Lierde, Peter Canisius

**Van Lierde, Peter Canisius**
*See* Van Lierde, John

**Van Loenen, Gabrielle**
*See* Van Schaik-Willing, Jeanne
Gabrielle

**Van Loot, Cornelius Obenchain**
*See* Tarkington, [Newton] Booth

**Van Lorne, Warner**
*See* Tremaine, F[rederick] Orlin

**Van Lorne, Warner**
*See* Tremaine, Nelson

**Van Mattimore, Richard**
1899?-1976 [F2, FC]
*American actor*
* Arlen, Richard

**Van Mever, Piet**
*See* Van Mever, Pieter Adriaan

**Van Mever, Pieter Adriaan** 1899-
[IWM]
*Dutch musician*
* Van Mever, Piet

**Van, Mr.**
*See* Van Berg, Marion Harold

**Van Naerssen, Jan** 1580-1637 [PA]
*Author*
* Narssius

**Van Name, E. J.** 20th c. [SFP]
*Author*
* Vanny, Jim

**Van Niekerk, I. R.**
*See* Nienaber, Petrus Johannes

**Van Noppen, Ina [Faye]
W[oestemeyer]** 1906- [CA]
*American historian and author*
* Woestemeyer, Ina Faye

**Van Nuland, Wim**
*See* Mohlmann, [Father] Michael

**Van Offel, David** 1919-1975 [SC]
*British-born actor, director,
playwright*
* Daufel, Andre

**Van Oort, Jan** 1921- [CA]
*Dutch author and illustrator*
* Dulieu, Jean

**Van Oostsanen, Jakob**
*See* Cornelisz, Jakob

**Van Oranje, Christina**
*See* Maria Christina

**Van Orden, Robert E.** 1931-
[FC, SW]
*American actor*
* Smith, John

**Van P. Polanen** 1936?- [CW]
*Surinamese poet*
* Dandilo, Kwame

**Van Peteghem, Camille** 1935- [OP]
*Belgian opera singer*
* Meghor, Camillo

**Van Ree, Jean**
*See* Schloesser, Hendrik

**Van Rensburg, Jaco**
*See* Van Rensburg, Roelog Jacobus
Jansen

**Van Rensburg, Roelf**
*See* Van Rensburg, Roelog Jacobus
Jansen

**Van Rensburg, Roelog Jacobus
Jansen** 1935- [IAW]
*South African author*
* Van Rensburg, Jaco
* Van Rensburg, Roelf

**Van Rijn, Ignatius**
*See* Ingram, Forrest L[eo]

**Van Rijn [or Ryn], Rembrandt
Harmensz [or Harmenszoon]**
1606-1669 [WBD]
*Dutch painter*
* Rembrandt

**Van Robays, Bomber**
*See* Van Robays, Maurice Rene

**Van Robays, Maurice Rene**
1914-1965 [BE]
*American baseball player*
* Van Robays, Bomber

**Van Roemer, A.** 1940?- [CW]
*Surinamese poet*
* Zamani

**Van Roey, Leon** 1921- [GA]
*Danish cartoonist, illustrator, painter*
* Leon
* Van Roy

**Van Roomen, Adrian** 1561-1615
[FFF, RH]
*Mathematician*
* Andrianus Romanus
* [The] Roman

**Van Rooy, Anton**
See Van Rooy, Antonius Maria Josephus

**Van Rooy, Antonius Maria Josephus**
1879-1932 [MS]
*Dutch opera singer*
* Van Rooy, Anton

**Van Roy**
See Van Roey, Leon

**Van Ryssel, Paul**
See Gachet, Paul Ferdinand

**Van Saanen, Marie Louise**
See Gibson, Marice Louise

**Van Scelter, Helter**
See Ridley, James

**Van Schaik-Willing, Jeanne Gabrielle**
1895- [IAW]
*Dutch author*
* Van Loenen, Gabrielle

**Van Shaick, John** 1873- ? [NAA]
*American author and editor*
* Johannes

**Van Siller, Hilda** 20th c. [WW]
*Author*
* Siller, Van

**Van Sluijters, Georges Joseph**
1868-1943 [B10]
*French artist*
* De Feure, Georges

**Van Someren, Liesje**
See Lichtenberg, Elisabeth Jacoba

**Van Straubenzee, Clyde** 1867-1934
[THR]
*British theatrical manager*
* Meynell, Clyde

**Van Studdiford, Grace**
See Quivey, Grace

**Van Surdam, Dutch**
See Van Surdam, Henderson

**Van Surdam, Henderson** 20th c.
[FB]
*American football coach*
* Van Surdam, Dutch

**Van Tassell, Cora**
See Young, Mrs. Edwin

**Van Tijn, Maartje**
See Van Tijn, Mijntje Leentje

**Van Tijn, Mijntje Leentje** 1933-
[IAW]
*Dutch author*
* Van Tijn, Maartje

**Van Tricht, Elisabeth Emmy** 1911-
[IAW]
*Dutch author*
* De Jong-Keesing, Elisabeth

**Van Tuyl, Rosealtha** 1901-
[SFL, WGT]
*American author*
* Van Tuyl, Zaara

**Van Tuyl, Zaara**
See Van Tuyl, Rosealtha

**Van Twiller, Walter** 1580?-1656?
[SN]
*Dutch colonial governor in America*
* Walter the Doubter

**Van Valkenburg, Julia** [FFF]
*American writer*
* Wayne, Gladys

**Van Vechten, Abraham** 1762-1823
[FFF]
*American attorney*
* [The] Father of the New York Bar

**Van Vechten, Carl** 1880- ? [CAA]
*American author*
* Atlas

**Van Velthus, Jan**
See Brunken, Ernest

**Van Vleck, John** 1899?-1980
*American physicist*
* [The] Father of Modern Magnetism

**Van Vliet, Don** 1941- [PRS, RM]
*American singer and songwriter*
* Beefheart, Captain

**Van Vogt, A. E.**
See Van Vogt, Alfred Elton

**Van Vogt, Alfred Elton** 1912- [SF]
*Canadian-born author*
* Van Vogt, A. E.

**Van Vogt, Edna Mayne Hull**
1905-1975 [WGT]
*American author*
* Hull, E. Mayne

**Van Vormizeele, Eelco Voet** 1942-
[OP]
*German opera singer*
* Von Jordis, Eelco

**Van Wagener, Isabelle** 1797-1883
[IBW]
*American abolitionist*
* God's Fool
* [The] Libyan Sibyl
* Truth, Sojourner

**Van Wageningen, J.**
See Presser, [Gerrit] Jacob

**Van Walree, Mrs. E. C. W.** [PA]
*Author*
* Miller, Christine

**Van Weddingen, Marthe** 1924-
[CA]
*Belgian-born author*
* Dumas, Claire

**Van Winkle, Harold E.** 1939-
[ASC]
*American composer*
* Van Winkle, Rip

**Van Winkle, Rip**
See Van Winkle, Harold E.

**Van Woeart, Alpheus**
See Halloway, Vance

**Van Wolzogen, Lodowijk**
1642-1690 [PA]
*Author*
* Volzogenius

**Van Wynkyn, Jan** ?-1534? [WBD]
*British printer*
* Worde, Wynkyn de

**Van Zandt, E. F.**
See Cudlipp, Edythe

**Van Zeller, Claud** 1905- [CA]
*British clergyman and author*
* Brother Choleric
* Van Zeller, Hubert
* Venning, Hugh

**Van Zeller, Hubert**
See Van Zeller, Claud

**Van Zwienen, Ilse Charlotte Koehn**
1929- [CA]
*German-born American author and illustrator*
* Koehn, Ilse

**Vanags, Martin** 1947- [RO2]
*German singer*
* Kristian, Marty

**Vanardy, Varick**
See Dey, Frederic Van Rensselaer

**VanBebber, Blackjack**
See VanBebber, Jack Francis

**VanBebber, Jack Francis** 20th c.
[BBH]
*American wrestler*
* VanBebber, Blackjack

**Vanbrugh, [Dame] Irene**
See Barnes, Irene

**Vanbrugh, Prudence**
See Bourchier, Prudence

**Vanbrugh, Violet**
See Barnes, Violet

**Vance, Ag**
See Vance, Walter Addington

**Vance, Alfred Glenville**
See Stevens, Alfred Peck

**Vance, Charles**
See Goldblatt, Charles

**Vance, Clara**
See Denison, Mary Andrews

**Vance, Clarence Arthur** 1891-1961
[BE, PB, SR]
*American baseball player*
* [The] Dazzler
* Vance, Dazzy

**Vance, Clarice**
See Black, Clara Ella

**Vance, Cyrus Roberts** 1917-
*American attorney and diplomat*
* Cyrus the Gray

**Vance, Dazzy**
See Vance, Clarence Arthur

**Vance, Dazzy**
See Vance, Gene E.

**Vance, Edgar**
See Ambrose, Eric [Samuel]

**Vance, Ethel**
See Stone, Grace Zaring

**Vance, Gale**
See Van Horn, Dale R.

**Vance, Gene E.** 1947- [SMG]
*American baseball player*
* Vance, Dazzy
* Vance, Sandy

**Vance, Gerald** [joint pseudonym with Robert Silverberg] [house pseudonym, Ziff-Davis]
See Garrett, [Gordon] Randall [Philip David]

**Vance, Gerald** [house pseudonym, Ziff-Davis]
See Geier, Chester S.

**Vance, Gerald** [house pseudonym, Ziff-Davis]
See Graham, Roger Phillips

**Vance, Gerald** [joint pseudonym with Randall Garrett] [house pseudonym, Ziff-Davis]
See Silverberg, Robert

**Vance, John Holbrook [Jack]**
1916?- [CA, EMD, WGT]
*American author*
* Holbrook, John
* Wade, Alan

**Vance, Joseph Albert [Joe]** 1905-
[BE]
*American baseball player*
* Vance, Sandy

**Vance, Nina**
See Whittington, Nina Eloise

**Vance, Sandy**
See Vance, Gene E.

**Vance, Sandy**
See Vance, Joseph Albert [Joe]

**Vance, Stan**
See Vancini, Florestano

**Vance, Walter Addington** 20th c.
[BBH]
*American basketball player*
* Vance, Ag

**Vancel, Doris** 20th c. [WGT]
*Author*
* Thomas, Doris

**Vancini, Florestano** 1936- [FDG]
*Italian director*
* Vance, Stan

**Vanda, Harry**
See Wandan, Harry

**Vandegrift, Billy B.** 1870- ? [THR]
*American actor*
* Van, Billy B.

**Vandegrift, Margaret**
See Janvier, Margaret Thomson

**Vandemann, Frederick H.**
1873-1935 [BE]
*American baseball player*
* Abbott, Fred

**Vandenberg, Harold Harris** 1907-
[BE]
*American baseball player*
* Vandenberg, Hy

**Vandenberg, Hy**
See Vandenberg, Harold Harris

**Vandenberg, Simon** 1899- [BEW]
*Belgian-born actor*
* Abbott, Richard

**Vandenburgh, Theodore H.** [PA]
*Author*
* Bunsby, Jack

**Vandeputte, Roger** 1930-    [OP]
*Belgian conductor*
* Rossel, Roger

**Vander Linden, Anthony** 1924-
[BS]
*American magician and bookseller*
* [The] Continental Magician
* Presti, Tony

**Vander Meer, John Samuel** 1914-
[BE]
*American baseball player*
* Double No-Hit
* [The] Dutch Master

**Vander Zee, James** 1883-    [IBW]
*American photographer*
* [The] Dean of Black
  Photographers

**Vanderbilt, Commodore**
*See*  Vanderbilt, Cornelius

**Vanderbilt, Cornelius** 1794-1877
[WBD]
*American industrialist*
* Vanderbilt, Commodore

**Vanderbilt, Cornelius, Jr.** 1898-
[NAA]
*American author*
* Lane, R.

**Vanderbilt, Gloria** 1924?-
*American heiress*
* Vanderbilt, Little Gloria

**Vanderbilt, Little Gloria**
*See*  Vanderbilt, Gloria

**Vanderbilt, William Henry**
1821-1885    [SN]
*American industrialist*
* [The] Railway King

**Vanderbundt, Skip**
*See*  Vanderbundt, William Gerard

**Vanderbundt, William Gerard**
1946-    [SMG]
*American football player*
* Vanderbundt, Skip

**Vanderdecken**
*See*  Cooper, William

**Vanderpoel, Aaron** 1799-1871
[FFF]
*American politician*
* [The] Kinderhook Roarer

**Vanderpool, Sylvia** 1936-    [RO1]
*American singer*
* Little Sylvia

**Vandersteen, Willibrord Jan Frans
Maria** 1913-    [WECO]
*Belgian cartoonist*
* Vandersteen, Willy

**Vandersteen, Willy**
*See*  Vandersteen, Willibrord Jan
Frans Maria

**Vandivier, Fuzzy**
*See*  Vandivier, Robert

**Vandivier, Robert** 1903-    [NBA]
*American basketball player*
* Vandivier, Fuzzy

**Vandour, Cyril**
*See*  Surmelian, Leon [Zaven]

**[The] Vandyck of England**
*See*  Dobson, William

**[The] Vandyck of Sculpture**
*See*  Coysevox, Antoine

**Vane, Alice**
*See*  Templeton, Mrs. John

**Vane, Bret**
*See*  Kent, Arthur [William
Charles]

**Vane, Henry**    [SN]
* Pulteney's Toad-Eater

**Vane, Michael**
*See*  Humphries, Sydney Vernon

**Vane, Roland**
*See*  McKeag, Ernest L[ionel]

**Vane, Sutton**
*See*  Sutton-Vane, Vane Hunt

**Vane, Volet**
*See*  Howell, Jane L.

**Vaneuf, Andre**
*See*  Cohen, Sol B.

**Vanglon, Henri** 1875-1944    [CD]
*French playwright*
* Gheon, Henri

**Vanhoutte, Marie-Leonie** 20th c.
[EE]
*Intelligence agent*
* Charlotte

**Vanini, Giulio Cesare**
*See*  Vanini, Lucilio

**Vanini, Lucilio** 1585-1619    [WBD]
*Italian philosopher*
* Vanini, Giulio Cesare

**Vann, Joe**
*See*  Canzano, Joe

**Vanne, Marda**
*See*  Van Hulsteyn, Marda

**Vanner, John**
*See*  North, William

**Vannga, France** 1939-    [SW]
*French actress*
* Nuyen, France

**Vanni, Helen Elizabeth**
*See*  Spaeth, Helen Elizabeth

**Vannucci, Pietro** 1446-1523
[WBD]
*Italian painter*
* Della Pieve, Pier
* [Il] Perugino

**Vanny, Jim**
*See*  Van Name, E. J.

**Vanpeperstraete, Norbert** 1912-
[FDG]
*Belgian director*
* Benoit, Norbert

**VanSickle, V. A.**
*See*  Carhart, Arthur Hawthorne

**Vansittart, Jane**
*See*  Moorhouse, Hilda Vansittart

**Vansittart, Nicholas** 1766-1851
[HN]
*British politician*
* Old Bags

**Van't Sant, Mien**
*See*  Van't Sant-Van Bommel,
Aartje Wilhelmina

**Van't Sant-Van Bommel, Aartje
Wilhelmina** 1901-    [IAW]
*Dutch author*
* Van't Sant, Mien

**Vanzetti, Bartolomeo** 1888-1927
*Italian-born American political
radical*
* [The] Poor Fish Peddler

**Vanzi, Luigi** 20th c.    [WF]
*Director*
* Lewis, Vance

**Vanzina, Stefano** 1915-    [FDG]
*Italian director*
* Steno

**Vao Gogo, Emmanuel**
*See*  Fernandes, Millor

**Vaquerito [Little Cowboy]**
*See*  Soler y Gisbert, Manuel

**Varaigne, Dominique** 1948-    [FC]
*Actress*
* Sanda, Dominique

**Varconi, Victor**
*See*  Varkonyi, Mihaly

**Varden, Evelyn**
*See*  Hall, Evelyn

**Vardon, Richard**
*See*  O'Brien, David Wright

**Vardre, Leslie**
*See*  Davies, Leslie Purnell

**Vare y Garcia, Manuel** 1894-1921
[GS]
*Spanish bullfighter*
* Varelito [Little Vare]

**Varelito [Little Vare]**
*See*  Vare y Garcia, Manuel

**Varelli, Alfredo** 20th c.    [WF]
*Italian actor*
* Farrell, Fred

**Varelst, Simon**    [HN]
*Painter*
* [The] God of Flowers

**Varenov, Leonard** 1911-1960    [MS]
*American opera singer*
* Warren, Leonard

**Varesi, Gilda**
*See*  Conti, Gilda

**Varga, Judy**
*See*  Stang, Judit

**Vargas, Jose** 20th c.    [OBW]
*American baseball player*
* Vargas, Tetelo

**Vargas, Teresa** 1935-    [OP]
*Spanish opera singer*
* Berganza, Teresa

**Vargas, Tetelo**
*See*  Vargas, Jose

**Vargas y Gonzalez, Enrique**
1870-1930    [GS]
*Spanish bullfighter*
* Minuto [Minute]

**Vari, Giuseppe** 20th c.    [WF]
*Italian director*
* Warren, Joseph

**Varick**
*See*  Palmer, M.

**Varick, Alfred** 1881-1949    [F2, FC]
*British actor*
* Drayton, Alfred

**Varina**
*See*  Waryng, Jane

**Varkonyi, Mihaly** 1896-    [FC]
*Hungarian-born actor*
* Varconi, Victor

**Varley, John** 1947-    [CA]
*American author*
* Boehm, Herb

**Varley, John Philip**
*See*  Mitchell, Langdon [Elwin]

**Varnadow, Peggy** 1928-    [FC]
*American actress*
* Dow, Peggy

**Varnel, Marcel**
*See*  Le Bozec, Marcel

**Varner, Buck**
*See*  Varner, Glen Gann

**Varner, Glen Gann** 1930-    [BE]
*American baseball player*
* Varner, Buck

**Varney, Dike**
*See*  Varney, Lawrence Delano

**Varney, Lawrence Delano**
1880-1950    [BE]
*American baseball player*
* Varney, Dike

**Varney, Pete**
*See*  Varney, Richard Fred

**Varney, Richard Fred** 1949-    [SMG]
*American baseball player*
* Varney, Pete

**Varnum, Zoe Shippen** 1902-    [IAW]
*American author*
* Shippen, Zoe

**Varotari, Alessandro** 1590-1650
[WBD]
*Italian painter*
* [Il] Padovanino

**Varro, Marcus Terentius** 1st c. BC
[DNNF, DNNS, FFF]
*Roman scholar*
* Most Erudite of the Romans
* Most Learned of the Romans

**[The] Varro of Britain**
*See*  Camden, William

**Varro, Publius Terentius** 1st c. BC
[WBD]
*Roman poet*
* Atacinus

**Varro, William** 13th c.
[DNNF, RH, SN]
*British scholastic philosopher*
* Fundatus, Doctor
* [The] Thorough Doctor

**Vasarely, Jean-Pierre** 1934-    [CAR]
*French painter*
* Yvaral

**Vasaturo, Giuseppe** 1900?-1964
[BEW, FC]
*Italian producer*
* Amato, Giuseppe
* Amato, Peppino

**Vasek, Vladimir** 1867-1958
[CD, EWL]
*Czech poet*
* Bezruc, Petr

Vasili, [Comte] Paul
See Adam, Juliette

Vasili, Paul
See Casal, Julian del

Vasiliu, Gheorghe 1881-1957
[EWL, TCL]
Rumanian poet
* Bacovia, Gheorghe

Vasistha, Mohan
See Shastri, Prithvinath

Vasko, Elmer 1935-
[CEI, FHE, HK]
Canadian-born hockey player
* Vasko, Moose

Vasko, Moose
See Vasko, Elmer

Vassa, Gustavus
See Equiano, Olaudah

Vassallo, Aldo Mirabella
See Mirabella, Gesualdo

Vassilakis, Panayotis 1925- [CAR]
Greek sculptor
* Takis

Vassili, [Count] Paul
See Radziwill, Catherine

Vassy, Gaston [PA]
Author
* Punch

Vasu, Nirmala-Kumara
See Bose, Nirmal Kumar

Vasudeva, Vishnudayal
See Bissoondoyal, Basdeo

Vatel
See Deserres, Gaston

[Der] Vater des Deutschen Liedes
[The Father of German Songs]
See Albert, Heinrich

[Le] Vauban de la Marine
See Sane, Jacques Noel

[The] Vauban of Sweden
See Dahlberg [or Dahlbergh], Erik
Jonsson

Vaughan, Arky
See Vaughan, Joseph Floyd

Vaughan, Auriel Rosemary Malet
1923- [SFL, WGT]
Author
* Malet, Oriel

Vaughan, Carter A.
See Gerson, Noel Bertram

Vaughan, Dudley
See Johnson, Dudley Vaughan

Vaughan, Elizabeth
See Jones, Elizabeth Myfanwy

Vaughan, Frankie
See Abelsohn, Frank

Vaughan, Glenn Edward 1944-
[BE]
American baseball player
* Vaughan, Sparky

Vaughan, Henry 1622-1695
[DEL, DEP, DNNS]
Welsh poet
* [The] Silurist

Vaughan, Henry 1890- [BEW]
American actor and playwright
* Hull, Henry

Vaughan, Hilda
See Morgan, Hilda Campbell

Vaughan, Jack 1949- [IBW]
American magician
* Goldfinger

Vaughan, John Walker 1925-
[BEW]
American actor and director
* Vaughan, Stuart

Vaughan, Joseph Floyd 1912-1952
[AS, DGS, PB]
American baseball player
* Vaughan, Arky

Vaughan, Kate
See Candelin, Catherine

Vaughan, Lefty
See Vaughan, [Cecil] Porter

Vaughan, Leo
See Lendon, Kenneth Harry

Vaughan, Owen 20th c. [WGT]
Author
* Rhoscomyl, Owen

Vaughan, Pete
See Vaughan, Robert E.

Vaughan, Peter
See Ohm, Peter

Vaughan, [Cecil] Porter 1919- [BE]
American baseball player
* Vaughan, Lefty

Vaughan, Robert E. 20th c. [BBH]
American basketball coach
* Vaughan, Pete

Vaughan, Sarah [Lois] 1924-
[EPM, PMJ]
American singer
* [The] Divine One
* [The] Divine Sarah
* Vaughan, Sassy

Vaughan, Sassy
See Vaughan, Sarah [Lois]

Vaughan, Sparky
See Vaughan, Glenn Edward

Vaughan, Stuart
See Vaughan, John Walker

Vaughan, Susie
See Candelin, Susan Mary
Charlotte

Vaughan, Yvonne 1949-
[ECM, RO2]
American singer and songwriter
* Fargo, Donna

Vaughan Williams, Ralph
See Williams, Ralph

Vaughan Williams, Ursula 1911-
[WD]
British author, poet, librettist
* Wood, Ursula

Vaughn, Ace
See Vaughn, Ralph Lincoln

Vaughn, Cora
See Oakley, Mrs. J. R.

Vaughn, Farmer
See Vaughn, Harry Francis

Vaughn, Fred[erick Thomas]
1918-1964 [BE]
American baseball player
* Vaughn, Muscles

Vaughn, Harry Francis 1864-1914
[BE, PB]
American baseball player
* Vaughn, Farmer

Vaughn, Hippo
See Vaughn, James Leslie

Vaughn, James Clayton, Jr. 1950?-
American murder suspect
* Franklin, Joseph Paul

Vaughn, James Leslie 1888-1966
[AS, DGS, PB]
American baseball player
* Vaughn, Hippo

Vaughn, Jap
See Vaughn, Tommy

Vaughn, Kate
See Kestin, Helen

Vaughn, Muscles
See Vaughn, Fred[erick Thomas]

Vaughn, Ralph Lincoln 1918-
[BBH]
American basketball player
* Vaughn, Ace

Vaughn, Richard
See Thomas, Ernest Lewis

Vaughn, Theresa
See Mestayer, Mrs. W. A.

Vaughn, Thomas [PA]
Author
* Edwin

Vaughn, Tommy 20th c.
American football player
* Vaughn, Jap

Vaughn, Vivian 1902-1966 [SC]
American actress and singer
* Gould, Gypsy

Vaughn, William
See Von Brincken, Wilhelm

Vaulet, Clement 1876- ? [WGT]
French author
* Vautel, Clement

[The] Vaulting Vicar
See Richards, Robert [Bob]

Vautel, Clement
See Vaulet, Clement

Vaux, Patrick 20th c. [WGT]
Author
* Navarchus [joint pseudonym with
James Woods]

Vava
See Neto, Edvaldo

Vawter, L. P. 1885- [NAA]
American artist and writer
* Capooch, Tony
* Doogin, Skinny
* Goode, Uncle Abner
* Leisure, Piddleton

Vaz, Gil
See Lenoir, Carlos

Veach, Peek-A-Boo
See Veach, William Walter

Veach, William Walter 1863-1937
American baseball player
* Veach, Peek-A-Boo

Veal, Coot
See Veal, Orville Inman

Veal, Orville Inman 1932- [BE]
American baseball player
* Veal, Coot

Veale, Thomas 1896?-1964 [BEW]
Theatrical performer
* Leslie, Tom

Veary, Arthur T. 1894-1975
[BEW, F2, FC]
British actor
* Treacher, Arthur

Veazie, Joseph [PA]
Author
* J. V. Z.

[Il] Vecchio
See Amato, Giovanni Antonio d'

[Il] Vecchio [The Elder]
See Palma, Jacopo

Vecelli, Marco 1545-1616? [WBD]
Italian painter
* Marco di Tiziano

Vecelli [or Vecellio], Tiziano
1477-1576 [WBD]
Italian painter
* Titian

Vecelli, Tiziano 1579- ? [WBD]
Italian painter
* [Il] Tizianello

Vedder, John K.
See Gruber, Frank

Vedette
See Fitchett, William Henry

Vedette
See Hensman, Howard

Vedette
See Williams, [George] Valentine

Vee, Bobby
See Velline, Robert Thomas

Vega, Al
See Vagramian, Aram

Vega, David 20th c. [RO2]
American musician
* Vega, Dynamite

Vega, Dynamite
See Vega, David

Vega, Memo
See Coruelio, Memo

Vega Carpio, Lope Felix de
1562-1635 [HN, SN, WBD]
Spanish playwright and poet
* [The] Father of the Spanish
Drama
* [El] Fenix de Espana
* [El] Licenciado Tome de
Burguillos
* [The] Monster of Nature
* Padecopeo, Gabriel
* [The] Phoenix of Spain
* [The] Spanish Phoenix

Vega De Los Reyes, Francisco
1903-1931 [GS]
Spanish bullfighter
* Gitanillo de Triana [Little Gypsy
from Triana]

**Vegg, Samuel** 1827-1865 [BMH]
*British comedian, singer, music hall manager*
* Collins, Sam

**Veheyne, Cherry**
*See* Williamson, Ethel

**Veidt, Conrad**
*See* Weidt, Conrad

**Veigelsberg, Hugo** 1869- ? [CD]
*Hungarian critic, poet, publicist*
* Ignotus

**Veil, Bucky**
*See* Veil, Frederick William

**Veil, Frederick William** 1881-1931 [BE]
*American baseball player*
* Veil, Bucky

**[The] Veiled Prophet of Khorassan**
*See* Hakim ben Allah

**Veitch, Tom**
*See* Padgett, Ron

**Veits, Ulf**
*See* Lindberg, Karl Sivert

**Vejar, Chico**
*See* Vejar, Francis

**Vejar, Francis** 20th c. [SG]
*Boxer*
* Vejar, Chico

**Vel, Rob**
*See* Velter, Robert

**Velasco, Luis de** 1500?-1564 [FFF]
*Viceroy of Mexico*
* [The] Father of New Spain

**Velazco, Emil, Jr.** 1924- [ITA]
*American film executive*
* Velazco, Robert E.

**Velazco, Robert E.**
*See* Velazco, Emil, Jr.

**Velegra, Doris** 1904- [F2]
*Actress*
* Revier, Dorothy

**Veleriy, Ivan**
*See* Tarsis, Valerii Iakovievich

**Velez, Lupe**
*See* Velez De Villalobos, Guadelupe

**Velez, Otoniel** 1950- [ALR]
*Puerto Rican-born baseball player*
* Velez, Otto

**Velez, Otto**
*See* Velez, Otoniel

**Velez De Villalobos, Guadelupe** 1909-1944 [CED, CU, IPA]
*Mexican-born actress*
* [The] Mexican Spitfire
* Velez, Lupe

**Velikovsky, Immanuel** 1895-1979 [AW, CA]
*Russian-born author*
* [The] Grand Old Man of the Fringe
* Ram, Immanuel

**Velitchkova, Ljuba** 1913- [BBD]
*Bulgarian opera singer*
* Welitsch, Ljuba

**Vellejus, Andre Severin** 1542-1616 [PA]
*Author*
* Soerensen

**Velline, Robert Thomas** 1943- [EPM, RO1]
*American singer*
* Vee, Bobby

**Veloshkina, Irina** 1925- [OP]
*Russian opera singer*
* Arkhipova, Irina

**Velter, Robert** 20th c. [WECO]
*French cartoonist*
* Vel, Rob

**Veltman, Vera**
*See* Panova, Vera [Federovna]

**[The] Velvet Fog**
*See* Torme, Mel[vin Howard]

**[The] Velvet Frog**
*See* Torme, Mel[vin Howard]

**Vemian, Alex Kirk** 20th c. [WFA]
*American jewelry designer*
* Kirk, Alexis

**Venable, Clark** 1892- [SFL, WGT]
*Author*
* Clarke, Covington

**Venable, Lyn**
*See* Venable, Marilyn

**Venable, Marilyn** 20th c. [SFP]
*Author*
* Venable, Lyn

**Venafro, Mark**
*See* Pizzat, Frank J[oseph]

**Venance, Father**
*See* Dongados, Jean Francois

**Venatorini**
*See* Myslivecek [or Mysliweczek], Josef

**Vendome, Francois de** 1616-1669 [DNNS, FFF, HN]
*French officer and politician*
* Beaufort, Duc de
* [The] King of the Markets
* [Le] Roi des Halles

**Vendome, Philippe de** 1655-1727 [WBD]
*French army officer*
* [Le] Prieur de Vendome

**Vendrovskii, David Efimovich** 1879-1971 [CA]
*Russian author and translator*
* Wendroff, Zalman
* Wendrowsky, Zalman

**Vene-Cavanagh, Paul** 1895- [THR]
*British actor*
* Cavanagh, Paul

**Venerabilis, Doctor**
*See* Bede [Baeda, or Beda]

**Venerabilis, Doctor**
*See* Hildebert

**Venerabilis, Doctor**
*See* Occam [or Ockham], William of

**Venerabilis, Doctor**
*See* Peter [or Pierre] of Cluny

**Venerabilis Inceptor**
*See* Occam [or Ockham], William of

**[The] Venerable Bede**
*See* Bede [Baeda, or Beda]

**[The] Venerable Doctor**
*See* Peter [or Pierre] of Cluny

**[The] Venerable Doctor**
*See* William of Champeaux

**[The] Venerable Initiator**
*See* Occam [or Ockham], William of

**Venerandus, Doctor**
*See* Gregory of Fonts

**Veneris, James** 1922-
*American Korean War POW*
* Wen

**[The] Venetian**
*See* Andrew III

**[The] Venetian**
*See* Stirling, James

**[The] Venetian Addison**
*See* Gozzi, Gaspare

**Veneziano, Agostino**
*See* De Musi, Agostino

**Venezis, Ilias**
*See* Mellos, Ilias

**[El] Venezolano [The Man from Venezuela]**
*See* Gonzalez, Pedro

**Veni Vidi**
*See* Croly, Jane Cunningham

**Venison, Alfred**
*See* Pound, Ezra [Loomis]

**Venkateswaran, Taruvai Anantaramaseshan** 1953- [IAW]
*Indian poet*
* Ramanan

**Venn, Topsy**
*See* Cornell, Mrs. E. J.

**Venner, Arthur**
*See* Griswold, William McCrillis

**Venner, J. G.**
*See* Lewis, John Noel Claude

**Vennew, Norman R.**
*See* Wade, George Alfred

**Venning, Corey** 1924- [CA]
*American author*
* Hyde, Tracy Elliot

**Venning, Hugh**
*See* Van Zeller, Claud

**Venning, John** [HN]
* [The] Howard of Russia

**Venning, Michael**
*See* Randolph, Georgiana Ann

**Venning, Normandy**
*See* Shepheard-Walwyn, Hugh Wallwyn

**Venn's Principal Fireman at Windsor**
*See* Love, Christopher

**[The] Venomous Preacher**
*See* Traill, Robert

**Venora, Elena Sinaguglia** 1932- [BEW]
*American singer and actress*
* Venora, Lee

**Venora, Lee**
*See* Venora, Elena Sinaguglia

**Ventura, Charlie**
*See* Venturo, Charles

**Ventura, Lino**
*See* Borrini, Angelo

**Venturi, Denise Scott Brown**
*See* Brown, Denise Scott

**Venturi, Robert** 1925?-
*American architect*
* [The] Guru of Chaos

**Venturo, Betty Lou Baker** 1928- [CA]
*American author*
* Baker, Betty

**Venturo, Charles** 1916- [EJ, PMJ, WWJ]
*American jazz musician*
* Ventura, Charlie

**Venuta, Benay**
*See* Crooke, Venuta Rose

**Venuti, Giuseppe** 1904- [EJ]
*American jazz musician*
* Venuti, Joe

**Venuti, Joe**
*See* Venuti, Giuseppe

**Vequin, Capini**
*See* Quinn, Elisabeth

**Vera**
*See* Neumann, Vera

**Vera, Billy**
*See* McCord, William, Jr.

**Vera Ellen**
*See* Rohe, Vera-Ellen Westmeyr

**Verax**
*See* Dunckley, Henry

**Verax**
*See* Godwin, William

**Verban, Dutch**
*See* Verban, Emil Matthew

**Verban, Emil Matthew** 1915- [BE, PB]
*American baseball player*
* [The] Antelope
* Verban, Dutch

**Verbeck, Blanche Avicestill Harriman** 1890- [NAA]
*American author*
* Harriman, Blanche Avicestill

**Verble, Gene Kermit** 1928- [BE]
*American baseball player*
* Verble, Satchel

**Verble, Satchel**
*See* Verble, Gene Kermit

**Vercors** [code name used during World War II]
*See* Bruller, Jean Marcel

**Verd**
*See* Verdier, Ed

**Verdel, Al[bert Alfred]** 1921- [BE]
*American baseball player*
* Verdel, Stumpy

**Verdel, Stumpy**
*See* Verdel, Al[bert Alfred]

**Verdery, Emily**
*See* Battay, Emily Verdery

**Verdi, Giuseppe** 1813-1901    [SN]
*Italian composer*
* [The] Euripides of Italian Opera

**Verdier, Ed** 20th c.    [WECO]
*American cartoonist*
* Verd

**Verdon, Dorothy**
*See* Tralins, S[andor] Robert
[Bob]

**Verdon, Gwen**
*See* Verdon, Gwyneth Evelyn

**Verdon, Gwyneth Evelyn** 1926-
[AM, BEW, EMT]
*American actress, dancer, singer*
* Verdon, Gwen
* [The] World's Fastest Tapper

**Verdu, Matilde**
*See* Cela, Camilo Jose

**Vere, Margaret**
*See* Long, Gabrielle Margaret Vere
[Campbell]

**Verelius, Olaus**
*See* Werl, Olaf

**Veren, Gilbert**
*See* Keveren, A. G.

**Veresaev, Vikenti**
*See* Smidovich, Vikenti
Vikentievich

**Verett, E.**
*See* Evans, E. Everett

**Verett, H. E.** [joint pseudonym with
Thelma D. Hamm Evans]
*See* Evans, E. Everett

**Verett, H. E.** [joint pseudonym with
E. Everett Evans]
*See* Evans, Thelma D. Hamm

**Verghese, Paul** 1922-    [IAW]
*Indian clergyman and author*
* Gregorios, Paulos Mar

**Vergilius Maro, Publius** 1st c. BC
[DEP, FFF, SN]
*Roman poet*
* [The] Mantuan Bard
* [The] Mantuan Muse
* [The] Mantuan Swan
* [The] Price of Roman Poets
* [The] Prince of Poets
* [The] Swan of Mantua
* Virgil [or Vergil]

**Verginie, Jean Dimitre** 1904-1970
[WFA]
*French fashion designer*
* Desses, Jean

**Vergniaud, Pierre Victurnien**
1753-1793    [HN]
*French politician*
* [The] Mirabeau of the Gironde

**Verhagen, Jean** 1924-    [FC, ITA]
*American actress*
* Hagen, Jean

**Verhoeff, Nico**
*See* Verhoeff, Nicolaas Theodorus

**Verhoeff, Nicolaas Theodorus**
1904-    [IWM]
*Dutch musician*
* Verhoeff, Nico

**Verhuel**
*See* Bonaparte, Charles Louis
Napoleon

**Verin, Velko**
*See* Inkiow, [Janakiev] Dimiter

**Verissimus**
*See* Annius Verus, Marcus

**Verite sans Peur**
*See* Prouting, Frederick James

**Verkhovynetz, M.**
*See* Fedorovich, Nicholas

**Verkuyl, Gerrit** 1872- ?    [NAA]
*Dutch-born clergyman and author*
* Streefkerf, Hendrick

**Verlanger, Julia**
*See* Taieb, Heliane

**Verle, Emy**    [FFF]
*Entertainer*
* Fursch-Madi, Mme.

**Verlooghen, Corly**
*See* Van Bedacht, Rudy

**Vermeer, Jan** 1632-1675    [WBD]
*Dutch painter*
* Van der Meer van Delft, Jan

**Vermeule, Cornelius Clarkson, III**
1925-    [CA]
*Irish-born educator and author*
* Tsukinabe, Isao

**Vermilye, Kate** 20th c.    [ALY]
*Irish-born author*
* Jordan, Kate

**Vermretus**
*See* Vernerey, Jean

**Vern, David** 1924-
[ESF, SFL, WGT]
*American author*
* Blade, Alexander [house
pseudonym, Ziff-Davis]
* Ellis, Craig [house pseudonym]
* Horn, Peter [house pseudonym,
Ziff-Davis]
* Reed, David V.
* Woodruff, Clyde

**Verne, Adela**
*See* Wurm, Adela

**Verne, Alice**
*See* Wurm, Alice

**Verne, Karen**
*See* Klinckerfuss, Ingabor Katrine

**Verne, Mathilde**
*See* Wurm, Mathilde

**Verner, David** 1894-    [BS]
*Canadian-born magician*
* [The] Professor
* Vernon, Dai

**Verner, Gerald**
*See* Stuart, Donald

**Vernerey, Jean**    [PA]
*Author*
* Vermretus

**Verneuil, Louis**
*See* Collin Du Bocage, Louis
Jacques Marie

**Verney, Sarah**
*See* Holloway, Brenda W[ilmar]

**Vernieres, Francois**
*See* Baudovy, Michel-Aime

**Vernon, Ada**
*See* Dickinson, Susan E.

**Vernon, Anne**
*See* Vignaud, Edith Antoinette
Alexandrine

**Vernon, Bill**
*See* Slaughter, Marion T.

**Vernon, Claire**
*See* Breton-Smith, Clare

**Vernon, Dai**
*See* Verner, David

**Vernon, Dorothy** 1875-1970    [SC]
*German-born actress*
* Baird, Dorothy
* Burns, Dorothy

**Vernon, Eddie**
*See* Stone, Hoyt E[dward]

**Vernon, Edward**
*See* Coleman, Vernon

**Vernon, Edward** 1684-1757
[DEP, HN, SN]
*British naval officer*
* Old Grog

**Vernon, Edward** 1757-1847    [WBD]
*British prelate*
* Harcourt, Edward

**Vernon, Fanny**
*See* Sinclair, Mrs. Harry

**Vernon, Frank**
*See* Vernon-Humphrey, Frank

**Vernon, [Sir] George** 16th c.    [HN]
*British jurist*
* [The] King of the Peak

**Vernon, George S[hirra] G[ibb]**
1885-    [WGT]
*Author*
* George, Vernon

**Vernon, Ida**
*See* McGowan, Bridget

**Vernon, James Barton** 1918-
[DGS, PB, SMG]
*American baseball player and coach*
* Vernon, Mickey

**Vernon, Judge**
*See* Tuttle, E. C.

**Vernon, Max**
*See* Kellogg, Vernon Lyman

**Vernon, Mickey**
*See* Vernon, James Barton

**Vernon, Peter**
*See* Huddleston, Sisley

**Vernon, Richard** 1726-1800    [WBD]
*British sportsman*
* [The] Father of the Turf

**Vernon, Rose**
*See* Brant, Mrs. Luke

**Vernon, V.**
*See* Hersey, Harold

**Vernon-Humphrey, Frank**
1875-1940    [THR]
*British actor and producer*
* Vernon, Frank

**Vernor, D.**
*See* Casewit, Curtis

**Veron, Docteur**
*See* Veron, Louis Desire

**Veron, Louis Desire** 1798-1867
[WBD]
*French journalist*
* Veron, Docteur

**[The] Veronese of France**
*See* Delacroix, Ferdinand Victor
Eugene

**Veronese, Paolo**
*See* Cagliari [or Caliari?], Paolo

**Verpilleux, A. E.**
*See* Verpilleux, Emile Antoine

**Verpilleux, Emile Antoine**
1888-1964    [DBA]
*British painter, engraver, illustrator*
* Verpilleux, A. E.

**VerPlanck, Billy**
*See* VerPlanck, John Fenno

**Verplanck, Gulian Crommalin**
1786-1870    [PA]
*Author*
* Coody, Abimelech
* Herbert, Francis

**VerPlanck, John Fenno** 1930-
[ASC, EJ]
*American jazz musician*
* VerPlanck, Billy

**Verral, Charles Spain** 1904-
[CAP, SAT, WD]
*Canadian-born author*
* Eaton, George L.

**Verrall, A. W.**
*See* Verrall, Arthur Woollgar

**Verrall, Arthur Woollgar**
1851-1912    [LC]
*British educator and author*
* Verrall, A. W.

**Verret, Cajun**
*See* Verret, Irving

**Verret, Irving** 1906?-    [NOJ]
*American jazz musician*
* Verret, Cajun

**Verrill, A[lpheus] Hyatt** 1871-1954
[ESF, SFL, WGT]
*American naturalist, explorer,
author*
* Ainsbury, Ray

**Verrill, Virginia**
*See* McLean, Virginia Katherine

**Verrocchio [or Verocchio], Andrea
del**
*See* Di Michele Cione, Andrea

**Versace, Marie Teresa Rios** 1917-
[CA]
*American author*
* Rios, Tere

**Versalles, Zoilo Casanova** 1940-
[BE, PB]
*Cuban-born baseball player*
* Versalles, Zorro

**Versalles, Zorro**
*See* Versalles, Zoilo Casanova

**Versatile, Val**
*See* Enton, Harry

**Verschaffelt, Pierre Antoine**
1710-1793    [WBD]
*Flemish sculptor*
* Fiammingo, Pietro

**Versois, Odile**
See De Poliakoff-Baidaroff, Militza

**Vert Gallant [Devoted Admirer]**
See Henry IV [or Henri]

**Vertot, Abbe de**
See Aubert, Rene

**Vertov, Dziga**
See Kaufman, Denis Arkadievitch

**Vertue, George** 1684-1756 [SN]
British engraver and antiquary
* [The] Old Mortality of Pictures

**Verus, Lucius Aurelius**
See Commodus, Lucius Ceionius

**Veruschka**
See Von Lehndorff, Vera

**Verval, Alain** [joint pseudonym with Lawrence Montague Lande]
See Greenwood, Thomas

**Verval, Alain** [joint pseudonym with Thomas Greenwood]
See Lande, Lawrence Montague

**Verwer, Hans**
See Verwer, Johanna Elisabeth

**Verwer, Johanna Elisabeth** 1911-
[AW]
Dutch critic, editor, author
* Johanson, Elisabeth
* Verwer, Hans

**Verwey, Hans** 1648-1692 [PA]
Author
* Pharboeus

**Verwilghen, A[lbert-] Felix** 1916-
[CA]
British-born clergyman and author
* Yanagimura, Shimpu

**Vescia, George Milo** 1909- [ITA]
American film set decorator
* Milo, George

**Vesenyi, Paul E.** 1911- [CA]
Hungarian-born librarian and author
* Bod, Peter

**Vesey, George** [PA]
Author
* Beef Eater

**Vesey, Paul**
See Allen, Samuel [Washington]

**Vespasian, Titus Flavius Sabinus** 9-79 [HN, RH]
Roman emperor
* [The] Darling of Mankind
* Thaumaturgus

**Vesque von Puettlingen, Johann** 1803-1883 [WBD]
Austrian composer
* Hoven, J.

**Vessels, Billy W.** 1931- [FB]
American football player
* Vessels, Curly

**Vessels, Curly**
See Vessels, Billy W.

**Vestal, Herman Beeson** 20th c.
[SFP]
Author
* Beeson
* S. A. M.

**Vestal, Stanley** 1887-1957
[TC, WW]
American author
* Campbell, Walter Stanley

**Vestergard, Luther** 1902-1968
[SC]
American actor
* Power, Paul

**Vestris, Gaetano Apollino Balthazar** 1729-1808 [DNNS, FFF, RH]
Italian dancer
* [The] God of Dancing
* [The] King of Dance

**Vestvali, Felicita** [SN]
Opera singer
* [The] Magnificent Vestvali

**Vet, T. V.**
See Straiton, Edward Cornock

**Veteran Observer**
See Mansfield, Edward Deering

**Veto**
See Sedgwick, Theodore, Jr.

**[The] Veto Governor**
See Cleveland, [Stephen] Grover

**Veto, Madame**
See [Josephe Jeanne] Marie Antoinette

**[The] Veto Mayor**
See Cleveland, [Stephen] Grover

**Veto, Monsieur**
See Louis XVI

**[The] Veto President**
See Cleveland, [Stephen] Grover

**[The] Veto President**
See Johnson, Andrew

**Vetri, Victoria**
See Dorian, Angela

**Vetsch, Jakob** 20th c. [WGT]
Author
* Mundus, Jakob

**Vetus**
See Sterling, Edward

**Vexatus**
See Blair-Fish, Wallace Wilfrid

**Vexillum**
See Banner, Hubert Stewart

**Vey, Elinor**
See Glover, Mrs. Eliot

**Vezelay, Edith**
See Davis, Edith Vezolles

**Vezhinov, Pavel**
See Gougov, Nikola Delchev

**Vezina, Georges** 1888?-1926
[BBH, SR]
Canadian-born hockey player
* [The] Chicoutimi Cucumber

**Viadana, Lodovico**
See Grossi, Lodovico

**Vial, Gion**
See Deplazes, Gion

**Vialis, Gaston**
See Simenon, Georges [Joseph Christian]

**Vian, Boris** 1920-1959 [B10]
French author
* Sullivan, Vernon

**Viana, Nicholas** 20th c. [BLB]
American underworld figure
* [The] Choir Boy

**Vianney, Jean Baptiste Marie** 1786-1859 [WBD]
Saint
* [The] Cure of Ars

**Viard, Felix** 1882-1967 [CW]
Haitian author
* Saint Robert

**Viard, Henri Louis Luc** 1921-
[SFL, WGT]
French author
* Ward, Henry

**Viator**
See Bright, J. H.

**Viator**
See Forbes, Henry

**Viator**
See Taylor, Benjamin Ogle

**Viator, Scotus**
See Seton-Watson, Robert William

**Viator, Vacuus**
See Hughes, Thomas

**Viau, Lee**
See Viau, Leon

**Viau, Leon** 1866-1947 [BE]
American baseball player
* Viau, Lee

**Viau, Theophile de** 1590-1626 [SN]
French poet
* [The] Coryphaeus of his Day

**Viaud, Louis Marie Julien** 1850-1923 [CD, EWL, LC]
French author
* Loti, Pierre

**Vic the Stick**
See Correll, Victor Crosby

**[The] Vicar**
See Haig, Alexander Meigs

**Vicar, Henry**
See Felsen, Henry Gregor

**Vicar of Bray**
See Alleyn, Simon

**[The] Vicar of Hell**
See Borde, Andrew

**[The] Vicar of Hell**
See Bryan, [Sir] Francis

**[The] Vicar of Hell**
See Cromwell, Thomas [Earl of Essex]

**[The] Vicar of Hell**
See Skelton, John

**[The] Vicar of Hell**
See Wolsey, Thomas

**[The] Vicar of Wakefield**
See Wilson, Benjamin

**Vicarion, [Count] Palmiro**
See Logue, Christopher

**Vicars, Henry Edward** 1888-1942
[CEC]
British criminal
* Flannelfoot
* Williams, Henry

**Vicary, Dorothy**
See Rice, Dorothy Mary

**Vice Emperor**
See Rouher, Eugene

**Vice God**
See Borghese, Camillo

**Vice Pres Quinichette**
See Quinichette, Paul

**Vicente, Gil** 1480?-1557? [HN]
Portuguese playwright
* [The] Portuguese Plautus

**[The] Viceroy**
See Churchill, Sarah Jennings

**Vichard, Cesar** 1639-1692
[FFF, HN, RH]
French historian
* Saint Real, Abbe de
* [The] Sallust of France

**Vicious, Sid**
See Ritchie, John Simon

**Vick, Ernie**
See Vick, Henry

**Vick, Henry** 20th c.
American football player
* Vick, Ernie

**Vicker, Angus**
See Felsen, Henry Gregor

**Vickers**
See Kaufman, Wallace

**Vickers, Harry Porter** 1878-1958
[BE]
American baseball player
* Vickers, Rube

**Vickers, Martha**
See MacVicar, Martha

**Vickers, Mattie**
See Rogers, Mrs. Charles S.

**Vickers, Roy** 1899-1965
[AW, EMD, WW]
British author
* Durham, David
* Kyle, Sefton
* Spencer, John

**Vickers, Rube**
See Vickers, Harry Porter

**Vickers, Sarge**
See Vickers, Stephen James

**Vickers, Steady Steve**
See Vickers, Stephen James

**Vickers, Stephen James** 1951-
[SMG]
Canadian-born hockey player
* Vickers, Sarge
* Vickers, Steady Steve

**Vicky**
See Weisz, Victor

**Vico, George Steve** 1923- [BE]
American baseball player
* Vico, Sam

**Vico, Sam**
See Vico, George Steve

**Victoire** [code name used during World War II]
See Carre, Mathilde [Belard]

**Victor, Charles B.**
See Puechner, Ray

**Victor [or Victor-Perrin], Claude**
See Perrin, Claude Victor [Duc de Bellune]

**Victor Emmanuel II** 1820-1878
[DEP, HN, SN]
*King of Italy*
* [The] Gallant King
* Guaff
* [The] Hero of Palestro
* Honest Man King
* Re Galantuomo

**[The] Victor Hugo of Painting**
*See* Delacroix, Ferdinand Victor
Eugene

**Victor, Joan Berg** 1937-   [ICB]
*American author and illustrator*
* Berg, Joan

**Victor, Josephine**
*See* Guenczler, Josephine

**Victor, Lucia**
*See* Baker, Lucia Adelaide Victor

**Victor, Metta Victoria Fuller**
1831-1886   [FFF]
*American author and poet*
* Regester, Seeley
* [The] Singing Sibyl

**[The] Victor of a Hundred Battles**
*See* Bonaparte, Napoleon

**Victor II**
*See* Gebhard

**Victor III**
*See* Dauferius

**Victor IV**
*See* Conti, Gregorio

**Victor IV**
*See* Octavius

**Victoria [or Victorina]** 3rd c.
[DNNF, FFF]
*Mother of Victorinus, one of the
Thirty Tyrants of Rome*
* [The] Mother of the Camps

**Victoria** 1819-1901
[DEP, DNNS, HN]
*Queen of England*
* Empress of India
* [The] Mirror of Justice
* Wetter, Mrs.
* [The] Widow of Windsor

**Victoria, Guadalupe**
*See* Fernandez, Manuel Felix

**Victoria, [Sister] M.**
*See* Danforth, Ethel M.

**Victoria, Tomas** 16th c.   [FFF]
*Spanish missionary to Guatemala*
* [The] Elias of Guatemala

**Victoria, Vesta**
*See* Lawrence, Vesta

**[The] Victorious**
*See* Charles VII

**[The] Victorious**
*See* Frederick I

**[The] Victorious**
*See* Joseph I

**[The] Victorious**
*See* Khosru II [or Chosroes]

**[The] Victorious**
*See* Ladislaus [or Lancelot]

**[The] Victorious**
*See* Waldemar II

**Vida, Marco Girolamo** 1480?-1566
[DEP, DNNS, SN]
*Italian poet*
* [The] Christian Virgil
* Virgilius Redivivus

**Vidacovich, Irving J.** 1904-1966
[ASC, SC, WWJ]
*American jazz musician*
* Cajun Pete
* Vidacovich, Pinky

**Vidacovich, Pinky**
*See* Vidacovich, Irving J.

**Vidal, Eugene Luther, Jr.** 1925-
[CA, CC, EMD]
*American author*
* Box, Edgar
* Hargrave, Leoni?
* Vidal, Gore

**Vidal, Gore**
*See* Vidal, Eugene Luther, Jr.

**Vidal, Jose Nicolas** 1940-   [BE]
*Dominican-born baseball player*
* Vidal, Papito

**Vidal, Papito**
*See* Vidal, Jose Nicolas

**Videla, Jorge Rafael** 20th c.
*Argentinian military leader*
* [El] Hueso [The Bone]

**Videlbias, Johannes**
*See* Collin, Jacques Albin Simon

**Vidette**
*See* Doyle, Jefferson E. P.

**Vidette**
*See* Elliott, J. J.

**Vidi**
*See* Conant, William C.

**Vidocq**
*See* Hawkins, Charles Ashton

**Vidor, Florence**
*See* Arto, Florence

**Vieira da Cunha, Antonio Belisario**
1896-1956   [WEC]
*Brazilian cartoonist*
* Belisario

**[El] Viejo**
*See* Herrera, Francisco de

**[El] Viejo [The Old One]**
*See* Shoemaker, William [Willie]

**Viela, Paul**
*See* DeLucia, Felice

**Viele, Egbert Ludovicus** 1863-1937
[TC, WBD]
*American-born French poet*
* Viele-Griffin, Francis

**Viele-Griffin, Francis**
*See* Viele, Egbert Ludovicus

**Vien, Charles**   [PA]
*Author*
* Hall, Robert

**Viereck, G. S.**
*See* Viereck, George Sylvester

**Viereck, George Sylvester**
1884-1962   [HFF, NAA]
*German author*
* Corners, George F.
* Viereck, G. S.

**Vies, Jen** 1868-1949   [SC]
*French actor*
* Sinoel

**Vieschouwer, Johann** 1520-1562
[PA]
*Author*
* Carnarius

**Viespi, Alexander** 1931?-
[FC, HT, SW]
*American actor*
* Cord, Alex

**Viete [or Vieta], Francois**
1540-1603   [WBD]
*French mathematician*
* [The] Father of Algebra

**Vieth Von Golssenau, Arnold
Friedrich** 1889-1979
[CD, HDM, TC]
*German author*
* Renn, Ludwig

**Viett, George Frederic** 1868- ?
[NAA]
*French-born poet and playwright*
* Everett, Gifo G.
* Wegg De Norva, Silas

**Vieu, M.**   [HN]
*Author*
* Halt, Robert

**Vieux, Marie** 1917-1975   [CW]
*Haitian author and playwright*
* Colibri

**Vieux Renard**
*See* Soult, Nicolas Jean de Dieu

**Vigan, Luc**
*See* Ruellan, Andre

**Vigilans**
*See* Partridge, Eric Honeywood

**Vigilans**
*See* Rice, Brian K.

**Vigilant**
*See* Barker, Stanley

**Vigilant**
*See* Corlett, John

**Vigilant**
*See* Mitchell, R. C.

**Vigilant**
*See* Vosburg, F. W.

**Vigiola Del Torco, Serafin**
1889-1958   [GS]
*Spanish bullfighter*
* Torquito [Little Torco]

**Vignaud, Edith Antoinette
Alexandrine** 1925-
[FC, ITA, WEF]
*French actress*
* Vernon, Anne

**Vigne d'Octon**
*See* Vigne, Paul

**Vigne, John** 1885?-   [NOJ]
*American jazz musician*
* Vigne, Ratty

**Vigne, Paul** 1859-1943   [WBD]
*French author and politician*
* Kerhouel, Gaetan
* Vigne d'Octon

**Vigne, Ratty**
*See* Vigne, John

**Vignola, Giacomo da**
*See* Barocchio [or Barozzi],
Giacomo

**Vignoles, Etienne** 1387-1442   [HN]
*French general*
* [La] Hire [The Growler]

**Vignon, Claude**
*See* Bouvier, Mme.

**Vigo, Francis**
*See* Vigo, Joseph Maria Francesco

**Vigo, Jean**
*See* Almereyda, Jean

**Vigo, Joseph Maria Francesco**
1747-1836   [WBD]
*Italian-born fur trader and pioneer
in America*
* Vigo, Francis

**Viguers, Ruth Hill** 1903-1971
[CA, CAP, SAT]
*American editor and critic*
* Hill, Ruth A.

**Viking, Ted**
*See* Louwen, Jan

**Vikstedt, Toivo Alarik** 1891-1930
[WEC]
*Finnish cartoonist*
* Topi

**Vildrac, Charles**
*See* Messager, Charles

**Vile Lyle Nelson**
*See* Nelson, Lyle

**Vilelleschi, Marchese Francesco**
[PA]
*Author*
* Pomponio, Leto

**Vilenkin, Nikolai Maksimovich**
1855-1937   [CD]
*Russian poet and philosopher*
* Minski, Nikolai Maksimovich

**Viles, Walter** 20th c.   [MBF]
*British author*
* Beaumont, Brenchley

**Villa, Bobby**
*See* Villa, Roberto

**Villa, Francisco**
*See* Arango, Doroteo

**Villa, Joe**
*See* Francavilla, Joe

**Villa, Jose Garcia** 1914-   [CA]
*Filipino-born poet, author, editor*
* Doveglion

**Villa, Mrs. Samuel B.**   [FFF]
*Entertainer*
* Wallace, Agnes

**Villa, Pancho**
*See* Arango, Doroteo

**Villa, Pancho**
*See* Guilledo, Francisco

**Villa, Paul**
*See* DeLucia, Felice

**Villa, Roberto** 20th c.   [OBW]
*American baseball player*
* Villa, Bobby

**Villa y Arilla, Nicanor** 1869-1944
[GS]
*Spanish bullfighter*
* Villita [Little Villa]

**Villa y Mari, Francisco** 1884-    [GS]
*Spanish bullfighter*
* Rubio de Valencia [Redhead of Valencia]

**Villaard**
See   Beaumesnil, Henrietta Adelaide

**[The] Village Schoolmaster**
See   Dickinson, Charles M.

**[The] Village Shoemaker**
See   Dickinson, Charles M.

**Villagran, Ce'sar**
See   Cabral, Ce'sar Augusto

**Villain, Regardant**
See   Tozer, Basil

**Villain-Marais, Jean** 1913-
[BDF, WEF]
*French actor*
* Marais, Jean

**Villanueva Parma, Luis** 20th c.
[SG]
*Boxer*
* Azteca, Kid

**Villard, Frank**
See   Drouineau, Francois

**Villard, Henry**
See   Hilgard, [Ferdinand] Heinrich [Gustav]

**Villars, Elizabeth**
See   Feldman, Ellen [Bette]

**Villegaignon, Chevalier de**
See   Durand, Nicholas

**Villegas, Jose** 1868-1927   [GS]
*Spanish bullfighter*
* Potoco [Large Pot]

**Villehardouin, Geoffroi de**
1150?-1212?   [DEP, FFF, SN]
*French historian*
* [The] Father of French History
* [The] Father of French Prose

**Villemessant, Jean Hippolyte** 1812-
?   [PA]
*Author*
* Cartier

**Villette, Allis**
See   Ackerman, Forrest J[ames]

**Villiard, Paul** 1910-1974   [CAP]
*American author and photographer*
* DeGros, J. H.

**Villiers, George**
See   Tardieu, Andre Pierre Gabriel Amedee

**Villiers, George** 1592-1628
[DNNF, DNNS, HN]
*First Duke of Buckingham*
* [The] Sejanus of England
* Steenie

**Villiers, George** 1628-1687
[DEP, SN]
*Second Duke of Buckingham*
* [The] Alcibiades of his Time
* [The] Pindar of England

**Villita [Little Villa]**
See   Villa y Arilla, Nicanor

**Villon, Jacques**
See   Duchamp, Gaston

**Villon, Pierre**
See   Gintzburger, Pierre

**Vilmar**
See   Rodrigues, Vilmar Silva

**Vinal, William Gould** 1881- ?
[NAA]
*American naturalist and author*
* Cap'n Bill

**Vinard, F. N.**
See   Vincent, Nathaniel Hawthorne

**Vincens, Mme. Charles** 1840-1908
[WBD]
*French author and critic*
* Arvede Barine

**Vincent**
See   Napoli, Vincent

**Vincent** 19th c.    [HN]
*Welsh religious leader*
* [The] King of the Hills

**Vincent, Ann**
See   Ridings, Hope Dupre

**Vincent, Charles** 1851-1920    [SFL]
*Author*
* Mael, Peter [joint pseudonym with Charles Causse]

**Vincent, Clarence** 1899-1960
[NOJ]
*American jazz musician*
* Vincent, Little Dud

**Vincent de Paul** 1581?-1660
[RH, SN]
*Saint*
* [The] Father of Your Country
* [Le] Pere de la Patrie
* Thaumaturgus

**Vincent, E. L.**
See   Morris, Charles Smith

**Vincent, E[lizabeth] Lee** 1897-
[CAP]
*American psychologist and author*
* Vincent, Leona

**Vincent, Ellerton**
See   Logan, M. C.

**Vincent, Frank**
See   Kirkham, Reginald S.

**Vincent, Gene**
See   Craddock, Vincent Eugene

**Vincent, Harl**
See   Schoepflin, Harl Vincent

**Vincent, Heinrich Joseph**
See   Winzenhoerlein, Heinrich Joseph

**Vincent, Irving B.** 1909-    [MK]
*American baseball player*
* Vincent, Lefty

**Vincent, Isabeau**    [HN]
*Prophetess*
* [The] Shepherdess of Dauphiny

**Vincent, J. Harry**
See   Taurasi, James V., Sr.

**Vincent, Jacques**
See   Dussaud, Angele

**Vincent, John**
See   Alvarez Del Rey, Ramon Felipe San Juan Mario Silvio Enrico

**Vincent, John**
See   Farrow, R.

**Vincent, June**
See   Smith, Dorothy June

**Vincent, Katharine**
See   Vincenti, Ella

**Vincent, Lefty**
See   Vincent, Irving B.

**Vincent, Leona**
See   Vincent, E[lizabeth] Lee

**Vincent, Lina**
See   Tanner, Lina

**Vincent, Little Dud**
See   Vincent, Clarence

**Vincent, Mary Keith**
See   St. John, Wylly Folk

**Vincent, Monroe** 1919-    [BWW]
*American singer*
* Calhoun, Mr.
* Monroe, Vince
* Polka Dot Slim

**Vincent, Nathaniel Hawthorne**
1889-    [ASC]
*American composer and singer*
* Kenbrovin, Jaan
* Vinard, F. N.

**Vincent of Lerins** ?- 450?   [WBD]
*Saint*
* Peregrinus

**Vincent, Reggie** 20th c.    [RM]
*Musician*
* Vincent, Rockin' Reggie

**Vincent, Rockin' Reggie**
See   Vincent, Reggie

**Vincent, Sailor Billy**
See   Vincent, William J.

**Vincent, Walter**
See   Vinson, Walter Jacobs

**Vincent, William J.** 1896-1966
[SC]
*American actor, stunt performer, boxer*
* Vincent, Sailor Billy

**Vincent, William R.**
See   Heitzmann, W[illia]m Ray

**Vincenti, Ella** 1919-    [ITA]
*American actress*
* Vincent, Katharine

**Vinciguerra, Francesca** 1900-    [TC]
*American author*
* Winwar, Frances

**Vincson, Walter**
See   Vinson, Walter Jacobs

**Vindex**
See   Barker, Edmund Henry

**Vindex**
See   Buet, Charles

**Vindex?**
See   Francis, [Sir] Philip

**Vindex**
See   Gibbons, William

**Vindex**
See   Rogers, Henry

**Vindex**
See   Tefft, Lyman Beecher

**Vindicator**
See   Hopkinson, Henry Thomas [Tom]

**Vine, Sarah**
See   Rowland, D[onald] S[ydney]

**Vine, William**
See   Youd, Christopher Samuel

**Vinegar Bend Mizell**
See   Mizell, Wilmer David

**Vinegar Bill Essick**
See   Essick, William Earl [Bill]

**Vinegar Joe Stilwell**
See   Stilwell, Joseph W.

**Vinegar Roan Vamvoras**
See   Vamvoras, Clyde

**Vinegar, Tom**
See   Gregg, Andrew K.

**Vinest, Shaw**
See   Longyear, Barry Brookes

**Vingedal, Sven Erik Axel** 1906-
[IAW]
*Swedish author and poet*
* Redax

**Vinicombe, Walter** 1888-1971
[F2, FC]
*British actor*
* Patch, Wally

**Viniello, Danny** 1902-1958
[PMJ, WWJ]
*American jazz musician*
* Alvin, Danny

**Vining, Elizabeth Gray** 1902-    [CA]
*American author*
* Gray, Elizabeth Janet

**Vinning, Pamelia S.**    [FFF]
*Canadian writer*
* Emilia
* Xenette

**Vinokur, Grigory**
See   Weinrauch, Herschel

**Vinson, Carl** 1884?-1981
*American politician*
* Defense, Mr.
* [The] Swamp Fox

**Vinson, Cleanhead**
See   Vinson, Eddie

**Vinson, Eddie** 1917-
[EJ, PMJ, WWJ]
*American jazz musician*
* Cleanhead, Mr.
* Vinson, Cleanhead

**Vinson, Elaine**
See   Rowland, D[onald] S[ydney]

**Vinson, Ernest Augustus**
1879-1951   [BE]
*American baseball player*
* Vinson, Rube

**Vinson, Helen**
See   Rulfs, Helen

**Vinson, Kathryn**
See   Williams, Kathryn Vinson

**Vinson, Piano Sam**
See   Vinson, Sam

**Vinson, Rex Thomas** 1935-
[ESF, SFL]
*British author*
* King, Vincent

**Vinson, Rube**
See   Vinson, Ernest Augustus

**Vinson, Sam** 20th c.   [BWW]
*American musician*
* Vinson, Piano Sam

**Vinson, Walter Jacobs** 1901-1975
[BWW]
*American singer*
* Jacobs, Walter
* Vincent, Walter
* Vincson, Walter

**Viola**
See Downing, Fanny Murdaugh

**[Le] Viola**
See Picton, Thomas

**Viola**
See Thurston, Laura M. Hawley

**Violet, M.**
See Marryatt, Frederick

**Violet, Ultra**
See Collin-Dufresne, Isabelle

**Violetti**
See Eva, Marion

**[Il] Violino**
See Cortellini, Camillo

**Violinsky, Solly**
See Ginsberg, Sol

**Violis, G.**
See Simenon, Georges [Joseph Christian]

**VIP**
See Partch, Virgil Franklin, II

**[The] Viper Girl**
See Howard, Rosetta

**Vipont, Charles**
See Foulds, Elfrida Vipont

**Vipont, Elfrida**
See Foulds, Elfrida Vipont

**Vipsania Agrippina**
See Agrippina

**Virden, Katherine**
See Southerland, Katherine Virden

**Virdon, Quail**
See Virdon, William C. [Bill]

**Virdon, William C. [Bill]** 1931-
[PB]
*American baseball player*
* Virdon, Quail

**Virga Dei**
See Genseric

**Virgil [or Vergil]**
See Vergilius Maro, Publius

**[The] Virgil and Horace of the Christians**
See Prudentius, Aurelius Clemens

**Virgil, Laura**
See Mainhall, Mrs. Henry

**[The] Virgil of Dramatic Poets**
See Jonson, Ben[jamin]

**[The] Virgil of Prose**
See Stevenson, Robert Louis Balfour

**[The] Virgil of the French Drama**
See Racine, Jean Baptiste

**Virgil, Osvaldo Jose** 1933-
[BE, SMG]
*Dominican-born baseball player and coach*
* Virgil, Ozzie

**Virgil, Ozzie**
See Virgil, Osvaldo Jose

**[Le] Virgile au Rabot [The Virgil of the Plane]**
See Bellaut, Adam

**Virgilius Redivivus**
See Vida, Marco Girolamo

**[The] Virgin Mary**
See Mary

**Virgin Modesty**
See Wilmot, John

**[The] Virgin Queen**
See Elizabeth I

**Virginia**
See Davidson, Virginia E.

**[The] Virginia Confederate**
See Kelly, A. M.

**Virginia, Daisy**
See Van Horn, Dale R.

**[A] Virginian**
See Caruthers, William

**[A] Virginian**
See Tyler, R.

**Virginia's Tutelary Saint**
See Matoaka

**Virginius**
See Connett, Eugene Virginius, III

**Virlup, A. Kvazau**
See Ackerman, Forrest J[ames]

**Virtue, Lancaster**
See Virtue, Vivian

**Virtue, Vivian** 1911- [CW]
*Jamaican poet and translator*
* Virtue, Lancaster

**[The] Virtuous Genevese**
See Necker, Jacques [or James]

**Virza, Edvarts**
See Lieknis, Edvarts

**Vischer, Friedrich Theodor von**
1807-1887 [PA]
*German author*
* Mystifizinsky, Deutobold
  Symbolizetti Allegoriowitsch
* Schartenmeyer

**Visconti, Galeazzo II** 1320-1378
[SN]
*Duke of Lombardy*
* [The] Maecenas of His Time

**Visconti, Luchino**
See De Modrone, Luchino Visconti

**Visconti, Matteo** 1250-1323?
[DNNS, SN]
*Lord of Milan*
* [The] Great

**Visconti, Teobaldo** 1210-1276
[WBD]
*Pope*
* Gregory X

**Visee**
See Sitaramiah, Venkataramiah

**Visger, Jean A. Owen** 20th c.
[WWL]
*British author*
* Owen, J. A.
* [A] Son of the Marshes

**Visiak, E. H.**
See Physick, Edward Harold

**Viskardy, Nicholas** 20th c.
[WECO]
*Cartoonist*
* Cardy

**Visser, A. J. J.**
See Visser, Abraham Jacobus Johannes

**Visser, Abraham Jacobus Johannes**
1925- [IAW]
*South African author*
* Visser, A. J. J.

**Visser, Willem Johannes Conradie**
1920- [IAW]
*South African author*
* Klinikus
* Psigoloog
* Visser, Willie

**Visser, Willie**
See Visser, Willem Johannes Conradie

**[The] Vitagraph Girl**
See Turner, Florence

**Vital, David**
See Grossman, David

**[The] Vital Spark**
See Hill, Jenny

**Vitaliano, Genaro Louis** 1932-
[RO1]
*American singer*
* Vale, Jerry

**Vitalis**
See Sjoeberg, Erik

**Vitamin T Smith**
See Smith, Verda T.

**Vitamin Z**
See Brzezinski, Zbigniew

**Vitelleschi, Stella** 1886- [THR]
*British actress*
* Rho, Stella

**Vitellius, Aulus** 15- 69 [RH, SN]
*Roman emperor*
* [The] Flatterer
* [The] Glutton

**Viterbo, Dina Tiktiner** 20th c.
[WFA]
*French fashion designer*
* Tiktiner

**Vitesse, Grande**
See Walkerley, Rodney Lewis [De Burgh]

**Vitet, Louis** 1802-1873 [WBD]
*French author and politician*
* Vitet, Ludovic

**Vitet, Ludovic**
See Vitet, Louis

**Vitezovic, Tomislav**
See Kuehnelt-Leddihn, Erik [Ritter Von]

**[El] Viti**
See Martin Sanchez, Santiago

**Vitols, Valdis**
See Kikauka, Talis Talivaldis Tully

**[The] Vitruvius of England**
See Jones, Inigo

**Vitt, Oscar Joseph** 1890-1963 [AS]
*American baseball player*
* Vitt, Ossie

**Vitt, Ossie**
See Vitt, Oscar Joseph

**Vitti, Monica**
See Ceciarelli, Maria Luisa

**Vitti, Ralph** 1931?- [FC, SW]
*American actor*
* Dante, Michael

**Vittorino da Feltre**
See Ramboldini [or de Ramboldoni], Vittorino

**Viva**
See Williams, Eva

**Vivarelli, Piero** [FDG]
*Italian director*
* Murray, Donald

**Vivarini, Bartolommeo**
See Da Murano, Bartolommeo

**Vivers, Eileen Elliott** 1905- [CA]
*American home economist and author*
* Quigley, Eileen Elliott

**Vivian**
See Lewes, George Henry

**Vivian, Emily**
See Kernell, Mrs. John

**Vivian, Evelyn Charles H.**
1882-1947 [ESF, HFF, WGT]
*British author*
* Cannell, Charles
* Mann, Jack

**Vivian, Francis**
See Ashley, [Arthur] Ernest

**Vivian, Herbert** 1865- ? [WWL]
*British author*
* X.

**Vivian, Lila**
See Hicks, Edna

**Vivien**
See Shaw, Hollace

**Vivier, Colette**
See Duval, Colette

**Vizard, Stephen**
See James, [David] Burnett [Stephen]

**Vizardi, Ligio**
See Diaz Ordonez, Virgilio

**Vizetelly, Ernest Alfred** 1853-1922
[WBD, WWL]
*French author and journalist*
* [Le] Petit Homme Rouge

**Vizetelly, Francis Horace [Frank]**
1864- ? [ALY]
*British-born author*
* Syntax, Dr.

**Vlacic Ilir, Matija**
See Flacius Illyricus, Matthias

**Vladimir I** 956?-1015
[DNNS, SN]
*Grand Duke of Russia*
* [The] Great

**Vladimir II** 1053-1125 [WBD]
*Russian ruler*
* Monomachus

**Vladimirov, Leonid**
See   Finkelstein, Leonid
Vladimirovitch

**Vlady**
See   Zabache, Wladimiro Bas

**Vlady, Marina**
See   De Poliakoff-Baidaroff,
Marina

**Vlasek, June** 1915-   [FC]
*American actress*
* Lang, June

**Vlasic, Bob**
See   Hirsch, Phil

**Vlasto, John Alexander** 1877-1958
[WW]
*Author*
* Alexander, John
* Remenham, John

**Vocalis, Lambros Charles** 1928-
[BEW]
*American stage manager, director,
actor*
* Forsythe, Charles

**Vodnoy, Matthew**
See   Vodnoy, Max

**Vodnoy, Max** 1892-1939   [SC]
*Russian-born actor*
* Vodnoy, Matthew

**Voel, David**
See   Morgan-Jones, David Sylvanus

**Voelker, John Donaldson** 1903-
[CA, CC, WD]
*American author and jurist*
* Traver, Robert

**Voer, Jon Ur**
See   Jonsson, Jon

**Vogau, Boris Andreyevich**
1894-1938   [CD, EWL, TC]
*Russian author*
* Pilnyak, Boris

**Vogel, Big Ed**
See   Vogel, Eddie

**Vogel, Eddie** 20th c.   [PHM]
*American underworld figure*
* Vogel, Big Ed

**Vogel, Harry Benjamin** 1868- ?
[LAO]
*New Zealand-born author*
* Kinver, Richard

**Vogel, Otto** 20th c.   [BBH]
*American baseball coach*
* Vogel, Otts

**Vogel, Otts**
See   Vogel, Otto

**Vogelland, Rico** 1936?-   [CW]
*Surinamese poet, critic, editor*
* Kross, Rudy

**Vogelstein, Julie**
See   Braun-Vogelstein, Julie

**Vogenitz, David George** 1930-
[AW, CA]
*American author*
* George, David

**Vogt, Carl Henry** 1895-1956
[BDF, BEW, F2]
*American actor and director*
* Calhern, Louis

**Vogt, Marie**
See   Seckener, Mrs. James A.

**Voiart, Anne E. Petitpain**
1786-1866   [PA]
*Author*
* Elisa

**[The] Voice of Mission Control**
See   Powers, John A.

**[The] Voice of the Astronauts**
See   Powers, John A.

**[The] Voice of the Metropolitan**
See   Cross, Milton

**Voiceless Tim O'Rourke**
See   O'Rourke, Timothy Patrick

**Voight, Valeska**   [PA]
*Author*
* Stahr, Arthur

**Voigt** 20th c.   [DEP]
*Prussian shoemaker who
masqueraded as an army officer*
* [A] Captain of Koepenick

**Voigt, James Wesley** 1940-   [ECM]
*American singer and songwriter*
* Taylor, Chip

**Voigt, Olen Edward** 1899-   [BE]
*American baseball player*
* Voigt, Ollie

**Voigt, Ollie**
See   Voigt, Olen Edward

**Voiselle, Big Bill**
See   Voiselle, William Symmes

**Voiselle, William Symmes** 1919-
[BE, PB]
*American baseball player*
* Ninety Six
* Voiselle, Big Bill

**Voiture, Vincent** 1597-1648   [SN]
*French courtier, poet, author*
* [The] Great Letter-Writer

**Vojtech**
See   Adalbert [or Adelbert]

**Vokes, Harry**
See   Langlin, Henry

**Vokes, Rosina**
See   Clay, Mrs. Cecil

**Volk, Gordon** 1885-   [WW, WWL]
*British author*
* Knotts, Raymond
* Sussex, Gordon

**Volk, Hannah Marie**
See   Wormington, Hannah Marie

**Volkmann, Richard von** 1830-1889
[WBD]
*German surgeon, author, poet*
* Leander, Richard

**Volkoff, Vladimir** 1932-   [CA]
*French-born author, poet,
playwright*
* Barbare, Rholf
* Duloup, Victor

**Volodarsky**
See   Goldstein, Moisei Markovich

**Volonte, Claudio** 20th c.   [WF]
*Italian actor*
* Camaso, Claudio

**Voloshin, Maximilian Aleksandrovich**
See   Kirienko-Voloshin, Maximilian
Aleksandrovich

**Volpe, Mops**
See   Volpe, Tony

**Volpe, Tony** 20th c.   [BLB, PHM]
*American underworld figure*
* Volpe, Mops

**Volpone**
See   Godolphin, Sidney

**Voltaggio, Vic**
See   Voltaggio, Vito Henry

**Voltaggio, Vito Henry** 1941-
[ALR]
*Baseball official*
* Voltaggio, Vic

**Voltaire**
See   Arouet, Francois Marie

**[The] Voltaire of Chambermaids**
See   Restif, Nicolas Edme

**[The] Voltaire of Germany**
See   Goethe, Johann Wolfgang von

**[The] Voltaire of Germany**
See   Wieland, Christoph Martin

**[The] Voltaire of Poland**
See   Krasicki, Ignatius

**[The] Voltaire of Science**
See   Boerhaave, Hermann

**[The] Voltaire of the Sixteenth
Century**
See   Gerhards, Gerhard [or Geert]

**Volterra, Daniele da**
See   Ricciarelli, Daniele

**[Il] Volterrano**
See   Franceschini, Baldassare

**Voltige a la Richard**
See   Rastelli, Oreste

**[El] Voluntario [The Ready One]**
See   Serrano, Carlos

**Volusenus**
See   Wilson, Florence

**Volz, Jacob Phillip [Jake]**
1878-1962   [BE]
*American baseball player*
* Volz, Silent Jake

**Volz, Silent Jake**
See   Volz, Jacob Phillip [Jake]

**Volzogenius**
See   Van Wolzogen, Lodowijk

**Von**
See   Second element of name for
further listings

**Von Amyntor, Gerhard**
See   Gerhardt, Dagobert von

**Von An Der Lan-Hochbrunn, Paul
Eugen Josef** 1863-1914   [BBD]
*German conductor and composer*
* Hartmann, Pater

**Von Aschendorf, Ignatz**
See   Korzeniowski, Teodor Jozef
Konrad Nalecz

**Von Benewyck, Jan** 1594-1647
[PA]
*Author*
* Beverovicus

**Von Berweck, Carl Gustav** 1803- ?
[PA]
*Author*
* Von Guseck, Bornd

**Von Betz, Matthew** 1881-1938
[SC]
*American actor*
* Betz, Matthew

**Von Block, Bela** 20th c.   [CA]
*Author*
* Chambertin, Ilya [joint
pseudonym with Sylvia Von
Block]

**Von Block, Sylvia** 1931-   [CA]
*American author*
* Beaumont, Beverly
* Chambertin, Ilya [joint
pseudonym with Bela Von Block]
* Clifford, Theodore
* Hennessey, Caroline
* Randolph, Gordon
* Sprague, W. D.

**Von Bolanden, Conrad**
See   Bischoff, Joseph E. Carl

**Von Bolvary, Geza**
See   Von Bolvary-Zahn, Geza
Maria

**Von Bolvary-Zahn, Geza Maria**
1897-1961   [FDG]
*Hungarian director*
* Von Bolvary, Geza

**Von Bonewell, Hendrick** ?-1542
[PA]
*Author*
* Bonemelus

**Von Boyle, Ackland**
See   Boyle, Acland

**Von Brandenburg, Hugo**   [SN]
*German aristocrat*
* [The] Great Baron

**Von Brincken, Wilhelm** 1891-1946
[SC]
*German-born actor and director*
* Beckwith, Roger
* Vaughn, William

**Von Buttlar-Brandenfels, Johannes**
1940-   [IAW]
*German author*
* Buttlar, Johannes

**Von Castelhun, Friedl**
See   Marion, Frieda

**Von Chelius, Oskar** 1859-1923
[BBD]
*German composer*
* Berger, Siegfried

**Von Dalberg, Johann Kamera**
1445-1503   [PA]
*Author*
* Dalburgius

**Von Den Steinen, Robert**
See   Graf Wickenburg, Erik

**Von Der Ahe, Chris**
See   Von Der Ahe, Christian
Frederick Wilhelm

**Von Der Ahe, Christian Frederick
Wilhelm** 1851-1913   [BE]
*German-born baseball manager*
* Von Der Ahe, Chris

**Von Der Belin, Charles** 1885-1936
[SC]
*Belgian-born actor, producer,
director*
* Fallon, Charles

**Von Der Butz, Philip** 1883-1964
[F2]
*Actor*
* August, Edwin

**Von der Clana, Heinrich**
See Weiss, Albert Maria

**Von der Linde, Philander**
See Mencke [or Mencken], Johann
Burkhard

**Von Dombrowski zu Papros und
Krusvic, Kathe** 1881- ? [SFL]
*Author*
* Dombrowski, Katrina
* K. O. S.

**Von Drey, Howard**
See Wandrei, Howard Elmer

**Von Economo, C.**
See Economo, Constantin

**Von Einsiedel, R.**
See Tetzner, Martha Helene

**Von Fehmarn**
See Lafrentz, Ferdinand William

**Von Furstenberg, Betsy**
See Von Furstenberg-Hedringen,
Elizabeth Caroline Maria Agatha
Felicitas

**Von Furstenberg-Hedringen,
Elizabeth Caroline Maria Agatha
Felicitas** 1931?- [BEW, TR]
*German-born actress*
* Von Furstenberg, Betsy

**Von Gerber, Francesca Mitzi
Marlene** 1930- [FC, SW, WEF]
*American actress*
* Gaynor, Mitzi

**Von Grau, Wernher**
See Schoeb, Erika

**Von Grofe, Ferdinand Rudolph**
1892-1972 [PMJ]
*American composer and musician*
* Grofe, Ferde

**Von Gunther, Ilse [or Inge?]** 1891-
[BBD]
*Hungarian opera singer*
* Ivoguen, Maria

**Von Guseck, Bornd**
See Von Berweck, Carl Gustav

**Von Hassia, Henricus**
See Langenstein, Heinrich

**Von Heine, Baroness Gustav** [FFF]
*Opera singer*
* Klein, Regina

**Von Hernreid, Paul George Julius**
1908- [BDF, WEF]
*Austrian-born actor and director*
* Henreid, Paul

**Von Hildebrand, Dietrich**
1889-1977 [CA]
*German-born educator and author*
* Ott, Peter

**Von Himmel, Ernst**
See Petersilea, Carlyle

**Von Hohenberg, Luli** 1909- [FIR]
*German-born actress*
* Deste, Luli

**Von Hohenheim, Theophrastus
Bombastus** 1493?-1541 [WBD]
*Swiss-born physician*
* Paracelsus, Philippus Aureolus

**Von Holst, Gustavus Theodore**
1874-1934 [BBD, WBD]
*British composer and musician*
* Holst, Gustav Theodore

**Von Homberg, Otto**
See Geise, [Dr.] Otto

**Von Horn, Eylard Theodore**
?-1948 [AS]
*American auto racer*
* Horn, Ted

**Von Horn, W. O.**
See Oertel, Philipp Friedrich
Wilhelm

**Von Ingerslaven, Emma** [PA]
*Author*
* Von Rotherfels, E.

**Von Jordis, Eelco**
See Van Vormizeele, Eelco Voet

**Von Kaschnitz-Weinberg, Marie
Luise** 1901-1974 [CA]
*German poet, author, playwright*
* Kaschnitz, Marie Luise

**Von Keller, Adalbert** 1820-1882
[WBD]
*Hungarian conductor and composer*
* Keler, Bela

**Von Klopp, Vahrah**
See Malvern, Gladys

**Von Koerber, Hans Nordewin**
1886- [CA]
*German-born educator and author*
* Euphemides, Aristes

**Von Kolnitz, Alfred Holmes**
1893-1948 [BE]
*American baseball player*
* Von Kolnitz, Fritz

**Von Kolnitz, Fritz**
See Von Kolnitz, Alfred Holmes

**Von L., Detlev**
See Liliencron, Friedrich [Axel
Adolf]

**Von Lang, Jochen**
See Von Lang-Piechocki, Joachim

**Von Lang-Piechocki, Joachim**
1925- [CA]
*German author, editor, producer*
* Von Lang, Jochen

**Von Lauchen, Georg Joachim**
1514-1576 [WBD]
*German astronomer and
mathematician*
* Rhaeticus [or Rheticus]

**Von Lehndorff, Vera** 1943-
*Actress and artist*
* Veruschka

**Von Lewinski, Fritz Erich** 1887-
[WBD]
*German army officer*
* Mannstein, Fritz Erich von

**Von Losch, Marie Magdalene**
See Dietrich, Marie Magdalene

**Von Muench-Bellinghausen, Eligius**
1806-1871 [WBD]
*German poet and playwright*
* Halm, Friedrich

**Von Nordenwald, Erich Oswald Hans
Carl Stroheim** 1885-1957
[BEW, F1, FC]
*Austrian-born actor and director*
* Von Stroheim, Erich

**Von Oberndorff, Carl**
See Oberndorff, [Count] Charles

**Von Ohl, Adele** 1885-1966 [SC]
*American actress, stunt and rodeo
performer*
* Parker, Adele

**Von Ohlen, Baron**
See Von Ohlen, John

**Von Ohlen, John** 1941- [EJ7]
*American jazz musician*
* Von Ohlen, Baron

**Von Oleuschtaeger, Johann Daniel**
1711-1778 [PA]
*Author*
* Olearius

**Von Opel, Maria-Christina** 1951?-
*German heiress involved in drug
smuggling operation*
* Von Opel, Putzi

**Von Opel, Putzi**
See Von Opel, Maria-Christina

**Von Ost, Henry Lerner** 1915- [CA]
*American author, radio and
television performer, comedian*
* Morgan, Henry

**Von Rachen, Kurt**
See Hubbard, Lafayette Ronald

**Von Redlich, Marcellus Donald A. R.**
1893- [NAA]
*Austrian-born author and legal
scholar*
* Comes
* Diplomat
* Donaldus
* Redlich, Marcellus Donald

**Von Reinhold, Calvin**
See Von Reinhold Lutz, Calvin
Jack

**Von Reinhold Lutz, Calvin Jack**
1927- [BEW]
*Canadian dancer, choreographer,
singer*
* Von Reinhold, Calvin

**Von Richthofen, Manfred Freiherr**
1892-1918 [NN]
*German military aviator*
* [The] Red Baron

**Von Rotherfels, E.**
See Von Ingerslaven, Emma

**Von Rudloff, Alfred Felix** 1902-
[CAT]
*German-born American author and
clergyman*
* Rudloff, Leo

**Von Scherler, Sasha**
See Von Schoeler,
Alexandra-Xenia Elizabeth Anne
Marie Fiesola

**Von Schmidt, Ferdinand** [PA]
*Author*
* Dranmor

**Von Schoeler, Alexandra-Xenia
Elizabeth Anne Marie Fiesola**
1939- [TR]
*American actress*
* Von Scherler, Sasha

**Von Schwarzenfeld, Gertrude**
See Cochrane De Alencar,
Gertrude Emanuela Luise

**Von Sechten**
See Siegen, Ludwig von

**Von Seyffertitz, Gustav** 1863-1943
[SC]
*Austrian-born actor and director*
* Clonblough, G. Butler

**Von Sittewald, Philander**
See Moscherosch [or Mosenrosh],
Johann Michael

**Von Stackelberg-Treutlein, Freda
Fanny Erica** 1929- [AW]
*Estonian-born author*
* Genter, Harry

**Von Stade, Flicka**
See Von Stade, Frederica

**Von Stade, Frederica** 1945?-
*American opera singer*
* Von Stade, Flicka

**Von Sternberg, Josef**
See Sternberg, Jonas

**Von Storch, Anne B.** 1910-
[CAP, SAT]
*American author*
* Malcolmson, Anne

**Von Strensch, Gunther** 1889-1963
[SC]
*American actor, opera singer,
director*
* L'Estrange, Dick

**Von Stroheim, Erich**
See Von Nordenwald, Erich
Oswald Hans Carl Stroheim

**Von Suttner, Bertha** 20th c.
*Austrian baroness*
* Von Suttner, Peace Bertha

**Von Suttner, Peace Bertha**
See Von Suttner, Bertha

**Von Sydow, Carl Adolf** 1929-
[BDF, IPA, OCF]
*Swedish actor*
* Von Sydow, Max

**Von Sydow, Max**
See Von Sydow, Carl Adolf

**Von Teller, Ivan Dahl** 20th c.
[BLB]
*American swindler*
* Anderson, Dutch
* Anderson, George

**Von Tempski, Armine**
See Ball, Armine

**Von Theumer, Ernst** 20th c. [WF]
*German director*
* Welles, Mel

**Von Tilzer, Albert**
See Gumm, Albert

**Von Tilzer, Harry**
See Gumm, Harry

**Von Tromlitz, A.**
See Von Witzleben, Karl Friedrich

**Von Vohning**
*See* Howard, Mrs. A. W. M.

**Von Walhofen, Baroness** [FFF]
*Entertainer*
* Lucca, Pauline

**Von Watt, Joachim** 1484-1551
[WBD]
*Swiss religious leader*
* Vadianus, Joachim

**Von Witzleben, Karl Friedrich**
1773-1839 [PA]
*Author*
* Von Tromlitz, A.

**Von Wohl, Ludwig** 1903-1961
[SFL]
*Author*
* De Wohl, Louis

**Von Zaytz, Giovanni**
*See* Zajc, Ivan

**Von Zesen, Philipp** 1619-1689
[PA]
*Author*
* Coesius

**Vonnegut, Kurt, Jr.** 1922- [WGT]
*American author*
* Ferdinand

**Voo-chee** 7th c. [FFF, HN, RH]
*Widow of King Tae-tsong of China*
* [The] Katherine de Medici of
China
* [The] Queen of Heaven

**Vorhees, Cy**
*See* Vorhees, Henry Bert

**Vorhees, Henry Bert** 1874-1910
[BE]
*American baseball player*
* Vorhees, Cy

**Vormius**
*See* Worm, Olaus

**Vorobeva, Maria** 1892- [B10]
*French artist*
* Marevna

**Vorster, Balthazar Johannes** 1915-
*South African prime minister*
* Vorster, Jackboot John

**Vorster, Jackboot John**
*See* Vorster, Balthazar Johannes

**Vorwarts, Marschall**
*See* Bluecher, Gebhard Leberecht
von

**Vos, Anna Beyera** 1919- [IAW]
*South African author*
* Minnaar-Vos, Anna

**Vos, Tonny**
*See* Vos-Dahmen Von Buccholz,
Tonny

**Vos-Dahmen Von Buccholz, Tonny**
1923- [IAW]
*Dutch author*
* Vos, Tonny

**Vosburg, F. W.** [FFF]
*American writer*
* Vigilant

**Vosburgh, Alfred**
*See* Whitman, Gayne

**Vosburgh, Alfred** 1890- [F1, F2]
*Actor*
* Whitman, Alfred

**Voskovec, George**
*See* Voskovec, Jiri

**Voskovec, Jiri** 1905- [BEW]
*Czech-born actor, playwright,
director*
* Voskovec, George

**Voss, Fatty**
*See* Voss, Frank

**Voss, Frank** 1888-1917 [SC]
*American actor*
* Voss, Fatty

**Voss, Tillie**
*See* Voss, Walter

**Voss, Walter** 20th c. [SMG]
*American football player*
* Voss, Tillie

**Voss, Werner** 1897-1917
*German fighter pilot*
* [The] Flying Hussar
* [The] Hussar of Krefeld

**Votre Solidite**
*See* D'Aubigne, Francoise

**Voudel, Jesse Vanden** 1587-1679
[PA]
*Author*
* Justus

**Vovsky, Salomon Mikhailovich**
1890-1948 [BEW]
*Russian actor and producer*
* Mikhoels, Salomon

**Vowinkel, John Henry** 1884-1966
[BE]
*American baseball player*
* Vowinkel, Rip

**Vowinkel, Rip**
*See* Vowinkel, John Henry

**Vox, Valentine**
*See* Walsh, John Henry

**[A] Voyager**
*See* Hill, George

**Voyageur**
*See* Allen, Cecil J[ohn]

**Voyant, Clair**
*See* Ackerman, Forrest J[ames]

**Voyle, Mary**
*See* Manning, Rosemary Joy

**Voynich, E. L.**
*See* Voynich, Ethel Lilian Boole

**Voynich, Ethel Lilian Boole**
1864-1960 [LC]
*British author*
* Voynich, E. L.

**Vradinnos, Zefiros**
*See* Hatzidakis, Nicholas

**Vrchlicky, Jaroslav**
*See* Frida, Emil

**Vredenburg, Mona** 1918- [THR]
*British dancer and choreographer*
* Inglesby, Mona

**Vriendt, Frans de** 1520?-1570
[DNNS, HN, WBD]
*Flemish painter*
* [The] Flemish Raphael
* Floris, Frans

**Vrijman, Jan**
*See* Hulsebos, Jan

**Vronsky, Victoria** 1909- [BBD]
*Russian musician*
* Vronsky, Vitya

**Vronsky, Vitya**
*See* Vronsky, Victoria

**Vroom, Paul**
*See* O'Sullivan, Paul

**Vrugt, J. P.** 1905-1960 [EWL]
*Dutch author*
* Blaman, Anna

**Vucerovich, William** 1918-1955
[AS, EAR]
*American auto racer*
* [The] Fresno Flash
* [The] Mad Russian
* Vukovich, Bill

**Vugteveen, Verna Aardema** 1911-
[CA]
*American author*
* Aardema, Verna

**Vujovic, Vladimir** 1922- [FC]
*French actor*
* Auclair, Michel

**Vukovich, Bill**
*See* Vucerovich, William

**Vulliamy, C[olwyn] E[dward]**
1886-1971 [CC, EMD, WW]
*British author*
* Rolls, Anthony

**Vulpius, Paul**
*See* Fodor, Ladislaus

**[The] Vulture**
*See* Regan, Phil[lip Raymond]

**Vuyk, Beb**
*See* De Willigen, Elisabeth

**Vynne, Eustace** 1921?- [B10]
*American yachtsman*
* Vynne, Sunny

**Vynne, Sunny**
*See* Vynne, Eustace

**Vyse, Bertie**
*See* Beckett, Arthur

# W

**W.**
See Prime, William Cowper

**W. C.**
See Chambers, [Sir] William

**W. C.**
See Cowley, William

**W. C. C.**
See Coward, William C.

**W. D.**
See Dudeney, Wilfred

**W. D.**
See Ness, Richard Derby

**W. E. F.**
See Flaharty, W. E.

**W. E. S.**
See Simmons, William E.

**W. H.**
See Herbert, William

**W. H. H.**
See Haseltine, W. H. H.

**W. H. R**
See Rule, William Harris

**W. J. D.**
See De La Mare, Walter [John]

**W. J. F.**
See Fitzpatrick, William John

**W. K.**
See Kingsford, William

**W. L. K.**
See Keese, William Linn

**W. P. H.**
See Hodgkinson, Wilfred Philip

**W. R. G.**
See Greg, William Rathburn

**W. R. H.**
See Hearst, William Randolph

**W. S.**
See Haring, G. W. H.

**W. S.**
See Spaulding, William

**W. S. L. S.**
See Lach-Szyrma, Wladislaw Somerville

**W. S. R.**
See Raleigh, Walter S.

**W. T. P.**
See Palmer, William Thomas

**W. U. R.**
See Richards, William Upton

**W. W.**
See Bloom, William

**Wa-hun-sen-a-cawh [or Wahunsonacook]** 1550?- 1618 [WBD]
*American Indian chieftain*
* Powhatan

**Wa-Sha-Quon-Asin** 1888-1938 [WBD]
*Canadian-Indian author*
* Grey Owl

**Wabash George Mullin**
See Mullin, George Joseph

**Wabbes, Maria** 20th c. [IBY]
*Illustrator*
* Florence

**Wabun [East Wind]**
See James, Marlise Ann

**Wace, Robert** 1120-1180 [PA]
*Author*
* Wistace, Grace

**Wachenheimer, Fred** 1915- [JL]
*American television executive and producer*
* Friendly, Fred W.

**Wacher, August** 1862- ? [BE]
*American baseball player*
* Sunday, Art[hur]

**Wachsmann, Franz** 1906-1967 [FC, PMJ, WEF]
*German-born composer*
* Waxman, Franz

**Wachtel, Robert** 20th c. [RM]
*Musician*
* Wachtel, Waddy

**Wachtel, Waddy**
See Wachtel, Robert

**Waddel, Charles Carey** 1868-1930 [WW]
*Author*
* Carey, Charles

**Waddell, Evelyn Margaret** 1918- [CA, SAT, WD]
*Canadian author*
* Cook, Lyn

**Waddell, George Edward** 1876-1914 [AS, BE, PB]
*American baseball player*
* Waddell, Rube

**Waddell, James** 1739-1805 [FFF]
*Irish-born American clergyman*
* [The] Blind Preacher

**Waddell, Rube**
See Waddell, George Edward

**Waddell, Samuel J.** 1879-1967 [LC]
*Irish playwright*
* Mayne, Rutherford

**Waddington, Miriam** 1917- [CA]
*Canadian author*
* Merritt, E. B.

**Waddles, Charleszetta Campbell** 1913- [IBW]
*American clergywoman*
* Detroit's Black Angel

**Wade, A. E.**
See Wade, Arthur Edward

**Wade, Abraham Lincoln** 1880-1968 [BE]
*American baseball player*
* Wade, Ham

**Wade, Alan**
See Vance, John Holbrook [Jack]

**Wade, Arthur Edward** 1895- [ART]
*Welsh painter*
* Wade, A. E.

**Wade, Bill**
See Barrett, Geoffrey John

**Wade, Doc**
See Wade, Harold

**Wade, Gale**
See Wade, Galeard Lee

**Wade, Galeard Lee** 1929- [BE]
*American baseball player*
* Wade, Gale

**Wade, George Alfred** 1863- ? [WWL]
*British author*
* [The] Scholar Gypsy
* Vennew, Norman R.

**Wade, George Edward** 1869-1954 [BEW, EMT, F1]
*British comic actor*
* [The] Prime Minister of Mirth
* Robey, [Sir] George

**Wade, Ham**
See Wade, Abraham Lincoln

**Wade, Harold** 20th c. [RO2]
*American musician*
* Wade, Doc

**Wade, Henry**
See Aubrey-Fletcher, [Sir] Henry Lancelot

**Wade, Herbert**
See Wales, Hugh Gregory

**Wade, Jacob Fields** 1912- [BE]
*American baseball player*
* Wade, Whistlin' Jake

**Wade, Jake**
See Wade, Julius Jennings

**Wade, Jennifer**
See Wehen, Joy DeWeese

**Wade, Joanna**
See Berckman, Evelyn Domenica

**Wade, John** [PA]
*Author*
* J. W.

**Wade, John Stevens**
See Stevens, Clysle

**Wade, Julius Jennings** 20th c. [BBH]
*American sportswriter and columnist*
* Wade, Jake

**Wade, Kit**
See Carson, Xanthus

**Wade, Malcolm** 1914- [BB]
*American basketball player*
* Wade, Sparky

**Wade, Richard Frank** 1899-1957 [BE]
*American baseball player*
* Wade, Rip

**Wade, Rip**
See Wade, Richard Frank

**Wade, Robert**
See McIlwain, David

**Wade, Robert [Bob]** 1920- [EMD, WW]
*American author*
* Masterson, Whit [joint pseudonym with Bill Miller]
* Miller, Wade [joint pseudonym with Bill Miller]
* Wilmer, Dale [joint pseudonym with Bill Miller]

**Wade, Rosalind Herschel** 1909-
[CAP, WD]
*British author and poet*
* Carr, Catharine

**Wade, Sparky**
*See* Wade, Malcolm

**Wade, Whistlin' Jake**
*See* Wade, Jacob Fields

**Wadekin, Karl-Eugen**
*See* Waedekin, Karl-Eugen

**Wadelton, Maggie Jeanne** 1896-
[SFL]
*Author*
* Wadelton, Maggie-Owen

**Wadelton, Maggie-Owen**
*See* Wadelton, Maggie Jeanne

**Wadinasi, Sedeka**
*See* Nall, Hiram Abiff

**Wadkar, Hansa** 1924-1971    [SC]
*Indian actress*
* Wadkar, Swan

**Wadkar, Swan**
*See* Wadkar, Hansa

**Wadkins, Jerry Lanston** 1951-
[EG]
*American golfer*
* Wadkins, Lanny

**Wadkins, Lanny**
*See* Wadkins, Jerry Lanston

**Wadlow, M. Marie** 20th c.    [BBH]
*American softball player*
* Wadlow, Waddy

**Wadlow, Waddy**
*See* Wadlow, M. Marie

**Wadman, Elmer E.**    [FFF]
*American writer*
* Ellsworth

**Waedekin, Karl-Eugen** 1921-    [CA]
*German educator and author*
* Wadekin, Karl-Eugen

**Wagenhurst, Elwood Otto**
1863-1946    [BE]
*American baseball player*
* Wagenhurst, Woodie

**Wagenhurst, Woodie**
*See* Wagenhurst, Elwood Otto

**Wager, Mary A. E.**    [FFF, PA]
*Author*
* Mintwood

**Wager, Michael**
*See* Weisgal, Emanuel

**Wager, Walter Herman** 1924-
[IAW]
*American author*
* Tiger, John

**Waggamon, Mary T.**    [FFF]
*American writer*
* Fairie, Fanny
* Queerquill

**Waggner, George**
*See* Waggoner, George

**Waggoner, George** 1894-    [FD]
*American director*
* Waggner, George

**Waghorn, H. L.**
*See* Horn, Holloway

**Wagman, Naomi** 1937-    [CA]
*Irsaeli-born writer*
* Newmar, Rima

**Wagmann, Adam** 1905-    [EWL]
*Polish poet and author*
* Wazyk, Adam

**Wagmuller, Charlotte** 20th c.
*Actress*
* Susa, Charlotte

**Wagner, Albert** 1869-1928    [BE]
*American baseball player*
* Wagner, Butts

**Wagner, Aubrey** 20th c.
*American industrialist*
* Wagner, Red

**Wagner, Broadway**
*See* Wagner, Charles Thomas

**Wagner, Bull**
*See* Wagner, William George

**Wagner, Butts**
*See* Wagner, Albert

**Wagner, C[harles] Peter** 1930-
[CA]
*American author and editor*
* Epafrodito
* Underwood, Lewis Graham

**Wagner, Charles F.** 1881-1943
[BE]
*American baseball player*
* Wagner, Heinie

**Wagner, Charles Thomas** 1912-
[BE]
*American baseball player*
* Wagner, Broadway

**Wagner, Cheekie [or Cheeks]**
*See* Wagner, Leon Lamar

**Wagner, Daddy Wags**
*See* Wagner, Leon Lamar

**Wagner, Danny, Jr.** 1968-    [IBW]
*American karate expert*
* Wagner, Little Man

**Wagner, Eddie** 20th c.    [EJS]
*American boxer*
* Wagner, Kid

**Wagner, Emmet** ?-1977    [FIR]
*Actor*
* Wagner, Kid

**Wagner, Ernest B.** 20th c.    [BBH]
*American basketball coach*
* Wagner, Griz

**Wagner, Frank**
*See* Wagner, Franklin A.

**Wagner, Franklin A.** 20th c.
[BEW]
*American choreographer, director,
educator*
* Wagner, Frank

**Wagner, George Raymond**
1915-1963    [SC, SR]
*American wrestler*
* Gorgeous George

**Wagner, Griz**
*See* Wagner, Ernest B.

**Wagner, Gustav Franz** 1912?-
*German Nazi police official*
* [The] Human Beast

**Wagner, Hans**
*See* Wagner, John Peter

**Wagner, Hans** 1872- ?    [LAO]
*German author*
* Wagner-Schoenkirch, Hans

**Wagner, Heinie**
*See* Wagner, Charles F.

**Wagner, Honus**
*See* Wagner, John Peter

**Wagner, John Peter** 1874-1955
[AS, BAB, BE]
*American baseball player*
* [The] Flying Dutchman
* Wagner, Hans
* Wagner, Honus

**Wagner, Kid**
*See* Wagner, Eddie

**Wagner, Kid**
*See* Wagner, Emmet

**Wagner, Leon Lamar** 1934-
[BE, DGS, PB]
*American baseball player*
* Wagner, Cheekie [or Cheeks]
* Wagner, Daddy Wags
* Wagner, Wag

**Wagner, Little Man**
*See* Wagner, Danny, Jr.

**Wagner, Mark Duane** 1954-
[SMG]
*American baseball player*
* Wagner, Peanut

**Wagner, Peanut**
*See* Wagner, Mark Duane

**Wagner, Red**
*See* Wagner, Aubrey

**Wagner, [Wilhelm] Richard**
1813?-1883?    [HN]
*German composer*
* [The] Michael Angelo of Opera
* [The] Shakespeare of Harmony

**Wagner, Wag**
*See* Wagner, Leon Lamar

**Wagner, William George**
1887-1967    [BE]
*American baseball player*
* Wagner, Bull

**Wagner-Schoenkirch, Hans**
*See* Wagner, Hans

**Wago, Bob Allotey** 1943-    [RBE]
*Ghanaian boxer*
* Allotey, Bob

**[The] Wagon Boy**
*See* Corwin, Thomas

**Wagon Tongue Adams**
*See* Adams, Joseph Edward [Joe]

**Wagon Tongue Keister**
*See* Keister, William Hoffman

**Wagoner, Hank**
*See* Mosher, L. E.

**Wagstaff, Harold** 1891-1939
[OCS]
*British rugby player*
* [The] Prince of Centres

**Wagstaff, Theophile**
*See* Thackeray, William
Makepeace

**Wagstaffe, Launcelot, Jr.**
*See* Mackay, Charles

**Wahl, Lou**
*See* Schaffenberger, Kurt

**Wahl, Thomas [Peter]** 1931-    [CA]
*American clergyman and author*
* Caedmon, [Father]

**Wahl, Walter Dare**
*See* Kalwara, Walter

**Wahloo, Per** 1926-1975    [CA]
*Swedish author*
* Wahloo, Peter

**Wahloo, Peter**
*See* Wahloo, Per

**[The] Wahoo Barber**
*See* Crawford, Samuel Earl

**Wahoo Sam Crawford**
*See* Crawford, Samuel Earl

**Wainer, Cord**
*See* Dewey, Thomas B[lanchard]

**Wainewright, Thomas Griffiths**
1794-1852    [WBD]
*British art critic and forger*
* Weathercock, Janus

**Wainscott, Cricket**
*See* Blakely, Paul Lendrum

**Wainwright, Gordon Ray** 1937-
[AW, WD]
*British educator and author*
* Gordon, Ray

**Wainwright, Ken**
*See* Tubb, Edwin Charles

**Wainwright, Marie**
*See* James, Mrs. Louis

**Wait**
*See* Frankenstein, George L.

**Wait, Frona Eunice**
*See* Colburn, Frona Eunice Wait

**Waite, A. E.**
*See* Waite, Arthur Edward

**Waite, Arthur Edward** 1857-1942
[LC]
*British poet and author*
* Waite, A. E.

**Waite, Charles** ?-1951    [SC]
*Actor*
* Levance, Cal

**Waite, Deacon**
*See* Waite, Frank E.

**Waite, Frank E.** 1906-    [CEI]
*Canadian-born hockey player*
* Waite, Deacon

**Waite, Victor**
*See* Makgill, [Sir] George

**[The] Waiter**
*See* DeLucia, Felice

**Waitford, Hannah**
*See* Hume, David

**Wajcieckowski, Earl** 1898-1926
[BLB, MM, PHM]
*American underworld figure*
* Hymie the Polack
* [The] Perfume Burglar
* Weiss, Earl
* Weiss, Hymie
* Weiss, Little Hymie

**Wajditsch Verbovac Von Doenhoff,
[Baron] Gabriel** 1888-1969 [BBD]
*Hungarian-born American composer*
* Wayditch, Gabriel

**Wajsowna, Jadwiga**
*See* Weiss, Pana

**[The] Wake**
*See* Hereward

**Wake, Nancy** 1916- [BDW]
*Australian-born journalist and
intelligence agent*
* Andree, Madame
* Carlier, Lucienne

**Wakefield, Elizabeth**
*See* Montgomery, Mamie
Elizabeth

**Wakefield, Jean L.**
*See* Laird, Jean E[louise]

**Wakefield, John**
*See* Darling, John

**Wakefield, [Father] John**
*See* Walsh, James Anthony

**Wakefield, R. I.**
*See* White, Gertrude M[ason]

**Wakeford, William** 1863- ? [THR]
*British theatrical manager*
* Albert, William

**Wakenshaw, Janet Mackie** 1951-
[IAW]
*Scottish journalist*
* Fielding, Ann

**Wako, Mdogo**
*See* Nazareth, Peter

**Wakoski, Diane** 1937- [CA]
*American poet*
* Wakoski-Sherbell, Diane

**Wakoski-Sherbell, Diane**
*See* Wakoski, Diane

**Walasiewicz, Stella** 1911- [OCS]
*Polish-born American sprinter*
* Walsh, Stella

**Walberg, George Elvin** 1899-
[BE, PB]
*American baseball player*
* Walberg, Rube

**Walberg, Rube**
*See* Walberg, George Elvin

**Walbrook, Anton**
*See* Wohlbrueck, Adolf

**Walch, Jakob**
*See* Barbari, Jacopo de'

**Walcott, Eugene** 20th c. [SG]
*Boxer*
* Meehan, Willie

**Walcott, Jersey Joe**
*See* Cream, Arnold Raymond

**Walcott, Joe** 1872-1935
[BX, RBE]
*Barbadian-born boxer*
* [The] Barbados Demon

**Walcott, Louis Gene** 1934- [IBW]
*American actor, musician, author*
* Farrakhan, Louis
* Louis X

**Walczak, Ed[win Joseph]** 1915-
[BE]
*American baseball player*
* Walczak, Husky

**Walczak, Husky**
*See* Walczak, Ed[win Joseph]

**Wald, Jerry**
*See* Wald, Jervis

**Wald, Jervis** 1918?-1973 [PMJ]
*American musician*
* Wald, Jerry

**Waldbauer, Albert Charles** 1898-
[BE]
*American baseball player*
* Waldbauer, Doc

**Waldbauer, Doc**
*See* Waldbauer, Albert Charles

**Waldemar [or Valdemar]**
1281?-1319 [DNNS, WBD]
*Margrave of Brandenburg*
* [The] Great

**Waldemar I** 1131-1182
[DNNS, SN, WBD]
*King of Denmark*
* [The] Great

**Waldemar II** 1170-1241 [WBD]
*King of Denmark*
* [The] Victorious

**Walden, Walter** 1870- ? [NAA]
*American author*
* Irving, Miles

**Walder, Herman** 20th c. [IEJ]
*American jazz musician*
* Walder, Woody

**Walder, Jimmy** 20th c. [AES]
*American soccer official*
* [The] Dean of Referees

**Walder, Woody**
*See* Walder, Herman

**Waldeyer, Wilhelm** 1836-1921
[WBD]
*German anatomist*
* Waldeyer-Hartz, Wilhelm von

**Waldeyer-Hartz, Wilhelm von**
*See* Waldeyer, Wilhelm

**Waldmueller, Robert**
*See* Duboc, Edouard

**Waldo, Cedric Dane**
*See* Wolff, Cecil Drummond

**Waldo, Dave**
*See* Clarke, D[avid] Waldo

**Waldo, E. Hunter**
*See* Waldo, Edward Hamilton

**Waldo, Edward Hamilton** 1918-
[CA, ESF, HFF]
*American author*
* Ewing, Frederick R.
* Hunter, E. Waldo
* Sturgeon, Theodore Hamilton
* Waldo, E. Hunter
* Watson, Billy

**Waldo, James Curtis** 1835-1901
[FFF]
*American writer*
* Linkinwater, Tim

**Waldo, Pierre** 1120-1170 [HN]
*Leader of religious sect*
* [The] Morning Star of
Reformation

**Waldo, Ralph Emerson, III** 1944-
[CA]
*American author, musician,
composer*
* Waldo, Terry

**Waldo, Terry**
*See* Waldo, Ralph Emerson, III

**Waldorf, Lynn O.** 1902- [FB]
*American football coach*
* Waldorf, Pappy

**Waldorf, Pappy**
*See* Waldorf, Lynn O.

**Waldron, Colin** 1948- [SMG]
*British soccer player*
* Waldron, Waldo

**Waldron, D'Lynn**
*See* Waldron-Shah, Diane Lynn

**Waldron, George** 1755-1840?
[WBD]
*Irish author*
* Barrington, George

**Waldron, Jack**
*See* Baum, Jacob Kestem

**Waldron, Kenny** 20th c. [RBE]
*American boxer*
* Weldon, Kenny

**Waldron, Marion Patton** 20th c.
[NAA]
*American author*
* Patton, Marion

**Waldron, Waldo**
*See* Waldron, Colin

**Waldron-Shah, Diane Lynn** 1936-
[CA]
*American author*
* Waldron, D'Lynn

**Waldrop, Gid**
*See* Waldrop, Gideon William
Winthrop, Jr.

**Waldrop, Gideon William Winthrop,
Jr.** 1919- [ASC, BEW]
*American composer, conductor,
educator*
* Waldrop, Gid

**Waldstein, Charles** 1856-1927
[WBD, WWL]
*American-born archaeologist*
* Seymour, Gordon
* Walston, [Sir] Charles

**Waldus, Edythe**
*See* Sudlow, Elizabeth Williams

**Wale, Henry** 1891-1970 [FC]
*British actor*
* Oscar, Henry

**Walenn, Cecil** 1865?-1949 [THR]
*British theatrical manager*
* Barth, Cecil

**Walentoski, Norman Edward**
1917- [BE]
*American baseball player*
* Wallen, Norm[an Edward]

**Wales, Geoffrey** 1912- [ART]
*British engraver*
* G. W.

**Wales, Hubert**
*See* Pigott, William

**Wales, Hugh Gregory** 1910- [CA]
*American educator and author*
* Wade, Herbert

**Wales, Nym**
*See* Snow, Helen Foster

**Wales, Peleg**
*See* Croffut, William A.

**Wales, Wally**
*See* Alderson, Floyd Taliaferro

**Walesa, Lech** 1943?-
*Polish labor leader*
* Walesa, Leszek

**Walesa, Leszek**
*See* Walesa, Lech

**Waley, Arthur**
*See* Schloss, Arthur David

**Walford, Bessy G.** [PA]
*Author*
* Walford, Flora

**Walford, Christian**
*See* Dilcock, Noreen

**Walford, Cornelius** [FFF, PA]
*Writer*
* Junius

**Walford, Flora**
*See* Walford, Bessy G.

**Walford, J. H.** [FFF]
*British writer*
* Detached Badger

**Walker, Aaron Thibeaux**
1910-1975 [BWW, DAM, EJ]
*American singer and songwriter*
* [The] Daddy of the Blues
* Oak Cliff T-Bone
* Walker, T Bone

**Walker, Albert Bluford** 1926-
[BE, PB, SMG]
*American baseball player, manager,
coach*
* Walker, Rube

**Walker, Alvin** 1954- [SMG]
*American football player*
* Walker, Skip

**Walker, Anna** 1891- [THR]
*Irish actress*
* O'Doherty, Eileen

**Walker, Barbara K[erlin]** 1921-
[CA, SAT]
*American author*
* Kilreon, Beth

**Walker, Bee**
*See* Walker, Bertha

**Walker, Bertha** 1908- [ASC]
*American composer*
* Walker, Bee

**Walker, Bessie**
*See* Henry, Bessie Walker

**Walker, Big**
*See* Walker, Edsell

**Walker, Blind Willie**
*See* Walker, Willie

**Walker, Blue**
*See* Walker, Tim

**Walker, Bob** 20th c. [GW]
*American rodeo performer*
* Walker, Cowboy

**Walker, Bronc Man**
*See* Walker, Enoch

**Walker, Charles Herbert**
1867-1947 [SC]
*American actor*
* Walker, Tex

**Walker, Chet** 1940- [BB]
*American basketball player*
* [The] Jet

**Walker, Clarence** 1951-
[NBA, SMG]
*American basketball player*
* Walker, Foots

**Walker, Clarence William**
1889-1959 [AS, BE, PB]
*American baseball player*
* Walker, Tilly

**Walker, Clifton Reginald** [SFL]
*Author*
* Dixon, Richard

**Walker, Cowboy**
*See* Walker, Bob

**Walker, Curt**
*See* Walker, William Curtis

**Walker, Dimples**
*See* Wolke, Lillian

**Walker, Dixie**
*See* Walker, Ewart Gladstone

**Walker, Dixie**
*See* Walker, Frederick E.

**Walker, Dixie**
*See* Walker, James Roy

**Walker, [Ewell] Doak, Jr.** 1927-
[FB]
*American football player*
* Walker, Doaker

**Walker, Doaker**
*See* Walker, [Ewell] Doak, Jr.

**Walker, Douglas C.** 1899?-1970
[AS, CFH, FB]
*American football coach*
* Walker, Peahead

**Walker, Edmund** 1934?- [FC, TR]
*British actor*
* Kemp, Jeremy

**Walker, Edsell** 20th c. [OBW]
*American baseball player*
* Walker, Big

**Walker, Edward Patrick**
1901-1981 [BX, RBE]
*American boxer*
* [The] Toy Bulldog
* Walker, Mickey

**Walker, Elocution**
*See* Walker, John

**Walker, Emily Kathleen** 1913-
[AW, WD]
*British author*
* Ash, Pauline
* Devon, Sarah
* Durham, Anne
* Ellis, Louise
* Lester, Jane
* Murray, Jill
* Tilbury, Quenna
* Treves, Kathleen
* Winchester, Kay

**Walker, Emmeline Lisle** [FFF]
*Author*
* Lisle, Lester

**Walker, Enoch** 20th c. [GW]
*American rodeo performer*
* Walker, Bronc Man

**Walker, Ewart Gladstone**
1887-1965 [BE]
*American baseball player*
* Walker, Dixie

**Walker, Fleet**
*See* Walker, Moses Fleetwood

**Walker, Foots**
*See* Walker, Clarence

**Walker, Frederick E.** 1910-
[BE, DGS, PB]
*American baseball player*
* [The] People's Cherce
* Walker, Dixie

**Walker, Frederick Mitchell**
1884-1958
*American baseball player*
* Walker, Mysterious

**Walker, Gee**
*See* Walker, Gerald Holmes

**Walker, George** 1915-1967 [MK]
*American baseball player*
* Walker, Schoolboy

**Walker, George Alfred** 1807-1884
[FFF]
*Welsh physician*
* Walker, Graveyard

**Walker, Gerald Holmes** 1908-1981
[BE, PB]
*American baseball player*
* Walker, Gee

**Walker, Glenn** 20th c. [IBW]
*American scientist*
* Walker, Sonny

**Walker, Graveyard**
*See* Walker, George Alfred

**Walker, Harry**
*See* Waugh, Hillary Baldwin

**Walker, Harry William** 1918-
[BE, PB, SMG]
*American baseball player, manager, team owner*
* [The] Hat

**Walker, Harvey Willos** 1906- [BE]
*American baseball player*
* Walker, Hub

**Walker, Heather Eulalie** 1908-
[CED]
*American actress*
* Walker, Polly

**Walker, Holly Beth**
*See* Bond, Gladys Baker

**Walker, Hookey**
*See* Walker, John

**Walker, Hoss**
*See* Walker, Jesse

**Walker, Hub**
*See* Walker, Harvey Willos

**Walker, Ira**
*See* Walker, Irma Ruth [Roden]

**Walker, Irma Ruth [Roden]** 1921-
[CA]
*American author*
* Walker, Ira

**Walker, J.**
*See* Crawford, John Richard

**Walker, J. Donald** 1927- [NAD]
*Spiritual teacher*
* Kriyananda, [Swami]

**Walker, Jack**
*See* Thayer, Frederick C[lifton], Jr.

**Walker, James** 1912?-1949 [WWJ]
*American jazz musician*
* Walker, Jim Daddy

**Walker, James Roy** 1893-1962
[BE]
*American baseball player*
* Walker, Dixie

**Walker, Jerry Jeff**
*See* Crosby, Ronald

**Walker, Jesse** 20th c. [OBW]
*American baseball player*
* Walker, Hoss

**Walker, Jim Daddy**
*See* Walker, James

**Walker, John** [DNNF, FFF]
*British clerk*
* Walker, Hookey

**Walker, John** 1732-1807 [DEL]
*British lexicographer*
* Walker, Elocution

**Walker, John** 1861- ? [LAO]
*British author*
* Thirlmere, Rowland

**Walker, John Mayon [Johnny]**
1929- [BWW]
*American singer*
* Big Moose
* Moose John

**Walker, Junior**
*See* DeWalt, Autrey, Jr.

**Walker, Katherine C.** [FFF]
*Writer*
* Kind, K. K.

**Walker, Kenneth Francis** 1924-
[CA]
*British-born physician and author*
* Gifford-Jones, W.

**Walker, Kenneth MacFarlane**
1882-1966 [CA]
*British physician and author*
* MacFarlane, Kenneth

**Walker, Lillian**
*See* Wolke, Lillian

**Walker, Lucy**
*See* Sanders, Dorothy Lucie

**Walker, Mickey**
*See* Walker, Edward Patrick

**Walker, Mildred**
*See* Schemm, Mildred Walker

**Walker, [Addison] Mort[imer]**
1923- [WECO]
*American cartoonist*
* Addison

**Walker, Moses Fleetwood**
1857-1924 [BE, IBW, OBW]
*American baseball player*
* Walker, Fleet

**Walker, Mrs. D. M. F.** [FFF, PA]
*Author*
* Mar, Helen

**Walker, Mysterious**
*See* Walker, Frederick Mitchell

**Walker, Nancy**
*See* Swoyer, Anna Myrtle

**Walker, Peahead**
*See* Walker, Douglas C.

**Walker, Peter Norman** 1936-
[AW, CA]
*British author*
* Coram, Christopher
* Ferris, Tom
* Manton, Paul
* Rhea, Nicholas

**Walker, Polly**
*See* Walker, Heather Eulalie

**Walker, Rachel**
*See* Lenoir, Lucie

**Walker, Rose**
*See* Dowsey, Rose Walker

**Walker, Rowland** 20th c.
[MBF, WWL]
*British author*
* Blair, Anthony
* Kenworthy, Hugh

**Walker, Rube**
*See* Walker, Albert Bluford

**Walker, Schoolboy**
*See* Walker, George

**Walker, Shel**
*See* Sheldon, Walt[er J.]

**Walker, Sidney** 1921-
[BX, IBW, RBE]
*American boxer*
* [The] Battlin' Shoeshine Boy
* Battling Beau Jack
* Beau, Jack

**Walker, Skip**
*See* Walker, Alvin

**Walker, Sonny**
*See* Walker, Glenn

**Walker, Stella Archer** 20th c.
[WD]
*British author*
* Archer-Batten, S.

**Walker, Syd**
*See* Kirkman, Sidney

**Walker, T Bone**
*See* Walker, Aaron Thibeaux

**Walker, T Bone, Jr.**
*See* Rankin, R. S.

**Walker, T. Michael** 1937- [CA]
*American author*
* White Elk, Michael

**Walker, Tex**
*See* Walker, Charles Herbert

**Walker, Thomas** 1850?-1934
[BEW]
*Entertainer*
* Walker, Whimsical

**Walker, Tilly**
*See* Walker, Clarence William

**Walker, Tim** 20th c. [RBE]
*American boxer*
* Walker, Blue

**Walker, Whimsical**
*See* Walker, Thomas

**Walker, William Curtis** 1896-1955 [DGS]
*American baseball player*
* Walker, Curt

**Walker, William Marvin [Billy]** 1929- [ECM, FCW]
*American country-western performer*
* [The] Masked Singer of Country Songs
* [The] Traveling Texan

**Walker, William Sidney** 1795-1846 [PA]
*Author*
* Haselfoot, Edward

**Walker, William Sylvester** 1846- ? [WWL]
*Scottish author*
* Coo-Ee

**Walker, Willie** 1896-1933 [BWW]
*American singer*
* Walker, Blind Willie

**Walkerley, Rodney Lewis [De Burgh]** 1905- [CAP]
*British author*
* Athos
* Vitesse, Grande

**Walkin' Joe Teasdale**
*See* Teasdale, Joseph

**Walkin' Lawton Chiles**
*See* Chiles, Lawton

**Walkin' Slim**
*See* Minter, Iverson

**[The] Walking Gallows**
*See* Hepenstall, Edward

**[A] Walking Gentleman**
*See* Grattan, Thomas Colley

**[A] Walking Library**
*See* Hales, John

**[The] Walking Library**
*See* Longinus, Dionysius Cassius

**[The] Walking Man**
*See* Yost, Edward Frederick Joseph

**[The] Walking Morgue**
*See* Harper, Lucius Clinton

**[The] Walking Museum**
*See* Longinus, Dionysius Cassius

**[The] Walking Polyglot**
*See* Agnesi, Maria Gaetana

**[The] Walking Polyglot**
*See* Mezzofanti, Giuseppe

**Walkinshaw, Colin**
*See* Reid, James Macarthur

**Walkley, A. B.**
*See* Walkley, Arthur Bingham

**Walkley, Arthur Bingham** 1855-1926 [LC, WWL]
*British drama critic*
* Spectator
* Walkley, A. B.

**Walkup, Fairfax Proudfit**
*See* Proudfit, Fairfax

**Wall, Barbara** 1911- [CAT]
*British author*
* Lucas, Barbara

**Wall, Corinna** 1910-1965 [SC]
*Actress and singer*
* Mura, Corrine

**Wall, Gummy**
*See* Wall, Joseph Francis [Joe]

**Wall, John William** 1910- [ESF, SFL, WGT]
*British author*
* Sarban

**Wall, Joseph Francis [Joe]** 1873-1936 [BE]
*American baseball player*
* Wall, Gummy

**Wall, Max**
*See* Lorimer, Maxwell George

**Wall, Mrs. Henry** [FFF]
*Entertainer*
* Holt, Elise

**Wall, Murray Wesley** 1926-1971 [BE]
*American baseball player*
* Wall, Tex

**Wall Street Bear in Europe**
*See* Young, Samuel

**Wall, Tex**
*See* Wall, Murray Wesley

**Wallace, Agnes**
*See* Villa, Mrs. Samuel B.

**Wallace, Alexander Fielding** 1918- [CA, WD]
*British author and translator*
* Fielding, A. W.
* Fielding, Xan

**Wallace, Babe**
*See* Wallace, Emmitt

**Wallace, Bad News**
*See* Wallace, Edgar

**Wallace, Beulah Thomas** 1898- [BWW]
*American singer*
* [The] Texas Nightingale
* Wallace, Sippie

**Wallace, Bill**
*See* Lally, William

**Wallace, Bobby**
*See* Wallace, Roderick John

**Wallace, Clarence Eugene** 1890-1960 [BE]
*American baseball player*
* Wallace, Jack

**Wallace, Cookie**
*See* Wallace, Roy Dean

**Wallace, D. I. M.**
*See* Wallace, Donald Ian Mackenzie

**Wallace, David** 1948-
*American author*
* Wallechinsky, David

**Wallace, Dexter**
*See* Masters, Edgar Lee

**Wallace, Doc**
*See* Wallace, Frederick Renshaw

**Wallace, Donald Ian Mackenzie** 1933- [ART]
*British artist*
* Wallace, D. I. M.

**Wallace, Doreen**
*See* Rash, Dora Eileen Agnew [Wallace]

**Wallace, [Richard Horatio] Edgar**
*See* Wallace, Walter

**Wallace, Edgar** 20th c. [RBE]
*American boxer*
* Wallace, Bad News

**Wallace, Emmitt** 20th c. [IBW]
*American entertainer and composer*
* Wallace, Babe

**Wallace, F. L.**
*See* Wallace, Floyd L.

**Wallace, Floyd L.** 20th c. [SF]
*American author*
* Wallace, F. L.

**Wallace, Frederick Renshaw** 1893-1964 [BE]
*American baseball player*
* Wallace, Doc

**Wallace, Gordon**
*See* Shaw, Stanley Gordon

**Wallace, Harry Clinton** 1882-1951 [BE]
*American baseball player*
* Wallace, Huck
* Wallace, Lefty

**Wallace, Helen** 20th c. [WWL]
*British author*
* Roy, Gordon

**Wallace, Henry** 20th c. [WWL]
*Scottish author*
* Chalom, John
* O'Dreams, John

**Wallace, Huck**
*See* Wallace, Harry Clinton

**Wallace, Ian**
*See* Pritchard, John Wallace

**Wallace, Jack**
*See* Wallace, Clarence Eugene

**Wallace, James Harold** 1921- [BE]
*American baseball player*
* Wallace, Lefty

**Wallace, Jean**
*See* Wallasek, Jean

**Wallace, Jennie**
*See* Dobson, Mrs. Frank

**Wallace, Jerry** 1933- [ECM]
*American singer and songwriter*
* Smooth, Mr.

**Wallace, John** 20th c. [WW]
*Author*
* Aintree
* Grantham, Gerald
* Texas Ranger

**Wallace, Laura**
*See* Mourdaunt, Mrs. Frank

**Wallace, Lefty**
*See* Wallace, Harry Clinton

**Wallace, Lefty**
*See* Wallace, James Harold

**Wallace, Lewis** 1827-1905 [DNNS, FFF, SN]
*American army officer, attorney, author*
* Louisa

**Wallace, May**
*See* Maddox, May

**Wallace, Mike**
*See* Wallace, Myron

**Wallace, Myron** 1918- [IPA]
*American television interviewer*
* Wallace, Mike

**Wallace, Nellie**
*See* Liddy, Eleanor Jane

**Wallace, Nigel**
*See* Hamilton, Charles Harold St. John

**[The] Wallace of Persia**
*See* Nadir Shah

**[The] Wallace of Switzerland**
*See* Hofer, Andreas

**[The] Wallace of Wales**
*See* Glendower, Owen

**Wallace, Pat** 1929- [CA]
*American author and poet*
* Cloud, Patricia
* Latner, Pat Wallace
* Lord, Vivian
* Strother, Pat Wallace

**Wallace, Paul**
*See* Willens, Paul Norton

**Wallace, Rhody**
*See* Wallace, Roderick John

**Wallace, Richard**
*See* Ind, Allison

**Wallace, Robert**
*See* Champion, D. L.

**Wallace, Roderick John** 1873-1960 [AS, BE, DGS]
*American baseball player and manager*
* Wallace, Bobby
* Wallace, Rhody

**Wallace, Roger**
*See* Charlier, Roger H[enri]

**Wallace, Roy Dean** 20th c. [RBE]
*American boxer*
* Wallace, Cookie

**Wallace, Ruby Ann** 1924- [BEW, FC, IPA]
*American actress*
* Dee, Ruby

**Wallace, Sippie**
*See* Wallace, Beulah Thomas

**Wallace, Sylvan**
*See* Ippoliti, Silvano

**Wallace, Ted**
*See* Kirkeby, Wallace Theodore

**Wallace, Vince**
*See* Gambino, Vincenzo

**Wallace, Walter** 1875-1932 [WGT]
*British author*
* Freeman, Richard [Dick]
* Wallace, [Richard Horatio] Edgar

**Wallace, [Sir] William** 1270?-1305 [DNNS, HN, RH]
*Scottish patriot*
* [The] Hammer and Scourge of England

**Wallace-Clarke, George** 1916- [WD]
*British author*
* Jaffa, George

**Wallach, [Dr.] Louis C.** 1886-1957
[BX, EJS, RBE]
*American boxer*
* Cross, Leach

**Wallach, Meir** 1867-1951    [JL]
*Russian government official*
* Litvinov, Maxim M.

**Wallack, John Johnstone**
1820-1888    [FFF, WBD]
*American-born actor and playwright*
* Field, Allan
* Wallack, Lester

**Wallack, Lester**
See   Wallack, John Johnstone

**Wallasek, Jean** 1923-    [FC]
*American actress*
* Wallace, Jean

**Wallechinsky, David**
See   Wallace, David

**Wallek, Lee**
See   Johnson, Curt[is Lee]

**Wallen, Norm[an Edward]**
See   Walentoski, Norman Edward

**Wallenberg, Gustav** 1904-1966
[SC]
*Swedish-born actor and producer*
* Wally, Gus

**Waller, Brown**
See   Fraser, Waller Brown

**Waller, Christopher Edward** 1948-
[DC]
*British cricketer*
* Waller, Wal

**Waller, Edmund** 1606-1687    [SN]
*British poet*
* [The] Father of English Numbers
* [The] Parent of English Verse

**Waller, Fats**
See   Waller, Thomas Wright

**Waller, John Francis** 1810-1894
[DEL, PA]
*Irish author and poet*
* Iota
* J. F. W.
* Slingsby, Jonathan Freke

**Waller, John Francis** 1883-1915
[BE]
*American baseball player*
* Waller, Red

**Waller, Leslie** 1923-
[CA, WGT, WW]
*American author*
* Cody, C. S.
* Mann, Patrick

**Waller, Lewis**
See   Lewis, William Waller

**Waller, M. E.**
See   Waller, Mary Ella

**Waller, Mary Ella** 1855-1938    [LC]
*American author*
* Waller, M. E.

**Waller, Red**
See   Waller, John Francis

**Waller, Thomas Wright** 1904-1943
[ASC, BBD, WWJ]
*American jazz musician*
* Waller, Fats

**Waller, Virginia Harmon**
See   Sefrit, Sallie Mulholland

**Waller, Wal**
See   Waller, Christopher Edward

**Waller, [Sir] William** 1597?-1668
[SN]
*British army officer*
* William the Conqueror

**Walley, David Gordon** 1945-
[IAW]
*American author*
* Tombs, Harry

**Wallin, Gunilla Lovisa** 1938-    [OP]
*Swedish opera singer*
* Slaettegard, Gunilla Lovisa

**Walling, R. A. J.**
See   Walling, Robert Alfred John

**Walling, Robert Alfred John**
1869-1949    [LC]
*British author*
* Walling, R. A. J.

**Wallington, George**
See   Figlia, Giorgio

**Wallington, Lord**
See   Figlia, Giorgio

**Wallis, B. and G. C.**
See   Wallis, George C.

**Wallis, Blanche** 1891-1918    [SC]
*American actress*
* Seelos, Annette

**Wallis, George C.** 20th c.
[ESF, MBF, SF]
*British author*
* Heath, Royston
* Stanton, John
* Wallis, B. and G. C.

**Wallis, Geraldine McDonald** 1925-
[CA, SAT]
*American author and actress*
* Campbell, Hope
* Hughes, Virginia
* McDonald, Cathy
* Wells, Helen

**Wallis, Harold Joseph** 1952-
[SMG]
*American baseball player*
* Wallis, Tarzan

**Wallis, Henry Marriage** 20th c.
[WWL]
*British author*
* Hilliers, Ashton

**Wallis, Ik**
See   Laughton, Thomas R.

**Wallis, Tarzan**
See   Wallis, Harold Joseph

**Wallmann, Jeffrey M[iner]** 1941-
[CA]
*American author*
* Baxter, Phyllis
* Carter, Nick [house pseudonym]
* DaSilva, Leon
* Douglass, Amanda Hart
* Goering, Helga
* Graham, Carlotta
* Granby, Milton
* Heflin, Donald
* Jensen, Peter
* Miner, Matthew
* Mountbatten, Richard
* Reskind, John
* Robard, Jackson
* Roberts, Grant
* Saxon, Bill
* Sheldon, Scott

**Wallmann, Jeffrey M[iner]**
(Continued)
* Simmons, Blake
* Sinclair, Grace
* Townsend, Mark
* Van Dorne, R.
* Wilson, Carole

**Wallner, Christian Johannes** 1948-
[IAW]
*Austrian author*
* Winkler, Johannes

**Wallner, Franz**
See   Leidersdorf, Franz

**Wallop, Lucille Fletcher** 1912-
[CA]
*American author*
* Fletcher, Lucille

**Wallopin Willie McCovey**
See   McCovey, Willie Lee

**Wallraff, Guenter** 20th c.
*German journalist*
* Esser, Hans

**Walls, Peter** 1926?-
*Zimbabwe Rhodesian army officer*
* Walls, Tommy

**Walls, Tommy**
See   Walls, Peter

**Wally, Gus**
See   Wallenberg, Gustav

**Walmesley, Charles** 1722-1797
[PA]
*Author and clergyman*
* Pastorini, Signor

**Walmoden**
See   Yarmouth, Countess of

**Walmsley, Arnold Robert** 1912-
[CA]
*British author*
* Roland, Nicholas

**Walmsley, Leo** 1892-    [WWL]
*British author*
* March Hare

**Walneerg**
See   Knox, Thomas

**Walpole, Horace**
See   Walpole, Horatio [Fourth Earl
of Orford]

**Walpole, Horatio [First Baron
Walpole of Wolterton]** 1678-1757
[SN]
*British diplomat*
* Old Horace

**Walpole, Horatio [Fourth Earl of
Orford]** 1717-1797
[FFF, SN, WBD]
*British politician and author*
* [The] Last of the Romans
* Marshall, William
* Tydeus
* Ultimus Romanorum
* Walpole, Horace

**Walpole, [Sir] Robert [First Earl of
Orford]** 1676-1745
[DNNF, HN, SN]
*British statesman*
* Bluestring, Robin
* [The] Grand Corrupter
* [The] Leviathan
* [The] Norfolk Gamester
* Sidrophel, Sir
* Sir Bob

**Walraven**
See   Kaler, James Otis

**Walsby, Charnock**
See   Heald, Leslie V.

**Walser, Sam**
See   Howard, Robert Ervin

**Walsh, Big Ed**
See   Walsh, Edward Augustine

**Walsh, Buck**
See   Walsh, Charles S.

**Walsh, Charles** 20th c.    [SMG]
*American football coach*
* Walsh, Chile

**Walsh, Charles S.** 20th c.    [BBH]
*American rowing coach*
* Walsh, Buck

**Walsh, Chile**
See   Walsh, Charles

**Walsh, Dee**
See   Walsh, Thomas L.

**Walsh, Edward Augustine**
1881-1959    [BBH, BE, PB]
*American baseball player*
* Walsh, Big Ed
* Walsh, Moose

**Walsh, Flat**
See   Walsh, James

**Walsh, Flora**
See   Hoyt, Mrs. Charles H.

**Walsh, Frank**
See   March, Miles Standish

**Walsh, J. M.**
See   Walsh, James Morgan

**Walsh, James**
See   Robinson, Frank M[alcolm]

**Walsh, James** 1897-    [CEI]
*Canadian-born hockey player*
* Walsh, Flat

**Walsh, James Anthony** 1867-1936
[CAT]
*American author and clergyman*
* Wakefield, [Father] John

**Walsh, James Gerald** 1919-    [BE]
*American baseball player*
* Walsh, Junior

**Walsh, James Morgan** 1897-1952
[ESF, WGT, WW]
*Australian-born author*
* Hill, H. Haverstock
* Maddock, Stephen
* Walsh, J. M.

**Walsh, Jimmy**
See   Walsh, Michael Timothy

**Walsh, John Henry** 1826- ?
[DEL, FFF, PA]
*British author*
* Stonehenge
* Vox, Valentine

**Walsh, Joseph Patrick [Joe]** 1917-
[BE]
*American baseball player*
* Walsh, Tweet

**Walsh, Junior**
See   Walsh, James Gerald

**Walsh, M. M. B.** 20th c.    [CA]
*American author*
* Walsh, Marnie

**Walsh, Marie A.** 19th c.   [PA]
*Author*
* Sandette

**Walsh, Marnie**
*See* Walsh, M. M. B.

**Walsh, Michael Timothy**
1886-1947   [BE]
*American baseball player*
* Walsh, Jimmy
* Walsh, Runt

**Walsh, Moose**
*See* Walsh, Edward Augustine

**Walsh, Mrs. John**   [FFF]
*Entertainer*
* Coleman, Kitty

**Walsh, Runt**
*See* Walsh, Michael Timothy

**Walsh, Stella**
*See* Walasiewicz, Stella

**Walsh, Thomas L.** 1892-   [BE]
*American baseball player*
* Walsh, Dee

**Walsh, Tweet**
*See* Walsh, Joseph Patrick [Joe]

**Walsh, William W.** 1858- ?   [PA]
*Author*
* Fenwood, Harry
* Gellert

**Walshe, Douglas** 20th c.   [MBF]
*British author*
* Carr, Adams

**Walsingham**
*See* Stewart, Clinton

**Walston, [Sir] Charles**
*See* Waldstein, Charles

**Walston, Joseph**
*See* Walston, Marie

**Walston, Marie** 1925-   [CA]
*American author*
* Walston, Joseph

**[The] Walt Whitman of American Music**
*See* Harris, Roy

**Waltari, Mika [Toimi]** 1908-1979
[CA]
*Finnish author*
* Nauticus
* Ritvala, M.

**Walter**
*See* Henry VIII

**Walter** 11th c.   [HN, RH, SN]
*Leader of the First Crusade*
* [The] Penniless

**Walter, Bruno**
*See* Schlesinger, Bruno Walter

**[The] Walter Camp of Brown Football**
*See* Robinson, Edward N.

**Walter, Charles Russell** 20th c.
[BBH]
*American basketball player*
* Walter, Rut

**Walter, Charles T.** 19th c.   [FFF]
*American author*
* Peck, Wallace

**Walter, Dorothy Blake** 1908-
[CAP]
*American author*
* Blake, Katherine
* Blake, Kay
* Ross, Katherine

**Walter, Henry**
*See* Rocken, Kurt Walter

**Walter, Nancy**
*See* Hagberg, Nancy

**Walter of Evesham** 14th c.   [WBD]
*British monk*
* Odington, Walter

**Walter, Rut**
*See* Walter, Charles Russell

**[The] Walter Scott of Belgium**
*See* Conscience, Hendrick

**[The] Walter Scott of Hungary**
*See* Josika, Miklos Nicholas

**[The] Walter Scott of the Middle Ages**
*See* Froissart, Jean

**Walter the Doubter**
*See* Van Twiller, Walter

**Walters, Alfred John** 1892-1956
[BE]
*American baseball player*
* Walters, Roxy

**Walters, Big Stan**
*See* Walters, Stan

**Walters, Bucky**
*See* Walters, William Henry

**Walters, Chad**
*See* Smith, Richard Rein

**Walters, Frankie** 1859-1953   [SC]
*American actress*
* Bailey, Frankie
* [The] Girl with the Million Dollar Legs

**Walters, Fred James** 1912-   [BE]
*American baseball player*
* Walters, Whale

**Walters, Gordon**
*See* Locke, George [Walter]

**Walters, Hugh**
*See* Hughes, Walter Llewellyn

**Walters, J.** 20th c.   [MBF]
*British author*
* Owen, Norman

**Walters, John** 1949-   [DC]
*British cricketer*
* Walters, Welder

**Walters, Kirby** 20th c.   [GW]
*American rodeo performer*
* Walters, Popcorn

**Walters, Marvin M.** 1882-   [NAA]
*American clergyman and writer*
* Brinker, Martin

**Walters, Maud** 1910-   [THR]
*American actress and dancer*
* Walters, Polly
* Walters, Teddy

**Walters, Mule**
*See* Walters, Stan

**Walters, Nell**
*See* Muse, Patricia [Alice]

**Walters, Polly**
*See* Walters, Maud

**Walters, Popcorn**
*See* Walters, Kirby

**Walters, Rick**
*See* Rowland, D[onald] S[ydney]

**Walters, Robert**   [PA]
*Author*
* Roberts, George

**Walters, Roxy**
*See* Walters, Alfred John

**Walters, Shelly**
*See* Sheldon, Walt[er J.]

**Walters, Stan** 1948-   [SMG]
*American football player*
* Walters, Big Stan
* Walters, Mule

**Walters, T. B.**
*See* Rowe, John Gabriel

**Walters, Teddy**
*See* Walters, Maud

**Walters, W. G.**
*See* Steffens, Arthur

**Walters, Welder**
*See* Walters, John

**Walters, Whale**
*See* Walters, Fred James

**Walters, William Henry** 1909?-
[B10, DGS, PB]
*American baseball player*
* Walters, Bucky

**Walther, George** 1946?-1974   [B10]
*American boat racer*
* Walther, Skipp

**Walther, Skipp**
*See* Walther, George

**Walton**
*See* Thorpe, Henry

**Walton, Bill** 1952-
*American basketball player*
* [The] Mountain Man
* [The] Stranger

**Walton, Bryce** 1918-   [ESF, WGT]
*American author*
* Franklin, Paul
* O'Hara, Kenneth
* Sands, Dave? [house pseudonym?]

**Walton, Daniel James** 1947-   [BE]
*American baseball player*
* Walton, Mickey

**Walton, Douglas**
*See* Duder, J. Douglas

**Walton, Evangeline**
*See* Ensley, Wilma Evangeline

**Walton, Francis**
*See* Hodder, Alfred

**Walton, Fred**
*See* Heming, Frederick

**Walton, Harry** 20th c.   [WGT]
*Author*
* Collier, Harry

**Walton, Izaak** 1593-1683
[DEL, FFF, PA]
*British author*
* Chalkhill, John
* [The] Father of Angling

**Walton, Izaak** (Continued)
* [The] Gentle
* Piscator

**Walton, Lloyd** 1953-   [SMG]
*American basketball player*
* Walton, Speedy

**Walton, Luke**
*See* Henderson, Bill

**Walton, Mercy Dee** 1915-1962
[BWW]
*American singer*
* Dee, Mercy

**Walton, Michael Robert** 1945-
[HR]
*Canadian-born hockey player*
* Walton, Shakey

**Walton, Mickey**
*See* Walton, Daniel James

**Walton, Shakey**
*See* Walton, Michael Robert

**Walton, Speedy**
*See* Walton, Lloyd

**Walton, W. H.**   [PA]
*Author*
* Mansfield, Walworth

**Walton, Zach**
*See* Zachary, Jonathan Thompson Walton

**Waltz, J. Jacques** 1873- ?   [LAO]
*French author*
* Hansi

**[The] Waltz King**
*See* King, Wayne

**Walworth, Alice**
*See* Graham, Alice Walworth

**Walworth, Mrs.**   [PA]
*Author*
* Haderman, Jeanette

**Walz, Audrey** 20th c.   [CC, WW]
*Author*
* Bonnamy, Francis

**Wambsganss, William Adolph**
1894-   [BE]
*American baseball player*
* Wamby, William Adolph

**Wamby, William Adolph**
*See* Wambsganss, William Adolph

**Wampum, King**
*See* Pemberton, Israel

**Wan Chia-Pao** 1905-   [MWD]
*Chinese playwright*
* Ts'ao Yu

**Wan, [Mme.] Sul Te**
*See* Conley, Nellie

**Wandan, Harry** 1947-   [RO2]
*Dutch musician*
* Vanda, Harry

**[The] Wanderer**
*See* Barker, Matthew Henry

**Wanderer**
*See* Gilbert, Jean

**[The] Wanderer**
*See* Goethe, Johann Wolfgang von

**Wandering Eric Brook**
*See* Brook, Eric F.

**Wanderone, Rudolf, Jr.** 20th c.
*American pool player*
* Minnesota Fats

**Wandrei, Howard Elmer**
1909-1965 [WGT]
*American author*
* Coley, Robert
* Garron, Robert A.
* Graham, Howard
* Guernsey, H. W.
* Von Drey, Howard

**Waner, Lloyd James** 1906-
[BE, DGS, PB]
*American baseball player*
* Little Poison

**Waner, Paul Glee** 1903-1965
[BE, DGS, PB]
*American baseball player*
* Big Poison

**Wang, C. T.**
*See* Wang Cheng-t'ing

**Wang Chao-ming** 1884-1944
[WBD]
*Chinese politician*
* Wang Ching-wei

**Wang Cheng-t'ing** 1882-1961
[WBD]
*Chinese politician*
* Wang, C. T.

**Wang, Ching Hsien** 1940- [CA]
*Chinese-born educator and author*
* Mu, Yang
* Shan, Yeh

**Wang Ching-wei**
*See* Wang Chao-ming

**Wang, Hui-Ming** 1922- [CA]
*Chinese-born wood engraver,
calligrapher, translator*
* H. M. W.

**Wang Mang** ?- 23 [WBD]
*Chinese emperor*
* [The] Usurper

**Wang Shou-jen** 1472-1528?
[WBD]
*Chinese philosopher*
* Wang Yang-ming

**Wang Yang-ming**
*See* Wang Shou-jen

**Wangara, Harun Kofi**
*See* Lawrence, Harold G.

**Wangara, Malaika Ayo**
*See* Lawrence, Joyce Whitsett

**Wangchuk, Anangavajra Khamsum**
*See* Govinda, Anagarika

**Wanger, Beatrice** 20th c. [NAA]
*American-born writer*
* Nadja

**Wanger, Walter**
*See* Feuchtwanger, Walter

**Wangner, Ellen D.** 1874- ? [NAA]
*Canadian-born editor and author*
* Jeffrey, Ellen

**Wanlass, Chris**
*See* Wanlass, Cravens

**Wanlass, Cravens** 1926-
*American inventor, engineer,
computer scientist*
* Wanlass, Chris

**Wannamaker, Bruce**
*See* Moncure, Jane Belk

**Wanner, Clarence Mellert**
1884-1962 [BE]
*American baseball player*
* Wanner, Jack

**Wanner, Jack**
*See* Wanner, Clarence Mellert

**Wanninger, Paul Louis** 1902- [BE]
*American baseball player*
* Wanninger, Pee Wee

**Wanninger, Pee Wee**
*See* Wanninger, Paul Louis

**Wanostrocht, Nicholas** [PA]
*Author*
* Felix, M.

**Wanstall, Ken**
*See* Green-Wanstall, Kenneth

**Wantage, Baron**
*See* Lindsay, Robert James

**Wapens, Piet [Pete Weapons]**
*See* Botha, Pieter

**War Horse**
*See* Nicholson, James William
Augustus

**[The] War Poet**
*See* Boker, George Henry

**War Whoop Page**
*See* Page, Alan

**[The] Warbeck of the North**
*See* Otrepieff, Gregory

**Warbeck, Perkin** 1474-1499
[HN, RH, SN]
*Pretender to the crown of England*
* [The] White Rose of England

**Warbler, J. M.**
*See* Cocagnac, Augustin
Maurice-Jean

**[The] Warbler of Poetic Prose**
*See* Sidney, [Sir] Philip

**Warburg, James Paul** 1896-1969
[ASC, CAP]
*American author*
* James, Paul

**Warburg, Sandol Stoddard** 1927-
[SAT]
*American author*
* Stoddard, Sandol

**Warburton, Cotton**
*See* Warburton, Irvine E.

**Warburton, Irvine E.** 1911- [FB]
*American football player*
* Warburton, Cotton

**Warburton, Joan** 1920- [ART]
*Scottish-born artist*
* J. W.

**Warburton, William** 1698-1779
[SN]
*British prelate*
* [A] Colossus of Literature
* [The] Literary Bull-Dog
* [A] Mountebank in Criticism
* [A] Quack in Commentatorship
* [The] Scaliger of the Age

**Ward, A. Sarsfield**
*See* Ward, Arthur Henry

**Ward, Artemus**
*See* Browne, Charles Farrar

**Ward, Arthur Henry** 1883-1959
[ESF, HFF, SFL]
*British author*
* Furey, Michael
* Rohmer, Sax
* Ward, A. Sarsfield

**Ward, Bud**
*See* Ward, Marvin Harvey

**Ward, Burt**
*See* Gervis, Burt

**Ward, Carrie**
*See* Clarke-Ward, Carrie

**Ward, Charles Dexter**
*See* Taylor, John [Alfred]

**Ward, Craig** 1892-1979 [CA]
*American astrologer and author*
* MacCraig, Hugh

**Ward, Diane**
*See* Bunce, Corajane Diane

**Ward, Don[ald G.]** 1911- [CA]
*American editor*
* Tracy, Powers

**Ward, Elizabeth Campbell** 1936-
[CA]
*American author*
* Allen, E. C.

**Ward, Elizabeth Honor [Shedden]**
1926- [CA, WD]
*British author*
* Leslie, Ward S.

**Ward, Elizabeth Rebecca** 1881- ?
[LC]
*Author and poet*
* Inchfawn, Fay

**Ward, Elizabeth Stuart [Phelps]**
1844-1911 [FFF, WGT]
*American author*
* Adams, Mary
* Onyx
* Phelps, Elizabeth Stuart
* Trusta

**Ward, Fannie**
*See* Buchanan, Fannie

**Ward, Ferdinand** 19th c. [FFF]
*American speculator*
* [The] Napoleon of Finance

**Ward, Frank Gray** 1867-1912 [BE]
*American baseball player*
* Ward, Piggy

**Ward, Frederick William Orde** 1843-
? [WWL]
*British author*
* Williams, F. Harald

**Ward, H. D.** [PA]
*Author*
* Harvard Senior

**Ward, Hap**
*See* O'Donnell, John Thomas, Sr.

**Ward, Hap, Jr.**
*See* O'Donnell, John Thomas, Jr.

**Ward, Harold** 20th c. [SFL, SFP]
*Author*
* Zorro

**Ward, Harry**
*See* De Michele, Angelo

**Ward, Harry** 20th c. [IBW]
*American athlete*
* Ward, Wu Fang

**Ward, Henry**
*See* Viard, Henri Louis Luc

**Ward, Ideal**
*See* Ward, William George

**Ward, Jackie** [RO1]
*American singer*
* Ward, Robin

**Ward, James Warner** 1807-1873
[FFF]
*Writer*
* Yorick

**Ward, Janet**
*See* Werner, Janet Anne

**Ward, Jennie**
*See* Williams, Mrs. Odell

**Ward, John A.** 20th c. [BE]
*American baseball player*
* Ward, Rube

**Ward, John C.** 20th c. [WWL]
*Irish author and translator*
* Mac An Bhaird, Seaghan

**Ward, John Montgomery**
1860-1925 [AS]
*American baseball player*
* Ward, Monte

**Ward, Jonas**
*See* Ard, William [Thomas]

**Ward, Jonas**
*See* Garfield, Brian [Francis]
Wynne

**Ward, Jonathon**
*See* Stine, Whitney Ward

**Ward, Joshua** 18th c. [HN, SN]
*British physician*
* Ward, Spot

**Ward, Kirwan**
*See* Kirwan-Ward, Bernard
Edward

**Ward, [Sir] Leslie** 1851-1922 [LC]
*British illustrator*
* Spy

**Ward, Mabella Ann** 19th c. [PA]
*Author*
* Dashaway, Kate

**Ward, Maisie**
*See* Ward, Mary Josephine

**Ward, Marian**
*See* Williams, Mrs. Tony

**Ward, Marion**
*See* Stephens, Harriet Marion

**Ward, Marion Inez Douglas** 1885-
[LAO]
*British author*
* Fox, Marion

**Ward, Marvin Harvey** 1913-1968
[AS, EG, GF]
*American golfer*
* Ward, Bud

**Ward, Mary**
*See* Holton, Mary Ward

**Ward, Mary Jane**
*See* Quayle, Mary Jane Ward

**Ward, Mary Josephine** 1889-1975
[CA]
*British-born author and publisher*
* Ward, Maisie

**Ward, Melanie**
See Lynch, Marilyn

**Ward, Monte**
See Ward, John Montgomery

**Ward, Mrs. H. O.**
See Moore, Mrs. Bloomfield H.

**Ward, Nathaniel** 1578?-1652
[FFF, PA, WBD]
*British-born clergyman and author*
* De La Guard, Theodore

**Ward, Ole**
See Ward, Richard [Dick]

**Ward, Peter**
See Faust, Frederick [Schiller]

**Ward, Philip** 1938-　[CA]
*British author*
* Greenfield, Darby

**Ward, Piggy**
See Ward, Frank Gray

**Ward, Polly**
See Poluski, Byno

**Ward, R. H.**
See Ward, Richard Heron

**Ward, R. Patrick**
See Holzapfel, Rudolf Patrick
[Rudi]

**Ward, Richard [Dick]** 1909-1966
[BE]
*American baseball player*
* Ward, Ole

**Ward, Richard Heron** 1910-1969
[LC]
*British author and playwright*
* Ward, R. H.

**Ward, Robert**
See Howard, Robert Ervin

**Ward, Robin**
See Ward, Jackie

**Ward, Roger** 20th c.
*Auto racer*
* Roger the Dodger

**Ward, Rose Elizabeth Knox** 1886-
[SFL, WGT]
*American author*
* Knox, Lisbeth
* Rohmer, Elizabeth Sax

**Ward, Rube**
See Ward, John A.

**Ward, Sam**
See Jacobs, George Herman

**Ward, Sam[uel]** 1814-1884
[FFF, PA, SN]
*American politician*
* [The] King of the Lobby
* S. W.
* Ward, Uncle Sam

**Ward, Seth** 1928-　[CME]
*American country-western performer*
* Dean, Jimmy

**Ward, Spot**
See Ward, Joshua

**Ward, Sylvia** 1900-　[THR]
*British actress and singer*
* Leslie, Sylvia

**Ward, Thomas** 1847- ?　[PA]
*Author*
* Draw, Thom
* Flaccus

**Ward, Tom**
See Sellers, Connie Leslie, Jr.

**Ward, Townsend**　[PA]
*Author*
* Logan

**Ward, Uncle Sam**
See Ward, Sam[uel]

**Ward, Vera Hall**
See Hall, Vera

**Ward, Warwick**
See Mannon, W.

**Ward, William [Willie]** 1893-
[BX, RBE]
*Panamanian-born boxer*
* Norfolk, Kid

**Ward, William George** 1812-1882
[DEP, WBD]
*British theologian*
* Ward, Ideal

**Ward, Wu Fang**
See Ward, Harry

**Ward Thomas, Evelyn Bridget
Patricia** 1928-　[AW, CA]
*British author*
* Anthony, Evelyn
* Evelyn, Anthony

**Warde, Beatrice Lamberton**
1900-1969　[SFL, WGT]
*Author*
* Beaujon, Paul

**Warde, Margaret**
See Dunton, Edith Kellogg

**Warde, William F.**
See Novack, George [Edward]

**Wardell, Dean**
See Prince, Jack Harvey

**Wardell, Edith** 1869-1947　[BEW]
*British actress*
* Craig, Edith

**Wardell, Etelka**
See Heaton, Eva

**Wardell, Henry Edward Gordon
Godwin** 1872-1966　[OCF]
*British stage designer*
* Craig, Edward Gordon

**Warden, Colonel** [code name used
during World War II]
See Churchill, Winston S.

**Warden, Florence**
See James, Florence Alice [Price]

**Warden, Francis**
See Harrison, Mary Bennett

**Warden, Jon[athan Edgar]** 1946-
[BE]
*American baseball player*
* Warden, Warbler

**Warden, Warbler**
See Warden, Jon[athan Edgar]

**Wardle, Dan**
See Snow, Charles Horace

**Wardle, Jane**
See Hueffer, Oliver Madox

**Wardrop, Bert**
See Wardrop, Robert

**Wardrop, Robert** 1932-　[SWI]
*British swimmer*
* Wardrop, Bert

**Ware, Eugene Fitch** 1841-1911
[WBD]
*American poet*
* Ironquill

**Ware, Helen**
See Remer, Helen

**Ware, John**
See Mabley, Edward [Howe]

**Ware, Mary Harris**　[FFF]
*Author*
* Glenn, Gertrude

**Ware, Monica**
See Marsh, John

**Ware, Wallace**
See Karp, David

**Wares, Buzzy**
See Wares, Clyde Ellsworth

**Wares, Clyde Ellsworth** 1886-1964
[BE]
*American baseball player*
* Wares, Buzzy

**Warfield, Sandra**
See Bornstein, Flora-Jean

**Wargar, Kurt**
See Ruellan, Andre

**Warhol, Andy** 1927-
*American painter and filmmaker*
* Drella

**Warhol, Minnie**
See Warhol, Ted

**Warhol, Ted** 20th c.　[GW]
*American rodeo performer*
* Warhol, Minnie

**Warhop, Chief**
See Wauhop, John Milton

**Warhop, Crab**
See Wauhop, John Milton

**Warhop, John Milton**
See Wauhop, John Milton

**Waring, Barbara**
See Gibb, Barbara

**Waring, Herbert**
See Rutty, Herbert Waring

**Waring, Marcus H.**
See Manning, William Henry

**Waring, Richard**
See Stephens, Richard Waring

**Warland, Allen**
See Wollheim, Donald A[llen]

**Warland, John**
See Buchanan-Brown, John

**Warlick, Ernie** 1933-　[IBW]
*American football player*
* Warlick, Hands

**Warlick, Hands**
See Warlick, Ernie

**[The] Warlike**
See Charles XII

**[The] Warlike**
See Frederick I

**[The] Warlike**
See Henry II [or Henri]

**Warlock, Peter**
See Heseltine, Philip

**Warmerdam, Cornelius** 1915-　[TF]
*American track and field athlete*
* Warmerdam, Dutch

**Warmerdam, Dutch**
See Warmerdam, Cornelius

**[The] Warming Pan Child**
See Stuart, James Francis Edward

**[The] Warming Pan Hero**
See Stuart, James Francis Edward

**Warmley, Ernst**
See Manson, James B.

**Warmoth, Cy**
See Warmoth, Wallace Walter

**Warmoth, Wallace Walter**
1893-1957　[BE]
*American baseball player*
* Warmoth, Cy

**Warneford, Lieut.**
See Gunter, Archibald Clavering

**Warneke, Lonnie** 1909-　[BE]
*American baseball player*
* [The] Arkansas Humming Bird

**Warner, Albert**
See Eichelbaum, Albert

**Warner, Anna Bartlett** 1827-1915
[DEL, DNNF, RH]
*American author*
* Lothrop, Amy

**Warner, Augustine**
See Byars, William Vincent

**Warner, B. Ellison**　[FFF, PA]
*American writer and clergyman*
* Pascarel

**Warner, B. F.**
See Bowers, Warner Fremont

**Warner, Charles**
See Lickfold, Charles

**Warner, Connie**
See Warner, Cornell

**Warner, Cornell** 1948-　[SMG]
*American basketball player*
* M
* Warner, Connie

**Warner, Edgar** 20th c.　[NAD]
*Psychic healer*
* Karmu

**Warner, Esther S.**
See Dendel, Esther [Sietmann
Warner]

**Warner, Frances Lester**
See Hersey, Frances Lester
Warner

**Warner, Frank**
See Richardson, Gladwell

**Warner, Frank A.** [house
pseudonym] [Stratemeyer
Syndicate]
See Stratemeyer, Edward L.

**Warner, [George] Geoffrey John**
1923- [CA, WD]
*British author and artist*
* Johns, Geoffrey

**Warner, Glenn Scobey** 1871-1954
[AS, FB, OCS]
*American football coach*
* Warner, Pop

**Warner, Gloria**
*See* Kelly, Gloria

**Warner, Harry Morris**
*See* Eichelbaum, Harry Morris

**Warner, Henry Bryon**
*See* Lickfold, Henry Bryon

**Warner, Hoke Hayden** 1894-1947
[BE]
*American baseball player*
* Warner, Hooks

**Warner, Hooks**
*See* Warner, Hoke Hayden

**Warner, Indian**
*See* Warner, Thomas

**Warner, Jack**
*See* Waters, John

**Warner, Jack L.**
*See* Eichelbaum, Jack L.

**Warner, Jessie**
*See* Clarance, Mrs. Edward

**Warner, Kenneth [Lewis]** 1915-
[CAP]
*British author*
* Morel, Dighton

**Warner, L. T.** [PA]
*Author*
* Leigh, Larry

**Warner, Matt**
*See* Christiansen, Williard

**Warner, Matt**
*See* Fichter, George S.

**Warner, [Sir] Pelham Francis**
1873-1963 [OCS]
*British cricketer*
* Warner, Plum

**Warner, Plum**
*See* Warner, [Sir] Pelham Francis

**Warner, Pop**
*See* Warner, Glenn Scobey

**Warner, Reginald Ernest** 1905-
[SFL]
*Author*
* Warner, Rex

**Warner, Rex**
*See* Warner, Reginald Ernest

**Warner, Samuel Louis**
*See* Eichelbaum, Samuel Louis

**Warner, Susan** 1819-1885
[DEL, PA]
*American author*
* Wetherell, Elizabeth

**Warner, Thomas** ?-1675 [WBD]
*Governor of Dominica*
* Warner, Indian

**Warner, Virginia**
*See* Brodine, Virginia Warner

**Warner, William** 1558?-1609 [SN]
*British poet*
* Our English Homer

**Warner-Crozetti, R.**
*See* Crozetti, Ruth G. Warner
[Lora]

**Warnes, Carlos** 20th c. [WECO]
*Cartoonist*
* Bruto, Cesar

**Warnow, Harry** 1909?-
[ASC, EJ, PMJ]
*American bandleader*
* Scott, Raymond

**Warren, Andrew** [joint pseudonym
with Warren (Stanley) Tute]
*See* Rosenthal, Andrew

**Warren, Andrew** [joint pseudonym
with Andrew Rosenthal]
*See* Tute, Warren [Stanley]

**Warren, Arthur** [FFF]
*American journalist*
* Quill, Timothy

**Warren, Baby Boy**
*See* Warren, Robert Henry

**Warren, Betty**
*See* Hogan, Babette Hilda

**Warren, Brett**
*See* Breitberg, Louis

**Warren, Charlie**
*See* Mueller, Marvin

**Warren, Dave**
*See* Wiersbe, Warren Wendell

**Warren, David** 1943- [CA]
*American author*
* Featherstone, D.

**Warren, Earle** 20th c. [NP]
*American jazz musician*
* Warren, Smiley

**Warren, Edith** [IBW]
*American actress, singer, dancer*
* Washington, Fredi

**Warren, Eliza**
*See* Sutton, Eliza Warren

**Warren, Elizabeth**
*See* Supraner, Robyn

**Warren, Fiddlin' Kate**
*See* Warren, Margie Ann

**Warren, Francis Emroy** 1844-1929
[WBD]
*American politician*
* [The] Father of Reclamation

**Warren, Frederick H.** 1888-
[WWL]
*British author*
* Warren, Henry

**Warren, Harold**
*See* Schwartz, Charles Henry

**Warren, Harry**
*See* Guaragna, Salvatore

**Warren, Henry**
*See* Warren, Frederick H.

**Warren, Henry** 1903- [ECM]
*American country-western performer*
* Warren, Uncle Henry

**Warren, Jeff**
*See* Jones, George Warren

**Warren, John Byrne Leicester [Baron
de Tabley]** 1835-1895 [DEL]
*British poet*
* Lancaster, William

**Warren, John Russell** 1886- [WW]
*Author*
* Coverack, Gilbert

**Warren, Joseph**
*See* Vari, Giuseppe

**Warren, Leonard**
*See* Varenov, Leonard

**Warren, Margie Ann** 1922-
[CWG, DAM]
*American country-western performer*
* Warren, Fiddlin' Kate

**Warren, Mary**
*See* Campion, Katherine

**Warren, Mary Douglas**
*See* Greig, Maysie

**Warren, Peter Whitson** 1941- [CA]
*American author and artist*
* Whitson

**Warren, Red**
*See* Warren, Robert Penn

**Warren, Robert Henry** 1919-1977
[BWW]
*American singer*
* Warren, Baby Boy
* Williams, Johnny

**Warren, Robert Penn** 1905-
*American author*
* Warren, Red

**Warren, Smiley**
*See* Warren, Earle

**Warren, Uncle Henry**
*See* Warren, Henry

**Warren, Vernon**
*See* Chapman, George Warren
Vernon

**Warrick, Dionne** 20th c. [LRR]
*American singer*
* Warwick, Dionne

**Warriner, Cornelia** 20th c. [WW]
*Author*
* Crockett, James [joint pseudonym
with James A. MacPhail]

**Warriner, Thurman** 20th c. [CC]
*Author*
* Troy, Simon

**Warrington**
*See* Robinson, William Stevens

**Warrington, Dan**
*See* Reed-Smith, Ida

**Warrington, Maris**
*See* Billings, Edith S.

**[The] Warrior**
*See* Friend, Robert Bartmess

**[The] Warrior**
*See* Michael VI Stratioticus

**[The] Warrior Lady of Latham**
*See* Charlotte

**[The] Warrior of Freedom**
*See* Garibaldi, Giuseppe

**[The] Warrior of Today**
*See* Jordan, Vernon Eulion, Jr.

**Warrren, Charlie**
*See* Donaldson, Dan

**Warsh**
*See* Warshaw, Jerry

**Warshaw, Jerry** 1929- [CA]
*American illustrator*
* Warsh

**Warshofsky, Isaac**
*See* Singer, Isaac Bashevis

**Warstler, Harold Burton**
1903-1964 [BE]
*American baseball player*
* Warstler, Rabbit

**Warstler, Rabbit**
*See* Warstler, Harold Burton

**Wart, Helen**
*See* Miserocchi, Anna

**Wartenegg, Hanna**
*See* Warzilek, Johanna

**Warter, John Wood** 1806-1878
[DEL, PA]
*British author and clergyman*
* Old Vicar
* Oldacre, Cedric, of Saxe
Normanby

**Warton, Thomas** 1728-1790 [SN]
*British poet and critic*
* Honest Tom

**Wartski, Maureen [Ann Crane]**
1940- [CA]
*Japanese-born American author*
* Crane, M. A.

**Warwick**
*See* Ryer, Frederick R.

**Warwick, A. H.** 20th c. [CFH]
*Canadian football player, coach,
executive*
* Warwick, Bert

**Warwick, Alan Ross** 20th c. [MBF]
*British author*
* Ross, Allan
* Sidney, Frank
* Sydney, Frank

**Warwick, Anne**
*See* Cranston, Ruth

**Warwick, Bama**
*See* Warwick, William Carl

**Warwick, Bert**
*See* Warwick, A. H.

**Warwick, Bill**
*See* Warwick, Firman Newton

**Warwick, Charles**
*See* McDonough, C. J.

**Warwick, Dionne**
*See* Warrick, Dionne

**Warwick, Dolores**
*See* Frese, Dolores Warwick

**Warwick, Eden**
*See* Jabet, George S.

**Warwick, Elsie**
*See* Fullilove, Mrs. E. J.

**Warwick, Firman Newton** 1897-
[BE]
*American baseball player*
* Warwick, Bill

**Warwick, Francis Alister** 20th c.
[MBF]
*British author*
* Clifford, Martin [house
pseudonym]
* Jardine, Warwick [house
pseudonym]

**Warwick, Francis Alister**
(Continued) .
* Sidney, Frank
* Spencer, Roland [joint
   pseudonym with Geoffrey Prout]
* Sydney, Frank

**Warwick, George**
See Deeping, George Warwick

**Warwick, Grant David** 1921-
[CEI, FHE, HK]
*Canadian-born hockey player*
* Warwick, Knobby

**Warwick, Jarvis**
See Garner, Hugh

**Warwick, John**
See Beattie, John McIntosh

**Warwick, Knobby**
See Warwick, Grant David

**Warwick, Pauline**
See Davies, Betty Evelyn

**Warwick, Robert**
See Bien, Robert Taylor

**Warwick, Sidney** 1870-1953
[MBF]
*British author*
* Drayson, A. W.
* Sidney, Frank
* Sydney, Frank

**Warwick, William Carl** 1917-
[EJ, WWJ]
*American jazz musician*
* Warwick, Bama

**Waryng, Jane** 17th c.   [SN]
*Friend of British satirist, Jonathan
Swift*
* Varina

**Warzilek, Johanna** 1939-   [OP]
*Austrian scenic and costume
designer*
* Wartenegg, Hanna

**Wash, Martha** 20th c.   [IBW]
*American singer*
* Two Tons of Fun

**Wash, R.**
See Cowlishaw, Ranson

**[The] Washboard King**
See King, Ernest

**Washboard Sam**
See Brown, Robert

**Washboard Willie**
See Hensley, William Paden

**Washburn, Bryant**
See Ludlow, Dwight

**Washburne, Country**
See Washburne, Joe

**Washburne, Joe** 1904-1974
[ASC, PMJ]
*American musician*
* Washburne, Country

**Washburne, Mary B.**   [PA]
*Author*
* Morrison, Mary

**Washer, Buck**
See Washer, William

**Washer, William** 1882-1955   [BE]
*American baseball player*
* Washer, Buck

**Washington, Alex**
See Finkelstein, Mark

**Washington, Berwell**
See Cabell, James Branch

**Washington, Buck**
See Washington, Ford Lee

**Washington, C.**
See Pharr, Robert D[eane]

**Washington, Clyde** 20th c.   [RBE]
*American boxer*
* Washington, Kid

**Washington, D. C.**
See Bender, D. C.

**Washington, Diamond**
See Washington, Leon

**Washington, Didimus**
See Washington, Richard

**Washington, Dinah**
See Jones, Ruth [Lee]

**Washington, Edward** 1902-1964
[NOJ]
*American jazz musician*
* Washington, Son White

**Washington, Edward Emmanuel**
See Hill, David

**Washington, Ford Lee** 1903-1955
[EJ, SC, WWJ]
*American jazz musician and
comedian*
* Buck, Ford
* Washington, Buck

**Washington, Fredi**
See Warren, Edith

**Washington, George**
See Thomas, George Henry

**Washington, George**
See Washington, Sloane Vernon

**Washington, George** 1732-1799
[DHA, FAP, SN]
*American president*
* [The] American Cincinnatus
* [The] American Fabius
* [The] Atlas of America
* [The] Cincinnatus of the
   Americans
* [The] Cincinnatus of the West
* [The] Deliverer of America
* [The] Fabius of America
* [The] Farmer President
* [The] Father of His Country
* [The] Father of Pittsburgh
* [The] Flower of the Forest
* [The] Lovely Georgius
* [The] Old Fox
* [The] Sage of Mount Vernon
* [The] Savior of His Country
* [The] Stepfather of His Country
* [The] Surveyor President
* [The] Sword of the Revolution

**Washington, George** 20th c.
[BWW]
*American entertainer*
* Washington, Oh Red

**Washington, Gladys J[oseph]** 1931-
[CA]
*American author and educator*
* Curry, Gladys J.

**Washington, Grover, Jr.** 1943-
[IBW]
*American jazz musician*
* [The] Crossover King

**Washington, Herbert** 1941-   [IBW]
*American leader of military
deserters organization*
* Washington, Wash

**Washington, Isabel** 1871-1944
[THR]
*American actress*
* Irving, Isabel

**Washington, Isidoe** 20th c.   [BWW]
*American entertainer*
* Washington, Tuts

**Washington, Jack**
See Washington, Ronald

**Washington, Joe** 1953-   [SMG]
*American football player*
* Washington, Joe Boy

**Washington, Joe Boy**
See Washington, Joe

**Washington, Kid**
See Washington, Clyde

**Washington, Leon** 1909-   [WWJ]
*American jazz musician*
* Washington, Diamond

**Washington, Leon H., Jr.**
1907-1974   [IBW]
*American publisher*
* Washington, Wash

**Washington, Mack**
See Washington, William

**Washington, [Catherine] Marguerite
Beauchamp** 1892-1972   [CAP]
*American author*
* Beaton, Anne
* Beauchamp, Pat
* Washington, Pat Beauchamp

**[The] Washington of Africa**
See Wilberforce, William

**[The] Washington of Colombia**
See Bolivar, Simon

**[The] Washington of South America**
See Bolivar, Simon

**[The] Washington of the West**
See Harrison, William Henry

**Washington, Oh Red**
See Washington, George

**Washington, Ora** 1898-1971   [IBW]
*American tennis player*
* [The] Queen of Tennis

**Washington, Pat Beauchamp**
See Washington, [Catherine]
Marguerite Beauchamp

**Washington, Richard** 20th c.   [RM]
*Musician*
* Washington, Didimus

**Washington, Rocky**
See Washington, Roscoe

**Washington, Ronald** 1912-1964
[NP, WWJ]
*American jazz musician*
* Washington, Jack
* Washington, Weasel

**Washington, Roscoe** 20th c.   [IBW]
*American police officer*
* Washington, Rocky

**Washington, Russell** 1946-   [FB]
*American football player*
* Mount Washington

**Washington, Sloane Vernon** 1907-
[BE]
*American baseball player*
* Washington, George

**Washington, Son White**
See Washington, Edward

**Washington, Sylvester** 1906-1971
[IBW]
*American police officer*
* Two Gun Pete

**Washington, Tuts**
See Washington, Isidoe

**Washington, Val**
See Washington, Valores James

**Washington, Valores James** 1903-
[IBW]
*American politician and journalist*
* Washington, Val

**Washington, Wash**
See Washington, Herbert

**Washington, Wash**
See Washington, Leon H., Jr.

**Washington, Weasel**
See Washington, Ronald

**Washington, William** 1908-1938
[WWJ]
*American jazz musician*
* Washington, Mack

**Wasmansdoff, Joyce** 1928?-1972
[FIR]
*American actress*
* Lansing, Joi
* Loveland, Joy

**Wason, Betty**
See Hall, Elizabeth Wason

**Wasself, Lucille** 1887?-1921
[BBD]
*American opera singer*
* Marcel, Lucille

**Wasserburg, Phillipp**   [PA]
*Author*
* Laicus, Phillipe

**Wassersug, Joseph D.** 1912-   [CA]
*American physician and writer*
* Bradford [M.D.], Adam

**Wast, Hugo**
See Martinez Zuviria, Gustavo
Adolfo

**Wastle, William**
See Lockhart, John Gibson

**[The] Watch Dog of the Treasury**
See Holman, William Steele

**Watchman**
See Draper, Warwick Herbert

**[The] Water Drinker**
See Montague, Basil

**[The] Water Poet**
See Taylor, John

**[The] Water Rat**
See Jones, Stephen [Phillip]

**Water, Silas**
See Loomis, Noel M[iller]

**Waterfield, Buckets**
See Waterfield, Robert S.

**Waterfield, Rifle**
See Waterfield, Robert S.

**Waterfield, Robert S.** 1920- [FB]
*American football player*
* Waterfield, Buckets
* Waterfield, Rifle

**Waterhouse, Arthur**
See Fearn, John Russell

**Waterhouse, Keith [Spencer]** 1929-
[CA]
*British author, journalist,
playwright*
* Froy, Herald [joint pseudonym
with Guy (Stephen) Deghy]
* Gibb, Lee [joint pseudonym with
Guy (Stephen) Deghy]

**[The] Waterloo Hero**
See Hill, Rowland [First Viscount
Hill]

**Waterman, Bic**
See Joseph, Stephen M.

**Waterman, Ida**
See Francoeur, Ida Shaw

**Waters**
See Russell, William

**Waters, Augustus** [PA]
*Author*
* Belshazzar

**Waters, Blizzard**
See Waters, Charlie

**Waters, Bucky**
See Waters, Raymond

**Waters, Charlie** 20th c.
*American football player*
* Waters, Blizzard

**Waters, Chocolate**
See Waters, Marianne

**Waters, Chris**
See Waters, Harold A[rthur]

**Waters, Clear**
See Waters, Eddie

**Waters, Daisy**
See Waters, Doris

**Waters, Doris** 1904?-1978 [FIR]
*British entertainer*
* Waters, Daisy

**Waters, Eddie** 20th c. [NBB]
*American singer*
* Waters, Clear

**Waters, Ethel** 1896-1977 [BWW]
*American singer and actress*
* America's Foremost Ebony
  Comedienne
* Baby Star
* [The] Ebony Nora Bayes
* Jones, Mamie
* [The] Original Dinah
* Pryor, Martha
* [The] Queen of the Blues
* Sweet Mama Stringbean

**Waters, Frank** 20th c.
*American football coach*
* Waters, Muddy

**Waters, Harold A[rthur]** 1926-
[CA]
*American educator and author*
* Waters, Chris

**Waters, John**
See Carey, Henry

**Waters, John** [PA]
*Author*
* Flaccus

**Waters, John** 1894- [B10, BF, FC]
*British actor*
* Warner, Jack

**Waters, Marianne** 1949- [CA]
*American poet*
* Waters, Chocolate

**Waters, Monty**
See Waters, Monville Charles

**Waters, Monville Charles** 1938-
[EJ7]
*American jazz musician*
* Waters, Monty

**Waters, Muddy**
See Morganfield, McKinley

**Waters, Muddy**
See Waters, Frank

**Waters, Muddy, Jr.**
See Buford, George

**Waters, Raymond** 1935- [BB]
*American basketball coach*
* Waters, Bucky

**Waters, Rosemary Elizabeth** 1920-
[AW]
*British television producer and
writer*
* Horstmann, Rosemary

**Waters, Thomas?**
See Russell, William

**Watford, Joel Albert** 1906- [AW]
*British author*
* Essex, Jon

**Wathan, Duke**
See Wathan, John David

**Wathan, John David** 1949- [SMG]
*American baseball player*
* Wathan, Duke

**Watjen, Carolyn L. T.** 20th c. [CA]
*American author*
* Stafford, Caroline

**Watkins, A. T. L.**
See Watkins, Arthur Thomas Levi

**Watkins, Alex** 20th c. [WW]
*Author*
* Linklater, J. Lane

**Watkins, Arthur Thomas Levi**
1907-1965 [CA, LC]
*Welsh-born playwright*
* Watkins, A. T. L.
* Watkyn, Arthur

**Watkins, Frances Jane Grierson**
1919- [ART, DBA]
*British artist*
* Milligan, Frances J. G.
* Watkins, Peggy

**Watkins, Gino**
See Watkins, Henry George

**Watkins, Henry George** 1907-1932
[B10]
*British explorer*
* Watkins, Gino

**Watkins, Joan C.**
See Casale, Joan T[herese]

**Watkins, Joe**
See Watson, Mitchell

**Watkins, Maurice** 1956- [RBE]
*American boxer*
* Watkins, Termite

**Watkins, Mel** 1940- [CA]
*American author*
* Jackson, Franklin Jefferson

**Watkins, Mrs. Charles A.** [FFF]
*Entertainer*
* Gray, Ada

**Watkins, Paula** 1937- [BEW]
*American actress and singer*
* Wayne, Paula

**Watkins, Peggy**
See Watkins, Frances Jane
Grierson

**Watkins, Termite**
See Watkins, Maurice

**Watkins-Pitchford, D. J.**
See Watkins-Pitchford, Denys
James

**Watkins-Pitchford, Denys James**
1905- [CA, SAT, TCC]
*British author and illustrator*
* B B
* Traherne, Michael
* Watkins-Pitchford, D. J.

**Watkinson, Frank** 1925- [ART]
*British sculptor, potter, painter*
* Meretricious

**Watkinson, Valerie**
See Elliston, Valerie Mae
[Watkinson]

**Watkyn, Arthur**
See Watkins, Arthur Thomas Levi

**Watling, Dilys**
See Rhys-Jones, Dilys

**Watney, Bernard Martyn** 1922-
[AW]
*British author*
* Dolley, Marcus, J.

**Watney, John B[asil]** 1915- [CA]
*British author*
* Roberts, Anthony

**Watre, Antony** [PA]
*Author*
* Nemesis

**Watson, A.** [PA]
*Author*
* De Younge, A.

**Watson, A. J.**
See Watson, Abram Joseph

**Watson, Abram Joseph** 1924-
[EAR]
*American auto racer*
* Watson, A. J.

**Watson, [John Hugh] Adam** 1914-
[CA]
*British diplomat and author*
* Scipio

**Watson, Alan**
See Watson, William Alexander
Jardine

**Watson, Arthel** 1923- [DAM]
*American singer*
* Watson, Doc

**Watson, Billy**
See Levie, Isaac

**Watson, Billy**
See Waldo, Edward Hamilton

**Watson, Bobby**
See Knucher, Robert Watson

**Watson, Bootsie**
See Watson, Douglas C.

**Watson, [Sir] Brook** 1735-1807
[FFF]
*British soldier*
* [The] Wooden Legged
  Commissary

**Watson, Bryan Joseph** 1942-
[FHE, SMG]
*Canadian-born hockey player*
* Watson, Bugsy

**Watson, Bugsy**
See Watson, Bryan Joseph

**Watson, Bull**
See Watson, Robert Jose

**Watson, Charles** 20th c.
*American murderer*
* Watson, Tex

**Watson, Charles John** 1885-1950
[BE]
*American baseball player*
* Watson, Doc

**Watson, Claire**
See McLamore, Claire

**Watson, Deek**
See Watson, Ivory

**Watson, Doc**
See Watson, Arthel

**Watson, Doc**
See Watson, Charles John

**Watson, Douglas C.** 20th c. [IBW]
*American engineer*
* Watson, Bootsie

**Watson, Edmund Henry Lacon** 1865-
? [LAO]
*British author*
* Lacon

**Watson, Elizabeth**
See Boles-Watson, Elizabeth

**Watson, Eve** 1918- [THR]
*British actress and singer*
* Lister, Eve

**Watson, Evelyn Mabel** 1886-
[NAA]
*American author and poet*
* Palmer, Halleck

**Watson, Fly**
See Watson, Thomas Sturges

**Watson, Frank**
See Ames, Francis H.

**Watson, Frederick**
See Porter, Frederick

**Watson, Gayle Hudgens**
See Hudgens, A[lice] Gayle

**Watson, Guitar**
See Watson, Johnny

**Watson, Guy**
See Sisson, Jack

**Watson, Harold** 1912?- [CW]
*Jamaican poet and author*
* Merson, H. A.

**Watson, Harry E.** 1898-1957 [HK]
*Canadian-born hockey player*
* Watson, Moose

**Watson, Henrietta**
See Boles-Watson, Henrietta

**Watson, Ivory** 1909-1969 [SC]
*American singer and actor*
* Watson, Deek

**Watson, J[ames] Wreford** 1915-
[CA, WD]
*British poet, author, geographer*
* Wreford, James

**Watson, James** 19th c. [SN]
*British author and editor*
* [The] Doctor

**Watson, James Lopez** 1922- [IBW]
*American politician and jurist*
* Watson, Skiz

**Watson, Jane Werner** 1915-
[CA, SAT, WW]
*American author*
* Bedford, A. N.
* Bedford, Annie North
* Hill, Monica
* Nast, Elsa Ruth
* Werner, Jane

**Watson, Jimmy**
See Watson, Johnny

**Watson, Joe** 1943- [SMG]
*Canadian-born hockey player*
* Watson, Pumpkin
* Watson, Thundermouth

**Watson, John** 1850-1907 [LC]
*British-born author*
* Maclaren, Ian

**Watson, John H., MD**
See Farmer, Philip Jose

**Watson, John Reeves** 1896-1949
[BE]
*American baseball player*
* Watson, Mule

**Watson, Johnny** 1867-1963
[BWW, NBB]
*American singer*
* Daddy Stovepipe
* Pitts, [Rev.] Alfred
* Sunny Jim
* Watson, Jimmy

**Watson, Johnny** 1935-
[BWW, RO1]
*American singer*
* Watson, Guitar

**Watson, Joseph K.**
See Koff, Joseph

**Watson, Julia** 1943-
[AW, CA, WD]
*British author*
* De Vere, Jane
* Fitzgerald, Julia
* Hamilton, Julia

**Watson, L. J.**
See Watson, Leslie Joseph

**Watson, Le. De W.**
See Wood, Richard Kennedy
[Dick]

**Watson, Lee**
See Watson, Leland Hale

**Watson, Leland Hale** 1926- [BEW]
*American theatrical lighting designer*
* Watson, Lee

**Watson, Leslie Joseph** 1906-
[ART]
*British painter and landscape architect*
* Watson, L. J.

**Watson, Lillian Debra** 1950-
[BBH, SWI]
*American swimmer*
* Watson, Pokey

**Watson, Mabel** 1875?-1953 [BEW]
*British actress*
* Love, Mabel

**Watson, Margaret**
See Boles-Watson, Margaret

**Watson, Mary** 20th c. [WWL]
*Scottish author*
* Tubalcain

**Watson, Mitchell** 1900-1969
[NOJ]
*American jazz musician*
* Watkins, Joe

**Watson, Moose**
See Watson, Harry E.

**Watson, Mother**
See Watson, Walter L.

**Watson, Mule**
See Watson, John Reeves

**Watson, O[scar] Michael** 1936-
[CA]
*American anthropologist and author*
* Shears, Billie

**Watson, Pauline** 1925- [CA]
*American author and columnist*
* POLA

**Watson, Pokey**
See Watson, Lillian Debra

**Watson, Pumpkin**
See Watson, Joe

**Watson, Reatha** 1896?-1926
[BEW, F2, FC]
*American actress*
* La Marr, Barbara

**Watson, Richard F.**
See Silverberg, Robert

**Watson, Robert Jose** 1946-
[B10, BE, PB]
*American baseball player*
* Watson, Bull

**Watson, Robert R[utherford]** 1917-
[CA]
*American psychologist and author*
* Holt, Robert R[utherford]

**Watson, Rosamund [Ball] Marriott**
1863-1911 [B10]
*British poet*
* Tomson, Graham R.

**Watson, St. John**
See Clarke, Percy A.

**Watson, Skiz**
See Watson, James Lopez

**Watson, Solomon Lancelot Inglis**
1901- [THR]
*British actor*
* Lister, Lance

**Watson, Tex**
See Watson, Charles

**Watson, Thomas Sturges** 1949-
*American golfer*
* Watson, Fly

**Watson, Thundermouth**
See Watson, Joe

**Watson, Tom**
See Slaughter, Marion T.

**Watson, Vernon** 1886?-1949
[BEW]
*Theatrical performer*
* King, Nosmo

**Watson, Violet** 1900-1972 [FC]
*British actress*
* Lyel, Viola

**Watson, Virginia Cruse** 20th c.
[NAA]
*American editor and author*
* West, Roger

**Watson, Walker** 1752-1854 [PA]
*Author*
* [The] Poet of Kirkintilloch

**Watson, Walter L.** 1865-1898 [BE]
*American baseball player*
* Watson, Mother

**Watson, Will**
See Floren, Lee

**Watson, Will**
See Stivers, Jeremiah

**Watson, William Alexander Jardine**
1933- [CA]
*Scottish educator and author*
* Watson, Alan

**Watson, William Lorimer** 20th c.
[WWL]
*British author*
* Lorimer, Adam

**Watson, William Robinson**
1799-1864 [FFF]
*American politician and writer*
* Hamilton

**Watson, Wylie**
See Robertson, John Wylie

**Watt, Elsie Gowans** 1902- [IAW]
*Canadian writer*
* Gowans, Elsa

**Watt, Esme Violet** 20th c. [AW]
*British author*
* Jeans, Angela

**Watt, Frank Marion** 1902-1956
[BE]
*American baseball player*
* Watt, Kilo

**Watt, Kilo**
See Watt, Frank Marion

**Watt, Mr.** [code name used during
World War II]
See Wilson, [Sir] Henry Maitland

**[The] Watt of America**
See Evans, Oliver

**Watt, William**
See Scott, Will[iam Matthew]

**Watt-Evans, Lawrence**
See Evans, Lawrence Watt

**Watters, Barbara H.**
See Hunt, Barbara

**Watterson, Henry** 1840?-1921
[FFF, PA, WBD]
*American politician and journalist*
* Marse Henry
* Trenchard, Asa

**Watterson, John William** 1878- ?
[WWL]
*British author*
* Cowley, Ramsay

**Wattie**
See Chisholm, Walter

**Watts, [Anna] Bernadette** 1942-
[CA, SAT]
*British author and illustrator*
* Bernadette

**Watts, Charles H.** 1902-1968 [SC]
*American actor*
* Watts, Cotton

**Watts, Clem**
See Trace, Al[bert J.]

**Watts, Cotton**
See Watts, Charles H.

**Watts, Cueball**
See Watts, Don[ald Earl]

**Watts, Dodo**
See Watts, Dorothy Margaret

**Watts, Don[ald Earl]** 1951-
[IBW, NBA, SMG]
*American basketball player*
* Watts, Cueball
* Watts, Slick

**Watts, Dorothy Margaret** 1910-
[THR]
*British actress*
* Watts, Dodo

**Watts, Elizabeth [Bailey] Smithgall**
1941- [CA]
*American anthropologist and author*
* Smithgall, Elizabeth

**Watts, Herman** 20th c. [OBW]
*American baseball player*
* Watts, Lefty

**Watts, Joan Alwyn** 1921- [ART]
*British painter*
* J. A. W.

**Watts, John** 1922- [TR]
*Canadian singer and actor*
* Hanson, John

**Watts, Lefty**
See Watts, Herman

**Watts, Lou[is Thomas]** 1934-1970
[BWW]
*American singer*
* Lewis, Tommy
* Louis, Tommy
* Thomas, Kid

**Watts, Mabel Pizzey** 1906-
[CA, SAT]
*British-born author*
* Lynn, Patricia

**Watts, Marilyn** 1932- [FC, SW]
*American actress*
* Corday, Mara

**Watts, Noble** 20th c. [RO1]
*American musician*
* Watts, Thin Man

**[The] Watts of Wales**
See Williams, William

**Watts, Peter Christopher** 1919-
[CA]
*British author*
* Chisholm, Matt
* James, Cy
* Mackinlock, Duncan
* Owen, Tom

**Watts, Slick**
*See* Watts, Don[ald Earl]

**Watts, Thin Man**
*See* Watts, Noble

**Watts, Thomas** 1811-1869    [PA]
*Author*
* P. P. C. R.

**Watts, Walter Theodore**
1932-1914    [LC]
*British author*
* Watts-Dunton, [Walter]
  Theodore

**Watts-Dunton, [Walter] Theodore**
*See* Watts, Walter Theodore

**Wattson, Lewis Thomas**
1864-1940    [B10]
*American clergyman*
* Paul James Francis, [Father]

**Watzke, Alex** 1880?-1918    [NOJ]
*American jazz musician*
* Watzke, King

**Watzke, King**
*See* Watzke, Alex

**Wauch, Mansie**
*See* Moir, David Macbeth

**Waud, Elizabeth**
*See* Tattersall, Muriel Joyce

**Waugh, Edwin** 1817-1890
[PA, WBD]
*British poet*
* [The] Lancashire Burns
* [The] Lancashire Poet

**Waugh, Hillary Baldwin** 1920-
[CA, CC, EMD]
*American author*
* Grandower, Elissa
* Taylor, H. Baldwin
* Walker, Harry

**Waughburton, Richard** [joint
pseudonym with Christopher (Hugh)
Sykes]
*See* Byron, Robert

**Waughburton, Richard** [joint
pseudonym with Robert Byron]
*See* Sykes, Christopher [Hugh]

**Wauhop, John Milton** 1884-1960
[BE, PB]
*American baseball player*
* Warhop, Chief
* Warhop, Crab
* Warhop, John Milton

**Waverley, Edward Bradwardine**
*See* Croker, John Wilson

**Waverly**
*See* Wilson, A. J.

**Wax, Rosalie [Amelia] H.** 1911-
[CA]
*American anthropologist and author*
* Hankey, Rosalie A.

**Waxem of Wayback, Jedge**
*See* Lampton, W. J.

**Waxman, Albert** 1875-1962
[BMH, THR]
*Australian-born comedian*
* [The] Australian Entertainer
* Whelan, Albert

**Waxman, Franz**
*See* Wachsmann, Franz

**Way, Fanny**
*See* Way, Frances Elizabeth

**Way, Frances Elizabeth** 1871- ?
[DBA]
*British painter*
* Way, Fanny

**Way, Isabel Stewart**
*See* Bonnard, Isabel Stewart Way

**Way, Robert E[dward]** 1912-    [CA]
*South African-born author*
* Black, David

**Way, Wayne**
*See* Humphries, Adelaide M.

**Wayde, Bernard** 20th c.    [WW]
*Author*
* Collier, Old Cap

**Wayditch, Gabriel**
*See* Wajditsch Verbovac Von
Doenhoff, [Baron] Gabriel

**Waye, Ellen Jeanne** 20th c.    [AW]
*Australian author*
* Jose, Ellen J.

**Waylan, Mildred**
*See* Harrell, Irene B[urk]

**Wayland, Frederic Gregson** 1906-
[WWJ]
*American jazz musician*
* Wayland, Hank

**Wayland, Hank**
*See* Wayland, Frederic Gregson

**Wayland, Patrick**
*See* O'Connor, Richard

**Wayman, Dorothy [Godfrey]**
1893-1975    [B10, CA, NAA]
*American journalist, librarian,
author*
* Geoffrey, Theodate

**Wayman, Tony Russell** 1929-    [CA]
*British-born author*
* Cardui, Van
* Cardui, Vanessa
* Rahman, Abdul

**Waymon, Eunice Kathleen** 1933-
[EJ, IBW, SSS]
*American singer*
* [The] High Priestess of Soul
* Simone, Nina

**Wayne, Alice**
*See* Ressler, Alice

**Wayne, Anderson**
*See* Dresser, Davis

**Wayne, Anthony** 1745-1796
[DNNS, FFF, SN]
*American army officer*
* Wayne, Dandy
* Wayne, Mad Anthony

**Wayne, Bobby**
*See* Weintrop, Reuben

**Wayne, Charles Stokes** 1858- ?
[NAA]
*American author and playwright*
* Hazeltine, Horace

**Wayne, Chuck**
*See* Jagelka, Charles

**Wayne, Dandy**
*See* Wayne, Anthony

**Wayne, Daphne** 1895?-    [FC]
*American actress*
* [The] Biograph Blonde
* Sweet, Blanche

**Wayne, David**
*See* Balsiger, David W[ayne]

**Wayne, David**
*See* McMeekan, Wayne James

**Wayne, Donald**
*See* Dodd, Wayne [Donald]

**Wayne, Frances**
*See* Bertocci, Chiarina Francesca

**Wayne, Frances**
*See* Wedge, Florence

**Wayne, Gladys**
*See* Van Valkenburg, Julia

**Wayne, John**
*See* Morrison, Marion Michael

**Wayne, Joseph**
*See* Overholser, Wayne D.

**Wayne, Kyra Petrovskaya** 1918-
[SAT]
*Russian-born author*
* Petrovskaya, Kyra

**Wayne, Mad Anthony**
*See* Wayne, Anthony

**Wayne, Michael A.**
*See* Morrison, Michael A.

**Wayne, Naunton**
*See* Davies, Naunton

**Wayne, Patricia**
*See* Cutts, Patricia

**Wayne, Paula**
*See* Watkins, Paula

**Wayne, Philip**
*See* Powell, Philip Wayne

**Wayne, Richard**
*See* Decker, Duane

**Waynflete [or Wainfleet], William of**
*See* Patyn, William

**Ways, C. R.**
*See* Blount, Roy [Alton], Jr.

**Wazyk, Adam**
*See* Wagmann, Adam

**wbassett, Marnie**
*See* Bassett, Flora Marjorie

**Weadon, Percy**
*See* Preston, Frank

**Weafer, [Kenneth] Al[bert]** 1914-
[BE]
*American baseball player*
* Weafer, Hal

**Weafer, Hal**
*See* Weafer, [Kenneth] Al[bert]

**Weale, Anne**
*See* Blake, Andrea

**Weale, B. L. Putnam**
*See* Simpson, Bertram Lennox

**Weary, Ogdred**
*See* Gorey, Edward [St. John]

**[The] Weasel**
*See* Bessent, Fred Donald

**[The] Weasel**
*See* Cecil, William [First Baron
Burleigh]

**[The] Weasel**
*See* Fratianno, James [Jimmy]

**[That] Weather Cock**
*See* Pulteney, William [Earl of
Bath]

**[The] Weather Glass of His Time**
*See* Pepys, Samuel

**[The] Weathercock**
*See* Aswad, al-

**[The] Weathercock**
*See* Romaine, Lawrence B.

**[The] Weathercock**
*See* Townshend, Charles

**Weathercock, Janus**
*See* Wainewright, Thomas
Griffiths

**Weatherford, William** 1780?-1824
[WBD]
*American Indian chieftain*
* Red Eagle

**Weatherly, [Cyril] Roy** 1915-
[BE, PB]
*American baseball player*
* Weatherly, Stormy

**Weatherly, Stormy**
*See* Weatherly, [Cyril] Roy

**Weathers, Felicia Frances Theresa**
1937-    [IBW]
*American opera singer*
* Weathers, Frankie

**Weathers, Frankie**
*See* Weathers, Felicia Frances
Theresa

**Weathers, Philip Joseph** 1908-
[IAW]
*British director, playwright, author*
* Sherwood, Michael

**Weathers, Winston** 1926-    [CA]
*American author*
* Palmer, Tobias

**Weathersby, Eliza**
*See* Goodwin, Mrs. Nat C.

**Weatherspoon, Nick** 1950-    [SMG]
*American basketball player*
* Weatherspoon, Spoon [or
  Spoonie]

**Weatherspoon, Spoon [or Spoonie]**
*See* Weatherspoon, Nick

**Weatherstone, June Irene** 1935-
[CA]
*Australian-born author*
* Collins, June

**Weaver, Bertrand** 1908-1973    [CA]
*Clergyman and writer*
* Hunter, Paul

**Weaver, Big Jim**
*See* Weaver, James Dement

**Weaver, Blind Curley**
*See* Weaver, Curley James

**Weaver, Buck**
*See* Weaver, George Davis

**Weaver, Charles** 1940-  [EJ7]
*American jazz musician*
* Abdullah, Shakur

**Weaver, Charley**
See  Arquette, Cliff[ord]

**Weaver, Curley James** 1906-1962
[BWW]
*American singer*
* Gordon, Slim
* Weaver, Blind Curley

**Weaver, Earle**
See  Willets, Walter E.

**Weaver, Effie**
See  McVicker, Mrs. Horace

**Weaver, Ella**
See  Whiteley, Mrs. John H.

**Weaver, Elviry**
See  Weaver, June

**Weaver, Farmer**
See  Weaver, William B.

**Weaver, Fluss**
See  Weaver, James Brian [Jim]

**Weaver, George Davis** 1890-1956
[AS, BE, PB]
*American baseball player*
* Weaver, Buck

**Weaver, Gertrude Renton** 1884-
[SFL, WGT]
*British author*
* Colmore, G[eorge]
* Dunn, Gertrude

**Weaver, Gustine Courson** 1873- ?
[NAA]
*American author*
* Lady Gustine

**Weaver, James Brian [Jim]** 1939-
[BE]
*American baseball player*
* Weaver, Fluss

**Weaver, James Dement** 1903-  [BE]
*American baseball player*
* Weaver, Big Jim

**Weaver, June** 1891?-1977  [FIR]
*Entertainer*
* Weaver, Elviry

**Weaver, Katherine Grey Dunlap**
1910-  [CA]
*American author*
* Weaver, Kitty

**Weaver, Kitty**
See  Weaver, Katherine Grey
Dunlap

**Weaver, Lapland Willie**
See  Weaver, William [Bill]

**Weaver, Mateman**
See  Greene, Alvin Carl

**Weaver, Monte**
See  Weaver, Montgomery Morton

**Weaver, Montgomery Morton**
1906-  [BE, PB]
*American baseball player*
* Weaver, Monte
* Weaver, Prof

**Weaver, Orlie**
See  Weaver, Orville F.

**Weaver, Orville F.** 1888-  [BE]
*American baseball player*
* Weaver, Orlie

**Weaver, Pat**
See  Weaver, Sylvester L., Jr.

**Weaver, Paul Ford** 1901-
[BEW, TR]
*American actor*
* Ford, Paul

**Weaver, Phoenix Donald**
See  Weaver, William [Bill]

**[The] Weaver Poet of Inverurie**
See  Thom, William

**Weaver, Prof**
See  Weaver, Montgomery Morton

**Weaver, Robert G.** 20th c.  [CA]
*American author*
* Weber, Rubin [joint pseudonym
  with S(amuel) Leonard
  Rubinstein]

**Weaver, Sylvester L., Jr.** 20th c.
[ET]
*Television executive*
* Weaver, Pat

**Weaver, Ward**
See  Mason, F[rancis] Van Wyck

**Weaver, William [Bill]**  ?-1954
[BLB]
*American robber*
* Weaver, Lapland Willie
* Weaver, Phoenix Donald

**Weaver, William B.** 1865-1943
[BE]
*American baseball player*
* Weaver, Farmer

**[The] Weazel**
See  Van Buren, Martin

**Web, Dan**
See  Millsaps, Daniel W., III

**Webb, A. C.**
See  Webb, Augustus Caesar

**Webb, Ada**  [BMH]
*Entertainer*
* Queen of the Crystal Tank

**Webb, Anthony** [joint pseudonym]
See  Wilson, N[orman] Scarlyn

**Webb, Arthur Patterson** 1889-
[WWL]
*British author*
* Simpkin

**Webb, Augustus Caesar** 1894-
[SFL]
*American author*
* Webb, A. C.

**Webb, Baby**
See  Webb, James

**Webb, Bill** 1926-  [BWW]
*American singer*
* Webb, Boogie Bill

**Webb, Blanche A.**  [SFL]
*Author*
* Draper, Blanche A.

**Webb, Boogie Bill**
See  Webb, Bill

**Webb, Brenda Gail** 1951-
*American country-western performer*
* Gayle, Crystal

**Webb, Charles Henry** 1834?-1905
[FFF, PA, WBD]
*American poet and journalist*
* Paul, John

**Webb, Charles Hull**  [FFF]
*American writer*
* Caqueteur
* Cutting, Pierce

**Webb, Chick**
See  Webb, William

**Webb, Christopher**
See  Wibberley, Leonard [Patrick
O'Connor]

**Webb, Cleon Earl** 1885-1958  [BE]
*American baseball player*
* Webb, Lefty

**Webb, Clifton**
See  Hollenbeck, Webb Parmelee

**Webb, Cornelius** 19th c.  [PA]
*Author*
* [A] Person about Town

**Webb, Dora**
See  Webb, Mahala Theodora

**Webb, Dorothy Anna Maria** 20th
c.  [WW]
*Author*
* March, Jermyn

**Webb, Ellsworth** 1931-  [BX]
*American boxer*
* Webb, Spider

**Webb, Ethel** 1925-  [IAW]
*British-born author*
* Roch, Dalby

**Webb, Eve [Rudd]** 1940?-
*American artist*
* Webb, Sasha

**Webb, Forrest**
See  Forrest-Webb, Robert

**Webb, Godfrey Edward Charles**
1914-  [AW]
*British author*
* England, Norman
* Godfrey, Charles

**Webb, Harold** 1940-  [FC, LRR]
*British singer*
* Richard, Cliff

**Webb, Jack** 1920-  [WW]
*Author*
* Farr, John
* Grady, Tex

**Webb, James** 20th c.  [OBW]
*American baseball player*
* Webb, Baby

**Webb, James Laverne** 1909-  [BE]
*American baseball player*
* Webb, Skeeter

**Webb, Jean Francis** 1910-
[CA, WD, WW]
*American author*
* Hamill, Ethel
* Morrison, Roberta

**Webb, Joseph** 19th c.  [PA]
*Author*
* Tela, Josephus

**Webb, Lawrence Arthur** 1906?-
[WWJ]
*American jazz musician*
* Webb, Speed

**Webb, Lefty**
See  Webb, Cleon Earl

**Webb, Lionel**
See  Hershman, Morris

**Webb, Lizbeth**
See  Wills-Webber, Lizbeth

**Webb, Lucas**
See  Burgess, Michael Roy

**Webb, Mahala Theodora** 1887-
[DBA]
*British painter and sculptor*
* Webb, Dora

**Webb, Mary**  [WWL]
*British author*
* Meredith, Mary G.

**Webb, Mary Haydn** 1938-  [CA]
*American author*
* Ross, Leah

**Webb, Neil**
See  Rowland, D[onald] S[ydney]

**Webb, Red**
See  Webb, Samuel Henry

**Webb, Richard Wilson**
[CC, EMD, WW]
*British-born American author*
* Patrick, Q. [joint pseudonym with
  Mary L. Aswell, Martha Kelly,
  and Hugh Wheeler]
* Quentin, Patrick [joint
  pseudonym with Hugh
  Callingham Wheeler]
* Stagge, Jonathan [joint
  pseudonym with Hugh
  Callingham Wheeler]

**Webb, Robert Forrest**
See  Forrest-Webb, Robert

**Webb, Ruth Enid Borlase Morris**
1926-  [AW, CA, WD]
*Australian author*
* Morris, Ruth

**Webb, Samuel Henry** 1924-  [BE]
*American baseball player*
* Webb, Red

**Webb, Sasha**
See  Webb, Eve [Rudd]

**Webb, Skeeter**
See  Webb, James Laverne

**Webb, Speed**
See  Webb, Lawrence Arthur

**Webb, Spider**
See  Gohman, Fred Joseph

**Webb, Spider**
See  Webb, Ellsworth

**Webb, Spider**
See  Webb, Travis

**Webb, Travis** 20th c.
*Auto racer*
* Webb, Spider

**Webb, W. H.** 19th c.  [PA]
*Author*
* Magpie

**Webb, W. T.**
See  Webb, William Thomas

**Webb, William** 1902?-1939
[DAM, EJ, PMJ]
*American jazz musician*
* Webb, Chick

**Webb, William Thomas** 1918-
[HFF]
*British author*
* Webb, W. T.

**Webbe, Gale D[udley]** 1909-   [CA]
*American clergyman and author*
* Cole, Stephen

**Webber, Bert**
*See*   Webber, Ebbert T[rue]

**Webber, Ebbert T[rue]** 1921-   [CA]
*American author*
* Webber, Bert

**Webber, George Harris** 1882-
[NAA]
*American educator and author*
* Sig

**Webber, Stawford**
*See*   Pile, D. W.

**Weber, Annemarie** 1918-   [IAW]
*German author*
* Henning, Katja

**Weber, Hulda** 1909-   [IAW]
*American author, poet, painter*
* Katz, Hilda

**Weber, Joe**
*See*   Weber, Morris

**Weber, Lisa**
*See*   Mullaly, Mrs. W. S.

**Weber, Morris** 1867-1942   [PMJ]
*American entertainer*
* Weber, Joe

**Weber, Nancy** 1942-   [CA]
*American author*
* Harmston, Olivia
* Rose, Jennifer
* West, Lindsay

**Weber, Rubin** [joint pseudonym with
Robert G. Weaver]
*See*   Rubinstein, S[amuel] Leonard

**Weber, Rubin** [joint pseudonym with
S[amuel] Leonard Rubinstein]
*See*   Weaver, Robert G.

**Weber, Sarah Appleton** 1930-   [CA]
*American educator and author*
* Appleton, Sarah

**Webfoot**
*See*   Phelps, W. D.

**Webley, Pelagian**
*See*   Morgan, William Sacheus

**Webster, Alice Jane Chandler**
1876-1916   [LC, TC]
*American author*
* Webster, Jean

**Webster, Chick**
*See*   Webster, John Robert

**Webster, Daniel** 1782-1852
[DNNS, HN, SN]
*American statesman*
* [The] Demosthenes of America
* [The] Expounder of the
Constitution
* [A] Traitor to Freedom

**Webster, David Endicott** 1929-
[CA]
*American author*
* Strongblood, Casper

**Webster, Edith Smith** 20th c.
[NAA]
*American author*
* Smith, Edith Lillian

**Webster, Ester Luise** 1898-   [NAA]
*American writer, editor, columnist*
* Paul, Genay

**Webster, Ester Luise** (Continued)
* Skillman, Ester Webster

**Webster, Frank V.** [house
pseudonym] [Stratemeyer
Syndicate]
*See*   Stratemeyer, Edward L.

**Webster, Gary**
*See*   Garrison, Webb B[lack]

**Webster, Jean**
*See*   Webster, Alice Jane Chandler

**Webster, Jennie Ellis Burdick**
1882-   [NAA]
*American author and editor*
* Burdick, Jennie Ellis

**Webster, Jesse**
*See*   Cassill, Ronald Verlin

**Webster, John Robert** 1921-   [CEI]
*Canadian-born hockey player*
* Webster, Chick

**Webster, Lizzie**
*See*   Nunnemacher, Mrs. Jacob

**Webster, Lucille** 1886-1947   [F2]
*American actress*
* Gleason, Lucille

**Webster, Mamie**
*See*   Smith, Mabel Louise

**Webster, Marvin** 1952-   [SMG]
*American basketball player*
* [The] Human Eraser

**Webster, Mrs. John**   [FFF]
*Entertainer*
* McHenry, Nellie

**Webster, Noah**
*See*   Knox, William [Bill]

**Webster, Noah** 1758-1843
[DNNS, FFF, SN]
*American lexicographer and author*
* Candor
* [The] Schoolmaster of the
Republic

**Webster, Paul Frank** 1909-   [MY]
*American jazz musician*
* Webster, Webb

**Webster, Robert N.**
*See*   Palmer, Raymond A[rthur]

**Webster, Speck**
*See*   Webster, William

**Webster, Webb**
*See*   Webster, Paul Frank

**Webster, William**   [OBW]
*American baseball player*
* Webster, Speck

**Wechsler, Moe**
*See*   Wechsler, Morris Louis

**Wechsler, Morris Louis** 1920-   [EJ]
*American jazz musician*
* Wechsler, Moe

**Weda [or Wegner], Richard**
*See*   Dallwitz-Wegner, Richard Von

**Wede**
*See*   Espy, Willard Richardson

**Wedecee**
*See*   Caroe, William Douglas

**Wedekind, Benjamin Franklin**
1864-1918   [BEW, LC]
*German playwright, producer, actor*
* Wedekind, Frank

**Wedekind, Frank**
*See*   Wedekind, Benjamin Franklin

**Wedell, Carl Heinrich** 1712-1782
[DNNF, FFF, SN]
*Prussian army officer*
* Wedell, Leonidas

**Wedell, Leonidas**
*See*   Wedell, Carl Heinrich

**Wedemeyer, Albert C.** 1897-
[CND]
*American military leader*
* White, Mr. [code name used
during World War II]

**[The] Wedge**
*See*   Turnesa, William P.

**Wedge, Florence** 1919-   [CA]
*Canadian author*
* Wayne, Frances

**Wedgwood, [Dame] C. V.**
*See*   Wedgwood, Cicely Veronica

**Wedgwood, Cicely Veronica** 1910-
[LC]
*British author*
* Wedgwood, [Dame] C. V.

**Wedgwood, Josiah** 1730-1795
[DNNS, HN, SN]
*British potter*
* [The] Father of English Pottery
* [The] Father of the Potteries

**Wee Bea Booze**
*See*   Nicholls, Muriel

**Wee Ben Sayers**
*See*   Sayers, Bernard

**Wee Bobby Cruickshank**
*See*   Cruickshank, Bobby

**Wee Bonnie Baker**
*See*   Nelson, Evelyn

**Wee Georgie Wood**
*See*   Bramlett, George

**[The] Wee Iceman**
*See*   Hogan, Benjamin William

**Wee Johnny**
*See*   Wilson, John

**[The] Wee Scot**
*See*   Cruickshank, Bobby

**[The] Wee Scot**
*See*   MacKay, Duncan McMillan

**Wee Tommy Leach**
*See*   Leach, Thomas W.

**Wee Willie Clark**
*See*   Clark, William Otis

**Wee Willie Damman**
*See*   Damman, William Henry
[Bill]

**Wee Willie Keeler**
*See*   Keeler, William Henry

**Wee Willie Ludolph**
*See*   Ludolph, William Francis
[Willie]

**Wee Willie Mains**
*See*   Mains, Willard Eben

**Wee Willie Messino**
*See*   Messino, William

**Wee Willie Mills**
*See*   Mills, William Grant [Willie]

**Wee Willie Powell**
*See*   Powell, William Ernest

**Wee Willie Robyn**
*See*   Robyn, William

**Wee Willie Sherdel**
*See*   Sherdel, William Henry

**Wee Willie Sudhoff**
*See*   Sudhoff, John William

**Wee Willie Wilkin**
*See*   Wilkin, Wilbur

**Weed, Buddy**
*See*   Weed, Harold Eugene

**Weed, Cy**
*See*   Weed, Randolph W.

**Weed, Harold Eugene** 1918-
[EJ, PMJ]
*American jazz musician*
* Weed, Buddy

**Weed, Leland T.** 1901-1975   [SC]
*American actor and singer*
* Baker, Bob

**Weed, Randolph W.** 1883?-1964
[AS]
*American rowboat racer*
* Weed, Cy

**Weed, Thurlow** 1797- ?   [PA]
*Author*
* T. W.

**Weegee**
*See*   Fellig, Arthur

**Weekes, Agnes Russell** 1880- ?
[TC, WW]
*British author*
* Pryde, Anthony

**Weekley, Maurice Arden**   [WGT]
*Author*
* Arden, Rice

**Weeks, Ada Mae** 1900-   [THR]
*American actress and dancer*
* May, Ada

**Weeks, Bill** 20th c.   [GW]
*American rodeo performer*
* Weeks, Crotcho

**Weeks, Black Hoss**
*See*   Weeks, Guy

**Weeks, Constance Tomkinson**
1915-   [CA]
*Canadian-born author*
* Tomkinson, Constance

**Weeks, Crotcho**
*See*   Weeks, Bill

**Weeks, Guy** 20th c.   [GW]
*American rodeo performer*
* Weeks, Black Hoss

**Weeks, Helen C.** 19th c.   [FFF, PA]
*Author*
* Campbell, Helen
* Wheaton, Campbell

**Weems, Ted**
*See*   Weymes, Wilfred Theodore

**[The] Weeping Greek from Cripple
Creek**
*See*   Zaharias, George

**[The] Weeping Philosopher**
*See*   Heraclitos [or Heraclitus]

**[The] Weeping Saint**
*See*   Swithin

**Weeping Willie Willoughby**
See   Willoughby, Claude William

**Weer, William**
See   Kaufman, Isadore

**Weertz, Louis** 1926-   [EPM]
*American musician*
* Williams, Roger

**Wees, Frances Shelley** 1902-   [CA]
*Canadian author*
* Shelley, Frances

**Wef [Wild Eyed Fellow]**
See   Clifford, Christopher Craven

**Wegg De Norva, Silas**
See   Viett, George Frederic

**Wegier, Bayla** 1927-1971   [FC]
*Polish-French actress*
* Darvi, Bella

**Wehde, Biggs**
See   Wehde, Wilbur

**Wehde, Wilbur** 1906-   [BE]
*American baseball player*
* Wehde, Biggs

**Wehen, Joy DeWeese** 20th c.   [CA]
*Malaysian-born author*
* Wade, Jennifer

**Wehmeyer, Lillian [Mabel] Biermann**
1933-   [CA]
*American author and educator*
* Biermann, Lillian

**Wehr, Werner**
See   Gartmann, Heinz

**Wei, Rex Yue-Tien** 1933-
[AW, WD]
*British author and poet*
* Williams, Rex

**Weichbrodt, Rudolph C.**
1871-1958   [BE]
*American baseball player*
* Roach, Skel

**Weidenfeld, Jesse Marc** 1919-
[BEW]
*American actor and comedian*
* White, Jesse

**Weidman, George E.** 1861-1905
[AS, BE]
*American baseball player*
* Weidman, Stump

**Weidman, Stump**
See   Weidman, George E.

**Weidt, Conrad** 1892-1943   [WEF]
*German-born actor*
* Veidt, Conrad

**Weigel, Ralph Richard** 1921-   [BE]
*American baseball player*
* Weigel, Wig

**Weigel, Wig**
See   Weigel, Ralph Richard

**Weight, Frank**
See   Tubb, Edwin Charles

**Weightman, Wild Bill**
See   Weightman, William E.

**Weightman, William E.** 20th c.
[EAR]
*American auto racer*
* Weightman, Wild Bill

**Weigle, Marta**
See   Weigle, Mary Martha

**Weigle, Mary Martha** 1944-   [CA]
*American folklorist and author*
* Weigle, Marta

**Weigle, Ross** 1901-1961
*American actor*
* Ross, Churchill

**Weigum, Patricia Millicent** 1929-
[EJ]
*American singer*
* Yankee, Pat

**Weihe, John Garibaldi** 1862-1914
[BE]
*American baseball player*
* Weihe, Podgie

**Weihe, Podgie**
See   Weihe, John Garibaldi

**Weik, Legs**
See   Weik, Richard Henry

**Weik, Richard Henry** 1927-   [BE]
*American baseball player*
* Weik, Legs

**Weil, Josef** 1828-1889   [WBD]
*Bohemian-born poet and playwright*
* Weilen, Josef von

**Weil, Joseph R.** 1875?-1976   [B10]
*American swindler*
* Weil, Yellow Kid

**Weil, Roman L[ee]** 1940-   [CA]
*American educator and author*
* Worman, Eli

**Weil, Yellow Kid**
See   Weil, Joseph R.

**Weiland, Cooney**
See   Weiland, Ralph

**Weiland, Lefty**
See   Weiland, Robert George

**Weiland, Ralph** 1904-
[CEI, FHE, HK]
*Canadian-born hockey player*
* Weiland, Cooney

**Weiland, Robert George** 1905-
[BE]
*American baseball player*
* Weiland, Lefty

**Weilen, Josef von**
See   Weil, Josef

**Weilenmann, Carl Woolworth**
1889-1924   [AS, BE]
*American baseball player*
* Weilman, Carl Woolworth
* Weilman, Zeke

**Weiler, Phyllis** 1914-   [FC]
*American actress*
* Brooks, Phyllis

**Weill, Rene** 1868-1952   [WBD]
*French playwright*
* Coolus, Romain

**Weilman, Carl Woolworth**
See   Weilenmann, Carl Woolworth

**Weilman, Zeke**
See   Weilenmann, Carl Woolworth

**Weimer, Jacob** 1873-1928
[AS, BE]
*American baseball player*
* Weimer, Tornado Jake

**Weimer, Marguerite Josephine**
1787-1867   [WBD]
*French actress*
* George, Mlle.

**Weimer, Tornado Jake**
See   Weimer, Jacob

**Weinbaum, Helen**
See   Kasson, Helen Weinbaum

**Weinbaum, Stanley G[rauman]**
1900?-1935   [ESF, WGT, WOA]
*American author*
* Jessel, John
* Stanley, Marge

**Weinberg, Abe** ?-1935   [PHM]
*American underworld figure*
* Weinberg, Bo

**Weinberg, Bo**
See   Weinberg, Abe

**Weinberg, Charles** 1889-1955
[ASC]
*American composer and conductor*
* Wynn, Charles

**Weinberg, Janet Hopson**
See   Hopson, Janet L[ouise]

**Weinberg, Melvin** 1925?-
*American swindler and government
witness in Abscam trials*
* [The] McDonald's of Con Men

**Weinberger, Caspar** 1917?-
*American government official*
* Cap the Cup
* Cap the Knife
* Cap the Shovel
* Cap the Suitcase

**Weinberger, Harry** 1924-   [ART]
*German-born artist*
* H. W.

**Weinberger, Moshe** 1908-   [CA]
*Hungarian-born American author*
* Carmilly, Moshe

**Weinblatt, Mike**
See   Weinblatt, Myron

**Weinblatt, Myron** 20th c.   [ET]
*Television executive*
* Weinblatt, Mike

**Weiner, Doc**
See   Stacher, Joseph

**Weiner, Edith** 1943-   [CA]
*American journalist and editor*
* Lederer, Edith Madelon

**Weiner, Henri**
See   Longstreet, [Henry] Stephen
[Weiner]

**Weiner, Margery Sarah** 20th c.
[AW]
*British author*
* Lake, Sarah

**Weiner, Skip**
See   Weiner, Stewart

**Weiner, Stewart** 1945-   [CA]
*American author and editor*
* Lebreo, Steward
* Lebreo, Stewart
* Weiner, Skip

**Weiner, Yehudi** 1929-   [BBD]
*American composer*
* Wyner, Yehudi

**Weinert, Charley** 1895-   [BX]
*Hungarian-born boxer*
* [The] Newark Adonis

**Weinert, Lefty**
See   Weinert, Philip Walter

**Weinert, Philip Walter** 1901-1973
[BE]
*American baseball player*
* Weinert, Lefty

**Weingarten, David** 1902-   [ASC]
*American composer*
* Gardner, Dave

**Weingartner, Dutch**
See   Weingartner, Elmer William

**Weingartner, Elmer William** 1918-
[BE]
*American baseball player*
* Weingartner, Dutch

**Weinig, Jean Maria** 1920-   [CA]
*American writer and poet*
* Mary Anthony, [Mother]
* Weinig, [Sister] Mary Anthony

**Weinig, [Sister] Mary Anthony**
See   Weinig, Jean Maria

**Weinrauch, Herschel** 1905-   [CAP]
*Russian-born American author*
* Vinokur, Grigory

**Weinrich, Anna Katharina Hildegard**
1933-   [CA]
*German-born anthropologist and
author*
* Mary Aquina, [Sister]

**Weinstein, Aaron** 1898-1967
[WGT]
*American author*
* Wyn, A. A.

**Weinstein, Ellen R.** 1939-   [BEW]
*American actress*
* Weston, Ellen

**Weinstein, Nathan Wallenstein**
1903?-1940   [LC, TC, TCL]
*American author*
* West, Nathanael
* West, Pep

**Weinstein, Sam** 1914-   [BBH]
*American radio and television
broadcaster*
* [The] Tenpin Tattler

**Weinstock, Helen** 1910-   [CA]
*American author*
* Lewis, Francine
* Wells, Helen

**Weinstock, Jack** 20th c.
*American playwright and
screenwriter*
* Mareth, Glenville [joint
pseudonym with William Gilbert
Gomberg]

**Weintraub, Mickey**
See   Weintraub, Philip

**Weintraub, Philip** 1907-   [BE, EJS]
*American baseball player*
* Weintraub, Mickey

**Weintraub, Wiktor** 1908-   [IAW]
*Polish-born author*
* Quidam
* Theates

**Weintrop, Reuben** 1896-1968
[BMH]
*British comedian and singer*
* Fargo the Boy Wizard
* Flanagan, Bud
* Wayne, Bobby
* Winthrop, Robert

**Weir, Alice M.**
*See* McLaughlin, Emma Maude

**Weir, Ike O'Neil** 1867-1908
[BX, RBE]
*Irish-born boxer*
* [The] Belfast Spider

**Weir, John**
*See* Cross, Colin [John]

**Weir, Mordred**
*See* Long, Amelia Reynolds

**Weir, Rosemary** 1905- [TCC]
*South African-born author*
* Bell, Catherine

**Weir, Roy**
*See* Weir, William Franklin [Bill]

**Weir, Stan** 1952- [SMG]
*Canadian-born hockey player*
* Weir, Stash

**Weir, Stash**
*See* Weir, Stan

**Weir, William Franklin [Bill]** 1911-
[BE]
*American baseball player*
* Weir, Roy

**Weir, Woodrow** [BBH]
*American basketball player and coach*
* Weir, Woody

**Weir, Woody**
*See* Weir, Woodrow

**[The] Weird Guitar Player**
*See* Bell, Ed[ward]

**Weis, Arthur John** 1903- [BE]
*American baseball player*
* Weis, Butch

**Weis, Butch**
*See* Weis, Arthur John

**Weis, Isaac Mayer** 1819-1900
[WBD]
*American clergyman*
* Wise, Isaac Mayer

**Weisberg, Roy B.** 1893-1975 [SC]
*Russian-born actor, director, screenwriter*
* West, Billy

**Weisenfreund, Muni** 1895-1967
[F2, FC, IPA]
*Austrian-born actor*
* Muni, Paul

**Weiser, Bud**
*See* Weiser, Harry Budson

**Weiser, Harry Budson** 1891-1961
[BE]
*American baseball player*
* Weiser, Bud

**Weisgal, Emanuel** 1925-
[BEW, TR]
*American actor and director*
* Wager, Michael

**Weisgard, Leonard [Joseph]** 1916-
[CA, SAT]
*American author and illustrator*
* Green, Adam

**Weisinger, Mort[imer]** 1915-
[SFP, WGT]
*American author*
* Garth, Will [house pseudonym]
* Geris, Tom Erwin
* Rectez, Ian
* Saturn, Sergeant [house pseudonym]

**Weisman, Alfred** 1883-1972 [SC]
*American actor*
* White, Alfred H.

**Weiss, Albert Maria** 1844-1925
[WBD]
*German-born theologian and author*
* Von der Clana, Heinrich

**Weiss, Amalie**
*See* Schneeweiss, Amalie

**Weiss, Earl**
*See* Wajcieckowski, Earl

**Weiss, Edna**
*See* Barth, Edna

**Weiss, Ehrich** 1874-1926
[BS, FC, THR]
*American magician*
* [The] Handcuff King
* Houdini, Harry
* [The] King of Cards

**Weiss, Emanuel** ?-1944 [PHM]
*American underworld figure*
* Weiss, Mendy

**Weiss, Francesca** 1885?-1975
[FIR]
*Television performer*
* Weiss, Mama

**Weiss, George Martin** 1894-1972
[BAB]
*American baseball executive*
* Weiss, Lonesome George

**Weiss, Henry George** 1898-1946
[NAA, SF]
*Canadian-born writer*
* Flagg, Francis

**Weiss, Howard Peter** 1927- [BEW]
*American musician*
* Howard, Peter

**Weiss, Hymie**
*See* Wajcieckowski, Earl

**Weiss, Irving J.** 1921- [CA]
*American editor and writer*
* Forio, Robert

**Weiss, Little Hymie**
*See* Wajcieckowski, Earl

**Weiss, Lonesome George**
*See* Weiss, George Martin

**Weiss, Louis** 1907- [FC, ITA, SW]
*American actor*
* Taylor, Kent

**Weiss, Mama**
*See* Weiss, Francesca

**Weiss, Mendy**
*See* Weiss, Emanuel

**Weiss, Miriam**
*See* Schlein, Miriam

**Weiss, Morris S[amuel]** 1915- [CA]
*American author and illustrator*
* Higgins, Ink
* Sirrom, Wes

**Weiss, Pana** 20th c. [EJS]
*Polish discus thrower*
* Wajsowna, Jadwiga

**Weiss, Theo** 20th c. [BMH]
*American magician*
* Hardeen
* Hardin

**Weisse, Clifford Stevens** 1936-
[BEW]
*American talent representative*
* Stevens, Clifford

**Weissenberg, Alexis** 1929- [MS]
*Bulgarian-born musician*
* Weissenberg, Sigi

**Weissenberg, Sigi**
*See* Weissenberg, Alexis

**Weisshaus, Imre** 1904-
*Hungarian composer*
* Arma, Paul

**Weissman, Jack** 1921- [CA]
*American author*
* Anderson, George

**Weissman, Solly**
*See* Weissman, William

**Weissman, William** 20th c. [BLB]
*American underworld figure*
* Weissman, Solly

**Weisz, Herbert** 1924- [TR]
*Austrian-born director and actor*
* Wise, Herbert

**Weisz, Victor** 1913-1966 [LC]
*German-born cartoonist*
* Vicky

**Weitz, George** 1888?-1968
[EMT, PMJ]
*American producer, director, writer*
* White, George

**Weitzel, Mrs. S. W.** [PA]
*Author*
* Winthrop, Sophy

**Wejp-Olsen, Werner** 1938- [WEC]
*Danish cartoonist*
* WOW

**Welber, Del**
*See* Wilber, Delbert Quentin

**Welburn, Vivienne**
*See* Furlong, Vivienne Carole

**Welby, Henry** [SN]
*British eccentric*
* [The] Hermit of Grub Street

**Welby, Horace**
*See* Timbs, John

**Welby, Thomas Earle** 1881-1933
[LC]
*British author and journalist*
* Stet

**Welch, Alfred** 1899-1952 [SC]
*American actor*
* Bond, Jack

**Welch, Ann Courtenay Edmonds**
1917- [CA]
*British author*
* Douglas, Ann C.
* Edmonds, Ann C.

**Welch, Bugger**
*See* Welch, Frank Tiguer

**Welch, Charles Scott**
*See* Smith, LeRoi Tex

**Welch, Dutch**
*See* Welch, Herb[ert M.]

**Welch, Edgar L[uderne]** 1855- ?
[SFL, WGT]
*Author*
* Gay, J. Drew
* Grip

**Welch, Frank Tiguer** 1897-1957
[BE]
*American baseball player*
* Welch, Bugger

**Welch, Hawley** 1907- [BBH, FH]
*Canadian football player*
* Welch, Huck

**Welch, Herb[ert M.]** 1900-1967
[BE]
*American baseball player*
* Welch, Dutch

**Welch, Huck**
*See* Welch, Hawley

**Welch, Jean-Louise**
*See* Kempton, Jean Welch

**Welch, Louise** 1896-1980 [F1, F2]
*American actress*
* Carbasse, Louise
* Lovely, Louise

**Welch, Marilyn** 1933- [ASC]
*American composer and entertainer*
* Welch, Mitzie

**Welch, Michael F.** 1859-1941
[AS, DGS, PB]
*American baseball player*
* Welch, Mickey
* Welch, Smiling Mickey

**Welch, Mickey**
*See* Welch, Michael F.

**Welch, Mitzie**
*See* Welch, Marilyn

**Welch, Pauline**
*See* Bodenham, Hilda Morris

**Welch, Raquel**
*See* Tejada, Raquel

**Welch, Ronald**
*See* Felton, Ronald Oliver

**Welch, Rowland**
*See* Davies, Leslie Purnell

**Welch, Smiling Mickey**
*See* Welch, Michael F.

**Welch, Timothy L.** 1935- [CA]
*American author*
* Cake, Patrick

**Welcher, Rosalind** 1922- [CA]
*American author and illustrator*
* Slavic, Rosalind Welcher

**Welcome, John**
*See* Brennan, John N[eedham] H[uggard]

**Weld, Susan Ker** 1943-
[BDF, FC, HT]
*American actress*
* Weld, Tuesday

**Weld, Tuesday**
*See* Weld, Susan Ker

**Welday, Lyndon Earl** 1879-1942
[BE]
*American baseball player*
* Welday, Mike

**Welday, Mike**
*See* Welday, Lyndon Earl

**Weldon, [Sir] Anthony** 1590-1655
[PA]
*Author*
* A. W., Sir

**Weldon, Casey Bill**
*See* Weldon, Will

**Weldon, John** 1875?-1963
[BEW, LC]
*Irish actor, playwright, author*
* MacNamara, Brinsley

**Weldon, Kenny**
*See* Waldron, Kenny

**Weldon, Lillian**
*See* Martin, Elizabeth

**Weldon, Marvelous Mel**
*See* Weldon, Melvin

**Weldon, Melvin** 20th c.    [IBW]
*American basketball player*
* Weldon, Marvelous Mel

**Weldon, Rex**
*See* Rimel, Duane [Weldon]

**Weldon, Robert** 20th c.    [WWL]
*Irish poet*
* Weldon, Roibeard

**Weldon, Roibeard**
*See* Weldon, Robert

**Weldon, Will** 1909-    [BWW]
*American singer*
* [The] Hawaiian Guitar Wizard
* Kansas City Bill
* Levee Joe
* Weldon, Casey Bill

**Welitsch, Ljuba**
*See* Velitchkova, Ljuba

**Welk, Ehm**
*See* Trimm, Thomas

**Welker, John Paul Pater** 1946-
*American entertainer*
* Attle, John C.

**[The] Well Beloved**
*See* Charles VI

**[The] Well Beloved**
*See* Louis XV

**[The] Well Founded Doctor**
*See* Aegidius [or Giles] of Colonna

**[A] Well Known Author**
*See* Lang, Andrew

**Well Languaged Daniel**
*See* Daniel, Samuel

**[The] Well of English Undefiled**
*See* Chaucer, Geoffrey

**Wellen, Edward [Paul]** 1919-
[CA, SFL]
*American author*
* Felder, Paul
* Gellert, Lew
* Killian, Larry

**Weller, Bernard Williams** 1870- ?
[LAO]
*British author, critic, journalist*
* B. W.

**Weller, Calamity**
*See* Weller, Luman Hamlin

**Weller, George [Anthony]** 1907-
[CA]
*American-born author and translator*
* Wharf, Michael

**Weller, Luman Hamlin** 1833-1914
[FFF]
*American politician*
* Weller, Calamity

**Welles, Mel**
*See* Von Theumer, Ernst

**Wellesley, Arthur** 1769-1852
[DEP, DNNS, SN]
*British army officer and statesman*
* [The] Achilles of England
* [The] Captain of the Age
* [The] English Achilles
* Europe's Liberator
* [The] Great Duke
* [The] Hero of a Hundred Fights
* [The] Hero of the Peninsula
* [The] Iron Duke
* Nosey
* Old Douro
* [The] Saviour of the Nations
* Wellington, Duke of

**Welling, Sylvia**
*See* Galloway, Sylvia

**Wellington, Arthur** 1885-1968
[SC]
*American actor*
* Page, Arthur W.

**[Le] Wellington des Joueurs**
*See* Woodville, Anthony [Lord Rivers]

**Wellington, Duke of**
*See* Wellesley, Arthur

**Wellington, John**
*See* Farnill, Barrie

**[The] Wellington of Gamblers**
*See* Rivers, Lord

**Wellman, Bert J.** 20th c.    [WGT]
*Author*
* [A] Law Abiding Revolutionist

**Wellman, Manly Wade** 1903-
[ESF, HFF, SFL]
*American author*
* Barclay, Gabriel [house pseudonym]
* Cotton, John
* Crow, Levi
* Ferney, Manuel
* Field, Gans T.
* Garth, Will [house pseudonym]
* Perez, Juan
* Wells, Hampton
* Wells, Wade

**Wellman, Pearl** 1910-    [THR]
*South African-born dancer*
* Argyle, Pearl

**Wells, Amos**
*See* Blackmore, Amos

**Wells, Barry**
*See* Richards, Dick

**Wells, Basil** 1912-    [ESF, WGT]
*American writer*
* Ellerman, Gene

**Wells, Billy** 1887-1967    [BX, RBE]
*British boxer*
* Wells, Bombardier Billy

**Wells, Bombardier Billy**
*See* Wells, Billy

**Wells, Braxton**
*See* Wollheim, Donald A[llen]

**Wells, Carolyn** 1870?-1942
[CC, EMD, WW]
*American author*
* Wright, Rowland

**Wells, Charles Jeremiah**
1799?-1879    [DEL, WBD]
*British poet and author*
* Howard, H. L.

**Wells, Dee**
*See* Ayer, Alberta Constance [Chapman]

**Wells, Devil**
*See* Wells, Willie James

**Wells, Dicky**
*See* Wells, William

**Wells, H. G.**
*See* Wells, Herbert George

**Wells, Hampton**
*See* Wellman, Manly Wade

**Wells, Helen**
*See* Wallis, Geraldine McDonald

**Wells, Helen**
*See* Weinstock, Helen

**Wells, Herbert George** 1866-1946
[CC, LC, SF]
*British author*
* Bliss, Reginald
* [The] Shakespeare of Science Fiction
* Wells, H. G.

**Wells, Hondo**
*See* Whittington, Harry

**Wells, Hubert George**
*See* Ackerman, Forrest J[ames]

**Wells, J. Wellington**
*See* De Camp, L[yon] Sprague

**Wells, Jacqueline** 1917-    [SW]
*American actress*
* Bishop, Julie

**Wells, Jane Warren**
*See* Picken, Mary Brooks

**Wells, Jessica**
*See* Buckland, Raymond

**Wells, John Jay** [joint pseudonym with Juanita Ruth Wellons Coulson]
*See* Bradley, Marion Zimmer

**Wells, John Jay** [joint pseudonym with Marion Zimmer Bradley]
*See* Coulson, Juanita Ruth Wellons

**Wells, Julia Elizabeth** 1935-
[BDF, BEW, CA]
*British actress, singer, author*
* Andrews, Julie
* Edwards, Julie

**Wells, June**
*See* Swinford, Betty [June Wells]

**Wells, Junior**
*See* Blackmore, Amos

**Wells, Kitty**
*See* Deason, Muriel Ellen

**Wells, Little Junior**
*See* Blackmore, Amos

**Wells, Mary P.**    [PA]
*Author*
* Thorne, P.

**Wells, Michael John** 1946-    [EJ7]
*British jazz musician*
* Wells, Spike

**Wells, Robert**
*See* Welsch, Roger L[ee]

**Wells, Robert** 1922-    [ASC]
*American composer and producer*
* Levinson, Bob

**Wells, [Frank Charles] Robert**
1929-    [IAW]
*British author*
* Roberts, Martin

**Wells, Roy**
*See* Downey, Raymond Joseph

**Wells, Sadie**
*See* O'Day, Mrs. William

**Wells, Spike**
*See* Wells, Michael John

**Wells, Susan**
*See* Siegel, Doris

**Wells, Thornton**
*See* Williams, T.

**Wells, Tobias**
*See* Forbes, DeLoris [Florine] Stanton

**Wells, Viola Gertrude** 1902-
[BWW]
*American singer*
* Rhapsody, Miss
* Underhill, Viola

**Wells, Wade**
*See* Wellman, Manly Wade

**Wells, William** 1820- ?    [FFF, PA]
*American author*
* Uncle Will

**Wells, William** 1910-    [ASC]
*American jazz musician*
* Wells, Dicky

**Wells, William Charles** 1757-1817
[PA]
*Author*
* Marius

**Wells, Willie James** 1908-    [MK]
*American baseball player*
* Wells, Devil

**Welsch, Roger L[ee]** 1936-    [CA]
*American folklorist and author*
* Wells, Robert

**Welser, Albert**
*See* Graw, William P.

**Welsh, Freddy**
*See* Thomas, Frederick Hall

**Welsh, H.** 20th c.    [CSH]
*Canadian football promoter*
* Welsh, Huck

**Welsh, Huck**
*See* Welsh, H.

**Welsh, James J.** 1866- ?    [BE]
*American baseball player*
* Welsh, Tub

**Welsh, Robert**
*See* Roberts, John Peter

**[The] Welsh Shakespeare**
*See* Williams, Edward

**Welsh, Susan**
See Collins, Margaret [Brandon James]

**Welsh, Tub**
See Welsh, James J.

**[The] Welsh Wizard**
See Lloyd George, David

**[The] Welsh Wizard**
See Meredith, Billy

**[The] Welsh Wizard**
See Thomas, Frederick Hall

**Welskopf, Liselotte Elisabeth Charlotte** 1901- [IAW]
German author
* Welskopf-Henrich, Liselotte

**Welskopf-Henrich, Liselotte**
See Welskopf, Liselotte Elisabeth Charlotte

**Welter, Blanca Rosa** 1923?-
[FC, IPA, ITA]
Mexican-born actress
* Christian, Linda

**Welty, S. F.**
See Welty, Susan F.

**Welty, Susan F.** 1905- [CAP, SAT]
American author
* Welty, S. F.

**Welwood**
See Moncrieff, [Sir] Henry

**Welzenbach, Lanora F.**
See Miller, Lanora

**Wemlinger, Claire** 1909?-
[FC, OCF]
American actress
* Trevor, Claire

**Wemyss, Nigel** 1913- [BF]
British actor and director
* Patrick, Nigel

**Wen**
See Veneris, James

**Wenceslas of Luxembourg**
1337-1383
Duke of Brabant
* [The] Blue Duke

**Wenceslaus [or Wenceslas]**
1359?-1419 [DNNS, RH, SN]
King of Bohemia and Germany
* [The] Drunkard
* [The] Nero of Germany
* [The] Sardanapalus of Germany
* [The] Worthless

**Wendelken-Wilson, Charles**
See Wilson, Charles Edwin

**Wendell, Bullet**
See Wendell, Percy L.

**Wendell, Percy L.** 1889-1932 [FB]
American football player and coach
* Wendell, Bullet

**Wenden, Michael** 1949- [SWI]
Australian swimmer
* [The] Swimming Machine

**Wender, Dorothea** 1934- [CA]
American educator and author
* Schmidt, Dorothea

**Wendig, Dr.**
See Schwend, Friedrich

**Wendolin**
See Durben, Wolfgang Johannes Maria

**Wendorff, Arnold** 1928?-1962
[BEW]
Theatrical performer
* Arnold, Eddie

**Wendroff, Zalman**
See Vendrovskii, David Efimovich

**Wendrowsky, Zalman**
See Vendrovskii, David Efimovich

**Wendt, Fats**
See Wendt, George

**Wendt, George** 1909?-1973 [FIR]
American jazz musician
* Wendt, Fats

**Weng, Hsing Ching**
See Weng, Wan-go

**Weng, Wan-go** 1918- [CA]
Chinese-born American author and filmmaker
* Weng, Hsing Ching

**Wenger, Rose August** 1892-
[F1, F2, FC]
American actress
* Gibson, Helen

**Wenham, Jane**
See Figgins, Jane

**Wenkart, Henni**
See Wenkart, Henny

**Wenkart, Henny** 1928- [CA]
Austrian-born publisher and author
* Wenkart, Henni

**Wennerstrom, Genia Katherine**
1930- [IBY, ICB]
American illustrator
* Genia

**[The] Wensleydale Poet**
See Barker, George William Michael Jones

**Wensloff, Butch**
See Wensloff, Charles William

**Wensloff, Charles William** 1915-
[BE]
American baseball player
* Wensloff, Butch

**Wentworth, Barbara**
See Pitcher, Gladys

**Wentworth, Bessie**
See Andrews, Elizabeth

**Wentworth, Charles** [house pseudonym]
See Bradley, Albert W.

**Wentworth, Charles** [house pseudonym]
See Clarke, Percy A.

**Wentworth, Charles** [house pseudonym]
See Shute, Walter

**Wentworth, Charles** [house pseudonym]
See Steffens, Arthur

**Wentworth, Cy**
See Wentworth, Marvin

**Wentworth, Fanny**
See Evans, Fanny Wentworth Osborn Porteus

**Wentworth, Herbert**
See James, Herbert Wentworth

**Wentworth, John** 1815?-1888
[FFF]
American politician
* Long John

**Wentworth, Mae**
See Ostrander, Mrs. Clarence

**Wentworth, Martha**
See Wentworth, Verna

**Wentworth, Marvin** 1905- [CEI]
Canadian-born hockey player
* Wentworth, Cy

**Wentworth, Patricia**
See Turnbull, Dora Amy Elles Dillon

**Wentworth, Robert**
See Hamilton, Edmond [Moore]

**Wentworth, Verna** ?-1974 [SC]
American actress
* [The] Actress of One Hundred Voices
* Wentworth, Martha

**Wentworth, William Charles**
1793-1872 [WBD]
Australian politician
* [The] Australian Patriot

**Wenz, Fireball**
See Wenz, Frederick Charles, Jr.

**Wenz, Frederick Charles, Jr.** 1941-
[SMG]
American baseball player
* Wenz, Fireball

**Wenzlaff, George** 1946- [FC]
American actor
* Winslow, Foghorn
* Winslow, George

**Wep**
See Pidgeon, William Edwin

**Werata, Tota**
See Gadd, David Bernard Hallard

**Werblin, David** 20th c. [EJS]
American football team owner
* Werblin, Sonny

**Werblin, Sonny**
See Werblin, David

**Werden, Percival Wheritt**
1865-1934 [BE]
American baseball player
* Werden, Perry

**Werden, Perry**
See Werden, Percival Wheritt

**Werdna, Retnyw**
See Wynter, Andrew

**Wergeland, Henrik Arnold**
1808-1845 [SN, WBD]
Norwegian poet, playwright, patriot
* [The] Betrayer of the Fatherland
* [The] Holberg of Norway
* Sifadda, Siful

**Werhas, John Charles [Johnny]**
1938- [BE]
American baseball player
* Werhas, Peaches

**Werhas, Peaches**
See Werhas, John Charles [Johnny]

**Werheim, John**
See Fearn, John Russell

**Werkman, Nick** 1942- [BB]
American basketball player
* Nick the Quick

**Werl, Olaf** 1618-1682 [SN]
Swedish antiquary and historian
* [The] Coryphaeus of Northern Lore
* Verelius, Olaus

**Werle**
See Werle, Dan

**Werle, Bugs**
See Werle, William George

**Werle, Dan** 20th c. [ITA]
American costume designer
* Werle

**Werle, William George** 1920- [BE]
American baseball player
* Werle, Bugs

**Werner, Buddy**
See Werner, Wallace

**Werner, E.**
See Burstenbinder, Elisabeth

**Werner, Franz von** 1836-1881
[WBD]
Austrian-born poet and playwright
* Murad Efendi

**Werner, Herma** 1926- [CA]
American author
* Cowen, Eve
* Pinner, Joma

**Werner, Isaiah**
See Douglass, Ellsworth

**Werner, Jane**
See Watson, Jane Werner

**Werner, Janet Anne** 20th c. [BEW]
American actress
* Ward, Janet

**Werner, K.**
See Casewit, Curtis

**Werner, Oskar**
See Bschliessmayer, Josef

**Werner, Sacher S.** 1898- [EJS]
Austrian horse trainer and harness racer
* Werner, Satch

**Werner, Satch**
See Werner, Sacher S.

**Werner, Victor Emile** 1894-
[CA, WD]
American author
* Dallas, Vincent

**Werner, Wallace** 1935?-1964 [AS]
American skier
* Werner, Buddy

**Werper, Barton** [house pseudonym]
See Scott, Peg O'Neill

**Werper, Barton** [house pseudonym]
See Scott, Peter T.

**Werschkul, Gordon M.** 1927-
[FC, ITA, SW]
American actor
* Scott, Gordon

**Wertenbaker, G. Peyton** 1907-
[WGT]
*American author*
* Peyton, Green

**Wertenbaker, Lael Tucker** 1909-
[CA]
*American author*
* Tucker, Lael

**Werter, Max**
*See* Smyth, Frank

**Wertham, Fredric**
*See* Wertheimer, Frederick Ignace

**Wertheimer, Frederick Ignace**
1895- [SFL]
*German-born author*
* Wertham, Fredric

**Wertheimer, Leo** 1862-1937
[WBD]
*German philosopher*
* Brunner, Constantin

**Wertmueller, Lina**
*See* Wertmueller Von Elgg,
Arcangela

**Wertmueller Von Elgg, Arcangela**
1928- [CA, FDG]
*Italian director and screenwriter*
* Brown, George
* Wertmueller, Lina

**Werty, Quentin**
*See* Stone, Peter

**Wertz, Del**
*See* Wertz, Dwight Lewis

**Wertz, Dwight Lewis** 1891- [BE]
*American baseball player*
* Wertz, Del

**Wertz, Henry Levi** 1898- [BE]
*American baseball player*
* Wertz, Johnny

**Wertz, Johnny**
*See* Wertz, Henry Levi

**Wesander, Bjoern Kenneth** 1914-
[CA]
*British-born journalist and author*
* Cox, P[atrick] Brian
* Stuart, Kenneth
* Tantrist

**Weschcke, Carl L[ouis]** 1930- [CA]
*American author and publisher*
* Gnosticus

**Wescott, Frederick** 1866-1941
[THR]
*British comedian, author, theatrical
manager*
* Karno, Fred

**Weslager, C. A.**
*See* Weslager, Clinton Alfred

**Weslager, Clinton Alfred** 1909-
[WYA]
*American author*
* Weslager, C. A.

**Wesley, Art**
*See* Grennell, Dean A.

**Wesley, Charles** 1707-1788 [FFF]
*British clergyman and hymn writer*
* [The] Poet of Methodism

**Wesley, Elizabeth**
*See* McElfresh, [Elizabeth]
Adeline

**Wesley, James**
*See* Rigoni, Orlando [Joseph]

**Wesley, Mary**
*See* Eady, Mary Aline

**Weslock, Nick**
*See* Wisnock, Nick

**Wessel, Johann [or John]**
1419-1489 [DNNF, DNNS, RH]
*Dutch theologian and religious
reformer*
* Lux Mundi
* Magister Contradictionum
* [The] Master of Contradiction
* Sapiens, Doctor
* [The] Wise Doctor

**Wessel, Peder** 1691-1720
[HN, RH]
*Norwegian naval officer*
* [The] Danish Nelson
* Tordenskiol [Thunder Shield]

**Wesselmann, Tom** 20th c.
*American artist*
* Stealingworth, Slim

**Wessler, Bernard** 1918- [BEW]
*American actor*
* West, Bernard

**Wesso, Hans**
*See* Wessolowski, Hans Waldemar

**Wessolowski, Hans Waldemar**
1882- [SF]
*German-born illustrator*
* Wesso, Hans

**West, Adam**
*See* Anderson, William

**West, Adam**
*See* Garrett, Sam

**West, Al**
*See* Hubbard, Al[len]

**West, Angela** 1933- [THR]
*British actress*
* Glynne, Angela

**West, Anthony C.** 1910- [CN]
*Irish author*
* MacGrian, Michael

**West, Barbara**
*See* Price, Olive

**West, Belf**
*See* West, D. Belford

**West, Bernard**
*See* Wessler, Bernard

**West, Betty** 1921- [CA, SAT]
*Author and illustrator*
* Bowen, Betty Morgan

**West, Big Jim**
*See* West, Jim

**West, Billy**
*See* Weisberg, Roy B.

**West, Buck**
*See* West, Milton Douglas

**West, Buster**
*See* West, James

**West, C. P.**
*See* Wodehouse, Pelham Grenville

**West, Charles [Charlie]** 1899-
[IBW]
*American football player*
* West, Prunes

**West, Charles [Charlie]** 1914-1976
[BWW]
*American singer*
* Poor Charlie

**West, Charles Converse** 1921-
[CA]
*American author and theologian*
* Barnabas

**West, Chinese Tommy**
*See* West, Thomas

**West Country**
*See* Dawson, Charles Kenneth

**[A] West Country Doctor**
*See* Cooper, Robert Andrew

**West, Curly**
*See* West, Granville

**West, D. Belford** 1896- [FB]
*American football player*
* West, Belf

**West, Doc**
*See* West, Harold

**West, Dorothy Marie [Dottie]**
1932- [ECM]
*American country-western performer*
* [The] Country Sunshine

**West, Douglas**
*See* Tubb, Edwin Charles

**West, Edgar**
*See* Carr, Gordon

**West, Gertrude Ida** 20th c. [AW]
*Belgian-born journalist and author*
* West, Trudy

**West, Granville** 1915?-1978 [FIR]
*American country-western performer*
* West, Curly

**West, Harold**
*See* Wilson, Roger C.

**West, Harold** 1915-1951
[EJ, WWJ]
*American jazz musician*
* West, Doc

**West, Hi**
*See* West, James

**West, James**
*See* Withers, Carl A.

**West, James** 1884-1963 [BE]
*American baseball player*
* West, Hi

**West, James** 1902-1966 [SC]
*American actor*
* West, Buster

**West, Jerry** [house pseudonym]
[Stratemeyer Syndicate]
*See* Stratemeyer, Edward L.

**West, Jerry** [house pseudonym]
[Stratemeyer Syndicate]
*See* Svenson, Andrew E.

**West, Jerry** 1938- [SMG]
*American basketball player and
coach*
* Clutch, Mr.

**West, Jim** 20th c. [RBE]
*Australian boxer*
* West, Big Jim

**West, John**
*See* Pentelow, John Nix

**West, Joyce [Tarlton]** 20th c.
[TCC]
*New Zealand author*
* Gilbert, Manu

**West, Julian**
*See* Mueller, Ernst

**West, Katherine** 1883-1936 [SC]
*American actress*
* Morton, Maxine
* Westner, Lillian

**West, Keith**
*See* Lane, Kenneth Westmacott

**West, Kenyon**
*See* Howland, Frances Louise

**West, Kirkpatrick**
*See* Harris, F[rank] Brayton

**West, Lefty**
*See* West, Weldon Edison

**West, Lillie** 1860-1939
[BEW, NAA]
*American actress and drama critic*
* Leslie, Amy

**West, Lindsay**
*See* Weber, Nancy

**West, Luther Shirley** 1899- [IAW]
*American author and poet*
* Praeceptor Humilis

**West, Mae** 1893-1980
*American actress*
* [The] Baby Vamp

**West, Mark**
*See* Runyon, Charles W.

**West, Mary**
*See* Rochester, George Ernest

**West, Michael**
*See* Derleth, August [William]

**West, Milton Douglas** 1860-1929
[BE]
*American baseball player*
* West, Buck

**West, Morris L[anglo]** 1916-
[CA, WD]
*Australian author and playwright*
* East, Michael
* Morris, Julian

**West, Mrs. William** [FFF]
*Entertainer*
* Templeton, Fay

**West, Nancy Richard**
*See* Westphal, Wilma Ross

**West, Nathanael**
*See* Weinstein, Nathan
Wallenstein

**West, Pep**
*See* Weinstein, Nathan
Wallenstein

**West, Prunes**
*See* West, Charles [Charlie]

**West, Rebecca**
*See* Fairfield, Cecily Isabel

**West, Richard** 18th c. [SN]
*Friend of British poet, Thomas Gray*
* Favonius

**West, Roger**
*See* Watson, Virginia Cruse

**West, Speedy**
*See* West, Wesley Webb

West, Thomas 1577-1618 [WBD]
*British colonial administrator in America*
* De La Warr, Third Baron
* Delaware, Lord

West, Thomas 1859-1932 [SC]
*American actor*
* West, Chinese Tommy

West, Token
*See* Humphries, Adelaide M.

West, Tom
*See* Reach, James

West, Tristram Frederick 1911-
[IAW]
*British scientist and writer*
* Prospero

West, Trudy
*See* West, Gertrude Ida

West, Uta 1928- [CA]
*Polish-born American author*
* Auden, Renee

West, Virgil Clifford 1931- [IBW]
*American dancer*
* Beaver, Flash

[The] West Virginia Hillbilly
*See* Snead, Sam[uel Jackson]

West, Wallace 20th c. [SFP]
*Author*
* Barlow, Roger

West, Ward
*See* Borland, Harold Glen [Hal]

West, Weldon Edison 1915- [BE]
*American baseball player*
* West, Lefty

West, Wesley Webb 1924-
[CWG, DAM]
*American country-western performer*
* West, Speedy

West, William H.
*See* Flinn, William H.

West-Watson, Keith Campbell 20th
c. [WW]
*Author*
* Campbell, Keith

Westbrook, Chauncey Leon 1921-
[EJ]
*American jazz musician*
* Westbrook, Lord

Westbrook, Lord
*See* Westbrook, Chauncey Leon

Westbrook, Walter J. 20th c.
[BWW]
*American singer*
* Little Walter J.

Westcombe, Charles
*See* Carr, Gordon

Westcott, Charles S. [FFF, PA]
*Author*
* Homo

Westcott, Helen
*See* Hickman, Myrthas Helen

Westcott, Kathleen
*See* Abrahamsen, Christine Elizabeth

Westcott, Netta
*See* Lupton, Netta

Westcott, Thompson [PA]
*Author*
* Miller, Joe, Jr.

Westcott-Jones, K[enneth]
*See* Jones, Kenneth Westcott

Wester, Doris 1917-1960 [SC]
*American actress*
* Weston, Doris

Westerham, S. C.
*See* Alington, Cyril Argentine

Western, Barry
*See* Evans, Gwnfil Arthur

[The] Western Hangman
*See* Jeffreys, George [First Baron Jeffreys of Wem]

Western, Mark
*See* Crisp, Anthony Thomas [Tony]

[The] Western Spy
*See* Dillon, John M[yles]

Westerzil, George J. 1891-1964
[BE]
*American baseball player*
* Westerzil, Tex

Westerzil, Tex
*See* Westerzil, George J.

Westfall, Eddie
*See* Westfall, Edwin Vernon

Westfall, Edwin Vernon 1940-
[FHE]
*Canadian-born hockey player*
* Westfall, Eddie

Westfield, Rick 20th c. [RO2]
*American musician*
* Westfield, West

Westfield, West
*See* Westfield, Rick

Westford, Susanne
*See* Leonard, Susan

Westgate, John
*See* Bloomfield, Anthony John Westgate

Westgate, Lady
*See* Din, Salima

Westheimer, David 1917- [CA]
*American author*
* Smith, Z. Z.

Westlake, Donald E[dwin] 1933-
[AW, CA, WGT]
*American author*
* Clark, Curt
* Coe, Tucker
* Culver, Timothy J.
* Cunningham, J. Morgan
* Stark, Richard

Westlake, Waldon Thomas 1920-
[BE]
*American baseball player*
* Westlake, Wally

Westlake, Wally
*See* Westlake, Waldon Thomas

Westland, Lynn
*See* Joscelyn, Archie Lynn

Westley, Helen
*See* Manney, Henrietta

Westley, John
*See* Conroy, John

Westmacott, Charles Malloy [PA]
*Author*
* Blackmantle, Bernard

Westmacott, Mary
*See* Christie, Agatha [Mary Clarissa]

Westman, Hab'k O.
*See* Ewbank, T.

Westmore, Buddy
*See* Westmore, Hamilton

Westmore, Hamilton 20th c.
[BEW]
*American makeup consultant*
* Westmore, Buddy

Westmoreland, Maria Elizabeth
[Jourdan] 1815- ? [FFF]
*American author*
* Mystery

Westmoreland, Reg[inald] [Conway]
1926- [CA, WD]
*American author and journalist*
* Conway, Ward

Westmoreland, William Childs 1914-
*American army officer*
* Westy

Westner, Lillian
*See* West, Katherine

Weston, Agatha 1943- [IBW]
*American singer and actress*
* Weston, Kim

Weston, Allen [joint pseudonym with Alice Mary Norton]
*See* Hogarth, Grace Weston

Weston, Allen [joint pseudonym with Grace Weston Hogarth]
*See* Norton, Alice Mary

Weston, Ann
*See* Pitcher, Gladys

Weston, Dick
*See* Slye, Leonard

Weston, Doris
*See* Wester, Doris

Weston, Ellen
*See* Weinstein, Ellen R.

Weston, Helen Gray
*See* Daniels, Dorothy

Weston, James
*See* Step, Edward

Weston, Kim
*See* Weston, Agatha

Weston, Paul
*See* Wetstein, Paul

Weston, Philip
*See* De Filippi, Amedeo

Weston, Robert P.
*See* Harris, Robert P.

Weston, Ruth
*See* Shillaber, Ruth West

Weston, W. Garfield 1898?-1978
*Canadian business executive*
* [The] Barnum of Bread

Weston, Warren
*See* Gale, Linn A. E.

Weston, William
*See* Milsom, Charles Henry

Westover, Charles 1939- [RO1]
*American singer*
* Shannon, Del

Westphal, Paul 1950- [SMG]
*American basketball player*
* Westphal, Westy

Westphal, Westy
*See* Westphal, Paul

Westphal, Wilma Ross 1907- [CA]
*American author*
* West, Nancy Richard

Westridge, Harold
*See* Avery, Harold

Westrup, Enrique Tomas 1879- ?
[NAA]
*Mexican educator and author*
* Wycliff

Westwater, [Sister] Agnes Martha
1929- [CA]
*American-born author*
* Earley, Martha

Westwick, Harry 1876-1957
[FHE, HK]
*Canadian-born hockey player*
* Westwick, Rat

Westwick, Rat
*See* Westwick, Harry

Westwood, N. J.
*See* Millard, Joseph

Westy
*See* Westmoreland, William Childs

Wetcheek, J. L.
*See* Feuchtwanger, Lion

Wethered, M. L.
*See* Wethered, Maud Llewellyn

Wethered, Maud Llewellyn 1898-
[ART]
*British sculptor, engraver, painter*
* Wethered, M. L.

Wetherell, Elizabeth
*See* Warner, Susan

Wetherell, Mrs. E. 1850-1891
[FFF]
*American opera singer*
* Abbott, Emma

Wetherell-Pepper, Joan Alexander
1920- [CA]
*British author*
* Alexander, Joan
* Pepper, Joan

Wetmore, Joan
*See* Deery, Joan

Wetstein, Paul 1912- [PMJ]
*American arranger and conductor*
* Edwards, Jonathan
* Weston, Paul

Wettach, Adrien 1880-1959
[BEW, FC]
*Swiss clown*
* Grock

Wetter, Mrs.
*See* Victoria

Wetterbergh, Carl Anton
1804-1889 [FFF, WBD]
*Swedish author*
* Onkel Adam

**Wetton, Mary** 1936- [TR]
*British actress and singer*
* Millar, Mary

**Wetzel, Buzz**
*See* Wetzel, Charles Edward

**Wetzel, Buzz**
*See* Wetzel, Franklin Burton

**Wetzel, Charles Edward**
1894-1941 [BE]
*American baseball player*
* Wetzel, Buzz

**Wetzel, Franklin Burton**
1893-1942 [BE]
*American baseball player*
* Wetzel, Buzz

**Wetzel, George William**
1868-1899 [BE]
*American baseball player*
* Wetzel, Shorty

**Wetzel, Shorty**
*See* Wetzel, George William

**Weverka, Robert** 1926- [CA]
*American author*
* McMahon, Robert

**Wexisnensis**
*See* Magnus, Jonas

**Wexler, Irving** 20th c. [BLB, MM]
*American underworld figure*
* Gordon, Waxey

**Wexler, Jerome [LeRoy]** 1923-
[CA]
*American author, illustrator,
photographer*
* Delmar, Roy

**Wexler, Morris** 20th c. [MM]
*American underworld figure*
* Wexler, Mushy

**Wexler, Mushy**
*See* Wexler, Morris

**Weyand, Alexander M.** 1892- [FB]
*American football player*
* Weyand, Babe

**Weyand, Babe**
*See* Weyand, Alexander M.

**Weyerhaeuser, Frederick**
1834-1914 [WBD]
*German-born industrialist*
* [The] Lumber King

**Weygand, James Lamar** 1919- [IA]
*American author*
* [The] Indiana Kid
* James, Westbrook

**Weyhing, August** 1866-1955
[AS, PB]
*American baseball player*
* Weyhing, Cannonball
* Weyhing, Gus

**Weyhing, Cannonball**
*See* Weyhing, August

**Weyhing, Gus**
*See* Weyhing, August

**Weyl, Fernand** 1874?-1931 [BEW]
*Playwright and critic*
* Noziere, Fernand

**Weyler, Joseph** ?-1919 [BLB]
*American underworld figure*
* Spanish, Johnny

**Weymes, Wilfred Theodore**
1901-1963 [PMJ]
*American bandleader*
* Weems, Ted

**Weymouth, Elizabeth Graham** 1943-
*American author*
* Weymouth, Lally

**Weymouth, Lally**
*See* Weymouth, Elizabeth Graham

**[The] Whacky Warbler**
*See* Turner, Joan

**[The] Whale**
*See* Hemmings, Edward Ernest
[Eddie]

**Whalen, Michael**
*See* Shovlin, Joseph Kenneth

**Whaley, Barton Stewart** 1928-
[CA]
*American educator and author*
* Barton, S. W.

**Whaling, Thornton** 1858- ? [ALY]
*American clergyman and author*
* Pipper, Pippia
* [The] Professor

**Whalley, Dorothy** 1911- [CAP]
*British author*
* Cowlin, Dorothy

**Wharf, Michael**
*See* Weller, George [Anthony]

**Wharmby, Margot** 1910-
[AW, CA]
*British author*
* Winn, Alison [Osborn]

**Wharton, Anthony**
*See* McAllister, Alister

**Wharton, Baby Ray**
*See* Wharton, Ray

**Wharton, Buck**
*See* Wharton, Charles M.

**Wharton, Charles M.** 1868-1949
[AS, FB]
*American football player*
* Wharton, Buck

**Wharton, Grace**
*See* Thomson, Katherine Byerley

**Wharton, Henry** 17th c. [PA]
*Author*
* Harmer, Anthony

**Wharton, Jim** 1813-1856 [IBW]
*American-born boxer*
* Molineaux, the Morocco Prince

**Wharton, Len**
*See* Wharton, Thomas

**Wharton, Philip**
*See* Thomson, John Cockburn

**Wharton, Ray** 20th c. [GW]
*American rodeo performer*
* Wharton, Baby Ray

**Wharton, Thomas** 1927- [CEI]
*Canadian-born hockey player*
* Wharton, Len

**Wharton, Virginia**
*See* Ratigan, Eleanor Eldridge

**Whately, Richard** 1787-1863
[DEL, FFF, SN]
*Irish author and clergyman*
* [A] Country Pastor

**Whately, Richard** (Continued)
* Konx Ompax
* Newlight, Aristarchus
* Search, John
* [The] White Bear

**Whatley, David** 20th c. [OBW]
*American baseball player*
* Whatley, Speed

**Whatley, Fess**
*See* Whatley, John Tuggle

**Whatley, John Tuggle** 1895- [IBW]
*American bandleader*
* Whatley, Fess

**Whatley, Speed**
*See* Whatley, David

**What's the Use**
*See* Chiles, Pearce Nuget

**Whatshisname**
*See* Massey, E. C.

**Whattaman**
*See* Shires, [Charles] Art[hur]

**Whear, [Dr.] Rachael** 1923- [AW]
*British author*
* Low, Rachael

**Wheat, Buck**
*See* Wheat, Zachariah Davis

**Wheat, Mack**
*See* Wheat, McKinley Davis

**Wheat, McKinley Davis** 1893-
[BE]
*American baseball player*
* Wheat, Mack

**Wheat, Patte** 1935- [CA, IAW]
*American author*
* Mahan, Pat
* Mahan, Patte Wheat

**Wheat, Zachariah Davis**
1888-1972 [BE, DGS]
*American baseball player*
* Wheat, Buck
* Wheat, Zack

**Wheat, Zack**
*See* Wheat, Zachariah Davis

**Wheatbread, Paul** 1946- [RO2]
*American musician*
* Wheatbread, Private
* Wheatbread, Wheaty

**Wheatbread, Private**
*See* Wheatbread, Paul

**Wheatbread, Wheaty**
*See* Wheatbread, Paul

**Wheatcroft, Mrs. Nelson** [FFF]
*Entertainer*
* Stanhope, Adeline

**Wheatley, Agnes**
*See* Cantor, Eli

**Wheatley, H. B.**
*See* Wheatley, Henry Benjamin

**Wheatley, Henry Benjamin**
1838-1917 [LC]
*British author*
* Wheatley, H. B.

**Wheatley, Jane**
*See* Simpson, Jane

**Wheatley, Richard** 19th c. [FFF]
*Author*
* Gotham

**Wheatley, William [Bill]** 1909-
[BB, BBH]
*American basketball player*
* [The] Galloping Ghost

**Wheaton, Campbell**
*See* Weeks, Helen C.

**Wheaton, Elwood Pierce** 1914-
[BE]
*American baseball player*
* Wheaton, Woody

**[The] Wheaton Ice Man**
*See* Grange, Harold E.

**Wheaton, Woody**
*See* Wheaton, Elwood Pierce

**[The] Wheatpicker**
*See* Smith, J. D.

**Wheatstraw, Little Peetie**
*See* Hogg, Andrew

**Wheatstraw, Peetie**
*See* Bunch, William

**Whedon, Julia**
*See* Schickel, Julia Whedon

**Wheeler, Albert** 1895- [BEW]
*American actor*
* Wheeler, Bert

**Wheeler, Andrew Carpenter**
1835?-1903 [FFF, PA]
*American journalist*
* Crinkle, Nym
* Trinculo

**Wheeler, Arthur L.** 1872-1917
[AS, FB]
*American football player*
* Wheeler, Beef

**Wheeler, Babe**
*See* Wheeler, Harold

**Wheeler, Beef**
*See* Wheeler, Arthur L.

**Wheeler, Bert**
*See* Wheeler, Albert

**Wheeler, C. C.** [FFF, PA]
*American writer*
* Crispus

**Wheeler, C. R.**
*See* Wheeler, Carol Rosemary

**Wheeler, Captain**
*See* Ellis, Edward S[ylvester]

**Wheeler, Carol Rosemary** 1927-
[ART]
*British painter*
* Wheeler, C. R.

**Wheeler, Charles S.** 19th c. [PA]
*Author*
* Wheeler, Stern

**Wheeler, Don[ald Wesley]** 1922-
[BE]
*American baseball player*
* Wheeler, Scotty

**Wheeler, Emily Frances** [FFF]
*Author*
* Winter, June

**Wheeler, Fanny**
*See* Stell, Mrs. Martin

**Wheeler, Floyd Clark** 1898-1968
[BE]
*American baseball player*
* Wheeler, Rip

**Wheeler, George Dryden**
1863-1939 [BMH]
*British singer*
* Dryden, Leo

**Wheeler, George Harrison**
1881-1918 [BE]
*American baseball player*
* Wheeler, Heavy

**Wheeler, George L.**
*See* Heroux, George L.

**Wheeler, Greyhound**
*See* Wheeler, Wayne

**Wheeler, Harold** 20th c. [BBH]
*American basketball coach*
* Wheeler, Babe

**Wheeler, Heavy**
*See* Wheeler, George Harrison

**Wheeler, Hugh Callingham** 1913-
[CC, EMD, WW]
*Author*
* Patrick, Q. [joint pseudonym with Richard Wilson Webb]
* Quentin, Patrick [joint pseudonym with Richard Wilson Webb]
* Stagge, Jonathan [joint pseudonym with Richard Wilson Webb]

**Wheeler, Janet D.** [house pseudonym] [Stratemeyer Syndicate]
*See* Stratemeyer, Edward L.

**Wheeler, Jimmy**
*See* Remnant, Ernest

**Wheeler, Joseph Trank** 1868- ?
[ALY]
*American author and editor*
* Michael

**Wheeler, Mary Jane** 20th c. [CA]
*American author*
* Fowler, Mary Jane
* Simonson, Mary Jane

**Wheeler, Mrs. James** [FFF]
*Entertainer*
* Valdeau, Vintie

**Wheeler, Mrs. S. T.** [FFF]
*Entertainer*
* Olive, May

**Wheeler, Richard [Dick]**
*See* Maynard, Richard Wheeler

**Wheeler, Rip**
*See* Wheeler, Floyd Clark

**Wheeler, Scotty**
*See* Wheeler, Don[ald Wesley]

**Wheeler, Stern**
*See* Wheeler, Charles S.

**Wheeler, Teresa** ?-1975 [SC]
*Actress*
* Cabaret Tess

**Wheeler, Wayne** 1950- [FB]
*American football player*
* Wheeler, Greyhound

**Wheeler-O'Bryen, Wilfrid James**
1898- [THR]
*British theatrical manager*
* O'Bryen, W. J.

**Wheelhouse**
*See* Semple, Dugald

**Wheelock, Bobby**
*See* Wheelock, Warren H.

**Wheelock, Martha E.** 1941- [CA]
*American educator and author*
* Alinder, Martha Wheelock

**Wheelock, Warren H.** 1864-1928
[BE]
*American baseball player*
* Wheelock, Bobby

**Wheelton, Brooke**
*See* Sladen, Douglas

**Wheelwright, W.** [PA]
*Author*
* Old Bushman

**Wheezer**
*See* Hutchins, Bobby

**Whelan, Albert**
*See* Waxman, Albert

**Whelan, John**
*Author*
* O'Faolain, Sean

**Whellier, Alexander** [RH]
*Author*
* Gifford, John, Esq.

**Whelpton, [George] Eric** 1894-
[CA]
*French-born author*
* Lyte, Richard
* Parry, John

**Whetham, William Cecil Dampier**
1867-1952 [TC1]
*British historian and author*
* Dampier, [Sir] William Cecil

**Wheway, John W.** 20th c. [MBF]
*British author*
* Armitage, Vincent
* Richards, Hilda

**Whicker, Kemp Caswell**
*See* Wicker, Kemp Caswell

**Whidby, Lulu** 20th c. [BWW]
*American entertainer*
* White, Ella

**[The] Whig Johnson**
*See* Parr, Samuel

**[A] Whig of the Revolution**
*See* George III

**Whilk, Nat**
*See* Lewis, Clive Staples

**Whim Wham**
*See* Curnow, [Thomas] Allen [Munro]

**[The] Whip**
*See* Blackwell, Ewell

**Whipem, Benedick**
*See* Harris, Richard

**Whipper, Frances E. Rollin** [IBW]
*American author*
* Rollin, Frank A.

**[The] Whipping Post**
*See* Livingston, William

**Whipple, Henry Benjamin**
1822-1901 [FFF]
*American clergyman*
* Straight Tongue

**Whipple, Nelson S.** 1882-1923
[SC]
*American actor*
* Dean, Nelson

**Whipple, Squire** 1804-1888 [FFF]
*American engineer*
* [The] Father of Iron Bridges

**Whipple, Wade**
*See* Stevens, George

**Whips, Andrea** ?-1972 [SC]
*American actress*
* Feldman, Andrea

**Whisenton, Larry** 1957- [SMG]
*American baseball player*
* Whisenton, Whizzer

**Whisenton, Whizzer**
*See* Whisenton, Larry

**Whiskey Van**
*See* Van Buren, Martin

**[The] Whispering Baritone**
*See* Smith, Jack

**Whispering Bill Anderson**
*See* Anderson, Bill

**Whispering Bill Barrett**
*See* Barrett, William Joseph

**Whispering Jack Smith**
*See* Smith, Jack

**Whispering Jimmie**
*See* Ketcham, James

**[The] Whispering Pianist**
*See* Gillham, Art

**Whispering Roy Hughes**
*See* Hughes, Roy John

**[The] Whispering Tenor**
*See* Lucas, Eugene

**Whistlecraft, William and Robert**
*See* Frere, John Hookham

**[The] Whistler**
*See* Engressia, Joe

**Whistler, Laurence** 1912- [ART]
*British engraver*
* L. W.

**Whistler, Lew[is]**
*See* Wissler, Lewis

**Whistlin' Jake Wade**
*See* Wade, Jacob Fields

**Whistling Alex Moore**
*See* Moore, Alexander Herman

**Whistling Bob Smith**
*See* Smith, Robert A.

**[The] Whistling Coster**
*See* Mason, Fred

**Whitaker, Charles Orbie**
1893-1960 [SC]
*Actor*
* Whitaker, Slim

**Whitaker, E. E.** 20th c. [ITA]
*American theatre executive*
* Whitaker, Whit

**Whitaker, Louis Rodman** 1957-
[SMG]
*American baseball player*
* Whitaker, Sweet Lou

**Whitaker, Pat**
*See* Whitaker, William H.

**Whitaker, Popsie**
*See* Whitaker, Rogers Ernest Malcolm

**Whitaker, Rod** 1931- [CA]
*American author and educator*
* Seare, Nicholas

**Whitaker, Rogers Ernest Malcolm**
1900-1981 [B10]
*American editor and railroad buff*
* Frimbo, E[rnest] M[alcolm]
* J. W. L.
* R. E. M. W.
* R. W.
* Whitaker, Popsie
* [The] World's Greatest Railroad Buff

**Whitaker, Slim**
*See* Whitaker, Charles Orbie

**Whitaker, Sweet Lou**
*See* Whitaker, Louis Rodman

**Whitaker, Thomas** 1883-1937
[BMH]
*British ventriloquist*
* Coram
* [The] Great Coram
* [The] Military Ventriloquist
* [Le] Roi

**Whitaker, Whit**
*See* Whitaker, E. E.

**Whitaker, William H.** 1865- ? [BE]
*American baseball player*
* Whitaker, Pat

**Whitbread, Samuel** 1758-1815
[SN]
*British statesman*
* [The] Brewer

**Whitby, Sharon**
*See* Peters, Maureen

**Whitcher, Frances Miriam**
1814-1852 [FFF, PA]
*American author*
* Bedott, [Widow] Priscilla P.

**Whitcomb, Ian** 1941- [CA]
*British writer, singer, composer*
* Bubb, Mel
* Murphy, Buck
* Newton, Stu
* Nouveau, Arthur

**Whitcomb, Joshua**
*See* Thompson, Denman

**Whitcomb, Kenneth G.** 1926-
[ASC]
*American composer, conductor, arranger*
* Kenny, George

**White**
*See* Anglus, Thomas

**[The] White**
*See* Clitus

**[The] White**
*See* Hugh [or Hugues]

**White, Abe**
*See* White, Adel

**White, Adam** [PA]
*Author*
* Arachnophilus

**White, Adel** 1906- [BE]
*American baseball player*
* White, Abe

White, Alan 20th c.
[AW, CA, WD]
*British author*
* Fraser, James
* Whitney, Alec

White, Albert Eugene 1918-  [BE]
*American baseball player*
* White, Fuzz

White, Alexina B.  [FFF, PA]
*American author*
* Alba

White, Alfred H.
*See* Weisman, Alfred

White, Alice
*See* White, Alva

White, Alva 1907-  [F2]
*American actress*
* White, Alice

White, Andy
*See* White, Elwyn Brooks

White, Babe
*See* White, Harold A.

White, Babington
*See* Maxwell, Mary Elizabeth
[Braddon]

White, Barry 1945-  [IBW]
*American orchestra leader, singer,
composer*
* [The] Pied Piper of Love

[The] White Bear
*See* Whately, Richard

White, Beatrice 1901?-1963
[BEW]
*Theatrical performer*
* Curtis, Beatrice

White, Bill
*See* Rattenberry, William A.

White, Bob
*See* Slaughter, Marion T.

White, Bob
*See* White, Floyd Lester

White, Booker T. Washington
1906-1977  [BWW]
*American singer*
* [The] Singing Preacher
* White, Bucca [or Bukka]

White, Bucca [or Bukka]
*See* White, Booker T. Washington

White, Buck
*See* White, O'Neal

White, Byron Raymond 1917-
[FB, OCS]
*American football player and
Supreme Court Justice*
* White, Whizzer

White, Cecil 1900-  [WEC]
*Australian cartoonist*
* Unk
* White, Unk

White, Cecil B.
*See* Christie, William H.

White, Celia 20th c.  [AW]
*British author*
* Tustin, Elizabeth

White, Century
*See* White, John

White, Charles Albert  [FFF]
*Songwriter*
* Birch, Harry

White, Charles William 1906-
[ANT]
*American author*
* White, Max

White, Charley
*See* Anchowitz, Charles

White, Clara
*See* McCoy, Viola

White, Cleve 1928-  [BWW]
*American singer*
* Schoolboy Cleve

White, Dale
*See* Place, Marian T[empleton]

White, Deacon
*See* White, James Laurie

White, Deke
*See* White, George Frederick

[The] White Devil of Wallachia
*See* Castriot [or Castriota?],
George

White, Doc
*See* White, Guy Harris

White, Duck
*See* White, James

White, Dwight 1949-  [SMG]
*American football player*
* White, Mad Dog

White, E. B.
*See* White, Elwyn Brooks

[The] White Eagle
*See* McCoy, Tim

White, Eliza A. 19th c.  [PA]
*Author*
* Alex

White Elk, Michael
*See* Walker, T. Michael

White, Ella
*See* Crippen, Catherine [Katie]

White, Ella
*See* Whidby, Lulu

White, Ellerton Oswald 1917-1971
[DAM, EJ, PMJ]
*American jazz musician*
* White, Sonny

White, Elwyn Brooks 1899-
[IPA, LC, TC]
*American author*
* White, Andy
* White, E. B.
* White, En

White, En
*See* White, Elwyn Brooks

White, Eric 20th c.  [BBH, CSH]
*Canadian lacrosse player*
* White, Rusty

[The] White Eyed Kaffir
*See* Chirgwin, George H.

[The] White Eyed Musical Moke
*See* Chirgwin, George H.

White, Father
*See* White, Harry Alexander

[The] White Flower
*See* Alighieri, Durante

White, Floyd Lester 1932-  [CWG]
*American country-western performer*
* White, Bob

White Fox
*See* Hargrave, John

[The] White Friar
*See* Sabine, William Henry Waldo

White, Fruit
*See* White, Morris

White, Fuzz
*See* White, Albert Eugene

White, G. A.
*See* Millar, James Primrose
Malcolm

White, George
*See* Weitz, George

White, George Frederick
1872-1957  [BE]
*American baseball player*
* White, Deke

White, Gertrude M[ason] 1915-
[CA]
*American author*
* Wakefield, R. I.

White, Gladys
*See* Henderson, Rosa [Rose]

White, Grace
*See* Moore, Monette

White, Guy Harris 1879-1969
[BE, DGS, PB]
*American baseball player*
* White, Doc

White, H. T.
*See* Engh, Rohn

White, Harold A. 1894-1973  [FB]
*American football player*
* White, Babe

White, Harry
*See* Whittington, Harry

White, Harry Alexander
1898-1962  [EJ, WWJ]
*American jazz musician*
* White, Father

White, Herbert [Martyn] Oliver
1885-  [WW]
*Author*
* Martyn, Oliver

White, Hubert
*See* Cobb, J. Storer

White, Hy
*See* White, Hyman

White, Hyman 1915-  [WWJ]
*American jazz musician*
* White, Hy

White, J. H.
*See* White, John Henry

White, James  [HN]
*British politician*
* [The] Plymouth Sound

White, James 1953-  [SMG]
*American football player*
* White, Duck

White, James Blanco 1775-1841
[PA]
*Author*
* Doblado, Don Lucadio

White, James Dillon
*See* White, Stanley

White, James Laurie 1847-1939
[AS, BE, PB]
*American baseball player*
* White, Deacon

White, Jesse
*See* Weidenfeld, Jesse Marc

White, Jo Jo
*See* White, Joseph

White, Jo-Jo
*See* White, Joyner Clifford

White, John 1574-1648
[DNNF, DNNS, SN]
*British clergyman*
* [The] Patriarch of Dorchester
* White, Patriarch

White, John 1590-1645
[DNNS, FFF, RH]
*Welsh barrister and political writer*
* White, Century

White, John 1893-  [BMH]
*Scottish singer*
* MacGregor, Sandy

White, John Henry 1909-  [ART]
*British sculptor*
* White, J. H.

White, John I[rwin] 1902-
[CA, CWG]
*American country-western performer*
* Johns, Whitey
* [The] Lone Star Ranger
* [The] Lonesome Cowboy
* Price, Jimmie

White, John S.
*See* Schwarzkopf, Hans

White, Johnny
*See* Bimstein, Morris

White, Joseph 1946-  [BB]
*American basketball player*
* White, Jo Jo

White, Joseph Blanco 1775-1841
[DEL]
*British author*
* Leucadio Doblado, Don

White, Joseph M.
*Singer*
* [The] Silver Masked Tenor

White, Josh[ua Daniel] 1915-1969
[BWW]
*American singer*
* Barton, Tippy
* Pinewood Tom
* [The] Singing Christian

White, Joyner Clifford 1909-  [BE]
*American baseball player*
* White, Jo-Jo

White, Katharine S. ?-1977
*American author*
* K. S. W.

White, Katherine Elizabeth
1916-1972  [FC]
*American actress*
* Wilson, Marie

White, Kevin Hagan 1929?-
*American politician*
* King Kevin
* Mayor De Luxe

[The] White King
See  Charles I

White, [Oliver] Kirby 1884-1943
[BE]
American baseball player
* White, Redbuck

[The] White Knight
See  Hunyadi, Janos [or Huniades, John]

White, Lasses
See  White, Lee Roy

White, Lee Roy 1888-1949    [SC]
American actor
* White, Lasses

White, Leonard
See  Farjeon, J[oseph] Jefferson

White, Leonard Arthur 1919-
[CEI]
Canadian-born hockey player
* White, Moe

White Lightning
See  Donley, Doug

White, M. Robert
See  Montero, Roberto Bianchi

White, Mad Dog
See  White, Dwight

White, Manster
See  White, Randy

White, Mary Helen  ?-1923  [BEW]
Playwright
* Collingham, G. G.

White, Max
See  White, Charles William

White, Melvin 1921-  [IBW]
American actor and comedian
* White, Slappy

White, Meryon 20th c.  [WWL]
British author
* White-Winton, Meryon

[The] White Milliner
See  Jennings, Frances

White, Mr. [code name used during World War II]
See  Wedemeyer, Albert C.

White, Moe
See  White, Leonard Arthur

White, Morris 1911-  [WWJ]
American jazz musician
* White, Fruit

White, Mrs. Charles O.   [FFF]
Entertainer
* Howard, Lillian

White, Mrs. Frank   [FFF]
Entertainer
* Hall, Pauline

White, Mrs. Legrand   [FFF]
Entertainer
* Maddern, Minnie

White, O'Neal 1911-  [GF]
American golfer
* White, Buck

White, Patriarch
See  White, John

White, Paul Hamilton Hume 1910-
[CA]
Australian physician and author
* Jungle Doctor

White, Phyllis [James] 20th c.
[B10]
British author
* James, P. D.

White Pine Thomson
See  Thomson, Floyd Harvey

[The] White Poet
See  Olaf

White, Princess 1881-1976   [BWW]
American singer
* [The] International Entertainer

White, Priscilla 20th c.   [LRR]
British singer
* Black, Cilla

[The] White Queen
See  Mary, Queen of Scots

White, Quinten 1952-   [EJ7]
American jazz musician
* White, Rocky

White Rabbit
See  Yeo-Thomas, Forest Frederick Edward

White, Ramy Allison [house pseudonym] [Stratemeyer Syndicate]
See  Stratemeyer, Edward L.

White, Randy 20th c.
American football player
* White, Manster

White, Ray
Boxer
* White, Windmill

White, Redbuck
See  White, [Oliver] Kirby

White, Richard Alan 1944-  [CA]
American author
* Cabral, Alberto

White, Richard Grant 1821-1885
[DEL, FFF, PA]
American author and critic
* Outis, U. Donough
* R. G. W.
* Saint Benjamin
* [The] Shakesperian Scholar
* [A] Yankee

White, Rocky
See  White, Quinten

[The] White Rose
See  Elizabeth

[The] White Rose of England
See  Warbeck, Perkin

[The] White Rose of Raby
See  Neville, Cecily [or Cicely]

[The] White Rose of Scotland
See  Gordon, [Lady] Catherine

[The] White Rose of York
See  Courtney, Edward

White, Rusty
See  White, Eric

[The] White Saint of India
See  Bowen, George

White, Sam
See  White, Sanford B.

White, Sanford B. 1888-1964   [FB]
American football player
* White, Sam

White Shoes Johnson
See  Johnson, Billy

White, Sidney 1864-1919
[BEW, FC]
American actor
* Drew, Sidney

White, Slappy
See  White, Melvin

White, Solomon 1868-1955   [MK]
American baseball player
* King Solomon

White, Sonny
See  White, Ellerton Oswald

White, Stanhope 1913-
[AW, CA, IAW]
British author
* Bana, Dan
* Sabiad

White, Stanley 1913-   [CA]
British author
* Krull, Felix
* Peto
* Peto, James
* White, James Dillon

White, Terence Hanbury
1906-1964   [CA, SAT]
British author
* Aston, James

White, Tex
See  White, Wilfred

White, Theodore Edwin [Ted]
1938-   [CA, ESF, SFP]
American author
* Archer, Ron [joint pseudonym with Dave Van Arnam]
* Edwards, Norman [joint pseudonym with Terry (Gene) Carr]

White, Thomas 1582-1676   [FFF]
British philosopher and clergyman
* Candidus

White, Trentwell Mason 1901-
[WWL]
American author
* Trant, Martin

White, Unk
See  White, Cecil

White, Whizzer
See  White, Byron Raymond

White, Whizzer
See  White, Wilford

White, Whoop-La
See  White, William Henry

[The] White Widow
See  Tyrconnel, Duchess of

White, Wilford 20th c.  [FB, SMG]
American football player
* White, Whizzer

White, Wilfred 20th c.   [CEI]
Hockey player
* White, Tex

White, Wilfrid 1903-  [BEW]
British actor
* Hyde-White, Wilfrid

White, William [Bill] 1934-   [IBW]
American sportscaster
* [The] Jackie Robinson of Broadcasting

White, William A[nthony] P[arker]
1911-1968   [CA, CC, EMD]
American author and critic
* Boucher, Anthony
* Holmes, H. H.
* Mudgett, Herman W.

White, William Allen 1868-1944
[WBD]
American author and journalist
* [The] Sage of Emporia

White, William Hale 1831-1913
[LC]
British author
* Rutherford, Mark

White, William Henry 1854-1911
[BE]
American baseball player
* White, Whoop-La

White, William Jack 20th c.
[BLB, PHM]
American underworld figure
* Three Fingered Jack

White, William, Jr. 1934-
[CA, WD]
American author, translator, poet
* Spinossimus

White, Windmill
See  White, Ray

White, Zita
See  Denholm, Therese Mary Zita White

White-Winton, Meryon
See  White, Meryon

Whitebird, J[oanie]
See  Green, Joan Elizabeth

[The] Whitechapel Whirlwind
See  Bergman, Judah

[The] Whitechapel Windmill
See  Bergman, Judah

Whitefeather, [Captain] Barabbas
See  Jerrold, Douglas William

Whitefield, Ann
See  Stone, Susan Berch

Whitefield, George 1714-1770
[FFF, RH]
British religious leader
* Squintum, Doctor

Whiteford, Blackie
See  Whiteford, John P.

Whiteford, John P. 1873-1962
[SC]
American actor
* Whiteford, Blackie

Whitehall, Harold 1905-  [CAP]
British author, educator, playwright
* Fritz

Whitehead, Burgess Urquhart
1910-  [BE]
American baseball player
* Whitehead, Whitey

Whitehead, John Henderson
1909-1964  [BE]
American baseball player
* Whitehead, Silent John

Whitehead, John L., Jr. 1925-
[IBW]
American air force officer and engineer
* Death, Mr.

Whitehead, Kate 1896-    [WWL]
*British author*
* Oxley, Kate

Whitehead, Margaret della Rovere
[ART]
*British artist*
* M. della R. W.

Whitehead, Mrs. C. B.    [PA]
*Author*
* Jackson, Josephine

Whitehead, Silent John
See   Whitehead, John Henderson

Whitehead, Whitey
See   Whitehead, Burgess Urquhart

Whitehill, Walter Muir 1906?-1978
*American historian and man of letters*
* Boston, Mr.

Whitehorn, Arthur Lee
See   Daney, Lee

Whitehorn, Katharine
See   Lyall, Katharine Elizabeth

Whitehouse, Arch
See   Taylor, W. T.

Whitehouse, Arch
See   Whitehouse, Arthur George Joseph

Whitehouse, Arthur George Joseph
1895-1979    [CA, WW]
*British-born author, cartoonist, journalist*
* Whitehouse, Arch

Whitehouse, Charles Evis [Charlie]
1894-1960    [BE]
*American baseball player*
* Whitehouse, Lefty

Whitehouse, Flight
See   Whitehouse, John

Whitehouse, John 1949-    [DC]
*British cricketer*
* Whitehouse, Flight

Whitehouse, Lefty
See   Whitehouse, Charles Evis [Charlie]

Whitehouse, W. F. 19th c.    [PA]
*Author*
* Agricola

Whiteing, E.    [PA]
*Author*
* Sprouts

Whiteing, Richard 1840- ?    [WWL]
*British author*
* Thorne, Whyte

Whiteley, John Peter 1955-    [DC]
*British cricketer*
* Whiteley, Nimmo

Whiteley, Mrs. John H.    [FFF]
*Entertainer*
* Weaver, Ella

Whiteley, Nimmo
See   Whiteley, John Peter

Whiteley, William 1831-1907
[WBD]
*British department store owner*
* [The] Universal Provider

Whitelock, Louise [Clarkson] 1865-
?    [WGT]
*Author*
* Clarkson, L.

Whitelocke, Bulstrode 1605-1675
[SN]
*British politician*
* [The] Temporizing Statesman

Whiteman, Paul 1890-1967    [PMJ]
*American jazz musician*
* [The] King of Jazz

Whiteman, Sydney 1877-1958
[THR]
*Australian-born critic, author, journalist*
* Carroll, Sydney W.

Whitewell, A. M.
See   Close, John

Whitfield, Howard
See   Smith, Howard Whitfield, Jr.

Whitfield, John Humphreys 1906-
[AW, CA]
*British educator and author*
* Pilio, Gerone

Whitfield, Malvin Greston 1924-
[IBW]
*American rack and field athlete*
* Whitfield, Marvelous Mal

Whitfield, Marvelous Mal
See   Whitfield, Malvin Greston

[The] Whitfield of the Stage
See   Garrick, David

[The] Whitfield of the Stage
See   Quin, James

Whitfield, Raoul 1898-1945
[CC, EMD]
*American author*
* Decolta, Ramon

Whitford, Joan 1922?-    [MBF]
*British author*
* Ford, Barry
* Oldham, Hugh R.

Whitford, Lawrence W. 20th c.
[BBH]
*American baseball coach*
* Whitford, Mon

Whitford, Lee
See   Coates, Walter John

Whitford, Mon
See   Whitford, Lawrence W.

Whithorne, Emerson
See   Whittern, Emerson

Whiting, Ed[ward C.]
See   Zieber, Harry

Whiting Spilhaus, M.
See   Spilhaus, Phyllis Margaret

Whitinger, R. D.
See   Place, Marian T[empleton]

Whitley, Crane
See   Wilenchick, Clem

Whitley, George
See   Chandler, Arthur Bertram

Whitley, Jonas E. 1849- ?    [PA]
*Author*
* Nick

Whitlock, Billy
See   Essex, Frederick

Whitlock, Bob
See   Whitlock, Von Varlynn

Whitlock, Buck
See   Whitlock, Roy

Whitlock, John
See   Codner, John

Whitlock, Ralph 1914-    [CA, WD]
*British author*
* [The] Countryman
* Reynolds, John
* Reynolds, Madge

Whitlock, Roy 20th c.    [SMG]
*Canadian-born hockey player*
* Whitlock, Buck

Whitlock, Von Varlynn 1931-    [EJ]
*American jazz musician*
* Whitlock, Bob

Whitly, Jonas E. 1849- ?    [PA]
*Author*
* J. E. W.

Whitman, Alfred
See   Vosburgh, Alfred

Whitman, [Walter] Frank[lin]
1924-    [BE]
*American baseball player*
* Whitman, Hooker

Whitman, Gayne 1890-1958    [SC]
*American actor and screenwriter*
* Vosburgh, Alfred

Whitman, Hooker
See   Whitman, [Walter] Frank[lin]

Whitman, Jerry
See   Winters, June

Whitman, Otis Dewey, Jr. 1924-
[CME, CWG, DAM]
*American country-western performer*
* Whitman, Slim

Whitman, Sarah Helen Power
1803-1878    [FFF]
*American poet*
* Helen

Whitman, Slim
See   Whitman, Otis Dewey, Jr.

Whitman, Walt[er] 1819-1892
[DNNS, FFF, SN]
*American poet*
* [The] Good Gray Poet

Whitmore, Cilla
See   Gladstone, Arthur M.

Whitner, Edward Clarence 1916-
[BE]
*American baseball player*
* Levy, Ed[ward Clarence]

Whitney, Alec
See   White, Alan

Whitney, Arthur Carter 1906-
[BE, PB]
*American baseball player*
* Whitney, Pinky

Whitney, Cornelius Vanderbilt 20th
c.
*American sportsman and industrialist*
* Whitney, Sonny

Whitney, David
See   Malick, Terrence

Whitney, Elliott [joint pseudonym
with Harry Lincoln Saylor]
See   Bedford-Jones, Henry [James O'Brien]

Whitney, Elliott [joint pseudonym
with Henry Bedford-Jones]
See   Sayler, Harry Lincoln

Whitney, Frank Thomas
1856-1943    [BE]
*American baseball player*
* Whitney, Jumbo

Whitney, Grasshopper Jim
See   Whitney, James E.

Whitney, Hallam
See   Whittington, Harry

Whitney, J. L. H.
See   Trimble, Jacquelyn W[hitney]

Whitney, James E. 1856-1891
[AS, DGS, PB]
*American baseball player*
* Whitney, Grasshopper Jim
* Whitney, Long Jim

Whitney, Jock
See   Whitney, John Hay

Whitney, John Hay 1905?-1982
*American diplomat and newspaper publisher*
* Whitney, Jock

Whitney, Jumbo
See   Whitney, Frank Thomas

Whitney, Long Jim
See   Whitney, James E.

Whitney, Lucia
See   Kelley, Ethel [May]

Whitney, Moxam 1919-    [ASC]
*Canadian musician*
* Whitney, Moxie

Whitney, Moxie
See   Whitney, Moxam

Whitney, Mrs. A. T. 1824- ?    [PA]
*Author*
* Garney, Faith

Whitney, Peter
See   Engle, Peter King

Whitney, Pinky
See   Whitney, Arthur Carter

Whitney, Reid
See   Armour, R. Coutts

Whitney, Sonny
See   Whitney, Cornelius Vanderbilt

Whitney, Spencer
See   Burks, Arthur J.

Whiton, James Nelson 1932-    [CA]
*American author and screenwriter*
* Bolo, Solomon
* Boylan, Boyd

Whitshaw, Stella 1887-    [THR]
*Russian-born actress*
* Arbenina, Stella

Whitson
See   Warren, Peter Whitson

Whitson, John H. 1854-1936
[EMD]
*Author*
* Carter, Nicholas?

Whitstable, George
See   Lissenden, George B.

**Whittaker, A.** 17th c.   [HN]
*American clergyman*
* [The] Apostle of Virginia

**Whittaker, Doc**
*See* Whittaker, Walt[er Elton]

**Whittaker, Hudson**
*See* Woodbridge, Hudson

**Whittaker, Lucian**   [SMG]
*American basketball player*
* Whittaker, Skippy

**Whittaker, Norman** 20th c.   [BLB]
*American swindler*
* [The] Fox

**Whittaker, Skippy**
*See* Whittaker, Lucian

**Whittaker, Walt[er Elton]**
1894-1965   [BE]
*American baseball player*
* Whittaker, Doc

**Whitted, George Bostic** 1890-1942
[AS, BE]
*American baseball player*
* Whitted, Possum

**Whitted, Possum**
*See* Whitted, George Bostic

**Whittemore, Don** 20th c.   [CA]
*American author and film critic*
* Norman, Louis

**Whitten, Wilfred** ?-1942
[LC, WWL]
*British author and editor*
* O'London, John

**Whittenton, Jesse**
*See* Whittenton, Urshell

**Whittenton, Urshell** 1934-   [FB]
*American football player*
* Whittenton, Jesse

**Whittern, Emerson** 1884-1958
[DAM]
*American composer*
* Whithorne, Emerson

**Whittet, George Sorley** 20th c.
[IAW]
*Scottish-born author*
* Jok
* Kerr, John O'Connell
* Monkland, George

**Whittier, John Greenleaf**
1807-1892   [DEL, PA]
*American author and poet*
* [The] Quaker Poet

**Whittier, Matthew F.** 1812-1883
[FFF]
*American author*
* Spike, Ethan

**Whittingham, Charlie** 1913-   [BBH]
*American horse trainer*
* [The] Bold Eagle

**Whittingham, Mary**
*See* Skuse, Mrs.

**Whittington, Harry** 1915-   [CA]
*American author*
* Harrison, Whit
* Holland, Kel
* Myers, Harriet Kathryn
* Phillips, Steve
* Stuart, Clay
* Wells, Hondo
* White, Harry
* Whitney, Hallam

**Whittington, Nina Eloise** 20th c.
[BEW]
*American producer and director*
* Vance, Nina

**Whittington, Peter**
*See* Mackay, James [Alexander]

**Whittington [or Whitynton?], Robert**
15th c.   [SN]
*British grammarian and poet*
* Protovates Angliae

**Whittington-Egan, Richard** 1924-
[IAW]
*British author*
* Barrington, Nicholas
* Curzon, Charles
* Doughty, Nigel

**Whittle, Emma**
*See* Clark, Mrs. J. P.

**Whittle, Tyler**
*See* Tyler-Whittle, Michael Sidney

**Whittlebot, Hernia**
*See* Coward, [Sir] Noel [Pierce]

**Whittlesey, Oscar C.**   [PA]
*Author*
* Bloomer, Ben

**Whittridge, Irwin Thomas**
1908-1971   [SC]
*American actor*
* Goode, Jack

**Whitwell, O'Brien** 1870-1915
[BBD]
*Irish composer*
* Butler, O'Brien

**Whiz, Walter**
*See* Johnson, Curt[is Lee]

**Whoa Bill Phillips**
*See* Phillips, William Corcoran

**[The] Whole Duty of Man**
*See* Moncrieff, [Sir] James
Wellwood

**[The] Whopper**
*See* Paultz, Billy

**Whyatt, Frances**
*See* Boyd, Shylah

**Whye, Felix**
*See* Dixon, Arthur

**Whyms, Bo**
*See* Whyms, Ronald

**Whyms, Ronald** 20th c.   [RBE]
*American boxer*
* Whyms, Bo

**Whyte, Donald** 1926-   [IAW]
*Scottish author*
* Sennachie

**Whyte, Henry** 1852?-1913   [WWL]
*British author and folklorist*
* Fioun

**Whyte, Jerome**
*See* Jerchower, Jerome Victor

**Whyte, Rollin** 20th c.   [BBH]
*American sailboat racer*
* Whyte, Skip

**Whyte, Sibley**
*See* Stein, Henry Eugene

**Whyte, Skip**
*See* Whyte, Rollin

**Whyte, [Mr.] Thomas**
*See* Elliott, C. W.

**Whyte Tye**
*See* Wingfield, Lewis

**Whyte, [Viscount] Y. Melton**
*See* Anderson, G. J. B.

**Whytforde, Richard**   [SN]
* [The] Wretch of Sion

**Whytock, Ora** 1893-1955   [SC]
*American actress*
* Carew, Ora

**Wibberley, Leonard [Patrick
O'Connor]** 1915-   [CA, EMD, SAT]
*Irish-born author*
* Holton, Leonard
* O'Connor, Patrick
* Webb, Christopher

**Wicher, Ernie**
*See* Witcher, Ernie

**Wick, Air**
*See* Wick, Charles Z.

**Wick, Carter**
*See* Wilcox, Collin

**Wick, Charles Z.** 20th c.
*American government official*
* Wick, Air

**Wickdahl, Lillian** 20th c.   [ASC]
*American composer*
* Sandell, Lynn

**[The] Wicked**
*See* Pickett, Wilson

**[The] Wicked Lord Lyttelton**
*See* Lyttelton, Thomas [Second
Baron Lyttelton]

**[The] Wickedest Man in San
Francisco**
*See* Bierce, Ambrose [Gwinett]

**[The] Wickedest Man in the World**
*See* Crowley, Edward Alexander

**Wickenden, William**   [PA]
*Author*
* [The] Bard of the Forest

**Wickenhauser, Mary** 1916-   [FC]
*American actress*
* Wickes, Mary

**Wicker, Ireene** 1905-
*American singer*
* [The] Singing Lady

**Wicker, Kemp Caswell** 1906-1973
[BE]
*American baseball player*
* Whicker, Kemp Caswell

**Wicker, Randolfe Hayden**
*See* Hayden, C[harles] Gervin

**Wicker, Thomas Grey** 1926-
[B10, CA, WD]
*American author and journalist*
* Connolly, Paul

**Wickersham, Ned**
*See* Wickersham, Ray

**Wickersham, Ray** 20th c.   [BBH]
*American softball player*
* Wickersham, Ned

**Wickes, Mary**
*See* Wickenhauser, Mary

**Wickham, Geoffrey Earle** 1919-
[ART]
*British painter and sculptor*
* G. E. W.

**Wickham, Hilary Judith** 1912-
[ART]
*British artist*
* Hilary

**Wickham, Jean** 1903-   [CA]
*American author*
* Gordon, Jean

**Wickham, John** 1923-   [CW]
*Barbadian author, critic, editor*
* Wilsden, Clemensford

**Wickham, M. F.**
*See* Wickham, Mabel Frances

**Wickham, Mabel Frances** 1901-
[ART]
*British painter*
* Wickham, M. F.

**Wickham, Mary Fanning**
*See* Bond, Mary Fanning Wickham

**Wickham, Tony**
*See* Wickham-Jones, Anthony

**Wickham-Jones, Anthony**
1922-1948   [BEW]
*British actor*
* Wickham, Tony

**Wickloe, Peter**
*See* Duff, Douglas Valder

**Wicks, Katharine Gibson**
1893-1960   [IA]
*American author*
* Gibson, Katharine

**Wictorin, John** 1907-1969   [BBH]
*Swedish-born skiing organization
supporter and tournament official*
* Swix, Mr.

**Widdemer, Mabel Cleland**
1902-1964   [CA, SAT]
*American author*
* Cleland, Mabel
* Ludlum, Mabel Cleland

**Widdemer, Margaret**
*See* Schauffler, Margaret
Widdemer

**Widdrington, Roger**
*See* Preston, Roger

**[The] Wide Awake**
*See* Louis VI

**Widenhofer, Robert** 1943-   [SMG]
*American football coach*
* Widenhofer, Woody

**Widenhofer, Woody**
*See* Widenhofer, Robert

**Widerman, Robert** 1926-   [BEW]
*French-born actor and singer*
* Clary, Robert

**Widforss, Gunnar Mauritz**
1879-1934   [WBD]
*Swedish-born painter*
* [The] Painter of the National
Parks

**Widing, Juha Markku** 1947-
[FHE, HK, HR]
*Finnish-born hockey player*
* Widing, Whitey

**Widing, Whitey**
*See* Widing, Juha Markku

Widmer, Mrs. Harry [FFF]
*Entertainer*
* Mayhew, Katie

Widner, Arthur L. 20th c. [WGT]
*Author*
* Lambert, Arthur

Widner, Wild Bill
See Widner, William Waterfield

Widner, William Waterfield
1867-1908 [BE]
*American baseball player*
* Widner, Wild Bill

[The] Widow Capet
See [Josephe Jeanne] Marie
Antoinette

[The] Widow of Windsor
See Victoria

Wieand, Franklin Delano Roosevelt
1933- [BE]
*American baseball player*
* Wieand, Ted

Wieand, Ted
See Wieand, Franklin Delano
Roosevelt

Wiechmann, Ferdinand Gerhard
1858- ? [ALY]
*American chemist and author*
* Monroe, Forest

Wieder, Robert S[hannon] 1944-
[CA]
*American author*
* Shannon, Robert

Wiederrecht, Martha Lucile 20th
c. [BEW]
*American actress and singer*
* Wright, Martha

Wiederump, Trotzhard
See Steiner, Gerolf

Wiegand, Ursula 1930- [IAW]
*German author*
* Sonntag, Uschi

Wieland, Christoph Martin
1733-1813 [DNNF, DNNS, HN]
*German poet and author*
* [The] German Voltaire
* [Der] Meister
* [The] Voltaire of Germany

Wieman, Elton E. 1896-1971
[BBH, FB]
*American football coach*
* Wieman, Tad

Wieman, Tad
See Wieman, Elton E.

Wienecke, Gretchen Patricia 1932-
[BEW]
*American singer, dancer, actress*
* Wyler, Gretchen

Wiener, Francis de [or Franz]
1877-1937 [CD, WBD]
*Belgian-born French playwright*
* Croisset, Francis de

Wiener, Joan
See Bordow, Joan [Wiener]

Wiener, Norbert 1894-1964
[ESF, JL, WGT]
*German-born mathematician and
author*
* [The] Father of Cybernetics
* Norbert, W.

Wiener, Sam
See Dolgoff, Sam

Wiener, Thomas G[ustav] 1917-
[CA]
*Czech-born author*
* Winner, Thomas G[ustav]

Wieniawska, Irene Regine
1880-1932 [BBD]
*Belgian-born composer*
* Poldowski

Wier, Johannes 1515-1588 [PA]
*Author*
* Piscinarius

Wier, Stuart Austin 1894- [NAA]
*American author*
* Austin, Stuart

Wiersbe, Warren Wendell 1929-
[CA]
*American clergyman and author*
* Warren, Dave

Wiersma, Stanley M[arvin] 1930-
[CA]
*American author and poet*
* Buning, Sietze

Wiesengrund, Theodor 1903-
[BBD]
*German music theorist*
* Adorno, Theodor
* Wiesengrund-Adorno, Theodor

Wiesengrund-Adorno, Theodor
See Wiesengrund, Theodor

Wiesner, Portia
See Takakjian, Portia

Wiest, Grace L.
See Deloughery, Grace L.

Wietelmann, Whitey
See Wietelmann, William
Frederick

Wietelmann, William Frederick
1919- [BE, SMG]
*American baseball player and coach*
* Wietelmann, Whitey

Wigan, Christopher
See Bingley, David Ernest

[The] Wigan Nightingale
See Booth, James

Wiggen, Henry J.
See Finkelstein, Mark

Wigger, Ralf Harolde 1899-1952?
[FC]
*American actor*
* Harolde, Ralf

Wiggins, Ava June 1934- [OP]
*British opera singer*
* June, Ava

Wiggins, David 1933- [AW]
*British author and educator*
* Priestley, Robert

Wiggins, Gerald Foster 1956-
[EJ7]
*American jazz musician*
* Wiggins, J. J.

Wiggins, J. J.
See Wiggins, Gerald Foster

Wigglesworth, Margaret McKean
20th c. [BBH]
*American skier*
* Wigglesworth, Marian

Wigglesworth, Marian
See Wigglesworth, Margaret
McKean

Wigglesworth, Martin Francis
1926- [AW]
*British television and radio script writer*
* Worth, Martin

Wiggs, Big Jim
See Wiggs, James Alvin [Jimmy]

Wiggs, James Alvin [Jimmy]
1876-1963 [BE]
*Norwegian-born baseball player*
* Wiggs, Big Jim

Wiggs, Johnny
See Hyman, John Wigginton

Wight, James Alfred 1916- [B10]
*Scottish veterinarian and author*
* Herriot, James

Wight, James Ambrose [FFF]
*American clergyman and writer*
* Ambrose

Wight, Lefty
See Wight, William Robert

Wight, William Robert 1922- [BE]
*American baseball player*
* Wight, Lefty

Wightman, Frieda 1901?-1976
[HCA, THR]
*Scottish-born actress*
* Inescort, Frieda

Wighton, David 1863- ? [THR]
*British entertainer*
* Devant, David

Wigmore
See Price, Charles

Wignall, Anne 1912- [CA]
*British author*
* Acland, Alice
* Marreco, Anne

Wignall, Trevor 1883-1958 [MBF]
*Welsh-born author*
* Dene, Alan
* Rees, David

Wigniolle, Yvonne 1898- [BEW]
*French actress and singer*
* Printemps, Yvonne

Wigoder, Thelma 1925- [TR]
*British actress*
* Ruby, Thelma

Wigram, S. R. 19th c. [FFF]
*American author*
* Bee, Hookanit, Esq.

Wijnstroom, Christy
See Hoppen-Ram, Henderika
Wilhelmina Christina

Wikstrom, Maud 1946- [SW]
*Swedish-born fashion model and
actress*
* Adams, Maud

Wilber, Babe
See Wilber, Delbert Quentin

Wilber, Bill
See McCoy, Joe

Wilber, Delbert Quentin 1919-
[BE]
*American baseball player*
* Welber, Del
* Wilber, Babe

Wilberforce, Robert Isaac
1802-1857 [FFF]
*British author and clergyman*
* Theophilus Secundus

Wilberforce, Samuel 1805-1873
[DEP, DNNS, SN]
*Bishop of Oxford and Winchester*
* Soapy Sam

Wilberforce, William 1759-1833
[DNNF, RH]
*British religious leader and
antislavery crusader*
* [The] Friend of Man
* [The] Washington of Africa

Wilborn, Nelson 1907- [BWW]
*American singer*
* Dirty Red
* Red Devil
* Red Nelson

Wilbur, Anna T. 1817- ? [PA]
*Author*
* Leigh, Florence

Wilbur, Gilligan
See Wilbur, John

Wilbur, Homer
See Lowell, James Russell

Wilbur, John 20th c.
*American football player*
* Wilbur, Gilligan

Wilby, Basil Leslie 1930-
[AW, WD]
*British author*
* Knight, Gareth

Wilby, R. Hunt
See Eyster, William Reynolds

Wilc
See Wilczynski, Katerina

Wilcox, Collin 1924- [CA]
*American author*
* Wick, Carter

Wilcox, David 1942- [FB]
*American football player*
* [The] Intimidator

Wilcox, Don 1908- [ESF, WGT]
*American author*
* Atomcracker, Buzz-Bolt
* Blade, Alexander [house
pseudonym, Ziff-Davis]
* Eldon, Cleo
* Overton, Max
* Shelton, Miles

Wilcox, Hannah Simms
See Miner, Virginia Scott

Wilcox, Harry 20th c. [WW]
*Author*
* Derby, Mark

Wilcox, Howard 20th c. [BBH]
*American auto racer*
* Wilcox, Howdy

Wilcox, Howdy
See Wilcox, Howard

Wilcox, Jess
See Hershman, Morris

Wilcox, L. A.
See Wilcox, Leslie Arthur

Wilcox, Leslie Arthur 1904- [ART]
*British artist*
* Wilcox, L. A.

**Wilcoxon, Harry** 1905-   [ITA]
*British actor and producer*
* Wilcoxon, Henry

**Wilcoxon, Henry**
*See* Wilcoxon, Harry

**Wilczynski, Katerina** 1894-
[ART, DBA]
*British painter and etcher*
* Wilc

**Wild Bill Connelly**
*See* Connelly, William Wirt [Bill]

**Wild Bill Cummings**
*See* Cummings, Bill

**Wild Bill Davis**
*See* Davis, William Strethen

**Wild Bill Davison**
*See* Davison, William

**Wild Bill Donavan**
*See* Donavan, William

**Wild Bill Donovan**
*See* Donovan, William Edward

**Wild Bill Donovan**
*See* Donovan, William Joseph

**Wild Bill Douglas**
*See* Douglas, William Orville

**Wild Bill Elliott**
*See* Elliott, Gordon

**Wild Bill Ezinicki**
*See* Ezinicki, William

**Wild Bill Hallahan**
*See* Hallahan, William Anthony

**Wild Bill Hancock**
*See* Hancock, Bill

**Wild Bill Hickok**
*See* Hickok, James Butler

**Wild Bill Hickok**
*See* Hickok, William O.

**Wild Bill Hunnefield**
*See* Hunnefield, William Fenton

**Wild Bill Hutchison**
*See* Hutchison, William Forrest

**Wild Bill Kelly**
*See* Kelly, William

**Wild Bill Leard**
*See* Leard, William Wallace [Bill]

**Wild Bill Lovett**
*See* Lovett, W. L.

**Wild Bill Luhrsen**
*See* Luhrsen, William Ferdinand
[Bill]

**Wild Bill Mehlhorn**
*See* Mehlhorn, William

**Wild Bill Miller**
*See* Miller, William Francis [Bill]

**Wild Bill Morgan**
*See* Morgan, William

**Wild Bill Piercy**
*See* Piercy, William Benton

**Wild Bill Pierro**
*See* Pierro, William Leonard [Bill]

**Wild Bill Pierson**
*See* Pierson, William Morris [Bill]

**Wild Bill Weightman**
*See* Weightman, William E.

**Wild Bill Widner**
*See* Widner, William Waterfield

**[The] Wild Boar of the Ardennes**
*See* La Marck, Guillaume [or
William] de

**Wild Bull McEver**
*See* McEver, Eugene T.

**[The] Wild Bull of the Pampas**
*See* Firpo, Luis Angel

**[The] Wild Bull of the Pampas**
*See* Gonzalez, Froilan

**Wild Child Butler**
*See* Butler, George

**[The] Wild Elk of the Wasatch**
*See* Heusser, Edward Burleton

**Wild, Henry** 1684?-1734
[DEP, DNNF, DNNS]
*British tailor who mastered seven
foreign languages*
* [The] Arabian Tailor
* [The] Learned Tailor

**Wild Horse Annie**
*See* Johnston, Velma B.

**Wild Horse Crosby**
*See* Crosby, Bob

**[The] Wild Horse of the Osage**
*See* Martin, John Leonard

**Wild Horse Sheridan**
*See* Sheridan, Neill Rawlins

**Wild, Johann** 1485-1554   [PA]
*Author*
* Ferus

**Wild Man Fischer**
*See* Fischer, Larry

**[The] Wild Man of Brooklyn**
*See* Barney, Rex

**[The] Wild Man of Pop**
*See* Hendrix, James Marshall
[Jimi]

**[The] Wild One**
*See* Cottrell, Morganna Roberts

**Wild, Reginald Leonard** 1912-
[AW]
*British author*
* Edwards, Leonard

**Wild Willie Chaney**
*See* Chaney, Willie

**Wild Willie Moore**
*See* Moore, Willie

**Wildbore, Charles**   [FFF]
*Writer*
* Amicus

**Wilde, D. Gunther**
*See* Hurwood, Bernhardt J[ackson]

**Wilde, Hilary**
*See* Breton-Smith, Clare

**Wilde, James [Jimmy]** 1892-1969
[BX, OCS, RBE]
*British boxer*
* [The] Ghost with a Hammer in
His Hand
* [The] Mighty Atom

**Wilde, Jane Francesca Elgee** 1806-
?   [CEC]
*Irish author*
* Speranza

**Wilde, Jennifer**
*See* Huff, Tom Elmer

**Wilde, Jimmy**
*See* Creasey, John

**Wilde, Kathey**
*See* King, Patricia

**Wilde, Larry**
*See* Wildman, Larry

**Wilde, Oscar Fingal O'Flahertie
Wills** 1854-1900   [FFF, LC]
*Irish poet and playwright*
* Melmoth, Sebastian
* [The] New Dress-Improver

**Wilde, Robert** 17th c.   [SN]
*Author*
* [The] Withers of the City

**Wilde, Susie**
*See* Adams, Mrs. Mark

**Wilde, Vyvyan Beresford**
1886-1967   [CA]
*British author and translator*
* Holland, Vyvyan [Beresford]

**Wildeblood, Joan**
*See* Murray, Joan

**Wilder, Alexander** 19th c.   [FFF]
*American journalist*
* Merlin
* Plautus

**Wilder, Billy**
*See* Wilder, Samuel

**Wilder, Cherry**
*See* Grimm, Cherry Barbara

**Wilder, Gene**
*See* Silberman, Jerome

**Wilder, Katherine Loving Buell**
1889-   [WWL]
*American author*
* Buell, Wilder

**Wilder, Rose**
*See* Lane, Rose Wilder

**Wilder, Samuel** 1906-   [FC, FD]
*Austrian-born writer and director*
* Wilder, Billy

**Wilder, William West**
*See* Patten, William George

**Wildfire**
*See* Wyndham, [Sir] William

**[The] Wildflower of the Linden Field**
*See* Clement, Lewis

**Wilding, Anthony F.** 20th c.   [OET]
*New Zealand-born tennis player*
* Little Hercules

**Wilding, Eric**
*See* Tubb, Edwin Charles

**Wilding, Philip** 20th c.
[ESF, SFL, WGT]
*British author*
* Fraser, Jefferson?
* Haynes, John Robert
* Marshall, Lloyd?
* Russell, Erle?
* Stanton, Borden?
* Stewart, Logan
* Stuart, Logan?

**Wilding, Sten**
*See* Liljenfors, Bennie Mads Carl

**Wildman, Larry** 1928-   [JL]
*American comedian and author*
* Wilde, Larry

**Wildwood, Will**
*See* Pond, Frederick Eugene

**Wilenchick, Clem** ?-1958   [SC]
*Actor*
* Whitley, Crane

**Wiles, Domini**
*See* High-Smith, Domini

**Wiley, Bell**
*See* Strauss, Frances

**Wiley, Carl A.** 20th c.   [WGT]
*Author*
* Saunders, Russell

**Wiley, Coyote**
*See* Wiley, Mark Eugene

**Wiley, Doc**
*See* Wiley, Washeba

**Wiley, John**
*See* Graham, Roger Phillips

**Wiley, Margaret L.**
*See* Marshall, Margaret Lenore
Wiley

**Wiley, Mark Eugene** 1948-   [SMG]
*American baseball player*
* Wiley, Coyote

**Wiley, Stan**
*See* Hill, John S[tanley]

**Wiley, Washeba**   [OBW]
*American baseball player*
* Wiley, Doc

**Wilford, Charles**
*See* Dukes, Charles W.

**Wilfred, Wilf**
*See* Cude, Wilfred

**Wilhelm**
*See* Brewer, William A.

**Wilhelm, C.**
*See* Pitcher, William John Charles

**Wilhelm, Charles Ernest** 1929-
[BE]
*American baseball player*
* Wilhelm, Spider

**Wilhelm, Irvin Key** 1874-1936
[AS, BE, BN]
*American baseball player*
* Wilhelm, Kaiser
* Wilhelm, Little Eva

**Wilhelm, James Hoyt** 1923-   [SMG]
*American baseball player*
* Wilhelm, Knuckles

**Wilhelm, Kaiser**
*See* Wilhelm, Irvin Key

**Wilhelm, Kate**
*See* Knight, Kate Wilhelm

**Wilhelm, Knuckles**
*See* Wilhelm, James Hoyt

**Wilhelm, Little Eva**
*See* Wilhelm, Irvin Key

**Wilhelm, Spider**
*See* Wilhelm, Charles Ernest

**Wilhelmina**
*See* Cooper, Wilhelmina
[Behmenburg]

**Wilhoite, Donald MacRae, Jr.**
1909- [ASC, PMJ]
*American songwriter*
* Raye, Don

**Wilkening, Howard [Everett]** 1909-
[CA]
*American psychologist and author*
* Stokes, Robert [Bob]

**Wilkens, Maybritt** 1933?-
[FC, SW]
*Swedish actress*
* Britt, May

**Wilkes, Ada**
*See* McLeod, Mrs. J. F.

**Wilkes, Jamaal** 1953- [SMG]
*American basketball player*
* Wilkes, Silk

**Wilkes, Jim** 20th c.
*American baseball player*
* Wilkes, Junior

**Wilkes, Junior**
*See* Wilkes, Jim

**Wilkes, Silk**
*See* Wilkes, Jamaal

**Wilkes, Thomas**
*See* Derrick, Samuel

**Wilkes, W.** 20th c. [MBF]
*British author*
* Evelyn, A. W.

**Wilkes-Hunter, Richard** 1906-
[AW, CA]
*Australian author and journalist*
* Ballard, Dean
* Brody, Marc
* Conrad, Tod
* Crane, Alex
* Douglas, Shane
* Dunn, James
* Gordon, Peter
* Mitchell, Kerry
* O'Neill, C. M.
* Sanders, Kent
* Shulberg, Alan

**Wilkie, Aldon Jay** 1914- [BE]
*Canadian-born baseball player*
* Wilkie, Lefty

**Wilkie, [Sir] David** 1785-1841
[DEP, RH, SN]
*Scottish painter*
* [The] Raphael of Domestic Art
* [The] Scottish Teniers

**Wilkie, F. B.** 1830- ? [FFF]
*American author*
* Poliuto

**Wilkie, Lefty**
*See* Wilkie, Aldon Jay

**Wilkie, William** 1721-1772
[DEL, FFF, RH]
*Scottish poet*
* [The] Homer of Scotland
* [The] Scottish Homer

**Wilkin, Wee Willie**
*See* Wilkin, Wilbur

**Wilkin, Wilbur** ?-1973 [FB]
*American football player*
* Wilkin, Wee Willie

**Wilkins, Alan Haydn** 1953- [DC]
*Welsh cricketer*
* Wilkins, Wilki

**Wilkins, Alonzo** 1939-1972
[BBH, IBW]
*American wheelchair basketball
player*
* Wilkins, Willie [or Willy]

**Wilkins, Aminda Ann Badeau** 20th
c. [IBW]
*American social worker*
* Wilkins, Minnie

**Wilkins, Dominique** 1960?-
*American basketball player*
* Dunk, Dr.

**Wilkins, E. G. P.** [PA]
*Author*
* Personne

**Wilkins, H. A.** 19th c. [FFF]
*Canadian poet*
* Harriet Annie

**Wilkins, Isaac** 1741-1830 [PA]
*Author*
* Farmer, A. W.

**Wilkins, Mary E.**
*See* Freeman, Mary Eleanor
Wilkins

**Wilkins, Mary Huiskamp Calhoun**
1926- [TBJ]
*American author*
* Calhoun, Mary

**Wilkins, Minnie**
*See* Wilkins, Aminda Ann Badeau

**Wilkins, Peter**
*See* Paltock, Robert

**Wilkins, [Robert] Tim[othy]** 1896-
[BWW, NBB]
*American singer*
* Keghouse
* Oliver, Tim

**Wilkins, Wilki**
*See* Wilkins, Alan Haydn

**Wilkins, William A.** [PA]
*Author*
* Greene, Hiram

**Wilkins, Willie [or Willy]**
*See* Wilkins, Alonzo

**Wilkinson, Anna** 1942- [TR]
*British actress*
* Carteret, Anna

**Wilkinson, Bonara**
*See* Overstreet, Bonaro Wilkinson

**Wilkinson, Bud**
*See* Wilkinson, Charles B.

**Wilkinson, Buzz**
*See* Wilkinson, Richard

**Wilkinson, Charles B.** 1916-
[FB, OCS]
*American football coach*
* Wilkinson, Bud

**Wilkinson, Cyril Theodore
Anstruther** 1884-1970 [OCS]
*British field hockey player and
cricketer*
* Wilkinson, Wilkie

**Wilkinson, Fred** 1894-1966 [THR]
*British theatrical press
representative*
* Gratton, Fred

**Wilkinson, Henry, Jr.** 17th c. [SN]
*British politician*
* Long Harry

**Wilkinson, Iris Guiver** 1906-1939
[LC, TCL]
*New Zealand poet and author*
* Hyde, Robin

**Wilkinson, Jan** 1931- [TR]
*British actress*
* Holden, Jan

**Wilkinson, Jennie Gaudio** 20th c.
[IWM]
*American musician*
* Gaudio, Jennie

**Wilkinson, John [Donald]** 1929-
[CA]
*British clergyman and author*
* Ironmaster, Maximus

**Wilkinson, Lorna Hilda Kathleen**
1909- [CAP]
*British author*
* Deane, Lorna

**Wilkinson, Louis Umfreville**
1881-1966 [LC]
*British author*
* Marlow, Louis

**Wilkinson, Mrs. Arthur P.** [FFF]
*Entertainer*
* Dudley, Perle

**Wilkinson, Mrs. R. O.** [FFF]
*Entertainer*
* Quinn, Kitty

**Wilkinson, Percy Francis Hamilton**
1912- [AW, WD]
*British author*
* Wilkinson, Tim

**Wilkinson, Richard** 1932- [BB]
*American basketball player*
* Wilkinson, Buzz

**Wilkinson, Ronald** 1920- [CA]
*British physician and author*
* Scott Thorn, Ronald

**Wilkinson, Tim**
*See* Wilkinson, Percy Francis
Hamilton

**Wilkinson, Wilkie**
*See* Wilkinson, Cyril Theodore
Anstruther

**Wilks, Brian** 1933- [CA]
*British educator and playwright*
* Hughes, Sam

**Wilks, Cork**
*See* Wilks, Theodore [Ted]

**Wilks, Madge** 1880- ? [THR]
*British actress*
* Fabian, Madge

**Wilks, Theodore [Ted]** 1915-
[BE, PB]
*American baseball player*
* Wilks, Cork

**Will**
*See* Lipkind, William

**Will, Butch**
*See* Will, Robert Lee

**Will o' the Wisp**
*See* Papaleo, William

**Will R.**
*See* Roberts, Will

**Will, Robert Lee** 1931- [BE]
*American baseball player*
* Will, Butch

**Willadsen, Gene**
*See* Lynn, Jane Thursten

**Willamow, Johann Gottlieb**
1736-1777 [SN]
*Prussian poet*
* [The] Prussian Pindar

**Willard, C. D.**
*See* Diffin, Charles W[illard]

**Willard, Charles**
*See* Armstrong, John Byron

**Willard, Cowboy Jess**
*See* Willard, Jess

**Willard, Jess** 1881-1968
[BX, RBE, WBC]
*American boxer*
* [The] Pottawatomie Giant
* Willard, Cowboy Jess

**Willard, John**
*See* Clawson, John

**Willard, John**
*See* Ray, James Earl

**Willard, Josiah Flynt** 1869-1907
[EMD, TC, WW]
*American author*
* Flynt, Josiah

**Willard, Mrs. Charles** [FFF]
*Entertainer*
* Sothern, Ella

**Willard, Portman**
*See* Norwood, Victor G[eorge]
C[harles]

**Willcox, J. K. Hamilton** [PA]
*Author*
* Fawcette, Wyliaume

**Willcox, Orlando Bolivar**
1823-1907 [FFF, PA]
*American army officer and author*
* March, Major
* March, Walter

**Willebrands, Johannes** 1910?-
*Dutch cardinal*
* [The] Flying Dutchman

**Willeford, Charles [Ray, III]** 1919-
[CA, WD]
*American author, poet, playwright*
* Charles, Will

**Willemer, Marianne von**
1784-1860 [WBD]
*Friend of German poet, Johann
Wolfgang von Goethe*
* Zuleika

**Willenan, M. W.** [PA]
*Author*
* Prairie Bird

**Willens, Paul Norton** 1938- [BEW]
*American actor, dancer, singer*
* Wallace, Paul

**Willer?**
*See* Emshwiller, Ed[mund
Alexander]

**Willes, Irwin** ?-1871 [FFF, RH]
*British journalist*
* Argus
* Argus the Exile

**Willes, Jean**
*See* Donahue, Jean

**Willet, Mittens**
See   Aveling, Mrs. Henry

**Willet, Slim**
See   Moore, Winston Lee

**Willets, Walter E.** 1924-   [CA]
*American editor and author*
* Weaver, Earle

**Willett, [Brother] Franciscus** 1922-
[CA]
*American author*
* Premont, [Brother] Jeremy
* Primm, [Brother] Orrin

**Willetts, R. F.**
See   Willetts, Ronald Frederick

**Willetts, Ronald Frederick** 1915-
[WYA]
*Author*
* Willetts, R. F.

**Willey, Abby**
See   Chamberlain, Mrs. R. B.

**Willey, Bill**
See   Willey, David

**Willey, Carl**
See   Willey, Carlton Francis

**Willey, Carlton Francis** 1931-   [BE]
*American baseball player*
* Willey, Carl

**Willey, Chin**
See   Willey, Peter

**Willey, David** 20th c.   [B10]
*American collector*
* Willey, Bill

**Willey, Peter** 1949-   [DC]
*British cricketer*
* Willey, Chin
* Willey, Will

**Willey, Robert**
See   Ley, Willy

**Willey, Will**
See   Willey, Peter

**William**
See   Evarts, Jeremiah

**William** 1143-1214
[FFF, HN, RH]
*King of Scotland*
* [The] Lion

**William** 1196-1226   [DHA, DNNS]
*Earl of Salisbury*
* Longsword

**William** 15th c.   [SN]
*Duke of Austria*
* [The] Delightful

**William, Arnold**
See   Meadowcroft, Ernest
[William]

**William August Charles Frederick
Adolf** 1817-1905   [WBD]
*Duke of Nassau*
* Adolf of Nassau

**William Augustus** 1721-1765
[DEP, DNNF, SN]
*Duke of Cumberland*
* Billy the Butcher
* [The] Bloody Butcher
* [The] Butcher of Culloden

**William, David**
See   Williams, David

**William Frederick** 1776-1834
[DNNS, HN]
*Duke of Gloucester*
* Silly Billy

**William, Joseph** 1878-1939   [SC]
*Actor*
* Ranger Bill

**William of Champeaux**
1070?-1121   [DNNF, FFF]
*French philosopher*
* [The] Pillar of Doctors
* [The] Venerable Doctor

**William Powlett, Katherine** 1911-
[ART]
*British painter*
* K. W. P.

**[The] William Tell of the Tyrol**
See   Hofer, Andreas

**William the Conqueror**
See   Waller, [Sir] William

**William the Red**
See   Wright, William Simmons

**William, Warren**
See   Krech, Warren William

**William I** ?- 943
[DNNS, FFF, RH]
*Duke of Normandy*
* Longsword

**William I** ?-1166
[DNNS, HN, SN]
*King of Sicily*
* [The] Bad

**William I** 886- 918   [WBD]
*Duke of Aquitaine*
* [The] Pious

**William I** 1027-1087
[DNNS, HN, RH]
*King of England*
* [The] Bastard
* [The] Conqueror
* [The] Norman

**William I** 1533-1584
[DNNS, FFF, RH]
*Prince of Orange*
* [The] High Born Demosthenes
* [The] Silent

**William I [Wilhelm Friedrich Ludwig]**
1797-1888   [HN, RH, SN]
*Emperor of Germany*
* [The] Emperor of the German
  Kingdoms
* Kartaetschenprinz
* Tartuffe, Kaiser

**William II** 1056?-1100
[HN, RH, SN]
*King of England*
* [The] Red King
* Rufus

**William II** 1154-1189
[DNNS, HN, SN]
*King of Sicily*
* [The] Good

**William II [Friedrich Wilhelm Viktor
Albert]** 1859-1941   [DEP]
*Emperor of Germany*
* [The] Talkative

**William III** 1650-1702
[DEP, DHA, SN]
*King of England*
* [The] Gallic Bully
* Old Glorious

**William IV**
See   Friso, Charles Henry

**William IV** 1532-1592   [WBD]
*Landgrave of Hesse-Cassel*
* [The] Wise

**William IV** 1765-1837
[DNNS, FFF, HN]
*King of England*
* [The] Sailor King
* Silly Billy

**William V** 960?-1030   [WBD]
*Duke of Aquitaine*
* [The] Great

**Williams**
See   Grover, William

**Williams**
See   Townley, Michael Vernon

**Williams, A. B.** 1897?-1964   [BEW]
*Theatrical performer*
* Williams, Racehorse

**Williams, A. C.** 20th c.   [IBW]
*American disc jockey and glee club
director*
* Williams, Moohah

**Williams, Ace**
See   Bamber, Wallace Eugene

**Williams, Ace**
See   Williams, Robert Fulton

**Williams, Al**
See   Williams, Almon Edward

**Williams, Alan Moray** 1915-
[IAW]
*British author and journalist*
* Robert the Rhymer

**Williams, Alma Claire** 1928-   [OP]
*American opera singer*
* Barlow, Klara

**Williams, Almon Edward**
1914-1969   [BE]
*American baseball player*
* Williams, Al

**Williams, Alva Mitchel** 1882-1933
[BE]
*American baseball player*
* Williams, Rip

**Williams, Andre** 1936?-   [BWW]
*American singer*
* Rhythm, Mr.
* Williams, Bacon Fat

**Williams, Andrew** 1906?-   [PMJ]
*American jazz musician*
* Williams, Sandy

**Williams, Andrew** 20th c.   [OBW]
*American baseball player*
* Williams, Stringbean

**Williams, Annabelle**
See   Rucker, Annabelle

**Williams, August** 1888-1964   [BE]
*American baseball player*
* Williams, Gloomy Gus

**Williams, Augustine H.** 1870-1890
[BE]
*American baseball player*
* Williams, Gus

**Williams, Avril** 1932-   [TR]
*British actress*
* Elgar, Avril

**Williams, Bacon Fat**
See   Williams, Andre

**Williams, Barney**
See   Lebrowitz, Barney

**Williams, Barney**
See   O'Flaherty, Barney

**Williams, Bay Boy**
See   Williams, Matthew

**Williams, Bearcat**
See   Williams, John Overton

**Williams, Benjamin** 1831-1923
[WBD]
*British painter*
* Leader, Benjamin Williams

**Williams, Berl** 1919?-1978   [FIR]
*Comedian*
* Funny, Mr.

**Williams, Bert**
See   Williams, Egbert Austin

**Williams, Beryl**
See   Epstein, Beryl [Williams]

**Williams, Bessie**
See   Henderson, Rosa [Rose]

**Williams, Bessie**
See   McCoy, Viola

**Williams, Big Boy**
See   Williams, Guinn

**Williams, Big Cat**
See   Williams, Clarence

**Williams, Big Joe**
See   Williams, Joe

**Williams, Bill**
See   Crawford, William [Elbert]

**Williams, Bill**
See   Katt, William Henry

**Williams, Billy**
See   Williams, Paul B.

**Williams, Billy Dee**
See   December, William, Jr.

**Williams, Blazer**
See   Williams, Cecil

**Williams, Blind Boy**
See   McGhee, Walter Brown

**Williams, Blinky**
See   Williams, Sondra

**Williams, Booker**
See   Fleischer, Leonore

**Williams, Bransby** 1870-1961
[BMH]
*British entertainer*
* [The] Actor Mimic
* [The] Hamlet of the Halls

**Williams, Brian** 1904-1969   [BF]
*British actor*
* Williams, Hugh

**Williams, Bullet**
See   Williams, Jim

**Williams, Buster**
See   Williams, Charles Anthony, Jr.

**Williams, Butch**
See   Williams, Warren Milton

**Williams, Buttons**
See   Williams, James Thomas

**Williams, Cadillac**
See Williams, Nelson

**Williams, Campbell**
See Smith, Campbell Sherston

**Williams, Cap**
See Williams, Marshall
McDiarmid

**Williams, Cara**
See Kamiat, Bernice

**Williams, Carol** 1929- [WD]
*American author*
* Fenner, Carol

**Williams, Cecil** 1936?- [CW]
*West Indian poet and playwright*
* Williams, Blazer

**Williams, Charles**
See Collier, James L[incoln]

**Williams, Charles Anthony, Jr.**
1942- [EJ7]
*American jazz musician*
* Williams, Buster

**Williams, Charles Hanbury**
1709-1759 [FFF]
*British author and diplomat*
* Carl

**Williams, Charles Henry**
1896-1952 [MK]
*American baseball player*
* Williams, Lefty

**Williams, Charles J.** [PA]
*Author*
* Blue Jay

**Williams, Charles Melvin** 1908-
[ASC, DAM, EJ]
*American jazz musician*
* Williams, Cootie

**Williams, Charles Prosek** 1947-
[SMG]
*American baseball player*
* Williams, Knuck-Z

**Williams, Chester**
See Schechter, William

**Williams, Chickie**
See Smik, Jessie Wanda

**Williams, Chino** 1934- [IBW]
*American actor*
* Williams, Fats

**Williams, Claerwen** 1938- [CA]
*Australian-born author*
* Lang, Maud

**Williams, Clancy**
See Williams, Clarence

**Williams, Clarence** 1942- [FB]
*American football player*
* Williams, Clancy

**Williams, Clarence** 1946- [SMG]
*American football player*
* Williams, Big Cat

**Williams, Claude** 1908- [EJ7]
*American jazz musician*
* Williams, Fiddler

**Williams, Claude Preston**
1893-1959 [AS, BE, PB]
*American baseball player*
* Williams, Lefty

**Williams, Clyde C.** 1881-1974
[CAP, SAT]
*American author*
* Williams, Slim

**Williams, Colonel Bill**
See Williams, William [Bill]

**Williams, Cootie**
See Williams, Charles Melvin

**Williams, Craig** [OBW]
*American baseball player*
* Williams, Stringbean

**Williams, Cris**
See DeCristoforo, Romeo John

**Williams, Cy**
See Williams, Fred

**Williams, Cyclone**
See Williams, Joseph

**Williams, D.**
See Ronald, David William

**Williams, D.** 20th c. [WBD]
*British author*
* Williams, Patry [joint pseudonym
with M. Patry]

**Williams, D. E.** [PA]
*Author*
* Publicola

**Williams, Dale**
See Williams Elisha Alphonso

**Williams, Dave** 1954- [SMG]
*Canadian hockey player*
* Williams, Tiger

**Williams, David** 1926- [TR]
*British actor and director*
* William, David

**Williams, David** 1946- [EJ7]
*West Indian jazz musician*
* Williams, Happy

**Williams, David Carter** 1891-1962
[BE]
*American baseball player*
* Williams, Mutt

**Williams, David Rhys** 20th c.
[WGT]
*Author*
* Gan Index

**Williams, Dee**
See Williams, Dewey Edgar

**Williams, Denny**
See Williams, Evon Daniel

**Williams, Dewey Edgar** 1916- [BE]
*American baseball player*
* Williams, Dee

**Williams, Diamond**
See Williams, James

**Williams, Dib**
See Williams, Edwin Dibrell

**Williams, Dino**
See Williams Don[ald Reid]

**Williams, Doc**
See Smik, Andrew J., Jr.

**Williams, Doc**
See Williams, Henry L.

**Williams Don[ald Reid]** 1935- [BE]
*American baseball player*
* Williams, Dino

**Williams, Dootsie**
See Williams, Walter, Jr.

**Williams, Dorian** 1914- [IAW]
*British author*
* Pied Piper

**Williams, E. C.**
See Williams, Eric Cyril

**Williams, E. N.**
See Williams, Ernest Neville

**Williams, Earl A.** 1928- [IBW]
*American businessman*
* Williams, Skip

**Williams, Earl Craig** 1948- [SMG]
*American baseball player*
* Williams, Heavy

**Williams, Edith** 1906- [THR]
*American actress*
* Barrett, Edith

**Williams, Edward** 1745-1826
[DEP, DNNS, WBD]
*Welsh poet*
* Iolo Morgannwg
* [The] Welsh Shakespeare

**Williams, Edward Francis**
1903-1970 [CA]
*British author and journalist*
* Francis Williams, Lord

**Williams, Edwin Alfred** 1910-
[AW, CC, WW]
*British author*
* De Caire, Edwin
* Moodie, Edwin

**Williams, Edwin Dibrell** 1910-
[BE]
*American baseball player*
* Williams, Dib

**Williams, Egbert Austin**
1874?-1922 [BEW, CED, IBW]
*West Indian-born composer, actor,
singer*
* [The] Greatest Comedian on the
American Stage
* [The] King of Laughter
* Rogers, Duke?
* Williams, Bert

**Williams, Eirlys O[lwen]** 20th c.
[CAP]
*Welsh author*
* Trefor, Eirlys

**Williams Elisha Alphonso**
1855-1939 [BE]
*American baseball player*
* Williams, Dale

**Williams, Elizabeth**
See Dohen, Dorothy

**Williams, Emery H.** 1931- [BWW]
*American singer*
* Detroit Jr.
* Williams, Little Junior

**Williams, Eric Cyril** 1918- [SFL]
*British author*
* Williams, E. C.

**Williams, Ernest Neville** 1917-
[WYA]
*Author*
* Williams, E. N.

**Williams, Ethlyne** 1908- [F2]
*Actress*
* Claire, Ethlyne

**Williams, Eva** [FFF]
*American writer*
* Viva

**Williams, Evon Daniel** 1899-1929
[BE]
*American baseball player*
* Williams, Denny

**Williams, F. Harald**
See Ward, Frederick William Orde

**Williams, Fats**
See Williams, Chino

**Williams, Fats**
See Williams, Frederick Richard

**Williams, Feab. S.** 20th c. [SG]
*Boxer*
* Godfrey, George
* Old Chocolate

**Williams, Ferelith Eccles** 1920-
[SAT]
*British author and illustrator*
* Eccles

**Williams, Fess**
See Williams, Stanley R.

**Williams, Fiddler**
See Williams, Claude

**Williams, Floyd** 20th c. [NP]
*American jazz musician*
* Williams, Horsecollar

**Williams, Fly**
See Williams, James

**Williams, Franc**
See Williams, Francis

**Williams, Frances**
See Jellinek, Frances

**Williams, Frances B.**
See Browin, Frances Williams

**Williams, Francis** 1910- [EJ7]
*American jazz musician*
* Williams, Franc

**Williams, Fred** 1888-
[BE, DGS, PB]
*American baseball player*
* Williams, Cy

**Williams, Fred** 1913- [BE]
*American baseball player*
* Williams, Pap

**Williams, Fred J.**
See Smith, Bernard

**Williams, Frederick** 1865-1930
[BEW]
*American actor*
* Williams, Fritz

**Williams, Frederick Richard** 1956-
[SMG]
*Canadian-born hockey player*
* Williams, Fats

**Williams, Frisky**
See Williams, Ron

**Williams, Fritz**
See Williams, Frederick

**Williams, Fritz**
See Williams, Ron

**Williams, Froggy**
See Williams, James

**Williams, G. Mennen** 1911-
*American politician*
* Williams, Soapy

**Williams, George Dale** 1917-
[EJ, PMJ]
*American arranger and composer*
* [The] Fox

**Williams, George Henry**
1823?-1910   [FFF]
*American politician*
* Williams, Landaulet

**Williams, George W.** 19th c.   [PA]
*Author*
* G. W. W.

**Williams, Giggy**
See   Williams, Norwood

**Williams, Gilbert M.** 1917-   [CA]
*American author and director*
* Wolfe, Michael

**Williams, Gloomy Gus**
See   Williams, August

**Williams, Gorgeous**
See   Williams, Nature

**Williams, Graeme** 20th c.   [MBF]
*British author*
* Dent, Denis

**Williams, Guinn** 1900?-1962
[BEW, F1, FC]
*American actor*
* Williams, Big Boy

**Williams, Gus**
See   Williams, Augustine H.

**Williams, Gus** 20th c.
*American basketball player*
* [The] Wizard

**Williams, Hank**
See   Williams, Hiram King

**Williams, Happy**
See   Williams, David

**Williams, Harrison** 1920?-
*American politician*
* Williams, Pete

**Williams, Harry Millard**
1928-1969   [SC]
*American actor and producer*
* Millard, Harry W.

**Williams, Hawley**
See   Heyliger, William

**Williams, Heavy**
See   Williams, Earl Craig

**Williams, Henry**
See   Manville, William Henry

**Williams, Henry**
See   Vicars, Henry Edward

**Williams, Henry**
See   Williamson, Henry

**Williams, Henry L.** 1869-1931
[FB]
*American football coach*
* Williams, Doc

**Williams, Herb**
See   Billerbeck, Herbert Schussler

**Williams, Herbert** 1914-   [SFL]
*Author*
* H. W.

**Williams, Hiram King** 1923-1953
[ECM, PAC]
*American country-western performer*
* [The] Hillbilly Shakespeare

**Williams, Hiram King** (Continued)
* [The] King of Western Country
  Music
* Luke the Drifter
* Williams, Hank

**Williams, Honolulu Johnny**
See   Williams, John Brodie
[Johnny]

**Williams, Horsecollar**
See   Williams, Floyd

**Williams, Hugh**
See   Williams, Brian

**Williams, Hugh Ernest Leo** 1903-
[BEW]
*British actor*
* Williams, John

**Williams, Idris Elgina** 20th c.
[ART]
*British artist*
* Aeron, Idris

**Williams, Ike**
See   Williams, Isaiah

**Williams, Irene**
See   Gibbons, Irene

**Williams, Isaiah** 1912-   [RBE]
*American boxer*
* Williams, Ike

**Williams, J. R.**
See   Williams, Jeanne

**Williams, J. Walker**
See   Wodehouse, Pelham Grenville

**Williams, J. X.**
See   Ludwig, Myles Eric

**Williams, J. X.** [house pseudonym,
Greenleaf Classics]
See   Offutt, Andrew Jefferson

**Williams, Jac Lewis** 1918-   [IAW]
*Welsh author*
* Arthfab
* Isambard

**Williams, James** 1928-   [FB]
*American football player*
* Williams, Froggy

**Williams, James** 1946-1973   [IBW]
*American lacrosse player*
* Williams, Poopie

**Williams, James** 20th c.   [B10]
*American basketball player*
* Williams, Fly

**Williams, James** 20th c.   [RO2]
*American musician*
* Williams, Diamond

**Williams, James Edwards Lee**
[IBW]
*American composer*
* Lee, Bill

**Williams, James Thomas**
1876-1965   [BE, PB]
*American baseball player*
* Williams, Buttons

**Williams, Jay** 1914-1978
[SAT, WD]
*American author*
* Delving, Michael

**Williams, Jay Jerome**   [WECO]
*American cartoonist*
* Alger, Edwin, Jr.

**Williams, Jeanne** 1930-
[CA, SAT, WD]
*American author*
* Crecy, Jeanne
* Michaels, Kristin
* Rhys, Megan
* Rowan, Deirdre
* Williams, J. R.

**Williams, Jim**   [OBW]
*American baseball player*
* Williams, Bullet

**Williams, Jo Jo**
See   Williams, Joseph

**Williams, Joan Mary Eileen** 1916-
[OP]
*British programing advisor for opera
company*
* Ingpen, Joan

**Williams, Joe**
See   Goreed, Joseph

**Williams, Joe** 1903-
[BWW, DAM, EJ]
*American singer*
* Hill, King Solomon
* Mississippi Big Joe
* Williams, Big Joe
* Williams, Po Joe

**Williams, Joel**
See   Jennings, John [Edward, Jr.]

**Williams, John**
See   Williams, Hugh Ernest Leo

**Williams, John** 1582-1650   [SN]
*British prelate and statesman*
* [The] Statesman Bishop

**Williams, John** 1664-1729
[DNNF, DNNS, SN]
*American clergyman*
* [The] Redeemed Captive

**Williams, John** 1761-1818
[SN, WBD]
*British-born author*
* Pasquin, Anthony [Tony]

**Williams, John** 1773-1845   [PA]
*Author*
* Publicola

**Williams, John** 1883-1951   [SC]
*American actor*
* Arthur, Johnny

**Williams, John Babington** 20th c.
[WW]
*Author*
* Brampton, James?

**Williams, John Brodie [Johnny]**
1889-1963   [BE]
*American baseball player*
* Williams, Honolulu Johnny

**Williams, John H.**   [PA]
*Author*
* Dadd, B.

**Williams, John Joseph** 1920-
[BEW]
*Canadian actor and playwright*
* McLiam, John

**Williams, John Overton** 1905-
[WWJ]
*American jazz musician*
* Williams, Bearcat

**Williams, Johnny**
See   Hooker, John Lee

**Williams, Johnny**
See   Warren, Robert Henry

**Williams, Johnny** 1906-   [BWW]
*American singer*
* Williams, Uncle Johnny

**Williams, Jolan**   [ART]
*Austrian-born painter and graphic
artist*
* Polatschek-Williams, Jolan

**Williams, Joseph** 1876- ?   [MK]
*American baseball player*
* Williams, Cyclone
* Williams, Smokey Joe

**Williams, Joseph** 1920-   [BWW]
*American singer*
* Williams, Jo Jo

**Williams, Joseph Leon [Joe]** 1935-
[BWW]
*American singer*
* Little Papa Joe
* Williams, Sugar Boy

**Williams, Josephine** 1864-1950
[SC]
*American actress*
* Winthrop, Joy

**Williams, Jumpin' Joe**
See   Goreed, Joseph

**Williams, June Deniece** 1951-
[IBW]
*American singer and songwriter*
* Williams, Niecy

**Williams, Katherine**
See   Buck, Laura A.

**Williams, Kathryn Vinson** 1911-
[WD]
*American author*
* Vinson, Kathryn

**Williams, Kid**
See   Gutenko, John

**Williams, Knuck-Z**
See   Williams, Charles Prosek

**Williams, L. C.** 1930-1960   [BWW]
*American singer*
* Lightnin' Jr.

**Williams, Landaulet**
See   Williams, George Henry

**Williams, Lee** 1938-   [BWW]
*American singer*
* Williams, Shot

**Williams, Lefty**
See   Williams, Charles Henry

**Williams, Lefty**
See   Williams, Claude Preston

**Williams, Leroy** 20th c.   [RBE]
*American boxer*
* Williams, Roy

**Williams, Lester** 1920-   [NBB]
*American singer*
* Wintertime, Mr.

**Williams, Little Junior**
See   Williams, Emery H.

**Williams, Liza** 1928-   [CA]
*American author*
* Lehrman, Liza

**Williams, Louis** 1938-   [OP]
*American opera singer*
* Hagen-William, Louis

**Williams, Lucinda** [IBW]
*American track and field athlete*
* Williams, Lucy

**Williams, Lucita Squier** 1899-
[NAA]
*American author*
* Squier, Lucita

**Williams, Lucy**
*See* Williams, Lucinda

**Williams, Lynn**
*See* Hale, Arlene

**Williams, M. B.**
*See* Beresford-Williams, Mary E.

**Williams, Marietta** 1911-
[PMJ, WWJ]
*American singer*
* Sullivan, Maxine

**Williams, Marsh**
*See* Williams, Marshall
McDiarmid

**Williams, Marshall McDiarmid**
1893-1935 [BE]
*American baseball player*
* Williams, Cap
* Williams, Marsh

**Williams, Mary**
*See* Barnes, Mrs. J. H.

**Williams, Mary Lou**
*See* Winn, Mary Elfrieda

**Williams, Matthew** 20th c. [IBW]
*American artist*
* Williams, Bay Boy

**Williams, Meurig Mon** 1925-
[AW]
*Welsh author*
* Carrington, Michael

**Williams, Michael**
*See* St. John, Wylly Folk

**Williams, Mike**
*See* Ferrara, Romano

**Williams, Moohah**
*See* Williams, A. C.

**Williams, Morris** [PA]
*Author*
* Nicander

**Williams, Mrs. B. W. J.** [FFF]
*Writer*
* Constance

**Williams, Mrs. Jesse** [FFF]
*Entertainer*
* Tracy, Hetty

**Williams, Mrs. Odell** [FFF]
*Entertainer*
* Ward, Jennie

**Williams, Mrs. Tony** [FFF]
*Entertainer*
* Ward, Marian

**Williams, Mutt**
*See* Williams, David Carter

**Williams, Myrna** 1905-
[BDF, F2, FC]
*American actress*
* Loy, Myrna

**Williams, Nature** 20th c. [IBW]
*American clown*
* Williams, Gorgeous

**Williams, Ned** 1909- [CA]
*South African-born author*
* Harbin, Robert

**Williams, Nelson** 1917- [EJ]
*American jazz musician*
* Williams, Cadillac

**Williams, Niecy**
*See* Williams, June Deniece

**Williams, No Neck**
*See* Williams, Walter Allen

**Williams, Nolan** 1902?-1942?
[NOJ]
*American jazz musician*
* Williams, Shine

**Williams, Norman Neale, III** 1943-
[SW]
*American actor*
* Kincaid, Aron

**Williams, Norwood** 1880?- ?
[NOJ]
*American jazz musician*
* Williams, Giggy

**Williams, Orlando Cyprian**
1883-1967 [LC]
*British author and critic*
* Williams, Orlo

**Williams, Orlo**
*See* Williams, Orlando Cyprian

**Williams, Otis**
*See* Miles, Otis

**Williams, Pap**
*See* Williams, Fred

**Williams, Patrick J.**
*See* Butterworth, William
Edmund, III

**Williams, Patry** [joint pseudonym
with D. Williams]
*See* Patry, M.

**Williams, Patry** [joint pseudonym
with M. Patry]
*See* Williams, D.

**Williams, Paul** 1934- [RO2]
*American singer*
* Paul, Billy

**Williams, Paul B.** 20th c. [BBH]
*American baseball coach*
* Williams, Billy

**Williams, Paulette** 1949-
*American poet and playwright*
* Shange, Ntozake

**Williams, Pete**
*See* Faulknor, Cliff[ord Vernon]

**Williams, Pete**
*See* Reach, James

**Williams, Pete**
*See* Williams, Harrison

**Williams, Po Joe**
*See* Williams, Joe

**Williams, Poopie**
*See* Williams, James

**Williams, Pop**
*See* Williams, Walter Merrill

**Williams, Priscilla** 1943- [IBW]
*American trapeze artist*
* Williams, Toni

**Williams, Pug**
*See* Williams, T. Ralph

**Williams, R. D.** [PA]
*Author*
* Shamrock

**Williams, Rabbit's Foot**
*See* Coleman, Burl C.

**Williams, Racehorse**
*See* Williams, A. B.

**Williams, Ralph** 1872-1958 [BBD]
*British composer*
* Vaughan Williams, Ralph

**Williams, Rees Gephardt** 1892-
[BE]
*American baseball player*
* Williams, Steamboat

**Williams, Reginald Gordon** 1885-
[WWL]
*British librarian and author*
* Montana

**Williams, Rendall**
*See* Riddell, William Renwick

**Williams, Renwick** ?-1790
[DNNS, HN, RH]
*British criminal*
* [The] Monster

**Williams, Rex**
*See* Wei, Rex Yue-Tien

**Williams, Richard** [house
pseudonym]
*See* Baker, William Arthur
Howard

**Williams, Richard** [house
pseudonym]
*See* Chambers, Philip

**Williams, Richard** [house
pseudonym]
*See* Dolphin, Reginald Charles
[Rex]

**Williams, Richard** [house
pseudonym]
*See* Francis, Stephen D.

**Williams, Richard** [house
pseudonym]
*See* Franes, S. O.

**Williams, Richard** [house
pseudonym]
*See* Hopkins, B.

**Williams, Richard** [house
pseudonym]
*See* Marquis, M.

**Williams, Richard**
*See* Reach, James

**Williams, Richard Valentine**
1877-1947 [DIL, SFL]
*Irish poet and playwright*
* Rowley, Richard

**Williams, Rip**
*See* Williams, Alva Mitchel

**Williams, Robert** 1928- [IBW]
*American actor*
* Guillaume, Robert

**Williams, Robert** 20th c. [RBE]
*American boxer*
* Williams, Songbird

**Williams, Robert** 20th c.
*American management consultant*
* Williams, Rusty

**Williams, Robert Fulton** 1917-
[BE]
*American baseball player*
* Williams, Ace

**Williams, Robert Moore**
1907-1977 [CA, ESF, SF]
*American author*
* Browning, John S.
* Harmon, H. H.
* Jarvis, E. K. [house pseudonym,
Ziff-Davis]
* Moore, Robert
* Storm, Russell

**Williams, Roger**
*See* Weertz, Louis

**Williams, Ron** 1944- [BB, SMG]
*American basketball player*
* Williams, Frisky
* Williams, Fritz

**Williams, Rose**
*See* Ross, William Edward Daniel

**Williams, Roswell**
*See* Owen, Frank

**Williams, Rowland** 1818-1870
[PA]
*Author*
* Garonva, Camlan

**Williams, Rowland** 1823-1905
[WBD]
*Welsh poet*
* Hwfa Mon

**Williams, Roy**
*See* Williams, Leroy

**Williams, Rubberlegs**
*See* Williamson, Henry

**Williams, Rusty**
*See* Williams, Robert

**Williams, S. L.**
*See* Williams, Stephen Lionel

**Williams, Sampson N.** 1921- [IBW]
*American singer*
* Williams, Viloski

**Williams, Sandra** [RO2]
*American singer*
* Blinky

**Williams, Sandy**
*See* Williams, Andrew

**Williams, Scott T.** 1898-1967 [SC]
*American actor*
* Thundercloud, Chief

**Williams, Sherley Anne** 1944- [CA]
*American author and poet*
* Williams, Shirley

**Williams, Shine**
*See* Williams, Nolan

**Williams, Shirley**
*See* Williams, Sherley Anne

**Williams, Shot**
*See* Williams, Lee

**Williams, Skip**
*See* Williams, Earl A.

**Williams, Slim**
*See* Williams, Clyde C.

**Williams, Smokey Joe**
*See* Williams, Joseph

**Williams, Soapy**
*See* Williams, G. Mennen

**Williams, Sol** 1917-
[CME, CWG, DAM]
*American country-western performer
and actor*
* Williams, Tex

**Williams, Sondra** 20th c.   [IBW]
*American singer*
* Williams, Blinky

**Williams, Songbird**
*See*   Williams, Robert

**Williams, Speedy**
*See*   Smith, L. H.

**Williams, Stanley R.** 1894-1975
[B10, PMJ, WWJ]
*American bandleader*
* Williams, Fess

**Williams, Steamboat**
*See*   Williams, Rees Gephardt

**Williams, Stephen Lionel** 20th c.
[ART]
*British artist*
* Williams, S. L.

**Williams, Stringbean**
*See*   Williams, Andrew

**Williams, Stringbean**
*See*   Williams, Craig

**Williams, Sugar Boy**
*See*   Williams, Joseph Leon [Joe]

**Williams, Susan**
*See*   McCoy, Viola

**Williams, T.**   [PA]
*Author*
* Wells, Thornton

**Williams, T. Ralph** 20th c.   [BBH]
*American wrestling coach*
* Williams, Pug

**Williams, Tennessee**
*See*   Williams, Thomas Lanier

**Williams, Terrible Ted**
*See*   Williams, Theodore Samuel
[Ted]

**Williams, Tex**
*See*   Williams, Sol

**Williams, Theodore Samuel [Ted]**
1918-   [BE, DGS, PB]
*American baseball player*
* [The] Kid
* [The] Splendid Splinter
* [The] Thumper
* Williams, Terrible Ted

**Williams, Thomas** 1779-1876
[FFF]
*American clergyman and writer*
* Egomet, Demens

**Williams, Thomas [Andrew]** 1931-
[CA]
*American educator, author,
columnist*
* Andreas, Thomas

**Williams, Thomas Charles** 1951-
[SMG]
*Canadian-born hockey player*
* Williams, Vanderbilt

**Williams, Thomas Lanier** 1911-
[BEW, IPA, LC]
*American playwright, author, poet*
* Williams, Tennessee

**Williams, Tiger**
*See*   Williams, Dave

**Williams, Tina**
*See*   High-Smith, Domini

**Williams, Tom**
*See*   Thomas, William B. [Bill]

**Williams, Toni**
*See*   Williams, Priscilla

**Williams, Uncle Johnny**
*See*   Williams, Johnny

**Williams, [George] Valentine**
1883-1946   [WW]
*British author*
* Valentine, Douglas
* Vedette

**Williams, Vanderbilt**
*See*   Williams, Thomas Charles

**Williams, Viloski**
*See*   Williams, Sampson N.

**Williams, Violet M.**
*See*   Boon, Violet Mary

**Williams, Vivian Claud Craddock**
1936-   [ART]
*British author and illustrator*
* V. C. C. W.

**Williams, W.**   [PA]
*Author*
* [A] Philadelphian

**Williams, W. F.**   [PA]
*Author*
* Blondell

**Williams, W. R.** 1867-1954   [ASC]
*British-born American composer*
* Rossiter, Will

**Williams, Walter Allen** 1943-
[BE, PB]
*American baseball player*
* Williams, No Neck

**Williams, Walter, Jr.** 20th c.
[IBW]
*American record company owner*
* Williams, Dootsie

**Williams, Walter Merrill**
1874-1959   [BE]
*American baseball player*
* Williams, Pop

**Williams, Warren Milton** 1952-
[HR, SMG]
*American hockey player*
* Williams, Butch

**Williams, Wash**
*See*   Williams, Washington J.

**Williams, Washington J.** 20th c.
[BE]
*American baseball player*
* Williams, Wash

**Williams, [Margaret] Wetherby**
[CA, CC, WW]
*Canadian-born British author*
* Erskine, Margaret

**Williams, William** 1717-1791
[FFF, PA]
*Welsh hymn writer and clergyman*
* Caledfryn, Gwilym
* [The] Watts of Wales

**Williams, William [Bill]** 1898-1973
[BWW]
*American singer*
* Williams, Colonel Bill

**Williams, William Francis** 1836- ?
[FFF, PA]
*American writer*
* Trovatore
* Wirt

**Williams, William Holt [Billy]**
1878-1915   [BMH]
*Australian-born comic singer*
* [The] Man in the Velvet Suit

**Williams, Willie**
*See*   Ford, Aleck

**Williams, Woodrow Wilson** 1912-
[BE]
*American baseball player*
* Williams, Woody

**Williams, Woody**
*See*   Williams, Woodrow Wilson

**Williamson, A. M.**
*See*   Williamson, Alice Muriel
[Livingston]

**Williamson, Alice Muriel [Livingston]**
1869-1933   [LC, WW]
*American-born author*
* De Crespigny, [Capt.] Charles
   [joint pseudonym with Charles
   Norris Williamson]
* De Savallo, Teresa [Marquesa
   d'Alpens]
* Revere, M. P.
* Stuyvesant, Alice [joint
   pseudonym with Charles Norris
   Williamson]
* Williamson, A. M.
* Williamson, [Mrs.] Harcourt

**Williamson, B. L.** 1927-   [CM]
*American recording executive*
* Williamson, Slim

**Williamson, C. N.**
*See*   Williamson, Charles Norris

**Williamson, Charles Norris**
1859-1920   [LC, WW]
*British author*
* De Crespigny, [Capt.] Charles
   [joint pseudonym with Alice
   Muriel L. Williamson]
* Stuyvesant, Alice [joint
   pseudonym with Alice Muriel
   (Livingston) Williamson]
* Williamson, C. N.

**Williamson, Claude C[harles] H.**
1891- ?   [CAP]
*British author*
* Hope, Felix

**Williamson, Connie** 1930-1963
[SC]
*American actress*
* Pryor, Jacqueline

**Williamson, Edward N.** 1857-1894
[AS]
*American baseball player*
* Williamson, Ned

**Williamson, Ellen Douglas** 20th c.
[CA]
*American author*
* Douglas, Ellen

**Williamson, Ethel** 20th c.
[SFL, WGT]
*Author*
* Cardinal, Jane
* Veheyne, Cherry

**Williamson, Fred R.** 1938?-
[B10, FB]
*American football player and actor*
* [The] Hammer
* Williamson, Hammer

**Williamson, Geoffrey** 1897-   [CA]
*British author*
* Hastings, Alan

**Williamson, H. S.**
*See*   Williamson, Harold Sandys

**Williamson, Hammer**
*See*   Williamson, Fred R.

**Williamson, [Mrs.] Harcourt**
*See*   Williamson, Alice Muriel
[Livingston]

**Williamson, Harold Sandys** 1892-
[ART]
*British painter and designer*
* Williamson, H. S.

**Williamson, Henry** 1907-1962
[BWW]
*American singer*
* Williams, Henry
* Williams, Rubberlegs

**Williamson, Ivan B.** 1911-1969
[AS, FB]
*American football coach*
* Williamson, Ivy

**Williamson, Ivy**
*See*   Williamson, Ivan B.

**Williamson, J. A.**
*See*   Williamson, James Alexander

**Williamson, J. R.**
*See*   Williamson, John

**Williamson, James**
*See*   Henderson, John William

**Williamson, James Alexander**
1886-1964   [LC]
*British author and educator*
* Williamson, J. A.

**Williamson, John** 20th c.   [SMG]
*American football player*
* Williamson, J. R.

**Williamson, John A.**
*See*   Henderson, John William

**Williamson, John Lee** 1914-1948
[DAM, EJ, NBB]
*American musician*
* Williamson, Sonny Boy
* Williamson, Straw

**Williamson, John Stewart [Jack]**
1908-   [CA, WD]
*American author and critic*
* Stewart, Will

**Williamson, LaVerne** 1923-   [ECM]
*American country-western performer*
* Lee, Dixie
* Mountain Fern
* O'Day, Molly

**Williamson, Mrs. J. C.**   [FFF]
*Entertainer*
* Moore, Maggie

**Williamson, Ned**
*See*   Williamson, Edward N.

**Williamson, Paul**
*See*   Butters, Paul Theophilus
William

**Williamson, Slim**
*See*   Williamson, B. L.

**Williamson, Sonny Boy**
*See* Ford, Aleck

**Williamson, Sonny Boy**
*See* Williamson, John Lee

**Williamson, Sonny Boy, Jr.**
*See* Anderson, Clarence

**Williamson, Straw**
*See* Williamson, John Lee

**Williamson, Thames Ross** 1894-
[TC, WBD]
*American author*
* Dragpmet, edward
* Fleming, Waldo
* Morgan, De Wolfe
* Smith, S. S.
* Trent, Gregory

**Williamson, William Henry** 1870-
? [LAO]
*British author*
* Bank, W. Dane
* Heath, W. Shaw

**Williamson, Willie**
*See* Ford, Aleck

**Willibald, Graf**
*See* Durben, Wolfgang Johannes
Maria

**Willibrord** 658- 739
[DNNS, FFF, SN]
*Saint*
* [The] Apostle of the Frisians
* Clement

**Willie, Albert Frederic**
*See* Lovecraft, Howard Phillips

**Willie B**
*See* Borum, William [Willie]

**Willie C**
*See* Cobbs, Willie

**Willie C.**
*See* Crawford, Willie Murphy

**Willie the Actor**
*See* Sutton, William Francis
[Willie]

**Willie the Knuck**
*See* Ramsdell, James Willard

**Willie the Lion**
*See* Smith, William Henry Joseph
Berthol Bonaparte Bertholoff

**Willing, Foy**
*See* Willingham, Foy

**Willing, Squaretoes**
*See* Willing, Thomas

**Willing, Thomas** 18th c.
*American merchant*
* Willing, Squaretoes

**Willingham, Foy** 1915- [ECM]
*American country-western performer*
* Willing, Foy

**Willingham, Saundra** 1942- [IBW]
*American community organizer*
* Melanie, [Sister]

**Willis, Aaron** 1932- [BWW, NBB]
*American singer*
* Willis, Little Son

**Willis, [George] Anthony Armstrong**
1897-1976 [CA, CC, EMD]
*Canadian-born author and
playwright*
* A. A.

**Willis, [George] Anthony Armstrong**
(Continued)
* Armstrong, Anthony

**Willis, Browne** 1682-1760 [SN]
*British archeologist*
* Old Wrinkle-Boots

**Willis, Charles**
*See* Clarke, Arthur C[harles]

**Willis, Charles William** 1905-1962
[BE]
*American baseball player*
* Willis, Lefty

**Willis, Chet**
*See* Willis, Clarence

**Willis, Chuck** 1928-1958 [RO1]
*American singer and songwriter*
* King of the Stroll

**Willis, Clarence** 20th c. [RO2]
*American musician*
* Willis, Chet

**Willis, Corinne Denneny** 20th c.
[CA]
*American author*
* Denning, Patricia

**Willis, Goose**
*See* Willis, Robert George Dylan

**Willis, Guy**
*See* Willis, James Ulysis

**Willis, Harold**
*See* Willis, Robert George Dylan

**Willis, Hope**
*See* Mannix, Mary Walsh

**Willis, J. H.**
*See* Willis, John Henry

**Willis, Jack**
*See* Willis, Joshua F.

**Willis, James Ulysis** 1915-
[CWG, DAM]
*American country-western performer*
* Willis, Guy

**Willis, John Henry** 20th c. [ART]
*British painter*
* Willis, J. H.

**Willis, Joshua F.** 1920- [NOJ]
*American jazz musician*
* Willis, Jack

**Willis, Julia A.**
*See* Kempshall, Julia A.

**Willis, Lefty**
*See* Willis, Charles William

**Willis, Lefty**
*See* Willis, Les[ter Evans]

**Willis, Les[ter Evans]** 1908- [BE]
*American baseball player*
* Willis, Lefty
* Willis, Wimpy

**Willis, Little Son**
*See* Willis, Aaron

**Willis, Little Son**
*See* Willis, Malcolm

**Willis, Malcolm** 20th c. [BWW]
*American musician*
* Willis, Little Son

**Willis, Maud**
*See* Lottman, Eileen

**Willis, Namby Pamby**
*See* Willis, Nathaniel Parker

**Willis, Nathaniel Parker**
1806-1867 [FFF, PA, SN]
*American author and editor*
* Roy
* Slingsby, Philip
* Willis, Namby Pamby
* Willis, Penciller

**Willis, Penciller**
*See* Willis, Nathaniel Parker

**Willis, Robert George Dylan** 1949-
[DC]
*British cricketer*
* Willis, Goose
* Willis, Harold
* Willis, Swordfish

**Willis, Samuel**
*See* Parker, Hershel

**Willis, Swordfish**
*See* Willis, Robert George Dylan

**Willis, Walt** 20th c. [SFP]
*Author*
* Bryan, Walter

**Willis, Wimpy**
*See* Willis, Les[ter Evans]

**Willis, Woodrick, Jr.** 1941- [IBW]
*American television newscaster*
* Willis, Woody

**Willis, Woody**
*See* Willis, Woodrick, Jr.

**Willkomm, Otto** 1887-1941 [SC]
*American actor and acrobat*
* Nevaro

**Willman, Tony** 20th c.
*Auto racer*
* [The] Flying Dutchman

**Willmore, Alfred** 1899-1978 [DIL]
*Irish playwright, actor, author*
* MacLiammoir, Micheal

**Willoughby, Barrett**
*See* O'Conner, Barrett Willoughby

**Willoughby, Cass**
*See* Olsen, Theodore Victor

**Willoughby, Claude William** 1898-
[BE]
*American baseball player*
* Willoughby, Weeping Willie

**Willoughby, Elaine Macmann**
1926- [CA]
*American author*
* Macmann, Elaine

**Willoughby, George**
*See* Goldring, Douglas

**Willoughby, Hugh**
*See* Harvey, Nigel

**Willoughby, Weeping Willie**
*See* Willoughby, Claude William

**Willoughby-Higson, Philip John**
1933- [WD]
*British historian and poet*
* Higson, Philip John Willoughby

**Wills, Bob** 1906- [CWG]
*American country-western performer*
* [The] Daddy of Western Swing

**Wills, Brember**
*See* Le Couteur, Brember

**Wills, Bump**
*See* Wills, Elliot Taylor

**Wills, Chester**
*See* Snow, Charles Horace

**Wills, Elliot Taylor** 1952- [SMG]
*American baseball player*
* Wills, Bump

**Wills, Garry** 1935?-
*American author*
* Roman, William

**Wills, Harry** 1892-1958 [BX]
*American boxer*
* [The] Black Panther

**Wills, Helen Newington** 1907-
[OET]
*American tennis player*
* Little Miss Poker Face

**Wills, Maurice Morning** 1932-
[SMG]
*American baseball player*
* Wills, Maury
* Wills, Mouse [or Mousey]

**Wills, Maury**
*See* Wills, Maurice Morning

**Wills, Mouse [or Mousey]**
*See* Wills, Maurice Morning

**Wills, Nat M.**
*See* McGregor, Edward

**Wills, Oscar** 1916-1969
[BWW, NBB]
*American singer*
* TV Slim

**Wills, Ronald**
*See* Thomas, Ronald Wills

**Wills, Thomas**
*See* Ard, William [Thomas]

**Wills-Webber, Lizbeth** 1926-
[THR]
*British actress and singer*
* Webb, Lizbeth

**Willson, Frank Hoxie** 1895-1964
[BE]
*American baseball player*
* Willson, Kid

**Willson, Kid**
*See* Willson, Frank Hoxie

**Willson, Meredith**
*See* Reiniger, Robert Meredith

**Willson, Wingrove**
*See* Light, Walter Herrod

**Willy**
*See* Gauthier-Villars, Henri

**Willy, Colette**
*See* Colette, Sidonie Gabrielle

**Willy the Wisp**
*See* Lindstrom, Willy

**Wilma, Dana**
*See* Faralla, Dorothy W.

**Wilman, Buck**
*See* Wilman, Joseph

**Wilman, Joseph** 1905-1969 [AS]
*American bowler*
* Wilman, Buck

**Wilmer, Dale** [joint pseudonym with
Robert (Bob) Wade]
*See* Miller, Bill

**Wilmer, Dale** [joint pseudonym with Bill Miller]
*See* Wade, Robert [Bob]

**Wilmore, Alfred** 20th c. [OBW]
*American baseball player*
* Wilmore, Apple

**Wilmore, Apple**
*See* Wilmore, Alfred

**Wilmot, Anthony** 1933- [CA]
*British author*
* Raoul, Anthony

**Wilmot, Frank Leslie Thomson** 1881-? [LAO]
*Australian author*
* Furnley, Maurice

**Wilmot, James Reginald** 1897- [WW]
*Author*
* Stewart, Frances
* Trevor, Ralph

**Wilmot, John** 1647-1680 [DNNF, FFF, RH]
*British courtier and poet*
* Rochester, Earl of
* Virgin Modesty

**Wilmott**
*See* Price, Charles

**Wilmshurst, Zavarr**
*See* Bennett, William

**Wilna, Elijah [or Elias]** 1720-1797 [WBD]
*Scholar*
* Ben Solomon, Elijah [or Elias]
* Gaon Elijah of Wilna

**Wilsden, Clemensford**
*See* Wickham, John

**Wilsey, Jay** 1902- [F2]
*Actor*
* Buffalo Bill, Jr.

**Wilshere, Vernon Sprague** 1912- [BE]
*American baseball player*
* Wilshere, Whitey

**Wilshere, Whitey**
*See* Wilshere, Vernon Sprague

**Wilshin, Sunday [or Sundae]**
*See* Horne-Wishin, S.

**Wilson, A. J.** [FFF]
*British cyclist and writer*
* Waverly

**Wilson, Ace**
*See* Wilson, James [Jimmy]

**Wilson, Al H.** 1868-? [CED]
*Actor*
* Wilson, Metz

**Wilson, Albert W.** 1897-1949 [WWJ]
*American jazz musician*
* Wilson, Buster

**Wilson, Albert William** 1909- [AW]
*British author*
* Wilson, Yates

**Wilson, Alexander [Douglas Chesney]** 1893- [WW]
*Author*
* Spencer, Geoffrey

**Wilson, Alexander Galbraith** 1924- [BEW, EMT]
*British composer, lyricist, librettist*
* Wilson, Sandy

**Wilson, Alice** 20th c. [THR]
*British actress*
* De Winton, Alice

**Wilson, Angus**
*See* Johnstone-Wilson, Angus Frank

**Wilson, Art** 1920- [IBW]
*American baseball player*
* Wilson, Octopus

**Wilson, Arthur** ?-1953 [IBW]
*American actor and singer*
* Wilson, Dooley

**Wilson, Arthur Earl** 1885-1960 [BE]
*American baseball player*
* Wilson, Dutch

**Wilson, Barbara**
*See* Harris, Larry M[ark]

**Wilson, Barbara** 1932- [IAW]
*British author*
* Grayson, Laura

**Wilson, Belting Bert**
*See* Wilson, Bertwin Hilliard

**Wilson, Benjamin** [SN]
*Clergyman*
* [The] Vicar of Wakefield

**Wilson, Bertwin Hilliard** 1949- [SMG]
*Canadian-born hockey player*
* Wilson, Belting Bert

**Wilson, Big Potatoes**
*See* Wilson, Homer

**Wilson, Black Jack**
*See* Wilson, John Francis

**Wilson, Bojum**
*See* Wilson, Ernest Judson

**Wilson, Bubbles**
*See* Robertson, Mary Imogene

**Wilson, Bud**
*See* Wilson, Montgomery S.

**Wilson, Buster**
*See* Wilson, Albert W.

**Wilson, Camilla Jeanne** 1945- [CA]
*American author and journalist*
* Wilson, Cammy

**Wilson, Cammy**
*See* Wilson, Camilla Jeanne

**Wilson, Carol** 1893-? [CEI, FHE]
*Hockey player*
* Wilson, Cully

**Wilson, Carole**
*See* Wallmann, Jeffrey M[iner]

**Wilson, Charles** 1884-1966 [FC]
*American actor*
* Crehan, Joseph

**Wilson, Charles Edward** 1886-1972
*American industrialist*
* Wilson, Electric Charlie

**Wilson, Charles Edwin** 1938- [OP]
*American conductor*
* Wendelken-Wilson, Charles

**Wilson, Charles Erwin** 1890-1961
*American automobile executive and government official*
* Wilson, Engine Charlie

**Wilson, Charles McMoran** 1882-1977 [CA, CAP]
*British physician and author*
* Moran, Charles McMoran Wilson

**Wilson, Charles Woodrow [Charlie]** 1905- [BE]
*American baseball player*
* Wilson, Swamp Baby

**Wilson, Chief**
*See* Wilson, [John] Owen

**Wilson, Chink**
*See* Wilson, Howard William

**Wilson, Christine**
*See* Geach, Christine

**Wilson, Claude** 20th c. [GW]
*American rodeo performer*
* Wilson, Whip

**Wilson, Clerow** 1933- [IPA, SSS, SW]
*American comedian*
* Wilson, Flip

**Wilson, Constance** 20th c.
*American actress*
* Lewis, Connie

**Wilson, Cora**
*See* Conner, Mrs. J. W.

**Wilson, Crane**
*See* O'Brien, Cyril C[ornelius]

**Wilson, Cully**
*See* Wilson, Carol

**Wilson, Dave**
*See* Floren, Lee

**Wilson, David**
*See* MacArthur, D[avid] Wilson

**Wilson, Derek Alan** 1935- [IAW]
*British author*
* Preston, Hugh

**Wilson, Desemea** 20th c. [WWL]
*British author*
* Patrick, Diana

**Wilson, Diana**
*See* Hunt, Diana

**Wilson, Dick**
*See* Wilson, Louis Sibbett

**Wilson, Doc**
*See* Wilson, Rudolph

**Wilson, Don** 20th c. [GW]
*American rodeo performer*
* Wilson, Spider

**Wilson, Dooley**
*See* Wilson, Arthur

**Wilson, Doris Marie Claire Baumgardt Pohl** 20th c. [WGT]
*Author*
* Perri, Leslie

**Wilson, Duke**
*See* Wilson, Robert Earl

**Wilson, Dunc**
*See* Wilson, Duncan Shepherd

**Wilson, Duncan Shepherd** 1948- [CEI]
*Canadian-born hockey player*
* Wilson, Dunc

**Wilson, Dutch**
*See* Wilson, Arthur Earl

**Wilson, Edith** 1906- [BWW]
*American singer and actress*
* Aunt Jemima

**Wilson, Edwin P.** 1929?-
*American intelligence agent*
* [The] Ice Man

**Wilson, Electric Charlie**
*See* Wilson, Charles Edward

**Wilson, Elizabeth**
*See* Ivison, Elizabeth

**Wilson, Engine Charlie**
*See* Wilson, Charles Erwin

**Wilson, Erasmus** 19th c. [FFF]
*British surgeon and author*
* Quiet Observer

**Wilson, Ernest Judson** 1899-1963 [MK]
*American baseball player*
* Wilson, Bojum
* Wilson, Jud

**Wilson, Ethiop**
*See* Wilson, William J.

**Wilson, F. P.**
*See* Wilson, Frank Percy

**Wilson, Flea**
*See* Wilson, Peter Hugh L'Estrange

**Wilson, Flip**
*See* Wilson, Clerow

**Wilson, Florence** 1500-1547 [PA]
*Author*
* Volusenus

**Wilson, Florence** 1894- [BBD]
*Australian opera singer*
* Austral, Florence

**Wilson, Florence Roma Muir** 1891-1930 [LC, TC]
*British author*
* Marichaud, Alphonse
* Wilson, Romer

**Wilson, Francis Edward [Frank]** 1902- [BE]
*American baseball player*
* Wilson, Squash

**Wilson, Frank Ealton** 1869-1928 [BE]
*American baseball player*
* Wilson, Zeke

**Wilson, Frank Percy** 1889-1963 [LC]
*British author and educator*
* Wilson, F. P.

**Wilson, Fred**
*See* Girolami, Marino

**Wilson, G. L.** [PA]
*Author*
* Falkland, Frank

**Wilson, Gary**
*See* Wilson, James Garrett

**Wilson, Gene** ?-1962 [BEW]
*Theatrical performer*
* Lafferty, Wilson

**Wilson, George**
*See* McNally, Walter

**Wilson, George** ?-1951 [BF]
*British director*
* Wilson, Rex

**Wilson, George Archibald** 20th c.
[BE]
*American baseball player*
* Wilson, Hickie

**Wilson, George Frank** 1889-1967
[BE]
*American baseball player*
* Wilson, Squanto

**Wilson, George Peacock**
1912-1973 [BE]
*American baseball player*
* Wilson, Icehouse

**Wilson, George Pepper** 1876-1902
[BE]
*American baseball player*
* Prentiss, George Pepper
* Prentiss, Kitten

**Wilson, George Washington**
1925-1974 [BE]
*American baseball player*
* Wilson, Ted [or Teddy]

**Wilson, Giuseppe** 1945- [AES]
*British-born Italian soccer player*
* Wilson, Pino

**Wilson, Gomer Russell** 1901-1946
[BE]
*American baseball player*
* Wilson, Tex

**Wilson, Gordon Allan** 1895-1970
[BBH, HK]
*Canadian-born hockey player*
* Wilson, Phat

**Wilson, Gregory**
*See* DeLamotte, Roy Carroll

**Wilson, Guthrie Edward** 1914-
[WD]
*New Zealand-born author*
* Paolotti, John

**Wilson, Gwendoline**
*See* Ewens, Gwendoline Wilson

**Wilson, Hack**
*See* Wilson, Lewis Robert

**Wilson, Hackenschmidt**
*See* Wilson, Lewis Robert

**Wilson, Hamilton K.** 1922-
[CWG, DAM]
*American country-western performer*
* Wilson, Smiley

**Wilson, Hank** 1941- [RO2]
*American singer*
* Russell, Leon

**Wilson, Harding** 1921-1975
[BWW]
*American singer*
* Poppa [or Poppy] Hop
* Wilson, Hop

**Wilson, Harry E.** 1902- [BB, FB]
*American basketball and football
player*
* Wilson, Light Horse Harry

**Wilson, Harry Warden** 1904-1966
[SC]
*American actor*
* Wilson, Ward

**Wilson, Helen Helga** 1902- [IAW]
*Australian author*
* Mayne, H. H.

**Wilson, Henry**
*See* Colbath, Jeremiah Jones

**Wilson, [Sir] Henry Maitland**
1881-1964 [CND]
*British military leader*
* Watt, Mr. [code name used
during World War II]
* Wilson, Jumbo

**Wilson, Hickie**
*See* Wilson, George Archibald

**Wilson, Highball**
*See* Wilson, Howard P.

**Wilson, Homer** 20th c. [BLB]
*American bank robber*
* Wilson, Big Potatoes

**Wilson, Hop**
*See* Wilson, Harding

**Wilson, Howard P.** 20th c. [BE]
*American baseball player*
* Wilson, Highball

**Wilson, Howard William** 20th c.
[BE]
*American baseball player*
* Wilson, Chink

**Wilson, Icehouse**
*See* Wilson, George Peacock

**Wilson, Imogene**
*See* Robertson, Mary Imogene

**Wilson, J. Arbuthnot**
*See* Allen, [Charles] Grant
[Blairfindie]

**Wilson, J. G.**
*See* Wilson, John Gideon

**Wilson, Jack**
*See* Wovoka

**Wilson, James [Jimmy]** 1900-1947
[AS, BE, PB]
*American baseball player and
manager*
* Wilson, Ace

**Wilson, James** 1933?-1977 [FIR]
*Film executive*
* Wilson, Skeet

**Wilson, James Edwin** [PA]
*Author*
* Zinn, Sargeant

**Wilson, James F.** 20th c. [BBH]
*American sports information
director*
* Wilson, Pepper

**Wilson, James Garrett** 1877-1969
[BE]
*American baseball player*
* Wilson, Gary

**Wilson, Jerry**
*See* Miali, Roberto

**Wilson, John** [SN]
*Scottish artist*
* Old Jock

**Wilson, John** 1785-1854
[DEL, HN, PA]
*British author and poet*
* Crusty Christopher
* J. W.
* Mullion, Mordecai
* North, Christopher

**Wilson, John** (Continued)
* [That] Old Man Eloquent

**Wilson, John** 1802-1868 [SN]
*Scottish-born printer and author*
* Wee Johnny

**Wilson, John [Anthony] Burgess**
1917- [AW, CA, CN]
*British author, translator, critic*
* Burgess, Anthony
* Kell, Joseph

**Wilson, John E.** 20th c. [BBH]
*American basketball player*
* Wilson, Jumpin' Johnny

**Wilson, John Francis** 1912- [BE]
*American baseball player*
* Wilson, Black Jack

**Wilson, John Gideon** 1876-1963
[LC]
*Scottish-born bookseller*
* Wilson, J. G.

**Wilson, John Nicodemus**
1890-1954 [BE]
*American baseball player*
* Wilson, Lefty

**Wilson, John Park** 1867-1932
[MBF]
*British author*
* Jackson, Julian

**Wilson, Johnny**
*See* Panica, John

**Wilson, Joyce M[uriel Judson]** 20th
c. [CA]
*British author*
* Stranger, Joyce

**Wilson, Jud**
*See* Wilson, Ernest Judson

**Wilson, Juice**
*See* Wilson, Robert Edward

**Wilson, Julia**
*See* Fox, Mrs. Charles F.

**Wilson, Jumbo**
*See* Wilson, [Sir] Henry Maitland

**Wilson, Jumpin' Johnny**
*See* Wilson, John E.

**Wilson, June**
*See* Badeni, June

**Wilson, Kid**
*See* Wilson, Wesley

**Wilson, Kitty**
*See* Wilson, Mary K.

**Wilson, Lank**
*See* Wilson, William Clarence

**Wilson, Lee**
*See* Lemmon, Laura Elizabeth

**Wilson, Lefty**
*See* Wilson, John Nicodemus

**Wilson, Lefty**
*See* Wilson, Ross Ingram

**Wilson, Lefty**
*See* Wilson, Roy Edward

**Wilson, Lena** 1898?-1939? [BWW]
*American singer*
* Coleman, Nelly

**Wilson, Les[ter Wilbur]** 1885-1967
[BE]
*American baseball player*
* Wilson, Tug

**Wilson, Lewis Robert** 1900-1948
[AS, PB, SR]
*American baseball player*
* [The] Hacker
* Wilson, Hack
* Wilson, Hackenschmidt

**Wilson, Light Horse Harry**
*See* Wilson, Harry E.

**Wilson, Louis Sibbett** 1903-1965
[GF]
*American golf course architect*
* Wilson, Dick

**Wilson, Louise Bruguiere Church**
1902- [NAA]
*American writer and poet*
* Ramsay, Joan

**Wilson, Mamie** [PA]
*Author*
* Clayton, May

**Wilson, Margaret Campell** 1912-
[IAW]
*British author*
* Stewart, Margaret

**Wilson, Marie**
*See* White, Katherine Elizabeth

**Wilson, Marie B[eatrice]** 1922-
[CA]
*American author*
* Marie, Jeanne

**Wilson, Marilla** 1945- [IAW]
*Australian author and poet*
* North, Marilla

**Wilson, Martha**
*See* Morse, Martha Wilson

**Wilson, Mary Ann Ward** 20th c.
[CWG]
*American country-western performer*
* Worth, Marion

**Wilson, Mary K.** 1927- [DAM]
*American singer and songwriter*
* Wilson, Kitty

**Wilson, Matthias** 1580-1656
[DEL, PA]
*Author*
* Knott, Edward

**Wilson, Metz**
*See* Wilson, Al H.

**Wilson, Michael** 20th c. [RM]
*Musician*
* Mick

**Wilson, Mike**
*See* Wilson, Samuel Marshall

**Wilson, Mitchell A.** 1913- [WW]
*Author*
* Hogarth, Emmett [joint
pseudonym with Abraham
Polonsky]

**Wilson, Montgomery S.**
1910?-1964 [BBH]
*Ice skater*
* Wilson, Bud

**Wilson, Moose**
*See* Wilson, Robert Earl

**Wilson, Mrs.** 1787-1846 [PA]
*Author*
* Fry, Caroline

**Wilson, Mrs. A. J.** 1836- ? [PA]
*Author*
* Evans, Augusta

**Wilson, Mutt**
See Wilson, William Clarence

**Wilson, N[orman] Scarlyn** 1901-
[CA]
*British author*
* Norman, W. S.
* Webb, Anthony [joint pseudonym]

**Wilson, Neil**
See Wilson, Sammy O'Neil

**Wilson, Norris D.** 1938- [CM]
*American country-western performer, songwriter, music publisher*
* Wilson, Norro

**Wilson, Norro**
See Wilson, Norris D.

**Wilson, Octopus**
See Wilson, Art

**Wilson, [John] Owen** 1883-1954
[BE, PB]
*American baseball player*
* Wilson, Chief

**Wilson, Pat**
See Olney, Ross Robert

**Wilson, Penelope Coker**
See Hall, Penelope C[oker]

**Wilson, Pepper**
See Wilson, James F.

**Wilson, Peter Hugh L'Estrange** 1958- [DC]
*British cricketer*
* Wilson, Flea

**Wilson, Phat**
See Wilson, Gordon Allan

**Wilson, Philip Whitwell** 1875- ?
[WWL]
*American author*
* P. W. W.

**Wilson, Pino**
See Wilson, Giuseppe

**Wilson, R. A.**
See Keiser, Robert

**Wilson, R. A.**
See Wilson, Robert Arthur

**Wilson, Red**
See Wilson, Robert James

**Wilson, Reg.**
See Thomas, Reginald George

**Wilson, Rex**
See Wilson, George

**Wilson, Richard** 1713-1782
[HN, RH, SN]
*British painter*
* [The] English Claude

**Wilson, Richard** 1920-
[ESF, WGT]
*American author and journalist*
* Halibut, Edward
* Towers, Ivar [house pseudonym]

**Wilson, Robb**
See Royer, Robb

**Wilson, Robert** 1889- [DBA]
*Scottish-born painter*
* Scottie
* Wilson, Scottie

**Wilson, Robert A.** [FFF]
*American writer*
* Maglone, Barney

**Wilson, Robert Arthur** 20th c.
[ART]
*British painter*
* Wilson, R. A.

**Wilson, Robert E. [Bobby]** 20th c.
[FB]
*American football player*
* [The] Mighty Midget of Corsicana

**Wilson, Robert Earl** 1935- [SMG]
*American baseball player*
* Wilson, Duke
* Wilson, Moose

**Wilson, Robert Edward** 1904-1964
[DAM, EJ, WWJ]
*American jazz musician*
* Wilson, Juice

**Wilson, Robert James** 1929- [BE]
*American baseball player*
* Wilson, Red

**Wilson, Robert McNair** 1882-
[CC, WW, WWL]
*British author*
* Wynne, Anthony

**Wilson, Roberta**
*American actress*
* Kane, Diana

**Wilson, Robin S[cott]** 20th c.
[WGT]
*Author*
* Scott, Robin

**Wilson, Roger**
See Nelson, Earle Leonard

**Wilson, Roger C.** 1912- [ASC]
*American composer, conductor, arranger*
* Ahrens, Thomas
* London, Stewart
* Price, Benton
* Price, Walter
* Rogers, Lee
* West, Harold

**Wilson, Roger Harris Lebus** 1920-
[CA]
*American author*
* Harris, Roger

**Wilson, Romer**
See Wilson, Florence Roma Muir

**Wilson, Ross Ingram** 1919-
[CEI, SMG]
*Canadian-born hockey player*
* Wilson, Lefty

**Wilson, Rossiere** 1919-1959
[EJ, PMJ, WWJ]
*American jazz musician*
* Wilson, Shadow

**Wilson, Roy Edward** 1896-1969
[BE]
*American baseball player*
* Wilson, Lefty

**Wilson, Rudolph** 20th c. [IBW]
*American magician*
* Wilson, Doc

**Wilson, Sammy O'Neil** 1935- [BE]
*American baseball player*
* Wilson, Neil

**Wilson, Samuel** 1766-1854 [WBD]
*American meat packer*
* Uncle Sam

**Wilson, Samuel Marshall** 1896-
[BE]
*American baseball player*
* Wilson, Mike

**Wilson, Sandra** 1944- [CA]
*British author*
* Heath, Sandra

**Wilson, Sandy**
See Wilson, Alexander Galbraith

**Wilson, Scottie**
See Wilson, Robert

**Wilson, Shadow**
See Wilson, Rossiere

**Wilson, Skeet**
See Wilson, James

**Wilson, Smiley**
See Wilson, Hamilton K.

**Wilson, Socks [or Sox]**
See Wilson, Wesley

**Wilson, Spider**
See Wilson, Don

**Wilson, Squanto**
See Wilson, George Frank

**Wilson, Squash**
See Wilson, Francis Edward [Frank]

**Wilson, Stanley Kidder** 1879- ?
[WW]
*Author*
* Pliny the Youngest

**Wilson, Swamp Baby**
See Wilson, Charles Woodrow [Charlie]

**Wilson, Ted [or Teddy]**
See Wilson, George Washington

**Wilson, Tex**
See Wilson, Gomer Russell

**Wilson, Thornton Arnold** 1921?-
*American business executive*
* [The] Old Shoe

**Wilson, Tug**
See Wilson, Les[ter Wilbur]

**Wilson, Virginia De Luce** 1921-
[BEW]
*American actress, singer, dancer*
* De Luce, Virginia

**Wilson, Ward**
See Wilson, Harry Warden

**Wilson, Warren** 1909- [ITA]
*American screenwriter, producer, actor*
* Burke, Warren

**Wilson, Wesley** 1893-1958
[BWW, DAM]
*American singer*
* Jenkins
* Pigmeat Pete
* Wilson, Kid
* Wilson, Socks [or Sox]

**Wilson, Whip**
See Wilson, Claude

**Wilson, William** 1801-1860
[FFF, PA]
*American journalist*
* Alpin
* Grant, Allan

**Wilson, William Carl** 1885-1946
[IA]
*American columnist*
* Starr, Tramp

**Wilson, William Clarence** 1896-1962 [BN]
*American baseball player*
* Wilson, Lank
* Wilson, Mutt

**Wilson, William J.** 20th c. [IBW]
*Journalist*
* Wilson, Ethiop

**Wilson, [Thomas] Woodrow** 1856-1924 [FAP]
*American president*
* [The] Coiner of Weasel Words
* [The] Phrasemaker
* [The] Professor
* [The] Schoolmaster of Politics

**Wilson, Yates**
See Wilson, Albert William

**Wilson, Zeke**
See Wilson, Frank Ealton

**Wilt the Stilt**
See Chamberlain, Wilt[on]

**Wiltbye, John**
See Blakely, Paul Lendrum

**Wilton, Arthur** 1944-
[PRS, RM, RO2]
*British musician*
* Brown, Arthur
* [The] God of Hell Fire

**Wilton, Hal**
See Pepper, Frank S.

**Wilton, [Capt.] Mark**
See Manning, William Henry

**Wilton, Robb**
See Smith, Robert Wilton

**Wiltse, George LeRoy** 1880-1959
[AS, BE, PB]
*American baseball player*
* Wiltse, Hooks

**Wiltse, Harold James [Hal]** 1903-
[BE]
*American baseball player*
* Wiltse, Whitey

**Wiltse, Hooks**
See Wiltse, George LeRoy

**Wiltse, Lewis DeWitt** 1871-1928
[BE]
*American baseball player*
* Wiltse, Snake

**Wiltse, Snake**
See Wiltse, Lewis DeWitt

**Wiltse, Whitey**
See Wiltse, Harold James [Hal]

**[The] Wiltshire Bard**
See Duck, Stephen

**Wiltshire, George** 1939- [IBW]
*American auto racer*
* [The] Lonesome Road Racer

**[The] Wily**
See Ferdinand V [or Ferdinand II of Aragon]

Wimar, Carl
See Wimar, Karl Ferdinand

Wimar, Karl Ferdinand 1828-1862
[WBD]
German-born painter
* Wimar, Carl

Wimhurst, Cecil Gordon [Eugene]
1905- [AW, WW]
British author
* Brent, Nigel

Wimp, Kathryn Elizabeth 1920-
[EJ]
American singer
* Davis, Kay

Winans, Katharine Brush 1903-
[NAA]
American author
* Brush, Katharine

Winar, Ernst
See Eichhorn, Wilhelm

Winch, Evelyn M.
See Winch, Marie Elizabeth Agnes

Winch, John
See Long, Gabrielle Margaret Vere
[Campbell]

Winch, Marie Elizabeth Agnes 20th
c. [WW]
Author
* Winch, Evelyn M.

Winchcomb, John 16th c.
[DNNS, HN, SN]
British clothier
* [The] Clothier of England
* Jack of Newbury

Winchell, Fred[erick Russell]
See Cook, Frederick Russell

Winchell, Prentice 1895-
[CC, WW]
Author
* Collans, Dev
* De Bekker, Jay
* Dean, Spencer
* Sterling, Stewart

Winchester
See Henry III

Winchester, Carroll
See Curtis, Caroline G.

Winchester, Clarence 1895-
[IAW, MBF, WWL]
British author
* Ornis
* Tanner-Rutherford, C.

Winchester, Hugh E.
See Wuensche, Edward Hugh

Winchester, Kay
See Walker, Emily Kathleen

Winchevsky, Morris
See Novachovitch, Lippe Benzion

Windaybank, Stephen James 1956-
[DC]
British cricketer
* Windaybank, Windy

Windaybank, Windy
See Windaybank, Stephen James

Winder, Mavis Areta 1907-
[CA, WD]
New Zealand author
* Areta, Mavis
* Wynder, Mavis Areta

Windermere
See Hurd, Percy Angier

Windermere, Charles
See Todd, Charles

Windham, Basil
See Wodehouse, Pelham Grenville

Windisch, Gerard Roland
See Hill, Roy Leeuwenhoek
Aloysius

Windle, Bill
See Windle, Willis Brewer

Windle, Willis Brewer 1904- [BE]
American baseball player
* Windle, Bill

[The] Windmill with a Weathercock
Atop
See Goodwin [or Goodwyn], John

Windsor
See Henry VI

Windsor, Annie
See Shull, Margaret Anne Wyse

Windsor, Barbara
See Deeks, Barbara

Windsor, Claire
See Cronk, Claire Viola

Windsor, Claire
See Hamerstrom, Frances

Windsor, Ernest Victor 1886-
[WWL]
British writer
* Bartlemy

Windsor, Frank
See Birnage, Derek A. W.

Windsor, Marie
See Bertelson, Emily Marie

Windsor, Mary Catherine
1830-1914 [IBW]
American Civil War spy
* Aunt Kitty

Windsor, Rex
See Armstrong, Douglas Albert

Windsor-Garnett, John Raynham
1899- [LAO, WWL]
Welsh-born author
* Othere

Wine, Dick
See Posner, Richard

Wine Head Bender
See Bender, D. C.

Wine, Robert Paul [Bobby] 1938-
[PB, SMG]
American baseball player and coach
* Wine, Wino

Wine, Wino
See Wine, Robert Paul [Bobby]

Wine-Gar, Fran
See Wine-Gar, Frank

Wine-Gar, Frank 1901- [ASC]
American composer and educator
* Wine-Gar, Fran

Wineapple, Edward 1906- [EJS]
American baseball player
* Wineapple, Lefty

Wineapple, Lefty
See Wineapple, Edward

Winfield, Allen?
See Stratemeyer, Edward L.

Winfield, Arthur M.
See Stratemeyer, Edward L.

Winfield, Dick
See Perry, Dick

Winfield, Edna
See Stratemeyer, Edward L.

Winfield, Leigh
See Youngberg, Norma Ione
[Rhoads]

Winfindale, Judy 1914- [THR]
British actress
* Gunn, Judy

Winford, Cowboy
See Winford, James Head

Winford, James Head 1909- [BE]
American baseball player
* Winford, Cowboy

Winfrey, Mule
See Winfrey, Stan

Winfrey, Stan 20th c. [SMG]
American football player
* Winfrey, Mule

Winfrid [or Winfrith] 680- 755
[DNNS, FF, FFF]
Saint
* [The] Apostle of Germany
* Boniface

Wing, Frances [Scott] 1907- [CAP]
American author
* Scott, Frances V.

Wing, James Egerton
See Bayfield, William John

Wingate, Charles F. 1847- ?
[FFF, PA]
Author
* Carlfried

Wingate, George Wood 1840-1928
[FFF]
American attorney and National
Guard officer
* [The] Father of Rifle Practice

Wingfield, Frederick Davis
1899-1975 [BE]
American baseball player
* Wingfield, Ted

Wingfield, Lewis [FFF]
British journalist
* Whyte Tye

Wingfield, Sheila [Viscountess
Powerscourt] 1906- [WD]
British author and poet
* Powerscourt, Sheila

Wingfield, Susan
See Reece, Alys [Tracy]

Wingfield, Ted
See Wingfield, Frederick Davis

Wingham, Charles Wing 1882- ?
[WWL]
British journalist
* Davids, Charles

Wingo, Absalom Holbrook
1898-1964 [BE]
American baseball player
* Wingo, Al
* Wingo, Red

Wingo, Al
See Wingo, Absalom Holbrook

Wingo, Ed[mund Armand]
See LaRiviere, Edmond

Wingo, Ivey Brown 1880-1941
[BE, PB]
American baseball player
* Wingo, Ivy

Wingo, Ivy
See Wingo, Ivey Brown

Wingo, Red
See Wingo, Absalom Holbrook

Wingrave, Anthony
See Wright, Sydney Fowler

Wingrove, Sybil Westmacott 1891-
[F2]
Actress
* Grove, Sybil

Winham, Lafayette Sylvester 1881-
? [BE]
American baseball player
* Winham, Lave

Winham, Lave
See Winham, Lafayette Sylvester

Winiki, Ephriam
See Fearn, John Russell

Wininger, Bo
See Wininger, Francis G.

Wininger, Francis G. 1922-1967
[GF]
American golfer
* Wininger, Bo

Winkelman, Donald M. 1934- [CA]
American author and poet
* Moshe, David

Winkler, Bull
See Winkler, Martin

Winkler, C. G. T. [PA]
Author
* Hell, Theodore

Winkler, Johannes
See Wallner, Christian Johannes

Winkler, Martin 1890?-1955?
[NOJ]
American jazz musician
* Winkler, Bull

Winkles, Bobby Brooks 1932- [PB]
American baseball manager
* Winkles, Winks

Winkles, Winks
See Winkles, Bobby Brooks

Winkworth, Derek William 1924-
[AW]
British writer
* 5029

Winn, Alison [Osborn]
See Wharmby, Margot

Winn, Anona
See Winn-Wilkins, Anona

Winn, Breezy
See Winn, George Benjamin

Winn, George Benjamin 1897-1969
[BE]
American baseball player
* Winn, Breezy
* Winn, Lefty

**Winn, Lefty**
See Winn, George Benjamin

**Winn, Mary Elfrieda** 1910-1981
[EJ, PMJ]
*American jazz musician*
* Burleigh, Mary Lou
* Williams, Mary Lou

**Winn, William Edwin** 20th c.
[IBW]
*American producer, educator, actor*
* Alexandros, Alexis

**Winn-Wilkins, Anona** 20th c.
[THR]
*Australian-born actress and singer*
* Winn, Anona

**Winn-Winter, Jessie** 20th c.  [THR]
*British actress*
* Winter, Jessie

**Winnard, Frank**
See Tubb, Edwin Charles

**Winne, Robert Bruce** 1920-
[FC, ITA, SW]
*American actor*
* Hutton, Robert

**Winnefred**
See Gibson, Mary Frances

**Winner, Polly**
See Temple, Mrs. Edward P.

**Winner, Septimus** 19th c.  [PA]
*Author*
* Hawthorne, Alice

**Winner, Thomas G[ustav]**
See Wiener, Thomas G[ustav]

**Winner, Viola Hopkins** 1928-  [CA]
*American author*
* Hopkins, Viola

**Winney, Ken**
See Marks, Winston K[itchener]

**Winnifrith, Joanna** 1914-  [FC]
*British-born actress*
* Lee, Anna

**Winninger, Charles**
See Winninger, Karl

**Winninger, Karl** 1884-1969  [BEW]
*American actor*
* Winninger, Charles

**Winogradsky, Barnet** 1909-
[BEW, EMT, TR]
*Russian-born producer and theatre manager*
* Delfont, Bernard

**Winogradsky, Lew** 1906-  [JL]
*Russian-born British television and film executive*
* Grade, [Sir] Lew

**Winpisinger, William** 1925?-
*American labor leader*
* Winpisinger, Wimpy

**Winpisinger, Wimpy**
See Winpisinger, William

**Winscott, Edwin C.** 1874-1947
[SC]
*American actor*
* Armand, Teddy V.

**Winsett, John Thomas** 1909-  [BE]
*American baseball player*
* Winsett, Long Tom

**Winsett, Long Tom**
See Winsett, John Thomas

**Winship, Elizabeth** 1921-  [CA]
*American author and columnist*
* Beth

**Winslow, Barry** 20th c.  [RO2]
*American musician*
* Winslow, Snoopy

**Winslow, Dean Hendricks, Jr.**
1934-1972  [CA]
*American author, poet, journalist*
* Winslow, Pete

**Winslow, Donald**
See Zoll, Donald Atwell

**Winslow, Dorian**
See Winston, Daoma

**Winslow, Foghorn**
See Wenzlaff, George

**Winslow, George**
See Wenzlaff, George

**Winslow, Mrs. Irving**  [FFF]
*Entertainer*
* Reignolds, Kate

**Winslow, Paul**
See Mullaly, Charles J.

**Winslow, Pete**
See Winslow, Dean Hendricks, Jr.

**Winslow, Snoopy**
See Winslow, Barry

**Winslowe, John**
See Richardson, Gladwell

**Winsor, Alfred** 1881- ?  [BBH]
*American hockey coach*
* Winsor, Ralph

**Winsor, Ralph**
See Winsor, Alfred

**Winstanley, William** 1628?-1698
[WBD]
*British author*
* Poor Robin

**Winsted, Huldah Lucile** 20th c.
[NAA]
*Swedish-born poet and author*
* Dakotan

**Winston, Bobby**
See Winston, Clarence

**Winston, Clarence** 20th c.  [OBW]
*American baseball player*
* Winston, Bobby

**Winston, Daoma** 1922-  [SFL]
*Author*
* Winslow, Dorian

**Winston, Harry** 1896?-1978
*American jewel merchant*
* [The] King of Diamonds

**Winston, Lena**
See Chaffin, Lillie D.

**Winston, Mike**
See King, Florence

**Winston, Moonie**
See Winston, Roy C.

**Winston, Robert Alexander**
1907-1974  [CAP]
*American author and aviator*
* Fox, [Colonel] Victor J.

**Winston, Roy C.** 1940-  [FB]
*American football player*
* Winston, Moonie

**Winston, Sarah** 1912-  [CA, WD]
*American author and poet*
* Lorenz, Sarah E.

**Winteler de Weindeck, U. M. C.**
[SFP]
*Author*
* Fighton, George Z.

**Winter, Abigail**
See Schere, Monroe

**Winter, Andrew** 1819- ?  [PA]
*Author*
* Retnyw, Werdna

**Winter, Bevis** 1918-  [CA, WW]
*British author*
* Bocca, Al
* Cagney, Peter
* Shayne, Gordon

**Winter, Bud**
See Winter, Lloyd

**Winter, Faith** 1927-  [ART]
*British sculptor*
* Ashe, Faith

**Winter, Fred** 1922-  [BB]
*American basketball player*
* Winter, Tex

**Winter, George Lovington**
1878-1951  [AS, BE]
*American baseball player*
* Winter, Sassafrass

**Winter, H. G.** [joint pseudonym with
Desmond W. Hall]
See Bates, Harry Arthur

**Winter, H. G.** [joint pseudonym with
Harry Arthur Bates]
See Hall, Desmond Winter

**Winter, Herbert**
See Ellingford, Herbert Frederick

**Winter, Holmes Edwin Cornelius**
1851-1935  [DBA]
*British painter*
* Rowland, W.

**Winter, Jessie**
See Winn-Winter, Jessie

**Winter, John Strange**
See Palmer, Henrietta Eliza
Vaughan

**Winter, Johnny** 1944-  [BWW]
*American singer*
* Texas Guitar Slim

**Winter, June**
See Wheeler, Emily Frances

**[The] Winter King**
See Frederick V

**Winter, Lloyd** 20th c.  [BBH]
*American track and field coach*
* Winter, Bud

**[The] Winter Queen**
See Elizabeth

**Winter, R. R.**
See Winterbotham, Russell Robert

**Winter, Sassafrass**
See Winter, George Lovington

**Winter, Tex**
See Winter, Fred

**Winter, William** 1836-1917
[FFF, PA]
*American poet and critic*
* Mercutio

**Winterbotham, Russell Robert**
1904-1971  [CA, SAT]
*American author*
* Addy, Ted
* Bond, J. Harvey
* Hadley, Franklin
* Winter, R. R.

**Winterfeld, Henry** 1901-  [TBJ]
*German-born author*
* Michael, Manfred

**Winterfeld, Max** 1879-1942
[BBD, BEW]
*German composer*
* Gilbert, Jean

**Winterfield, Carl Georg August**
1794-1852  [PA]
*Author*
* De Virigens

**Wintergreen, Warren**
See Adamson, Joseph, III [Joe]

**Wintermute, Slim**
See Wintermute, Urgel

**Wintermute, Urgel** 1917-  [BB]
*American basketball player*
* Wintermute, Slim

**Winternitz, Roland** 1904-  [BEW]
*Actor*
* Winters, Roland

**Winters, Bayla**
See Winters, Bernice

**Winters, Bernice** 1921-  [CA]
*American poet and editor*
* Winters, Bayla

**Winters, Coddy**
See Winters, Frank J.

**Winters, Frank J.** 1884-1944
[BBH]
*American hockey player*
* Winters, Coddy

**Winters, Jack**
See Talent, Leo

**Winters, Janet Lewis** 1899-  [CAP]
*American author and poet*
* Lewis, Janet

**Winters, Jesse** 1899-1971  [MK]
*American baseball player*
* Winters, Nip

**Winters, Jesse Franklin** 1893-  [BE]
*American baseball player*
* Winters, T-Bone

**Winters, June** 1918-  [ASC]
*American composer and singer*
* Whitman, Jerry

**Winters, Linda** 1918-1971  [SC]
*American actress*
* Comingore, Dorothy

**Winters, Marjorie**
See Henri, Florette

**Winters, Nip**
See Winters, Jesse

**Winters, Rae?**
See Palmer, Raymond A[rthur]

**Winters, Roland**
See Winternitz, Roland

**Winters, Rosemary**
See Breckler, Rosemary

**Winters, Shelley**
See Schrift, Shirley

**Winters, T-Bone**
See Winters, Jesse Franklin

**Wintertime, Mr.**
See Williams, Lester

**Winterton, Paul** 1908-
[CA, CC, EMD]
*British author and journalist*
* Bax, Roger
* Garve, Andrew
* Somers, Paul

**Winthorpe, Winifred** [FFF]
*Author*
* Augusta, Clara

**Winthrop, Elizabeth**
See Mahony, Elizabeth Winthrop

**Winthrop, Fitz-John**
See Winthrop, John

**Winthrop, John** 1638-1707 [WBD]
*American colonial governor*
* Winthrop, Fitz-John

**Winthrop, Joy**
See Williams, Josephine

**Winthrop, Laura** 1825- ? [FFF]
*American author*
* Hare, Emily

**Winthrop, Robert**
See Weintrop, Reuben

**Winthrop, Sophy**
See Weitzel, Mrs. S. W.

**Wintle, Alfred Daniel** 20th c. [SFL]
*Author*
* Cobb, Michael

**Wintle, Anne** 20th c. [CA]
*British author*
* Ellis, Olivia
* Francis, Anne

**Wintle, Elizabeth Rhoda** 1943-
[SFL]
*British author*
* Lawrence, Louise

**Wintle, Justin [Beecham]** 1949-
[CA]
*British author*
* Beecham, Justin

**Winton, John**
See Pratt, John

**Winwar, Frances**
See Vinciguerra, Francesca

**Winwood, Brent**
See Denny, John Thomas

**Winwood, Estelle**
See Goodwin, Estelle

**Winwood, Mervyn** 1943- [RO2]
*British musician*
* Winwood, Muff

**Winwood, Muff**
See Winwood, Mervyn

**Winwood, Rett**
See Corey, Frank

**Winzenhoerlein, Heinrich Joseph**
1819-1901 [BBD]
*German composer, singer, musical
theorist*
* Vincent, Heinrich Joseph

**[The] Wire Master**
See Stuart, John [Third Earl of
Bute]

**Wireker, Nigel**
See Nigel

**Wirt**
See Williams, William Francis

**Wirt, William** 1772-1834 [PA]
*American politician and author*
* [The] British Spy
* Old Bachelor

**Wirt, Winola Wells** 20th c. [CA]
*American author*
* Frazier, Sarah

**Wirtanen, Atos Kasimir** 1906-
[IAW]
*Finnish author*
* Finn, Huck
* Musketoeren
* Sawyer

**Wirth**
See Haspinian, Jean

**Wirtz, Elwood Vernon** 1897-1968
[BE]
*American baseball player*
* Wirtz, Kettle

**Wirtz, Kettle**
See Wirtz, Elwood Vernon

**Wisbar, Frank**
See Wysbar, Franz

**[The] Wisconsin Wrath**
See Rebholz, Russ

**Wisdom, Kenny**
See Grogan, Emmett

**[The] Wise**
See Aben-Ezra [or Esra]

**[The] Wise**
See Albert II

**[The] Wise**
See Albert IV

**[The] Wise**
See Alfonso X [or Alphonso]

**[The] Wise**
See Charles V

**[The] Wise**
See Che-Tsou

**Wise**
See Djang, Yuan Shan

**[The] Wise**
See Duns Scotus, Johannes

**[The] Wise**
See Frederick II

**[The] Wise**
See Frederick III

**[The] Wise**
See Gildas [or Gildus]

**[The] Wise**
See James I

**[The] Wise**
See John V [or Jean]

**[The] Wise**
See Las Cases, Emmanuel
Augustin Dieudonne de

**[The] Wise**
See Leo VI

**[The] Wise**
See Robert of Anjou

**[The] Wise**
See Saemund Sigfusson

**[The] Wise**
See Scotus, Johannes [or John]

**[The] Wise**
See William IV

**Wise, Arthur** 1923- [CA, CC]
*British author*
* McArthur, John

**Wise, Buddy**
See Wise, Robert Raymond

**Wise, Casey**
See Wise, Kendall Cole

**Wise, Daniel** 1813- ? [FFF, PA]
*American author and clergyman*
* Cousin Clara
* Forrester, Francis, Esq.
* Lancewood, Lawrence

**[The] Wise Doctor**
See Wessel, Johann [or John]

**[The] Wise Duchess**
See Churchill, Sarah Jennings

**Wise, Ernie**
See Wiseman, Ernest

**Wise, Harry**
See Factor, John

**Wise, Henry Augustus** 1819-1869
[DEL]
*American author*
* Gringo, Harry

**Wise, Herbert**
See Weisz, Herbert

**Wise, Isaac Mayer**
See Weis, Isaac Mayer

**Wise, James Waterman** 1901-
[NAA]
*American author*
* Analyticus

**Wise, John S.** [FFF, PA]
*American writer*
* Plover

**Wise, Jonathan B.**
See Colwell, Stephen

**Wise, Kendall Cole** 1932- [BE]
*American baseball player*
* Wise, Casey

**Wise, Modoc**
See Wise, Samuel W.

**Wise, Ray** 1906-1952 [JL]
*American actor*
* Mala

**Wise, Robert A.**
See Gebhart, Fred J.

**Wise, Robert Raymond** 1928-1955
[EJ]
*American jazz musician*
* Wise, Buddy

**Wise, Samuel W.** 1857-1910 [PB]
*American baseball player*
* Wise, Modoc

**Wise, Vic**
See Bloom, David Victor

**[The] Wise Wife of Keith**
See Simpson [or Sampson?],
Agnes

**Wiseman, Ann [Sayre]** 1926- [CA]
*American author*
* Denzer, Ann Wiseman

**Wiseman, Ernest** 1925- [FC]
*British comedian*
* Wise, Ernie

**Wiseman, Mac**
See Wiseman, Malcolm B.

**Wiseman, Malcolm B.** 1925-
[ECM]
*American country-western performer*
* Wiseman, Mac

**Wiseman, Myrtle Eleanor Cooper**
1913- [CWG]
*American country-western performer*
* Lulu Belle

**Wiseman, Richard** 1622?-1676
[HN]
*British surgeon*
* [The] Father of English Surgery

**Wiseman, Scott** 1909-
[CWG, DAM]
*American country-western performer*
* Skyland Scotty

**[The] Wisest, Brightest, Meanest of
Mankind**
See Bacon, Francis [First Baron
Verulam]

**[The] Wisest Fool in Christendom**
See James I

**[The] Wisest Man of Greece**
See Socrates

**Wishart [or Wiseheart?], George**
1513?-1546 [SN]
*Scottish clergyman and martyr*
* Sophocardus

**Wishner, Sam** 20th c. [BS]
*American magician*
* [The] Sultan of Magic
* Zovello

**Wisnock, Nick** 1918- [CSH]
*Canadian golfer*
* Weslock, Nick

**Wissler, Lewis** 1868-1959 [BE]
*American baseball player*
* Whistler, Lew[is]

**Wist, Olav**
See Rinnan, Henry Oliver

**Wistace, Grace**
See Wace, Robert

**Wistert, Albert A.** 1920- [FB]
*American football player*
* Wistert, Ox

**Wistert, Francis M.** 1912- [FB]
*American football player*
* Wistert, Whitey

**Wistert, Ox**
See Wistert, Albert A.

**Wistert, Whitey**
See Wistert, Francis M.

[The] Witch of Eye
See   Jourdemain, Marjory

Witcher, Ernie 20th c.    [RBE]
American boxer
* Wicher, Ernie

[The] Witchfinder
See   Hopkins, Matthew

Witcombe, Rick Trader 1943-
[AW]
British screenwriter
* Marker, Clare

Witcover, Walt
See   Scheinman, Walter Witcover

Witek, Mickey
See   Witek, Nicholas Joseph

Witek, Nicholas Joseph 1915-    [BE]
American baseball player
* Witek, Mickey

Witham, Marjorie Alexandra
1902-1970    [THR]
British actress
* Aubrey, Madge

Withem, Gary 1946-    [RO2]
American musician
* Withem, Private

Withem, Private
See   Withem, Gary

Withers, Carl A. 1900-1970
[CA, SAT]
American author and editor
* North, Robert
* West, James

Withers, E. L.
See   Potter, George William, Jr.

Withers, Georgette Lizette 1917-
[OCF, TR]
British actress
* Withers, Googie

Withers, Googie
See   Withers, Georgette Lizette

Withers, Jane 1926-    [AM]
American actress
* Dixie's Dainty Dewdrop

[The] Withers of the City
See   Wilde, Robert

Witherspoon, Irene Murray 1913-
[CA]
American author
* Murray, Irene

Witherspoon, J. J.
See   Wyman, Walter Forestus

Witherspoon, James [Jimmy] 1923-
[BWW, SSS]
American singer
* [The] Spoon

Witherspoon, John 1722-1794
[FFF]
Scottish-born clergyman and author
* Druid

Witherspoon, Matilda 1914-
[BWW]
American singer
* Mississippi Matilda

Witherspoon, Naomi Long
See   Madgett, Naomi Long

Witherup, Anne Warrington
See   Bangs, John Kendrick

Withington, Leonard 1789- ?
[FFF]
American author
* Oldbug, Jonathan

Withrow, Corky
See   Withrow, Raymond Wallace

Withrow, Frank Blaine 1891-1966
[BE]
American baseball player
* Withrow, Kid

Withrow, Kid
See   Withrow, Frank Blaine

Withrow, Raymond Wallace 1937-
[BE]
American baseball player
* Withrow, Corky

Witkacy
See   Witkiewicz, Stanislaw Ignacy

Witkiewicz, Stanislaw Ignacy
1885-1939    [MWD, WOA]
Polish author, playwright,
philosopher
* Witkacy

Witkins, Alexander 1907-1961
[BEW, BMH]
South African-born theatrical
performer
* Afrique

Witkowski, Daisy 1881- ?    [THR]
American-born comedienne
* Jerome, Daisy

Witkowski, Maximilian 1861-1927
[JL]
German editor
* Harden, Maximilian

Witkowski, Sadie 1876-1950
[BEW]
American actress
* Jerome, Sadie

[The] Witling of Terror
See   Barere de Vieuzac, Bertrand

Witt, George Adrian 1933-    [BE]
American baseball player
* Witt, Red

Witt, Lawton Walter
See   Wittkowski, Ladislaw
Waldemar

Witt, Red
See   Witt, George Adrian

Witt, Shirley Hill 1934-    [CA]
American author
* Thundercloud, Katherine

Witt, Whitey
See   Wittkowski, Ladislaw
Waldemar

Witte, Glenna Finley 1925-    [CA]
American author
* Finley, Glenna

[The] Wittenberg Monk
See   Luther, Martin

Wittermans, Elizabeth [Pino]    [CA]
Indonesian-born educator and
author
* Pino, E.

Wittgenstein, Oberleutenant
See   Khokhlov, Nicolai

Wittig, Hans
See   Wittig, John Carl

Wittig, John Carl 1914-    [BE]
American baseball player
* Wittig, Hans

Wittinghoff, Julienne 1764-1824
[HN]
Russian author and mystic
* [The] Grey Sister of Hearts

Wittkowski, Ladislaw Waldemar
1895-    [BE, PB]
American baseball player
* Witt, Lawton Walter
* Witt, Whitey

Wittlin, Tadeusz 1909-    [CA, WD]
Polish-born American author, poet,
historian
* Karniewski, Janusz
* Wittlin, Thaddeus [Andrew]

Wittlin, Thaddeus [Andrew]
See   Wittlin, Tadeusz

Wittman, Steve
See   Wittman, Sylvester J.

Wittman, Sylvester J. 1904-    [OCS]
American aviator
* Wittman, Steve

Wittop, Freddy
See   Koning, Fred Wittop

Witweyke
See   Oliver, Hugh

Witzleben, Karl August Friedrich von
1773-1839    [WBD]
German author
* Tromlitz, A. von

Wixom, Emma 1859-1940
[BBD, FFF]
American opera singer
* Nevada, Emma

Wizard
See   Corlett, John

[The] Wizard
See   Gibbons, Mike

[The] Wizard
See   Hoff, Bobby

[The] Wizard
See   John III Sobieski

[The] Wizard
See   Schaefer, Jacob, Sr.

[The] Wizard
See   Williams, Gus

[The] Wizard Earl
See   Percy, Henry

Wizard, Mr.
See   Herbert, Don

[The] Wizard of Berkeley
See   Heinrich, Edward Oscar

[The] Wizard of Kinderhook
See   Van Buren, Martin

[The] Wizard of Manton
See   Taylor, Alec

[The] Wizard of Menlo Park
See   Edison, Thomas Alva

[The] Wizard of Spirit Lake
See   Gilbert, Fred

[The] Wizard of the Albany Regency
See   Van Buren, Martin

[The] Wizard of the Italian
Renaissance
See   Da Vinci, Leonardo

[The] Wizard of the North
See   Scott, [Sir] Walter

[The] Wizard of the North
See   Scott, John

[The] Wizard of the Sea
See   Kidd, [Captain] William

[The] Wizard of the Winged-T
See   Hollis, Wilburn

Wizbor, Jakub Horczak
See   Paszkiewicz, Mieczyslaw

Wjconnon
See   Connon, William John

Wobbly Willie
See   McKinley, William

Wockenfuss, Fuss
See   Wockenfuss, Johnny Bilton

Wockenfuss, Johnny Bilton 1949-
[SMG]
American baseball player
* Wockenfuss, Fuss

Woddis, Hillel Chayim Keith 1914-
[IAW]
British author
* Woddis, Jack

Woddis, Jack
See   Woddis, Hillel Chayim Keith

Wodehouse, John 1826-1902    [HN]
British statesman
* Kimberley, Earl of
* Slumber, Baron

Wodehouse, P. G.
See   Wodehouse, Pelham Grenville

Wodehouse, Pelham Grenville
1881-1975    [ASC, BEW, CA]
British author, playwright, lyricist
* Brooke-Haven, P.
* Grenville, Pelham
* Plum, J.
* West, C. P.
* Williams, J. Walker
* Windham, Basil
* Wodehouse, P. G.

Woden, George
See   Slaney, George Wilson

Wodge, Dreary
See   Gorey, Edward [St. John]

Woelflein, Heinrich 1470-1532
[PA]
Author
* Lupulus

Woestemeyer, Ina Faye
See   Van Noppen, Ina [Faye]
W[oestemeyer]

Wofford, Chloe Anthony 1931-
[CA]
American author
* Morrison, Toni

Wohl, Burton 20th c.    [SFL]
Author
* Hills, Baldwin

Wohl, James P[aul] 1937-    [CA]
American author
* Coltrane, James

**Wohlbrueck, Adolf** 1900-1967
[BDF, F2, OCF]
*Austrian-born actor*
* Walbrook, Anton

**Wohlford, James Eugene [Jim]**
1951-  [BE]
*American baseball player*
* Wohlford, Wolfie

**Wohlford, Wolfie**
*See*  Wohlford, James Eugene [Jim]

**Wojciechowicz, Alexander** 1915-
[FB]
*American football player*
* Wojciechowicz, Wojie

**Wojciechowicz, Wojie**
*See*  Wojciechowicz, Alexander

**Wojciechowska, Maia [Teresa]**
1927-  [CA, SAT]
*Polish-born American author*
* Larkin, Maia
* Rodman, Maia

**Wojcieszko, Jan** 1888-  [THR]
*Polish-born dancer*
* Oyra, Jan

**Wojnilower, Albert** 20th c.
*American economist*
* Gloom, Dr.

**Wojtek, Emerich Josef** 1898-
[FDG]
*Austrian director*
* Emo, E. W.

**Wojtyla, Karol** 1920-
*Pope*
* John Paul II

**Wolcot, John** 1738-1819
[DEL, PA, WBD]
*British author and poet*
* Pindar, Peter

**Wolcott, Mary Adella** 1874?- ?
[CW]
*Jamaican poet*
* Tropica

**Wolcott, Ona** 1906?-1955  [F2, FC]
*American actress*
* Munson, Ona

**Wolf, Chicken**
*See*  Wolf, William Van Winkle

**Wolf, Dieter**
*See*  Thomas, Michael Wolf

**Wolf, Frederick**
*See*  Dempewolff, Richard
F[rederic]

**Wolf, George** 1777-1840  [FFF]
*American politician*
* [The] Father of the Public School
System of Pennsylvania

**Wolf, Jay**
*See*  Wolf, Julius Rosenthal

**Wolf, Julius Rosenthal** 1929-
[BEW]
*American talent representative*
* Wolf, Jay

**Wolf, Lefty**
*See*  Wolf, Walter Francis

**Wolf, Markus** 1923?-
*East German intelligence agent*
* Wolf, Mischa

**Wolf, Miriam Bredow** 1895-  [CAP]
*American medical secretary and
author*
* Bredow, Miriam

**Wolf, Mischa**
*See*  Wolf, Markus

**[The] Wolf of America**
*See*  Montgomery, Richard

**[The] Wolf of Badenoch**
*See*  Steward, Alexander

**[The] Wolf of Plinlimmon**
*See*  Gwenwyn

**Wolf, Walter Francis** 1900-  [BE]
*American baseball player*
* Wolf, Lefty

**Wolf, William Van Winkle**
1862-1903  [BE, PB]
*American baseball player*
* Wolf, Chicken

**Wolfe, Cedric**
*See*  Alais, Ernest W.

**Wolfe, Charles Keith** 1943-  [CA]
*American author*
* Henricks, Kaw

**Wolfe, Eddie** 20th c.  [EJS]
*American boxer*
* Wolfe, Kid

**Wolfe, George** 1908-  [EJS]
*American basketball player*
* Wolfe, Red

**Wolfe, Harold** 1931-  [BB]
*American basketball player*
* Wolfe, Herc

**Wolfe, Herc**
*See*  Wolfe, Harold

**Wolfe, Kid**
*See*  Wolfe, Eddie

**Wolfe, Lilian Lauferty** 1887-1958
[IA]
*American columnist*
* Fairfax, Beatrice

**Wolfe, Michael**
*See*  Williams, Gilbert M.

**Wolfe, Polly**
*See*  Wolfe, Roy Chamberlain

**Wolfe, Red**
*See*  Wolfe, George

**Wolfe, Reginald**
*See*  Dibdin, Thomas Frognall

**Wolfe, Roy Chamberlain**
1888-1938  [BE]
*American baseball player*
* Wolfe, Polly

**Wolfenden, George**
*See*  Beardmore, George

**Wolff, Carl [or Karl?]** 1860-1934
[CW]
*Haitian author*
* Carolus

**Wolff, Cecil Drummond** 20th c.
[WGT]
*Author*
* Waldo, Cedric Dane

**Wolff, Frank**
*See*  Hermann, Frank

**Wolff, Mary Evaline** 1887-1964
[CAT, TC]
*American author and poet*
* Madeleva, [Sister] M.
* Mary Madeleva, [Sister]

**Wolff, Perry** 20th c.  [ET]
*Television writer and producer*
* Wolff, Skee

**Wolff, Skee**
*See*  Wolff, Perry

**Wolff, Victoria** 1910-  [IAW]
*German-born author*
* Martell, Claudia

**Wolff, Wilhelm**  [SN]
*German sculptor*
* [Der] Thier Wolff

**Wolff, William Deakin** 1902-
[AW, WD]
*British author and poet*
* Martindale, Spencer

**Wolffe, Jabez** 1877-1943  [EJS]
*British distance swimmer, coach,
and trainer*
* Wolffe, Jappy

**Wolffe, Jappy**
*See*  Wolffe, Jabez

**Wolffe, Katherine**
*See*  Scott, Marian [Gallagher]

**Wolfgang, Meldon John**
1890-1947  [BE]
*American baseball player*
* Wolfgang, Mellie

**Wolfgang, Mellie**
*See*  Wolfgang, Meldon John

**Wolfgang, Otto** 1898-  [IAW]
*Austrian-born author and poet*
* Hill, Tom
* Roy, Percy Gordon

**Wolfington, Iggie**
*See*  Wolfington, Ignatius

**Wolfington, Ignatius** 1920-  [BEW]
*American actor*
* Wolfington, Iggie

**Wolfman Jack**
*See*  Smith, Robert

**Wolfson, Victor** 1910-  [CA, WW]
*American author and playwright*
* Dodge, Langdon

**Wolgast, Ad**
*See*  Wolgust, Adolphus

**Wolgast, Midget**
*See*  Loscalzo, Joseph Robert

**Wolgust, Adolphus** 1888-1955
[BX, RBE, WBC]
*American boxer*
* [The] Cadillac Wildcat
* [The] Dutchman
* [The] Michigan Wildcat
* Wolgast, Ad

**Wolinski, David** 20th c.  [RO2]
*American musician*
* Wolinski, Hawk

**Wolinski, Hawk**
*See*  Wolinski, David

**Wolinsky, Dimples**
*See*  Wolinsky, Moey

**Wolinsky, Moey**  ?-1943?
[BLB, PHM]
*American underworld figure*
* Wolinsky, Dimples

**Wolk, George** 20th c.  [SFL]
*Author*
* Graat, Heinrich

**Wolke, Lillian** 1888-1975
[CU, FIR, SC]
*American actress*
* Walker, Dimples
* Walker, Lillian

**Wolkers-Ransome, J. E. M.**
*See*  Wolkers-Ransome, Joan
Elizabeth Margaret

**Wolkers-Ransome, Joan Elizabeth
Margaret** 1928-  [ART]
*British painter*
* Wolkers-Ransome, J. E. M.

**Wollersen, Florence** 1893-  [THR]
*British actress*
* Buckton, Florence

**Wollheim, Donald A[llen]** 1914-
[CA, ESF, WGT]
*American author*
* Cooke, Arthur [joint pseudonym
with C. Kornbluth, R. Lowndes, J.
Michel, E. Balter]
* Gordon, Millard Verne
* Grinnell, David
* Pearson, Martin [joint pseudonym
with Cyril M. Kornbluth]
* Warland, Allen
* Wells, Braxton
* Woods, Lawrence [joint
pseudonym with Robert
Augustine Ward Lowndes, John
Michel]

**Wollstoncroft**
*See*  Godwin, Mary

**Woloweki**
*See*  Szymonowska, Marie

**Wols**
*See*  Schulze, Alfred Otto Wolfgang

**Wols, Frits**
*See*  Wong loi Sing, Eugene Wilfred

**Wolseley, Faith**
*See*  Tower, Stella Mary [Hodgson]

**Wolseley, Garnet Joseph [First
Viscount Wolseley]** 1833-1913
[DNNS]
*British army officer*
* Our only General

**[The] Wolsey of Hungary**
*See*  Martinuzzi, George

**Wolsey, Thomas** 1475?-1530  [SN]
*British prelate and statesman*
* Hough No
* [The] Vicar of Hell

**Wolstenholme, Stuart John** 1947-
[PRS]
*British musician*
* Wolstenholme, Woolly

**Wolstenholme, Woolly**
*See*  Wolstenholme, Stuart John

**Wolston, Henry**
*See*  Twinberrow, William Henry

**Wolters, Reinder Albertus**
1842-1917  [BE]
*Dutch-born baseball player*
* Wolters, Rynie

**Wolters, Rynie**
See Wolters, Reinder Albertus

**Wolton, Edward** 1492-1555 [PA]
*Author*
* Ododonus

**Wolverton, Fighting Harry**
See Wolverton, Harry

**Wolverton, Harry** 1873-1937
*American baseball manager*
* Wolverton, Fighting Harry

**Womack, David A[lfred]** 1933-
[CA]
*Canadian-born clergyman and author*
* Buchan, David

**Womack, Dooley**
See Womack, Horace Guy

**Womack, Horace Guy** 1939- [BE]
*American baseball player*
* Womack, Dooley

**Womack, Sid[ney Kirk]** 1896-1958
[BE]
*American baseball player*
* Womack, Tex

**Womack, Tex**
See Womack, Sid[ney Kirk]

**[The] Woman Flogger**
See Haynau, Julius Jakob von

**[The] Woman who Knows**
See Scott, Malcolm

**Won-Sik, Lim** 1919- [IWM]
*Korean conductor and educator*
* Unpa

**Wonder, Alvin**
See Lourie, Dick

**[The] Wonder Boy of the Speedways**
See Fengler, Harlan

**[The] Wonder Boy Preacher**
See Burke, Solomon

**[The] Wonder Child**
See Hajos, Magdalena [or Marishka]

**Wonder, Little Stevie**
See Cauthen, Steve

**Wonder, Little Stevie**
See Morris, Steveland

**[The] Wonder of the Age**
See Sullivan, Dan

**[The] Wonder of the World**
See Albert IV

**[The] Wonder of the World**
See Frederick II

**[The] Wonder of the World**
See Gerbert

**[The] Wonder of the World**
See Otto III [or Otho]

**Wonder, Stevie**
See Morris, Steveland

**Wonder, Wally**
See Jones, Walter [Wally]

**Wonder, William**
See Kirwan, Thomas

**[The] Wonder Worker**
See Gregory of Neocaesarea

**[The] Wonderful**
See Gongora y Argote, Luis de

**[The] Wonderful Baritone**
See De Melvin, Henri

**[The] Wonderful Boy of Devizes**
See Lawrence, [Sir] Thomas

**[The] Wonderful Doctor**
See Bacon, Roger

**[A] Wonderful Quiz**
See Lowell, James Russell

**[The] Wonderful Soprano**
See De Melvin, Henri

**Wonderful Walter Payton**
See Payton, Walter Jerry

**Wonderful Willie Smith**
See Smith, Willie

**Wonderlich, Jerry** 20th c.
*Auto racer*
* [The] Sheik of Hollywood

**Wonders, Anne**
See Passel, Anne W[onders]

**[The] Wondrous Maid**
See Joan of Arc [or Jeanne d'Arc]

**Wondrous Wilma Rudolph**
See Rudolph, Wilma Glodean Ward

**Wong, Anna May**
See Wong Liu Tsong

**Wong, Elizabeth** 1937- [AW]
*Chinese writer*
* Lien, Chi

**Wong, Hin** 1888- [LAO]
*Journalist*
* Huang Hsin Chao

**Wong Liu Tsong** 1907-1961
[BEW, F1, FC]
*Chinese-American actress*
* Wong, Anna May

**Wong loi Sing, Eugene Wilfred** 20th
c. [CW]
*Surinamese poet and author*
* Wols, Frits

**Wong Tung Jim** 1899- [FC, WEF]
*Chinese-born cinematographer*
* Howe, James Wong

**Wonso, Pamela** 1942- [SW]
*American actress*
* Tiffin, Pamela

**Woo, Chun Hoi** 1936- [IAW]
*Chinese author*
* Four, Yer

**Wood, Alice** 1873?-1949
[BEW, BMH]
*Theatrical performer*
* Lloyd, Alice

**Wood, Anthony** 1632-1695 [SN]
*British antiquary*
* [The] Ostade of Literary History

**Wood, Audrey Donella** 1927-
[BEW]
*American choreographer, dancer, actress*
* Wood, Deedee

**Wood, Barry**
See Rapp, Louis

**Wood, Barry**
See Wood, William B.

**Wood, Barry** 1942- [DC]
*British cricketer*
* Wood, Sawdust

**Wood, Batman**
See Wood, Richard

**Wood, Bootie**
See Wood, Mitchell, Jr.

**Wood, Buddy**
See Wood, Carl

**Wood, Carl** 1905-1948 [SC]
*American actor*
* Wood, Buddy

**Wood, Carole**
See Du Barry, Camille

**Wood, Charles Asher** 1909- [BE]
*American baseball player*
* Wood, Spades

**Wood, Charles Spencer** 1900-1974
[BE]
*American baseball player*
* Wood, Doc

**Wood, Christopher [Hovelle]** 1935-
[CA]
*British author*
* Dixon, Rosie
* Grape, Oliver
* Lea, Timothy
* Sutton, Penny

**Wood, Clement** 1888-1950
[NAA, WW]
*American author and poet*
* Dubois, Alan

**Wood, Daisy** 1877-1961 [BMH]
*British entertainer*
* Lancashire's Own Principal Boy

**Wood, Dandy**
See Wood, George A.

**Wood, David Duffield** 1838-1910
[DAM]
*American organist and educator*
* Wood, Duffle

**Wood, Deedee**
See Wood, Audrey Donella

**Wood, Del**
See Hazelwood, Adelaide

**Wood, Doc**
See Wood, Charles Spencer

**Wood, Doc**
See Wood, John B.

**Wood, Dorothy Adkins**
See Adkins, Dorothy C.

**Wood, Duffle**
See Wood, David Duffield

**Wood, Edgar A[llardyce]** 1907-
[CA, SAT, TCC]
*Canadian author and illustrator*
* Wood, Kerry

**Wood, Eric**
See Campling, F. Knowles

**Wood, Esther**
See Brady, Esther Wood

**Wood, Geoffrey**
See Russell, C.

**Wood, George** 1799-1870 [PA]
*Author*
* Schlemihl, Peter

**Wood, George A.** 1858-1924
[AS, BE, PB]
*American baseball player*
* Wood, Dandy

**Wood, Gloria** 1919- [FC, ITA]
*American actress*
* Stevens, K. T.

**Wood, Gordon D.**
See DeMain, Gordon

**Wood, Grant** 1892-1942 [WBD]
*American painter*
* [The] Painter of the Soil

**Wood, James Playsted** 1905-
[SAT]
*American author*
* St. Briavels, James
* Soudley, Henry

**Wood, Jane**
See Bokenham, Jane

**Wood, Joan Wentworth**
See Morgan, Joan

**Wood, John B.** ?-1883? [FFF, SN]
*American printer and journalist*
* [The] Great American Condenser
* Wood, Doc

**Wood, John George** 1827-1889
[RH]
*British author and clergyman*
* Forrest, George

**Wood, John H., Jr.** 1916?-1979
*American jurist*
* Wood, Maximum John

**Wood, Joseph** 1889- [BE, PB]
*American baseball player*
* Wood, Smokey Joe

**Wood, Julia A.** [PA]
*Author*
* Lee, Minnie Mary

**Wood, Ken**
See Cianfriglia, Giovanni

**Wood, Kerry**
See Wood, Edgar A[llardyce]

**Wood, Kirk**
See Stahl, Le Roy

**Wood, Larry**
See Wood, Marylaird

**Wood, Laura N[ewbold]**
See Roper, Laura Wood

**Wood, Lillian**
See Ross, Mrs. W. S.

**Wood, Mary**
See Bamfield, Veronica [Grissell]

**Wood, Marylaird** 20th c. [CA]
*American writer*
* Wood, Larry

**Wood, Matilda Alice Victoria**
1870-1922 [BEW, BMH, THR]
*British theatrical performer*
* [The] Bernhardt of the Music Halls
* Delmere, Bella
* Lloyd, Marie
* Our Marie

**Wood, [Sir] Matthew** 1768-1843
[HHF, HN, SN]
*British jurist*
* Absolute Wisdom

**Wood, Maximum John**
See Wood, John H., Jr.

**Wood, Mitchell, Jr.** 1919- [EJ]
*American jazz musician*
* Wood, Bootie

**Wood, Mrs. G. M.** [FFF]
*Entertainer*
* Saint John, Marguerite

**Wood, Natalie**
See Gurdin, Natasha

**Wood, Patricia E. W.** 20th c.
[AW, WD]
*British poet and playwright*
* Ross, Patricia

**Wood, Quality**
See Wood, Violet

**Wood, Richard** [SMG]
*American football player*
* Wood, Batman

**Wood, Richard Kennedy [Dick]** 20th
c. [NAA]
*American writer*
* Baker, Lon
* DuBois, Dick
* Watson, Le. De W.

**Wood, Robert Paul** 1931- [WD]
*British film critic*
* Wood, Robin

**Wood, Robin**
See Wood, Robert Paul

**Wood, Roland A.** [PA]
*Author*
* Beaulien

**Wood, Rose**
See Morrison, Mrs. Lewis

**Wood, Rosie** 1879-1944
[BMH, THR]
*British entertainer*
* Lloyd, Rosie

**Wood, Roy Winton** 1892- [BE]
*American baseball player*
* Wood, Woody

**Wood, Samuel Andrew** 1890-
[MBF, WW]
*British author and journalist*
* Cross, Thomson
* Ravenglass, Hal
* Temple, Robin

**Wood, Sara Bard Field** 1882-
[NAA]
*American author and poet*
* Field, Sara Bard

**Wood, Sawdust**
See Wood, Barry

**Wood, Serry**
See Freeman, Graydon La Verne

**Wood, Smokey Joe**
See Wood, Joseph

**Wood, Spades**
See Wood, Charles Asher

**Wood, Starr** 1870-1944 [DBA]
*British caricaturist*
* [The] Snark

**Wood, Stuart** 1957- [RO2]
*Scottish musician*
* Wood, Woody

**Wood, Sue**
See Taylor, Mary Virginia

**Wood, Tommy**
See Noack, Armond A.

**Wood, Ursula**
See Vaughan Williams, Ursula

**Wood, Violet** 1898- [AW]
*British author*
* Wood, Quality

**Wood, W. S.** [PA]
*Author*
* Merchant, Matthew

**Wood, Wee Georgie**
See Bramlett, George

**Wood, Wilbur** 1941- [SMG]
*American baseball player*
* Wood, Woody

**Wood, William B.** 1910-1971 [FB]
*American football player*
* Wood, Barry

**Wood, William McDonald** 1847- ?
[PA]
*Author*
* Jarvie, Nichol

**Wood, Woody**
See Wood, Roy Winton

**Wood, Woody**
See Wood, Stuart

**Wood, Woody**
See Wood, Wilbur

**Wood De Vere, Clementine Duchene**
1864-1954 [BBD]
*French-born opera singer*
* De Vere, Clementine Duchene

**Wood-Smith, Noel** ?-1955? [MBF]
*British author and editor*
* Clifford, Martin [house
pseudonym]
* Conquest, Owen [house
pseudonym]
* Richards, Frank [house
pseudonym]
* Taylor, Norman
* Terry, Noel

**Woodard, J. H.** [FFF]
*American writer*
* Jayhawker

**Woodbine Willie**
See Kennedy, G. A. Studdert

**Woodbridge, Anne**
See Fletcher, Frances

**Woodbridge, Elizabeth**
See Morris, Elizabeth Woodbridge

**Woodbridge, Hudson** 1900?-1981
[BWW]
*American singer*
* Eager, Jimmy
* [The] Guitar Wizard
* Smith, Honey Boy
* Tampa Red
* Whittaker, Hudson

**Woodbridge, Ruth**
See Law, Ruth Helen

**Woodbridge, Timothy** 1784-1862
[FFF]
*American clergyman*
* [The] Blind Preacher

**[The] Woodchopper**
See Moody, Clyde

**Woodcock, John** 1924- [ART]
*British artist*
* J. W.

**Woodcock, Leonard** 1911?-
*American labor leader and diplomat*
* [The] Professor
* [The] Undertaker

**Woodcott, Keith**
See Brunner, John [Kilian
Houston]

**Wooden Joe Nicholas**
See Nicholas, Joseph [Joe]

**Wooden, John** 1910- [BB]
*American basketball player and
coach*
* [The] India Rubber Man

**[The] Wooden Legged Commissary**
See Watson, [Sir] Brook

**Woodfall, Memory**
See Woodfall, William

**Woodfall, William** 18th c. [SN]
*British journalist*
* Woodfall, Memory

**Woodfern, Winnie**
See Gibson, Mary W. Stanely

**Woodfield, Harry** 20th c. [BBH]
*American horseshoe pitcher*
* Woodfield, Pop

**Woodfield, Pop**
See Woodfield, Harry

**Woodford, [Irene] Cecile** 1913-
[AW, IAW]
*British author*
* Barrie, Jane
* Douglas, Kim
* Lee, Veronica

**Woodford, Jack**
See Woolfolk, Josiah Pitts

**Woodfork, Robert** 1925-
[BWW, NBB]
*American singer*
* Poor Bob

**Woodfull, William Maldon**
1897-1965 [EC]
*Australian cricketer*
* [The] Great Unbowlable

**Woodham-Smith, Cecil Blanche
[Fitzgerald]** 1896-1977 [CA, TC1]
*British historian and author*
* Gordon, Janet

**Woodhead, James** 1851-1881 [BE]
*British-born baseball player*
* Woodhead, Red

**Woodhead, Red**
See Woodhead, James

**Woodhouse, C. M.**
See Woodhouse, Christopher
Montague

**Woodhouse, Christopher Montague**
1917- [MBL]
*British author*
* Woodhouse, C. M.

**Woodhouse, Henry**
See Casalegno, Mario Terenzio
Enrico

**Woodhouse, Martin** 1932- [CA]
*British author*
* Charlton, John

**Woodin, H. L.** 20th c. [SMG]
*American football player*
* Woodin, Whitey

**Woodin, Whitey**
See Woodin, H. L.

**Woodland, Waif**
See Blair, Caroline

**Woodlawn, Holly**
See Ajzenberg, Harold

**Woodleigh, Dorma** 1893- [THR]
*British actress and dancer*
* Leigh, Dorma

**Woodley, David** 20th c.
*American football player*
* Woodstrock

**Woodley, Letitia Matilda** 1869- ?
[THR]
*British comedienne*
* Pryde, Peggy

**Woodley, Winifred**
See Hedden, Worth Tuttle

**Woodman, Cocoa**
See Woodman, Dan[iel Courtenay]

**Woodman, Dan[iel Courtenay]**
1893-1962 [BE]
*American baseball player*
* Woodman, Cocoa

**Woodman, Thomas** 20th c. [MBF]
*British author*
* Quilter, Eddie

**Woodpecker, Woody**
See Brzezinski, Zbigniew

**Woodrich, Mary Neville** 1915-
[CA, SAT]
*American author*
* Neville, Mary

**Woodrook, R. A.**
See Cowlishaw, Ranson

**Woodruff, Burt**
See Woodruff, William H.

**Woodruff, Clyde**
See Vern, David

**Woodruff, George** 20th c. [BBH]
*American football coach*
* Woodruff, Kid

**Woodruff, John** 1915- [BBH]
*American track and field athlete*
* Woodruff, Long John

**Woodruff, Josephine Constance**
1909- [F2, FC]
*American actress*
* Booth, Edwina

**Woodruff, Julia Louisa Matilda**
[PA]
*Author*
* Jay, W. L. M.

**Woodruff, Kid**
See Woodruff, George

**Woodruff, Long John**
See Woodruff, John

**Woodruff, Orville** 1876-1937 [BE]
*American baseball player*
* Woodruff, Sam

**Woodruff, Philip**
See Mason, Philip

**Woodruff, Sam**
See Woodruff, Orville

**Woodruff, William H.** 1856-1934 [SC]
*American actor*
* Woodruff, Burt

**Woods, A. H.**
See Herman, Aladore

**Woods, Al**
See Dreeke, Frederick Ludwig

**Woods, Al**
See Woods, Alvis

**Woods, Albert Herman**
See Herman, Aladore

**Woods, Alvis** 1953- [ALR]
*American baseball player*
* Woods, Al

**Woods, Big Boy**
See Collins, Samuel

**Woods, Buddy**
See Woods, Oscar

**Woods, C. H.** [PA]
*Author*
* Otis, Belle

**Woods, Charles Robert** 1827-1885 [FFF]
*American army officer*
* Woods, Susan

**Woods, Constance**
See McComb, Katherine Woods

**Woods, Ethel** 1878- ? [BEW]
*British actress*
* Griffies, Ethel

**Woods, Frederick** 1932- [CA]
*British author*
* Ives, Lawrence

**Woods, George Rowland** 1915- [BE]
*American baseball player*
* Woods, Pinky

**Woods, Granville T.** 1856-1910 [IBW]
*American inventor*
* [The] Dean of American Inventors

**Woods, James** 20th c. [WGT]
*Author*
* Navarchus [joint pseudonym with Patrick Vaux]
* Yexley, Lionel

**Woods, James Jerome [Jim]** 1939- [BE]
*American baseball player*
* Woods, Woody

**Woods, Jonah**
See Woods, Olwen Spencer

**Woods, Kate Tannant** [FFF]
*Writer*
* True, Kate

**Woods, Lawrence** [joint pseudonym with Donald A(llen) Wollheim]
See Lowndes, Robert Augustine Ward

**Woods, Lawrence** [joint pseudonym with Donald A(llen) Wollheim]
See Michel, John B.

**Woods, Lawrence** [joint pseudonym with Robert Augustine Ward Lowndes, John Michel]
See Wollheim, Donald A[llen]

**Woods, Lawrence J.** 20th c. [IBW]
*American manufacturer*
* [The] Chicago Carpet King

**Woods, Nat**
See Stratemeyer, Edward L.

**Woods, Nick**
See Schaber, Nicholas

**Woods, Olando** 1951- [RO2]
*American musician*
* Woods, Terrell

**Woods, Olwen Spencer** 1913- [AW]
*British-born author*
* Woods, Jonah

**Woods, Oscar** 1900-1956? [BWW]
*American singer*
* [The] Lone Wolf
* [The] Street Rustler
* [The] Troubadour
* Woods, Buddy

**Woods, P. F.**
See Bayley, Barrington J[ohn]

**Woods, Percy** 1909- [MY]
*American singer*
* Woods, Sonny

**Woods, Pinky**
See Woods, George Rowland

**Woods, Ross**
See Story, Rosamond Mary

**Woods, Sara**
See Bowen-Judd, Sara [Hutton]

**Woods, Sonny**
See Woods, Percy

**Woods, Stuart**
See Lee, Stuart

**Woods, Susan**
See Woods, Charles Robert

**Woods, Terrell**
See Woods, Olando

**Woods, William J.** 1937-1968 [RO1]
*American singer*
* Little Willie John

**Woods, Woody**
See Woods, James Jerome [Jim]

**Woodsley, H. Austin**
See Mittelholzer, Edgar

**Woodson, Carter Godwin** 1875-1950 [IBW]
*American historian, author, editor*
* [The] Father of Modern Black History

**Woodson, Jeff**
See Oglesby, Joseph

**Woodson, Kittie**
See Mack, Mrs. Will H.

**Woodson, Mary Blake** 1886- [NAA]
*American journalist*
* Mayo, Mary

**Woodson, Meg**
See Baker, Elsie

**Woodson, Mrs. W. L.** [FFF]
*Entertainer*
* Fay, Lottie

**Woodson, Richard Lee [Dick]** 1945- [BE, PB]
*American baseball player*
* Woodson, Woody

**Woodson, Woody**
See Woodson, Richard Lee [Dick]

**Woodstrock**
See Woodley, David

**Woodthorpe, Georgie**
See Cooper, Mrs. Fred

**Woodthorpe, Patricia Mariella** 1928- [ART]
*British painter and draftsman*
* M. W.

**Woodville, Anthony [Lord Rivers]** [SN]
* [Le] Wellington des Joueurs

**Woodville, Jennie**
See Stabler, J. L.

**Woodward, A. A.** [PA]
*Author*
* Auber, Forrestier

**Woodward, Edward [Emberlin]** 20th c. [WW]
*Author*
* Grierson, Jane

**Woodward, Grace Steele** 1899- [CAP]
*American author*
* Doane, Marion S.

**Woodward, Henry Lovett** [PA]
*Author*
* H. L. W.

**Woodward, Joseph Janvier** 1833-1884 [FFF]
*American physician and author*
* Janvier

**Woodward, Lilian**
See Marsh, John

**Woodward, Patti** 1880-1967 [BDF, F1, FC]
*American actress*
* Darwell, Jane

**Woodward, Tena Garrison** 1883-1968 [IA]
*American author*
* Garrison, Anet

**Woodward, Thomas Jones** 1940- [IPA, RO2, SW]
*Welsh-born singer*
* Jones, Tom
* Scott, Tommy
* Tiger Tom
* [The] Twisting Vocalist

**Woodward, William Frederick** 1942- [BE, PB]
*American baseball player*
* Woodward, Woody

**Woodward, Woody**
See Woodward, William Frederick

**Woodworth, Samuel** 1784-1842 [SN]
*American printer, journalist, author*
* [The] American Goldsmith

**Woody, Regina Jones** 1894- [CA]
*American dancer and author*
* Devi, Nila

**[The] Wool Carder President**
See Fillmore, Millard

**Wooldridge, George B.** [PA]
*Author*
* Quick, Tom

**Wooldridge, Lestocq Boileau** 1851?-1920 [BEW]
*Actor, theatre manager, playwright*
* Lestocq, William

**Wooler, Thomas Jonathan** 1786-1853 [PA]
*Author*
* Black Dwarf

**Woolery, Clarence** ?-1978 [FIR]
*Singer*
* Woolery, Pete

**Woolery, Pete**
See Woolery, Clarence

**Wooley [or Woodley?], Charles** [PA]
*Author*
* C. A. M. W.

**Wooley, Sheb**
See Wooley, Shelby F.

**Wooley, Shelby F.** 1921- [ASC, CWG, DAM]
*American singer, composer, actor*
* Colder, Ben
* Wooley, Sheb

**Woolf, George** 1910-1946 [BBH, CSH]
*Canadian-born jockey*
* [The] Iceman

**Woolf, Walter** 1899- [THR]
*American actor and singer*
* King, Walter Woolf

**Woolfolk, Josiah Pitts** 1894-1971 [CA, NAA, WW]
*American author*
* Britt, Sappho Henderson
* Kennedy, Howard
* Sayre, Gordon
* Woodford, Jack

**Woollcott, Alexander** 1887-1943 [B10]
*American author and journalist*
* [The] Town Crier

**Woolley, Catherine** 1904- [AW, CA, MJA]
*American author*
* Thayer, Jane

**Woolley, Edgar Montillion** 1888-1963 [BEW, EMT, FC]
*American actor and director*
* Woolley, Monty

**Woolley, Monty**
See Woolley, Edgar Montillion

**Woolman, David S.** 1916- [CA]
*American author and journalist*
* Vaidon, Lawdom

**Woolmer, Robert Andrew [Bob]** 1948- [DC]
*British cricketer*
* Woolmer, Woolly

**Woolmer, Woolly**
See Woolmer, Robert Andrew [Bob]

**Woolrich, Cornell**
See Hopley-Woolrich, Cornell George

**Woolrich, Daniel** 20th c. [SFP]
*Author*
* Homes, Geoffrey

**Woolridge, Anna Marie** 1930-
[IBW, SW]
*American singer, actress, educator*
* Lee, Gabby
* Lincoln, Abbey
* Moseka, Aminata
* Woolridge, Gabby

**Woolridge, Gabby**
*See* Woolridge, Anna Marie

**Woolsey, Maryhale** 1899- [ASC]
*American author*
* Hale, Eugenia
* Hale, Mary
* Snow, Terry

**Woolsey, Sarah Chauncey**
1835-1905 [FFF]
*American author and poet*
* Coolidge, Susan

**Woolson, Constance Fenimore**
1840-1894 [WBD]
*American author*
* March, Anne

**Woolwine, Laura** [FFF]
*Entertainer*
* Bellini, Laura

**Woon**
*See* Wotherspoon, Ralph

**Wooten, Earl Hazwell** 1924- [BE]
*American baseball player*
* Wooten, Junior

**Wooten, Junior**
*See* Wooten, Earl Hazwell

**Wootten, Lawrence B.** 1922- [EJ]
*American jazz musician*
* Wootten, Red

**Wootten, Red**
*See* Wootten, Lawrence B.

**Worblefister, Petunia**
*See* Gribbin, Lenore S.

**Worboys, Anne Eyre**
*See* Worboys, Annette Isobel

**Worboys, Annette Isobel** 20th c.
[AW, CA, WD]
*New Zealand-born author*
* Eyre, Annette
* Maxwell, Vicky
* Worboys, Anne Eyre

**Worcester, Donald E[mmet]**
*See* Makemson, Donald Emmet

**Worcester, N.** [PA]
*Author*
* Philopacificus

**[The] Worcester Speculator**
*See* Fiske, Nathan

**[The] Word Catcher**
*See* Ritson, Joseph

**[The] Word King**
*See* Partridge, Eric Honeywood

**Worde, Wynkyn de**
*See* Van Wynkyn, Jan

**Worden, Helen** 1896- [B10]
*American author and journalist*
* Brummel, Belle

**Wordsdale, James** ?-1767 [RH]
*British painter and playwright*
* Jemmy

**Wordsworth, Christopher**
1774-1846 [FFF]
*British clergyman and scholar*
* [The] Master of Trinity

**Wordsworth, Favel Perry**
1851-1888 [BE]
*American baseball player*
* Wordsworth, Red

**Wordsworth, Red**
*See* Wordsworth, Favel Perry

**Wordsworth, William** 1770-1850
[DEL, FFF, SN]
*British poet*
* [The] Bard of Rydal Mount
* [The] Cumberland Poet
* [The] Poet of the Excursion

**Worfel, W. G.** 20th c. [SFL]
*Author*
* [The] Baron

**Workman, Charles** 20th c.
[BLB, MM, PHM]
*American underworld figure*
* [The] Bug

**Workman, Harry Hall** 1899-1972
[BE]
*American baseball player*
* Workman, Hoge

**Workman, Hoge**
*See* Workman, Harry Hall

**Workman, James** 20th c. [SFL]
*Author*
* Dark, James

**Workman, Raymond** 1909?-1966
[AS]
*American jockey*
* Workman, Sonny

**Workman, Sonny**
*See* Workman, Raymond

**Works, Judge**
*See* Works, Ralph Talmadge

**Works, Ralph Talmadge**
1888-1941 [BE]
*American baseball player*
* Works, Judge

**World Destroyer**
*See* Hamilton, Edmond [Moore]

**[The] World Renowned Coon Shouter**
*See* Abuza, Sophie

**[The] World Wrecker**
*See* Hamilton, Edmond [Moore]

**[The] World's Champion Moaner**
*See* Smith, Clara

**[The] World's Fastest Human**
*See* Paddock, Charles W.

**[The] World's Fastest Tapper**
*See* Verdon, Gwyneth Evelyn

**[The] World's Fastest Woman**
*See* Rudolph, Wilma Glodean
Ward

**[The] World's Greatest Blues Shouter**
*See* Turner, Joseph [Vernon]

**[The] World's Greatest Blues Singer**
*See* Johnson, Alonzo

**[The] World's Greatest Dribbler**
*See* Haynes, Marques Oreole

**[The] World's Greatest Gospel Singer**
*See* Jackson, Mahalia

**[The] World's Greatest Pickpocket**
*See* Perry, Vic[tor]

**[The] World's Greatest Railroad Buff**
*See* Whitaker, Rogers Ernest
Malcolm

**[The] World's Greatest Salesman**
*See* Girard, Joe

**[The] World's Most Perfectly Developed Man**
*See* Siciliano, Angelo

**[The] World's Most Pulchritudinous Evangelist**
*See* McPherson, Aimee Semple

**[The] World's Number One Wisecracker**
*See* Rogers, Will[iam Penn Adair]

**[The] World's Richest Cop**
*See* Gilbert, Daniel A.

**[The] World's Strongest Teen-Ager**
*See* Gubner, Gary

**[The] World's Sweetheart**
*See* Smith, Gladys Mary

**[The] World's Tallest Man**
*See* Hibe, Henry

**[The] World's Wildest Tenor Man**
*See* Cobbs, Arnette

**[The] World's Wonder**
*See* Elizabeth I

**[The] World's Worst Guitarist**
*See* Bowman, Don

**Worloou, Lambros** 1915- [FC]
*Greek-Egyptian singer*
* Guetary, Georges

**[The] Worm**
*See* McCarter, Willie

**Worm, Olaus** 1588-1654 [PA]
*Author*
* Vormius

**Worman, Eli**
*See* Weil, Roman L[ee]

**Wormington, Hannah Marie** 1914-
[CA]
*American archaeologist and author*
* Volk, Hannah Marie

**Wormley, Cinda**
*See* Kornblum, Cinda

**Wormser, Richard [Edward]** 1908-
[SFL, SFP]
*Author*
* Carter, Nick [house pseudonym]
* Friend, Ed

**Worne, John**
*See* Wylie, James

**Worner, Philip Arthur Incledon**
1910- [AW]
*British author*
* Incledon, Philip
* Sylvester, Philip

**Wornum, Miriam** 1898- [AW]
*American author*
* Dennis, Eve

**Worrell, Everil** 1893-1969
[HFF, WGT]
*American author*
* Monett, Lireve

**Worrell, Jennie**
*See* Hatfield, Mrs.

**Worsley, Bruce**
*See* Digby-Worsley, Bruce

**Worsley, Gump**
*See* Worsley, Lorne John

**Worsley, Lorne John** 1929-
[CEI, FHE, SR]
*Canadian hockey player*
* [The] Gumper
* Worsley, Gump

**Worsnop, Wilfrid** 1900-1966 [FC]
*British actor*
* Lawson, Wilfrid

**[The] Worst Pope**
*See* Borgia, Rodrigo [or
Rodriguez]

**Worters, Roy** 1900-1957 [FHE]
*Canadian-born hockey player*
* Worters, Shrimp

**Worters, Shrimp**
*See* Worters, Roy

**Worth, Amy**
*See* Keller, David H[enry]

**Worth, Billie**
*See* Rothmund, Wilhelmino

**Worth, Constance**
*See* Howarth, Jocelyn

**Worth, Dan**
*See* Cruger, Paul

**Worth, Margaret**
*See* Arvonen, Helen

**Worth, Marion**
*See* Wilson, Mary Ann Ward

**Worth, Martin**
*See* Wigglesworth, Martin Francis

**Worth, Nicholas**
*See* Page, Walter Hines

**Worth, Nigel**
*See* Wright, Noel

**Worth, Peter** [house pseudonym,
Ziff-Davis]
*See* Geier, Chester S.

**Worth, Peter** [house pseudonym,
Ziff-Davis]
*See* Graham, Roger Phillips

**Worth, Valerie**
*See* Bahlke, Valerie Worth

**Worthington, Allan Fulton** 1929-
[BE]
*American baseball player*
* Worthington, Red

**Worthington, Mabel**
*See* Blake, Mrs. O. W.

**Worthington, Red**
*See* Worthington, Allan Fulton

**Worthington, Red**
*See* Worthington, Robert Lee
[Bob]

**Worthington, Robert Lee [Bob]**
1906-1963 [BN]
*American baseball player*
* Rhubarb, Colonel
* Worthington, Red

**Worthington Ball, John**
See Totten, W. Fred

**Worthington-Stuart, Brian Arthur**
20th c. [WW]
*Author*
* Meredith, Peter
* Stuart, Brian

**[The] Worthless**
See Wenceslaus [or Wenceslas]

**Wortis, Avi** 1937- [CA, SAT]
*American author*
* Avi

**Wortman, Buster**
See Wortman, Frank

**Wortman, Chuck**
See Wortman, William Lewis

**Wortman, Frank** 1903-1970 [BLB]
*American underworld figure*
* Wortman, Buster

**Wortman, William Lewis** 1892-
[BE]
*American baseball player*
* Wortman, Chuck

**Worts, George Frank** 1892-
[WGT, WW]
*American author*
* Brent, Loring

**Wosmek, Frances** 1917- [CA]
*American author and illustrator*
* Brailsford, Frances

**Wotherspoon, Ralph** 1897- [WWL]
*British author*
* Woon

**Wouil, George**
See Slaney, George Wilson

**[The] Wounded Wonder**
See Criqui, Eugene

**Wovoka** 1856?-1932 [WBD]
*American Indian religious leader*
* Wilson, Jack

**WOW**
See Wejp-Olsen, Werner

**Wow the Wizard**
See Fox, Karrell

**Woxholt, Greta** 1916- [FC]
*Norwegian actress*
* Gynt, Greta

**Woy, Bucky**
See Woy, William

**Woy, William** 1938- [B10]
*American sports agent*
* Woy, Bucky

**Woyda**
See Adamowicz, Adam

**Wrangel, Friedrich Heinrich Ernst von** 1784-1877 [SN, WBD]
*Prussian army officer*
* Wrangel, Papa

**Wrangel, Papa**
See Wrangel, Friedrich Heinrich Ernst von

**[The] Wrangler**
See Henry II

**Wraxall, [Sir] Frederick Charles L.**
1828-1865 [PA]
*Author*
* Wraxall, Lascelles

**Wraxall, Lascelles**
See Wraxall, [Sir] Frederick Charles L.

**Wray, James R. Ludlow**
1894-1967 [AS, FB]
*American football player and coach*
* Wray, Lud

**Wray, John**
See Malloy, John

**Wray, John** 1628?-1705
[DNNS, WBD]
*British naturalist*
* [The] Father of English Natural History
* Ray, John

**Wray, Lud**
See Wray, James R. Ludlow

**Wray, Reginald**
See Home-Gall, William Benjamin

**Wray, Roger**
See Marriott, James William

**Wray, W. Fitzwater** 20th c.
[WWL]
*British author*
* Kuklos

**[The] Wrecker**
See Hrechkosy, David John

**Wreford, James**
See Watson, J[ames] Wreford

**Wren, Ellaruth**
See Elkins, Ella Ruth

**Wren, M. K.**
See Renfroe, Martha Kay

**Wren, P. C.**
See Wren, Percival Christopher

**Wren, Percival Christopher**
1885-1941 [LC]
*British author*
* Wren, P. C.

**Wrencher, Big John**
See Wrencher, John Thomas

**Wrencher, John Thomas**
1923-1977 [BWW, NBB]
*American singer*
* One Armed John
* Wrencher, Big John

**[The] Wretch of Sion**
See Whytforde, Richard

**Wrexe, Charles**
See Hardinge, Charles Wrexe

**Wright, Ab**
See Wright, Albert Owen

**Wright, Albert** 1912-1957
[AS, BX, RBE]
*Mexican-born boxer*
* Wright, Chalky

**Wright, Albert Owen** 1905- [BE]
*American baseball player*
* Wright, Ab

**Wright, Alexander** ?-1940 [BMH]
*Australian impressionist*
* Navarre, Andre

**Wright, Archibald Lee** 1916?-
[BX, IBW, RBE]
*American boxer*
* [The] Magnificent Mongoose
* Moore, Archie
* Ol' Man River

**Wright, Arleta** 1923- [CA]
*American author*
* Richardson, Arleta

**Wright, Armand Vincent**
1896-1965 [SC]
*American actor*
* Wright, Curly

**Wright, Bill**
See Wright, Burnis

**Wright, Bruce McMarion** 1918-
[IBW]
*American jurist and poet*
* Turn 'Em Loose Bruce

**Wright, Buckshot**
See Wright, Forest Glenn

**Wright, Buggy**
See Wright, Clarence

**Wright, Burnis** 20th c. [OBW]
*American baseball player*
* Wright, Bill

**Wright, Cat**
See Wright, Rayfield

**Wright, Ceylon**
See Wright, Edward Yatman

**Wright, Chalky**
See Wright, Albert

**Wright, Charles** 1927- [EJ]
*American jazz musician*
* Wright, Specs

**Wright, Clarence** 20th c. [OBW]
*American baseball player*
* Wright, Buggy

**Wright, Clyde** 1943- [PB]
*American baseball player*
* Wright, Skeeter

**Wright, Curly**
See Wright, Armand Vincent

**Wright, Damon**
See Ackerman, Forrest J[ames]

**Wright, Dancer**
See Wright, Elmo

**Wright, Deacon**
See Wright, William Simmons

**Wright, Dick**
See Wright, William James

**Wright, Edward H.** 20th c. [IBW]
*American politician*
* [The] Iron Master

**Wright, Edward Yatman** 20th c.
[BE]
*American baseball player*
* Wright, Ceylon

**Wright, Elinor Bruce** 1921- [IAW]
*British author*
* Lyon, Elinor

**Wright, Elizur** 1804-1885 [WBD]
*American actuary*
* [The] Father of Legal-Reserve Life Insurance

**Wright, Elmo** 1949- [FB]
*American football player*
* Wright, Dancer

**Wright, Elsie**
See Kaplan, Leigh Wright

**Wright, Elsie N.** 1907- [WW]
*Author*
* Grayson, [Capt.] J. J.

**Wright, Enid Meadowcroft [LaMonte]** 1898-1966 [CAP, SAT]
*American author*
* Meadowcroft, Enid LaMonte

**Wright, Eugene Joseph [Gene]**
1923- [EJ7]
*American jazz musician*
* Wright, Senator

**Wright, Farnsworth** 1888-1940
[WGT]
*American author*
* Hard, Francis

**Wright, Faye** 1914- [CA]
*American author*
* Mata, Daya

**Wright, Forest Glenn** 1901-
[BE, PB]
*American baseball player*
* Wright, Buckshot

**Wright, Frances** 1795-1852 [PA]
*Author*
* [An] Englishwoman

**Wright, Frances J.**
See Crothers, Jessie F[rances]

**Wright, Francesca**
See Robins, Denise [Naomi]

**Wright, Franklin**
See Farmer, Henry

**Wright, Frosty**
See Wright, Paul W.

**Wright, G. B.**
See Wright, Gordon Butler

**Wright, George** 1877-1931 [THR]
*British actor*
* Bealby, George

**Wright, Georgie**
See Henley, Georgina

**Wright, Gilbert Munger** 1901-
[SFL]
*Author*
* Lebar, John

**Wright, Gordon Butler** 1925-
[ART]
*British artist*
* Wright, G. B.

**Wright, Harry**
See Wright, William Henry

**Wright, Harry Wendell** 1916-1954
[SC]
*American actor and stunt performer*
* Wright, Wen

**Wright, Jack R.**
See Finkelstein, Mark

**Wright, James Richard** 1883-
[NAA]
*British-born writer*
* Hart, J. E. T.

**Wright, John Geoffrey** 1954-    [DC]
*New Zealand-born cricketer*
* Wright, Wrighty

**Wright, Joseph** 1734-1797
[HN, WBD]
*British painter*
* Wright of Derby

**Wright, Joseph, Jr.** 1906-    [CSH]
*Canadian rowboat racer*
* Wright, Young Joe

**Wright, Joseph, Sr.** 1864-1950
[CSH]
*Canadian rowboat racer*
* Mr. Joe

**Wright, Joseph X.**    [FFF]
*American writer*
* Tukesbury, Joe

**Wright, Judith Grovner**
*See* Bull, Lois

**Wright, Julia McNair**    [FFF]
*Author*
* Aunt Sophronia

**Wright, Kenneth**
*See* Alvarez Del Rey, Ramon
Felipe San Juan Mario Silvio Enrico

**Wright, Lan**
*See* Wright, Lionel Percy

**Wright, Lionel Percy** 1923-
[ESF, SFL, WGT]
*British author*
* Wright, Lan

**Wright, Little Stevie**
*See* Wright, Steve

**Wright, Lucky**
*See* Wright, William Simmons

**Wright, M. Jane** 20th c.    [OP]
*American opera singer*
* Nelson, Jane

**Wright, Mabel Osgood** 1859-1934
[ALY, WGT, WWL]
*American author*
* Barbara
* Russell, Sarah

**Wright, Martha**
*See* Wiederrecht, Martha Lucile

**Wright, Mary Kathryn** 1935-
[EG, GF, GME]
*American golfer*
* Wright, Mickey

**Wright, Mary M.** 1894-    [NAA]
*American poet and author*
* Lorraine, Lilith

**Wright, Mary Pamela [Godwin]**
1917-    [AW, CAP]
*British author*
* Bawn, Mary

**Wright, Mickey**
*See* Wright, Mary Kathryn

**Wright, Nathan Edward** 1943-
[CWG, DAM]
*American country-western performer*
* Wright, Sonny

**Wright, Nathan, Jr.** 1923-    [CA]
*American educator and author*
* Wright, Nathaniel, Jr.

**Wright, Nathaniel, Jr.**
*See* Wright, Nathan, Jr.

**Wright, Noel** 1890-1975
[SFL, WGT]
*Author*
* Worth, Nigel

**Wright of Derby**
*See* Wright, Joseph

**Wright, Orlando** 1921-    [EJ]
*American jazz musician*
* Kaleem, Musa

**Wright, [Mary] Patricia** 1932-
[CA]
*British author*
* Napier, Mary

**Wright, Paul W.** 20th c.    [BBH]
*American collegiate athletic director*
* Wright, Frosty

**Wright, Paula Ramona** 20th c.
[ITA]
*American actress*
* Raymond, Paula

**Wright, R. R.**
*See* Wright, Richard Robert, III

**Wright, R. W.**    [PA]
*Author*
* Quevedo

**Wright, Rasty**
*See* Wright, Wayne Bromley

**Wright, Rasty**
*See* Wright, William S.

**Wright, Rayfield** 1945-    [SMG]
*American football player*
* [The] Big Cat
* Wright, Cat

**Wright, Richard Robert, III** 20th c.
[IBW]
*American banker*
* Wright, R. R.

**Wright, Rita** 1946-    [IBW]
*American singer, lyricist, songwriter*
* Wright, Syreeta

**Wright, Robert** [joint pseudonym
with Robert Augustine Ward
Lowndes]
*See* Ackerman, Forrest J[ames]

**Wright, Robert** [joint pseudonym
with Forrest J. Ackerman]
*See* Lowndes, Robert Augustine
Ward

**Wright, Robert B.** 1915-    [ASC]
*American musician*
* Bruce, Robert

**Wright, Rowland**
*See* Wells, Carolyn

**Wright, Royston** 1927-    [CAR]
*British artist*
* Adzak, Roy

**Wright, Ruth**
*See* Kauffman, Ruth [Hammitt]

**Wright, S. A.**    [PA]
*Author*
* Cousin Sue

**Wright, Samuel**
*See* Murray, Charles T.

**Wright, Senator**
*See* Wright, Eugene Joseph [Gene]

**Wright, Sewell Peaslee** 1897-
[NAA]
*American author*
* Andrew, Thomas
* Cameron, Leigh
* Spencer, Parke

**Wright, Skeeter**
*See* Wright, Clyde

**Wright, Sonny**
*See* Wright, Nathan Edward

**Wright, Specs**
*See* Wright, Charles

**Wright, Steve**    [RO2]
*British singer*
* Wright, Little Stevie

**Wright, Sydney Fowler** 1874-1965
[ESF, LC, WGT]
*British author and poet*
* Fowler, Sydney
* Seymour, Alan
* Wingrave, Anthony

**Wright, Syreeta**
*See* Wright, Rita

**Wright, Taffy**
*See* Wright, Taft Shedron

**Wright, Taft Shedron** 1913-
[BE, PB]
*American baseball player*
* Wright, Taffy

**Wright, Tennessee**
*See* Wright, V. Richard

**Wright, Thomas** 1859- ?
[FFF, WWL]
*British author*
* Journeyman Engineer
* Riverside Visitor
* [A] Trinity Man

**Wright, V. Richard** 1921?-1966
[AS]
*American horse trainer*
* Wright, Tennessee

**Wright, W. George** 20th c.    [MBF]
*British editor*
* Bouchard, William
* Bryant, Bruce
* Grant, Howard
* Masterson, Val
* Quinton, Paul
* Rishton, William

**Wright, Wayne Bromley**
1895-1948    [BE]
*American baseball player*
* Wright, Rasty

**Wright, Weaver**
*See* Ackerman, Forrest J[ames]

**Wright, Wen**
*See* Wright, Harry Wendell

**Wright, Willard Huntington**
1888-1939    [CC, EMD, LC]
*American author, journalist, editor*
* Van Dine, S. S.

**Wright, William Henry** 1835-1895
[AS, BAB, BBH]
*American baseball player and
manager*
* [The] Father of Professional
Baseball
* Wright, Harry

**Wright, William James** 1890-1952
[BE]
*American baseball player*
* Wright, Dick

**Wright, William S.** 1863-1922
[BE]
*American baseball player*
* Wright, Rasty

**Wright, William Simmons**
1880-1941    [BE]
*American baseball player*
* William the Red
* Wright, Deacon
* Wright, Lucky

**Wright, Winifred** 1910?-1950
[BEW]
*Actress*
* Melville, Winifred

**Wright, Wrighty**
*See* Wright, John Geoffrey

**Wright, Young Joe**
*See* Wright, Joseph, Jr.

**Wright-Cooper, Richard**
1893-1947    [THR]
*British actor*
* Cooper, Richard

**Wrigley, George Watson**
1873-1952    [BE]
*American baseball player*
* Wrigley, Zeke

**Wrigley, Zeke**
*See* Wrigley, George Watson

**Wroblewski, Jan**
*See* Wroblewski, Ptaszyn

**Wroblewski, Ptaszyn** 1936-    [EJ]
*Polish jazz musician*
* Wroblewski, Jan

**Wrong Way Marshall**
*See* Marshall, Jim

**Wrong Way Riegels**
*See* Riegels, Roy

**Wronker, Lili Cassel** 1924-    [SAT]
*German-born illustrator*
* Cassel, Lili

**Wronski, Jozef Maria**
*See* Hoene, Jozef Maria

**Wrottesley, Arthur John Francis**
1908-    [CA]
*British barrister and author*
* Staffordshire Knot

**Wroughton, Julia** 1934-    [ART]
*British painter*
* J. W.

**Wroughtwell, Faith**
*See* Helphingstine, Mary J[ane]

**Wroxham, Cecil**
*See* Belfield, Harry Wedgwood

**Wry-Mouthed**
*See* Boleslav III

**Wrzaskala, Richard**
*See* Wrzaskala, Ryszard Jozef

**Wrzaskala, Ryszard Jozef** 1932-
[IWM]
*Polish-born musician*
* Wrzaskala, Richard

**Wrzos, Joseph Henry** 1929-    [CA]
*American author and editor*
* Ross, Joseph

**Wu, C. C.**
See Wu Ch'ao-ch'u

**Wu Ch'ao-ch'u** 1886-1934 [WBD]
*Chinese statesman*
* Wu, C. C.

**Wu, Nelson I[kon]** 1919- [CA]
*Chinese-born educator and author*
* Lu ch'iao

**Wu Wen-Hsiu** 1935- [OP]
*Taiwanese opera singer*
* Wu, William

**Wu, William**
See Wu Wen-Hsiu

**Wuelcker, Richard Paul**
1845-1910 [WBD]
*German theologian and author*
* Wuelker, Richard Paul

**Wuelker, Richard Paul**
See Wuelcker, Richard Paul

**Wuensche, Edward Hugh** 20th c.
*American underworld figure and government witness*
* Winchester, Hugh E.

**Wuestling, George** 1903-1970
*American baseball player*
* Wuestling, Yatz

**Wuestling, Yatz**
See Wuestling, George

**Wul, Stefan**
See Pairault, Pierre

**Wulff, Edgun Valdemar** 1913-
[IBY, ICB]
*American illustrator*
* Edgun

**Wulff, Sigismund** [PA]
*Author*
* Sieg, W. M.

**Wunnakyawhtin U Ohn Ghine**
See Maurice, David [John Kerr]

**Wunsch, Josephine M.** 1914- [WD]
*American author*
* McLean, J. Sloan [joint
   pseudonym with Virginia M(ary)
   Gillette]

**Wupperman, Claudeigh Louise**
1912- [BEW]
*American actress*
* Morgan, Claudia

**Wupperman, Francis Philip**
1890-1949 [F1, F2, FC]
*American actor*
* Morgan, Frank

**Wupperman, Georgiana [Iversen]**
20th c. [BEW]
*American actress*
* Arnold, Grace

**Wupperman, Raphael Kuhner**
1882?-1956 [BEW, F2, SC]
*American actor*
* Morgan, Ralph

**Wurm, Adela** 1877-1952 [BBD]
*British musician*
* Verne, Adela

**Wurm, Alice** 1868-1958 [BBD]
*British musician*
* Verne, Alice

**Wurm, Mathilde** 1865-1936 [BBD]
*British musician*
* Verne, Mathilde

**Wurman, Claude Olin** 1927-1974
[SC]
*American actor*
* Justin, Morgan

**Wurmbrand, Richard** 1909- [AW]
*Rumanian-born clergyman and author*
* Moses, Ruben

**Wursteisen, Christian** 1544-1588
[PA]
*Author*
* Urtisius

**Wurzbach, Constant** 1818-1893
[WBD]
*Austrian poet and author*
* Constant, W.

**Wyandotte, Steve**
See Thomas, Stanley

**Wyant, Andrew R[obert] E[lmer]**
1873-1964 [FB]
*American football player*
* Wyant, Polyphemus

**Wyant, Polyphemus**
See Wyant, Andrew R[obert]
E[lmer]

**Wyatt, B. D.**
See Robinson, Spider

**Wyatt, Ben**
See Young, Fred W.

**Wyatt, Joe**
See Wyatt, Loral John

**Wyatt, John Whitlow** 1907- [BE]
*American baseball player*
* Wyatt, Whit

**Wyatt, Loral John** 1901- [BE]
*American baseball player*
* Wyatt, Joe

**Wyatt, Pepper**
See Wyatt, Ralph Arthur

**Wyatt, Ralph Arthur** 1920- [MK]
*American baseball player*
* Wyatt, Pepper

**Wyatt, Wesley Butler**
See Torme, Mel[vin Howard]

**Wyatt, Whit**
See Wyatt, John Whitlow

**Wyatt, Wilma Winifred**
1910?-1952 [CED, F2]
*American actress*
* Crosby, Dixie Lee
* Lee, Dixie

**Wybraniec, Peter F[rank]** 1882-
[WGT]
*Author*
* Leonhart, [Dr.] Raphael W.

**Wycherley, Bus**
See Wycherley, Ralph

**Wycherley, Ralph** 1920- [CEI]
*Canadian-born hockey player*
* Wycherley, Bus

**Wycherley, Richard Newman** 20th
c. [LC]
*Author*
* Murray, Gilbert

**Wycherly, Margaret**
See De Wolfe, Margaret

**Wycherly, William** 1640?-1716
[SN]
*British playwright*
* [The] Plain Dealer

**Wyckham, John**
See Suckling, John

**Wyckoff, Robert Fletcher** 1923-
[BEW, TR]
*American theatrical designer and producer*
* Fletcher, Robert

**Wycliff**
See Westrup, Enrique Tomas

**Wycliffe, Bubba**
See Wycliffe, Nathaniel Morton

**Wycliffe, John**
See Bedford-Jones, Henry [James
O'Brien]

**Wycliffe [or Wyclif], John**
1324-1384 [DEP, RH, SN]
*British religious reformer*
* [The] Evangelic Doctor
* Evangelicus, Doctor
* [The] Father of English Prose
* [The] Gospel Doctor
* [The] Morning Star of the
   Reformation

**Wycliffe, Nathaniel Morton** 1934-
[SMG]
*American baseball player*
* Wycliffe, Bubba

**Wycoff, Leon** 1903-
[BEW, ITA, SW]
*American actor*
* Ames, Leon

**Wyeth, N. C.**
See Wyeth, Newell Convers

**Wyeth, Newell Convers** 1882-1945
[WYA]
*American author*
* Wyeth, N. C.

**Wykham, Helen**
See Evans, Pamela

**Wylcotes, John**
See Ransford, Oliver Neil

**Wylde, Katharine**
See Colvill, Helen Hester

**Wyler, Gretchen**
See Wienecke, Gretchen Patricia

**Wyler, Richard** 1934- [FC]
*American actor*
* Stapley, Richard

**Wyler, Rose**
See Ames, Rose Wyler

**Wylie, Dirk** [joint pseudonym with
C. Kornbluth, F. Kummer, F. Pohl]
See Dockweiler, Joseph Harold

**Wylie, Dirk** [joint pseudonym with
Joseph Harold Dockweiler and
Frederik Pohl]
See Kornbluth, Cyril M.

**Wylie, Dirk** [joint pseudonym with
Joseph Harold Dockweiler]
See Kummer, Frederic Arnold

**Wylie, Dirk** [joint pseudonym with
Joseph Harold Dockweiler and Cyril
M. Kornbluth]
See Pohl, Frederik

**Wylie, Francis E[rnest]** 1905- [CA]
*American author*
* Wylie, Jeff

**Wylie, I. A. R.**
See Wylie, Ida Alexa Ross

**Wylie, Ida Alexa Ross** 1885-
[LC, TC]
*Australian-born author*
* Wylie, I. A. R.

**Wylie, James** 1875- ? [LAO]
*British barrister and author*
* Worne, John

**Wylie, James Renwick** 1861-1951
[BE]
*American baseball player*
* Wylie, Ren

**Wylie, Jeff**
See Wylie, Francis E[rnest]

**Wylie, Julian**
See Samuelson, Julian

**Wylie, Lauri**
See Samuelson, Morris Laurence

**Wylie, Ren**
See Wylie, James Renwick

**Wylie, Wiggy**
See Wylie, William Vance

**Wylie, William Vance** 1928- [CEI]
*Canadian-born hockey player*
* Wylie, Wiggy

**Wyllie, George Ralston** 1921-
[ART]
*Scottish sculptor*
* G. R. W.

**Wylwynne, Kythe**
See Hyland, M. E. F.

**Wyman, Jane**
See Fulks, Sarah Jane

**Wyman, Marc**
See Howith, Harry

**Wyman, Walter Forestus** 1881- ?
[NAA]
*American author*
* Chapman, John
* Johnson, H. B.
* Maxwell, Herbert M.
* Witherspoon, J. J.

**Wymark, Patrick**
See Cheesman, Patrick

**Wyn, A. A.**
See Weinstein, Aaron

**Wyn, Marjery**
See Yeomans, Marjery

**Wynd, Oswald [Morris]** 1913-
[AW, CA, WW]
*Scottish author*
* Black, Gavin

**Wynder, Mavis Areta**
See Winder, Mavis Areta

**Wyndham, [Sir] Charles**
See Culverwell, Charles

**Wyndham, Esther**
See Lutyens, Mary

**Wyndham, J.** [PA]
*Author*
* Merry, Doctor

**Wyndham, John**
*See* Harris, John [Wyndham Parkes Lucas] Beynon

**Wyndham, Lee**
*See* Hyndman, Jane Andrews [Lee]

**Wyndham, Poppy**
*See* Mackay, Elsie

**Wyndham, Robert**
*See* Hyndman, Robert Utley

**Wyndham, [Sir] William**
1687-1740 [SN]
*British statesman*
* Wildfire

**Wynegar, Butch**
*See* Wynegar, Harold Delano, Jr.

**Wynegar, Harold Delano, Jr.**
1956- [SMG, WWB]
*American baseball player*
* Wynegar, Butch

**Wyner, Yehudi**
*See* Weiner, Yehudi

**Wynette, Tammy**
*See* Pugh, Wynette

**Wynn, Alfred**
*See* Brewer, Fredric [Aldwyn]

**Wynn, Cannon**
*See* Wynn, James Sherman [Jim]

**Wynn, Charles**
*See* Weinberg, Charles

**Wynn, Doris**
*See* Rink, Doris

**Wynn, Early** 1920-
[B10, DGS, PB]
*American baseball player*
* Wynn, Gus

**Wynn, Ed**
*See* Leopold, Isaiah Edwin

**Wynn, Gus**
*See* Wynn, Early

**Wynn, James Sherman [Jim]** 1942-
[BE, PB, SMG]
*American baseball player*
* [The] Toy Cannon
* Wynn, Cannon

**Wynn, May**
*See* Hickey, Donna Lee

**Wynn, Roberta Lee** ?-1978 [FIR]
*Acrobatic dancer*
* [The] Dancing Doll of the South

**Wynne, Anthony**
*See* Wilson, Robert McNair

**Wynne, Brian**
*See* Garfield, Brian [Francis] Wynne

**Wynne, Frank**
*See* Garfield, Brian [Francis] Wynne

**Wynne, May**
*See* Knowles, Mabel Winifred

**Wynne, May**
*See* May, Winifred Jean

**Wynne, Pamela**
*See* Scott, Winifred Mary

**Wynne-Tyson, Esme** 1898-
[AW, CA]
*British author, journalist, playwright*
* Amanda
* De Morny, Peter
* Diotima

**Wynne-Tyson, [Timothy] Jon [Lyden]**
1924- [CA]
*British author*
* Fourest, Michel
* Pitt, Jeremy

**Wynter, Andrew** [PA]
*Author*
* Werdna, Retnyw

**Wynter, Dagmar** 1930?- [FC]
*British actress*
* Wynter, Dana

**Wynter, Dana**
*See* Wynter, Dagmar

**Wynter, Sylvia** 1932?- [CW]
*Cuban-born critic, playwright, author*
* Carew, Wynter

**Wynyard, Diana**
*See* Cox, Dorothy Isobel

**Wynyard, Talbot**
*See* Hamilton, Charles Harold St. John

**Wyre, Alfred** 20th c. [BBH]
*American athletic trainer*
* Wyre, Duke

**Wyre, Duke**
*See* Wyre, Alfred

**Wysbar, Franz** 1899-1967
[FD, FDG, WEF]
*German director*
* Wisbar, Frank

**Wyse, Henry Washington** 1918-
[BE, PB]
*American baseball player*
* Wyse, Hooks

**Wyse, Hooks**
*See* Wyse, Henry Washington

**Wyseman, Demetrius**
*See* Dicke [or Duke?], Willis

**Wyshner, Peter J.** 1917-
*American baseball player*
* Gray, Pete

**Wysong, Biff**
*See* Wysong, Harlin

**Wysong, Harlin** 1905-1951 [BE]
*American baseball player*
* Wysong, Biff

**Wyspianski, Stanislaw** 1869-1907
[MWD]
*Polish poet and playwright*
* [The] Creator of Modern Polish Drama

**Wytske**
*See* Nederveen Hendriks, Wietske

**Wyvill, Fanny Susan** [FFF]
*American poet*
* Brook, Fanshawe

**Wyvis, Ben**
*See* Munro, [Macfarlane] Hugh

**Wyzewski, Theodore** 1862-1917
[BBD]
*Polish-born musicologist*
* De Wyzewa, Theodore

# X

**X.**
*See* Budgell, Eustace

**X**
*See* Fawkes, Frank Attfield

**X**
*See* Fox-Davies, Arthur Charles

**X**
*See* Raymond, William Lee

**X.**
*See* Vivian, Herbert

**X. L.**
*See* Field, Julian Osgood

**X 22**
*See* Magriel, Paul

**X. Y. Z.**
*See* De Quincey, Thomas

**Xanrof, Leon**
*See* Forneau, Leon

**Xanthopalus**
*See* Callistus, Nicephorus

**Xanthus, Xavier**
*See* Laumer, March

**Xariffa**
*See* Townsend, Mary Ashely [Van Voorhis]

**Xavier**
*See* Boniface, Joseph Xavier

**Xavier, [Father]**
*See* Hurwood, Bernhardt J[ackson]

**Xavier, Adro**
*See* Rey-Stolle, Alejandro

**Xavier, Francis**
*See* Fish, Horace

**Xavier, Francis [or Francisco]**
1506-1552 [DNNS, FFF, HN]
*Spanish missionary*
* [The] Apostle of the Indies

**Xenette**
*See* Vinning, Pamelia S.

**Xenophon** 4th c. BC
[DEP, RH, SN]
*Greek historian*
* [The] Attic Muse
* [The] Muse of Greece
* [The] Syren of Antiquity

**Xenophon XIII**
*See* Maurras,
Charles-Marie-Photius

**Xerxes I** 5th c. BC [WBD]
*King of Persia*
* [The] Great

**Xixx, [Ms.] Jezebel Q.**
*See* Borgmann, Dmitri A[lfred]

**Xylander, Wilhelm**
*See* Holtzmann, Wilhelm

# Y

**Y. O.**
See Russell, George William

**Y. S. L.**
See Saint Laurent, Yves [Henri Donat Mathieu]

**Y. Y.**
See Lynd, Robert

**Yabes, Leopoldo Y[abes]** 1912-
[CA]
*Philippine author and editor*
* Christian, A. B.
* Ibarra, Crisostomo
* Silangan, Manuel

**Yablok, Indian**
See Yablok, Julius

**Yablok, Julius** 20th c.   [EJS]
*American football player*
* Yablok, Indian

**Yablonski, Jock**
See Yablonski, Joseph A.

**Yablonski, Joseph A.** 1910-1969
*American labor leader*
* Yablonski, Jock

**Yacconetti, Carlo** 20th c.   [SG]
*Boxer*
* Duane, Carl

**Yack, Baby**
See Yack, Norman

**Yack, Norman** 20th c.   [BBH]
*Boxer*
* Yack, Baby

**Yaeger, Bart**
See Strung, Norman

**Yaffe, Kadish** 1897-   [NAA]
*Polish-born journalist*
* Jaffe, Charles
* Kadish, I.

**Yaffe, Morris** 1921-   [ITA]
*American producer, director, actor*
* Barr, Anthony

**Yaffe, Richard** 1903-   [CA]
*American journalist*
* Chanan, Ben

**Yager, Anna** 1879-1954
[BBD, BEW]
*Austrian-born opera singer*
* Scheff, Friederike
* Scheff, Fritzi

**Yaho**
See Kitabatake, Miyo

**Yahsin-che [Dumb Walking Man]**
See Chiang Yee

**Yakobson, Helen B[ates]** 1913-
[CA]
*Russian-born American educator and author*
* Bates, Helen L. Z.

**Yakoub Beg** 19th c.   [DHA]
*Led revolt against China in Kashgar*
* Attalik Ghazi

**Yakovlev, Aleksandr Ivanovich**
1812-1870   [WBD]
*Russian author*
* Herzen [or Hertzen], Aleksandr Ivanovich
* Iskander

**Yakub, Tasnim**
See Memon, Fahmida

**Yakumo, Koizumi**
See Hearn, [Patricios] Lafcadio [Tessima Carlos]

**Yale, Ad**
See Yale, William M.

**Yale, Frankie**
See Uale, Frank

**Yale, William M.** 1870-1948   [BE]
*American baseball player*
* Yale, Ad

**Yallup, Pat** 1929-   [ART]
*South African-born painter and graphic designer*
* Harvey, Pat

**Yama**
See Sur, Atul Krishna

**Yamaguchi, Gogen** 1909-   [OCS]
*Japanese karate expert*
* [The] Cat

**Yamasaki, Takeo** 1905-   [IAW]
*Japanese author*
* Shibukawa, Gyo

**Yamashita, Tomoyuki** 1885-1946
[BDW, WWW]
*Japanese army officer*
* [The] Tiger of Malaya
* [The] Tiger of the Philippines

**Yamashita, Tsutomu** 1947-   [BBD]
*Japanese musician*
* Yamash'ta, Stomu

**Yamash'ta, Stomu**
See Yamashita, Tsutomu

**Yamauchi, Tetsu** 20th c.   [RM]
*Musician*
* Tetsu

**Yambo**
See Novelli, Enrico

**Yan**
See Almeida Prado, Joao Fernando

**Yanagimura, Shimpu**
See Verwilghen, A[lbert-] Felix

**Yancey, Estella** 1896-
[BBW, WWJ]
*American singer*
* Yancey, Mama

**Yancey, James Edward [Jimmy]**
1898-1951   [BWW]
*American singer*
* Yancey, Papa

**Yancey, Joseph J., Jr. [Joe]** 1906-
[IBW]
*American track and field coach*
* [The] Coach of Champions

**Yancey, Mama**
See Yancey, Estella

**Yancey, Papa**
See Yancey, James Edward [Jimmy]

**Yancey, William J.** 1904-1971
[MK]
*American baseball player*
* Yancey, Yank

**Yancey, Yank**
See Yancey, William J.

**Yaney, Clyde A.** 1910?-1978
[CWG]
*American country-western performer*
* Yaney, Skeets

**Yaney, Skeets**
See Yaney, Clyde A.

**Yang, C. K.**
See Yang, Chuan-Kwang

**Yang, Chuan-Kwang** 1935-   [TF]
*Formosan track and field athlete*
* Yang, C. K.

**Yang-jen**
See Shu, Austin Chi-wei

**Yanger, Benny**
See Angone, Frank

**[A] Yankee**
See Ingraham, Joseph Holt

**[A] Yankee**
See Mitchell, John Kearsley

**[A] Yankee**
See White, Richard Grant

**[The] Yankee Clipper**
See DeMaggio, Giuseppe Paolo, Jr.

**[The] Yankee Empire Builder**
See Barrow, Edward Grant

**[A] Yankee Farmer**
See Lowell, John

**Yankee Irishman**
See Nowlan, George

**Yankee Jonathan**
See Hastings, Jonathan

**[The] Yankee Killer**
See Lary, Frank Strong

**Yankee, Pat**
See Weigum, Patricia Millicent

**Yanks, Byron** 1928-   [BBD]
*American musician*
* Janis, Byron

**Yanne, Jean**
See Gouye, Jean

**Yannis, Michael**
See Cacoyannis, Michael

**Yannopoulos, Dino**
See Yannopoulos, Konstantin

**Yannopoulos, Konstantin** 20th c.
[OP]
*Greek-born producer and stage-lighting designer*
* Yannopoulos, Dino

**Yanovsky, Basile S.**
See Yanovsky, Vassily Semenovich

**Yanovsky, V. S.**
See Yanovsky, Vassily Semenovich

**Yanovsky, Vassily Semenovich**
1906-   [CA]
*Russian-born American author*
* Yanovsky, Basile S.
* Yanovsky, V. S.

**Yap, Diosdado M.** 1907-   [IAW]
*Filipino-born author*
* Doc

**Yapp, Alexander**   [DEL]
*Author*
* Page, H. A.

**Yapp, Frederick Francis** 1878-1970 [BE]
*American baseball player and manager*
* Mitchell, Frederick Francis

**Yar-Shater [or Yarshater], Ehsan O[llah]** 1920- [CA, IAW]
*Iranian-born educator and author*
* Rahsepar

**Yarborough, Cale**
See Yarborough, William Caleb

**Yarborough, Jim** 20th c.
*American football player*
* Yarborough, Punjab

**Yarborough, Punjab**
See Yarborough, Jim

**Yarborough, William Caleb** 1939-
[IPA]
*American auto racer*
* Yarborough, Cale

**Yardley, Alice** 1913- [IAW]
*British educator and author*
* Young, Angela

**Yarmouth**
See Bailey, Isaac H.

**Yarmouth, Countess of** 18th c.
[SN]
*Mistress of King George II*
* Walmoden

**Yarnall, Rusty**
See Yarnall, Waldo Ward

**Yarnall, Waldo Ward** 1902- [BE]
*American baseball player*
* Yarnall, Rusty

**Yaroslava**
See Mills, Yaroslava Surmach

**Yaroslavsky, Yemelyan**
See Gubelman, Yemelyan

**Yaroslaw, Bernard** 1916- [IPA]
*American radio interviewer*
* Gray, Barry

**Yarosz, Teddy**
See Yarosz, Thaddeus

**Yarosz, Thaddeus** 1910-1974
[WBC]
*American boxer*
* Yarosz, Teddy

**Yarrison, Byron Wardsworth**
1896- [BE]
*American baseball player*
* Yarrison, Rube

**Yarrison, Rube**
See Yarrison, Byron Wardsworth

**Yaryan, Clarence Everett**
1893-1964 [BE]
*American baseball player*
* Yaryan, Yam

**Yaryan, Yam**
See Yaryan, Clarence Everett

**Yashima, Taro**
See Iwamatsu, Jun Atsushi

**Yasin, Erol**
See Ozdenak, Yasin Erol

**Yasin, Khalid**
See Young, Larry

**Yastrzemski, Carl Michael** 1939-
[BE, PB, SMG]
*American baseball player*
* Yaz

**Yates, A. G.**
See Yates, Alan Geoffrey

**Yates, Al[bert Arthur]** 1945- [BE]
*American baseball player*
* Yates, Bunny

**Yates, Alan Geoffrey** 1923- [CA]
*British-born author*
* Brown, Carter
* Yates, A. G.

**Yates, Bill**
See Yates, Floyd Buford

**Yates, Bunny**
See Yates, Al[bert Arthur]

**Yates, Dornford**
See Mercer, Cecil William

**Yates, Edmund Hodgson**
1831-1894 [FFF, PA]
*British author and journalist*
* Flaneur
* Lounger at the Clubs
* Q.

**Yates, Elizabeth** 1905- [CA]
*American author*
* McGreal, Elizabeth

**Yates, Floyd Buford** 1921- [WEC]
*American cartoonist and editor*
* Yates, Bill

**Yates, Frederic B.** 19th c. [PA]
*Author*
* Roscoe, Deane

**Yates, George Worthing** 20th c.
[WW]
*Author*
* Hunt, Peter [joint pseudonym with Charles Hunt Marshall]

**Yates, Mary E.**
See Madigan, Mrs. H. P.

**Yates, Mrs. Benjamin** [FFF]
* Zoe, Mlle.

**Yates, Raymond Francis** 1895-
[NAA]
*American author*
* Pioneer

**Yates, Robert** [FFF]
*American author*
* Rough Hewer

**Yatron, Michael** 1921- [CA]
*American author*
* Sorel, Byron

**Yaukey, Grace S[ydenstricker]**
1899- [ANT, CA, SAT]
*American author*
* Spencer, Cornelia

**Yavits, Doc**
See Yavits, Isadore

**Yavits, Isadore** 20th c. [EJS]
*Basketball player*
* Yavits, Doc

**Yavorska, Lydia**
See De Hubbenet, Lydia

**Yaz**
See Yastrzemski, Carl Michael

**Ybarra, Jose** 1892-1957 [BX, SG]
*American boxer*
* [The] Mexican Wildcat
* Rivers, Joe

**Yeabsley, Bert**
See Yeabsley, Robert Watkins

**Yeabsley, Robert Watkins**
1893-1961 [BE]
*American baseball player*
* Yeabsley, Bert

**Yeager, Buddy**
See Yeager, John

**Yeager, John** 1918- [MY]
*American jazz musician*
* Yeager, Buddy

**Yeager, Joseph F.** 1875-1937 [BE]
*American baseball player*
* Yeager, Little Joe

**Yeager, Little Joe**
See Yeager, Joseph F.

**Yeakley, Marjory Hall** 1908- [CA]
*American author*
* Blair, Lucile
* Hall, Marjory
* Morse, Carol

**Yeamans, Annie**
See Griffiths, Annie

**Yeamans, Eugenia Marguerite**
1862-1906 [BEW]
*Australian-born actress*
* Yeamans, Jennie

**Yeamans, Jennie**
See Yeamans, Eugenia Marguerite

**Yeargin, Grapefruit**
See Yeargin, James Almond [Jim]

**Yeargin, James Almond [Jim]**
1902-1937 [BE]
*American baseball player*
* Yeargin, Grapefruit

**Yearsley, Ann** 1756-1806
[HN, PA]
*British poet*
* Lactilla
* [The] Milkwoman of Bristol
* [The] Poetical Milkmaid

**Yeary, Lee** 1939-
*American actor*
* Majors, Lee

**Yeates, Mabel**
See Pereira, Harold Bertram

**Yeatman, R. J.**
See Yeatman, Robert Julian

**Yeatman, Robert Julian** 1898-1968
[LC]
*British author*
* Yeatman, R. J.

**Yeaton, Charles Kendall** 1911-
[BEW]
*American educator and director*
* Yeaton, Kelly

**Yeaton, Kelly**
See Yeaton, Charles Kendall

**Yeats, W. B.**
See Yeats, William Butler

**Yeats, William Butler** 1865-1939
[LC]
*Irish poet and playwright*
* Yeats, W. B.

**Yeats-Brown, F. C.**
See Yeats-Brown, Francis Charles Claypon

**Yeats-Brown, Francis Charles Claypon** 1886-1944 [LC]
*British author*
* Yeats-Brown, F. C.

**Yeghiayan, Luisa Anais** 1936- [OP]
*French opera singer*
* Bosabalian, Luisa Anais

**Yeh, Wei-lien**
See Yip, Wai-lim

**Yehoash**
See Blumgarten, Solomon

**Yehonala**
See Tzu Hsi [or Tze-hsi]

**Yeiser, Sarah C. [Smith]** [FFF]
*American writer*
* Aunt Charity
* Azelee

**Yeldam, Walter S.** [PA]
*Author*
* Cham, Aliph

**Yellen, Jack**
See Yellen, Selig

**Yellen, Selig** 1892- [BEW]
*Polish-born lyricist and playwright*
* Yellen, Jack

**Yellott, Barbara Leslie** 1915-
[IAW]
*American author and poet*
* Jordan, Barbara Leslie

**[The] Yellow Doctress**
See Seacole, Mary

**Yellow Kid Weil**
See Weil, Joseph R.

**Yellowhorse, Chief**
See Yellowhorse, Moses J.

**Yellowhorse, Moses J.** 1900-1964
[PB]
*American baseball player*
* Yellowhorse, Chief

**Yellowplush, Charles James**
See Thackeray, William Makepeace

**Yen Hui-ch'ing** 1877-1950 [WBD]
*Chinese statesman*
* Yen, W. W.

**Yen, James Y. C.**
See Yen Yang-ch'u

**Yen, W. W.**
See Yen Hui-ch'ing

**Yen Yang-ch'u** 1894- [WBD]
*Chinese scholar*
* Yen, James Y. C.

**Yendys, Sydney**
See Dobell, Sydney

**Yeo-Thomas, Forest Frederick Edward** 1902-1964 [BDW, WWW]
*British intelligence agent*
* Shelley
* White Rabbit

**Yeomans, Louisa**
See King, Louisa Yeomans

**Yeomans, Marjery** 1909- [THR]
*British actress and singer*
* Wyn, Marjery

**Yepremian, Garabed S.** 1944-    [FB]
*Cyprian-born football player*
* Yepremian, Garo

**Yepremian, Garo**
*See* Yepremian, Garabed S.

**Yerby, Frank Garvin** 1916-    [IBW]
*American author*
* King of the Costume Novel

**Yerex, Cuthbert**
*See* Cuthbert, Estella Y.

**Yerke, T. B.**
*See* Yerke, Theodore Bruce

**Yerke, Theodore Bruce** 20th c.
[WGT]
*Author*
* Fassbinder, Carlton J.
* Yerke, T. B.

**Yerkes, Charles Carroll** 1903-1950
[BE]
*American baseball player*
* Yerkes, Lefty

**Yerkes, Lefty**
*See* Yerkes, Charles Carroll

**Yerrick, William John** 1873-1936
[BE]
*American baseball player*
* Banks, William John [Bill]

**Yerushalmi, Chaim**
*See* Lipschitz, [Rabbi] Chaim U.

**Yerushalmi, Gershon**
*See* Harkavy, Zvi

**Yerxa, Leroy** 1915-1946
[ESF, SFP, WGT]
*American writer*
* Arno, Elroy
* Blade, Alexander [house
   pseudonym, Ziff-Davis]
* Casey, Richard [house
   pseudonym, Ziff-Davis]

**Yewcic, Kibby**
*See* Yewcic, Thomas J. [Tom]

**Yewcic, Thomas J. [Tom]** 1932-
[BE]
*American baseball player*
* Yewcic, Kibby

**Yewrownckie, Aunt**
*See* Blinn, Mrs. Henry G.

**Yexley, Lionel**
*See* Woods, James

**[The] Yiddish Curver**
*See* Pelty, Barney

**[The] Yiddish Mark Twain**
*See* Zevin, Israel Joseph

**[The] Yiddish Sarah Bernhardt**
*See* Simon, Mae

**[Der] Yiddisher Vild-Kat**
*See* Loeb, Albert Lorch

**Yifter, Miruts** 20th c.
*Ethiopian track and field athlete*
* Yifter the Shifter

**Yifter the Shifter**
*See* Yifter, Miruts

**Yigal the Printer**
*See* Hurvitz, Yigal

**Yin, Leslie Charles Bowyer** 1907-
[CC, EMD, LC]
*Chinese-born author*
* Charteris, Leslie
* Taylor, Bruce

**Yingling, Chink**
*See* Yingling, Earl Hershey

**Yingling, Earl Hershey** 1888-1962
[BE]
*American baseball player*
* Yingling, Chink

**Yingst, Henry Z.** 1924-    [CWG]
*American country-western performer*
* Zack, Jimmie

**Yip, Wai-lim** 1937-    [CA]
*Chinese-born educator, author, poet*
* Yeh, Wei-lien

**Yizhar, S.**
*See* Smilansky, Yizhar

**Ylla**
*See* Koffler, Camilla

**Ynetchi, Paul**
*See* Ryder, Elliot

**[The] Yodeling Cowgirl**
*See* Blevins, Rubye

**[The] Yodeling Ranger**
*See* Snow, Clarence Eugene

**Yodeling Slim Clark**
*See* Clark, Raymond Le Roy

**Yoelson, Asa** 1886-1950
[BDF, BEW, EMT]
*American singer and actor*
* Jolson, Al

**Yoffe, Shlomo**
*See* Yoffe, Solomon

**Yoffe, Solomon** 1909-    [IWM]
*Israeli composer*
* Yoffe, Shlomo

**Yogiji, Harbhajan Singh Khalsa**
1929-    [CA]
*Indian-born religious leader and
author*
* Bhajan, Yogi

**Yokely, Laymon Samuel** 1906-
[MK]
*American baseball player*
* Yokely, Norman

**Yokely, Norman**
*See* Yokely, Laymon Samuel

**Yoki**
*See* King, Yolanda

**Yong-Tching** 1677?-1735    [SN]
*Emperor of China*
* [The] Immortal

**Yonge, Remington**
*See* Doherty, Robert R.

**Yoo, Grace S.**
*See* Yoo, Young H[yun]

**Yoo, Young H[yun]** 1927-    [CA]
*Korean-born librarian and author*
* Yoo, Grace S.

**Yorick**
*See* Ferrigni, Pietro C.

**Yorick**
*See* Hodgson, Ralph

**Yorick**
*See* Ivens, Michael William

**Yorick**
*See* Ward, James Warner

**Yorick, A. P.**
*See* Tindall, William York

**Yorick, Mr.**
*See* Sterne, Laurence

**York, Amanda**
*See* Dial, Joan

**York and Albany, Duke of**
*See* Frederick Augustus

**York, Andrew**
*See* Nicole, Christopher Robin

**York, Anton**
*See* Zagat, Arthur Leo

**York, Cardinal**
*See* Stuart, Henry Benedict Maria
Clemens

**York, James E.** 1895-    [BE]
*American baseball player*
* York, Lefty

**York, Jeremy**
*See* Creasey, John

**York, Lefty**
*See* York, James E.

**York, Simon**
*See* Heinlein, Robert A[nson]

**York, Wesley Simon**
*See* Platt, Kin

**Yorke, Carol**
*See* Bjorkman, Carol

**Yorke, Carras**
*See* Marshall, Arthur C.

**Yorke, Edith**
*See* Byard, Edithe

**Yorke, Henry Vincent** 1905-1974
[EWL, LC, TC1]
*British author*
* Green, Henry

**Yorke, Margaret**
*See* Nicholson, Margaret Beda
[Larminie]

**Yorke, Oliver, Esq.**
*See* Mahony, Francis

**Yorke, Onslow**
*See* Dixon, William Hepworth

**Yorke, Philip [First Earl of
Hardwicke]** 1690-1764    [SN]
*British jurist*
* Gripus, Judge

**Yorke, Roger**
*See* Bingley, David Ernest

**Yorke, Susan**
*See* Telenga, Suzette

**Yorkel, Hans**
*See* Hall, Abraham Oakey

**Yorkin, Alan** 1926-    [FC, FD, ITA]
*American director*
* Yorkin, Bud

**Yorkin, Bud**
*See* Yorkin, Alan

**Yorkist**
*See* Morrah, Dermot [Michael
Macgregor]

**York's Tall Son**
*See* Porter, William Trotter

**[The] Yorkshire Lad**
*See* Foy, Tom

**[The] Yorkshire Ripper**
*See* Sutcliffe, Peter

**Yoseloff, Thomas** 1913-    [CA]
*American author*
* Young, Thomas

**Yoshikawa, Takeo** 20th c.    [EE]
*Japanese intelligence agent*
* Morimura, Tadasi

**Yoshinobu**
*See* Hitotsubashi

**Yoshkin, Nicolai** 1907-    [FC]
*Russian actor*
* Kosleck, Martin

**Yosimura, Huyukiko**
*See* Terada, Torahiko

**Yost, Charles W.** 1908?-1981
*American diplomat*
* [The] Gray Ghost

**Yost, Edward Frederick Joseph**
1926-    [BE, SMG]
*American baseball player and coach*
* [The] Walking Man

**Yost, Fielding H.** 1871-1946
[AS, FB]
*American football coach*
* Yost, Hurry Up

**Yost, Herbert A.** 1880-1945
*American actor*
* O'Moore, Barry

**Yost, Hurry Up**
*See* Yost, Fielding H.

**You, Dominique** 1775-1830    [FFF]
*Pirate*
* Johnness

**Youd, C. S.**
*See* Youd, Christopher Samuel

**Youd, Christopher Samuel** 1922-
[CA, DLE, SF]
*British author*
* Christopher, John
* Ford, Hilary
* Godfrey, William
* Graaf, Peter
* Nichols, Peter
* Rye, Anthony
* Vine, William
* Youd, C. S.

**[The] Young**
*See* Fulk V

**[The] Young**
*See* Louis II [or Ludwig]

**[The] Young**
*See* Louis VII

**Young, A. S.**
*See* Young, Andrew Sturgeon
Nash

**Young, Ado**
*See* Young, M. Adrian

**[The] Young Adventurer**
*See* Stuart, Charles Edward Louis
Philip Casimir

**Young, Agatha**
*See* Young, Agnes [Brooks]

**Young, Agnes [Brooks]** 1898-1974 [B10]
*American author*
* Young, Agatha

**Young, Alan**
*See* Young, Angus

**Young, Alexander**
*See* Youngs, Basil Alexander

**[A] Young American**
*See* Slidell, Alexander

**[The] Young American Roscius**
*See* Cowell, Sam

**[The] Young and Happy Husband**
*See* Dowty, A. A.

**Young, Andrew Jackson, Jr.** 1932-
*American diplomat*
* Motor Mouth

**Young, Andrew Sturgeon Nash** 1924- [LBA]
*American author and editor*
* Young, A. S.
* Young, Doc

**Young, Angela**
*See* Yardley, Alice

**Young, Angus** 1919-
[FC, ITA, SW]
*British-born actor*
* Young, Alan

**[The] Young Apollo**
*See* Shakespeare, William

**Young, Austin** 1885?-1954? [NOJ]
*American jazz musician*
* Young, Boots

**Young, Babe**
*See* Young, Norman Robert

**Young Barney Aaron**
*See* Aaron, Barney

**Young, Billie** 1936- [CA]
*American author*
* Ashe, Penelope [joint pseudonym]

**Young, Billy**
*See* D'Arcy, Colin

**Young Blood Russell**
*See* Russell, William Ellis [Bill]

**Young, Boots**
*See* Young, Austin

**Young, Buddy**
*See* Young, Claude H.

**Young, Bull**
*See* Young, John W.

**Young, Candy**
*See* Young, Canzetta

**Young, Canzetta** 1963- [IBW]
*American track and field athlete*
* Young, Candy

**Young, Carter Travis**
*See* Charbonneau, Louis [Henry]

**Young, Catfish**
*See* Young, Granville

**Young, Catherine**
*See* Klinckerfuss, Ingabor Katrine

**Young, Charles A.** 1865-1951 [AS]
*American trapshooter*
* Young, Sparrow

**Young, Charlie** 1951- [IBW]
*American football player*
* Young, Tree

**Young, Chesley Virginia** 1919-
[CA]
*American author*
* Barnes, Chesley Virginia

**[The] Young Chevalier**
*See* Stuart, Charles Edward Louis Philip Casimir

**Young, Chic**
*See* Young, Murat Bernard

**Young, Clarence** [house pseudonym]
[Stratemeyer Syndicate]
*See* Stratemeyer, Edward L.

**Young, Claude H.** 1926- [FB]
*American football player*
* Young, Buddy

**Young, Collier**
*See* Bloch, Robert [Albert]

**[The] Young Cub**
*See* Fox, Charles James

**Young, Cy**
*See* Young, Denton True

**Young Cy**
*See* Young, Irving Melrose

**Young, Denton True** 1867-1955
[AS, IPA, OCS]
*American baseball player*
* Young, Cy

**Young, Doc**
*See* Young, Andrew Sturgeon Nash

**Young, Donnie** .
*See* Lytle, Donald

**Young, Dorothea Bennett** 1924-
[CA]
*British author*
* Bennett, Dorothea

**Young, Duke**
*See* Young, John Thomas

**Young, E. H.**
*See* Young, Emily Hilda

**Young, Edward**
*See* Reinfeld, Fred

**Young, Edward** 1683-1765 [SN]
*British poet*
* [The] Hoary Bard of Night

**Young, Edward** 20th c. [OBW]
*American baseball player*
* Young, Pep

**Young, Eileen** 20th c. [ART]
*British artist*
* E. Y.

**Young, Elaine L.**
*See* Schulte, Elaine L[ouise]

**Young, Elizabeth Jane** 1910- [F2]
*American actress*
* Blane, Sally

**Young, Emily Hilda** 1880-1949
[LC]
*British author*
* Young, E. H.

**Young, Eric Brett** 20th c.
[CC, WW]
*Author*
* Leacroft, Eric

**Young, Ernest A.** 20th c. [WW]
*Author*
* Rockwood, Harry

**Young, Eugene Edward** 1919-
[EJ, NP, WWJ]
*American jazz musician*
* Young, Rabbit
* Young, Snookie

**Young, Everett**
*See* Cosby, Yvonne Shepard

**Young, Faron** 1932- [ECM]
*American country-western performer*
* [The] Sheriff

**Young, Fay**
*See* Young, Frank A.

**Young, Frank A.** 20th c.
[IBW, OBW]
*American sportswriter and baseball player*
* [The] Dean of Black Sportswriters
* Young, Fay

**Young, Frank W.**
*See* Young, Fred W.

**Young, Fred W.** 20th c. [MBF]
*British author*
* Arnold, Frank
* Newcome, Colin
* Scott, Hedley
* Wyatt, Ben
* Young, Frank W.

**Young, G. M.**
*See* Young, George Malcolm

**Young, George** 1910-1972 [CSH]
*Canadian swimmer*
* [The] Catalina Kid

**Young, George Malcolm** 1882-1959 [LC]
*British author*
* Young, G. M.

**Young, Gig**
*See* Barr, Byron Ellsworth

**Young, Gladys** ?-1975 [NN]
*Actress*
* [The] First Lady of the Air

**Young, Granville** [WWJ]
*American jazz musician*
* Young, Catfish

**Young, Gretchen Michaela** 1913-
[BDF, F1, FC]
*American actress*
* Young, Loretta

**Young, Harley E.** 20th c. [SR]
*American baseball player*
* Cy the Third

**Young, Harold** 1881-1936 [SC]
*American actor*
* North, Bob

**[A] Young Hercules**
*See* Sheridan, Richard Brinsley

**Young Hickory**
*See* Pierce, Franklin

**Young Hickory**
*See* Tyler, John

**Young Hickory**
*See* Van Buren, Martin

**[The] Young Horace**
*See* Jonson, Ben[jamin]

**Young Hotspur**
*See* Ingersoll, Ralph Isaacs

**Young, Irving Melrose** 1877-1935
[BE]
*American baseball player*
* Cy the Second
* Young Cy

**[The] Young Isis**
*See* Cleopatra

**Young Jack Hearne**
*See* Hearne, John William

**Young Jack Thompson**
*See* Thompson, Cecil Lewis

**Young, James Osborne** 1912-
[EJ, PMJ, WWJ]
*American jazz musician*
* Young, Trummy [or Trummie]

**Young, Jan[et Randall]** 1919-
[CA, SAT, WD]
*American author*
* Randall, Janet [joint pseudonym with Robert W(illiam) Young]

**Young, Jesse Colin**
*See* Miller, Perry

**Young, Jessica May Brewer** 20th c.
[NAA]
*American poet*
* Young, Jessica Morehead

**Young, Jessica Morehead**
*See* Young, Jessica May Brewer

**Young Joe Shugrue**
*See* Shugrue, Joe

**Young Joe Wright**
*See* Wright, Joseph, Jr.

**Young, John** 1773-1837 [FFF, PA]
*Canadian writer*
* Agricola

**Young, John O. [Johnny]**
1918-1974 [BWW]
*American singer*
* Young, Man

**Young, John Russell** 1840-1899
[FFF]
*American journalist*
* Bizarre

**Young, John Thomas** 1949- [SMG]
*American baseball player*
* Young, Duke

**Young, John W.** ?-1913 [SC]
*American boxer and actor*
* Young, Bull

**Young, Johnny** 1943- [BWW]
*American singer*
* Taylor, Johnny Lamar
* Taylor, Little Johnny

**Young, Joseph** ?-1888 [FFF]
*American master of many trades and professions*
* [The] Learned Weaver

**Young, Joseph** 1927- [BWW]
*American singer*
* Young, Mighty Joe

**[The] Young Juvenal**
*See* Lodge, Thomas

**Young Juvenal**
*See* Nash [or Nashe?], Thomas

**Young Klondyke**
*See* Moore, Harry R.

**Young, Larry** 1940-1978
[EJ7, IBW]
*American jazz musician*
* Yasin, Khalid

**Young, Lee**
*See* Young, Leonidas Raymond

**Young, Lemuel Floyd** 1907-1962
[BE]
*American baseball player*
* Young, Pep

**Young, Leonidas Raymond** 1917-
[EJ, PMJ, WWJ]
*American jazz musician*
* Young, Lee

**Young, Lester Willis** 1909-1959
[DAM, EJ, IBW]
*American jazz musician*
* [The] Father of Modern Jazz
* Young, Prez

**Young, Loretta**
*See* Young, Gretchen Michaela

**Young, M. Adrian** 1946- [FB]
*Irish-born football player*
* Young, Ado

**Young, Man**
*See* Young, John O. [Johnny]

**Young, Marian**
*See* Deane, Martha

**[The] Young Marshal**
*See* Chang Hsueh-liang

**Young, Martha** 20th c. [ALY]
*American author*
* Sheppard, Eli

**Young, Mary Elizabeth** 1901?-1981
*American columnist*
* Haworth, Mary

**Young, Mighty Joe**
*See* Young, Joseph

**Young, Mrs. Duncan** [FFF]
*Entertainer*
* Braham, Leonora

**Young, Mrs. Edwin** [FFF]
*Entertainer*
* Van Tassell, Cora

**Young, Murat Bernard** 1901-1973
[CA]
*American cartoonist*
* Young, Chic

**Young, Nacella**
*See* Tate, Velma

**Young, Nedrick**
*See* Bessie, Alvah

**Young, Noel** 1922- [CA]
*American author*
* Elder, Leon

**Young, Norma** 1889-1974 [SC]
*Actress*
* Prudence Penny

**Young, Norman Robert** 1915- [BE]
*American baseball player*
* Young, Babe

**Young, Patricia Helena** 1922-
[IAW]
*British author*
* Ross, Helena

**Young, Pep**
*See* Young, Edward

**Young, Pep**
*See* Young, Lemuel Floyd

**Young, Pep**
*See* Young, Ralph

**Young, Pep**
*See* Young, William P.

**Young, Percy M[arshall]** 1912-
[CA]
*British author*
* Marshall, Percy

**[The] Young Pretender**
*See* Stuart, Charles Edward Louis
Philip Casimir

**Young, Prez**
*See* Young, Lester Willis

**Young, R.** [PA]
*Author*
* Guyon

**Young, Rabbit**
*See* Young, Eugene Edward

**Young, Ralph** 1890-1965
*American baseball player*
* Young, Pep

**Young, Raymond A.**
*See* Jones, Vernon

**Young, Robert**
*See* Payne, [Pierre Stephen]
Robert

**Young, Robert W[illiam] [Bob]**
1916-1969 [CA, SAT]
*American author*
* Randall, Janet [joint pseudonym
with Jan(et Randall) Young]

**[The] Young Roscius**
*See* Betty, William Henry West

**Young, Rose**
*See* Harris, Marion Rose [Young]

**Young, Sammy** 1874- ? [THR]
*Scottish comedian*
* Shields, Sammy

**Young, Samuel** ?-1854 [PA]
*Author*
* Wall Street Bear in Europe

**Young Sanford Houpe**
*See* Houpe, Sanford

**Young, Snookie**
*See* Young, Eugene Edward

**Young, Sparrow**
*See* Young, Charles A.

**Young, Stephen**
*See* Levy, Stephen

**Young, Stewart**
*See* Burrage, Alfred McLelland

**Young Subtlety**
*See* Fiennes, Nathaniel

**Young, Sugar Bear**
*See* Young, Willie Lull

**[The] Young Swan**
*See* Chenier, Andre Marie de

**Young, Terry**
*See* Samperi, Anthony

**Young, Thomas**
*See* Yoseloff, Thomas

**Young Tom Morris**
*See* Morris, Thomas, Jr.

**Young, Tree**
*See* Young, Charlie

**Young, Trummy [or Trummie]**
*See* Young, James Osborne

**[The] Young 'Un**
*See* Burnham George P.

**Young, Waddy**
*See* Young, Walter R.

**Young, Walter R.** 1916-1945
[AS, FB]
*American football player*
* Young, Waddy

**Young, Warwick**
*See* Parsons, B.

**Young, Welton** 20th c. [RO1]
*American singer and songwriter*
* Dean

**Young, Will**
*See* Home-Gall, William
Bolinbroke

**Young, William P.** 20th c. [OBW]
*American baseball player*
* Young, Pep

**Young Willie Dunn**
*See* Dunn, Willie

**Young, Willie Lull** 1943- [SMG]
*American football player*
* Young, Sugar Bear

**[The] Young Wolf**
*See* Jenkins, Gus

**Young Zoilus**
*See* Dennis, John

**[The] Young Zulu Kid**
*See* Dimelfi, Giuseppe

**Youngberg, Norma Ione [Rhoads]**
1896- [CA]
*American author*
* Winfield, Leigh

**Youngblood, Arthur Clyde**
1900-1968 [BE]
*American baseball player*
* Youngblood, Chief

**Youngblood, Chief**
*See* Youngblood, Arthur Clyde

**[The] Younger**
*See* Cato, Marcus Porcius

**[The] Younger**
*See* Danton, Jean Pierre

**[The] Younger**
*See* James

**[The] Younger**
*See* Justin II

**[The] Younger**
*See* Medici, Lorenzo de

**[The] Younger**
*See* Pliny [Gaius Plinius Caecilius
Secundus]

**[The] Younger**
*See* Pompeius Magnus, Sextus

**[The] Younger**
*See* Scipio Aemilianus Africanus
Numantinus, Publius Cornelius

**[The] Younger**
*See* Teniers, David

**[The] Younger**
*See* Tintoretto, Domenico

**[The] Younger Brother of
Oehlenschlaeger**
*See* Grundtvig, Nikolai Frederik
Saverni

**Younger, Cole**
*See* Younger, Thomas Coleman

**Younger, Elizabeth** 1913-
[AW, CC]
*British author*
* Hely, Elizabeth

**Younger, John Leo** 1912?-1962
[BEW]
*Theatrical performer*
* Grant, Barney

**Younger, Paul** 1928- [FB, SMG]
*American football player*
* Younger, Tank

**[The] Younger Pitt**
*See* Pitt, William

**Younger, Tank**
*See* Younger, Paul

**Younger, Thomas Coleman**
1844-1916 [B10]
*American outlaw*
* Younger, Cole

**Younger, William Anthony**
1917-1962 [CC, WW]
*Scottish poet and author*
* Mole, William

**[The] Youngest Interlocutor in the
World**
*See* Thomas, Lillian

**Youngs, Basil Alexander** 1920-
[OP]
*British opera singer*
* Young, Alexander

**Youngs, John** 1951?-
*American actor*
* Savage, John

**Youngs, Joseph, Jr.** 1870-1948
[AS, BX, RBE]
*American boxer*
* Ryan, Tommy

**Youngs, Pep**
*See* Youngs, Ross Middlebrook

**Youngs, Ross Middlebrook**
1897-1927 [BAB, CBS, DGS]
*American baseball player*
* Cobb, Ty, Jr.
* Youngs, Pep

**Youngstrom, Adolph F.** 1897-1968
[FB]
*American football player*
* Youngstrom, Swede

**Youngstrom, Swede**
*See* Youngstrom, Adolph F.

**Yount, Ducky**
*See* Yount, Herbert M.

**Yount, Herbert M.** 1889- [BE]
*American baseball player*
* Yount, Ducky

**Your Gospel Singer**
*See* MacHugh, Edward

**Yourcenar, Marguerite**
*See* De Crayencour, Marguerite

**Youssef-Ahmabadabi, Henry** 1949-
[SMG]
*Iranian-born football player*
* Abadi, Henry

**[The] Youth**
*See* Almagro, Diego de

**Yowa**
*See* McMurray, Nancy
A[rmistead]

**Yowell, Carl Columbus** 1902-    [BE]
*American baseball player*
* Yowell, Sundown

**Yowell, Sundown**
*See* Yowell, Carl Columbus

**Yowlachie, Chief**
*See* Simmons, Daniel

**Yoxall, Harry W[aldo]** 1896-    [CA]
*British author*
* Partington, F. H.

**Yrjo-Koskinen, Yrjo Sakari**
*See* Forsman, Georg Zachris

**Yu, Charles**
*See* Torgownik, William

**Yu Jih-chang** 1882-1936    [WBD]
*Chinese Christian leader*
* Yui, David Z. T.

**Yui, David Z. T.**
*See* Yu Jih-chang

**Yuki**
*See* Inoue, Yukitoshi

**Yukteswar Sri Babajhan, [Yogi]**
*See* Douglas, John Lee

**Yule, Joe, Jr.** 1920-
[ASC,  BDF,  FC]
*American actor*
* McGuire, Mickey
* Rooney, Mickey

**Yuma, Dan**
*See* Dunham, Robert [Bob]

**Yun, Mu**
*See* Fee, Benjamin J.

**Yunkel, Ramar**
*See* Martin, Jose L[uis]

**Yuriko**
*See* Amemiya, Yuriko

**Yurka, Blanche**
*See* Jurka, Blanche

**Yuro, Rosemarie** 1941-    [RO1]
*American singer*
* Yuro, Timi

**Yuro, Timi**
*See* Yuro, Rosemarie

**Yusolfsky, John Gary** 1937-
[FC,  HT]
*American actor*
* Lockwood, Gary

**Yussel the Muscle**
*See* Jacobs, Joe

**Yusuke, Suga** 1942-    [WFA]
*Chinese-born hairstylist*
* Suga

**Yvaral**
*See* Vasarely, Jean-Pierre

**Yvars, Sal**
*See* Yvars, Salvador Anthony

**Yvars, Salvador Anthony** 1924-
[BE]
*American baseball player*
* Yvars, Sal

**Yver, Colette**
*See* Huzard, Antoinette

**Yves of Brittany** 1253-1303    [WBD]
*Saint*
* [L']Avocat des Pauvres

# Z

**Z**
See  Jefferys, William Hamilton

**Z.**
See  Moore, Hannah

**Z.**
See  Prosner, G. W.

**Z.**
See  Zetti, Italo

**[The] Z Man**
See  Zanders, Emanuel

**Z. P.**
See  Mansfield, L. W.

**Z. Z.**
See  Zangwill, Louis

**[The] Za Zu Girl**
See  Spivey, Elton Island

**Zabache, Wladimiro Bas** 1929-
[EJ]
*Spanish jazz musician*
* Vlady

**Zabel, George W.** 1891-1970   [AS]
*American baseball player*
* Zabel, Zip

**Zabel, Steve G.** 1948-   [FB]
*American football player*
* Zabel, Zabe

**Zabel, Zabe**
See  Zabel, Steve G.

**Zabel, Zip**
See  Zabel, George W.

**Zabelle, Flora**
See  Mangasarian, Flora

**Zabotin, Colonel** 20th c.   [EE]
*Russian intelligence agent*
* Grant

**Zabriskie, F. N.**   [PA]
*Author*
* Old Colony

**Zabunyan, Serkis** 1938-   [CAR]
*Turkish artist*
* Sarkis

**Zac, Pino**
See  Zaccaria, Pino

**Zaccaria, Nicola Angelo**
See  Zachariou, Nicolas Angelos

**Zaccaria, Pino** 1930-   [WEC]
*Italian cartoonist and animator*
* Zac, Pino

**Zacchini, Edmondo** 1894?-1981
*Italian-born circus clown*
* Zacchini, Papa

**Zacchini, Papa**
See  Zacchini, Edmondo

**Zachak, Anna** 1897-1973   [SC]
*Hungarian-born actress*
* Grey, Olga

**Zacharias, Basileios** 1850-1936
[CBS]
*Turkish-born British financier and munitions manufacturer*
* Zaharoff, Basil

**Zacharias, Lee**
See  Zacharias, Lela Ann

**Zacharias, Lela Ann** 1944-   [CA]
*American author*
* Zacharias, Lee

**Zachariou, Nicolas Angelos** 1923-
[OP]
*Greek opera singer*
* Zaccaria, Nicola Angelo

**Zachary, Albert Myron** 1917-   [BE]
*American baseball player*
* Zachary, Chink

**Zachary, Chink**
See  Zachary, Albert Myron

**Zachary, Elizabeth**
See  Zachary, Hugh

**Zachary, Hugh** 1928-
[CA, SFL, WD]
*American author*
* Gorman, Ginny
* Hughes, Zach
* Kane, Pablo
* Kanto, Peter
* Pilgrim, Derral
* Rangely, Olivia
* Van Heller, Marcus
* Zachary, Elizabeth

**Zachary, Jonathan Thompson Walton** 1897-1969   [BE, DGS]
*American baseball player*
* Walton, Zach
* Zachary, Tom

**Zachary Leo, [Brother]**
See  Meehan, Francis Joseph

**Zachary, Tom**
See  Zachary, Jonathan Thompson Walton

**Zacher, Elmer Henry** 1883-1944
[BE]
*American baseball player*
* Zacher, Silver

**Zacher, Silver**
See  Zacher, Elmer Henry

**Zacherle, John** 1918-   [RO1]
*American singer and television performer*
* Roland

**Zacherle, John C.** 1919-
[SFL, WGT]
*Author*
* Zacherley

**Zacherley**
See  Zacherle, John C.

**Zachos, John C.**   [FFF]
*Author*
* Cadmus

**Zack**
See  Keats, Gwendoline

**Zack, Jimmie**
See  Yingst, Henry Z.

**Zadkiel**
See  Morrison, Richard James

**Zafon, Silvino** 1908-   [GS]
*Spanish bullfighter*
* Nino de la Estrella [Child of the Star]

**Zag**
See  Zagorski, Jerzy

**Zagat, Arthur Leo** 1895-1948
[SFP, WGT]
*American author*
* Alzee, Grendon?
* Conyers, Latham
* York, Anton

**Zagorski, Jerzy** 1907-   [IAW]
*Russian-born poet, author, playwright*
* Magister, Juras
* Zag

**Zaharias, Babe Didrikson**
See  Zaharias, Mildred Didrikson

**Zaharias, George** 20th c.
*American wrestler*
* [The] Weeping Greek from Cripple Creek

**Zaharias, Mildred Didrikson**
1914-1956   [AS, GF, MEB]
*American golfer and track and field athlete*
* Didrikson, Babe
* Zaharias, Babe Didrikson

**Zaharoff, Basil**
See  Zacharias, Basileios

**Zahava, Irene** 1951-   [CA]
*American author*
* Levinson, Irene

**Zahir ud-Din Muhammad**
1483-1530   [WBD]
*Emperor of India*
* Baber [Babur or Babar]

**Zaidys, Pranas**
See  Gaida-Gaidamavicius, Pranas

**Zain, C. C.**
See  Benjamin, Elbert

**Zajc, Ivan** 1831-1914   [BBD]
*Croatian composer*
* Von Zaytz, Giovanni

**Zale Gale**
See  Abbott, Wenonah Stevens

**Zale, Tony**
See  Zaleski, Anthony Florian

**Zalega**
See  Balucki, Michal

**Zaleski, Anthony Florian** 1913-
[BX, RBE]
*American boxer*
* [The] Man of Steel
* Zale, Tony

**Zamacois, Eduardo**
See  De Zamacois y Quintana, Eduardo

**Zamani**
See  Van Roemer, A.

**Zambock, George**
See  Glasser, Allen

**[The] Zamboni Machine**
See  Reitz, Kenneth John

**Zamenhof, Lazarus Ludwig**
1859-1917   [JL]
*Polish oculist and philologist*
* Esperanto, Dr.
* [The] Father of Esperanto

**Zametkin, Laura K.** 20th c.   [IPA]
*American author*
* Hobson, Laura Z.

**Zamora, Blackie**
See Zamora, Porfiro

**Zamora, Porfiro** 1940- [RBE]
*American boxer*
* Zamora, Blackie

**Zampieri, Domenico** 1581-1641
[HN, WBD]
*Italian painter*
* Domenichino
* [The] Ox

**Zanardi-Landi, Elizabeth Marie**
1904-1948 [FC]
*Italian-born actress, playwright,
author*
* Landi, Elissa

**Zanchin, Nino** 20th c. [WF]
*Italian director*
* Andrews, Robert

**Zanco, Manuel** 1929- [NOJ]
*American jazz musician*
* Zanco, Moose

**Zanco, Moose**
See Zanco, Manuel

**Zanders, Emanuel** 1951- [SMG]
*American football player*
* [The] Z Man

**Zanders, Roosevelt Smith** 1915-
[IBW]
*American chauffeur to celebrities*
* [The] Czar

**Zane, Frank** 1942?-
*American body builder*
* Olympia, Mr.

**Zanelli, Carlos** 1897- [BBD]
*Chilean-born opera singer*
* Morelli, Carlo

**Zangwill, Louis** 1869- ? [LAO]
*British author*
* Z. Z.

**Zanni, Dom**
See Zanni, Dominick Thomas

**Zanni, Dominick Thomas** 1932-
[BE]
*American baseball player*
* Zanni, Dom

**Zanville, Bernard** 1913- [FC]
*American actor*
* Clark, Dane

**[The] Zany of Debate**
See Canning, George

**[The] Zany of His Age**
See Henley, John

**[El] Zapatero [The Shoemaker]**
See Shoemaker, William [Willie]

**Zapolska, Gabrjela**
See Korwin-Piotrowska, Gabrjela

**Zara, Louis**
See Rosenfeld, Louis Zara

**Zarchy, Harry** 1912- [CA]
*American educator and author*
* Lewis, Roger

**Zarchy, Rubin** 1915- [EJ]
*American jazz musician*
* Zarchy, Zeke

**Zarchy, Zeke**
See Zarchy, Rubin

**Zardis, Chester** 1900- [WWJ]
*American jazz musician*
* Zardis, Little Bear

**Zardis, Little Bear**
See Zardis, Chester

**Zarello, Florian**
See Painton, Ivan Emory

**Zarilla, Allen Lee** 1919- [BE, PB]
*American baseball player*
* Zarilla, Zeke

**Zarilla, Zeke**
See Zarilla, Allen Lee

**Zarumba, Louis**
See Rothkopf, Louis

**Zarzel**
See Starr, Mrs. George O.

**Zass, Aleksandr** [BL]
*Russian strong man*
* Zass, Samson

**Zass, Samson**
See Zass, Aleksandr

**Zastrow, Erika**
See Massey, Erika

**Zauchin, Norbert Henry** 1929-
[BE]
*American baseball player*
* Zauchin, Norm

**Zauchin, Norm**
See Zauchin, Norbert Henry

**Zauner, Franz Paul** 1876- ? [LAO]
*German writer*
* Pezet, [Dr.] F.

**Zavavi, Aboul-Halcon** 1168-1230
[PA]
*Author*
* Ibn-Maat

**Zawadsky, Patience** 1927- [CA]
*American writer*
* Hartman, Patience
* Lynne, Becky

**Zawoluk, Robert** 1930- [BB]
*American basketball player*
* Zawoluk, Zeke

**Zawoluk, Zeke**
See Zawoluk, Robert

**Zayanskovsky, John Kremchek**
1907- [BEW]
*American producer*
* Kenley, John

**Zbyszko, Stanislaus**
See Cyganiewicz, Stanislaus

**Zdenek, Marilee** 1934- [CA]
*American author and actress*
* Earle, Marilee

**[The] Zealous Doctor**
See Sacheverell, Henry

**Zeani, Virginia**
See Zehan, Virginia

**Zed**
See Dienes, Zoltan Paul

**Zedekiah**
See Mattaniah

**Zeffirelli, Franco**
See Corsi, Gian Franco

**Zeglio, Primo** 1906- [FDG]
*Italian director*
* Creepy, Anthony
* Hopkins, Omar

**Zehan, Virginia** 1928- [OP]
*Italian opera singer*
* Zeani, Virginia

**Zehringer, Richard** 1947- [RO2]
*American singer and songwriter*
* Derringer, Rick

**Zeidel, Lawrence [Larry]** 1928-
[FHE]
*Canadian-born hockey player*
* [The] Rock

**Zeider, Bunions**
See Zeider, Rollie Hubert

**Zeider, Rollie Hubert** 1883-1967
[BE, PB]
*American baseball player*
* Zeider, Bunions

**Zeidler, Leatrice Joy** 1899-
[F2, FC]
*American actress*
* Joy, Leatrice

**Zeiem, Lyle** 1905-1967 [SC]
*American actor*
* Latell, Lyle

**Zeiger, Henry A[nthony]** 1930-
[CA]
*American author*
* Peterson, James

**Zeiger, Sophia** 1926- [IBY, ICB]
*American illustrator*
* Sofia

**Zeigerman, Gerald** 1939- [CA]
*American author and columnist*
* Gerald, Ziggy

**Zeigfreid, Karl**
See Fanthorpe, R[obert] Lionel

**Zeigle, Kate M.** 1850- ? [PA]
*Author*
* Stewart, Catherine

**Zekowski, Arlene** 1922- [CA]
*American author and poet*
* Berne, Arlene
* Jans, Zephyr

**Zelazny, Roger [Joseph]** 1937-
[ESF, WGT]
*American author*
* Denmark, Harrison

**Zelenski, Tadeusz** 1874-1942 [CD]
*Polish critic, author, translator*
* Boy

**Zelide**
See Charriere, Isabelle de

**Zelig, Big Jack**
See Alberts, William

**Zelig, Jack**
See Alberts, William

**Zelinsky, Joseph F.** 1901- [BBH]
*Hungarian-born bowler*
* Kissoff, Joseph F.

**Zell, Ira**
See Roosevelt, Robert Barnwell

**Zell, Mrs.** [FFF]
*Entertainer*
* Mann, Rheta

**Zelle, Margarete Gertrude**
1876-1917 [BL, CBS, LC]
*Dutch-born intelligence agent for
Germany*
* Mata Hari

**Zelmanowitz, Gerald Martin** 20th c.
*American underworld figure and
government witness*
* Maris, Paul

**Zelver, Patricia [Farrell]** 1923-
[CA]
*American author*
* Farrell, Patricia

**Zemach, Harve**
See Fischtrom, Harvey

**Zemach, Margot**
See Fischtrom, Margot Zemach

**Zeman, Antonin** 1843-1931 [CD]
*Czech author*
* Stasek, Antal

**Zeman, Kamil** 1882-1952
[CD, EWL]
*Czech author*
* Olbracht, Ivan

**Zemaria**
See Dos Santos, Zemaria

**Zena, Harry**
See Butler, George H.

**Zenea, Juan Clemente** 1832-1871
[CW]
*Cuban poet, author, playwright*
* [Un] Amigo de la Juventud
* Azucena, Adolfo de la
* Ego-Queque

**Zenobia** ?- 273
[DEP, DNNF, HN]
*Queen of Palmyra*
* [The] Pearl of the East
* [The] Queen of the East

**Zenon [or Zeno], George Louis
Francis** 1900-1968 [WWJ]
*American jazz musician*
* Lewis, George

**Zentner, Carola** 1927- [CA]
*German-born author and journalist*
* Mason, Carola

**Zequiera y Arango, Manuel de**
1764-1846 [CW]
*Cuban poet*
* Armuna, Ezequiel
* Raquenue, Izmael

**Zerby, Deborah [or Derby?]** 1948-
[HT, ITA, SW]
*American actress*
* Darby, Kim

**Zere, Al**
See Ablitzer, Alfred G.

**Zerilli, Joseph** 1898?-1977
*American underworld figure*
* Mr. Joe

**Zernial, Gus Edward** 1923-
[BE, PB]
*American baseball player*
* Ozark Ike

**Zernoudjy**
See Eddya, Borhan

**Zero**
See Schleger, Hans

**Zero, Commander**
See  Pastora Gomez, Eden

**Zero, Kid**
See  Brimsek, Francis Charles
[Frank]

**Zero, Mr.**
See  Brimsek, Francis Charles
[Frank]

**Zeromski, Stefan** 1864-1925
[CD, EWL]
*Polish author and playwright*
* Katerla, Jozef
* Zych, Maurycy

**Zeta**
See  Cope, [Vincent] Zachary

**Zeta**
See  Froude, James Anthony

**Zetford, Tully**
See  Bulmer, [Henry] Kenneth

**Zetti, Italo** 1913-  [ART]
*Italian artist*
* Z.

**Zettlein, George** 1844-1905  [BE]
*American baseball player*
* [The] Charmer

**Zevin, Israel Joseph** 1872-1926
[WBD]
*Russian-born journalist and author*
* Tashrak
* [The] Yiddish Mark Twain

**Zhuchenko, Yar** 1918-  [CA]
*Russian-born author*
* Slavutych, Yar

**Ziar, E. R.**
See  Ziar, Elizabeth Rosemary

**Ziar, Elizabeth Rosemary** 1919-
[ART]
*British painter*
* E. R. Z.
* Ziar, E. R.

**Zibelman, Charles** 1891-  [EJS]
*American swimmer*
* Zimmy, Charles

**Zieber, Harry** 20th c.  [BE]
*American baseball player*
* Whiting, Ed[ward C.]

**Ziegfeld, Flo**
See  Ziegfeld, Florenz

**Ziegfeld, Florenz** 1869-1932  [PMJ]
*American producer*
* Ziegfeld, Flo

**Ziegler, Alan** 1947-  [CA]
*American author and poet*
* Bona, Mercy

**Ziegler, Anne**
See  Eastwood, Irene Frances

**Ziegler, Buster**
See  Ziegler, John

**Ziegler, Edward William** 1932-
[ESF, SFL, WGT]
*American author*
* Tyler, Theodore

**Ziegler, John** 20th c.  [BBH]
*American softball player*
* Ziegler, Buster

**Ziegler, Karen** 1942-  [SW]
*American actress*
* Black, Karen

**Ziegler, Shotgun**
See  Goetz, Fred

**Zif, Jay Jehiel**
See  Silberstein, Jay Jehiel

**Zigis**
See  Skujins, Zigmunds

**Zigzag**
See  Sykes, Arthur Alkin

**Zilberg, Veniamin A.** 1902-  [EWL]
*Russian author*
* Kaverin, Veniamin

**Zillah**
See  Macdonald, Zillah K[atherine]

**Zilles, Antoine** 1868-1932  [BEW]
*Dutch-born actor*
* Corrigan, Emmett

**Zilveritch, Fanny** 1909-  [FC]
*Hungarian actress*
* Gaal, Franceska

**Zim, Sonia Bleeker** 1909-1971
[AW, CA]
*Russian-born American author*
* Bleeker, Sonia

**Zimeas, John**
See  Tzimeas, John

**Zimm, Louise Hasbrouck** 1883-
[NAA]
*American author*
* Hasbrouck, Louise Seymour

**Zimmer, Charles Louis** 1860-1949
[AS, BE, PB]
*American baseball player*
* Zimmer, Chief

**Zimmer, Chief**
See  Zimmer, Charles Louis

**Zimmer, Don[ald William]** 1931-
[PB, SMG]
*American baseball player and
manager*
* Zimmer, Zim

**Zimmer, Jill Schary**
See  Robinson, Jill

**Zimmer, Zim**
See  Zimmer, Don[ald William]

**Zimmerman, Arthur A.** 1869-1936
[BBH]
*American bicycle racer*
* [The] Flying Yankee
* King of the Wheel
* Zimmerman, Zimmie

**Zimmerman, Elizabeth S.**
1884-1959  [SC]
*American actress*
* Stoddard, Betsy

**Zimmerman, Ethel Agnes** 1909-
[BEW, EMT, ITA]
*American singer and actress*
* Merman, Ethel

**Zimmerman, Gerald Robert** 1934-
[SMG]
*American baseball coach*
* Zimmerman, Zim

**Zimmerman, Heinie**
See  Zimmerman, Henry

**Zimmerman, Henry** 1887-1969
[BE]
*American baseball player*
* Zimmerman, Heinie

**Zimmerman, Robert** 1941-
[CA, DAM, LRR]
*American singer and composer*
* Dylan, Bob
* Grunt, Blindboy

**Zimmerman, Zim**
See  Zimmerman, Gerald Robert

**Zimmerman, Zimmie**
See  Zimmerman, Arthur A.

**Zimmermann, Werner** 20th c.
[SFL]
*Author*
* Douglas, Drake

**Zimmerwal, Edmond**
See  Lozzi, Edmondo

**Zimmy, Charles**
See  Zibelman, Charles

**Zinberg, Leonard** 1911?-1968
[CC, EMD]
*American author*
* Lacy, Ed

**Zincke, Hans** 1837-1922  [BBD]
*German composer*
* Sommer, Hans

**Ziner, Feenie**
See  Ziner, Florence

**Ziner, Florence** 1921-  [CA]
*American author*
* Ziner, Feenie

**Zingale, Carl** 1895?-
*American billiard player*
* Kelly, Cue Ball

**Zingara, Professor**
See  Leeming, Joseph

**[Il] Zingaro**
See  Solario, Antonio

**Zink, John Smith** 1929-  [EAR]
*American auto racer*
* Zink, Junior

**Zink, Junior**
See  Zink, John Smith

**Zinken**
See  Hopp, Signe Marie

**Zinkler, Christiane**
See  Moeckl, Christiane

**Zinn, Sargeant**
See  Wilson, James Edwin

**Zinoviev, Grigori Evseevich**
See  Apfelbaum, Hirsch

**Zipfel, Bud**
See  Zipfel, Marion Sylvester

**Zipfel, Marion Sylvester** 1938-
[BE]
*American baseball player*
* Zipfel, Bud

**Zipoli, Perlone**
See  Lippi, Lorenzo

**Zippo, Mr.**
See  Blaisdell, George G.

**Ziraldo**
See  Pinto, Ziraldo Alves

**Zisca, John** 1360?-1424  [SN]
*Bohemian army officer*
* [The] One Eyed

**Ziska**
See  Cummings, Amos Jay

**Zitelmann, Konrad** 1854-1897
[WBD]
*German poet and author*
* Telmann, Konrad

**Zito, Salvatore** 1933-  [ASC]
*American composer*
* Zito, Torrie

**Zito, Torrie**
See  Zito, Salvatore

**Zivic, Charlie**
See  Affif, Charles

**Zivic, Ferdinand Henry John** 1913-
[B10]
*American boxer*
* Zivic, Fritzie

**Zivic, Fritzie**
See  Zivic, Ferdinand Henry John

**Zmaj**
See  Jovanovic, Jovan

**Zmich, Ed[ward Albert]** 1884-1950
[BE]
*American baseball player*
* Zmich, Ike

**Zmich, Ike**
See  Zmich, Ed[ward Albert]

**Zmogas**
See  Rodziewiczowna, Marja

**Zobbau, M.**  [PA]
*Author*
* Castorim

**Zobeltitz, Hanns von** 1853-1918
[WBD]
*German author*
* Spielberg, Hanns von

**Zocato [Left-Handed]**
See  Borrego Ruiz, Carlos

**Zoe, Mlle.**
See  Yates, Mrs. Benjamin

**Zoeller, Frank Urban** 1952?-
*American golfer*
* Zoeller, Fuzzy

**Zoeller, Fuzzy**
See  Zoeller, Frank Urban

**Zoffani, John** 1733-1810  [SN]
*German-born painter*
* [The] Dutch Hogarth

**Zog I [or Zogu]**
See  Ahmed Bey Zogu

**[The] Zoilos of Quinault**
See  Boileau-Despreaux, Nicolas

**Zoilus**
See  Dennis, John

**Zoilus**
See  Lovecraft, Howard Phillips

**Zoilus**
See  Stuart, Gilbert

**Zoilus [or Zoilos]** 4th c. BC
[DNNS, HN, RH]
*Greek grammarian*
* Homeromastix
* Homer's Scourge
* [The] Scourge of Homer
* [The] Thracian Dog

**Zolar**
See  King, Bruce

**Zoldak, Sad Sam**
See  Zoldak, Samuel Walter

**Zoldak, Samuel Walter** 1918-1966
[BE]
*American baseball player*
* Zoldak, Sad Sam

**Zolf, Larry** 1934- [CA]
*Canadian author and television journalist*
* Jaded Observer

**Zoll, Donald Atwell** 1927- [CA]
*American educator and author*
* Winslow, Donald

**Zolotow, Charlotte [Shapiro]** 1915-
[B10, TCC]
*American author and editor*
* Abbot, Sara
* Bookman, Charlotte

**Zomerdijk, Hein**
See Zomerdijk, Henricus Jacobus

**Zomerdijk, Henricus Jacobus**
1918- [IWM]
*Dutch musician*
* Zomerdijk, Hein

**Zomphier, Charles** 1906-1973
[MK]
*American baseball player*
* Zomphier, Zomp

**Zomphier, Zomp**
See Zomphier, Charles

**Zonik, Eleanor Dorothy** 1918-
[CA, WD]
*British playwright*
* Glaser, Eleanor Dorothy

**Zonis, Stuart Michael** 1937-
[BEW, FC]
*American actor and singer*
* Damon, Stuart

**Zoolactaf [or Dsulaktaf]**
See Shapur II [or Sapor]

**Zoophilus**
See Blyth, Edward

**Zorilla, Jose** 1829- ? [FFF]
*Spanish poet*
* [The] Spanish Victor Hugo

**Zorina, Vera**
See Hartwig, Eva Brigitta

**Zorio, Vincent Edward** 1928- [FC]
*American actor*
* Edwards, Vince

**Zoroaster [or Zarathustra]**
[DEP, FFF, SN]
*Founder of the Magian religion*
* [The] Bactrian Sage

**Zorro**
See Ward, Harold

**[El] Zorzal Crillo [The Native Thrush]**
See Gardes, Charles Romuald

**Zoschokke** 1771-1848 [RH]
*Swiss author*
* [The] Swiss Walter Scott

**Zovello**
See Wishner, Sam

**Zsigmond, Vilmos** 20th c. [WF]
*Cinematographer*
* Zsigmond, William

**Zsigmond, William**
See Zsigmond, Vilmos

**Zuber, Goober**
See Zuber, William Henry

**Zuber, William Henry** 1913- [BE]
*American baseball player*
* Zuber, Goober

**Zuccari, Anna Radius** 1846-1918
[CD]
*Italian author*
* Neera

**Zuck, Alexandra** 1942- [FC, SW]
*American actress*
* Dee, Sandra

**Zucker, Dolores Mae Bolton** [CA]
*American author and columnist*
* Hill, Dee
* Hill, Devra

**Zuckerman, Buck Henry** 1930-
[CA, SW]
*American screenwriter and actor*
* Henry, Buck

**Zuckerman, Norma Anna Bella**
1931-1973 [SC]
*American actress*
* Crane, Norma

**Zuckermann, Augusta** 1890- [BBD]
*American musician*
* Mana-Zucca

**Zudekoff, Moe**
See Zudekoff, Muni

**Zudekoff, Muni** 1919-
[EJ, PMJ, WWJ]
*American jazz musician*
* Morrow, Buddy
* Zudekoff, Moe

**Zuker, Barney**
See Zuker, William

**Zuker, William** 20th c. [EJS]
*American swimming coach*
* Zuker, Barney

**Zukerman, Pinchas** 20th c.
*Israeli musician*
* Zukerman, Pinky

**Zukerman, Pinky**
See Zukerman, Pinchas

**[The] Zula Kid**
See Flammia, Michael

**Zulawski, Juliusz** 1910- [IAW]
*Polish author and poet*
* J. Z.

**Zulawski, Marek** 1908-
[ART, DBA]
*Italian-born painter*
* Marek

**Zuleika**
See Willemer, Marianne von

**[The] Zulu Queen**
See Chaka

**Zumwalt, Elmo Russell, Jr.** 1920-
*American naval officer*
* Zumwalt, Zoomie

**Zumwalt, Oral** 20th c. [GW]
*American rodeo performer*
* Zumwalt, Zumie

**Zumwalt, Zoomie**
See Zumwalt, Elmo Russell, Jr.

**Zumwalt, Zumie**
See Zumwalt, Oral

**Zunich, Ralph** 1910- [CEI]
*American hockey player*
* Zunich, Ricky

**Zunich, Ricky**
See Zunich, Ralph

**Zuniga Villquiran, Jose** 1950- [GS]
*Colombian bullfighter*
* Josellilo de Colombia [Little Joe from Colombia]

**Zunser, Eliakim** 1836-1913
*Yiddish poet*
* Badchen, Eliakim

**Zupo, Frank Joseph** 1939- [BE]
*American baseball player*
* Zupo, Noodles

**Zupo, Noodles**
See Zupo, Frank Joseph

**Zuppke, Robert C.** 1879-1957
[AS, BBH, FB]
*German-born football player and coach*
* [The] Little Dutchman
* [The] Rembrandt of the Prairies
* Zuppke, Zupp

**Zuppke, Zupp**
See Zuppke, Robert C.

**Zurhorst, Charles [Stewart, Jr.]**
1913- [CA, SAT]
*American author*
* Stewart, Charles

**Zurito [Little Wild Dove]**
See De La Haba, Antonio

**Zurito [Little Wild Dove]**
See De La Haba Vargas, Gabriel

**Zurndorfer, Dorothy Paula** 1933-
[BEW]
*American actress and singer*
* Stewart, Paula

**Zuta, Jack** ?-1928 [BLB]
*American underworld figure*
* Goodman, J. H.

**Zvi, H.**
See Harkavy, Zvi

**Zweibelsharf, David** 1895- [BEW]
*Russian-born actor*
* Dank, David

**Zweit, Adam**
See Lovin, Roger Robert

**Zwerbach, Max** 1882-1908 [BLB]
*American underworld figure*
* Twist, Kid

**Zwerenz, Gerhard** 1925- [CA]
*German author*
* Tarrok, Peer

**Zwibak, Jacques** 1902- [CA]
*Russian-born American author*
* Sedych, Andrei

**Zwilling, Dutch**
See Zwilling, Edward Harrison

**Zwilling, Edward Harrison** 1888-
[BE]
*American baseball player*
* Zwilling, Dutch

**Zwillman, Abner** 1899-1959
[BLB, MM, PHM]
*American underworld figure*
* Zwillman, Longy

**Zwillman, Longy**
See Zwillman, Abner

**Zwingli, Carl** [PA]
*Author*
* Carlopago

**Zwingli, Ulrich** 1484-1531 [SN]
*Swiss religious reformer*
* [The] Martin Luther of Switzerland

**Zych, Maurycy**
See Zeromski, Stefan

**Zylberberg, Regina** 1929- [B10]
*French singer, dancer, cabaret owner*
* Regine

**Zylis, Teresa Geralda** 1935- [MS]
*Polish opera singer*
* Zylis-Gara, Teresa

**Zylis-Gara, Teresa**
See Zylis, Teresa Geralda

**Zyskind, Bruno** 1901-1939 [JL]
*Polish author*
* Jasienski, Bruno

**Zyx**
See Hurtubise, Jacques

**ZYX**
See Sykes, Arthur Alkin